GROOT WOORDEBOEK

AFRIKAANS · ENGELS

Dertiende Uitgawe
Versorg deur L. C. Eksteen

Vroeëre samestellers
M. S. B. Kritzinger,
P. C. Schoonees, U. J. Cronjé

J. L. van Schaik

J. L. van Schaik (Edms) Bpk,
Librigebou, Kerkstraat, Pretoria
Alle regte voorbehou

Eerste uitgawe 1926
Tweede uitgawe 1928
Derde uitgawe 1937
Vierde uitgawe 1946
Vyfde uitgawe 1951
Sesde uitgawe 1954
Sewende uitgawe, eerste druk 1956, tweede druk 1957
Agtste uitgawe, eerste druk 1959, tweede druk 1960, derde druk 1961
Negende uitgawe, eerste druk 1963, tweede druk 1966
Tiende uitgawe, eerste druk 1968, tweede druk 1969, derde druk 1970
Elfde uitgawe, eerste druk 1972, tweede druk 1977
Twaalfde uitgawe 1981
Dertiende uitgawe 1986

ISBN 0 627 01491 7

Geset, gedruk en gebind
deur Nasionale Boekdrukkery,
Goodwood, Kaap

VOORWOORD BY DIE DERTIENDE UITGAWE

Hierdie uitgawe is grondig hersien en aansienlik uitgebrei.
Meer idiomatiese uitdrukkings het bygekom.
Daar is probeer om nuwe woorde wat in die daaglikse pers ingang vind, op te neem.
My waardering aan dié gebruikers wat besondere woorde of lyste aan my gestuur het, of wat op een of ander wyse hulp verskaf het.
My dank aan mev. A. Smith vir haar hulp met die lees van die galeiproewe.

L.C.E.
Pretoria
Julie 1986

AFKORTINGS

b	=	byvoeglike naamwoord	telw	=	telwoord
bw	=	bywoord	vgw	=	voegwoord
mv	=	meervoud	vs	=	voorsetsel
s	=	selfstandige naamwoord	vw	=	voornaamwoord
tw	=	tussenwerpsel	w	=	werkwoord

..   word gebruik waar die laaste lettergreep van 'n woord verander is, bv.
    geklee, (..klede) vir **geklede;**

~- waar 'n koppelteken gebruik word, bv.
    see: ~-eend vir **see-eend;**

~ (los) dui aan dat die sleutelwoord op die betrokke plek kom,
   bv. **agting:** uit ~ vir = *uit agting vir;*

~ (vas aan 'n woord) dui aan dat die sleutelwoord en die ander woord vas geskryf word, bv.
   rooibok: ~**vel** = **rooibokvel;**

~ na sekere Afrikaanse werkwoorde dui aan dat daardie werkwoord geen *ge-* of *-ge-* vir die verlede tyd
   kry nie, bv. **voorspel, (~)** bly **voorspel;**

= aan die end van 'n reël dui aan dat die betrokke woorddeel vas aan die volgende geskryf moet word;

' word gebruik om aan te dui dat die klem by die uitspreek van 'n woord val op die sillabe wat die
   aksentstreep voorafgaan, bv. **dia'ken, poli'tikus, mu'sici.**

A

A¹, a, (s), (-'s), A, a; *geen A van (voor) 'n B KEN nie,* not know a B from a battledore; ~ *KRUIS,* A sharp; *as 'n mens A sê, MOET jy ook B sê,* in for a penny, in for a pound; ~ *MOL,* A flat; *VAN A tot Z,* from beginning to end, from A to Z.

a², (tw), ah, oh! ~ *JA* ~, certainly, of course; ~ *NEE* ~, not at all! oh no! by no means! of course not!

a³, (vs), at, (@); ~ *PARI,* at par; ~ *20 SENT stuk,* at 20 cents each; *VYF* ~ *ses,* five to six, five or six.

a⁴, (w), *(kinderwoord),* **(ge-),** go to stool. *See* **akka.**

aag, (tw) pooh; ~ *FOEI tog!* what a pity! ~ *WAT!* pshaw! go on!

aai, (w) **(ge-),** stroke, caress, chuck (under the chin), pat; flatter; (tw) ah! oh!

aak, (ake), barge.

aak′lig, (b, bw) **(-e),** horrible, nasty, macabre; awful, bad, dreary, miserable, bleak, dismal; lurid (tales); gruesome, ghastly, grisly, gaunt; *'n* ~ *e gesig,* a terrible sight; ~ *e GEWOONTES,* nasty habits; *ek VOEL* ~ *daarvan,* it has upset me, it made me feel sick; ~ **heid, (. . hede),** dreariness; horribleness, nastiness; miserableness; grisliness, gruesomeness, ghastliness; ~ *hede van HONGERS-NOOD,* miseries of starvation; *die* ~ *hede van OORLOG,* the horrors of war.

aal, (ale), eel; *so GLAD soos 'n* ~, as slippery as an eel; ~ *is geen PALING nie,* every like is not the same; *'n* ~ *aan die STERT vang,* tackle a slippery customer; ~ **agtig, (-e),** eel-like.

a′älawa, aa lava, block lava.

aal′bessie, (black, red, white) currant; ~ **bos,** currant bush; ~ **sap,** currant juice; ~ **vla,** currant custard; ~ **wyn,** currant wine.

aal′fuik, (-e), eelpot.

aal′moes, (-e), alms, charity, dole; largesse, maundy money; *van* ~ *e LEWE,* live on charity; live by begging; *om 'n* ~ *VRA,* ask for charity.

aalmoesenier′, (-s), almoner; ~ **shuis,** almshouse, almonry; ~ **skap,** almonership.

aal′moes, (-e), gewer, almoner; ~ **kassie,** almsbox.

aal: ~ **pastei,** eel-pie; ~ **skêr,** eelspear; ~ **skolwer,** cormorant; ~ **so(e)p,** eel soup; ~ **streep, (. . strepe),** list, belt of colour (animal); ~ **vel,** eelskin; ~ **tjies,** nematodes; little eels; eel-worms; ~ **verkoper,** eelmonger; ~ **vissery,** eel-fishing; ~ **vormig, (-e),** eel-shaped, anguilliform.

aal′wee, (-s), aloe; ~ **agtig, (-e),** aloetic.

aal′wurm, eel-worm; nematode; potato disease; ~ **doder,** nematicide; ~ **middel,** nematode preparation; nematicide.

aal′wyn, (-e), aloe; *hy het* ~ *getap,* he is in a bad mood; ~ **agtig, (-e),** aloetic; ~ **bitter,** aloin; ~ **boom,** aloe tree; ~ **hars,** aloetic resin; ~ **hout,** eaglewood; ~ **pil,** aloe drop (laxative); *met 'n* ~ *pil in jou kies loop,* move about with a sour mouth; look down in the mouth; ~ **sak,** aloe bag; ~ **sap,** aloe juice; ~ **tapper,** aloe-juice collector; poor person.

aam, (ame), aum.

aam′beeld, (-e), anvil; incus (in ear); *altyd op dieselfde* ~ *slaan (hamer),* keep on harping on the same string; ~ **beentjie,** incus; ~ **beitel,** hardy; ~ **blok,** anvil bed (block, stand, stock); ~ **horing,** anvil beak; ~ **voël,** red-fronted tinker barbet *(Pogoniulus pusillus).*

aam′bei, (-e), piles (disease), haemorrhoids, emerods; *BLOEIENDE* ~ *e,* bleeding (wet) piles; *DROË* ~ *e,* dry piles; ~ **bos,** Christmas berry, wild gentian *(Chironia baccifera, Teucrium africanum, Acorus leucura, Indigofera hedyantha);* ~ **poeier,** pile powder; ~ **salf,** pile ointment.

aambors′tig, (-e), asthmatic, short-winded, wheezy; ~ **heid,** breathlessness; asthma.

aan¹, (b, bw) on, in, upon, onwards; *ons moet weet waar ons* ~ *of AF is,* we must know where we stand; *daar is IETS van* ~, there is something in it; *jy IS* ~, it's your turn; *dit KOM nie daarop* ~ *nie,* it does not matter; *daar is NIKS* ~ *nie,* that is quite easy, there is nothing in it; *daar is NIKS van* ~ *nie,* there is not a word of truth in it; *ons het daar NIKS* ~ *nie,* it is useless to us; *die SKOOL is* ~, the school has begun; *dit is weer* ~ *TUSSEN hulle,* they have made it up again.

aan², (vs) at, against, for, in, by, near, next to, on which; ~ *BOORD,* on board (ship); ~ *(die) BRAND,* on fire; ~ *(die) KANT,* tidied, neat; ~ *die LYKANT,* under the lee; ~ *die MUUR,* on the wall; ~ *TAFEL,* at table; ~ *die WERK wees,* be busy, be at work.

aan-aan′, touch (game); ~ **speel,** play at touch.

aan′bak, (-ge-), stick to (the pan); cake together (coal); ~ **sel,** crust.

aan′behoort, (~), belong to.

aan′bel, (-ge-), ring (doorbell).

aan′beland, (~), come to, arrive at.

aan′belang, (s) importance; (w) (~), concern, regard.

aan′besteder, (-s), contractor.

aan′besteding, (-e, ′-s), giving out, contracting for work; contract, tender; *by* ~, by contract, by tender; ~ **som,** contract price; ~ **stelsel,** contract system; ~ **svoorwaarde,** condition of contract (tender), ~ **swerk,** work let out on contract.

aan′bestee, (~), invite tenders, contract for; give out on contract; *aanbestede werk,* contract work.

aan′besterf, . . sterwe, (~), fall to someone by inheritance.

aanbester′wing, inheritance; succession.

aan′betref, (~), concern; *wat dit* ~, as far as this is concerned, as to this, as regards this.

aan′betrou, (~), entrust to; confide in; confide to; trust with.

aan′beur, (-ge-), struggle along; exert oneself.

aan′beveel, (~), recommend, commend; advocate; *vir op- en AANMERKINGS hou ek my* ~, all comments will be welcome; *ek HOU my* ~, I beg to recommend myself; ~ **baar, (. . bare), . . velenswaar′dig, (-e),** commendable (plan); recommendable (article), laudable.

aan′bevelend, (-e), commendatory.

aan′beveling, (-e, -s), (re)commendation; committal; introduction; reference; *'n* ~ *DOEN,* make a recommendation; *GOEIE* ~ *s,* good recommendations (references); *OP* ~ *van,* on the recommendation of; *dit VERDIEN* ~, it is recommendable (advisable); ~ **sbrief,** letter of introduction (recommendation).

aan′bevole, recommended; *jou* ~ *hou by,* commend oneself to; ~ **ne, (-s),** person (thing) recommended.

aanbid′, (~), adore; worship; idolize (a girl); ~ **baar, (. . bare),** ~ **delik, (-e),** adorable; divine; ~ **baarheid,** ~ **delikheid,** adorableness; divinity; ~ **der,** worshipper; adorer; admirer; ~ **ding, (-e, -s),** worship, adoration, admiration.

aan′bied, . . bie(ë), (-ge-), offer, proffer; propose; propound; present (bill); tender (evidence); volunteer (services); apply; *iem. 'n GESKENK* ~, make a presentation; *jou HULP* ~, offer one's services; *as die KANS hom* ~, if the opportunity offers itself; *iem. 'n SOM geld* ~, offer someone money.

aan′bieder, (-s), offeror, presenter, profferer; master of ceremonies; programme presenter, announcer.

aan′bieding, (-e, -s), offer, proposal, tender, presentation, presentment; overture; ~ **sdatum,** date of presentation.

aan′bind, (-ge-), tie, fasten, bind; moor (boat); *die STRYD* ~, take up the cudgels; *die STRYD* ~ *met,* try conclusions with.

aan′blaas, (-ge-), fan (a flame), stir up, rouse (passions); *die vuur van twee dra* ~, foment discord.

aan′blaf, (-ge-), bark at, bay at.

aan′blaser, (-s), instigator, inciter.

aan′blasing, (-e, -s), aspiration, inspiration, afflation, afflatus; blowing; instigation.

aan′blik, (s) sight, view, aspect, look; *by die eerste* ~, at first sight; (w) **(-ge-),** glance at; beam upon.

aan′bly, (-ge-), continue, remain, last; *bly AAN asb.,* hang on please; *laat die HEMP* ~, keep on your shirt; *hulle sal vir drie JAAR* ~, they will hold office for three years; *laat jou SKOENE maar* ~, you need not take off your shoes; *die VERGADE-*

RING sal nie lank ~ *nie*, the meeting won't last long.
aan'bod, (..**biedinge**, ..**biedings**), offer, proffer, proposal; supply; *'n* ~ *AFSLAAN*, refuse an offer; turn down a proposal.
aan'boer, (-ge-), farm progressively.
aan'bons, (-ge-), bump against, bounce against.
aan'boor, (-ge-), begin boring; continue boring; strike (mineral); tap, broach (a cask).
aan'boring, strike (oil, water).
aan'bot, (-te) = **aanbod**.
aan'bots, (-ge-), collide with, clash together, strike against; ~**ing**, (-e, -s), collision.
aan'bou, (s), annex(e); construction; *die huis is in* ~, the house is under construction; (w) (-ge-), add to by building, build on to; ~**ing**, construction; ~**program**, building programme; ~**sel**, (-s), annex(e), addition.
aan'brand, (-ge-), burn (food); stick to (the pan); ~**ing**, burning; ~**sel**, (-s), crust caused by burning; scorched part of meat, etc.; *moenie al die* ~ *sel uit jou pot krap nie*, don't put all your eggs in one basket; ~**steker**, lighter.
aan'breek, (s) beginning; dawn (of an epoch); fall (of dusk); *by die* ~ *van die dag*, at daybreak; (w) (-ge-), dawn, come (day); broach (cask); arrive (time); *die dag sal* ~, the day will come.
aan'brei, (-ge-), add by knitting; continue knitting; ~**sel**, (-s), newly knitted part.
aan'bring, (-ge-), bring near; affix (stamps); bring on, announce, introduce (innovations); effect, introduce, make (improvements); impart (knowledge); bring about (change); install (apparatus); let (a door into a wall); construct (a wall); bring, inform, tell, say; denounce (at law); ~**er**, (-s), denouncer, denunciator, informer, tale-bearer; carrier, bringer; feeder; applier; common informer, applicator *(jur.)*; ~ *geld*, commission; ~**ing**, introduction, installation; ~**lyn**, feeder line; ~**premie**, commission; reward (for denouncing).
aan'bruis, (-ge-), come rushing (roaring) along.
aan'brul, (-ge-), roar (growl) at.
aan'byt, (-ge-), bite (into); *'n aangebyte appel*, a bitten apple.
aand, (-e), evening, eve; *'n GESELLIGE* ~, a social (evening); *die* ~ *van die LEWE*, old age; *dis NOG nie* ~ *nie*, don't bless the day until it is over; ~ *ROOI*, *môre water in die sloot*, red sky at night is the shepherd's delight; *die* ~ *voor die SLAG*, the eve of the battle; *TEEN die* ~, at nightfall; *die* ~ *voor my VERJAARSDAG*, the eve of my birthday.
aanda'dig, (-e), accessory, accessary, implicated (in), instrumental (in, to); ~**heid**, complicity, guilt.
aan'dag, attention, heed, notice; advertance, advertancy; devotion, family prayers; *BENEDE iem. se* ~ *nie*, not worth taking notice of; *die* ~ *BOEI*, arrest the attention; *EEN en al* ~ *wees*, be all ears; ~ *GEE aan*, pay attention to; ~ *GENIET*, receive attention; *ONDER die* ~ *bring*, bring to the notice of; *die* ~ *ONTGAAN*, escape attention (notice); *OP* ~, attention; ~ *begin TREK*, begin to attract notice; *die* ~ *VESTIG op*, direct (draw) the attention to; ~ *WY aan*, devote attention to; ~**streep**, dash; ~'**tig**, (-e), attentive(ly); ~'**tigheid**, attentiveness; ~'**tiglik**, attentively.
aand: ~**baadjie**, dinner jacket; ~**besoek**, evening visit (call); ~**bestelling**, evening delivery; ~**blad**, evening paper; ~**blom**, evening flower (species of *Hesperantha*, Gladiolus, Freesia and *Iridaceae)*; ~**bos**, *Gnidia wilmsii*; ~**brood**, supper; ~**byeenkoms**, evening meeting; ~**diens**, evening service; evensong; ~**dou**, (evening) dew; ~**drag**, evening dress, black tie, dinner jacket; dinner suit, dinner wear, evening wear; glad rags; ~**edisie**, evening edition.
aan'deel, (..**dele**), share; portion, part, quota, allotment; communion; concern; *EK vir my* ~, as far as I am concerned; *GEWONE (preferente)* ~, ordinary (preference) share; ~ *HE in*, have a share in; ~ *op NAAM*, nominal share; *'n* ~ *NEEM in*, participate in, take part in; *VOORLOPIGE* ~, scrip;

~**bewys**, share certificate; ~**hebber**, (-s), ~**houer**, (-s), shareholder; ~**mark**, sharemarket.
aan'dele: ~**besit**, shareholdings; ~**handel**, dealing in shares; ~**kapitaal**, share capital, capital stock; ~**maatskappy**, joint-stock company; ~**omset**, turnover of shares; ~**portefeulje**, share portfolio; ~**register**, (transfer) register; ~**transaksie**, share deal; ~~**uitgifte**, share issue.
aan'denking, (-e, -s), remembrance, favour, keepsake, memento, souvenir; ~**sdiens**, commemoration service.
aand: ~**ete**, supper, evening meal; *ligte* ~ *ete*, (high) tea; ~**gebed**, evening prayer; ~**gesang**, evensong, evening hymn, vespers; ~**geselligheid**, evening social; ~**gloed**, sunset glow, afterglow; ~**godsdiens**, evening prayers, evening worship; ~**grou**, twilight; ~**hemp**, dress shirt; ~**huwelik**, evening wedding.
aandiekaak'stelling, (-e), exposure.
aan'dien, (-ge-), announce (by name), usher in; *'n BESOEKER* ~, announce a visitor; *jou* ~ *BY 'n minister*, send in your name to a minister; ~**ing**, (-s), announcement, declaration.
aan'dig, (-ge-), impute; ~**ting**, (-s), imputation.
aan'dik, (-ge-), make thicker; underline, emphasize, stress; *'n PUNT* ~, emphasize a point; *iem. se WOORDE* ~, dot the i's and cross the t's; exaggerate; ~**king**, (-s), emphasis, stressing, underlining, exaggeration.
aand: ~**japon**, evening dress; ~**jie**, (-s), social evening; night-out; ~**kerk**, evening service; ~**klas**, evening (night) class; *hy loop* ~ *klas*, he goes courting; ~**klere**, dress clothes, evening dress, evening wear; ~**klok**, evening bell, curfew; ~**koelte**, cool of evening; ~**koerant**, evening (afternoon) paper; ~**kostuum**, evening dress; *A* ~ **land**, the Occident, the West; ~**lied**, evensong; vespers; hymn; ~**lig**, evening light, dusk, twilight, ~**lug**, evening (night) air; ~**mantel**, opera-cloak; ~**newel**, evening mist.
aan'doen, (-ge-), call at (a port); (-ge-, ..**gedaan**), cause, render, affect, move; *sy naam EER* ~, do honour to his name; *die waarheid GEWELD* ~, stretch the truth; *die KAAP* ~, touch (call) at the Cape; *ONAANGENAAM* ~, offend, displease, jar (grate) upon; *SMART (las)* ~, cause grief (trouble); *aangedaan VOEL*, be moved; ~**ing**, emotion, feeling; affection; touch (of illness); ~**lik**, (-e), touching, pathetic; affectionate; impressionable, emotional; ~**likheid**, pathos; sensitiveness.
aan'donker, (-ge-), become (grow) dark; darken.
aand: ~**pak**, evening suit, dress suit, black tie; tuxedo; ~**party**, evening party, soiree; ~**pos**, evening post; ~**praatjies**: *sy* ~ *praatjies en môrepraatjies kom nie ooreen nie*, his word is quite unreliable; ~**pypie**, gladiolus; large brown afrikaner.
aan'dra, **aan'draag**, (-ge-), bring on, carry to; tell, inform; *nuus* ~, tell tales.
aan'draai, (-ge-), screw tighter, fasten by twisting; switch on; turn on; *rem* ~, put on the brake, proceed more slowly (warily); ~**knoppie**, switch (button).
aan'draer, carrier, bearer; tale bearer, telltale.
aan'draf, (-ge-), come (go) trotting along, run on; run faster.
aan'drang, pressure, entreaty, insistence, impulse, impulsion; instance; urge, prompting; ~ *van BLOED*, afflux of blood; *uit EIE* ~, of one's own accord; *die* ~ *van die HART*, promptings of the heart; *op* ~ *van my VRIEND*, at the instigation (instance) of my friend.
aan'drawwe, (-ge-), *kyk* **aandraf**.
aan'drentel, (-ge-), come (go) sauntering along.
aan'dreun, (-ge-), come roaring along.
aan'dribbel, (-ge-), toddle (dribble) along.
aan'drif, instigation, urge, impulse, instinct, impetus; drift.
aan'dring, (-ge-), urge, press on, push, importune, enforce, insist on; *op 'n saak* ~, insist on a matter; ~**erig**, (~**e**), insistent, importunate.
aand'rok, evening dress.
aan'drom, (-ge-), flock together.
aand'rooi, evening glow, sunset.
aan'druis, (-ge-), come roaring along; clash; *dit*

druis teen alle reëls in, it sets all the rules at naught.
aan'druk, (-ge-), press against (on); clasp (to one's heart), hug (a child); hurry on; *julle moet ~ vorentoe,* you must hurry ahead; **~ker,** presser, squeezer.
aan'dryf, (-ge-) = **aandrywe;** **~as,** propeller shaft; **~skroef,** propeller screw; **~staaf,** accelerator.
aan'drywe, (-ge-), float along; press on, drive on, urge, goad, incite; move, actuate; hammer; float ashore; egg on; *deur edele beginsels aangedryf,* prompted by noble principles; **~r,** instigator; driver *(mech.,);* pusher, hustler.
aan'drywing, (-e, -s), instigation, incitement, urge, actuation; drive (engine); floating along.
aand: **~sakkie,** (lady's) evening bag; **~sang,** evensong; **~sitting,** night (evening) session; **~skemering,** dusk, twilight, nightfall, gloaming; **~skoen,** evening shoe; **~skof,** evening (night) shift; **~skofry,** visit a girl; **~skool,** night school, evening (night) classes; *~skool hou by,* court, make love to; **~snapsie,** nightcap; **~son,** setting sun; **A~ster,** evening star, Venus; Hesperus; **~stilte,** evening quiet (calm); **~stond,** evening (hour); **~student,** night-class student; **~tabberd,** evening dress; **~tee,** evening tea; **~toilet,** evening dress, evening toilet.
aan'du, (-ge-), push forward.
aan'dui, (-ge-), indicate, point out, intimate; denote, designate, qualify, describe; denominate; express; hint, adumbrate; betoken; mark; *nader ~,* specify; **~dend, (-e),** denominative, denotative; prognostic; **~ding, (-e, -s),** pointing, indication, designation, hint, intimation, sign; denotation; **~er,** denominator; denotation.
aand: **~uitgawe,** evening (afternoon) edition; **~uitvoering,** evening performance.
aan'durf, (-ge-), dare; be game for; risk, venture; *'n TAAK ~,* have the courage to undertake a task; *'n TAAK nie ~ nie,* shrink from a task; *die VYAND ~,* dare to fight (oppose) the enemy.
aan'duur, (-ge-), continue.
aand: **~uur,** evening hour, vespertide; **~vergadering,** evening meeting (session); **~visite,** evening visit; **~vrede,** evening quiet (calm); **~wag,** evening watch; **~wandeling,** evening walk; **~wind,** night wind.
aaneen', (b) together, connected; (bw) consecutively, continuously; close together; *tien dae ~,* ten days at a stretch.
aaneen'bind, (-ge-), tie together.
aaneen'brei, (-ge-), knit together.
aaneen'flans, (-ge-), patch up; piece together; **~ing,** patching up; piecing together.
aaneen'geskakel, (-ge-), connected, concatenated; *~de KABELVERVOER,* endless haulage; *'n ~de VERHAAL,* a connected story.
aaneen'geslote, clannish; connected, serried, united; *~ geledere,* serried ranks.
aaneen'geslotenheid, clannishness; coherence.
aaneen'gesluit, clannish; connected, serried.
aaneen'giet, (-ge-), cast together (iron).
aaneen'groei, (-ge-), grow together, **~ing,** growing together.
aaneen'hang, (-ge-), adhere, cling to, hang together; *~ soos droë sand,* hang together like grains of sand.
aaneen'heg, (-ge-), fasten together, connect, link together, **~ting,** linking, fastening, connecting; conglutination.
aaneen'kitting, cementation.
aaneen'kleef, (-ge-), stick together.
aaneen'klink, (-ge-), clinch (clench) together; rivet.
aaneen'knoop, (-ge-), tie together.
aaneen'koek, (-ge-), stick together.
aaneen'koppel, (-ge-), couple; link together; **~ing,** coupling (linking) together.
aaneen'las, (-ge-), join (seam, stitch) together; **~sing,** joining, seaming, stitching.
aaneen'lopend, (-e), continuous.
aaneen'lym, (-ge-), glue together.
aaneen'mou, magyar sleeve.
aaneen'plak, (-ge-), glue (paste) together, conglutinate.

aaneen'rye, ..ryg, (-ge-), tack (string) together, baste.
aaneen'skakel, (-ge-), link together; interlink, connect up, link up, concatenate; **~end, (-e),** copulative; linked; **~ing,** concatenation, linkage, series; *'n ~ing van ongelukke,* a concatenation (series) of accidents.
aaneen'skryf, (-ge-), write in one (as one word); join up (letters).
aaneen'sluit, (-ge-), fit; link together; close, join, close the ranks; **~ing,** closing, joining, linking.
aaneen'smee, (-ge-), weld together.
aaneen'snoer, (-ge-), string together, link.
aaneen'soldeer, (-ge-), solder together.
aaneen'tabberd, one-piece dress.
aaneen'vleg, (-ge-), braid (plait, twist) together.
aaneen'voeg, (-ge-), put together, join, unite, connect.
aaneen'vries, (-ge-), regelate; **~ing,** regelation.
aan'erd, (-geërd), earth up (of plants), tump; **~ploeg,** tumping-plough.
aan'fiets, (-ge-), cycle along.
aan'fladder, (-ge-), flit (flutter) along.
aan'fluit, (-ge-), mock, flout, taunt; **~ing,** byword, taunt, mockery.
aan'frons, (-ge-), frown at.
aan'gaan, (-ge-), concern; begin; conclude, make (contract); enter (into an agreement); proceed, continue, go ahead, carry on; call (visit); tease; happen; *die BOER gaan goed aan,* the farmer is doing very well; *BY iem. ~,* call at somebody's; *Meneer, die KINDERS gaan met my aan,* Sir, the children are teasing me; *KOSTE ~,* incur expenses; *'n LENING ~,* negotiate a loan; *met 'n NOOI ~,* court a girl; *'n OOREENKOMS ('n huwelik) ~,* conclude an agreement (a marriage); *die SKOOL gaan om agtuur aan,* the school commences at eight o'clock; *SO kan dit nie ~ nie,* that won't do, that is (just) too much; *die kinders het VREESLIK aangegaan,* the children were very unruly; *WAT my ~,* as far as I am concerned; **~'de,** concerning, with reference to, as regards, regarding, anent; as for; **~plek,** visiting place, house (place) one visits.
aan'gaap, (-ge-), stare at, gape at; gaze.
aan'galop, (-ge-): *aangegalop kom,* come galloping along; come at a gallop.
aan'gang, commencement, beginning.
aan'gaper, (-s), gazer.
aan'gebede, adored, idolized, worshipped; **~ne, (-s),** adored one, idol.
aan'geblaas, aspirated; instigated.
aan'gebode, offered, proffered.
aan'gebonde: *kort ~,* short-tempered, irritable.
aan'gebore, innate, inborn, connate, connatural, constitutional; congenital (disease); natural (taste); native; *~ talent,* innate ability; *~ vermoë,* innate ability (competence).
aan'gebrand, (-e), burnt; quick-tempered, touchy; tipsy; discomfited.
aan'gedaan, moved, affected, touched; *diep ~ wees,* be deeply moved.
aan'gedrewe, driven; *elektries ~,* electrically driven (powered).
aan'gee, (s) (..geë), pass (rugby); (w) **(-ge-),** hand to, pass, reach, hand on; mention, notify (disease); allege (as reason); give notice; report (oneself); declare (customs); set (fashion); denote (meaning); *die MAAT ~,* mark the time, give the beat; *die PAS ~,* set the pace; *'n SAAK ~,* report a matter (case); lay information; denounce; *die TOON ~,* set the fashion (example, tone); **~beweging,** passing bout (movement) (rugby).
aan'geër, denunciator, informer; notifier; declarant; passer (sport).
aan'geërf, (-de), inherited.
aan'gegewe, given; stated, reported, recorded.
aan'gegroei, (-de), increased (population); accumulated (capital); grown.
aan'gehaal, (-de), quoted.
aan'geheg, (-de, -te), attached, affixed, adjunct; *die ~ te (~de) verslag (tjek),* the attached report (cheque).
aan'gehoudene, (-s), person arrested (held in custody); person in custody.

aan'gehuud, (..hude), related by marriage.
aan'gekap, (-te), tipsy; grieved.
aan'geklaagde, (-s), accused, defendant, prisoner at the bar.
aan'geklam, (-de), moistened; tipsy, tight, half intoxicated, squiffy, in one's cups, half-seas-over.
aan'gekomene, (-s), arrival; person who has arrived.
aan'gelê, (..legde), disposed, inclined; *musikaal* ~, with a bent (gift) for music.
aan'geleë, adjoining, adjacent.
aan'geleentheid, affair, concern, incident, matter; *'n saak van die GROOTSTE* ~, a matter of the greatest importance; *'n PRIVAAT (private)* ~, a private affair.
aan'geleer, (-de), acquired (by learning); *~ de refleks*, conditioned reflex.
aan'gemaak, (-te), prepared, made up (medicine); diluted.
aan'gemeet, (..mete), tailored, made to measure.
aan'genaam, (..name; ..namer, -ste), congenial, pleasant (circumstances), pleasurable, agreeable, comfortable; acceptable (gift); enjoyable (time); likeable (person); *..name KENNIS*, pleased to meet you; how do you do? how are you?; *jou by iem. ~ MAAK*, make yourself agreeable to a person; *'n ..name MENS*, an agreeable person; ~**heid**, pleasantness, agreeableness; pleasure, comfort.
aan'genome, (b), accepted (opinion); received (impression); approved (model); adscititious; adoptive; fictitious (name); adopted; *'n ~ kind*, an adopted child; ~! agreed, adopted!; (vgw), supposing, granted; ~ *dat dit waar is*, supposing it is true.
aan'gepak, (-te), coated, furred, furry (kettle).
aan'gepas, (-te), fitted; adapted; ~ *by*, conditioned to.
aan'geplant, (-e), planted; ~ *e weiding*, artificial pasture.
aan'gesetene, (-s), guest (at meal), diner.
aan'gesien, seeing that, as, whereas, since, considering, for as much as, in as much as; ~ *dit al so laat is, moet ons vertrek*, seeing that (as) it is so late, we must leave.
aan'gesig, (-te), face, countenance; *net van ~ KEN*, know by face only; *iem. met TWEE ~ te*, a double-faced person (double face); *VAN ~ tot ~*, face to face, personally; ~**senuwee**, facial nerve; ~**spyn**, face-ache, facial pain, neuralgia.
aan'gesit, put on, applied; crusted (wine); sharpened (razor); ~ *kom*, arrive unexpectedly.
aan'geskote, wounded (buck); tipsy, tight, slightly intoxicated.
aan'geskrewe, **aan'geskryf**, noted, reputed, known, estimated; *GOED (sleg) ~ staan*, be in good (bad) repute; *SLEG ~ staan by iem.*, be in someone's bad books.
aan'geskryf, (-de), charged; fined.
aan'geslaan, (..slane), coated, furred (with morbid matter); moistened; taxed, assessed; tarnished (copper); estimated (taxes); *hy het die BAL ~*, he has knocked-on the ball; *die pasiënt se TONG is ~*, the patient's tongue is furred.
aan'geslane, (-e), person assessed.
aan'geslote, joined, connected; affiliated; conjoint.
aan'gesnyde, cut; ~ *brood*, a married woman.
aan'gespe, ..**gesper**, (-ge-), buckle on, gird on.
aan'gespoel, (-de), alluvial; washed up.
aan'gesproke, addressed; ~**ne**, (-s), person addressed, addressee.
aan'gesteek, (-te), alight; infected; ~**te**, (-s), infected person.
aan'gestel, (-de), appointed; ~ *de argitek*, commissioned architect.
aan'gestorwe, inherited.
aan'getas, infected.
aan'geteken, (-de), noted, on record; registered (letter); ~ *wegstuur*, send by registered post.
aan'getrokke, attracted, charmed; *jou ~ voel tot*, feel attracted (drawn) to(wards).
aan'getroud, (-e), related by marriage; *'n ~ e BROER*, brother-in-law; ~ *e FAMILIE*, the in-laws, relatives by marriage.
aan'gevogtene, (-s), distressed person.

aan'gevreet, (..vrete), carious; corroded.
aan'gewaai: *êrens ~ kom*, turn up unexpectedly, hitch up.
aan'gewer, complainant; reporter.
aan gewese, obvious, right, proper, appropriate; ideal; ~ *OP*, committed to; *OP mekaar ~*, thrown on each other's company; *die ~ PERSOON*, the person delegated; the right person; *die ~ STAATSPRESIDENT*, the state president designate; *die ~ WEG*, the proper (obvious) course.
aan'gewing, information (to the police).
aan'gewys, dependent on; *hulle is op hulleself ~*, they are thrown on their own resources.
aan'gifte, (-s), declaration (customs); denunciation, denouncement; information; notification; entry (for a competition); ~ *doen van*, give notice of; declare (at customs).
aan'gluur, (-ge-), ogle, peep at, leer (at); look crossly at.
aan'gly, (-ge-), slip on; glide on.
aan'golf, ..**golwe**, (-ge-), come rolling (surging); billowing along.
aan'golwing, surging (billowing) (along).
aan'gons, (-ge-), come (go) buzzing along.
aan'gooi, (-ge-), fling along; level (a gun); cast (throw) against (to); *'n GEWEER op iem. ~*, take aim at somebody; *sy KLERE ~*, dress quickly.
aan'gord, (-ge-), gird (buckle) on; *jy MOET jou ~*, you must gird (up) your loins; *die WAPENS ~*, take up arms; ~**ing**, girding on (up).
aan'grens, (-ge-), border on, adjoin, be contiguous on.
aangren'send, (-e), adjacent, bordering on, adjoining, abutting, neighbouring, contiguous; ~ *e goed*, abutting properties.
aan'grensing, contiguity.
aan'groei, (-ge-), grow, swell; accrue, increase (profits); develop (business); redouble (efforts); *die been sal ~*, the bone will set; ~**end**, (-e), increasing, growing, accretive; ~**ing**, growth, increase; accretion; augmentation; waxing (moon); ~**sel**, accretion, increase, augmentation; grown part.
aan'gryns, (-ge-), grin (grimace) at; stare in the face; ~**ing**, grin, grimace.
aan'gryp, (-ge-), seize, catch hold of; attack, assail; stir (the heart); fasten upon (take hold of) (a pretext); *'n GELEENTHEID ~*, seize an opportunity; *iets met altwee HANDE ~*, jump at something; *die VYAND ~*, attack the enemy; ~**end**, (-e), touching, thrilling, moving, gripping, affecting (story); *'n ~ ende vertelling*, a touching tale; ~'**endheid**, impressiveness; ~**er**, (-s), attacker, assailant, aggressor; ~**ing**, embracement; attack; ~**ingspunt**, point of attack; point of application; abutment line.
aan'haak, (-ge-), hook on, fasten; hitch on; inspan; limber (cannon); ~**lyn**, line of hitch; ~**wa**, tender.
aan'haal, (-ge-), draw tighter, tauten, tighten; cajole, fondle, caress; quote; cite, adduce, instance (passages, cases); *BEWYSE ~*, produce proofs; *'n SKRYWER ~*, quote an author; *die TEUELS ~*, tighten the reins; *VERKEERD ~*, misquote.
aanha'l(er)ig, (-e), sweet, winning, attractive, caressive, cajoling, coaxing, cuddlesome; ~**heid**, winsomeness, cajolery, attractiveness, sweetness.
aan'haling, (-e, -s), citation, quotation, quoted passage (word); extract; ~**stekens**, quotation marks, inverted commas.
aan'hang, (s) followers, following; adherents, party, clique; dependency; adherence; *'n groot ~ hê*, have a large family; have a large following; (w) (-ge-), follow; hang on to, adhere to; append, attach; love; ~**er**, (-s), partisan, adherent, follower, hanger-on; votary, acolyte; water-shoot; ~'**ig**, (-e), pending; *'n SAAK ~ ig maak*, institute legal proceedings; bring up for consideration; ~ *ig WEES*, be under consideration, be sub judice; ~**motor**, outboard motor; ~**sel**, (-s), supplement, annexure, appendix; corollary; adjunct; dependence (state); affix *(gram.)*; appendage, appendant; codicil *(law)*; ~**wa**, trail car, trailer; side-car; ~**woonwa**, trailer caravan.

aanhank'lik, (-e), devoted, loyal (to throne); attached; clinging; ~**heid,** attachment, devotion; allegiance; adhesiveness.
aan'hardloop, (-ge-), run along; run faster.
aan'hark, (-ge-), rake along (up).
aan'hê, (..gehad), have on, wear.
aan'hef, (s), beginning, preamble, opening words (lines), exordium; intonation; *die* ~ *van 'n BRIEF,* the beginning of a letter; *die* ~ *van 'n WET,* the preamble of a law; (w), **(-ge-),** begin, set up, intone, intonate; strike up (a song); raise (a shout); *"hef aan" lê nog voor,* the greatest hurdle lies ahead.
aan'heg, (-ge-), affix, attach, fasten, adhibit; *die aangehegte kwitansie,* the attached receipt; ~**sel, (-s),** addendum; enclosure; affix, affixture; ~**ting,** adhibition, affixion; fixation, attachment; fastening; annexation (country); apposition; articulation; ~**tingspunt,** point of contact, juncture; ~**toestel,** attachment.
aan'help, (-ge-), help on with, assist, expedite; further (a cause); push.
aan'hink, (-ge-), hobble (limp) along.
aan'hits, (-ge-), incite, egg on, abet (a criminal); foment (discord); provoke bad blood; bait; halloo, set on (a dog); set by the ears; kindle (desires); instigate (a plot); stimulate (growth); ~**er, (-s),** abettor, instigator; setter-on; ~**ing, (-e, -s),** incitement, instigation, abetment, fomentation.
aan'hol, (-ge-), come running along; run faster; keep on running
aan'hoor, (-ge-), listen to; give a hearing to; ~**der, (-s),** listener, hearer.
aan'hore: *ten* ~ *van die hele klas,* in the presence (hearing) of the whole class.
aanho'rig, (-e), belonging (appertaining) to; dependent upon; ~**e, (-s),** retainer, dependant, servant; ~**heid,** appurtenance; dependence.
aan'hou, (-ge-), continue, insist, persist, persevere; keep (servants); arrest (a thief); challenge (by police); hold on (up); keep on (clothes); hold, sustain (a tone); *hou AAN!* hold the line! hang on! ~ *MET,* keep on with, persevere with; ~ *(met) SANIK,* keep on nagging; ~'**delik,** continual, repeated.
aanhou'dend, (b) (-e), perennial; continual, lasting, persistent, assiduous, insistent, persevering, continuous, incessant; (b, bw) continuously, constantly; *die* ~ *e DROOGTE,* the persistent drought; *hy LOL* ~ *met my,* he is constantly worrying me; ~ *e OPBRENGS,* sustained yield; *die* ~ *e slegte WEER,* the long spell of bad weather; ~**heid,** continuance, persistence; spell (weather).
aan'houding, holding up (of a ship); apprehension, detention, retention, arrest; continuance, persistence; hold-up (by robbers); ~**sbevel,** warrant for arrest; ~**sel,** detention cell; ~**stehuis,** home of detention.
aan'houer, (-s), perseverer; ~ *wen,* perseverance will be rewarded; dogged does it.
aan'houvermoë, perseverance.
aan'huppel, (-ge-), skip (hop) along; hop faster.
aan'hyg, (-ge-), come on panting.
aan'ja, ..jaag, (-ge-), hurry, urge, drive (oxen); bustle, drive on (people), hasten, hustle, hurry (on); supercharge, boost (an engine); *MOENIE my* ~ *nie,* don't hurry me; *iem. VREES* ~, intimidate (frighten) a person.
aan'ja(ag)druk, boost.
aanja(ag)masjien, (-e), booster, booster engine.
aan'ja(ag)pomp, (-e), booster pump.
aan'jaer, (-s), inciter, driver, booster, supercharger; starter (electr.).
aan'jaging, supercharging.
aan'kalk, (-ge-), fur (kettle); charge (account).
aan'kant, (-ge-): *hom* ~ *teen,* oppose; ~**ing,** opposition.
aankant', (b), neat.
aan'kap, (s) interference; (w) **(-ge-),** chafe; overreach, cut, click, interfere (with a horse); *die perd kap aan,* the horse interferes; ~**knieë,** knock-knees; *met* ~*knieë,* knock-kneed; ~**kussinkie,** hoof-pad; ~**plek,** crepance; ~**yster,** knocked-up shoe.

aan'karwei, (-ge-), transport (goods).
aan'keer, (-ge-), drive on; gather (people); round up (criminals); divert (water).
aan'kla, ..klaag, (-ge-), accuse, denounce, prefer a charge, charge with, arraign, indict, impeach; delate; *iem.* ~ *weens diefstal,* charge someone with theft.
aan'klaagbaar, (..bare), accusable, impeachable.
aan'klaagster, (-s), *vroulik van* **aanklaer.**
aan'klaer, (-s), accuser, complainant, impeacher, plaintiff; denouncer; prosecutor; *OPENBARE* ~, public prosecutor; ~ *WEES,* be plaintiff.
aan'klag, (-te), accusation, count, charge, indictment, impeachment, plaint, arraignment; action; presentment; delation; denouncement; *'n* ~ *INDIEN teen,* lodge (lay) a complaint against; *OP* ~ *van,* on a charge of; ~**akte,** charge sheet; ~**kantoor,** charge office.
aan'klam, (s) casing (tobacco); (w) **(-ge-),** moisten; condition (a tobacco leaf); become damp; intoxicate, make tipsy; *hy is aangeklam,* he is tipsy; ~**kelder,** conditioning cellar (tobacco).
aan'klamp, (-ge-), fasten with a clamp; board (a vessel); accost; *BY iem.* ~, cling to someone, sponge upon someone; accost, solicit for; *by 'n NOOI* ~, make love to a girl.
aan'klamtert, tipsy tart.
aan'klap, (-ge-), switch on; hurry up; increase (cattle).
aan'kleding, clothing, make-up, get-up; drapery; way of presenting, presentation, stage setting.
aan'klee(d), (-ge-), dress, attire, clothe, array; make up; present.
aan'kleef, ..klewe, (-ge-), stick to, adhere to, cling to, be attached to; *baie gebreke kleef hom aan,* he has many failings; ~**sel,** that which adheres; ..**klewer, (-s),** adherent; ..**klewing,** adhesion.
aan'klink, (-ge-), clinch, rivet; touch (glasses).
aan'klop, (-ge-), knock, beat on (at); appeal to; *by iem.* ~ *om geld,* apply to someone for money.
aan'klots, (-ge-), beat, dash (against).
aan'knip, (-ge-), click, switch on (electricity); cut on.
aan'knoop, (-ge-), button on; fasten, enter into; tie on to; establish (relations); open (negotiations); *ONDERHANDELINGE* ~, enter into negotiations; *'n PRAATJIE* ~, begin a conversation; ..**knoping,** linking up; ..**knopingspunt,** point of contact, starting point; joint.
aan'knyp(hoef)yster, feather-edged (horse)shoe.
aan'koling, carbonization.
aan'kom, (-ge-), arrive, come (on, along), approach, get at; acquire, obtain; drop in; call (on friends); be born (lambs); touch (with hands); *dit kom daar nie op AAN nie,* it does not matter; *BETYDS* ~, arrive in time; *as dit DAAROP* ~, when it comes to the push; *as dit daarop* ~, *kan hy dit DOEN,* if it comes to a pinch, he can do it; *met 'n EIS* ~, put forward a claim; *dit sal nie op GELD* ~ *nie,* money will be no object; *dit kom net op GOUIGHEID aan,* swiftness is the only thing required; *met 'n KLAG* ~, make a complaint; *iets SIEN* ~, see something coming, foresee something; *met allerhande VRAE* ~, come up with all kinds of questions; *te VROEG* ~, arrive too early; ~**de, aankomende,** coming; ~**eling, (-e),** comer, newcomer, beginner; ~**ende,** coming, incoming, prospective; next, following; budding (author); ~**ende (aankomde) MAAND,** next month; ~**ende ONDERWYSER,** prospective teacher; ~**ende TREIN,** approaching (incoming) train; ~**er,** arrival, newcomer; ~**plek,** place of destination; ~**s,** arrival; ~**shawe,** port of arrival; ~**stryd,** time of arrival.
aan'kondig, (-ge-), announce, publish, inform, presage, previse, notify; advertise, herald, portend, harbinger; review (a book); gazette; declare; adumbrate, foreshadow; annunciate; ~**er, (-s),** announcer, compère; reviewer; advertiser; ~**ing, (-e, -s),** announcement, notification; review (of book); advertisement; annunciation; hue.
aan'kool, (-ge-), carbonize.
aan'koop, (s) purchase; *BY* ~, when purchasing; *my NUWE* ~, my new acquisition (purchase); *VERKRY deur* ~, acquired by purchase; (w) **(-ge-),**

purchase, buy; acquire; ~ **koers**, purchasing price; buying rate (shares); ~ **koste**, buying expenses; ~ **opdrag**, instructions to buy; ~ **prys**, purchase price; ~ **som**, purchase price; ~ **waarde**, cost price.
aan′**koper**, purchaser, buyer.
aan′**koppel**, (-ge-), couple; join; leash; ~ **ing**, coupling.
aan′**kors**, (-ge-), form a crust, encrust; ~ **ting**, encrustation.
aan′**krui(e)**, (-ge-), bring on (in a wheelbarrow); struggle along; saunter along.
aan′**kruip**, (-ge-), crawl along; *teen iem.* ~ , nestle close to someone.
aan′**kry**, (-ge-), get on (clothing, etc.); get to burn (fire).
aan′**kuier**, (-ge-), saunter along; continue visiting.
aan′**kweek**, (-ge-), cultivate, grow, rear, raise; foster, nurture; foment; *'n goeie gewoonte* ~, cultivate a good habit; ~ **baar**, (. . **bare**), cultivable, growable; . . **kweker**, grower; . . **kweking**, cultivation, culture, growing, raising.
aan′**kwispel**, (-ge-): *aangekwispel kom*, come along fawning (wagging the tail).
aan′**kyk**, (-ge-), look at; face; *iem. NIE* ~ *nie*, cut someone; *iem. SKEEF* ~, look askance at a per= son; ~ **enswaardig**, (-e), worth seeing; ~ **er**, specta= tor, onlooker.
aan′**laat**, (-ge-), leave on; leave burning.
aan′**lag**, (-ge-), favour; smile on; *die fortuin lag hom aan*, fortune smiles on him.
aan′**land**, (-ge-), land, arrive; *ÊRENS onverwags* ~, find oneself somewhere unexpectedly; *niem. weet WAAR hy sal* ~ *nie*, no one (goodness) knows what will become of him; ~ **ing**, arrival, landing.
aan′**lap**, (-ge-), sew on, patch on; impose on.
aan′**las**, (-ge-), join, attach, dove-tail; exaggerate; em= broider (a tale); ~ **sing**, (-e, -s), joining, joint; at= tached part; ~ **tafel**, extension table.
aan′**lê** (-ge-), aim at, point (a rifle); apply (a bandage); address (a ball); lay (a cable, fire); take aim, level (a gun); moor, berth (a boat); plant (in a garden); plan, lay out (a township); build (a road); court (a girl); install, place in position for use; ~ *met 'n GEWEER*, take aim; *by 'n NOOI* ~, court a girl; *MUSIKAAL aangelê wees*, have a talent for music; *PRAKTIES aangelê wees*, be of a practical disposi= tion; *'n SPOORWEG* ~, construct a railway; *'n TUIN* ~, lay out a garden; *dit VERKEERD* ~, set about it the wrong way; *'n VUUR* ~, lay (set) a fire; *WATER* ~, lay on water; install water; ~ **er**, fitter; instigator, originator; plaintiff; builder, founder, constructor.
aan′**leer**, (-ge-), learn, acquire; master (language); continue one's studies; *'n aangeleerde smaak*, an ac= quired taste; ~ **der**, learner.
aan′**lees**, (-ge-), read further; continue reading.
aan′**leg**, (. . **lêe**, -te, -gings, -ginge), plan, arrangement, design (of a house); layout, construction, plan, groundplan (of a house); talent, (pre)disposition; quality; bent, flair, aptitude, capability; installa= tion (of a machine); ~ *hê vir musiek*, have a natural bent for music.
aan′**lêgeld**, jettage, quayage, wharfage.
aan′**legger**, (-s), plaintiff; originator.
aan′**leghawe**, . . **lêhawe**, (-ns), port of call.
aan′**leg**: ~ **kaai**, quay; ~ **mas**, mooring-mast; ~ **paal**, dolphin, bollard.
aan′**legplek**, . . **lêplek**, landing-stage, pier, jetty, moorage; place frequently visited.
aan′**leg**: ~ **steier**, landing-stage; ~ **toets**, aptitude test; ~ **vee**, foundation stock; ~ **verklikker**, aim correc= tor.
aan′**lei**, (-ge-), lead to, induce; cause; ~ **dend**, (-e), contributory, contributive; ~ *dende oorsaak*, pri= mary cause.
aan′**leiding**, (-e, -s), cause, reason, motive; call; pro= vocation; ~ *GEE tot*, give rise to, occasion; *by die GERINGSTE* ~, for the slightest reason; at the slightest provocation; *NA* ~ *van*, with reference to, in connection with; *SONDER die minste* ~, with= out the slightest provocation.
aan′**lêkoste**, cost of installation.

aan′**lêmas**, mooring mast.
aan′**leng**, (-ge-), dilute, weaken (whisky); become longer.
aan′**lêpaal**, . . **pale**, *see* **aanlegpaal**.
aan′**lêplaas**, . . **plek**, *see* **aanlegplek**.
aan′**leun**, (-ge-), lean against; *hom iets nie laat* ~ *nie*, not take something lying down; ~ **ing**, leaning against; ~ **ingspunt**, point of support.
aan′**lig**, (-ge-), dawn; clear up.
aanlig′**gend** (-e), adjacent, adjoining, contiguous; next to; ~ *e hoek*, adjacent angle.
aan′**lok**, (-ge-), attract, charm, invite; inveigle, de= coy, entice, (al)lure; tout; tempt; ~ **ker**, enticer, charmer, inveigler; ~ **king**, allure(ment), entice= ment, attraction; ~ **'lik**, attractive, charming, allur= ing, enticing, seductive, inviting; *'n* ~ *like vooruit= sig*, an attractive prospect; ~ **'likheid**, allurement, enticement, charm, attractiveness; ~ **sel**, decoy, bait, allurement, lure.
aan′**lonk**, (-ge-), ogle, smile at, make eyes at.
aan′**loop**, (s), patronage, custom (business); rush (on a trench); take-off, land (aeroplane); introduction, beginning, preamble; *hierdie winkel het 'n GOEIE* ~, this shop is well patronized; *'n GROOT* ~ *hê*, have many visitors, be well patronized; *'n* ~ *NEEM*, take off (a plane); take a run (for the long jump); (w), (-ge-), go on walking; walk faster; call in passing; *AGTER iem.* ~, follow someone; *IN Kaapstad* ~, put into Cape Town harbour; *agter MEISIES* ~, run after girls; *TEEN iem.* ~, run into someone; *loop 'n bietjie aan by die WINKEL*, please call at the shop; ~ **baan**, runway (aero= plane); ~ **hawe**, port of call; ~ **kleur**, annealing colour; ~ **lig**, approach light; ~ **plank**, spring board; ~ **plek**, visiting place; ~ **sprong**, flying jump.
aan′**luister**, (-ge-), listen to.
aan′**lym**, (-ge-), glue on; impose on.
aan′**maak**, (s) making, manufacture, fabrication; (w) (-ge-), prepare, mix (paint); lay (set, start) (a fire); dress; *MEDISYNE* ~, make up a prescription; *aangemaakte VERF*, ready-mixed paint; ~ **goed**, ingredients; ~ **hout**, dry twigs for starting a fire, kindling; ~ **sel**, mixture.
aan′**maan**, (-ge-), warn, admonish, exhort; dun (for payment); *tot betaling* ~, press for payment.
aan′**maker**, mixer; primer.
aan′**manend**, (-e), hortative, hortatory.
aan′**maning**, (-e, -s), warning, (ex)hortation, re= minder (to pay), (legal) demand; relapse, touch, recurrence (of a disease); *'n* ~ *om te BETAAL*, a reminder to pay; *GEREGTELIKE* ~, judicial summons; *'n* ~ *van PERDESIEKTE*, a recurrence of horse-sickness; *SONDER voorafgaande* ~, without any previous demand; *'n* ~ *van TAND= PYN*, a twinge of toothache; ~ **sbrief**, letter of demand.
aan′**mars**, (s) advance, approach (by marching).
aan′**marsjeer**, (-ge-), march on; march faster; advance.
aan′**marslyn**, line of advance.
aan′**matig**, (-ge-), arrogate to oneself; lay claim to, presume, pretend, usurp; assume; *jou 'n oordeel* ~, presume to give an opinion; ~ **end**, (-e), presump= tuous, proud-hearted, pretending, pretentious, ar= rogant, high-handed, hoity-toity, overbearing, pre= suming, assumptive, assuming; dogmatic; haughty; ~ **ing**, (-e, -s), presumption, pretentiousness, arro= gance, haughtiness; arrogation; assumption; self-assertion.
aan′**meet**, (-ge-), measure on to; *jou 'n PAK laat* ~, have a suit made (to measure); *'n aangemete PAK klere*, a made-to-measure suit.
aan′**mekaar**, together; connected; consecutively, continuously; ~ *PRAAT*, talk continuously; ~ *SKRYF*, write without a break; ~ *STAAN*, stand close together; *die TWEE is* ~, the two are fighting (are at it); *tien jaar* ~ *WERK*, work for ten years without leave.
aanmekaar′**bind**, (-ge-), tie together.
aanmekaar′**bly**, (-ge-), stick (remain) together.
aanmekaar′**brei**, (-ge-), knit together.

aanmekaar'giet, (-ge-), cast together (steel).
aanmekaar'groei, (-ge-), grow together.
aanmekaar'haak, (-ge-), hook together.
aanmekaar'hang, (-ge-), hang together; *soos droë sand* ~, hang together like grains of sand.
aanmekaar'heg, (-ge-), fasten (link) together.
aanmekaar'huis, semi-detached house, townhouse.
aanmekaar'kleef, ..**klewe**, (-ge-), stick (cling) together.
aanmekaar'klink, (-ge-), rivet, clinch together.
aanmekaar'klou, (-ge-), cling together, cleave to one another.
aanmekaar'knoop, (-ge-), tie (fasten) together.
aanmekaar'koek, (-ge-), stick together; ~**erig**, (-e), matted; cliquish.
aanmekaar'koppel, (-ge-), couple (link) together, concatenate.
aanmekaar'lap, (-ge-), piece together; fake, fudge.
aanmekaar'las, (-ge-), join together; mortise (wood); weld (metal).
aanmekaar'loop, (-ge-), form a whole; come to blows, clash.
aanmekaar'lym (-ge-), glue (paste) together.
aanmekaar'naai, (-ge-), sew (stitch) together.
aanmekaar'pak, combination suit.
aanmekaar'plak, (-ge-), glue (paste) together.
aanmekaar'pleister, (-ge-), plaster together.
aanmekaar'raak, (-ge-), start fighting (quarreling), come to blows.
aanmekaar'rok = **aanmekaartabberd**.
aanmekaar'rye, ..**ryg**, (-ge-), string (beads); baste, tack together (clothing).
aanmekaar'ryging, stringing together (of sentences).
aanmekaar'sit, (-ge-), put together, frame up, piece together; cause a fight.
aanmekaar'skakel, (-ge-), link together, concatenate; ~**ing**, concatenation (ideas).
aanmekaar'skryf, ..**skrywe**, (-ge-), write in one (as one word); join up (letters).
aanmekaar'sluit, (-ge-), close, join; close the ranks.
aanmekaar'smee(d), (-ge-), weld together.
aanmekaar'spring, (-ge-), start fighting, come to blows.
aanmekaar'spyker, (-ge-), nail together.
aanmekaar'tabberd, one-piece frock (dress).
aanmekaar'voeg, (-ge-), join (put) together, join, dovetail, mortise.
aanmekaar'vries, (-ge-), regelate, freeze together.
aanmekaar'werk, (-ge-), sew together.
aan'meld, (-ge-), announce, report; *jou vir 'n EKSAMEN* ~, enter for an examination; *jou LAAT* ~, send in your name (card), have yourself announced; ~**bare siekte**, notifiable disease.
aan'melding, (-e, -s), announcement, notice.
aan'merk, (-ge-), remark, observe, note; find fault with; *as 'n BELEDIGING* ~, consider an insult; *DAAR is niks op aan te merk nie*, no fault can be found with that; ~**enswaardig**, (-e), worthy of comment, worthy of consideration; **-erig**, (-e), fault-finding, captious.
aan'merking, (-e, -s), remark, comment; criticism; objection; arraignment, consideration; *in* ~ *KOM*, be considered; *hy KOM nie in* ~ *vir die betrekking nie*, he is not being considered for the position; *in* ~ *KOM vir pensioen*, qualify for a pension; *'n* ~ *MAAK op iets*, make a remark about something; *in* ~ *NEEM*, take into consideration; *UIT* ~ *van*, in consideration of.
aanmerk'lik, (b) (-e), considerable, notable (rise); (bw) **materially**; appreciably; ~ *e prysverhoging*, considerable rise in price; ~**heid**, importance.
aanmin'lik, (-e), charming, amiable, lovable, winning; ~**heid**, loveliness, charm.
aanmin'nig, (-e) = **aanminlik**.
aan'moedig, (-ge-), encourage, promote; foment, countenance (revolt); support morally, favour, lead on, tempt; animate; embolden; elate; fortify; hearten; ~**end**, (-e), encouraging; ~**er**, (-s), inspirer, encourager; ~**ing**, (-e, -s), encouragement; animation; fomentation; comfort; ~**ingsbonus**, incentive bonus; ~**ingsprys**, consolation prize.

aan'monster, (-ge-), enrol(l), enlist; sign on, recruit; ~**ing**, enlistment, enrolment, recruitment.
aan'munt, (-ge-), coin, mint, monetize; ~**ing**, coining, coinage, milling, minting; ~**ingskoste**, cost of coining.
aan'naai, (-ge-), sew on.
aan'name, (-s), acceptance; passing (bill of parliament); supposition; presupposition.
aan'neem, (-ge-), accept (situation); adopt (a child); assume airs (bearing); presuppose, presume; receive; admit (a statement); carry (a motion); make a contract (for work); take on (work); embrace (a religion); confirm (a new member); take (a name); engage (an expert); pass (a bill); espouse (a cause); affiliate (as a member); *ALGEMEEN word aangeneem*, it is generally believed; *die CHRISTENDOM* ~, embrace Christianity; *'n vriendelike HOUDING* ~, adopt a friendly attitude; *sy word aangeneem (in die KERK)*, she will be confirmed; *tot KIND* ~, adopt as child; *die NOTULE* ~, take the minutes as read, confirm the minutes; *'n OPDRAG* ~, undertake a commission; *dit word as REËL aangeneem*, it is generally accepted, it has the rule of force; *ek wil* ~ *dat dit SO is*, I assume that it is so; ~**'baar**, (..**bare**), acceptable, adoptable, assumable; ~**'lik**, (-e), acceptable, credible, plausible; reasonable (terms); admissible; accommodating; receivable; likely (story); ~**'likheid**, acceptability, credibility, reasonableness, plausibility, eligibility; ~**som**, contract price; ~**toets**, acceptance test; ~**tyd**, time allowed for acceptance; time for confirmation; ~**werk**, contract work.
aan'nemeling, (-e), candidate for confirmation.
aan'nemer, (-s), recipient; contractor; undertaker; accepter; *God is geen* ~ *v.d. persoon nie*, God is no respecter of persons; ~**saak**, contractor's (contracting) business; ~**sfirma**, firm of contractors, contractor, contracting firm.
aan'neming, acceptance, adoption (proposal); assumption; admission; affiliation; carriage (proposal); confirmation (church); passing, passage (bill); *by* ~, by contract.
aan'nemings: ~**diens**, confirmation service; ~**tabberd**, confirmation dress; ~**voorwaardes**, terms of contract.
aan'pak, (-ge-), seize, grip, take hold of; handle, take in hand; embark (on); engage, grapple; tackle (difficult work); attack (an enemy); encrust, fur, form a crust; adhere to; lay, pack, make, start (a fire); *'n aangepakte TONG*, a furred tongue; *'n saak VERKEERD* ~, set about a matter in the wrong way; *hy WEET van* ~, he knows how to tackle a thing; he is a hard worker; ~**king**, embarkation (on a scheme); attack; encrustation; ~**sel**, (-s), layer (of dirt, etc.), sediment, furring, coating, concretion; crust, encrustation, encrustment, incrustation; ~ *sel op tande*, tartar, plaque.
aan'pap, (-ge-): *met 'n meisie* ~, pick up a girl, flirt with a girl.
aan'pas, (-ge-), try on, fit (clothes), adapt (adjust) oneself; match; accommodate; acclimatize; *'n mens moet jou* ~ *by die OMSTANDIGHEDE*, one must adapt oneself to circumstances; *aangepaste TEENSTAND*, matched impedance; ~**baar**, (..**bare**), adaptable, adjustable; ~**kamer**, fitting-room; ~**send**, (-e), accommodating; ~**sing**, (-e, -s), matching; adaptation, conformation, adjustment; accommodation; acclimatization.
aan'passings: ~**klousule**, escalator clause; ~**leer**, adaptation theory, theory of adaptation; ~**proses**, process of adaptation, adaptation process; ~**vermoë**, adaptability; accommodation (of the eye).
aan'peil, (-ge-), home; start home (pigeons); direct by radio; ~ *op iets*, go in the direction of something; ~**baken**, homing beacon; ~**er**, homing device; ~**instink**, homing instinct; ~**stasie**, homing station; ~**toestel**, homing device; ~**wys(t)er**, homing indicator.
aan'piekel, (-ge-), carry with difficulty; go (move) laboriously; *die ou vroutjie moet alleen* ~ *met haar swaar sak*, the old lady must struggle on alone with her heavy bag.

aan'piets (-ge-), whip up.
aan'plak, (-ge-), post (up); stick (bills); placard; ~**biljet**, posting-bill, bill, poster, placard; ~**bord**, notice-board, billboard, hoarding; ~**ker**, poster, bill-sticker; ~**king**, affixing, pasting on.
aan'plant, (s), planting; plantation, (w), **(-ge-)**, plant, cultivate; add (by planting); ~**er**, planter, cultivator; ~**ing**, cultivation, planting; plantation; ~**koste**, cost of planting, planting costs.
aan'pleister, (-ge-), continue plastering; stick against, plaster to; apply copiously.
aan'ploeg, (-ge-), continue ploughing; add by ploughing.
aan'pluk, (-ge-), slip (put) on quickly (clothes).
aan'pomp, (-ge-), pump further; nudge.
aan'por, (-ge-), prod, rouse, urge, press, ginger up; instigate; egg on, arouse, actuate; stir up (a fire); ~**der, (-s)**, inciter, instigator; urger; ~**ring**, stimulation; instigation; rousing.
aan'pos, (-ge-), forward by post.
aan'praat, (-ge-): IEM. ~, rebuke someone; *iem. IETS ~*, talk someone into buying (believing, doing) something.
aan'preek, (-ge-), recommend; palm off; continue preaching.
aanpresenta'sie, (-s), offer.
aan'presenteer, (-ge-), offer, proffer; volunteer.
aan'prikkel, (-ge-), stimulate, goad on; ~**ing**, stimulation.
aan'prys, (-ge-), (re)commend, puff, extol, eulogize; *goeie ware prys homself aan*, good wine needs no bush; ~**er, (-s)**, praiser, extoller, eulogist; ~**ing, (-e, -s)**, commendation, eulogy, extolment, praising.
aan'punt, (-ge-), point, sharpen (a pencil).
aan'raai, (-ge-), advise, counsel, recommend, assuade; persuade; advocate; *ek wil jou sterk (dringend) ~ om*, I wish to urge (advise), persuade you earnestly to.
aanraai'ing = aanrading.
aan'raak, (-ge-), touch on, allude to; handle.
aan'rading, (-e, -s), advice; suggestion; *op jou ~*, on your advice.
aan'raking, (-e, -s), touch, contact; contiguity; *in persoonlike ~ BLY met*, keep in personal contact with; *in ~ BRING*, put into contact; *in ~ KOM met*, get in touch with; *geen PUNTE van ~ hê nie*, have nothing in common.
aan'rakings: ~**lyn**, pitch-line; contact line, line of contact; ~**punt**, point of contact; ~**veiligheid**, protection against accidental contact.
aan'rand, (-ge-), attack, assault, assail; outrage; invade; *iem. se eer ~*, impugn someone's honour; ~**er, (-s)**, assaulter, assailant, aggressor; invader; ~**ing, (-e, -s)**, assault, aggression; outrage; invasion; *'n ~ ing pleeg*, commit an assault.
aan'reg, (s) (-te), (kitchen) dresser, counter; set (prepared) table; (w), **(-ge-)**, serve up; *'n maaltyd ~*, prepare a dinner; ~**bank**, dresser, slab; preparing table; ~**kamer**, servery.
aan'reik, (-ge-), reach, pass, hand on.
aan'reken, (-ge-), blame for, lay to one's charge; credit; *dit sal my aangereken word*, I shall be blamed (held responsible) for this.
aan'rig, (-ge-), cause (damage); commit (wrong), do; prepare (a meal); *SKADE ~*, cause damage; *WAT het jy nou aangerig?* what have you done now? ~**ter, (-s)**, perpetrator; ~**ting**, causation, perpetration.
aan'roei, (-ge-), row along (on); row faster, keep on rowing, row against.
aan'roep, (s), (-e), call, challenge; (w) **(-ge-)**, invoke (the deity); call upon (a person); challenge (a passer-by); ~**er, (-s)**, invoker; ~**ing**, call, hail; invocation; challenge.
aan'roer, (-ge-), touch upon, allude to, hint at, mention (a subject); stir up; whip up (horses), hasten; *hy het die SAAK net so effentjies aangeroer*, he only made a slight allusion to the matter; *altyd dieselfde SAAK ~*, be continually harping on the same string; *'n tere SNAAR ~*, touch a sensitive spot; ~**ing**, mention.

aan'rol, (-ge-), roll along, roll towards.
aan'ruis, (-ge-), approach with a rustling sound.
aan'ruk, (-ge-), advance (forces); pull towards, tumble into; pull on forcibly (clothes); *die vyand het aangeruk*, the enemy advanced; ~**king**, advance.
aan'ry, (-ge-), drive (ride) faster; move, ride (drive) on; convey, bring (by car, truck); *ÊRENS ~*, touch in at, stop somewhere; *aangery KOM*, come riding (driving) along; *TEEN iets ~*, crash (drive, ride) into something; *TEEN iem. ~*, run into someone; ~**ding**, faster driving; conveyance, vehicle.
aan'rye, ..ryg, (-ge-), string (beads); lace up (boots); baste, tack (a dress).
aan'rykafee, road-house, drive-in café, drive-in.
aans, presently; perhaps; ~ *DINK hy dat ek dom is*, he would really think that I am stupid; *EK kom ~ weer*, I shall be back in a minute.
aan'saag, (-ge-), begin (continue) sawing; saw more quickly; run along.
aan'sê, (-ge-), announce, inform, notify, give notice; order, call upon; call (to arms); ~**brief**, written notice; ~**er, (-s)**, announcer; call-boy, page.
aan'segging, (-e, -s), notice, announcement, notification; order.
aan'seil, (-ge-), keep on sailing; sail faster; sail towards, make for; *aangeseil kom*, come sailing along; ~**ing**, collision (of yachts); ~**ingskade**, collision damage.
aan'send, (-ge-), forward, dispatch; ~**ing**, dispatch; expedition.
aan'set: ~**sel**, concretion, coating, crust; addition, extension piece; ~**skroef**, feedscrew; ~**ter**, instigator, inciter; ~**ting**, sharpening; starting; accretion; instigation.
aan'sien, (s), appearance; respect, credit, honour, note, prestige, distinction; esteem; consideration; *HOOG in ~ wees*, be highly respected; *ek KEN hom van ~*, I know him by sight; *'n MAN van ~*, a man of distinction; *dit gee die SAAK 'n ander ~*, that puts another complexion on the matter: *SONDER ~ des persoons*, without regard to persons; *UIT ~ van*, in view of; *TEN ~ van*, with regard to, regarding; (w) **(-ge-)**, look at; hold, regard; tolerate, put up with; *uit die HOOGTE ~*, look down upon; *ons MOES dit maar so ~*, we had to tolerate it; *iem. ‒ VIR*, mistake someone for; *WAARVOOR sien jy my aan?* what do you take me for? ~**'lik, (-e)**, respectable, honourable, notable; handsome; distinguished; personable; considerable, appreciable; great; ~*like FAMILIES*, notable (of, well-to-do) families; ~*like SKADE*, considerable damage; ~**'likes**, aristocracy; people of high standing; notable persons; nobility; ~**'likheid**, importance; handsomeness; distinction; considerableness (of a sum).
aan'sies = aans.
aan'sig, (-te), view, aspect; elevation (drawing).
aan'sirkel, escribed (described) circle.
aan'sit, (-ge-), sit down (at table); put on (a ring); actuate; instigate (an action); incite, egg on (dogs); set, strop (a razor); collar (a mine shaft); start (a motor); switch on; form a crust; begin to grow; *GEWIG ~*, put on weight; *êrens aangesit KOM*, turn up, arrive unexpectedly; ~**blad**, tarmac, apron (aerodrome); ~**bout**, thrust screw; ~**buis**, branch tube; ~**(druk)knop**, starter button; ~**ete**, formal (sit-down) dinner; ~**kraan**, starting cock; ~**magneet**, starting magneto; ~**masjien**, starting machine; ~**motor**, starting motor; self-starter; ~**pyp**, branch pipe; ~**riem**, (razor) strop; ~**sleutel**, ignition key; ~**slinger**, starting (crank) handle; ~**span**, starting crew; ~**sproeier**, starting jet; ~**staal**, steel sharpener (knife); ~**steen**, hone; ~**tafel**, dining-table; ~**tende, (-s)**, guest; ~**ter**, instigator, promptor; guest; sharpener, strop; starter self-starter (engine); rammer (gun); ~**toestel**, starting gear; ~**vyl**, safe-edge file; ~**weerstand**, starting resistance; ~**wiel**, starting wheel.
aan'sjou, (-ge-), haul (drag) along.
aan'skaf, (-ge-), procure, obtain, provide oneself with, acquire, purchase, buy, secure; ~**fer, (-s)**, procurer, provider, buyer; ~**fing**, acquisition, pro-

curing, buying, purchase, obtaining; ~**fingskoste**, initial outlay; ~**fingswaarde**, initial value.
aan'skakel, (-ge-), switch on, flick on; connect.
aan'skel, *(ong.)*, (-ge-), ring (doorbell).
aan'skerp, (-ge-), sharpen; intensify.
aan'skeur, (-ge-), begin to tear; tear further.
aan'skiet, (-ge-), throw on (clothes); slip on (coat); approach quickly; *sy verbeelding sal vleuels* ~ , his imagination will soar.
aan'skoffel, (-ge-), hoe on; dance on.
aan'skommel, (-ge-), waddle along; shake on (along).
aanskou', (~), see, look at, contemplate, view, eye, behold; *die LEWENSLIG* ~, be born; *TEN* ~*e van*, in the presence of; ~**baar**, (..**bare**), visible; ~**enswaardig'**, (-e), worth seeing; ~**er**, (-s), onlooker, spectator, eye-witness.
aanskou'ing, (-e, -s), contemplation, view; *innerlike* ~ , intuition.
aanskou'ings: ~**les**, object lesson; ~**onderwys**, object lesson, object teaching; ~**vermoë**, intuitive faculty (power).
aanskou'lik, (-e), visible, perceptible; graphic(al); spectacular; ~*e ONDERWYS*, object lesson, object teaching; '*n* ~*e TEKENING*, vivid (realistic) portrayal; ~ *VOORSTEL*, illustrate; ~**heid**, clearness, vividness, perceptibility; ~**heidshalwe**, for the sake of clearness.
aan'skraap, (-ge-), scrape nearer; sue (a person), summon.
aan'skroef, ..**skroewe**, (-ge-), screw on; *iem.* ~ , put the screw on someone.
aan'skry, (-ge-), stride on; *die* ~ *dende ouderdom*, approaching old age.
aan'skryf, ..**skrywe**, (-ge-), notify, send a letter of demand; keep on writing; escribe, describe (circle); *hy staan goed (sleg) aangeskryf (aangeskrewe) by my*, he is in my good (bad) books.
aan'skrywing, (-e, -s), notification, letter of demand; summons, writ.
aan'skuif, ..**skuiwe**, (-ge-), push (shove) on (nearer); draw up (chair).
aan'skyn, appearance, look; face.
aan'slaan, (s) (..**slane**), knock-on; (w) (-ge-), touch; start (an engine); overreach, interfere, click (a horse); tarnish (copper); strike (a note); assume (a pose); assess (tax); estimate; salute; knock on (rugby); knock against (something); flick on; switch on (an electric light); put up, nail up (a notice); become furred (the tongue); fur (a kettle); put on (a brake); hit; *vir R500 BELASTING* ~ , have your taxes assessed at R500; *jy slaan sy bekwaamheid te HOOG aan*, you overestimate his ability; *die RUITE is aangeslaan*, the panes (windows) are misted over; ~ *TEEN*, strike against; *die regte TOON* ~ , strike the right note; *'n ander TOON* ~ , sing another (smaller) tune; *'n hoë TOON* ~ , ride (mount) the high horse; ~**speletjie**, touch (game).
aan'slaer, (-s), assessor.
aan'slag, (..**slae**), stroke; attempt, attack (on life); touch (in music); rating, assessment (income tax); coating, deposit (on teeth); fur, furring, sediment, scale (of kettle); appearance (of plants); mildew (on plants); click (of heels); rabbet; impact (of a bullet); *'n* ~ *op iem. se EER*, an attack on somebody's honour; *'n* ~ *op iem. se LEWE*, an attack on someone's life; *'n* ~ *op 'n REKORD maak*, attempt to beat a record; ~**beampte**, assessor, assessing official; ~**bedrag**, amount assessed; ~**biljet**, notice of assessment; ~**jaar**, year of assessment; ~**kommissie**, assessment committee; ~**pen**, stop pin; ~**plaat**, striking plate, ~**waarneming**, spotting (by aeroplane).
aan'sleep, (-ge-), drag along (further).
aan'slenter, (-ge-), saunter along.
aan'sleur, (-ge-), drag along; make little progress.
aan'slib, (-ge-), silt up (soil, mud); accrete; ~**bing**, (-e, -s), alluvial soil (deposit), alluvion; ~**sel**, (-s), silt, deposit, alluvium.
aan'slik = **aanslib**.
aan'slinger, (-ge-), reel along; hurl at; fling forward.
aan'slof, (-ge-), shuffle along.

aan'sluip, (-ge-), approach stealthily; ~**ing**, sneaking along; stealthy approach.
aan'sluit, (-ge-), join; follow; enlist, enrol(l), join (soldier); connect; embrace; ~ *BY*, concur in (judgment); link up with (a railway); ~ *MET*, connect with, put through (on the telephone); *by 'n VERENIGING* ~ , join a society; ~**blokkie**, terminal block; ~**bus**, socket, plug socket; ~**draad**, branch wire, connecting wire; ~**er**, adaptor.
aan'sluiting, (-e, -s), junction, juncture, union; communication; connection, linking up; affiliation; *IN* ~ *by*, with reference to; *IN* ~ *met*, relayed from (radio, TV); ~ *KRY (mis) met 'n trein*, catch (miss) a train connection; ~**skoste**, installation charge(s); ~**spoorlyn**, ~**spoorweg**, junction; ~**spunt**, place (point) of connection.
aan'sluit: ~**kas**, junction box; terminal box; ~**spoor**, private siding; ~**stuk**, adaptor piece, nipple; ~**veer**, connection spring.
aan'slyk = **aanslib**.
aan'slyp, (-ge-), grind, sharpen, whet; *iets 'n punt* ~ , grind (sharpen) something to a point.
aan'smee, (-ge-), forge on (together).
aan'smeer, (-ge-), grease; apply (ointment); fob (foist, palm) off; *hy het my die gemors aangesmeer*, he palmed this worthless article off on me.
aan'smering, fadding (lacquer); application.
aan'smyt, (-ge-), throw (fling) against; put on (slip on) very quickly (clothes).
aan'snel, (-ge-), come rushing (racing) along.
aan'snoer, (-ge-), lace more tightly; pull tight.
aan'snor, (-ge-), come whizzing along.
aan'snou, (-ge-), snarl at.
aan'sny, (-ge-), give the first cut to (a loaf); continue cutting; add by cutting.
aan'soek, (-e), application (for a post); (re)quest (information); proposal (marriage); ~ *DOEN om 'n betrekking*, apply for a situation; *'n* ~ *RIG tot*, make an application to; apply to; ~**doener**, ~**er**, applicant; ~**vorm**, application form.
aan'soldeer, (-ge-), solder on.
aan'spanwa(entjie), trailer (of a motor); side-car.
aan'spat, (-ge-): ~ *teen*, splash against.
aan'speel, (-ge-), continue playing.
aan'sped(e), (-ge-), pin on.
aan'spoed, (-ge-), hasten (along).
aan'spoel, (-ge-), wash (cast) ashore; be washed up; ~**ing**, ~**sel**, alluvion, deposition, flotsam; drift.
aan'spoor, (-ge-), spur on, urge on, prompt, press, prick, goad (on), impel; chuck (a horse); exhort, arouse, encourage, quicken, incite, egg on; *iem. tot 'n daad* ~ , urge somebody to act; ~**der**, (-s), urger, impeller, inciter.
aan'sporend, (-e), (ex)hortative; encouraging, impellent.
aan'sporing, (-e, -s), stimulation, encouragement, animation, fillip, incitement, incentive; (ex)hortation, challenge, abetment; *op* ~ *van mnr. A.*, encouraged by (at the instigation of) Mr. A.; ~**sbonus**, incentive bonus.
aan'spraak, (..**sprake**), claim, title, right, pretence, pretension, company; ~ *KRY oor, op*, become entitled to; ~ *MAAK op iets*, lay claim to something; *ons het MIN* ~ , we have little company, we see few people; *SONDER* ~ *wees*, be without company; *alle* ~ *VERLOOR oor, op*, lose all claim to; ~**maker**, claimant, pretender, contender.
aan'spreek, (-ge-), address, speak to; accost; apostrophize; *nog 'n BOTTEL* ~ , crack another bottle; *ek wil my KAPITAAL nie* ~ *nie*, I do not wish to touch my capital; ~**lik**, (-e), responsible, answerable, liable; accountable; *iem.* ~ *lik hou vir die koste*, hold someone responsible for costs.
aanspreek'likheid, liability, responsibility; *BEPERKTE* ~ , limited liability; ~ *OPLOOP*, incur liability; ~ *UITSLUIT*, exclude liability; ~**sbeperking**, limitation of liability; ~**sgrens**, limit of liability.
aan'spreekvorm, form (mode) of address.
aan'spring, (-ge-), come leaping along.
aan'spyker, (-ge-), nail on (to).
aan'staan, (-ge-), please, like; suit; *die man staan*

my glad nie aan nie, I do not like that man at all.
aanstaan'de, (s) (-s), intended (spouse), fiancé (male), fiancée (female); (b) next (week); prospective; impending (changes); imminent (danger); forthcoming (elections); oncoming, future; expectant (mother); ~ *MAAND*, next month, proximo; *MY* ~, my bride (husband)-to-be; my prospective wife (husband); *my* ~ *SKOONMOEDER*, my prospective mother-in-law; ~ *VERKIESING*, next election; forthcoming election; ~ *WEEK*, next week.
aan'staar, (-ge-), stare at, gaze at, goggle at; ~ **der**, (-s), gazer.
aan'stalte, (-s), preparation; ~ *(s) maak*, get ready, take steps, make preparations.
aan'stamp, (-ge-), ram down (in); nudge; bump.
aan'stap, (-ge-), walk on; walk briskly; *BY iem.* ~, look in on someone; *aangestap KOM*, come walking along.
aan'staring, glare; gazing.
aan'steek, (-ge-), infect, attaint (with disease); fire; light; kindle (a fire); strike (a match); set fire to (a haystack); pin on (a buttonhole); put on (a ring); broach (a cask); *iem. met 'n siekte* ~, infect a person with a disease, ~ **'lik**, (-e), communicable, infectious, contagious, catching; ~ *lik werk op*, prove infectious to; ~ **'likheid**, contagiousness, infectiousness; ~ **streep**, lighting train; ~ **tyd**, period of infection; ~ **vlam**, pilot light (flame).
aan'steier, (-ge-), stagger along.
aan'steker, igniter, lighter.
aan'steking, lighting, igniting, ignition; infection, contagion.
aan'stel, (-ge-), appoint, employ, institute; instate; pretend, pose, give oneself airs; *hom soos 'n BEES* ~, make a beast of himself; behave like a beast; *MOENIE jou so* ~ *nie*, do not put on such airs; *hom SIEK* ~, pretend illness, malinger; ~ **ler**, (-s), appointer; constitutor; pretender, poseur, humbug, attitudinarian; ~ **lerig**, (-e), affected, ostentatious, bumptious, niminy-piminy, high and mighty, gushing, conceited, la-di-da; mannered; ~ **lerigheid**, affec(ta)tion, airs, conceit, play-acting, affectedness; ~ **lery**, pose, affectation, ostentation, conceit, gush, make-believe; appointment; hypochondria; ~ **ling**, (-e, -s), appointment, commission; *'n* ~ *ling MAAK*, appoint (someone); *'n VASTE* ~ *ling*, a permanent appointment.
aan'stellings, airs, conceitedness, affectation; ~ **brief**, letter of appointment; ~ **datum**, date of appointment; ~ **voorwaardes**, conditions of appointment; service conditions.
aan'stelskroef, adjustment screw.
aan'sterf, (-ge-), inherit.
aan'sterk, (-ge-), recuperate, recover, get stronger; ~ **ing**, convalescence, recuperation.
aan'stig, (-ge-), instigate, hatch (a plot), set on foot, start, begin; ~ **ter**, instigator, prime mover; ~ **ting**, instigation; *op* ~ *ting van*, at the instigation (instance) of.
aan'stik, (-ge-), stitch on.
aan'stip, (-ge-), jot down; touch lightly on, hint at; tick off; ~ **pel**, (-ge-), indicate by dots.
aan'stoker, (-s), agitator, firebrand, instigator, putter-on, prime mover, fomenter.
aan'stoking, instigation, incitement, fomentation; *op* ~ *van*, at the instigation of.
aan'stommel, (-ge-), approach stumbling; *aangestommel kom*, come stumbling along.
aan'stons, presently, directly, anon, by and by.
aan'stook, (-ge-), kindle (a fire); inflame, fan (dissension); egg on, foment (a riot); *TWIS* ~, sow discord; *iem.* ~ *om te VEG*, egg on (incite) a person to fight.
aan'stoom, (-ge-), come steaming along; get up more steam; ~ *teen*, collide with.
aan'stoot, (..**stote**), (s) push, bump; offence; ~ *gee (of NEEM)*, give (or take) offence; (w) (-ge-), push on, bump against; bestir oneself (when driving); nudge (with elbow); move forward (hands of clock); clink, touch (glasses); close (door); ~ **'lik**, (-e), offensive, indecent, scandalous, shocking, objectionable, invidious, obnoxious; exceptionable; ~ **'likheid**, offensiveness, indecency, obnoxiousness, scandalousness, invidiousness.
aan'storm, (-ge-), rush upon; *aangestorm kom*, come rushing (charging) along.
aan'streef, ..**strewe**, (-ge-), struggle along (forward).
aan'streep, (-ge-), mark, indicate, underline; come straggling along.
aan'strik, (-ge-), fasten with a knot (bow).
aan'strompel, (-ge-), come hobbling (stumbling) along; ~ **ing**, hobbling, stumbling.
aan'stroom, (-ge-), flow downstream; *aangestroom KOM*, come flowing (drifting) along; ~ *TEEN*, flow against.
aan'struikel, (-ge-), stumble along.
aan'stryk¹, (-ge-), continue walking; quicken (pace), walk on.
aan'stryk², (-ge-), paint, varnish, brush on; float (masonry); strike (a match); iron quickly; ~ **er**, brusher, varnisher.
aan'studeer, (-ge-), continue one's studies.
aan'stuif, ..**stuiwe**, (-ge-), come rushing along; continue drizzling.
aan'stuur, (-ge-), send on, redirect, forward (letter), pass on; direct, aim at, strive at; ~ *op LAND*, stand inshore; ~ *op LOONSVERBETERING*, aim at (strive for) wage improvement; ~ *OP*, set (course for); ~ **agent**, ~ **der**, forwarding agent.
aan'suis, (-ge-), rustle, buzz along.
aan'suiwer, (-ge-), pay off, settle (account); clear; *'n tekort* ~, make up a deficit; ~ **ing**, settlement, payment.
aan'sukkel, (-ge-), struggle (trudge) along, peg away; make shift; creep along.
aan'suring, acidulation, acidification.
aan'suur, (-ge-), sour, acidify, acidulate.
aan'sweef, ..**swewe**, (-ge-), come floating (gliding) along.
aan'sweep, (-ge-), incite, egg on (a crowd); whip up (horses).
aan'swel, (-ge-), swell, rise; increase (numbers); ~ **ling**, swelling.
aan'swem, (-ge-), swim on; *aangeswem kom*, come swimming along.
aan'swerm, (-ge-), approach in a swarm (in large numbers).
aan'swewe = **aansweef**.
aan'swoeg, (-ge-), struggle along; continue struggling.
aan'syn, existence, being; presence; *IN my* ~, in my presence; *in* ~ *ROEP*, create, call into existence; *sy* ~ *VERSKULDIG wees aan*, owe his life to; *in* ~ *wees*, exist.
aan'tal, (-le), number; bevy (of girls); course (of lectures); deal (of mistakes); head (of cattle); *die* ~ *punte*, the score; the marks.
aan'tas, (-ge-), touch; attack (of disease), affect, impair, injure; *sy GESONDHEID was aangetas*, his health was impaired; *jou KAPITAAL* ~, draw on one's capital; *iem. in sy SWAK* ~, attack someone in his weak spot; *die VYAND* ~, attack the enemy; ~ **'baar**, (..**bare**), vulnerable, attackable, assailable, pregnable; ~ **ting**, attack.
aan'teel, (s), breed(ing), (yearly) increase, offspring, progeny; rearing; (w) (-ge-), breed, rear, increase; ~ **aalwyn**, *Aloe claviflora;* ~ **bees**, ~ **ding**, brood (breeding, stock) animal; ~ **goed**, breeding (stock) animals; ~ **hokke**, breeding-pens (fowls); ~ **merrie**, brood-mare; ~ **ui**, pickle onion; ~ **vee**, breeding-stock (cattle), breeders.
aan'teken, (-ge-), note down, make a note of, annotate, record, log, mark (down), itemize; register (letter); score (sport); *AANGETEKEN stuur*, send by registered post; *hoër BEROEP* ~, appeal (in law); *'n BRIEF* ~, register a letter; *'n DRIE* ~, score a try; *PROTES* ~ *teen*, enter a protest against; ~ **aar**, recorder, commentator; ~ **geld**, registration money.
aan'tekening, (-e, -s), note, memo, record, memorandum, annotation; mark; registration; endorsement (licence); ~ *van APPÈL*, notice of appeal; *noukeurig* ~ *HOU*, keep strict note (record); ~

aanteken   11   *aanvlug*

MAAK, take down notes; ~ **boek**, notebook, scribbling- book; block, memorandum book; memopad.
aan'teken: ~ **kantoor**, registration office; ~ **inkie**, (-s), little (small) note, memo, jotting; ~ **koste**, registration fee, costs.
aan'tik, (-ge-), rap (tap) at; continue ticking (watch, clock); clink (glasses); touch the forelock, salute; ~ *aan 'n venster*, tap at a window.
aan'timmer, (-ge-), nail on; continue hammering; hammer faster.
aan'tjank, (-ge-), come howling along, howl at.
aan'tjokker, (-ge-), jog along.
aan'tog, approach, advance; *die vyand is in* ~, the enemy is advancing.
aanto'nend, (-e), indicative; ~ *e wys(e)*, indicative mood.
aan'toner, (-s), indicator.
aan'toon, (-ge-), show, evince, demonstrate, indicate; *met feite* ~, establish beyond doubt, prove; ~ **'baar**, (..**bare**), demonstrable.
aan'tou, (-ge-), come straggling along; come along in a queue.
aan'trap, (-ge-), pedal along; click.
aan'tree, (-ge-), line up, fall in; step up; ~ *met die linkervoet*, step off with the left foot; ~ **plek**, parade station.
aan'tref, (-ge-), meet, find, light on, come upon, fall on, stumble across; *'n vreemde PLANT* ~, come across a strange plant; *TUIS* ~, find in (at) home.
aan'trek, (-ge-), pull nearer; dress, don, garb, get into one's (put on) clothes; array, garment; tog (sports, e.g. rugby, soccer, tennis); attract; draw tighter (belt); gear; brace; take to heart; feel hurt; trek on, continue trekking; endue (with qualities); *jou IETS* ~, take something to heart; *jou iem. se LOT* ~, take someone's plight to heart; *ek trek dit MY nie aan nie*, it does not worry me; ~ **ding**, garment, (piece of) clothing; ~ **hokkie**, dressing-room; clothing-closet, dressing- (clothing-) cubicle; ~ **kamer**, cloakroom; ~ **kend**, (-e), attracting, attractive; ~ **king**, attraction, draw, affinity, allure; cynosure; ~ **kingsfeer**, centrosphere, directive sphere; ~ **kingskrag**, power of attraction; gravity, gravitation; appeal (of beauty); ~ **kingspunt**, centre of gravity; centre of attraction; ~ **kingsvermoë**, power of attraction.
aantrek'lik, (-e), sensitive; engaging, attractive, fascinating, prepossessing, catchy, catching; dinky, appetising; hypochondriac(al); touchy, oversensitive; ~ **heid**, attractiveness, attraction, grace, charm; amenity; sensitiveness.
aan'trekplek, parade station; shelter (room) for dressing.
aan'trippel, (-ge-), trip along; continue ambling; *aangetrippel kom*, come ambling along.
aan'trou, acquire (become related) by marriage; *aangetroude familie*, relations by marriage, in-laws.
aan'tuur, (-ge-), stare (gaze) at.
aan'tyg, (-ge-), impute, accuse, charge with, criminate; incriminate; ~ **ing**, (-e, -s), imputation, accusation, charge; incrimination.
aan'vaar[1], (-ge-), collide (ships); continue sailing; ~ *teen*, collide with.
aanvaar'[2], (~), accept (facts, a proposal, a bill of exchange); assume, enter upon (duties); accede to (a request); adopt (a resolution); embark (upon); embrace (an opportunity); set out on (a journey); face (a responsibility); *'n BETREKKING* ~, accept a post; assume duty; *'n ERFENIS* ~, enter upon an inheritance; *'n TENDER (aanneem)*, accept a tender; ~ **baar**, (..**bare**), acceptable; ~ **baarheid**, acceptableness, acceptability; ~ **der**, (-s), acceptor; ~ **ding**, beginning; reception, taking possession of; accession to, entrance upon (office); acceptance (of an inheritance); assumption (of duties); entry (in law).
aan'val, (s), attack, onset, offensive, onrush, onslaught, charge; aggression, raid, assault; (epileptic) fit, seizure; raid (by air); bout (illness); *AAN (OP) die* ~, on the attack; *'n* ~ *van AFSLAAN*, repel an attack; *'n* ~ *van BEROERTE*, an apoplectic stroke (fit); *die* ~ *HERNIEU*, return to the charge; *HEWIGE* ~, paroxysm; *'n* ~ *ONDERNEEM*, make an attack; *tot die* ~ *OORGAAN*, take the offensive; *tot die* ~ *OPROEP*, sound the charge; *'n* ~ *van WAANSIN*, a fit of madness; (w) (-ge-), attack, assail, charge, pounce, fall upon; go at it; impugn; invade (a country); *die AGTERHOEDE* ~, fall upon the rear; *die FLANK* ~, take in the flank; *die VOORHOEDE* ~, make a frontal attack; ~ **lend**, (-e), aggressive, assurgent; ~ *lend OP= TREE*, take the offensive; ~ *lende en verdedigende VERBOND*, offensive and defensive alliance; ~ **lenderwys(e)**, aggressively, offensively; ~ **ler**, (-s), assailant, assaulter, mugger; invader, attacker, aggressor; raider (by air).
aanval'lig, (-e), lovely, amiable, charming, bonny; ~ **heid**, loveliness, charm, amiableness, amiability, grace.
aan'valsdaad, aggression, aggressive act.
aan'valsdag, D-day, day of attack.
aan'valsein, signal for attack, attacking signal.
aan'vals: ~ **front**, front of attack; ~ **gees**, offensive spirit; ~ **geveg**, offensive battle (action); ~ **golf**, wave of attack, ~ **handeling**, offensive action, attack; ~ **kolonne**, attacking column; ~ **krag**, offensive energy; ~ **kreet**, war-cry; ~ **leër**, attacking force; ~ **middel**, means of attack; ~ **myn**, offensive mine; ~ **oorlog**, war of aggression, offensive war; ~ **plan**, plan of attack; ~ **punt**, point of attack; ~ **taktiek**, offensive tactics; ~ **teken**, signal to attack; ~ **terrein**, territory for attack; ~ **troepe**, attacking force; ~ **uur**, zero hour; ~ **verkenning**, offensive reconnaissance; ~ **vermoë**, offensive energy; ~ **vliegtuig**, attack plane (aircraft); ~ **wapen**, weapon of offence, offensive weapon.
aan'vang, (s), beginning, start, outset, commencement; inception; *BY die* ~, at the beginning; *'n* ~ *NEEM*, begin; (w) (-ge-), begin, commence; do; *met die werker kan 'n mens NIKS* ~ *nie*, this worker is quite useless; *WAT het jy aangevang?* what have you done? ~ **end**, (-e), inceptive, inchoative, incipient; ~ **er**, inceptor; ~ **salaris**, initial (commencing, minimum) salary.
aan'vangs: ~ **datum**, date of commencement; ~ **druk**, initial pressure; ~ **gebed**, opening prayer; ~ **kapitaal**, initial capital; ~ **klas**, beginners' class, tiro class; ~ **koers**, opening price; ~ **kolwer**, opening batsman; ~ **kondensasie**, initial condensation; ~ **letter**, initial letter; ~ **loon**, initial wage.
aan'vangsnelheid, initial velocity; muzzle velocity.
aan'vangs: ~ **onderwys**, infant teaching; ~ **probleme**, teething troubles; ~ **punt**, starting point; ~ **term**, first term *(maths.)*; ~ **uur**, opening hour; ~ **werk= saamheid**, initial (preliminary) work.
aanvank'lik, (-e), initial, incipient; primary, elementary; (bw) in the beginning, at first, at the outset; ~ *e onderwys*, elementary education.
aan'varing, collision (boats).
aan'vat, (-ge-), take hold of; begin; undertake; *die werk* ~, start work.
aan'vee(g), (-ge-), continue sweeping.
aan'veegsel, (-s), dirt; sweepings.
aan'veg, (-ge-), assail; tempt (passions); impugn (honour); contest, dispute (allegation); continue fighting; ~ **'baar**, (..**bare**), attackable, debatable, objectionable, contentious; impugnable; ~ **ting**, (-e, -s), temptation; sudden impulse; *vatbaar vir* ~ *ting*, open to dispute.
aan'verstorwe: ~ *goedere*, demised property.
aan'vertrou, (~), entrust to.
aan'verwant, (-e), relative, kindred, related (by affinity); allied, cognate; ~ *e tale*, cognate languages; ~ **skap**, relationship, affinity.
aan'vleg, (-ge-), continue to braid (plait); braid on.
aan'vlie, ..**vlieg**, (-ge-), fly at, rush upon; approach (by plane); jump down one's throat; *aangevlie(g) kom*, come flying (running) along.
aan'vlieg: ~ **baken**, landing-beam, beacon; ~ **duik**, approach dive; ~ **hoek**, angle of approach; ~ **hoogte**, approach height.
aan'vloei, (-ge-), flow along; keep on flowing.
aan'vlug, approach.

aan'vlug: ~**hoek**, angle of approach; ~**hoogte**, approach height.

aan'vly, (-ge-), nestle against; *hom* ~ *teen*, nestle himself against.

aan'voeg, (-ge-), join, add; ~*ende wys(e)*, subjunctive mood; ~**ing**, addition; ~**sel, (-s)**, addendum, appendage.

aan'voel, (-ge-), feel, touch; be attuned to; sense; *soos ek dit* ~, as I sense it; ~**ertjie**, semblance, trace; ~**ing**, touch; sensing, attunement.

aan'voer, (s), supply: *die* ~ *is veels te GROOT*, the supply is overabundant, the market is glutted; *die* ~ *van appels was ONVOLDOENDE*, apples were in short supply; **(w), (-ge-)**, supply, convey; conduct; bring (forward), allege (arguments); marshal (facts); advance, instance, put forward (reasons); adduce (evidence); produce (proofs); raise, array (objections); state (facts); command, lead (an army); captain (a team); *BEWYS* ~, adduce (bring forward) proofs; *'n LEËR* ~, command an army: *'n PUNT* ~, mention (state) a point; ~**'baar**, commandable, adducible; ~**band**, feed (conveyor) belt; ~**buis**, suction hose, supply pipe; afferent duct (in body); ~**der, (-s)**, commander, leader; chieftain; commodore *(navy)*; ringleader (riot); marshaller; ~**hawe**, port of entry; ~**ing**, lead, command, leadership; *onder* ~ *ing van*, led by, under the command of; ~**lyn**, line of supply; ~**pyp(ie)**, supply pipe, feedpipe; ~**stelsel**, supply system; ~**tang**, feeding-tongs; ~**tempo**, rate of feed; rate of supply; ~**voor**, supply furrow.

aan'voor, (-ge-), begin, commence (ploughing); break new ground; *te BREED* ~, undertake too much; take too much hay on one's fork; *'n SAAK* ~, take preliminary steps in a matter; ~**installasie**, pilot plant; ~**sel, (-s)**, beginning, point of contact; ~**werk**, initial steps.

aan'vra, (-ge-), apply for, request (samples); solicit (a testimonial); *'n OKTROOI* ~, take out a patent; *hoofdelike STEMMING* ~, demand a poll.

aan'vraag, (..vrae), application, request, requisition; demand; *daar is 'n GROOT* ~ *vir hierdie artikel*, there is a great demand for this article; *OP* ~, on demand (request); ~ *RIG tot*, make application to; ~**formulier**, application form; ~**wissel**, demand draft.

aan'vraer, (s), applicant; proposer *(insurance)*.

aan'vreet, (-ge-), damage (by eating); corrode.

aan'vreting, corrosion.

aan'vryf, ..vrywe, (-ge-), rub (against); smear on; accuse of, impute; *iem. 'n misdaad* ~, accuse someone of a crime.

aan'vul, (-ge-), fill up, replenish (stock); recruit, supplement; complete; justify (statement); complement; eke out; *MEKAAR* ~, be complementary; *met ligte WERKIES sy pensioen* ~, eke out his pension with odd jobs; ~**lend, (-e)**, complementary; complemental; supplementary; completive; supporting; ~*lende voer*, supplementary feed; ~**ler**, extension, filler (paint).

aan'vulling, (-e, -s), complement, replenishment, addition, amplification, completion; filling.

aan'vullings: ~**aanslag**, additional assessment; ~**bedrag**, supplementary sum; ~**begroting**, supplementary estimates; ~**bepalings**, supplemental provision; ~**blad**, supplement; ~**eksamen**, supplementary examination; ~**hoek**, complementary angle; ~**kleure**, complementary colours; ~**lys**, supplementary list; ~**onderwys**, supplemental instruction; ~**rapport**, supplementary report; ~**rekening**, supplementary account; ~**troepe**, reserves (troops), reserve troops; ~**voorraad**, supplementary supplies.

aan'vulsel, (-s), supplement, complement.

aan'vuring, incitement, stimulation.

aan'vuur, (-ge-), fire (imagination); encourage, inspire, incite, stimulate (zeal); inflame (passions); ~**der, (-s)**, stimulator, inciter; ~**inrigting**, firing mechanism.

aan'waai, (-ge-), be blown towards; arrive; *die DIPLOMA sal jou nie* ~ *nie*, the diploma won't just drop into your lap; *ÊRENS aangewaai kom*, arrive (blow in, drop in), arrive somewhere unexpectedly.

aan'waggel, (-ge-), come staggering along; *die dronklap kom aangewaggel*, the drunkard comes reeling (staggering) along.

aan'wakker, (-ge-), animate, fire, encourage, brisk up, quicken, energize; increase (trade); freshen (wind); foment (discord); fan (hatred); ~**ing**, stimulation, fanning, increase, freshening.

aan'wandel, (-ge-), walk (quickly, along).

aan'was, (s) growth, increase (population); deposit, alluvion; accrual (interest); accretion (soil); *verbeter deur* ~ *en AANSPOELING*, improved by accretion and alluvion; *reg van* ~, right of accrual (inheritance); right of accretion (soil); **(w) (-ge-)**, grow, increase; ~**send, (-e)**, growing, accretive; ~**sing**, accruement; increase.

aan'wen, (-ge-), contract (a habit), accustom oneself, habituate; reclaim (land); *jou rook* ~, accustom oneself to smoking.

aan'wend, (-ge-), use, employ, apply; adapt; appropriate (funds); exercise (one's right); convert; adopt; harness; *GELD* ~ *vir*, convert money for the use of; *'n POGING* ~, make an effort; ~**'baar**, (..**bare**), applicable, employable, adaptable; appropriable; ~**'baarheid**, adaptability; applicability; ~**ing**, employment, appropriation, use, application; adaptation; adhibition.

aan'wensel, (-s), (bad) habit, custom, habitude; mannerism.

aan'werf = **aanwerwe**.

aan'werk, (-ge-), continue working; sew on; *'n knoop* ~, sew on a button.

aan'werp, avulsion.

aan'werwe, (-ge-), recruit, (en)list, enrol(l), crimp, impress (soldiers); engage (labourers); ~**r**, recruiter, enroller, enlister, canvasser.

aan'werwing, recruiting, enlisting, enrol(l)ment.

aanwe'sig, (-e), present, attendant; existent, existing; to the fore; *DIE* ~*es*, those present; *alle* ~*es UITGESLUIT*, present company excluded; ~**heid**, presence, attendance; occurrence.

aan'wikkel, (-ge-), come (staggering) along; bestir oneself; go (run) fast.

aan'winning, reclamation (of land).

aan'wins, (-te), gain, profit, acquisition, asset, catch; accession; acquirement.

aan'wip, (-ge-), hop along; call in (on someone), pop in.

aan'worstel, (-ge-), struggle forward.

aan'wys, (-ge-), show, point out, indicate; assign, allot, allocate (funds); nominate; designate for (office); denote (time); *op jouself aangewys wees*, be thrown on your own resources; ~**bord**, markingtarget; notice-board; ~**end, (-e)**, indicating; demonstrative (pronoun); deictic; directory; presumptive; ~**er, (-s)**, indicator; pointer (petrol pump); exponent, tracer, index *(algebra);* annunciator; ~**ing, (-e, -s)**, indication, hint, assignation, assignment, allocation; reading (speedometer); instruction *(R.C.);* designation (contents); index (to character); clue; cue (for beginners); identification; ~**inge**, circumstantial evidence; ~**ingsnommer**, reference number; ~**stok**, pointer; dipstick.

aan'yl, (-ge-), hurry along, come tearing along.

aap, (ape), monkey, ape; fool, stupid person; *so min van iets weet as 'n* ~ *van GODSDIENS*, know as much as the man in the moon; *lyk of hy van die ape GEKUL is*, look perplexed and dismayed; *al dra 'n* ~ *'n GOUE ring, hy is en bly 'n lelike ding*, fine feathers do not make fine birds; *jy lyk 'n MOOI* ~*!* you look like doing it! *die* ~ *kom uit die MOU*, let the cat out of the bag; *'n* ~ *in die MOU hê*, have something up one's sleeve; *'n* ~ *in 'n PORSELEINKAS*, a bull in a chinashop; *hom 'n* ~ *SKRIK*, be frightened out of one's wits; *dit weet die* ~ *se STERT*, everybody knows it, that is self-evident; *nes 'n* ~ *op 'n STOKKIE sit*, seem to be at a loss; *dit kan jy aan die ape VERTEL*, tell that to the marines; *'n* ~ *WEES*, be stupid; ~**agtig, (-e)**, apish, pithecoid; ~**brood**, monkey bread; ~**gesig**, pug face; ~**kliere**, monkey glands; ~**kou**, monkey

aapsekos   *aartappel*

cage; ~**mens**, ape-man, pithecanthropus; ~**natuur**, monkeyism.

aap'sekos, *Rothmannia capensis;* candlewood.

aap'skeloeder, *(Ndl.)*, dirty fellow, mean creature; *jou* ~! you blackguard!

aap'stert, monkey's tail; sjambok; chain wrench; rascal; *iem.* ~ *GEE*, give someone a good hiding; *jou KLEIN* ~! you jackanapes!

aap'streke, monkey tricks, monkeyism.

aap'stuipe: *hy kan die* ~ *kry*, he is beside himself with rage.

aar[1], **(are)**, ear (of corn); spike; *in die* ~ *kom*, come into ear.

aar[2], **(are)**, are (square measure).

aar[3], **(are)**, vein (in body); shoot (chute) (ore); nerve, nervure (leaf); underground watercourse; ~**agtig**, **(-e)**, veiny.

aar'bei, **(-e)**, strawberry; hautboy *(Fragaria elatior);* ~**bedding**, strawberry bed; ~**blaar**, strawberry leaf; ~**boom**, strawberry tree *(Arbutus);* ~**konfyt**, strawberry jam; ~**kwekery**, strawberry cultivation; ~**limonade**, strawberry lemonade; ~**mandjie**, strawberry basket (punnet); ~**-oes**, strawberry harvest; ~**plant**, strawberry plant; *Arbutilon;* ~**rank**, strawberry tendril; ~**sap**, strawberry juice; ~**stroop**, strawberry syrup; ~**tyd**, strawberry time; ~**veld**, strawberry field; ~**verbouing**, strawberry culture; ~**wêreld**, strawberry-growing region.

aar: ~**beskrywing**, angiography, phlebography; ~**bloed**, venous blood; ~**bossie**, *Walafrida geniculata;* ~**breuk**, rupture of blood-vessel, phleborrhage.

aard[1], **(s)** nature, kind, disposition, character, description; colour; complexion; conformation; composition; make; quality, sort; *iets van DAARDIE* ~, something of that sort; *dit LÊ in die* ~ *van die saak*, it is in the nature of things, it stands to reason; *NIKS van dié* ~ *nie*, nothing of the kind; *UIT die* ~ *van die saak*, naturally; *UIT die* ~ *raak*, degenerate (plants); (w) **(ge-)**, take after (parents); take to; thrive (plants); *ek kan nie hier* ~ *nie*, it does not suit me here.

aard[2], (w) **(ge-)**, earth *(electr.);* ~ **agtig**, **(-e)**, earthy; ~**-alkali**, alkaline earth; ~**artisjok**, Jerusalem artichoke; ~**as**, the earth's axis; ~**baan**, orbit of the earth; ~**balletjie**, earthball, hard-skinned puff-ball *(Sclerodermaceae).*

aard'bewing, **(-e, -s)**, earthquake; *'n* ~ *in 'n miershoop (mishoop)*, much ado about nothing, a storm in a teacup.

aard'bewings: ~**gebied**, earthquake region; ~**golf**, seismic wave; ~**haard**, hypocentre; ~**leer**, seismology; ~**meter**, seismograph.

aard: ~**bewoner**, dweller on earth, tellurian, earthling, mortal; ~**bodem**, earth's surface, earth; *op dees* ~ *bodem!* good gracious! ~**bol**, globe; (the) earth; ~**boor**, earth drill; ~**brand**, subterranean fire; ~**by**, solitary bee; ~**deeltjies**, particles of earth; ~**draad**, earth wire *(electr.).*

aar'de, earth, ground; *die* ~ *nutteloos BESLAAN*, serve no purpose; *ter* ~ *BESTEL*, inter, bury; *op DEES* ~! oh my! *in GOEIE* ~ *val*, fall on fertile soil; *voel of jy in die* ~ *kan INSINK*, feel as if the earth could swallow you; *met die* ~ *KENNIS maak*, fall to the ground; *die* ~ *was te KOUD vir hom om op te trap*, nothing was too good for him; *NOG op* ~ *wees*, still be alive; *O (alla)* ~! oh my! *ONDER die* ~ *lê*, be dead and buried; *OP die* ~! good heavens! oh my! *toe was die hele* ~ *REG*, everything was in order; *onder die* ~ *RUS*, sleep in the grave, *SWART* ~, black soil; *WAT op* ~! what on earth! ~**baan**, earthwork, permanent way, foundation; ~**ling**, **(-e)**, earth dweller; ~**plaat**, ground plate; ~**poeier**, fuller's earth; ~**pot** = **erdepot**; ~**tjie**: *o* ~ *tjie!* oh, heavens! ~**vas**, **(-te)**, earthbound; ~**waarts**, **(-e)**, earthward; ~**werk** = **erdewerk**.

aard: ~**gas**, natural gas; ~**gees**, gnome, earth-spirit; ~**geleiding**, groundwire, earthing *(electr.);* **-globe**, earth globe, globe; ~**gonser**, power buzzer; ~**gordel**, zone; ~**grot**, cave, cavern; ~**hars**, bitumen; ~**hommel**, bumblebee; ~**hoop**, mound (of earth).

aar'dig, (b) **(-e)**, nice, agreeable, smart; funny, unpleasant, queer; strange; considerable (sum of money); fairly well; *dit sal te* ~ *LYK om nee te sê*, it will look so odd to refuse; *'n* ~ *e MEISIE*, quite a nice girl; *'n* ~ *e SOMMETJIE geld*, a considerable sum of money; *ek VOEL so* ~, I feel so queer (creepy).

aar'digheid, **(..hede)**, joke, fun, pleasantry; giddiness; ..**hede**, facetiae; *dis 'n HELE* ~ *om die kind te sien*, it is quite a treat to see the child; *NET vir die* ~, just for fun.

aar'ding, earthing *(electr.)*

aard'jie: *'n* ~ *na sy vaartjie*, like father, like son.

aard: ~**kabel**, earth (ground) cable; ~**kern**, core (of earth); ~**klem**, earth terminal *(electr.);* ~**kleur**, earth colour; ~**klomp**, clod of earth; ~**kluit**, clod; ~**kontak**, earth *(electr.);* ~**kors**, crust of earth; the earth's crust; ~**kruiper**, snail *(Neritidae);* ~**kunde**, geology, geognosy; ~**kun'dig**, **(-e)**, geologic(al); ~**kun'dige**, **(-s)**, geologist; ~**laag**, layer (of earth); ~**leiding**, earth wire (lead, electrode), ground connection *(electr.);* ~**lig**, earth shine; ~**lug**, earthy smell; ~**magneetveld**, magnetic field of the earth; ~**mannetjie**, brownie, gnome, goblin; ~**meetkunde**, ~**meting**, geodesy; ~**olie**, petroleum, rock oil; ~**oppervlak**, surface of the earth; ~**oppervlakte**, surface area of the earth; ~**pen**, earth pin *(electr.);* ~**pik**, bitumen; ~**pool**, terrestrial pole; ~**rook**, fumitory; ~**roos**, root parasite (e.g. *Hyobanche sanguinea).*

aard'druk, venous pressure.

aard'ryk, the earth; the world.

aard'rykskunde, geography; ~**onderwyser**, geography teacher.

aardrykskun'dig, **(-e)**, geographic(al); ~**e**, **(-s)**, geographer.

aards, **(-e)**, worldly, terrestrial; earthy, earthborn, mundane; ~**gesind**, **(-e)**, worldly-minded, earthly-minded, wordly; ~**gesindheid**, worldliness, earthliness.

aard: ~**skaduwee**, shadow of the earth; ~**skok**, earthquake, earth tremor, earth shock; ~**kors**, earth crust; ~**skudding**, earth tremor; ~**sluiting**, earth fault *(electr.);* ~**spleet**, earth fissure; ~**storting**, earth-fall, landslip, landslide; ~**stroom**, earth current *(electr.);* ~**terugleiding**, earth return *(electr.);* ~**trilling**, earth tremor; ~**tydperk**, geological age; ~**veil**, ground ivy; ~**verbinding**, earth contact (connection) *(electr.);* ~**verklikker**, ground detector; ~**verskuiwing**, landslide; ~**was**, mineral wax; ~**werke**, earthworks; ~**wolf**, aardwolf, maned jackal, maanhaar jackal *(Proteles cristatus).*

aar'erts, vein ore.

aar: ~**holte**, cavernous sinus; ~**inspuiting**, intravenous injection.

aar'kwarts, vein quartz.

aar: ~**laat**, **(-ge-)**, bleed, cup; phlebotomize; ~**lating**, bloodletting, cupping; phlebotomy; ~**ontstoking**, phlebitis.

aar'opteller, gleaner.

aar: ~**pers**, tourniquet; ~**pols**, venous pulse; ~**ryk**, **(-e)**, veined, veiny.

aars, **(-e)**, anus, arse, rectum.

aar'sel, **(ge-)**, hesitate, waver, hang back, demur; boggle; flinch; hum and haw; ~**end**, **(-e)**, hesitant, hesitative, vacillating; ~**ing**, hesitation, hesitancy, doubt, vacillation; demur; *sonder* ~ *ing*, unhesitatingly.

aar: ~**slag**, heartbeat; ~**spat**, varix, varicose vein; ~**stelsel**, neuration; venation.

aart'appel, potato; *hy skil sy* ~ *s nie twee KEER oor nie*, he does not cook his cabbage twice; ~ *s in sy KOUSE*, holes in his stockings; ~**akker**, potato field; ~**blaar**, potato leaf; ~**boer**, potato grower; ~**bredie**, Irish stew, potato stew; ~**drukker**, ~**fyndrukker**, potato masher; ~**gereg**, potato dish; ~**grond**, potato ground; ~**handel**, potato trade; ~**kewer**, Colorado beetle; ~**kop**, blockhead; ~**koper**, potato dealer; ~**kroket**, potato croquette; ~**kultivar**, potato cultivar; ~**land**, potato field; ~**lowwe**, potato stalks (leaves); ~**moel**, po-

tato flour; ~**messie**, potato peeler; ~**moer**, seed potato; ~**mot**, potato tuber moth; ~**oes**, potato crop; ~**pastei**, cottage (shepherd's) pie; ~**plaag**, potato blight; ~**plant**, potato plant; ~**repies**, potato chips; ~**roes**, potato blight; ~**sak**, potato bag; ~**siekte**, potato blight; potato rot; ~**skil**, potato peel; ~**skiller**, potato peeler; ~**skuur**, potato barn; ~**skyfie**, potato crisp; potato chip, chip; ~**skyfies**, potato chips, chips; ~**slaai**, potato salad; ~**snip= pertjie**, potato chip; ~**snyer**, potato chipper; ~**so(e)p**, potato soup; ~**stoel**, potato plant; ~**suurdeeg**, potato yeast; ~**veld**, potato field; ~**verbouing**, potato culture (cultivation); ~**voor= raad**, supply of potatoes, potato supply; ~**water**, water in which potatoes have been boiled.
aar'tjie¹, (-s), veinlet; venule.
aar'tjie², (-s), small ear (of corn); spikelet (of plant).
aar'tjie³: ~ *na sy VAARTJIE*, like father, like son.
aarts: ~**bedrieër**, arrant rogue; ~**bisdom**, archbish= opric; ~**biskop**, archbishop; primate; hierarch; metropolitan; ~**biskop'lik**, (-e), archiepiscopal; ~**deken**, archdeacon; ~**deugniet**, arrant rogue; ~**dief**, arrant thief; ~**dom**, as stupid as an ass; ~**engel**, archangel; ~**gek**, arrant fool; ~**gierig= aard**, miser; ~**hertog**, duke, archduke; ~**hertog= dom**, archduchy, duchy; ~**herto'gelik**, ducal, arch= ducal; ~**hertogin'**, duchess, archduchess; ~**huigelaar**, arch-hypocrite; ~**ketter**, arch-heretic; ~**leuenaar**, arrant (consummate) liar; ~**liefhebber**, passionate lover, devotee, votary, enthusiast; ~**lui**, very lazy; ~**luiaard**, inveterate idler; ~**luiheid**, ex= treme laziness; ~**moeder**, matriarch; ~**moederlik**, matriarchal; ~**priester**, high priest; ~**skelm**, ar= rant rogue; inveterate rascal, out-and-out rogue; ~**skobbejak**, consummate rascal; ~**skurk**, double-dyed villain; ~**vabond**, arrant rogue; ~**vader**, pa= triarch; ~**vaderlik**, (-e), patriarchal; ~**verleier**, arch-tempter; ~**vyand**, arch-enemy.
aar: ~**verkalking**, arteriosclerosis; ~**vernouing**, vaso= constriction; ~**verstopping**, phlebothrombosis; ~**verwyding**, vasodilatation.
aar'vormig, (-e), spicate, spiciform *(bot.)*.
aas¹, (ase), ace (of cards); *dubbele* ~, ambs-ace (dice).
aas², (s), carrion; (fish) bait; prey; *waar die* ~ *is, ver= gader die ARENDE*, where the carcase is, the vul= tures will gather; ~ *MAAK*, collect bait; *as jy aan* ~ *ROER, stink dit*, he that toucheth pitch shall be defiled therewith; *ROOI* ~, red bait (ascidian); (w) (ge-), feed on, prey on; covet; *iets te* ~ *(ase)*, some= thing to eat; something to turn to good account; ~**blom**, carrion flower, fetid-smelling stapelia *(Stapelia schinzii)*.
Aas'domsreg, Aasdom Law.
aas: ~**jag**, scavenger hunt; ~**joggie**, gilly, gillie; ~**kelk**, stapelia; ~**kewer**, carrion beetle, scaven= ger, scavenger beetle; ~**stok**, baithook; ~**(ver)gif**, botulism; ~**vlieg**, carrion fly *(Calliphora, Chryso= myia, Sarcophaga)*.
aas'voël, vulture, aasvogel; glutton; *die* ~ *s het hom BEETGEHAD*, he is tattered and torn; *lyk of die* ~ *s sy KOS afgeneem het*, look glum; *so LUI soos 'n* ~, very lazy; *hy hou sy LYF* ~, he is a sponger; *'n REGTE* ~, a glutton; *dis 'n SLEGTE* ~ *wat bly sit (nie wegvlieg nie) as hy gevreet het*, don't overstay your welcome; *WEGVLIEG soos* ~ *s*, depart im= mediately after eating or drinking; ~**bessie**, wild cherry *(Maurocenia)*; ~**bos(sie)**, *Pteronia pallens*; ~**dans**, type of ethnic dance; ~**krans**, steep cliff, precipice; ~**oë**, sharp eyes; eagle-eyes; ~**tarentaal**, vulterine guineafowl; ~**vet**, vulture fat.
aas'vretend, (-e), carrion-eating, necrophagous.
aas'vreter, scavenger; ~**y**, necrophagia.
ab, (-te), abbot.
a'bakus, (-se), abacus.
abattoir', (-s), abattoir, (municipal) slaughter house; ~**stelsel**, abattoir system.
ab'ba, (s), lean-to; (w) (ge-), carry on one's back (baby), carry pick-a-back (piggy-back); ~**(geskut)= vragwa**, porté lorry; ~**kaggel**, lean-to chimney, outside chimney; ~**oond**, lean-to (Dutch) oven; ~**skip**, aircraft carrier; ~**trekker**, mechanical horse; ~**vliegtuig**, pick-a-back (piggy-back) plane.

abbé', (-s), abbé.
abc', ABC, alphabet; *hy KEN nie die* ~ *nie*, he is an ignoramus; he is illiterate, he doesn't know the al= phabet; *vir iem. die* ~ *moet LEER*, teach someone elementary things; *dis NES* ~ *vir hom*, it's as easy as ABC to him; *die* ~ *van 'n VAK*, the first prin= ciples (elements) of a subject; ~**-boek**, primer.
abdika'sie, abdication.
abdikeer', abdiseer', (ge-), abdicate.
abdis', (-se), abbess, prelatess.
abdolka'ter, catch the hare (children's game); *see* **ablou**.
abdo'men, (..mina, -s), abdomen.
abdominaal', (..nale), abdominal.
abdominoskopie', abdominoscopy.
abduk'sie, abduction.
abdy', (-e), abbey, monastery.
abeel', (abele), aspen, trembling poplar.
a'bel: ~ *spel*, (mediaeval) secular drama.
aberra'sie, (-s), aberration.
Abessi'nië, Abyssinia; ~**r**, (-s), Abyssinian.
Abessi'nies, (-e), Abyssinian.
abi'ekwa(s)geelhout, tamarisk *(Tamarix articulata, T. austro-africana)*.
ab'intestaat, ab intestato.
abiogene'se, abiogenesis.
abissaal', (..sale), abis'sies, (-e), abyssal.
AB-jab', primer.
abja'ter¹, (-s), rogue, scamp; nonentity.
abja'ter², (-s), G-string.
ablakta'sie, ablactation, weaning.
abla'sie, ablation.
ablatief', (..tiewe), ablative.
ab'laut, ablaut, gradation, vowel substitution.
ablou' = abdolkater.
ablu'sie, ablution.
abnormaal', (..male), abnormal.
abnormaliteit', (-e), abnormality.
abnormiteit', (-e), abnormity.
aboel': *hasie* ~, castles are blue, catch the hare (chil= dren's game).
aboli'sie, abolition.
A-'bom, atom bomb, A-bomb, nuclear bomb.
abomina'bel, (-e), abominable.
abomina'sie, (-s), abomination.
abonnee', *(Ndl.)*, (-s), subscriber; ~**r'**, (ge-), sub= scribe to; *geabonneer wees op 'n tydskrif*, subscribe to (take in) a magazine.
abonnement', (-e), subscription; ~**s'geld**, subscrip= tion; ~**s'voorwaardes**, terms of subscription.
abonnent', (-e), subscriber.
abor'sie, abortion.
aborteer', (ge-), abort.
aborteur', (-s), abortist, abortionist.
abortief', (..tiewe), abortive.
abor'tus, abortion.
A'braham, Abraham; ~ *se SKOOT*, of Abraham's bosom; *in* ~ *se SKOOT grootword*, grow up in luxury; be pampered in childhood; *in* ~ *se SKOOT sit*, lead a happy life.
abrakada'bra, abracadabra.
abra'sie, (-s), abrasion.
abroga'sie, (-s), repeal (law), abrogation.
abrogeer', (ge-), abrogate, repeal.
abrup', (-te), abrupt.
absen'sie, absence, non-attendance.
absent', absent; ~**eer'**, (ge-), absent (oneself); ~**eïs'me**, ~**is'me**, absenteeism.
abses', (-se), abscess, ulcer.
absint', wormwood, absinthe; ~**ien'**, ~**i'ne**, absinthine.
ab'sis, (-se), abscissa *(maths.)*.
ab'skap, abbacy.
absolu'sie, absolution; ~ *van die instansie*, absolu= tion from the instance.
absolutis'me, absolutism.
absoluut', (b) (..lute), absolute; (bw) absolutely, quite; ~ *NIKS nie*, nothing at all; ~ *ONMOONT= LIK*, quite (absolutely) impossible; *absolute VOG= GEHALTE*, absolute humidity.
absorbeer', (ge-), absorb; ~**middel**, absorbent.
absorp'sie, absorption; ~**kromme**, absorption curve;

abstergeer   15   *adverbiaal*

~**poeier,** absorption powder; ~**strepe,** absorption bands; ~**vermoë,** absorptive power.
abstergeer', (ge-), absterge.
abstraheer', (ge-), abstract.
abstrak', (-te), abstract; ~ *GESPROKE,* spoken abstractly; ~*te OORWEGINGS,* imponderabilia; ~*te WISKUNDE,* abstract mathematics; ~**sie,** abstraction; ~**t'heid,** abstractness.
absurd', (-e), absurd, preposterous; ~**iteit', (-e),** absurdity.
abuis', mistake, error; *per* ~, by mistake, through an oversight.
abusief', (..siewe), mistaken, erroneous; ~**lik, abusie'welik,** by mistake, inadvertently.
achilie', achylia.
Achil'les, Achilles; ~**hiel,** tendon of Achilles, Achilles' heel; vulnerable spot; ~**pees,** hamstring.
acholie', acholia.
achondriet', achondrite.
achromaat', (..mate), achromat.
achromasie', achromation.
achroma'ties, (-e), achromatic, colourless.
achromatis'me, achromatism.
a'cre, (-s), acre; ~**voet,** acre-foot.
ac'ta: *A*~ *Synodi,* resolutions, acts of Synod.
ac'tiva, assets; ~ *en passiva,* assets and liabilities.
actua'rius, (..rii), *(L.): A*~ *Synodi,* actuary of the Synod; *see* **aktuarius.**
ada'gio, adagio *(music),* slow.
A'dam, Adam; ~ *en EVA se skoene aantrek,* go barefoot; *familie van* ~ *sê dis EVA en Eva sê dis die slang,* Adam blamed Eve, Eve in turn the snake; *verwant van* ~ *se KANT,* distantly related; *ek KEN hom nie van* ~ *af nie,* I do not know him from Adam; *die OU* ~ *aflê,* shake off the old Adam.
adamelliet', adamellite.
adamien', adamine.
Adamiet', Adamite.
adami'ne, adamine.
a'damsappel, Adam's apple; *Citrus medica.*
A'dams: ~**geslag,** mankind; ~**gewaad** = Adamsklere.
adamsiet', adamsite.
a'dams: ~**kind,** human being; ~**klere,** ~**kostuum,** ~**pak,** nature's garb; birthday suit; *in* ~*kostuum,* in nature's garb, nude.
a'damsvy, Adam's fig.
adapta'sie, adaptation.
adapteer', (ge-), adapt.
a'dat, adat, traditional law (of an Islamic region); ~**reg,** traditional law.
adden'dum, (-s, ..da), addendum.
ad'der, (-s), adder, viper, asp, serpent; *ek het 'n* ~ *aan my BORS gekoester,* I have cherished a serpent in my bosom; *daar skuil 'n* ~ *in die GRAS,* there is a snake in the grass; ~**gebroedsel,** breed of vipers; ~**geslag,** generation of vipers; bunch of crooks; ~**gif,** viper's venom; ~**tong,** viper's tongue; slanderer, backbiter.
addi'sie, (-s), addition; ~**stof,** additive.
addisioneel', (..nele), additional.
Ad'disonsiekte, Addison's disease.
adduk'tor, (-s), ~**spier,** adductor (muscle).
adekwaat', (..kwate), adequate.
a'del, (s) peerage, nobility; dignity; *hy is van die* ~, he is of noble birth; **(w) (ge-),** ennoble, raise to the peerage.
a'delaar, (-s), eagle; standard; *die dubbele* ~, the double eagle.
a'delaars: ~**blik,** eagle-eye; ~**nes,** eyrie, eyry; ~**neus,** aquiline nose; ~**oog,** sharp (eagle-) eye; ~**vlug,** flight of an eagle.
a'del: ~**boek,** peerage, red book, Debrett's; ~**bors, (-te),** naval cadet, marine cadet, midshipman, middy; ~**brief,** patent of nobility; ~**broer,** (maternal) brother; ~**dom,** nobility, aristocrats, aristocracy; ~**heerskappy,** aristocracy; ~**lik, (-e),** noble, aristocratic, highborn; ~*like BLOED,* noble blood; ~*like WILDSVLEIS,* high venison; ~**likheid,** nobleness, nobility.
a'delstand, nobility, aristocracy, peerage; *tot die* ~ *verhef word,* be raised to the peerage.

a'deltrots, aristocratic pride.
a'dem, (s), breath; *see* **asem; (w), (ge-),** breathe *(fig.); die boek* ~ *'n gesonde gees,* a healthy spirit emanates from the book; ~**haling,** breathing; ~**loos, (..lose),** breathless; ~**tog,** breath(ing), respiration; gasp.
adenografie', adenography.
adenoï'de, (-s), adenoïed', (-e), adenoid.
adenologie', adenology, study of glands.
adenoom', (..nome), adenoma.
adep', (-te), adept.
a'derlaat, a'derlating = **aarlaat, aarlating.**
a'derlik, (-e), venous.
adhe'sie, adhesion; ~**betuiging,** assurance of adhesion.
adiaba'ties, (-e), adiabatic.
adia'sie, adiation.
adieer', (ge-), adiate.
adieu', (-s), good-bye.
adinool', adinole.
adjektief', (..tiewe), adjective.
adjekti'wies, (-e), adjectival.
adjudant'¹, (-e), marabou stork, adjutant.
adjudant'², (-e), adjutant, aide-de-camp; equerry; **a**~**generaal,** Adjutant-General.
adjunk', (-te), adjunct, deputy, assistant; ~**-inspekteur,** deputy inspector; ~ **mediese direkteur,** deputy medical director; ~**-minister,** deputy minister; ~**-sekretaris,** assistant secretary.
administra'sie, administration, management; ~**gebou,** administrative building; ~**koste,** managing (administrative) expenses; ~**personeel,** administrative staff.
administrateur', (-s), administrator, ~**s'kantoor,** administrator's office.
administratief', (..tiewe), administrative.
administratri'se, (-s), administratrix.
administreer', (ge-), administrate; administer.
admiraal', (-s, ..rale), admiral; ~**skap,** admiralship; ~**skip,** admiral's ship, flagship; ~**skoe(n)lapper,** red admiral (butterfly) *(Vanessa atalanta);* ~**s'rang,** rank of admiral; ~**s'vlag,** admiral's flag.
admiraliteit', admiralty.
admis'sie, admission; ~**-eksamen,** admission examination (to D.R.C. Theological Seminary); entrance examination.
adolessen'sie, adolescence.
adolessent', (s, b), (-e), adolescent; ~ *e rivier,* adolescent river.
Ado'nis, Adonis; extremely handsome man.
adoons', monkey; ugly fellow.
adop'sie, adoption.
adopteer', (ge-), adopt.
adoptief', (..tiewe), adoptive.
adora'sie, adoration.
adoreer', (ge-), adore.
adrenalien', adrenali'ne, adrenaline.
adres', (-se), address; memorial; petition; *dit is AAN jou* ~, that refers to you, *iem. se* ~ *KEN,* know a person's pedigree; *PER* ~, care of; *dis aan die REGTE* ~, the shoe is on the right foot; *by die VERKEERDE* ~, at the wrong place; ~**boek,** address book; directory; ~**kaart,** dispatch label; ~**kaartjie,** business card; tag, trade card; ~**lys,** list of addresses; ~**plaatjie,** address stencil; ~**sant', (-e),** sender, petitioner; ~**seer', (ge-),** address, direct; ~**seermasjien,** addressograph; ~**sy,** address side; ~**verandering,** change of address.
adret', (-te), spruce, smart; stately.
Adria'ties, (-e), Adriatic.
adsorbeer', (ge-), adsorb.
adsorp'sie, adsorption.
adstrin'gens, (-e, ..gentia), astringent.
adstringe'rend, (-e), astringent; ~ *e middels,* astringents.
adulaar', (..lare), adular.
A'-dur, *(ong.),* A major.
advek'sie, advection.
Ad'vent, Advent.
adventief', (..tiewe), adventitious.
Adventis', (-te), Adventist.
adverbiaal', (..biale), adverbial.

adver'bium, (..bia), adverb.
adversatief', (..tiewe), adversative.
adverteer', (ge-), advertise; puff; *iem.* ~ *homself*, advertise oneself.
adverten'sie, (-s), advertisement; ~ **afdeling**, advertisement department (section); ad department (section); ~ **agent**, press agent, advertising agent, ad agent; ~ **agtig**, (-e), catchpenny, like an advertisement; ~ **bestuurder**, advertisement manager; ~ **blad**, advertiser, advertising paper; ~ **bord**, hoarding; ~ **buro**, advertising agency, ad agency; ~ **kolom**, advertisement column; ~ **kontrak**, advertising contract; ~ **koste**, advertising expenses, cost of advertisement; ~ **lawaai**, ballyhoo; ~ **tarief**, advertising rate; ~ **werwer**, advertisement canvasser.
advies', (-e), advice, information; opinion (of a lawyer); *iem. van* ~ *DIEN*, advise a person; ~ *IN-WIN*, seek advice; *OP* ~ *van*, on the advice of; *REGSKUNDIGE* ~, legal advice; ~ **boot**, tender; aviso; ~ **brief**, letter of advice; ~ **geld**, fee for (legal) advice; ~ **jag**, advice boat.
adviseer', (ge-), advise.
advise'rend, (-e), consulting, advisory; *in* ~ *e HOE-DANIGHEID*, in an advisory capacity; ~ *e LIG-GAAM*, consulting body.
adviseur', (-s), adviser.
advokaat[1], egg flip (with brandy).
advokaat'[2], (..kate), advocate, counsel, barrister-at-law, lawyer; *'n* ~ *KRY*, brief counsel; *soos 'n* ~ *LIEG*, be a smart (clever) liar; *soos 'n* ~ *PRAAT (pleit)*, have the gift of the gab; *as* ~ *TOELAAT*, call to the bar; *VIR* ~ *studeer*, read for the bar; ~ **generaal**, attorney-general; advocate-general; ~ **peer** = **avokadopeer**; ~ **s'beroep**, legal profession; ~ **s'toga**, barrister's gown.
advoka'testreek, lawyer's trick, clever trick.
aëra'dio, aeradio.
aëra'sie, aeration.
aëreer', (ge-), aerate.
aë'ro: ~ **baat'**, aerobat; ~ **batiek'**, aerobatics; ~ **biologie'**, aerobiology; ~ **bio'se**, aerobiosis; ~ **dina'mies**, (-e), aerodynamical; ~ **dina'mika**, aerodynamics; ~ **di'ne**, aerodyne; ~ **foon'**, aerophone; ~ **grafie'**, aerography; ~ **liet'**, (-e), aerolite; ~ **logie'**, aerology; ~ **lo'gies**, (-e), aerological; ~ **mega'nika**, aeromechanics; ~ **meter**, aerometer; ~ **metrie'**, aerometry; ~ **nomie'**, aeronomy.
aëroob', (aërobe), aerobe.
aëro: ~ **sfeer'**, aerosphere; ~ **sol'**, aërosol; ~ **staat'**, (..state), aerostat; ~ **sta'ties**, (-e), aerostatic; ~ **sta'tika**, aerostatics.
af, off, down, from; completed, perfect(ed), finished; broken (engagement); ~ *en AAN*, to and fro; *ek wil weet waar ek* ~ *of AAN (AAN of* ~ *) is*, I want to know where I stand; I want to know whether the deal is off or on; *hy het 'n* ~ *ARM*, he is one-armed; he has only one arm; *op die DAG* ~, to the very day; *hy is van sy EETLUS* ~, he has lost his appetite; *ek is daar GELUKKIG van* ~, that is good riddance; *iem. te GLAD* ~ *wees*, be one too many for someone; *iem. te GOU* ~ *wees*, be too quick for someone; *ek voel HEELTEMAL* ~, I am quite exhausted; *HOEDE* ~*!* hats off! *van sy JEUG* ~, since his (early) youth; *sy is van haar MAN* ~, she is a divorcee; *van die PAD* ~, off the road; *sy RUG is* ~, his back is broken; *die SKILDERY is* ~, the painting has been completed; *SLEG* ~ *wees*, be badly off; *van TOE* ~, since then; ~ *en TOE*, now and again; *van iets* ~ *WEES*, not be sure of (a fact); *van die drank* ~ *wees*, have given up drink; *VAN die President* ~, from the President downwards.
af'arm, (partially) armless; with a broken arm; ~ **werker**, one-armed worker.
afasie', aphasia.
af'baan, (ge-), mark out (off), mark.
af'baard, (ge-), (de)burr.
af'babbel, (ge-), talk a lot, chatter, babble.
af'baken, (ge-), divide; demarcate; define; beacon off (roadstead); mark out, delimit; ~ **ing**, demarcation, delimitation; division, location (in mines); ~ **ingsgeknoei**, gerrymandering; ~ **ingskommissie**, delimitation commission; ~ **ingswerksaamhede**, delimitation work (duties).
af'bars, (-ge-), crack (burst) off.
af'bedel, (-ge-), obtain by begging, wheedle out of.
af'beeld, (-ge-), picture, portray, draw, paint, depict, delineate, describe; ~ **er**, delineator; ~ **ing**, (-e, -s), picture, portrait(ure); depiction, portrayal, image, representation, delineation; ~ **sel**, (-s), portrait, image, effigy; counterfeit.
af'been, cripple(d); (partially) legless; having a broken leg; ~ **man**, one-legged man.
af'beitel, (-ge-), chisel off.
af'bel, (-ge-), ring off; ~ **sein**, clearing signal.
af'bestel, (~), countermand; cancel an order; ~ **ling**, counter-order, cancellation.
af'betaal, (~), pay off (workmen); settle (account); pay on account; amortise; ~ **staat**, pay-off sheet; ~ **stelsel**, instalment system.
af'betaling, (-e, -s), payment, settlement; instalment; *op* ~ *KOOP*, buy on the instalment system; ~ *op TERMYNE*, payment by instalments; ~ **stelsel**, instalment system, hire-purchase system, system of deferred payments; ~ **stermyn**, period of repayment; ~ **svoorwaardes**, terms of repayment.
af'beul, (-ge-), worry to death; slave, fag out, work to death.
af'beur, (-ge-), force away (off), drag off.
af'bid, (-ge-), deprecate, pray for, invoke; obtain by prayer (blessing); ~ **dend**, (-e), deprecative, deprecatory; ~ **der**, deprecator; ~ **ding**, deprecation.
af'bie, (-ge-), haggle.
af'biggel, (-ge-), trickle down (tears).
af'bind, (-ge-), tie up (a vein), ligate, ligature; string; ~ **ing**, ligation.
af'blaar, (-ge-), husk (mealies); blister (paint); exfoliate.
af'blaas, (-ge-), blow off (dust); exhaust, deflate; let off (steam); ~ **klep**, eduction (blow-off) valve, stop valve; ~ **kraan**, blow cock, purging cock; stop cock; ~ **pyp**, blow-off (exhaust) pipe, blast pipe; eduction pipe; waste-steam pipe.
af'blaring, husking; blistering, popping (paint); exfoliation.
af'bly, (w) (-ge-), leave alone; keep off; (tw) hands off!
af'boek, (-ge-), write off (debt); close (account).
af'boen, (-ge-), rub, scrub; polish.
af'boender, (-ge-), drive (chase) down from.
af'bons, (-ge-), bang (bounce) down.
af'borsel, (-ge-), brush (off); rebuke.
af'bou, (s) stoping (mining); catabolism *(biol.)*; (w) (-ge-), finish (building); stope; ~ **er**, stoper; ~ **front**, stopeface; ~ **ing**, stoping; ~ **lengte**, back (mine); ~ **plek**, stope; ~ **sluis**, stopebox; ~ **wydte**, stoping width.
af'braak, demolition; rubble, debris; *vir* ~ *verkoop*, sell for demolition; ~ **koste**, expense of demolition, demolition costs; ~ **produk**, degradation product; byproduct; ~ **werksaamhede**, (work of) demolition.
af'brand, (-ge-), burn down (away, off); be burnt down, set on fire; *tot die grond toe* ~, burn to the ground; ~ **ing**, burning down (away), flame-cleaning.
af'breek, (-ge-), pull down, destroy, raze, demolish (building); part, break off, sever (friendship); stop (talking); strike (camp); divide (a word); disconnect (current); interrupt (conversation); crack; discontinue (friendship); intermit (fever); *'n GESPREK* ~, break off a conversation; *'n VERHAAL* ~, cut short a story; ~ **geweer**, ~ **roer**, *(hist.)*, breech-loader; ~ **sel**, debris.
af'brekend, (-e), destructive; ~ *e kritiek*, destructive criticism.
af'breker, demolisher.
af'breking, demolition, dismantlement, razing; disconnection, discontinuity, disengagement; fault (reef); ~ **steken**, break, dash, hyphen.
af'breuk, damage (trade); detraction (from reputation); reduction (beauty); impairment (influence); injury; ~ *DOEN aan*, injure, prejudice, be derogatory (detrimental) to, mar, cheapen, dis-

afbring   17   *affêre*

count, detract (derogate) from; *dit DOEN ~ aan die skoonheid van die gedig*, this mars the beauty of the poem; *dit doen ~ aan jou REPUTASIE*, it is detrimental to your reputation; *SONDER om ~ te doen aan*, without detracting from, without reducing (diminishing) the credit due to.
af'bring, (-ge-), bring down, reduce (weight); cause (abortion); come off (with honour); *iem. van 'n DWALING ~*, reason a person out of an error; *dit daar GOED van ~*, be successful; *iem. van die GOEIE pad ~*, lead a person astray; *dit daar HEELHUIDS ~*, come off without a scratch; *dit daar LEWEND ~*, escape with one's life; *iem. van 'n PLAN ~*, make someone give up a plan; *die VRUG ~*, cause abortion.
af'brokkel, (-ge-), crumble away; deteriorate; chip; ~**ing**, crumbling away, deterioration.
af'bruis, (-ge-), roar down.
af'buie, ..**buig**, (-ge-), bend down; deviate (a road); turn aside.
af'buiging, deviation; bending (down).
af'buitel, (-ge-), tumble down.
af'byt, (-ge-), bite off, pickle (metals with acid); *meer ~ as wat jy kan KOU*, undertake too much; *'n kort afgebyte (afgebete) STYL*, a snappy (terse) style; *jou WOORDE ~*, clip one's words.
af'daal, (-ge-), descend, go down; declass; *in BESONDERHEDE ~*, go into details; *tot IEM. ~*, come down to the level of, condescend to; *~ TOT*, stoop to.
af'dak, shed, lean-to, penthouse; hovel; drip-stone.
af'daling, descent; condescension.
af'dam, (ge), dam up (stream), dike; ~**ming**, (-e, -s), damming up, diking; dam, barrage, dike.
af'dank, (-ge-), disembody, disband (troops); pay off, dismiss, discharge, fire, cashier (a clerk); discard; cast off (clothing); *die troepe word afgedank*, the troops are being disbanded; ~**ing**, (-e, -s), discharge, dismissal, disbandment, demission, mittimus.
af'deel, (-ge-), divide, classify, parcel out; detach *(mil.)*; graduate (an instrument).
af'dek, (-ge-), remove (the cloth); cover, thatch; *die tafel ~*, clear the table; ~**king**, removing the cloth; clearing the table.
af'deling, (-e, -s), divison, section, detachment; draft (soldiers); compartment, partition, canton (province, country); corps (army); department; graduation (of instrument); *'n ~ RUITERY*, a body of horsemen (cavalry); *'n ~ SOLDATE*, a detachment of soldiers; *~ VIR mans*, men's ward; men's section; ~**'sbestuurder**, system manager; ~**shoof**, departmental head; section head; ~**sekretaris**, departmental secretary; ~**sraad**, divisional council.
af'demp, (-ge-), muffle, deaden the sound of (musical instrument); mute; ~**ing**, muting.
af'dig, (-ge-), seal, close (a can); ~**ring**, objurating ring; gastight joint; sealing ring; packing ring; ~**ting**, sealing; ~**vet**, sealing grease
af'ding, (-ge-), haggle, chaffer, higgle, beat down the price; *ek wil NIKS op sy verdienste ~ nie*, I do not wish to disparage his merits; *duar VAL niks op af te ding nie*, there is nothing to be said against it; ~**er**, haggler; ~**ing**, haggling, beating down.
af'dobbel, (-ge-), rob by gambling.
af'doen, (-ge-, -gedaan), finish, complete; lay aside; take off (a hat); dispatch, expedite (business); dispose of; reduce (prices); pay (a debt); cover, get through (work); *dit sal daar NIKS aandoen of ~ nie*, that will not alter the matter; *die SAAK is afgedaan*, the matter is settled; ~**de**, decisive; final; condign; effective; conclusive, adequate; up to the hilt; *'n ~ de BEWYS*, a conclusive proof; *~ de MAATREËLS*, decisive measures; ~**dheid**, finality, conclusiveness; decisiveness; ~**ing**, dispatch, disposal; settlement (of business); payment (of a debt).
af'donder, *(plat)*, (-ge-), fling, hurl, chuck down, clatter down; tumble down; *van die muur ~*, fall down from a wall.
af'dop, (-ge-), shell, hull; peel; blister, pop (paint); undress.

af'dra, (-ge-), wear out (clothes); hand over; carry down; pay over.
af'draad, (-ge-), fence in; string (beans).
af'draai, (-ge-), turn off (a tap); furcate, branch off (a road); turn away (at a crossroad); twist off; reel off (a film); strip (a thread); turn (a lathe); unwind (a roll); ~**sel**, (-s), turning(s) (of a metal).
af'draand, (-e, -es), **af'draande**, (-s), slope, decline, descent, declivity; descending grade; *op die ~ wees met die BRIEK los*, be the cause of one's own downfall; *op die ~ WEES*, going downhill.
af'draand, (-e), **af'draans**, descending, downhill, sloping; prone; *altyd die ~ e pad kies*, follow the line of least resistance.
af'draf, ..**drawwe**, (-ge-), trot off; finish in haste (quickly).
af'dreig, (-ge-), blackmail, extort; *iem. iets ~*, blackmail someone; ~**ing**, blackmail.
af'dreun, (-ge-), rattle off (poetry, a speech).
af'drifsel = **opdrifsel**.
af'dring, (-ge-), push (hustle) off; force from (promise).
af'drink, (-ge-), settle it over a glass; drink away (down).
af'droë, ..**droog**, (-ge-), dry (dishes); wipe off (away) (tears); become dry (a road).
af'droging, rubbing down, wiping off; drying off.
af'droog: ~**kraal**, draining-pen (dipping); ~**lap**, glass cloth, dish cloth.
af'druip, (-ge-), trickle down, fall in drops; go away stealthily, slink away; ~**sel**, (-s), guttering; drippings.
af'druis, (-ge-), roar down.
af'druk, (s), (-ke), copy, impression, counterfeit, press copy; reproduction (of a painting); imprint; (w) (-ge-), push off; push away; force down (prices); print (a photo); cast (in a foundry); press down (a lever); impress; off-print; ~**kas**, printing-box *(photog.)*; ~**ker**, cutter; depressor; ~**papier**, transfer paper; ~**raam**, printing-frame; ~**sel**, (-s), impress, impression, print, mark.
af'drup, (-ge-), ~**pel**, (-ge-), trickle down.
af'drup: ~**blad**, draining-board; ~**sel**, (-s), guttering; winding sheet (candle); dripping(s).
af'dryf, ..**drywe**, (-ge-), drive down (away); drift off; blow over (clouds); float downstream; repulse (the enemy); purge (a body); cause (an abortion); liquate; refine (gold).
af'dryfsel, (-s), flotsam, jetsam.
af'drywend, (-e), purgative; abortifacient.
af'drywing, (-e, -s), floating down; expulsion, purgation; abortion; liquation; deviation; drift; ~**smiddel**, purgative, ecbolic.
af'duik, (-ge-), dive down.
af'duiwel, (-ge-), tumble off, fall off (down).
af'dun, (-ge-), taper; ~**ning**, tapering.
af'dwaal, (-ge-), stray, err, deviate; digress, ramble, lose the thread, wander; aberrate; divagate; *~ van die onderwerp*, wander from the subject.
af'dwaling, (-e, -s), deviation, error, lapse; digression, divagation; aberration; aberratio ictus *(law)*.
af'dwarrel, (-ge-), whirl down; float (spin) down.
af'dweil, (-ge-), mop, mop down, mop up.
af'dwing, (-ge-), extort (money, a promise), force from; compel (admiration); constrain; enforce (discipline); *EERBIED ~*, command respect; *~ OP*, force upon; ~**baar**, (..**bare**), enforceable, constrainable, compellable; ~**bare eis**, actionable claim; ~**er**, (-s), extorter; ~**ing**, extortion, enforcement, exaction
af'eet, (afgeëet), eat off, browse.
af'eg, (afgeëg), harrow away.
af'eis, (afgeëis), demand.
afe'lium = **aphelium**.
af'ent, (afgeënt), graft on; inoculate on (into).
afere'se, **afe'resis**, aphaeresis.
affek', affect.
affek'sie, affection.
affekta'sie, (-s), affectation, mannerism.
affekteer', (-ge-), affect; **geaffekteerd**, affected.
affê're, **affê'ring**, (-s), affair, thing, matter; a nice how-do-you-do; business.

afferent   *afgooi*

afferent', (-e), afferent.
affida'vit, (-s), affidavit, oath.
af'fiks, (-e), affix.
affilia'sie, affiliation.
affilieer', (ge-), affiliate; ~ **met**, affiliate with, to.
affineer', (ge-), refine; ~ **dery**, (-e), refinery.
affiniteit', (-e), affinity.
affodil', (-le), daffodil.
affront', (-e), affront; ~**a'sie**, (-s), affront, insult; ~ **eer'**, (ge-), insult, affront; ~ **eer'speletjie**, come-sit-by-me.
affuit', (-e), (gun) carriage; mount; ~**slee**, gun slide.
af'gaan, (s), passage (movement) of the bowels; (w) (-ge-), go down, descend; leave (the road); depend (on) (a promise); get loose; subside, decrease; go off (alarm); discharge; be discharged (a gun); wear off (paint); go to stool; *hier moet DRIE sent ~*, three cents must be deducted here; ~ *de GETY*, ebb-tide; *die GLANS sal gou ~*, the lustre will soon be lost; *waar IS, moet ~*, when you have something you must expect losses; ~ *de KOORS*, remittent fever; ~ *de MAAN*, waning moon; *OP iem. se woord ~*, rely on the word of someone; *REG op iets ~*, make straight for something; *VAN mekaar ~*, separate, get divorced.
Afgaan', (..gane), Afghan; ~**s'**, Afghan.
af'gang, descent, declivity; stool, faeces.
Afga'nistan, Afghanistan.
af'gebete, abrupt, harsh; *'n ~ styl*, a snappy (terse) style; ~ **nheid**, abruptness, harshness.
af'gebeul, fagged out, jaded.
af'gebroke, interrupted; intermittent, discontinuous; incoherent, abrupt; broken.
af'gedaan, (..dane), finished; foregone.
af'gedank, (-te), discarded; dismissed.
af'gedankste, confounded, severe; *'n ~ DWAAS*, a blatant fool; *'n ~ LOESING (pak slae)*, a severe thrashing.
af'gedruk, (-te), printed.
af'gedwaal, (-de), strayed, astray; ~ *de lid*, lapsed (church) member.
af'gee, (-ge-), deliver, hand over (letters); be deprived of (by death); come off, issue; give off (paint, heat); give out (heat); give forth, emit (smell); mingle with (inferiors); result in, cause; *die BANK gee af*, the paint on the bench comes off; *die BRUID ~*, give away the bride; *jou ~ MET iets*, meddle with something; *jou ~ MET iem.*, have truck with someone; *TWIS ~*, cause dissension.
af'gehaal, (-de), humiliated, insulted, snubbed; *ek voel ~*, I feel insulted.
af'geheg, (-de, -te), cast-off (knitting).
af'gekant, (-e), chamfered.
af'gekeur, (-de), condemned.
af'geklim, dismounted.
af'geknot, (-te), stunted, maimed, pruned, truncated, doddered.
af'gekoel, (-de), cooled; chilled; iced.
af'gelas, (~), call off; countermand; ~ **ting**, calling-off.
af'geleë, (~ **ner**, ~ **nste; meer** ~ , **mees** ~), remote, distant, out-of-the-way, far outlying, lonely.
af'geleef, (-de), worn out, decrepit; aged; effete; ~ **dheid**, decrepitude, caducity, senility.
af'geleënheid, remoteness.
af'gelei, (-de), derived, concluded; ~ *de RIVIER*, diverted (beheaded) river; ~ *de WOORD*, derivative, derivation.
af'geloop, (-te), at an end.
af'gelope, finished; past; *die ~ jaar*, the past year.
af'geluister, (-de), overheard.
af'gemartel, (-de), tortured.
af'gemat, (-te), tired, fatigued, weary, exhausted, jaded, forspent, languorous; ~**heid**, fatigue, exhaustion.
af'gemete, measured; dignified, stately, formal, stiff, aloof; ~**nheid**, formality, stiffness, aloofness.
af'gepas, (-te), apportioned; measured (distance); exact (sum of money).
af'geplat, (-te), flattened, oblate, tabular, bevelled; ~ *te bol*, spheroid.
af'gerand, (-e), skirted (wool).

af'gerem, (-de), worn out; ~ *lyk*, look worn out.
af'gerig, (-te), trained, drilled; fit.
af'gerond, (-e), well-rounded (period); complete; ~ *e GEHEEL*, rounded whole; ~ *e SINNE*, well-rounded sentences.
af'geroom, (-de), skimmed; ~ *e melk*, skim(med) milk.
af'gesaag, (-de), sawn off (gun); banal, hackneyed, trite, stale (phrase); corny, hard-worked (joke); well-worn; beaten; *'n ~ de GESEGDE*, a trite saying; *'n ~ de GRAP*, a stale joke; ~**dheid**, triteness.
af'gesant, (-e), envoy, messenger, ambassador.
af'gesien: ~ *van*, notwithstanding, irrespective of, except for.
af'geskaf, (-te, -de), abrogated, abolished.
af'geskeidene, (-s), dissenter, nonconformist; separatist.
af'geskeidenheid, seclusion, privacy.
af'geskeie, separated, detached; divided; *die ~ KERK*, the Reformed (Nonconformist) Church; ~ *VAN*, apart from.
af'geskerf, (-de), chipped; ~ *de breekgoed*, chipped crockery.
af'geskrewe, written off.
af'geskrik, (-te), frightened off (away).
af'geslete, worn off; trite, stereotype.
af'gesloof, (-de), wearied out, worn out, jaded, careworn, fagged.
af'geslote, closed, secluded, isolated; *'n ~ geheel*, a complete whole; ~**nheid**, seclusion.
af'geslyt, (-e), worn out, attrited.
af'gesny, (-de), cropped, cut.
af'gesonder, (-de), isolated, retired, lonely, recluse, claustral; abstracted, disjunct; sequestered, private, close; ~**dheid**, isolation, insulation.
af'gespe, (-ge-), unbuckle, unclasp.
af'gesper, (-de), fenced off, barricaded.
af'gesproke, agreed, arranged.
af'gestomp, (-te), blunted, deadened, dulled.
af'gestorwe, deceased, dead; necrotic; ~ **ne**, (-s), deceased, dear departed, late lamented.
af'getakeldheid, decay.
af'getob, (-de), worn out, weary, careworn.
af'getredene, (-s), retired person.
af'getrokke, absentminded, preoccupied, absent, distracted; abstract; ~ *selfstandige naamwoord*, abstract noun; ~**nheid**, absence of mind; absent-mindedness, preoccupation; abstraction, abstract=edness; detachment.
af'gevaardigde, (-s), deputy, delegate; ~ **s**, delegacy, delegation.
af'geval, (-de, -le), fallen; ~ *de APPELS*, fallen apples; ~ *le LID*, renegade member, turncoat.
af'gevallene, (-s), apostate, renegade.
af'gewas, (-te, -de), washed away; *iem. hou hom ~*, he pretends to know nothing.
af'gewerk, (-te), finished, completed (sculpture); haggard, worn out, tired, overworked, tired out.
af'gewese, refused, rejected, dismissed.
af'gewronge, extorted (confession).
af'giet, (-ge-), cast, mould; strain (pour) off; pour down; ~ **sel**, cast, mould; copy; ~ **seldiertjies**, infusoria.
af'gifte, delivery; issue (of certificate); *by ~ van die telegram*, on delivery of the telegram.
af'glip, (-ge-), slip down; ~ **ping**, slipping down.
af'glooi, (-ge-), slope down; ~ **ing**, slope, sloping.
af'gly, (-ge-), glide down, slide down, slip (down); ~ **ding**, sliding down; glissade (down a snow slope); ~ **draai**, slipping turn *(aeron.)*.
af'god, idol; fetish; *'n ~ van KLEI*, a clay idol; *'n ~ MAAK van*, idolise, worship.
af'gode: ~ **aanbidder**, ~ **dienaar**, idolator; ~**diens**, ~ **ry**, (-e), idolatry.
afgo'dies, (-e), idolatrous.
afgodis', (-te), idolator.
af'gods: ~ **beeld**, idol, (molten, graven) image; ~**dienaar**, idolator; ~ **dienares**, idolatress; ~ **tempel**, temple of an idol.
af'goël, (-ge-), obtain by trickery.
af'gooi, (-ge-), throw down; drop (golf-ball); dump;

afgord   *afknip*

cast off (the yoke of slavery); decant (wine); un=horse; slip (a calf); fling aside (care).

af'gord, (-ge-), lay aside (weapon); unbuckle.

af'graaf, ..**grawe**, (-ge-), dig down, level.

af'gradeer, (-ge-), grade down, degrade.

af'grens, (-ge-), mark out, delimit.

af'grond, precipice, abyss, pit, chasm, gulf; hell; *'n GAPENDE ~*, a yawning gulf; *op die RAND van die ~*, on the edge of the precipice; *iem. in die ~ STORT*, ruin someone; *~beleid*, brinkmanship.

af'grou, (-ge-), speak rudely to, snarl at.

af'gryp, (-ge-), grab, seize.

af'gryse, horror, abhorrence; *met ~ vervul*, horror-struck; fill with horror.

afgrys'lik, (-e), horrible, ghastly, hideous, monstrous, atrocious, dreadful; *~heid*, hideousness, horribleness, dreadfulness, ghastliness, grisliness, atrocity.

af'guns, envy, grudge, jealousy, spite, heart-burning; *~'tig*, (-e), envious, jealous, spiteful, jaundiced; *~'tigheid*, envy, enviousness, jealousy, grudge, spite.

af'guts, (-ge-), stream down.

af'haak, (-ge-), let go, let loose; unhook, detach (railway carriage); pull (trigger); stop work; unhitch; get married; *wanneer gaan julle twee ~?* when are you two getting married?

af'haal, (-ge-), take off, take down, fetch down; meet, call for (a person); insult, snub (a person); dismount, dismantle (a tyre); collect (letters); strip (beds); doff (a cap); *BOONTJIES ~*, string beans; *IEM. ~*, insult a person; *~koste*, collection charges; *~wa*, collecting van (lorry).

af'haar, (-ge-), depilate, remove the hair; string (beans).

af'hak, (-ge-), chop off, lop off.

af'halerig, (-e), insulting.

af'handel, (-ge-), settle, terminate, finalize, bring to a close; despatch; *~ing*, settling, termination, settlement; dismissal.

afhan'dig: *iem. iets ~ maak*, pilfer (filch) something from someone.

af'hang, (-ge-), hang down, droop, decline; lop; depend (up)on; *alles hang van jou af*, everything depends on you; *~end*, (-e), drooping, hanging; reclinate *(bot.)*.

afhank'lik, (-e), dependent, depending; *~e*, (-s), dependent; *~heid*, dependence.

af'hap, (-ge-), bite off.

af'haring, depilation.

af'hark, (-ge-), rake away.

af'haspel, (-ge-), rattle off; bungle.

af'hê, (-gehad), complete, finish; reduce; *ek wil vanmiddag ~*, I want this afternoon off.

af'heg, (-ge-), cast off (knitting); finish; *~knoop*, crown-knot; *~ting*, finish (cordage).

af'heid, finish, completeness.

af'hein, (-ge-), fence in (off).

af'hel, (-ge-), decline, slope down, fall, dip, slant; *~lend*, (-e), sloping down, declivitous, declivous; *~ling*, slope, declivity, declination, dip.

af'help, (ge), help down; rid (of something).

af'hok, (-ge-), put in pen, shed, kennel, etc.; isolate, separate.

af'hol, (-ge-), rush (run) down (from a hill).

af'hou¹, (s) down stroke; (w) (-ge-), keep off (a hat); keep from; fend off; hinder; withhold, deduct (money); turn; *die BABETJIE ~*, hold the baby out; *die HANDE van iem. ~*, not interfere with someone; not touch someone; *van die LAND ~*, stand from the (off-) shore; *REGS ~*, turn to the right; *iem. van sy WERK ~*, keep someone from his work.

af'hou², (-ge-), cut off, chop off, lop off.

af'hys, (-ge-), hoist down, lift off.

afillie', aphylly.

af'ja(ag), (-ge-), chase off (a hen from a nest); race over (a stretch of road); hasten through (a narrative); force down (prices); rush at; perform hurriedly; *op die vyand ~*, rush upon the enemy.

af'jaart(s), (-ge-), measure off in yards.

af'jak, (s) (-ke), rating, insult, rebuff; scolding; (w) (-ge-), rate, scold, chide; snub, rebuff, insult, affront.

af'jakker, (-ge-), overdrive (a horse); worry to death; exhaust (wear out) oneself (with pleasure), play, play around; bungle.

af'kabbel, (-ge-), wear (wash) away; burble (purl, ripple) along; *~ing*, (-e, -s), scouring; rippling along.

af'kalf, ..**kalwe(r)**, (-ge-), cave in, fall in, crumble away (soil).

af'kalwing, caving in.

af'kam, (-ge-), comb off; run down, flay, belittle (by criticism); *~mery*, disparagement, depreciation; *~ming*, combing off; decrial.

af'kamp, (-ge-), fence off, impark, rail in.

af'kant, (-ge-), bevel off, edge, chamfer; *~boor*, chamferbit.

af'kantel, (-ge-), tumble down.

af'kant: *~gereedskap*, bevelling tools; *~ing*, chamfer; *~ingsbeitel*, finishing chisel; *~skaaf*, chamferplane.

af'kap, (-ge-), cut off (down); chop off (down); chip, chisel; break (off), apostrophize (a word); *~ en uitsleep*, felling and slipping (forestry); *~ping*, cutting off, truncation, felling; aphaeresis (at beginning of a word); apocope (at end of a word); *~pingsteken*, apostrophe.

af'karring, (-ge-), churn; rattle off (a speech); masturbate.

af'karteling, fret.

af'keer, (s) aversion (to); odium, repugnance (against); loathing, horror, abhorrence (of); disinclination, disrelish; hate, dislike (to, for, of); side furrow; *'n HÊ van*, have a dislike of; *~ INBOESEM*, inspire aversion; *met ~ VERVUL*, fill with aversion; *~ VOEL teenoor*, feel dislike towards; (w); (-ge-), avert (danger); ward off (blow); turn away (aside); *'n VUISSLAG ~*, ward off (parry) a blow with the fist; *die WATER (in die sloot) ~*, turn away (aside) the water (in the furrow).

af'kerf, ..**kerwe**, (-ge-), carve (off); cut (tobacco); die.

afke'rig, disaffected; disinclined; *~ van*, averse to; *~heid*, dislike, aversion, disaffectedness.

af'kets, (-ge-), glance off, ricochet (bullet); reject, defeat (a motion).

af'keur, (-ge-), disapprove, find fault with, frown upon; veto; condemn, blame, denounce, deprecate; reject, declare unfit; discard, scrap; disallow, disavow, discommend; decry, animadvert; *~baar*, (..bare), condemnable, rejectable; *~end*, (-e), condemnatory, dispraising; *jou ~ end uitlaat oor*, comment adversely upon; *~enswaar'dig*, (-e), censurable, condemnable, objectionable, blameworthy, reprehensible; *~ing*, disapprobation, disapproval, condemnation, censure, denouncement; stricture; decrial; animadversion; *'n mosie van ~ing aanneem*, pass a vote of censure; *~ingsreg*, veto right; *~merk*, condemned (mark).

af'klaar, (-ge-), clarify; clear; decant.

af'klap, (-ge-), pop off; peg out; *doppie ~*, miss fire; *~skoot*, misfire.

af'klaring, decantation.

af'klim, (-ge-), climb down, descend; get off, get down (from a vehicle); unmount, dismount (from a horse); rebuke; *OP iem. ~*, rebuke a person; *van sy PERDJIE ~*, come down a notch or two; *~plek*, halt, alighting-point.

af'klink, (-ge-), pop off; drink as friends (after a quarrel); *DIT ~*, settle a matter over a glass; *te VROEG ~*, die too soon.

af'klits, (-ge-), finish beating (eggs); shoot down.

af'kloof, (-ge-), split (wood).

af'klop, (-ge-), beat (carpets); thrash; die, peg out.

af'klouter, (-ge-), scramble (climb) down.

af'kluif, ..**kluiwe**, (-ge-), pick (a bone); gnaw at (off).

af'knaag, (-ge-), gnaw off (away).

af'knabbel, (-ge-), browse on; gnaw (away), nibble at.

af'knak, (-ge-), snap (break) off.

af'knap, (-ge-), snap.

af'knibbel, (-ge-), gnaw off; haggle down (price).

af'knip, (-ge-), cut off, lop, snip (clip) off; switch off; die; *~sel*, clipping, cutting; trimming.

af'knot, (-ge-), lop off, truncate; poll (horns); ~ **ting**, truncation; polling.
af'knou, (-ge-), hurt, bully, play roughly with, man= handle; ~**er**, (-s), bully; ~**erig**, (-e), bullying; ~**ery**, ~**ing**, bullying.
af'knyp, (-ge-), pinch off; poll (horns); shoot; *'n paar rand* ~, scrape up a rand or two, cut down by a couple of rands; economize.
af'koel, (-ge-), cool down; chill, refrigerate; calm down; ~**er**, (-s), cooler.
af'koeling, calming down; refrigeration, cooling; cooling system; cracking (oil).
af'koelings: ~**installasie**, cooling plant; ~**middel**, cooling agent; ~**oond**, annealing oven (furnace); ~(**opper**)**vlak**, cooling surface; ~**politiek**, détente; ~**pyp**, flue; ~**vlak**, cooling surface; ~**wet**, law of refrigeration.
af'koel: ~**middel**, cooling medium; ~**rak**, cooling rack (shelf, tray); ~**stelsel**, cooling (refrigeration) system.
af'kom, (-ge-), come down, descend; reduce (prices); come off; get rid off; meet unexpectedly, strike; issue (from ancestry); *met 'n BOETE daarvan* ~, get off with a fine; *daar GENADIG van* ~, get off lightly; ~ *OP*, meet unexpectedly (a wild animal); discover, catch; *die RIVIER sal* ~, the river will be in flood (come down); *met die SKRIK daarvan* ~, get off with a fright; *hy het daar SLEG van afge= kom*, he came off badly; ~ *TOT op*, come down to; ~ *VAN*, get off; ~**eling**, (-e), descendant.
af'koms, parentage, descent; derivation (of word); extraction, birth, family, ancestry, origin(ation); pedigree; *GOEIE* ~, gentility, good stock; *HOË* ~, noble ancestry, gentlehood; *VAN goeie (hoë)* ~, gently born; be of noble birth.
afkoms'tig, (-e), derived from; originating from; *HARE van 'n dier* ~, hair belonging to an animal; *UIT Rusland* ~, of Russian origin.
af'kondig, (-ge-), proclaim (a republic); declare (a moratorium); promulgate (a law); call; publish; *die gebooie* ~, publish the banns; ~**er**, proclaimer; ~**ing**, (-e, -s), proclamation, declaration, promul= gation, publication.
af'konkel, (-ge-), coax away, entice from; persuade in an underhand way; alienate; ~**ing**, alienation.
af'kook, (-ge-), decoct (herbs); parboil (tough meat); boil down to; ~**sel**, (-s), decoction, pot liquor; ex= tract (of meat); ptisan; compilation, summary (of a book); elixir.
af'koop, (s), buying off; ransom; redemption; surren= der (a policy); (w) (-ge-), buy off, ransom, redeem; pay out; commute (pension); ~**baar**, (..**bare**), re= deemable; corruptible; venal; ~**baarheid**, redeema= bility; corruptibility; ~**boete**, spot fine; ~**geld**, ransom; hushmoney; ~**prys**, indemnity; ~**som**, ransom, redemption money; hushmoney; ~**waarde**, surrender value (of policy).
af'kop, without head, decapitated, headless.
af'kopend, (-e), redemptive.
af'koper, redeemer; corrupter.
af'koping, composition; ransom, redemption.
af'koppel, (-ge-), uncouple; disconnect (a telephone); disengage (a clutch); unhook; ~**ing**, uncoupling, disconnection.
af'korrel, (-ge-), pick off grapes (from a bunch); aim, measure.
af'korsing, decrustation.
af'kort, (-ge-), shorten; abbreviate (a word); abridge (a story); ~**ing**, abbreviation, abridgement; *op ~ing betaal*, pay on account; in part payment; ~**ingsteken**, abbreviation mark; apostrophe.
af'kou, (-ge-), chew off.
af'krabbel, (-ge-), scribble (down).
af'krap, (-ge-), scrape off, scratch away (off); scribble down; scold; ~**per**, scraper; ~**sel**, scrapings.
af'kronkel, (-ge-), wind down (a road).
af'kruie, (-ge-), trundle along (down); trudge along.
af'kruip, (-ge-), creep (crawl) down.
af'krummel, (-ge-), crumble off.
af'kry, (-ge-), get down (from a shelf); remove, separ= ate; complete (work); *'n vlek* ~, remove a stain.
af'kwansel, (-ge-), obtain in exchange.

af'kweking, subculture.
af'kwyl, (-ge-), dribble down.
af'kyk, (-ge-), observe, spy; copy, crib; look down; learn by looking at; await, wait for; *'n KANS* ~, wait for an opportunity; *iem. se WERK* ~, copy the work of someone, crib someone's work; ~**ery**, cribbing; ~**papiertjie**, crib, cab; ~**werk**, cribbing.
af'laai, (-ge-), unload, unship; off-load; discharge, dump; disburden; *werk op iem. anders* ~, pass your work on to someone else; ~**koste**, off-loading charges.
af'laat, *(R.K.)*, (s), (**aflate**), indulgence; pardon; *volle* ~, plenary indulgence; (w), (-ge-), leave off; let down (a curtain); desist; lower; ~**brief**, letter of in= dulgence; ~**geld**, indulgence money; ~**handel**, sale of indulgences; ~**kramer**, seller of indulgences; ~**prediker**, preacher selling indulgences; ~**ver= koper**, pardoner; ~**week**, week of Corpus Christi.
af'lag, (-ge-), laugh away (off).
aflan'dig, (-e), off-shore.
af'las, (-ge-), call off, cancel.
af'lê, (-ge-), lay down (aside); part with, discard (an overcoat); lay out (a body for burial); take (an oath); pass (an examination); cover (a distance); layer (a plant); give (evidence); pay (a visit); *'n AF= STAND* ~, cover a distance; *'n BESOEK* ~, pay a visit, call; *'n EED* ~, take an oath; *'n EKSAMEN* ~, write, undergo an examination; *GETUIENIS* ~, give evidence; *die LEWE* ~ *vir jou land*, lay down one's life for one's country; *die MASKER* ~, throw off the mask; *hy moes dit teen sy MEDE= DINGER* ~, he was no match for his rival.
af'leer, (-ge-), unlearn, forget; cure of; *ek sal jou dié gewoonte laat* ~, I shall cure you of this habit.
af'lêer, dropper (for a fence); layer, offshoot (of a plant).
af'lees, (-ge-), call (read) out; *die ~ van 'n termo= meter*, the reading of a thermometer; ~**skaal**, measuring-scale.
af'legging, laying down, taking of (oath); laying aside; kenosis.
af'lei, (-ge-), lead down; deduce, infer, educe; evolve; conclude; distract, divert (attention, water); derive (words); conduct *(electr.)*; *wat moet ek uit jou woorde* ~?, what must I infer from your words? ~**baar**, (..**bare**), educible, deducible, inferable; constructive (permission); ~**buis**, fistula.
af'leiding, distraction, diversion (mind); deduction (logic); derivation (words); corollary; deducement; deviation (water); derivative; ~ *SOEK*, seek diver= sion (distraction); *TENNIS is 'n goeie ~ na al jou studie*, tennis is a good recreation after all your study; ~**saanval**, diversion (attack); ~**skanaal**, drain; ~**smiddel**, distraction; diversion; ~**svorm**, derivative form(ation), derivation form, derivative.
af'lei: ~**er**, (lightning) conductor; dropper (for fenc= ing); ~**kanaal**, drain; ~**kunde**, etymology; ~**ska= kelaar**, drainage switch; ~**voor**, drain; derivation furrow.
af'lek, (-ge-), lick (with the tongue); trickle down (water).
af'lewer, (-ge-), deliver; hand over; ~**ing**, (-s), deliv= ery; part, number, volume (of a magazine); *'n werk in ~ inge*, a serial publication; ~**ingsbrief**, delivery note; ~**ingskoste**, delivery charges; ~**ingstaat**, de= livery sheet; ~**ingstasie**, cartage station; ~**ingswa**, delivery van (lorry, vehicle).
af'lig, (-ge-), lift off; light down (the steps); free from.
af'loer, (-ge-), spy, watch; ~**der**, (-s), Peeping Tom, peeper; ~**dery**, peeping; spying.
af'lok, (-ge-), entice away; ~**king**, enticing, entice= ment.
af'loop, (s), end, result, issue; run-off (water); rill; run (of a candle); slope; speening (of grapes); denoue= ment (of a drama); expiry (of time); termination (of a contract); drain, gutter; outlet; gully; *'n ONGE= LUK met dodelike* ~, a fatal accident; *na ~ van die VERGADERING*, after the meeting; (w) (-ge-), end, expire, terminate; flow; run down, decline; run off; ebb; eventuate; walk down; foot (a distance); slope; deviate; cause to grow downward (plants); loot; wear out (shoes); gutter (a candle); measure

aflopend   21   *afransel*

(by walking); launch (a ship); *ek het my BENE afgeloop om die ding te koop*, I walked from shop to shop to buy the article; *GOED* ~, turn out well; *dit IS afgeloop met hom*, he is dying; *die KLOK is afgeloop*, the clock has run down; *die KONTRAK loop af*, the contract expires; *die TAPYT is afgeloop*, the carpet is worn; ~**bedding**, launching way, ramp; ~**gang**, draining-race (for cattle); ~**groefies**, rill marks; ~**kraal**, drying-pen; ~**plank**, gangway; draining-board; ~**slootjies**, runnels, rill marks; ~**water**, tail water, tailings; run-off; drainage-water.

af′lopend, (-e), decurrent, decursive, expiring.

af′los, (-ge-), relieve (a guard); redeem (a bond); discharge (a debt); *MEKAAR* ~, take turns; *sal jy my NOU* ~? will you take my place (relieve me) now? *sy SKULD* ~, pay his debts; ~**baar, (..bare)**, redeemable; terminable; ~*baar teen pari*, redeemable at par; ~**klerk**, relief clerk; ~**ser**, substitute, stand-in; ~**sing**, relief; redemption; call; ~**singsgewyse**, in relays; ~**(sing)som**, amount redeemed; ~**personeel**, relief staff; ~**(sings)plan**, redemption scheme; ~**(sings)reg**, right of redemption; ~**(sings)troepe**, relief (troops); ~**(sings)voorwaardes**, terms of redemption; ~**(sings)waarde**, redemption value; ~**wedloop**, relay race; ~**(sings)werk**, relief work; ~**suster**, relief sister; ~**vliegtuig**, relief aeroplane (aircraft).

af′lui, (-ge-), ring off; ~**ing**, ringing off.

af′luister, (-ge-), overhear; eavesdrop; bug; ~**aar**, eavesdropper; bugger; ~**y**, eavesdropping, phone-tapping; bugging.

af′lyn, (-ge-), mark, line out; delimit.

af′maai, (-ge-), mow (wheat); cut down, kill (with a sword); *deur die dood afgemaai*, cut off by death.

af′maak, (-ge-), kill, finish (off), destroy; thresh (maize); bring to a conclusion; remove (stains); scrape off; settle (a dispute); run down (a book); *jou met 'n GRAP van iets* ~, pass off as a joke; *MET iem.* ~, make friends again with someone; *MIELIES* ~, shell mealiecobs; *hy het hom van die SAAK afgemaak*, he backed out of the matter.

af′maal, (-ge-), grind.

af′maker, (-s), sheller, husker.

af′making, disengagement; settlement.

af′mars, departure, marching off (of troops).

af′marsjeer, (-ge-), march off, file off.

af′martel, (-ge-), torture, torment, worry, fret; ~**ing**, torture.

af′mat, (-ge-), tire, fatigue, fag, exhaust, harass, override; ~**tend, (-e)**, tiresome, wearisome, fatiguing; ~**ting**, weariness, fatigue, exhaustion; ~**tingsoorlog**, war of attrition.

af′meet, (-ge-), gauge, measure off; proportion, mensurate; ~**baar, (..bare)**, measurable.

af′merk, (-ge-), measure (off); mark (sports field, parking-site); ~**tou**, marking-tape.

af′meting, (-e, -s), measurement, measure, admeasurement, dimension; *'n GEBOU van reusagtige* ~*e*, a building of gigantic proportions; *GROOT* ~*s aanneem*, assume huge proportions; *van VIER* ~*s*, of four dimensions, fourdimensional.

af′monster, (-ge-), sign off; discharge; ~**ing**, discharging.

af′muur, (-ge-), separate by means of a wall.

af′nael, (-ge-), run off (away).

af′name, decrease, diminution, decline, decay, drop, reduction (in trade); record, noting down.

af′neem (-ge-), take from; take down (off); remove (a hat); deprive of (money); lessen; decrease, shrink (trade); take a photo, photograph; cut (cards); conduct (an examination); clear (the table); ebb (away); *die DAE neem af*, the days are becoming shorter; *iem. 'n EED* ~, administer an oath to someone; *'n EKSAMEN* ~, examine; conduct an examination; *sy KRAGTE neem vinnig af*, his strength is rapidly ebbing, he is sinking; *die MAAN neem af*, the moon is on the wane; *'n ROK laat* ~, shorten a dress; ~**baar, (..bare)**, detachable, removable; ~*bare dele*, removable parts, movable (moving) parts; ~**toestel**, camera.

af′nek, with a broken neck.

af′nemend, (-e), decreasing, diminishing, fading; *die* ~ *e maan*, the waning moon.

af′nemer, photographer; buyer, customer; ~**y, (-e)**, photographing; photographer's studio.

af′neming, decline, decay; Descent (from the Cross).

af′nerf, (-ge-), peel off the outer skin; grain (leather); thrash.

af′nerwing, graining.

af′nommer, (-ge-), number off (down).

af′oes, (-ge-), reap, harvest.

afonie′, aphony, loss of voice.

af′oor, crop-eared; ~**koppie**, cup without a handle.

aforis′me, (-s), aphorism, epigram.

aforis′ties, (-e), aphoristic, epigrammatic.

af′paal, (-ge-), peg (stake) out; fence in; delimit, define.

af′paar, (-ge-), pair off.

af′pak, (-ge-), unpack, unload.

af′palm, (-ge-), fob; ~ *op*, fob off (up)on.

af′paring, pairing-off.

af′pas, (-ge-), measure, count, apportion; *'n afgepaste som geld*, an exact sum of money.

af′patrolleer, (-ge-), patrol.

af′peil, (-ge-), fathom, gauge.

af′pel, (-ge-), shell, peel.

af′pen, (-ge-), lay out (a garden, an area); peg off (a claim); ~**ning**, pegging-off.

af′perk, (-ge-), enclose, shut off; limit, circumscribe; fence in; ~**ing**, limitation, demarcation; enclosure.

af′pers, (-ge-), extort (money); force from; rack (off); exact from (a promise); *GELD van iem.* ~, blackmail a person; *TRANE* ~, draw tears; ~**bende**, gang of extortioners (blackmailers), ~**end, (-e)**, extortive, extortionary; ~**er**, extorter, racketeer, extortioner; ~**ing**, extortion, exaction, chantage, blackmail.

af′peul, (-ge-), shell (peas).

af′peusel, (-ge-), pick at (one's food).

af′piekel, (-ge-), carry (drag) down; saunter along.

af′piets, (-ge-), flick (hit) off; rattle off.

af′pik, (-ge-), peck off.

af′plat, (-ge-), flatten, bevel; ~**ting**, flattening.

af′pleister, (-ge-), plaster, cover with plaster.

af′ploeg, (-ge-), plough off (roots); finish ploughing.

af′plof, (-ge-), tumble down.

af′plooi, (-ge-), pleat.

af′pluis, (-ge-), pick off (fluff); give off (fluff).

af′pluk, (-ge-), pick off, gather (fruit); pull down (from a wall); ~**ker**, gatherer, picker.

af′poeier, (-ge-), powder; *iem.* ~, dust someone's jacket.

af′poets, (-ge-), scour, clean, polish.

af′pomp, (-ge-), pump down.

af′poot, with a broken leg; without a leg, legless.

af′praat, (-ge-), arrange (a matter); agree upon; dissuade from (an undertaking).

af′prewel, (-ge-), mumble (prayers), mutter.

af′pulwer, (-ge-), crumble.

af′punt, (-ge-), remove the point(s), bevel.

af′pyl, (-ge-), run straight for something; make a beeline for someone; *die voertuig het op my afgepyl*, the vehicle came straight at me.

af′pynig, (-ge-), torture; rack (one's brain).

af′raai, (-ge-), dissuade from, discommend, caution (advise) against; *hy het my dit afgeraai*, he cautioned me against it; he advised me not to do it; ~**end, (-e)**, dissuasive; ~**ing**, dissuasion.

af′raak, (-ge-), get away from, go astray; get rid of; be broken off; *van die DRANK* ~, drop the drink habit; *van sy ONDERWERP* ~, lose the thread of one's discourse; *van die PAD* ~, lose one's way; leave the road; *hy het van sy VROU afgeraak*, he has become estranged from his wife.

af′rafel (-ge-), ravel out.

af′rammel, (-ge-), prattle, rattle off; patter; *die Onse Vader* ~, rattle off the Lord's Prayer.

af′rand, (-ge-), edge (off); skirt (fleece); ~**saag**, edger; ~**sels**, skirtings.

af′ransel, (-ge-), thrash, flog, belabour, pepper, punish, cudgel, curry, lace, larrup, bang; horsewhip, belt; ~**ing**, whipping, thrashing, flogging, spanking, lacing.

af'raspe(r), (-ge-), rasp off.
af'rasping, rasping off.
af'raster, (-ge-), rail off; ~ing, railing.
af'ratel, (-ge-), rattle off, gabble.
af'reën, ..reent, (-ge-), get washed off by rain (paint); rain down.
af'reis, (s), departure; (w) (-ge-), depart, leave; *die hele land* ~, travel all over the country.
af'reken, (-ge-), pay, settle (debts); get even with; deduct; *ek het goed met hom afgereken*, I have paid him out; ~**ing**, settling of accounts, settlement, liquidation; *dag van* ~*ing*, day of reckoning.
af'rem, (-ge-), apply brakes; break by pulling; tire out, exhaust; *daar afgerem uitsien*, look very tired.
Africa'na, Africana; ~**veiling**, auction of Africana; ~**versamelaar**, collector of Africana.
af'rig, (-ge-), train, coach; exercise; produce (a play); break in, dress (a horse); turn away (the eyes); ~**ter** (-s), trainer, coach; producer (a play); director (a play, film); ~**ting**, training, coaching; producing, directing.
Af'rika, Africa; ~*tale*, African languages.
Afrikaan', (..kane), African.
Afrikaans', (s) Afrikaans (language); (b) (-e), Afrikaans; ~**gesind**, Afrikaans-minded; pro-Afrikaans; ~**heid**, something characteristic of Afrikaans or the Afrikaner; Africanism; ~**kun'dig, (-e)**, conversant with Afrikaans; ~**sprekend**, Afrikaans-speaking.
afrika'ner¹, (-s) anyone of various wild flowers, e.g. *Gladiolus, Homoglossum.*
Afrika'ner², (-s), Afrikaner; South African (white man); ~**bees**, Afrikan(d)er (breed of cattle peculiar to South Africa); ~**bloed**, Afrikaner blood; ~**bul**, Afrikan(d)er bull; ~**dogter**, Afrikaner girl; ~**dom**, Afrikanerdom; ~**gesin**, Afrikaner family; ~**hart**, Afrikaner heart (soul); ~**kind**, Afrikaner child; ~**nasie**, Afrikaner nation; ~**seun**, Afrikaner boy; ~**skaap**, fat-tailed South-African sheep.
afrika'nertjie, (-s), ornamental plant *(Tageus erecat).*
afrika'nertroos, coffee.
Afrika'nervolk, Afrikaner nation.
Afrikanis', (-te), student of the Afrikaans language; student of African languages.
Afrikanisa'sie, Afrikaansification.
Afrikanis'me Afrikaans expression (idiom).
Afrikanistiek, African Studies.
af'rit, (-te), off-ramp (traffic); ramp; departure.
af'rits, (-ge-), rattle off; break off.
af'rittel, (-ge-), rattle off, gabble.
Af'ro-Asia'ties, (-e), Afro-Asian; ~**e blok**, Afro-Asian bloc; ~**e lande**, Afro-Asian countries.
afrodiet', (-e), hermaphrodite.
af'roei, (-ge-), row down; cover by rowing; *'n lang AFSTAND* ~, row over a long distance; *die RIVIER* ~, row down the river.
af'roep, (-ge-), call out; call over (roll); announce (a strike); call away (dog); ~**er**, crier; ~**ing**, proclamation.
af'roes, (-ge-), rust away (off).
af'roffel, (-ge-), rough-plane; bungle (one's work); scold.
af'rokkel, (-ge-), coax away, wheedle away, juggle out of, inveigle out of; *iem. se bediendes* ~, coax away someone's servants.
af'rol, (-ge-), roll down, unroll (a cloth); uncoil, lay out (a wire); cyclostyle, duplicate, gestetner; ~**ink**, duplicator ink; ~**masjien**, duplicator, gestetner.
af'romer, (-s), (cream) separator.
af'rond, (-ge-), round off; blunt; complete; camber (road); skirt (wool); ~**beitel**, rounding-tool; ~**ing**, rounding-off, finish; ~**ingsmasjien**, rounding-machine; ~**sels**, skirtings; ~**tafel**, skirting-table.
af'room, (-ge-), skim, cream, separate (milk); *afgeroomde melk*, skimmed (separated) milk, skim milk.
af'ros, (-ge-), thrash, lick, wallop.
af'roskam, (-ge-), rub down; run down, slate; curry-comb.
af'ruim, (-ge-), clear away, clear (a table).
af'ruk, (-ge-), tear off, snatch away; pull down; march on; *op die vyand* ~, bear down upon the enemy.

af'ry, (-ge-), drive (ride) down (off); cover by riding (driving); transport, convey; *die motorhuis se deur* ~, ride off the garage door.
af'rye, af'ryg, (-ge-), unlace, unstring.
af'rypaal, starting-place.
af'saag, ..sae, (-ge-), saw off, poll (horns); *'n balk* ~, snore.
af'saal, (-ge-), off-saddle; unsaddle; bait; rest; *êrens* ~, go courting somewhere.
af'sak, (-ge-), sink, go down; slip down, sag (clothes); settle, clarify (sediment); float (sail) down; deteriorate, weaken; ~**king**, sagging; slipping down; prolapse; ~**sel**, (-s), dregs, lees (wine); silt, sediment, sludge, grout, ooze, (alluvial) deposit; ~**selbak**, sump.
af'sê, (-ge-), throw over, sack (your fiancée); countermand; cancel (an order); *sy meisie het hom afgesê*, his fiancée broke the engagement (gave him the sack).
af'seep, (-ge-), clean with soap.
af'segging, sacking (throwing over) (a fiancée); countermand, cancellation.
af'seil, (-ge-), sail, put to sea, sail down (canal); slip down; make for.
af'send, (-ge-), send off, forward, consign, dispatch; ~**er**, sender, consignor; despatcher; ~**ing**, consignment, despatch, forwarding; (~**ing**)**stasie**, forwarding station.
af'set, (s), turnover, sale: market ~ *VIND*, find a market; *maklike* ~ *VIND*, find a ready sale; (w) (-ge-), victimize, swindle, overcharge, cheat; sell; deposit (mud); trim, set off; ~**baar, (..bare)**, disposable, marketable; ~**gebied**, market, outlet, sales area; ~**masjien**, offset machine; ~**metode**, marketing (sales) method; ~**plan**, sales (marketing) scheme; ~ **plek**, market(place); ~**sel** (-s), sediment, layer, deposit.
af'setter, (-s), swindler, cheat; copycatcher; ~**y**, swindling, cheating.
af'setting, (-e, -s), deposition, dismissal, dethronement, degradation; amputation (of a limb); precipitation; sediment, deposit; sedimentation; demission; layer; ablation.
af'settingsgesteente, sedimentary rock.
af'setvraagstuk, marketing problem
af'sien, (-ge-), look down; give up, abandon (a plan); relinquish, waive (claim); *van 'n plan* –, give up a plan.
afsien'baar, (..bare), measurable; *binne* ~ *bare tyd*, in the foreseeable future, within a measurable space of time, shortly.
af'sif, (-ge-), sift away; trot off.
afsig'telik, (-e), ugly, frightful, hideous, ghastly, gruesome, grim; grisly; ~**heid**, hideousness, ghastliness, ugliness, frightfulness, gruesomeness.
af'sink, (-ge-), sink down; descend; lose status.
af'sit, (s), start; *by die* ~, at the start; (w), (-ge-), put down; amputate (a limb); deprive (of office); disestablish, dismiss (from office); depose, dethrone, discrown; run away; start, begin, dash away; defrock, unfrock (a clergyman); drop (a passenger); guard; trim (a dress); degrade, cashier (an officer); break by sitting (leg of a chair); switch off (the light); deposit (mud); sell (produce); take off (aircraft); face (with ribbon); *'n BEEN* –, amputate a leg; *voor DAGBREEK* ~, set off (go) before daybreak; ~**baar, (..bare)**, deposable; ~**putjie**, first hole *(golf);* ~**ter**, starter; dethroner; ~**ting**, amputation.
af'skaaf, ..skawe, (-ge-), plane away; rub away (rusticity); excoriate, graze, abrade (skin); skive (leather); ~**sel** shaving; filings.
af'skaal, (-ge-), exfoliate.
af'skadu, (-ge-), shadow forth, foreshadow, adumbrate; typify, silhouette; ~**wing**, adumbration, shadowing, shadow, silhouette.
af'skaf, (-ge-), abolish (a practice); do away with; abrogate, repeal (a law); part with; abstain from, cut out, give up (drink), ~ **fer**, abstainer, prohibitionist, teetotaller; abolitionist; abolisher; ~**fershotel**, temperance hotel.

afskaffing 23 *afslaan*

af'skaffing, abolition, abolishment; prohibition, teetotalism; abrogation; repeal (a law).
af'skaffings: ~**beweging**, temperance movement; ~**genootskap**, temperance society.
af'skakel, (-ge-), change down (gears); switch off (a light); ~**ing**, switching off.
af'skawe = **afskaaf**.
af'skawing, planing (of a board); excoriation, abrasion (of skin).
af'skeep, (-ge-), ship, forward, despatch; do work in a slipshod manner; skimp (work); treat shabbily (person); *die MAN het weer lelik afgeskeep*, the man has done his work in a very slipshod manner again; *die NOOI het my afgeskeep*, the girl treated me shabbily; ~**goed**, inferior goods; ~**werk**, slapdash, slipshod work.
af'skeer, (-ge-), shear (wool); shave (beard); graze off (grass).
af'skei, (-ge-), separate, sever from; exude, secrete, educe; dissent, dissever; partition off; divide; comb out; excrete; *jou ~ van*, break away from; dissociate oneself from; ~**(d)baar**, (..**bare**), separable.
af'skeid, parting, departure, farewell, leave-taking; *BY die ~*, at parting; *plotseling ~ NEEM*, take leave suddenly; *vertrek sonder om – te NEEM*, take French leave; *TEN ~*, for taking leave; ~**TOEWUIF**, wave farewell; ~**end, (-e)**, excretive, excretory; ~**ing**, separation; recrement, secretion (bile); secession (party) dissociation (chemistry); segregation (race); excretion; disruption; dissent; ~**jie**, farewell party; parting drink; ~**sbeweging**, secession movement; ~**ingslyn**, line of demarcation, dividing line; ~**ingsmuur**, partition wall; ~**ingsorgaan**, secreting (secretive, secretory) organ, secrement, emunctory; ~**ingsprodukte**, waste products; differentiation products; ~**ingsteken** diaeresis; ~**ingstowwe**, excreta.
af'skeids: ~**beker**, grace cup; ~**besoek**, farewell visit; ~**boodskap**, farewell message; ~**dinee**, farewell dinner; ~**dronk**, parting (stirrup-) cup; ~**glasie**, doch-an-doris, stirrup-cup, parting cup; ~**groet**, farewell, last greeting; ~**kaartjie**, p.p.c. card (*pour prendre congé* = to take leave); ~**kus**, parting kiss; ~**lied**, parting song; ~**maal**, farewell dinner.
af'skeidsoen, farewell kiss.
af'skeids: ~**party**, farewell party; ~**plegtigheid**, farewell ceremony; ~**preek**, farewell (valedictory) sermon; ~**rede**, farewell address; ~**resepsie**, farewell reception; ~**toespraak**, valedictory address; ~**woord**, parting word.
af'skeier, (-s), separator.
af'skeisel, (-s), secretion.
af'skep, (-ge-), skim, scoop off.
af'skeper, (-s), botcher; ~**ig, (-e)**, inclined to work in a slipshod manner; shabby, mean; ~**y**, bad treatment; slipshod work, botching.
af'skerf, (-ge-), chip off (from); *afgeskerfde breekgoed*, chipped crockery.
af'skerm, (-ge-), screen, shade (a light); ward off, parry, bully *(hockey)*; ~**bus**, screen can; shield can; ~**ing**, screening off.
af'skets, (-ge-), sketch; adumbrate.
af'skeur, (-ge-), tear off; secede (from a church); drag down (away); ~**ing**, severing, tearing off; schism; abscission; secession; avulsion (of land); ~**tang**, avulsion forceps.
af'skiet, (-ge-), discharge (a rifle), fire, let off (a gun); shoot off (a bird's wing); shoot down (aircraft); penetrate into (roots); catapult; *~ met 'n katapult*, catapult; starting staff (aircraft); ~**er**, discharger; ~**ers**, starting crew; ~**span** starting crew.
af'skil, (-ge-), peel; rind (trees); pare; decorticate, excoriate.
af'skilder, (-ge-), depict, paint, describe; *met swart KLEURE ~*, paint in sombre colours; *na die LEWE afgeskilder*, drawn from life; ~**ing**, picture, representation, description; delineation *(fig.)*.
af'skilfer, (-ge-), scale, flake, peel off, chip; desquamate *(med.)*; exfoliate; ~**ing**, flaking, shelling (of rocks); desquamation; peeling, scaling off; exfoliation.

af'skilling, peeling; decortiction; excoriation.
af'skink, (-ge-), pour off; decant.
af'skoffel, (-ge-), hoe away (off); dance.
af'skommel, (-ge-), shake down (off); saunter along.
af'skop, (s), centre kick; kick-off (rugby); (w) **(-ge-)**, kick off; kick down (stairs).
af'skort, (-ge-), partition off, box; ~**ing, (-e, -s)**, partition, brattice; bulkhead (of a ship); ~**inkie, (-s)**, cubicle.
af'skot, (-te), brattice; partition.
af'skraap, (-ge-), scrape off; rasp off (away); scale (fish); excoriate; ~**sel**, scrapings, shavings.
af'skram, (-ge-), graze, glance off, deflect.
af'skrap, (-ge-), scratch out, delete; ~**er**, scraper.
af'skraping, scraping off; excoriation; scaling (fish).
af'skreeu, (-ge-), call out loudly (names); call down (from upstairs).
af'skrif, copy, duplicate, estreat (a law); exemplification; *GEWAARMERKTE ~*, certified copy; *'n ~ MAAK van*, make a copy of.
af'skrik, (s), horror, aversion, determent; *'n ~ HÊ van*, have an aversion to; *TOT ~ van*, as a warning; (w) **(-ge-)**, frighten away, terrify, scare away, deter, dishearten, daunt, discourage; *hy het hom nie laat ~ nie*, he did not allow himself to be disheartened (frightened off); ~**kend, (-e)**, frightening, terrifying; forbidding; deterrent; ~**king**, horror, aversion; (s); ~**middel**, deterrent; ~**wek'kend, (-e)**, terrifying; deterrent; forbidding.
af'skroef, ..**skroewe, (-ge-)**, unscrew; screw off.
af'skroei, (-ge-), singe off.
af'skrop, (-ge-), scrub (scour) off (dirt); scrub (a floor).
af'skryf, ..**skrywe, (-ge-)**, copy, transcribe; crib; write off, cancel (a debt); countermand; *R5 op 'n REKENING ~*, write R5 off an account; *SKULD ~*, write off as a bad debt; ~**baar**, (..**bare**), bad (debts); expendable (forces).
af'skrywer, amanuensis, copier.
af'skrywing, (-e, -s), copy(ing); cancellation; write-off; ~ *vir waardevermindering*, written off for depreciation.
af'skrywings: ~**bedrag**, amount written off; ~**fonds**, depreciation fund; ~**pos**, amount written off; ~**rekening**, depreciation account.
af'sku, abomination, horror, abhorrence, detestation, aversion; *'n ~ HÊ van iets*, abhor (loathe) a thing; *'n VOORWERP van ~*, an abomination.
af'skub, (-ge-), scale.
af'skud, (-ge-), shake off; disregard (troubles); get rid of.
af'skuif = **afskuiwe**.
af'skuim, (-ge-), scum, skim; despumate; ~**ing**, despumation; ~**lepel**, skimming-spoon; ~**sel, (-s)**, scummings.
af'skuins, (-ge-), chamfer, bevel; ~**hoek**, bevel angle; ~**ing**, bevel, bevelled edge; embrazure.
af'skuiwe, (-ge-), push off, shove off; slide down; exculpate; *iets van 'n MENS ~*, put something out of one's mind; *hy wil al die SKULD van hom ~*, he wants to exculpate himself completely; *WERK op iem. unders ~*, push work on to someone else.
af'skuiwing, landslide; (normal) fault (mines); downthrow; ~**shoek**, hade; ~**svlak**, sheer plane.
af'skuring, scouring, abrasion; attrition; sanding; corrosion.
af'skut, (-ge-), partition off, screen off; ~**ting, (-e, -s)**, partition, fence; railing.
af'skuur, (-ge-), scour off; buff (a tyre); graze, abrade; ~**sel**, off-scourings.
afskuwek'kend, (-e), horrific, hideous, gruesome.
afsku'welik, (-e), abominable, nefarious, monstrous, grisly, hideous, detestable, abhorrent, horrible (crime); execrable (weather); heinous (misdeed); ~**heid**, horribleness, abomination, detestableness, enormity, hideousness, nefariousness.
af'skyn, (-ge-), shine (down) upon; ~**sel**, reflection.
af'slaaf = **afsloof**.
af'slaan, (s), delivery, service *(tennis)*; tee shot *(golf)*; (w) **(-ge-)**, decline, refuse (an offer); discount; beat off, repulse (an attack), counter (a blow); abate, rebate, reduce (a price); knock off (a

afslaer 24 *afstand*

hat); hit off, serve *(tennis);* tee off *(golf);* switch off (lights); branch off (a road); *'n AANBOD ~*, refuse an offer; *'n AANVAL ~*, repulse an attack; *die PRYS ~*, reduce the price; *WATER ~*, urinate; ~**baan**, service court; ~**bank**, adjustable bunk; ~**hou**, service *(tennis);* tee shot *(golf);* ~**kant**, serving side; ~**kap**, folding hood; ~**koepee**, convertible coupé; ~**lyn**, service line; ~**monster**, chip sample; ~**motor**, convertible; ~**paal**, bolster bar; ~**platform**, striking platform; ~**sylyn**, service sideline; ~**tafel**, adjustable table.

af´slaer, (-s), auctioneer; ~**saak**, auctioneering firm, firm of auctioneers.

af´slag, (s), excoriation; discount, reduction, abatement; fall; allowance; rebate; *by ~ verkoop*, sell by Dutch auction; (w) (-ge-), flay, skin; excoriate; flench, flense (whale); ~**mes**, flaying-knife; ~**ter**, flayer; ~**winkel**, discount store.

af´slaner, server *(tennis)*.

af´sleep, (-ge-), drag down; pull off (rocks).

af´slenter, (-ge-), knock about (in the city), saunter along.

af´slib, (-ge-), wash away.

af´slinger, (-ge-), sling off; reel down; fling off, toss off, hurl off; branch off; meander down.

af´slof, (-ge-), shuffle down; wear out.

af´slons (-ge-), wear out through slovenliness.

af´sloof, ..**slowe**, (-ge-), fag, drudge, slave, toil, wear out; *ek het my afgesloof vir JOU*, I have worn myself to the bone for your sake; *'n afgesloofde LIGGAAM*, a worn-out body.

af´sluip, (-ge-), slink down, sneak away.

af´sluit, (-ge-), close, block; close the door upon; shut off, patrol; fence in, rail in: seclude; effect (insurance); balance, close (accounts); cut out, disconnect (electricity); cut off (steam); conclude (a bargain); lock; interlock; *die BOEKE ~*, close (balance) the books; *JOU ~*, cut oneself off, seclude oneself; *'n KONTRAK ~*, enter into a contract; *die TOEVOER ~*, cut off the supply; ~**deksel**, insulating lid; ~**blokkie**, stop block; ~**boom**, boom, bar, gate bar; ~**dam**, barrage, levee; coffer dam; ~**doppie**, valve cap; terminal plug; ~**er**, cut-out; bolt; obturator; regulator; sluice valve; starting valve, boiler stop valve (of a steam engine); ~**ing**, enclosure, fence; road block; obturation; closing, cutting off; stopping (a current); conclusion (of an agreement); barrier; *ter –ing van*, in conclusion; ~**ingsbalans**, closing balance; ~**ingsdatum**, closing date; ~**ingstelsel**, block system; ~**klep**, throttle (valve); stop (check, cut-off) valve; ~**kraan**, stopcock; ~**orgaan**, (..**gane**), sealing member; ~**ring**, obturator; ~**ruit**, glass guard; ~**skakelaar**, lock-out switch; ~**tyd**, block time.

af´sluk, (-ge-), swallow down.

af´slyp, (-ge-), grind away (off); polish; ~**ing**, grinding down; polishing.

af´slyt, (-ge-), wear out; waste; fret; ~**ing**, detrition, wearing away, decay; attrition; denudation; ~**sel**, detritus.

af´smeek, (-ge-), implore, beseech, beg, invoke; impetrate.

af´smeer, (-ge-), palm off on; foist on; *hy het 'n stokou kar aan my afgesmeer*, he palmed off a very old car on me.

af´smekend,(-e), impetratory, supplicatory.

af´smeker, (-s), supplicator.

af´smeking, supplication, invocation; impetration.

af´smelt, (-ge-), smelt off (down); ~**masjien**, sealing-off machine.

af´smoor, (-ge-), choke off.

af´smyt, (-ge-), fling (throw) off (down).

af´snel, (-ge-), hurry down, rush down; *~ op*, rush at.

af´snipper, (-ge-), tear (cut) into shreds.

af´snoei, (-ge-), prune, lop off.

af´snoer, (-ge-), abstrict, tie off; ligate; ~**ing**, abstriction; ligature.

af´snou, (-ge-), speak harshly to, snub, bluff, choke off; ~**ing**, snub.

af´sny, (s), cropping; (w) (-ge-), cut off, curtail, cut short, crop (hair); lop off, pare; (de)truncate; dock (a tail); amputate, prescind; chip, foreclose; intercept; sever; clip (a cigar); *sy LEWENSDRAAD is afgesny*, his thread of life is cut; he is dead; *iem. die PAS ~*, bar a person's passage; ~**ding**, cutting off, abscission; amputation; interception; ~**er**, sloper; ~**masjien**, cropping machine; ~**sel**, (-s), cuttings, parings, clippings; trimmings; ~**skêr**, paring scissors.

af´soek, (-ge-), search all over, scour (the country).

af´soen, (-ge-), kiss away (tears); become reconciled (with a kiss).

af´sonder, (-ge-), isolate, separate; set apart, detach, detail; quarantine; enisle; segregate; cloister; draft; insulate; reserve; prescind; appropriate; earmark; *jou –*, seclude oneself, retire (detach oneself) from; ~**ing**, seclusion, retirement; recluse, reclusion, privacy; detachment; quarantine; separation; insulation; ~**ingsaal**, isolation ward; ~**ingshospitaal**, isolation hospital.

afson´derlik, (b), (-e), separate, (in)dividual; asunder, distinct, isolated; discrete; *~e gevalle*, isolated cases; (bw), separately, individually; ~**heid**, exclusiveness.

af´span, (-ge-), fence off.

af´spat, (-ge-), spatter off, be dashed from; chip, crack; ~**ting**, chipping (of rock).

af´speel, (-ge-), finish, play off (a game); enact, play to the end (drama); take place, happen; *wat DAAR afgespeel is, weet niemand nie*, what took place there, no one knows; *'n DRAMA het hom daar afgespeel*, dramatic events took place there; *die HANDELING sal ~ in Natal*, the scene will be laid in Natal.

af´speen, ablactate (fruit); wean.

af´spel, (-ge-), spell out.

af´speld, (-ge-), pin off.

af´sper, (-ge-), block; close (a road); rope off; ~**ring**, blocking; roping off.

af´spieël, (-ge-), reflect, mirror; ~**ing**, reflection.

af´spit, (-ge-), dig away (off).

af´splinter, (-ge-), splinter off, chip, spall; ~**ing**, splintering off.

af´splits, (-ge-), split off; branch off (a road); ~**ing**, splitting off.

af´spoel, (-ge-), rinse; wash away; float down; ~**ing**, ablution; washing away (by a flood); ~**sel**, wash.

af´spons, (-ge-), sponge down; ~**ing**, sponging, sponge-down.

af´spraak, (afsprake), agreement, appointment, engagement; date (a girl); committal; *LUKRAAK (onbeplande) ~*, blind date; *ek het môre 'n ~ MET hom*, I have an appointment with him tomorrow; *VOLGENS ~*, according to agreement; ~**boek(ie)**, appointment book; ~**oproep**, fixed-time call.

af´spreek, (-ge-), agree upon, preconcert, arrange, settle; *cf. afgesproke.*

af´spring, (-ge-), jump off (a wall), jump down from (a table); parachute, bale out; crack, burst, chip off; alight (from a horse); break down, come to nothing (negotiations); *~ op 'n HAAS*, jump (rush) at a hare; *die ONDERHANDELINGE het afgespring*, the negotiations have broken down; ~**plek**, starting point.

af´spuit, (-ge-), hose down, squirt; ~**gat**, cleaning aperture.

af´staan, (-ge-), stand away from; give up, yield (one's place); cede (a territory); surrender (a privilege); hand over, deliver up (one's rights); sell; *kan jy dit ~?* can you spare it?

af´stam, (-ge-), descend, spring from; be derived from (a word; language); ~**meling**, (-e, -s), descendant; issue; *~ meling in die REGTE lyn*, lineal descendant; *~ meling in die SYLINIE*, collateral descendant; ~**ming**, descent (of man); genealogy, ancestry; extraction; derivation (of words); pedigree; filiation; ~**mingsleer**, descent theory, evolution theory.

af´stamp, (-ge-), bump (knock) off; churn.

af´stand, abdication, demission; (re)cession; surrender; abdication, renunciation; cession (of a territory); waiver (of rights); interval (of a tone); (-e), distance, length, range; elongation; perspective; *op 'n ~ BESTUUR*, remote-controlled; *die ~ BE=*

WAAR, keep the distance, be aloof; *op 'n* ~ *BLY*, keep aloof (at a distance); ~ *DOEN van sy boedel*, assign one's property to the creditors; ~ *DOEN van die wêreld*, renounce the world; ~ *DOEN van 'n eis*, abandon a claim; ~ *DOEN van die troon*, abdicate (the throne); *op kort* ~ *SKIET*, shoot at short range; ~**doening**, abandonment (of claim), quit claim; renouncement, cession; abdication; ~**sbediening**, ~**sbeheer**, remote control; ~**sbepaling**, ascertainment of distance; ~**sgeskut**, long-range guns; ~**shuls**, spacer (distance) sleeve; ~**sin**, distance perception; ~**skaal**, range scale; ~**skakelaar**, remote-control switch.

af'**stands**: ~**klousule**, waiving clause; ~**mars**, route march; ~**meter**, (h)odometer; range-finder; ambulator; speedometer; telemeter; viameter.

af'**standsoeker**, rangefinder.

af'**stands**: ~**opnemer**, range taker; ~**rekord**, long-distance record; ~**rit**, long-distance run; ~**toets**, cross-country test; ~**verligting**, distance lighting; ~**verskil**, horizontal equivalent; ~**vliegtuig**, long-distance aeroplane; ~**wyser**, scale of distance.

af'**stap**, (**-ge-**), step down, alight; detrain; walk (a distance); change; drop (a subject); *van 'n onderwerp* ~, change a subject or topic; ~**ping**, getting (walking) off; changing, dropping; ~**trap**, gangway.

af'**steek**, (**-ge-**), contrast with; cut off; deliver (a speech); bevel (with a chisel); chisel (woodwork); peg out (a foundation), mark off; lay out (a terrace); push off (from ashore); *GUNSTIG* ~ *by*, compare favourably with; *iem. die LOEF* ~, outdo (get the better of) someone; *SKERP* ~ *teen*, stand out in bold relief against; *'n TOESPRAAK* ~, fire off (hold) a speech; ~**beitel**, parting-tool; cross-cut chisel.

af'**steel**, (**-ge-**), steal from, rob of.

af'**stel**, (s), cancellation, abandonment; postponement, delay; (w) (**-ge-**), put off, abandon, give up, cancel; disconnect (current); adjust; ~**baar**, (..**bare**), adjustable; ~**hefboom**, trimming lever; ~**knip**, releaser.

af'**stem**, (**-ge-**), reject, vote against, blackball, negative; tune; ~ *OP*, tune in to (the radio); *die VOORSTEL is afgestem*, the motion was rejected; ~**knop**, tuning control; ~**lamp**, turning lamp; ~**mer**, tuner *(radio)*; ~**ming**, rejection (of a proposal); tuning; ~**skakelaar**, tuning switch.

af'**stempel**, (**-ge-**), stamp; postmark, obliterate, cancel (a document); shade (prints); ~**ing**, postmark(ing); cancellation.

af'**sterf**, ..**sterwe**, (**-ge-**), die (off); lose touch with (relatives); *hy het van sy familie afgesterwe*, he has become estranged from his relations (family).

af'**sterwing**, death, departure (from life); decay; necrosis; gangrene; estrangement.

af'**stig**, (**-ge-**), form (a new congregation), secede; disestablish; ~**ter**, devolutionist; ~**ting**, disestablishment; new formation.

af'**stippel**, (**-ge-**), mark by dotted line, dot.

af'**stof**, (**-ge-**), dust; thrash; ~**kwas**, dusting brush; ~**lap**, duster.

af'**stommel**, (**-ge-**), stumble down (stairs).

af'**stomp**, (**-ge-**), (make) blunt; dull (feeling); weaken; deaden (the conscience); truncate; ~**ing**, blunting, obtusion; deadening; dulling; truncation.

af'**stook**, (**-ge-**), distil (from).

af'**stoom**, (**-ge-**), steam off (away, down).

af'**stoot**, (**-ge-**), push off (down); knock off (down); repulse, repel; *die GLAS van die tafel* ~, knock the tumbler off the table; *jy stoot al jou VRIENDE van jou af, you alienate all your friends*; ~**lik**, (**-e**), repulsive, repellent; ~**likheid**, repulsiveness; ~**mes** scraper, scraping-knife.

af'**storm**, (**-ge-**), storm, rush down (at); ~ *op*, charge at.

af'**stort**, (**-ge-**), tumble down; rush down (water); ~**ing**, fall.

afsto'**tend**, (**-e**), repelling, repellent, repulsive, antipathetic, grim, forbidding.

af'**stoting**, (**-e, -s**), rebuff; pushing off.

af'**straal**, (**-ge-**), radiate, reflect; beam; be radiant with; *vreugde straal van sy gelaat af*, his face beams with joy.

af'**straf**, (**-ge-**), punish; thrash; correct; reprove, lecture; ~**fing**, reprimand; punishment.

af'**straling**, reflection, radiation.

af'**stromend**, (**-e**), defluent, effluent; flowing down.

af'**stroming**, effluent.

af'**strompel**, (**-ge-**), stumble down (stairs).

af'**stroom**, (**-ge-**), flow down, stream down.

af'**stroop**, (**-ge-**), strip off, flay, skin; stem (tobacco); trash (sugarcane leaves); pillage, lay waste, ransack.

af'**stroping**, denudation, stripping off, ransacking.

af'**stry**, (**-ge-**), dispute; beat (opponent in finals); *hy het my verklaring afgestry*, he disputed (the accuracy of) my statement.

af'**stryk**, (**-ge-**), iron off; wire off; cover (distance); float (plaster); transfer (a pattern); strike (a match); ~**patroon**, transfer.

af'**studeer**, (**-ge-**), complete one's studies.

af'**stuif**, ..**stuiwe**, (**-ge-**), fly off; ~ *op*, rush at (upon).

af'**stuit**, (**-ge-**), rebound, recoil; be rebuffed by; be frustrated (by opposition); ~ *op*, glance off (the cuirass).

af'**stuur**, (**-ge-**), dispatch, send off, forward (a parcel); expedite, send; bear down (upon); direct; send down; draft (troops); ~ *OP*, make head for; ~ *van die SKOOL*, send away (expel) from school.

af'**styg**, (**-ge-**), alight, descend, dismount, get off; ~**ing**, descent, alighting.

af'**suie**, ..**suig**, (**-ge-**), suck down (off).

af'**suig**: ~**filter**, suction filter; ~**pomp**, scavenger pump; ~**stelsel**, scavenging system.

at'**sukkel**, (**-ge-**), get down (do something) with difficulty; become exhausted.

af'**swaai**, (**-ge-**), turn aside, branch off (road); stumble down.

af'**swakker**, (**-s**), reducer; attenuator.

af'**sweef**, ..**swewe**, (**-ge-**), glide down.

af'**sweer**[1], (**-ge-**), rot off, fall off by ulceration.

af'**sweer**[2], (**-ge-**), abjure; adjure, renounce; forswear; ~**der**, adjurer; abjurer.

af'**swem**, (**-ge-**), swim down; cover by swimming.

af'**swenk**, (**-ge-**), branch off, turn aside.

af'**swerf**, ..**swerwe**, (**-ge-**), wander away from.

af'**swering**, abjuration, renunciation; adjuration.

af'**swoeë**, ..**swoeg**, (**-ge-**), slave, overwork (oneself); toil.

afsy'**dig**, (**-e**), aloof; neutral; ~**heid**, aloofness; indifference.

af'**syfer**, (**-ge-**), seep down; ~**ing**, seepage.

af'**tak**, (**-ge-**), branch off, shunt (*electr.*); ~**draad**, tapping wire.

af'**takel**, (**-ge-**), unrig (a ship); dismantle (a tower); be on the decline, grow decrepit; *iem. lelik* ~, criticize someone severely; ~**ing**, dismantling; unrigging; decay.

af'**tak**: ~**kas**, header, distribution box; ~**ker**, (**-s**), adapter; ~**king**, branching, shunting; ~**kingsdraad**, derivative wire; ~**paal**, forking (bifurcation) pole; ~**rol**, shunt coil, ~**stasie**, branching-off station; siding

af'**tandig**, af'**tands**, (**-e**), aged, with long teeth.

af'**tap**, (**-ge-**), draw off, rack (wine), bottle; trickle down (tears); tap; drain; ~**klep**, drain-valve; ~**kraan**, cylinder (drain) cock, radiator cock; petcock; ~**ping**, tapping, draining, punction; aspiration; ~**prop**, drain plug (gas); ~**pyp**, drain (pipe).

af'**tas**, (**-ge-**), feel all over; scan *(radar, television)*; ~**elektronmikroskopie'**, scanning electron microscopy; ~**ter, scanner**; ~**ting**, feeling all over; scanning *(radar, television)*.

af'**teken**, (**-ge-**), mark, draw, delineate (features); depict; describe; sign off (after work); copy; visé (passport); endorse; *die berge staan afgeteken teen die lug*, die mountains are outlined against the sky; ~**ing**, sketch; delineation; signing off; viséing (passport); ~**ings**, markings.

af'**tel**[1], (**-ge-**), count out; *afgetelde geld*, counted sum of money.

af'**tel**[2], (**-ge-**), lift off.

af'**telling**, count-down; count-off.

af'telrym(pie), counting-out rhyme.
af'tik, (-ge-), tick off; type (on typewriter); tap out (telegram).
af'timmer, (-ge-), knock up (off).
af'tob, (-ge-), tire out, fatigue, fag.
af'tog, retreat, decampment; *die ~ BLAAS*, sound the retreat; *take to one's heels*; *die ~ DEK*, cover the retreat; *~sein*, signal for retreat.
af'toom, (-ge-), unbridle.
af'top, (-ge-), prune, top, lop.
af'torring, (-ge-), unrip.
af'transformeer, (-ge-), step down.
af'trap, (-ge-), wear out (heels); step down; break by treading; cause to go off (a trap); cycle; kick away; *'n lelike stel ~*, make an awful blunder; have an awful experience.
af'trede, af'treding, resignation; retirement; abdication.
af'tree, (-ge-), pace, measure by pacing (a course); resign; abdicate; retire, go out; *as LID van die bestuur ~*, retire as member of the executive; *van die TONEEL ~*, leave (retire from) the stage; *~grens*, pensionable age.
af'trek, (s), sale, demand; rebate; deduction (of charges); subtraction; *die BOEK kry baie ~*, the book is a good seller; *die WINKEL kry baie ~*, the store is well patronized; (w) **(-ge-)**, deduct, recoup, subtract; discount; abstract; pull off, strip, pull down, move down, pitch down; press (a trigger); divert (attention); retreat (an army); trace (an outline); *jou van die WÊRELD ~*, retire from the world; *~baar (..bare)*, deductable; divertible; traceable; *~film*, stripping film; *~fout*, mistake in subtracting, subtraction mistake; *~getal*, subtrahend; *~ker*, subtrahend; abductor (muscle); *~king*, subtraction, deduction; *~(kings)teken*, minus sign; *~magtiging*, stop-order deduction; *~order*, stop order; *~papier*, tracing paper; *~sel*, extract, essence; stock *(cookery)*; decoction (herbs, tealeaves), tincture; abstract; *'n ~ sel maak*, brew, draw, infuse, steep; *~som*, subtraction sum; *~spier*, abductor muscle; *~tal*, minuend; *~teken*, minus sign; *~tou*, lanyard *(artil.)*; *~wiel*, tracing-wheel.
af'trippel, (-ge-), amble; trip down.
af'troef, (-ge-), trump; get the better of.
af'troggel, (-ge-), entice away, wheedle out of.
af'trommel, (-ge-), strum (on piano)
af'tuie, ..tuig, (-ge-), outspan (horses), unharness; unrig (a ship).
af'tuimel, (-ge-), tumble down.
af'vaar, (-ge-), sail, put to sea, depart; sail down (river).
af'vaardig, (-ge-), delegate, return (to parliament), depute, send; *~er*, sender; *~ing*, deputation, delegation, delegacy; embassy.
af'vaarhawe, port of departure.
af'vaart, departure; sailing; *~datum*, date of sailing; *~lys*, sailing list; *~sbevel*, sailing orders.
af'val, (s), head, tripe and trotters (of sheep); offal; giblets (of fowl); garbage, refuse (of an animal); draff, waste; trash; scraps, dog's meat, chippings; scrap (metal); dross; stuff (of mines); foots (of an oil refinery); flotsam and jetsam; attle (of ore); forsaking (a political party); apostasy, desertion (of a faith); revolt, defection; coom (of soot); deads (of coal); effluent (of a factory); leavings (food); loopings; (w) **(-ge-)**, fall off, tumble down; forsake (a party); secede from (a church); drop out (from a race); lose weight (flesh), be in bad condition; apostasize; garble; *~afbou*, waste mining; *~bak*, garbage (refuse) bin; *~bos*, (forest) litter; *~erts*, attle, gangue; *~goed*, scraps, waste; *~hoop*, scrap heap, tip-mound, kitchen-midden; *~houer*, waste (refuse) container; *~hout*, scrap wood; *~katoen*, cotton waste; *~kole*, dross; *~kooks*, coke waste; *~lend, (-e)*, caducous; deciduous; *~'lig, (-e)*, faithless, recreant, apostate; disloyal; *~'lige, (-s)*, renegade, pervert, recreant, apostate; adulterer; *~'ligheid*, desertion, defection, apostasy; disloyalty; *~opvanger*, tailings elevator; *~produk*, by-product, residual product; *~stowwe*, sewage;

waste product; fall-out; *~stukkies*, scraps, orts; *~vleis*, scraps, pieces; *~waarde*, scrap value; *~water*, mill effluents, stickwater, industrial waste water (effluent); *~wol*, pieces.
af'vang, (-ge-), snatch away; remove by catching; catch from.
af'vat, (-ge-), clear (a table); take away.
af'vee(g), (-ge-), wipe off, dry; polish; dust; *jou aan iets ~*, treat something with contempt.
af'veegsels, sweepings.
af'veër (-s), wiper.
af'veging, wiping off.
af'verhuur, (~), sublet; let a portion of (a farm).
af'verhuring, subletting.
af'verkoop, (~), sell a part.
af'vlak, (-ge-), smooth.
af'vlie(g), (-ge-), fly down (off, away); cover distance by air; take off (aeroplane).
af'vloei, (s), drainage, flowing-off; (w) **(-ge-)**, flow down; *~ing*, drainage, defluxion.
af'voer, (s), conveyance (of goods); discharge (from glands); eduction (of liquid); drainage; output *(electr.)*; (w) **(-ge-)**, convey, transport; lead away, carry off, conduct away; drain (water); cut (oats) for feeding.
af'voer: *~buis*, outlet (pipe); *~der*, abductor; *~end (-e)*, conveying; emunctory; efferent; excurrent; *~gat*, exhaust port; *~geut*, spillway; *~grippie*, drain ditch; *~hospitaal*, clearing hospital; *~ing*, eduction, drainage; outlet; *~kanaal*, transport canal; emissary vessel; emunctory; outlet, drainage canal; *~klep*, escape (exhaust) valve; *~koste*, transport charges; *~kraan*, discharge cock; *~middel*, aperient, laxative; *~pyp*, waste pipe, drain(pipe), eduction pipe; outlet (pipe, duct); exhaust pipe; delivery pipe; over-flow pipe; drain-pipe; *~sloot*, catch-water drain; gutter; *~sluis*, waste gate; *~water*, effluent (water).
af'vorder, (-ge-), demand, wring from; command (respect); *~ing*, exaction.
af'vra, (-ge-), ask, request; demand; *EK het my dikwels afgevra*, I often wondered; *iem. op die MAN ~*, ask someone point-blank.
af'vreet, (-ge-), eat away (animals), crop; browse (off).
af'vries, (-ge-), freeze off.
af'vrot, (-ge-), rot away.
af'vry, (-ge-), oust (in courting), cut out.
af'vryf, ..vrywe, (-ge-), rub down (off), scour, abrade, polish; fret; *~lap*, dishcloth.
af'vuur, (-ge-), fire (off), discharge (a gun).
af'vyl, (-ge-), file off (away).
af'waai, (-ge-), blow down (off); be blown off (down); rush down (along).
af'waarts, (-e), downward(s).
af'wag, (-ge-), await, abide, wait for, lie doggo; *sy BEURT ~*, await his turn; *'n ~tende HOUDING aanneem*, temporize, adopt a waiting attitude; *~ting*, expectation; *in ~ting van die finale reëling*, pending the final settlement (arrangement); *~rekening*, suspense account.
af'waggel, (-ge-), stagger down, waddle along (the street).
af'wandel, (-ge-), walk down (away).
af'was, (-ge-), wash away (off); cleanse (of sin); *~baar, (..bare)*, washable; *~sing*, washing; ablution; swab (a wound); *~stokkie*, dishmop; *~water*, dishwater.
af'water, (-ge-), drain; pour off; water down; weaken, make less effective *(fig.)*; *'n BESLUIT deur 'n toegewing ~*, weaken a decision by a concession; *afgewaterde KOOL*, drained cabbage.
af'watering, drainage; drain.
af'waterings: *~buis*, drainpipe; *~gebied*, drainage area; *~geut*, drain; drainage cutting; *~kanaal*, drain-outlet; *~pomp*, drainpump; *~put, (-te)*, drain; *~pyp*, drainpipe.
af'weë, ..weeg, (-ge-), weigh.
af'weef, (-ge-), finish (by weaving).
af'week, (-ge-), soak off; unglue.
af'weer, (s), defence; (w) **(-ge-)**, ward off, fend, counter, parry (a blow); avert (danger); prevent

(disease); stave (keep) off; fence (hive) off; ~ '**baar**, (..**bare**), preventible, avertible, avoidable; ~ **geskut**, ~ **kanon**, anti-aircraft gun; ~ **middel**, repellent.

af'wei(e), (-ge-), graze off, (de)pasture, feed.

af'wen¹, (-ge-), unlearn, disaccustom; break a person of a habit; *'n slegte gewoonte* ~, get out of a bad habit.

af'wen², (-ge-), unwind (a windlass); unreel.

af'wen³, (-ge-), win from (at cards); get the better of.

af'wend, (-ge-), turn aside, head off; divert; avert; parry, ward off; deprecate (by prayer); obviate; *die GELAAT* ~ *van*, turn the face away from; *die GEVAAR* ~, avert the danger; ~ '**baar**, (..**bare**), avertible; ~**ing**, diversion; turning aside; deprecation.

af'wenning, disuse; unlearning.

af'wentel, (-ge-), roll down (away); shift off; ~**ing**, rolling away.

af'wering, prevention; resistance; parry.

af'werk, (-ge-), complete, finish; work off (a debt); get through (a programme); put finishing touches to (a painting); overwork oneself; remove, take away from; bring down slowly (sheep); trim (windows); dress (a stone); *'n PROGRAM* ~, get through a programme; *ek VOEL afgewerk*, I feel overworked; ~**er**, finisher, fabricator; ~**ing**, finish; completion; trimming; workmanship; elaborateness; ~**ing van KLIP**, dressing of stone (rock); *MAT* ~**ing**, dull finish; ~**rand**, fair edge.

af'werp, (-ge-), throw off, shake off (a feeling); fling aside; hurl down; cast (a skin); exuviate; produce (a harvest); yield (a profit); drop (fruit); *die MASKER* ~, throw off the mask; *baie WINS* ~, yield much profit.

afwe'sig, (-e), away, absent; absent-minded; ~**e**, (-s), absentee, defaulter; casualty (army); missing person; ~**heid**, absence, default; non-appearance, non-attendance; preoccupation; *skitter deur sy* ~**heid**, be conspicuous by his absence.

af'wikkel, (-ge-), unroll, unwind; wind up, liquidate (estate); break (by twisting); ~**ing**, unwinding; winding up, liquidation.

af'wimpel, (-ge-), fob off, cancel.

afwip, (-ge-), skip down; jerk off; tip off.

af'wissel, (-ge-), change, alternate; relieve one another; take turns; vary (colours); interchange, diversify (menu).

af'wisselend, (b), (-e), alternative, diversified, varying; intermittent (fever); intercurrent; ~ *van AARD*, varying in character; ~*e BLARE*, alternate leaves *(bot.)*; ~*e KLEURE*, variety of colours; ~*e REËNBUIE*, intermittent showers; ~*e VOEDSEL*, diversified food; (bw), alternately, in turns.

af'wisseling, (inter)change, alternation, succession; diversification; relief; diversity, variety, fluctuation; *vir (ter)* ~, by way of a change, to relieve the monotony.

af'wit, (-ge-), whitewash; ~**ting**, whitewashing.

af'woel, (-ge-), fidget (work) off; unwind.

af'wring, (-ge-), wring (wrench) off; wrest from, extort (secret).

af'wurg, (-ge-), gulp down; eat without relish.

af'wyk, (-ge-), deviate, depart from, differ from (conclusions); deflect, decline (needle of compass); diverge, vary; digress; aberrate; *geen DUIMBREEDTE* ~ *nie*, not budge an inch; *van die regte PAD* ~, go astray; *van die WAARHEID* ~, swerve from the truth; ~**end**, (-e), deviating, divergent; different (readings); dissenting (judg(e)ment); anomalous; dissident, dissentient (views); declinatory; devious; erroneous; aberrant (forms); ~*ende kinders*, deviate children; ~**er**, (-s), deviator.

af'wyking, (-s), deviation, departure, deflection, declination; divergence; anomaly; digression; evection (of moon); excursion; variation, difference (in text); aberration (heavenly bodies); eccentricity; *in* ~ *van die gewone reëls*, in contravention of the ordinary rules; ~**sdruk**, deflection pressure.

af'wyk: ~**grootte**, magnitude of deflection; ~**ingshoek**, angle of declination (deflection); ~**ingsirkel**, circle of declination (deflection); ~**skaart**, deviation card; ~**smeter**, declinator, declination metre.

af'wys, (-ge-), reject, refuse, rebuff, decline (offer); repudiate (responsibility); dismiss (appeal); disallow; fail (examination); ~ *by die AANNEMING*, reject as communicant; ~ *van 'n AKSIE*, discharge of an action; ~**end**, (-e), recusant, negative; declinatory; ~*end beskik oor*, reject, refuse; ~**ing**, (-e, -s), rejection, refusal, declination (of a request); dismissal (of appeal).

ag¹, (s), attention, care, regard; *GEE* ~*!* attention! *ek GEE (slaan)* ~ *op*, I pay attention to; *in* ~ *NEEM*, take into consideration; *jou in* ~ *NEEM vir*, be careful, be on your guard; (w) (ge-), esteem, deem; value; *iets NODIG* ~, consider something necessary.

ag², (tw), oh, ah, alas! ~ *NEE!* is that so! well, I never; ~ *NEE wat*, oh, never mind; please don't; *cf.* **aag**.

ag³, (telw), (-s, -te), see **agt**.

agaat', (**agate**), agate; ~**bontperd**, roan (odd-coloured) horse; ~**kleur**, agate (colour); ~**horing**, shell of a land snail; ~**roos**, *Rosa provincialis*; ~**slak**, land snail *(Achatina)*.

aga'mi, (-'s), trumpeter (bird), agami *(Psophia crepitans)*.

agamie', agamy, celibacy.

agapant', (-e), agapanthus.

aga'pe, (-s), agape, spiritual love.

a'gar-a'gar, agar-agar; ~**streep**, agar-agar streak.

ag'armig, (-e), octopod.

aga'we, (-s), agave.

ag'baar, (..**bare**), respectable, creditable, venerable, honourable; ~**heid**, respectability; venerableness.

ageer', (ge-), act; *agerende hoof(onderwyser)*, acting principal (headmaster).

agen'da, (-s), agenda, order paper; *die* ~ *afhandel*, finish the business of the meeting, complete the agenda; ~**punt**, item on the agenda.

agens', (-e, ..**entia**), (chemical) agent; doer.

agent', (-e), agent; constable; emissary; procurator, factor; ~-**generaal**, agent-general; ~**skap**, (-pe), agency; procuratorship, factorship.

ag'gewing, attentiveness, attention.

ag'gie, (-s), little (small) eight; (tw), oh! oh no! shucks!

agglomeraat', (..**rate**), agglomeration, agglomerate.

agglutina'sie, agglutination.

agglutineer', (ge-), agglutinate.

aggrada'sie, aggradation.

aggregaat', (..**gate**), aggregate; ~**polarisasie**, ~**polarisering**, aggregate polarization.

aggregaats'tekstuur, aggregate structure.

aggrega'sie, aggregation; ~**toestand**, aggregate state (of matter).

aggres'sie, aggression; ..**sief'** (..**siewe**), aggressive; ~**oorlog**, war of aggression.

aggressiwiteit', aggressiveness.

aggres'sor, (-s), aggressor.

ag'hoek = **ag(t)hoek**.

a'gie, (-s): *NUUSKIERIGE* ~, quidnunc, Paul Pry, inquisitive person; *NUUSKIERIGE* ~ *s hoort in die wolwehok*, curiosity killed the cat; *'n ORIGE* ~, a bumptious child; ~**rig**, (-e), inquisitive, curious.

a'gio, (-'s), premium, agio; ~**ta'ge**, stock jobbing, agiotage.

agita'sie, (-s), agitation; excitement.

agita'tor, (-s), agitator.

agiteer', (ge-), agitate; ~**der**, (-s), agitator.

ag'jarig, *ens.*, = **ag(t)jarig**, *etc*.

agnaat', (**agnate**), agnate.

agni'sie, acknowledgement (of drafts), agnition.

agnos'ties, (-e), agnostic.

agnos'tikus, (-se, ..**tici**), agnostic.

agnostisis'me, agnosticism.

agonie', *(digt.)*, agony.

ago'nies, (-e), agonic.

agorafobie', agoraphobia.

agrafie', agraphia.

agrammatis'me, agrammatism.

agra'riër, (-s), agrarian.

agra'ries, (-e), agrarian.

agret'jie, (-s), mayflower *(Tritonia scillaris)*; *Spiraea prunifolia*; aigrette.

agrikoliet', agricolite.
agrimonie' = **akkermonie.**
agroëkologies, agro-ecological.
agronomie', agronomy.
agrono'mies, (-e), agronomic.
agronoom', (..nome), agronomist.
ag'saam, (..same), careful, considerate; ~**heid**, care, considerateness.
ag(t), (-e, -s), eight; *oor 'n DAG of* ~, within a week; *Maandag oor* ~ *DAE*, Monday week; *KWART voor* ~, 7.45, a quarter to eight; ~ *MAAL*, eight times; ~ *UUR*, eight hours.
ag'tal, group (team) of eight, octad; eight.
ag(t)'arm, octopus; ~**ig, (-e),** with eight arms, octopod.
ag(t): ~**benig, (-e),** eight-legged; ~ *benige poliep*, octopus; ~**blarig, (-e),** octopetalous; ~**daags, (-e),** eight-day; for a week; ~**daegeneesbos,** *Hermannia hyssopifolia;* ~**delig, (-e),** consisting of eight parts (volumes); ~**dubbeld, (-e),** eightfold.
ag'teloos, (..lose), careless, mindless, indifferent, inattentive, inobservant; ~**heid**, carelessness, indifference, inattention.
agtelo'sig, (-e), careless, perfunctory; headless; ~**heid**, carelessness; perfunctoriness.
agtenswaar'dig, (-e), respectable, estimable, honourable; ~**heid**, respectability.
ag'ter¹, (bw, b), behind, at the back, in the rear; late; *van* ~ *BESKOU*, seen in retrospect; *my HORLOSIE is* ~, my watch is slow; ~ *wees (raak) met die HUUR*, be in arrears with the rent; ~ *in die KAMER*, at the back of the room; *iets wat* ~ *LÊ*, something of the past; *LOOP* ~ *om*, go round the back; ~ *RAAK by iem.*, lag behind someone; ~ *UITGAAN*, go out at the back(door).
ag'ter², (vs), behind, at the back; ~ *iem. AAN wees*, pursue; imitate someone; *van* ~ *BETER lyk as van voor*, be ugly; ~ *'n HUIS wees*, try to find a house; ~ *MEKAAR*, one behind the other; tandem; ~ *MEKAAR loop*, walk in Indian file, walk in a row; ~ *'n NOOI wees*, be interested in a girl; *sit 'n PUNT* ~ *die woord*, place a fullstop behind the word; *daar SKUIL (sit, steek) iets* ~, there is something behind that; ~ *die TYD wees*, be old-fashioned, be behind the times.
ag'teraan, behind, at the back; ~ *KOM*, bring up the rear, come last; ~ *LOOP*, follow, walk behind.
ag'teraansig, backview, rear view.
ag'teraf, out-of-the-way; backward, poor; secretly; *van* ~ *BESKOU*, considered in the light of what has happened; *iets* ~ *DOEN*, do something on the sly; ~ *MENSE*, poor (uneducated) people; ~**heid**, neglect, poverty, lack of good breeding; ~**kapping**, apocope.
ag'ter-agterkleinkind, great-great-grandchild.
ag'teras, rear axle; trailing axle.
ag'terbaan, backcourt *(tennis)*; backpanel (of a skirt); ~**spel**, backcourt play; ~**speler**, backcourt player.
ag'terbak, (-ke), boot, dickey.
agterbaks', (-e), sly, underhand, secret, secretive, clandestine, hole-and-corner, behind one's back; *iets* ~ *doen*, do something in an underhand manner; ~**heid**, underhandedness, secretiveness.
ag'terbalkon, (-ne, -s), rear platform (of a train, tram); rear balcony (of a house).
ag'terband, back (hind) tyre.
ag'terbank, backbench; ~**er, (-s),** backbencher (in parliament).
ag'terbeen, hind leg.
ag'terbeweging, passing movement among backs, backline movement (rugby).
ag'terbly, (-ge-), remain behind, straggle, hang behind; drag; survive; *die KINDERS sal hulpeloos* ~, the children will be left helpless; *WIE* ~ *WEN*, the loser wins; ~**er**, laggard, straggler; back number; misfire (dynamite).
ag'terblywende, (-s), survivor, surviving spouse.
ag'terboeg, stern post.
ag'terboom, rear arch, cantle (of a saddle), rear fork.
ag'terborg, rear surety.
ag'terboud, hindquarter.

ag'terbroeksak, hip pocket.
ag'terbuurt, (-e), ~**e, (-s),** backstreet, slum(s), purlieu, low quarter(s).
ag'terbuurt: ~**huise**, slum houses; ~**maniere**, slum (uncouth) manners; ~**toestande**, slum conditions; ~**woning**, slum house.
ag'terdeel, hindquarters, buttock(s), hind part; rear part.
ag'terdek, quarter deck, poop, awning.
ag'terdeur, (s), backdoor, postern (gate); *by die* ~ *INKOM*, gain a position by favouritism; *op iem. se* ~ *LÊ*, visit someone very often; *'n* ~ *OOPHOU*, keep a loophole open; (bw, vs), through at the back, through the back.
ag'terdier, wheeler (horse).
ag'terdoek, backcurtain; backdrop.
ag'terdog, suspicion, distrust, mistrust(fulness); *met* ~ *AANSIEN*, look askance at; ~ *KOESTER*, entertain (foster) suspicion; ~ *KRY*, become suspicious; *iem. met* ~ *VERVUL*, arouse someone's suspicions; ~ *WEK*, rouse suspicion; ~**'tig, (-e),** suspicious; distrustful; ~**'tigheid**, suspiciousness, distrust.
ag'terdorp, back part of a town (village); town slum; dilapidated houses; backward (unprogressive) town (village).
ag'tereb, neap tide.
agtereen', consecutively; *dit het drie DAE* ~ *gereën*, it rained for three days; *drie MAAL* ~, three times running; *drie UUR* ~, three hours on end (consecutively).
agtereenvol'gende, consecutive, successive.
agtereenvol'gens, successively, consecutively.
agterend, ..ent, (-e), hind part; rear; backside, anus; posterior; cloaca (of a bird).
ag'tererf, backyard.
ag'tergalery, stern gallery.
ag'tergang, backpassage.
ag'tergeblewene, (-s), person left behind; relative of a deceased; survivor.
ag'tergebou, backpremises.
ag'tergedeelte, (-s), back part; hind end (of an insect).
ag'tergewel, backgable.
ag'tergrond, back(ground), rear; backdrop; *op die* ~ *BLY*, remain in the background; *'n gepaste* ~ *VORM*, be a fitting background; ~**inligting**, background information.
agterhaal', (~), overtake; hunt down.
ag'terhand, back part of the hand; *ek sit in (aan) die* ~, I am the last player *(cards)*.
ag'terhek, postern gate; backgate.
ag'terhelfte, backhalf, forte (of sword).
ag'terhoede, (-s), rear(guard); backline *(rugby)*; ~**geveg**, rearguard action.
ag'terhoef, hind hoof.
ag'terhoek, outlying (out-of-the-way) part (of the country).
ag'terhoof, back part of the head, occiput; ~**s, (-e),** occipital; *'n* ~ *se gedagte*, an idea at the back of one's mind; ~**sgewrig**, occipital joint.
ag'terhou, (-ge-), keep behind; keep back, retain, hold back (over); reserve (forces); ~**'dend, (-e),** reserved, close, incommunicative; reticent, secretive; ~**'dendheid**, secretiveness, closeness, reticence; reserve; ~**ding**, retainment; concealment; detention (by police).
ag'terin, at the back (of a book); in the back; ~ *sit*, sit in the rear seat (of car).
ag'teringang, rear entrance, back entrance.
ag'terjuk, hind (rear) yoke.
ag'terkam, rear (nape) comb.
ag'terkamer, backroom.
ag'terkant, back, backpart; rear (end); reverse side (of coin); *jou* ~ *vir iem. TOEKEER*, turn your back on someone; *die WÊRELD staan met sy* ~ *na my*, I am having bad luck; *ons net sy* ~ *WYS*, show us his worst side only.
ag'terklas, (-se), slum dwellers, lower class.
ag'ter: ~**kleindogter**, greatgranddaughter; ~**kleinkind**, greatgrandchild; ~**kleinseun**, greatgrandson.
ag'terkom, (-ge-), discover, find out, get wind of, suspect; penetrate.

agterkop, back part of the head, occiput; poll (of a horse).
ag'terkopholte, nape of the neck.
ag'terkwart, hind quarter.
ag'terlaaier, (hist.), breechloading gun, breechloader; frock-coat.
ag'terlaat, (-ge-), leave behind; maroon; *sy vrou onversorg* ~, leave his wife unprovided for.
ag'terlaer, rear bearing.
ag'terlamp, tail light, rear light, backlight.
ag'terland, hinterland, interior, the country.
ag'terlas, freight (in afterhold); ~ *hê*, be loaded in stern.
ag'terlating, leaving behind, abandonment; *met ~ van*, leaving behind.
ag'terleen, *(hist.)*, mesnetenure; ~**man**, mesnelord; rear vassal.
ag'terleisel, hind rein.
ag'terlengte, length of back.
ag'terlig, rear light, tail light, backlight.
ag'terlik, (-e), backward, mentally deficient, (mentally) retarded; behindhand; undeveloped (region); ~**heid**, backwardness; mental deficiency, (mental) retardation.
ag'terlosig = agtelosig.
ag'terluik, rear hatch.
ag'terlyf, abdomen (insect); hindquarters, buttocks, behind, dèrriere.
ag'terlyn, base line; backline, threequarter line *(rugby)*.
ag'termas, jigger mast; miz(z)en mast.
agtermekaar', in order, orderly; capital; well-groomed, dressy; neat, spruce, dapper; in form; ready; without a stop, at a stretch; in succession; *'n ~ BOER*, a progressive farmer; *DRIE dae reën ~*, three days rain in succession, *'n ~ KÊREL*, a fine fellow; *iets ~ SIT*, put something in order.
agtermid'dag, afternoon; ..*dae*, ~**s**, in (during) the afternoon.
ag'termodderskerm, rear mudguard.
ag'termuur, backwall, rear wall.
agterna', after, later, subsequently; behind; *EK is toe ~*, then I followed; *~ RY*, follow (by car); *~ STUUR*, send after; redirect (letters).
ag'ternaaf, rear hub.
ag'ternaam, second name, surname.
agterna'doen, (-ge-), imitate.
agterna'draai, result, consequence(s).
agterna'loop, (-ge-), follow, run after (in pursuit); flock after; curry favour; dance attendance on.
agterna'praat, (-ge-), repeat (another's words), echo.
agterna'sit, (-ge-), pursue, give chase; *iem. ~*, make after one; hound someone down.
ag'terneef, grandnephew (cousin).
ag'ternig(gie), grandniece (cousin).
ag'terom, round the back, behind; *~ kyk*, look back.
ag'teromspring, (-ge-), cheat; jump round.
agteroor', backward(s), supinely.
agteroor'druk, (-ge-), bend backwards.
agteroor'gooi, (-ge-), throw back(wards).
agteroor'hang, (-ge-), hang (slant) back.
agteroor'lê, (-ge-), lie back, recline, lean back(wards).
agteroor'leun, (-ge-), lean back(wards); ~**end**, (-e), recumbent.
agteroor'siekte, agteroorsiekte (cattle disease).
agteroor'slaan, (-ge-), somersault backwards; loop.
agteroor'val, (-ge-), fall backward(s).
agteroor'vlieg, (-ge-), loop the loop.
agteroor'vlug, loop (in flying).
ag'terop, behind, at the back; *~ ry*, ride pillion.
agterop'skop, (-ge-), kick (fling) up the heels, frisk; be unmanageable, revolt; *~ van vreugde*, be mad with joy.
ag'teros, hind ox; *~ kom ook in die kraal*, slow but sure; ~**sambok**, heavy sjambok (whip).
ag'terpad, backroad; country road.
ag'terpant, backpanel (gore) (of a skirt).
ag'terperd, hindhorse, wheeler.
ag'terplaas, backyard; buttocks.
ag'terpoort, postern, gate, backentrance (gate).

ag'terpoot, hind leg; *op sy ..pote STAAN*, rear (up); become unmanageable (horse); *gou op die ..pote WEES*, be quick-tempered.
ag'terpunt, backend; rear (of procession).
ag'terraak, (-ge-), drop behind, lag behind, get into arrears, fall behind, fall astern.
ag'terrat, sprocket (of a bicycle).
ag'terrem, backbrake, rear brake.
ag'terruim, stern hold.
ag'terruiter, rear horseman; also-ran.
ag'terryer, attendant on horseback; henchman; obsequious follower; flunkey; batman; outrider; gillie; hanger-on; ~**y**, flunkeyism.
ag'terrym, end rhyme.
ag'tersaal, pillion, flapper bracket (motorcycle); ~**ryer**, pillion rider, pillion passenger (rider).
ag'tersak, backpocket; hippocket.
ag'terseil, jigger.
ag'tersitter, backbencher.
ag'terskeeps, (-e), astern, aft.
ag'terskip, stern, poop.
ag'terskot, (-te), arrear (deferred, back) payment, final payment (by a co-operative society), supplementary pay; tailboard (of a cart).
ag'terspel, backplay; ~**er**, back, backplayer.
ag'terstaan, (-ge-), be inferior; be behind; *by niemand ~ nie*, be inferior to nobody, stand back for no one; ~**der**, backstand (of a motor cycle).
agterstal'lig, (-e), in arrear, overdue, back (rent); behindhand; ~*e PAAIEMENTE*, arrear instalments; ~*e RENTE*, interest still outstanding; ~*e SKULDE*, arrears.
ag'terstand, arrears, arrearage; backward position; backlog; handicap; *die ~ inhaal*, make up leeway (lost ground).
ag'terste, (s), (-s), hind part, hindquarters, backside, endmost, the lattter end, bottom, bum; fundament; last one; (b), last, endmost, rearmost, hind(er)most, posterior.
ag'terstel[1], (s) tail-end (wagon); rear part (chassis); trailing truck.
ag'terstel[2], (w), (-ge-), put (place) behind, put in the background; discriminate against; *~ by*, pass over for, slight; ~**ling**, slight, neglect; subordination.
agterstevoor', hind part foremost; topsy-turvy, upside down, wrong; *'n perd ~ RY*, put the cart before the horse; *~ SUINIG*, penny wise pound foolish; *in alles ~ WEES*, set about everything in the wrong way.
ag'terstewe, (-ns), sternpost, stern (ship); poop; ~**ring**, stern ring.
ag'terstraat, backstreet, slum street.
ag'terstring, wheel trace.
ag'terstuk, backpiece, backpart; heel; breech, breechblock (cannon).
ag'terswaar, tail-heavy; ~**te**, tailheaviness.
ag'tertand, backtooth, molar.
ag'tertang, afterguide (of a wagon).
ag'tertoe, astern; towards the back (rear); *baie kos gaan ~*, much food goes to the kitchen.
ag'tertoon, backtoe (of a bird).
ag'tertrap, backstairs.
ag'tertuin, backgarden.
ag'tertuig, wheel harness.
agteruit', (s), reverse (gear); (b) backward(s), abaft, aback; counterclockwise; *die PASIËNT gaan ~*, the patient is becoming worse; *dit is 'n STAP ~*, that is a retrograde (backward) step.
agteruit'boer, (-ge-), go downhill; farm at a loss.
agteruit'deins, (-ge-), start back, shrink from, recoil.
agteruit'dring, (-ge-), force back, supersede; put into the shade.
agteruit'gaan, (-ge-), go backward(s), reverse (gear); give ground; grow worse, decline (patient); be on the downgrade; deteriorate (fruit); degenerate (morals); back; fall off (numbers); dwindle; ~**d**, (-e), failing.
agteruit'gang[1], decay, retrogression, deterioration, dilapidation, labefaction; derogation; fall(ing-off), decline, drop; recession.
ag'teruitgang[2], rear exit, backdoor, rear door.
agteruit'gly, (-ge-), tailslide, slide backward(s).

agteruitkrabbel 30 *akkerwerk*

agteruit'krabbel, (-ge-), back out of, climb down, cry off.
agteruit'kykspieël, rear-vision mirror, rear mirror.
agteruit'loop, (-ge-), walk backward(s); lose ground.
agteruit'raak, (-ge-), become poorer; deteriorate.
agteruit'ry, (-ge-), sit with the back to the engine (train); ride (drive) backwards; reverse, back (a motor).
ag'teruitsig, rear view, backview.
agteruit'sit, (-ge-), put back (watch); sit back; make worse, cause to deteriorate; retard progress.
agteruit'skuif, ..skuiwe, (-ge-), push back.
agteruit'spring, (-ge-), jump backward(s).
agteruit'staan, stand back, yield.
agteruit'stap, (-ge-), walk backwards, step back.
agteruit'stel, (-ge-), retard, set back (clock); over= look, pass over.
agteruit'trap, (-ge-), step back; back-pedal.
agteruit'tree, (-ge-), step backwards.
agteruit'trek, (-ge-), pull back.
agteruit'vaar, (-ge-), sail backwards.
agteruit'versnelling, reverse gear.
agteruit'vlieg, (-ge-), fly (start) back.
agteruit'wyk, (-ge-), start back, shrink back; retreat, fall back (army).
ag'terveer, rear spring, backspring.
ag'terveld, backveld; backcountry; ~er, backvelder.
ag'tervenster, rear window, tonneau window, back= window.
ag'terverhemelte, soft palate.
ag'tervertrek, backroom.
ag'tervin, backfin.
ag'tervlak, backface.
ag'tervoeg, (-ge-), affix, postfix, subjoin; ~ing, ad= dition (to the end); paragoge; ~sel, (-s), suffix, af= fix, postfix.
ag'tervoet, hind foot; *aan die ~ UITGEVANG wees*, be very backward; *iem. se ~ VAT*, give someone a hiding.
agtervolg', (~), follow, chase, pursue, hunt (a crimi= nal); dog; persecute; haunt (by thoughts); ~ens, in turn, successively; ~er, (-s), pursuer; chaser; ~ing, chase, pursuit, persecution; full cry.
ag'tervurk, backfork, rear fork (of a bicycle).
ag'terwa, van; trailer.
ag'terwaarts, (b), (-e), backward, rearward; (bw), backwards; ~*e BEWEGING*, backward move= ment; ~*e PEILING*, tail-bearing *(aeron.)*.
ag'terwand, backwall, rear wall.
agterwe'ë, aside, behind; ~ *BLY*, fail to appear; re= main in abeyance; ~ *HOU*, keep back, withhold; *iets ~ LAAT*, drop (omit) something.
ag'terwêreld, rear world; backveld; buttocks.
ag'terwerk¹, stern (of a ship); backside.
ag'terwerk², inferior-quality raisins.
ag'terwiel, backwheel, hindwheel, rear wheel.
ag'terwyk, slum.
ag(t)'hoek, octagon; ~ig, (-e), octagonal, octangular.
ag'tien = agt(t)ien.
ag'ting, regard, esteem, deference, honour; respect; consideration; duty; ~ *AFDWING*, compel re= spect; *in iem. se ~ DAAL*, sink in someone's es= teem; *die ~ GENIET van*, enjoy the esteem of; ~ *HÊ vir iem.*, respect someone; *UIT ~ vir*, out of consideration for; *iem. se ~ VERBEUR*, forfeit someone's respect; *iem. se ~ VERWERF*, earn someone's respect.
ag(t)'jarig, (-e), eight years old; octennial.
ag(t)'kantig, (-e), octagonal, octahedral.
ag(t)'lettergrepig, (-e), octosyllabic.
ag(t)'ostou, *Aspalathus mollis*.
ag(t)'potig, (-e), octopod.
ag(t)'puntig, (-e), with eight points.
ag(t)'reëlig, (-e), of eight lines.
ag(t)'ryig, (-e), in eight rows.
ag(t)'silindermotor, eight-cylinder car.
ag(t)'sitplekmotor, eightseater.
ag(t)'snarig, (-e), octochord.
ag(t)'ste, (-s), eighth.
ag(t)'steman, (-ne), eighth man, no. 8 (forward).
ag(t)'sydig, (-e), octahedral, octagonal.

ag(t)'syfertoets, figure-of-eight test.
ag(t)'tal, team of eight, octad; eight; octave.
ag(t)'tallig, (-e), octonal.
agt'(t)ien, eighteen; ~de, eighteenth; ~de-eeus, (-e), eighteenth-century.
agt'uur, eight o'clock; breakfast; ..*urige werkdag*, eight-hour working day.
ag(t)'vlak, octahedron; ~kig, (-e), octahedral.
ag(t)'voetig, (-e), octopod, with eight feet; octameter (verse).
ag(t)'voud, eightfold; ~ig, (-e), eightfold, octuple.
agurk', (-e), ~ie, (-s), gherkin; ~iekonfyt, gherkin preserve.
aha'! ah! aha!
ahorn', maple; ~blaar, maple leaf; ~suiker, maple sugar; ~stroop, maple syrup.
ai¹, (s), (-'s), sloth.
ai²! (tw), ah! oh! by Jove!
aide-de-camp', (aides-de-camp), aide-de-camp.
aigret'te, (-s), aigrette.
ai'kôna, no, not at all.
air, (-s), air, appearance; ~*s AANNEEM*, put on side; *hom (haar) ~s GEE*, give himself (herself) airs.
aispaai', I spy, hide-and-seek.
ait's(a)! look out! hallo! ~ *maar sy's mooi!* my word, she is pretty!
aits'atjie, (-s), drink, tot.
ajo'sie, (-s), puffball *(Phellorina)*.
ajuin', sliced and pickled onions; squill *(Urginea maritima)*.
akade'mie, (-s), academy; college, university; ~bur= ger, collegeman, universityman; gownsman; ~jaar, academic year; ~lewe, college life, universi= ty life; ~lid, academy member; ~raad, council of the academy; ~s, (-e), academical(ly); ~*se GRAAD*, university degree; ~*se VRAAG*, aca= demic question; ~stad, university town; ~vriend, college (university) friend.
akade'mikus, (-se, ..mici), academic.
akant', (-e), akan'tus, (-se), acanthus, bear's breech.
aka'sia, (-s), acacia.
akatalek'ties, (-e), acatalectic (verse).
akelei', (-e), columbine.
A'ken, Aix-la-Chapelle.
a'keriet, akerite.
ak'ka, *(kinderwoord)* (s), faeces, dirt; (w) (ge-), have bowel movement.
akkedis', (-se), lizard; gecko; *groen ~*, lacerta; ~ag= tig, (-e), lizard-like, lacertian; ~dier, saurian; ~leer, lizardskin; ~vanger, lizard buzzard.
ak'kel: *'n ~ MAAK*, achieve something, make a bar= gain; ~*s MAAK*, put on airs, cut capers.
ak'ker¹, (-s), field, plot (of land); acre; *elke MAN op sy ~*, every man to his post; *die SAAD het in 'n vrugbare ~ geval*, the seed has fallen on fertile soil; *nie omgee oor watter ~s die WATER loop nie*, not care what one says or does.
ak'ker², (-s), acorn; oak(tree); *sy ~s BRAND*, his chestnuts are in the fire; *jou ~ sal KRAAK*, you are in for a hard time; *laat jy jou met ~s in, word jy van VARKE gevreet*, pitch defiles.
ak'keraarde, humus; ground suitable for cultivation.
ak'kerboom, oak(tree).
ak'kerbou, agriculture; agronomy; field cropping, field husbandry.
ak'ker: ~dop, acorncup; ~doppie, acornshell; ~draend, (-e), glandiferous; ~druiwe, Waltham Cross, acorn-shaped grape.
ak'kerertjie, pea *(Pisum arvense)*.
ak'kergans, bean goose *(Anser arvensis)*.
ak'kerhout, oak(wood).
ak'kerklawer, hopclover *(Trifolium)*.
ak'kerklokkie, bluebell.
ak'kerkoffie, acorn coffee.
ak'kermannetjie, wagtail.
akkermo'nie, agrimony *(Agrimonia eupatoria)*.
ak'kertjie¹, (-s), garden bed.
ak'kertjie², (-s), small acorn.
ak'kervormig, (-e), glandiform, acorn-shaped.
akkerwa'nie, cuscus (-grass).
ak'kerwerk, farming, agricultural work.

ak'kerwinde, convolvulus.
akklama'sie, acclamation.
akklimatisa'sie, acclimatization.
akklimatiseer', (ge-), acclimatize.
akklimatise'ring, acclimatization.
akkola'de, accolade; brace (bracket).
akkommoda'sie, accommodation; ~ **vermoë**, power of accommodation; ~ **wissel**, accommodation bill.
akkommodeer', (ge-), accommodate.
akkoord', (s), agreement, harmony; chord *(music)*; composition; ~ *met SKULDEISERS*, composition with creditors; *OP 'n* ~, continuously, incessantly; (b), correct, in order; ~ *!* agreed, that's a bargain! ~ *BEVIND*, find correct; ~ *GAAN met*, agree (concur) with.
akkordeer', (ge-), agree; get on with; thrive (plants); *komkommer* ~ *nie met my nie*, cucumber does not agree with me.
akkor'deon, (-s), accordion.
akkrediteer', (ge-), accredit.
akkultura'sie, acculturation.
akkultureer', (ge-), acculturize, acculturate.
akkumula'sie, accumulation.
akkumula'tor, (-e, -s), accumulator, storage battery; *ontlaaide* ~, discharged battery.
akkumuleer', (ge-), accumulate.
akkuraat', (..rate), accurate; ~ **heid**, accuracy, precision.
akkusatief', (..tiewe), accusative; accusatival.
A-klein'terts, *(ong.)*, A minor.
ak'me, acme.
akmiet', acmite.
ak'nee, acne.
akoestiek', acoustics.
akoes'ties, (-e), acoustic.
akoes'tikus, (-se, ..tici), acoustician.
akoliet', (-e), acolyte.
akoniet', aconite, wolf's bane.
akonitien', **akoniti'ne**, aconitine.
akranie', acrania; **akra'nies**, acranial.
akriel'suur, acrylic acid.
akriflavien', acriflavine.
akrobaat', (..bate), acrobat; posture maker (master); ..**ba'ties**, (-e), acrobatic.
akrogeen', (..gene), acrogen.
akropetaal', (..tale), acropetalous.
akro'polis, (-se), acropolis.
akros'ties, (-e), acrostic.
akros'tigon, (-s), acrostic.
akroto'mies, (-e), acrotomous.
aks, (-e), eighth (of an inch); tiny bit (part), fraction.
akselera'sie, acceleration.
akselera'tor, (-s), accelerator.
akselereer', (ge-), accelerate.
aksent', (-e), accent; cadence; *akuut* ~, acute accent; (stress); ~ **loos**, (..lose), unaccentuated; ~ **teken**, accent mark; ~ **ua'sie**, accentuation, ~ **ueer'**, (ge-), accent, accentuate, stress.
aksep, (-te), acceptance (of a bill); promissory note; ~ **bank**, merchant bank, acceptance house (bank).
aksepta'bel, (-e), acceptable.
akseptant', (-e), acceptor.
aksepta'sie, (-s), acceptation (of a bill).
aksepteer', (ge-), accept.
aksiaal', (aksiale), axial.
ak'sie[1], (-s), tiny bit, minute quantity, little; *'n* ~ *groter*, slightly (a fraction) larger.
ak'sie[2], (-s), action; suit; campaign; *'n* ~ *HÊ teen iem.*, have a bone to pick with someone; *'n* ~ *INSTEL*, take legal proceedings; ~ *uit KONTRAK*, action arising from contract, actio ex contractu vel ~*s WEES*, be affected; ~ **diens**, communion (service); ~ **komitee**, action committee; ~ **lied**, action song; ~ **radius**, action radius; ~ **reg**, law of procedure.
aksillêr', (-e), axillary.
aksiniet', axinite.
aksio'ma, (-s), axiom, postulate; ..**ma'ties** (-e), axiomatic.
aksiona'bel, (-e), actionable; disgusting; silly.
aksiona'ris, (-se), shareholder.
aksioom', (aksiome) = **aksioma**.

aksyns', excise, inland duty; ~ **belasting**, excise duty; ~ **kantoor**, excise office; ~ **meester**, excise officer; ~ **pligtig**, (-e), excisable; ~ **reg**, excise duty; ~ **vry**, (-e), non-excisable, duty-free; ~ **wet**, excise law.
ak'te, (-s), deed; certificate; act; document; ~ *van BESKULDIGING*, indictment; ~ *van OORDRAG*, deed of conveyance; ~ *van OPRIGTING*, memorandum of association; *REGISTRATEUR van* ~*s*, registrar of deeds; ~ *van SUPERSKRIPSIE*, act of superscription; ~ *van VERKOOP*, deed of sale; ~ **besorger**, conveyancer; ~ **besorging**, conveyancing; ~ **makery**, conveyancing; ~ **skantoor**, deeds office; ~ **tas**, attaché case, brief case, despatch case; ~ **trommel**, deeds box; ~ **-uitmaker**, conveyancer.
akteur', (-s), actor, player; showman; mummer; ~ **s'kamer**, greenroom.
aktief', (**aktiewe**), active, energetic; *in ..tiewe DIENS*, on active service; *'n ..tiewe LID*, a live wire; *..tiewe OFFISIER*, combatant officer; *..tiewe VULKAAN*, active volcano.
akti'nieë, sea-anemones.
akti'nies, (-e), actinic.
aktinis'me, actinism, intensity of solar radiation.
akti'nium, actinium.
aktinografie', actinography.
aktinoliet', actinolite.
aktinome'ter, actinometer.
aktinometrie', actinometry.
aktiveer', (ge-), activate; ~ **middel**, activator.
aktive'ring, activation.
aktivis', (-te), activist; ~ **me**, activism; ~ **ties**, (-e), activistic.
aktiwiteit', (-e), activity.
aktri'se, (-s), actress.
aktualisa'sie, actualization.
aktualiseer', (ge-), actualize.
aktualiteit', (-e), actuality, topicality, timeliness; ~ **sprogram**, actuality (news) programme (radio; TV).
aktuarieel', (..riële), actuarial.
aktua'ris, (-se), actuary.
aktua'rius, registrar (of a Synod).
aktueel', (..tuele), actual, real; topical, timely, of present interest; *'n artikel oor 'n aktuele onderwerp*, a topical article.
aktueer', (ge-), actuate.
akuïteit', acuity.
akupunktuur', acupuncture.
akuut', (akute), acute.
akwaduk', (-te), aqueduct.
akwamaryn', (-e), aquamarine.
akwarel', (-le), water-colour painting, aquarelle; ~ **lis'**, (-te), water-colour painter.
akwa'rium, (-s), aquarium.
a'kwatint, aquatint.
al[1], (s), all, everything; universe; *die* ~ *deur GOD geskape*, the universe created by God; *al HAWERKLAP*, every now and then; regularly, often; ~ *wat dit LEES*, all who read this; *sy LOOP so* ~ *wat sy kan*, she runs for all she is worth; *MET dit* ~, for all that, nevertheless; ~ *wat OPDAAG (kom)*, *is hy*, he never turned up; and still he does not come; *met SKIL en* ~, skin and all; *dis* ~ *wat ek WEET*, that is as much as I know; (b, telw), all, every; only; ~ *die ANDER*, all the others; ~ *DAG wat ek kan kom*, the only day I can come; ~ *DRIE*, all three; ~ *MANIER om dit te doen*, the only way to do it; ~ *PERSOON wat beswaar het*, the only person who objects; ~ *le REDE hê om te glo*, have every reason to believe; *k. k TYD*, at all times, ~ *die TYD*, all the time; *dis* ~ *VIR my of*, I have an inkling, I feel as if; (bw), already, yet; continually; ~ *DAN nie*, whether or not; *dit DWING* ~ *soontoe*, it keeps on going that way; ~ *EERDER*, before now; ~ *GAANDE*, while walking along; ~ *HOE meer mense*, more and more people; ~ *IN die 12de eeu*, as early as the 12th century; ~ *LANKAL*, long ago; ~ *NA dit val*, however things may turn out; ~ *OM die ander week*, every other week; ~ *SINGENDE*, singing (all the while); *TOE* ~, even then; (vgw), (al)though, even if, even though; ~ *is hy nog*

so *ARM*, however poor he may be; ~ *HELP dit nie, dan troos dit*, even if it does not help, it comforts.
al-², pan-, all-.
alaba'ma, (-s), puggree; something big.
Al'-Amerikaans, Pan-American.
a la car'te, a la carte, per item (menu).
alarm', (-s), alarm; tumult; ~ *BLAAS*, sound the alarm; *'n VALS (blinde)* ~ *gee*, sound (create) a false alarm; ~ eer', (ge-), alarm; alert; ~ e'rend, (-e), alarming; ~ fluit, alarm whistle; ~ is', (-te), alarmist, scaremonger; ~ is'ties, (-e), alarmist; ~ jaer, ~ jagvliegtuig, interceptor (plane); ~ kanon, alarm gun; ~ klok, alarm bell, tocsin; ~ kreet, cry of alarm, hue; ~ kwartiere, close bil=lets; ~ plek, alarm post; ~ pos, action post; ~ sein, alarm (signal); ~ skoot, alarm gun; ~ toestel, alarm, alarum; ~ trom, alarm drum.
Albaans', (-e), Alban.
al'bakoor, (..kore), albacore.
Albanees', (..nese), Albanian.
Alba'nie, Albany (Cape Prov.).
Alba'nië, Albania.
Alba'nies, (-e), Albanian.
albas' = albaster.
albas'ter, (-s), marble; *hy staan of hy 'n* ~ *ingesluk het*, he seems to have lost his tongue; ~ gips, ala=baster (gypsum); ~ speler, marble(s) player; ~ spel=(etjie), marble game; ~ tyd, time for marbles, mar=ble season.
al'batros, (-se), albatross.
al'be, (-s), alb, stole (R. C. Church).
al'bedil, (-le), faultfinder, caviller, busybody, meddler.
al'beheersend, (-e), all-ruling, all-dominating.
Al'behoeder, the All-Preserver, God.
al'bei, both; ~ *die KINDERS*, both children; *ONS* ~, both of us.
al'beskikking, supreme providence.
al'bestuur, supreme rule.
al'bies, (-e), albian.
Albigens', (-e), Albigensian; ~ e, Albigenses; ~ ies, (-e), Albigensian.
albi'no, (-'s), albino.
Al'bion, Albion, England.
albitiet', albitite.
alboliet', albolite, albolith.
al'bum, (-s), album; ~ blad, album leaf.
albumina'te, albuminates.
albumien', albumi'ne, albumin.
alchemie', alchemy.
alchemis', (-te), alchemist; ~ ties, (-e), alchemistic.
aldaar', there, at that place.
al'dae, al'dag, all day; every day; daily; *HEELDAG en* ~, continually; *liewer* ~ *WAT as een dag sat*, waste not, want not.
al'dagse, everyday; *nie 'n* ~ *kêrel nie*, an outstanding fellow.
aldehi'de, (-s), aldehied', (-e), aldehyde.
al'deur, continually, all the time; ~ dringend, (-e), piercing, penetrating.
al'disvisier, aldis sight.
aldo'se, (-s), aldose, aldehyde sugar.
Al'-Duits, (-e), Pan-German.
aldus', thus, so, in this manner.
aleer', before, ere.
alei'send, (-e), exacting.
Aleksan'drië, Alexandria (Egypt).
aleksandriet', alexandrite.
aleksandryn', (-e), alexandrine.
Aleksandryns',(-e), Alexandrian.
aleksie', alexia.
aleksi'ne, alexin.
alembiek', (-e), alembic, distilling-retort.
aleuronaat', aleuronate.
ale'wig, (-e), continual, incessant; ~ *DEUR*, continu=ally, incessantly; ~ *LAAT wees*, be continually late.
Alexan'dria, Alexandria (C.P.).
Alexan'drialae, Alexandria beds.
Alexan'drië, Alexandria (Egypt).
al'fa, alpha; *die* ~ *en die OMEGA*, the alpha and the omega (beginning and end); *van – tot OMEGA*, from beginning to end.
alfaam' = halfaam.
al'fabet, (-te), alphabet, ABC; ..be'ties, (-e), alpha=betic(al); abecedarian; ~ iseer', (ge-), alphabetize.
al'fa: ~ deeltjies, alpha particles; ~ gras, esparto; ~ strale, alpha rays.
alfeni'de, (-s), alfenied', (-e), alfenide.
alg, (-e), alga.
algaan'de, gradually, by degrees.
al'gar, all, everybody.
al'ge, (-s) = alg.
Al'gebieder, God.
al'gebra, algebra; *dit is vir my* ~, it is Greek to me; ..bra'ïes, (-e), algebraic.
al'geheel, (..hele), total(ly), entire(ly); all-round; al=together; utter (nonsense); whole-hearted; ..*hele oorgawe*, total surrender; ..*hele slibbing*, complete sliming.
al'gemeen, (..mene), general(ly), universal(ly); cath=olic; current, prevalent, public, prevailing, popular, common(ly), generic; rampant, pandemic; *dit is* ~ *BEKEND*, it is common knowledge; *die algemene BELANG*, public interest; ~ *in GEBRUIK (swang)*, in common use, in vogue; *IN (oor) die* ~, on the whole, in general; *algemene KENNIS*, gen=eral knowledge; *algemene KOSTE*, overhead ex=penses; *'n ONDERWERP baie* ~ *behandel*, discuss a subject in broad outlines; *algemene PROKURA=SIE*, general power of attorney; *algemene RENDE=MENT*, overall efficiency (of a machine); *met alge=mene STEMME*, unanimously; *algemene VER=BAND*, general bond; *algemene VERKOOPBELASTING (AVB)*, general sales tax (GST); *algemene WERKSMAN*, handyman; *A* ~ *-Beskaaf*, standard language; ~ heid, univer=sality, commonness; prevalence, prevalency; plati=tude; generality; ~ making, generalization; ~ tjie, (-s), general news-item.
al'genoegsaam, (..same), all-sufficient; ~ heid, all-sufficiency.
Alge'rië, Algeria.
Al'-Germaans, (-e), Pan-Germanic.
Algeryn', (-e), Algerian; ~ s', (-e), Algerian.
Algiers', Algiers (city).
al'godedom, pantheism.
Al'goede: *die* ~, the All-Bountiful.
algoris'me, algorit'me, algorism, algorithm (integral calculus).
al'heilig, (-e), all-holy.
al'heilmiddel, panacea.
alhier', here, local; *mnr. N.*, ~, Mr. N., Local.
alhoewel', (al)though, albeit.
al-hondered-en-tien', even if it is so; notwithstanding, all the same.
a'lias, (s), (-se), alias; (bw) alias, otherwise.
aliba'ma = alabama.
a'libi, (-'s), alibi; *jou* ~ *bewys*, establish one's alibi.
a'lidade, alidade.
aliëna'sie, alienation.
aliëneer, (ge-), alienate.
alifa'ties, (-e), aliphatic.
a'likreukel, (-s), periwinkle.
a'likwant, aliquant.
a'likwot, aliquot.
alimenta'sie, alimentation; allowance, ~ plig, ali=mentary obligation.
alimentêr', (-e), alimentary; ~ *e kanaal*, digestive tract.
ali'nea, (-s), paragraph; subsection.
alisarien', alisari'ne, alizarin.
aljan'der, oranges and lemons (game).
aljim'mers, always, ever, repeatedly.
alk, (-e), auk, razorbill.
alka'li, (-ë, -'s), alkali.
alka'lies, (-e), alkaline; ~ *e aarde*, alkaline earth.
alka'li: ~ gesteente, alkaline rock; ~ meter, alkali=meter; ~ niteit', alkalinity; ~ waarde, alkali content.
alkaloï'de, (-s), alkaloïed', (-e), alkaloid.
al'kant, on all sides; *'n ou BOETIE* ~, hypocrite; ~ *RUGSTRING wees*, be very lean; ~ *SELFKANT*,

six of the one and half-a-dozen of the other; ~ **byl,** double(-bitted) axe.
al′kante, on both (all) sides; ~ *van die pad loop,* be tipsy.
al′kantig, (-e), all-sided, versatile.
al′kantslot, reversible lock.
alklaps′, every now and then; continually.
al′kohol, alcohol; ~ **gebruiker,** alcohol user, drinker; ~ **gehalte,** alcohol content; . . **ho′lies, (-e),** alcoholic; ~ *e drank,* alcoholic beverage; ~ **inhoud,** alcohol content; ~ **is′, (-te),** alcoholic; ~ **isa′sie,** alcoholization; ~ **iseer′, (ge-),** alcoholize; ~ **is′me,** alcoholism; ~ **meter,** alcohol meter; ~ **toetser,** alcotester; ~ **vergiftiging,** alcoholic poisoning; ~ **vry, (-e),** non-alcoholic, non-intoxicant.
alkoof′, (alkowe), alcove, recess.
al′la! gracious! upon my word!
Al′lah, Allah.
al′la: ~ **krag′tie!** ~ **krag′tig!** ~ **mag′(gies)!** ~ **mag′tig!** ~ **map′stieks!** ~ **mas′kas!** ~ **mas′tig!** ~ **mat′jies!** ~ **mat′jiesgoed!** ~ **men′sig!** ~ **min′tig!** ~ **wêreld!** oh! oho! I say! goodness! good gracious! upon my word! heigh-ho! gee whiz! great Scott!
allaniet′, allanite.
allantoïen′, allantoï′ne, allantoin.
al′lawêreld, *see* **alla.**
al′le, every, all.
alledaags′, (-e), daily, common (event); ordinary, trivial; workaday, humdrum, characterless; familiar; pedestrian; prosaic, prosy, platitudinarian; colloquial, plain, banal, trite; hackneyed; *klere vir ~ e GEBRUIK,* clothes for everyday wear; ~ *e OP= MERKINGS,* commonplaces, platitudes; ~ *e VOORVALLE,* common events; ~ **heid,** commonness, triviality, banality; pedestrianism.
allee′, (-s, alleë), avenue, alley, walk.
alleen′, alone, by oneself, single, lonely; mere(ly); bare; single-handed; friendless; only; ~ *die DIEF vang,* catch the thief single-handed; *die GEDAGTE* ~ , the mere thought; *die HUIS staan* ~ , the house stands in its own grounds; *HY, heeltemal* ~ , all by himself; *hy IS nie ~ nie,* he is tipsy; ~ *MAAR om= dat,* only because; *MAN* ~ , all by himself; without any aid; *ons MOES die kinders ~ laat,* we had to leave the children unattended; *iem.* ~ *SPREEK,* talk to someone in private; ~ *STAAN,* have no supporter; be unique; ~ *VOEL,* feel lonely; ~ **agent,′** sole agent; ~ **beheer,** sole management; ~ **besit,** sole possession; ~ **handel,** monopoly; ~ **heerser,** absolute monarch, dictator, monocrat; autocrat; ~ **heerskappy,** absolute monarchy, dictatorship, autocracy, autocratic rule; absolutism.
alleen′heid, loneliness, solitude.
alleen′invoerder, sole importer.
alleen′lik, only, merely.
alleen′lopend, (-e), single, unmarried; solitary.
alleen′loper = **alleenstaner.**
alleen′reg, sole right, exclusive right.
alleen′saligmakend, (-e); *die ~ e kerk,* the Roman Catholic Church – with no salvation outside it.
alleen′sang, monody.
alleen′spraak, soliloquy, monologue; *dramatiese* ~ , monodrama, dramatic monologue.
alleen′staande, single, solitary, isolated (case); detached, separate (buildings).
alleen′staner, bad mixer; lone fighter, loner.
alleen′verkoop, monopoly; sole agency; . . **koper,** sole agent, sole seller.
alleen′verteenwoordiger, sole representative (agent).
alleen′verteenwoordiging, sole agency.
alleen′vlug, solo flight.
allegaar′tjie, (-s), mixed grill; chow-chow, jumble, pot-pourri, farrago, medley, hodge-podge; scratch team.
al′legenugtig! good gracious!
allegorie′, (-ë), allegory.
allego′ries, (-e), allegoric(al).
allegret′to, allegretto, fairly lively (music).
alle′gro, allegro, lively (music).
al′le: ~ **mag′(gies),** ~ **mag′tig,** ~ **men′sig,** ~ **min′tig,** *see* **alla.**
al′leman, everybody, people; *Jan en* ~ , Tom, Dick and Harry; ~ **sgeheim,** open secret; ~ **sgek,** simpleton, Simple Simon; ~ **sgoed,** government property; common property; ~ *sgoed is niemandsgoed,* everybody's responsibility is nobody's responsibility.
al′lemansvriend, hail-fellow-well-met, everybody's friend; ~ *is niemandsvriend,* a friend to all is a friend to none.
allengs′(kens), gradually, by degrees.
alle′nig, alone, lonely; sole; *nie ~ wees nie,* be intoxicated.
al′ler¹, of all; *dis ons ~ (almal se) wens,* it is our united wish.
al′ler=², of the highest degree, exceptionally, most.
alleraar′digs, (-te,) most charming(ly).
allerarm′ste, (-s), the very poorest.
allerbekoor′liks, (-te), most attractive (charming).
allerbelag′liks, (-te), most ridiculous(ly).
allerbespot′liks, (-te), most ridiculous.
allerbes′te, very best, tiptop.
allerdring′end(ste), most pressing (urgent).
allerdroe′wig(ste), (most) lamentable, deplorable.
allerdruk′(ste), busiest.
allereers′(te), very first, first of all, first and foremost; primitive, elementary; *hy het ~ te GEKOM,* he came first of all; *~ te LEWENSBEHOEFTES,* bare necessities of life.
allererg′s(te), very worst, worst of all.
allerfraai′s(te), most beautiful.
allerfyn′s(te), finest of all.
allergeen′, (s), (. .gene), allergen; (b) (. .gene), allergenic.
allergena′digs, (-te), most gracious; most merciful.
allergerings′, (-te), least possible; most trifling.
allergetrous′, (-te), most faithful.
allergie′, (-ë), allergy.
aller′gies, (-e), allergic; ~ *vir (teenoor),* allergic to.
allergroots′, (-te), very largest, very greatest.
allerguns′tigs, (-te), most favourable.
al′lerhande, all sorts, all kinds, sundry, omnifarious.
Allerhei′lige, All Saints' Day, All Hallows, Hallowmas.
allerhei′ligs, (-te), most holy; *die Allerheiligste,* the holy of holies.
allerhoogs′te, supreme, highest of all.
Allerhoog′ste: *die ~ ,* the Supreme Being, the Almighty; God.
allerjam′merliks, (-te), most wretched, most regrettable.
Allerkin′derdag, Innocents' Day, Childermas.
allerlaags′, (-te), lowest, exceptionally low.
allerlaas′, (-te), very last, ultimate; *OP allerlaas,* finally, at the very end; *môre OP die allerlaaste,* not later than tomorrow.
al′lerlei, of all kinds, miscellaneous; ~ **tjie,** pot-pourri.
allerliefs′, (-te), (b), most charming (lovable); sweetest, dearest; (bw), preferably.
allerlief′ste, (-s), most beloved, very dearest; my dearest, my very own.
allermees′, (te), most of all, very most, mostly.
allermins′, (-te), least of all, very least.
allermoderns′, (-te), most modern.
allernaas′te, nearest of all; *ELKEEN is homself die* ~ , charity begins at home; *in die ~ TOEKOMS,* in the very near future.
allerno′digs, (-te), most necessary; *die ~ te voedsel,* the barest necessities of food.
allernuut′ste, very newest, very latest.
alleroud′ste, very oldest.
Allersie′le, All Soul's Day.
al′lersyds, on all sides.
allerui′ters, (-te), most extreme, very utmost, last; *as die ~ te gebeur,* if the worst happens.
allervoorde′ligs, (-te), most advantageous.
allervroegs′, (-te), very earliest.
al′lerweë, everywhere, in all respects, on all sides.
al′les, (s), all, everything; *BO* ~ , above all; *DIT* ~ , all this; *daar is van ~ te KRY,* a large variety is in stock; *MET dit ~ ,* notwithstanding; ~ *EN ~ ,* all in all; *en dis NOG nie ~ nie,* that's not all; *tot ~ in STAAT wees,* be able to do everything; bad enough for anything; ~ *op sy TYD,* there is a time for

everything; ~ *VEILIG*, all clear; ~ *VIR iem. wees*, be everything to somebody; *VOOR (bo)* ~, above all; ~ *goed en WEL, maar*, all very well, but ..; ~ *WEL*, all's well; (bw), everywhere; *dis* ~ *water waar 'n mens kyk*, one sees nothing but water.
al'lesbehalwe, anything but, not at all, far from.
al'lesbeheersend, (-e), predominating, of paramount importance.
al'lesetend, (-e), omnivorous.
al'leseter, omnivore.
al'lesins, in every respect, completely; *dit is* ~ *billik*, this (it) is quite fair.
al'lesomvattend, (-e), comprehensive, exhaustive.
al'lesoorheersend, (-e), predominant.
al'lesvernielend, (-e), all-destroying.
al'lesverslindend, (-e), omnivorous.
al'lesvretend, (-e), omnivorous.
al'lesvreter, (-s), omnivore.
allewê'reld = **allawêreld**.
allian'sie, (-s), alliance.
allia'sie, alloy.
allieer', (ge-), ally; alloy; *die Geallieerdes*, the Allies.
allig', perhaps, maybe, probably, peradventure.
alliga'tor, (-s), alligator.
allitera'sie, alliteration.
allitereer', (ge-), alliterate.
allo'! hallo!
allochtoon', (..tone), allochtonous.
allodiaal', (..diale), allodial, freehold.
allofaan', allophane.
allogaam', (..game), allogamous.
allogamie', allogamy.
allogeen', (..gene), allogenic.
alloku'sie, (-s), allocution.
allomorf', ** allomorph; ~ **is'me, allomorphism.
allooi', alloy; standard, quality (material); sort (people); *van die SUIWERSTE* ~, of the finest quality; *van VERDAGTE* ~, of a suspicious character; ~ **metaal**, alloy metal; ~ **staal**, alloy steel; ~ **suier**, alloy piston.
allopaat', (..pate), allopathist.
allopatie', allopathy.
allopa'ties, (-e), allopathic.
allotigeen', (..gene), allothigenous.
allotrofie', allotrophy.
allotroop', (..trope), allotrope.
allotropie', allotrophy, allotropism.
allotro'pies, (-e), allotropic.
allu're, (-s), air, manner, style.
alluviaal', (..viale), alluvial.
allu'vium, alluvium, alluvion.
al'maardeur, continually, the whole time.
al'mag, omnipotence, almightiness; ~ '**tig, (-e)**, almighty, all-powerful, omnipotent; *die Almagtige*, the Almighty (Omnipotent).
al'mal, all, everybody; all ranks; one and all; all= comers; *ons* ~, all of us.
al'ma ma'ter, Alma Mater.
almanak', (-ke), almanac, calendar; *hy DRUK* ~ *ke*, he is an expert liar; *hy is GEEN* ~ *nie*, you can't expect him to remember everything; *LIEG soos 'n* ~, lie like a gasmeter; *hy het UIT die* ~ *weggeloop*, he has taken French leave.
almandien', almandi'ne, almandine (ruby, garnet).
almaskie', all the same; notwithstanding, nevertheless; even so; *dis nie* ~ *nie*, of that you can be quite sure.
al'melewe, always, the whole time; ~ *laat wees*, be continually late.
al'middel, panacea.
almo'ënd, (-e), almighty; *die Almoënde*, the Almighty; ~ **heid**, almightiness, omnipotence.
alnoïet', alnoite.
aloïen', (-e), aloï'ne, (-s), aloin.
alom', everywhere; by all people; ~ *bekend*, known by (to) all.
al'omteenwoordig, (-e), omnipresent; ~ **heid**, omni= presence, ubiquity.
alomvat'tend, (-e), all-embracing, comprehensive.
aloud'heid, antiquity, antiqueness.
alou'e, ancient, antique.
alpak'ka¹, alpaca (animal, wool cloth).

alpak'ka², German silver, nickel silver.
alp'bok, ibex.
Al'pe, Alps; ~ **flora**, alpine flora; ~ **gloed**, Alpine glow; ~ **horing**, alpenhorn; ~ **klimmer**, Alpinist; ~ **kraai**, chough; ~ **pas**, Alpine pass; ~ **plant**, Al= pine plant; ~ **roos**, rhododendron; ~ **sport**, Alpine sports; ~ **stok**, alpenstock; ~ **streek**, Alpine region; ~ **top**, top of the Alps; ~ **vergeet-my-nietjie**, Alpine forget-me-not; ~ **viooltjie**, cyclamen, sowbread.
Alpien', Alpi'nies, Alpine.
Alpinis', (-te), Alpinist; ~ **me**, Alpinism.
Alpyns', (-e), Alpine.
alras', (vero.), very soon.
alreeds', already.
al'rigting, in every direction; ~ **svliegveld**, multidirec= tional-landing aerodrome.
alruin', mandragora, mandrake; ~ **wortel**, mandrake.
Al-Russies, (-e), Pan-Russian.
als, wormwood; bitterness; *so bitter soos* ~, as bitter as gall; ~ **brandewyn**, absinth(e).
al'sem, wormwood; *die pen in* ~ *doop*, dip one's pen in gall; ~ **beker**, cup of bitterness; ~ **bitter**, absin= thine; ~ **drank**, absinth(e); ~ **kruid**, wormwood (*Artemisia absinthium*).
alsien'de, all-seeing; omniscient, *die A* ~, the All-seeing.
alsiend'heid, omniscience.
also', thus, in this way, so.
alsy'dig, (-e), many-sided; all-round (sportsman); versatile (entertainer); all-purpose; ~ **heid**, many-sidedness, versatility.
alt, (-e), contralto, alto; counter-tenor.
al'taar, altaar', (altare), altar; *wie die* ~ *BEDIEN, moet van die* ~ *lewe*, one's calling should provide one with a comfortable living; *altare vir iem. of iets BOU*, build a shrine to; *VOOR die* ~, at the altar; ~ **brood**, altarbread; ~ **dienaar**, acolyte; ~ **diens**, mass; ~ **doek**, altarcloth, frontlet, frontal; ~ **gewaad**, chasuble; ~ **kelk**, chalice; ~ **kleed**, stole, chasuble; ~ **knaap**, altarboy; ~ **lamp**, sanctuary lamp; ~ **skerm**, reredos; ~ **skildery**, altarpiece; ~ **stuk**, predella.
altans', at least, anyway, at any rate, that is to say; *hy het nie opgedaag nie;* ~ *ek het hom nie gesien nie*, he has not turned up; at least I have not seen him.
al'te, too; *jy weet maar* ~ *GOED*, you know only too well; *ek voel nie – wel nie*, I don't feel too well; *hulle WOON* ~ *ver*, they live too far away; *nie* ~ *WYD nie*, not too wide.
al'teenwoordig, omnipresent.
al'tegaar, al'tegader, altogether.
altemit(s)', perhaps, maybe; *dis nie* ~ *nie*, there is no doubt about it.
al'ter e'go, alter ego, second self.
alternatief', (s, b), (..tiewe), alternative.
alterna'tor, (-e, -s), alternator.
alterneer', (ge-), alternate; *alternerende dae*, alternat= ing days.
al'tesaam, al'tesame, altogether, together.
alt'hobo, English horn, cor anglais.
alt'horing, althorn.
altigraaf', (..grawe), altigraph.
al'timeter, altime'ter, (-s), altimeter.
altimetrie', altimetry.
al'tiskoop, (..skope), altiscope.
al'toos, (-e), always, ever; ~ *deur*, continually; ~ **durend, (-e)**, everlasting.
alt'party, contralto part.
altruïs', (-te), altruist; ~ **me**, altruism; ~ **ties, (-e)**, altruistic.
alt: ~ **sangeres**, contralto; ~ **sleutel**, alto clef; ~ **speler**, violist; ~ **stem**, alto, contralto; counter (voice, singer); ~ **viool**, (alto) viola.
al'twee, both; *ons* ~, both of us.
al'tyd, always, ever, aye; continually; *NOG* ~, still; *SOOS* ~, as ever, as usual; *VAN* ~ *af*, from the very beginning; *VIR* ~, for ever; *die WERK word* ~ *moeiliker*, the work becomes continually more difficult; ~ **blommetjie**, immortelle; ~ **bos**, *Staavia radiata*; ~ **deur**, continually, always; ~ **durend (-e)**, everlasting; perennial (plant); ~ **groen**, evergreen.

alu'del, (-s), earthen retort.
aluin', (-e), alum; ~**aarde,** alum earth, alumina; hornblende schist; ~**agtig, (-e),** aluminous; ~**erts,** alum ore; ~**houdend, (-e),** aluminous; ~**leer,** leather prepared with alum; ~**looiery,** tawery, tawing; ~**oplossing,** alum solution; ~**poeier,** powdered alum; ~**steen,** alumstone, alunite.
aluminiseer', (ge-), aluminize.
alumi'nium, aluminium; ~**agtig, (-e),** aluminous; ~**blad,** aluminium foil; ~**houdend, (-e),** aluminiferous, ~**verf,** aluminium paint; ~**ware,** aluminium ware.
aluminotermie', aluminothermy.
alum'nus, (-se, ..ni), alumnus, ex-student.
Al'vader: *die* ~, the All-Father.
alvas', meanwhile.
alveolaar', (s), (..lare), alveolar (sound).
alveolêr, (b), (-e), alveolar.
alveo'lus, (-se), alveool', (alveole), alveolus.
al'verdelgend, (-e), all-destroying.
al'verdelger, all-destroyer.
al'vermoë, omnipotence; ~**nd, (-e),** omnipotent.
al'vernielend, (-e), all-destroying.
al'vernieling, total destruction.
al'verslindend, (-e), omnivorous, all-devouring.
al'vleisklier, pancreas.
al'vleissap, pancreatic fluid.
alvo'rens, *(form.),* before, until; previous to; ~ *hierdie gewigtige stap te doen,* before taking this important step.
alwaar', where, wherever.
al'weldadig, (-e), all-bounteous.
al'wertjie, (-s), ablet, bleak.
alwe'tend, (-e), all-knowing, omniscient; ~**heid,** omniscience.
al'weter, (-s), know-all, quidnunc; ~**y,** self-conceit.
al'wys, (-e), all-wise; *die Alwyse,* the All-Wise; ~**heid,** supreme wisdom.
amaas', sour milk beverage; alastrim; form of smallpox.
A-majeur, A major.
amalai'ta, *(vero.),* amalaita; ~**bende,** amalaita gang.
amalgaam', (..game), amalgam; ~**plaat,** amalgam plate; ~**roller,** apron roll, ~**vulsel,** amalgam filling.
amalgama'sie, amalgamation.
amalgama'tor, (-e, -s), amalgamator.
amalgameer', (ge-), amalgamate; ~**der, (-s),** amalgamator; ~**plaat,** apron plate; ~**vat,** amalgamating barrel.
amalgamis', (-te), amalgamist.
aman'del, (-s), almond; tonsil; amygdala *(geol.); jou* ~ *sal kraak,* you'll get it in the neck; ~**agtig, (-e),** almond-like, amygdaline; ~**bas,** almond rind; ~**blom,** almond blossom; ~**boom,** almond tree; ~**boord,** almond orchard; ~**deeg,** almond paste; ~**draend, (-e),** amygdaloidal; ~**gebak,** almond cake; ~**groen,** almond green; ~**houdend, (-e),** amygdaloidal; ~**klier,** *(ong.),* tonsil; ~**koek,** almond cake; ~**koekie,** macaroon, ratafia; ~**likeur,** ratafia, ~**makrolletjie,** macaroon; ~**melk,** orgeat; almond emulsion; ~**oë,** almond-shaped eyes; ~**olie,** almond essence; oil of almonds; ~**ontsteking,** tonsilitis; ~**pit,** almond; ~**skil,** almond peel; ~**steen,** amygdaloidal; ~**tameletjie,** hard bake; ~**vla,** almond custard; ~**vormig, (-e),** almondshaped, amygdaloid; ~**vulsel,** almond paste; ~**water,** almond water.
amanuen'sis, (-se), assistant, amanuensis.
ama'ra, bitter medicine.
amarant', (-e), amaranth (flower), love-lies-bleeding; ~**hout,** purplewood, blue ebony.
amaril', emery; ~**bord,** emery board, ~**doek,** emery cloth; ~**katoen,** ~**linne,** emery cloth; ~**papier,** sandpaper; emery paper; ~**pasta,** emery paste; ~**poeier,** emery powder; ~**skyf,** glazer, emery wheel; ~**slyper,** emery grinder; ~**steen,** emery (wheel), ~**vyl,** emery stick.
amasoem'biesie, *(gew.),* edible root.
Amaso'ne¹, Amazon (river).
amaso'ne², (-s), amazon; ~**kleed,** riding habit; ~**steen,** amazonite, amazon stone.
amasoniet', amazonite, amazon stone.

amateur', (-s), amateur; ~**agtig, (-e),** amateurish; ~**band,** amateur band *(radio);* ~**geselskap, (-pe),** amateur (dramatic) society; ~**is'me,** amateurism; ~**is'ties, (-e),** amateurish; ~**s'wedstryd,** amateur match; ~**toneel,** amateur theatricals.
am'bag, (s), (-te), trade, profession, (handi)craft, business; *'n* ~ *LEER,* learn a trade; *SMID van* ~, a blacksmith by trade; *'n man van TWAALF* ~ *te en dertien ongelukke,* Jack of all trades, master of none; *'n* ~ *UITOEFEN,* follow a trade; (w), (ge-), do, be busy with; *wat* ~ *jy vanaand?* what are you doing tonight?
am'bags: ~**baas,** master craftsman; ~**gesel,** improver, journeyman; ~**jonge,** apprentice.
am'bagskool, trade (industrial) school, technical school.
am'bags: ~**kwekeling,** artisan trainee; ~**leerling,** apprentice; ~**lui,** artisans, mechanics, workmen; ~**man,** workman, artisan, (handi)craftsman; ~**onderwys,** technical instruction.
ambag'telik, (-e), professional; technical.
ambassa'de, (-s), embassy.
ambassadeur', (-s), ambassador; ~**s'vrou,** wife of an ambassador.
ambassadri'se, (-s), ambassadress, ambassador's wife.
am'ber, amber; ~**agtig, (-e),** amber-like; ~**boom,** ambertree, sweetgum; ~**geur,** odour of amber; ~**grys,** ambergris; ~**iet',** amberite; ~**kleur,** amber (colour); ~**kleurig, (-e),** amber (-coloured); ~**reuk,** amber odour; ~**saad,** seed of *Abelmoschus moschutus;* ~**steel,** amber stem; ~**steen,** amber.
am'bidekster, (-s), ambidexter; ~**iteit',** ambidexterity.
ambidekstrie', ambidextrousness.
ambieer', (ge-), aspire after.
ambigeer', (ge-), doubt, vacillate.
ambi'sie, ambition, push.
ambisieus', (-e), ambitious.
ambivalen'sie, ambivalence.
ambivalent', (-e), ambivalent.
ambligoniet', amblygonite.
ambraal', (s), person who is feeling ill, chronic patient; nonentity; bungler, stick-in-the-mud; children's game; (b, bw), sick, ailing; showy; ~**voel,** be ailing, not feel very well; *die VROU is net* ~, the lady is very swanky; ~**stuk,** showpiece.
ambra'kel, (-s), good-for-nothing.
ambroos', ambro'sia, ambrosia.
ambro'sies, (-e), ambrosial.
ambrosyn', ambrosia.
ambulans', ambulans; *soos 'n* ~ *wees,* be a slow-coach; ~**diens,** ambulance service; ~**trein,** ambulance (hospital) train; ~**vliegtuig,** ambulance aircraft; ~**wa,** ambulance wagon.
ambulant', (-e), ambulatory.
ambuleer', (ge-), ambulate.
ame'be, (-s), amoeba; ~**agtig, (-e),** amoeboid; ~**dis-enterie,** amoebic dysentery; ~**vormig, (-e),** amoeboid.
ame'bies, (-e), amoeboid.
ameboïed, (-e), amoeboid.
ameg'tig, (-e), breathless, panting for breath; ~**heid,** breathlessness.
a'men, (-s), amen; *op ALLES* ~ *sê,* agree to everything; *so seker soos* ~ *in die KERK,* as sure as fate; *iem. wat nie* ~ *kan SÊ nie,* a long-winded person; *daar kan jy* ~ *op SÊ,* you can concur to that; *die – UITSPREEK,* conclude.
amendeer', (ge-), amend.
amendement', amende'ring, (-e), amendment.
America'na, Americana.
Ame'rika, America.
Amerikaan', (..kane), American Indian, Amerindian, Rooihuid.
Amerikaans', (-e), American; ~*e, BOLWURM,* American boll-worm; ~*e RYPERD (SAALPERD),* American saddler (saddlehorse).
Amerika'ner, (-s), American.
amerikanisa'sie, Americanization.
amerikaniseer', (ge-), Americanize.
amerikanise'ring, Americanization.

Amerikanis'me, (-s), Americanism, Yankeeism.
ameri'kium, americium.
ametis', (-te), amethyst; **-agtig, (-e),** amethystine.
ametrie', ametria.
ameublement', (-e), set of furniture; furniture.
am'fi=, both, of both kinds, on both sides, around.
amfibie', (-ë), amphibious animal, amphibian.
amfi'bies, (-e), amphibious.
amfibiologie', amphibiology.
amfibo'lies, (-e), amphibolous; amphibological.
amfiboliet', amphibolite.
amfibologie', amphibology, ambiguity.
amfibool', amphibole.
amfibrag', (-ge), amphibrach; **~gies,** amphibrachic.
amfitea'ter, (-s), amphitheatre; **~sgewys(e),** in the form of an amphitheatre.
amfo'ra, (-s), amphora.
ami'ce, (dear) friend, amice.
amiel', amyl.
amikaal', (..kale), friendly, amicable.
amila'se, amylase.
amiloï'de, (-s), amiloïed', (-e), amyloid.
amilopsien', amilopsi'ne, amylopsin.
amilo'se, amylose.
A-mineur, A minor.
am'meter, am(pere)meter.
ammo'niak, ammonia; **~agtig, (-e),** ammoniacal; **~oplossing,** spirits of hartshorn; **~vergiftiging,** ammonia poisoning.
ammoniet', ammonite.
ammo'nium, ammonium.
am'monshoring, ammonite; cornu ammonis.
ammuni'sie, ammunition; **~ insamel,** get ready for action; **~ fabriek,** (am)munition(s) factory; **~fa= brikant,** manufacturer of (am)munition(s); **~ kis,** limber chest; (am)munition(s) box; **~ voorraad,** supplies of (am)munition(s); **~ voorsiening,** (am)= munition(s) supply; **~ wa,** caisson.
amnesie', amnesia, loss of memory.
amnestie', (-ë), amnesty; pardon; *ALGEMENE ~ afkondig,* issue an amnesty (general pardon); *~ VERLEEN,* grant an amnesty (pardon).
amok', amok, amuck; *~ maak,* run amok!
A'-mol, A flat.
A'mor, Amor, god of love.
amoralis'me, amoralism.
amoreel', (..rele), amoral.
amorf', (-e), amorphous; **~ ie',** amorphy; **~ is'me,** amorphism.
amortisa'sie, amortization; **~ fonds,** redemption fund, sinking fund; **~ lening,** sinking-fund loan; **~ plan,** plan of redemption; **~ rekening,** redemp= tion account.
amortiseer', (ge-), sink (debt), amortize, redeem; **~ baar, (..bare),** redeemable, repayable.
amosiet', amosite.
amouret'te, (-s), love affair, amour(ette).
amoureus', (-e), amorous.
amp, (-te), office, post, employment, charge, duty, dignity, function; berth; *'n ~ AANVAAR,* assume an office (duty); *'n ~ BEKLEE,* hold an office; *in sy ~ HERSTEL,* reinstate in office; *jou ~ UIT= OEFEN,* discharge one's duties.
am'pas, bagasse.
am'pel, (-e), ample, amply, enough, more than enough.
ampelografie', ampelography.
am'per, nearly, almost, within an inch, narrowly; all but; *~ is op die BLOK se stamper, was ~ nie daar nie, dan het hy hom GEHAD, ~ is honderd MYL van Amsterdam, ~ maar nog nie STAMPER nie,* a miss is as good as a mile; *~ NOOIT,* hardly ever; *SO ~,* touch-and-go; *~ WIT,* off-white; **~ broe= kie,** scanty-pantie, scanties.
ampè're, (-s), ampere; **~ meter,** am(pere)meter; **~ tal,** amperage.
am'perhoekig, (-e), sub-angular.
am'perkook, scald.
am'perraakskoot, near-miss.
am'pertjies = amper.
am'perwit, off-white.
amp'genoot, (..note), colleague; **~ skap,** colleague= ship.

Am'pie¹, (-s), poor white.
am'pie², (-s), small job (post).
amp'jagter, job hunter.
amplia'sie, amplification *(legal).*
amplifika'sie, amplification.
amplifiseer', (ge-), amplify.
amplitu'de, (-s), amplitude.
amps: ~ aanvaarding, accession to office, assumption of duty; **~ bediening,** (tenure of) office; **~ bejag,** of= fice hunting; **~ bekleder,** incumbent (of office); of= fice bearer; **bekleding,** tenure of office; **~ bekleër,** incumbent (of office), officeholder; **~ benaming,** official title (designation); **~ besighede,** official du= ties; **~ beslommeringe,** cares of office; **~ besoek,** of= ficial visit; **~ broer,** colleague; **~ draer,** office bear= er; **~ duur,** term of office; **~ dwang,** official coercion; **~ eed,** oath of office.
amp'seël, seal of office.
amp'serp, sash of office.
amps: ~ gebied, jurisdiction (magistrate); **~ geheim,** professional (official) secret; **~ sgenoot,** colleague; **~ gewaad,** robes of office, livery; **~ halwe,** of= ficially, ex officio; **~ handeling,** official action; **~ jaar,** year of office; **~ ketting,** chain of office; **~ kleed,** official dress (wear); **~ misbruik,** abuse of office; **~ misdryf,** official misdemeanour; **~ oor= treding,** malfeasance; abuse of power.
amp'sorge, cares of office.
amps: ~ plig, official duty; function; **~ reis,** official journey; **~ termyn,** term of office; **~ titel,** official title; **~ toelae,** official allowance; **~ toga,** robes of office; **~ tyd,** term (tenure) of office; **~ verlies,** loss of office; **~ verrigting,** ministry; **~ versuim,** mispri= sion; **~ vervulling,** discharge of one's official duties; **~ waardigheid,** dignity of office; **~ wag,** serjeant-at-arms; Black Rod; **~ weë:** *van ~ weë,* officially; ex officio; **~ woning,** official residence.
amp'telik, (-e), official(ly); ministerial; formal.
amp'teloos, (..lose), out of office, retired; **~ heid,** retirement.
amp'tenaar, (..nare), official, officer, clerk, func= tionary, civil servant; *VERTROUDE ~,* confiden= tial clerk; **~ salaris,** salary of an official.
amp'tenaars: ~ gees, bureaucracy; **~ kringe,** official circles; **~ lewe,** official life; **~ loopbaan,** official ca= reer; **~ wêreld,** official world; officialdom.
amp'tenaartjie, (-s), jack-in-office.
amp'tenaredom, amptenary', bureaucracy, red tape; officialdom.
am'pul, (-le), ampulla.
amputa'sie, (-s), amputation.
amputeer', (ge-), amputate.
amulet, (-te), amulet, charm, periapt, phylactery.
amusant', (-e), amusing, entertaining.
amuseer', (ge-), amuse, entertain; *julle moet julle maar ~,* you must enjoy yourselves.
amusement', (-e), amusement, entertainment.
anaal', (anale), anal; *anale opening,* anus.
Anabaptis', (-te), Anabaptist; **~ me,** Anabaptism; **~ ties, (-e),** Anabaptist(ic).
anabolie', anabolis'me, anabolism.
a'naboom, ana tree *(Acacia albida).*
anachoreet', (..rete), anchorite, hermit.
anachronis'me, (-s), anachronism.
anachronis'ties, (-e), anachronous, anachronistic.
anaërobiont', (-e), anaëroob', (..robe), anaerobe.
anaëroob', (..robe), anaerobian, anaerobic.
anafalanti'sis, baldness.
anafilak'se, anaphylaxis.
anafilak'ties, (-e), anaphylactic.
anafoor', anafo'ra, anaphora.
anaglief', anaglyph.
anago'ge, anagoge.
anagram', (-me), anagram; **~ ma'ties, (-e),** anagram= matic(al).
anakoloet', (-e), anacoluthon.
anakon'da, (-s), anaconda.
anakreon'ties, (-e), anacreontic.
analek'te, analects.
analfabeet', (..bete), analphabete, illiterate (person).
analfabetis'me, illiteracy.
analgesie', analgie', analgesia.

analis', (-te), analyst.
analisa'tor, (-e, -s), analyser.
anali'se, (-s), analysis.
analiseer', (ge-), analyse.
anali'ties, (-e), analytic.
anali'tikus, (..tici, -se), analyst.
analogie', (-ë), analogy.
analo'gies, (-e), analogical.
analogiseer', (ge-), analogize.
analoog', (..loë), similar, analogous.
anamne'se, anamnesie', anamnesis.
anamorfis'me, anamorphism.
anamorfo'se, anamorphosis.
a'nanas, (Ndl.), (-se), pineapple.
anan'dries, (-e), anandrous.
anapes', (-te), anapaest; ~**ties**, (-e), anapaestic.
anaplasmo'se, anaplasmosis.
anaplastiek', anaplasty.
anaplas'ties, (-e), anaplastic.
anaplero'se, anaplerose.
anaplero'ties, (-e), anaplerotic.
anapodik'ties, (-e), anapodictic.
anargie', anarchy.
anar'gies, (-e), anarchic.
anargis', (-te), anarchist; ~**me**, anarchism; ~**ties**, (-e), anarchist.
anar'tries, (-e), anarthrous.
anastasie', anasta'sis, convalescence.
anasta'ties, (-e), anastatic.
anastigmaat', anastigmat.
anastigma'ties, (-e), anastigmatic.
anastomo'se, anastomosis.
anastomoseer', (ge-), anastomose.
anataas', anatase.
anatek'sis, anatexis.
ana'tema, anate'ma, (-s), anathema, curse.
anatomie', anatomy.
anato'mies, (-e), anatomical.
anatomiseer', (ge-), anatomize.
anatoom', (..tome), anatomist.
Andalu'sia, Andalusia (C.P.).
Andalu'sië, Andalusia (Spain); ~ **r**, (-s), Andalusian; ..**sies**, (-e), Andalusian.
andan'te, andante, slow (*music*).
andanti'no, (*mus.*), andantino, fairly slow.
an'der, (s, b), (-e), other, another; different; *BY 'n ~ koop*, buy from someone else; *die ~ DAG*, the next day; *'n ~ DAG*, another day; some days ago; *die EEN en ~*, one thing and another; *die EEN met die ~*, taken as a whole; *jy is weer 'n ~ EEN*, you're a nice one! *die EEN die ~*, one another; *EK voel 'n ~ mens*, I veel a different person; *my ~ EK*, my other self; *die ~ GESLAG*, the oppposite sex; *aan die ~ KANT*, on the other hand, *'n ~ MENS sal eers vra*, any other (ordinary) person would have asked; *NA 'n ~ gaan*, go elsewhere (to someone else); *al OM die ~ week*, every other week; *ONDER ~(e)*, among others; among other things; *TEN ~ e*, in the second place; *in die ~ TYD*, in the family way; *VAN 'n ~ hoor*, hear somewhere else; *VIR 'n ~ mens was*, take in washing; *~ WEEK*, next week; *met ~ WOORDE*, in other words.
an'derdaags: ~ *-e koors*, tertian fever.
an'derdag, some other day, later.
anderdagmô're: *die ~*, the next morning.
an'derdeels: *eensdeels, ~, partly ... partly*.
an'derhalf, one and a half; ..*halwe DAG*, a day and a half; ~*stylige DUBBELDEKKER*, one and a half strutter; ~ *UUR*, an hour and a half.
an'derkant, (bw), on the other side, opposite; (vs), on the other side of, across (from), opposite (to); *~ se*, ~**ste**, opposite.
an'derland, foreign country; ~ *toe gaan*, go abroad; ~**er**, (-s), foreigner.
an'derling, (-e), blood relation in second degree.
an'dermaal, again, a second time, once again.
an'derman, someone else; stranger; ~ *se goed*, someone else's property.
an'derpad, by another road; in a different direction; elsewhere; ~ *kyk*, look away (in a different direction).
an'ders, otherwise, else, different; failing which; at other times, usually; ~ *AS sy familie*, not like his relations; *IEM. ~*, someone else, some other person; *heeltemal IETS ~*, something quite different; ~ *IS daar altoos baie plek*, otherwise there is always plenty of room; *dit KAN nie ~ nie*, it cannot be done in any other way; there is no help for it; *hoe KNAP hy ~ ook is*, however clever he is (may be) otherwise...; *NIEMAND ~ nie*, no one else; *dit is NIKS ~ as*, this is nothing else but...; *dis NOOIT ~ nie*, undoubtedly; *dis OOK nie ~ nie*, exactly, precisely; ~ *SAL ek gaan*, otherwise I shall go; *ek sou dit nie ~ WENS nie*, I should not wish it otherwise; *WIE ~ glo dit?* who else believes this?
an'derdenkend, (-e), dissenting (in religion); of a different opinion, dissentient; ~ **e**, (-s), dissident, dissentient; dissenter.
an'dersgesind, (-e), otherwise-minded, dissenting, dissentient.
an'dersheid, otherness.
an'dersins, otherwise, in another way.
an'dersom, the other way about; *dit is net ~*, just the reverse (contrary).
an'dersoortig, (-e), of another (different) kind.
an'derste(r) = **anders**.
an'dersyds, on the other hand.
an'dertalig, (-e), speaking a different language.
andoe'lie, (-s), andouille sausage; andouille.
androgien', (-e), androgynous.
androginie', androgyny.
andy'vie, endive *(Cichorium endivia)*.
anekdo'te, (-s), anecdote; ~**tjie**, little anecdote.
anekdo'ties, (-e), anecdotic(al), anecdotal.
anemie', anaemia.
ane'mies, (-e), anaemic.
anemofiel', anemophilous.
anemofobie', anemophobia.
anemograaf', (..grawe), anemograph.
anemografie', anemography.
anemologie', anemology.
anemo'meter, anemome'ter, anemometer.
anemometrie', anemometry.
anemoon', (..mone), anemone.
anemoskoop', (..skope), anemoscope.
aneroï'de, (-s), aneroïd', (-e), aneroid (barometer).
anesteseer', (ge-), anaesthetize.
anestesie', anaesthesia, insensibility.
aneste'ties, (-e), anaesthetic.
aneste'tikum, (-s), (..tetika), anaesthetic.
aneste'tikus, (..tetici, -se), anaesthetist.
anetol', anethol.
aneuris'me, (-s), aneurism.
anfraktuositeit', anfractuosity.
angarie', angary.
an'gel, (-s), sting (of a bee); barb (of an arrow); awn, beard (of grain); fish hook; tongue (of a rifle); *die ~ sit agter in die by*, the sting is in the tail; ~**draer**, stinger.
angelier', (-e), carnation *(Dianthus)*; *wilde ~*, wild pink; ~**geur**, carnation scent; ~**tentoonstelling**, carnation show.
ange'lika, (-s), angelica.
angelofanie', angelophany.
angelologie', angelology.
an'gelrig, (-e), full of awns.
Angel-Sak'ser, (-s), Anglo-Saxon.
Angel-Sak'sies, (-e), Anglo-Saxon.
an'gelus, angelus.
angi'na, angina, ~ *pectoris*, angina pectoris, constriction of the heart.
angiografie', angiography.
angiologie', angiology.
angiopatie', angiopathy.
Anglikaan', (..kane), Anglican; ~ **s'**, (-e), Anglican; *die ~ se kerk*, the Anglican Church.
Anglis', (-te), Anglis.
angliseer', (ge-), Anglicize.
anglise'ring, Anglicizing.
Anglisis'me, (-s), Anglicism.
anglisis'ties, (-e), English; containing Anglicisms.
Anglistiek', English studies.
An'glo-Amerikaans', Anglo-American.
Anglofiel', Anglophile.

Anglofilie, Anglophily.
Anglofobie', Anglophobia.
Anglomaan', (..**mane**), Anglomaniac.
Anglomanie', Anglomania.
Ango'la: Angola; ~**boere**, Angola Boers; ~**-ertjie**, Angola peanut, Bambara groundnut, pigeon pea.
Angolees', (..**lese**), Angolese.
Angools', (-e), of Angola, Angolan.
ango'ra, (-s), Angora; ~**boer**, Angora farmer; ~**boerdery**, Angora farming; ~**bok**, Angora goat; ~**haar**, Angora wool, mohair; ~**konyn**, Angora rabbit; ~**ooi**, Angora ewe; ~**ram**, Angora ram; ~**wol**, Angora wool, mohair.
angostu'ra, angostura.
angs, (-te), anxiety, fear, pang, terror, anguish, funk; agony (mental); *met* ~ *en BEWING*, in fear and trembling; *UIT* ~ *vir*, for fear of; *dodelike* ~ *UIT= STAAN, in dodelike* ~ *VERKEER*, be in mortal fear; ~**geroep**, ~**geskrei**, cry of distress; ~**gevoel**, feeling of anxiety; qualm; ~**kreet**, agonised cry; cry of distress; ~**sweet**, cold perspiration (of terror).
angs'tig, (-e), afraid, terrified, fearful; anxious (time); ~*e oomblikke*, anxious moments; ~**heid**, anxiety, fear.
angs'toestand, state of anxiety.
angsval'lig, (-e), anxious, timid, timorous; scrupu= lous, conscientious; meticulous; ~**heid**, anxiety; timidity; scrupulousness, conscientiousness.
angs'vol, (-le), anxious, full of fear.
angswek'kend, (-e), alarming, fearsome, frightening; ~**heid**, alarming nature.
anhe'dries, (-e), anhedral.
anhe'dron, anhedron.
anhidri'de, (-s), **anhidried'**, (-e), anhydride.
anhidreer', (-e), dehydrate.
anhi'dries, (-e), anhydrous.
anhidriet', anhydrite.
anhidrobi'ose, anhydrobiosis.
anil', anil; indigo plant; indigo dye.
anilien', **anili'ne**, aniline; ~**bereiding**, aniline pro= duction; ~**produkte**, aniline products; ~**verf**, ani= line dye; ~**vergiftiging**, aniline poisoning.
animaliseer', (ge-), animalize.
animalis'me, animalism.
animaliteit', animality.
animeer', (ge-), animate, inspire; urge on.
animis'me, animism.
animis'ties, (-e), animistic.
a'nimo, gusto, zest; *met* ~ , with spirit (zest).
animositeit', animosity.
animo'so, (*mus.*), animoso.
anioon', (**anione**), anion.
aniset', anisette.
anisol', anisol.
anisome'tries, (-e), anisometric.
anisotro'pies, (-e), anisotropic.
an'kas, (*gew.*), silly; proud.
an'ker¹, (s), (-s), anker (measure).
an'ker², (s), (-s), anchor; brace; armature *(electr.)*; stay *(mech.)*; *êrens* ~ *GOOI*, go courting some= where; *voor* ~ *KOM*, moor; *voor* ~ *LÊ*, be at anchor; *die* ~ *LIG*, weigh anchor; *die* ~ *laat VAL*, cast anchor; (w), (ge-), anchor (a ship); moor (an airship); cramp (a wall); ~**arm**, anchor arm; ~**baar**, (..**bare**), girder stay; crown stay (boiler); ~**blad**, fluke; ~**boei**, anchor buoy; ~**boot**, chain boat; ~**bout**, tie bolt; stay bolt (rod); ~**draad**, di= agonal wire; stay wire; guy wire *(electr.)*; ~**draaier**, stay driver (tool); ~**eindplaat**, armature head; ~**gat**, stay hole; ~**geld**, anchorage (dues); harbour dues; ~**grond**, anchoring ground; ~**haak**, cathook; ~**hand**, palm of anchor; ~**horlosie**, *see* **ankeroorlosie**; ~**kabel**, ~**ketting**, chain; mooring; ~**klou**, bill; fluke; ~**kluis**, hawse; ~**kraan**, anchor crane, cat; ~**lamp**, ~**lantern**, anchor lamp; ~**lat**, grounds; ~**lig**, riding light; ~**mas**, mooring mast, pylon; ~**masjien**, capstan engine; ~**moer**, stay nut; ~**oorlosie**, lever watch; ~**paal**, straining post (in fencing); ~**pen**; anchor pin; picketing pin; ~**plaat**, anchor plate; girder stay; crown stay (of a boiler); ~**plek**, moorings, road(stead), anchorage; ~**reg**, anchorage right; ~**ring**, anchor ring; ~**spoel**, ar=

mature coil; ~**staaf**, armature bar; ~**stang**, truss rod, steady-rest rod; ~**steun**, anchorage bracket; ~**tand**, fluke; abutment tooth; ~**tou**, cable, haw= ser; picketing rope *(aeron.)*; guy; ~**wikkeling**, ar= mature winding (coil).
an'na, (-s), anna (Indian coin).
annabergiet', annabergite.
anna'le, annals; ~**geskiedenis**, annals history; ~**skrywer**, annalist.
annate', *(mv.)*, annates.
annalien', **annali'ne**, annalin.
annalis', (-te), annalist.
annat'to, annatto (dye),
anneks', (-e), annexe.
anneksa'sie, (-s), annexation; ~**planne**, designs of annexation, annexation plans; ~**politiek**, policy of annexation.
annekseer', (ge-), annex; mediatize.
annihileer', (ge-), annihilate; rub out; extinguish.
annonseer', (ge-), announce.
annota'sie, (-s), annotation.
annoteer', (ge-), annotate; ~**der**, (-s), annotator.
annuïteit', (-e), annuity; ~**tafels**, annuity tables; ~**versekering**, annuity insurance.
annuleer', (ge-), annul, cancel.
annule'ring, annulment.
Annunsia'sie, The Annunciation, Lady Day.
ano'de, (-s), anode; ~-**katodespanning**, anode-cathode voltage; ~**spanningsapparaat**, high-tension supply unit.
anoë'se, anoesis.
anoë'ties, (-e), anoetic.
ano'feles(muskiet), (-e), anopheles (mosquito).
anomaal', (..**male**), anomalous.
anomalie', (-ë), anomaly, irregularity.
anoniem', (-e), anonymous.
anonimiteit', anonymity.
ano'nimus, (-se, ..**mi**), anonymous person; anon.
an'organies, (-e), inorganic.
anortosiet', anorthosite.
anosmie', anosmia.
ansiënniteit', (ong.), priority; seniority.
ansjo'vis, (-se), anchovy; ~**smeer**, anchovy paste.
antafrodi'ties, (-e), antaphroditic.
antagonis', (-te), antagonist; ~**eer'**, (ge-), antag= onize; ~**me**, antagonism; ~**ties**, (-e), antagon= istic(al).
Antark'ties, (-e), Antarctic.
Antark'tika, Antarctica.
antedateer', (ge-), antedate (cheque).
antediluviaal', (..**viale**), **antediluviaans'**, (-e), antediluvian.
anten'ne, (-s), aerial (wire); antenna; ~**aansluiting**, aerial terminal; ~**kring**, aerial circuit; ~**mas**, aerial mast; ~**raam**, aerial frame; ~**stroomkring**, aerial circuit; ~**toring**, aerial tower; ~**verbindings**, aerial connections; ~**wenas**, aerial winch.
antenupsiaal', (..**siale**), antenuptial.
an'ter, (-s), anther (of flower).
antesedent', (-e), antecedent.
anthe'lion, (..**lia**), anthelion.
an'ti-apartheid, anti-apartheid; ~**sbetoger**, anti-apartheid demonstrator; ~**groep**, anti-apartheid group.
an'tibioties, (-e), antibiotic.
antibio'tikum, (-s, ..**tika**), antibiotic.
anticham'bre, (-s), antechamber, anteroom.
an'tichloor, antichlor.
An'tichris, Antichrist.
an'tichristelik, antichristian.
an'tidemokraties, (-e), antidemocratic.
antidoot', (..**dote**), **antido'tum**, (-s), antidote.
antiek', (-e), antique; *die A~e*, the classics; antique times; ancient times; (b), (-e), antique; ~*e KUNS*, antique art; ~*e MEUBELS*, period furniture, an= tique furniture; *die A~e WÊRELD*, the Ancient World; ~**handelaar**, antique-dealer, antiquarian; ~**versamelaar**, collector of antiques; ~**winkel**, an= tique-shop.
antifebrien', **antifebri'ne**, antifebrine.
antiflogisti'ne, (-s), antiphlogistine.
antifoon', (..**fone**), antiphony.

antigeen', (s), (..gene), antigen; (b), (..gene), antigenic.
an'tigly, non-skid; ~**loopvlak**, non-skid surface.
antikiteit' = **antikwiteit**.
an'tiklimaks, anticlimax.
an'tiklinaal, anticlinal.
an'tiklop, antiknock.
antikwariaat', (..riate), dealer in antiques; second-hand bookseller; antiquarian; antique-dealer.
antikwa'ries, (-e), antiquarian; second-hand; *die boek is net ~ verkrygbaar*, the book is only obtainable second-hand.
antikwiteit', (-e), curio, relic, antiquity; ~**ewinkel**, curiosity shop.
an'tilegomena, (-s), antilegomena.
an'tiliggaam, antibody.
Antil'le, Antilles.
an'tilogaritme, antilogarithm.
an'tiloop, (..lope), antelope.
antimakas'sar, (-s), antimacassar.
an'timilitaris, (-te), antimilitarist; pacifist; ~**me**, antimilitarism; pacifism.
an'timoesson, (-s), antimonsoon.
an'timonargies, (-e), antimonarchic.
an'timonargis, (-te), antimonarchist.
an'timonargisme, antimonarchism.
antimoniet', antimonite.
antimo'nium, antimony, stibium.
antimoon', antimony; ~**glans**, antimonite; ~**streep**, antimony line.
antinomie', (-ë), antinomy.
an'tipassaatwind, antitrade (wind).
antipatie', (s), (-ë), antipathy; ~**k'**, (b), (-e), antipathetic(al), unsympathetic.
antipersoneel'myn, antipersonnel mine.
an'tipireties, antipyretic.
antipirien', **antipiri'ne**, antipyrin.
antipo'de, (-s), antipode.
antipo'dies, (-e), antipodal.
an'tireligieus, (-e), antireligious.
an'tirepublikein, (-e), antirepublican; ~**s**, (-e), antirepublican.
an'tirevolusionêr, ..**rewolusionêr**, (s) (-es), antirevolutionist; Calvinist; (b) (-e), antirevolutionary.
an'tirojalis, (-te), antiroyalist; ~**me**, antiroyalism; ~**ties**, (-e), antiroyalistic.
an'ti-Rooms, (-e), anti-Roman Catholic.
an'ti-Sabbatariër, anti-Sabbatarian.
an'ti-Semiet, anti-Semite.
anti-Semi'ties, (-e), anti-Semitic.
anti-Semitis'me, anti-Semitism.
antisep'sis, antisepsis.
antisep'ties, (-e), antiseptic.
antisep'tikum, (-s, ..tika), antiseptic.
antisikloon', anticyclone.
antisipa'sie, anticipation.
antisipeer', (ge-), anticipate.
an'tiskeurbuikmiddel, antiscorbutic.
antiskorbu'ties, (-e), antiscorbutic.
an'tisosiaal, (..sosiale), antisocial.
an'tisosialis, antisocialist; ~**me**, antisocialism; ~**ties**, (-e), antisocialistic.
antite'se, (-s), antithesis.
antite'ties, (-e), antithetic(al).
antite'tika, antithetics.
an'titipe, antitype.
antitoksien', (-e), **antitoksi'ne**, (-s), antitoxin.
an'tivenene, antivenene.
an'tivries, antifreeze.
An'tjie: ~ *Somers*, bogeyman; ~ *Tattcrat*, gossip, chatterbox.
antoniem', (-e), antonym; (b), (-e), antonymous.
antonimie', antonymy.
Anto'nius, Anthony; ~**vuur**, St. Anthony's fire, erysipelas.
antonoma'sia, antonomasia.
antrakno'se, anthracnosis, black rust; *Gloecosporium ampelophagum*.
antrako'se, anthracosis.
an'traks, anthrax; carbuncle.
antraseen', anthracene.
antrasiet', anthracite; ~**vorming**, anthracitization.
antrisi'de, (-s), **antrisied'**, (-e), antrycide.
antri'tis *(med.)*, antritis.
antropofaag', (..fae), anthropophagite, cannibal.
antropofagie', cannibalism.
antropofobie', anthropophobia.
antropogenie', anthropogeny.
antropoglot', (-te), anthropoglot.
antropografie', anthropography.
antropoï'de, (-s), **antropoïed'**, (-e), anthropoid.
antropolatrie', anthropolatry.
antropoliet', anthropolite.
antropologie', anthropology.
antropolo'gies, (-e), anthropological.
antropoloog', (..loë), anthropologist.
antropometrie', anthropometry.
antropome'tries, (-e), anthropometric.
antropomorf', (-e), anthropomorphous; ~**ies**, (-e), anthropomorphic; ~**is'me**, anthropomorphism.
antropopatie', anthropopathy.
antropopa'ties, (-e), anthropopathic.
antroposen'tries, (-e), anthropocentric.
antroposentris'me, anthropocentrism.
antroposofie', anthroposophy; ..**poso'fies**, (-e), anthroposophical.
antropotomie', anthropotomy.
an'trum, (-s), antrum.
ant'woord, (s), (-e), answer, reply, response; counter, counterblast; echo; reaction; *iem. van ~ DIEN*, reply to someone; *'n GEVATTE ~*, (witty) repartee; *IN ~ op*, in reply to; *gou met 'n ~ KLAAR wees*, be quick to reply; *'n ~ OP 'n ~*, rejoinder; *'n SKEWE ~ gee*, give an insulting answer; *tem. die ~ SKULDIG bly*, be unable to reply to someone; *TELEGRAM met ~ betaal*, prepaid telegram; *om 'n ~ VERLEË wees*, not to have an answer ready; *op 'n ~ WAG*, wait for a reply; (w), (ge-), answer, reply; *BEVESTIGEND ~*, reply in the affirmative; ~ *op 'n HEILDRONK*, respond to a toast; *ONTKENNEND ~*, reply in the negative; ~ *OP 'n vraag*, reply to a question; ~**berig**, reply message; ~**betaal(d)**, (-e), reply paid; ~**eboek**, answer book; script; examination book.
anurie', anuria.
a'nus, (-se), anus, arse; vent (of a bird).
anys, anise; ~ *en koljander, die een is soos die ander*, as like a dock as a daisy; ~**beskuit**, anise rusk; ~**boegoe**, *Rutaceae;* ~**brandewyn**, aniseed (liqueur) brandy; ~**likeur**, anisette, aniseed liqueur; ~**olie**, aniseed oil; ~**plant**, aniseed (plant); ~**saad**, aniseed; ~**sopie**, anisette; ~**wortel**, *Annesorrhiza macrocarpa*.
aoris', (-te), **aoris'tus**, (-se), aorist.
aor'ta, (-s), aorta.
aor'ties, (-e), aortic.
Apa'che[1], (-s), Apache.
apa'che[2], -s, hooligan, apache.
apana'ge, (-s), apanage.
apantropie', apanthropy.
apart', (-e), apart, separate; distinct; discrete; aloof; ~ *BEHANDEL*, treat separately; ~ *HOU*, keep separate, ~ *NEEM*, take aside; *ek wil jou ~ SPREEK*, I wish to see you private.
apart'heid, separateness; segregation, apartheid; ~**sbeleid**, policy of segregation (of separate development), apartheid policy.
apart'jie, (-s), heart-to-heart talk; aside.
apatie', apathy.
apa'ties, (-e), apathetic.
apatiet', apatite (calcium phosphate).
a'pe: ~**bakkies**, monkey-face; ~**broodboom**, monkeybread tree, baobab; ~**dom**, monkeys in general; the mob; ~**gape**: *op ~ gape lê*, be at the last gasp; ~**geslag**, monkey tribe; ~**hok**, monkey cage; ~**klier**, monkey gland; ~**kleuter**, tiny tot; ~**kool**, rubbish, nonsense; ~**kop**, monkey head; stupid person; ~**liefde**, blind love; ~**neute**, monkeynuts, peanuts; ~**pak**, dress-suit; ~**rig**, (-e), monkeyish, foolish; imitative.
aperio'dies, (-e), aperiodic; ~*e kompas*, aperiodic compass.
aperiodisiteit', aperiodicity.

aperitief', (..tiewe), aperient, laxative; aperitif, appetiser.
a'pery, (-e), foolish action (behaviour); apery.
a'pe: ~ **spel**, buffoonery, tomfoolery; ~ **streek**, apery, monkeytrick; ~ **tronie**, monkeyface.
aphe'lium, aphelion.
a pie, (-s), little monkey; infant; cane; ~! fooled! ~ *kyk vir KERRIEKOS*, how do you like that! *hy LAG hom 'n ~*, hy laughs heartily; *iem. ~ MAAK*, make a fool of someone; ~ *op 'n STOKKIE*, jackanapes; *toe jy nog 'n ~ WAS*, before you were born; when you were still very young; ~ *WEES, be the ass;* ~ **sdoring**, Acacia galpinii; ~ **skos** = **aapsekos**.
aplomb', aplomb.
apodik'ties, (-e), apodictic(al).
apofi'se, (-s), apophysis.
apoge'um, apogee.
apokalips', apocalypse; *A* ~, The Revelation(s) (Apocalypse).
apokalip'ties, (-e), apocalyptic.
apo'kopee, (-s), apocope.
apokrief', (..kriewe), apochryphal; *Apokriewe Boeke*, Apochrypha.
Apol'lo: *'n ~*, an Apollo.
apologeet', (..gete), apologist.
apologetiek', apologetics.
apologe'ties, (-e), apologetic(al)
apologie', (-ë), apology.
apomorfien', **apomorfi'ne**, apomorphine (emetic).
apoplek'sie, apoplexy.
apoplek'ties, (-e), apoplectic.
aposie', aposia.
aposiope'sis, aposiopesis.
apositie', apositia.
apostaat', (..tate), apostate.
apostasie', apostasy.
apos'tel, (-s), apostle; *dis nie almal ~s wat wandelstokke dra nie*, it is not every cowl that hides a friar; ~ **amp**, apostolate; ~ **lepel**, apostle spoon; ~ **perde**: *met ~perde ry*, go on Shanks's mare (pony); go on foot; ~ **skap**, apostleship.
apostolaat', (..late), apostolate, apostleship.
aposto'lies, (-e), apostolic.
apostrofeer', (ge-), apostrophize.
apostroof', (..strowe), apostrophe.
apote'ma, (-s), apophthegm.
apoteo'se, apotheosis, deification.
apparaat', (..rate), apparatus.
apparatuur', hardware (computer).
appèl', (-le, -s), appeal; roll-call; parade; ~ *AANTEKEN*, lodge an appeal; *op die ~ ONTBREEK*, not to answer to one's name; *REG van ~*, right of appeal.
ap'pel, (-s), apple; apple, pupil (eye); fist; *die ~ val nie ver v.d. BOOM nie*, like father, like son; a chip of the old block; *'n ~ tjie vir die DORS bewaar*, provide against a rainy day; *vir 'n ~ en 'n EI*, for a mere song (trifle), dirt-cheap; *met sy ~s GOOI*, use his fists; *die GOUE ~ wegdra*, be the fairest of all; *~s MAAK*, show off; *ek het 'n ~tjie met jou te SKIL*, I have a bone to pick with you; *'n SUUR ~ deurbyt*, make the best of a bad bargain; *een VROT ~ steek al die ander aan*, one scabby sheep infects the whole flock; ~ **asyn**, cider vinegar; ~ **barssiekte**, apple-cracking disease; ~ **bloedluis**, apple aphis; ~ **bloeisel**, apple blossom; ~ **blou**, dapple-grey; ~ **blouskimmel**, dapple-grey horse; ~ **boer**, apple grower; ~ **bol**, apple dumpling; ~ **boom**, apple tree; ~ **boor**, apple corer; ~ **boord**, apple orchard; ~ **boorder**, apple borer, codling moth; apple corer; ~ **bruinperd**, dapple-bay horse; ~ **compote**, compote of apples; ~ **de(r)liefde**, *see* **appelliefie**; ~ **drank**, cider.
appelgaai'erig, *(inform.)*, (-e), proud, boastful; smart.
appèl'geding, appeal proceedings.
ap'pelgroen, apple green.
appèl': ~ **grond**, ground of appeal; ~ **hof**, court of appeal; appellate division (court).
ap'pelkoekie, apple fritter.
appelkoos', (..kose), apricot; *appelkose vir die goddelose*, the wicked must pay for their sins; ~ **boom**, apricot tree; ~ **boord**, apricot orchard; ~ **geel**, apricot (colour); ~ **konfyt**, apricot jam; ~ **maag**, *see* **appelkoossiekte**; ~ **perske**, plumcot; ~ **pit**, apricot stone; ~ **pruim**, plumcot, cotplum; ~ **siekte**, gastro-enteritis, (summer) diarrhoea; ~ **smeer**, apricot leather; ~ **tert**, apricot tart.
appellant', (-e), appellant.
appelleer', (ge-), appeal (in law); ~ *na 'n hoër hof*, appeal to a higher court.
appellie'fie, (-s), Cape gooseberry; ~ **konfyt**, Cape gooseberry jam.
ap'pel: ~ **moes**, mashed apples, apple pulp; ~ **mot**, apple borer, codling moth; ~ **oes**, apple crop; ~ **pastei**, apple pie; ~ **pit**, apple pip.
appèl': ~ **plek**, venue of appeal; ~ **reg**, right of appeal; ~ **regter**, judge of the appeal court, judge of appeal.
ap'pelring, apple ring.
appèl'saak, appeal case.
ap'pel: ~ **sap**, apple juice; ~ **skil**, apple peel; ~ **skimmel**, dapple-grey; ~ **skuim**, apple whip; ~ **skurfte**, apple scab; ~ **skyfie**, apple chip; ~ **soort**, variety of apple; ~ **suur**, malic acid; ~ **tameletjie**, apple leather; ~ **tert**, apple tart; ~ **tjie**, (-s), little apple; ~ **tyd**, apple season; ~ **vink**, hawfinch, grosbeak; ~ **vormig**, (-e), pomiform; ~ **vrug**, pome; ~ **wyn**, cider.
appendektomie', appendectomy.
appen'diks, (-e), appendix.
appendisi'tis, appendicitis.
appersep'sie, apperception.
appersipieer', (ge-), apperceive.
appliek'werk, appliqué (work).
applikant', (-e), applicant.
applika'sie, (-s), application (for a post).
applikee', appliqué (work).
applikeer', (ge-), appliqué.
appliseer', (ge-), apply (bandage).
apploudisseer', (ge-), applaud.
applous', applause, plaudits, hand(clapping); ~ *vir die wenner*, give the winner a hand.
apporteer', (ge-), fetch and carry back (in training dogs), retrieve.
apporteur', (-s), retriever.
apposi'sie, apposition.
appren'tjiesreën, (gew.), rain in December (out of season) (in the Western Province).
appresia'sie, appreciation.
appresieer', (ge-), appreciate.
approba'sie, approbation; *op ~ stuur*, send on appro(bation).
approksima'sie, approximation.
approksimeer', (ge-), approximate.
approviandeer', (ge-), provision.
April', April; *so taai soos ~ se vlieë*, very sticky; ~ **blom**, chrysanthemum; ~ **gek**, April fool; ~ **grap**, April-fool joke; ~ **maand**, month of April; ~ **perske**, April peach; ~ **(s)'vlieg**: *nes 'n ~(s)vlieg wees*, be extremely troublesome.
a prio'ri, a priori.
aprioris'ties, (-e), aprioristic.
apropos', apropos, to the purpose.
apsi'de, (-s), *(sterrek.)*, apsis.
ap'sis, (-se), *(argit.)*, apse.
apteek', (..teke), chemist, chemist's shop, pharmacy, dispensary, drug store.
apte'ker, (-s), pharmacist, dispenser, pharmaceutical chemist, dispensing chemist, chemist, druggist; ~ **es'**, (-se), female chemist.
aptekers: ~ **bediende**, chemist's assistant; ~ **bedryf**, chemist trade, chemist business; ~ **boek**, pharmacopoeia; ~ **maat**, apothecaries' measure; ~ **paraffien**, liquid paraffin; ~ **winkel**, drug store.
aptyt', appetite; ~ **lik**, (-e), appetizing, savoury, tempting; ~ **loosheid**, loss of appetite; ~ **snapsie**, appetiser; aperitif; ~ **verlies**, loss of appetite; ~ **wekkertjie**, appetizer.
Apu'lië, Apulia; ~ **r**, (-s), Apulian.
a'ra, (-s), ara, macaw.
arabesk', (-e), arabesque.
Ara'bië, Arabia.
Arabier', (-e), Arab; ~ **perd**, Arab (horse).

Ara'bies, (s), Arabic (language); (b), (-e), Arabian; ~ *e GOM*, gum arabic; ~ *e SYFERS*, Arabian numerals.
aragoniet', aragonite.
arak', (ar)rack; ~ **pons**, (ar)rack punch.
Arame'ër, (-s), Aramean.
Aramees', (s), Aramaic (language); (b), (..mese), Aramic.
arapapegaai', macaw.
a'raroet, arrowroot.
ar'bei, (ge-), work, labour, toil; *hulle* ~ *en hulle spin nie*, they toil not, neither do they spin.
ar'beid, work, labour, toil; pursuits; ~ *ADEL*, labour ennobles; *BESKUTTE* ~, protected industry; *aan die* ~ *GAAN*, set to work; *GESKOOLDE* ~, skilled labour; *aan die* ~ *WEES*, be at work; ~ **besparend**, (-e), labour-saving; ~ **end**, (-e), working, labouring, toiling, operative; *die* ~ *ende klas*, the working class; ~ **er**, (-s), labourer, workman, worker; operator; *'n* ~ *er is sy loon werd*, a labourer is worthy of his hire; **A** ~ **er**, Labourite.
ar'beiders: ~ **belange**, interests of workers; ~ **bevolking**, working-class population; ~ **beweging**, labour movement; ~ **buro**, labour exchange; ~ **buurt**, working-class district; ~ **eise**, demands of labour; ~ **gesin**, working-class family; ~ **huisie**, labourer's cottage; ~ **kaartjie**, labourer's ticket; ~ **klas**, working class; ~ **organisasie**, labour organisation.
Ar'beidersparty, Labour Party.
ar'beiders: ~ **vakunie**, labour trade-union; ~ **verhoudings**, labour relationships; ~ **woning**, labourer's dwelling.
arbeid'saam, (..same), industrious, hardworking, diligent, laborious; ~ **heid**, industry, diligence.
ar'beids: ~ **besparing**, saving of labour; ~ **betrekkinge**, industrial relations, labour relations; ~ **beurs**, ~ **buro**, labour exchange, employment bureau; ~ **dag**, working-day; **A** ~ **dag**, Labour Day; ~ **diagram**, indicator diagram ~ **dwang**, forced labour; ~ **eenheid**, unit of work; erg(on), joule; ~ **geskil**, labour (trade) dispute; ~ **intensief**, labour intensive, ~ **kolonie**, labour colony; ~ **kontrak**, labour contract; ~ **koste**, labour costs; ~ **kragte**, manpower.
ar'beidsku, (-we), work-shy.
ar'beids: ~ **loon**, wages, pay, hire; ~ **loos**, (..lose), out of work, unemployed; ~ **loosheid**, unemployment; ~ **mark**, labour market; ~ **omset**, labour turnover; ~ **onwillig**, (-e), work-shy; ~ **ooreenkoms**, labour agreement; ~ **periode**, cycle of action (work); ~ **potensiaal**, energy; labour potential; ~ **raad**, labour council.
ar'beidstaat, worksheet.
ar'beidstempo, power (of a machine); rate of work.
ar'beids: ~ **terapie**, occupational therapy; ~ **toestande**, working conditions; ~ **toevoer**, labour supply; ~ **tyd**, working-hours; ~ **veld**, sphere of action, field of activity; ~ **verbruik**, input; ~ **verdeling**, division of labour; ~ **vermoë**, (working) power, energy; ~ *vermoë van BEWEGING*, kinetic energy; ~ *vermoë van PLEK*, potential energy; ~ *vermoë van WATER*, duty of water; ~ **voorraad**, labour reservoir; ~ **voorwaardes**, working conditions, conditions of labour; ~ **vraagstuk**, labour question (problem); ~ **week**, working week; ~ **wet**, labour law; ~ **wetgewing**, labour legislation.
arbi'ter, (-s), arbiter, arbitrator.
arbitraal', (..trale), arbitral.
arbitra'sie, arbitration; ~ **beding**, arbitration clause; ~ **hof**, court of arbitration; ~ **koste**, arbitration expenses; ~ **uitspraak**, arbitration award.
arbitreer', (ge-), arbitrate; umpire.
arbitrêr', (-e), arbitrary.
archego'nium, (..gonia), archegonium; ~ **draend**, (-e), archegoniate.
arduin'(steen), free stone, ashlar.
a're, (-s), are.
a'rea, (-s), area.
are'ka, (-s), areca; ~ **neut**, areca nut; ~ **palm**, areca palm.
are'na, (-s), arena.

a'rend, (-e), eagle; mandrel (of a lathe); erne; tang, spike (of a file); eagle *(golf)*; *die een* ~ *BROM nie teenoor 'n ander nie*, hawks will not pick hawks' eyes out; *'n* ~ *vang nie VLIEË nie*, an eagle does not catch flies; ~ **jie**, (-s), eaglet.
a'rends: ~ **blik**, eagle eye; ~ **klou**, eagle's talon; rapacity; ~ **kuiken**, eaglet; ~ **nes**, eagle's nest, aerie (aery, eyrie, eyry); ~ **neus**, aquiline nose; ~ **oog**, eagle's eye; sharp eye(s); ~ **vleuel**, eagle's wing; ~ **vlug**, eagle's flight.
areome'ter, **a'reometer**, (-s), areometer, hydrometer.
arga'ïes, (-e), archaic; ~ *e tydperk*, archaic era.
Arga'ïes, *(geol.)*, (-e), Archaen.
argaïseer', (ge-), archaize.
argaïsme, (-s), archaism.
argaïs'ties, (-e), archaic, archaistic.
ar'g(e)loos, (..lose), unsuspecting, unsuspicious, innocent, guileless; ~ **heid**, harmlessness, innocence.
argentaan', German silver, nickel silver, argentan.
argentiet', argentite.
Argenti'nië, Argentine.
Argentyn', (-e), Argentinian; ~ **s'**, (-e), Argentine.
argeologie', archaeology.
argeolo'gies, (-e), archaeologic(al).
argeoloog', (..loë), archaeologist.
argief', (..giewe), archives, records, rolls; record room, record office; muniment room; filing cabinet; ~ **bewaarder**, keeper of the archives; ~ **bewaarplek**, archives; ~ **gebou**, archive building; ~ **kamer**, chamber of archives; ~ **klerk**, record clerk; ~ **navorser**, research worker in the archives; ~ **stuk**, archival document; ~ **wese**, archives, public records.
argilliet', argillite.
ar'gipel, (-s), **argipel'**, (-le), archipelago.
argitek', (-te), architect; ~ **to'nies**, (-e), architectural; ~ **tuur**, architecture; ~ **tuurvereniging**, architectural society.
argitraaf', (..trawe), architrave, epistyle.
argivaal', (..vale), **argiva'lies**, (-e), archival.
argiva'lia, archivalia, public records.
argiva'ris, (-se), recorder, keeper of the archives, archivist.
arglis'tig, (-e), crafty, cunning; insidious; designing; ~ **heid**, craft, craftiness, guile, malice, insidiousness.
arg'loos = **argeloos**.
ar'gon, argon.
Argonout', (-e), Argonaut.
argot', argot, slang.
argument', (-e), argument, plea; ~ **a'sie**, (-s), argumentation; ~ **eer'**, (ge-), argue; ~ **shalwe**, for the sake of argument.
Ar'gusoë: *met* ~, Argus-eyed.
arg'waan, suspicion, mistrust; searchings of the heart; distrust; doubt; misgiving; presumise; ~ *HÊ (* ~ *KOESTER) teen*, harbour (have) a suspicion against; *sonder die MINSTE* ~, with never a suspicion; ~ *WEK*, rouse suspicion.
arg'wanend, (-e), distrustful, suspicious.
a'ria, (-s), air, tune, song, aria.
Ariaan', (Ariane), Arian; ~ **s'**, (-e), Arian.
Arianis'me, Arianism.
A'riër, (-s), Aryan.
A'ries, (-e), Aryan.
a'rig, (-e), unwell, queer, strange; unfriendly; awkward, uncomfortable; ~ *e MENSE*, unfriendly people; *ek voel* ~, I feel ill (giddy); *dit sal te* ~ *WEES om so iets te sê*, it will be too odd to say such a thing; ~ **heid**, indisposition, giddiness.
a'rikreukel = **alikreukel**.
a'ring, graining; veining, venation.
aristokraat', (..krate), aristocrat.
aristokrasie', aristocracy.
aristokra'ties, (-e), aristocratic.
Aristo'teles, Aristotle.
Aristoteliaans', (-e), Aristotelian.
aritme'ties, (-e), arithmetic(al).
ark, (-e), ark; *uit die* ~ *se DAE*, from time immemorial; *dit LYK of dit uit die* ~ *kom*, it looks antediluvian; *die* ~ *is OOP*, many visitors have called (are calling); *die Ark v.d. VERBOND*, the Ark of the Covenant

arka'de, (-s), arcade.
Arka'dië, Arcadia.
Arka'dies, (-e), Arcadian.
ark'mark, petshop.
Ark'ties, (-e), Arctic.
arko'se, arcose.
arm[1], (s), (-s), arm; limb; crank, lever; beam (of a balance); jib (of a crane); web (of a horseshoe); bracket (of a machine); gab lever; outrigger *(naut.)*; horn (of inlet); *met 'n nooi AAN sy ~*, with a girl on his arm; *iem. onder die ~ HÊ*, pull the wool over someone's eyes; *die ~s KRUIS*, to submit; be unconcerned; *LANG ~s hê*, have far-reaching power; *iem. die ~ LEEN*, lend a hand; *sy ~ LIG*, take strong drink; *in die ~ NEEM*, enlist the aid of someone; secure support; *met OPE (oop) ~s ontvang*, receive with open arms; *die ~ teen iem. OPHEF*, threaten violence against someone; *onder iem. se ~ gaan RUIK*, recognize someone as your superior; *die ~s oor mekaar SLAAN*, fold the arms; *die ~s SLAP laat hang*, lose courage; *iem. in die ~s SLUIT*, embrace someone; *die STERK ~ gebruik*, use (armed) force; *op iem. se ~ STEUN*, lean on someone else; *die ~s tot (na) iem. UITSTEEK*, come to someone's assistance; *iem. se ~s trek WATER*, someone is becoming tired; *die WÊRELDLIKE ~*, temporal power; *jou in iem. se ~s WERP*, fling yourself into someone's arms.
arm[2], (b), (-er, -ste), poor, needy, indigent; (-e), unfortunate; *~ AAN digters, vee*, poor as regards poets, cattle; *~ AAN fosfate*, deficient in phosphates; *die ~ man se BAADJIE*, the sun; *so 'n ~e ou DROMMEL*, such an unfortunate wretch (beggar); *~ maar EERLIK*, poor but honest.
arma'da, (-s), armada.
armadil', (-le), armadillo.
armatuur', (..ture), armature.
arm'band, bracelet; armlet; brassard; *~oorlosie*, wrist(let) watch.
arm: *~been*, arm bone; *~bedekking*, covering for the arm(s).
arm'bestuur, (..sture), poor-relief board.
arm'beurs, poorbox.
arm'blaker, branch candlestick.
armblan'ke, (-s), poor white; *~dom*, poor-whiteism; *~nedersetting*, poor-white settlement; *~vraagstuk*, poor-white problem.
arm'breuk, fracture of the arm.
arm: *~bus*, poor-box, charity box, alms box; *~buurt*, poor quarter(s).
arm: *~dik*, as thick as an arm; *~draagdoek*, arm sling; *~dryfkrag*, arm drive.
ar'me, (-s), pauper; *~begrafnis*, pauper burial; *~belasting*, poor-rate.
Armeens', (s), Armenian (language); (b), (-e), Armenian.
ar'megestig, alms house.
Arme'nië, Armenia; -r, (-s), Armenian; ..nies, (-e), Armenian.
arm'erig, (-e), rather (somewhat) poor.
ar'mes, have-nots, paupers, the poor; *die ~ het julle ALTYD by julle*, the poor are always with us; *die ~ van GEES*, the poor in spirit; *die ~ en die RYKES*, the poor and the rich.
ar'mesorg, care for the poor; parochial relief; (system of) poor-relief; *~kommissie*, poor-relief committee.
ar'meversorging, poor relief.
arm'fonds, poor-relief fund.
arm: *~greep*, arm-grip; *~holte*, armpit.
arm'huis, alms house, workhouse.
Arminiaan', (..niane), Arminian, adherent of the doctrine of Arminius.
arm'kandelaar, sconce.
arm'ketting, wrist chain.
arm'kolonie, pauper colony.
arm'kussing, pillow arm-rest.
armlas'tig, (-e), chargeable to the community; indigent; *~e*, (-s), pauper; *~heid*, pauperism.
arm: *~lengte*, arm's length, reach; *~leuning*, armrest.
arm: *~lik*, (-e), poor, shabby, indigent; *~mansbaad*jie, the sun; *~manskind*, poor man's child; *~manskoek*, poor man's cake; *~mansrib*, chuck rib; *~mansvriend*, poor man's friend.
ar'moede, poverty, destitution, penuriousness, penury, pennilessness, pauperism, want; paucity (of words); *~ leer BENE kou*, necessity is the mother of invention; hunger will break through stone walls; *tot ~ BRING*, reduce to poverty; *~ is geen SKANDE nie*, poverty is no disgrace; *as ~ by die VOORDEUR inkom, gaan liefde by die agterdeur uit*, when poverty enters the door, love flies out at the window; *tot ~ VERVAL*, decline (lapse) into poverty.
armoe'dig, (-e), poor, needy, indigent, penurious; poky (house); mangy; *in -e OMSTANDIGHEDE*, in poor (reduced) circumstances; *daar ~ UITSIEN*, look shabby; *~heid*, poverty, penury.
ar'moedsaaier, pauper, starveling; agitator.
arm: *~paal*, cantilever mast; *~pie*, (-s), armlet; *~pyp*, brachial bone.
arm'rig, (-e), rather poor.
arm'ring, manilla, armlet, bangle.
armsa'lig, (-e), pitiful, poor(ly), pitiable, miserable; mangy, measly; beggarly; paltry; *~heid*, pitifulness, pitiableness, miserableness, paltriness.
arms'gat, armhole, sleevehole.
arm'sieraad, trinket (ornament) for the arm, bracelet, bangle.
arm'skool, charity school, poor school; *~kind*, charity child.
arm'slag, swing of arm.
arms'lengte, arm's length; reach; *op ~ hou*, keep at arm's length.
arm'stoel, easy chair, elbow chair; armchair.
arm'versorger, deacon; almoner.
arm'vol, (armsvol), armful.
arm: *~wese*, pauperism; poor-relief; *~wet*, poor-law.
ar'nika, arnica.
aroe'na, variety of *Stapelia* (with stout spines); *Caraluma incarnata*.
aro'ma, aroma, fragrance; *~'ties*, (-e), aromatic.
a'ronskelk, arum lily, pig lily, wakerobin; *Arum maculatum*.
arrangeer', (ge-), arrange; orchestrate.
arrangement', (-e), arrangement; scoring, orchestration.
ar'ren: *(vero.), in ~ moede*, in anger, in an angry mood.
arres', arrest, custody; *in ~ GEE*, give up (to police); *in ~ NEEM*, take into custody, place under arrest; *~bevoegdheid*, power of arrest; *~tant'*, (-e), arrested person, prisoner; *~ta'sie*, arrest; *~teer'*, (ge-), arrest, take prisoner, put (take) into custody, pinch.
ar'rie! I say! heigh!
arriveer', (ge-), arrive.
arrogan'sie, arrogance.
arrogant', (-e), arrogant.
arrondissement', *(Eur.)* (-e), district; *~s'regbank*, district court.
arseen', arsenic; *~houdend*, arsenical; *~piriet*, mispickel, arsenopyrite; *~suur*, arsenic acid; *~vergiftiging*, arsenical poisoning.
arseer', (ge-), shade (in), hatch (over).
arsenaal', (..nale), arsenal.
arsenaat', (..nate), arsenate.
arseni'de, (-s), **arsenied'**, (-e), arsenide.
arseniet', (-e), arsenite.
arse'nigsuur, arsenous acid.
ar'senik, arsenic; *~kies*, mispickel.
arse'nikum, arsenic; *~vergiftiging*, arsenical poisoning.
arse'ring, hatching, shading (in line drawings).
arsien', **arsi'ne**, arsine.
ar'sis, (arses), arsis.
artefak', (-te), artefact.
arte'rie, (-ë), artery; *..rieel'* (..riële), arterial.
arte'riosklero'se, arteriosclerosis.
arteriotomie', arteriotomy.
arte'sies, (-e), artesian; *~e put*, artesian well.
arties', (-te), artist; *~tekamer*, greenroom.

arti'kel, (-s), article, clause; item; commodity; line; story *(journalism);* clause (of a bill); section (of a law); *die Twaalf A~s van ons geloof,* the Apostles' Creed; **~reeks,** series of articles; **~sgewys(e),** each clause separately, clause by clause.
artikula'sie, articulation; **~basis,** articulation basis.
artikulato'ries, (-e), articulatory; **~e fonetiek,** articulatory phonetics.
artikuleer', (ge-), articulate.
artillerie', artillery; **~aanval,** artillery attack; **~afdeling,** artillery section; **~battery,** artillery battery; **~depot,** artillery base (depot); **~kaserne,** artillery quarters; **~-offisier,** artillery officer; **~skietbaan,** gunnery range; **~skool,** artillery school; **~trein,** artillery train; **~tweegeveg,** artillery duel; **~vuur,** artillery fire; **~waarneming,** artillery observation; **~werk,** artillery co-operation; **~werkplaas,** ordnance factory; **~wetenskap,** gunnery (science).
artilleris', (-te), artillery man, gunner.
ar'tisjok, (-ke), artichoke.
artistiek, artis'ties, (-e), artistic, tasteful.
artistie'kerig, (-e), would-be artistic, sham; **~heid,** pseudo-art.
artistisiteit', artisticity.
artri'tis, arthritis.
arts, (-e), physician, doctor, curer; **~eksamen,** medical examination.
artseny', (-e), medicine, medicament, physic; **~bereiding,** pharmacy; **~bereider,** pharmaceutist, druggist; **~bereikunde,** pharmacy, pharmaceutics; **~kunde,** pharmacology; **~kun'dig, (-e),** pharmaceutical; **~kun'dige, (-s),** pharmacologist; **~leer,** pharmacology; **~middel,** drug; medicine.
as¹, (s), ash(es), cinders, *jou by KOUE ~ warm maak,* rejoice without reason; *in die ~ LÊ,* reduce to ashes; *soos ~ in die MOND,* very, unpleasant; *uit die ~ OPTEL,* raise from a humble position; *laat sy ~ in vrede RUS,* peace to his ashes; *in die ~ SIT,* wear sackcloth and ashes; *jy kan hom uit die ~ SKOP,* he is a nonentity; *daar is ~ op jou TOON,* your fly is open; *is VERBRANDE hout,* if ifs and ands were pots and pans; *uit die ~ VERRYS,* rise from the ashes; *WARM ~,* embers.
as², (s), (-se), shaft, spindle, axle; axletree; axis; *~ van ELASTISITEIT,* axis of elasticity; *die ~ SMEER,* grease the axle; do the dirty work; *sy ~ het VASGEBRAND,* he got into a fix.
as³, *(ong., mus.),* A flat.
as⁴, (vgw), if, in case when; on condition that; except; but; as; *'n baie GROOT ~,* very unlikely (risky); *GROTER ~,* bigger than; *~ arm MAN sterf,* die a poor man; *NIKS ~ onkruid nie,* nothing but weeds; *~ PREDIKANT,* as (in the capacity of) minister; *~ dit REËN,* in case it rains; *~ jy hom SIEN,* if (when) you see him; *SO goed ~,* practically; *~ SODANIG,* as such; *~ VOLG,* as follows; *~ 't WARE,* as it were.
as'afstand, wheel base; axial distance.
as'agtig, (-e), ash-like, ashy.
asa'lea, (-s), azalea.
as'arm, (axle) arm.
as: ~baan, dirt (cinder) track; **~bak,** ash bucket, dustbin; **~bakkie,** ash tray; **~balk,** axle beam, axle bed; **~beeld,** axial image.
as'bek, donkey, ass.
as'belasting, axle (axial) load, load on axle.
asbes', asbestos, earth flax; **~draad,** asbestos thread; **~sement,** asbestos cement; **~solder,** asbestos loft (cciling), **~tose,** asbestosis; **~tou,** asbestos cord; **~verf,** asbestos paint; **~verpakking,** asbestos packing; **~verwarmer,** asbestos heater; **~vocl,** asbestos thread; **~vormig, (-e),** asbestiform.
as: ~beuel, U-bend bolt (for axle); **~beweging,** axle float.
as'blik, ash (dust, rubbish) bin.
as'blokvoering, bushing, pillow.
as'blom, cineraria.
as'blond, ashy (coloured), ash-blond.
as'bok, axle stand.
as'bos, lyebush.
as'bus, shaft bush.
asdan', (ong.), then, at that moment; in that case.

as'draaibank, axle lathe.
a'se, *see* **aas** (w): *hier is niks te ~ nie,* here is nothing to eat, find, take away.
a'seksueel, (..suele), asexual.
a'sem, (s), (-s), breath; *in EEN ~,* in one breath, without a break; *die ~ inhou,* hold one's breath; *op ~ KOM,* get one's breath; *die LAASTE ~ uitblaas,* die, expire; *LANK van ~ wees,* be long-winded; *op iem. se ~ LÊ,* disturb a busy person; *~ SKEP,* take breath; *sy ~ MORS,* waste one's breath; *in een ~ NOEM,* mention in one breath; *jou ~ OPHOU,* be on tenterhooks; (w), (ge-), breathe; fetch (draw) a breath; **~beheersing,** breath control; **~benemend, ~berowend, (-e),** astounding; breathtaking.
a'semhaal, (-ge-), breathe, fetch (draw) a breath; *DIEP ~,* take a deep breath, breathe deeply; *WEER kan ~,* enjoy a breathing space.
a'semhaling, (-e, -s), breathing, respiration.
a'semhalings: ~apparaat, breathing apparatus; **~oefening,** breathing exercise; **~orgaan,** respiratory organ; **~opening,** spiracle; **~toestel,** respirator; **~werking,** respiration.
asemie', asemia.
a'semloos, (..lose), breathless.
a'sem: ~meter, spirometer; **~opening,** lenticle; **~porie,** breathing pore; **~pouse,** breathing space; **~pyp,** breather tube; **~rig,** breathy; **~rowend, (-e),** breathtaking; **~stoot,** breath; **~teken,** breathing mark *(mus.);* **~toetser,** breath analyser; **~tog,** breath; **~weerstand,** breathing resistance.
asepsie', asep'sis, asepsis.
aseptien', aseptin'e, aseptin(e).
asep'ties, (-e), aseptic.
asetaat', (..tate), acetate.
asetileen', acetylene; **~lamp,** acetylene lamp; **~sweiswerk,** acetylene welding; **~verligting,** acetylene lighting.
ase'timeter, (-s), acetimeter.
asetoon', aceton.
as'falt, asphalt; **~baan,** asphalt court *(tennis);* **~bestrating,** asphalt paving; **~eer', (ge-),** asphalt, asphaltize; **~iet',** asphaltite; **~linne,** bituminized linen; **~pad,** asphalt road, tarmac; **~plaveisel,** asphalt pavement; **~straat,** asphalt(ed) (tarred) street; **~sypaadjie,** asphalt pavement.
asfiksia'sie, asphyxiation.
asfiksie', asphyxia, asphyxy.
asgaai' = **assegaai.**
as: ~gat (-e), ash hole; **(-te),** *(plat),* ne'er-do-well, nincompoop, rascal, good-for-nothing, scamp, blighter; **~gehalte,** ash content; **~grou,** ashy grey, cinereous; **~grys,** griscent.
as: ~hals, journal; axle neck; **~helling,** chamber; caster; **~hoek,** axial angle; **~hoogte,** ground clearance (vehicle).
as'hoop, ash heap, scrap heap, dumping ground, dirt heap, rubbish dump; midden; *iets op die ~ GOOI,* relegate to the rubbish heap; *op die ~ SIT,* wear sackcloth and ashes; *uit die ~ kan SKOP,* to be had for the asking.
as'hulsel, axle housing.
Asiaat', (Asiate), Asian.
Asia'ties, (-e), Asiatic.
asiditeit', acidity.
asido'se, acidosis.
A'sië, Asia; **~r, (-s),** Asian.
asiel', (-e), asylum, place of refuge, shelter, sanctuary; *~ VRA,* request asylum; **~reg,** right of sanctuary.
asimmetrie', asymmetry.
asimme'tries, (-e), asymmetric(al).
asimptoot', (..tote), asymptote.
asimpto'ties, (-e), asymptotic.
a'simut, azimuth; **~kompas,** azimuth compass; **~sirkel,** azimuth circle.
asinde'ties, asyndetic.
asin'deton, (-s), asyndeton.
as'jas, (-se), ne'er-do-well, blighter, joker, good-for-nothing, nincompoop.
as'kanteling, camber.
aska'ri, (-'s), askari.
as'kas, axle box.

askeet', (..kete), ascetic.
askena'wel, *(ong.),* **(-e),** libellous; repulsive; exactly; silly; old-fashioned; cheeky; intolerable.
aske'se, ascesis.
aske'ties, (-e), ascetic.
asketis'me, asceticism.
as'kleur, ash colour; ~ig, ashen, ash-coloured, cinereous.
as'klip, tuff.
as'koek, ash cake; ne'er-do-well, rascal; ~ **slaan,** dance a Khoi-Khoi jig.
as: ~**koker,** axle housing (tube); ~**koppeling,** axle coupling; ~**kraan,** ash cock; ~**kruik,** urn; ~**laer,** axle bearing; ~**lyn,** axial line, axis.
as'ma, asthma; ~**aanval,** asthma attack; ~**-ag'tig, (-e),** asthmatic; ~**lyer,** asthma sufferer, asthmatic; ~**'ties, (-e),** asthmatic.
asme'de, *(form.),* as also, besides, as well as.
as: ~ **moer,** axle nut; ~**naaf,** journal.
asnog', as yet.
asof', as if; *ek het GEVOEL* ~ *ek haar kon slaan,* I felt like hitting her; *dit lyk* ~ *dit gaan HAEL,* it looks like hail; *maak* ~ *jy TUIS is,* make yourself at home.
asook', also, as well as.
Aso're: *die* ~, the Azores.
asosiaal', (..siale), asocial.
aspaai', *(vero.),* I spy (hide-and-seek game).
as'pan, ash pan.
as'patat, numskull, ass, fool.
aspek', (-te), aspect.
asper'sie, (-s), asparagus; ~**bed,** ~ **bedding,** asparagus bed; ~**punte,** asparagus tops; ~**so(e)p,** asparagus soup; ~**water,** asparagus water.
aspidis'tra, (-s), aspidistra.
aspiek', aspic.
aspirant', (-e), aspirant, probationer, prospective applicant; ~**-kandidaat,** prospective candidate; ~**-onderwyser,** teacher in training, prospective teacher.
aspira'sie, (-s), aspiration.
aspireer', (ge-), aspire; aspirate.
aspirien', (-e), aspiri'ne, (-s), aspirin (registered trade name).
as'pis, (-se), asp; aspic; ~**slang,** asp.
As poestertjie, (-s), Cinderella.
aspres', aspris' = **ekspres.**
as'punt, earth pole.
as'put, ash pit.
as'reëler, fly governor.
as'ryer, dustman.
As'sam, Assam; ~**ees, (..mese),** Assamese.
asseblief', please, if you please; *van* ~ *en DANKIE lewe,* live on charity; *met* ~ *en DANKIE kom jy deur die wêreld,* all doors open to courtesy; *HOU nou* ~ *op,* please stop it now; ~ *NIE!* please don't! ~ *TOG!* do please! ~ *is 'n groot WOORD,* I come hat in hand.
as(se)gaai', (-e), assegai; ~**hout,** assegai wood (*Curtisia faginea*).
as'serig, (-e), ashy.
asses'sor, (-e, -s), assessor; *A* ~ *Synodi,* Assistant Chairman of the Synod; ~**lid,** assessor member.
as'sevlak, axial plane.
as'sies, small quantity of ashes.
assignant', (-s), drawer of bill.
assigna'sie, (-s), assignation, bill of exchange.
assigneer', (ge-), assign.
assimila'sie, assimilation.
assimileer', (ge-), assimilate.
assimile'rend, (-e), assimilative, assimilatory.
assimile'ring, assimilation.
assinjaat', (..jate), assignat.
Assi'rië, Assyria; ~**r, (-s),** Assyrian; **..ries, (-e),** Assyrian.
assisteer', (ge-), assist, help.
assisten'sie, assistance.
assistent', (-e), assistant; ~**-bestuurder,** assistant manager; assistant driver; ~**-hoofbestuurder,** assistant general manager; ~**e, (-s),** (lady-) assistant; ~**-landdros,** assistant magistrate.
as: ~**(skop)graaf,** ash shovel; ~**soda,** kelp.

assonan'sie, assonance.
assoneer', (ge-), assonate.
assone'rend, (-e), assonant.
assosiaat', (..ate), associate (of an institute); ~**lidmaatskap,** associate membership.
assosia'sie, (-s), association.
assosieer', (ge-), associate.
assorteer', (ge-), assort.
assortiment', *(ong.),* **(-e),** assortment.
assous', (-e), smelt (fish); whitebait (*Atherina breviceps; Engraulis capensis*).
as: ~**spy,** shaft key; ~**staal,** axle steel; ~**standig, (-e),** axial.
as'steen, breeze brick, ash brick.
assumeer', (ge-), co-opt.
assump'sie, (-s), assumption, co-optation; *met mag van* ~, with the right to co-opt.
assuradeur', *(ong.),* **(-s),** insurer, insurance broker, underwriter.
assuran'sie, insurance, assurance; ~**-agent,** insurance agent; ~**kantoor,** insurance (company) office; ~**koste,** costs of insurance; ~**maatskappy,** insurance company; ~**polis,** insurance policy; ~**premie,** insurance premium; ~**tarief,** insurance rate (tariff); ~**wese,** insurance, assurance.
assureer', (ge-), insure, assure.
as'tap, stop axle, shaft journal.
astasie', state of being astatic, astasia.
asta'ties, (-e), astatic.
astatisis'me, astaticism.
Asteek', (..teke), Aztec; ~**s', (-e),** Aztec.
astenie', asthenia, astheny, debility; **aste'nies, (-e),** asthenic.
as'ter, (-s), aster, chrysanthemum; girl, fiancée.
asterisk', (-e), asterisk.
asteroïdaal', (..dale), asteroidal.
asteroïed', (-e), asteroï'de, (-s), asteroid.
astigma'ties, (-e), astigmatic.
astigmatis'me, astigmatism.
astraal', (astrale), astral; ~**lig,** astral light; ~**liggaam,** astral body.
astragaal', (..gale), astragal.
astra'galus, (-se), astragalus.
as'trakan, astrakhan (cloth).
astrant', (-e), cheeky, impudent, audacious, bold, over-confident, free-and-easy, cool, devil-may-care, daring, presumptuous, impudent, pert, precocious; perky, brazen, fresh; ~**erig, (-e),** rather (somewhat) cheeky; ~**heid,** cheek(iness), pertness, backchat, effrontery, over-confidence, audacity, assurance, daring.
as'tro: ~ **fotografie',** astrophotography; ~ **genie',** astrogeny; ~**grafie',** astrography; ~**la'bium, (-s),** astrolabe; ~**latrie',** astrolatry, star worship.
astrologie', astrology.
astrolo'gies, (-e), astrologic(al).
astroloog', (..loë), astrologer.
as'trometer, astrometer.
astrometrie', astrometry.
astronomie', astronomy.
astrono'mies, (-e), astronomic(al).
astronoom', (..nome), astronomer.
as'uitwerper, ash ejector.
asuriet', azurite.
asuur', (s), vault of heaven; (b), azure, sky-blue; ~**steen,** lapis lazuli, lazulite, azurite.
as'vaal, pallid, ashy, deathly pale; *jou* ~ *skrik,* (become) pale with fright.
as: ~ **vlak,** axial plane; ~**vormig, (-e),** axiform.
as'wenteling, axle rotation.
asyn', vinegar; ~**agtig (-e),** acetous, sour, vinegary; ~**bottel,** vinegar bottle; ~**ekstrak,** essence of vinegar; ~**flessie,** vinegar cruet; ~**gees,** aceton(e); ~**kan,** vinegar jug; ~**kuip,** vinegar cask, ~**smaak,** vinegar taste; ~**sout,** acetate; ~**stander(tjie),** ~**stel,** cruet (stand); ~**suiker,** oxysaccharum; ~**suur, (s),** acetic acid; (b), acetous; *dit is* ~, this is vinegar itself (as sour as vinegar); ~**suurgisting,** acetic fermentation; ~**suurhoudend, (-e),** acetous; ~**suurmeter,** acetimeter; ~**vaatjie, (-s),** ~**vat, (-e),** vinegar vat.
ataksie', ataxy.

atak'sies, (-e) ataxic.
atavis'me, atavism; reversion (to type); throwback.
atavis'ties, (-e), atavistic.
ateïs', (-te), atheist; ~**me,** atheism; ~**ties, (-e),** atheistic.
ateljee', (-s), studio, workshop; ~**kamera,** studio camera; ~**orkes,** studio orchestra.
aterosklero'se, atherosclerosis.
At(h)eens', (-e), Athenian.
At(h)e'ne, Athens; ~**r, (-s),** Athenian.
athene'um, (-s), athenaeum.
at'jar, pickles; ~**fles,** pickle jar; ~**smeer,** relish; ~**vis,** pickled fish; ~**vurk,** pickle fork.
a"tjie, (-s), small a.
Atlan'ties, (-e), Atlantic; ~**e Oseaan,** Atlantic Ocean.
at'las[1], (-se), atlas.
at'las[2], satin twill; ~**hout,** satin wood; ~**papier,** satin paper; ~**spaat,** satin spar.
at'lasvlinder, atlas moth.
atleet', (atlete), athlete.
atletiek', athletics; ~**byeenkoms,** athletic meeting.
atle'ties, (-e), athletic.
atletisis'me, athleticism.
atmoli'se, atmolysis.
atmologie', atmology; ..**lo'gies,** atmological.
atmosfeer', (..sfere), atmosphere.
atmosfe'ries, (-e), atmospheric(al).
atol', (-le), atoll.
ato'mies, (-e), atomic; corpuscular.
atomiseer', (ge-), atomize.
atomis'me, atomism.
atomistiek', atomicity.
atomis'ties, (-e), atomistic.
atonaal', (..nale), atonal; ..**naliteit',** atonality.
atonie', atony, debility.
ato'nies, (-e), atonic, weak.
atoom', (atome), atom; ~**beheer,** atomic control; control of atomic energy; ~**bom,** atomic bomb; ~**bou,** atomic structure; ~**desintegrasie,** atomic disintegration; ~**eeu,** atomic age; ~**energie,** atomic energy; ~**gedrewe,** atom-powered; ~**geheime,** atomic secrets; ~**gewig,** atomic weight; ~**kern,** atomic nucleus; ~**krag,** atomic energy; atomic power; ~**leer,** atomic science; ~**navorser,** nucleur physicist; ~**neerslag,** atomic fall-out; ~**ondersoek,** atomic research; ~**oorlog,** atomic warfare; ~**pie, (-s),** small atom; ~**splitsing,** splitting of the atom; atomic fission; ~**suil,** atomic pile; ~**teorie,** atomic theory; ~**toets,** atomic test; ~**tydperk,** atomic era; ~**wapens,** atomic weapons.
OPM. In baie van die bostaande woorde is *atoom-* tans vervang met *kern-*.
a'trium, (-s), auricle *(anat.)*; atrium *(archit.)*.
atrofie', atrophy.
atrofieer', (ge-), atrophy.
atro'fies, (-e), atrophied.
atropien', atropi'ne, atropin(e).
atsjie', atsjoe', (tw.), achoo.
attaché, (-s), attaché (at legation); ~**tas,** attaché case.

at'tarolie, attar (otto) of roses.
atten'sie, (-s), attention, considerateness; ~**s,** considerations; ~**s bewys,** call on (a girl).
attent', (-e), attentive; considerate; *iem. op iets ~ maak,* draw someone's attention to something.
attes', (vero.), (-te), certificate, testimonial, attestation
attestaat', (..tate), certificate; testimonial; ~ *van LIDMAATSKAP,* certificate of membership (of a church); *jou ~ LIG,* obtain your certificate on leaving; *(fig.)* to inquire about your antecedents.
attesta'sie, (-s), testimonial, certificate, attestation, certification.
attesteer', (ge-), attest, certify; ~**der,** attestant.
At'ties, (-e), Attic; ~*e sout,* Attic salt (wit).
attrak'sie, (-s), attraction.
attribueer', (ge-), attribute.
attributief', (..tiewe), attributive; ..*tiewe byvoeglike naamwoord (adjektief),* attributive adjective.
attribuut', (..bute), attribute, quality, characteristic.
au, (tw.), ow, ouch.
auba'de, (-s), aubade.
au'erhaan, capercaillie, mountain cock *(Tetrao urogallus).*
Au'giasstal, stable of Augeas; *die ~ reinig,* cleanse the Augean stable.
Augs'burg: *die ~se Geloofsbelydenis,* the Augsburg Confession.
au'gur, (-s), augur.
Augus'tus, August; ~**maand,** (the month of) August.
Augusty'ner, (-s), Augustinian, Augustinian friar.
auk, (-s), auk, guillemot, puffin, razor-bill, great (little) auk.
au'la, (-s), aula, hall; court.
Auro'ra, Aurora, goddess of dawn.
austraal', (australe), austral, southern.
Australasië, Australasia; ..**sies,** Australasion.
Austra'lië, Australia; ~**r (-s),** Australian.
Austra'lies, (-e), Australian.
australiet', australite.
Aus'tralorp, (-s), Australorp.
auto-da-fé, auto-da-fé.
aval', (-le), (written) guarantee for (payment of) bill (of exchange), aval.
aviatiek', aviatics, aviation.
avoirdupois', avoirdupois
avoka'do, (-'s), ~**peer,** avocado (pear), alligator pear (U.S.A.)
A'vondmaal = Awendmaal.
avonturier', (-s), adventurer; ~**ster, (-s),** adventuress.
avontuur', (..ture), adventure; ~**lik, (-e),** adventurous, enterprising; ~**roman,** adventure (picaresque) novel.
a'wegaar(boor), auger.
A'wendland, *(ong.),* the Occident, the West.
A'wendmaal, *(ong.),* the Lord's Supper, Holy Communion.
a'weregs, (-e), wrong, preposterous; purl (knitting).
awery', average (at sea); damages (marine insurance); ~*oploop,* incur damages.

B

b, (-'s), b.
ba (tw.) pshaw, phew, bah.
baad'jie, (-s), coat jacket; *sy al vir 'n ANDER aantrek,* be very kind-hearted; *BO jou ~,* beyond you; *prosedeer oor 'n ~ en hou jou BROEK klaar vir die onkoste,* law is a bottomless pit; *iem. op sy ~ GEE,* dust someone's jacket; *die GEEL ~ aanhê,* be very jealous; *op jou ~ KRY,* get a licking (beating); *sy ~ PAS hom nie,* he is unfit for the job; *moenie iem. op sy ~ TAKSEER nie,* don't judge anyone by appearances; *iem. se ~ vir hom UITBORSEL,* dust someone's jacket; *sy ~ vir 'n ander UITTREK,* take one's shirt off one's back for another; ~ *UITTREK vir 'n saak,* roll up one's sleeves; throw oneself heart and soul into a cause; ~**hanger,** coat hanger; ~**hemp,** bush shirt; ~**knoop,** coat button; ~**kraag,** coat collar; ~**mou,** coat sleeve; ~**pak,** coat and skirt; ~**pant,** (coat) tail; ~**sak,** coat pocket; **skouer,** ~**stok = baadjiehanger;** ~**tjie, (-s),** small coat (jacket).
baai[1], (s), baize.
baai[2], (s), (-e), bay, inlet, gulf, cove; **(w), (ge-),** bathe (in the sea); foment (swelling); ~**broek,** bathing-trunks; ~**er, (-s),** bather.
baai'erd, chaos.
baai: ~**hokkie,** bathing-booth, cubicle; ~**klere,** ~**kostuum,** bathing-costume (suit); ~**mus,** bathing-cap; ~**plek,** bathing-place; ~**sout,** bay-salt; ~**tabak,** Maryland (tobacco); ~**tjie, (-s),** cove.

baak, (**bakens**), beacon; landmark; seamark; ~**hout**, bottlebrush (*Grevia sutherlandii*).
Ba'äl, (**-s**), Baal; *DOOF bly soos* ~, be hard of hearing; *voor* ~ *die KNIE buig*, bow the knees unto Baal.
baal, (s), (**bale**), bale, pack; (w), (**ge-**), bale (lucerne); ~**draad**, baling wire; bundling wire; ~**masjien**, baler; ~**pers**, baling press, baler; ~**sak**, woolsack.
Ba'älsprofeet, false prophet.
baan, (s), (**bane**), course, path, way, race (of moon), orbit (stars); trajectory (shell); court (tennis); rink (bowls, skating); floor (dancing); track (athletics); breadth, width, panel (cloth); permanent way, roadbed; lane (traffic); circuit (electr.); guide-way; gore (skirt); ~ *BREEK*, pave the way; pioneer; *op die* ~ *BRING*, bring on the tapis; *op 'n GLADDE* ~, on a slippery path; *iem. v.d.* ~ *KNIKKER*, oust someone; *op die LANGE* ~, postponed indefinitely; shelved; *'n* ~ *OPSKOP*, kick up a row; *die* ~ *OPEN*, open the dance; *die* ~ *RUIM*, clear the way; clear the floor; *VAN die* ~ *wees*, be shelved; *VRYE* ~ *hê*, have been given the right of way; *v.d.* ~ *WEES*, have been put off (shelved); (w), (**ge-**), clear, pave (the way); *die GEBAANDE weg*, the beaten track; *'n PAD* ~, open a way; ~**bed**, permanent way; ~**blad**, roadbed; pitch, wicket; ~**brekend**, (**-e**), pioneering; ~**breker**, pioneer, pathfinder; trail-blazer; ~**brekerswerk**, pioneering, pioneer('s) work.
baan'derheer, (hist.), banneret.
baan: ~**geld**, entrance money; green fee (golf); ~**kennis**, court craft (tennis); ~**meester**, clerk of the course; plate-layer; ganger; ~**nommer**, track (flat) event (athletics) ~**opsigter**, track steward; greenkeeper, green-ranger; ~**rekord**, lap (track) record; course record; ~**ruimer**, ~**skuiwer**, track-clearer, cow-catcher; ~**stang**, tie rod; ~**streep**, lane line; ~**syfer**, bogey, par (golf).
baan'tjie, (**-s**), employment, job, billet; ~*s vir BOETIES*, jobs for pals; *'n LEKKER* ~, a soft job; ~**houer**, placeman; ~**jaer**, place (job, office) hunter; careerist; ~**jaery**, job hunting; ~**soeker** = **baantjiejaer**.
baan: ~**vak**, railway section; ~**veër**, cow-catcher sweeper; iceman; ~**vernuf**, court craft; ~**versnelling**, course acceleration; ~**vyl**, valve file; ~**wagter**, line-keeper; flagman; groundman; linesman; ~**wagtershuis(ie)**, line-keeper's cottage; lodge box; ~**wedloop**, flat race; track item; ~**werker**, track-worker; surfaceman; ~**wydte**, rail gauge.
baar¹, (s), (**bare**), (vero.), wave (in sea); billow.
baar², (s), (**bare**), bier (for corpse); stretcher; litter (for patient).
baar³, (s), (**bare**), ingot, bar (of gold).
baar⁴, (**bare**), (ong.), sea-barbel, catfish *(Galeichthys feliceps)*.
baar⁵, (w), (**ge-**), give birth to, bring into the world; bring forth; bear, produce; breed; create; cause; *OEFENING* ~ *kuns*, practice makes perfect; *ONRUS* ~, create unrest; cause uneasiness; *OPSIEN* ~, create a stir.
baar⁶, (b, bw), (**-der, -ste**), uncivilized, unskilled, raw, untrained, green; ready, hard (cash); undisguised; *die bare DUIWEL*, the very devil, the devil himself; ~ *WEES*, be a greenhorn; be unskilled.
baard, (**-e**), beard; whiskers; web, ward, bit (key); byssus (biol.); awn (wheat); barb (hook); burr (plates and holes); cirrus (clouds); *in die* ~ *BROM*, mutter in one's beard; *waar jy self nie kan kom nie, word jou* ~ *nie GESKEER nie*, a man far from his goods is near his harm; *in jou* ~ *GLIMLAG*, smile slyly; *die* ~ *sit in sy keel*, his voice is beginning to crack; *bietjie* ~, *maar KLIPSTEENHARD*, not as green as he looks; *hy moet nog* ~ *KRY*, he has lots to learn; *ROOI* ~, *duiwelsaard*, a red beard, like the devil to be feared; *die* ~ *laat STAAN*, grow a beard; *iem. iets in die* ~ *VRYWE*, take someone to task; ~**aar**, bearded ear (of wheat); ~**angelier**, sweetwilliam; ~**brander**, nose-warmer (short pipe); ~**draer**, full-grown man; protea (*Protea barbigera*); ~**gras**, bearded grass; ~**haar**, hair of beard; ~**jie**, (**-s**), little beard; barbule; ~**keep**, ward (of key); ~**koring**, bearded wheat; ~**loos**, (..lose), beardless; ~**man**, bearded man; hippie; rocker; ~**mannetjie**, barbel fish (*Umbrina capensis*); tassel fish (Natal); white fish; bearded finch (*Sporopipes squamifrons*).
baar'draer, (ong.), ambulance man, stretcher bearer.
baard: ~**siekte**, ~**skurfte**, sycosis; ~**stoppels**, stubbly beard; ~**suikerbos**, sugar bush (*Protea barbigera*); ~**uitslag**, barber's itch; ~**vis**, mullet; ~**voël**, wattled bird (*Capitonidae, Megalaemidae*); ~**vyl**, warding file; ~**wurm**, skin disease (*Herpes tonsurans*).
baar'goud, gold in bars.
baar'heid, rawness, inexperience.
baar'kleed, pall, hearse cloth.
baar'lik, (**-e**): *die* ~*e duiwel*, the devil himself (incarnate).
baar'moeder, womb, uterus, matrix; ~**hals**, cervix uteri; ~**krans**, pessary; ~**ontsteking**, metritis; ~**ring**, pessary; ~**uitsnyding**, hysterectomy.
baars, (**-e**), bass, perch.
baas, (**base**), master, foreman, chief, manager, lord, gaffer, governor, boss; employer; champion, crack (-player); *die* ~ *BLY*, remain master; *daar is altyd* ~ *BO* ~, every man meets his match (master); *jou EIE* ~ *wees*, be one's own master; *elkeen is* ~ *op sy eie WERF (plaas)*, a man's home is his castle; *wie* ~ *is, moet* ~ *bly*, hold fast when you have it; *eers* ~ *en dan KLAAS*, first the master, then the slave; *klein* ~ *is beter as groot KNEG*, lean liberty is better than fat slavery; *jou* ~ *KRY*, meet one's match; *die* ~ *maak die PLAAS*, a farm is made by the master; ~ *SPEEL oor iem.*, rule the roost; *as die* ~ *nie TUIS is nie, word sy baard nie geskeer nie*, a man far from his property is near his harm; *iem. die* ~ *WEES*, be another's match; *hy wil altyd* ~ *WEES*, he always wants to rule the roost; *iets* ~ *(meester) WORD*, master something; ~**agtig**, (**-e**), domineering; ~**bakker**, master-baker; ~**bakleier**, champion fighter; ~**drukker**, master-printer; ~**jaer**, champion racer, ace; ~**kaart**, master-card; ~**kleremaker**, master-tailor; ~**messelaar**, mastermason; ~**navorser**, masterly research-worker; ~**raak**, (**-ge-**), master, subdue, get the better of, cope successfully, manage, overcome; ~**seeman**, leading seaman (rating); ~**seeman(sgraad)**, leading rating; ~**skap**, championship, mastery; supremacy, mastership; paramountcy; ~**skrywer**, master writer; ~**skut**, champion shot.
baas'speel, (**-ge-**), bully, domineer, lord it over, hector, wear the breeches (wife); *oor iem.* ~, domineer (boss) someone; ~**geaardheid**, domineering disposition.
baas: ~**speler**, bully, bluster, dominator; hector; crack-player; ~**spelerig**, (**-e**), masterful, overbearing, domineering, overweening, blustering; ~**spelerigheid**, imperiousness; ~**spelery**, hectoring; ~**timmerman**, master-carpenter; ~**vlieënier**, ~**vlieër**, flying ace; ~**voorman**, chargeman.
baat, (s), (**bate**), profit, gain, asset; benefit; *te* ~ *NEEM*, avail oneself of, use; *TEN bate van*, on behalf of, in aid of; ~ *VIND by*, obtain relief from; *see* **bate**; (w), (**ge-**), avail, help; profit; *daarmee is EK nie gebaat nie*, that is of no benefit to me; *dit sal net NIKS* ~ *nie*, that will be of no use; *WAT* ~ *dit om hom raad te gee*, of what use is advice to him?
baat'sug, selfishness; self-interest; ~**tig**, (**-e**), selfish, egotistic(al), mercantile; ~**'tigheid**, selfishness, egotism.
baat'wissel, bill receivable.
ba'ba, (**-s**), baby; babe; child; sweetheart, love, darling; ~**bedjie**, cot; ~**bottel**, feeder, feeding-bottle; ~**broekie**, pilch; ~**doek**, napkin; ~**kos**, baby food.
babalaas' = **babelas**.
ba'ba: ~**lief**, baby dear; *die* ~*(tjie) met die BADWATER uitgooi*, throw out the baby with the bathwater; *die* ~*tjie op 'n ander se DRUMPEL sit*, pass the buck; *van iem. 'n* ~*tjie MAAK*, molly (-coddle) someone; *so ONSKULDIG soos 'n PASGEBORE*

~ *tjie*, as innocent as a newborn babe; *'n* ~ *tjie VANG*, assist at a confinement; *iem. sal die* ~ *tjie moet VASHOU*, someone will have to nurse the baby; ~ **uitrusting**, ~ **uitset**, layette; ~ **wagter**, baby-sitter; ~ **wedstryd**, baby competition.

bab'bel, (ge-), tattle, chatter, prate, talk, gossip, gabble), clack, jabber, jaw, gibber, confabulate, cackle, chat, prattle (child); patter; ~ **aar**, ~ **aarster, (-s)**, tattler, chatterer, gossip, cackler, chatterbox, prattler, prater, telltale; ~ **agtig, (-e)**, talkative, loquacious; ~ **(a)ry**, chattering; ~ **bek**, chatterbox; ~ **end, (-e)**, jabbering, chattering, gossiping, confabulatory.

babeljoen'tjie, (-s), (vero.), canopy bed; fourposter.

bab'bel: ~ **kous**, rattle, chatterbox; ~ **rig, (-e)**, chattering, talkative; gossipy, loquacious; ~ **siek, (-e)**, loquacious, gossipy; ~ **sug**, loquacity, talkativeness, garrulity; ~ **sug'tig, (-e)**, loquacious, talkative, garrulous.

Ba'bel, Babel; ~ **s**, Babylonian.

babelas', (s), hangover; (b), drunk.

ba'ber, (-s), barbel; bagger (*Clariidae*); ~ **bek**, person with a large mouth; ~ **bekploeg**, type of plough.

ba'betjie — **babatjie**.

Ba'bilon, Babylon.

Babilo'nië, Babylonia; ~ **r, (-s)**, Babylonian.

Babilo'nies, (-e), Babylonian.

babiroe'sa, babirussa.

ba'bo: *iem van* ~ *na bibo stuur*, send someone from pillar to post.

baccalau'reus, (..rei, -se), bachelor; ~ *Artium*, Bachelor of Arts (B.A.); ~ **Scientiae**, Bachelor of Science (B.Sc.).

baccarat', baccarat

Bacchana'lia, Bacchana'lieë, bacchanals; Bacchanalia.

bacchana'lies, (-e), bacchanal(ian).

bacchan'te, (-s), Bacchante, priestess (votary) of Bacchus, maenad.

Bac'chus, Bacchus, god of wine; ~ **fees**, Bacchanals; ~ **lied**, bacchanalian song, dithyrambic; ~ **priester**, bacchant; ~ **staf**, thyrsus.

bad, (s), (-de, -dens), bath, bath tub; **(baaie)**, swimming-bath; mineral bath, hot spring, mineral spring; *die baaie GEBRUIK*, take the waters; *die KIND 'n* ~ *gee*, bath the child; *'n* ~ *NEEM*, have a bath; *'n WARM* ~, a hot bath; (hot) mineral spring; (w), **(ge-)**, take a bath, give a bath; ~ **bande**, bath straps; ~ **benodigdhede**, bathing requisites (requirements); ~ **broek**, bathing drawers; ~ **dery**, bathing; ~ **gas**, visitor to a watering place; ~ **greep**, grab bar; ~ **handdoek**, bath towel; ~ **handskoene**, bath gloves; ~ **hokkie**, bathing-cubicle (box); ~ **huis(ie)**, bathing booth; bath; bagnio.

badineer', (ge-), banter.

bad: ~ **inrigting**, bathing-establishment; ~ **jie**, little bath; ~ **kaartjie**, bathing-ticket; ~ **kamer**, bathroom; ~ **ketel**, geyser; hot-water installation; ~ **klere**, bathing-wear; ~ **kom**, bath basin; ~ **kostuum**, bathing-costume; ~ **kraal**, bathing-enclosure; ~ **kuip**, bathtub; ~ **kussinkie, (-s)**, bath pad(s); ~ **kuur**, bathing cure; ~ **mat**, bath mat.

badmin'ton, badminton.

bad'mus, bathing-cap; ~ **olie**, bath oil; ~ **pak**, see **badkostuum**; ~ **plaas**, ~ **plek**, bath; bathing-place; watering-place; health resort; seaside resort; ~ **seep**, bath soap; ~ **seisoen**, bathing-season; ~ **(s)huis**, bathhouse; bathing-booth; **bads'kamer** = **badkamer**; ~ **skoen**, bathing-shoe; ~ **sout**, bathsalts; ~ **spons**, bath sponge; ~ **water**, bath water.

baedeker, (-s), Baedeker.

baf'aro, (-'s), *Polyprion prognathus*.

baf'ta, coarse blue material.

baf'tablou, blue, lead-coloured.

baga'sie, baggage, luggage; *oortollige* ~ *dra*, be corpulent; ~ **-afdeling**, baggage (luggage) department; ~ **bak**, luggage container, boot; ~ **bewys**, luggage receipt; ~ **biljet**, luggage slip; ~ **buro**, luggage office; ~ **draer**, luggage carrier; parcel carrier, porter; ~ **geleibrief**, luggage waybill; ~ **kaartjie**, luggage ticket; ~ **kamer**, cloakroom; ~ **kantoor**, luggage office; ~ **lys**, baggage list; ~ **net**, cradle, luggage rack; ~ **rak**, luggage rack, carrier; ~ **ruim**, baggage compartment; ~ **trein**, baggage train; ~ **wa**, luggage van.

bagasse', bagasse

bagatel', (-s), bagatelle (game); trifle.

bagatel'le, *(mus.)*, **(-s)**, bagatelle.

bag'ger, (s), dredgings; slush (street); (w), **(ge-)**, dredge; ~ **boot**, dredger, dredging boat; ~ **maatskappy**, dredging company; ~ **masjien**, dredging machine, (mud)dredger, dredge; ~ **net**, dredging net, dredger; ~ **skuit**, dredger, dredging boat; ~ **werk**, dredging work (operations).

bai'e, (meer, meeste), very (much), (a good) many, abundant, endless; frightfully, greatly, a great deal, muckle; far; frequently; ~ *BELANGRIKE PERSOON (BBP)*, very important person (VIP); *'n BIETJIE* ~, rather (somewhat) much; ~ *DANKIE*, many thanks, thank you very much; *hy KOM* ~ *daar*, he often goes there; ~ *MINDER*, much less, far fewer; ~ *SÊ so*, many say so; ~ **keer**, ~ **maal**, many a time, frequently, often.

bajonet', (-te), bayonet; *met gevelde* ~, with fixed bayonets; ~ **aanval**, bayonet attack; ~ **geveg**, bayonet tight; ~ **gloeilamp**, bayonet bulb; ~ **kling**, bayonet blade; ~ **lamphouer**, bayonet lamp-holder; ~ **nok**, sword bar; ~ **skede**, bayonet scabbard; ~ **sluiting**, bayonet catch; ~ **steek**, bayonet thrust.

bak¹, (s), (-ke), basin, bowl; vat, trough; body (of a carriage); (snake's) hood; dustbin; ash bucket; parterre, pit (theatre); forecastle (fo'c's'le); hutch (ore); tray; *hulle EET nie uit een* ~ *nie*, they do not see eye to eye; *'n* ~ *MAAK*, be getting on well; *in die* ~ *RAAK*, get in arrears; *vinnig by die* ~, *lui by die VAK*, said of a lazy worker with a good appetite; *iem. in die* ~ *WERK (spit, skoffel, ploeg, ens.)*, work faster than someone; beat him hollow; (b, bw), cup-shaped, cupped; baggy (trousers); protruding; *sy BENE staan* ~, he is bandy-legged; *jou hande* ~ *HOU*, cup one's hands; ~ *STAAN*, stand with bent legs (for a heavy load); work hard; *'n plank wat* ~ *TREK*, a warped board (plank).

bak², (w), (ge-), bake (bread); fry (fish, egg); roast (meat); fire (pottery); mess; *sy laat die mense maar* ~ *en BROU*, she allows the people to do as they please; *hulle* ~ *en BROU oor die aanstelling*, they are intriguing about the appointment; *toe maar, môre* ~ *ons KOEKIES*, never mind, daddy will bring you the moon; *in die SON* ~, bask in the sun.

bakatel', (-le), trifle, futility; *see* **bagatel**.

bak: ~ **baard**, side-whiskers; ~ **barometer**, cistern (mercury) barometer; ~ **bees**, giant; whopper; ~ **bene**, bandy (bow) legs.

bak'boek, mess book.

bak'boord, larboard; port(side); *iem. van* ~ *na stuurbood stuur*, send someone from pillar to post; ~ **kant**, portside; ~ **lig**, port light; ~ **wal**, port shore.

bak: ~ **bou**, body-building; ~ **bouer**, bodymaker; ~ **bout**, body bolt.

Bakchos = **Bacchus**.

bak'dag, baking day.

bakellet', bakelite.

ba'ken, (-s), beacon, cairn, buoy; landmark; ~ *STEEK*, come a cropper; tent pegging; *die* ~ *VERSIT*, strike out a new line; ~ **landing**, beacon landing; ~ **lig**, beacon light; cresset; ~ **punt**, beacon point; ~ **stasie**, beacon station; ~ **stok**, beacon pole; ~ **toring**, beacon tower; ~ **vuur**, beacon light.

ba'ker, (s), (-s), (dry) nurse; (w), **(ge-)**, (dry) nurse; ~ **kind**, infant in arms; ~ **luier**, child's napkin; ~ **mat**, cradle; (fig.) birthplace, origin; ~ **sprokie**, *(ong.)*, nursery tale.

bak: ~ **gat**, (sl.), fine, exellent; ~ **geleentheid**, messing (on board ship); ~ **goed**, bread-stuff; ~ **hoender**, roaster; ~ **huis**, bakery.

bak'kebaard = **bakbaard**.

bak'ker, (-s), baker.

bak'kerig, (-e), floppy.

bak'kers: ~ **brood**, baker's loaf; ~ **graaf**, peel; ~ **jeuk**, baker's itch; ~ **kar**, baker's cart; ~ **kneg**, baker's man; ~ **leerling**, baker's apprentice; ~ **trog**, baker's trough; ~ **winkel**, baker's shop, bakery.

bak'kery, (-e), bakery; baking.
bak'kie, (-s), small tray (basin, bowl); punnet; small fishing boat; light delivery van, LDV, pick-up van.
bak'kies, (-e), face, mug, dial, phiz(og).
bak'kies: ~ **blom,** red disa (Pride of Table Mountain) (*Disa uniflora, D. grandiflora*); ~ **draai, (-ge-),** spin round while holding hands; ~ **pomp,** bucket pump, Persian wheel, tub wheel.
bak: ~ '**kis,** baker's trough; ~ '**kool,** baking coal.
bak'kop(slang), ringed cobra.
baklei', (ge-), fight, scrap, quarrel; ~ **er, (-s),** fighter, combatant; performer (boxing); ~ **erig, (-e),** pugnacious, fond of fighting, quarrelsome, with his hackles up; ~ **erigheid,** pugnacity; ~ **ery,** fighting, affray, scrap, set-to; ~ **slag,** fight, scrap, fisticuffs.
bak'loon, baking-fee.
bak'maat¹, messmate.
bak'maat², volume; capacity (dam).
bak'maker, bodymaker.
bak: ~ **meester,** caterer; baker; ~ **mengsel,** baking mix; ~ **olie,** oil for baking, cooking oil.
bak'ontwerp, body design.
bak'oond, oven; *sy sit op die* ~ , she is an old maid (on the shelf)
bak'oor(jakkals), bat-eared jackal.
bak'ore, large, prominent ears.
bak'pan, bread pan; frying pan, fryer.
bak'paneel, body panel.
bak: ~ **plaat,** bread plate; ~ **poeier,** baking powder.
bak'pypie, Caledon bluebell.
bak: ~ **sel, (-s),** batch, baking; ~ **seun,** mess orderly; ~ **skottel,** baking dish; casserole.
bak: ~ **skuif,** (common) slide valve; ~ **spel,** backgammon; ~ **spoor,** camber (wheel); ~ **stag,** backstay (on ship); ~ **stapel,** clamp.
bak'steen, brick, burnt brick; bat; *HALWE* ~ , bat; *dit reën bakstene,* it is raining cats and dogs; *soos 'n* ~ *SAK,* fail badly (ignominiously); *soos 'n* ~ *SWEM,* be unable to swim; sink like a brick; ~ **oond,** brick kiln; ~ **rooi,** brick red; ~ **huis,** brick dwelling.
bak'ster, (-s), female baker.
bak: ~ **tafel,** mess table; ~ **tand,** grinder (tooth); ~ **tent,** mess tent.
bakte'rie, (-ë, -s), bacterium; ~ **el', (..riële),** bacterial; ~ **melk,** yoghurt; ~ **s, (-e),** bacterial; ~ **telling,** bacterial count(s).
bakteriologie', bacteriology.
bakteriolo'gies, (-e), bacteriological.
bakterioloog', (..loë), bacteriologist.
bak'trens, gag-snaffle.
bak: ~ **trog,** *see* **bakkerstrog;** ~ **vet,** baking fat; ~ **vis,** baking fish.
bak'vis(sie), flapper, chit of a girl.
bak'vorm, baking mould.
bak'werk, coachwork, bodywork; baking.
bal¹, (s), (-le), ball (tennis, etc.); testicle; *wie KAATS, moet die* ~ *verwag,* if you play at bowls you must look out for rubbers; *die* ~ *misslaan,* be mistaken; ~ *NA* ~ , ball-to-ball (billiards); *die* ~ *aan die ROL sit,* set the ball rolling; (w), (ge-), clench.
bal², (s), (-s), ball, dance; *GEMASKERDE* ~ , masked ball; *die* ~ *OPEN,* open the ball.
balans', balance; *die* ~ *opmaak,* draw up the balance sheet; ~ **arm,** balancing arm (machinery).
balanseer', (ge-), balance, poise; ~ **ballas',** trim ballast; ~ **stok,** balancing pole.
balanse'ring, balancing.
balans': ~ **hefboom,** balance lever; ~ **opmaking,** balancing the accounts (books); ~ **opruiming,** stocktaking sale; ~ **rekening,** balance account; ~ **staat,** balance sheet; ~ **tenk,** trimming tank; ~ **tou,** tail rope; ~ **veer,** balance (steadying-) spring.
bal-bal', ball game.
bal'beheer, ball-control (sport).
bal'bytermier, ball-biter (ant) (*Camponotus*).
balda'dig, (-e), mischievous, malicious, wanton; rowdy; frisky; ~ **heid,** mischievousness, maliciousness, wantonness; rowdiness.
baldakyn', (-e), baldachin, canopy; pylon.
bal'dans, ballroom dancing.
bal'derjan, valerian (*Valeriana capensis*).

Balea're, Balea'riese Eilande, Balearic Islands.
balein', (-e), whalebone; busk (corset); bone.
bal: ~ **-en-klou'pote,** ball and claw feet; ~ **-en-pot'jiegewrig,** ball and socket joint; ~ **gooier,** pitcher (baseball).
balho'rig, (-e), refractory, unruly, headstrong, intractable; ~ **heid,** refractoriness; unruliness.
ba'lie¹, bar, barristers; *tot die* ~ *toegelaat word,* be called to the bar.
ba'lie², (-s), tub; kit; *hy is 'n regte ou* ~ , he is as round as a barrel.
ba'lieraad, bar council.
ba'lievormig, (-e), tub-shaped.
baljaar, (ge-, ~ **),** make much noise, play noisily, frolic, gambol, rampage, rollick, racket; ~ **der, (-s),** romper; ~ **derig, (-e),** playful; ~ **dery,** noisy play, gambolling, racket, ~ **pakkie,** romper; play-suit.
balju', (-'s), bailiff, sheriff, messenger of the court; ~ **skap,** post of messenger of the court; bailiwick; ~ **vandisie,** ~ **veiling,** ~ **vendusie,** sheriff's sale.
balk¹, (s), (-e), beam; rafter; girder; flitch; joist (floor); share beam (plough); scantling (timber); staff, stave, bar (music); bend, fesse (her.); *'n* ~ *AFSAAG,* snore; *HAAL eers die* ~ *uit jou eie oog,* first cast out the beam out of your own eye; ~ *e na NOORWEË stuur,* send coal to Newcastle; *nie die* ~ *in eie OOG sien nie,* not see the beam in one's own eye; *'n* ~ *in iem. se OOG wees,* be a thorn in someone's side; ~ *e SAAG,* be driving one's hogs to market; snore; *tot aan die* ~ *e SPRING,* jump for joy.
balk², (w), bray.
balk'aksie, beam action.
Bal'kan, Balkans.
balkaniseer', (ge-), balkanize.
Bal'kanstate, Balkan states.
balk: ~ **anker,** crompon; ~ **arm,** beam (drilling machine); ~ **band,** key (building); ~ **bedding,** girder bed; ~ **brug,** girder bridge; ~ **draer,** corbel; ~ **hoogte,** as high as the roof (building); ~ **hout,** beamwood; ~ **huis,** log cabin; ~ **ie, (-s),** bar (rugby boot); bail (cricket); ~ **iesbal,** bailer (cricket); ~ **iesdakrand,** slatted eaves; ~ **kraan,** cantilever crane; ~ **laag,** framing of joists; joist frame.
bal'klep, ball valve.
balkon', (-ne, -s), balcony, gazebo, open gallery; platform, bridge (train); dress-circle (theatre); ~ **deur,** balcony door; ~ **kamer,** balcony room; jutty room; ~ **netjie, (-s),** balconet; ~ **venster,** balcony (jut) window.
bal'kostuum, ball dress.
bal'kraan, ball tap.
balk: ~ **skrif,** staff notation; ~ **stapel,** crib; ~ **stel,** set (of timbers); ~ **yster,** bar shoe.
balla'de, (-s), ballad; ~ **digter,** ballad poet, balladeer; ~ **versameling,** minstrelsy.
bal'las¹, mv. van **bal¹,** testicles.
ballas'², ballast.
ballas'mandjie, bushel basket.
ballas': ~ **sand,** ballast sand; ~ **skip,** ballast ship; ~ **trein,** ballast train; ~ **yster,** kentledge.
balleri'na, (-s), ballerina; ~ **romp,** ballerina skirt.
balleri'no, (-s), ballerino, male (ballet) dancer.
ballet', (-te), ballet; ~ **dans,** ballet dance; ~ **danser,** ballet dancer; ~ **danseres,** ballet dancer; chorus girl, dancing girl, figurant(e).
bal'letjie, (-s), small ball; *'n* ~ *opgooi,* throw out a feeler.
ballet': ~ **meester,** ballet master; ~ **musiek,** ballet music.
balletomaan, (..mane), balletomane, devotee of ballet.
bal'ling, (-e), exile, outlaw, outcast; ~ **skap,** exile, banishment; captivity; ~ **skrywer,** exiled author; ~ **soord,** place (land) of exile.
ballistiek', ballistics.
ballis'ties, (-e), ballistic.
ballon', (-ne, -es), balloon; *bestuurbare* ~ , dirigible balloon; ~ **afdeling,** balloon section; ~ **anker,** balloon anchor; ~ **band,** balloon tyre; ~ **gas,** balloon gas; ~ **gordyn,** balloon apron; ~ **mandjie,** balloon basket; ~ **vaarder,** balloonist; ~ **versperring,** balloon barrage.

ballotasie   49   *bankier*

ballota'sie, voting by ballot.
balloteer', (ge-), vote by ballot.
bal'ontsteking, orchitis.
bal'poot, ball foot.
bal'rok, balldress.
bal'roos, guelder rose.
bal'ruiter, children's ball game.
bal'saal, ballroom.
bal'sahout, balsa wood.
bal'sak, scrotum, cod.
bal'sem, (s), (-s), balm, balsam, ointment; ~ *GI-LEADS,* the Balm of Gilead; ~ *in iem. se WONDE giet,* comfort someone; pour balm onto someone's wounds; (w), **(ge-),** embalm; **~agtig, (-e),** balmy; **~er, (-s),** embalmer; **~geur,** balsamic odour; **~hars,** balsamic resin.
balsemiek', (ong.), (-e), hot, oppressive, balsamic.
bal'sem: ~ing, embalming, embalmment; **~i'nie,** garden balsam, balsamine; **~kopi'va,** copaiva balsam (medicine); **~kruid,** basil.
bal'skoene, pumps.
bal'spel, ballgame.
bal'stikker, East Indian plant *(Sansevieria languinosa).*
balstu'rig, (-e), obstinate, unruly, intractable; **~heid,** obstinacy, intractability, unruliness.
Balt, (-e), Balt.
Bal'tiese See, Baltic Sea.
balus'ter, (-s), baluster, ban(n)ister.
balustra'de, (-s), balustrade.
bal'vorming, (-e), ball-shaped, round.
bambar'ra-grondboontjie, Bambarra nut *(Voandzeia subterranea),* 'njugo bean.
bamboes', (-e), bamboo, rat(t)an; **~beer,** panda; **~berg,** bamboo (-covered) mountain; **~bos,** bamboo wood; **~gordyn,** bamboo curtain; *agter die ~ gordyn,* behind the bamboo curtain (in Communist China); **~mandjie,** bamboo basket; **~mat,** bamboo mat; **~riet,** kind of (S.A.) reed; **~suiker,** cane sugar; **~vis,** gold-stripe fish *(Sarpa salpa).*
ban, (s), excommunication, ban, banishment; *in die ~ doen,* excommunicate; ostracize; (w), **(ge-),** exile, banish, expel.
banaal', (..nale), banal, vulgar, trite, platitudinarian, commonplace, trivial.
banaliteit', (-e), banality, triteness, vulgarity, platitude; ¹⁻e, inanities.
bana'na, (-s), banana; **~handel,** banana trade; **~plantasie,** banana plantation.
ban'bliksem, anathema.
band, (-e), band (of skirt, hat, etc.); tape; lace; braid (bonnet); cord; belt; girdle, cincture; ribbon, fillet (for hair); fascia; fraenum (anat.); nexus; strap; hoop; tyre (motor); sling (for arm); truss; binding (book); volume; attachment, bond, tie (of blood); copula; cord, ligament (anat.); vinculum; cushion; cush (billiards); tape (recording); *iem. se ~ AAN-DRAAI,* force someone to do something; *ALMAL se ~ wees,* surpass every one; *BO sy ~,* beyond him; *die ~e BREEK,* sever connections; *~e v.d. DOOD,* the throes of death; *aan ~e LÊ,* keep in check; *IN v d ~ af,* in off the cush (billiards); *die ORIGE ~ aansit,* put the spare tyre on; *SLAP ~,* limp cover, paperback; *uit die ~ SPRING,* get out of hand, kick over the traces; **~ trek,** relieve nature; **~aandrywing,** belt drive; **~aanvoering,** belt feed.
banda'na, (-s), bandan(n)a.
band: ~anker, band stay; **~breuk,** tyre failure; **~defek, (tyre)** puncture; tyre defect; **~doek,** diaper; **~druk,** tyre pressure.
bandelier', (-e, -s), bandoleer, shoulder (cartridge) belt.
ban'deloos, (..lose), unrestrained, unbounded, turbulent, riotous; dissolute; orgiastic; **~heid,** lawlessness; turbulence, riotousness, lack of restraint; licentiousness.
band: ~garnering, tape trimming; **~grootte,** tyre size.
bandiet', (-e), prisoner, convict; bandit; **~jiespampoen,** turk's cap (kind of lily); **~klere,** convict's clothes.

band: ~koppeling, belt coupling; **~legging,** marriage ceremony; **~ligter,** tyre lever; **~lintsaag,** endless saw; **~maat,** tape measure; **~nael,** belt rivet.
band'om, belted (banded) ox *or* cow; banded stone; **~slang,** cross-barred snake.
band: ~ontwerp, cover design; **~opname,** tape recording; **~opneemtoestel, ~opnemer,** tape recorder; **~oteek, (..teke)** tape library; **~rem,** band brake; **~reparasie,** tyre repairs; **~roller,** traveller; **~saag,** band saw, belt saw; **~skyf,** belt pulley; **~staal,** strip steel; **~trekker,** caterpillar tractor; **~vat, (ge-),** hold tight; scold; **~ventiel,** tube vent; valve; **~verbinder,** belt fastener; **~versiering,** cover design, cover ornamentation; **~vormig, (-e),** ribbon-shaped; **~wand,** tyre wall; **~wewer,** tape weaver; **~wewery,** tape factory; **~wiel,** pulley; **~wipper,** tyre lever; **~yster,** hoop iron, band iron.
bang, (-, -e), afraid, frightened, timorous, henhearted, pigeon-hearted, funky, pavid, timid (disposition); anxious (days); *so ~ soos die DOOD vir,* mortally afraid of; *iem. ~ MAAK,* frighten (intimidate, bluff) someone; *'n ~e OOMBLIK,* a terrifying moment; *iem. ~ PRAAT,* intimidate someone; *~ VIR,* afraid of; *~ WORD,* become scared; **~broek,** coward, scrimshanker, poltroon, funk(y); mouse; **~erd, (-s),** coward; **~erig, (-e),** afraid; fairly frightened; nervous; skittish (horse); **~(-er)igheid, ~heid,** awe, anxiety; timidity; eeriness, fear; cowardice; terror; poltroonery, dastardliness; **~gat,** (plat), funk, coward.
Bangladesh', Bangladesh.
bang'pratery, intimidation.
bang'skyter, (plat), funk, poltroon.
baniaan', (baniane), banyan.
banier', (-e), banner, flag, standard, pennon; *die ~ HOOG hou,* keep the colours flying; *hom onder iem. se ~ SKAAR,* become a follower of someone; **~draer,** standard-bearer; **~kop,** banner headline.
ban'jo, (-'s), banjo, **~bout,** banjo bolt; **~snaar,** banjo string; **~speler,** banjo player.
bank¹, (-e), bank; bank building; *GELD in die ~ sit,* bank (deposit) money; *so VEILIG soos die ~,* as safe as the Bank of England; (w), **(ge-),** bank (money).
bank², (-e), seat; bench; settee; desk; pew (church); protrusion (sea, road); shoal; compact mass; strip (of unploughed soil); box (in court); dock (in court); ridge; shelf *(geog.); DEUR die ~,* on an average, as a rule; *~ PLOEG,* leave strips unploughed; rib; **~aambeeld,** stake-bench anvil.
bank: ~aangeleentheid, banking matter, **~amptenaar,** bank official; **~balans,** bank balance; **~beampte,** bank official; **~bedryf,** banking; banking practice; **~bestuurder,** bank manager; **~biljet,** banknote; **~boek,** pass book; **~bronne,** banking sources; **~dekking,** bank cover; **~deposito,** bank deposit; **~diskonto,** bank rate.
ban'kerig, (-e), bumpy, jolty.
banket', confectionery; confection; **(-te),** banquet; banket, auriferous conglomerate; **~bakker,** confectioner, pastrycook; **~bakkery,** confectioner's shop; **~kock,** fancy cake, fine pastry, (w), **~teer,** (ge-), banquet, feast; **~teer'der, (-s),** reveller; **~winkel,** confectioner's shop, confectioner.
ban'keveld, broken veld; scarped plane.
Ban'keveld, Bankeveld.
bank: ~fasiliteite, banking facilities; **~garansie,** bank(er's) guarantee; **~gebou,** bank building; **~gebruik,** banking custom (usage).
bank: ~geld, pew rent, pewage; **~haak,** bench claw; **~hamer,** bench hammer; fitter's hammer; **~hoogte,** seat height.
bank'houer, banker (gambling); **~huis,** bank (manager's) house.
bank'huur, (-e), pew rent(al).
ban'kie, (-s), small bench, seat; ridge (eye); *KAAL ~ ry,* be disappointed; *~ SIT,* court; *~s SPIT,* dig unploughed patches.
bankier', (-s), banker; **~saak,** banking business; **~sigwissel,** banker's sight draft; **~s'kantoor,** bank; banker's office; **~s'kommissie,** bank commission.

ban'kiespad, corrugated road.
bank'instelling, banking house.
bank'klem, bench clamp.
bank'klerk, bank clerk.
bank'klou, bench clamp.
bank: ~**kluis,** safe deposit; ~**koers,** bank rate; ~**kommissie,** bank commission; ~**krediet,** bank credit.
bank'lengte, seat length.
bank: ~**lening,** bank(er's) loan; ~**meester,** bank manager; ~**noot,** banknote; flimsy (slang); (mv) paper money, banknotes.
ban'koelneut, bankul nut, candle nut.
bank'oortrekking, overdraft.
bank'oortreksel, seat cover.
bank: ~**outomaat,** automatic teller, bank automat; ~**papier,** paper currency; ~**personeel,** bank staff; ~**referensie,** bank reference; ~**rekening,** banking account.
bank'reling, seat rail.
bank'rente, bank interest.
bankroetier', (-s), bankrupt, insolvent.
bankrot' (s) (-te), bankrupt; (b) bankrupt, insolvent, without funds; ~ *speel,* go bankrupt, go bang; ~**skap,** bankruptcy; insolvency, non-solvency, failure; ~*skap was die voorland,* bankruptcy was the order of the day, ~**speler,** bankrupt, insolvent; ~**vandisie,** ~**vendusie,** bankruptcy sale; ~**wurm,** bankrupt worm (*Trichostrongylus*).
bank: ~**sake,** banking, banking matters; ~**saldo,** bank balance.
bank: ~**skaaf,** jack plane; ~**skroef,** bench vice.
bank: ~**skuld,** overdraft; ~**staat,** bank statement.
bank'stasie, banking station (railway).
bank: ~**stelsel,** banking (pool) system; ~**tarief,** tariff of banking charges; ~**vakansiedag,** bank holiday.
bank'vas, (-te), packed, close together, massed.
bank: ~**verslag,** bank report; ~**voorskot,** bank(er's) advance (loan); ~**waardig** (-e), bankable; ~**verwysing,** bank reference; ~**wêreld,** banking world.
bank'werk, bench work; ~**er,** engine turner, fitter; bench-worker; ~**ery,** fitting shop.
bank: ~**wese,** banking; ~**wissel,** bank bill.
bank'ys, shelf-ice.
ban'neling, (-e), exile, outcast, expatriate; ~**skap,** state of exile; ~**skrywer,** expatriate author (writer).
ban'tam, bantam; ~**gewig,** bantam-weight; ~**gewigskampioen,** bantam-weight champion; ~**haantjie,** bantam cock; small cocky person; ~**hoendertjie,** bantam (fowl); ~**vliegtuig,** ultralight aeroplane, baby aeroplane.
ban'opleêr, excommunicator.
Bantoe: ~**folklore,** African folklore; ~**kunde,** African studies; ~**tale,** African languages.
bant'om, *see* **bandom.**
ban: ~**vloek,** anathema, ban; ~**vonnis,** exile order, interdiction; ~**werk,** compulsory service (work).
ba'obab, (-s), baobab, cream-of-tartar tree (*Adansonia digitata*).
Baptis', (-te), Baptist; ~**gesinde,** (-s), Baptist; ~**tekerk,** Baptist Church; ~**ties,** (-e), Baptist.
bar¹, (s) (-s), bar (unit of pressure).
bar², (b) (-re), barren; inclement; grim; gruff; *die* ~ *re winter,* the severe winter; (bw) horribly; *dit is* ~ *koud,* it is terribly cold.
barak', (-ke), barracks, hut(ment) for soldiers; (mv) cantonment; ~**keer',** (ge-), barrack; ~**kekamp,** hutments; ~**ruimte,** barrack space.
baratea', barathea.
baratteer', (ge-), commit barratry.
baratterie', barratry.
barbaar', (..bare), barbarian, savage; ~**s',** (-e), barbarous, barbarian; Gothic; ~**s'heid,** (..hede), barbarity, barbarousness; Gothicism.
barba'redom, barbarians.
barbaris'me, barbarism.
Barbary'e, Barbary.
Bar'bertonse ma'deliefie, (-s), Barberton daisy.
barbier', (-s), barber; coiffeur; friseur; ~**s'paal,** ~**stok,** barber's pole; ~**s'winkel,** barber's shop.
barbital', barbital.
barbituraat', barbiturate.

bar'bot, burbot (fish).
barcarol'le, (-s), barcarole.
bard, (-e), bard.
ba'rensnood, labour, travail.
ba'renswee, labour-pains, (birth-)throes, pangs of parturition.
baret', (-te), beret; biretta (priest's cap); barret; cap.
bargoens', jargon, gibberish, double-dutch, lingo; thieves' language.
bar'heid, inclemency; barrenness.
bariet', barytes (heavy spar); ~**aarde,** baryta.
ba'ring, (child)birth, parturition.
ba'risfeer, barysphere.
ba'riton, (-s), baritone.
ba'rium, barium (metal); ~**nitraat,** barium nitrate; ~**oksied,** ~**oksied,** baryta.
bark, (-e), barge, barque; boat.
barkaan', (..kane), barkan.
barkas', (-se), launch, long-boat.
barkentyn', (-e), barquentine, barkentine.
bark'haan, ptarmigan.
barlewiet', barley wheat.
barmhar'tig, (-e), merciful, charitable, compassionate; ~**heid,** mercy, charitableness, compassion.
barmits'wa, barmitzvah.
barn'steen, amber; ~**pyp,** amber pipe.
baro(e)', one of several plants of the genus *Cyphia*.
barograaf', (..grawe), barograph.
barogram', (-me), barogram.
barok', grotesque; baroque; ~**styl,** baroque style.
Ba'rolong, (-s), Barolong.
ba'rometer, barome'ter, (-s), barometer, rain (weather) glass; ~**huis,** barometer casing; ~**stand,** barometer reading (height).
barome'tries, (-e), barometric(al); ~*e minimum,* minimum barometric pressure.
baron', (-ne, -s), baron; ~**es',** (-se), baroness; ~**ie',** (-ë), barony.
baroskoop', (..skope), baroscope.
barotro'pies, barotropic.
barra'ge, barrage.
bar'revoets, (vero.) barefooted.
barriè're, (-s), barrier, fence, gate.
barrika'de, (-s), barricade.
barrikadeer', (ge-), barricade; bar (door).
bars¹, (s) (-te), burst, crack, cleft, cranny, fissure; flaw; sand-crack (hoof); chap (of hands); blow-out (tyre); *sy LIEG 'n* ~, she is a great (damned) liar; *hy SLAAN 'n* ~, he is a terrific hitter; (w) (ge-), burst; fly (to pieces); crack, chap (hands); disrupt; explode (shell); *JY sal* ~ (plat), you'll catch it; *my KOP wil* ~, I have a splitting headache; ~ *v.d. LAG,* split one's sides with laughter; *VEG dat dit* ~, fight like lions (mad).
bars², (-ie), (b, bw) harsh, rough; grim, forbidding (countenance); stern (look); gruff (voice); offhand, unfriendly (manner); *dit sal* ~ *GAAN,* it will be a tough job; *'n* ~ *WERK,* work like a Trojan; ~**heid,** sternness, harshness, grimness, gruffness; ~**hou,** fine shot; *hy speel 'n* ~**hou,** he is a crack player.
bars: ~**ie,** (-s), small crack (chap), *sy kop het 'n* ~*ie,* he has a screw loose; ~**lek,** blowout; ~**tend** (-e), bursting; *'n* ~*tende hoofpyn,* a splitting headache.
bars'tens: *dit het* ~ *GEGAAN,* it was a tough job; *TOT* ~ *toe,* to bursting point.
bars'terig, (-e), full of cracks; ~**heid,** state of being full of cracks.
bars'vorming, cracking (paint).
Bartholome'üsnag, massacre of St. Bartholomew.
bas¹, (-se), bass (music); bass singer.
bas², (-te), bark (tree), cortex; rind, husk (fruit); bast; body; hull; *hy hom sal jy GEEN* ~ *afmaak nie,* you wil get nothing out of him; *iem. op sy* ~ *GEE,* tan someone's hide, a tanning; *alles aan sy* ~ *HANG,* spend everything on clothes; *op jou* ~ *KRY,* be given a thrashing; come off second best; *tussen die* ~, *meer LOS as vas,* so-so.
basaal', (..sale), basal, basilar.
basaan'gans, gannet.
basaar', (-s), bazaar; ~**winkel,** bazaar (store).

bas: ~-**af,** without bark; ~**agtig, (-e),** fibrous; bark-like.
basalt', basalt; ~**blok,** block of basalt; ~**gesteente,** basalt rock; ~**glas,** byalite; ~**groewe,** basalt quarry; ~**ien',** ~**ine,** basaltine; ~**ies, (-e),** basaltic; ~**lawa,** basalt(ic) lava; ~**rots,** basalt rock; ~**suil,** basaltic pillar.
basaniet', basanite, touchstone.
bas'bariton, bass baritone.
bas: ~**boer,** wattle farmer; ~**boom,** wattle (tree); ~**broekie,** hotpants.
Ba'sedow se siek'te, Basedow's disease, goitre.
baseer', (ge-), base, ground.
Ba'sel¹, Basle, Basel, Bâle.
ba'sel², (ge-), talk nonsense, twaddle; ~**aar, (-s),** twaddler.
base'la = pasella.
bas'enting, rind grafting.
ba'serig, (-e), domineering.
ba'sie, (-s), young master; youngster, young boy.
bas'fluit, bass flute.
ba'sies, (-e), basic; ~*e RANTSOEN,* basic ration(s); ~*e SOUT,* basic salt.
basil', (-le), bacillus; ~**draer,** germ carrier.
basiliek', (-e), basi'lika, (-s), basilica.
basi'likum, basil (unguent).
basilisk', (-e), basilisk, cockatrice; ~**eier,** basilisk egg.
basil'ledraer, carrier (of disease).
basillêr', (-e), bacillary; ~*e wit diarree,* bacillary white diarrhoea.
basillo'se, bacillosis.
basil'vormig, bacilliform.
ba'sis, (-se), basis, base; foothold, grounding, *op ~ van,* on the basis of; ~**iteit,** basicity; ~**kleur,** primary colour; ~**loon,** basic pay; ~**lyn,** base-line; ~**metaal,** base (parent) metal; ~**snede,** basal section; ~**soldy,** basic pay; ~**stasie,** base-station; ~**tyd,** basic time; ~**vlak,** basal plane.
bas'jan, (-ne), blusterer, bungler.
Bask, (-e), Basque.
bas'kewer, bark beetle.
Bas'kies, (-e), Basque.
basku'le, (-s), bascule, platform scale.
bas'noot, bass note.
Basoetoponie, Basuto pony.
bas'rand, wany edge.
bas'-reliëf, bas(s)-relief.
bas'sanger, bass (singer).
bassin', (-ne), basin.
bas'sleutel, bass clef.
basson', (-s), (ong.) bassoon.
bas'stem, bass (voice).
bas'ta, (tw) enough! stop!; *en DAARMEE ~!* and that is the end of it!; *en NOU ~!* and now, that is that!; *~ NOU met jou lollery!* stop bothering me!; ~ *RAAS!* keep quiet!
bas'ter, (s) (-s), (neerh.) bastard, half-caste, half-breed; mulatto; quadroon; hybrid (animal, plant); mongrel (dog); *iem. ~ maak,* disinherit; (w) **(ge-),** hybridize; interbreed; (b) cross-bred, half-bred; (bw), rather, somewhat; *dis ~ 'n GELOL,* it is rather a nuisance; *dis ~ KOUD vandag,* it is fairly cold to-day; ~**eland,** roan antelope; ~**esel,** mule; ~**galjoen,** parrot fish; ~**geelhout,** *Podocarpus elongata;* ~**gemsbok,** roan antelope; ~**geslag,** mongrel breed, degenerate descendants; ~**grootte,** bastard size; ~**hond,** mongrel; ~**hartbees,** tsessebe; ~**hottentot,** kind of rock fish; ~**klawer,** Alsike clover; ~**koedoe,** nyala *(Tragelaphus angasie);* ~**makou,** half-bred duck; ~**mielie,** hybrid mealie (maize); ~**perdepis,** *Hippobromus alatus;* ~**ras,** hybrid breed (race); ~**saffraan,** wild tree *(Pleurostylia capensis);* ~**skaap,** cross-bred sheep; ~**skap,** bastardy; ~**soort,** hybrid (type); ~**suiker,** bastard sugar; ~**taal,** barbarism (language); lingua franca; mixed jargon; ~**vloek(woord),** disguised (mild) oath; ~**vorm,** hybrid (form); ~**vyl,** bastard file; ~**waterbok,** lechwe; ~**witysterhout,** wild tree *(Cyclostemon argutus);* ~**woord,** hybrid (word); ~**ysterhout,** forest tree *(Olea foveolata).*
bastiet', bastite.
bastion', (-s), bastion.
bastonna'de, bastinado.
basuin', (-e), trumpet, bassoon, trombone; bombardon(e); *jou eie ~ blaas,* blow one's own trumpet; ~**blaser,** trumpet-player; trombonist; ~**geluid,** sound of trumpets; ~**geskal,** trumpet blast.
bas'vesel, bast fibre.
bas'toon, bass note.
bas'viool, contrabass, bass violin; ~**speler,** bassist.
Bataaf', (..tawe), Batavian; ~**s', (-e),** Batavian; ~*se teëls,* Batavian tiles.
bataljon', (-ne, -s), battalion; ~**kommandant,** major, battalion commander.
Bata'via, Batavia; **(-se),** of Batavia.
Bata'viër, (-e), Batavian.
ba'te, assets, effects; credit; ~ *en laste,* assets and liabilities; *NATUURLIKE ~s,* natural resources; *TEN ~ van,* in aid of; ~**sy,** credit side.
ba'tig: ~*e saldo,* credit balance.
ba'tik, batik; (w) **(ge-),** batik; ~**werk,** batik (work).
batis', (s) batiste, lawn, cambric; (b) **(-te), (of)** cambric.
batiskoop', (..skope), bathyscape.
batoliet', batholite.
ba'tometer, bathometer.
ba'tos, bathos.
battery', (-e), battery; *DROË ~,* dry battery; *GALVANIESE ~,* galvanic battery; *van ~ VERANDER,* change front; ~**bord,** plotting table; ~**dek,** gun deck; ~**geskut,** battery pieces (guns); ~**grondstasie,** battery ground station; ~**houer,** battery carrier; ~**kabel,** battery cable; ~**laaier,** battery charger; ~**ontsteking,** battery ignition; ~**plate,** battery plates; ~**sel,** battery cell; ~**stukke,** ~**geskut,** battery pieces (ordnance); ~**suur,** battery acid, electrolyte; ~**toetser,** battery tester; ~**vuller,** battery filler; ~**winkel,** battery shop.
bauhi'nia, (-s), bauhinia.
bauxiet', bauxite.
bazaar', (-s), *see* **basaar.**
bdel'lium, bdellium (gem); resin; resin tree.
B'-dur, (ong.), B major.
bê, baa (sheep).
beaam', (~), assent to, approve of, corroborate; say ditto to.
bea'ming, assent, assentation, approval, corroboration.
beamp'te, (-s), employee, functionary, official, (civil) officer.
beangs', (-te), anxious, afraid, uneasy; fearful; ~**t'heid,** uneasiness, anxiety, fear.
beangs'tig, (~), cause alarm, make uneasy, frighten; ~**end,** causing alarm, frightening.
beant'woord, (~), answer, reply to; respond to (toast); return (call); reciprocate (feelings); acknowledge (greetings); pay; *aan die DOEL ~,* answer (fulfil) the purpose; *'n GROET ~,* acknowledge a greeting (salute); *LIEFDE ~,* return love; *aan die VERWAGTING ~,* come up to expectations; ~**baar, (..bare),** answerable; ~**ing,** answer, reply; reciprocity, reciprocation; acknowledg(e)ment; *ter ~ing,* in reply to; ~**ingsein,** answering signal.
bear'bei, (~), work at; cultivate, till; do religious work; minister to the spiritual needs; canvass (constituency); ~**der,** worker; ~**ding,** cultivation; elaboration; ministration; religious work; canvassing.
bea'ring, venation.
bebaard', (-e), bearded, hirsute.
beblaar', (-de), leafy, blistered (hands).
bebloed', (-de), blood-stained, bloody, covered with blood, gory.
beboet', (~), fine, penalize; amerce, mulct; *iem. met R20 ~,* fine someone R20; ~**baar, (..bare),** finable; ~**ing,** fining.
bebos', (w) (~), afforest; (b) **(-te),** wooded, ~**sing,** afforestation.
bebou', (w) (~), cultivate, till; build (up) on, construct, fill with buildings; (b) cultured; built up (area); ~**baar, (..bare),** cultivable, cultivatable, arable, tillable; ~**baarheid** cultivatability; arabil-

bebril 52 *bedieningstasie*

ity; ~**de gebied,** built-up area; ~**er,** cultivator, tiller; ~**ing,** cultivation, tillage.
bebril', (-de), spectacled.
bebroei', (-e), partly hatched (hard-set) (eggs).
bebroei'de-eiers, strawberry plant *(Abutilon venosa)*.
bebrou', (~), mess (muddle) up, spoil.
bed, (-de, -dens), bed, berth, couch; kib; layer (mines); *vroeg uit die* ~ *maak die BEURSIE vet,* early to bed and early to rise makes a man healthy, wealthy and wise; *die* ~ *van EER,* field of honour; battlefield; *kinders v.d. EERSTE* ~, children of the first marriage; *dit het my in die* ~ *GESIT,* that was too much for me; *die* ~ *HOU,* be laid up; *IN die* ~ *bly,* remain in bed; *sy moet in die* ~ *KOM,* she is an expectant mother; *laat NA* ~ *gaan,* keep late hours; *OM sy* ~, round his bed; ~ *en ONTBYT,* bed and breakfast; *'n* ~ *OORTREK,* change bedlinen; *'n* ~ *OPMAAK,* make a bed; *geen* ~ *van ROSE nie,* not a bed of roses; *iem. se* ~ *SKEND,* commit adultery; *tussen* ~ *en TAFEL skei,* separate *a mensa et thora.*
bedaag', (-de), old, aged, elderly.
bedaar', (~), quiet, tranquillize, appease; subside, fall (wind); abate (storm); drop (wind); calm down (temper), cool down (off); allay, alleviate (pain); becalm; ~**middel,** tranquillize.
bedaard', (-e), calm, easy, sedate, composed; quiet, quiescent, tranquil; dispassionate; collected, deliberate; canny; ~**heid,** composure, collectedness, evenness (of temper); deliberateness; calmness, quiescence, quiet(ness); tranquillity; deliberation; ~**weg,** calmly, dispassionately.
bedag', careful, aware, mindful; prepare; ~ *wees op,* be mindful of, be prepared for.
bedags', during the day, by day, in the daytime.
bedag'saam, (..same), thoughtful, circumspect, obliging, considerate; deliberate; ~**heid,** thoughtfulness, circumspection, considerateness, consideration; deliberateness, prudence.
bedank', (~), thank; decline (invitation); refuse (offer); resign (office); give up (post); *vir 'n BEROEP (betrekking)* ~, refuse a call (post); *HARTLIK vir iets* ~, *(iron.),* catch me doing that; *wat jy* ~, *is jy KWYT,* what one refuses, one loses; *as LID* ~, resign one's membership; *uit 'n PARTY* ~, resign membership of a party; ~**ing,** refusal; resignation; expresion of gratitude; acknowledgement; ~**ings: brief,** letter of resignation.
beda'rend, (-e), pacificatory, calming, soothing.
beda'ring, appeasement, pacification, abatement, calming down; *tot* ~ *BRING,* pacify, calm down; *tot* ~ *KOM,* become tranquil, calm down.
bed: ~**baadjie,** bed jacket; ~**bewaarder,** eunuch; chamberlain.
bed'degoed, bedding; bed-linen; bed-clothes; litter (for animals); ~**beampte,** bed-steward; ~**kaartjie,** bedding ticket.
bed'deken, blanket; counterpane.
bed'(de): ~**kussing,** pillow; ~**laken,** bed-sheet.
bed'ding, (-s), river bed, channel; flower bed, garden bed; layer, seam, stratum (matter); seat (valve); ~**rand,** (flower) bed border.
bed'dinkie, (-s), verkleinwoord van **bedding.**
be'de, (-s), prayer, petition, appeal, entreaty, request; cry; ~**dag,** day of intercession.
bedeel', (w) (~), endow with, bestow; (b) (-de), favoured; ~*d met aardse goedere,* blessed with worldly goods; ~**de,** (-s), beneficiary.
bedees', (-de), timid, bashful, coy, demure; backward; ~**d'heid,** bashfulness, timidity, shyness.
be'dehuis, place of worship.
bedek', (w) (~), cover up, bury, conceal; hide; overlie; deck; cap; cloak, mantle, coat; clothe; blanket; fleece (with down); (b) (-te), hidden, covered, euphemistic; ~*te DAGSOOM,* sub-outcrop; ~ *MET,* overlain, covered with; *OP* ~ *te wyse,* covertly; *'n* ~ *te SEËN,* a blessing in disguise; ~**bloeiend,** (-e), cryptogamic, cryptogamous; ~**king,** cover(ing), tegument; occultation (star); cope (mines); *onder* ~ *king van die nag,* under cover of night; ~**kingsweefsel,** epithelium.
be'deklok, angelus.

bedek': ~**sadig,** (-e), angiospermous; ~**sel,** cover(ing), integument; ~**telik,** indirectly; secretly, covertly.
be'del, (ge-), beg, ask alms; cadge.
be'delaar, (-s), beggar, mendicant; cadger; ~**sko: lonie,** tramps' colony; ~**slewe,** beggar's life; ~**ster,** (-s), beggarwoman.
be'delagtig, (-e), beggarly, begging.
bedelares', (-se), beggarwoman.
bedelary', beggary, begging, mendicancy, mendicity.
be'delbrief, begging letter.
be'delbroeder, mendicant (begging) friar.
bedelf', (~), bury; cover with soil.
bede'ling, dispensation; order; endowment; supply; allocation; *die ou* ~, the old dispensation.
be'del: ~**kind,** child beggar; ~**meisie,** beggar girl; ~**monnik,** mendicant friar; begging friar; dervish (Mohammedan); ~**orde,** mendicant order; ~**ry,** *see* **bedelary:** ~**-ry,** (w) (ge-), hitch-hike; ~**sak,** beggar's wallet; ~**staf,** beggar's staff; *tot die* ~ *staf bring,* reduce to beggary; ~**vrou,** beggarwoman.
bedel'we = bedelf.
beden'king, (-e, -s), consideration, reflection, remark; misgiving, doubt; objection, demur; *in* ~ *GEE,* give one something to think about; *geen* ~ *HÊ teen,* have no objection to; *in* ~ *NEEM,* take into consideration.
bedenk'lik, (-e), critical (condition); risky (venture); dangerous; serious, grievous, grave, alarming (state); doubtful (look); precarious; *'n* ~ *e verskynsel,* a grave phenomenon, a matter that must give pause; ~**heid,** criticalness, danger; seriousness, gravity, precariousness.
bedenk'sel, (-s), figment, myth; contrivance, excogitation, device, notion, conceit, invention, myth.
bedenk'tyd, time for reflection.
be'de: ~**oord,** place of worship; ~**plaas,** ~**plek,** shrine.
bederf', (s) corruption, depravity (morals), demoralization; depravation; deterioration; rot (wood); poison; decay, decomposition (meat); *AAN* ~ *onderhewig,* perishable; *tot* ~ *OORGAAN,* decay, go bad; *die* ~ *van 'n persoon WEES,* be a person's ruin; (w) (~), *see* **bederwe;** (b) (-de), rotten; blown; cankered; ~**baar,** (..bare), perishable; ~**lik,** (-e), corruptible (morals); perishable (food); ~**likheid,** corruptibility; liability to perish; ~**weermiddel,** preservative; ~**werend,** (-e), antiseptic, preservative.
beder'we, (~), spoil, cocker, pamper (child); mess up; damage, putrefy, go bad (goods); taint, vitiate, deteriorate (air); queer (chances); derange, upset (stomach); demoralize; corrupt, pervert, deprave (morals); crab, blight, ruin (one's prospects); disfeature, disfigure (beauty); adulterate; perish; flaw; *'n kind* ~, spoil a child; ~**nd,** (-e), corruptive, damaging; tainting; demoralizing; ~**r,** (-s), corrupter, seducer, spoiler.
be'devaart, pilgrimage; ~**ganger,** pilgrim; ~**soord,** ~**splek,** place of pilgrimage.
bed: ~**genoot,** (..note), bed-fellow; ~**gordyn,** bed curtain.
bedien', (~), serve, attend to (customers); wait upon (guests); groom, help; administer (last sacrament); minister (unto); operate, tend (machine, cannon); actuate; *hom* ~ *van 'n MIDDEL,* avail oneself of a means; *aan TAFEL* ~, wait at table.
bedie'naar, minister, parson.
bedien'de, (-s), menial, (serving) man, employee, servant; assistant (shop); attendant; ~**kamer,** servant's room; ~**kappie,** maid's cap.
bedie'ner, (-s), servicer, operator; attendant.
bedie'ning, service, attendance (by servants); serving (at table); function (office); (ad)ministration (sacraments); operation, attention (machines); teamwork, crew (guns); actuation; *die* ~ *neerlê,* resign the ministry.
bedie'nings: ~**as,** operating shaft; ~**geld,** service charge, tip; ~**hefboom,** control lever; ~**knop,** control (radio); ~**koste,** service charges (hotel); ~**manskappe,** artillerists: ~**middels,** controls.
bedie'ningstasie, service station.

bedien

bedien': ~ **tafel**, dinner wagon; ~ **venstertjie**, service hatch.
bedil', (~), find fault with, carp at; criticize, censure; boss; ~ **al**, (-**le**), caviller, fault-finder, busy-body; ~ **ler**, (-**s**), caviller, fault-finder; ~ **lerig**, ~ **siek**, (-**e**), faultfinding, captious; censorious; ~ **lerigheid**, ~ **sug**, faultfinding, censoriousness.
beding', (s) condition, stipulation; *BY uitdruklike* ~, by express stipulation; *MET* ~ *van boete*, with a penal stipulation; *ONDER* ~ *dat*, on condition that; (w) (~), stipulate; bargain; *tensy anders* ~, unless otherwise stated; ~ **ing**, condition, stipulation; ~ **ingsmag**, bargaining power.
bedink', (~), consider, reflect, bear in mind; contrive; fabricate, devise (plan); invent (story); change one's mind; *HOM* ~, think over, reconsider; *ek het MY* ~, I have changed my mind; *iets NUUTS* ~, devise something novel; '*n PERSOON in jou testament* ~, remember a person in one's will; ~ **tyd**, time for reflection.
bedis'sel, (~), arrange, manage (matters); ~ **ing**, arrangement.
bed: ~ **jakkie**, bed jacket; ~ **kaartjie**, bedding ticket; ~ **kassie**, bedside chest; ~ **kruik**, hotwater bottle; ~ **laken**, (bed-)sheet; ~ **lamp**, bed-lamp; **lê'end**, (-**e**), bedridden, confined to bed; ~ **lê'endheid**, confinement to one's bed; illness; ~ **lê'erig**, (-**e**), inclined to stay in bed, fond of staying in bed; bedridden, laid up.
Bedoeïen', (-**e**), Bedouin.
bedoel', (~), mean, intend, aim at, destine, drive at, purpose; *GOED* ~ *d*, well meant; *ek het dit NIE* ~ *nie*, I didn't mean it; *die* ~ *de PERSOON*, the person referred to; *ek het dit nie SO* ~ *nie*, that is not what I meant.
bedoe'ling, (-**e**, -**s**), meaning, intent(ion), plan, purport, purpose, object, intendment, implication, aim; *sonder BEPAALDE* ~, undesignedly; *met die BESTE* ~, with the best intentions; *sonder SLEGTE* ~, with no evil intent; no harm being meant.
bedol', (-**de**), mad, crazy.
bedol'we, buried; covered with soil; *onder die stof* ~, covered with dust.
bedom'pig, (-**e**), suffocating, close, stuffy; fuggy; frowzy; ~ **heid**, stuffiness, closeness, fug, frowst.
bedon'der, (-**de**), (plat), full of nonsense, daft; churlish; *jy is* ~, you are out of your mind; ~ **dheid**, cussedness.
bedon'ge, stipulated; *see* **beding**.
bedor'we, spoiled, corrupt, depraved; putrid; rotten; addled (egg); peccant; '*n* ~ *KIND*, a spoilt child; ~ *LUG*, foul air; '*n* ~ *MAAG*, an upset stomach; '*n* ~ *SMAAK*, depraved taste; ~ **nheid**, corruption, pravity, evil; depravity; badness (food).
bedot', (~), befool, trick, beguile, cozen; ~ **tery**, trickery, hanky-panky.
bedou', (w) (~), bedew; (b) (-**de**), dewy.
bed'predikasie, curtain lecture.
bedra', **bedraag'**, **bedra'e**, (~), amount to, number.
bedraad', (w) (~), wire (elect.); (b) (. . **drade**), bad-tempered; wired (elect.)
bedra'ding, wiring.
bedrag', (. . **drae**), amount, quantum; '*n* ~ *STORT*, deposit an amount; *TEN* bedrae van, to the amount of, amounting to.
bedreig', (w) (~), threaten, menace; brood; comminate; (b) (-**de**), threatened; ~ **end**, (-**e**), threatening, comminatory; ~ **er**, menacer; ~ **ing**, (-**e**, -**s**), threat, menace, commination; *DEUR* ~ *ing*, by threats; *ONDER* ~ *ing*, under threats; '*n* ~ *ing VIR*, a threat to.
bedrem'meld, (-**e**), confused, perplexed; ~ **heid**, confusion, perplexity.
bedre'we, (-**ner**, -**nste**), skilled, expert, skilful, accomplished, great; cunning; practised, proficient, experienced, versed; ~ **nheid**, skill, proficiency, efficiency; cunning; craftsmanship, expertness; ~ **nheidstoelae**, proficiency allowance.
bedrie'ë = **bedrieg**.
bedrie'ër, (-**s**), fraud, deceiver, swindler, spiv, guller, hoaxer, humbug, impostor, deluder, dodger, embezzler, cheat; four-flusher; *die* ~ *bedroë*, the biter bit; ~ **y**, (-**e**), deception, cheating, deceit, imposture, fraud, bamboozlement, humbuggery, bilking.
bedrieg', (w) (~), cheat, deceive, defraud, dupe, mislead, impose upon, take in, blind, crook, gull, bamboozle, humbug, lead up the garden path, hoodwink, jockey, juggle; betray, bilk, befool, counterfeit; circumvent; delude; diddle; double; *skyn* ~, appearances are deceptive; ~ **lik**, (-**e**), deceptive, fraudulent, deceitful, delusive, elusive, false, fallacious, guileful, imposing, illusory, illusive, double-hearted; dishonest; false-hearted; captious; ~ *like insolvensie*, fraudulent insolvency; ~ **likheid**, fraud, deceptibility, dishonesty, fallaciousness, captiousness, delusiveness, fraudulence, fraudulency, deceptiveness; ~ **ster**, (-**s**), female impostor (cheat).
bedrink', (~), fuddle, booze; *jou* ~, take a drop to many.
bedro'ë, deceived, taken in; *in sy verwagtinge* ~ *UITKOM*, his hopes were dashed.
bedroef', (w) (~), grieve, afflict, pain, lacerate, distress; *dit sal my* ~, that will grieve me; (b) (-**de**; -**der**, -**ste**), sorrowful, sad; (ag)grieved, distressed, disconsolate, heavy-hearted; afflicted; bereaved; ~ *wees oor*, grieved at; (bw) precious, awfully, frightfully; ~ *min*, precious little; ~ **d'heid**, sorrow, sadness, affliction, grief.
bedro'ëne, (-**s**), dupe, victim.
bedroe'we = **bedroef**, (w).
bedroe'wend, (-**e**), distressing, saddening, pitiable, deplorable, pitiful, sad.
bedrog', (**bedrieërye**), deceit, deception, counterfeit, delusion, circumvention, foul-dealing, fraud, ramp, cheating, dishonesty, chambering, imposture, hoax, humbug, guile; *deur LIS en* ~, by ruse and trickery; ~ *loon sy MEESTER*, the deceiver pays for his deceit; ~ *PLEEG*, practise deceit, cheat.
bedruip', (~), moisten by dripping, baste (meat); pay one's own way; *HOMSELF* ~, fend for one self; '*n saak wat HOMSELF* ~, an undertaking which pays for itself.
bedruk', (w) (~), print on; sadden, depress; (b) (-**te**), printed; oppressed, dejected, downhearted; clouded (face); glum; ~ **t'heid**, depression, dejectedness, dejection, dumps.
bedrup'pel, (~), besprinkle.
bed'rusbank, bed sofa.
bedryf', (s) (..**drywe**), (branch of) industry; (line of) business, calling, profession, trade; works; doing(s); act (of play); *buite* ~ *STEL*, put out of commission; *in* ~ *STEL*, set in motion; '*n* ~ *UITOEFEN*, follow a calling, practise a trade; (w) *see* **bedrywe**.
bedryfs': ~ **administrasie**, business administration; ~ **bates**, current assets; ~ **belasting**, trade tax; ~ **bemanning**, operating crew; ~ **benodigdhede**, trading goods (stores); ~ **beperking**, trading restriction(s); ~ **dockindes**, trade (business) purposes; ~ **drukte**, briskness of trade; ~ **eenheid**, business unit.
bedryf'seker, reliable, foolproof (machine).
bedryfs': ~ **ekonomie**, business economics; ~ **ervaring**, business experience; ~ **groep**, group of trades; ~ **hoof**, head of business.
bedryf'siekte, occupational disease.
bedryfs': ~ **ingenieur**, works engineer; efficiency expert; ~ **inkomste**, trade income; ~ **inrigting**, operating (business) plant; ~ **installasie**, working plant; ~ **jaar**, business year; ~ **kapitaal**, working capital; ~ **klaar**, in working order; ~ **kollege**, business college; ~ **koste**, working expenses; running costs; ~ **laste**, current liabilities; ~ **leer**, business management; ~ **leier**, works manager; ~ **materiaal**, working stock; ~ **moeilikhede**, trade difficulties; ~ **omvang**, extent of trade; ~ **ontvangste**, trading receipts (income); ~ **organisasie**, trade organization; ~ **personeel**, operating staff; ~ **plan**, working plan; ~ **raad**, industrial council; ~ **rekening**, trade account; ~ **risiko**, trade risk.
bedryf'steuring, (industrial) break-down.
bedryfs': ~ **toestande**, working conditions; ~ **uitrus**

ting, plant; ~**verhoudinge**, industrial relations, labour relations; ~**verlies**, operating loss; ~**vrede**, industrial peace; ~**voorskrifte**, service instructions; ~**wese**, trade; industry; ~**wins**, working profit.

bedry'we, (~), commit, perpetrate; *ROU* ~, mourn; *VREUGDE* ~, rejoice; *bedrywende VORM,* active voice; ~**r, (-s),** doer, perpetrator.

bedry'wig, (b) (-e), active, busy, humming, bustling; (bw) busily; ~**hede**, goings-on; ~**heid**, activity, stir, bustle; engagement.

bed: ~**sermoen**, curtain lecture; ~**sitkamer**, bed-sitting-room; bed-sitter; ~**skroef**, coach-screw; ~**sprei**, bed-spread; ~**stut**, bed-rest; ~**styl**, bed post; ~**tafel**, bedside table; ~**toegaantyd**, bedtime, ~**tyd**, bedtime.

bedug', afraid, apprehensive; ~ *vir*, apprehensive of (trouble); apprehensive for (his freedom); ~**t'heid**, fear, apprehension, dread.

bedui'dend, significant, appreciable.

bedui'denis, meaning, signification; sign, token.

bedui'(e), (~), signify, mean, imply, portend, give to understand; point out, indicate; direct to (a place); gesticulate; *iem. die pad* ~, point out the road to someone.

bedui'ery, pointing out, directing; gesticulation.

bedui'mel, (w) (~), thumb; finger; (b) **(-de),** thumbed, soiled; *'n* ~ *de boek,* a thumbed book.

bedui'wel, (~), make crazy; spoil, bungle; *hy het die hele saak* ~, he has bungled (spoiled) the whole affair; ~**d, (-e),** possessed by an evil spirit; churlish, daft; ~**dheid**, craziness; ~**ing**, bedevilment.

bed: ~**veer**, bed-spring; ~**verpleging**, nursing in bed; ~**verwarmer**, bed-warmer; hot-water bottle; ~**vriend(in)**, husband (wife); ~**waarts**, to bed.

bedwang', control, repression, restraint, controlment, curb, subjection, coercion; *HOM in* ~ *hou*, control oneself; *IN* ~ *hou*, keep under control.

bed'watering, bedwetting, incontinence (of urine), enuresis.

bedwelm,' (w) (~), stun, stupefy (with liquor or blow); render insensible; drug, intoxicate; (b) **(-de),** benumbed, stunned, intoxicated, stupefied, giddy; ~**end, (-e),** intoxicating, stunning; ~ *ende middels,* narcotics, drugs; ~**ing**, stunned state; stupefaction, daze, intoxication, coma; ~**middel**, drug.

bed'wieg, bed cradle.

bedwing', (~), curb, check; quell (mutiny); reduce, suppress (desires), hold in check; govern; restrain (passions); control (fire); coerce; refrain, keep down (under); *hy kon hom NIE* ~ *nie,* he could not restrain himself, he could not control his temper; *'n OPROER* ~, quell a rebellion; ~**baar, (..bare),** restrainable, controllable, repressible; ~**baarheid**, restrainability, repressibility; ~**er**, coercer, suppressor; restrainer; controller.

bedwon'ge, restrained, subdued.

beë'dig, (w) (~), swear to, attest, objure, confirm with oath, put upon oath; make a person take the oath; (b) **(-de),** sworn; ~ *de VERKLARING,* sworn statement; affidavit; ~ *de VERTALER,* sworn translator; ~ *WAARDEERDER,* sworn appraiser; ~**er, (-s),** attestor; ~**ing**, swearing-in; confirmation with an oath, attestation; putting on oath (of witnesses).

beef, (ge-), tremble (with fear), cower; flutter (heart); shiver (with cold); shudder (with horror); quake, dither, quiver; dodder; *ek* ~ *by die GEDAGTE,* I tremble at the thought; ~ *soos 'n RIET,* tremble like an aspen-leaf; *bewende van WOEDE,* trembling with rage.

beef'aal, (ong.) electric eel, gymnotus.

beëindig, (~), finish off, make an end to, terminate; ~**ing**, finishing, conclusion, (de)termination.

beek, (beke), (ong.) brook, rill, rivulet.

beeld, (s) (-e), image, likeness, picture, portrait; reflection; idol, statue, figure(head); figure of speech; metaphor; effigy; icon; notion, idea; ~ *na BUITE,* public image; *'n DUIDELIKE* ~ *van die toestand,* a clear picture of the circumstances; *'n* ~ *van 'n MEISIE,* a perfect beauty, a picture of a girl; *SUID-AFRIKA se* ~ *in die buiteland,* South Africa's image overseas; *VOORSTELLINGS in* ~, pictorial representations; *'n* ~ *VORM van,* picture to oneself, realize; (w) **(ge-),** portray, depict; form, make a likeness of; *die* ~ *ende KUNSTE,* the plastic arts; ~**beskrywing**, iconography; ~**bouing**, image building; ~**eaanbidder**, ~**edienaar**, image worshipper; iconolater; ~**ediens**, idolatry, image worship, iconolatry; ~**egalery**, statue gallery; ~**egroep**, statuary; ~**enaar, (-s),** effigy, head (on coin); ~**end, (-e),** plastic (art); expressive; formative; figurative; ~**erig, (-e),** beautiful, lovely, sweet; ~**estorm**, iconoclasm, image-breaking; ~**estormer**, iconoclast; ~**estormery**, iconomachy; ~**everering**, image worship; idolatry; ~**gieter**, founder of statues; ~**gietery**, statue foundry.

beeld'hou, (ge-), sculpture, carve, chisel; ~**er, (-s),** sculptor; ~**eres, (-se),** sculptress; ~**ershamer**, bush hammer; ~**ery**, statuary workshop; sculpture; ~**kuns**, sculpture; ~**ster, (-s),** sculptress; ~**werk**, sculpture; work of sculpture; carving.

beeld: ~**ig, (-e),** beautiful; picturesque; ~**ing**, portrayal; ~**jie, (-s),** image, statuette, figurine; ~**mooi**, pretty, beauteous; ~**radio**, television; ~**ryk, (-e),** figurative, imaginative, ornate, flowery (style); ~**rykheid**, imagery, ornateness; ~**send, (ge-),** (ong.) radio (pictures); televize; ~**sending**, (ong.) telecast; ~**skerpte**, sharpness, clearness, definition (of picture); ~**skoon, (..skone),** beautiful as a picture; ~**skrif**, picture writing, pictograph(y); hieroglyphics; ~**snyer**, figure carver; ~**snykuns**, (art of) image carving; ~**snywerk**, figure carving; ~**soeker**, viewer, view-finder (camera); ~**spraak**, figure of speech; figurative (metaphorical) language; metaphor; tropology; imagery; ~**storm**, iconoclasm; iconoclastic riots; ~**stormend, (-e),** iconoclastic; ~**stormer**, iconoclast; ~**versiering**, polychromy; ~**vorming**, image forming (building); ~**werk**, imagery, statuary, sculpture, intaglio.

Beël'sebub, Beël'sebul, Beelzebub.

beel'tenis, (-se), image, portrait, likeness, effigy; *iem. in* ~ *verbrand,* burn someone in effigy.

been, (bene, beendere), bone; **(bene),** leg; limb; *'n AF= GELEKTE* ~, a flirt; widow(er); *die bene onder die ARMS neem,* take to flight; *met die verkeerde* ~ *uit die BED klim,* get out of bed on the wrong side; *op die* ~ *BLY,* keep on one's feet; *sy* ~ *BREEK oor 'n nooi,* be in love with a girl; *op die* ~ *BRING,* raise; set up; *sy bene DRA,* take to one's heels; *met die een* ~ *in die GRAF staan,* have one foot in the grave; *vir iem. 'n* ~ *GOOI,* tip someone the wink; *met albei bene op die GROND staan,* stand on one's feet; *iem. op die* ~ *HELP,* set someone on his legs again; *op die* ~ *HOU,* keep going; *onder op die* ~ *KOM,* recover one's legs again; *harde bene KOU,* suffer hardships; *ou bene KOU,* rake up unpleasant bygones; *bene KRY,* to have sprouted wings; *op sy LAASTE bene loop,* he is on his last legs; *sy bene is LAM,* he can't stand up straight; *bene in die LUG lê,* lie flat on one's back; *hy sal nie ou bene MAAK nie,* he will not make old bones; *die hele dorp is OP die* ~, the whole town is astir; *iem. op een* ~ *tjie laat SPRING,* give someone a spanking; *nie op een* ~ *kan STAAN nie,* be intoxicated (drunk); ~ *van ons* ~ *VLEES van ons vlees,* bone of our bone and flesh of our flesh; *VROEG op die* ~ *wees,* be about (up) early; *sterk bene kan alleen die WEELDE dra,* much wealth makes wits waver; *op die* ~ *WEES,* be on one's feet all the time; ~**aarde**, bone earth; ~**-af**, with a broken leg; in love; ~**-af raak oor 'n nooi**, fall in love with a girl; ~**agtig, (-e),** bony, osseous; ~**as**, bone ash; ~**band**, puttee; ~**bank**, bone bank; ~**bankie**, leg-rest; ~**bederf**, caries, necrosis; ~**bek**, (gew.) cock; ~**beskermer**, shinguard; ~**beskrywer**, osteographer, osteologist; ~**beskrywing**, osteography; ~**bevattend, (-e),** ossivorous; ~**boeie**, leg irons; ~**boor**, bone drill; ~**brand**, caries; ~**breker**, ossifrage, osprey (fishhawk); ~**breuk**, fracture of the leg; ~**dere-urn**, bone urn, ossuary; ~**dergrot**, ossuary; ~**derhuis**, charnel-house; ~**dokter**, osteopath, orthopaedic surgeon; ~**droog, (..droë),** bone-dry; ~**dryfkrag**, arm drive; ~**etend, (-e),** ossivorous; ~**etter**, caries, necrosis; ~**ettering**, caries, necrosis; ~**geswel**, swelling of leg; ~**greep**, leghold; ~**holte**, bone cavity; antrum; ~**honger**, osteophagia; ~**kanker**, osteosarcoma; ~**kant**, (ong.) leg-side; on side (cricket); ~**knoop**, bone button; ~**kouery**, osteopagy; ~**kunde**, ~**leer**, osteology; ~**loos**, (..lose), boneless; legless; ~**lym**, gluten, bone glue; ~**malery**, bone milling; ~**meel**, bone meal; frame meal; ~**meul(e)**, bone mill; ~**mis**, bone manure; ~**murgontsteking**, osteomyelitis; ~**naat**, suture; ~**ontsteking**, ostitis; ~**ontwikkeling**, osteogenesis; ~**oud**, (..oue), very old; ancient; ~**paaltjie**, (ong.) leg-wicket; ~**plaat**, jamb; greaves; ~**pyp**, leg bone; ~**ruimte**, leg room; ~**saag**, bonesaw; ~**skerms**, leg guards; ~**skurfte**, malanders; ~**skut**, leg pad; ~**spalker**, bone-setter; ~**spat**, bone spavin; ~**splinter**, bone splinter; ~**stelsel**, skeleton, osseous system; ~**suur**, phosphoric acid; ~**swart**, bone-black, ivory-black, velvet-black; bone-charcoal; ~**sweer**, ulcerated leg; ~**tering**, caries, necrosis.

been'tjie, (-s), little leg; small bone; ossicle, osselet; *die BESTE* ~ *voorsit*, put the best foot forward; *KORT* ~, double (crochet); *LANG* ~, treble (crochet); *iem. op een* ~ *laat SPRING*, give someone a hiding; ~**passer**, inside and outside caliper.

been: ~**uitwas**, bony excrescence; ~**verharding**, osteosclerosis; ~**versagting**, osteosarcoma; ~**vertoning**, leg parade; ~**vlies**, periosteum; ~**vliesontsteking**, periostitis; ~**vorming**, bone-formation, ossification, osteogenesis; ~**vreter**, caries, necrosis; ~**weefsel**, osseous tissue, bony tissue, ossein; ~**windsel**, puttee; ~**ysters**, leg irons (for cripples; for criminals).

beer, (**bere**), bear; boar (pig); mole, pier, weir (in stream); buttress, counterfort (wall-support); *die GROOT B*~, the Great Bear; *die KLEIN B*~, the Lesser Bear; *'n ONGELEKTE* ~, unlicked cub; *die* ~ *se VEL verkoop voordat hy geskiet is*, count one's chickens before they are hatched.

beërf', **beër'we**, (~), inherit.

beer: ~**klou**, bear's foot; acanthus; ~**mus**, (-se), muff-cap; ~**put**, cesspool; ~**tjie**, (-s), little bear; little boar; teddy bear; ~**vel**, bearskin.

beër'we, (~) = **beërf**.

beer'wyfie, she-bear, female bear.

bees, (-te), beast; neat, bovine (animal); (mv) cattle; brute, bugger; *die* ~ *te het in die BRAND geloop*, we have run out of milk; the milk has a bad taste (a taste of burning); *jou soos 'n* ~ *GEDRA*, behave like a brute; *JOU* ~, you brute! *geen* ~ *KOOP voor jy hom gesien het nie*, never buy a pig in a poke; *'n* ~ *van 'n KROKODIL*, a giant crocodile; *ou* ~ *te OPGRAWE*, rake up the past; *OU* ~, splendid! stout fellow! *'n* ~ *van 'n VENT*, a brute of a fellow; ~**ag'tig(-e)**, brutal, bestial, beastly, feral, ferine; ~**ag'tigheid**, bestiality, beastliness, brutality; ~**bak**, big, enormous; *'n* ~ *bak van 'n woning*, a very big dwelling; ~**boer**, cattle farmer; rancher; ~**boerdery**, cattle farming; ranching; ~**byter**, mamba snake; ~**filet**, fillet of beef; ~**gal**, ox gall; ~**ga'sie**, (-s), monster; ~**gras**, course grass *(Aristida)*; ~**haas**, fillet of beef; ~**harslag**, ox pluck; ~**hart**, ox heart; ~**ka'sie** = **beesgasie**; ~**klits**, weed *(Xanthium strumarium)*; ~**klou**, leg of ox; ox plant *(Eriospermum cernuum)*; ~**kool**, kale; ~**koper**, cattle dealer; drover; ~**kraal**, cattle kraal (fold, pen); ~**leer**, neat's leather; ~**lende**, sirloin (of beef); ~**lenderol**, rolled sirloin of beef; ~**mark**, cattle market; ~**mis**, cow dung; ~**nier**, ox kidney; ~**pens**, ox tripe; ~**plaas**, cattle ranch; ~**poot**, cow heel, neat's foot; ~**ras**, breed of cattle; ~**stal**, cowshed; cattle stable; ~**stapel**, stock (cattle); ~**stert**, oxtail; ~**stertsop**, oxtail soup; ~**stroop**, treacle (cattle lick), molasses; ~**sult**, brawn; ~**swart** = **besoar**.

bees'telik, (-e), beastly; ~**heid**, beastliness, brutishness.

bees'teteelt, cattle breeding.

bees'tong, neat's tongue, ox-tongue.

bees'vel, oxhide; ~ *GOOI*, toss in a blanket; ~ *RY*, throw into the air with an oxhide (punishment); ~**skild**, oxhide shield.

bees: ~**vet**, suet; ~**vleis**, beef; ~**vleisolywe**, beef olives; ~**vleisrol**, beef roll; ~**vlieg**, warble fly; ~**voer**, cattle fodder; ~**wagter**, cattle-herd, neat-herd; ~**wêreld**, cattle country; ~**wors**, beef sausage.

beet¹, (**bete**), beetroot.

beet², (**bete**), bite, hold, grip.

beet'gryp, (-ge-), seize, lay hold of.

beet'hê, (-gehad), have hold of; cheat, deceive; *iets aan die verkeerde ent* ~, get hold of the wrong end of the stick.

beet'kry, (-ge-), get hold of; seize, grasp, grip.

beet'lowwe, beet tops.

beet'neem, (-ge-), get hold of, seize; deceive, cheat, delude, bamboozle.

beet'nemery, imposture; deception.

beet'pak, (-ge-), grab, get hold (of); grip, clasp, clutch; tackle.

beet'slaai, beet(root) salad.

beet'spinasie, spinach beet; Swiss chard.

beet'suiker, beet sugar; ~**nywerheid**, beet-sugar industry.

beet'vat, (-ge-), seize, grab.

beet'wortel, beetroot; ~**suiker**, beet(root) sugar.

bef, (-fe, bewwe), bands (of a person); bib (child's); chemisette, front (lady's).

befaamd', (-e), notorious; famous; well-known; ~**heid**, fame, renown, notoriety.

bef'fie, (-s), small bib.

befie'del, (-de), (geselst.) full of nonsense; draft; whimsical.

befloers', (w) (~), muffle; (b) (-te), muffled, *met* ~ *te trom*, with muffled drum.

befoe'ter, (~), spoil, make a mess of; bedevil; ~**d**, (-e), full of nonsense, perverse, cantankerous, churlish, daft, troublesome; spoilt; *moenie jou so* ~ *d hou nie*, don't be so damn foolish; ~**d'heid**, craziness, perversity, cussedness.

begaaf', (-de), talented, gifted; (well-)favoured; ~**d'heid**, talent, ability, accomplishment, gift(edness).

begaan', (s) perpetration; (w) (~), commit, make, perpetrate; treat, walk on; *'n FOUT* ~, make a mistake; *LAAT hom maar* ~, let him have his way, leave him alone; ~ *WEES oor*, be concerned about; (b) (..gane), beaten, trodden; upset, worried; enthusiastic; *weer op begane GROND wees*, be on firm ground once again; *die begane PAD*, the beaten track; ~ *oor die UITSLAG*, worried about the result; ~**baar**, (..bare), passable (road); practicable; commitable (blunder); ~**baarheid**, passability; ~**heid**, anxiety, concern.

begaap', (~), gape at, gaze at.

begas', (w) (~), (contaminate with) gas; (b) (-te), gassed; ~**sing**, gassing.

begeef', (~), abandon, forsake, fail (courage); repair to, betake oneself to; resort to, proceed to; *jou in GEVAAR* ~, expose oneself to danger; *jou in die HUWELIK* ~, get married; *sy KRAG* ~ *hom*, his strength fails him; *die MOED* ~ *hom*, he loses heart, his courage fails him; *jou ter RUSTE* ~, (plegt.) go to bed; *jou na die STAD* ~, go to the city; *WAARIN het ek my* ~, what have I let myself in for?

begeer', (~), desire, wish for, want, covet, set one's heart on; aspire to; *al wat 'n mens se hart maar kan* ~, everything one could wish for; ~**baar** (..bare), desirable; ~**der**, cherisher; ~**lik**, (-e), desirable; tempting, enticing, greedy, eager; covetous; ~**likheid**, desirability; cupidity; ~**te**, (-s), desire, wish, pleasure; greed, hankering, avidity; anxiety; ~**tedoop**, baptism of desire.

begees'ter, (~), inspire, fill with enthusiasm; ~**ing**, inspiration, enthusiasm.

begelei', (~), accompany (on piano); chaperon, gallant (lady), escort (home); convoy; ~**dend**, (-e), accompanying, covering (letter), appendant; ~**ende minerale**, associated minerals; ~**er**, (-s), companion, attendant, accompanist (on piano); ~**ding**, accompaniment; escort; ~**dingsflens**, companion flange; ~**d'ster**, (-s), accompanist (female); chaperon; female companion.

begena'dig, (w) (~), forgive, pardon, reprieve; *'n mis=*

begerig 56 **behaag**

dadiger ~, reprieve a criminal; (b) **(-de)**, reprieved, pardoned; *'n ~ de kunstenaar*, artist by the grace of God; gifted artist; ~**ing**, pardon, reprieve, amnesty.

bege'rig, (-e), desirous, covetous, anxious, eager, keen; greedy, esurient, devouring, appetent, avid, acquisitive; ~ *na GELD*, keen on money; ~*om te WEET*, anxious to know; ~**heid**, eagerness, covetousness, avidity, cupidity, greed(iness).

bege'we, (~), = **begeef**.

begiet', (~), water, sprinkle, perfuse, douse; ~**ing**, watering, sprinkling, affusion, perfusion.

begif'tig, (~), endow, present, dower, donate; confer upon; ~ *met*, endow with; ~**de, (-s)**, donatory, presentee, donee; ~**er, (-s)**, donor, endower; ~**ing**, endowment, donation, dotation; ~**ingspolis**, endowment (insurance) policy.

begin', (s), beginning, origin, prime (of life), prelude, commencement, outset, start, onset, first opening, go-off, forepart, inception; *AL in die ~*, from the outset; *v.d.* ~ *tot die END*, from beginning to end, from first to last; *waar 'n ~ is, is 'n END*, every beginning has an end; *betyds* ~ *is 'n goeie GEWEER*, well begun is half done; *'n GOEIE ~ sit voordeel in*, a good beginning is half the battle; *'n GOEIE ~ is halfpad gewin*, well begun is half done: *in die ~*, in the beginning, at the outset; *dit is maar 'n ~*, it is but a beginning; *'n ~ MAAK*, make a start; *'n mens MOET by die ~*, one must start at the beginning; *VAN DIE ~ af*, from the start (beginning); (w) **(~), begin'ne, begint'**, begin, commence, start; originate; initiate; ~ *BY*, begin at; *KLEIN ~, aanhou win*, perseverance wins from small beginnings; *met hom kan jy NIKS ~ nie*, you can't do anything with him (he is useless); *OM te ~*, to start with; as a beginning; *van VOOR af ~*, start afresh; start at the beginning; ~**datum**, date of commencement; entry date; ~**druk**, initial pressure; ~**gebrek**, incipient flaw; ~**kapitaal**, initial capital; ~**kraak**, incipient flaw; ~**leerlingeskader**, ab initio training squadron; ~ **letter**, initial (letter); ~**neling, (-e)**, beginner, novice, acolyte, neophyte, amateur; ~**nend, (-e)**, inchoate; ~**ner, (s), beginner**, novice, amateur, rabbit (tennis, gholf); ~**noot**, (..**note**), first note; ~**opleiding**, ab initio training; ~**paal**, starting post; ~**produksie**, flush production; ~**punt**, starting point; ~**reël**, first line, opening line; ~**salaris**, initial salary.

begin'sel (-s), principle, element, rudiment (chemistry); plank (politics); beginning; *die EERSTE ~ s van 'n vak*, the rudiments (elements) of a subject; *IN ~*, in principle; *UIT ~*, on principle; ~**kwessie**, matter of principle; ~**loos, (..lose)**, unprincipled, without principle; ~**loosheid**, lack of principles; ~**vas, (-te)**, of firm principles; principled; ~**vastheid**, firmness of principle; backbone; ~**verklaring**, statement of principles; ~**versaking**, abandonment of principles.

begin': ~**sillabe**, first syllable; ~**skop**, kick-off; ~**snelheid**, initial velocity; ~**stadium**, initial stage; ~**traktement**, initial salary; ~**voorraad**, initial stock.

beglans', (~), illuminate, light up.

begloor', (~), (ong.) illuminate, shine on.

begluur', (~), ogle, eye; pry upon, spy upon; ~**der**, peeper, ogler.

bego'gel, (~), bewitch, throw a spell upon; hallucinate; deceive, delude; ~**ing, begoëling**, bewitchment, spell; glamour, charm, delusion, illusion.

bego'nia, (-s), begonia.

begon'ne, begun; *goed ~, half gewonne*, well begun, half done.

begraaf', *see* **begrawe;** ~**plaas,** ~**plek**, cemetery, graveyard, burial ground, necropolis.

begraf'nis, (-se), burial, funeral (obsequies), interment, entombment; *vir sy eie ~ te LAAT wees; te STADIG vir sy eie ~ wees*, be too late for his own funeral; be too slow to catch a snail; ~**dag**, day of burial; burial day; ~**diens**, burial service (office); ~**fonds**, burial fund; ~**formulier**, office of the dead; ~**koste**, funeral expenses; ~**lys**, list of people present at the funeral; ~**maaltyd**, funeral feast; funeral dinner; ~**ondernemer**, undertaker; ~**onderneming**, undertaker; ~**onkoste**, funeral expenses; ~**pas**, slow (funeral) march; ~**plegtigheid**, funeral ceremony; exequies; ~**rys**, rice with turmeric (and raisins); yellow rice; ~**stoet**, cortege, funeral procession; ~**vereniging**, burial society.

begra'we, (w) (~), bury, entomb, earth, inter; (b) buried; low-laid; *hom LEWENDIG in 'n ou dorpie ~*, bury oneself alive in a little village; ~ *ONDER WERK*, inundated with work; *die VERLEDE ~*, bury the past; *dood en ~ WEES*, be dead and buried.

begra'wing, burial, entombment.

begrens', (w) (~), limit, bound; border; confine; define; (b) **(-de)**, limited, confined; definite, mensurable, circumscribed; finite; ~**baar, (..bare)**, limitable; ~**d'heid**, limitedness, circumscription; ~**ing**, limitation; abutment; bounds.

begre'pe, understood; included; ~?, is that understood?

begrip', (-pe), idea, notion; grasp; insight, conception; (ap)prehension; intelligence; concept; *binne die ~ BRING*, bring within the comprehension; *nie die FLOUSTE ~ nie*, not the faintest notion; *dit GAAN MY ~ te bowe*, it passes my understanding; *'n GOEIE ~ het maar 'n halwe woord nodig*, a word to the wise is enough; *'n ~ KRY*, gain some understanding; *SWAAR van ~ wees*, be slow on the uptake; ~ *TOON*, show understanding; *TRAAG van ~*, slow of comprehension; *'n diep ~ VERRAAI*, reveal a profound insight (comprehension); *VLUG van ~*, quick of apprehension; intelligent; *'n ~ van iets VORM*, form an idea of something.

begrips': ~**vermoë**, faculty of comprehension; intelligence; ~**verwarring**, confusion of concepts, mental confusion; ~**werkwoord**, notional verb; ~**woord**, abstract noun, notional word.

begrip'skrif, ideography.

begrip'teken, ideogram, ideograph.

begroei', (~), overgrow; (b) **(-de)**, overgrown.

begroet', (~), greet, welcome, hail, salute; *met APPLOUS ~*, greet with applause; *hom as REDDER van sy land ~*, acclaim him as saviour of his country; *met VREUGDE ~*, greet with joy; ~**ing**, salutation, greeting, accosting.

begroot', (~), estimate, compute, budget; ~ *op, (vir)*, budget for.

begro'ting, (-s), estimate, approximation; budget.

begro'tings: ~**debat**, debate on the budget; budget debate; ~**jaar**, financial year; **B**~**komitee**, Select Committee on the Budget; ~**oorskot**, budget surplus; ~**pos**, budget item; ~**raming**, estimates on the budget; ~**rede**, budget speech; ~**tekort**, budget deficit; ~**voorstel**, budget proposal; ~**wet**, appropriation act.

begryp', (~), understand, conceive, apprehend, comprehend, perceive, get, grasp (with the mind); compass; ~ *IN*, contained in (maths.); ~ *jou AAN!* ~ *JOU!*, just imagine! ~ *JY my?*, do you understand what I am saying? *om alles te ~, is om alles te VERGEWE*, to understand all is to forgive all; ~**baar**, graspable; ~**er, (-s)**, one who understand; *'n goeie ~er het maar 'n halwe woord nodig*, a word to the wise is enough; ~**lik, (-e)**, understandable, apprehensible, fathomable, perceivable, intelligible, conceivable, comprehensible; *dis ~lik*, it is easy to understand; ~**likerwys(e)**, obviously, evidently; ~**likheid**, comprehensibility, intelligibility.

begun'stig, (~), favour, patronize; befriend; countenance (resistance); ~**de, (-s)**, allottee; beneficiary (policy); (con)cessionaire; *mees ~de NASIE*, most favoured nation (trade relations); ~*de VERWERING*, differential weathering; ~**er, (-s)**, protector, patron; furtherer; ~**ing**, favour, protection; patronage; differentiation, favouritism, preferential treatment, nepotism; *onder ~ing van*, favoured by.

begyn', (-e), begyn'tjie, (-s), (ong.) lay sister not bound by vows, beguine; ~**hof**, beguinage.

behaag', (~), please, delight; *dit het die ALMAGTIGE ~ om*, the Almighty has been pleased to; *BELOFTES om die kiesers te ~*, promises to

behaal   57   **beitel**

please the voters; ~**lik**, **(-e)**, pleasant, agreeable, cosy, comfortable, comfy; ~**likheid**, pleasantness; ~**siek**, **(-e)**, over-anxious to please; coquet(tish); ~**sug**, coquetry, flirtation.

behaal', (~), obtain (degree); achieve; get, win (prize); gain (one's desires); score (points); fetch (good prices).

behaar(d)', **(-de)**, hairy, hirsute; ~**d'heid**, hairiness.

beha'e, delight, pleasure, liking; ~ *skep in*, find pleasure in, take delight in.

beha'ling, obtaining, acquiring, acquisition.

behal'we, except, save, beside(s), but; in addition to; *hy het alles* ~ *GELD*, he has everything except money; ~ *hierdie NADELE is daar nog ander*, besides these disadvantages there are still others; ~ *my was daar drie PERSONE*, in addition to me there were three persons; ~ *die lang TOESPRAAK was alles interessant*, except for the long speech, everything was interesting.

behan'del, (~), treat; handle (correspondence); manipulate; manage (affairs); tend, attend on (sick person); treat, deal with (subject); ~**aar**, manipulator; ~**ing**, treatment, manipulation, handling; attendance (on patient); discussion (bill); hearing (court case); *die saak is in* ~ *ing*, the matter is being dealt with.

behang', (s) papering; hanging(s); arras; furniture; (w) (~), paper, cover; adorn; dress up; (b) overhung; *met sierade* ~, adorned with trinkets; ~**er**, **(-s)**, paperhanger; ~**ery**, paper-hanging.

behang'sel, (wall)paper, paper, hangings; drapery; ~**papier**, wallpaper.

beha'ring, hairiness, pilosity.

behar'tig, (~), have at heart, take care of, further (someone's interests); manage (affairs); ~**enswaar'dig**, **(-e)**, worthy of consideration; ~**ing**, care, furthering, promotion (interests); management (affairs).

beheer', (s) management, direction, administration; husbandry, governance, control; dispensation; rule; *die* ~ *HÊ oor iets*, have control of something; *ONDER* ~ *van*, under the control (administration) of; *RAAD van* ~, board of control; ~ *VERLOOR*, lose control; (w) (~), manage, administer, handle, govern, control; *'n beherende LIGGAAM*, a board of control; *die STAAT* ~ *die spoorweë*, the state administers the railways; ~**baar**, (..**bare**), manageable, controllable, manoeuvrable; commandable; ~**der**, **(-s)**, manager, director; curator (estate); operator; ruler; ~ *der van 'n fonds*, administrator of a fund; ~**knop**, control knob; ~**middels**, controls; ~**raad**, governing body.

beheers', (w) (~), rule, govern, manage (country); command (passions); dominate (man); possess, lord it over (someone); control (oneself), contain (anger); keep in hand; be master (of a language); *jou DRIFTE* ~, control your passions; *'n vreemde TAAL volkome* ~, be master of a foreign language; (b) **(-te)**, controlled, restrained; *met* ~ *te stem*, with restrained voice; ~**er**, **(-s)**, ruler, dominator; ~**eres'**, **(-se)**, curatrix; ~**ing**, command, rule, government, possession, sway, control.

beheer'skakel, control.

beheers'onkoste, administrative expenses.

beheer'stasie, control station.

beheerst'heid, control; mastery.

beheks' (w) (~), bewitch; (b) **(-te)**, hag-ridden; ~**ing**, bewitching; ~**t'heid**, bewitchment.

behelp', (~), make shift, resort to, manage in a way; *ek moet my met min* ~, I must manage with very little.

behels', (~), contain, embrace, purport, imply, incorporate; *die kontrak* ~ *dat*, the contract contains...

behen'dig, **(-e)**, dexterous, deft, crafty, cunning, adroit, able, skilful; handy; clever; ~**heid**, dexterity, skill, handiness, knack; sleight, sleight of hand, cunning; diplomacy; feat; ~**heidstoets**, test of skill.

behep': ~ *WEES met*, be possessed with; *met voordele* ~ *WEES*, possessed by prejudices.

behoed', (~), preserve, guard, protect; *GOD* ~ *e die koningin*, God save the Queen; *iem. VIR (van) gevaar* ~, protect someone from danger; ~**er**, **(-s)**, preserver, protector; ~**ing**, prophylaxis; ~**middel**, periapt, prophylactic.

behoed'saam, (..**same**), (pre)cautious, circumspect, circumspective, prudent, wary; ~**heid**, cautiousness, carefulness, prudence, wariness.

behoed'ster, **(-s)**, protectress.

behoef', (~), want, need, require; *jy* ~ *nie te gaan nie*, (ong.) you need not go.

behoef'te, **(-s)**, want, need, poverty, necessity; demand; *jou* ~ *doen*, (ong.) go to stool; ~ *HÊ aan*, be in want of; *in* ~ *s VOORSIEN*, satisfy wants; ~**peil**, bread-line, poverty margin.

behoef'tig, **(-e)**, poor, needy, indigent, distressed, penniless, penurious, destitute; ~**e**, **(-s)**, pauper; ~**heid**, indigence, distitution, need(iness), necessity, penuriousness, penury, pauperism.

behoe'we: *ten* ~ *van*, on behalf of (a person); for the benefit of, in aid of (a cause).

behoor'lik, (b) **(-e)**, proper, fit, fitting, due, becoming (answer); decent, seemly (clothes); sizeable (room); congruous; *ek was* ~ *BANG*, I was quite scared; *jy moet jou* ~ *GEDRA*, you must behave properly; (bw) properly; fairly; duly; thoroughly; decently; ~**heid**, propriety, respectability; sufficiently; ~**heidseise**, propriety standards; ~**heidshalwe**, for decency's sake.

behoor(t), (~), belong to; behove, ought; be proper; *dié sleutels* ~ *AAN my*, these keys belong to me; *hulle* ~ *BY mekaar*, they belong together; *jy* ~ *te GAAN*, you ought to go; *dit* ~ *nie HIER nie*, it doesn't belong here; *sy* ~ *nie in hierdie KLAS te wees nie*, she ought not to be in this class; *SOOS dit* ~, as it ought to be; *iets wat tot die VERLEDE* ~, a thing of the past.

beho're: *na* ~, as it should be, properly, decently.

behou', (~), keep, retain, preserve, save, maintain.

behoud', preservation, safety; conservation (energy); salvation (soul); retention (of conquerred territory); conservatism (politics); anchor; ~ *VAN arbeidsvermoë*, conservation of energy; *dit WAS sy* ~, that was his salvation; ~**end**, **(-e)**, conservative; ~**endheid**, conservatism, conservativeness.

behou'denis, salvation.

behou'dens, save, except, but for; without prejudice to (rights); subject to (his approval); ~ *'n paar wysiginge*, with the exception of a few changes; ~**gesind**, **(-e)**, conservative.

behouds': ~**man**, conservative; ~**party**, conservative party.

behou': ~**e**, safe (and well); unscathed, unhurt; ~**er**, maintainer, preserver; ~**ering**, containerization.

behuil(d)', **(-de)**, tear-stained.

behuis', **(-de)**, housed; *skraps* ~, cramped for space.

behui'sing, housing, house; ~**skema**, ~**splan**, housing scheme; ~**vraagstuk**, housing problem.

behulp', aid, help; shift; *met* ~ *van*, with the aid of.

behulp'saam, (..**same**), helpful, useful, instrumental, assistant, adjuvant; ~ *wees met*, assist with; ~**heid**, helpfulness.

bei, **(-s)**, bey (title).

bei'aard, **(-s)**, chimes, carillon; ~**ier'**, (s), carillon player.

bei'de, both; *EEN van* ~, either, one of the two; *GEEN van* ~, neither; *ons* ~ *r VRIEND*, our mutual friend.

bei'derlei, of both kinds; *op* ~ *wyse*, in both ways.

bei'dersyds, on both sides.

Bei'er¹, (s), **(-e)**, Bavarian.

bei'er², (w), **(ge-)**, chime, play a carillon; dingle.

Bei'ere, Bavaria.

Bei'ers, **(-e)**, Bavarian.

beige, beige.

beïn'druk, (~), impress, affect (influence) deeply.

beïnvloed', (~), influence, affect, bias; *kunsmatig* ~, manipulate (market); ~**ing**, influencing, influence.

bei'tel, (s) **(-s)**, chisel; (w) **(ge-)**, chisel; chip; ~**hef**, chisel handle; ~**houer**, tool post; ~**lem**, chisel blade; ~**staaf**, tool bar; ~**staak**, hatchet-stake; ~**vormig**, **(-e)**, chisel-shaped, scalpriform; ~**werk**, chiselling.

beits, (s) stain, dye; mordant; **(w) (ge-),** stain (wood), etch; mordant; ~**kleurstof,** mordant dye; stain.
bejaard', (-e), aged, old, elderly; ancient; ~**heid,** old age.
bejag', striving after, pursuit (of gain).
bejam'mer, (~), deplore, lament, bewail; commiserate; *ek ~ jou,* you have my sympathy, I pity you; ~**enswaar'dig, (-e),** deplorable, commiserable, lamentable; ~**ing,** commiseration.
beje'ën, (~), treat, act towards; use; *iem. vriendelik ~,* be friendly towards someone; ~**ing,** treatment.
bejok', (~), lie to (a person).
bejo'sie, possessed (by the devil).
bek, (-ke), beak (bird); jaws (lion); muzzle (of gun); snout, mouth (animal); mouth (derogatory); pit (mine); neb, jet; *'n ~ soos 'n ADVOKAAT hê,* have the gift of the gab; *meer ~ as BINNEGOED,* more beef than brain; *'n DIK ~ hê,* have the sulks, be sulky; *met 'n DROË ~ (droëbek) sit,* have had nothing to eat or drink; be dissatisfied; without a partner (e.g. at a dance, party); *nie op sy ~ GEVAL nie,* have a ready tongue; *GLAD van ~ wees,* have a glib tongue; *'n GROOT ~ hê,* have plenty of jaw; *sy ~ HANG,* be down in mouth; *HARD (taai) in die ~,* hard-mouthed (of a horse); ~ *HÊ,* have a ready wit; *baie ~ HÊ,* be all mouth; *HOU jou ~!,* shut (dry) up!; *so 'n bek moet JEM kry,* such a remark (person) must be praised; *jou ~ nie verniet KOS gee nie,* have the gift of the gab; *hy is NET ~,* he is all jaw; *al wat ~ en POTE het,* all without exception; *so moet 'n ~ PRAAT!,* you can say that again; *PURE ~ wees,* be all jaw; *iem. in die ~ RUK,* pull someone up short; *'n ~ soos 'n SKEERMES hê,* have a tongue like a razor; ~ *lek en STERT swaai,* cringe and fawn; *TAAI in die ~ wees,* be hard to handle; *met 'n ~ vol TANDE sit,* not say a word; *sonder om 'n ~ te TREK,* without batting an eyelid; *jou ~ VERBRAND,* put one's foot in it; *sy ~ VERBYPRAAT,* say more than one should have.
bekaaid': *daar ~ van afkom,* come away with a flea in one's ear.
bek'-af, downhearted; chap-fallen, glum, down in the mouth.
bekalk', (~), plaster (with lime).
bekamp', (~), combat, fight against, stand up against, oppose, withstand.
bekap'¹, (~), hew (stone); *'n ~te klip,* a hewn stone.
bekap'², (~), roof in; cope.
bek'bestuurder, (spot.) back-seat driver
bekeer', (~), convert, reform; proselytize; *hy het hom ~,* he has become converted; ~**d', (-e),** converted; ~**de, (-s),** convert; ~**der, (-s),** converter; ~**ling, (-e),** convert, proselyte.
beken', (~), confess, own up, admit, avouch; acknowledge, avow, recognize; know, have intercourse with (a woman); *KLEUR ~,* follow suit (cards); show one's colours (politics); *nie KLEUR ~ nie,* revoke (at cards).
bekend', (-e), known, noted, familiar; *dit is ALGEMEEN ~,* it is a matter of common knowledge; ~*wees AS,* be known by the name of; ~ *MAAK,* make known, announce, proclaim; publish; ~ *MET,* known to; conversant with; ~ *RAAK,* become acquainted with; become known; *SOVER my ~,* to the best of my knowledge; as far as I know; ~ *STAAN,* be known; ~ *STEL,* introduce, make known; *dit kom my ~ VOOR,* it seems familiar to me; ~ *WEES met,* be acquainted with, know; ~**e, (-s),** acquaintance (person); well-known person; ~**heid,** acquaintance, knowledge; notoriety, name; familiarity; ~**making, (-e, -s),** notice, publication, promulgation, notification, announcement; declaration (of poll); manifest; ~**stel, (ge-),** introduce; ~**stelling, (-e, -s)** introduction; ~**stellingsbrief,** letter of introduction.
bek-en-klou'seer, foot-and-mouth disease.
beken'tenis, (-se), confession, avowal, admission.
be'ker, (-s), cup, drinking vessel; jug, bowl; chalice (Holy Communion); goblet; sports trophy; plate; *'n bitter ~ tot op die BODEM moet drink (ledig),* drain a bitter cup to the dregs; *tussen LIP en ~ is soveel (lê 'n groot) onseker,* there is many a slip between the cup and the lip; *hy LOOP vir die ~,* he runs with might and main; *my ~ is VOL,* my cap is full; ~**houer, (-s),** cup holder.
beke'ring, (-e, -s), conversion; repentance; reclamation; *tot ~ BRING,* convert; *tot ~ KOM,* become converted.
beke'rings: ~**werk,** proselytization, conversionist work; missionary work; ~**ywer,** conversionist zeal, proselytism; missionary zeal.
be'ker: ~**lappie,** doily; ~**mos,** cupmoss, cup weed; ~**plant,** pitcher plant; ~**reëls,** cup rules; ~**vormig, (-e),** cup-shaped; ~ *vormige kraakbeen,* arytenoid; cartilage; ~**wedstryd,** cup match; ~**wenner,** cup winner.
bek'fluitjie, (spot.) mouth organ.
bekis', (~), box in (concrete); shutter; encase; ~**ting,** boxing, shuttering, formwork; moulds.
bek'ken, (-s), pelvis; basin; catchment area; font (christening); cymbal; ~**been,** pelvic bone; ~**beenbreuk,** fracture of pelvis, pelvic fracture; ~**eel', (..ele),** (ong.) skull; ~**gordel,** pelvic girdle; ~**holte,** pelvic cavity; ~**is', (-te),** cymbal player; ~**vliesontsteking,** pelvic peritonitis; ~**vormig, (-e),** basin-shaped.
bek'kie, (s) (-s), little beak; little mouth; kiss; **(w) (ge-),** kiss (nursery term).
bek'kig, (-e), impudent, cheeky, pert.
bekla', bekla'e, (~), lament, deplore, complain, bemoan (hard times); pity (someone), condole; *jou ~ oor,* complain of.
beklaag': ~de, (-s), accused; defendant; ~**debank,** (ong.) dock (court); ~**lik, (-e),** lamentable, pitiable; ~**likheid,** pitiableness.
beklaenswaar'dig, (-e), pitiable, lamentable; ~**heid,** pitiableness.
beklad', (~), stain, sully, blot, fling, dirt, besmirch; slander, denigrate, asperse; bespatter; ~**ding,** aspersion, slander, mud-slinging, dirt-flinging.
beklaenswaar'dig, (-e), lamentable, deplorable.
beklag', complaint; ~ *DOEN,* make complaint, complain; *REDE vir ~ hê,* have reason for complaint.
beklamp', (~), clamp, cleat.
beklant', (-e), *'n goed ~e winkel,* a well-patronized shop.
bekle'de, upholstered; trousered; ~ *onderstel,* trousered undercarriage; ~**r, (-s),** holder (of office).
bekle'ding, (-e, -s), covering (floor); upholstering, upholstery; sheathing; vestiture; facing; liner (pipe); tenure (office); investiture (with office); cap, casing, lagging, clothing (steam engine); fairing (cables); ~**sbuis,** casing, drive pipe; ~**smuur,** retaining wall; ~**splaat,** clothing plate; ~**stof,** material for upholstery; ~**swal,** breast wall.
beklee', (~), invest (with); fill, hold, occupy (office); *'n pos (betrekking, amp) ~,* occupy (a post, office).
beklee(d)', (~), cover, clothe, attire; trim, upholster; case; pitch (boat); revet (engineering); face (with tiles); endue, indue; ~ *met MAG,* endued (indued) with power.
bekleed'sel, covering, upholstery, trimming.
bekle'ër, (-s), upholsterer; holder (office); incumbent (church); fabric worker; ~**swinkel,** fabric shop, trimming shop.
beklee'werk, trimming; upholstery, upholstering.
beklem', (~), oppress, distress, straiten; stress, emphasize; ~**d', (-e),** oppressed, distressed; ~*de BREUK,* strangulated hernia; *met 'n ~de GEMOED,* in great distress, greatly distressed; ~**d'heid,** oppression, sinking of the heart; ~**ming,** oppression, tightness, heaviness; angina; impaction (of tooth); incarceration (of hernia).
beklem'toon, (~), accentuate, emphasize, stress.
beklem'toning, accentuation.
beklets', (~), (ong.) spread rumours; slander, talk scandal.
beklim', (~), ascend (mountain); climb (tree); mount (throne); scale (wall); cover, serve (ewe); *iem. se bed ~,* commit adultery; ~**baar, (..bare),** climbable, scalable; ~**ming,** climbing; ascent, mounting, escalade.

beklink', (~), clinch, rivet; arrange, settle; drink to; *'n saak ~*, settle an affair.
beklon'ke, settled, arranged; *'n ~ saak*, a settled matter.
beklon'ter, (~), clot.
beklop', (~), knock on, tap on; sound (chest), percuss; ~ **ping**, tapping; sounding; percussion.
beklou', (~), hug, squeeze.
beklou'ter, (~), climb up, scale, clamber up.
beknaag', (~), gnaw at.
beknab'bel, (~), nibble (at).
beknel', (~), oppress, pinch, constrict; *deur sorge ~*, oppressed by care.
beknib'bel, (~), stint, barter down, cut down.
beknies', (~), fret about.
beknop', (-te), succinct, contracted, compendious, cramped, compact, concise (style); summarised, abridged; small, poky (room); narrow (space); ~ **t'heid**, conciseness, compression, succinctness, briefness, compactness, compendiousness, contractedness, brevity, brachylogy.
beknor', (~), scold, rebuke, chide.
bekoe'ël, (~), pelt with, pepper.
bekoel', (~), (ong.) cool (down); labate, quench; flag; *die vriendskap het ~*, the friendship has cooled down; ~ **ing**, cooling, flagging.
bekom', (~), obtain, get; agree (with the stomach); recover from (fright); *dit sal jou sleg (suur) ~*, you will rue it (be sorry for it); ~ **baar, (..bare)**, accessible; available.
bekom'mer, (w) (~), trouble, worry, be anxious (uneasy) about, be solicitous about; *ek ~ my daaroor*, I am worried about it; (b) ~ **d, (-e)**, worried, uneasy, anxious; solicitous; ~ **dheid**, anxiety, solicitude; concern; ~ **ing, (-e, -s)**, ~ **nis, (-se)**, uneasiness, worry, care, anxiety.
bekoms', satisfaction, bellyfull, fill, satiety; *jou ~ EET*, eat more than one's fill; *jou ~ HÊ van iets*, be fed up with something.
bekon'kel, (w) (~), plot, scheme, concoct, wangle; (b) ~ **(d), (-de)**, muddled up; full of whims and fancies (nonsense); daft; ~ **aar**, plotter, schemer.
bekook', (~), wangle, concoct.
bekoop', (~), pay dearly for; *iets met die dood ~*, pay for something with one's life.
bekoor', (~), charm, enchant, fascinate, ravish, bewitch, captivate, enamour, tempt; ~ **der, (-s)**, charmer, tempter; enchanter; fascinator; ~ **lik, (-e)**, charming, tempting, enchanting, glamorous, attractive, graceful, fascinating; ~ **likheid**, charm, enchantment, attractiveness, grace(fulness); ~ **ster, (-s)**, enchantress, temptress, charmer, enslaver.
beko'ring, charm, temptation, fascination; allurement, bewitchment, captivation, enchantment, glamour.
bekors', (~), become encrusted; encrust; ~ **ting**, encrustment; encrustation.
bekort', (~), shorten, cut short; abridge; ~ **ing**, shortening, abridgement, condensation; guillotine (in parliament).
bekos'tig, (~), defray, pay; afford; *ek kan 'n MOTOR ~*, I can afford a car; *ek kan dit nie ~ om 'n MOTOR aan te hou nie*, I cannot afford a car; ~ **er**, defrayer; ~ **ing**, defrayal, defrayment, meeting (expenses).
bek'praatjies, boasting, bragging; empty promises.
bek'prater, (-s), boaster, braggart; ~ **y**, boasting.
bekrab'bel, (~), scribble, scrawl all over.
bekrag', (~), energize (elec.); boost.
bekrag'tig, (~), confirm (sentence); validate; sanction (compact); ratify (treaty); bind, approve; affirm, authenticate, corroborate, enforce; enact; ~ **er, (-s)**, approver, affirmant, enforcer, ratifier; ~ **ing**, confirmation, affirmation, authentication, corroboration, sanction, ratification, convalidation, enforcement.
bekrans', (~), wreathe, crown with laurel, garland; *'n ~ te spreker*, a garlanded speaker; ~ **ing**, laureation, crowning.
bekrap', (~), scribble all over; bescratch; prick up (plaster).
bekras', (~), scribble over; scratch on.

bekreun', (~), mind, care for, be concerned, worry; *hy ~ hom daar min oor*, he is very little concerned about that.
bekrimp', (~), (ong.) curtail, cut down (expenses); *ons moet ons ~*, we have to cut down expenses; ~ **ing**, curtailment, stinting.
bekrip', (~), crib, (with timber).
bekritiseer', (~), disparage, decry, criticize.
bekrom'pe, straight-laced, insular, narrow-minded, provincial (person); parochial; bigoted, petty; narrow (principles); limited (outlook); claustral; poky, contracted; ~ **nheid**, narrow(minded)ness, contractedness, insularity, pettiness, philistinism; parochialism.
bekro'ning, crowning; reward of merit, award.
bekroon', (w) (~), crown, pinnacle; laureate; cap, award; ~ **de, (s) (-s)**, prize-winner, laureate; (b) **(-de)**, prize, laureate; laurelled; *'n ~ de opstel*, a prize essay.
bekruip', (~), creep upon, steal upon, surprise, stalk; ~ **bossie**, trailing bush (*Euphorbia rectirama*); ~ **er, (-s)**, stalker, trailer; ~ **mus**, stalking cap.
bekruis', (~), mark with a cross; cruise over.
bekryg', (~), (ong.) make war upon.
bek: ~ **sak**, nose bag; ~ **snyer**, slasher, stabber; ~ **stuk**, nose band; ~ **vegter**, braggart; ~ **vriend**, false friend.
bekwaald', (b) (-e), sickly, diseased; (bw) scarcely; *hy kan ~ loop*, he can scarcely walk.
bekwaam', (w) (~), qualify, make able, capacitate, train; *jou vir 'n beroep ~*, train for a profession; (b) **(bekwame)**, able, capable, clever, competent, qualified, proficient, efficient; fit; mature, ripe (fruit); sober; *met bekwame SPOED*, as soon as possible, *te bekwamer TYD*, in due course; ~ **WORD**, mature (e.g. potatoes).
bekwaam'heid, (..hede), ability, capability, capacity, qualification; acquirement; faculty; maturity (fruit); proficiency, efficiency; address; ~ **hede**, capabilities, parts; *met GROOT ~*, with great efficiency; *SALARIS volgens ~*, salary according to qualifications.
bekwyl', (~), beslaver.
bekyk', (~), look at (over), view, inspect, examine.
bekyks': *veel ~ hê*, be the focus of attention.
bel, (s) (-le), bell; lobe (of ear); wattle (bird); caruncle (of turkey); bubble; mucus (nose); (w) **(ge-)**, ring (telephone, door bell); *daar word ge ~*, there is a ring.
belaag', (~), waylay, set traps for, lay snares for; slander; *die onskuld ~*, persecute innocence.
belaai', (w) (~), load, burden; *'n swaar ~ de voertuig*, a heavily laden vechile; (b) heavy; ~ **met**, fraught with.
belab'berd, (-e), (ong.) miserable, rotten.
bela'de, laden, loaded, burdened.
bela'ding, freight(ing); weighting; load; ~ **skuld**, lien, contingent debt.
hela'er, (-s), ensnarer.
belag'lik, (-e), ridiculous, laughable, farcical, grotesque, absurd, ludicrous; *IETS ~ maak*, hold something up to ridicule, pour derision on something; *JOU ~ maak*, make oneself ridiculous; ~ **heid**, ridiculousness, absurdity; farcicalness, risibility; ~ **hede**, ridiculous things.
beland', (~), land; get to, arrive; *waar het die BOEK ~?* what has become of the book?; *iem. in moeilikheid LAAT ~*, land someone in trouble.
belang', (-e), importance; consequence; interest, concern; moment; account; (mv) interests; *GEMEENSKAPLIKE ~ e*, common interests, *die HOOGSTE ~*, the utmost (prime) importance; *IN jou eie ~*, in, for your own interest; *'n SAAK van ~*, a momentous matter; ~ *STEL, see* **belangstel**; *in die ~ VAN*, in the interest(s) of; ~ *VERKRY by*, acquire an interest in; *van WEINIG ~*, of little consequence; ~ **egemeenskap**, community of interest, common interests; ~ **egroep**, interest group.
belan'geloos, (..lose), disinterested; without interest; unselfish; ~ **heid**, disinterestedness; unselfishness.
belan'gende, concerning, regarding.

belan'gesfeer, sphere of interest.
belangheb'bend, (-e), interested; ~*e EENHEDE,* interested units; ~*e VOORWERP,* indirect object; ~**e, (-s),** interested party; person concerned.
belang'rik, (-e), important, material, eventful, capital, considerable; notable (occasion); essential; ~**heid,** importance, gravity, magnitude; ~**ste,** premier, most important.
belang'stel, (w) (-ge-), take an interest in; be interested in; ~**lend, (-e),** interested, keen; concerned; ~**lende, (-s),** person taking an interest; those interested.
belang'stelling, interest; keenness; *BLYKE van* ~, tokens of sympathy (funeral); signs of interest (concern); proof of interest (wedding); ~ *INBOESEM vir,* rouse interest in (for); *SONDER* ~, without interest; *UIT* ~, out of interest; ~ *VERLOOR in,* lose interest in; ~ *WEK* arouse interest.
belangwek'kend, (-e), interesting; ~**heid,** source of interest.
belap', (~ **), (ong.)** put patches on.
belas', (w) (~ **),** burden, tax, rate; debit, excise, assess; encumber, charge with; load (machine, vehicle); (b) **(-te),** charged, laden; burdened, taxed, ~ *en BELADE,* heavily laden; *iem. MET iets* ~, put one in charge of; *erftik* ~ *WEES,* be tainted with heredity.
belas'baar, (..bare), taxable, ratable, exciseable, dutiable, assessable, liable to taxation; ..*bare goedere,* dutiable articles (goods); ~**heid,** taxability, liability to taxation, ratableness.
belas'ter, (~ **),** slander, backbite, calumniate, asperse, defame, libel, malign, detract, traduce, vilify; ~**aar, (-s),** slanderer, backbiter, libeller, calumniator; detractor; ~**ing,** slander, calumniation, aspersion, defamation, detraction.
belas'ting, (-s), tax, rate, duty, impost, taxation; load (elect., engineering, vehicles); ~ *HEF op,* levy a tax on; ~ *LÊ op,* put a tax on; *ONTVANGER van* ~ *s,* receiver of revenue; ~ *OP beroepswedders,* bookmakers' tax; *VOLLE* ~, complete load (elect.); ~**aanslag,** assessment; ~**amptenaar,** revenue officer; ~**betaler,** tax payer; rate payer; ~**betaling,** payment of taxes; ~**biljet,** tax form; ~**bron,** source of taxes (revenue); ~**diensjaar,** financial year; ~**druk,** burden of taxation; ~**gaarder,** tax collector; receiver of revenue; ~**grens,** tax(able) limit; ~**grondslag,** basis of taxation; ~**heffer,** assessor; ~**hervorming,** tax(ation) reform; ~**inkomste,** tax(ation) revenue(s); ~**jaar,** year of assessment, fiscal year; ~**kantoor,** office of the receiver of revenue; tax office; ~**kundige,** tax expert; ~**kwytskelding,** remission of taxes; ~**maatreël,** taxation measure; ~**ontduiker,** tax dodger (evader); ~**ontduiking,** tax dodging (evasion); ~**opbrengs,** tax revenue; ~**plan,** taxation scheme; ~**pligtig, (-e),** ratable: taxable; ~**pligtige, (-s),** tax (rate) payer; ~**pligtigheid,** ratableness; ~**raming,** (taxation) estimates; ~**s,** rates and taxes; ~**seël,** revenue stamp; ~**sfaktor,** load factor; ~**skuldig, (-e),** ratable; ~**sproef,** load test; ~**stelsel,** system of taxation; tax(ation) system; ~**toeslag,** surtax; ~**verdeler,** load-despatcher; ~**verhoging,** tax(ation) increase; ~**verlaging,** ~**vermindering,** reduction in taxation; tax reduction; ~**voet,** rate of taxation; tax rate; ~**vorm,** tax form; ~**vry, (-e),** tax (duty) free; ~**wet,** fiscal law.
belat', (~ **),** lath, batten, slat; ~**ting,** lathing; battening; slatting; strapping (of wall).
bel'boei, bell buoy.
belê, (~ **),** convene, convoke, call (meeting); trim (dress); cover; invest (capital); place (money); compound; overlay (woodwork); *belegde GELD,* invested money; *'n VERGADERING* ~, convene a meeting.
bele'de, professed, avowed; confessed; ~*sondes,* confessed sins.
bele'dig, (~ **),** insult, offend, injure; affront, pique, abuse, flout, outrage, give offence; ~**de, (-e),** the offended party; ~**end, (-e),** offensive, injurious, opprobrious; abusive, outrageous, insulting; ~**er, (-s),** offender, insulter; ~**ing, (-e, -s),** insult, abuse,

outrage, offence, affront; *iem. 'n* ~*ing AANDOEN,* give offence to a person; *as 'n* ~*ing OPNEEM,* take as an insult; *'n* ~*ing VERKROP,* swallow an insult.
bele'ë, mature (wine); ripe (cheese), mellow; ~ *maak,* season (wood).
beleef', (w) (~ **),** live to see, witness, experience; live through (hard times); experience emotionally (poem); *ek het nog NOOIT sowat* ~ *nie,* I have never seen anything like it; *ek sal dit NOOIT* ~ *nie,* I will never live to see it; *baie VREUGDE van sy kinders* ~, live to enjoy a great deal of pleasure from his children; (b, bw) **(-de),** polite, mannerly, civil, courteous, genteel, obliging; *iem.* ~ *groet,* greet someone politely; ~**delik,** civilly, politely.
beleefd'heid, civility, politeness, mannerliness, complaisance; compliment, courteousness, comity, courtesy; amenity; ~ *BEWYS,* show courtesy; *die* ~ *self WEES,* be courtesy itself; ..**hede,** compliments, attentions; civilities, amenities.
beleefd'heids: ~**besoek,** courtesy call; duty call; ~**betuigings,** civilities, compliments; ~**halwe,** by way of compliment, out of politeness; ~**titel,** courtesy title; ~**vorm,** form of etiquette, formality; honorific; ~**woord,** honorific.
beleen', (~ **), (ong.)** pawn; mortgage; enfeoff; ~**baar, (..bare),** pawnable.
bele'ënheid, mellowness, maturity (of cheese, wine).
beleer', (~ **),** teach.
belê'er, (-s), depositor, investor; convener; overlayer.
bele'ër, (-s), besiege, lay siege to; ~**aar (-s),** besieger; beleaguerer; ~**de, (-s),** besieged; ~**ing, (-e, -s),** siege; ~**ingsgeskut,** siege-artillery; ~**ingsoorlog,** siege-warfare; ~**ingstrein,** siege-train; ~**ingstroepe,** besieging forces; ~**ingswerke,** siege-works; ~**ingswerktuig,** siege implement.
beleg', (s) (..leëringe, ..leërings), siege; *die* ~ *OPHEF,* raise the siege; *STAAT van* ~, state of siege; (w) *see* **belê;** ~**baar, (..bare),** available for investment; ~**band,** false piece, trimming; ~**ger = beleër;** ~**ging, (-e, -s),** convening, convocation (meeting); investment (money); deposit; deposition; ~**gingsfondse,** investment funds; ~**klamp,** cleat; ~**laag,** overlay; ~**lat,** strip (ceiling); ~**sel, (-s),** covering, trimming, facing (uniform); ~**stuk,** lining-piece; ~**werk,** overlay work; trimming.
beleid', tact, skill, discretion, prudence; policy; *met* ~ *te werk gaan,* act with discretion; ~**bepaler,** policy maker; ~**loos, (..lose),** without a policy; ~**saak,** matter of policy; ~**s'aankondiging,** announcement of policy; ~**vol, (-le), (ong.)** prudent, cautious, discreet, prudential, tactful, politic; ~**vormer,** policy maker.
belek', (~ **),** lick (all over).
belem'mer, (~ **),** encumber, impede, bar, handicap, impair, block, obstruct (the view); hamper, interfere with; halter, cumber, cramp; choke (canal); foul, clog (wheels); stunt (growth); make unfit for use; arrest, check; embarrass; estop (law); fetter; cripple (intentions); intercept; ~**d, (-e),** impeded, obstructed, hampered, stunted; ~*de groei,* stunted growth; stunting; ~**end, (-e),** obstructive, hampering; embarrassing; ~**ing, (-e, -s),** encumbrance; impediment (in speech); obstruction, hindrance, obstacle, hitch, hold-back, handicap, cramp; stunting, dwarfing (in growth); block, check, clogging, embarrassment; estoppel (law); drag; interception; fetter; rebuff.
belen'dend, (-e), abutting on, adjacent.
belen'ding, (-e, -s), abuttal, adjacency.
bele'ning, (-e, -s), mortgage; pawning; loan on pledge; enfeoffment.
bele'se, well-read; erudite; book-learned; ~ *in die wet,* learned in law; ~**nheid,** state of being well-read, extensive reading, range of reading, erudition.
belet', (~ **),** hinder, prevent, prohibit, ban, preclude, forbid; ~ *vra,* enquire whether a visit will be convenient; ~**sel, (-s),** obstacle, hindrance, impediment, hold-back, hitch; ~**tend, (-e),** inhibitory, preventative; ~**ter, (-s),** preventer; ~**ting,** prohibition, ban.

bele'we, *see* **beleef.**
bele'wenis, (-se), experience.
bele'wing, experience.
Belg¹, (-e), Belgian.
belg², (ge-): *ERG ge~ wees,* be highly offended; *hom OOR iets ~,* be incensed at a thing.
Bel'gië, Belgium.
Bel'gies, (-e-), Belgian.
Belgra'do, Belgrade.
belham'bra, belhambra (tropical tree) *(Phytolaca dioica).*
bel'hamel, bell-wether, ringleader.
bel'hoender, guinea-fowl
Be'lialskind, child of the devil, limb of Satan.
belief', (~), (ong.) please; *om sy vrou te ~,* to please his wife.
belieg', (~), belie, lie to; *hy het my gruwelik ~,* he told me a pack of lies.
belie'we, pleasure; *na sy ~,* at his pleasure.
belig', (~), lighten up; throw a light on, illuminate; expose (photo); explain.
belig'gaam, (~), embody, incorporate; exteriorize, externalize; body forth.
belig'gaming, embodiment, incorporation; incarnation; picture.
belig'hefboom, exposure lever.
belig'ting, illumination, lighting; exposure (photo).
belig'tings: ~ **duur,** exposure time; ~ **fout,** exposure error; ~ **grens,** terminator; ~ **meter,** exposure meter; ~ **tabel,** exposure table; ~ **tyd,** exposure time.
bel'korhaan, bel'kraanvoël, wattled crane *(Burgeranus carunculatus).*
belladon'na, belladonna, banewort, bear's foot, deadly nightshade; ~ **lelie,** *Amaryllis belladonna;* ~ **pleister,** belladonna plaster; ~ **vergiftiging,** atropism.
bel'letjie, (-s), little bell; small lobe; bead; ~ **heide,** royal heath *(Erica regia).*
belletrie', (ong.) literature, belles-lettres.
belletris', (-te), (ong.) belletrist; ~ **ties,** (-e), pertaining to belles-lettres, belletristic.
belliet', bellite.
beloer', (~), watch, spy upon, peep at.
belof'te, (-s), promise; committal; augury; faith; *'n ~ AFLÊ (doen),* make a promise; *'n ~ BREEK,* break a promise; *'n ~ HOU,* keep one's promise; *iem. aan sy ~ HOU,* hold a person to his promise; *'n ~ NAKOM,* fulfil one's promise; *ONDER ~ van,* under the promise of; *~ maak SKULD (en wie daarop wag, is gekuld),* promises are like piecrust, made to be broken; *VOLGENS ~,* as promised.
belol', (~), worry, trouble.
belom'mer, (~), shade; ~ **ing,** shade.
belo'ner, (-s), rewarder.
beloniet', belonite.
belo'ning, (-e, -s), reward, award, consideration, recompense, premium, prize, guerdon, gratification, remuneration, pay; *TER ~ van,* in reward of; *'n ~ UITLOOF,* offer a reward.
beloof', (~), promise; bid fair; plight (troth); *BAIE ~ vir die toekoms,* promise a great deal for the future; *oor die ~de JARE,* over threescore years and ten.
beloon', (~), reward, remunerate, recompense, pay.
beloop', (s) course (things); sweep (ship); *sy ~ NEEM,* let it take its course; *'n SAAK op sy ~ laat,* let the matter take its course; *dis die WÊRELD se ~,* it is the way of the world; (w) (~), amount to, run into, aggregate.
belo'pe: *bloed~ oë,* bloodshot eyes.
belo'we, (~), *kyk* **beloof;** ~ **nd,** (-e), promising; promissory.
bel'roos, erysipelas, St. Anthony's fire; ~ **lyer,** erysipelas sufferer (patient).
bels, medicinal herb *(Osmitopsis asteriscoides).*
Belt: *die GROOT ~,* the Great Belt; *die KLEIN ~,* the Little Belt.
Bel'tel, Beltel; ~ **stelsel,** Beltel system.
belug', (~), aerate (soil); ventilate; ~ **ting,** ventilation, aeration.
beluik', (~), shutter; ~ **ing,** shuttering.
belui'ster, (~), listen to; eavesdrop, overhear; listen (with one's mind); auscultate (doctor); ~ **aar,** listener, eavesdropper; ~ **ing,** listening to, overhearing; (mental) listening; auscultation.
belus', longing for, eager for, greedy; appetent; ~ *wees op,* be eager for (keen on); have a craving for; ~ **t'heid,** longing, lust.
bely', (~), confess, avow (one's guilt); profess (religion); ~ **denis,** (-se), confession, profession, creed; *–denis doen (aflê),* be confirmed (as church member); ~ **(d)er,** (-s), confessor; professor (of a religion); ~ **denisskrifte,** articles of faith.
belyn', (~), outline; define; rule (paper); line (a street); ~ **ing,** outline; lines, lining.
bemaak', (~), bequeath; demise (law); devise; *geld ~,* bequeath money; ~ **baar,** (..**bare**), demisable.
bemag'tig, (~), master, conquer, seize, usurp, take possession of, possess; make oneself master of, learn (a language); ~ **ing,** seizure, taking possession of.
bema'ker, bequeather.
bema'king, (-e, -s), bequest, endowment, bequeathment, devise; demise.
beman', (w) (~), man, equip, garrison; (b) (-de), manned; ~ **ning,** (-s), crew; garrison (fort); complement (ship); company.
beman'tel, (~), cover; veil; palliate, mask, gloss over; ~ **ing,** cloaking; palliation, glossing over; veiling; sheathing.
bemark', (~), market; sell; ~ **baar,** (..**bare**), marketable; saleable; ~ **ing,** marketing; selling.
bemas', (~), mast (ship).
bemees'ter, (~), get hold of; find fault with; gain; ~ **ing,** mastering, conquering, conquest.
bemerk', (~), observe, notice, perceive; ~ **baar,** (..**bare**), perceptible, noticeable, perceivable; ~ **baarheid,** perceptibility; ~ **ing,** (-e, -s), observation, remark.
bemes', (~), manure, dung; fatten; fertilize; ~ **ting,** manuring; fertilization; ~ **tingsdoeleindes,** manuring purposes; ~ **tingswaarde,** manurial value.
bemid'del, (~), mediate, intercede; ~ **aar,** (-s), (inter)mediator, intercessor; intermediary; compounder; conciliator; ombudsman;' ~ **aarster,** (-s), mediatress, mediatrix.
bemid'deld, (-e), well-to-do, wealthy, rich, moneyed, affluent.
bemid'delend, mediatorial, conciliatory; ~ *optree,* act as mediator, intercede.
bemid'deling, medium; intercession, procurement, (inter)mediation, good offices, interposition, intervention, intermediary; agency; *deur ~ van,* by the agency (mediation, kind offices) of.
bemid'delings: ~ **aanbod,** offer of mediation; ~ **plan,** scheme of mediation; ~ **poging,** attempt at mediation; ~ **voorstel,** proposal of mediation.
bemin', (~), love, be fond of; cherish; ~ **d',** (-e), loved, popular, beloved, endeared; cherished; *jou ~ maak,* endear oneself; ~ **de,** (-s), loved one, love(r), sweetheart, fiancé.
bemin'lik, (-e), lovely, lovable, amiable, likable, kind, goodly; endearing, affectionate; ~ **heid,** loveliness, lovableness; affectionateness; amiability, goodliness.
bemin'naar, (-s), (ong.) lover; amateur (actor).
beminnenswaar'dig, (-e), amiable, lovable, lovely; ~ **heid,** amiability, lovableness.
bemis', (~), manure; befoul; misted (over); ~ **ting,** *see* **bemesting.**
bemod'der, (~), (be)mire, besmirch; splash with mud; drabble; ~ **d,** (-e), bedrabbled, bemired, bedraggled, mud-stained.
bemoe'der, (~), mother; ~ **ing,** mothering.
bemoe'dig, (~), encourage, inspire, hearten, console; animate; ~ **end,** (-e), encouraging, cheering; ~ **ing,** encouragement.
bemoei', (~), meddle, interfere; ~ *jou met jou eie sake,* mind your own business; ~ **al,** (-le), busybody, meddler; Nosy Parker; ~ **enis,** concern, meddlement; *daar geen ~ enis mee hê nie,* have nothing to do with it; ~ **gees,** meddlesomeness; ~ **ing,** (-e, -s), meddling, interference; effort (on someone's behalf); ~ **lik,** (~), obstruct, embarrass,

hinder, hamper, handicap, impede; oppose; ~**siek**, (**-e**), meddlesome, interfering, pragmatic, officious; ~**sug**, meddlesomeness, officiousness; ~**sug'tig**, (**-e**), meddlesome, officious.
bemoont'lik, (~), make possible.
bemors', (~), soil; foul, stain, drabble, dirty, begrime, draggle, beslaver, beslubber.
bemos', (**-te**), mossy, moss-grown, lichened.
bemy'mer, (~), ponder about, brood on.
benaars'tig, (~), (ong.): *hom* ~, exert (apply) oneself, do one's utmost.
bena'deel, (~), derogate (reputation); adversely affect; damage (trade); aggrieve; harm, hurt, injure, damn, prejudice (interests); damnify; ~ *de persoon*, aggrieved party.
bena'deling, prejudice (law); injury, damage; lesion (path.).
bena'der, (~), approach; estimate, approximate; ~**end**, approximate; ~**ing**, (**-e, -s**), approximation, rough estimate; approach (to position); *by* ~*ing*, approximately, more or less.
bena'druk, (~), emphasize, stress.
bena'ming, (**-e, -s**), name, title, appellation, appellative, denomination.
benard', (**-e**), distressed, critical, trying; embarrassed; *in* ~ *e omstandighede*, in straitened circumstances; ~**heid**, distress, stringency.
benat', (~), wet; ~ **baar** (..**bare**), wettable; irrigable; ~**ting**, wetting; irrigation.
ben'de, (**-s**), band, troop; gang, pack (of thieves); horde, mob; clan, body, confraternity; ~ *van Kardoes*, riotous meeting; a gang of robbers; ~**hoof**, leader of a gang; ~**lid**, member of a gang, gangster.
be'nebreek, difficult, hard; *dit gaan maar* ~, it is very difficult.
bene'de, below, beneath, under, downstairs; *DIS* ~ *my*, it is beneath me; ~ *KRITIEK*, beneath criticism; ~ *PARI*, at a discount; ~**buurman**, neighbour on the lower storey; ~**dek**, lower deck; ~**gedeelte**, lower portion; ~**hoek**, bottom corner; ~**huis**, (dwelling on) ground floor; ~**kaak**, lower jaw; ~**liggend**, (**-e**), underlying (rock); ~**loop**, lower course (river); tail race (below waterwheel); ~**mas**, housing; ~**ruim**, lower hold; ~**stad**, lower town; ~**verdieping**, ground floor; basement; ~**vertrek**, ground floor; (b) downwards; (bw) downward(s); ~**wêreld**, underworld.
benedik'tekruid, naval-wort.
benediktien', **benedikti'ne**, benedictine (liqour).
benedik'sie, (**-s**), benediction.
Benediktyn', (**-e**), **Benedikty'ner**, (**-s**), Benedictine.
Benedikty'ne(r): ~**klooster**, Benedictine monastery; ~**monnik**, Benedictine monk.
be'nedy, (**ge-**), bless.
beneem', (~), take away, deprive; *die EETLUS* ~, take away the appetite; *die GELEENTHEID* ~, deprive of the opportunity; *die LUS* ~, take away the desire; *die MOED* ~, discourage, dishearten; *die UITSIG* ~, obstruct the view.
benefi'ce, (regst.), benefit; *onder* ~ *van inventaris*, assuming curatorship without prejudice.
benefi'cium, (..**cia**), (regst.), benefice.
benefi'sie, (ong.) benefice.
be'nehandelaar, dealer in bones.
Be'nelux, Benelux, ~**lande**, Benelux countries.
bene'pe, distressed, perplexed; petty, small-minded, mean-spirited; ~**nheid**, embarrassment, perplexity, small-mindedness, pettiness.
be'nerig, (**-e**), bony.
benet', (~), reticulate; ~**ting**, reticulation.
beneuk', (plat), (w) (~), damage, spoil; (b) (**-te**), cantankerous; daft.
bene'wel, (w) (~), cloud, darken, obscure, dim, befog, bemuse, purblind, obfuscate, fuddle, stupefy; (b) ~ (**d**), (**-de**), foggy, misty; besotted; muzzy, obfuscated, hazy; tipsy; ~*de verstand*, clouded (foggy) mind; ~**dheid**, haze, stupefaction.
bene'wens, together with, besides, in addition to; *'n goeie salaris* ~ *'n vrye woning*, a good salary in addition to a free house.
Bengaals', (**-e**), Bengal; ~*e vuur*, Bengal lights.
Benga'le, Bengal.

Bengalees', (..**lese**), Bengalese, Bengali.
ben'galiet, bengalite.
ben'gel[1], (s) (**-s**), ungainly youngster, unruly boy.
ben'gel[2], (s) (**-s**), clapper (of bell); (w) (**ge-**), swing to and fro, dangle; ring (bell).
benieu', (~): *dit sal my* ~, I wonder whether; that will make me curious; ~**d**, (**-e**), anxious (to know), curious, inquisitive; *ek is baie* ~ *d om te hoor wat gebeur het*, I am very anxious to know what has happened; *cf.* **benuwe**.
be'nig, (**-e**), bony; large-boned, osseous.
Ben'jamin, Benjamin.
ben'ning, (**-s**), (gew.) band (musical).
beno'dig, (**-de**), wanted, required; *ekstra hulp word* ~, extra help is needed; ~**dhede**, necessaries, equipage, equipment, lay-out; implements; requisites; requirements; properties (stage); ~**dheid**, (..**hede**), requirement, necessity, requisite, want.
benoem', (w) (~), nominate (for post); appoint, gazette; name; *in 'n AMP* ~, appoint to a post; ~ *tot HOOGLERAAR (PROFESSOR)*, appoint as professor; *as KANDIDAAT* ~, nominate as a candidate; *in 'n RAAD* ~, appoint to a council; (b) ~ (**d**), (**-de**), nominated, appointed; ~ *de getal*, concrete (appointed) number; ~**baar**, (..**bare**), eligible; ~**de**, (**-s**), nominee; ~**er**, (**-s**), nominator; ~**ing**, (**-e, -s**), appointment, designation, denomination; nomination; naming; ~*ing vir die parlement*, nomination for parliament; ~**ingsdag**, nomination day; ~**ingsvergadering**, nomination meeting; primary (meeting) (U.S.A.); ~**ingsvoorwaardes**, terms of appointment.
benom'mer, (~), give numbers to, number.
benoor'de, (to the) north of.
benou', (~), oppress, cause anxiety.
benoud', (**-e**), anxious, oppressed, afraid (person); stifling, suffocating, pressed, close, sultry; stuffy (room); tight in the chest, with difficult breathing; ~*e oomblikke*, anxious moments; ~**ebors**, asthma; croup; ~**heid**, (..**hede**), anxiety, pang; closeness, stuffiness; oppression, anguish.
benou'end, (**-e**), oppressive.
benou'enis, (**-se**), anxiety, anguish.
benou'ing, oppression.
benseen', benzene, benzol; ~**heksachloride**, ~**heksachloried**, benzene hexachloride.
bensidien', **bensidi'ne**, benzidine.
bensien', **bensi'ne**, benzine; petrol; ~**lamp**, blow-lamp; ~**opslagplek**, petrol dump; ~**reservoir**, petrol tank; ~**toevoer**, petrol supply.
bensoaat', benzoate.
benso'ësuur, benzoic acid.
bensoïen, **bensoï'ne**, benzoin.
bensol', benzol.
bentoniet', bentonite.
benul', notion, idea, conception; *ek het nie die FLOUSTE* ~ *nie*, I have not the faintest idea; *nie die MINSTE* ~ *hê nie*, not to have the slightest notion.
benut'baar, (..**bare**), tenable (bursary); serviceable, usable, useful.
benut'(tig), (~), utilize, use, avail oneself of, make use of, turn to account, harness, exploit.
benut'tiging, **benut'ting**, utilization.
beny', (~), envy, be jealous of, (be)grudge; *liewer* ~ *as beklaag*, better envied than pitied; ~**baar**, (..**bare**), enviable; ~**denswaar'dig**, (**-e**), enviable; ~(**d**)**er**, (**-s**), envious person, envier; ~**ding**, envy, jealousy.
beoe'fen, (~), practise, study (history); pursue (studies); profess, practise (virtue); cultivate (the arts); *'n BEROEP* ~, practise a profession; *GEDULD* ~, exercise patience; *'n VAK* ~, ply one's trade; ~**aar**, (**-s**), votary, student; cultivator; ~**ing**, practice, study, pursuit, cultivation, exercitation.
beo'lie, (~), oil.
beoog', (~), aim at, have in view, purpose, drive at, design; ~**de**, contemplated, planned.
beoor'deel, (~), judge, criticize, adjudicate (merits); evaluate, assess; review (books); rate, value.
beoor'delaar, (**-s**), judge (at a show); reviewer (of a book); critic (art); adjudicator (merit); ~**ster**, (**-s**), *vroulik van* **beoordelaar**.

beoor'delend, (-e), critical.
beoor'deling, (-e, -s), criticism, appreciation; judgement; review, critique; adjudication.
beoor'log, (~), make war upon.
beoos'te: ~ van, (to the) east of.
Beotië, Boiotia, Boeotia.
bepaal', (~), determine (conditions); define (boundaries); assign, circumscribe, condition, stipulate, limit (payments); fix (date); appoint (time); modify (grammar); provide, lay down (by law); localize, locate (enemy's position); orientate (opinion); decree (regulations); ascertain; articulate; destine; identify; ~ *jou tot die SAAK*, confine yourself to the matter (subject); *VOORUIT* ~, stipulate (arrange) beforehand; ~ **baar, (..bare)**, determinable, predicable, definable, assignable; ~ **baarheid**, determinability; localization.
bepaald', (b) (-e), fixed, stated (time); appointed, specified; positive, definite; given; particular (person); frank, distinct, determinate (answer); (bw) positively, decidedly, especially; unmistakably, expressly, by all means, really; ~ *e lidwoord*, definite article; *nie* ~ *MOOI nie*, not exactly pretty; ~ *ONMOONTLIK*, simply impossible; *die spoed op 'n* ~ *e OOMBLIK*, the speed at a given time; *OP* ~ *e ure*, at stated hours; *jy moet* ~ *PRAAT*, you must certainly speak; ~**heid**, definiteness, positiveness, distinctness, peremptoriness.
bepak', (~), pack; ~ **king**, pack; equipment; *met volle* ~ *king*, carrying full packs.
bepa'lend, (-e), definite, definitive; defining, determining; determinant, determinative; constitutive.
bepa'ling, (-e, -s), fixing; stipulation, orientation; appointment, determination; provision, proviso, decree, regulation (law); clause (of contract); ascertainment; extension (grammar); definition; fixture (sports); institution.
bepan', (~), tile; ~ **ning**, tiling (of roof).
bepant'ser, (~), armour, bemail; ~ *de trein*, armoured train; ~ **ing**, armour-plating.
bepeil', (~), fathom, gauge.
bepeins', ~ (pre)meditate, ponder, brood, muse (on); pore (over), cogitate; ~ **ing, (-e, -s)**, meditation, musing, brooding.
bepê'rel, (-de), pearled, adorned with pearls.
beperk', (w) (~), limit, bound, confine, abridge, restrict; circumscribe (area); modify; qualify (sense of a word); cramp; *uitgawes* ~, cut down expenses; (b) **(-te)**, restricted, finite, confined, determinate, incapacious, limited; ~ *te AANSPREEKLIKHEID*, limited liability; in a limited sense; ~ *TOT*, restricted to; ~ **end, (-e)**, limiting, qualitative, restrictive, limitative; ~ *ende voedingsfaktor*, limiting nutritional factor; ~ **ing, (-e, -s)**, limitation, restriction, restraint; reduction (arms), qualification, modification; abridgement; control, check; circumscription; cramp; confinement, ~ *inge stel op*, set limits to; ~ **ingshonorarium**, retaining fee (barrister); ~**ingsmaatreël**, restrictive measure; ~**ingsteken**, restriction notice; ~**t'held**, limitedness, restrictedness, confinement; finiteness.
bepeu'ter, (~), damage; tamper with.
bepik'¹, (~), cover with pitch.
bepik², (~), peck at.
beplaat', (~), sheet.
beplak', (~), paste over, paper (room); daub.
beplan', (~), plan, arrange beforehand; ~ **ning**, planning.
beplank', (~), plank, cover with planks, board; ~ **ing**, boarding.
beplant', (~), plant; ~ **er**, planter; ~ **ing**, planting.
bepla'ting, sheeting.
beplei'ster, (~), plaster; daub; ~ **ing**, plastering.
bepleit', (~), champion, plead (a scheme); advocate; ~ **er**, pleader, advocate; ~ **ing**, pleading, advocacy, championship.
beploe'ë, beploeg', (~), plough.
beploeg'baar, (..bare), ploughable.
bepoei'er, (~), powder.
bepraat', (~), discuss, talk over; commune; discourse; persuade, talk round; *hom laat* ~, allow himself to be persuaded.

bepreek', (~), read a homily to, preach a sermon to.
beprik', (~), prick.
beproef', (w) (~), try, test, prove, attempt, essay, experiment; visit (with affliction); (b) **(-de)**, tried, tested; trusty; ~ *ALLE dinge*, test (try) all things; *jou GELUK* ~, try one's luck; *'n* ~ *de MIDDEL*, an efficacious remedy; *SWAAR* ~ *de familie*, sorely-tried family; sadly bereaved family; ~ **baar, (..bare)**, triable.
beproe'we, (~), see **beproef**, (w).
beproe'wing, (-e, -s), trial, test, probation; visitation; affliction.
beprut'tel, (~), scold.
beraad', deliberation, consideration; *in* ~ *NEEM*, give careful thought to; *na RYP* ~, after mature deliberation.
beraad'slaag, (~), deliberate, take counsel, consult, commune, confer, consult with; ~ *MET*, take counsel with; ~ *OOR*, deliberate upon.
beraad'slagend, (-e), deliberative, consulting.
beraad'slaging, (-e, -s), deliberation, consultation, discussion, counsel, conference, indaba.
beraam', (~), plan, hatch (plot); contrive (means); frame (estimates); devise (plan); plot, conspire; concoct; calculate, forecast, project, compass; estimate (cost); lay (trap).
beraap', (~), render, plaster (walls).
bera'de, thoughtful, careful, considerate; ~**nheid**, resoluteness, deliberateness.
bera'der, (-s), councillor (psychology, social work).
bera'mer, (-s), projector.
bera'ming, (-e, -s), planning, plotting, forecast, calculation; estimate.
berand', (~), kerb, ~ **ing**, kerbing.
berank', (~), cover (with a creeper).
bera'ping, rendering, plastering (walls).
berberien', berberi'ne, berberine.
ber'beris, barberry (tree).
berceu'se, (-s), berceuse, cradle-song.
her'de: *te* ~ *bring*, bring on the carpet, broach a subject.
bê're, (ge-), store, save, put aside; house; garner; pigeon-hole, file (papers); bestow; *hy* ~ *sy lyf baie*, he is very lazy; *cf.* **berg¹**.
bered'der, (~), manage, arrange; wind up; administer (estate); ~ **aar, (-s)**, arranger; executor (testamentary); administrator; ~ **ing**, arrangement; administration; recovery.
bere'de, mounted; ~ *DIENS*, mounted service; ~ *MILISIE*, yeomanry; ~ *POLISIE*, mounted police; ~ *SOLDAAT*, yeoman, mounted soldier.
beredeneer', (~), reason about (upon), discuss, argue out, ~ **d', (-e)**, rational, logical, reasoned, argumentative; *'n* ~ *de oorsig*, a reasoned summary.
beredene'ring, deliberation, discussion, reasoning, argumentation.
bere'ën, (~), rain on; sprinkle; ~ **ing**, raining on; sprinkling.
bereg', (~), administer the last sacraments to; try, adjudicate (cause); ~ **baar, (..bare)**, triable, cognizable, justiciable.
bê'regeld, savings; storage fee.
bê'regoed, goods to be saved (stored away).
bereg'ting, administration of last sacraments; adjudication, trial.
bê'rehokkie, cubby-hole, pigeon-hole.
berei', (~), prepare (meal); dress (leather, tools); preserve (foodstuffs); cure (tobacco); concoct.
bereid', ready, prepared, disposed, game, willing; preserved, cured; ~ *e spek*, cured bacon; ~ **er, (-s)**, preparer; blender (tea); curer; ~ **heid**, readiness; gameness; ~ **ing**, preparation, dressing, seasoning; ~ **ingswyse**, process; ~ **s'**, already; ~ **vaar'dig, (-e)**, ready, willing; ~ **vaar'digheid**, readiness, willingness; ~ **wil'lig, (-e)**, ready, willing; ~ **wil'ligheid**, willingness, readiness; alacrity.
bereik', (s) reach, radius, range (guns); grasp; ken; *BINNE almal se* ~, within reach of all; *onder die* ~ *van die GESKUT*, within range; ~ *te HOOGTEGRENS*, absolute ceiling; (w) **(~)**, reach, attain, get to (a place); gain, compass; achieve (one's desires); grasp; ~ **baar, (..bare)**, attainable, within

reach; achievable; get-at-able; accessible; ~ **baar=
heid,** attainability; ~ **ing,** attainment, achievement.
bereis', (w) (~), travel over; tour; (b) **(-de),** experi=
enced (in travelling); (much) travelled (frequented)
(country), journeyed; *'n ~ de persoon,* person who
has travelled much; globe-trotter; ~ **baar, (..bare),**
fit to be travelled on (over, in).
bê'rekamer, store-room, box-room.
bêre'kas, (-te), locker, filing cabinet.
bere'ken, (w) (~), calculate, estimate, figure, com=
pute; charge, cast up (account); rate, evaluate; *te
veel* ~, overcharge; (b) **(-de),** suitable, calculated;
deliberate; ~ *vir sy taak,* equal to his task; ~ **aar,**
calculator; computer; ~ **baar, (..bare),** calculable;
computable; ~ **aarheid,** computability.
bere'kend, (-e), calculating, deliberate.
bere'kening, (-e, -s), calculation, estimation, evalu=
ation, gauge, computation, deliberation; ex=
pedience, cast (figure); *na ALLE* ~, according to
all reckoning(s); ~ *van SKADEVERGOEDING,*
computation of damages; *VOLGENS* ~ , as per ac=
count; as calculated; ~ **swyse,** method of com=
putation.
bê'reklere, best clothes, Sunday best.
be'reklou, bear's wort, Hercules' all-heel *(Heracleum
spondilium).*
bê'rekopie¹, lay-by.
bêrekopie'², file-copy.
be're: ~ **kuil,** bear-pit; ~ **leier,** bear-leader; ~ **mus,**
bearskin (cap).
bêrendlang'asem, hammer-head (bird) *(Scopus
umbretta).*
bê're: ~ **plek,** store-room, storage room; promp=
tuary; ~ **skoene,** best shoes.
be'retuin, beargarden.
bê'revrugte, fruit which can be stored.
berg¹, (w) **(ge-),** salve, salvage (cargo); store; *cf.* **bêre.**
berg², (s) **(-e),** mountain, mount; ~ *op,* ~ *AF,* up hill
and down dale; *goue ~e BELOWE,* promise
mountains of gold; *oor* ~ *en DAL,* over hill and
dale; ~ *e en DALE ontmoet mekaar nooit maar
mense wel,* this is a small world; ~ *toe GAAN,* be
visited by the stork; *iem. GOUE ~e beloof,* prom=
ise the moon; *dit lyk of hy uit die ~ e KOM,* he looks
like a tramp; *'n* ~ *van iets MAAK,* make a moun=
tain of something; *'n* ~ *van 'n MOLSHOOP maak,*
make mountains out of mole-hills; *as die* ~ *nie na
MOHAMMED wil kom nie, dan moet Mohammed
na die* ~ *gaan,* if the mountain won't come to Mo=
hammed, Mohammed must go to the mountain;
die ~ *het 'n MUIS gebaar,* the mountain brought
forth a mouse; *so OUD soos die ~e,* as old as the
hills; *'n* ~ *van iem. se SKOUERS af,* a weight from
one's shoulders; ~ *e VERSIT,* move mountains;
die VERSTE ~ *e is altyd die blouste,* distance lends
enchantment to the view; ~ **aalwyn,** mountain
aloe; ~ **aarde,** ochre; ~ **adder,** mountain-adder;
~ **affuit,** mountain carriage; ~ **afskuiwing,** moun=
tain slide, lock slide; ~ **afwaarts,** downhill; ~ **ag'=
tig, (-e),** mountainous, hilly, montane, montanic;
~ *agtige terrein,* mountainous country.
bergamot', bergamot (pear); ~ **olie,** bergamot oil.
berg: ~ **angelier,** mountain shrub *(Lachnaea pur=
purea; Dianthus monticolus);* ~ **artillerie,** moun=
tain artillery.
berg'baar, (..bare), salvable, salvagable.
berg: ~ **bas,** bark bush; ~ **battery,** mountain battery;
~ **(be)klimmer,** mountain climber, Alpinist;
~ **beskrywing,** orography; ~ **bewoner,** mountain=
eer, mountain dweller, hillman; ~ **blou,** mountain-
blue, bice, lapis lazuli; ~ **boegoe,** mountain buchu
(Ratuceae); ~ **brand,** mountain fire; ~ **bruin,** um=
ber; ~ **dorp,** mountain village; ~ **druk,** weight
pressure; ~ **eend,** sheldrake; ~ **engte,** mountain
pass, defile; ~ **enaar, (-s),** mountain dweller.
ber'ger, (-s), salvor, wrecker; hoveller.
berg: ~ **forel,** mountain trout; ~ **gans,** mountain
goose *(Anatidae);* ~ **geel,** yellow ochre; ~ **gees,**
mountain goblin, gnome.
berg'geld, salvage fee (money).
berg: ~ **gesig,** mountain view; ~ **geskut,** mountain
guns (artillery, battery, ordnance); ~ **gevaarte,**
gigantic mountain; ~ **grond,** hill (mountain) soil;
~ **grot,** mountain cave; ~ **haan,** bateleur eagle
(Terathopius ecaudatus); ~ **haas,** rock hare;
~ **hang,** mountain slope; ~ **hars,** bitumen; ~ **hel=
ling,** mountain (hill) slope; ~ **hoender,** francolin;
~ **hoog, (..hoë),** as high as a mountain; mountain-
high; ~ **ie, (-s),** small mountain; hill; mountain
tramp; ~ **iep,** witch elm, wich-elm, wych-elm.
ber'ging, salvage, salvaging; stowage; storage; re=
covery of stores.
ber'gings: ~ **afdeling,** recovery section; ~ **boot,** sal=
vage boat; ~ **diens,** salvage organization; ~ **een=
heid,** salvage unit; ~ **gereedskap,** salvage plant;
~ **maatskappy,** salvage company; wrecking associ=
ation; ~ **offisier,** salvage officer; ~ **onderneming,**
salvage concern; ~ **vaartuig,** salvage steamer; sal=
vage vehicle; ~ **werk,** salvage (work); ~ **werksaam=
hede,** salvage operations.
berg'kam, mountain crest (ridge).
berg'kamer, store-room.
berg: ~ **kamille,** mountain camomile *(Gamolepis pec=
tinata);* ~ **kanarie,** peach canary; ~ **ketting,** moun=
tain range, mountain chain; ~ **klimaat,** mountain
climate; ~ **klimmer,** mountaineer, mountain-
climber, Alpinist; cliffsman; ~ **klimmery,** moun=
taineering; ~ **klimstewel,** grampon; ~ **kloof,** gorge,
chasm, canyon, coomb, ravine; gully; ~ **kristal,**
rock-crystal, pebble (crystal); ~ **kruin,** mountain
top (crest); ~ **kurk,** mountain cork; ~ **kwagga,**
mountain zebra; ~ **land,** mountainous (hilly)
country; highlands; ~ **landskap,** mountain scenery;
~ **leer,** rock ladder; ~ **leeu,** puma; ~ **lelie,** Knysna
lily *(Vallota purpurea).*
berg'loon, storage charges; stowage; salvage; salvage
money.
berg: ~ **loop,** upper course (river); ~ **lug,** mountain
air; ~ **mannetjie,** (hob)goblin; gnome; ~ **massa,**
mountain mass; ~ **massief,** massif; ~ **meel,** rock-
meal; ~ **meer,** mountain lake; ~ **mis,** mountain fog;
~ **muis,** lemming; ~ **naeltjie,** *Lachenalia rubida;*
~ **nek,** col; ~ **nimf,** mountain nymph, oread; ~ **olie,**
petroleum; ~ **oorlogvoering,** mountain warfare;
~ **opwaarts,** uphill; ~ **pad,** mountain road; ~ **pas,**
mountain pass; gorge; ~ **patrys,** gray-wing par=
tridge; ~ **piek,** mountain peak; ~ **pik,** asphalt;
~ **plaas,** mountain (hill) farm; ~ **plato,** mountain
plateau; ~ **pos,** mountain post; B ~ **predikasie,** Ser=
mon on the Mount; ~ **punt,** mountain peak; ~ **py=
pie,** painted lady, white africander; ~ **rand,** moun=
tain ledge; B ~ **rede,** Sermon on the Mount;
~ **reeks,** mountain range; mountain chain; ~ **reus,**
large mountain; ~ **rooi,** cinnabar, red ochre;
~ **roos,** mountain rose *(Protea rosacea);* ~ **rot,**
dormouse; ~ **rug,** mountain ridge.
berg'ruimte, storage room.
berg: ~ **sapree,** mountain cypress *(Widdringtonia
cupressoides);* ~ **siekte,** mountain sickness;
~ **skaap,** moufflon; ~ **skilpad,** mountain tortoise,
leopard tortoise; ~ **skool,** initiation school;
~ **slang,** mountain snake (e.g. *Vipera inornata).*
berg'solder, storage loft.
berg: ~ **sout,** rock-salt; ~ **spelonk,** mountain cave;
~ **spits,** mountain peak; ~ **spleet,** gap (split) in the
mountain, mountain gap; ~ **spoor(weg),** mountain
railway; ~ **sport,** mountain sports; ~ **stad,** moun=
tain city; ~ **steilte,** mountain rise.
berg'stelsel¹, mountain system.
berg'stelsel², filing system.
berg: ~ **storting,** landslide, landslip, mountain slide;
rock slide; ~ **streek,** mountainous region;
~ **stroom,** mountain stream (torrent); gill; ~ **stut=
ting,** walling; props and stays; ~ **swa(w)el,** bee-
eater; ~ **sysie,** kind of linnet *(Serinus albigularis);*
~ **tee,** bush tea (e.g. *Cyclopia);* ~ **teer,** maltha;
~ **toegang,** adit; ~ **top,** mountain top (peak);
~ **troepe,** mountain troops; ~ **verskuiwing,** land=
slip, landslide; ~ **vesting,** hill fortress, mountain
fortress; ~ **voet,** foot of the mountain; ~ **volk,**
mountain people; ~ **vorming,** orogenesis; ~ **waarts,**
towards the mountain; ~ **wagter,** (mountain) chat;
~ **wand,** mountain side; precipice; ~ **wêreld,** moun=
tainous (hilly) country; ~ **wind,** mountain wind.

berig', (s) (-te), tidings, intelligence, report, notice, message, news, news report; advertisement; advice; *NAGEKOME* ~ te, stop-press; *SONDER voorafgaande* ~, without (previous) notice; *TOT nader* ~, until further notice; (w) (~), inform, report, notify, send word, acquaint, advise, let (someone) know; apprise, acknowledge; ~ **gewer**, reporter; correspondent; informant; communicant; ~ **gewing**, news service; ~ **vorm**, message form.
beril', (-le), beryl; ~ **draend**, (-e), ~ **houdend**, (-e), berylliferous; ~ **steen**, aquamarine.
berin', (-ne), she-bear.
beris'pe, (~), reprimand, reprove, rebuke, censure, blame, criminate, dress down, correct; condemn, chide, objurgate; animadvert; ~ **lik**, (-e), censurable, blamable, blameworthy, rebukable, impeachable, reprehensible; ~ **likheid**, sensurableness, blameworthiness; ~ **nd**, (-e), censorious, rebukeful; ~ **r**, (-s), censor, rebuker.
beris'ping, (-s, -e), rebuke, reproof, lecture; reprimand, censure, crimination, objurgation, correction; check; blame, animadversion.
ber'k(eboom), birch (tree).
berliniet', berlinite.
Berlyn', Berlin; ~ **er**, (-s), Berliner; ~ **s'**, (-e), Berlin (as adj.).
berlyns'blou, Prussian blue.
berlynsil'wer, German silver.
berm, (-e, -s), (Ndl.) verge (of road).
bermot'peer, bergamot pear.
bermotsersan'peer, *kyk* bermotpeer.
Bern, Berne; *die* ~ *Konvensie*, the Berne Convention.
beroem', (~), boast, brag, glory (in); *hy* ~ *hom op sy wreedheid*, he glories in his cruelty.
beroemd', (-e), famous, renowned, celebrated, famed, historical, great, illustrious, noted; ~ *om, vir, weens*, famous for; ~ **heid**, fame, renown, eminence, prominence; (..**hede**), celebrity; star (screen); *'n ONBEKENDE* ~ *heid*, an unknown celebrity; *'n SEKERE* ~ *heid geniet*, enjoy a certain (amount) of celebrity; *'n* ~ *heid in die SPORTWÊRELD*, a celebrity in sporting circles.
beroep', (s) (-e), profession, trade, business, occupation, calling; call, invitation (minister of religion); vocation; function; employment; appeal; *vir 'n* ~ *BEDANK*, refuse a call; *'n* ~ *DOEN op*, make an appeal to; *in hoër* ~ *GAAN*, appeal to a higher court; *PROKUREUR van* ~, an attorney by profession; *SONDER* ~, of no occupation; *onder* ~ *STAAN*, have had a call; *'n* ~ *UITBRING*, call (a minister of religion); *'n* ~ *UITOEFEN*, follow a profession; (w) (~), call (church minister); nominate; appeal to; *ek* ~ *my op*, I rely on; ~ **baar**, (..**bare**), callable, eligible; *die predikant stel hom* ~ *baar*, the minister is willing to receive a call (nomination); ~ **loos**, (..**lose**), without vocation (work).
beroeps': ~ **aanbrenger**, common informer; ~ **bedelaar**, professional beggar; ~ **besigheid**, professional duty; ~ **bokser**, prize fighter; ~ **danser(es)**, professional dancer; ~ **eed**, professional oath; ~ **eer**, professional honour.
beroep'seer, occupational sore.
beroeps': ~ **gedrag**, professional conduct; ~ **geheim**, professional secret; ~ **gids**, career guide; trade directory; ~ **halwe**, by virtue of one's profession; professionally.
beroep'siekte, occupational disease.
beroeps': ~ **jaloesie**, professional jealousy; ~ **keuse**, choice of a profession; ~ **kriekketspeler**, professional (cricketer); ~ **kunstenaar**, ~ **kunstenares**, professional artist; ~ **leiding**, career guidance; ~ **offisier**, professional officer.
beroep'skrywer, professional writer; full-time writer.
beroep's: ~ **leër**, regular army; ~ **naywer**, professional jealousy; ~ **opleiding**, vocational (occupational) training.
beroep': ~ **spekulant**, professional speculator; ~ **speler**, professional (player), pro; ~ **sport**, professionalism; professional sports.
beroeps': ~ **reëls**, professional rules; ~ **risiko**, occupational hazard; ~ **ryer**, professional rider; ~ **terapie**, occupational therapy.
beroep'stoei, professional wrestling; all-in wrestling; ~ **er**, professional wrestler; all-in wrestler.
beroeps': ~ **toneel**, professional (legitimate) theatre; professional (legitimate) stage; ~ **verandering**, change of profession (occupation); ~ **voorligter**, career (vocational) guide; ~ **voorligting**, career (vocational) guidance; ~ **vrou**, career woman; ~ **wedder**, bookmaker, bookie.
beroer', (~), disturb, trouble, affect; agitate.
beroerd', (-e), rotten, wretched, miserable, pesky; ~ *voel*, feel upset (rotten); ~ **er**, (-s), mischiefmaker; agitator; ~ **heid**, wretchedness, rottenness, miserableness.
beroe'ring, (-e, -s), commotion, disturbance, unrest, agitation, perturbation, cataclysm; *in* ~ *BRING*, stir up; ~ *VEROORSAAK*, cause unrest, create a disturbance; *in* ~ *WEES*, be all agog.
beroer'ling, (-e), rotter, blighter, trouble-maker.
beroer'te, apoplexy, palsy, paralysis; *'n aanval van* ~, a paralytic stroke, an apoplectic fit.
bero'king, fumigation; ~ **skoste**, fumigation fee; ~ **smiddel**, fumigant.
berok'ken, (~), cause, create; *iem. LEED* ~, bring misery upon someone; *iem. SKADE* ~, cause damage to someone; ~ **ing**, causing.
beroof', (~), *see* berowe.
berooid', (-e), poor, indigent, beggarly, necessitous; *daar* ~ *van afkom*, come off second-best.
berook', (w) (~), blacken (with smoke); fumigate; (b) (-te), reeky; smoked; *~ te glas*, smoked glass.
berou', (s) repentance, penitence, remorse; contrition, contriteness, attrition; depreciation, compunction; *KNEGTELIKE* ~, regret born of fear; ~ *is 'n goeie ding, maar hy kom altyd te LAAT* (~ *KOM altyd te laat)*, remorse always comes too late; *ONVOLMAAKTE* ~, attrition; (w) (~), repent, regret; deprecate; rue; *dit sal jou* ~, you will live to regret it; ~ **hebbend**, (-e), ~ **vol**, (-le), repentant, contrite, compunctious, penitent, penitential, remorseful.
bero'we, (~), deprive, bereave; divest, despoil, denude, rob; dispossess; *'n BANK* ~, rob a bank; *iem. van die LEWE* ~, rob someone of his life; ~ *VAN*, deprived of, divested of; ~ **nd**, (-e), privative; ~ **r**, robber, despoiler.
bero'wing, (-e, -s), robbery, hold-up; (de)privation, dispossession, pillage, despoliation.
ber'rie-ber'rie, beriberi; ~ **lyer**, beriberi sufferer.
berserk', (~ **te**), furious, berserk; ~ *van woede*, furious (berserk) with rage.
ber'serker, berserk(er); ~ **woede**, furious rage.
ber'tramkruid, pyrethrum.
berug', (-te), notorious, infamous, ill-famed; improper; flagrant; disreputable; ~ *om (weens, vir)*, notorious for; ~ **t'heid**, ill fame, notoriety, disrepute, flagrancy, disreputableness.
beruik', (~), smell at.
berus', (~), rest upon; be vested in; be in the keeping of; acquiesce; submit to; *in die ONVERMYDELIKE* ~, resign oneself to the inevitable; ~ *OP*, be based on; *laat die SAAK daarby* ~, let the matter rest there; *in die VONNIS* ~, abide by the judicial decision; ~ **tend**, (-e), acquiescent, resigned; ~ **ting**, acquiescence, resignation; consent, quiescence, quietism.
bery', (~), ride over (on); ride (a horse), bestride; ~ **baar**, (..**bare**), passable (road); ridable (animal); ~ **er**, (-s), rider, horseman.
berym', (~), rhyme, versify; ~ **de**, rhymed, versified; ~ *de Psalms*, rhymed Psalms (Psalm book); ~ **er**, rhymer; ~ **ing**, (-s), rhymed version.
beryp', (-te), covered with frost.
bes[1], (s) (ong., mus.) B flat minor.
bes[2], (s) best, utmost; *ALLES ten* ~ *te*, good luck; *jou UITERSTE* ~ *doen;* try one's utmost; (bw) very well; quite; ~ *MOONTLIK*, quite possible; ~ *MOONTLIK, hoor*, quite possible, I dare say.
besaai', (~), strew, sow (over), overspread, besprinkle, dot, bespangle; ~ **d**, (-e), strewn, sewn.

besaan', miz(z)en; ~**mas**, miz(z)en-mast; ~**seil**, miz(z)en-sail.
besa'dig, (-de; -der, -ste), composed, staid, soberminded, level-headed, sedate, calm, deliberate; cool-headed; moderate (views); dispassionate; ~**(d)heid**, sedateness, quiet manner, sobriety of judgment, composure; level-headedness, dispassionateness.
besak', (~), settle down, subside.
besand', (~), fill up with sand; cover with sand.
beseël', (~), seal, put the seal on; clinch (clench); *die KOOP* ~, clinch the bargain (sale); *sy LOT is* ~, his fate is sealed; ~**ing**, sealing.
beseer', (~), hurt, injure; ~**de**, (-s), injured person, casualty.
besef', (s) idea, notion, conception, perception, realization, consciousness, awareness; *iem. onder die* ~ *BRING*, make someone realize; *iem. tot die* ~ *BRING*, bring something home to someone; *tot die* ~ *KOM*, realize, come to the realization; (w) (~), realize, comprehend; be awake to.
be'sem, (-s), broom; besom (of twigs); *nuwe* ~*s vee skoon*, new brooms sweep clean; ~**bos**, broom bush (e.g. *Rhus dregeana*); mountain heath; ~**goed**, ~**gras**, broom-corn; coarse grass (e.g. *Eragrostis betschuana*); ~**koring**, broomcorn; ~**maker**, broom maker; ~**riet**, reed *(Restio triticeus);* ~**siekte**, witches' broom; ~**steel**, broomstick.
be'semstok, broomstick; *onder die* ~ *STAAN*, be hen-pecked; *onder die* ~ *STEEK*, belabour with a broomstick; *oor die* ~ *TROU*, co-habit, jump the broomstick.
besen'ding, (-e, -s), consignment.
bese'ring, (-e, -s), injury, trauma; *'n* ~ *opdoen*, sustain an injury.
bese'ringstyd, injury time (rugby).
beset', (w) (~), occupy, seize (territory); engage (chair); man, garrison; cast (a play); set (with diamonds); trim (a dress); line (with trees); (b) pregnant (animal), with young, in calf; occupied, engaged; busy; ~*te GEBIED*, occupied territory; *die LYN is* ~, the line is engaged; *die POS is nou* ~, the post has now been filled; *die SAAL is goed* ~, the hall is well-filled; *die SITPLEK is* ~, the seat is engaged; *my TYD is baie* ~, I am very busy.
bese'te, possessed (of evil spirits), maniacal, demoniacal, fiendish, obsessed.
bese'tene, (-s), one possessed, maniac, demoniac, fiend, energumen.
bese'tenheid, posession (by the devil), madness.
beset'heid, busyness, state of being occupied, engaged.
beset'sel, (-s), trimming.
beset'ting, (-e, -s), occupation (city, town); occupancy; garrison; cast (of play); strength (of orchestra); output; filling (of accommodation).
beset'tings: ~**leër**, occupation army; ~**(on)koste**, costs (expenses) of occupation; ~**troepe**, occupying forces.
be'shu, beshu.
be'sie, (-s), small bovine (animal); cricket, insect; buggy.
besiel, (~), animate, quicken, inspire, energize, inspirit, ensoul; *wat het JOU* ~ *om dit te doen*, what possessed you to do it?; *iem. met MOED* ~, inspire a person with courage; ~**(d)'**, (-de), animated, inspired, possessed (of good intentions), dithyrambic; ~**end**, (-e), inspiring, elevating, enthusiastic; ~**er**, invigorator; ~**ing**, inspiration, animation.
besien', (~), look at, inspect, examine, view; *dit staan nog te* ~, it still remains to be seen.
besiens: ~**waar'dig**, (-e), worth seeing, remarkable; ~**waar'dighede**, sights (of a town); ~**waar'digheid**, something worth seeing.
be'sig, (w) (ge-), use, employ (words); (b) (-e), occupied, busy, engaged; (bw) busily; ~ *BLY*, remain busy; *DRUK* ~, very busy, hard at work.
be'sigheid, (..hede), business, line; pursuit(s), occupation, employ, employment, affair, doing(s), activity; ~**klas**, business class (air travel); ~**sentrum**, business (city) centre; ~**splek**, business place; ~**sreis**, business trip.

be'sig hou, **(besig gehou)**, keep busy, exercise; engage (attention); keep at work (occupied); *jou* ~ *met lees*, occupy one's time with reading.
be'siging, using, usage, use, employing.
besig'tig, (~), inspect, view, look at (curiosities); survey; ~**ing**, inspection, examination, survey; *ter* ~*ing lê*, lie open for inspection.
besi'klometer, **besiklome'ter**, besiclometer.
besim'peld, (-e), daft, foolish, simple, silly; ~**heid**, daftness, silliness.
besin', (~), reflect, come to one's senses; ~ *eer jy BEGIN*, look before you leap; *hy het HOM* ~, he bethought himself (changed his mind); *jy moet jou* ~ *oor die SAAK*, you must think the matter over.
besing', (~), chant, sing of (about), celebrate (in song), poetize.
besink', (~), settle, subside, form a sediment, precipitate, clarify; ~**er**, settler, precipitator; ~**ing**, subsiding; precipitation; ~**ingsgesteente**, sedimentary rock; ~**put**, settling tank; ~**sel**, (-s), sediment, dregs, grounds, foots; lees (wine); residue, settlings; deposit (river); sludge; faeces.
besin'ning, reflection, consciousness; recollection; *tot* ~ *BRING*, bring (a person) to his senses; *tot* ~ *KOM*, come to one's senses; *sy* ~ *VERLOOR*, lose consciousness; lose one's head.
besit', (s) possession, demesne; holding, occupation; asset(s); appanage; ~ *ter BEDE*, tenancy at will; precarious possession; *in* ~ *HOU*, retain possession of; *in* ~ *NEEM*, take possession of; *in* ~ *STEL*, place in possession (of); (w), own, possess, have; *die* ~*tende KLASSE*, the moneyed (proprietary) classes; *die KOEI is* ~, the cow is in calf (covered); ~**lik**, (-e), possessive; ~*like voornaamwoord*, possessive pronoun; ~**nemer**, occupant; ~**neming**, occupation; ~**reg**, right of ownership, possessory right; dominion.
besits': ~**aksie**, possessory action; ~**interdik**, possessory interdict; rights of ownership, possessory rights; ~**mag**, power of possession; ~**reg**, right of ownership; possessory right; dominion.
besit': ~**ster**, (-s), female owner; ~**tend**, (-e), possessive; ~**ter**, (-s), possessor, owner, holder, proprietor; *salig is die* ~*ters*, possession is nine points of the law; ~**terig**, (-e), possessive; ~**terskap**, proprietary; proprietorship; ~**ting**, (-e, -s), possession, property, estate; (mv) effects, chattels, havings, goods.
beskaaf', (w) (~), plane; educate, cultivate, refine, civilize, reclaim; (b) (-de), cultivated, genteel, well-spoken, polished, refined, educated (person), accomplished; civilized, cultured (people); gentlemanly, courteous, polite (manners); ~**d'heid**, polish, refinement, gentility, good breeding; education, civilization; culture.
beskaam', (w) (~), abash, put to shame, mortify; falsify (one's expectations); (b) ~**(d)'**, (-de), ashamed, shamefaced; bashful; *iem.* ~ *MAAK*, put someone to shame; *iem.* ~ *laat STAAN*, make someone feel small; ~ *STAAN* stand ashamed; ~**d'heid**, bashfulness; shame, abashment.
beska'dig, (w) (~), damage, injure, harm, mar, impair; damnify; (b) (-de), damaged, impaired; ~**baar**, (..bare), damageable; ~**ing**, damage, harm, injury, impairment; lesion.
beska'du(wee), (~), overshadow, shade, adumbrate.
beska'duwing, overshadowing; shading; shadow.
beska'mend, (-e), humiliating, mortifying; shamed.
beska'ming, confusion, shame, discomfiture, mortification.
beskans', (~), fortify; ~**ing**, fortification.
beska'we, (~) see beskaaf.
beska'wend, (-e), cultural, civilizing.
beska'wer, (-s), (fig.), cultivator.
beska'wing, (-e, -s), civilization, culture, refinement; polish, politeness, accomplishment; polishing (manner).
beska'wings: ~**bolwerk**, bulwark of civilization; ~**peil**, standard of civilization; cultural level.
beskeid', (vero.) answer; document, record; ~ *BRING*, bring a reply; ~ *GEE*, send word.
beskei'denheid, discretion, discreetness; pudency,

beskeie 67 *beslote*

modesty; *met alle* ~, with all due deference; in all modesty.
beskei'e, discreet, humble, modest; unassuming; allotted; *elkeen sy* ~ *DEEL*, everyone his due; *na my* ~ *MENING*, in my humble opinion.
beskenk', (~) (ong.): ~ *met*, present with, endow with (funds); ~**ing**, (-e, -s), (ong.) present, endowment.
beskerm', (~), protect, save, shelter, defend, guard, preserve, screen; chaperon; patronize; ~ *de WILD*, (protected) game; ~ *TEEN (vir)*, protect against (from); ~**eling** = **beskermling**; ~**end**, (-e), patronizing; defensive; protective (duties); protectionist (system); ~**engel**, guardian angel, tutelary angel; ~**er**, (-s), protector, defender, guardian, patron; ~**gees**, tutelary spirit; genius; ~**heer**, patron; protector; ~**heerskap**, protectorship; patronage; ~**heilige**, patron (saint); patroness.
besker'ming, protection; patronage, auspices; cover; guard; aegis; conservancy; *onder* ~ *van die NAG*, under cover of the night; *in* ~ *NEEM*, take under one's protection; *ONDER* ~ *van*, under the auspices of; *ONDER* ~ *van die burgemeester*, under the patronage of the mayor.
besker'mings: ~**beleid**, policy of protection; ~**laag**, protective coating; ~**maatreël**, protective measure; ~**tarief**, protective tariff.
beskerm': ~**ling**, (-e), protégé; ~**middel**, protective remedy; means of protection; guard; ~**reling**, protection rail; ~**ster**, (-s), protectress, chaperon; ~**vrou**, patroness.
beskiet', (~), fire at, bombard, shell, pound (with cannon), batter; shoot (at); cover (by cannon fire); ~**er**, (-s), bombarder; shot; ~**ing**, bombarding, shelling, bombardment.
beskik, (~), manage, arrange, dispose (by testament); ~ *oor*, have at one's disposal; ~**al**, (-le), busy-body; ~**baar**, (..**bare**), available, forthcoming, at one's disposal, on hand; ~ *baar stel (maak)*, make available; release (film); ~**baarheid**, availability; ~**baarstelling**, the making available of; ~**ker**, (-s), disposer; ~**king**, (-e, -s), disposal, arrangement; appointment; command; dispensation; *die* ~ *king OOR lopende water*, the command over running water; *TER* ~ *king*, available; *TOT sy* ~ *king hê*, have at his disposal; ~**kingsreg**, right of disposal.
beskil'der, (~), paint; blazon; ~ *de vensters*, stained-glass windows; ~**ing**, painting.
beskim'mel, (~), grow mouldy (musty); mildew; ~(**d**), (-**de**), mouldy, musty, mildewed, mildewy; bashful, shy, timid (maiden); ~**dheid**, mouldiness; shyness.
beskimp', (~), mock, jeer at, revile, scorn, flout, scoff at, quip, gibe (at); ~**er**, (-s), reviler, scoffer, giber; ~**ing**, (-e, -s), insult, abuse, jeering, mockery, flouting.
beskin'der, (~), slander, denigrate, malign, detract, decry, disparage, defame, backbite, calumniate; ~**aar**, (-s), slanderer, maligner, defamer, backbiter, calumniator, disparager; ~**ing**, slander(ing), defamation, calumniation.
beskon'ke, intoxicated, inebriated, tipsy, drunk(en), in liquor, worse for liquor; ~**ne**, (-s), inebriate, alcoholic, drunk; ~**nheid**, drunkenness, intoxication, tipsiness.
besko're, granted to, allotted; *dit was my nie* ~ *nie*, it was not my fortune.
beskot, (-te), partition, wainscot; party wall; bulkhead (of ship); panelling; dado; boarding; ~**reling**, fence rail; ~**werk**, lining, wainscoting.
beskou', (~), view, look at, eye, behold; rate, hold; consider (offer); presume, envisage; apprehend; count (a blessing); contemplate; *OP sigself* ~, taken by itself; *as VERLORE* ~, give up for lost; *alles WEL* ~, all things considered, after all; ~**end**, (-e), speculative; ~**enswaardig**, (-e), worth looking at; ~**er**, (-s), looker-on, spectator; contemplator; ~**ing**, (-e, -s), consideration; contemplation; opinion, study; review, critique (of book, work of art); thoughts (on a subject); *buite* ~ *ing LAAT*, leave out of consideration (account); ignore; *by NADER(E)* ~*ing*, on closer inspection (examination).
beskreeu', (~), shout at.
beskrei', (-de), tear-stained; *met* ~ *de oë*, with tear-stained eyes.
beskroomd', (-e), timid, pigeon-hearted, timorous, bashful, diffident, shy; ~**heid**, diffidence, shyness, timidity, timorousness, bashfulness.
beskry', (~), bestride.
beskryf', **beskrywe**, (~), describe, define, picture, depict; write on, cover with writing; draw up in writing (deed); '*n sirkel* ~, move in a circle; draw (describe) a circle; ~**baar**, (..**bare**), describable.
beskry'wend, (e), descriptive.
beskry'wing, (-e, -s), description; ~**spunt**, point for discussion, item (on the agenda).
beskub', (-de), scaly, covered with scales.
beskuit', (-e), rusk; ~**blik**, rusk tin; ~**kleur**, biscuit (colour).
beskul'dig, (~), accuse, charge, blame; inculpate, impeach; arraign; denunciate, criminate; ~ *van*, accuse of; ~**de**, (-s), accused; defendant; ~**debank**, dock; ~**end**, (-e), accusatory, denunciatory, imputative, inculpatory, criminative; ~**er**, (-s), accuser; plaintiff: impeacher, denunciator; ~**ing**, (-e, -s), accusation, charge, impeachment, complaint, inculpation, arraignment; denunciation, imputation, crimination; inculpation; *AKTE van* ~*ing*, indictment; '*n* ~*ing INBRING teen*, lay a charge against.
beskut', (~), protect, shelter, screen; guard, shield; fence, cover; ~**ting**, protection, shelter; fence; (ankle) guard, lee (slip), coverture.
beskyn', (~), shine on.
beslaan', (w) (~), stud (with nails); mount (with metal); occupy, fill, comprise (pages); cover, extend over (space); dim with moisture (panes); shoe (horse); fur (tongue); (b) (-**de**, **beslane**), coated, furred (tongue, kettle); *goed* ~ *wees*, be very well prepared; ~**hamer**, farrier's shoeing hammer.
beslaap', (~), (ong.) sleep on; sleep with; *ek sal my daarop* ~, I'll sleep on it.
beslag', seizure (of person); distraint (on property); embargo (on ship); fittings, mount(ing) (with ornamental metal); dough paste, batter; ferrule; metal work (on furniture, door); escutcheon (keyhole); clasps (family Bible); chape (on sword); fur (on tongue); '*n Bybel met KOPER* ~, a Bible with copper mountings (clasps); *sy* ~ *KRY*, get into a settled state; ~ *LÊ op iem. se goed*, attach (seize, confiscate) someone's property; *in* ~ *NEEM*, take up (room); engross (attention); take possession of; ~**bak**, mash-tub; ~**deeg**, batter; ~**dop**, ferrule (of cane); ~**lêer**, distrainer, appropriator; ~**legging**, attachment; confiscation; execution, distress; seizure, distraint; ~ *legging op iem. se BOEDEL*, levying a distress on someone's estate; '*n saak sy* ~ *GEE*, clinch a matter; ~ *legging op GOED*, arrest (attachment) of property; ~**leggingsbevel**, order of attachment; ~**lyn**, gasket; knitting yarn; ~**meel**, flour for batter; ~**neming**, capture; ~**reling**, garnish-rail; ~**ring**, ferrule; ~**skuldenaar**, garnishee; ~**spyker**, stud.
besleg', (~), decide, settle (dispute); ~**ting**, (-e, -s), settlement, decision.
beslis', (w) (~), settle, determine, decide; award, adjudicate; conclude; (b) (-**te**), decided, crisp (manner); positive, pronounced, resolute; (bw) decidedly, definitely; positively; categorically; ~**send**, (e), decisive, final, crucial, conclusive (proof); determinative, determinate, definitive, fateful, peremptory, determinant (factor); ~*sende OOMBLIK*, critical moment; ~*sende STEM*, casting vote; ~**sing**, decision, award, adjudication, ruling, determination, resolution; finish; ~**singswedstryd**, deciding match; decider; ~**t'heid**, peremptoriness, determination, firmness, decisiveness, resoluteness, crispness.
beslob'ber, (~), beslubber.
beslom'mer, (~), annoy, vex, trouble; ~**ing**, (-e, -s), ~**nis**, (-se), vexation, trouble, bother; (mv) cares (of office).
beslo'te, resolved, determined; private; close (corpo-

ration); ~ *TESTAMENT*, closed will; *in 'n* ~ *VERGADERING*, in a private meeting; ~**nheid**, resoluteness, determination.
beslui'er, (-de), veiled, foggy, filmy.
be'sluip, (~), steal upon, stalk (game).
besluit', (s) (-e), resolution (of meeting); decree; ordination; decision, conclusion, close; *tot 'n* ~ *BRING*, bring to a close; *INGEVOLGE* ~ *VAN . . .*, in accordance with the resolution of . . .; *tot 'n* ~ *KOM*, *'n* ~ *NEEM*, make up one's mind; arrive at a decision; *tot* ~ *OPMERK*, remark in conclusion; *TEN* ~*e*, *TOT* ~, in conclusion; *hieruit TREK ek die* ~ *dat . . .*, from this I infer (conclude) that . . .; *van* ~ *VERANDER*, change one's mind; (w) (~), resolve, make up one's mind; conclude (speech); wind up; decide, determine (on doing); infer; *hy kon nie DAARTOE* ~ *nie*, he could not decide to act; *DAARUIT* ~ *ek dat . . .*, from this I infer that . . .; *OOR 'n saak* ~, take a decision about a matter; ~ *TOT*, decide on; ~**eloos**, (..**lose**), irresolute, wavering, hesitant; ~**eloosheid**, indecision, wavering, irresolution, hesitancy; ~**nemer**, decision taker; ~**neming**, decision-taking.
beslyk', (~), bemire, cover with mud.
besmeer, (~), soil, smear, besmear; mess (up); grease; grime; bedraggle; plaster, (be)daub; dirty, smudge; foul, grime; ~(**d**)', (-**de**), (be)smeared, soiled, dirty, bedrabbled, full of dirt, grimy.
besmet', (w) (~), infect, contaminate, pollute, attaint, defile; stain; blur; taint (milk); (b) (-**te**), infected, polluted, contaminated; infested; *met maaiers* ~, fly-blown; ~**lik, (-e)**, contagious, infectious, catching; epidemic; zymotic; ~ *like MISGEBOORTE*, contagious abortion; ~ *like ONVRUGBAARHEID*, infectious sterility; ~ *like SIEKTE*, infectious disease; ~ *te SKENKER*, infected donor; ~**likheid**, infectiousness, contagiousness; ~**ting**, infection, contamination, contagion; vitiation; sepsis; defilement; infestation (weeds); ~**tingsbron**, source of infection; ~**ingsgevaar**, danger (risk) of infection; ~**tingshaard**, nidus,,seat of infection.
besnaar', (~), string; ~(**d**)', (-**de**), strung; *'n fyn* ~ *de gemoed*, a sensitive (highly strung) mind.
besne'de, circumcized; cut; *fyn* ~ *gelaatstrekke*, clear-cut (delicate) features; ~**ne, (-s)**, circumcized person.
besnoei', (~), curtail; retrench, pare, axe (expenses); cut (salaries); clip (hedge); prune (tree); ~**ing**, curtailment, retrenchment; pruning; concision; cut.
besnuf'fel, (~), smell at, sniff at; pry into (secrets).
besny', (~), circumcize; cleanse (Bible); cut, carve; pare; ~ **denis**, ~ **ding**, circumcision; concision; ~**er**, circumcizer; ~**werk**, clipping.
be'soar, (-s), bezoar; ~**poeier**, bezoar powder.
besoe'del, (~), stain, contaminate, sully, smudge, dirty, befoul, blacken, besmirch, grime, attaint, blemish, pollute, defile; ~(**d**), (-**de**), stained, contaminated, sullied; polluted (air); guilty (conscience); ~**ing**, contamination, sullying; blemish; defilement, pollution.
besoek', (s) (-e), visit, call; visitors; attendance; *'n* ~ *AFLÊ*, make a call, pay a visit; *'n* ~ *BEANTWOORD*, return a call; *VERPLIGTE* ~, duty call; *op* ~ *WEES*, be on a visit; (w) (~), (pay a) visit, call on, come around; try, afflict; attend (church); frequent (bioscope); *die Here het ons met droogte* ~, the Lord has visited (afflicted, tried) us with drought; ~**dag**, at-home day; visiting day; ~**er, (-s)**, visitor, caller, frequenter, guest; ~**ersboek**, visitors' book; ~**ersburo**, visitors' bureau; ~**erskamer**, drawing-room; ~**ing, (-e, -s)**, visitation, affliction, trial; ~**reg**, right to visit (children); ~**ster, (-s)**, female visitor.
besoe'tjie, (-s), zinnia.
besog', (-te), (vero.) visited, frequented; afflicted; *'n goed* ~ *te vergadering*, a well attended meeting.
besol'dig, (w) (~), pay, (give) salary; remunerate; (b) **(-de)**, salaried, paid, stipendiary; remunerated; ~**ing**, pay, wages, salary, stipend, emolument; remuneration; ~*ing v.d. sonde is die dood*, the wages of sin is death.

beson'der, (b) (-e), particular, special; peculiar, strange; red-letter, rare, exceptional; *'n* ~ *e GUNS*, a special favour; *IN die* ~, especially, particularly; *IN* ~, especially; (bw) exceptionally, particularly; excessively; extremely; keenly; eminently; ~ *knap*, exceptionally smart (clever); ~**heid, (..hede)**, detail, particular, item; particularity; (mv) minutiae; *in nader(e)* ~ *hede tree*, enter into details; ~**lik** = **besonder** (bw); ~**s, (-e)**, particular, special; apart; *niks* ~ *s nie*, nothing uncommon, nothing out of the ordinary.
beson'dig, (~), commit (sin), be guilty of, perpetrate; *jou aan IEM.* ~, wrong a person; *hom* ~ *aan iem. se LEWE*, (ong., vero.), take someone's life.
beson'ke, well-considered; *sy* ~ *oordeel*, his well-considered judgment.
beson'ne, considerate, sedate, level-headed, thoughtful (person); well-considered (view); ~**nheid**, cautiousness, circumspection.
beson'ning, insolation.
beso'pe, fuddled (with drink), worse for drink, drunk; drunken, intoxicated, under the influence of alcohol; ~**nheid**, drunkenness.
besô're, (~), see **besorg**.
besorg', (w) (~), have a care of, attend to (animals); give cause (trouble); deliver (letters); procure, find, furnish (someone with); *ek sal die PAKKIE veilig* ~, I will deliver the parcel safely; *'n kind TUIS* ~, take a child home; (b) **(-de)**, anxious, solicitous, concerned, uneasy; ~**d'heid**, anxiety, solicitude, care, concern, worry, searchings of the heart, disquietude; ~**er, (-s)**, procurer; provider; delivery man; ~**ing**, delivery.
bespaar', (~), economize, save (money); ~ *jou die moeite*, save yourself the trouble; ~**der**, economizer.
bespan', (~), harness to (horse); inspan; string; (b) **(-ne)**, animal-drawn; strung; ~**ning**, inspanning, harnessing, draught; stringing.
bespa'ring, saving, economy; ~**srit**, economy run.
bespat', (~), spatter, splash, bedabble; drabble; ~**ting**, splashing.
bespeel', (~), finger, play (on an instrument); ~**baar**, (..**bare**), fit to be played on, playable.
bespek', (~), lard.
bespe'ler, player (on an instrument).
bespe'ling, playing (on).
bespeur', (~), perceive, descry, observe, detect, discover, notice; ~**baar, (..bare)**, perceivable, noticeable, detectable; ~**ing**, detection.
bespied', (~), spy, watch; descry; espy; ~**er, (-s)**, spy, espier, watcher; ~**ing**, spying, espionage, espial.
bespie'ël, (~), philosophize.
bespie'ëlend, bespie'gelend, (-e), speculative, reflective, contemplative; ~*e wysbegeerte*, (ong.), speculative philosophy.
bespie'ëling, bespie'geling, (-e, -s), speculation, contemplation.
bespioeneer', (~), spy on.
bespik'kel, (~), speckle.
bespoed', (~) *see* **bespoedig**.
bespoe'dig, (~), accelerate (motion); hasten, push on; precipitate; speed up, dispatch, expedite (business); ~**ing**, acceleration, hastening, precipitation, speeding up; expedition.
bespoeg', (~), spit on, spit at; bespit.
bespoel', (~), wash (the shores of); irrigate.
bespot', (~), mock, laugh at, ridicule, gibe (at); flout, deride; ~**lik, (-e)**, ridiculous, ludicrous, farcical; preposterous; *hom* ~ *lik maak*, make an ass of himself; ~**likheid**, ridiculousness; ~**tend, (-e)**, mocking, burlesque; ~**ter, (-s)**, mocker, derider, giber; ~**ting**, mockery, derision, ridicule; *aan die* ~ *ting prysgee*, hold up to ridicule.
bespraak', (-te), (ong.), eloquent; ~**t'heid, (ong.)**, eloquence; verbosity.
bespreek', (w) (~), discuss, talk about, talk over, argue, engage, palaver; review (book); bespeak (clothes); exorcize (evil spirits); book, reserve (seats); canvass; discourse; retain (counsel); (b)

(-te), bespoken; reserved (seat); ~geld, booking fee; ~kantoor, booking office, box office.
bespre'king, (-e, -s), discussion, discursion, palaver; conference; debate; booking, reservation (of seats); '*n voorstel in* ~ *BRING*, bring up a motion for discussion; '*n* ~ *HOU met*, hold a consultation with; *PUNT van* ~, subject of consideration (debate); ~ *WY aan*, give consideration to; ~sgeld, booking fee; ~skantoor, booking office, box office.
bespring', (~), spring upon, leap upon, assail; cover (mare); ~er, (-s), assailant.
besprin'kel, (~), (be)sprinkle (with water); dredge (with flour); perfuse; asperse (ritual); ~ing, aspersion; affusion; perfusion; sprinkling.
besproei', (~), irrigate, water; spray, sprinkle; ~baar, (..bare), irrigable; ~er, (-s), spray, irrigator; ~ing, irrigation; ~ingsdepartement, department of irrigation; ~ingsdoeltreffendheid, irrigation efficiency; ~ingskema, irrigation scheme; ~ingsraad, irrigation board; ~ingsvermoë, irrigability; ~ingswerke, irrigation works; ~ingswet, irrigation act.
besproet', (-e), freckled.
bespro'ke, (vero.), discussed; booked (seat).
bespu', (~), spit upon, spit at, bespit.
bespuit', (~), squirt (water upon); spray; ~ing, spraying; ~ingsmiddel, spray.
bespuug', (~), *see* bespu.
bespy'ker, (~), nail, stud with nails; board.
bes'semerstaal, Bessemer steel.
bes'sie, (-s), berry; jujube; bramble; *hy het te veel* ~ *s geëet*, he has had a drop too much; boom, bos, berrybush *(Rhus dregeana)*; ~sap, currant juice; ~vormig, (-e), bacciform; ~was, berry wax.
bestaan', (s) existence, livelihood, bread-winning, subsistence, living; being, life; *die HONDERD-JARIGE* ~, the hundredth anniversary; '*n* ~ *MAAK uit*, make a livelihood from; *die STRYD om die* ~, the struggle for existence; '*n goeie* ~ *VIND*, earn a good living; have a fair competency; (w) (~), be, exist; live, subsist; make a living; consist of; ~ *IN*, consist in; ~ *UIT*, consist of, be composed of; ~ *VAN*, live on; ~baar, (..bare), reconcilable, compatible (with); consistent (with); reasonable (offer); possible; congruent; ~baarheid, compatibility; possibility; congruency; ~de, existing, existent, extant, going (concern); *AL die* ~*de*, all that is; '*n* ~ *de SAAK*, a going concern; ~sekerheid, social security.
bestaans': ~ekonomie, subsistence economy; ~grond, reason for existence; ~landbou, subsistence agriculture; ~middel, livelihood; ~minimum, breadline; ~reg, right of existence; ~veiligheid, social security; ~voorwaarde, condition of existence; ~vorm, substantive form (of a verb).
bestand', (s) permanence; true; *Twaalfjarige B*~, 12 Year's Peace; (b) proof (against); match for, equal to; *teen DROOGTE* ~, drought resisting; *teen VUUR* ~, fire-proof; ~ *teen die WEER*, weather proof; ~ *WEES teen*, be equal to, be able to cope with; ~deel, ingredient, element, component (constituent, constitutive) part; ~heid, resistance; ~*heid teen siekte*, resistance to disease.
bes'te, (s) (-s), best, pick; champion; (b) best choice, premier, crack, excellent; dear (in beginning letters); *ALLES ten* ~!, goodbye!; *Alles van die* ~!, everything of the best!; *DIE* ~, the pink; *die EERSTE die* ~ *vat*, take the first that comes, choose at random; *net die* ~ *s GAAN verder*, only the very best (champions) go further; *iets ten* ~ *GEE*, render; put something across; *die* ~ *HOOP*, hope for the best; ~ *JAN*, My dear John; *sy het 'n LIED ten* ~ *gegee*, she obliged us with a song; *MY (ou)* ~, my better-half; *OP sy* ~, at his (its) best; at most; *na my* ~ *VERMOË*, to the best of my ability.
beste'ding, expenditure, spending (money); use (time); bestowal (care); devotion to (of energy).
bestee', (~), spend (money), expend on; use (time); bestow (care) on; devote (energy) to; lay out (money); ~baar, spendable.
besteek'band, headband (of book).

besteel', (~), rob, steal from.
bestek', (-ke), compass, space, purview; builder's estimate, specifications; bill of quantities; check point; radius (of action); *BUITE die* ~ *van hierdie boek*, outside the scope of this book; *die* ~ *te buite GAAN*, exceed the limit(s) (of a scheme); *baie in 'n KLEIN* ~, a great deal in a small compass; *OPMAAK van* ~*ke*, quantity surveying; *VOLGENS* ~, according to specifications; *binne die* ~ *van een WEEK*, within the compass (space) of one week; ~opmaker, quantity surveyor; ~tekening, plan.
bestel', (s) dispensation; ordination; scheme of things; *Gods* ~, God's ordination; (w) (~), order (goods); bespeak, indent; arrange, ordain (by Providence); deliver (letters); serve (summons); '*n dagvaarding* ~ *AAN*, serve a summons on; *GOEDERE wat* ~ *is*, goods on order; *op die* ~ *de UUR*, on the appointed hour; ~afdeling, delivery department (section); ~baar, (..bare), deliverable; ~biljet, order form; ~boek, order book; ~briefie, order (note); ~dag, call-day; ~diens, delivery (cartage) service; parcel service(s); ~diensaannemer, cartage contractor; ~driewiel, carriage (carrier) tricycle; delivery tricycle; ~fiets, delivery cycle; ~gebied, cartage area; ~huis, express company; ~kaart, order card; ~kantoor, order office, forwarding office, parcel office; ~klerk, indent clerk; ~koste, carriage (fee); cartage charge; ~kring, cartage radius (area); ~ler, (-s), one who orders; indenter; delivery man (boy); commissionaire; ~lerig, (-e), whimsical, capricious.
bestel'ling, (-e, -s), order; indent; delivery (letters); *OP* ~ *gemaak*, made to order; '*n* ~ *OPNEEM*, take an order; '*n* ~ *PLAAS*, place an order; '*n* ~ *UITVOER*, execute an order; *VOL* ~ *s wees*, be full of whims and fancies, hard to please; *VOLGENS* ~, as per order; as ordered; ~sboek, order book; ~swerwer, canvasser.
bestel': ~motor, delivery van (vehicle); ~offisier, indent officer; ~tarief, cartage rate; ~vorm, order form; ~wa, delivery van (vehicle).
bestem', (~), destine, mark out, earmark; bound for (boat); fix (time); apportion, appropriate, set apart; ordain; design; designate; *dié skip is vir Kaapstad* ~, this ship is bound for Cape Town.
bes'temaats: *met algar* ~ *wees*, be hail-fellow-well-met with everybody.
bestemd', (-e), intended, destined, set apart, appropriated, ear-marked; *die* ~ *e DAG*, the day fixed upon, the appointed day; *die* ~ *e PLEK*, the appointed place.
bestem'ming, destination; destiny, fate; designation; *plek van* ~, destination; ~swyser, destination sign.
bestem'pel, (~), stamp; label; name, call (names), designate as; ~ing, stamping; naming, designation.
besten'dig, (w) (~), make permanent, confirm; perpetuate; (b) (-e), lasting, durable, permanent, constant, stable, dependable (rainfall); consistent (play); ~*e RIVIER*, antecedent river; ~*e WEER*, settled weather; ~heid, permanence, permanency, stability, constancy; continuity; perpetuity; ~ing, continuance, perpetuation.
besterf', bester'we, (~) (ong.): *sy KLEUR het* ~, he became pale; *die WOORDE het op sy lippe* ~, the words died (away) on his lips.
bes'tevaar, (vero.) good old man.
bestiaal', (..tiale), (vero.) bestial.
bestialiseer', (ge-), bestialize.
bestialiteit', bestiality.
bestier', guidance, dispensation (of God); *see* bestuur; ~der, *see* bestuurder; ~ing, guidance, act of Providence; *dit was 'n* ~*ing*, it was an act of divine Providence.
bestik', (~), stitch, embroider.
bestik', bestik'pel, (~), stitch, embroider.
bestip', bestip'pel, (~), dot, speckle.
besto'lene, (-s), robbed person.
bestook', (~), harass, batter, press hard; bombard, pelt (with questions, stones); pepper; pound, ply, assail, cannonade (a fortress); *met vrae* ~, bombard (ply) with questions.

bestorm', (~), storm, assail, assault (fortress); rush at, make a dash; besiege (with requests); *die bank is* ~, there was a run on the bank; ~**er**, (s), assailant; ~**ing**, storming, assault, attack, onslaught; rush (on a bank).
bestor'we, (ong.) deadly pale, livid; ~ *boedel*, deceased estate.
bestraal', (~), irradiate, beam upon, illuminate; X-ray.
bestraat', (w) (~), pave, revet (with stones); pitch (dam wall); (b) **(bestrate)**, paved.
bestraf', (~), punish; rebuke, censure, animadvert, correct, reprove, amerce; ~**baar**, (..**bare**), rebukable; ~**fing**, *kyk* **bestrawwing**.
bestra'ling, (-e, -s), (ir)radiation; X-ray treatment; insolation.
bestra'ting, paving, pavage; pavement.
bestraw'wing (-e, -s), rebuke, reprimand, reproof, scolding, censure; punishment.
bestre'de, opposed, contested (election).
bestreep', (-te), striped.
bestrik', (~), adorn with knots (bows, ties).
bestrooi', (~), strew (on), bestrew, dust, sprinkle; powder.
bestry', (~), combat, fight against (person); arraign, controvert, contest (statement); dispute, oppose (proposal); cover, meet, defray (expenses); ~**baar**, (..**bare**), contestable, disputable, opposable; ~**(d)er**, (-s), antagonist, adversary, opponent, impugner; combatant; ~ *(d)er van verkwisting*, antiwaster; ~**ding**, combating, contest(ing), impugnment; antagonism; defrayment, defrayal; control (weeds, pests).
bestryk', (~), stroke (with hand); coat, spread over; command, cover, rake; range, sweep (artillery); *die BOEK* ~ *die hele gebied*, the book covers the whole subject; *met KALK* ~, coat with lime; *met PIK* ~, smear with pitch; ~**ing**, stroking; spreading, covering; raking (gun-fire).
bestudeer', (~), study (a book); investigate (a matter); *'n* ~ *de houding aanneem*, strike an attitude, adopt a studied attitude; ~**der**, (-s), student.
bestude'ring, study; examination.
bestuif', **bestui'we**, (~), cover with dust; pollinate, pollenize; dust; spray.
bestui'wer, insufflator; pollinator; sprayer.
bestui'wing, pollination; ~ *met poeier*, dusting (with powder); spraying; ~**sbewerker**, pollination agent; ~**stadium**, pollination stage.
bestu'rend, (-e), managing, directive, administrative; ~*e direkteur*, managing director.
bestu'ring, management, control, guidance; driving, steering (car); piloting (plane).
bestuur', (s) **(besture)**, management, direction; directorate, (managing) body, board; committee; guide, guidance; government; control; governance; *in die* ~ *dien*, serve on the committee (in the management); (w) (~), govern, manage, conduct, direct, administer, handle, operate, rule, guide; steer, drive (motor car); contrive, pilot (aeroplane); navigate (vessel); ~**baar**, (..**bare**), dirigible, manageable, guidable; navigable, steerable; ..*bare BALLON*, dirigible; ..*bare SKROEF*, controllable pitch propellor; ~**baarheid**, navigability; ~**der**, (-s), manager, director, administrator; administratrix; entrepreneur (trade, commerce); governor; head; driver (of motor car, train); conductor, motorman; pilot (aeroplane); ~**der-direkteur**, managing director; ~**deres'**, (-se), manageress; conductress; ~**dersertifikaat**, pilot's (driving) certificate; ~**derskap**, (-pe), managership; ~**derskunde**, management ability; programming; ~**derslisensie**, driver's licence; ~**lik**, (-e), administrative; ~**sake**, management matters.
bestuurs': ~**amp**, executive post; ~**besluit**, decision (resolution) of committee; ~**hervorming**, government reform; ~**kamer**, committee room; ~**komitee**, management committee; ~**kunde**, public administration; ~**lid**, committee member, board member, member of the board; ~**liggaam**, governing body; ~**moeilikhede**, administrative difficulties (problems); ~**(on)koste**, cost of administration;

~**plig**, management duty; ~**pos**, managerial post; ~**raad**, governing board; ~**reg**, administrative law; ~**vergadering**, board meeting, committee meeting; ~**verkiesing**, election of board (committee); ~**vorm**, form of government.
bestyg', (~), mount (throne, horse); bestride (horse); ascent (mountain); ~**baar**, (..**bare**), mountable; ~**ing**, ascension, ascent; mounting.
besui'de, (to the) south of.
besui'ker, (~), sugar; sweeten.
besui'nig, (~), economize; retrench, axe, cut down (expenses); husband (one's strength); ~**er**, (-s), economizer; ~**ing**, (-e, -s), economy, saving; economizing, retrenchment; ~**ingsmaatreël**, measure of economy; ~**ingsplan**, plan to economize; ~**ingspoging**, effort at economy; ~**ingsug**, desire for economy.
besuip', (~), get drunk, booze; *hy het hom* ~, he is drunk.
besuur', (~), (ong.), rue, suffer, pay for; *hy sal dit nog* ~, he will rue it yet.
beswaar', (s) (..**sware**), objection, demur, grievance; gravamen; difficulty, scruple; drawback; *besware HÊ*, have objections, object; *besware MAAK (opper)*, raise objections; (w) (~), burden, trouble, demur, clog; oppress; weight (figures); load; burden; *die GEWETE* ~, burden one's conscience; *GROND* ~, mortgage ground; ~**(d)'**, (-de), burdened, encumbered, heavy, uneasy; ~ *de GEMIDDELDE*, weighted average; *met 'n* ~ *de GEMOED*, with a heavy heart; ~ *(d) VOEL*, have misgivings; ~**de**, (-s), objector; ~**gronde**, grounds of objection; ~**lik**, with difficulty, hardly, scarcely; *ek kan dit* ~ *lik glo*, I can hardly believe it; ~**maker**, objector, protester, demurer; ~**skrif**, petition, complaint, remonstrance; gravamen.
beswad'der, (~), calumniate, slander, asperse, besmirch (character); ~**ing**, defamation, slandering, mud-slinging.
beswag'tel, (~), swathe.
beswan'ger, (~), impregnate, make pregnant; ~**d**, (-e), impregnated; laden, fraught (with).
beswa'rend, (-e), cumbersome, burdensome; aggravating, damning, damaging; incriminating (evidence).
beswa'ring, (-e, -s), encumbrance, mortgaging, charge (on estate); oppression.
beswa'(w)el, (~), treat with sulphur.
besweer', (~), swear, make oath, adjure, objure; exorcise, lay (ghosts); conjure up (ghosts); entreat earnestly; charm (snake).
besweet', **(beswete)**, perspiring; in a sweat.
beswe'ring, adjuration, invocation, objuration, conjuration; incantation, exorcism; ~**sformulier**, (formula of) incantation.
beswer'noot, mad, daft, bedevilled.
bes'wil: *vir jou EIE* ~, in your own interests; for your own good; *'n LEUENTJIE om* ~, a white lie.
beswyk', (~), succumb (to wounds); yield (to temptation); die; give way, collapse; *AAN 'n siekte* ~, die of a disease; *onder die LAS* ~, sink beneath the load; *voor die OORMAG* ~, yield to superior numbers; *TOT* ~ *ens toe*, to death; ~ *vir (voor) die VERLEIDING*, yield to temptation; ~**ing**, succumbing, yielding.
beswym', (~), (ong.), faint, swoon; ~**ing**, swoon, fainting fit.
besy'de, alongside, beside, next to; ~ *die waarheid*, beside the truth.
besy'fer, (~), figure out, compute, evaluate; ~**ing**, (-e, -s), calculation, figuring out, reckoning.
bet, **(ge-)**, bathe (wound), dab.
betaal', (w) (~), pay, foot (the bill), settle (debt); discharge (obligation, debt); disburse; *betalende GAS*, paying guest; *met geen GELD te* ~ *nie*, priceless; *KONTANT* ~, pay cash; *LAAT* ~, charge; make a person pay; *met jou LEWE* ~, pay with one's life; *die ONKOSTE is nog te* ~, the expenses are still outstanding (due); *die SAAK* ~ *goed*, the concern pays well; *te VEEL laat* ~, overcharge; *VOORUIT* ~, pay in advance; (b) **(-de)**, paid; *met* ~ *de antwoord*, reply prepaid; ~**baar**, (..**bare**), due,

betaam

payable; ~**beampte,** pay(ing) officer; ~**bestelling,** payment indent; ~**dag,** pay day; due date; quarter day; ~**datum,** due date; ~**diens,** pay corps; ~**kantoor,** pay-office; ~**lys,** pay bill (sheet); ~**meester,** paymaster; purser (ship); ~**meester-generaal,** paymaster-general; quartermaster; quaestor; ~**middel,** (legal) tender, currency, money, circulating medium; *STERK* ~ *middel,* hard currency; *SWAK* ~ *middel,* soft currency; ~**rol,** pay bill, pay sheet, pay list, pay roll; ~**staat,** pay list, pay sheet; ~**tyd,** time for (date of) payment; ~**venster,** ticket window, cash aperture; ~**vermoë,** solvency; ~**wyse,** method of payment.

betaam', (~), become, (be)fit, behove, be proper, suit, beseem; *dit ~ jou nie,* it is not for you to; ~**lik, (-e),** becoming, comely; due; (be)fitting, beseeming, decent, seemly, proper; ~**likheid,** decency, decorum, seemliness, propriety, convenance, becomingness, fitness.

beta'kel, (~), dirty, besmear; begrime, bedraggle.
beta'lend, (-e), paying, rewarding, profitable.
beta'ler, (-s), payer; paymaster.
beta'ling, (-e, -s), payment, defrayal, pay; salary; settlement; *GELYKE* ~ *vir gelyke werk,* (equal) rate for the job; *TEEN* ~ *van,* on payment of.
betalings: ~**balans,** balance of payments; ~**mandaat,** pay warrant; ~**termyn,** term of payment, prompt; ~**vermoë,** ability (capacity) to pay; ~**voorwaarde,** condition of payment; ~**wyse,** method of payment.
betas', (~), finger, touch, feel, handle; cuddle; paw; palpate (doctor); ~**ting,** handling, feeling; palpation; fingering.
be'te, (-s), (vero.) morsel.
bete'ël, (~), pave with tiles, tile; ~**ing,** tiling.
beteer', (~), tar.
bete'ken, (~), mean, signify, amount, betoken, denote, import, imply; convey (meaning); spell (ruin), portend (disgrace); serve (summons); count for; *'n DAGVAARDING* ~ *aan,* serve a summons on; *hy* ~ *nie VEEL nie,* he does not count for much; ~**ing, (-e, -s),** service (of summons).
bete'kenis, (-se), meaning, sense, signification, purport, significance, importance, consideration; denotation; connotation; note; account; *van GEEN* ~ *nie,* of no importance (account); ~ *HEG aan,* attach importance to; *MANNE van* ~, men of note; ~**leer,** semasiology, semantics; ~**loos, (..lose),** meaningless; empty, void; ~**vol, (-le),** significant, important; meaningful.
be'tel, betel; ~**neut,** areca (betel) nut; ~**palm,** betel (areca) palm.
be'ter, better; superior, ~ *AF wees,* be *in a better position; DES te* ~, so much the better; *NIKS* ~ *s nie,* nothing better; *dit maak die SAAK nie* ~ *nie,* that does not improve matters; *dis maar* ~ *SO,* it is just as well; *daar* ~ *aan TOE wees,* be better situated; *hy WEET van* ~, he knows better than that; ~ *WORD,* recover (from illness).
be'terhand: *die pasiënt is aan die* ~, the patient is recovering.
be'terskap, convalescence; improvement, rally, recovery; *ALLE* ~*!* I hope you will soon be well again!; ~ *BELOOF,* promise to turn over a new leaf.
be'terste, (skerts.), best; *die meer* ~ *manne,* picked men; the best.
be'ter: ~**wete:** *teen sy* ~**wete,** against his better judgement; ~**weter, (-s),** pedant, wiseacre, know-all; ~**weterig** = **betweterig.**
beteu'el, (~), restrain, check, moderate, control, refrain, bridle, hold in, guard, curb (passions); ~**aar,** checker; ~**end, (-e),** coercive; ~**ing,** restraint, curb, check, control.
beteu'ter(d), (b) (-de), confused, embarrassed, perplexed, puzzled, sheepish; (bw) blankly; perplexed; ~**dheid,** confusion, perplexity, embarrassment, puzzlement.
Bet'hlehem, Bethlehem (O.F.S.).
betig', (~), accuse, charge; correct (a child); *iem.* ~ *van,* accuse a person of; charge a person with; ~**ter, (-s),** accuser; ~**ting,** accusation, imputation, aspersion.

betreklik

betik', (-te), type-written, typed.
betim'mer, (~), board, wainscot; hammer; ~**ing,** wainscot(ing), boarding, timbering (in mines).
beti'tel, (~), name, style, give a title to, entitle, denominate; ~**ing,** naming; style, title, designation.
betjoins', perverse, cantankerous, contrary, impossible.
Bet'lehem, Bethlehem (Israel).
beto'gend, (-e), argumentative.
beto'ger, (-s), demonstrator, demonstrant.
beto'ging, (-e, -s), demonstration.
betok'kel, (~), play (strings).
beton', concrete; *gewapende* ~, reinforced concrete; ~**blok,** concrete block; ~**gebou,** concrete building; ~**gruis,** aggregate.
betonie', (-s), betony (plant).
beto'ning, (-e, -s), demonstration, manifestation; accentuation, stress.
beton': ~**laag,** concrete layer; ~**lorrie,** concrete mixing lorry; ~**masjiengeweernes,** pillbox; ~**menger,** concrete mixer; ~**vloer,** concrete floor; ~**werk,** concrete work.
betoog', (s) (betoë), argument(ation); expostulation; allegation; *dit BEHOEF geen* ~ *nie,* it stands to reason, it is self-evident; *'n lang* ~ *HOU,* expound at length; (w) (~), demonstrate, argue, prove, maintain, contend; hold forth; ~**baar,** (..**bare),** demonstrable; ~**grond,** (ground for) argument; ~**krag,** argumentative power; ~**skrif,** argumentative paper; ~**trant,** style of argument.
betoom', (~), *see* **beteuel.**
betoon'[1], (s) manifestation, demonstration; (w) (~), show, evince, manifest (joy), *hulde* ~, pay tribute.
betoon'[2], (w) (~), stress, accentuate.
betoor', (~), = **betower.**
bet'oorgrootmoeder, (..**vader),** great-great grandmother (grandfather).
beto'ring, (-de), towered.
beto'wer, (~), enchant, charm, fascinate, ravish, bewitch, enthral(l); spellbind; captivate; ~**aar, (-s),** enchanter; ~**end, (-e),** charming, fascinating, bewitching, enchanting, glamorous; ~**ing,** enchantment, glamour, captivation, charm, magic, fascination, spell; witchery.
betraan', (-de), tearful, tear-filled (eyes), tear-stained (cheeks).
betrag', (~), perform, observe, practise; consider; look at; *jou plig* ~, do your duty; ~**ting,** consideration, reflection, performance, discharge (of duty).
betra'lie, (~), rail in, lattice.
betrap', (~), tread; catch, surprise, entrap, detect; nail; *iem. op DIEFSTAL* ~, catch someone in the act of stealing; *op HETER daad* ~, catch redhanded; *iem. op 'n LEUEN* ~, catch someone out in a lie; ~**ping,** catching, detection.
betre'ding, treading (up)on; climbing.
betree', (~), tread upon, enter (church); foot, set foot upon (land).
betref', (~), concern, relate to, touch, affect; *wat DIT* ~, as for that, as far as that is concerned; *wat MY* ~, as for me; as far as I am concerned; ~**fende,** concerning, regarding, relative to, anent.
betrek', (~), occupy, move into, enter, take possession of (house); involve, implicate (in affair); mount guard (in trenches); cloud over, become overcast (sky); trick, cheat; obtain, get (goods); stalk (game); *iem. in 'n saak* ~, involve someone in a matter.
betrek'king, (-e, -s), relation (family); billet, situation, post, office, position, job; connection, reference; concern; ~ *op iets HÊ,* have a bearing on; ~*e AANKNOOP met,* enter into relations with; *watter* ~ *het dit op JOU?,* how does that concern you?; *SONDER* ~, out of employment; *met* ~ *TOT,* with reference to, regarding.
betrek'lik, (b) (-e), relative; comparative (poverty); (bw) comparatively, relatively; *ALLES is* ~, all things are relative; ~*e VOGGEHALTE,* relative humidity; ~*e VOORNAAMWOORD,* relative pronoun; ~*e WRINGINGSHOEK,* torsional strain; ~**heid,** relativity, relativeness.

betreur', (~), regret, lament, rue, deplore (one's incapacity); bewail, bemoan; condole; mourn for (lost friend); *sy lot* ~, pity oneself, bemoan one's fate; ~**enswaar'dig**, (-e), deplorable, pitiable, regrettable, lamentable; ~**enswaar'digheid**, deplorableness.

betrok'ke, relative; cloudy, overcast, gloomy, dull (sky); *die* ~ *AMPTENAAR*, the official concerned; *IN iets* ~ *wees*, be concerned in (mixed up with) something; ~**nheid**, involvement; ~**ne**, (-s), person concerned, drawee.

betrou', (~), trust.

betrou'baar, (..bare), trustworthy, creditable; dependable (person); reliable; authentic; ~**heid**, reliability; authenticity; trustworthiness; ~**heidsrit**, reliability run; ~**heidstoets**, reliability trial; ~**heidswedstryd**, reliability competition.

betuig', (~), testify, declare, assure, show; aver, protest, attest, profess (regard); express (sympathy); *sy dank* ~, render (express his) thanks.

betui'ging, (-e, -s), declaration (of one's feelings); protestation, profession (of friendship), expression (grief).

bet'weter, (-s), wiseacre, pedant, know-all; ~**ig**, (-e), pedantic; ~**y**, pedantry.

betwis', (w) (~), contest (point); challenge (statement); dispute (debt); contend, controvert; impeach (character); *'n setel* ~, contest a seat; (b) (-te), disputed; *'n lank* ~ *te saak*, a long-contested issue, a very vexed question; ~**baar**, (..bare), questionable, debatable, challengable, controversial, exceptionable, contestable, arguable, controvertible, contentious, moot (point), impugnable; ~**baarheid**, disputableness, contestability; ~**ter**, (-s), contester; challenger; impugner; ~**ting**, challenge, contestation.

beu: ~ *van iets wees*, sick (tired) of something.

beu'el, (-s), bugle, trumpet; horn; shackle (of padlock); gimbal (compass); trigger guard (rifle); joint; contact bow; bridle (in a mine); buckle (spring); clevis (on a wagon-pole); headsman; loop; brace; *sy eie* ~ *BLAAS*, blow one's own trumpet; *dit KAN nie deur die* ~ *nie*, it won't pass muster; ~**geblaas**, bugle-call; ~**blaser**, bugler; ~**perd**, vaulting horse; ~**sluiting**, swing-wire stopper; ~**tas**, chatelaine bag; ~**tjie**, spring catch; ~**trap**, loop step.

beuk¹, (s) (-e), aisle; nave.

beuk², (w), beat, thrash; pound (waves); *die golwe – die rotse*, the waves batter the rocks.

beuk³, (s) (-e), beech; ~**eboom**, beech (tree); ~**ebos**, beech wood; ~**ehout**, beech.

beu'kelaar, (-s), buckler.

beu'keneut, beech nut, beech-mast.

beu'kesbossie, aromatic shrub *(Lantana caffra)*.

beuk'hamer, mallet.

beul, (-e, -s), hangman, executioner; tormentor; *deur* ~ *shande*, (ong.) by the hangman; ~**s'kneg**, hangman's assistant.

beun'haas, (..hase), pettifogger, dabbler, bungler, quack.

beunhasery', quackery, pettifoggery.

beur, (ge-), pull with force, strain at, force one's way; exert oneself; struggle, strive; *opwaarts* ~, struggle upwards.

beurs, (-e), purse, pouch; scholarship, bursary; stock exchange; bursa (anat.); *GEMENE* ~ *maak*, pool resources; *'n LEE* ~ *hê*, have an empty purse; *'n STYWE* ~ *hê*, be well to do; have a long purse; ~**agent**, stockbroker; ~**berig**, stock list; ~**geswel**, cyst; ~**houer**, foundationer; exhibitioner; bursary holder; ~**ie**, (-s), small purse; ~**kringe** (stock) exchange circles; ~**krisis**, stock exchange crisis; ~**lid**, member of the stock exchange; ~**makelaar**, stockbroker; ~**notering**, stock market quotation; ~**sake**, stock exchange business; ~**spekulant**, stockjobber; ~**spekulasie**, stockjobbing; agiotage; ~**stelsel**, system of scholarships; ~**trekker**, bursary holder; ~**vakansie**, bank holiday; ~**vol**, purseful; ~**wenner**, bursary winner.

beurt, (-e), turn; bout; over, innings (cricket); *BY* ~ *e*, ~ *OM* ~, by turns, in turn; *aan die* ~ *KOM*, get one's turn; *OP sy* ~, in his turn; *iem. PRAAT uit sy* ~, someone has spoken out of turn; *te* ~ *VAL*, fall to the lot of; *VOOR sy* ~, out of his turn.

beur'telings, by turns, alternately, in rotation.

beurt'sang, antiphony, catch; respond; melibean song.

beurt'spel, foursome (golf).

beu'sel, (ge-), trifle, fribble, idle, dawdle, peddle, fiddle-faddle; ~**aar**, (-s), trifler, dilettante; dawdler; ~**ag'tig** (-e), trifling, trivial, puerile, potty, quotidian, footling, frivolous; fiddling, nugatory; ~**ag'tigheid**, (..hede), triviality, trifle, frivolity; small beer; ~**(a)ry'**, (-e), trifle, kickshaw, fiddle-faddle; ~**ing**, trifle; ~**praatjies**, piffle, nonsense; ~**werk**, trifling, dawdling.

bevaar', (~), navigate, sail (the ocean); *bevare SEEMAN (matroos)*, able-bodied seaman; *bevare VLIEËR*, experienced flyer; ~**baar**, (..bare), navigable; ~**baarheid**, navigability.

beval¹, (~), please; like; *die KIND* ~ *my*, the child appeals to me (attracts me); *hierdie PLEK* ~ *my*, I like this place.

beval'², (~), be confined; *sy is van 'n seun* ~ *(le)*, (ong.), she has given birth to a son.

beval': ~**lig**, (-e), gracious, charming; handsome, comely, graceful, pretty, elegant; ~**ligheid**, beauty, charm, grace(fulness), elegance, graciousness, comeliness.

beval'ling, (-e, -s), confinement, delivery (of a child), accouchement, parturition, lying-in; *ontydige* ~, premature confinement; ~**skoste**, confinement fees; ~**suitrusting**, layette.

bevang', (~), overcome, seize; ~**e**, seized; stiff, grain-sick, foundered (horse); *die PERD is* ~ *e*, the horse is foundered; the horse has collapsed owing to overwork; *van SKRIK* ~ *e*, seized with fear; ~**enheid**, seizure, constraint, embarrassment; founder(ing), heaves (horses), laminitis.

beva'rene, (-s), able rating.

bevark', (~), dirty, besmear; treat meanly.

bevat', (~), contain, carry, comprise, comprehend, conceive, grasp; imply; compass; ~**lik**, (-e), intelligent, intelligible, comprehensible, apprehensible, apprehensive; ~**likheid**, intelligence, comprehension, apprehensiveness, mental grasp; ~**tend**, (-e), comprising, inclusive of; ~**ter**, (-s), container; ~**ting**, (com)prehension, grasp; ~**tingsvermoë**, comprehensive faculty, mental grasp, comprehension.

beveel', (~), order, command, charge, direct, bid, enjoin, adjure, commend (spirit to God).

beveer', (~), feather.

beveg', (~), combat, contest, fight against; ~**ter**, (-s), opponent; ~**ting**, combating, fighting (against).

bevei'lig, (~), shelter, protect, safeguard, ensure, house, secure; ~**er**, (-s), safety device; ~**ing**, protection, security, safeguarding; ~**ingstoestel**, safety device.

bevel', (-e), order, command, precept, prescript(ion), mandate, charge, dictation, direction, injunction (judicial); bidding, behest; warrant, writ; dictate (of reason); enactment (government); *'n* ~ *tot AANHOUDING*, warrant of arrest; *'n* ~ *GEE*, give an order; ~ *tot HUISSOEKING*, search warrant; ~ *NISI*, rule nisi; *die* ~ *VOER oor*, be in command of; *OP* ~ *van*, by order of; *'n* ~ *UITREIK*, rule, order.

beve'lend, (-e), commanding, peremptory, preceptive.

bevel': ~**hebber**, (-s), commander; ~**hebberskap**, commandership; commanding office; chieftaincy; ~**s'gebied**, command; ~**skrif**, mandate, precept, edict; warrant, writ, mandamus, fieri facias; ~*skrif tot AANHOUDING*, warrant of arrest; *KRAGTENS 'n* ~*skrif*, under an order of court; ~**soldy**, command pay; ~**s'wisseling**, change of command; ~**voerder**, (-s), commander; officer commanding, commanding officer; ~**voerend**, (-e), commanding; ~*voerende offisier*, commanding officer, officer in command; ~**voering**, command.

beve'ring, feathering.

beverf', (~), paint on; cover with paint.

beves'tig, (~), confirm, attest, corroborate, bear out;

ordain, install, induct (new clergyman); predicate, affirm, approve, endorse (opinion); assert; fix (in wall); fasten (with string); consolidate; solemnize; perform (marriage); *in 'n AMP* ~, install in an office; *met 'n EED* ~, swear to (a statement), affirm with an oath; *'n HUWELIK* ~, perform a marriage ceremony; *die SYFERS* ~ *dit*, the figures prove it; ~**end, (-e)**, affirmative; predicative, positive, confirmative; corroboratory; declarative; *'n* ~*ende antwoord*, a reply in the affirmative; ~**er, (-s)**, approver; inductor.
beves'tiging, corroboration, confirmation, installment, installation, affirmation, verification; induction, predication, averment; ascertainment, fixation; consolidation; establishment (of crops); fixing, fastening.
beves'tigings: ~**diens, (-te)**, induction service; ~**eed**, affirmative oath; ~**middel**, means of attachment; ~**pen**, attachment pin; ~**plaat**, tie, adaptor plate.
beves'tiging: ~**skroef**, attachment screw; ~**stuk**, fastening, adaptor fitting.
bevind', (~), find; *jou in MOEILIKHEID* ~, find oneself in difficulty; *nagesien en in ORDE* ~, audited and found correct; *na* ~ *van SAKE*, according to circumstances; *SKULDIG* ~, find guilty; ~**ing**, experience; finding; ruling.
bevin'ger, (~), finger, thumb.
bevit', (~), cavil at, find fault with.
bevlag', (~), dress with flags, flag.
bevlek', (~), stain, soil, defile, pollute, contaminate; sully (character); imbrue; maculate; ~**king**, soiling, defilement, pollution, contamination, maculation.
bevlie', **bevlieg'**, (~), fly at, attack.
bevlie'ging, (-e, -s), caprice, sudden fancy, whim; *'n* ~ *van die HUMEUR*, a fit of temper; *'n – KRY*, experience a sudden fancy; have an inspiration.
bevloei', (~), irrigate; ~**baar**, (..**bare**), irrigable; ~**ing**, irrigation.
bevloer', (~), floor, flag; ~**ing**, flooring.
bevoeg', (-de), competent, qualified, able; authorised; *van* ~ *de sy*, on good authority.
bevoegd'heid, (..**hede**), competence, power, competency; capability; qualification; *kragtens die* ~ *my VERLEEN*, by virtue of the authority vested in me; ~ *VERLEEN*, empower; ~**sertifikaat**, competency (proficiency) certificate; ~**s'oortreding**, infringement of power (authority); ~**verklaring**, certification.
bevoel', (~), feel, finger, touch; cuddle; handle; palpate (med.); ~**ing**, fingering; palpation.
bevog'tig, (~), moisten, wet, bedew, damp; ~**er**, humidifier; ~**ing**, dampening, wetting, irrigation, moistening; ~**ingsmiddel**, wetting agent.
bevolk', (w) (~), people, populate; (b) **(-te)**, populous, populated; *dig* ~, thickly populated.
bevol'king, (-c, -s), population.
bevol'kings: ~**aanwas**, increase in population; ~**aanwins**, gain in population; ~**afname**, decrease in population, ~**buro**, registry office; ~**digtheid**, density of population; ~**groep**, section of population; ~**leer**, theory of population; demography; ~**massa**, population mass; ~**ontploffing**, population explosion; ~**oorskot**, surplus population; ~**register**, population register.
bevol'kingstatistiek, population (vital) statistics.
bevol'kingsyfer, population returns; number of inhabitants; census.
bevoog', (~), act as guardian; ~**de, (-s)**, ward.
bevoor'deel, (~), favour, promote, advance, benefit; ~**de, (-s)**, gainer.
bevoor'oordeel(d), (-de), prejudiced, bias(s)ed, partial, prepossessed, jaundiced.
bevoor'raad, (~), supply, stock; ..**rading**, stocking, supply.
bevoor'reg, (w) (~), further, favour; privilege; charter; (b) **(-te)**, privileged; preferential; favoured; ~ *te MEDEDELING*, privileged communication; ~ *te SKULDEISER*, preferent creditor; ~**ting**, favour(ing); preference, advantage.
bevor'der, (~), promote; advance (plans); forward, help on, expedite, prefer, further (cause); assist, push, contribute to; foster; aid, stimulate (digestion); benefit (health); preach; ~ *tot*, move up (standard), promote to (higher rank); ~**aar, (-s)**, promoter, furtherer, sponsor, patron; fosterer; ~**ing**, promotion; furtherance, forwarding, advancement, advance; preferment; facilitation, fosterage; ~**ingskans**, prospect of advancement; ~**ingstelsel**, system of promotion; ~**lik, (-e)**, conducive, conducible; instrumental; favourable; useful for, of benefit (to), beneficial, promotive, adjuvant; advantageous; ~**likheid**, conduciveness.
bevraag'teken, (~), query; doubt; ~**ing**, query.
bevrag', (~), load, charter, freight (ship); burden; ~**ter, (-s)**, carrier; charterer; ~**ting**, freighting, loading; ~**tingsooreenkoms**, charter party, contract of affreightment.
bevre'dig, (~), satisfy (appetite), content; placate, gratify (desire); indulge (one's passions); appease (hunger); meet (demands); conciliate; calm; ~**end, (-e)**, satisfactory; gratifying; ~**ing**, satisfaction, gratification; conciliation.
bevreem(d)', (~), surprise, astonish; *dit* ~ *my*, it surprises me; ~**dend, (-e)**, surprising; ~**ding**, surprise, astonishment; ~*ding veroorsaak*, cause surprise.
bevrees', (~), afraid, apprehensive; anxious; ~ *vir GEVAAR*, apprehensive of danger; ~ *vir 'n PERSOON*, apprehensive for a person; ~**d'heid**, fear, apprehension.
bevriend', (-e), friendly, intimate, on good terms, pally; ~ *wees met*, be a friend of; ~ *WORD met*, become friends with.
bevries', (w) (~), freeze, frost, congeal; *krediete* ~, freeze credits, (b) **(-de)**, iced, frozen, frost-bitten; ~**baar**, (..**bare**), congealable; ~**ing**, freezing; deep-freezing; glaciation, gelation, congealment, congelation; frost-bite.
bevrind' = **bevriend**.
bevroed', (~), (vero.), suspect, surmise, presume, realize.
bevro're, frozen; ~ *vleis*, frozen meat.
bevrug', (w) (~), impregnate, make pregnant; fecundate, pollinate, fertilize; milt (fishes); inseminate, (b) **(-te)**, fertilized; pregnant; ~**ting**, conception, impregnation, pollination, fertilization; fructification; *KUNSMATIGE* ~**ting**, artificial insemination (A.I.); ~**ting van OVUM**, insemination; fertilization of ovum.
bevry', (w) (~), free, deliver, liberate, set free, rescue (from danger); ransom, release (from confinement); emancipate (from yoke); exempt (from control); extricate, disentangle; enfranchize; affranchize; *jou* ~ *van*, get rid of; (b) (**dc**), free, at liberty, liberated; disengaged; ~**(d)er, (-s)**, deliverer, ransomer, rescuer; emancipator; ~**ding**, deliverance, release, ransom, rescue; disencumbrance, disengagement, disentanglement, disenthral(l)ment; redemption (from sins); enfranchizement; ~**dingsoorlog**, war of liberation.
bevryf', **hevry'we**, (~), rub on.
bevuil', (~), dirty, sully, soil, (be)foul, draggle, besmear; begrime; *jou eie nes* ~, foul one's own nest.
bewaak', (~), watch, guard; keep watch over; ~**ster**, watcher (female).
bewaar', (~), keep (commandment); preserve, maintain (poise); save (for a rainy day); conserve; protect, defend; keep on file; guard; ~ *vir GEVAAR*, keep safe from danger; *O* ~ *my!*, o dear me!; ~ *my SIEL!*, bless my soul!; ~ *my van my VRIENDE*, God defend me from my friends; from my enemies I can defend myself; ~**biblioteek**, copyright (depository)library; ~**dam**, catchment (storage) dam; ~**der, (-s)**, keeper, custodian; depositary; preserver, conservator; warder; caretaker; ~**engel**, guardian angel; ~**gebied**, conservancy (forestry); ~**geld**, storage (dues); ~**gewer**, depositor; ~**gewing**, bailment; deposit (jewels).
bewaar'heid, (~), prove true, verify, confirm; justify; ~ *word*, be proved true.
bewaar'kamer, cloak-room; ~**kaartjie**, cloak-room ticket; ~**koste**, cloak-room charges.
bewaar'kluis, safe-deposit, safe.
bewaar'nemer, bailee, depositary.

bewaarplaas / *bewonder*

bewaar'plaas, ..plek, depository, storehouse; dumping place for debris (from mines); crèche; conservatory.
bewaar'skool, infant school, kindergarten; crèche; ~**juffrou,** nursery-school teacher, kindergarten mistress.
bewaar'ster, (-s), wardress, female custodian.
bewa'ker, (-s), keeper, watchman, guard(ian).
bewa'king, watch, guard(ing); custody; *onder ~, under guard.*
bewa'kings: ~**beampte,** preventive officer (customs); ~**diens,** preventive service.
bewal', (~), (ong.) surround with ramparts.
bewan'del, (~), walk upon.
bewa'pen, (~), arm, provide with arms, equip.
bewa'pening, armament, equipment, armature; reinforcing.
bewa'penings: ~**konferensie,** armament (arms) conference; ~**planne,** plans for re-armament; ~**program,** re-armament programme; ~**verhouding,** relative armaments; ~**voorstel,** re-armament proposal; ~**wedloop,** armaments (arms) race.
bewa'ring, keep(ing), preservation, conservation, custody; charge; *met die ~ BELAS wees,* have the custody of; *in ~ BLY,* remain in charge (custody); *in ~ GEE,* deposit; *in ~ HÊ,* have in custody; hold in trust; *in ~ HOU,* retain under custody; *iem. in ~ NEEM,* take someone into custody; *iets in ~ NEEM,* take something into safe keeping; *ter VEILIGE ~,* for safe keeping; *in VERSEKERDE ~ gee (neem),* give (take) into safe custody; ~**sbewus,** conservation conscious; ~**sbewustheid,** conservation consciousness; ~**sboerdery,** conservation farming; ~**swerk,** conservation (work).
bewa'sem, (~), cover with vapour, dim with moisture.
bewa'ter, (~), water, irrigate; wet (bed); ~**ing,** watering, irrigation.
be'we, (ge-) = beef.
beweeg', (~), move, stir, locomote, persuade; actuate; commove; agitate; animate; determine; motive; shift, budge; *g'n DUIMBREED ~ nie,* not budge an inch; *HEEN en weer ~,* move (shift) about.
beweeg': ~**baar, (..bare),** movable; *..bare anker,* flexible stay (boiler); ~**baarheid,** movability, mobility; ~**brood,** wave loaf; ~**grond,** motive; ~**krag,** (loco)motive power, motivity, impetus; ~**lik, (-e),** movable, mobile, lively, vivacious; flexible; ~**likheid,** mobility, liveliness, sprightliness; ~**loos, (..lose),** immovable, motionless; ~**offer,** wave offering; ~**rede,** motive, reason, cause; ~**ruimte,** elbow-room; room for manoeuvring.
beween', (~), weep over, deplore, mourn, lament, bemoan, bewail.
beweer', (~), assert, contend, affirm, profess, predicate, purport, maintain, aver; pretend; argue, allege; *~ en BEWYS is twee,* assertion is no proof; *die ~ de MOORD,* the alleged murder; *SO ~ hy,* that is what he claims; ~**baar, (..bare),** assertable, predicable; ~**der, (-s),** affirmant.
bewe'gend, (-e), moving, dynamic; motive, motorial; kinetic; ~*e mas,* transporter mast.
bewe'ger, (-s), mover.
bewe'ging, (-e, -s), movement, motion, gesture; exercise (physical); commotion; emotion; stir, agitation; *ARBEIDSVERMOË van ~,* kinetic energy; *in ~ BRING,* set in motion; *uit EIE ~,* of one's own accord; *in ~ HOU,* keep going; *in ~ KOM,* start moving; take off; *VRYHEID van ~,* freedom of movement; ~**loos, (..lose),** motionless; ~**loosheid,** inertia; ~**sdraaipunt,** centre of motion; ~**senuwee,** motory nerve.
bewe'gings: ~**hoek,** angle of movement; ~**hoeveelheid,** moment, momentum; ~**leer,** kinematics; kinetics, dynamics; eurithmics; ~**metamorfisme,** dynamic metamorphism; ~**moment,** impetus; ~**oorlog,** mobile war(fare); ~**organe,** locomotive organs; ~**prikkel,** motor impulse; ~**ruimte,** elbow-room; manoeuvring space; ~**terapie,** kinesitherapy; ~**vryheid,** freedom of movement; elbow-room; ~**wette,** laws of (loco)motion.

bewei', (~), graze; ~**baar, (..bare),** pasturable; ~**ding,** grazing.
bewelda'dig, (~), (ong.) (confer) benefit(s); favour; ~**ing,** benefaction, favouring.
be'wend, (-e), trembling, quaking.
bewe'ner, (-s), mourner.
bewe'ning, lamentation, mourning.
be'wer, (-s), beaver; castor; mobile.
bewera'sie, rigor, trembling fit, shivering; jim-jams; *die ~ kry,* get the funks; ~**siekte,** the funks; *cf.* **bibberasie.**
be'wer: ~**bont,** beaver fur; ~**dam,** beaver dam; ~**geil,** castoreum; ~**hoed,** beaver hat.
be'werig, (-e), shaking, trembling; quaky, quavery, quivering; groggy; creepy; tremulous (voice); doddering, shaky (hand); ~**heid,** trembling; tremulousness (voice); shakiness; jumpiness.
bewe'ring, (-e, -s), assertion, allegation, claim, contention, predication, averment; *volgens ~,* allegedly.
be'werjagter, beaver hunter.
bewerk', (~), work; process; dress, fashion, shape, manipulate; treat, prepare (material); till (the ground); adapt, edit, remodel (book); use one's influence with, canvass (voters); exploit (a person); effect, contrive, bring about; *~ te GROND,* prepared soil; *HOE het jy dit ~?,* how did you manage it?; ~**baar, (..bare),** arable, tillable (soil); adaptable; ~**baarheid,** adaptability; arableness; ~**er,** worker (of mischief); compiler (of a book); rewriter; editor (of a book); agent, adapter; actor; tiller (soil); originator (scheme); ~**ing,** workmanship; manipulation; exploitation; dressing (skins); preparation, cultivation, tilling (of ground); tillage; revision; adaptation; ~**lik, (-e),** (ong.) laborious, toilsome; *baie ~ lik,* requiring a great deal of very careful attention.
bewerkstel'lig, (~), effect, cause, bring about, accomplish, manage, effectuate; ~**ing,** effectuation, bringing about, accomplishment; ~**te,** processed.
bewerk'tuig, (-de), (ong.) organic; organized; ~**ing,** (ong.), organization; state of being organic.
be'wertjie, (-s), mobile.
be'wertjies, totter grass, quiver (quaking) grass *(Briza maxima).*
be'wervel, beaver skin.
bewe'se, *see* **bewys;** proved, proven, demonstrated, established; rendered; *vir ~ dienste,* for services rendered.
bewes'te, (to the) west of.
bewie'roking, incense, incensing; open flattery, lauding; praising; thurification.
bewie'rook, (~), incense, cense, burn incense to fume; adulate, praise, flatter; *iem. ~,* shower compliments on someone; praise someone to the skies.
bewil'lig, (~), consent, acquiesce in, assent; vote (money); allow; ~**ing,** consent, assent; voting (of money).
bewim'pel, (~), disguise, palliate (unpleasant fact); gloss over; hide (truth), conceal; colour; mince (matters); *'n saak ~,* becloud the issue; ~**ing,** palliation, glossing over, disguising.
bewind', government, administration, rule; *AAN die ~ wees,* be in office (power); *die ~ AANVAAR,* assume office; *aan die ~ BLY,* remain in power; *aan die ~ KOM,* assume office; come into power; *ONDER die ~ van,* during the reign of; *die ~ VOER,* rule; ~**hebber,** ~**voerder, (-s),** director, ruler, administrator, commander, governor; ~**voerend, (-e),** administrative; governing; ~**voering,** government, administration.
be'wing, trembling, shudder, quake, quaking, trepidation, shaking, quivering, dither.
bewoë', moved, affected; agitated (times); *BYNA ~,* almost persuaded; *tot TRANE ~,* moved to tears; ~**nheid,** emotion; compassion.
bewolk', (w) (~), cloud over, become cloudy; (b) (-te), cloudy, clouded, overcast; ~**ing,** cloudiness becoming clouded; ~**t'heid,** cloudiness.
bewon'der, (~), admire, adore; ~**aar, (-s),** admirer, adorer; fan; ~**enswaar'dig, (-e),** admirable; ~**ing,** admiration, adoration.

bewo'ner, (-s), inhabitant, dweller; inmate; occupant, occupier; resident; denizen.
bewo'ning, (in)habitation; occupation, occupancy.
bewoon', (~), occupy, inhabit, reside; ~**baar,** (..**bare**), habitable; ~**baarheid,** habitability; ~**reg,** right of occupancy; ~**ster,** (-s), (female) in= habitant, occupant, occupier.
bewoord', (~), word, express (in words), phrase.
bewoor'ding, (-e, -s), wording, expression; *in alge= mene* ~, in general terms.
bewus', (-te), aware, conscious; knowingly, alive (to); ~ *of ONBEWUS,* wittingly or unwittingly; *die* ~ *te PERSOON,* the person in question (con= cerned); *ten VOLLE* ~ *van,* fully aware of; ~ *WORD van,* become aware of; ~ **syn,** conscious= ness; knowledge; *weer tot sy* ~ *syn KOM,* regain consciousness; *by sy volle* ~ *syn,* quite conscious; ~**synswerking,** functioning (workings) of the mind; ~**teloos,** (..**lose**), unconscious, insensible; ~ *teloos wees,* be in a swoon (faint), be uncon= scious; ~**teloosheid,** unconsciousness, insensibil= ity; coma; ~**t'heid,** consciousness, full knowledge, awareness, cognition.
bewys', (s) (-e), proof, evidence, sign, testimony, clue, demonstration; voucher; receipt; promissory note, acknowledg(e)ment, attestation; token, mark; averment; certificate; ~ **AANVOER,** adduce evi= dence; *AFGELEIDE* ~, indirect evidence; *'n DEURSLAANDE* ~, conclusive proof; *die* ~ *e LEWER,* produce evidence, prove; ~ *van LID= MAATSKAP,* certificate of membership; ~ *TOE= LAAT,* admit evidence; (w) ( ), prove, demon= strate, circumstantiate, justify; establish; show (respect); make good (your words); manifest; sub= stantiate (charge); render (service); do (favour); ap= prove; evince (interest); *iem. 'n DIENS* ~, render someone a service; *die laaste EER* ~, pay the last tribute of respect; *HULDE* ~, pay homage; ~**baar,** (..**bare**), demonstrable, declarable, prov= able, capable of proof; ~**baarheid,** demonstrabil= ity, provability; ~**boek,** reference book; ~**end,** (-e), demonstrative; evidential; ~**grond,** argument, proof; ~**ie,** (-s), promissory note (for a small amount); sign, proof; indication; *GEEN* ~ *ie van reën nie,* not the slightest sign of rain; *daar is GEEN* ~ *ie van nie,* there is not the slightest proof; *SONDER 'n* ~ *ie van angs,* without a trace (sem= blance) of fear; ~**krag,** demonstrative power, co= gency, conclusiveness; ~**las,** burden of proof; onus probandi; ~**leer,** law of evidence; ~**lewering,** fur= nishing of proof; ~**materiaal,** body of evidence, documentary evidence; ~**middel,** means of prov= ing, proof; ~**plaas,** quotation, reference, ~**plek,** authority; ~**reëls,** rules of evidence; ~**stuk,** docu= ment(ary evidence); counterfoil; exhibit (law); ~**voerder,** demonstrator; ~**voering,** ratiocination, argumentation; ~**waarde,** evidential value.
bey'wer, (~), endeavour, apply oneself, exert oneself, do one's best; campaign; *ek sal my daarvoor* ~, I shall do my best to accomplish that; ~**ing,** zeal, exertion, endeavour.
bib'ber, (ge-), shiver, dither, tremble; ~**a'sie,** *see* **bewerasie.**
bibliofiel', (-e), bibliophil(e); ~*e uitgawe,* edition de luxe, bibliophile edition.
bibliofilis'me, bibliophilism.
bibliograaf', (..**grawe**), bibliographer.
bibliografie', (-ë), bibliography.
bibliogra'fies, (-e), bibliographic(al).
bibliolatrie', bibliolatry.
bibliomaan', (..**mane**), bibliomaniac.
bibliomanie', bibliomania.
biblioman'sie, bibliomancy.
biblioteek', (..**teke**), library; book collection; ~**amp,** librarianship; ~**beampte,** library official; ~**boek,** library book; ~**diens,** library service; ~**kunde,** li= brarianship; library science; ~**leer,** library science; ~**organiseerder,** library organiser; ~**owerheid,** li= brary authority; ~**skema,** library scheme; ~**wese,** library service, librarianship.
bibliotekares'se, (-s), (lady) librarian.
biblioteka'ris, (-se), librarian.

biblis', (-te), Biblical scholar.
biblisis', (-te), Biblicist; ~**me,** Biblicism.
biblistiek', Biblical scholarship.
bichromaat', bichromate.
bid, (ge-), pray, beseech, beg; ask a blessing, say grace (at meal); say one's prayers; ~ *jou AAN!,* just fan= cy!; *om REËN* ~, pray for rain; *die ROSEKRANS* ~, tell one's beads; *TOT God* ~, pray God; ~**ban= kie,** prayer desk (stool); priedieu; ~**dag,** day of prayer; ~**dend,** (-e), precatory, prayerful; ~**der,** (-s), prayer, supplicant, one who prays; ~**dery,** praying; ~**kaartjie,** memorial card (R.C.); ~**kamer,** oratory; ~**matjie;** prayer rug; ~**plek,** or= atory, place for prayer; ~**snoer,** rosary; ~**ster,** fe= male prayer; ~**stoel,** kneeling chair; priedieu; ~**stond,** (-e), ~**uur,** prayer meeting; intercession service; ~**vertrek,** oratory; ~**wiel,** prayer-mill; prayer wheel.
bie, (ge-), bid (at sale); call (cards); *HOËR* ~ *as,* out= bid; ~ *OP,* (make a) bid for.
bie'bies, (geselst.) vermin, lice (on head).
bied, (ge-), offer (assistance); present, tender; extend (hand); *iem. die HAND* ~, hold out one's hand to a person; *die HOOF* ~, *TEENSTAND* ~, offer re= sistance; ~**baar,** (..**bare**), biddable (cards); ~**er,** (-s), bidder, offerer; ~**ery,** ~**ing,** bidding (at auc= tion sale).
bie'ë, *see* **bie;** ~**r,** (-s), *see* **bieder;** ~**ry,** *see* **biedery.**
bief: ~**burger,** steakburger; ~**ekstrak,** beef extract; ~**skyf,** ~**stuk,** beefsteak; ~**stuk-en-niertjiepastei,** steak and kidney pie; ~**tee,** beef tea.
bieg, (s) (-te), confession, shrift; *iem. die AF= NEEM,* cross-question someone; *te* ~ *GAAN,* go to confession; *uit die* ~ *KLAP,* tell tales out of school; *iem. die* ~ *VOORLEES,* read someone a lecture; (w) (ge-), confess; *liewer* ~ *as LIEG,* open confession is good for the soul; ~**geheim,** con= fessional secret; ~**stoel,** confessional chair, confes= sionary; ~**teling,** (-e), confessant, penitent; ~**vader,** confessor; conscience keeper.
bie'lie, (-s), stalwart; whopper; *jy is darem 'n OU* ~*!,* you're really a brick!; *dis 'n* ~ *van 'n WAATLE= MOEN,* it's a whopping watermelon.
biep, (ge-), bleep; ~**er,** bleeper.
bier, beer; ale; ~**agtig,** (-e), beery, beer-like; ~**ak= syns,** excise duty on beer; ~**asyn,** beer-vinegar; ale= gar; ~**blik,** beer tin; ~**bottel,** beer bottle; ~**brouer,** brewer; ~**brouery,** brewery; ~**buik,** beer-barrel (belly); pot-belly; ~**drinker,** beer drinker; ~**fees,** ale party; beer festival; ~**geld,** money for beer; ~**glas,** beer glass; ~**hal,** beerhall, beerhouse; ~**handel,** beer trade; ~**huis,** ale-house, porter- house, pot-house, pub; ~**kan,** beer jug; ~**lug,** smell of beer; ~**maag,** (..**mae**), pot-belly; ~**party,** beer-drink; ~**pomp,** beer pump; ~**pot,** beer pot; ~**reuk,** smell of beer; ~**skuim,** barm; ~**soort,** kind of beer; ~**suiper,** beer drinker; froth-blower; ~**tapper,** ale-house keeper; ~**tapster,** barmaid; ~**tjie,** (-s), glass of beer; ~**vat,** beer cask, beer bar= rel; ~**wa,** dray, brewer's cart.
bies[1], beestings, colostrum.
bies[2], pipe, piping; facing (by piping); *broek met 'n rooi* ~, trousers with a red stripe.
bie's(e)roei, rush used for fruit baskets *(Bobartia spathacea).*
bie'sie, (-s), rush; reed; *jou* ~*s (biese) pak,* clear (dash) off; ~**goed,** ~**gras,** *Cyperus sexangularis;* ~**mandjie,** frail; ~**mat,** rush mat, ~**pol,** hassock, tussock of rush; pretty (peach of a) girl; *jou* ~ *pol!,* you are a brick!; ~**varing,** quil wort; ~**wieg,** wicker cradle.
bies'melk, beestings, colostrum.
bie'tjie, (s) (-s), a little, small quantity, grain; modi= cum; moment; *ALLE* ~ *s help,* every little helps, many a pickle makes a mickle; *BY* ~ *s,* bit by bit; *'n* ~ *ENGELS,* a smattering of English; *WAG 'n* ~, wait a bit (moment), half a mo (colloq.); (b) few, little; ~ *ALBASTERS,* a few marbles; (bw) please; rather, slightly, somewhat; *'n* ~ *BAIE,* rather much; *kom* ~ *HIER,* please come here; *'n* ~ *KOUD,* rather cold; *'n* ~ *baie LANK,* rather too long; ~ *WARMER,* slightly warmer; ~**s-bie=**

bietou 76 **binne**

tjie(s), a little at a time, bit by bit; ~ **sgewys,** little by little; bit by bit; a little at a time.
bie'tou, bush-tick berry (fam. *Compositae*).
bifokaal', (..**kale**), bifocal; ..**kale bril,** bifocal glasses; ..**kale lens,** bifocal lens.
bifurka'sie, bifurcation.
big, (-ge), young pig, piglet.
bigamie', bigamy.
biga'mies, (-e), bigamous(ly).
bigamis', (-te), bigamist.
big'gel, (ge-), trickle (tears); *trane ~ langs (oor) haar wange,* tears trickle down her cheeks.
bigno'nia, (-s), bignonia.
bigotterie', bigotry.
bi'jou, (-'s), bijou.
bik, (ge-), chip (stone); scrape (boiler); dress (millstone).
bi'kameraal, (..**rale**), bi-cameral.
bikarbonaat', bicarbonate.
bik'beitel, scaling tool, chipping chisel.
bik'hamer, boiler-scaling hammer; chipping (brick) hammer.
biki'ni, (-'s), bikini.
bikonkaaf', (..**kawe**), biconcave.
bikonveks', (-e), biconvex.
bikwadraat', (..**drate**), biquadratic.
bil, (-le), buttock.
bilabiaal', (s) (..**biale**), bilabial; **(b)** (..**biale**), bilabial; ..**biale klank,** bilabial sound.
bilal', (-s), muezzin.
bilateraal', (..**rale**), bilateral.
bilhar'zia, bilharzia (parasite).
bilharzia'se, (med.) (meerv.), bilharzia(sis), bilharziosis (disease); red water.
Bi'liamsesel, Balaam's ass (an ill-treated animal).
bilineêr', (-e), bilinear.
biljart', (s) billiards; **(w) (ge-),** play billiards; ~ **bal,** billiard ball; ~ **band,** billiard cushion; ~ **bok(kie),** (cue) rest, jigger; ~ **kamer,** billiard room; ~ **kampioen,** billiards champion, champion at billiards; ~ **kryt,** billiard (cue) chalk; ~ **saal,** billiard room; ~ **sak,** pocket (of billiard table); ~ **spel,** (game of) billiards; ~ **speler,** billiard player, billiardist; ~ **stok,** cue; ~ **tafel,** billiard table.
biljet', (-te), ticket; (bank)note; (hand)bill; poster; ~ **plakker,** bill-sticker (-poster).
biljoen', (-e), billion.
bil'lik, (w) (ge-), approve of; **(b) (-e),** reasonable, moderate (price); fair, just, equitable, fair-minded; *nie MEER as ~ nie,* no more than fair; *e SLYTASIE,* fair wear and tear; **erwys(e),** with(in) reason, reasonably, in all fairness; ~ **heid,** equity, reasonableness; reason, justness, fairness; justice; ~ **heidsgevoel,** sense of fairness; ~ **heidshalwe,** for the sake of equity; in justice; ~ **heidsreg,** equity; ~ **ing,** approval.
bil'naat, perineum; ~ **streek,** perineal region.
bil'stuk, (Ndl.), rump (piece), rump cutlet.
bil'tong, (-e), biltong (dried meat), jerky, jerked venison (beef) (Amer.); *hy DINK hy kan 'n ~ saamneem,* he thinks he can take it with him; be attached to one's worldly goods; *'n DROË ~,* dry old stick; *so DROOG soos ~,* as dry as dust; ~ *MAAK van iem.,* make mincemeat of someone; *dis so MAKLIK as ~ eet,* it's as easy as pie; *meer ~ SNY as wat jy kan opeet,* have too many irons in the fire; ~ *SNY voor die bees geslag is,* count one's chickens before they are hatched; ~ **koek,** (ong.) pemmican; ~ **skyfie,** slice of biltong; ~ **vleis,** silverside (beef); fillet; meat for biltong.
bim'bam, (ge-), ring, toll, ding-dong.
bimetaal', (..**tale**), bimetallic.
bimetallis'me, bimetallism.
bind, (ge-), tie, fasten, leash; bind (book); thicken (gravy, soup); harden, set (cement); enfetter; *iem. aan 'n BELOFTE ~,* hold someone to his promise; *iem. iets op die HART ~,* impress something on a person; *jou ~ OM ...,* commit oneself to ...
bind: ~ **balk,** tie-beam, cross-tie; binding joist; binder, bond timber; hammer beam; ~ **beuel,** lashing handle (loop); ~ **draad,** thin wire; binding wire; ~ **end (-e),** binding; *die ooreenkoms is ~ end vir al*=

bei partye, the agreement is binding for both parties; ~ **er, (-s),** binder; ~ **ery, (-e),** bindery; binding; ~ **garing,** string twine; ~ **geld,** retainer, retaining fee; commitment fee; ~ **ing,** binding; linkage; bond; fixation; weave; cementing; ~ **ketting,** lashing chains; ~ **klip,** parpen; ~ **krag,** binding force, setting strength; ~ **laag,** binder course (road); ~ **masjien,** binder; ~ **middel,** binding agent, binder; cement; styptic; ~ **plaat,** fishplate (railway); ~ **rib,** lierne; ~ **sel,** bandage, ligature; binding; band, binder, lashing, mortar; ~ **slaai,** cos lettuce; ~ **spier,** ligament; ~ **staaf,** tie-bar; ~ **stang,** tie-rod; ~ **steek,** binder; ~ **steen,** bonder, bond-stone; ~ **stof,** cement; ~ **strook,** binding slip; ~ **tou,** binder twine; lasher; lashing; ~ **vlies,** conjunctiva; ~ **vliesontsteking,** conjunctivitis; ~ **weefsel,** connective tissue; ~ **weefselgewas,** scirrhus; ~ **weefselontsteking,** phlegmon; ~ **woord,** conjunctive.
binêr', (-e), binary.
bin'ne, in, within; inside; *jou te ~ BRING,* recall, recollect; *van ~ en van BUITE,* inside and outside; ~ *'n paar DAE,* within a few days; *na ~ GAAN,* enter, go in; *KOM ~!,* come in!, *te ~ SKIET,* flash into one's mind; ~ **aars, (-e),** intravenous; ~ **-antenne,** inside aerial; ~ **as,** axle-shaft; ~ **bal,** bladder (football); ~ **band,** tube; inner tube; bandeau (hat); ~ **bandklep,** valve of tube; ~ **bas,** inner bark, bast; ~ **bediende,** housemaid; ~ **bly (-ge-),** remain indoors; keep down, remain (in stomach); ~ **boords, (-e),** inboard; ~ **boud,** topside (beef); ~ **brandmotor,** internal combustion engine; ~ **bring, (-ge-),** bring in; ~ **buis,** inner tube; ~ **deur, (s),** inner (inside) door; (bw) ~ *deur gaan,* take a short cut; ~ **deurkosyn,** door casing; ~ **deurs, (-e),** within doors; ~ **dring, (-ge-),** penetrate, invade, force one's way into; ~ **dringend, (-e),** incursive; penetrating; ~ **duin,** inner dune; ~ **dyk,** inner dike; ~ **gaan, (-ge-),** enter, go in; ~ **galery,** inner gallery; ~ **gang,** inner passage; ~ **gebruik,** on-consumption (liquor); ~ **goed,** intestines, entrails; works (of a watch); innards; ~ *goed van 'n hoender uithaal,* draw a fowl; ~ **gordyn,** glass (sash) curtain; ~ **haal, (-ge-),** bring (fetch) in; gather; ~ **handel,** inland trade; ~ **hawe** inner harbour; inland port; ~ **hoek,** interior angle; ~ **hof,** inner court; patio; ~ **hou, (-ge-),** keep indoors; keep in, retain (food); ~ **huis,** interior; ~ **huisversiering,** interior decoration; ~ **hulp,** domestic servant; inside servant (aid); ~ **huls,** inner sleeve; ~ **-in,** inside, within; ~ **kamer,** inner room; *na die ~ kamer gaan,* go to pray; ~ **kant,** interior, inside; ~ **kas,** inner case (of watch); ~ **kom, (-ge-),** come in, walk in, make one's entrance; enter; ~ **komende,** incoming; ~ **koms,** entrance, entry; ~ **komsbaan,** aerial corridor; ~ **koors,** low fever; ~ **kort,** shortly, soon, before (ere) long; ~ **kring,** inner circle; ~ **kringskoot,** inner (target shooting); ~ **kruip, (-ge-),** creep in; ~ **kry, (-ge-),** get down (food, medicine); get in; ~ **laag,** inner layer; ~ **laat, (-ge-),** let in, admit.
bin'neland, interior, country, hinterland, midland; ~ **er, (-s),** inlander, countryman; ~ **s, (-e),** inland, home, domestic, home-made (grown); interior; internal; midland; ~ *se HANDEL,* home trade; ~ *se LUGDIENS,* internal air service; *MINISTER van B~ se Aangeleenthede,* Minister for Interior Affairs; ~ *se OORLOG,* civil war; ~ *se SENDING,* home mission; ~ *se VERKEER,* internal traffic.
bin'ne: ~ **lei, (-ge-),** usher (lead) in; ~ **leisel,** checkrein; *sy ~ leisels is te kort,* he is cock-eyed; ~ **lig,** interior light; ~ **linie,** interior line (mil.); ~ **loods, (-ge-),** pilot (into port); ~ **loop, (s)** putting into port (ship); (..**lope**), inner course (river); inner barrel (cannon); **(w) (-ge-),** enter; put into port; draw in (train); ~ **lopend, (-e),** incoming (boat); ~ **maat,** inside measurement; ~ **meer,** inland lake; ~ **muur,** inner wall; ~ **muurs, (-e),** intramural; ~ **naat,** inner seam; ~ **naatvelskoen,** home-made shoe; velskoen; ~ **nshuis, (-e),** indoors, within doors, in the house; ~ *huise versiering,* interior decoration; ~ **nslands, (-e),** at home, in the country; ~ **nsmonds, (-e),** between the teeth, mumblingly; under one's breath;

binokel 77 *bivak*

~nste = binneste; ~(n)stebuite, inside out; ~nstyds, within the appointed time; ~-om, round the inside; ~omslag, inside cover; ~oppervlak, inner surface; ~pakstuk, internal gasket; ~palm, (-ge-), appropriate; palm, sweep in (winnings); ~pasiënt, inpatient; ~passer, inside callipers; ~plaas, inner court, quad(rangle); ~plein, quad(rangle); inner court; ~rem, internal brake; ~roep, (-ge-), call in; summon; ~ruk, (-ge-), march into (enemy's territory); jerk in; ~ry, (-ge-), ride in, drive in; ~sak, inside pocket; bladder; ~see, inland sea; lake; ~seil (-ge-), sail in(to); approach; ~seilbaan, approach path; ~seilbaken, approach beacon; ~seillig, approach light; ~seillyn, approach line; ~seisoen(s), in-season; ~skeepvaart, inland navigation; ~skil, inner rind; white pith, albedo; ~skuif, (-ge-), push in; ~sleep, (-ge-), tow in, drag in(to); ~sluip, (-ge-), enter stealthily; ~smokkel, (-ge-), smuggle in(to); foist in(to); ~sool, inner sole; gaiter (tyre); ~soom, inner seam, inseam; ~spelers, inside players; ~spiers', (-e), intramuscular; ~stad, inner town; ~stap, (-ge-), walk into; ~stasie, approach station; ~ste, innermost; core, heart; *in sy* ~*ste,* in his heart of hearts; ~stoom, (-ge-), steam in(to); ~storm, (-ge-), rush (burst) in(to); ~string, inner (inside) trace; ~stroming, in rush; ~stroom, (-ge-), stream in(to); flock in; ~sweef, (-ge-), *see* binneseil; ~swewing, approach (aircraft); ~sy, inside; ~tandrat, annual ring gear; ~telefoon, house telephone, intercom; ~toe, in(side); inward(s); ~tredende, (-s), entrant; ~treding, entry, entrance; ~tree, (go), step in(to), enter; ~trek, (-ge-), march (trek, move) into (country); pull in(to); ~vaar, (-ge-), sail in; ~vaart, inland navigation; river (canal) navigation; ~val, (-ge-), fall in(to); drop in (for a visit); attack, invade; irrupt; ~veermatras, inner-spring mattress; ~verbranding, internal combustion; ~verspanning, internal bracing; ~vertanding, internal gear; ~vet, intestinal fat; lard; axunge; *iem. die* ~*vet van die boud gee,* give someone the benefit of the doubt; *op jou* ~*vet teer,* draw on one's capital; ~vetter, (-s): *hy is 'n* ~*vetter,* he does not parade his virtues; he does not display all his wares in the shop-window; still waters run deep; ~voering, inner lining; ~vorm, core (foundry); ~vra, (-ge-), ask in; invite; ~vuurketel, internally fired boiler; ~vuurmasjien, internally fired engine; ~waai, (-ge-), blow in; drop in (on a visit); ~waarts(e), inward(s); into; ~wag, inlying picket; ~water, internal waterway; river, canal; ~welf, (..welwe), intrados (mine); ~welwing, soffit; ~werk, inner work; inside works (of watch); insertion (needlework); ~wip, (-ge-), skip into; drop (pop) in (visit); ~wydte, inside width.
bino'kel, (-s), (ong., vero.) binocle, binoculars, fieldglass; opera-glass.
binomiaal', (..miale), binomial.
bino'mies, (-e), binomial (theorem).
binominaal', (..nale), binominal.
bino'mium, binoom', binomial.
bint, (-e), tie-beam.
biochemie', biochemistry; **bioche'mies**, (-e), biochemical; **bioche'mikus**, biochemist.
biodina'mika, biodynamics.
bioëlektrisiteit', bio-elektrisiteit', bio-electricity.
biofi'sika, biophysics.
biogene'se, biogenesis.
biogene'ties, (-e), biogenetic.
biograaf', (biograwe), biographer.
biografie', (-ë), biography.
biogra'fies, (-e), biographic(al).
bioingenieurs'wese, bio-ingenieurs'wese, bio-engineering.
bioliet', biolite.
biologie', biology.
biolo'gies, (-e), biological; ~**e beheer**, biological control; ~**e plaagbeheer**, biological pest control.
bioloog', (..loë), biologist.
biomagnetis'me, biomagnetism.
biomas'sa, biomass.
biometrie', biometry.

biome'tries, (-s), biometrical.
biome'trikus, (-se, ..trici), biometrician.
bionomie', bionomy, bionomics.
bioplas'ma, bioplasm.
biop'sie, (..sieë, -s), biopsy.
biosinte'se, biosynthesis.
bioskoop', (bioskope), bioscope, cinema, picture-palace, (motion-) pictures; ~besoeker, ~ganger, picture-goer, cinema-goer; ~sensuur, film censorship; ~voorstelling, bioscope entertainment, cinema show.
biostatistiek', vital statistics.
biotiek', biotic.
bio'tika, biotics.
bipiramidaal', (..midale), bipyramidal.
bi'piramide, bipyramid.
bipirami'dies, (-e), bipyramidal.
bipolêr, (-e), bipolar.
Bir'ma, Burma; ~an', (..mane), Burmese; ~ans', (s) Burmese (language); (b) (-e), Burmese.
bis, twice; again, encore; B sharp.
bi'samrot, musk-rat; musquash (fur).
Bisan'tium, Byzantium.
Bisantyns', (-e), Byzantine.
bisar', (-re), bizarre, grotesque; ~heid, bizarrerie.
bis'dom, (-me), bishopric, diocese, episcopate; ~'lik, (-e), diocesan.
biseksueel', (..suele), bisexual.
bisek'triks, (-e), bisectrix (mines).
bi'seps, (-e), biceps.
bisk, bisk; bisque.
Bisla'je, Biscay.
bis'kop¹, (-pe), steenbras, musselcracker (fam *Sparidae*).
bis'kop², (-pe), bishop, pontifex; diocesan; ~'lik, (-e), pontifical, episcopal; ~samp, episcopacy; episcopate; ~setel, bishop's see; ~shoed, ~smyter, mitre; ~staf, crosier, bishop's staff, crook; ~stoel, cathedral, throne of a bishop.
bis'ley, (-s), Bisley, rifle contest.
bis'mut, bismuth; ~as, bismuth oxide; ~iet', bismuthite; ~oker, bismuth ochre.
bi'son, (-s), bison.
bisseux'tjie, (-s), zinnia.
bis'ter, bistre.
bistouri', (-'s), bistoury.
bisulfaat', bisulphate.
bisulfiet', bisulphite.
bits, bit'sig, (-e), harsh, sharp (answer); biting, pungent, acrimonious, peppery, cutting, crusty, acid, acrid, tart; ~heid, (..hede), acerbity, snappishness, acrimony, acridity; acidity; pungency.
bit'ter, (s) bitter; bitters; (b) ((-e); -der, -ste), bitter, acrid, grievous; acerb, acrimonious; sardonic; atrabillious; (bw) bitterly; *IN* ~*e nood verkeer,* be in sore distress; ~ *MIN,* precious little; ~ *in die MOND maak die hart gesond,* the bitter goes before the sweet and makes the sweet the sweeter; ~*SLEG,* extremely bad; ~aarde, magnesia; ~agtig, (-e), bitterish; ~amandel, bitter almond (*Pygeum africanum*); ~appel, bitter apple (*Citrullus colocynthis*); apple of Sodom; ~bas, bitter bark (*Bersama tysoniana*); ~bessie(bos), bitter berry; ~boela, bitter (wild) melon (fam. *Cucurbitacea*); ~bossie, wild gentian; Christmas berry (*Chrysocoma tenuifolia*); ~duif, large dove (*Streptopelia semitorquata*); ~einder, (-s), die-hard, bitter-ender; ~heid, bitterness, pungency, acridity, acerbity, gall, acrimony; ~hout, quassia; ~koekie, macaroon; ~lemoen, grape-fruit, pomelo; ~lik, bitterly; ~loog, bitter waters; ~soet, bittersweet; ~sout, Epsom salts, magnesium sulphate; ~steen, jade; nephrite; ~tjie, (-s), gin-and-bitters; appetizer; ~waatlemoen, ~wartlemoen, ~waterlemoen, bitter (wild) melon; ~wortel, bitterwort.
bitu'men, bitumen.
bitumineer', (ge-), bituminize.
bitumine'ring, bituminization.
bitumineus', (-e), bituminous.
bivak', (-ke), bivouac, camp; ~keer', (ge-), bivouac; ~mus, knitted helmet, Balaclava (cap); ~vuur, campfire.

blaad'jie, (-s), small leaf (of book), leaflet; sheet (of paper); small magazine, newspaper; petal (flower); disc (gunpowder); *in 'n GOEIE ~ staan by iem.*, be in someone's good books; *'n NUWE ~ omslaan*, turn over a new leaf.
blaai, (ge-), turn over leaves (pages).
blaak, (ge-), burn, scorch; glow with; flame; *~ van woede*, burn with rage.
blaam, blame, blemish, dispraise, censure; *iem. van alle ~ ONTHEF (suiwer)*, exonerate a person from all blame; *sonder SMET of ~*, without speck or spot, flawless.
blaar¹, (blare), blister, bleb, blain.
blaar², (blare), leaf (of a plant); blade; *waar die blare ROER, waai daar 'n windjie*, where there is smoke, there is fire; *onderste blare UITBREEK*, prime (tobacco plants); ~ **aar,** leaf vein; ~ **agtig, (-e),** leafy, leaf-like, foliaceous; foliate; ~ **bedekking,** leaf cover; vegetative growth; ~ **beet,** spinach beet, Swiss chard; ~ **brand,** leaf scorch; ~ **dak,** leaf canopy; ~ **dos,** foliage.
blaar'gas, blister gas.
blaar: ~ **geel,** xanthophyll; ~ **groente,** greens; green (leafy) vegetables; ~ **grond,** leaf mould; ~ **houdend, (-e),** evergreen; ~ **knop,** leaf bud; gemma; ~ **kors,** flaky pastry; ~ **koers,** leaf crinkle; ~ **kroon,** leaf crown; ~ **loos** (..lose), leafless, aphyllous; ~ **loosheid,** aphylly; ~ **luis,** greenfly; ~ **moes,** mesophyll; ~ **myner,** leaf miner; ~ **pens,** omasum, manyplies, leaf stomach; ~ **pootwants,** leaf-footed bug, squash bug; ~ **rand,** margin of leaf; ~ **ryk, (-e),** leafy; ~ **sel,** leaf cell; ~ **siekte,** leaf blight; ~ **skede,** leaf sheath; ~ **skilfer,** leaf blister; ~ **slaai,** lettuce; ~ **spil,** rachis; ~ **stand,** disposition of leaves, phyllotaxy; ~ **steel,** leaf stalk; ~ **stingel,** leaf stem; stipule, petiole; ~ **tabak,** leaf tobacco; ~ **tee,** whole leaf tea; ~ **tert,** puff pastry.
blaar'tjie¹, (-s), small leaf, plumule, lamella; foliole.
blaar'tjie², (-s), pustule (abscess); small blister, bleb, blain.
blaar: ~ **trekkend, (-e),** raising blisters; epispastic; vesicating; ~ **trekkende vog,** blistering fluid; ~ **trekker,** epispastic, vesicant; ~ **trekking,** vesication.
blaar: ~ **vlek,** leaf spot; tomato canker; ~ **vlug,** falling leaf (aircraft); ~ **vorm,** leaf-form; ~ **vormig (-e),** leaf-shaped; ~ **vorming,** foliation; ~ **vreter,** defoliator.
blaas¹, (s) (blase), bladder (of body, of football); bubble; blob; cyst, blister; *skrik vir 'n ~ met ERTJIES*, start at one's shadow, be easily frightened; *vir 'n ~ met ERTJIES op loop sit*, take fright easily.
blaas², (w) (ge-), blow, puff, hiss; huff (draughts); *LAAT ~*, allow a breather; *iem. iets in die OOR ~*, whisper something into someone's ear.
blaas'aandoening, bladder complaint (illness).
blaas: ~ **balk,** bellows; ~ **balkbroek,** riding breeches.
blaas'breuk, rupture of the bladder.
blaas; ~ **gas,** cloud gas; ~ **gat,** blowhole; ~ **horing,** horn; ~ **instrument,** wind instrument; ~ **kaak,** gasbag, braggart; hector; ~ **kakery,** bragging, swagger, braggadocio; ~ **kans,** breathing space, breather.
blaas; ~ **katar,** catarrh of the bladder; ~ **klier,** prostate gland; ~ **kwaal,** bladder ailment.
blaas: ~ **lamp,** blowlamp; ~ **masjien,** blowing engine; ~ **mond,** tuyere.
blaas'ontsteking, inflammation of the bladder; cystitis.
blaas'op, (-pe), poisonous toad-fish (*Tetrodon honckeni*); green bladder grasshopper; frog (*Breviceps*).
blaas'operasie, cystotomy.
blaas; ~ **orkes,** brass band; wind orchestra; ~ **pootjie,** thrips; ~ **pyp,** blast pipe; blowpipe; peashooter; ~ **pypknop,** exhaust nozzle; ~ **roer,** pea shooter; ~ **skoot,** blow-out (charge).
blaas': ~ **steen,** calculus (stone in the bladder), urolith; ~ **vormig, (-e),** bladdershaped; cystiform; ~ **vorming,** vesiculation; blistering (paint); ~ **wurm,** defoliator; bladderworm; hydatid cyst.
blad, (blaaie), shoulder (of animal); top (of table); surface (of tennis court); leaf (of book): sheet (of newspaper); newspaper; blade (of spring); flake;

bowl (of oar); shoulder (of meat); *geen ~ voor sy MOND neem nie*, be outspoken; *sy skeur blaaie uit haar boek*, she is mutton dressed like lamb; *met 'n skoon ~ begin*, begin with a clean slate; ~ *SKUD (gee)*, shake hands; *van die ~ SPEEL*, play at sight (music); ~ **aar,** leaf-vein; nerve (bot.); ~ **aarde,** leaf mould; mulch; ~ **aarstelsel,** nervation; ~ **aluminium,** aluminium foil; ~ **anker,** palm stay; ~ **been,** shoulder-blade; ~ **breker,** scarifier (on road); ~ **erig, (-e),** foliated; ~ **erosie,** sheet erosion; ~ **geel,** leaf yellow (colour); xanthophyll; ~ **goud,** gold-leaf, gold-foil; leaf metal; ~ **groen,** leaf green, chlorophyll; ~ **groente,** greens, green vegetables; ~ **groentetablette,** chlorophyll tablets; ~ **ham,** shoulder ham; ~ **houdend, (-e),** evergreen.
bla'dig, (-e), foliate(d); ~ **heid,** foliation.
blad: ~ **jie, (-s),** small shoulder (of meat); ~ **knop,** gemma; ~ **koper,** sheet copper; copper-foil; ~ **laag,** carpet (of road); ~ **lees, (-ge-),** do sight-reading, sight read; ~ **lood,** lead-foil; sheet lead; ~ **luis,** aphis, plant louse; greenfly; ~ **metaal,** foil, leaf metal; ~ **moes,** mesophyll; ~ **neus,** vampire (*Rhinolophus*); ~ **rank,** leaf tendril; ~ **sak,** knapsack, gamebag; ~ **silwer,** leaf silver; silver foil; ~ **skroei,** leafscorch; ~ **spieël,** type page, printing surface; ~ **springer,** leaf hopper, jassid; ~ **steek, (-ge-),** shake hands; ~ **steel,** petiole, leaf stalk; ~ **stil:** *dit was ~ stil*, there was not the slightest breeze; ~ **stuk,** bolo (beef); ~ **sy,** page, folio; ~ **synommering,** pagination; ~ **syproef,** page proof; ~ **tin,** tinfoil; ~ **veer,** flat (blade) spring; leaf spring, laminated spring; ~ **vernuwing,** resurfacing; filler; ~ **vet,** leaf fat, flare fat; ~ **vleis,** shoulder (mutton); ~ **vormig, (-e),** foliaceous; ~ **vreter,** leaf cutter; ~ **vulling,** stop gap, titbit, padding, filler; ~ **wagter,** catchword (in printing); ~ **wisselend, (-e),** deciduous; ~ **wisseling,** shedding of leaves; ~ **wyser,** bookmark, index; ~ **yster,** sheet iron.
blaf, (s) bark; tongue; **(w) (ge-),** bark, give tongue; cough; *moenie te HARD ~ nie*, don't brag so much; *hy ~ HARDER as wat hy byt*, his bark is worse than his bite; ~ **fer, (-s),** barker, boaster, ~ **ferig, (-e),** fond of barking, inclined to bark.
bla'kend, (-e), burning, glowing, ardent; *in ~ e gesondheid*, in radiant health.
bla'ker¹, (s) (-s), candlestick; **(w) (ge-),** burn, bake, scorch.
bla'ker², (w) (ge-), hit, strike; *iem. op die oor ~*, give someone a blow on the ear.
blameer', (ge-), blame, cast the blame on; *ek word daarvoor ge~*, I am blamed for that.
blanc-man'ge, blancmange.
blan'je, white.
blank, (-e), white; fair; blank (verse); innocent, unstained; naked (sword); *~ e OPREGTHEID*, genuine uprightness, unquestioned integrity.
Blan'ke, (-s), white (person); ~ **dom,** whites.
blanket¹, (s) blanquette, white fricassée.
blanket'², (w) (ge-), paint, rouge; ~ **sel,** paint, cosmetic, rouge; make-up; grease-paint.
blank'heid, whiteness, fairness; purity, pureness.
blan'ko, blank; oop; *'n ~ tjek*, a blank cheque.
blansjeer', (ge-), bleach, blanch.
blaps, (-e), mistake, bloomer, howler.
bla're, foliage; ~ **dak,** leaf canopy; ~ **dos,** foliage; ~ **kroon,** crown of leaves; ~ **stand,** phyllotaxis, disposition of leaves; ~ **tooi,** foliage.
blas, dark brown, sallow (complexion); swarthy.
blasé', blasé, cloyed with pleasure.
bla'send, (-e), puffing.
bla'ser, (-s), blower; braggart.
blas'heid, sallowness; swarthiness.
bla'sie, (-s), bubble; bead; vesicle; bleb, blain; follicle.
bla'sies; ~ **koper,** blister (copper); ~ **rig, (-e),** vesicular; ~ **uitslag,** herpes.
blasoen', (-e), blazon, banner, coat of arms; ~ **eer', (ge-),** (em)blazon.
blastoder'mies, (-e), blastodermic.
blastogene'se, blastogenesis.
blastokar'pies, (-e), blastocarpous.
blat'jang, chutney; ketchup, relish.
bled'die, (plat), bloody; *jou ~ skaap*, you bloody fool.

bleek, (w) (ge-), bleach, whiten; (b) pale, pallid, discoloured, colourless, wan, white, ashen (cheeks); faint; *so* ~ *soos die DOOD*, as pale as death; ~ *WORD*, lose colour; ~**agtig**, wan, rather pale; ~**blou**, pale blue; ~**geel**, pale yellow; ~**gesig**, pale face, puttyface; ~**groen**, pale green; ~**heid**, pallor, paleness; ~**kol**, blister (cold-storage meat); ~**neus**, pale face; ~**pap**, see **bleikpap;** ~**poeier**, see **bleikpoeier;** ~**rooi**, pale red; ~**siekte**, anaemia, chlorosis, chloraemia; ~**sug**, anaemia; greensickness; chlorosis; ~**sug′tig**, (-e), chlorotic, anaemic; ~**vlerkspreeu**, pale-winged starling ~**vos**, light chestnut (horse).
blei, (-e), white bream (*Abramis*).
bleik, (ge-), bleach; ~**er**, (-s), bleacher, laundryman; ~**aarde**, fuller's earth; ~**middel**, bleaching agent; ~**pap**, bleaching paste; ~**poeier**, bleaching powder; ~**veld**, bleaching field; ~**water**, bleaching liquid.
blek, (ge-), blaze, mark (for felling).
ble′kerig, (-e), rather pale, wan.
blen′de, blende (ore).
blêr, (ge-), bleat; bellow; howl (of child); ~**arm**, extremely poor; ~**fliek**, talkies; ~**kas**, (-te), juke box; ~**lelik**, (-e), very ugly.
blerts, (s) (-e), spattering; stain; (w) (ge-), splash, bespatter, spatter.
bles, (-se), blaze (on horse); bald head; *hy is al HEELTEMAL* ~, he is already quite bald; *as ek dit doen, is my naam B* ~, I'm a Dutchman if I'll do that; ~**bok**, blesbuck, blesbok; ~**hoender**, red-knobbed coot; African coot; ~**kop**, baldhead, baldpate; ~**mol**, star (sand) mole; ~**perd**, bald-horse, horse with a blaze.
blesseer′, (ge-), wound, injure.
blessuur′, (..sure), wound; injury.
bleu, (ong.) blue.
blief, please; *as jou* ~, if you please.
bliek, bleak (fish).
bliep, (ge-), bleep; ~**er**, bleeper.
blik¹, (-ke), glance, glimpse, look, peep, view; *in EEN* ~, at a glance; *'n HELDER* ~ *op sake*, a keen insight into matters, keenness of discernment; *RUIM van* ~ *wees*, be broadminded; *'n* ~ *SLAAN (werp) op*, cast a glance at; *sy* ~ *VERRUIM*, broaden one's views; *VLUGTIGE* ~, (fleeting) glance.
blik², (s) (-ke), tin (plate); bin; white iron; pelf (money); *dis* ~ *of ek dit sal DOEN*, I am blowed if I'll do it; *IN* ~, canned; *JOU* ~!, you blighter!; *LEË* ~*ke raas die meeste*, empty vessels make the most noise; *so SEKER as* ~, as sure as fate; *SONDER* ~ *wees*, be out of cash; *met 'n* ~ *aan sy STERT huis toe kom*, come home after having been given his congé.
blik³, (w) (ge-), look, glance; *sonder (om te)* ~ *of (te) bloos*, unblushingly; without batting an eyelid.
blik: ~**beker**, tin mug; ~**bord**, tin plate; *'n* ~*bord voor sy kop hê*, be as bold as brass; be thickskinned; ~**doos**, canister; ~**emmer**, tin pail; ~**god:** *hy dink hy is 'n* ~ *op wiele*, he thinks he is a tin-god; ~**houer**, rascal, scoundrel; ~**huis**, galvanized iron house; tin shanty; ~**kantien**, tin can, *dis laaste sien van die* ~*kantien*, that's the last you'll see of it.
blik′ker, (ge-), sparkle, glare, flash.
blik′kerig, (-e), tinny.
blik′kering, glare.
blik′kie, (-s), small tin; hole (golf); *dit gaan jou* ~*s!*, good luck to you!, good-bye!, cheerio!
blik′kies: ~**biltong**, (tinned) chipped beef; ~**dorp**, tin town; the slums; ~**groente**, tinned vegetables; ~**kos**, tinned food(stuffs); ~**melk**, tinned (condensed) milk; ~**vleis**, army-beef, bully-beef, tinned meat.
blik: ~**motor**, flivver; ~**ners**, saddle-sore; *jou* ~*nery*, get saddle-sore; ~**oopmaker**, tinopener.
Blik′oor¹, nickname for a Free Stater.
blik′oor², fool, block-head, lout.
blik′sem, (s) (-s), lightning; *JOU* ~! (plat), you scoundrel (blackguard)!; *na die* ~ *GAAN*, go to the devil (the dogs); *die* ~ *IN wees vir iem.*, be furious with someone; *geen* ~ *OMGEE nie*, not care a damn; *SOOS die* ~, like blazes; like lightning; (w) (ge-), lighten, flash; fulminate; ~**afleier**, lightning conductor; chaperone; ~**buis**, lightning tube, fulgurite; ~**end**, (-e), fulminating; ~**flits**, lightning flash; ~**lig**, flashlight; ~**oë**, flashing eyes; ~**poeier**, vegetable brimstone; ~**s**, (b) (-e), accursed, confounded; damn it!; ~**skig**, thunderbolt; ~**slag** (..**slae**), thunderclap; flash of ligtning; ~**snel**, quick as lightning; meteoric; ~**snelheid**, lightning speed; ~**stofhoudend**, (-e), idioelectric; ~**straal**, flash of lightning; bolt of thunder; ~**trein**, (geselst.) lightning express; ~**vry**, (-e), lightningproof.
blik′skater(s), dash it!, hang!
blik: ~**skêr**, plate shears; ~**skottel**, tin dish; fool, silly ass; scoundrel; ~**skottels!**, the deuce!, hang it!, dash it! ~**slaer**, (-s), tinsmith, white smith, tinman; scoundrel, rascal, blighter; ~**slaerswerk**, tinware; ~**slaerswinkel** tinsmith's shop; ~**snyer**, tin-opener; ~**soldaat**, tin soldier.
blikveld, (field of) vision.
blik: ~**vuur**, blue light; ~**ware**, tinware; ~**werker**, tin plater.
blind, (-e), blind(ly); eyeless; buried (stone); ~*e AANVLUG*, blind approach; ~*e BAL*, no-ball (cricket); ~*e FLENS*, blind flange; ~*vir iem. se FOUTE*, blind to someone's faults; ~*e GALERY*, blind drift; winze; blind shaft; ~*GANG*, dead end, blind alley; ~*e HOEK*, blind angle (corner); ~*e HOOFPYN*, migraine; *'n* ~*e HOOGTE (bult)*, a blind rise; *IN die* ~*e*, at random; ~*e KAART*, skeleton map; ~*e KANT*, blind side, ~*e MONSTER*, grab sample; ~*e MUUR*, dead (blank) wall; ~*e PASSASIER*, stowaway; *niem. is so* ~ *as dié wat nie wil SIEN nie*, none so blind as those who do not wish to see; ~*e SKOOT*, snap shot; ~*e STEEG*, blind alley; ~*e STRAAT(JIE)*, blind alley; *'n* ~*e SUIDOOSTEWIND*, blind south-easter; ~*e TOEVAL*, mere (blind) chance; ~*e VENSTER*, dummy window; ~*e VERTROUE*, implicit faith; ~*e VINK*, beef olive; ~*e VLEK*, blindspot; ~**doek**, (s) eye bandage; (w) (ge-), blindfold; hoodwink, deceive; ~**druk**, blind printing.
blin′de, (-s), blind person; *een* ~ *kan nie 'n ander LEI nie*, the blind cannot lead the blind; *in die* ~ *RONDTAS*, grope in the dark; ~**derm**, appendix; blind-gut, caecum; ~**dermontsteking**, appendicitis; ~**dermoperasie**, appendectomy; ~**hand**, dummy (cards); ~**-instituut**, institute for the blind, blind school; ~**kantvyl**, safe-edge file; ~**kas**, (-te), wall cupboard; ~**lings**, blindly, implicitly; baldheaded, blindfold; ~**man**, blind man; dummy (at cards); ~**mannetjie**, blind-man's-buff; ~**mol**, blind mole; hoodman blind; mole rat; ~**molletjie**, blind-man's-buff.
blin′der, (-s), stymie (golf); blind (window); huge wave.
blin′dering, blindage.
blin′de: ~**skool**, school for the blind, ~**skrif**, braillewriting; ~**slang**, blind snake; ~**sorg**, care of (for) the blind; ~**speler**, dummy (player at cards); ~**vlek**, blind spot; ~**vlieë**, tabanids; ~**vlieg**, blind fly; sting fly; *nes 'n* ~*vlieg wees*, be a pest; ~**wurm**, hazelworm, slowworm, blind worm.
blind: ~**gebore**, blind-born; ~**heid**, blindness, cecity; *met* ~*heid geslaan*, struck blind, blinded.
blin′ding, (-s), blind (of window).
blind: ~**landing**, blind landing; ~**tik**, touch typing, ~**vlieg**, blind fly; ~**vliegtoets**, blind flying test; ~**weg**, blindly, rashly.
blink, (w) (ge-), shine, gleam; (b) shining, polished (floor); gleaming, glittering; glazy; sleek (hair); glossy, lustrous; *'n* ~ *GEDAGTE*, a brain-wave, an inspiration; (bw): ~ *en bles lieg*, lie like a gasmeter; ~**blaarboom**, *Pterocarpus rotundifolius*; ~**blaarwag-'n-bietjie**, mimosa with glossy leaves (*Ziziphus mucronata*); ~**bout**, bright bolt; ~**end**, (-e), glossy, glittering, phosphorescent, shiny; ~**er**, (-s), sequin, spangle; cat's eye; ~**erig**, (-e), shiny; ~**etjie**, (-s), small diamond; ~**goed**, shiny ornaments; ~**heid**, shine, brilliance, glossiness; ~**kool**, glossy coal, blind coal; ~**leer**, patent leather; ~**maak**, (-ge-),

polish up; ~**nuut, (..nuwe),** brand-new; ~**ogie,** cat's eye (road sign); ~**oog,** lizard, diamond; *ou ~ oog,* the devil; ~**verhaar,** in good condition; ~**vet,** plump, very fat; ~**water,** will-o'-the-wisp.
blits, (s) (-e), lightning; flash; dop brandy; *soos 'n vetgesmeerde ~ LOOP,* run like greased lightning; *SOOS 'n ~,* like a shot, quick as ligtning; **(w) (ge-),** flash; *DAAR ~ dit,* the cannon has just fired; there's a flash of lightning; *sy OË ~,* his eyes shoot fire; ~**aanval,** lightning attack; ~**ig, (-e),** quick as ligthning; hot-tempered; ~**lig,** flashlight; *bedekte ~ lig,* concealed flashlight; ~**ligopname,** flashlight portraiture; ~**lont,** instantaneous fuse; ~**lyn,** hotline; ~**motor,** flying-squad car; ~**oorlog,** blitzkrieg; ~**patrollie,** flying squad; ~**poeding,** hasty (quick) pudding; ~**poeier,** magnesium powder; ~**rekenaar,** ready reckoner; ~**snel,** quick as lightning; ~**staking,** lightning strike; ~**trein,** fast express; ~**verkiesing,** snap election; ~**verkoper,** bestseller; ~**vinnig, (-e),** like greased lightning, at lightning speed.
blo¹, (w) = beloof.
blo², (b), (geselst.) cowardly; *liewer ~ Jan as do(oie) Jan,* better a living dog than a dead lion.
bloed, blood; strain (in cattle); *van ADELLIKE ~,* having blue blood in one's veins; *iem. se ~ in sy are laat stol,* make someone's blood turn cold; *nuwe ~ BRING in,* introduce fresh (new) blood in(to); *BLOU ~ hê,* be of noble birth; have blue blood; *na ~ DORS,* thirst for blood; *EIE ~,* one's own (flesh and) blood; *daar kleef ~ aan die GELD,* it is blood-tainted money; *daar kleef ~ aan sy HANDE,* his hands are stained with blood; *laat sy ~ op ons en ons KINDERS ~,* his blood be on us, and on our children; *~ uit 'n KLIP wil tap,* try to squeeze blood from a stone; *in KOELE, ~* in cold blood; *van KONINKLIKE ~,* of royal blood; *sy ~ KOOK,* he is furiously angry, his blood boils; *~ KRUIP waar dit nie kan loop nie,* blood is thicker than water; *KWAAD ~ sit,* create ill-feeling; *werk dat die ~ onder die NAELS uitloop,* work one's fingers to the bone; *dit SIT my in die ~,* it runs in my blood; *~ SWEET,* sweat blood; *iem. se ~ TAP,* bleed someone dry; *~ is dikker as WATER,* blood is thicker than water; *ten ~ e toe WEERSTAND bied,* resist to the bitter end; ~**aandrang,** congestion of blood; ~**aar,** blood vein; ~**agtig, (-e),** bloodlike; ~**appel,** blood apple; ~**arm,** anaemic, exsanguine; ~**armoede,** poverty of blood, anaemia, chlorosis; ~**KWAADAARDIGE ~ armoede,** pernicious anaemia; *MENSLIKE ~ armoede,* oligaemia; ~**bad, (baaie),** massacre, slaughter; blood-bath; carnage; pogrom; battue; *'n ~ bad aanrig,* massacre; ~**bank,** blood bank; ~**belope,** bloodshot; ~**blaar,** blood blister; ~**blaas,** haematoma; ~**blom,** blood flower (*Haemanthus natalensis*); ~**broer,** blood-brother.
Bloed'bruilof, Massacre of St. Bartholomew, 1572.
bloed: ~**dors,** blood-lust; ~**dor'stig, (-e),** bloodthirsty; bloody; bloody-minded; ~**dor'stigheid,** blood-thirstiness; ~**dronk,** blood-thirsty; ~**druk,** blood-pressure; ~**drukmeter,** sphygmomanometer; ~**druppel,** drop of blood; ~**eie,** very own (by blood relationship); german; ~**end, (-e), bloeding: ~ens:** *tot ~ens toe mishandel,* ill-treat severely; ~**erig, (-e),** bloody; blood-stained; ~**erigheid,** bloodiness; ~**etter,** sanies; ~**gebrek,** poverty of blood; ~**geld,** price of blood; blood money; ~**geswel,** h(a)ematocele; ~**gierig (-e),** blood-thirsty; ~**groep,** blood group; ~**hond,** bloodhound; man of blood; ~**hormoon,** blood hormone; ~**hormoonvlak,** blood-hormone level; ~**ig, (-e),** sanguinary, gory; bloody, homicidal; scorching; *die ~ ige SON,* the scorching sun; *ek het my ~ ig VERERG,* I was extremely annoyed; ~**ing,** haemorrhage; bleeding; ~**jie, (-s),** young child, urchin; poor mite; ~**jong,** ~**jonk,** very young; ~**kanker,** leukemia; ~**kleur,** blood colour, crimson; ~**kleurstof,** haemoglobin; ~**klont,** thrombus, blood-clot; ~**koek,** clot; ~**koraal,** red coral; ~**kruid,** lythrum; ~**kunde,** h(a)ematology; ~**laat, (ge-),** let blood, bleed, cup; phlebotomize; exsan-

guinate; venesect; *iem. ~laat,* fleece someone; ~**lating,** bloodletting, cupping; bleeding; phlebotomy; venesection; ~**lelie,** haemanthus; ~**lemoen,** blood orange; ~**liggaampie,** blood corpuscle; ~**loos, (..lose),** bloodless; exsanguine; anaemic; ~**loosheid,** anaemia; ~**luis,** woolly aphis, blood louse; ~**lyn,** line, strain (in breeding); ~**menging,** mixture of blood; ~**min,** precious little; ~**neef,** first cousin; ~**neus,** bloodstained (bleeding) nose; *iem. ~neus slaan,* blood someone's nose; ~**nier,** pulpy kidney, enterotoxaemia; ~**ondersoek,** blood-test; ~**oortapping,** blood transfusion; ~**parsie =** ~**persie;** ~**pens,** bloody dysentery (lamb disease); ~**perd,** thoroughbred horse; ~**persie,** bloody diarrhoea; bloody flux; ~**plas,** pool of blood; ~**plaatjie,** blood plate; ~**plasma,** bloodplasm; ~**produk,** blood product; ~**pruim,** Satsuma plum; ~**prys,** price of blood; blood-money; ~**puisie,** anthrax; **B~raad,** Council of Blood; ~**reinigend, (-e),** blood purifying (medicine); ~**reinigingsmiddel,** blood purifier; ~**ring,** blood ring (in eggs); ~**rooi,** blood-red; scarlet, crimson; pillar-box red; ~**rou,** underdone (meat); ~**ryk, (-e),** sanguineous, full-blooded, plethoric, rich in blood; ~**sap,** genuine SAP-man; ~**serum,** blood serum; ~**sisteem,** circulatory system; ~**skande,** incest; ~**skender,** incestuous person; ~**skendig, (-e),** incestuous; ~**skenker,** donor of blood, blood donor; ~**skoon,** spotless; ~**sku, (-we),** haemophobe, averse to (sight of) blood; ~**skuld,** blood-guilt; ~**skuldig, (-e),** guilty of blood; ~**skyfie,** blood disc; ~**smeer,** blood-stain; blood-smear (of sick animals); ~**s'omloop,** circulation of the blood; ~**spat,** blood spavin; ~**spoor,** blood trail; ~**spuwing,** spitting of blood; haemorrhage of the lungs; ~**steen,** bloodstone, haematite; ~**stelpend, (-e),** astringent, styptic; ~**stelper,** ~**stelpmiddel,** styptic, astringent; ~**storting,** bloodshed; effusion of blood; flux; haemorrhage (of uterus); ~**stroom,** blood stream; ~**stuwing,** congestion; ~**suier,** leech, blood-sucker; hunks; horseleech; usurer, extortioner; ~**suiker,** blood-sugar; ~**suiweraar,** blood-purifier; abstergent; ~**suiwerend, (-e),** purifying the blood, abstergent; ~**suiwering,** blood purification; ~**sweet,** bloody sweat; ~**telling,** blood count; ~**transfusie,** blood transfusion; ~**vat,** blood-vessel; ~**vatestelsel,** vascular system; ~**vergieter,** murderer; ~**vergieting,** bloodshed; ~**vergiftiging,** blood-poisoning; toxaemia; ~**verlies,** loss of blood; ~**vermenging,** miscegenation; **verwant, (-e),** relative kinsman; agnate; bloodrelation; consanguine; ~**verwantskap,** kinship, (blood-)relationship; consanguinity; propinquity, proximity of blood; ~**verwig, (-e),** bloody, red; ~**vete,** blood feud; ~**vin, (-ne),** ~**vint, (-e),** boil, furuncle; ~**vintagtig, (-e),** furuncular; ~**vlek,** blood-stain; ~**vog,** ichor; ~**vorming,** blood-forming; sanguification; ~**warmte,** blood-heat; ~**water,** lymph, ichor; haematuria; ~**wei,** lymph; serum; ~**weinig,** precious little; ~**wors,** blood polony; black pudding; blood pudding; ~**wraak,** revenge of blood; vendetta, blood feud; ~**wurm,** bloodworm.
bloei¹, (s), bloom, florescence; flourishing condition, prosperity, (ef)florescence; bleeding (paint); *in die ~ van sy JARE,* in the prime of his life; *in VOLLE ~,* in full bloom; **(w) (ge-),** bloom, blossom, effloresce, flower, flourish; prosper.
bloei² (w) (ge-), bleed; *my neus ~,* my nose is bleeding.
bloei'as, rachis.
bloei'end¹, (-e), flowering; green; flourishing; florescent; prosperous; *'n ~ende vereniging,* a flourishing society (association).
bloei'end² (-e), bleeding.
bloei'er¹, (-s), flowerer.
bloei'er², (-s), bleeder; ~**siekte,** haemophilia.
bloei: ~**maand,** (Ndl.) flowering month, spring month (October); ~**periode,** golden age; flourishing period; flowering season; ~**sel, (-s),** blossom, flower; flow; efflorescence; ~**tyd,** (ef)florescence; flowering time; flourishing period, prime; golden

bloekom 81 **blou**

age; ~**tydperk**, flowering time; palmy days; ~**wyse**, inflorescence.
bloe'kom, (-s), eucalyptus, blue-gum (tree); ~**boom**, blue-gum tree; ~**olie**, eucalyptus oil.
bloem: *see* **blom**: ~**is'**, (-te), florist; ~**istery'**, floristry; ~**istewinkel**, florist's shop; ~**kolf**, spadix; ~**lesing**, anthology; analecta, delectus, excerption; chrestomathy; garland; florilegium; culling; ~**ryk**, (-e), florid, ornate, flowery (style); ~**rykheid**, floridness, ornateness; floweriness; euphuism.
bloes, (-e), **bloe'se** (-s), blouse.
bloe'sem, (-s), blossom, bloom.
bloe'send, (-e), rosy, ruddy.
blok[1], (s) (-ke), block, log (of wood); poppet (lathe head); clog, stock (for leg); pig (of iron); die; climp; cliché (printing); hobble; '*n* ~ *aan die BEEN hê*, be handicapped; ~ *en TAKEL*, block and fall; block and tackle; '*n* ~ *van 'n VENT*, a giant of a fellow; '*n* ~ *of drie verder WOON*, live about three blocks further on.
blok[2], (w) (ge-), block.
blok[3], (w) grind at, cram, swot (for examination).
blok: ~**bedryf**, block working; ~**boek**, dummy (in library); ~**druk**, block printing; ~**gat**, (-e), block; ~**hamer**, mallet; ~**huis**, blockhouse; loghouse.
blokka'de, (-s), blockade; ~**breker**, blockade runner; ~**breuk**, running the blockade; ~**lyn**, blockade line.
blok'kedoos, box of bricks; brick box.
blok'keer, (ge-), blockade; ~**der**, blockader.
blok'ker, (-s), plodder, grinder, crammer.
blokke'ring, blockading.
blok'kery, cramming.
blok: ~**ketting**, block chain; ~**kie**, (-s), little square; little log, cube; ~**kiesgoed**, check; ~**kiesraaisel**, crossword puzzle; ~**kiesuiker**, loaf sugar, cube sugar; ~**kiesvloer**, block-floor; parquet floor; ~**koppeling**, jaw clutch; ~**las**, (-se), block-joint; ~**letter**, blockletter; ~**maker**, block maker; ~**rand**, blocked rand; ~**rem**, block-brake; *B*~*sberg*: *ek wou dat jy op B*~*sberg sit*, go to Jericho; I'd rather see you in Hades; ~**sein**, block signal; ~**seintoestel**, block signalling apparatus; ~**silwer**, block silver; ~**skaaf**, jack (double) plane, jointing plane; smoothing plane; ~**skoen**, clog; sabot; wooden sandal; ~**skrif**, block writing (letters); ~**skyf**, (block) sheaf; ~**staal**, ingot steel.
blok'stelsel[1], block system.
blok'stelsel[2], cramming system.
blok: ~**telefoon**, block telephone; ~**tin**, bar tin; ~**toediening**, block application (e.g. insecticides).
blok'tyd, cramming time.
blok: ~**vas**, (-te), close together, solidly; ~**venster**, block-window; ~**vyl**, square file; ~**wagter**, block signalman; ~**wiel**, web wheel; ~**woning**, flats, block of flats.
blom, (s) (-me), flower, blossom; elite, flour; '*n* ~ *MAAK*, do exceptionally well; *dis nie altyd die MOOISTE* ~ *wat die by om draai nie*, looks are not everything; *die* ~ *van die NASIE*, the choice (pride) of the nation; '*n* ~ *van 'n NOOI*, a very pretty (peach of a) girl; ~*me RANGSKIK*, arrange flowers; ~ *van SWA(W)EL*, flowers of sulphur; (w) (ge-), flower, blossom, floriate; ~**agtig**, (-e), flower-like; ~**akkertjie**, flower bed; ~**as**, floral axis; ~**bak**, flower bowl, vase; ~**bedding**, flower bed; ~**bekleedsel**, perianth; ~**blaar**, petal; *sonder* ~*blare*, apetalous; ~**blaarvormig**, (-e), petaline; ~**bodem**, receptacle; ~**bol**, (flower) bulb; ~**bolhandelaar**, bulb dealer; ~**bolkweker**, bulb grower; ~**briefkaart**, (flower) picture postcard; ~**dek**, perianth; ~**draend**, (e), floriferous; ~**ertjie**, sweet pea; ~**figuur**, knot (of flowers); ~**geur**, fragrance of flowers; ~**handel**, flower trade; ~**hart**, corolla; ~**hofie**, flower head; ~**houer**, flower holder; ~**huisie**, conservatory; ~**kelk**, calyx; bell (of flower); ~**kenner**, florist, flower expert; ~**knop**, flower bud; ~**kolf**, spadix; ~**kool**, cauliflower; ~**krans**, wreath, garland; ~**kroon**, corolla; ~**kweker**, nurseryman, florist; ~**kwekery**, (flower) nursery; ~**kweper**, flowering quince; ~**luis**, green-fly.

blom'me: ~**handel**, flower trade; ~**handelaar**, florist; ~**hulde**, floral tribute; ~**liefhebber**, flower lover; ~**mandjie**, flower basket; ~**meisie**, flower-girl; ~**prag**, beauty of flowers; ~**rangskikking**, flower arrangement; ~**skat**, wealth of flowers; ~**stalletjie**, flower (seller's) stall; ~**taal**, language of flowers; ~**teelt**, floriculture; ~**tentoonstelling**, flower show; ~**tjie**, (-s), floweret, small flower; lover; ~**weelde**, wealth of flowers.
blom: ~**patroon**, diaper pattern; ~**pens**, honeycomb stomach, reticulum; ~**perk**, flower bed, parterre; ~**perske**, flowering peach; ~**plant**, flowering plant; ~**pluim**, panicle; ~**poeier**, pollen; ~**pot**, vase; (flower)pot; ~**pruim**, flowering plum; ~**rand**, flower border, herbaceous border; ~**riet**, canna; ~**ruiker**, nosegay; bouquet; ~**ryk**, (-e), flowery; florid, flamboyant, figurative; ~**rykheid**, floweriness; floridity, floridness; ~**saad**, flower seed; ~**simboliek**, language of flowers; ~**skede**, spathe; ~**skerm**, umbel; ~**skilpadjie**, ladybird; ~**skoot**, fine (good) shot; ~**slinger**, garland of flowers; ~**stand**, inflorescence; ~**stander**, flower stand; ~**steel**, peduncle, pedicel, pedicle; ~**stingel**, flower stalk; ~**stof**, pollen; ~**struik**, flowering shrub; ~**swael**, ~**swawel**, flowers of sulphur; ~**taal**, language of flowers; ~**tafel**, flower stall; flower stand; ~**tee**, (flower) bush tea; ~**tros**, raceme; ~**tuin**, flower garden; ~**tyd**, flowering time (season); ~**vaas**, (flower) vase; ~**verkoopster**, flowergirl, flower seller; ~**versiering**, floral decoration; ~**vormig**, (-e), flower shaped; ~**werk**, flower work.
blond, (-e), fair, light, blond; ~**harig**, (-e), fair-haired; ~**held**, fairness; ~**i'ne**, (-s), fair woman, blonde.
bloos, (ge-), blush, colour, redden, flush, change countenance; crimson; ~ *tot agter die ORE*, blush to the roots of one's hair.
bloot, (blote), naked, bare; bald (facts); mere(ly); *die blote FEITE*, the bald facts; *met die blote HAND veg*, fight with bare fists (knuckles); *onder die blote HEMEL*, in the open air; *met die blote OOG*, with the naked eye; *blote VERBOD*, nude prohibition (jur.); '*n blote VERMOEDE*, a mere supposition; ~ **gee**, (-ge-): *hom* ~*gee*, commit oneself; expose oneself; ~**heid**, bareness; ~**lê**, (-ge-), lay bare, exhibit; expound; enucleate, open, expose, disclose, reveal; ~**legging**, denudation; exposure; ~**s**, bare-back(ed); *iem.* ~*s ry*, make it hot for someone; ~**s'hoof(s)**, bare-headed; ~**s'perd**, bare-backed horse; ~**s'rug**, bare-back; ~**staan**, (-ge-), be exposed; ~**stel**, (-ge-), expose; compromise; commit; *hom aan gevaar* ~*stel*, expose oneself to danger; ~**stelling**, exposure; exposé; ~**s'voet(s)**, barefoot(ed); ~**weg**, merely; ~**wol**, skin wool, slipe wool.
blos, (-se), blush, bloom, flush, glow.
blo'send, (-e), blushing, flushed, rosy, ruddy, aglow, erubescent.
blou, blue; ~ *BABA*, blue baby; ~ *BLOED hê*, be of noble descent; *een maal in 'n* ~ *JAAR*, very seldom, once in a blue moon; ~ *van die KOUE*, blue with cold; *LIEG dat jy* ~ *word*, lie like a trooper; ~ *MAAK*, blue (metal); ~ *van MAERTE*, very lean; *PRAAT tot jy* ~ *word*, talk till you are blue in the face; *die B*~ *TREIN*, the Blue Train; ~**aap**, ~**apie**, vervet monkey; marmoset (Amer.); *Cercopithecus aethiops;* ~**agtig**, (-e), bluish; ~**apiestuipe**: ~*apiestuipe kry*, be taken aback, be flabbergasted; ~**asbes**, blue asbestos, crocidolite; ~**baadjie**, (vero.) blue-jacket; *B*~**baard**, Bluebeard; ~**bek**, tribulosis (sheep disease); ~**bessie** (bos), whortleberry, huckleberry; ~**biskop**, stone bass; ~**blasie**, bluebottle, Portuguese stone bass, ~**blasie**, bluebottle, Portuguese man-of-war *(Physalia arethusa);* ~**blindheid**, blueblindness; ~**blommetjie**, tittle-tattle story, feeble excuse; ~**blomsalie**, wild sage; ~-**blou**, as it is; *iets* ~*-blou laat*, leave well alone, let the matter rest; ~**boek**, blue-book; ~**bok**, bluebuck; ~**boontjie**, bullet, blue pill; *iem. leer hoeveel* ~*boontjies vyf MAAK*, tell someone what's what; *die VYAND* ~*boontjies gee*, give the enemy a leaden pill; ~**borsie**, *Luscinia svecica;* ~**bosbessie**, bilberry; ~**bosluis**, blue tick;

~ **bottel**, castor oil; ~ **brander**, blue-flame burner; ~ **bul**, nilgai; ~ **dissel**, Mexican poppy; ~ **draad**, galvanized wire; ~ **druk**, blue print.
blou'duiwel[1], Mexican poppy.
blou'duiwel[2], delirium tremens.
blou: ~ **e, (-s)**, blue one; blue horse; ~ **erig, (-e)**, bluish; ~ **geruit**, blue-checkered; ~ **glas**, cobalt glass; ~ **gras**, blue grass; ~ **groen**, blue green; aquamarine; caesious; ~ **grond**, blue ground; kimberlite; ~ **grys**, griseous; ~ **haai**, blue shark; ~ **haak**, kind of mimosa, e.g. *Acacia detinens;* ~ **heid**, blueness; ~ **hottentot**, *Sparidae;* ~ **hout**, logwood, campeachy; ~ **ig, (-e)**, bluish; ~ **klip**, blue-stone; ~ **knoop**, teetotaller; ~ **koos**, the devil; ace of spades; chamber-pot; ~ **kopkoggelmander**, blue-headed lizard; tree-lizard *(Agama articollis);* ~ **kopsiekte**, blue tongue (a sheep's disease); ~ **korhaan**, blue bustard; ~ **kous**, bluestocking, literary woman, savante; ~ **kwint** = **bloublasie;** ~ **lelie**, agapanthus; ~ **oog, (s)** blue-eyed person; mouse; (b) blue-eyed; *iem.* ~ *oog slaan*, give someone a black eye; ~ **oognooi**, blue-eyed girl; ~ **potklei**, blue clay; ~ **reën**, wistaria; ~ **reier**, grey heron *(Ardea cinerea);* ~ **renoster**, blue rhinoceros; ~ **rok**, adherent of Latter Rain sect; ~ **saadgras**, variety of grass *(Diptachne, Eragrostis, Panicum);* ~ **seep**, mottled (blue) soap; ~ **sel**, (laundry) blue, bluing; ~ **siekte**, blue disease, cyanosis; ~ **skilder**, blue-speckled; ~ **skimmel**, blue mould (citrus); ~ **skimmel(perd)**, blue roan, bluish grey horse; ~ **slik**, blue mud; ~ **spaat**, lazulite; ~ **steen**, bluestone, copper sulphate, blue vitriol; ~ **sug**, blue jaundice; ~ **suur**, prussic acid; hydrocyanic acid; ~ **suursout**, prussiate; ~ **swart**, blue black; ~ **sysie**, blue siskin *(Uraeginthus angolensis);* ~ **te**, blueness; blue; ~ **tjie, (-s)**, carbon paper; carbon copy; *'n* ~ *tjie loop*, be refused (by a girl); get the mitten; ~ **tong**, blue tongue (a sheep's disease); ~ **-uier**, mastitis; ~ **valk**, black-shouldered kite; ~ **visvanger**, half-collared kingfisher *(Alcedo semitorquata);* ~ **vitrioel**, chalcanite, copper sulphate; ~ **vlamstoof**, blue-flame stove; ~ **vlieg**, blue fly; ~ **walvis**, blue whale; ~ **wildebees**, blue wildebeest, brindled gnu *(Gorgon taurinus).*
bluf, (s) bragging, boasting; bluff, gas, bounce, swank, gasconade; (w) **(ge-)**, brag, boast, bluff; puff; gasconade; ~ **fer, (-s)**, braggart, boaster, gasbag; ~ **ferig, (-e)**, boastful, boasting; ~ **fery**, boasting, braggadocio, bluffing.
blus, (ge-), extinguish (fire); quench, put out; slacken, slake (lime); become floury (mealy) (potato); *sy* ~ *is uit*, he is done for (totally exhausted); ~ **aartappel**, mealy potato; ~ **baar, (..bare)**, extinguishable, quenchable; ~ **emmer**, fire bucket; ~ **gereedskap**, extinguishing appliance(s); ~ **masjien**, extinguisher; ~ **middel**, fire extinguisher; ~ **ser, (-s)**, extinguisher, quencher; ~ **sing**, quenching, extinguishing; extinction; ~ **toestel**, extinguisher, annihilator.
bly[1], (w) **(ge-)**, stay, remain, abide; live, dwell; keep; *ek* ~ *DAARBY*, I stick to it, I persist in saying; *LAAT maar* ~, never mind; *hy* ~ *by sy OPINIE*, he sticks to his opinion; *op 'n PLAAS* ~, live on a farm; ~ *van die SAAG af weg*, keep clear of the saw; ~ *SIT*, remain seated; stick; *in die SLAG* ~, be killed in battle; be a victim; ~ *STAAN*, remain standing; get stuck (vehicle); ~ *STIL!*, be quiet!
bly[2], (b) **(-e)**, glad, joyful, joyous, cheerful, happy, pleased, jocund; *iem. twee maal* ~ *MAAK*, outstay one's welcome; *in* ~ *e VERWAGTING*, expecting a baby, in the family way.
bly'de, mangonel.
blyd'skap, joy, happiness; gladness, cheer.
bly: ~ **-ein'dend, (-e)**, with a happy ending; ~ **gees'tig, (-e)**, happy-natured, gay, cheerful; ~ **gees'tigheid**, cheerfulness; joviality; ~ **har'tig, (-e)**, glad-hearted, joyful; ~ **har'tigheid**, joyfulness; ~ **heid**, gladness, joy, jocundity.
blyk, (s) (-e), proof, mark, token, sign; ~ *gee van*, give proof of; (w) **(ge-)**, appear, seem, emerge, be evident (obvious); *dit sal GOU* ~, it will soon become evident; *LAAT* ~, betray, give away; show (feelings); reveal; ~ **baar, (..bare)**, apparent(ly),

obvious, evident, manifest; to all appearances; ostensible; ~ **baarheid**, ostensibility; ~ **ens**, according to, as is apparent, as appears from.
bly'makertjie, tot, drink.
bly'mare, glad tidings.
blymoe'dig, (-e), joyful, cheerful, glad, gay, blithe, with a glad heart; ~ **heid**, joyfulness, cheerfulness, gladness, gaiety.
bly'spel, (-e), comedy; ~ **digter**, ~ **skrywer**, writer of comedies.
blystaan'plek, place where a vehicle got stuck.
bly'wend, (-e), enduring, lasting (impressions); abiding (sorrow); permanent (improvement); perennial (plant); *'n* ~ *e INDRUK*, a lasting impression; ~ *e KLEURE*, fast colours.
B'-majeur, B major.
B'-mol, B minor.
bo, above, upstairs, aloft; up, upon; over, beyond; ~ *aan (boaan) die BLADSY*, at the top of the page; *DAAR* ~, up there; ~ *EN behalwe*, over and above; ~ *die veertig JAAR*, past forty years; *NA* ~, up; upstairs; *van* ~ *tot ONDER*, from top to toe (bottom); ~ *vyf RAND*, more than five rand; *SOOS* ~, as above; *VAN* ~, from above; ~ *alle VERWAGTING*, beyond all expectations; *VRYHEID* ~*!*, freedom for ever!; ~ *WATER wees*, have overcome one's difficulties.
bo'a, (-s), boa (fur); boa constrictor (snake).
bo'aan, at the top; at the head; ~ *die KLAS staan*, be at the top of the class; ~ *die LYS*, at the top (head) of the list.
bo'aards, (-e), heavenly, celestial, supermundane, extramundane.
bo'akonstriktor, (-s), boa constrictor.
bo'al = **bowenal.**
bo'arm, upper arm; ~ **been**, humerus.
bo'baadjie, jacket, coat.
bo'baas, master, superior, top-dog; top-notcher; ~ *wees*, be top-dog, boss the show, be second to none, excel.
bobbejaan', (..jane), monkey, baboon; (monkey-)pipewrench; goose (person); ~ *kry BERG (krans)*, be bragging about one's achievements; *die* ~ *agter die BULT gaan haal*, meet your troubles half-way; *van iets soveel weet as 'n* ~ *van GODSDIENS*, know as much about something as the man in the moon; *die* ~ *tjies HARDLOOP*, the heat-waves are dancing; *hulle IS ..jane*, they are a lot of sheep (fools); *JOU* ~*!*, you silly ass!; *die* ~ *het daar 'n KIERIE nodig*, the road is impassable; *elke* ~ *op sy KRANS*, each one to his proper sphere; birds of a feather flock together; *hy is 'n MAL* ~, he is a madcap; *jy is (lyk) 'n MOOI* ~*!*, you're a fine one!; *toe jy NOG 'n* ~ *was*, before you were born; ~ *OPPASSER van die vyeboom maak*, set the fox to keep the geese; *so vry soos 'n* ~ *aan 'n PAAL*, as free as the monkey on his pole; *so lelik as die* ~ *sy SLAAPPLEK*, as ugly as sin; *as die* ~ *sy STERT verbrand, byt hy sy baas*, take it out on someone else; *hy is 'n UITGEBYTE* ~, he has been sent to Coventry; has been ostracized; *jy kan dit vir die ..jane gaan WYSMAAK*, tell that to the marines; ~ **agtig, (-e)**, monkeyish; ~ **appel**, gall on *Asparagus striatus;* fruit of the shrub *Rothmannia capensis;* ~ **bakkies** (person with) ugly face; ~ **bek**, (monkey-)wrench; ~ **boud**, old-fashioned musket; ~ **druiwe**, wild (grape) berries; ~ **hartseer**, crocodile tears; ~ **klier**, monkey gland; ~ **leer**, pegladder; ~ **liefde**, feigned love; calflove; ~ **mannetjie**, male baboon; foolish (stupid) person; ~ **oor**, elephant's ear *(Eriosperum);* ~ **sleutel**, monkeywrench; ~ **snuif**, puff-ball; ~ **spinnekop**, baboon spider *(Harpactira);* ~ **stert**, baboon's tail; *Barbacenia retinervis;* ~ **streke**, monkey tricks; buffoonery; ~ **stuipe**, hysterics, fits; ~ **tjie, (-s)**, small baboon; wild tulip, *Babiana villosa; 'n* ~ *tjie vang*, assist at childbirth; ~ **tou**, wild vine; bush-rope *(Vitis capensis);* ~ **verdriet**, monkeypuzzle *(Araucaria).*
bob'bel, (s) (-s), bubble, blister; (w) **(ge-)**, bubble; blister.
bo'bed, upper bed (bunk).

bo'bedoel(d), (-de), (referred to) above.
bo'been, upper leg, thigh.
bo'belasting, supertax, surcharge.
bo'bemes, (~), top-dress; **~ting,** top-dressing.
bobo'tie, curried mincemeat, bobotie.
bo'bou, superstructure.
bo'bramseil, royal sail.
bo'bramsteng, royal mast.
bo'bring, (-ge-), take (bring) up.
bo'broek, trousers.
bo'brug, overhead bridge.
bob'slee, bob-sled, bob-sleigh.
bo'buik, epigastrium.
bobyn', (-e), bobbin.
bod, bot, (botte), offer, bid; call (cards); *gee my 'n ~,* make me an offer.
bo'de, (-s), messenger, page; peon; dispatch-runner; commissionaire; herald.
bo'deel, upper part.
bode'ga, (Ndl.), bodega.
bo'dek, upper (main) deck.
bo'deloon, messenger's fee.
bo'dem, (-s), bottom; soil, ground; surface, territory; ship; *tot die ~ DRINK,* drain to the dregs; *uit die ~ van sy HART,* from the depths of his heart; *iets die ~ INSLAAN,* knock on the head; frustrate a plan; *die vrag is van die sinkende ~ na 'n ander OORGEBRING,* the cargo was transferred to another from the sinking ship; *op die ~ van die SEE,* at the bottom of the sea; *op VADERLANDSE ~,* in the mother country; on native soil; *op VASTE ~,* on firm ground; *die ~ van sy VERWAGTINGS inslaan,* dash (knock the bottom out of) his hopes; *op VREEMDE ~,* on a foreign shore; **~ armoede,** poverty of the soil; **~ beskerming,** soil protection; **~ beslag,** sheathing; **~ bestanddeel,** soil ingredient; **~ biologie,** soil biology; **~ diepte,** depth of soil; **~ drukmeter,** pressure bomb; **~ eienskappe,** qualities of the soil.
bodemery', bottomry, **~ brief,** bottomry (respondentia) bond.
bo'dem: ~ gesteldheid, soil conditions, state of soil; **~ hoogte,** ground level; **~ klep,** foot valve; **~ kunde,** pedology, soil science; **~ kun'dige, (-s),** soil expert; **~ lae,** basal beds; **~ loos, (..lose),** bottomless; fathomless; **~ opbrengs,** soil yield; **~ opname,** soil survey; **~ rykdom,** mineral wealth; **~ stampmasjien,** bottom-ramming machine; **~ vas, (-te),** attached to one's native land; rooted in the fatherland's traditions; **~ verbetering,** improvement of the soil; **~ vergiftiging,** soil poisoning; **~ vlak,** ground surface; **~ water,** soil water; **~ wind,** surface wind.
Bo'denmeer, Lake Constance.
bo'deur¹, (s) upper half of door.
bo'deur², (bw) through at the top.
bo'deveiling, (court) messenger's sale.
bo'dop, carapace.
bo'dorp, upper town.
bo'drumpel, door head.
bo'dryf, ..drywe, (-ge-), float on the top (surface).
boe, (tw) bo(h); *g'n ~ of bu sê nie,* not able to say bo to a goose.
Boe'dapest, Budapest.
Boed'dha, Buddha.
Boeddhis', (-te), Buddhist; **~me,** Buddhism; **~ties, (-e),** Buddhist(ic).
boe'del, (-s), estate, property, assets; **~ OORGEE,** surrender one's estate; lay all before one; *uitgestorwe ~,* deceased estate; **~ afstand doen,** assign an estate; surrender; cession (of estate); assignment (of estate); **~ afstand,** assignment (of an estate); **~ afstander,** assignor; **~ agent,** estate agent; **~ beheerder,** trustee; **~ belasting,** probate duties; estate dury; **~ beredderaar,** executor, administrator (of an estate); **~ beskrywing,** inventory (of estate); **~ besorger,** executor; **~ gelde,** estate fee; **~ houer,** estate holder; **~ lys,** inventory (of estate); **~ oorgawe,** surrender(ing) of estate; **~ redder,** assignee; **~ reg,** right of inheritance; **~ regte,** estate duties; **~ skeiding,** division of an estate; **~ skulde,** debts of estate; **~ staat,** inventory (of estate); **~ vereffening,** winding up of estate; **~ verkoping,** sale of estate; **~ vorderinge,** debts due to estate.
boef, (boewe), thug, rogue, villain, cut-throat, tough, knave; **~ agtig, (-e),** villainous, knavish; **~ ag'tigheid,** roguery, knavery, knavishness, villainy; **~ ie, (-s),** little rogue; street arab.
boeg, (boeë), bow, prow; stem (of ship); shoulder point (of horse); *oor 'n ander ~ GOOI,* try another angle; hawse; *oor een ~ PRAAT,* talk incessantly; *oor een ~ WERK,* work without a break; **~ anker,** bow-anchor; **~ beeld,** figure-head; **~ golf,** backwash; **~ kajuit,** cockpit; **~ lam,** tired out; fatigued, dead beat, exhausted; *jou ~ lam skrik,* be frightened out of one's wits; *iem. WERK hom ~ lam,* he works himself to a frazzle; **~ lyn,** bow-line.
boe'goe, buchu *(Barosma, Agathosma, Diosma); dit is sy ~,* that is the death of him; *hy RUIK na ~,* he reeks of the bottle; *sy ~ is UIT,* he is exhausted; **~ asyn,** buchu vinegar; **~ blare,** leaves of the buchu; **~ brandewyn,** buchu brandy; **~ tjie, (-s),** tot of buchu brandy.
boegseer', (-ge-), tow (boat); **~ lyn,** tow-line.
boeg'spriet, bowsprit; bolt sprit.
boeg'swaar, bow heavy; **~ te,** bow-heaviness.
boei, (s) (-e), shackle, fetter; pinion; handcuff; buoy; (mv) chains; irons; darbies; (w) **(ge-),** handcuff; chain; (en)fetter, captivate, enthrall, grip, attract, hold (attention); *iem. in ~ e SLAAN,* handcuff someone; *die ~ e VERBREEK,* break the chains (fetters); **~ ekoning,** handcuff king; escapologist; **~ end, (-e),** captivating, engrossing, gripping, fascinating, interesting, arresting, absorbing, attractive; *'n ~ ende verhaal,* a gripping story.
boek, (s) (-e), book; quire (of paper); *die ~ e AFSLUIT,* balance the books; *iem. het BAIE op sy ~ e,* he has a lot to answer for; *in iem. se ~ e BLAAI,* pry into another's affairs; *die ~ DER ~ e,* the Book of books, the Bible; *iem. se ~ e is DEURMEKAAR,* he is in a fix; *iem. se ~ e DEURMEKAAR krap,* make things difficult for someone; *DIT is nou 'n ~,* that is a dead certainty; *anderman se ~ e (briewe) is DUISTER om te lees,* the lives of others are a closed book; *'n GESLOTE ~,* a sealed book; *in iem. se GOEIE ~ e wees,* be in someone's good books; *die GROOT ~,* the Good Book; *iem. soos 'n ~ LEES,* read someone like a book; *die ~ e NASIEN,* audit the books; *soos 'n ~ PRAAT,* speak like a book; *uit die ~ e PRAAT,* speak by the book; *iets op die ~ SIT,* charge to one's account; *dit SPREEK soos 'n ~,* it goes without saying; *te ~ STAAN as,* be known as; *te ~ STEL,* commit to paper; *so WAAR as 'n ~,* as true as fate; (w) **(ge-),** book, enter; **~ aanbiddend, (-e),** bibliolatrous; **~ aanbidder,** bibliolater; **~ aanbidding,** bibliolatry; **~ aankondiging,** booknotice (review); press notice; **~ agtig, (-e),** bookish.
boekanier', (-s), buccaneer; filibuster.
Boe'karest, Bucharest.
boek: ~ antikwariaat, antiquarian bookseller; **~ band,** cover, binding (book); **~ beoordelaar,** reviewer, critic; **~ beoordeling, ~ bespreking,** review, criticism; critique; **~ bewys,** book token; **~ binder,** bookbinder; **~ bindersperkament,** for(r)el; **~ bindery,** bookbinding; bookbinder's shop; **~ deel,** volume, part; *dit spreek ~ dele,* it speaks volumes; **~ drukker,** printer; **~ drukkersaak,** printing business; **~ drukkersbedryf,** printing trade; **~ drukkery,** printing works; **~ drukkuns,** printing art, typography; **~ egek,** bibliomaniac; **~ ekamer,** bookroom; **~ ekas,** bookcase; **~ ekennis,** book-learning; **~ ekoors,** bibliomania; **~ elys,** list of books, catalogue; **~ e-nasien,** audit.
boe'kenhout, wood of *Rapanea melanophleas;* S.A. (Cape) beech.
boe'kereeks, series of books.
boe'kery, boekery', (-e), library.
boe'ke: ~ sensuur, censorship of books; **~ skat,** wealth of books; **~ stut,** book-end.
boeket', (-te), bouquet, bunch of flowers; bouquet (of wine).
boe'k(e)taal, bookish (stilted) language.
boe'ketas, satchel, book-bag.

boe'kevat, (s) family devotions; (w) (-ge-), observe divine service at home; ~**tyd**, time for family prayers.
boe'k(e)wysheid, book-learning.
boek: ~**geleerdheid**, see **boekekennis**; ~**geskenk**, book(s) as a present, gift of books; ~**handel**, book trade; bookseller's shop; ~**handelaar**, bookseller.
boek'hou, (s) bookkeeping; *DUBBEL* ~, bookkeeping by double entry; *ENKEL* ~, bookkeeping by single entry; (w) (-ge-), keep books, keep account of; ~**ding**, bookkeeping; ~**er**, book-keeper; accountant; ~**kunde**, accountancy; ~**-onderwyser**, book-keeping teacher.
boe'kie, (-s), small book, booklet; *buiten sy* ~ *GAAN*, exceed one's instructions; *baie op sy – hê*, have a great deal to answer for; *'n* ~ *OOPMAAK oor iem.*, discuss somebody's character; *iem. se* ~ *is VOL*, he should be brought to book.
boek: ~**ing**, booking; entry; ~**jaar**, financial year; ~**keurder**, publisher's reader; ~**klub**, bookclub; ~**kolporteur**, colporteur; ~**lêer**, bookmark(er); ~**liefhebber**, bibliophil(e), lover of books; ~**long**, book-lung; ~**lys**, list of books; ~**mark**, book market; ~**merk**, book-plate; ex-libris; ~**omslag**, book-cover; ~**oortreksel**, book-covering.
boek'pens = **boepens**.
boek: ~**pos**, book post; ~**prys**, price of a book; book prize; prize-book; ~**rak**, bookshelf, bookcase; ~**sak**, school bag, satchel, case; ~**skrywer**, author, writer of books; biliographer; ~**skuld**, book debts; ~**smous**, colporteur; ~**staaf**, (ge-), place on record, commit to paper; ~**stalletjie**, bookstall; ~**stander**, book stand; ~**stut**, bookrest; ~**taal**, bookish (stilted) language; ~**verkoper**, bookseller; ~**verkoping**, book auction (sale); ~**versamelaar**, book collector; bibliophil(e); ~**versameling**, collection of books; ~**versiering**, book ornament (ornamentation); ~**vink**, chaffinch *(Fringilla coelebs)*; ~**vorm**, book form; ~**vriend**, book lover, bibliophil(e); ~**waarde**, book value; ~**werk**, book, printed work; ~**winkel**, book shop; ~**woord**, bookish word; ~**wurm**, bookworm; ~**wysheid**, book lore, mere theory.
boel[1], crowd, lot, heap, fleet, a great many, mint (of money); *die HELE* ~, the whole lot (caboodle); *'n hele* ~ *MENSE*, a large number of people; *die* ~ *in die WAR stuur*, make a mess of everything.
Boel[2]: ~ *PRYS sy eie stert*, he blows his own trumpet; *VRA vir* ~ *se stert*, don't ask me!
boeleer', (ge-), commit adultery.
boeljon', bouillon, beef tea, broth.
boel'tjie, (ong.), belongings; *pak jou* ~, pack up your traps!
boem!, boom!
boe'man, (-s), bog(e)y man, bogle.
boe'mel, (ge-), spree, booze, go the pace; carouse; loaf about; *aan die* ~ *wees*, be on the spree; ~**aar**, (-s), reveller; loafer; carouser; loafer, tramp; ~**party**, spree, jollification; ~**straat**, Skid Row; ~ **(straat)alkoholis**, Skid-Row alcoholic; ~ **(straat)drinker**, Skid-Row drinker; ~**trein**, slow train; mixed train.
boe'merang, (-s), boomerang.
boen, (ge-), scrub; rub, polish.
boen'der, (s) (-s), scrubbing brush; (w) (ge-), scrub, rub, polish; bundle (drive) away; *iem. uit die kamer* ~, thrust (bundle) someone out of the room.
bo'-en-on'derdeur, Dutch door; stable door.
bo'-ent, head (of table); top side; upper end.
boen'was, floor (furniture) wax.
boe'pens, (s) (-e), paunch; pot belly, corporation (stomach), bulge (in barrel); (b) (plat), in the family way; pot-bellied.
boe'pie, (-s), pot-belly, corporation.
boep'maag, pot-belly.
Boer[1], (-e), Boer, Afrikaner; *die* ~ *in hom is dood*, he has become anglicized.
boer[2], (s) (-e), farmer, peasant, husbandman, grower, agriculturist; knave, jack (of cards); *waar die* ~ *nie is nie, word sy BAARD nie geskeer nie*, the eye of the master makes the cattle thrive; *gee die* ~ *KOS, dan loop hy*, when a farmer has eaten, he's off; *die* ~ *die KUNS afvra*, try to worm a secret out of someone;

---

pump someone; *die beste* ~ *woon in die STAD*, old maids' children and bachelors' wives are the best trained; *die* ~ *met sy VARKE*, a school of porpoises; (w) (ge-), farm; remain; frequent; *AGTERUIT* ~, go downhill; *ERENS* ~, frequent a place; *hy* ~ *by die NOOI se huis*, he simply lives at the girl's house; *waar het jy al die TYD ge* ~ ? where have you been all the time? *VORENTOE* ~, make a success of things; ~**agtig**, (-e), boorish; ~**beskuit**, boerbeskuit, rusk; ~**blits**, home-made, extra strong brandy; ~**boel**, Bull mastiff; ~**bok**, Boer goat; ~**bokkapater**, castrated boer goat; ~**boontjie**, broad bean; ~**botter**, farm butter; ~**brood**, home-made bread, brown bread.
boer'dery, (-e), farm, farming; husbandry; *jou met jou eie* ~ *besig hou*, to mind your own business; ~**bedrywighede**, pastoral pursuits, farming; ~**belange**, farming interests; ~**kolonie**, farm colony.
boer: ~**dogter**, farmer's daughter; B~**dogter**, Boer girl; ~**dorp**, village.
boe're: ~**bank**, agricultural bank; ~**bedrieër**, confidence trickster; spiv (slang); pettifogger; mountebank; ~**bedrog**, swindling, humbug, clap-trap, charlatanism, charlatanry; ~**bedryf**, agriculture, farming; ~**bevolking**, farming population (community); ~**dans**, barn dance; dance on a farm; ~**drag**, farmer's dress (clothing); ~**familie**, farmer's family; ~**fopper**, see **boerebedrieër**; ~**gesin**, farmer's family; B~**hater**, hater of Afrikaners; ~**jongens**, brandied raisins; B~**kerk**, Dutch Reformed Church; ~**kneg**, farmhand; ~**knoop**, figure-of-eight knot; B~**kommando**, Boer commando; ~**kruishout**, thumb gauge; ~**matriek**, confirmation (church); ~**mense**, farmers, country folk; ~**middel**, home remedy; ~**musiek**, popular (South African) music.
Boe'renasie, Afrikaner (Boer) nation.
boe're: ~**ooreenkoms**, gentleman's agreement; B~**orkes**, Boer orchestra; B~**krygsgevangene**, Boer prisoner of war; ~**pastei**, cottage pie; ~**raat**, home remedy; ~**seun**, country lad; ~**stand**, farming community, peasantry, farmer class; ~**troos**, coffee; ~**vereniging**, farmers' association; ~**verneuker**, see **boerebedrieër**.
Boe'revolk, see **Boervolk**.
boe'revriend, farmer's friend.
boe'revrou = **boervrou**.
boe'rewors = **boerwors**.
boergon'je(wyn), (ong.), burgundy.
boer'hond, mongrel.
boerin', (-ne), woman farmer.
Boerkakie, hands-upper, Boer renegade.
boer: ~**kêrel**, young farmer; ~**kind**, farmer's child; ~**kool**, borecole; kale; ~**kos**, (-se), country fare; ~**kwagga**, country bumpkin; young fellow; ~**lewe**, country life; ~**manna**, boer millet; ~**meel**, unsifted meal; boer meal; ~**meisie**, country girl, peasant girl, wench; ~**mense**, country people.
boer'noes, burnous(e).
boer: ~**noi**, ~**nooi**, see **boermeisie**; ~**pampoen**, common pumpkin; ~**perd**, (strong) farm horse; ~**plaas**, farm; ~**plek**, haunt, favourite spot; den (of robbers); ~**pot**, jackpot (poker); ~**s**, (-e), boorish, rustic, agrestic, countrified; ~**seep**, home-made soap; B~**seun**, Afrikaner (Boer) boy; ~**seun**, farm lad, country boy; ~**s'heid**, rusticity, boorishness; ~**tabak**, boer tobacco; ~**tannie**, country woman.
boer'tig, (-e), jocose, jocular, comical; ~**heid**, jocularity.
Boer'volk, Boer (Afrikaner) nation.
boer: ~**vrou**, country woman; farmer's wife, peasant wife; ~**woning**, farmhouse, farmstead; ~**wors**, boerwors, home-made (boer) sausage.
boe'sel, (-s), bushel; ~**mandjie**, bushel basket.
boe'sem, bosom, breast; auricle (of heart); *verdeeldheid in eie* ~, division in the camp; ~**sonde**, secret sin, besetment, besetting sin; ~**vriend**, chum, bosom (intimate) friend, boon companion, confidant, crony; ~**vriendin**-, female bosom friend, confidante.
Boes'man, (-s), (vero.), Bushman, San; *hy het 'n* ~ *tjie*

boestroentjie   85   *bokant*

dood geslaan, his conscience is troubling him; he has had a spot; ~ **gif,** Bushman poison; **b** ~ **gras,** Bushman gras *(Aristida brevifolia);* ~ **huis,** ~ **hut,** Bushman hut; ~ **kers,** candle-bush *(Sarcocaulon burmanni);* ~ **klip,** Bushman stone; ~ **land,** Bushmanland; **b** ~ **mielie,** Cincinnati (mealie); ~ **pyl,** (poisoned) Bushman arrow; **b** ~ **pyltjies,** blackjacks, beggar-ticks, sweethearts *(Bidens pilosa);* **b** ~ **rys,** larva of termites; ~ **skildery,** Bushman painting; **b** ~ **sriet,** *Berkheya radula;* ~ **taal,** Bushman language; ~ **tekening,** Bushman drawing.
boestroen'tjie, (-s), tunic, pelisse.
boet¹, (s) brother; comrade, crony.
boet², (w) (ge-), atone, redeem, expiate, make amends; forfeit, pay; *met jou LEWE* ~, pay with one's life; *vir sy SONDE* ~, pay for one's sins.
boet³, (w) (ge-), repair (fishing net).
boe'ta, (-s), brother; old chap, my friend; *ek sal jou wys,* ~ *!* I'll show you, old chap!
boe'tabessie, wild cherry *(Osteospermum moniliferum).*
boe'te, (-s), fine, penalty, cost, penance; forfeit; ~ *DOEN,* do penance; *ONMIDDELLIKE* ~, spot fine; *OP* ~ *van,* on penalty of; ~ *OPLÊ,* impose a fine; *tot 'n* ~ *VEROORDEEL,* condemn to a fine; ~ **bessie,** (geselst.), meter maid; ~ **bossie,** burweed *(Xanthium spinosum);* ~ **dag,** day of atonement; ~ **doening,** penance, atonement; penitential exercise; expiation; asceticism; ~ **kaartjie,** fine-ticket; ~ **keuse,** option of a fine; ~ **kleed, (..klede),** hair shirt, haircloth; penitential robe; ~ **ling, (-e),** penitent; ~ **nd, (-e),** expiatory; ~ **oplegging,** imposition of fine; ~ **seël,** penalty stamp; ~ **stelsel,** system of fines.
boet: ~ **gesant,** *see* **boetprediker;** ~ **gewaad,** penitential garment.
boe'tie, (-s), little brother; confidant, pal; ~ *ie-* ~ *ie SPEEL,* be hand in glove.
boetiek', (-e), boutique.
boet: ~ **kleed, (..klede),** penitential garment; ~ **predikasie,** exhortation to repentance, homily; lecture; ~ **prediker,** preacher of penitence; ~ **profeet,** prophet of repentance; ~ **psalm,** penitential psalm, miserere; ~ **seël,** postage-due stamp.
boetseer', (ge-), model, mould; ~ **der, (-s),** modeller; ~ **klei,** modelling clay, plasticine (registered trade name); ~ **kuns,** (art of) modelling; ~ **was,** modelling wax; ~ **werk,** modelling (work).
boet'son, bumblefoot (poultry disease).
boetvaar'dig, (-e), penitent, penitential, contrite; ~ **e, (-s),** penitent; ~ **heid,** repentance, contriteness, penitence.
boe'we: ~ **bakkies,** gallows-face; ~ **bende,** gang of rogues (robbers), pack of knaves; ~ **gesig,** rogue's face; ~ **ry,** ~ **streek,** villainy, roguery, roguishness; ~ **taal,** thieves' slang, cant, argot; ~ **tronie,** hangdog face, gallows-face.
bof¹, (s) fluke; (w) **(ge-),** be lucky (fortunate), turn up trumps.
bof², (s) (bowwe), tee (golf); base (baseball); den, home (catch-games); (w) **(ge-),** tee; ~ **bal,** baseball; ~ **bulliga, (-s),** baseball league ~ **balspel,** baseball; ~ **balspeler,** baseball player; ~ **balveld,** baseball field.
bof'fie, a children's game.
bof: ~ **lopie,** home run; ~ **perk,** tee; ~ **rympie,** counting-out rhyme; ~ **skyfie,** teeing disc.
bog¹, (s) (-te), bend, incurvation, elbow (in road); bay, creek, inlet (sea); *dubbele* ~, hairpin bend.
bog², (s) tripe, bunkum, trash, moonshine, poppycock, piffle, punk, picayune, drivel, twaddle; bushes and shrubs, litter (as stable bedding); **(-te),** nincompoop, crook, fool, blighter; *AAG,* ~ *met jou!* oh, stop your nonsense! *iem. is 'n* ~, a nincompoop; *jou KLEIN* ~, you little fool (rascal); *KOM bog!* oh rubbish! *jy lyk 'n MOOI* ~, you look like it! *hy PRAAT* ~, he is talking nonsens; *dis PURE* ~, it's all nonsense (bunkum) it's all tommy rot.
bog³, (b) bad, useless, rotten, worthless, trashy; ~ **ding,** useless article; picayune.
bo'gedeelte, upper part.
bo'gemelde, bo'genoemde, above-mentioned.

bog'gel, (-s), hump, hunch, crook-back; huckle, huckleback; *hy EET hom 'n* ~ *tjie,* he guzzles; *jou 'n* ~ *(tjie) LAG,* split one's sides, be convulsed with laughter; ~ **agtig,** gibbous; ~ **mannetjie,** hunchback; ~ **rig, (-e),** humped; ~ **rug,** hunchback; camel-back; ~ **terrein,** hump yard; ~ **tjie, (-s),** hunchback.
bog'gie, (-s), little blighter; mere child.
bog'gom = **bôgom.**
bo'gie, (-s), bogie; picot; small bow; small arch; ~ **masjien,** bogie engine; ~ **raamwerk,** bogie frame; ~ **rand,** picot edging; ~ **wa,** bogie carriage.
bog: ~ **kind,** mere child, (young) brat; ~ **koning,** kingling.
bô'gom!, (baboon) bark.
bog'praatjies, twaddle, trash, tripe, nonsense, piffle.
bo'grens, high limit.
bo'grond, top-soil.
bo'gronds, (-e), elevated; overhead; overground; ~ *e DELE,* aerial parts; ~ *e SKAGWAGTER,* bankman; ~ *e WERK,* grass work (mining).
bog: ~ **rympie,** limerick; doggerel; ~ **snui'ter,** little blighter; ~ **spul,** absurd business, mad scheme; ~ **terig, (-e),** paltry, nonsensical, piffling, feeble.
bog'tery, (-e), nonsense, bunk, bunkum; *dit sal 'n* ~ *AFGEE,* that will end in a mess, will cause trouble; *dis nou vir jou 'n MOOI* ~ *!,* this is a fine how-d'ye-do!; *laat STAAN jou* ~ *!,* stop your nonsense!
bog'tig, (-e), tortuous, winding, sinuous; flexuose, flexuous; ~ **heid,** anfractuosity, sinuesity, sinuousness.
bohaai', fuss, hubbub, noise; *'n* ~ *maak,* make a fuss about nothing.
bo'hand, upper hand; *die* ~ *kry,* get the upper hand.
Boheems', (-e), Bohemian.
Bohe'me, Bohemia; ~ **r, (-s),** Bohemian.
behémien', (-s), Bohemian (person of free-and-easy habits (morals)).
bo'hou, (-ge-), keep on top (afloat); *'n DRENKELING* ~, keep a drowning person afloat; *die blink KANT* ~, keep smiling.
bo'huis, upper flat, top flat.
boi'kot, (s) boycott; (w) **(ge-),** boycott; ~ **aksie,** boycott movement (action); ~ **beweging,** boycott movement; ~ **ter, (-s),** boycotter.
Boiotia = **Beotië.**
bo'-in, (in) at the top.
bo'jan = **bobaas.**
bok¹, (s) (-ke), goat; antelope (buck); driving box; box (coach); trestle; test (for cue); (vaulting) horse; frame (printing); *- ke AANJA,* be tipsy; *'n ou* ~ *lus ook wel 'n groen BLAARTJIE,* old men like tender chicken; *hy is 'n BONT* ~, he is a black sheep; *ou* ~ *ke pluk die hoogste DORINGPEULE,* old age has its advantages; fine tunes are played on old fiddles; *so bang soos 'n* ~ *vir 'n skoot HAEL,* as scared as the devil of holy water; *hoe ouer die* ~, *hoe harder die HORING,* old age brings experience; ~ *kie op die KLIP wees,* be proud; ~ *sal sy KOOL afvreet,* he will be ousted by someone else; *daar is 'n* ~ *in die LAND,* your shirt is hanging out; *MAER* ~ *ke dip,* ply the cane; ~ *op die MUUR wees,* sit on the fence; ~ *ke gaan OPPAS;* ~ *RY,* attend a masonic meeting; *so wild vir iets wees soos 'n* ~ *vir 'n SKOOT hael,* be as timid as a fawn; *hy het die* ~ *aan die STERT gehad,* he had a brush with death; *hy is soos 'n* ~, *waar hy VREET groei niks meer nie,* he is a bird of ill omen: die; ~ *in die WINGERD laat loop,* give the wolf the wether to keep.
bok², (s) (best) girl; (w) **(ge-),** (stud.), spoon, court, flirt.
bok³, (s) (-ke), (fig.) blunder, howler, bloomer; *'n* ~ *skiet,* make a blunder.
Bok⁴, (-ke), Springbok rugby player; Bok; Springbok player (at various sports).
bo'kaak, upper jaw, maxilla.
bokaal', (..kale), beaker, goblet.
bok'agtig, (-e), capric, caprine, goatish, hircine; rammish, rammy; rude, surly.
bo'kakebeen = **bokaak.**
bo'kamer, upper room; room upstairs.

bo'kant, (s) upper side, top(side); (vs) over, above; ~ *die DEUR,* over (above) the door; *nie* ~ *die WIND kom nie,* keep away from the windward side, keep to the leeside (of game); (b), ~**se,** ~**ste,** upper.
bo'kas, upper case, capitals (printing).
bok'baaivygie, Bokbaai vygie, *Dorotheanthus criniflorus.*
bok'baard, beard of goat; Vandyke beard; goatee; ~**jie,** billy-goat beard, French cut, goatee, imperial.
bok'balk, side beam (of ox-wagon).
bok'bier, bock.
bok'boer, mohair farmer.
bok-bok-staan-styf', high cockalorum.
bok'doring, *Lycium horridum.*
bo'kerf, top-notch, top-hole; top gear; ~ *trek,* have a very hard time; be progressive.
bok'haar, mohair; ~**mark,** mohair market.
bok'hael, buck-shot; ~**skoot,** large tot.
bok'horings, goat's horns; stapilia *(Asclepiadaceae);* ~ *maak,* take an oath.
bo'kiestand, upper grinder.
bok'jol, sheepskin, wild party.
bok'kapater, castrated goat.
bok'kem, (-s), kippered herring, Cape herring, red herring; bloater; *nie* ~ *kan BRAAI nie,* not have the know-how; *hy is 'n DROË* ~, he is a dry stick; ~**smeer,** bloater paste.
bok'ker, (-s), (plat.), bugger.
bok'kesprong, antic, caper, capriole, gambade, gambado, caracol(e); ~ *e maak,* cut capers; try to wriggle out of a difficulty.
Bok'keveld: *die KOUE* ~, the Cold Bokkeveld; *die WARM* ~, the Warm Bokkeveld.
bok'kie¹, (-s), buggy.
bok'kie², (-s), kid; small buck; trestle.
bok'knie, goat's knee; *'n broek wat* ~ *ē maak,* baggy-kneed (baggy) trousers.
bok'kom = **bokkem.**
bok: ~**koors,** Malta fever; lovesickness; ~**kos,** food for goats; *Kleinia radicans;* lettuce; ~**kraan,** gantry crane; ~**lam,** kid.
bo'kleed, overdress, outer garment.
bok'leer, buckskin, kid.
bo'klere, upper clothes, outer garments.
bokmakie'rie, (-s), bush shrike, green shrike; *Telophorus zeylonus.*
bok'man, (-ne), leveller.
bok: ~**'melk,** goat's milk; ~**'mis,** goat manure (dung).
bo'kom, (-ge-), rise (to the surface), surface (submarine), come to the top.
bok'ooi, she-goat, nanny goat.
bo'kop, sinciput.
bo: ~**kors,** upper crust; ~**koste,** overhead expenses, overheads.
bok'pokkies, goat-pox.
bok'ram, he-goat; ~**kuif,** exceptionally big curl on forehead.
bok: ~**rug,** trestle-bridge; ~**ryer,** goatrider; nickname for a Freemason.
boks, (s) boxing; (w) (ge-), box.
bok'saag, buck-saw.
boks'afriger, boxing (fighting) coach, trainer; ~**afrigting,** coaching, training.
boks'boon, buck-bean.
bok'seil, bucksail, tarpaulin, cover (wagon).
bok'semdais, bok'sendais, (geselst.), everybody, everything; *die hele* ~, the whole caboodle.
bok'ser, (-s), boxer, pugilist; ~**y,** pugilism, fighting, fist fighting.
boks'geveg, boxing match, fight, fist fight.
boks'handskoen, boxing glove; muffler.
boks'kryt, boxing ring; prize-ring.
bok'skyn, buckskin.
boks'plooi, box-pleat(ing).
boks'spoor, track of goat or buck.
boks'poot, goat's foot; the devil; Pan.
bok'spring, (s) bucking, prance, caper; (w) (ge-), caper, buck, prance, capriole, caracol(e), curvet, jump (about); cut capers; look for excuses; *JY sal* ~, you will get a hiding; ~*e MAAK,* try to wriggle out of a difficulty; *hy* ~ *weer VANDAG,* he is showing off again today; ~ *van VREUGDE,* jump for joy; ~**ery,** antics, gambols; prevarication.
bok'stert, goat's tail.
boks: ~**vernuf,** ring-craft; ~**wedstryd,** boxing match; glove-fight; ~**yster,** knuckleduster, brass knuckles.
bok'tafel, trestle table.
bo'kussing, top pillow (cushion).
bok'vel, goatskin; kid.
Bok'veld, part of the Karoo.
bok'veld, goat pasture; *hy IS* ~ *toe,* he is dead; he has gone west (gone to the Happy Hunting Grounds); ~ *toe GAAN,* hop the twig, kick the bucket; ~ *toe STUUR,* send to glory.
bok: ~**vet,** goat suet; ~**vleis,** goat's meat.
bok'wa, buck-wagon; hustings; *êrens met 'n* ~ *en 'n span osse kan DRAAI,* one can drive a coach-and-four through it; *OP die* ~ *wees,* be on the stump; ~**toespraak,** stump oratory.
bok'wagter, goatherd; old maid; bachelor; ~ *word,* be left on the shelf; ~**sny,** very thick slice of bread.
bok'wavrag, big (buck-wagon) load; large quantity.
bok'wiet, buckwheat; ~**pap,** flummery.
bol, (s) (-le), ball, globe; clew (wool); crown (hat); star, planet; brain; orb; bulb, corm (plant); *in die* ~ *GEPIK wees,* have a screw loose; *HOOG met die* ~ *wees,* be in an advanced state of pregnancy; (w) (ge-), bulge, gather into a mass; (b) round, convex; bulgy; gibbous; ~ *staan,* bulge.
bo'laag, upper layer, top coat; surface course; superstratum, overburden; ~**gis,** barm.
bol'agtig, (-e), bulbous; bulb-shaped.
bo'laken, upper sheet, top sheet.
Bo'land, Boland, Western Province; ~**er,** (-s), inhabitant of the Boland or Western Province; *so bang soos 'n* ~ *er vir donderweer,* to be as afraid of something as of the devil himself; ~**is'me,** (-s), Western Province (Boland) expression (pronunciation, etc.); ~**s,** (-e), of the Western Province.
bo'langs, superficially, lip-deep, skin-deep.
bo'las, deck cargo.
bol: ~**bedding,** spherical seat; ~**bliksem,** fire ball; globe lightning; ~**blom,** bulbous flower; ~**buis,** bulb-tube.
bol'der, (-s), bollard.
bol'derwa, rumbling cart.
bol'dop, spherical cover.
bol'draend, (-e), coniferous; bulbiferous; ~*e bome,* conifers.
bol'driehoek, spherical triangle; ~**smeting,** spherical trigonometry.
bo'leer, upper leather, uppers, top.
bo'leiding, contact-wire.
bole'ro, (-'s), bolero.
bol: ~**gewas,** bulbous plant; ~**gewrig,** ball and socket joint; ~**graniet,** ball granite; ~**hamer,** ball hammer, peen hammer; ~**handelaar,** bulb-dealer; ~**heid,** convexity; gibbosity; ~**hol,** convexo-concave.
bo'lig, skylight, fan-light; batten light (theatre).
bo'liggend, (-e), overhead, top; superincumbent.
bo'lip, upper lip; muffle (rodents).
Boli'via, Bolivia.
Boliviaan', (..viane), Bolivian.
Boli'viaans, (-e), Bolivian.
bol: ~**kalander,** boll-weevil; ~**klep,** ball valve, globe-valve; ~**konkaaf,** convex-concave; ~**kweker,** bulb grower.
bol'la, (-s), chignon, bob, bun (hair); knot; ~ *begin dra,* put up the hair.
bol'laer, spherical bearing.
bollemakie'sie = **bolmakiesie.**
bol'letjie, (-s), bun; croquette (meat, fish); globule, bulblet.
bolmakie'sie, head over heels, somersault, flip-flap; cartwheel; Catherine wheel; volte face; ~ *SLAAN,* turn somersualt; change front suddenly; ~ *VLIEG,* loop the loop; ~**hou,** purler; ~**slag,** somersault.
bo'lo, (-'s), bolo (beef).

boloop 87 *boodskap*

bo'loop, upper course (reach), head waters.
bol: ~ **penhamer,** ballpeen hammer; ~ **plant,** bulbous plant; ~ **puntpen,** ballpoint pen; ~ **rond, (-e),** convex, spherical; globular; conglobate; ~ **rondheid,** convexity; ~ **rond-holrond,** convexo-concave; ~ **sektor,** sector of sphere.
Bolsjewiek', (-e), *see* **Bolsjewis.**
Bolsjewis', (-te), Bolshevist; ~ **me,** Bolshevism; ~ **ties, (-e),** Bolshevistic.
bol'skarnier, ball-and-socket joint.
bol'skyf, frustum (of sphere).
bol'ster, (-s), shell, husk; bolster, underpillow (for bed).
bo'lug, upper air.
bol'vorm, globular (spherical) shape; ~ **ig, (-e),** globular, spherical, obicular, conglobate, globoid; globose, glomerate; convex (glass); ~ **igheid,** globosity; sphericity; convexity.
bol'vrot, ball rot (cotton).
bol'waster, spherical washer.
bol'werk, (s), bulwark, earthwork, palladium, bastion, counterguard, rampart, sconce, fence; (w) **(ge-),** manage, arrange.
bol'wurm, brain-worm *(Taenia coenurus)* (in sheep); boll-worm, boll-weevil.
bo'lyf, body above the hips; ~ **ie,** bodice; ~ **portret,** kit-cat portrait.
bo'lyn, upper line; balk, baulk (fishing net).
bom, (-me), bomb, shell; round (mortar fire); bung (of cask); *die* ~ *het GEBARS,* the fat is in the fire; *'n* ~ *LOS,* drop a bomshell; ~ **aanslag,** bomb-outrage; ~ **aanval,** bombing attack (raid).
bo'maat, oversize, outsize.
bom'afstand, bombing range.
bo'mate, exceedingly, beyond measure.
boma'tig, (-e), exceeding, extreme; ~ **heid,** excessiveness.
bo'matras, mattress, overlay.
Bom'baai, Bombay.
bom'baan, bombing straight.
bombardeer', (ge-), shell, bomb(ard), pepper, pound.
bombardement', (-e), bombardment.
bombardier', (-s), bombardier.
bomba'rie, fuss, noise; *'n* ~ *opskop,* cause a row.
bom'bas, bombast, rant, brag, humbug, fustian; ~ **'ties, (-e),** bombastic, grandiloquent, highfalutin(g), magniloquent, puffed up.
bombasyn', bombasine, fustian.
bombel'la, (-s), truck, lorry.
bom'dop, bomb shell.
bo'melk, top milk.
bo'menslik, (-e), superhuman, preterhuman.
bom: ~ **eskader,** bomber-squadron; ~ **gat,** bunghole; bomb crater; ~ **gooier,** bomb thrower, dynamitard; ~ **hyser,** bomb hoist; ~ **kop,** war-head; ~ **krater,** bomb crater; ~ **losser,** bomb-dropper; bomber; ~ **lostoestel,** bomb-release; ~ **maxim,** pom-pom; ~ **ontploffing,** bomb explosion (burst); ~ **rak,** bomb carrier (aeroplane); ~ **rigter,** bomb aimer; ~ **skade,** bomb(ing) damage; ~ **skerf,** bomb splinter; ~ **skok,** bomb shock; ~ **splinter,** shell splinter; ~ **tregter,** bomb crater; ~ **vas, (-te),** bombfree; ~ **vliegtuig,** *see* **bomwerper;** ~ **vrag,** bomb load; ~ **vry, (-e),** shell-proof, bomb-proof; ~ **werper,** bomber, bombing machine; ~ **werping,** bombing.
bon, (-s, -ne), bon, slip, ticket, token, coupon.
bo'na fi'de, bona fide; ~ **-boer,** bona fide farmer; ~ **-student,** bona fide (enrolled) student.
bo'natuurlik, (-e), preternatural, supernatural; transcendent; ~ **heid,** supernaturalness, preternaturalness.
bonbon', (-s), bonbon.
bonchré'tienpeer, bon-chrétien pear.
bond, (-e), confederation, association, union, league, fellowship; entrepôt; *die B* ~, the Bond (train between Cape Town and Worcester).
bon'del, (s) (-s), parcel; pack; bunch; bundle (washing); sheaf (papers); cluster, fascicle (bot.); faggot; *sy dra 'n* ~, she is pregnant; (w) **(ge-),** bunch, bundle; huddle; club; ~ **draer,** pedlar, tramp, cadger, chapman; ~ **koop,** package deal; ~ **tjie,**

(-s), little bundle; fascicle; ~ **transaksie,** package deal; ~ **vormig, (-e),** fascicular.
bond'genoot, (. . note), ally (in war); confederate, accomplice (in crime); ~ **skap, (-pe),** alliance, confederacy, coalition.
bon'dig, (-e), concise, brief, terse, succint; sententious; laconic; close; *kort en* ~, short and to the point; ~ **heid,** succinctness, conciseness, terseness; laconicism, concision, briefness, brevity.
Bonds'ark, Ark of the Covenant.
bond'seël, sacrament, seal of covenant.
Bonds'man, adherent of the Afrikander Bond.
bonds'raad, federal diet.
bonds'republiek, federal republic.
bond'staat, federal state.
bonds'volk, chosen people; the chosen.
bo'nekstuk, scrag end.
bonk, (s) (-e), lump (mud); chuck (ice); stocky person; (w) **(ge-),** thump, beat; ~ **ig, (-e),** bony, lumpy, stocky.
bons, (s) (-e), bump, bang, thud, clash, thump; *iem. die* ~ *GEE,* give someone the sack; *die* ~ *KRY,* be given the sack; (w) **(ge-),** dash, knock; beat, palpitate; bash, clash; jounce.
bon'sai, (bonsai), bonsai, dwarfed potted plant.
Bonsma'ra, Bonsmara.
bont^1, (s) fur, flix (beaver).
bont^2, (b) (-e), many-coloured, multi-coloured (flower); spotted (cow); pied, piebald (horse); punctuate; parti-coloured, variegated (colour); motley (crowd); *dis 'n BIETJIE te* ~ *, that is a bit* thick; (bw) all over; ~ *en BLES,* right and left; ~ *en BLOU slaan,* beat (someone) black and blue; *dit te* ~ *MAAK,* lay it on too thick(ly); *rond en* ~ *PRAAT,* wander away from the point, discuss irrelevant matters; ~ *STAAN,* do all in one's power; ~ **beenbosluis,** bont-leg(ged) tick; ~ **blaar,** mottle leaf; ~ **ebok,** bontebok *(Damaliscus dorcas);* ~ **elsie,** avocet *(Recurvirostra avosetta);* ~ **erig, (-e),** many-coloured; spotted; ~ **etjie, (-s),** small spotted animal (thing); *'n* ~ *wees,* be cock of the walk.
bont'garnering, fur trimmings.
bont: ~ **goed,** cotton prints; ~ **haai,** tiger shark *(Galeocerdo articus).*
bont'handelaar, furrier.
bont'heid, variegation (variety) of colours.
bont'jas, fur coat.
bont: ~ **joubert,** spotted dog (pudding), plum duff; ~ **kleurig, (-e),** many-coloured.
bont'kraag, fur collar.
bont: ~ **kraai,** pied crow *(Corvus scapulatus);* ~ **kwartel,** harlequin quail; ~ **kwagga,** Burchell's zebra; ~ **lê, (-ge-),** coax, beg; ~ **loop,** jaywalking; ~ **loper,** jay-walker.
bont'mantel pelisse, fur (coat).
honton', bon ton, good breeding; the fashionable world.
bont: ~ **papier,** mottled paper; ~ **pootbosluis,** bont-leg tick; ~ **praat, (-ge-),** ramble, talk incoherently, wander in discourse; contradict oneself; ~ **rokkie,** ~ **rokwagter,** stonechat; ~ **seep,** mottled soap; ~ **sinnig, (-e),** fickle, unreliable; ~ **slang,** parti-coloured snake; ~ **span,** span of oxen of different colours; motley crowd; ~ **spring, (-ge-),** jump about, prevaricate, grope for excuses; *lelik* ~ *spring,* resort to devious devices; ~ **springer,** hedger; ~ **springery,** hedging; ~ **staan, (-ge-),** stamp about; bestir (exert) oneself (against odds); prevaricate; ~ **stefanie,** toad fish *(Tetrodon honckeni);* ~ **vat, (-ge-),** make uncertain, clumsy movements; grope.
bont'vel, pelt.
bont'veld, open country (with shrubs).
bont: ~ **visvanger,** pied kingfisher; ~ **werk,** fur goods, peltry, furriery; ~ **werker,** furrier; ~ **winkel,** fur store (shop).
bo'nus, (-se), bonus; ~ **aanbod,** bonus offer; ~ **aandeel,** bonus share; ~ **jaar,** bonus year; ~ **obligasie,** bonus bond; ~ **verklaring,** declaration of bonus.
bonvivant', (-s), man about town; happy-go-lucky person; bon vivant, gourmand.
bood'skap, (s) (-pe), message, errand; *die BLYE* ~,

boog   88   *boor*

the glad tidings (gospel); ~ *pe DOEN*, run errands; give messages; *'n KIND met 'n* ~ *stuur*, take ineffective measures; (w) (ge-), announce; send word, inform; ~ **jong**, messenger, errand-boy; ~ **per**, (-s), messenger, harbinger, announcer; ~ **perstaf**, caduceus; ~ **seun**, messenger-boy.

boog[1], (s) **(boë)**, (arrow) bow; (rain)bow; curve; arch (in building); arc (of circle); arch (of foot); *die* ~ *kan nie altyd GESPAN wees nie*, all work and no play makes Jack a dull boy.

boog[2], (w) (ge-), boast, brag; ~ *op jou rykdom*, brag about one's money.

boog: ~ **brug**, viaduct; arched bridge; arc gap; ~ **dak**, arched roof; ~ **draer**, impost; ~ **duiker**, arched culvert; ~ **erker**, bow window; ~ **gewelf**, arched vault; ~ **graad**, degree of arc; ~ **haak**, brace; ~ **handvatsel**, bow handle; ~ **hout**, hornbeam; ~ **kap**, bow truss; ~ **lamp**, arc lamp; ~ **lampsender**, arc transmitter; ~ **lig**, (electric) arc light; ~ **lyn**, bowline, curvature; ~ **maker**, bowyer; ~ **passer**, bow compasses; ~ **pees**, bowstring; ~ **raam**, bow window; arched (bay) window; ~ **rib**, curved rib; ~ **saag**, bow (circular) saw; ~ **s'(ge)wys(e)**, archwise; ~ **skiet**, archery; ~ **sko(o)t**, bow shot; ~ **skutter**, archer; toxophilite; *die B* ~ *skutter*, Sagittarius; ~ **slag**, pitch; ~ **snaar**, bowstring; ~ **spring**, curver; ~ **staaf**, arch bar; ~ **steen**, compass brick; ~ **sweising**, arc welding; ~ **veer**, spring bow; ~ **venster**, arched window; bay-window; ~ **verkoper**, bowyer; ~ **visier**, arch sight; ~ **vonking**, arcing (electr.); ~ **vormig**, (-e), arched, arcuate, curviform; ~ **weerstand**, curve resistance.

bo′-om, round the top.

boom[1], (s) (..**bome**), bottom (of barrel); seat (of trousers); *sy verwagting die* ~ *INSLAAN*, baffle his expectations; frustrate his plans; *op sy* ~ *RAAK, op die* ~ *WEES*, be stony broke; ~ (w) (ge-), punt.

boom[2], (s) **(bome)**, tree; bar, beam (for shutting off); boom (naval); thill (wagon); *tussen die* ~ *en die BAS*, betwixt and between; *deur die bome die BOS nie sien nie*, not see the wood for the trees; *'n dik* ~ *met 'n klein BYLTJIE kap*, try to make bricks without straw; *die* ~ *v.d. KENNIS van goed en kwaad*, the tree of the knowledge of good and evil; *'n* ~ *van 'n KÊREL*, a strapping fellow; *algar moenie in een* ~ *NESMAAK nie*, there should not be too much intermarriage between two families; *'n* ~ *gooi altyd 'n SKADUWEE*, parents influence their children; *soos die* ~ *VAL, bly hy lê*, in the place where the tree falleth, there it shall be; *hoe groter die* ~, *hoe swaarder die VAL*, the highest tree hath the greatest fall; *v.d. VERBODE* ~ *eet*, eat forbidden fruit; *'n ou* ~ *word nie maklik VERPLANT nie*, you can't teach an old dog new tricks; *die* ~ *aan die VRUGTE ken*, know a tree by its fruit; *hoë bome vang die meeste WIND*, high winds blow on high hills; the wind blows coldest through the top of the tree; ~ **aalwyn**, tree aloe; ~ **aanplanting**, tree-planting; ~ **agaat**, tree agate; ~ **agtig**, (-e), tree-like, dendriform, aboraceous, arborescent, arboreal; ~ **arm**, poor in trees; ~ **bas**, (tree) bark; ~ **bassteen**, forest-blend; ~ **beskrywing**, dendrology; ~ **bewoner**, arboreal (tree) animal; ~ **blare**, tree leaves; ~ **dassie**, bush dassie (*Dendrohyrax arboreus*); ~ **enter**, inoculator; ~ **gaard**, (-e), orchard; ~ **gans**, brent (goose); wild goose; ~ **geitjie**, tree lizard; ~ **gom**, resin; ~ **grens**, tree line; ~ **groei**, growth of trees; ~ **groep**, clump of trees; ~ **kano**, dug-out; ~ **kenner**, arborist; ~ **klimmer**, tree climber; ~ **kogelmander** = **bloukopkoggelmander**; ~ **kunde**, dendrology; tree lore; ~ **kun′dig**, (-e), arboricultural; ~ **kweker**, arborist, nurseryman, arboriculturist; ~ **kwekery**, (tree) nursery; arboriculture; ~ **loos**, (..lose), treeless; bottomless; ~ **luis**, tree louse; ~ **meter**, dendrometer; ~ **mos**, tree moss; lichen; ~ **nimf**, tree nymph; dryad; hamadryad; ~ **operateur**, boom operator (TV); ~ **padda**, tree frog; ~ **palm**, tree palm; ~ **pampoen**, pa(w)paw; ~ **pie**, (-s), young tree, sapling; *die* ~ *pie BUIG solank as dit nog jonk is*, young twigs are sooner bent than old trees; bend the twig while it is tender; ~ *pie*

GROOT plantertjie dood, the tree flourishes though the one who planted it is dead; ~ **plaas**, (well-)wooded farm; **B** ~ **plantdag**, Arbor Day; ~ **planter**, tree planter; ~ **ryk**, (-e), abounding in trees, wooded; ~ **saag**, pit saw; long saw; ~ **singertjie**, cicada, scissor-grinder; ~ **skors**, bark; ~ **skraap**, almost finished (empty); hard-up; *dit het* ~ *skraap GEGAAN*, it was a close thing; ~ *skraap WEES*, be hard-up; ~ **skraapsel**, scrapings; ~ **slang**, tree snake; ~ **snoeier**, pruner; ~ **soort**, kind of tree; ~ **stam**, (tree) trunk, bole; ~ **stomp**, (tree) stump; ~ **stoter**, tree dozer; ~ **styf**, very stiff; stiff as a poker; ~ **swaaier**, boom swinger (TV); ~ **swam**, agaric; tree fungus; ~ **tak**, branch of a tree; ~ **top**, tree top; ~ **tou**, swifter; ~ **valk**, hobby (bird); ~ **varing**, tree fern; ~ **verering**, tree worship; ~ **vormig**, (-e), tree-shaped; arborescent; dendriform, dendroid; dendritic; ~ **vrug**, fruit of a tree; ~ **was**, tree wax; ~ **wol**, wood-wool; cotton; cotton wool; ~ **wortel**, root (of tree).

boon, (bone), (nie alg.) bean; *iem. in die bone JAAG*, land someone in trouble; *in die bone RAAK*, land in trouble; *in die bone VAL*, strike it lucky; *in die bone WEES*, be in trouble, be at wit's end, be in a fix.

boon′op, moreover, besides, in addition to, furthermore; ~ *ALLES*, to crown everything; *DOM en* ~ *astrant*, stupid and in addition cheeky.

boon′ste, (s) (-s), top, upper part; (b) top, uppermost, highest; ~ *dooie punt*, top dead centre.

boon′tjie, (-s), bean; *iem. beduie hoeveel BLOU* ~ *s vyf is*, tell someone what's what; *HEILIGE* ~, goody-goody; *die* ~ *s IN wees*, be in a fury; *daar KOM* ~ *s van*, nothing will come of that; *iem. in die* ~ *s KRY*, play someone false; ~ *kom om sy LOONTJIE*, chickens come home to roost; one's sins always find one out; ~ *kry sy LOONTJIE*, everybody receives his just deserts; *soos twee* ~ *s na mekaar LYK*, be as like as two peas; *in die* ~ *s RAAK*, get into hot water; *hy kan sy eie* ~ *s wel UITDOP*, he can fight his own battles; *ek is 'n* ~ *as dit nie WAAR is nie*, I'll eat my hat if it is not true; ~ **akker**, bean field; ~ **bredie**, bean stew (bredie); ~ **kerwer**, bean slicer; ~ **peul**, bean pod; ~ **so(e)p**, bean soup; ~ **stoel**, beanstalk.

boon′toe, to the top, up(wards); upstairs; ~ *roep*, call to heaven; swear.

bo′-oor, over the top, right over.

bo′-op, on top, atop; superficial; ~ *die kind val*, fall on top of the child.

boor[1], (s) boron (B).

boor[2], (s) **(bore)**, jumper boring machine; broach; borer, piercer, drill, brace (and bit); gimlet; *groot* ~, auger; (w) (ge-), bore, drill; core (fruit); *in die grond* ~, sink (ship); ~ **beitel**, jumper, boring tool; drill bit; ~ **beuel**, drill socket; drill clamp; drilling post; ~ **blad**, drill table; ~ **buis**, drill pipe.

boord[1], (-e), orchard.

boord[2], (-e), border, edge, brim (cup); board (ship); *aan* ~ *GAAN*, go aboard; *oor* ~ *GOOI*, fling overboard, throw to the winds; ~ **apteek**, first aid case; ~ **e(nste)vol**, brimful; ~ **er**, (-s), borer, driller; ~ **ery**, boring; drilling; ~ **ingenieur**, flight engineer.

boord′jie (-s), collar; *SAGTE* ~, soft collar; *STYWE* ~, hard (starched) collar; ~ **gaas**, buckram; ~ **knoop**, collar stud.

boord: ~ **kapelaan**, naval chaplain; ~ **lint**, lace, galloon, facing; ~ **personeel**, air-going crew; ~ **predikant**, naval chaplain; ~ **skietbaan**, gunnery range; ~ **skutter**, air gunner; ~ **vry**, (-e), free on board; free overside; ~ **werktuigkundige**, flight mechanic.

boor′eiland, (-e), (off-shore) oil rig, (floating) drilling rig, drilling platform.

boor′flennie, boracic lint.

boor: ~ **gat**, (-e), borehole; *'n* ~ *gat slaan (stamp)*, sink a borehole; ~ **gereedskap**, boring apparatus; drilling tools; ~ **gruis**, dril cuttings, drillings; ~ **hamer**, jack-hammer; ~ **houer**, drill (chuck) socket; ~ **kern**, drill-core; ~ **kewer**, (stalk) borer; ~ **klembus**, drill chuck; ~ **kop**, cutter-block; drill socket; ~ **kroon**, crown (of drill); ~ **lem**, drill blade.

boor′ling, (-e), native (of a country, place).

boor: ~ **man**, borer, driller; jumper man; ~ **masjien**,

boring (drilling) machine; ~**monster**, drill core; boring sample; ~**mossel**, stone borer; ~**omslag**, bit brace, drill brace; ~**(on)koste**, drilling costs; ~**pit**, drill core.
boor: ~**pluksel**, boracic lint; ~**poeier**, boracic powder; ~**salf**, boracic ointment.
boor'sel¹, (-s), borings; frass (of insects).
boor'sel², edging, lacing, facing; purl; ~**soom**, roll hem.
boor: ~**skaaf**, side fillister; ~**skulp**, drill; ~**slik**, sludge; ~**slyk**, sludge; ~**slyper**, drill sharpener; ~**spil**, cutter bar; boring bar; drill spindle; ~**staaf**, boring rod; ~**staal**, bore bit; ~**stang**, drill pole, drill rod.
boor'suur, boracic acid.
boort, diamond powder, bort.
boor: ~**tjie**, (-s), gimlet; small drill; ~**toring**, derrick, boring tower; ~**voering**, drill socket; ~**vuur**, plunging fire; ~**vyl**, auger file.
boor'water, boracic lotion.
boor: ~**werk**, drilling; ~**wurm**, borer; ~**wydte**, bore; ~**yster**, (drill) bit, boring tool, brace bit.
boos, (bose; boser, -ste), angry, cross; wicked, evil (spirit); malignant (ulcer); *bose KRINGLOOP*, vicious circle; *iem.* ~ *MAAK*, anger a person; ~ *WEES op*, be angry with; be angry at; *die WÊRELD is* ~, the world is a wicked place; ~**aar'dig**, (-e), malicious, vicious; cankered; spiteful; evil-minded; felonious; malignant, malevolent; flagitious; ill-natured; hellish; destructive; ~**aar'digheid**, ill-nature, malice, maliciousness, malignity, malignancy, malevolence; ~**doener**, (-s), evil-doer, evil-worker, malefactor, villain, criminal, ~**held**, anger; impiety; wickedness; ~**wig**, (-te), villain, criminal.
boot, (bote), boat, bark, canoe; ship; *eerste in die* ~, *keur van RIEME*, first come, first served; *VINNIGE* ~, ocean greyhound; ~**geleentheid**, passage accommodation; ~**huis**, boat-house; ~**huur**, boat hire; ~**lading**, boat load; ~**lengte**, boat's length; ~**s'haak**, boathook gaff; ~**s'man, (-ne)**, boatswain; ~**steier**, (landing) stage; ~**s'volk**, crew, sailors; ~**tog**, boat excursion (trip); ~**transport**, boatage; ~**trein**, boat train; ~**verhuurder**, boatman; ~**vor'mig**, (-e), boat-shaped, navicular; cymbiform; ~**werker**, docker, dock worker (labourer).
bo: ~**pad**, upper road; ~**perd**, top dog.
Bophu'thatswana, Bophuthatswana.
bo: ~**plaat**, top plate; ~**punt**, top (end); head (of procession); ~**raam**, upper window.
boraat', (..rate), borate.
bo'raks, borax; ~**pêrel**, borax head.
borasiet', boracite.
bord, (-e), plate (for meals); trencher (of wood); (black)board; board (material); name plate; *'n* ~ *voor die kop hê*, be brazen.
Bordeaux', Bordeaux.
bordeaux', ~**mengsel**, Bordeaux mixture (against fungi); ~**wyn**, red wine (from Bordeaux in France), claret.
bor'de: ~**borsel**, plate brush; ~**doek**, dishcloth.
bordeel', (..dele), brothel, house of ill-fame; bagnio, bawdy-house, bordello, whorehouse; ~**houdster**, brothel-keeper (female); ~**houer**, brothel-keeper.
bor'derak, plate-rack.
bordes', (-se), (Ndl.) flight of steps (outside a house); landing (of stairs).
bor'de: ~**verwarmer**, plate warmer; ~**wasser**, plate (dish) washer; ~**wassery**, dish-washing.
bord'jie, (-s), small plate; notice-board; *die* ~ *is verhang*, the tables have been turned; ~**sdraai**, an indoor game (catch-me-quick); ~**skilder**, signwriter, sign-painter.
bord'papier, cardboard, millboard, pasteboard, board; ~**houer**, carton.
bord'politoer, plate polish.
borduur', (ge-), embroider, purl, lace; ~**der**, (-s), embroiderer; ~**draad**, purl (knitting); ~**gaas**, embroidery canvas (gauze); ~**garing**, embroidery cotton; ~**kant**, purfle; ~**kuns**, embroidery; ~**lap**, sampler; ~**naald**, embroidery hook (needle); ~**patroon**, embroidery pattern; ~**raam**, embroidery frame; tambour; ~**sel**, embroidery; ~**skêr**, embroidery scissors; ~**ster**, (-s), embroideress; ~**sy**, embroidery silk; ~**werk**, embroidery, crewel work; ~**wol**, crewel (yarn), zephyr yarn.
bord: ~**verwarmer**, plate-warmer; ~**wisser**, blackboard duster (eraser).
boreaal', (boreale), **borea'lies**, (-e), boreal.
bo'register, upper register (music).
borg, (s) (-e), surety, security, guarantee, hostage, bail; bailsman; sponsor (radio, sport); guarantor; guard (for valve); prop (fence); ~ *e baar SORGE*, debt creates anxiety, he who goes a-borrowing goes a-sorrowing; ~ *STAAN (teken, wees)*, become surety, stand bail; vouch for; guarantee; *daarvoor sal ek* ~ *STAAN*, I'll vouch for that; (w) **(ge-)**, sponsor; guarantee; give (get) credit; ~**akte**, (bail) bond; recognisance; ~**bout**, securing bolt; ~**draad**, locking wire; ~**geld**, bail, caution (money); ~ *geld verbeur*, estreat (forfeit) bail; ~**moer**, safety nut (lock); ~**pen**, keeper pin; ~**plaat**, bridge plate; lock plate; ~**ring**, circlip; ~**skap**, suretyship; sponsorship; ~**skroef**, keeper screw; ~**som**, surety, bail; ~**steller**, surety; ~**stelling**, suretyship; surety, bail; guaranty; hostage; *akte van* ~**stelling**, deed of suretyship; surety; ~**tog**, bail, surety; recognizance pledge; *op* ~ *tog uit*, admitted to bail, out on bail; ~**toghouer**, bailee.
bo'riem, upper part of harness; upper strap.
bo'ring¹, boring; bore (of gun).
bo'ring², (-e), upper ring.
bo'rium, boron.
Bor'neo, Borneo.
borneol', borneol.
borniet', bornite (kind of copper ore).
bo'rok, (over)skirt; dress.
bor'rel, (s) (-s), bubble, fizz; drop, tot; (w) **(ge-)**, bubble, popple; tipple; ~**ing**, bubbling, gush; ~**siekte**, decompression disease; ~**stevol**, fed up; ~**tyd**; ~**uur**, time for a drink; ~**vink**, red bishop bird *(Pyromelana orynx)*.
bor'rie¹, (-s), stretcher, bier.
bor'rie², tumeric, curcuma; borge; ~**geel**, deep yellow; jaundiced; ~**hout**, wild lemon, lemon-wood; ~**kweper**, variety of quince *(Cydonia vulgaris)*; ~**patat(ta)**, yellow sweet-potato; ~**rys**, yellow rice.
bor'rievel, skin stretcher; skin apron.
bor'rievink = **borrelvink**.
bors, (-te), breast, mamma; chest; thorax; bosom; bust; counter (horse); brisket (beef); (shirt) front; dickey; *sy* ~ *begin AFSAK*, he is developing a paunch; *iem. aan jou* ~ *DRUK*, press a person to one's bosom; *'n kind die* ~ *GEE*, suckle a child; *iem. voor die* ~ *LOOP*, affront someone; *uit volle* ~ *SING*, sing lustily; *dit STUIT my teen die* ~, it goes against the grain with me; *sy* ~ *UITSTOOT*, puff up one's chest with pride; *iem. aan die* ~ *VAT*, throw down the gauntlet; ~**aandoening**, affection of the chest; ~**aar**, thoracic vein; ~**baba**, breast-fed baby; ~**beeld**, bust; effigy, head (on coin); ~**been**, (..bene), breastbone, chest-bone; sternum; ~**boor**, breast drill; ~**bout**, collar bolt; ~**breedte**, chest measurement; ~**drankie**, ~**druppels**, pectoral (potion), cough mixture.
bor'sel, (s) (-s), brush; bristle; (w) **(ge-)**, brush; dust someone's jacket (ragging among students); ~**agtig**, (-e), bristly; ~**baard**, hard (bristly) beard; ~**draad**, brushwire; wire bristle; ~**gras**, mat weed; ~**hare**, bristles; ~**houer**, brush holder; ~**kontak**, brush contact; ~**kop**, crew-cropped head; crew-cut; ~**koppeling**, brush-coupling; ~**maanhare**, hog-mane; ~**maker**, brushmaker; ~**plaat**, brush plate; ~**rig**, (-e), bristled, bristly, horrent; ~**sak**, brush bag; ~**stert**, bushy tail; ~**tjie**, (-s), small brush; ~**veer**, brush spring; ~**ware**, brushware; ~**wurm**, chaetopod worm.
bors: ~**hal**, breast-stroke; ~**harnas**, cuirass; corslet; breastplate; habergeon; ~**hemp**, dress shirt; ~**holte**, chest (thoracic) cavity; ~**hoog**, breast high; ~**ie**, (-s), little breast; shirt front; dickey; plastron; ~**kanker**, cancer of the breast; ~**kas**,

(-se), chest, thorax; ~**ketting**, pole chain; ~**kind**, breast-fed baby; ~**klier**, thoracic gland; mammary gland; ~**klontjie**, lung lozenge; ~**knopie**, breast stud; ~**kruis**, pectoral cross; ~**kwaal**, chest complaint; ~**lap**, breastpiece (harness); feeder bib; ~**leer**, plastron; ~**leuning**, head-rail; ~**lyer**, pulmonary (chest) sufferer; ~**lyfie**, bust bodice; ~**maat**, chest measurement, girth; ~**melk**, mother's milk; ~**middel**, pectoral (chest) remedy; ~**omloper**, breast collar (harness); ~**plaat**, breastplate; hames; breastpiece (of harness); plastron; sternum; butterscotch, fudge; ~**plooi**, apron (of sheep); ~**pomp**, breast pump; breast reliever(s); ~**pote**, thoracic feet; ~**remmer**, breast strap (harness); ~**riem**, pole strap; breast strap; ~**rok**, corset, stays; ~**rokveter**, stay lace; ~**sak**, breast-pocket; ~**siekte**, chest disease; ~**skans**, breast work; ~**skild**, breast shield; ~**slag**, breaststroke; ~**speld**, brooch; ~**spier**, pectoral muscle; ~**stuk**, breast-cut, brisket (beef); breastplate (harness); plastron; thorax (insect); pectoral; ~**suiker**, lollipop, sugarstick; barley sugar; ~**tap**, haunch joint; ~**tapmasjien**, haunching machine; ~**tepel**, (breast) nipple, teat; ~**trok** = **borsrok**; ~**vere**, breast feathers; ~**vin**, pectoral fin; ~**vleis**, brisket.
bors'vlies, pleura; ~**ontsteking**, pleuritis, pleurisy.
bors: ~**voeding**, breast feeding; ~**wapen**, bard (for horse); ~**water**, pleural effusion; ~**wering, (-s)**, breastwork, parapet, breast wall, rampart, balustrade; redan; ~**werwel**, thoracic vertebra; ~**wydte**, chest measurement(s).
bort, urticaria.
bo: ~**rug**, upper back; ~**ruimte**, headway; overhead clearance.
bos, (-se), bundle, bunch, cluster; hand (of leaves); holt; head (flax); wood, forest; shrub, bush; shock (hair); *die ~ vanweë die BOME nie sien nie*, not to see the wood for the trees; *om die ~ DRAAI (spring)*, look for excuses; *agter die – GETROUD (spring)*, married over the broomstick; *agter die ~ GROOTGEWORD*, ill-bred, unmannered; *iem. in die ~ JAAG*, get the better of an argument; *om die ~ LEI*, lead by the nose; *agter een ~ SIT*, be hand in glove; *in die ~ TRAP*, take to one's heels; *jy kan dit agter elke ~ UITSKOP*, you can find it everywhere (in abundance).
bo'saai, (-ge-), sow before the plough.
bo'saal, upper hall.
bos: ~**aanplanting**, afforestation; ~**aap**, thick-tailed lemur, bushbaby *(Otolemur crassicaudatus)*; ~'**agtig**, woody, bosky; ~**anemoon**, (wood) anemone; windflower; ~**baadjie**, lumber jacket; ~**beampte**, forest official; ~**bedryf**, forestry; ~**beheer**, forest administration, forest management; ~**bessie**, cranberry; ~**bewoner**, woodsman; hatter (Australia); ~**bok**, bushbuck; ~**bontrokkie**, Cape batis; ~**boom**, forest-tree; ~**bou**, forestry; silviculture; *Departement van B~bou*, Department of Forestry; ~**bouafdeling**, forestry department; ~**boukunde**, forest craft; silviculture; ~**bouskool**, school of forestry; ~**brand**, forest fire, bush fire; ~**bult**, holt; ~**dassie**, tree dassie *(Procavia arborea)*; ~**druif**, wild creeper *(Rhoicissus capensis)*; ~**duif**, wood (rock) pigeon; ~**duiwel**, mandrill.
bo'se: *DIE B~*, the Evil One; *uit die ~*, inspired by the Evil One; odious; evil; *VERLOS ons van die ~*, deliver us from evil.
bos'fisant, francolin.
bosga'sie, see **boska'sie**.
bos: ~**ghwarrie**, *Euclea lanceolata*; ~'**god**, faun, sylvan deity; ~**godin'**, wood nymph; ~**hemp**, bush shirt.
bo'sinlik, (-e), supersensual.
boska'sie, (-s), unkempt hair; mop (hair); copsewood, thicket, grove.
bos: ~**kat**, wild cat; ~**koning**, lion; ~**korhaan**, bush korhaan; ~**kraai**, hornbill *(Bucerotidae)*; ~**krapper**, terrestrial bulbul; ~**kwartel**, button-quail.
bo'slagwaterwiel, overshot water-wheel.
bos'land, woodland; ~**skap**, woodscape.
bos: ~'**lanser**, bush whacker, country cousin; coward; ~'**loerie**, narina trogon *(Apaloderma narina)*.

bos'luis, (bush)tick; *hy het die ~ nou AFGESKUD*, he has rid himself of the bad habit; ~ *SPEEL*, be a scrounger; ~**boom**, tick tree *(Ricinus communis)*; ~**koors**, East Coast fever (cattle); tick fever (humans); ~**verlamming**, tick paralysis; ~**voël**, tick-bird, white heron, ox-pecker.
bos: ~**mens**, forest dweller; orang-outang; ~**musikant**, bush musician, forest weaver *(Ploceus bicolor)*; *B~***neger**, maroon; ~**netel**, archangel (plant).
Bos'nië, Bosnia; ~**r, (-s)**, Bosnian.
Bos'nies, (-e), Bosnian.
bos'nimf, woodland nymph.
bos: ~**opsigter**, forester; ~**opstand**, forest stand; ~**pad**, forest road; ~**peper**, *Piper capense*; ~**pik**, pick-axe; ~**plant**, hylophyte; ~**rand**, edge of forest; woody ridge; ~**reservaat**, forest reserve; ~**reus**, forest giant (man, elephant, tree); ~**ruigte**, jungle, tangled undergrowth; ~**ryk, (-e)**, woody, wooded; ~**rykheid**, woodiness.
bosseer', (ge-), mould, model; shape roughly (stone); ~**beitel**, boaster; ~**werk**, boasting.
bosseleer', (ge-), emboss; ~**stok**, embossing stick.
bos'sie, (-s), shrub, copse; bunch (carrots); bob (of hair); herb; tuft, fascicle; floccus (hair); grove; frutex; *dis ALLES ~s*, that's all nonsense!; *~s toe GAAN*, go to stool; *agter die ~s OPGEGROEI*, be dragged up, not brought up; have bad manners; *~s het OË*, *~s het ORE*, walls have ears; *dit SKOP 'n mens agter elke ~ uit*, it is as common as dirt; *nie agter elke ~ UITGESKOP nie*, not easily come by; *WERK soos ~s*, piles of work; ~**agtig, (-e)**, fruticose; ~**dokter**, herbalist; ~**kop**, pony with bushy mane, nag; shock head, mop head; person with untidy hair; ~**smaak**, taste of herbs; ~**stee**, bush tea; ~**stroop**, sugar-bush syrup; ~**veld**, shrub veld.
bos'sing, (-s), bush(ing) box (of door); rabbet joint; border, edge.
bos'skuif, piston valve.
bos: ~**sprinkaan**, bush locust; ~**stertmuis**, dormouse.
bo: ~**staande**, above(-mentioned), foregoing; ~**stad**, upper city; ~**stamkultivar**, scion cultivar; ~**standig, (-e)**, superior (bot.); ~**stel**, body (of a carriage); upper denture (set).
bos'tongreep, Boston grab.
bo: ~**straat**, upper street; ~**strooms, (-e)**, up-stream; ~**stuk**, upper piece (part), top piece.
bos: ~**uil**, bush owl; ~**vark**, bush pig.
bos'veld[1], bush country; ~**patrys**, crested partridge.
Bos'veld[2], Bushveld; ~**plaas**, farm in the Bushveld; **bosveldplaas**, farm in bushy country.
bos: ~**voël**, sombre bulbul; ~**wagter**, ranger, gamekeeper; ~**wêreld**, forest country, woodland; bushveld; ~**werker**, lumberman; ~**wese**, forest service; forestry (department).
bot[1], (s) (-te), flounder; fluke (fish).
bot[2], (s) (-te), bone; *jy kan sy –te tel*, you can count his ribs.
bot[3], (s) (-te), = **bod**.
bot[4], (s) (-te), sprout, bud; (w) (ge-), sprout, bud.
bot[5], (b) (-te), blunt (knife); obtuse; dull, stupid; blockish; *moenie vir jou so ~ HOU nie*, don't pretend to be so stupid; *wat 'n ~ te SKEPSEL!*, what a stupid person!; ~ *toe*, tightly closed; *'n ~ te WEIERING*, a flat refusal.
bot'-af, bluntly, flatly, point-blank; impolite, curt; *'n versoek ~ weier*, refuse a request bluntly.
bo'tallig, (-e), supernumerary.
bo'tand, tooth in upper jaw.
botanie', botany.
bota'nies, (-e), botanic(al).
bota'nikus, (-se, ..nici), botanis', (-te), botanist.
botaniseer', (ge-), botanize; ~**trommel**, vasculum.
bot'heid, bluntness; stupidity; obtuseness; lethargy; leaden-heartedness.
bot'jie, small coin; *~ by ~ sit*, club together, throw into common fund.
Bot'nië, Bothnia.
bo'toon, overtone; dominant; *die ~ voer*, dominate; boss the show.
bo'trapping, tread (of horse).
botri'tis, botrytis (disease).

bots, (s) shock, collision; conflict; (w) **(ge-),** collide, clash, strike, jostle; impinge; ~ *MET,* collide with; be contrary to; ~ *TEEN,* bump against.
bot'sel, (-s), bud.
bot'sing, (-e, -s), collision, smash, crash, clash, impact; conflict; crush; impingement; percussion; concussion; *in* ~ *kom,* clash, collide.
bot'sinkie, (-s), slight collision.
bot'stil, motionless, quite still, stock-still, very quiet; ~ **stand,** complete standstill.
Botswa'na, Botswana.
bot'tel, (s) (-s), bottle, flask; *al BARS die* ~ , by hook or by crook; come what may; *hy het die* ~ *se BOOM gesien,* he is tipsy; *so dig soos 'n* ~ *BRANDEWYN,* close as an oyster; *te veel van die* ~ *HOU, in die* ~ *KYK, LIEF vir die* ~ *wees, iem. SPREEK die* ~ *aan,* ply the bottle; (w) **(ge-),** bottle; ~ **aar, (-s),** bottler; ~ **ary', (-e),** place for bottling; bottling-works; ~ **baba,** bottle-fed child (baby); ~ **bier,** bottled beer; ~ **etiket,** bottle label; ~ **groen,** bottle green; ~ **heide,** bottle heath; ~ **ier', (-s),** steward (ship's); butler; ~ **kind,** bottle-fed baby; ~ **omslag,** bottle wrapper; ~ **ring,** jar ring; ~ **skei,** bottle-shaped jukskei (for game); ~ **tjie, (-s),** phial; nip, small bottle.
bot'ter, butter; *AFGELEKTE* ~ , jilted girl; ~ *sal tussen die twee nie AFKOM nie,* they will never hit it off; *dis* ~ *tot by die BOOM,* they are as thick as thieves; *die* ~ *sal BRAAI,* it will come to light; *dit is* ~ *op sy BROOD,* it is grist to his mill; *so maklik soos* ~ *en BROOD,* it is mere child's play; *hy laat* ~ *nie van sy BROOD eet nie,* he is not easily taken in; *dis* ~ *aan die GALG gesmeer,* it is to little purpose; *die* ~ *het alleen GESLAAP,* the butter won't spread; *so GLAD soos* ~ , as slippery as soap; ~ *aan sy HANDE hê,* have butter-fingers; *dis* ~ *op 'n warm KLIP,* it is not worth the effort; *OMGEWERKTE* ~ , remade butter; ~ *sal nie in sy mond SMELT nie,* butter won't melt in his mouth; *so sterk soos OU* ~ , only his odour is strong; *in die* ~ *VAL,* strike it lucky; ~ *by die VIS,* cash down; cash on the nail; *so WAAR as* ~ *en brood,* as true as faith; ~ **agtig,** butyrous; ~ **bereiding,** butter= making; ~ **blom,** buttercup; goldilocks, Cape daisy; kingcup; bachelor's buttons; ~ **boer,** dairy farmer; ~ **boom,** butter tree *(Cotyledon panicu= lata);* ~ **boontjie,** butter-bean; ~ **boor,** butter sampler; ~ **broodjie,** scone; ~ **doek,** buttermuslin; ~ **-en-brood,** bread-and-cheese *(Malva parviflora);* ~ **fabriek,** creamery; ~ **gebrek,** butter shortage; ~ **hambalk,** filch-beam; ~ **ham(metjie),** sandwich; ~ **hampapier,** grease-proof paper; ~ **hande,** butter= fingers; ~ **handel,** butter trade; ~ **ik, (e),** dunce; ~ **karamel,** butterscotch; ~ **karring,** butter churn; ~ **kelk,** Californian poppy; ~ **kleur,** buttercolour; ~ **koeler, (-s),** butter-cooler; ~ **kop,** dolt; block= head; dunderhead; hinny; garron (mule); ~ **koper,** butter dealer; ~ **koppie,** hinny; ~ **mark, (-te),** but= ter market; ~ **mes, (-se),** butter-knife; ~ **opbrengs,** butter yield; ~ **papier,** butter paper; ~ **peer, (..pere),** beurre, butter pear; ~ **pot(jie);** butter dish; ~ **proeër,** butter trier; ~ **skorsie,** butternut (squash); ~ **sous,** butter sauce; ~ **sout,** table salt; ~ **spaan,** butter pat; ~ **stof,** butter fat; ~ **suur,** butyric acid; ~ **tand:** *die* ~ *tande uittrek,* have to do with= out butter; ~ **vaatjie,** butter firkin (tub); ~ **verval= sing,** butter falsification; ~ **vet,** butter fat; ~ **vorm,** butter mould; ~ **woorde,** deceptive (smooth) words; *glad is die* ~ *woorde van sy mond,* the words of his mouth were smoother than butter.
bot: ~ **ting,** foliation; ~ **tyd,** blossom-time.
botulis'me, botulism.
bot'vellig, (-e), thick-skinned, dull.
bot'vier, (-ge), give reins to (passions, etc.); indulge; ~ **ing,** giving reins to.
bot'weg, flatly, straight out, plump, point-blank; *iets* ~ *weier,* refuse something point-blank.
bou, (s) construction, build, structure; conformation, anatomy; (w) **(ge-),** raise (an edifice), build, con= struct; ground; *op iem.* ~ , rely on someone; ~ **aan= nemer,** (building) contractor; ~ **baas, (..base),** master builder; ~ **bedryf,** building trade; ~ **beheer,** building control ~ **bepalings,** building restrictions; ~ **bord,** building board.
boud¹, (s) **(-e),** buttock; joint of meat, leg (of mutton), haunch (animal); hind quarters, buttocks; nates.
boud², (b) bold.
boud: ~ **jie, (-s),** little buttock; drumstick (of fowl); ~ **jiespampoen,** Turkish cap (pumpkin); ~ **karme= naadjie,** chump chop; ~ **naat,** perineum.
bou'doos, (..dose), box of bricks (toy).
boud: ~ **sak, (-ke),** hip-pocket; ~ **vet,** cod fat.
boud'weg, (ong.) boldly.
bou'ksiet, bauxite.
bou: ~ **er, (-s),** builder, constructor; ~ **ersbaas,** mas= ter builder; ~ **ery,** building; ~ **fonds,** building fund.
bougainvil'lea, bougainvill(a)ea.
bou: ~ **genootskap,** building society; ~ **gereedskap,** building implements; ~ **grond,** building site; arable land; ~ **hout,** building timber; ~ **-ingenieur,** struc= tural engineer; ~ **-inspekteur,** building inspector.
bo'-uit, out at the top (above); louder; *sy stem klink* ~ , his voice sounds louder than all the rest.
bou: ~ **kalk,** building lime; ~ **klip,** building stone; ~ **kommissie,** building committee; ~ **kontrak,** building contract; ~ **koors,** building mania; ~ **koste,** building expenses; ~ **kunde,** architecture; ~ **kun'dig, (-e),** tectonic; architectonic; architec= tural; constructive; ~ **kun'dige, (-s),** architectural expert; ~ **kuns,** architectural art, tectonics.
boul, (ge-), bowl (cricket).
bou'land, arable land.
boulbeurt, over; *leë* ~ , maiden (over).
boulo, buhl work.
bou'ler, (-s), bowler.
bou'levard, (-s), boulevard.
boul: ~ **lyn,** bowling crease; ~ **manier,** delivery (cricket); ~ **ontleding,** bowling analysis; ~ **skerm,** bowling net; ~ **streep,** *see* **boullyn;** ~ **werk,** bowling.
bou: ~ **maatskappy,** building company; ~ **materiaal,** building material; ~ **meester,** architect; builder; constructor; ~ **nywerheid,** building industry; ~ **on= dernemer,** builder and contractor; ~ **opsigter,** clerk of works; ~ **orde,** style of architecture; ~ **perseel,** building plot; ~ **plan,** building project; plan (of building); ~ **program,** building programme; ~ **re= gulasie,** building regulation; ~ **rekenaar,** quantity surveyor.
bourgeois', bourgeois; ~ **ie',** bourgeoisie.
bourrée', (-s), bourrée.
Bourgog'ne, (ong.) Burgundy (wine).
bou: ~ **sel, (-s),** structure; ~ **staal,** structural steel; ~ **steen,** building stone; ~ **stof,** building material; (fig.) sources, ~ **styl,** style of building, architectural style; architecture.
bout, (-e), (s) bolt (iron); pin (wooden); pintle; (sol= dering-) iron; (w) **(ge-),** bolt.
bouta'de, (-s), witticism, sally.
bout'boor, (..bore), bolt auger.
bou'terrein, building site.
bout'gat, (-e), bolt hole.
bout'jie, (-s), small bolt.
bout'kop, bolt head.
bou: ~ **trant,** architecture; build; ~ **trein,** construc= tion train.
bout: ~ **skag,** bolt body, bolt shank; ~ **snyer,** stock and dies; bolt cutter.
bou'vak, building trade.
bou'val, (-le), ruin(s); ~ **'lig, (-e),** tumble down, ram= shackle, dilapidated, decayed, tottering; ~ **'ligheid,** decayed state, dilapidation.
bou: ~ **vereniging,** building society; ~ **verordening,** building regulation; building bylaw; ~ **voorman,** foreman of works; ~ **voorskot, (-te),** building loan; ~ **vorm,** structure; ~ **werk,** building; building oper= ations; construction, constructional work; ~ **woede,** building mania.
bo'venster, upper window.
bo'verdieping, (-s), upper storey; *daar is iets verkeerd in sy* ~ , there is something wrong in his upper storey.
bo'vermeld, above-mentioned.
bo: ~ **vlak, (-ke),** surface, top (side); ~ **vlerk,** top

wing; ~ **voortand,** upper front tooth; ~ **water,** mill-head.
bo'we, *see* **bo:** *te ~ GAAN,* exceed; *te ~ kom,* get the better of; ~ **aards** = **boaards;** ~ **al** = **bowenal;** ~ **buurman,** (..**bure),** upstairs neighbour; ~ **genoemd, (-e),** above-mentioned; ~ **hand,** upper hand; *die ~ hand kry,* get the upper hand; ~ **maans, (-e),** celestial, heavenly; ~ **mate,** beyond measure; ~ **ma'tig** = **bomatig.**
bo'wenal, above all (things).
bowe: ~ **natuur'lik (-e),** supernatural; metaphysical; miraculous ~ **natuur'likheid,** miraculousness.
bowendien', moreover, besides, further, furthermore.
bo'we: ~ **sin'lik,** supersensual; ~ **staande** = **bostaande;** ~ **watervaartuig,** surface craft.
bo'werk, superstructure.
bowe: ~ **toon** = **botoon;** ~ **wig'tig, (-e),** top-heavy; ~ **wig'tigheid,** top-heaviness; ~ **woning,** upstairs dwelling (lodging).
bo'wind, upper wind.
Bo'windse Eilande, Windward Islands.
boy'senbessie, boysen berry.
bra, (bw.) really, actually, rather, somewhat, very; *dit kan nie ~ ANDERS nie,* it can hardly be different; *hy is maar ~ DOM,* he is rather stupid; ~ *baie DRINK,* drink heavily; *jy kan ~ baie LIEG,* you are a bare-faced liar; *ek het nie ~ LUS nie,* I do not really feel inclined.
bra, (s) **(-'s),** bra, brassière.
braaf, (brawe), honest, virtuous, good, upright; *jou ~ GEDRA,* behave virtuously; *'n brawe Hendrik,* a goody-goody; ~ **heid,** honesty, integrity; *cf.* **dapper.**
braai, (ge-), roast (on spit); fry (in pan); grill, broil (on gridiron); bake (in oven); scorch (in sun); toast (bread); *IEM.* ~, take someone in; tell someone what you think of him; *in die OOND ~,* roast; *in VET ~,* fry; ~ **boud,** (roast) leg of mutton; ~ **brood,** fried bread; ~ **broodblokkie,** croûton; ~ **gereg, (-te),** grill; ~ *geregte ALTYD verkrybaar,* grills at all hours; *GEMENGDE ~ gereg,* mixed grill; ~ **hoek,** barbecue; ~ **hoender,** roaster; ~ **huis,** steakhouse; ~ **kaas,** Welsh rarebit (rabbit); ~ **kuiken,** griller; ~ **mielie,** mealie for roasting; ~ **olie,** frying-oil; ~ **oond,** roasting oven; ~ **pan,** frying pan, fryer; dripping pan; ~ **plek,** barbecue; ~ **restourant,** steak-house; ~ **ribbetjie,** roast(ed) rib; ~ **rooster,** gridiron; ~ **skottel,** roasting dish; ~ **spit,** (roasting) spit; ~ **stoof, (ge-),** braize; ~ **vet,** dripping; ~ **vleis,** roasted meat, roast; grilled meat; ~ **vleis,** braai, barbecue; ~ **vleisaand,** braaivleis gathering, barbecue; ~ **vleisgeleentheid,** braai, barbecue.
braak¹, (w) **(ge-),** break up, plough, fallow; (b) fallow; *die land lê ~,* the land lies fallow.
braak², (w) **(ge-),** vomit, belch; regurgitate.
braak'land, fallow land; land ploughed for the first time.
braak: ~ **middel,** emetic, vomitive; ~ **neut,** nux vomica.
braak'ploeg, subsoil cultivator
braak'sel, vomit.
braak: ~ **tand,** tusk (horse); ~ **teenmiddel,** anti-emetic; ~ **tyd,** fallowing time.
braak: ~ **wek'kend, (-e),** emetic, vomitory; ~ **wortel,** ipecacuanha (root); ~ **wyn,** emetic wine.
braam, (brame), bramble; dewberry; blackberry; burr (of chisel); ~ **bos, (-se),** bramble bush; ~ **bosbes(sie),** blackberry.
Bra'bander, (-s), Brabantine.
Bra'bant, Brabant; ~ **s, (-e),** Brabantine.
brab'bel, (ge-), jabber, mutter, cant, gibber; ~ **aar, (-s),** ~ **kous,** jabberer, sputterer; ~ **latyn,** dog latin; ~ **taal,** jabbering, gibberish; jargon, lingo, patois.
brag, (veroud.) brought.
Bra'ga, Bra'gi, Braga.
braggiet', braggite.
bragike'faal, (..fale), bragisefaal', (..fale), bragisefa'lies, (-e), brachycephalic.
Brah'ma, Brahma; ~ **an', (..mane),** Brahman; ~ **ans',** (b) Brahman; ~ **nis'me,** Brahmanism; ~ **is'ties, (-e),** Brahmanic(al).

brail'leskrif, braille writing (for the blind).
brak¹, (s) **(-ke),** dog (of small stature, e.g. the Pomeranian); mongrel, cur; *hoe kleiner ~ hoe groter geraas,* empty vessels make the most noise.
brak², (s) salt-lick, brackish spot; *op die ~ wees,* be without a sweetheart; (b) brackish, briny; alkaline; *'n ~ kol,* a brackish spot.
brak: ~ **bossie,** lye bush; ~ **grond,** brackish ground; ~ **heid,** brackishness, alkalinity.
brak'hond, brak'kie, (-s), (small) mongrel (dog); beagle.
bra'king, vomiting.
brak'kie, (-s), small dog, pooch, tyke; ~ **sakkie,** doggy bag.
brak: ~ **lek,** deer-lick; ~ **pan,** pond with brackish water; ~ **plek,** brackish spot, salt-lick, deer-lick; *'n groot ~ plek hê,* have a bald patch; ~ **slaai,** ice plant *(Mesembryanthemum crystallinum).*
braktee', (..teë), bract.
brak: ~ **veld,** brackish land; ~ **vyg,** fruit of the *Mesembryanthemum;* ~ **water,** brack(ish) water.
bram: ~ **seil,** topgallant sail; ~ **steng,** topgallant mast.
brand, (s) (-e), fire, conflagration, blaze; combustion; flame; brand (on cattle); burnt patch of veld; mildew, blight; ergot; smut (in wheat); gangrene; burning (tingling) sensation; burn; eruption; *AAN die ~!* all right! get going! agreed! *BEDEKTE ~,* loose smut; *aan (die) ~ RAAK,* catch fire; *ons SIT in die ~,* we are in a fix; *aan die ~ STEEK,* set on fire; *SWART ~,* burnt area of veld; *iem. UIT die ~ help,* get someone out of a fix; *aan die ~ WEES,* to be all agog; (w) **(ge-),** burn, scald, blaze, scorch, cauterize; brand (cattle); glow; calcine (bones); roast; *KOFFIE ~,* roast coffee; ~ *van VERLANGE,* yearn; *'n ~ ende VRAAGSTUK,* a burning question; acute problem; ~ **aar,** smut-ear (wheat); ~ **alarm,** fire-alarm; ~ **arm,** penniless, indigent, destitute; ~ **assie,** midge; ~ **assuransie,** fire-insurance; ~ **baar, (..bare),** combustible; ~ **baarheid,** combustibility; ~ **beskerming,** protection against fire; ~ **bestryder,** fire-fighter; protoman (mining term); ~ **bestryding,** fire fighting; ~ **bestrydingsmaatreëls,** fire-fighting precautions; ~ **bestrydingspan,** prototeam; ~ **bewaking,** fire watching; ~ **blaar,** blister (from a burn); kind of anemone; ~ **blusapparaat,** fire extinguisher; ~ **blusgereedskap,** fire-extinguishing implements; ~ **blusser,** ~ **blustoestel,** fire-extinguisher; ~ **bom,** incendiary (fire) bomb; napalm; ~ **bos,** aromatic fern *(Mohria caffrorum);* ~ **byl,** fireman's axe; ~ **dam,** reservoir for fire extinguisher; ~ **deur,** emergency door; ~ **dig, (-te),** fire-proof; ~ **emmer,** fire-bucket; ~ **end, (-e),** burning, live (coals); flaming, pyrotic; ardent, yearning, fervid.
bran'der¹, (-s), large wave, breaker; ~ *ry,* surf.
bran'der², (-s), burner (of lamp).
bran'der³, (-s), reprimand, rebuke; letter of demand; *iem. 'n ~ stuur,* send someone a scorcher.
brand: ~ **erig, (-e),** burning; irritant, smarting; burnt (taste); ~ **erigheid** irritation; heat, fire.
bran'der: ~ **merkies,** ripple marks; ~ **plank,** surfboard; aquaplane; ~ **vlak,** plane of marine erosion.
bran'dery, (-e), burning (of lime); lime-kiln.
bran'dewyn, brandy; eau-de-vie; *OORGEHAALDE ~,* rectified spirits; ~ *RAAS gewoonlik as dit uit die vat kom,* drunkards are usually noisy; ~ *en VROUERAAD is goeie dinge, maar jy moet dit bietjies-bietjies gebruik;* ~ **bos,** brandy bush *(Grewia cana);* ~ **bottel,** brandy bottle; ~ **glas,** brandy glass; ~ **handel,** brandy trade; ~ **handelaar,** (wholesale) brandy dealer; ~ **ketel,** potstill; ~ **maatskappy,** brandy company; ~ **moed,** pot valour; ~ **neus,** bottle-nose; ~ **ketel,** brandy still; ~ **smokkelaar,** brandy smuggler; ~ **stokery,** (brandy) distillery; ~ **tjie, (-s),** tot of brandy; ~ **vat,** brandy barrel; ~ **vlieg,** tippler, toper, boozer.
brand: ~ **gang,** fire-passage; ~ **gans,** brent-goose; ~ **gat, (-e),** fuse hole; ~ **gevaar,** fire-risk, danger from fire; ~ **glas,** burning-glass; lens; ~ **goed,** firing; ~ **gordel,** fire-belt; ~ **granaat,** incendiary shell; ~ **haak,** fire-hook; ~ **haar,** stinging hair; ~ **hout,**

branding   93   **breek**

firewood; *hulle breek nie ~hout van dieselfde tak nie*, they don't hit it off with one another.
bran'ding, surge, surf, breakers; ~**boot**, surf-boat; ~**serosie**, marine erosion.
brand: ~**jeuk**, nettle-rash; ~**kamer**, strong-room; ~**kas, (-te)**, safe, strong-box; ~**kasbreker**, yegg; ~**kelder**, strong-room (bank); ~**klok**, fire-alarm, fire-bell; ~**kluis**, safe; ~**koeël**, fire-ball; incendiary bullet; ~**kolle**, necrotic patches; burnt patches; ~**koring**, black-ear, burnt-ear; ~**kors**, eschar; ~**kraan**, fire-hydrant, fire-cock; ~**lasser**, acetylene welder; ~**leer**, fire-ladder; scaling ladder; escape ladder; pompier ladder; ~**lekker**, extra-strong (peppermint); ~**lelie**, dobo-lily *(Cyrtanthus angustifolius)*; ~**lont**, "slow match", fuse; ~**lug**, smell of burning; ~**maer**, skinny, as lean as a rake, raw-boned, scraggy; ~**meester**, chief fire-brigade officer; fire-master; ~**merk**, (s) brand, stigma; (w) (ge-), brand; stigmatize; *iem. ~ merk vir iets*, impute something to someone; ~**middel**, pyrotic, caustic; incendiary; ~**muur**, fire-proof wall; ~**nekel, (-s)**, stinging nettle; ~**net**, fire-system; ~**netel, (-s)**, stinging nettle; ~**oefening**, fire-drill; ~**offer**, burnt offering; holocaust; ~**olie**, furnace oil, fuel oil; ~**opsporingsapparaat**, fire-detecting appliance; ~**opsporingstoestel**, fire-detection device; ~**paal**, stake; ~**pad**, fire-path, fire-break; ~**plaat**, baffle-plate; ~**plek**, burn; ~**polis**, fire-policy; ~**pomp**, fire-pump; ~**punt**, focus (of lens); burning-point; centre (of interest); *gelykwaardige ~ punt*, equivalent focus; ~**puntafstand**, depth of focus; focal distance; ~**puntlamp**, focus lamp; ~**pyl**, Congreve rocket; ~**ramp**, disastrous fire; ~**rissie**, chili; ~**rosie**, eschar; ~**ruik**, smell of burning (fire); ~**seer**, veld sore; ~**sel¹, (-le)**, stinging cell; ~**sel², (-s)**, quantity (of coffee) roasted; ~**siek**, (s) sheep scab; (b) scabby; ~**siekbok**, scab-infected goat; ~**siekluis**, scab mite; ~**siekte**, scab; mange; ~**siekte-inspekteur**, scab inspector; ~**siektemyt** scab (itch) mite; ~**sinjaal**, fire-signal; ~**skade**, damage caused by fire; ~**skat, (ge-)**, lay under contribution; ~**skatting**, war levy, ransom, (war) contribution; ~**skerm**, iron (fire-) curtain; safety curtain; ~**skilder**, (s) enameller, glass-stainer; poker drawer; (w) **(ge~)**, enamel; stain; *gebrandskilderde venster*, stained window; ~**skilderwerk**, enamelled work; ~**skildery**, poker drawing; ~**skimmel**, smut-blight; ~**skot**, fire-proof bulkhead; fire-partition; ~**slaner**, fire-beater; ~**slang**, fire-hose; ~**smaak**, burnt flavour; ~**solder**, fire-proof ceiling; ~**spieël**, burning mirror; ~**spiritus**, methylated spirits; ~**spuit**, fire-engine; fire-hose; ~**stapel**, stake, pile, balefire; funeral pile; pyre (for cremation); *tot die ~ stapel veroordeel*, condemn to the stake; ~**steen**, lunar caustic; ~**stigtend, (-e)**, incendiary; ~**stigter**, incendiary: arsonist; ~**stigting**, incendiarism, arson.
brand'stof, fuel; petrol; combustible; ~ *aanvul (in neem)*, refuel; ~**bespaarder**, (fuel) economizer; ~**kamer**, fuel-chamber; ~**leiding**, fuel-line; ~**meter**, fuel-gauge; ~**pomp**, fuel-pump; ~**ruimte**, fuel-capacity; ~**tenk**, fuel-tank; ~**toevoer**, fuel supply; ~**verbruik**, fuel (petrol) consumption; ~**voorraad**, fuel supply; ~**vuldiens**, refuelling facilities; ~**wa**, fuel-tanker.
brand: ~**strook**, fire-belt, fire-break; ~**trap**, fire-escape; emergency stair; ~**vas (-te)**, fire-proof; ~**verf**, enamel; ~**versekering**, fire-insurance; ~**versekeringsmaatskappy**, fire insurance company; ~**vertragend, (-e)**, fire-retarding; ~**vry, (-e)**, fire-proof, apyrous; ~**wa**, fire engine; ~**wag**, watch, guard, outpost, sentry, picket; fire-watch; ~**wag staan**, mount duty, be on picket duty; ~**wagdiens**, picket duties; ~**weer, (..were)**, fire-brigade; ~**weerhoof**, fire-master; ~**weerman**, fire-man; ~**weeroefening**, fire-drill; ~**weerpersoneel**, fire-brigade; ~**weerstasie**, fire-station; ~**weerstrook**, fire-break, fire-belt; ~**weeruitrusting**, fire-equipment; ~**weerwa**, fire-engine; ~**werend, (-e)**, fire-resisting; ~**werk**, poker work; enamel; ~**werking**, incendiary effect; ~**wese**, fire-service; ~**wond**, burn, scald; ~**wondverband**, burn-dressing; ~**yster**, branding iron, searing iron; cautery (med.).
brangiopo'de, branchiopod(e).
bras¹, (s) brace; *groot ~*, main brace; (w) **(ge-)**, brace.
bras², (w) **(ge-)**, carouse, revel, booze.
bra'sem, (-s), bream (fish).
brasiel'hout, brazil (wood).
Brasiliaan', (..liane), Brazilian.
Brasiliaans', (-e), Brazilian.
Brasi'lië, Brazil.
Brasi'liër, (-s), Brazilian.
brasilien', brasili'ne, brazilin (colouring matter); ~**suur**, brazilinic acid.
bras'party, debauchery, carouse, carousal, orgy.
bras'ser, debauchee: carouser; ~**y, (-e)**, feasting, revelry, gluttony, debauch(ery).
brassie're, (-s), brassière, bra.
brava'de, (-s), bravado, boast.
braveer', (ge-), defy, brave.
bravo', (-'s), bravo! hear! hear!
bravour', (F.), bravura.
brec'cia, breccia.
bre'de: *in den ~*, at length, in detail.
bre'die, bredie, stew (vegetables and meat), ragout, haricot; *van iem. ~ maak*, make mincemeat of a person.
bre'ëblaarwoud, broad-leaf forest.
breed (breë; breër, -ste), broad, wide; expansive; ample; *~ AANVOOR*, begin on a large scale; *wie dit ~ het, kan dit ~ HANG*, those who have plenty of butter can lay it on thick; *dit nie ~ HÊ nie*, find it difficult to make both ends meet; *breë KOMMISSIE*, plenary committee; *dis net so ~ as wat dit LANK is*, it is six of the one and half a dozen of the other; *~ OPGEE van iets*, make much ado; *in breë TREKKE*, in broad outline; *iets ~ UITMEET*, exaggerate; ~**borstig, (-e)**, broad-chested; ~**gebou, (-de)**, sturdy, square-built; ~**gerand, (-e)**, broad-brimmed; ~**gesind, (-e)**, broad-minded; ~**geskouer, (-de)**, broad-shouldered; ~**heid**, broadness, breadth, width; ~**hoof'dig, (-e)**, platycephalic, brachicephalous; ~**neu'sig, (-e)**, platyrrhinous; ~ **saai**, (w), broadcast; ~**spra'kig, (-e)**, verbose, diffuse, voluble; circuitous; ~**spra'kigheid**, verbosity, circumlocution, diffuseness, prolixity, volubility.
breed'te, (-s), breadth, width, latitude; *iets tot op die ~ van 'n haar weet*, know something extremely well; *in die ~*, broadwise (on); ~**-as**, lateral axis; ~**bepaling**, determination of latitude; ~**boog**, traversing arc; ~**graad**, degree of latitude; ~**helling**, latitudinal incline; ~**lamp**, clearance lamp; ~**pord**, vaulting horse; ~**rigveld**, traverse (cannon); ~**sirkel**, parallel of latitude; ~**sy**, broadside.
breedvoe'rig, (b) (-e), circumstantial, detailed; exhaustive; (bw) at length, in detail; amply; ~**heid**, fullness of detail, minuteness, circumstance, copiousness, ampleness; ~ **wer'pig, (b)**, broadcast.
bree'fok, (Ndl.), lug sail
breek, (s) break, fracture (of bone); crushing (measles); fault (reef); (w) **(ge-)**, break, go to pieces, break down, smash, crush; refract (light); snap (twig); shatter (glass); fracture (bone); make an opening (football); *jou DORS ~*, quench one's thirst; *met 'n GEWOONTE ~*, break oneself of a habit; *sy oë ~*, his eyes become glassy; ~**baar, (..bare)**, breakable, brittle, fragile, refractable (light); ~**baarheid**, fragility; ~**bal**, break; ~**beitel**, ripping (crooked) chisel; ~**belasting**, breaking-load, breaking-weight; ~**bord**, (earthenware) plate; ~**goed**, crockery; earthenware; china; ~**grens**, breaking point; ~**hamer**, maul; ~**klip**, quarry stone; ~**klippaadjie**, crazy pavement; ~**krag**, tensile strength (wool); ~**las, (-te)**, breaking burden; ~**lyn**, line of (punch) fracture; ~**masjien**, crusher; ~**mielies**, samp; ~**plek**, place of fracture; ~**punt**, breaking point; ~**skade**, breakage; ~**slaan**, (w), **(breekge-)**, break by hitting; ~**slag**, break (rugby); ~**spanning**, breaking stress; ~**spul**, smash; *dit is 'n ~ spul*, it's a pretty kettle of fish; it's a sad mess; ~**vastheid**, breaking strength; ~**vlak**, fault plane; ~**vry, (-e)**, crash-proof; ~**ware**, crock-

breërandhoed   *bring*

ery; ~**water**, breakwater; hard labour; ~**yster**, crowbar; hand spike; inch bar; jemmy.
bre'ërandhoed, broad-brimmed hat; sun hat.
bre'ëspoor, broad (normal) gauge (railway).
brei¹, (ge-), prepare, dress, cure, curry (skins); coach (football); train (athlete); put through his paces, harden (for life); knead (clay); *ge~de ATLETE*, trained athletes; *ge~ WEES*, have been through the mill.
brei², (ge-), knit.
brei'del, (s) (-s), bridle; (w) **(ge-)**, bridle, check, curb; ~**loos**, (..**lose**), unbridled, unchecked; ~**voeg**, bridle-joint.
breier'¹, (-s), coach (sport); skin dresser.
brei'er², (-s), knitter.
brei: ~**gare**, ~**garing**, knitting yarn, cotton; ~**goed**, implements for knitting; knitting; knitted articles.
brei'hout, pole used in preparing riems.
brei'klas, tutorial; knitting class.
brei'klip, weight stone (dressing stone) for preparing riems.
brei: ~**kous**, knitted sock; boring person; tedious conversation; ~**les**, knitting lesson; ~**mandjie**, knitting basket; ~**masjien**, knitting machine, knitter.
brein, (-e), brain, intellect; *iets op die ~ hê*, have something on the brain.
brei'naald, knitting needle; ~**ekoker**, knitting case; knitting needle container.
brein: ~**bloeding**, cerebral haemorrhage; ~**floute**, blackout; ~**holte**, cerebral cavity; ~**kas, (-se)**, brain case; cranium; ~**ontsteking**, brain fever, cerebritis, cephalitis; ~**spesialis**, brain specialist; ~**spoeling**, brain-washing; ~**trust**, brain(s) trust; ~**verlamming**, cerebral palsy; ~**versagting**, ~**verweking**, softening of the brain; ~**vlies**, cerebral membrane; *die ~ vliese*, the meninges; ~**vliesontsteking**, meningitis; ~**werk**, brain work; ~**werking**, cerebration.
brei'paal, pole for preparing riems.
brei: ~**patroon**, knitting pattern; ~**pen**, knitting needle.
brei'riem, dressed riem.
brei: ~**skede**, knitting sheath; ~**steek**, knitting stitch; ~**ster, (-s)**, female trainer (coach); ~**werk**, knitting; ~**wol**, knitting wool; fingering.
breka'sie, breakage.
bre'kend, (-e), refractive.
bre'kens: *tot ~ toe*, near breaking point.
bre'ker, (-s), crusher; breaker; wave; ~**y**, crusher station.
brek'fis: *dit is net 'n ~ vir my*, that's child's play; that's chicken feed.
bre'king, (-e, -s), breaking; fraction; fracturing (leg); glazing (eyes); plunge (golf); refraction (light).
bre'kings: ~**afwyking**, aberration; ~**eksponent**, refractive index; ~**hoek**, angle of refraction; ~**indeks**, refractive index; ~**vermoë**, power of refraction; ~**vlak**, plane of refraction; ~**wet**, law of refraction.
brek'sie, (-s) = **breccia**.
brem, broom (plant); gorse.
bre'merblou, blue ashes.
brems, tabanid.
bren'ger = **bringer**.
Bren'geweer, Bren'masjiengeweer, Bren gun.
bres (-se), breach, gap (in fortification); *in die ~ SPRING vir*, step into the breach for; *in die ~ TREE vir iem.*, take up the cudgels for someone.
Bretag'ne, Brittany.
Breton', (-ne), Breton; ~**s, (b)**, Breton.
breuk, (-e), breach (peace); break, fracture; failure; schism; fraction; rupture, hernia; hiatus; fault (in rock); *EGTE ~*, proper fraction; *GEWONE ~*, vulgar (common) fraction; *ONEGTE ~*, improper fraction; *SAMEGESTELDE ~*, compound fracture (of leg); complex (compound) fraction; *TIENDELIGE ~*, decimal fraction; *~ van TROUBELOFTE*, breach of promise (of marriage); ~**band**, truss; ~**bandmaker**, truss maker; ~**beklemming**, strangled hernia; ~**instrument**, rupture appliance; ~**kuil**, cauldron, fault-pit; ~**poeiers**, hernia pow-

ders; ~**spalk**, splint; ~**splyting**, fracture cleavage; ~**steen**, face-stone; ~**vlak**, fracture surface.
breva'rium, (-s), breviary; brevier.
bre've, brief.
brevet', (-te), brevet, commission (officer).
brevier', (-s), brevier (type); breviary.
brief, (briewe), letter, epistle; missive; *'n ander man se briewe is DUISTER om te lees*, no one but the wearer knows where the shoe pinches; *die OUDSTE briewe hê*, have the greatest right to; *PER ~*, by letter; *'n RONDGAANDE ~*, a circular (letter); *~ van VOORNEME*, letter of intent; ~**aanhef**, beginning of a letter, salutation; ~**besteller**, postman; ~**draer**, letter carrier; ~**hoof**, letter-head; ~**ie, (-s)**, note(let), line, letterette; docket; short letter; chit; *daarvoor kan ek jou 'n ~ ie gee*, I can vouch for it; ~**kaart**, letter-card; ~**lêer**, letter file; ~**omslag**, envelope; ~**papier**, notepaper; ~**porto**, postage; ~**pos**, letter-post; ~**priem**, spike (for letters); ~**skaal**, letter-balance; ~**skrywer**, letter-writer; correspondent; ~**skrywery**, letter-writing; ~**sorteerder**, letter sorter; ~**stempelmasjien**, franking machine; ~**styl**, epistolary style; ~**telegram**, cable-letter; ~**vorm**, epistolary form; ~**weër**, letter balance; ~**wisseling**, correspondence.
briek, (s) (-e), brake; (w) **(ge-)**, apply the brake(s); *iem. se ~ AANDRAAI*, keep a tight rein on someone; *hy BLY maar by die ~*, he keeps on the safe side; *hy DRAAI die ~*, he is at the bottom (of the class); *sy ~ is LOS*, he is busy ruining himself; ~**balk**, beam to which brake blocks are attached; ~**blok**, brake block; ~**slinger**, brake handle, Vgl. **rem**.
brie'kwa, brindle(d) (animal); hybrid watermelon.
bries¹, (s) (-e), breeze.
bries², (w) (ge-), snort; fret; roar.
brie'send, (-e), snorting, furious, wild with rage, as cross as two sticks, in an awful bate (rage).
brie'we: ~**besteller** = **briefbesteller**; ~**boek**, letter book; ~**bus**, post-box; letter-box; ~**hoof** = **briefhoof**; ~**mandjie**, letter basket; ~**mes**, paper-knife; ~**pers**, letterpress; ~**rak**, letter-rack; ~**sak**, letter-bag; postbag, mailbag; ~**skaal**, letter balance; ~**stempel**, letter stamp; ~**tas**, wallet; postman's bag.
briga'de, (-s), brigade; ~-**generaal**, brigadier-general.
brigadier', (-s), brigadier; ~-**generaal**, brigadier-general.
brigantyn', brigantine.
brik, (-ke), brig.
briket', (-te), briquet(te), coal briquet(te); ~**te'ring**, briquetting.
bril, (s) (-le), (pair of) spectacles; gig-lamps; seat (of water-closet); *hy kyk deur 'n BLOU ~*, he sees only the gloomy side of things; *as jy deur 'n BLOU ~ kyk, is alles blou*, dark glasses make everything seem dark; *hy DRA 'n ~*, he wears spectacles; *iem. 'n ~ GEE*, insult a person; *'n ~ op die NEUS sit*, cheat a person; *iem. 'n ~ OPSIT*, take someone in; *alles deur 'n ROOSKLEURIGE ~ bekyk*, see everything through tinted spectacles; *TWEE ~ le*, two pairs of spectacles; *TWEE ~ le op hê*, see double; *hy het sy ~ VERLOOR*, he can't see straight; (w) **(ge-)**, wear glasses (spectacles); ~**doos**, spectacle case; ~**duiker**, golden-eye garrot (bird); ~**glas**, lens, spectacle glass; ~**glaslyper**, spectacles grinder optician; ~**huisie**, spectacle case.
briljant', (s) (-e), brilliant; cut diamond; (b) **(-e)**, brilliant, clever; ~**ien'**, ~**i'ne**, brilliantine (registered trade name).
bril: ~**maker**, optician; ~**pikkewyn**, jackass penquin; ~**raam**, spectacle frame; ~**skans**, lunette; ~**skuifie**, spectacle case; ~**slang**, spectacled snake, cobra *(Naia)*; ~**verkoper**, optician; ~**wewer**, spectacled weaver *(Ploceus ocularius)*.
bring, (ge-), bring, take, carry, convey; fetch; land (in difficulties); *tot die BEDELSTAF ~*, reduce to beggary; *te BERDE ~*, broach (a matter); *'n BESOEK ~*, pay a visit; *iem. DAARTOE ~*, get someone so far as to; *dit tot HOOFONDERWYSER ~*, rise to a principalship (of school); iem.

'n OFFER ~, make a sacrifice; *hy* ~ *'n RAMP oor homself*, he is courting disaster; *onder REËLS* ~, subject (made liable) to rules; *iem. na die TREIN* ~, take someone to the station; *dit VER* ~, go far, rise to something great; *tot WANHOOP* ~, drive to despair; ~ *my 'n bietjie WATER*, please get me some water; ~**er, (-s),** bringer, bearer.
brin'jal, (-s), brinjal, egg-plant, egg-fruit, aubergine *(Solanum melongena)*.
brioche', brioche.
brisant', high explosive; ~**bom,** high-explosive bomb; bursting bomb; ~**fabriek,** high-explosive factory; ~**granaat,** high-explosive shell; live grenade; ~**lading,** high-explosive charge.
Brit, (-te), Briton, Britisher; *die* ~ *te,* the British; ~**s, (-e),** British; ~*se warmte-eenheid*, British thermal unit.
britan'niametaal, Britannia metal.
Britan'nies, (-e), Britannic.
Brittan'je, Britain, Britannia.
broc'coli, broccoli.
brod'delwerk, bungle, bungling.
bro'de: *om den* ~, for a living, for money.
bro'deloos, (..lose), breadless, without a living; *iem.* ~ *maak,* bring someone to ruin.
broed, brood.
broe'der, (-s), brother; *'n* ~ *van die NAT gemeente,* a toper; ~*s en SUSTERS,* (my) brethren; brothers and sisters; ~ *in die VERDRUKKING,* fellow-sufferer; ~**band,** fraternal bond; ~**haat,** fraternal hatred; ~**hand,** fraternal hand; hand of friendship (fellowship); ~**huis,** brother's house; ~**liefde,** brotherly love; ~**lik, (e),** brotherly, fraternal; ~**moord,** fratricide; ~**moordenaar,** fratricide; ~**oorlog,** civil war; ~**plig,** brother's (brotherly) duty; ~**skap,** brotherhood; (con)fraternity; ~**trou,** fraternal fidelity; ~**twis,** quarrel between brothers, fraternal discord (quarrel).
broei, (ge-), brood, hatch, incubate; ferment (tobacco); ponder on, ruminate; get (over)heated; *DAAR* ~ *iets,* something is brewing; ~**bak,** garden frame; ~ -**eiers,** setting, sitting (eggs); ~**er, (-s),** hatcher; ~**erig, (-e),** close, sultry, grumpy; ~**ery,** hatching; hatchery; ~**hen,** brood-hen; ~**hitte,** sweltering heat; ~**hok,** hatching pen; ~**huis,** hatching room; ~**kamp,** breeding camp; ~**kas, (-te),** hothouse, conservatory, hotbed, greenhouse, forcing house; brood-chamber (bees); incubator; ~**kasbaba,** incubator baby; ~**kasplant,** hothouse plant; ~**kragtigheid,** hatchability; ~**kuip,** mashtub; ~**masjien,** incubator; ~**nes,** hotbed; plague-spot; nidus; cloaca; ~**oond,** hatching oven; ~**paar,** breeding pair (of ostriches); ~**periode,** incubation period (of disease); ~**plek,** hatchery; mating ground; breeding ground; spawning ground (fish); ~**raam,** forcing frame, ~**s,** broody; clucking; surly, grumpy; *'n* ~*s hen,* a broody hen; ~**sel, (-s),** hatch, clutch, sitting (of eggs); brood (of chicks); batch; aerie (bird of prey); ~**sheid,** broodiness; ~**toom,** breeding pen; ~**tyd,** breeding (hatching) time; ~**voël,** breeding bird; ~**warm,** suffocating(ly) hot.
broek, (e), (pair of) trousers, breeches; nether garments, drawers, knickers, pants, panties, bloomers; back part, breeching, buttock (of harness); ~ *AANPAS (afstof),* give someone a dressing down; *met* ~ *en BAADJIE,* (potatoes) in their jackets; *DIEP in die* ~ *gespring,* he is wearing his trousers half-mast, *die* ~ *DRA,* wear the breeches; *GROOT in die* ~ *WEES,* be portly; be too big for one's boots; *in die* ~ *HANG,* act as a drag; *sy* ~ *op die KOOP wil toegee,* be pleased with his bargain; *KORT* ~ *dra,* wear shorts; *LIG in die* ~ *wees,* be of slender build (a light-weight); be of little importance; *net MAN omdat hy 'n* ~ *dra,* a milksop; *aan sy* ~ *se NAAT voel,* feel it in his bones; *dit SIT nie in sy* ~ *nie,* he is not up to it; *sy* ~ *sit in sy SKOENE,* he has cold feet; *te vinnig deur die* ~ *SPRING,* wear very short trousers; *diep in die* ~ *STAAN,* a huge man; *sy* ~ *vir iem. wil UITTREK,* be generous to a fault; *hy kan nie eers* ~ *VASMAAK nie,* he cannot even tie his shoelaces; ~ *VERBIND (losmaak),* go to stool; *hy kon sy* ~ *VUILMAAK,* he was in a funk; *iem. se* ~ *WARM maak,* give someone a hiding; *hy is 'n* ~ *vol WIND,* he is a windbag; ~**band,** waist band; ~**goed,** trousering(s); ~**ie, (-s),** small (pair of) trousers; pilcher; ~**knyper,** trouser clip; ~**man(netjie),** little man; ~**ophouer,** hip strap; ~**pers,** trouser press; ~**plaat,** throat plate (harness); ~**sak,** trouser pocket; ~**s'ferweel,** corduroy; ~**s'gulp,** (trouser) fly; ~**skeur, (s)** tear in the trousers; (bw) hard, difficult; *dit sal net* ~ *skeur GAAN,* it wil be a near thing; ~*skeur deur 'n eksamen KOM,* pass an examination by the skin of one's teeth; ~**s'knoop,** trouser button; ~**s'plooi,** trouser crease.
broeks'pyp, trouser leg; *sy* ~ *speel ghitaar,* he trembles in his shoes; *dit LÊ nie in sy* ~ *e nie,* he hasn't it in him; *hy sal sy* ~ *e moet OPROL,* he will have to pull up his socks; *dit gaan nie sommer in sy* ~ *e SIT nie,* he will not put up with that.
broek'wol, breeches.
Broenei, Brunei.
broer, (-s), brother; *hy het met sy* ~ *SAAMGELOOP,* he is tipsy; *OU* ~, old chap, my friend; *onder* ~*s is dit seker R5 werd,* it is cheap at R5; ~**lief,** dear brother; ~**s'dogter,** niece; ~**seun,** nephew; ~**skap,** fellowship; ~**s'kind** nephew; niece.
broer'tjie, (-s), little brother; *aan werk het hy 'n* ~ *dood,* he hates work.
broes, (-e), rose (of watering-can).
broe'sa, (ong.), devil.
brok, (ke), piece, fragment, lump, chunk, bit.
brokaat', brocade.
brok'kel,(ge-), crumble, fritter; ~**ig,** ~**rig, (-e),** crumbly, friable, brittle, crisp; ~**rots,** broken rock (mines); brash.
brok'kie, (-s), bit, piece, crumb, morsel; *'n bedorwe* ~, a spoilt brat.
brok'kiespoeding, trifle.
broks'gewys(e), piece by piece, piecemeal.
brok'stuk, fragment; fraction, piece; snatch (of song).
brom, (ge-), grumble, mutter, carp, grouse (person); growl (animal); drone, hum, buzz (insect); *hy begin al te* ~, he is beginning to take an interest in girls.
bromaat', (..mate), bromate.
brom'bas, bourdon, bombardon(e).
brom'beer, growler, grouser.
bromeer', (ge-), brominate.
brom'fiets, buzz bike, moped.
bromi'de, (-s), bromied', (-e), bromide; ~**papier,** bromide paper.
bro'migsuur, bromous acid.
bro'mium — broom.
brom'kewer, horn-beetle.
brom'mend, (-e), grumbling.
brom'mer, (-s), grumbler, grouser; blowfly; horsefly, bluebottle; drone-fly; flesh-fly; ~**ig, (-e),** angry, grumpy, cross-tempered; disgruntled; surly, cantankerous; ~**plaag,** blowfly menace (plague); ~**vanger,** fly-catcher; ~**y,** growling, grumbling.
brom: ~**ponie,** (motor) scooter; ~**pot,** growler, grouser, curmudgeon, Dutch uncle, splenetic, grumbler; ~**tol,** humming top; ~**toon,** humming (radio); ~**voël,** turkey-buzzard *(Bucorvus cafer);* ground hornbill.
bron, (-ne), source, origin; fount(ain), fountain-head, spring (water); (water) head; cause (of evil); means (of living); mint (fig.); ~ *van BESTAAN,* means of living; *uit goeie* ~ *iets VERNEEM,* have it from a reliable source; ~**aar,** source, fountain-head.
brongiaal', (..giale), bronchial.
brongi'tis, bronchitis.
bron'gras, *Bromus mollis.*
bron'kors, watercress *(Nasturtium officinale);* ~**bredie,** watercress stew.
bron'ne: ~**kennis,** knowledge of sources; ~**materiaal,** sources; ~**-opgawe,** list of sources; ~**publikasie,** source publication (book); ~**studie,** research work, original research; ~**vermelding,** statement of sources; ~**versameling,** source book.
brons[1], (s) rut, heat, oestrus.
brons[2], (s) bronze; (w) **(ge-),** bronze; tan; ~**bruilof,** eighth anniversary of marriage, bronze wedding;

~busse, bronze bushing; ~gieter, brass founder; ~gietery, brass foundry; ~iet′, bronzite; ~itiet′, bronzitite; ~kleurig, (-e), bronze-coloured.
bron′slaai, watercress.
brons: ~laer, bronze bearing; ~medalje, bronze medal.
Brons′periode¹, Bronze Age.
brons′periode², rutting season.
brons: ~poeier, shell gold; bronze powder; ~siekte, Addison's disease.
brons′siklus, oestrum.
brons′tig, (-e), ruttish, on heat, oestrous; ~heid, heat, rut, ruttishness.
brons′tyd¹, rutting season.
Brons′tyd², Bronze Age; ~perk, Bronze Age.
bron: ~water, well-water, spring-water; ~wel, (digt.), spring.
brood, (brode), bread, loaf; *klae met wit ~ onder die ARM*, complain when you have everything your heart desires; *met iem. ~ BREEK*, break bread with someone; *DROË ~ eet*, live from hand to mouth; *DRIE brode*, three loaves; *dit EET nie ~ nie*, it makes you no poorer; *op sy ~ KRY*, be reprimanded; *'n mens kan nie alleen van ~ LEWE nie*, man cannot live by bread alone; *vir iem. ~ uit die MOND spaar*, do oneself short for another; *iem. se ~ uit sy MOND neem*, rob someone of his livelihood; *so NODIG as ~*, simply cannot be done without; *~ OPMAAK*, shape loaves; *die ~ begin RYS*, she is pregnant; *~ der SMARTE eet*, eat the bread of adversity; *hy SMEER die ~ dik*, he exaggerates; *dit elke dag op sy ~ SMEER*, cast it in his teeth daily; *dit kan jy op jou ~ SMEER*, put that in your pipe and smoke it; *iem. se ~ vir hom SMEER*, take someone to task; *SUUR ~ eet, hy VERDIEN skaars sy ~*, he scarcely earns a living; *jou ~ VERDIEN*, earn a living; *van ~ en WATER lewe*, live on crusts and crumbs; *jou ~ op die WATERS werp*, cast one's bread upon the waters; *wie se ~ 'n mens eet, dié se WOORD 'n mens spreek*, one does not quarrel with one's bread and butter; ~agtig, (-e), panary; ~bak, bread trough; ~bakker, baker; ~bakkery, bread-baking, panification; bakery; ~blik, bread tin (bin); ~boom, bread-fruit tree *(Artocarpus intergrifolia)*; ~bord, bread platter (plate); ~braaier, toaster; ~deeg, (bread) dough.
brooddronk′, wanton, extravagant; ~enheid, wantonness.
brood′eter, bread eater.
brood′gebrek, lack of bread; *~ ly*, starve.
brood′jie, (-s), roll; small loaf; *soet (mooi) ~s bak*, try to get into someone's good books.
brood: ~kaas, loaf cheese; ~kar, breadcart; ~kas, ~kis, (-te), bread chest (bin); *vir iem. die ~ kis hoog hang*, curtail someone's expenditure; ~koek, beebread; ~koring, bread grain; ~kors(ie), bread crust; ~krummel, (bread) crumb; ~krummelaar, bread crumber; ~meelblom, bread flour; ~loos, (..lose), breadless; ~mandjie, bread basket; ~mes, bread knife; ~mielie, variety of early mealie; ~nodig, (-e), indispensable, essential; badly needed; ~*nodig wees*, be a must; ~nood, dearth of bread; ~nyd, professional jealousy; ~pan, ~plaat, bread pan; baking pan; ~pap, bread poultice; ~plank, bread trencher (platter); ~poeding, bread-and-butter pudding; ~rolletjie, (bread)roll; ~rooster, toaster; ~rug; *rug maak*, arch the back (said of a horse); ~sak, bread bag; ~(s)′gebrek, destitution, want, penury, starvation; ~skimmel, mildew on bread; ~skrywer, penny-a-liner, pot-boiler, ink-slinger, hackwriter; literary hack; garreteer; ~skrywery, literary pot-boiling; ~smeer, sandwich spread; ~snyer, bread slicer; ~sop, bread soup, panada; ~struif, bread omelette; ~suiker, loaf-sugar; ~tou, bread queue; ~trommel, bread (bin) tin; ~vergiftiging, bread-poisoning; ~vraag, question of livelihood; ~vrug, bread-fruit; ~wa, baker's van; ~weinig, precious little; ~winkel, baker's shop; ~winner, bread-winner; ~winning, livelihood, means of subsistence; living; ~wortel, cassava root, maniok, manihot, yarn.

broom, bromine; ~kali(um), bromide of potassium; ~natrium, bromide of soda; ~silwer, silver bromide; ~sout, bromic salt; ~suur, bromic acid.
broos¹, (s) (brose), buskin.
broos², (b) (brose; broser, -ste), frail, brittle, fragile; short (metals); ~heid, fragility, frangibility, frailty.
bros¹, (s) (-se), bradawl.
bros², (b) brittle; crisp (lettuce); crumbly; friable; frail; ~brood, shortbread; ~doring, *Acacia robusta; Phaeoptilum spinosum*; ~heid, brittleness, crispness; frailty; friableness; ~heidmeter, shortometer.
bro′sjeer, (ge-), stitch; *ge~de boek*, paper-covered book.
brosju′re, (-s), (spr. u. bro-sju′re), brochure, pamphlet.
bros: ~koek, shortbread; ~kors, short-crust; ~lekker, frittle; ~tertdeeg, short pastry; ~wording, embrittlement.
brou, (ge-), brew (beer); bungle, botch (matters); concoct, hatch (mischief); ~er, (-s), brewer; ~ersgraan, brewer's grain(s); ~ery, (-e), brewery; *lewe in die ~ery bring*, stir things up, make things hum; ~gereedskap, brewing utensils; ~kuip, brewing vat; ~sel, (-s), brew, brewage; farrago; concoction; decoction; muddle; ~spul, mess, muddle; ~werk, bad work, bungling.
brug¹, bridge (card game).
brug², (-ge, brûe(ns)), bridge; parallel bars (gymnastics); gangway (ship); ga(u)ntry (crane); *'n ~ slaan oor*, throw a bridge across; ~balans, bascule; weighbridge; ~balk, baulk (bridge); ~boog, arch of a bridge; ~bou, bridge construction; ~dek, floor (of bridge).
Brug′ge, Bruges.
brug: ~(ge)hoof, bridgehead; ~leuning, bridge railing; ~pad, road across a bridge.
brug′party(tjie), bridge drive.
brug: ~pilaar, bridge pillar; ~reling, bridge rail; ~slag, bridge launching; ~spanning, bridge span.
brug′speler, bridge player.
brug′stander, bridge standard.
brug′tafel(tjie), bridge table.
brug: ~wagter, bridgeman; ~yster, bar-shoe.
bruid, (-e), bride; *het jy met die ~ GEKOM?* haven't you got anything to do? *die ~ is in die SKUIT, nou is al die mooi woordjies (praatjies) uit*, the bride is gotten, the promises forgotten; all sweet promises cease with marriage.
brui′degom, (-s), bridegroom.
bruids′: ~bed, nuptial couch; ~blom, bridal bouquet; ~boeket, bride's bouquet; ~goed, trousseau; ~jonker, bestman.
bruid′skat, marriage portion; dowry.
bruids: ~koek, wedding-cake; ~koekwerk, gingerbread work.
bruid′sluier, bruids′krans, bridal wreath, bridal veil.
bruids: ~meisie, bridesmaid; ~paar, bridal pair (couple); ~rok, ~tabberd, wedding dress; ~teeparty, tea shower.
bruid′stoet, bridal procession.
bruids: ~tooi, bridal array; ~trane, hippocras; mountain-rose (W.Indies); volubilis (flower); ~uitrusting, ~uitset, trousseau; ~wa, nuptial coach.
bruik′baar, (..bare), serviceable, useful; efficient; adaptable; employable; fit; ~heid, usefulness, adaptability; ~heidsduur, life (loan); period of efficiency.
bruik′huur, leasing; ~der, leaseholder.
bruik′leen, loan (for use); lease-lend, leasing; commodation; *in ~ AFSTAAN (gee)*, make a loan of (for use); *in ~ HÊ*, have on loan; ~bestelling, loan indent.
bruik′lening, the loan of the use of a thing.
brui′lof, (-te), wedding, espousals; nuptials, marriage; *GOUE ~*, golden wedding; *~ HOU*, celebrate a wedding.
brui′lofs: ~dag, wedding day; ~dig, epithalamium; ~fees, wedding party; ~gas, (-te), wedding guest; ~gedig, wedding song; hymeneal; ~kleed, wedding dress; *hoe het jy hier ingekom sonder 'n ~kleed aan?*, how comest thou in hither not having a wed=

ding garment?; ~**lied**, wedding song, hymeneal; prothalamium; ~**maal**, wedding banquet, wedding breakfast; ~**mars**, wedding march; ~**plegtigheid**, marriage ceremony.

bruin, (s) brown; bruin (bear); *die* ~ *slaan toe*, it is getting dark; (b) brown; bay (horse); coloured (people); ~**brand**, (s) tan; (w) **(ge-)**, tan, get tanned; brown (by roasting, frying); ~**agtig**, **(-e)**, brownish; ~**arend**, small eagle *(Aquila wahlbergi)*; ~**baardsuikerbos**, **(-se)**, brown-bearded protea; ~**beer**, brown bear; ~**boek**, brown book; ~**brood**, brown bread; ~**e**, **(-s)**, brown one; brown horse; ~**eend**, southern pochard.

bruineer', **(ge-)**, burnish; make brown; ~**der**, **(-s)**, ~**naald**, burnisher; ~**sel**, browning; burnishing; ~**staal**, burnisher, burnishing iron.

brui'nerig, **(-e)**, brownish.

bruine'ring, browning; frosting; burnishing.

brui'netjie, **(-s)**, small brown one.

bruin'geel, brownish yellow; tawny; sorrel (horse); filemot, lurid (bot.); ~**bekbees**, dark bovine with yellow ring round the mouth.

bruin: ~**goed**, brown articles; ~**groen**, brownish green; ~**harig**, **(-e)**, brown-haired; ~**heid**, brownness; ~**ing**, browning (of meat); ~**kapel**, brown cobra; ~**kleurig**, **(-e)**, brown; ~**kommetjiegatkat**, (kind of) skunk; ~**kool**, brown coal, lignite; ~**koollaag**, layer of lignite; B~**man**, Coloured man; ~**mense**, Coloured people; ~**oog**, person with brown eyes; ~**oog-**, brown-eyed; ~**rooi**, bay, maroon; reddish brown; ~**sel**, browning; ~**skimmel**, brown roan (horse); ~**sous**, brown sauce; ~**spaat**, brown spar; ~**sprinkaan**, brown locust *(Locustana pardalina)*; ~**steen**, manganese; ~**suiker**, muscovado, brown (government) sugar; ~**swart**, brownish black; B~**tjie**, **(-s)**, Bruin (bear); "Brown"; *dit kan* ~ *nie trek nie*, it is more than I can afford; ~**valk**, steppe buzzard; ~**verbrand**, **(-e)**, tanned; ~**vis**, porpoise; dolphin; puffing-pig; B~**volk**, Coloured people; ~**vrot**, fungous tomato disease; B-**vrou**, Coloured woman; ~**vy**, brown fig.

bruis, **(ge-)**, foam, froth, seethe, churn; roar (wind); effervesce, bubble, fizz, fizzle; ~**bron**, soda-fountain; ~**end**, **(-e)**, foaming, roaring, seething; fizzy; ~**limonade**, (effervescent) lemonade; ~**meel**, self-raising flour; ~**melk**, milk-shake; ~**poeier**, Seidlitz powder; effervescent powder; fruit salts; ~**water**, sea spray; mineral waters; ~**wyn**, sparkling wine.

brul, (s) **(-le)**, roar, bellow, blare; (w) **(ge-)**, roar, bellow; ~**aap**, howling monkey *(Alonatta)*; ~**bek**, cry-baby; ~**boei**, whistling buoy; ~**lag**, roaring laugh; ~**os**, yak; ~**padda**, bullfrog; ~**sand**, roaring sand; ~**voël**, bittern.

brunet', (s) **(-te)**, brunette; (b) melanous.

Bruns'wyk, Brunswick.

brusello'se, brucellosis, Malta fever, undulant fever.

Brus'sel, Brussels; ~**s**, **(-e)**, Brussels; ~*se KANT*, Brussels lace; ~*se LOF*, chickory; ~*se SPRUITJIES*, Brussels sprouts.

brutaal', (..tale), cheeky, saucy, forward, graceless, impertinent, pert, petulant, perky, impudent, insolent; glaring; malapert, ~**weg**, insolently, boldly, impertinently.

bruta'lerig, **(-e)**, cheeky, insolent.

brutaliseer', **(ge-)**, treat with insolence, insult, affront, cheek.

brutaliteit', **(-e)**, impudence, cheek, effrontery, impertinence, petulance, petulancy.

bru'to, gross; ~ *GEWIG*, gross weight; ~ *INKOMSTE*, gross income; ~ *KOSTE*, gross charges; ~ *ONTVANGS*, gross receipts; ~ *OPBRINGS*, gross proceeds; ~ *TONNEMAAT*, gross tonnage; ~ *UITGAWE*, gross expenses; ~ *VOLKSPRODUK*, gross national product; ~ *WINS*, gross winnings; gross profit.

bruusk, **(-e)**, brusque, abrupt, blunt (person), off-hand; ~**heid**, brusqueness.

bruut, **(brute)**, brute (force); *met brute geweld*, with brute force.

bry[1], (s) broth, pulp, mush, porridge.

bry[2], (s) burr (in speech); (w) **(ge-)**, roll the "r", burr, speak with a burr.

bryn, brine.

b'tjie, **(-s)**, small **b**.

bubo'nepes, bubonic plague.

bud'jie, **(-s)**, budgie, budgerigar.

buf'fel, **(-s)**, buffalo *(Syncerus caffer)*; rude fellow; churl, boor; ~**agtig**, **(-e)**, rude, churlish, boorish; ~**agtigheid**, rudeness, churlishness; ~**(s)doring**, buffalo-thorn (tree) *(Zizyphus mucronata)*; ~**(s)gras**, buffalo grass; ~**svel**, guff; ~**(s)voël**, ~**(s)vriend**, beef eater (bird); ~**vlieg**, buffalo gnat *(Simulium)*.

buf'fer, **(-s)**, buffer, bumper; cushion; ~**plakker**, bumper sticker; ~**staat**, buffer state.

buffet', **(-te)**, sideboard; (refreshment) bar, buffet; ~**ete**, finger supper, buffet meal, sit-down meal.

bui', **(-e)**, shower (of rain); flurry (snow); gush; whim, humour, mood; (coughing) fit; *BY (met)* ~ *e*, by fits and starts; *in 'n GOEIE* ~ *wees*, be in a good mood.

bui'del, **(-s)**, pouch, purse; ~**das**, bandicoot *(Perameles)*; ~**dier**, pouched animal, marsupial; ~**draend**, **(-e)**, marsupial; ~**kreef**, purse-crab, rubber-crab; ~**mees**, penduline tit (mouse); ~**rot**, opossum; ~**sak**, paunch, pouch; ~**vormig**, **(-e)**, sacciform; ~**wa**, straddle truck; ~**wolf**, zebrawolf.

bui'e, **(ge-)** = **buig**.

bui'erig, **(-e)**, showery; gusty (weather); capricious, whimsical, moody, fickle, disgruntled, crotchety, fitful; ~**heid**, capriciousness, moodiness, fickleness; showeriness.

bui'ewolk, cumulo-nimbus.

buig, **(ge-)**, bend; bow (head); stoop, curve; buckle; bob (the head); lean (over); decline; deflect (gram.); dip; ~ *of BARS*, bend or break, by hook or by crook; *wat nie* ~ *nie, moet BREEK*, either bend or break; ~ *VOOR*, bow to (the inevitable).

buig'baar, (..**bare**), flexible, bendable, pliable, ductile, supple; declinable (noun); *'n buigbare kierie*, a flexible walking-stick; ~**heid**, pliability, flexibility.

buig: ~**beuel**, jim-crow; ~**bok**, bending horse; ~**breuk**, greenstick fracture; flex break (tyre); ~**ing**, **(-e**, **-s)**, bend(ing), flexure; curts(e)y, bow, bob (the head); flexion (in grammar); curvature (earth's); curve (contour); modulation (voice); dip.

bui'gings: ~**druk**, bending stress; ~**hoek**, angle of curvature; ~**leer**, accidence; ~**uitgang**, flexional ending; ~**vorm**, flexional form.

buig: ~**krag**, bending power; ~**masjien**, bending machine; ~**moment**, bending moment; ~**-my-nie**, Cape boxwood *(Buxus macowani)*; ~**prisma**, deflecting prism; ~**proef**, bending test; ~**punt**, inflection point (curve).

buig'saam, (..**same**), flexible, pliant; flexile; ductile; lithe(some), lissom(e), limber; pliable; adaptable, compliable; *'n buigsame wil*, a flexible will; ~**heid**, flexibility, pliability, pliancy, litheness.

buig: ~**sening**, back tendon (horse); ~**spanning**, bending stress; ~**spier**, flexor (muscle); ~**stuk**, bend (in pipes); ~**tang**, bending pliers; ~**vastheid**, flexural strength; ~**veer**, flexion spring.

buik, **(-e)**, stomach, paunch, belly, abdomen; venter (anat.); bilge (of ship); platform, floor, buck (waggon); bunt; *van sy* ~ *'n AFGOD maak*, make a god of one's belly; *'n hongerige* ~ *het nie ORE nie*, hungry bellies have no ears; *'n* ~ *KRY*, become corpulent; ~**asemhaling**, abdominal respiration; ~**band**, belly band; ~**breuk**, abdominal hernia; ~**dienaar**, gourmand; ~**gord**, girth cinch; belly band; girdle; *die* ~ *gord styf moet trek*, have to tighten one's belt; ~**holte**, abdominal cavity; ~**ig**, **(-e)**, paunchy, paunch-bellied, corpulent; ~**ingewande**, entrails; ~**kramp**, gripes, colic; ~**landing**, belly landing; ~**loop**, diarrhoea, cholerine, dysentery; ~**lyer**, stomach sufferer; ~**naat**, belly suture; ~**operasie**, abdominal operation; ~**plank**, bed-plank; floor plate (wagon); bottom plank, platform-board; ~**poot**, clasper (of insect); ~**potig**, **(-e)**, gastropodous; ~**pyn**, stomach-ache; ~**riem**, belly band; girth; ~**senuwee**, abdominal nerve; ~**slagaar**, coeliac artery; ~**speekselklier**, pancreas; ~**spek**, belly fat; ~**spier**, abdominal

buil   98   **buite**

muscle; ~**spraak,** ventriloquy, ventriloquism; ~**spreek, (ge-),** ventriloquize, ~**spreker,** ventriloquist; ~**sprekery,** ventriloquy; ~**streek,** abdominal region; ~**stuk,** futtock; ~**sug,** abdominal dropsy; ~**suier,** ventral sucker; ~**tapnaald,** abdominal trocar; ~**tifus,** typhoid fever; abdominal typhus; ~**treksaag,** felling saw; ~**versakking,** abdominal ptosis; ~**vin,** ventral fin; ~**vleg,** solar plexus; ~**vlies,** peritoneum; ~**vliesontsteking,** peritonitis; ~**vol,** fed up; ~ *vol wees van (vir) iets,* be fed up with something; ~**vyl,** bellied file; ~**wand,** abdominal wall; ~**watersug,** ascites; ~**wurm,** round worm, maw worm (ascaris).

buil¹, (s) **(-e),** boil; swelling.

buil², (s) bolter, sieve; (w) **(ge-),** bolt, sieve; ~**doek,** bolting cloth.

bui'lepes, bubonic plague.

buil: ~**linne,** bolting-cloth; ~**meule,** bolting-mill.

buis, (-e), tube, pipe; duct; canal; meatus (anat.); sleeve; fistula (insects); ~ **ag'tig, (-e),** tube-shaped; ~**baba,** tube baby; ~**blom,** tubular floret; ~**chirurgie,** fallopian-tube operation; ~**dop,** fuse cap; ~**gat,** fuse hole; ~**granaat,** fuse shell; ~**holte,** lumen; ~**ie, (-s),** small tube; duct; ~**leiding,** piping, pipeline; ~**lig,** fluorescent light; ~**loos,** (..lose), ductless; tubeless; endocrine; ~**masjien,** tubing machine; ~ **poot,** tube foot; ~ **prop,** fuse hole plug; ~**slaner,** fuse mallet; ~**vor'mig, (-e),** fistulous; tubular; ~**wasser,** ~**waster,** tube washer.

buit, (s) booty, prize, prey, loot, plunder; *vir goeie* ~ *verklaar,* condemn (a ship) as a prize; (w) **(ge-),** rob, loot, pillage, plunder, ravin (poet.), maraud, seize, carry off.

bui'te, (bw) outside, out of doors; *na* ~ *GAAN,* go outside; *jou te* ~ *GAAN,* overstep the mark; indulge too freely (food or drink); *van* ~ *KEN,* know by heart; *van* ~ *LEER,* learn by heart; *VAN* ~, from the outside; externally; (vs) out of, beyond, outside; ~ *BEDRYF stel,* put out of commission; ~ *en BEHALWE,* over and above; ~ *GEVEG stel,* disable; ~ *die KWESSIE,* beyond all question; ~ *my OM,* without my knowledge; ~ *WERKING,* out of order; ~ *homself van WOEDE,* beside himself with rage; ~**-aan,** on the outside; ~**aards, (-e),** extraterrestrial; ~**-af:** *van* ~*-af,* from the outside; ~**afdruk,** external cast; ~**afmeting,** outside measurement; ~**amptelik, (-e),** non-official, private; ~**antenne,** outside aerial; ~**baantotalisator,** off-course totalizator; ~**bakoond,** outside oven; ~**band,** outer cover; tyre; ~**beampte,** outdoor officer; ~**beentjie,** by-blow; side-slip; ~**belange,** outside interests; ~**blad,** cover (of magazine); ~**boordmotor,** outboard motor; ~**boords, (-e),** outboard; ~**deur,** outer door; ~**diens,** *see* **buitekerk;** ~**distrik,** outlying district; country district; ~**dyk,** outer dike; ~**-egtelik, (-e),** extra-marital; illegitimate, bastard, out of wedlock; illicit, natural; ~**-egtelike verhouding,** extra-marital affair; ~**flank,** outer flank; ~**gebou,** out-building, outhouse; ~**gebruik,** off-consumption; ~**gedeelte,** outer part; ~**gereg'telik, (-e),** extrajudicial; ~**geveggestelde, (-s),** casualty; ~**grens,** outside boundary; ~**hawe,** outer port, outport; ~**hek,** outer gate; ~**hoek,** exterior angle; outer corner, quion; ~**huid,** outer skin; ~**-inkomste,** extra income; ~**-inspekteur,** outdoor inspector; ~**kaliber,** external gauge; ~**kamer,** outside room; ~**kans(ie),** godsend, unexpected advantage, windfall; ~**kant,** (s) outside, exterior; perimeter; (bw) outside, out of doors: out of, beyond; abroad; extrinsic; *loop speel* ~, go and play outside; (vs) outside, beyond; ~**kants(t)e, (s)** outside (surface); (b) outside, outermost; external; ~**kerk,** church service in the country; ~**klub,** country club; ~ **kors,** outer crust.

bui'tel, (ge-), tumble, fall head over heels.

bui'telaag, outer layer.

bui'telaar, tumbler.

bui'telaer, outer bearing.

bui'teland, foreign country; foreign parts; *IN die* ~, abroad; *NA die* ~ *gaan,* go abroad; ~**er, (-s),** foreigner; ~**s, (-e),** foreign; exotic; abroad; *MINISTER van B* ~ *se Sake,* Minister of Foreign Affairs; *'n* ~ *se REIS,* a journey abroad; ~ *se VOERTUIG,* foreign vehicle.

bui'te: ~**leerling,** day scholar; country scholar; ~**leisel,** outside rein; ~**lewe,** country life; outdoor life; ~**lid,** country member.

bui'teling, somersault, flip-flap.

buite: ~**linie,** exterior line (troops); ~**linkervleuel,** outside left (wing); ~**lisensie,** off-sales licence; ~**lug,** open air; country air; ~**lugskool,** open-air school; ~**lugteater,** open-air theatre; ~**lyn,** touch-line (rugby); perimeter; profile (face); outer boundary; ~**maat,** outsize; outside measurement; ~**mag'tig, (-e),** ultra vires; ~**man,** country dweller, outsider; ~**mars,** route march; ~**mate,** beyond measure, exceedingly, extremely; ~**ma'tig (-e),** excessive, extremely; ~**mense,** country people; ~**middellyn,** over-all diameter; ~**muur,** outer wall; ~**muurs, (-e),** extramural.

bui'ten, besides, except; beyond; save; other than; ~ *en BEHALWE,* over and above; *ek GAAN nie,* ~ *as jy belowe,* I won't go unless you promise; ~ *HOOP,* too far gone, past recovery, beyond hope.

bui'tenaatskoen, welted shoe.

bui'ten: ~**dien',** moreover, besides; in addition to; farther, further, furthermore; ~**egtelik, (-e),** *see* **buite-egtelik;** ~**gemeen, (..mene),** unusual, uncommon; ~**geveggestelde, (-s),** casualty; ~**gewoon, (..wone),** extraordinary, peculiar, phenomenal, out of the common, extra; exceedingly, exceptionally, exquisite; awful.

buitenis'sig, (-e), out of the common, eccentric; ~**heid, (..hede),** thing out of the commmon, fad, eccentricity.

bui'tensdeur, (-e), outdoor.

bui'tenshuis, (b) (-e), outdoor; ~*e werk,* work away from home; (bw) out of doors.

buitenshui'sig, (-e), outdoor; ~*e mense,* outdoor people.

bui'tenslands, abroad.

buitenspo'rig, (-e), extravagant, excessive, immoderate, intemperate, exorbitant; dissipated; ~*e PRYS,* excessive charge, exorbitant price; ~*e SLYTASIE,* excessive wear; ~*e SNELHEID (spoed),* excessive speed; ~**heid,** extravagance, excessiveness, excess, immoderation, exorbitance, extravaganza, rampancy.

bui'tenste, outermost, exterior, outer (darkness).

bui'tenstraat, (..strate), off-street; ~*se parkering,* off-street parking.

bui'ten(s)tyds, (-e), out of season; after hours.

bui'tentoe, outwards, outside; *iem. gaan* ~, someone goes outside (into the open).

bui'teom, round the outside; ~ *loop,* go round the outside way (on the outside).

bui'teonderwyser, country teacher.

bui'teoogvlies, sclera.

bui'teoor, outer ear.

bui'te: ~ **op,** on the outside of; ~**pad,** farm road; outside road; ~**parogie,** out-parish; ~**party,** alfresco party; outsider; ~**pasiënt,** outpatient; ~**passer,** outside calipers; ~**perd,** outsider; outrunner (horse); *'n* ~ *perd het die wedren gewen,* an outsider won the race; ~**personeel,** outside (field) staff; ~**plaas,** country seat; outlying farm; ~**portaal,** porch; ~**pos,** outpost, outstation, picket.

bui'ter, (-s), pillager, looter.

buite: ~**rand,** outer edge; ~**rem,** external brake; ~**ring,** outer race (ball bearing).

bui'tery¹, outside row.

bui'tery², looting, robbing, plundering.

bui'te: ~**sak,** outside pocket; ~**seisoen,** off-season; out of season; ~**silinder,** outside cylinder; ~**skil,** outer rind; ~**skool,** country school; ~**skop, (s)** touch kick; (w) **(-ge-),** kick out, find touch; eject; ~**sluit, (-ge-),** exclude, shut out, lock out; eject; ~**sluiting,** locking out, exclusion; ~**spel,** wing play; ~**spieël,** outside mirror; ~**staander, (-s),** outsider; ~**stasie,** outstation; ~**stedelik, (-e),** peri-urban; ~**steen,** face-brick; ~**straat,** outer street; ~**stut,** outside buttress; ~**sy,** outer side; exterior (side); ~**trap,** outside staircase; ~**veld,** outlying veld; outfield (cricket); ~**verblyf,** country seat (res-

buitjie   99   *busseltjie*

idence), chateau; ~**verbruik,** off-consumption; ~**verkoop,** off-sales; ~**vlies,** outer membrane; ~**voorspeler,** wing forward; ~**vriend,** country friend; ~**vuurmasjien,** externally-fired engine; ~**waarts, (-e),** outward(s); ~**wand,** outer wall; ~**wêreld,** outer world, outside world; ~**werk,** outside work; outdoor work; fieldwork; ~**werke,** outworks; ~**werkingstelling,** putting out of operation; lapse (of Act); ~**werp, (-ge-),** cast out; ~**wetlik, (-e),** illegal; ~**winkel,** country store; ~**wyk,** country district, outlying part, outskirts, purlieus.

bui′tjie, (-s), small (light) shower.

buit′maak, (-ge-), seize, capture, confiscate, carry off; ..**maker,** captor.

buit: ~**stelsel,** spoils system; ~**verdeling,** division of booty; melon-cutting.

buk, (ge-), stoop, bend, bow; *ge*~ *gaan onder,* be bowed (weighed) down by.

buko′lies, (-e), bucolic.

buks, (-e), buk′sie, (-s), saloon rifle, carbine; small person, dwarf, chit, slip.

buks: ~**boom,** boxtree; ~**hout,** boxwood.

buks′spyker, stub nail.

bul¹, (-le), (papal) bull; diploma.

bul², (-le), bull; thumper, whopper, corker; *die B*~ *(Stier),* Taurus; *soos 'n* ~ *in 'n GLA(A)SHUIS,* like a bull in a china shop; *die* ~ *by die HORINGS pak,* take the bull by the horns; tackle a difficult task bravely; *gaan kyk waar die* ~ *die KOEI gestoot het,* go to stool; *hy IS 'n* ~, he is a ripper; *die KOEI het* ~ *gevat,* the cow has been served; *OU* ~*!, old top! good for you! die* ~ *aan die STERT hê,* be like a bear with a sore head; *nou is dit* ~ *TEEN* ~, when Greek meets Greek, then comes the tug of war.

bulbêr′, (-e), bulbar.

bul′byter, bulldog, mastiff.

bul′der, (ge-), roar, boom; bellow; rage; ~**end, (-e),** roaring; booming; raging; ~**lag,** roar(ing) laugh, bellowing laugh.

Bulgaar′, (..gare), Bulgarian, bulgar; ~**s′, (-e),** Bulgarian.

Bulgary′e, Bulgaria.

bul: ~**geveg,** bullfight; ~**hond,** bulldog.

bulk, (ge-), low, bellow, moo; blare; break wind.

bul′kalf, bull-calf.

bul′kend, (-e), blatant; bellowing.

bulla′rium, (..ria), bullary (collection of papal bulls).

bul′lebak, surly person, bully; ruffian; hoodlum (Amer.); ~**kery,** bullying.

bulletin′, (-s), notice bulletin.

bul′letou, guy (of boom).

bulletyn′, (-e) = **bulletin.**

bul′perd, a great one, stunner, champion, first-rater, out-and-outer.

buls, on heat (cow).

bul′sak, feather-bed, bolster.

bult, (s) (-e), hill(ock), ridge, rising ground, hummock, boss, gibbosity, knoll; height; bulge; hunch, hump (on back); knob, knobble, protuberance, prominence, lump; node; *net AGTER die* ~, just round the corner; *ons is AMPER oor die* ~, the worst is nearly over; (w) **(ge-),** dent, indent; bulge; ~**agtig, (-e),** bumpy, lumpy; hilly; ~**enaar, (-s),** hunchback.

bul′tergery, bull-baiting.

bult: ~**erig, (-e),** uneven, hilly; bossy, gibbous; hummocky, humpy, knobbly; ~**eveld,** hilly country; ~**igheid,** unevenness; gibbosity; ~**jie, (-s),** hillock, monticle, monticule; ~**klopper,** panelbeater; ~**terrein,** ~**werf,** hump yard (railway).

bul′vegter, toreador.

bun′del, (s) (-s), volume (verse); fascicle (bot.); (w) **(ge-),** publish in book form; collect in a volume; ~**sgewys(e),** fascicular; ~**tjie, (-s),** small volume; fascicle.

bun′du, bundu.

bun′ker, (s) (-s) bunker; mill bin; (w) **(ge-),** bunker; ~**doeleindes,** bunkering; ~**kole,** bunker coal.

bun′senbrander, Bunsen burner.

bu′regerug, breach of the peace, disturbance.

buret′, (-te), measuring glass, burette.

burg¹, (-e, -te), castle, acropolis, citadel.

burg², (-e), castrated boar, hog, barrow.

bur′gemeester, mayor; burgomaster; ~**es′, (-se),** (lady) mayor; ~**lik, (-e),** mayoral.

bur′gemeesters: ~**amp,** office of mayor, mayoralty; ~**buik,** corporation; ~**dame,** mayoress; ~**kamer,** mayor's parlour.

bur′gemeesterskap, mayoralty.

bur′gemeestersketting, mayoral chain.

Bur′gemeestersondag, mayoral Sunday.

bur′gemeesters: ~**onthaal,** mayoral reception; ~**ontvangskamer,** mayor's parlour; ~**vrou,** mayoress.

bur′ger, (-s), citizen, civilian, burgess; burgher; commoner; plebian; (mv) nationals; ~**afkoms,** middle-class descent; ~**bandradio,** citizen band radio; ~ *e BESKERMING,* civil defence; ~**bevolking,** civilian population; ~**deug, (-de),** civic virtue; ~**drag,** mufti, civilian clothes, civvies; ~**es′, (-se),** citizeness; ~**klas,** middle class; ~**klere,** civilian clothes, civvies; *in* ~*klere,* in plain clothes, in mufti; ~**kryg,** civil war; ~**kunde,** civics; ~**leer,** civics; ~**lewe,** ordinary life.

bur′gerlik, (-e), civil, civilian; middle class, bourgeois, plebian; ~ *e BESKERMING,* civil protection (defence); ~ *e GESAG,* civic authorities; ~ *e REG,* civil law; municipal law; ~ *e VERDEDIGING,* civil defence; ~ *e WETBOEK,* civil code.

bur′ger: ~**lugvaart,** civil(ian) aviation: ~**lugvaartraad,** civil aviation board; ~**lugvaartskool,** civil aviation school; ~**mag,** defence force; armed civilians; militia; ~**moord,** murder of citizens; ~**oorlog,** civil war; domestic war; ~**oproer,** civil tumult (riot); ~**owerheid,** civil authority; ~**plig,** civic duty.

bur′gerreg, right of citizenship, civic right(s), freedom (city); burgher-right; ~ *VERKRY,* have become accepted; *die* ~ *VERLEEN aan,* enfranchize; admit to freedom (of city); *die WOORD het* ~ *gekry,* that word has been adopted into the language; ~**crf,** burgher-right plot.

bur′ger: ~**regering,** democracy, civil government; ~**sentrum,** civic centre; ~**sin,** civil (public) spirit; ~**skap,** citizenship; ~**stand,** middle class, bourgeoisie; ~**trots,** civic pride; ~**trou,** civil loyalty; ~**twis,** civil strife; ~**vliegwese,** civil aviation; ~**wag,** guard of citizens; civic guard; ~**y′,** citizens; commonage, citizenry.

burg′graaf, viscount; ..**gravin,** viscountess.

burg′heer, castellan.

burg′vark, hog.

burg: ~**voog,** castellan; ~**vrou,** chatelaine; ~**wal,** castle-moat.

burin′, (-ne) = **buurvrou.**

burlesk′, (s) (-e), burlesque; (b) **(-e),** ludicrous, burlesque.

buro′, (-'s), office; desk; bureau; *B* ~ *vir Standaarde,* Bureau of Standards; ~**kraat, (..krate),** bureaucrat, red-tapist; ~**krasie′,** red tape, red-tapism, bureaucracy, officialdom; ~**kra′ties, (-e),** bureaucratic, red-tapey.

bursi′tis, (med.), bursitis, housemaid's knee.

buryn′, (-e), graver, burin.

bus¹, (s) (-se), box, bin, tin; drum (in mines); bearing; bush(ing) (wheel); socket; *so GESLOTE soos 'n* ~, as close as an oyster; *die* ~ *LIG,* collect the letters; *SLUIT soos 'n* ~, fit perfectly, fall into place; *sy* ~ *is UITGEBRAND,* he is done for; (w) **(ge-),** bush (a wheel).

bus², (-se), (omni)bus; ~**bestuurder,** bus driver; ~**boor,** bow drill; ~**diens,** bus service; ~**geld,** bus fare; ~**halte,** bus stop; ~**huisie,** bus shelter; ~**kaartjie,** bus ticket; ~**kondukteur,** bus conductor.

bus′kruit, gunpowder; *hy het nie die* ~ *uitgevind nie,* he will not set the Thames on fire; he is not very clever; ~**fabriek,** powder works.

bus′ligting, clearance (of pillar-boxes), collection (of letters).

bus: ~**loods,** bus shed; ~**maatskappy,** bus company; ~**motor,** station-wagon; ~**passasier,** bus passenger.

bus′seltjie, (-s), bustle (pad for skirt).

bus: ~sie, (-s), castor; ~skroef, hollow screw.
bus: ~trek, (bus) stage; ~verkeer, bus traffic.
butirien', butiri'ne, butyrin.
buur, (ong.), **(bure),** neighbour; *dis jammer dat jou bure nie tuis is nie,* self-praise is no recommendation; ~**dorp,** neighbouring town; ~**kind,** neighbour's child.
buur'man, (bure), neighbour; *'n goeie ~ is beter as 'n BROER wat ver is,* we can live without our friends, but not without our neigbours; *as dit by my ~ reën, val die DRUPPELS ook op my,* your neighbour's good fortune is also yours; *alte GOED is ~ sgek,* all lay the load on the willing horse; *moenie dat jou ~ se HONDE vir jou blaf nie,* don't haunt your neighbour's doorstep; *as jou ~ se HUIS aan brand is, moet jy op jou eie pas,* when thy neighbour's house doth burn then look to your own; *beter 'n goeie ~ as 'n verre VRIEND,* we can live without our friends but not without our neighbours.
buur: ~**praatjie,** neighbourly talk, gossip; ~**skap,** neighbourliness, neighbourly intercourse.
buurt, (-e), buur'te, (-s), neighbourhood, quarter, vicinity; *in die ~ van,* approximately.
buur'vrou, (-e, -ens), neighbour's wife; female neighbour.
buus'te, (-s), bust; ~**houer, (-s),** bra(ssière), bust-bodice; bust-sculptor; ~**lyfie,** bust-bodice, brassière; ~**maat,** size of bust.
by¹, (s) **(-e),** bee; *die ~ wat lekker HEUNING maak, steek seer,* the prettiest girls break the most hearts; bees that have honey on their mouths, have stings in their tails; *waar die ~ sy HEUNING uitsuig, suig die spinnekop sy gif uit; so tussen die ~ en die KOEK,* betwixt and between; *tussen die ~ e, maar nog nie by die KOEKIE nie,* so near and yet so far.
by², (bw) present, there; *waar EK ~ was,* in my presence; *sy is NOG nie ~ nie,* she has not come round (to) yet; *goed ~ WEES in geskiedenis,* be well-read in history; *~ WEES met jou boeke,* be up to date with one's books.
by³, (vs), at, near, by, with; *~ sy AANKOMS,* on his arrival; *~ sy AFWESIGHEID,* in his absence; *iem. ~ sy BELOFTE hou,* keep someone to his promise; *~ DAG en ~ nag,* by day and by night; *DAG ~ dag erger word,* get worse day by day; *~ sy DOOD,* at his death; *~ jou HÊ,* have with (on) one; *~ HONDERDE,* by the hundred; *~ die HUIS,* at home; *~ al sy KENNIS,* with all his knowledge; *~ KERSLIG,* by candlelight; *~ die LEËR aansluit,* join the army; *~ die LEES,* when reading, at the reading; *~ sy LEWE,* during his life; *~ haar MOEDER,* with her mother; *~ ONTVANGS,* on receipt; *die partye ~ 'n OOREENKOMS,* the parties to an agreement; *~ al sy RYKDOM is hy ongelukkig,* notwithstanding all his money he is unhappy; *die SLAG ~ Colenso,* the battle of Colenso; *~ 'n koppie TEE,* over a cup of tea; *so ~ TIENUUR,* about ten o'clock; *~ TYE,* at times.
by'angel, sting, bee-sting.
by'as, secondary axis.
by'baantjie, side line; extra work.
by'bedoeling, side purpose, ulterior aim; *~ e hê,* have an axe to grind.
by'bedryf, side-line; subsidiary business.
by'behoorsels = **bybehorens.**
by'behore, (-ns, -s), attachments, accessories, appurtenances, accompaniment; garniture; garniture; ~**nd, (-e),** belonging to, corresponding, accessional to, matching; accessory.
By'bel, (-s), Bible; *sy ~ vir 'n ALMANAK verruil,* exchange better for worse; *met die ~ onder die ARM loop,* be a holy Joe; *die ~ met 52 BLAAIE,* a pack of cards; *hy loop met die ~ in sy MOND,* he is always quoting scripture; ~**genootskap,** Bible society; ~**kennis,** scriptural knowledge; ~**kritiek,** criticism of the Bible; higher criticism; ~**lande,** biblical lands; ~**leer,** scriptural doctrine; ~**leser,** Bible reader; ~**lesing,** Bible reading; ~**onderrig,** instruction in the Scriptures; ~**s (-e),** biblical, scriptural; ~**spreuk,** scriptural maxim; ~**studie,** Bible study; ~**styl,** biblical style; ~**taal,** biblical language; ~**teks, (-te),** text from Scripture; ~**uit-**
lêer, exegete; ~**uitlegging,** exegesis; ~**vas, (-te),** well-read in (conversant with) the Bible; ~**verhaal,** biblical narrative; ~**verklaarder,** exegete, interpreter of the Bible; ~**verklaring,** exegesis; ~**verspreiding,** distribution of the Bible; ~**vertaling,** Bible translation; ~**woord,** Scriptural word.
by'benodigdhede, accessories.
by'bestel, (~), order in addition.
by'betaal, (~), pay in addition, pay extra.
by'betaling, excess fare, extra payment.
by'betekenis, secondary (additional) meaning, implication, connotation.
by'bie, (-s), "baby" (diggings).
by'blad, (byblaaie), supplement (of newspaper).
by'bly, (-ge-), keep pace with (the times); be able to follow (a speaker); remember; stick to.
by'boek, (s) subsidiary book; **(w) (-ge-),** book up to date, write up, enter.
by'boerdery, (farming) side-line.
by'breek, leg break; ~**bouler,** leg-break bowler.
by'bring, (-ge-), bring forward (evidence); collate; adduce; afford; bring round, restore to consciousness; instill (ideas); *'n mens kan HOM dit nie ~ nie,* one can not make him understand it; *ons kan dit NIE ~ nie,* we cannot afford it; *hulle kon hom nie WEER ~ nie,* they could not bring him to (round) again.
by'dam, (-ge-), accost, approach (with a request); tackle.
byderhand', close by, near, at hand; smart, quick-witted; handy.
byderwets', (-e), with it, in tune.
by'diens, (-te), accessory service.
by'dra, (-ge-), contribute; club; be instrumental in, aid.
by'draad, auxiliary wire.
by'draai, (-ge-), come round; heave to (ship); gradually give in (fig.).
by'drae, (-s), contribution, subscription; *'n ~ lewer tot,* make a contribution to; contribute; ~**nd, (-e),** contributory, contributive; ~**r, (-s),** contributor; ~**tjie, (-s),** small contribution.
by'druk, (s) surcharge; **(w) (-ge-),** print in addition.
by'e: ~**angel,** sting of a bee; ~**boer,** apiarist, hiver; ~**boerdery,** apiculture, bee-farming, bee-keeping; ~**brood,** bee-bread, cerago.
byeen', together.
byeen'behoort, (~), see **byeen'hoort.**
byeen'bring, (-ge-), collect, gather; club; ~**ing,** rally.
byeen'hoort, belong together.
byeen'kom, (-ge-), meet, gather, assemble; convene; ~**s, (-te),** gathering, meeting, chapel, assembly, assemblage, meet, rally, conference, bee (for spelling or sewing).
byeen'roep, (-ge-), call together, convene, assemble; ~**ende KENNISGEWING,** notice convening a meeting; ~**ing,** convocation.
byeen'samel, (-ge-), collect, gather.
byeen'skraap, (-ge-), scrape together.
byeen'trek, (-ge-), adduct, bring together.
byeen'voeg, (-ge-), join, unite, fit (together).
by'e: ~**houer,** apiculturist; ~**hok,** ~**huis,** apiary; ~**kas, (-te),** beehive; ~**kolonie,** colony of bees; ~**koningin,** queen bee; ~**korf,** beehive; ~**korfoond,** beehive oven; ~**korfvormig, (-e),** beehive-shaped; ~**kos,** bee-bread; ~**nes,** beehive; ~**sel,** bee cell; ~**stal,** apiary; ~**steek,** bee-sting; ~**swerm,** hive, swarm (bees); ~**teelt,** bee culture, apiculture; ~**vanger,** bee-pirate; ~**vreter,** bee-eater; ~**was,** ~**werk,** propolis, (bees)wax; ~**werkpleister,** beeswax plaster, plaster of bee glue.
by'faktor, additional (subsidiary) factor.
by'figuur, minor character (in a novel); secondary figure (in a drawing).
by'gaande, accompanying, enclosed (cheque); annexed; ~ **minerale,** associated minerals.
by'gebou, annex(e), outhouse.
by'gedagte, by-thought, afterthought.
by'geloof, superstition.
by'gelowig, (-e), superstitious, bigoted; ~**heid,** superstitiousness, bigotry.
by'geluid, by-tone, secondary sound.
by'genaamd, nicknamed; surnamed.

by'gereg, side-dish.
by'geur, off-flavour.
by'geval, in case, if by any chance.
by'gevoeg, (-de), additional, appendant, adscititious; adjunct.
by'gevolg, consequently, in consequence, therefore, hence, ergo, accordingly.
by'gewig, additional weight; rider weight.
by'gooi, (-ge-), add (by pouring, by throwing).
by'groei, (-ge-), grow to.
by'haal, (-ge-), bring (drag) in; bring near.
by'heffing, surtax.
by'hou, (-ge-), keep up with, keep pace with; post; enter, keep up to date (books); *ek kan nie meer ~ nie*, I cannot cope with things anymore.
by'huur, (-ge-), hire in addition.
by'ja(ag), (-ge-), drive to(gether).
by'kaart, inset map.
by'kans, nearly, almost; *~ al die lede was teenwoordig*, nearly all the members were present.
by'kant, leg-side, on-side (cricket); *~ dryfhou*, on-side drive.
by'kantoor, branch office, sub-office.
by'kelk, epicalyx.
by'kies, (-ge-), choose in addition.
by'klank, secondary sound; *~ e*, sound effects.
by'knip, (-ge-), trim (hair).
by'knop, adventitious bud.
by'kom, (-ge-), come up with; revive, recover, regain (consciousness); reach, rally, get at; gain weight; be added; *as EK hom ~!*, when I get hold of him!; *daar kom NOG by dat*, and besides (this); *daar KAN hy nie ~ nie*, he cannot afford that; *nou KOM dit ook nog by*, this is the last straw.
by'kombuis, scullery.
by'komeling, (-e), newcomer.
by'komend, (-e), additional, incidental (expenses), accessional; minor; adventitious; extrinsic; supporting; *~ e AARD*, accessory nature; *~ e NALATIGHEID*, contributory negligence; *~ e OMSTANDIGHEDE*, attendant circumstances.
bykom'stig, (-e), accessory, minor, incidental; circumstantial; adventitious; episodic(al); collateral (security); *~ e loot*, epicormic shoot; *~ heid, (..hede)*, mere accident (incident); non-essential matter; accessory.
by'koop, (-ge-), buy in addition.
by'kos, side dish.
by'koste, incidental expenses.
by'kroon, corona (bot.)
by'kry, (-ge-), add, get in addition; bring to (after fainting), revive (a patient).
by'kweek, (-ge-), cultivate in addition.
byl, (-e), axe, hatchet, chopper; *met die growwe ~ KAP*, mangle; apply the axe; be living as lords; *~ e van TANDE*, large (front) teeth; *die ~ lê ook al teen die WORTEL*, the axe is about to fall; *die ~ aan die WORTELS lê*, lay the axe to the roots.
hy'lae, (-s), appendix, supplement, enclosure, accompanying paper (document), annexure, addendum, inset, schedule.
bylan'dig, (-e), near-shore.
bylang'e: *~ na nie*, not by a long way.
by'las, (-ge-), add, append.
byl: *~ brief*, mortgage of ship; *~ bundel*, fasces, *~ draer*, lictor.
by'lê, (-ge-), lay (additional egg); reconcile, compose, settle (differences); bury
by'legging, settlement (of quarrel).
byl: *~ kop*, axe-head; *~ neus*, aquiline nose.
by'loslopie, leg-bye.
byl: *~ pik*, mattock; *~ slag*, axe-stroke; *~ snee*, axe bit; *~ steel*, axe handle; *~ steen*, jade; *~ tjie, (-s)*, little axe, chopper; *die ~ tjie BEGRAWE*, bury the hatchet; *die ~ tjie daarby NEERLÊ*, throw up the sponge; leave it there; *~ vormig, (-e)*, axe-shaped; securiform.
by'lyn, (telephone) extension; extension line.
by'maak, (-ge-), make in addition.
by'maan, mock (second) moon, paraselene.
bymekaar', together.
bymekaar'behoort, (~), belong together.

bymekaar'bly, (-ge-), remain (stay) together.
bymekaar'bring, (-ge-), bring together, collect (money); gather; raise (army).
bymekaar'dryf, ..drywe, (-ge-), drive together.
bymekaar'flans, (-ge-), quilt; patch up, rig up.
bymekaar'gooi, (-ge-), throw together; match.
bymekaar'hang, (-ge-), hang together.
bymekaar'hou, (-ge-), keep together; *jou positiewe ~*, keep one's head, keep your wits about you.
bymekaar'jaag, (-ge-), drive together, round up.
bymekaar'keer, (-ge-), round up.
bymekaar'kom, (-ge-), come together, congregate, foregather, meet; *~ plek*, meeting-place; rendezvous, trysting place, venue; junction (of rivers); *~ slag*, (occasion) of meeting.
bymekaar'kry, (-ge-), get together.
bymekaar'lê, (-ge-), lie together.
bymekaar'maak, (-ge-), collect; compile; glean; save (money); round up (cattle); assemble (people); amass (riches).
bymekaar'raap, (-ge-), scrape together.
bymekaar'reken, (-ge-), add up, tot up.
bymekaar'roep, (-ge-), call together, convene (meeting).
bymekaar'sit, (-ge-), sit together; put together; assemble (machine).
bymekaar'skraap, (-ge-), scrape (scratch, rake) together.
bymekaar'slaan, (-ge-), compile (runs).
bymekaar'smyt, (-ge-), throw together, chuck together.
bymekaar'soek, (-ge-), gather, collect.
bymekaar'speld(e), (-ge-), pin together.
bymekaar'staan, (-ge-), stand together, join issue; unite forces.
bymekaar'sukkel, (-ge-), collect, round up (with difficulty).
bymekaar'tel, (-ge-), add together, count up.
bymekaar'trek, (-ge-), add together total; concentrate (troops), contract.
bymekaar'voeg, (-ge-), join together, unite; *~ ing*, joining.
bymekaar'woon, (-ge-), live together.
by'meng, (-ge-), mix with; *~ ing*, admixture; *~ sel*, admixture.
by'middel, additive.
by'mot, bee-moth *(Acherontia atropos)*.
by'motief, ulterior aim.
by'na, nearly, almost, full nigh; *nog ~ 'n KIND*, little more than a child; *~ NIKS*, next to nothing; *~ NOOIT*, hardly ever.
by'naam, nickname; agnomen, cognomen, epithet, sobriquet.
by'nes, beehive.
by'nier, adrenal gland (body); suprarenal gland; *~ stof*, adrenaline.
hy'omstandigheid, necessary circumstance.
by'oogmerk, side purpose, private end; ulterior motive; *'n ~ he*, have an axe to grind.
by'oorsaak, secondary cause, incidental cause.
by'paaltjie, leg-stump.
by'pad, by-road.
by'pas, (-ge-), add; pay the difference, make up; *vader sal die GELD ~*, father will pay the rest; *ROK met ~ sende hoed*, dress with hat to match; *~ sing*, contingent; *~ singstoelae*, contingent allowance.
by'planeet, satellite.
by'portret, inset (photo).
by'poskantoor, subpostoffice.
by'produk, by-product.
by'rat, laygear.
by'reken, (-ge-), add in, include, reckon in.
by'rivier, tributary.
by'roep, (-ge-), call in (for assistance).
by'rol, supporting part.
by'saaier, share-cropper.
by'saak, side issue, secondary matter, matter of minor importance, mere detail; *geld is ~*, money is no object.
by'saal, minor hall; hall annex(e).
by'sê, (-ge-), say in addition; *bygesê as*, provided (that), not forgetting (that).

bysien'de, short-sighted, near-sighted, myopic, beetle-eyed, moon-eyed, purblind.
bysiend'heid, short-sightedness, near-sightedness, purblindness, myopia, myopy.
by'sin, dependent (subordinate) clause.
by'sirkel, epicycle.
by'sit¹, (s) (-te), concubine, paramour, mistress; courtesan.
by'sit², (w) (-ge-), place (put) near; deposit (money); inter (corpse); help; add (money); *hand* ~, give (lend) a hand.
by'sit³, (-ge-), sit near; *ek het bygesit toe hy beswyk,* I was looking on (sat next to him) when he died.
by'skaduwee, penumbra.
by'skerm, cyme (bot.).
by'skilder, (-ge-), paint in, touch up.
by'skildklier, parathyroid (gland).
by'skink, (-ge-), pour in more; add, fill up.
by'skrif, inscription (tombstone); caption, subtitle (films); legend (charts); postscript; device, motto (shield); letterpress.
by'skryf, (-ge-), add something (in writing); bring up to date.
by'skuif, (-ge-), push nearer; pull (draw) up (one's chair).
by'slaap, bed-fellow; copulation, coition.
by'slag, leg-hit; excess charge; allowance.
by'sleep, (-ge-), drag in (to), lug in.
by'smaak, after-taste, peculiar (off) flavour; tang (of sea air); taint (in food); tinge (figuratively); ~ *wekkende EIENSKAPPE,* taint-producing properties; *OPPERVLAKKIGE* ~, toppiness (in butter).
by'smyt, (-ge-), throw in with.
by'sny, (-ge-), trim.
by'son, parhelion, mock sun.
by'speler, supporting actor.
by'spier, accessory muscle.
by'spring, (-ge-), help, assist, lend a hand; attack.
by'staan, (-ge-), assist, help, abet, succour, back up; stand near.
by'stand, assistance, help, support, abetment, aid; ~ *verleen,* render (lend) assistance; ~ **er,** bystander, spectator; stand-by; ~ **sfonds,** benefit-fund; ~ **sraad,** board of aid.
by'steek, bee-sting.
by'ster: *nie* ~ *GELUKKIG nie,* not very (particularly) happy.
by'stort, (-ge-), make additional payment; ~ **ing,** (-s, -e), additional payment.
by'stroom, tributary.
by'stuur, (-ge-), send in addition.
by'syn, presence; *in die* ~ *van,* in the presence of.
byt, (s) (-e), bite, nip; chunk; champ; (w) (ge-), bite, nip, snap at; burn (on the tongue); *na 'n MENS* ~, snap at a person; *NET* ~ *aan iets,* nibble at something; *PERDE* ~ *op die stang,* horses champ the bit; *in die STOF* ~, bite the dust; *op jou TANDE* ~, clench one's teeth; be very determined; *WAT het jou gebyt?* what has bitten you?; *hy WOU nie* ~ *nie,* he would not bite; ~ **alkali,** caustic alkali.
byt'-byt: *net* ~ *aan iets,* nibble at something.

by'teken, accidental (mus.).
by'tel, (-ge-), count in, include.
by'tend, (-e), biting, caustic, poignant; pyrotic, corrosive, cutting; morodacious, mordant; pungent; nippy; nipping; trenchant; ~ *e soda,* caustic soda; ~ **heid,** mordacity, trenchancy, pungency.
by'ter, (-s), biter; tooth; blenny (fish); ~ **ig,** (-e), pugnacious; biting; snappish.
byt: ~ **gif,** (..giwwe), corrosive poison; ~ **ig,** (-e), keen; ~ **kalk,** quicklime; ~ **middel,** corrosive, mordant, caustic.
by'toon, subsidiary (secondary) tone, by-tone.
byt'potas, caustic potash.
by'trek, (-ge-), drag (person) in; attack; pull up (nearer) (chair); ~ **spier,** adductor.
byt: ~ **ring,** teething ring; ~ **soda,** caustic soda; ~ **suur,** corrosive acid; ~ **vermoë,** corrosive power; ~ **wond,** wound caused by biting.
by'vak, minor (secondary, subsidiary) subject.
by'val, (s) applause, acclamation, approval, approbation; *GEEN* ~ *vind nie,* fall flat; *groot* ~ *VIND,* meet with general approval; (w) (-ge-), remember, call to mind; recur, occur; *dit val my nou by,* I remember, it just occurs to me now; ~ **sbetuiging,** mark of approbation, applause.
by'vanger, (-s), drongo.
by'verdienste, side-line, extra earnings; perquisite.
by'vergadering, overflow-meeting.
by'vertoning, side-show.
by'voeding, supplementary feeding (livestock).
by'voeg, (-ge-), add, annex, append; compliment; ~ **ing,** (-e, -s), addition; apposition; ~ **'lik,** (-e), adjectival; ~ *like naamwoord,* adjective; ~ **sel,** (-s), supplement, appendix, complement, epithet, appendage, addition, adjunct; inset; ~ *sel tot,* supplement to.
by'voer, additive.
by'voetwol, moxa (med.).
byvoor'beeld, for example, for instance.
by'voordele, fringe benefits, perquisites, perks.
by'vorm, additional (subsidiary) form.
by'vreter, bee-eater.
by'vrou, concubine, mistress.
by'vul, (-ge-), add by filling, top up.
by'was, beeswax.
by'werk¹, propolis, bee-glue.
by'werk², (s) work of minor importance; (w) (-ge-), work up (a picture); bring up to date (books); retouch; ~ **ing,** retouching.
by'woner, sub-farmer, bywoner; squatter; *êrens* ~ *wees,* not have much influence somewhere; peasant type of farmer.
by'woning, attendance; ~ **sregister,** attendance register.
by'woon, (-ge-), be present at, attend; witness.
by'woord, adverb.
bywoor'delik, (-e), adverbial.
by'wortel, adventitious root.
by'wyf, (bywywe), concubine, mistress.
bywy'le, sometimes, off and on, now and then, occasionally.

C

c, (-'s), c; sent; *C drie,* C₃.
cachalot' (-te), cachalot, sperm whale; = **kasjelot.**
cachet', (-te), seal, signet (on documents); cachet; stamp (of distinction); = **kasjet.**
cachou, cachou.
cactoblas'tis, cactoblastis.
cadeau', (-s), *see* **kado.**
caden'za, (It. mus.) (-s), cadenza.
Cae'sar, Caesar.
caesaris'me, Caesarism.
cae'saronkruid, caesar weed (*Urena lobata*).
caesa'ropapisme, caesaropapism, caesaropapacy.
café'-chantant, (-s), café-chantant.
café'-restaurant, restaurant, cafe.
cairn'gorm, cairngorm.
caisson', (-s), caisson.
calain', leaf lead.
calan'do, calando (music).
cal'culus, calculus.
calè'che, (-s), calash.
calde'ra, (-s), caldera.
Caledo'nië, Caledonia, Scotland.
Caledo'nies, (-e), Caledonian.
Cal'edonner, (-s), inhabitant of Caledon.
calembour', (-s), calembour, pun; ambiguous joke.

Calvinis', (-te), Calvinist; ~**me**, Calvinism; ~**ties**, (-e), Calvinistic(al).
Calvyn', Calvin.
camaril'la (Sp.) (-s), camarilla.
cambiaal'reg, law of bills of exchange.
ca'mera: in ~, in camera, in private, behind closed doors.
camoufla'ge, camouflage; = **kamoeflage**.
campani'le, (-s), campanile.
campeche'hout, campeachy wood, logwood.
canai'lle, canaille; ragtag and bob-tail.
cana'sta, canasta
cancan', (F.), cancan.
Canos'sa: *na* ~ *gaan*, go to Canossa; go on hands and knees.
can'yon, (-s), canyon.
ca'pita: *per* ~, per capita.
capri'ce, (-s), caprice (music); freak, whim; *see* **kaprise**.
carboli'neum, carbolineum (registered trade name).
Carbona'ri, Carbonari (Italian police).
carbone'um, carbon oxide.
carmagno'le, carmagnola, carmagnole (dance).
car'men, **(carmina)**, carmen, song.
carni'vora, carnivora, flesh-eaters.
carra'ramarmer, Carrara (marble).
carrie're, (-s), career; *'n* ~ *KIES*, choose a career; ~ *MAAK*, make a name for oneself.
car'ronolie, carron oil.
car'te blan'che, carte blanche, free hand; unconditional power.
Cartesiaans', (-e), Cartesian; ~*e duikertjie*, Cartesian devil (diver), bottle imp.
Carte'sies = **Cartesiaans**.
Carthaags', (-e), Carthaginian.
Cartha'ger, (-s), Carthaginian.
Cartha'go, Carthage.
casi'no, (-'s), casino.
castore'um, castoreum (used in medicine).
ca'sus, *casc* (grammar).
cataw'badruif, (..**druiwe**), Catawba grape.
cause célè'bre, cause célèbre, notorious court-case.
causerie', (-ë), causerie, talk.
causeur', conversationalist, causeur.
cau'tie, (-s), surety, bail, *die* ~ *is verbeur*, the bail is estreated.
cavati'na, (-s), cavatina, short air (music).
cayen'nepeper, cayenne pepper.
C'-dur, C major.
cedil'le, (-s), cedilla.
Cele'bes, Celebes.
celes'ta, celesta (mus.)
cel'slustermometer, centigrade (Celsius) thermometer.
centa'vo, (-'s), centavo.
centiem', (-s), centime.
cen'tumtaal, (..**tale**), centum language.
cen'tumvir, (-i, -s), centumvir; ~**aat'**, centumvirate.
Cer'berus, Cerberus, the Hound of Hell
cerebel'lum, cerebellum.
ce'rebrum, cerebrum.
Ce'res, Ceres.
cerise', cerise (colour).
Ceylon', (vero.), Ceylon; ~**ees'** (..**nese**), Ceylonese; **-s'**, Ceylonese.
chacon'ne, (-s), chaconne (mus.).
chalcedoon', (..**done**), chalcedony (gem).
chalkografic', chalcography.
chalkopiriet', chalcopyrite, copper pyrite(s).
Chalde'ër, (-s), Chaldean.
Chaldeeus', (-e), Chaldean.
chalet', (-s), Swiss cottage.
chambray', chambray.
champ'sodon, champsodon (fish).
chanson', (-s), chanson, song.
chanta'ge, chantage, blackmail.
chanteu'se, (-s), singer (lady).
cha'os, chaos.
chao'ties, (-e), chaotic.
chaperon', (-s), chaperon, duenna; ~**neer'**, (**ge-**), chaperon.
Chap'mansebra, (-s), Chapman's zebra

char-à-banc' = **janplesier**.
chara'de, (-s), charade.
chargé d'affai'res, chargé d'affaires.
charis'ma, -s, charisma.
chariva'ri (-'s), charivari, mock serenade; watch triket, charm.
charlatan', (-s), charlatan, mountebank, quack, humbug.
charmeur', (-s), charmer.
charmeu'se, (-s), (female) charmer; charmeuse (material).
Charol(l)ais', Charol(l)ais; ~ **beeste**, Charol(l)ais cattle; ~**teler**, Charol(l)ais breeder.
Cha'ron, Charon, Hell's ferryman (mythology).
char'ter, (s) (-s), charter; (w) (**ge-**), hire (ship), charter.
chartreuse', chartreuse (liquor).
Charyb'dis, Charybdis: *van* ~ *in Scilla val*, fall from the frying-pan into the fire.
chassis', chassis (motor-car); plate holder (camera).
chauffeur', (-s), chauffeur, (car) driver.
chauvinis', (-te), chauvinist, jingo; ~**me**, chauvinism; ~**ties**, (-e), chauvinistic.
ched'darkaas, Cheddar (cheese).
chef, (ong.) chief; (superior) officer; (departmental) head; principal; = **sjef**.
chemie', chemistry.
che'mies, (-e), chemical; ~**e plaagbeheer**, chemical pest control.
chemigrafie', chemigraphy.
chemika'lieë, chemicals, chemical preparations.
che'mikus, (..**mici**, -**se**), scientific chemist, analyst.
chemoterapie', chemotherapy.
chemurgie', chemurgy; **chemur'gies** (-e), chemurgic(al).
chenil'le, chenille.
chevron', (-s), strip (on arm of officer); chevron (heraldry).
chias'ma, chiasmus.
chic, chic, fashionable, stylish; = **sjiek**.
chica'ne, (-s), chicane, chicanery; sharp practice, litigation.
chiffon', chiffon.
chignon', (-s), chignon.
Chileen', (..**lene**), Chilean; ~**s'** (-e), Chilean,
Chi'li, Chili.
chilias', (-te), chiliast; ~**me**, chiliasm; ~**ties**, (-e), chiliastic.
chi'lisalpeter, Chili saltpetre.
chime'ra, (-s), chimera, idle fancy.
Chi'na, China; = **Sjina**.
chinchil'la, (-s), chinchilla (rabbit); ~**bont**, chinchilla (fur); ~**konyn**, chinchilla rabbit.
Chinees', (s, b) (..**nese**), Chinese; *Chinese tee*, China tea; = **Sjinees**.
chirograaf', (..**grawe**), chirograph.
chirologie', chirology, deaf-and-dumb alphabet.
chiromansie', chiromancy, palmistry.
chiropodic', chiropody.
chiropodis', (-te), chiropodist.
chiroprak'ties, (-e), chiropractic.
chiropraktisyn', (-s), chiropractor.
chiropraktyk', (-s), chiropractics.
chirurg' (-e), surgeon; ~**ie'**, surgery; ..**rur'gies** (-e), surgical.
chirurgyn', (-s), ship's doctor.
chitien', **chiti'ne**, chitin.
chloor, chlorine; ~**ammonium**, sal ammoniac; ~**dioksiedmengsel**, enchlorine; ~**etiel'**, ethylchloride; ~**goud**, gold chloride; ~**kalk**, chloride of lime, bleaching powder; ~**natrium**, sodium chloride, common salt; ~**stikstof**, bichloride of nitrogen; ~**suur**, chloric acid; ~**suursout**, chlorate; ~**waterstofsuur**, hydrochloric acid.
chloraal', chloral, chloral hydrate.
chloraat', (..**rate**), chlorate.
chloreer', (**ge-**), chlorinate.
chlori'de, (-s), **chloried**, (-e), chloride.
chloriet', chlorite; ~**lei**, chlorite slate.
chlo'rofil, chlorophyll.
chlo'roform, chloroform; ~**kap**, ~**masker**, chloroform mask.

chlorose

chloro'se, chlorosis, greensickness.
cho'lera, cholera; ~**basil**, cholera germ; ~**besmet=ting**, cholera infection; ~**epidemie**, cholera epidemic; ~**gordel**, cholera belt; ~**kiem**, comma bacillus; ~**lyer**, cholera patient.
cholerien', **choleri'ne**, cholerine, British cholera.
chole'ries, (-e), choleric, hasty, ill-tempered.
cholesterol', cholesterol.
choreograaf', (..grawe), choreographer.
choreografie', choreography.
choreogra'fies, (-e), choreographic(al).
chrestomatie', (-e), chrestomathy, anthology.
chris'ma, chrism, holy unction, consecrated ointment.
chrisoliet', chrysolite.
chri'soot, chrysote.
chrisopraas', chrysoprase (mineral).
chrisotipie', chrysotype.
Chris'telik, (-e), Christian (-like); *die* ~*e jaartelling*, the Christian era; ~**heid**, Christianity.
Chris'ten, (-e), Christian; ~**dom**, Christendom, Christianity; ~**heid**, Christianity, Christendom; ~**mens**, Christian (person); ~**siel**, Christian (soul).
Christin', (-ne), Christian (woman).
Christianiseer', (ge-), Christianize.
Chris'tosentries, (-e), Christocentric.
Chris'tus, Christ; *NA* ~, Anno Domini (A.D.); *VOOR* ~, before Christ (B.C.); ~**beeld**, image of Christ; crucifix; ~**doring**, Christ's thorn; ~**kind**, Christ-child; ~**kop**, head of Christ (painting).
chro'ma, chroma; colour.
chromaat'geel, chrome ochre.
chromatiek', chromatics.
chroma'ties, (-e), chromatic (colours; music); ~*e toonladder*, chromatic scale, semi-tonic scale.
chromatofoor', colour-bearer (physics).
chromatografie', chromatography.
chromatologie', chromatology.
chroma'tometer, **chromatome'ter**, chromatometer.
chromofotografie', chromophotography.
chromolitografie', chromolithography.
chromopsie', colour-blindness.
chromosfeer', chromosphere.
chromosoom', (..some), chromosome.
chromu'le, chromule.
chro'nies, (-e), chronic; ~*e siekte*, chronic disease.
chro'no: ~**fotografie'**, chronophotography; ~**graaf'**, (..grawe), chronograph; ~**grafie'**, chronography; ~**gram'**, chronogram; ~**logie'**, chronology; ~**lo'gies** (-e), chronological; ~**loog'**, (..loë), chronologist; ~**meter**, chronometer (navigation); ~**skoop'**, (..skope), chronoscope (astronomy).
chroom, chrome, chromium; ~**draend**, (-e), chromiferous; ~**geel**, *see* **chromaatgeel**; ~**leer**, chrome leather; ~**staal**, chrome steel; ~**suur**, chromic acid; ~**suursout**, chromate; ~**vernikkeling**, chromium plating; ~**ystersteen**, chromite.
chtoni'soterm, (-e), chthonisotherm (geology).
chyl, chyle.
chym, chyme.
cicero'ne, (-s), cicerone, guide.
Ciceroniaans' (-e), Ciceronian.
cinera'ria, (-s), cineraria.
Ci'pries, (-e), Cyprian.
Ciprioot', (Cipriote), Cyprian, Cypriot.
Ci'prus, Cyprus.
cir'ca, circa, about, nearly.
Cirkas'sies, (-e), Circassian.
cir'rus, (cirri), cirrus (cloud).
cis, C sharp (music).
Cisalpyns', (-e), Cisalpine.
cis-dur', C sharp major.
Cis'kei, Ciskei.
cis-mol', C sharp major.
Cistercïen'ser, (-s), Cistercian (monk).
clairvoyan'ce, clairvoyance.
clairvoyant', (-s), clairvoyant, medium.
clan, (-s), clan.
clas'sis, (classes), convocation (of Protestant clergymen), classis; = **klassis**.
clema'tis, clematis; *wilde* ~, virgin's bower.

Cyrillies

cliché', (-s), cliché; stereotype plate, block; ~**maker**, block-maker.
cloa'ca, cloaca; = **kloaka**.
Cloe'te: *die rondte van vader* ~ *doen*, do the rounds; *c* ~**-se-oor**, shoulder cartilage.
cochenil'le, cochineal; ~**-insekte**, cochineal insects.
Cock'ney, (-s), Cockney, Londoner.
cocot'te (-s), cocotte.
co'da, (-s), coda (music).
coiffeur', (-s), hairdresser.
coiffu're, coiffure; head-dress.
co'itus, coitus, coition, copulation (sexual); = **koïtus**.
Colise'um, **Colos'seum**, Coliseum, Colosseum.
Colora'dokewer, potato beetle.
collo'quium, colloquy, dialogue; ~ *doctum*, oral examination of clergymen.
commu'ne, (-s), commune.
communiqué', (-s), communique, news bulletin.
compo'te, fruit compote, stewed fruit.
concer'to, (-'s, ..ti), concerto (music).
confet'ti, confetti.
Confu'cius, Confucius.
congé', leave, permission; dismissal, congé.
connoisseur', (-s), connoisseur.
con'sols, consols, British government bonds.
Constan'tiawyn, Constantia wine.
consommé', consommé.
con'tra, contra, versus, against; = **kontra**.
contrami'ne: *in die* ~ *wees*, be contrary.
convol'vulus, (-se), convolvulus (flower).
Copernicaans', (-e), Copernican.
Coper'nicus, Copernicus.
coro'na, (sun's) corona.
corps, corps, body; *esprit de* ~, esprit de corps, team spirit.
cor'pus, body: ~ *DELICITI*, corpus delicti (material evidence); *HABEAS* ~, habeas corpus (you must have the body) (legal); ~ *JURIS*, corpus juris (systematized Roman Law).
corrigen'da, corrigenda, list of errors.
corrigen'dum, (..da), corrigendum.
corsa'ge, corsage, bodice.
Cor'tes, Cortes, Spanish Parliament.
coulis'se, (-s), coulisse, side-scene, movable scene, wing (theatre); *agter die* ~, behind the scenes, in secret.
coulomb' (-s), coulomb.
cou'lemeter, **couleme'ter**, coulometer.
coun'try, (mus.), country; ~**fees**, country festival; ~**musiek**, country (music).
coup, (-s), coup, stroke; ~ *d'ETAT*, coup d'etat; ~ *de GRACE*, death-blow.
courtisa'ne, (-s), courtesan.
cow'boy, (Amer.), cowboy; ~ **film**, cowboy film; ~**musiek**, cowboy music; ~**storie**, cowboy story.
crayon', (-s), crayon; ~**portret**, portrait in crayon.
crèche, (-s), crèche, day-nursery.
cre'do, (-'s), credo, belief.
crème, (-s) cream, crème; (b) cream (-coloured).
cremo'na, (-s), Cremona violin, Stradivarius.
crêpe, crêpe; ~**-de-chine**, crêpe de Chine.
crescen'do, (-'s), crescendo.
cri'men: ~ *injuria*, crimen injuria.
Croe'sus, Croesus.
cro'quet, croquet; ~**veld**, croquet lawn.
croupier', (-s), croupier.
c''tjie, (-s), small c.
cum: ~ *GRANO salis*, with some allowance, with a grain of salt; ~ *LAUDE*, with distinction, cum laude; ~ *SUIS*, with his following (confreres), cum suis.
cu'mulus, (..li), cumulus (cloud).
Cu'pido, cupid; ~**'tjie**, (-s), little Cupid.
cura'tor, (-es): ~ *BONIS*, curator bonis; ~*ad LITEM*, curator ad litem.
cu'rie[1], curia, the Holy See; curie.
curie'[2], (-s), curie (unit).
curio'sum, (..sa), curiosity, curio.
cus'tos, (ong.) (..todes), keeper, guardian, custodian.
cy'ma, cyma.
Cyril'lies, (-e), Cyrillic.

D

d, (-'s), d.

daad, (dade), deed, act, action, exploit, feat, performance, achievement; *op heter ~ BETRAP*, catch red-handed (in the act); *ou dade kom op ons HOOFDE neer*, our sins will be visited upon us; *'n MAN van die ~*, a man of action; *tot die ~ oorgaan*, take action; *OP die ~*, at once, on the spot; *geen ~ of RAAD weet nie*, be at a loss; *met die ~ STEUN*, support actively; *'n goeie ~ VERRIG*, do a good deed; *die ~ by die WOORD voeg*, suit the action to the word; *dade tel meer as WOORDE*, actions speak louder than words; *~ krag*, energy, drive, go; *~ krag'tig*, energetic; *~ lie'wend, (-e)*, practical, energetic; *~ lie'wendheid*, practicality; *~ lus*, urge for action; *~ mens*, practical person; *~ saak*, fact, reality; *~ sonde*, sin of commission; *~ werklik, (-e)*, real, actual; actively; *~ werklike lewering*, actual delivery.

daag¹, (ge-), summon (before court); challenge; arraign.

daag², (ge-), dawn; appear; *dit begin te ~*, the day is dawning.

daag'baar, (..bare), citable.

daag'liks, (-e), daily, every day, quotidian, diurnal; *~e BESTUUR*, executive committee; *~e GANG*, diurnal motion; *vir ~e GEBRUIK*, for daily use.

daags, in the daytime, by day; daily; on the day; *~ daarna*, on the following day.

daai'! (w) please! give! ta! (said to babies).

daai², (vnw) (geselst.) that; *hoe's ~?* how's that?

daal, (ge-), descend, sink, fall, decline, go down, drop (price); break (price, market); *in iem. se AGTING ~*, sink in someone's estimation (esteem); *in die GRAF ~*, sink into the grave.

daal'der, (-s), (vero.), old money unit; *dis darem te dik vir 'n ~*, difficult to believe; too expensive.

daal: *~ gang*, winze; *~ hoek*, angle of descent; *~ koper*, bear; *~ slag*, downstroke; *~ snelheid*, sinking speed; *~ stroom*, down current; *~ wind*, fall-wind.

Daan'tjie, Danny, Daniel; *sê GROETE vir oom ~*, enough of that; drop the subject; *tot by oom ~ in die KALWERHOK*, the whole hog; *~ Knakstert*, the devil.

daar, (bw) there; then; *~ IS hy*, there he is; *~ SIEN ek dit toe*, then suddenly I saw it; *TOT ~*, as far as that; *as die TYD ~ is*, when the time comes; *van ~ UIT*, beginning from there; *VAN ~ tot ~*, from there till there; as far as that; *sy VERJAARSDAG is al weer ~*, his birthday is here again; (vgw) since, as, because; *dit sterk reën, bly ek tuis*, as it is raining heavily, I am staying at home; *~ aan*, by that; on it; to that; *GOED ~ aan toe wees*, be in good condition; *WAT het ek ~ aan?*, of what use is that to me?; *~ aanvol'gend*, following on that; *~ ag'ter*, behind it (that); *eindelik is ek nou ~ agter*, at last I have solved the mystery; *~ bene'de*, under that; down below; *~ bene'wens*, in addition to, besides; *~ bin'ne*, inside (it), within; *~ bo'*, up there, above; *kinders van tien jaar en ~ bo*, children of ten years and upwards; *~ boon'op*, in addition to that; *~ bui'te*, outside; outside of it.

daarby', thereto, besides, in addition; *dit BLY ~*, the matter remains there; *hy BLY ~*, he still maintains, he sticks to it; *~ KOM nog*, and besides that; *'n mooi vrou en RYK ~*, a pretty woman and rich into the bargain (to boot).

daar: *~ deur*, thereby, by that means; through (there); for that reason; *~ deur kom dit*, that is why; *~ die*, that; those; *~ enbo'we*, moreover, besides, furthermore; in addition to; *~ ente'ë*, *~ enteen'*, on the contrary, on the other hand; *~ e'we*, just a minute ago; *~ gelate*, leaving aside, let alone, not to mention; ginds', *~ gun'ter*, (vero.) over there; yonder; *~ heen*, thither, there, to that place; *~ heen'*, gone, lost; departed; *ALLES is ~ heen*, everything is lost; *MOEDER is ~ heen*, mother is no more; *~ in*, therein, in that; inside; *~ juis'*, a moment ago; *~ laat, (-ge-)*, leave aside, pass over; *DIT sal ek maar ~ laat*, I shall just leave it at that; *NOG ~ gelate dat...*, quite apart from the question whether

...; *~ langs*, past there, along that; somewhere there; *~ mee*, therewith, with that.

daarna', after (that), afterwards; by that; accordingly; next; subsequently; at that; *KORT ~*, soon afterwards; *dit MAAK ~*, look for it; *~ OPTREE*, act according to that; *ek VOEL ~*, that is how I feel; I feel inclined.

daar: *~ naas'*, next to that (it); adjoining; next door; *~ natoe*, there, thither, in that direction; *dis tot ~ natoe*, so be it; it's over and done with; *~ net'*, a moment ago; *ek het hom ~ net sien verbyloop*, I saw him passing this minute; *~ ne'wens*, besides that; over and above that; *~ om*, therefore, hence, for that reason; *~ omheen'*, around (it), round about it; *~ om'streeks*, somewhere there; about that time; thereabouts; *~ omtrent*, thereabout, concerning that; *~ on'der*, under that, down there by that; among them.

daar'oor, daaroor', about that; therefore; across that; *~ GAAN dit juis*, that is just the point; *hy kan nie ~ KOM nie*, he can't forget it.

daar'op, daarop', thereupon, upon that; on it; *~ SÊ hy*, thereupon he said; *die JAAR ~*, the following year; *~ of DAARONDER*, win or lose.

daar: *~ opvol'gend, (-e)*, ensuing; (the) very next; *~ rond'om*, round that; *~ so*, there, yonder; *~ son'der*, without it (that); *~ sonder klaarkom*, manage (do) without; *~ stel, (-ge-)*, (Germ.) bring about, cause, accomplish, establish; *~ stelling*, bringing about, causing; creation; founding; accomplishment; *~ te'ë*, *~ teen'*, against that; *ek stem ~ teen*, I vote against; *~ teenoor*, opposite; on the other hand; over against that; *~ toe*, for it, for that purpose, to that end; *~ toe het dit gelei*, it has led to that; *~ tus'sen*, between that, in between; *~ uit*, thence, out of that; *~ uit volg dat*, from this it follows that; *~ uit'!*, get out!; *~ van*, of that, about that, thereof; *niks ~ van nie*, nothing of the sort; nothing about that; *~ vandaan*, from there, thence; *~ vandaan AF*, from there; after that; *toe ons ~ vandaan GAAN*, when we left there; *~ vol'gens*, according to that.

daar'voor, for that (reason); *~ het ons gekom*, that's why we came; *~*, before that; in front of it; previous to that; *die DAG ~*, the previous day; *ek KAN nie ~ nie*, it is not my fault.

da'ba(gras), long thatch grass.

da'da, dada; **Da'da,** Dada (art form).

dadaïs', (-te), Dadaist; *~ me*, Dadaism.

da'del, (-s), date, *DIS ~s met jou!*, that's all nonsense!; *iem. ~s GEE*, give someone beans; *~ boom*, date tree; *~ brood*, date loaf; *daar KOM ~s van*, nothing will come of it.

da'delik, immediate(ly), at once, readily, instantly, this minute, forthwith, direct(ly); *ek het al ~ getwyfel*, I had my doubts from the first; *~ hede*, blows, *van woorde het hulle na (tot) ~ hede oorgegaan*, from words they came to blows.

da'deloos, inactive; *~ heid*, inactivity.

da'del: *~ palm*, date palm; *~ pit*, date stone; pip; *~ pruim*, date plum; persimmon; *~ rol*, date roll; *~ vulsel*, date filling; *~ wyn*, date wine.

da'der, (-s), doer, perpetrator, actor, offender; *word ~s v.d. woord*, be ye doers of the word; *~ es', (-se)*, female doer.

da'ding, compromise, settlement.

da'do, (-'s), dado.

da'elange, lasting several days.

da'eliks = daagliks.

da'eraad = da(g)eraad.

dag¹, (w) verl. tyd van **dink**; *ek ~ so*, that's what I thought.

dag² (s) (dae), day, day-time; daylight; *~ AAN ~*, day by day; *moenie die ~ voor die AAND prys nie*, don't bless the day before it is over; *die ANDER ~*, the other day; *al om die ANDER ~*, every other day; on alternate days; *BAIE dae*, many a day; very often; *hy BEKOMMER hom nie oor die ~ van môre nie*, he does not worry about the morrow; *hy het BETER dae geken*, he has known better days;

dag-en-nagewening

aan die ~ *BRING*, bring to light; *voor die* ~ *BRING*, bring forth; *BY dae*, at times; ~ *en DATUM noem*, fix the date; ~ *DER dae*, Doomsday; the Day of Judgment; *DEURDRUK* ~ *toe*, carry on throughout the night; *hoe meer dae hoe meer DINGE (neukery)*, every day brings new problems; *voor* ~ *en DOU*, before the break of day; *elke* ~ *'n DRAADJIE is 'n hempsmou in 'n jaar*, every little makes a mickle; *van EEN* ~ *in die ander lewe*, live from day to day; *EEN van die dae*, one of these fine days; *die een* ~ *FEES, die ander* ~ *vas*, stuff today and starve tomorrow; *iem. dae GEE*, give someone grey hairs; *sy dae is GETEL*, his days are numbered; his end is approaching; *ek onthou dit soos die* ~ *van GISTER*, I remember it as if it were yesterday; *op 'n GOEIE* ~, one fine day; *'n GOEIE* ~ *hê*, be in affluent (easy) circumstances; *'n GROOT* ~, a great occasion; a red-letter day; *voor die* ~ *HAAL*, produce, bring to light; *'n HEERLIKE* ~ *hê*, have a glorious time; *HEDEN ten dae*, nowadays; *die HELE* ~, the whole day; all day; *die* ~ *van die HERE*, the Lord's day; *ten HUIDIGE dae*, to this day; *by die* ~ *HUUR*, hire by the day; ~ *in* ~ *uit*, day in, day out; *die JONGSTE* ~, the Day of Judgment; *so KLAAR soos die* ~, as clear as crystal; *verag die* ~ *van KLEIN dinge nie*, great things have small beginnings; *voor die ('n)* ~ *KOM*, appear; *sy* ~ *sal KOM*, his day of reckoning will come; *iem. sal sy* ~ *KRY*, his day will come; *elke* ~ *het genoeg aan sy eie KWAAD*, sufficient unto the day is the evil thereof; *'n KWAAIE* ~, an evil day; *KWAAI dae*, evil (bad) days; *dit was 'n KWADE* ~ *vir ons*, it was a bad day for us; *die KWADE* ~ *uitstel*, put off the evil day; *die LAASTE der dae*, the last days; *aan die* ~ *LÊ*, display, evince, manifest; *nooit in my* ~ *des LEWENS nie*, never in my day; *MEER as een* ~, on more than one occasion; *MET die* ~, by the day; *een v.d. MOOI dae*, one of these days; *die* ~ *van MORE*, tomorrow; ~ *NA* ~, day by day; *die* ~ *kom uit die NAG*, out of evil good will come; *NOU die* ~, the other day; *NUUS van die* ~, current news; *Sondag OOR agt dae*, Sunday week; *op my OU* ~, in my old age; *in die OU dae*, in the olden days; *hy PRYS die* ~ *nooit voor twaalfuur in die aand nie*, he never blesses the day before it is over; *een mooi* ~ *maak nie SOMER nie*, one swallow doesn't make a summer; *die dae TEL*, to count the days; *TEN dae van*, in the days of; *die* ~ *TEVORE*, the day before; *VAN dié* ~ *af*, from that day on; *VAN* ~ *tot* ~, from day to day; *VERAG die* ~ *van klein dinge nie*, great things have small beginnings; *die* ~ *van VERGELDING*, the day of reckoning; *soos* ~ *en nag VERSKIL*, differ like day and night; be poles apart; ~ *VIR* ~, day by day; every day; *die een* ~ *VOLOP, die ander* ~ *skoon op*, stuff today and starve tomorrow; ~**bestuur**, ex(ecutive) co(mmittee), emergency committee; ~**bevel**, daily orders; ~**blad**, daily paper, journal; ~**bladartikel**, newspaper article; ~**bladpers**, daily press; ~**bladskrywer**; journalist, publicist; ~**blind**, day-blind; ~**blindheid**, dayblindness; hemeralopia; ~**boek**, diary, logbook, memorandum, journal, day-book; ~**boekskrywer**, diarist; ~**bomwerper**, day(light) bomber; ~**boog**, diurnal arc; ~**bou**, open mining, open cast; ~**breek**, day-break, cockcrow, peep of dawn; *met* ~ *breek*, at daybreak; ~**breker**, (sicklewinged) chat *(Emarginata sinnata; Cercomela familiaris)*; ~**dief**, time-thief, idler, lazy-bones; ~**diens**, day duty (service); ~ *diens doen*, be on day duty; ~**diewery**, idling, loitering; ~**dromer**, daydreamer; ~**droom**, day-dream; ~**dromery**, daydreaming, mind-wandering.

dag-en-nag'ewening, (vernal and autumnal) equinox.

da'(g)eraad¹, (. . **rade**), dawn, aurora, day-spring.

da'(g)eraad², (-s), (brightly coloured) Cape fish *(Chrysoblephus cristiceps)*.

dag'ga, dagga *(Cannabis sativa)*, Cape hemp, hashish (hasheesh), marijuana; *wilde* ~, minaret flower *(Leonotis leonurus)*; ~**pyp**, dagga-pipe; ~**rook**, dagga smoke; ~**roker**, dagga smoker; *hy is 'n* ~ *roker*, he is a layabout; ~**sigaret**, reefer, dagga smoke.

dag: ~**gang**, daily fluctuation; ~**geld**, day's pay, daily wages (allowance); call-money; ~**getyeboek**, diurnal (R.C.); ~**gie**, (-s), (short) day; *'n* ~*gie OUER word*, get a little older; *'n ou* ~ *gie VRY hê*, have a day off.

da'gha, clay, mortar, dagha.

da'ging, cital, citation.

dag: ~**kaartjie**, day-ticket; ~**kant**, face; ~**leerling**, day-scholar; ~**lelie**, asphodel, tigridia; ~**lening**, call loan.

dag'lig, daylight; *by* ~ *BEKYK*, study carefully; *in die* ~ *BRING*, bring to light; *die* ~ *SIEN*, be born; be published; *in 'n ander* ~ *STEL*, put a different complexion on; *in 'n helder* ~ *STEL*, put a different complexion on; *dit kan nie die* ~ *VERDRA nie*, it cannot bear the light of day; *die* ~ *nie WERD wees nie*, be past redemption.

dag: ~**ligbesparing**, daylight saving; ~**loner**, (-s), day-labourer; journeyman; peon; ~**loon**, day's wages, daily pay; ~**loseerder**, table-boarder; ~**lumier**, daybreak, dawn; ~**mars**, day's march; ~**myn**, opencast workings.

da'gon, idol; pipe (colloq.).

dag: ~**orde**, order of the day; order-paper; ~**order**, order of the day (mil.); ~**oud**, day old; ~**pak**, lounge suit; ~**ploeg**, day shift; ~**register**, day-book, journal; ~**reis**, day's journey; ~**sê**, (-ge-), say good-day; greet; ~**sê!**, good-day!, I greet you; ~**sirkel**, diurnal circle; ~**skof**, day shift; day's journey; ~**skolier**, day-scholar; ~**skool**, day-school; ~**skuheid**, photophobia; ~**soom**, exposure; outcrop (geol.); ~**stempel**, datestamp; ~**suster**, day-nurse; ~**taak**, daily task; ~**tarief**, daily tariff; ~**teken**, (ge-), date; ~**tekening**, date; ~**trein**, day(light) train.

daguerreoti'pe, daguerreotype.

dag'vaar, (ge-), summon, subpoena, garnish (law); cite; ~**ding**, (-e, -s), summons, warrant, writ, cital, citation, assignation; *'n* ~*ding bestel*, serve a summons.

dag'varend, (-e), citatory.

dag: ~**verblyf**, day haunt; ~**verbruik**, daily consumption; ~**verdeling**, division of the day; ~**verhaal**, journal, daily account, diary; ~**verpleegster**, day-nurse; ~**verslag**, daily report; ~**vlieg**, day-fly, ephemeron; ~**vlinder**, lepidopter, diurnal, rhopolacera, (diurnal) butterfly; ~**vlug**, day flight; ~**vors(tin)**, sun; ~**wag**, morning watch; ~**werk**, day work; daily work, char; journey-work; ~**werker**, day labourer.

dah'lia, (-s), dahlia; ~**bol**, dahlia bulb.

Dail Ei'reann, Dail Eireann.

dak, (-ke), roof; hanging wall (mines); *op iem. se* ~ *AFKLIM*, give someone a dressing down; *onder* ~ *BRING*, give shelter; accommodate; *'n* ~ *bo jou HOOF hê*, have a roof over one's head; *te veel* ~ *op die HUIS hê*, walls have ears; *dit KRY ek op my* ~, I shall have to answer for that; *ONDER* ~ *wees*, have a roof over one's head; *ONDER een* ~ *sit*, have common interests; *SONDER* ~, roofless; *van die* ~*ke af VERKONDIG*, proclaim from the housetops; ~**balk**, roof beam; ~**bedekking**, roofing, roofage; ~**bindbalk**, principal beam; ~**bint**, roof-tie; ~**boog**, carline, hoopstick, roof (bow) stick; ~**dekker**, tiler; thatcher; ~**drup**, eaves, eaves-drip; ~**fees**, wetting the roof; ~*fees vier*, wet the roof; ~**gesteente**, roof wall; hanging rock; ~**geut**, eaves-gutter, eaves; cullis; ~**hanger**, roof pendant; roof hanger (loco.); ~**hoog**, as high as the roof; ~**huis**, penthouse; ~**juk**, ashlar; ~**kamertjie**, attic, garret; ~**kap**, roof truss; principal; ~**kiel**valley; ~**lamp**, roof lamp; dome lamp; ~**lat**, roof lath; ~**leer**, cat ladder; ~**lei**, roof(ing) slate; ~**lig**, skylight; ~**loos**, (..**lose**), roofless, homeless; ~**lose**, (-s), waif, homeless person; ~**luik**, garret window; rooflight; ~**lys**, eaves; ~**materiaal**, roofing; ~**nok**, ridge of roof; ~**ondersoeker**, hanging inspector; ~**pan**, tile; ~**panligging**, imbrication, overlap (of tiles); ~**pansgewyse**, imbricate; ~*pansgewyse lê*, overlap, imbricate; ~**plankie**,

daktiel — **dans**

shingle; ~**prys**, ceiling price, upper limit of prices; ~**pyp**, gutter pipe; drain; ~**rak**, roof carrier; ~**rand**, drip, eaves; ~**randlat**, eaves purlin; ~**randlys**, eaves moulding; ~**reling**, roof rack, roof rail; ~**rib**, roof stick; ~**spaan**, shingle; clapboard; ~**spar**, rafter, eaves lath; ~**spyker**, roofing nail; ~**steunrib**, carline; ~**stoel**, roof truss; ~**strooi**, thatch; ~**stut**, roof support; ~**styl**, principal post.

daktiel', (-e), dactyl.
dakti'lies, (-e), dactylic.
dakti'lus, (-se, ..tili) = daktiel.
dak: ~**tuin**, roof garden; ~**venster**, garret window, skylight, luthern, dormer window; ~**vilt**, roofing felt; ~**vink**, roof clutch; ~**vors**, ridge of roof; ~**werk**, slating, roofing, thatching, roofage; ~**werker**, roofer; ~**woning**, penthouse.
dal, (-e), valley, vale, dale, dell; glen; *die AARDSE* ~, this vale of sorrows; *die* ~ *van DOODSKADUWEE*, the valley of the shadow of death; ~**bewoner**, dalesman, dweller in a valley.
da'ling, descent (from mountain); fall, drop, gradient; fall (in prices); slump (of market); winze (in mines).
dalk, perhaps, maybe, perchance, possibly; ~ *DAAG hy nog op*, perhaps he will still turn up; ~ *LIEG hy*, what if he lies?, possibly he is merely lying.
dal'kies, by-and-by, presently; perhaps, possibly.
dal'lelie, lily of the valley.
Dalma'sië, Dalmatia.
Dalma'tjies, (-e), Dalmation.
dalma'tika, (-s), dalmatic.
Dal'ton, Dalton, D~is'me, Daltonism, colourblindness; ~**skool**, Dalton School.
dal'weg, thalweg.
dam¹, (s) (-me), dam, pond, reservoir; cistern; barrage; weir (in river); perineum; *die GROOT (blou)* ~, the sea; *'n* ~ *OPWERP teen*, dam up; stem the tide; (w) (ge-), dam up, pond; crowd.
dam², king (draughts); *'n* ~ *maak*, make a king.
Da'mara, (-s), Damara.
Da'marabees, (-te), Damara cattle.
damas', damask; diaper; ~**blom**, rocket; ~**kusrooi**, damask rose; ~**linne**, damask linen; ~**pruim**, damson, damask-plum, damascene; ~**roos**, damask rose.
damasseer', (ge-), damaskeen (damascene).
damasse'nerstaal, Damascus steel.
damas'sy, damask silk.
dam'bord, draught board; chequer board; ~**skyf**, draughtsman; ~**spel**, checkers, draughts; ~**speler**, draughts player; ~**stuk**, draughts piece.
da'me, (-s), lady, queen (chess); ~*s en here!*, ladies and gentlemen!.
da'mes: ~**agtig**, (-e), ladylike; ~**gambiet**, queen's gambit; ~**kroeg**, ladies' bar; ~**opening**, queen's gambit (opening); ~**ruiter**, horsewoman, equestrienne.
da'me: ~**saal**, (-s), side saddle; ~**sakkie**, lady's bag, vanity bag.
da'mes: ~**baadjie**, coatee; ~**broekie**, pantie(s); ~**drag**, ladies' wear; ~**dubbelspel**, ladies' doubles; ~**enkelspel**, ladies' singles; ~**fiets**, lady's bicycle; ~**gek**, lady's man, lady-killer; ~**geruit**, zephyr (dress material); ~**hand**, lady's hand; ~**hangkas**, lady's wardrobe; ~**hoedemaker**, man milliner; ~**kamer**, boudoir; ~**kapmantel**, capuchin; ~**kleremaker**, ladies' tailor; ~**koepee**, ladies' coupé; ~**koor**, ladies' choir; ~**kostuum**, lady's costume; ~**mantel**, lady's coat, cardinal; ~**party**, ladies' (hen) party; ~**perd**, lady's mount, palfrey; ~**piesang**, lady's finger (banana); ~**poeiersakkie**, vanity bag; ~**rykleed**, (lady's) riding-habit; ~**ryperd**, palfrey; ~**tassie**, lady's handbag; ~**vertrek**, bower; ~**vriend**, lady's man; ~**werksakkie**, lady's work-bag; housewife (hussif).
da'metjie, (-s), little lady.
dam'gooi, (-ge-), dam up; stem the progress of.
dam'hert, fallow deer; *jong* ~, fawn.
dam'ketting, stud-link chain.
dam'kokker, (-s), blue hottentot *(Sparidae)*.
damma'r(a), dammar (resin).

Da'mokles, Damocles.
damp, (s) (-e), vapour, steam; smoke, puff, fume; reek, exhalation; (w) (ge-), emit steam; puff (at a pipe); smoke, fume, reek; ~**agtig**, vaporous; ~**bad**, vapour bath; Turkish bath; ~**ie**, (-s), smoke; *'n* ~ *ie slaan*, have a smoke; ~**digtheid**, vapour density; ~**druk**, vapour-pressure; ~**er**, (-s), smoker; ~**ig**, (-e), vaporous, hazy; ~**igheid**, haziness; broken-windedness; ~**kring**, atmosphere; ~**kringslug**, atmospheric air; ~**meter**, vaporimeter.
dam'pomp, outlet pipe (of dam); dam pump.
damp: ~**vormig**, (-e), vaporiform; ~**vorming**, vapour formation, vaporization.
dam: ~**pyp**, outlet pipe (of dam); ~**skraper**, ~**skrop**, damscraper.
dam: ~**skyf**, draughtsman; ~**spel**, (ong.) draughts.
dam: ~**vlak**, dam level; ~**wal**, dike, embankment (of a dam); ~**water**, water from a dam; wish-wash.
Dan¹, Dan; *van* ~ *tot Berseba*, from Dan to Beersheba; throughout the land.
dan², (bw), then; *is daar* ~ *GLAD niks*, is there really nothing at all?; *as dit* ~ *MOET*, if needs must; *tot MÔRE* ~, until tomorrow then; *so NOU en* ~, now and then; *SELFS* ~ *nog*, but even so; *loop* ~ *TOG!*, do go!; *TOE* ~ *!*, come on!; *TOT* ~, until then; *en jou VRIEND* ~*?*, and what about your friend?, ~ *en WAN*, now and then, occasionally.
dan³, (vgw) than; *AL* ~ *nie*, whether or not; *hy was groter as teoloog* ~ *AS politikus*, he was a better theologian than politician.
da'nebol, (gew.) fir cone.
Da'niëlsbende, small but brave band, the faithful few.
da'nig, (b) (-e), exuberant, effusive; familiar, overfriendly; intimate; (bw) much rather; awfully; *nie* ~ *GOED nie*, not too good; ~ *met HAAR*, intimate with her; *hom* ~ *HOU*, give himself airs; *jy HOU jou verniet so* ~ *!*, don't give yourself airs, *maar* ~ *LUI*, lazy enough.
da'nigheid, effusiveness, intimacy; *dit was 'n HELE* ~, it was quite a to-do; *dis 'n* ~ *MET hulle!*, it's quite a business with them!; *dis 'n* ~ *TUSSEN hulle*, they are very close.
dank, (s) thanks, acknowledgement, gratitude; *met* ~ *AANNEEM*, accept gratefully; *in* ~ *ONTVANG*, received with thanks, ~ *BETUIG*, express thanks; *GOD sy* ~ *!*, thank God!; ~ *VERSKULDIG wees aan*, owe a debt of gratitude to; (w) (ge-), thank, give thanks, return thanks; say grace; ascribe, owe (to); ~ *jou die DUIWEL*, well I like that! well I never!, *ek* ~ *my WELSLAE aan*, I owe my success to; ~**altaar**, votive altar; ~**baar**, (..bare), thankful, grateful; ~**bare AARDE**, fertile soil; *nie 'n* ~*bare WERK nie*, a thankless task; ~**baarheid**, thankfulness, gratefulness, gratitude; ~**betuiging**, expression (vote, letter) of thanks; ~**brief**, letter of thanks; ~**dag**, thanksgiving day; ~**diens**, thanksgiving service.
dan'ke: *te* ~ *AAN*, due to, thanks to; *NIE te* ~ *nie*, don't mention it; *te* ~*e aan sy MOED*, owing to (thanks to) his courage; *dit was aan sy VLYT te* ~, it was due to his diligence.
dank: ~**fees**, thanksgiving feast; ~**gebed**, thanksgiving (prayer); grace.
dan'kie! thank you! thanks! *BAIE* ~ *!*, many thanks!; *NEE* ~ *!*, no thanks!; *hy kan* ~ *SÊ!*, he will have to wait a long time for it!; *hy kan* ~ *SÊ*, he can forget about it; he can whistle for it; ~ *SÊ vir niks*, thanks for nothing; ~ *TOG!*, thank goodness!; ~**bly**, thankful; relieved; *jy kan* ~ *bly wees*, you can thank your stars; ~**blyverlossing**, good riddance.
dank: ~**lied**, song of thanksgiving; paean; ~**offer**, thank-offering; votive offering; ~**sê**, (ge-), thank, return thanks; say grace; ~**segging**, thanksgiving; grace; ~**seggingsdiens**, thanksgiving service; ~**stond**, thanksgiving service; ~**sy**, as a result of; thanks to; ~*sy haar hulp*, thanks to her help; ~**woord**, word of thanks.
dans, (s) (-e), dance, ball; ballet; ballroom dancing; *die* ~ *ontspring*, escape unhurt; have a narrow escape; (w) (ge-), dance, shake a leg; trip it on the

light fantastic toe; ~ **akademie**, dancing academy; ~**baadjie**, tuxedo (coat), dance coat; ~**beer**, dancing (performing) bear; ~**beskrywing**, choreography; ~**boekie**, dance-card; ~**er**, (-s), dancer; ~**eres'**, (-se), dancer, female dancer; ballerina; ~**ery**, dancing, ~**eu'se**, (-s), (ong.) ballet dancer; ~**genoot**, dancing partner; ~**huis**, dance hall; ~**ie**, (-s), dance; (little) hop; ~**inrigting**, ~**instituut**, dancing academy; ~**kamer**, dance room; ~**klepper**, castanet; ~**klere**, dancing clothes; ~**klub**, dance-club; ~**kuns**, art of dancing; orchestics; ~**les**, dancing lesson; ~**lied**, dancing song; ~**lustig**, (-e), fond of dancing; ~**maat**, (-s), (dancing) partner; ~**meester**, dancing master; ~**meisie**, dancing girl; ~**musiek**, dance music; ~**onderwyser**, dancing instructor; ~**ontwerper**, choreograph(er); ~**orkes**, dance band; ~**paar**, dancing couple; ~**party**, ball, dance; ~**pas**, (dance-)step; ~**rok**, evening (dancing) frock, ball-dress; ~**saal**, ball-room; ~**saalkryt**, French chalk; ~**skoen**, dancing shoe; pump; ~**skool**, school of dancing; dancing academy; ~**tabberd**, ball-dress; ~**vloer**, dancing floor; ~**woede**, rage (passion) for dancing; dancing mania; tarantism; ~**wysie**, dance tune.

dap'per¹, (s): *met* ~ *en STAPPER*, on foot; *met* ~ *en STAPPER reis*, ride Shanks's mare.

dap'per², (b) (-der, -ste), brave, valiant, gallant, plucky, doughty, valorous, manful, game; *hom* ~ *HOU*, make a gallant stand, bear up bravely; *HOU jou* ~!, never say die!; *jou* ~ *WEER*, offer a stout resistance; *cf*. **braaf**; ~**heid**, bravery, valour, gallantry, doughtiness, prowess.

dar, (-re), drone (bee).

Dardanel'le, Dardanelles.

da'rem, though, all the same, after all, surely; in spite of, notwithstanding; really; *ek sal dit* ~ *DOEN*, I'll do it after all; *JY*, ~!, ah, but you! *dis* ~ *alte LAAT*, it is really too late; ~ *maar TOESTEM*, give one's consent after all.

dario'le, (-s), dariole.

dar'tel, (w) (ge-), frisk, gambol, dally, frolic; disport; galumph; (b) playful, skittish, sportive; rompish, gleeful, boisterous, frisky, frolicsome, wanton, kittenish, full of play; ~**heid**, playfulness, wantonness, frolicksomeness, friskiness; boisterousness.

Darwinis', (-te), Darwinist; ~**me**, Darwinism; ~**ties**, (-e), Darwinian.

das¹, (-se), neck-tie, bow.

das², (-se), badger (*Meles meles* in Europe; *Taxidea taxus* in N. Amer.).

das³, (-se), rock-fish, blue hottentot (*Diplodus sargus*).

das⁴, (-se), rock rabbit (*Procavia capensis*); hyrax, con(e)y; ~**adder**, dragon; *see also* **likkewaan**.

das'sie¹, (-s), small neck-tie, bow.

das'sie², (-s), rock rabbit; hyrax; *elke* ~ *prys sy KWASSIE*, every cook praises his own broth; *SOOS* ~ *s in die SON sit*, bask in the sun; ~ *het 'n STERT gekry*, he is as pleased as Punch; *as* ~ *STERT kry*, when pigs fly; *'n* ~ *aan sy STERT vang*, milk the ram; ~**bergwagter**, mocking chat; ~**hond**, basset; dachshund; badger-dog; ~**pis**, hyraceum (secretion of the hyrax); ~**vanger**, black eagle; coney catcher (*Pteroaetus verreauxi*).

das'speld, tie pin, scarf pin.

das'vel, skin of the rock rabbit.

dat, (b) (eufem.): *jou dit-en-datse kind*, you damn rascal!; (vgw) that, so that, in order that; *ons het 'n BRIEF gekry* ~ . . ., we received a letter to the effect (stating, to say) that . . .; *hy is so DOM* ~ *hy niks begryp nie*, he is so stupid that he does not understand anything; *die FEIT* ~ *hy nie daar was nie*, the fact that he was not present; *dis nou sewe JAAR* ~ *ek hom laas gesien het*, it is now seven years since I last saw him; *PLEKS* ~ *jy my help*, instead of helping me; *oor dit en* ~ *gesels*, talk about this and that.

da'ta, data; information, facts; ~**bank**, databank; ~**gehalte**, data quality; ~**korpus**, data corpus; ~**punt**, data point; ~**verspreiding**, data dissemination.

dateer', (ge-), date; ~ *uit (van) die vorige EEU*, date from the previous century; ~ *VAN*, date from; *VOORUIT* ~, postdate; *VROEËR* ~, antedate, predate.

date'ring, date; dating.

da'tief, (**datiewe**), dative.

dat'jie, (-s), trifle; *ditjies en* ~*s*, trifles.

da'to, date; *onder* ~, (ong.) dated.

da'tum, (-s), date; *tot op* ~ *BRING*, bring up to date; *van GELYKE* ~, of the same (even) date; *SONDER* ~, undated; ~**grens**, ~**lyn**, date-line; ~**loos**, (. . lose), without a date; ~**lys**, fixture (sports); list of dates; ~**masjien**, date press; ~**stempel**, date stamp.

dauphin', (-s), dauphin; ~**e**, (-s), dauphiness.

da'vit, (-s), davit.

dawee', (-s), tamarisk.

da'wer, (ge-), rumble, roar, thunder, boom, crash; ~**end**, (-e), thundering, booming; *iem.* ~ *end toejuig*, greet someone with loud cheers (roars of applause); ~**lag**, booming laughter.

dawib' = **dawee**.

Da'wid, David; *soos* ~ *en JONATHAN*, like David and Jonathan (bosom-friends); *weet waar* ~ *die WORTELS graaf*, know what is what; know how many beans make five; *iem. wys waar* ~ *die WORTELS gegraaf het*, teach someone a thing or two.

da'widjies, daw'wetjies, shrub (*Antizoma capensis*) used for snake-bite.

da'wie, word of honour; *op my* ~, on my honour.

dè, (w) take! here you are! ~, *vat hier*, here, take this.

de, (bw) the (used for emphasis instead of *die*); *om* ~ *DOOD nie*, on no account; never; *wat* ~ *DUIWEL makeer jou*, what the deuce is the matter with you?; *wat* ~ *ONGELUK vang jy nou aan*, what the deuce are you doing now?

dê, (tw) now! see!; *jy sal niks kry nie*, ~, you'll get nothing, so there!

deba'kel, (-s), debacle, smash, collapse, crash, crack-up.

deballota'sie, (-s), blackballing.

deballotteer', (ge-), blackball.

debarkeer', (ge-), (ong.) debark.

debat', (-te), debate, discussion, argument; ~**sluiting**, closure (parliament); ~**s'vereniging**, debating society; ~**teer'**, (ge-), debate, discuss; *oor 'n rekening* ~ *teer*, debate an account; ~**teer'der**, (-s), debater; ~**teerset**, debating point (trick).

de'bet, debet', (-s, -te), (Ndl.) *ongewone vorm vir* debiet (*s.d.*).

debiel', (-e), debile, feeble.

debiet', (-e), debit, (record of) sum owing (on account); (sum on) debit side (of account); (*NB* Die vorm *debet* word ook gebruik, maar is Ndl.) (Vgl. **krediet**); ~**boek**, debit book; ~**brief**, debit note; ~**fout**, debit error; ~**kant**, debit side; ~**kredietverhouding**, debit-credit relation; ~**nota**, debit note; ~**pos**, debit entry; ~**saldo**, debit balance; ~**sy**, debit side.

debiliteit', debility, feebleness.

debiteer', (ge-), debit, charge with; retail; *grappies* ~, crack jokes.

debite'ring, debit.

debiteur', (-e, -s), debtor; ~**s'(groot)boek**, debtor's ledger.

debs, (ge-), (geselst.) grab; appropriate, take.

debutant', (-e), débutant; ~**e**, (-s), debutante ~**ebal**, debutante ball.

debuteer', (ge-), make one's debut.

debuut', (**debute**), first appearance, debut; *jou* ~ *maak*, make one's début; ~**bundel**, first volume; ~**vlug**, maiden flight.

decem'vir, (-i, -s), decemvir; ~**aat'**, decemvirate.

décolleté, décolleté, décolletage.

decrescen'do, decrescendo.

dedika'sie, (-s), dedication.

dedolomitisa'sie, . . **tise'ring**, dedolomitization.

deduk'sie, (-s), deduction, inference.

deduktief', (. . tiewe), deductive.

deeg, dough; paste; pastry; ~ *in iem. se hande wees*, clay in someone's hands; ~**agtig**, (-e), doughy; ~**frikkadel**, rissole; ~**karmenaadjie**, chop in bat-

ter; ~**kartelaar**, pastry crimper (pincer): ~**kwassie**, pastry brush.
deeg'lik, (-e), solid, thorough; sterling; sound (reason); ~ *ONDERSOEK (nasien)*, overhaul (investigate) thoroughly; *WEL ~ waar*, really true; *sy het WEL ~ ja gesê*, she really did say yes; ~**heid**, solidity, soundness, thoroughness, efficiency.
deeg: ~**plank**, pastry board, dough board; ~**roller**, pastry roller, rolling-pin; ~**snyer**, pastry cutter; ~**stadium**, dough stage; ~**toespys**, Yorkshire pudding; ~**wieletjie**, pastry cutter.
deel¹, (s) (dele), deal, plank, board.
deel², (s) (dele), part, portion, share, division, section; moiety (of inheritance); volume (book); dole; *die grootste ~ BYDRA*, contribute the largest share; *vir 'n GROOT ~*, to a large extent; *~ HÊ aan*, be a party to; *jou ~ ONTMOET*, meet one's mate; *TEN dele*, partly; *~ UITMAAK van*, form a part of; *ten ~ VAL*, fall to one's share (lot); *VIR 'n ~*, partly; *dit WAS sy ~*, that was his lot; (w) (ge-), divide; share (house, view); participate (in joy, sorrow); *gelykop ~*, share equally; ~**ag'tig, (-e)**: *iets ~ agtig word*, participate in something; acquire something; ~**baar, (..bare)**, divisible; composite (number); ~**baarheid**, divisibility; ~**besitter**, part-owner; ~**boer**, share-cropper; ~**fout**, mistake in dividing; ~**genoot**, partner, sharer, participator; partaker; *ek maak jou ~ genoot van my geluk*, I share my happiness with you; ~**genootskap**, (co)-partnership, fellowship; ~**geregtig, (-de)**, entitled to a share, entitled to participate; ~**geregtigheid**, right of participation; ~**hebber, (-s)**, participant; co-partner; partaker; part owner; stake-holder; ~**hebberskap**, participation; ~**huis**, apartment house; ~**kristallyn**, hypo-crystalline; ~**lyn**, bisector (of angle); ~**name**, participation; ~**neem, (-ge-)**, participate in, partake, sympathize with, take part in; *~ neem aan*, take a hand in, be a party to; enter (a war); ~**nemend, (-e)**, sympathetic, compassionate, ~**nemer**, participant, competitor, entrant, participator, contestant; sympathizer; ~**nemersverband**, sectional title; ~**neming**, sympathy; participation; *~ neming betuig*, condole with, sympathize with, express sympathy; ~**punt**, point of division.
deels, partly, in part.
deel: ~**saaier**, share cropper; ~**s'genitief**, partitive genitive; ~**s'gewys(e)**, piecemeal, bit by bit; ~**skyf**, division plate; ~**som**, division sum; ~**tal**, dividend (arith.); ~**teken**, diaeresis; division sign (arith.); ~**titel**, sectional title; subtitle; ~**tjie, (-s)**, small part, particle; ~**tyds, (-e)**, part-time; ~**vruggie**, mericarp; ~**woord**, participle; *teenwoordige (verlede) ~ woord*, present (past) participle.
dee'moed, meekness, humility, submissiveness.
deemoe'dig, (-e), humble, meek, submissive; ~**heid**, humbleness, meekness; ~**ing**, humiliation, mortification (of the flesh).
Deen, (Dene), Dane; ~**s, (s)** Danish (language); (b) (-e), Danish; *~ se hond*, Great Dane.
deer, (ge-), hurt, harm; ~**lik, (-e)**, pitiful, miserable, sad, sore; sorely, badly, profound; *jou ~ lik vergis*, make a grave blunder, be sorely mistaken; ~**nis**, commiseration, pity; *~ nis hê met*, have pity on; ~**nisvol, (-le)**, compassionate, pitiful; ~**niswaar'dig, (-e)**, pitiable, commiserable; ~**niswek'kend, (-e)**, pitiful.
dees, (verb.) this; *op ~ aarde!*, oh my! good gracious!; ~**dae**, nowadays; *~ dae se kinders*, children of today.
défaitis', (-te), defeatist; ~**me**, defeatism; ~**ties, (-e)**, defeatist.
defek', (s) (-te), defect, fault, breakdown; (b) (-te), defective; punctured (tyre); *~ RAAK*, break down, become defective; *~ WEES*, be out of order, be defective.
defeka'sie, defecation.
defektief', (..tiewe), defective, faulty.
defensief', (..siewe), defensive; *~ optree*, be on the defensive; ~**pleister**, *emplastrum defensivi Vigonis*.
defeseer', (ge-), (ong.) defecate.
defibrineer', (ge-), defibrinize.

défilé', (-s), defile, march past (in file).
defileer', (ge-), defile, march (file) past; ~**mars**, march past.
definieer', (ge-), define; ~**baar, (..bare)**, definable.
defini'sie, (-s), definition.
definitief', (..tiewe), definite, decisive, final.
deflagra'sie, (-s), deflagration.
deflagra'tor, (-s), deflagrator.
defla'sie, deflation.
deflasioneer', (ge-), deflate.
deflasionis'ties, (-e), deflationary.
deflek'sie, deflection; ~**hoek**, angle of deflection.
deflekteer', (ge-), deflect, deviate from; lose endings; *die deflekterende tale*, the deflecting languages.
deflora'sie, defloration.
defloreer', (ge-), deflower; deprive of virginity.
deforma'sie, (-s), deformation.
deformeer', (ge-), deform.
def'tig, (-e), grand, stately, matronly, grave, smart, fashionable, classy, formal, elegant; dignified, orotund (speech); fine (clothes); portly; *~ GEKLEED*, elegantly dressed; *by ~e GELEENTHEDE*, on formal occasions; *iem. 'n ~e PAK slae gee*, give someone a sound thrashing; ~**heid**, stateliness, dignity, distinction, gravity; fashionableness; gentility; lordliness; portliness.
defungeer', (ge-), die; lay down office; stop functioning.
degausseer', (ge-), degauss.
de'gel, platen; ~**drukker**, platen man; ~**pers**, platen press.
de'gen, (-s), sword; foil; blade.
degenera'sie, degeneracy, degeneration.
degeneratief', (..tiewe), degenerative.
degenereer', (ge-), degenerate.
de'genstok, sword-cane (stick).
de'gerig, (-e), doughy.
degrada'sie, degradation; demotion; disrating; reduction to the ranks.
degradeer', (ge-), degrade, reduce in rank; disrate.
degrade'ring, demotion, reduction to the ranks; disrating.
dehidra'sie, dehydration.
dehidrateer', (ge-), dehydrate.
dehidrate'ring, dehydration.
dehidreer', (ge-), = **dehidrateer**.
dei, (-s), dey.
deïfika'sie, deification.
deik'ties, (-e), deictic.
dein, (ge-), heave, surge, swell; billow; cockle; ~**ing, (-e, -s)**, heave, swell, surge.
deins, (ge-), shrink (back); recoil, retreat.
deïs', (-te), deist; ~**me**, deism; ~**ties, (-e)**, deistic.
dek, (s) (-ke), deck; floor (of bridge); cover; (w) (ge-), cover, clothe; foliate; protect (bill); shield (a person); defray (costs); be at stud, cover, serve (cow, mare); make good (loss); thatch (a house); cap (fuse); *die AFTOG ~*, cover the retreat; *KOSTE ~*, defray expenses, *TAFEL ~*, lay the table; *jou teen VERLIES ~*, cover oneself against loss.
dekaan', (dekane), dean; ~**skap**, deanship.
deka'de, (-s), decade.
dekaden'sie, decadence.
dekadent', (-e), decadent.
deka'dies, (-e), decadal, decadic.
dekagonaal', (..nale), decagonal.
dekagoon', (..gone), decagon.
de'kagram, (-me), decagram(me).
de'kaliter, (-s), decalitre.
Dekaloog', (..loë), Decalogue, Ten Commandments.
de'kameter, (-s), decametre.
dekanaat', (..nate), diaconate, deanship, deanery.
dekanie', (-ë), deanery.
dekanteer', (ge-), decant, pour off.
dekapita'sie, decapitation, beheading.
dekapiteer', (ge-), behead, decapitate.
dekarboniseer', (ge-), decarbonize.
dekat'lon, (-s), decathlon.
dek: ~**balk**, deck beam, crossbeam; roadbearer (of bridge); ~**band**, cover strip; ~**beitel**, covering iron; ~**beslag**, coating batter; ~**blaar**, bract(eal), floral leaf; (cigar) wrapper.

dek'blad¹, (..blaaie), fly-leaf; cover-slab, deckslab; overthrust mass, nappe (geol.).
dek'blad², (..blare), floral leaf; (cigar) wrapper.
de'ken¹, (-s), counterpane, quilt, coverlet; blanket, blanketing.
de'ken², (-s), doyen (of ambassadors); dean (church); ~ **aat'**, deanery; ~ **skap**, deanship.
de'kenstof, blanketing.
dek: ~ **geld**, stud fee, service fee; thatching costs; ~ **gewas**, cover crop; ~ **glas**, glass cover; cover glass; ~ **gras**, thatch(ing grass); ~ **hamer**, claw wrench; ~ **hare**, coat (beast's hair, fur); ~ **hings**, stallion, studhorse; ~ **huid**, integument; ~ **kend**, (-e), covering; ~ **kende magtiging**, covering authority; ~ **ker**, (-s), thatcher, roofer, tiler.
dek'king, cap; cover, shelter, guard; coverture; margin (stock exchange); security; hedge (betting); heave (in mines); coping; ~ **soek**, seek cover.
dek'kings: ~ **afdeling**, covering detachment; ~ **mag**, covering force; ~ **troepe**, covering troops; ~ **vuur**, covering fire.
dek: ~ **kleed**, (..klede), cover, body cloth; casing; ~ **kleedjie**, overlay; ~ **kraan**, deck crane; ~ **laag**, overburden; covering (surface) layer; overlay; coping, burden (in mines); mulch; apron (of concrete); cap; final coat (paint); seal coat (road); ~ **lading**, deck cargo.
deklama'sie, declamation, recitation.
deklama'tor, (-s), reciter; elocutionist.
deklameer', (ge-), declaim, recite.
dek'landing, deck landing.
deklarant', (-e), declarant.
deklara'sie, (-s), declaration; intendit (legal).
deklareer', (ge-), declare.
dek'las, deck load (cargo).
deklasseer', (ge-), declass.
dek: ~ **lat**, thatching lath; lag (mine); ~ **lei**, roofing-slate.
deklina'sie, (-s), declination; variation (of compass); ~ **hoek**, angle of declination; ~ **kaart**, deviation card; ~ **naald**, declination needle; ~ **sirkel**, circle of declination.
deklinatoor', (..tore), declinatory; *deklinatore eksepsie*, declinatory exception.
deklineer', (ge-), decline.
dek: ~ **lood**, sheet lead; ~ **lys**, cock-bead, cover beading; fillet (arch.); ~ **manskap**, deckhand; ~ **mantel**, cloak, mantle; excuse, pretext, mask, colour; disguise; *onder die ~ mantel van*, under the cloak of; ~ **matroos**, deck-hand; ~ **naald**, thatching needle; ~ **naat**, deck-seam.
dekodeer', (ge-), decode.
dek'offisier, petty officer.
dekolleteer', (ge-), wear a low-necked dress.
dekolonisa'sie, decolonization.
dekompres'sie, decompression.
dekor', (-s), scenery (stage), décor.
dekora'sie, (-s), decoration; order (knighthood); ~ **skilder**, scenic artist, scene-painter.
dekorateur', (-s), decorator.
dekoratief', (..tiewe), decorative, ornamental.
dekoreer', (ge-), decorate.
deko'rum, decorum, the proprieties.
dek: ~ **papier**, protective paper; ~ **passasier**, deck passenger; ~ **plaat**, cap(ping); coping, (cover)plate; top iron; deck plate; ~ **punt**, cover point (cricket).
dekreet', (dekrete), decree, edict.
dekrement', (-e), decrement.
dekrepiteer', (ge-), decrepitate.
dekreta'le, decretal.
dekreteer', (ge-), decree, enact, ordain.
dek: ~ **riet**, thatch reed; ~ **ring**, deck quoits; ~ **ruimte**, deck space; ~ **seil**, tarpaulin; ~ **sel**, (-s), cap; cover, lid; flap; *JOU ~ sel!* you wretch! *WAT die ~ sel!* what the dence! ~ **selhorlosie**, hunter (watch).
dek'sels, (b) (-e), blessed, confounded; very, exceedingly; *'n ~ gelol*, a darned nuisance; (bw) confoundedly, darned; ~ **hard**, dashed hard; (tw) dash it! hang it!
dek'selslot, lid lock.
dek: ~ **serk**, (ong.), covering slab (bridge); ~ **skild**, wing-cover, elytron; ~ **skub**, calypter; squama; ~ **sous**, coating (masking) sauce; ~ **spaan**, thatch spade; ~ **steen**, topstone, cope (coping-)stone; ~ **stoel**, deckchair.
dekstrien', **dekstri'ne**, dextrine, British gum.
dek: ~ **strooi**, thatch (grass); ~ **strook**, cover strip.
dekstro'se, grape-sugar, dextrose.
dek: ~ **stuk**, apron cover; apron-piece, cap(ping) piece; entablature; abacus (archit.); ~ **teël**, coping-tile; ~ **tennis**, deck tennis; ~ **terrein**, overburden (in mines); ~ **tyd**, time for service (animals); ~ **veer**, feather-spring; ~ **veld**, (kriek.), (the) covers, cover field; ~ **venster**, deck-light (passenger coach); ~ **vere**, coverts, tectrices; ~ **verf**, second coat; body colour; ~ **vermoë**, covering power, opacity, body (of paint); ~ **vlerk**, elytron; ~ **vlies**, coat, tectorial membrane; ~ **weefsel**, epithelium.
Delago'abaai, Delagoa Bay.
delegaat', (..gate), delegate.
delega'sie, (-s), delegation.
delegeer', (ge-), delegate; depute.
de'ler, (-s), divider; divisor; factor; *grootste gemene ~*, greatest common factor.
delf, (ge-), dig, mine, delve; *na minerale ~*, dig for minerals.
delfinien', **delfini'ne**, delphinine.
delf: ~ **plek**, stope; working; ~ **skag**, sinking shaft.
delf'stof, mineral; ~ **kunde**, mineralogy; ~ **kun'dig**, (-e), mineralogical; ~ **kun'dige**, (-s), mineralogist; ~ **ryk**, rich in minerals.
delf'stowweryk, mineral kingdom.
Delfts, (-e), Delft; *~ e erdewerk*, Delft ware.
delg, (ge-), discharge, pay off; wipe out, extinguish; redeem, amortize; ~ **ing**, payment, discharge, redemption, amortization; ~ **ingsfonds**, amortization fund, sinking fund, redemption fund.
delibera'sie, deliberation.
delibereer', (ge-), deliberate, consider.
delik', (-te), delict, offence.
delikaat', (..kate), delicate, delicious, tender; ticklish, difficult (undertaking).
delikates'se, (-s), delicacy, savoury (bit); ~ **winkel**, delicatessen.
delik'tereg, law of torts.
delimita'sie, delimitation; ~ **kommissie**, delimitation commission.
delimiteer', (ge-), fix boundaries, delimit(ate).
delinea'sie, (-s), delineation.
de'ling, (-e, -s), division; partition; fission; *lang ~*, long division.
delinkwent', (-e), (ong.) delinquent.
deli'ries, (-e), delirious.
deli'rium, delirium; ~ *tremens*, delirium tremens.
del'ta, (-s), delta; ~ **eiland**, delta island; ~ **'ies**, (-e), deltoid; ~ **meer**, delta lake; ~ **metal**, delta metal; ~ **spier**, deltoid muscle; ~ **vormig**, (-e), deltoid; ~ **vorming**, deltafication.
del'we, (ge-), dig, mine, delve; ~ **r**, (-s), digger, delver; ~ **ry**, digging; ~ **rye**, diggings (alluvial).
demagnetiseer', (ge-), demagnetize.
demagogie', demagogy.
demago'gies, (-e), demagogic.
demagoog', (..goë), demagogue.
demarka'sie, demarcation.
demarkeer', (ge-), demarcate.
demaskeer', (ge-), unmask.
demen'sie, (ong.), dementia, insanity.
demen'ti, (-'s), denial.
demi', demy (paper).
demilitarisa'sie, demilitarization.
demilitariseer', (ge-), demilitarize.
demilitarise'ring, demilitarization.
demi'-mondai'ne, (-s), demi-mondaine.
demi'-mon'de, demi-monde.
demis'sie, demission; dismissal.
demitteer', (ge-), dismiss; grant demission.
demobilisa'sie, demobilization.
demobiliseer', (ge-), demobilize.
demograaf', (..grawe), demographer.
demografie', demography; ..**grafies**, (-e), demographic.
demokraat', (..krate), democrat.

demokrasie', democracy.
demokra'ties, (-e), democratic
demokratiseer', (ge-), democratize; ..**kratise'ring**, democratization.
de'mon, (-e), demon, devil.
demo'neleer, demonology.
demonetisa'sie, demonetization.
demonetiseer', (ge-), demonetize; ..**tise'ring**, demonetization.
demo'nies, (-e), fiendish, devilish, ghoulish, diabolic(al).
de'mon: ~ **iseer'** (ge-), demonize; ~ **is'me**, demonism; ~ **ologie'**, demonology; ~ **omanie'**, demonomania.
demonstrant', (-e), demonstrator.
demonstra'sie, (-s), demonstration; ~ **veld**, demonstration plot (small holding); ~ **vlug**, demonstration flight.
demonstrateur', (-s), demonstrator.
demonstratief', (..tiewe), demonstrative.
demonstreer', (ge-), demonstrate; ~ **der, (-s)**, demonstrator.
demonteer', (ge-), dismantle (gun); dismount; devitalize (elec.); take to pieces.
demoralisa'sie, demoralization.
demoraliseer', (ge-), demoralize; deprave.
demoralise'rend, (-e), demoralizing.
demo'sie, demotion.
Demos'thenes, Demosthenes.
demo'ties, (-e), demotic.
demoveer', (ge-), demote.
demp, (ge-), fill up with earth; quell (riot); quench (fire); mute, deaden, muffle (sound); cushion (mech.); subdue, dim (light); tone down, soften (colours); ge ~ te LIG, subdued light; met ge ~ te STEM, in a muffled voice; ~ **baar**, (..**bare**), quenchable; ~ **er, (-s)**, quencher; attenuator; absorber; silencer; choke; damper; muffler (engine); mute, sordine (mus); ~ **glas**, dimming glass (music); ~ **ing**, extinction, quenching, stamping out; silencing, absorption (sound); damping; attenuation (elec.); ~ **klep**, damper valve; ~ **punt**, cushion point; ~ **trommel**, baffle drum; ~ **veer**, damper spring.
den¹, (s) (-ne), pine, fir (tree); ~ **agtig, (-e)**, firry.
den²: in ~ BREDE, in full detail; om ~ BRODE, for a living; for one's bread and butter.
denasionalisa'sie, denationalization.
denasionaliseer', (ge-), denationalize.
denaturalisa'sie, denaturalization.
denaturaliseer', (ge-), denaturalize.
denatureer', (ge-), denature; ..**ture'ring**, denaturation.
dendriet', (-e), dendrite.
dendri'ties, (-e), dendritic; ~ e mangaan, dendritic manganese.
dendroï'de, dendroïed', (-e), dendroid.
dendroliet', (-e), dendrolite (fossil).
dendrologie', dendrology.
dendroloog', (..loë), dendrologist.
De'nemarke, Denmark.
Den Haag, The Hague.
denitreer', (ge-), denitrate.
den'gue(koors), dengue (fever).
denk'baar, (..bare), imaginable, thinkable, conceivable; ~ **heid**, conceivability.
denk'beeld, (-e), idea, imagination, notion; view, opinion; fancy; iem. op 'n ~ BRING, put an idea into someone's head; suggest to someone; jou 'n ~ VORM van, form an idea (image) of.
denkbeel'dig, (-e), imaginary, chimerical, hypothetical; fictitious; fanciful, fantastic, illusive, illusory; ideal; ~ **heid**, fictitiousness.
denk: thought, (act of) thinking; ~ **beeldvorming**, ideation; ~ **end, (-e)**, thinking, sentient; ~ **er, (-s)**, thinker, reasoner, meditator; philosopher; ~ **fout**, error of reasoning; ~ **krag**, thinking power; ~ **lik**, **(-e)**, probable, conceivable, possible; ~ **oefening**, mental exercise; ~ **rigting**, school (way) of thinking; ~ **vermoë**, intellectual capacity; thinking faculty; brain power; ~ **wyse**, way of thinking, opinion; mental attitude.
den'ne: ~ **agtig, (-e)**, piny; ~ **bier**, spruce beer; ~ **bol**,

fir-cone, pine-cone; ~ **bolvormig, (-e)**, pineal; ~ **boom**, fir (tree), pine (tree); ~ **bos**, pine grove, fir forest.
den'nebros, dandy-brush.
den'ne: ~ **gom**, ~ **hars**, fir-resin; ~ **hout**, pine (wood), fir(wood); ~ **naald**, pine-needle, fir-needle; ~ **pap**, pulp-wood; ~ **pit**, fir-cone pip; ~ **plantasie**, pinery; ~ **suur**, pinic acid; ~ **tak**, pine bough.
denominaal', (..nale), denominal.
denomina'sie, denomination.
denominatief', (..tiewe), denominative.
denota'sie, denotation.
denoteer', (ge-), denote.
dénou'ement, dénouement.
den'simeter, densime'ter, (-s), densimeter.
densiteit', density.
dentaal', (..tale), dental.
dentien', denti'ne, dentine.
denti'sie, teething, dentition.
denuda'sie, denudation.
denudeer', (ge-), denude.
de'odar, (-s), deodar.
dep, (s) = **depper**; (w) (ge-), swab (medical).
departement', (-e), department; office.
departementeel', (..tele), departmental.
departement': ~ **sekretaris**, secretary of a department; departmental secretary; ~ **s'hoof**, head of a department; departmental head.
dêpê'che, (-s), dispatch, telegram.
depolarisa'sie, depolarization.
depolarisa'tor, (-e, -s), depolariser.
depolariseer', (ge-), depolarize.
deponeer', (ge-), place, put down, pay in, deposit (money); lodge (document); make a statement (law).
deponent', (-e), deponent; depositor.
deport', backwardation.
deporta'sie, deportation.
deporteer', (ge-), deport.
deport'handel, backwardation.
deposant', (-e), depositor.
deposita'ris, (-se), depository, depositee.
depo'sito, (-'s), deposit; lodg(e)ment (law); ~ **bank**, deposit bank; ~ **bewys**, receipt of deposit; ~ **gelde**, deposits; ~ **nemend, (-e)**, deposit-receiving; ~ **rekening**, deposit account; ~ **strokie**, deposit slip.
depot', (-s), depot; dump.
dep'per, (-s), swab (medical).
depresia'sie, depreciation.
depresieer', (ge-), depreciate.
depres'sie, depression; ~ **f', (..siewe)**, depressive; ~ **gebied**, cyclonic area; area of low pressure; ~ **hoek**, depression angle.
deprimeer', (ge-), depress, dispirit; ..**prime'rend, (-e)**, depressing.
de'proklameer, (ge-), deproclaim.
deputaat', (..tate), (church) delegate, deputy; ~ **skap, (-pe)**, deputation.
deputa'sie, (-s), deputation.
deputeer', (ge-), depute.
der, (vero.) of (the); die HEILIGE ~ Heilige, the Holy of Holies; die HERE ~ here, the Lord of lords; JARE ~ jare, many years; in ~ WAARHEID, in very truth, truly.
derailleer', (ge-), run off the rails, be derailed, leave the metals, jump the rails.
derda'e, long ago.
der'de, third; AANSPREEKLIKHEID teenoor ~ s, third party risk; 'n ~ DEEL, a third part (volume); ~ GELUI, third ringing (church bell); ~ KLAS reis, travel third class; D ~ STRAAT, Third Street, TEN ~, in the third place; UIT die ~ hand, at third hand; ~ **daags, (-e):** ~ **daagse koors**, tertian fever; ~ **dagaand**, evening of the third day; ~ **graads, (-e)**, third grade; ~ **half**, two and a half; ~ **jaars, (-e)**, third year (student); ~ **klas**, inferior, third-class; ~ **klaskaartjie**, third-class ticket; ~ **lesingsdebat**, third-reading debate; ~ **mag**, cube; ~ **magsvergelyking**, cubic equation; ~ **magswortel**, cube root.
der'demannetjie, twos and threes (game); ~ speel, play gooseberry.
der'departyversekering = **derdeversekering**.

der'depersoonrisiko, third-party risk.
der'derangs, (-e), third-rate.
der'deversekering, third-party insurance.
derdui'sende, many thousands.
derdui'wel, brute; vicious (ill-tempered) person; brave person, daredevil; *soos 'n ~ veg*, fight like mad; *~ s*, (bw) very, exceedingly; *dis ~ s koud*, it is exceedingly cold; *~ s*, (tw) my word!
derf, (ge-), *see* **derwe**
der'gelik, (-e), such, the like, similar; *in ~ e GE= VALLE*, in such cases; *IETS ~ s*, something like that.
der'halwe, therefore, so, consequently, hence.
derivaat', (..vate), derivative.
deriva'sie, derivation.
derivatief', (..tiewe), derivative.
derja're, many years.
derm, (-s), gut; *~ s*, intestines, bowels, entrails; casing (for sausage); *hy het ~ s in sy kop*, he is very clever (very brainy).
dermaal', (..male), dermal.
derm: *~* **aandoening**, intestinal complaint; *~* **afslui= ting**, ileus.
der'mate, in such a manner, to such an extent.
dermatologie', dermatology; *..tolo'gies, (-e)*, derma= tological.
dermatoloog', (..loë), dermatologist, skin specialist.
dermato'se, dermatosis.
derm: *~* **been**, ilium, iliac bone; *~* **beklemming**, gut= tie; *~* **beweging**, peristalsis; *~* **breuk**, enterocele, rupture of the intestines; *~* **instulping**, intussuscep= tion; *~* **jig**, ileus, iliac passion; *~* **kanaal**, intestinal canal (tube); *~* **knoop**, ileus; volvulus; *~* **kronkel**, twist of the bowels; volvulus; *~* **net**, caul; *~* **ont= steking**, enteritis; *~* **pie, (-s)**, little gut; *~* **skeil**, me= sentery; *~* **snaar**, catgut, gut string; *~* **uitspoeling**, enema; *~* **vet**, gut fat, ruffle fat; *~* **vlies**, perito= neum; *~* **vliesontsteking**, peritonitis; *~* **vlokkie**, villus.
derogeer', (ge-), derogate.
der'rie, blue material (dress).
der'tien, thirteen; a baker's dozen; *~* **de**, thirteenth; *~* **de-eeus**, (b) **(-e)**, of the thirteenth century; *~* **jarig, (-e)**, of thirteen years; thirteen years old; *~* **jarige, (-s)**, thirteen-year-old.
der'tig, thirty; *hy is IN die ~*, he is in his thirties; *in die JARE ~*, in the thirties; *~* **er, (-s)**, person between 30 en 40 years old; Afrikaans poet of the period 1930-40; *~* **erjare**, (in) the thirties; *~* **jarig, (-e)**, of thirty years; thirty years old; *~* **jarige, (-s)**, thirty- year-old; *~* **ste**, thirtieth; *~* **tal**, (about) thirty; *~* **voud**, thirty times.
der'waarts, thither.
der'we, (ge-), lack, miss, want, be deprived of.
der'wing, privation, want, lack; loss.
der'wisj, (-e), dervish.
des¹, (s) D flat minor (mus.).
des², (bw, lw) of the, so much the; *~ te BETER*, all the better, so much the better; *~ te MEER omdat*, the more so because.
des'alnietemin, nevertheless, still.
des'betreffend, (-e), relating to the matter concerned; relevant.
de'se, this; *BY ~*, herewith, hereby; *~ en GENE*, each and everybody; *MITS ~*, herewith; *NA ~*, after this.
Desem'ber, December; *~* **maand**, the month of De= cember.
Desem'berpeer, pear ripening in December.
desen'nium, (..nnia, -s), decennium, decade.
desentralisa'sie, decentralization.
desentraliseer' (ge-), decentralize.
de'ser, of this; *~ DAE*, these days; *DIE 10de ~*, the 10th instant.
deser'sie, (-s), desertion.
deserteer' (ge-), desert, run away.
deserteur', (-s), deserter.
de'ses, (ong.) of this; *skrywer ~*, the writer of this (letter, article).
des'gelyks, likewise, accordingly.
des'gewens, if need be; if (so) desired.
deshabillé', undress, deshabille.

deshonoreer', (ge-), dishonour (a bill).
de'siaar, (desiare), deciare.
de'sibel, (-s), decibel.
desideer', (ge-), decide.
desidera'tum, (..ta), desideratum.
de'sigram, (-me), decigram(me).
desikka'sie, desiccation.
desikka'tor, (-s), desiccator.
desilika'sie, desilication.
de'siliter, (-s), decilitre.
des'illusie, (-s), disillusion(ment).
desillusioneer', (ge-), disillusion(ize).
desimaal', (..male), decimal; *..male breuk*, decimal fraction; *..male punt*, decimal point; *~* **punt**, deci= mal point; *~* **stelsel**, decimal system.
desimalisa'sie, decimalization.
desimaliseer', (ge-), decimalize.
desimeer', (ge-), decimate.
de'simeter, (-s), decimetre.
desinfek'sie, disinfection; *~* **middel**, disinfectant.
desinfekteer', (ge-), disinfect.
desintegra'sie, disintegration.
desintegreer', (ge-), disintegrate.
deskriptief', (..tiewe), descriptive.
deskun'dig, (-e), expert; adept; *~ e getuie*, expert wit= ness; *~* **e, (-s)**, expert, adept, specialist; *~* **heid**, expertness.
desmotropie', desmotropy, desmotropism.
des'nieteenstaande, for all that, nevertheless, even so.
des'nietemin, nevertheless, for all that.
desnoods', if need be; in case of need, at a pinch.
desolaat', (..late), (ong.) desolate, disconsolate; ruined; wretched.
des'ondanks, nevertheless.
desorganisa'sie, disorganization.
desorganiseer', (ge-), disorganize.
desoriënta'sie, disorientation.
desoriënteer', (ge-), lead astray, bewilder, dis= orientate.
desoriëntering, disorientation.
desperaat', (..rate), desperate, despairing.
despera'do, (-'s), desperado.
despereer', (ge-), despair.
despoot', (despote), despot, tyrant.
despo'ties, (-e), despotic, tyrannic(al).
despotis'me, despotism, tyranny.
dessert', (-e), dessert; *~* **bord**, dessertplate; *~* **happies**, friandises; *~* **lepel**, dessertspoon; *~* **mes**, dessert= knife; *~* **vurk**, dessertfork.
dessin', (-s), (ong.) design, pattern.
destina'sie, destination.
destruktief', (..tiewe), destructive.
des'tyds, (-e), at that time, then; *die ~ e hoof*, the then head master.
des'verkiesend, if so wished (desired).
des'weë, on that account, for that reason.
detail', (-s), detail; *~* **leer', (ge-)**, detail, specify.
detasjeer', (ge-), detach, draft off.
detasjement', (-s), detachment.
detasje'ring, (-e, -s), detachment, secondment, draft= ing off.
detek'tor, (-s), detector.
deten'sie, detention.
détente, (F.) détente.
determinant', (-e), determinant.
determina'sie, determination.
determineer', (ge-), determine, define.
determinis', (-te), determinist.
determinis'me, determinism.
determinis'ties, (-e), deterministic.
detoneer', (ge-), be out of the picture (out of tune, keeping, place); detonate.
detritaal', (..tale), detrital.
detri'tus, detritus.
deug, (s) (-de), virtue, excellence, probity; (good) quality; *LIEWE ~! good gracious! twee ~ de van hierdie MATERIAAL*, two good qualities pos= sessed by this material; (w) (ge-), be good for, serve a purpose, befit, be of use; *dit ~ nie*, this won't pay; this is no good (is useless, bad, unsuitable, worth= less).

deug'delik, (-e), solid; valid (argument); durable (material); genuine; sound; ~**heid,** validity, solidity, durability, soundness.
deug'liewend, (-e), virtuous, worthy.
deug'niet, (-e), rascal, good-for-nothing, ne'er-do-well, blackguard.
deug'saam (..same), virtuous, honest; gracious; ~**heid,** virtuousness, honesty, probity, worthiness.
deuk, (s) (-e), (ong.), dent; (w) (ge-), dent; ~**hoed,** crush-hat, fedora, soft (Homburg) hat; ~**mielie,** dent mealie.
deun'tjie, (-s), air, tune, ditty, chime; *die ~ goed KEN,* to have heard it before; *dieselfde OU ~,* the same old story; *'n ander ~ SING,* sing a different tune, sing small; ~**klok,** door-chimes.
deur[1], (s) (-e), door; portal, gate; *van ~ tot ~ GAAN,* go from door to door; *agter GESLOTE ~e,* in camera; behind closed doors; *met die ~ in die HUIS val,* blurt something out; plunge into a matter; *'n ~ voor iem. se NEUS toemaak,* shut the door in someone's face; *'n OOP ~ intrap,* force an open door; *die OOP ~ roep die dief,* opportunity makes the thief; *die ~ altyd OOP vind,* find the doors always open; *die ~ OOPMAAK vir iets,* give an opportunity for something; *iem. buite die ~ SIT,* show someone the door; *dit STAAN ons voor die ~,* it is at hand (upon us); *as jy self agter die ~ STAAN, dan soek jy 'n ander ook daar,* you measure another man's corn by your own bushel; *agter die ~ STAAN,* not to come out in the open; *jou ~ STAAN oop,* your fly is open; *alle ~e STAAN vir hom oop,* all doors are open to him; *aan 'n oop ~ STOOT,* force an open door; *as elkeen voor sy eie ~ VEE, sal die straat skoon wees,* if each would sweep before his own door, we should have a clean city; *voor jou eie ~ VEE,* sweep before one's own door; *by die VERKEERDE ~ klop,* knock at the wrong door; *iem. die ~ WYS,* show someone the door.
deur[2], (vs) through; throughout; across; by; on account of; *~ die BANK,* all, without exception; *BO ~,* through at the top; *hy IS ~,* he has passed (his examination); *die hele JAAR ~,* all through the year, all the year round; *iem. ~ en ~ KEN,* know someone through and through (thoroughly); *die hele LAND ~,* throughout (all over) the country; *~ die MIS opgehou,* delayed by the mist, fog-bound; *~ die SKRYWER,* by the author; *~ die pos STUUR,* send by post; *~ die lug VERVOER,* airborne; *~ die WATER afgeslyt,* water-worn; *~ die WEER opgehou (vertraag),* delayed by the weather, weather-bound; *~ die WIND gesorteer,* wind-sorted.
deur'aanslag, doorstop.
deuraar', deura'der, (-de), veined, veiny.
deur'baan, door runner (guide).
deur'babbel, (-ge-), continue talking (chatting).
deur'bak, (-ge-), bake through; continue baking, *deurgebakte vleis,* well-done meat.
deur'bars, (-ge-), burst through.
deur'bel,[1] (s) doorbell.
deur'bel,[2] (w) (-ge-), phone through.
deur'beslag, metal-work on door.
deur'bind, (-ge-), divide by binding.
deur'blaai, (-ge-), turn over the leaves of a book, skim, leaf through (the pages of a book).
deur'blaas, (-ge-), blow through; ~**klep,** blow-through valve; ~**kraan,** petcock.
deur'bloeier, (-s), perennial (plant).
deur'boer, (-ge-), continue farming.
deurboor'[1], (w) (~), pierce, stab, transfix; riddle (with bullets); impale; penetrate; gore (with horns); (b) (-de), penetrated, pertused.
deur'boor[2], (w) (-ge-), drill through, bore, pin; perforate.
deur'boring[1], perforation, tunnelling.
deurbo'ring[2], impalement.
deur'bout, door-nail.
deur'braak, breach (of sea dikes); penetration, breakthrough (of enemies' lines); gap; holing through; eruption (teeth); rupture, breaking through.
deur'brand, (-ge-), burn through; continue burning.

deur'breek[1], (-ge-), break through; hole through.
deurbreek'[2], (~), penetrate, break through (fig.)
deurbre'king, penetration.
deur'bring, (-ge-), pass, idle away (one's time); spend, squander, prodigalize (money); expend; ~**er,** (-s), spendthrift, prodigal, wastrel, spend-all; devourer; ~**erig** (-e), wasteful, prodigal, extravagant; ~**erigheid,** wastefulness.
deur'buiging, flexure, sag, deflection.
deur'byt, (-ge-), bite through; get over; persist, persevere.
deurdag', (-te), well thought-out, considered (opinion).
deur'dans, (-ge-), dance through (the night); wear out (shoes) by dancing.
deur'dat, because, as; *~ hy lank moes wag, het hy ...,* because he had to wait so long, he ...
deur'dink[1], (-ge-), continue thinking; think out.
deurdink'[2], (~), consider fully.
deur'draai, (-ge-), keep on turning; turn through.
deur'draf, ..drawwe, (-ge-), trot through; go on trotting; treat (a matter) superficially; settle (complete) quickly; *'n stuk werk gou ~,* rush through work.
deurdrenk', (~), saturate, impregnate, steep; *~ van water,* saturated with water; ~**ing,** saturation.
deur'drif, ford.
deur'dring[1], (-ge-), penetrate into, enter into; ooze through; push through; *die waarheid het tot hom deurgedring,* the truth dawned upon him.
deurdring'[2], (~), permeate; pervade; impress; pierce; plunge through; *iem. van iets ~,* make someone realise; ~**baar,** (..bare), penetrable, permeable, pervious; ~**baarheid,** penetrability, permeability, perviousness; ~**end,** (-e), shrill, piercing, penetrating, searching; pungent; soaking, penetrant; keen; pervasive; ~**endheid,** penetrative power, permeation, pervasion; ~**ing,** infiltration, pervasion, penetration, permeation; ~**ingsvermoë,** penetrative power.
deurdron'ge: *~ van,* impressed with, fully convinced of, alive to.
deur'druk, (-ge-), press through, force one's way; persist; go on printing; mackle (paper); punch; *~ tot die end,* keep right on to the end; ~**ker,** go-getter, pusher, persister; ~**lyn,** perforated line, line of punch (fracture); ~**steek,** stab stitch (needlework).
deur'drumpel, threshold, door-sill.
deur'dryf, ..drywe (-ge-), force through, enforce, persist, carry one's point; *jou wil ~,* have one's way; ~**hamer,** drift hammer.
deur'drywer, persistent person; hustler; thrusting person; live wire; ~**y,** persistence.
deureen'meng, (-ge-), mix thoroughly; ~**ing,** promiscuity.
deureen'vleg, (-ge-), implicate; interlace.
deur'eet, (deurgeëet), eat through, corrode; keep on eating; cat to satiety.
deur en deur, through and through, thoroughly, out and out, all-round; *~ eerlik,* thoroughly honest, honest to the core; *~ KEN,* know thoroughly; *~ 'n SKELM,* an out-and-out scoundrel.
deur'entyd, always, continually, throughout.
deur'gaan, (-ge-), pass, go through; experience; examine; wear through (clothes, shoes); clinch (bargain); proceed; go over, ford (river); *die KOOP kan nie ~ nie,* the sale must be cancelled; *~ MET 'n plan,* go through with a plan; *vir die PRINS ~,* pass (masquerade, pose) as the prince; *~ 'baar,* (..bare), passable; ~**de,** non-stop (train); *~ de verkeer,* through traffic; ~**plek,** ford.
deur'gaans, commonly, usually, generally, mostly, passim, as a rule; all the way through.
deur'gang, (right of) passage, thoroughfare; gangway, corridor; slot; *GEEN ~,* no thoroughfare; *'n NOU ~,* a bottle-neck.
deur'gangsreg, wayleave, right of way.
deur'gee, (-ge-), pass on (information), relay.
deur'gelê, (deurgelegde), bed-sore; addled; *die eier is ~,* the egg is addled.
deur'geloop, (-te), foot-sore, foot-worn; worn-out (shoes).
deur'gery, (-de), saddle-sore.

deur'gesak, (-te), sagged; ~ *te vlerk*, stalled wing.
deur'gestoke: *'n ~ kaart*, a pre-arranged matter, a frame-up.
deurgeur', (~), perfume.
deur'giet, (-ge-), pour through, filter, strain.
deur'glip, deur'gly, (-ge-), slip through.
deur'gooi, (-ge-), pour through, throw through; filter.
deur'gordyn, portière.
deurgraaf¹, ..grawe (~), pierce.
deur'graaf², ..grawe, (-ge-), dig through, cut through, tunnel, honeycomb; continue digging.
deur'grawing, (-e, -s), digging through, cutting through; cutting, tunnel; canalization.
deur'grendel, door-bolt.
deur'groei, (-ge-), grow through; continue growing; ~ **end**, (-e), perennial; ~ **ing**, intergrowth.
deurgrond', (w), (~), fathom (one's mind); penetrate, see through; understand, get to the bottom of (a thing); ~ **elikheid**, penetrability.
deur'haak, cabin (door) hook.
deur'haal, (-ge-), bring through; strike (cross, scratch) out, strike through, delete, cancel, erase (word); pull (a patient) through, cure.
deur'hak, (-ge-), cut through; solve.
deur'haling, (-e, -s), cancellation, erasure, deletion, obliteration.
deur'handvatsel, door-handle.
deur'hardloop, (-ge-), run through; hurry through.
deurheen', through.
deur'helling, door-ramp (truck).
deur'help, (-ge-), help (one) through.
deur'hol, (-ge-), run (hurry) through.
deur'ja(ag), (-ge-), rush through; drive through.
deur'kam, (-ge-), comb through; examine (records, facts).
deur'kap, (-ge-), cut through, split.
deur'klief¹, (-ge-), cleave (in two).
deurklief'², (~), cleave (the air); plough through (waves).
deur: ~ **klink**, door-pawl; door-latch; ~ **klok**, door-bell; ~ **klopper**, door-knocker.
deur'knaag¹, (-ge-), gnaw through (on).
deurknaag'², (~), torture, torment.
deur'knee¹, deur'knie¹ (-ge-), knead thoroughly; keep on kneading.
deurknee'², deurknie'², well-read, versed in, steeped in (ancient lore).
deurkneed'heid, intimate (thorough) knowledge, conversance, conversancy.
deur'knip¹, (s) door-catch; thumb-latch.
deur'knip², (w) (-ge-), cut through (with scissors); perforate; ~ **ping**, perforation.
deur'knop, door-knob, door-handle.
deur'kom, (-ge-), get through, pass (an examination); survive; tide over; erupt (teeth); *die KIND se tande wil ~*, the child is beginning to cut its teeth; *'n KRI= SIS ~*, survive a crisis; *genoeg OM deur te kom*, enough to see us through, enough to last; ~ **plek**, exit, place to slip out.
deur'kook, (-ge-), boil (cook) thoroughly; keep on boiling.
deur'kosyn, door-frame, door-case.
deur'krap, (-ge-), cross out; scratch through; ~ **ping**, erasure.
deur'kruip, (-ge-), creep through; wear out by creeping.
deurkruis', (~), traverse, intersect; ramble over, scour; cross (the mind).
deur'kry, (-ge-), get (a pupil, needle) through; pull (a patient) through; get accepted (plan).
deur'kyk, (s) (-e), through view, vista; (w) (-ge-), look over (through), skim, peruse; examine closely; sum up (person); *ek het hom goed deurgekyk*, I know his tricks, I summed him up thoroughly.
deur'laat, (s) culvert; passage, outlet; (w) (-ge-), let through, allow to pass; *LIG ~*, be translucent; *geen WATER ~ nie*, be watertight (-proof); ~ **'baar**, (..bare), permeable, porous; ~ **'baarheid**, permeability; ~ **sel**, transfusion cell.
deur'latend, (-e), permeable, pervious; ~ **heid**, permeability.
deur'lating, permeation; transmission.

deur'lê, (-ge-), become bedsore; *deurgelegde eier*, stale (addled) egg, broken yolk; *deurgelegde STOF*, perished material.
deur'leef¹, ..**le'we**, (w) (-ge-), continue to live, survive.
deurleef'² deurle'we, (w) (~), experience, pass through.
deurleef' (b) (-de), experienced, based on experience.
deur'lees, (-ge-), read through, peruse; read on.
deur'lek¹, (-ge-), leak through.
deur'lek², (-ge-), lick through (on).
deur'lêseer, bedsore.
deur'lesing, perusal.
deur'lig¹, (s) (-te), door-light; screen (med.).
deurlig'² (w) (~), illuminate; X-ray
deurlig'ting, (-e, -s), transillumination; X-ray examination.
deur'loer, (-ge-), peep through.
deur'loods, (-ge-), pilot through, guide.
deur'loop¹, (s) arcade; passage; thoroughfare; culvert; enjambment; (w) (-ge-), move on, walk through, wear out (one's shoes) by walking; chafe the legs (by walking); become foot-sore; reprimand, punish; follow through (billiards); examine; check (accounts); *laat ~ DAG toe*, carry on till daybreak; *iem. LAAT ~*, make someone run the gauntlet; *my SALARIS loop deur*, my salary continues; *die STRAAT loop deur tot*, the street continues (extends) to; *onder die VOORSLAG ~*, run the gauntlet.
deurloop'², (w) (~), traverse; cover (distance); pass through (school).
deur'loopstoot, (-ge-), run-through (billiards).
deur'lopend, deurlo'pend, (-e), continuous story, uninterrupted; through (service); running (commentary); non-stop; ..**lopendheid**, continuity.
deurlug', (~), ventilate (soil), aerate; ~ *te water*, aerated water.
deurlug'tig, (-e), illustrious; glorious; ~ **heid**, illustriousness; *sy D~heid*, His Serene Highness.
deurlug'ting, aeration; ventilation.
deur'lys, door-moulding; architrave (moulding).
deur'maak, (-ge-), go (pass) through, experience.
deur'mars, march-through (of troops); ~ **jeer**, (-ge-), march through.
deur'mat, door-mat; *iem op die ~ laat staan*, leave someone standing on the threshold (doorstep).
deurmekaar', (-der, -ste), together, mixed, miscellaneous; pell-mell, in disorder (confusion); higgledy-piggledy; puzzled, puzzle-headed; flurried; on the average; delirious; blowzed, blowzy; littered (with junk); crisscross; distracted; dishevelled (hair); farraginous; fey; huddled; *'n ~ GEVEG*, a scuffle; *'n ~ SPUL*, a mixed lot; a chaotic business; omnium gatherum, jumble, medley, mix-up; *dit WAS glad ~*, everything was topsy-turvy; ~ **WEES met iem.**, be at loggerheads with someone; have an understanding (with a girl); ~ **boerdery**, mixed farming; mixing of races; ~ **boom**, *Terminalia prunioides*, *T. porphyrocarpa*; ~ **draad**, mass fibre; ~ **heid**, confusion, jumbled condition, mix-up; chaos, flurry, hurry-scurry; ~ **maak** (-ge-), mix; muddle; confuse; ~ **praat**, (-ge-), be delirious; talk incoherently; ~ **raak**, (-ge-), get mixed up (confused); become delirious; clash with (the law); ~ **skud**, (-ge-), shake up (together), hustle; ~ **spul**, mix-up, confusion, hugger-mugger; chaos; ~ **strengel**, (-ge-), interlace, intertwine; ~ **vleg**, (-ge-), intertwine, interwind; ~ **weef**, (-ge-), interweave; ~ **woon**, (-ge-), live together (with other races).
deur'naai, (-ge-), sew on (through); quilt; ~ **werk**, quilting.
deur'nat, thoroughly wet, soaked.
deur'neem, (-ge-), take through.
deur: ~ **nommer**, door number; ~ **opening**, doorway.
deur'pad, freeway, throughway, speedway, motorway.
deur'paneel, door-panel.
deurpeil', (~), probe, gauge.
deur'plaat, finger-plate.
deur'ploeë, ..**ploeg**, (-ge-), plough through (on).

deurploeg', (~), furrow, wrinkle; *'n gesig ~ van smart*, a face wrinkled by sorrow.
deur'pos, door-post, door-jamb.
deur'praat, (-ge-), continue talking; discuss thoroughly.
deur'prik, (-ge-), prick through; perforate.
deur'pyl, (-ge-), rush through.
deur'raam, door-frame.
deur'rammel, ..ratel, (-ge-), rattle off; go on rattling.
deur'reën, ..reent, (-ge-), rain through; continue raining.
deur'reis¹, (s) passage; through-journey; *op die ~, en route*; (w) (-ge-), travel (pass) through.
deurreis'² (w), (~), travel all over.
deur'rit, passage.
deur'roei, (-ge-), row through (on).
deur'roer, (-ge-), stir well.
deur'roes, (-ge-), rust through, corrode.
deur'rol, (-ge-), roll through.
deurrook'¹, (~), fumigate.
deur'rook², (-ge-), continue smoking; *'n pyp ~*, colour a pipe; *ek is al deurgerook*, I am accustomed to smoking, I am a confirmed smoker.
deur'ry, (-ge-), pass through; gall (a horse); wear through by riding; *hy is deurgery*, he is saddle-sore; *~straat*, through-street.
deur'saag, (-ge-), saw through.
deur'sak, (-ge-), sag, sink; pancake, stall (aeroplane); ~**king**, sag; sinking; ~**landing**, pancake landing; ~**punt**, stalling point; ~**snelheid**, stalling speed; ~**vlug**, stalled flight
deur'seil, (-ge-), sail through.
deur'sein, (-ge-), signal through; transmit.
deur'settingsvermoë, persistence, perseverance, push, doggedness, drive.
deur'sien¹, (-ge-), see into, penetrate, check; glance over, skim, peruse.
deursien'², (~), see through (disguise); sum up (person); fathom; penetrate.
deur'sif, (-ge-), sift out, strain; filter.
deur'sig, view, perspective; insight, discernment, penetration; ~**'tig**, (-e), transparent, lucid; obvious (reason, excuse); ~**'tigheid**, transparency, lucidity.
deur'sit, (-ge-), sit through; sit oneself sore; have one's will, persist, persevere; see through (war); negotiate, put through (deal, telephone-call); *jou broek ~*, wear through the seat of one's trousers.
deur'skaaf, (-ge-), plane through; chafe.
deur'skakel, (-ge-), put (switch) through (telephone); ~**ing**, through-switching.
deur'skarnier, butt hinge.
deur'skawe = **deurskaaf**.
deur'skemer, (-ge-), glimmer through; *laat ~*, hint at, give to understand, intimate.
deur'skeur, (-ge-), tear (rend) asunder.
deur'skiet¹, (-ge-), shoot through; go on shooting.
deurskiet'², (~), interleave, interpage.
deursko'te, interfoliated, interleaved; *'n ~ eksemplaar*, an interleaved book.
deurskou', (~), fathom, see through.
deur'skrap, (-ge-), scratch (strike) out, delete.
deur'skryf, ..skrywe, (-ge-), continue writing.
deur'skud, (-ge-), shake up; shuffle (cards).
deur'skuif, (s) bolt; (w) (-ge-), push through.
deur'skuiwe, (-ge-), push through.
deur'skuur, (-ge-), rub (scour) through; chafe.
deur'skyn, (-ge-), shine (show) through; ~**aansig**, phantom view; ~**'end**, (-e), transparent, translucent, glassy, diaphanous, pellucid, liquid; ~**'endheid**, pellucidity, translucency; ~**papier**, transparent paper.
deur'slaan, (-ge-), punch, hit through, smash (pane); break into (a canter); soak through; change colour, ripen (fruit); break (voice); knock in two; force one's way; skid (locomotive); *in AFRIKAANS ~*, change over (from another language) into Afrikaans; *JOU ~ deur*, make one's way through; *die MOTOR het deurgeslaan*, the car jolted; *die MUUR slaan deur*, the wall is damp (is not weather-proof); *die SKAAL laat ~*, tip the scales.
deur'slaande: *~ bewys*, conclusive proof (evidence).
deur'slaap, (-ge-), sleep on.

deur'slag, moist soil, boggy ground, quag(mire); decisive factor; slough; average; (..**slae**), punching tool, punch (tool); carbon copy; flimsy; *~ GEE aan iets*, settle the matter; decide the issue; clinch matters; *IN ~ geneem*, on the average; ~**gewend**, (-e), decisive; *~ gewend vir*, vital to; ~**grond**, boggy land; ~**kopie**, flimsy (copy); ~**kussing**, bump rubber; ~**mens**, average person; ~**papier**, carbon paper; flimsy (copy); ~**'tig**, (-e), marshy, boggy, muddy, waterlogged; quaggy; ~**'tigheid**, marshiness, bogginess; ~**veer**, bump spring; ~**yster**, punch bar.
deur'sleep, (-ge-), drag (pull) through; trail through.
deur'slot, door-lock.
deur'sluip, (-ge-), steal (sneak) through.
deur'sluk, (-ge-), swallow down.
deur'slyt, (-ge-), wear through.
deur'smelt, (-ge-), fuse.
deur'smokkel, (-ge-), smuggle through.
deur'snede, (-s), **deur'snee**, (..**sneë**), section (transverse); cross-section; intersection; transection; diameter; caliber (of gun); profile; *in ~*, on an average; in section.
deur'snee: ~**aansig**, sectional view; ~**mens**, man in the street; ~**prys**, average price; ~**tekening**, sectional drawing.
deur'snel, (-ge-), hurry through.
deur'snork, (-ge-), continue snoring.
deur'snuffel, (-ge-), hunt through, ferret, rummage, ransack; ~**ing**, rummaging, ransacking.
deur'sny¹, (ge), out through, dissect; intersect.
deursny'², (~), cross, traverse.
deursny'ding¹, decussation.
deur'snyding², intersection.
deursoek'¹, (~), rake through; examine, search (fig.); *~ jou hart*, search one's heart.
deur'soek², (-ge-), examine, search, explore; beat (bushes for game); ransack (house); rummage (desk); ~**ing**, search, rummaging, ransacking.
deur'spartel, (-ge-), struggle through.
deur'speel, (-ge-), play to the end.
deurspek', (w) (~), interlard; intersperse; (b) (-te), interlarded, larded; honeycombed; marbled (meat); *~ met lesse*, full of lessons.
deur'spoel, (-ge-), flush, rinse; ~**ing**, flush.
deur'spring, (-ge-), jump through.
deur'staan, (-ge-), **deurstaan'**, (~), endure, suffer, bear; weather (storm); pass, stand (the test); *deurgestane ANGS*, anxiety which has been endured; *die PROEF ~*, stand the test; *die STORM ~*, weather the storm; *'n VERGELYKING ~ met*, bear comparison with.
deur'stap, (-ge-), walk through, continue walking.
deur'steek¹, (-ge-), pierce, pike, make a hole in, prick; put through (needle); take a straight course.
deursteek'², (~), stab, pierce; cut (dyke); impale.
deur'steker, (pipe-)cleaner; probe.
deur'stik, (-ge-), stitch through; quilt; -**werk**, quilting.
deur'stoot, (s) push-stroke (billiards); (w) (-ge-), push through; broach.
deur'stop, (-pe), door-stop, doorstopper.
deur'storm, (-ge-), rush (storm) through.
deur'straal¹, (-ge-), shine through; *laat ~*, hint at, give to understand.
deurstraal'², (~), illuminate, irradiate.
deur'straat, through street, thoroughfare.
deurstra'ling, illumination; motion (of bowels).
deur'streep, (-ge-), cross out, draw the pen through.
deurstren'gel, (~), intertwine, interweave.
deur'stroom, (-ge-), flow through (water); flush.
deur'stryk, (-ge-), continue ironing; walk on; delete.
deur'studeer, (-ge-), continue studying.
deur'stuiter, door-stop, doorstopper.
deur'stuur, (-ge-), pass (ball); forward (letter); send on, transmit; direct through.
deur'styl, door-post, jamb.
deur'suig, (-ge-), aspirate (gas); suck through.
deur'sukkel, (-ge-), struggle through; jog along; muddle through.
deur'swaai, (-ge-), follow through (golf).
deur'sweet, (-ge-), sweat through, transpire.

deurswerf

deur'swerf, (-ge-), rove (roam) through.
deur'swoeg, (-ge-), toil on.
deur'syfer, (-ge-), trickle (ooze) through; permeate, filter through, percolate; ~**ing**, seepage; filtration; filtering; percolation.
deur'syg, (-ge-), filter, strain (through); ~**er**, (-s), strainer; ~**sakkie**, jelly-bag.
deur'sypel, (-ge-), ooze through; percolate, filter; ~**ing**, percolation.
deurtas', (~), search (pockets); *'n gevangene* ~, search a prisoner.
deurtas'tend, (-e), energetic, decisive, sweeping, drastic (steps); resolute, vigorous; thorough (search); ~**heid**, resoluteness; thoroughness.
deur'tel[1], (-ge-), lift through.
deur'tel[2], (-ge-), continue counting, count through.
deur'tik, (-ge-), type through; continue typing.
deurtin'kel, (~), thrill.
deur'tog, passage; march-through; *'n* ~ *baan*, force a passage (through).
deur'trap[1] (w) (-ge-), tread through; pedal on.
deurtrap'[2], (b) (-te), sly, crafty, foxy; out-and-out; arrant; artful; engrained; ~**t'heid**, slyness, cunning, craftiness, skill, artfulness.
deur'trein, non-stop train, express (train).
deurtrek'[1], (w) (~), permeate, pervade, imbue, soak, saturate, alive with, leaven, impregnate; (b) (-te-), honeycombed; ~ *van BEDROG*, filled with deceit; ~ *van VROOMHEID*, steeped in piety; *VRUG* ~ *met maaiers*, fruit alive with maggots.
deur'trek[2], (-ge-), pass through; trek through; pull through; carry forward; extend, produce (line); trace (copy); cross (plain); waste, squander.
deurtrek'baar, (..bare), permeable, pervious; ~**heid**, permeability.
deurtrek'kend, (-e), pervasive.
deur'trekker, passer through; spendthrift; pull-through (rifle); jock-strap; G-string.
deurtrek'king, impregnation, pervasion.
deur'trekpapier, tracing-paper.
deurtril', (~), thrill.
deurtrok'ke, permeated, saturated (with); imbued (with), steeped (in); ~ *van 'n verkeerde gees*, imbued with a wrong spirit.
deur'vaar, (-ge-), sail (stem) through.
deur'vaart, passage, transit (by water).
deur'val[1], (s) booby-trap.
deur'val[2], (w) (-ge-), fall through.
deur'vat, (-ge-), take through; convey.
deur'veer, door-spring.
deur'veg, (-ge-), fight through; continue fighting.
deur'verbinding, through-connection.
deur'verkeer, through-traffic.
deur'vleg, (w) (-ge-), intertwine, interweave, entwine, interlace, pleach, plash, enwreathe; (b) (-te), inwrought.
deur'vlieg, (-ge-), fly through; continue flying; rush (gallop) through.
deur'vloei, (-ge-), flow through.
deur'vlug, non-stop flight.
deurvoed', (-e), well-fed.
deurvoel', (~), feel deeply.
deur'voer, (s) transit; (w) (-ge-), carry through; follow out (a plan); go ahead with; conduct through; ~**goed(ere)**, transit goods; ~**handel**, transit trade; ~**hawe**, transit port; ~**ing**, execution (of plan); ~**regte**, transit dues.
deurvors', (~), investigate; probe; ~**end**, (-e), searching, heart-searching, probing.
deur'vrag, through-freight.
deur'vreet, (-ge-), eat till satisfied; eat through, corrode.
deur'vryf, ..**vrywe**, (-ge-), rub through; rub sore, chafe.
deur'vyl, (-ge-), file through.
deurwaad', (~), ford, wade through; ~**baar**, (..bare), fordable.
deurwaai[1], (-ge-), blow through; keep on blowing.
deurwaai'[2], (~), penetrate by blowing (fig.).
deur'waak, (-ge-), watch through, keep vigil.
deur'waarder, ..**wagter**, janitor, door-keeper, porter, apparitor, concierge; commissionaire, court messenger.

dialek

deur'wandel, (-ge-), ramble (walk) through.
deurwas', (-te), streaky; marbled; *die vleis was mooi* ~, the meat was finely marbled.
deurweef', (~), interweave; (b) (-de), interwoven.
deurweek', (w) (~), soak, moisten, saturate; (b) (-te), soaked, sodden, waterlogged, soggy; ~ *van die reën*, drenched with rain.
deur'weg, passage; through-way.
deur'werk[1], (w) (-ge-), work through, mix (concrete); quilt; impregnate; *iets laat* ~, let something have its effect (make itself felt).
deurwerk'[2], (~), elaborate, interweave.
deur'werwel, door-button.
deur'wewe, (-ge-), inweave, enweave.
deurwin'ter, (~), get through the winter.
deurwoel', (-ge-), root up.
deur'worstel, (-ge-), struggle through, labour through.
deurwrog', (plegt.), (-te), elaborate, studied, well-worked.
deur'wurg, (-ge-), swallow with difficulty; suffer, endure (pain); struggle through.
deus ex machina, deus ex machina, providential intervention (intercession).
deus'kant, (-se, -ste), (on) this side of.
deute'ries, (-e), deuteric.
deute'rium, deuterium.
Deuterono'mium, Deuteronomy.
devalua'sie, devaluation.
devalueer', (ge-), devaluate.
deverbatief', (..tiewe), deverbative.
devia'sie, deviation; ~**hoek**, angle of deviation.
devies', (-e), motto, device, impress; logo.
deviese', (pl) foreign bills of exchange.
devolu'sie, *see* **dewolusie**.
devo'nies, (-e), devonian.
Devoon', (**Devone**), Devonian (rocks, era).
devoot', (**devote**), devout, pious.
devo'sie, devotion, piety.
dewolu'sie, devolution.
dewyl', because, since, as.
Dex'ter(bees), Dexter (cattle).
dhal'boontjie, pigeon pea.
di'a, (-s), (ong.), colour slide; *see* **diapositief**.
diabaas', diabase, diorite.
diabe'tes, diabetes.
diabe'ties, (-e), diabetic.
diabe'tikus, (-se, ..tici), diabetic.
diabe'tometer, **diabetome'ter**, diabetometer.
diabo'lies, (-e), diabolic(al).
diabolis'me, diabolism.
diabro'se, diabrosis.
diachro'nies, (-e), diachronic.
diadeem', (..deme), diadem.
dia'de, (-s), dyad; **dia'dies**, (-e), dyadic.
diafaan', (..fane), diaphanous.
diafrag'ma, (-s), diaphragm; ~**breuk**, hiatus hernia.
diagno'se, (-s), diagnosis.
diagnoseer', (ge-), diagnose.
diagnostiek', diagnostics.
diagnos'ties, (-e), diagnostic.
diagnos'tikus, (..tici, -se), diagnostic.
diagonaal', (..nale), diagonal.
diagraaf', (..grawe), diagraph.
diagram', (-me), diagram; ~**ma'ties**, (-e), diagrammatic.
dia'ken, (-s), deacon; ~**sbank**, deacon's pew; ~**skap**, deaconship; deaconate; ~**swyk**, deacon's ward.
diaklaas', diaclase.
diakoestiek', diacoustics.
diakoes'ties, (-e), diacoustic.
diakonaat', (..nate), deaconate.
diakones', (-se), deaconess; ~**sehuis**, (Ndl.), deaconesses home, nursing home.
diakonie', (-e), parochial charity (board); body of deacons.
diakri'ties, (-e), diacritical.
diakti'nies, (-e), diactinic.
dialek', (-te), dialect; patois; ~**atlas**, dialect atlas; ~**leer**, dialectology; ~**tiek'**, dialectics; ~**ties**, (-e), dialectic(al); ~**tograaf'**, dialectographer; ~**tografie'**, dialectography; ~**toloog'**, (..loë), dialectologist; ~**woordeboek**, dialect dictionary.

dialektologie — *diens*

dialektologie', dialectology.
diali'se, dialysis.
dialo'gies, (-e), dialogic.
dialoog', (..loë), dialogue.
diamagne'ties, (-e), diamagnetic.
diamagnetis'me, diamagnetism.
diamant', (-e), diamond; *hy is 'n ongeslypte* ~, he is a rough diamond; *ruwe* ~, rough diamond; ~**agtig, (-e)**, adamantine; ~**boor**, diamond drill; ~**bruilof**, diamond wedding; ~**delwer**, (diamond) digger; ~**delwery**, (diamond) diggings; ~**druk**, diamond (letter-type); ~**gaasdraad**, diamond mesh wire; ~**glans**, diamond (adamantine) lustre; ~**grint**, diamond grit; ~**grond**, diamondiferous (diamond-bearing) ground (soil); ~**gruis**, diamond dust; bort; ~**handel**, diamond trade; *onwettige* ~*handel*, I(llicit) D(iamond) B(uying); ~**handelaar**, diamond merchant (dealer); ~**houdend, (-e)**, diamondiferous; ~**koper**, diamond buyer; ~**letter**, brilliant, diamond (printing); ~**myn**, diamond mine; ~**poeier**, diamond powder; ~**pyp**, diamond pipe; ~**slyper**, diamond cutter; ~**slypery**, diamond polishing (cutting) works; ~**veld**, diamond field; ~**vergrootglas**, loupe; ~**werker**, diamond cutter; ~**werkerskyf**, skive; ~**winning**, diamond production.
diame'ter, (-s), diameter.
diametraal', (..trale), diametric(al), diametral.
diapa'son, diapason (music).
diapositief', (..tiewe), diapositive; colour slide.
diarree', diarrhoea; scour (in cattle)
dia'spora, diaspora.
diasta'se, diastase.
diasta'ties, (-e), diastatic.
diasto'le, diastole.
diasto'lies, (-e), diastolic.
diastro'fies, (-e), diastrophic.
diatermie', diathermy.
diater'mies, (-e), diathermal.
diate'se, diathesis.
diato'mies, (-e), diatomic.
diatomiet', diatomite.
diato'nies, (-e), diatonic(al).
diatoom', (diatome), diatom.
diatri'be, (-s), diatribe.
dic'tum, (..ta), dictum.
didaktiek', didactics.
didak'ties, (-e), didactic.
didak'tikus, (..tici, -se), didactic (writer).
dié, (vnw) this; that; *dis* ~ *DAT ek self wou kom*, that is why I wanted to come myself; *MET* ~, just then, at that moment; *MET* ~ *dat*, just at that moment; ~ *Jan is darem 'n PLATJIE*, isn't John an imp! ~ *SNYER van ons dorp*, the leading tailor in our village; ~ *moet jy WEET*, you can be sure of that.
die, (lw) the; that, those, this; *10 SENT* ~ *pond*, 10 cents per pound; ~ *pure SPIERE*, all muscle; *een UIT* ~ *tien*, one out of ten.
die'derdae, die'dertyd: *van* ~ *af*, from time immemorial, from distant days.
die'derik, (-e, -s), cuckoo *(Cuculus cupreus)*.
dic'driks: *op sy* ~ *kry*, get a thrashing.
dieet', (diëte), diet, regimen; *op* ~ *GAAN*, go on diet; ~ *van sagte KOS*, bland diet, slops; *iem. op* ~ *STEL*, diet somebody; put someone on diet; ~**behandeling**, dietary treatment; ~**kunde**, dietetics; ~**kun'dig, (-e)**, dietetic; ~**kun'dige**, dietician; ~**matig, (-e)**, dietary; ~**reeling**, dietary.
dief, (diewe), thief, lurcher, larcener, pug (slang), pilferer, crook; *een* ~ *met 'n ANDER* ~ *vang*, set a thief to catch a thief; *diewe BESTEEL mekaar nie*, there is honour amongst thieves; *daar is 'n* ~ *aan die KERS*, the candle-wax is dripping; *soos 'n* ~ *in die NAG*, like a thief in the night; *elkeen is 'n* ~ *in sy NERING*, everyone is a thief in his trade; everybody looks after number one; *wie een maal STEEL, is altyd 'n* ~, once a knave, always a knave; *op die diewe TOESLAAN*, swoop down on the thieves; *klein diewe het YSTERKETTINGS, groot diewe goue kettings*, small thieves are hanged, big ones go free; ~**agtig, (-e)**, thievish, furtive; larcenous; ~**agtigheid**, thievish disposition; ~**dig,** **(-te)**, burglar-proof; ~**draad**, burglar-proof wire.
dief'stal, theft, robbery, larceny; *LETTERKUN= DIGE* ~, plagiarism; *POGING tot* ~, attempted theft; *SKULDIG aan* ~ *van geld*, guilty of theft of money.
dief: ~**te**, theft; ~**verklikker**, burglar alarm; ~**vry, (-e)**, burglar-proof; ~**wering**, burglar-proofing; ~**yster**, burglar-bars.
die'gene, he, she; that (the) one, those; ~ *onder julle wat ontevrede is*, those of you who are dissatisfied.
die'kant, on this (that) side of; ~**s(t)e**, on this side.
diëlek'tries, (-e), dielectric; ..**trikum**, dielectric.
die'mit, dimity.
dien¹, (w) (ge-), serve, wait on, attend; suit; follow; *van ADVIES* ~, give (offer) advice; *tot BEWYS* ~, serve as proof (evidence); *NÊRENS toe* ~ *nie*, serve no purpose; *die SAAK sal op P.* ~, the case is set down for hearing at P.; *die SONDE* ~, lead a sinful life; *WAARMEE kan ek u* ~, can I do anything for you? can I serve you in any way? *met iets nie gedien WEES nie*, be dissatisfied (annoyed) with something, to be having none of that.
dien², (vnw): *met* ~ *verstande dat*, provided that, on condition that.
dien'aangaande, as for that, regarding (respecting) that.
die'naar, (-s, ..nare), servant, pursuivant (poet.); valet, servitor; henchman; ministrant; ~ *van die GE= REG*, officer of the law; *U dienswillige* ~, Your obedient servant.
dien: ~**ares', (-se)**, female servant; ~**bord**, service-plate; ~**der, (-s)**, (geselst.), policeman, constable, peace officer; ~**end, (-e)**, serving; ministrant, ministering; ~ *ende dag van bevel nisi*, return day of rule nisi; ~**er, (-s)**, server (at tennis); waiter; ~**ing**, service; ~**lik, (-e)**, serviceable; hard-wearing; ~**luik**, service-hatch.
dien'ooreenkomstig, accordingly; correspondingly.
dien'periode, period in office.
diens, (-te), service; function; duty; employ, employment; ministration; office; *voordat sy* ~ *BEGIN*, before he comes on duty; *'n* ~ *BEWYS*, do (someone) a service (a good turn); ~ *in die BUITE= LAND*, foreign service; ~ *DOEN*, be on duty; ~ *HÊ*, be in service; *die* ~ *HERVAT*, return to duty; *tot HOËR* ~ *opgeroep word*, be called to higher service; ~ *LEI*, conduct a service; *NA die* ~, after (divine) service; *in* ~ *NEEM*, take into service; engage; *die* ~ *OPSÊ*, give notice; *SONDER* ~, be out of employment; *in* ~ *STEL*, place in commission, put into use; *buite* ~ *STEL*, relieve someone of his duties; *TEN* ~ *te wees*, be of service; *TOT u* ~, at your service (disposal); *uit die* ~ *TREE*, retire; *VAN* ~ *wees*, be of use; *VRY van* ~ *wees*, be off duty; *op* ~ *WEES*, be on duty; *van* ~ *WEES*, be off duty; *die een* ~ *is die ander WERD*, one good turn deserves another; ~**aanbieding**, offer of service; ~**aangeleentheid**, official business; ~**aanvaarding**, entrance upon office; ~**aanwysing**, official instruction, direction.
diens'baar, (..bare), serviceable; subservient; employable, ancillary; base, menial; ~ *maak aan*, make subservient to; ~**heid**, serviceableness; servitude, thraldom, bondage.
diens: ~**bak**, service-utility body; ~**bare, (-s)**, servant, menial; ~**bataljon**, spesiale ~ bataljon, special service battalion; ~**berig**, service message; ~**betoon**, rendering of service; ~**beurt**, tour (turn) on duty; ~**bode**, servant, domestic, menial; ~**bodevraagstuk**, servant problem; ~**brief**, official letter; minute; ~**bus**, duty bus, courtesy bus; ~**doende**, on duty; acting; officiating; on the establishment; *die* ~*doende suster*, the nurse on duty; ~**geheim**, official secret; ~**geleentheid**, employment; ~**geweer**, service rifle; ~**heffing**, service charge; ~**hyser**, service lift; ~**ie, (-s)**, short (church) service; small service; ~**ingang**, tradesmen's entrance; ~**jaar**, official year; year of service; ~**kaart**, service-record card; ~**kneg**, servant, manservant, domestic; ~**koevert**, official envelope; ~**kontrak**, service contract; ~**lading**, ~**las**,

dienstig   118   *Diets*

duty load; ~**maagd**, handmaid(en); ~**meisie**, maid, servant girl, abigail; ~**meisie-alleen**, maid-of-all-work; ~**neming**, enlistment; acceptance of service; ~**onderbreking**, break in service; ~**oortreding**, transgression of (service) rules; ~**opsegging**, notice of termination of service; ~**perd**, regulation charger; ~**personeel**, domestic staff; ~**plig**, compulsory (military) service, conscription; ~**plig'tig, (-e)**, conscript, liable to serve (military); ~**plig'tige, (-s)**, conscript; ~**plig'tigheid**, liability to military service; ~**reëling**, timetable; ~**regulasies**, (service) regulations; ~**reis**, official journey (tour); ~**rewolwer**, service revolver; ~**rooster**, timetable; duty-roster; ~**sertifikaat**, certificate of service; ~**staat**, record of service; establishment; ~**telegram**, service (official) telegram; government despatch; ~**stewel**, service boot; ~**trap**, service stairs; ~**termyn**, period of service; *nuwe* ~ *termyn*, re-engagement; new term of office.

diens'tig, (-e), serviceable, useful; conducive; fit; expedient; effective; advisable; ~ *e vliegtuig*, serviceable aeroplane; ~**heid**, usefulness, serviceableness; conduciveness, effectiveness; expediency.

diens: ~ **tyd**, term of office (official); duration of service; ~ **ure**, hours of attendance; ~**vaar'dig, (-e)**, obliging, helpful; ~**vaar'digheid**, readiness to serve; helpfulness; ~**verbreking**, breaking of contract; ~**verlating**, abandoning of (one's) post, desertion (from duty, employment); ~**verlenging**, extension of service; ~**vernuwing**, re-engagement; ~**verrigting**, ~**vervulling**, discharge of one's duties; ~**vliegtuig**, service aeroplane; ~**vlug**, service flight; ~**voorwaardes**, conditions of service; ~**vroue**, service women; ~**vry, (-e)**, off duty; exempt from (military) service; ~**waarnemer**, officiant; ~**wei'eraar**, conchy; conscientious objector (to military service); ~**wei'ering**, conscientious objection; refusal to obey orders; ~**wil'lig, (-e)**, assiduous, ready to serve; obedient, dutiful; *U* ~ *willige dienaar*, Your obedient servant; ~**woning**, official dwelling; ~**woonstel**, service flat; ~**ywer**, official (professional) zeal.

dien'tafel, dinner-wagon, dumbwaiter.

dien'tengevolge, in consequence of this, hence, therefore.

dien'volgens, (form.), accordingly, consequently.

dien'waentjie, dinner-wagon, dumbwaiter.

diep, (b) (-er, -ste), deep; profound (interest); intense (disgust); low (obeisance); close (secret); intensive (research); grave; ~ *windbarsies*, crazing (paint); (bw) deeply, profoundly; ~ *in GEDAGTE*, deep in thought; lost to everything around; ~ *op iets INGAAN*, consider a matter very thoroughly (in detail); ~ *in die NAG*, far into the night; ~ *ONGELUKKIG*, profoundly unhappy; ~ *in sy SAK vat*, dig deeply into his pocket; pay dearly; ~ *in die SESTIG*, well over sixty; ~ *in die SKULD*, deeply in debt; ~**bakvoertuig**, high-sided vehicle; ~**bedorwe**, very corrupt; ~**bedroef, (-de)**, deeply afflicted; ~**blou**, deep blue, mazarine; ~**bord**, soup plate; porridge plate, porringer; ~**bou**, underground engineering (construction); ~**braai**, deep frying; ~**breker**, subsoiler.

diep'denkend, (-e), deep-thinking, profound; ~**heid**, profoundness, penetration.

diep'druk, intaglio, recess.

die'perig, (-e), rather deep.

diep'gaande, profound, deep, thorough, intimate (knowledge); deep-drawing (ship); searching, probing; *'n* ~ *ONDERSOEK*, a searching enquiry; *'n* ~ *SKIP*, ship with deep draught.

diep'gang, (depth of) draught (ship); immersion; dip; load mark; gauge; depth, profundity; ~**smerk**, Plimsoll's mark, Plimsoll line.

diep: ~**gevoel(d), (-de)**, heartfelt; ~**gewortel(d), (-de)**, deep-rooted; ~**glans**, deep shine; ~**hoek**, depression angle; ~**liggend, (-e)**, deep-seated; deep-set; ~**lood, (..lode)**, sounding (deep-sea) lead, plummet; plumb (bob); fathom line; ~**ploeg**, trench plough; ~**rooi**, scarlet.

diep'see, deep sea; ~**duiker**, ocean diver, deep-sea diver; ~**gewas**, pelagic vegetation; ~**lood**, clam; ~**-ondersoek**, deep-sea exploration; ~**peiling**, deep-sea fathoming (sounding); ~**slenk**, oceanic deep.

diepsin'nig, (-e), deep, profound, abstruse (reasoning); recondite, abstract; ~**heid**, depth, profoundness, profundity (mind), abstruseness, abstractedness.

diep'te, (-s), depth; profundity; deep place, pocket, bottom; altitude; *na die* ~ *GAAN*, go down (to the bottom); *OP 'n* ~ *van*, at a depth of; *'n ROMAN sonder* ~, superficial novel; ~**bom**, depth-charge; submarine bomb; ~**film**, three-dimensional film; ~**gesteente**, plutonic rock; ~**hoek**, altitude angle; ~**lading**, depth charge; ~**lyn**, isobath; ~**maat**, depth gauge; ~**meter**, fathoming lead, sea gauge, bathometer; ~**peiling**, sounding; ~**sielkunde**, psycho-analysis; ~**syfer**, depth.

diep'tuin, sunken garden.

diep'vetbraai, deep-fat frying.

diep'vries, deep-freeze; ~**kas**, deep-freezer; ~**behandeling**, hypothermy.

dier¹, (ong.) that; *in* ~ *voege*, in that (such a) manner, so that, to that effect.

dier², (s) (-e), animal; brute; *mens en* ~, man and beast; ~**afbeelding**, zoomorph; ~**a'sie, (-s)**, monster; vixen, (she-)devil.

dier'baar, (..bare), dear, beloved; ~**heid**, dearness; ~**making**, endearment.

dier'bare, (-s), loved one, beloved.

die're: ~**aanbidding**, animal worship; ~**beskerming**, animal protection; *Vereniging vir D* ~ *beskerming*, Society for the Prevention of Cruelty to Animals; ~**beskrywer**, zoographer; ~**doder**, animal killer; humane killer; ~**epos**, animal epic; ~**fabel**, animal fable; ~**fossiel**, zoolith; ~**geneeskunde**, veterinary (animal) science; ~**geografie**, zoogeography; ~**kenner**, zoologist; ~**koning**, king of animals, lion; ~**koor**, animal concert; ~**kweller**, tormentor of animals; ~**lewe**, animal life; ~**liefhebber**, animal lover; ~**mishandeling**, cruelty to animals; ~**opsetter**, ~**opstopper**, taxidermist; ~**riem**, zodiac; ~**ryk**, animal kingdom; ~**sage**, animal saga.

dière'se, (-s), di(a)eresis.

die're: ~**siekte**, animal disease; ~**skilder**, animal painter; ~**storie**, animal story; ~**taal**, animal language; ~**temmer**, wild-beast tamer, animal tamer; ~**tuin**, zoo(logical garden); game reserve (preserve); ~**vel**, skin of an animal; ~**verhaal**, animal story; ~**versameling**, menagerie; ~**versorging**, animal care; ~**vet**, animal fat; ~**voeding**, animal nutrition; ~**vriend**, animal lover; ~**wêreld**, animal world, fauna; ~**winkel**, pet-shop.

dier: ~**kunde**, zoology; ~**kun'dig, (-e)**, zoological; ~**kun'dige, (-s)**, zoologist.

dier'lik, (-e), animal, bestial, brutal, carnal; boarish; feral; ~ *e STYSEL*, glycogen, animal starch; ~ *e VET*, animal fat; ~**heid**, animality, animalism; animal nature; bestiality, brutality.

dier: ~**mens**, brute; ~**ontleder**, zootomist; ~**ontleding**, zootomy; ~**park**, zoo; ~**soort**, species of animal; ~**storie**, animal story; ~**stysel**, glycogen; ~**tjie, (-s)**, little animal, animalcule; *elke* ~ *tjie het sy plesiertjie*, everybody enjoys himself in his own way; ~**vet**, adipose, animal fat.

dies, (vnw) there; those; *en wat* ~ *MEER sy*, and so on, and so forth; ~ *wat nie WIL nie*, those who are unwilling.

die'sel: ~**brandstof**, diesel fuel; ~**elektries**, diesel-electric.

dieself'de, the same, idem, identical; *presies* ~, exactly the same; the exact copy.

die'sel: ~**enjin**, diesel engine; ~**lokomotief**, diesel locomotive; ~**motor**, diesel engine (motor); ~**olie**, diesel oil.

Dies'man, (-ne), Dutchman; European.

diesul'ke(s), such.

Dies'volk, Dutchmen; Europeans.

diëtetiek', dietetics.

diëte'ties, (-e), dietetic(al).

diets¹: *iem. iets* ~ *maak*, make someone believe the moon is made of green cheese.

Diets², (s) Middle (Mediaeval) Dutch; Dutch in the

broadest sense, including Flemish and Afrikaans; (b) (-e), Mediaeval Dutch; *die ~e beweging*, the Pan-Dutch movement; ~**er, (-s)**, protagonist of the Pan-Dutch movement.

dieveg′ge, (-s), (ong., vero.) (female) thief.

die′we: ~**bende**, gang (pack) of thieves; ~**hol, (-e)**, thieves' den; ~**kruid**, clematis, traveller's joy; ~**lantern**, dark lantern; ~**ry, (-e)**, theft, thieving, robbery; ~**sleutel**, pick-lock, skeleton key, master key, pass-key; ~**streek**, thief's trick; ~**taal**, language of thieves, thieves' Latin, argot, flash language.

differensiaal′, (..siale), differential; ~**rekening**, differential calculus; ~**takel**, block of differential pulley.

differensia′sie, differentiation.

differensieel′, (..siële), differential; ~*siële BEWEGINGS*, differential movements; ~*siële VERWERING*, differential weathering.

differensieer′, (ge-), differentiate.

differensie′ring, differentiation.

diffrak′sie, diffraction.

diffundeer′, (ge-), diffuse.

diffunde′ring, diffusion.

diffu′sie, diffusion; ~**vermoë**, diffusibility.

diffuus′, (..fuse; ..fuser, -ste), diffuse; *diffuse lig*, diffused light.

difterie′, diphtheria.

difte′ries, (-e), diphtheritic.

difteri′tis = **difterie**.

dif′tong, (-e), diphthong; ~**eer′, (ge-)**, diphthongize.

diftonge′ring, diphthong(iz)ation.

dig¹, (s) poetry; ~ *en ondig*, poetry and prose; (w) (ge-), write poetry, compose, versify.

dig², (w) (ge-), seal, stop up; join (pipes); (b), **(-te)**, tight, shut, close; near; dense, compact; thick (fog); impermeable; *iets* ~ *HOU*, keep something mum; *so* ~ *soos 'n POT*, very close; as close as an oyster.

dig: ~**aar**, ~**ader**, poetic vein.

dig′behos, (-te), thickly wooded.

dig′bundel, volume of verse.

dig: ~**by**, close by, near, anigh; ~*by die dorp*, close to the village; ~**byopname**, close-up (photo).

diges′tie, digestion; ~**f′, (..tiewe)**, digestive; ~**visite**, after-dinner call.

dig′genootskap, (-pe), poetical society.

dig: ~**gooi, (-ge-)**, close by throwing, slam (door); fill up (with earth); ~**groei, (-ge-)**, grow densely; heal (up); close (up); ~**hou, (-ge-)**, keep secret.

digitalien′, digitali′ne, digitalin.

digita′lis, foxglove (flower); digitalis.

dig: ~**klap, (-ge-)**, slam (door); ~**knoop, (-ge-)**, button up; ~**korrelig, (-e)**, close-grained.

dig′kunde, poetics.

dig′kuns, poetry, poetic art, poesy.

dig′maak, (-ge-), close, plug, stop (up), join.

dig′maat, metre, poetic measure.

dig′naai, (-ge-), sew up (tightly).

dignita′ris, (-se), dignitary.

digoto′mie, dichotomy.

dig′plak, (-ge-), seal up.

dig′reël, line of poetry.

dig: ~**ring**, expanding washer; ~**skroei, (-ge-)**, cauterize, sear.

dig′soort, kind of poetry.

dig′splytbaar, (..bare), fissile; ~**heid**, fissility.

dig′stop, (-ge-), close up, fill.

dig: ~**stuk**, poem; ~**talent**, poetic talent.

dig′teby, (s) (-s), bird of the fam. *Laniidae*; (bw) hard by, near by.

dig′ter, (-s), poet; ~**es′, (-se)**, poetess; ~**lik, (-e)**, poetic(al); ~*like vryheid*, poetic licence; ~**likheid**, poeticalness, poetic art; ~**y**, doggerel.

digt′heid, density, denseness, consistency, compactness; ~**smeter**, densimeter.

dig′ting, closing up; seal(ing).

dig′tings: ~**mengsel**, sealing compound; ~**middel**, sealing agent; packing; ~**ring**, sealing ring.

dig: ~**trant**, poetic style; ~**vorm**, poetic form; *in* ~*vorm*, in verse.

dig′vou, (-ge-), fold up (tightly).

dig′vries, (-ge-), freeze up (over); freeze solid.

dig: ~**vuur**, poetic fire; ~**werk**, poetical work.

dik, thick, bulky, stout, pudsy, pudgy, plump, fleshy, obese, portly, corpulent, burly; crass; pea-soupy, dense (fog); gross; great; swollen; satiated (animal); *dit* ~ *AANMAAK*, pile it on; spread it thick; *deur* ~ *en DUN*, through thick and thin; *jou* ~ *EET*, eat one's fill, gorge oneself; ~ *van die GELD wees*, be very rich; ~ *van die LAG*, be highly amused; *iets te* ~ *OPLÊ*, lay it on too thick; overdo something; *daar* ~ *in SIT*, be well-to-do; ~ *SOP*, thick soup; *hulle is* ~ *VRIENDE*, they are intimate friends; ~ *WEES vir iem.*, be sick of someone; ~ *WORD*, put on flesh; grow stout; thicken; set (milk); ~**agtig, (-e)**, thickish; ~**bas**, wild pear *(Dombeya rotundifolia)*.

dik′bek, sulky (person), pouter; ~**kerig, (-e)**, rather sulky; ~**kie, (-s)**, panga (fish); ~**kig, (-e)**, rather sulky; ~**sysie**, white-throated sead-eater.

dik′biltong, thick biltong.

dik′bloedig, (-e), thick-blooded.

dik′buik, pot-belly, paunch; ~**ig, (-e)**, pot-bellied, big-bellied.

dik′dei, (-s), lizard *(Mabuia)*.

dik′derm, large intestine, colon; ~**ontsteking**, colitis.

dikdik′, (-ke, -s), Damara dikdik *(Rhynchotragus damarensis)*.

dik: ~**dood**, very lazy, slow; ~**ent**, bulb end, butt-end (pole); ~**gevreet, (..vrete)**, satiated, glutted; ~**heid**, plumpness; satiety; ~**hoofdig, (-e)**, thick-headed.

dik′huid, thick-skinned person; nachyderm; ~**ig (-e)**, thick-skinned; ~**igheid**, callosity, pachydermia.

dikkeden′sie, trouble, muddle, fix; confusion; *in die* ~ *raak*, get into a fix; be in the soup.

dik: ~**keel**, bottle-jaw (cattle disease); ~**kerd, (-s)**, fatty, podge, pudge, plump person; ~**kerig, (-e)**, fattish, rather stout; rather thick.

dik′kop, thick-head; blockhead; curmudgeon; form of horse-sickness; cheese head (rivets); hangover; **(-pe)**, Cape dikkop *(Burhinops capensis capensis)*; small fish; ~**korhaan**, Karoo korhaan *(Otis vigorsii)*; ~**pie, (-s)**, species of *Gobius*; skipper (butterfly); ~**pig, (-e)**, obstinate; stupid; ~**spyker**, hob(nail); ~**voël**, thick-knee(d) plover.

dik′lies, thick flank.

dik′lip, thick-lipped (person); sulky (person); ~**pig, (-e)** thicklipped, negroid.

dik′lywig, (-e), corpulent.

dik′maag, pot-belly.

dik′maals, (ong.), often.

dik′melk, curdled milk; clabber(ed) milk; *as* ~ *KAAS geword het*, set a beggar on horseback and he will ride to the devil; *SOET* ~, junket; ~**kaas**, cottage cheese; ~**seep**, curd soap; ~**water**, whey.

dik: ~**mond**, sulky (person); ~*mond wees*, sulk; ~**nek**, with a thick neck; aggressive, cheeky; proud; ~**neus(ig)**, thick-nose(d), bottle-nose(d); ~**oulap**, cart-wheel penny; ~**pens**, swag-belly, paunch-belly; ~**rib**, thick rib (mutton, pork); chuck (beef); ~**ribskyf**, chuck steak; ~**sak**, stout person, fatty, paunch, podge, humpty-dumpty.

dik′sic, diction.

dik′stem, (bw) in a threatening tone.

dik′stert, with a thick tail; ~**geitjie**, lizard of the genus *Oedura*; ~**muishond**, polecat *(Viverridae)*.

diktaat′, (..tate), (professor's) notes; dictation.

diktafoon′, (..fone), dictaphone.

diktak′kig, (-e), with thick branches.

dikta′tor, (-s), dictator; ~**iaal′, (..riale)**, dictatorial; ~**skap**, dictatorship; Caesarism.

diktatuur′, (..ture), dictatorship.

dik′te, (-s), thickness, swollenness; grist (of rope); consistency; burliness; crassitude; gauge.

diktee′, (-s), dictation.

dikteer′, (ge-), dictate; ~**der, (-s)**, dictator; ~**masjien**, dictaphone.

dik′temeter, calliper; plate gauge.

dik′tepasser, outside callipers, micrometer callipers, crooked compass.

diktograaf′, (..grawe), dictograph.

dik′tong(ig), (b) (-e), thick-tongued; *hy praat* ~, his speech is slurred.

dik'vel, pachyderm; thick-skinned animal; ~ **lig, (-e)** thick-skinned, pachydermatous; unfeeling, callous; ~ **ligheid**, insensitiveness.
dik'vleis, ball (of hand); buttock(s); thick flank (beef).
dik'vloeibaar, viscous.
dik'voet, club-root (disease of cabbage, turnips).
dik'wangig, (-e), chubby-cheeked.
dik'wels, often, frequently, constantly.
dik'wors, polony.
dilata'sie, dilatation.
dilata'tor, (-s), dilator, dilatator.
dilem'ma, (-s), dilemma, puzzle.
dilettant', (-e), dilettante, amateur; ~ **erig, (-e)**, ~ **ies, (-e)**, dilettantish; amateurish; ~ **erigheid**, amateurishness; ~ **is'me**, dilettantism.
diligen'ce, (-s), diligence, coach.
dil'le, dill *(Anethum graveoleus)*; ~ **sous**, dill sauce.
diluviaal', (..viale), diluvial.
dilu'vium, diluvium.
dimen'sie, (-s), dimension.
dimensionaal', (..nale), dimensional.
diminuen'do, diminuendo.
diminutief', (..tiewe), diminutive.
dimorf', (-e), dimorphous; ~ **ie'**, ~ **is'me**, dimorphism.
dinamiek', dynamics; dynamism.
dina'mies, (-e), dynamic; ~ *e LUGVAART*, dynamic aviation; ~ *e METAMORFISME (metamorfose)*, dynamic metamorphism; ~ *e SWEEFVLIEG*, sail-planing; ~ *e WEERKUNDE*, dynamic meteorology.
dinamiet', dynamite; ~ **aanslag**, dynamite outrage; ~ **doppie**, dynamite cap; ~ **fabriek** dynamite factory; ~ **kers**, stick of dynamite; ~ **lading**, blast, dynamite charge; ~ **man**, dynamiter, dynamitard; ~ **patroon**, dynamite cartridge; ~ **skieter**, blaster; dynamiter.
dina'mika, dynamics.
dinamis'me, dynamism.
dina'mo, di'namo, (-'s), dynamo; generator (elect.); ~ **-aandrywing**, dynamo drive; ~ **band**, dynamo strap; ~ **bediener**, dynamo assistant (attendant); ~ **dryfrat**, dynamo driving gear; ~ **-elektries, (-e)**, dynamoelectric; ~ **koppeling**, generator coupling; ~ **meter**, dynamometer; ~ **me'tries, (-e)**, dynamometric(al); ~ **spil**, dynamo spindle; ~ **skyf**, dynamo pulley.
di'nar, (-s), dinar.
dinastie', (-ë), dynasty.
dinastiek', dinas'ties, (-e), dynastic.
di'ne, (-s), dyne.
dinee', (-s), dinner; ~ **baadjie**, dinner-jacket; ~ **-dans**, dinner-dance; ~ **pak**, dinner-suit; ~ **pouse**, dinner interval.
dineer', (ge-), dine, have dinner.
dinee'servies, dinner-service.
ding¹, (s) (-e), thing, object; affair, matter; contraption; *dit sal 'n ~ AFGEE*, that will cause trouble; *ARME ~! poor thing! die een ~ DOEN en die ander nie nalaat nie*, apply oneself to one thing without neglecting another; *alle goeie ~e bestaan uit DRIE*, there is luck in odd numbers; *alle GOEIE ~ e kom langsaam*, all good things come to those who wait; *daar LÊ die ~*, there's the rub; *'n ~ by sy NAAM noem*, call a spade a spade; *sy is SOMMER 'n ~*, she is rather a bad lot; *VOL ~e wees*, be full of tricks (pranks, airs).
ding², (w) (ge-), vie, try (for); compete (for); aspire to; *na die hand van 'n dame ~*, sue for the hand of a lady.
dingaans'appel(koos), kei apple *(Doryalis caffra)*.
Dingaans'dag, (vero.), Dingaan's Day; *see* **Geloftedag**.
din'ger, (-s), competitor, aspirant.
din'ges, what-do-you-call-it, thingummy, thingumajig, thingumbob; ~ **ie, (-s)**, gadget; trifle, oddment.
din'getjie, (-s), little thing; little child, etc.; term of endearment.
din'go, (-'s), dingo.
dink, (dag, dog, ge-, gedag, gedog), think, consider, ponder; deem, reckon; *AAN iets ~*, think of a thing, remember something; *ek kan daar nie AAN ~ nie*, I can't bear the thought of it; *ANDERS ~*, take a different view; *jy kan ~ hoe BLY ek was*, you can imagine how glad I was; *stof tot ~ GEE*, be food for thought; *ek HET so ge ~*, I thought so; I expected as much; *LAAT ~ aan*, remind one of; *'n MENS laat ~*, set one thinking; *~ nou NET*, just imagine that; *OOR iets ~*, think about (of, on) a thing; *ek sou SO ~*, I should think so; *jou SUF ~*, cudgel one's brains; *daar VAL nie aan te ~ nie*, it is out of the question; *wat ~ jy VAN my?* what do you take me for?
dink: ~ **ery**, thinking; ~ **fout**, mistake in thought; ~ **gewoonte**, habit of thought; ~ **krag**, thinking power; ~ **proses**, process of thought; ~ **skrum**, think-tank; ~ **tyd**, thinking time; ~ **vermoë**, faculty of thought; rationality; ~ **werk**, thinking, mental work; ~ **wyse**, way of thought.
dinosou'rus, (-se, ..ri), dinosaur.
Dins'dae, on Tuesdays.
Dins'dag, Tuesday; ~ **s**, on Tuesdays.
dioksi'de, (-s), dioksied', (-e), dioxide.
dioptaas', dioptase, emerald copper.
diop'ter, (-s), diopter, sight vane.
dioptriek', dioptrics.
diop'tries, (-e), dioptric.
diora'ma, (-s), diorama.
diora'mies, (-e), dioramic.
dioriet', diorite, greenstone.
diosees', (diosese), (ong.) diocese.
diosesaan', (..sane), (ong.) diocesan.
dip, (s) (-pe), dip; *gelyktydige ~*, simultaneous dipping; (w) (ge-), dip; ~ **bak, (-ke),** ~ **gat, (-e)**, dipping-tank; ~ **hok**, ~ **kraal**, dipping-pen.
diplo'ma, (-s), diploma, certificate.
diplomaat', (..mate), diplomat, diplomatist.
diplo'makandidaat, diploma candidate.
diplomasie', diplomacy, diplomatic service.
diplomatiek', (-e), diplomatic; ~ **e diens**, diplomatic (foreign) service.
diploma'ties, (-e), diplomatic.
diplomeer', (ge-), get a diploma; certify.
dip'per, (-s), dipper (of cattle); ~ **y**, dipping.
dipsomaan', (..mane), dipsomaniac.
dipsomanie', dipsomania.
dipsoma'nies, (-e), dipsomaniac(al).
dip'stof, dip.
dipteraal', (..rale), dipterous.
diptiek', (-e), diptych.
direk', (b) (-te), direct, straight; (bw) straight away; at once; ~ **te koers**, direct course.
direk'sie, (-s), direction; management, managing board; ~ **verslag**, directors' report.
direkteur', (-e, -s), director, manager; executive; ~ *van burgerlugvaart*, director of civil aviation; ~ **-generaal, (direkteurs-..)**, director-general; ~ **s'geld(e)**, director's fee(s); ~ **skap, (-pe)**, directorship; ~ **s'lessenaar**, executive desk; ~ **s'verslag**, director's report.
direkt'heid, directness.
direktief', (..tiewe), directive.
direktoraat', (..rate), directorate, directorship.
direktri'se, (-s), directress, manageress.
dirigeer', (ge-), conduct (music); ~ **stok**, baton, conductor's stick.
dirigent', (-e), (music) conductor, choir-master.
dirkdir'kie, (-s), spotted cloud warbler *(Hemipteryx textrix)*.
dirnd'l, dirndl.
dis¹, it (that) is; ~ *te sê*, that is (to say).
dis², (ong.), (s) D sharp (music).
dis³, (s) (-se), (deftig), table, board.
dis⁴, (s) (-se), food, plate of food.
di'sa, (-s), disa (flower).
dis'agio, disagio.
disassimila'sie, disassimilation.
disenterie', dysentry.
disente'ries, (-e), dysenteric.
dis'genoot, (..note), table companion.
disharmonie', disharmony, discord.
disharmonieer', (ge-), disharmonize.
disharmo'nies, (-e), unharmonious, discordant.

disintegra'sie, disintegration.
disintegreer', (ge-), disintegrate.
disjunk', (-te), disjunctive; ~ **sie**, disjunction; ~ **tief'**, (..tiewe), disjunctive.
diskant', (-s), descant, treble, soprano.
dis'ko, (-'s), disco(theque).
disko'bolos, (-se), discobolus.
dis'kodanser, disco dancer.
diskoers', (-e), discourse.
dis'kofiel, (-e), (gramophone) record collector.
dis'komusiek, disco music.
dis'konnekteer, (ge-), disconnect.
diskonteer', (ge-), discount, ~ **baar**, (..bare), discountable; ~ **bank**, discount house (bank).
diskontinu', (-e), discontinuous; ~ **ïteit'**, discontinuity.
diskon'to, (-'s), discount; ~ **bank**, discount(ing) bank; ~ **koers**, rate of discount; ~ **verhoging**, raising the rate of discount (bank rate); ~ **voet**, discount rate; ~ **wissel**, bill of discount.
dis'kordansie, unconformity.
diskordant', (-e), uncomformable; discordant.
dis'kosanger, disco singer.
diskoteek' (..teke), (grammophone) record library; disco(theque).
diskoteka'ris, (-se), record librarian.
dis'krediet, discredit; *in* ~ *BRING*, bring discredit (up)on; *in* ~ *RAAK*, fall into disrepute.
diskrediteer', (ge-), discredit, bring into discredit.
diskreet', (diskrete), discreet, considerate, modest.
diskre'sie, discretion; considerateness.
diskresionêr', (-e), discretionary.
diskrimina'sie, discrimination.
diskrimineer', (ge-), discriminate.
dis'kus, (-se), discus, disc; ~ **gooi**, throwing the discus; ~ **gooier**, (-s), discus thrower; ~ **gooister**, (-s), female discus thrower.
diskusseer', (ge-), discuss, argue.
diskus'sie, (-s), discussion, argument; *in* ~ *bring*, bring under discussion.
dis'kuswerper, discobolus, discus thrower.
diskuta'bel, (-e), debatable, arguable.
diskuteer', (ge-), debate, argue.
dis'kwalifikasie, (-s), disqualification.
diskwalifiseer', (ge-), disqualify.
dislek'sie, dyslexia.
dislojaal', disloyal.
dislojaliteit', disloyalty.
disloka'sie, dislocation.
dis'nis: ~ *LOOP*, beat thoroughly, outdistance; ~ *SLAAN*, knock out (unconscious).
disorganisa'sie, disorganization.
disoriënteer', disorientate.
disparaat', (..rate), disparate (in age); incongruous.
dispariteit', disparity, incongruity.
dispens', (-e), (vero.) pantry.
dispensa'sie, (-s), dispensation, special licence; indult (R.C.).
dispenseer', (ge-), dispense; *iem. van iets* ~, exempt someone from.
dispep'sie, dyspepsia; *lyer aan* ~, dyspeptic.
dispep'ties, (-e), dyspeptic.
disper'sie, dispersion.
dispnee', dyspnoea.
disponeer', (ge-), dispose.
disponi'bel, available, at disposal.
disposi'sie, disposition.
disputant', (-e), disputant, arguer.
disputa'sie, (-s), disputation, dispute.
disputeer', (ge-), dispute.
dispuut', (dispute), dispute, controversy, argument.
dissek'sie, (-s), dissection.
dissekteer', (ge-), dissect.
dis'sel¹, (s) (-s), adze; addice; (w) (ge-), adze.
dis'sel², (-s) = **distel**.
dis'selboom, shaft, thill, beam (of wagon); pole (of cart); *iem. teen die* ~ *GOOI*, go one better than another; *aan dieselfde* ~ *TREK*, to be hand in glove; ~ **bout**, pole-pin; ~ **ketting**, pole-chain; ~ **kram**, pole-lug; ~ **riem**, back-band strap; ~ **stut**, pole-prop, prop-stick.
dissemina'sie, dissemination.

dissemineer', (ge-), disseminate.
disserta'sie, (-s), dissertation, thesis.
dissimila'sie, dissimilation.
dissimula'sie, dissimulation, deceit, hypocrisy.
dissimuleer', (ge-), dissimulate.
dissi'pel, (-s), disciple; ~ **in'**, (-ne), female disciple; ~ **skap**, discipleship.
dissipli'ne, discipline; *'n strenge* ~ *handhaaf*, maintain a strict (rigid) discipline.
dissiplineer', (ge-), discipline.
dissipli'nemaatreël, disciplinary measure.
dissiplinêr', (-e), disciplinary.
dissipli'nesaak, affair of discipline.
dissonan'sie, (-s), discordance, dissonance.
dissonant', (s) discord; discordant note; (b) (-e), discordant, dissonant, jarring.
dissoneer', (ge-), discord, be dissonant, jar.
dissosia'sie, dissociation.
dissosieer', (ge-), dissociate.
distan'sie, (-s), distance.
distansieer', (ge-), distance; *jou van iets* ~, dissociate oneself from something.
distansië'ring, dissociation; placing at a distance.
dis'tel, (-s), thistle; ~ **agtig**, (-e), thistly; ~ **doring**, thistle *(Berkheya)*; ~ **vink**, gold-finch, thistle-finch; ~ **wol**, thistle-down.
distem'per, distemper.
dis'tigon, (-s), distich (poem).
distillaat', (..late), distillate.
distilla'sie, distillation.
distilleer', (ge-), distil; rectify; ~ **der**, (-s), distiller; ~ **dery**, (-e), distillery, ~ **fles**, distilling flask, ~ **kamer**, still-room; ~ **ketel**, still; ~ **kolf**, alembic; ~ **matras**.
distingeer', (ge-), distinguish.
distink'sie, distinction, refinement.
distinktief', (..tiewe), distinctive.
distor'sie, distortion.
distrak'sie, (-s), distraction.
distribueer', (ge-), distribute; ~ **der**, (-s), distributor.
distribu'sie, distribution.
distrik', (-te), district.
distriks': ~ **dokter**, ~ **geneesheer**, district surgeon; ~ **gevaar**, action warning (air raids); ~ **kommandant**, district commandant (officer).
disurie', dysuria.
dit, this, it, these; *hy BESIT nie* ~ *nie*, he possesses nothing; *ek moet nog* ~ *en dat DOEN*, I must still do this, that and another thing; *nie* ~ *vir iets GEE nie*, not to give tuppence for something; ~ *is my GOED*, these are my possessions; *oor* ~ *en dat PRAAT*, talk of this and that; ~ **heid**, thisness, haecceity.
ditiram'be, (-s), dithyramb.
ditiram'bies, (-e), dithyrambic.
dit'jie: *oor* ~ *s en datjies gesels*, talk about this and that (trifles).
di'to, ditto, the same.
dit'sem! dit'sit! that's it!
ditsy', either; ~ *in geld of in goed*, either in money or in kind.
dit'to = **di'to**.
diure'se, diuresis.
diure'ties, (-e), diuretic.
di'va, (-s), diva.
divaga'sie, (-s), wandering, roaming, dilation (on subject), divagation.
di'van, divan', (-s), divan; sofa, ottoman.
divariant', (-e), divariant.
divergeer', (ge-), diverge.
divergen'sie, divergence.
diverge'rend, (-e), divergent.
diver'se, sundries; incidental expenses.
diversiteit', diversity.
dividend', (-e), dividend; *'n* ~ *AANKONDIG*, declare a dividend; *'n* ~ *UITKEER*, pay a dividend; ~ **bewys**, dividend warrant; ~ **draend**, (-e), dividend-bearing; ~ **geregtigde**, (-s), person entitled to a dividend; ~ **uitkering**, distribution of dividends; ~ **vasstelling**, dividend declaration.
divina'sie, divination.

divi'sie, (-s), division; *ligte* ~, mobile division; ~**kommandant**, divisional commander.
diwan' = divan.
diwidend' = dividend.
dob'bel, (ge-), gamble, play at dice, plunge (slang); ~**aar**, (-s), gamester, gambler, plunger, dicer, dice-player; ~**(a)ry'**, dicing, gamble, gambling; ~**beker**, ~**dosie**, dice-box; ~**huis**, gambling-house; ~**kantoor**, bucket-shop; ~**plek**, gaming house; ~**siek**, gamblesome; ~**spel**, (-e), hazard; gambling, dice-playing; fa(h)fee; ~**steen**, die, cube; bone; hazard; ~**steenkruit**, cube gunpowder; ~**sug**, gambling spirit; ~**tafel**, gaming table; gambling table; ~**tolletjie**, teetotum.
dob'ber, (s) (-s), float, carburettor float; cork; buoy; (w) (ge-), go up and down, bob, float; fluctuate; ~**end**, (-e), fluctuating; ~**ing**, fluctuation; ~**klep**, float-valve; ~**tjie**, (-s), float; Cape dabchick *(Poliocephalus ruficollis capensis)*.
Do'bermann-pin'scher, (-s), Dobermann pinscher.
dod'der, dodder (weed), cuscuta.
do'de, (dode, -s), dead; *uit die* ~ *opstaan*, rise from the dead; ~**akker**, God's acre, cemetery; ~**boek**, book of the dead; *in die* ~ *boek geskryf staan*, to be past history; ~**dans**, dance of death, danse macabre; ~**huis**, mortuary; charnel house.
dodekaë'der, (-s), dodecahedron.
dodekaë'dries, (-e), dodecahedral.
dodekagonaal', (..nale), dodecagonal.
dodekagoon', (..gone), dodecagon.
do'deklaaglied, elegy.
do'delik, (-e), mortal (fear, wound); fatal (mistake); lethal (weapon, dose); pernicious, killing; deadly (earnest; poison); *'n ongeluk met* ~*e afloop*, a fatal accident; ~**hede**, mortal blows; ~**heid**, deadliness, mortalness.
do'de: ~**lys**, death-roll; ~**mars**, dead (funeral) march; ~**masker**, death-mask; ~**mis**, requiem mass.
do'der, (-s), killer; *pynlose* ~, humane killer.
do'de: ~**register**, death-roll; death-register; ~**ryk**, realm of death; ~**sel**, condemned cell; ~**stad**, necropolis; ~**tal**, death-roll, mortality; ~**vallei**, valley of death; ~**verbranding**, cremation; ~**wa**, hearse; ~**waak**, death-watch.
do'ding, killing; mortification (of flesh).
do'do, (-'s), dodo.
doea'ne, custom house, customs; *Departement van D* ~ *en Aksyns*, Department of Customs and Excise; ~**amptenaar**, ~**beampte**, customs officer; ~**formaliteit**, customs formality; ~**inklaringsbrief**, customs bill of entry (import); ~**kantoor**, custom house; ~**klaring**, customs clearance; ~**ooreenkoms**, customs agreement; ~**pakhuis**, bond-store; ~**regte**, customs duties; ~**seël**, customs seal; ~**uitklaringsbrief**, customs bill of entry (export); ~**verklaring**, customs declaration; ~**visenteerkantoor**, customs searcher's office; ~**vliegveld**, customs aerodrome; ~**vorm**, customs form.
doebleer', (ge-), double, round (a cape); double (at cards); ~**der**, (-e), understudy; ~**proses**, doubling process.
doeblet', (-te), doublet.
doe'del, (ge-), play the bagpipe, skirl; ~**sak**, bagpipes; ~**sakmelodie**, pibroch; ~**sakspeler**, piper.
doe'doe, (s) (-s), dormy (golf); hushaby; (w) (ge-), sing (hush) to sleep; go to sleep.
doef! thud! puff! ~-~ *gaan*, go puff-puff (thud-thud), go pit-a-pat.
doek, (-e), cloth; fabric; sling (for arm); napkin (for baby), diaper; canvas, painting, curtain; screen; *ARM in 'n* ~, arm in a sling; *op die* ~ *BRING*, put onto canvas; bring to the screen; *op die* ~ *GOOI*, screen; ~**baan**, gore (of skirt); ~**baanlengte**, gore length; ~**bak**, fabric body; ~**ie**, (-s), piece of cloth, little rag; *nie* ~*ies omdraai nie*, speak in plain words, not to mince matters; ~**ies**, (ge-), go to sleep (nursery term); ~**poeding**, plum-pudding; duff; boiled pudding; ~**ring**, grummet washer; ~**sif**, lawn-sieve; ~**speld**, napkin pin; tommy pin); ~**steen**, asbestos; ~**voet**, noiselessly.
doel, (s) (-eindes), purpose, aim, end, object, mark,
point, goal; ambition; bourn(e); drift; (-e), goal (football); *'n* ~ *BEOOG (najaag)*, aim at an object; *sy* ~ *BEREIK*, achieve one's object; *die* ~ *heilig die MIDDELE*, the end justifies the means; *jou* ~ *MIS*, miss one's aim (object); *'n* ~ *NAJAAG*, pursue an object; *REGUIT op die* ~ *afgaan*, go straight to the point; *jou ten* ~ *STEL*, make it one's object to; *die* ~ *TREF*, hit the mark; *sy* ~ *VERBYSTREWE*, defeat one's own object; (w) (ge-): ~ *op*, aim at; refer to; allude to; ~**aanwysend**, (-e): ~ *aanwysende bysin*, final clause; ~**beoordelaar**, goal judge; ~**bewus**, (-te), purposeful, purposive; ~**bewustheid**, fixity of purpose; ~**einde**, (-s), purpose, end, aim, object; ~**gebied**, goal area; ~**gerig**, (-te), purposeful; single-minded; ~**gerigtheid**, purposefulness; ~**grenslyn**, goal touch-line; ~**kring**, goal circle.
doel'loos, (..lose), aimless, motiveless, inane, objectless, purposeless, useless; ~**heid**, aimlessness, uselessness.
doel'lyn, goal-line.
doelma'tig, (-e), efficacious, efficient, practical, fit for a purpose, appropriate, adequate; ~**heid**, efficacy, efficiency, effectiveness, expedience, finality, adequacy, suitability.
doel: ~**paal**, goal-post; ~**punt**, aim, goal; ~**skieter**, goal getter; ~**skop**, goal-kick; ~**skopper**, goal-kicker; goal-shooter.
doel'stelling, (-e), aim; object in view; objective; ~ *van wet*, considerans (of act).
doel'streepagterlyn, goal-line.
doeltref'fend, (-e), effective, efficient, effectual, efficacious, adequate, pertinent; ~**heid**, effectiveness, efficaciousness; efficacy, efficiency; ~**heidsdeskundige**, efficiency expert.
doel: ~**verdediger**, goalkeeper, goalie; ~**verdediging**, goalkeeping; ~**wagter**, goalkeeper, goalie; ~**wit**, (-te), aim, view, goal, object; target; ~**witbestuur**, management by objectives (MBO).
doem, (s) doom; (w) (ge-), doom, condemn.
doemdoem'pie, (-s), small variety of gnat.
doe'melaklontjie, bull's-eye (sweet).
doe'meling, (-e), condemned person.
doem'vonnis, doom, condemnation.
doemwaar'dig, (-e), condemnable, damnable; ~**heid**, damnability.
doen, (s) doing; *my* ~ *en LATE*, my activities; my goings out and comings in; *in iem. se* ~ *en LATE*, in one's comings and doings; *uit jou gewone* ~ *RAAK*, get out of one's usual routine; (w) (ge-, gedaan), do; make (promise); take (oath); effect, perform; act; *ons het te* ~ *met 'n GEVAL van*, .., we have to deal with a case of ..; *GEWIGTIG* ~, affect importance; *jou te GOED* ~, do oneself proud; *wie GOED* ~, *goed ontmoet*, virtue is its own reward; *niks te* ~ *HÊ nie*, be at a loose end; *veel te* ~ *HÊ*, be very busy; *'n KAMER* ~, tidy a room; *wat KOM jy hier* ~? what do you want here? *te* ~ *KRY met*, have to deal with; come up against; *iets gedaan KRY*, get something done; *iem. KWAAD* ~, do someone harm; *iets LAAT* ~, have something done; *dit* ~ *'n MENS nie*, this isn't done; *te NIET* ~, destroy; *daar is NIKS aan te* ~ *nie*, there is nothing to be done about it; *aan POSSEËLVERSAMELING* ~, collect stamps; go in for stamp collecting; *ons weet wat ons te* ~ *STAAN*, our course is clear; we know how to act; *dit WIL gedoen wees*, that takes some doing; ~**de**, ~**ig**, doing; busy; *ALTYD* ~**de wees**, be always busy (on the go); *al* ~*de LEER 'n mens*, practice makes perfect; ~**er**, (-s), doer; ~**igheid**, doings, activity; ~**ing**, act, deed; behaviour; activity.
doen'lik, (-e), feasible, possible, practicable; ~**heid**, feasibility, practicability.
doe'pa, (s) (-s), dope; love potion, charm; (w) (ge-), bewitch, charm; drug, administer dope to; noble; ~**gebruiker**, dope fiend.
doer, doer'die, doe'rie, (gesell.), over there, far away; *daar* ~, far away.
doe'rian, durian *(Durio zibethinus)*.
doe'ria(s), printed muslin.
doeri'ne, dourine *(Polyneuritis infectiosa)*.

doe'sel, (ge-), be drowsy, doze; stump (-drawing); ~ **aar, (-s)**, stump-drawer; ~ **ig, (-e)**, hazy; (feeling) tired, drowsy, worn out; ~ **ing**, drowsiness; ~ **poeier**, stumping-powder.

dof, (dowwe; dowwer, -ste), dull, faint, pale, lustreless; dim, blurred (light); lack-lustre (eyes); dead (colour); matt (surface); dud; indistinct; full-mouthed; foggy; blear; undeveloped (fruit); *'n dowwe GELUID*, an indistinct sound; *'n dowwe HERINNERING*, a vague recollection; *'n dowwe KLEUR*, a dull colour; ~ *in die KOP voel*, feel thick-headed; ~ **agtig, (-e)**, rather dull (dim, faint); ~ **fies**, faintly, indistinctly; ~ **geel**, buff; ~ **grys**, dull grey, neutral tint; ~ **heid**, dullness, deadness, dimness, faintness, haziness; ~ **lampie**, parking light; ~ **skakelaar**, dim switch; ~ **wit**, dull white.

dog¹, (s) (-ge), mastiff; *Deense* ~, great Dane.

dog², (w) verl. tyd van **dink**, think; *EK ~ so*, I thought so; *jy MOENIE ~ nie*, don't presume.

dog³, (vgw) but, yet, still, however.

dogares'sa, (-s), dogaressa.

Do'ge, (-s), Doge (of Venice); ~ **paleis**, Doges' Palace.

dog'ma, (-s), dogma; ~ **tiek'**, dogmatics; ~ **'ties, (-e)**, dogmatic(al), pragmatic.

dogma'tikus, (..tici, -se), dogmatist.

dogmatiseer', (ge-), dogmatize.

dogmatis'me, dogmatism.

dog'ter, (-s), daughter; girl; *'n ~ van EVA*, a daughter of Eve; *as jy die ~ wil hê, moet jy eers na die MOEDER vry*, he that would the daughter win, must with the mother first begin; ~ **kerk**, daughter church; ~ **lik, (-e)**, daughterly; ~ **maatskappy**, subsidiary company; ~ **tjie, (-s)**, little daughter; girlie.

doi'lie, (-s), doily, doyley.

dok, (-ke), dock; *drywende* ~, floating dock; (w) **(ge-)**, dock; ~ **geld**, dock dues.

Doketis' = **Dosetis'**.

Doketis'me = **Dosetis'me**.

dok'kies, game of marbles; game with tops; – *hou*, hold the knuckles for another to shoot at with a marble; hold top for knocks.

doksologie', (-ë) doxology.

dok'ter, (s) (-s), doctor, medical practitioner, physician; medico; *die ~ GAAN oor hom*, the doctor is treating (examining) him; *daar HELP geen ~ aan nie*, it is past cure; *die KAAPSE ~*, southeaster; *sagte ~s maak stinkende WONDE*, spare the rod and spoil the child; (w) **(ge-)**, doctor; physic; nurse; edit, correct (for publication); adulterate; *'n RENPERD ~*, dope a racehorse; *WYN ~*, adulterate wine.

dok'ters: ~ **behandeling**, medical treatment; ~ **besoek**, doctor's visit; ~ **boek**, medical book; ~ **geld**, medical fee; ~ **hande:** *onder* ~ **hande wees**, be receiving medical treatment; ~ **kis**, medical pannier; ~ **koste**, medical expenses (fees); ~ **mes**, scalpel, gorget; ~ **praktyk**, medical practice; ~ **rekening**, doctor's bill; ~ **vrou**, doctor's wife.

dok'tor, (-e, -s), doctor (in literature, law, science, etc.); ~ **aal', (..rale)**, doctoral; *..torale eksamen*, examination for degree of doctor; ~ **aat'**, doctorate; *doctor's degree*; ~ **an'dus, (-se, ..di)**, candidate for doctor's degree (who has passed the examination, but not written a dissertation); ~ **eer', (ge-)**, obtain the doctor's degree; ~ **sgraad**, doctor's degree.

dok'trein, dock train.

doktrinêr', (s) pedant; (b) **(-e)**, doctrinaire, rigid; doctrinal.

dokument', (-e), document, record; ~ **e**, papers; ~ **a'sie**, documentation; ~ **eer', (ge-)**, give documentary proof, document; ~ **êr', (-e)**, documentary.

dokumente'ring, documentation.

dokument'tassie, attaché case.

dok'werker, docker, dock labourer, longshoreman, navvy.

dol¹, (s) (-le), thole; rowlock.

dol², (w) (ge-) = **dolwe**.

dol³, (b) (-le), mad, crazy, delirious, frenzied, frantic; ridiculous; worn-out (thread of nut); ~ *ler as KOP=*

AF kan dit nie, one can only be killed once; *in ~ le VAART*, in headlong career; *dis om ~ van te WORD*, it is enough to drive one mad; ~ **WEES** *op*, be crazy about; be keen on; be very fond of; ~ **bly**, mad with joy; ~ **boord**, gunwale, port last.

dol'ce far nient'e, sweet idleness, dolce far niente.

dol'dapperheid, dare-devilry.

dol'draai, (-ge-), strip (the thread of a screw)

dol'dries, (-te), dare-devil, foolhardy.

dol'driftig, (-e), furious; hot-headed; ~ **heid**, fury, frenzy.

dolean'sie, (hist.), complaint, charge; Protestant dissenting movement (in Holland, 1886).

doleer', (vero.) (ge-), grieve; dissent; *dolerende kerk*, (Dutch) nonconformist Church.

do'lend, (-e), wandering, errant; ~ *e ridder*, knight-errant.

doleriet', dolerite, whinstone.

dolf, (ge-) = **dolwe**; ~ **land**, deeply ploughed land; ~ **voor**, deeply trenched furrow.

dolfyn', (-e), dolphin.

dol'graag, with the greatest pleasure; delightedly; with the greatest eagerness.

dol: ~ **heid**, madness; foolishness, frenzy, rampage, folly; ~ **huis**, (ong.) lunatic asylum, bedlam, madhouse.

dolk (-e), dagger, poniard; dirk; bodkin; ~ **gat, (-e)**, stab hole.

dol'kop, mad person, reckless person.

dolkruid, henbane.

dolk: ~ **steek**, dagger stab; ~ **steekduif**, bleeding heart; **vormig, (-e)**, dagger-shaped.

dol'land = **dolfland**.

dol'lar, (-s), dollar; ~ **gebied**, dollar area; ~ **wisselkoers**, dollar exchange.

dol'leeg, (..leë), absolutely empty.

dol'lerig, (-e), rather mad.

dol'ligheid, madness; *dis eenvoudig ~*, it is sheer folly (madness).

dolliwa'rie, confusion, chaos; *in die ~ wees*, be in trouble, be confused; be in high feather, as proud as Punch.

dol'man, (-s), dolman; ~ **mou**, dolman sleeve.

dol'men, (-s), dolmen.

dolomiet', dolomite.

dol'os, (-se), ball of ankle-joint, knuckle bone, astragalus; talus; harbour (armour) block, dolos; ~ **GOOI**, throw the bones; *jou ~se agtermekaar SPAN*, put on one's thinking cap; ~ **gooier**, witch-doctor, soothsayer, diviner; ~ **gooiery**, bone-throwing; soothsaying; ~ **skarnier**, two-way knuckle joint.

dol'pen, thole, rowlock.

dol'ploeg, subplough, subsoiler.

dolsin'nig, (-e), rash, headlong, hare-brained; ~ **heid**, rashness, frenzy.

dol'verlief, madly in love, head over heels in love.

dol'vlieëry, crazy flying.

dol'voor = **dolfvoor**.

dol'we, (ge-), dig very deep; delve; trench; ~ **voor** = **dolfvoor**.

dom¹, (s) (-me), cathedral; dome.

dom², (b) stupid, fatuous, dull, dense, feather-brained, fat-headed, addle-headed, addle-pated, empty-headed, mindless; anserine; asinine; backward; bovine; pig-headed, block-headed; cloddish; doltish; goofy; Boeotian; *hy is te ~ om voor die DUIWEL te dans*, very stupid; he is a regular dolt; *hom ~ HOU*, pretend to know nothing; *nie so ~ as hy LYK nie*, not as green as he is cabbage-looking; ~ *vang vir SLIM*, even a clever person is caught out; *my VINGERS is ~*, my fingers are clumsy (benumbed); ~ **astrant, (-e)**, impudent, cheeky; insolent; ~ *astrant wees*, be bumptious; ~ **astrantheid**, impudence, cheek, dumb insolence, effrontery.

domein', (-e), domain, crown-land, demesne; ~ **goed**, crown land, demesne.

dom'heer, canon, prebendary; ~ **skap**, canonry.

dom'heid, stupidity, doltishness, dullness, denseness, hebetude, silliness, obtuseness.

domici'lium, (..lia), *see* **domisilie**.

dominan'sie, dominance.

dominant', (-e), dominant.
do'minee, (-s), clergyman, minister, parson; *ds. S.*, the Rev(erend) Mr. S.; ~ **agtig**, (-e), parsonic, preachy.
domineer', (ge-), predominate; domineer, dominate, lord it over.
domine'rend, (-e), dominating, domineering.
Dominikaan', (..kane), **Dominika'ner**, (-s), Dominican, Black friar.
Dominikaans', (-e), Dominican; ~*e Republiek*, Dominican Republic.
domi'nium, (-s), dominion.
do'mino, (-'s), domino; ~ **spel**, (game of) dominoes; ~ **steen**, domino (piece).
domisi'lie, (-ë, -s), domicile, home.
domisilieer', (ge-), domicile, settle.
dom: ~ **kapittel**, (dean and) chapter; ~ **kerk**, minster, cathedral (church).
dom: ~ **kiewiet**, dott(e)rel; ~ **kop**, blockhead, stupid, dud, ignoramus, fool, blunderer, ninny, nit-wit, clod, pudding head, dolt, dunderhead, gull, juggins, fat-head, chuckle-head, ass, donkey; ~ **krag**, jack screw, (lifting) jack; *so sterk soos 'n* ~ *krag*, as strong as a horse.
dom'mel, (ge-), doze, drowse, be half asleep; ~ **ig**, (-e), dozy, drowsy; ~ **igheid**, drowsiness; ~ **ing**, doze, doziness, dozing.
dom: ~ **merig**, (-e), rather stupid; ~ **merik**, (-e), stupid, fat-head, dud; ~ **migheid**, stupidity; ~ **-onnosel**, inane; ~ **oor**, dunce, blockhead, dud, ignoramus.
domp, (ge-), dip (lights of car), lower; smother.
dom'pel, (ge-), plunge, dive, dip, immerse; *in ellende* ~, plunge into misery; ~ **aar**, (-s), plunger; immersion heater; ~ **bad**, (-de(ns)), soak-bath; ~ **battery**, plunge battery; ~ **doop**, baptism by immersion; ~ **ing**, immersion, duck; ~ **pomp**, submersible pump; ~ **verwarmer**, immersion heater.
dom'per, damper; (-s), extinguisher; obscurant (fig.); *iem. die* ~ *OPSIT*, put the damper on someone; *iets die* ~ *OPSIT*, put the damper on something; ~ **sug**, obscurantism.
domp'hoek, angle of depression.
domp'skakelaar, dip-switch.
dom'siekte, pregnancy disease (in sheep).
dom'slim, silly-clever; ~ *wees*, betray one's ignorance.
dom'toring, cathedral tower.
dom'weg, in a stupid way.
don, (-s), don.
dona'sie, (-s), donation, gift.
donateur', (-s), contributor, patron; donor.
donatri'se, (-s), donor (female).
Do'nou, Danube.
don'der, (s) (-s), thunder; wretch; *GAAN na die* ~ *(plat)*, go to pot; *asof deur die* ~ *GETREF*, as if thunderstruck; *die* ~ *IN wees*, be in a rage; *g'n* ~ *OMGEE nie*, not to give a damn; (w) (ge-), thunder, boom; fulminate; ~ **besie**, tree cricket *(Cicada)*; ~ **bui**, thunderstorm; ~ **buis**, detonator (hand-grenade); ~ **bus**, blunderbus.
Don'derdae, on Thursdays.
Don'derdag, Thursday; *hy sal nog sy* ~ *teëkom*, he will meet his match; ~ **s**, on Thursdays.
don'der: ~ **end**, (-e), fulminating, fulminatory; ~ **gerommel**, rumbling of thunder; ~ **god**, thunderer; Thor; ~ **goud**, fulminating gold; ~ **jaag**, (ge-), bully; ~ **jaer**, bully; ~ **knal**, clap of thunder; ~ **kop**, thunder-head; blockhead; ~ **lug**, stormy sky; ~ **padda**, bull-frog; ~ **poeier**, fulminating powder; ~ **s**, (-e), cursed; damned; (tw) the deuce! ~ **silver**, fulminating silver; ~ **slag**, thunderclap, peal of thunder; ~ **steen**, belemnite; ~ **stem**, voice like thunder; ~ **storm**, thunderstorm; ~ **vlaag**, thunder with rain; ~ **weer**, thundery weather; ~ **wolk**, thunder cloud.
don'ga, (-s), donga, ravine, gully, gulch.
doniet', donite.
Don Ju'an, Don Juan, rake, seducer.
don'ker, (s) dark(ness); dark colour; *in die* ~ *is al die KATTE grou*, in the dark all cats are grey; *NA* ~, after dark; ~ *het nie OË nie*, no one can see in the dark; *in die* ~ *TAS*, grope in the dark; *VOOR* ~, before dark; (b) ((-e); -**der**, -**ste**), dark, dusky, lightless, dingy, opaque; dim, deep, gloomy, obscure, fuliginous; murky, melanous; cloudy; fuscous; dull (colour); grave (condition); ~ *word voor die oë*, turn black before one's eye's; ~ **aand**, late in the evening; ~ **agtig**, (-e), darkish; ~ **blou**, dark blue; perse; mazarine; ~ **bruin**, dark brown, dun, puce, nigger-brown; ~ **dag**, before daybreak; very early in the morning; ~ **geel**, deep yellow; ~ **groen**, dark green; ~ **grys**, dark grey; ~ **heid**, darkness; dimness, opacity; depth; obscurity; ~ **ig**, (-e), darkish; ~ **ing**, darkness; ~ **kamer**, dark-room; ~ **maan**, new moon; *met* ~ *maan*, on a moonless night; ~ **oog**, dark-eyed (person); ~ **pers**, dark purple; modena; ~ **rooi**, dark red, prune (colour), maroon; ~ **sien**, night vision; ~ **te**, darkness; gloom.
don'kervat, lucky dip.
don'kervellig, (-e), dark-skinned.
don'kerwerk, work in the dark; ~ *is konkelwerk*, bunglers work in the dark.
don'kie, (-s), donkey; dunce; mop; low gear; *'n* ~ *se BEEN afpraat*, talk the hind leg off a donkey; *as 'n* ~ *eenmaal GROENVOER geëet het, is dit moeilik om hom daaruit te hou*, forbidden fruit once tasted will always be desired; *van 'n* ~ *moet jy 'n SKOP verwag*, one can only expect a kick from a donkey; *'n* ~ *stamp hom twee maal aan dieselfde STEEN*, a fox is not taken twice in the same snare; ~ *VASMAAK*, hang up one's hat; ~ **ketel**, donkey boiler; ~ **kraan**, donkey crane; ~ **melk**, ass's milk; ~ **merrie**, she-ass, jenny; ~ **pomp**, donkey pump.
don'na, (-s), donna (Spanish).
donquichotterie', quixotry; quixotism.
donquichot'terig, (-e), quixotic.
dons¹, (w) (ge-), hit; *op die grond* ~, fling to the ground.
dons², (-e), down, fluff, floss, flue; fuzz; nap (fruit); ~ **agtig**, (-e), fluffy, downy; ~ **erig**, (-e), fluffy, downy, flossy, fuzzy, lanuginous; pubescent; lofty (wool); ~ **gans**, eider duck; ~ **haartjies**, down, pile, fluff (beard); pubescence (bot.); ~ **hael**, fine shot; ~ **ie**, (-s), fluff; plumule; ~ **harig**, (-e), pubescent; ~ **ies** = **donshaartjies**; ~ **ig**, (-e), fluffy, downy, fuzzy, lanuginous; pubescent; lofty (wool); ~ **kombers**, (eiderdown) quilt; ~ **luis**, fluff louse; ~ **papier**, fluffy paper; ~ **vere**, floss (of ostrich); plumules; powder down; ~ **vlokkie**, floccus; ~ **wol**, fleecy wool, downy wool.
dood, (s) death, decease, demise; passing, quietus, Great Divide, the latter end; *by die* ~ *AF*, at death's door; *so BANG as die* ~ *vir*, mortally afraid of; *nie BANG vir die* ~ *nie, maar vir die lank wegbly*, it is not death I fear but the fact that I'll be dead so long; ~ *en BEGRAWE*, dead and buried; *ter* ~ *BRING (veroordeel)*, put (condemn) to death; *die een se* ~ *is die ander se BROOD*, one man's meat is another man's poison; *BY sy* ~, on his death; *die* ~ *kom soos 'n DIEF in die nag*, death keeps no calendar; *DIS sy* ~, that will cause his downfall (death); *DUISEND dode sterf*, die a thousand deaths; *die* ~ *maak almal GELYK*, death is the great leveller; *tot in die* ~ *GETROU*, faithful (un)to death; *net goed om die* ~ *te gaan HAAL*, be as slow as a funeral; *iem. haal hom die* ~ *op die HALS*, someone courts his own death; *so bleek soos die* ~ *van IEPERE*, as pale as death; *die* ~ *is nie te KEER nie*, death will have no denial; *nog LANK nie* ~ *nie*, there's life in the old dog yet; *meer* ~ *as LEWENDIG*, more dead than alive; *iem. die* ~ *op die LYF ja*, put the fear of death into somebody; *liewer* ~ *as uit die MODE*, rather out of this world than out of fashion; ~ *is jou NAAM*, you are playing with death; *'n NATUURLIKE* ~ *sterf*, die a natural death; *iem. die* ~ *voor OË hou*, threaten someone with the worst; *OM die* ~ *nie*, not for anything, not for the life of me; *by die* ~ *OMDRAAI*, be at death's door; ~ *moet 'n OORSAAK hê*, there is an excuse for everything; *die* ~ *is in die POT*, the food is poisoned; all activity has come to a standstill; *so SEKER as die* ~, as sure as fate; *net een* ~ *SKULDIG wees*, man can only die once; *daar uitsien soos die* ~ *in SLUITERS*, be all skin

doodloop

and bones; *die* ~ *SOEK*, be courting one's death; *die SWART D*~, the Black Death; *TEN dode gedoem*, doomed (to death); *die* ~ *kan enige TYD kom*, death keeps no calendar; ~ *en VERDERF*, death and destruction; ~ *is jou VOORLAND*, you are doomed; *ek was eerder my* ~ *te WAGTE*, that is totally unexpected; *op iem. se* ~ *WAG*, wait for dead men's shoes; *dit sal nog sy* ~ *WEES*, that will be the end of him; *van die* ~ *in die WÊRELD gekom het, is 'n mens nie van sy lewe seker nie*, we don't know what the future may hold; (b) **(dooi(e))**, dead, deceased, defunct, extinct; insensitive (from cold); worthless, unproductive (capital); dull (colour); out of action (games); slow (affair); *dooie KAPITAAL*, non-productive capital; *die regulasie is 'n dooie LETTER*, that regulation is a dead letter; *meer* ~ *as LEWENDIG*, more dead than alive; *liewer* ~ *as uit die MODE*, rather out of this world than out of fashion; ~ *is die MOSSIE*, the cat is out of the bag; ~ *soos 'n MOSSIE*, as dead as a doornail; ~ *is die MOSSIE*, the cat's been let out of the bag; ~ *in die NOOD wees*, be mortally afraid; *op die dooie PUNT*, at a deadlock; *dooie PUNT*, dead centre; stalemate; *dooie SKULD*, bad debts; *'n dooie VENT*, a slow coach; ~**aankondiging**, announcement of a person's death; ~**advertensie**, obituary notice; ~**-af**, dead-beat; ~**alleen**, all alone; ~**arm**, extremely poor, indigent; ~**baar**, bier; ~**baklei, (-ge-)**, fight to death; *liewer* ~ *baklei as doodeet*, rather die a soldier's than a glutton's death; ~**bang**, very much afraid; ~**bed**, deathbed; ~**bedaard, (-e)**, very (quite) calm, cool-headed; ~**benoud**, in deadly fear; ~**berig, (-te)**, death notice, obituary, necrology; ~**blaas (-ge-)**, extinguish (candle); ~**bloei, (-ge-)**, bleed to death; ~**boek**, book of death; *op die* ~ *boek skryf*, put off (postpone) indefinitely; write something off; ~**brand, (-ge-)**, burn to death; cauterize (wound); ~**byt, (-ge-)**, bite to death; ~**doener**, clincher, corker, catch word, knock-out argument; ~**drink, (-ge-)**, drink to death; ~**druk, (-ge-)**, press (squeeze) to death, squash, silence; suppress (riot); touch down (rugby); ~**eenvoudig**, quite simple, plain sailing; *om die* ~ *eenvoudige rede*, for the simple reason; ~**eerlik**, honest; ~**eet, (doodgeëet)**, overeat, gormandize; eat ravenously; kill oneself by eating; *jou* ~ *eet*, make a glutton of oneself; ~**ernstig, (-e)**, in dead earnest, deadly serious; ~**gaan, (ge-)**, die, perish, go west; stop working; peter out; croak; go out (fire); ~ *gaan oor 'n nooi*, be infatuated with a girl; ~**gebore**, still-born; ~**gegooi**; ~ *gegooi wees op 'n nooi*, be madly in love with a girl; ~**gerus**, perfectly calm; quite unconcerned; ~**geryp, (-te)**, killed by frost; very slow; lifeless; listless; ~**getrek**: ~ *getrekte opstyging*, stalled start; ~**gewaan, (-de)**, presumed dead; ~**gewoon, (..gewone)**, very simple, very common; ordinary; ~**goed, (..goeie)**, very kind; kind to a fault; ~**gooi, (-ge-)**, kill by throwing; extinguish (fire by water); bombard; snow under, overwhelm with (work); put out of action by throwing (games); ~**gooier**, stunner; clincher; dumpling; something indigestible; ~**grawer, (-s)**, grave-digger; ~**honger, (w) (-ge-)**, starve to death, famish; (b) starving, famished; ~**hou**, death-blow, smash; smasher; corker, clincher; ~**jammer**, very sorry; *dit is* ~ *jammer*, it is a great pity; ~**kaartjie**, memorial card; ~**kalm**, very calm; ~**kis**, coffin; *so skaars soos 'n tweedehandse* ~ *kis*, as scarce as can be; not to be had for love or money; ~**(kis)kleed, (..klede)**, shroud; ~**knies, (-ge-)**, fret (to death); ~**knip**, ~**knyp, (-ge-)**, pinch to death; snuff (put) out; ~**kook**, overcook, overdo; ~**koud**, icy cold; ~**krap, (-ge-)**, delete; ~**kry, (-ge-)**, kill; succeed in killing; *my* ~ *kry is min*, I defy all comers (killers); ~**kwyn, (-ge-)**, pine away; ~**lag, (-ge-)**, laugh (oneself) to death; *ek wou my* ~ *lag*, I was tickled to death; ~**lê, (-ge-)**, overlie; kill by lying (on it); lie dead; numb; *sy ma moes hom klein* ~ *gelê het*, he should have died young.

doodˈloop, (-ge-), tire oneself out by walking; come to a dead end (street); peter out, fizzle out (revolt);

doods

~**baantjie**, blind-alley occupation; ~**paadjie**, blind alley; ~**punt**, cul-de-sac, dead end; ~**spoor**, dead end; ~**straat(jie)**, blind alley, cul-de-sac; impasse.

dood: ~**luiters**, free and easy; with innocent expression; *jou* ~ *luiters hou*, seem blissfully unaware; ~**lyn**, dead-line (sport); ~**maak, (-ge-)**, kill, finish off, douse, despatch; *wat nie* ~ *maak nie, maak vet*, what does not kill fattens; ~**maakkamer**, lethal chamber; ~**mak**, very tame; ~**maker**, killer; ~**maklik**, very easy; ~**mare**, tidings of death; ~**martel, (-ge-)**, torture to death; ~**moeg, (..moeë)**, dead-beat, dog-tired, tired to death; done up; ~**nugter**, completely sober; objectively; ~**ongelukkig**, utterly miserable; ~**onskuldig**, completely innocent; ~**op** = **doodmoeg**; ~**praat, (-ge-)**, hush up, talk out (away); talk to death; ~**redeneer, (-ge-)**, out-argue; ~**reën, (-ge-)**, be killed by rain; be washed out (sport); ~**reg**, perfectly right; ~**register**, death register; ~**ry, (-ge-)**, ride to death; ride down (horse); knock over and kill (in road accident).

doodˈryp¹, (w) (-ge-), be killed by frost.
doodˈryp², (b) overripe
doods, (-e), desolate, dreary; death-like; dull; ~*e stilte*, dead silence.
doodˈsake, matter(s) of life and death.
doods: ~**angs**, agony, mortal fear; pangs of death; ~**baar**, hearse; ~**bang** = **doodbang**; ~**beendere**, deadman's bones; ~**begeleiding**, care for the dying; ~**benoud** = **doodbenoud**; ~**berig** = **doodberig**; ~**bleek**, ghastly (deadly) pale, ashy; livid, pallid, ashen; ~**bleekheid**, lividness; ~**brief**, obituary notice.
doodˈseker, quite certain; absolutely sure.
doodsˈengel, angel of death.
doodˈsertifikaat, death-certificate.
doods: ~**gevaar**, peril of death; deadly danger; ~**gewaad** = ~**skleed**; ~**haas**, deadly haste; ~**heid**, desolateness, dreariness, deadness, inanimation; ~**hemp**, shroud, cerecloth; winding sheet; ~**hoof**, death's-head, skull; ~**hoofvlinder**, death's-head moth.
dood: ~**siek, (-e)**, dangerously ill; moribund; ~**sit, (-ge-)**, get the better of, outwit; kill by sitting on; ~**skaam, (w) (-ge-)**, be very shy; die of shame; (b) painfully shy; ~**skaduwee**, shadow of death; ~**skiet, (-ge-)**, (kill by) shoot(ing); fusillade; grass.
doods: ~**kleed, (..klede)**, pall, shroud, winding-sheet; *die* ~ *kleed het geen sakke nie*, you can't take it with you; ~**klere**, death clothes; grave clothes; ~**kleur**, colour of death; livid colour; ~**klok**, death bell, knell.
dood: ~**skok, (-ge-)**, electrocute; ~**skoot**, mortal wound; clincher; ace (tennis).
doodsˈkop¹, (s) death's head; monkey fish.
doodˈskop², (w) (-ge-), kick to death.
dood: ~**skreeu, (-ge-)**, shout down; ~**skrik, (s)** mortal fright; *iem. die* ~ *skrik op die lyf ja*, frighten someone out of his wits; (w) (ge-), be frightened to death; ~**slaan, (-ge-)**, beat to death, kill, slay; *AL slaan jy my dood*, even if it costs my life; *VUUR* ~ *slaan*, extinguish a veldfire; ~**slaap**, sleep of death; ~**slag**, manslaughter, homicide, killing; ~**slaner**, killer; clincher; ~**sˈmare** = **doodmare**; ~**smoor, (-ge-)**, stifle, smother; ~**snik**, last gasp.
doodsˈnood, imminent danger; agony of death.
doodˈsonde, deadly (mortal) sin.
doodsˈoorsaak, cause of death.
doodˈspuit, (-ge-), kill (weeds, pests) by spraying; anaesthetize.
doodsˈroggel, death rattle.
dood: ~**stadig**, dead slow; ~**steek, (s)** deathblow, coup de grâce; *Latyn was sy* ~ *steek*, Latin made him fail; (w) (-ge-), stab to death; dirk; ~**stem, (-ge-)**, outvote; ~**still**, very still, quiet as a mouse; ~**stonde**, hour of death; ~**straal**, death-ray; ~**straf**, capital punishment; ~**stryd**, death-struggle, last agony; flurry (whale); ~**stuipe**, pangs of death.
doodsˈtyding, death-notice.
doodˈsukkel, (-ge-), plod, struggle.
doods: ~**uur**, hour of death; ~**vallei**, valley of death;

dood — **doppie**

~veragting, contempt of death; ~vermoeidheid, (deadly) exhaustion; ~vrees, fear of death; ~vyand, mortal enemy; ~wa, hearse; ~waak, death-watch.

dood: ~swak, extremely weak; ~sweet, (s) cold sweat of death; (w) (-ge-), perspire very freely; ~swoeg, (-ge-), exhaust (overstrain) oneself; ~s'worsteling, death-struggle; ~swyg, (-ge-), ignore, not talk about; *'n boek (saak)* ~ *swyg,* form a conspiracy of silence about a book (matter); ~tevrede, perfectly content; ~trap, (-ge-), trample to death; ~trappers, navvies (boots); ~trek, (-ge-), delete; overstrain; -treur, (-ge-), grieve to death; ~vak, baulk (billiards); *dubbele* ~ *vak,* double baulk; ~val, (-ge-), fall (drop down) dead; *ek kan* ~ *val as dit nie so is nie,* strike me dead if that is not true; ~vat, (-ge-), hold (tackle) firmly; ~vee, (-ge-), wipe out, obliterate, erase; ~veilig, (-e), quite safe; gilt-edged (investment); ~vererg, (~), become mortally vexed (incensed).

dood'verf¹, (-ge-), paint over.

dood'verf², (ge-), mark out; put on ground-paint; designate for (a post); *hy is gedoodverf as die minister se opvolger,* he has been marked out for the minister's successor.

dood: ~verlief, lovesick; ~vervelend, (-e), deadly dull (boring); ~verwonderd, quite astonished; ~voël, barn (screech) owl; ~vonnis, sentence of death, death-warrant; ~vries, (-ge-), freeze to death; ~waterpas, plumb centre; ~werk, (-ge-), work to death; overwork oneself; ~wurg, (-ge-), choke to death.

doof¹, (w) (ge-), extinguish, put out (light); deaden (noise).

doof², (b) (dowe; dower, -ste), deaf; *niemand is so* ~ *as wie nie wil HOOR nie,* none are so deaf as those who will not hear; *HORENDE* ~ *en siende blind wees,* blind and deaf to all around one; *jou* ~ *HOU, jou Oos-Indies* ~ *HOU,* sham deafness; *so* ~ *soos 'n KWARTEL,* as deaf as a post; ~ *WEES vir,* turn a deaf ear to; ~heid, deafness; ~middel, drug, narcotic, anaesthetic.

doof'pot, extinguisher; *die SAAK is in die* ~ , the matter is being hushed up; *iets in die* ~ *STOP,* hush up something; suppress a matter.

doof'stom, deaf mute, deaf and dumb; ~heid, deafmutism; ~inrigting, ~instituut, deaf-and-dumb asylum; ~me, (-s), deaf mute; ~me-inrigting = doofstominrigting; ~metaal, finger-alphabet.

doog, (ge-), tolerate, brook; *geen teëpratery word ge* ~ *nie,* no objections are tolerated.

dooi, (ge-), thaw.

dooi'e, (-s), the dead, the deceased; ~bal, ball-inhand; dead ball; ~bloed, clotted (bruised) blood; ~gang, backlash, lost motion; ~gewig, dead load, dead weight.

dooi'(e)lam, still-born lamb; ~ *afgooi,* throw a still-born lamb.

dooi'elas, dead weight, dead load.

dooi'elug, bad air.

dooi'elyn, dead-line (rugby).

dooi'(e)mansdeur: *aan* ~ *KLOP,* knock in vain; *voor* ~ *KOM,* find nobody at home.

dooie'punt, deadlock.

dooi'er, (-s), yolk (of an egg).

dooi'erd, (-s), lazy-bones, dotard.

dooi'erig, (-e), lifeless, listless, slow; ~heid, lifelessness, listlessness, apathy.

dooi'ersak, yolk sack.

dooi'(e)rus, rifle rested.

dooi'es, fatalities.

dooie'skuld, bad debts.

dooi'(e)vul, still-born foal; ~ *afgooi,* throw a still-born foal.

dooi'gewig = dooiegewig.

dooi'gety, neap-tide.

dooi'lik, (-e), dead-alive, lifeless.

dooi'weer, thaw.

dool, (ge-), wander, ramble, roam, meander; err; ~hof, maze, labyrinth; ~weg, wrong way; *op* ~ *weë raak,* go astray.

doop, (s), christening, baptism; naming; ducking; dipping; *ten* ~ *hou,* present at the font; (w) (ge-), christen, baptize; sop, dip; dub; initiate (a student); ~bak, ~bekken, baptismal font; ~belofte, baptismal vow; ~boek, register of baptism; ~borg, baptismal sponsor; ~dag, christening day; ~formulier, christening ritual (formulary); ~gelofte, baptismal vow; ~getuie, godfather, godmother; ~kapel, baptistry; ~kleed, (..klede), chrison; ~klere, christening robes; ~komitee, initiation committee; ~maal, christening feast; ~naam, Christian (baptismal) name, given name; ~ouers, parents of child to be baptized; ~plegtigheid, christening ceremony; ~register, church (baptismal) register; ~rok, christening robe; ~seel, baptismal certificate; *iem. se* ~ *seel lig,* lay bare a man's past; ~sel, baptism; ~sertifikaat, baptismal certificate.

Doops'gesind, (-e), Baptist; ~e, (-s), Baptist.

doop'skoene: ~ *aanhê,* be ill at ease.

doop'sondag, christening Sunday.

doop: ~vont, baptismal font, baptistry; ~water, baptismal water.

door, (dore) = dooier.

Door'nik, Tournay.

doos, (dose), box, case, etui; carton, packet; *uit die OU* ~ , old-fashioned; out of date; *die* ~ *van PANDORA,* pandora's box; ~barometer, aneroid barometer; ~vormig, (-e), capsular; ~vrug, capsule.

dop, (s) (-pe), shell (egg); husk (seeds); peel (fruit); pod (pea); cup (of acorn); sheath (of bomb); cover (of tobacco-pipe); carapace (tortoise); hull; cap; head; integument; tot, drink; *'n paar stywe* ~ *pe agter die BLAAIE hê,* have a spot or two; ~ *en DAM,* brandy and water; *in die* ~ *GEKYK,* have been at the bottle; *hy het net die* ~ *GEPIK,* he is hardly out of the shell; *in sy* ~ *GEPIK wees,* be crazy; *IN die* ~ , in the making; in the bud; *daar sal* ~ *pe van KOM,* nothing will come of it, it will be a failure; *in sy* ~ *KRUIP,* draw in one's horns; withdraw into one's shell; *'n LEË* ~ , an empty shell; *iem. met 'n LEË* ~ , an addlepate; a numbskull; ~ *pe MAAK van iem.,* beat someone hollow; *OUD uit die* ~ *gekruip,* born clever; *hoe droër* ~ *, hoe soeter SOP,* never judge by appearances; *IN STYWE* ~ *steek,* be a hard drinker; *skaars uit die* ~ *WEES,* be hardly out of the shell; (w) (ge-), shell (peas), peel; *in 'n eksamen* ~ , be ploughed in an examination; fail; ~beitel, shelling chisel; ~bout; cap stud; ~brandewyn, dop brandy; ~diertjie, scale insect.

do'peling, (-e), child to be baptized.

dop'emmer, small milk-pail.

do'per, (-s), baptizer; *Johannes die D* ~ *,* John the Baptist.

dop'-ertjie, green pea; chick-pea.

do'pery, christening; initiation (of new students).

dop: ~hard, (w) (-ge-), case-harden; ~hard, (b) (-e), case-hardened; ~harding case-hardening; ~heide, bottle heath, bell heath(er); ~hoed, bowler; derby; ~hou, (-ge-), keep an eye on, watch; hold the milk-pail.

do'ping, immersion.

dop: ~klier, shell gland; ~luis, scale (insect); *HARDE* ~ *luis,* armoured scale; *ROOI* ~ *luis,* red scale; *SAGTE* ~ *luis,* soft scale; *VERDERFLIKE* ~ *luis,* pernicious scale; ~masjien, husker; ~moer, acorn nut.

dop'peling, (-e), failure, student who has failed.

Dop'per, (-s), Dopper; ~ *ag'tig,* (-e), like a Dopper, conservative.

dop'perig, (-e), full of husks.

Dop'perkerk, Dopper Church.

dop'perkiaat, round-leaf kiaat *(Pterocarpus rotundifolius).*

dop'permaniere, (vero., skerts.,) uncouth manners.

dop'pie, (-s), detonator, (percussion) cap; primer, shell; cover (of pipe); capsule; quencher, tot (liquor); button; cupule (bot.); dab (compass); silver fish *(Argyrozona argyrozona);* ~ *AFKLAP,* refuse (gun); die; *jy kan gaan* ~ *s BLAAS,* you are wasting your time; go and boil your head; *dis* ~ *in die EMMER met hom,* he is done for; his number is up; *sy* ~ *het GEKLAP,* he has had his chips; his knell has

dop

been rung; ~**lont,** capped fuse; ~**patroon,** primer cartridge; ~**sgeweer,** ~**sroer,** muzzle loader.
dop: ~**rys,** paddy rice; ~**skroef,** cap screw; ~**sleutel,** box spanner; ~**smeer,** cup grease; ~**steker,** drunkard, toper; ~**stelsel,** tot system for labourers; ~**uittrekker,** ~**uitwerper,** cartridge ejector; ~**verhard,** (~), carburize, case-harden; ~**vormig, (-e),** cup-shaped; ~**vrug,** achene; ~**vuller,** cup filler.
dor, (w) **(ge-),** dry; (b) **(-re; -der, -ste),** dry, barren, withered, desert, arid.
dora'do¹, (-'s), dorado (fish).
Dora'do², (-'s), El Dorado.
dor'bank, hardpan.
dor'heid, dryness, barrenness, aridity.
Do'ries, (-e), Doric, Dorian.
do'ring, (-s), thorn, spine, prick(le); barb (weapon); cock; tang (of knife); mandrel; ripper, dab, go-getter, stunner, topper, adept, first-rater; stout fellow; *'n ~ in die OOG,* an eyesore; *jy is 'n OU ~,* you are a brick; *hy SIT op ~ s,* he is sitting on thorns; *op ~ s slaap,* have one's path strewn with thorns; *'n ~ in die VLEES,* a thorn in one's side; (tw) good chap! ~**agtig, (-e),** thorny, spinous; acanaceous; ~**appel,** thorn-apple; ~**blad,** prickly pear *(Opuntia);* ~**boom,** mimosa, thorntree; ~**bos,** thicket of thorns; thornbush; ~**draad,** barbed-wire; fiery liquor; ~**draadversperring,** barbed-wire entanglement; ~**haai,** spiny dogfish *(Squalidae);* ~**holtevis,** coelacanth; ~**kraal,** zareba; ~**kroon,** crown of thorns; ~**loos,** (..**lose),** spineless; ~*lose turksvy,* spineless cactus; ~**peer,** (kind of) thorntree; ~**rig, (-e),** thorny, prickly; braky; ~**righeid,** prickliness; ~**stomp,** stump of thorntree; ~**struik,** thornbush; briar, brier; ~**tak,** bough of a thorntree; ~**tangetjie,** tweezers; ~**tee,** *Cliffortia ilicifolia;* ~**veld,** thornbush country; ~**vormig, (-e),** spinate; ~**vygie,** *Eberlanzia spinosa, E. intricata.*
do'rinkie, (-s), small thorn, prick, spinute.
Dor'kas: 'n ~, a Dorcas.
Dor'mer, (-s), Dormer (sheep).
dorp, (-e), village, town; *op (in) die ~ woon,* live in town.
dor'pel, (-s), head (of door).
dorp: ~**eling, (-e),** ~**enaar, (..nare, -s),** villager, town-dweller.
Dor'per¹, (-s), Dorper (sheep).
dor'per², (-s), villein.
dorp: ~**eraad,** village council; ~**ie, (-s),** hamlet.
dorps, (-e), rustic, boorish, ~**aanleg,** town planning; village extension; ~**bestuur,** village management board; ~**bewoner,** townsman, villager; ~**boer,** village (town) farmer; ~**gas, (-te),** villager; ~**gebied,** township; municipal area; ~**geestelike,** pariah priest; ~**grens,** town boundary; ~**grond,** village ground, commonage, town lands; ~**huis,** house in a village; town house; ~**kinders,** town children.
dorp'skool, village school, town school.
dorps: ~**lewe,** village life, town life; ~**meent,** commonage; ~**ontwikkeling,** township development; ~**praatjies,** village gossip; ~**sraad = dorperaad;** ~**veld,** commonage; ~**veldwagter,** town ranger; ~**wet,** bye-law.
dor're bank = **dorbank.**
dors¹, (s) thirst; desert country; *ek HET ~,* I am thirsty; *KRY,* get thirsty; *jou ~ LES,* quench one's thirst; *die ~ na ROEM,* the thirst for glory; (w) **(ge-),** be thirsty; ~ *na,* thirst after; (b) **(-er, -ste),** thirsty; dry; *sy is ~,* she is thirsty.
dors², (s) threshing, thrashing; (w) **(ge-),** thresh, thrash; shell (maize).
dorsaal', (..**sale),** dorsal.
dor'ser, (-s), thresher; ~**y,** threshing.
Dor'sie, (-s), Dorsian, Dorper (sheep).
Dors'land, Thirstland (waterless region); **d~plant,** xerophyte, eremophyte; ~**trek,** Dorslandtrek (1874-1905).
dors: ~**masjien,** threshing-machine; ~**stillend, (-e),** thrist-quenching.
dor'stig, (-e), thirsty, athirst, adry; droughty; ~**heid,** thirstiness, thirst.
dors: ~**stok,** flail; ~**trek,** journey through waterless regions; ~**tyd,** threshing-time; ~**verwekkend, (-e),**

producing thirst; ~**vleël, (-s),** flail; ~**vloer,** threshing floor, barn floor.
dor'te = dorheid.
dor'telappeltjie, apple of Sodom *(Solanum sodomaeum).*
dos, (s) attire, array, raiment; feather; (w) **(ge-),** clothe (in fine raiment), attire, deck out.
doseer'¹, (ge-), teach, lecture; ~**pos,** lecturing post.
doseer'², (ge-), dose (animals); ~**spuit,** dosing syringe.
dosent', (-e), teacher, lecturer, reader.
dose'ring¹, lecturing, teaching.
dose'ring², (-s), dosage.
Dosetis', Docetist.
Dosetis'me, Docetism.
do'sie, (-s), *verkleinwoord van doos,* small box; pyxis; casket; *'n ~ vuurhoutjies,* a box of matches.
dosiel', (-e), docile.
do'sis, (-se), dose, dosage; *te groot ~,* overdose.
dossier', (-e, -s), dossier, docket; file, brief.
dosyn', (-e), dozen; *~e MALE,* dozens of times; *drie ~ PIESANGS,* three dozen bananas.
dota'sie, (-s), dotation, endowment.
doteer', (ge-), dotate, endow.
dot'jie, (-s), little dear; dot; soft-brimmed hat.
dot'terblom, marshmarigold *(Caltha).*
dou, (s), dew; *van die ~ lewe,* live on air; (w) **(ge-),** dew; ~**blom,** sundew *(Drosera).*
douairiê're, (-s), dowager.
douche, (-s), douche.
dou: ~**druppel,** dewdrop; ~**erig, (-e),** dewy; ~**meter,** drosometer; ~**punt,** dew point; ~**spoor,** track in the dew, ~**tjie,** *verkleinwoord van dou;* drizzle; ~**trapper,** early riser (walker); ~**voordag,** very early in the morning, before daybreak.
dou'wurm, ringworm, eczema; lichen; seborrhoeic dermatitis; annelid; ~**salf,** ringworm ointment.
do'we, (-s), deaf person; *dit het jy aan geen ~ gesê nie,* that didn't fall on deaf ears; ~**mansdeur:** *aan ~ mansdeur klop,* knock in vain; find no hearing; find no one at home.
do'werig, (-e), somewhat deaf; ~**heid,** partial deafness.
do'we: ~**skool,** school for the deaf; ~**toestel,** hearing-aid.
dow'we: ~ *koringaar,* blank ear of wheat; ~**neute,** empty (shrivelled) nuts; *cf. dof.*
dow'wel, (ge-), dig up, burrow.
dow'werig, (-e), rather dull (dim), dimmish, indistinct.
dow'wigheid, something indistinct; dullness, dimness.
do'yen, (-s), doyen.
dra, (ge-), carry (on shoulder); wear (clothes); bear (expenses); reach (voice); discharge; suppurate (wound); crop (wheat); support (roof, masonry); *HAAT ~,* be resentful, bear malice; *jou JARE goed ~,* carry one's years well; *'n KIND ~,* be pregnant; *sy KNIEË ~,* take to one's heels; ~ *dit soos 'n MAN,* take it like a man; *'n ver draende STEM,* a carrying voice, *VRUG ~,* bear fruit.
draad, (drade), (s), wire; fence; yarn, thread (of material, sermon); strand (of cotton); ply (wool); filament (of root); string (of pod); grain (wood); clue; line (telephone); *geen DROË ~ aan die lyf hê nie,* be drenched to the skin; *sy ~ is op 'n END,* he is at the end of his tether; *GROF van ~,* coarse-grained; *'n ~ in HANDE kry,* discover a clue; *alle drade in HANDE hê,* have the matter well in hand; *aan 'n dun ~ HANG,* hang by a thread; *tem. se ~ KNIP,* put a spoke in someone's wheel; *KORT van ~,* short-tempered; ~ *KOU,* be homesick; *die ~ van iets KRY,* get the hang of; *nie 'n ~ van iem. KRY nie,* not to get a penny from someone; *die ~ KWYT wees,* have lost the thread (of an argument); *LANK van ~ wees,* be long-winded; *geen ~ aan die LYF hê nie,* not have a rag on; *'n ~ vir elke NAALD hê,* have a ready tongue; *'n ~ in die NAALD steek,* thread a needle; *sy ~ RAAK op,* he is getting impatient; *op die ~ SIT,* blow hot and cold; sit on the fence; *met die ~ SNY,* cut on the square; *TEEN die ~ sny,* cut against the grain; *TOT op die ~ afgesly,* worn to a thread; *drade TREK,* pull strings; *die brood TREK drade,* the

draad

draadloos   *draak*

bread is ropy (stringy); (w) **(ge-)**, fence, wire; string (beans); ~ **anker**, wire-wound armature; wire anchor, fence anchor; ~ **berig**, telegram, wire; ~ **boor**, wire-drill; ~ **borsel**, wire brush; scrubber; ~ **buier**, wire bender; ~ **dikte**, wire gauge; ~ **duweltjie**, caltrop; ~ **gaas**, wire gauze; ~ **haarborsel**, wire hairbrush; ~ **heg**, (-ge-), wire-stitch; ~ **heining**, wire fence; ~ **hindernis**, wire obstacle; ~ **jie**, (-s), thin thread; filament; short piece of wire; ~ **kabel**, wire cable; ~ **klankopnemer**, wire recorder; ~ **knipper**, wire clipper; ~ **kouer**, homesick internee; ~ **leiding**, wiring (elect.).

draad'loos, (s), (..lose), (vero.), wireless, radio; (b) (..lose), without wires, wireless; ~ *lose telegrafie,* wireless telegraphy.

draad: ~ **loper**, tight-rope walker; ~ **maas**, wire mesh; ~ **maat**, wire gauge; ~ **mandjie**, wire basket; ~ **monteur**, wireman (teleg.); ~ **net**, wiring; ~ **nommer**, wire gauge (thickness); ~ **opnametoestel**, (vero.), wire recorder; ~ **paal**, fencing standard; ~ **perske**, mango; ~ **pop**, puppet; ~ **rol**, wire roll; ~ **sitter**, (-s), one who sits on the fence; temporizer; mugwump; ~ **sittery**, temporization; ~ **skêr**, wire cutters, nippers; ~ **skilder**, (ge-), grain (wood); ~ **skildering**, graining; ~ **sny**, (-ge-), screw; ~ **snyer**, wire-cutter, screw cutter; ~ **snymoer**, die nut; ~ **spanner**, wire strainer; turn-buckle; wireman; ~ **spanning**, fencing; ~ **speekwiel**, wire wheel; ~ **spoel**, solenoid; ~ **spyker**, wire nail; ~ **stoel**, doolie, dooly; ~ **tang**, wire pliers (cutters); ~ **tou**, wire rope; ~ **trekker**, wire-puller, fence maker; intriguer (in politics); masturbator; ~ **trekkery**, wire-pulling; intrigue; ~ **trekwerk**, drawn work (embroidery); ~ **trommel**, coiling drum; ~ **versperring**, barbed-wire entanglement; ~ **vlegwerk**, wiring; ~ **vorm**, wire shape; ~ **vormig**, (-e), filamentary; filiform; ~ **werk**, wiring; wire grate, filigree work; nonsense; *vol* ~ *werk wees,* be full of fads and fancies; ~ **winding**, helix; ~ **wol**, wire wool; ~ **wurm**, wire-worm, round worm, nematode.

draag, (ge-), = dra.
draag'as, carrying shaft.
draag'baar, (s) (..bare), bier, hand-barrow; litter (for wounded person); stretcher; bearer; brancard; (b) (..bare), bearable (pain); wearable (clothes); portative, portable; ~ **dril**, stretcher drill; ~ **heid**, portability.

draag: ~ **balk**, supporting (bearer) beam, girder; transom (of bridge); ~ **band**, arm (gun) sling; suspensor(y); ~ **doek**, sling; ~ **draad**, carrying (lift) wire; ~ **duur**, life (clothes); ~ **ent**, support end; ~ **golf**, carrier wave; ~ **hout**, neck bar; cross-bar (foreshaft of a cart); ~ **klamp**, bracket; ~ **knop**, stud; ~ **koëffisiënt**, lift coefficient; ~ **krag**, strength to bear (loads); supporting power (foundation); carrying capacity (ship); working load (beam); range (gun); import, carrying quality (voice); ~ **laer**, journal bearing; ~ **lik**, (-e), endurable, livable (conditions), passable, bearable, tolerable; ~ **loon**, porterage; ~ **lys**, impost; bearing-ledge; ~ **mandjie**, pannier; ~ **pak**, lounge-suit; ~ **plaat**, bearing plate; ~ **plek**, bearing; ~ **pot**, general box; axle box; journal (of axle); ~ **potvurk**, horn-plate, horn-guards; ~ **punt**, fulcrum; ~ **rand**, ground service (horseshoe); ~ **riem**, strap (for forshaft of cart); lanyard; ~ **rok**, utility dress; ~ **skakel**, hanging link; ~ **spanning**, bearing stress; ~ **steen**, padstone, bedstone; corbel, impost, console bracket; ~ **ster**, (-s), female bearer, wearer; ~ **stoel**, sedan chair; gestatorial chair (pope); palanquin (palankeen); ~ **stok**, carrying pole; cowl-staff; ~ **stuk**, templet; standard; ~ **tap**, trunnion; ~ **tyd**, (period of) gestation; ~ **veer**, carrying (bearer) spring; ~ **verband**, (arm-)sling; suspensory bandage; ~ **vermoë**, bearing power; (carrying) capacity; ~ **verspanning**, lift bracing; ~ **vlak**, bearing-surface; area; plane; air foil, aerofoil; ~ **weerstand**, lift; ~ **wydte**, range; import (of words), bearing; carry; scope.

draai, (s) (-e), turn, twist; corner; bend; curve; whorl (shell); throw (silk); coil; boggle; dodge; *'n* ~ *aan iets GEE,* twist something; put another face on something; ~ *e HÊ,* be full of fads and fancies; *êrens 'n* ~ *GOOI,* pay a short visit somewhere; *KAAPSE* ~ *e maak,* take sharp turns; *jou* ~ *e KEN,* know the ropes; *met 'n* ~ *KOM,* beat about the bush; *daar kan nog 'n* ~ *KOM,* something unforeseen may still happen; *hy kan sy* ~ *nie KRY nie,* run out of time; *met 'n* ~ *LOOP,* make a detour; (fig.) be crooked (dishonest); *'n* ~ *by iem. MAAK,* make a quick call on someone; *in 'n NOU* ~ *kom,* get into a tight corner; *OM die* ~ *wees,* be near (close); *die agterste* ~ *kom met ROK en kabaai,* the sting is in the tail; *met* ~ *e en SWAAIE loop,* chose a roundabout way; *jy sal jou* ~ *VERLOOR by my,* you will find out your mistake; *'n* ~ *aan iem. se WOORDE gee,* misrepresent (twist the meaning of) somebody's words; (w) **(ge-)**, turn, hinge; revolve (round a point), rotate; roll (pills); wind (rope); veer round, shift (wind); whirl; slew; tarry, linger (dilly-dally), dawdle, lag, loiter; hesitate; spin, twist (ball); gyrate; change (one's opinion); court (girl); lay (rope); grind (organ); *ALLES* ~ *om hierdie feit,* everything hinges on this fact; *by (om) 'n NOOI* ~, be courting a girl; *OM iem.* ~, buzz about someone; pester someone; *al om 'n PUNT* ~, beat about the bush; *die nuwe ROLPRENT* ~ *nou,* the new film is showing now; *jou UIT iets* ~, wriggle out of a thing; *VERSIES* ~, spin verses.

draai: ~ **baar**, (..bare), rotatable, revolving; ~ **baken**, rotating beacon; ~ **bank**, lathe; ~ **bankklou**, lathe-dog; ~ **bankwerk**, lathe-work; ~ **blok**, swivel block; ~ **boek**, script; scenario; ~ **boekrak**, revolving book-case; ~ **boekskrywer**, scenario-writer; ~ **boom**, turnpike, turnstile; ~ **boor**, auger; rotary drill; ~ **bord**, bogie centre, pivot centre; raffling board; catch-me-quick (indoor game); ~ **brug**, swing (swivel, pivot) bridge; ~ **deur**, swing (revolving) door; ~ **duik**, tail dive; ~ **end**, (-e), gyratory, revolving, rotating; ~ **er**, (-s), turner; loiterer, laggard; prevaricator; ~ **erig**, (-e), loitering, dilatory; giddy, dizzy; ~ **erigheid**, dilatoriness; dizziness; ~ **ery**, turning shop; loitering, delay; ~ **gewrig**, wheel-and-axle joint; ~ **hals**, red-breasted wryneck *(Jynx ruficollis);* ~ **hek**, turnstile; swing gate; kiss-gate, turnpike; ~ **ing**, turning, rotation, spin (tennis, etc.), torsion, gyration; convolution; ~ **ingsas**, axis of revolution; pivotal axis; ~ **ingshoek**, angle of torsion (rotation); ~ **ingstraal**, radius of torsion; ~ **jakkals**, long-eared fox *(Octocyon megalotis);* silver jackal *(Cynalopex chama);* ~ **klep**, revolving valve; ~ **kolk**, whirlpool; swirl; vortex; ~ **kom**, turning basin; ~ **koord**, flex; ~ **koppeling**, flexible joint; ~ **kous**, loiterer; dawdler; ~ **kraan**, rotary crane; ~ **kruis**, moulinet; ~ **lamp**, swivel lamp, spotlight; ~ **lig**, revolving light; changing light; ~ **masjien**, wringer; ~ **moment**, turning moment; torque; ~ **orrel**, barrel-organ; handorgan, hurdy-gurdy; ~ **pen**, screw picket; ~ **plek**, room to turn; place where a turn can be made; ~ **pomp**, rotary pump; ~ **pot**, journal box; ~ **potlood**, self-propelling pencil; propeller pencil; ~ **punt**, turning point; fulcrum, pivot, centre of rotation; ~ **rigting**, direction of rotation; ~ **saag**, circular saw; bow-saw; ~ **sein**, turn signal; ~ **siekte**, gid, (mad) staggers; ~ **sif**, revolving screen; ~ **skop**, screw (kick); ~ **skyf**, revolving target; turning platform, turntable (railw.); lathe; dial (of telephone); ~ **sleutel**, bent spanner; ~ **spieël**, revolving mirror; cheval-glass; ~ **spier**, rotator; ~ **spil**, pivot; ~ **spit**, revolving spit; ~ **stel**, bogie; ~ **steltrok**, bogie wagon; ~ **stoel**, revolving chair; ~ **stroom**, rotary (electric) current; rotating current; ~ **suiker**, barley-sugar; ~ **tafel**, turn-table; ~ **tjie**, (-s), small turn; *'n* ~ *tjie loop,* go for a short walk (to relieve nature); ~ **tol**, spinning top; whipping top; ~ **toring**, revolving turret; ~ **trap**, winding (spiral) staircase; caracol(e); ~ **trommel**, revolving drum; ~ **venster**, whirling window; ~ **verhoog**, revolving stage; ~ **vlerk**, rotor; ~ **vurk**, swivel fork; ~ **werk**, nittery; ~ **wind**, whirlwind; ~ **wissel**, turning points; ~ **wurm**, maggot *(Muscidae).*

draak, (drake), dragon; basilisk; *sommer 'n OU* ~, a real old bugbear; a perfect horror; *die* ~ *STEEK*

met iem., poke fun at somebody; ~ **ag'tig, (-e)**, dragonish; ~ **bloedboom**, dragon-tree *(Dracaena)*.
draal, (ge-), hang fire, tarry, linger, loiter, procrastinate, dawdle; ~ **skoot**, hang fire.
dra'baadjie, lounge-coat.
dra'bok, darnel, rye-grass.
dra'boog, relieving arch.
dra'derig, (-e), fibrous, stringy; filamentous; ropy (bread); ~ **heid**, ropiness, stringiness; fibrousness.
dra'e = dra(ag).
dra'end, (-e), bearing, carrying; ~ *e buitehuid*, stressed outer skin.
dra'er, (-s), bearer, carrier, holder, porter; cropper; wearer (of clothes); carrier (of disease); host (plant); ~ **werwel**, atlas, uppermost cervical vertebra.
draf', (s) swill, draff, hogwash.
draf², (s) trot; *dit GAAN op 'n* ~ *fie*, things are jogging along; *op 'n* ~ *LEI*, run (a horse); *OP 'n* ~, at a trot; (w) **(ge-)**, trot; run; ~ - ~ *wen*, win at a trot; ~ **hoender**, guinea-fowl, pintado bird; ~ **karretjie**, sulky; ~ **stap**, (s) piaffe, jog-trot; (w) **(ge-)**, go at a slow trot; ~ **wedstryd**, trotting match.
drag, pus, discharge (wound); gun-range; bearing; **(-te)**, load, burden; dress, fashion, apparel; faggot (of wood); crop; litter, farrow; *'n* ~ *HOUT*, a bundle of (fire)wood; *'n* ~ *SLAE*, sound thrashing.
dragant'(gom), gum-dragon, tragacanth.
drag'gie, (-s), small bundle (load).
drag'lyn, water-line (of ship).
drag'me, (-s), dra(ch)m; drachma (Greek coin).
dra'goman, (s), dragoman, interpreter.
dragon', tarragon; ~ **asyn**, tarragon vinegar.
dragon'der, (-s), dragoon.
dragonna'de, (-s), dragonnade.
drag'tig, (-e), pregnant, with young; in foal; in pig; in calf; ~ **heid**, gestation, pregnancy.
drag'tyd, gestation period.
dra'hout = draaghout.
dra'ke: ~ **bloed**, dragon's blood; bloodwort; ~ **kop**, gargoyle.
dra'kerig, (-e), of the blood-and-thunder type; hair-raising, melodramatic.
dra'ketand: ~ *e saai*, sow dragon's teeth.
Drako'nies, (-e), Draconic, Draconian, harsh, cruel.
drakoniet', draconite (mineral).
dra'koste, overheads.
dra'krag, carrying (financial) capacity; means; range (of voice).
dra'lend, (-e), loitering, hesitating.
dra'ler, (-s), laggard, procrastinator, loiterer; ~ **ig**, **(-e)**, slow; loitering.
dra'ma, (s), drama, play; ~ **skrywer**, dramatist, playwright; ~ **tiek'**, dramatics, (the) drama; ~ **'ties, (-e)**, dramatic; ~ **tiseer', (ge-)**, dramatize; ~ **tise'ring**, dramatization; ~ **turg', (-e)**, dramatist, playwright; ~ **turgie'**, dramaturgy, playwriting.
drang, (-e), urgency, pressure; instancy; impulse, urge; craving; imperiousness; bias; exigence; *ONDER die* ~ *van omstandighede*, under the stress of circumstances; ~ *UITOEFEN op*, bring pressure to bear upon; *SOSIALE* ~, social instinct, ~ *na VRYHEID*, urge towards liberty; ~ **rede**, urgent reason.
drank, (-e), drink, liquor, spirits, potables; beverage; drench, potion; *aan die* ~ *RAAK*, take to drink; *die* ~ *laat STAAN*, give up drinking; *STERK* ~, strong drink, alcoholic liquor; *aan die* ~ *VERSLAAF wees*, be addicted to alcohol; ~ **bestryding**, temperance worker, drink fighter; ~ **bestryding**, temperance movement; ~ **buffet**, bar; ~ **duiwel**, drink demon; ~ **gebruik**, use of alcohol; ~ **handel**, liquor trade; ~ **huis**, pub(lic house); ~ **ie, (-s)**, tot, quencher, spot; potion; draught; *'n* ~ *ie maak*, have a drink; ~ **kabinet**, cocktail (wine) cabinet; ~ **kelner**, bar waiter; ~ **lisensie**, liquor licence; ~ **lug**, alcoholic smell; ~ **lus'tig, (-e)**, intemperate; ~ **lus'tigheid**, intemperance; ~ **menger**, cocktail-mixer; ~ **misbruik**, excessive drinking; ~ **neus**, grogblossom; ~ **offer**, libation; drink-offering; ~ **saal**, drinking-hall; ale-house; ~ **smokkelaar**, liquor runner; ~ **smokkel(a)ry**, liquor running (smuggling); ~ **sug**, craving for a drink; dipsomania; ~ **sug'tig, (-e)**, bibulous; addicted to drink; dipsomaniac; ~ **sug'tige, (-s)**, dipsomaniac; drink addict; ~ **verbod**, prohibition; ~ **verbruik**, drink consumption; ~ **vergunning**, liquor licence; ~ **verkoop**, liquor traffic; ~ **verkoper**, licensed victualler; ~ **wet**, liquor law; ~ **winkel**, bottle-store, liquor shop, gin-shop.
dra'pak, lounge-suit.
drapeer', (ge-), drape; ~ **der, (-s)**, draper.
draperie', (-ë), drapery, hangings.
drape'ring, draping.
dra: ~ **radio**, portable radio; walkie-talkie, transistor (radio); ~ **rok**, dress for daily wear, utility dress; ~ **skoen**, shoe for daily wear.
dras'land, swamp, marshland.
dras'sig, (-e), marshy, boggy, swampy; waterlogged; ~ **heid**, marshiness, bogginess.
dras'ties, (-e), drastic; ~ *optree*, take drastic steps.
dra: ~ **tap**, trunnion (pin); ~ **veer**, bearing (carrying) spring; ~ **vermoë**, (carrying) capacity; deadweight (cargo); lift capacity (aeroplane); bearing strength.
draviet', dravite.
dra: ~ **vlak**, bearing surface; ~ **wieg(ie)**, carrycot.
draw'we = draf.
draw'wer, (-s), trotter, hackney; courser (bird); jogger.
draw'wertjie, (-s), courser (bird); girl belonging to youngest group of Voortrekkers.
dreef, (drewe), alley; pasture; meadow; form; *op* ~ *HELP*, set going; *aan die* ~ *KOM*, get going; *op* ~ *WEES*, be in one's stride, be in excellent form; ~ **reg**, right to drive cattle over another's land.
dreg, (s) (-ge), drag, grapnel; dredge; (w) **(ge-)**, dredge, drag; ~ **anker**, grapnel; ~ **haak**, drag-hook, grapple; ~ **net**, dragnet, trawl.
dreig, (ge-), threaten, menace, impend; lour, lower (clouds); comminate; *die HUIS* ~ *om in te val*, the house is in imminent danger (on the point) of falling down; *ek* ~ *al LANKAL*, I have long intended; *met 'n pak SLAE* ~, threaten to cane; ~ **brief**, threatening letter; ~ **ement', (-e)**, threat, menace; ~ **end, (-e)**, threatening, pressing, menacing; grim; minacious, minatory, ominous; impending (catastrophe; imminent (danger); comminatory; ~ **ing, (-e, -s)**, threat, menace; commination; impendence.
drein, (ge-), whine, worry, whimper, pule.
dreineer', (ge-), drain; ditch; ~ **band**, seton (med.); ~ **buis**, drainage tube; ~ **put**, French drain; absorbing well; ~ **pyp**, drain pipe.
drei'nerig, (e), whining, puling.
dreine'ring, drainage.
drek, muck, dirt; dung; faeces; ~ **god**, image, idol (Bible); ~ **steen**, coprolite; ~ **stowwe**, excrements.
drel, (-le), indecent woman, slut, slattern; slow-coach; obnoxious person; ~ **kous**, slow person, dawdler; ~ **lerig, (-e)**, slow, dawdling; ~ **letjie, (-s)**, little slut.
drem'pel, (-s), threshold; ~ **waarde**, minimum value, limit.
drenk, (ge-), drench, steep (in liquid); soak, impregnate; imbue, saturate with; water, allow to drink (animal).
dren'keling, (-e), drowned (drowning) person; *'n* ~ *gryp na 'n strooihalmpie*, a drowning man clutches at a straw.
dren'king, drenching; soaking; impregnation.
dren'tel, (ge-), loiter, lounge, saunter; ~ **aar, (-s)**, saunterer, loiterer; ~ **gang**, saunter, lounge; ~ **kous**, loiterer, lingerer.
dresseer', (ge-), train, break in (horse); drill; coach (boys); ~ **der, (-s)**, coach; trainer.
dresse'ring, dressuur', training, coaching; dressage.
dreun, (s) rumble, roar, boom(ing); chant, sing-song (way of reciting); drone; (w) **(ge-)**, rumble, roar, roll, bellow, boom; chant; *hy loop dat dit so* ~, he runs very fast (for all he is worth); ~ **ing**, rumble, roar, boom(ing); thunder; *sy* ~ *ing teëkom*, meet one's match.
dreun'stem, monotonous voice (tone).
dre'wel, (-s), drift-pin; mandrel.

dria′de, (-s), dryad.
drib′bel, (ge-), dribble (football).
drie, (s) (-ë, -s), three; try (rugby); *'n ~ AANTEKEN (behaal)*, score a try; *'n ~ VERVYF*, convert a try; (telw) three; *alle goeie DINGE bestaan uit ~*, there is luck in odd numbers; *so EEN, twee, ~*, in a trice; *~ MAAL*, three times; *~ -~*, in threes; *geen ~ kan TEL nie*, be very stupid; *~ UUR*, three hours; ~**agtdaereën**, soaking summer rain, general rain; ~**-agtste**, (-s), three eighths; ~**aks**, three eighths (of inch); ~**akter**, (-s), three-act play; ~**assig**, (-e), triaxial; ~**(bal)kuns**, hat trick; ~**been**, triad; tripod, trivet; three-legged; ~**blaar**, trefoil; ~**blarig**, (-e), tripetalous; ~**daags**, (-e), three day, of three days' duration; ~**daesiekte**, three days' (cattle) disease; ~**deel**, (ge-), trisect; ~**dekker**, three-decker, triplane; ~**delig**, (-e), tripartite; ~**deling**, dividing into three, tripartition; ~**dimensionaal**, (..nale), three-dimensional; ~ *dimensionale meetkunde*, solid geometry; ~**dissel**, carline; ~**doring**, *Dalbergia melanoylon*; Karoo shrub, *Rhigozum trichotomum*; ~**draads**, (-e), three-ply; ~**dubbel(d)**, (-de), threefold, treble, triple; ~**duims**, three inch; ~**duimspyp**, three-inch pipe.
Drie-een′heid, Trinity; ~**sleer**, Trinitarianism.
drie-eeu′efees, tercentenary.
drie: ~**-e′nig**, (-e), triune; ~**-enigheid**, triunity; ~**ër′lei**, of three kinds; ~**fasig**, (-e), three-phase; ~**gatkontak**, (-te), three-way socket; ~**hoek**, triangle; *die EWIGE ~hoek*, the eternal triangle; *REGHOEKIGE ~hoek*, right-angled triangle; ~**hoekghitaar**, balalaika; ~**hoekig**, (-e), triangular; deltoid; ~**hoeksbaken**, trigonometrical beacon; ~**hoekskakeling**, mesh connection; ~**hoeksmeting**, trigonometry; triangulation; trigonometrical survey; ~**hoekspar**, arris-rafter; ~**hoeksverkiesing**, triangular election contest; three-cornered contest; ~**hoekverband**, triangular bandage; ~**hokkig**, (-e), trilocular; ~**hoofdig**, (-e), three-headed; ~*hoofdige spier*, triceps (muscle); ~**jaarliks**, (-e), triennial; ~**jaaroud**, three-year-old; ~**jarig**, (-e), of three years; ~**kaart**, tierce, sequence of 3 cards; ~**kantig**, (-e), three-sided, trilateral; ~**kantshoek**, trihedral angle; ~**klank**, triphthong; triad (music); ~**kleppig**, (-e), trivalvular; ~**kleur**, tricolour; ~**kleurig**, (-e), tricoloured; ~ *kleurige winde*, convolvulus; ~**kleursiener**, trichromato; **D**~**koninge**, Epiphany; ~**kopspier**, triceps; ~**kroon**, tiara; ~**kuns**, hat trick; ~**kwart**, three-quarter (rugby); three fourths; ~**kwartbed**, three-quarter bed; ~**kwartsmaat**, three-four time; ~**laaghout**, threeply; ~**ledig**, (-e), threefold; of three parts, trifurcate, tripartite; ~**lettergrepig**, (-e), trisyllabic; ~**ling**, (-e), triplet; ~**lip**, harelip; ~**lobbig**, (-e), trilobate; ~**loop**, three-barrelled; ~**luik**, triptych; ~**maandeliks**, (-e), quarterly; ~**man**, triumvir; ~**manskap**, triumvirate; ~**master**, (-s), three-master; ~**moondhede-**, three-power; ~**mylgrens**, three-mile limit; ~**oog-**, three-eyed; ~**persoonsmotor**, three-seater; ~**ponder**, three-pounder; ~**poot**, tripod; ~**poot-**, three-legged; ~**poottafel**, trivet table; ~**puntig**, (-e), three-pointed; tricuspid; ~**raskruising**, triangular cross; ~**reëlig**, (-e), of three lines; ~**riemsgalei**, trireme; ~**rigtingskakelaar**, three-way switch.
dries[1], (s) fallow land; (w) (ge-), plough virgin land, break new ground; (b) fallow.
dries[2], (b) (-te; -ter, -ste), audacious, bold, rash.
drie: ~**saadlobbig**, (-e), tricotyledonous; ~**sadig**, (-e), trispermous; ~**sang**, trio; ~**slagmaat**, triple time; ~**slagsteek**, triple treble; ~**snarig**, (-e), three-stringed; trichord; ~**soor′tig**, (-e), of three kinds; ~**span**, threesome; team of three; ~**spel**, three-some (golf); ~**spletig**, (-e), trifid; ~**sprong**, junction of three roads; hop, skip and jump; *op die ~ sprong*, at the parting of the ways; *op die ~sprong STAAN*, have come to the crossroads; ~**stemmig**, (-e), for three voices, three-part; ~**ster**, asterism.
driest′heid, rashness, boldness, daring, audacity.
drie: ~**stukrok**, three-piece frock; ~**sydig** (-e), threesided, trilateral; ~**tal**, (number of) three, trio; ~**talig**, (-e), trilingual; ~**tallig**, (-e), ternary; ~**tand**, trident; ~**term**, trinomial; ~**tjie**, (-s), three (sport); magpie (target); ~**uur**, three o'clock; ~**valshoek**, solid angle; ~**vertrek-**, three-roomed; ~**vlakkig**, (-e), trihedral; ~**vlaksshoek**, trihedral angle; ~**voet**, tripod, trivet; ~**voetbok**, tripod rest; ~**voethysblok**, gyn; ~**voetig**, (-e), three-legged; ~**voud**, treble; triple; ~**voudig**, (-e), threefold, triple; ~**waardig**, trivalent; ~**weekliks**, (-e), triweekly; every three weeks; ~**wegkraan**, three-way (stop)cock; ~**werf**, three times, thrice; ~**wiel(er)**, (-s), tricycle; ~**wywery**, trigamy.
drif[1], **(driwwe)**, ford, drift.
drif[2], (-te), anger, hot temper, passion, hastiness, headiness, heat, fury, fervidness, fieriness; *jou ~ BETEUEL*, keep one's temper, curb (control) one's passion; *IN ~*, in an angry mood (in a fit of temper); *daar is ~ in (by) die WEER*, everything predicts rain.
drif′aanwyser, drift indicator.
drif: ~**bui**, fit of passion; ~**kop**, hothead, spitfire.
drif′sel, (-s), flotsam.
drif′tig, (-e), angry, hasty, irascible, heated, fiery, choleric, quick-tempered, impatient, heady, hot-headed, hot-tempered; passionate, in a passion; *~ word*, fly into a temper (passion); ~**heid**, hot temper, irascibility, passionateness, choler, impatience, abruptness.
dril[1], (s) drill (material.)
dril[2], (s) drill (implement, exercise); (w) (ge-), bore, drill; exercise; train; quiver, shake (like jelly); cram, coach (children); enregiment; ~**baas**, coach; ~**boog**, drill bow (spindle); ~**boor**, drill, wimble; bow (drill); ~**gras** = **dronkgras**; ~**grond**, quagmire; ~**kostuum**, gym (tunic); ~**kuns**, art of drilling; ~**ler**, (-s), coach; ~**lerig**, (-e), jellylike; shaking; ~**meester**, drill sergeant; coach; ~**plek**, drilling ground; ~**sel**, jelly; ~**siekte** = **dronksiekte**: ~**vis**, electric ray (fish); ~**vleis**, aspic.
dring, (ge-), press, urge, impel, force; throng, crowd, elbow, jostle, push; *dit ~ ons tot VERSIGTIGHEID*, this compels us to be cautious; *VORENTOE ~*, push (press) forward.
drin′gend, (b) (-e), urgent, pressing, crying (need), peremptory, instant, emergent; exigent; imperative; (bw) urgently; *iets ~ nodig hê*, be in urgent need of something; ~**heid**, urgency, pressure, instancy, importunity.
drink, (ge-), drink; imbibe, be addicted to liquor, carouse, booze; *op die BRUID ~*, propose a toast to the bride; *iem. iets te ~e GEE*, give someone something to drink; *op iem. se GESONDHEID ~*, drink (to) someone's health; *'n GLAS leeg ~*, empty a glass; *~ soos 'n VIS*, drink like a fish; ~**baar**, (..bare), drinkable, potable; ~**baarheid**, potability; ~**bak**, watering-trough; ~**beker**, goblet, beaker, mug, tankard; ~**ebroer**, boon companion, toper, tippler, pot-companion; ~**emmer**, bucket for drinking-water; ~**er**, (-s), drinker, boozer, quaffer, tippler; *'n kwaai ~er*, a hard drinker; ~**ery**, drinking; ~**fontein**, drinking-fountain; scuttle-butt; ~**gat**, (-e), waterhole; ~**gelag**, drinking-bout, carouse, carousal, potation; ~**geld**, tips, drink-money; ~**glas**, (-e), tumbler, drinking-glass, ~**goed**, booze, drinks; drinkables; ~**horing**, drinking-horn; ~**huis**, beershop; ~**kan**, tankard; ~**lied**, drinking-song; ~**lustig**, (-e), boozy; ~**maat**, pot-companion; ~**party**, drinking party; booze-party, potation, randan; orgy; ~**plek**, tap-room, bar; drinking-place; ~**saal**, pump-room; ~**strooitjie**, straw; ~**toestel**, drencher; ~**ware**, drinks, potables; ~**water**, drinking-water; *~water vra by 'n nooi*, make advances to a girl; ~**watertenk**, drinking-water tank; ~**watervoorsiening**, water supply.
dro′ë, (s) dry land; *op die ~*, on dry land; (w) (ge-), dry, make dry; become dry; fire (tea); set (cement); evaporate; season (wood); cure (tobacco).
dro′ëbek: ~ *SIT*, go hungry; be disappointed; ~**bone**, dried beans, dry beans; field beans; ~ *TUISKOM*, come home disappointed.
droe′daskruid, medicinal herb (*Pharnaceum lineare*).
droef, **(droewe; droewer, -ste)**, sad, dejected, in low spirits; *dit GAAN ~ met ons*, we are having a diffi-

droefgeestig   *druil*

cult time; *droewe HERINNERINGE*, sad memories; ~ *MIN van sy werk weet*, know very little about his work.

droefgees'tig, (-e), melancholy, dejected, gloomy, sad, glum, mirthless, pensive; ~**heid**, pensiveness, melancholy, gloom(iness), melancholia.

droef'heid, sadness, sorrow, affliction, dole, mourning; *o ~ op note!*, what a pity! alack and alas!

droef'nis, sadness, sorrow, affliction, grief.

dro'ë: ~**koekie**, biscuit; ~**kompas**, dry compass.

droë'land, dry land; ~**boerdery**, dry-land farming.

dro'ë: ~**lewer**, (s) thirsty soul; tippler; bore; *Cassine tetragona;* (b) dry-throated; ~**maat**, dry measure; ~**melk**, powdered milk; ~**mond** = **droëbek**; ~**perske**, dried peach; ~**plaatkoppeling**, dry-plate clutch (motor).

dro'ër, (-s), drier; curer, salter; ~**ig, (-e)**, rather dry; ~**y, (-e)**, drying (place); (ong.), drug; chemical.

droes¹, the devil; *die ~ haal jou*, may the devil take you!

droes², glanders; farcy (in horse's nose), strangles.

droes³, druse (geol.).

droes⁴, dross.

dro'ëselbattery, dry-cell battery.

droe'sem, dregs, sediment; lees; *tot die ~ ledig*, drink to the lees.

droe'sig, (-e), glandered, glanderous.

dro'ë: ~**voer**, dried forage; ~**vrot**, dry-rot; ~**vrugte**, dried-fruit.

droe'wenis, (-se), sadness, grief.

droe'wig, (-e), sad (person); funereal, mournful (countenance); baleful, doleful, pitiful, sorrowful (sight); ~*e AFLOOP*, sorry end; *'n ~ e FIGUUR slaan*, cut a sorry figure; ~*e RESULTATE*, poor results; ~**heid**, mournfulness, dolefulness.

dro'ë: ~**wors**, dried sausage; ~**ys**, dry ice.

drog'beeld, illusion, chimera, eidolon.

dro'gery = **droëry**.

drogery', (-e), = **droëry**; ~**handel**, (ong.), drug trade.

dro'gies, drily, impassively.

dro'ging, drying, seasoning (wood), curing (tobacco).

dro'gingsinstallasie, drying plant.

drogis', (-te), (ong.), druggist; pharmacist; ~**tery, (-e)**, drugstore, druggist's shop.

drog'rede, sophism, fallacy, false reasoning; paralogism; ~**naar**, sophist, casuist; caviller; ~**nering**, sophistry.

drol, (-le), turd, dropping; shit; *hy's 'n regte ou ~*, (plat), he's a real shit (turd); ~**letjie, (-s)**, little turd.

drol'peer, wild pear *(Dombeya rotundiflora)*.

drom, (s) (-me), troop, crowd, throng, multitude; (w) **(ge-)**, crowd together.

dromeda'ris, (-se), dromedary.

dro'mer, (-s), dreamer, visionary, fantast; ~**ig, (-e)**, dreamy; far-away; ~**igheid**, dreaminess; vagueness; ~**y, (-e)**, day-dreaming, reverie.

drom'mel, (-s), deuce, devil; wretch; dickens; *ARME ~*, poor wretch; *wat d(i)e ~ wil jy HÊ?*, what the deuce do you want?

drom'mels, (-e), confounded, darned; (bw) very extremely; *hy is ~ laat*, he is very late; ~*!*, (tw), the deuce! goodness gracious!

dronk, (s) draught (medicine); drink; *'n ~ instel*, propose a toast; (b) drunk(en), intoxicated, (gone) in drink; giddy, dizzy; ~ *in die kop VOEL*, feel giddy; *tot ~ WORDENS toe*, into a state of drunkenness; ~**aard, (-s)**, drinker, drunkard, inebriate; ~**aardsaslel**, inebriate reformatory; ~**bessie**, berry of *Chymococca empetroides;* ~**bestuur**, driving while under the influence of drink; drunken driving; ~**emansrusie**, ~**emanstandjie**, drunken brawl; ~**enskap**, drunkenness, inebriety, insobriety, drinking; ~**erig, (-e)**, boozy, fuddled; giddy; ~**geslaan**, agape, confused, amazed, struck all of a heap; ~**gras**, horse-tail, *(e.g. Melica decumbens);* ~**heid**, drunkenness.

dron'kie, (-s), (vero.); drink; drunk(en person); *'n ~ water*, a glass of water.

dronk: ~**lap**, drunkard, inebriate; Bacchanal; ~**makend, (-e)**, inebriant; ~**manspraatjies**, ~**manstories**, idle (drunken) talk; ~**manswaansin**, delirium tremens, the horrors; ~**nes**, drinking bout; ~**nes** *hou*, have a booze party; ~**party**, drinking party; ~**siekte**, sturdy, gid (sheep); turnside (dogs); staggers (horses); goggles.

dronk'slaan, (-ge-), flabbergast, confuse, dumbfound, flummox; amaze, floor, strike dumb, astonish, astound; beat one's comprehension; *IEM. ~*, floor someone; *dit slaan MY dronk*, it beats me, I don't understand it.

dronk'slaner, clincher, irrefutable argument.

dronk'tou, *Solanum quadrangulare.*

dronk'verdriet, alcoholic remorse.

droog, (ge-), (w) = **droë**; (b) **(droë; droër, -ste)**, dry, adry, parched; rainless, arid; chippy; husky (voice); dull (story); not in milk; chicane (at cards); *droë BESKUIT*, rusk; *as dit ~ BLY*, if the weather keeps dry; *droë BONE*, dried beans; *'n droë HOTEL*, hotel without a liquor licence; *droë MAAT*, dry measure; *so ~ soos SAND*, as dry as dust; *droë WYN*, dry wine; ~**bed, (-de)**, drying bed; ~**braai, (-ge-)**, dry-fry; ~**dok**, dry (graving) dock; ~**gewig**, dry weight; ~**heid**, dryness; ~**hopie**, cock (of hay); ~**kamer**, ~**kas**, drying room; ~**komiek, (s) (-e)**, dryboots, dry humorist; (b) drolly, with dry humour, drily; ~**kook, (-ge-)**, boil dry; ~**lê, (-ge-)**, drain, reclaim; make (a country) dry (by prohibiting the sale of intoxicants); ~**legging**, draining; reclaiming, reclamation; ~**loop, (-ge-)**, run dry; ~**lyn**, washing-line; ~**maak, (s)** reclamation; (w) **(-ge-)**, dry; reclaim (land); air (clothes); drain-cure (tobacco); accomplish nothing; talk nonsense, ~**masjien**, drying machine; drier; hydroextractor; ~**middel**, drying agent; drier; ~**my-keel bessie**, dry-my-throat-bush *(Scutia commersonii, Cissus cirrhosa, Rhoicissus rhomboidea);* ~**oond**, drying kiln; oast; ~**oondskuur**, flue barn; ~**plank**, drying board; ~**pomp, (-ge-)**, pump dry; ~**pruim**, dry-stick; ~**raam**, ~**rak**, (clothes-)drainer; clothes-horse; drying frame; flake (for fish); ~**sit, (-ge-)**: *iem. ~ sit*, outwit someone; get the better of (oust) someone; ~**skoonmaak, (-gemaak)**, dry-clean; **skoonmaker**, drycleaner; ~**skoonmakery**, drycleaning (works); ~**skuur**, flue barn; curing shed; ~**solder**, loft; ~**stoppel**, dry old stick, a wet blanket; matter-of-fact person; ~**te, (-s)**, drought, dryness; ~**tebestand**, drought-resistant; ~**tegeteisterde**, drought-stricken; ~**toestel**, drying tower (apparatus); ~**tou**, clothes-line; ~**vloer**, barbecue; ~**voets**, dry-shod; ~**weg**, dryly, with dry humour.

droom, (s) (drome), dream; *drome kom altyd ANDERSOM uit*, dreams go by contraries; *drome is BEDROG*, lay no store on dreams; dreams are but fantasies; *ult die ~ HELP*, disillusion someone; *nie in my STOUTSTE drome nie*, not in my wildest dreams; (w) **(ge-)**, dream; moon; *wie het dit kon ~*, who could have dreamt of such a thing? ~**agtig, (-e)**, dreamlike, vague; ~**beeld**, illusion, chimera, phantasm, phantom; phantasmagoria; ~**boek**, dream book; ~**gesig**, vision; ~**laaitjie**, bottom-drawer; ~**land**, dreamland; *'n kind ~ land toe stuur*, send a child to the Land of Nod; ~**lewe**, dreamlife; ~**loos, (..lose)**, dreamless; ~**uitleêr**, oneirocritic; interpreter of dreams; ~**uitlegging**, oneiromancy, interpretation of dreams; ~**uitlegkunde**, oneirology; ~**wêreld**, dream world.

drop, (Ndl.), liquorice (licorice); ~**lekker**, liquorice; ~**pille**, liquorice pills; ~**poeier**, liquorice powder; ~**water**, liquorice water.

dros, (ge-), run away, abscond, bunk (lecture), desert, take French leave.

drosdy', (-e), magistrate's residence, residency, drosdy.

dros'sery, (-e), desertion, running away.

dros'ter, (-s), runaway, absconder, deserter, fly-by-night; ~**y** = **drossery**.

Druï'de, (-s), Druid.

Druï'dies, (-e), Druidic(al).

druif, (druiwe), grape; *druiwe na die BOLAND bring*, carry coals to Newcastle; *suur druiwe EET*, take a nasty knock; *die druiwe is SUUR*, sour grapes; *sy druiwe TEËKOM*, meet one's match; ~**luis**, vine pest, phylloxera.

druil, (ge-), mope; pout; ~**erig, (-e)**, moping; mopy, *druip* 132 *druppel*

pouting; ~**kop**, pepper-pot (fig.); ~**oor**, mope; dunce.
druip, (ge-), drip, trickle, fall in drops; fail (in examination); *in die eksamen* ~, fail in an examination; ~**eling, (-e)**, failure (in examination).
drui'per, gonorrhoea, clap; gleet.
druip, ~**groef**, water-drip; ~**grot**, ~**kelder**, stalactite cave; ~**lys**, drip; ~**nat**, dripping wet, soaked; ~**ogig (-e)**, bleary-eyed.
druip'steen, dripstone; *HANGENDE* ~, stalactite; *STAANDE* ~, stalagmite; ~**grot**, stalactite cave.
druip'stert, sneaking; ashamed; ~ *weggaan*, slink off (with the tail between one's legs).
druip'vak, failing subject; compulsory subject.
druip'vet, dripping.
druis, (ge-), roar, swirl.
drui'we: ~**agtig, (-e)**, grapy; ~**asyn**, grape-vinegar; ~**blaar**, vine leaf; ~**brandewyn**, grape-brandy; ~**dop**, grape-skin; (mv) grape; ~**-eksportasie**, grape-export; ~**god**, god of wine, Bacchus; ~**handel**, grape-trade; ~**kar**, grape-cart; *met die* ~ *kar gery hê*, be half seas over; be intoxicated; ~**kissie**, grape-box; ~**konfyt**, grape-jam; ~**korrel**, grape; ~**kuur**, grape-cure; ~**mandjie**, grape-basket; ~**oes**, grape-harvest; vintage; ~**pakker**, grape-packer; ~**pers**, winepress; ~**pit**, grape-stone; ~**plukker**, vintager, grape-gatherer; ~**prieel**, vine-bower, (vine) pergola; ~**rank**, vine tendril; ~**sap**, grapejuice; wine; ~**skêr**, grape-scissors; ~**soort**, species of grape; ~**steen**, botryolite; ~**steggie**, ~**stiggie**, vine cutting; ~**stok**, vine; *die* ~ *stokke werk met hom*, he is tipsy; he is well primed; ~**suiker**, dextrose; glucose; grape-sugar; ~**suur**, racemic acid; ~**trapper**, wine-treader; ~**tros**, bunch of grapes; ~**tyd**, grape-season; ~**uitvoer**, grape-export; ~**witluis**, grape-mealybug.
druk, (s) press(ure); weight; print, type; printing; thrust (of engine); squeeze (of hand); stress, incidence (taxes); **(-ke)**, edition (of book); *HOË (lae)* ~ high (low) pressure; *onder HOË* ~ *werk*, work at high pressure; *UIT* ~, out of print; ~ *UITOEFEN op*, bring pressure to bear upon; *in* ~, *VERSKYN*, be published; appear in print; (w) (ge-), press, print (books); squeeze; elbow (your way through); hustle (in crowd); weigh (heavy) upon; oppress; push (rugby); cramp; depress; *in jou ARMS* ~, clasp in your arms; *'n DRIE* ~, score a try; *iem. die HAND* ~, shake hands with someone; *iem. se HAND* ~, squeeze someone's hand; *die SKOEN* ~ *my*, the shoe pinches me; *op 'n WOORD* ~, emphasize a word; (b, bw), busy (street); lively, fussy (person); crowded; *dit BAIE* ~ *hê*, be very busy; be under pressure; *die kerk is* ~ *BESOEK*, the service was well attended; ~ *aan die GANG wees*, be in full swing; ~ *in GESPREK wees*, deep in conversation with; *jou* ~ *MAAK*, work oneself up; ~ *SAKE*, brisk business; ~**baar**, (..bare), printable; ~**balk**, compression beam; ~**bars**, pressure burst; ~**belasting**, compression strain; ~**blad**, thumb piece; ~**doel**, try (rugby); ~**doenery**, to-do, fuss; ~**dop**, thrust-cap; ~**draai**, diving turn; ~**effek**, punching effect; ~**fout**, printer's error; misprint; erratum; ~**gang**, crush (for cattle); ~**gelaagdheid**, schistose structure; ~**golf**, surge (metereology); ~**groep**, pressure group; ~**hoek**, depression angle; ~**ink**, printer's ink; ~**kajuit**, pressurized cabin; ~**kastrol**, pressure cooker; ~**kend, (-e)**, oppressive (heat); heavy, burdensome, grievous, depressing; onerous (taxes); sultry; carking; ~**ker, (-s)**, printer; plunger; pusher; presser.
druk'kers: ~**baas**, master printer; ~**duiwel**, printer's devil; ~**merk**, printer's (imprint) mark; ~**naam**, publisher's imprint; ~**piekniek**, wayzgoose; ~**proef**, slip copy, galley proof, proof-sheet, printer's proof; ~**uitstappie**, wayzgooze.
druk'kertjie, (-s), press-stud.
druk'kery[1], squeezing; pushing; process of printing; *die* ~ *v.d. boek is nou aan die gang*, the book is now being printed.
drukkery'[2], (-e), printing works, press.

druk: ~**kie, (-s)**, little squeeze; ~**king**, pressure, weight; incidence; ~**kingsmeter**, piezometer; ~**knop**, push button; press button; bell-push; ~**knopie**, press-stud; fastener; ~**koker**, pressure cooker; ~**koste**, printing expenses; ~**kraag**, thrust collar; ~**kraan**, push tap; ~**krag**, compression strain; ~**kuns**, printing typography; ~**laer**, thrust bearing; ~**lamp**, pressure lamp; ~**leiding**, pressure lead; ~**letter**, primer, type, print letter; ~**lug**, compressed air; ~**lugboor**, pneumatic drill; ~**meter**, pressure gauge; manometer; piezometer; ~**model**, dummy (of book); ~**moer**, gland nut; ~**olie**, pressure oil; ~**oliepyp**, pressure oil-pipe; ~**ontlaspyp**, pressure relief valve; ~**papier**, printing paper; ~**pers**, printing-machine, printing-press; ~**plaat**, printing-plate, stereotype; follower plate, block; ~**pomp**, pressure pump; ~**proef**, proof-sheet, printer's proof; ~**punt**, pressure point; ~**raam**, printing-frame; ~**reëling**, pressurization; ~**rib**, compression rib; ~**ring**, follower ring, pressure ring, junk ring; ~**silinder**, printing-cylinder; ~**skakelaar**, press switch; ~**skeur**, pressure burst; ~**skilfer**, pressure flake; ~**skrif**, print; typewritten matter; ~**skroef**, thrust-screw; ~**slot**, thumb lock; ~**smering**, forcefeed (pressure) lubrication; ~**spanning**, compressive strain; pressure, stress; ~**spieël**, type page, printing-surface; ~**sproeipomp**, pressure spray-pump; ~**spuit**, pressure hose; ~**spyker(tjie)**, drawing pin; ~**staaf**, compression member; ~**stelletjie**, printing-set; ~**stempel**, rubber stamp; die-stamp; ~**sterkte**, compression strength; ~**stof**, print, printed fabric; ~**stoof**, pressure stove; ~**stoom**, pressure steam; ~**stuifpomp**, pressure spray-pump; ~**stuk**, printout (computer); follower; gland (mech.); ~**sweising**, pressure welding; ~**tafel**, platen.
druk'te, stir, rush (of business); press(ure), buzz, bustle, fuss, to-do; racket, commotion; *'n* ~ *maak*, make a fuss.
druk: ~**telegraaf**, teletype machine, writing telegraph, recording telegraph, teleprinter; telex; ~**telegraafdiens**, ticker service; ~**telegraafsentrale**, teleprinter exchange; ~**telegram**, telex message; ~**temaker**, fussy (noisy) person; ~**toevoer**, pressure (force) feed; ~**vas, (-te)** pressurized; incompressible; ~**vastheid**, compressive strength; ~**veer**, pressure spring; ~**veld**, pressure field; ~**verband**, pressure bandage; ~**verdeling**, distribution of pressure; incidence (taxes); ~**verligting**, decompression; ~**vlak**, pressure face; ~**voetjie**, presser foot (of machine); ~**vorm**, (printing-) chase; former; ~**wapening**, compression reinforcement; ~**waterspuit**, water-blast; ~**waster**, thrust washer; ~**werk**, printing, printed matter, letterpress; book post; ~**wyser**, pressure indicator.
drum'pel (-s), threshold; doorsill, doorstep; sole piece; *iem. se* ~ *PLATLOOP*, frequent someone's house; haunt someone's doorstep; *die* ~ *TRAP*, be a constant caller; *vir iem. jou* ~ *WYS*, show someone the door; ~**trapper**, troublesome visitor, persistent caller.
drup, (s) drip, eaves; dribble; (w) (ge-), drip, drop, trickle; *dit* ~ *AL*, the rain is beginning to fall; ~**bak**, drip-tray; ~**besproeiing**, drip-irrigation; ~**bottel**, drop bottle; ~**buisie**, dropper; ~**dig, (-te)**, drip-proof; ~**fles**, drop bottle; ~**kelder** = **druipkelder**; ~**koffie**, drip-coffee; ~**lepel**, basting-spoon; ~**lys**, drip-mould, drip-stone; label (arch.); weather-drip.
drup'pel, (s) (-s), drop, dribble, globule (welding); bead (of perspiration); blob; *'n* ~ *in die EMMER*, a drop in the ocean; *die* ~ *wat die EMMER laat oorloop*, the straw that breaks the camel's back; *wie die laaste (onderste)* ~ *uit die KAN wil hê, kry die deksel op sy neus*, covet all, lose all; *tot die LAASTE* ~ *bloed*, to the last drop of blood; *'n SOET* ~ *in iem. se beker*, comfort in the hour of sorrow; *'n* ~ *WATER in die see*, a drop in the ocean; *soos twee* ~*s WATER na mekaar lyk*, be as like as two peas in a pod; (w) (ge-), drop, trickle; ~**aar, (-s)**, dropper; ~**fles**, drop bottle; ~**ing**, dripping; trickling; ~**prop**, drop-stopper; ~**sgewys(e)**, by drops, in

drupper 133 *duidelik*

drops; at a snail's pace; ~**ring,** drip-loop; ~**tjie, (-s),** drib(b)let, droplet.
drup'per, (-s), dropper.
drup: ~**plaat,** drip-tray; ~**rak,** dish drainer; ~**tregter,** dropping funnel.
dryf, (w) (ge-), see **drywe;** ~**anker,** floating anchor; drogue; kite; ~**as,** back axle-shaft; cardan shaft; driving shaft (axle); pinion shaft; ~**baken,** floating beacon; ~**band,** endless belt; driving band, driving belt; ~**beitel,** chasing chisel; ~**brug,** floating bridge; ~**dok,** floating dock; pontoon; ~**eenheid,** drive unit; ~**haard,** refining furnace, cupel furnace; ~**hek,** caisson; ~**hou,** drive (tennis, golf); *'n ver ~ hou,* a long drive; ~**hout,** flotsam, driftwood; ~**jag,** drive, battue; ~**katrol,** driving pulley; ~**ketting,** driving chain; ~**klou,** driving dog; ~**koppeling,** cardan joint; ~**kraan,** floating crane; ~**krag,** motive (moving) power, drive; propelling force, propellent; driving power (force), propulsion; impulse; impeller; mainspring; buoyancy, floating power; ~**lading,** propellent charge; ~**middel,** propellent; ~**myn,** floating mine; ~**net,** drift net; ~**netboot,** drifter; hang net; ~**olie,** motor fuel; petrol; ~**paraffien,** power paraffin; ~**pen,** driving pin; ~**plaat,** driving plate; ~**plank,** embossing board; ~**rat,** driving wheel; impeller; lantern wheel; pinion; swing wheel; ~**riem,** driving belt; leather belt; band; ~**rondsel,** driving pinion; ~**sand,** drift-sand, quicksand; ~**skoot,** drive; ~**stang,** connecting rod, main rod, propelling rod, beam, driving rod; ~**stok,** driver (golf); ~**stroom,** drift, ~**tap,** drive lug; ~**tapvoeg,** chase mortise joint; ~**tol,** whip-top; ~**tou,** driving rope; buoy; ~**veer,** motive, incentive, reason, mainspring; ~**vermoë,** buoyancy, floating power; floatage.
dryf'werk[1], raised work; chasing; embossed work.
dryf'werk[2], transmission; driving gear; gear(ing); mill-gearing; driving-shaft assembly.
dryf: ~**wiel,** driver, driving wheel, pinion; flywheel; ~**ys,** drift-ice, floe; ~**yster,** driving bolt; rail drift.
dry'we, (ge-), float, swim; raft, drift; impel, propel; drive (cattle); actuate, prompt (to an action); conduct, run (business); *HANDEL ~* (conduct) trade; *iem. in 'n HOEKIE ~,* drive someone into a corner; *die SPOT ~,* mock; *deur STOOM gedrywe,* steam-driven; *iem. tot die UITERSTE ~,* drive someone to extremes; *iets te VER ~,* go too far; *deur die VERLANGE gedrywe,* actuated by the longing; ~**nd, (-e),** floating, adrift, afloat, awash; propellent, propelling.
dry'wer, (-s), driver, wagon-driver; propeller; beater (game); hustler, zealot, fanatic; float (seaplane); embosser; driver (golf); ~**y,** driving; fanaticism, bigotry.
dry'wing, power (engineering); ~**svermoë,** power rating.
d'tjie, (-s), small d.
du, (s) (e), push, thrust; (w) **(ge-),** push, shove.
duaal', (duale), dual.
dua'lis[1], dual (Greek grammar).
duaïs'[2]**, (-te),** dualist; ~**me,** duallsm; ~**tïes, (-e),** dualistic.
dualiteit', duality.
dub'bel, (-e), double, dual; duplex; twice, double; geminate; *'n ~ e DRAAI,* hairpin bend; *~ so DUUR,* twice as expensive; *~ en DWARS,* over and over again; *~ en DWARS verdien,* more than deserved; *~ e KEN,* double chin; *~ e PLOOI,* quilling; *~ SIEN,* see double; *~ SPOOR loop,* be tipsy; ~**afdruk,** double printing; ~**bank,** double seat; ~**bed,** double bed; ~**beksleutel,** double-ended spanner; ~**besturing,** dual control; ~**binding,** double bond (link) (chem.); ~**bol,** biconvex, convexo-convex; ~**heid,** biconvexity; ~**borspak,** double-breasted suit; ~**brandpuntig, (-e),** bifocal; ~**brekend, (-e),** birefringent, double refracting; ~**byl,** twibill; ~**d = dubbel;** ~**dekker,** double-decker; ~**dekkerpad,** double-deck road; ~**deur,** double door; folding doors; ~**doel,** dual purpose; ~**doelras,** dual-purpose breed; ~**dooier,** egg with double yolk; ~**druk,** mackle; ~**ganger,** double, second self, fetch, wraith (of person); ~**gelidmotor,**

two-row engine; ~**geslagtelik,** bisexual; ~**geveer, (-de),** bipinnate; ~**greep,** double stop; ~**han'dig, (-e),** ambidextrous; ~**har'tig, (-e),** false, double-minded, hypocritical; ~**har'tigheid,** double-dealing, duplicity; ~**heid,** duality; ~**hol,** biconcave, concavo-concave; ~**holheid,** biconcavity; ~**huls,** double sleeve; ~**joe:** *in die ~ joe wees,* be uncertain, be in a quandary; ~**jukkig, (-e),** bi-jugate, bijugous; ~**kamer,** double room; ~**kantig, (-e),** reversible; ~**karbonaat,** bicarbonate; ~**kastrol,** double boiler; ~**kernig, (-e),** diploid; ~**kolom,** double column; ~**ketting,** duplex chain; ~**kleppig, (-e),** bivalvular; ~**konkaaf = dubbelhol;** ~**konveks = dubbelbol;** ~**koolsuur,** bicarbonate; ~**koppigheid,** bicephaly; ~**kramjuk,** double-staple yoke; ~**kruis,** double sharp (music); ~**kruishout,** mortise gauge; ~**kruising,** scissors crossing; ~**langbeentjie,** double treble (crochet stitch); ~**letter,** digraph; ~**lewerik,** lark *(Calendula magnirostris);* ~**longontsteking,** double pneumonia.
dub'belloop=, double-barrel(led); ~**haelgeweer,** double-barrelled shotgun.
dub'bel: ~**medium,** double medium, dual medium; ~**meter,** duplex gauge; ~**mol,** double flat (music); ~**noot,** breve; ~**ontsteking,** dual ignition, double ignition; ~**pad,** double road; ~**penkruishout,** mortise gauge; ~**penvoeg,** bridle-joint; ~**polig, (-e),** bipolar; ~**punt,** colon; ~**puntig, (-e),** bicuspid; ~**rat,** double-gear; ~**rym,** rich rhyme.
dubbelsin'nig, (-e), ambiguous, equivocal, double; oracular; ~**heid,** ambiguity, amphibology; quibble, prevarication, equivocalness, equivocation, equivoke; double entendre
dub'bel: ~**skakelaar,** two-way switch; ~**skroef,** twin-screw (boat); ~**slag,** double action; ~**slagbeentjie,** double treble (stitch); ~**slagsteek,** double-treble stitch; ~**slag'tig, (-e),** gynandrous; hermaphrodite; ~**slag'tigheid,** hermaphroditism; ~**soetvyl,** deadcut file; ~**spel,** doubles (tennis), ~**spelbaan,** double court; ~**speler,** understudy; doubles player; ~**spelling,** two spellings; ~**spoor,** double track (railway), double line; ~**spruit,** dual manifold; ~**ster,** binary (star); ~**stuurvliegtuig,** dual-control aeroplane; ~**stuurvlug,** dual flight; ~**sweep,** whip folded double; ~**tal,** double number; two (nominees); ~**ta'lig, (-e),** bilingual.
dub'beltjie, (-s), penny, pence; *'n ~ in die ARMBUS gooi,* also to have something to say; *dit was 'n ~ op sy KANT,* it hung in the balance; *elke ~ OMKEER,* turn every penny over twice; *loop voor die PAD vol ~s is,* be quick about it; *'n ~ ROL wonderlik,* the unexpected often happens; *'n ~ in die VIOOL hê,* have a finger in the pie.
dub'beltjiesroman, (ong.), penny horrible.
dub'bel: ~**ton'gig, (-e),** double-tongued; ~**verdieping,** double storey; ~**verdiepingpad,** double-deck road; ~**verdiepingwoonstel,** duplex flat; ~**voorploeg,** double-sheared plough; gang plough; ~**vorm,** doublet (word derivation); ~**werkend, (-e),** double-acting.
dubieus', (-e), doubtful, dubious, questionable.
du'bio, doubt; *in ~ wees,* be in doubt, waver.
dubloen', (-e), doubloon.
duel', (-le), duel; ~**leer', (ge-),** fight a duel; ~**lis', (-te),** duellist.
duen'na, (-s), duenna, chaperon.
duet', (-te), duet; ~**sanger,** double-part singer, duettist.
duf, (duwwe; duwwer, -ste), close, stuffy, fusty, musty.
duf'fel, duffel (duffle) (coarse woolen cloth); frieze; ~**s, (-e):** *'n ~ se baadjie,* a duffel coat.
duf'heid, closeness, stuffiness; fustiness, mustiness; mildew.
dug, (ge-), dread, fear, apprehend; *niks te ~ te hê nie,* have nothing to fear; ~**tig, (-e),** fearful; strong, hard; thorough; *'n ~ tige pak SLAE,* a sound thrashing; *~ tig WEERSTAND bied,* put up (offer) stout resistance.
dui, (ge-), point (to), suggest; *ten kwade (euwel) ~,* take amiss, take (it) in bad part.
dui'delik, (b) (-e), clear, distinct, plain, obvious, overt, patent, perceptible, perspicuous, evident, ex-

duiding / **duiwel**

plicit, express; legible (writing); marked, pronounced; graphic(al); *so ~ as DAGLIG, so ~ as TWEE maal twee vier is,* as plain as a pikestaff; (bw) broadly; plainly; ~ **heid,** clearness, ostensibility, obviousness, plainness, conspicuousness, clarity, perspicuity, distinctness, explicitness; ~**heidshalwe,** for the sake of clearness.
dui'ding, interpretation.
dui'e¹, (s) *mv. van* **duig.**
dui'e², (w) (ge-), = **dui.**
duif, (duiwe), pigeon, dove; culver; *onder iem. anders se duiwe SKIET,* poach on another's preserves; *gebraaide duiwe VLIEG niemand in die mond nie,* success does not come the easy way; ~ **agtig,** (-e), columbine; ~ **eier,** pigeon's egg; ~ **ertjie,** pigeon pea, Congo pea *(Cajanus indicus)*, njugo-bean.
dui'fie, (-s), columbine; small pigeon; ~ *sonder gal,* sweet innocent.
duif'kruid, scabious.
duig, (duie), stave; *in duie val,* fall through, miscarry (plan); ~ **saag,** barrel-saw; ~ **vormig,** (-e), pulvinate(d)
duik, (s) (-e), dent; indent; depression (of ground); dive; (w) (ge-), dive, duck, plunge, douse, dip; pitch (boat); nose-dive (aero.); dent; tackle low; ~ **aangee,** dive pass; ~ **bal,** yorker; ~ **bombardement,** ~ **bombardering,** dive-bombing; ~ **bomwerper,** dive-bomber.
duik'boot, submarine, U-boat; ~ **basis,** submarine base; ~ **jaer,** submarine destroyer, anti-submarine vessel; ~ **moederskip,** submarine tender; ~ **ontdekker,** asdic; ~ **oorlog,** submarine warfare; ~ **opspoorder,** asdic.
duik: ~ **bril,** diving-goggles; ~ **doodvat,** dive tackle (rugby); ~ **draai,** diving turn; ~ **eend,** snew *(Anatidae)*.
dui'kel, (ge-), tumble forward, turn somersault; ~ **aar,** (-s), diver; tumbler (pigeon); ~ **ing,** tumble, somersault; *'n ~ ing maak,* turn a somersault.
dui'kend, (-e), diving; ~ *e sinkline,* pitching syncline.
duiker, (-s), diver, plunger; duiker (antelope); culvert; dabchick, dipper, didapper, (Cape) cormorant; yorker (cricket); ~ **gans,** merganser; goosander; ~ **klok,** diving-bell; ~ **pak,** diving-dress; ~ **s,** confounded; ~ **siekte,** caisson disease; ~ **spak,** armour (diver); ~ **tjie,** (-s), small duiker; dabchick; cat-tail; *Cartesiaanse* ~ *tjie,* Cartesian diver, bottle imp; ~ **wortel,** plant of the genus *Grielum;* ~ **y,** diving.
duik: ~ **hamer,** raising-hammer; ~ **helling,** dip slope; ~ **helm,** diving-helmet; ~ **hoender,** guillemot; ~ **ing,** (-s), pitch (aeroplane); ~ **klok,** diving-bell; ~ **klopper,** panel-beater; ~ **long,** aqualung; ~ **pak,** diving-dress; ~ **pitmielie,** dent maize; ~ **plank,** diving-board; ~ **rigting,** line of dip; ~ **roer,** immersion rubber; ~ **skyf,** vanishing target; ~ **sloot,** culvert; ~ **sluis,** culvert, flood-gate; ~ **stoel,** diving-chair; ~ **tenk,** immersion tank; ~ **toestel,** diving apparatus; ~ **toets,** diving test; ~ **uitklopper,** panel-beater; ~ **vlug,** nose-dive (aero.); ~ **weg,** subway, underpass (Amer.).
duim, (-e), thumb; inch; cam (mining); *iem. om sy ~ DRAAI,* twist someone round one's finger; *op sy ~ FLUIT vir iets,* whistle for something; *met die ~ GOOI,* hitchhike; *iem. onder die ~ HE,* have someone under one's thumb; *goed onder die ~ HOU,* keep under strict control; *met die ~ in die PAD val,* cadge a lift; hitch-hike; *op sy ~ SIT,* have to sit on the floor; *met sy ~ e staan en SPEEL,* twiddle one's thumbs; *iem. die ~ op die KEEL hou,* have a person under one's thumb; *iets uit die ~ SUIG,* suck something from one's thumb; *vir iem. ~ VASHOU,* keep your fingers crossed for someone; ~**afdruk,** thumb-print; ~ **bal,** ball of thumb, thenar; ~ **breed,** (breadth of) an inch; *geen* ~ *breed padgee nie,* not to yield an ich; ~ **breedte,** (width of) inch; ~ **dik,** an inch deep; ~ **drukker,** drawing-pin; ~ **eling,** ~ **elot,** thumb (nursery term); ~ **gooi,** (-ge-), thumb a lift; ~ **gooier,** hitchhiker; ~ **greep,** thumb index; ~ **handskoen,** mitten; ~ **klink,** ~ **knip,** latch; ~ **kole,** nuts; ~ **kruid,** money, tip, palm-oil; *iem. ~ kruid gee,* oil a person's palm; ~ **maat,** inch-tape; ~ **pie,** (-s), little (small) thumb; *iets op sy ~ pie*

KEN, have a thing at one's fingertips; *KLEIN D ~ pie,* Tom Thumb; ~ **ring,** cam ring; ~ **ry,** (-ge-), hitchhike; ~ **ryer,** hitchhiker; ~ **ryery,** hitch hiking; ~ **skroef,** thumb-screw; *iem. die ~ skroef aansit,* put on the screw; ~ **spil,** camshaft; ~ **spyker,** nail of one inch; ~ **spykertjie,** drawing-pin; push-pin; ~ **s'pyp,** inch pipe; ~ **stok,** inch measure, foot-rule; carpenter's measure; ~ **suiery,** thumb-sucking; lies, untruthful assertions.
duin, (-e), sand-hill (sand-)dune, down; ~ **agtig,** (-e), resembling a dune; ~ **ebesie,** beach buggy; ~ **eboef,** uneducated person; ~ **eveld,** sandy (hilly) country; dunes; ~ **gras,** beach grass, lyme-grass; ~ **grond,** dune ground; ~ **kerk,** (ge-), retreat, flee; **D ~ kerken,** Dunkirk; ~ **meer,** dune lake; ~ **mol,** sand-mole, dune-mole; ~ **pou,** S.A. bustard; ~ **roos,** dune rose, Scotch rose; ~ **sand,** sand (of the dunes); ~ **skilpad,** angulated tortoise; ~ **spreeu,** dune starling; ~ **tjie** (-s), small dune.
dui'sel, (ge-), grow giddy (dizzy); reel; ~ **ig,** (-e), giddy, queer, dizzy, groggy; ~ *ig word,* become dizzy; ~ **igheid,** giddiness, vertigo, dizziness, megrims; ~ **ing,** giddiness, dizziness; vertigo; ~ **ingwek'kend,** (-e), dizzy, giddy, vertiginous.
dui'send, (-e), thousand; chiliad; *'n MAN (uit) ~ ,* a very fine man, one in a thousand; *'n MES ~ ,* the best of knives; *OOR die ~ ,* more than a thousand; ~ **blad,** milfoil; ~ **erlei,** of a thousand kinds; ~ **hoofdig,** (-e), thousand-headed; ~ **jarig,** (-e), millennial, millenarian, millenary; *die ~ jarige ryk,* the millennium; ~ **knoop,** knotweed, polygonum; ~ **koppig,** (-e), = **duisendhoofdig;** ~ **kunstenaar,** magician, wizard; ~ **miljoen,** billion; ~ **poot,** millipede, multiped, pillworm; myriapod; ~ **skoon,** sweet william; ~ **ste,** (-s), thousandth; ~ **tal,** a thousand; ~ **voud,** multiple of thousand; ~ **voudig,** (-e), thousandfold; ~ **werf,** thousand times.
duis'koring, (vero.) wheat.
duis'ter, (s), dark(ness); *in die ~ tas,* grope (about) in the dark; (b) dark, obscure, blear, murky, cloudy, dusk(y); cryptic (remark), ambiguous, recondite, abstruse; mystic, oracular; *die saak bly ~ ,* the matter remains inexplicable; ~ **heid,** darkness, opacity, duskiness; mystery; obscurity, abstruseness; dinginess, dimness, gloom(iness); ~ **ling,** obscurantist.
duis'ternis, dark(ness), murk; obscurity; hell; crowd, large number; *BUITENSTE ~ ,* outer darkness; *EGIPTIESE ~ ,* Egypt's night; *'n ~ van MENSE,* very many people, some crowd, people galore.
duit, (-e), penny, cent; farthing; (mv) money; rap, blunt (slang); *jou ~ e MORS,* squander; spend, money like water; *jou ~ e RONDGOOI,* play ducks and drakes with one's money; *'n ~ in die ARMBEURS gooi,* contribute your share (to the discussion), shove in one's oar; *geen ~ besit nie,* be moneyless; *geen BLOU ~ werd nie,* not worth a bean (brass button).
Duits, (-e), German; ~ *e MASELS,* German measels; ~ *e MERINO,* German merino; ~ *e SIS,* printed calico.
Duit'ser, (-s), German.
Duits'gesind, (-e), pro-German.
Duits'land, Germany.
dui'we: ~ **boon,** pigeon pea; ~ **-eier,** pigeon's egg; ~ **-ertjie** = **duifertjie;** ~ **handelaar,** pigeon fancier; ~ **hok,** pigeonry, pigeon house, dovecot(e); pigeon loft; ~ **jag,** pigeon shooting.
dui'wel¹, (s) (-s), devil, Satan; enemy; the Evil One; Old Nick; deuce, dickens; *die ~ met BEËLSEBUB uitdryf,* cast out the devil by Beelsebub; *v.d. ~ BESETE wees,* be possessed by the devil; *BID jou die ~ aan,* bless my soul! *by die ~ gaan BIEG,* make the devil one's father confessor; *die ~ se BRIEWE lees,* to be reading the Devil's book; *DANK jou die ~ !* well, I like that! no wonder! *te dom om vir die ~ te DANS,* very stupid; *DIK die ~ in,* in a huff; *GEE die ~ wat hom toekom,* give the devil his due; *die ~ het in hom GEVAAR,* he seems possessed of the devil; *die ~ HAAL jou!* the devil take you! *soos die ~ dit wou HÊ,* as luck would have it; *die ~ IN wees,* be in a temper; *hy IS 'n ~ ,* he is a brute; he is

the very deuce of a fellow; *die ~ stap weer met sy KRULSTERT hier rond*, there's the very devil to pay; *v.d. – geen KWAAD weet nie*, pretend to be blissfully ignorant; *op sy ~ KRY*, get a sound thrashing; *LOOP of die ~ agter hom is*, run like the wind; *die ~ is LOS*, the fat is in the fire; *hoe MEER die ~ het, hoe meer wil hy hê*, the more one has, the more one wants; *die ~ en sy MOER*, all the world and his wife; *die ~ sit agter sy nek*, he is in a huff; *geen ~ OMGEE nie*, not to care a rap; *PRAAT van die ~ (dan trap jy op sy stert)*, talk of angels and you hear (the flutter of) their wings; *die ~ se PRENTEBOEK*, playing cards; *die ~ sal jou RY!* you are in for it; *die ~ RY hom bloots*, he is as black as thunder; *die ~ by SATAN verkla*, complain to satan about the devil; *die ~ preek vir SATAN*, the devil rebukes sin; *oor iets wees soos 'n ~ oor 'n SIEL*, desire something madly; *wie met die ~ uit een SKOTTEL eet, moet 'n lang lepel hê*, he should have a long spoon who sups with the devil; *die ~ te SLIM wees*, be wide-awake; *op sy ~ SPEEL*, give someone a drubbing; *vir geen ~ STUIT nie*, stop at nothing; *VLIEG na die ~*, go to the devil; *die ~ sit sy VOETE reg*, the devil looks after his own; *die ~ staan klaar met sy VURK*, the devil is waiting to take you; *so bang soos die ~ vir 'n SLYPSTEEN*, fear something like the very devil; *die ~ word altyd SWARTER gesmeer as wat hy is*, the devil is not so black as he is painted; *stille WATERS diepe grond onder draai die ~ rond*, still waters run deep; *'n ~ om te WERK*, a glutton for work; *die ~ alleen WEET, the devil only knows, WIE die ~!* who the dickens? *daar kan die ~ niks uit WYS word nie*, one cannot make head or tail of it.

dui'wel², (w) (ge-), fall (down), tumble; throw.

dui'wel: ~ **aanbidding**, diabolism; ~ **agtig** (-e), devilish, fiendish, diabolical; ~ **ary'**, deviltry, diablerie; ~ **banner**, exorcist; ~ **banning**, exorcism; ~ **besweerder**, exorcist; ~ **beswering**, exorcism; ~ **dienaar**, demonist; ~ **in'**, (-ne), she-devil; ~ **-in-diebos**, love-in-a-mist; ~ **-in-'n-dosie**, jack-in-the-box; ~ **jaer**, troublesome (quarrelsome) person; ~ **jagter**, devil-dodger; ~ **kunde**, diablerie; ~ **leer**, demonology.

dui'wels, (-e), devilish, diabolic(al), demoniac(al), hell-born; Mephistophelean; fiendish; ~ *BITTER*, extremely bitter; ~ *GOED weet*, know very well; ~ **advokaat**, devil's advocate; ~ **bek**, monkeywrench; ~ **brood**, toadstool; ~ **by**, social wasp (*Polistes marginalis*); ~ **dood**, extremely well; *'n man wat hom ~ dood werk*, an excellent worker; ~ **doring**, grapple-thorn; ~ **drek**, asafoetida; ~ **kerwel**, black-jack, sweetheart (*Bidens pilosa*); ~ **kind**, child of the devil, imp of hell; ~ **klou**, devil's grip, wall-knot; ~ **kos**, mushroom; ~ **kring(loop)**, vicious circle; ~ **kunste**, the black art, sorcery, witchcraft; ~ **kunstenaar**, magician, sorcerer; ~ **kunstenary**, magic, sorcery, witchcraft; ~ **naaigaring**, dodder (*Cuscuta*).

dui'wel: ~ **snuif**, puff-ball, ~ **sterk**, (s) barbed-wire cloth, corduroy, whipcord, ceiling calico; fearnought (cloth), drill; (b) very strong, lasting; ~ **stoejaer**, factotum, jack-of-all-work; ~ **swerk**, devil's work, diabolism; ~ **tjie**, (-s), little devil; imp; *see* **dubbeltjie** (plant); ~ **verering**, demonolatry, satanism; ~ **vis**, devil-fish (fam. *Mobulidae*).

dui'we: ~ **melk**, pigeon's milk; ~ **pastei**, pigeon-pie, ~ **pos**, pigeon post, pigeon service; ~ **sport**, pigeon flying; ~ **tand**: *so skaars soos ~ tande*, not to be had for love or money; ~ **vlug**, flight of pigeons; ~ **wedvlug**, pigeon race.

dukaat', (dukate), ducat.

dukaton', (-s), ducatoon.

duktiel', (-e), ductile.

duktiliteit', ductility.

duld, (ge-), bear, tolerate, permit, endure, put up with; digest; *dit ~ geen uitstel nie*, this brooks no delay; ~ **baar**, (..bare), bearable, tolerable; ~ **eloos**, (..lose), unbearable.

dul'sies, dulcis (old country, folk remedy).

dul'simer, (-s), dulcimer.

dum-dum'koeël, dum-dum bullet.

dump, (ge-), dump; ~ **ing**, dumping (trade); ~ **ingreg**, dumping duty.

dun, thin, rarefied (air); rare, sparse (vegetation); attenuated, slender (waist); washy, watery (soup); flimsy; ~ *GESAAI wees*, be very scarce; *ek VOEL net ~*, I am hungry; ~ **bevolk**, (-te), thinly (sparsely) populated; ~ **bier**, washy beer, swipes; ~ **derm**, ileum, small intestine; ~ **doek**, bunting; ~ **drukpapier**, India paper; ~ **drukuitgawe**, omnibus edition.

dungree', dungaree

dun: ~ **heid**, thinness; flimsiness; slenderness, tenuity; sparseness; rarity (air); ~ **hout**, matchboard; ~ **huidig**, (-e), thin-skinned.

duniet', dunite.

dunk, opinion, idea; *'n hoë ~ hê van*, think much of, have a high opinion of.

dun: ~ **kop**, horse-sickness; ~ **lies**, thin flank; ~ **lippig**, (-e), thin-lipped; ~ **loop**, (-ge-), taper; ~ **nerig**, (-e), thinnish; rather watery.

dun'netjies, thinly; indifferent; *dit GAAN maar ~*, things are poorly; *die WERK is maar ~*, the work is rather poorly (done).

dun: ~ **rib**, flat rib (beef); ~ **siekte**, senecio poisoning (in horses); ~ **te**, thinness; ~ **vel'lig**, (-e), thin-skinned; ~ **vleis**, thin flank (beef).

du'o, (-'s), duo, duet.

duodenaal', (..nale), duodenal; *duodenale sweer*, duodenal ulcer.

duode'num, duodenum.

duode'simo, (-'s) duodecimo

du'pe, (-s), dupe, victim; *die ~ word van iets*, become the dupe of.

dupeer', (ge-), dupe, deceive; disappoint.

du'pleks, duplex; ~ **woonstel**, duplex flat.

dupliek', rejoinder, rebuttal.

duplikaat', (..kate), duplicate.

duplika'sie, (-s), duplication.

duplika'tor, (-s), duplicator.

dupliseer', (ge-), duplicate; rejoin (legal).

du'plo, double; *in ~ opstel*, draw up in duplicate.

dupteek', rejoinder; ~ **lewer**, rejoin.

dur, sharp (music).

dura'bel, (-e), durable, lasting; expensive.

duralumi'nium, duralumin.

dura'men, duramen, heartwood.

dura'sie, (geselst.) (-s), duration.

duratief', (..tiewe), intensive (verb).

Durbaniet', (-e), inhabitant of Durban.

dur'bar, durbar.

du'rend, (-e), lasting; *'n ~ e vrede*, a lasting peace.

durf, (s) pluck, daring, nerve, guts, grit, dash, gameness; enterprise; (w) (ge-), dare, venture; risk; ~ **al** (-le), daredevil; ~ **krag**, daring.

duriet', durite.

du'rumkoringsaad, durum wheat seed.

dur'we, *see* **durf** (w).

dus, thus, so, therefore, ergo, accordingly; *ek is nie genooi nie*, ~ *GAAN ek nie*, I have not been invited, therefore I am not going; ~ *GESÊ en gedoen*, no sooner said than done; ~ **danig**, (-e), such; in such a way; ~ **doende**, so doing; ~ **kant** = **deuskant**.

dus'ketyd: (geselst.), *om ~*, (about) this time.

dus'ver: *tot ~*, so far up to the present, up to now.

dut, (s) nap, snooze; (w) (ge-), nap, doze, snooze; ~ **jie**, (-s), nap, doze, snooze; forty winks, cat-nap; *'n ~ jie doen*, take a nap.

duur¹, (s) duration; life (of mine); currency (notes); permanence, permanency; length; *van LANGE ~*, of long duration; *OP die (lange) ~*, in the long run; *VIR die ~ van*, for the duration of; (w) (ge-), last, continue, extend; *mag die vrede lank ~*, may peace last a long time.

duur², (b, bw) (dure); -der, -ste), dear, costly, expensive, high; *baie ~ BETAAL*, pay through the nose; *'n dure EED sweer*, vow a solemn oath; *HOE ~ is dit?* how much is this! *ons dure PLIG*, our bounden duty; *dit sal jou ~ te STAAN kom*, it will cost you dearly; you will rue it; *dis TE ~ vir my*, I can't afford it; *sy lewe ~ VERKOOP*, sell one's life dearly.

duur'golf, perm(anent wave).
duur'heid, expensiveness.
duur'kamp, permanent training camp.
duur'koop, expensive.
duur'rekord, endurance record
duur'saam, (..same), durable; lasting, abiding, permanent, perdurable; consistent, enduring; hard-wearing, wearing well (material); ~ *same gebrek,* permanent defect; ~**heid,** durableness, durability, perdurability, permanence, permanency, life (machine); fixity.
duur'te, dearness, expensiveness; duration; lifetime, currency (of contract); *rus nòg* ~ *ken,* be restless, unsettled; ~**toeslag,** cost-of-living allowance.
duur: ~ **toets,** endurance test; ~ **tyd,** duration, lifetime; ~ **vermoë,** endurance.
duur: ~ **verwerf,** (-de), ~ **verworwe,** dearly-bought.
duur'vlug, endurance flight; duration flight.
duus'man = **diesman.**
duus'volk = **diesvolk.**
duvet', (-s), duvet.
du'wel, (-s), devil; bee-moth.
duw'wel(d) = **dubbel(d).**
duw'weltjie, (-s), devil's thorn *(Emex australis, Tribulus terrestris)*
dux, (duces), dux; ~**student,** dux scholar; dux student.
dwaal, (ge-), err; wander, roam; *dit is menslik om te* ~, to err is human; ~ **begrip,** false notion; fallacy; erroneous idea (notion); misconception; idolum; ~**gees,** wandering spirit; ~ **leer,** false (erroneous) doctrine, heresy; ~ **lig,** will-o'-the-wisp, fen-fire, friar's lantern, march fire; jack-o'-lantern, firedrake, ignis fatuus; ~**spoor,** false (wrong) track; *op 'n* ~ *spoor bring,* lead astray; put off the scent; ~**ster,** planet; comet; ~**weg,** false (wrong) way.
dwaas, (s) **(dwase),** fool, silly fellow; ass; *een* ~ *kan meer vrae vra as sewe wyse kan beantwoord,* a fool may ask more questions than a wise man can answer in seven years; (b) **(dwase; dwaser, -ste),** foolish, silly, absurd, preposterous, boobyish, daft; doltish; (bw) foolishly, stupidly, absurdly; ~**heid,** folly, absurdity, hebetude; stupidity; fatuity, daftness, preposterousness; ~ **lik,** foolishly.
dwa'lend, (-e), errant, erratic, planetary, wandering.
dwa'lerolifant, rogue-elephant.
dwa'ling, (-e, -s), error, mistake; miscarriage (of justice); hallucination; *iem. uit die* ~ *HELP,* put someone right; *die LAASTE* ~ *is erger as die EERSTE,* the last error is worse than the first; *REGTERLIKE (geregtelike)* ~, miscarriage of justice; *in 'n* ~ *VERKEER,* be on the wrong track.
dwang, compulsion, coercion, force, constraint, durance, enforcement; coaction; *onder* ~ *handel,* act under duress; ~ **arbeid,** compulsory labour; hard labour; penal servitude; ~ **arbeider,** convict, lag; ~ **bevel,** warrant, writ; fieri facias; ~ **buis,** strait jacket; ~ **gedagte,** obsession; ~ **handskoen,** muffle; ~ **koopstelsel,** truck system; ~ **maatreël,** ~ **middel,** coercive measure; ~ **nael,** hangnail; ~ **neurose,** compulsive neurosis; ~ **voeding,** force-feeding; ~ **voorstelling,** obsession, fixed idea; ~ **wet,** coercive law; ~ **waansin,** compulsive insanity.
dwar'rel, (s) eddy; whirligig, reel; (w) (ge-), whirl, reel; eddy; flutter; ~ **cumulus,** dynamic cumulus; ~ **gebied,** wake; ~ **ing,** whirling, eddying; ~ **wind,** whirlwind, tornado, cyclone; eddy.
dwars, (-er, -ste), across, transverse, diagonal, abeam, athwart, aslant; contrary, peevish, pig-headed, cross-grained, perverse; *dit SIT my* ~, it goes against the grain with me; ~ *VENT,* a cross-grained fellow; ~ **afskuiwing,** shearing (geol.); ~ **anker,** cross-stay; ~ **as,** lateral (transverse) axis; cross-shaft; ~ **baanrok,** tiered skirt; ~ **balk,** stringer; purling; joist; collar-beam; crossbeam, girder-beam; ledger; transom; (bridge) girder; rail, cross-member (chassis); bar, fess(e) (herald.). ~ **balk,** belt; transverse seat (motor); cross bench (in parliament); ~ **banker,** cross-bencher; ~ **bestuuring,** lateral control; ~ **beweging,** traverse; ~ **boog,** transverse arch; ~ **boom,** (s) slip-rail; (w) **(ge-),** thwart, abstruct, counterwork, cross, put one's foot down; frustrate; block; ~ **bout,** collar key; cross-bolt.
dwars'deur, right across, right through, all along the line; *iem.* ~ *kyk,* stare at a person; look daggers at someone; ~ **snee,** cross-section.
dwars'draad, cross-fibre, woof; shot (in grain bags); cross-grain; ~ **s,** (-e), cross-grained, against the grain.
dwars'dradig, (-e), cross-grained.
dwars'draer, flood-beam (of bridge); cross bearer (motor).
dwars'drywer, obstructor, thwarter; ~ **y,** obstruction, contrariness.
dwars: ~ **duik,** cross dip, cross drain (road); ~ **fluit,** German flute; flute; fife; ~ **galery,** traverse; ~ **gang,** cross-cut; transverse dyke, cross passage (way); ~ **gesny,** (-de), cross-cut; ~ **geut,** drain, scupper (in road); ~ **gly,** (-ge-), skid; ~ **haakhou,** cross-cut (tennis); ~ **heid,** peevishness, irritability; perverseness, contrariness; ~ **helling,** latitudinal incline; bank (aero.); ~ **hellingmeter,** cross-level; ~ **hellingshoek,** bank angle; ~ **hofie,** cross-heading; ~ **hou,** crosspass (hockey); by-blow; ~ **hout,** cross-arm (bar), futchel(l); capping; ~ **kop,** self-willed person; hothead, opinionist; ~ **kophamer,** crosspeen hammer; ~ **koppig,** (-e), cantankerous; perverse, cussed, contrary; ~ **kyker,** grumbler, grouser; ~ **lat,** transom; cross-bar; ~ **lêer,** sleeper (under the rails); cross-tie (architecture); ~ **lig,** cross-light; ~ **ligging,** cross-birth; ~ **loper,** crab (mech.); ~ **lyn,** cross-line; transversal (mathematics); ~ **mars,** cross-tie (nautical); ~ **naat,** circumferential (cross-) seam; ~ **oor,** right across, right over; ~ **paal,** cross-bar; ~ **pad,** cross-way; ~ **pen,** crosskey; toggle; ~ **penhamer,** crosspane hammer; ~ **pyp,** cross-tube; ~ **reling,** cross-rail; ~ **rif,** cross-reef; ~ **saag,** cross-cut saw; ~ **saal,** (-s), side-saddle; ~ **skeeps,** abeam; athwartships; ~ **skip,** transept; ~ **skoot,** cross-shot; ~ **skop,** tally-ho (kick), cross-kick; ~ **sloot,** cross-ditch; ~ **sne(d)e,** cross-section; ~ **sny,** cross-cut; ~ **snysaag,** cross-cut saw; ~ **spy,** cotter(pin); ~ **spleet,** joint; ~ **stabiliteit,** lateral stability; ~ **stang,** cross-bar (bicycle); ~ **steek,** ladder stitch; ~ **steun,** cross-tie; ~ **stok,** perch; ~ **straat,** cross-street; ~ **streep,** bar, cross-line; ~ **stroom,** cross-current; ~ **stuk,** cross-piece; cross-bar; yoke (of dress); puncheon prop; toggle; ~ **stukkie,** riffle (in sluice box); ~ **styl,** bier.
dwars'te, *in die* ~, crosswise, across, athwart.
dwars'tonnel, offset tunnel.
dwars'trek, (-ge-), thwart, squabble, quarrel; cross; ~ **ker,** squabber, obstructionist, maverick, thwarter; ~ **kerig,** (-e), cross-grained, thwarting, obstructive, contrary; maverick; ~ **kerigheid,** contrariness, perverseness; ~ **kery,** contrariness, perverseness.
dwars: ~ **trilling,** transverse vibration; ~ **veer,** transverse spring; ~ **vleuel,** cross-aisle; ~ **voeding,** cross-feed; ~ **vuur,** enfilade (fort); ~ **wal,** traverse (fort); mole; diversion; ~ **waterpas,** cross-level.
dwars'weg, (s) cross-road; (bw) abruptly; *iem.* ~ *antwoord,* give someone a surly answer; be abrupt with someone.
dwars'wind, crosswind.
dweep, (ge-), be infatuated, be fanatical; be an enthusiast, rave about, fanaticise, dote, enthuse; gush; ~ *met voetbal,* rave about football; ~ **agtig,** (-e), fanatic(al); (over-)enthusiastic; ~ **siek,** (-e), fanatic(al), bigoted; ~ **ster,** (-s), (female) fanatic; ~ **sug,** fanaticism, zealotry; ~ **sug'tig,** (-e), enthusiastic, fanatic.
dweil, (s) (-e), mop, floor-swab, deck-swab; (w) **(ge-),** mop, swab (deck); wipe; ~ **kop,** mop head; ~ **stok,** mop-stick.
dwelm: ~ **middel,** drug; ~ **pistool,** dart-pistol; ~ **slaaf,** ~ **verslaafde,** drug addict; ~ **smous,** drug pedlar (pusher).
dwelms, drugs.
dwe'pend, (-e), fanatical.
dwe'per, (-s), fanatic, bigot, faddist, enthusiast, gusher, zealot, devotee, fan; energumen, ideologist; ~ **ig,** (-e), bigoted; ~ **y,** bigotry, raving, fanaticism, ideology, gush.

dwerg, (-e), dwarf, pygmy, midget, manikin; minim; elf; troll; ~**agtig**, (-e), dwarfish, elfin, pygmean; gnomish; ~**agtigheid**, dwarfishness; ~**beuk**, dwarf beech; ~**boom**, dwarf tree; ~**duikboot**, midget submarine; ~**gans**, dwarf goose (*Nettapus auritus*); ~**gewig**, midget-weight; ~**ie**, (-s), gnome; ~**muis**, dwarf mouse; **D**~**neger**, Negrillo; ~**palm**, palmetto; ~**plant**, dwarf plant; ~**tennis**, tennisette; ~**volk**, pygmean race; dwarfs.

dwing, (ge-), (en)force, compel, press, constrain, coerce, make, necessitate; drive; coact; be on the point of; nag; *iem.* ~ *om te BETAAL*, dun a person, force a person to pay; *iem.* ~ *om te GAAN*, compel someone to go; *IEM.* ~, force someone's hand; *die KIND* ~ *om dit te hê*, the child is nagging about it; *hom nie LAAT* ~ *nie*, refuse to be driven; *hy* ~ *altyd om SIEK te word*, he is always on the point of getting ill.

dwin'geland, (-e), tyrant, despot; ~**y'**, tyranny, despotism.

dwing: ~**end**, (-e), compelling, compulsive; coercive; ~**er**, coercer; ~**erig**, (-e), insistent, nagging, bothersome; ~**ery**, nagging, compulsion.

dy¹, (s) (-e), thigh; silverside (meat); ham.

dy², (w) (ge-), thrive, prosper; swell, expand; *die PLANT* ~ *hier nie*, the plant does not thrive here; *RYS* ~ *altyd*, rice always swells.

dy'been, femur, thigh-bone; ~**breuk**, femoral hernia; ~**draaier**, rochanter.

dyk, (-e), dike, embankment, mole, bank; ~**breuk**, rupture of the dike; dike-burst; ~**werker**, dikemaker; ~**wese**, diking system.

dyn, thine; *myn en* ~, mine and thine.

dyn's(er)ig, (-e), misty, cloudy, hazy; ~**heid**, cloudiness, mistiness, atmospheric haze.

dy: ~**slagaar**, femoral artery; ~**spier**, thigh muscle; ~**stuk**, cuisse, fillet; silverside (of beef).

E

e, (-'s), e.
eau-de-colog'ne, eau-de-Cologne.
eb, (s) ebb; ~ *en vloed*, ebb-tide and flood-tide, ebb and flow; (w) (**geëb**), ebb, flow (away).
eb'behoom, ebony tree.
eb'behout, ebony (wood), black ivory.
Ebenhaë'ser, Ebenezer.
eb'gety, ebb-tide.
eboniet', vulcanite, ebonite.
ebullioskoop', (..skope), ebullioscope.
echappement', (-e), escapement.
echec', (-s), defeat, setback, failure, reverse, rebuff, check; *'n* ~ *ly*, meet with a rebuff.
echelon', (-s), echelon; *in* ~, in echelon.
eclat', éclat; *baie* ~ *maak*, cause a great stir.
ecru', ecru.
E'cuador, Ecuador; ~**iaan'**, (s) (..riane), Ecuadorian; (b) ~**iaans'**, (-e), Ecuadorian.
E'dam, Edam; ~*se kaas*, Edam cheese; ~**merkaas**, Edam cheese.
Ed'da, (-s), Edda.
edeem', (edeme), oedema.
e'del, (-, -e), noble, high-minded, honourable, generous; precious (stones); handsome; *DIE E*~*e*, the Honourable; *SY E*~*e*, His Honour; ~**aar'dig**, (-e), noble-hearted; ~**ag'baar**, (..bare), honourable, worshipful (mayor); ~**ag'bare**, my lord (judge); ~**denkend**, (-e), noble-minded; high-souled; ~**e**, (-s), nobleman; (mv) the nobility; ~**gas**, rare gas; ~**gebore**, noble, high-born; ~**gesind**, (-e), nobleminded; ~**gesteente**, precious stone, gem; ~**gestreng**, (-e), honourable; ~**heid**, nobleness, nobility; ~**hert**, red deer; ~**knaap**, page; ~**man**, (-ne, ..liede, ..lui), nobleman, peer; *dis by hulle* ~ *man of bedelman*, with them it is either a feast or a fast; ~**marter**, pine-marten; ~**metaal**, noble (precious) metal; bullion.
edelmoe'dig, (-e), generous, magnanimous, large-minded; ~**heid**, generosity, magnanimity, handsomeness.
e'del: ~**sement**, supercement, high-grade cement; ~**smeedkuns**, art-metalwork; ~**smid**, art-metalworker; ~**steen**, gem, precious stone; ~**steenagtig**, (-e), gem-like; ~**valk**, lanner falcon (*Falco biarmicus*); ~**vrou**, noble lady, noblewoman, gentlewoman.
e'delweiss, edelweiss (Alpine flower), lion's foot.
e'delwyn, noble wine.
ede'mies, (-e), oedemic.
E'den, Eden.
E'denburg, Edenburg (O.F.S.).
e'dik¹, vinegar; *soos* ~ *op salpeter wees*, make things worse.
edik'², (-te), edict, decree; ~**taal'**, (..tale), edictal.
E'dinburg, Edinburgh (Scotland).

edi'sie, (-s), edition; issue (of newspaper).
edog', however, yet.
eduka'sie, education.
eduk'sie, eduction.
e'e, (s) = **egge**, mv van **eg**.
ê'e, (w) (**geëe**), harrow.
eed, (ede), oath, adjuration; *'n* ~ *AFNEEM*, administer an (the) oath; *met 'n* ~ *BEKRAGTIG*, *onder* ~ *BEVESTIG*, affirm (confirm) on oath, swear to; *'n* ~ *op die BOEK neem*, swear on the Bible; *sy* ~ *BREEK*, break one's oath; perjure oneself; *'n* ~ *DOEN (aflê)*, take an (the) oath; *'n HEILIGE* ~ *neem*, take a solemn oath; *ONDER* ~ *(ede)*, on oath; ~ *van TROU*, oath of allegiance; ~**aflegger**, oath-taker; ~**aflegging**, taking the oath, swearing in; ~**afneming**, administering (administration of) the oath, attestation; ~**breekster**, ~**breker**, perjurer; ~**breuk**, breach of oath, perjury; ~**genoot**, (..note), confederate, conspirator; ~**genootskap**, confederacy; ~**helper**, compurgator; ~**hulp**, compurgation; ~**oplegging**, adjuration; ~**skender**, *see* **eedbreker**; ~**skending**, *see* **eedbreuk**.
eek'horing: ~**bont**, calaber, minever, miniver; ~**hondjie**, butterfly spaniel.
eek'horinkie, (-s), squirrel, chipmuck, chipmunk.
eelt, (-e), horny skin, callosity, callus; ~**agtig**, (-e), ~**erig**, (-e), callous; horny; ~**agtigheid**, callosity; ~**sweer**, bunion.
een, (-s, ene), (s, vnw) one, someone; something; ~ *en AL*, one and all; *die* ~ *of ANDER*, someone or other; *die* ~ *en ANDER weet*, know a thing or two; *dis* ~ *en DIESELFDE*, it is one and the same; ~ *uit DUISEND*, one in a thousand; *die* ~ *MET die ander*, this way or that; some way or other; ~ *MET die ander*, one with another; ~ *vir MY en* ~ *vir jou*, one for me and one for you; *sy is nie* ~ *OM te lieg nie*, it is not like her to tell a lie; *OP* ~ *na*, all but one; *soos jy SÊ* ~, in a trice; *UIT* ~ *en ander volg*, from the above it follows; (b, bw) one, a certain (one); the same; *in* ~ *ASEM*, in the same breath; *die veld was (die) ene BLOM (een blom aanmekaar)*, the veld was covered with flowers; ~ *van die DAE*, one of these days, soon; *van* ~ *GESLAG wees*, be of the same sex; *jou* ~ *GEVOEL met*, agree with someone; *IN* ~ *woord*, in a word, briefly; *van* ~ *LEEFTYD*, of the same age; *soos* ~ *MAN*, with one voice; *ene MNR. X*, a (certain) Mr. X; *die pad was die ene MODDER*, the road was one continuous stretch of mud; *dis* ~ *MOEITE*, it is no extra trouble; ~ *en al OOR*, all ears; *net* ~ *PYP op 'n dag rook*, smoke all day; *om die* ~ *of ander REDE*, for some reason or other; ~ *RIGTING*, one way; ~ *teen TIEN*, ten to one; ~, *TWEE*, *drie*, in a moment; in a trice; ~ *van TWEE*, one of two; *hy het* ~ *te VEEL in*, he has had a drop too much;

eend   138   *eenselwig*

~ **te** *VEEL* vir *ons*, one too many for us; ~ *VIR* ~, one by one; singly, separately; ~ **akter, (-s)**, one-act play; ~ **armig, (-e)**, one-armed; ~ **assig, (-e)**, uniaxial; ~ **atomig, (-e)**, monoatomic; ~ **basies, (-e)**, monobasic; ~ **bedryf**, one-act play; ~ **been**, on one leg; ~ **beentjie**, on one leg; ~ *beentjie SPEEL*, play hopscotch; *nie* ~ *beentjie kan STAAN nie*, be tipsy; ~ **bladig,** ~ **blarig, (-e)**, unifoliate, monophyllous, monopetalous, one-leaved; ~ **blommig, (-e)**, monanthous, uniflorous; ~ **broederig, (-e)**, monadelphous.

eend, (-e), duck; *dis maklik gesê, maar die* ~ *lê die EIER*, talk is cheap, but money buys the whisky, fair words butter no parsnips; *soos* ~ *e agter mekaar LOOP*, walk in single file; *so gelukkig soos 'n* ~ *in WATER*, as happy as the day is long.

een'daags, (-e), lasting a day; ephemeral; ~ *e ekskursie*, one-day excursion.

een'dag, once, one day; some day; ~ *is* ~, some day it will happen; the day will come; ~ **mooi**, morning glory; ~ **skuiken**, day-old chick; ~ **svlieg**, ephemera, mayfly.

eend: ~ **ag'tig, (-e)**, duck-like; ~ **bekdier**, duck-bill, duck-mole, platypus *(Ornithorynchus anatinus)*; ~ **eboud**, leg of a duck; ~ **edam**, duckpond; ~ **eeier**, duck's egg; ~ **egeweer**, duck-hunting gun.

een'dejag, wild-duck shooting; ~ **ter**, duck-hunter.

een'dekker, (-s), monoplane; single decker.

een'de: ~ **kooi**, decoy; ~ **kroos**, duckweed; ~ **kuiken**, duckling, ~ **mossel**, swan-mussel, goose-barnacle, ship's barnacle; ~ **nes**, duck's nest.

een'delig, (-e), monomeric, monomerous.

een'ders, similar, the same, equally, alike; *dis vir my MAAR* ~, it is all the same to me; *PRESIES* ~ *lyk*, look exactly the same (alike).

een'dersdenkend, (-e), of the same opinion, like-minded; ~ **e, (-s)**, person of the same opinion.

een'dersheid, similarity, sameness.

een'deweer, rainy weather.

een'dimensionaal, (..nale), one-dimensional.

eend'jie, (-s), duckling; various plants *(Crassulaceae, Sutherlandia)*; *so DRONK soos 'n* ~, as drunk as a lord; *die LELIKE E* ~, the Ugly Duckling.

eend'kuif, ducktail (boy).

een'dradig, (-e), unifilar.

een'drag, concord, union, unity, harmony; peace; ~ *maak mag*, union is strength; ~ **'tig(lik), (-e)**, unanimous; united, harmonious, in unison, as one man.

eend: ~ **stert**, ducktail; teddyboy, ducktail (boy); ~ **vliegtuig**, canard; ~ **voël**, wild duck.

een'-een, one by one, one at a time; in single file.

een'eiig, (-e), uniovual.

een'fasig, (-e), monophase.

een'gewas, single crop; ~ **stelsel**, single-crop system.

een'godedom, monotheism.

een'hand, single-handed, with one hand; having one hand; ~ **ig, (-e)**, one-handed.

een'heid, uniformity, unanimity; entity; oneness; (..**hede**), unity; unit (electricity); *die DRIE eenhede*, the three (dramatic) unities; *'n gevoel van* ~ *met die NATUUR*, a feeling of oneness with nature.

een'heids: ~ **aksent**, unity accent; ~ **band**, bond of union; ~ **front**, united front; ~ **koste**, cost per unit; unit cost; ~ **maat**, module; ~ **metode**, unitary method, rule of three; ~ **prys**, unit-price; ~ **verpakking**, unitization.

een: ~ **helmig, (-e)**, monandrous; ~ **hoewig, (-e)**, one-hoofed, soliped, ungulate; ~ **hoofdig, (-e)**, monocephalous (plant); monarchical (state); ~ **horing**, unicorn; ~ **huisig, (-e)**, monoecious.

een'jarig, (-e), of one year, one year old, annual; ~ *e DIER*, yearling; ~ *e GEWASSE*, annual crops; ~ *e PLANT*, annual.

een'jukkig, (-e), unijugate.

een'kamer, unicameral.

een'kamerig, (-e), monothalamous (botany).

een'kamerwoning, single-roomed dwelling; bachelor's flat.

een'kant, aside; on one side; partly; *dit moet nou* ~ *toe of ANDERKANT toe*, a definite decision must now be reached; it will have to be settled one way or another; *hy HOU hom* ~, he stands aloof; *dit was* ~ *my SKULD*, it was partly my fault.

een'keer, once, one day; *dis nou* ~ *te ERG*, that is really too bad; *dis nou* ~ *SO*, that can't be altered; that is how it is.

eenken'nig, (-e), shy, timid; obedient to one master only (of animals); ~ **heid**, shyness, timidity; vgl. **inkennig**.

een'kernig, (-e), uninuclear.

een: ~ **klank**, unison, monophthong; ~ **kleppig, (-e)**, univalve, univalvular; ~ **kleurig, (-e)**, of one colour, monochrome, monochromic.

een'lêer: ~ **bou**, ~ **konstruksie**, monospar construction; ~ **vlerk**, monospar wing.

een'lettergrepig, (-e), monosyllabic.

een: ~ **ling, (-e)**, individual; peculiar person, eccentric individual; individual crystal; ~ **lippig, (-e)**, unilabiate; ~ **littig, (-e)**, uninodal; ~ **lobbig, (-e)**, mono-cotyledonous; ~ **loop**-, with one barrel (gun); ~ **lopend, (-e)**, unmarried, single; not gregarious, solitary-natured; ~ **loper**, a bad mixer; a lone wolf.

een'maal, once, one day; *dit is nou* ~ *so*, there is no getting away from it, that is how it is; ~ **bloeiend, (-e)**, monocarpous.

een'malig, (-e), single; unique.

een'man, consisting of one man; one person; intended for one person; ~ *KOMMISSIE*, one-man commission.

een'manier, continually; actually.

een'mannig, (-e), monandrous, monandrian.

een: ~ **manskool**, single-teacher school; ~ **mantelig, (-e)**, unipetalous; ~ **master**, ship (boat) with one mast; ~ **meeldradig, (-e)**, concentric; ~ **motorig, (-e)**, single-engined; ~ **ogig, (-e)**, one-eyed, single-eyed, monoptic, monocular.

Een'oog, Cyclop(s).

een'oog, one-eyed person.

een'oog-, one-eyed.

eenpa'rig, (-e), unanimous, by common consent; consentaneous; *ons is* ~ *van OPINIE*, we are unanimously of opinion; *met* ~ *e STEMME aanneem*, carry unanimously; ~ **heid**, unanimity, uniformity, consentaneity.

een'persoons-, for one person; ~ **bed**, single bed; ~ **vliegtuig**, single-seater (plane); ~ **woonstel**, bachelor flat.

een'pittig, (-e), monopyreneous.

een'polig, (-e), unipolar; ~ **heid**, unipolarity.

een'ponder, (-s), object weighing 1 lb.

een-pond-tien'-bene, badger-legged.

een'-pot-in-die-ander, hodge-podge (hotch-potch).

een'rassig, (-e), of one race.

een're: *ter* ~, of the one part; *ter* ~ *bindend*, unilateral (contract).

een'rigting-, one-way; ~ **pad**, one-way road; ~ **straat**, one-way street; ~ **verkeer**, one-way traffic.

eens, once; even; unanimous, of the same opinion; ~ *en vir ALTYD*, once and for all; *DIT* ~ *word*, come to an agreement; *hy het nie* ~ *DANKIE gesê nie*, he did not even say thank you; *ek sê NOG* ~, I say once more; *OP* ~, (all) at once; ~ *so VEEL*, twice as much; as many again; *dit nog nie met homself* ~ *WEES nie*, be in two minds.

een'saadlobbig, (-e), monocotyledonous; ~ **e, (-s)**, monocotyledon.

een'saam, (..**same**), solitary, recluse, lonely, remote (place); secluded; desolate; ~ **heid**, ~ **te**, solitude, loneliness, seclusion, reclusion, privacy; desolateness.

een'sadig, (-e), monospermic.

een'samig = **eensaam**.

eens'deels, partly on the one hand; ~ . . ., *anderdeels* . . ., partly this . . ., partly that . . .

eens'denkend, at one, of one mind.

een'selfde, one and the same; *van* ~ *mening wees*, hold the same opinion.

een'sellig, (-e), unicellular, unilocular; **E** ~ **es**, Protozoa.

eensel'wig, (-e), similar, monotonous; solitary, self-contained; *die* ~ *e roetine*, the monotonous routine; ~ **e, (-s)**, reserved person, introvert; ~ **heid**, solitariness, reserve; monotony.

eens'gesind, (-e), unanimous, in harmony; harmonious; ~**heid,** unanimity, harmony, harmoniousness; entente.
een'sitplekmotor, one-seater (car).
eens'klaps, suddenly, all of a sudden.
een'skulp, barnacle; ~**ig, (-e),** univalvular.
een'slag, one day, once.
een'slagtig, (-e), unisexual (flowers).
eens'luidend, (-e), verbally identical; *'n ~ e AF= SKRIF,* a true copy; *dit is ~ MET die oorspronk= like,* it agrees with the original.
een'snarig, (-e), one-stringed.
een'soortig, (-e), of one kind; homogeneous; ~**heid,** homogeneity.
een'spaaier, (-s) lone wolf; bad mixer; ~**ig, (-e),** of a quiet (retiring) disposition; keeping aloof; keeping oneself to oneself.
een: ~**spoortrein,** monorail; ~**stammig, (-e),** monophyletic.
eenstem'mig, (-e), for one voice; unanimous, concurrent; ~ *e liedere,* unison songs; ~**heid,** harmony, consensus of opinion; ~ *heid bereik,* reach agreement.
een'stroom=, belonging to one stream (race); ~**beleid,** conciliation policy.
een: ~**stryk,** continuously; ~**stuk,** one-piece (dress); ~**styler, (-s),** one-strutter; ~**stylig, (-e),** monogynous.
eensy'dig, (-e), one-sided, lop-sided, biassed, partial; unilateral; *ex parte* (law); ~**heid,** one-sidedness, partiality; unilaterality; narrow-mindedness.
een'tandig, (e), monodont.
eenta'lig, (-e), unilingual; monoglot; ~ **e, (-s),** monoglot; ~**heid,** unilingualism.
een'term, monomial; ~**ig, (-e),** monomial.
een'tjie, one; *NOG ~ ?* have another drink? *OP sy ~ sit,* sit all alone (all by oneself).
een'tonig¹, (-e), monodactylous.
eento'nig², (-e), monotonous, tedious, dull; drab; ~**heid,** monotony; tedium, drab(ness).
een'toon, monotone.
een-twee-drie', in a very short time, in a trice.
een: ~ **uur,** one o'clock; ~**verdiepinghuis,** house of one storey; ~**vertrekwoonstel,** bachelor's flat; ~**vingerig, (-e),** monodactylous; ~**vinnig, (-e),** ~**vlerkig, (-e),** monopteral; ~**voetig, (-e),** one-legged, uniped; ~**voorploeg,** single-furrow plough.
eenvor'mig, (-e), uniform; monotropic (maths.); monomorphic, monomorphous; ~**heid,** uniformity; monotropism.
een'voud, simplicity, plainness, homeliness, primitiveness; ~ *is die kenmerk van die ware,* simplicity is the hallmark of truth.
eenvou'dig, (b) (-e), simple, homely, singular; credulous; popular; plain (food); artless; flat; austere; primitive; elementary (method); inferior; stupid; incapable; (bw) quietly, without any ceremony; plainly, mere; *dis ~ MALLIGHEID,* it is sheer madness, that is mere folly; *jy sê ~ NEE,* you just (simply) refuse, ~ *e VERGELYKING,* equation of the first degree; ~**heid,** simplicity, primitiveness, plainness, homeliness; austereness, austerity; credulity; innocence; *in sy ~ heid,* in his innocence, credulous as he is; ~**heidshalwe,** for the sake of simplicity; ~**weg,** in a simple manner.
een'vrugtig, (-e), monocarpous.
een'waardig, (-e), univalent; monad; ~**heid,** univalence.
een: ~**wangversperring,** single-apron fence; ~**wegklep,** throughway valve; ~**wiel=,** one-wheeled; ~**wieler, (-s)** one-wheeled cycle, unicycle; ~**wording,** unification; ~**wywery,** monogamy, monogyny.
een'wywig, (-e), monogamous, monogynous.
eer¹, (s) honour, repute, reputation, credit, merit; *iem. in sy ~ AANTAS,* injure a person's good name= (honour); *die ~ AAN God,* glory to God; *met ~ van iets AFKOM,* acquit oneself honourably; *iem. alle ~ GEE vir,* give someone full credit for; ~ *van iets HÊ,* have the honour of; *iem. in sy ~ HERSTEL,* clear a person's reputation (honour); *in ~ (ere) HOU,* hold in esteem; *die LAASTE ~ bewys,* render funeral honours; pay one's last respects; *'n MAALTYD alle ~ aandoen,* do full justice to a meal; *met MILITÊRE ~ begrawe,* bury with military honours; *ek het die ~ OM,* I have the honour to, I beg to; *OP my (woord van) ~,* on my (word of) honour; *'n PUNT van ~,* a point of honour; *daar 'n ~ in STEL om . . .,* regard it as an honour to . . .; *dit sal jou tot ~ STREK,* it will redound to your credit; *iem. in sy ~ TAS,* injure someone's pride; *ere wie ere TOEKOM,* honour to whom honour is due; (w) (geëer), honour, praise, revere, respect; *iem. se nagedagtenis ~,* honour someone's memory.
eer², (bw), rather, sooner; *see* **eerder.**
eer³, (vgw) before; *besin ~ jy begin,* look before you leap.
eer'baar, (..bare), virtuous, chaste, honest; ~**heid,** honesty, honour; chastity, pudency, pudicity, virtue; decency; integrity.
eer'betoon, eer'betuiging, eer'bewys, mark of honour, homage; **eer'bewyse,** honours.
eer'bied, respect, regard; devoutness, reverence, veneration; consideration; ~ *AFDWING,* command respect; ~ *HÊ vir,* have respect for; *UIT ~ vir,* in deference to.
eerbie'dig, (w) (geëer-), respect; defer to; revere; (b) (-e), respectful, reverent, devout, deferential; ~**heid,** respect, deference; ~**ing,** respect, deference; devotion; acknowledgement; observance (Sunday).
eer'biedloos, (..lose), disrespectful.
eer'biedshalwe, out of respect.
eerbiedwaar'dig, (-e), respectable, venerable; ~**heid,** respectability, venerableness.
eerbiedwek'kend, (-e), imposing, awful, solemn, impressive.
eer'dat, before.
eerder, sooner, rather; first, earlier, prior; *HOE ~ hoe beter,* the sooner the better; ~ *MEER as minder,* rather more than less.
eer: ~**dief,** defamer; ~**gestoelte,** seat of honour.
eer'gevoel, sense of honour; ~**ig, (-e),** proud, sensitive (on the point of honour); ~**'igheid,** sensitiveness, touchiness; sense of honour.
eergie'rig, (-e), ambitious; ~**heid,** ambition.
eer'gister, the day before yesterday; ~ **aand,** ~**middag,** ~ **môre (~ more,** ~ **oggend),** the night, afternoon, morning before last.
eer'herstel, rehabilitation.
eer'lang, ..lank, before long, ere long, soon.
eer'lik, (-e), honest, upright, fair; with clean hands, plain-dealing; guileless, frank, plain-spoken, candid (opinion); ~ *BLY,* keep straight; ~ *soos die DAG,* honest as daylight; ~ *DUUR die langste,* honesty is the best policy; *alles GAAN ~ toe,* everything is above-board; ~ *GESÊ,* frankly speaking, to be honest; *so ~ soos GOUD,* as true as steel; *iem. 'n ~ e KANS gee,* give someone a fair chance; *die geld KOM my ~ toe,* the money is justly due to me; ~ *het 'n OS geslag,* your honesty is a mere pretence; ~ *SPEEL,* play fair; *'n ~ e STUK= KIE brood verdien,* turn an honest penny; ~ *WAAR,* honestly, to tell the truth; *dis ~ WAAR die geval,* truly, that is the case; ~**heid,** honesty, probity, fair-dealing; fairness; bona fides; candidness; square-dealing, integrity; directness; plain-dealing; bluntness; ~ *heid duur die LANGSTE,* honesty is the best policy; *iem. is die ~ held SELF,* he is the soul of honour; ~**heidshalwe,** in fairness; ~**heidswaarborg,** bond of guarantee.
eer'loos, (..lose), infamous; dishonourable; ~**heid,** infamy.
eer: ~**roof,** defamation, calumny; ~**rowend, (-e),** defamatory, slanderous, libellous; ~**rower,** defamer, slanderer; ~**rowing,** defamation, slander, calumny.
eers, firstly, formerly; even; only; at first, at the outset; *BETER as ~,* better than formerly; *GISTER ~,* not until yesterday; only yesterday; *NIE ~ 'n sent nie,* not even a cent; *NOU ~,* only now; ~ *in die laaste TYD,* only recently; *sy WEET dit nie ~ nie,* she does not even know this.

eer'saam, (..same), honourable, honest, respectable; ~**heid**, chastity, honesty, virtue; integrity.
eers'barend, (-e), primiparous; ~**e**, (-s), primipara.
eers'daags, soon, shortly; within the next few days.
eers'geboorte, priority of birth, primogeniture; ~**reg**, birthright, right of primogeniture; *sy* ~*reg vir 'n bord lensiesop verkoop*, sell one's birthright for a mess of pottage.
eers: ~**gebore**, first-born; ~**geborene**, (-s), first-born (child); ~**genoemde**, the former, the first-mentioned.
eer: ~**skennend**, (-e), defamatory; ~**skennis**, defamation.
eers'komend, (-e), next, following.
eer'soekerig, (-e), ambitious; ~**heid**, ambition, ambitiousness.
eers'sterwende, first deceased.
eers'te, (s) dux; (b) first, premier; prime (minister), prima(l); chief; fontal; leading (shops); initial (expenses); maiden (speech); original; primordial, pristine, former, primeval (inhabitants); primary (truths); *die* ~ *die BESTE boek*, the first book at hand; ~ *BESTUURDER*, first pilot; ~ *BEURT*, first innings; *die* ~ *BOD*, the opening bid; ~ *BURGER*, chief citizen; ~ *INSNYDING*, holding (in coal mine); *in die* ~ *KLAS slaag*, get a first-class pass; ~ *KWALITEIT*, best quality; *baie* ~*s sal die LAASTE wees*, many that are first shall be last; *v.d.* ~ *tot die LAASTE*, from first to last; *die* ~, *die LAASTE*, the former, the latter; ~ *LEESBOEK*, primer; ~ *MINISTER*, prime minister, premier; *in die* ~ *PLEK*, in the first place; *die* ~ *REIS (van 'n skip)*, maiden voyage; *op* ~ *sig*, at first sight; ~ *STEM*, soprano; *TEN* ~, first of all; in the first place; *sy* ~ *TOESPRAAK*, his maiden speech; ~ *VLUG*, maiden flight; ~**beurt**, first innings (cricket); ~**beurttotaal**, first-innings total; ~**dagkoevert**, first-day cover; ~**graads**, (-e), of the best grade, first-class, first-grade.
eer'stehands, (-e), first-hand; ~**kennis**, first-hand knowledge.
eer'stehulp, first aid; ~**kassie**, first-aid box.
eer'stejaar, (-s), **eer'stejaarstudent**, first-year student, freshman.
eer'steklas, first-rate, first-class, excellent; top-quality, prime; capital; *dit gaan nog* ~, we are getting on first-class; ~**kaartjie**, first-class ticket; ~**wa**, first-class coach.
eers'teling, (-e), firstling, first-born; first-fruit(s); first work (artist); phenocryst; ~**toespraak**, maiden speech.
eers'telinievliegtuig, first-rate aircraft.
eer'stemagsfaktor, ..**funksie**, ..**vergelyking**, linear factor, function, equation.
eer'steministers-, of the prime minister; ~**kantoor**, prime minister's office.
eer'steministerskap, prime ministership.
eer'stens, first(ly), in the first place.
eers'te-oortreder, first-offender.
eer'sterangs, (-e), first-rate, first-class; ~*e werk*, work of the greatest value; first-rate work.
eer'sug, ambition.
eersug'tig, (-e), ambitious; ~**heid**, ambitiousness.
eer'suil, column in honour (of).
eers'volgende, following, next.
eer'tyds, (-e), former(ly), anciently, one-time.
eer'vergete, vile, devoid of honour.
eer'verlies, loss of honour; attainder.
eer'vol, (-le), honourable, honorific, creditable; ~*le ONTSLAG*, honourable dismissal; ~*VERMELD*, mentioned in dispatches; ~*le VERMELDING*, honourable mention.
eerwaar'de, reverend; *Eerw. X.*, the Reverend X.
eerwaar'dig, (-e), venerable; honourable; ~**heid**, venerableness.
eet, (geëet), eat; have one's meals; dine; taste; *van sy* ~ *AF wees*, be off his food, have lost his appetite; *LEKKER* ~, enjoy one's food; ~ *wat jy LUS en ly wat daarop volg*, eat what you like and suffer the consequences: *UIT* ~, dine out; *die druiwe* ~ *VORENTOE*, the grapes have a wonderful flavour; *by VRIENDE* ~, have one's meal(s) with friends; ~**aartappel**, table potato; ~**baar**, (..bare), eatable, edible, esculent; ~**baarheid**, eatableness, edibility; ~**bak**, feeding trough; ~**blik**, mess-tin; ~**ding**, something to eat; ~**druiwe**, table-grapes; ~**-en-drink**, face, mouth; stomach; ~**gereedskap**, ~**gerei**, dinner-ware, crockery; cutlery; ~**goed**, edibles, foodstuffs, eats (slang), eatables; ~**hoekie**, dinette; ~**huis**, eating-house; restaurant; ~**kajuit**, cuddy; ~**kamer**, dining-room, refectory; ~**kamerstel**, diningroom suite; ~**lepel**, tablespoon; ~**lus**, appetite; belly, *geen* ~*lus HÊ nie*, have no appetite; *die* ~*lus WEK*, stimulate the appetite; ~**luswekkend**, (-e), appetizing; ~**luswek'kertjie**, (-s), appetizer; ~**maal**, (..**male**), meal; dinner; banquet; ~**party**, junket; feast; ~**plek**, cook-shop; restaurant; cafe; ~**saal**, dining-hall; messroom; refectory (in monastery); ~**salon**, dining-saloon (-car), diner; ~**servies**, dinner-set (-service); ~**staking**, hunger strike; ~**stokkie**, chopstick; ~**tafel**, dining-table; mess-table; ~**tent**, mess-tent; ~**uur**, dinner-hour; ~**vis**, table fish; ~**voorhuis**, dining-room, parlour; ~**wa**, dining-saloon; diner; ~**ware**, victuals, provisions; food (stuffs), supplies, eatables, comestibles, edibles.
eeu, (-e), century, age, aeon; *dit bestaan AL* ~*e lank*, it has existed for centuries; *iem. in GEEN* ~ *gesien hê nie*, not have seen someone for ages; *die GOUE* ~, the golden age; *IN die* ~ *van koning Karel*, in the time of King Charles.
eeu'elang, (-e), ..**lank**, age-long; *'n* ~ *lange gewoonte*, an age-old custom.
eeu'e-oud, (..**oue**), **eeu'e-ou**(**e**), centuries old, age-old, time-honoured.
eeu'fees, centenary.
e'fa, (-s), epha(h).
efemeer', (**efemere**), ephemeral.
Efe'siër, (-s), Ephesian.
Efe'sies, (-e), (b), Ephesian.
ef'fe, (b, bw) even, level, flat, smooth; plain (material); flush (with the ground); calm, undisturbed; slightly, a little; *iets* ~ *AANRAAK*, touch something lightly; *'n* ~ *GETAL*, an even number; ~ *te GROOT*, slightly too big; *'n* ~ *PAD*, a level road; *in* ~ *SWART*, in plain black; *iets op 'n* ~ *TOON sê*, say something calmly (in a level voice); ~**draads**, (-e), even-threaded.
effek', (-**te**), effect, result; *te (tot) dien* ~*te*, to this effect; screw (billiards); ~**bejag**, playing to the gallery; claptrap; straining after effect; ~**te**, stocks, bonds, shares, securities; ~**tebeurs**, stock exchange; ~**tehandel**, stockjobbing; ~**tehandelaar**, stockjobber; ~**tehouer**, stock-holder; ~**tehuur**, backwardation; ~**tekoers**, price of stocks; ~**temakelaar**, stockbroker; ~**temark**, stockmarket; ~**tetrust**, share's trust, growth fund; mutual trust, unit trust.
effektief', (..**tiewe**), effective, real, actual; ~*tiewe PERDEKRAG*, actual horsepower; ~*tiewe RANG*, substantive rank; ~*tiewe SPANNING*, virtual voltage; ~*tiewe VERMOË*, effective output.
effek'vol, (-**le**), effective.
ef'fen, (**geëffen**), smooth (down, over), make even, equalize, level; *die baan* ~ *vir*, pave the way for; ~**aar**, (-s), equalizer; ~**heid**, smoothness, evenness; ~**ing**, levelling.
ef'fens, **ef'fentjies**, (b) (-e), slight, hardly noticeable; (bw) slightly, a moment; a little, just; ~ *GROTER*, a little larger; *'n* ~*e OPDRAAND*, a slight rise; *WAG* ~, half a mo(ment), wait a bit; *die WATER is maar* ~, the water is not plentiful; *die WERK is baie* ~ *gedoen*, the work has not been well done.
efferent', (-e), efferent.
effi'gie, (-s), effigy.
effisiën'sie , (ong.), efficiency.
effisiënt', (-e), efficient.
effloresseer', (ge-), effloresce.
effloressen'sie, efflorescence.
effu'sie, effusion; ~**f'**, (..**siewe**), effusive; ~**gesteente**, volcanic effusive rock.
e'fod, (-s), ephod.

eg 141 *eier*

eg¹, (s) (-ge, êe), harrow, drag; (w) (geëg), harrow, drag.
eg², (s) marriage, wedlock, matrimony; *in the* ~ *tree*, enter into wedlock (matrimony); (w) (geëg), legitimate, legitimize; marry; *'n kind* ~, legitimize a child.
eg³, (b) (-te; -ter, -ste), authentic, pure, real; genuine (friendship); legitimate (child); intrinsic (value); fast, fadeless (colour); honest; devout (belief); *'n* ~ *te flerrie*, a regular (real) flirt.
e'ga, (-s), spouse, consort.
egaal', (egale), level, smooth, even, uniform.
ega'lig, (-e), even, equal, homogeneous; uniform, level; ~ *e wind*, constant wind; ~ **heid**, evenness, levelness, smoothness, uniformity; balance.
egalitaris'me, egalitarianism.
egalitaris', egalitarist; ~ **me**, egalitarism; ..**ris'ties**, (-e), egalitaristic.
eg'band, bond of matrimony.
eg'breek, commit adultery; ~ **ster**, (-s), adulteress.
eg'breker, adulterer.
eg'breuk, adultery.
Ege'iese See, Aegean Sea.
e'gelvis, globe-fish, swell-fish.
eg'genoot, (..**note**), husband, spouse.
eg'genote, (-s), wife, spouse.
eg'ger, harrower.
eg'go, ('s), echo.
eg'go: ~ **lood**, (..**lode**), echo sounder; ~ **mens**, imitator, echo.
eggolalie', echolalia.
Egip'te, Egypt; ~ **naar**, (..**nare**, -s), Egyptian; **tics**, (-e), Egyptian.
Egiptologie', Egyptology.
Egiptoloog', (..**loë**), Egyptologist.
e'go, (-'s), self; *sy alter* ~, his alter ego, his other self, his intimate friend.
egoïs', (-te), egotist; ~ **me**, egotism; ~ **ties**, (-e), egotistic(al), selfish.
egosen'tries, (-e), egocentric.
egosentrisiteit', egocentricity.
egotis'me = **egoïsme**.
egotis'ties = **egoïsties**.
eg'paar, married couple.
eg'raam, harrow-frame.
egret', (-te), egret; ~ **reier**, aigrette (egret) *(Casmerodius albus)*.
egrotat'eksamen, aegrotat.
eg'skeiding, divorce, marital separation; ~ *verkry*, get a divorce; ~ **saak**, divorce case.
eg'skeidings: ~ **bevel**, divorce order; ~ **grond**, ground for divorce; ~ **proses**, divorce suit.
eg'tand, harrow-pin; ~ **ing**, harrow perforation.
eg'telik, (-e), conjugal, matrimonial, connubial, marital; *die* ~ *e staat*, the married (wedded) state.
eg'teloos, (..**lose**), unmarried; ~ **heid**, unmarried state.
eg'ter, however, yet, notwithstanding; *Jan is slim; Koos* ~ *baie dom*, John is clever; James, however, very stupid.
egt'heid, genuineness; legality, authenticity, legitimacy; canonicity; pureness; ~ **stempel**, hallmark.
eg'verbintenis, marriage.
ei'der: ~ **dons**, eiderdown; ~ **eend**, eider duck *(Somateria)*.
eidograaf', (..**grawe**), eidograph.
eidografie', eidography.
ei'e, own, private; personal; natural, native; peculiar, specific, distinct, friendly, familiar, intimate; ~ *AAN*, peculiar to; *uit* ~ *BEWEGING*, of one's own free will (one's own accord); ~ *DOEN* ~ *geen skade nie*, dog does not eat dog; *die* ~ *EK*, the self, ego; *vir* ~ *GEBRUIK*, for one's private use; *in* ~ *GELD*, in the local currency; *IETS wat hom* ~ *is*, something characteristic of him; *in* ~ *KRING*, in one's own circle, privately; *jou* ~ *MAAK*, master something; get the better of something; make something one's own; ~ *wees MET iem*., be intimate with someone; *op* ~ *NAAM*, in one's own name; *hulle is* ~ *NIGGIES (neefs)*, they are first cousins; *in* ~ *PERSOON*, personally, in person; *'n* ~ *SAAK begin*, set up business on one's own account; ~ *STABILITEIT*, inherent stability; *sy was 'n nooi N. VAN haar* ~, her maiden name was N.; *sy* ~ *WOORDE*, his very words; ~ **baat**, self-interest; personal gain; self-seeking; egoism; ~ **belang**, self-interest; expedience; ~ **dunk**, self-esteem, self-conceit, egotism; ~ **gebak**, (-te), home-made; ~ **geërf**, (-de), allodial, freehold; ~ **geërfde**, (-s), freeholder; ~ **gemaak**, (-te), home-made; ~ **gereg'tig**, (-de), self-righteous; high-handed; ~ **gereg'tigheid**, self-righteousness; ~ **geweef**, (-de), home-spun; ~ **gewig**, dead-weight; tare; ~ **goed**, own (cultural) possessions; ~ **han'dig**, (-e), autographic, with one's own hand, per himself; ~ **heid**, familiarity, intimacy; ~ **hulp**, self-help; ~ **lands**, (-e), endemic; belonging to one's own country; ~ **liefde**, self-love; egotism; ~ **lof**, self-praise, self-advertisement; ~ *lof stink (is uielof)*, self-praise is no recommendation; ~ **mag'tig**, (-e), arbitrary, high-handed, autocratic; on one's own authority; ~ **mag'tigheid**, arbitrariness; ~ **mon'dig**, (-e), with one's own mouth.
ei'en, (geëien), recognize (person), identify; *hom aan sy stap* ~, recognize him by his gait (step).
eie'naam, proper name.
ei'enaar, (-s, ..**nare**), proprietor, possessor, owner; *van* ~ *verwissel*, change hands; ~ -**bestuurder**, owner-manager; owner-driver; ~ -**boer**, owner-farmer; ~ -**bouer**, owner-builder.
eienaar'dig, (-e), peculiar, singular, quaint, novel; *dis* ~ !, that's funny! ~ **heid**, peculiarity, characteristic, idiosyncrasy, particularity, singularity, feature, kink.
ei'enerereg, royalty (mining).
eienares', (-se), owner (woman), proprietress.
ei'endom, (-me), property, holding, demesne, estate, belongings, possession(s); ownership; *die* ~ *BERUS by*, the right of property vests in; *INGEKOOPTE* ~, property in possession (building soc.); *die geleerde tot jou* ~ *MAAK*, assimilate what you learn; *die* ~ *word VAN*, become the property of; *die* ~ *VERKRY van*, acquire the ownership of; *in VOLLE* ~ *afstaan aan*, grant the full ownership to; ~ **lik**, (-e), peculiar; singular; ~ **'likheid**, peculiarity.
ei'endoms-: proprietary (company); ~ **afdeling**, estates branch; ~ **agent**, (real-)estate agent; ~ **belasting**, assessment rate, land-and-property tax; ~ **beperking**, restriction of ownership; ~ **besitter**, property-owner; ~ **beskikking**, disposition of property; ~ **bewys**, title-deed; ~ **lyn**, property line; ~ **maatskappy**, proprietary company; ~ **mark**, property market; ~ **plaas**, freehold farm; ~ **reg**, right of possession, proprietary right(s); freehold (of land); ownership, copyright (of book); ~ **vordering**, vindicatory action.
ei'enheid, (..**hede**), individuality, characteristic.
ei'ening, identification; ~ **sparade**, identification paradc.
ei'enskap, (-pe), quality, property, attribute; characteristic, feature (of country); appanage; *dit gee* ~, that is self-evident.
ei'er, (-s), egg; grain (silkworm); ovum; *hy is so bang (benoud) dat 'n* ~ *in sy AGTERSTE kan kook*, he has the blue funk; *op 'n* ~ *BROEI*, be hatching something; *altyd 'n* ~ *tjie BYLÊ*, be continually chipping in; *'n halwe* ~ *is beter as 'n leë DOP*, half a loaf is better than no bread at all; *a bird in hand is worth two in the bush*; *'n GEBAKTE (gekookte)* ~, a fried (boiled) egg; *moenie al jou* ~ *s onder aan HEN sit nie*, don't put all your eggs in one basket; *op* ~ *s LOOP*, tread warily; *die* ~ *wil SLIMMER wees as die hen*, try to teach your grandmother to suck eggs; ~ **albumien**, ~ **albumine**, ovalbumin; ~ **blom**, iris, fritillary; ~ **boer**, poultry-farmer; ~ **boor**, ovipositor (locust); ~ **brandewyn**, egg-flip, egg-nog; ~ **broodjie**, brioche; ~ **dans**, egg-dance; ~ **dooier**, ~ **door**, yolk; ~ **dop**, egg-shell; ~ **drankie**, *kyk eierbrandewyn*; ~ **eter**, egg-eater; ~ **frikkadel**, Scotch eggs; ~ **geel**, (..**gele**), yolk; ~ **geld**, egg-money; ~ **gereg**, (-te), dish made with eggs; ~ **glans**, egg-shell gloss; ~ **handgranaat**, egg-grenade; ~ -**in-die-hoed**, egg-in-the-hat (ball-game); ~ **in-die-lepel**, egg-and-spoon race; ~ **kelkie**, egg-

eieselwig / *ek*

cup; ~**kiem**, embryo of egg; ~**kissie**, egg-box; ~**klitser**, ~**klopper**, egg-whisk; egg-beater; ~**koek**, egg-cake; ~**kokertjie**, egg-boiler, sand-glass, hour-glass; ~**koper**, egg-dealer; ~**kring**, egg-circle; ~**kunde**, oology; ~**laai**, egg-tray; ~**lêend, (-e)**, oviparous; ~**legging**, oviposition; ~**leier**, Fallopian tube, oviduct; ~**lepeltjie**, egg-spoon; ~**lys**, chaplet, egg-moulding (arch.); ~**mandjie**, egg-basket; ~**mussie**, egg-cosy; ~**nes**, egg-nest; ~**pannekoek**, omelet(te); ~**plant**, egg-plant, brinjal; ~**poeier**, egg-powder; powdered egg; ~**produk**, egg product; ~**pruim**, egg-plum; ~**rakkie**, egg-rack; ~**raper**, egg-collector; ~**rond, (-e)**, egg-shaped; oval; ~**sak(kie)**, ovisac, egg-sac; ~**sel**, egg-cell, ovicell; ~**skuim**, white-of-egg froth; ~**slaai**, egg salad; ~**snyer**, egg-slicer; ~**sous**, egg-sauce; ~**spaan**, egg-slice; ~**stander**, egg-stand; ~**steen**, oolite; ~**stelletjie**, egg-stand; ~**stok**, ovary, ovarium; ~**ontsteking**, ovaritis; ~**struif**, omelet(te); ~**tjie, (-s)**, small egg; ovule; ~**uitstoting**, ovulation; ~**versameling**, collection of eggs; ~**vla**, egg-custard; ~**vlies**, egg-membrane; amnion; integument (bot.); ~**vormig, (-e)**, ovate; egg-shaped; ovoid; ~**vreter**, egg-eater; ~**vrug**, brinjal, egg-fruit; ~**wit**, albumen, white of egg; ~**witgehalte**, percentage of albumen; albumen content; ~**witpulp**, egg-white pulp.

eiesel'wig, (-e), individual.

ei'eroem, self-praise; ~ *stink*, self-praise is no recommendation.

eiesin'nig, (-e), wilful, refractory, obstinate, capricious, contrary, self-willed, pigheaded; ~**heid**, wilfulness, obstinacy, self-will, pigheadedness, capriciousness.

eiesoor'tig, (-e), peculiar to itself (oneself); distinctive, separate, particular, special, specific; autogenous; ~**heid**, peculiar character, character of its own, peculiarity; distinctiveness.

ei'etyds, (-e), contemporary.

eievaar'dig, (-e), very large, terrific, huge.

ei'evormig, (-e), idiomorphic, automorphic.

ei'ewaan, self-conceit, conceitedness.

ei'ewaarde, self-esteem, proper pride, self-respect.

ei'ewerfbeslissing, home-town decision.

eiewet'lik, (-e), autonomous.

eiewil'lig, free(ly), according to one's own wish, of one's own free will; wilful, obstinate.

eiewys', ei'ewys, opinionated, self-willed, priggish, headstrong, perverse; cocky; ~**heid**, headstrongness, obstinacy, conceitedness; priggishness.

eik, (-e), oak (tree); ~**aring**, oak graining; ~**ebalk**, oak beam (rafter); ~**eboom**, oak-tree; ~**ebos, (-se)**, oak forest; ~**ehout**, oak(-wood).

ei'kel, (-s), acorn; glans penis.

ei'ke: ~ **laan**, avenue of oaks; ~**rosie**, Chinese rose (hibiscus); ~**stad**, city of oaks; **Eikestad**, name for Stellenbosch; ~**tak**, oak branch.

ei'land, (-e), island, isle; ~**berg**, inselberg; ~**bewoner**, ~**er, (-s)**, islander; ~**esee** = **eilandsee**; ~**groep**, archipelago, group of islands; ~**platform**, island platform; ~**ryk**, island empire; ~**see**, archipelago, ~**vormig, (-e)**, insular.

ei'na, (-s), pain; (b) painful; poor, weak; ~ *KRY*, get hurt; *die OES is maar* ~, the harvest is very poor; *die ROK is darem te* ~, the dress is far too short; *gou* ~ *SKREE*, be touchy (querulous); (tw), oh! ow! (exclamation of pain); ~**beentjie**, funny-bone; ~**eina**, painful, weak; *dit gaan maar* ~~ *met die werk*, poor progress is being made; ~**seer**, very painful; ~**tjies**, poorly, weakly.

eind: ~ **analise**, ultimate analysis; ~**balans**, final balance; ~**bedrag**, final sum; ~**begrensing**, termination; ~**beslissing**, final decision; ~**besluit**, final decision; ultimatum; ~**bestemming**, final destination; ~**diploma**, final certificate; ~**doel**, final purpose, goal, finality, ultimate object, aim, consummation; ~**drukking**, terminal pressure; ~**duik**, terminal dive (velocity).

ein'de, (-s), end, conclusion, ending, termination; cesser; *tot die BITTER* ~ *toe*, to the bitter end; *te DIEN* ~, with that in view; *eind(e) GOED alles goed*, all's well that ends well; *ten* ~ *LOOP*, draw to a close; *ten* ~ *RAAD wees*, be at one's wits' end; *die* ~ *van sy RYKDOM nie ken nie*, be rolling in money; have money to burn; *die* ~ *v.d. STORIE was*, the end of the story was; *TEN* ~, with a view to, in order to; *TOT die* ~ *toe*, till the end; *die* ~ *kroon die WERK*, the end crowns the work.

eind'eksamen, final examination.

ein'delik, finally, at (long) last, ultimately, eventually, at length; ~ *(en) ten laaste*, at long last.

ein'deloos, (..lose), endless, infinite, interminable; ~**heid**, endlessness, infinity.

ein'der, (-s), horizon.

eind: ~ **fluitjie**, final whistle; ~**halte**, terminus; ~**hawe**, port of destination.

ein'dig, (w) (geëindig), end, conclude; determine; close (book); eventuate, come to an end; terminate; ~ *IN*, end in; *die JAAR geëindig 28 Febr.*, the year ending Feb. 28 (in the past); *die JAAR* ~*ende 28 Febr.*, the year ending Feb. 28 (in the future); ~ *MET*, end in; finish up with; ~ *OP*, end in (on); (b) finite; mortal; ~*e wesens*, mortal beings; ~**heid**, finiteness.

eind: ~ **klinker**, final vowel; ~**konsonant**, final consonant; ~**letter**, last letter; ~**lettergreep**, final syllable; ~**loop**, final race; ~**medeklinker**, final consonant; ~**oogmerk**, ultimate object, final purpose; ~**oordeel**, final judgment; ~**oorsaak**, final cause; ~**oorwinning**, final victory; ~**paal**, goal, winning-post; limit; bourn(e); ~**produk**, final product; ~**punt**, terminus, end; ultimate aim; ~**reëling**, final settlement; ~**repetisie**, full-dress rehearsal; ~**resultaat**, sum total; final result; ~**ronde**, final(s) (sport); last round; ~**rym**, (final) rhyme; ~**salaris**, maximum salary; ~**sertifikaat**, leaving-certificate; ~**sitting**, closing sitting (session); last meet; ~**skikking**, see **eindreëling**; ~**snelheid**, final velocity; ~**spel**, final game; ~**stand**, final position; ~**standig, (-e)**, end; terminal (botany); ~**stasie**, terminus; ~**stemming**, final voting; ~**streep**, finish; ~**stryd**, final struggle; final, final match (sport); ~**syfer**, final figure; ~**telling**, final score; ~**term**, last term; ~**tyd**, end of the world; ~**uitdunwedloop**, final heat; ~**vlak**, base, terminal; ~**vonnis**, final judgment; ~**vokaal**, final vowel; ~**voorraad**, closing stock; ~**waarde**, final value; ~**wedstryd**, final(s), final match; ~**wedstrydspeler**, finalist.

ein'ste, same; identical, self-same; *die* ~ *MAN*, the very same man; *op die* ~ *OOMBLIK*, at that very moment.

eint'lik, (b) (-e), proper, real, actual; *die* ~*e bedoeling*, the real aim; (bw) properly, really, actually; *dit is* ~ *JAMMER*, it is rather a pity; *NIE* ~ *nie*, not exactly, not really; hardly; *ek is* ~ *SAT daarvan*, in fact I'm absolutely sick of it.

Eire, Eire.

eis, (s) (-e), demand, claim, postulation, postulate, call, requirement, exigency; *teen iem. 'n* ~ *INSTEL*, sue someone for damages; *'n* ~ *INWILLIG*, grant a claim; *sy* ~ *LAAT vaar (daarvan afsien)*, waive one's claim; *'n* ~ *STEL*, make a demand; put in a claim; sue; *hoë* ~*e STEL*, demand a high standard; *aan die* ~*e VOLDOEN*, meet the requirements; *VOLGENS* ~, as required, properly; (w) **(geëis)**, demand (apology); claim (damages); require (care); sue, exact; *te veel* ~ *van 'n KIND*, demand too much from a child; *hoër LONE* ~, demand higher wages; ~**afdeling**, claims-section.

ei'ser, (-s), plaintiff, claimant, demander, demandant, exactor, complainant; suer; ~**es', (-se)**, plaintiff (woman), prosecutrix.

eistedd'fod, (-au, -s) eisteddfod.

ei'wit, albumen, white of egg; ~**agtig, (-e)**, glaireous; albuminous; ~**houdend, (-e)**, albuminous; ~**ryk, (-e)**, nitrogenous; ~**stof**, albuminoid, protein, glair.

ejakula'sie, (-s), ejaculation.

ejekteur', (-s), (ong.), ejector.

ek, I, ego; *ARME* ~!, poor me!; *sy BETER* ~, his better self; *sy EIE* ~, the great I am; number one; ~ *EN jy*, you and I; ~ *SELF het dit gedoen*, I did it myself; ~ *VIR my*, I for one; ~**heid**, the ego, the *eklampsie*

self; ~ **ke**, I (with stress); ~ **kerig**, (-e), egotistic; ~ **kerigheid**, egotism.
eklampsie', eclampsia.
ekklesias'ties, (-e), ecclesiastic.
eklek'ties, (-e), eclectic.
eklek'tikus, (-se, ..tici), eclectic.
eklektisis'me, eclecticism.
eklips', (-e), eclipse; ~ **eer'**, (geëk-), eclipse.
eklip'ties, (-e), ecliptic.
eklip'tika, ecliptic.
ekologie', ecology; ..**lo'gies**, ecological.
ekoloog', (..loë), ecologist.
ekonomie', economy; economics.
ekono'mies, (-e), economic(al); ~ *e lewensduur*, economical life.
Ekono'miese: ~ **Adviesraad**, Economic Advisory Council; ~ **Ontwikkelingskorporasie**, Economic Development Corporation.
ekonomiseer', (geëk-), economize.
ekonoom', (..nome), economist.
e'kostelsel, ecosystem.
ek'roman, novel in the first person.
eks-, ex; *eks-Keiser*, ex-Kaiser; ex-Emperor.
eksak', (-te), exact; ~ **t'heid**, exactness, precision.
eksalta'sie, exaltation.
eksalteer', (geëk-), (ong.) exalt, become exalted.
eksa'men, (-s), examination; *'n ~ AFLÊ*, write an examination, sit for an examination; *'n ~ met goeie gevolg AFLÊ*, pass an examination; ~ *AFNEEM*, examine; ~ *DOEN*, sit for an examination; *in sy ~ SAK (druip)*, fail his examination; *in sy ~ SLAAG*, pass his examination; ~ **boek**, prescribed book; ~ **geld**, examination fee; ~ **kommissie**, examining board; examination committee; ~ **koors**, examination fever; ~ **nommer**, examination number; ~ **opgawe**, examination paper (return); ~ **posisie**, examination position; ~ **rooster**, examination time-table; ~ **sentrum**, examination centre; ~ **skrif**, examination book; ~ **stelsel**, examination system; ~ **syfer**, examination mark; ~ **toets**, examination test; ~ **tyd**, time of examination; ~ **uitslae**, examination results; ~ **vak**, subject of examination; ~ **vraag**, examination question; ~ **vrae(stel)**, examination paper; ~ **vrees**, examination fright; ~ **werk**, examination work.
eksaminan'dus, (-se, ..di), examinee.
eksamina'tor, (-e, -s), examiner.
eksaminatri'se, (-s), femal examiner.
eksamineer', (geëk-), examine.
ekseem', eczema.
eksegeet', (..gete), exegete.
eksege'se, exegesis.
eksege'ties, (-e), exegetic(al).
ekseku'sie, (-s), execution; ~ **verkoping**, sale in execution.
eksekuta'bel, (-e), executable (goods); enforceable.
eksekutant', (-e), executant.
eksekuteer', (geëk-), execute.
eksekuteur', (-e, -s), executor; ~ **sbrief**, letter of administration; ~ **s'kamer**, board of executors; ~ **skap**, (-pe), executorship.
eksekutief', (tiewe), executive.
eksekutri'se, (-s), executrix.
eksekwa'tur, (-s), exequatur.
eksellen'sie, (-s), excellency.
eksellent', (-e), excellent.
eksemplaar', (..plare), specimen, copy, example.
eksentriek', (-e), eccentric, queer, odd, ~ **as**, eccentric shaft; ~ **ring**, eccentric ring; ~ **stang**, eccentric gab (rod); ~ **toestel**, eccentric gear.
eksen'tries, (b) (-e), eccentrical; (bw) eccentrically.
eksentrisiteit', (-e), eccentricity.
eksep'sie, (-s), exception; challenge; demurrer (law); ~ *NEEM teen*, take exception to; *'n ~ OPWERP*, raise an objection.
eksepsioneel', (..nele), exceptional.
ekserp', (-te), excerpt, extract.
ekserpeer', (geëk-), make an excerpt; ~ **der**, maker of excerpts.
ekserp'temaker, excerptor.
ekserseer', (geëk-), drill, exercise.
eksersi'sie, military drill, exercise; ~ **patroon**, dummy

eks-president

(blank) cartridge; ~ **terrein**, ~ **veld**, parade (drilling) ground.
eksfolia'sie, exfoliation.
ekshala'sie, exhalation.
ekshibeer', (geëk-), exhibit.
ekshibi'sie, (-s), exhibition.
ekshibisionis', (-te), exhibitionist; ~ **me**, exhibitionism; ~ **ties**, (-e), exhibitionistic.
ek'sieperfek'sie, perfect; very particular; *iets ~ doen*, do something to perfection.
eksistensialis', (-te), existentialist; ~ **me**, existentialism; ~ **ties**, (-e), existentialist(ic).
eksisten'sie, existence.
eksistensieel', (..siële), existential.
eksklu'sie, exclusion; ~ **f'**, (..siewe), exclusive.
eksklusivis'me, eksklusiwiteit', exclusiveness.
ekskommunika'sie, excommunication.
ekskommuni(s)eer', (geëks-), excommunicate.
ekskrement', (-e), excrement; ~ **e**, excreta.
ekskre'sie, (-s), excretion.
ekskre'ta, excreta, faeces.
ekskur'sie, (-s), excursion, outing; ~ **kaartjie**, excursion ticket; ~ **trein**, excursion train.
ekskuseer', (geëk-), excuse, pardon.
ekskuus', (..kuse), excuse, apology, pardon; *as ~ AANVOER*, plead as an excuse; ~ *MAAK*, apologize; ~ *VRA*, apologize, beg pardon; ~ **dans**, leap-year dance.
ek'sodus, (-se), exodus.
eksogaam', (..game), exogamous, exogamic.
eksogamie', exogamy.
eksogeen', (..gene), exogenous.
eksoge'nies, (-e), exogenic.
eksor'dium, (-s, ..dia), exordium.
eksote'ries, (-e), exoteric.
eksoter'mies, (-e), exothermic.
ekso'ties, (-e), exotic, maverick.
eksotis'me, exoticism.
ekspan'sie, expansion; ~ **f'**, (..siewe), expansive; ~ **kamer**, expansion chamber; ~ **klep**, expansion valve; ~ **koppeling**, expansion joint; ~ **politiek**, policy of expansion; ~ **pyp**, expansion pipe; ~ **stoom**, expansion steam.
ekspatria'sie, expatriation.
ekspatrieer', (geëks-), expatriate.
ekspedi'sie, (-s), expedition; ~ **kantoor**, shipping-office; ~ **klerk**, shipping-clerk; ~ **leër**, expeditionary force.
ekspediteur', (-e, -s), forwarding agent.
eksperiment', (-e), experiment; ~ **eel'**, (..tele), experimental; ~ **eer'**, (geëks-), experiment, ~ **eer'der**, (-s), experimenter.
eks'pert, (-e), expert.
eksplana'sie, (-s), explanation.
eksplisiet', explicit(ly).
eksploitant', (-e), operator (of airlines); entrepreneur.
eksploita'sie, exploitation; *in ~* , under development; ~ **koste**, working expenses; ~ **maatskappy**, development company; ~ **rekening**, working-costs account; trading account.
eksploiteer', (geëk-), exploit, work (a mine); trade on (someone's feelings); exploit (someone's ignorance); ~ **der**, (-s), entrepreneur.
eksplora'sie, (-s), exploration.
eksploreer', (geëk-), explore.
eksplo'sie, (-s), explosion; ~ **f'**, (..siewe), explosive; ~ **stowwe**, explosives.
eksponeer', (geëk-), expose.
eksponensiaal', (..siale), exponential; ~ **vergelyking**, exponential equation.
eksponent', (-e), exponent; index (figure).
eks'port, export(ation); ~ **eer'**, (geëk-), export; ~ **eur'**, (-s), exporter; ~ **handel**, export trade.
eksposant', (-e), exhibitor.
eksposeer', (geëks-), exhibit.
eksposi'sie, exposition; exhibition, show.
ekspres'[1], (s) (-se), express (train).
ekspres'[2], (bw), expressly, on purpose, intentionally, purposely, by design; *jy het dit ~ GEDOEN*, you did this on purpose; *ek het ~ SELF gekom*, I purposely came myself.
eks'-president, ex-president

ekspres'sie, (-s), expression; ~ f', (..siewe), expressive.
ekspressionis', (-te), expressionist; ~ me, expressionism; ~ ties, (-e), expressionistic.
ekspres'trein, express (train).
ekspropria'sie, expropriation.
eksproprieer', (geëks-), expropriate.
ekspul'sie, (-s), expulsion; ~ f', (..siewe), expulsive.
ekspurga'sie, expurgation.
ekspurgeer', (geëks-), expurgate.
eksta'se, ecstacy, rapture; *in* ~ *raak*, go into raptures.
eksta'ties, (-e), ecstatic, enraptured; ecstatically.
ekstempora'sie, (-s), extemporization.
ekstemporeer', (geëks-), extemporize.
eksten'sie, (-s), extension.
ekstensief', (..siewe), extensive.
ek'ster, (-s), magpie.
eksterieur', (-e), exterior.
ekstern', (-e), extern.
eksterritoriaal', (..riale), exterritorial.
eksterritorialiteit', exterritoriality.
ek'stra, (s) (-s), spare, extra; (b) extra, additional; ~ *wiel*, spare wheel; (bw) additionally, specially; ~ **blad**, special edition.
ekstradi'sie, extradition.
ekstra: ~ **fyn**, superfine; ~ **groot**, extra large; king-size.
ekstraheer', (geëk-), extract.
ekstrak', (-te), extract; essence; summary; strong coffee; ~ **sie**, extraction.
ek'straport, surcharge.
ek'stratjie, (-s), extra, some small thing in addition, perquisite; backhander.
ek'stratrein, special train.
ekstreem', (ekstreme), extreme.
ekstremis', (-te), extremist; out-and-outer; ~ ties, (-e), extremist(ic).
ekstremiteit', (-e), extremity.
ekstrovers', (b) (-e), extrovert.
ekstrover'sie, extroversion.
ekstrovert', (s) (-e), extrovert.
ekstru'sie, extrusion; ~ **gesteentes**, extrusive (volcanic) rocks.
ek'sug, egotism, selfishness; ~ 'tig, (-e), selfish.
eksulta'sie, exultation.
ektoplas'ma, ectoplasm.
ekume'nies, (-e), ecumenical.
ekwa'tor, equator; ~ **iaal'**, (..riale), equatorial; ..*riale stiltegordel*, doldrums.
e'kwinoks, equinox; ~ **iaal'**, (..siale), equinoctial.
ekwipa'sie, (-s), equipage.
ekwitei'te, equities, shares.
ekwivalent', (-e), equivalent.
el, (-le), ell; *by die* ~, by the yard.
élan', élan, vivacity, impetuous rush.
e'land, (-e), elk (Europe); eland *(Tragelaphus oryx)* (S.A.); ~ **sboontjie**, *Elephantorrhiza elephantina*; ~ **svel**, eland skin.
elastiek', (-e), elastic.
elas'ties, (-e), elastic; ~ *e SLUITMOER*, elastic stop-nut; ~ *e WASTER*, elastic washer.
elastisiteit', elasticity; ~ **s'grens**, limit of elasticity, yield-point.
elaterien', **elateri'ne**, elaterin.
elateriet', elaterite.
Elber'ta, (-s), Elberta (peach).
el'ders, elsewhere; *ÊRENS* ~, somewhere else; *NÊRENS* ~, nowhere else.
Eldora'do, **eldora'do**, (-'s), El Dorado.
elefantia'se, elephantiasis.
elegan'sie, elegance.
elegant', (-e), elegant.
elegie', (-ë), elegy.
ele'gies, (-e), elegiac.
elek'sie, (-s), election; ~ **belofte**, election promise; ~ **stryd**, election contest; ~ **tyd**, election time; ~ **vergadering**, election meeting; ~ **verhoog**, hustings.
elektoraat', electorate.
elek'tries, (-e), electric(al); ~ *e AANLEG*, electric installation; ~ *e BELASTING*, electrical load; ~ *e DRYFKRAG*, electric power; ~ *e EENHEID*, electrical unit; ~ *e ENERGIE*, electrical energy; ~ *e HORLOSIE*, electrical clock; ~ *e KRAG*, electrical power; ~ *e KRAGPROP*, powerplug; ~ *e LADING*, electric charge; ~ *e ONTLADING*, electric discharge; ~ *e REMME*, magnetic brakes; ~ *e SENTRALE*, power-station; ~ *e SNOER*, flex, flexible cord; ~ *e STOEL*, electric(al) chair; ~ *e STORM*, electric storm; ~ *e STROOM*, electric current; ~ *e SWEISING*, electric welding; ~ *e UITRUSTING*, electrical equipment; ~ *VERLIG*, lighted by electricity; ~ *e VERWARMING*, electric heating; ~ *e WA*, electric van.
elektrifika'sie, electrification.
elektrifiseer', (geël-), electrify; ~ **baar**, (..**bare**), electrifiable; ~ **masjien**, electrifying machine; ..**fise-ring**, electrification.
elektrise'ring, electrification.
elektrisiën', (-s), electrician.
elektrisiteit', electricity.
elektrisiteits': ~ **eenheid**, coulomb; ~ **leer**, electrology; electricity; ~ **meter**, electricity meter.
elek'tro-: ~ **analise**, electrolytic analysis; ~ **bedekker**, electroplater; ~ **biologie'**, electrobiology; ~ **chemie'**, electrochemistry.
elektro'de, (-s), electrode.
elek'tro-: ~ **dinamika**, electrodynamics; ~ **enkefalograaf'**, electro-encephalograph; ~ **enkefalogram'**, electro-encephalogram.
elektrofoor', (..**fore**), electrophorus.
elektrografie', electrography.
elektrokardiograaf', (..**grawe**), electrocardiograph.
elektrokardiogram', electrocardiogram.
elektroku'sie, electrocution.
elektrokuteer', (geëlek-), electrocute.
elektroli'se, electrolysis.
elektroliseer', (geëlek-), electrolyse.
elektroli'ties, (-e), electrolytic.
elektromagneet', electromagnet.
elektromagne'ties, (-e), electromagnetic.
elektromagnetis'me, electromagnetism.
elektromega'nies, (-e), electromechanical.
elektrometallurgie', electrometallurgy, galvaniplastics.
elek'trometer, **elektrome'ter**, electrometer.
elek'tromotor, **elektromo'tor**, electromotor.
elektromoto'ries, (-e), electromotive.
elek'tron, (-e), electron.
elektrone'gatief, (..**tiewe**), electronegative.
elektro'neleer, electronics.
elektro'nies, (-e), electronic.
elektro'niese: ~ **dataverwerking**, electronic data processing; ~ **redigeerder**, electronic editor; ~ **rekenaar**, electronic computer.
elektron: ~ **ika**, electronics; ~ **mikroskoop**, electron(ic) microscope.
elektropo'sitief, (..**tiewe**), electropositive.
elektroplateer', (geël-), electroplate.
elektroplate'ring, electroplating.
elektroskoop', (..**skope**), electroscope.
elektrosko'pies, (-s), electroscopic(al).
elektrosta'ties, (-e), electrostatic.
elektrosta'tika, electrostatics.
elektrotegniek', electrotechnics.
elektroteg'nies, (-e), electrotechnical.
elektroteg'nikus, electrical technician, electrotechnician.
elektroterapie', electrotherapy.
elektrotipie', electrotypy, electrotype.
elektrotropie', electropism.
element', (-e), element; cell; *in sy* ~ *wees*, be in one's element, be perfectly at home; ~ **aal'**, (..**tale**), elemental.
elementêr', (-e), elementary; abecedarian; ~ *e analise*, ultimate analysis (chem.).
eleva'sie, elevation; ~ **hoek**, angle of elevation.
eleva'tor, (-s), elevator, lift.
elf[1], (s) (**elwe**), elf, fairy, puck.
elf[2], (s) (**elwe**), elf, shad *(Pomatomus saltator)*.
elf[3], (s) (-e, -s, elwe), eleven; *die* ~, the eleven (disciples); (telw.) eleven.
elf: ~ **agtig**, (-e), elfin, elfish; ~ **dans**, fairy dance.

elf: ~ de, eleventh; *ter* ~ *der ure*, at the eleventh hour; ~-en-dertigste: *op sy* ~-*en-dertigste*, at a snail's pace; ~ hoek, hendecagon; ~ ie, (-s), verkleinwoord van elf; (small) elf; ~ hoe'kig, (-e), hendecagonal; ~ lettergrepig, (-e), hendecasyllabic; ~ tal, (number, team of) eleven.
elf'uur, eleven o'clock; ~ tee, ~ tjie, eleven o'clock tea.
elf'vlak, undecahedron; ~ kig, (-e), undecahedral.
elf'voud, (-e), multiple of eleven; ~ ig, (-e), elevenfold.
elideer', (geël-), elide (letter).
elik'ser, (-s), elixir.
E'limheide, Elim heath *(Erica regia)*.
elimina'sie, elimination.
elimineer', (geël-), eliminate.
eli'sie, (-s), elision.
Eli'sies, (-e), Elysian.
eli'te, élite, the upper ten, smart set.
elk¹, (s) (-e), elk.
elk², (vnw) (-e), each, every; any; ~ *en IEDER*, each and everyone; ~ *WAT wils*, something for everyone; (b) (-e), each, every; *in* ~ *e GEVAL*, in every case; ~ *e OOMBLIK*, every minute; any moment.
elkaar', elkan'der = mekaar.
elk'een, everybody, everyone, each, every man jack; *(dis)* ~ *se gouigheid*, anybody's chance, first come first served.
el'kers, every now and again.
el'lelang, ..lank, long-drawn: ..*lange woorde*, sesquipedalian words, words measured by the yardstick.
ellend', wretch; *trap, jou* ~!, be off, you wretch!; *see* **ellende.**
ellen'de, misery, wretchedness, distress, extremity; *in die diepste* ~, in most dire distress; ~ ling, (-e), wretch, miserable fellow; abject creature; miscreant.
ellen'dig, (b) (-e), wretched, miserable; poorly; piteous; distressful; plaguey, accursed; paltry; forlorn; (bw) confoundedly, ~ *sleg*, bad beyond words; ~ heid, miserableness, piteousness, wretchedness, paltriness.
el'lepyp, ulna.
el'leridder, (ong.), knight of the yard-stick, counter-jumper.
el'lie, (-s), alley (marble).
ellierous', child's game, Early (Ellie) Rose.
ellips', (-e), ellipse; ellipsis (gramm.); ~ oïdaal', (..dale), ellipsoid(al).
ellipsoï'de, (-s), ellipsoid.
ellips'passer, trammel.
ellip'ties, (-e), elliptic(al); ~ *e ROMP*, elliptical hull; ~ *e VLERK*, elliptical wing.
el'maat, ell-measure.
elm'boog, (..boë), elbow; *hy KOM altyd met 'n elmboog na 'n mens*, he is always out to do one; *die* ~ *LIG*, lift the elbow; be addicted to drink; ~ *in die WIND steek*, make a hurried departure; ~ beentjie, funny-bone; ~ lengte, cubit; ~ ligter, drunkard; ~ stuk, elbow; ~ swaai, elbow bend; dog-leg (golf); *die rivier maak 'n* ~ *swaai*, the river has a sharp bend.
El'm(u)svuur, St. Elmo's fire.
eloku'sie, elocution.
elokusionis', (-te), elocutionist.
elonga'sie, elongation.
el'pebeen, ivory.
els¹, (e), awl, prod, pricker, bodkin, broach (boring bit).
els², (-e), alder (tree).
El'sas, Alsace; ~-Lo'tharinge, Alsace-Lorraine; ~ 'ser, (-s), Alsatian; ~ 'sies, (-e), Alsatian.
els: ~ bos, alder-bush; ~ hout, alderwood.
el'sie, (-s), small awl; *BONT* ~, avocet.
els'vormig, (-e), awl-shaped.
el'wedans, fairy dance.
em, (-s, -me), m; em (printing).
emalange'ni, emalangeni (pl. of **lilangeni,** Swaziland note equal to one rand).
emal'je, (-s), enamel.
emaljeer', (geëm-), enamel; ~ der, (-s), enameller; ~ werk, enamelling.

emal'je: ~ kastrol, enamel saucepan; ~ verf, enamel paint; ~ ware, enamelware.
emana'sie, (-s), emanation.
emaneer', (geëm-), emanate.
emansipa'sie, emancipation.
emansipeer', (geëm-), emancipate.
emaskula'sie, emasculation, castration.
emaskuleer', (geëm-), emasculate.
embar'go, (-'s), embargo.
embleem', (embleme), emblem.
emblema'ties, emblematic(al).
embolie', embolism (of blood vessel).
embo'lus, (-se), embolus.
em'brio, (-'s), embryo; ~ logie', embryology; ~ lo'gies, (-e), embryologic(al): ~ loog', (..loë), embryologist; ~ naal', (..nale), ~ nêr', (-e), ~ 'nies, (-e), embryonic; ~ tomie', embryotomy; ~ terugplasing, embryo replacement.
embroka'sie, embrocation.
embui'a, embuia.
emenda'sie, (-s), emendation.
emendeer', (geëm-), emend.
emeritaat', superannuation, clergyman's pension.
eme'ritus, (-se, ..ti), emeritus, retired; ~-predikant, retired clergyman, pastor emeritus; ~-professor, retired professor.
emer'sie, (-s), emersion.
eme'tikum, (-s, ..ka), emetic (medicine).
emfa'se, emphasis.
emfa'ties, (-e), emphatic.
emigrant', (-e), emigrant
emigra'sie, emigration.
emigreer', (geëm-), emigrate.
eminen'sie, eminence; *Sy E*~, His Eminence.
eminent', (-e), eminent.
e'mir, (-s), emir; ~ aat', (..rate), emirate.
emis'sie, emission; issue (shares); ~ koers, price of issue.
emitteer', (geëm-), issue.
Em'mausgangers, disciples of Emmaus.
em'mer, (-s), pail, bucket; *IN die* ~ *sit*, be drunk; *twee* ~ *KORING*, two pailfuls of wheat; *iem. in die* ~ *SIT*, take someone in; do someone down; ~ ketting, bucket-chain; ~ koring, *Triticum dicoccum*; ~ leer, bucket-elevator; ~ stelsel, bucket-system; ~ vol, (-svol), a bucketful, pailful.
e'moe, (-s), emu.
emolumen'te, emoluments; perquisites.
emo'sie, (-s), emotion.
emo'sievol, (-le), emotion-laden, emotional.
emosionaliseer', (geëm-) emotionalize
emosionalis'me, emotionalism.
emosionaliteit', emotionality.
emosioneel', (..nele), emotional, affective.
Empi'restyl, Empire style.
empirie', empiricism.
empi'ries, (-e), empiric(al).
empi'rikus, (-se, ..rici), empiris', (-te), empiric(ist)
empiris'me, empiricism.
emplojeer', (geëm-), employ.
empo'rium, (-s, ..ria), emporium.
emula'sie, emulation.
emuleer', (geëm-), emulate.
emulgeer', emulseer', (geëm-), emulsify; ~ baar, emulsifiable; ~ middel, emulgent.
emulge'ring, emulsification.
emul'sie, emulsion; ~ blywend, (-e), emulsion persistent.
emulsifiseer', (geëm-) = **emulgeer.**
en¹, (s) (-ne, -s), n; en (printing).
en², (vgw) and; **èn** .. **èn**, both ... and; *STAAN* ~ *praat*, stand talking; ~ *TOE?*, well?; *verlede WEEK* ~ *Vrydag*, on Friday last week.
en³, (vs) (French), in, ~ *PASSANT*, in passing; ~ *ROUTE*, en route, on the way.
E'nakskind, giant, son of Anak.
enan'tiomorf, enantiomorph(ic).
enargiet', enargite.
end, (s) (ente, eindes), end, termination, close; extremity; distance; length (string); colophon; last; death; result; cue (queue); *AAN die* ~ *van*, at the close (end) of; *tot 'n* ~ *BRING*, terminate; *dit is my*

endekagoon 146 enkel

DOOIE (DROË) ~, it is beyond me; that beats me; ~ *GEE*, stop; *daar is GEEN* ~ *aan nie*, there is no end to it; *die* ~ *van die GELD*, the last of the money; ~ *GOED, alles goed*, all's well that ends well; *'n HELE* ~, a good distance; *nooit die* ~ *van iets HOOR nie*, never hear the last of something; *aan alles KOM 'n* ~, there is an end to everything; *aan sy* ~ *KOM*, meet his death; *aan die KORTSTE* ~ *wees*, get the worst of it; ~ *KRY*, come to an end; *aan die LANGSTE* ~ *wees*, have the best of it; *die* ~ *sal die LAS dra*, the sting is in the tail; *'n* ~ *MAAK aan*, put an end to; settle; *dit LOOP op 'n* ~, it is drawing to a close; *op die OU* ~, at long last; finally; in the end; *iets by die REGTE* ~ *hê*, be right about something; *die* ~ *van die SAAK was*, the result of the matter was; *iets se* ~ *wil SIEN*, be wanting to see the last of something; *nie die* ~ *van iets SIEN nie*, not to know how it will end; *hy is SONDER* ~, he never gets tired; he never stops teasing (talking, etc.); *iets by die VERKEERDE* ~ *hê*, be wrong about something; *op die* ~ *WEES*, to be at an end; have come to an end; *die* ~ *v.d. WÊRELD*, the end of the earth; (w) (geënd), end, come to an end; ~**balk**, end-plate; ~**derm**, blind-gut; ~**deur**, end door.
endekagoon', (..gone), hendecagon.
en'delderm, rectum.
endemie', endemic (disease).
ende'mies, (-e), endemic.
end: ~**fluitjie**, final whistle; ~**hout**, end-grain; ~**jie**, (-s), short distance; a short piece (of string); *see* **entjie**; ~**moreen**, end-moraine; ~**noot**, final note.
endoder'mis, endodermis.
endogamie', endogamy.
endogeen', (..gene), endogenic.
endogene'ties, (-e), endogenetic.
endokardi'tis, endocarditis.
en'dokarp, endocarp.
endokrien', (-e), endocrine, secreting internally, ductless.
endokrinologie', endocrinology.
endomorf', endomorph(ic); ~**ie'**, ~**is'me**, ~**o'se**, endomorphism.
endosmo'se, endosmosis.
endossant', (-e), endorser.
endosseer', (geën-), endorse.
endossement', (-e), endorsement.
endosse'ring, endorsing.
end'raam, end frame.
en'dresdruppels, type of country (folk) medicine.
end: ~**rym**, final (end) rhyme; ~**snelheid**, terminal speed; ~**stasie**, terminus; ~**streep**, finish; ~**syfer**, last figure, final figure; ~**-uit**, to the end; ~**-uit hou**, persevere to the last; ~**voorraad**, closing stock.
e'ne, *see* **een**; *ten* ~ *MALE*, entirely, absolutely, completely; *ten* ~ *male VERNIET*, absolutely in vain.
ene'ma, (-s, -ta), enema.
enem'mel, enamel; *kyk* **emalje**; ~**beker**, enamel jug (mug, beaker).
energie', energy, mettle, go; ~**k'**, (-e), energetic, active.
e'nerlei, of the same kind.
e'ners = **eenders**.
e'nersyds, on the one hand.
en fa'ce, full face; face to face.
enfila'de, (-s), enfilade.
eng, (-e), narrow, tight, contracted; insular; narrow-minded; ~*e reëls*, strict rules.
eng'borstig, (-e), narrow-chested.
en'gel, (-e), angel; peri (mythology); *van 'n* ~ *'n DUIWEL maak*, tease the life out of someone; *soos 'n* ~ *uit die HEMEL kom*, drop like an angel from heaven; *al kom daar 'n* ~ *uit die HEMEL*, even if an angel should drop from heaven; *as jy dink jy het 'n* ~ *aan die KOP, dan het jy 'n duiwel aan die stert*, appearances are deceptive; ~**agtig**, (-e), angelic, seraphic; ~**agtigheid**, angelic nature.
En'geland, England.
en'gel: ~**bewaarder**, guardian angel; ~**ebak**, upper gallery (of a theatre), gods; ~**ediens**, angelolatry; ~**egeduld**, patience of an angel; ~**ekoor**, choir of angels; ~**esang**, hymn of angels; ~**eskaar**, host of angels; ~**haai**, angel-fish; ~**in'**, (-ne), female angel; ~**koppie**, cherub's head; ~**rein**, (-e), of angelic purity.
En'gels, (-e), English; ~ *EENTALIG*, unilingual in English; *GERADBRAAKTE (krom)* ~, broken English; *die* ~*e OORLOG*, the Boer War; ~ *PRAAT*, talk English; be cursing; be in one's cups; ~*e SIEKTE*, rickets (rachitis); ~*e SOUT*, Epsom salt(s); *SUIWER* ~, good English; the King's (Queen's) English; ~*e VLAG*, Union Jack.
En'gels: ~**gerus**, quite at ease; ~**gesind**, (-e), Anglophile, pro-English; ~**heid**, (..hede), English expression (custom); ~**man**, **(Engelse)**, Englishman; *'n MAK* ~*man*, an Englishman who has adopted Afrikaans ways, etc.; *'n ROU* ~*man*, Englishman fresh from England; ~**medium**, English medium; ~**sprekend**, (-e), English-speaking; ~**sprekende**, (-s), English-speaking person; ~**talig**, (-e), English-speaking.
en'geltjie, (-s), little angel, cherub; *praat van 'n* ~ *en jy hoor sy vlerke klap*, talk of the devil and he is sure to appear; ~**smaker**, baby-former.
en'gelwortel, angelica, archangel (nettle).
enggees'tig, (-e) = **enghartig**.
enghar'tig, (-e), narrow-minded; ~**heid**, narrow-mindedness.
eng'heid, narrowness; tightness, constriction; parochialism; insularity; narrow-mindedness.
engram', (-me), engram.
eng'te, strait, neck, defile (in mountains); isthmus; difficulty; gut; *iem. in die* ~ *dryf*, drive someone into a corner; ~**vrees**, claustrophobia.
enharmo'nies, (-e), enharmonic (notes).
e'nig, (-e), only, sole, any; unique; ~ *en ALLEEN*, that and only that; ~*e BOME*, a few trees; ~*e DAG*, any day; ~ *in sy SOORT*, unique (of its kind); ~**een**, anyone; ~**er**: *te* ~ *er tyd*, at any time; ~**erlei**, any (kind of); of some or other kind; ~**ermate**, somewhat, to some extent; ~**gebore**, only-begotten.
e'nigheid, loneliness, solitude; unanimity; *IN my* ~, by myself; *ek het in my* ~ *gedink*, I thought to myself.
e'nigiets, anything.
enig'ma, (-s), enigma, puzzle; ~**'ties**, (-e), enigmatic.
e'nigsins, somewhat, rather, slightly; at all; *as dit* ~ *KAN*, if (it is) at all possible; *hy was* ~ *VERBAAS*, he was somewhat surprised.
e'nigste, only, sole.
enjambeer': *..berende versreël*, unstopped line.
enjambement', (-e), enjambment.
en'jin, (-s), engine; *die* ~ *slaan terug*, the engin backfires; ~**bedding**, engine bed; ~**blok**, engine block; ~**draaimoment**, engine torque; ~**kap**, hood, bonnet (of engine); ~**koeling**, engine cooling; ~**nokas**, engine camshaft; ~**nommer**, engine number; ~**olie**, engine oil; ~**smering**, engine lubrication; ~**spoed**, engine speed; ~**vermoë**, engine power; ~**weiering**, engine failure.
enkefali'tis, encephalitis.
enkefalograaf', (..grawe), encephalograph.
enkefalogram', (-me), encephalogram.
en'kel¹, (s) (-s), ankle.
en'kel², (b) (-e), single; a few, some; alone; ~*e BEWEGING*, single action (revolver); ~*e BOME*, some (a few) trees; *GEEN* ~*e nie*, not a single one; ~ *(e) KRISTAL*, individual crystal; ~ *ONSIN*, sheer nonsense; ~*e REIS*, single journey; (bw) solely, mere(ly), only; separately; ~ *en ALLEEN*, solely; ~ *ter wille van sy KIND*, solely for the sake of his child; ~**bank**, single seat; ~**bed**, single bed.
en'kelbeen, ankle-bone; talus.
en'kel: ~**beentjie**, slip-stitch; ~**breedte**, single width; ~**d**, (-e), single; ~**dekker**, monoplane.
en'kel: ~**diep**, up to the ankles; ~**gewrig**, ankle-joint.
en'keling, (-e), individual.
en'kel: ~**kaartjie**, single ticket; ~**kwartiere**, single quarters; ~**lewend**, solitary-living (e.g. locusts); ~**loop(geweer)**, single-barrelled gun; ~**lopend**, single, unmarried; ~**mediumskool**, single-medium

school; ~**plooi**, monocline (reef); ~**reis**, single journey.
en'**kelskut**, ankle-guard.
en'**kel:** ~**skyfkoppelaar**, single plate clutch; ~**spel**, singles (tennis); ~**speler**, singles player; ~**spoor**, single track; ~**steek**, single chrochet, slip-stitch.
en'**kelverband**, anklet.
en'**kelverdiepinghuis**, single-storey house.
en'**kelverstuiting**, sprain of ankle.
en'**kelvoor**, single furrow (track); ~**ploeg**, single-furrow plough.
en'**kelvoud**, (-e), singular; ..**vou'dig**, (-e), singular; simple; ..*voudige rente*, simple interest; ~'**igwerkend**, (-e), single-acting; ~**vorm**, singular form.
en'**kelwoonstel**, bachelor flat.
en'**kelwoord**, simplex.
enkla've, (-s), enclave.
enkli'se, enkli'sis, enclisis.
enkli'ties, (-e), enclitic.
enkoustiek', encaustic.
enologie', oenology.
enolo'gies, (-e), oenologic.
enoloog', (..loë), oenologist.
enorm', (-e), enormous; ~**iteit'**, (-e), enormity; monstrous wickedness.
enquê'te, (-s), inquiry, investigation, enquête.
ensceneer', (geën-), stage-manage, stage; ..**ne'ring**, (-e, -s), staging.
ensefali'tis = **enkefalitis**.
ensem'ble, (-s), ensemble.
ensiem', (-e), enzyme.
ensikliek', (-e), encyclic(al) letter.
ensiklopedie', (-ë), encyclopaedia; *hy is 'n wandelende* ~, he is a walking encyclopaedia, has a great fund of general knowledge.
ensiklope'dies, (-e), encyclopaedic; ~*e kennis*, encyclopaedic (general) knowledge.
ensileer', (geën-), ensilage.
en'**sovoort(s)**, et cetera, and so forth.
enstatiet', cnstatite.
ent[1], (s) (-e), graft; inoculation; serum; vaccination (mark); (w) (**geënt**), graft, inoculate, bud; vaccinate.
ent[2], (s) (-e), piece, length; distance; end; stretch (of road); extremity; *see* **end**; *'n* ~ *tou*, a piece of string.
enta'sis, entasis.
entablement', entablement.
en'**-teken**, ampersand (&).
entelegie', entelechy.
enten'te, entente.
en'**ter**[1], (s) (-s), inoculator, grafter; vaccinator.
en'**ter**[2], (w) (**ge-**), board (ship); ~**byl**, pole-axe; ~**haak**, (..**hake**), grappling iron; ~**ing**, boarding (of a ship).
enteri'tis, enteritis.
en'**tery**, en'**ting**, vaccination; grafting; inoculation.
ent'**hout**, budwood.
en'**titeit**, (-e), entity.
en'**tjie**, (-s), end, stub; bit, piece, length; short (little) distance; *see* **end(jie)**; *'n snaakse* ~ *MENS*, an odd specimen of humanity; *gaan 'n* ~ *SAAM*, accompany me a little way; *'n* ~ *TOU*, a piece of string.
ent: ~**kussing**, vaccination pad; ~**loot**, graft scion; ~**merk**, vaccination mark; ~**mes**, grafting-knife.
entoesias', (s) (-te), enthusiast; ~**me**, enthusiasm; ~**ties**, (-e), enthusiastic.
entomograaf', (..**grawe**), entomographer.
entomografie', entomography.
entomologie', entomology.
entomolo'gies, (-e), entomologic.
entomoloog', (..loë), entomologist.
entoura'ge, entourage; surroundings, environment.
entree', (-s), entry, entrance; admission; entrée; ~**geld**, entrance fee; admission; ~**kaartjie**, (admission) ticket; ~**skottel**, entrée dish.
entrepot', (-s), bonded warehouse, bond, entrepôt; emporium.
entrepreneur', (-s), entrepreneur.
entropie', entropy.
ent: ~**saag**, grafting-saw; ~**spleet**, graft; ~**steggie**, ~**stiggie**, graft; ~**stof**, serum, vaccine; ~**verbinding**, graft union; ~**was**, grafting-wax.

enumera'sie, enumeration.
enumereer', (geën-), enumerate.
enure'se, enuresis.
envelop', (-pe), envelope.
Eo'lies, (-e), Aeolian.
eoliet', (-e), eolith.
Eo'lusharp, Aeolian harp.
Eoseen', Eocene Period.
eosoön, (**eosoa**, **eosoë**), eozoon.
epak'ta, epact, age of moon on 1 Jan.
epente'se, epenthesis.
epente'ties, (-e), epenthetic.
epide'mie, (-s), **epidemie'**, (-ë), epidemic.
epide'mies, (-e), epidemic.
epidemiologie', epidemiology.
epidemiolo'gies, (-e), epidemiological.
epidemioloog', (..loë), epidemiologist.
epidermaal', (..**male**), epidermal, epidermic(al).
epider'mies, (-e), epidermic, epidermal.
epider'mis, (-se), epidermis.
epidiaskoop', (..**skope**), epidiascope.
epidoot', epidote.
epidosiet', epidosite.
epidotiseer', (geëp-), epidotize.
epiek', epic poetry.
e'pies, (-e), epic.
epifiet', (-e), epiphyte, aerophyte.
epifi'se, epiphysis, pineal gland (body).
epifi'ties, (-e), epiphytic.
epigeen', (..**gene**), epigene.
epigene'se, epigenesis.
epigene'ties, (-e), epigenetic.
epiglot'tis, (-se), epiglottis.
epigoon', (..**gone**), epigone.
epigram', (-me), epigram; ~**ma'ties**, (-e), epigrammatic; ~**skrywer**, epigrammatist.
epiklas'ties, (-e), epiclastic.
epikri'se, epicrisis (of disease).
epiku'ries, (-e), epicurean.
epikuris', (-te), epicure; ~**me**, epicurism; ~**ties**, (-e), epicurean.
e'pikus, (**epici**, -**se**), epic poet.
epilep'sie, epilepsy.
epilep'ties, (-e), epileptic.
epilep'tikus, (..**tici**, -**se**), epileptic.
epiloog', (..loë), epilogue.
episen'trum, epicentre.
episi'klies, (-e), epicyclic.
episikloïdaal', (..**dale**), epicycloidal.
episikloï'de, (-s), epicycloid.
episkoop', (..**skope**), episcope.
episkopaal', (..**pale**), ~**s**, (-e), episcopalian.
episkopaat', (..**pate**), episcopate, bishopric.
episo'de, (-s), episode.
episo'dies, (-e), episodic.
episoö'ties, (-e), epizootic.
epis'tel, (-s), epistle.
epistemologie', epistemology.
epiteel', epithelium.
epite'ton, (..**teta**, -**s**), epithet, adjective.
epivagini'tis, epivaginitis.
epog', (-ge), epoch; ~**makend**, epoch-making.
e'pos, (-se), epic (poem), epopee.
epoulet', (-te), epaulette (of officer); shoulder knot (on livery).
e'ra, (-s), era.
erbarm', (~): *hom* ~ *OOR*, have pity on; *HERE* ~ *u OOR ons*, Lord have mercy upon us; ~**ing**, pity, compassion; ~**lik**, (-e), pitiable, piteous, lamentable, miserable, deplorable, wretched; ~**likheid**, wretchedness, pitiableness, deplorableness, piteousness.
er'bium, erbium.
erd[1], (-e), fireplace, hearth.
erd[2], (s) earth; clay; earthenware; (w) (**geërd**), earth up; mould up.
er'de-: ~**bad**, porcelain bath; ~**goed**, crockery; ~**kastrol**, caserole; ~**kruik**, ~**pot**, earthenware pot; ~**pyp**, clay pipe; ~**skottel**, earthenware basin (dish); ~**ware**, ceramics; ~**werk**, earthenware, pottery, crockery, clayware; ~**werkfabriek**, pottery.
erd'mannetjie, ground-squirrel.

erd'slang, earth snake *(Typhlops bibronii)*.
erd'vark, ant-eater, ant-bear, aardvark; ~gat, (-e), hole made by ant-eater; ~jag, ant-eater hunting.
erd'wolf, aardwolf, maned jackal; hyena-dog.
erd'wurm, earthworm, lobworm.
e're, honour; *in* ~ *HOU*, honour; *iem. iets ter* ~ *NAGEE*, give someone credit for; ~ *SY God*, glory to God; *TER* ~ *van*, in honour of; ~ *wie* ~ *TOEKOM*, honour to whom honour is due; ~amp, ~baantjie, honorary post; ~blyk, mark of honour; ~boog, triumphal arch; ~burger, freeman, honorary burgess; ~burgerskap, freedom (of a city); ~dame, matron-of-honour; ~diens, public worship; cult; ~doktor, doctor honoris causa; ~doktoraat, honorary doctor's degree; ~gas, guest of honour; ~gawe, xenia; ~graad, honorary degree; ~ketting, chain of honour (office); ~kode, code of honour; ~kolonel, honorary colonel; ~konsul, honorary consul; ~krans, wreath of honour; ~kroon crown of honour; ~kruis, cross of merit; ~lid, honorary member; ~lidmaatskap, honorary membership; ~lys, roll of honour; ~medalje, medal of honour; ~naam, name of honour.
ê'rens, somewhere; *HIER* ~, somewhere here; ~ *van HOU*, like (be fond of) something.
e're: ~-ooreenkoms, gentleman's agreement; ~palm, palm of honour; ~penning, medal of honour; ~penningmeester, honorary treasurer; ~plaas, ~plek, place of honour; ~poort, triumphal arch; ~pos, place (position) of honour; ~president, honorary president.
e'reprys¹, prize.
e'reprys², veronica, speedwell (flower).
e're: ~raad, court of honour; ~rol, roll of honour; ~saak, affair (matter) of honour; ~saluut, ceremonial salute (gunfire); ~sekretaris, honorary secretary; ~skoot, salute; ~skuld, debt of honour; ~stoel, seat of honour; ~suil, column in honour of . . .; obelisk; ~swaard, presentation sword; ~tafel, principal table; ~teken, badge (mark) of honour, decoration; ~tempel, pantheon; ~titel, honorary title; honorific (oriental); ~toekenning, honorary award; ~voorsitter, honorary president; ~wag, guard of honour; ~woord, word of honour; faith; *op my* ~*woord*, (up)on my word of honour.
erf¹, (s) (erwe), erf, plot (of ground), stand, allotment; (back)yard; premises; *huis en* ~, house and grounds, premises; property; estate.
erf², (w) (geërf), inherit, succeed to, come into (an estate); ~adel, hereditary nobility; ~baar, (..bare), heritable; ~baarheid, hereditability.
erf'belasting, site rate.
erf: ~besit, hereditary possession; ~deel, hereditary portion, heritage, heritance; ~dekking, plot coverage; ~diensbaarheid, praedial servitude; ~dogter, heiress; ~dwang, prepotency.
erf'-en-diensstelsel, site and service system.
erf: ~enis = erfnis; ~faktor, gene; ~gebrek, inherited defect; ~geld, inherited money; ~*geld is swerfgeld*, easy come, easy go; ~genaam, (..name), heir; legatee; heritor; devisee; ~*gename en regsverkrygendes*, heirs and assigns; ~genaamskap, heirdom; ~gename, (-s), heritrix, heiress; ~geregtig, (-de), heritable; ~goed, patrimony, (in)heritance, estate; hereditament; ~*goed is swerfgoed*, lightly come, lightly go; ~grondbrief, original title-deed; ~laatster, (-s), testatrix; ~later, (-s), testator; legator; devisor; ~lating, testation, legacy; devise; bequest; ~leen, hereditary fief.
erf'lik, (-e), hereditary, hereditable, heritable; transmissible; congenital; ~ *belas*, the victim of one's heredity; with hereditary taints (of character); ~heid, heritability; heredity; ~heidsbepaler, gene; ~heidsleer, genetics; ~heidsnavorser, geneticist.
erf: ~nis, (-se), birthright; (in)heritance, heirdom, heirship; heritage; ~oom, uncle from whom one inherits; ~opvolger, successor, heir; ~opvolging, succession; ~pag, hereditary tenure, quitrent, long lease; copyhold; ~pagreg, emphyteusis (law); ~pagter, copyholder; emphyteuta; ~plaas, hereditary farm; ~porsie, inheritance, share of inheritance; ~prins, hereditary prince; ~reg, heredi-

tary right; law of succession; heirdom, heirship; ~siekte, hereditary disease; ~skuld, hereditary debt (sin); ~smet, ~sonde, original sin, hereditary sin; birth-sin; ~stelling, appointment of heir; ~stuk, heirloom; ~tante, aunt from whom one inherits; ~vyand, hereditary enemy; ~vyandskap, hereditary enmity.
erg¹, (s) mistrust, suspicion; *hy HET daar geen* ~ *in nie*, he does not notice it; he does not care for it, he has no interest in it; *SONDER* ~, unsuspectingly; unwittingly, unintentionally; (w) (geërg, geërge(r)), give offence, annoy; be vexed (annoyed); *ek het (my) bloedig geërg*, I was mortally vexed.
erg², (s) (-e, -s), erg, ergon (unit of electr. power).
erg³, (s) (-e), erg (desert).
erg⁴, (b) (-e; -er, -ste), bad, evil, ill; *DES te* ~*er*, so much the worse; *in 'n* ~ *e GRAAD*, to a severe degree; (bw) badly, severely, extremely, highly; *te* ~ *AANGAAN*, go too far, exceed the limits; ~ *oor IEM. wees*, like someone very much; to be serious over someone; *wat te* ~ *IS*, *is te* ~, too much is too much; *te* ~ *WEES*, be too much; ~ *oor iets WEES*, dote on; *iets te* ~ *MAAK*, exaggerate, overdo something; lay it on thick; *ek het dit* ~ *NODIG*, I need it very badly.
er'ger, (w) (geër-), annoy, pique, give offence, discompose, chagrin; be vexed (annoyed); ~end, (-e), vexatious.
er'gerlik, (-e), offensive, annoying, vexed; harrowing, provoking, exasperating; ~ *word*, become annoyed; ~heid, vexation, annoyance.
er'gernis, (-se), offence, annoyance, vexation, dudgeon; heart-burning, gall, grief; exasperation; nuisance; *iem.* ~ *gee*, be a source of annoyance; ~ *met sy GEDRAG gee*, cause annoyance by his behaviour; *tot GROOT* ~ *van*, to the great annoyance of; ~wekkend, (-e), provoking.
er'go, ergo, therefore.
ergot', ergot; ~is'me, ergotism; ~swam, ergot fungus; ~vergiftiging, ergotism.
erg'ste, worst; *IN die* ~ *geval*, if the worst comes to the worst; *die* ~ *KOM nog*, there is worse to come; *tot die* ~ *OORGAAN*, do the worst; *OP die* ~ *voorberei*, prepared for the worst; *om die* ~ *te VOORKOM*, to prevent the worst; *die* ~ *VREES*, fear the worst; *WEE diegene deur wie die* ~ *kom*, woe to the man by whom the offence cometh.
e'rika, (-s), heath, erica.
e'riometer, eriome'ter, (-s), eriometer (for wool).
Eritreër', (-s), Eritrean.
erken', (w) (~), acknowledge, recognize, profess, own, confess, admit (the truth); accredit; allow; avow; avouch; *'n KIND as wettig* ~, acknowledge a child; *ONTVANGS* ~, acknowledge receipt; (b) (-de), acknowledged, professed; approved (suitor); admitted (allegation); ~baar, (..bare), avowable; ~ning, (-e, -s), acknowledgement; exequatur (of consul); recognition; admission; cognisance; avowal; avouchment; ~*ning en bekentenis*, admission and confession; ~ningsbesluit, exequatur; ~ningspaaiement, token payment.
erken'tenis, acknowledgement; gratitude; admission (of guilt).
erkent'lik, (-e), grateful, thankful.
erkent'likheid, gratitude, thankfulness, gratefulness; *UIT* ~ *jeens*, in gratitude to; *uit* ~ *VIR*, in recognition of.
er'ker, (-s), bow window, bay window.
erlang', (~), obtain, acquire.
Er'meloër, (-s), inhabitant of Ermelo.
erns, earnest(ness), seriousness, gravity; *in ALLE* ~, in real earnest, in all seriousness; *IS dit ons* ~? do we really mean it?
erns'tig, (-e), serious, grave, grievous, earnest; *iets* ~ *opneem*, take a serious view of something; ~ *e droogte*, serious drought; ~heid, seriousness, earnest(ness), gravity.
erodeer', (geër-), erode.
E'ros, Eros.
ero'sie, erosion; ablation; ~basis, base level of erosion; ~berg, residual mountain; ~bestryding, fight against erosion.

erotiek', eroticism, erotism.
ero'ties, (-e), erotic.
ero'tikus, (-se, ..tici), eroticist.
erotis'me, erotism.
erotomaan', (..mane), erotomaniac, sex maniac.
erotomanie', erotomania, sex mania.
erra'tum, (..ta), erratum, printer's error, error in printing (writing).
er'tappel, = **aartappel**.
er'temeel, pea flour.
er'teso(e)p = **ertjieso(e)p**.
er'tjie[1], (-s), pea; *hy laat hom nie met BLOU ~ s op loop jaag nie*, you can't frighten him; *~ s en BOONTJIES èrens kan deurdruk*, as thin as muslin (gauze).
er'tjie[2], (-s), hole, mark (in top).
er'tjie: ~ **bos**, wild pea *(Podalyria, Rafnia)*; ~ **dop**, ~ **peul**, pea shell, pea pod; ~ **soep**, ~ **sop**, pea soup; ~ **(steen)kool**, peas (coal); ~ **vormig**, (-e), pisiform.
erts, (-e), ore; ~ *was*, buddle; ~ **aar**, mineral vein, lode; ~ **afkapping**, cobbing; ~ **afsetting**, ore deposit; ~ **bereiding**, ore dressing; ~ **breker**, ore crusher; ~ **brekery**, crushing station; ~ **draer**, ore-bearer (carrier); ~ **formasie**, ore formation; ~ **gang**, fissure lode; ~ **gehalte**, ore content; ~ **glybaan**, ore chute, ore passes; ~ **hoop**, tipple; ~ **houdend**, (-e), ore-bearing; ~ **kamer**, ore chamber; ~ **kas**, ore box; ~ **kol**, ore pocket; ~ **laag**, ore deposit; ledge (mining); ~ **meul**, ore-crusher; ~ **nes**, ore pocket; ~ **ondersoek**, ore assay; ~ **ondersoeker**, assayer; ~ **ontwikkeling**, development of ore (in nature); ~ **oond**, ore furnace; ~ **produksie**, ore production, through-put; ~ **pyp**, mineral (ore) pipe; ~ **reserwe**, ore reserve; ~ **sif**, (ore) jigger; griddle; ~ **stamper**, ore crusher; ~ **stof**, ore dust; ~ **strook**, ore shoot; ~ **uitgrawing(s)**, workings; ~ **uitskeidings**, ore segregation; ~ **wals**, ore roll; ~ **winning**, ore mining.
erudi'sie, erudition, learning.
erup'sie, (-s), eruption (volcano).
eruptief', (..tiewe), eruptive; *..tiewe gesteente*, igneous rock.
ervaar', (~), experience, undergo.
erva're, (-ner, meer ~, -nste, mees ~), experienced, practised, expert, conversant, adept, skilled; ~ **ne**, (-s), person of experience; ~ **nheid**, experience, skill.
erva'ring, (-e, -s), experience; *die ~ LEER dat*, experience shows that; ~ *OPDOEN*, gain (acquire) experience; *UIT ~*, by (from) experience; ~ **sleer**, empiricism, empirico; · **stoelae**, proficiency allowance.
er'we, (s) heritage; *die ~ van ons vaders*, the land of our fathers; (w) **(geërwe)**, *see* **erf**.
es[1], (-se), letter S; short turn, S-bend; ~ *se gooi*, take sharp turns with a vehicle.
es[2], (-se), fireplace, hearth, hob.
es[3], (-se), ash (tree).
Es[4], E flat.
esbattement', (-e), comedy (in Middle Ages).
eschschol'tzia, (-s), eschscholtzia.
escu'do, (-'s), escudo.
es'doring, sycamore maple *(Acer)*.
e'sel, (-s), ass, donkey; mule; blockhead; easel; *so DOM soos 'n ~*, as dense as a donkey; *iem. IS 'n ~*, he is an ass; *'n ~ van iem. MAAK*, make someone your drudge; *jy kan 'n ~ nie 'n PERD maak nie*, you cannot make a silk purse out of a sow's ear; *pas op, die ~ sal PRAAT*, don't ill-treat an animal; *van 'n ~ kan 'n mens altyd 'n SKOP verwag*, all one can expect from a pig is a grunt; *'n ~ STOOT hom nie twee maal aan dieselfde steen (klip) nie*, once bitten, twice shy; *soos 'n ~ WERK*, work like a slave; ~ **agtig**, (-e), asinine, stupid; ~ **ag'tigheid**, stupidity, asinity, mulishness; ~ **dom**, stupid, asinine; ~ **drywer**, ass-driver; ~ **hings**, jackass; ~ **in'**, (-ne), she-ass; ~ **melk**, asses' milk; ~ **merrie**, jenny, she-ass; ~ **pen**, easel-peg; ~ **(s)brug**, ass's bridge, memory aid; pons asinorum; ~ **skop**, ass's head; dunce (fig.); ~ **(s)kos**, *Euphorbia meloformis*; ~ **soor**, ass's ear; dunce (fig.); dog's ear (in book); *Cheiridopsis peculiaris*; ~ **werk**, drudgery, hard work; ~ **wa**, donkey-wagon.
es'hout, ash(wood).
eska'der, (-s), squadron; flotilla; ~ **kommandant**, squadron-commander; ~ **leier**, squadron-leader; ~ **stasie**, squadron station.
eskadriel'je, (vero.), (air) squadron.
eskadron', (-ne, -s), squadron.
eskala'de, (-s), escalade.
eskala'sie, (s), escalation; ~ **bepaling**, ~ **klousule**, escalation clause.
eskaleer', (w), escalate.
eskapa'de, (-s), escapade.
eskarp', (-e), escarp; escarpment; ~ **eer'**, (geëskarpeer), escarp.
eskatologie', eschatology; ..lo'gies, (-e), eschatological.
Es'kimo, (-'s), Eskimo.
eskort', (-e), escort; ~ **eer'**, (geës-), escort.
eskulaap', (..lape), physician, medico.
Eso'pus, Aesop.
esote'ries, (-e), esoteric.
esp, (-e), asp (tree); ~ **blaar**, aspen leaf.
espar'to(gras), Spanish (esparto) grass.
Esperantis', (-te), Esperantist.
Esperan'to, Esperanto.
esplana'de, (-s), esplanade.
essai', (-e), assay; ~ **duim**, assay inch; ~ **eer'**, (geësaieer), assay; ~ **ë'ring**, (-e, -s), assay; ~ **eur'**, (-s), assayer; ~ **waarde**, assay value.
es'say, (-s), essay; ~ *is'*, (-te), essayist; ~ **'isties**, essayistic.
es'sehout, Cape ash *(Ekebergia capensis)*, *Trichilia emetica*.
essens', (-e), essence.
essen'sie, essence.
essensieel', (..siële), essential.
es'sie, (-s), small s.
Est, (-e), Esthonian.
estcet', **(estete)**, aesthete.
es'ter, (-s), ester.
estesie', aesthesia.
estetiek', aesthetics.
este'ties, (-e), aesthetic(al).
este'tika, aesthetics.
este'tikus, (-se, ..tici), aesthetician.
estima'sie, estimation.
Est'land, Esthonia; ~ **er**, (-s) = **Est**; ~ **s**, (-e), Esthonian.
Est'nies, (-e), Esthonian.
estop'pel, (-s), estoppel.
estra'de, (-s), estrade.
es'trum, (-s), oestrum, oestrus.
estua'rium, (-s), estuary.
es'yster, andiron, firedog.
et, (-te), hole, mark (in top).
éta'ge, (-s), floor, storey; flat; ~ **woning**, apartment house.
etala'ge, (-s), display; show window.
etaleer', (geëtaleer), display (in windows); dress (window).
étaleur', (-s), window-dresser.
e'te, (-s), food, meal, dinner, fare; appetite; *ek is van my ~ AF*, I have lost my appetite; *BY die ~*, with meals; *at mealtime*; *jou ~ en DRINKE vir iets laat staan*, set everything aside for someone else; *die ~ is op TAFEL*, dinner is ready (being served); *VOOR ~*, before dinner; *iem. vir ~ VRA*, invite someone to dinner; ~ **bewys**, meal-ticket.
e'tens-: ~ **klok**, dinner-bell; ~ **onderbreking**, ~ **pouse**, meal-break, meal-interval; ~ **tyd**, dinner-time, mealtime; time for dinner; ~ **uur**, dinner-hour.
e'ter[1], (-s), eater; feeder; *'n groot ~*, a big eater; *'n swak ~*, a poor eater.
e'ter[2], ether, upper air; ~ **agtig**, (-e), ethereal; ~ **golf**, ether wave.
ete'ries, (-e), ethereal.
eterniet', asbestos cement.
e'tery, eating; meal.
Ethio'pië, Ethiopia; ~ **r**, (-s), Ethiopian.
Ethio'pies, (-e), Ethiopian.
etiek', ethics, moral philosophy.

etiel', ethyl.
e'ties, (-e), ethical.
e'tika, ethics.
etiket', (-te), etiquette; label; docket; *teen die ~ sondig*, commit a breach of etiquette; *~jie*, (-s), ticket, label; *~klem*, label (docket), clip; *~teer'*, (geëtiketteer), label.
etimologie', etymology.
etimolo'gies, (-e), etymologic(al).
etimoloog', (..loë), etymologist.
etioleer', (geëtioleer), etiolate.
etiologie', etiology.
etiolo'gies, (-e), etiologic(al).
etioloog', (..loë), etiologist.
e''tjie, (-s), small e.
et'like, several, some, divers.
et'maal, 24 hours; *~ diens*, 24 hour service.
et'nies, (-e), ethnological.
etnograaf', (..grawe), ethnographer.
etnografie', ethnography.
etnogra'fies, (-e), ethnographic(al).
etnologie', ethnology.
etnologie', ethnologic(al)
etnoloog', (..loë), ethnologist.
etologie', ethology.
etoloog', ethologist.
e'tos, ethos.
Etru'rië, Etruria; *~r, (-s)*, Etrurian.
Etru'ries, (-e), Etrurian.
ets, (s) (-e), etching; (w) (geëts), etch; *~er, (-s)*, etcher; *~figuur*, etch-figure; *~kuns*, art of etching; *~middel*, caustic; *~naald*, etching-needle; *~natron*, caustic potash; *~patroon*, etching structure; *~plaat*, etched plate; *~suur*, mordant; *~water*, etching-water; *~yster*, etching-iron.
et'ter, (s) (purulent) matter, discharge, pus; gleet; (w) (geëtter), suppurate, fester, ulcerate; *~agtig, (-e)*, purulent; *~end, (-e)*, festering, mattery; *~buil*, abscess; *~geswel*, ulcer; abscess; gathering; *~ig, (-e)*, mattery, pussy, purulent; gleety; *~igheid*, purulence, purulency; *~ing*, suppuration, maturation, gleet, discharge, purulence, ulceration; *~sak*, cyst; *~vergiftiging*, sepsis; *~vorming*, ulcerative process, suppuration; *~wond*, suppurating wound.
etu'de, (-s), etude.
étui', (-s), case (of cutlery); etui.
eubiotiek', eubiotics.
eucharis'tie, eucharist (R. C. Church).
eucharis'ties, (-e), eucharistic.
eufemis'me, (-s), euphemism.
eufemis'ties, (-e), euphemistic.
eufonie', euphony.
eufo'nies, (-e), euphonic.
euforie', euphoria.
Eufraat', Euphrates.
eugene'se, eugenetiek', eugenics.
eugene'ties, (-e), eugenic.
eukalip'tus, eucalyptus; *~olie*, eucalyptus oil.
Eukli'des, Euclid.
eu'nug, (-e, -s), eunuch.
Eurafrikaan', (..kane), Eurafrican; *~s', (-e)*, Eurafrican.
Eura'siër, (-s), Eurasian.
Eura'sies, (-e), Eurasian.
eure'ka, eureka.
euritmiek', eurhythmy, eurhythmics.
eurit'mies, (-e), eurhythmic.
Eu'romark, Euromart.
Euro'pa, Europe.
Europeaan', (..peane), European.
Europe'ër, (-s), European.
Europees', (..pese), European; *~pese mark*, European market.
Eustachiaans', (-e), Eustachian; *~e buis*, Eustachian tube.
Eusta'chius: *buis van ~*, Eustachian tube.
eutanasie', euthanasia.
eutek'ties, (-e), eutectic.
eu'wel, (s) (-s), evil; defect; *aan 'n ~ MANK gaan*, have a weakness; (bw): *iem. iets ~ dui*, take something amiss; *~daad*, evil deed, outrage, crime; *~moed*, insolence; wantonness.

E'va, Eve; (-s), woman.
evakua'sie, evacuation.
evakueer', (geëvakueer), evacuate.
evalueer', (geëvalueer), evaluate.
evalue'rend, (-e), evaluative.
evalua'sie, (-s), evaluation.
evange'lie, (-s), gospel, evangel; *vir ~ AANNEEM*, accept as gospel; *dit is vir hom ~*, he regards that as gospel; *dis die ~ in die KERK*, it is gospel; *dis NIE alles ~ nie*, it is not all gospel-truth; *~bediening*, ministry of the Gospel; *~boodskap*, gospel message; *~dienaar*, minister of the Gospel; *~leer*, doctrine of the Gospel; *~prediker*, evangelist, gospeller; *~s, (-e)*, evangelic(al); *~waarheid*, gospel truth; *~woord*, the Gospel.
evangelis', (-te), evangelist; *~a'sie*, evangelization; *~eer'*, (geëvangeliseer), evangelize; *~ties, (-e)*, evangelistic.
E'vasgeslag, daughter(s) of Eve.
E'vasgewaad: *in ~*, naked, in birthday suit, in the altogether.
evenement', (-e), (remarkable) occurrence, event.
eventualiteit', eventuality; contingency.
eventueel', (..tuele), eventual, possible; *as hy ~ mag KOM*, in case he should come; *by eventuele MOEILIKHEDE*, if any difficulties should arise.
evident', (-e), evident.
evoka'sie, evocation.
evokatief', (..tiewe), evocative.
evokeer', (geëvokeer), evoke.
evolueer', (geëvolueer), evolve.
evolu'sie, see **ewolusie**.
evoseer', (geëv-) = **evokeer**.
e'we, just as, even, equally; *~ GOED*, just as well, equally well; *'n ~ GROOT som*, an equal sum; *~ MIN*, no more than, just as little; *hy kon dit nie bereik nie en ek ~ MIN*, he could not reach it, nor could I; *dis vir my OM die* ('t) *~*, it is all the same (immaterial) to me; *~ of ONEWE*, odd or even; *~ ONGEËRG*, quite unconcerned; *~ OUD wees*, be of the same age; *~ VEEL*, (just) as much; *~ VER*, (just) as far; *~as*, just as; just like; *~beeld*, likeness, image, counterpart, picture; *~-eens*, see **eweneens**; *~handig, (-e)*, ambidextrous; *~kansig*, random; *~kansige monster*, random sample; *~kleurig, (-e)*, self-coloured; *~knie*, equal, match, peer, compeer; *~maat*, symmetry; *~ma'tig, (-e)*, symmetrical, proportional, aliquot (part); *~mens*, fellow(-being).
e'wenaar¹, (s) equator, line; compensator (mech.); *magnetiese ~*, aclinic line; (-s, ..nare), differential (motor); tongue (of a balance); beam (where the traces are fastened).
ewenaar'², (w) (geëw-), equal, be a match for; come up to.
e'wenaar: *~kruis*, differential cross; *~laer*, differential bearing; *~omhulsel*, differential casing; *~sratte*, differential gears; *~ster*, differential spider.
e'wenaaste, fellow(-being); neighbour.
e'wenag: *~slyn*, equinoctial line; equator; *~storm*, equinoctial gale.
e'wenas, just as, like.
e'weneens, similarly, in the same manner, likewise, also, just as well, too.
e'wenwel, ewenwel', however, yet, still, nevertheless, even so.
ewere'dig, (-e), proportionate, proportional; commensurate, equal; pro rata; homologous; equable; equivalent, aliquot, adequate; *die PRYS is ~ met die kwaliteit*, the price is proportionate to the quality; *~e VERTEENWOORDIGING*, proportional representation; *~e, (-s)*, proportional (maths.).
ewere'digheid, proportion; commensuration; homology; equibility; proportionality; *NA ~ van*, in proportion to; *OMGEKEERDE ~*, inverse proportion; *na ~ TOENEEM*, increase proportionately, increase on a corresponding scale.
e'we: *~seer*, (just) as much; equally; *~so*, likewise, just as; *~wel = ewenwel*.
e'wewig, equilibrium, libration, equation, (counter)-

poise, (equi)poise, (counter)balance; *die ~ BEWAAR,* keep one's balance; *uit die ~ BRING,* throw out of balance; *in ~ HOU,* keep in equilibrium; *LABIALE (wankelbare, onvaste) ~,* unstable equilibrium; *die STAATKUNDIGE ~,* the balance of power; *STABIELE (vaste) ~,* stable equilibrium; *die ~ VERLOOR,* lose one's balance; **~sklep,** balance valve; **~skrag,** equilibrant; **~sleer,** statics; **~smoment,** balance moment; **~sorgaan,** organ of equilibrium; **~spunt,** centre of gravity; centre of equilibrium; **~stand,** equilibrium position; **~steentjie,** otolith, statolith; **~stoestand,** equilibrium.
ewewig'tig, (-e), evenly (well) balanced; equilibrious; level-headed; **~heid,** (mental) balance, level-headedness.
ewewy'dig, (-e), parallel; collateral; *~e plooi,* parallel fold; **~heid,** parallelism.
e'wig, (-e), for ever (and a day), evermore, eternal, everlasting, abiding, perpetual; incessant; *~ en ALTYD,* for ever and ever; *dit is 'n ~e JAMMER,* it is a thousand pities; *die ~e RUS ingaan,* enter upon eternal rest; *VIR ~,* for ever; **~deur,** continually; **~durend, (-e),** everlasting, incessant, perpetual; for all time; **~durendheid,** perpetuity, perdurability.
e'wigheid, eternity, (the) everlasting, aeon; perpetuity; *die ~ INGAAN,* go to one's last account; *NOOIT in der ~ nie,* never; *TOT in (der) ~,* to all eternity, for ever and ever; *VAN ~ tot ~,* for ever and ever.
ewolu'sie, evolution; **~leer,** theory of evolution.
ewolusionis', (-te), evolutionist; **~me,** evolutionism; **~ties, (-e),** evolutionistic.
ew'wa-trew'wa, (-s), orchid *(Satyrium coriifolium).*
excel'sior, excelsior.
exequa'tur = eksekwatur.
ex-li'bris, ex-libris, book-plate.
Ex'odus, Exodus.
ex offi'cio, ex officio; **~ -lid,** ex officio member.
ex par'te, ex parte.
ex tem'pore, extempore, impromptu.

F

f, (-'e, -'s), f.
fa, (-'s), fa.
faal, (ge-), fail, be unsuccessful; default (payment); not hold good (argument); miscarry (plan), err (judgment); *sy kragte het ge~,* his strength failed him.
faam, reputation, fame, repute; **~rower, ~skender,** defamer.
faas¹, (fase), fesse.
faas², (fase), bevel.
fa'bel, (s) (-s), fable, legend, fiction; myth; *dis maar ~ s,* that is all stories; **~ aar,** fabulist, fibber; **~agtig, (-e),** fabulous; incredible; mythic(al), mythologic(al); **~agtigheid,** fabulosity, fabulousness; **~boek,** book of fables; **~dier,** fabulous animal; **~digter,** fabulist, writer of fables; **~kunde, ~leer,** mythology.
fabriek', (-e), factory; mill; works; (w) (ge-), concoct, fabricate; **~ma'tig, (-e),** manufactured, machine-made; mechanical.
fabrieks': ~ arbeid, factory work; **~arbeider,** factory hand; **~artikel,** manufactured article; **~baas,** factory owner; foreman (in factory); **~bevolking,** factory population; **~botter,** creamery butter; **~fluit,** factory hooter; **~gebied,** manufacturing area; **~gebou,** factory (building); **~geheim,** trade secret; **~goed,** manufactured goods; **~huis,** prefabricated house; **~kaas,** factory cheese; **~hotel,** stationary boiler.
fabriek'skip, factory ship.
fabrieks': ~meisie, factory girl; factory hand (female); **~merk,** trade mark; **~nommer,** factory number; **~nywerheid,** manufacturing industry; **~opsigter,** (factory) foreman, overseer; **~prys,** cost (factory) price.
fabriek'stad, manufacturing town.
fabrieks': ~vel, mill sheet; **~ware,** factory goods; **~werk,** factory work; manufactured goods; machine work; **~werker,** factory hand (worker); mill-hand; **~wese,** manufacturing industry; **~wet,** factory act; **~wyk,** industrial quarter.
fabrikaat', (..kate), fabric; manufacture, make, brand.
fabrikant', (-e), manufacturer.
fabrika'sie, manufacture, manufactured goods, fabrication.
fabriseer', (ge-), manufacture, produce; fabricate, concoct (stories).
fabuleus', (-e), fabulous, incredible.
fae'ces, faeces.
fa'ëton, (-s), phaeton.
fagosiet', (-e), phagocyte.
fagositêr', fagosi'ties, (-e), phagocytic.
fagot', (-te), bassoon; **~tis', (-te),** bassoonist.
fah'foe, fahfoo.
Fah'renheit, Fahrenheit.
faïen'ce, faïence.
fai'konta, as if (it were), quasi; afraid to play further.
faillissement', bankruptcy, insolvency.
fa'kir, (-s), fakir.
fak'kel, (-s), torch, flare, flambeau; **~baan,** flare-path; **~bom,** flare-bomb; **~dans,** torch-dance, **~draer,** torch-bearer, light-bearer; **~houer,** flare-carrier; **~lig,** torchlight; **~loop,** torch-race; **~optog,** torchlight procession; **~sein,** flare signal; **~stok,** cheesa (dynamite-loading) stick; **~tjie, (-s),** small torch.
fak'sie, (-s), faction.
faksi'milee, (-s), facsimile, autotype.
fak'ties, (-e), factual.
faktitief', (..tiewe), factitive.
faktoor', (..tore), agent, factor.
fak'tor, (-e), factor; *ENKELVOUDIGE ~,* prime factor; *in ~ e ontbind,* factorize, **~ Isa'sle,** factorization; **~iseer', (ge-),** factorize; **~ise'ring,** factorizing.
faktory', (-e), factory.
fakto'tum, (-s), factotum, handyman.
faktureer', (ge-), invoice.
faktuur', (..ture), invoice, bill; **~bedrag,** amount of invoice; **~boek,** invoice book; **~klerk,** invoice clerk; **~prys,** invoice price; **~waarde,** invoice value.
fakultatief', (..tiewe), optional, facultative.
fakulteit', (-e), faculty; **~s'vergadering,** faculty meeting.
fa'lanks, (-e), phalanx.
fal'bala, (-s), falbala.
faldisto'rium, (-s, ..storia), faldstool.
fa'lie, (-s), shawl, mantle.
faljeer', (ge-), become insolvent (bankrupt).
faljiet', bankrupt, insolvent; **~ gaan,** go bankrupt, become insolvent; **~verklaring,** adjudication order.
falkoen', (-e), falcon.
falkonet', (-te), falconet.
fal'lies, (-e), phallic.
fallis'me, phallism.
fal'lus, (-se), phallus.
falsa'ris, (-se), forger, falsifier.
falset', falset'to, falsetto.
fal'sitas, falsiteit', (-e), fraud, falsitas.
fameus', (-e), famous; enormous, glorious; notorious.
familiaal', (..liale), (belonging to a) family.
familiaar', (..liare), intimate, familiar; *baie ~ wees*

met iem., be very intimate (take liberties) with someone.
familiariteit', (-e), familiarity, intimacy.
fami'lie, (s) (-s), family, kindred, blood relations, relatives; (b) related; *AANGETROUDE* ~, relations (related) by marriage; ~ *van ADAM se kant af*, very distantly related; *dis IN die* ~, it runs in the family; *so ver* ~ *dat 'n mens dit nie met 'n KLIP kan raakgooi nie*, distantly related; *VER langs* ~, remotely related; ~ *WEES van*, be related to; ~**aangeleenthede**, family affairs; ~**argief**, family archives; ~**band**, family tie; ~**berigte**, births, deaths, marriages column (in newspaper); ~**betrekking**, relationship; relative; ~**bybel**, family Bible; ~**drama**, domestic drama; ~**fees**, family gathering (feast); ~**gek**, (over)fond of one's relations; ~**gelykenis**, family likeness; ~**genootskap**, private company; ~**goed**, family belongings; ~**graf**, family vault; family grave; ~**kring**, family circle, home circle; ~**kwaal**, hereditary malady; *dis 'n* ~ *kwaal*, it runs in the family; ~**lewe**, family life; ~**lid**, member of a family; ~**naam**, family name; patronymic; surname; ~**omstandighede**, family affairs.
familiêr', (-e), familiar, free-and-easy.
fami'lie: ~**raad**, family council; ~**sake**, family matters (affairs); ~**siek** = **familiegek**; ~**skandaal**, family skeleton; skeleton in the cupboard; ~**skap**, kinship, relationship; ~**stam**, (family) stock; ~**stuk**, heirloom; ~**swak**, family failing; ~**trek**, singularity peculiar to a family; family likeness (trait); ~**trots**, family pride; ~**twis**, family quarrel; ~**vas**, (-te), strongly attached to the family; ~**voël**, sociable weaver *(Philetairus socius)*; ~**wapen**, family (coat-of-)arms, escutcheon.
Fanagalo', **Fanakalo'**, Fanakalo, Fanagalo.
fanatiek', **fana'ties**, (-e), fanatic(al), phrenetic.
fana'tikus, (-se, ..tici), fanatic.
fanatis'me, fanaticism.
fandan'go, fandango, (Spanish) dance.
fanerogaam', (..game), phanerogam.
fanfa're, (-s), flourish of trumpets, fanfare; ~**korps**, brassband.
fantas', (-te), fantast, visionary; castle-builder; ~**eer'**, (ge-) imagine, fancy, invent; improvise (music).
fanta'sia, (-s), fantasia (music).
fantasie', (-ë), imagination, phantasy, fancy; fantasia (music); ~**artikel**, fancy article; ~**goed**, fancy articles; ~**kostuum**, fancy dress; ~**loos**, (..lose), unimaginative; ~**naam**, fancy name, book name; ~**pak**, fancy suit (of clothes); ~**stof**, fancy-dress materials; ~**ware**, fancy goods, novelties.
fantas'ma, (-s, -ta), phantasm; hallucination; ~**gorie'**, (-ë), phantasmagoria; ~**go'ries**, (-e), phantasmagoric.
fantastery', (-e), fantasticality, figment.
fantas'ties, (-e), fantastic, bizarre; wild (ideas).
fanto'mig, (-e), phantomlike.
fantoom', (**fantome**), phantom.
fa'rad, (-s), farad.
fara'dies, (-e), faradaic.
faradis'me, faradaism.
Fa'rao, Pharaoh; ~ *se PLAE*, the plagues of Egypt; *tussen* ~ *en die ROOI See*, between the devil and the deep blue sea; ~**'nies**, (-e), pharaonic.
fa'raorot, ichneumon.
fardegalyn', (-e), farthingale.
farineus', (-e), farinaceous, farinose.
faringi'tis, pharyngitis, sore throat.
fa'rinks, (-e), pharynx.
Farise'ër, Pharisee.
farise'ër, (-s), pharisee, hypocrite; concealed stone (in road).
farise'ëragtig, (-e), **farisees'**, (..sese), pharisaic(al), hypocritical.
Fariseïs'me, Pharisaism.
fariseïsme, hypocrisy, pharisaicalness.
farmakologie', pharmacology; ..lo'gies, pharmacologic(al).
farmakoloog', (..loë), pharmacologist.
farmakopee', pharmacopoeia.
farmaseut', (-e), druggist, pharmacist.

farmaseu'ties, (-e), pharmaceutical.
farmasie', pharmacy, pharmaceutics.
fa'ro¹, faro (card-game).
fa'ro², (-'s), fern *(Pellaca calomelanos)*.
farseer', (ge-), stuff; force (meat).
fasa'de, (-s), facade.
fas'cia, (-e), fascia.
fasci'ne, (-s), fascine.
Fascis', (-te), Fascist; ~**me**, Fascism; ~**ties**, (-e), Fascist.
fa'se, (-s), phase, stage.
faseer', (ge-), phase; **fase'ring**, phasing.
fa'sel, (-s), ravel, frayed or loose end.
faset', (-te), facet (of diamond); bezel.
fa'sie, (-s), face, physiognomy, mug, phiz.
fasiel', (-e), facile, easy.
fasiliteit', (-e), facility; ~**e**, amenities.
fassina'sie, fascination.
fassineer', (ge-), fascinate.
fat, (-te), dandy, swell, nut, snob, buck, blood.
fataal', (**fatale**), fatal.
fatalis', (-te), fatalist; ~**me**, fatalism; ~**ties**, (-e), fatalistic.
fataliteit', (-e), fatality.
fa'ta morga'na, fata morgana, mirage.
fatsoen', (-e), shape, form; cut, style (clothes); fashion; manners, good form, etiquette; *HOU jou* ~*!* behave yourself! *sy* ~ *OPHOU*, keep up appearances; *UIT sy* ~, out of shape; *VIR die* ~, for form's sake; ~**eer'**, (ge-), shape, mould, pattern, fashion; block (hat); ~**eer'der**, (-s), shaper; ~**lik**, (-e), decent, proper, respectable, parliamentary (language); behaved, presentable, decorous; gentlemanly; genteel; ~**likheid**, decency, propriety; decorum; gentility; ~**s'halwe**, for decency's sake.
fat'terig, (-e), dandified, dandyish, foppish, snobbish; ~**heid**, dandyism, foppishness.
fa'tum, (**fata**), fate.
faun, (-e), faun.
fau'na, fauna.
fauteuil', (-s), fauteuil, easy chair, arm-chair.
faveur': *ten* ~ *e van*, in favour of.
favoriet', (-e), favourite.
favoritis'me, favouritism.
febriel', (-e), febrile.
Fe'bruarie, February.
federaal', (..rale), federal.
federalis', (-te) federalist; ~**me**, federalism.
federa'sie, (-s), federation.
federatief', (..tiewe), federative.
federeer', (ge-), federate.
fee, (**feë**), fairy; peri; ~**agtig**, (-e), fairy-like, elfin.
feeks, (-e), vixen, virago, shrew, jade, beldam(e), catamaran, gipsy, gimalkin, harridan, hell-cat; ~**ig**, (-e), shrewish.
feërie', (-ë), fairyland; fairytale.
feëriek', (-e), fairy-like, elfin.
fe'ërig, (-e), fairy-like.
fe'ëryk, fairyland.
fees, (-te), feast, festival, fête, gala; function; beanfeast; banquet; spread; *DIS 'n* ~, it is a great occasion (pleasure); *'n* ~ *vir die OË*, feast (treat) for the eyes; *'n* ~ *VIER*, celebrate a feast; ~**aand**, eve of a festival; festive evening; ~**artikel**, novelty; ~**dag**, festival, holiday, festive day, day of rejoicing; ~**dis**, special (festive) dish; ~**dos**, festive (festal) attire; ~**dronk**, toast; ~**drukte**, festivities; ~**ganger**, one who attends a festival; ~**gelag**, (..lae), revel; symposium; ~**genoot**, (..note), guest; ~**gesang**, festive song; ~**gety**, festive season; ~**gewaad**, festive attire, festal dress; gala costume; ~**huis**, festive building; ~**jaar**, festive year; ~**klere**, festive garments; ~**kommissie**, fête (celebration) committee; ~**lied**, festive song; ~**maal**, ~**maaltyd**, banquet; dinner; festive spread; ~**mars**, festive march; ~**nommer**, special issue (paper); ~**offer**, festive sacrifice; ~**program**, programme of the festivities; ~**rede**, speech of the day; inaugural speech; ~**redenaar**, speaker of the day; ~**saal**, festive hall; ~**seël**, jubilee stamp; ~**stemming**, festive mood; ~**telik**, (-e), festive, festal; convivial; ~*telik onthaal*, entertain lavishly; ~**telik**=

heid, festivity, fiesta, jollity, conviviality; shindig; ~**terrein,** celebration site; ~**tyd,** festive season; ~**uitgawe,** jubilee issue; ~**vier, (-ge-),** feast, celebrate, junket, jollify, make cheer, banquet; ~**vierder, (-s),** merry-maker, reveller; ~**viering,** festival, feast, carnival; ~**vreugde,** festive mirth, merrymaking, revelry, festivity; ~**week,** festive week.
fee'tjie, (-s), (small) fairy.
feil¹, (s) (-e), fault, error; (w) **(ge-),** go wrong, err.
feil², (s) mop, polishing cloth; (w) **(ge-),** mop, scrub.
feil: ~**baar, (..bare),** fallible; ~**baarheid,** fallibility; ~**loos, (..lose),** faultless; ~**loosheid,** faultlessness.
feit, (-e), fact; *'n* ~ *ERKEN,* admit a fact; *deur* ~ *e GESTAAF,* supported by facts; *IN* ~ *e,* in fact, really; *'n VOLDONGE* ~, an accomplished fact.
fei'te: ~**dwaling,** error of facts; ~**film,** documentary film; ~**fout,** error of fact; ~**kennis,** knowledge of facts; ~**materiaal,** body of facts.
feit'lik, (b) (-e), real, actual, in fact, factual; (bw) actually, indeed, truly, virtually, really, practically; ~**heid, (..hede),** reality, actuality.
fekaal', (fekale), faecal.
feka'lieë, night-soil, faeces.
fel, (-le), violent, fierce, sharp, intense, grim, severe (cold); glaring (colour, light); ~**heid,** fierceness, violence, severity; glare.
felisita'sie, (-s), congratulation; ~**brief,** letter of congratulation.
felisiteer', (ge-), congratulate.
fel'lah, (-s), fellah.
feloek', (-e), felucca.
felonie', (-ë), felony.
fels, (s) (-e), welt; (w) **(ge-),** welt.
felsiet', felsite.
fels'naat, welted joint.
fe'mel, (ge-), cant; snivel; ~**aar, (-s),** hypocrite, pharisee; precisian; ~**(a)ry',** cant, hypocrisy.
feminis', (-te), feminist; ~**me,** feminism; ~**ties, (-e),** feminist(ic).
fenasetien', fenaseti'ne, phenacetin.
fe'negriek, fenugreek.
Feni'cië, Phoenicia; ~**r, (-s),** Phoenician.
Feni'cies, (-e), Phoenician.
feniel', phenyl.
fe'niks, phoenix.
fe'nokris, phenocryst.
fe'nol, phenol (carbolic acid).
fenologie', phenology.
fenomeen', (..mene), phenomenon.
fenomenaal', (..nale), phenomenal.
fenomenologie', phenomenology.
fenoti'pe, phenotype.
feodaal', (feodale), feudal.
feodaliseer', (ge-), feudalize.
feodalis'me, feudalism.
ferm, (-e), firm, solid, strong; energetic.
ferment', ferment.
fermenta'sie, fermentation.
fermentatief', (..tiewe), fermentative.
fermenteer', (ge-), ferment.
ferm'heid, firmness, solidity; vigour.
fer'plie, (geselst.), fair play; really, straight (out); honestly; *sy is* ~ *MOOI,* she is really pretty; *dis NIE* ~ *nie,* that is not fair play.
ferraat', (ferrate), ferrate.
Ferrei'ra: *vat jou goed en trek* ~*!,* take your things and go!
ferromagne'ties, (-e), ferromagnetic.
ferromangaan', ferromanganese.
ferrotipie', ferrotype.
ferrugineus', (-e), ferruginous.
fertiel', (-), fertile.
fertiliseer', (ge-), fertilize.
fertiliteit', fertility; ~**smiddel,** fertility drug.
ferweel', corduroy (whipcord); ~**broek,** corduroy (whipcord) trousers; ~**tjie, (-s),** sparaxis.
fes, (-se), fez, tarboosh.
festiwiteit', (-e), festivity.
festoen', (-e), festoon; ~**eer', (ge-),** festoon; scallop (collar).
feston', (-ne), (floral) border; festoon; ~**neer',** festoon.

festyn', (-e), feast, banquet.
fetaal', (fetale), f(o)etal.
fête, (-s), fête.
fêteer', (ge-), fête, make much of.
fe'tisj, (-e), fetish; ~**dienaar,** fetish worshipper; ~**is', (-te),** fetisher; ~**is'me,** fetishism; ~**is'ties,** fetishistic.
fe'tus, (-se), f(o)etus.
feudaal', feudale = **feodaal.**
feuilleton', (-s), serial (story); ~**nis', (-te),** ~**skrywer,** serial writer, serialist.
fiancé', (-s), fiancé; **fiancée', (-s),** fiancée.
fias'ko, (-'s), fiasco, wash-out, failure; *op 'n groot* ~ *uitloop,* result in a complete failure.
fi'at, fiat.
fibreus', (-e), fibrous.
fibrien', fibrin(e).
fibril', (-le), fibril.
fibri'ne = **fibrien.**
fibroïen', fibroï'ne, fibroine.
fibroom', (fibrome), fibroma.
fibrosi'tis, fibrositis.
fi'bula, (-e), fibula.
fichu, (-'s), fichu.
fideel', (fidele), jolly, jovial, merry.
fi'deicommis'sum = **fideïkommis.**
fideïkommis', fideicommissum; *iem.* ~ *MAAK,* cut someone off with a shilling; *dis* ~ *MET jou,* it's all over with you.
Fidjiaan', (..jiane), Fiji(an); ~**s',** Fijian (language); ~**s', (-e),** Fijian.
Fi'dji-eilande, Fiji Islands.
fidu'sie, confidence, reliance, trust.
fidusiêr', (-e), fiduciary.
f'ie, (-s), small f.
fie'del, (s) (-s), fiddle, violin; (w) **(ge-),** fiddle, play the violin.
fie'lafooi, ring-finger.
fielt, (s) (-e), rascal, scoundrel, rogue, villain; (w) **(ge-),** copy, cheat, crib; ~**agtig, (-e),** villainous; ~**estreek,** roguery, villainy, rascality.
fie'mies, capriciousness, freakishness, whims; nonsense; affectation; caprice; *vol* ~ *wees,* be full of whims and fancies; ~**rig, (-e),** capricious.
fier, (-e), proud, high-spirited, noble-minded, gallant; lofty (carriage); ~**heid,** pride, dignity, élan.
fieterja'sies, superfluous ornaments, flourishes; fads.
fiets, (s) (-e), bicycle; (w) **(ge-),** cycle, pedal; ~**afdak,** bicycle shed; ~**baan,** cycle lane; cycle track; ~**band,** cycle tyre; ~**er, (-s),** cyclist; ~**klokkie,** bicycle bell; ~**pad,** cycle path; ~**pomp,** bicycle pump, ~**rak,** bicycle rack; ~**ry,** cycling; ~**ryer,** cyclist; ~**tog,** cycle tour; ~**wedren,** cycling race; ~**winkel,** cycle-shop.
figurant', (-e), cipher, mute, puppet, stooge, utility man; extra (in theatre).
figura'sie, figuration.
figuratief', (..tiewe), figurative, metaphorical.
figureer', (ge-), figure, pose.
figuur', (figure), shape, figure; character (drama); diagram (drawing); *jou* ~ *probeer RED,* try to save one's face; *'n DROEWIGE* ~ *slaan,* cut a sorry figure; *iem. 'n MAL* ~ *laat maak,* make someone look silly; ~**dans,** figure-dance; ~**lik, (-e),** figurative(ly); metaphoric(ally); ~**saag,** fret(-saw), scroll-saw, compass-saw, coping-saw; jigsaw; ~**werk,** scrollwork, fretwork.
fiks, (-e), quick, strong; thorough; buxom, fit, robust, healthy; dapper; *die een dag* ~, *die ander dag niks,* wilful waste makes woeful want.
fiksa'sie, (-s), fixation.
fiksatief', (..tiewe), fixative.
fikseer', (ge-), fix (camera film); stare at; ~**bad,** fixing-bath; ~**middel,** fixative; ~**sout,** fixing-salts (solution).
fikse'ring, fixing.
fiks'heid, robustness, push, go; fitness.
fik'sie, fiction; untruth.
fiktief', (..tiewe), fictitious, imaginary.
filakterie', (-ë), phylactery.
filament', (-e), filament; ~**agtig, (-e),** filamentous.
filantroop', (..trope), philanthropist, humanitarian.

filantropie 154 **flank**

filantropie', philanthropy
filantro'pies, (-e), philanthropic, humanitarian.
filatelie', philately, stamp collecting.
filate'lies, (-e), filatelis'ties, (-e), philatelic.
filatelis', (-te), philatelist, stamp collector.
filatuur', (..ture), filature.
fileer', (ge-), fillet (meat); twist (silk) into threads, throw.
file'ring, throwing (of silk); filleting.
filet'¹, (-te), fillet; undercut.
filet'², filet; ~ **kant**, filet lace; ~ **net**, filet net.
filet'skyf, fillet steak.
filharmo'nies, (-e), philharmonic.
filhelleen', (..lene), philhellene.
filiaal', (s) (filiale), branch (office); (b) **(filiale)**, filial; ~ **bank**, branch bank; ~ **kantoor**, branch office; ~ **maatskappy**, subsidiary company; ~ **winkel**, chain store.
filibus'ter, (-s), filibuster.
filigraan'(werk), filigree (work).
Filippen'se, Philippians.
filippien', philippine (philippina); almond or other nut with double kernel.
filip'pika, (-s), philippic.
filippyn' = **filippien**.
Filippy'ner, (-s), Filipino.
Filippyns', (-e), Philippine; ~ *e Eilande*, Philippine Islands.
filis'ter, (-s), philistine; townee; ~ **agtig, (-e)**, philis= tine; ~ **y**, philistinism.
Filistyn', (-e), Philistine; ~ **s', (-e)**, Philistine.
fillogene'ties, (-e), phyllogenetic.
fillok'sera, phylloxera.
film, (s) (-s), film screen; (w) (ge-), screen; film; ~ **ak= teur**, film (screen) actor; ~ **aktrise**, film (screen) ac= tress; ~ **drama**, picture play; ~ **houer**, film cage; ~ **ies, (-e)**, filmic, filmish, belonging to (character= istic of) a film; ~ **kamera**, film camera; ~ **keuring**, film censorship; ~ **klem**, film clip; ~ **operateur**, film operator, cinematographer; ~ **oteek', (..teke)**, film library; ~ **pak**, film pack; ~ **pie, (-s)**, filmlet; ~ **projektor**, film projector; ~ **rol**, cartridge; ~ **ster**, film (screen) star; ~ **uitreiking**, film release.
filogene'se, phylogenesis, phylogeny.
filogene'ties, (-e), phylogenetic.
filogenie' = **filogenese**.
filologie', philology.
filolo'gies, (-e), philologic.
filoloog', (..loë), philologist.
filomeel', (..mele), nightingale (Philomel).
filosofeer', (ge-), philosophize.
filosofie', philosophy.
filoso'fies, (-e), philosophic(al).
filosoof', (..sowe), philosopher.
fil'ter, (-s), filter, percolator; ~ **dop**, filter cap; ~ **ele= ment**, filter element; ~ **haar**, filter hair; ~ **pan**, filter tray; ~ **pit**, filter cartridge; ~ **romp**, filter body.
filtraat', (filtrate), filtrate.
filtra'sie, filtration; percolation.
filtreer', (ge-), filter, filtrate; percolate; ~ **der, (-s)**, fil= ter; ~ **kan**, percolator; ~ **masjien**, filtering ma= chine; percolator; ~ **papier**, filter(ing) paper; ~ **toestel**, filtering apparatus.
filtre'ring, filtration, filtering.
fi'lum, (-s, fila), phylum.
Fin¹, (-ne), Finn.
fin², (-ne), bladderworm.
finaal', (finale), final, total; *finale BALANSERING*, final balance (wheels); *finale UITVERKOPING*, winding-up sale.
fina'le, (-s), finale; final (match).
finalis', (-te), finalist.
finaliteit', finality.
finansieel', (..siële), financial, pecuniary, monetary; ~ **siële bestuurder**, financial manager; *finansiële KOMITEE*, finance committee; ~ *ONAFHANK= LIK*, of independent means.
finansieer', finansier', (w) (ge-), finance.
finansier', (s) (-s), financier, banker.
finansie'ring, finansië'ring, financing; ~ **smaatskap= py**, finance company.

finan'sies, finance; *Departement van F~*, Depart= ment of Finance.
finan'siewese, finance(s).
fineer', (ge-), veneer; refine (metals); ~ **hout**, veneer; decorative wood; ~ **stel**, veneer; ~ **werk**, veneer= ing.
fines'se, (-s), finesse, nicety, finer points; subtleties.
finesseer', (ge-), finesse (cards).
fingeer', (ge-), feign, simulate, pretend, sham, invent.
Fin'go, (-'s), Fingo.
Fin'land, Finland; ~ **er, (-s)**, Finn.
Fins, (-e), Finnic, Finnish, Ugrian, Ugric.
fiool', (fiole), phial; *die fiole van toorn*, the vials of wrath.
fir'ma, (-s), firm, house (of business); ~ **blad**, house journal.
firmament', firmament, sky; ~ **aal', (..tale)**, firma= mental.
fir'manaam, business name; style (title) of firm.
firmant', (-e), partner of a firm.
Fis, F sharp (music).
fisant', (-e), pheasant; francolin; ~ **ehok**, pheasantry; ~ **eier**, pheasant egg; ~ **haan**, cock pheasant; ~ **hen**, hen pheasant; ~ **jag**, pheasant hunt; ~ **nes**, pheasant's nest; ~ **veer**, pheasant's feather.
fisia'ter, (-s), naturopathist; physiatrician.
fisiatrie', physiatrics, naturopathy.
fisiek', (s) physique; (b) **(-e)**, physical; *'n ~ e onmoont= likheid*, a physical impossibility.
fi'sies, (-e), physical; ~ *e aardrykskunde*, physical ge= ography.
fi'sies-chemies, physico-chemical.
fi'sika, physics.
fi'sikus, (-se, fisici), physicist.
fisiogenie', physiogeny.
fisiografie', physiography.
fisiogra'fies, (-e), physiographic(al).
fisiologie', physiology.
fisiolo'gies, (-e), physiological.
fisioloog', (..loë), physiologist.
fisionomie', physiognomy.
fisiono'mies, (-e), physiognomical.
fisioterapeut', physiotherapist; ~ **ies, (-e)**, physio= therapeutic(al).
fisioterapie', physiotherapy.
fiskaal', (s) (..kale, -s), butcher-bird; water-superin= tendent; (b) **(..kale)**, fiscal.
fis'kus, treasury, exchequer, revenue department.
fis'tel, (-s), fistula (channel for pus); ~ **agtig, (-e)**, fistulous.
fitogene'se, phytogeny.
fitografie', phytography.
fitosanitêr', (-e), phytosanitary.
fitotok'sies, (-e), phytotoxic.
fjord, (-s, -e), fiord (fjord).
flad'der, (ge-), flutter, flit, flap, hover; ~ **ing**, hover= ing.
flagel'lum, (-s), flagellum.
flageolet', (-te), flageolet (musical instrument).
flagrant', (-e), flagrant, glaring.
flair, flair, selective instinct for good quality.
flambojant', (-e), (s) flamboyant *(Poinciana regia)*; (b) flamboyant.
flambou', (-e), torch.
Flamingant', (-e), Flamingant, fighter for the rights of the Flemish.
flamink', (-e), flamingo.
flaneer', (ge-), stroll, laze about, lounge, saunter.
flanel', flannel; ~ **broek**, flannel trousers, flannels.
flanelet', flannelette.
flaneur', (-s), idler, lounger.
flank, (-e), flank, side; ~ **aanval**, flank attack; ~ **bat= tery**, flank battery; ~ **beveiliging**, flank protection; ~ **beweging**, flank movement; ~ **borswering**, flank= ing parapet; ~ **dekking**, flank covering, flankers.
flankeer', (ge-), flank; saunter about; stroll; flirt; *met die nooiens ~*, flirt with the girls; ~ **dery**, flirting, strolling.
flank: ~ **grens**, flanking boundary; ~ **hoede**, flank guard; ~ **mars**, flank march; ~ **patrollie**, flanking patrol; ~ **regiment**; flank regiment; ~ **seksie**, flank section; ~ **verdediging**, flank defence; ~ **versterker**,

flanker; ~**versterking,** flanker; reinforcement of the flank; ~**vuur,** flank fire.
flans, (ge-), patch up, knock together; *vgl.* **saamflans.**
flap, (s) (-pe), window-bird, sakabula *(Diatropura progne)*; flag, iris (flower); flap; (w) **(ge-),** flap; ~**dosie,** flapjack; ~**-flap'pie, (-s),** Cape wren, warbler *(Prinia maculosa)*; ~**hoed,** slouch-hat; ~**kan,** tankard, flagon; ~**ore,** drooping ears, lop-ears.
flap'per, (ge-), flicker; flap; ~**tjie (-s),** crumpet.
flaps! flops!
flap'teks, (-te), blurb.
flapuit', (-e), chatterbox, blabber; enfant terrible.
flard, (-e), rag, tatter; *aan* ~*e skeur,* tear to pieces.
fla'ter, (-s), blunder, mistake, gaffe; *'n* ~ *BEGAAN,* slip up; drop a brick; *GROOT* ~, howler; great blunder; ~**water,** (geselst.), typing fluid, type-removing fluid.
flatteer', (ge-), flatter.
flatte'rend, (-e), flattering.
flavi'ne, flavin.
fleem, (ge-), coax, cajole.
fleg'ma, phlegm; apathy; stolidity; ~**'ties, (-e),** phlegmatic, stolid.
fleim, slime, mucus, phlegm.
flek'sie, flection, flexion; ~**loos, (..lose),** without inflection (inflexion), uninflected.
flekteer', (ge-), inflect.
fle'mer, (-s), fawner, cajoler, coaxer.
flen'nie, flannel; ~**agtig, (-e),** flannely; ~**bord,** flannel board; ~**onderklere,** flannel underwear; ~**verband,** flannel bandage.
flens, (s) (-e), flange, bead (of tyre); (w) **(ge-),** flange; ~**band,** clincher tyre; ~**hiel,** bead-heel.
flen'sie, (s), thin pancake.
flens: ~**juk,** flange yoke; ~**koppeling,** flange coupling; ~**masjien,** flanging press; ~**moer,** flange nut; ~**pakking,** gasket; ~**pyp,** flange pipe; ~**sleutel,** flange wrench; ~**verbinding,** flange union.
flen'ter¹, (w) (ge-), stroll; gad about.
flen'ter², (s) (-s), rag, small piece; dud; *AAN* ~*s,* in tatters; *g'n* ~ *OMGEE nie,* not to care a straw (rap); ~**baadjie,** ragged coat; ~**dorper,** slumdweller; ~**fyn,** in small bits; ~**hoed,** ragged hat; ~**ig, (-e),** ragged, torn, tattered; ~**igheid,** raggedness; ~**kind,** ~**kous,** ragamuffin; ~**papiertjie,** scrap of paper; ~**s,** flinders; in rags (tatters), in smithereens; *iets aan* ~*s SLAAN,* smash something up; ~**tjie,** morsel, small piece; fragment; *'n* ~*tjie vleis,* a small piece of meat.
fler'rie, (s) (-s), flirt; gadabout (girl), hussy; (w) **(ge-),** flirt; gad about.
flerts, (-e), splash; loose flap (of dress).
fles, (-se), flask, bottle, jar; *Leidse* ~, ~**sie, (-s),** small flask (bottle), phial; *'n klein* ~*sie medisyne,* a small bottle of medicine.
flets, (-e), faded, pale, dim (eyes); washed-out (person); ~**heid,** fadedness, paleness, wishy-washiness.
flet'ter, (ge-), flutter.
Flett'nerskip, rotor.
fleur, prime, bloom; hey-day; *die* ~ *is daarvan AF,* the bloom is off; *IN die* ~ *van sy lewe,* in the prime of his life; *OP sy* ~ *wees,* be in the prime of life; ~**ig, (-e),** sprightly, lively, happy; ~**igheid,** prime, brightness, bloom.
fliek, (s) (-e), bio, movies, bioscope; (w) **(ge-),** go to a bioscope; ~**ganger,** visitor to a bioscope; ~**vlooi,** movie fan.
flik'flooi, (ge-), coax, fawn, flatter, cozen, wheedle; blarney, cajole; ~**er, (-s),** flatterer, wheedler, backscratcher, cajoler; ~**erig, (-e),** cajoling, wheedling; ~**ery,** coaxing, flattery, blarney, fawning, adulation.
flik'ker, (s) (-s), atom, grain (of truth); leap, prank, caper; ~*s GOOI,* cut capers; show off; *geen* ~ *HOOP nie,* no sign of hope; ~*s UITHAAL by 'n nooi,* dance attendance on a girl; (w) **(ge-),** flicker, glitter, twinkle, flash, flare, glint; glance, glare; scintillate; prank, bicker; flutter (candle); gleam, glimmer; coruscate; ~**end, (-e),** glary, sparkling, coruscant, flaring, glimmering; glittering; ~**ing, (-e, -s),** flittering, gleam, glare, glimmer, glimmering; glance, coruscation; blink; flickering, twinkling (of star); ~**lamp,** flickering lamp; ~**lig,** flickering light, flash(ing) light; flare.
flink, (b) (-e), robust, stalwart, energetic, thorough, brisk, spirited, hearty, game, gallant, vigorous; generous, considerable (amount); buxom (bodybuild); fine (player); (bw) thoroughly, soundly, vigorously, briskly, firmly; *iem.* ~ *AFRANSEL,* give someone a sound thrashing; ~ *EET,* eat heartily; *iem.* ~ *die WAARHEID vertel,* give someone a piece of one's mind; ~**gebou, (-de),** well-built, strong, robust; ~**heid,** thoroughness, élan, dash, vigour, gallantry, hardiness, lustiness, soundness; ~**weg,** without mincing matters; fluently; without hesitation.
flint, flint; ~**geweer,** flint-lock (gun).
flirt, (s) (-e, -s), flirt, philanderer; (w) **(ge-),** flirt; ~**a'sie, (-s),** flirtation; ~**ery,** flirting.
flits, (s) (-e), (lightning) flash; torch: blink; glint; (w) **(ge-),** flash; ~**apparaat,** flash gun; ~**berig,** news flash; ~**kaart,** flashcard; ~**lamp,** flasher, flashlamp; ~**lig,** flash-light, torch; ~**punt,** flash point (oil); ~**seiner,** flasher (signaller).
flod'der, (s) mud; slush, sludge; grout; *ligte* ~ *van sement,* a light coating of (unmixed) cement; (w) **(ge-),** splash in (through); grout; flush; ~**broek,** wide trousers, Oxford bags; ~**ig, (-e),** baggy (clothes); ~**kous,** slut; dowdy; slattern(ly woman); ~**mus,** mob-cap; ~**myn,** gunpowder mine.
floëem, phloem.
floep, (ge-), cloop.
floers, crêpe; veil; mist (before eyes); ~**kleed,** crêpe cloth.
flogis'ties, (-e), phlogistic.
flogis'ton, phlogiston.
flogoskoop', (..skope), phlogoscope.
flokkula'sie, (-s), flocculation.
flokkuleer', (ge-), flocculate; *..le'ring,* flocculation.
floks, (-e), flok'sie, (-s), phlox (flower).
flon'ker, (ge-), sparkle; twinkle; ~**ing,** sparkling; ~**lig,** sparkling light, ~**ster,** twinkling star.
flo'ra, flora.
floreer', (ge-), flourish, thrive, boom, prosper.
Floren'ce, Florence.
Florentyns', (-e), Florentine.
flore'rend, (-e), flourishing, thriving.
floret'¹, (-te), foil.
floret'², floret silk; ~**band,** ferret; ~**sy,** floret silk.
florissant', (-e), flourishing, prosperous.
floryn', (-e), florin.
flota'sie, floatation.
floteer', (ge-), float (company).
flote'ring, floatation (of company).
flotta'sie, (-s), floatation (miner.).
flotteer', (ge-), float (miner.).
flottiel'je, (-s), flotilla.
flou, (-e), faint, qualmish; weak; unconscious, insensible; dead-tired, jaded; insipid (food); dim (recollection, light); vapid (conversation), pointless, poor (joke); spent (bullet); flat, easy (market); pale; *geen* ~ *BENUL hê nie,* not have the vaguest idea; ~ *KOFFIE,* weak coffee; *die MARK is* ~, the market is dull; *'n PERD* ~ *jaag,* override a horse; ~ *VAL (word),* have a fainting fit; ~**erig, (-e),** rather weak, dim, etc.
flouhar'tig, (-e), faint-hearted; ~**heid,** fainthearted ness.
flou'heid, faintness, insipidity, dimness, deadness.
flouiteit', (-e), foolish talk, insipid (poor) joke.
flou'kop, broken-winded horse.
flous, (ge-), cheat, deceive, trick, hoodwink, diddle; dupe; feint (football); ~**ery,** cheating; ~**vry, (-e),** foolproof.
flou'te, (-s), swoon, faint, insensibility; ~**-aanval,** fainting fit, blackout.
flou'tjies, feeble, poor; faintly, poorly.
flou'vallery, fainting.
fluï'dum, (-s), effluvium.
fluim, *see* **fleim.**
fluis'ter, (ge-), whisper; breathe; hiss; ~**aar, (-s),** whisperer; hisser; ~**end, (-e),** in a (half-)whisper; under one's breath; susurrant; ~**gewelf,** whispering gallery; ~**ing,** whisper(ing); susurration;

~stem, ~toon, whisper(ing voice), undertone; ~veldtog, whispering campaign.
fluit, (s) (-e), flute; quill (musical); whistle; hooter; chanter; *goue ~ my storie is uit*, that is the end of my story; (w) (ge-), whistle; play on the flute; whiz, zip; inoculate; wheeze; make water, piddle; *iem. LAAT ~*, let someone whistle for something; *NA iets ~*, have to whistle for something; *as ek jou NODIG het, sal ek vir jou ~*, I'll whistle when I need you; ~blaser, flute-player, flautist; fifer; ~boei, whistle buoy; ~bord, whistle-board; ~eend, widgeon; ~er, (-s), whistler; ~ery, whistling; ~-fluit, easily; *~-fluit deur 'n eksamen kom*, pass an examination easily (with flying colours); ~glas, flute, flute-(glass); ~is', (-te), flute-player; ~jie, (-s), mouth-organ; whistle; *~tjie blaas*, act as referee, umpire; ~jiesriet, common reed; ~ketel, whistling kettle; ~maker, flute-maker; ~plek, place for urinating; urinal; ~skip, flute, flyboat; ~speler, flutist, flute-player, flautist; piper.
fluks, ((-e); -er, -ste), quick, hard-working, rapid; diligent; spry, go-ahead; *~ LEER*, learn well, study diligently; *~ VOORUITGAAN*, make rapid progress; ~heid, diligence, industry, go (colloq.).
fluktua'sie, (-s), fluctuation (of the market).
fluktueer', (ge-), fluctuate.
flu'oor, fluorine.
flu'oor: ~lamp, fluorescent lamp; ~lig, fluorescent light; ~waterstof, hydrofluoric acid; ~waterstofsuur, hydrofluoric acid.
fluoresseer', (ge-), fluoresce.
fluoressen'sie, fluorescence.
flus, flus'sies, just, directly, just now; in a moment; a moment ago.
fluviaal', (..viale), fluvial.
flu'viometer, fluviome'ter, (-s), fluviometer.
fluweel', velvet, plush; ~agtig, (-e), velvety; ~blom, amaranth(h); *Sparaxis, Nemesia barbata*; ~boontjie, velvet bean; ~gogga, mite *(Trombidium tinctorum)*; ~koord, chenille; ~tjie, (-s) = ferweeltjie.
fluwe'lig, (-e), velvety.
fnuik, (ge-), clip the wings, break, cripple; frustrate.
fobie', (-ë), phobia.
foedraal', (foedrale), case, cover, sheath.
foe'fie, (-s), dodge, trick; hanky-panky; gimmick.
foei! pish, pshaw, pooh; *~ tog!* for shame! poor thing! fie!
foei'lelik, very ugly.
foe'lie, (s) mace (of the nutmeg); (tin)foil; (w) (ge-), foil; silver; foliate; ~laag, foil; ~sel, tin foil.
foe'sel, fusel (oil).
foe'ter, (ge-) bother, pester; tamper; trouble; hurt; strike; rush, tumble; rail at; *~ HOM!* hit him! *MOENIE daarmee ~ nie*, don't tamper with that; *TEEN iem. ~*, rail at someone; *WAT ~ jy so?* why are you so troublesome? ~y, botheration.
fok, (s) (-ke), foresail; jib.
fokaal', (fokale), focal.
fok'mas, (-te), foremast.
fok'seil, foresail; jibsail.
fok'sia, (-s), fuchsia.
fok'stag, (-ge, -stae), forestay.
Foks'terriër, (-s), fox terrier.
fo'kus, (-se), focus; ~seer', (ge-), focus.
fokusse'ring, focussing.
foliant', (-e), folio (volume).
folia'sie, foliation.
folieer', (ge-), foliate (leaves of book), page.
folië'ring, foliation.
fo'lio, (-'s), folio; ~formaat, folio size; ~papier, foolscap paper; ~uitgawe, folio edition; ~vel, foolscap sheet.
folk'lore, folklore.
folkloris', (-te), student of (authority on) folklore; folklorist.
folkloris'ties, (-e), according to folklore, folkloristic.
fol'likel, (-s), follicle.
follikulêr', (-e), follicular.
fol'ter, (ge-), torture, torment, rack, agonize, harrow; excruciate; put on the rack; ~aar, (-s), torturer, tormentor; ~bank, rack; ~end, (-e), excruciating, harrowing; splitting (headache); ~ing, torture; anguish, pang; excruciation; ~kamer, torture room; ~paal, stake; ~tuig, instrument of torture.
fomenta'sie, fomentation.
fomenteer', (ge-), foment.
fonda'sie, (-s), foundation.
fon, (-e), phon (physics).
fondament', (-e), foundation; basis; fundament, anus, rectum, bottom; ~balk, ground beam; ~klip, bed stone; ~steen, foundation stone.
fondant', (-e, -s), fondant.
fondeer', (ge-), found, lay the foundation.
fonde'ring, (-e, -s), foundation, grounding.
fonds, (-e), fund, foundation; money, means; *nie oor die nodige ~ e BESKIK nie*, not have the necessary funds available; *'n LAS teen 'n ~*, a charge upon a fund; ~artikels, publisher's own editions; ~katalogus, ~lys, publisher's trade list (catalogue).
foneem', (foneme), phoneme.
fonetiek', phonetics.
fone'ties, (-e), phonetic,
fone'tikus, (..tici, -se), phonetician.
fo'nies, (-e), phonic.
fonograaf', (..grawe), phonograph.
fonografie', phonography.
fonogra'fies, (-e), phonographic(al).
fonogram', (-me), phonogram.
fonologie', phonology.
fonolo'gies, (-e), phonologic(al).
fonoloog', (..loë), phonologist.
fo'nometer, fonome'ter, (-s), phonometer.
fonoskoop', (..skope), phonoscope.
fontanel', (-le), fontanel(le).
fontein', (-e), fountain, spring; ~tjie, (-s), little fountain; *'n mens moet nooit sê: ~ tjie ek sal nooit weer van jou drink nie*, never is a long day; don't say I'll never drink of this water how dirty so ever it be; ~water, spring water;
fooi, (s) (-e), gratuity, tip; perquisite; douceur; (w) (ge-), tip; ~stelsel, tipping system; ~tjie, (-s), tip.
foon¹, (s) (-s) = fon.
foon², (s) (fone), phone; ~boek, telephone directory; ~flerrie, ~snol, call-girl.
fop, (ge-), hoax, cheat, fool, outwit, bamboozle, pigeon, deceive, dodge, gull, hoodwink, chicane, diddle; ~medisyne, placebo; ~afpenning, dummy-pegging; ~myn, booby trap; ~per, (-s), cheat, hoaxer; faker.
fop'pertjie, (-s), baby's dummy; soother, comforter; falsie.
fop'pery, hoax(ing), fooling, cheating, mystification; doing (someone) down, chicanery, hoodwinking, deception.
fop: ~room, mock cream; ~sak, mock pocket; ~sloop, sham, pillow sham; ~speen = foppertjie.
forel', (-le), trout; *rooi ~*, char; ~kwekery, trout farm, trout hatchery; ~skimmel, flea-bitten horse; ~vangs, trout fishing.
foren'sies, (-e), forensic.
for'ma, form; *IN ~ pauperis*, in forma pauperis (pauper's suit at law); *PRO ~*, for form's sake.
formaat', (..mate), size, shape; format; ~boek, dummy.
formaldehi'de, formaldehied', formaldehyde.
formalin', formalin.
formalis', (-te), formalist; ~me, formalism; ~ties, (-e), formalistic.
formaliteit', (-e), formality, matter of form.
forma'liter, formally.
formans', (..mantia), affix, prefix, suffix.
forma'sie, (-s), formation; configuration; measure (geol.).
formatief', (..tiewe), formative.
formeel'¹, (s) (..mele), centre.
formeel'², (b) (..mele), formal; ..*mele reg*, adjective law.
formeer', (ge-), form, shape, mould, create; ~der, (-s), creator, moulder.
forme'ring, forming, moulding, shaping.
formida'bel, (-e), formidable.
Formosaan', (s) (..sane), Formosan; -s', (b) (-e), Formosan.
formu'le, (-s), formula.

formuleer', (ge-), formulate.
formule'ring, formulation; framing, drawing up, drafting.
formulier', (-e), formulary; form; *'n ~ invul*, fill in a form; **~gebed**, collect (prayer).
fornuis', (-e), cooking-range, furnace.
fo'rometer, forome'ter, (-s), phorometer.
fors, ((-e;) -er, -ste), robust, strong, powerful, burly, masculine; vigorous (style).
forseer', (ge-), force, press, compel; *sake ~*, force the issue; **..se'ring**, forcing.
fors: **~gebou**, (-de), strongly built; **~heid**, robustness, strength, vigour.
fort, (-e), fortress, fort; *die ~ hou*, hold the fort; **~ifika'sie**, (-s), fortification; **~ifiseer'**, (ge-), fortify.
fortis'simo, fortissimo.
fortuin', (-e), luck, fortune; wealth; pile (of money); **~hou**, hole-in-one (golf); **~lik**, (-e), lucky; fortunate; **~soeker**, adventurer; fortune-hunter; chevalier; *vreemde ~soekers*, foreign adventurers; **~soekster**, (-s), adventuress, gold-digger.
fo'rum, (-s, fora), forum.
fosfaat', (..fate), phosphate; **~kunsmis**, phosphatic fertilizer.
fos'for, phosphorus; **~agtig**, (-e), phosphorous; **~esseer'**, (ge-), phosphoresce; **~essen'sie**, phosphorescence; **~essent**, (-e), phosphorescent; **~esse'rend**, (-e), phosphorescent.
fosfo'ries, (-e), phosphoric.
fosfor: **~iet'**, phosphorite; **~pasta**, phosphorous paste; **~sout**, microcosmic salt; **~suur**, phosphoric acid.
fosgeen'(gas), phosgene (gas).
fossiel', (s) (-e), fossil; (b) (-e), fossil, fossilized; **~afdruk**, fossil imprint; **~boom**, dendrolite; **~eier**, ovulite; **~houdend**, (-e), fossiliferous; **~jagter**, fossil hunter; **~kenner**, fossilist.
fossilisa'sie, fossilization.
fossiliseer', (ge-), fossilize; **..se'ring**, fossilization.
fossoriaal', (..riale), fossorial.
fotis'me, (-s), photism.
fo'to, (-'s), photo(graph); **~afdruk**, blueprint; **~album**, photograph album; **~ateljee**, photographic studio; **~blad**, photo page; **~brief**, airgraph; **~chemie**, photochemistry; **~chemigrafie**, process engraving; **~-elektries**, (-e), photo-electric; **~-ets**, (-e), photo-engraving; (w) (ge-), photo-engrave; **~etswerk**, photo-engraving; **~fobie'**, photophobia; **~geen'**, (..gene), photogenic object, organ; **~ge'nies**, (-e), photogenic.
fotograaf', (..grawe), photographer.
fotografeer', (ge-), photograph, take a photo; *jou laat ~*, have one's photo taken.
fotografie', photography.
fotogra'fies, (-e), photographic.
fo'to: **~gram**, photogram; **~gram'meter**, photogrammeter; **~grammetrie'**, photographic survey; **~gramme'tries**, (-e), photogrammetric; **~gravu're**, photogravure; **~kopie'**, photo print, photo copy; **~kopieer'**, (ge-), photocopy; **~litografie'**, photolithography; **~logie'**, photology; **~meter**, photometer; **~metrie'**, photometry.
fo'ton, (-e), photon.
fo'to: **~sel**, photocell; **~sfeer'**, photosphere; **~sintese**, photosynthesis; **~staat**, (..state), photostat; **~staatafdruk**, photostat copy; **~sta'ties**, (-e), photostatic; **~statiese afdruk**, photostat copy; **~teek**, photo library; **~telegrafie'**, phototelegraphy; **~terapie'**, phototherapeutics; **~tipie'**, (-ë), phototype; phototypy; **~tjie**, (-s) snap, small photo; **~troop**, (..trope), phototropic; **~tropie'**, phototropism, heliotropism; **~verveelvoudbuis**, photomultiplier tube.
fout, (s) (-e), mistake, error; failure, demerit, fault; blunder, oversight, faux pas; failing; flaw; defect; *'n ~ begaan*, make a mistake, commit an error; (b) mistaken; *jy het dit ~*, you have got it wrong; **~bal**, no-ball (cricket); **~druk**, misprint (stamp); **~eer'**, (ge-), err, make a mistake; **~eloos**, (..lose), faultless; **~eteorie**, theory of errors; **~grens**, permissible error; margin of error; **~ief'**, (..tiewe), faulty, erroneous, wrong; **~opnemer**, black box,

flight recorder; **~sein**, fault-tone (teleph.); **~soeker**, fault-finder, caviller; **~speurder**, trouble shooter; **~speurdery**, trouble shooting; **~speuring**, trouble shooting; **~tjie**, (-s), slight error.
fout'vind, (-ge-), find fault; **~er**, (-s), fault-finder; **~ery**, fault-finding.
fout: **~vrag**, dead freight; **~vry**, (-e), free from faults.
foyer', (-s), foyer.
fraai, (-, -e), fine, handsome, elegant, beautiful; brave; artistic, fancy; **~handwerk**, fancywork; **~heid**, beauty, prettiness, handsomeness, elegance.
fraai'igheid, (..hede), nicety, fine things; *dis gedwonge ~ met hom*, he had to do it willynilly.
fraai'skrif, copy-book writing.
fraai'tjies, handsome, beautiful.
fragiel', (-e), fragile.
fragment', (-e), fragment, piece; **~a'ries**, (-e), fragmentary, scrappy; **~a'sie**, fragmentation; **~eer'**, (ge-), break up; **~êr'**, (-e), fragmentary; **~e'ring**, fragmentation.
frai'ing, (-s), fringe, tassel, aglet; fimbria; **~poot**, phalarope.
frak'sie, diffraction (of light); (-s), fraction (of political party).
fraksioneel', (..nele), fractional.
fraksioneer', (ge-), fractionate, break up (into constituent parts); **..nering**, fractionation.
fraktuur', (..ture), fracture.
framboe'sia, framboesia, yaws.
framboos', (..bose), raspberry; **~stroop**, raspberry syrup; **~struik**, raspberry bush.
Franciskaan', (..kane), **Franciska'ner**, (-s), Franciscan, Grey friar.
frangipa'ni, (-'s), frangipani, temple flower.
Frank¹, (s) (-e), Frank.
frank², (s) (-e), franc.
frank³, (b) frank, candid; *~ en vry*, frank and free.
frankeer', (ge-), frank, prepay (postage); stamp; **~koevert**, reply-paid envelope; **~koste**, postage; carriage.
franke'ring, prepayment; stamping.
Fran'kies, (-e), Franconian.
fran'ko, franco, post-free; prepaid.
frankofiel', (-e), Francophile.
Frank'ryk, France.
Frans, (s) French; Francis; *'n vrolike ~*, a jolly dog, a boon companion; (b) (-e), French; *~e KNOPIES*, French knots; *OP ~e manier*, à la française; *~e SLAAISOUS*, French dressing.
frans: *~'brandewyn*, French brandy, cognac; *~'druiwe*, French grapes.
Frans'gesind, (-e), pro-French; **~e**, (-s), Francophil; **~heid**, Francophilism.
Franskiljon', (-s), pro-French Belgian.
frans'madam, (-me, -s), *Boopsoidea inornata* (fish).
Frans'man, (Franse), Frenchman.
Frans'sprekend, (-e), French speaking.
fransspies', (-e), frontispiece (architecture).
frappant', (-e), striking, remarkable; *dit lyk ~*, it is a striking resemblance.
trappeer', (ge-), strike, impress; cool, chill, freeze.
fra'se, (-s), phrase; hollow word.
fraseer', (ge-), phrase (in music).
fraseologie', phraseology.
frase'ring, phrasing.
fraseur', (-s), coiner of hollow phrases, phrasemonger.
fra'ter, (-s), (Christian) brother; **~niseer'**, (ge-), fraternize; **~niteit'**, fraternity.
frats, freak, caprice, whim, buffoonery, joke; *vol ~e wees*, be mischievous; be full of pranks; **~emaker**, buffoon, clown; **~vlieër**, aerobat, stuntflyer; **~weer**, freak weather.
frauduleus', (-e), fraudulent.
Fraun'hoferlyne, Fraunhofer lines.
frees, (s) milling cutter (lathe); fraise; (w) (ge-), mill; fraise.
free'sia, (-s), freesia.
frees'masjien, milling machine; spindle machine.
fregat', (-te), frigate; **~voël**, hurricane-bird (*Fregatidae*).

frekwen'sie, (-s), frequency.
frekwent', (-e), frequent.
frekwentatief', (..tiewe), frequentative.
frenesie', phrenitis, frenzy.
frenologie', phrenology.
frenoloog', (..loë), phrenologist.
fre'ser, (-s), millwright; ~y, (-e), mill; milling.
fres'ko, (-'s), fresco.
fret¹, (-te), ferret (*Putorius furo*).
fret², (-te), finch (*Ploceidae*).
fret³, (-te), gimlet; ~**boor**, gimlet; ~**saag**, fret-saw.
Freudiaans', (-e), Freudian.
freu'le, (-s), young lady of noble birth, freule.
frie'mel, (ge-), fumble, fidget.
fries¹, (s) (-e), frieze.
Fries², (s) (-e), Frieslander; Frisian (language); (b) (-e), Frisian; ~**bees**, Frisian (cattle); ~**in'**, (-ne), Frisian; ~**land**, Friesland.
fries: ~**lys**, frieze moulding; ~**reling**, frieze rail.
Fri'gië, Phrygia; ~**r**, (-s), Phrygian.
Fri'gies, (-e), Phrygian.
frikassee', fricassee; ~**r**, (ge-), fricassee.
frikatief', (..tiewe), fricative; aspirate, aspirant.
frik'boortjie, gimlet.
frikkadel', (-le), minced-meat ball, fricandel(le), rissole; ~ *maak van iets*, smash something to pieces; make mincemeat of something; ~**broodjie**, hamburger; ~**letjie** (-s), small rissole.
frik'keboortjie, gimlet.
frik'sie, friction; ~**skyf**, clutch (of motor).
fris, ((-se); -ser, -ste) fresh; cool; strong, stout, hale, healthy, hefty; green; crispy; ~ *en GESOND*, hale and hearty; *'n* ~ *LUGGIE*, a cool breeze; *'n* ~ *VENT*, a muscular, well-built fellow; *so* ~ *soos 'n VIS in die water*, as fit as a fiddle; as fresh as a daisy; ~ *VOEL*, feel fit.
friseer', (ge-), curl, frizz, crisp; crimp; ~**tang**, crimping-iron; curling-tongs.
frise'ring, curling, crimping.
friseur', (-s), hairdresser.
fris: ~**gebou**, (-de), able-bodied, strongly built, well-built, athletic; beefy; ~**heid**, freshness; strength, bloom; crispness; ~**sies**, rather cold, fresh; ~**te**, freshness; strength.
frit, (s) frit; (w) (ge-), frit (glass-making); ~**ter**, (-s), coherer (telegraphy).
frituur', (friture), fritter, puff; ~**yster**, snackle iron.
frivoliteit', (-e), frivolity.
frivool', (frivole), frivolous.
Frö'belskool, Froebel school.
froe'tang, (-s), fruit of an edible herb (*Romulea rosea*).
frok, (-ke), ~**kie**, (-s), singlet; vest.
frok'kiehemp, T-shirt.
from'mel, (s), (-s), crumpled (creased, rumpled) mass; home-made vermicelli; (w) (ge-), fumble; crease; rumple, crumple; ~**aar**, (-s), fumbler; ~**oor**, cauliflower ear; ~**s**, crumbles.
frons, (s) (-e), frown, scowl; (w) (ge-), frown, scowl, knit the brows, knot, purse (forehead), lour, corrugate (forehead), pucker (brow); *met ge* ~ *te voorkop*, frowning (forehead).
front, (-e), front, frontage; facing; ~ *MAAK teen*, take a stand against something; *van* ~ *VERANDER*, change front; ~**aal'**, (..tale), frontal; ~**aansig**, full face (photo); front view; ~**aanval**, frontal attack; ~**behoeftes**, field stores.
fronteljak'druiwe, Frontignac grapes.
front'gebied, front area.
frontispies', (-e), frontispiece.
front: ~**linie**, line (of fortifications) at the front; ~**lyn**, front line (of military operations); ~**offisier**, regimental officer, combatant officer.
fronton', (-s), fronton, pediment.
front: ~**troepe**, front-line troops; ~**vegter**, front-line fighter; ~**verandering**, change of front (attitude); volte face; ~**vuur**, frontal fire; ~**werk**, stoping; ~**wydte**, frontage.
frot, touch (children's game).
fruktivo're, frugivorous animals.
frukto'se, fructose, fruit-sugar.
frum'mel, (ge-) = **frommel**.

frum'melplooie, smocking.
frum'meltjies = **frommels**.
frustra'sie, frustration.
frustreer', (ge-), frustrate.
frut'tel, (ge-), fumble.
fti'sis, phthisis.
fuch'sia = **foksia**.
fu'ga, (-s), fugue (music); ~**komponis**, fuguist.
fuif, (s) (**fuiwe**), spree, carousal, debauch, binge, shindig, feast, junket, bean-feast, merry-making, wassail; *aan die* ~ *gaan*, go on the spree; (w) (ge-), spree, feast, carouse, booze, junket.
fuik, (-e), bow-net, tunnel-net, fish-trap, kiddle; hencoop; *in die* ~ *loop*, run one's head into a noose; ~**blom**, trap-flower.
fui'wer, (-s), carouser, reveller; ~**y**, feasting, carousing, revelry.
fulguriet', fulgurite.
fulminaat', (..nate), fulminate.
fulmineer', (ge-), fulminate, thunder, inveigh against.
fumiga'sie, (-s), fumigation.
fumigeer', (ge-), fumigate.
fundamentalis', (-te), fundamentalist (in religion); ~**me**, fundamentalism; ~**ties**, (-e), fundamentalist.
fundamenteel', (..tele), fundamental, basal, basic, radical.
funda'sie, seating (under cannon); foundation (of association); ~**bout**, foundation bolt.
fundeer', (ge-), found, ground (a right); fund (debt).
funde'ring, founding (of rights); grounding.
funes', (-te), fatal, disastrous.
fungeer', (ge-), act, officiate, perform duties, function, serve as.
funge'rend, (-e), acting, deputy.
funge'ring, acting; functioning (limbs, regulations).
fungoïed', (-e), fungoid.
fun'gus, (-se, ..gi), fungus.
funikulêr', (-e), funicular.
funk'sie, (-s), function; *in* ~ *tree*, assume duty, ~**loos**, (..lose), functionless; ~**verandering**, change of function.
funksiona'ris, (-se), functionary.
funksioneel', (..nele), functional.
funksioneer', (ge-), function.
funksione'ring, functioning.
fu'rie, (-ë, -s), fury; she-dragon.
furieus', (-e), furious.
furo're, furore; ~ *maak*, cause a stir (furore), make a hit.
fu'sie, fusion, merger.
fusilla'de, (-s), fusillade.
fusilleer', (ge-), execute, shoot, hang, fusillade.
fusillier', fusilier.
fustein', fustian.
fustiek', fustic
fut, mettle, dash, vim, pep, élan, go, ginger, guts, grit, verve; *sy* ~ *is uit*, he has lost his spirit.
futiel', (-e), futile.
futiliteit', (-e), futility.
fut'loos, (..lose), spiritless, pithless, without grit; ~**heid**, lack of grit (spirit).
fut'sel, (ge-), trifle, tamper; ~**aar**, (-s), bungler, trifler; ~(**a)ry'**, fiddling, trifling; ~**werk**, trifling work.
futuris', (-te), futurist; ~**me**, futurism; ~**ties**, (-e), futurist(ic).
futuroloog', (..roloë), futurologist.
futu'rum, (..tura), future (tense).
fyn, (-e), fine, delicate (ear); refined, subtle, lady-like, dainty; exquisite; choice (wine); pulverous, pulverulent; small (print); tender (skin); pure (gold); sensitive; natty; smooth (jam); ~ *AARTAPPELS*, mashed potatoes; ~ *BESNAARD wees*, be touchy; ~ *BESNEDE*, finely cut (features); ~ *van DRAAD wees*, be touchy; ~ *en FLENTERS slaan*, smash to smithereens (bits); ~ *LOOP*, tread warily; ~ *MIELIESEMELS*, hominychop; ~ *OPLET*, take careful note, attend carefully; *die* ~ *e van die SAAK*, the essence (ins and outs) of the matter; ~ *UITGEVAT*, smartly dressed; *die* ~ *e UITHANG*, play the saint; ~**bedag**, (-te), deeplaid, cunningly conceived; ~**besnaard**, (-e), highly-

strung; ~**besnede**, finely chiselled, fine-cut; ~**blaarvaring**, maiden-hair fern; ~**bos**, machia; natural scrub vegetation; ~**brood**, white bread; ~**draaier**, precision turner; ~**dradig**, (-e), fine-grained; ~**druk**, (-ge-), press (until fine); crush; mash; ~**gelaag**, (-de), laminate(d); ~**gesaag**, (-de), serrulate(d); ~**gemasjineer**, (-de), precision machined; ~**gereedskap**, precision tools (instruments); ~**getand**, (-e), denticulate(d); ~**gevat**, (-te), smartly dressed, nifty; sensitive.

fyn'gevoelig (-e), sensitive, delicate; ~**heid**, delicacy, sensitiveness.

fyn: ~**goed**, fines (mining); fine (dainty, delicate) plants, materials; ~ *goed maak van*, make matchwood of; ~**heid**, fineness, delicacy, nicety; daintiness; cuteness; exquisiteness; ~**hout**, kindling; ~ *hout maak van*, make mincemeat of; ~**igheid**, (..hede), fineness; particular (fine) detail; *die* ~ *ighede v.d. saak*, the ins and outs (particulars) of the matter; ~**kam**, (s) nit-comb; fine-tooth comb; (w) (ge-), make a thorough search, comb; toothcomb; ~**kap**, (-ge-), hash; chop finely; ~**karteling**, crenulation; ~**klerasie**, lingerie; ~**kole**, fines; ~**konfyt**, (smooth) jam; ~**kook**, (-ge-), boil until soft (to pieces); ~**kool**, duff; ~**korrel**, fine-sight (of rifle); ~**korrelrig**, (-e), fine-grained; ~**kou**, (-ge-), masticate thoroughly; ~**linne**, long cloth; ~**maak**, (-ge-), pulverize; mince; mash; levigate; ~**maakploeg**, pulverator plough; ~**maal**, (-ge-), grind to powder, pulverize; ~**meel**, flour; ~**monteur**, precision fitter; ~**plooiing**, puckering, plication; ~**proewer**, connoisseur; gourmet; ~**ruigte**, undergrowth; underbrush; coppice; ~**saag**, (s) fret-saw; (w) (-ge-), do fretwork; ~**saagwerk**, fretwork; ~**semels**, pollard; ~**sin'nig**, (-e), sensitive, delicate; ~**skut**, marksman; ~**skutkuns**, marksmanship; ~**skuur**, (-ge-), buff; ~**skuurder**, buff; ~**skuurskyf**, buff; ~**slaan**, (-ge-), knock to pieces; ~**slyp**, (-ge-), lap; ~**slyper**, precision grinder, lap; ~**sny**, cut up finely; ~**sout**, table salt; ~**spinnasjien**, mule (jenny); ~**staal**, sheer steel; ~**stamp**, (-ge-), pound, pulverize, bray (with pestle); ~**stamping**, pulverization; ~**steenkool**, duff; ~**stelling**, fine adjustment; ~**stopper**, invisible mender; ~**stopwerk**, invisible mending; ~**strepig**, (-e), pencilled, finely lined; ~**talk**, French chalk; ~**te**, fineness; ~**tjies**, smartly, cleverly; fastidiousl(y); ~**tuin**, kitchen-garden, garden for small plants; ~**vrywe**, (-ge-), rub (to powder); ~**vrywing**, levigation.

fyt, whitlow, felon.

G

g, (-'s), g.

ga! phew! ~, *maar dit stink!*, phew, what a smell!

gaaf, (gawe; gawer, -ste), good, nice, likeable, excellent; whole, undamaged (teeth); friendly; entire (bot.); *dis ALTE* ~ *van jou*, that's very kind of you; *'n gawe KÊREL*, a pleasant fellow, a brick; ~ *en ONGESKEND*, whole and entire; ~**heid**, soundness, etc.

gaai[1], (-e), fool, idiot; backside.

gaai[2], (e), small crow.

gaan, (ge-), go, move, walk; *dit* ~ *jou nie AAN nie*, it does not concern you; *die verf* ~ *AF*, the paint comes off; ~ *BARS*, ~ *na die hoenders*, go to blazes; *dit* ~ *om 'n groot BEGINSEL*, an important principle is involved; *jou goed* ~ *BESIN*, ponder well; *BO alles* ~, to top all; to cap everything; *dit* ~ *BO my middele*, I can't afford it; *dit* ~ *BO alles*, it is of the utmost importance; *daar* ~ *2 pinte in die BOTTEL*, the bottle holds (contains) 2 pints; *hy* ~ *BUITE sy bevoegdheid*, he exceeds his competency; *as alles GOED* ~, if all goes well; *dit* ~ *GOED met die pasiënt*, the patient is doing well; *dit* ~ *jou GOED (blikkies)*, good luck to you; ~ *HAAL*, go and fetch; *HOE* ~ *dit?*, how do you do?; *dit KAN* ~ *soos dit wil, come what may*; *die KLEUR* ~ *nie saam met jou hoed nie*, this colour does not go with your hat; *jou LAAT* ~, let oneself go; *die koring* ~ *LÊ*, the corn is lodging; *so* ~ *dit in die LEWE*, such is life; *dit* ~ *baie MAKLIK*, it is very easy; *dit* ~ *OOR hierdie saak*, this is the point at issue; *OP iets* ~, depend on something; *jy moet hom* ~ *OPSOEK*, you must look him up; *my PLIG* ~ *voor alles*, my duty takes precedence; *al sy SAKGELD* ~ *aan (vir) lekkers*, all his pocket money is spent on sweets; *oor 'n SIEKE* ~, attend a patient; ~ *SIT*, land (aeroplane); go and sit down; ~ *SLAAP*, go to bed; ~ *STIK*, go to blazes; *SO* ~ *dit maar*, that's the way of things; *van* ~ *en STAAN*, *kom niks gedaan*, long demurs breed new delays; procrastination is the thief of time; *waar jy ook al* ~ *of STAAN*, wherever you may find yourself; *my TREIN* ~ *om 2-uur*, my train goes (is due to leave) at 2 o'clock; *die TREIN het al gegaan*, the train was already moving; *ons* ~ *TREK*, we are going to move; *VEILIGHEID* ~ *bo alles*, safety is the paramount consideration; *te VER* ~, go too far; *so* ~ *die VERHAAL*, so the tale goes; *die VERSLAG* ~ *hierby*, the report is enclosed; *die tyd* ~ *VINNIG*, time passes quickly; *die wind* ~ *WAAI*, the wind is going to blow; *dit sal WEL* ~, *meen ek*, I think I can manage it; *die WIND* ~ *lê*, the wind is dying down (dropping).

gaan'de, going; excited; *'n BEDRAG R5 nie te bowe* ~ *nie*, an amount not exceeding R5; *DAAR is iets* ~, there's something the matter (afoot); ~ *HOU*, keep going; ~ *MAAK*, get going, stir up, excite; ~ *RAAK oor 'n saak*, get excited (enthusiastic) about a matter; *WAT is* ~?, what is going on?; ~**ry**, (-e), gallery; ~**weg**, by degrees, gradually.

gaans: *'n uur* ~, an hour's walk.

gaanslaap'tyd, bed-time.

gaansla'pery, going to bed (sleep).

gaap, (s) (**gape**), yawn; (w) (ge-), yawn; gape; ~**been**, hyoid bone; ~**siekte**, the gapes; ~**skulp**, clam; ~**wurm**, gape-worm.

gaar[1], (w) (ge-), gather, collect.

gaar[2], (b) (-der, -ste), sufficiently cooked, done (meat), worn-out (clothes); perished (rubber); *iets* ~ *DRA*, wear something threadbare; *GOED* ~, well done; *NET* ~, done to a turn; *TE* ~, overdone; ~**bak**, (w) (-ge-), bake until done.

gaar'boord, garboard; ~**gang**, garboard stroke.

gaar'de, (-s), (digt.), garden.

gaar'der, (-s), receiver (of revenue).

gaar'heid, state of being done (cooked); temper (of steel).

gaar'kook, (-ge-), cook, cook until done.

gaar'koper, rose (refined) copper.

gaar'maak, (-ge-), cook, bake; prepare food; ~**metode**, method of cooking.

gaar'ne, (Ndl.) gladly, willingly.

gaar'oond, refining furnace.

gaas, gauze, netting; lawn; lint; canvas; ~**agtig**, (-e), gauzy; ~**borduurwerk**, canvas embroidery; ~**doek**, gauze; cheese-cloth; ~**draad**, wire gauze; gauze wire; ~**kant**, point de gaze; ~**vlieg**, lacewing fly; ~**weefsel**, gauze tissue.

gaat'jie, (-s), little hole; puncture; prick, perforation; aperture; foramen; orifice; loop-hole; ventage (of flute); ~**kamera**, pin-hole camera; ~**knipper**, punch plier; ~**prop**, breather plug; ~**ring**, breather ring; ~**s**, drills (for vegetables).

gaat'jies: ~**agtig** = **gaatjiesrig**; ~**bak**, colander; ~**borduurwerk**, eyelet embroidery; ~**dier**, rhizopod *(Foraminifera)*; ~**goed**, eyelet material; ~**plaat**, perforated plate; ~**pyp**, perforated tube; ~**rig**, (-e), full of holes, holey.

gaat'jie: ~**steek**, punching; ~**swam**, pore-bearing

fungus *(Polyporaceae);* ~**visier,** peep sight; aperture sight.
gaats! o dear!, goodness!
gaat'steen, perforated brick.
gabardien', gabardi'ne, gabardine; ~**broek,** gabardine trousers.
Gaboen, Gaboon; g ~ **adder,** gaboon adder *(Bitis gabonica);* ~**ees',** (s) *(..* **nese),** Gaboonese.
ga'de, (-s), spouse, consort, wife; husband.
ga'deslaan, (-ge-), observe, watch, regard, eye.
ga'ding, liking, inclination; *ALLES is van sy* ~, all is grist that comes to his mill; *IETS van sy* ~, something to his taste (his liking).
gadoliniet', gadolinite.
Gae'lies, (-e), Gaelic.
gaf'fel, (s) (-s), (pitch)fork, prong; bifurcation; gaff (ship); (w) **(ge-),** poke at (with horns); toss; ~ **aar,** (-s), animal inclined to poke; ~**bok,** prong-buck; ~**hanger,** drop-hanger frame; ~**ploeg,** forked plough; ~**seil,** trysail; ~**splitsing,** dichotomy; ~**vormig,** (-e), forked, pronged, bifurcated.
gag'gel, (ge-), quack, croak.
gaip', (-e), lubber, churl, boor.
gajaal', (**gajale),** gayal *(Bos frontalis frontalis).*
gal¹, gall, bile; ~ *AFGAAN,* make a fuss, get into a rage; *dis BO sy* ~, it is beyond his capabilities; *nooit iem. se* ~ *RUIK nie,* be no match for someone; *sy* ~ *UITBRAAK,* vent one's spleen; *sy* ~ *sal WAAI,* he wil know all about it; he'll catch it; *met iem. se* ~ *WERK,* fix someone.
gal², (**-le**), gall (painful swelling); excrescence (produced by an insect on trees).
ga'la, (-s), gala, festive occasion; *gaste moet in* ~ *kom,* guests must wear full dress; ~ **bal,** gala ball; ~ **dag,** gala day; ~ **dinee,** gala dinner, state dinner.
gal: ~ **afdrywend,** choleretic; ~ **afdrywer,** cholagogue, choleretic; ~ **afskeiding,** secretion of bile.
gal'agtig, (-e), bilious; choleric (fig.); ~ **heid,** biliousness; choler.
ga'la: ~ **klere,** gala dress, full dress; ~ **konsert,** command performance; ~ **kostuum,** gala dress, full dress.
galak'ties, (-e), galactic.
galaktiet', galactite.
galakti'ne, galactine.
galak'tometer, galaktome'ter, galactometer.
galakto'se, galactose.
ga'lambotter, shea butter.
galant', (s) (-e), suitor, fiancé; gallant; (b) (-e), gallant, polite, courteous; ~**erie',** gallantry, courtesy; ~**erie'ë,** ~**erie'ware,** small wares, fancy goods; ~**erie'winkel,** fancy-goods shop.
galantien', galanti'ne, galantine.
gal'appel, gall-nut.
Gala'siërs, Galatians.
ga'lavoorstelling, gala performance.
ga'lawedstryd, gala (match).
gal: ~ **berou,** *see* **naberou;** ~ **bessie,** *see* **nastergal;** ~ **bitter,** bitter as gall; ~ **blaas,** gall-bladder; ~ **brakery,** ~ **braking,** exhibition of hatred; outpour of malignity; ~ **buis,** gall-duct, bile-duct; ~ **bult,** nettle-rash, urticaria, heat-bump; ~ **drywer,** cholagogue.
galei', (-e), galley; ~ **boef,** galley-convict; ~ **proef,** galley proof (printing); ~ **slaaf,** galley-slave; ~ **straf,** labour in the galleys.
galeniet', galena.
galery', (-e), gallery; balcony; gate; heading (mine); driftway; circle (theatre); ~ **bou,** post-and-stall work, drifting; ~ **leuning,** gallery girder; ~ **raam,** gallery frame.
galg, (-e), gallows, gibbet; scaffold; *BOU 'n* ~ *vir 'n ander, dan hang jy self daaraan,* harm watch, harm catch; hoist (a man) with his own petard; *lyk of hy van die* ~ *GEWAAI is,* look very pale and thin; *'n kind vir die* ~ *GROOTMAAK,* rear a child in vice (for the gallows); *as jy vir die* ~ *gebore is, sal jy nie deur 'n KOEËL sterf nie,* he that is born to be hanged shall never be drowned; ~ *en RAD aan mekaar lieg,* be a consummate liar, tell whoppers; *vir* ~ *en RAT opgegroei,* grow up for the gallows; ~ **aas,** gallows-bird; scoundrel.
galgant', galingale.
galg: ~ **berou,** false remorse; *see* **naberou;** ~ **ehumor,**

grim humour; ~**emaal,** last (parting) meal; ~(e)**tronie,** gallows-face; hangdog look; ~ **paal,** gallows-tree; ~ **stut,** gallows-tree; ~ **tou,** hennep; ~ **voël,** hangdog.
gal'hoofpyn, bilious headache.
Galile'a, Galilee.
Galile'ër, (-s), Galilean.
Galilees', (.. **lese),** Galilean.
galjas', (-se), galleon.
galjoen', (-e), galleon; blackfish, galjoen *(Dipterodon capensis);* ~ **pomp,** bow-pump; ~ **vangs,** galjoen catch.
galjoot', (.. **jote),** gal(l)iot.
gal: ~ **koliek,** biliary colic; ~ **koors,** bilious fever, biliary fever; ~ **lamsiekte,** splenic fever (cattle); ~ **leier,** bile-conductor, bileduct.
gal'lerig, (-e), bilious; ~ **heid,** biliousness.
Gal'lië, Gaul; ..**lies,** (-e), Gallic, Gaulish.
Gallisis'me, (-s), Gallicism; ..**sis'ties** (-e), Gallican.
gal'lium, gallium.
Gallomanie', Gallomania.
gallon', (-s), gallon.
gal'lussuur, gallic acid.
galm', (s) (-e), peal, clangour, (booming) sound; reverberation; echo; (w) **(ge-),** sound, resound, reverberate; bawl (voice); ~ **bord,** sounding-board.
galmei', calamine.
galm: ~ **gat,** sounding-hole; ~ **stem,** parson's bellow.
gal'neut, oak-apple; gall(-nut).
galon', (gold or silver) lace, braid, galloon; ~ **neer',** (ge-), lace, galloon, braid; ~ **werk,** braiding; braidwork.
galop', (s) gallop; pitch (of locomotive); galop (dance); *op 'n* ~, at a gallop; be moving fast; (w) (ge-), gallop; pitch (of van); galop (a dance); ~ **dans,** gallopade; ~ **draf,** canter; ~ **peer',** (ge-), gallop; ~ **peer'der,** (-s), galloper; ~ **tering,** galloping consumption.
galpeer', (ge-), (gew.), gallop.
gal'pil, liver pill.
gal'rooi, bilirubin.
gal'serig, (-e) = **galsterig.**
gal'siekte, bilious complaint; gallsickness; anaplasmosis; ~ **bos,** *Chenopodium anthelminticum.*
gal: ~ **sout,** bile salts; ~ **steen,** gall-stone, biliary calculus.
gal'sout, bile salts.
gal'steen, gall-stone, biliary calculus.
gal'sterig, (-e), rancid, olid, musty, rank, fetid, strong; loathsome, offensive; ~ **heid,** randicity, rankness.
gal'sug, bilious complaint.
galva'nies, (-e), galvanic.
galvanisa'sie, galvanization.
galvaniseer', (ge-), galvanize.
galvanise'ring, galvanization.
galvanis'me, galvanism; voltaism.
galva'no, (-'s), electrotype, galvano; ~ **grafie',** galvanography; ~ **meter,** current indicator; galvanometer; ~ **plastiek',** electrodeposition; electroplating; galvanoplasty; ~ **skoop',** (..**skope),** galvanoscope; ~ **tipie',** galvanotypy.
gal: ~ **verdrywend,** (-e), antibilious; ~ **vlieg,** gall-fly.
Gam, Ham.
Gama'liël, Gamaliel *(Acts* 5:34).
gaman'der, germander.
gam'ba, gam'be, (viola da) gamba.
gambiet', (-e), gambit (chess).
gameet', (**gamete),** gamete.
gam'ma, (-s), (Greek letter) gamma; gamut, scale (music).
gam'mat, (neerh.) (-s, -te), Malay child (young man); Coloured person.
gamut', gamut, scale; *die hele* ~, (over) the whole gamut (scale).
gang¹, (s) (-e), gait, walk; rack, pace (of a horse), amble; progress; passage, corridor; race (for classing animals); alley, gallery, aisle; escapement (watch); canal, duct; (level) drive, dyke, heading, level (in mine); speed, velocity (of machine); course (of disease); course (of story); *aan die* ~ *BLY,* keep on the go, continue (working, etc.); *aan die* ~ *HOU,* keep

going; *op jou eie* ~ *AANGAAN*, go one's own way about things; *sy eie* ~ *GAAN*, go one's own way; *GAAN jou* ~!, do as you please!; go ahead!; *iem. sy* ~ *laat GAAN*, let someone go his own way; *op* ~ *KOM*, get going; *KRY jou* ~!, go away!; *aan die* ~ *KRY*, get going; *ek sal sy gange NAGAAN*, I shall watch his movements (behaviour); *die* ~ *van SAKE*, the course of events; *aan die* ~ *SIT*, set going; *die SKOOL is al aan die* ~, school has already begun; *in VOLLE* ~, in full swing; *hy is WEER aan die* ~, he is at it again; *aan die* ~ *WEES*, be going on, be in progress.

gang²! (tw) *see* **ga!**

gang'baar, (..bare), passable (bills); approved, valid; current (money); *die KAARTJIE is nie meer* ~ *nie*, the ticket is no longer valid; *in die gangbare SIN van die woord*, in the accepted sense of the word; ~**heid**, currency, validity; ~**heidstudie**, feasibility study.

gang: ~**bank**, passage seat, gangway seat; ~**boord**, gangway; ~**deur**, passage door; ~**erts**, veinstone; ~**etjie**, (-s), small passage; jogtrot (horse); gully (cricket); *dit GAAN so op 'n* ~*etjie*, things are jogging along; *die GEWONE* ~*etjie*, the usual routine; ~**gesteente**, dyke rock; gangue; ~**kant**, selvedge; ~**kapstok**, hall stand; ~**klok**, hall clock; ~**lamp**, hall lamp.

gan'glion, (..glië), ganglion.

gang: ~**loopgraaf**, gangway trench; ~**loper**, hall carpet; pacer, ambler (horse); ~**maker**, pace-maker (setter); ~**massa**, *see* **gangsteen**; ~**mat**, hall (passage) mat.

gangreen', gangrene.

gangreneus', (-e), gangrenous.

gang: ~**spil**, capstan bar, ~**stander**, hall stand; ~**steen**, gangue, veinstone; ~**swerm**, dyke swarm; ~**tapyt**, passage carpet; ~**trein**, corridor (train); ~**verskuiwing**, dyke fault; ~**werk**, driving gear; ~**wissel**, gear (lever); transmission; ~**wisseling**, gear change.

gan'na, lyebush *(Salsola)*; ~**-as**, ash of lyebush; ~**bos**, lyebush.

gans¹, (s) (-e), goose; stupid person; sweetheart; ~*e AANJA*, be tipsy; *stadige* ~ *verloor sy KANS*, faint heart ne'er won fair lady; ~*e sonder VERE soek*, go courting.

gans², (b, bw) (-e), whole, entire; all; quite, completely; ~ *en AL nie*, by no means; ~ *ANDERS*, totally different; ~ *en GAAR*, completely; ~ *en GAAR nie*, not by a long chalk; *die* ~*e LAND*, the whole country; ~ *ONBEKWAAM*, quite incapable.

gans: ~**afval**, goose giblets; ~**agtig, (-e)**, goosey; ~**bek**, goose's bill; ~**blom**, ox-eye (daisy); ~**bord**, (royal) game of goose; ~**bors**, (s) breast of goose; (b) hoarse; ~**boud**, leg of goose.

gan's(e)gaar, (gans en gaar), at all; completely, quite; even; *dis* ~ *onmoontlik*, it is quite impossible.

gans'eier, goose's egg.

gan's(e)lik, quite, totally.

gan'semars: (ong) *in die* ~, in single (goose) file.

gan'ser: *van* ~ *harte*, with all one's heart.

gan'serik, goosegrass, silver weed *(Potentilla)*.

gans: ~**hok**, goose pen; ~**ie, (-s)**, gosling; one of several wild flowers (e.g. *Asclepias fruticosa*); girl; ~**jag**, goose hunt (chase).

gans'ke, (geselst.) whole; *die* ~ *liewe dag*, the livelong day.

gans'klip: *hy gooi met 'n* ~, he draws a long bow; he lays it on thick.

gans: ~**kop**, goose head; ~**lewer**, goose liver, foie gras; ~**lewerpastei**; pâté de foie gras; goose liver pie; ~**loper**, jay-walker; ~**mannetjie**, gander; ~**mark**, goose market; ~**mars**, Indian file; goosestep; ~**nek**, gooseneck; ~**nekploeg**, old-fashioned (single-furrow) plought; ~**nes**, goose's nest; ~**ogies**, huckaback; ~**oog**, goose's eye; ~**pastei**, goose pie; ~**pennetjie**, goose quill; ~**poot**, web(bed foot) of goose; ~**spele(tjie)**, game of goose; ~**stem**, hoarse voice; ~**veer**, goose-quill; goose feather; ~**vet**, axunge; ~**vleis**, goose-flesh; ~**voet**, pigweed; goose-foot; ~**wagter**, gooseherd.

gap, (ge-), grab, pinch, steal, filch, snitch.

ga'pend, (-e), yawning; ~*e AFGROND*, yawning abyss; ~*e WOND*, gaping wound.

ga'per, (-s), gaper, yawner; ~**ig, (-e)**, yawny; sleepy.

ga'ping, (-e, -s), gap, hiatus, lacuna; heave (in mines); gash; jump (in series); gape.

ga'pingsaar, gash vein.

gaps, (ge-) = **gap**.

gara'ge, (-s), garage, motorhouse.

garandeer', (ge-), guarantee, warrant; ~**der**, guarantor, gaurantee.

garande'ring, guarantee.

garan'sie, (-s), guarantee, security; ~**bewys**, warranty; ~**verdrag**, guarantee pact.

garant', (-e), underwriter; guarantor.

gar'de, (-s), guard, bodyguard; *die ou* ~, the old school (guard).

garde'nia, gardenia, Cape jasmine.

gar'de-offisier, guardsman, guard officer.

gar'derobe, (-s), wardrobe; cloak room.

ga're, thread, yarn, cotton thread; *'n tolletjie* ~, a reel of cotton; ~**boom**, agave, American aloe, Mexican aloe *(Agave americana)*; loom tree; ~**draad**, thread of cotton.

gareel', harness, yoke; *in die* ~ *draf*, be in harnes.

ga'reklip = **garingklip**.

ga'respoeletjie, thread bobbin.

garibal'di, (-'s), (vero.) Garibaldi (blouse).

ga'ring, *see* **gare**; ~**biltong**, biltong from the loin; ~**draer**, bobbin; ~**insteker**, needle-threader; ~**kant**, mercerized cotton; ~**klip**, asbestos; ~**klos**, pirn; ~**ogie**, loop; earth-flax; ~**suiker**, spun sugar, sugar threads; ~**tolletjie**, cotton reel; ~**vleis**, stringy meat

garnaal', (..nale), shrimp; ~**broodjie**, shrimp roll; ~**geheue**, memory like a sieve; ~**net**, shrimp net; ~**pastei**, shrimp pie; ~**visser**, shrimp fisher.

garneer', (ge-), trim, garnish; decorate; ~**papier**, lacey paper; ~**sel, (-s)**, garnish, trimming; ..**ne'ring, (-s)**, trimming, garnishment, garniture, decoration.

garnisoen', (-e), garrison.

garnisoens': ~**diens**, garrison duty; ~**dokter**, regimental doctor; ~**lewe**, garrison life; ~**mag**, garrison force; ~**magasyn**, garrison magazine; ~**order**, garrison order.

garnisoenstad, garrison town.

garnisoens': ~**troepe**, garrison troops; ~**verwisseling**, change of garrison; ~**wag**, garrison guard.

garnituur', (..ture), trimming, garniture (gown); set of jewels (lady's wear); side mirrors (mantlepiece).

garrot', (-te), garrotte; ~**teer', (ge-)**, garrotte

gars: ~**bier**, barley(corn) beer; ~**gerf**, sheaf of barley; ~**gort**, barley groats; ~**koffie**, barley coffee; ~**korrel**, grain of barley; barleycorn; ~**land**, barley field; ~**meel**, barley flour; ~**mout**, barley malt; ~**saad**, barley seed; ~**semels**, barley bran; ~**so(e)p** barley-broth (soup); ~**suiker**, barley sugar; ~**water**, barley-water, ptisan.

gas¹, (s) (-te), guest, visitor; *ongenooide* ~ *te hoort agter die deur*, uninvited guests should not expect to be accommodated; an unbidden guest knows not where to sit.

gas², (s) (-se), gas; *op* ~ *kook*, cook by gas; (w) (ge-), gas; ~**aanlêer**, gas-fitter; ~**aanval**, gas attack; ~**afsluiting**, gas check (valve); ~**agtig, (-e)**, gaseous; gassy; ~**agtigheid**, gaseity; ~**alarm**, gas alarm; ~**arm**, gas bracket; ~**bedwelming**, gassing; ~**bek**, gas jet; ~**beskerming**, gas protection; ~**besmetting**, gas contamination; ~**bespaarder**, gas economizer; ~**blasie**, gas-bubble; vesicle; ~**bom**, gas-bomb; ~**brander**, gas-burner; ~**buis**, gas-pipe (cylinder); ~**damp**, gaseous vapour, gas-fume.

gas'dier, inquiline (e.g. cuckoo).

gas: ~**dig, (-te)**, gas-tight; ~**dirigent**, guest conductor; ~**dissipline**, gas discipline; ~**draad**, gas thread; ~**drank**, explosive (gaseous) drink; gas cooldrink.

gasel', (-le), gazelle; ariel; ~**oog**, hazel eye.

gas'enjin, gas engine.

gas-en-ontbrandingsmengsel, gas and ignition mixture.

gaset', (-te), gazette.

gas: ~**fabriek,** gas-works; ~**fabrikant,** gas-man; ~**gordyn,** gas-curtain; ~**granaat,** gas-shell.
gas'heer, host; entertainer; ~**plant,** host plant.
gas: ~**holte,** blow-hole; pocket of gas; ~**houer,** gas-holder, gasometer.
gas: ~**huis,** hospice; ~**huisprediker,** (hist.) knight hospitaller.
ga'sie, reward, pay; wages, salary.
ga'sig, (-e), gauzy; ~**heid,** gauziness.
gas: ~**installasie,** gas installation; ~**kaggel,** gas (-heating) stove; ~**kennis,** knowledge of gas; ~**klep,** gas-valve; ~**kooks,** gas-coke; ~**kousie,** gas-man-tle; ~**kraan,** gas-cock; ~**kroon,** gas chandelier; gaseleer, gas pendant (pendent); ~**lamp,** gas-lamp; ~**leiding,** gas main; ~**lek,** escape of gas; ~**lig,** gaslight; ~**lug,** smell of gas.
gas'maal, banquet, feast.
gas: ~**masjien,** gas (engine) machine; ~**masker,** gas-mask, respirator, gas-helmet; ~**maskersak,** respiratory bag; ~**mengsel,** gas mixture; ~**meter,** gas-meter; ~**motor,** gas engine; ~**myn,** gas mine; fiery mine.
gasolien', gasoli'ne, gasoline.
gas: ~**ontleding,** atmolysis; ~**ontploffing,** gas explosion; ~**ontsmetting,** gas decontamination; ~**oond,** gas-oven; ~**oorlog,** gas-warfare; ~**ornament,** gas-fixture; ~**pedaal,** accelerator; ~**pipet,** gas-sampling tube; ~**pistool,** gas-pistol; ~**pit,** gas-jet; ~**pomp,** gas-pump; ~**prop,** air (vapour) lock; ~**pyp,** gas-pipe; ~**reëlaar,** gas governor; ~**reën,** spray attack; ~**reinigingspos,** gas-cleaning centre; ~**sak,** gas-bag; ~**serig, (-e),** gassy; flatulent; ~**siek,** gassed; ~**silinder,** gas-cylinder; ~**skildwag,** gas sentry; ~**sleepwa,** gas-trailer; ~**spreker,** guest speaker; ~**sproeier,** gas-spayer (aircraft); ~**stel,** ~**stoof,** gas-stove; ~**sweising,** gas-welding; ~**tang,** gas-pliers.
gas'te: ~**boek,** guestbook; ~**handdoek,** guest towel.
gas'toevoer, gas-supply.
gas'tries, (-e), gastric.
gastri'tis, gastritis.
gas'troënteritis, gastro-enteritis.
gastroliet', (-e), gastrolith.
gastrologie', gastrology.
gastronomie', gastronomy; ..**no'mies, (-e),** gastronomic; ..**noom', (..nome),** gastronomer.
gas: ~**uitlaatklep,** bleeder valve; ~**uitlaatpyp,** bleeder (in mines); ~**verbruik,** gas consumption; ~**verdediging,** gas defence; ~**vergiftiging,** gas poisoning; gassing; ~**verkenning,** gas reconnaissance; ~**verklikker,** gas-detector; ~**verligting,** gaslighting; ~**verstikking,** gassing; ~**vlam,** gas flame; gas-jet.
gas'voorstelling, guest performance.
gas: ~**vormig, (-e),** gaseous; aeriform; gasiform; ~**vorming,** gasification.
gas: ~**vriend,** guest; ~**vrou,** hostess, chatelaine.
gas'vry, (-e), hospitable; ~**heid,** hospitality; *iem. se* ~*heid beantwoord*, return hospitality.
gas: ~**wa,** gas van; ~**wapen,** gas weapon; ~**weermaatreëls,** anti-gas measures; ~**werker,** gas-worker; ~**werper,** gas projector.
Gat¹, Gath; *verkondig dit nie in* ~ *nie*, tell it not in Gath.
gat²,(-e), hole, opening, gap, pit; socket; eye; hole of a place, unattractive place, room, etc.; *daar is 'n* ~ *in sy BEURSIE*, he throws money about; *'n* ~ *in die DAG slaap*, sleep until the sun is high in the sky; *'n* ~ *EET*, eat a lot; *'n* ~ *vir iem. GRAWE en daar self in val*, be hoist with one's own petard; *alle* ~*e en HOEKE deursoek*, look in all corners; *in die* ~*e HOU*, not to let someone out of one's sight; *iem. 'n* ~ *in die KOP praat*, talk someone into something; *iets in die* ~*e KRY*, get wind of something; *een* ~ *MAAK om 'n ander te vul*, rob Peter to pay Paul; ~*e MAAK*, make tracks; ~-~ *SPEEL*, play holey-holey (marbles); *vir elke* ~ *'n SPYKER hê*, know all the answers; *'n* ~ *TOESTOP (opvul)*, plug a hole; pay a debt; ~*e UIT (slaap, werk)*, like mad; no end; *hulle het* ~*e UIT gespeel (geniet, gewerk)*, they had the time of their lives.
gat³, (-te), arse, bottom, anus, backside; seat (of trousers); *dit was by die* ~ *AF*, it was a near thing,

touch and go; *in sy* ~ *GEKNYP wees*, be scared; *in iem. se* ~ *INKRUIP*, iem. se ~ *LEK*, toady to someone.
ga'temasjien, mortise machine.
ga'terig, (-e), full of holes (road, clothes); honeycombed.
gat'grawer, post-hole digger.
gat'jie, (-s), little anus; ~**ponder,** frock-coat; nickname for member of the N.G. Church; one who digs for diamonds while on holiday.
gat'kant, tail side, rear; *die wêreld staan met sy* ~ *na my toe*, everything goes against me.
gat'kruip, (-ge-), toady (to); ~**er,** toady; ~**ery,** toadyism.
gat'lekker, (-s), toady; ~**y,** toadyism.
gat'oorkop, head over heels; ~ *slaan*, turn somersault.
gats! gat'ta! goodness!, gracious me!
gat'someter, gatsome'ter, gatsometer (registered trade name).
gat'tang, belt punch.
gat'vel, skin of buttocks; skin-covering for buttocks, beshu.
gavot'te, (-s), gavotte.
ga'we, (-s), gift, donation; talent; dower; *die* ~ *van die woord hê*, have the gift of the gab.
ga'werig, (-e), excellent, nice, first-rate; rather nice.
ga'wie, (-s), churl, boor, bumpkin.
gê, (s) piffle; trash; (w) **(ge-),** jest; (tw) nonsense!
geaar', (-de), veined; grained; grainy; striated; streaked, streaky.
geaard', (-e), natured, tempered; earthed (electr.); ~**heid,** temper, nature, disposition; habit, habitude; education; refinement, composition; configuration (of coast).
geabonneer'de, (-s), subscriber.
geadresseer'de, (-s), addressee; consignee.
geaffekteerd', (-e), affected, false, pretended; prim; ~**heid,** affectation.
geag', (-te), respected; esteemed; *G*~*te Heer (Meneer)*, Dear Sir.
geakkrediteer', (-de), accredited; ~**de verteenwoordiger,** accredited representative.
geakkrediteer'de, (-s), accredited person.
geallieer', (-de), allied; *Die Geallieerdes*, The Allies.
geanimeer', (-de), animated; ~**d'heid,** animation.
gea'ppel, (-de), dappled, dapple-grey.
gearm', (-de), arm-in-arm.
gearresteer', (-de), arrested; ~**de misdadiger,** arrested criminal.
gearresteer'de, (-s), arrested person.
gearseer', (de-), shaded, hatched (in drawing); ~**de lyn,** hatched line.
geassureer'de, (-s), insured person.
geavanseer', (ong.) **(-de),** advanced; (ultra) modern.
gebaan', (-de), beaten; *die* ~ *de pad*, the beaten track.
gebaar', (gebare), gesture, gesticulation; *gebare MAAK*, gesticulate; *'n MOOI* ~, a fine gesture.
gebaard', (-e), bearded.
gebab'bel, babble, prattle, gossip, chatter, prate, rattle, chat; cackle; confabulation, gabble, jabber, patter, chit-chat; clack.
gebak', (s) pastry, cake, baked product; baking; (b) **(-te),** baked (bread); fried (eggs); roasted (meat); *met sy* ~ *te pere bly sit*, be left holding the baby.
geba'ker: *kort (heet)* ~ *wees*, be hasty (short-tempered, touchy).
gebak'kie, (-s), tartlet, cake, biscuit.
gebal', (-de), clenched; *met* ~ *de vuiste*, with clenched fists.
gebalanseer', (-de), balanced; ~**de HOOGTEROER,** balanced elevator; ~**de RIGTINGSNOER,** balanced rudder.
gebalk', braying.
geband'heid, banding.
geba're, gestures; ~**kuns,** mimics, mimic art; ~**maker,** mime; ~**nd, (-e),** gesticulatory; ~**spel,** gesticulation, pantomime, dumb-show; ~**taal,** gesticulatory language, dumb-show; sign-language, chirology.
gebars', (-te), burst (pipe); chapped (hands); cracked, split.

geba'sel, twaddle, silly talk.
gebed', (-e), prayer; orison; benediction; grace; *'n ~ DOEN*, pray, say (offer) a prayer; *die ~ van die HERE*, the Lord's prayer.
gebe'deboek, prayer-book, book of common-prayer.
gebe'del, begging.
gebeds': *~ mantel*, prayer-shawl; *~ riem*, phylactery; *~ verhoring*, answer to prayer.
gebeef', trembling.
gebeen'te, bones; skeleton; *wee (bewaar) jou ~!*, beware!
gebei'er, ringing.
gebei'tel, (-de), chiselled.
gebeits', (-te), stained (wood).
gebek', (-te), beaked; *elke voëltjie sing soos dit ~ is*, every one talks after his own fashion.
gebel', ringing.
gebelg', (-de), incensed, offended; *~d'heid*, anger, pique.
gebenedy', (-de), blessed.
geben'gel, ringing, chiming, clangour.
geberg'te, (-s), mountain chain, mountains; *~ kunde*, *~ leer*, orology; *~ vorming*, mountain building; orogenesis.
gebe'te: *op iem. ~ wees*, bear a grudge against someone; be embittered against someone; *~ nheid*, embitterment.
gebeuk', battering, pounding.
gebeur', (~), happen, occur, come to pass; chance; fall out; come about; *wat ook AL ~*, come (happen) what may; *what's done is done*; *om te VERHINDER dat dit weer ~*, to ensure that it does not happen again; *WAT ~ het, het ~*, the past is irrevocable.
gebeur'de: *die ~*, what (has) happened, the occurence.
gebeu're, (chain of) events.
gebeur'lik, (-e), possible, contingent; potential, eventual; *~ heid*, possibility, potentiality, probability; eventuality, contingency, emergency, chance; *~ heidsfonds*, emergency (contingency) fund; *~ heidskans*, contingent probability, contingency.
gebeur'tenis, (-se), event, occurrence, circumstance; *ryk aan ~se*, eventful; *~ roman*, novel of adventure.
gebeur'woord, verb.
gebeu'sel, piffle, twaddle, dalliance, dallying.
gebied'¹, (s) (-e), territory, area, domain, range, precinct, confine, district; sphere, field, province (of art, science, etc.); realm, empire, jurisdiction; compass; dominion; *hom op 'n ~ BEGEWE*, enter a field (sphere); *op DAARDIE ~*, in that area; in that line; *BUITE die ~ van die GESKIEDENIS*, outside the pale of history; *op die ~ van die KUNS*, in the realm of art; *dit VAL buite my ~*, this is not my province (outside my scope).
gebied'², (w) (~), dictate, command, order, direct; bid; *die gesonde verstand ~*, common sense dictates.
gebie'dend, (-e), imperious, imperative, compelling, preceptive, dictatorial, peremptory, commanding; *~ NOODSAAKLIK*, urgently necessary; *~ e WYS(E)*, imperative mood.
gebie'denderwys(e), imperiously, authoritatively.
gebie'dendheid, imperativeness.
gebie'der, (-s), ruler, master, lord, boss, dictator.
gebieds'afstand, surrender of territory.
gebied': *~ skeiding*, territorial separation; partition, *~ skending*, violation of territory.
gebieds'owerheid, territorial authority.
gebied'ster, (-s), mistress, female ruler.
gebieds'uitbreiding, extension of territory.
gebier', (-de), tipsy.
gebil'lik, (-te), approved.
gebint', cross-beams.
gebit', (-te), set of teeth, denture; bit (of bridle); *~ rand*, bar (in horse's mouth); *~ formule*, dental formula; *~ plaat*, dental plate; *~ s'regulasie*, orthodontics.
geblaar', (-de), foliate; stripped (tobacco); blistered; *~ te*, foliage.
geblaas', blowing, hiss(ing), puff(ing).

geblaat', bleating.
gebla'der, (-de), lamellar; *~ te*, foliage, leaves.
geblaf', barking; coughing; bragging.
geblaseer', (-de), blasé, bored; *~d'heid*, the state of being blasé or bored; boredom, satiety.
gebleik', (-te), bleached.
geblêr', bleating; howling (of children).
geble'we, *(verlede deelwoord van bly)*, remain.
geblik', (-te), tinned; *~ te vis*, tinned fish.
geblik'ker, glare.
geblind'doek, (-te), blindfolded.
geblits', lightning; flicker.
gebloem(d)', (-de), floral (dress); flowered, floriated, flowery; figured (fabric); *~ de taal*, flowery language.
geblok', swotting, grind.
geblokkeer', (-de), blocked.
geblom' = **gebloem(d)**.
gebloos', blushing.
gebluf', bragging, boast(ing).
geblus', (-te), extinguished (fire); slaked (lime).
gebod', (gebooie), commandment, command, edict, dictate, order, decree; bidding; *sonder GOD en Sy ~ leef*, live a godless life; *hulle STAAN onder gebooie*, they are to be married; *iem. die TIEN gebooie voorlees*, read someone a lecture.
gebo'de, *(verlede deelwoord van bied*, offer, *en gebied*, demand); offered; demanded; ordered; *drastiese optrede is ~*, drastic steps are imperative.
gebo'ë, curved, bent, arched; *met ~ hoof*, with bowed head; *~ ne*, (s), distressed person; *~ nheid*, distress.
geboei', (-de), handcuffed; captivated, interested, engrossed.
geboe'mel, loafing, revelling.
gebog'gel, (-de), hunchbacked, humpbacked, huckle-backed; crooked; *~ de*, (-s), hunchback.
gebom', booming, ringing (bells).
gebon'de, tied, bound; attached; latent (heat); *~ AAN*, committed to; obliged; *~ huis*, tied house; *~ STYL*, poetic style.
gebon'del, glomerate; bundled.
gebon'denheid, state of being tied down, bondage, lack of freedom; consistency.
gebons', bouncing, throbbing, battering, banging.
gebooi'e, *mv. van gebod*, banns; *~ brief*, banns certificate.
geboom'te, (clump of) trees.
geboor'te, (-s), birth; ancestry; nativity; nascency; parentage; *KRAGTENS sy ~*, by right of his birth; *NA die ~*, post-natal; *in die ~ (kiem) SMOOR*, nip in the bud, *VAN ~*, by birth; *VAN sy ~ af*, from his birth; *VOOR die ~*, pre-natal; *~ aanwas*, increase in births; *~ beperking*, birth-control; contraception; *~ berig*, (-te), birth notice; *~ bewys*, birth-certificate; *~ dag*, birthday; *~ datum*, date of birth; *~ grond*, native soil, homeland; *~ jaar*, year of birth; *~ kerk*, Church of the Nativity; *~ land*, native land, fatherland; *~ plek*, birth-place; *~ pyn*, birth pang; labour pain(s); *~ reg*, birthright; *~ register*, birth-register, *~ registrasie*, registration of births; *~ sang*, nativity ode; *~ sertifikaat*, birth-certificate; *~ stad*, home(town); *~ syfer*, birth-rate; natality; *~ uur*, hour of birth; *~ van*, maiden name; *~ vlek*, birth-mark; *~ wee*, labour pains, birth throes.
geboor'tig: *~ uit X*, native of X, hailing from X.
geborduur', (-de), brocaded; embroidered.
gebo're, born; *'n ~ ENGELSMAN*, an Englishman by birth; *~ en GETOË*, born and bred; *MEV. A. ~ B.*, Mrs. A. born (née) B; *'n ~ ONDERWYSER*, a born teacher; *nie ~ in STAAT nie om*, be totally unable to, be wholly incapable of.
geborg', (-de), sponsored.
gebor'ge, safe; provided for; *~ nheid*, safety, freedom from care.
geborneerd, (-de), (ong.), narrow-minded, stupid.
gebor'rel, gurgling, bubbling, hubble-bubble, popple.
gebors', (-te), chested.
gebor'sel, (-de), aristate.
gebos'seleerd, (-e), embossed.

gebot′ter, (-de), buttered.
gebou′, (s) (-e), building, structure; fabric; premises, edifice; construction; (b) **(-de),** built; *'n sterk ~ de atleet,* a well-built athlete; **~ e-inspekteur,** building inspector; **~ ekompleks,** block (pile) of buildings; **~ eopsigter,** caretaker; clerk of works.
gebraai′, (-de), roasted, grilled, fried, broiled; tipsy; *~ de BEESVLEIS,* roast beef; *~ de BROOD,* fried bread; *~ de EIER,* fried egg; *~ de RIBBETJIE,* roast(ed) rib; *~ de SKAAPLEWER,* lamb's fry; *in die SON ~,* parched in the sun; sun-tanned.
gebraak′, (-te), fallowed.
gebrab′bel, jargon, gibberish.
gebrag′, (vero.), brought.
gebral′, bragging, boasting.
gebrand′, (-e), burnt (by sun); stained (glass); roasted (coffee); *~ e AMANDELS,* burnt almonds (sweets); *BRUIN ~,* sun-tanned; *~ e GIPS,* plaster of Paris.
gebreek′, (-te), broken, fractured (leg); fractional; *~ te HAWER,* crushed oats; *~ te MIELIES,* crushed mealies.
gebrei′, (-de), knitted; hardened, inured; trained; *'n ~ de span,* a trained team.
gebrek′, (-e), defect, fault, flaw, blemish; deficiency; default; deformity; disability; lack, absence, privation, need, paucity; penury; want; failure; destitution, dearth, scarcity, famine; poverty; *weens ~ aan BEWYS,* for want of evidence; *in ~ e BLY om . . , fail to . .; by ~ aan BROOD eet 'n mens korsies van pastei,* if water cannot be had, we must make shift with wine; *BY ~ aan,* for want of; failing; *~ HÊ aan,* be in want of, be short of; *aan niks ~ HÊ nie,* want for nothing; *~ LY,* suffer, want; *die ~ e van die OUDERDOM,* the infirmities of old age; *~ aan RUIMTE hê,* be cramped for room; *SPRAAK~,* speech impediment; *in 'n ~ VOORSIEN,* fill a want; *~ aan WERKERS,* scarcity of labour(ers).
gebrek′kig, (-e), defective, faulty; deficient, inadequate; impotent; *hom ~ uitdruk,* express oneself badly (imperfectly); **~ heid,** defectiveness, faultiness.
gebrek′lik, (-e), disabled, crippled, decrepit; abnormal, deformed, afflicted; infirm; *~ e, (-s),* disabled person; **~ heid,** infirmity, crippled state, affliction; abnormity.
gebrek′siekte, deficiency disease.
gebril′, (-de), bespectacled.
gebroe′ders, brothers; *die ~ Van Tonder,* Van Tonder Bros.
gebroed′sel, (-s), brood; rabble, scum.
gebro′ke, broken; broken-hearted; ruined; *~ ENGELS,* broken (poor) English; *~ GETAL,* fraction; *'n ~ HART,* a broken heart; *~ TERREIN,* broken ground; *~ VELD,* broken veld, mixed pasturage.
gebro′kehartjies, bleeding heart *(Dicentra spectabilis).*
gebro′kenheid, brokenness.
gebrom′, buzz(ing), growl(ing), grumbling; humming (of motor engine); drone.
gebrons′, (-de), bronzed, tanned (by sun).
gebrou′, concoction; mess; botching, slapdash.
gebruik′, (s) (-e), use; usage, practice, exercise; convention; habit, custom; praxis, consuetude; employment; ethos; consumption (of food); application; *volgens ALOUE ~,* according to time-honoured usage (custom); *die ~ BESLIS,* usage decides; *uit ~ GAAN,* pass out of use; *IN ~,* in use; *~ MAAK van,* make use of, avail oneself of; *NA ~,* when done with, when it has served its purpose; *in ~ NEEM,* bring into use, put into service; *buite ~ RAAK,* go out of use; *slegs vir UITWENDIGE ~,* for external use only; *VRYE ~ hê van,* have the free use of; (w) (~), use, employ; take, touch (liquor); enjoy (food); (b) **(-te),** used, secondhand (vehicle); **~ er, (-s),** user; consumer; usuary; **~ goed,** articles in daily use.
gebruik′lik, (-e), usual, customary; accustomed, conventional; habitual; consuetudinary; ordinary; **~ heid,** use, usage, conventionality.

gebruik′making, use, using, utilization, making use of; *by ~ van,* when using.
gebruik′mielies, mealies for own consumption.
gebruiks′: ~ aanwysing, directions for use; **~ boek,** customary (R.C.); **~ duur,** period of use; life cycle.
gebruik′sfeer, sphere of use.
gebruiks′: ~ kode, code of practice, instruction (operating) manual; **~ lading,** normal charge; **~ reg,** right of use; **~ taal,** colloquial language; **~ voorwerp,** implement; object of utility; **~ waarde,** use-value (of money); utilitarian value; **~ wyse,** method of use.
gebruin′, (-de), sunburnt, tanned; brown.
gebruis′, effervescence (of lemonade); roar (of the ocean.
gebrul′, roaring, howling, bellow, cry, growl.
gebuig′, (-de), bent, crooked.
gebuk′, (-te), gebuk′kend, (-e), croaching, stooping; *~ gaan onder 'n las,* bowed down by a burden, be heavily burdened.
gebul′der, rumbling, booming, roar; blustering, bellow.
gebulk′, lowing, bellowing, bleat.
gebult′, (-e), dented; hunch-backed; bulged (sheets).
gebun′del, (-de), collected (poems).
gebuur′te, (-s), neighbourhood.
gebyt′, (-e), bitten; struck (on), smitten (fond of).
gedaag′de, (-s), defendant, respondent.
gedaan′, (gedane), done, finished; exhausted; worn out; *ons KOS is ~,* we have no food left; *niks ~ KRY nie,* get nothing done; not have one's way; *'n MOTOR ~ ry,* wear out a car; *~ WEES,* be dead tired; *~ VOEL,* feel done up (exhausted); *dit WIL ~ wees,* it takes some doing.
gedaan′te, (-s), shape, form, aspect; configuration; spectre, apparition; face; *IN menslike ~,* in human shape; *IN die ~ van,* in the shape of; *van ~ VERANDER,* undergo a change of form; *hom in sy ware ~ VERTOON,* reveal himself in his true colours; **~ leer,** morphology; **~ verandering, ~ verwisseling,** metamorphosis, transformation; transfiguration; **~ vorming,** figuration; **~ wisseling:** *'n ~ wisseling ondergaan,* undergo a change of form.
gedag′, *(verlede deelwoord van dink): ek het so ~ (gedink),* I thought so.
gedag′te, (-s), thought, idea, notion, opinion; mind; reflection; *'n BLINK ~,* a bright idea; *BY die ~ aan,* at the thought of; *sy ~ s nie bymekaar HÊ nie,* be absent-minded; *DIEP in ~ s versink,* absorbed in thought; *die ~ laat GAAN oor iets,* reflect upon something, ponder over something; *hulle ~ is so kort as hulle NEUSE,* they have short memories; *op twee ~ s HINK,* be in two minds; *in ~ HOU,* remember; bear in mind; *IN ~ wees,* be in a brown study; *op die ~ KOM,* come to mind; *die ~ KRY,* get the idea; *SOOS 'n ~,* quick as thought; *~ s in TOLVRY,* one may think what one likes; *van ~ VERANDER,* change one's mind; *sy ~ s VERSAMEL,* collect one's thoughts; *VOLGENS my ~,* to my mind; *van ~ WEES om,* think of, mean to; *van ~ WEES dat,* be of the opinion that; *~ s WISSEL oor,* exchange views on; **~ armoede,** poverty of thought; **~ beeld,** thought image; idea, thought; **~ gang,** order of thought, line of thought; **~ inhoud,** thought content; **~ kring,** range of thought; **~ lees,** thought-reading; **~ leser,** thought reader; clairvoyant, mindreader; **~ lesery,** mindreading; clairvoyancy; **~ loop,** train of thought.
gedag′teloos, (..lose), thoughtless, absent-minded; reckless; **~ heid,** thoughtlessness, absent-mindedness.
gedag′tenis, remembrance, memory; memento, keepsake; favour; memorial; *SALIGER ~,* of blessed memory; *TER ~ aan (van),* in memory of; as a memorial to; **~ diens,** memorial service.
gedag′te: ~ prikkelend, (-e), thought-provoking; **~ rigting,** train (trend) of thought; **~ ryk, (-e),** thought-provoking; **~ skool,** school of thought; **~ streep,** dash, horizontal stroke; **~ verband,** context; **~ vlug,** flight of fancy; **~ vormer,** opinion former; **~ wending,** turn of thought; **~ wêreld,**

gedagtig / gedruk

realm (sphere) of thought; ~ **wisseling**, interchange of thoughts (views, ideas), discussion, discourse.
gedag'tig, mindful; ~ *aan*, mindful of.
gedag'vaarde, (-s), person summoned.
gedamasseer', (-de), damascened (steel); well-built; thorough.
gedans', dancing; frolicking.
gedar'tel, dalliance, frolic.
geda'wer, booming, resounding; thundering, peal, clangour; *die* ~ *van kanonne*, the booming of cannon.
gede'ë, solid; pure; native (element).
gedeel', (-de), divided, dividual, shared, partite.
gedeel'te, (-s), part, section, portion, moiety, share, instalment; *vir 'n GROOT* ~, largely, to a great extent; *OORBLYWENDE* ~, balance, remainder, rest.
gedeel'telik, (b) (-e), partial; fractional; fractionary; ~ *e VAKUUM*, partial vacuum; ~ *e VERBRAN*= *DING*, incomplete combustion; (bw) partly, partially.
gedegenereer', (-de), degenerate.
gedegenereer', (-de), degraded; *'n* ~ *de*, a degraded person; a soldier reduced in rank.
gedein', rolling, heaving, swell.
gedek', (-te), covered; pregnant (animal); guarded, secured; thatched (roof); ~ *wees teen brandskade*, insured against fire.
gedekolleteer', (-de), low-necked (dress), décolleté.
gedelegeer'de, (-s), delegate, representative.
gedemp', (-te), filled up; dim (light); *te LIG*, dimmed light; ~ *PRAAT*, murmer; *op* ~ *te TOON*, in a muffled voice.
gedenk', (~), remember, commemorate, bear in mind; ~ **boek**, memorial book, remembrance book; album; ~ **dag**, anniversary; memorial day; ~ **diens**, memorial service; ~ **fonds**, memorial fund; ~ **jaar**, memorial year; ~ **naald**, obelisk, monument; ~ **offer**, commemorative offering; ~ **penning**, commemorative medal; ~ **plaat**, memorial tablet; ~ **rol**, annals, record; ~ **saal**, memorial hall; ~ **seel**, phylactery; ~ **seël**, memorial stamp; ~ **skrif**, memoir; ~ **spreuk**, apophthegm, aphorism; ~ **steen**, memorial stone; slab; cenotaph; ~ **stuk**, memorial; record; ~ **suil**, commemorative pillar; ~ **teken**, memorial, monument; ~ **tuin**, garden of remembrance; ~ **uitgawe**, commemorative publication (edition).
gedenkwaar'dig, (-e), memorable; red-letter, commemorable, never-to-be-forgotten; ~ **hede**, memorabilia; ~ **heid**, memorableness; memorability; monument.
gedeponeer', (-de), deposited (amount).
gedeporteer'de, (-s), deported person, deportee.
gedeputeer'de, (-s), delegate, deputy, representative.
gederm'te, entrails.
gedetailleer', (-de), detailed, in detail.
gedetermineer', (-de), determined; identified; ~ **d'**, firm, resolute; *•d om sy sin te kry*, firmly resolved to have his way; ~ **d'heid**, determination, resoluteness.
gedlend': *nie van (met) iets* ~ *wees nie*, not be pleased with something, not prepared to tolerate something.
gediens'tig, (-e), officious; obliging; ~ **heid**, officiousness; obligingness, readiness to oblige.
gedier'te, (-s), animals, beasts; insects, vermin; monster.
gedifferensieer', (-de), differentiated; ~ **d'heid**, differentiation.
gedig', (-te), poem; ~ **sel**, (-s), thoughts.
geding', (-e), lawsuit, action, case; quarrel; *in* ~ *tree*, join issue; ~ **koste**, costs of suit; ~ **voerend (-e)**: ~ *voerende partye*, contending parties; ~ **voering**, litigation.
gediplomeer', (-de), provided with diploma (teacher); chartered (accountant); qualified, certificated.
gedisponeer', (-de), disposed of (by testament).
gedissemineer', (-de), disseminated; ~ *de erts*, disseminated ore.
gedissiplineer', (-de), disciplined.
gedistilleer', (-de), distilled.

gedistingeer', (-de), distinguished, refined-looking; striking; ~ **d'heid**, refinement, distinction.
gedob'bel, gambling.
gedo'de, (-s), killed person, casualty.
gedoe', bustle, noise, hubbub, fuss.
gedo'ë, (~), tolerate, permit, suffer, allow; *see* **ge= doog**.
gedoe'del, skirling.
gedoef', thudding.
gedoem', (-de), doomed.
gedoen'te, (-s), fuss, noise, business, to-do, affair, ado, hullabaloo; contraption.
gedog', (*verl. dw. van* **dink**), thought.
gedok'ter, (s) (medical) treatment: (b) (-de), (medically) treated; *'n ge* ~ *de verslag*, a doctored report.
gedokumenteer', (-de), documented (finding); documentary (film).
gedo'mie = **gedorie(waar)**.
gedomisilieer', (-de), domiciled.
gedomp', (-te), dipped (light); ~ *te lig*, passing beam; dipped light.
gedon'der, thunder(ing); botheration; fulmination.
gedoog', (~) = **gedoë**.
gedop', (-te), tipsy; shelled (peas); failed (in examination).
gedo'rie(waar), really, upon my word.
gedors', (-te), threshed (grain).
gedra', (~), behave, conduct, act; deport; carry; demean; *hy* ~ *hom GOED*, he behaves well; *'n mens* ~ *jou nie net voor vreemde MENSE nie*, one should always be on one's best behaviour; *hy* ~ *hom SLEG*, he behaves badly.
gedraai'¹, (s) lingering, tarrying, delay.
gedraai'², (s) turning, rotation, twisting; (b) (-de), convoluted; turned, twisted; ~ **d'heid**, torsion; twistedness.
gedraal', loitering, delay.
gedra'e, sustained (style); legato (mus.); ~ **nheid**, sustention, sustaining; loftiness.
gedrag', (-inge), behaviour, conduct, demeanour; air; deportment; governance; doings; *'n bewys van goeie* ~, testimonial (of good behaviour); ~ **boek**, conduct book; ~ **inge**, actions, doings, course of conduct.
gedrags': ~ **afwykend**, (-e), deviate; ~ **kode**, code of ethics; ~ **leer**, behaviourism.
gedrags'lyn, line of conduct, course; cue; *sy* ~ *BE= PAAL*, decide on (define) one's line of action; *te WERK gaan volgens 'n sekere* ~, follow a certain course; ~ **norm**, norm of conduct; ~ **orde**, order of conduct.
gedrags'reël, rule of conduct.
gedrag'syfer, conduct mark.
gedrang', crowd, throng; crush, push, press, jam; *in die* ~ *kom*, become hard pressed; suffer; become involved; come under fire.
gedrenk', (-te), saturated; imbued.
gedren'tel, lounging, dallying, sauntering.
gedresseer', (-de), trained (horses).
gedreun', droning, drone, sing-song; din; boom; drumming; *die* ~ *van die GOLWE*, the booming of the waves; *die* ~ *van VLIEGTUIE*, the drone (droning) of aeroplanes.
gedre'we, driven; actuated; embossed (metals); ~ *deur die BEGEERTE om*, actuated by the desire to; ~ *KETTINGRAT*, driven sprocket; ~ *PLAAT*, driven plate; ~ *RAT*, driven gear; *deur STOOM* ~, steam-driven.
gedrib'bel, dribbling.
gedril', drilling; quivering.
gedrink', (-te), tipsy, drunk.
gedrog', (-te), monster.
gedrog'telik, (-e), monstrous, misshapen; ~ **heid**, monstrosity.
gedron'ge, compact, terse (style); thick-set, stumpy; ~ *voel om*, feel obliged to; ~ **nheid**, compactness, terseness.
gedroog', (-de), dried.
gedroom', dreaming.
gedros', desertion.
gedruis', (-e), noise, stir, bustle, rumbling.
gedruk', (s) squeeze; squeezing; (b) (-te), printed; de=

gedrup

pressed, dejected; pressed; heavy-laden; ~**t'heid**, depressedness; depression; dullness.
gedrup', drip; *'n gedurige* ~ *maak 'n gat in 'n klip*, constant dropping wears the stone; the drop hollows the stone not by force but by often falling.
gedryf', driven; propelled; urged, actuated; forced.
gedug', (-te), formidable, redoubtable; tremendous, severe; feared, dreaded; *'n* ~ *te PAK*, a sound thrashing; *'n* ~ *te VYAND*, a formidable enemy; ~**t'heid**, formidableness; formidability; awe.
gedui'wel, botheration.
geduld', patience, forbearance; ~ *HÊ (gebruik)*, have patience; *net 'n OOMBLIKKIE* ~, just a moment, please; *my* ~ *is OP*, my patience is exhausted; ~ *VERLOOR*, lose patience; ~**igheid**, patience; ~**spel**, patience (game); jigsaw puzzle.
gedu'rende, during, for a time, pending.
gedurf', (-de), daring, risky; improper (joke); risque; ~**d'heid**, recklessness, bravado.
gedu'rig, (b) (-e), constant, continual, frequent, incessant; (bw) constantly, continually, always, incessantly, frequently.
gedu'rigdeur, gedu'riglik = **gedurig**, (bw).
gedwaal', wandering, roaming.
gedwar'rel, whirl(ing).
gedwee', (..**dweë**, ..**dweër**, -ste), submissive, pliant, conformable, tractable, meek; governable; *so* ~ *soos 'n lam*, as meek as a lamb; ~**heid**, meekness, submissiveness, mansuetude, conformability.
gedweep', fanaticism, excessive enthusiasm, raving.
gedwerg', (-de), stunted.
gedwon'ge, forced (laugh); compulsory (service); farsought (conclusion); enforced (visit); constrained (manner); unnatural (pose); ~ *sekwestrasie*, compulsory sequestration; ~**nheid**, constraint; unnaturalness.
gedy', (~), prosper, thrive, flourish, do well; result.
gee, (ge-), give, confer, present with, allow, grant (permission); yield (fruit); lay down (rules); cause (trouble); afford (opportunity); impart (colour); administer (medicine); bear (interest); place (orders); deal (cards); *dit* ~ *'n totale BEDRAG van*, this makes a total amount of; *te DINK(E)* ~, be food for thought; *EERS ge* ~ *en weer geneem, is erger as 'n DIEF gesteel*, to give a thing and take a thing is to wear the devil's gold ring; *wie GOU* ~, ~ *dubbel*, he gives twice who gives in a trice; *EENS gegee (gegewe), bly gegee (gegewe)*, a gift remains a gift; *dit GEWONNE* ~, yield the point, give in; *aan die wat HET, sal gegee word*, whoever has, to him shall be given; *te KENNE* ~, intimate; allege; *hom MOEITE* ~, take great pains; *'n mens moet* ~ *en NEEM*, one has to give and take; *dit* ~ *NIKS*, it is of no use; nothing will come of it; *ek* ~ *nie OM nie*, I don't mind; ~ *PAD!* stand clear! *REKEN-SKAP* ~ *van*, account for; give an account of; *'n SUG* ~, heave a sigh; *iem. TYD* ~ *om*, allow a person time to; *al sy TYD* ~ *aan*, devote all his time to; *VERLIGTING* ~, bring relief; *iem. iets te VERSTAAN* ~, give someone to understand, bring someone under the impression.
geëelt', (-e), calloused.
geëer', (-de), honoured.
geef: (vero.) *wie* ~ *wat hy heef (het), is waardig dat hy leef*, give and spend and God will send; ~**ster**, (-s), vroulik *van* **gewer**, donatress.
geëis', (-te), demanded; *die* ~ *te bedrag*, the amount demanded.
geëksalteer', (-de), overwrought, overstrung.
geel, (s) (**gele**), yolk (of an egg); yellow; yellowness; yellow-dun (horse); *die* ~ *van twee eiers*, the yolks of two eggs; (b) yellow; *hoe geler, hoe JA-LOERSER*, the jealous favour yellow; *die* ~ *PERS*, the yellow press; ~ *SKOENE*, tan shoes; ~**agtig**, (-e), yellowish; carroty; flavescent; ~**baadjie**: *die* ~ *baadjie aanhê*, be jealous; ~**bek**, Cape salmon; yellow-billed duck *(Anas undulata)*; half-caste; ~**bek(bos)duif**, *Columba arquatrix arquatrix*; ~**bekeend**, yellow-bill duck; ~**bekooievaar**, wood stork; ~**bekwou**, *see* **kuikendief**; ~**blom(metjie)**, Cape saffron; ~**boek**, yellow book (official publication); ~**boom**, Port Jackson;

gees

~**borsie**, icterine warbler; ~**bruin**, tan, tawny; fawn; ochre; bridle(d); sienna; ~**dikkop**, tribulosis (ovium) (sheep disease); ~**gat**, bulbul; ~**gietery**, brass foundry; ~**gom**, gamboge; ~**goud**, antique gold; ~**granaat**, *see* **driedoring**; ~**groen**, yellowish green; flavovirens; ~**grond**, yellow ground; kimberlite; ~**haak**, *Acacia senegal*; ~**haarvrou**, platinum blonde; ~**heid**, yellowness; ~**hout**, yellowwood *(Podocarpus)*; fustic; citron wood; ~**kalossie**, *Ixia maculata*; ~**kapel**, yellow cobra; ~**klei**, ochre, yellow clay; ~**koors**, yellow fever; ~**koper**, (yellow) brass; ~**koperband**, brass tape; ~**koperbeslag**, brass furnishings; ~**koperlynstafie**, brass rule; ~**koperplaat**, brass sheet; ~**koppie**, mountain dahlia *(Liparia sphaerica)*; ~**kuifpikkewyn**, rock-hopper; ~**magriet**, yellow daisy; ~**meerkat**, thick-tailed mongoose; yellow meercat; ~**mielie**, yellow mealie; *vol* ~ *mielies wees*, be full of beans (high spirits); ~**patrys**, spotted sandgrouse; ~**perske**, yellow clingstone peach; ~**perskereën**, rain during canning (fruit-drying) season; ~**piesang**, *Strelitzia regina*; ~**rooi**, saffron; ~**rys**, "yellow" rice, rice with turmeric; ~**seep**, yellow soap; ~**sel**, yellow colouring; ~**siekte**, jaundice (in cattle); ~**slang**, yellow cobra, Cape cobra; ~**spreeu**, oriole; ~**stert**, yellowtail, albacore *(Seriola lalandii)*; ~**stroop**, golden syrup.
geel'sug, jaundice; icterus; chlorosis (in plants); ~**kuur**, jaundice cure; ~**lyer**, icteric; ~**middel**, jaundice cure (medicine); ~**'tig**, (-e), jaundiced; icteric; ~**wortel**, root of curcuma.
geel: ~**suiker**, yellow sugar; ~**sysie**, yellow seedeater; ~**vel'lig**, (-e), yellow-skinned; ~**vink**, masked weaver; golden sovereign; ~**vlek**, yellow spot (in plants); ~**wortel**, carrot.
geëmaljeer', (-de), enamelled.
geëmansipeer', (-de), emancipated.
geëmplojeer'de, (-s), employee.
geen¹, (s) (**gene**), gene.
geen², (vnw, b) none, no; ~ *ANDER as hy nie*, nobody else but he; ~ *van BEIDE*, neither of them; *daar is glad* ~ *GEVAAR by nie*, it is not in the least dangerous; ~ *INGANG*, no entry; ~ *die MINSTE verskil*, no difference whatever; ~ *PARKERING*, no parking; *g'n STUK (gestuk) lollery nie!* not the slightest nonsense! ~ *U-DRAAI*, no U-turn.
geëndosseer'de, (-s), endorsee.
geeneen', no one, not one; none; *ek ken* ~ *van die kinders nie*, I don't know any of the children.
geen'sins, by no means, not at all, in no wise; *dit is* ~ *nodig nie*, this is by no means necessary.
geënt', (-e), grafted; inoculated, vaccinated; ~ *e rivier*, engrafted river.
geep, (gepe), hornbeak; garfish *(Scomberesox saurus)*.
ge'ër, (-s), giver, donor; ~**y**, giving (alms), donating.
geer, (s) (**gere**), gore (skirt); gusset; (w) (**ge-**), gore.
geërf', (-de), inherited; patrimonial; ~ *de DREINERING*, superimposed drainage; ~ *de RIVIER*, superimposed river.
geer'rok, gored skirt, skirt with gores.
gees, (-te), spirit, ghost; mettle; essence; animus; mind, psyche, wit, intellect; tendency; tone; genie, python; bog(e)y, peri; *ARM van* ~, poor in spirit; *hoe groter* ~, *hoe groter BEES*, master minds are often ill-mannered; *iem. se* ~ *BLUS*, dampen a person's enthusiasm; ~ *van BRANDEWYN*, spirits of wine; *voor die* ~ *BRING (roep)*, call to mind; *in DIESELFDE* ~, in the same spirit (strain); *die* ~ *GEE*, give up the ghost, die; *in die* ~ *van die GRONDWET*, in accordance with the constitution; *'n GROOT* ~, a master spirit; *daar HEERS 'n slegte* ~ *op dié skool*, there is a bad tone in that school; *die HEILIGE* ~, the Holy Ghost; *'n verslag IN hierdie* ~, a report on these lines; *voor die* ~ *KOM*, spring to mind; *soos die* ~ *LEI*, as the spirit moves; *na die* ~ *en die LETTER*, in letter and in spirit; *soos 'n* ~ *LYK*, look like a ghost, be as thin as a lath; *iets in dieselfde* ~ *OPVAT*, take something in the same spirit; *voor die* ~ *STAAN*, to be seen in the mind's eye; *in die* ~ *TEENWOORDIG wees*, be present in spirit; *TRAAG van*

~, slow-witted, mentally slack; *die ~ van die TYD*, the spirit (tendency) of the times; *as die ~ in hom VAAR*, when the spirit moves him; *die ~ is gewillig, maar die VLEES is swak*, the spirit is willing but the flesh is weak; *in ~ en in WAARHEID*, in spirit and in truth; ~ **besweerder**, exorcist, conjurer, conjuror; ~ **do'dend, (-e)**, monotonous, dull; ~ **do'dendheid**, monotony, dullness.

gees'drif, enthusiasm, ardour, zeal; zest; ecstasy; ~ *VERWEK*, stir up enthusiasm; *VOL ~ wees oor*, be most enthusiastic about; ~**'tig, (-e)**, enthusiastic, zealous, ecstatic.

gees'drywer, fanatic; bigot; ~**y**, fanaticism, bigotry.

gees'genoot, (..note), kindred soul; congenial spirit.

gees'krag, spirit, strength of mind, mental power; nerve; energy.

gees'ryk, (-e), witty, ardent, ingenious; spirituous; ~*e dranke*, spirituous liquors; ~**heid**, wit, wittiness; strength (of liquor).

geëssaieer', (-de), assayed.

gees'te: ~ **banner**, ~ **besweerder**, exorcist; necromancer; ~ **beswering**, exorcism; psychomancy; ~ **dom**, the spirit world; ~ **klopper**, spirit rapper; ~ **kloppery**, spirit rappings; ~ **leer**, spiritualism; demonology; pneumatology.

gees'telik, (-e), spiritual; mental, intellectual (gifts); sacred (songs); religious, clerical, ecclesiastical (duties); ghostly; moral; ~*e voorbehoud*, mental reservation; ~ **e, (-s)**, clergyman, minister, parson, abbé, ecclesiastic, priest, ablate, cleric; ~ **heid**, clergy; spirituality; clerisy; church.

goos'toloos, (..lose), spiritless, senseless, pointless; dull, inane, insipid; ~**heid**, insipidity

gees'teryk, spirit realm, invisible world.

gees'tes: ~ **adel**, mental nobility; ~ **arbeid**, mental work; ~ **armoede**, poverty of mind; ~ **beeld**, mental image; ~ **beskawing**, refinement of the mind; ~ **dissipline**, mental discipline; ~ **gawe(s)**, intellectual gift(s); ability; ~ **gebrek**, mental disorder; ~ **gesteldheid**, mental indisposition; state of mind, mentality; ~ **higiëne**, spiritual hygiene; ~ **houding**, attitude of mind.

gees'te: ~ **sieke**, mental patient; ~ **siekte**, mental disease; ~ **siener**, visionary; one who sees ghosts; spiritist.

gees'tes: ~ **inspanning**, mental exertion; ~ **kind**, brain-child; ~ **krank**, mentally sick; ~ **kranke**, mental patient; ~ **krankheid**, mental disease; ~ **kwelling**, mental torture; ~ **lewe**, mental life; culture; ~ **lyding**, mental suffering; ~ **oog**, the mind's eye; ~ **rigting**, spiritual bent, mental tendency; ~ **toestand**, state of mind, mental condition.

gees'testoornis, mental derangement.

gees'testroming, cultural (spritual) trend.

gees'tes: ~ **vermoëns**, mental faculties; ~ **vervoering**, exaltation; ecstasy; ~ **verwarring**, mental derangement; ~ **voedsel**, mental pabulum, food for the mind; ~ **werksaamheid**, mental activity; G ~ **wetenskaplike Navorsing, Raad vir**, Human Sciences Research Council; ~ **wetenskappe**, humanities, human sciences.

gees'te-uur, ghostly hour

gees'tewêreld, spirit world.

gees'tig, (-e), witty, facetious, humorous; pointed, right, smart, keen-witted; ~**heid**, wit, quip, witticism, humour; ~ **hede**, facetiae.

gees'verheffend, (-e), elevating (the mind); noble, edifying, sublime

gees'vermoë(ns), intellectual power; power of the mind; *gekrenkte ~*, unsound mind.

gees'verrukking, rapture, ecstasy; trance.

gees'verskyning, apparition, ghost, phantasm, spectre.

gees'vervoering, exaltation, rapture; *in ~ bring*, hold entranced.

gees'verwant, (s) (-e), kindred spirit; adherent (politics); (b) **(-e)**, congenial; ~ **skap**, mental affinity, congeniality.

geeu, (s) (-e), yawn; (w) **(ge-)**, yawn; ~ **honger**, bulimia, canine hunger.

geëwere'dig, (-de), commensurate; ~ *wees aan*, be commensurate to.

gefarseer', (-de), forced, stuffed (meat).

gefatsoeneer', (-de), moulded; shaped.

gefe'mel, cant.

gefingeer', (-de), fictive, fictitious, feigned.

geflad'der, flutter(ing); flitter.

geflap', flapping.

geflatteer(d)', (-de), flattered; flattering (photo).

geflens', (-de), flanged; ~ *de ent*, flanged end.

geflik'flooi, coaxing, wheedling.

geflik'ker, twinkling, flashing; flicker(ing).

geflirt', flirting, flirtation.

geflits', flashing.

geflon'ker, sparkling, sparkle.

gefluis'ter, whispering; rustling; buzzing.

gefluit', whistling, piping, warbling (of birds); wheezing (of chest); hiss(ing); pinging; hoot(ing); catcalls; passing water.

gefnuik', (-te), crippled; frustrated.

gefoe'lie, (-de), foliate; foiled.

gefoe'ter(y), nonsense; teasing; botheration.

gefolieer', (-de), foliated.

geforseer', (-de), forced, constrained; ~ *de mars*, forced march.

gefortuneer', (-de), rich, wealthy.

gefrankeer(d)', (-de), prepaid, post-paid, stamped.

gefrom'mel, (-de), crumpled.

gefundeer', (-de), funded.

gefuif', feasting.

gegaap', yawning, gaping.

gega'digde, (-s), prospective (intending) buyer, tenant; interested party

gegaf'fel(d), (-de), dichotomous; forked.

gegalm', bawling, (monotonous) chant.

gegalvaniseer', (-de), galvanised; ~ *de yster*, galvanised iron.

gegarandeer', (-de), warranted, guaranteed.

gege'we, (s) (-ns), datum, information; premise, premiss; (b) given; *EENS ~, bly ~*, a gift (always) remains a gift; *in die ~ OMSTANDIGHEDE*, in the (existing) circumstances; *op 'n ~ UUR*, at a given hour; *jou aan jou ~ WOORD hou*, stick to one's word.

gegier', yell(ing), scream(ing).

gegig'gel, giggling, tittering.

gegil', scream(ing), yell(ing).

gegin'negaap, sniggering.

gegis¹, (s) guessing; (b) **(-te)**, guessed; ~ *te bestek*, dead reckoning.

gegis², (s) fermentation; (b) fermented.

geglans', (-de), glacé; glazed.

geglaseer', (-de), glazed (paper); glacé (kid); sugared (fruits).

geglasuur(d)', (-de), glazed (tile).

gegleuf', (-de), slotted; fluted.

gegoed', (-e), well-to-do, well-off, moneyed; ~ **heid**, ease, competency, wealth.

gego'ël, gego'gel, juggling.

gegolf', (-de), set in waves, waved (hair); corrugated (road); undulating (hills); crispate; ~ *de yster*, corrugated iron.

gegom', (-de), gummed.

gegons', buzz(ing), whirr, hum, drone; ping(ing).

gegor'rel, (s) gargling; gurgle; (b) **(-de)**, fenced in.

gego'te, cast (steel); pressed (glass); molten (image); ~ *yster*, cast iron.

gegrab'bel, scramble; grabbing.

gegradeer', (-de), graded.

gegradueer', (-de), graduated.

gegradueer'de, (-s), (post-)graduate.

gegranuleer', (-de), granulated.

gegratineer', (-de), au gratin (cookery).

gegraveer(d)', (-de), engraved.

gegren'del, (-de), barred, bolted, interlocked.

gegrens', whining, howling, puling.

gegrief', (-de), annoyed, vexed; ~ **d'heid**, annoyance.

gegrif', (-te), graven, incised.

gegrin'nik, grinning.

gegroef', (-de), grooved (beams); fluted (columns); splined (shaft); furrowed (brow); lined (countenance); slotted (gun); canaliculated; groovy.

gegroet'! hail!

gegrom', rumbling; growl.

gegrond', (-e), well-founded; sound; ~ *e redes*, sound reasons; ~ **heid**, soundness, justness.
gegruis', (-de), gravelled.
gehaaihoei', rowdiness.
gehaak', (-te), hooked; crocheted.
gehaas', (s) hurry; (b) (-te), hurried; ~ *wees*, be in a hurry; ~ **t'heid**, hurry, haste.
gehaat', (gehate), hated, detested.
gehak'¹, (s) minced (meat); (b) (-te), chopped, minced.
gehak'², (b) (-te), heeled; *hoog* ~ *te skoentjies*.
gehak'kel, stammering, stuttering.
gehal'te, quality, standard, calibre; fineness, content, grade (of ore); alloy (of gold); proof, strength (alcohol); *van GERINGE* ~, of low grade, of a low standard; *van HOË* ~, of a high standard; *INNERLIKE* ~, intrinsic value; ~ **beheer**, quality control.
geha'mer, (s) hammering; (b) ~ (d), (-de), hammerdressed.
gehand'haaf, (-de), maintained; ~ *de rivier*, antecedent river.
gehand'skoen, (-de), gloved.
gehard', (-e), hardened, hardy; ~ *teen*, inured to; ~ **heid**, hardiness, inurement; temper (steel).
gehar'nas, (-te), in armour, mailed, panoplied, mailclad; protected.
gehar'rewar, gehar'war, bickering(s), wrangling.
Geha'sie: *van waar* ~? from where do you come so unexpectedly? what brings you here so suddenly?
gehas'pel, pother, annoyance; botheration.
geha'wend, (-e), battered, dilapidated.
geheel', (s) (gehele), whole, entireness, entirety; aggregate; entirety; ensemble; *as* ~, as a whole; *IN die* ~ *nie*, not al all; *iets in sy* ~ *NEEM*, look at a matter as a whole; *OOR die* ~, on the whole, in the main; *een* ~ *VORM*, form an integral part of; (b) (geheel), whole entire, quite, complete; ~ *en AL*, completely, wholly, totally; all over; *GLAD en* ~ *nie*, under no circumstances; ~ *die UWE*, yours sincerely; ~ **beeld**, complete view, total image; ~ **getal**, integer, whole number; ~ **heid**, wholeness, entirety, totality.
geheel'onthouding, total abstinence, teetotalism.
geheel'onthouer, teetotaller, total abstainer, Good Templar.
geheel'opname, full shot (film).
geheg', (-te), attached, fond; ~ **t'heid**, fondness, attachment; adhesion.
gehei'lig, (-de), hallowed, consecrated; ~ **de**, (-s), saint.
geheim', (s) (-e), secret; privacy; *'n* ~ *BEWAAR*, keep a secret; *IN die* ~, in secret, secretly; *geen* ~ *van iets MAAK nie*, make no secret of something; *'n* ~ *OPHELDER*, clear up a mystery; *'n* ~ *VERKLAP*, let the cat out of the bag; (b, bw) (-e), privy, secret; covert; cabbalistic, recondite, cryptic, esoteric; private, close; ~ *e DIENS*, secret service; ~ *HOU*, keep secret; *G~e RAAD*, Privy Council; *in* ~ *e SITTING*, in secret session; ~ *e STEMMING*, voting by (secret) ballot.
geheim'doenery, secrecy, mysteriousness.
gehei'menis, (-se), mystery; ~ **vol**, (-le), mysterious.
geheim': ~ **houding**, secrecy; concealment; ~ **middel**, secret remedy; nostrum; ~ **pie**, (-s), (little) secret; ~ **raad**, privy councillor; ~ **seël**, privy seal.
geheimsin'nig, (-e), mysterious, secretive; daedal; esoteric; ~ **heid**, mystery, mysteriousness.
geheim'skrif, cryptogram; cipher, secret characters; ~ **kun'dig**, (-e), cryptographic.
geheim'taal, cant; code.
gehe'kel, (s) fault-finding, cavilling, satirizing; (b) (-de), crocheted.
gehelm', (-de) helmeted; galeate (bot.).
gehe'melte, (-s), palate, roof of mouth; ~ **klank**, palatal (sound).
Gehen'na, Gehenna.
geher'kou, rehash.
geher'rie, noise, clamour.
geheu'e, memory, recollection; *as my* ~ *my nie BEDRIEG nie*, if my memory does not deceive me; *KORT van* ~ *wees*, have a short memory; *jou* ~ *OPFRIS*, refresh one's memory; *iets in die* ~ *PRENT*, impress something on the memory; *iets in die* ~ *ROEP*, call something to mind; ~ **leer**, mnemotechny, mnemonic; ~ **verlies**, loss of memory, amnesia; ~ **werk**, memory work.
gehe'we, raised (tax); demanded; *cf.* **hef**.
gehik', hiccoughing, hiccups.
gehink', halting; limping; ~ *op twee gedagtes*, vacillation.
gehin'nik, whinnying, neighing.
gehoe'hoe, hoot(ing) (owl).
gehoef', (-de), hoofed.
gehoek', (-te), angulate.
gehoes', coughing.
gehol', running.
gehol'pe, helped, provided with; *gou* ~ *RAAK*, be served quickly; ~ *WEES*, provided for; served.
gehoon', derision, mockery.
gehoor', (gehore), hearing; audience, ear; *BUITE* ~ *wees*, be out of earshot; ~ *EIS*, demand a hearing; ~ *GEE aan*, give someone a hearing; give heed to something; *geen* ~ *KRY nie*, get no reply; not be given a hearing; *ONDER sy* ~ *wees*, be one of his audience; *SLEG van* ~ *wees*, be hard of hearing; *op die* ~ *SPEEL*, play by ear; ~ *VERLEEN*, give a hearing; lend an ear; give an audience; ~ *gee aan 'n VERSOEK*, comply with a request; ~ **aandoening**, ear complaint; ear (hearing) disorder; ~ **beentjie**, ossicle (of the ear), malleus; ~ **buis**, ear-trumpet; ear-piece, receiver (telephone); ear-duct; ~ **de**, what one has heard; ~ **gang**, auditory canal; ~ **gebrekkige**, (-s), hearing-defective; ~ **gewing**, compliance; listening; ~ **leer**, acoustics; ~ **meter**, audiometer; ~ **oefening**, ear-training; ~ **orgaan**, auditory organ; ~ **pyp**, stethoscope; ~ **saal**, (..sale), audience chamber; auditorium, auditory.
gehoor'saam, (w) (~), obey, submit to; follow (orders); answer to (steering-wheel); (b) (..same), obedient, submissive, docile; dutiful, duteous; biddable; law-abiding; ~ *wees aan jou meerderes*, be obedient to one's superiors; ~ **heid**, obedience, submissiveness, duteousness, dutifulness; ~ **heid is beter as offerande**, obedience is better than sacrifice.
gehoors'afstand, hearing distance; *op* ~, within earshot.
gehoor': ~ **sentrum**, auditory centre; ~ **senuwee**, auditory nerve; ~ **toestel**, otophone, hearing aid; ~ **toets**, ear test; ~ **vlies**, tympanum.
geho're: *ten* ~ *bring*, present; render (song).
geho'rig, (-e), sounding, resounding; *die huis is baie* ~, in this house one can hear everything; this house is far from sound-proof; ~ **heid**, resonance.
geho'ring, (-de), horned.
gehou', obliged, bound; ~ *wees om...*, be obliged to...
gehou'denheid, obligation.
gehu'de, (-s), married person.
gehug', (-te), hamlet.
gehuggie, (-s), (small) town, hamlet; (small) dilapidated house.
gehui'gel, (s) hypocrisy, dissembling; (b) (-de), pretended, feigned.
gehuil', yelling, howling (of dogs, etc.); crying (of a child).
gehuis'ves, (-te), lodged, domiciled.
gehumeur(d)', (-de), in a humour (temper); *goed* ~, good humoured; ~ **d'heid**, bile, temper.
gehun'ker, hankering, craving.
gehup'pel, hopping, skipping, frisking.
gehurk', (-te), in squatting posture.
gehuud', (gehude), married; *die gehude staat*, the married state.
gehuud', (-de), hired.
gehyg', panting.
gei'gertelbuis, gei'gerteller, Geiger counter.
geil, (-er, -ste), rank, rampant (in action); rich, fertile (land); luxuriant (growth); unfertilized (egg); sensual; ~ *KOS*, rich food; ~ *REËNS*, plentiful rains; ~ **heid**, richness; rankness, fertility; sensuality.
geïllustreer', (-de), illustrated; ~ *de boek*, illustrated book; picture book.
geil'siekte, prussic acid; poisoning (stock disease).

geïmporteer   169   *geknutsel*

geïmporteer', (-de), imported.
geïmproviseer', (-de), improvized.
geïnspireer', (-de), inspired.
geïnteresseer', (-de), interested.
geïnterneer'de, (-s), interned person, internee.
gei'ser, (-s), geyser.
gei'sja, (-s), geisha (girl).
geïsoleer', (-de), isolated; ~ *de borsel*, insulated brush.
geit, (-e), goat; girl; whim, fancy.
geit'jie, (-s), gecko; vixen, shrew, minx; ~**rig**, (-e), quarrelsome, shrewish.
gejaag', (s) hurry, bustle; (b) (-de), hurried, hasty, flurried, restless; ~**d'heid**, hurry, press, flurry, rest= lessness, fidget; fever-heat; distraction; hastiness, fluster.
gejak'ker, romping, scramble.
gejam'mer, lamentation, lamenting; dolefulness; moaning, wailing.
gejas', (-te), coated.
gejeremieer', lamentation, wailing.
gejeuk', itch(ing), pruritus.
gejil', teasing, joking.
gejodeer', (-de), iodized.
gejo'del, gejoe'del, yodelling.
gejoel', shouting, cheering, jubilation.
gejok', fibbing, storytelling.
gejol', merrymaking.
gejool', revelling, merrymaking.
gejou', hooting, booing (at meeting) hiss(ing)
geju'bel, shouting, cheers, jubilation.
gejuig', rejoicing, cheers, applause, jubilation.
gejy'-en-jou, disrespectful mode of address.
gek, (s) (-ke), fool, madman, booby; ~ *ke en DWASE skryf hulle name op deure en glase*, fools' names and donkeys' faces are to be seen in public places; a white wall is a fool's paper; *elke ~ het sy GEBREK*, every rose has its thorn; every bean has its black; *iem. vir die ~ HOU*, make a fool of someone; *die ~ ke kry die KAARTE*, fortune favours fools; *staan en KYK soos 'n ~*, stare like an idiot; *dit is nog LANK nie so ~ nie*, it is not a bad idea; *iem. vir die ~ laat LOOP*, send someone on a fool's errand; *die ~ SKEER met iem.*, make a fool of someone; *soveel WERD as 'n ~ daaroor wil gee*, it is worth as much as a fool would give for it; *een ~ kan meer vra as 'n honderd WYSES kan beantwoord*, one fool can ask more questions than ten wise men can answer; (w) (ge-), play the fool; (b, bw) (**[-ke]; -ker, -ste**), foolish, mad, queer, crazy; fond (of); ~ *wees van ANGS*, be frantic with anxiety; ~ *GENOEG, sy . . .*, oddly enough she . . .; ~ *na sy KIND wees*, dote on his child; *dis te ~ om LOS te loop*, that is most absurd; it does not bear thinking of; *nie so ~ as wat hy LYK nie*, he is not as green as he is cab= bage-looking; *iem. ~ MAAK*, drive a person crazy; ~ *NA*, mad about (on); *jou ~ SOEK*, hunt high and low; *die ~ ste van die TOESTAND*, the oddest feature of the situation; ~ *na VIS wees*, be very partial to fish; ~ *van WOEDE*, mad with rage; ~ *WORD*, go mad.
gekaard', (-e), aristate; carded.
gekab'bel, babbling, clack.
gekalibreer', (-de), calibrated.
gekam', (-de), combed (hair); crested (wave).
gekan'fer, (-de), camphorated.
gekan'ker, nagging.
gekant': ~ *teen*, dead against, hostile to.
gekanteel' (-de), crenellated, embattled.
gekant'heid, hostility.
gekap', (s) chopping, thumping; pawing; (b) (-te), chopped (wood); dressed (stone); done, set (hair); *hy is ~ maar nie geskaaf nie*, he is a rough diamond.
gekar'ring, churning; nagging.
gekar'tel, (-de), milled (coins), crenate (leaves); waved, wavy (hair); jagged (rocks); castellated.
gekef', yelping, yapping.
gekek'kel, cackling; tittle-tattle; cackle, gab(bling).
gekelk', (-te), cup-shaped; cupped.
geke'per, (de), twilled.
gekerf', (-de), sliced, cut (biltong); crenate (bot.).

gekerk', (-te), married.
gekerm', groan(ing), lamentation, moan(ing).
gekeur' (-de), selected; seeded (sportsman).
gekeu'wel, chat(ting), gossip; cooing (of baby).
gek'heid, (..hede), folly, foolishness; madness, luna= cy; joke, pleasantry; nonsense; ~ !, fiddlesticks!; *ALLE ~ op 'n stokkie*, all joking apart (aside); and now to be serious; *SONDER ~*, jesting apart, real= ly; *UIT ~*, for fun.
gekib'bel, bickering, squabbling.
gekie'lie, tickling.
gekin'kel, (-de), knotted, twisted.
gekir', cooing.
gekit'tel, tickling, titillation.
gek'ke: ~ **dag**, (ong.), All Fools' Day; ~ **dokter**, mad doctor; ~ **dom**, foolocracy; ~ **getal**, fool's number, number eleven; ~ **huis**, lunatic asylum, bedlam; ~ **mat**, fool's mate (chess); ~ **nommer**, fool's num= ber, eleven; ~ **paradys**, fool's paradise; ~ **praatjies**, nonsense; ~ **rny**, (-e), jesting, joking; tomfoolery; ~ **werk**, madness, folly.
gek'kie, (-s), little fool.
gek'kigheid, (..hede), foolishness, folly.
gek'ko, (-'s) = **geitjie**.
geklaag', complaining, lamentation(s).
geklad', (-de), blotted; blurred.
gekla'(e), geklag' = **geklaag**.
geklak', clacking.
geklank', sounding, sound (of words); clangour; *onder die ~ wees* among those present (in church).
geklap', crack(ing) (whip); clapping (hands); clack; tittle-tattle, ~ **per**, chattering (of the teeth); clutch; flapping (wings).
gekla'ter, clatter(ing), splashing, patter.
geklee', (..klede), dressed; dressy; clad; *goed gekleed wees*, be well-dressed; ~ **d'heid**, dressiness.
geklep', tolling (of bell); clanging.
geklep'per, clattering; clip-clop (of hoofs).
geklets', tattle, rattle, twaddle, chatter, flapdoodle, gossip, tosh, palaver, gab(ble), blether, fudge.
geklet'ter, clattering, clang, clash(ing), clangour; pat= tering (rain); (pitter-)patter.
gekleur', (-de), coloured; of mixed blood; ~ *de BRIL*, tinted glasses; ~ *de GLAS*, stained glass; ~ *de PLATE*, coloured plates (pictures); **G~de**, (-s), Coloured person.
geklief', (-de), cloven, cleft.
geklik'¹, (s) tale-telling; pattering; clicking.
geklik'², (b) (-e), foolish, silly; ~ **heid**, foolish= ness.
geklik'klak, click-clack, clattering, clicking.
geklin'gel, jingling, tinkling, clink.
geklink', jingling; clinking.
gekloek', **geklok'**, clucking (of hen); gurgle.
gekloof', (-de), cloven, cleft.
geklop', knocking; throbbing (of the pulse); hammer= ing (bearings).
geklots', dashing, beating, lapping, popple.
geklou'ter, clambering.
geknaag', gnawing.
geknab'bel, nibbling, munching, crunch(ing).
geknak', (-te), broken; impaired (health); crippled; wrecked.
geknal', report (gun); popping, banging.
geknars', gnashing (of teeth); grinding, creak(ing) (wheel); crunch.
gekneg', (-te), enslaved, subdued.
gekners' = **geknars**.
geknet'ter, crackling; ping-ping (musketry).
gekneus', (-de), bruised.
geknib'bel, haggling.
gekniel', (-de), kneeling, prostrate.
geknies', fretting, sulkery.
geknip', (-te), cut out (scissors), snipped.
geknoei', messing, botching, bungling; scheming, plotting, intriguing.
geknoes', (-te), gnarled, knotty.
geknoop'¹, (s) cursing.
geknoop'², (b) (-te), meshy, knotted.
geknor', grunt(ing) (pig); grumbling, growl(ing) (dog); scolding.
geknut'sel, pottering; niggling; patch-work.

geknyp 170 *geld*

geknyp', (s) pinching; (b) (**-t**), pinched; ~ *wees*, be in a fix; be afraid.
gekoek', (**-te**), matted; ~ *te GROND*, matted soil; ~ *te HARE*, matted hair; ~ *te WOL*, lumpy wool.
gekoer', cooing.
gekog', (**-te**), bought; *see* **koop**.
gekol', (**-de**), spotted.
gekommitteer'de, (**-s**), deputy, delegate; person committed.
gekompliseer', (**-de**), complicated; ~**d'heid**, complexity.
gekompromitteer', (**-de**), compromised.
gekondenseer', (**-de**), condensed.
gekondisioneer', (**-de**), conditioned.
gekonfyt'[1], (**-e**), preserved; ~ *e vrugte*, preserved fruit.
gekonfyt'[2]: ~ *wees in*, be clever at; be at home in; be well versed in.
gekon'kel, botching; intriguing (for a post); underhand doings.
gekonsentreer', (**-de**), concentrated.
gekonsinjeer'de, (**-s**), consignee.
gekonsolideer', (**-de**), consolidated.
gekook', (**-te**), boiled; cooked; ~ *te eier*, boiled egg.
gekoop', (**-te**), bought; ~ *te klere*, ready made clothes.
gekop', (**-te**), capped; capitated.
gekop'pel, (**-de**), coupled, linked.
geko'ring, (**-de**), drunk, tipsy.
gekor'rel, (**-de**), granulated; pelleted.
gekorrigeer', (**-de**), corrected.
gekors', (**-te**), crusted, furfuraceous.
geko'se, chosen, elected, selected; *see* **kies**, (w); ~ *komitee*, select committee; ~ *ne*, (**-s**), person elected.
gekostumeer', (**-de**), in costume; ~ *de BAL*, fancydress ball; ~ *de OPTOG*, pageant.
gekots', vomiting.
gekou', chewing.
gekraag', (**-de**), collared.
gekraai', crowing.
gekraak', (s) creak(ing), cracking, crunch(ing); (b) (**-te**), cracked; high, slightly tainted (meat); sour (wine).
gekraal'[1], (**-de**), kraaled (animals); fenced in.
gekraal'[2], (**-de**), beaded.
gekrab'bel, scratching; scrawl, illegible writing.
gekrakeel', wrangling, bickering.
gekrap', cacography, scrawl; scratching.
gekras', croaking, scratching (of pen), shrieking, caw, screeching.
gekrenk', (**-te**), offended, hurt, aggrieved, mortified; deranged (mentally); ~**t'heid**, mortification, despite.
gekreu'kel, (**-de**), creased; puckered.
gekreun', groaning, moaning.
gekrie'bel, tickling, itching; crawling.
gekriek', chirping.
gekrie'wel = **gekriebel**.
gekrin'kel, (**-de**), crinkled; ~ *de rubber*, crêpe rubber.
gekrioel', swarming, crowding.
gekroes', (**-te**, **-de**), crisped, curly, wool-like, woolly (hair); crispate.
gekrom', (**-de**), curved; *met* ~ *de rug*, with bent back.
gekron'kel, (**-de**), winding, twisted, meandering; contorted.
gekrook', (ong.), (**-te**), broken; bruised; *'n* ~ *te riet*, a bruised reed.
gekroon', (**-de**), crowned; *'n* ~ *de naarheid*, a calamity, terrible state of affairs.
gekrui', (**-de**), seasoned (meat); spicy, high (jokes).
gekruis', (**-te**, **-de**), crossed; cross-bred; crucified; ~ *te* (~ *de*) *tjek*, crossed cheque; ~ **ig**, (**-de**), crucified.
gekruk', (**-te**), crocked; cranked; ~ *te AS*, cranked axle; ~ *te SKAKEL*, cranked link.
gekrul', (**-de**), curled; curly, crisp, frizzled; crispate (bot.).
gekrys', screeching.
gekryt', lamentation.
gek'skeer, (**-ge-**), jest, joke, fool, banter; footle; play the giddy goat; kid; *hy laat nie met hom* ~ *nie*, he is not to be trifled with; he will stand no joking; ~ **der**, (**-s**), joker; ~ **dery**, fooling, jesting, banter, buffoonery.

gekug', coughing, clearing the throat.
gekuif', (**-de**), crested; tufted, cristate.
gekuil', (**-de**), bunkered (golf); ~ *de voer*, silo fodder.
gekuip', intriguing, scheming.
gekuis', (**-te**), pure, chaste; *'n* ~ *te smaak*, a refined taste.
gekul', (**-de**), cheated, deceived, done down.
gekun'stel(d), (**-de**), artificial, mannered; sophisticated, prim; finical; laboured; ~**dheid**, artificiality, mannerism; art, sophistication.
gekus', kissing; smooching (colloq.).
gekwaak', quack-quack; croaking, quacking.
gekwalifiseer', (**-de**), qualified, certificated.
gekwan'sel, bartering; haggling.
gekwarteer', quarted, separated in quarts.
gekwartier', (**-de**), quartered.
gekwartileer', (**-de**), quarted.
gekwas'[1], (**-te**), knotty (wood).
gekwas'[2], (**-te**), tufted; tasselled.
gekweel', warbling.
gekwel', possessed (by spirits); worried; ~**d'heid**, worry, vexation.
gekwes', (**-te**), wounded; disabled.
gekwets', (**-te**), hurt, offended; *in sy eer* ~ , wounded in his honour; dishonoured; ~**t'heid**, pique, sense of grievance.
gekwet'ter, twittering, chirruping.
gekwinkeleer', warbling, twittering.
gekwis'pel, (tail-)wagging.
gekwyl', slobber, drivelling, dribbling.
gekyf', squabbling, bickering.
gelaag', (**-de**), stratified; ~**d'heid**, stratification.
gelaai', (**-de**), loaded (gun); tense (atmosphere); live (elec.).
gelaars', (**-de**), booted; ~ *en GESPOOR*, booted and spurred; *die G* ~ *de KAT*, Puss in Boots.
gelaat', (**gelate**), face, countenance; mine; front; ~**kunde**, physiognomy; ~ **kun'dig**, (**-e**), physiognomic; ~ **kun'dige**, (**-s**), physiognomist.
gelaats': ~**hoek**, facial angle; ~**kleur**, complexion; colour (of face); ~**trek**, feature; lineament; ~**uitdrukking**, countenance, facial expression.
gela'de, charged (with emotion, meaning); tense; ~**nheid**, tenseness; meaningfulness.
gela'er, (**-de**), camped, laagered.
gelag'[1], laughter, laughing.
gelag'[2], drinks, feasting; score; *die* ~ *betaal*, pay the score (lit); pay the piper; ~**kamer**, bar(room), saloon, taproom.
gelammelleer(d)', (**-de**), laminated.
gelang': *NA* ~ *van*, in accordance with; *na* ~ *van OMSTANDIGHEDE*, according to circumstances.
gelap', (**-te**), patched.
gelardeer', (**-de**), larded.
gelas'[1], (w) (~), order, instruct, command; direct, charge; *'n ondersoek* ~ , direct that an enquiry be held.
gelas'[2], (b) (**-te**), welded, joined; ~ *te yster*, welded iron.
gelas'tigde, (**-s**), mandatory, proxy, deputy.
gela'te, (**-ner**, **-nste**), resigned, submissive; patient; ~**nheid**, equanimity, resignation, aquiescence.
gelatien', **gelati'ne**, gelatin(e); ~**agtig**, (**-e**), gelatinous; ~**papier**, gelatin(e) paper; ~**plaat**, collotype.
geld'[1], (s) (**-e**), money, cash; currency; pelf; chink (sl.) (filthy) lucre; *AGTER* ~ *wees*, be after money; *staan of hy* ~ *in die BANK het*, behave as if one owned the Bank of England; be idle (inactive, nonchalant); *dis met geen* ~ *te BETAAL nie*, it is not to be had for love or money; it is worth its weight in gold; *met* ~ *speel soos 'n BOBBEJAAN met waboomblare*, play ducks and drakes with one's money; ~ *soos BOSSIES*, money to burn; heaps of money; *op* ~ *BROEI*, sit on one's money; *agter* ~ *wees soos die DUIWEL agter 'n siel*, sell one's soul for money; *vir* ~ *kan 'n mens die DUIWEL laat dans*, money makes the mare to go; ~ *wat GEEL is, maak reg wat skeel is*, love does much, but money does all; ~ *stop geen GIERIGHEID nie*, the miser is always in want; *GOEIE* ~ *na slegte* ~ *gooi*, (Angl.) throw good money after bad; *met* ~ *GOOI*,

throw money away; *waar ~ IS, wil ~ wees*, money begets money; *'n mens moenie al jou ~ op een KAART sit nie*, don't put all your eggs in one basket; *~ in KAS*, cash in hand; *KONTANT ~*, cash, ready-money; *rondloop vir KWAAD ~*, wander about idly; *~ uit iem. LOSSLAAN*, get money out of someone; *te ~ e MAAK*, convert into cash; *sy ~ PLA hom*, he is playing ducks and drakes with his money; *met sy ~ geen RAAD weet nie*, not to know what to do with one's money; *~ moet ROL*, money is round and rolls away; *~ is ROND*, money is there for the spending; *~ groei nie op jou RUG nie*, money does not grow on trees; *dit RUIK na ~*, it reeks of wealth; *~ uit iem. se SAK ja*, cause someone to spend money; *die ~ brand in sy SAK*, his money burns a hole in his pocket; *~ SKIET*, advance cash; *~ SLAAN uit iets*, make money out of something; *~ wat SLEG is, maak krom wat reg is*, muck and money go together; *~ is maar SLYK*, money is filthy lucre; *met ~ SMYT*, throw money about; *~ SOEK ~*, money begets money; *~ STEEK in*, invest money in; *daar STEEK ~ in*, there's money in that; *STIK in die ~*, have money to burn; *~ wat STOM is, maak reg wat krom is*, ready money is a ready medicine; love does much but money does all; *in ~ SWEM*, swim in money; *meer ~ as VERSTAND hê*, have more money than brains; *VUIL ~*, tainted money; *~ soos WATER verdien*, coin money; *~ in die WATER gooi*, waste money; *dit is ~ WERD*, it is worth a lot of money; *vir geen ~ ter WÊRELD nie*, not for the wealth of all the world; *vir geen ~ of goeie WOORDE nie*, not to be had for love or money; *met ~ en goeie WOORDE kry mens alles gedaan*, money and kindness will open all gates.

geld'2, (w) (ge-), be valid, be in force; hold good; hold; obtain (laws); concern (interests); apply to; assert oneself; *die KOEPONS ~ net vir een maand*, the coupons are valid for one month only; *sy invloed LAAT ~*, bring one's influence to bear; *sy regte LAAT ~*, enforce one's rights; *dit ~ jou LEWE*, your life is at stake; *dit ~ VAN (vir) ons almal*, it holds good for us all, it is true of all of us; *die beurs ~ VIR een jaar*, the bursary is tenable for one year.

geld: ~**aanbidding**, plutolatry; ~**adel**, moneyed aristocracy, plutocracy; ~**afperser**, blackmailer; ~**afpersing**, extortion (of money); blackmail; ~**baas**, magnate, capitalist, plutocrat; ~**bedrag**, sum (amount) of money; ~**bejag**, mercenariness; ~**belegging**, investment; ~**besparing**, saving of money; ~**beurs**, purse; ~**beursie**, small purse; soldier in the-box *(Albuca cahadensis)*; ~**boekie**, wallet; ~**boete**, fine; mulct; ~**bussie**, collection box; ~**dors**, thirst for money; greed for gold; ~**duiwel**, money demon, mammon; ~**eenheid**, monetary (currency) unit.

gel'delik, (-e), monetary, financial, pecuniary.
gel'deloos, (..lose), moneyless, impecunious.
gel'dend, (-e), ruling, current (ideas); accepted (opinion).
geld'fonds, monetary fund.
geld'gebrek, want of money, lack of funds, penury; financial stringency; impecuniosity; *~ hê*, be short of money.
geldgie'rig, (-e), covetous, money-grubbing, miserly; ~**heid**, covetousness, miserliness, avarice.
geld'gif, (ong.) gift of money.
geld'god, mammon.
geld'handel, money-market (business), banking; ~**aar**, banker, money-dealer.
geld'heerskappy, plutocracy.
gel'dig, (-e), legal, valid, binding (in law); admissible; available; in force; *~ VERKLAAR*, validate; *nie meer ~ WEES nie*, lapse, become void; *~ WORD*, take effect; ~**heid**, validity; legality; availability; ~**heidsduur**, period of availability, currency; ~**heidstermyn**, currency (licence); ~**verklaring**, validation.
geld'inflasie, monetary inflation.
gel'ding, legal force; ~**sdrang**, impulse of self-assertion.
geld: ~**insamelaar**, collector; ~**insameling**; collection of money; ~**jaar**, financial year; ~**jag**, lust for money; ~**jies**, pittance; petty cash; a little money; ~**kas**, safe, coffer; money-chest; ~**kissie**, cashbox; ~**koers**, rate of exchange; money (interest) rate; ~**koning**, millionaire, magnate, plutocrat; ~**koors**, lust for money; ~**kragtig**, (-e), moneyed; ~**kwessie**, question of money; ~**laai**, cash-drawer; till; ~**lening**, loan; ~**lotery**, money (cash) lottery; ~**makelaar**, money-broker; ~**maker**, profiteer; guinea-pig; ~**makery**, profiteering; ~**man**, capitalist, financier; magnate; ~**mark**, money-market, circulation of money; ~**middele**, finances, pecuniary resources; money; ~**nood**, lack of money; financial difficulty; *in ~nood verkeer*, be in want of money; ~**omloop**, circulation of money; ~**onttrekking**, withdrawal of funds (money); ~**oormaking**, transmission (remittance) of money; ~**opbrengs**, money return; ~**opnemer**, borrower; ~**prys**, money prize; ~**rugby**, professional rugby; Rugby League; ~**saak**, money matter; ~**sak**, moneybag; ~**sake**, financial (pecuniary) affairs; ~**sending**, remittance; payment; ~**skaarste**, scarcity (tightness) of money; deflation; ~**skieter**, moneylender; financier; ~**skietery**, money-lending; ~**skip**, argosy; ~**snoeier**, money-clipper; ~**som**, sum of money; capital amount; ~**soort**, kind of money; coinage; ~**sorge**, money cares, financial worries; ~**stelsel**, monetary (financial) system; ~**storting**, deposit of money; ~**straf**, fine; ~**stuk**, coin; ~**sug**, covetousness; lust for money; ~**(s)'waarde**, money value; ~**(s)'waardig**, (-e), valuable; ~**waardige prestasie**, valuable consideration; ~**trommel**, money-box; ~**trots**, purse-pride; ~**uitlener**, money-lender; ~**verduistering**, embezzlement, defalcation, malversation; ~**verering**, mammonism; ~**verkwisting**, waste of money; ~**verleentheid**, pecuniary embarrassment; ~**verlies**, loss of money; ~**versending**, remittance; despatch of money; ~**verspilling**, waste of money; ~**voorraad**, stock of money; ~**vordering**, financial claim; ~**waarde**, money value; value in money; ~**wêreld**, world of finance; ~**wese**, finance, money matters; ~**winning**, money-making; ~**wissel**, money order; ~**wisselaar**, money-changer; money-agent; ~**wolf**, miser, money-grabber.

gele'de, (b) suffered; *die ~ onreg*, the injustice suffered; (bw) past, ago; back; *vyftig JAAR ~*, fifty years ago; *tot KORT ~*, until recently.
gele'dere, *(mv van gelid)*, ranks; *uit EIE ~*, one from their number; *ENKELE ~*, single file; *GESLOTE ~*, closed ranks.
gele'ding, (-e, -s), articulation (bones); joint, hinge (armour); segment.
gele'ë, located; situated; convenient; opportune; *~ wees AAN*, be dependent on; be beholden to; *SENTRAAL ~*, in a central position; *VERAF ~*, distantly situated; *dit ~ VIND*, find something convenient; *~ WEES in*, be contained in.
geleed', (gelede), indented (coastline); articulated, jointed (animals); *gelede ketel*, sectional boiler; ~**heid**, articulation; ~**loos**, (..lose), anarthrous; ~**potig**, (-e), arthropod(al); *~potige diere*, arthropoda; ~**potige**, (-s), arthropod.
geleen', (s) borrowing; (b) (-de), borrowed; seconded (official); *met ~ de vere pronk*, strut about in borrowed plumes.
gele'ëner: *te(r) ~ tyd*, in due course, in good season, all in good time.
geleent'heid, (..hede), opportunity, scope, occasion; facility; function; *'n ~ BEETPAK (aangryp)*, seize an opportunity; *BY die een of ander ~*, as the opportunity occurs; *by ~ van sy HUWELIK*, on the occasion of his marriage; *~ maak die DIEF*, opportunity makes the thief; *van die ~ GEBRUIK maak*, avail oneself of the opportunity; *iem. die ~ GEE*..., give someone the opportunity to...; *~ maak GENEENTHEID*, propinquity breeds love; *~ by die HARE gryp*, take time by the forelock; *die ~ vir iets KRY*, find an opportunity for something; *~ KRY*, get a lift; *MET dié ~*, on this occasion; *in die ~ STEL om*, afford an opportunity to; *iets met 'n ~ STUUR*, send when an op-

geleentheids

portunity offers; *die* ~ *laat VERBYGAAN*, let the opportunity (chance) slip.
geleent'heids: ~ **bankie**, occasional seat; ~ **gedig**, topical poem; ~ **lisensie**, occasional licence; ~ **tafel**, occasional table; ~ **toespraak**, speech for the occasion; after-dinner speech.
geleent'heid: ~ **spreker**, guest speaker; ~ **stuk**, something written (composed) for a special occasion.
geleent'heids: ~ **verlof**, occasional leave; ~ **woord**, nonce-word.
geleer'¹ (-de), trained (animal).
geleer'² (-de), laddered (stocking).
geleerd', (-e, -er, -ste), learned, scholarly, bookish; highbrow, erudite; *HOE* ~ *er, hoe verkeerder,* a mere scholar, a mere ass; *dit is TE* ~ *vir my,* that is Greek to me; *die* ~ *e WÊRELD,* the scholastic world; ~ **doenery**, pedantry.
geleer'de, (-s), scholar; learned person; man of letters; clerk, savant; ~ **s**, scholars; literati.
geleerd'heid, learning, erudition; *iem. LUG sy* ~ , air one's knowledge; *jou* ~ *bring jou tot RASERNY,* much learning do make thee mad; ~ **svertoon**, showing off one's erudition.
gelees', read; *die verslag as* ~ *beskou,* take the report as read.
geleg', (-de), laid; *pas* ~ *de eiers,* new-laid eggs.
gele'gener = geleëner.
gelei¹, (ong.), (s) jelly.
gelei'², (w) (~), conduct (heat); escort, accompany; convoy (ships); ~ **baar, (..bare)**, conductible; ~ **baarheid**, conductibility; ~ **brief**, letter of safe conduct, permit; waybill; entry; ~ **buis**, conduit; duct; ~ **de**, attendance; convoy, escort, envoy; *iem.* ~ *de DOEN, iem. onder sy* ~ *de NEEM,* escort someone; accompany someone; *ONDER* ~ *de van,* escorted (chaperoned) by; ~ **dehond**, (ong.), guide-dog.
gelei'delik, (-e), gradual(ly), by degrees; little by little; ~ *e OORSKRYDING (transgressie),* progressive transgression; *UITERS* ~ , by imperceptible degrees; ~ *e VERSNELLING,* gradual acceleration; ~ **heid**, gradualness, progressive graduation.
gelei'dend, (-e), conductive; ~ *e neerslae,* conducting deposits.
gelei'ding, (-e -s), leading; wiring, connection, conducting (wire); conduit; fair-lead; main (of pipe line, etc.).
gelei'dings: ~ **diagram**, wiring diagram; ~ **draad**, conducting wire; ~ **koëffisiënt'**, coefficient of conduction; ~ **net**, wiring.
gelei'dingstroom, convection current.
gelei'dingsvermoë, conductivity, conductive power.
gelei'draad, conducting wire, conductor.
geleid'ster, (ong.), (-s), *vroulik van geleier;* conductress.
gelei'er, (-s), attendant, guide, conductor; *slegte* ~ , non-conductor.
gelei'; (ong.), ~ **gees**, guardian spirit; ~ **gleuf**, ~ **groef**, featherway; ~ **plaat**, guide-plate; ~ **ring**, guide-ring; ~ **rol**, fixed pulley; ~ **skip**, escort vessel, convoy, consort; ~ **stang**, bus-bar.
gelek', licking; toadyism; leaking.
ge'lerig, (-e), yellowish, flavescent.
gele'se, read; *as* ~ *(gelees) BESKOU,* taken as read; *DIE* ~ *ne,* the things (books) read; the lesson (in church).
gelet': ~ *op,* taking into account; with a view to.
ge'letjie, (-s), small yellow one.
gelet'terd, (-e), lettered; literacy; *'n* ~ *e,* a man of letters; ~ **heid**, literacy.
gelid', (s) (geledere), rank, file, line; generation; *hy is ALTYD in die* ~ , he is always present where he is not wanted; *GESLOTE geledere,* serried (closed) ranks; *in* ~ *STEL,* draw up in line; *uit die* ~ *TREE,* fall out of line; *die TWEEDE* ~ , the second generation; *in die* ~ *VAL,* fall into line.
gelief', (-de), dear, beloved; favourite; fancied (girl); *hom* ~ *MAAK by,* endear himself to; *sy* ~ *de UITDRUKKING,* his pet saying; ~ **de**, **(-s)**, beloved one, dearest, sweetheart, darling, inamorata (fem.); inamorato.

geluid

gelief'hebber, dabbling (in); tinkering (with); amateurism; dilettantism.
gelief'koos, (-de), favourite, fancy (girl); caressed, fondled.
gelie'we, (vero., plegt.), please; ~ *my per omgaande te antwoord,* please reply by return of post.
geligniet', gelignite.
gelinieer', (-de), ruled; lineated; lined.
gelip', (-te), labiate.
gelisensieer', (-de), licenced.
gelis'pel, lisping; rustling (leaves).
gelit', (-te), articulate, jointed.
gel'ling, (-s), gallon.
gelob', (-de), lobed, lobate.
geloei', roar(ing), bellowing.
geloer', spying, peeping.
gelof'te, (-s), vow, solemn promise; *'n* ~ *aflê,* take a vow.
Gelofte: ~ **dag**, Day of the Covenant; ~ **kerk**, Church of the Covenant.
gelok'¹, (s) enticement, allure; (b) **(-te)**, enticed.
gelok'², (b) (-te), curly.
gelokaliseer', (~ de), localized.
gelol', worry, botheration.
gelonk', ogling.
geloof', (s) credit, credence, trust, faith; **(..lowe)**, belief, profession, religion; creed; persuasion; *'n* ~ *BELY,* profess a creed; ~ *kan BERGE versit,* faith can move mountains; *'n BLINDE* ~ *hê in,* have a blind faith in, trust implicitly; *iem. van DIESELFDE* ~ , a person of the same persuasion; *op GOEIE* ~ *aanneem,* accept on trust; *elkeen sal deur sy* ~ *SALIG word,* everyone believes what he likes to believe; ~ *SLAAN (heg) aan,* give credence to; (w) (~), believe; vgl. **glo.**
geloof'baar, (..bare), credible, believable; ~ **heid**, credibility.
geloof'lik, (-e), believable, credible; ~ **heid**, credibility.
geloof'saak, matter of faith.
geloofs': ~ **artikel**, article of faith; ~ **belydenis**, creed, confession of faith; credo, belief; ~ **beproewing**, trial (for one's faith); ~ **beswaar**, religious scruple; ~ **brief**, credential, letter of credence; ~ **daad**, act of faith; ~ **dwang**, religious coercion; ~ **formulier**, creed; ~ **geneser**, faith-healer; ~ **genesing**, faith-healing; ~ **genoot**, co-religionist; ~ **geskil**, religious difference; ~ **grond**, ground for belief; ~ **held**, religious hero; ~ **krag**, religious strength; ~ **kwessie**, matter of faith (religion); ~ **leer**, doctrine (of faith); ~ **lewe**, religious life; inner life; ~ **onderwys**, religious instruction; ~ **oortuiging**, religious conviction; ~ **punt**, doctrinal point; ~ **reël**, canon, rule of faith; ~ **verdedigingsleer**, apologetics; ~ **versaker**, apostate; ~ **versaking**, apostasy; ~ **vertroue**, trust in God; ~ **vervolging**, religious persecution; ~ **vrede**, religious peace; ~ **vryheid**, religious freedom; ~ **ywer**, religious zeal.
geloofwaar'dig, (-e), trustworthy, credible, authentic; ~ **heid**, veracity, credibleness, credibility, reliability, authenticity.
geloop', walking.
gelou'er, (-de), laurelled; ~ **de, (-s)**, prizewinner, laureate.
gelo'wer, (-s), believer.
gelo'wig, (-e), believing, faithful, pious; ~ **e, (-s)**, true believer; ~ **heid**, piety, faithfulness.
gelui', tolling, ringing, pealing, clang; *'n derde* ~ *wees,* be a slow-coach.
geluid', (-e), sound, noise; ~ *gee (voortbring),* emit sound; ~ **breking**, catacoustics; ~ **dempend, (-e)**, sound-proof, sound-insulating; ~ **demper, (-s)**, silencer; muffler; sordine, mute (on violin); ~ **demping**, silencing; ~ **dig, (-te)**, soundproof; ~ **digting**, sound-proofing; ~ **film**, soundfilm; ~ **gewend, (-e)**, sound-producing; ~ **gewer**, soundbox; ~ **golf**, soundwave; ~ **grens**, soundbarrier; ~ **loos**, (..lose), soundless; dumb; ~ *lose klank,* silent sound; ~ **loosheid**, soundlessness; ~ **meetgroep**, sound-ranging group; ~ **meter**, audiograph, sound-ranger; ~ **meting**, sound-ranging; ~ **reëling**, volume control; ~ **sein**, soundsignal; ~ **(s)'golf**,

sound (acoustic) wave; ~ **s'leer**, acoustics; ~ **snelheid**, velocity of sound; ~ **s'trilling**, sound-vibration; ~ **s'verswakking**, fading; ~ **vinder**, sound-locator; ~ **voorbrenging**, sound-production; ~ **vry, (-e)**, sound-proof; ~ **weergawe**, sound-reproduction; ~ **werend, (-e)**, sound-proofing.

gelui'er, idling.

geluim', (-de): *GOED* ~, good-tempered, amiably disposed; *SLEG* ~, bad-tempered.

geluk', (s) joy, happiness, bliss; good luck; fortune; felicity; **(-ke)**, fluke, chance; bonanza; *jou* ~ *BEPROEF*, try one's luck; ~ *BO* ~, the greatest luck of all; ~ *is maar 'n DAG lank*, happiness does not last long; *op GOEIE* ~ *afgaan*, trust to chance; *soos die* ~ *dit wou HÊ*, as luck would have it; *die* ~ *LOOP hom na*, fortune dogs his footsteps; *die* ~ *LOOP hom onderstebo*, he is overwhelmed by good fortune; fortune smiles on him; *daar is altyd 'n* ~ *by 'n ONGELUK*, an accident is never so bad, but it might have been worse; every cloud has a silver lining; ~ *en ONGELUK woon onder een dak*, even the most fortunate are sometimes unfortunate; *van* ~ *kan PRAAT*, you may thank your lucky stars; *die* ~ *het hom die RUG toegekeer*, he is down on his luck; ~ *kom in die SLAAP*, good fortune comes when least expected; *met die* ~ *SPEEL*, tempt fate; *VEELS* ~, hearty congratulations; *sy* ~ *VERBYHARDLOOP*, force one's luck; *jou* ~ *met die VOETE vertrap*, spurn one's good fortune; *WAT 'n* ~ !, what a fluke!; *meer* ~ *as WYSHEID*, more by good luck than by good guiding; (w) (~), succeed, prosper, come off; *AS dit hom* ~, if he succeeds; *dit HET my* ~, I succeeded in doing it; I managed to ..; *NIKS* ~ *hom nie*, he has no luck; he fails in everything; ~ **bringer**, mascot, talisman, lucky charm; ~ **kie, (-s)**, piece of good luck.

geluk'kig, (-e), happy, fortunate, lucky, auspicious; blissful, blessed; good; godly; prosperous; felicitous; providential, fluky; *jy kan jou* ~ *AG*, you can consider yourself lucky; *dit* ~ *TREF*, be lucky; *'n* ~ *e VOORTEKEN*, a good omen; ~ **e, (-s)**, lucky person; ~ **erwys(e)**, luckily, fortunately, as luck would have it.

geluksa'lig, (-e), blessed, happy, beatific, blissful; Elysian; ~ **heid**, beatitude, bliss(fulness); blessedness, felicity; ~ **heidsleer**, eudemonism.

geluks': ~ **beentjie**, wish-bone; merry-thought; ~ **dag**, red-letter (lucky, field) day; ~ **getal**, lucky number; ~ **godin**, goddess of fortune; ~ **kind**, fortune's favourite, lucky dog; ~ **klawer**, Trifolium.

geluk': ~ **skoot**, lucky shot; fluke; windfall; *die volmaakte* ~ *skoot*, hole in one (golf); ~ **slag**, stroke of fortune; fluke; ~ **soeker**, adventurer, fortune-hunter; ~ **s'pakkie**, lucky packet; ~ **spel**, game of hazard (chance); ~ **spinnekop**, money spinner; ~ **s'pop**, mascot; ~ **staat**, state of bliss (beatitude); ~ **steentjie**, amulet; ~ **ster**, lucky star.

geluks'voël, very successful (fortunate) person, lucky dog.

geluk'wens, (s) **(-e)**: ~ **e**, congratulations; (w) **(ge-)**, congratulate; compliment; felicitate; ~ **end, (-e)**, congratulatory, complimentary; ~ **er, (-s)**, congratulator; ~ **ing, (-e, -s)**, congratulation, felicitation.

gelyk', (s) right; ~ *BY* ~, like will to like; *jy HET* ~, you are right; *iem.* ~ *GEE*, grant that someone is right; ~ *met* ~ *VERGELD*, pay back in the same coin; (b, bw) **(-e)**, equal, even, quits, similar, identical; flush; level, smooth; adequate; equiponderant; equally, alike; as we lie (golf); simultaneously, at the same time; fifty-fifty; ~ *AFSNY met*, cut flush with; *met* ~ *e munt BETAAL*, pay in the same coin; *jouself* ~ *BLY*, be like yourself; *van* ~ *e DATUM*, of the same date; *onder origens* ~ *e OMSTANDIGHEDE*, all other things being equal; *ONS is* ~, we are quits (even); *my OORLOSIE is* ~, my watch is right; *'n* ~ *PAD*, a level road; ~ *VERDEEL*, divide equally; ~ *VOL*, filled to the brim; *op* ~ *e WYSE*, in the same way.

gelyk'benig, (-e), like-sided; ~ *e driehoek*, isosceles triangle.

gelyk'betekenend, (-e), synonymous.

gelyk'draads, (-e), even-grained.

gely'ke, (-s), equal, like, peer, compeer, match; *geen* ~ *hê nie*, have no peer; be unequalled; ~ **nd, (-e)**, like; *'n* ~ *nde portret*, a good likeness; ~ **nis, (-se)**, resemblance, likeness; parable; *'n groot* ~ *nis vertoon met*, bear a close resemblance to.

gely'kerwys(e), just as, like(wise).

gelykgereg'tig, (-de), with equal rights; of equal status; ~ **dheid**, state of having equal rights.

gelyk'gesind, (-e), like-minded; ~ **heid**, unanimity.

gelyk': ~ **gesteld, (-de)**, equalized, adjusted; ~ **golf**, continuous wave; ~ **heid**, equality, similarity, likeness, identity, evenness; equability; co-equality; parity (in years); congeniality; par; *op voet van* ~ *heid met*, on an equal footing with; ~ **heidsteken**, sign of equality; equation sign; ~ **hoekig, (-e)**, equiangular; isogonic; ~ **jarig, (-e)**, equally old, even-aged; ~ **kleurig, (-e)**, isochromatic; ~ **klinkend, (-e)**, homophonous; ~ **knip, (-ge-)**, trim off; ~ **korrelrig, (-e)**, equigranular; ~ **lastig, (-e)**, on an even keel; ~ **lik**, equally; ~ **luidend, (-e)**, consonant (notes); true, exact (copy); consistent (descriptions); verbally identical; assonant; homophonous, homonymic; ~ **lui'dendheid**, assonance, consonance.

gelyk'maak, (-ge-), level, planish, equalize, equate, assimilate; raze (to the ground); float (plastering, mining); ..**makend, (-e)**, assimilative, assimilatory; ..**maker**, leveller; equalizer; ..**making**, equalization, levelling, razing; equation; normalization; assimilation.

gelykma'tig, (-e), equable, uniform, regular, even; uniform (motion); continuous; unruffled (temper); ~ *e DRAAIMOMENT*, even torque; ~ *e POLE*, like poles; ~ **heid**, evenness, uniformity; equanimity.

gelyk'middelpuntig, (-e), concentric.

gelykmoe'dig, (-e), contented, placid (mind), equanimous, even-tempered; ~ **heid**, contentedness, equanimity.

gelykna'mig, (-e), homonymous; analogous; having the same denominator; of the same name; ~ *e breuke*, fractions with a common denominator; ~ **heid**, homonymy.

gelyk'op, deuce (tennis); drawn (game); peel (bowls); equally; ~ *DEEL*, divide equally; ~ *SPEEL*, draw, tie (in games); ~ **spel**, drawn game.

gelyk'rig, (-ge-), rectify (radio); ~ **ter, (-s)**, rectifier (radio); directing funnel; honeycomb.

gelyk'rigting, rectification (radio).

gelykslag'tig, (-e), homogenous; congeneric, homogamous; ~ **heid**, homogeny.

gelyksoor'tig, (-e), similar, homogeneous; congenerous, congenial; ~ **heid**, similarity, congeniality, homogeneity.

gelyk'spanning, direct voltage (pressure).

gelyk'speel, (-ge-), tie, draw (in games).

gelyk'spel, draw, tie (in games).

gelyk'staan, (s) scratch, (w) **(-ge-)**, be equal, be on a level; be scratch (athletics); ~ *met*, amount to be equivalent to; ~ **de**, equivalent, equal; *iets* ~ *de met*, something that amounts to; something equal to.

gelyk'stel, (-ge-), put on a level, equalize; place on an equal footing, on an equality (with); co-ordinate; identify; ~ **ling**, equalization, levelling; ~ **lingsbeleid**, policy of equal rights.

gelyk'stroom, direct (electric) current, DC.

gelyk'stryk, (-ge-), smooth (with iron).

gelyksy'dig, (-e), equilateral; ~ **heid**, equilateralness.

gelyk'tallig, (-e), of the same number, even-numbered.

gelyk'te, (-s), level, plain, flat.

gelyk'teken, equation sign.

gelykto'nig, (-e), concordant; ~ **heid**, concordance.

gelykty'dig, (-e), simultaneous, concurrent, contemporaneous, co-instantaneous, isochronous, synchronous; ~ *ingeslote*, connate (leaves); ~ **heid**, synchronism, simultaneousness; contemporaneity, contemporaneousness; simultaneity.

gelykvler'kig, gelyk'vleuelig, (-e), isopterous, homopterous.

gelyk'vloers, (-e), on the ground floor; plain, homely; flat; ~ *e uitgrawing,* flat working (in mines).
gelykvor'mig, (-e), uniform, of like form, homomorphic; analogical, analogous; congruent; equal; ~ *e plooi,* similar fold; ~ **heid,** uniformity, conformity; analogy, conformability, equability.
gelykwaar'dig, (-e), equivalent to, of equal value to; equipollent; ~ **heid,** equipollence, equivalence.
gelyk'weg, evenly; together.
gelyk'wigtig, (-e), equiponderant.
gelyn', (-de), lined (paper).
gelys', (-te), listed; framed; *'n* ~ *te kommunis,* a listed communist.
gemaak', (-te), affected, sham, forced (laugh); precious; niminy-piminy, mincing (speech); ready-made; coined (word); *so* ~ *en so laat staan,* a stick-in-the-mud; uncouth person; ~ **t'heid,** affectation, affectedness, primness, apishness, mannerism.
gemaal'¹, (s) whirling; grind; milling about, rough-and-tumble; mêleé; bother: (b) **(-de),** ground; minced (meat); ~ *de KOFFIE,* ground coffee; ~ *de MIELIES en hawer,* provender; ~ *de VLEIS,* minced meat.
gemaal'², (s) (gemale), husband, consort, spouse.
gemag', genitals; anus.
gemagnetiseer', (-de), magnetized.
gemag'tig, (-de), authorized; ~ **de, (-s),** holder of power of attorney; proxy, deputy; commissary, assignee.
gemak', ease, convenience, leisure, comfort; facility, ease, easiness; freedom; *iem. op sy* ~ *BRING,* put someone at ease, make one feel at home; *op sy DOOIE* ~, in his own good time; at his leisure; *iets met die GROOTSTE* ~ *doen,* do something with the greatest of ease, do something with very little effort; *'n HUIS met al die moderne* ~ *ke,* a home with all the modern conveniences; *MET* ~, with ease; *OP sy* ~, at ease; leisurely; *VIR die* ~, for convenience; ~ **huisie,** convenience, W.C., toilet, latrine, loo.
gemak'lik, (-e), easy, convenient, comfortable; handy; *dit* ~ *OPNEEM,* take it easy; *'n* ~ *e STOEL,* an easy chair; ~ *VOEL,* feel comfortable; ~ **heid,** ease, comfortableness; facility, easiness.
gemak'pan, lavatory pan, bedpan.
gemaks'halwe, for the sake of ease, for convenience sake.
gemaks'huisie = gemakhuisie.
gemak'stoel, commode; easy chair.
gemak'sug, love of ease; indolence; ..**sug'tig, (-e),** ease-loving, lazy, easy-going, easeful.
gemalin', (-ne), wife, consort, spouse.
gemanierd', (-e), well-mannered, mannerly, courtly; affected; ~ **heid,** mannerliness, courtliness, good-breeding.
gemaniëreerd', (-e), mannered; unnatural; ~ **heid,** mannerism.
gemarineer', (-de), marinated.
gemar'mer, (-de), marbled (stone); mottled (soap); grained (wood).
gemar'tel, (s) tormenting, torture; (b) **(-de),** tortured, tormented.
gemas'ker, (-de), masked; ~ *de bal,* masked ball.
gema'tig, (-de), moderate, temperate; ~ **dheid,** moderation; temperateness.
gemeen', (gemene; gemener, -ste), common, plebeian, mean, abject, despicable, foul, low, dirty, obscene; vulgar; ordinary; *iem.* ~ *BEHANDEL,* treat a person shabbily; *gemene BOEDEL,* joint estate; *grootste gemene DELER,* greatest common factor (divisor); *NIKS* ~ *hê nie,* have nothing in common; *gemene REG,* common law; *gemene SPEL,* foul play; *kleinste gemene VEELVOUD,* least common multiple; ~ **goed,** common property; ~ **heid,** vulgarity, meanness; commonness; despicableness; abjectness, lowness, foulness, dirt; ~ **lik,** usually, commonly; ~ **plaas,** commonplace, platitude; generality; ~ **plasig, (-e),** trite, hackneyed; platitudinarian; ~ **regtelik, (-e),** concerning, pertaining to common law.
gemeen'saam, (..same), familiar (with person); in a familiar way; conversational, colloquial; intimate; ~ **heid,** familiarity.
gemeen'skap, (-pe), community; intercourse, connection; commune; commonalty; collectivity; communication; commerce; fellowship; intimacy; ~ *van BREINKRAG,* brains' trust; *met (in)* ~ *van GOEDERE getroud,* married in community of property; *die* ~ *van die HEILIGES,* the communion of saints; *met iem.* ~ *HOU (hê),* associate with someone; keep company with; *VLEESLIKE* ~, carnal relationship; sexual intercourse; ~ **'lik, (-e),** common, joint; conjointly; mutual, collective; ~ *lik HANDEL,* act in common; take concerted action; ~ *like SANG,* community singing; ~ **'likheid,** (inter)community; collectivity; ~ **'likheidsgevoel,** communal sense; ~ **sentrum,** community centre; ~ **sgevoel,** communal sense; ~ **sin,** sociality, communal sense.
gemeen'skaps: ~ **kas,** community chest; ~ **kuns,** popular art.
gemeenslag'tig, (-e), of common gender; epicene.
gemeen'te, (-s), community, congregation; parish; commune; *as die* ~ *dans, slaap die duiwel,* it is when the congregation revels that the devil sleeps; ~ **basaar,** bazaar held by congregation; church bazaar; ~ **grond,** parish lands; ~ **kas,** parish treasury; ~ **lewe,** parish life; ~ **lid,** parishioner, church member; ~ **lik, (-e),** parish, congregational; ~ **motor,** church car; ~ **raad,** parish council; ~ **vergadering,** parish meeting.
gemeet', (gemete), measured.
gemeganiseer', (-de), mechanized; ~ *de vervoer,* mechanized transport.
gemeld', (-e), mentioned.
ge'melik, (-e), sullen, peevish, morose, fretful; ~ **heid,** peevishness, moroseness, sullenness.
geme'nebes, (-te), commonwealth; republic; ~ **telik, (-e),** of a commonwealth.
geme'nerd, (-s), blackguard, cad.
gemeng', (-de), mixed, promiscuous, miscellaneous; motley; amalgamated; farraginous; impure; ~ *de BAAIERY,* mixed bathing; ~ *de BOERDERY,* diversified (mixed) farming; ~ *de BOU,* composite construction; ~ *de DUBBELSPEL,* mixed doubles; *met* ~ *de GEVOELENS,* with mixed feelings; ~ *de GETALLE,* mixed numbers (fractions).
geme'nigheid, (..hede), geme'niteit, (-e), meanness, scurrility.
gemerceriseer', (-de), mercerized.
gemerk', (-te), marked; earmarked.
gemes', (-te), fatted; *die* ~ *te kalf,* the fatted calf.
gemeubeleer', gemeubileer', (-de), furnished; ~ *de woonstel,* furnished flat.
gemi'a(a)u, mewing (of cats).
gemid'deld, (-e), average, mean, on an average; aggregate, mediate; ~ *e KOLFSYFER,* batting average; ~ *e SNELHEID,* average velocity (speed); ~ *e SPOED,* average speed; ~ *e SUIERSNELHEID,* mean piston velocity; ~ *e TEMPERATUUR,* mean temperature; ~ **e, (-s),** average, mean; *die* ~ *de neem,* take an average.
gemina'sie, gemination.
gemis', want, lack; *by* ~ *van BETER,* for want of (something) better; *die* ~ *aan goeie BOEKE,* the lack of good books; *BY* ~ *van,* in the absence of; *in 'n* ~ *VOORSIEN,* supply a lack (want).
gem'mer, ginger; ~ **agtig, (-e),** gingery; ~ **bier,** ginger beer; ~ **brandewyn,** ginger brandy; ~ **brood,** gingerbread; ~ **essens,** ginger essence; ~ **kleur,** ginger (colour); ~ **koekie,** ginger nut; ~ **konfyt,** preserved ginger; ~ **limonade,** ginger ale; ~ **plant,** ginger plant; ~ **stroop,** ginger syrup; ~ **wortel,** ginger-root, ginger-race; ~ **wyn,** ginger wine.
gemmologie', gemmology.
gemod'der, scheming, intriguing, plotting; muddling.
gemodereer', (-de), moderated.
gemoed', (-ere), mind, heart; *die* ~ *ere tot BEDARING bring,* calm the ruffled feelings; *iem. iets op die* ~ *DRUK,* impress something on one's mind; *met 'n GERUSTE* ~, with a clean conscience; *diep in sy* ~ *OORTUIG wees,* be convinced in one's heart of hearts; *sê wat jy op jou* ~ *HET,* speak one's

gemoedelik *mind; sy ~ LUG*, vent one's feelings; *die ~ere OPSTOOK*, incite the public mind; *sy ~ SKIET vol*, he is deeply moved.
gemoe'delik, (-e), kind-hearted, genial; comforting; informal; jovial; **~heid**, good nature, bonhomie; joviality.
gemoeds': ~**aandoening**, emotion, excitement; ~**aard**, nature, disposition; ~**beswaar**, conscientious scruple; ~**ewewig**, poise; ~**gesteldheid**, disposition, humour; frame (attitude) of mind; ~**lewe**, inner life; ~**rus**, tranquillity of mind, peace of mind.
gemoed'stemming, mood, humour, frame of mind.
gemoeds'toestand, state of mind, mental condition.
gemoed'stryd, mental struggle.
gemoeid', concerned, at stake; *baie GELD is daarmee ~*, a big sum is involved (at stake); *die hele TOEKOMS is daarmee ~*, the whole future is at stake.
gemom'pel, muttering, grumbling, mumbling, murmuring, hum.
gemop'per, grumbling, grousing.
gemor', grumbling, murmuring.
gemoraliseer', moralizing(s).
gemors', (s) mess; failure; puddle; something of inferior quality; wash-out; (b) **(-te)**, spilt; wasted.
gemotiveer', **(-de)**, motivated.
gemotoriseer', **(-de)**, motorized, mobile.
gems, **(-e)**, chamois *(Rupicapra)*.
gems'bok, gazelle, roebuck (Bible); *Gazella dorcas, G. arabica; oryx, gemsbuck (Oryx gazella)*; ~**muis**, dormouse *(Graphiurus)*.
gemuf', **(-te)**, musty, mouldy.
gemuil'band, **(-e)**, muzzled.
gemum'mel, mumbling; munching.
gemunt', **(-e)**, coined; ~*e GELD*, specie; ~ *OP*, aimed at.
gemur'mel, gurgling, murmuring, babbling, gurgle, purl.
gemurmureer', murmuring, grumbling.
gemuts': *nie goed ~ nie*, be in a bad mood.
gemy'mer, reverie, meditation.
gena' = **genade**.
genaak', **(~)**, approach, come near.
genaak'baar, **(..bare)**, accessible, approachable; easy of access; ~**heid**, accessibility.
genaald', **(-e)**, bearded, aristate.
genaamd', called, by name, entitled.
gena'de, mercy, grace, favour, clemency; quarter; *AAN iem. se ~ oorgelewer wees*, be delivered up to someone's tender mercies; *~ BETOON*, pardon, show clemency; *om ~ BID*, beg for mercy; *iets op ~ DOEN*, take a chance; trust to luck; *~ is nie GEVRA of gegee nie*, quarter was neither asked nor given; *GOEIE ~!*, good gracious!; *~ het nie HORINGS nie*, mercy without any strings attached; *aan iem. se ~ OORGELEWER*, be at someone's mercy; *~ maak 'n PLAN*, necessity is the mother of invention; *SONDER ~*, without mercy; *UIT ~*, out of pity; *dit is jou uit VRYE ~ toegestaan*, it has been granted to you purely as an act of grace; *~ VIND*, find favour; ~**bewys**, act of grace; ~**brief**, letter of pardon (grace); ~**bron**, fount(ain) of grace; ~**brood**, bread of charity; ~*brood eet*, eat the bread of charity; ~**doder**, humane killer; ~**dood**, euthanasia; ~**gif**, free gift; a gift of grace; ~**lappie**, G-string; ~**leer**, doctrine of grace; ~**loos**, (..**lose**), pitiless, ruthless; ~**loosheid**, ruthlessness; ~**middel**, means of grace; ~**slag**, final stroke, death-blow, coup de grâce; finisher; *die ~slag ONTVANG*, receive a death-blow; *iem. die ~slag TOEDIEN*, give someone the coup de grâce; ~**staat**, state of grace; ~**stoel**, mercy seat; ~**tjie**, (-s), favour; ~**troon**, throne of grace; propitiatory; mercy-seat; ~**verbond**, covenant of grace.
gena'dig, **(-e)**, merciful, lenient; clement; *daar ~ AFKOM*, be let off lightly; *met 'n ~e GLIMLAG*, with a condescending smile; ~**heid**, mercy, leniency; ~**lik**, mercifully.
genael(d)', **(-de)**, clawed, ungulate (bot.); armed, unguled (her.).
genant', **(-e)**, namesake; comrade; name-child.
genap'pe(sajet), genappe.

ge'ne, (bw) yonder; *aan ~ syde van die graf*, beyond the grave.
genealogie', **(-ë)**, genealogy; ..**lo'gies**, **(-e)**, genealogic(al); ..**loog'**, **(..loë)**, genealogist.
gene'ë, inclined, disposed; *~ om 'n AANBOD aan te neem*, inclined to accept an offer; *iem. nie ~ WEES nie*, be unfavourably disposed towards someone; have no liking for someone.
Geneefs', **(-e)**, Genevan.
geneent'heid, inclination, disposition, attachment, kindness, love, heart, fondness; *~ vir iem. koester (opvat, voel)*, feel affection for, take a liking to.
geneer', **(ge-)**, inconvenience, embarrass; *JOU ~*, feel embarrassed, be ill at ease; *MOENIE jou ~ nie*, make yourself at home.
genees', **(~)**, cure, heal, recover; *ek is DAARVAN ~*, I am cured of that; *iem. ~ VAN*, cure a person of; ~**al**, panacea; ~**baar**, (..**bare**), curable; medicable; ~**baarheid**, curability; ~**blaar**, *Withania somnifera; Solanum giganteum*; ~**bossie**, *Hermannia cuneifolia*; ~**heer**, physician, doctor; ~*heer, genees jouself*, physician heal thyself; ~**heer-generaal** (..**here-generaal**), surgeon-general; ~**inrigting**, sanatorium.
genees'krag, healing (curative) power; ~'**tig**, **(-e)**, medicinal, curative.
genees'kruid, drug, medicinal herb.
genees'kunde, medical science; medicine; physic.
geneeskun'dig, **(-e)**, medical; ~**e**, **(-s)**, doctor, physician, medical practitioner; ~*e ONDERSOEK*, medical examination; ~*e PERSONEEL*, medical staff.
genees'kuns, art of healing.
genees'lik, **(-e)**, curable, remediable, medicable.
genees'middel, **(-s, -e)**, remedy, medicine, physic, cure, medicament; ~**ebereiding**, pharmacy; ~**eleer**, pharmacology.
genees'wyse, curative (medical) method, cure.
geneig', **(-de)**, inclined, proclivitous, proclivous; prone; disposed; *'n mens is so LIG ~ om dit te vergeet*, one is so apt to forget this; *~ tot ONGELUKKE*, accident-prone; *~ tot die VERKEERDE*, prone to wrong; ~**d'heid**, inclination, propensity, proneness; aptitude, facility.
ge'nepoel, gene pool.
ge'ner: *van nul en ~ waarde*, null and void; absolutely worthless, of no value whatever.
generaal'¹, (s) **(-s)**, general.
generaal'², (b) **(..rale)**: ..**rale repetisie**, dress rehearsal.
generaal': ~**-majoor**, **(-s)**, major-general; ~**skap**, ~**s'rang**, generalship.
generalis', generalist.
generalisa'sie, **(-s)**, generalization.
generaliseer', **(ge-)**, generalize; ..**se'ring**, **(-s)**, generalization.
generalis'simus, **(-se, ..mi)**, generalissimo.
generaliteit', generality.
genera'sie, **(-s)**, generation; ~**wisseling**, metagenesis.
generatief', (..**tiewe**), generative, sexual.
genera'tor, **(-e, -s)**, dynamo; generator.
genereer', **(ge-)**, generate, produce.
generf', **(-de)**, nervate, veined, grained.
generiek', **gene'ries**, **(-e)**, generic.
ge'nerlei, not at all, not in the least.
gene'se¹, (s) genesis, origin.
gene'se², (w) verl. dw. van **genees**, healed; *'n ~ wond*, a healed wound.
gene'send, **(-e)**, medicinal; healing, convalescent; curative.
gene'sene, **(-s)**, cured patient.
gene'ser, **(-s)**, curer.
gene'sing, recovery, restoration to health; cure; healing; convalescence; *~ bring*, bring about a cure.
ge'nesis, genesis.
genet', (s) **(-te)**, garnet, jennet.
gene'ties, **(-e)**, genetic; ~*e konstitusie*, genetic constitution.
gene'tika, genetics.
gene'tikus, **(-se, ..tici)**, geneticist.
geneug'te, **(-s)**, joy; enjoyment, pleasure.

geneuk', botheration, annoyance; trouble.
geneul', nagging.
geneu'rie, hum(ming).
Genè've, Geneva.
geniaal', (..niale), very gifted, brilliant, ingenious; *'n geniale gedagte*, a stroke of genius.
genialiteit', genious, giftedness, brilliance.
genie', (-ë), genius; military engineering; ~**kompanjie**, engineer company; ~**korps**, corps of engineers; sappers; ~**offisier**, engineer officer.
geniep': *in die* ~, on the quiet.
geniep'sig, (-e), on the sly, in an underhand way, purposely hurting, mean, bullying; false; ~**erd, (-s)**, bully; ~**heid**, bullying (in an underhand way); maliciousness, malice.
genies', sneezing.
genie'skool, military engineering school.
geniet', (~), enjoy; possess; partake (food); *ek het die AAND* ~, I enjoyed the evening; I enjoyed myself this evening; *die vrug van jou ARBEID* ~, enjoy the fruits of your labour; ~ *VAN iets*, enjoy something; ~**baar**, (..**bare**), enjoyable; ~**er, (-s)**, one who enjoys; epicurean; ~**ing, (-e, -s)**, enjoyment; amenity; gratification; *die* ~ *inge van die vlees*, the pleasures of the flesh; ~**lik, (-e)**, happy, joyous, enjoyable.
genie'troepe, (military) engineers, sappers.
genie'werk, engineering duties; ~**e**, engineer(ing) services.
genitaal', (..**tale**), genital.
genita'lieë, genitals.
ge'nitief, (..**tiewe**), genitive.
ge'nius, (**genii**) genius (protective spirit).
genoe'ë, (-ns), pleasure, delight; joy; satisfaction, delectation; amenity; *dit DOEN my* ~, it gives me pleasure, I am pleased (to ...); *MET* ~, with pleasure; *NA* ~, to one's satisfaction (liking); ~ *NEEM met*, content oneself with; ~ *SKEP in*, take pleasure in.
genoeg', enough, sufficient, plenty; ~ *BRANDSTOF*, enough (sufficiency of) fuel; *DAARAAN het ek* ~, that will keep me going; *DIT is nou* ~, that will do now; ~ *HÊ van iem.*, have enough of someone; *MEER as* ~, more than enough; ~ *is OORVLOED*, enough is as good as a feast; *VREEMD* ~, strangely enough; ~**doening**, satisfaction, indemnification, reparation.
genoeg'lik, (-e), agreeable, pleasant, pleasurable, enjoyable, comfortable; ~**heid**, pleasantness, agreeableness.
genoeg'saam, (..**same**), sufficient; condign; ~**heid**, sufficiency, competence, competency; fill.
genoem', (-**de**), named, called; just mentioned, abovementioned.
genologie', genology.
geno'me, taken; *die* ~ *MOEITE*, the trouble taken; *STRENG* ~, strictly speaking.
genomineer'de, (-s), nominee.
genom'mer, (-de), numbered.
genooi'de, (-s), guest, one invited; ~ *spreker*, guest speaker.
genoop', obliged; *ek voel my* ~ *om*, I feel obliged to.
genoot', (**genote**), fellow (of an institute); associate, partner; ~**skap, (-pe)**, society, company, association, sodality; academy; ~**skap'lik, (-e)**, of a society, associate.
genot', (**genietinge, genietings**), enjoyment, delight, joy, pleasure; possession; delectation; fruition; gratification; gusto; *dit is 'n* ~ *OM . . .*, it is a pleasure (treat) to . . .; *ONDER die* ~ *van*, while enjoying; *TOT* ~ *van*, to the delight of; ~ *VERSKAF*, afford pleasure; ~**e**, enjoyed; *vir rente genote*, for interest received.
ge'notipe, genotype.
genot': ~**leer**, hedonism; ~**middel**, article of luxury; ~**reg**, usufruct; ~**ryk, (-e)**, enjoyable; delightful; ~**siek**, pleasure-loving; ~**soekend, (-e)**, pleasure-seeking, pleasure-loving, epicurean; ~**soeker**, pleasure-lover; ~**sug**, epicurism, love of pleasure; ~**sug'tig, (-e)**, pleasure-loving; hedonic, hedonistic; ~**sug'tige, (-s)**, hedonist; ~**vol, (-le)**, delightful, enjoyable, delectable.

gen're, (-s), kind, genre; ~**skilder**, painter of genre pieces; ~**stuk**, genre piece, painting of incident.
gens'bok = **gemsbok**.
Gent, Ghent; ~**enaar, (-s, ..nare)**, inhabitant of Ghent.
gentiaan', gentian.
Ge'nua, Genoa.
Genuees', (..**nuese**), Genoese.
genug'tig: *my* ~ *!*, goodness me!, good gracious!
ge'nus, (-se, ..nera), genus.
ge'nuskoop, generic sale.
genut', use, profit; *geen* ~ *uit iets haal nie*, derive no advantage (benefit) from.
geo'de, (-s), geode.
geodeet', (**geodete**), geodesist.
geodesie', geodesy.
geode'ties, (-e), geodetic (survey); ~*e konstruksie*, geodetic structure.
geoe'fen, (-de), trained, practised, exercised, adept, expert, drilled; ~**dheid**, efficiency.
geofaag', (**geofae**), geophagist.
geofagie', geophagy.
geofiet', (-**e**), geophyte.
geofi'sies, (-e), geophysical; *internasionale* ~*e jaar*, international geophysical year.
geofi'sika, geophysics.
geofi'sikus, (-se, ..sici), geophysicist.
geogenie', geogeny.
geognos', (-**te**), geognost.
geognosie', geognosy.
geograaf', (**geograwe**), geographer.
geografie', geography.
geogra'fies, (-e), geographic(al); ~*e KOERS*, true course; ~*e LENGTE*, longitude; ~*e LIGGING*, geographical position; ~*e NOORDE*, true north; ~*e POOL*, true pole.
geologie', geology; ..*'gies*, (-e), geologic(al).
geoloog', (..**loë**), geologist.
geometrie', geometry; ..*'tries*, (-e), geometric(al).
geomorfologie', geomorphology.
geonomie', geonomy.
geoor'loof, (-de), allowed, allowable, admissible, permissible, lawful.
geopolitiek', (s) geopolitics; (b) (-e), geopolitical.
geor'den, (-de), regulated; ordained.
Georg', George; *die Heilige* ~, Saint George.
georget'te, georgette.
Geor'gia, Georgia (U.S.A.).
Geor'gië, Georgia (Russia).
georiënteer', (-de), orientated.
geosen'tries, (-e), geocentric.
geosta'ties, (-e), geostatic.
geosta'tika, geostatics.
geoter'mies, (-e), geothermal; ~*e bron*, geothermal spring.
geotroop', (**geotrope**), geotropic.
geotropie', geotropism.
geotro'pies, (-e), geotropic.
geoutoriseer', (-**de**), authorized; ~ *de uitgawe*, authorized edition.
gepaard', (-**e**), coupled, mated, in pairs; conjugate; germinate; ~ *AAN (met)*, coupled with; accompanying; ~ *GAAN met*, attended with (by), coupled with, fraught with.
gepaneer', (-**de**), crumbed.
gepant'ser, (-**de**), iron-clad (ship); armoured (car); mailed (fist); ~ *de kabel*, armoured cable.
geparenteer(d)', (-**de**), connected, related.
geparfumeer(d)', (-**de**), perfumed.
gepars', (-**te**), pressed.
gepas', (-**te**), becoming, suitable, apt, seemly, appropriate; competent; congruous; fitting, proper; comely; in good time; fit; pertinent.
gepassioneer(d)', (-**de**), impassioned, passionate.
gepasteuriseer(d)', (-**de**), pasteurized.
gepast'heid, propriety, aptness, suitability, seemliness, becomingness; expedience; convenance, grace; pertinence.
gepatenteer', (-**de**), patented; ~ *de medisyne*, patent medicine; ~ *de ontwerp*, patented design.
gepeins', musing, meditation, pensiveness, reverie.

gepensioneer(d)', (-de), pensioned; ~**de, (-s),** pensioner, annuitant.
gepe'per, (-de), peppered, peppery; seasoned.
gepêrel, (-de), pearled, pearly.
geperforeer(d)', (-de), perforated; ~ *de rolroer*, perforated aileron.
gepers', (-te), pressed; ironed.
gepeu'pel, mob, populace, rabble, hoi polloi, plebs, riff-raff, rascaldom, ragtag and bobtail, proletariat, canaille; crowd; ~ **heerskappy,** mob rule, mobocracy, ochlocracy.
gepeu'sel, nibbling.
gepeu'ter, fumbling, trifling.
gepie'ker, worry, fretting.
gepiep'¹, (s), chirp(ing); squeak(ing); cheep, peep; pampering.
gepiep'², (b) (-te), spoilt, pampered (child).
gepier', (-de), cheated, diddled; ~ *wees,* be taken in.
gepik', (s) picking, pecking; **(b) (-te),** cracked (egg); mad, dotty; *jy is glo* ~!, you must be mad!
gepikeer', (-de), offended, nettled, piqued; ~ **d'heid,** pique.
gepikkewaan', (geselst.) (-de), mad, abnormal.
geplaag', (-de), vexed, tormented; possessed (by evil spirits); ~ *wees met,* be troubled (plagued) with, be suffering from.
geplaas', (-te), placed; sold.
geplas', splashing.
geplatteer', (-de), plated.
geplavei', (-de), paved.
gepleis'ter, (-de), plastered.
geplet', (-te), rolled (steel).
geploe'ter, drudging, toiling.
geplof', thud, thumping.
geplons', plunge, splashing.
geplooi', (s) compromise, arrangement; **(b) (-de),** folded; pleated (skirt); puckered (forehead); plicate; liny; ~ *de streek,* folded belt (in country-side).
gepluim', (-de), plumose, plumed.
gepluis', (-de), picked, unravelled; teased (hair, wool); ~ *de tou,* oakum.
gepluk', (-de), plucked (wool); picked (flowers).
gepoets', (-te), polished.
gepof', (-te), puffed.
gepolariseer', (-de), polarized.
gepolitoer', (-de), polished.
gepons', (-te), punched.
gepo'pel, flutter.
geposjeer', (-de), poached (egg).
gepraat', talking, talk, tattle, chit-chat, prate.
gepreek', preaching, sermonizing.
gepremediteer', (-de), premeditated; ~ *de kwaad,* malice aforethought.
gepre'se, praised, lauded.
gepre'wel, muttering, mumbling.
geprik'kel, (-de), irritated; ~ **dheid,** (sense of) irritation.
geprivilegieer', gepriviligeer', (-de), privileged.
geproes', snorting; laughter.
gepromoveer', (-de), promoted (to degree); ~ **de, (-s),** graduate; doctor.
gepronk', ostentation, showing-off.
geprononseer', (-de), pronounced (views); striking (difference); ~ **d'heid,** markedness.
gepruik', (-te), bewigged.
geprut'tel, grumbling, muttering; simmering (kettle).
geprys', (-de), priced; praised; *see* **geprese.**
gepubliseer', (-de), printed, published.
gepunt', (-e), pointed, sharpened; cuspidal; peaked; mucronated (biol.); punctuate (path.).
gepyp'kan, dummied (rugby); cheated, diddled.
geraai', ~ **ery,** guesswork.
geraak', (w) (~) reach; **(-te),** vexed, piqued, offended; hit; moved, touched; ~ **t'heid,** peevishness, irritability, huff.
geraam', (-de), framed (picture); estimated (cost); ~ *de koste,* estimated costs.
geraam'te, (-s), skeleton, anatomy, carcass; shell; framework (of building); fuselage; *'n wandelende* ~, a walking skeleton.
geraas', (gerase), noise, din, hubbub, bluster, pother, hullabaloo, hurly burly, clutter, racket, rave (wind); rattling; crash; *meer* ~ *as wol,* much ado about nothing.
geraas'kal, divagation, raving.
geraas'maker, noisy person.
geradbraak, (-te), mutilated; ~ *te taal,* broken language.
gera'de, advisable; *dit* ~ *ag,* think (deem) advisable.
gera'fel, (-de), frayed, fuzzy, ragged.
geraffineer', (-de), refined (sugar); consummate (rogue); ~ *de goud,* fine gold; ~ **d'heid,** refinement; cunning.
geram'mel, clank(ing), rattling, clatter, clash, rattle.
gerand', (-e), flanged; milled (coin); bordered, marginated.
gera'nium (-s), geranium, pelargonium.
geras'per, (-de), grated; ~ *de kaas,* grated cheese.
gera'tel, rattling, clack, clang, clatter; peal.
gere'dekawel, arguing, argumentation, hair-splitting.
gere'delik, (b) (-e), ready, prompt; **(bw)** readily, promptly; *iets* ~ *toegee,* admit something readily.
geredeneer' arguing.
gere'detwis, wrangling, disputation.
gereed', ready, prepared; *gerede BETALING,* ready cash; ~ *vir GEBRUIK,* ready for use; ~ *om te HELP,* willing to help; *jou* ~ *HOU,* be prepared; *MAAK jou* ~, get ready (set); ~ *STAAN,* hold oneself in readiness, be at the ready; ~ **heid,** standby (mil.); preparedness; *in* ~ *heid bring,* get (make) ready; ~ **heidshouding,** alert position.
gereed'making, preparation.
gereed'skap, (-pe), tools, tackle, apparatus, kit, implements, utensils; *'n stuk* ~, a tool; ~ **bankwerker,** tool-fitter; ~ **houer,** tool-holder; ~ **inspeksie,** tool-inspection; ~ **kamer,** tool-room; ~ **kar,** tool-cart; ~ **kis,** toolbox; ~ **maker,** toolmaker; ~ **sak,** toolbag, kitbag, ditty-bag; ~ **(s)kis,** tool-box (-chest); ~ **skuur,** tool-shed; ~ **slyper,** tool-sharpener; ~ **smit,** tool smith; ~ **stuk,** tool; ~ **wa,** tool-wag(g)on; ~ **winkel,** tool-shop.
gere'ël, (-de), arranged; *'n goed* ~ *de wedstryd,* a well-organized match.
gereeld', (-e), regular, orderly; ~ *e BERIG,* routine message; ~ *e DIENS,* scheduled service; ~ *e WEIERING,* consistent failure (of engine); ~ **heid,** regularity, orderliness.
gereformeerd', (-e), reformed; Calvinistic; orthodox.
gereg'¹, (s) (-te), course, dish.
gereg'², (s) justice, court; tribunal; *voor die* ~ *DAAG (bring),* summon before court; *voor die* ~ *VERSKYN,* appear in court; **(b) (-te),** righteous; *sy* ~ *te straf ontvang,* receive his just punishment; ~ **saal,** law-court; hall (court) of justice.
geregenereerd', (-e), regenerate; reclaimed (rubber).
geregistreer', (-de), registered; ~ *de verpleegster,* registered nurse.
geregs': ~ **amptenaar,** officer of the court; ~ **bode,** beadle, usher; messenger of the court; ~ **dienaar,** law-officer; bailiff; officer of the court; minion of the law; ~ **hof,** court of justice, tribunal; ~ **koste,** law charges, legal expenses.
gereg'telik, (-e), judicial, forensic, edictal; legal; ~ *e BESTUUR,* judicial management; ~ *e DWALING,* miscarriage of justice; ~ *e GENEESKUNDE,* forensic medicine, medical jurisprudence; ~ *e LYKSKOUER,* coroner; ~ *e LYKSKOUING,* inquest; ~ *e VEILING,* sale in execution; ~ **-geneeskundig,** medico-legal.
gereg'tig, (-de), entitled, qualified; justifiable; ~ *wees op,* be entitled to; ~ **dheid,** entitlement, justness; ~ **heid,** justice.
geregver'dig, (-de), justified, warranted.
gerei', gear, utensils, implements.
gereis', travelling, travel.
gerek', (-te), stretched; tedious, long-winded (sermon); long-drawn, protracted (negotiations).
gere'ken, (-de), prominent, esteemed (people).
gerekt'heid, long-windedness, tedium; protractedness.
gerem', braking; restraint, opposition.
geren', running (about).
gere'se, risen.

gereserveer', (-de), reserved (seat); aloof, reticent; ~ d'heid, reticence; aloofness.
gereu'tel, death-rattle, ruckle.
gerf, (gerwe), sheaf; bundle; ~ hoop, stook.
geria'ter, (-s), geriatrician.
geriatrie', geriatry.
geria'tries, (-e), geriatric.
gerib', (-de), ribbed; costate; fluted, nervate.
gerib'bel, (-de), rippled.
gerief', (s) (geriewe), comfort, convenience, amenity; accommodation; commodity; *ten geriewe van*, for the convenience of; (w) (~), be of use (service), convenience; ~ baan, convenience circuit; ~ huisie, W.C.; ~ ie, (-s), convenience; ~ kring, convenience circuit; ~ lik, (-e), convenient, comfortable, com= modious; accommodative; appropriate, handy; ~ likheid, convenience, comfort, commodiousness; ~ (likheid)shalwe, for the sake of convenience.
gerie'we, facilities.
gerif'fel, (-de), corrugated (road), ribbed; furrowy; ~ *de plooi*, composite fold; ~ dheid, corrugation.
gerig'¹, (s) (-te), judgment, court; *die JONGSTE* ~, judgment-day, doomsday; *met iem. in die* ~ *TREE*, take someone to court, take legal action against someone.
gerig'², (b) (-te), directed, aimed; directional; ~ *te DRUK*, directed pressure; ~ *te ONTVANGER*, di= rectional receiver; ~ *te PROJEKTIEL*, guided mis= sile; ~ *te SENDER*, directional transmitter (wire= less); ~ t'heid, alignment.
gerik'ketik, ticking; tick-tock.
gerim'pel, (-de), wrinkled, puckered, furrowed, fur= rowy; liny.
gering'¹, (-e), small, slight, trifling (amount); petty; faint, poor; low (price); ~ *e AFKOMS*, of humble birth (descent); ~ *e HOOGTE*, low alti= tude; ~ *e KERSKRAG (kerssterkte)*, low candle- power; *van* ~ *e WAARDE*, of trifling value.
gering'², (-de), ringed, banded.
gering'ag, (-ge-), slight, hold cheap, underestimate; have a poor (low) opinion of, disparage; ~ ting, underestimation, slighting, disdain, disregard.
geringeleer', girdled (trees); ringed (birds).
gering'heid, smallness, scantiness, modicity, exiguity, paucity.
gering'skat, (-geskat), hold cheap, disesteem, under= estimate, minify, disparage; contemn; ~ tend, (-e), slighting, derogatory, depreciatory; *hom* ~ *tend uitlaat oor*, express oneself disparagingly (slight= ingly) about; ~ ting, disdain, slight, disregard, disesteem.
gerin'kel, jingling, clank, clink, tintinnabulation, crash.
gerinkink', noise; romping, obstreperousness; merry- making.
gerit'sel, rustling, rustle, frou-frou.
gerit'tel, trembling, shaking.
Germaan', (..mane), Teuton; ~ s', (-e), Teutonic, Germanic.
Germa'nië, Germania.
Germanis', (-te), Germanic scholar; g ~ eer', (ge-), make German, germanize; ~ me, Germanism; ~ tiek', Germanic (Teutonic) studies.
germa'nium, germanium.
germina'sie, germination.
geroep', (s) calling, shouting; outcry, clamour; (b) called; *kom of hy* ~ *is*, come in the nick of time, come as if called.
geroe'pe, called, chosen; *Paulus*, '*n* ~ *APOSTEL*, Paul, called to be an apostle; *ek VOEL my nie* ~ *om*, I don't feel called upon to; ~ ne, (-s), person called, chosen one.
geroer', (-de), moved, affected.
geroes', (-te), rusty, corroded.
geroe'semoes, buzz, din, hum, bustle.
geroetineer', (-de), experienced, skilled; ~ d'heid, skill, expertness.
gerof'fel, roll (of a drum).
gerog'gel, rattling (in throat), death-rattle.
gerom'mel, rumble, rumblings.
gerond', (-e), rounded; ~ *e DAK*, cambered roof; ~ *e PAD*, cambered road.

geronk', snoring (sleeper); snorting, roar (engine).
geron'ne, clotted (blood); curdled (milk).
gerontis'me, gerontism, senescence.
gerontokrasie', gerontocracy.
gerontokra'ties, (-e), gerontocratic.
gerontologie', gerontology.
gerontolo'gies, (-e), gerontological.
gerontoloog', (..loë), gerontologist.
gerook', (-te), smoked; bloated; tipsy; busy; cured (ham); ~ *te haring*, kipper, kippered herring.
geroos'ter, (-de), roasted, toasted; broiled; ~ *de brood*, toast.
Gert, Gerard; ~ *Erf*, ~ *Swerf*, easy come, easy go.
ge'rub, (-im, -s), gerubyn', (-e), cherub.
gerug', (-te), rumour, report; noise; *DAAR is 'n* ~, there is a rumour, rumour has it; *die* ~ *doen die RONDE*, there is a rumour doing the rounds; *in 'n SLEGTE* ~ *staan, be in a bad odour*; ~ *te VER= SPREI*, spread rumours; ~ makend, (-e), sen= sational.
gerug'steun, assisted, backed up, strengthened.
gerui'me, long, considerable; '*n* ~ *tyd*, for a consider= able time.
geruis', rustling, murmur, tinkling, noise; frou-frou; ~ loos, (..lose), noiseless, silent; ~ *loos inskakel*, change gears noiselessly; ~ makend, (-e), noisy; ~ peilerboei, sonobuoy.
geruit', (a) gingham; plaid; check; (b) (-e), checkered, tessellated; ~ *e PAPIER*, squared (graph) paper; ~ *e PLAAT*, chequered plate.
gerun'dium, (-s, ..dia), gerund.
gerun'nik, bray(ing), neighing.
gerus', (b) (-te), quiet, calm, peaceful; easy (in mind); cocksure; (bw) safely, really; *jy kan dit* ~ *DOEN*, you can safely do it; *sy GEWETE is* ~, his con= science is clear; *HEELTEMAL* ~, quite at ease; *KOM* ~, do come; *hy LEWE* ~, he lives a peaceful life; ~ *te (~ tige) NAG!*, good night!; *jy kan* ~ *maar ROOK*, you are welcome to smoke.
geru'sie, (prolonged) quarrelling.
gerus'stel, (-ge-), quiet, reassure, soothe, relieve; make easy; *weer* ~, reassure; ~ lend, (-e), reassur= ing, soothing, easing; ~ ling, (-e, -s), (re)assurance, consolation, relief. ·
gerust'heid, peace of mind, security, safety; con= fidence.
gery', riding, driving; (noisy) bustle of traffic.
geryg', (-de), laced.
gery'mel, rhyming, doggerel.
geryp', (-te), matured, mellow; covered with frost.
gerys', (-de), risen (cake).
gesaag', (s) sawing; snoring; (b) (-de), sawn.
gesaai'de, (-s), crop; growth.
gesag', authority, power, influence; puissance; pres= tige; rule, dominion; *op EIE* ~ *handel*, act off one's own bat, act on one's own authority; *jou* ~ *laat GELD*, enforce one's authority; *OP* ~ *van*, on the authority of; *met* ~ *PRAAT*, speak with authority (authoritatively); ~ *UITOEFEN oor*, exercise authority over; '*n man VAN* ~, a man of authority; ~ draer, person in authority; ~ heb'bend (-e), auth= oritative, influential; *van* ~ *hebbende kant verneem*, learn on good authority; ~ heb'bende, (-s), auth= ority; ~ hebber, (-s), commander; master mariner; ~ s'draer, authority, one in whom authority is vested; ~ s'posisie, position of authority; ~ staat, authoritarian state; ~ s'weë: *van* ~ *sweë*, by the government, officially; ~ voerder, (-s) = gesagheb= ber.
gesak', (-te), ploughed, failed (in examination); sagged; let down (milk); ~ te, (-s), failure (in exam= ination).
gesalarieer', (-de), salaried.
gesalf'de, (-s), anointed.
gesa'ligde, (-s), saint.
gesa'mentlik, (b) (-e), joint (owners); united (forces); total (amount), aggregate; collective; concerted (action); (bw) jointly, conjoint(ly); in common; col= lectively, together; ~ *e AANKLAG*, joint charge; ~ *e BESKERMING*, collective protection; ~ *e KOMITEE*, joint committee; ~ *e OPTREDE*, combined operations (action); ~ *OPTREE*, act in

gesang concert, take joint action; ~*e VERHOOR*, joint trial.

gesang', (-e), song, hymn; singing; *die* ~ *INSIT*, start the hymn; start crying; *hy SING altyd dieselfde* ~, he is always singing the same tune; *sy* ~ *is UIT*, he has nothing more to say, he has had his innings; ~**digter**, hymnographer; ~**digting**, hymnody; ~**(e)boek**, hymn-book, hymnal; ~**kunde**, hymnology.

gesa'nik, bother, worry, nagging, prate.

gesant', (-e), ambassador, minister plenipotentiary, legate, deputy; *POUSLIKE* ~, papal nuncio; *sy* ~*e en TRAWANTE*, his aiders and abettors; his henchmen.

gesant'skap, (-pe), embassy, legation; mission; chancellory; ~**sekretaris**, secretary of an embassy; ~**s= gebou**, embassy.

gesê: *hom nie laat* ~ *(geseg) nie*, not to listen to reason, be intractable.

gese'ën, (-de), blessed, fortunate; ~ *met goeie GE= SONDHEID*, blest with good health; *in* ~ *de OM= STANDIGHEDE*, pregnant, expecting, enceinte, in the family way; *in 'n* ~ *de OUDERDOM sterf*, die at a ripe old age.

geseg', (-de), (afore)mentioned; called; *see* **gesê**.

geseg'de, (-s), saying, adage, expression; predicate (grammar).

geseg'lik, (-e), docile, obedient, tractable; commandable, biddable; amenable; *iem. is* ~, someone listens to reason; ~**heid**, docility, meekness, amenability.

gesegmenteer', (-de), segmented, annulate.

gesel'¹, (s) (-le), companion, mate; journeyman.

ge'sel'², (s) (-s), scourge, whip; lash; (w) (ge-), scourge, whip, flagellate, lash; ~**aar**, (-s), whipper; ~**broeder**, flagellant; ~**draend**, (-e), flagellate; ~**ing**, (-e, -s), scourging, flagellation; flogging.

gesel'lig, (-e), sociable (people); chummy; homelike; convivial; gregarious; conversable; genial, conversational; cosy, snug (room); ~*e BYEEMKOMS*, social gathering; *GLAD nie* ~ *wees nie*, be most unsociable; ~*e HOEKIE*, cosy corner; *'n* ~ *e PER= SOON*, good company; ~**heid**, sociability; conviviality; social, party; companionableness; cosiness, snugness (of a room).

gesellin', (-ne), companion (feminine).

ge'sel: ~**paal**, whipping-post; ~**roede**, scourge, lash.

gesels', (~), chat, converse, talk; discuss; ~**erig**, (-e), talkative, loquacious, chatty; ~**ery**, chatting, confabulation, talking; ~**kamer**, common-room.

gesels'radio, (-'s), walkie-talkie.

gesel'skap, (-pe), company; party; conversation; companionship; fellowship; circle; *iem.* ~ *HOU*, keep a person company; *goeie* ~ *maak kort MYLE*, good company on the road is the shortest cut; *SLEGTE* ~ *bederwe goeie sedes*, evil communications corrupt good manners; *in VERKEERDE* ~ *raak*, fall into bad company; *VOL* ~ *wees*, be talkative; be in one's cups; ~**kamer**, commonroom; ~**saal**, lounge; ~**sjuffrou**, lady companion; ~**skring**, social circle; ~**speletjie**, indoor (party, social) game, parlour game; ~**sreis**, party tour.

gesels'taal, colloquial language; vernacular; ~**uit= drukking**, colloquialism.

gesertifiseer', (-de), certified; diplomated, certificated.

geset', (-te), stout, corpulent, plump; set, defined (hours); composed (in type); formed; *OP die* ~ *te tyd, TE* ~ *ter tyd*, at the appointed time.

gese'te, mounted; seated; (man) of means.

geset'heid, stoutness, corpulence, ventricosity, embonpoint, plumpness.

gesid'der, trembling.

gesien', (-e), seen, visé; esteemed, respected; ~ *die FEIT dat*, in view of the fact that; *'n* ~*e MAN*, a respected man; ~ *die RESULTATE*, considering the results.

gesig', (-te), face, features, phiz (vulgar), physiognomy (col.); sight, view; vision, apparition; eyesight; *die* ~ *BENEEM*, obscure the view; *op die EERSTE* ~, at first sight; on the face of it; *waar jy nie self by is nie, word jou* ~ *nie GEWAS nie*, the eye of the master makes the cattle thrive; *IN die* ~ *van*, in view of; *iem. in die* ~ *kan KYK*, look someone squarely in the face; *'n* ~ *wat net 'n MOEDER kan liefhê*, a face that only a mother can love; *iem. in sy* ~ *PRYS*, praise someone to his face; *iets in iem. se* ~ *SÊ*, say something straight to his face; *'n SKEWE* ~ *trek*, make a wry face; *iem. in die* ~ *SLAAN*, slap someone in the face; *SLEG van* ~ *wees*, have bad eye-sight; *jou* ~ *sal so bly STAAN*, your face will stay like that; *iem. deur sy* ~ *STREEP*, bid defiance to someone; *'n* ~ *soos 'n SUURLEMOEN*, a sour face; *sonder om 'n* ~ *te TREK*, without batting an eyelid; *'n lang* ~ *TREK*, pull a long face; ~*te TREK*, pull faces; *iem. met TWEE* ~ *te*, a double-faced person; *UIT die* ~, out of sight; *in die* ~ *VAT*, rebuke, reprimand; insult; *uit die* ~ *VERDWYN*, disappear from sight; ~**doekie**, face cloth, tissue.

gesig'gie, (-s), little face; pansy, heart's-ease.

gesig'kunde, optics; optometry; ~**kun'dige**, (-s), optician, optometrist; oculist.

gesig: ~**lap**, facecloth; ~**pap**, face pack.

gesigs': ~**afstand**, eye-shot; ~**as**, visual axis; ~**be= drog**, optical illusion, phantasm; ~**doekie**, face cloth; tissue; ~**einder**, horizon, skyline.

gesig'senu(wee), optical nerve.

gesigs': ~**grens**, kenning (at sea), limit of vision; ~**hoek**, optic(al) (facial, visual) angle, viewpoint; ~**indruk**, visual impression.

gesig'; sintuig, sense of sight, visual sense; ~**skerm**, facial shield; ~**skerpte**, acuity of vision.

gesigs'kring, horizon; field of vision, purview.

gesigs'kuur, face-lift(ing).

gesig'slagaar, facial artery.

gesigs': ~**lyn**, line of sight; ~**masker**, facial mask (pack); ~**meetkunde**, optometry; ~**meetkundige**, (-s), optometrist; ~**meter**, optometer; ~**oorspanning**, eyestrain; ~**orgaan**, organ of sight; ~**pap**, face pack; ~**poeier**, face powder; ~**punt**, point of view, standpoint, aspect; angle; ~**purper**, rhodopsin; visual purple; ~**room**, face cream; ~**veld**, field of vision; ~**veldkromming**, curvature of field of vision; ~**verjonging**, facelift; ~**verlamming**, facial paralysis; ~**verlies**, loss of eyesight; ~**vermoë**, visual faculty, eyesight.

gesimuleer', (-de), disguised; ~ *de regshandeling*, disguised transaction.

gesin', (-ne), household, family, home; children.

gesinchroniseer(d)', (-de), synchronized; ~ *de ratkas*, synchromesh transmission.

gesind', (-e), disposed, minded, inclined; *iem. gunstig* ~ *wees*, be favourably disposed towards someone; ~**heid**, disposition, inclination; (religious) denomination, persuasion; animus; spirit; attitude; *die werklike* ~*heid v d volk*, the real mind of the nation, the true disposition of the population.

gesind'te, (-s), denomination, persuasion, sect.

gesing', singing; ~**ery**, bawling.

gesins': ~**band**, family tie; ~**begroting**, family budget; ~**beperking**, birth-control; **G**~**dag**, Family Day; ~**fees**, family celebration; ~**hof**, family court; ~**hoof**, head of the family, householder; ~**lewe**, family life; ~**lid**, member of a family; ~**loon**, family wages; ~**toelae**, family allowance; ~**vermeerdering**, increase of one's family, addition to the family.

gesis', hiss(ing), fizz.

gesit', seat; patch.

gesitueer', (-de), situated.

gesjabloneer', (-de), stencilled.

gesjirp', chirping.

gesjor', pulling.

gesjou', (Ndl.), toiling, fagging.

geskaaf', (-de), planed (wood), smoothed.

geskaak'¹, (-te), abducted.

geskaak'², chequered (her.).

geskakeer', (-de), chequered, pied, shaded, variegated (soil); ~**d'heid**, variegation.

geskal', sound, clangour; braying; flourish, blare (of trumpets).

geskand'vlek, (-te), stigmatized, disgraced.

geskape 180 *geslinger*

geska'pe, created; *hoe staan dit ~?* what is the position? *~ne*, created, creation.
geskar'rel, flirting; rummaging.
geska'ter, burst of laughter, peals of laughter.
geskeer', (-de), shaven; shorn (sheep).
geskei', (-de, -e), divorced, separated; *~de AANWYSING*, distant reading; *'n ~ (d)e VROU*, divorcee; *~dene*, (-s), divorced person, divorcee.
geskei'denheid, separation, separate state.
geskel', abuse.
geskenk', (s) (-e), present, gift, bounty, donation, largesse; *as ~ GEE, ten ~e GEE*, give as present, make a gift of; *~ in GELD*, gift of money; (b) (-te), donated, donative, presented; *~boek*, gift-book.
geskep', (-te), handmade (paper); scooped, ladled (water).
geskerm', fencing; *~ met woorde*, high-sounding talk, verbiage.
geskermut'sel, skirmishing.
gesket'ter, flourish (of trumpets), blare.
geskeur', (-de), torn, ragged.
geskied', (~), happen, occur, chance; befall, take place; *laat U wil ~*, Thy will be done; *~blaaie*, historical records, annals; *~boeke*, annals (of history).
geskie'denis, (-se), history, story; *tot die ~ BEHOORT*, be a thing of the past; *GEWYDE ~*, sacred history; *die ~ HERHAAL hom*, history repeats itself; *OU ~*, ancient history; *dis die OU ~*, it's the old story; *daar is ~ aan VERBIND*, it has historical value; thereby hangs a tale; *~boek*, history book; *~les*, history lesson; *~onderwyser*, history teacher; *~vervalsing*, falsification of history.
geskied'kunde, history, historical science; historiography.
geskiedkun'dig, (-e), historical; *~e*, (-s), historian.
geskied': *~rol*, historical record; (mv) archives, annals; *~skrywer*, (-s), historian; historiographer; *~skrywing*, historiography; *~verhaal*, history; *~vorser*, historical research worker; *~vorsing*, historical research work.
geskiet', shooting, firing.
geskif', (-te), curdled (milk); perished (material); sifted, sorted out.
geskik', (-te), fit, suitable, proper, adequate, opportune, convenient, expedient, efficient, competent, qualified, appropriate (measures, instruments); capable (persons); apt (retort); suitable, answerable (for purpose); appropriate (to occasion); eligible (candidate); tame, well-trained (animal); proper (time); arranged; settled; *~ om te EET*, fit to be eaten; *~ MAAK vir 'n doel*, adapt for a purpose; *~t'heid*, fitness, suitability, adequacy, congeniality, convenience; eligibility; expedience; propriety; capability; aptitude; competence, competency; expediency; goodness; opportuness; pertinence; efficiency; *~t'heidsertifikaat*, competency certificate.
geskil', (-le), quarrel, difference, dispute; conflict; *'n ~ besleg (bylê, skik)*, settle a dispute; *~punt*, point of difference, question at issue, disputed point.
geskim'mel (-de), mouldy; grey.
geskimp', insinuation; gibing.
geskip'per, temporizing.
geskit'ter, glitter(ing), sparkling.
geskoei', (-de), shod.
geskof'fel, (s) weeding; dancing; (b) (-de), weeded; cultivated.
geskok', (-te), shocked.
geskom'mel, jolting, pitching; swinging.
geskon'de, damaged, violated, disfigured; defiled (honour); infringed (rights); *~nheid*, defectiveness; violated condition.
geskon'ke, granted, presented.
geskool', (-de), trained, skilled, schooled; *~de arbeiders*, skilled labourers; *~d'heid*, skill.
geskoor(d)', (-de), supported.
geskop', kicking.
gesko're, lost, stranded, inconvenienced; left without resources; *ek IS so ~ sonder my bril*, I am lost (helpless) without my glasses; *daar SIT hy mee ~*, he is saddled with it; *~ WEES*, be in hot water.
geskors', (-te), suspended (official).

geskraap', scraping; grabbing.
geskrap', (-te), cancelled, deleted; *'n ~ te lid*, a member who has been struck off the roll.
geskreeu', shouting, crying, outcry, hoot, clamour, shrieking; braying; *veel ~ en weinig wol*, much ado about nothing.
geskrei', weeping, crying; wailing.
geskre'we, written; *~ reg*, statute law; *~ne*, what has been written.
geskrif', (-te), writing, document; publication; *IN ~ te*, in writing; *in ~ STEL*, put in writing.
geskryf', **geskry'we**, writing, polemic writing, war of words; *al die ~ en gevryf*, this endless writing (scribbling).
geskub', (-de), scaly; imbricate; squamous.
geskud', (s) jumble; shaking; (b) (-de), jumbled, shaken.
geskui'fel, shuffling, scraping (of feet).
geskuins', (-te), bevelled; canted; slanted; splayed.
geskulp', (-te), scalloped; engrailed; *~te aartappels*, scalloped potatoes.
geskut', cannon, artillery, guns, ordnance; *LIGTE ~*, small arms (artillery); *'n STUK ~*, a piece of ordnance; *~ammunisie*, ordnance ammunition; *~bank*, barbette; *~brons*, gun-metal; *~dek*, gun-deck; *~fabriek*, gun-factory; *~gieter*, gun-founder; *~gietery*, gun-foundry; *~kuil*, gun-pit; *~metaal*, gun-metal; *~mond*, gun-tube; *~offisier*, gunnery officer; *~park*, artillery park; *~poort*, porthole; gun-port; *~stand*, position of the guns; gun emplacement; *~toring*, gun-turret; *~vuur*, gun-fire; *~werf*, ordnance yard.
geslaaf', slaving, drudgery, toiling, toiling and moiling.
geslaag', (-de), successful; passed (examination); *~de*, (-s), pass; *~d'heid*, success.
geslaan', (-de, geslane), beaten; coined (money).
gesla'e, beaten (gold); afflicted, tried; *~ne*, (s) (-s), afflicted person; (b) livelong; *die hele ~ne dag*, the livelong day; *~nheid*, affliction, despondency.
geslag'¹, (s) (-te), gender; sex; lineage, clan, house, race; generation (men); gender (masculine); genus; species (of animals, plants); *die ANDER ~*, the opposite sex; *die MENSLIKE ~*, mankind; *die OPKOMENDE ~*, the rising generation; *die SKONE ~*, the fair sex; *die SWAK ~*, the weaker sex.
geslag'², (b) (-te), slaughtered; butchered.
geslag': *~bepaler*, sexer; *~bepaling*, sexing; *~kunde*, genealogy; *~kun'dig*, (-e), genealogical; *~kun'dige*, (-s), genealogist; *~loos*, (..lose), asexual (plants); neuter, sexless; genderless.
geslags': *~afwyking*, sex perversion; *~begeerte*, libido; *~boom*, genealogical tree, pedigree; *~dele*, genital organs, genitals; private parts; *~drang*, sex urge; *~drif*, sexual passion, sex-urge; *~gemeenskap*, sexual intercourse, coition; *~hare*, pubes; *~hormoon*, sex hormone.
geslag'siekte, venereal disease.
geslags': *~kenmerk*, sexual characteristic; *~kliere*, sexual glands; *~kunde*, genealogy; *~lys*, genealogical table; pedigree; *~maniak*, sex maniac; *~misdaad*, sex crime; *~naam*, family name; surname; genus; *~opening*, sexual orifice; *~organe*, sexual organs; *~prikkel*, aphrodisiac; *~register*, genealogical register; genealogy; pedigree; *~rekening*, genealogy; *~ryp*, pubescent; *~rypheid*, puberty, pubescence; *~uitgang*, ending indicative of (grammatical) gender; *~verandering*, change of sex; *~verhouding*, sexual relations; *~verwantskap*, genetic affinity; *~voorligting*, sex education; *~vooroordeel*, sexism; *~wapen*, family crest, coat of arms; armorial bearings; armory.
geslag': *~telik*, (-e), sexual; *~telikheid*, sex(uality).
gesleep', (s) dragging; (b) (-te), dragged, towed.
geslen'ter, lounging, sauntering.
gesle'pe, sly, cunning; cute; astute, crafty, politic, knowing; *'n ~ KALANT*, a sly dog, a cunning fellow; *~ WEES*, be an old hand at something; *~nheid*, slyness, cunning, astuteness, cuteness, finesse.
gesle'te, spent; worn-out, second-hand.
geslin'ger, rolling (ship); staggering; dangling; oscillation.

geslobber

geslob'ber, slobbering.
gesloer', dawdling, postponing.
geslof', shuffling.
gesloof', toiling and moiling, drudgery.
geslo'te, shut, locked, closed; reticent; private; concluded (treaty); *'n ~ BOEK*, a sealed book; *agter ~ DEURE*, behind closed doors, in committee, in camera; *in ~ GELEDERE*, with closed ranks; *~ GRONDWATEROPPERVLAK*, piezometric surface; *~ geledere-ooreenkoms*, closed shop agreement; *~ nheid*, reserve, reticence.
geslui'er, (-de), veiled; foggy (photo).
gesluip', prowling, creeping.
gesluit', (-e), closed (doors); secured (screws); concluded (treaty).
geslurp'¹, (s) gobbling.
geslurp'², (b) (-te), with a trunk.
geslyp', (-te), sharpened; cut (glass); ground; polished.
geslyt', (-e), worn (shoes); rolled (stones).
gesmaal', scoffing, contumely, reviling.
gesmak', smacking (of lips).
gesmee', (gesmede), forged; wrought.
gesmeek', entreaty, supplication(s).
gesmeer', (-de), oiled; greased; *'n ~ de plaat*, a buttered baking-sheet.
gesmelt', (-e), molten (lead); melted (snow); *~ e vet oorgooi*, baste (with fat).
gesmeul', smouldering.
gesmoor', (-de), suppressed; strangled; stewed, fried; braised; *~ de BIEFSTUK*, braised steak; *~ de HOENDER*, sauté of chicken; *~ de KALFS= VLEIS*, sauté of veal.
gesmok'kel, smuggling.
gesmous', bartering.
gesmul', banqueting, feasting.
gesmyt', banging; waste (money).
gesnaar', (-de), stringed; strung.
gesnak', gasping.
gesnap', chattering.
gesna'ter, chattering, palaver, gabble, patter, prattle.
gesna'wel, (-de), beaked.
gesne'de, engraved, graven; *'n ~ beeld*, a graven image; *~ ne, (-s),* castrated person, eunuch.
gesnerp', grating (of wheels).
gesneu'wel, (-de), killed (in action); *~ de, (-s),* one killed in action; casualty; *lys van ~ des*, casualty list.
gesnik', sobbing, weeping.
gesnip'per, (-de), shredded (fruit).
gesnoef', bragging, boasting.
gesnoei', pruning, lopping, topping.
gesnoep', eating of dainties.
gesnor', whir(ring), whizzing, purr(ing).
gesnork', snoring.
gesnot'ter, snivelling.
gesnou', snarling; scolding.
gesnuf'fel, ferreting, rummaging.
gesnuif', sniffing.
gesny', (-de), emasculated; castrated; cut, sliced; *in repies ~*, cut into strips; *~ de, (-s),* eunuch.
gesoe'bat, begging and praying, imploring.
gesoek', search, hunt; searching.
gesoem', buzzing, humming, zooming.
gesoen', kissing.
gesog', (-te), forced, far-fetched; popular, (much) in demand; precious, sought-after; *~ t'heid*, mannerism, straining after effect; preciosity.
gesond', (-e), healthy, sound, hale, fit, blooming (health); wholesome, healthful (food); sane (views); bracing, balmy (air); hearty, *FRIS en ~*, hale and hearty; *~ e VERSTAND*, common sense; *weer ~ WORD*, recover one's health.
geson'de, (-s), healthy person.
gesond'heid, health, healthiness, soundness; lustiness; *sy ~ gaan AGTERUIT*, he is failing in health; *op iem. se ~ DRINK*, drink to someone's health; *MINISTER van G ~*, Minister of Health; *NIE vir hulle ~ nie*, not for their health; *met die OOG op sy ~*, for reasons of his health; *~ in die RONDHEID (mooi meisies in die blomtyd)!*, here's luck! here's health to everybody!; *~ is die grootste SKAT*,

gespuis

health is better than wealth; *met jou ~ SPEEL*, play with one's health; *~ sbeampte*, medical officer of health, health-officer; *~ sdiens*, sanitary service; *~ sdruiwesuiker*, medical glucose; *~ sertifikaat*, certificate of health.
gesond'heids: *~ halwe*, for health's sake; *~ koffie*, medicated coffee; *~ kommissie*, board of health; health-committee; *~ leer*, hygiene; *~ maatreël*, sanity (health) measure; *~ oord*, health-resort; *~ raad*, board of health, health-committee; *~ redes*, reasons of health; *~ reël*, health-rule, regimen; *~ toestand*, (state of) health; *~ voorskrif*, health rule (regulation); *~ wandeling*, constitutional.
gesond': *~ maker, (-s),* healer; *~ making*, healing, cure.
geson'ge, sung; *see* **sing**.
geson'ke, depraved; sunk(en); *~ ne, (-s),* rake, roué, debauchee; *see* **sink**.
gesons', buzzing, humming.
gesorteer', (-de), assorted, graded.
gesoteer', (-de), sauté.
gesous'¹, (s) continual rain.
gesous'², (b) perfumed, scented; sauced (tobacco).
gesout', (-e), salted, seasoned, cured (ham); corned (beef); immune; accustomed; experienced; *'n ~ e PERD*, a horse immune from horse-sickness; *~ teen 'n SIEKTE*, be immune to.
gespan'ne, tense, rapt (attention), strained; tight, taut (rope); *met ~ AANDAG*, with rapt attention; *~ SENUWEES*, highly-strung nerves; *op ~ VOET lewe*, live in strained relations; *~ nheid*, tenseness, tension, intentness, keen expectation; strained relations.
gespar'tel, struggling, sprawling.
gespasieer', (-de), spaced; leaded.
gespat', splashing.
ges'pebroek, trousers that fasten with a clasp.
gespeel', playing.
gespeen', (-de), weaned (child); stripped of buds (owing to drought, etc); *van IETS ~ wees*, have been weaned of something; *van WEELDE ~*, not used to luxury.
gespek', (-te), larded.
ges'pe(r), (s) (-s), buckle, clasp; (w) (ge-), buckle, clasp; strap (on); *~ broek*, knickerbockers; *~ tjie, (-s),* small buckle.
gespesialiseer', (-de), specialized.
gespesifiseer', (-de), specified.
gespier(d)', (-de), muscular, athletic, brawny; vigorous (style); powerful; *~ d'heid*, muscularity; brawniness; vigour.
gespik'kel, (-de), speckled, spotted, guttate; dapple, pied, brindle(d); grey; flecked.
gespits', (b) (-te), pointed; divaricate; bifid; erect; cloven; *met ~ te ore*, with ears erect (lit); be all ears; with rapt attention (fig.); (bw) attentively.
gesple'te, split, cloven (hooves); slotted; cleft (palate); *die ~ klou*, the (devil's) cloven hoof; *~ nheid*, dividedness.
gesplits', (-te), forked, cleft, split.
gespog', bragging.
gespon'ne, spun.
gespons', (-te), sponged.
gespook', haunting; fighting, struggle, scuffle.
gespoor', (-de), spurred; aligned.
gespot', mocking, jeering.
gesprek', (-ke), conversation, talk, discourse; interview; interlocution; colloquy; call (telephone); *'n ~ AANKNOOP*, begin a conversation; *die ~ BRING op*, turn the talk to; *die ~ GAANDE hou*, keep the conversation alive; *'n ~ VOER met*, converse with; *in ~ WEES*, engaged in conversation; *~ stof*, material for conversation; *~ storing*, cross-talk (teleph.); *~ taal*, colloquial language; *~ toon*, conversational tone; *~ vorm*: *in ~ vorm*, in the form of a conversation.
gesprik'kel, (-de), speckled, spotted.
gespro'ke, spoken; *oor die ALGEMEEN ~*, speaking generally; *MENSLIK ~*, humanly speaking.
gespuis', rabble, mob, scum, rascaldom, riff-raff, hooligans; populace, herd; *~ reg*, mob law.

gespuit', spouting, squirting.
gestaaf', (-de), confirmed (fact).
gestaag = **gestadig**.
gestaal', (-de), steeled, hardened.
gesta'dig, (-e), steady, constant, regular, continual; ~ *e weer*, settled weather; ~**heid**, steadiness, constancy.
gestal'te, (-s), build, stature, figure; size; attitude; configuration; ~ *gee aan*, give form to, create.
gestal'tenis, (-se), figure, shape.
gesta'mel, muttering; stammering.
gestamp', (s) pitching; pounding (of bearings), thumping, stamping; (b) (-te), crushed; ~ *te mielies*, samp.
gestand': *sy woord* ~ *doen*, keep one's word; redeem a promise.
gesta'pel, (-de), stacked.
Gesta'po, Gestapo (German secret police).
gestasioneer', (-de), stationed.
ges'te, (vero.), (-s), gesture.
gesteel', (s) thieving; (b) (-de), stolen; ~ *de geld*, stolen money.
gesteeld', (-e), stalked, pedunculate.
gesteen'te, (-s), rock, rocky boulder; (precious) stone; ~ **leer**, ~ **studie**, petrology, petrography.
geste'kel, (-de), echinate; spiny.
gestel'¹, (s) (-le), constitution, system, structure; *die POLITIEKE* ~, the political structure; *iem. met 'n STERK* ~, someone with a strong constitution.
gestel'², (b) (-de), placed; phrased; laid down; *'n goed* ~ *de BRIEF*, a well composed letter; *die oor ons* ~ *de MAGTE*, the powers that be; *die deur die vyand* ~ *de VOORWAARDES*, the conditions laid down by the enemy.
gestel³, (vgw) suppose, supposing; ~ *DAT*, suppose that; ~ *hy WEIER*, supposing he refuses.
gesteld: *HOE is dit daarmee* ~? how do matters stand? *dit is TREURIG* ~ *met hom*, he is in a very bad way; *op sy WAARDIGHEID* ~, stand on ceremony (on one's dignity); *op iets* ~ *WEES*, be fond of, be insistent upon (getting things well done); ~ **heid**, condition, state, nature; constitution (soil); habitude.
gestem', (-de), disposed; tuned; *gunstig* ~ *teenoor*, be well-disposed towards; ~ **d'heid**, mood, temper; tendency.
gestem'pel, (-de), printed, stamped, post-marked.
gesteriliseer', (-de), sterilized.
gestern'te, (-s), constellation, stars; asterism; *onder 'n gelukkige* ~ *gebore*, born under a lucky star.
gestert', (-e), caudate, tailed.
gesteun'¹, (s) moaning, groan(ing), grunt(ing).
gesteun'², (b) (-de), supported.
gesteur', (-de), offended, piqued; ~ **d'heid**, pique.
geste'wel, (-de), booted; ~ *en gespoor*, booted and spurred; ready.
gestig'¹, (s) (-te), institution, (lunatic) asylum; home (for helpless); building, establishment.
gestig'², (b) (-te), established, built; edified; *oor iets nie* ~ *wees nie*, be greatly displeased at something.
gestik'¹, (-te), smothered, suffocated.
gestik'², (-te) stitched.
gestikula'sie, (-s), gesticulation.
gestikuleer', (ge–), gesticulate, make gestures.
gestileer', (-de), in good style, styled.
gestip'pel, (-de), mottled; punctate.
gestoei', romping, mêlée.
gestoel'te, (-s), chair, seat, pulpit.
gestoffeer', (-de), furnished, upholstered.
gestol', (-de), congealed; clotted, coagulated.
gesto'le, stolen.
gestom'mel, cluttering (feet), stumbling.
gestoof', (-de), stewed; ~ *de GEREG*, stew; ~ *de HAAS*, jugged hare; ~ *de PENS*, stewed tripe; ~ *de VLEIS*, stew, stewed meat.
gestook', (-te), fired, distilled; *iem. het* ~, he has been boozing.
gestoom', (-de), steamed.
gestoot', pushing.
gestort', (-e), paid-in (capital); spilt (milk).
gestor'we, dead, deceased.
gestot'ter, stuttering, stammering.

gestraat', (gestrate), paved.
gestrand', (-e), stranded; ashore, aground, castaway.
gestre'de, fought.
gestreel', caressing, stroking; ~ **d**, flattered; (-de), ~ *d voel oor iets*, feel flattered about something.
gestreep', (-te), striped, streaked, streaky; ~ *te KWARTSIET*, banded quartsite; ~ *te YSTERSTEEN*, banded ironstone; ~ **t'heid**, banding.
gestrek', (-te), stretched; ~ *te DRAF*, full trot; ~ *te HOEK*, straight angle; ~ *te VOET*, linear foot.
gestrem(d)', (-de), retarded, impeded; curdled (milk); ~ **d'heid**, retardation; *serebrale* ~ **dheid**, cerebral palsy.
gestreng', (-e), severe, austere, rigorous; ~ **heid**, severity, austerity, rigour.
gestrib'bel, wrangling; haggling.
gestrom'pel, stumbling.
gestroom'lyn, (-de), streamlined.
gestru'wel, quarrelling.
gestry', quarrelling, wrangling, bickering.
gestryk', (-te), ironed.
gestudeer', (-de), studied; *'n* ~ *de houding*, a studied pose.
gestuik'sweis, (-te), butt-welded.
gestuk' = **geen stuk**.
gestyf', (-de), starched; ~ *de kraag*, starched collar.
gesug', sighing, groaning.
gesui'ker, (-de), sugared; ~ *de vrugte*, sugar(ed) fruit.
gesuip', drinking, drunkenness.
gesuis', buzzing, tinkling, singing; sough (of wind); murmur (of the heart).
gesui'wer, (-de), purified, refined; ~ *de goud*, fine gold; **G** ~ **de**, (-s), (hist.), member of purified National Party.
gesuk'kel, botheration; constant trouble (with officials); small progress; pottering; *dis 'n* ~ *met sy GESONDHEID*, he is constantly ailing; he has trouble with his health; *'n* ~ *van die ander WERELD*, much fuss and bother.
gesus'ters, (ong.), sisters.
gesuur', (-de), leavened.
geswaai', swinging, reeling.
geswael, (-de) = **geswawel**.
geswam', tosh, drivel.
geswa'wel, (-de), sulphured; drunk; groggy, tipsy, hazy.
gesweis', (-te), welded.
geswel', (s) (-le), swelling, protuberance, tumour, abscess, growth; (b) (-de), swollen, puffy.
geswen'del, swindling, fraud.
geswets', bragging, bluster, (talking) rubbish; swearing, cursing.
geswiep', swishing.
geswind', (-e), rapid, quick, swift, nimble.
geswoeg', drudging, toiling, grind.
geswol'le, swollen; stilted, bombastic, orotund, magniloquent, declamatory, pompous (language); bellied; ~ **nheid**, swollenness; puffiness, intumescence; bombast, magniloquence, pomposity.
geswo're, sworn (enemies).
getak', (-te), forked; branched, ramose.
getal', (-le), number; count; *'n BENOEMDE (onbenoemde)* ~, a concrete (abstract) number; *EWE en onewe* ~ *le*, even and odd numbers; *'n ONDEELBARE* ~, a prime number; *in RONDE* ~ *le*, in round figures; *TEN* ~ *le van*, to the number of; ~ **leleer**, science of numbers, arithmetic; ~ **lereeks**, series of numbers; ~ **letjie**, (-s), small number.
getalm', lingering, loitering, dawdling, dallying, procrastination.
getal'sterk, (-e), numerically strong; numerically superior; ~ **te**, numerical strength, establishment (army).
getals'vermindering, wastage (army).
getal'waarde, numerical value.
getand', (-e), edged, serrated; toothed (saw); cogged (wheel); dentate, crenate (leaves); jagged; fanged; ~ *e KETTINGRAT*, sprocket-wheel; ~ *e WIEL*, toothed wheel; ~ **heid**, serration.
getap', (-te), tapped; dowelled.
gete'ël, (-de), tiled.
geteem', drawl(ing).

geteer', (-de), tarred.
geteis'ter, (-de), afflicted, devastated; damaged.
gete'ken, (-de), signed; drawn (picture).
getem'per, (-de), temperate, moderate.
geteoretiseer', theorizing.
gete'pel, (-de), papillate, mamillate.
geterg', (s) teasing; (b) (-de), teased, provoked.
getier', clamour, noise, bluster.
getik'[1], (s) ticking, click(ing), tapping.
getik'[2], (b) (-te), moony, mellow, loony, dotty, balmy, crackbrained; tipsy, merry; typewritten; *so EFFENS* ~, a bit crazy; ~ *WEES*, be slightly tipsy.
getik'-tak, tick-tack.
getikt'heid, craziness.
getim'mer, carpentering; ~ **te**, (-s), structure.
getin'gel, getin'kel, tinkling, jigling.
getint', (-e), coloured.
getin'tel, sparkling, twinkling; tingling.
geti'tel, (-de), named, called, entitled; titled (person); headed (chapter).
getjank', yelping, whining, blubber, bleat howl(ing), puling.
getjilp', chirping, chirruping, cheep.
getjin'gel, tinkling.
getjom'mel, grousing, grumbling.
getob', bother, worry; drudgery; ~ *oor sake*, business worries.
getoë: *gebore en* ~, born and bred.
getoet', getoe'ter, tooting, hoot(ing).
getoets', (-te), tested.
getok'kel, thrumming (on a harp); plunk.
getop', (-te), lopped, topped.
getor'ring, teasing, nagging, worry; unstitching.
getra'lie, (-de), grated, cross-barred, trellised.
getrap', (-te), trodden; ~ *te pad*, (beaten) track.
getrap'pel, trampling, pitter-patter, clatter, patter.
getrek', (s) trekking, moving; pulling; (b) (-te), drawn.
getreur', mourning, sadness.
getreu'sel, dawdling.
getril', flickering.
getrip'pel, trippling; pitter-patter (of feet).
getroef', (-de), trumped.
getrof'fe, moved, touched; taken, arranged.
getrok'ke, attracted; drawn; *tot iem.* ~ *voel*, feel attracted to someone.
getrom'mel, drumming, strumming, beating, rataplan.
getroos', (w) (~), submit, bear, resign (oneself); *jou baie moeite* ~, spare no pains; (b) (-te), comforted, consoled; *so ewe* ~ *sit*, sit perfectly at ease (coolly).
getrou', (-e), faithful, true, reliable, trusty; *'n* ~ *e afskrif*, a true copy.
getroud', (-e), married; *hulle IS gister* ~, they were married yesterday; *MET iets* ~, wedded to something; ~ **e**, (-s), married person.
getrou'e, (-s), adherent, follower; stalwart, loyal (faithful) supporter.
getrou'heid, fidelity, faithfulness, loyalty, allegiance.
getui'e, (s) (-s), witness; deponent; attestor; godfather, godmother; *as* ~ *DAGVAAR*, summon as witness; *iem. tot (as)* ~ *ROEP*, call someone to bear witness (give evidence); *vir iem.* ~ *WEES*, bear witness for someone; ~ *WEES van*, be witness of; (w) (~), testify, give evidence, bear witness; confess; ~ **bank**, witness box; ~ **geld**, witness-money; conduct-money.
getui'enis, (-se), evidence, testimony, attestation; deposition; ~ *AFLÊ van*, bear witness to, give evidence of; ~ *INWIN*, take (collect) evidence; *VOLGENS eie* ~, on his own evidence.
getui'e: ~ **stelsel**, tally system; ~ **verhoor**, examination of witnesses; ~ **verklaring**, deposition, evidence.
getuig, (~), see **getuie** (w); *almal* ~ *van sy BEKWAAMHEID*, all testify to his ability; *DAAR VAN kan ek* ~, I can confirm this; *die FEITE* ~ *daarvan*, the facts prove it; *vir iem. in die HOF* ~, bear witness in court in favour of someone; *sulke dade* ~ *TEEN hom*, such actions bear witness against him; ~ **skrif**, testimonial, certificate; chit, character, reference.
getuit'[1], (s) tingling.
getuit'[2], (b) (-e), with a nozzle, nozzled.
getuur', poring; peering.
getweng', twang.
getwis', quarrelling, wrangling; controversy.
gety', (-e), tide; *as die* ~ *verloop, versit 'n mens die BAKENS*, one must trim one's sails to the wind; *met die* ~ *SAAMGAAN*, swim (go) with the stream; *die* ~ *laat VERLOOP*, let the opportunity slip; *die* ~ *WAARNEEM*, take the tide at the flood; ~ **amplitude**, tide amplitude; ~ **beweging**, tidal (tide) movement.
gety'(de)boek, breviary, hour-book.
gety': ~ **golf**, tidal wave; ~ **hawe**, tidal harbour (basin); ~ **hoogte**, high-tide level; ~ **konstante**, tide constant; ~ **lesing**, tide reading; ~ **lug**, tidal air; ~ **meter**, tide-gauge; ~ **rivier**, tidal river; ~ **sluis**, tide-lock; ~ **stroom**, tidal current; ~ **tafel**, tide-table; ~ **vry**, (-e), tideless, tide-free; ~ **water**, tide-water.
geul, (-e), gully, narrow channel.
geur, (s) (-e), fragrance, smell, flavour, savour, scent, odour, essence, perfume, aroma; redolence; bouquet (wine); *'n* ~ *AFGEE (versprei)*, emit (diffuse) an odour; *iets in* ~ *e en KLEURE vertel*, relate in great detail; (w) (ge-), emit scent (perfume), smell; aromatize; flavour (a cake); season (a dish); *hy* ~ *met sy kennis*, he flaunts his knowledge.
geu'rig, (-e), fragrant, odorous, balmy, perfumed, redolent, aromatic; savoury (food); racy (wine); flavoursome, flavorous; ~ **heid**, fragrance, perfume, redolence; raciness (of flavours).
geur: ~ **ing**, flavour(ing); ~ **loos**, (..lose), flavourless; ~ **middel**, flavouring, aromatic substance; ~ **pilletjie**, cachou; ~ **sel**, seasoning, flavour, flavouring (essence).
geur'tjie, (-s), flavour; *daar is 'n* ~ *aan*, there is something fishy about it.
geur'tyd, rut, rutting time.
geus[1], jack(-flag).
Geus[2], (-e), Protestant, Beggar of the Sea; ~ **epenning**, Beggar's medal; ~ **verbond**, Beggar's League.
geut, (-e), gutter, sewer; chute; duct; channel; grip; ~ **bak**, leader (rain-water) head; hopper; ~ **dissel**, spout adze; ~ **lys**, cyma recta; ~ **put**, cesspool; ~ **pyp**, gutter pipe, down-pipe; ~ **spuit**, gargoyle; ~ **werk**, guttering.
gevaar', (gevare), danger, peril, risk, exposure; distress; *jou in* ~ *BEGEWE*, imperil oneself; *aan* ~ *BLOOTSTEL*, expose to danger; *in* ~ *BRING*, endanger; *BUITE* ~, out of danger (a patient); ~ *LOOP*, run a risk; *OP* ~ *van*, at the risk of; ~ *SOEK (uitlok)*, court danger; *SONDER* ~, without danger (risk); *jou in* ~ *STORT*, plunge oneself into danger; ~ **gebied**, dangerous area, danger zone.
gevaar'lik, (-e), dangerous, perilous, precarious, risky (speculation); grave; chanceful; hazardous; ~ **heid**, dangerousness, perilousness, hazardousness.
gevaar': ~ **loos**, (..lose), safe, without danger; ~ **punt**, danger point; crisis; ~ **sein**, danger signal; ~ **strook**, danger zone (area).
gevaar'te, (-s), colossus, monster.
gevaar': ~ **teken**, danger sign (signal); ~ **'vol**, (-le), perilous, hazardous, dangerous.
geval', (s) (-le), case, event, instance, matter; predicament, plight; *BY* ~, in case; by chance; *in die ERGSTE* ~, if the worst comes to the worst; *in GEEN* ~, not in any case; *in HIERDIE* ~, in this instance; *IN alle* ~, in any case, at all events, at any rate; *in JOU* ~, as far as you are concerned; *in* ~ *VAN*, in case of; (w) (~), please, suit; *DIT* ~ *my nie*, I don't like it; *jou iets LAAT* ~, put up (agree) with something; (b) (-le), killed (in action); fallen (angel, woman); ~ **leboek**, case-book; ~ **lene**, (-s), fallen person; person killed in action; ~ **lestudie**, case history; ~ **lig**, (-e), agreeable; ~ **ligheid**, agreeableness.
gevang', (-de), caught.

gevan'ge, captive; collared; *hom* ~ *GEE*, surrender himself, give himself up; ~ *HOU*, hold captive; keep prisoner; ~ *NEEM*, take prisoner; ~ *SIT*, be in a prison; ~**bewaarder**, gaoler, jailer, warder, turnkey; ~**houding**, detention, imprisonment, detainment; ~**kamer**, detention-room.
gevan'gene, (-s), prisoner, captive, convict.
gevan'genemer, captor.
gevan'geneming, arrest, capture, caption, apprehension.
gevan'genis, (-se), prison, gaol; cage; hold; ~**buitepos**, prison outpost; ~**klere**, gaol clothes; ~**kos**, prison food; ~**regulasies**, prison regulations; ~**straf**, imprisonment, confinement; ~**wese**, prison system, prison administration.
gevan'ge(n)skap, captivity, imprisonment, confinement, bondage, chains; custody; duress; fetters.
gevan'gesetting, imprisonment, commitment.
gevank'lik, as a prisoner, captive; ~ *wegvoer*, carry into captivity.
gevat'¹, (b) (-te), shrewd, clever, smart, apt, acute, ready-witted, quick-witted; quick (at repartee).
gevat'², (b) set; *diamante in platina* ~, diamonds set in platinum.
gevat'heid, shrewdness, smartness (at repartee); ready wit.
geve'der, (-de), feathered; ~**te**, feathers, plumage.
geveer'¹, (b) (-de), feathered, pinnate, plumose.
geveer'², (b) (-de), with springs, sprung (car).
geveerd'heid, plumosity.
geveg', (-te), fight, battle, action, engagement, fray, combat; *buite* ~ *stel*, put out of action; knock out; disable.
gevegs': ~**afstand**, fighting distance; ~**behoeftes**, fighting needs; ~**bomvliegtuig**, fighter-bomber (plane); ~**eenheid**, fighting unit; ~**eskader**, fighting squadron; ~**formasie**, fighting formation; ~**front**, battle front; ~**hoedanighede**, fighting qualities; ~**kaart**, battle map; ~**linie**, fighting line, front; ~**loopgraaf**, front-line trench; ~**nasievlag**, battle-ensign; ~**oefening**, battle exercise; ~**onderskeiding**, battle honours; ~**pos**, action station.
geveg': ~**staat**, fighting state; ~**sterkte**, fighting strenght.
gevegs': ~**trein**, fighting train; ~**troepe**, fighting troops; ~**veld**, operating area; ~**vermoë**, fighting power; ~**vliegtuig**, fighter plane; ~**vlug**, fighter flight; ~**voorpos**, battle outpost; ~**waarde**, fighting value; ~**warreling**, mêlée.
geveins', (s) hypocrisy; (b) (-de), pretended, false, feigned, dissembling, simulated, hypocritical; ~**de**, (-s), hypocrite; ~**d'heid**, hypocrisy, cant, dissimulation.
gevel', (-de), sentenced; felled; couched (arms).
geventileer', (-de), ventilated.
geverf', (-de), painted.
gevernis', (-te), varnished.
geves', (-te), hilt.
geves'tig, (-de), fixed, established; ~*de REGTE*, vested rights; *'n* ~*de SAAK*, old-established business.
gevier', (-de), fêted, made much of; celebrated.
gevie'rendeel, (-de), divided into four, quartered; riftsawn; ~ *de hout*, quarterings.
gevin', (-de), finned; pinnate (leaf).
gevit', fault-finding, carping cavilling.
gevitamineer', (-de), vitaminized.
gevlag', flag-flying.
gevlam', (-de), watered, flamed (silk); grained, marbled; figured.
gevleg', (-te), plaited, braided; ~ *te patroon*, braided pattern.
gevlei', flattering; *in die* ~ *kom by iem.*, get into someone's good books; win someone's favour.
gevleis', (-de), fleshy.
gevlek', (-te), spotted, speckled, blurred, stained; dappled; stretched (skin); cut open (up) (fish); guttate.
gevlerk', (-te), winged, pinnate.
gevleu'el, (-de), pennate, winged; alated; ~ *de woorde*, winged words.
gevloek', cursing, swearing, profanity.

gevoeg': (Ndl., ong.), *sy* ~ *doen*, evacuate one's bowels.
gevoeg'lik, (-e), appropriate, fit, suitable, proper; *dit kan* ~ *weggelaat word*, this may as well be omitted; ~**heid**, propriety, appropriateness, decorum.
gevoel', (-ens), feeling, sentiment, pathos, perception, sentience, sense, sensation, emotion; *op* ~ *AF*, by the touch (feel); *sy* ~ *van EER*, his sense of honour; *iem. met* ~ *vir HUMOR*, somebody with a sense of humour; *met* ~ *PRAAT*, speak feelingly; *die* ~ *SPEEL daarby geen rol nie*, sentiment plays no part in it.
gevoe'le, (-ns), opinion, impression, view; *die ALGEMENE* ~ *is*, the consensus of opinion is; *VOLGENS my* ~, in my opinion; *van* ~ *WEES dat ..*, be of opinion that ..; ~**ntheid**, feeling.
gevoe'lerig, (-e), (rather) touchy, sentimental; ~**heid**, sentimentality; touchiness.
gevoe'lig, (-e), tender, sensitive, delicate, reactive, alive; emotional; touchy; *iem. 'n* ~*e LES leer*, teach someone a painful lesson; ~ *MAAK*, sensitize (film); *'n* ~*e NEERLAAG*, a severe defeat; *'n* ~*e SLAG*, a severe blow; ~ *VIR*, sensitive to (kindness); *erg* ~ *WEES oor iets*, be very touchy about something; ~**heid**, sensitiveness, tenderness, impressibility, impressionability (mind); passibility; sensibility, emotionality; ~**heidsgrens**, limit of sensibility.
gevoel'loos, (..lose), unfeeling, apathetic, callous, heartless; insensitive (to emotion); insensible (to fear); numb, benumbed (with cold); cloddish; ~*maak*, anaesthetize; ~**heid**, apathy, insensibility; anaesthesia; numbness; callousness, cloddishness.
gevoel': ~**s'afstomping**, blunting of feelings; ~**senuwee**, sensory nerve; ~**sin**, sense of touch (feeling), tactile sense.
gevoels': ~**kwessie**, question of sentiment; ~**lewe**, emotional (inner) life; ~**mens**, man of feeling, sentimentalist; ~**orgaan**, sensory organ; ~**uitbarsting**, display of emotion; ~**uiting**, expression of feeling; ~**waarde**, emotional value; feeling-tone; connotation (of word).
gevoel': ~ **te**, (-s), feeling; ~**vol**, (-le), tender, full of feeling, pitiful, compassionate.
gevoer'¹, (-de), lined (cloak).
gevoer'², (-de), fed (chicken).
gevoet', (-e), pedate.
gevo'gelte, (ong.), birds, fowl; bird life.
gevolg', (-e), consequence, result, product; entailment; effect; entourage, train, equipage, following; retinue, followers; progeny; cortège; suite; *met ALLE* ~ *e*, come what may; ~ *GEE aan*, give effect to, comply with; obey; grant; *met GOEIE* ~, with great success; *OORSAAK en* ~, cause and effect; *SONDER* ~, without success; without retinue; *TEN* ~*e van*, in consequence of; as a result of; ~**aanduidend**, (-e), consecutive; ~**gewing**, compliance; ~**lik**, consequently, as a consequence; eventual; resultant; accordingly; ~**s'omvang**, incidence.
gevolg'trekking, (-e, -s), conclusion, deduction, inference, illation, ratiocination, corollary; consequence; *tot 'n* ~ *KOM*, arrive at a conclusion; *oorhaastige* ~*e MAAK*, jump to conclusions.
gevolmag'tigde, (-s), plenipotentiary (of a country); procurator; proxy, holder of a power of attorney; delegate; mandatory; assignee; warrantee.
gevon'de, found; *die saak is* ~, the problem has been solved.
gevon'kel, sparkling, twinkling.
gevon'niste, (-s), condemned prisoner.
gevor'der, (-de), advanced; ~ *de GELD*, money demanded; *op* ~ *de LEEFTYD*, at an advanced age; ~ *de VLIEGKUNS*, advanced flying.
gevorm(d)', (-de), formed, shaped; mature.
gevou', (-de), folded, plicate; ~ *de arms*, crossed arms.
gevra', (gevraagde), gevraag', (-de), wanted, demanded; *die gevraagde antwoord*, the required answer.
gevrees', (-de), dreaded, redoubtable; feared; ~ *de siekte*, dreaded disease; ~ *de teenstander*, feared opponent.

gevreet', gnawing pain; gorging; ~, (gevrete), face, mug, phiz.
gevrek', (-te), dead (of animals); slow, dull, uninteresting.
gevries', (-de), frozen
gevry', wooing; love-making; *lank ~, maar niks gekry,* after all the wooing there is nothing doing.
gevryf', (-de), polished, rubbed.
gevul', (-de), well-filled, well-lined (purse); full, full-bodied (figure).
gevulkaniseer(d)', (-de), vulcanized.
gevurk', (-te), forked; pronged; dichotomous; (bi)furcate(d); *~ te dryfstang,* forked connecting rod.
gevuur', shooting, firing.
gewaad', (gewade), garb, garment, dress, habiliments, habit, apparel, raiment, attire.
gewaag'¹, (w) (~), mention, make mention of; *met lof van iets ~,* speak highly of.
gewaag'², (b) (-de), risky, dangerous, chanceful, chancy, perilous; adventurous; hazardous, bold; equivocal; offending against propriety, risqué (story, joke); *fris ~, is half gewonne,* well begun is half done; **~d'heid,** riskiness, hazardousness, perilousness.
gewaai', (-de), blown; *~de grond,* aeolian soil.
gewaand', (-e), supposed, feigned, pretended, fancied, putative.
gewaar', (w) (~), notice, perceive, see, descry; *jy sal dit ~,* you'll catch it.
gewaardeer', (-de), valued, appreciated.
gewaar'merk, (-te), hallmarked; certified (as correct); attested.
gewaar'word, (-ge-), become aware of, perceive, notice.
gewaar'wording, (-e, -s), sensation, perception; experience; aura; feeling; percipience; *'n ONAANGENAME ~,* an unpleasant sensation; *jou ~ VERBERG,* hide one's feelings.
gewag', mention, reference; *~ maak van,* make mention of, refer to.
gewag'gel, staggering.
gewalm', smoking; smoke.
gewals'¹, (s) waltzing.
gewals'², (s) rolling; (b) (-te), rolled; *~te BRONS,* rolled bronze; *~ te STAAL,* hard-drawn steel.
gewan'del, walking.
gewa'pen, (-de), armed; prepared; reinforced (concrete); *~de mag,* armed force; mailed fist; *~ wag,* armoured guard.
gewa'penderhand, (ong., plegt.), by force of arms.
gewap'per, fluttering (of flags).
gewar'rel, whirling.
gewas'¹, (s) (-se), harvest, crop; plant; growth, tumour (in body); *tropiese ~se,* tropical plants.
gewas'², (b) (-te), washed; *~te wol,* scoured wool.
gewas'³, (b) (-te), waxed (silk).
gewas'se: *daarteen is geen kruid ~ nie,* there is no remedy for that.
gewa'ter, (-de), moiré (silk); watered; *~de sy,* watered silk, moiré.
gewatteer', (-de), wadded (quilt), padded (counterpane).
gewa'wel, drivel, rot.
geweb', (-de), webbed.
geweef', (-de), woven.
geweeg', (-de), weighed; *~de gemiddelde,* weighted mean (average).
geweek', (-te), soaked; *~te brood,* sippet.
gewee'klaag, lamentation, wailing.
geween', weeping, wailing.
geweer', (gewere, -s), rifle; fire-arm, piece, gun; *met 'n ~ AANLÊ, die ~ AANGOOI (rig),* point a gun; *na die ~ GRYP,* take up arms; *PRESENTEER ~!* present arms! *PROBEER is die beste ~,* there's nothing like trying; **~band,** sling; **~beslag,** mountings (gun); **~boontjie, ~doppie,** percussion cap; **~fabriek,** small-arms factory; **~koeël,** bullet, musket-ball; **~koek,** gun-stock; **~kolf,** butt(-end); **~laaimaker,** stocker; **~loop,** gunbarrel; **~magasyn,** arsenal; **~maker,** gunsmith; **~metaal,** gun-metal; **~prop,** tampion; **~rak,** arms-rack; gun-rack; **~riem,** rifle-sling; **~sak,** gun-bag; **~skoen,** gun-pocket (on saddle); **~skoot,** rifle-shot; **~sku, (-we),** gun-shy; **~slot,** gunlock; firelock; **~smokkelaar,** gun-runner; **~smokkelary,** gun-running; **~standertjie,** musket-rest; **~val,** spring gun; **~vuur,** musketry fire, gun-fire, rifle-fire, fusillade, gunnery.
gewees', been; vgl. **gewese.**
gewei', (Ndl.), (-e), antlers, horns, head; **~draend, (-e),** antlered.
gewei'fel, vacillation, wavering.
ge'wel, (-s), gable, façade; front; **~breedte,** frontage.
geweld', force, violence; coaction; *homself ~ AANDOEN,* force oneself; *iem. ~ AANDOEN,* do violence to someone; *met ALLE ~,* come what may; by hook or by crook; *BRUTE ~,* brute force; *met ~ kan 'n mens die DUIWEL die krans (berg) afja,* force will make even the devil budge; *MET ~ iets wil doen,* insist upon doing something; do something by force; *MET ~,* by force; *~ PLEEG,* commit violence.
ge'weldak, gabled roof.
geweld'daad, deed of violence, outrage.
gewelddadig, (-e), violent; forcible; **~heid, (..hede),** violence, outrage; violent conduct.
gewel'denaar, (-s), tyrant, usurper, oppressor.
geweldenary', (-e), tyranny.
gewel'dig, (b) (-e), violent, severe, enormous, mighty, forcible, forceful, vehement; plaguy; (bw) greatly, dreadfully, intensely, awfully; *~ duur,* wickedly expensive; **~heid,** vehemence, violence.
geweld'loos, (..lose), non-violent; **~heid,** non-violence.
geweld': *~ pleging,* violence; *~staat,* police state.
gewelf', (s) (gewelwe), vault(ing); dome; cove; cope; *die ~ van die hemele,* the canopy (vault) of heaven; (b) (-de), domed, vaulted, arched; convexed; **~d'heid,** convexity; **~boog,** vaulted arch; **~rib,** arch-rib; **~vorming,** doming.
ge'wel: *~laag,* barge-course; **~lys, (-te),** cornice; **~muur,** gable-end; **~plaat,** facia; **~spits,** gable-end; **~top,** gable; **~trap(pie),** corbie step; **~venster,** gable-window.
gewe'mel, swarming, teeming.
gewen', (~), accustom, inure, harden; *jou aan iets ~,* accustom oneself to something.
gewend'¹, accustomed, used to; *ons is dit NIE van hom ~ nie,* we are not used to that from him; *NIKS ~ wees nie,* be accustomed to nothing; *~ RAAK (word) aan,* become accustomed to.
gewend'², turned; *met die hoof na links ~,* with the head turned to the left.
gewen'ning, (ong.), accustoming, inurement.
gewens', (-te), wished, desirable; desired; welcome; **~t'heid,** desirability.
gewen'te, habit; *die ~ maak die gewoonte,* habit becomes second nature.
gewen'tel, rotation.
ge'wer, (-s), giver, donor, presenter.
gewer'skaf, bustle, ado, to-do.
gewer'wel, (-de), vertebrate; *~de dier,* vertebrate (animal).
ge'wery, giving.
gewes', ~te, province, region, country; clime; *betere ~te,* abode of the blessed; *so in DIE ~te,* in that region; in those parts; approximately.
gewe'se, former, ex-, later; retired; *~ HOOF,* ex-principal, *~ KONING,* former (late) king, *~ne, (-s),* former fiancé(e).
gewes'spraak, gewes'taal, (ong., vero.), (regional) dialect.
gewes'telik, (-e), provincial, regional; *~e segswyse,* dialect.
gewe'te, (-ns), conscience; breast; *met 'n GERUSTE ~,* with a clear conscience; *heelwat op sy ~ HÊ,* have much on his conscience; *'n goeie ~ is 'n sagte KUSSING,* who has a clear conscience sleeps well; *'n RUIM ~ hê,* have an elastic conscience; *sy ~ KWEL (pla) hom,* his conscience pricks him; *'n SKULDIGE ~,* a guilty conscience; *'n SUIWER ~,* a clean conscience; *jou ~ sus,* appease one's conscience; *sy ~ is TOEGESKROEI,* he has no

gewete(n)loos

conscience; *in SY ~ kan 'n WA en span osse draai*, his conscience is pretty elastic.
gewe'te(n)loos, (..lose), unscrupulous, unprincipled; conscienceless; **~heid**, unscrupulousness.
gewe'te(n)saak, matter (case) of conscience.
gewe'tens: ~-angs, pangs of conscience; **~artikel**, conscience clause; **~beswaar**, conscientious objection (scruple); **~dwang**, religious (moral) constraint; **~geld**, conscience money; **~getrou, (-e)**, conscientious, conscionable; **~halwe**, for conscience sake; **~klousule**, conscience clause; **~knaging**, compunction, pricks of conscience, remorse; **~mens**, precisian; **~ondersoek**, examination of conscience; **~vraag**, question of conscience; **~vryheid**, liberty of conscience; **~wroeging**, qualms (pangs) of conscience.
gewet'tig, (-de), entitled; well-founded, justified, legitimate; **~d'heid**, legitimateness.
gewe'we, woven.
gewie'bel, wobbling.
gewie'gel, rocking.
gewiek', (-te), winged; vaned.
gewig', (-te), weight, importance, moment; consequence; concernment; poise; gravity; impost (horse-racing); load; ponderosity, heaviness; onerousness; ~ **AANSIT**, put on weight; *sy ~ in GOUD werd*, worth one's weight in gold; **~ HEG aan**, attach weight to; *jou ~ INGOOI*, throw in one's weight; **~ van LOS uitrusting**, removable equipment weight; *'n MAN van ~*, a man of standing; **~ te OPTEL**, lift weights; *'n saak van ~*, a weighty matter; *baie ~ in die SKAAL lê*, be of great import; carry much weight; **SKOON ~**, dressed weight; **SOORTLIKE ~**, specific gravity; *die ~ van 'n STAP besef*, realize the importance (gravity) of a step; *by die ~ VERKOOP*, sell by weight; *met gelyke ~ te WEEG*, hold the scales even; *jou ~ in die skaal WERP*, throw in one's weight; **~druk**, weight pressure; **~loos, (..lose)**, weightless; **~loosheid**, weightlessness; **~optel**, weight-lifting; **~opteller**, weight-lifter.
gewigs': ~analise, gravimetric analysis; **~bepaling**, assize; **~eenheid**, unit of weight; **~grens**, 'weight limit; **~leer**, barology; **~lys**, weight schedule; **~reëlaar**, weighted governor; **~toename**, increase in weight.
gewig'stoot, (s) putting the shot; **(w) (-gestoot)**, put the shot.
gewig'stoter: shot-putter.
gewigs': ~verdeling, weight distribution; centrage; **~verlies**, loss of weight; **~vermindering**, reduction of weight; **~verskil**, difference in weight.
gewig'tig, (-e), important, momentous, consequential, grave, ponderous, heavy, weighty; *hom erg ~ voel*, feel the weight of his own importance; **~doenery**, pomposity; **~heid**, importance, weightiness, momentousness, consequence, gravity.
gewik', deliberation; *na baie ~ en (ge)weeg*, after long deliberation.
gewik'kel, wobbling; hurrying.
gewiks', (-te), sharp, smart, clever, quick; **~t'heid**, shrewdness, smartness.
gewild', (-e), wished-for; in demand, popular, favoured; far-fetched; *~ by sy BURE*, a great favourite with his neighbours; *'n ~e GEESTIGHEID*, a forced joke; *die KOFFIE is ~*, the coffee is in great demand; **~heid**, favour; demand; popularity.
gewil'lig, (-e), willing, ready; docile; free; **~heid**, willingness, readiness.
gewin', (s) gain, profit, advantage; *die eerste ~ is KATTEGESPIN*, win at first and lose at last; *VUIL ~*, ill-gotten gains; (w) (~), gain; beget; **~siek, (-e)**, avaricious, eager for gain; **~soeker**, profiteer; **~sug**, covetousness; lust for gain; **~sug'tig, (-e)**, covetous, avaricious.
gewir'war, confusion, swirl.
gewis', (b) (-se) sure, certain; forsooth; (bw) undoubtedly, certainly, surely; **~heid**, surety, certainty.
gewo'ë, weighed; *~ (geweeg) en te lig bevind*, weighed and found wanting.

gewoel', bustle, stir, tumult, crowd.
gewond', (-e), wounded, disabled; **~ e, (-s)**, wounded (person), casualty, case.
gewon'ne, won; *dit ~ GEE*, yield the point; *so ~ so GERONNE*, lightly come, lightly go.
gewoon', (gewone), accustomed; common, plain, usual; everyday; habitual, pedestrian; ordinary; vulgar (fraction); popular, general; *gewone AANDELE*, ordinary shares; *van meer as gewone BEKWAAMHEID*, of unusual ability; *die gewone LOOP van sake*, the usual run of things; *die gewone MENS (man)*, the ordinary person, the man in the street.
gewoond', used, accustomed; *hy is daaraan ~*, he is accustomed to it; **~wording**, inurement.
gewoon'heid, commonness, ordinariness.
gewoon'lik, usually, habitually, ordinarily; *soos ~*, as usual.
gewoon'te, (-s), habit, custom, usage, practice; mode; habitude; convention; consuetude; mannerism; *'n ~ AANNEEM*, fall into (pick up) a habit; *'n ~ AFLEER*, give up a habit; break oneself of a habit; *'n ~ word 'n GEWENTE*, habit becomes second nature; *die ~ HÊ om*, be in the habit of; *daar 'n ~ van MAAK*, make a habit of it; *NA (volgens) ~*, according to custom; *~ word tweede NATUUR*, habit becomes second nature; *OUDER ~*, according to (ancient) custom; **~drinker**, compulsive drinker; **~dronkaard**, habitual drunkard; **~kramp**, tic; **~misdadiger**, habitual criminal; **~reg**, customary (common, consuetudinary) law; prescription; **~werklose**, habitually unemployed.
gewoon'weg, downright, plain(ly); normally; *dit is ~ dwaasheid*, it is simply (nothing less than) foolishness.
geword', became; came into being.
gewor'stel, struggle, struggling.
gewor'tel, (-de), rooted, ingrained (customs); *~ de stiggies*, rooted cutting(s).
gewraak', (-te), challenged; *~ te JURIELID*, challenged juryman; *~ te WOORDE*, words complained of.
gewrie'mel, swarming.
gewrig', (-te), joint; wrist; **~loos, (..lose)**, anarthrous.
gewrigs': ~aandoening, arthrosis; **~band**, ligament; **~breuk**, fracture of a joint; **~holte**, articular cavity, cotyle; **~knobbel**, condyle; **~knop**, condyle; **~koppeling**, flexible coupling; **~ontsteking**, arthritis; **~rumatiek**, rheumatoid arthritis; **~vergroeiing**, ankylosis; **~verstywing**, arthrosclerosis; **~vlies**, synovial membrane; **~vog**, synovial fluid.
gewroet', burrowing.
gewrog', (-te), production, creation, structure, masterpiece.
gewron'ge, distorted; **~nheid**, distortion.
gewuif', waving.
gewurg', (-de), strangled, choked, throttled.
gewyd', (-e), sanctified, consecrated; sacred (music); holy; devotional.
gewys'de, (-s), sentence, judgment; decided case.
gewy'sig, (-de), qualified.
geyk', (-te), assized; stamped; *'n ~ te term*, a standing (stereotyped) phrase.
geys', (-de), iced; covered with ice; frozen; *~ de koffie*, iced coffee.
gezoem', buzzing.
ghaap, (ghape), succulent, wild plant, e.g. *Hoodia bainii, Trichocaulon piliferum*.
ghallaghie'lie, (gew.), (-s) tadpole; small fish.
gham'pie, (-s), rise; rut (in road).
Gha'na, Ghana.
Ghanees', (Ghanese), Ghanaian.
ghannaghoe'tjie, (-s), tapping beetle.
ghan'tang, (-s), suitor, lover.
ghar'ra, (-s), edible berry *(Rhus undulata)*.
ghar'tjie = graatjiemeerkat.
ghei'ta, *Monsonia ovata*.
ghek'ko, (-'s), gecko, tree-lizard.
ghet'to, (-'s), ghetto, Jewish quarter.
ghie'lie, (-s), gillie.
ghie'nie, (-s), guinea.

ghitaar', (-s, ghitare), guitar.
ghoe'lasj, goulash.
ghoem, (-e, -s), **ghoe'ma**, (-s), whopper.
ghoem'pie, (-s), fag-end (of cigarette); pipe with short stem.
ghoem'psie, (-s), corporation, tummy.
ghoen, (-e, -s), large marble; pipe; chucking stone (in play); ironie; *hy is 'n* ~, a man in a million; a Trojan.
ghoe'na, (-s), sour fig *(Carpobrotus)*.
ghoe'ra, (-s), gorah (musical instrument).
ghoe'roe, (-s), guru, teacher, expert, pundit.
ghô'kum, sour fig.
gholf, golf; ~**baan**, golf course; (golf) links; ~**bal**, golf ball; *geverfde* ~*bal*, repaint; ~**borg**, golf sponsor; ~**joggie**, caddie; ~**kampioenskap**, golf championship; ~**klub**, golf club; ~**klubhuis**, golf clubhouse; ~**kompetisie**, golf competition; ~**sak**, golf bag; ~**skoen**, golf shoe; ~**smous**, ringer; ~**speler**, golfer; ~**stok**, golf club; ~**swaai**, golf swing; ~**veld**, golf links; ~**wedstryd**, golf match.
gholm, (-s), crowd, multitude.
ghom'ma, (-s), drum; ~**lied**, picnic song.
ghong, (-e, -s), gong.
ghon'nel, (-s), gunwale, gunnel.
ghries, grease; dope; ~**dop**, ~**kop**, grease-cap; ~**nippel**, grease-nipple, greaser; ~**pot**, grease-cup; ~**skerm**, grease-protector; ~**spuit**, grease-gun; ~**vry**, (-e), grease-proof.
ghrie'tel, (-s), iron bucket.
ghrok — grok
ghrop, (s) (-pe), cultivator; (w) (ge-), cultivate.
ghwa'no, guano.
ghwar, (-re), lout, boor, uncouth fellow.
ghwar'rieboom, guarri tree *(Euclea undulata)*; ..**bos**, guarri bush; ..**hout**, guarri wood.
ghwar'rieko(e), shrub *(Fockea crispa)*.
gib'bon, (-s), gibbon *(Hylobates)*.
gibus', (-se), gibus, opera-hat, crush-hat.
Gi'deonsbende, small brave band.
gids, (-e), guide, directory; pilot; conductor, cicerone; manual, handbook; ~ *tot die GESKIEDENIS*, guide to the history; ~ *vir LUGVARENDES*, air pilot; *as* ~ *na 'n PLEK dien*, serve as guide to a place; ~**aartjie**, leader (mine); ~**fossiel**, index fossil, ~**hond**, guide-dog; ~**kromme**, index curve; ~**laag**, key-bed; ~**lyn**, guide-line; ~**pleister**, screed; ~**rif**, leader (reef); ~**stippel**, guide-dot.
gie'gel, (ge-), giggle, titter; ~**aar**, (-s), giggler.
giek, (-e), gig (light boat).
gier[1], (s) (-e), vulture *(Aegypiidae)*.
gier[2], (s) (-e), yaw; (w) (ge-), yaw.
gier[3], (s) (-e), fancy, caprice, fad, freak; craze; yell, scream; (w), (ge-), scream (with laughter); howl (wind); *vol* ~ *e en GRILLE*, full of whims and fancies; *die* ~ *KRY*, have a sudden fancy (whim); *die* ~ *ende STORM*, the howling storm; *die WIND het om die huis ge* ~, the wind howled round the house.
gier[4], (s) liquid manure.
gier: ~**aanwyser**, yaw indicator; ~**as**, yaw-axis; ~**beweging**, yawing; ~**brug**, flying bridge.
gie'rig, (-e), avaricious, niggardly, miserly; close, close-fisted; ~**aard**, (-s), miser, niggard, grabber; pincher, cheeseparer; curmudgeon.
gie'righeid, avarice, niggardliness, miserliness, covetousness, rapacity, rapaciousness; *hy is die* ~ *in PERSOON*, he is avarice personified; ~ *is die wortel van alle kwaad*, avarice is the root of all evil.
giers, (vero.), millet *(Panicum miliaceum)*.
gier'valk, gerfalcon.
gier'vlak, yawing plane.
giet, (ge-), pour; cast (metals); found; mould; water; *REEN dat dit* ~, come down in sheets (rain); *in beleefde VORM* ~, couch in courteous language; ~**blok**, ingot; ~**eling**, (-e), pig (of metal).
gie'ter, (-s), watering-can; founder; ~**kop**, rose; ~**kraakbeen**, arytenoid; ~**y**, (-e), foundry (works); casting yard.
giet: ~**gat**, pouring hole; sprue; ~**kas**, casting box (frame); ~**kuil**, casting pit; ~**lepel**, casting ladle; ~**lood**, piglead; ~**messing**, cast brass; ~**model**, casting pattern; ~**opening**, pouring hole; ~**pan**, ladle; ~**rand**, pouring edge; ~**sand**, founder's sand; ~**sel**, (-s), cast(ing), founding; casting-metal; ~**staal**, cast-steel; ~**stuk**, casting; ~**vorm**, frame; casting mould; ingot mould; matrix; chill; proplasm; ~**ware**, castings; ~**werf**, casting yard; ~**werk**, loan casting; cast work; ~**yster**, cast-iron.
gif[1], (ong., vero.), (-te), present, gift, donation; bounty; benevolence.
gif[2], (-te, giwwe), poison, venom, toxin; *die* ~ *AFDRINK*, get it over and done with; *hulle is soos* ~ *op MEKAAR*, they hate each other like poison; ~**SPOEG**, spit venom at; ~**aas**, poison bait; ~**appel**, apple of Sodom; ~**beker**, poisoned cup; ~**bessie**, poisonous berry; ~**blaar**, ~**blom**, poisonous shrub *(Dichapetalum cymosum)*; ~**boek**, poison register; ~**bol**, a bulb *(Buphane disticha)*; ~**boom**, *Acokanthera venenata*; ~**bos**, poisonous shrub; ~**buis**, poison duct; ~**dampe**, poison fumes; ~**drank**, poison(ed) draught, potion; ~**gas**, poison gas; ~**goed**, poisonous vegetation (animals); ~**hout**, logwood; ~**inhoud**, toxic content; ~**klier**, poison gland; ~**kun'dig**, (-e), toxicologic(al); ~**kun'dige**, (-s), toxicologist; ~**leer**, toxicology; ~**menger**, poisoner; ~**moord**, murder by poisoning; ~**pil**, poison pill; ~**plant**, poisonous plant; ~**pyl**, poisoned arrow; ~**rook**, toxic smoke; ~**sakkie**, venom bag; poison bladder; ~**seer**, malignant ulcer; ~**siek(te)**, anthrax; ~**stof**, toxin; ~**sweer**, malignant ulcer; ~**tand**, poison fang; ~**tig**, (b) (-e), poisonous, venomous; toxic; virulent; antibiotic; (tw) *o* ~ *tig!* good gracious! ~**tigheid**, poisonousness, venomousness; virulence; ~**vry**, (-e), non-poisonous; ~**werend**, (-e), antitoxic, antidotal; ~**werking**, toxic influence (action).
gigant', (ong.), (-e), giant; ~**ies**, (-e), gigantic; ~**is'me**, gigantism.
gig'gel, **gig'gelgaggel**, (ge-), giggle, titter; snigger; ~**aar**, (..lare, -s), giggler; ~(**a**)**ry**, ~**ing**, giggling.
gi'golo, (-'s), gigolo.
gigue, (-s), gigue.
gil, (s) (-le), yell, scream, cry, howl, shriek; (w) (ge-), yell, scream, shriek.
gil'de, (-s), guild; company; fraternity; craft; ~**broer**, freeman of a guild; ~**huis**, guild-hall; ~**meester**, guild-master; ~**wese**, system of guilds.
gil'letjie, (-s), small scream.
gil'ling, (-s), roach.
gimka'na, (-s), gymkhana.
gimnas', (-te), gymnast; ~**iaal'**, (..siale), pertaining to a gymnasium; ~**ium**, (-s), gymnasium, gym.
gimnastiek', gymnastics; ~**bal**, medicine ball; ~**les**, lesson in gymnastics; ~**kostuum**, gymnastic costume, gym; ~**lokaal**, gymnastic room; ~**meester**, gymnastic instructor; ~**oefening**, gymnastic lesson; physical jerks; ~**onderwyser**, gym(nastics) teacher (instructor); ~**rok**, gym (costume); ~**skoen**, gym shoe; ~**uitvoering**, gymnastic display; ~**vereniging**, gymnastic society.
gimnas'ties, (-e), gymnastic.
gimnastra'de, gymnastrade.
gim'nosperm, (-e), gymnosperm.
gimp, (-e), gimp, gymp; ~**spyker**, gimp pin.
ginan'dries, (-e), gynandrous.
ginds, (plegt.), yonder, over there; *aan* ~ *e sy van die graf*, in the hereafter.
ginekologie', gynaecology.
ginekolo'gies, (-e), gynaecologic(al).
ginekoloog', (..loë), gynaecologist.
gin'gang, gingham.
gink'go, (-'s), ginkgo.
gin'negaap, (ge-), pass the time in small talk; giggle, titter, snigger.
gips, gypsum, plaster of Paris; gesso; gypsophila; ~**aarde**, gypsum; ~**afgietsel**, plaster cast; ~**agtig**, (-e), gypseous; like gypsum; plaster-like; ~**beeld**, plaster image; ~**houdend**, (-e), gypsiferous; ~**kruid**, gypsophila; ~**model**, plaster of Paris model; plaster cast; ~**verband**, plaster of Paris bandage; ~**vorm**, plaster mould.
giraf', (-fe, -s), giraffe; ~**nek**, long neck.
girandool', (..dole), girandole.

gi'robank, (Ndl.), transfer (clearing) bank.
giroskoop', (..skope), gyroscope.
girosko'pies, (-e), gyroscopic.
gis[1], (s) (-te), yeast, ferment, barm; (w) (ge-), ferment, rise, work; *AAN die ~*, fermenting; *in 'n ~tende TOESTAND*, in a ferment.
gis[2], (s) (-se), guess; (w) (ge-), guess, conjecture, divine; *~ laat MIS*, a guess is usually wrong; guessing gets one nowhere; *ons kan daar SLEGS na ~*, we can only make a guess.
gis: ~ **baar**, (..**bare**), fermentable; ~ **balie**, fermenting vat; gyle.
gis'bestek, dead reckoning.
gis: ~ **houdend**, (-e), yeasty; ~ **kuip**, fermenting vat; ~ **middel**, ferment, leavening agent.
gisp, (ge-), censure, blame, denounce; ~ **end**, (-e), denunciatory; ~ **ing**, censure.
gis: ~ **poeier**, yeast powder; ~ **sel**, yeast cell.
gissend, (-e), guessing.
gissing (-e, -s), conjecture, supposition, divination; guess; *op ~ BERUS*, based on guesswork; *NA ~*, at a guess, approximately; *'n ~ WAAG*, hazard a conjecture.
gis'stof, ferment.
gis'ter, yesterday; *het jy my ~ GEHUUR, het jy my vandag gehad*, I am under no obligation to you; *jy het maar ~ GEKOM*, you are a mere chicken; *HY is nie van ~ nie*, he is not born yesterday; *nie ~ se KIND nie*, no chicken; *OUER as ~ wees*, not born yesterday; *nie VAN ~ nie*, not since yesterday; *sy ~ en VANDAG se praatjies kom nie ooreen nie*, you can't trust a thing he says; *VANDAG is nie ~ nie*, circumstances have changed; ~ **aand'**, yesterday evening, last night; ~ **middag**, yesterday afternoon; ~ **môre**, yesterday morning; ~ **nag**, last night; ~ **oggend**, yesterday morning.
gis'ting, zymosis, effervescence, fermentation; ferment; excitement; ~ **sproses**, fermentative process.
git, jet.
gits! *o ~!* oh dear! oh my! by gosh!
git'swart, jetblack.
gitta! = **gits!**
gla(a)s: ~ **agtig**, (-e), vitreous; ~ **agtigheid**, vitreosity; ~ **dak**, glass roof; ~ **deur**, glass (sash) door; ~ **goed**, glassware, glass things; ~ **industrie**, glass industry; ~ **kap**, glass shade; globe (lamp); ~ **kas**, (-te), glazed cabinet, glass case; ~ **krale**, glass beads.
glaas'ogie, (-s), Cape white-eye *(Zosterops)*.
gla(a)s: ~ **oog**, artificial (glass) eye; ~ **oond**, glass oven; ~ **ruit**, (glass) pane; ~ **skerf**, glass splinter; ~ **skilder**, painter on glass; ~ **slag**, floss; ~ **slyper**, glass-grinder; ~ **snyer**, glass cutter; ~ **splinter**, *see* **gla(a)sskerf**; ~ **traan**, Rupert's drop, glass tea; ~ **winkel**, glass shop.
glacé, glacé; kid; patent leather; ~ **handskoene**, kid gloves.
glad, (b) (-de; -der, -ste), smooth, slippery (road); sleek (hair); glib; deep; glabrous; (bw) smoothly; quite, altogether; cleanly; evenly; glibly; *iets ~ AFSNY*, make a clean cut; *~ de DRAAD*, plain wire; *'n ~ de KÊREL*, a slippery customer; *~ MAAK*, smooth; *~ MAL*, quite crazy; *~ NIE*, not at all; *so ~ soos SEEP*, as slippery as an eel; *~ van STAPEL* loop, go off smoothly; *~ van TONG*, glib, voluble, fluent; ~ **beitel**, paring chisel; ~ **dekantvyl**, safe-edge file; ~ **delyfram**, plainbodied ram; ~ **deperske**, nectarine; ~ **derig**, (-e), rather slippery; ~ **(dig)heid**, smoothness; glibness; slipperiness; ~ **geskeer**, (-de), clean-shaven; ~ **heid**, smoothness; evenness; glibness; slipperiness; ~ **hout**, sleekstick; polishing stick.
gladia'tor, (-e, -s), gladiator.
gladio'lus, (..li, -se), **gladiool'**, (..diole), gladiolus, sword-lily.
glad'maker, planer.
glad'making, smoothing.
glad'skaaf, (..skawe), smoothing plane.
glad'verhaar, (-de), smooth and shining; prosperous.
glad'weg, flatly, bluntly; smoothly.
glans, (s) (-e), gloss, lustre, brilliance, finish; brightness (eyes); glory, gleam, radiancy, splendour; sheen, polish; glare, glitter, glossiness, fulgency, effulgence; blink; flash; ~ **verleen aan**, lend lustre to; (w) (ge-), shine, gleam, glisten; gloss; hot-press; ~ **bordpapier**, glazed cardboard; ~ **druk**, calendering; ~ **end**, (-e), luminous, fulgent, bright, glazed, gleaming, glossy; sleek; ~ **er**, (-s), hot-presser; ~ **erig**, (-e), glittering, shining; ~ **garing**, glazed yarn; ~ **kant**, shiny side, back (of photographic plate); ~ **katoen**, glazed cotton; ~ **kool**, bright coal; ~ **leer**, glacé leather; ~ **leerskoene**, patent-leather shoes; pumps; ~ **loos**, (..**lose**), lustreless; lacklustre (eyes); ~ **masjien**, calender; ~ **nommer**, star turn; ~ **oplossing**, glazing solution; ~ **papier**, glazed paper; ~ **pen**, highlighter, highlight pen; ~ **periode**, noonday (heyday) of its glory; golden age; ~ **program**, feature programme; ~ **punt**, acme, crowning feature, highlight, grand climax; ~ **rol**, star turn.
glans'ryk, (-e), glorious, brilliant, resplendent, lustrous, effulgent, radiant; refulgent; ~ **heid**, resplendence, splendour; refulgence.
glans: ~ **spreeu**, Cape starling; ~ **stof**, lustre cloth; ~ **sy**, lustrine; ~ **verf**, gloss (enamel) paint; ~ **vrugte**, glacé fruit.
glas, (-e), glass, tumbler; chimney (lamp); *DEURSIGTIG soos ~*, as clean as day; perfectly transparent; *iem. is van ~ GEMAAK*, he is fragile; his father was not a glazier; *GESLYPTE ~*, cutglass; *so HELDER as ~*, as clear as daylight; *hy KYK in die ~*, he drinks; *~ in LOOD*, leaded glass work; *'n ~ MELK*, a glass of milk; *in iem. se ~ VAL*, butt in; chip in; *meer mense VERDRINK in ~ as in die see*, drink causes more deaths than drowning; *see also* **gla(a)s**; ~ **afval**, cullet; ~ **agtig**, (-e), glassy, glazy, vitreous; hyaline; ~ **agtigheid**, vitreosity, glassiness; ~ **beker**, glass beaker; ~ **bereiding**, glass-making; ~ **beton**, ferroglass; ~ **blaser**, glassblower; ~ **blaserseep**, manganese; ~ **blaserspyp**, blowing iron; ~ **blasery**, glass works; ~ **dig**, (-te), glass-enclosed; ~ **draad**, glass thread; ~ **druppel**, *see* **gla(a)straan**.
glaseer', (ge-), glaze (pottery); ice; sugar (fruit); ~ **sel**, frost, glaze, glacé.
glas'elektrisiteit, vitreous electricity.
gla'serig, (-e), glassy; glazed, glazy.
glas: ~ **'fabriek**, glass-works; ~ **fabrikant**, glass-manufacturer; ~ **glans**, vitreous lustre; ~ **'helder**, clear as crystal (glass), explicit; hyaline.
glas'huis, glass house, conservatory; *wie in 'n ~ woon, moenie met klippe gooi nie*, people who live in glass houses should not throw stones.
gla'sie, (-s), small glass; *te diep in die ~ kyk*, be fond of the bottle.
gla'sig, (-e), vitreous, glass-like, hyaline.
glas'industrie, *see* **gla(a)sindustrie**.
glasiaal', (..siale), glacial.
glasiologie', glaciology.
glas: ~ **kap**, globe (for lamp); ~ **knoop**, bull's-eye; ~ **kolf**, bulb; ~ **kraal**, bugle (glass bead).
glas'maker, glazier; *was jou pa 'n ~ maker?* was your father a glazier? ~ **smes**, putty-knife; ~ **sdiamant**, glass-cutter.
glas: ~ **mengsel**, batch; ~ **ogie**, white-eye; ~ **oog**, glass eye; ~ **opaal**, hyalite; ~ **opaalagtig**, (-e), hyalite; ~ **papier**, cellophane (trade name); glass-paper; ~ **poeier**, glass dust; ~ **ruit**, glass pane; ~ **skerf**, fragment of glass.
glas'skilder, painter on glass; ~ **ing**, glass-painting.
glas'snyer, (-s), (cutting) diamond; glass-cutter; ~ **sdiamant**, glass-cutter.
glas'splinter, splinter of glass.
glas'spuit, glass-irrigator.
glas'steen, hyalite.
glas'tregter, glass-funnel.
glasu'ring, glazing.
glasuur', (s) (**glasure**), enamel (teeth); glazing (pottery); icing (cake); (w) (ge-), glaze; ~ **der**, (-s), glazer; ~ **glans**, glaze; ~ **laag**, glaze coat; ~ **suiker**, icing-sugar; ~ **steen**, glazed brick; ~ **verf**, enamel paint; ~ **vrug**, glacé fruit.
glas: ~ **venster**, glass window; ~ **vernis**, enamel paint;

glattendal — *gnostisisme*

~**vesel**, glass fibre; ~**vol**, glassful; ~**ware**, glassware; ~**watte**, glass wool; ~**werk**, glass-ware; ~**werker**, glazier; ~**wol**, spun glass, glass wool.
glat'tendal, completely, totally; really, actually.
glau'bersout, Glauber's salts.
gles, (-se), flaw (in diamond).
glet'ser, (-s), glacier; ~**afsetting**, glacier deposit; ~**kloof**, crevasse; ~**kunde**, glaciology; ~**periode**, glacial period; ~**moreen**, (glacier) moraine; ~**puin**, moraine debris; drift; ~**rivier**, river formed by glacier; ~**skrape**, glacial striae; ~**spleet**, crevasse; ~**vloer**, glacial pavement; ~**vorming**, glaciation.
glet'werk, box-casting.
gleuf, (s) **(gleuwe)**, groove, slot, recess, slit, aperture; bezel; (w) (ge-), slot; groove, flute; ~**deler**, riffle; ~**deurslag**, slot-punch; ~**gat**, slot hole; ~**hout**, coulisse; ~**koppeling**, slotted joint; ~**masjien**, slotting machine; ~**moer**, slotted nut; ~**pen**, slotted peg; ~**ring**, bezel; ~**sak**, slit pocket; ~**siekte**, stem-pitting; ~**werk**, slotting.
glib'ber, (ge-), slither, slip.
glib'berig, (-e), slippery, slimy; lubricious; ~**heid**, slipperiness, lubricity.
glief, **(gliewe)**, glyph.
glieps, (-e), = **glips**.
glifogeen', glyphogene.
glifografie', glyphography.
glikogeen', glycogen.
glim, (ge-), glimmer, smoulder, phosphoresce, glow (faintly); ~**buis**, luminous tube; ~**hout**, touch wood; ~**kompas**, luminous compass, ~**korrel**, luminous foresight.
glim'lag, (s) (-ge), smile; (w) (ge-), smile; ~**gie**, (-s), half smile, grin.
glim'mend, (-e), luminous, gleaming; glowing; shining.
glim'mer, (s) mica; (w) (ge-), glimmer, glow, shine; ~**agtig**, (-e), micaceous; glimmering.
glim'ming, phosphorescence.
glimp, (-e), glimpse; gleam; colour (of truth), glimmering, glint; semblance; *'n ~ van waarheid gee aan*, lend verisimilitude to, give some semblance of truth to.
glim: ~**strook**, reflector-strip; ~**teken**, luminous sign; ~**verf**, luminous paint; ~**visier**, luminous back-sight; ~**wurm**, glow-worm.
glin'ster, (ge-), glitter, glisten, radiate, sparkle, glint; effulge; glimmer; coruscate; ~**end**, (-e), glittering, radiant; coruscant; lambent; ~**ig**, (-e), glittering, ~**ing**, glint, glittering, glistening, coruscation; lambency; glare; ~**stof**, brilliant dust.
glip, (s) slip; *die ~ pe*, the slips (cricket); (w) (ge-), slip, slide; *'n kans laat ~*, let an opportunity slip; ~**druif**, Isabella (grape), Catawba.
glip'pens, slip, mistake, oversight.
glip'perig, (-e), slippery; ~**heid**, slipperiness.
glip'pertjie, (-s), Isabella (grape), Catawba.
glips, (-e), slip, mistake.
glip'steek, slip-stitch, single crochet.
gliptiek', glyptics, glyptography.
glip'weg, slipway; sneak away road.
gliserien', **gliseri'ne**, glycerine.
gliserol', glycerol.
glo, (w) (ge-), believe, credit, trust; reckon; accredit; *AAN iem. ~*, believe in somebody; *die wat ~, is nie HAASTIG nie*, those who have faith are in no hurry, *wil jy ~, dis 'n goeie PLAN, believe me, it's a good plan*; *as jy nie wil ~ nie, kan jy PROE*, if you don't believe it, see for yourself; *aan SPOKE ~*, believe in ghosts; *ek WIL ~*, I should think (so); (bw) seemingly, evidently, allegedly, presumably; *dis ~ nie so ERG nie*, apparently it is not so bad; *jy is ~ MAL*, you're obviously mad.
globaal', (b) **(globale)**, rough, general; global; (bw) roughly, broadly, in the gross; ~ *GENEEM*, taking it roughly; *'n globale SOM*, a lump sum; *globale SYFERS*, round figures.
glo'be, (-s), globe.
globulien', **globuli'ne**, globulin (in blood).
gloed, glow, heat; ardour, fervour, fervency, fire, blush, passion; flame; blaze; (in)candescence; *'n ~ van GESONDHEID*, a glow of health; *die ~ van*

die SON, the glare of the sun; ~**nuut**, (..**nuwe**), brand-new; ~**vol**, (-le), glowing, perfervid.
gloei, (ge-), glow, be red-hot; burn; frit; ~**draad**, filament; ~**end**, (-e), glowing, incandescent, phosphoric; scorching, ardent, blazing, aglow, ablaze, fiery; flagrant; live (coals); candescent; afire; aflame; ~ *end heet*, red-hot; ~**hitte**, incandescence, red heat, white heat; ~**ing**, glow, heat, phosphorescence, candescence; ~**kousie**, incandescent (gas-) mantle; ~**lamp**, (electric) bulb, globe; incandescent lamp; glow-lamp; ~**lamphouer**, bulb holder; ~**lig**, incandescent light; ~**oond**, annealing oven; calcining furnace; calciner; ~**pers**, hot-press.
glooi, (ge-), slope; ~**end**, (-e), sloping, shelving; ~**ing**, (-e, -s), slope, gradient, glacis; declivity.
gloor, (s) gleam, glitter, glimmer; (w) (ge-), glitter, glimmer.
glo'ria, glory; ~ *hou*, spree, carouse.
glo'rie, glory, lustre, fame; *in sy ~ wees*, be in one's glory; ~**dag**, day of glory; ~**kroon**, crown of glory; aureole; ~**ryk**, (-e), glorious, brilliant, splendid; ~**tyd**, golden epoch, heyday.
glorieus', (ong.), (-e), **glorievol**, *see* **glorieryk**.
glos, (-se), gloss, note, explanation, comment; marginal note.
glossa'rium, (..**ria**, -s), glossary.
glosseer', (ge-), gloss (a text).
glossi'tis, glossitis.
glossolalie', glossolalia.
gloukoom', glaucoma.
glulp, (ge-), sneak, skulk, spy, ~**erd**, (-s), spy, sneak, ~**erig**, (-e), sneaking, furtive.
glu'kose, glucose.
glukosi'de, (-s), glucoside.
glukosu'ria, glucosuria.
glun'der, (w) (ge-), beam; (b) cheerful, jovial.
glu'ten, gluten.
glutien', **gluti'ne**, glutin(e).
gluur, (ge-), peer, peep at, stare; glint; spy; blink; gloat.
gly, (ge-), glide, slip, skid; slide; *iets LAAT ~*, let something go; *oor 'n SAAK ~*, treat a matter lightly; *iets in die SAK laat ~*, slip something into a pocket; ~**dende SKAAL**, sliding scale; ~**baan**, slide (artil.); chute; glide-path; ~**beweging**, sliding motion; ~**blom**, *Drosera cistiflora*; ~**boot**, hydroplane; ~**ding**, (-e, -s), shear; ~**draad**, wire slide.
gly: ~**er**, (-s), glider; continuant; ~**erig**, (-e), slippery; ~**erigheid**, slipperiness, glibness; ~**geut**, chute; ~**gewrig**, arthrodial joint; ~**helling**, gliding slope; ~**hoek**, gliding angle; ~**jakkals**, bilker, ~**klep**, sleeve valve; ~**kontak**, sliding contact; ~**laer**, plain bearing; ~**merk**, skid mark; ~**passing**, gliding (sliding) fit; ~**ryer**, skid kid; ~**skaal**, sliding-scale; ~**snelheid**, gliding speed; ~**spanning**, shearing stress; ~**toestel**, glider; ~**vas**, (-te), nonskid; ~*vaste band*, non-skid tyre; ~**verhouding**, gliding ratio; ~**vlak**, sliding surface.
gly'vlieër, glider (person); volplanist; glider kite; ~**y**, gliding.
gly'vlieg, (ge-), glide; ~**draai**, gliding turn; ~**klub**, gliding club; ~**lisensie**, gliding licence; ~**sertifikaat**, gliding certificate; ~**skool**, gliding school; ~**terrein**, gliding site; ~**tuig**, glider (aeroplane); ~**tuigtroepe**, glider troops.
gly'vlug, volplane, glide; gliding flight; *in ~ DAAL*, glide downwards; *'n ~ MAAK*, glide.
gly'vry, (-e), non-skid; ~**band**, non-skid tyre (tread).
gly'-yster, railskid (rail car).
gmf, humph!
g'n, not; *see* **geen**: *ek sal ~ werk nie*, I shall simply not (do any) work.
gneis, gneiss.
gno'me, (-s), gnome, aphorism.
gno'mies, (-e), gnomic, aphoristic.
gno'mon, gnomon, sun-dial.
gnomo'nies, (-e), gnomic.
gnoom, **(gnome)**, gnome, goblin, elf, dwarf.
gno'se, **gno'sis**, gnosis.
gnos'ties, (-e), gnostic.
gnos'tikus, (-se, ..**tici**), gnostic.
gnostisis'me, gnosticism.

gô¹, (-'s), bogey-man (to frighten children); bugbear.

gô², pep, go, vim, vigour; *sy ~ is uit*, he is completely exhausted; he is worn out.

gobelin', (-s), gobelin; ~**steek**, gobelin stitch.

God, God; the Lord; *as dit ~ BEHAAG*, if God wills; *~ sy DANK*, thank God; *wat ~ DOEN, is welgedaan*, what God does is well done; *met ~ en met EER*, with honour and glory; *aan ~ nòg Sy gebod GLO*, be without religion; *~ die HERE*, the Lord God; *IN ~s naam*, in the name of God; *~ gee KRAG na kruis en kruis na krag*, God shapes the back for the burden; *aan ~ s SEEN is alles geleë*, all is dependent on God's mercy; *~ SLAAP nie*, God does not sleep; *vir ~ en VADERLAND*, for God and country; *~s WATER oor ~s akker laat loop*, let things slide (take their course); *as ~ WIL*, God willing; *iets om ~s WIL doen*, do something out of charity; *om ~s WIL*, for God's sake; *~s WOORD*, Word of God, the Bible.

god, (-e), idol, god; *GROTE ~e!* good heavens!; *die MINDERE gode*, the smaller fry; lesser gods; *in die SKOOT van die ~e*, in the lap of the gods; *hom VERBEEL dat hy 'n ~ jie is*, regard himself as a tin god.

god'dank, thank God (the Lord).

God'delik, (-e), divine, of God.

god'delik, sublime, glorious; ambrosial; *elke ~e dag laat wees*, be late every blessed day.

God'delikheid, divineness, divinity.

goddeloos'¹, (b) (..lose), naughty, mischievous; shameless; *dit is 'n baie ..lose KIND*, this is an extremely naughty child; (bw) extremely; *dit is ~ MOEILIK*, it is inconceivably difficult.

god'deloos², (b) (..lose), godless, wicked, impious; profane; graceless; *vloek is ~*, swearing (cursing) is wicked.

god'deloosheid¹, wickedness, impiety, ungodliness, evil.

goddeloos'heid², naughtiness, mischief, profanity.

goddeloos'lik, wickedly, impiously, mischievously; *~ stout*, extremely naughty.

goddelo'se, (-s), impious (wicked) person.

go'de: ~**bloed**, ichor; ~**dom**, the gods, pantheon; ~**drank**, nectar; ambrosia; ~**leer**, mythology; ~**skemering**, twilight of the gods; ~**spys**, ambrosia; ~**taal**, divine language (accents); ~**verering**, idol worship; ~**wêreld**, pantheon.

god'gans(elik): *die ~e dag*, the livelong day.

God'gegewe, God-given.

god'geklaag: *dit is ~*, it cries to high heaven.

god: ~**geleerd**, (-e), theological; ~**geleerde**, (-s), divine theologian; ~**geleerdheid**, theology; ~**gevallig**, (-e), pleasing to God; ~**gewyd**, (-e), sacred, hallowed; ~**heid**, deity; divinity; *die G~heid*, Godhead, the Divinity.

godin', (-ne), goddess.

god'jie, (-s), little tin god.

god: ~**lik**, livelong, blessed; *ek het die hele ~like middag gewag*, I waited the whole blessed afternoon; ~**loënaar**, (-s), atheist; ~**loëning**, unbelief, atheism; ~**lof**, God be praised; *G~loos*, (..lose), without God; *G~mens*, Godman.

gods'akker, god's-acre, graveyard, churchyard, cemetery.

godsa'lig, (-e), pious, godly; *~e*, (-s), pious person; ~**heid**, godliness.

gods'begrip, notion (idea) of God.

gods'diens, (-te), divine worship; religion; faith; ~**dwepery**, religiosity; ~**haat**, religious hatred; ~**leraar**, clergyman; ~**loos**, (..lose), irreligious; ~**loosheid**, irreligion; ~**oefening**, divine service; devotion(s); religious exercise; ~**onderwys**, religious instruction; ~**oorlog**, religious war; ~**plegtigheid**, religious ceremony; ~**plig**, religious duty; ~**sin**, piety.

godsdiens'tig, (-e), religious, pious; devout; devotional; *~e onverskilligheid*, indifferentism; ~**e**, (-s), devotionalist; ~**heid**, religiousness, piety, devotion.

gods'diens: ~**toets**, religious test; ~**twis**, religious dissension (discord); ~**vryheid**, religious freedom; ~**waansin**, religious fanaticism (mania); ~**wetenskap**, theology; ~**ywer**, religious zeal.

gods: ~**gawe**, deodand; ~**gebou**, church, ~**gerig**, ordeal; *G~gesant*, divine messenger; apostle; ~**huis**, place of worship, church; ~**jammerlik**, (-e), pitiable, miserable; ~**las'teraar**, blasphemer; ~**las'tering**, profanity, blasphemy; ~**las'terlik**, (-e), blasphemous, profane; ~**las'terlikheid**, blasphemy, profanity; ~**man**, man of God, prophet.

gods'onmoontlik, (-e), absolutely impossible.

Gods'oordeel, trial by ordeal, judgment of God.

gods'penning, earnest money.

god'spraak, prophecy, oracle.

gods: ~**regering**, theocracy; *G~ryk*, kingdom of God; ~**vrede**, the peace of God; ~**vrug**, piety, devotion, devoutness.

god: ~**vergete**, God forsaken; graceless; ~**versaker**, (-s), atheist; ~**versaking**, atheism; ~**vre'send**, (-e), godfearing, pious; ~**vre'sendheid**, piety.

godvrug'tig, (-e), devout, pious; ~**heid**, devoutness, piety.

goed¹, (s) (-ere), goods, stuff, fabric; commodities, merchandise, property, things; *AARDSE ~ere*, earthly goods; *~ en BLOED*, life and property; *GELD te ~ hê*, have money outstanding; *GESTEELDE ~ gedy nie*, ill-gotten gains do not thrive; *ONREGVERDIGE (gesteelde) ~ gedy nie*, ill-gotten gains seldom prosper; *ONROERENDE (vaste) ~ere*, real (fixed) property; *ROERENDE ~ere*, movables; *ver van jou ~, naby jou SKADE*, the eye of the master makes the horse fat; *VAT jou ~ en trek!*, be off! be going!; *VUIL ~*, washing, dirty linen; dirty articles.

goed², (s) good; *jou te ~ DOEN aan*, do oneself well; feast upon; *die HOOGSTE ~*, the greatest good; *ten ~e HOU*, to be said in one's favour; *IETS ~s*, something good; *ten ~e KOM*, be to the good of; *~ met KWAAD vergeld*, return evil for good; *~ en KWAAD*, good and evil; *ten ~e en ten KWADE*, for good or evil; *sou ons die goeie ontvang en nie die KWADE nie?*, shall we receive good and shall we not receive evil?; *iets ten ~e OPNEEM*, take in good spirit; *die goeie met die SLEGTE neem*, take the good with the bad; *ten ~e STREK*, be of advantage; *TEN ~e*, for the good; *VIR ~*, for good; (b, bw) (**goeie, beter; beste**), good, kind, right, all right, well, proper; *daar ~ van AFKOM*, come well out of something; *~ AG*, think fit; *dit sal nie ~ BLY nie*, this won't keep; *alte ~ is BUURMAN se gek*, everyone rides a willing horse; *op 'n goeie DAG*, one fine day; *DIS ~ so!*, it serves you right!, well done!; *die lug DOEN my ~*, the air benefits me; *so ~ as DOOD*, all but (practically) dead; *so ~ soos GOUD*, as good as gold; *dit ~ HÊ*, be well off; *jou ~ HOU*, keep oneself in control; *hy IS ~ vir R1 000*, he is safe for R1 000; *so ~ en so KWAAD*, for good or ill; *dit is MAAR ~ om . . .*, it is just as well to . . .; *MY ~*, it suits me; *jy kan NET so ~*, you may just as well; *NIE so ~ nie*, not so well (good); *so ~ as NIEMAND*, next to nobody; *vir NIKS ~ nie*, good for nothing; *daar kan NIKS ~s van kom nie*, no good can come of that; *goeie REIS!*, pleasant journey!; *so ~ as SEKER*, almost certain; *dit SMAAK ~*, this tastes good; *~ SO!*, serves you right!; *~ daaraan TOE wees*, be well off; *goeie TROU*, bona fides, good faith; *te ~er TROU*, bona fide, in good faith; *die goeie ou(e) TYD*, the good old days; *'n goeie UUR*, a full hour; *VEEL ~s in iets vind*, find much to praise in something; *hy is ~ VIR so 'n bedrag*, his name is good (enough) for such a sum; *WEES so ~ om . . .*, be good enough to . . .; *~ en WEL*, well and good; *alles ~ en WEL, maar . . .*, that is all very well but . . .; *hy moet maar weer ~ WORD*, he must become friends again.

goedaar'dig, (-e), good-natured, benign; ~**heid**, good nature, mildness.

goed'beklant, (-e), cliented, well-patronized.

goed'dink, (-ge-), think fit, consider desirable.

goed'doen, (-ge-), do good; cheer up.

goed'dunk, (-ge-), think fit; *~e*, opinion, discretion; *na ~e optree*, use one's own discretion.

goe'dere: ~**hysbak,** ~**hyser,** goods lift; ~**kantoor,** goods (luggage) office; ~**klerk,** goods clerk; ~**loods,** goods shed; ~**omset,** turnover of goods; ~**rekening,** goods account; ~**ruil,** exchange of commodities; ~**stasie,** goods station; ~**terrein,** goods yard; ~**trein,** goods train; ~**trok,** goods wagon (truck); ~**verbruik,** consumption of goods; ~**verkeer,** ~**vervoer,** goods traffic; ~**vliegtuig,** freight aircraft; ~**voertuig,** goods vehicle; ~**voorraad,** stock-in-trade; stock of goods; ~**vrag,** goods freight; ~**wa,** goods truck, goods van; delivery van.
goedertie're, (vero.) merciful, clement, gracious; ~**nheid,** mercy, clemency, grace, loving-kindness.
goed'geefs, (-e), liberal, generous; ~**'heid,** generosity, liberality.
goedgehumeur', (-de), good-humoured (-tempered).
goed'gekeur, (-de), approved, confirmed; adopted.
goed'gelowig, (-e), credulous; ~**heid,** credulity.
goed'geplant, (-e), well-planted; *'n ~e bal,* well-pitched (well-placed) ball.
goed'gesind, (-e), favourable, kind, well-meaning, sympathetic; ~**e,** (-s), well-wisher; ~**heid,** kindness, sympathy, goodwill.
goedguns'tig, (-e), well-disposed, kind; ~**heid,** kindness; graciousness; ~**lik,** kindly, graciously.
goedhar'tig, (-e), kind-hearted, kindly, humane, good-hearted; ~**heid,** kind-heartedness, kindliness.
goed'heid, kindness, goodness; *GROTE ~!,* goodness mc!, *IN ~s naam, for goodness' sake.*
goed'hou, (-ge-), keep fair (good); last (perishables); continue; *hom ~,* control oneself; ~**eienskappe,** ~**vermoë,** keeping qualities.
goe'dig, (-e), good-natured, kind; ~**heid,** kindness, good nature.
goed'jies, goods, things, knick-knacks.
goed'karoo, goedkaroo', *Phymosphermum parvifolium; Pentzia globosa, Pincana.*
goed'keur, (-ge-), approve, confirm, ratify, think proper, deem fit, endorse, consent; adopt (minutes); pass (person for service); accept; homologate; ~**end,** (-e), approving; approbative, approbatory; ~**enswaar'dig,** (-e), approvable.
goed'keuring, approval, approbation, consent; adoption; endorsement, confirmation (minutes); ratification (of treaty); assent (king's); *MET die ~ van,* with the sanction (approval) of; *voorstelle ter ~ VOORLÊ aan,* present proposals for approval to; *vir ~ VOORLÊ,* submit for approval; *sy ~ WEGDRA,* win (meet with) his approval.
goed'koop, (..**koper, -ste),** inexpensive, cheap, low-priced; *~ is DUURKOOP,* a bad bargain is dear at a farthing; ~ *EFFEK soek,* play to the gallery; ~ *WINKEL,* cheap store; ~**heid,** ~**te,** cheapness.
goed'lags, easily amused.
goed: ~**maak,** (-ge-), make good; make up for; counterbalance, offset; prove; redeem; put right, retrieve (one's fault); *'n belofte ~maak,* keep a promise; ~**moe'dig,** (-e), good-hearted, kind; ~**praat,** (-ge-), gloss over, varnish (it) over, explain (it) away.
goed'rond, (-e), frank, candid, straightforward.
goed'skiks, willingly, with a good grace; ~ *of kwaadskiks,* willing or unwilling; willy-nilly.
goeds'moeds, cheerfully, of good cheer; with a glad heart; calmly, without fuss; deliberately.
goed'staan, (-ge-), guarantee; vouch for.
goed'vertrouend, (-e), trusting, trustful; ~**heid,** trustfulness.
goed'vind, (-ge-), think fit, deem fit, approve of; agree to; put up with, submit to; ~**e,** ~**ing,** approbation; discretion; *handel na eie ~e,* exercise one's own discretion.
goedwil'lig, (-e), willing, with a good grace; obliging; ~**heid,** willingness, goodwill.
goei'e: ~ *GENADE!,* good gracious!, oh, goodness me!; ~ *WEET!,* goodness knows!
goeiechris'tenpeer, Bon Chrétien pear.
goeie: ~**mid'dag,** good afternoon; ~**mô're,!** ~**more!,** good morning!; ~**nag'!,** good night!

goeienaand'! good evening!; ~**sê, (-gesê),** say good evening.
goei'en: ~**dag!,** good day!; ~**dag'sê,** (..**gesê),** greet, say good day.
goei'erig, (-e), goodish, kind; *'n ~e soort kêrel,* a good-natured fellow, a decent sort of chap.
Goeie Vry'dag, Good Friday.
goei'igheid, kindness; kindliness; *uit SKONE ~,* out of sheer kindness; *eintlik SLEG van ~,* kind to a fault.
goei'ste: *MY ~!,* dear me!; ~ *WEET!,* goodness knows!
go'ël, (ge-), juggle, conjure; hocus-pocus; practise magic; do tricks; ~**aar,** (-s), juggler, conjurer; prestidigitator; illusionist; ~**bal,** googly (cricket); ~**ery,** juggling, conjuring, conjuration; hanky-panky; hocus-pocus; prestidigitation; white magic; ~**toer,** legerdemain, sleight-of-hand; juggling (conjuring) trick; ~**woord,** magic word.
goe'terig, (-e), fairly good, goodly, goodish.
goe'ters, things, small fry.
goe'tertjies, odds and ends, small fry.
goewerment', (-e), government.
goewerments': ~**amptenaar,** government official; ~**beleid,** government policy; ~**diens,** government service; ~**dokter,** district surgeon; ~**garage,** government garage; ~**gebou,** government building; ~**koerant,** government gazette, ~**kontrak,** government contract.
goewerment': ~**skool,** government school; ~**suiker,** brown sugar.
goewernan'te, (-s), governess; duenna.
goewerneur', (-s), governor; *hy dink hy is die ~ se hond,* he regards himself as a tin god; he thinks that the king is his uncle; ~**-generaal** (~**s-generaal),** governor-general; ~**lik,** (-e), belonging to the governor; ~**s'huis,** government house; ~**skap,** governorship; ~**s'trein,** vice-regal train; ~**s'woning,** government house.
go'fer, gopher.
gog, (-ge), = **gogga.**
gog'ga, (-s), insect, vermin; bogey; eidolon; rail-bender; *~ maak vir BABA bang,* as ugly as sin; he will frighten the child; *van die ~ GEPIK wees,* be bitten by the bug; ~**bie'** (-s), bogeyman; vermin; ~**dokter,** entomologist; ~**soeker,** bug-hunter; ~**tjie,** little bug (insect); (my) darling.
goi, (gojiem), goy.
goi'ing, jute, gunny; ~**sak,** gunny bag; hessian; burlap.
golf, (s) (golwe), wave, billow; bay, gulf; corrugation, crinkle, ~ *in voortplantingsrigting,* longitudinal wave; (w) (ge-), wave, undulate; corrugate; crinkle; *jou hare laat ~,* have one's hair waved; ~**agtig,** (-e), wave-like, wavy; ~**band,** wave-band (radio); ~**beweging,** wavelike motion, undulation; ~**breker,** cut-water, breakwater; ~**dal,** wave trough; ~**duur,** period of wave; ~**gedruis,** ~**geklots,** dashing of the waves; booming; ~**le,** (-s), wavelet; ~**kode,** wave-code; ~**kruin,** wave crest; ~**lengte,** wave-length; ~**lyn,** wave-line; waved rule (in printing); ~**masjien,** corrugating machine; ~**meter,** wave-meter; ~**ry,** (s) surfing; (w) (-ge-), surf; ~**plank,** surfing board; ~**s'gewys(e),** wave-like, in waves; ~**slag,** wash, dash, chop (of the waves); ~**stroom,** gulf-stream; ~**veld,** wave-range; ~**vlies,** undulating membrane; ~**vormig,** (-e), undulating, undulatory; ~**vorming,** corrugation; ~**yster,** corrugated iron.
Go'liat, Goliath; *g~***kewer,** giant-beetle; *g~***skraper,** bulldozer.
gol'we, (ge-), = **golf.**
gol'wend, (-e), waving, wavy, flowing, curly (hair); undulating (wheat); surging (crowd); billowy; gyrose.
gol'wing, (-e, -s), waving, undulation; corrugation; ~**steorie,** wave-theory; undulatory theory.
gom, (s) (-me), gum, glue; paste; *Arabiese ~,* gum Arabic; (w) (ge-), gum; ~**agtig,** (-e), gummy; ~**boom,** gumtree; ~**kwas,** paste-brush; ~**laag,** gum ply; ~**lak,** shellac.
gomlastiek', elastic, India rubber; elastical caout=

chouc; gutta-percha; eraser; ~**band**, rubber band; ~**breukband**, rubber belt for hernia; ~**buisie**, rubber tubing; ~**hak**, rubber heel; ~**skoen**, rubber shoe; ~**tandvulsel**, gutta-percha filling for tooth; ~**weefsel**, gutta-percha tissue.
gom: ~**lekker**, gumdrop; ~**pot**, gum-pot.
gom'pou, kori bustard *(Ardeotis kori kori)*.
gom: ~**siekte**, gum disease; ~**snuif**, gum sniffing; ~**strook**, gum strip; ~**tor**, (-re), uncouth person, lout, churl, clodhopper; ~**vlek**, gum spot (in fruit).
gona'de, (-s), gonad.
gon'del, (-s), gondola; nacelle; ~**ier'**, (-s), gondolier; ~**lied**, barcarole; ~**vaart**, gondola trip.
gonidiaal', (..diale), gonidial.
goni'dium, (-s), gonidium.
goniometrie', goniometry; ..**me'tries**, goniometric; ~**se funksie**, trigonometrical function.
gon'na: *o ~!*, oh my!, oh dear!; ~**beentjie**, funny-bone.
gonorree', clap, gonorrhoea.
gons, (ge-), buzz, zip, hum, drone; *leer dat dit ~*, study very hard; ~**er**, (-s), buzzer; ~**geluid**, buzz-(ing); ~**groep**, buzz group; ~**tol**, humming-top; *soos 'n ~ tol draai*, spin like a top.
gooi, (s) (-e), throw, fling, shy, put, chuck; (w) (ge-), throw, cast, pitch, fling, hurl, chuck; peg; pelt, cock-shy; serve (tennis); *met GELD ~*, fling one's money about; *HEEN en weer ~*, throw backwards and forwards; *met KLIPPE ~*, throw stones; *uit die SAAL ~*, throw out of the saddle; unseat; *'n TAAL maklik (lekker) ~*, speak a language fluently; *'n VUL ~*, throw a foal; ~**ding**, missile; ~**er**, (-s), thrower; pelter; ~**ery**, throwing, pelting; ~**goed**, missiles; ~**pleister**, daub; ~**pyltjie**, dart; ~**ring**, quoit; ~**skyf**, quoit; ~**ster**, (-s), female thrower; ~**tou**, lasso.
goor, (gore; -der, -ste), dirty, filthy; nasty, rancid; threadbare; *die klere is ~ gedra*, the clothes have been worn to shreds; ~**appel**, dwarf shrub *(Pachystigma zeyheri)*; *see* **grysappel**; ~**derig**, (-e), slightly dirty; *see* **goor**; ~**heid**, nastiness; dinginess; ~**maag**, congestion of the stomach.
Goot, (Gote), Goth.
gops, (-e), slum (area); ~**erig**, slummy.
gora'¹, (-'s), water-hole.
go'ra², (-'s) = **ghoera**.
gord, (s) (gorte), band, belt, girdle; cincture; (w) (ge-), gird; *jou vir die geveg ~*, gird oneself for the fight; *cf.* **gort¹**.
gor'del, (-s), belt, girdle; zone; fascia; *die ~ stywer trek*, tighten one's belt; ~**kruiser**, belted cruiser; ~**pantser**, belt-armour; ~**roos**, shingles, herpes zoster; ~**vormig**, (-e), zonal.
Gordiaans', (-e): *die ~ e knoop deurkap (deurhak)*, cut the Gordian knot.
gor'ding, (-s), purlin.
gord'reling, belt rail.
gordyn', (-e), curtain; blind; apron (balloon barrage); *die ~ GAAN op*, the curtain rises; *die ~ SAK*, the curtain falls; *die ~ oor iets laat VAL*, draw a curtain over; ~**band**, curtain tape; ~**goed**, curtaining, curtain material; ~**haak**, curtain hook; ~**kap**, pelmet; ~**koord**, curtain cord; apron (balloon barrage); ~**paal**, curtain rod; tringle; ~**ring**, curtain ring; ~**tjie**, fringe; ~**tjiekapsel**, fringe; ~**tjiekop**, (girl with a) fringe (bang); ~**valletjie**, valance, pelmet; ~**vuur**, protective fire, curtain fire, barrage.
gorê', (-s) = **gora**.
gor-gor', grunter (fish) *(Pomadasys bennettii)*.
goril'la, (-s), gorilla.
gor'let: ~**beker**, jug, ewer; ~**kom**, wash-stand basin.
gor'ra(tjie), (-s), small hole in a dry river-bed (to collect subterranean water).
gor'rel, (s) (-s), throat, pharynx; gullet (of horse); (ge-), gargle, gurgle; waffle (exam.); fence in (road); ~**drank**, ~**goed**, gargle, mouth-wash; ~**pyp**, wind-pipe, weazand.
gort¹, (-e), (s), band, belt, girdle; cincture; (w) (ge-), gird; *jou vir die geveg ~*, gird oneself for the fight.
gort², (s) groats, grits; barley; *die ~ is gaar*, the fat is in the fire; ~**so(e)p**, barley soup; ~**water**, barley-water.

Gotiek', Gothic style.
Go'ties, (-e), Gothic.
got'tabeentjie, funny-bone.
gou¹, (s) (-e), region, district.
gou², (b, bw) quick, rapid, ready, soon; facile; agile, brisk, expeditious; like fun; in haste, presto, post, pronto (slang); hastily; winged; ~ *BY wees*, be close at hand; *so ~ as NOU*, on the spot; ~ *MAAK*, haste(n), make haste; ~ *met die PEN*, a good penman; ~ *SPEEL!*, be quick!
goua'che, (-s), gouache.
goud, gold; *met ~ BEKROON*, award a golden medal; *iets soos ~ BEWAAR*, treasure something like gold; *alles wat BLINK, is nie ~ nie*, all is not gold that glitters; *met geen ~ te BETAAL nie*, not to be had for love or money; *so EERLIK soos ~*, as true as steel; *o, die ding is seker van ~ GEMAAK*, one would think it was made of gold; *'n mens kan ~ ook te duur KOOP*, even gold can be bought at too high a price; *dis seker van ~ GEMAAK!*, mind, it is made of gold!; ~ *of silwervrye OPLOSSING*, barren solution; *teen ~ OPWEEG*, to regard as being as good as gold; *geen ~ sonder SKUIM nie*, there is no gold without dross; ~ *op SNEE*, gilt-edged; *in ~ SWEM*, be rolling in wealth; *van ~ WEES*, be worth its weight in gold; ~**aar**, gold-lode, gold-vein.
gou'dakaas, Gouda cheese, sweetmilk cheese.
goud: ~**amalgaam**, (gold) amalgam; ~**bedding**, deposit of gold; ~**blaar**, gold-leaf; ~**blad**, gold-leaf, gold-foil; ~**blond**, (-e), golden (blond); ~**boorsel**, gold lace; ~**borduursel**, gold embroidery; ~**brokaat**, gold brocade; kincob; ~**brons**, goldbronze, shell gold; ~**bruin**, auburn; old-gold, golden brown; ~**delwer**, gold-digger; ~**dors**, gold-fever; thirst (greed) for gold; avarice; ~**draad**, gold thread, gold wire; ~**draend**, (-e), auriferous; ~**druk**, gold printing; ~**duiwel**, avarice, mammon; ~**erts**, gold ore; ~**fisant**, golden pheasant; ~**fraiing**, bullion, gold fringe; ~**galon**, gold lace; ~**geel**, golden, as yellow as gold, aureate; ~**gehalte**, gold-content, gold-grade; ~**geld**, gold coin; ~**gepunt**, (-e), gold-tipped; ~**glans**, golden lustre; ~**glassteen**, aventurine; ~**glimmer**, yellow mica; ~**grawer**, gold-digger; ~**haas**, agouti; ~**harig**, (-e), golden-haired; ~**houdend**, (-e), gold-bearing, auriferous.
gou'dief, pickpocket, sneak-thief; ~**diewery**, pocket-picking.
goud: ~**kleur**, gold colour; ~**kleurig**, (-e), gold-coloured; golden; ~**kleurstof**, gold dye; ~**klomp**, gold nugget; ~**klont**, gold nugget; ~**klousule**, gold clause; ~**koning**, gold-bug; ~**koors**, gold-fever; ~**korrel**, grain of gold.
Goud'kus, Gold Coast.
goud: ~**laag**, gold-bearing layer (of rock); gold-plating; ~**lak**, gold lacquer; ~**laken**, (gold) brocade; cloth of gold; ~**land**, gold-producing country; country on the gold standard; ~**leer**, gilt leather; ~**legering**, gold alloy; ~**magnaat**, magnate, capitalist; ~**maker**, alchemist; ~**mark**, gold-market; gold mark (coin); ~**myn**, gold-mine; bonanza; gold-dust plant *(Alyssum saxatile)*; ~**mynwese**, gold-mining; ~**neerslag**, precipitate of gold; ~**ondersoek**, assay of gold; ~**ontdekking**, gold-strike; ~**opbrengs**, *see* **goudproduksie**; ~**oplossing**, gold solution; ~**pap**, gold-slime; ~**papier**, gilt paper; ~**pariteit**, gold parity; ~**poeier**, gold powder; ~**produksie**, gold-production; ~**proef**, gold-test; ~**prys**, gold price; ~**punt**, specie point; ~**ranonkel**, gaillardia; ~**reën**, golden rain; ~**renet**, golden rennet; ~**reserwe**, gold reserve; ~**rif**, gold reef.
Gouds, (b) (-e), Gouda; ~*e kaas*, Gouda cheese, sweetmilk cheese.
goud: ~**sertifikaat**, gold certificate; ~**servies**, gold plate; ~**skaal**, assay balance; gold-slime; ~**smedery**, goldsmith's art; goldsmith's workshop; ~**smid**, goldsmith; ~**snee**, gilt edge (of book); ~**snip**, painted snipe; ~**soeker**, prospector (for gold); ~**staaf**, bar (ingot) of gold; ~**standaard**, gold standard; ~**steen**, chrysolite; gold brick; ~**stof**, gold-dust; ~**stormloop**, gold-rush; ~**stuk**,

gold piece; ~**uitvoer**, gold export; ~**vaal**, golden dun; ~**veld**, gold-field; ~**verf**, gold paint; ~**verlak, (-te)**, gold-lacquered; ~**vernis**, gold lacquer; ~**vink**, bullfinch; ~**vis**, goldfish; dory; ~**vlies**, gold beater's skin; ~**vonds, (-te)**, gold-strike; ~**voorraad**, gold supply; ~**vulling**, gold stopping, gold filling (dental); ~**wasser**, gold-washer; ~**weefsel**, gold tissue; ~**werk**, gold work (ware); gold plate; ~**wesp**, cuckoo fly; chrysidid; ~**winning**, gold-mining.

gou'e, gold (coin); golden; ~ *BRUILOF*, golden wedding; *die* ~ *EEU*, the golden age; ~**man'netjie**, gold-dust plant; ~**reën**, laburnum; ~**stroop**, golden syrup.

gou'gaar, quick-cooking; ~ *kos*, quick-cooking food.

gou'-gou, very soon, in a moment, quickly; in a trice.

gou'igheid, quickness, dexterity; *dis ELKEEN se* ~, first come, first served; *in die* ~ *iets DOEN*, do a thing hurriedly.

gous'blom, calendula; daisy; marigold; species of Compositae.

gou'siekte, cattle (or sheep) disease; ~**bossie**, *Pachystigma pygmaeum*.

graad, (grade), degree; rate; stage; grade; gradation; *'n* ~ *BEHAAL*, take a (university) degree; *in die HOOGSTE* ~, to the last degree; *in LIGTE* ~, lightly; *'n NEEF in die eerste* ~, a cousin once removed; *5 grade RYP*, five degrees of frost; ~**boog**, graduated arc; protractor, Jacob's staff; ~**liniaal**, protractor; ~**meter**, graduator, protractor, gauge; ~**meting**, gradimetry; ~**verdeling**, grad(u)ation; calibration; ~**verlening**, capping (conferring of degree); ~**verskil**, difference in degree.

graaf¹, (s), (grawe), count, earl.

graaf², (s) (grawe), spade; (w) (ge-), dig, sink (hole); burrow (of rabbits); cut; *na diamante* ~, dig for diamonds; ~**dopluis**, burrowing scale; ~**emmer**, grab

graaf'lik, (-e), of a count, count-like.

graaf: ~**masjien**, excavator; ~**pik**, entrenching implement.

graaf'skap, county; shire, earldom.

graaf: ~**steel**, spade handle; ~**stok**, digging stick; dibber; ~**toestel**, digger; ~**werk**, digging, tunnelling, excavating, excavation(s).

graag, (liewer, liefste, -ste), gladly, readily, freely, willingly; eager; fain; *hulle wil maar ALTE* ~, they are only too anxious to; *ek GLO dit* ~, I quite believe it; *ek sou NET so* ~, I would just as soon; *hoe ~ ek OOK al wil*, much as I should like to; *gaan jy SAAM!? G*~, are you going with us? Rather (please); *ek wil* ~ *WEET*, I should very much like to know; ~**heid**, ~**te**, eagerness.

graai, (ge-), rummage; grab.

graal, grail. *G*~**ridder**, Knight of the Round Table, *G*~**roman**, romance of the Holy Grail; *G*~**sage**, saga of the Holy Grail.

graan, (grane), grain, corn, wheat; (mv) cereals; ~**aar**, ear of grain; ~**afval**, grain sweepings; ~**agtig, (-e)**, corny; ~**beurs**, corn exchange; ~**boer**, wheat farmer, agriculturist; ~**bou**, agriculture, corn-growing, cereal culture; ~**distrik**, corn-growing district; ~**doppie**, glume; ~**gewasse**, cereals; ~**handel**, corn-trade; ~**handelaar**, corn-dealer, corn-chandler; ~**hoop**, grain stack, cock; ~**koper**, corn-merchant; ~**korrel**, grain seed; ~**kos**, cereal food; ~**lym**, gluten; ~**maat**, dry measure; ~**mark**, corn-market; ~**mied**, grain stack; ~**oes**, grain harvest (crop); ~**silo**, grain elevator; ~**skuur**, granary; ~**solder**, corn-loft; ~**sorghum**, grain-sorghum; ~**stingel**, corn-stalk; ~**suier**, (grain) elevator; ~**suierstortgeut**, grain elevator chute; ~**uitvoer**, grain export; ~**vlok**, cornflake; ~**voggehalte**, grain moisture-content; ~**voorraad**, stock of grain; ~**vrug**, caryopsis; ~**wet**, corn-law.

graas, (ge-), graze, feed.

graat, (grate), fishbone; arris; very lean person; *so maer soos 'n* ~ *(tjie)*, as thin as a rake.

graat'jie, (-s), small fish-bone; (exceptionally) thin child; ~**meerkat**, true meercat, suricate.

graat'rib, (-bes), groin.

graat'spar, hip rafter.

grab'bel, (ge-), scramble for (a thing); grabble; ~**sak**, lucky-dip.

grada'sie, gradation; grading.

gra'dedag, degree (graduation) day.

gradeer', (ge-), graduate, gradate, grade; ~**der, (-s)**, grader; ~**masjien**, grader; graduator.

gra'deplegtigheid, graduation ceremony.

grade'ring, (-e, -s), grading, graduation; scaling.

gradiënt', (-e), gradient.

graduan'dus, (-se, ..duandi), graduand; graduate student.

gradua'sie, (-s), graduation.

gradueel', (..duele), gradual; *graduele verskil*, slight difference, difference in degree.

gradueer', (ge-), graduate; take a degree.

graf, (-te), grave, tomb; pit, sepulchre; cell; *ANDERKANT die* ~, beyond the grave; *dit sal hom in die* ~ *BRING*, that will be the death of him; *BY die* ~, at the grave-side; *so DUISTER soos die* ~, as mysterious as the grave; *GEPLEISTERDE* ~*te*, whitened sepulchres; *so GESLOTE soos die* ~, as close as an oyster; *'n GEWITTE* ~, a whitened sepulchre; *vir 'n ander 'n* ~ *GRAWE*, dig someone else's grave; bring about someone else's ruin; *sy eie* ~ *GRAWE*, dig one's own grave; *die* ~ *MAAK algar gelyk*, death levels all; *hy sou in sy* ~ *OMDRAAI*, he would turn in his grave; *daar LOOP iem. oor my* ~, somebody is walking over my grave; *'n ONTYDIGE* ~ *vind*, find an early grave; *so STIL soos die* ~, *as quiet as the grave; soos die* ~ *SWYG*, remain silent as the grave; *met die een VOET in die* ~, with one foot in the grave; aged; ~**blom**, candytuft; ~**delwer**, *see* **grafgrawer**; ~**doek**, cerecloth.

graf'fito, (graffiti), graffito.

graf: ~**gewelf**, sepulchral vault; ~**grawer**, grave-digger; ~**heuwel**, barrow, grave-mound; tumulus.

gra'fie, (-s), small spade.

grafiek', graphic art; (-e), graph; ~**boek**, graph book.

gra'fies, (-e), graphic; ~*e vergroeiing*, graphic intergrowth.

grafiet', graphite; plumbago; ~**ghries**, graphite grease.

grafi'ties, (-e), graphitic.

graf: ~**kelder**, vault; ~**kuil**, grave; ~**legging**, interment, sepulture; ~**lug**, sepulchral smell; ~**maker**, grave-digger; ~**naald**, sepulchral obelisk.

grafologie', graphology.

grafolo'gies, (-e), graphological.

grafoloog', (..loë), graphologist.

graf: ~**rede**, funeral oration; ~**skender**, ghoul; ~**skending**, ~**skennis**, violation of a tomb; gravedesecration; ~**skrif**, epitaph; ~**steen**, gravestone, tombstone; headstone; ~**steenmaker**, monumental mason; ~**stem**, sepulchral voice; ~**suil**, memorial column; ~**urn**, sepulchral urn; ~**waarts**, to the grave.

grag, (-te), canal, ditch, moat, fosse.

Gra'hamstad, Grahamstown, ~**ter, (-s)**, inhabitant of Grahamstown; Grahamstown waggon, Grahamstadter.

gram, (-me), gramme.

gramadoe'las, the back of beyond, backwoods, rough country; inhospitable country; *hy kom uit die* ~, he comes from the backwoods.

gramkalorie', (-ë), gramme-calorie.

gramma'ties, (-e), grammatic(al).

gramma'tika, (-s), grammar.

grammatikaal', (..kale), grammatical.

gramma'tikus, (-se, ..tici), grammarian.

gram'-meter, gram-metre.

gram'mofoon, (..fone), gramophone; ~**naald**, gramophone needle; ~**plaat**, gramophone record.

gram'radio, radiogram.

gram'skap, anger, ire, wrath.

gramsto'rig, (-e), angry, wrathful; ~**heid**, wrath.

granaat', (..nate), pomegranate; garnet (gem), Cape ruby; round (artil.); grenade, pip-squeak, shrapnel; ~**afdeling**, bombing section; ~**appel**, pomegranate; ~**dop**, shell case; ~**gooier**, bomber; ~**grip**, shell slit; ~**haak**, shell hook; ~**hok**, shell room; ~**kartets**, shrapnel; ~**krater**, shell crater; ~**mag-**

neet, shell trap; ~**raket**, shell rocket; ~**skerf**, bomb splinter; ~**skieter**, bomber; ~**skok**, shell-shock; ~**steen**, garnet; ~**stroop**, grenadine; ~**tregter**, shell crater; ~**vas, (-te)**, ~**vry, (-e)**, shellproof; ~ *vaste (~ vrye) skuiling*, shell-proof shelter; ~**vuur**, shellfire.
grenadil'la, = **grenadella**.
gran'de, (-s), grandee.
grandioos', (..diose), grandiose.
graniet', granite; *hulle kou op ~* , they are trying to cut blocks with a razor; ~**agtig, (-e)**, granitoid; ~**blok**, block of granite; ~**rots**, granitic rock; ~**suil**, column of granite.
grani'ties, (-e), granitic.
granofier', granophyre.
granoliet', granolite.
granoli'ties, (-e), granolithic.
granula'sie, granulation.
granuleer', (ge-), granulate.
granulêr', (-e), granuleus', (-e), granular.
granuliet', granulite; ..**li'ties, (-e)**, granulitic.
grap, (s) (-pe), joke, jest, quip; fun; prank, lark; *hom daar met 'n ~ pie van AFMAAK*, turn it into a joke; *dis GEEN ~ nie*, it is no laughing matter; *'n ~ en 'n HALF*, a good joke; *dis 'n MOOI ~ met jou!* you are a fine one! *SONDER ~ pies*, all joking aside; *alle ~ pies op 'n STOKKIE*, all joking aside; *~ pe UITHAAL*, play jokes (pranks); *die ~ gaan te VER*, that is beyond a joke; *VIR die ~* , for fun, as a joke; (w) **(ge-)**, joke, make fun; ~**jas, (-se)**, joker; clown; ~**maker**, joker, buffoon, clown, comic, jester, larker, merry-andrew, wag; comedian; ~**makery**, jesting, joking, buffoonery.
grap'penderwys(e), comically, humorously, facetiously, jocularly.
grap'perig, grap'pig, (-e), funny, comic(al); droll; burlesque, quizzical, diverting; frolicsome; humorous, facetious, jocose, jocular; *iets ~ vind*, be amused by something; ~**heid**, drollery, fun, frolicsomeness, facetiousness, jocularity, pleasantry.
grap'prentjies, comic strips, comics; cartoons.
graps'gewys, see **grappenderwys(e)**.
gras, (-se), grass; *van die ~ AF wees*, be dead and gone; *die ~ aan die BRAND steek*, set the world on fire; *in die ~ BYT*, bite the dust; *geen ~ oor iets laat GROEI NIE*, not to let the grass grow under one's feet; *daar ~ oor laat GROEI*, let bygones be bygones; *dis nie alles ~ wat GROEN is nie*, appearances are deceptive; *iem van die ~ af MAAK*, do away with someone; *daar is 'n SLANG in die ~*, there is a snake in the grass; *die VERSTE ~ is die groenste*, distance lends enchantment to the view; *geen ~ onder die VOETE laat groei nie*, not let the grass grow under one's feet; *die ~ voor iem. se VOETE wegmaai*, cut the ground from under someone's feet; ~**agtig, (-e)**, grassy; graminaceous; ~**angelier**, Indian pink; ~**baan**, grass court; ~**blom**, *Dicrama ensifolium*; ~**bouleer**, agrostology; ~**brand**, grass fire; *soos 'n ~ brand versprei*, spread like wildfire; ~**bult**, down; grassy hill; ~**deskundige**, agrostologist; ~**draer**, termite, harvester termite; ~**duin, (ge-)**, enjoy; *êrens in ~ duin*, browse among (books); ~**etend, (-e)**, herbivorous; graminivorous; ~**groen**, grass-green; ~**halm**, blade of grass; culm; ~**helling**, grassy slope; ~**huisie**, grass hut; bagworm (*Ceromitia, Psychidae, etc.*); tussock-moth.
gra'sie, grace, favour; pardon, reprieve; *die DRIE Grasieë*, the three Graces; *by die ~ GODS*, by the grace of God; *~ VERLEEN aan*, grant (a) pardon to; *by iem. in die ~ WEES*, be in someone's good graces.
grasieus', (-e), graceful, elegant, gracious.
gra'sig, (-e), grassy.
gras: ~**kenner**, agrostologist; ~**klipvis**, *Clinus graminis*; ~**klokkie**, harebell; ~**kunde**, agrostology; ~**kun'dig, (-e)**, agrostological; ~**kun'dige, (-s)**, agrostologist; ~**land**, grassland; ~**linne**, grasscloth, holland, grassliner; ~**loos, (..lose)**, grassless; ~**maaier**, lawn-mower; ~**mat**, grassed surface; greensward; ~**mossie**, hedge sparrow; ~**parkiet**, budgerigar, budgie; ~**perk**, lawn, green,

grassy plot; ~**pol**, tuft of grass; hassock; tussock; ~**rand**, grass border; ~**ryk**, grassy; graminaceous; ~**rykheid**, grassiness; ~**saad**, grass seed; ~**sakkie**, ballonet; ~**slang**, grass snake; ~**snyer**, grass-cutter; lawn-mower; ~**sooi**, sod; ~**soort**, kind of grass, grass-type; ~**spriet**, blade of grass; ~**sproeier**, lawnsprinkler; ~**stoel**, cane chair; ~**tapyt**, carpet of grass; ~**uil**, grass-owl; ~**veld**, sward, green, grassy field; ley, lea; ~**veldhaakwurm**, grassveld hookworm (*Bunostonum trigonocephalum*); ~**vlakte**, meadow, plain, prairie; ~**voël**, grassbird; ~**vuur**, veld-fire; ~**weduwee**, grass widow; ~**wewenaar**, grass widower.
gra'terig, (-e), full of bones (fish).
gratifika'sie, (-s), gratuity.
gratineer', (ge-), gratinate; *ge ~* , au gratin.
gra'tis, gratis, free; free of charge; no charge, eleemosynary; *ons DOEN dit ~* , we make no charge for this; *~ MONSTER*, free sample; *~ VERSPREIDING*, free distribution.
grava'men, (..mina), gravamen.
graveer', (ge-), engrave, chase; carve; sink (dies); ~**der, (-s)**, engraver; ~**kuns**, (art of) engraving; ~**naald**, ~**stif**, engraver's needle (tool); graver; burin; ~**werk**, engraving; ~**yster**, engraver's chisel.
grave'ring, (-s), (en)graving, chasing.
graveur', (-s), (en)graver, chaser.
gra'vimeter, gravime'ter, gravimeter; ..**me'tries, (-e)**, gravimetric.
gravin', (-ne), countess, duchess.
gra'visaksent, grave accent.
gravita'sie, gravitation; ~**tenk**, dash-tank (motor).
graviteer', (ge-), gravitate.
gravu're, (-s), engraving, copperplate.
gra'we, (ge-), dig, sink, burrow, delve.
graweel', gravel (disease), calculus, stone; nephrite; ~**agtig, (-e)**, calculous; ~**stene**, urinary calculi; nephrite, gravel-stone; ~**wortel**, medicinal herb (*Berkheya artractyloides*).
gra'wer, (-s), digger, delver, grubber.
Green'wichtyd, Greenwich (mean) time.
greep, (grepe), grasp, bite; handle; snatch; stock (of gun); hold; grip (of a weapon); clutch; cleat; hilt (of sword); grab; grapple; handgrip; knack; *'n ~ uit die GESKIEDENIS*, a dip into history; *LOSKOM uit die ~ van*, slip out of the grip (grasp) of.
Gregoriaans', (-e), Gregorian.
grein, (-e), grain; *grof van ~* , coarse-grained; ~**eer', (ge-)**, granulate; grain; ~**eer'der, (-s)**, grainer; ~**hout**, white pine-wood; *AMERIKAANSE ~ hout*, American pine (oregon); *BALTIESE ~ hout*, Baltic deal, northern pine; ~**houtplank**, deal board.
grein'tjie, (-s), grain; particle, atom, scrap, shred; *geen ~ nie*, not an atom (a trace); not a shred (of evidence); not a spark (of shame).
Grekis', (-te), Greek scholar; ~**me**, Graecism.
grenadel'la, (-s), granadilla, passion fruit (-flower).
grenadier', (-s), grenadier.
gren'del, (s) (-s), sliding bolt, bolt, bar; fastener; breech-bolt (of gun); hasp; (w) **(ge-)**, bolt, hasp, interlock, bar; ~**bak**, locking tray (railw.); ~**deur**, bolted door; ~**hefboom**, fastening lever; ~**ing**, interlocking; bolting; ~**kamgroewe**, bolt camgrooves; ~**kopskroeftop**, bolt-head tenon; ~**sluiting**, stock-locking; ~**toestel**, interlocking apparatus.
grens¹, (s) (-e), boundary; border, bourn(e), compass, divide, line; march; pale; reach, limit; circuit; frontier; margin; *die ~e van sy BEVOEGDHEID te buite gaan*, exceed one's authority; *BINNE sekere ~ e*, within certain limits; *g'n ~ e KEN nie*, know no bounds; *die ~ OORSKRY*, go beyond the bounds; go too far; *OP die ~ van*, on the verge (border) of; *~ e STEL aan*, set bounds to; *TOT 'n sekere ~* , up to a certain point; *êrens 'n ~ TREK*, draw the line somewhere; *die ~ e TREK TUSSEN*, draw up the line between; *die UITERSTE ~ e*, the uttermost confines; *oor die ~ e VERBAN*, banish from the country; (w) **(ge-)**, bound, border on, abut on; *dit ~ aan parmantigheid*, this borders on cheek.
grens², (w) (ge-), cry, blubber, howl, pule, bawl.

grens'afbakening, demarcation, delimitation.
grens'bal, (-le), boundary (cricket).
grens'balie, cry-baby.
grens: ~**bewoner**, frontiersman, frontier resident, marchman; ~**dorp**, frontier village.
grens's(e)loos, (..lose), boundless, infinite; ~**heid**, boundlessness.
grens: ~**erig (-e)**, always crying; crying weakly; ~**ery**, crying, puling, mewling.
grens: ~**gebied**, border(land), confines; ~**geskil**, boundary dispute; ~**geval**, border-line case; ~**heining**, boundary fence; ~**hersiening**, boundary revision; ~**hou**, boundary (cricket); ~**laag**, boundary layer; ~**land**, borderland; march-land; ~**lig**, boundary light; ~**loos, (..lose)**, limitless; ~**lyn**, perimeter (of aerodrome); precinct, boundary line, line of demarcation; limit; *oor die ~lyn*, out of bounds; ~**maat**, limit gauge; ~**merk**, boundary mark; ~**nywerheid**, border industry; ~**paal**, boundary post; goal; ~**plaas**, boundary farm; ~**pos**, frontier post; ~**reëling**, boundary settlement; ~**regter**, linesman (football); ~**skeiding**, boundary line; frontier; ~**stad**, frontier town; ~**teken**, boundary mark; ~**traktaat**, boundary treaty; ~**troepe**, frontier troops; ~**veld**, deep field (cricket); ~**verbetering**, rectification of frontiers; ~**verdediging**, frontier defence; ~**verligting**, boundary lighting; ~**vesting**, frontier fortress; ~**voordele**, fringe benefits; ~**waarde**, limit value; marginal value; ~**wag**, frontier watch; ~**waardeleer**, theory of marginal value, ~**weer**, frontier (protective) force; ~**wysiging**, change of frontier.
gre'pie, (-s), extract; selection; *~s uit die geskiedenis*, selections from history.
grep'pel, (-s), trench, furrow, ditch.
Gresis', (-te) = Grekis: ~**me, (-s)**, Graecism.
gre'tig, (-e), eager, desirous, greedy; keen; avid; athirst; hot; ~ *na mag*, anxious for power; ~**heid**, eagerness, greediness, avidity; alacrity; greed; keenness; ~**lik**, eagerly, avidly.
grief, (s) (griewe), grievance; gravamen; grouse; (w) **(ge-)**, grieve, aggrieve, hurt, gall.
Griek, (-e), Greek, ~**eland**, Greece; ~**s, (s)** Greek; *dis ~s vir my*, I do not understand it; it is Greek to me; (b) **(-e)**, Grecian.
Grie'kwa, (-s), Griqua; ~**land**, Griqualand.
**griekwalandiet', griqualandite.
griep, influenza, flu(e); grippe; *Asiatiese ~*, Asiatic flu; ~**aanval**, attack of flu; ~**erig, (-e)**, influenzal; *ek voel so ~erig*, I feel I have a touch of flu.
grie'sel, (ge-), shudder, get goose-flesh; ~**lg, (-e)**, creepy, gruesome, weird, nasty; ~**igheid**, gruesomeness, creepiness; ~**roman**, horror story, penny-dreadful.
grie'seltjie, see **krieseltjie**.
gries'meel, pollard, semolina.
griet¹, (-e), godwit (bird); brill (fish).
Griet', *grote ~!* Great Scott!
grie'wend, (-e), grievous, hurtful, bitter; *~e TELEURSTELLING*, grievous disappointment; *~e WOORDE*, offensive (hurtful) words.
grif¹, (w) (ge-), scratch, engrave.
grif², (Ndl.) **(bw)**, promptly, readily.
grif'fel, (-s), slate-pencil; pencil; ~**doos**, pencil box.
grif'fie, (-s), slate-pencil; *'n stomp ~*, a dull fellow; a numbskull.
griffier', (-s), registrar, recorder, clerk.
griff(i)oen', (-s), griffin.
grif'weg, promptly.
gril¹, (s) (-le), caprice, whim, freak, fad, fancy, vagary, kink; humour; fantasy; fit; gadfly; *deur 'n ~ van die NOODLOT*, by some strange stroke of destiny; *aan iem. se ~le VOLDOEN*, gratify someone's whims.
gril², (w) **(ge-)**, shudder, shiver.
gril'lerig, (-e), whimsical, queer; hair-raising, creepy, arabesque; ~**heid**, creepiness; whimsicality.
gril'lig, (-e), fantastic, whimsical, fanciful, faddy, freakish, bizarre; ~**heid**, whimsicality, fantasticality; fantasticalness; freakishness, quaintness.
gril: ~**prent**, thriller; ~**toneelstuk**, thriller (play); ~**verhaal**, penny-horrible, thriller (story).

grimas', (-se), grimace; ~**maker**, grimacer.
grimeer', (ge-), make up (for stage); ~**der, (-s)**, make-up artist; ~**sel**, grease-paint; ~**tassie**, vanity case.
grime'ring, make-up.
grim'lag, (s) (-ge), grin, sneer; (w) **(ge-)**, grin, sneer.
grim'mig, (-e), angry, enraged, furious, austere; grim; ~**heid**, fury, wrath.
grin'nik, (ge-), sneer, mock; grin, chuckle, chortle; grimace.
grint, gravel; shingle; cobblestone, grit (uncemented); ~**erig**, gritty, gravelly; ~**pad**, gravel(led) road; ~**spat, (ge-)**, rough-cast; ~**spatpleister**, rough-cast plaster; ~**steen**, grit (cemented); ~**weg**, gravel road.
grip, (-pe), furrow, ditch, drain, drill; slit-trench; grip.
grip'pie, (-s), small furrow, drill.
groef, (s) (groewe), groove; flute (in a column); furrow (in the skin); grave; recess, chase, slot (of gun); guttering; undercut (welding); rut; riffle; channel; chamfer; guideway; *by die geopende groewe*, at the graveside; (w) **(ge-)**, groove, flute, chase; channel; ~**hoek**, groove angle; ~**ie (-s)**, small groove; bezel; striation; ~**katrol**, grooved pulley; ~**lys**, quirk moulding; ~**maker**, slotter; ~**masjien**, paring machine; key seater; channeller; ~**naat**, slot seam; ~**rat**, splined gear (wheel); ~**saag**, grooving saw; ~**skaaf**, grooving (dado) plane; ~**snyer**, dado-cutter; ~**staal**, hollowing plane; ~**sweislas**, groove-weld; ~**taster**, pickup; ~**versiering**, fluting; ~**vyl**, riffler; ~**werk**, channelled work, channelling (bullets); fluting; ~**wiel**, spurwheel; ~**yster**, grooving tool, groover.
groei, (s) growth; (w) **(ge-)**, glow, increase, evolve; pullulate; ~ *en BLOEI*, grow and thrive; *uit sy KLERE ~*, grow out of one's clothes; *teen VERDRUKKING in ~*, flourish in adversity; ~**bodem**, hotbed; ~**end, (-e)**, growing, accrescent; ~**er (-s)**, grower; ~**fonds**, growth fund; ~**hand**, green fingers; *'n ~hand hê*, have green fingers; ~**klier**, thymus; ~**koors**, growing pains; ~**krag**, power to grow, vitality, natural strength; ~**kromme**, ~**kurwe**, sigmoid curve; ~**laag**, cambium; ~**meel**, growing meal; ~**plek**, habitat (of plant); ~**proses**, process of growth; ~**punt**, growing-point; growth-point; ~**pyne**, growing pains; ~**saam, (..same)**, favourable to growth; fertile; ~**saamheid**, fertility; ~**seisoen**, growing-season.
groei'sel¹ (-s), growth.
groei'sel², (-le), vegetative cell.
groei: ~**vorm**, habitus; ~**wyse**, habit of growth.
groen, (s) green; (b) green, verdant; fresh; unripe, immature; ~ *van AFGUNS*, green with envy; *dit word vir hom ~ en GEEL voor die oë*, his head begins to swim; *ek is nie so ~ dat 'n KOEI my sal eet nie*, I am not as green as I am cabbage-looking; ~**aarde**, green earth; celadonite; ~**agtig, (-e)**, greenish; viridescent; greeny; ~**agtigheid**, viridescence, ~**amandel**, pistachio nut; ~**amara**, *Vernonia elaeagnoides*; ~**bemesting**, green manure; ~**blou**, greenish blue; ~**blywend, (-e)**, indeciduous; evergreen; ~**boontjie**, green (haricot) bean; ~**bosnimf**, the butterfly *Macna hampsoni*; ~**brommer**, green blowfly *(Lucilia sericata, L. cuprina)*; ~**bruin**, greenish brown; ~**druiwe**, variety of grape; ~**e, (-s)**, freshman, fresher; ~**erig, (-e)**, greenish; greeny; aeruginous; ~**erigheid**, greenishness; ~**ertjie**, green pea; ~**kader**, ab initio training-squadron; ~**geel**, greenish yellow; ~**goed**, greens; ~**heid**, green(ness), verdancy, viridity; ~**igheid**, greenness; greens; greenery; ~**kaas**, green cheese; ~**kalossie**, *Ixia viridiflora*; ~**kleurig, (-e)**, greenish; ~**koekoek**, green cuckoo *(Chrysococcyx cupreus sharpei)*; ~**kwarts**, plasma.
Groen'land, Greenland; ~**er, (-s)**, Greenlander; ~**s, (-e)**, Greenlandish.
groen: ~**mamba**, green mamba *(Dendraospis augusticeps)*; peppermint liqueur; ~**mielie**, green mealie; ~**modder**, green mud; ~**pampoentjie**, hubbard squash; ~**poortruiter**, greenshank *(Tringa nebularia)*; ~**pruim**, greengage; ~**sand**, green sand; ~**seep**, soft soap; ~**skimmel**, green mould (citrus);

~ **slik,** green mud; ~ **spaan,** verdigris; ~ **staar,** glaucoma; ~ **steen,** greenstone, diorite.

groen'te, vegetables; greens; pot-herb; green food; ~ **atjar,** pickled vegetables; pickles; ~ **boer,** market (vegetable) gardener; ~ **boerdery,** vegetable grow=ing; market-gardening; ~ **eter,** vegetarian; ~ **han=delaar,** greengrocer; ~ **kar,** vegetable cart; ~ **mark,** vegetable (fresh) market; ~ **pille,** vegetable pills; ~ **skottel,** vegetable dish; ~ **so(e)p,** vegetable soup; ~ **smous,** vegetable hawker; ~ **stalletjie,** vegetable stall; ~ **tuin,** kitchen garden, vegetable garden; kale-yard; ~ **winkel,** greengrocer's shop.

groen'tjie, (-s), freshman, greenhorn; ham; fag; *cf.* **jangroentjie.**

groen: ~ **tyd,** noviciate; initiating period; period of freshmanship; ~ **viooltjie,** *Lachenalia orchioide;* ~ **vitrioel,** green vitriol, copperas; ~ **vlerkduif,** emerald-spotted dove; ~ **vlieg,** Spanish fly, cantharis.

groen'voer, fresh fodder; soilage, soiling crop; green barley (crop); *ook nog* ~ *op die land hê,* to be vul=nerable too; ~ **gewasse,** green-fodder crop.

groenvy'ekonfyt, green-fig preserve.

groep, (-e), group; section; clump; classis; ~ **eer',** **(ge-),** group, form groups; assort; ~ **e'ring, (-e, -s),** grouping; classification; ~ **ie, (-s),** small group (people); cluster (crochet; trees); ~ **leier,** group-leader; ~ **s'belange,** sectional interests; ~ **gelykes,** peer group; ~ **s'gebied,** group area; ~ **s'gewys(e),** in groups, in batches; ~ **s'kaptein,** group-captain; ~ **taal,** slang, cant; social dialect.

groes'bebouing, sod culture.

groet, (s) (-e), salute, greeting; (w) **(ge-),** greet, salute, shake hands, say goodbye; *met die hand* ~ , shake hands; ~ **end, (-e),** greeting; with kind regards.

groe'te, groet'nis, compliments, regards, greetings; *sê* ~ *aan oom DAANTJIE,* lets cut it out (drop it), shall we? *die* ~ *TUIS,* love to all at home; *sê* ~ *aan die VRATE,* what a glutton you are; (my) greetings to the gluttons; *VRIENDELIKE* ~ , kind regards.

groe'tery, farewell, leave-taking.

groe'we = **groef, (s).**

groe'wing, grooving, fluting.

grof, (growwe; growwer, -ste), coarse, hard; large-boned (build); hard-mouthed; rough, rude (language); gruff (voice); crude (style); gross (injus=tice); roughhewn (statue); heavy; crass (ignorance); *'n growwe FLATER,* a glaring error; *'n growwe LEUEN,* a shameless lie; *growwe SUIKER,* granu=lated sugar; ~ **breking,** spalling; ~ **dradig, (-e),** course-fibred (threaded); coarse-grained; ~ **gebou, (-de),** large-limbed; ~ **geskut,** big guns, cannon, heavy artillery; ~ **grein,** grogram; ~ **heid,** coarse=ness, rudeness; broadness; crassitude; grossness; crassness; ~ **korrelig (-e),** coarse-grained; ~ **linne,** crash; ~ **skaaf,** jack-plane; ~ **smid,** blacksmith; ~ **spat, (-ge-),** rough-cast; ~ **spatpleister,** rough-cast; ~ **stelling,** coarse adjustment; ~ **stelskroef,** coarse adjuster.

grok, (-ke), grog; ~ **neus,** grog blossom.

grom¹, (s) dregs, lees, sediment.

grom², (w) **(ge-),** grumble, grouse (person, bear); ~ **pot,** grumbler, growler.

grond, (s) (-e), ground, soil; dirt (road); land; bottom; reason; cause; *tot in die* ~ *BEDERWE,* spoil utter=ly; *in die* ~ *BOOR,* send (a ship) to the bottom; *die* ~ *BRAND onder sy voete,* he is on hot coals; *op DROË* ~ *val,* fall on barren ground; ~ *EET,* bite the dust; *staan of jy in die grond GENAEL is,* stand as if rooted to the ground; *op GEVAARLIKE* ~ *staan,* be on slippery ground; *in die* ~ *van my HART,* in the depths of my soul; *ONBEBOUDE* ~ , virgin (undeveloped) land; *van alle* ~ *ontbloot,* without any foundation; *OP* ~ *van,* by virtue of, by reason of, on (the) grounds of; *(in) die* ~ *PLOEG,* come a cropper; *aan die* ~ *RAAK,* ground; *deur die* ~ *wil SINK,* wish that the earth will swallow one; *SONDER* ~ *wees,* without foun=dation; *ONDER die* ~ *STOP,* bury; *op gevaarlike* ~ *TREE,* be skating on thin ice; *op VASTE* ~ *staan,* be on firm ground; *nie eers kans kry om* ~ *te VAT nie,* before you even know where you are; ~ *VERLOOR,* lose ground; *op droë* ~ *VISVANG,* fish on dry ground; *vaste* ~ *onder die VOETE hê,* be on firm ground; *geen* ~ *onder die VOETE hê nie,* have no leg to stand on; ~ *WEN,* gain ground; (w) **(ge-),** found, ground, base; prime (paint); *op waarheid gegrond,* based on truth; ~ **aanwas,** allu=vion; ~ **afweer,** anti-aircraft defence; ~ **agtig, (-e),** earthy; ~ **antenne,** ground aerial; ~ **baan,** ground track; bottoming; ~ **bal,** grounder; ~ **baron,** land-baron; ~ **bedryf,** key-industry; ~ **bedryfsleer,** soil utilization; soil use; ~ **beeld,** prototype; ~ **beginsel,** first (basic) principle, rudiment; ground; funda=mental; essence; ~ **begrip,** fundamental idea; ~ **be=lasting,** land-tax; ~ **besit,** system of land-tenure; domain; landed property; real estate; ~ **besitter,** landed proprietor, landowner; ~ **besitters,** landed gentry; ~ **bestanddeel,** element, essence, fundamen=tal part; ~ **betekenis,** primary sense; basic meaning; ~ **bewaring,** soil conservation; ~ **bodem,** soil sur=face; ~ **bewerking,** tillage; ~ **bonetameletjie,** pea=nut-brittle; ~ **boontjie,** peanut, monkeynut; ground (earth-)nut; ~ **boontjiebotter,** peanut butter; ~ **boontjiedopper,** peanut sheller; ~ **boontjieolie,** arachis-oil; ~ **boor,** spiral dril; ~ **breker,** subsoiler; ~ **brief,** conveyance; ~ **bus,** bottom-stuffing box; ~ **dam,** earth dam; ~ **diens,** ground service (duties); ~ **dienswa,** mobile ground-station; ~ **doel,** ground objective.

gron'de: *te* ~ *GAAN,* go to rack and ruin, be ruined; *te* ~ *RIG,* wreck, raze to the ground.

grond: ~ **eekhoring,** gopher; ~ **eenheid,** non-flying unit.

grondeer', (ge-), prime, ground, give a priming coat.

grond: ~ **eienaar,** *see* **grondbesitter;** ~ **eiendom,** free=hold tenure; landed property.

gron'del, goby, gudgeon (fish); *Gobius nudiceps.*

gron'deloos, (..lose), bottomless, unfathomable; abysmal; ~ **heid,** bottomless depth.

grond: ~ **erig, (-e),** earthy; ~ **erosie,** soil erosion; ~ **eter,** geophagist; ~ **ertjie,** hugo bean (*Voandzeia subterranea*); ~ **etery,** geophagia; ~ **feite,** basic facts; ~ **formasie,** ground formation; ~ **gebied,** ter=ritory; ~ **gedagte,** leading thought, root-idea; ~ **ge=laagdheid,** soil profile; ~ **geriewe,** ground facilities; ~ **gesteldheid,** nature of the soil; relief; ~ **getal,** ra=dix; basic number; base; ~ **geut,** surface drain; ~ **golf,** ground swell; ~ **herwinning,** land reclama=tion; ~ **hoek,** ground angle; ~ **honger,** land hunger; ~ **hoogte,** clearance (of vehicle); ground level; ~ **hoop,** earth mound (dump); ~ **horison,** soil hori=zon; ~ **hou,** ground stroke, carpet drive (golf); ~ **huur,** ground rent; ~ **idee,** basic idea.

gron'dig, (-e), thorough, sound, valid, fundamental, intimate, deep, profound, well-founded; searching; ~ *e redes hê,* have sound reasons; ~ **heid,** thor=oughness, profoundness.

grond: ~ **invloed,** ground interference; ~ **kaart,** soil map; key map; ~ **klep,** foot valve; ~ **kleur,** primary (basic) colour; ground-colour; ~ **kombers,** (soil) mulch; ground dressing; ~ **krummels,** aggregates (soil); ~ **kunde,** pedology; ~ **laag,** bed, bottom lay=er; bedrock; priming, first coating (paint); ~ **lêer,** ~ **legger,** founder; ~ **legging,** foundation; ~ **lig=gend, (-e),** basic, fundamental; ~ **loon,** basic wage; ~ **loos, (..lose),** without ground; ~ **lose kweking,** hydroponic culture; ~ **lus,** geophagy; ~ **lyn,** ground (base) line, base (triangle); ~ **massa,** ma=trix; ~ **mis,** ground fog; ~ **missiel,** ground missile; ~ **moreen,** ground moraine; ~ **onderrig,** ground in=struction; ~ **ondersoek,** soil research; ~ **oorsaak,** primary cause; underlying cause; ~ **opbrengs,** em=blement(s), profits of sown land; ~ **oppervlak,** soil surface; ~ **opsigter,** groundsman; ~ **organisasie,** ground organization; ~ **pad,** earth road; ~ **peilsta=sie,** ground direction-finding station; ~ **personeel,** ground staff; ~ **plan,** ground plan lay-out; ~ **pligte,** ground duties; ~ **profiel,** soil profile; ~ **reël,** prin=ciple, maxim; fundamental rule; ~ **reg,** land right; basic right; ~ **register,** land registry; ~ **salaris,** ba=sic salary; ~ **seiltjie,** ground-sheet; ~ **sein,** ground signal; ~ **servituut,** pr(a)edial servitude; ~ **sig,** ground visibility; ~ **skeikundige,** soil chemist;

~**skenking**, donation of land; ~**skool**, ground instruction school; ~**slag**, fundamental, ground, foundation, basis, principle; *die beginsel wat daaraan ten ~ slag lê,* the underlying principle; ~**sluiting**, earth (elect.); ~**snelheid**, ground speed; ~**snuitkewer**, vegetable weevil; ~**snuittor**, ground weevil; ~**soort**, kind of soil; ~**sop**, dregs, grounds, sediment; ground-yeast; draff; lees, *die ~ sop is vir die goddelose,* the dregs fall to the wicked; ~**spekulant**, landjobber; property speculator; ~**stelling**, fundamental axiom; ~**stof**, element, radical, raw material; ~**storting**, landslip; landslide; ~**taal**, original language; language of origin; ~**tal**, basic number, base, basis, radix (maths.); ~**tarief**, basic rate; ~**teiken**, ground target; ~**teks**, original, basic text; ~**tipe**, type of soil; archetype; ~**toestand**, state of ground; ~**toon**, pitch tone; key-note; dominant note; fundamental tone; ~**-tot-lug-missiel**, ground-to-air missile; ~**-tot-lugprojektiel**, ground-to-air projectile; ~**trek**, characteristic feature, trait; ~**troepe**, ground troops; ~**vak**, ground subject.

grond'vat, (-ge-), alight, arrive; *geen kans kry om grond te vat nie,* get no opportunity to rest; *met die ~ slag,* as soon as he alighted.

grond: ~**verdieping**, ground floor; ~**verf**, (s) ground-colour; first coat(ing); distemper; grounding, priming; (w) (ge-), prime, give a priming coat, ground; ~**versakking**, subsidence, depression; ~**verskuiwing**, landslide; ~**verspoeling**, (soil) erosion; ~**ves**, (ge-), found; ground; base; ~**veste**, foundations; ~**vester**, (-s), founder; ~**vesting**, foundation; groundwork; ~**vlak**, horizontal plane; ~**vloer**, earthen floor; ~**vog**, soil humidity; ~**voggehalte**, soil-moisture content; ~**vogtoestand**, soil-moisture condition; ~**voorwaarde**, primary condition; ~**vorm**, primitive (fundamental) form; archetype; ~**vreter**, excavator; ~**vrugbaarheid**, fertility of soil; ~**vryhoogte**, ground clearance; ~**waarheid**, fundamental truth; axiom; ~**wal**, mound; ~**water**, ground water; phreatic water, subsoil water; ~**waterstand**, ~**watervlak**, watertable; ~**weefsel**, ground tissue, parenchyma; ~**werk**, groundwork; permanent way; ~**werktuigkundige**, ground engineer; ~**wet**, (written) constitution, fundamental law; ~**wet'lik** (-e), constitutional; ~**wetlike bedeling**, constitutional dispensation; ~**wetshersiening**, revision of the constitution; ~**wet'tig**, (-e), constitutional; ~**wind**, ground wind; ~**wolf**, land-grabber, land-shark; ~**woord**, radical word, primitive word, etymon; ~**ys**, ground ice; anchor ice.

groos, (geselst.), (**groser, -ste**), proud; ~ *wees op,* be proud of; *see* **groots.**

groot, (s): *in die ~,* wholesale; (b) (**[grote]**; **groter, -ste**), great, large, big, tall, immense; gross, vast; grown-up; exquisite; grand; important; *voor sy EIE mense is niemand ~ nie,* a prophet has no honour in his own country; ~ *GRONDBESITTER,* large landowner; *die ~ ste HELFTE,* the bigger half; ~ *LEWE,* live in grand style; *by die ~ MAAT,* wholesale; in bulk; *n ~ MAN,* a tall (corpulent) man; a great man; *die ~ MOONDHEDE,* the Great Powers; *die ~ PUBLIEK,* the general public; *TE ~ lewe,* live beyond one's means; *die ~ ste van die TWEE,* the bigger of the two; *VANDAG ~, môre dood,* here today, gone tomorrow; *iets ~ s VERWAG,* expect something great; *die ~ WÊRELD,* society, the élite; ~**albatros**, wandering albatross; ~**as**, major axis; ~**baas**, chief, master; leader, manager; *DIE ~ baas,* honours (cards); *DIE G ~ baas,* the Lord; ~**baas** *SPEEL,* lord it (over); ~**bedryf**, the large industries; ~**bek**, popinjay, braggart; ~**boek**, ledger; ~**boekhouer**, ledger clerk; ~**boekklerk**, ledger clerk; ~**boekrekening**, ledger account; ~**boog**, instep; major arc; ~**bram**, maintop gallant; ~**bring**, (-ge-), rear, raise, bring up (children).

Groot-Brittan'je, Great Britain.

groot: ~**by**, death's-head moth; ~**byl**, felling axe; ~**derm**, colon, large intestine.

groot'doener, (-s), swaggerer; ~**ig**, (-e), swanky, snobbish; ~**y**, swagging.

groot: ~**doop**, adult baptism; ~**flamink**, greater flamingo; ~**grondbesit**, large landed interests.

groot'handel, wholesale (trade); ~**aar**, wholesale merchant; dealer in gross; ~**aarslisensie**, wholesale licence; ~**prys**, wholesale price; ~**verkoping**, wholesale selling.

groot'harsings, cerebrum.

groothar'tig, (-e), magnanimous, high-minded; ~**heid**, magnanimity.

groot'heid, greatness, largeness, magnitude, burliness; grossness; grandeur; *'n ONBEKENDE ~,* an unknown quantity; ~ *van SIEL,* magnanimity; ~**swaansin**, megalomania, paranoia.

groot'hertog, grand duke; ~**dom**, grand duchy; ~**in'**, grand duchess.

groothertog'gelik, (ong.) (-e), grand-ducal.

groothoof'dig, (-e), megacephalic, macrocephalic; ~**heid**, megacephaly, macrocephaly.

groot'hou, (-ge-), show a brave front; pretend to be big.

groot'industrie = **grootbedryf**.

groot: ~**industrieel**, leader of industry; ~**inkwisiteur**, grand inquisitor.

groot'jie, (-s), great grandmother (grandfather); granny; beldam; *LOOP na jou ~!* go to the devil! *NA sy ~,* gone to Jericho.

groot: ~**kanselier**, (ong.), Lord High Chancellor; ~**kap**, grand slam (at cards); ~**kern**, macronucleus; ~**koffer**, cabin trunk.

groot'kop, master mind; bigwig; leader; big bug; important person; big end (mech.); ~ **spyker**, clout.

groot: ~**kruis**, grand cross; ~**lawaai**, noisy person; four-flusher, bluffer, humbug; ~**letter**, cock-up (typog.), capital letter; ~**liks**, greatly, to a great extent, to a high degree; ~**losie**, grand lodge; ~**maak**, (-ge-), bring up, rear, raise, foster (children); ~**maattoets**, bulk test; ~**mag'tig**, (-e), all-powerful.

groot'man: *hom ~ HOU,* pretend to be somebody (rich or important); ~ *SPEEL,* lord it over others.

groot'mars, maintop; ~**seil**, maintop sail; ~**steng**, maintop mast.

groot: ~**mas**, mainmast; ~**meester**, grand master; past master.

groot'meneer, big bug; *hy hou vir hom ~,* he throws his weight around.

groot'mens, adult, grown-up (person); *eers ~ e dan langore,* first the grown-ups and then the children.

groot: ~**mes**, carver, carving knife; gully; ~**moeder**, grandmother, granny.

grootmoe'dig, (-e), magnanimous; large-hearted; high-minded; handsome; generous; ~**heid**, magnanimity, generosity.

Groot'mogol, Great Mogul.

groot: ~ **mufti**, grand mufti; ~**muisvoël**, grey lourie (*Corythaixoides concolor*); ~**nôi**, ~**nooi**, (vero.) lady of the house; ~**oktavo**, royal octavo.

groot'oog ~ *LOER,* show surprise; *..oë MAAK,* show disapproval; glare at.

groot: ~**ouers**, grandparents; ~**pad**, high road, main road; highway; ~**pawiljoen**, grand stand; ~**pens**, rumen.

groot'praat, (-ge-), brag, boast; rant; gas; talk through one's hat; gasconade; ~ *is nie 'n KUNS nie,* there is no art in boasting; ~ *is niem. se MAAT nie,* talk is cheap, but money buys the whisky; Brag is a good dog, but Hold Fast is a better.

groot: ~**prater**, boaster, braggart; ranter, popinjay, four-flusher; ~**pratery**, bragging, boasting; great brag (students); bluff; ~**ra**, (-'s), mainyard.

Groot'rivier, Orange River.

groots, (-e; -er, -ste), grand, majestic, proud; august; magnificent; exalted; ambitious; grandiose; ~ *wees op,* be proud of.

groot: ~**seël**, Great Seal; ~**seil**, mainsail.

groots'heid, grandeur, majesty, augustness, exaltedness, grandiosity.

groot: ~**skaals**, (-e), large-scale; ~**skeeps**, (-e), grand, copious, elegant, royal, on a grand scale; ~**skrif**, text-hand; ~**slag**, grand slam (cards); ~**spraak**, boasting, swaggering, rant(ing), gasconade; magniloquence, grandiloquence; ~**sprakig**, (**-e**), grandiloquent, bombastic, magniloquent; ~**sproeier**, main jet; ~**stad**, large city; ~**stag**, mainstay; ~**ste**, biggest (*see* groot); main; ~*ste HOOGTE*, overall height; ~*ste LENGTE*, overall length; ~**steeds**, (**-e**), fashionable, pertaining to (life in big) cities; ~**steek**, herringbone stitch; gasconade.

groot'te, (**-s**), size, extent, magnitude; tallness; greatness; dimension; bulk; length; amount; area; *van GERINGE* ~, of limited size; *man van MIDDELMATIGE* ~, a man of medium build; *volgens* ~ *SORTEER*, sort according to size, size; *op die VERLANGDE* ~ *sny*, cut to the desired size (length).

groot'tenue, full dress.
groot'terts-toonladder, major scale (music).
groot: ~**toon**, big toe; ~**totaal**, grand total; ~**trommel**, bass drum; ~**uier**, in calf; in lamb; ~**uierooi**, springing ewe, ewe with lamb; ~**vader**, grandfather; grandsire; ~**vaderlik**, (**-e**), grandfatherly; ~**vee**, (bovine) cattle; ~**veer**, mainspring; ~**verlof**, furlough, long leave; ~**verlofganger**, person on long leave; ~**vis**, game-fish; ~**vishengelary**, game-fishing; ~**visier**, grand vizier; ~**vors**, grand duke; ~**vurk**, the Devil's fork; carving fork; ~**vuur**, Hades, hell; ~**waardigheidsbekleër**, high dignitary; ~**want**, main shroud; ~**wild**, big game; ~**woord**, swear-word, curse; ~**word**, (**-ge-**), grow up, ~**wulp**, curlew.

gros, (**-se**), gross; majority; *die grootste* ~ *weet dit nie*, most people do not know it; ~**lys**, nomination roll; list of candidates; short list, panel.

grot, (**-te**), cave, grotto; ~**bewoner**, cave-dweller; troglodyte.
gro'tendeels, for the greater part, principally, chiefly, mainly, largely, to a large extent.
gro'ter, bigger; ~ *maak*, enlarge.
gro'terig, (**-e**), fairly big; in the teens; sizeable, largish.
grotesk', (**s**) (**-e**), grotesque; (**b**) (**-e**), bizarre, absurd; fanciful; ~**heid**, grotesqueness, grotesquerie.
gro'tetjie, (**-s**), fairly large one.
gro'tigheid, fuss, ado; *van 'n kuier 'n* ~ *maak*, consider a visit an important affair.
grou¹, (s) growl, snarl; (w) (**ge-**), growl, snarl.
grou², (w) (**ge-**), dig, burrow, *see* grawe.
grou³, (w) (**ge-**), grey; (b) grey; grizzly; old, monotonous; ~**erig**, (**-e**), greyish; ~**heid**, greyness.
grou: ~**kat**, wild cat (*Felis libyca caffra*); ~**staar**, cataract; ~**tjie**, (**-s**), donkey; ~**vomitief**, tartar emetic; ~**wak**, greywacke.
grow'we: ~**brood**, brown bread, coarse bread; ~**handdoek**, Turkish towel; ~**rig**, (**-e**), rather coarse (rough); ~**skilsuurlemoen**, rough lemon.
grow'wigheid, roughness (of road).
gru, (**ge-**), shudder (at); *dit laat my* ~, it makes me shudder.
gruis, (s) gravel; grit; roughly-ground meal; crushed mealies; (w) (**ge-**), macadamize; gravel; ~**baan**, gravel court.
gruis'elemente, fragments, bits; *in* ~, in fragments (bits).
gruis: ~**erig**, (**-e**), gritty, sandy; gravelly; ~**gat**, (**-e**), gravel pit, (gravel) quarry; ~**gesteente**, fragmental rocks; ~**pad**, gravel(led) road (path); ~**sif**, (sifting) screen; ~**skerm**, chip-guard, chip-shield (motor); ~**steenkool**, duff-coal; ~**stroke**, runs of gravel.
gru'saam, (**grusame**), gruesome, horrible, heinous; ~**heid**, gruesomeness, horridness, horribleness.
gru'wel, (**-e**, **-s**), horror, abomination; crime; enormity; *so 'n KLEIN* ~, such a little rascal; *die* ~ *van 'n OORLOG*, the horrors of war; ~**daad**, crime, atrocity, outrage.
gru'welik, (**-e**), horrible, abominable, atrocious; very, extremely; mischievous (child); ~ *vererg*, extremely annoyed; ~**heid**, horribleness, atrocity, horror, naughtiness.
gru'welkamer, chamber of horrors.
gruweloos'(lik) = **gruwelik**.
gru'welstuk, atrocity, thriller, prank.
gryns, (s) (**-e**), grin, sneer, grimace; leer; (w) (**ge-**),

grin, sneer; grimace, leer; ~**lag**, (s) grin, sneer; (w) (**ge-**), grin sneer.
gryp, (**ge-**), seize, snatch, grab, clutch; grabble; pot; pounce; grapple, claw; *hy* ~ *dit uit my HANDE*, he snatches it out of my hands; *te HOOG* ~, overreach oneself; *iets wat jou in die SIEL* ~, something which touches one to the quick; ~**aanval**, smash-and-grab attack; ~**baar**, (..**bare**), prehensile; ~**dief**, (..**diewe**), pickpocket, snatch-and-grab thief; ~**er**, (**-s**), grabber, gripper; holder; ~**haak**, grapnel, grapple; ~**handvatsel**, grab-handle; ~**inbraak**, smash-and-grab raid; ~**kant**, flank (of a tooth); ~**klou**, dog; ~**kraan**, grab crane; ~**mark**, snatch-and-grab sale; ~**stert**, prehensile tail; ~**sug**, avarice, greed; ~**sug'tig**, (**-e**), avaricious, grasping; ~**voël**, griffin; vulture.
grys, (**]-e**]; **-er**, **-ste**), grey; hoar(y), grizzly, grizzled; clever, smart, precocious; *KINDERS wat glad te* ~ *is*, children who are too precocious; *dit sal my nie* ~ *MAAK nie*, that won't worry me much; that won't give me grey hairs; ~ *voor sy TYD wees*, be prematurely grey; be precocious; be conceited, put on airs; *die* ~ *e VERLEDE*, hoary antiquity; *in die* ~ *e VERLEDE*, in the remote past; ~**aard** (**-s**), old man, greybeard; ~**ag'tig**, (**-e**), greyish, grizzled (hair); ~**appel**, sandapple (*Parinari capense*); ~**baard**, greybeard; ~**beer**, grizzly bear; ~**blou**, greyish blue, perse; azurine; ~**bok**, grysbok (*Raphicerus melanotis*); ~**bont**, greyish mottled; ~**erig**, (**-e**), rather grey; grizzly; ~**heid**, greyness, hoariness, old age; ~**kleurig**, grizzly; ~**kop**, grey-head; ~**loerie**, grey lourie; ~**mark**, grey market; ~**mol**, mole-rat; ~**muishond**, Cape ichneumon (*Herpestes caffer*); ~**stof**, grey matter.
g'tjie, (**-s**), small g.
guajak'hars, guaiac resin.
guana'co, (**-'s**), guanaco.
gua'no = **ghwano**.
Guatema'la, Guatemala.
Guatemalaan', (..**lane**), Guatemalan; ~**s'**, (**-e**), Guatemalan.
guerril'la, (**-s**), guerrilla; ~**oorlog**, guerrilla warfare); ~**vegter**, guerrilla fighter.
Guia'na, Guiana.
Guianees', (**s**, **b**) (..**nese**), Guianan.
guilloti'ne, (**-s**), guillotine; ..**tineer'**, (**ge-**), guillotine.
Guinee', Guinea.
guipu're, guipure.
guirlan'de, (**-s**), garland, wreath.
guit, (**-e**), rogue; ~**ig**, (**-e**), roguish; ~**igheid**, roguishness, devilment.
gul, (**-le**; **-ler**, **-ste**), generous, liberal, cordial, genial, free(-handed); ~*le gasvryheid*, cordial hospitality.
gul'de, golden; *'n* ~ *GELEENTHEID*, a golden opportunity; *die* ~ *MIDDE(L)WEG*, the golden mean.
gul'den, (**-s**), (Dutch) guilder; (Australian) florin.
gul'desnee, median section (maths.).
gulhar'tig, (**-e**), frank, cordial; bluff; ~**heid**, cordiality, bonhomie.
gul'heid, generosity, liberality.
Gul'lik, Jülich.
gulp¹, (s) (**-e**), fly (of trousers).
gulp², (s) large mouthful; sudden stream (blood); (w) (**ge-**), spout, gush.
guls: ~**aard**, glutton, gormandizer; ~**bek**, glutton.
gul'sig, (b) (**-e**), gluttonous, greedy, rapacious; edacious; (bw) greedily; ~**aard**, (**-s**), glutton, guttler, gormandizer, pig, gobbler; ~**heid**, gluttony, greediness, gulosity.
guls'sak, glutton.
gul'weg, frankly, liberally, genially.
gum'mi, Indiarubber, caoutchouc; ~**band**, elastic band; rubber tyre (of carriage); ~**oorskoen**, galosh; ~**slang**, tubing; ~**spons**, rubber sponge; ~**stok**, (policeman's) truncheon; ~**verpakking**, rubber packing.
gun, (**ge-**), not grudge; grant; *ek* ~ *jou DIT*, you are welcome to it; *'n MENS moet 'n ander ook iets* ~, one must live and let live; *NIEM. ooit iets* ~ *nie*, (be)grudge everybody everything; *hy* ~ *hom geen RUS nie*, he allows himself no rest.

guns, (-te), favour, goodwill, good graces; privilege, grace; '*n* ~ *BEWYS,* do a favour, do a good turn; *deur* ~ *te en GAWE kry,* obtain through favouritism; *met* ~ *te en GAWE,* through the kindness of others; *van* ~ *te en GAWE lewe,* live on charity; *IN die* ~ *wees (staan),* be in a person's good books; *in iem. se* ~ *probeer KOM,* curry favour with someone; *van* ~ *ste en gawe LEWE,* live on charity; *O* ~ *! goeie* ~ *!* dear me! oh dear! *uit die* ~ *RAAK by,* fall into disfavour with; *TEN* ~ *te van,* in favour of; *iem. om 'n* ~ *VRA,* beg a favour from someone; ~**bejag,** favour-hunting (currying); ~**betoon,** favour(ing), favouritism; nepotism; ~**bewys,** mark of favour (grace), ~**genoot,** (..**genote),** favourite; ~**passasier,** indulgence passenger; ~**teling, (-e),** favourite, fancied candidate; minion; pet.
guns'tig, (-e), favourable, advantageous, fair, fortunate, auspicious, propitious; ~ *BEKEND staan,* enjoy a good reputation; *'n* ~*e LIGGING,* a favourable site (situation); *'n* ~*e WIND,* a favourable wind; ~**heid,** favourableness, auspiciousness.
gun'ter, far away, in the distance; *daar* ~, yonder, over there; ~**se,** distant, far away; *agter* ~ *se berg,* behind yonder mountain.
gus, sterile, barren (cattle); dry; *sy loop* ~ *vanjaar,* she won't foal (lamb, calve) this year; ~**ooi,** sterile (barren) ewe; dry ewe, ewe not with lamb; ~**skape,** dry sheep.
gus'tang, leather punch.
guts¹, (-e), (s) gush; (w) **(ge-),** spout, gush.
guts², (s) **(-e),** gouge; (w) **(ge-),** gouge; ~**beitel,** gouge.
guttaper'tsja, gutta-percha.
gutturaal', (..rale), guttural.
guur, (-der, -ste), bleak, cold, raw, harsh, inclement (weather); ~**heid,** bleakness, inclemency.
gy'selaar, (..lare, -s), hostage; prisoner for debt, civil debtor.
gy'seling, imprisonment (for debt); *siviele* ~, (vero.), civil imprisonment.
gy'selreg, right of imprisonment for debt.

H

h, (-'s); h; *die* ~ *nie uitspreek nie,* drop one's aitches.
ha! ha! ah!
Haag¹: *Den* ~, The Hague.
haag², (hage, hae), hedge; ~**doring,** hawthorn; ~**preek,** open-air sermon; ~**prediker,** hedge priest.
haai¹, (s) **(-e),** shark; *na die* ~*e GAAN,* go down to Davy Jones' locker; *vir die* ~*e GOOI,* throw to the dogs.
haai², (b) desolate, barren; *die* ~ *vlakte,* the desolate flats.
haai³! (tw) heigh! I say! hoy!; ~ *is in die see,* hallo yourself.
haai'-hoei, (s) fuss, noise; (b) dishevelled; bushy.
haai: ~**beksleutel,** shark-jaw spanner, alligator wrench; ~**net,** shark-net; ~**tande,** shark's teeth; protruding teeth; ~*tande hê,* have buck-teeth.
haak, (s) (hake), hook, hasp; angle; barb; drag; clevis; bracket; gaff (grappling); crook (kettle); square; composing stick (printing); catch (door); hanger; chape; clench; hitch; clencher (clincher); grip; clutch; clasp; loop (saw); *AAN die* ~, on the hook; *in die* ~ *BRING,* square, arrange; true up; *IN die* ~, square, in order; true; ~ *en KRAM,* hook and staple; *daar SIT die* ~, there's the rub; *aan die* ~ *VERKOOP,* sell on the hook; (w) **(ge-),** hook, heel (rugby); gaff; crochet; catch; be delayed; *hy* ~ *AF,* he is getting married; he is firing; *iem.* ~ *met GELD,* assist someone with money; ~ *NA,* hanker after, pant for; ~**bout,** hook-bolt; ~**bus,** (h)arquebus, blunderbuss; ~**doring,** grapple-plant; hookthorn *(Acacia detinens, A. burkei);* ~**-en-steek,** umbrella thorn *(Acacia heteracantha);* ~**greep,** hook grip; ~**hou,** hook; ~**kierie,** shepherd's crook; ~**kruis** = **hakekruis;** ~**mes,** hooked knife; ~**neus,** hooked (Roman) nose; ~**patroon,** crochet pattern; ~**pen,** crochet needle.
haak'plek, obstruction, difficulty, hitch; contretemps; *daar sit die* ~, there's the snag (rub).
haaks, (-e), right-angle(d), square(d), *hulle is ALTYD* ~, they are continually at loggerheads; ~ *MAAK,* square; ~**heid,** squareness, discord; ~**kant,** face-edge.
haak: ~**skoot,** hook (stroke); ~**sleutel,** hook-spanner; claw-spanner (wrench); ~**soldeerbout,** hatched soldering-iron; ~**speld,** safety-pin; ~**spyker,** dogspike; ~**stok,** clearing rod; gaff; hoodstick; ~**stoot,** hook (golf); ~**tand,** corner tooth (in gelding); ~**tou,** hook-rope; ~**veerbout,** toggle bolt; ~**vormig, (-e),** hook-shaped, hooked; unciform, uncate, uncinate, hamuted, hamiform; ~**werk,** crochet work; ~**wurm,** hook-worm; ~**wurmsiekte,** hookworm disease; ~**yster,** dog-iron.
haal, (s) (hale), stroke, lash, dash; wale, weal; draw, puff (pipe); *met lang hale AANKOM,* approach with long strides; *met een* ~ *van die PEN,* with one stroke of the pen; (w) **(ge-),** fetch, reach, catch; dash; recover; realize (price); *hy sal nie die DORP* ~ *nie,* he will not reach the town (alive); *waar moet ek die GELD vandaan* ~*?,* where am I to get the money?; *jy moet* ~ *so wat jy KAN,* you must race for all you're worth; *ek KOM jou* ~, I am coming to fetch you; ~ *om daar te KOM,* race to get there; *LAAT* ~, send for; *die sieke sal MÔRE nie* ~ *nie,* the patient will not live through the night; *NIE by iem.* ~ *nie,* not to be a patch on someone; *die TREIN* ~, catch the train; *WAAR* ~*jy dit vandaan?,* where do you get that from?; *WEER gaan* ~, start afresh.
haal-en-betaal, cash and carry.
haam, (vero.) hames (harness).
haan, (hane), cock, rooster, chanticleer; hammer (of gun); *elke* ~ *is BAAS op sy eie ashoop,* every cock crows best on his own dunghill; *JONG* ~, cockerel; *sy* ~ *moet altyd KONING kraai,* he always wants to be cock of the walk; *elke* ~ *is KONING op sy mishoop,* every cock crows on his own dunghill; *die* ~ *KRAAI baie harder as die hen wat die eier gele het,* the cock crows louder than the hen that laid the egg; *voor die hane KRAAI,* before cockcrow; *geen* ~ *sal daarna KRAAI nie,* nobody will be the wiser; *hy is 'n OU* ~*!,* he is all there!; *die ROOI* ~, fire; *lyk soos 'n* ~ *waarvan die STERTVERE uitgepluk is,* look like a plucked chicken; ~**gekraai,** cock-crow(ing); ~**geweer,** shotgun with hammer.
haan'tjie, (-s), cockerel, cock; quarrelsome fellow; *hy HOU hom* ~, play the gallant; be a cock-sparrow; ~ *die VOORSTE,* cock of the walk; the ringleader.
Haan'tjiepik, Old Nick.
haar¹, (s) **(hare),** hair; *sy hare het te BERGE gerys,* his hair stood on end; *iets by die hare BYSLEEP,* drag something in by the hair; *iem. se hare goed DEUR- MEKAARKRAP,* give someone a dressing down; *aan die hare DEURSLEEP,* drag (pull) someone through an examination; *iem. het deur sy hare GE- GROEI,* he has lost all his hair; *dit het geen haar GESKEEL nie,* it was a close thing; *sy hare het GEWAAI,* he had the stuffing knocked out of him; *die hare het GEWAAI,* the fur flew; *GRYS hare kry van* ..., turn grey over ...; *dit het my GRYS hare gegee,* it gave me grey hairs; *soos hare op 'n HOND,* as thick as hops; *iets by die hare INSLEEP,* drag something in; discuss an irrelevant subject; *geen bang* ~ *op sy KOP nie,* very brave, afraid of nothing; *geen* ~ *op sy KOP sal gekrenk word nie,* not a hair of his head shall perish; *g'n lui* ~ *op sy KOP hê nie,* without a lazy bone in his body; *OP 'n* ~, by a hair's breadth; *OP 'n* ~ *to a hair; sy hare het ORENT gestaan,* his hair stood on end; *sy hare*

haar

is SEER, he has a hang-over; *gekrulde hare, gekrulde SINNE*, fly-away curls cover fly-away wits; curly heads are quick-tempered; *mekaar in die hare SIT*, be at loggerheads; *soveel SKULD soos hare op sy kop*, over his ears in debt; *alles op hare en SNARE sit*, turn everything topsy-turvy; leave no stone unturned; *meer SPYT hê as hare op sy kop*, be bitterly remorseful; *hare op die TANDE hê*, have plenty of grit; *mekaar in die hare VLIEG*, come to blows; *die hare laat WAAI*, make the sparks fly; *WILDE hare*, wild oats; *geen ~ WYSER nie*, none the wiser.

haar², (b) right off; *~ om*, to the right, clockwise.

haar³, (vw) her; *DIT is hare*, it is hers; *dit is ~ HOED*, it is her hat.

haar'-af, skerm, hairless, depilated; *iets nie help ~ MAAK nie*, to have no effect; *dit kan niks ~ MAAK nie*, it is of no use.

haar'agter, right hind; *~ dier*, off-wheeler.

haar: *~ agtig*, (-e), hairy, hair-like, hirsute, piliform, crinite, crinose; *~ band*, chaplet, fillet, snood, hair-ribbon, alice band; *~ barsie*, chink, hair-crack; *~ binder*, bandeau; *~ boetehemp*, cilice; *~ bol*, ball of hair (in stomach of ruminating animals); *~ borsel*, hairbrush; *~ bos*, shock (bush) of hair; *~ bossie*, verricule; *~ breedte*, hairbreadth; *~ buis*, capillary tube; *~ buiswerking*, capillarity.

haard, (-e), hearth, fireside; focus (of disease); source, nidus; *eie ~ is goud waard*, there is no place like home; *~ kleedjie*, hearth-rug; *~ kool*, cobble coal; *~ mat*, hearth-rug.

haar'dos, wealth of hair; fleece.

haard'plaat, hob, hearth-plate.

haar'drag, hair-style.

haard'rand, fender.

haar'droër, hair drier.

haard: *~ skerm*, fire-screen; fender; *~ stede*, (-s), ..stee, (..steë), hearth, fireside; *~ steen*, hearthstone; *~ vuur*, fire on hearth, ingle; *~ yster*, andiron; fender.

haar: *~ fyn*, as fine as hair; in detail; subtle; minute; *iets ~ fyn beskryf*, describe something minutely (in detail); *~ gaas*, pouffe; *~ ghries*, hair-cream; *~ golwer*, hair waver; *~ golwing*, hair-waving; *~ gom*, hair-fixing cream; fixature; *~ grens*, hair-line; *~ groei*, growth of hair; *~ groeimiddel*, hair-restorer; *~ kam*, comb.

haar'kant, off-side; right side.

haar': *~ kapper*, hairdresser, barber; *~ kappery*, hairdressing (saloon); *~ kapsel*, hair-do; *~ kapster*, (-s), female hairdresser; *~ kartelmiddel*, wave-setting lotion; *~ kies*, millerite; *~ kleed*, cilice; *~ klein*, minute; *~ klem*, hairclip; *~ kleursel*, hair dye; *~ kloof*, *~ klowe*, (ge-), split hairs, quibble; *~ klower*, hypercritic, hairsplitter; casuist; quibbler; *~ klowery*, cavilling, hairsplitting, hypercriticism; micrology; pettifogging; pettigoggery; casuistry; quiddity; *~ knip*, (hair) slide; hair clip; *~ knipper*, pair of hair-clippers; hair-dresser, barber; *~ knoop*, hair-knot; *~ krul*, quiff, curl (of hair); *~ kruller*, hair curler; *~ kunde*, trichology; *~ kun'dig*, (-e), trichological; *~ kun'dige*, (-s), trichologist; *~ laat*, (ge-), get into trouble, be rebuked.

haarlemen'sis, haar'lemmerolie, haarlemensis, Dutch drops.

haar: *~ lint*, hair-ribbon; *~ lok*, lock of hair; *~ loos*, (..lose), hairless, bare; *~ lym*, fixative hair-cream; *~ lyn*, sighting vane (of compass); *~ massa*, chignon; *~ middel*, hair-restorer; *~ naald*, hairpin.

haar'naasagter, second right hind (ox).

haar'naasvoor, second right front.

haar: *~ net*, hair-net; *~ olie*, hair-oil, pomade.

haar: *~ omhoo*, pull (to leg); slice (golf); *~ omslaan*, (-ge-), pull (cricket).

haar: -op-ag(t), eight on the right (fourth yoke); *~-op-ses*, sixth on the right (third yoke); *~ os*, ox on the right.

haar: *~ passer*, hair dividers; *~ pluis*, papus; *~ poeier*, hair-powder; *~ pyn*, hang-over, hot coppers (morning-after-the-night-before), headache; *~ sak-*

haglik

kie, hair-tidy; hair sac; *~ salf*, pomade; *~ sel*, hair-cell.

haar: *~ self*, herself; *~ s'gelyke*, her equal.

haar: *~ siekte*, disease of the hair; *~ skeerder*, (barber-)spider (species of *Solifuga*); *~ skikkertjie*, *~ skuifie*, hair-slide; *~ sneller*, hair trigger; *~ snit*, hair style; *~ snyer*, hairdresser; coiffeur; friseur; *~ speld*, hairpin; bobby-pin; bodkin; *~ spoelmiddel*, hair rinse; *~ string*, plait; *~ sproeier*, hair spray; *~ styl*, hair style; *~ swiep*, fall; *~ tang*, pair of tweezers; curling tongs; *~ tjie*, (-s), tiny hair; *~ tooisel*, head-dress; *~ vat*, capillary vessel; *~ vatverwyding*, capilarectasia; *~ vatwerking*, capillarity; *~ veer*, filoplume; *~ verf*, hair-dye; *~ verwyderingsmiddel*, hair-remover, depilatory; *~ vlegsel*, plait; pigtail; braid.

haar'voor, right front; *~ dier*, off-leader.

haar: *~ vormig*, capilliform; *~ was*, *~ wasmiddel*, hair-wash, shampoo; *~ waspoeier*, shampoo powder; *~ water*, hair-wash; *~ wortel*, root of a hair; hair-root; *~ wrong*, knot of hair, bun; *~ wurm*, wireworm (in sheep) (*Haemonchus contortus*).

haas¹, (s) (**hase**), hare; *so bang soos 'n ~ vir 'n HOND*, be mortally afraid; *SLAAP soos 'n ~*, be a light sleeper; be on the alert.

haas², (ong., Ndl.), (s), fillet.

haas³, (s) haste, hurry; speed; *daar is geen ~ BY nie*, there is no great hurry; *IN ~*, haste; *hoe meer ~*, *hoe minder SPOED*, more haste, less speed; (w) (ge-), hurry, make haste; *ek HOEF my nie te ~ nie*, I can take my time; *~ jou LANGSAAM*, make haste slowly; *jy MOET jou ~*, you must hurry up.

haas⁴, (bw) almost, nearly; before long; *hulle moet ~ KOM*, they ought to be here soon; *~ elke MAAND*, almost every month; *~ WORD dit weer winter*, soon it will be winter again.

haas: *~ bek*, hare-lip; with a tooth (teeth) missing; *~ gras*, hare's grass (*Danthoria purpurea*); *~ hael*, fairly fine shot.

haas'hak, curb (horse).

haas: *~ lip*, hare-lip; *~ oog*, lagothalmos; *~ oor*, *Stapelia grandiflora*; *~ pootjie*, hare's foot; *Trifolium arvense*; *~ pastei*, hare pie.

haas'tig, (-e), hasty, hurried in a hurry; cursory, fleet; hot-foot; expeditious, rash; quick; (bw), hastily; *~ heid*, hastiness, hurry, precipitation; cursoriness; *van ~ heid kom lastigheid*, more haste, less speed.

haat, (s) hatred; malice, grudge; rancour; *~ teen iem. hê*, have hatred for (towards) someone; hate someone; (w) (ge-), hate, detest, abominate.

haatdra'end, (-e), revengeful, resentful, hateful, rancorous, malicious, vindictive; *~ heid*, revengefulness, malice, rancour, vindictiveness.

haat'lik, (-e), hateful, detestable, malicious; abhorrent; odious; obnoxious; *~ heid*, malice, spite, hatefulness; odiousness; obnoxiousness; (..hede), gibe; objectionable thing; spiteful remark.

haatwek'kend, (-e), invidious.

habilita'sie, (-s), habilitation.

habiliteer', (ge-), habilitate.

ha'bitat, (-s), habitat.

habitué', (-s), habitué, regular customer.

had, (ong., vero., gew.) verl. tyd van hê.

haché, hashed meat, hash.

Ha'des, Hades.

ha'dida, (-s), hadeda (*Hagedashia hagedash*).

had'jie, (-s), hadji.

ha'el, (s) hail; shot; *iem. skiet met ~*, make wild accusations; (w) (ge-), hail; *~ boor*, shot drill; *~ bui*, shower of hail, hailstorm; *~ geweer*, shot gun; *~ korrel*, grain of shot; pellet; small hailstone; *~ loop*, shot-barrel (of combination gun); *~ patroon*, shot-cartridge; *~ skade*, damage caused by hail; *~ snoer*, chalaza; *~ steen*, hailstone; *~ storm*, hailstorm; *~ streek*, hail-belt; *~ wit*, snow-white.

Ha'genaar, (-s), inhabitant of The Hague.

hagiograaf', (..grawe), hagiographer.

hagiografie', hagiography; ..gra'fies, (-e), hagiographic(al).

hag'lik, (-e), critical, risky, perilous, precarious; *~ heid*, critical state, precariousness.

(h)ai'kôna, no, not at all.
Haï'ti, Haiti; ~ **aan'**, **(Haïtiane)**, Haitian; ~ **aans'**, **-e**, Haitian.
hait's(a), hallo! I say!
hak¹, (s) **(-ke)**, heel, hock (of animals); bullet (of horse); *nie by iem. se ~ ke KOM nie*, be put in the shade by someone; not to be a match for another; *die ~ ke LIG*, run away, take to one's heels; *op iem. se ~ ke SIT*, follow closely on another's heels; *van die ~ op die TAK spring*, jump from one subject to another.
hak², (w) **(ge-)**, cut; mince (meat).
hak'been, calcaneum.
hak'bord, chopping-board; dulcimer.
ha'ke-kruk'ke, boy's leg-hooking game; *dit gaan maar ~*, progress is slow.
ha'kekruis, swastika; fylfot.
hak'-en-tak, quarrelsome, fault-finding; ~ *LEWE*, live like cat and dog; ~ *WEES*, be at loggerheads.
ha'ker, **(-s)**, hooker (rugby).
ha'kerig, **(-e)**, having hooks, hooked; inclined to stick; cantankerous.
ha'kery, discord, disagreement.
hak'gal, soft curb (horse); ~ *en vlotgal*, thorough-pin.
hak'gewrig, **(-te)**, hock (of horse); tarsal joint.
hak: ~ **hamer**, creasing hammer; ~ **hou**, cut (in cricket); ~ **hout**, coppice, copse.
ha'kie, **(-s)**, bracket; little hook; ~ *s en OGIES*, hooks and eyes; *TUSSEN ~ s*, in parenthesis, parenthetically, by the way, incidentally.
ha'kiesdoring = **haakdoring**.
ha'kiesdraad, barbed wire; horsemackerel, masbanker; home-distilled brandy.
hak'kejag, hot pursuit.
hak'kel, **(ge-)**, stammer, stutter; hum and ha; ~ **aar**, (-s, ..are), stammerer; ~ **ary'**, ~ **ry**, stammering; ~ **bout**, rag-bolt; ~ **rig**, **(-e)**, stammering, stuttering.
hak: ~ **mes**, chopping (hacking) knife, cleaver; ~ **ploeg**, clearing plough; ~ **saag**, hack-saw; ~ **sel**, chopped feed; liver-dish, prepared liver.
hak'sening, Achilles' tendon; hamstring.
hak'skeen, heel; *die ~ LIG (laat klap)*, run away, show a clean pair of heels; take to one's heels; *sy ..skene word al ROOI*, he is beginning to take an interest in girls; *op iem. se ..skene TRAP*, follow someone closely; tread upon someone's heels; ~ **byter**, yapper; backbiter; ~ **pleister**, blueback; ~ **sening**, Achilles' tendon, hough, hock.
hak'stuk, counter (shoe), heel-piece (tap).
hak'vleis, chopped (minced) meat.
hal, **(-le)**, hall.
ha'ler, **(-s)**, pullwire (signal); fetcher.
half, **(halwe)**, half; semi-; *halwe BAKSTEEN*, half bat; ~ *ult ARMOEDE*, partly from poverty; ~ *en ~ BEGRYP*, understand partially; ~ *en ~ DEEL*, go halves; *SO ~ en ~*, nearly, not quite; ~ *en ~ op iets VOORBEREI wees*, be more or less prepared for something; ~ *SALARIS*, half-pay; *daar SLAAN dit ~*, the half-hour is striking; *ek het nou ~ SPYT daaroor*, I am rather sorry about it now; *'n halwe TOON*, a semitone; ~ **aam'**, half aum; ~ **aamp'ie**, pot-belly; *'n kêrel met 'n ~ aampie*, a fellow with a pot-belly (paunch); ~ **aap**, half-ape, lemur; ~ **ag(t)'**, half past seven; ~ **amptelik**; semi-official; ~ **bakko**, half cooked, half baked; not thorough (plan); ~ **bevangenheid**, laminitis; ~ **bewus**, semi-consious; ~ **blind**, half-blind; ~ **blindheid**, hemianopsia; ~ **bloed**, **(-e)**, half-caste; ~ **bloedrei= siesperd**, cocktail (horse); ~ **botteltjie**, half bottle, nip; ~ **broekie**, pantie; ~ **broer**, half-brother; ~ **by**, mid-on (cricket); ~ **dag**, half-day; ~ **dagkursus**, half-day course; ~ **dek**, quarterdeck; ~ **deursigtig**, **(-e)**, semi-transparent; ~ **donker**, semi-dark(ness); ~ **dood**, half-dead, all but dead; ~ **dosyn**, half-dozen; ~ **drie**, half past two; ~ **dronk**, half-drunk, tipsy; ~ **duim**, half-inch; ~ **duimspyp**, half-inch pipe; ~ **edel**, semi-precious; ~ **een**, half past twelve; ~ **eeufees**, jubilee; ~ **eiervormig**, **(-e)**, hypidiomor= phic; ~ **eind(ronde)**, semifinal; ~ **elf**, half past ten; ~ **-en- ~**, half-and-half; shandy; ~ **ernstig**, **(-e)**, se=

riocomic; ~ **fabrikaat**, semi-manufactured article; ~ **gaar**, half-baked, half-done; underdone (meat); slack-baked; dotty, not all there; ~ *gaar KOOK*, parboil; ~ *gaar MAAK*, precook; ~ **gebak**, **(-e)**, half-baked (lit.), raw; ~ **gebied**, half (of football-field), ~ **geleerd**, **(-e)**, half-taught, semi-educated; ~ **geleerde**, **(-s)**, half-educated person, sciolist; ~ **geleier**, semiconductor; ~ **geleiermateriaal**, semi-conducting material; ~ **gemonteer**, semi-mounted; ~ **geskoold** **(-e)**, semi-skilled; ~ **god**, semi-god; hero; ~ **har'tig**, **(-e)**, half-hearted, luke-warm; ~ **hartig'heid**, half-heartedness; ~ **heid**, indecision, irresoluteness; ~ **ie**, **(-s)**, half (cup, glass); nip; ~ **jaar**, half year; semester; ~ **jaarliks**, **(-e)**, half-yearly; ~ **klaar**, half-finished (done); ~ **klik**, sam= my (golf); ~ **klinker**, semivowel; ~ **kolskyf**, tin-hat target; ~ **koord**, albacore; ~ **korrel**, shot; ~ **kristal= lyn**, hemicrystalline; ~ **kroon**, half-a-crown; ~ **langbeen**, half-treble (crochet); ~ **leer**, half-bound; half leather; ~ **linne**, half cloth; ~ **lyf**, half-length; ~ **maan**, crescent, semicircle; lune (math.); *met 'n ~ maan kom*, not to be straightforward; beat about the bush; ~ **maandeliks**, **(-e)**, half-monthly, fortnightly; ~ **maanlens**, meniscus; ~ **maantjie**, **(-s)**, half moon; crescent-shaped earmark (of cattle, sheep, etc.); ~ **maanvenster**, lunette; ~ **maanvor= mig**, **(-e)**, lunate; semi-lunar; ~ **marathon**, half mar= athon; ~ **mas**, half-mast; between long and short; ~ **masbroek**, three-quarter trousers; jeans; ~ **mat**, semi-matt; ~ **mens**, semi-human; a succulent *(Pa= chypodium namaquanum)*; ~ **mes**, paring knife; ~ **myl**, half mile; ~ **mylloper**, half-miler; ~ **naat'jie**, **(-s)**, half-caste; mulatto; bastard; ~ **ne'ge**, half past eight; ~ **-om-half**, half and half, fifty-fifty; from equal quantities; ~ **onderrok**, underskirt, half-pet= ticoat; ~ **-outomaties**, **(-e)**, semi-automatic; ~ **pad**, half-way; partially; ~ **pennie**, halfpenny; ~ **prys**, half-price; ~ **rok**, skirt; ~ **rond**, (s) hemisphere; apse; (b) **(-e)**, half round, hemispherical; ~ **ronde= vyl**, half-round file.
half'rou¹, half-mourning.
half'rou², underdone.
half: ~ **ryp**, underripe; ~ **saaldak**, single-pitch roof; ~ **salaris**, half-pay; ~ **sewe**, half past six; ~ **sirkel**, semicircle; ~ **skaduwee**, penumbra; ~ **slag**, (s) half-blood, half-breed; (b) of medium size; ~ **slag'tig**, **(-e)**, amphibious; half-hearted, diffident; ~ **slag= tigheid**, amphibiousness; half-heartedness, diffi= dence; ~ **slyt**, second-hand, partly worn; ~ **soet**, semi-sweet (wine); ~ **soldy**, half-pay; ~ **sool**, (s) half sole; (w) **(ge-)**, half-sole; recap (tire); ~ **stede= lik**, **(-e)**, semi-urban; ~ **steen**, half-brick; ~ **stok**, half-mast; ~ **suster**, half-sister; ~ **sy**, half-silk; ~ **te**, (-s), half; ~ **tint**, half tint; ~ **twee**, half past one; ~ **ty**, half tide; ~ **uur**, half an hour; ~ **vaste**, mid-lent; ~ **verhewe**, bas-relief; ~ **vers**, hemistich; ~ **vloeibaar**, (..bare), semi-fluid; ~ **vrystaande**, semi-detached; ~ **vokaal**, semi-vowel; ~ **vol**, half-full; ~ **was**, half-grown, medium; ~ **waskuikens**, started chicks; ~ **wasrivier**, adolescent river; ~ **weekliks** **(-e)**, bi-weekly, ~ **weg**, mid-off (cricket); half-way; ~ **wild**, half-wild; ~ **woestyn**, semi-desert; ~ **wolstof**, linsey-woolsey; ~ **wys**, half-witted; ~ **yster**, mid-iron.
hallelu'ja, **(-s)**, hallelujah; ~ **boek**, hymn (song) book.
hal'lo, **(-'s)**, hallo, hullo.
hallusina'sie, **(-s)**, hallucination.
hallusinato'ries, **(-e)**, hallucinatory.
hallusineer', **(ge-)**, hallucinate.
halm, **(-e**, **-s)**, blade, stalk, ha(u)lm
halm'pie, **(-s)**, small blade, stalk.
ha'lo, **(-'s)**, halo.
halofiet', **(-e)**, halophyte.
halogeen', (..gene), halogen.
hals, **(-e)**, neck; throat; journal (in mines); *jou iets op die ~ HAAL*, bring something upon one's own head; *iem. om die ~ HANG*, make a nuisance of oneself; *met ~ en MAG*, with might and main; *'n ROK met 'n lae ~*, a low-cut dress; *iem. iets op die ~ SKUIWE*, saddle someone with something; *iem. om die ~ VAL*, fall on someone's neck; ~ **aar**, jugular vein; ~ **band**, collar; neckband; collet;

~**bout,** throat bolt; ~**brekend, (-e),** breakneck; ~**doek,** neckcloth; neckerchief; ~**ketting,** necklace, neck chain; ~**klier,** jugular gland; ~**knopie,** stud; ~**kraag,** collar, frill, ruff; gorget (armour); fraise; ~**lengte,** neck length; neck (in racing); ~**lyn,** neckline; ~**maat,** neck measurement; ~**misdaad,** capital crime; ~**oorkop,** head over heels; hurry-scurry; slap-dash; flurried; precipitate; helter-skelter; harum-scarum; ~**opening,** neck opening; ~**reg,** power of life and death; ~**regter,** criminal judge; ~**riem,** neckband; ~**sieraad,** neck ornament; ~**slagaar,** carotid; ~**snoer,** necklace, gorget.

halsio'nies, (-e), calm, still.

halsstar'rig, (-e), obstinate, stiff-necked, headstrong, pertinacious, stubborn, intractable; ~**heid,** obstinacy, stubbornness, intractability, pertinacity.

hals: ~**straf,** capital punishment; ~**stuk,** neck-piece, neck (of gown); collar (of stay); ~**tou,** neck-rope.

hals'werwel, cervical vertebra; *eerste* ~, atlas.

halt! halt! stop! ~ *HOU,* come to a standstill; ~ *MAAK,* stop; ~ *ROEP,* call a halt.

hal'te, (-s), halt, stop, halting-place; siding.

hal'ter, (s) (-s), halter; *iem. die* ~ *AANSIT,* bridle someone; *die* ~ *AFHAAL,* turn loose (adrift); *die* ~ *is van die KOP,* he is free to do as he pleases; *sy* ~ *is LOS,* he has a free rein; (w) (ge-), halter; ~**ketting,** halter chain; ~**riem,** halter strap.

halveer', (ge-), halve, divide into halves, bisect; ~**der, (-s),** bisector; ~**lyn,** bisector; ..**ve'ring,** halving, bisection.

hal'we, (-s), half; ~ *EFFEKKANON,* half-ball cannon; ~ *EFFEKSTOOT,* half-ball shot; *TWEE* ~ *s maak 'n hele,* two halves make a whole; ~ **maan,** *see* **halfmaan.**

hal'werweë, half-way.

ham, (-me), ham.

ham'burger, (-s), hamburger.

ha'mel, (-s), wether, hamel; ~**boud,** leg of mutton; ~**gras,** *Eragrostis denudata;* ~**stertgeitjie,** variety of lizard *(Pachydactylus).*

ha'mer (s) (-s), hammer, mallet; striker (firearms); malleus (ear); *tussen* ~ *en AAMBEELD,* between the devil and the deep sea; *vir iem. die* ~ *IN wees,* be very angry with someone; *onder die* ~ *KOM,* be sold by auction; (w) (ge-), hammer; *iem.* ~, give someone a severe hiding; *OP iets* ~, harp on something; ~**baar, (..bare),** malleable; ~**boor,** jackhammer; pneumatic drill; ~**bout,** hookbolt; key bolt; ~**byl,** axe-hammer; ~**gooi,** throwing the hammer; ~**haai,** hammerheaded shark; ~**kop,** hamerkop *(Scopus umbretta);* ~**meule,** hammer-mill; ~**pik,** poll pick; ~**slag,** blow of a hammer; clinker; *op die* ~ *slag,* at the stroke of; ~**steel,** handle of a hammer; ~**vormig, (-e),** hammer-shaped.

Hamiet', (-e), Hamite.

Hami'ties, Hamitic.

ham'kewer copra beetle *(Necrobia rufipes).*

ham'ster, (-s), hamster.

hand, (-e), hand; ~ *AAN* ~, hand in hand; *AAN die* ~ *van,* at the hand of; *iem. se* ~ *e is AFGEKAP,* his hands are tied; *die* ~ *van iem. AFHOU,* leave someone alone; *liewer jou* ~ *AFKAP as om iets te doen,* refuse to have a hand in something; *sy* ~ *e van iem. AFTREK,* give someone no further assistance; *my* ~ *e kan AFVAL as dit nie so is nie,* may my hands drop off if it isn't the truth; *jou* ~ *e van iem. AFWAS,* wash one's hands of someone; ~ *in die AS slaan,* oust someone; *iem. die* ~ *BIED,* offer someone a hand; *iem. se* ~ *e BIND,* tie someone's hands; *in die* ~ *BLAAS,* spit on one's hands; *die* ~ *in eie BOESEM steek,* search one's heart; *BY die* ~ *wees,* be at hand; ~ *BYSIT,* lend a hand; *hy het 'n* ~ *DAARIN gehad,* he had a finger in the pie; he was at the bottom of it; *DOEN wat jou* ~ *vind om te doen,* do whatever comes to hand; *iets aan die* ~ *DOEN,* make a suggestion; *so DONKER dat jy jou* ~ *nie voor jou kan sien nie,* so dark that one cannot see one's hand before one's face; *iem. op die* ~ *e DRA,* make much of someone; *iets met EEN* ~ *kan doen,* do something with one hand tied; *uit die EERSTE* ~, at first hand; *uit iem. se* ~ *EET,* eat from someone's hand; *dit GAAN deur baie* ~ *e,* it passes through many hands; ~ *aan* ~ *GAAN,* go hand in hand; *van* ~ *tot* ~ *GAAN,* pass from hand to hand; *sy* ~ *e is GEBONDE,* his hands are tied; *sy* ~ *e GEBRUIK,* use one's hands; *iets aan die* ~ *GEE (doen),* suggest something; hint at something; *aan die* ~ *van sekere GEGEWENS,* on the basis of certain data; *my* ~ *e het eintlik gejeuk,* my fingers itched; ~ *e vol GELD,* fistfuls of money; *in die* ~ *e v.d. GEREG gee,* hand over to the police; *'n GESONDE* ~ *hê,* have green fingers; *met GEVOUDE* ~ *e sit,* sit with one's hands folded; *iets uit 'n GOEIE* ~ *verneem,* learn from a reliable source; *die* ~ *e slap laat HANG,* remain inactive; *met die* ~ *in die HARE sit,* be at one's wits' end; *met die* ~ *op die HART,* truly, sincerely; *iets by die* ~ *HÊ,* have something at hand (ready); *'n* ~ *in iets HÊ,* have a hand in something; *'n HELPENDE* ~ *bied,* offer a helping hand; *net so min as wat jy met jou* ~ *aan die HEMEL kan raak,* as impossible as to touch the sky with one's hand; *met die* ~ *aan die HEMEL probeer raak,* reach for the sky; *iem. die* ~ *bo die HOOF hou,* hold a protecting hand over someone; *iets agter die* ~ *HOU,* hold something back; *die* ~ *HOU aan,* look after, take care of; *die* ~ *e INEENSLAAN,* clap one's hands together in amazement; *sy* ~ *e JEUK,* his fingers are itching; *so KAAL soos iem. se* ~, as bare as one's hand; *in die* ~ *KLAP,* clap hands; *in ander* ~ *e KOM,* change hands; *in die* ~ *e KOM,* be caught; *die* ~ *oor iem. se KOP hou,* protect someone; ~ *e KORTKOM,* be short of hands; *KOUE* ~ *e, warm liefde,* cold hands, warm heart; *op jou* ~ *e KRY,* win someone over; *in die* ~ *e KRY,* get hold of; gain control of; *die LAASTE* ~ *lê aan,* put the finishing touches to; *agter die* ~ *LAG,* laugh up one's sleeve; *dit LÊ voor die* ~, it is obvious; it goes without saying; *die* ~ *op iem. LÊ,* lay hands on someone; *die* ~ *op iets LÊ,* lay one's hands on something; *dit LÊ voor die* ~, it is self-evident; *met LEË* ~ *e,* empty-handed; *die* ~ *aan eie LEWE slaan,* lay violent hands on himself, commit suicide; ~ *e aan die LYF hê,* have a useful pair of hands; *met die* ~ *e oor die MAAG gevou,* with one's hands folded in one's lap; *die* ~ *op die MOND lê,* place one's hand over one's mouth; *met* ~ *en MOND belowe,* promise faithfully; *van die* ~ *na die MOND val die pap op die grond,* there's many a slip betwixt the cup and the lip; *v.d.* ~ *na die MOND lewe,* live from hand to mouth; *die* ~ *e uit die MOU steek,* put one's shoulder to the wheel; *ter* ~ *NEEM,* take in hand; *iem. onder* ~ *e NEEM,* take someone to task; *iets by die (ter)* ~ *NEEM,* take up something; ~ *om die NEK sit,* have one's arm around another's neck; *geen* ~ *voor jou OË kan sien nie,* be unable to see one's hand before one's face; *sy* ~ *e nie vir iets OMDRAAI nie,* not to lift a finger; *ONDER die* ~, in an underhand manner; *'n OOP* ~ *hê,* be openhanded; *OP* ~ *e wees,* be near at hand; *sy* ~ *e daaroor OPSTEEK,* take an oath on something; *ek is so OUD soos my* ~ *e, maar nie so oud soos my tande nie,* my age is my own business; *geen* ~ *op PAPIER sit,* don't commit your hand to paper; *die* ~ *aan die PLOEG slaan,* put one's shoulder to the wheel; *uit die* ~ *RAAK,* get out of hand; *die REDDENDE* ~ *bied,* offer someome a helping hand; *iem. die* ~ *REIK,* lend a hand; *die* ~ *e SAAMSLAAN,* stand aghast; *jou* ~ *uit iem. se SAK hou,* want nothing from another; *sy* ~ *in sy eie SAK steek,* foot the bill; dip into one's own pocket; *die* ~ *in die SAK steek,* bear the expense oneself; dip into one's pocket; ~ *e in die SAK staan,* stand about with one's hands in one's pockets; *van die* ~ *SIT (doen),* dispose of; *met die* ~ *e oormekaar SIT,* sit with folded hands; *op jou* ~ *e SIT en kyk,* twiddle one's thumbs; *jou* ~ *e nie aan iets SIT nie,* keep one's hands off something; *haar* ~ *SKENK aan iem.,* give her hand in marriage; *SKOON* ~ *e hê,* have clean hands; *die* ~ *e in die SKOOT lê,* lay one's hands in one's lap; *met die* ~ *e in die SKOOT sit,* be sitting with one's hands in one's lap; *'n mooi* ~ *SKRYF,* write a fair hand; *die* ~ *e in mekaar SLAAN,* clap one's hands together in amazement; ~ *e aan iem. SLAAN*, lay violent hands on someone; *die ~ e SLAP laat hang*, throw up one's hands in despair; *die ~ e SMEER*, grease someone's hands; *'n los ~ SPEEL*, establish a hand (at cards); *iem. iets in die ~ SPEEL*, play into someone's hands; *'n ~ in die SPEL hê*, have a hand in something; *in die ~ e SPOEG*, spit on one's hands; *ter ~ STEL*, hand over; *iem. se ~ e STERK*, strengthen someone's hands; *iem. iets in die ~ STOP*, thrust something in someone's hands; *sy ~ is SWAAR*, he has a heavy hand; he yields much influence; *SWAAR op die ~ wees*, be heavy on the hand; *v.d. ~ na die TAND val die pap in die sand*, there is many a slip 'twixt the cup and the lip; *van die ~ in die TAND*, from hand to mouth; *met ~ en TAND verdedig*, defend tooth and nail; *'n TOE ~ hê*, be close-fisted; *~ oor ~ TOENEEM*, spread riotously, progress hand over fist; *hou jou ~ e TUIS*, hands off; *as TWEE ~ e mekaar was, word altwee skoon*, one good turn deserves another; *net maar TWEE ~ e hê*, have only one pair of hands; *uit die TWEEDE ~*, secondhand; *UIT die eerste ~*, at first hand; *geen ~ UITSTEEK nie*, not to lift a finger; *in iem. se ~ e VAL*, fall into someone's hands; *in VREEMDE ~ e val*, fall into the hands of strangers; *aan die ~ VAN*, according to; from; *iem. se ~ VASHOU*, hold someone's hand; encourage someone; *met VASTE ~*, with a firm hand; *VAT my ~!*, here's my hand!; *jou ~ e VERBRAND*, burn one's fingers; *sy ~ e staan vir niks VERKEERD nie*, he is good at everything; *uit die ~ VERKOOP*, sell by private treaty, sell out of hand; *soos 'n ~ vol VLIEË*, like a pinch of snuff; *op die ~ e en VOETE*, on all fours; *aan ~ e en VOETE gebind wees*, be bound hand and feet; *die ~ e VOL hê*, have one's hands full; *aan die ~ van VOORBEELDE*, at the hand of examples; *'n meisie om haar ~ VRA*, ask for a girl's hand in marriage; *in VREEMDE ~ e val*, fall into the hands of strangers; *die ~ e VRY hê*, have a free hand; *jou ~ e VRYWE*, rub one's hands; *jou ~ e nie aan iets VUIL wil maak nie*, refuse to dirty one's hands; *as jy nie ~ e het, kan jy nie VUIS maak nie*, one cannot make an omelet without breaking eggs; *met 'n WARM ~ gee*, bequeath something during one's lifetime; *sy ~ e in onskuld WAS*, wash one's hands of something; *as die een ~ die ander WAS, word albei skoon*, one good turn deserves another; *sy steek nie haar ~ e in koue WATER nie*, she never has to lift a finger; *bang wees om jou ~ e in koue WATER te verbrand*, be afraid of burning one's fingers; *hy die ~ WEES, bo at hand; iets in die ~ WERK*, promote something; *baie ~ e maak ligte WERK*, many hands make light work; *van die ~ WYS*, turn down.

hand-: hand-(operated), hand-(driven).
hand: ~ **aambeeld**, stake; ~ **aansetting**, handfeed; ~ **aansitter**, hand-starter; ~ **afdruk**, palm print; ~ **badsproeier**, telephone shower; ~ **bal**, handball (game); ~ **balsem**, hand-cream; ~ **bedieningskanon**, hand-worked gun; ~ **beweging**, gesture, motion of the hand; ~ **boeie**, handcuffs; manacles; ~ **boek**, manual, hand-book, textbook; ~ **boog**, hand-bow; crossbow; ~ **boom**, handspike; ~ **boor**, hand-drill; gimlet; ~ **boortjie**, cuff; ~ **borsel**, bannister-brush; ~ **breed(te)**, hand's breadth; ~ **byl**, chopper, hatchet; ~ **da'dig, (-e)**, instrumental; implicated; ~ **doek**, towel; ~ **doeklinne**, huckaback; crash; ~ **doekrak**, towel-horse (roller); ~ **doekroller**, towel-rack (-rail); ~ **doekstof**, towelling; ~ **druk**, handshake, handclasp, grip.
hand'dearbeid, manual labour; handicraft, handiwork, hand-work.
hand'el, (s) trade, commerce, business, traffic; proceed; *in die ~ BRING*, put on the market; *~ DRYF (drywe)*, carry on a trade; trade; *in die ~ GAAN*, go into business; *NIE in die ~ nie*, not supplied to the trade; *~ en WANDEL*, conduct in life; **(w) (ge-), act**; deal, trade, carry on business; *die BOEK ~ oor*, the book deals with (treats of); *~ uit PLIGSGEVOEL*, act from a sense of duty; *~ met 'n SAAK*, dispose of a matter; *~ in STRYD met*, contravene; *by 'n WINKEL ~*, deal at a shop; ~ **aar, (-s)**, merchant, dealer, trader; ~ **baar, (..bare)**, tractable, manageable, docile, ductile; pliant, flexible; ~ **baarheid**, tractability, docility, ductility; manageability; pliancy; flexibility.
han'deldrywe, trading; ~ **nd, (-e)**, commercial; trading; mercantile.
han'delend: ~ *optree*, take action.
han'deling, (-e), action, act, conduct, handling; proceeding; transaction; *H~e van die APOSTELS*, Acts of the Apostles; *~ onder LEWENDES*, act inter vivos; *EENHEID van ~*, unity of action (in drama); ~ **bevoeg**, capable of contracting; ~ **bevoegdheid**, contractual capacity.
han'delsaak, business concern, commercial matter.
han'dels: ~ **aangeleentheid**, business matter; ~ **aardrykskunde**, commercial geography; ~ **adresboek**, commercial directory; ~ **afslag**, trade allowance; ~ **agent**, commercial agent; ~ **agentskap**, commercial agency; ~ **artikel**, commodity, article of commerce; ~ **attaché**, commercial attaché; ~ **balans**, trade balance, balance of trade; ~ **bank**, commercial bank; ~ **bedryf**, branch of trade; ~ **belang**, commercial interest; ~ **berig**, commercial news; market report; ~ **betrekking**, commercial relation (connection); ~ **blad**, trade journal; ~ **carrière**, business career; ~ **dag**, trading day; ~ **drukker**, job printer; ~ **drukwerk**, jobbing, job printing; ~ **ekonomie**, commercial economy.
han'delsekretaris, commercial secretary.
han'delsender, commercial transmission.
han'dels-Engels, commercial English.
han'delsentrum, (..tra, -s), entrepôt.
han'dels: ~ **firma**, trading house (firm); ~ **gebied**, domain of trade; *op ~ gebied*, in business; ~ **gebruik**, commercial custom, trade usage; ~ **gees**, commercial spirit; mercantilism; commercialism; ~ **gewoonte** *see* **handelsgebruik**; ~ **hawe**, shipping (trading) port; ~ **hoogty**, boom; ~ **huis**, commercial house, business firm (establishment).
han'delsink, spilter.
han'delskeepvaart, mercantile marine.
han'del: ~ **skip**, merchantman, trading vessel, trader; ~ **skool** commercial school, business college.
han'dels: ~ **korrespondensie**, business correspondence; ~ **korting**, trade discount; ~ **kringe**, commercial circles; ~ **krisis**, commercial crisis; ~ **kuns**, commercial art; ~ **kunstenaar**, commercial artist; ~ **kwessie**, business matter.
han'delslapte, (trade) depression, recession.
han'dels: ~ **lugvaart**, commercial aviation; ~ **maatskappy**, trading company; ~ **merk**, trade mark; ~ **monopolie**, trade monopoly; ~ **naam**, trade name; ~ **onderneming**, commercial enterprise; ~ **onderwys**, commercial education (training); ~ **onderwyser**, commercial teacher; ~ **ooreenkoms**, commercial agreement; ~ **oorlog**, trade-war; merchant warfare; ~ **perseel**, trading site; ~ **plek**, emporium; ~ **politiek**, commercial policy; ~ **pos**, trading post; ~ **prys**, trade-price; ~ **rabat**, trade discount; ~ **reg**, commercial (mercantile) law; ~ **reisiger**, commercial traveller; bagman; ~ **rekene**, ~ **rekenkunde**, commercial arithmetic; ~ **roete**, trade route.
han'delstad, commercial town, trading centre.
han'dels: ~ **tak**, line (branch) of business; ~ **tarief**, commercial tariff.
han'delstatistiek, trade statistics (returns).
han'delstand, merchant class.
han'delstekene, commercial art.
han'delstelsel, commercial system, mercantile system.
han'dels: ~ **term**, business term (word); ~ **traktaat**, commercial treaty; ~ **transaksie**, business transaction; ~ **tydskrif**, trade journal; commercial journal (magazine); ~ **vaartuig**, merchantman, trading vessel; ~ **vennootskap**, trade (business) partnership; co-partnership; ~ **verdrag**, commercial treaty; ~ **vereniging**, trading association; ~ **verkeer**, commercial intercourse; ~ **vlag**, merchant flag; ~ **vlieër**, commercial pilot; ~ **vliegtuig**, commercial (aero)plane; ~ **vloot**, merchant fleet; mer-

handelwyse   204   *hang*

cantile marine; ~**vooruitsigte**, trade prospects; ~**vors**, merchant prince; ~**vriend**, business friend; ~**vryheid**, freedom of trade; free trade; ~**waarde**, goodwill; ~**ware**, merchandize; ~**weg**, trade route; ~**wêreld**, business world; ~**wet**, commercial law; ~**wetboek**, mercantile code; ~**wetenskap**, commercial science; ~**wetgewing**, trade legislation; ~**wins**, trade profit; ~**wissel**, trade bill; ~**woordeboek**, commercial dictionary.

han'delwyse, procedure, action, process, proceeding; conduct, course of action, demeanour, behaviour.

han'deversorger, manicurist.

han'deversorging, manicure, manicuring.

hande-vier'voet, on all fours.

han'dewassing, washing of hands.

han'dewerk, handiwork, hand-work.

hand: ~**galop**, canter; ~**gat**, hand hole; ~**gebaar**, gesture, motion of the hand; ~**ge**, (-ge-), shake hands; ~**geklap**, applause; plaudits, clap(ping); ~**geld**, earnest(-money); han(d)sel; ~**gemaak**, (-te), handmade; ~**gemeen**, hand-to-hand fight; scuffle; ~*gemeen raak*, come to blows; ~**gereedskap**, non-power tools; ~**geselser**, walkie-talkie; ~**geweer**, hand gun; ~**gewig**, dumb-bell; ~**gewrig**, (-te), wrist; ~**gif**, arrha; earnest(-money); han(d)sel; ~**granaat**, hand-grenade; ~**greep**, grip, grasp, hold; ~**haaf**, (ge-), maintain (authority, condition, position) uphold, vindicate (rights); assert; preserve; administer; *jou* ~*haaf teen*, hold one's own against; maintain oneself against; ~**hamer**, hammer; ~**harmonika**, accordion.

hand'hawer, (-s), maintainer, upholder; protector; ~**sbond**, maintainers league.

hand'hawing, maintenance, assertion, preservation, stubborn defence, vindication.

hand'hefboom, handlever.

hand'hotnotjies, carpal bones.

han'dig, (-e), handy, clever, skilful, agile, adroit, dexterous, deft; ~ *wees met*, be a good hand at; ~**heid**, handiness, adroitness, sleight-of-hand; cleverness, skill, legerdemain, agility, dexterity; dodge.

hand'jie, (-s), small hand; *'n* ~ **HELP** *(bysit)*, assist, lend a hand; ~-~ *SPEEL*, hold hands.

han'djiesklap, handy-handy (game).

hand'jievol, handful; a few; *die KIND is 'n* ~, the child is a handful; *'n* ~ *MENSE*, a mere handful of people.

hand: ~**kaarte**, playing cards; ~**kar**, push-cart; ~**karwats**, riding whip; ~**klem**, handscrew; ~**kloofsaag**, rip (jack) saw; ~**koevoet**, moil, tommy-bar; ~**koffer**, case, portmanteau, handbag; ~**kus**, handkiss; *'n* ~*kus gooi*, blow a kiss; ~**kyker**, palmist; ~**kykery**, palmistry; ~**langer**, (-s), helper, handyman; journeyman; abettor; aid; assistant; bottlewasher; bottle-holder; myrmidon; emissary; stall; famulus; factotum; gilly; utility man; tool, accessory, accompliice; hodman; henchman; ~**leiding**, (-s), handbook; manual (of instruction), textbook; ~**leser**, palmist, handreader; ~**lesery**, palmistry, handreading; ~**ligting**, emancipation; ~**ligter**, handlever; ~**lyn**, hand line (angling), line in a hand; ~**meule**, handmill; quern; ~**moer**, finger nut; ~**moffie**, mitten; ~**monster**, handspecimen; ~**omslag**, handbrace; ~**oplegging**, laying on of hands; ~**opsteking**, show of hands (voting); ~**palm**, palm of the hand; ~**perd**, ledhorse; second string (to someone's bow); *iem. vir 'n* ~*perd hou*, keep someone as a standby; ~**pers**, hand press; ~**pik**, hand pickaxe; ~**pomp**, handpump; ~**ponsmasjien**, punching bear; ~**pop**, puppet; ~**reiking**, assistance; ~*reiking doen*, render assistance; lend a hand; ~**rem**, handbrake; ~**riem**, handstrap.

hand'rug, backhand; ~**hou**, backhand stroke; ~**speler**, backhand player; ~**spieël**, handmirror; ~**vat**, backhand grip; ~**vlughou**, backhand volley.

hand: ~**saag**, handsaw; ~**sak(kie)**, handbag; ladies' vanity bag; attaché case; ~**sein**, handsignal; ~**setter**, handcompositor; ~**skaaf**, jackplane; ~**skêr**, small scissors; snips (for metals).

hand'skoen, glove; gauntlet; *die* ~ *vir iem. OPNEEM*, espouse someone's cause; take up the cudgels on someone's behalf; *die* ~ *OPNEEM*, take up the gauntlet; *nie iem. om sonder* ~ *e aan te PAK nie*, he cannot be handled with velvet gloves; *iem. die* ~ *TOEWERP*, throw down the gauntlet; *met die* ~ *TROU*, marry by proxy; ~**doos**, glove box; ~**hakie**, glove hook; ~**huwelik**, proxy-marriage; ~**maker**, glover; ~**rekker**, glove stretcher; ~**tjies**, small gloves; honeysuckle.

hand: ~**skrif**, hand(writing); manuscript; copy; codex; ~**skrifdeskundige**, handwriting expert; ~**skrifkunde**, graphology; ~**skrifkun'dige**, (-s), graphologist; ~**skroef**, hand-screw (vice); ~**slag**, slap (with hand); ~**smering**, handlubrication; ~**sortering**, handsorting; ~**spaak**, handspike; ~**spieël**, handmirror; ~**spuit**, handsyringe; handpump; ~**stand**, handstand; ~**stelarm**, handspeed change lever; ~**steun**, handrest; ~**stoffertjie**, whisk broom; ~**stok**, swagger cane; dip-rod; ~**stoking**, hand-firing; ~**stuur**, manual steering; ~**tas**, handbag.

handtas'telik, (-e), palpable, obvious, evident; ~**heid**, violence; battery; *tot* ~ *hede kom*, come to blows.

hand: ~**tekening**, signature; autograph; ~**telefoon**, hand-microtelephone; ~**telegraaf**, manual telegraph; ~**tertjie**, tartlet; ~-**uit**, out of control; ~-*uit ruk*, get out of control (hand); ~**uitgesoek**, (-te), hand-picked; ~**vaardigheid**, dexterity; handiness; ~**vatsel**, grip, handle; ear (ewer); crutch (spade) sleeve (of crank); loom (oar); haft; hilt (of sword); helve; ~**versneller**, throttle; ~**ves**, (-te), charter, grant; covenant; ~**vislyn**, handline.

handvol, **(handevol)**, handful; *hulle is nie* ~ *nie, maar LANDVOL*, there is legion; they are not the only pebbles on the beach; *'n* ~ *RAAK*, become a handful; *soos 'n* ~ *VLIEË*, of doubtful value; of little worth; *met 'n* ~ *VLIEË*, with empty hands, disappointed.

hand: ~**vorm**, shape of hand; ~**vormig**, (-e), handshaped, palmate; digitate; ~**vulling**, namptissement, provisional sentence; ~**vuurwapen**, small arm; ~**vyl**, flat file; handfile; ~**waarsêer**, (-s), chiromancer, palmist; ~**waarsêery**, chiromancy; ~**wapens**, small arms; ~**waterpas**, handlevel; ~**werk**, hand-work, craft, handiwork; needlework; ~**werker**, manual labourer; craftsman; ~**werkgesel**, journeyman; ~**werkie**, piece of needlework; ~**werksman**, (-ne, werksmense); artisan; workman; labourer; artificer; handicraftsman; mechanic; ~**werkster**, workwoman; ~**woordeboek**, pocket (desk) dictionary; ~**wortel**, carpus; ~**wyser**, signpost, guide-post, fingerpost.

ha'ne: ~**balk**, collar beam; rafter; purlin; top beam; ~**gekraai**, crowing (of cocks); *met* ~ *(ge)kraai*, at cockcrow; ~**geveg**, cockfight(ing); ~**kam**, cock's comb; cockscomb; celosia (flower); ~**mat**, cockpit; ~**pas**, goose-step.

ha'nepoot, pot-hook; crow-foot; ~**druiwe**, honeypot, hanepoot (variety of grape, muscat of Alexandria).

ha'nepote, boat slings.

ha'nerig, (-e), cocky, impudent, cock-a-hoop; ~**heid**, cockiness.

ha'ne: ~**spat**, spring-halt; ~**spoor**, cock's spur; ~**treetjie**, (-s), short distance, stone's throw; ~**veer**, cock's feather; ~**voet**, crow foot.

hang, (s) (-e), slope; ramp; poise; *SKOTIGE* ~, a back-slope; *sy* ~ *na STUDIE*, his inclination towards study; (w) **(ge-)**, hang; suspend; sag; droop; be hanged; *nie SLAP laat* ~ *nie*, not to relax one's efforts; *dit* ~ *SWAAR aan 'n mens*, it is a heavy burden to bear; *aan MEKAAR* ~, be greatly attached to each other; *tussen* ~ *(e) en WURG(E)*, with the greatest difficulty; between two fires.

hang: ~**band**, sling; ~**berger**, hangberger (edible fish) *(Pachymetopon blochii)*; ~**beuel**, tieband of kingpost; ~**bout**, hanging (suspension) bolt; ~**brug**, suspension bridge; ~**draad**, (-e), dropper (elect.).

han'gend, (-e), pending; hanging; unsettled; penduline, pendulous, pensile, pendant; in abeyance; *die beslissing*, pending the decision.

hang: ~**er**, (-s), hanger; pendant; eardrop; dropper;

~erig, (-e), sagging; pendulous; listless; ~ertjie, (-s), locket; dropper; pendant; clothes hanger; ~gewelf, pendentive; ~haak, hanging hook; ~heup, dropped hip; ~kaatser, dangle tag, glow bracelet; ~kajuit, underslung carriage (cabin); ~kas, wardrobe; ~klip, overhanging rock; ~klok, wall clock; ~kruis, gooserump (defect in sheep); ~lamp, hanging lamp; ~lip, hanging lip; sulky; pendulous lip; ~*lip wees*, be in the sulks; ~lipjaghond, jowler; ~lippe, flews (blood hound); ~mat, hammock; dandy (India); ~oor, lop-ear; drop-ear; ~*oor wees*, be downcast; ~ornament, pendant; ~paaltjie, dropper; ~plaatjie, glass plate; ~punt, point of suspension; ~skouer, dropped shoulder; ~slot, padlock; ~snor, drooping moustache; ~spoor, suspension railway; ~stang, hanger; ~steier, cradle scaffold; ~styl, kingpost; queenpost (wagons); truss-post; ~veer, elbow spring; ~verband, sling; ~verkoeler, underslung radiator; ~voet, dropfoot; ~wang, baggy cheek; jowl; ~wieg, hanging cradle.

ha'nou! stop! halt! (to draught animals).

hans, orphan; hand-fed; ~ *GROOTMAAK*, bottle-rearing, rear by hand; *die LAM is* ~, this is an orphan lamb; ~babatjie, bottle-baby; ~dier, pet.

Hans'ard, Hansard.

Han'se, (hist.), league of the Hanse-towns; ~stede, Hanse-towns; ~verbond, Hanseatic League.

han'sie-my-kneg, handyman, factotum; ~ speel, carry out orders.

hans: ~kakie, (hist.), National Scout; renegade; ~kalf, (~kalwers), hand-fed calf; orphan calf, pet calf; ~lam, pet lamb, orphan lamb; cade, cosset.

hans'wors, (-e, -te), clown, jester, punch, harlequin; ~tery, (-e), clownishness, clowning.

hanteer', (ge-), handle, manage; operate; ply (needle); ~baar (..bare), manageable, easy to handle; ~der, (-s), manipulator, operator; ~koste, handling charges.

hante'ring, manipulation, handling, working.

hap, (s) (-pe), bite; piece, bit, morsel; snap; *in EEN* ~, in one bite; *'n HELE* ~ *uit my salaris*, a big slice out of my salary; (w) (ge-), bite, snap.

ha'per, (ge-), ail; be impeded; not function correctly; falter; haw; *dit* ~ *altyd aan GELD*, there is always a lack of money; *haar STEM het ge* ~, her voice broke; *WAAR* ~ *dit?* what is amiss? where is the hitch? ~ing, (-e, -s), impediment, hitch; hesitation; disturbance; *sonder* ~ *ing*, without a hitch.

haplografie', (-ë), haplography.

hap'masjien, mechanical shovel.

hap'p(er)ig, (-e), eager, keen; hackly, jagged; snappish (dog).

hap'pie, (-s), small bite (mouthful); titbit, morsel, snack.

hap'pig, eager, keen; ~ *wees op iets*, be keen on something; ~heid, eagerness, keenness.

hap'stokkie, cocktail stick.

haraki'ri, happy dispatch; harakiri, suicide.

hard, (w) (ge-), harden, steel (one's nerves); temper (steel); (b, bw), (-e), hard; loud (voice); stern (fact); glaring (colours); unkindly (feelings); harsh, grim (measure); heavily, fast (run); apace; severely, harshly; loudly; *iem. is* ~ *in die BEK*, someone is rebellious; ~ *BESIG*, very busy; ~*e BLOUGROND*, hard blue; ~*e DOPLUIS*, armoured scale; ~ *GEKOOK*, hard-boiled (eggs); ~ *HARDLOOP*, run fast; *PRAAT* ~*er*, speak up (more loudly); *SKREEU so* ~ *as 'n mens kan*, shout at the top of one's voice; *dis* ~ *TEEN* ~, it is a clash of wills; *dit VAL my* ~ *om te besluit*, I find it difficult to decide; ~ *van die VET*, very fat; ~*e WOORDE*, harsh words; ~ *WORD*, harden, become hard, set; ~bek'kig, (-e), hard in the mouth; hard-mouthed; hardbitten.

hard'drawwer, (-s), trotter; ~y, trotting match.

har'de: ~bolkeil, billcock, bowler; ~bord, hardboard; ~hout, hardwood; brandy; ~koejawel, (s) tough customer; (b) headstrong, cheeky; hard-boiled; ~kool, leadwood; combretum; ~kop, (s) stubborn (pig-headed) person; maverick; (b) stubborn; ~kwas, (s) tough customer; (b) hard-boiled;

~pad, hard road; hard labour, penal servitude; *iem. het* ~ *pad gekry*, someone was sentenced to hard labour; ~peer, hard pear *(Olinia cymosa)*.

har'der¹, (s) (-s), (Cape) herring; mullet *(Mugilidae); 'n ongeskraapte* ~, an ill-mannered oaf.

har'der², (b) harder, louder.

har'derig, (-e), rather hard (loud); ~heid, hardness, callosity.

har'de: ~soolsiekte, hardpad disease; ~versiersel, royal icing; ~veld, stony veld, hardeveld; ~vet, suet; hard fat; *nes* ~ *vet wees*, to be hard-hearted.

hard: ~gebak, (-te), hard-boiled; ~gebaker, (-de), hard-boiled; ~gekook, (-te), hard-boiled.

hardhan'dig, (-e), rough, rude, hard-handed; ~heid, roughness, hardhandedness.

hardhar'tig, hard-hearted; ~heid, hardheartedness.

hard'heid, hardness; sternness, asperity; loudness; temper (of metals).

hard'heid: ~sgraad, temper of metals; ~skaal, scale of hardness; ~smeter, sclerometer; ~s'toets, hardness test.

hardhoof'dig, (-e), stubborn, obstinate; ~heid, obstinacy, stubbornness.

hard: ~ho'rend, ~ho'rig, (-e), hard (dull) of hearing, deaf; ~ho'rendheid, hardness of hearing.

har'digheid, hardness; something hard, callosity.

har'ding, hardening; ~smengsel, hardening mixture; ~soplossing, hardening (solution).

hardkop'pig, (-e), obstinate, hard-headed; ~heid, obstinacy.

hard'leers, (-e), slow to learn, dull-witted.

hard'lood, hardened lead.

hard'loop, (ge-), run, hurry, race, make haste.

hard'loper, runner; sprinter; racer; goer; estafette; ~y, running, racing; footrace.

hardly'wig, (-e), constipated, costive; ~heid, constipation, costiveness.

hard'maak, (-ge-), temper (steel).

hardnek'kig, (-e), stubborn, obstinate, refractory; perverse; persistent (cold); dogged; hard-mouthed; obdurate; ~heid, stubbornness, obstinacy, obduracy; perversity; persistence, pertinacity.

hard'op, aloud, in a clear voice.

hard'roeper, (-s), megaphone.

hard'soldeer, (-ge-), braze; hard-solder; ~sel, brazing-wire; spelter.

hard: ~soldering, brazing; ~staal, hardened steel; ~steen, freestone, ashlar; ~vet, very fat.

hardvog'tig, (-e), unfeeling, callous, hard, hard-hearted, heartless; flint-hearted; hard-boiled; ~heid, heartlessness, hardheartedness.

hard'vrieskas, deep-freeze(r).

hardwer'kend, (-e), hard-working; industrious, diligent; ~heid, diligence.

hard'wording, solidification; hardening.

ha're, (vnw) hers; *dit is* ~, it is hers.

ha'reborsel = haarborsel.

ha'rekleed, coat (animals).

ha'rem, (-s), harem; ~broek, divided skirt.

ha'r(er)ig, (-e), hairy, haired, piliferous, pilose, pilous, hirsute, hispid, crinose, comose; ~heid, hairiness, pilosity.

ha'resnyer, hairdresser, barber.

ha'ring, (-s), herring; *gerookte* ~, kippered herring; ~bootjie, herring smack; ~buis, herring-buss; ~graat, herring-bone; ~graatsteek, herring-bone stitch; ~haai, porbeagle, mackerel-shark; ~kaker, herring-curer; ~net, herring-net; ~pakker, herring-packer; ~roker, herring-curer; ~tyd, herring-season; ~vaatjie, herring-barrel; ~vanger, herring-fisher; ~vangs, herring-catch; ~visser, herring-fisher; ~vissery, herring-fishing; ~vloot, herring-fleet.

hark, (s) (-e), rake; (w) (ge-), rake; ~er, (-s), raker; ~masjien, raker.

harlaboer'la, (s) hurly-burly, noise; chaos; bear-garden; rat race; (bw) in disorder, chaotic; hurry-scurry.

harlekina'de, (-s), harlequinade.

harlekyn', (-e), buffoon, harlequin, clown, jester; ~s'pak, motley, fool's dress; ~streke, buffoonery.

har'mansdrup, Dutch drops; slowcoach; *dit GAAN*

(soos) ~, it goes slowly; *'n* ~, a slow coach; a sluggard.
harmat'tan, harmattan.
harmonie', (-ë), harmony, accord, diapason; concord.
harmonieer', (ge-), harmonize; chime; agree; ~ **met,** go well together.
harmonie'leer, harmonics, theory of harmony.
harmonië'ring, harmonizing.
harmo'nies, (-e), symmetrical, harmonious.
harmonieus', (-e), harmonious.
harmo'nika, harmonica; concertina.
harmoniseer', (ge-), harmonize (mus.); ~ **nise'ring,** harmonization.
harmo'nium, (-s), harmonium.
har'nas, (s) (-se), armour, cuirass; *iem. in die* ~ *jaag,* rouse someone's ire; put someone's back up; (w) (ge-), armour; harness; *jou* ~ *teen,* arm oneself against; ~ **mannetjie,** miller's thumb (fish).
harp, (-e), harp, ~ **bout,** shackle bolt; ~ **enaar,** (-s, ..**nare),** ~ **enis',** ~ **is',** (-te), harpist, harper, harp-player.
harpoen', (-e), harpoon; gig; (w) (ge-), ~ **eer',** (ge-), harpoon; peg; ~ **ier',** (-s), harpooner; ~ **kanon,** whaling-gun; harpoon-gun.
harp'speelster, (lady) harpist.
harp'spel, harp-playing; ~ **er,** harp-player, harpist, harper.
harpuis', resin, rosin; colophony; copal; (w) (ge-), resin; ~ **agtig,** (-e), resinous; rosiny; bituminous; ~ **boom,** ~ **bos,** resin tree *(Euryops multifidus);* ~ **olie,** resin oil; ~ **seep,** resin soap.
harpy', (-e), harpy.
hars, resin, rosin; ~ **agtig,** (-e), rosiny; ~ **elektrisiteit,** resinous electricity.
har'sing, *see* **har'sings;** ~ **arbeid,** brain work; ~ **bloeding,** cerebral bleeding; ~ **-en-rugmurg(vlies)ontsteking,** encephalomyelitis; ~ **gimnastiek,** mental gymnastics; ~ **helfte,** cerebral hemisphere; ~ **holte,** cerebral cavity; ~ **kas,** skull, brain pan, cranium; ~ **klier,** pineal gland; ~ **koors,** brain fever; ~ **loos,** (..**lose),** brainless; ~ **ontsteking,** inflammation of the brain, cerebritis, phrenitis, encephalitis; ~ **pan,** cranium; ~ **panboor,** trepan.
harsings, brain, brains, cerebrum, grey matter; *die* ~ *INSLAAN,* dash out the brains; *hoe minder* ~ *in sy KOP, hoe hoër pluiskeil sit hy op,* great boast, small roast.
har'sing: ~ **rugmurgvog,** cerebrospinal fluid; ~ **senuwee,** cranial nerve; ~ **skudding,** concussion of the brain; ~ **siekte,** brain disease; ~ **skors,** cerebral cortex; ~ **skudding,** cerebral concussion; ~ **slymklier,** pituitary gland; hypophysis; ~ **stam,** brain stem; ~ **stoornis,** brain storm; ~ **vermoeienis,** brain fag; ~ **verweking,** softening of the brain; encephalomalacia; ~ **vlies,** cerebral membrane; ~ **vliese,** meninges; ~ **vliesontsteking,** meningitis; cephalitis; ~ **werk,** brain work; ~ **winding,** convolution (of the brain).
hars'koek, resinous disc (of electrophore).
har'slag, (-te), entrails, haslet, pluck; purtenance.
hars'lak, resinous lac.
hars'pan, cranium, brain pan, skull, head, pate; *iem. se* ~ *inslaan,* crack someone's nut; knock out someone's brains.
hart, (-e), heart; mind; courage; core; pith; bosom; *hy dra sy* ~ *op sy AANGESIG,* his face gives him away; *van iem. se* ~ *AFGAAN,* part with someone reluctantly; *AS jy die* ~ *daartoe het,* if you have the heart to do it; *iem. iets op die* ~ *BIND,* bring something home to someone; *uit die DIEPTE van sy* ~, from the bottom of his heart; *iem. op die* ~ *DRA,* think much of someone; *iets op die* ~ *DRA,* have something at heart; *iem. iets op die* ~ *DRUK,* make someone take something to heart; *dit GAAN hom ter* ~ *e,* it touches him deeply; *dit GAAN van my* ~ *af,* I part with it with a heavy heart; *van GANSER* ~ *e,* with all one's heart; *met 'n GEBROKE* ~, with a broken heart; *'n GOEIE* ~ *hê,* have a kind heart; *'n* ~ *van GOUD,* a heart of gold; *'n GROOT* ~ *hê,* be stout-hearted; be big-hearted; ~ *en HAND aanbied,* offer one's hand and heart; *sy* ~ *HANG daar-*

aan, he has set his heart on it; *'n* ~ *vir iets HÊ,* have the heart for something; *iets op sy* ~ *HÊ,* want to tell something; *as jy die* ~ *daartoe HET,* if you have the heart for it; *'n HOË* ~ *hê,* be overweening; *my* ~ *het in my KEEL geklop,* my heart leapt into my mouth; *sy* ~ *is in sy KEEL,* his heart is in his mouth; *sy* ~ *is maar KLEIN,* he has a small heart; *nie oor die* ~ *KRY nie,* not to have the heart to; *dit LÊ hom na aan die* ~, it is close to his heart; *sy* ~ *op sy LIPPE hê,* come out with what is on one's mind; *sy* ~ *LUG (uitpraat),* give vent to one's feelings; *waar die* ~ *van vol is, loop die MOND van oor,* out of the abundance of the heart, the mouth speaketh; *met* ~ *en MOND belowe,* promise whole-heartedly; *vuil* ~ , *vuil MOND,* foul-minded, foul-mouthed; *iem. dra sy* ~ *nie op sy MOU nie,* he does not wear his heart on his sleeve; *nie van sy* ~ *'n MOORDKUIL maak nie,* speak one's mind freely; *'n man NA my* ~, a man after my own heart; *ter* ~ *e NEEM,* take to heart; *in* ~ *en NIERE,* in pith and marrow; in the marrow of one's bones; *sy* ~ *OPHAAL aan iets,* indulge in something to one's heart's content; *sy* ~ *sit op die regte PLEK,* his heart is in the right place; *met* ~ *en SIEL,* with heart and soul; *een van* ~ *en SIEL wees,* be of one mind; *sy* ~ *op iets SIT,* set one's heart on something; *sy* ~ *sink (sak) in sy SKOENE,* his heart sinks into his boots; *'n* ~ *in SKROEF,* the body of a screw; *elke* ~ *het sy SMART,* every heart has its sorrow; *dit SPREEK tot die* ~, it touches the heart; *sy* ~ *het byna gaan STAAN,* his heart missed a beat; *iem. se* ~ *STEEL,* steal someone's heart; *'n* ~ *van STEEN,* a heart of stone; *sy* ~ *lê op sy TONG,* he wears his heart on his sleeve; *UIT jou* ~ *uit,* from the depth of one's heart; *sy* ~ *UITSTORT (uitpraat),* unbosom oneself; *VAN* ~ *e,* heartily; most sincerely; *jou* ~ *VASHOU,* hold one's breath; *sy* ~ *is VERDEEL,* his feelings are divided; *sy* ~ *VERLOOR,* lose one's heart; *die* ~ *VERRUIM,* ease one's feelings; *haar* ~ *is nog VRY,* she is fancy-free; *een WARM* ~ *steek die ander aan brand,* love is catching; *'n WARM* ~ *hê,* have a warm heart; *'n* ~ *van YSTER,* a heart of stone; ~ **a,** darling, my dear; ~ **aandoening,** cardiac affection; heart trouble; ~ **aar,** aorta, life artery; pulse (fig.); ~ **bars,** heart-shake.
hart'bees, hartebeest (antelope); kaama *(Alcelaphus buselaphas, A. lichtensteini);* ~ **huis,** wattle-and-daub house.
hart: ~ **beklemming,** angina pectoris; ~ **binnevlies,** endocardium; ~ **boesem,** atrium, auricle; ~ **brekend,** (-e), heart-breaking.
har'te: *'n saak wat my ter* ~ *GAAN,* a matter which I have at heart; *van GANSER* ~, with all one's heart; *van* ~ *GELUK,* hearty congratulations; *iets ter* ~ *NEEM,* take a thing to heart; ~ **aas,** ace of hearts; ~ **bloed,** heart's blood, life-blood; ~ **boer,** knave of hearts; ~ **dief,** darling; heart of my heart; enslaver; ~ **heer,** king of hearts; ~ **leed,** deepfelt grief, great sorrow.
har'teloos, (..lose), heartless; ~ **heid,** heartlessness.
har'telus, heart's desire; *na* ~, to one's heart's delight.
har'te: ~ **(n)aas,** ace of hearts; ~ **ns,** hearts (cards); ~ **nsaas,** ace of hearts; ~ **pyn,** heartache; ~ **veroweraar,** lady-killer; ~ **vrou,** queen of hearts; ~ **wee,** heartache, grief; ~ **wens,** fondest wish; ~ **wond,** heart's wound.
hart: ~ **gebrek,** heart ailment; ~ **geruis,** cardiac murmur; ~ **gordel,** heart girth.
hartgron'dig, (-e), heartfelt, cordial, sincere; ~ **heid,** cordiality.
har'tig, (-e), hearty; ~ *e woorde wissel,* speak strongly (plainly); ~ **heid,** heartiness.
har'tjie, (-s), little heart; darling, sweetheart, love; *in die* ~ *van die NAG,* at dead of night; *dankie, my* ~, *'n SOENTJIE en 'n kwartjie,* bless you! *in die* ~ *van die STAD,* in the centre of the city; *in die* ~ *van die WINTER,* in the heart of winter.
hart: ~ **kamer,** ventricle; ~ **klep,** cardiac (heart) valve; ~ **klop,** heartbeat; ~ **kloppings,** palpitation, heart-beating; ~ **kolk,** heart pit; anti-cardium;

~kramp, spasm of the heart; angina pectoris; ~kwaal, heart disease; cardionosis; ~lam, lady-love, darling, dearest, dearly-beloved, popsy (-wopsy), ~land, centre, heartland; ~lief, darling.

hart'lik, (b) (-e), cordial, hearty, sincere, genial; heartfelt; affectionate; ex animo; (bw) heartily; ~heid, heartiness, cordiality, affectionateness; geniality.

hart: ~-long'masjien, heart-lung machine; ~lyer, heart sufferer, cardiac; ~lyn, centre line, axis; ~massering, heart massage; ~meting, cardiometry; ~oorplanter, heart transplanter; ~oorplanting, heart transplantation; ~oorplantingspionier, heart-transplant pioneer; ~roer'end, (-e), touching, pathetic, heart-stirring, moving; ~sak(kie), pericardium, cardiac sac; ~sakontsteking, pericarditis; ~seer, (s) grief, sorrow, disconsolateness, disconsolation; (b) heartsore, sad; ~senuwee, cardiac nerve.

harts'geheim secret of the heart.

hart: ~siekte, heart disease; ~slag, heartbeat, pulsation of the heart; ~snare, heart-strings; ~spesialis, heart specialist, cardiologist; ~spier, heart muscle; ~sterking, cordial, tonic, stimulant; ~stilstand, cardiac arrest.

harts'tog, (-te), passion, fire, rage; ~'telik, (-e), passionate, impassioned, hot-blooded, fervid, fervent, ardent; ~'telikheid, passionateness, passion.

hart: ~steek, cardiac region; ~s'vanger, cutlass, dirk; ~s'vergroting, dila(ta)tion of the heart; ~s'vriend, bosom friend; ~vorhoffend, (-e), uplifting, exalting; ~verlamming, heart-failure, paralysis of the heart, heart-seizure; ~versaking, heart-failure; ~verskeurend, (-e), heart-rending, heart-breaking, harrowing; ~versterkertjie, ~versterkinkie, (-s), elixir; pick-me-up, tot, cordial, drink; ~versterking, heart stimulant, cordial; cardiac; ~vervetting, fatty heart; ~vlies, pericardium; endocardium; ~vliesontsteking, endocarditis; pericarditis; ~voorkamer, atrium; ~vormig, (-e), heart-shaped, cordiform; cordate (of leaves); ~wand, heart wall; ~water, heart-water (in animals); dropsy; ~werking, heart action.

har'war, squabbling, confusion, rumpus; in 'n ~ wees, be confused, upset.

ha'sardspel, (ong.), game of chance.

ha'selhout, hazel.

ha'selneut, hazel-nut, cobnut, filbert; ~boom, filbert.

ha'sepad: die ~ kies, take to one's heels.

ha'se: ~peper, jugged hare, ragout; ~slaap, forty winks, catnap

ha'sie, (-s), young hare; catch the hare (children's game); ~-oor, leap-frog.

ha'sie-ablou, catch the hare (children's game).

hasjee', hash.

has'jisj, hashish (Cannabis sativa).

has'pel, (s) (-s), reel, windlass; sounding-post (violin); (w) (ge-), wind, reel; potter; wrangle; ~aar, winder; spindle; bungler; -ary', bickering; ~oond, reel oven.

ha'ter, (-s), hater, detester.

ha'terig, (-e), inclined to hate, revengeful.

ha'tig, (-e), spiteful, malicious.

ha'tigheid, hatred, spite, vengefulness.

Havan'na, Havana.

havan'na: ~sigaar, Havana cigar; ~tabak, Havana tobacco.

ha'vikklou, grapple fork.

Hawai'i, Hawaii; ~ër, (-s), Hawaiian.

Hawai'ies, (-e), Hawaiian.

ha'we¹, goods, property, chattels, stock; ~ en GOED, goods and chattels; LEWENDE ~, livestock.

ha'we², (-ns), harbour, port, dock; haven; die ~ binnevaar, put into port; ~arbeider, dock worker; ~bank, port bar; ~beampte, port official; ~bedryf, port business; ~bestuur, port authority; ~boom, harbour bar; ~bou, harbour construction; ~dokter, port doctor; ~geld, harbour dues; dock charges, pierage, pier dues, dockage, wharfage; groundage; ~geleentheid, ~geriewe, port facilities; ~hoof, pier, jetty, mole; quay; breakwater; bulwark; ~ingenieur, harbour engineer; ~-inrigtings, port facilities, dock facilities; ~kantoor, harbour(-master's) office; ~kaptein, port captain; ~kom, basin; ~kommandant, port admiral; ~loods, harbour pilot; ~loodsvaartuig, harbour pilot vessel.

ha'weloos, (..lose), poor, ragged, tattered; ~heid, raggedness, poverty.

ha'we: ~meester, harbour-master; ~plaas, ~plek, seaport town; ~polisie, harbour-police.

ha'wer, oats; iets van ~ tot GORT ken, know something inside out.

ha'we: ~reglement, ~regulasies, port regulations; ~regte, port dues.

ha'wer: ~gerf, oat sheaf; ~gort, grits; groats.

ha'werklap: om die ~, on the slightest provocation; at the drop of a hat; often, every now and then.

ha'wer: ~koek, oat cake; ~korrel, oat grain.

ha'wer: ~land, oat field; ~meel, oatmeal, ~meelkoek, oatmeal cake; parkin; ~mout, rolled oats; ~moutpap, oatmeal porridge; ~pluim, panicle (of oats); ~saad, seed oats; ~sak, oat bag; nose-bag (horse); ~wortel, salsify; oysterplant (Tragopogon porrifolius.)

ha'we: ~stad, port, seaport town; ~staking, dock strike; ~werker, dock labourer.

ha'wik, (-e), hawk; ~sneus, Roman nose, hook(ed) nose, aquiline nose.

H'-bom, hydrogen bomb, H-bomb.

hè! oh! my!

hê¹, (w) (had, gehad), have, possess; 'n mens weet nooit wat jy AAN hom het nie, one never knows where one is with him; iets AAN iem. ~, know what someone means to you; DAAR het jy dit, there you are; wat sal jy DAARAAN ~? what will you gain by it? iedereen het dit DAAROOR, it is on everybody's lips; DIT het jy daarvan, that's what you get for it; DIT ~, be having a time of it; waaroor het hy DIT? what is he talking about? aan wie het, sal GEGEE word, unto him who has it shall be given; GELYK ~, be right; daar HET jy dit nou! there you are! HOE het ek dit met jou? what is wrong with you? ~ is ~, maar KRY is die kuns, possession is nine points of the law; het jy dit of KRY jy dit? what's tickling you? hoe MEER 'n mens het, hoe meer wil hy hê, the more we have, the more we want; dit MIS ~, be (in the) wrong; het jy NOG iets? have you ever? is that all? NOU het ek jou, now I have you; het jy nou OOIT? did you ever! well I never! daar niks op TEË ~ nie, have nothing against it; WAT het jy? what is wrong with you? WEET wat jy aan iem. het, know where one stands with someone; iem. WIL jou ~, you are wanted, someone wants (to see) you; ek WIL dit ~, I want it; I quite believe it; iem. het, know where one stands with someone; dit WIL ek hê, I quite believe it.

hê², (tw) hey? what is it?

heb'be: (vero.), met sy ~ en HOUE, with all his posessions, iem. se ~ en HOUE, one's goods and chattels.

heb'belikheid, (..hede), habit, peculiarity, trick, habitude.

Hebra'ïkus, (-se, ..ïci), Hebraïs', (-te), Hebraist.

Hebraïs'me, (-s), Hebraism.

Hebre'ër, (-s), Hebrew.

Hebreeus', (s) (-e), Hebrew (language); (b) (-e), Hebrew.

heb'sug, covetousness, greed, avidity, cupidity, avarice; acquisitiveness; rapaciousness, rapacity; ~'tig, (-e), covetous, rapacious, greedy, grasping, avaricious, acquisitive; ~'tigheid, see hebsug.

he'de¹, (s) the present, this day; van hierdie ~ AF, from this very moment; ~ ten DAE, this day and age; VANAF ~, from today, on and after this date, from now on; die ~ en die VERLEDE, the present and the past; (bw) today, at present.

he'de²! (tw) o ~! oh my! oh heavens!

he'den: ~ten DAGE, nowadays; OP hierdie ~, on this very day.

he'dendaags, (-e), modern, present-day, contemporary; hodiernal, nowadays, at present; latter-day.

hedonis', (-te), hedonist; ~**me**, hedonism; ~**ties**, (-e), hedonistic.
heel¹, (w) (ge-), heal, cure; granulate (wound).
heel², (w) (ge-), receive (stolen goods).
heel³, (b) (**hele**), whole, entire, complete, unbroken, undamaged; sound; repaired, mended; *'n hele AANTAL*, quite a (large) number; *die hele DAG*, all day; the whole day; *'n ~ KOPPIE*, an unbroken cup; *een RUIT is nog ~*, one pane is still intact; *my SKOENE is nou weer ~*, my shoes have been repaired; (bw) very; quite; *~ ANDERS*, totally different; *~ in die BEGIN*, at the very outset; *~ EENVOUDIG*, quite simple; plain-sailing; *~ MOONTLIK*, quite possible; *SLUK dit ~*, swallow it whole; *~ WAARSKYNLIK*, quite probable.
heel'aand, during the whole evening, through the evening.
heel'agter, (-s), full-back (rugby).
heelal', universe, macrocosm; cosmos; creation; ~**vaarder**, astronaut; cosmonaut; ~**vaart**, astronautics, interplanetary aviation.
heel'baar, (..**bare**), curable; ~**heid**, curableness.
heel'dag, the whole day, all day; always, constantly.
heel'eierpulp, whole-egg pulp.
heel'getal, whole number, integer.
heelhar'tig, (-e), wholeheartedly, cordially.
heel'huids, unscathed; without injury; *daar ~ van afkom*, get off unscathed (scot-free).
heel: ~**konfyt**, conserve; whole preserve; ~**koring**, whole wheat; ~**krag**, healing (curative) power; ~**krag'tig**, (-e), healing, curative; ~**kunde**, surgery; ~**kun'dig**, (-e), surgical; ~**kun'dige**, (-s), surgeon; ~**kuns**, art of healing; ~**maak**, (-ge-), mend; ~**maker**, (-s), mender.
heel'meester, surgeon; *SAGTE ~s maak stinkende wonde*, desperate diseases must have desperate cures.
heel'nag, through the night.
heel'olie, healing oil.
heel: ~**middag**, all afternoon; ~**môre**, all through the morning; ~**nag**, all night; ~**pad**, all the way.
heel'party, a good few, quite a large number.
heel'tal, integer, whole number.
heel'temal, quite, altogether, entirely; outright; absolute; to the full; clean; every bit; *~ AGTER in die saal*, right at the back of the hall; *~ ALLEEN*, quite alone; *iets ~ VERGEET*, forget something completely; *~ VREEMD hier*, a complete stranger here; *iets WEER ~ oordoen*, do something all over again.
heel'tyd, always, continually, the whole time; ~**s**, (-e), whole-time.
heel: ~**vrugkonfyt**, whole-fruit jam; ~**vyekonfyt**, fig preserve.
heel'wat, quite a lot, a good deal, a considerable number, appreciably; *~ tyd*, considerable time.
heem'kunde, (ong.), local folklore.
heem'raad, (..**rade**), (hist.), heemraad (member of a country court).
heems'wortel, hibiscus.
heen, away; thither, thence; *DEUR alles heen*, through it all; *~ en TERUG*, there and back; *iem. is VER ~*, someone is far gone; *WAAR moet dit ~?* where will this end? *WAAR wil hy ~?* what is he driving at? *~ en WEER*, to and fro.
heen'-en-terugreis, forward and return journey.
heen'-en-weer'diens, shuttle service.
heen'-en-weer'pratery, palaver; evasive talk.
heen'-en-weer'steek, feather (herring-bone) stitch.
heen'-en-weerstelsel, shuttle system.
heen'-en-weertjie, a moment or two, very short time.
heen'gaan, (s) departure; death, demise, passing away; exit; (w) (-ge-), go away, depart; die; *daar sal 'n WEEK mee ~*, that will take a week; *nie WEET waar dinge ~ nie*, not know what things are coming to.
heen'kabel, outgoing cable.
heen'kome, refuge, escape; shelter; livelihood; *êrens 'n ~ vind*, find a refuge (means of livelihood) somewhere.
heen'reis, forward journey.
heen'sit, (-ge-): *jou oor iets ~*, get over something.

heen'skeer, (-ge-), flee (scurry) away, hurry off; *jy KAN ~!* make yourself scarce! *oor jou WERK ~*, scamp one's work.
heen: ~**sluip**, (-ge-), sneak away; ~**snel**, (-ge-), run (speed, fly) away.
heen'stap, (-ge-), walk away; *oor besware ~*, pass over (ignore) objections.
heen: ~**swerf**, ~**swerwe**, (-ge-), wander away; ~**vlug**, outward flight; ~**weg**, forward journey.
Heer¹, the Lord, God; *die ~ der (v.d.) heerskare*, the Lord (God) of hosts; *in die ~ ONTSLAPE*, departed in the Lord; *as die ~ WIL*, God willing.
heer², (**here**), host, army.
heer³, (**here**), gentleman; lord; master; king (at cards); *wat die here wys, moet die GEKKE prys*, he who pays the piper calls the tune; *die here eet en die GEKKE sing*, while masters dine fools sing; *die GROOT ~ uithang*, do the grand; lord it over; *die ~ des HUISES*, master of the house; *so ~, so KNEG*, like master, like man; *liewer klein ~ as groot KNEG*, lean liberty is better than fat slavery; *~ en MEESTER*, lord and master; *hoe kaler ~, hoe groter MENEER*, great boast, small roast; *NUWE here, nuwe wette*, new masters, new laws; *die ~ tjie SPEEL*, give oneself airs; swagger; *die here van die SKEPPING*, the lords of creation; *niem. kan TWEE here dien nie*, nobody can serve two masters; *die WELEDELE heer X*, X Esquire.
heer'agtig, (-e), in a lordly (grand) manner.
heer'baan, mainroad.
heer'boontjie, civet bean; Lima bean.
heer'lik, (-e), glorious, delightful, pleasant (day); delicious (fruit); lovely (time); ambrosial, delectable; ~! oh dear! great Scott! ~**heid**, glory, splendour; magnificence; deliciousness, gorgeousness.
heers, (ge-), reign, govern, dominate, rule; prevail, be rampant, be rife (dissatisfaction); obtain (condition); be prevalent (disease); be in force, be operative (system, tariff); *'n vrou wat oor die MAN ~*, a woman who dominates her husband; *daar ~ VREDE in die land*, there is peace in the country.
heer'send, (-e), dominant, hegemonic, ruling; rampant, prevailing, prevalent; *~e MARKWAARDE*, ruling market-value; *~e MENING*, prevailing opinion; *~e PRYSE*, ruling prices; *~e SIEKTE*, prevalent disease; *~e WIND*, prevailing wind.
heers: ~**er**, (-s), ruler; potentate; dynast; ~**eres'**, (-se), (woman) ruler.
heer'sersras, master-race, dominating race.
heer'skaar, see **heerskare**.
heer'skap, (-pe), gent, fellow; *'n snaakse ~*, a funny fellow, an odd type (of person).
heerskappy', (-e), power, reign, authority, dominion, domination, mastery; empire; government; supremacy; *~ voer oor*, rule over.
heer'skare, (vero.), hosts.
heers'sug, imperiousness, ambition; lust for power; ~'**tig**, (-e), imperious, ambitious; lordly; overbearing; ~'**tigheid**, imperiousness.
heer'tjie, (-s), young gentleman; young blood; dandy.
hees, (**heser**, -**ste**), hoarse, husky; raucous; raspy; ~**heid**, hoarseness, huskiness, frog-in-the-throat, raucity.
hees'ter, (-s), shrub.
heet¹, (w) (ge-), be called; name; bid; *hy ~ na sy PA*, he is called after his father; *iem. WELKOM ~*, bid someone welcome.
heet², (b) (**hete**; **heter**, -**ste**), hot; burning; bitter (tears); torrid; *op heter DAAD betrap*, caught in the act (red-handed); *die hete LUGSTREEK*, the torrid zone.
heet: ~**gebaker**, (-de), hasty, hot-tempered; ~**heid**, heat, warmth.
heet'hoof, hothead; ~'**dig**, (-e), hotheaded, passionate; ~'**digheid**, hotheadedness.
heet'oond, reverberating furnace.
hef¹, (s) (-te, **hewwe**), handle, haft, hilt; *die ~ in hande hê*, be in full control; hold the cards.
hef², (w) (ge-), raise, lift; heave; levy, impose; charge; *~ AAN lê nog voor*, the worst is still to come; *BELASTINGS ~*, impose taxes; *jou HANDE hemelwaarts ~*, raise one's hands to heaven; *~ arm*, lift-

ing-bracket; ~**baar**, (..**bare**), leviable; ~**bok**, screw-jack.

hef'boom, lever; fulcrum; prize; cuddy (for stones); jack; ~ *van 'n rem*, brake lever; ~**as**, lever pivot; ~**krag**, leverage; ~**steun**, lever bracket; ~**uitskakelaar**, lever switch; ~**werking**, leverage; gearing (of a company).

hef'brug, autohoist, dock-lift.

hef'fer, (-s), cog; lift; collector; raiser.

hef'fing, (-e, -s), levy, imposition, collection; arsis (in prosody); ~**sfonds**, levy fund; ~**skommissie**, ~**sloon**, raising fee.

hef: ~**haak**, lifting wire, lifting hook; ~**kraan**, lifting crane; ~**krag**, lift (aero.); purchase; ~**offer**, heave offering.

hef'skroef, jack-screw; lifting air-screw; ~**vliegtuig**, helicopter.

hef: ~**spier**, levator; elevator, ~**tand**, cog.

hef'tig, (-e), violent, vehement, extreme; hot, heated (argument); fierce; forcible; hard; impetuous; ~**heid**, violence, vehemence, brunt, fury, impetuosity.

hef: ~**vermoë**, lifting power; ~**vlak**, elevating plane; ~**voordeel**, mechanical advantage; ~**wa**, lifting truck.

heg[1], (s) (-ge), hedge; *GEEN ~ of steg ken nie*, be a complete stranger; *oor ~ en STEG*, up hill and down dale.

heg[2], (w) (ge-), fasten, attach, affix; stitch up; *hom AAN iem. ~*, attach oneself to someone; grow fond of someone; *geen WAARDE ~ aan nie* attach no value to; (b) (-te), firm, solid, strong; staunch (friendship); *op ~te fondament*, on firm foundation; ~**bosdruif**, clematis; ~**draad**, band string.

hegemonie', hegemony.

heg: ~**gat**, tackling hole; ~**lat**, baten; ~**lint**, adhesive tape; ~**middel**, fixative; adhesive; ~**plaatjie**, tag; ~**pen**, attachment pin; ~**pleister**, sticking (adhesive) plaster; courtplaster; ~**rank**, tendril; ~**sel**, (-s), fastener.

heg'skêr, hedge shears.

heg: ~**spyker**, tack-nail; ~**stuk**, fastening, fixture.

heg'tenis, custody, imprisonment, detention; *in ~ neem*, arrest (a person), take into custody.

hegt'heid, solidity, firmness.

heg'ting, (-e, -s), stitching (wounds); adhesion; suture.

heg'wortel, crampon.

hei[1], (s) (-e), pile-driver; (w) (ge-), ram, drive (piles); pitch (ship).

hei[2], (ong.), (s) = **heide**.

hei[3]! (tw) hey! hallo!

hei'agtig, (-e), heathery, moorish.

hei'blok, monkey, beetle; pile-driver; ram, rammer.

hei'de, (-s), erica; heath, heather; moorland; ~**agtig**, (-e), heathery; ~**blommetjie**, heather-bell, heath, heather; ~**kleur**, heather (colour); ~**kruid**, erica.

hei'den, (-e, -s), heathen, pagan; gipsy; *MY ~ wat makeer jy?*, good gracious what is wrong with you? *aan die ~e OORGELEWER wees*, delivered to the Gentiles; at the mercy of bad people; ~**dom**, heathendom, paganism, heathenry; ~**s**, (-e), pagan, savage, heathenish, heathen; *'n ~se herrie*, an infernal commotion.

hei'dewortel, brier, briar; ~**pyp**, briar pipe.

heidin', (-ne), female heathen.

hei: ~**er**, (-s), pile-driver; ~**hamer**, pile-hammer; ~**hock**, pitch angle.

heil, welfare, good, prosperity; (spiritual) salvation; bliss; hail! *êrens geen ~ in SIEN nie*, unable to see the good of something; see no good in something; *H~ die LESER*, Lectori Salutem; *~ en SEËN!* best wishes! good luck! *TOT ~ van*, to the benefit of; *sy ~ in VLUG soek*, seek safety in flight.

Hei'land, Saviour, Redeemer.

hei'land: *jou ~ leer ken*, be having a hard time of it.

heil: ~**bede**, good wishes; ~**begerig**, (-e), desirous of salvation.

heil'bot, (-te), halibut.

heil'bron, fountain of bliss.

heil'dronk, toast; pledge; *'n ~ instel*, propose a toast.

heil'gimnastiek, physical culture, hygienic gymnastics, Swedish drill, remedial gymnastics.

hei'lig, (w) (ge-), sanctify, consecrate, hallow; keep holy; *laat U NAAM ge~ word*, hallowed be Thy name; (b, bw) (-e), holy, sacred; sacrosanct; hieratic; ~ *BLY*, be held sacred; ~*e DAE*, holy days; *die H~e GEES*, the Holy Ghost; *iets ~ GLO*, believe implicitly; accept something as gospel; *die H~e HART*, the Sacred Heart; *hom ~ HOU*, be sanctimonious; *hulle is nie almal ~ wat baie KERK toe gaan nie*, the cowl does not make the monk; *die H~e LAND*, the Holy Land; *vir hom is NIKS ~ nie*, nothing is sacred to him; *ons ~e REGTE*, our sacred rights; *die H~e SKRIF*, Holy Writ, Holy Scripture; ~ *VERKLAAR*, canonize; *haar WENSE is vir my ~*, her wishes are sacred to me; *die ~e WAARHEID*, gospel truth; *baie ~ WEES op*, hold sacred; regard as sacred; ~**dom**, (-me), sanctuary, holy shrine, preserve; penetralia; presbytery; sanctum.

hei'lige, (-s), saint; *hy is GEEN ~ nie*, he is no saint; *die ~ UITHANG*, pretend to be a saint; ~**beeld**, image of a saint; ~**been**, sacrum; ~**dag**, saint's day; ~**kalender**, menology; ~**krans**, aureole, halo, nimbus; ~**lewe**, life of a saint; ~**verering**, saint-worship, hagiolatry, hierolatry.

hei'lig: ~**heid**, holiness, sanctity; *Sy Heiligheid*, His Holiness: ~ *U Heiligheid*, Your Holiness; ~**ing**, sanctification; ~**makend**, (-e), sanctifying; ~**making**, sanctification; ~**skenner**, sacrilegist; ~**skennis**, blasphemy desecration, sacrilege, profanation, profanity; ~**verklaring**, canonization.

heil'loos, (..**lose**), impious, baleful, pernicious, wretched, bad; *'n ..lose kringloop*, a vicious circle; ~**heid**, balefulness, badness.

heil'ryk, (-e), beneficial, salutary.

heil'saam, (..**same**), beneficial, salutary, salubrious, benign, benignant; healthful, wholesome; ~**heid**, beneficial influence, benignity, benignancy; healthiness.

heils: ~**belofte**, promise of salvation; ~**leer**, doctrine of salvation.

Heils'leër, Salvation Army.

Heil'soldaat, Salvationist.

heil: ~**staat**, ideal state, Utopia; ~**wens**, congratulation.

hei'masjien, pile-engine.

heim'lik, (-e), secret, private, clandestine; furtive; privy; collusive; in secret; ~**heid**, secrecy, privacy.

heim'wee, homesickness, nostalgia.

hein'der, (-s), *en ver*, (from) far and wide.

hei'ning, (-s), fence, hedge, enclosure; *op die ~ sit*, sit on the fence; ~**paal**, fence pole; ~**planter**, hedger; ~**skêr**, garden shears; ~**sloot**, limit ditch.

hei'ninkie, (-s), small fence.

Hein'tjie Pik, (ong.), Old Nick.

hei'paal, pile.

hei'sa! I say, you!

hei: (ong.), ~**veld**, moor, heath; ~**werk**, piling.

hek, (-ke), gate, hurdle; turnpike; stern; wicket (in cricket); *die ~ is van die KRAAL*, they are running wild; *op die ~ SIT*, sit on the fence; be in two minds; *by die ~ STAAN*, be the keeper of the gate; *soos hulle by die ~ UITKOM*, as they come; *die ~ke is VERHANG*, the tables are turned.

hekatom'be, (-s), hecatomb.

hek'balk, transom (of ship).

he'kel[1], (s) dislike, hatred, grudge; pique; *'n ~ aan iem. HÊ*, dislike someone very much; *'n ~ in iets HÊ*, to be unable to bear; have no liking for; *'n ~ KRY aan*, take a dislike to.

he'kel[2], (s) comb, hackle (flax); *iem. oor die ~ haal*, haul someone over the coals; (w) (ge-), heckle; crochet; satirize, censure severely; lampoon; *'n kandidaat op 'n vergadering ~*, heckle a candidate at a meeting; ~**aar**, (-s), satirist; heckler; lampooner; ~**dig**, (-te), satire; ~**digter**, satirist; ~**garing**, crochet cotton; ~**ing**, heckling; satirizing; ~**kantwerk**, needle-lace; ~**naald**, crochet needle; ~**patroon**, crochet pattern; ~**pen**, crochet needle; ~**rede**, philippic; ~**skrif**, satire; skit; diatribe;

~ **steek**, tricot stitch; ~ **vers**, satiric poem; ~ **werk**, crochet-work.
hek'geld, gate(-money).
hek'kie, (-s), small gate; hurdle; *120 m* ~ *s*, 120 m hurdles; ~ **shardloper**, hurdler; ~ **sloop**, (s) (..**lope**), hurdle-race; (w) (**-ge-**), hurdle; ~ **springer**, hurdler; ~ **sreisies**, ~ **wedloop**, hurdle-race.
hek: ~ **man**, gate-keeper; ~ **ontvangste**, gate (-money); ~ **paal**, gatepost; *hy het op 'n* ~ *paal gesit toe sy ouers getrou het*, he is very precocious.
heks, (s) (-e), witch, hag; vixen; charmer; crone; harpy; *ou* ~ , hag; witch; (w) (**ge-**), practise witchcraft; *ek kan nie* ~ *nie,* I am not a conjurer.
heksaë'der, (-s), hexahedron.
heksaë'dries, (-e), hexahedral.
heksagonaal', (..**nale**), hexagonal.
heksagoon', (..**gone**), hexagon.
heks'agtig, (-e), haggish.
heksa'meter, (-s), hexameter.
hek'sateug, hexateuch.
hek'se: ~ **besem**, witches' broom; ~ **dans**, witches' dance; ~ **ketel**, witches' cauldron; ~ **kring**, fairy ring; ~ **meester**, sorcerer; ~ **proses**, witches' trial; ~ **ry**, witchcraft, sorcery; bedevilment; ~ **sabbat**, witches' sabbath; ~ **toer**, tough job; ~ **vleg**, elflock; ~ **werk**, sorcery; witchcraft; difficult job.
hek'sluiter, (-s), last-comer, rear man; youngest child, Benjamin, minimus.
hektaar', (..**tare**), hectare.
hek'to: ~ **graaf** (..**grawe**), hectograph; ~ **grafeer'** (**ge-**), duplicate, make manifold copies; ~ **gram**, hectogramme; ~ **liter**, hectolitre; ~ **meter**, hectometre.
Hek'tor, Hector; a hero.
hek'wagter, wicket-keeper; gate-keeper.
hek'wiel, stern wheel; ~ **er**, (-s), stern-wheeler.
hel[1], (s) hell, Gehenna, inferno; ~ *op AARDE hê*, have hell on earth; *ter* ~ *le DAAL*, descend into the grave; ~ *DEURMAAK*, go through hell.
hel[2], (w) (**ge-**), lean, incline, slope, slant; list; lean over; *die rotse* ~ *na hierdie kant*, the rocks incline to this side.
hel[3], (b) (**-le; -ler, -ste**), bright, glaring; *in die* ~ *le sonlig*, in the glaring sunlight.
helaas'! ailas! alack!
hel'bakkie, hell-box.
held, (-e), hero; *hy is 'n* ~ *met die MOND*, he is all hot-air; *tot* ~ *VERHEF*, heroize; *'n* ~ *in VREDESTYD*, a shy cock.
hel'de: ~ **bloed**, heroic blood; ~ **daad**, feat, heroic deed (exploit); **H** ~ **dag**, Heroes' Day (Oct. 10), now named Krugerdag; ~ **dig**, (-te), epos, epopee, heroic poem, heroics, epic poem; ~ **digter**, epic poet; ~ **dood**, hero's death, heroic death; ~ **eeu**, heroic age; ~ **gees**, heroic spirit; ~ **geslag**, heroic race; race of heroes; ~ **moed**, heroic courage; heroism, prowess.
hel'der, ((-e), -der, -ste), clear, bright, lucid, serene, distinct; pellucid, vivid; glassy; limpid; luminous, perspicuous, clean; fine (fluid); sonorous; clearheaded; fair (weather); ~ *DRUK*, clear type; ~ *van GEES*, clear-headed; *'n* ~ *KOP hê*, have a clear head; ~ *LUG*, clear sky; *'n* ~ *OOMBLIK*, a lucid moment; ~ *OORDAG*, in broad daylight; ~ *RYSSOP*, clear rice soup; ~ *WAKKER*, wide awake; ~ **blou**, bright (vivid) blue; ~ **denkend**, (-e), clearheaded; ~ **heid**, clearness, limpidity, lucidity, lucency, pellucidity, clarity, brightness; perspicuity; ~ **horend**, (-e), clairaudient; ~ **horende**, (-s), clairaudient; ~ **horendheid**, clairaudience; ~ **klinkend**, (-e), clear, ringing; ~ **ogig**, (-e), bright-eyed.
hel'derrooi, bright red.
hel'de: ~ **ry** line of heroes; ~ **sang**, epic poem (song).
hel'der: ~ **sap**, clarified juice; ~ **siende**, clairvoyant, clear-sighted; ~ *siende wees*, have second sight; be clairvoyant; ~ **siendheid**, clairvoyance, clearsightedness; ~ **siener**, clairvoyant.
hel'de: ~ **skaar**, heroic band; ~ **stryd**, heroic struggle; ~ **stuk**, heroic deed; ~ **tyd**, heroic age; ~ **verering**, hero-worship; ~ **volk**, nation of heroes.
heldhaf'tig, (-e), courageous, heroic, brave; ~ **heid**, heroism, bravery.

heldin', (**-ne**), heroine; amazon.
Hele'navuur, St. Helen's Fire.
he'ler[1], (-s), receiver (of stolen goods); fence; fencingcully; *die* ~ *is so goed soos die steler*, the receiver is as bad as the thief.
he'ler[2], (-s), healer.
helf'te, (-s), half; moiety; *sy BETER* ~ *(-helf)*, his better half; *die* ~ *MEER*, half as much again; *die* ~ *MINDER*, less by half; *OM die* ~ , half and half; *vir die* ~ *van die PRYS*, at half-price.
Hel'goland, Heligoland.
hel'hond, hell-hound, Cerberus, Garm.
He'likon, Helicon.
helikop'ter, (-s), helicopter; ~ **blad**, heliport.
he'liks, (-e), helix.
he'ling[1], receiving (stolen goods).
he'ling[2], henology.
heliodoor', (..**dore**), heliodor.
he'liofiet, (-e), heliophyte.
heliofobie', heliophobia.
heliograaf', (..**grawe**), heliograph.
heliografeer', (**ge-**), heliograph.
heliografie', heliography; ..**gra'fies**, (-e), heliographic.
heliogram', (-me), heliogram.
heliogravu're, (-s), heliogravure.
helioli'ties, (-e), heliolithic.
he'liometer, heliome'ter, (-s), heliometer.
heliosen'tries, (-e), heliocentric.
helioskoop', (..**skope**), helioscope.
helioterapie', heliotherapy.
heliotroop', (..**trope**), heliotrope; cherry-pie.
heliotro'pies, (-e), heliotropic.
heliotropis'me, heliotropism.
he'lium, helium (metal).
hel'lebaard, (-e), halberd, battle-axe; twibill; ~ **ier'**, (-s), halberdier.
Helleen', (**Hellene**), Hellene; ~ **s'**, (-e), Hellenic, Greek.
hel'lend, (-e), sloping, inclined; aslope; ~ *e vlak*, inclined plane.
Hellenis', (-te), Hellenist; ~ **me**, Hellenism; ~ **ties**, (-e), Hellenistic.
hel'le: ~ **poort**, gate of hell; ~ **pyn**, torments of hell; ~ **vaart**, descent into hell.
hel'leveeg, (..**veë**), hell-cat, termagant, virago, shrew, fury.
hel'(le)vuur, hell-fire.
hel'ling, (-e, -s), slope, incline, inclination, acclivity, declivity; hade; fall; grade; gradient; up-grade; raise (rise); down-grade; dip, cant, pitch (of roof); plane; slip(s), slipway (ship); glacis; *van die* ~ *LOOP*, leave the slips; *MET 'n* ~ *van 2 op 100 meter*, with a drop of 2 in 100 meter; *NATUURLIKE* ~ , angle of repose (rest); ~ **bult**, convex slope; ~ **diepte**, run; ~ **gewing**, grading; ~ **hoogte**, lift; ~ **meter**, gradiometer, gradient meter; inclinometer; ~ **meting**, gradiometry; ~ **sbreuk**, gradient; ~ **shoek**, gradient, angle of dip; ~ **slyn**, line of dip; ~ **snaat**, dip-joint; ~ **splank**, grade-board; ~ **srigting**, line of dip; ~ **strepie**, hachure; ~ **svlak**, plane of dip; incline shaft; ~ **swyser**, gradient post.
helm, (-e, -s), caul; helmet; galea; headpiece; helm, bas(i)net; casque; dome (loco); *met die* ~ *gebore*, born with a caul; have second sight; ~ **band**, pug(a)ree; ~ **draad**, filament (of flowers); ~ **draend**, (-e), galeate.
hel'met, (-te, -s), helmet.
helm: ~ **gras**, sea reed; ~ **hoed**, (sun-)helmet; pith helmet.
helmint', (-e), helminth.
helmintologie', helminthology.
helmintoloog', (..**loë**), helminthologist.
helm: ~ **kam**, crest; ~ **kleed**, lambrequin; ~ **klep**, beaver; ~ **knopskimmel**, anthermould; ~ **kruid**, figwort; ~ **knoppie**, anther; ~ **laksman**, helmet-shrike (*Prionopidae*); ~ **pluim**, panache; ~ **spits**, helmet spike; ~ **stok**, tiller, helm; ~ **stylig**, (-e), gynandrous; ~ **styligheid**, gynandry; ~ **teken**, crest; ~ **visier**, visor; ~ **vor'mig**, (-e), galeate.
helofiet', (-e), helophyte.
helloot', (**helote**), helot.

help, (ge-), help, assist, aid, succour; be of use; avail; serve (at table); lend a hand; abet; *is u AL ge ~ ?*, have you been attended to (served)?; *iem. aan 'n BETREKKING ~*, get a situation for someone; *~ JOUSELF, dan ~ God jou*, the Lord helps those that help themselves; *al my gepraat het NIKS ge ~ nie*, all my talking was not a bit of use; *dit ~ NOU nie*, you can't get away from it; *~ my ONTHOU*, remind me; *dit ~ vir TANDPYN*, it is good for toothache; *al ~ dit nie, dit TROOS darem*, even if it does not help it comforts; *~ jouself, dan het jou VRIENDE jou lief*, help yourself; don't be shy; *WAT ~ dit?*, what is the use (good) of it?; *iem. na die ander WÊRELD ~*, send someone to Kingdom Come; ~ **end**, (-e), helping; *'n ~ ende hand*, a helping hand.
hel'pen, sansevieria; tartar, violent person.
hel'peper, cayenne (pepper).
hel'per, (-s), helper, assistant; aid; co-agent; auxiliary.
Help'mekaarvereniging, Helpmekaar Society.
help-my-krap', scabies, the itch.
hel'poort = **hellepoort**.
help'ster, (-s), female helper (assistant), coadjutrix.
hels, (-e), hellish, devilish, infernal, fiendish, hellborn; *'n ~ e LAWAAI*, a hell of a noise; *iem. ~ MAAK*, infuriate someone; *die ~ se VUUR*, hellfire.
hel'steen, lunar caustic, silver nitrate; caustic holder.
Helve'sië, Helvetia; *~ r*, (-s), Helvetian; ~ **ve'ties**, (-e), Helvetian.
hel; ~ **vuur**, hell-fire; ~ **waarts**, towards hell.
hemaal', (hemale), haemal.
hemataal', (..tale), haematic.
hematien', haematin (in blood).
hematiet', haematite.
hematiet'vorming, hematise'ring, haematization.
hemati'ne = **hematien**.
hematogeen', (..gene), haematogenous.
hematologie', haematology; ..**lo'gies**, (-e), haematologic(al).
hematoloog', (..loë), haematologist.
hematurie', haematuria.
hem'degoed, shirting.
he'mel, (-e), heaven; firmament, sky; Elysium; (-s), tester, canopy (of bed); ~ **en AARDE beweeg**, move heaven and earth; ~ *op AARDE hê*, (have) heaven on earth; *so ver uitmekaar as ~ en AARDE*, as far apart as heaven and earth; *geen ~ of AARDE kan beken nie*, not to be able to see a thing; *dit lyk of ~ en AARDE vergaan*, it seems as if they are trying to waken the dead; *nie van ~ of AARDE weet nie*, not to know a thing; *die ~ BEWAAR my!*, heaven help me! *onder die BLOTE ~*, under the open sky; *so seker as die ~ BLOU is*, as sure as fate; *uit die BLOU ~*, out of the blue; *die ~ sy DANK, thank heavens! DANK die ~*, thank heavens! *in die DERDE ~ wees*, be in one's seventh heaven; *mag die ~ GEE*, would to heaven; *in die ~ KOM*, go to heaven; *LIEWE ~!*, good heavens (gracious)! *tot aan die ~ REIK*, touch the sky; *dit ROEP (skrei, skreeu) na die ~*, it cries to high heaven; *in die SEWENDE ~ wees*, be in one's seventh heaven; *TUSSEN ~ en aarde*, between heaven and earth, in mid-air; *as die ~ VAL, is algar dood*, (kry almal 'n blou mussie), the heavens may fall and we may have lark-pie for supper; *uit die ~ VAL*, drop from the skies; *iets (iem.) tot die ~ VERHEF*, laud something (someone) to the skies; *die ~ WEET, goodness knows*; ~ **bed**, tester-bed, fourposter; ~ **bedekking**, cloudiness of the sky; ~ **beskrywing**, uranography; ~ **bestormer**, (-s), heaven-stormer, Titan; ~ **bewoner**, celestial, dweller in heaven; ~ **blou**, blue of the sky; ~ **bode**, angel; heavenly messenger; ~ **bol**, celestial globe (orb); ~ **boog**, vault of heaven; ~ **boom**, tree of heaven *(Ilanthus altissima)*; ~ **breedte**, celestial latitude; ~ **dak**, dome of (the) heaven(s); ~ **dou**, dew of heaven, manna; ~ **dragonder**, sky pilot; devil-dodger; ~ **gewelf**, celestial vault; firmament; ~ **globe**, celestial globe; H ~ **heer**, Host of Heaven; Lord of Heaven; ~ **hof**, court of heaven; paradise; ~ **hoog**, (..hoë), towering to the sky, sky-high; ~ *hoog prys*, laud to the skies; ~ **ing**, (-e), angel, celestial being; ~ **kaart**, astronomical map; planisphere; H ~ **koningin**, Queen of Heaven; ~ **ledekant**, canopy bedstead; tester-bed; ~ **lig**, heavenly (celestial) light; ~ **liggaam**, celestial (heavenly) body; ~ **lyn**, midheaven; ~ **poort**, heaven's gate; ~ **rein**, (b), pure as heaven; ~ **ruim**, expanse of heaven (the heavens); ~ **ryk**, Kingdom of Heaven.
he'mels, (-e), heavenly, celestial; ethereal; spheric; heaven-born; goluptious; *die H ~ e Ryk*, the Celestial Empire (China); ~ **blou**, sky-blue, azure; cerulean, celeste.
he'mels: ~ **breed**, (..breë), wide as heaven; *dit MAAK 'n ~ breë verskil*, differ like chalk and cheese; ~ **breedte**, astronomical latitude; ~ **gesind**, (-e), pious, heavenly-minded; ~ **gesindheid**, heavenliness.
he'melsnaam: *in ~*, for heaven's sake!
hemel: ~ **stad**, the Celestial City; ~ **straat**, the Milky Way.
he'melstreek, zone (region) of heaven; climate; ..**streke**, points of the compass; zones, climates.
he'melswil: *om ~*, for goodness' sake, for heaven's sake.
he'mel: ~ **taal**, celestial accents; ~ **teken**, sign of the zodiac; ~ **tergend**, (-e), crying to heaven, blasphemous, shameful; ~ **tjie!**, good heavens!; ~ **trans**, canopy of heaven, firmament.
He'melvaart, Ascension; ~ **sdag**, Ascension Day.
he'mel: H ~ **vader**, Heavenly Father; ~ **vreug(de)**, heavenly joy; ~ **vuur**, celestial fire, lightning; ~ **waarts**, heavenward(s); ~ **water**, rain.
hemimorfiet', hemimorphite.
hemiplegie', hemiplegia.
he'misfeer, hemisphere.
hemofilie', haemophilia.
hemoglobien', hemoglobi'ne, haemoglobin.
hemostaat', (hemostate), haemostat.
hemp, (hemde), shirt; *iem. die ~ van die LYF vra*, cross-question someone closely; *iem. die ~ v.d. LYF stroop*, strip someone bare; *nie 'n ~ aan sy LYF hê nie*, have no shirt to one's back; *die ~ is nader as die ROK*, charity begins at home; near is my shirt, but nearer is my skin; *jou ~ vir iem. UITTREK*, be free-hearted; ~ **baadjie**, bush shirt; ~ **bloes(e)**, shirt-blouse; ~ **broek**, combination; cami-knickers; ~ **ie**, (-s), small shirt; *sy ~ ie is KORT*, he is short-tempered; *in sy ~ ie STAAN*, be helpless; be deprived of everything; ~ **kraag**, collar; ~ **linne**, shirting; ~ **rok**, shirt-frock; shirt-waister; ~ **s'boordjie**, shirt collar; ~ **skakel**, link (for cuff); ~ **s'knoop**, ~ **s'knope**, shirt button; stud; ~ **slip**, skirt of shirt; shirt tail; ~ **s'mou**, shirt sleeve; *in sy ~ smoue rondloop*, walk around in his shirt-sleeves.
hen, (-ne), hen; *die ~ wat goue EIERS lê*, the goose that lays the golden eggs; *'n eiewys ~ lê die EIER opsy*, one who goes his own way may well go astray; *loop soos 'n ~ wat 'n EIER wil lê*, fuss like a broody hen; *die ~ netjie wat eerste gekekkel het, het die EIER gelê*, a guilty conscience needs no accusers; *die ~ ne wat die meeste kekkel, lê nie die meeste EIERS nie*, the greatest talkers are always the least doers; big boast, small roast; *'n blinde ~ kry ook partykeer 'n MIELIEPIT*, you never know your luck; *'n ~ wat kraai, word die NEK omgedraai, 'n meisie wat fluit, word uit die huis uitgesmyt*, a whistling maid, a crowing hen is neither good for God nor men; *loop soos 'n ~ wat NES soek*, go about aimlessly; *'n REGTE ou ~*, a broody hen; *'n ~ met SPORE*, a termagant; a virago.
hendi'adis, (-se), hediadys.
hen'dikep, (geselst.), (s) (-s), handicap; (w) (ge-), handicap.
hen'(d)sop, (ge-), hands-up, put up one's hands, surrender; ~ **per**, (-s), hands-upper, one who surrenders.
he'ne = **hede**.
hen'-en-kuikens, nest of tables.
hen-en-kui'kentjie, pincushion (plant).
hen'gel, (ge-), (catch) fish, angle; loiter around; vacillate; *~ na 'n kompliment*, angle (fish) for a compli-

ment; ~ **aar**, (-s), angler; ~ **ary'**, fishing; ~ **gerei**, fishing tackle; ~ **klub**, angling club; ~ **kuns**, halieutics; ~ **paradys**, angler's paradise; ~ **stok**, angling rod.
Heng'stebron, (hist.), Hippocrene.
hen'na, henna.
hen'nep, hemp; ~ **olie**, hempseed oil; ~ **oes**, hemp crop; ~ **saad**, hemp seed.
hen: ~ **nerig**, (-e), henny, fussy; ~ **netjie**, (-s), pullet.
heparien', hepari'ne, heparin.
hepa'ties, (-e), hepatic.
heptaan', heptane.
heptaë'der, (-s), heptahedron; .. **ë'dries**, (-e), heptahedral.
heptagonaal', (..nale), heptagonal.
heptagoon', (..gone), heptagon.
hep'tateug, heptateuch.
heptargie', heptarchy.
her, hither; ~ **en DERWAARTS**, hither and thither; *van JARE* ~, from years past.
her=, re=.
heraan'pas, (-ge-), readjust; ~ **sing**, readjustment.
her'aanstelling, reappointment.
her'absorpsie, reabsorption.
hera'dem, (~), breathe again; ~ **ing**, relief.
her'adresseer, (~), readdress, reconsign, redirect; divert.
heradresse'ring, (~), readdressing; diversion.
her'aflewer, (~), redeliver; ~ **ing**, redelivery; ~ **ings= koste**, redelivery charges.
He'rakles, Hercules.
heraldiek', heraldry.
heral'dies, (-e), heraldic.
heral'dikus, (..dici, -se), herald, blazoner.
her'anneksasie, reannexation.
her'annekseer, (~), reannex.
herba'rium, (..ria, -s), herbarium.
her'bebos, (~), reforest; ~ **sing**, reafforestation.
her'bedraad, (~), rewire; ..**drading**, rewiring.
her'begraaf, ..grawe, (~), rebury, reinter.
her'begrafnis, reburial, reinterment.
her'bekragtig, (~), reconfirm.
her'belas, (~), recharge.
her'beleef, her'belewe, (~), relive.
her'benoem, (~), reappoint; ~ **baar**, (..bare), eligible for reappointment; ~ **ing**, (-e, -s), reappointment.
her'berg, (s) (-e), inn, hotel, tavern; accommodation; public house; hostelry; house; (w) (ge-), shelter, lodge, accommodate; harbour (criminal); ~ **ganger**, (-s), hosteler; ~ **ier'**, (-s), innkeeper, host; ~ **ier'= ster**, (-s), hostess, landlady.
herberg'saam, (..same), hospitable; ~ **heid**, hospitableness, hospitality.
her'besnaar, (~), restring; ..**snaring**, restringing.
her'bevestig, (~), reaffirm.
her'bewapen, (~), rearm; ~ **ing**, rearmament.
her'bewoording, rephrasing.
herbivoor', (s) (..vore), herbivore; (b) (..vore), herbivorous.
her'bloei, (~), reflourish.
herbo're, reborn, regenerate, born again.
herbo'ring, reboring.
herboris', (-te), herborist; ~ **eer'**, (ge-), herborize.
her'bou, (s) rebuilding; reconstruction; (w) (~), rebuild, reconstruct; re-edify; *'n* ~ *de kerk*, a rebuilt church; ~ **er**, (-s), rebuilder; ~ **ing**, rebuilding.
Her'cules, Hercules.
herd, (-e), fireplace, hearth.
herdenk', (~), commemorate, memorialize; celebrate; ~ **ing**, (-e, -s), commemoration, remembrance; *ter* ~ *ing van*, in commemoration of; ~ **ingsdiens**, (religious) commemorative service; ~ **ingskaartjie**, memorial card; ~ **ingsplaat**, memorial tablet; ~ **ingsprentjie**, memorial card.
her'der, (-s), shepherd; clergyman; *GOEIE* ~ !, *O* ~ !, good gracious! *as die* ~ *dwaal, dool die SKAPE*, when the leaders err the followers are confused; *terwyl die* ~ *s twis, roof die WOLF die skape*, while the dogs are snarling at each other the wolf devours the sheep; ~ **in'**, (-ne), shepherdess; ~ **lik**, (-e), pastoral; ~ **loos**, (..lose), without a minister; shepherdless; ~ **roman**, pastoral novel; ~ **samp**, pastorate; ~ **sang**, pastoral poem (song); bucolic; idyll; eclogue.
her'ders: ~ **dig**, (-te), bucolic(s), idyll, pastoral poem; eclogue; ~ **fluit**, shepherd's reed; ~ **haak**, shepherd's crook; ~ **hond**, shepherd's dog; ~ **lewe**, shepherd's (pastoral) life; ~ **lied**, pastoral song; ~ **pastei**, cottage pie; ~ **poësie**, bucolics.
her'der: ~ **skap**, pastorate; ~ **spel**, pastoral play; ~ **staf**, shepherd's crook; (bishop's) crosier; ~ **stam**, nomadic tribe; ~ **svolk**, pastoral people.
herd'hoekie, inglenook.
herdiskonteer', (~), rediscount.
herdiskon'to, rediscount.
herd'kool, cobble-coal.
her'doop, (s) rebaptism.
herdoop', (w) (~), rebaptize, rename, rechristen.
her'doping, (-e, -s), rebaptism.
her'druk, (s) reprint, new edition.
herdruk', (w) (~), reprint.
herd: ~ **steenkool**, cobbles; ~ **yster**, fire-dog, andiron.
He're, the Lord, God; *die DAG van die* ~, the Lord's day, the Sabbath; *in die JAAR van ons* ~, in the year of our Lord; *in die* ~ *ONTSLAPE*, departed in the Lord; *jou aan die* ~ *OORGEE*, give oneself to God; ~ ~ *SÊ*, say "Lord, Lord"; *die TAFEL van die* ~, the communion table; *ons kan die* ~ *nie VOORUITLOOP nie*, we must leave it in the hands of the Lord; *by die* ~ *WEES*, be with the Lord, dead; *as die* ~ *WIL*, God willing.
he're: ~ **afdeling**, (gentle)men's department; ~ **boer**, gentleman-farmer; ~ **boontjie** = **heerboontjie**; ~ **dienste**, compulsory labour, corveé.
hereditéit', heredity.
hereditêr', (-e), hereditary.
he're: ~ **huis**, manor house; ~ **kleding**, men's clothing.
her'eksamen, re-examination.
hereksamineer', (~), re-examine.
here'nig, (~), reunite; rally; ~ **ing**, reunion; rally; reconciliation; ~ **ingsbeweging**, movement for reunion; ~ **ingskongres**, congress for reunion.
her'ent, (~), revaccinate; regraft (trees); ~ **ing**, revaccination; regrafting.
he'reparty, bachelor party.
he'reregte, transfer dues.
Here'ro, (-'s), Herero.
He'retjie, good Lord!
herfs, (-te), autumn, fall; ~ **aand**, autumn evening; ~ **agtig**, (-e), autumnal; ~ **blare**, autumn leaves; ~ **blom**, autumn(al) flower; ~ **blommetentoonstelling**; autumn flower-show; ~ **dag**, autumn day; ~ **draad**, air-thread, gossamer; ~ **kleur**, filemot; autumn colour; ~ **landskap**, autumn(al) landscape; ~ **maneuwers**, autumn manoeuvres; ~ **nag**, autumn night; ~ **nagewening**, autumnal equinox; ~ **sering**, phlox; ~ **son**, autumn sun; ~ **storm**, equinoctial gale; ~ **telik**, (-e), autumnal; ~ **tint**, autumn(al) tint; ~ **ty**, ~ **tyd**, autumn(al) (season); ~ **versameling**, autumn collection (fashion); ~ **vrug**, autumn(al) fruit; ~ **weer**, autumn weather; ~ **wind**, autumn wind.
her'gevangesetting, recommittal.
her'giet, (~), recast, remould.
her'gradeer, (~), regrade; ..**de'ring**, regrading.
hergraveer', (~), recut.
her'groei, regrowth.
hergroepeer', (~), reorganize; realign; regroup; ..**pe'ring**, reorganization.
herhaal', (~), repeat, (re)iterate, recur; rehearse; recapitulate; *die geskiedenis* ~ *hom*, history repeats itself; ~ **bestelling**, repeat order; ~ **delik**, repeatedly, over and over; frequent(ly); ~ **(d)**, **(-de)**, repeated, successive; ~ *de male*, repeatedly; ~ **nommer**, encore; ~ **sinjaal**, repeat signal; ~ **toestel**, ..**ha'ler**, (-s), repeater.
herha'ling, (-e, -s), repetition, recapitulation; recurrence; rehearsal; iterance, iterancy; (re)iteration; reduplication; *by* ~, repeatedly, time and again, on a repitition (of the offence); ~ **samestelling**, iterative.
herha'lings: ~ **getal**, multiplicative (recurring) num=

ber; ~**les,** repetition lession; ~**kursus,** refresher course; ~**oefening,** repetition (recapitulatory) exercise; ~**teken,** repeat sign (music); ~**woord,** frequentative.
her'inbesitneming, resumption of possession.
her'indeel, (-ge-), redistribute; reclassify; remuster; ..**deling,** redistribution; reorganization; reclassification, reapportionment.
herin'ner, (~), remember, recollect; (re)call to mind; ~ *AAN,* remind of; recall; *vir sover ek my KAN* ~, as far as I can remember.
herin'nering, (-e, -s), remembrance, recollection, reminiscence, memory; reminder; keepsake, memento, souvenir; anamnesis; memorial; *in* ~ *BRING,* recall; *TER* ~ *aan,* in memory of; as a memorial to; ~**sbeeld,** memory, image; ~**smedalje,** commemorative medal; ~**svermoë,** memory, recollective power.
her'inskeping, re-embarkation.
her'inskryf, (~), re-enter.
her'inskrywing, re-entry.
her'invoer, (s) reimportation; (w) (~), reimport.
herken', (~), identify, recognize; *iem.* ~ *AAN,* recognize a person by; *iets as jou EIENDOM* ~, identify something as one's property; ~**baar,** (..**bare),** recognizable; ~**ning,** recognition; ~**ningsein,** recognition signal.
herken'nings: ~**parade,** identification parade; ~**plaatjie,** identity disc; ~**teken,** distinctive mark, sign of recognition; countersign; ~**woord,** password, countersign.
herkeur', (~), re-examine, retest; ~**ing,** re-examination, retesting.
herkies', (~), re-elect; ~**baar (..bare),** re-eligible; eligible for re-election; *hy is* ~ *baar,* he is re-eligible; ~**baarheid,** eligibility for re-election; ~**ing, (-e, -s),** re-election.
her'kleur, (~), retint.
her'koms, origin, descent, source, extraction; derivation (of word); provenance; ~'**tig,** descended (born, sprung) from, a native of; originating from.
herkoop', (s) repurchase; (w) (~), buy back, repurchase.
herkou', (ge-), ruminate, chew the cud; repeat; ~*ende DIER,* ruminating animal (ruminant); *'n SAAK* ~, turn something over in one's mind; ponder over a subject; ~**er, (-s),** ruminant; ~**ery,** ~**ing,** pondering; chewing the cud; wearisome repetition.
herkou'tjie, (-s), cud (of animal); *sy* ~ *spring in sy KEEL,* he has a bone in the throat; *iem. het sy* ~ *VERLOOR,* he is out of sorts.
herkry', (~), get back, regain, recover; recuperate (health); resume (liberty); ~**g'baar, (..bare),** recoverable; ~**ging,** regaining, recovery; recuperation.
Her'kules, Hercules.
herku'lies, (-e), Herculean; ~*e taak,* Herculean task.
herlaai', (~), recharge (elect); reload; ~**koste,** reloading-charges.
herlê, (s) relay; ~ *van dwarsleers,* resleepering; (w) (~), relay.
herleef' = **herlewe.**
herlees', (~), reread, read over again.
her'legging, relaying.
herlei', (~), reduce; simplify; convert; transform; deduce; ~**baar, (..bare),** reducible; ~**baarheid,** reducibility; ~**ding,** reduction; conversion; deduction; reducement; ~*ding van breuke,* simplification of fractions; ~**dingsformule,** deduction formula; ~**dingstafel,** reduction table; plotting scale; ~**passer,** reducing compass.
her'lesing, rereading.
herle'we, (~), revive; live again; relive; ..**le'wing,** revival, reanimation, quickening.
hermafrodiet', (-e), hermaphrodite; ..**di'ties, (-e),** hermaphroditic; bisexual; ..**ditis'me,** hermaphroditism.
hermeet', (~), measure again, remeasure.
hermelyn', ermine; ~**bont,** ermine (fur); ~**vlekke,** ermine marks.
hermeneutiek', hermeneutics.
hermeneu'ties, (-e), hermeneutic(al).

herme'ties, (-e), hermetic, air-tight.
hermiet', (-e), hermit.
hermita'ge, hermityk', hermitage.
her'moeskruie, horse-tail, bottle-brush *(Equisetum arvense).*
her'munt, (~), recoin; ~**ing,** recoinage; reminting.
herneem', (~), take again, recapture; resume.
herne'ming, retaking, recapture; resumption.
herneu'termes, bowie knife, Hernhuter knife.
hernieu', (w) (~), renew, renovate; (b) **(-de),** renewed; resumed; *'n* ~ *de kontrak,* a renewed contract; ~**baar,** (..**bare),** renewable.
hernoem', (~), rename; ~**ing, (-e, -s),** renaming.
hernu'baar = **hernieubaar.**
hernu'de = **hernieude.**
hernu(i)'termes = **herneutermes.**
hernu'we, (~), renew, renovate; ~**r, (-s),** renewer.
hernu'wing, renewal, renovation.
Hero'dotos, Herodo'tus, Herodotus.
heroïek', hero'ïes, (-e), heroic.
heroïen', heroï'ne, heroin; ~**handel,** heroin trade; ~**smokkelary,** heroin smuggling; ~**verslaafde,** heroin addict.
heroï'sme, heroism.
her'ondersoek, (s) reinvestigation; (w) (~), reinvestigate.
her'ondervraging, re-examination (of witness).
her'ontmoeting, second meeting; ~**swedstryd,** return fight; return match.
her'ontwaak, (~), reawake.
her'ontwerp, (~), redesign; redraft.
her'oorweging, reconsideration; *'n saak in* ~ *neem,* take a matter into reconsideration.
her'opbou, (s) reconstruction; (w) (~), reconstruct.
hero'pen, (~), reopen; ~**ing,** reopening.
her'oplewing, recrudescence.
her'opname, readmittance.
her'opvoering, repeat performance.
her'oriëntasie, reorientation.
he'ros, (-se, heroë), demigod, (Greek) hero.
herout', (-e), herald.
hero'wer, (~), reconquer, recapture, recover (lost ground); ~**aar, (-s),** reconqueror; ~**ing,** reconquest, recapture.
her'pes, herpes.
herpetologie', herpetology; ..**lo'gies, (-e),** herpetologic(al).
herpetoloog', (..loë), herpetologist.
herplaas', (~), replace; reinsert (advertisement).
herplant', (~), replant; ~**ing,** replanting.
herpla'sing, replacement; reinsertion.
her proviandeer, (~), revictual.
her'rangskikking, rearrangement.
herre'ël, (~), rearrange; ~**ing,** rearrangement.
her'registrasie, second registration.
herre'se, rerisen, revived; *see* **herrys;** ~ **ne, (-s),** person risen.
her'rie, confusion, noise, uproar, row; *na die* ~ *GAAN,* go to the devil; *iem. op sy* ~ *GEE,* give someone a thrashing; *'n HEIDENSE* ~, a devil of a row; *die* ~ *IN wees,* be furious, be in a rage; *op sy* ~ *KRY,* to be given what for; ~ *MAAK,* kick up a row; *'n* ~ *OPSKOP,* raise Cain; cause a commotion; ~**maker,** noisy fellow, rowdy; ~**makery,** rowdyism.
Herrn'hutter, (-s), Herrnhuter, Moravian Brother.
herroep', (~), revoke, repeal, abolish, abrogate; reclaim; abjure; cancel; redesignate (appointment); annul (laws); countermand (order); recall (to mind); recant (statement); retract (promise); ~**baar,** revocable, recallable, repealable; defeasible; ~**baarheid,** revocability; ~**ing,** repeal (of law); revocation; recantation, retraction; abrogation; palinode; defeasance, reclaim.
herrys', (~), rise from the dead; arise; ~**enis,** resurrection.
hersê', (~), repeat, say over again.
herseg'ging, repetition.
her'senskim, phantasm, chimera, dream, illusion, phantom, fantasy, hallucination; ~'**mig, (-e),** chimerical, fanciful, phantomatic.
her'senskudding, *see* **harsingskudding.**

hersien', (~), revise, review, reconsider; (re)adjust; ~ er, (-s), reviser, revisor; ~ ing, revision, review; *Hof van H~ ing,* Revision Court; ~ ingsbeampte, revising officer.
herska'pe, transformed, reborn.
herskat', (~), revalue; reassess; ~ ting, revaluation, reassessment.
herskep', (~, **herskape**), recreate, regenerate; convert, transform; ~ pend, (-e), recreative; ~ ping, recreation, regeneration; conversion.
herskik', (~), reorganize; ~ king, reorganization.
herspo'ring, rerailment.
herstel', (s) reparation, repair (of what is broken); resituation; redress (of wrongs); convalescence, recovery, rally, restoration (of health); reinstatement (official); rectification; recruitment; refit; recomposition; ~ *van huweliksregte,* restitution of conjugal rights; (w) (~), recover, convalesce, pull oneself together, get over; rectify, make good; restore, rehabilitate; restitute; remedy; overhaul (machine); readjust; re-establish; refit; redintegrate; recruit; rebuild; redress; recondition; repair, mend (shoes); ~ !, as you were! *die aandele het* ~ , the shares rallied; ~ **afdeling**, repair section; ~ **baar**, (..bare), reparable; retrievable; ~ **betaling**, reparation-payment; ~ **depot**, repair depot; ~ **gewas**, (-se), ley, restorative crop; ~ **kans**, chance of recovery; ~ **koste**, cost of repairs; ~ **kuil**, pit, ~ **lende**, (-s), convalescent; ~ **ler**, (-s), repairer; replacer; mender; rebuilder.
herstel'ling, recovery, rehabilitation; restitution, reclamation; convalescence; instauration, restoration; reinstatement (of discharged official); repair; readjustment; re-establishment; redintegration.
herstel'lings: ~ **oord**, health-resort, convalescent home; ~ **teken**, natural sign (music); ~ **verlof**, recuperative leave; ~ **vermoë**, recuperative power; ~ **werk**, repairs, repair work; ~ **werkplaas**, (repair) workshop.
herstel': ~ **put**, drop-pit; ~ **wa**, breakdown lorry.
herstel'werk, repairs, repair work, mending; ~ **bestelling**, repair indent; ~ **plaas**, repair shop.
herstel'winkel, repair shop.
herstem', (~), vote again; tune again (musical instrument); ~ **ming**, second ballot; retuning.
hert, (-e), hart, stag, deer; *hygend* ~ !, oh, goodness!, ~ **ejag**, deer-stalking.
herte'ken, (~), sign again.
hertel', (~), recount; ~ **ling**, recount.
her'tevel, doeskin.
hert'hond, stag-hound, deer-hound.
her'tog, (..toë), duke; ~ **dom**, (-me), duchy; ~ **in'**, (-ne), duchess.
hertrou', (~), remarry, marry again; ~ **e**, remarriage; ~ **ing**, remarriage.
herts: ~ **horing**, hartshorn; ~ **leer**, buckskin, deerskin.
Hertzogis'me, Hertzogism.
her'uitbreking, recrudescence.
her'uitgawe, reissue, republishing.
her'uitreiking, reissue.
her'uitsend, (~), relay; rebroadcast; ~ **ing**, relay(ing).
her'uitvoer, (s) re-exportation; (w) (~), re-export.
her'vasstelling, re-enactment.
hervat', (~), resume, repeat, recommence, begin again; reassume; ~ **ting**, recommencement, reassumption, resumption, renewal; revivor (lawsuit).
her'verbinding, reattachment, recombination.
her'verdeel, (~), redistribute, reapportion, redivide.
her'verdigting, recondensation.
her'verhoor, (s) rehearing; retrial; (w) (~), bring to trial again, retry.
her'verkoop, (s) resale; (w) (~), resell.
her'verseker, (~), reinsure; ~ **ing**, reinsurance.
her'verskyn, (~), reappear; ~ **ing**, reappearance, re-emergence.
herves'tig, (~), resettle; rehouse; ~ **ing**, resettlement.
hervind', (~), find again, recover; *sy kalmte* ~ , recover his composure.
hervon'de, refound; *see* **hervind**.
hervorm', (~), reform, reshape; reclaim; reconstruct (company); ~ **baar**, reformable; ~ **(d)**, **(-de)**, reformed; *die H~ de Kerk,* the Reformed Church; ~ **end**, **(-e)**, reformative, reformatory; ~ **er**, **(-s)**, reformer; ~ **ing**, **(-e, -s)**, reformation, reform; reconstruction.
Hervor'ming: *die* ~ , the Reformation; ~ *sdag,* Reformation Day (Oct. 31st).
hervor'mingsgesind, **(-e)**, reformist(ic); ~ **e**, **(-s)**, reformist.
hervul', (~), refill; recharge; ~ **ling**, refill.
her'waardasie, revaluation.
her'waardeer, (~), revalue.
her'waardering, revaluation, reassessment.
her'waarts, in this direction, hither, this way, hitherward; ~ *en derwaarts dwaal,* wander hither and thither.
herwa'pen, (~), rearm; ~ **ing**, rearmament.
herwin', (~), regain, reconquer, recover (lost ground); retrieve (lost property); retake; reclaim (waste land); ~ **ner**, **(-s)**, recoverer; reclaimer; ~ **ning**, recovery, reclaiming, recapture; reclamation (of soil).
herwon'ne, recovered, regained; reclaimed; ~ *wol,* mungo.
herwy', (~), reconsecrate; ~ **ding**, reconsecration.
heryk', (~), regauge; recalibrate; ~ **ing**, regauging; recalibration.
he'serig, **(-e)**, slightly hoarse, husky; ~ **heid**, hoarseness, huskiness.
Hesperi'de, Hesperides.
Hespe'rië, Hesperia.
Hes'sies, **(-e)**, Hessian.
het, *see* **hê**.
he'te = **hede**.
he'ter: *op* ~ *daad betrap,* catch in the act; catch red-handed.
hete're, **(-s)**, hetaera, courtesan.
heterodoks', **(-e)**, heterodox; ~ **ie'**, heterodoxy.
heterofiet', **(-e)**, heterophyte.
heterogaam', (..game), heterogamous.
heterogamie', heterogamy.
heterogeen', (..gene), heterogeneous.
heterogene'se, heterogenesis.
heterogeniteit', heterogeneity.
heteromorf', **(-e)**, heteromorphic; ~ **ie'**, heteromorphism.
heteroniem', (s) **(-e)**, heteronym; (b) **(-e)**, heteronymous.
heteronomie', heteronomy.
heteronoom', (..nome), heteronomous.
heteropatie', heteropathy.
heteropa'ties, **(-e)**, heteropathic.
heteroseksualiteit', heterosexuality.
heteroseksueel', (..suele), heterosexual.
heterosigoot', (..gote), heterozygous.
het'man, hetman (Cossacks).
het'se! hetsê! hallo there! I say!
hetsy': ~ .. ~ , either .. or; whether .. or.
het'tété = **hittete**.
heug, (s): *teen* ~ *en meug,* willy-nilly; reluctantly; (w) **(ge-)**: *dit* ~ *my,* I remember; I recall.
heu'genis, remembrance, recollection, memory.
heug'lik, **(-e)**, memorable; glad; joyful, pleasant; ~ **heid**, joyfulness, pleasantness; memorability.
heul, **(ge-)**: ~ *met,* collude with, hold secret intercourse with, collaborate with (the enemy); ~ **ing**, collusion.
heu'ning, honey, ~ *in die MOND, gal in die hart,* bees that have honey in their mouths have stings in their tails; *iem.* ~ *om die MOND smeer,* soft-soap someone; butter someone up; ~ *in die MOND dra,* drip honey; be honey-tongued; ~ *is nie SOET genoeg vir hom nie,* butter won't melt in his mouth; *SOETER as* ~ , sweeter than honey; *wie* ~ *wil eet, moet STEKE verdra,* no grains without pains; no pains no grains; no sweet without sweat; ~ *uit iets SUIG,* get the best out of something; ~ *op die TONG hê,* be honey-tongued; ~ **agtig**, **(-e)**, honied (honeyed); like honey; ~ **bakkie**, hectary (botany); ~ **beer**, honey-bear *(Helarctos malayanus)*; ~ **bekkie**, honey-bird; ~ **bier**, mead; ~ **blom**, candytuft; ~ **bos**, *Melobobium canescens, Euryops aspara*

goide; ~**by**, honeybee; ~**das**, honey-badger; ~**dou**, blight; honeydew; ~**draend, (-e)**, melliferous; ~**drank**, hydromel, mead; ~**etend, (-e)**, melliphagous; ~**graat**, honeycomb; ~**graatsteek**, honeycomb-stitch; ~**graatverkoeler**, honeycomb radiator; ~**gras**, soft (sweet) grass; ~**kas**, super-hive; ~**kelk**, ectary; ~**klier**, nectar (honey) gland; ~**koek**, honeycomb; ~**koekag'tig, (-e)**, favose, alveolate, alveolar; ~**koekpoeding**, honeycomb cream; ~**koekspons**, honeycomb sponge; ~**koeksteek**, honeycomb stitch; *kwas: die* ~*kwas gebruik*, flatter, coax; ~**merk**, nectar guide; ~**nes**, beehive; ~**pot**, honey jar; *met die* ~*pot rondloop*, soft-soap a person; drip honey; ~**sakkie**, nectary; honey-bag; ~**saphoudend, (-e)**, nectariferous; ~**seem**, virgin honey; ~**slurp**, proboscis; ~**soet**, sweet as honey; honeyed (words); ~**sous**, honey sauce; ~**steen**, mellite; ~**suiker**, invert sugar; ~**tee**, bush-tea (*Cyclopia vogelii*); ~**voël**, honey-guide; ~**water**, hydromel, ~**wyn**, honey wine, hydromel; mulse; ~**wyser**, honey-guide (*Indicatoridae*).

heup, (-e), hip, haunch (of animal); huckle; *iem.* ~ *en skenkel slaan*, smite someone hip and thigh; ~**been**, hip-bone; ilium; hucklebone; haunch-bone; innominate bone; ~**beenstuk**, aitch-bone (beef); saddle of mutton; ~**breuk**, fracture of the hip; ~**doek**, loincloth; ~**erig, (-e)**, with big hip-bones, ~**gewrig (-te)**, hip-joint, coxa; ~**gewrigsontsteking**, coxitis; ~**jas**, jigger; ~**jig**, hip-gout, ischias, sciatica; ~**knop**, point of hip; ~**kom**, hip cavity; lyn, hip line, • maat, hip-measurement; ~**potjie**, hip-cavity; ~**pyn**, pain in the hip; sciatica; ~**riem**, hip-strap; ~**rok**, skirt; ~**sak**, hip-pocket; ~**senuwee**, sciatic nerve; ~**siekte**, hip-disease; ~**skoot**, shot through the hips; ~**spier**, hip-muscle; ~**stuk**, hip-yoke; ~**swaai**, swing of hips; ~**val**, peplum.

heuristiek', heuristics.
heuris'ties, (-e), heuristic.
heu'wel, (-s), hill; mound; ~**agtig, (-e)**, hilly; downy; ~**agtigheid**, hilliness; ~**hang**, hillside; ~**ketting**, chain of hills; ~**landskap**, hilly landscape; ~**rem**, hill-holder; ~**rug**, ridge of hill; ~**tjie, (-s)**, small hill, hummock; ~**top**, hilltop.
he'wel, (s) (-s), siphon; crane; (w) **(ge-)**, draw off, siphon; crane; ~**barometer**, siphon barometer; ~**ing**, siphonage; ~**kraan**, siphon cock; ~**pyp**, siphon pipe; ~**werking**, siphonage.
he'wig, (-e), severe, violent, fierce; exquisite (pain); acute; fell, grim; high; hard, intense (cold); vehement; heavy (rain); sharp (fight); ~**heid**, violence, vehemence; acuteness, acuity, exquisiteness; intenseness, intensity.
hiaat', (hiate), hiatus, gap.
hialiet', hyalite; hiali'ties, (-e), hyalitic.
hiasint', (-e), hyacinth.
hiberneer', (ge-), hibernate.
Hiber'nies, (-e), Hibernian.
hibis'kus, (-se), hibiscus.
hibri'de, (-s), hybrid.
hibri'dies, (-e), hybrid.
hibridisa'sie, hybridism.
hibridiseer', (ge-), hybridize.
hibried', (-e), hybrid.
hidal'go, (-'s), hidalgo.
hi'dra, (-s), hydra.
hidraat', (hidrate), hydrate; ~**suur**, hydrated acid.
hi'drant, (-e), hydrant.
hidra'sie, hydration.
hidrateer', (ge-), hydrate; ..**te'ring**, hydration.
hidreer', (ge-), hydrogenate; **hidre'ring**, hydrogenation.
hi'drochloorsuur, hydrochloric acid.
hi'drodinamies, hydrodynamic.
hi'drodinamika, hydrodynamic.
hi'droëlektries, (-e), hydro-electric.
hidrofiel', (-e), hydrophilic.
hidrofiet', (-e), hydrophyte.
hidrofi'ties, (-e), hydrophytic.
hidrofobie', hydrophobia.
hidrofoon', (..fone), hydrophone.
hidrogeen', hydrogen.

hidrogeneer', (ge-), hydrogenate; ..**gene'ring**, hydrogenation.
hidrograaf', (..grawe), hydrographer.
hidrografie', hydrography; ~**k'**, hydrograph; ..**gra'fies, (-e)**, hydrographic(al).
hi'drokoolstof, hydrocarbon.
hi'droksi'de, hidroksied', hydroxide.
hidroli'se, hydrolysis.
hidroliseer', (ge-), hydrolize.
hidrologie', hydrology.
hi'drometer, hidrome'ter, hydrometer.
hidropatie', hydropathy; ..**pa'ties, (-e)**, hydropathic.
hidropo'nika, hydroponics.
hidropsie', hydropsy.
hi'drosiaansuur, prussic acid.
hidrosfeer', hydrosphere.
hidroskoop', (..skope), hydroscope.
hidrosta'ties, (-e), hydrostatic.
hidrosta'tika, hydrostatics.
hidroterapie', hydrotherapy.
hidrotroop', (..trope), hydrotropic.
hidrotropie', hydrotropism.
hidrou'lies, (-e), hydraulic; ~*e KALK*, hydraulic lime; ~*e KRAAN*, hydraulic crane; ~*e REM*, hydraulic brake.
hidrou'lika, hydraulics.
hie'ha, hee-haw.
hiel, (-e), heel, shoe (of lace); bead(s); *die* ~ *van ACHILLES*, Achilles' heel; *die* ~*e LIG*, show a clean pair of heels; *iem. op die* ~*e SIT*, be close on the heels of someone; *op iem. se* ~*e WEES*, follow close on someone's heels; ~**bande**, beaded-edge tyres; ~**ing, (-s)**, hawser bend; heel (of mast); ~**kussing**, heel-pad; ~**ojief**, cyma reversa; ~**rus**, heel-rest; ~**stoel**, heel-chair.
hie'na, (-s), hyena.
hiep! hip! (hip, hip, hurrah!).
hier, here; ~ *en DAAR*, here and there; ~ *of DAAR*, somewhere or other; ~ *JY!* I say! hallo! ~ *te LANDE*, in this country; ~ *OM*, round this way; ~ *ROND*, round about here; ~ **aan**, to, by this; here(un)to; ~ **af**, from this; ~ **agter**, behind this.
hiërarg', (-e), hierarch; ~**ie', (-ë)**, hierarchy; ~**iek', (-e)**, official (church); *die* ~*ieke weg*, official (church) channels; ~**ies, (-e)**, hierarchic(al).
hier: ~**benede**, here below; ~**benewens**, besides this; ~**binne**, within (here), in here; ~**bo**, up here; ~**buite**, outside; without this; ~ **by**, herewith, hereby, enclosed, included; ~ *by kom nog*, in addition to this, moreover; ~ **deur**, through here; through this; owing to; by this; hereby; by these presents; ~**die**, this; ~**heen**, this way, to this side, hither; ~**in**, in this; herein.
hier'jy, (s) (-s), lout, boor, yokel; (w) **(ge-)**, order about; *ek laat my nie* ~ *nie*, I don't allow anyone to order me about; (bw); ~**grootword**, grow up without (parental) discipline; ~**mense**, low-class people; ~**vent**, hooligan, uncouth fellow, lout.
hier: ~**lang(e)s**, along here, past here, somewhere here; ~**mee**, with this, herewith, hereby; ~**na**, after this, hereafter, hereinafter, hereunder; ~**naas'**, next door; next to this; ~**na'maals**, hereafter, in the beyond; in the next life; *die* ~*namaals*, the hereafter, the great beyond.
hier'natoe, this way; here; *dis nie* ~ *en ook nie DAARNATOE nie*, it is neither here nor there; it is not to the point; *KOM* ~, come here; *NIE* ~ *nie*, super; out of this world.
hiëroglief', (..gliewe), hieroglyph.
hiërogli'fies, (-e), hieroglyphic.
hier: ~**om**, for this reason; round here; ~*om en daarom*, for this and that reason; ~**omheen**, round this; ~**omstreeks**, hereabout(s); ~**omtrent**, hereabout(s); about this; ~**onder**, underneath, under here; at the foot (of the page); among these.
hier'oor, about this, over this; ~ *en DAAROOR*, this and that; ~ *of DAAROOR*, about this and that.
hier: ~**oorheen'**, over this; ~**op**, (up)on this, after this; hereupon; ~**opvolgend**, following (on this); ~**so**, here, at this place; *(kom)* ~ *so!* come here! ~**son'der**, without this.

hiert = **hierts**.
hier: ~ **teen**, against this; ~ **teenoor**, opposite; against this; ~ **tevore**, hereinbefore; ~ **toe**, for this end; thus far; up till now, hereto; *TOT* ~ *toe,* so far; thus far; *tot* ~ *toe en nie VERDER nie,* thus far and no further.
hierts! hallo! what's this!
hier: ~ **tussen**, between (among) these; ~ **uit**, out of (from) this, hence; ~ **van**, herefrom, of this, about this; ~ *van en daarvan praat,* talk about this, that and the other thing; discuss miscellaneous matters; ~ **vandaan**, from here, hence, from this point; in future; ~ **volgend**, (-e), following; ~ **volgens**, according to this; ~ **voor**, for this, in return (for this); ~ **voor**´, before this place, in front.
hiet[1], (s) (nie alg.), time; ~ *vir* ~, time after time.
hiet[2], (w) (ge-), order; *iem.* ~ *en gebied,* order someone about.
hi´fe, (-s), hypha.
higië´ne, hygiene.
higië´nies, (-e), hygienic.
higrafiet´, (-e), hygrophyte.
higrofobie´, hygrophobia.
higrograaf´, (..grawe), hygrograph.
hi´grometer, higrome´ter, hygrometer.
higrometrie´, hygrometry.
higrome´tries, (-e), hygrometric.
higroskoop´, (..skope), hygroscope.
higroskopie´, hygroscopy.
higrosko´pies, (-e), hygroscopic.
hik, (s) (-ke), hiccough; *die* ~ *hê,* have the hiccups; (w) (ge-), hiccough; *nie* ~ *of KIK nie,* not to utter as much as a murmur; *sonder om te* ~ *of te KIK,* without saying a word; *SLAAN dat hy so* ~, strike him a stunning blow; ~ **kerig**, (-e), hiccoughing.
hilariteit´, hilarity.
hilofiet´, (-e), hylophyte.
Himala´jagebergte, Himalaya mountains.
Himala´jas, the Himalayas.
hi´men, (-s), hymen.
him´ne, (-s), hymn.
hin´de, (-s), doe, hind.
hin´der, (s), trouble, impediment, hindrance, discomfort; obstacle; *'n* ~ *wegruim,* clear away an obstacle; (w) (ge-), hinder, hamper, impede, disturb, embarrass, entrammel, annoy; clog (wheels); trouble; ~ **laag**, ambush; ambuscade; ~ **lik**, (-e), annoying, troublesome (people); inconvenient, disturbing, cumbrous; awkward; cumbersome (things).
hin´dernis, (-se), obstacle, impediment, hindrance, encumbrance; obstruction; block; annoyance; embarrassment; hazard (golf); *wedloop met* ~ *se,* obstacle-race; steeplechase; ~ **wedren**, steeplechase; obstacle-race.
hin´derpaal, (..pale), obstacle; bar, impediment, stumbling-block; hedge; drawback, stumbling-stone; barrier.
Hin´doe, (-s), Hindu; ~ **is´me**, Hinduism; ~ **s**, (-e), Hindu; ~ **stan**, Hindustan; ~ **sta´ni**, Hindustani (language).
hin´gel, (ge-), hesitate, shrink back.
hings, (-te), stallion, stud-horse; entire; *as die* ~ *te vul en die merries horings kry,* on the Greek calends; when pigs fly.
hing´sel, (-s), handle, (drop-)handle; hinge; loop (between whip and stick); bow; ~ **mandjie**, basket with handle.
hings´terig, hings´tig, (-e), on heat, ruttish, oestrous; lewd.
hings´vul, colt (foal).
hink, (ge-), limp, hobble; halt; vacillate; ~ *op twee GEDAGTES,* vacillate (halt) between two opinions; hesitate; shrink back.
hin´kel, (ge-), play hopscotch.
hink: ~ **ende-pink(ende)**, ~ **epink**, dot and go one; limping, lame; ~ **spel**, hopscotch.
hink´-stap´-spring´, hop, skip and jump.
hink´vers, choliamb.
hin´nik, (ge-), neigh, whinny.
hin´terland, hinterland.
hip, (ge-), hop.
hipabassaal´, (..sale), hypabyssal.

hi´per-Afrikaans, (-e), ultra-Afrikaans.
hiper´baton, (-s), hyperbaton.
hi´perbeleef, (-de), over-polite.
hi´perbeskaaf, (-de), over-civilized, over-refined.
hiperbo´lies, (-e), hyperbolic, exaggerated.
hiperbool´, (..bole), hyperbole; exaggeration; hyperbola; ~ **rat**, hypoid gear.
hiperestesie´, hyperaesthesia.
hiperiet´, hyperite.
hiperkri´ties, (-e), hypercritical.
hi´permark, -te, hypermarket.
hipermetropie´, hypermetropia.
hi´permodern, (-e), hypermodern.
hipertrofie´, hypertrophy.
hipidiomorf´, hypidiomorphous; ~ **ies**, (-e), hypidiomorphic.
hipno´se, hypnosis; ~ **behandeling**, hypnosis treatment.
hipno´ties, (-e), hypnotic.
hipnotiseer´, (ge-), hypnotize.
hipnotiseur´, (-s), hypnotist.
hipnotis´me, hypnotism, animal magnetism.
hi´po=, under, below.
hipochon´drie, hypochondria.
hipochon´dries, (-e), hypochondriac(al).
hipoder´mies, (-e), hypodermic.
hipofi´se, (-s), hypophysis, pituitary gland.
hipofosfiet´, hypophosphite.
hipogeen´, (..gene), hypogene.
hipokon´ders, hypochondria; whims, caprices; ~ *hê,* be a hypochondriac.
hipokriet´, (-e), hypocrite.
hipokristallyn´, (-e), hypocrystalline.
hipokri´ties, (-e), hypocritic(al).
hiposen´trum, hypocentre.
hipoteek´, (..teke), (ong.), mortgage; hypothec; encumbrance; ~ **aflossing**, mortgage redemption; ~ **bank**, mortgage bank; ~ **gewer**, mortgagor; ~ **houer**, mortgagee; encumbrancer; ~ **nemer**, mortgagee.
hipotekêr´, (-e), hypothecary.
hipotenu´sa, (-s), hypotenuse.
hipotermie´, hypothermy.
hipotermaal´, (..male), hypothermal.
hipote´se, (-s), hypothesis, postulate.
hipote´ties, (-e), hypothetic(al).
hip´pies, (ong.), (-e), hippic, equine; ~ *e sport,* horse-racing.
hippodroom´, (..drome), hippodrome.
hip´pokras, hippocras.
Hippokra´ties, (-e), Hippocratic.
Hippokreen´, Hippocrene.
hippopo´tamus, (-se), hippopotamus.
hip´someter, hipsome´ter, (-s), hypsometer.
hipsometrie´, hypsometry.
hipsome´tries, (-e), hypsometric.
hirsu´ties, (-e), hirsute.
hi´sop, hyssop.
histere´se, hysteresis.
histe´rie, hysteria, hysterics.
histe´ries, (-e), hysterical.
histogene´se, histogenesis.
histogene´ties, (-e), histogenetic.
histologie´, histology; ..**lo´gies**, (-e), histological.
histoloog´, (..loë), histologist.
histo´rie, (vero.), (-ë, -s), history, story; ~ **s**, (-e), historic(al).
histo´rikus, (..rici, -se), historian; recorder.
historiografie´, historiography; ..**gra´fies**, (-e), historiographical.
historisis´me, historicism.
historis´me, historism.
historisiteit´, historicity.
histrio´nies, (-e), histrionic.
histrionis´me, histrionism.
Hit´land, Shetland; ~ **er**, Shetland pony.
Hitleris´me, Hitlerism, Nazi-ism.
Hit´lertydperk, Hitler era.
hits, (w) (ge-), make red-hot (iron); (b) red-hot; ~ **broekie**, hot-pants.
hit´sig, (-e), hot; lewd; ruttish, on heat (animals); ~ **heid**, heat; ruttishness, rut.

hits'tjor, (-re), hot rod.
hit'te, heat; fervour; flame; ~ **afleiding**, heat dissipation; ~ **bereik**, heat-range; ~ **beroerte**, heat-stroke; ~ **bestand**, heat-resistant; ~ **damp**, hot vapour; ~ **golf**, heat-wave; ~ **graad**, degree of temperature; ~ **keerplaat**, heat-shield; ~ **kraak**, fire crack; ~ **kunde**, pyronomics; ~ **liewend**, (-e), thermophilic; ~ **meter**, heat-meter; pyrometer; ~ **puisies**, summer rash, heat-spot, heat-rash; miliaria; ~ **skerm**, heat-shield; ~ **steek**, heat-stroke.
hit'tete: *so ~*, touch and go; a near thing.
hit'te: *~-uitslag*, prickly heat, heat-rash; ~ **vas**, (-te), heat-resisting, heat-proof; ~ **vloei**, heat-flow; ~ **vloeitempo**, heat-flow rate; ~ **weerstand**, heat-tolerance; ~ **wyser**, heat-indicator.
hit'tig, (-e), hot; ruttish; heated; ~ **heid**, heat; ruttishness.
h'm, h'm, hem!
hmf, umph!
ho, ho! stop!
hob'bel, (ge-), rock, (go) see-saw; hobble; ~ **aar**, (-s), circular plane; ~ **agtig**, (-e), uneven, rugged, bumpy; ~ **ig**, (-e), bumpy, uneven, rough, rugged; ~ **patroon**, crazy pattern (crochet); ~ **perd**, cock-horse, hobble-horse; rocking horse; ~ **rig**, (-e), uneven, bumpy; ~ **skaaf**, compass (circular) plane; ~ **vyl**, riffler.
ho'bo, (-'s), hautboy (music), oboe (hobo); ~ **is'**, (-te), ~ **speler**, (-s), oboist.
hock'(wyn), hock.
hodograaf', (..grawe), hodograph.
ho'dometer, hodome'ter, (-s), hodometer.
hoe, how; what (in exclamations); ~ *DAN ook*, anyhow, somehow; ~ *DAN*? how then? ~ *'s DIT*? how's that? ~ *EERDER*, ~ *beter*, the sooner the better; ~ *HET ek dit met jou*? what have I to make of you? ~ *JAMMER!* what a pity! ~ *LAAT is dit*? what is the time? ~ *LANGER* ~ *erger*, the longer it is left, the worse it becomes; ~ *NOU*? what now? *of ~ SÊ ek*? or what am I saying? ~ *SO*? what's that? ~ *dit ook SY*, however this may be; be that as it may; *nie weet ~ of WAT nie*, not know how or what.
hoë, *see* **hoog**.
hoed¹, (s), (-e), hat, bonnet; *sy ~ AFHAAL vir iem.*, take off one's hat to someone; *hy sit sy ~ so EENKANT toe*, he swanks; he plumes himself; *iem. sy ~ GEE*, send someone packing; *jou ~ ook nog agterna GOOI*, shake hands with yourself; you should be delighted; *met die ~ in die HAND kom 'n mens deur die hele (ganse) land*, courtesy costs nothing, but it goes a long way; it pays to be civil; *HOF ~ tophat*, *iets onder die ~ HOU*, keep it under one's hat; *eers jou ~ INGOOI*, you had better first throw in your hat; *jou ~ in die LUG gooi*, toss one's hat in the air; *met die ~ in die OË*, abashed; shamefaced; *~ oor die OË druk*, hide one's face in shame; *sy ~ OPEET as dit so is*, eat one's hat if it is so; *êrens ~ OPHANG*, go courting somewhere; *die ~ laat RONDGAAN*, send round the hat; *sy ~ SKEEF opsit*, put on side; swank; *sy ~ uit die oë STOOT*, push out one's chest; *VASDRUK*, take to one's heels; *sy ~ VAT*, take one's hat and go.
hoed², (w) (ge-), guard, take care of, protect, tend: ~ *jou vir die versoeking*, guard against the temptation.
hoeda'nig, (-e), how, what kind of, what; ~ **heid**, quality, capacity; attribute; adjunct; character.
hoed: ~ **band**, hatband; ~ **bol**, crown of hat.
hoe'de, guard, care, keeping, protection; aegis; guardianship; heed; *iem. onder sy ~ NEEM*, take someone into one's care; *ONDER die ~ van*, under the guardianship of, in the care of; *in VEILIGE ~*, in safe keeping; *op sy ~ WEES*, be on one's guard; *nie op sy ~ wees nie*, be off one's guard.
hoe'de: ~ **aap**, bonnet-monkey; ~ **blok**, hatblock; ~ **bol**, crown of hat; ~ **borsel**, hatbrush; ~ **doos**, hatbox; bandbox; ~ **draadsteek**, wire stitch; ~ **fabrikant**, hatter; ~ **handelaar**, hatter; ~ **kapstok**, hatrack, hatstand; ~ **knoopsteek**, tie-stitch, milliner's knot; ~ **maakster**, milliner; ~ **maker**, hatter; ~ **makery**, millinery; hat factory; ~ **naald**, straw-needle.

hoe'der, (-s), keeper; guardian; *is ek my broer se ~*?, am I my brother's keeper?
hoe'de: ~ **rak**, hatstand; ~ **rand**, brim of hat; ~ **speld**, hatpin; ~ **stander**, hallstand; ~ **styfgaas**, buckram; ~ **winkel**, hatshop, milliner's shop, hatter's shop.
hoë'digtheid, high density; ~ **sbehuising**, high-density housing; ~ **sbevolking**, high-density population; ~ **sgebied**, high-density area.
hoed: ~ **jie**, (-s), little hat (bonnet); ~ **lint**, hatband, bonnet string.
ho'ëdruksilinder, high-pressure cylinder.
hoed: ~ **loos**, (..lose), hatless; ~ **vormig**, (-e), pileate; ~ **windsel**, puggaree.
hoef¹, (s) (hoewe), hoof; heel; landslide (plough).
hoef², (w) need; *jy ~ nie te gaan nie*, you need not go.
hoef: ~ **angel**, caltrop; ~ **bal**, ball of heel; ~ **been**, coffin bone; ~ **beslag**, shoeing; ~ **bevangenheid**, laminitis, founder; ~ **blad**, coltsfoot (flower); ~ **dier**, ungulate; ~ **getrappel**, clatter of hoofs; ~ **gewrig**, (-te), foot joint; coffin joint; ~ **hamer**, farrier's hammer; ~ **ie**, (-s), small hoof; landslide; ~ **kanker**, cancer of the hoof; ~ **magneet**, horseshoe magnet; ~ **mes**, paring-knife, parer; drawing knife; ~ **meter**, pedometer; ~ **salf**, hoof ointment; ~ **seer**, founder; canker; laminitis; ~ **slag**, hoof beat; ~ **smid**, farrier; ~ **smidvoorskoot**, basil apron; ~ **spyker**, horseshoe nail; ~ **vormig**, (-e), hoof-shaped, ungular; ~ **yster**, horseshoe; ~ **ysterboog**, horseshoe arch; ~ **ystermagneet**, horseshoe magnet; ~ **ystermpen**, ox-bow lake; ~ **ysterpen**, calk; ~ **ystervormig**, (-e), horseshoe-shaped.
hoe'genaamd: *het jy ~ IETS*? have you anything at all? ~ *NIE*, not at all; ~ *NIKS*, nothing whatever (at all).
ho'ëgraads, (-e), high-grade; ~ **e produk**, high-grade product.
hoegroot'heid, quantity; amount; size; extent.
ho'ëhakskoen, high-heeled shoe.
hoe(i)haai', fuss, to-do, commotion; *'n ~ maak oor niks*, make a fuss about trifles; *see* **haaihoei**.
hoek, (-e), corner (of room); angle (of triangle); elevation; edge; hook, fish-hook; recess; coign; *om elke ~ en DRAAI*, at every turn; *alle ~ e en GATE deursoek*, look into every nook and cranny; *die ~ van INVAL*, the angle of incidence; *iem. in 'n ~ JA*, drive someone into a corner; *iets van ~ tot KANT ken*, know something inside out; *KLEIN in die ~*, maar groot in die broek, small but plucky; *uit watter ~ KOM hy*? where does he hail from? *om die ~ KYK (loer)*, peep round the corner; *die ~ OM*, round the corner; *die ~ van UITVAL*, the angle of reflection; ~ *in die WATER gooi*, fish for; *weet uit watter ~ die WIND waai*, know how the land lies.
hoe'ka, long ago; already, indeed; *van ~ (se tyd) AF*, from time immemorial; *ek het ~ nie lus gehad om saam te gaan nie*, as a matter of fact I did not want to accompany them.
hoek: ~ **afstand**, angular distance, ~ **anker**, angle tie; dragon tie, angle brace; ~ **baken**, corner beacon; ~ **balk**, (roof) hip; ~ **bankie**, corner seat; ~ **beampte**, corner judge; ~ **boon**, hip rafter, ~ **beoordelaar**, corner judge; ~ **beweging**, angular motion; ~ **boor**, angle brace; ~ **deler**, angle dividers.
hoe'ke, (geselst.) what kind of.
hoek: ~ **er**, hooker (boat); ~ **erig**, (-e), angular; jagged; ~ **hoogte**, angular elevation; ~ **hou**, corner hit (cricket); ~ **huis**, corner house.
hoe'kie, (-s), little corner, nook; *uit ALLE ~s en gaatjies*, from every nook and corner; *iets om die ~ DOEN*, do something on the sly; *iem. in 'n ~ DRYF*, drive someone into a corner; *alle ~s en GAATJIES*, every nook and cranny; *die ~ van die HAARD*, the ingle-nook; *IN 'n ~*, in a tight corner; *iem. in 'n ~ JA*, drive someone into a corner; *in 'n ~ KRUIP*, creep into a corner; *iem. in 'n ~ SPEEL*, drive someone into a corner; *in 'n ~ WEES*, be in a tight corner.
hoe'kig, (-e), angular; rugged; bevelled; cornered; gruff, morose, crusty; ~ **e blaarvlek**, angular leaf-spot; ~ **heid**, angularity; gruffness.
hoek'inlating: ~ *op halwe hout*, corner half-lap.

hoek: ~**kas**, corner cupboard; ~**klamp**, angle cleat; ~**lappie**, gusset; ~**las**, bracket (corner, angle) joint; ~**lyn**, diagonal; ~**lys**, corner moulding; angle bead; ~**magneet**, horseshoe magnet; ~**meetkunde**, goniometry; ~**meter**, quadrant; protractor; graphometer; goniometer; battery director; bevel; ~**meterstand**, director setting; ~**meterstander**, director stand; ~**meting**, goniometry; ~**nok**, hip (of roof), hip ridge; ~**nokrol**, hip roll.

hoe'kom, why, for what reason; *omdat* ~ *'n DRAAI is, omdat* ~ *nie REGUIT is nie*, because Y is a crooked letter (and you can't make it straight); ~ *VRA jy?* what makes you ask?

Ho'ë Kommissaris, (-se), High Commissioner.

hoek: ~**omslag**, angle brace; ~**paal**, corner post, angle standard; ~**pilaar**, corner pillar; ~**plaat**, gusset plate; corner plate; ~**plek**, corner seat; ~**punt**, angular point; vertex of angle; ~**puntlyn**, diagonal; ~**pyler**, corner pillar; ~**ronding**, corner radius; ~**s**, **(-e)**, diagonal; ~**skaaf**, angle plane; ~**skop**, corner kick; ~**snelheid**, angular velocity; ~**snytand**, canine incisor; ~**spar**, (roof) hip; ~**staaf**, angle bar; ~**stand**, angularity; ~**stander**, corner boy.

hoek'steen, corner (foundation) stone, keystone; quoin; ~**legging**, laying of the corner (foundation) stone.

hoek: ~**steun**, gusset; ~**steunplaat**, gussetstay; ~**stoel**, box, angle bar; corner chair; ~**stoot**, hook (boxing); ~**stuk**, angle piece; ~**stut**, angle brace; corner post; ~**styl**, corner post; ~**sweislas**, fillet weld; ~**tand**, eye-tooth, canine, corner-tooth (in mares); herringbone tooth (of wheel); ~**tandrat**, herringbone gear; ~**venster**, corner window; ~**verbinding**, gusset; ~**versnelling**, angular acceleration; ~**vlag**, corner flag; ~**vlak**, spandrel; ~**vlek**, angular leaf-spot (tobacco disease); ~**vormig**, (-e), angulated; ~**yster**, corner iron.

hoe-lan'ger-hoe-liewer, kiss-me-at-the-garden-gate (*Saxifraga umbrosa*); woody nightshade *(Solanum dulcamara)*.

hoëlisien'mielies, high-lysine maize.

ho'ëlui, aristocracy, upper ten, elite.

ho'ëmode, high fashion, haute couture.

hoen'der, (-s), fowl; chicken; *'n* ~ *in die BANK hê*, brag; show off; take it easy; *dis beter om vandag die* ~ *te hê as môre die EIER*, a bird in the hand is worth two in the bush; *iem. na die* ~*s laat GAAN*, tell someone to go to blazes; let someone go to hang; *die* ~*s aan die JAKKALS toevertrou*, give the wolf the wether to keep; *loop gee die* ~ *s KOS*, clear off! *'n blinde* ~ *vind ook 'n KORRELTJIE*, even the least fortunate may have a stroke of luck; *die* ~*s het sy KOS afgeneem*, he is crest-fallen; *LOOP na die* ~ *s!* begone! *'n gebraaide* ~ *vlieg niem. in die MOND nie*, no gains without pains; *soos 'n NATGEREËNDE* ~, out of countenance; *loop soos 'n* ~ *wat NES soek*, fuss about like a broody hen; *met die* ~*s OPSTAAN*, rise with the lark; *so SIEK soos 'n* ~ *wees*, be as sick as a dog; *met die* ~*s gaan SLAAP*, go to bed with the chickens; *die* ~ *s TANDE KRY*, on the Greek calends; *gaan TEL die* ~ *s!* buzz off! *soos 'n VERKLUIMDE* ~ *lyk*, look like a drowning duck; *gaan VERTEL dit aan die* ~ *s*, tell that to the marines; *die* ~ *s in WEES*, be in a rage; *soos 'n* ~ *van die WERF af*, unprepared; ~**afval**, fowl giblets; ~**ag'tig**, (-e), gallinaceous; ~**bel**, *Sutherlandia frutescens;* ~**binnegoed**, fowl giblets; ~**boer**, poultry farmer; ~**boerdery**, poultry farming; ~**bors**, chicken breast; pigeon breast (fig.); ~**boud**, drumstick, leg of a fowl; ~**brandsiekte**, deplumiing itch; ~**cholera**, fowl cholera; ~**dief**, poultry thief; ~**eier**, hen's egg; ~**haan**, cock; ~**hemel**: *in die* ~ *hemel wees*, be under the weather; ~**hen**, hen; ~**hennerig**, (-e), henlike; ~**hok**, fowl house; coop, fowl run; hencoop, henhouse, hennery; poultry-yard; ~**huis**, poultry house; ~**jaer**, hawk; ~**kamp**, poultry yard; ~**kop**, (s) fowl's head; (b) muzzy, half-seas-over, tipsy, (fuddled); ~**koper**, poulterer; ~**kos**, poultry food; ~**kraai**, (s) crowing; (bw) cock-crow; very early; ~**luis**, chicken tick; ~**maag**, gizzard; ~**mark**,

poultry market; ~**mis**, fowl droppings; ~**nes**, hen's nest; ~**pastei**, chicken pie; ~**pes**, fowl cholera; ~**pokkies**, chicken pox (in animals); ~**poot**, fowl's foot; bad writing; *soos 'n* ~ *poot krap*, scrawl; ~*s*, poultry; ~**slaapplek**, hen-roost; ~ **so(e)p**, chicken broth; ~**spoor**, broad arrow; crowfoot (grass); *die* ~ *spoor dra*, be a gaolbird; ~**stok**, fowl perch; ~**stuitjie**, pope's (parson's) nose; ~**tande**: *so skaars soos* ~ *tande*, not to be had for love or money; not to be had at any price; ~**teelt**, poultry farming; ~**tifus**, fowl typhoid; ~**tifus-entstof**, fowl-typhoid vaccine; ~**veer**, fowl's feather; ~**vel**, fowl's skin; goose pimples, goose-flesh; ~*vel word (kry)*, have cold shivers down one's spine; be given goose-flesh; ~**verkoue**, roup; ~**verkouepille**, roup pills; ~**vleis**, (flesh of) chicken (fowl); goose-flesh, crispation, horripilation; *ek kry daarvan* ~ *vleis (* ~ *vel)*, it makes my flesh creep; it gives me goose-flesh; ~**voer**, fowl's food, poultry food.

ho'ënektrui, polo-neck jersey, turtle-neck sweater.

hoe'pel, (s) (-s), hoop; *iem. se* ~*s AANKLINK*, take someone to task; *dis nog maar die EERSTE* ~, it is only the first ditch; *die eerste* ~ *om die VAATJIE*, the firstborn; (w) (ge-), hoop (vat); trundle a hoop, play with hoops; ~**been**, bandy leg(s); ~**hamer**, driver; ~**kap**, calash; ~**rok**, hoop petticoat, crinoline; farthingale; ~**stok**, hoop-stick; ~**yster**, hoop iron.

hoep-hoep' (-e), hoopoe (*Upupa africana*).

hoep'la! hoopla!

ho'ëpriester, high priest; pontiff; pontifex; ..**pries'terlik**, (-e), pontifical; high-priestly; ~**skap**, pontificate.

ho'ër, *see* **hoog**; superior; excelsior; ~ *ONDERWYS*, higher education; ~ *OP*, higher up; ~ *in RANG*, senior (officer, etc.).

hoer, (s) (-e), prostitute, harlot, whore, adulteress, fornicatress; (w) (ge-), whore; ~ *en rumoer*, gallivant, play about.

hoera'! (-'s), **hoerê!** (-s), hurrah! hurray! *moenie* ~ *skree voor jy oor die brug is nie*, do not halloo till you are out of the wood.

hoereer', (ge-), commit adultery; ~**der**, (-s), adulterer, fornicator.

hoe'rery, (-e), adultery, prostitution, fornication, harlotry.

Ho'ërhand: *van* ~, from God.

Hoër: ~**hof**, Supreme Court; ~**huis**, Upper House, Senate; House of Lords (England).

hoer'huis, brothel, bordello, house of ill-fame, whorehouse.

ho'ërisikogeval, high-risk case.

hoe'ri, (-'s), houri.

hoer'kind, illegitimate child, bastard.

hoërmei'sieskool, girls' high school.

hoërseunskool, boys' high school.

ho'ërskool, ho'ër skool, high (secondary) school; academy.

ho'ërskoolleerling, high-school pupil.

ho'ërug-, high-backed.

hoërvlieg'skool, advanced (senior) flying-school.

hoes, (s) (-te), cough, bark; hack; (w) (ge-), cough; sputter (engine); ~ *en proes*, cough and sneeze; ~**aanval**, coughing fit; ~**bonbon**, cough lozenge; cough drop; ~**bui**, coughing fit; ~**drank**, cough mixture.

hoesee'! huzza!

hoeseer', hoe'seer, how(ever) much, much as.

hoe'-se-naam, (-s), what-d'ye-call-him (-her, -it).

hoes: ~**erig**, (-e), inclined to cough, coughing; ~**ery**, (fit of) coughing; ~**ie**, (-s), short cough; hem; ~**klontjie**, ~**lekker**, cough lozenge; ~**middel**, cough remedy; cough elixir; ~**pepperment**, cough (peppermint) lozenge; ~**pille**, cough tablets; ~**stillend**, (-e), pectoral, cough-relieving, soothing; ~**stroop**, cough syrup; ~**terig**, (-e), inclined to cough, coughing; ~**tery**, (spell of) coughing.

hoe'veel, how much, how many; ~ *is DIT?* what do I owe you? ~ *te MEER sal* . . ., how much more shall . . .

hoeveel'heid, (..hede), quantity, amount; quantum;

~sbepaling, quantification; ~slys, bill of quantities.
hoe'veelste: vir die ~ KEER, for the umpteenth time; die ~ van die MAAND? what day of the month?
Ho'ëveld, Highveld.
hoever're, how far; in ~ dit juis is, as to how far this is correct.
hoe'we, (-s), small holding, allotment (of land); plot.
hoewel', though, although, albeit.
hof, (howe), court; courtyard; garden; ~ van APPÈL, court of appeal; die ~ van EDEN, the garden of Eden; ~ toe GAAN, go to law; 'n meisie die ~ MAAK, pay court to someone; die ~ is op REIS, the court is on (its) circuit; die ~ SIT, the court is in session; ~amp, function at court; ~arts, court physician; ~bal, state ball; ~beampte, groom, court functionary; ~bediende, court attendant; ~bevel, order of the court; ~dame, court lady; lady-in-waiting, maid of honour; ~digter, poet laureate; ~digterskap, laureateship; ~etiket, court etiquette; ~fees, court fête, festivity at court.
hoffmannsdruppels, Hoffmann's drops (Dutch medicine).
hof: ~geld, court fees; ~geneesheer, court physician; ~guns, court favour; ~houding, court household.
ho'fie, (-s), small head; head(ing); ~vormig, (-e), capitate.
hof: ~kabaal, intrigues at court; ~kapel, court chapel; ~kapelaan, court chaplain; ~kapper, court hairdresser; ~kliek, court clique; ~knaap, page; ~kostuum, court dress; ~kringe, court circle; ~lewe, court life; ~leweransier, purveyor (by royal appointment).
hof'lik, (-e), courteous, obliging, polite; complaisant; fair-spoken; ~heid, courtesy, politeness; complaisance, comity; gallantry; ~heidshalwe, out of courtesy.
hof: ~lug, court air; ~maarskalk, court marshal; ~maker, gallant; ~makery, courtship, love-making; ~meester, steward, purser; major-domo; seneschal; ~meesteres, stewardess; air hostess; ~nar, court fool, jester; ~ordonnans, court orderly; ~prediker, court chaplain; ~rou, court mourning; ~saak, court case, lawsuit; legal action; ~saal, court room; ~sanger, court singer; willow-wren (*Phylloscopus trochilus*); ~skoen, court shoe; ~stad, court capital; ~stoet, entourage, court retinue; ~termyn, court term; ~verslae, law reports.
Hog'genheimer, (-s), Hoggenheimer, unscrupulous capitalist.
ho'haai = hoeihaai.
hoi-hoi'! come (call to oxen when yoking).
hoipolloi', rabble, riff-raff, hoi polloi.
hok, (s) (-ke), pen (fowl); shed (cattle); crate; kennel (dog); sty (pig); hutch (rabbit); cage (bird); enclosure (fowls); ~ toe gaan, going to be cooped up; in die ~ HÊ, have someone cornered; in die ~ SIT, be behind bars; in die ~ SPIT, get the better of; get the upper hand; (w) (ge-), (put into) pen, shut in, enclose; gate (scholars); ~! go away! (to calf when milking).
ho'kaal! whoa! stop! (to oxen).
hok: ~agtig, (-e), loculose, loculous (bot.); ~kerig, (-e), poky.
hok'kie¹, (-s), small shed; cell; pigeon-hole; sentrybox; cubicle; 'n benoude ~, a poky little hole, a stuffy corner.
hok'kie², hockey; ~speler, hockey player; ~stok, hockey stick.
hok'slaan, (-ge-), beat calf off (when milking); deprive someone of a pleasure; keep someone away from; iem. ~, dash the cup from someone's lips.
hok'spoor, bay (railway).
hok'stok, milking-stick (used to keep calves away when milking).
hok'stut, sleeper-crib.
ho'kus-po'kus, hocus-pocus; cheating.
hok'vas, (-te), fond of staying at home; ~ wees, be a homebird.
hol¹, (s) (-le), anus, arse.
hol², (s) (-e), cave, cavern, cavity (within solid body); hole, den (of animal); in sy ~ kruip, go to earth.

hol³, (w) (ge-), run, rush, career, bolt; op ~ GAAN, bolt; run away; op ~ WEES, run riot (amuck).
hol⁴, (b), (-le), hollow (tooth); sunken (eyes); empty (stomach); concave (lens); inane (talk); gaunt; IN die ~ste van die nag, at the dead of night; ~ KLANKE, hollow words; ~aar, vena cava; ~as, tube shaft; ~beitel, gouge.
hol'bewoner, cave-dweller.
hol: ~bol, concavo-convex; ~-bol struktuur, ball-and-socket structure; ~boor, hollow drill, tubular drill.
hol'derstebolder, topsy-turvy, head over heels, pell-mell, helter-skelter, harum-scarum.
hol: ~ding, (-e, -goed), scooping utensil, bailer; ~-endol'voeg, joggle; ~guts, firmer-gouge; ~heid, hollowness; emptiness; concavity; inanity; ~horing, cavicorn.
holis', (-te), holist; ~me, holism; ~ties, (-e), holistic.
hol'klinkend, (-e), hollow-sounding; hollow.
hol'knie, calf-knee.
hol'krans, cave (in mountain); ~sandsteen, cave sandstone.
Hol'land, Holland; the Netherlands; dis ~ en Seeland, that's all I have; ~er, (-s), Dutchman, Hollander; die VLIEËNDE ~er, the Flying Dutchman; ~is'me, (-s), Dutch idiom.
Hol'lands, (s) Dutch, High Dutch; die KAAP is (nou weer) ~, everything is tops (ship-shape) again; ~ met iem. PRAAT, not to mince matters; tell someone the plain truth; dit is nou PRONT ~, that is the plain truth; (b) (-e), Dutch; ~e sous, sauce hollandaise; ~s-Afrikaans, Dutch South-African.
hol'landslinne, holland (cloth); ongebleikte ~, brown holland.
hol'lerig, (-e), fairly empty (hollow).
hol'ligheid, hollowness, cavity; iem. in die ~ van jou hand hê, have someone in the hollow of one's hand.
hol: ~lys, cavetto (casement) moulding; ~moer, capnut; ~muur, hollow wall; ~nek, ewe neck (vet.).
holoë'dries, (-e), holohedral, holohedric.
holofiet', (-e), holophyte.
holofi'ties, (-e), holophytic.
holoë'der, (-s), holohedron.
holograaf', (..grawe), holograph; ..gra'fies, (-e), holographic; ..grafiese testament, holograph will.
ho'lohialyn, holohyaline.
ho'lokristallyn, (-e), holocrystalline.
hol'oog, hollow-eyed, with sunken eyes.
Ho'loseen, Holocene.
hol: ~passer, spherical compasses; ~pypie, (-s), (shoe-making) punch; hollow-punch; ~pyptang, punching pliers.
hol'rond, (-e), concave; ~-bolrond, concavo-convex; ~heid, concavity.
hol'rug, (s) hollow back; saddle tool (blacksmith); saddleback; (b) hollow-backed; hackneyed, trite (fig.); 'n TEORIE ~ ry, ride a theory to death; hackney; ~ WOORDE, trite (hackneyed) phrases; cliché's; ~saag, skewback saw.
hol: ~saag, concave saw; ~senter, cup centre; ~skaaf, hollow plane; ~skraper, hollow scraper; ~slytasie, hollow-wear.
hol'spaat, macle, chiastolite.
hol'steen, oilstone slip.
hol'ster, (-s), holster, pistol case.
hol'te, (-s), hollow, cavity; concavity; hollowness; socket (eye); pit (stomach); belly; recess; pocket (in gold mines); in die ~ van iem. se HAND, in the hollow of one's hand; in die ~ v.d. NAG, at the dead of night; ~agtig, (-e), pockety; ~dier, coelenterate.
hol'voor, centre furrow.
hom¹, (s) milt (fish).
hom², (vnw) him; it; hy verbeel ~ BAIE, he is very conceited; ek het ~ SELF gesê, I told him myself; hy SKEER ~, he is shaving.
hom(e)opaat', (..pate), homoeopath.
hom(e)opatie', homoeopathy.
hom(e)opa'ties, (-e), homoeopathic.
Home'ries, (-e), Homeric; ~e GELAG, Homeric laughter; ~e VERGELYKING, a Homeric simile.

Home'ros, Home'rus, Homer; ~ *dut (slaap) ook soms,* even Homer nods.
homileet', (..lete), homilist.
homiletiek', homiletics.
homile'ties, (-e), homiletic.
homilie', (-ë), homily.
hom'mel, (-s), hom'melby, drone, bumble-bee.
hom'mer, milter.
homofoon', (s) (..fone), homophone; (b) (..fone), homophonous (words); homophonic (music).
homogaam', (..game), homogamous.
homogamie', homogamy.
homogeen', (..gene), simple (minerals); homogeneous.
homogene'se, homogenesis.
homogene'ties, (-e), homogenetic.
homogeniseer', (ge-), homogenize.
homogenise'ring, homogenization.
homogeniteit', homogeneity, homogeneousness.
homologeer', (ge-), homologate.
homologie', homology.
homologiseer', (ge-), homologize.
homoloog', (s) (..loë), homologue; (b) (..loë), homologous.
homomorf', homomor'fies, (-e), homomorphic.
homoniem', (s) (-e) homonym; homonymic; (b) (-e), homonymous.
homopaat', homopatie', homopa'ties = hom(e)o= paat, hom(e)opatie, hom(e)opaties.
homoseksualiteit', homosexuality.
homoseksueel', (s) (..suele), homosexual; (b) (..suele), homosexual.
homosen'tries, (-e), homocentric.
homosigoot', (..gote), homozygote.
homoti'pe, homotype.
homp, (-e), lump, hunk, chunk.
homself', himself; *BUITE* ~, beside himself, out of his wits; *die KIND kan* ~ *al aantrek,* the child can put on his own clothes; ~ *WEES,* be himself, be normal.
hom'vis = hommer.
hond, (-e), dog; hound; *elke* ~ *is BAAS op sy eie werf,* every dog crows best on his own dunghill; *twee* ~ *e veg om een BEEN, die derde loop daarmee heen,* while two dogs are fighting, a third takes the spoil; *iem. soos 'n* ~ *BEHANDEL,* treat someone like a dog; *'n* ~ *BLAF tog,* even a dog will bark; *die* ~ *e BLAF nie meer vir hom nie,* the dogs no longer bark at him; *jy kan 'n* ~ *die BLAF nie belet nie,* you cannot forbid a person the right of speech; *haastige* ~ *verbrand sy BEK,* hasty climbers have sudden falls; *dié wat agter my BLAF, is my* ~, my dog is he who barks behind my back; *agter elke* ~ *aan BLAF,* echo what everybody else says; *bekend soos 'n BONT* ~, as notorious as a pye dog (pariah); *blaffende* ~ *e BYT nie,* great barkers are no biters; *dooie* ~ *e BYT nie,* dead men tell no tales; *mak (eie)* ~ *e BYT die seerste,* to be bitten by one's own dogs hurts most; *DAG,* ~*!,* don't you say hullo!; *elke* ~ *kry sy DAG en 'n brakkie twee,* every dog has his day; *DANKIE,* ~*!,* can't you say "thank you"?; *van jou eie* ~ *e GEBYT word,* to have been bitten by those you feed; ~ *se GEDAGTES kry,* smell a rat; become suspicious; *'n GEMENE* ~, a mean dog, a cur; *nie eers 'n* ~ *HAAR-AF maak nie,* accomplish nothing; *baie* ~ *e is 'n HAAS se dood,* many hands make light work; *met onwillige* ~ *e kan niemand HASE vang nie,* you may take a horse to the water but you cannot make him drink; *wie* ~ *e HOU, blaf nie self nie,* do not keep a dog and bark yourself; *hy laat geen* ~ *of KAT met rus nie,* he leaves nobody in peace; *hoe meer 'n* ~ *te KERE gaan, hoe banger is hy,* the louder the barking, the greater the fear; *KOMMANDEER jou eie* ~ *e en blaf self,* do your own dirty work; *hy lyk of die* ~ *e sy KOS afgeneem het,* he looks down in the mouth; *iem. is soos 'n* ~, *waar hy kos kry daar bly (blaf) hy,* he likes abusing hospitality; *KWAAI* ~ *e blaf nie,* great barkers are no biters; *KWAAI* ~ *e byt mekaar nie,* dog will not eat dog; *'n lewendige* ~ *is beter as 'n dooie LEEU,* discretion is the better part of virtue; a living dog is better than a dead lion; *'n kind* ~ *MAAK,* treat a child like a dog; *die* ~ *in die POT kry,* dine with Duke Humphry; come too late for dinner; *oor die* ~ *se RUG wees,* be over the worst; *met alle* ~*e SAAMBLAF,* echo what all others say; *so SIEK soos 'n* ~, as sick as a dog, very ill; *moenie SLAPENDE* ~*e wakker maak nie,* let sleeping dogs lie; *elke* ~ *prys sy eie STERT,* every cook praises his own broth; *oor die* ~ *se STERT wees,* be over the worst, have finished the most difficult part of a task; *kom 'n mens oor die* ~, *dan kom jy ook oor die STERT,* once one is over the worst, the rest is easy; *as 'n mens 'n* ~ *wil slaan, kry jy maklik 'n STOK,* a stick is quickly found to beat a dog with; *soos 'n* ~ *wat VET gesteel het,* with a hang-dog air (look); *blaf met die* ~*e en huil met die WOLWE,* run with the hare and hunt with the hounds; ~ **ag= tig, (-e),** canine.
hon'de: ~ **baantjie,** rotten (wretched) job; ~ **belasting,** dog-tax; ~ **beskuit,** dog-biscuit; ~ **bloed,** liquorice; ~ **boer,** dog-fancier; ~ **brood,** dog-cake; ~ **byt,** dog-bite; ~ **draffie,** easy trot; hobble; dog-trot; ~ **geblaf,** barking of dogs, bark; ~ **gesig,** dog-face; *Phylica stipularis;* ~ **haar,** dog-hair; ~ **geveg, (-te),** dog-fight; ~ **halsband,** dog-collar; ~ **hok, (-ke),** dog-kennel; ~ **hokvloeistof,** kennel fluid; ~ **kar,** dog-cart; ~ **kenner,** dog-fancier; ~ **ketting,** dog-chain; slip; ~ **kop,** dog's head; ~ **kos,** dog's food; ~ **lewe,** wretched life; *'n* ~ *lewe lei,* lead a dog's life; ~ **liefhebber,** dog-fancier; ~ **oor,** *Cotyledon orbiculata;* ~ **pisbossie,** *Exomix microphylla; Artiplex albicans;* ~ **ras,** dog-breed.
hon'derd, hundred; ~ *teen EEN,* a hundred to one; *alles is IN die* ~, everything is at sixes and sevens; *'n MAN* ~, a man in a million; ~ **delig, (-e),** centesimal (balance); centigrade (thermometer); ~ **dui= send,** hundred thousand; ~ **-en-een:** ~ *-en-een moeilikheidjies hê,* have a thousand and one troubles; ~ **-en-tien,** hundred and ten; *al* ~ *-en-tien,* all the same; in spite of your excuses; I'll believe you but thousands wouldn't; ~ **gradig, (-e),** centigrade; ~ **poot,** centipede; ~ **jarig, (-e),** centennial, centenary; ~ *jarige fees,* centenary; ~ **jarige, (-s),** centenarian; ~ **ogig, (-e),** with a hundred eyes; ~ **ste,** hundredth, centesimal; ~ **tal,** a hundred; ~ **voud,** centuple; ~ **voudig, (-e),** hundredfold.
hon'de: ~ **reisies,** greyhound races; ~ **siekte,** dog-disease; distemper (in dogs); ~ **sweep,** dog-whip; ~ **teler,** dog-breeder; ~ **tentoonstelling,** dog-show; ~ **tou,** lead; ~ **vanger,** dog-catcher; ~ **vel,** dog's skin; ~ **vleis,** dog's meat; dog's flesh; ~ **wag,** (first) dog-watch, middle watch; ~ **wedrenne,** greyhound racing; ~ **weer,** weather not fit to turn a dog into, bad weather.
hond'jie, (-s), little dog, pup(py); *van die* ~ *GEBYT wees,* be as vain as a peacock; *nie so erg om die* ~ *as om die HALSBANDJIE nie,* the child is being kissed for the nurse's sake; *MY* ~*!,* my pet!
hond'lelik, (-e), as ugly as sin, dog-ugly.
hond'mak, as tame as a dog; completely beaten; *hy is* ~, he is eating out of my hand.
honds, (-e), brutal, churlish, cynical; doggish; ~ **dae,** dog-days; canucular days; ~ **dolheid,** rabies; hydrophobia; ~ **haai,** spotted dogfish; tope; pike-dog; ~ **heid,** currishness; cynicism; ~ **honger,** (b), very hungry; ~ **luis,** dog's tick; ~ **roos,** dog-rose, dogbriar; ~ **taai,** dogged; ~ **tand,** dog's tooth.
Hond'ster, Dog Star, Sirius.
honds: ~ **tong,** dog's tongue; ~ **vot,** rascal.
Hondu'ras, Honduras.
Hondurees', (..rese), (s, b) Honduran.
ho'nend, (b) (-e), derisive, derisory; insulting; contumelious, mocking; (bw) gibingly, mockingly.
Hongaar', (..gare), Hungarian; ~ **s'**, (s) Hungarian; (b) (-e), Hungarian; ~ **..gary'e,** Hungary.
hon'ger, (s) hunger; ~ *maak rou BENE soet,* hunger is the best sauce; *die* ~ *buite die DEUR hou,* keep the wolf from the door; ~ *is die beste KOK (sous),* hunger is the best sauce; ~ *LY,* starve; *hy SKREE v.d.* ~, he is starving; *van* ~ *STERF,* die of hunger; *sy* ~ *STIL,* appease one's hunger; ~ *is 'n skerp SWAARD,* hunger is a sharp goad; hunger fetches the wolf out of the wood; *VAAL van die* ~, maar

vrek van die aanstel, faint with hunger, but full of pretence; (w) (ge-), hunger; ~ en dors na die geregtigheid, hunger and thirst after righteousness; (b) hungry; *so ~ dat jy 'n spyker se kop kan AFBYT*, be as hungry as a hunter; ~ *WEES*, be hungry; *so ~ soos 'n WOLF*, be as ravenous as a wolf; ~**beto= ging**, hunger-march; ~**blokkade**, hunger-blockade; ~**blom**, *Senecio arenarius;* ~**dood**, death from starvation.
hon'gerig, (-e), hungry, esurient; peckish; ~**heid**, hungriness.
hon'ger: ~**holte**, hunger-groove; ~**kuur**, hunger-cure; ~**loon**, starvation wage; ~**loonstelsel**, sweating system; ~**lyer**, starveling; ~**opstootjie**, hunger-riot; ~**pyn**, pang of hunger.
hon'gersnood, famine; dearth.
hon'gerstaker, hunger-striker; ..**staking**, hunger-strike.
hon'ger: ~**erte**, hunger; ~**tee**, *Leyssera gnaphaloides;* ~**tifus**, hunger-typhus; ~**wol**, lean wool.
honk'bal, rounders.
honneurs', honours; ~ *BEHAAL*, obtain honours; *GELYKE ~* , honours easy; *VIER ~* , four honours; *die ~ WAARNEEM*, do the honours; ~**eksamen**, honours examination; ~**graad**, honours degree.
honora'rium, (..ria, -s), honorarium, fee; royalty (of authors); *vaste ~*, retaining fee.
honoreer', (ge-), honour (a bill); cash (a cheque).
honorêr', (-e), honorary.
hono'res = **honneurs** (universiteitsgraad).
hono'ris cau'sa, honorary, honoris causa; *'n graad as toeken*, confer an honorary degree.
ho'nou, see **hanou**.
hoof¹, (-de), head; boss; chieftain, chief, leader; heading (of letter); principal, headmaster; headmistress; headline (newspaper); *waar die ~ nie is nie, word die BAARD nie geskeer nie*, a man far from his goods is near his harm; *die ~ BIED aan*, offer resistance to; *sy ~ BREEK oor*, rack one's brains about; *die ~ BUIG*, bow one's head; *iem. se ~ laat DRAAI*, make someone feel dizzy; *deur die ~ GAAN*, think of something; *na die ~ GAAN*, go to one's head; *sy ~ is daarmee GEMOEI*, his life is at stake; *die ~ van die GESIN*, the head of the family; *'n GESWOLLE ~ hê*, have a swollen head; *iem. iets na die ~ GOOI*, throw something in someone's teeth; *iem. oor die ~ GROEI*, outstrip someone; *jou iets in die ~ HAAL*, take something into one's head; *wat jou bo die ~ HANG*, what is hanging over your head; *jou ~ laat HANG*, hang one's head in shame; *met HANGENDE ~*, crest-fallen; chapfallen; *iem. se ~ op HOL bring*, turn a person's head; *die ~ HOOG hou*, hold one's head high; *iets uit die ~ LEER*, learn something by heart; *met die ~ teen die MUUR loop*, run one's head against a brick wall; *op die ~ van iem. NEERKOM*, be visited upon someone; come down on someone's head; *die ~ NEERLÊ*, lay down one's head; *die ~ ONTBLOOT*, uncover (one's head); *met OPGEHEWE ~* , with head held high; *die ~ OPSTEEK*, make a stand against; *iem. iets uit die ~ PRAAT*, talk someone out of something; *'n RAND per ~* , a rand per head; ~ *REGS!*, eyes right!; *iem. oor die ~ SIEN*, ignore someone; not promote someone; *iets oor die ~ SIEN*, overlook something; *soveel ~ de, soveel SINNE*, so many men, so many minds; *iets uit jou ~ SIT*, put something out of one's mind; *die ~ van die SKOOL*, the principal of the school; *die ~ in die SKOOT lê*, bow one's head in submission; *iem. iets teen die ~ SLINGER*, throw something into someone's teeth; *uit die ~ SPEEL*, play from memory; *aan die ~ STAAN van*, be at the head of; *sy ~ STAAN nie daarna nie*, he is not so inclined; he is not in the mood for it; *die ~ de bymekaar STEEK*, put heads together; take counsel; *na die ~ STYG*, let something go to one's head; *UIT die ~*, by heart; *UIT dié ~ de*, for that reason; on these grounds; *uit ~ de VAN*, on account of, owing to; *VERBRUIK per ~*, consumption per capita; *v.d. ~ tot die VOETE*, from top to toe; *die ~ VOL hê van*, have one's head full of; *die ~ bo WATER hou*, keep one's head above water; *see also* **kop**.

hoof²=, main, chief, principal.
hoof: ~**aandryfmasjien**, prime mover; ~**aanklag**, major charge; ~**aansluiting**, main connection; ~**aantogsweg**, main avenue of approach; ~**aanval**, main attack; ~**aanvoerder**, commander-in-chief.
hoof'aar, cephalic vein; mid-rib.
hoof: ~**afdeling**, principal (main) division (section); ~**agent**, chief agent; ~**agentskap**, general agency; ~**aksent**, chief accent; ~**aksyns**, poll excise; ~**altaar**, high altar; ~**amptenaar**, chief officer; high official, head of a department; head official; ~**artikel**, leader, leading article, editorial; ~**as**, main axis; ~**balk**, main girder, principal; main beam; architrave.
hoof: ~**band**, headband, fillet; ~**bedekking**, headgear, covering for the head; headdress.
hoof: ~**bediende**, butler; pug; ~**bedrag**, principal amount; ~**beginsel**, cardinal principle; ~**begrip**, principal notion; first principle.
hoof'belasting, headtax; capitation, poll tax.
hoof: ~**bestanddeel**, main constituent; principal ingredient; ~**bestuur**, head office; head committee; ~**bestuurder**, general manager, chief director; ~**bestuurslid**, member of the head committee; ~**beswaar**, chief objection; ~**betekenis**, principal meaning; ~**betrekking**, chief post; ~**blad**, leader page, principal page; chief paper; main blade (plate); ~**bladsy**, leader page; front page (newspaper); ~**bout**, kingbolt; ~**brandweerpyp**, fire main.
hoof: ~**brekens**, ~**brekings**, brain-racking.
hoof: ~**bron**, main spring; head-spring; ~**buis**, main pipe, main; ~**buro**, head office; ~**deel**, major (main) part; ~**dek**, main deck; ~**dekking**, main guard.
hoofdeksel, headgear; hood.
hoofdelik, (-e), per head, per capita; ~ *AANSPREEKLIK*, severally liable; ~*e STEMMING hou*, take a poll (division).
hoof: ~**denkbeeld**, principal idea; ~**deug**, cardinal virtue; ~**deur**, main door; ~**dieet**, staple diet.
hoof'dig, (-e), obstinate; ~**heid**, obstinacy.
hoof: ~**direkteur**, chief director, director-in-chief; ~**doel**, main object; ~**dra(ag)vlak**, main plane; ~**dryfstang**, main connecting-rod; ~**dryfveer**, chief motive; ~**eienskap**, principal quality; main proposition (in mathematics).
hoof: ~**einde**, top-head; ~**end**, lip (of spring).
hoof: ~**ertsliggaam**, mother-lode; ~**faktor**, chief factor; ~**feit**, main fact; ~**figuur**, principal figure, dominant figure; ~**gebeurtenis**, chief event; ~**gebou**, main building; ~**gebrek**, main fault; ~**gedagte**, leading idea.
hoof'geld, poll tax.
hoof: ~(**ge**)**leiding**, main (line); ~**gereg**, principal dish; ~**getal**, cardinal number; ~**getuie**, chief witness; ~**geveg**, main battle; ~**grond**, main cause (argument); ~**grootboek**, main ledger.
hoof'haar, hair of the head.
hoof: ~**idee**, motif; ~**ingang**, main entrance; ~**ingenieur**, chief engineer; ~**inhoud**, chief contents; argument; ~**inspekteur**, chief inspector; ~**kaas**, (ong.), brawn; ~**kabel**, main (electr.); ~**kanonnier**, master gunner; ~**kantoor**, head office; ~**kaptein**, paramount chief; ~**karakter**, main character (in novel); ~**kelner**, chief steward; head waiter; ~**kerk**, cathedral, chief church; ~**klem**, main stress (accent); ~**klerk**, chief clerk; ~**kleur**, main colour; basic dye; major suit (cards); ~**klok**, master clock.
hoof'knik, nod of the head.
hoof: ~**kok**, chef; ~**kolonne**, main column; ~**komitee**, head committee; ~**kommandant**, chief commandant; ~**kommando**, chief commando; ~**kommissaris**, chief commissioner; ~**kommissie**, general committee; ~**kompartement**, main compartment; ~**kondukteur**, chief guard (conductor); ~**konstabel**, chief constable; head constable; ~**kraal**, great place (of African chief); ~**kraan**, main switch, main tap.
hoof'kussing, pillow.
hoof: ~**kussingblok**, main bearings; pillow block; brasses; ~**kwartier**, headquarters; ~**laer**, main

hoofpyn — *hoogkonjuntuur*

bearing; principal laager; ~ lêer, main girder; main file; ~ leiding, supreme direction; main (line, circuit); power main; ~ leier, chief leader; chief, boss; supremo; ~ letter, capital letter; ~ lyn, main line, trunk line; ~ lyngesprek, trunk call; long-distance conversation; ~ lynoproep, trunk call; ~ maaltyd, principal meal; ~ mag, main body; ~ man, headman, chief, leader, captain; centurion; ~ marslyn, main line of advance; ~ middel, chief means (of livelihood); ~ misdadiger, principal offender; ~ motief, *see* hoofdryfveer; ~ nerf, mid-rib (of leaves); ~ offisier, chief officer; field officer; ~ offisiersrang, field rank; ~ omroep, high change; ~ ondervraging, examination-in-chief; ~ onderwyser, head master; principal; ~ onderwyseres, head mistress; ~ oogmerk, chief aim; ~ oorsaak, principal (main) cause; ~ opsigter, head overseer; ~ pad, high (main) road; ~ parade, principal parade; ~ persoon, leader; hero; protagonist; leading character (in novel); ~ poskantoor, general post office; ~ produkte, major produce; ~ punt, main point; gravamen.

hoof'pyn, headache; cephalalgia; *'n BARSTENDE* ~, a splitting headache; *'n BLINDE* ~, migraine; *aan ~ LY*, suffer from headaches; ~ pil, headache pill (tablet); ~ poeier, headache powder.

hoof: ~ pyp, main (pipe); ~ raad, main council; ~ rat, master wheel; ~ redakteur, editor-in-chief, chief editor; ~ rede, main reason; ~ reël, principal rule; headline; ~ regter, chief justice; ~ reken(e), ~ rekening, ~ rekenkunde, mental arithmetic; ~ rif, main reef; ~ rifweg, main reef road; ~ rigstraal, main beam-track; ~ rivier, principal river; ~ rol, chief role (part), lead; *die ~ rol speel*, play the leading part; ~ rolspeler, star, principal player.

hoofs, (-e), courtly, ceremonious.

hoof'saak, main point (thing); essentials; gist; pivotal question; *IN die ~*, in the main; *in ~ VERKEERD*, substantially wrong; ~ 'lik, chiefly, mainly, principally, essential(ly), mostly, primarily.

hoof: ~ seil, mainsail, head sail; ~ sekretaris, chief (general) secretary; ~ setel, chief seat; head office; headquarters.

hoofs'heid, courtliness, ceremoniousness.
hoof'sieraad[1], ornament for the head.
hoof'sieraad[2], chief ornament.

hoof: ~ silinder, master cylinder; ~ sin, principal (main) clause; principal (main) sentence; ~ skakelaar, main switch; master switch; ~ skap, principalship, headmastership.

hoof'skedel, skull, cranium.
hoof'skottel, principal (main) dish, pièce de résistance; principal item.
hoof'skud, head shake.

hoof: ~ skuld, principal debt; chief guilt; ~ skuldenaar, principal debtor; ~ skuldige, (-s), principal offender.

hoof'slagaar, main artery, aorta.

hoof: ~ som, capital sum, principal (money); substance, summary (of argument); ~ sonde, capital sin, mortal sin; ~ spoorweg, main (railway) line; ~ stad, capital; metropolis; ~ stam, bole; ~ stander, kingpost; ~ stasie, main station; ~ stelling, principal position; main position; ~ straat, main street; ~ streke, main points (of the compass); ~ stroom, main current; ~ stuk, chapter; ~ swarigheid, principal difficulty.

hoof'sweer, ulcer in the head.

hoof: ~ tafelbediende, chief steward; ~ tak, main branch; ~ telwoord, cardinal number; ~ tema, leitmotif; burden (of song); master theme.
hoof'tooisel, head dress, head gear; coif.

hoof: ~ toon, main stress; keynote; ~ trek, chief feature, salient feature; outline; principal trait; ~ troepe, main body; ~ tyd, principal tense; ~ uitgang, main exit; ~ vak, chief (major) subject; ~ valskerm, main parachute; ~ veer, master spring.

hoof'verband, head bandage.

hoof: ~ verdedigingslyn, main line of defence; ~ verdedigingsplan, main plan of defence; ~ verdeelpyp, distributing main; ~ verdienste, chief merit; bulk of the income; ~ vereiste, chief requisite; ~ verkeerspad, ~ verkeersweg, main (arterial) road, trunk road; main line of traffic; ~ verpleegster, head nurse, sister-in-charge; matron; nursing sister; ~ vlieër, master pilot; ~ voedsel, staple food, main article of food; ~ vorm, main (principal) feature; ~ vraag, main question; ~ vyand, chief enemy; ~ waarheid, cardinal truth; ~ wag, main guard; ~ want, main rigging.

hoof: ~ wassing, washing of head; shampoo; ~ watersug, dropsy in the head; hydrocephaly.
hoof: ~ weerstand, main resistance; ~ weerstandstrook, main resistance-area; ~ weg, main road, highroad; main route; trunk road.
hoof'werk[1], mental work, head work.
hoof'werk[2], chief business; principal work.
hoof: ~ wind, cardinal wind; ~ windstreke, *see* hoofstreke.
hoof'wond, wound in the head; head wound.
hoof'wortel, main root, tap-root.

hoog, (b), (hoë; hoër, -ste), high (opinion); tall (tree); lofty (ideals); exalted (eminent personage); exorbitant (prices); aloft; (s), high, high-pressure system; *~ AAN wees*, be the worse for liquor; *van hoë AFKOMS*, of high (noble) descent; *ewe ~ en DROOG sit*, be quite unconcerned; sit high and dry; *iets te ~ INSIT*, begin on too high a note; *'n hoë KLEUR*, a high colour; flushed; *~ en LAAG sweer*, swear by all that one holds sacred; *~ in LAAG trap*, be unsteady on one's feet; *of jy ~ of LAAG spring*, if you like it or not; *dit kan nie hoër of LAER nie*, there is no alternative; no excuse will be accepted; *'n hoë LEEFTYD*, a great age; *~ LEWE*, be living in style; *dit is ~ NODIG*, it is absolutely necessary; *die hoë NOORDE*, the extreme north; *~ OPGEE oor iets*, make much of something; *hoë POLITIEK*, high politics; *~ SING*, sing in a high key; *~ in sy SKIK*, very pleased, delighted; *~ STUKKEND wees*, be blind drunk; *dit is vir my TE ~*, it is above my comprehension; *hoë VERWAGTINGS hê*, have high hopes; *~s WAARSKYNLIK*, very probable; most probably, as likely as not; ~ aangeskrewe, highly respected; ~ adellik, (-e), very noble.

hoog'ag, (-ge-), esteem highly, hold dear, respect; *~ tend die uwe*, yours truly (respectfully); ~ ting, respect, esteem, regard.

hoog: ~ altaar, high altar; ~ bejaard, (-e), very old, advanced in years; ~ blond, (-e), very fair; sandy (colour); ~ blou, deep blue; ~ dag, late in the morning; red-letter day; ~ dekker, high-wing monoplane.

hoogdra'wend, (-e), bombastic, grandiloquent, pompous, stilted, highflown; orotund; declamatory; altisonant; heroic; *~e taal*, pompous, (highflown) language; heroics; ~ heid, pompousness, gradiloquence, fustian.

hoog: ~ drawwer, high-stepper; ~ druk, high pressure; embossing; letterpress; ~ drukgebied, anticyclone; ~ druksmering, high-pressure lubrication; ~ drukstelsel, high-pressure system, high; ~ duikaanval, high-dive attack; H ~ duits, High German; ~ edelagbare, right honourable; ~ edele, right honourable; ~ eerwaarde, right reverend; ~ gaande, high (words); heavy (sea); ~ geag, (-te), highly esteemed; ~ gebergte, (high) mountains; ~ gebore, highborn; noble; ~ geel, bright yellow; ~ geëerd, (-e), highly honoured; ~ geleë, high-lying, situated at high elevation; ~ geleerd, (-e), very learned; ~ geplaas, (-te), highly placed, high in authority; ~ geregshof, Supreme Court; High Court; ~ geskat, (-te), (highly) valued; ~ gespan, (-ne), tense (expectation); highly strung; wrought up; ~ gestem, (-de), high-pitched; ~ gewaardeer, (-de), highly appreciated; ~ groen, bright green.

hooghar'tig, (-e), proud, haughty; cavalier; stand-offish; proud-spirited; high and mighty; lofty; ~ heid, pride, haughtiness, hauteur, loftiness.

hoog'heid, highness, majesty, grandeur; elevation; greatness; *Sy H ~*, His Highness, His Eminence.
Hoog'hollands, (South African) High Dutch.
hoog'hou, (-ge-), uphold, maintain; live up to.
hoog'konjuntuur, (ong.), boom, trade boom.

hoog'land, highland, plateau.
Hoog'lande, Highlands (of Scotland); ~**r**, (-s), Highlander; ~**rbroek**, trews.
hoog'leraar, professor; ~**samp**, professorship.
Hoog'lied, Song of Solomon, Canticles.
hoog'liggend, (-e), high-lying; ~*e gruis*, high-level gravel.
hoog: ~**lopend**, (-e), high (words); heavy (seas); ~**lugkunde**, (ong.), aerology; ~**mis**, high mass.
hoog'moed, pride, haughtiness, hauteur; ~ *kom voor die val*, pride comes before a fall.
hoogmoe'dig, (-e), overbearing, proud, haughty, prideful; ~**heid**, haughtiness.
hoog'moedswaan(sin), megalomania.
hoog: ~ **mo'ënd**, (-e), high and mightly; ~**nodig**, (-e), most necessary; urgently needed; ~**oond**, blast furnace; ~**oondslak**, blast-furnace slag; ~**pas**, col; ~**peil**, high-water mark; ~**reliëf**, high relief; ~**rooi**, bright red; crimson; ~**s**, very, extremely, eminently, highly, best possible; ~*s GEHEIM*, top secret; ~*s WAARSKYNLIK*, most probably.
hoogs'eie: *in* ~ *persoon*, in his own person.
hoog'skat, (-ge-), esteem highly, think much of; ~**ting**, (high) esteem, regard.
hoog: ~**slaan**, (-ge-), lob (in tennis); serve overhead; ~**slag**, lob; ~**spanning**, high tension; ~**spanningskabel**, high-tension cable; ~**spanningsleiding**, high-tension wire; ~**sprakig**, (-e), bombastic; ~**spring**, (s) high jump; (w) (-ge-), jump high; do the high jump; ~**staande**, of high standing, eminent; high-minded; outstanding; chief.
hoog'ste, highest; senior, chief; culminant; maximum, top (price); paramount; *OP sy* ~, at most; ~ *in RANG*, most senior; ~ *RAT*, topgear.
hoog'stens, at most, at best, at the outside; not more than; ~ *'n week*, not more than a week.
hoog'swewer, altitudinarian; glider.
hoog'te, (-s), height; pitch (voice); highness (prices); level (social; water); altitude; plane; elevation, eminence; hill; hummock; *uit die* ~ *AANKYK*, look down upon; *uit die* ~ *AANSIEN*, look down upon someone (something); *iem. uit die* ~ *BEHANDEL*, regard someone with a lofty air; *op* ~ *BLY*, keep abreast of the times; be well-informed; *iem. op* ~ *BRING*, post (inform) someone; bring someone up-to-date; *iets uit die* ~ *DOEN*, do something high-handedly; *in die* ~ *GAAN*, go up; take off; *iem. op* ~ *HOU*, keep someone up-to-date (informed); *die* ~ *inskiet*, soar; shoot; up; *uit die* ~ *op iem. NEERSIEN*, look down on a person; *OP die* ~ *van Kaapstad*, off Cape Town; *op* ~ *van SAKE*, be up-to-date, be well informed; *tot op SEKERE* ~, to a certain extent; up to a point; *iem. in die* ~ *STEEK*, laud someone to the skies; *hom op* ~ *STEL van iets*, acquaint oneself with a thing; *TOT op sekere* ~, to a certain extent (height); *goed op* ~ *van sy TYD wees*, be well abreast of the times; *die VENSTER was op dieselfde* ~ *as die vloer*, the window was flush with the floor; ~**afstandmeter**, range-finder; ~**bepaling**, altimetry; ~**bombardement**, high-altitude bombardment; ~**graad**, elevation; ~**grens**, ceiling (aviation); ~**hoek**, elevation angle; ~**lyn**, perpendicular (of triangle); contour line (map); ~**lynkaart**, contour map; ~**merk**, (contour) mark; ~**meter**, hypsometer, altimeter; sextant; height computer; ~**meting**, hypsometry, altimetry; ~**punt**, culmination, culminating point; acme, high-water mark; zenith, meridian; climax, peak (of production); apogee; pinnacle (of fame); crisis; heat; ~**punte**, highlights; ~**reëlaar**, ~**reëling**, altitude control; ~**rekord**, altitude record; ~**rigting**, elevation (shooting); ~**roer**, elevator; ~**siekte**, mountain (altitude) sickness; ~**sirkel**, circle of altitude; parallel of latitude; ~**snypunt**, orthocentre; ~**son**, artificial sunlight; ~**stang**, elevating bar; ~**stelskroef**, elevating screw; ~**tjie**, (-s), monticle, monticule; ~**toets**, height test; ~**verskil**, difference in height (levels); ~**versneller**, altitude throttle; ~**vliegtuig**, high-altitude aeroplane; ~**vlug**, altitude flight; ~**vrees**, acrophobia.
hoog'trapsiekte, stilted-gait disease.
hoog'ty: ~ *vier*, reign supreme; be the order of the day.
hoog'tyd, high festival (R.C. Church).
hoog: ~**verhewe**, lofty, sublime, empyreal, empyrean; ~**verraad**, high treason; ~**vlakgruis**, high-level gravel; ~**vlakte**, plateau, tableland; ~**vlie'ënd**, (-e), highflying, highflown; ~**vlieër**, highflier; *hy is geen* ~*vlieër nie*, he is no genius; ~**vlug**, supersonic flight.
hoogwaar'dig, (-e), venerable, eminent; ~**heid**, eminence; ~**heidsbekleër**, dignitary.
hoog'water, high tide; flood tide; high water; ~ *en laagwater*, high water and low water; ~**lyn**, ~**peil**, high-water mark.
hooi, hay; *te* ~ *en te GRAS*, off and on; *te veel* ~ *op sy vurk NEEM*, bite off more than one can chew; ~**berg**, haystack, hayrick; ~**er**, (-s), haymaker; ~**gaffel**, hayfork; ~**gewas**, (-se), haycrop; ~**hopie**, haycock; ~**kamp**, stack-yard; ~**kis**, (-te), haybox; fireless cooker; ~**klou**, grapple fork; ~**koors**, hayfever; ~**land**, hayfield; ~**masjien**, haymaker; ~**mied**, haystack; hayrick; ~**pers**, haypress; ~**solder**, hayloft; ~**skuur**, haybarn; ~**tyd**, hay-making time; ~**veld**, hayfield; ~**vurk**, hayfork, pitchfork; ~**wa**, haywag(g)on; daddy-long-legs *(Phalangida)*.
hook! stop! (to oxen); ~**haai**, *see* **hokaai**.
hoon, (s) scorn, mockery, derision, taunt; insult; contumely; gibe; (w) **(ge-)**, sneer at, mock, gibe, jeer at, deride; flout; ~**lag**, scornful laughter.
hoop¹, (s) **(hope)**, heap, pile; group; bundle; cluster, crowd; stack (of hay); dollop; accumulation; mound; *hy het hope GELD*, he has heaps of money; *die GROOT* ~, the great majority; *hope-hope GROND aandra*, bring heaps of soil; *'n* ~ *LEUENS*, a pack of lies; *by die* ~ *VERKOOP*, sell in lump; *nog 'n* ~ *WERK hê*, still have any amount of work; (w) **(ge-)**, heap; *laste op iem. se skouers* ~, place burdens on someone's shoulders.
hoop², (s) hope; expectance; *die* ~ *BESKAAM nie*, hope maketh not ashamed; *op* ~ *van BETER*, in the hope of better things to come; *BUITE* ~ *lê*, be critically ill; *met GERINGE* ~ *op welslae*, with small hope of success; *IN die* ~ *dat*, in the hope (hoping) of; ~ *KOESTER*, cherish (entertain) hope; *die* ~ *laat LEWE*, if hope were not, heart would break; *OP* ~ *van*, in the hope (hoping) of; *die* ~ *OPGEE*, abandon hope; *die* ~ *OPWEK*, raise hopes; *sy* ~ *VESTIG op*, set one's hopes on; *op* ~ *van SEËN*, hoping for the best; *TEEN* ~ *op* ~, against all hope; *tussen* ~ *en VREES*, between fear and hope; (w) **(ge-)**, hope; *die BESTE* ~, hope for the best; *teen BETERWETE in* ~, hope against hope; *dis TE hope dat*, it is to be hoped that.
hoop: ~**dra**, **(ge-)**, stook, shock; ~**s'gewys(e)**, in heaps.
hoop'vol, (-le), hopeful, sanguine, confident, optimistic.
hoor, **(ge-)**, hear; listen; heed; learn; *volgens ALLES wat ek* ~, from all accounts; ~ *nou 'n BIETJIE*, just listen for a moment; *kom ons GAAN* ~, come, let us go and find out; *jouself GRAAG* ~, to like hearing one's own voice; ~, ~*!*, hear, hear!; *HORENDE doof wees*, sham deafness; *iem. net van* ~ *KEN*, know someone only by repute; *jy moet KOM, ge* ~*?*, you must come, did you hear me?; *jou LAAT* ~, make oneself heard; *jy sal nog MEER daarvan* ~, you will hear more about it; ~ *is MIN*, he simply will not listen; ~ *NA my*, listen to me; *NIE van iets wil* ~ *nie*, not wish to hear anything about something; *ek wil NIKS van jou* ~ *nie*, I do not wish to hear a word from you; *hy wou daar NIKS van* ~ *nie*, he turned a deaf ear to it; *van* ~ *en SÊ, lieg mens veel*, the tale runs as it pleases the teller; ~, *SIEN en swyg*, nature has given us two ears, two eyes, and but one tongue, to the end that we should hear and see more than we speak; *ek het* ~ *VERTEL*, I have heard it said; *wie nie wil* ~ *nie, moet VOEL*, those who will not be ruled by the rudder, must be ruled by the rock; he who refuses to obey must take the consequences; *nie van iets WIL* ~ *nie*, not to want to hear of it; ~**afstand**, earshot; ~**baar**, (..**bare**), audible; ~**baarheid**, audibility; ~**beeld**, (radio) feature programme;

hoornblende

~ **buis**, receiver (telephone); ~ **der**, (-s), hearer, listener; ~ **deres'**, (-se), hearer (woman); ~ **gang**, listening gallery.
hoorn'blende = **horingblende**.
hoor'sê, hearsay; *iets van* ~ *weet*, know by hearsay; ~ **getuienis**, hearsay evidence.
hoor'spel, (-e), radio drama.
hoort, (ge-), belong; be proper (fit); ought; *DIT* ~ *nie so nie*, it is improper; it is not done that way; *dit* ~ *nie HIERBY nie*, it does not belong to this; it is out of place here.
hoor: ~ **toestel**, hearing-aid, deaf-aid; ~ **vermoë**, audition.
hoos[1], (ong., Ndl.), (s) (**hose**), waterspout.
hoos[2], (w) (ge-), scoop, bail.
hop[1], (s) (-pe), hoopoe (bird).
hop[2], (s) hop(s).
hop[3], (w) (ge-), hop, jump; (tw) gee-up!
hop: ~ **agtig**, (-e), hoplike; ~ **akker**, hopfield, ~ **brood**, white baker's-bread, hopbread.
ho'pelik, as hoped; it is to be hoped, hopefully.
ho'peloos, (..lose), hopeless, without hope; past hope; desperate; ~ **heid**, hopelessness.
ho'pend, (-e), hoping, expectant.
ho'pie, (-s), small heap; ~ *s maak*, cock (hay); relieve nature.
hop'kweker, hopgrower.
hop: ~ **oond**, cast; ~ **plukker**, hop-picker, hopper; ~ **rank**, hop(-bine); ~ **sak**, hopsack(ing); ~ **teelt**, hop cultivation.
Ho'rak: *wat sê* ~ *?*, well, what's the news?, well what do you know?
hor'de, (-s), horde, band, troop, gang.
ho'rig, (-e), predial; ~ **e**, (-s), serf, villein, predial; ~ **heid**, serfdom, villeinage, bondage.
ho'ring, (-s), horn; hooter; mandrel (anvil); cornu (anat.); cone (for ice-cream); *iem. moes nog net* ~ *s gehad het, dan was hy 'n BUFFEL*, he is very rude; he is a churl; *ENGELSE* ~, cor anglais; *FRANSE* ~, French horn; *sy* ~ *s KOM uit*, he a quite a man now; *die* ~ *LIG*, show fight; show one's teeth; *op* ~ *s NEEM*, cause a shindy; raise the roof; *te veel op jou* ~ *s NEEM*, take too much on one's shoulders; *die* ~ *van OORVLOED*, the horn of plenty, cornucopia; *die* ~ *OPHEF*, face boldly; show a bold front; *die* ~ *s OPSTEEK*, show one's teeth; show fight; *slaan dat hy na* ~ *RUIK*, give him a good hiding; ~ *s SKERP maak*, sharpen one's claws; *iem. se* ~ *onder die TOU uithaal*, do someone a favour; ~ **agtig**, (-e), horny, horn-like, keratoid; cornuted; ~ **bal**, heel (horse's hoof); ~ **bekvoël**, hornbill; ~ **bewerker**, horner; ~ **blaser**, hornblower; horner; ~ **blende**, hornblende; ~ **bril**, horn-rimmed spectacles; ~ **bul**, bulb (on horse's foot); ~ **draaier**, horner; ~ **draer**, cuckold; ~ **droog**, (..droë), dry as dust, very dry; ~ **fels**, hornfels; ~ **fluit**, hornpipe; ~ **geskal**, mort; hornblast, hornblowing; ~ **huid**, cuticle; ~ **klip**, rock flint; ~ **laag**, horny layer; ~ **loos**, (..lose), hornless; ~ **manslang**, horned viper; ~ **musiek**, horn music; ~ **oud**, (..oue), as old as the hills, very old; ~ **pit**, horn core; ~ **rots**, hornfels; ~ **slang**, horned snake; ~ **sman**, horned adder; horned sheep; ~ **smanooi**, merino ewe with horns; ~ **speler**, horn-blower; ~ **steen**, rock-flint, hornstone; ceratite; chert; ~ **stof**, keratin; ~ **straal**, frog (in horse's hoof); horny frog; ~ **suil**, keratoma; ~ **uil**, horned owl, bubo; ~ **vee**, horned cattle; ~ **vis**, trigger fish; ~ **vlies**, cornea; ~ **vliesontsteking**, inflammation of the cornea, keratitis; ~ **vliesvlek**, nebula (of eye); ~ **vormig**, (-e), horn-shaped; ~ **vrat**, chestnut; ~ **weefsel**, ceratin; ~ **werk**, hornwork.
ho'rinkie, (-s), little horn; antenna; cone (ice-cream).
ho'rison, (-ne, -te), horizon; sky-line; ~ **taal'**, (..tale), horizontal, level; ~ **tale afbouing**, breast stoping.
horlo'sie, see **oorlosie**; (-s), watch; ~ **band**, watchband; ~ **blom**, passion-flower; ~ **glas**, watchglass; ~ **kas**, watchcase; ~ **ketting**, watch-chain; ~ **maker**, watchmaker; ~ **rakkie**, clock stand; ~ **sak**, fob; ~ **sleutel**, watchkey; ~ **veer**, watch-spring; ~ **winkel**, jeweller's (watch-maker's) shop; ~ **wyser**, hand of watch.

hottentots

hormoon', (**hormone**), hormone; ~ **vlak**, hormone level.
horoskoop', (..**skope**), horoscope; ascendant; ~ **trekker**, fortune teller.
horoskopie', horoscopy.
hor'relpoot, club-foot (animal).
hor'relpyp, hornpipe; jig; *iem. die* ~ *laat dans*, give someone a hiding (flogging).
hor'reltjies! time! (in children's games).
hor'relvoet, club-foot (human); talipes; varus.
hor'ries, delirium tremens; horrors, blue devils.
hors-d'oeu'vre, (-s), hors d'oevre.
hor'sel, (-s), hornet, gadfly.
hors'makriel, horse-mackerel.
hors'sweep, horsewhip.
hor'te, jolts, jerks; *met* ~ *en stote*, by fits and starts.
hor'tend (-e), lame; joltingly; jerky (style); ~ *en stotend*, hemming and hawing.
horten'sia, **horten'sie**, (-s), hortensia, hydrangea.
hor'terig, (-e), jerky; abrupt (style); joltingly.
hor'tjie, (-s), louvre, slat; ~ **sblinding**, Venetian blind; louvre; ~ **sruit**, louvre.
hortoloog', (..**loë**), horticulturist.
hortula'nus, (-se), conservator.
hor'tus, (-se), botanical garden.
hosan'na, (-s), hosanna; *vandag* ~, *more kruisig hom*, "hosanna" today, "crucify him" tomorrow.
hos'pita, (-s), landlady, hostess.
hos'pitaal, **hospitaal'**, (..**tale**), hospital; *in die* ~ *lê*, be in hospital; ~ **behandeling**, hospital treatment; ~ **broeder**, hospitaller; ~ **geld**, hospital fee; ~ **koors**, jail fever; ~ **linne**, surgical linen; ~ **personeel**, medical staff (army); ~ **ridder**, knight hospitaller; ~ **skip**, hospital ship; ~ **stelsel**, hospitalism; ~ **superintendent**, hospital superintendent; ~ **trein**, hospital train; ~ **verpleegster**, hospital nurse.
hospitalisa'sie, hospitalization.
hospitaliseer', (ge-), hospitalize; ..**lise'ring**, hospitalization.
hospiteer', (ge-), attend a lecture as visitor.
hos'tie, host, consecrated wafer; ~ **bord**, paten; ~ **kelk**, pyx.
hot, (s) lefthand; animal on near side; (bw) left (team of oxen); ~ *en HAAR stuur*, send from pillar to post; ~ *is* ~ *en HAAR is haar*, a fact is a fact; *nie weet wat* ~ *of HAAR is nie*, not to know what's what; *altyd* ~ *om wil KOM*, be contrary; ~ *HOU*, keep left; *dit net* ~ *KRY*, be having a hard time; *nie* ~ *of LINKS weet nie*, be at a loss; ~ *OM*, to the left, anti-clockwise; reverse (in dancing); backhand (bowls); ~ *om en haar om STAAN*, try to find a way out; ~ **agter**, hind left; *dit* ~ *agter kry*, be having a hard time; he hard pressed; ~ **agteros**, left hind-ox; on-wheeler.
hotel', (-le, -s), hotel; ~ **baas**, hotelier; hotel-keeper; hotel-owner; ~ **bedryf**, hotel business; ~ **bespreking**, hotel reservation; ~ **dief**, hotel thief; ~ **eienaar**, hotel proprietor (owner); ~ **houer**, (-s), hotel-keeper.
hotelier', (-s), hotel-keeper, hotelier.
hotel': ~ **joggie**, page (boy); ~ **koste**, hotel expenses; ~ **lewe**, hotel life; ~ **lisensie**, hotel license; ~ **pryse**, hotel tariffs; ~ **raad**, hotel board; ~ **register**, hotel register; ~ **rekening**, hotel bill; ~ **wese**, hotels, hotel-keeping.
hot: ~ **hand**, left hand; ~ **hou**, left; ~ **kant**, left side; ~ **klou**, left claw; southpaw, left-handed boxer; ~ **naasagter**, second left-hind; ~ **naasvoor**, second left-front.
hot'not, (-s), type of fish *(Cantharus blochii; Sargus hottentottus)*.
hot'notjie, (-s), carpal; tarsal; knuckle-bone.
hot: ~ **om**, porridge made from flour; ~ **omhou**, slice (cricket, golf); ~ **omslaan**, (-geslaan), slice (cricket, golf); ~ **op-ag(t)**, eighth on the left from behind (fourth yoke); ~ **op-ses**, sixth on the left from behind (third yoke); ~ **perd**, left horse.
hot'tentots: ~ **boontjie**, broad bean (*Schotia speciosa*); ~ **brood**, a yam (*Testitundinaria elephantipes*); ~ **got**, (-te), praying mantis; ~ **kersie**, berry of *Maurosenia capensis*; ~ **kooigoed**, soft woolly substance of *Helichrysum crispum*; ~ **kougoed**,

shrub *(Mesembryanthemum tortuosum)*; ~**tee**, wild tea *(Helichrysum orbiculare)*; ~**vy**, wild fig *(Carpobrotus edulis)*.

hot'voor, left front; ~**dier**, near leader; ~**perd**, near leader; near-leading horse.

hou¹, (s) (-e), blow, cut, stroke, lash; fib, gash, hack; hit; punch, sock; chop; *'n ~ in die DONKER slaan*, take a shot in the dark; *'n ~ in die LUG slaan*, beat the air (wind); *'n ~ LEER, werk, ens.*, study, work hard; *'n OU ~*, rather much; *'n ou (goeie) ~ SLAAN*, make a good shot; take a stiff tot; ~ *VIR* ~, time and again; blow by blow; *'n goeie ~ WEGSLAAN*, take a stiff tot; know how to put it down; (w) (ge-), hew, cut, hack; strike.

hou², (s): ~ *en trou sweer*, pledge fealty; (b); ~ *en trou*, loyal and faithful.

hou³, (w) (ge-), keep, hold; retain (shape, value); observe (Sunday); celebrate (Christmas); take place (examination); run, conduct (shop); wear (shoes); contain; fulfil (promise); deliver, make (speech); *hom AAN iets ~*, be true to one's word; *hy ~ hom ASOF...*, he pretends to...; *die BED ~*, keep to one's bed; *hom DOOF ~*, feign deafness; *hom GOED ~*, bear up; be good; ~ *wat jy HET (en kry wat jy kan)*, hold on to what you have and get what you can; *LINKS ~*, keep to the left; ~ *jou MOND*, hold your tongue; *MUISE ~ hier*, mice frequent this place; ~ *OP!* stop it! have done! *REGS ~*, keep to the right; *die SEËL wil nie ~ nie*, the stamp won't stick; *hy ~ hom SIEK*, he shams illness; *hy ~ hom maar SO*, he is shamming; *iets STAANDE ~*, maintain something; *TEN goede ~*, take in good part; *VAN iets ~*, like a thing; ~ *dit VIR jou*, keep it to yourself, keep it secret; keep it for yourself; *'n WINKEL ~*, run a shop; *WAARVOOR jy my?* what do you take me for?

hou(d)'baar, (..bare), tenable, maintainable; defensible; ~**heid**, tenability.

hou'ding, (-e, -s), conduct, bearing, behaviour, air, comportment, demeanour, mien, attitude, deportment; pose, position; posture; port, presence; poise; stance; *'n ~ AANNEEM*, strike a pose; adopt an attitude; *'n AFWAGTENDE ~ aanneem*, wait and see; *'n DREIGENDE ~*, a threatening attitude; *die ~ van haar HOOF*, the poise (carriage) of her head.

hou'e: *met sy hebbe en ~*, with all his worldly goods.

hou'er, (-s), holder; licensee (shop); container; stoper (in mines); ~**verpakking**, containerization; ~**vrag**, containers, containerization, container load.

hou-hou': ~**speel**, play keeps.

hou-jou-bek'-wet, shut-up law (act), discipline law (act, ordinance), gag-law.

hou'plek, haunt, habitat; grip; stamping ground.

houri', (-'s), houri.

hout, (s) (-e), wood, timber; *iem. met 'n lang ~ DOODSLAAN*, lay someone flat with whatever comes to hand; *DROË ~*, dead wood; *van dieselfde ~ GEKAP wees*, be of the same sort (kind); *uit goeie ~ GESNY wees*, have come of good stock; *as dit met die GROEN ~ gebeur, wat sal met die dorre geskied*, if that is done in the green tree, what will be done in the dry? ~ *KOU*, fritter away one's time; *OUD soos droë ~*, time-worn; hoary; *van dik ~ saag mens PLANKE*, those that have plenty of butter can lay it on thick; ~ *SAAG*, be driving hogs to market; *dit SNY geen ~ nie*, it cuts no ice; *alle ~ is nie TIMMERHOUT nie*, you cannot make a silk purse out of a sow's ear; *uit die ou ~ GESNY wees*, be a chip of the old block; *met nat ~ VUUR wil maak*, try to make bricks without straw, *droë ~ of 'n VUURTJIE wees*, try to be helpful; ~**afval**, chips, wood waste; ~**agtig**, (-e), woody, ligneous; ~**appel**, crab-apple; ~**appelboom**, crab-tree.

hout'as¹, wood ashes.

hout'as², (-se), wooden axle.

hout: ~**asyn**, pyroligneous acid; ~**bedryf**, timber-industry (-trade); ~**been**, wooden leg; ~**bekleding**, panelling; boxing; ~**beskot**, wainscot(ing); panelling; ~**bewerking**, woodwork; ~**blaasinstrument**, woodwind instrument; ~**blasers**, woodwind; ~**blok**, woodblock; chump; ~**boorder**, wood borer; ~**brandwerk**, poker-work; ~**bry**, woodpulp; ~**draaier**, turner (in wood); ~**druk**, lock-print(ing); ~**duif**, woodpigeon; ~**e**, woods (golf, bowls); ~**emmer**, wooden bucket; ~**erig**, (-e), wooden, stiff, clumsy; ~**erigheid**, woodenness, clumsiness; ~**gees**, wood alcohol, methyl alcohol; ~**gerus**, (-te), quite at ease, unsuspicious; ~**gerus wees**, be blissfully unaware; be quite unconcerned; ~**graveerkuns**, wood-engraving; xylography; ~**gravure**, woodcut; ~**hakker**, woodcutter; ~**hamer**, mallet; dresser; ~**handel**, timber trade; ~**handelaar**, dealer in wood; timber merchant; ~**hawe**, camber; ~**hoop**, woodpile; ~**huis**, wooden house; ~**industrie**, timber trade (industry); ~**inlegwerk**, tarsia.

hout'jie¹, (-s), bit of wood; *iets op eie ~ DOEN*, do something off one's own bat; *so slim soos die ~ van die GALG*, as sharp as a needle; *'n ~ met iem. SNY*, do business with someone; talk things over with someone; *sy ~ VERLOOR hê*, have lost one's touch.

hou'tjie², (-s), light blow, tap.

hout: ~**kapper**, (-s), barbet; (bird); forager; lumberman, lumberjack, woodcutter; ~ *kappers en waterdraers*, hewers of wood and drawers of water; ~**kappersbyl**, felling axe; ~**kapperskamp**, lumbercamp; ~**kappery**, lumbering, woodcutting; ~**katel**, wooden bedstead; ~**kewer**, death-watch beetle; ~**kis**, woodbox; ~**klower**, (-s), woodcutter; ~**kop**, blockhead, fathead; ~**koper**, wood merchant; ~**krulle**, turnings, woodshavings; ~**loods**, timbershed; ~**luis**, woodlouse; ~**masjienwerker**, wood machinist, ~**mark**, timber market; ~**molm**, dry rot; ~**mosaïek**, marquetry; ~**nael**, dowel; ~**pakhuis**, timber warehouse; ~**pap**, woodpulp; ~**perd**, cockhorse, wooden horse; ~**poeiertor**, powder-post beetle; ~**pop**, wooden doll; nonentity; marionette; ~*pop sit*, sit like a dummy; ~**raam**, crate, wooden framework; ~**ryk** (-e), well-wooded; ~**saag**, woodsaw; ~**saagmeule**, sawmill; ~**saer**, wood-sawyer, snorer; ~**saery**, sawmill; snoring; ~**sel**, woodcell; ~**skilder**, grainer; ~**skoen**, wooden shoe, sabot; ~**skool**, charcoal; ~**skoolbeskuit**, charcoal biscuit; ~**skoolyster**, charcoal iron; ~**skroef**, woodscrew; ~**skutting**, boarding; ~**skuur**, woodshed; ~**snee**, woodcut; ~**sneegravure**, woodcut; ~**sneekuns**, (art of) wood-engraving; ~**sneewerk**, woodcarving; ~**snip**, woodcock; ~**sny**, (-ge-), carve in wood; ~**snybeitel**, carving chisel; ~**snyer**, woodcarver (engraver); ~**snyguts**, carving gouge; ~**snykuns**, (art of) woodcarving (engraving), xylography; ~**solder**, woodloft; ~**soort**, kind of wood; ~**spaander**, chip of wood; ~**speekwiel**, artillery wheel; ~**spyker**, nog, dowel(-pin); ~**stapel**, woodstack, pile of wood; ~**steen**, lignite; wood-opal; ~**stof**, lignin, woodpulp, ~**(stok)**, wood (golf); ~**stoof**, stove for wood; ~**suiker**, xylose; ~**swam**, dry rot; woodfungus; lichen; ~**teelt**, sylviculture; ~**teer**, vegetable tar; ~**vat**, trachea (botany); ~**verduursaming**, timber preservation; ~**vervoervragwa**, timber lorry; ~**vesel**, wood fibre; ~**vester**, (-s), ranger, forester; ~**vestery**, forestry; ~**vlot**, raft, catamaran; ~**vorming**, lignification; ~**vuur**, woodfire; ~**vyl**, woodfile; ~**ware**, woodware; ~**weefsel**, woodtissue; ~**werf**, timber-yard; ~**werk**, woodwork; ~**werkfabriek**, wood-manufacturing plant; ~**wiel(e)**, artillery wheel(s); ~**wol**, woodwool, fine woodshavings; ~**wolvesels**, staple fibre; ~**wurm**, woodworm, borer, wood-(fretter-)mite.

hou'vas: hold; handle; hold-fast, foothold; handhold; grip, grasp; *iets wat ~ BIED*, something to rely on; *'n ~ HÊ op iem.*, have a hold on someone.

hou'vermoë, capacity; ability to last; keeping quality (foodstuffs).

houweel', (..wele), mattock, pick-axe.

houwit'ser, (-s), howitzer.

hovaar'dig, (-e), haughty, arrogant, proud.

hovaar'digheid, hovaardy', haughtiness, arrogance, pride.

ho'weling, (-e), courtier.

howenier', (vero.) (-s), gardener; ~**s'almanak**, gar=

deners almanac; ~s'kuns, (vero.) horticultural art.
h'′tjie, (-s), small **h**.
hu, (ge-), marry, wed; ~baar, (..bare), marriageable, nubile; ~baarheid, marriageableness, nubility.
hub'bardpampoen, Hubbard squash.
Hu'genoot, (..note), Huguenot.
huid, (-e), hide, skin; derm; *iem. die ~ AFSTROOP*, fleece someone; *BANG wees vir sy ~*, be afraid to risk his skin; think of his skin; *die ~ verkoop voor die BEER geskiet is*, count your chickens before they are hatched; *'n DIK ~ hê*, be thick-skinned; *op die blote ~ DRA*, wear next to the skin; *iem. op sy ~ GEE*, give someone a tanning; *met ~ en HAAR*, neck and crop; in hide and hair; *sy ~ WAAG*, risk his neck; ~aar, cutaneous vein; ~arts, skin specialist, dermatologist; ~bloeding, purpura; ~droes, farcy (vet.); ~ekoper, dealer in hides and skins; ~emark, skin (hide) market.
hui'dig, (-e), present, modern, recent, hodiernal; *ten ~e dae*, in these (modern) times, nowadays; *in die ~e tyd*, at present; in present times.
huid'jie, skin, cuticle.
huidjiehu', (-'s), green-bladder grasshopper *(Pneumora variolosa)*.
huid: ~kanker, cancer of the skin; ~kleur, skin colour, complexion; ~klier, skin (cutaneous) gland; ~leer, dermatology; ~mondjie, stoma; ~ontsteking, inflammation of the skin; dermatitis; ~opening, dermal pore; ~plooi, fold of the skin, plica; ~pyn, dermalgia; ~senuwee, cutaneous nerve; ~siekte, skin disease, cutaneous disease; ~siekteleer, dermatology; ~s'kleur, colour of the skin; complexion; ~skelet, exoskeleton; ~smeer, sebum; ~smeerklier, sebaceous gland; ~spesialis, skin specialist; dermatologist; ~spier, cutaneous muscle; ~uitslag, eruption of the skin, rash; hives; eczema; ~vlek, birth-mark, mole; ~water, lotion; ~wurm, Guinea worm.
huig, (-e), uvula; *my ~ hang*, my uvula is swollen; ~-R, uvular R.
hui'gel, (ge-), dissemble, feign, sham; counterfeit; dissimulate; ~aar, (-s), hypocrite, canter, pretender, pharisee, dissimulator; ~aarster, female hypocrite; ~agtig, (-e), hypocritical, dissembling; histrionic; insincere, sanctimonious; pretending; ~agtigheid, insincerity, hypocrisy; ~ares', (-se), female hypocrite; ~(a)ry', hypocrisy, dissimulation, double-dealing, histrionism, cant; counterfeit; disguiser; ~taal, cant, hypocritical language.
huik, (-e), hooded cloak; *die ~ na die wind hang*, trim one's sails to the wind.
huil, (s) crying, weeping; bleeding (of plants); whining; *aan die ~ GAAN*, start crying; *TOT ~ens toe*, on the verge of tears; (w) (ge-), cry, weep, blubber (humans); howl (wolves), pule; whine (dogs); bleed (vine); *ek KON ~*, I could sit down and cry; *SAAM met iem. ~*, weep with someone; *dis om VAN te ~*, it is enough to make one weep; ~-~WEGLOOP, walk away crying; *die ~ende WILDERNIS*, the howling wilderness; ~balie, cry-baby; whiner; ~boom, ~bos, African wattle *(Peltophorum africanum)*; ~bui, crying fit; ~ebalk, cry-baby; whiner; weeper; ~er, (-s), howler; ~erig, (-e), tearful, lachrymose; ~ery, crying; whining; sorrowing, weeping; ~stem, whining voice.
huis, (-e), (s) house, dwelling, household; cottage; home; institution; casing; *al is 'n ~ ook hoe ARM, hy dek warm*, home is home, though it be never so homely; *'n ~ se DAK opsit*, raise the roof; *~ en HAARD*, hearth and home; *die ~ van die Here*, the house of God; *die ~ op HORINGS neem*, turn the house upside-down; *daar is geen ~ met jou te HOUnie*, one can do nothing with you; your conduct is intolerable; *~ se KANT toe staan*, be thinking of going home; *by iem. aan ~ KOM*, visit a person's home; *as jy 'n ~ wil bou, moet jy eers die KOSTE bereken*, first consider, then begin; *hoe groter ~, hoe groter KRUIS*, content lodges oftener in cottages than palaces; *~e is KRUISE*, a house to be let for life or years, its rent is sorrow and its income tears; *elke ~ het sy KRUIS*, every family has its skeleton in the cupboard; no house but has its cross; *'n MEISIE ~ toe neem*, see a girl home; *OPE ~ hou*, entertain a great deal; *~ OPSIT*, start a home; *as jy 'n ~ na elkeen se RAAD bou, is hy krom*, too many cooks spoil the broth; *'n ~ op SAND bou*, build a house on sand; *TEN ~e van*, at the home of; *~ toe GAAN*, go home; *van ~ UIT*, of origin; by birth; *drie ~e VERDER*, three doors away; (w) (ge-), house, lodge; ~adres, home (private) address; ~agent, house agent; ~altaar, household altar; family devotions; ~apteek, medicine chest; ~arres, house arrest; ~baadjie, smoking jacket; ~baas, landlord, house-owner; ~bakkie, plain; narrow-minded; ~bediende, domestic servant; ~besoek, pastoral visit; house-to-house call; canvas; visitation; *op ~ besoek gaan*, do parish-visiting; ~bestuur, housewifery; domestic economy; ~bewaarder, caretaker; ~bewoner, householder, occupant of a house; ~bivakke, close billets; ~blad, house organ; ~bou, house-building; ~braak, housebreaking, burglary; ~braakgereedskap, housebreaking implements; ~bybel, family Bible; ~deur, house door; ~diensbaarheid, urban servitude; ~dier, domestic animal; ~dokter, family doctor; home-doctor; ~eienaar, house-owner, landlord; householder; ~gebrek, shortage of houses; ~genoot, (..note), house mate, inmate (of same house); ~gesin, family, household; ~goed, furniture; ~gode, household gods; Lares, Panates; teraphim; ~godsdiens, family prayers; ~heer, master of the house; landlord; ~hen, stay-at-home, home-bird; ~hoog, as high as a house; ~hospitaal, cottage hospital.
huis'hou, (s) (-ens), household, family; housekeeping; (w) (-ge-), keep house; *vreeslik ~ met 'n ander se GOED*, play havoc with the possessions of another person; *IEWERS vreeslik ~*, cause havoc somewhere; ~boek, house-keeping book; ~'delik, (-e), economical; domestic; housewifely; *'n ~delike vergadering*, a formal (private) meeting; ~geld, house-keeping allowance (money).
huis'houding, household; housekeeping; menage; establishment; economy (of the state); *'n ~ BEGIN*, set up house; start a home; *'n ~ van Jan STEEN*, an unruly household.
huis'houdkunde, domestic science (economy); home economics; homecraft; housewifery.
huishoudkun'dig, (-e), economical; ~e, (-s), household economist.
huis'houdskool, school for domestic science.
huis'houdster, (-s), housekeeper.
huis'hou: ~e, household affairs; ~er, (-s), householder; ~geld, money for housekeeping; ~kuns, housewifery.
huis: ~hulp, domestic assistant (servant); ~huur, house rent; ~huurder, tenant; ~huurtoelae, house allowance; ~ie, (-s), small house, cottage; shell; (spectacle) case; section (of orange); binnacle (of compass); ~ieslak, snail; ~industrie, home industry; ~inwyding, house-warming; ~jas, dressing gown; ~kamer, living-room; ~kat, domestic cat; ~kewer, *Hylotrupes bajulus*; ~kleding, ~klere, déshabillé, undress; indoor clothes; ~klok, house clock; ~kneg, footman; factotum; ~komitee, house committee; ~lid, house-committee member; ~kriek, (house) cricket; cricket on the hearth; ~kring, home circle; ~kruis, domestic nuisance; ~lêer, (-s), idler, stay-at-home.
huis'lik, (-e), homely, home-like, domestic; home-keeping, homy; home-bred; familiar; *~e AANGELEENTHEDE*, family affairs; *~e KRING*, home circle; *die ~e LEWE*, home life; *~e PLIGTE*, household duties; *~e VERKEER*, family intercourse; ~heid, homeliness; domesticity; home life.
huis: ~linne, household linen; ~mense, members of a family; household; ~middel, household remedy; empirical remedy; home remedy; ~moeder, mistress of the house, mother (of the family); matron; ~moederlik, matronly, housewifely; ~muis, ordinary small mouse; ~nommer, number of the house; ~nood, dearth of houses; ~nooi, lady of the house; ~olie, household oil; ~onderwyser, private

teacher; tutor; housemaster; governor; ~**onderwyseres**, governess; ~**opvoeding**, home education; ~**orde**, rules of the house; ~**orrel**, cabinet organ; harmonium; ~**party**, house-warming (party); ~**plaag**, house-pest; ~**raad**, furniture; goods; chattels; ~**rok**, morning frock, housedress; ~**ry**, row of houses; ~**saak**, domestic affair; ~**sitter**, (-s), home-bird; ~**sitterig**, (-e), housebound; ~**skaarste**, dearth of houses; ~**skilder**, housepainter; decorator; ~**skoonmaak**, house cleaning; ~**slaaf**, domestic slave; ~**sleutel**, housekey; ~**sloper**, housebreaker; ~**soeker**, househunter; ~**soekery**, househunting; ~**soeking**, house-search, search in a (of the) house; domiciliary visit; ~**speletjies**, indoor games; ~**swael(tjie)**, house-martin; ~**taal**, home language; ~**vader**, housemaster; father of a family; resident master (hostel); ~**vas**, (-te), homekeeping, stay-at-home; ~**verfraaiing**, home (interior) decoration; ~**verwer**, housepainter.

huis'ves, **(ge-)**, house, lodge, (give) board(ing); ~**ting**, lodging, boarding, housing, accommodation; harbourage.

huis: ~**vlieg**, housefly, domestic fly; ~**vlyt**, homecraft, housecraft, home-industry; domestic science; ~**vrede**, domestic peace; ~**vriend**, family friend; familiar; ~**vrou**, wife, housewife; dame; ~**waarts**, home(wards); ~**werk**, housework; homework, preparation (of scholar).

hui'tjie: met ~ en muitjie, bag and baggage; skin and all.

hui'wer, **(ge-)**, shiver, tremble; hesitate; ~ van AF-SKU, shudder with horror; ~ by die GEDAGTE aan, shudder at the thought of; ~ OM, be hesitant about; ~**ig**, (-e), timorous, timid, afraid; hesitant; ~ig wees om in te gryp, shrink from (be hesitant about) taking steps; ~**igheid**, hesitation; ~**ing**, (-e, -s), trepidation; horror; hesitation; ~**ingwekkend**, (-e), horrible, eerie, shuddering.

hul¹, (w) **(ge-)**, shroud, envelop; in geheimsinnigheid ge~, shrouded in mystery.

hul², (vnw) (skryftaal), they, them; their.

hul'de, tribute, homage, ovation; ~bring aan, pay a tribute to, do homage to; ~**betoon**, mark of esteem, homage; ~**blyk**, mark of respect, tribute.

hul'dig, **(ge-)**, do homage, honour; hold (view); ~**ing**, homage, show of respect, acknowledgement.

hul'le, they, them; their; DIS ~ s'n, it is theirs; JAN-~, John and his party; die MINISTER-~, the minister cum suis; ~ moet ~ oor die SAAK besin, they must think the matter over; ~ SÊ, people say, it is rumoured; ~**self**, themselves.

hulp, help, aid, support, assistance; relief (charity); assistant, helper; helping; coagency; adjutant; EERSTE ~, first aid; iem. se ~ INROEP, call in someone's aid; te ~ KOM, assist, come to the rescue of; om ~ ROEP, call (out) for help; SONDER ~, unaided; TYDIGE ~ is dubbele ~, he gives twice who gives quickly; ~ VERLEEN, render assistance; van ~ WEES, be of assistance; ~**aandrywing**, auxiliary drive; ~**as**, auxiliary shaft; ~**battery**, auxiliary battery; ~**beampte**, relief man; emergency man; ~**bediende**, between-maid; tweeny; ~**behoewend** (-e), requiring help, indigent, destitute, needy; helpless; impotent; ~**behoewendheid**, destitution, indigence; ~**betoon**, assistance, help; ~**brandstoftenk**, auxiliary fuel tank; ~**bron**, resource; ~**brug**, temporary bridge; ~**buikgordel**, steadying girth; ~**diens**, auxiliary service(s); ~**draad**, auxiliary wire; ~**dryfstang**, auxiliary connecting-rod; ~**drywer**, auxiliary float.

hul'peloos, (..lose), helpless; ~**heid**, helplessness.

hulp: ~**fonds**, emergency fund; ~**gat**, easer; ~**geroep**, cry for help; ~**hefboom**, auxiliary lever; ~**kerkie**, chapel of ease; ~**klas**, aid class; assistance class; ~**klep**, (-pe), auxiliary valve; ~**kruiser**, auxiliary cruiser; ~**landingstroepe**, auxiliary landing-forces; ~**leër**, auxiliary army; ~**lig**, auxiliary light; ~**lokomotief**, (..tiewe), banking engine; ~**lugmag**, auxiliary airforce; ~**lyn**, artificial line; ledger line; ~**masjien**, donkey-engine; ~**middel**, means, makeshift, expedient; aid; stepping-stone; ~**middele**, resources, facilities; implements; ~**motor**, auxiliary engine; ~**onderwyser**, (-s), assistant (teacher); ~**pomp**, donkey-pump; ~**prediker**, assistant minister; ~**priester**, curate; ~**pyp**, auxiliary pipe; ~**rigtingsroer**, auxiliary rudder; ~**rooster**, auxiliary grid; ~**sekretaris**, assistant secretary; ~**skag**, (-te), auxiliary shaft; ~**stoommasjien**, donkey-engine; ~**stoomtoestel**, (-le), auxiliary steam-engine; ~**stut** (-te), puncheon; ~**taal**, auxiliary language; ~**tenk**, auxiliary tank; ~**toelae**, grant-in-aid; ~**trein**, breakdown (rescue) train; ~**troepe**, auxiliary troops; auxiliaries; ~**tronk**, lock-up.

hulpvaar'dig, (-e), helpful, willing to assist; obliging; ~**heid**, helpfulness.

hulp: ~**vak**, ancillary subject; ~**veer**, overload spring; ~**vereniging**, benefit society; ~**wa**, breakdown lorry; ~**werkplek**, auxiliary workshop; ~**werkwoord**, auxiliary verb; ~**wetenskap**, auxiliary science.

huls¹, (-te), holly; ilex.

huls², (-e), (pea) pod; (walnut) shell; (cartridge) case; casing; sleeve (machinery).

hul'sel, (-s), wrap, cover(ing); envelope.

huls: ~**klep**, (-pe), sleeve-valve; ~**koppeling**, sleeve-coupling.

humaan', **(humane)**, humane; humane optrede, humane act.

humanio'ra, humanities.

humanis', (-te), humanist.

humaniseer', **(ge-)**, humanize.

humanis'me, humanism; **tiee**, (e), humanistic.

humaniteit', humanity.

humanitêr', (-e), humanitarian.

hu'merus, (-se), humerus.

humeur', temper, mood, humour; blood; uit sy ~ wees, be in a bad temper; ~**ig**, (-e), moody, sulky, capricious; humoursome; ~**igheid**, moodiness, capriciousness, sulkiness.

humiditeit', humidity.

humifika'sie, humification.

humifiseer', **(ge-)**, humidify.

hu'mor, humour; gevoel vir ~ hê, have a sense of humour; ~**es'ke**, (-s), humoresque.

humoris', (-te) humorist; comedian; ~**ties**, (-e), humorous, humoristic.

hu'morskrywer, (-s), humorist, humoristic writer.

hu'mus, vegetable earth, humus; garden mould; ~**agtig**, humous; ~**kool**, humic coal; ~**ryk**, humic; ~**suur**, humic acid.

Hun, (ne), Hun.

hu'nebed, giant's grave, cromlech, cairn, dolmen, barrow.

hun'ker, **(ge-)**, yearn, long (for), hanker (after); aspire; itch; covet; crave; ~ na eer, hanker after honour; ~**ing**, longing, yearning, hankering, pining, heart hunger, itch.

hun'nebed = **hunebed**.

hup, **(ge-)**, hop.

hup'pel, **(ge-)**, skip, hop, gambol, frisk, bound; ~**ing**, (-e), gambol; ~**rig**, (-e), frisky, skippy.

hups, (-e), lively, pretty, fine; courteous, obliging; die grysaard is nog ewe ~, the old man is still quite lively; ~**heid**, liveliness, prettiness, fineness; courtesy.

hup'stootjie, last push, last effort (in a scrum).

hurk, **(ge-)**, squat, crouch.

hur'ke, haunches; op sy ~ sit, squat on his haunches.

husaar', **(husare)**, hussar.

hus'se, pigeon's milk; dis ~ met lang ore, curiosity killed the cat (nonsense reply to an inquisitive child).

Hussiet', (-e), follower of John Huss, Hussite.

hut, (-te), hut, cottage, cot; cabin (on ship); booth (bathing); hovel; crib (mining); ~**bagasie**, cabin-luggage; ~**bewoner**, cottager; ~**huis**, bungalow; ~**jie**, (-s), small cottage; crib; ~jie en mutjie: see huitjie.

hut'ser, scrambler (computer).

huts'pot, hotch-potch, Irish stew; gallimaufry, hodge-podge; bubble-and-squeak.

hut'tefees, feast of tabernacles.

huur, (s) rent; tenancy (house); hire (labourer); wages (workmen); lease; *die ~ OPSÊ,* give notice (to quit); *huis TE ~,* house to let; (w) (ge-), hire, rent; engage; charter (vessel); freight; *as jy my gister ge~ het, het jy my vandag gehad,* whom are you ordering about? ~ **baas,** landlord; ~ **besit,** leasehold; ~ **der,** (-s), tenant, lessee; occupant; holder; hirer; ~ **diens,** (-te), charter service; ~ **geld,** rental rent; ~ **huis,** hired house; ~ **kamer,** room to let; ~ **kamerhuis,** tenement, ~ **koetsier,** cabman, cab-driver, cabby, flyman; ~ **kontrak,** (-te), (written) lease; ~ **koop**= **(stelsel),** hire-purchase (system), instalment sys= tem; ~ **leër,** hired (mercenary) army, mercenaries; ~ **ling** (-e), hireling; hackney; ~ **loon,** hire, wages; ~ **motor,** taxi; ~ **motorbestuurder,** taximan, taxi= driver; ~ **ooreenkoms,** (-te), hire agreement; agree= ment of lease; memorandum of agreement; ~ **op**= **brengs,** rental; ~ **opsegging,** notice to vacate; ~ **pag,** leasehold, huurbesit; ~ **perd,** hack, hack= ney; ~ **premie,** foregift; ~ **prys,** rent; H ~ **raad,** Rent Board; ~ **reg,** right to lease; ~ **rytuig,** (..**tuie),** cab, hackney-coach; fly; hired (leased) vehicle; ~ **soldaat,** mercenary (soldier); ~ **som,** rental; ~ **stal,** (-le), livery stable; ~ **termyn,** tenancy; ~ **tol,** royalties (mining); ~ **troepe,** mercenaries; ~ **verle**= **ning,** relocation; ~ **vliegdiens,** (-te), airhire service; ~ **vliegtuig,** (..**tuie),** air-taxi; ~ **voorwaardes,** terms of lease; ~ **waarde,** rental value; H ~ **wet,** Rent Act.

hu'welik, (s) (-e), marriage, wedding, wedlock; match; bed; double harness; alliance; *jou in die ~ BEGEWE,* contract a marriage, enter into matri= mony; *'n ~ BEVESTIG,* perform a marriage cer= emony; *BUITE die ~ gebore,* born out of wedlock, illegitimate; *BURGERLIKE ~,* civil marriage; *'n ~ om GELD,* a mercenary marriage; *~ in GE= MEENSKAP van goedere,* marriage in community of property; *~ met die HANDSKOEN,* marriage by proxy; *~ e word in die HEMEL gesluit,* matches are made in heaven; ~ *in KAMERAADSKAP,* companionate marriage; *'n ~ ONTBIND,* dissolve a marriage; *'n ~ SLUIT,* contract a marriage; *in die ~ TREE,* enter into matrimony; get married; *VOLTOOIDE ~,* consummated marriage; *'n vrou ten ~ VRA,* propose to a girl; (b) (-se), matri= monial; *~ e staat,* state of matrimony.

hu'weliks: ~ **aankondiging,** notice of marriage; ~ **aansoek,** offer of marriage, proposal; ~ **afkon**= **diging,** banns; ~ **akte,** marriage certificate; ~ **band,** matrimonial tie; marriage knot; nuptial tie; ~ **be**= **ampte,** marriage officer; ~ **bed,** marriage bed; ~ **be**= **letsel,** impediment to marriage; ~ **belofte,** promise of marriage; ~ **bemaking,** marriage settlement; ~ **bemiddelaar,** matrimonial agent; ~ **berig,** (-te), wedding notice; ~ **bevestiging,** marriage ceremony; ~ **bevoordeling,** marriage settlement; ~ **bootjie,** boat of Hymen; marriage; *in die ~ bootjie stap,* get married; take the plunge; ~ **buro,** (-'s), matrimonial agency; ~ **dag,** wedding day; ~ **diens,** marriage ser= vice; ~ **dig,** (-te), epithalamium.

hu'welikseën, marriage blessing.
hu'weliksertifikaat, (..**kate),** marriage certificate.
hu'weliks: ~ **fees,** (-te), wedding feast; ~ **formulier,** marriage formulary; ~ **gebooie,** banns; ~ **gedig** (-te), epithalamium; ~ **gelofte,** marriage vow; ~ **ge**= **luk,** conjugal bliss; ~ **geskenk,** wedding present; ~ **gif,** marriage portion; dowry; ~ **god,** Hymen, god of marriage; ~ **goed,** dowry, marriage portion; ~ **hater,** misogamist; ~ **herdenking,** wedding anni= versary; ~ **hof,** (..**howe),** matrimonial court; ~ **in**= **seëning,** solemnization of marriage; ~ **juk,** matri= monial yoke; ~ **knoop,** marriage tie; ~ **kontrak,** (-te), antenuptial contract; marriage contract; mar= riage settlement; ~ **lewe,** married life; ~ **lied,** (-ere), nuptial song (poem), epithalamium; ~ **liefde,** con= jugal love; ~ **liksens,** ~ **lisensie,** marriage licence; ~ **maat,** marriage partner; ~ **makelaar,** matri= monial agent; ~ **makelary',** matchmaking; ~ **mark,** (-te), marriage market; ~ **ontbinding,** divorce; ~ **ontrou,** conjugal infidelity; ~ **ooreenkoms,** (-te), marriage settlement; ~ **plegtigheid,** marriage cer= emony; ~ **plig,** conjugal (matrimonial) duty; ~ **reë**= **ling,** matchmaking; ~ **reg,** conjugal right; marital power; law of marriage; ~ **register,** marriage regis= ter; ~ **reis,** honeymoon trip.

hu'welikstaat, matrimony, wedlock, wedded (mari= tal, married) state.

hu'weliks: ~ **trou,** conjugal fidelity; ~ **verband,** affin= ity; ~ **verwantskap,** affinity; ~ **voltrekking,** *see* **huweliksinseëning;** ~ **voorligting,** advice about mar= riage; ~ **voorwaarde(s),** antenuptial contract, mar= riage articles.

hy, he; it; *dis NET ~!* that's it! *is dit 'n ~ of 'n SY,* is it a male or a female?

hyg, (ge-), pant, long (for), gasp (for breath); puff; blow; ~ **na,** pant for, yearn after; ~ **end,** (-e), gasping, panting, ~ **ing,** panting, gasping, heaving.

hys, (ge-), wind, hoist; heave; lift; ~ **baan,** skipway; ~ **bak,** (-ke), hoisting cage, lift, elevator, kibble; skip; tackle-block; ~ **bakwagter,** skipman; ~ **be**= **stuurder,** lift attendant; ~ **balk,** outrigger; ~ **blok,** (-ke), ginblock; tackle-block; ~ **emmer,** kibble; ~ **er,** (-s), lift; hauler; elevator; ~ **erbediende,** lift= man; ~ **erdeur,** elevator door; ~ **erhulsel,** elevator casing; ~ **erpyp,** elevator pipe; ~ **erskag,** (-te), lift= shaft; ~ **erwurm,** elevator worm; ~ **hok,** (-ke), skip; cage (mine); ~ **ing,** hoist(ing); ~ **kabel,** hoisting cable; ~ **kraan,** (..**krane),** elevator; crane; ~ **ma**= **sjien,** crane; davit; elevator; winding-engine; ~ **pomp,** elevator pump; ~ **takel,** winding tackle; ~ **tang,** crampon; ~ **toestel,** (-le), hoisting appar= atus, elevator, hoister, hoist; recovery gear; ~ **tou,** tackle-rope, hoist-rope, elevator cable; ~ **trap,** (-pe), escalator; ~ **trommel,** hoisting-drum; ~ **weg,** haulage; ~ **werk,** poppethead; ~ **werktuig,** (..**tuie),** hauling gear, hoist, winding-engine.

I

i, (-'s), i.
Ibe'rië, Iberia; ~ **r,** (-s), Iberian.
Ibe'ries, (-e), Iberian.
i'bis, (-se), ibis.
ideaal', (s) **(ideale),** ideal; *'n ~ verwesenlik,* realise an ambition; (a) ideal; abstract.
idealis', (-te), idealist; ~ **eer', (geïd-),** idealize; ~ **me,** idealism; ~ **ties,** (-e), idealistic.
idealiteit', ideality.
idee', (**ideë,** -s), idea, notion; *iem. op 'n ~ BRING,* suggest something to a person; *idée FIXE,* fixed idea, idée fixe; *op die ~ KOM,* get the idea (into one's head); *geen die MINSTE ~ van hê nie,* not have the slightest idea of; *dis 'n STOM ~,* that is a stupid idea; *VOLGENS my ~,* according to my mind.
ide'ëassosiasie, association of ideas.
ideëel', (ideële), pertaining to ideas, ideal, imaginary.
idee'tjie, (-s), a bit of an idea.
ide'ë, ~ **vorming,** ideation; ~ **wêreld,** world of thought (ideas).
i'dem, ditto, the same, idem.
identiek', iden'ties, (-e), identical; *~ aan (met) me= kaar,* identical with each other.
identifika'sie, identification.
identifiseer', (geï-), identify; ..**se'ring,** identification.
identiteit', (-e), identity; ~ **s'bewys,** ~ **s'kaart,** proof of identity, identity card; ~ **skyf,** identity disc.
ideografie', ideography.
ideogram', (-me), ideogram.
ideologie', ideology; ..**lo'gies,** ideologic(al); ..**logiese** *oorlogvoering,* ideological warfare.

ideoloog 229 *imponeer*

ideoloog', (..**loë**), ideologist.
idil'le, (-s), idyl(l).
idil'lies, (-e), idyllic.
idioma'ties, (-e), idiomatic; ~*e uitdrukking*, idiomatic expression, idiom.
idiomorf', (-e), idiomorphic, automorphic, euhedral.
idioom', (**idiome**), idiom.
idioot', (s) (**idiote**), idiot, imbecile, gander, gowk, cretin, cuckoo, nincompoop, gaby; (b) (**idiote**), idiotic; ~**agtig**, (-e), like an idiot; ~**heid**, idiocy.
idiopatie', idiopathy.
idiopa'ties, (-e), idiopathic.
idiosie', (ong.) idiocy.
idiosinkrasie', idiosyncrasy.
idio'terig, (-e), rather idiotic.
idio'tery, idiocy.
idio'ties, (-e), idiotic.
idio'tikon, (..**ka, -s**), dictionary of idioms, dictionary.
idiotis'me, idiocy, idiotism.
idolatrie', idolatry.
ie'der, (-e), each, everyone, every; *'n* ~ *en 'n ELK*, each and everybody; *in* ~ *GEVAL*, in any case; ~*e GEVAL moet ondersoek word*, each case must be investigated; ~**een**, everyone; everybody, anyone.
ie'gelik (vero.): *'n* ~, everyone, everybody.
ie'mand, someone, somebody, some person or other, anybody, a person.
iep, (-e), elm (tree).
Ie'per, Ypres.
ie'ples: *hy hei* ~, he is pretending illness.
Ier, (-e), Irishman; ~**land**, Ireland, Erin; ~**s**, (s) Irish, Erse; (b) (-e), Irish, Erse.
iesegrim', (-me, -s), grumbler, surly fellow, crosspatch, grouch, churl; ~**mig**, (-e), surly, ratty, querulous, churlish ~**migheid**, querulousness.
iet, aught.
ietermago', **ietermagô'**, (-'s), **ietermagog'**, (-ge, -s), scaly ant-eater, pangolin; *Amerikaanse* ~, armadillo.
iets, something, anything; a little, somewhat, slightly; *hy BESIT nogal* ~, he is fairly well-to-do; he has a penny or two; *IS daar* ~?, is anything the matter? what's up? ~ *MEER as 'n rand*, a trifle more than a rand; *met* ~ *VAN afguns in sy stem*, with something like envy in his voice; *dit gee daar* ~ *VER= NAAMS aan*, it adds a touch of distinction to; ~**ie**, little bit, very little; trifle, a smack (touch) of; atom; *'n* ~*ie BETER*, just a shade better; *'N* ~*ie*, a dash of; a touch of; *net 'n* ~*ie SOETER*, just a little (bit) sweeter.
iet'wat, somewhat, a little, slightly; ~ *bolvormig*, subglobose.
ie'werig, (-e), irritable, touchy; diligent; zealous; skittish, inclined to shy (horse); ~**heid**, irritability.
ie'wers, somewhere.
ifa'falelie, ifafa lily *(Cyrhanthus)*.
ig'loe, (-s), igloo.
igneu'mon, (-s), ichneumon, mongoose.
ignorant', (ong.), (-e), know-nothing, ignoramus.
ignoreer', (geïg-), ignore, take no notice (of).
igtiofaag', (s) (..**fae**), ichthyophagist; (b) (..**fae**), ichthyophagous.
igtiografie', ichthyography.
igtioliet', (-e), ichthyolite.
igtiologie', ichthyology.
igua'nodon, (-s, -tc), iguanodon.
I'kabod, Ichabod, the glory has departed.
i'kon, (-e), icon; ~**ografie'**, iconography; ~**oklas'**, (-te), iconoclast; ~**oklas'me**, iconoclasm; ~**oklas'= ties**, (-e), iconoclastic.
ikosaë'der, (-s), icosahedron.
ikositetraë'der, (-s), icositetrahedron.
ik'tus, (-se), ictus.
ila'lapalm, ilala palm.
ileï'tis, ileitis.
il'eum, (-s, **ilea**), ileum.
I'liade, **I'lias**, Iliad.
il'ium, (-s, **ilia**), ilium.
illegaal', (**illegale**), illegal.
illegaliteit', illegality.
illegitiem', (ong.), (-e), illegitimate.
illikied' = **illikwied**.
illikiditeit = **illikwiditeit**.
illegitimiteit', illegitimacy.
illikwied', (-e), illiquid.
illikwiditeit', illiquidity.
Illi'rië, Illyria; ..**ries**, (-e), Illyrian.
illo'gies, (-e), illogical.
illumina'sie, illumination.
illumineer', (geïll-), illuminate.
illu'sie, (-s), illusion; *hom geen* ~*s MAAK nie*, cherish no illusions; *iem. sy* ~*s ONTNEEM*, disabuse a person's mind, shatter someone's illusions.
illusionis', (-te), illusionist.
illus'ter, (-e), illustrious.
illustra'sie, (-s), illustration.
illustratief', (..**tiewe**), illustrative.
illustra'tor, (-s), illustrator.
illustreer', (geïll-), illustrate; ~**der**, (-s), illustrator; ..**stre'ring**, illustration.
illu'vium, illuvium.
ilmeniet', ilmenite carbon.
ima'go, (-'s), imago.
imam', (-s), imam; ~**aat'**, (..**mate**), imamate.
imbesiel', (s) (-e), imbecile; (b) (-e), imbecile, feebleminded.
imbesiliteit', imbecility, amentia.
imita'sie, (-s), imitation; ~**klip**, scagliola; ~**leer**, imitation leather.
imiteer', (geïm-), imitate.
im'ker, (vero.), (-s), bee-keeper.
immanen'sie, immanence.
immanent', (-e), immanent.
immaterieel', (..**riële**), immaterial.
immens', (-e), immense, huge; ~**iteit'**, immensity.
im'mer, always, ever; ~**groen**, evergreen; ~**meer**, ever, evermore; ~**s**, yet, but, indeed, though.
immer'sie, immersion.
immigrant', (-e), immigrant.
immigra'sic, immigration; ~**syfer**, number of immigrants.
immigreer', (geïmm-), immigrate.
imminent', (-e), imminent.
immobiel', (-e), immobile.
immobiliseer', (geïmm-), immobilize.
immoleer', (geïmm-), immolate.
immoralis', (-te), immoralist.
immoraliteit', immorality.
immoreel', (..**rele**), immoral.
immortel'le, (-s), immortelle, everlasting (flower).
immunisa'sie, (-s), immunization.
Immunlseer', (geïm-), Immunlze; ..**se'rlng**, Immunlzation.
immuniteit', immunity; ~**siekte**, immunity disease.
immuniteits'leer, **immunologie'**, immunolgy.
immuun', (**immune**), immune.
impa'la, (-s), impala; ~**lelie**, impala lily *(Adenium)*.
impas'se, (-s), impasse.
impas'to, impasto.
impedan'sie, (-s), impedance.
impediment', (-e), impediment.
imperatief', (..**tiewe**), imperative.
imperato'ries, (-e), authoritative, imperatorial.
imperfek', (-te), imperfect; ~**sie**, imperfection.
imperfek'tum, (-s, ..**ta**), imperfect (tense).
imperiaal', (..**riale**), imperial; ~**koffer**, imperial coffer; ~**papier**, imperial paper.
imperialis', (-te), imperialist; ~**me**, imperialism; ~**ties**, (-e), imperialistic.
impe'rium, (-s, ..**ria**), imperium.
impertinen'sie, impertinence.
impertinent', (-e), impertinent.
im'petus, (-se), impetus.
im'pie, (-s), impi.
impiëteit', impiety.
implement', (-e), implement.
implika'sie, (-s), implication.
impliseer', (geïm-), implicate.
implisiet', implicit(ly).
implosief', (..**siewe**), implosive.
impondera'bel, (-e), imponderable.
imponderabi'lia, imponderabilia, imponderables.
imponeer', (geïm-), impress forcibly, awe.

imponerend 230 **indemniteit**

impone′rend, (-e), imposing, impressive.
impopulariteit′, unpopularity.
impopulêr′, (-e), unpopular.
importa′sie, importation.
importeer′, (geïm-), import; ~ **der, (-s)**, importer; ~ **handel**, import trade; ..**te′ring**, importation.
importeur′, (-s), importer.
imposant′, (-e), imposing.
impoten′sie, impotence.
impotent′, (-e), impotent, powerless.
impregna′sie, impregnation.
impregneer′, (geïm-), impregnate; ..**ne′ring**, impregnation.
impresa′rio, (-'s), impresario.
impres′sie, (-s), impression.
impressief′, (..siewe), impressive.
impressionis′, (-te), impressionist; ~ **me**, impressionism; ~ **ties, (-e)**, impressionistic.
imprima′tur, (-s), imprimatur, imprint.
impromptu′, (-'s), impromptu.
improvisa′sie, (-s), improvization, extemporization.
improviseer′, (geïm-), improvize, extemporize; vamp; ~ **der, (-s)**, improviser.
im′puls, (-e), impulse; ~ **ief′, (..siewe)**, impulsive.
imputa′sie, (-s), imputation.
imputeer′, (geïm-), impute.
in¹, (w) (geïn), gather, collect.
in², (bw, vs), in, into; within; during; ~ *AG neem*, take account of (facts); observe (rules); ~ *BESIT neem*, take possession of; ~ *elk GEVAL*, in any case; ~ *elke GEVAL*, in each case; ~ *ENGELS vertaal*, translated into English; *GOED* ~ *sy soort*, good of its kind; ~ *'n KOMITEE dien*, be (sit) on a committee; *ek het hom* ~ *geen MAANDE gesien nie*, I have not seen him for months; ~ *die RAAD kies*, elect to the council; ~ *die SESTIG*, over sixty; *dit SIT* ~ *hom*, he has it in him; ~ *een SLAG*, at a blow; ~ *hierdie STADIUM*, at this stage; ~ *STAND hou*, maintain, keep up; ~ *STUKKE sny*, cut (in)to pieces; *goed* ~ *TALE*, good at languages; ~ *die VEERTIG*, in the forties, forty odd; over forty; ~ *VREDE lewe*, live in peace; ~ *VRYHEID stel*, release; *drie keer* ~ *die WEEK*, three times a week; ~ *WERKING tree*, take effect; *dit WIL by my nie* ~ *nie*, I won't believe it.
in′abba, (-ge-), carry in on one's back; get by influence; pitchfork into a post.
inadekwaat′, (..kwate), inadequate.
in′adem, see **inasem**.
inag′neming, observance, care, compliance.
inakkuraat′, (..rate), inaccurate.
inaktief′, (..tiewe), inactive.
inaktiwiteit′, inactivity.
in′asem, (-ge-), inhale, breathe in; draw; inspire (phonetics); *rook* ~, inhale smoke; ~ **ing**, inhalation, breathing; inspiration; ~ **toestel**, inhaler, inspirator.
in′baar, (..bare), leviable, collectable.
in′baker, (-ge-), wrap in swaddling clothes; tuck in, bind.
in′balsem, (-ge-), embalm.
in′bars, (-ge-), burst in; interrupt rudely.
in′bed, (-ge-), bed (in), embed.
inbedryf′stelling, starting.
in′beeld, (-ge-), imagine, fancy; *hy beeld hom NOGAL in*, he rather fancies himself; *ingebeelde SIEKTES*, imaginary diseases; ~ **ing**, conceit, arrogance; imagination, fantasy, fancy.
in′begrepe, included; *alles* ~, all-inclusive; all-found: no extras.
in′begrip: *met* ~ *van*, including, inclusive.
in′begryp, including, included.
in′beitel, (-ge-), chisel (in), engrave.
inbesit′neming, taking possession of, occupation, seizing, entry (upon).
inbeslag′neming, seizure, attachment (goods); embargo (ship); taking up (of time); engrossment.
in′betaal, (~**)**, deposit (money); pay in addition; ~ *de tjeks*, cheques deposited; ~ **strokie**, deposit slip.
in′betaling, payment; deposit.
in′beur, (-ge-), push in; force into.
in′bind, (-ge-), bind (books); furl; *jy sal jou moet* ~,

you wil have to restrain yourself; you wil have to come down a peg or two; ~ **ing**, binding; ~ **inggeld**, binding-fee.
in′blaas, (-ge-), blow into; prompt, suggest; insufflate; *nuwe lewe* ~, breathe new life into; ~ **instrument**, insufflator.
in′blasing, (-e, -s), suggestion, prompting, insinuation; insufflation; afflatus; *OP* ~ *van*, at the instigation of; ~ *e v.d. SATAN*, promptings of Satan.
in′blik, (-ge-), can (fruit); *ingeblikte vrugte*, canned fruit.
in′bly, (w) (-ge-), remain in(doors); stay in (school).
in′boedel, (-s), furniture and effects.
in′boek, (-ge-), book, enter, indenture (servant); ~ **eling, (-e)**, indentured person; ~ **ing**, indenture; apprenticing; booking.
in′boesem, (-ge-), inspire, fill; strike (with terror); instil(l); *iem. haat* ~ *teenoor*, instil hatred into a person's mind towards; ~ **ing**, inspiration, instillation.
in′boet, (-ge-), plant in between (by hand); replace (dead plants); reset; lose; *die lewe* ~, pay with one's life.
in′bondel, (-ge-), cram into, stuff into.
in′boorling, (-e), native, aboriginal, aborigine, one of the aborigines; autochthon; ~ **skap**, nativedom.
in′borrel, (-ge-), bubble into (water); stream into (people).
in′bors, character, nature, disposition; quality; *van goeie* ~, of good (sound) character.
in′bottel, (-ge-), can (fruit).
in′bou, (-ge-), build in; fit (engine); *ingeboude kaste*, built-in cupboards.
in′braak, (s) (inbrake), housebreaking, burglary; cut (in mines); irruption; (w) **(-ge-)**, plough into the soil; ~ **alarm**, burglar alarm; ~ **beskerming**, burglar proofing; ~ **gate**, cutholes; ~ **polis**, burglary policy; ~ **vry, (-e)**, burglar-proof; ~ **yster**, jemmy.
in′brand, (-ge-), burn in(to); ~ ′**steking**, firing.
in′breek, (-ge-), burgle; ~ **yster**, jemmy.
in′breker, (-s), housebreaker, burglar; picklock, cracksman.
in′brenging, (-e, -s), intromission; ingestion.
in′breuk, infringement, transgression; encroachment; infraction; inroad; ~ *maak op*, encroach upon, infringe; ~ **making**, encroachment.
in′bring, (-ge-), bring in; contribute; introduce; yield; produce; raise, put forward (argument); haul in; *BEWYS* ~ *van*, furnish proof of; *wat kan u DAARTEEN* ~? what objection can you offer to that? ~ **aandele**, vendors shares; ~ **er, (-s)**, depositor; vendor.
in′brokkel, (-ge-), break into little by little.
in′buie, in′buig, (-ge-), bend in(ward).
in′buiging, incurvation.
in′burger, (-ge-), become current (words), denizen, be(come) naturalized (person); accustom oneself to; ~ **ing**, naturalization, adaptation.
in′byt, (-ge-), bite into; eat into; corrode.
inchoatief′, (..tiewe), inchoative.
incog′nito, (-'s), incognito.
inda′ba, (-s), indaba, council; great occasion, powwow, to-do; ~ *HOU*, lay heads together; *dis JOU* ~, that's your problem.
indag′tig, mindful; ~ *AAN*, mindful of; ~ *MAAK aan*, remind of.
in′dam, (-ge-), embank; enclose; check; ~ **ming**, damming.
in′damp, (-ge-), evaporate down; concentrate; ~ **ing**, evaporation.
in′deel, (-ge-), divide, classify, group, incorporate; rank; arrange; grade (fruit); map out; ~ **baar, (..bare)**, classifiable.
in′deks, (-e), index; *op die* ~ *plaas*, place on the index; ~ **eer′, (geïn-)**, index; ~ **getal**, index number; ~ **syfer**, index figure.
indelikaat′, (..kate), indelicate.
in′deling, (-e, -s), division, classification; grouping; posting; arrangement; regimentation; graduation; ~ *by 'n ander vak*, remustering.
indemnisa′sie, indeminification.
indemniseer′, (geïn-), indemnify.
indemniteit′, (-e), indemnity, indemnification.

indent', (-e), indent; **~eer', (geïn-)**, indent.
independent', (-e), independent.
inderdaad', indeed, really, in fact, actually, in truth.
inderhaas', hurriedly, in haste.
indertyd', at the time, formerly; at one time.
indeterminis'me, indeterminism.
indeterminis'ties, (-e), indeterminist(ic).
in'deuk, (-ge-), cave in, make a dent in, dent, bash; **~ing, (-s)**, dent.
Indiaan', (Indiane), Red Indian; **~s', (-e)**, Red Indian.
In'dië, India.
in'dien¹, (w) (-ge-), hand in, tender (resignation); exhibit, lodge, lay, prefer (complaint); introduce, present (bill); table (report); file (petition); deliver.
indien'², (vgw) if, in case, in the event of; **~ NIE**, if not; **~ WEL**, if so.
in'diener, (-s), introducer; mover; proposer.
in'diening, presentation, lodging, presentment, introduction; lodgement (documents); **~sgeld**, lodging-fee.
indiens'neming, employment.
indiens'stelling, putting into service.
indiens'treding, commencement of (entering upon) one's duties.
in-die-oog'-lopend, (-e), salient, flagrant; **~heid**, flagrancy.
in'dieping, embrasure.
Indiër, (-s), Indian; Asian; **~bevolking**, Indian (Asian) population.
In'dies, (-e), Indian; **~e Oseaan**, Indian Ocean; **~e tee**, Indian tea.
indifferentis'me, indifferentism.
indiges'tie, indigestion.
in'digo, indigo; **~blou**, indigo blue; **~fabriek**, indigo factory.
in'dik, (-ge-), evaporate; **~king**, evaporation.
indika'sie, (-s), indication.
indikateur', (-s), indicator.
indikatief', (..tiewe), indicative.
indika'tor, (-e, -s), tracer; indicator.
in'dink, (-ge-), realize, understand; enter into the spirit of; *jou in iem. se GEVAL ~*, imagine oneself in someone's place; put yourself in someone else's shoes; *'n mens kan JOU dit ~*, it is conceivable; it can be imagined.
in'direk, (-te), indirect; **~te oorsaak**, remote cause.
indiskreet', (..krete), indiscreet.
indiskre'sie, indiscretion.
indisponi'bel, (-e), unavailable.
in'dium, indium.
individu', indiwidu', (-e, -'s), individual; **~alls', (-te)**, individualist; **~alis'me**, individualism; **~alis'ties, (-e)**, individualistic; **~aliteit'**, individuality; haecceity; **~a'sie**, individuation; **~eel', (..duele)**, individual.
in'doen, (-ge-), put in(to).
indoc'na, (-s), induna, councillor; mugwump; pundit.
In'do-Europees, (..pese), Indo-European; Eurasian.
In'do-Germaans, (-e), Indo-Germanic.
indoktrina'sie, indoctrination.
indoktrineer', (geïn-), indoctrinate; **..ne'ring**, indoctrination.
indolen'sie, indolence.
indolent', (-e), indolent.
Indologie', Indology.
Indoloog', (..loë), Indologian.
in'dommel, (-ge-), doze off, slumber.
in'dompel, (-ge-), immerse, plunge into; dip; merge; **~ing**, immersion, plunge, plunging; *doop deur ~ing*, baptism by immersion; **~ingsverwarmer**, immersion heater.
Indone'sië, Indonesia; **..sies, (-e)**, Indonesian.
in'dons, (-ge-), smash, plunge in.
in'doop, (-ge-), dip into.
in'doping, immersion, dipping into.
in'dra, (-ge-), carry in(to).
in'draai, (-ge-), wrap up (parcel); screw in (tube cap); turn into (road); **~pad**, road which turns in; **~prop**, capping, screw-cap.
in'drentel, (-ge-), saunter in.
in'dril, (-ge-), drum into (a person's head); inculcate.

in'dring, (-ge-), enter by force, penetrate (forest); insinuate oneself into; interlope; intrude (on privacy), encroach, gatecrash, barge in; invade (country); force in; *hy dring hom in waar hy nie genooi is nie*, he intrudes without being invited; **~er, (-s)**, intruder, gatecrasher, insinuator, interloper; **~erig, (-e)**, officious, intrusive, obtrusive; pushing, pushful, thrustful; **~erigheid**, intrusiveness, obtrusiveness; **~ing**, penetration; intrusion; encroachment; **~ingsvermoë**, power of penetration.
in'drink, (-ge-), drink in, imbibe, absorb; **~ing**, imbibition.
in'droë, in'droog, (-ge-), dry (by absorption); shrink, shrivel up.
in'druis, clash; (-ge-), ~teen, run counter to, clash with, be at variance with (truth), conflict with, interfere with.
in'druk, (-ke), (s) impression; **~ MAAK**, make an impression; *hy MAAK op my die ~ van 'n eerlike man*, he strikes me as being an honest man; *VATBAAR vir ~ke*, easily impressed; *ONDER die ~ verkeer*, be under the impression; *die ~ WEK dat*, create the impression that; (w) (-ge-), impress, imprint; force one's way in(to); press in (needle); crush (egg); **~wek'kend, (-e)**, impressive, commanding, forcible, grandiose, imposing; **~wek'kendheid**, impressiveness, grandiosity.
in'drup(pel), (-ge-), drop in; pour in drop by drop; instil(l); **~ing**, instillation, instilment.
in'dryf, in'drywe, (-ge-), drive into; force into; float into; impact.
in'duik, (-ge-), plunge, dive in(to); (in)dent; recess; dip into; *see also* **indeuk**; **~ing**, depression; groove; dent, recess.
in'duiwel, (-ge-), plunge in; act in a reckless manner.
induk'sie, induction; **~-elektrisiteit**, induction; faradism; **~klos**, induction coil; **~kompas**, induction compass; **~moment**, induced moment; **~stroom**, induction current; induced current; **~vermoë**, inductivity; **~vry, (-e)**, anti-induction.
induktan'sie, inductance.
induktief', (..tiewe), inductive.
induk'tor, (-e, -s), inductor.
induseer', (geïn-), induce.
industrialis', (-te), industrialist.
industrialiseer', (geïn-), industrialize.
industrialise'ring, industrialization.
industrialis'me, industrialism.
industrie', (-ë), industry; **..trieel', (..riële)**, (s) industrialist, manufacturer; (b) industrial; *industriële skool*, industrial school; **~bedryf**, industry; **~skool**, industrial school; **~stad**, factory town (city).
in'dut, (-ge-), doze off, drop off.
in'dyk, (-ge-), dike, embank; **~ing**, embankment.
in'ëe, (ingeëe), *see* **ineeg**.
ineen', *see* **inmekaar**.
ineen'gedoke, hunched up.
ineen'gedronge, thick-set (person); condensed, compressed.
ineen'gekrul, (-de), involuted.
ineen'gerol, (-de), convoluted; rolled up.
ineen'groei, (-ge-), grow together.
ineen'gryp, (-ge-), mesh, interlock, engage; dovetail; **~ing**, interlocking; engagement (of gears); dovetailing.
ineen'krimp, (-ge-), writhe (with pain), be doubled up; wince; shrink together; cower; **~ing**, contraction; writhing.
ineen'loop, (-ge-), run together, pass into each other (colours); meet (lines).
ineens', at once, at the same moment, suddenly; outright.
ineen'sinking, collapse.
ineen'smelt, (-ge-), blend, fuse; merge, melt (together); **~ing**, blending, fusing, merging.
ineen'stort, (-ge-), fall in, collapse; break down; **~ing**, collapse, crash, falling, debâcle; slump.
ineen'strengel, (-ge-), pleach, entwine, intertwine.
ineen'vleg, (-ge-), intertwine, interlace; **~ting**, intertwining, interlacing.
ineen'vloei, (-ge-), flow together, run into each other;

merge; coalesce; ~ing, confluence; fusion, blending, junction.
in'eg, (ingeëg), pass over with harrow, harrow in.
ineksak', (-te), inexact; ~t'heid, inexactitude.
in'ent, (ingeënt), inoculate, vaccinate; ~er, (-s), inoculator, vaccinator; ~ery, ~ing, vaccination, inoculation.
iner'sie, inertia.
infaam', (infame), infamous, shameful; 'n infame leuen, an outrageous lie.
infant', (-e), infante (prince).
infan'te, (-s), infanta (princess).
infanterie', infantry; foot(-soldiers); ~bataljon, infantry battalion; ~brigade, infantry brigade; ~leer, ~-opleiding, infantry training; ~patrollie, infantry patrol; ~wapen, infantry weapon.
infanteris', (-te), infantryman, foot-soldier, footman.
infantiel', (-e), infantile.
infantilis'me, infantilism.
infark', (-te), infarct.
infek'sie, (-s), infection; ~haard, nidus; ~siekte, contagious disease, zymosis.
infekteer', (geïn-), infect.
inferieur', (-e), inferior, poor (quality).
inferioriteit', inferiority; ~s'kompleks, inferiority complex.
infer'no, (-'s), inferno.
infertiliteit', infertility.
infiltra'sie, infiltration.
infiltreer', (geïn-), infiltrate.
infiltre'ring, infiltration.
infinitesimaal', (..male), infinitesimal; ~rekening, infinitesimal calculus.
infinitief', (..tiewe), infinitive.
inflamma'sie, inflammation.
in'flans, (-ge-), insert (anecdote); ingeflansde woorde, superfluous words.
infla'sie, inflation; ~tempo, inflation rate; ~verhoging, increase in inflation.
inflasionêr', inflasionis'ties, (-e), inflationist, inflationary.
inflek'sie, flection.
inflekteer', (geïn-), inflect.
influen'sa, influenza, flu(e); ~epidemie, epidemic of influenza, flu epidemic.
influenseer', (geïn-), influence.
in'fluister, (-ge-), whisper, prompt, suggest; ~ing, whisper, suggestion, prompting.
in'foeter, (-ge-), plunge in; act in a reckless manner; smash.
informaliteit', informality.
informa'sie, information; ~buro, (-'s), information bureau, inquiry office.
informatief', (..tiewe), informative.
informato'ries, (-e), informatory.
informeel', (..mele), informal; ..mele byeenkoms, informal gathering (meeting); ..mele taal, informal language; colloquial language.
informeer', (geïn-), inform; inquire.
infrak'sie, infraction.
in'frarooi, infra-red.
in'frastraler, infra-red lamp.
in'frastruktuur, infrastructure.
infu'sie, infusion; ~diertjie, infusorian, monad.
infuso'rieëaarde, infusorial earth, kieselguhr.
in'gaan, (s): jou ~ en uitgaan, one's comings and goings; (w) (-ge-), enter (room); consent (to an agreement); die DOOD ~, pass away; die EWIGHEID ~, die, pass into eternity; ~ OP iets, consider something, entertain some idea; go into the subject; op 'n VERSOEK ~, consider a request; ~de, ingoing; imported; ~de regte, import duties; ~de VANAF, dating from.
in'gaar, (-ge-), collect, gather.
in'gang, (-e), entrance, ingress, entry, gate(way); port; input; pylon (of temple); doorway, portal; introit (R.C.); MET ~ van 5 Junie, with effect (dating as) from June 5th; ~ VIND, be readily accepted; find favour (acceptance); ~stonnel, adit.
in'gebeeld, (-e), imaginary, fancied (complaints); fantastic, priggish, fanciful, chimerical; presumptuous; ~heid, fantasy.

in'gebonde, bound (book).
in'gebore, innate, inborn, inherent; ~nheid, innateness.
in'gebou, (-de), built-in; ~de kaste, wall cupboards.
in'gebrand, (-e), encaustic; burnt-in; etched.
ingebruik'neming, inauguration, consecration (church); adoption; introduction.
ingedag'te, absent-minded, absorbed in thought; ~ wees, be wrapped up in something.
in'geduik, (-te), depressed; (in)dented.
in'gee, (-ge-), administer (medicine), dose; dictate, suggest (idea); inspire with (idea); yield (the point), surrender; lodge, send in, present (petition); give way, collapse; GEDAGTES ingegee deur vrees, thoughts prompted by fear; sy GEHOOR begin ~, he is getting deaf; wat die GEWETE ~, the dictates of conscience.
in'gehoue, subdued (force); pent-up (rage); restrained.
in'gekanker, (-de), inveterate (hate); ingrained (fault), deep-rooted.
in'gekeep, (-te), grooved.
in'gekome, received; ~ stukke, documents received.
in'gekuil, (-de), ensilaged.
in'gekwartier, (-de), billeted.
in'gelaat, (..late), admitted; recessed; inserted.
in'gelas, (-te), inserted, added, interpolated, intercalary.
in'gelê, (..legde), ..leg, (-de), inlaid; canned, preserved, pickled; tessellated; ..legde houtwerk, marquetry.
in'gelig, (-te), informed.
in'gelyf, (-de), incorporated, embodied.
in'gemaak, (-te), canned, preserved, potted; bottled.
in'genaai, (-de), stitched (book), with paper cover.
ingenieur', (-s), engineer; ~sopleiding, engineering training; ~skool, engineering school; ~s'wese, engineering.
ingenieus', (ong.), (-e), ingenious.
in'genome, pleased, charmed, taken up (with); MET jouself ~, be self-satisfied; ~ wees TEEN iemand, be prejudiced (biased) against someone; ~nheid, satisfaction, pleasure.
in'geplooi, (-de), pleated.
in'gerig, (-te), arranged, equipped, prepared, managed, organized, furnished.
in'gerol, (-de), involuted.
in'geryg, (-de), gathered; stringed; ~ staan, stand close together; be packed like sardines.
in'geseën, (-de), consecrated.
in'gesetene, (-s), inhabitant, resident, citizen.
in'geskakel, (-de), coupled (trucks; clutch); linked, connected; in gear.
in'geskape, innate, inborn, connate.
in'geskrewe, enrolled, conscript; inscriptive, inscriptional; ~ LEERLINGE, enrolled pupils; ~ PROKUREURSKLERK, articled clerk, ~ne, (-s), conscript.
in'geslae, in'geslane: op die ~ weg voortgaan, continue in the old way.
in'geslote, in'gesluit, enclosed; inclusive, included; under cover (of letter); ALLES ~, everything included, all-found; ~ DOKUMENTE, enclosed paper, enclosures.
in'gesonde, contributed; ~ stukke, letters (articles) to the editor.
in'gesonke, sunken (eyes); hollow (cheeks).
in'gespanne, intense; strenuous; intent; ~ luister, listen intently.
in'gestel, (-de), institutional, established.
inges'tie, ingestion.
in'getoë, modest, discreet, retiring, sedate, restrained; ~nheid, discretion, modesty, restraint; pudency; reserve.
in'getrek, (-te), retracted, drawn in; ~te STAND, retracted position; ~te WIELE, retracted wheels.
in'geval, in case, in the event.
in'gevalle, sunken (eyes); hollow (cheeks).
in'gevoer, (-de), imported; peregrin(e); ~ de vrag, imported freight.
ingevol'ge, in pursuance of, as a result, in conse-

quence (of), pursuant (upon); under; ~ *die grondwet*, under the constitution.

in'gevou, (-de), folded (in); ~ *de spene*, inverted teats.

in'gewand, (-e), bowel, intestine; ~**e**, entrails, viscera, guts; intestines; ~**siekte**, intestinal disease.

in'gewands: ~**koors**, enteric fever; typhoid fever; ~**kwaal**, bowel (intestinal) complaint; ~**wurm**, intestinal worm, maw-worm *(Ascaris)*, helminth.

in'geweef, (-de), inwoven, inwrought.

in'gewikkeld, (-e), complicated, complex, intricate, involved; anfractuous; crabbed; involute; labyrinthine; *'n ~e saak*, a complicated matter; ~**heid**, intricateness, complexity, complicacy, complication; involution.

in'gewing (-e, -s), inspiration; suggestion; brainwave; prompting; afflatus; *ASOF by ~*, as if inspired; *op die ~ van die OOMBLIK handel*, act on the spur of the moment.

in'gewortel, (-de), inveterate (hatred); deep-rooted, firmly rooted (tradition); deep-seated, ingrained; radical; ~**dheid**, inveteracy.

in'gewy, (-de), initiated, adept; ~**de**, (-s), iniate; adept; insider; *die ~des*, those in the know, adepts.

in'giet, (-ge-), pour in; *nuwe LEWE ~*, infuse new life into; *iets met 'n TREGTER ~*, drum something into a person; ~**ing**, infusion, pouring-in.

in'glip, (-ge-), slip in; ~**pad**, glide-on road; ~**per**, step-in.

in'gly, (-ge-), slide in (into).

in gooi, (s) (-e), throw-in (rugby); (w) (-ge-), throw in; put in (sugar), pour in, smash (pane), hole.

in'gord, (-ge-), lace tightly, compress one's waist; economize (fig.).

in'graaf, in'grawe, (-ge-), dig in, entrench; burrow.

in grawing, entrenchment.

ingrediënt', (-e), ingredient.

in grif, (-ge-), engrave, imprint.

in'groef, (-ge-), groove.

in'groei, (-ge-), grow in(to); *'n ~ende nael*, an ingrowing nail; ~**ing**, (-e, -s), intrusion (bot.); ingrowth; ~**sel**, (-s), ingrowth.

in'gryp, (-ge-), intervene, act, step in; encroach (on someone's authority); mesh (cogwheel); *~ in die regte van 'n ander*, encroach upon the rights of another; *~'end*, (-e), far-reaching, radical, drastic; ~**ing**, (-e, -s), intervention, interference; ~**ingsboog**, arc of action.

in'haak, (-ge-), hook in, take someone's arm; *ingehaak loop*, walk arm-in-arm; ~**pan**, interlocking tile.

in'haal, (-ge-), overtake, catch up, gain (ground) upon; gather in; furl; strike (flag); receive in state (head of state); make up for (lost time); *agterstallige take ~*, work off arrears; ~**rem**, overrun brake; ~**sels**, gathers.

inhala'sie, inhalation; ~**toestel**, inhaler.

inhaleer', (geïn-), inhale; ~**der**, (-s), inhaler.

inha'lig, (-e), greedy, covetous, miserly, churlish, penurious; griping; gainful; mercenary, avaricious, niggardly, grasping; ~**heid**, greediness, greed, niggardliness, covetousness, avarice, penuriousness.

in'ham, (-me), inlet, creek, bay, cove.

in'hamer, (-ge-), hammer in, hammer home; drum into (a scholar's head).

in'handel, (-ge-), acquire; trade in.

in'hê, (ingehad), have in, contain, hold; *IETS ~*, be tipsy; to have had a spot or two; *NIKS ~ nie*, be valueless.

inheems', (-e), native, home, home-bred, indigenous, domestic; aboriginal; autochthonous; endemic (disease); *~ in*, indigenous to.

inheg'tenisneming, arrest(ation); imprisonment, committal, apprehension, attachment.

inherent', (-e), inherent; *~ aan*, inherent in.

inhibeer', (geïn-), inhibit.

inhibi'sie, inhibition.

in'hol, (-ge-), rush in(to); overtake by running.

in'hou, (-ge-), contain; restrain (one's temper); refrain, repress; keep in check (horse), draw (bridle, rope); catch (breath); hold, retain (in stomach); refuse (price); cancel (sale); keep in (after school); deduct (money); recoup; purport; forbear; signify, mean, imply; *dit hou 'n BELOFTE in*, it holds out a promise; *die FEITE hou 'n waarskuwing in*, the facts carry a warning; *'n HUIS ~*, withdraw a house (from sale); *JOU ~*, control oneself; keep a straight face; *die SIEKE kan niks ~ nie*, the patient cannot retain anything; *TRANE ~*, keep back tears.

in'houd, (-e), contents (book); content (cube); capacity (vessel); purport (letter); *KORT ~*, extract, summary; *KUBIEKE ~*, cubic content; ~**ing**, stoppage (pay): retaining; withdrawal; checking.

inhouds: ~**bepaling**, determination of content(s); connotation; ~**lys**, covering list; index; ~**maat**, cubic measure; measure of capacity; ~**meting**, cubature; cubage; ~**opgaaf**, ~**opgawe**, index, table of contents; ~**ruimte**, capacity; ~**tabel**, table of contents; ~**vermoë**, content, capacity.

in'huldig, (-ge-), inaugurate, install, instate; ~**ing**, inauguration; ~**ingseremonie**, inauguration ceremony.

inhumaan', (..mane), inhuman; ..**maniteit'**, inhumanity.

inisia'sie, initiation.

inisiatief', (..tiewe), initiative, lead; *op EIE ~ handel*, act on one's own initiative; *die ~ NEEM*, take the initiative; *OP ~ van*, at the instance of, on the initiative of.

inisieer', (geïn-), initiate.

in'ja(ag), (-ge-), drive into; overtake, catch up with; cause to take (medicine); pen (animals).

inja'la (-s) = njala.

injek'sie, (-s), injection; ~**spuit**, injection syringe.

injekteer', (geïn-), inject.

injekteur', (-s), injector.

injunk'sie, (-s), injunction.

ink, (s) (-te), ink; *goedkoop ~ is beter as 'n duur BOODSKAP*, it's better to put it on paper; *met ~ GOOI*, sling ink; *OORSKRYF met ~*, rewrite in ink; (w) (geïnk), ink, cover with ink.

In'ka, (-s), Inca.

inkag'tig, (-e), inky.

in'kalwe(r), (-ge-), cave in; undermine (by water).

in'kam, (-ge-), mesh; ~**ming**, meshing.

in'kamp, (-ge-), enclose, fence in, hedge in.

in'kanker, (-ge-), fester; corrode (metals); penetrate into, become rooted; *ingekankerde haat*, deeply rooted hatred; ~**ing**, festering, spreading (like a cancer).

in'kap, (-ge-), engrave; inscribe; hammer in, force into; eat, enjoy one's food.

inkapasiteit', incapacity.

in'kapsel, (-ge-), capsulate, encyst; ~**ing**, capsulation, encystation.

inkarnaat', (..nate), incarnadine, flesh-coloured.

inkarna'sie, incarnation.

inkarneer', (geïn-), incarnate.

inkasseer', (geïn-), cash, collect; encash.

inkasse'ring, cashing, collecting.

inkas'so, (ong.), collection; *'n bedrag ter (vir) ~ oorhandig*, hand over an amount for collection.

ink: ~**bos**, ink bush *(Suaeda fructiosa)*; ~**bottel**, ink-bottle.

in'keep, (-ge-), notch, indent; jag; nick.

in'keer, (s) repentance; resipiscence; *tot ~ kom*, repent; come to one's senses; (w) (-ge-), turn into (fold, kraal); *tot jouself ~*, commune with oneself; become introspective; ~**hok**, sorting-gate; ~**kraal**, sorting-pen.

inken'nig, (-e), shy, timid; ~**heid**, shyness, bashfulness, timidity; *see* **eenkennig**.

in'keping, notch, indentation, indent, cogging, groove, housing, grooving (fire-arms).

in'kerf, (-ge-), carve (in), engrail, hack; notch, incise.

in'kering, introversion; repentance.

in'kerker, (-ge-), incarcerate; ~**ing**, incarceration.

in'kerwe, (-ge-) = **inkerf**.

in'kerwing, (-s), incision.

ink: ~**fles**, ~**kan**, ink-bottle; ~**koker**, ink-well, ink-stand; ~**kol**, ink-blot; ~**kussing**, ink(ing)-pad, ink-dobber.

in'klaar, (-ge-), clear in, clear (goods through customs).

inklam

in'klam, (-ge-), sprinkle, damp(en) (washing before ironing).
in'klank, (-ge-), dub, provide (film) with new sound track; ~ **ing**, dubbing.
in'klaring, clearing (inwards); ~ **sbewys**, clearance certificate; ~ **slys**, bill of entry.
in'kleding, wording, phrasing; clothing (novice).
in'klee(d), (-ge-), express, phrase, couch (in language, words); represent; clothe (novice).
in'klim, (-ge-), climb into, get in; rebuke; go to bed; board (a vehicle); *iem.* ~, pitch into someone; ~ **gordel**, step-in.
inklina'sie, inclination, dip; ~ **hoek**, angle of inclination; ~ **kompas**, inclination compass, inclinometer; ~ **naald**, dipping-needle.
in'klink, (-ge-), hit in(to); nail in, rivet in; shrink (ground); ~ **ing**, shrinkage.
in'klok, (-ge-), clock in.
in'klouter, (-ge-), clamber in(to).
inkluis,' included, including.
inklusief', (..siewe), inclusive.
in'knip, (-ge-), clip; slit.
in'knyp, (-ge-), pinch (in).
in'koejawel, rotten, inferior, feeble.
inkohatief', (..tiewe) = **inchoatief**.
in'kom, (-ge-), come in(to), get in, enter; pull in (train); be returned (for parliament); be received (accounts); be published (press); arrive (train); ~ **e**, income; ~ **eling**, (-e), new arrival, new-comer; ~ **end**, (-e), incoming.
inkompeten'sie, incompetence.
inkompetent', (-e), incompetent; ~ **e werker**, incompetent worker.
inkompleet', (..plete), incomplete.
in'koms, entering, entry; income.
in'komste, (*soms* -s), income, earnings, revenue; receipts (railways); ~ **en uitgawe(s)**, receipts (income) and expenditure; ~ **belasting**, income-tax; ~ **bron**, source of income.
inkongruen'sie, incongruence; ..**gruent'**, (-e), incongruent.
inkonsekwen'sie, (-s), inconsistency.
inkonsekwent', (-e), inconsistent.
in'konstitusioneel, (..nele), unconstitutional.
inkontinen'sie, incontinence.
in'koop, (s) (**inkope**), purchase, buying; *inkope doen*, go shopping; (w) (-ge-), buy, purchase; secure admission by payment; ~ **boek**, purchase book; invoice book; ~ **(s)prys**, cost price, purchase price, prime cost; ~ **sak**, shopping bag.
in'koper, (-s), purchaser, buyer.
in'kopie, (-s), small purchase; ~ *s doen*, go shopping; ~ **sak**, shopping bag.
in'koppel, (-ge-), let in the clutch, engage gear; clasp; ~ **ing**, engagement (of gear).
inkorpora'sie, incorporation.
inkorporeer', (geïn-), incorporate.
inkorrek', (-te), incorrect.
in'kort, (-ge-), shorten; curtail (rights); abridge (book); dock (tail); reduce (services); ~ **ing**, shortening, curtailing, abridgement; ~ *ing van regte*, diminution of rights.
ink'pen, fountain-pen; inking pen.
ink'poeier, ink-powder.
ink'pot, ink-pot, ink-well; ~ **lood**, copying (indelible) pencil.
in'krap, (-ge-), scratch in; write in quickly, scribble in.
inkrement', (-e), increment.
inkrimineer', (geïn-), incriminate.
in'krimp, (-ge-), shrink, dwindle; retrench (staff); curtail (expenses); cut down, decrease, reduce; ~ **ing**, shrinking, shrinkage, dwindling; retrenchment.
ink'rol(ler), printing-roller, inker.
in'kromming, incurvature.
in'kruip, (-ge-), creep in(to), crawl in(to); fawn upon, seek favour with; go to bed; ~ **er**, (-s), toady, adulator; intruder; ~ **erig**, (-e), toadyish, fawning, insidious; ~ **ery**, fawning; insidiousness; toadyism; adulation; ~ **sel**, (-s), intrusion.
in'kruiwa, (-ge-), pitchfork into a position; seek favours for another.
in'krulling, (-s), involution.

234

inlewer

inkrusta'sie, incrustation.
in'kry, (-ge-), get in, collect, take in; get down (food); *water* ~, swallow water.
ink: ~ **sak**, ink-bag; ink-sac (cuttlefish); ~ **stander**, ink-stand; ~ **stel**, ink-stand; ~ **swart**, inky; ~ **tekening**, ink-drawing.
inkuba'sie, incubation; ~ **periode**, incubation period.
in'kuil, (-ge-), ensile; store in silo; pit; ~ **ing**, ensilage; ~ **voer**, (en)silage, silo fodder.
ink'uitveër, ink-eraser.
inkulpeer', (geïn-), inculpate.
inkuna'bel, (-e, -s), incunabulum.
in'kus, (-se), incus.
ink: ~ **vis**, cephalopod, cuttlefish, sepia, squid; ~ **vlek**, ink-stain, ink-blot.
in'kwartier, (-ge-), quarter, billet; ~ **ing**, quartering, billeting.
ink: ~ **wellusteling**, ink-tippler; ~ **werper**, ink-thrower.
inkwisi'sie, inquisition.
inkwisiteur', (-s), inquisitor.
inkwisitoriaal', (..riale), inquisitorial.
in'kyk, (-ge-), see (look) in; *vlugtig* ~, glance at, skim.
in'laai, (-ge-), load; emplane; entrain; gobble (food); ~ **ery**, loading; ~ **plaatjie**, clip; ~ **platform**, entraining platform; ~ **stasie**, entraining station.
in'laat, (s) (-late), induction box; countersink (in mines); inlet; intake; (w) (-ge-), let in, admit; consort, associate with; mortise; *jou met IEM.* ~, mix with someone; *jou met IETS* ~, let oneself in for something; ~ **druk**, inlet pressure; ~ **klep**, inlet valve; ~ **pyp**, admission valve; ~ **rand**, countersunk margin; ~ **slag**, induction stroke; ~ **slot**, mortise lock; ~ **sluis**, inlet sluice; ~ **stelsel**, induction system; ~ **voeg**, flush joint.
in'lading, loading, shipment.
in'lae, (-s), enclosure (document); deposit (money).
in'lander, (-s), native; aboriginal.
in'lands, (-e), inland, native; home-made, home-bred, indigenous.
in'las, (s) (-se), inset (photo); stop press; gag (theatre); (w) (ge-), insert, intercalate, interpolate; mortise; ~ **kant**, lace insertion; ~ **sing**, insertion; interpolation; intercalation; mortise; ~ **teken**, caret.
in'lating, admission; interference; dovetailing; recessing; *blinde* ~, stopped housing.
in'lê, (-ge-), can (fruit), preserve, pickle, cure; pot marinate; deposit (money); chase; hatch; lay in; layer (shoots); plant (shoots), inlay (with gold); *EER* ~, gain honour; *SAMBOK* ~, beat severely; ~ **boek**, deposit book; ~ **bottel**, preserving-bottle.
in'leef, *see* **inlewe**.
in'lêer, (-s), depositor; layer (of rose); layer-on; ~ **loot**, layer; ~ **y**, curing, canning; layering.
in'lêfles, *see* **inlêbottel**.
in'leg: ~ **blad**, loose leaf (of table); ~ **boek**, savings (pass) book; ~ **geld**, investment; entrance-money, stakes; pot-money; ~ **ger**, (-s), depositor; ~ **ging**, (-s), hatch (of eggs); ~ **hout**, veneer; ~ **kapitaal**, capital invested; ~ **sel**, (-s), inlay, inset; ~ **werk**, inlay work, marquetry, veneer; checker-work.
in'lei, (-ge-), introduce, preface, usher in; open (debate); prelude; ~ **buis**, inlet tube; ~ **dend**, (-e), introductory; exordial; prolegomenous; preliminary; isagogic; preparatory; proemial; precursory; prelusive.
in'leiding, introduction; preface, preamble; prolegomenon; exordium (of speech); foreword; opening; overture; prelude; primer; prodrome; *ter* ~, as an introduction; introductory; ~ **sartikel**, leading article, leader; ~ **sgesang**, introit (R.C.).
in'leier, (-s), introducer, opener (of debate); usher.
in'lek, (-ge-), leak in.
in'lêstrokie, deposit slip.
in'lewe, (-ge-), penetrate (with the mind); become steeped in; merge into; *jou* ~ *in die gevoelens van ander*, enter into the feelings of others.
in'lewer, (-ge-), deliver up; send in (contribution); hand in (resignation); deposit; lodge; ~ **aar**, (-s), deliverer, presenter (of complaint); ~ **ing**, handing in, lodging (resignation); delivery; lodgment (docu-

ments); *teen ~ing van*, against (upon) surrender of; ~**ingsdatum**, date of handing in (delivery).
in'lêwerk, inlay.
in'lig, (-ge-), inform, enlighten; *verkeerd ingelig omtrent*, misinformed about; ~**tend, (-e)**, informative.
in'ligting, (-e, -s), information, enlightenment; intelligence; ~ *INWIN*, make enquiries (about), obtain information; *TER ~ van*, for the information of.
in'ligtings: ~**afdeling**, intelligence section; information section; ~**attaché**, information attaché; ~**beampte**, information officer; ~**berig, (-te)**, intelligence report; ~**buro, (-'s)**, information bureau; ~**diens**, intelligence corps; intelligence service; ~**kantoor**, information (inquiry) office; ~**offisier**, intelligence officer; ~**pos**, intelligence post; ~**resumé**, intelligence summary.
in'ligtingstuk, information pamphlet; news item.
in'loer, (-ge-), peep in(to); *by iem. ~*, look in on someone.
in'lok, (-ge-), entice in(to).
in'loods, (-ge-), pilot in(to) (port).
in'loop, (s) mouth (of stream); intake (of dam); catchment-area; running in (engine); entrance; (w) (-ge-), walk into; enter (harbour); turn into (street); overtake; run in (motor); *iem. êrens LAAT ~*, land someone in trouble; *in 'n VAL ~*, walk into a trap.
in'los, (-ge-), redeem (pledge); repay; ~**baar**, (..**bare**), redeemable; ~**sing**, redemption; ~**singsreg**, equity of redemption.
in'lui, (-ge-), ring in; inaugurate; usher in, herald (new era).
in'luister, (-ge-), listen in; ~**aar**, listener.
in'lyf, (-ge-), incorporate, embody; engraft, annex; ~**baar**, (..**bare**), annexable.
in'lys, (-ge-), frame; ~**ting**, framing.
in'lywing, incorporation; annexation; initiation; ~**smetode**, method of initiation.
in'maak, (s) preservation; canning; (w) (-ge-), can, bottle, preserve; pickle; pot; tin; ~**bottel**, (canned-) fruit bottle; ~**fabriek**, canning factory; ~**fles**, preserving-jar; ~**tyd**, preserving-season; ~**uie**, pickled onions.
in'maker, preserver, canner; ~**y**, canning; cannery.
in'meet, (-ge-), measure in.
in'mekaar, inmekaar', into each other, the one in the other; together; aheap; bent, stooping; smashed, crumpled up; *hy sit ~*, he sits bent (crumpled up).
inmekaar'draai, (-gedraai), twist together, roll together, intertwine.
inmekaar'flans, (-geflans), patch together, knock together.
inmekaar'trommel, (-gefrommel), crumple up.
inmekaar'groei, (-gegroei), grow together (into one another).
inmekaar'gryp, (-gegryp), mesh, dovetail, fit together.
inmekaar'haak, (-gehaak), interlock.
inmekaar'krimp, (-gekrimp), shrink up; writhe, double up (with pain).
inmekaar'loop, (-geloop), pass (run) into each other, become one (colours); communicate (rooms).
inmekaar'pas, (-gepas), fit into each other, interlock.
inmekaar'rol, (-gerol), roll together.
inmekaar'sak, (-gesak), collapse; founder; crumple up.
inmekaar'sit¹, (-gesit), piece together, assemble, mount (machinery), fit together.
inmekaar'sit², (-gesit), cause to collapse; crush; go to pieces; *'n stoel ~*, cause a chair to collapse.
inmekaar'skuif, (-geskuif), slide into each other; telescope.
inmekaar'slaan, (-geslaan), knock together; dash to pieces; clasp (hands).
inmekaar'sluit, (-gesluit), fit into each other, interlock, dovetail.
inmekaar'smelt, (-gesmelt), fuse, merge together.
inmekaar'stort, (-gestort), collapse; topple down; go to pieces; ~**ing**, dilapidation; collapse, crash.
inmekaar'trap, (-getrap), tread (kick) to pieces.
inmekaar'val, (-geval), collapse.
inmekaar'vleg, (-gevleg), intertwine, interlace.
inmekaar'vloei, (-gevloei), flow together (into each other).

in'meng, (-ge-), meddle with, interfere; mix in; *jou ~ in 'n ander se sake*, interfere in (meddle with) another's business; ~**ing**, meddling, interference; mixing.
in'messel, (-ge-), build in; brick up; immure; ~**ing**, setting (of boilers); bricking up.
inmid'dels, in'middels, meanwhile, in the meantime.
in'mond, (-ge-), inosculate, anastomose; ~**ing**, inosculation, anastomosis.
in'naai, (-ge-), sew (stitch) in.
in'name, taking capture (of a town); collection; tucking-in.
in'neem, (-ge-), take (medicine; a fort); adopt; accommodate; gather in (folds); take in (lodger; a tuck); conquer; load; hold; capture, reduce (fort); take up; charm, captivate; fill (a post); collect (tickets); *KOLE ~*, coal; *die MENSE teen jou ~*, prejudice people against oneself; turn people against oneself; ~**baar**, (..**bare**), pregnable.
inne'mend, (-e), captivating, charming, fetching, prepossessing, pleasing, ingratiating, attractive, taking, fascinating, endearing, engaging; insinuative, insinuating; plausible; ~**heid**, charm, winsomeness, fascination, attractiveness.
in'neming, (-e, -s), capture, conquest; collection; taking in tucks, tucking.
in'ner, (-s), collector (of taxes); cashier.
in'nerlik, (-e), inner, inward, internal; intrinsic (value); ~ *bewoë*, sincerely moved; ~**heid**, inwardness; fervour.
in'neuk, (ge) infected.
in'nig, (-e), cordial, true, sincere, fervent, fervid, heart-to-heart, profound, fond(ly), heart-felt; close(ly); ~**heid**, sincerity, earnestness, heartiness, fervour, fervency; profoundness.
in'ning, collection; levy; receiving.
in'nooi, (-ge-), invite in.
innova'sie, (-s), innovation.
in'oes, (**ingeoes**), reap, gather (in); *roem ~*, gain honour.
inokula'sie, inoculation.
inokuleer, (**geïn-**), inoculate.
inontvangs'neming, taking delivery; acceptance.
inougura'sie, inauguration; ~**seremonie**, inauguration ceremony; ~**toespraak**, inaugural speech.
inougureel', (..**rele**), inaugural, inauguratory.
inougureer', (**geïn-**), inaugurate.
in'pak, (-ge-), pack, do up; encase; wrap up (parcel); ~**ker**, packer; ~**king**, packing-up.
in'palm, (-ge-), haul in (rope); gain possession of, carry, appropriate, bag, capsulate, fetch in; *'n KÊREL ~*, captivate a young man; *die WINS ~*, pocket the winnings; ~**ing**, appropriation, captivation.
in'pas, (-ge-), fit in; ~**sing**, fitting.
in'peil, (-ge-), set (compass); ~**ing**, setting.
in'pekel, (-ge-), souse, (put in) pickle, salt.
in'peper, (-ge-), pepper; rub in; *iem. iets ~*, lay it on heavily (thick), rub it in.
in'perk, (-ge-), hem in; restrict (movements); curtail; confine; ~**ing**, restriction, limitation, curtailment.
in'pers, (-ge-), press in(to); ~**ing**, intrusion; ~**rand**, countersunk margin.
in'pik, (-ge-), nip up; bag, collar, nab.
in'plak, (-ge-), paste in; ~**album**, scrapbook.
in'plant, (-ge-), plant; implant; pitch (wickets); ~**ing**, implantation.
in'ploeë, in'ploeg, (-ge-), plough in (under).
in'plooi, (-ge-), pleat, ruffle; ~**voetjie**, ruffler; ~**werk**, ruffling.
in'polder, (-ge-), reclaim (by dikes), polder; ~**ing**, reclamation, poldering.
in'pomp, (-ge-), pump in; cram; drum in; ~**er, (-s)**, crammer; ~**ery**, cramming; ~**stelsel**, cramming-system (for examinations).
in'praat, (-ge-), talk into (believing or doing); *iem. moed ~*, talk someone into (doing) something.
in'prent, (-ge-), imprint, impress; engraft, implant; engrave; inculcate; ~**ing**, inculcation, implantation.
in'prop, (-ge-), cram into; stuff into; bolt.
in'reën, in'reent, (-ge-), rain in(to).

in'reken, (-ge-), add to (include in) the account.
in'rig, (-ge-), arrange, organize; fit up, install, plan, equip, appoint, furnish (house); construct; *'n modern ingerigte woning*, a house furnished in the latest style; ~**ting, (-e, -s)**, arrangement, organization; establishment, institution; installation, assembly, works, plant; frame; equipment, fittings; apparatus; device, gadget; disposition; ~**tingskoste**, equipment expenses.
in'rit, way in; entrance road.
in'roep, (-ge-), call in, invoke; solicit; enlist; ~**ing**, invocation.
in'rol, (-ge-), roll in; roll up (parcel).
in'ruil, (-ge-), exchange, barter, trade in; ~**ing**, exchange, bartering; trade-in; ~**waarde**, trade-in value.
in'ruim, (-ge-): *plek* ~, make room; ~**ing**, making room.
in'ruk, (-ge-), pull in, snatch in, jerk in; march into (enemy country).
in'ry, (-ge-), drive in; ride in; bring in (by wagon e.g.); run in (motor car); ~**bioskoop**, drive-in (bioscope).
in'rye, in'ryg, (-ge-), lace in, lace tightly; tack (dress); string (beads), bead; gather (frill).
in'ryfliek, drive-in (theatre, bioscope).
inryg': ~**ing**, lacing; gathering; ~**steek**, gathering stitch.
in'ry: ~**hek**, entrance gate; lodge-gate; ~**teater**, drive-in (theatre); ~**tyd**, running-in period.
in'saag, (-ge-), saw in(to).
in'sae, inspection, perusal; *ter* ~ *lê*, be open to inspection, lie open for inspection.
in'sak, (-ge-), sink in(to), sag; give way, collapse, cave in; *ingesakte koek*, sunken cake.
insa'ke, re, in the matter of, concerning.
in'sakking, sinking in(to), giving way, collapse; subsidence (of ground).
in'samel, (-ge-), gather, collect; harvest; reap; ~**aar, (-s)**, collector; harvester; ~**ing**, collection; gleaning, reaping.
in'sê, (-ge-), scold, reprimand, tell off; *iem. lelik* ~, give someone a piece of one's mind, tell someone off.
in'seën, (-ge-), consecrate, dedicate, solemnize; ordain, induct; ~**ing**, consecration; ordination, induction (minister); dedication.
in'seep, (-ge-), soap, lather; *iem.* ~, tell someone off.
in'seil, (-ge-), sail into, enter.
in'sek, insek', (-te-), insect; ~**bestryding**, insect control; ~**dodend**: ~ *dodende middel*, insecticide; ~**ta'rium, (-s, ..ria)**, insectarium.
insek'te: ~**byt**, insect bite; ~**doder**, insecticide; ~**-eter**, insectivore; ~**gif**, insecticide; ~**kenner**, entomologist; ~**kunde**, insectology, entomology; ~**kun'dig, (-e)**, entomological; ~**kun'dige**, entomologist; ~**leer**, entomology; ~**middel**, insecticide; ~**plaag**, insect pest; ~**poeier**, insect powder; Persian powder; ~**versameling**, collection of insects.
insektologie', insectology.
insektoloog', (..loë), insectologist.
insekwent', (-e), insequent.
insemina'sie, insemination; *kunsmatige* ~, artificial insemination.
insemineer', (geïn-), inseminate; ~**der, (-s)**, inseminator.
in'send, (-ge-), send in, contribute (to newspaper); submit (sample); enter (exhibit); ~**er, (-s)**, correspondent, contributor; exhibitor; ~**ing, (-e, -s)**, contribution; exhibit (at show).
inser'sie, (ong.), (-s), insertion.
in'set, (-te), input (production); ante (racing); stake; pool; contribution; ~**sel, (-s)**, insertion, inset; gusset; ~**ting, (-e, -s)**, decree, ordination (of God).
ins'gelyks, in the same way, likewise, also; the same to you.
insiden'sie, (ong.), (-s), incidence; ~**hoek**, angle of incidence.
insident', (-e), incident; ~**eel', (..tele)**, incidental.
in'sien, (-ge-), look into; perceive, understand, recognize, realize; admit; *MYNS* ~ *s*, in my opinion; *by NADER* ~, on closer inspection.

in'sig, (-te), insight, opinion; discernment; perceptivity; *iem. met BAIE* ~, a man of considerable discernment; ~ *KRY in*, gain an insight into; *VOLGENS my* ~, to my mind, in my opinion; ~**gewend, (-e)**, illuminating; instructive, informative; ~**ryk, (-e)**, perceptive, perspicatious, penetrating.
insin'je, (vero.), (-s), badge.
in'sink, (-ge-), sink in, give way, sag, subside; ~**ing**, subsidence, collapse; relapse; slump, decline (of market); droop(ing).
insinua'sie, (-s), insinuation, hint, innuendo, indirect suggestion.
insinueer', (geïn-), insinuate, hint.
in'sit, (-ge-), set in, put in, start (bidding); begin, intone, strike up (song); stake; install, fit; ~**prys**, starting (upset) price; ~**tende, (-s)**, occupant (of vehicle), passenger.
in'skakel, (-ge-), switch on, connect up; throw into gear, engage (gears); mesh (cog wheel); plug in; tune in (radio); let in (clutch); link up with; ~ *op*, tune in to; ~**aar**, switch; gear; ~**ing**, insertion; inclusion; switching on; throwing into gear; ~ *ing by*, integration with; ~**veer**, engaging spring.
in'skeep, (-ge-), ship, take on board, embark, load; *jou* ~ *na*, embark for; ~**hawe**, port of embarkation.
in'skeer, (-ge-), reeve.
in'skep, (-ge-), ladle into; dish up (food).
in'skeping, embarkation; shipment; ~**sdiens**, embarkation duties; ~**shawe**, embarkation port; ~**soffisier**, embarkation officer; ~**sorder**, embarkation order; ~**sinrigting**, embarkation establishment; ~**staat**, embarkation return; ~**sverlof**, embarkation leave.
in'skerp, (-ge-), inculcate, impress; enjoin; *iem. iets* ~, impress something upon a person; bring something home to another; ~**er, (-s)**, enjoiner; ~**ing**, inculcation; enjoinment.
in'skeur, (-ge-), tear, slit; ~**ing**, tearing.
in'skiet, (-ge-), shoot into; cut in quickly, middle (rugby); find the range of (artillery); *GELD by iets* ~, lose money over a thing; *sy LEWE* ~ *by*, lose his life in.
inskik'lik, (-e), complying, compliable, compliant, ductile, facile, easy, pliant, yielding, willing, conformable, complaisant, obliging, accommodating, placable, affable; ~**heid**, compliancy, indulgence, readiness to oblige, affability; conformability, conformity; facility.
in'skink, (-ge-), pour (out); ~**er, (-s)**, pourer.
in'skop, (-ge-), kick in; *iem. se DEUR* ~, kick someone's door in; *iem. in 'n POS* ~, find a job for a pal.
in'skrif, (-te), inscription.
inskrip'sie, (-s), inscription.
in'skroef, in'skroewe, (-ge-), screw in.
in'skryf, (-ge-), inscribe; enroll, enlist, enter; subscribe (to a loan); tender; register; record; *jou laat* ~, be enrolled, have one's name entered; ~**geld**, entrance fee; ~**vorm**, entry form.
in'skrywe, (-ge-) = **inskryf**.
in'skrywer, applicant; tenderer; subscriber (loan).
in'skrywing, (-e, -s), subscription, enrolment, registration, entry; conscription; enlistment; tender; *die* ~ *oopstel*, call for (invite) tenders.
in'skrywings: ~**boek**, register; ~**geld**, entrance fee; registration fee; ~**letter**, registration letter; ~**merk**, registration mark; ~**nommer**, registration number; ~**vorm**, entry form.
in'skuif, (-ge-), push (squeeze) in, intercalate; ~**leer**, sliding ladder; ~**stoel**, tuck-away chair; ~**tafel**, extension table, telescope table; ~**tafeltjie**, nest of tables; ~**vlerk**, variable-span wing.
in'skuiwe, (-ge-) = **inskuif**.
in'slaan, (-ge-), drive in (nail); smash, strike; swallow (drink); turn in (edges); turn into (road); drive home (facts); be effective (arguments); catch on, make a hit; lay in (food); *sy hoop die BODEM* ~, dash his hopes; *'n vat die BOOM* ~, stave in a cask; ~ *by die PUBLIEK*, catch the popular fancy; gain public approval.
in'slaap, (-ge-), fall asleep, drop off to sleep; pass away; die; sleep (live) in.

in'slag, woof; shot (bags); tendency, strain, flavour; flap; ~ *VIND,* accepted, become popular; *SKERING en* ~, warp and woof; *VOORSTE (agterste)* ~, front (back) flap; ~**draad,** woof-thread; weft (in textile); ~**garing,** weft yarn.
in'sleep, (-ge-), drag in(to), involve (in affair); tow (car); *iem.* ~ *vir R1 000,* do someone out of R1 000.
in'slenter, (-ge-), saunter into.
in'sleur, (-ge-), drag in(to).
in'slinger, (-ge-), hurl in(to); stagger into.
in'sluimer, (-ge-), doze off, fall asleep; ~**ing,** slumbering, sleeping, dozing off.
in'sluip, (-ge-), steal in(to), sneak in (to), creep in(to); *foute wat ingesluip het,* errors which have crept in; ~**er,** intruder, trespasser; ~**ing,** stealing in.
in'sluit, (-ge-), enclose (in a letter); embody, include, connote; hem in (enemy), encircle, hedge in; gate; fold in; beset, besiege; encase; gird; encyst (med.); embay, embed; invest (fortress); involve; shut in; contain, comprise, comprehend, embrace (all costs); *jou testament sluit alles in,* your will includes everything; *vgl.* **ingeslote;** ~**end, (-e),** including, inclusive; ~**ing,** enclosure; comprisal; inclusion; blockade, investment (town); ~**sel, (-s),** enclosure.
in'sluk, (-ge-), swallow; bolt (food); engourge; gulp down; absorb; pouch; *ALLES wil* ~, be very greedy; *MOENIE my* ~ *nie,* don't swallow me (said to one who yawns); *iem. sy WOORDE laat* ~, make someone eat his words; ~**king,** absorption; swallowing.
in'slurp, (-ge-), drink noisily, gobble up, gulp down.
in'slyp, (-ge-), grind in, bed (valve).
in'smeer, (-ge-), rub in, grease; embrocate; soap.
in'smelt, (-ge-), melt (down).
in'smering, rubbing in; greasing; inunction.
in'smokkel, (-ge-), smuggle in; ~**ing,** smuggling (in).
in'smyt, (-ge-), throw in(to).
in'sneeu, (-ge-), become snowbound; snow in.
in'snel, (-ge-), rush in.
in'snoer, (-ge-), string (beads); constrict; ~**ing,** narrowing; stringing.
in'snuif, in'snuiwe, (-ge-), sniff up, inhale.
in'sny, (-ge-), cut in(to), engrave, incise; ~**ding,** incision, cut; scarification; incisure; indentation (coastline); ~**vyl,** feather-edge file.
insola'sie, insolation.
insolen'sie, insolence.
insolent', (-e), insolent.
insolied', (-e), not solid, unsound, unsteady, frail.
insolven'sie, (-s), insolvency; bankruptcy.
insolvent', (-e), insolvent, bankrupt; ~**skap, (-pe),** insolvency, bankruptcy.
insom'nia, insomnia, sleeplessness.
inson'derheid, especially, notably, particularly.
in'sout, (-ge-), salt, pickle, cure, dry-cure; initiate (new scholars); ~**er, (-s),** curer; ~**ing,** salting; initiation.
in'span, (-ge-), exert; inspan, harness (horses); yoke (oxen), strain (eyes); *IEM.* ~, rope someone in; make use of someone; *JOU* ~, do one's level best; exert oneself; *'n MENS kan nie gedurig ingespan wees nie,* all work and no play makes Jack a dull boy; ~**nend, (-e),** exerting, strenuous, trying; ~**ning, (-e),** exertion, strain; effort; *met die* ~*ning van al sy kragte,* by exerting all his powers.
in'spat, (-ge-) = **inklam.**
in'speel, (-ge-), play into; sink (putt); get one's hand in.
inspek'sie, (-s), inspection; ~**besoek,** inspector's visit; ~**deksel,** inspection cover; ~**kring,** inspection circuit; ~**luik,** inspection hatch; ~**oog,** access eye; ~**reis,** tour of inspection; ~**sak,** kit-bag.
inspekteer', (geïn-), inspect.
inspekteur', (-s), inspector; ~**skap, (-pe),** inspectorship.
inspektoraat', (..rate), inspectorate.
inspektri'se, (-s), inspectress.
in'spin, (-ge-), form a cocoon (round).
inspira'sie, inspiration; *'n* ~ *kry,* get a brain wave.
inspirato'ries, (-e), inspirational.
inspireer', (geïn-), inspire.
in'spit, (-ge-), dig into (spoil).

in'spoel, (-ge-), be washed into; flow in(to); ~**grond,** alluvium.
in'spraak, dictate(s) (of one's heart); (access to) consultation.
in'spreek, (-ge-): *iem. moed* ~, encourage, hearten a person.
in'spring, (-ge-), jump in(to); indent (line of printing); come to the rescue; ~*ende HOEK,* reflex angle; *REËLS laat* ~, indent lines (in printing); *VIR iem.* ~, assist (deputize for) a person; stand in for someone; ~**ing, (-e, -s),** indent, indention.
in'sprinkel, (-ge-), sprinkel (before ironing).
in'spuit, (-ge-), inject; infuse; ~**er, (-s),** injector; ~**ing,** infusion; injection; enema; *onderhuidse* ~*ing,* subcutaneous injection; ~**ingspuit,** injection syringe; ~**pomp,** priming-pump; ~**sel, (-s),** injection; ~**toestel,** priming-gear.
in'spyker, (-ge-), nail in (up).
in'staan, (-ge-), guarantee, warrant, vouch for; *VIR iem.* ~, stand surety for someone; vouch for someone; *vir die WAARHEID* ~, vouch for the truth.
instabiel', (-e), unstable.
instabiliteit', instability.
installa'sie, (-s), installation, plant; setting-up, erection; fittings; equipment; induction (clergy); ~**koste,** cost of installation.
installeer', (geïn-), install, instate; induct (clergy); inaugurate; fit (up), equip.
installe'ring, installing; installation.
in'stamp, (-ge-), ram in(to), down, hammer into; drum into (pupils); inculcate; impact.
instand'houding, maintenance, upkeep, conservation, preservation; perpetuation.
instan'sie, (-s), instance; place; body, authority; *'n BEVOEGDE* ~, a competent authority; *in (die) EERSTE* ~, in the first place; *jou op HOËR* ~ *s beroep,* appeal to higher authorities.
in'stap, (s) embussing; (w) (-ge-), walk (step) in; emplane, entrain, board (train); ~!, all seats!; ~**stasie,** entraining-station.
in'steek, (-ge-), stick in, put in; dip; dive; thread (needle); plug in; ~**blad,** (..**blaaie**), leaf (of extension table); ~**pyp,** socket pipe; ~**slot,** mortise (lock).
in'steking, (-e, -s), insertion.
in'stel, (s) adjustment, setting; (w) (-ge-), set up (precedent); form, create, institute (proceedings); establish; tune up (machine); tune in (radio); propose (toast); introduce; prefer (claim); install (an official); adjust, focus (camera); *ingestel wees op NUWIGHEDE,* be ready for innovations; *'n ONDERSOEK* ~, make (hold) an inquiry; *die RADIO* ~ *op,* tune (the radio) in to; ~**fout,** error in adjustment; ~**ler, (-s),** proposer (of toast); institutor, founder; ~**ling, (-e, -s),** institution, establishment; adjustment; focusing; ~**matglas,** focusing-screen; ~**punt,** focal point, adjusting-point, ~**spoel,** tuning-coil.
in'stem, (-ge-), agree, concur, accede, assent; tune (violin); ~ *met,* (concur) with; ~**mend, (-e),** consentient; assentient; ~**mend knik,** nod assent.
in'stem: ~**oog,** magic eye; ~**spoel,** tuning-coil.
in'stemming, agreement, accord, acquiescence; adhesion; concurrence, assent; *met ALGEMENE* ~, by common consent; *sy* ~ *BETUIG,* signify one's approval.
instiga'sie, instigation.
instigeer', (geïn-) instigate.
instink', (-te), instinct; ~**ma'tig, (-e),** instinctive; ~**tief,** (..**tiewe**), instinctive.
institueer', (geïn-), institute.
institu'sie, (-s), institution.
institusioneel', (..**nele**), institutional.
instituut', (..**tute**), institute.
in'stoom, (-ge-), steam in(to).
in'stoot, (-ge-), push in(to), force in.
in'stop, (-ge-), stuff, cram; tuck up; shower gifts on.
in'storm, (-ge-), rush in to.
in'stort, (-ge-), collapse, tumble down (house); fall; relapse (patient); ~**ing,** collapse, downfall; caving in; relapse; (nervous) breakdown.

in'stoter, (-s), pusher.
in'straal, (-ge-), shine in(to).
in'stroming, influx, inflow, inrush; ~**sbeheer**, influx control; ~**sbuis**, admission pipe.
in'strompel, (-ge-), stagger in(to).
in'strooi, (-ge-), strew in.
in'stroom, (-ge-), stream in(to), flock in(to), crowd in(to).
instrueer', (geïn-), instruct.
instruk'sie, (-s), instruction, direction; order; ~**ambulans**, training-ambulance; ~**bataljon**, training-battalion; ~**battery**, training-battery; ~**-eenheid**, training-unit; ~**-eskader**, training-squadron; ~**kader**, training-cadre; ~**korps**, training-corps.
instrukteur', (-s), instructor; trainer.
instruktief', (..tiewe), instructive.
instruktri'se, (-s), instructress.
instrument', (-e), instrument, tool, appliance, implement; ~**aal'**, (..tale), instrumental; ~**alis'**, (-te), instrumentalist; ~**bord**, dashboard, instrument panel; ~**eel'**, (..tele), instrumental; ~**eer**, (geïn-), orchestrate; instrument; ~**is**, (-te), instrumentalist; ~**kissie**, surgical case; ~**maker**, instrument-maker; ~**paneel**, see **instrumentbord**; ~**stand**, instrument-reading.
in'stryk, (-ge-), walk in(to); iron in; point (a wall); sweep in (money).
in'studeer, (-ge-), study, learn up; rehearse (a part in a play); practise (a piece of music); ..**dering**, preparation; studying; rehearsing.
in'stuif, in'stuiwe, (w) (-ge-), rush in(to); blow in(to).
in'stulp, (-ge-), invaginate; introvert; ~**ing**, introversion; invagination.
in'stuur, (-ge-), send in; contribute (to newspaper); steer into; ~**der**, (-s), contributor.
insubordina'sie, insubordination.
in'suie, in'suig, (-ge-), suck in; imbibe, absorb.
in'suigingskrag, power of absorption, absorptivity.
in'suigverdeelpyp, intake manifold.
in'sukkel, (-ge-), get in (down) with difficulty.
insulêr', (-e), insular.
insulien', insuli'ne, insuline (trade name).
Insulin'de, the Malay archipelago, Insulinde.
in'sult, (-ge-), cure, salt.
insurgen'sie, insurgency.
insurgent', (-e), insurgent.
insurrek'sie, (-s), insurrection.
in'suur, (-ge-), make yeast (sour dough); season (mortar); prime (lime); sour.
in'swaai, (-ge-), swing in(to), cut into (traffic).
in'sweef = **inswewe**.
in'swering, taking of the oath, swearing in; ~**sakte**, attestation paper; ~**staat**, attestation sheet.
in'swewe, (-ge-), glide in(to); sail into (room).
in'syfer, (-ge-), infiltrate; filter in; ~**ing**, infiltration.
in'syg, (-ge-), infiltrate; ~**ing**, infiltration.
in'sypel, (-ge-) = **insyfer**.
intag'lio, (-'s), intaglio.
intak', (-te), intact, unimpaired; ~**t'heid**, intactness.
in'tand, (-ge-), notch, nick, indent; ~**ing**, indent(ing), notching.
in'tap, (-ge-), let liquid into.
intar'sia, intarsia.
in'teel, (-ge-), breed in, inbreed; ~**t**, inbreeding, endogamy.
inteen'deel, on the contrary.
in'teer, (ong.), (-ge-), use up capital; *elke maand R5* ~, be R5 short every month.
integraal', (..grale), integral; integer; ~**rekening**, integral calculus.
integralisa'sie, integralization.
integra'sie, integration; ~**beleid**, integration policy.
integreer', (geïn-), integrate; ..*grerende DEEL*, integral part; ..*grerende FAKTOR*, integrating factor.
integriteit', integrity.
in'teken, (-ge-), subscribe; plot, mark; ~ *op 'n maandblad*, subscribe to a monthly (magazine);

~**aar**, (..**nare**, -s), subscriber; ~**biljet**, (-te), subscription ticket, prospectus; ~**geld**, subscription; ~**ing**, subscribing, subscription; ~**lys**, subscription list; ~**prys**, subscription price.
in'tel¹, (-ge-), count in (sheep as they enter the kraal).
in'tel², (-ge-), lift into (car).
intel'kliek, jetset.
intellek', (-te), intellect; ~**tualis'**, (-te), intellectualist; ~**tualis'me**, intellectualism; ~**tualis'ties**, (-e), intellectualistic; ~**tualiteit'**, intellectuality; ~**tueel'**, (..**tuele**), intellectual, highbrow, egghead; (b), intellectual.
intelligen'sie, intelligence; ~**kwosiënt**, intelligence quotient; ~**toets**, intelligence test.
intelligent', (-e), intelligent, bright, clever.
intelligent'sia, intelligentsia.
intendans', (-e), service corps; commissariat (of army).
intendant', (-e), intendant; quartermaster.
intens', (-e), intense.
inten'sie, (-s), intension.
intens: ~**ief'**, (..**siewe**), intensive; ascentive; ..*siewe afdeling*, intensive department; ~**ioneel'**, (..**nele**), intentional; ~**iteit'**, intensity; ~**iveer'**, (geïn-), intensify; ~**ive'ring**, intensification.
interdepartementeel', (..**tele**), interdepartmental.
interdik', (-te), interdict, ~**sie**, interdiction.
in'teres, (vero.), interest.
interessant', (-e), interesting; readable; intriguing; *veel* ~ *s*, much of interest; ~**heid**, interesting quality (nature) (of something); ~**heidshalwe**, as a matter of interest.
interes'se, (ong., gew.), interest; *by iets* ~ *hê*, have an interest in something.
interesseer', (geïn-), interest, be interested in; *iem.* ~ *VIR*, interest a person in; *finansieel geïn* ~ *WEES by 'n onderneming*, have a financial interest in a business.
interieur', (-s), interior.
in'terim, interim; ~**dividend**, interim dividend.
interjek'sie, (-s), interjection.
interkala'sie, (-s), intercalation, interpolation.
interkaleer', (geïn-), intercalate, interpolate.
interkerk'lik, (-e), interchurch, interdenominational.
interkollegiaal', (..**giale**), intercollegiate.
interkoloniaal', (..**niale**), intercolonial.
interkommunaal', (..**nale**), intercommunal.
interkommunikasie', intercommunication.
interkontinentaal', (..**tale**), intercontinental.
interlineêr', (-e), interlinear.
interli'nie, lead (in printing).
interlinieer', (geïn-), interline; lead.
interlu'dium, (-s, ..**dia**), interlude.
intermediêr', (-e), intermediate.
intermez'zo, (-'s), intermezzo.
intermis'sie, intermission.
intermitte'rend, (-e), intermittent.
intermolekulêr', (-e), intermolecular.
intern', (s) (-e), houseman, intern(e); (b) (-e), intern, internal; ~ *e EKSAMENS*, internal examinations; ~ *e VAKKE*, subjects examined internally.
internasionaal', (..**nale**), international; *Internasionale Monetêre Fonds*, International Monetary Fund (IMF).
internasionalisa'sie, internationalization.
internasionaliseer', (geïn-), internationalize.
internasionalis'me, internationalism.
interneer', (geïn-), intern.
interne'ring, internment; ~**skamp**, internment camp.
internis', (-te), specialist physician.
intern'skap, internship.
internun'tius, (-se, ..**tii**), internuncio.
interpagineer', (geïn-), interpage.
interparlementêr', (-e), interparliamentary.
interpellant', (-e), interpellant, interpellator.
interpella'sie, (-s), interpellation.
interpelleer', (geïn-), interpellate.
interplanetêr', (-e), interplanetary.
interpola'sie, (-s), interpolation.
interpola'tor, (-s), interpolator.
In'terpol, Interpol.
interpoleer', (geïn-), interpolate.

interponeer', (geïn-), interpose.
interpreta'sie, interpretation, reading.
interpreteer', (geïn-), interpret.
interprovinsiaal', (..siale), interprovincial.
interpungeer', (geïn-), punctuate.
interpunk'sie, punctuation.
interreg'num, (-s), interregnum.
interroga'sie, (-s), interrogation.
interrogatief', (..tiewe), interrogative.
interrompeer', **interrumpeer'**, (vero.), (geïn-), interrupt.
interrup'sie, (-s), interruption.
intersek'sie, intersection.
interses'sie, intercession.
interskool'wedstryd, interschool match.
interuniversiteits'wedstryd, intervarsity (match).
interuniversitêr', interuniversity.
in'terval, (-le), interval.
intervar'sitie, (-s), intervarsity (match).
interven'sie, (-s), intervention.
intervoka'lies, (-e), intervocal(ic).
intestaat', (..tate), intestate; *intestate boedel*, intestate estate.
intestinaal', (..nale), intestinal.
in'teuel, (-ge-), curb, restrain, check.
intiem', (-e), intimate; close (friends); ~ *wees met iem.*, be on terms of intimacy with someone.
intimida'sie, intimidation.
intimideer', (geïn-), intimidate, browbeat, cow.
intimiteit', (-e), intimacy.
in'tog, (-te), entry, entrance.
intoksika'sie, intoxication.
intoleran'sie, intolerance.
in'toming, restraint, curbing.
intona'sie, (-s), intonation; ~ **leer**, tonetics.
intoneer', (geïn-), intone.
in'toom, (-ge-), curb, restrain, rein in, bridle; cohibit, check.
intransigent', (-e), intransigent, irreconcilable.
intransitief', (..tiewe), intransitive.
in'trap, (s) beginning; *sommer met die* ~ *(slag)*, at the very beginning; (w) (-ge-), tread in; walk in; bring in on shoes (mud); arrive; begin (work).
intraveneus', (-e), intravenous.
in'trede, entrance, entry; introit (R.C.).
in'tree, (s) = **intrede**; *sy* ~ *DOEN*, set in (winter); make one's appearance; take up one's duties; (w) (-ge-), set in; commence; arise; enter, go in; *hiermee het 'n nuwe tydperk ingetree*, this marks the beginning of a new era; ~ **geld**, entrance fee; ~ **preek**, induction sermon; ~ **rede**, inaugural speech; ~ **toespraak**, maiden speech.
in'trek, (s) abode, residence; *jou* ~ *neem by*, take up residence at; (w) (-ge-), go in, move into (house); absorb, soak in; draw in, repeal (a law); cancel, recant, revoke; retract (claws); redesignate (appointment); abrogate; suspend (licence); inhale (smoke); cheat; *DIEPER die land* ~, penetrate into the interior; *die LAND* ~, occupy the country; *sy VRIEND* ~, cheat one's friend; ~ **baar**, (..bare), retractile, retractable; revocable; ~ **band**, drawstring; ~ **ker**, (-s), new-comer, new arrival; ~ **king**, withdrawal, revocation, repeal (law), retraction; recall; rescission; abrogation; ~ **koord**, drawstring; ~ **lug**, downcast air; ~ **luggang**, intake airway; ~ **skag**, (-te), downcast shaft; ~ **werk**, ruffling.
intrigant', (-e), plotter, schemer, intriguer, machinator, designer, contriver.
intri'ge, (-s), intrigue, scheme, cabal; plot.
intrigeer', (geïn-), intrigue, scheme, machinate; *dit* ~ *my*, it intrigues me; it makes me curious.
intri'geroman, novel with an intricate plot.
intrinsiek', (-e), intrinsic.
introduk'sie, (-s), introduction; ~ **aand**, guest-night; ~ **brief**, letter of recommendation (introduction).
introduseer', (geïn-), introduce.
introspek'sie, introspection.
introspektief', (..tiewe), introspective; reflex.
in'trou, (-ge-), intermarry; marry into.
introvers', (-e), introvertive; ~ **ie**, introversion.
introvert', (-e), introvert.

intru'sie, intrusion; ~ **gesteente**, intrusive rock; ~ **plaat**, sill.
in'tuimel, (-ge-), tumble in(to); cave in.
intuï'sie, (-s), intuition.
intuïtief', (..tiewe), intuitive(ly).
intus'sen, meanwhile, in the meantime.
in'tuur, (-ge-), peer at.
intwy'feltrekking, query.
intyds', in time.
inunda'sie, (-s), inundation, flooding.
inundeer', (geïn-), inundate, flood.
in'vaar, (-ge-), sail in(to); *die duiwel het in hom ingevaar*; he is possessed by a devil; ~ **t**, entrance (by ship).
in'val, (s) (-le), idea, thought, brain-wave; raid, incursion; inroad; foray; descent; irruption, invasion; incidence (science); fancy, fantasy, freak; *'n* ~ *DOEN in*, raid, invade; *'n GELUKKIGE* ~, a happy thought; a bright idea; *SNAAKSE* ~ *le*, strange (queer) ideas (whims); *'n SOETE* ~, a home from home; (w) (-ge-), fall in; collapse; occur; interrupt; become ill; become hollow; join in; invade; begin; strike up; start playing; *'n LAND* ~, invade a country; ~ *lende LIGSTRALE*, incident rays; *wanneer MOET jy* ~ *?*, when must you assume duty?; *dit het MY ingeval*, I remembered; the idea occurred to me; *by die verkeerde NOOT* ~, join in on the wrong note; *VIR iem.* ~, deputize for someone; *WEER* ~, have a relapse; *dit WIL my nie* ~ *nie*, I cannot recall it; ~ **ete**, pot luck.
invali'de, (s) (-s), invalid; (b) invalid, disabled (soldier); ~ **huis**, home for invalids; ~ **stoel**, wheel-chair, invalid's chair.
invaliditeit', invalidity; ~ **s'toelae**, disability allowance; ~ **s'wet**, disablement act.
in'val: ~ **ler**, (-s), invader, raider; substitute; unexpected visitor; ~ **party**, surprise party.
in'vals: ~ **as**, axis of incidence; ~ **hoek**, angle of incidence; ~ **leër**, invading army.
in'valtyd, time to commence work.
invaria'bel, (-e), invariable.
invariabiliteit', invariability.
inva'sie, (ong.), (-s), invasion.
in'vat, (-ge-), take in, carry in; set (jewels).
inventa'ris, (-se), inventory; contents; equipment; *die* ~ *opmaak*, take stock; ~ **a'sie**, stock-taking; making an inventory; ~ **eer'**, (geïn-), make an inventory, take stock; ~ **uitverkoping**, stock-taking sale; ~ **voorraad**, stock on hand.
invers', inverse.
inver'sie, inversion; ~ **straal**, radius of inversion.
inverta'se, invertase.
inverteer', (geïn-), invert.
in'vertsuiker, invert sugar.
investeer', (geïn-), invest.
investe'ring, investment.
investituur', (..ture), investiture.
in'vet, (-ge-), grease (oil) well
in'vitasie, (-s), invitation; ~ **kaartjie**, invitation card; complementary ticket.
inviteer', (geïn-), invite.
in'vleg, (-ge-), intertwine, interlace, plait in; insinuate (remark); ~ **greep**, interlock (golf).
in'vlieër, test pilot.
in'vlie(g), fly in(to); reprimand, rebuke; *DAAR* ~, fall into a trap; *IEM.* ~, give someone a telling off (a dressing down).
in'vloed, (-e), influence; prestige, puissance, authority, power; credit; effect; hold; *sy* ~ *AANWEND by*, exert one's influence with; *sy* ~ *laat GELD*, use one's influence; *ONDER die* ~ *van sterk drank*, under the influence of drink; *SONDER* ~, without any influence; *van* ~ *WEES op*, have an influence on; ~ **ryk**, (-e), influential; powerful; puissant; prepotent; ~ **sfeer**, sphere of influence.
in'vloei, (-ge-), flow in(to); ~ **end**, (-e), influent; ~ **ing**, inpouring, flowing in.
in'vlug, (-ge-), flee into; take refuge.
in'voeg, (-ge-), put in, insert, intercalate; mortise; ~ **ing**, (-e, -s), ~ **sel**, (-s), insertion; interpolation; ~ **laer**, insert-bearing; ~ **teken**, caret.
in'voel, (-ge-): *jou in 'n ander se posisie* ~, penetrate

(with the mind) into someone's position; ~ing, empathy.
in'voer, (s) import(ation), introduction (new ideas); (w) (-ge-), import; introduce; put into force (effect); ~artikel, article of import; ~baar, (..bare), importable; ~baarheid, importability; ~beheer, import control; ~belasting, import duty; ~bepaling, import regulation; ~beperking, import restriction; ~buis, inlet tube; ~der, (-s), importer; ~draad, drop wire; ~goedere, import goods, imports; ~handel, import trade; ~hawe, import harbour; ~ing, importation; introduction; ~premie, import premium; ~reg, import duty; customs; ~verbod, embargo on importation; ~verlof, import permit; ~waarde, import value; ~ware, imports.
invoka'sie, invocation.
involu'sie, (-s), involution.
in'vorder, (-ge-), collect (taxes); recover (debts); demand (payment); ~aar, (-s), collector; ~baar, (..bare), leviable, collectable; exigible; recoverable; ~ing, collection; recovery (of debts); ~ingsgelde, collection fees.
in'vou, (-ge-), fold in, enfold, enclose; ~ing, folding in; enclosure.
in'vreet, (-ge-), bite into, eat into, corrode; fester; fret; ~baar, (..bare), corrodible, corrosible; ~vermoë, corrosive power.
in'vretend, (-e), corrosive, erosive.
in'vreting, (-e, -s), erosion; corrosion; corrosiveness; grooving; pitting (in iron); bite.
in'vries, (-ge-), freeze in, become ice-bound.
in'vryf, (-ge-), rub in, embrocate.
invry'heidstelling, release, reprieve, liberation, discharge.
in'vrywe, (-ge), rub in, embrocate.
in'vul, (-ge-), fill in, fill up; insert, enter; complete (form); ~ling, filling in; completion.
in'waai, (-ge-), blow in, be blown in; come bustling in.
in'waarts, (b) (-e), inward; (bw) inward.
in'wag, (-ge-), wait for, await; *inskrywings word ingewag*, tenders will be received; ~ting, awaiting.
in'waggel, (-ge-), stagger in(to).
in'wals¹, (-ge-), waltz in.
in'wals², (-ge-), roll in, press in.
in'warrel, (-ge-), whirl in(to).
in'weef, (-ge-), weave in(to).
in'weeg, (-ge-), weigh into holder.
in'week, (-ge-), soak in.
in'wendig, (-e), internal, inner; interior; inward; *nie vir ~e GEBRUIK nie*, not to be taken internally; *~e SPANNING*, internal tension; *die ~e mens VERSTERK*, fortify the inner man; take refreshments; ~e, (-s), inside; *die ~e*, the inner man; ~heid, inwardness.
in'wentel, (-ge-), roll into.
in'werk, (-ge-), act upon, affect, influence; work in; mix with (soil); press into; insinuate (oneself); insert (by means of some process); take in (seam); make up (time); earn (by doing work); work off (debt); impress (design); *jou êrens ~*, get to know the ropes thoroughly; *jou in iets ~*, get thoroughly acquainted with a subject; ~ing, influence, action, effect; *~ing van mis in grond*, incorporation of manure into soil.
inwer'kingstelling, putting into operation.
inwer'kingtreding, coming into operation, taking effect; commencement, inurement (law).
inwerk'neming, employment.
in'werp, (-ge-), throw in (coin); interrupt; object.
in'wewe, (-ge-), weave in(to).
in'wig, (-ge-), socket.
in'wikkel, (-ge-), wrap up (parcel); envelop; enmesh; enfold; encase; involve, implicate (in affair); insinuate oneself; walk in(to); *'n BABA ~*, cover up a baby; *jou in iem. se GUNS ~*, ingratiate yourself; *in 'n TWIS ingewikkel raak*, get involved in a quarrel.
in'willig, (-ge-), grant, consent, agree, concede, comply, acquiesce, assent, meet half-way, accede; *~ om 'n TAAK te onderneem*, agree to undertake a task; *'n VERSOEK ~*, grant a request; ~ing, consent, assent, compliance, acquiescence.
in'win, (-ge-), obtain (information); take (legal advice); regain (time); ~ning, gathering, collection (of advice).
in'wip, (-ge-), skip (whisk) in(to); drop in (on a person).
in'wissel, (-ge-), exchange; cash; discount; *papiergeld ~ vir(teen) dollars*, exchange banknotes for dollars; ~baar, (..bare), discountable; convertible; ~baarheid, discountability; ~ing, cashing; exchange.
in'woel, (-ge-), burrow into; force in (nail); envelop; *jou in die hoë kringe ~*, worm one's way into the upper circles.
in'wonend, (-e), resident; immanent; *~e ONDERWYSER*, resident teacher; *~e PASIËNT*, inpatient.
in'woner, (-s), inhabitant, resident, inmate; occupant (house); denizen; ~es', (-se), female inhabitant; ~s, population; inhabitants; ~tal, number of inhabitants.
in'woning, lodging; immanence.
in'woon, (-ge-), lodge, board, live in, be resident.
in'wortel, (-ge-), take root, become deeply rooted.
in'wring, (-ge-), squeeze (worm) oneself into.
in'wurg, (-ge-), force down one's throat; swallow with difficulty.
in'wurm, (-ge-), force one's way in; insinuate oneself (into favour, office, etc.).
in'wy, (-ge-), open, initiate; ordain; consecrate; auspicate; inaugurate; dedicate; take into use; *in 'n geheim ~*, let into a secret; ~der, (-s), dedicator.
in'wyding, (-e, -s), opening, inauguration, initiation; ~seremonie, ~sfees, ~splegtigheid, inaugural ceremony; ~srede, inaugural (dedicatory) address.
in'wyfees, (-te), house-warming.
io'neteorie, ionic theory.
Io'nië, Ionia; ~r, (-s), Ionian.
Io'nies, (-e), Ionian.
ionisa'sie, ionisation.
ioniseer', (geïon-), ionize; ..se'ring, ionization.
io'nosfeer, (..sfere), ionosphere.
ioon', (ione), ion.
ipekakuan'ha, ipecacuanha.
ipekon'ders, *see* hipokonders.
Iraaks', (-e), Iraqi.
Iraans', (-e), Iranian.
Irak', Iraq; ~ees', (..kese), Iraqi; ~iër, (-s), Iraqi; ~s', (-e), Iraqi.
Iran', Iran; ~iër, (-s), Iranian; ~ies, (-e), Iranian.
ire'nies, (-e), irenic(al).
iri'dium, iridium.
i'ris, (-se), iris; ~eer', (geïr-), iridesce.
irise'rend, (-e), iridescent
irise'ring, iridescence; irisation.
Irokees', (..kese), Iroquois, Iroquoian.
ironie', irony.
iro'nies, (-e), ironical; bland.
ironiseer', (geïr-), ironize.
irradia'sie, irradiation.
irrasionaal', (..nale), irrational (maths).
irrasionalis', (-te), irrationalist; ~me, irrationalism; ~ties, (-e), irrationalist(ic).
irrasionaliteit, irrationality.
irrasioneel', (..nele), irrational.
irrealiteit', unreality.
irredentis', (-te), irredentist; ~me, irredentism; ~ties, (-e), irredentist.
irreëel', (irreële), unreal, fictitious.
irrelevant', (-e), irrelevant.
irriga'sie, irrigation; ~departement, irrigation department; ~kanaal, irrigation canal; ~skema, irrigation scheme; ~werke, irrigation works.
irriga'tor, (-e, -s), irrigator.
irrita'sie, irritation.
irriteer', (geïrriteer), irritate; rasp.
irrup'sie, (-s), irruption.
is, is; are; was; *GOD ~*, God exists; *dit ~ GEDOEN*, it has been done; *die HUIS ~ gebou*, the house was built.
isagogiek', isagogics.
isago'gies, (-e), isagogic.
ise'belsakkie, vanity bag.
is'kias, sciatica.

Is'lam, Islam; ~**iet'**, (-e), Islamite.
islamiseer', (geïs-), Mohammedanize; ..**se'ring**, Mohammedanization.
Is'lam: ~**is'me**, Islamism; ~**i'ties**, (-e), Islamic, Moslem.
is'me, (-s), ism.
is'mus, (-se), isthmus.
isobaar', (isobare), isobar.
isobaat', (isobate), isobath.
isoba'ries, isobarome'tries, (-e), isobaric.
isoba'sis, isobase.
isochroma'ties, (-e), isochromatic.
isochro'nies, (-e), isochronal, isochronous.
isochronis'me, isochronism.
isochroon', (..chrone), isochrone.
isodina'mies, (-e), isodynamic.
isofoon', (isofone), isophone.
isogonaal', (..nale), isogonic.
isogoon', (isogone), isogon.
isoklinaal', (..nale), isoclinal, isoclinic.
isola'sie, isolation; insulation; ~**band**, insulation tape; ~**hospitaal**, isolation hospital; ~**materiaal**, insulating material; ~**meter**, megger; ~**vermoë**, insulating power.
isolasionis', (-te), isolationist; ~**me**, isolationism; ~**ties**, (-e), isolationist.
isola'tor, (-e, -s), isolator, insulator.
isoleer', (geïso-), isolate; quarantine; insulate; lag (boiler); ~**band**, insulating tape; ~**kamer**, padded room; ~**steen**, insulating brick; ~**vermoë**, insulating ability.
isolement', isolation, detachment.
isole'ring, isolation; clothing (steam-engine); quarantine.
isomeer', (s) (isomere), isomer(e); (b) isomeric(al), isomerous.
isomerie', isomerism.
isome'ries, (-e), isomeric.
isomeriseer', (geïso-), isomerize.
isome'tries, (-e), isometric.
isomorf', (-e), isomorphous.
isoterm', (-e), isotherm; ~**ies**, (-e), isothermal.
isoto'nies, (-e), isotonic.
isotoop', (isotope), isotope.
isotopie', isotopy, isotopism.
isoto'pies, (-e), isotopic.
isotroop', (isotrope), isotrope.
isotropie', isotropism.
isotro'pies, (-e), isotropic.
Is'rael, Israel.
Israe'li, (-'s), Israeli.
Israe'lies, (-e), Israeli.
Israeliet', (-e), Israelite; 'n ~ in wie daar geen bedrog is nie, an Israelite indeed in whom is no guile.
Israeli'ties, (-e), Israelitic.
Italiaan', (Italiane), Italian; ~**s'**, (b) (-e), Italian; ~**se kewer**, Italian beetle.
Italia'ner, (-s) = **Italiaan**.
Ita'lië, Italy.
i'tem, (-s), item; ~**pie**, (-s), small item.
itera'sie, (-s), iteration, repetition, duplication; reduplication.
iteratief', (..tiewe), iterative, reduplication.
i'′tjie, (-s), small i.
ivoor', ivory; ~**agtig**, (-e), ivory-like; eburnean; ~**draaier**, ivory turner; ~**druk**, ivory head; ~**geel**, ivory-yellow; ~**kleur**, colour of ivory; ~**kleurig**, (-e), ivory-coloured; ~**neut**, vegetable ivory; ~**papier**, ivory paper; ~**swart**, ivory-black; ~**toring**, ivory tower; ~**werk**, ivory ware; ~**wit**, ivory-white.
ivo're, (ong.), (b) ivory; ~ *toring*, ivory tower.
i'xia, (-s), ixia (lily).

J

j, (-'s), j.
ja, yes, yea, ay(e); certainly; to be sure; indeed; in fact; oh, well; *op alles* ~ *en AMEN sê*, agree to everything; ditto to Mr. Pitt; ~ *en AMEN wees*, be final; *as jy so DINK*, well, if that is your opinion; ~ *EN nee*, yes and no; ~, *die ou LEWE is swaar*, yes, indeed, life is hard; *laat jou* ~ ~ *wees en jou NEE nee*, let your yea be yea and your nay nay; ~, *PRAAT v.d. ding*, that is very true; ~ *en amen SPEEL*, say yes to everything; *'n VRAAG met* ~ *beantwoord*, answer in the affirmative; ~, *WAT sal ek sê?*, well, what shall I say?
ja(ag), (ge-), chase, pursue; race, chevy, chivvy; post; drive hard; rush; step on the gas; flutter (heart); *na EER (geld)* ~, pursue honour (money); *as jy iem. (wie 'n ander jaag)* ~, *staan jy self nie stil nie*, evildoers are evil-thinkers; he who pursues another cannot himself stand still.
jaag: ~**baan**, race course, speedway, race track; ~**besem**, husk broom, winnowing fan; ~**duiwel**, speed-merchant, speed-maniac, hell driver; ~**lokval**, speed trap.
jaag'siekte, droning (in sheep); crotalariosis (in horses); ~ **bos**, *Crotalaria dura, C. globifera*.
ja(ag)'spinnekop, hunting-spider *(Solifuga* or *Palystes)*.
jaag: ~**strik**, (-ke), speed trap; ~**vlieër**, racing pilot; racer.
jaap, (jape), uneducated, uncouth person, lout; incision.
jaap-jaap', (..-jape), chat *(Cercomela familiaris)*.
jaar, (jare), year, season; *al om die ANDER* ~, every other year; *BLOU jare*, donkey's years; *in die* ~ *BLOU* ~, once in a blue moon; *met* ~ *en DAG*, as years go by; ~ *en DAG bepaal*, fix the date; *sedert* ~ *en DAG*, for years and years; *na* ~ *en DAG*, after many a year; ~ *en DAG*, the exact date; for a year and a day; *jare DER jare gelede*, years and years ago; *sy jare goed DRA*, carry one's years well; *die* ~ *EEN*, the year dot; *die EEN* ~ *met die ander*, taking one year with another; *in GEEN jare nie*, not in years; *nog nie die jare HÊ nie*, not have reached the years; *iem. se jare HÊ*, have seen as many years as someone; *die HELE* ~ *deur*, all the year round; *van jare HER*, in days of yore; *in die* ~ *van Onse HERE*, in the year of grace (Our Lord); *so elke HONDERD* ~, once in a hundred years; *die* ~ *HONDERD*, the year dot; *dit was nie HONDERD* ~ *nie*, not long after; ~ *IN en* ~ *uit*, from one year to another; year in and year out; *JONK van jare, maar oud van dae (snare)*, an old head on young shoulders; *op jare KOM*, be getting on in years, *die LOPENDE* ~, the current year; *MET die jare*, as the years go by; *iem. van MY jare*, someone of my age, ~ *NA* ~, year by year; *NIE baie jare nie*, not so many years; *NOG baie jare*, many happy returns; *in die* ~ *NUL (as die hingste vul)*, on the Greek calends; in the year dot; when two Sundays come together; *iets uit die* ~ *NUL*, something as old as the hills; *ONDER die jare wees*, be under age; *OM die twee* ~, in every other year; *vandag OOR 'n* ~, this day twelvemonth; *die jare van ONDER= SKEID*, the age of discretion; *OUD van jare*, old in years; *PER* ~, per annum; *baie jare agter die RUG hê*, have seen many years (summers); *SEDERT jare*, for a long time already; *SONDER* ~, no date (of book); *SINDS* ~ *en dag*, for years and years; *jare wat die SPRINKAAN opgevreet het*, lost years; the years that the locusts have eaten; *SWAAR* ~, hard times; *die* ~ *TOET*, the year dot; *iem. VAN jare*, of mature age; *VER in die jare*, advanced in years; ~ *VIR* ~, year by year; *sy jare VOORUIT wees*, be in advance of his years; *VROEËR jare*, earlier times; *die* ~ *VROEG*, very long ago; ~**berig**, (-te), annual report; ~**beurs**, annual fair;

~blad, (..blaaie), annual (publication); ~book, year-book, annual; ~boeke, annuals; ~dag, anniversary (day); ~dig, chronogram; ~duisend, millennium; ~fees, (-te), anniversary, yearly feast; ~gang, year's issues (of newspaper); file (of a periodical); vintage; *ou* ~*gange,* back volumes; ~geld, annuity; pension; ~geldtrekker, annuitant; ~gemiddelde, yearly average; ~gety, season; ~getyverskil, seasonal variation; ~gewasse, annual crops; ~herdenkingsdiens, anniversary service; ~honderd, century; ~kring, annual cycle; annual ring (of tree); ~kursus, year's course; ~lemoen, shaddock; pomelo *(Citrus grandis (maxima));* ~liks, (-e), yearly, annual; ~mark, (-te), annual fair; annual market; ~omset, annual turnover; ~oud, (..oue), one-year-old; ~plant, annual (plant); ~premie, annual premium; ~punte, annual marks; ~rapport, annual report; ~reënval, annual rainfall; ~rekening, yearly account; ~ring, annual ring, growth ring; ~staat, annual return(s); ~stempel, date mark; ~syfer, year mark, annual record.
jaart, (-s), yard; back yard.
jaar: ~tal, date; ~telling, era; chronology; ~totaal, yearly total.
jaart: ~ridder, counter-jumper; ~stok, yard-measure.
jaar: ~vergadering, annual meeting; ~verslag, (..slae), annual report; ~wedde, annual salary; ~wisseling, turn of the year.
jabot', (-s), jabot.
ja'broer, (-s), yes-man, toady, truckler.
ja'de, jade.
ja'er, (-s), pursuer, chaser; racer; fast driver, speeder; ~y, racing; pursuit.
jag¹, (s) (-te), yacht.
jag², (s) hunt, shoot, chase; pursuit; gunning; *die* ~ *is toe, maar die GEWEER se loop is oop,* it may be the close season, but a gun's barrel remains open; ~ *MAAK op effek,* strive for effect; *OP* ~ *wees,* be on the hunt, be hunting; *die* ~ *na RYKDOM,* the pursuit of wealth; (w) (ge-), hunt, shoot; chase; *gaan* ~, go hunting (shooting); ~bomwerper, pursuit bomber; ~eskader, pursuit squadron; ~gebied, hunting-field; ~geselskap, (-pe), hunting-party, meet; ~geweer, sporting rifle; ~godin, goddess of the chase; ~grond, hunting-ground; ~hond, hunting-dog; hound; pointer; setter; harrier; ~horing, hunting-horn; ~huis, hunting-box, lodge, shooting-box; ~instink, hunting-instinct; ~klere, hunting-clothes.
jag'klub¹, hunt-club.
jag'klub², yacht-club.
jag: ~kruiser, long-range fighter; ~kuns, art of hunting; ~lamp, hunting-lamp; ~liksens, ~lisensie, hunting-licence, game-licence; ~luiperd, cheetah; ~meester, master of the hounds; ~mes, hunting-knife, bowie-knife; ~ongeluk, hunting-accident; ~opbrengs, kill; ~opsigter, keeper, huntsman; ~party, hunting-party; ~patrone, sporting ammunition; ~perd, hunter (horse); ~plaas, shooting-box.
jags, (-e), ruttish, on heat; ~heid, heat, rut.
jag: ~sak, game-bag; ~seisoen, hunting-season; ~skottel, hotpot.
jag'sneeu, drifting snow.
jag: ~spinnekop, *see* ja(a)gspinnekop; ~sweep, hunting-crop; ~ter, (-s), hunter, huntsman; deerstalker; pursuit plane; ~terig, (-e), hurried, restless, fitful; ~tog, (-te), hunting-expedition.
jag'tyd¹, hunting-season; open season.
jag'tyd², rutting season, tupping season (sheep).
ja'guar, (-s), jaguar.
jag: ~veld, hunting-field; grass; ~verhaal, hunting-story; ~vermaak, pleasures of the hunt; ~vliegtuig, chaser-plane; pursuit aeroplane; ~vlug, pursuit flight; ~wet, game law.
Jahwe(h)', Yahveh.
Jahwis'me, Yahvism.
Jahwis'ties, Yahvistic.
Jak, (-ke, -s), yak.
jakaran'da, (-s), jacaranda.

jak'ka, (-s), jack-fruit *(Artocarpus integrifolia).*
jak'kals, (-e), jackal; sly person, prevaricator; pug; *dis BO my* ~, that has me beat; that is beyond me; *hy is 'n* ~ *met baie DRAAIE,* he is a sly fox; *as die* ~ *dik is, is die DRUIWE suur,* plenty is not dainty; *'n* ~ *verander van HARE, maar nie van nukke nie,* a leopard cannot change its spots; *'n* ~ *wat slaap, tel HOENDERS in sy drome,* in his sleep the fox counts chickens; *'N* ~, a wily fox; *'n KAAL* ~, a pauper; a beggar; *as die* ~ *die PASSIE preek, moet die boer sy ganse oppas,* beware of your geese when the fox preaches; *ek RUIK* ~, I hear someone blowing his trumpet; ~*e vang nie 'n SKAAP in die dag nie,* it is at night that jackals prowl; *vir* ~ *SKAAPWAGTER maak,* give the wolf the wether to keep; ~ *SKIET,* relieve oneself; *so SLIM soos 'n* ~, as cunning (sly) as a fox; ~ *vee sy SPORE met sy stert dood,* a rogue destroys all traces of his crime; ~ *prys sy eie STERT,* he blows his own trumpet; *hoe kaler* ~, *hoe groter STERT,* great boast, small roast; *'n* ~ *met twee STERTE,* a turncoat; *die* ~*e TROU,* ~ *TROU met wolf se vrou,* rain with sunshine; the monkeys are having a wedding; the fairies are baking; *dis die klein* ~*ies wat die WINGERDE verniel,* small mistakes cause endless trouble; it is the little foxes that spoil the vines; ~agtig, (-e), foxy; ~bessie, Transvaal ebony *(Diospyros mespiliformis);* white milkwood *(Sieroxylon inerme);* ~bont, fox fur; ~bos, *Dimorphoteca zeyheri;* ~bruilof, rain with sunshine; ~dig, (-te), jackal-proof; ~doutjie, slight drizzle; ~draad, jackal-proof wire, strong netting-wire; ~draai, sharp turn, evasion, prevarication, clever excuse; ~*draaie maak,* try to dodge the issue; look for excuses; ~draf, foxtrot; *dit gaan op 'n* ~ *draffie,* things are jogging along; ~gat, jackal's burrow; ~ghaap, the succulent *Hoodia bainii;* ~hond, foxhound; ~jag, foxhunt (chase); ~jagter, pink; ~kos, dead dog *(Hydnora africana);* ~pis, jackal's urine; ~pisbossie, *Zygophyllum foetidum;* ~pruim, Cape sumach *(Osyris abyssinica);* ~reëntjie, rain with sunshine; ~smaak, foxiness; ~stert, foxbrush; ~streke, cunning, shrewdness, slyness; artifices; *vol* ~ *streke wees,* be as wily as a fox; ~tolbos, *Royena pubescens;* ~trap, foxtrot; ~trou(weer), rain and sunshine at the same time; ~uitroeier, exterminator of jackals; ~uitroeiing, vulpicide; ~vaalbos, *Stachys burchellii;* ~volk, jackal buzzard; ~vanger, jackal catcher; ~voël, jackal buzzard.
jak'ker, (ge-), hurry, fag; romp, career.
jak'kie, (-s), jacket, coatee.
ja'ko, (-'s), African gray *(Psittacus erihacus).*
Ja'kob: ~ *vry na RACHEL om vir Lea te kry,* be disappointed; have to be satisfied with the next best; *die WARE* ~, Mr. Right, the right man; the real Mackay (McCoy).
Jakobeaans', (-e), Jacobean.
Jakobiet', (-e), Jacobite.
jakobreg'op, (-pe, -s), zinnia (flower).
ja'kobs: ~leer, Jacob's ladder; bucket elevator; rope ladder; ~lelie, sprekelia.
Jakobyn', (-e), Jacobin.
jakonet', jaconet.
jakope'wer, (-s), *Sebastosemus capensis;* ~oë, protruding eyes, lobster-eyes.
jak'vrug, jack-fruit.
jalap', jalap.
jaloers', (-e), jealous, envious, green-eyed.
jaloers'heid, jaloesie', jealousy, envy.
jam¹: *so 'n MOND moet* ~ *kry, sy MOND verdien* ~, hear! hear! encore! he can say that again!
jam², (-s), yam *(Dioscorea).*
Jamai'ka, Jamaica.
Jamaikaan', (..kane), Jamaican; ~s', (-e), Jamaican.
jamai'ka: ~gemmer, Jamaica ginger; ~peper, allspice, pimento.
jam'be, (-s), jamb(us); ..bies, (-e), jambic.
jam'boes, (-e), rose-apple *(Eugenia jambos).*
jam'mer, (s) pity; misery; (w) (ge-), lament, wail; (b) sorry; *dit is EWIG* ~, it is a thousand pities; hard

lines!; *HOE* ~!, what a pity!, hard lines!; **~dal,** vale of tears; dreary place; **~end, (-e),** lamenting, grieving; **~ geskrei,** lamentations; **~ har'tig, (-e),** compassionate; **~ har'tigheid,** compassion; **~ klag,** lamentation; moan; **~ lappie,** damp cloth, damp finger napkin; **~ lik, (-e),** miserable, pitiable, pitiful, woeful, doleful, wretched, piteous; **~ likheid,** piteousness, miserableness, deplorableness; **~ poel,** pool of misery; **~ te,** sorrow; pity; hard lines; *iets uit ~ te doen,* do something out of pity; **~ toon,** tone of lamentation.

Jan, John; *~ en ALLEMAN,* Tom, Dick and Harry; all the world and his wife; *liewer BANG ~ as dooie (oorlede) ~,* better a living dog than a dead lion; *~ BURGER,* John Citizen; *~ DOM,* an ass; a numbskull; *wie is nou DOM ~ en wie slim ~?,* who knows best now? *pas op as DOM ~ vir slim ~ vang,* don't try to be too clever; *~ DROMER,* a day-dreamer; *~ KALBAS,* a boaster; a madcap; *~ KIESER,* John Citizen; *~ KLAASSEN,* merry Andrew; *~ KLAASSEN en Tryn,* Punch and Judy; *~ KOMPANJIE,* John Company; *~ LAVENTEL,* dandy; *~ LUI het hom dood gedra,* don't overdo it; *MAL ~ onder die hoenders,* the only gentleman in ladies' company; *'n regte ou ~ PAMPOEN,* a weakling; a nonentity; a nincompoop; a nitwit; *~, PIET en Klaas,* Tom, Dick and Harry; *~ PUBLIEK,* the general public; *~ RAP en sy maat,* ragtag and bobtail; *~ SALIE,* stick-in-the-mud; nonentity; *~ TAKS,* the finance minister; the exchequer; *met ~ TUISBLY se karretjie gaan (ry),* have to stay at home.

jan: **~ blom', (-me, -s),** huge (rain-) frog *(Breviceps);* **~ boel',** muddle, mess; **~ bruin', (-e, -s),** John Brown *(Gymnocrotaphus curvidens; Pachymetopon grande).*

jandooi', (-s, -e), Weary Willie, lazy-bones, dead-alive person; **~ erig, (-e),** dead-alive; **~ erigheid,** state of being dead-alive.

jandor'ie, (-s), John Dory *(fam. Zeidae).*

ja-nee'!, sure! indeed! oh, well! *~, dis darem waar,* that is only too true.

jan: **~ fiskaal',** butcher-bird, fiscal shrike; **~ fre'derik,** Cape robin *(Cossypha caffra);* **~ groentjie, (-s),** malachite sunbird *(Nectarinia famosa);* peppermint liqueur, crème de menthe; **~-half-verniet,** Cheap Jack; **~ hen,** apron-husband; **~-in-die-sak',** plum-pudding, plum-duff.

janitsaar', (..sare), janissary.

jan: **~ klaas'senspel,** Punch-and-Judy show; **~ knaphand,** handyman; **~ maat', (-s),** jack tar.

jan'nas, jeans, denims.

jan'netjie, jealous.

jan'nie, (b) jealous, envious; *~ se baadjie aanhê,* be jealous.

jan: **~ pie'dewiet,** **~ pie'rewiet,** shrike *(Telephorus zeylonus);* **~ plooier, (-s),** char à banc.

janrap', riff-raff.

janreg'maak, handy man, Mr. Fix-it.

jansa'lie, simpleton, slacker, stick-in-the-mud; **~ agtig, (-e),** sloppish, sluggish, spiritless; **~ gees,** carefree (don't care) spirit, spirit of backbonelessness.

Jansenis', (-te), Jansenist; **~ me,** Jansenism; **~ ties, (-e),** Jansenistic.

janta'terat, janta'tara, (-s), *see* **janfrederik.**

Jan'tjie, Johnnie; *j~ se BAADJIE aanhê, j~ WEES,* be jealous; *'n ~ KONTRARIE wees,* to be contrary; *~ of WAENTJIE,* heads or tails.

jan'tjie-trapsoetjies, (-e), chameleon.

jan'tjie-van-alles, (jantjies-van-alles), man of all work, factotum.

Ja'nuarie, January; **~ bossie,** *Thymelaeacea;* **~ maand,** the month of January.

Ja'nusgesig, Janus face, double-faced.

jan-van-gent', (-e, -s), gannet.

Japan, Japan; **~ nees', (..nese),** Japonic, Japanese; **~ ner, (-s),** Japanese; **~ s',** (s) Japanese (language); (b) **(-se),** Japanese; *~ nese MANNA,* Japanese millet; *~ se PORSELEIN,* japan(ned) porcelain).

ja'perig, (-e), uncouth, uncivilized.

ja'pie, (-s), johnny; bumpkin, clodhopper, dolt; *'n simpel ~,* a simpleton, country cousin, bumpkin;

VAAL~, new wine; home-made (inferior) wine; **~ agtig, (-e),** **~ rig, (-e),** uncouth, doltish, block-headed.

japon', (-ne), dress, frock.

japon'ika, (-s), japonica, camellia.

japon'stof, dress material.

jap'snoet, (-e), inquisitive (impertinent) child; wiseacre, know-all; Nosy Parker, pipsqueak; **~ erig, (-e),** know-all, nosy.

jap'trap, short while; moment; short distance; *dis net 'n ~ na sy HUIS,* it's only a stone's throw to his house; *IN 'n ~,* in a jiffy; in a trice.

ja'relang, ja're lank, for years, for many (long) years; *ek KEN hom al jare lank,* I have known him for many years; *jarelange VRIENDSKAP,* friendship of many years' standing.

jar'gon, jargon, gibberish; cant; trade language.

jar'ig, (-e), of age, mature; *DIE ~ e,* the person celebrating his (her) birthday; *hy IS ~,* it is his birthday.

jarl, (-s), jarl, chieftain (Scandinavia).

jaroek', jaroep', (-s), kind of grapefruit from the East.

jarowisa'sie, jarovization, vernalization.

jarowiseer', (ge-), jarovize, vernalize.

jar'ra, jarra(h).

jas, (-se), overcoat, greatcoat; knave of clubs; *OU J~,* Old Nick; *sy ~ is in die WIEL,* he is in the soup; he is in trouble; **~ beskermer,** dress guard; **~ goed,** overcoating; **~ kraag,** coat collar.

ja'sêer, yesman.

jasint', hyacinth.

jasj'mak, (-s), yashmak

jasmyn', jasmine, jessamin(e); **~ geur,** scent of jasmine.

jas'pis, jasper.

jas: **~ sak, (-ke),** coat pocket; **~ sie, (-s),** small overcoat; **~ stof,** *see* **jasgoed.**

ja'sus, spiny lobster; Cape crawfish.

ja'tagan, yataghan.

Ja'va, Java.

Javaan', (Javane), Javanese; **~ s',** Javanese (language); (b) **(-se),** Javanese.

ja'vakoffie, Java coffee.

ja'vel, (-s), lout, clodhopper, nincompoop.

javel'water, javelle water.

jawel', yes, indeed; I dare say.

ja'woord, consent, promise of marriage; *die ~ kry,* be accepted (as lover).

jazz, jazz; **~ orkes,** jazz band.

jee: *o ~!,* oh dear! gee!

jeans, (Eng.), jeans, denims.

jeens, to, towards, by, against, over against; *vriendelik ~ iem. wees,* be friendly with a person.

Jeho'va, Jehovah; **~ sgetuies,** Jehovah's Witnesses (Russellites).

Je'hu, (-'s), Jehu, speed-maniac, furious driver.

jeju'num, (-s), jejunum.

Jek, jek, (-ke), rough person; anglicized Afrikaner.

jek'ker(t), (-s), jacket; service jacket; pea-jacket; lumber-jacket.

jel, (s), gel.

jelatien', jelati'ne = gelatien; gelatine.

jelei', (-e), jelly.

jel'lie, (-s), jelly; **~ agtig, (-e),** jelly-like; **~ bakkie,** jelly-mould; **~ boontjie,** jelly-bean; **~ kristalle,** jelly-crystals; **~ poeier,** jelly-powder; **~ rig, (-e),** jelly-like; **~ vorm,** jelly-mould.

Je'men, Yemen.

je'menie, oh dear!

Jemeniet', (-e), Yemenite; **..ni'ties, (-e),** Yemenite.

jen, (-s), yen.

jene'wer, gin, geneva; Hollands; **~ bessie,** juniper berry; **~ boom,** juniper tree; **~ bossie,** juniper bush; **~ bottel,** gin bottle; **~ brander,** gin distiller; **~ brandery,** gin distillery; **~ drinker,** gin drinker; **~ fles,** gin bottle; **~ grog,** gin grog; **~ moed,** Dutch courage, pot-valour; **~ neus,** bottle-nose, drunkard's nose; **~ paleis,** gin palace; **~ stoker,** gin distiller; **~ vat,** gin cask.

jen'telman, gentleman.

jen'toe, (-s), prostitute.

jerboa 244 *jonger*

jerbo'a, (-s), jerboa.
Jeremi'a, Jeremiah.
jeremia'de, (-s), jeremiad, woeful tale; screed.
jeremieer', (ge-), lament, wail.
je'rigoroos, Jericho rose *(Anastatica hierochuntia)*.
jerk, (-e), central beam.
Jero'beam, (-s), Jeroboam.
jeropi'go, jeropigo.
Jer'sey, (-s), Jersey; ~ **koei**, Jersey cow.
Jeru'salem, Jerusalem; *by* ~ **BEGIN**, begin at home; *die HEMELSE* ~, the heavenly Jerusalem; *'n NUWE* ~, a new Jerusalem.
jeru'salemponie, (-s), bed-bug.
Jesa'ja, Isaiah.
jese'belsakkie, jese'beltassie, vanity bag.
Jesuïet', (-e), Jesuit; ~ **eklooster**, Jesuit convent; ~ **eorde**, order of Jesuits.
Jesuï'ties, (-e), Jesuitic; . . **suïtis'me**, Jesuitism.
Je'sus, Jesus; *om* ~ *wil*, for Jesus' sake.
je'te = **hete**!
je'ti, (-'s), yeti, abominable snowman.
jeug, youth; *die* ~ *het geen DEUG nie*, youth will have its swing; *in sy PRILLE* ~, in the flower of his youth; *die RYPERE* ~, adolescents; *iem. se TWEEDE* ~, one's second lease of youthfulness; ~ **beweging**, youth movement; ~ **diens**, church service for young people; ~ **dig**, (-e), young, youthful; adolescent; juvenile, juvenescent; ~ **dige**, (-s), adolescent; ~ **digheid**, youth(fulness), juvenescence, juvenility; ~ **geskrifte**, juvenilia; ~ **herberg**, youth hostel; ~ **hof**, juvenile court; ~ **leier**, juvenile leader; ~ **lektuur**, books for juveniles; ~ **misdaad**, juvenile offence; ~ **misdadiger**, juvenile delinquent; ~ **misdadigheid**, juvenile delinquency; ~ **misdryf**, ~ **oortreding**, juvenile offence; J~**raad**, Juvenile Affairs Board; ~ **saamtrek**, youth rally; ~ **sentrum**, youth centre; ~ **vet**, baby-fat; ~ **vriend**, friend of one's youth; ~ **werke**, juvenilia.
jeuk, (s) itching; irritation; (w) (ge-), itch; ~ *waar 'n mens nie kan krap nie*, find oneself in an unpleasant situation; ~ **bol**, *Urginea altissima, Drimia ciliaris*; ~ **bulte**, prurigo; ~ **end**, (-e), itchy, prurient, pruriginous.
jeu'kerig, (-e), itchy, itching; ~ **heid**, itchiness; prurience, prickliness, pruritus.
jeuk: ~ **ery**, itching; ~ **ing**, itching; prurience; fornication; ~ **pampoen**, Karoo shrub *(Allenia urens)*; ~ **poeier**, itch-powder; ~ **salf**, itch-ointment; ~ **siekte**, eruption; scabies; rash, prurigo; ~ **te**, itching; ~ **uitslag**, uredo.
Jid'disj, (-e), Yiddish.
jig, gout; podagra; ~ **aanval**, (-le), attack of gout; ~ **agtig**, (-e), gouty; lumbaginous; ~ **knobbel**, chalk-stone; ~ **lyer**, gout sufferer; ~ **mengsel**, gout mixture; ~ **pyne**, gouty pains; ~ **t(er)ig**, (-e), gouty; ~ **tigheid**, goutiness.
jil, (ge-), jest, joke; ~ **lerig**, (-e), joking, jesting, sportive; ~ **lery**, joking, jesting; persiflage; ~ **letjie**, (-s), trick, joke.
jin'go, (-'s), jingo; ~ **blad**, jingo paper; ~ **is'me**, jingoism; ~ **is'ties**, (-e), jingoistic; ~ **party**, jingo party.
Job, Job; *so ARM soos* ~, as poor as Job; as poor as a churchmouse; ~ *se GEDULD en Salomo se wysheid*, much patience and great wisdom; *so GEDULDIG soos* ~, as patient as Job.
job'belsee, choppy sea.
jobs: ~ **bode**, Job's messenger; ~ **geduld**, patience of Job; ~ **trane**, Job's tears *(Coix lachryma-jobi)*; ~ **trooster**, Job's comforter; ~ **tyding**, tidings of ill-luck (ill-fortune); *'n* ~ *tyding kry*, be brought Job's news.
Jo'de: ~ **buurt**, Jew's quarter; ghetto; ~ **dom**, the Jews, Judaism, Jewry; ~ **genoot**, (. . **note**), Jewish proselyte; ~ **gesig**, Jewish face; ~ **haat**, hatred of Jews, anti-Semitism; ~ **kerk**, synagogue; ~ **kerkhof**, Jewish cemetery.
jodeer', (ge-), treat with iodine, iodize.
jo'del, (ge-), yodel.
Jo'de: **j**~**lym**, bitumen; ~ **moord**, pogrom; ~ **neus**, Jewish nose; ~ **skool**, Jewish school; ~ **ster**, star of David; ~ **taal**, Yiddish; ~ **vakansie**, Jewish holiday; ~ **vervolging**, Jew-baiting, persecution of the Jews; anti-Semitism; pogrom; ~ **volk**, Jewish nation; ~ **vrou**, Jewess; ~ **wyn**, sweet, unfermented wine.
jodh'pur, (-s), jodhpurs.
jodi'de, (-s), **jodied'**, (-e), iodide.
Jodin', (-ne), Jewess; ~ **netjie**, (-s), little Jewess.
jo'dium, iodine; ~ **stikstof**, nitrate of iodine; ~ **tinktuur**, tincture of iodine.
jo'doform, iodoform.
joe, oh dear! I say!
Joe'go-Slaaf, (. . **Slawe**), **Joego-Sla'wiër**, (-s), Jugoslav.
Joe'go-Sla'wië, Jugoslavia; . . **wies**, (-e), Jugoslav.
joejit'soe, ju-jitsu.
joel, (ge-), cheer, shout, yell, bawl; ~ **end**, (-e), cheering, bawling; ~ **ing**, shouting.
joepjoep', (-s), jujube.
joe'rie, (-s), ant-lion.
joernaal', (. . **nale**), journal, newspaper; logbook.
joernalis', (-te), journalist, pressman; publicist; *onafhanklike* ~, freelance; ~ **me**, ~ **tiek'**, journalism; (b) ~ **tiek'**, (-e), ~ **ties**, (-e), journalistic.
jo'ga, yoga.
jog'gel, (s) (-s), joggle (joint); (w) (ge-), joggle; ~ **voeg**, joggle joint.
jog'gemlangasem, locust *(Porthetis; Lamarckiana)*.
jog'gie, (-s), laddie, sonny, chappy; caddie; attendant; ~ **baas**, caddiemaster.
jog'gom, (-s), baboon.
jo'ghurt, yoghurt.
jo'gi, (-'s), yogi.
johan'nesbroodboom, carob, St. John's bread *(Ceratonia siliqua)*.
joho'!, yoho!
joi'ner, (hist.), (-s), National Scout.
jô-jô'! ow! oh!
jok, (ge-), lie, tell stories (fibs, untruths); ~ **ker**, (-s), fibber; ~ **kery**, story-telling, fibbing, lying.
jok'kie, (-s), jockey; ~ **agtig**, (-e), horsy.
jok'ster, (-s), fibber (woman).
jol¹, (s) (-le), jolly-boat, yawl, dinghy.
jol², (s) (-le), wild party (dance); (w) (ge-), make merry, have fun; woo, court.
jo'lig, (-e), jolly, merry, larky; ~ **heid**, jolliness, revelry.
jol: ~ **jantjie**, (-s), playboy; ~ **lery**, revelry, merry-making; ~ **sang**, sing-song.
jolyt', merry-making, feasting, joyfulness, jollity.
Jo'na, Jonah; *hy is 'n REGTE* ~, he is a regular Jonah, one who brings misfortune; *WIE is die* ~?, who is the Jonah?
jo'nas, (ge-), jettison.
jo'nasklip, dolomite.
Jo'natan, Jonathan; *Broer* ~, United States of America; American; *j*~*appel*, Jonathan apple.
jong, (-s) (-es), young (of animal); fellow; *HAAI*, ~ *!*, I say, old fellow! *NEE* ~, *moenie!*, no, don't (w) (ge-), bring forth young; farrow; cub; cast young; pup (dogs); (b) (attributive) young; *van* ~ *s AF*, from an early age; *die* ~ *ste BERIGTE*, the latest news (intelligence); *die* ~ *ste DAG*, judgement day, doomsday; *in die* ~ *ste TYD*, lately; ~ **by**, bee-larva, brood; ~ **byraampie**, brood chamber.
jon'ge, (-s), young one; something young.
jon'ge: ~ **da'me**, young lady; (vero.), ~ **dog'ter**, young girl, spinster; ~ **heer'**, young gentleman; Master (in address); ~ **juf'frou**, young lady; Miss (in address).
jon'geliede, young people; ~ **vereniging**, young peoples' association.
jon'geling, (-e), youth, young man; adolescent; ~ **sjare**, years of boyhood; ~ **skap**, youth, adolescence; young men; ~ **svereniging**, young men's association.
jon'gelui, *see* **jongeliede**.
jon'gens: ~ **agtig**, (-e), boyish; ~ **agtigheid**, boyishness; ~ **gek**, girl fond of boys, flirt; ~ **jare**, boyhood years; ~ **klere**, boys' clothing.
jon'genstreek, boyish trick.
jon'ger, younger, junior; ~ **e**, (-s), junior; disciple, follower; *die* ~ *es van Jesus*, Jesus' disciples; ~ **ig**, (-e), rather young, youngish.

jon'getjie¹, (-s), young one; something young; *vang 'n* ~, catch a young one.
jon'getjie², (-s), boy, youth, lover; ~**skind**, boy; ~**skool**, (vero.), boys' school; ~**smaniere**, boyish manners.
jong'gesel, bachelor, unmarried man.
jong'getroude, (-s), newly-married person; ~ *paar*, newly-married couple.
jon'gie, (-s), chappy, boy, laddie, sonny.
jong'kêrel, bachelor, young man; lover; *sy lyf* ~ *hou*, pose as a bachelor.
jongleer', (ge-), juggle; tour as minstrel.
jongleur', (-s), jongleur, minstrel; juggler.
jong; ~ **man**, young man, stripling; ~ **meisie**, young girl, adolescent; spinster.
jong'mens, (-e, jongelui), young person; *die* ~*e*, the young people.
jong'os, young ox; tolly; ~ *se inspan*, vomit; retch, throw up, shoot the cat; ~ **gras**, crow-foot, goose-grass, crab-grass *(Eleusine indica)*.
jong'perd, young horse (about 2 years old).
jongs: *van* ~ *af*, from an early age, from childhood.
jongs'lede, last; ~ *Dinsdag*, Tuesday last.
jong'span, young people, youngsters, kids.
jong'ste, youngest; minimus; ~ *in diensjare*, junior in length of service.
jonk¹, (s) (-e), junk.
jonk², (b) (predicative) young; recent; *'n mens is maar EEN maal* ~, one is young only once; ~ *GEWEND en oud gedaan (gedoen)*, use doth breed habit in a man; once a use and ever a custom; ~ *van JARE, maar oud van dae*, an old head on young shoulders; *wat* ~ *is, SPEEL graag*, - *wat oud is, neul graag*, children like playing, old people prefer complaining.
jon'kas, (gew.), fellow, chap.
jonk: ~**er**, (-e, -s), ~**heer**, "jonkheer" (Dutch); junker (German); squire; *'n KAAL* ~*er*, an upstart; a social pretender; *hoe KALER* ~ *er hoe groter pronker*, great boast, small roast; he that is full of himself is ever empty; ~**heid**, youth, juvenility; ~*heid is ydelheid*, youth pursues vanity; ~**man**, (-s), bachelor, young man; lover; ~**manskap**, bachelorship; ~**vrou**, young lady; maiden, damsel; honourable miss; ~**vroulik**, (-e), maidenly, coy.
Jood¹, (Jode), Jew; *twee Jode weet wat 'n BRIL kos*, it takes a thief to catch a thief; *HY is 'n* ~, he is a miser; *daar gaan weer 'n* ~ *HEMEL toe*, there is an angel passing over; *Jode en JODEGENOTE*, Jew and Gentile alike; *'n* ~ *KUL*, save a match and buy a farm; *aan die Jode OORGELEWER wees*, have been delivered into the hands of the Philistines; *Jode en SAMARITANE hou nie gemeenskap nie*, the Jews and Samaritans have no dealings with one another; *die WANDELENDE* ~, the wandering Jew.
jood² = **jodium**.
Joods, (-e), Jewish; *dit gaan soos in 'n* ~*e kerk*, it is like a Polish diet, it is like bedlam broken loose; ~**heid**, ~**kap**, state, quality of being a Jew.
jool, (s) (jole), (students') rag; fun, jollifications; (w) (ge-), frolic, ~**blad**, rag magazine.
joon, (jone), fishing-buoy, dan.
joos, devil, Old Nick; enraged person, animal; *mag die* ~ *jou HAAL*, the devil take you; *HOE die* ~ *het dit gebeur?*, how on earth did it happen?; *dit mag* ~ *WEET*, goodness knows; *see josie*.
jop, (sl.), job, task, work; *die* ~ *doen*, do the job; serve.
jop'pelsee = **jobbelsee**.
jop'(pie), (-s), job.
Jordaan', Jordan (river); *die* ~ *deurgaan*, die.
Jorda'nië, Jordan: ~**r**, (-s), Jordanian.
Jorda'nies, (b) (-e), Jordanian.
jo'sef¹, (-s), josup, elephant-fish *(Callorhynchus capensis)*.
Jo'sef², Joseph; *ALMAL is nie* ~*s nie*, all are not so discreet and wise as Joseph; *'n GESLAG wat* ~ *nie geken het nie*, a generation which knew not Joseph; *die REGTE* ~, Mr. Right; ~**skleed**, coat of many colours; **j**~**skleed**, plant with multi-coloured leaves *(Coleus)*.

jo'sie, (-s), the devil; *mag die* ~ *jou HAAL*, the devil take you; *die* ~ *IN wees*, be in a rage (fury); *'N* ~, a Tartar; *die* ~ *in MAAK*, make one's blood boil; ~**s**, (-e), devilish, confounded; *ek was* ~*s MOEG*, I was deadbeat; *'n* ~ *se VROUMENS*, a shrewish woman; ~**skind**, little devil, rascal, limb of Satan.
jo'ta, (-s), iota, jot; *geen* ~ *of titel(tjie) nie*, not one jot or tittle.
jou¹, (w) (ge-), boo; hoot.
jou², (w) (ge-), address familiarly; *iem. sommer* ~, speak familiarly (disrespectfully) to a person; ~**e**, yours; *dis* ~*e (joune)*, it is yours; (vnw) you; your; *hy het* ~ *waarlik waar toegestem*, he actually consented.
jou'ery, booing.
joule, (-s), joule.
jouself', yourself; *HOU een vir* ~, keep one for yourself; *WEES* ~, be yourself.
joviaal', (joviale), jovial, jolly.
jovialiteit', joviality.
j''tjie, (-s), small j.
ju'bel, (s) rejoicing, cheering, jubilation; (w) (ge-), rejoice, shout with joy, be jubilant, cheer, exult, jubilate; ~**end**, (-e), jubilant; ~**fees**, jubilee; ~**ing**, (-e), jubilation; ~**jaar**, jubilee year; ~**kreet**, jubilation, shout of joy; cry of delight, vociferous cheering; ~**lied**, song of rejoicing; ~**sang**, paean; ~**toon**, (tones of) jubilation, joyful accents.
jubila'ris, (-se), person celebrating his jubilee; hero of the feast.
jubileer', (ge-), jubilate; celebrate one's jubilee; le'**ring**, jubilation.
jubilc'um, (..lea, -s), jubilee, ~**nommer**, jubilee issue.
Ju'da, Judah; ~**ïes**, (-e), Judaic(al); ~**ïs'me**, Judaism.
Ju'das¹, Judas, Jude.
ju'das², (-se), betrayer, traitor; ~**bok**, judas goat; ~**boom**, Judas tree; ~**haar**, red hair; ~**kus**, the kiss of Judas; traitor's kiss; ~**lag**, treacherous laugh; ~**loon**, traitor's reward; ~**streek**, treachery of a Judas, betrayal, disloyal trick.
Jude'a, Judaea.
Jude'ër, (s) (-s), Judaean.
Judees', (b) (**Judese**), Judaean.
judikatuur', judicature.
judisieel', (..siële), judical.
ju'do, judo.
juf'fer, (-s), young lady, damsel, miss; dead-eye (naval); ~**agtig**, (-e), ~**sagtig**, (-e), like a young lady, prim; ~**tjie**, (-s), little miss (lass), missy, lassie; ~**tjie-in-die-groen**, love-in-the-mist *(Nigella damascena)*; ~**tjie-roer-by-die-nag**, cat's tail *(Struthiola)*.
juf'fie, (-s), young lady, missy.
juf'frou, (e-, -ens), miss, young lady, (lady) teacher; *soos die* ~ *sing, wil ook die diensmaagd sing*, like mistress, like maid; ~**tjie**, (-s), missy.
jug'leer, Russian leather.
juig, (ge-), rejoice, exult; jubilate; ~**end**, (-e), jubilant; ~**kreet**, shout of joy; ~**toon**, joyful tone, jubilation, merry shout.
juis, (b) (-te), accurate, exact, correct; right; precise; proper, appropriate; (bw) exactly, precisely; rightly; just(ly); aright; ~ *DAAROM*, for that very reason; *daar GAAN dit* ~ *om*, that is just the point; ~ *ter GESÊ*, to put it more precisely; *daar KOM hy* ~, there he himself comes; ~ *wat NODIG is*, just exactly what is needed; *dat dit NOU* ~ *moet gebeur*, that it should happen now of all times; *SEER* ~, exactly; *die* ~*te gedragslyn VOLG*, follow the proper course (of action); *ek WOU* ~, I was just going to.
juistement', **juis'tement**, exactly, certainly, quite so, precisely.
juist'held, correctness, exactitude, exactness, rectitude, precision, accuracy; propriety, appropriateness; *die* ~ *nagaan van*, verify the accuracy of.
juju'be, (-s), jujube *(Zizyphus)*.
juk, (s) (-ke), yoke; pile; pier (bridge); beam (balance); cross-bar; ~ *toe AANJAAG (aankeer)*, round up for work; *die* ~ *(AFGOOI) AFSKUD*, throw off the yoke; *onder die* ~ *BRING*, bring under the

joke; reduce to subjugation; *onder die* ~ *BUIG,* pass one's neck under the yoke; *'n* ~ *DRA,* bear the yoke; *IN die* ~, in harness; *die* ~ *in 'n mens se JEUG dra,* bear the yoke in one's youth; *nooit teen die* ~ *KOM nie,* never do a stroke of work; never to put one's shoulder to the wheel; *hom onder die* ~ *KROM,* bow one's neck to the yoke; *vas teen die* ~ *LOOP,* strain under the yoke; *die* ~ *NEERLÊ,* retire from service; *in dieselfde* ~ *TREK,* associate with, co-operate with; pull together; (w) **(ge-),** yoke, put the yoke upon; (w) **(ge-)** = **jeuk;** ~ **been,** cheekbone, yoke-bone, jugal bone; ~ **boog,** zygomatic arch; ~ **brug,** pile-bridge; ~ **bout,** trunnion; ~ **maat,** yokemate, yokefellow; partner in marriage; ~ **os,** draught-ox.

juk'skei, (-e), yoke-pin, yoke-skey; jukskei (game); ~ *BREEK,* refuse to co-operate; cut up rough; resign from a party; cause trouble; *'n klein* ~ *met 'n groot KOP (knop),* a person of many parts; a handyman; a thing of many uses; *'n ORIGE* ~, the fifth wheel to the coach; a fly on the wheel; *elkeen STAAN voor sy eie* ~, everyone must fend for himself; ~ **breker,** maverick; ~ **gat,** skey-hole; ~ **laer,** jukskei club; ~ **liga,** jukskei league; ~ **spel,** jukskei game.

jul, (verkorte vorm van **julle),** (skryft.), you; your.

Juliaan', Julian; ~ **s',** (-e), Julian; ~ *se tydrekening,* Julian calendar.

Ju'lie, July; ~ **maand,** the month of July; ~ **wedren** *(in Durban),* (Durban) July Handicap.

julien'ne, julienne (soup).

Ju'lies: *die* ~ *e Alpe,* the Julian Alps.

jul'le, you, your; ~ **self,** yourselves.

Ju'nie, June; ~ **maand,** the month of June.

ju'nior, (-es, -s), junior; ~ **sertifikaateksamen,** Junior Certificate Examination.

junk'sie, (-s), junction, joint.

Ju'no, Juno; **Ju'nies, (-e),** Junonian.

jun'ta, (-s), junta.

Ju'piter, Jupiter, Jove; ~ **agtig,** Jovian.

Juras'sies, (-e), Jurassic.

juri'dies, (-e), juridical; legal; forensic.

ju'rie, (-s), jury; *in die* ~ *dien,* serve on the jury; ~ **bank,** jurybox; ~ **diens,** jury service; ~ **lid,** juryman, juror, member of the jury.

juris', (-te), jurisconsult; barrister, lawyer; ~ **dik'sie,** jurisdiction; cognisance; ~ **pruden'sie,** jurisprudence; ~ **tery,** sophistry, legal quibblings.

jurk, (-e), frock, dress; night-dress; overall; ~ **ie, (-s),** little frock.

justeer', (s) weighing; (w) **(ge-),** weight (mint); justify (print); ~ **skaal,** assay-balance.

justifi'na, (-s), sore-eye flower *(Cyrtanthus obliques).*

Justiniaans', (-e), Justinian.

Justinia'nus, Justinian.

justi'sie, justice; judicature; *MINISTER van J* ~, Minister of Justice; *aan die* ~ *OORLEWER,* hand over to the law.

justisieel', (..siële), justiciable; judicial.

Jut¹, (-te), Jute.

jut²: *dowe* ~, davit; ~ **goed,** jetsam.

ju'te, jute; ~ **sak,** jute bag.

Jut'land, Jutland; ~ **er, (-s),** Jutlander; ~ **s, (-e),** Jutish, Jutland(ish).

juts, (gew.), boastful, showy; very prim and proper, nonchalant; *EWE* ~ *aangestap kom,* turn up quite unconcerned; ~ *RY,* cut a dash on horseback.

Juvena'lis, Juvenal.

juweel', (juwele), jewel, precious stone, gem; brilliant; ~ **kenner,** gemmologist; ~ **kunde,** gemmology; ~ **setwerk,** jewelling, jewelsettings.

juwe'le: ~ **halsband,** rivière; ~ **kissie,** jewel-box, trinket-box.

juwelier', (-s), jeweller; ~ **s'ware,** jewellery; ~ **s'winkel,** jeweller's shop.

jy; you; one, a person; ~ *kan nooit weet nie,* one never knows; ~ **-en-jou', (g-e):** *iem.* ~ *-en-jou,* address someone with undue familiarity (with disrespect).

K

k, (-'s), k.

kaä'ba, caaba.

kaag, (kae), ketch.

kaai, (-e), quay, wharf; ~ **geld,** wharfage, quayage, jettage; ~ **lyn,** tripping-line.

kaai'man, (-ne, -s), (S. American) alligator; cayman; ~ **sblom,** *Nymphaea capensis;* blue water-lily; ~ **sgat,** river-pool.

kaai: ~ **meester,** wharfinger; ~ **muur,** wharfside, quay-wall; ~ **ruimte,** quayside, wharfage, jettage; ~ **werker,** dock-labourer, longshoreman, quayporter.

kaak¹, (s) pillory; *aan die* ~ *stel,* expose to public contempt, show up.

kaak², (s) **(kake),** jaw; mandible (of insect); gill; jowl; *iem. uit die kake van die DOOD red,* save a person from the jaws of death; *KLEM in die kake,* lockjaw; (w) **(ge-),** gut, gill (fish); ~ **klem,** lock-jaw, tetanus; ~ **kramp,** lock-jaw; trismus; ~ **spier,** jaw muscle.

kaal, (kaler, -ste), bald, bare, naked (head); unfurnished (room); unfledged (bird); hairless; nude, naked (person); leafless (tree); arid, treeless, barren (waste); shabby (jacket); threadbare (trousers); penniless; glabrous; featherless; *daar* ~ *van AFKOM,* be cleaned out (of possessions); come out of something with dishonour; *hoe kaler, hoe BRUTALER,* the poorer, the cockier; *iem.* ~ *MAAK (dop),* win everything from another; fleece a person; clean someone out; *hoe kaler, hoe ROJALER,* great boast, small roast; *iem.* ~ *UITSKUD,* fleece someone; *iem.* ~ *UITTREK,* fleece someone; ~ **basloper,** streaker; ~ **blaar,** ~ **blad,** spineless cactus; ~ **duiker,** skindiver; ~ **eier,** poached egg.

kaal'gaar, kaal'gare, rope-yarn; *Passerina filiformis;* ~ **tou,** rope-yarn; thatching-twine, twisted rope.

kaal'gars, (beardless) barley, barley-wheat.

kaal'gat, (plat.), (s) **(-te),** impoverished (bankrupt) person, pauper; (b) naked; poor, impoverished; ~ **perske,** nectarine.

kaal'geskeer, (-de), clean-shaven.

kaal'hand(e), with bare hands, bare-handed; unarmed.

kaal'hardloper, streaker.

kaal'heid, baldness, alopecia; bareness, barenness; nakedness; threadbareness.

kaalhoof'dig, (-e), bare-headed, baldheaded; ~ **heid,** baldness.

kaal: ~ **kar,** hoodless cart; ~ **kook, (-ge-),** poach (egg).

kaal'kop, (s) baldpate, baldhead, bare head; tuskless elephant; (b, bw) hatless, baldheaded; boldly; *iem.* ~ *jou MENING meedeel,* let someone have it straight from the shoulder; *iem.* ~ *die WAAR= HEID sê (vertel),* reprimand a person without mincing matters, go for a person baldheaded.

kaal: ~ **loper,** nudist; streaker; ~ **maak, (-ge-),** denude; fleece; ~ **making,** denudation; ~ **nael,** streaking; ~ **naeler,** streaker; ~ **pak,** flesh tights; ~ **perske,** nectarine; ~ **rug,** bare-backed.

kaal'siekte, alopecia; ~ **bossie,** *Chrysocoma tenuifolia.*

kaal: ~ **te,** smoothness, bareness, baldness; bald spot; open patch (e.g. in the veldt); ~ **voet,** barefooted; discalceate(d); ~ **vreter,** locust; ~ **vuis,** bareknuckled; bluntly, without mincing matters; straight from the shoulder; ~ **wa,** tentless (open) wagon.

kaam'bessie, wild plum *(Pappea capensis).*

Kaap¹, the Cape (Province); the Cape Peninsula; Cape Town; *by die ~ DRAAI*, to be long-winded; *die ~ die GOEIE Hoop*, the Cape of Good Hope; *as dit hier so GAAN, hoe gaan dit nie in die ~ nie*, if this is how things are here, how must they be else‑ where? *jy het nog nie die ~ GESIEN nie*, you have seen nothing of the world yet; *iets by die ~ gaan HAAL*, take an age about something; *die ~ is weer HOLLANDS*, all is well again; everything in the garden is rosy once more; *juig omdat die ~ weer HOLLANDS is*, rejoice that all is well again; *by die ~ OMGAAN*, go a roundabout way; *so stomp dat 'n mens daarop ~ toe kan RY*, very blunt (knife); *eers die ~ SIEN*, want to see the world first; *iem. die ~ WYS*, pick someone up by the ears.

kaap², (s) **(kape)**, cape, promontory, head(land), naze; foreland; *'n ~ omseil*, double a cape.

kaap³, (w) **(ge-)**, practise piracy, steal, rob, filch, privateer; highjack (aeroplane).

Kaap: ~**kolonie**, Cape Colony (Province); ~**land**, the Cape (Province); ~**lander, (-s)**, person from the Cape; ~**provinsie**, Cape Province.

Kaaps, (s) (hist.), Cape (Province); Cape Dutch; Afri‑ kaans; (b) **(-e)**, Cape; *die ~ e DOKTER*, the south‑ easter; *~ e DRAAI*, long, wide turn; *~ e DRAAIE maak*, take wide turns; not utter your intentions (meaning) directly; be roundabout; *~ e MIDDEL‑ LANDE*, Cape Midlands; *~ e NOOI(E)NTJIE*, Cape lady; bluefish; *Monodactylus falciformis*; *Stromateus fiatola*; *~ e SLOPEEND*, Cape shovel‑ lor; *e TON*, short ton; *e VY — HOTTEN‑ TOTSVY*; *~ e WOLKIES*, Magellanic clouds; (s) ~**-Hollands**, (hist.), Afrikaans; Cape Dutch.

Kaap′stad, Cape Town.

kaap′stander, capstan.

kaap: ~**vaarder, (-s)**, privateer; ~**vaart**, privateering.

Kaap-Ver′diese eilande, Cape Verde Islands.

kaar, (kare), cirque.

kaard, (ge-), card, tease, comb (wool); ~**e, (-s)**, card (for wool); ~**er, (-s)**, carder, teaser, comber; ~**ery**, carding, combing; ~**garing**, woollen yarn; ~**mas‑ jien**, gig-mill; ~**ster, (-s)**, comber, carder (woman); ~**stof**, woollen fabric; ~**wol**, card-wool.

kaart, (s) **(-e)**, map, chart; card; diagram; plan; ticket (concert); *dis BOKANT my ~*, it has me beat; *in ~ BRING*, plot; map out; *'n DEURGESTOKE ~*, a trumped-up affair; a prearranged affair; *sy ~ e is DEURMEKAAR*, his affairs are in a mess; *~ e en KANNE maak arm manne*, gaming, women and wine, which they laugh, they make men pine; *die e ken*, know what's what; *in iem se ~ e KYK*, spy out someone's secrets; pry into another's affairs; *jou nie in die ~ e laat KYK nie*, not to show one's hand; *'n ~ in die MOU hê*, have something up one's sleeve; *'n PAK ~ e*, a pack of cards; *oop ~ e SPEEL*, lay one's cards on the table; *alles op een ~ SIT*, stake everything on one throw; *in iem. se ~ e SPEEL*, play into someone's hands; *'n mens moet SPEEL met die ~ e wat jy het*, one must make the best of the cards one holds; *moenie jou beste ~ e eerste SPEEL nie*, never play your best card first; *die beste ~ e eerste SPEEL*, play one's trump card first; *~ en TRANSPORT*, title-deeds; *die VER‑ KEERDE ~ speel*, play the wrong card; *iem. sy ~ e laat WYS*, make someone show his cards; (w) **(ge-)**, play at cards; chart, map; ~**aandjie**, card-party; ~**bakkie**, card-tray; ~**boekie**, card-case; ~**emaker**, cartographer; mapmaker; ~**ehuis**, house of cards; *soos 'n ~ huis inmekaarstort*, col‑ lapse like a house of cards; ~**jie, (-s)**, ticket, card; ~**jiesdatumpers**, ticket-dating press; ~**jies‑ kantoor**, booking-office; ticket-office; pay-box, box-office; ~**jiesknipper**, ticket-punch; conductor; ticket-collector; collector; ~**jiesloket**, ticket-hatch; ~**jiesondersoeker**, ticket examiner; ~**jiesverkoop**, sale of tickets; ticket sales; booking; ~**kamer**, card-room; map-room (at school); chart-room (on ship); ~**kas**, card-index cabinet; ~**lêer**, card-reader; ~**lêery**, card-reading, fortune-telling; ~**lees**, map-reading; ~**legster**, female card reader; ~**maker**, cartographer, map-maker; ~**mannetjie**, jack-in-the-box; jumping jack; clown; cheeky fel‑ low; ~**net**, skeleton map; ~**outomaat**, passimeter; ~**projeksie**, map-projection; ~**register**, card in‑ dex; ~**sisteem**, card-index system.

kaart′speel, (-ge), play cards; ~**ster**, (lady) card-player.

kaart′spel, game of cards, card-game, card-playing; ~**er**, card-player.

kaart: ~**stelsel**, card-index system; ~**tafel**, card-table; ~**tekenaar**, cartographer; ~**tekenkuns**, car‑ tography; ~**vuur**, firing by map; ~**waarsêry**, cartomancy.

Kaas, Kase, (geselst.), Hollander.

kaas, (kase), cheese; *hy laat hom nie die ~ van die BROOD eet nie*, he will not be done out of any‑ thing; *DINK dat hy ~ is en dan is hy nog nie eers dikmelk nie*, be very conceited; *hy EET ~*, he is courting; *hy het sy ~ GEHAD*, he has had enough; *LUS hê vir ~*, not to know quite what one wants; ~**agtig, (-e)**, cheesy, caseous; ~**bereiding**, cheese-making; ~**boor**, cheese-scoop, cheese-taster; ~**bord**, cheese-plate; ~**burger**, cheeseburger; ~**doek**, cheese-cloth; ~**fabriek**, cheese factory; ~**gereg, (-te)**, cheese dish; ~**gif**, tyrotoxin; ~**han‑ del**, cheese trade; ~**handelaar**, cheesemonger; ~**happie**, cheesenip; ~**kamer**, cheese-room; ~**kleursel**, cheese colouring, annatto; ~**kop**, fool, blockhead; **K~kop**, (skerts., geselst.), Hollander; ~**koper**, cheesemonger; ~**kors**, cheese rind; ~**kor‑ sies**, cheese-parings; ~**maaier**, cheese-mite, cheese-skipper; ~**maker**, cheese-maker; ~**makery**, cheese factory; cheese-making; ~**mark, (-te)**, cheese mar‑ ket; ~**melk**, cheese-milk; ~**mes**, cheese-cutter; ~**miet**, cheese-maggot; ~**omelet**, cheese omelette; ~**pakhuis**, cheese-store; ~**pers**, cheese press; ~**reuk**, smell of cheese; ~**skottel**, cheese dish; ~**soufflé**, cheese soufflé; ~**sous**, cheese sauce; ~**stof**, casein(e); ~**stokkie**, cheese straw; ~**stolp**, cheese cover; ~**stremsel**, rennet; ~**vorm**, cheese-mould; chessel; ~**winkel**, cheese-shop; ~**wurm**, cheese-maggot.

kaat′jie¹: *~ van die baan wees*, be cock of the walk.

Kaat′jie²: *~ Kekkelbek*, chatterbox; tattler.

kaatjievrek′, card game.

kaats, (ge-), play (at) ball; ~**baan**, fives court; dutch hand-tennis, court tennis.

kabaai′, (-e), loose gown, banian; sleeping gown.

kabaal′, noise, hubbub, clamour, rumpus; cabal; *daar was 'n HELSE ~*, bedlam broke loose; *~ MAAK (opskud)*, raise Cain; raise the roof; ~**maker**, rowdy person.

kabaret′, (-te), cabaret; ~**liedjie**, cabaret song; ~**san‑ ger(es)**, cabaret singer; ~**tis′, (-te)**, cabaret enter‑ tainer.

kabba′la, kab′bala, cabala.

kabbalis′, (-te), cab(b)alist; ~**ties, (-e)**, cab(b)alistic.

kab′bel, (s) ripple, babble, popple, purl; (w) **(ge-)**, babble, ripple, purl, lap; ~**ing, (-e, -s)**, rippling, lapping, purling, babbling.

ka′bel, (s) **(-s)**, cable; (w) **(ge-)**, cable; ~**a′ring, (-s)**, messenger (chain, rope); ~**baan**, wire-rope rail‑ way; cable road; ~**ballon**, captive balloon; ~**berig, (-te)**, cablegram; ~**boei**, cable buoy; ~**boor**, cable drill; ~**garing**, cable yarn; ~**geul**, cable trench; ~**gram, (-me)**, cablegram; ~**hangdraad**, cable sus‑ pension wire; ~**hanger**, cable suspender; ~**houer**, cable cramp; ~**hysing**, cable haulage; ~**inleistuk**, cable gland.

kabeljou′, (-e), Cape salmon (deep sea); *Johnius holo‑ lepidotus*; cod (fish) (*Gadus morrhua*); ~**kuit**, cod roe; ~**vangs**, cod-fishing; ~**visser**, cod-fisher; ~**vissery**, cod-fishing.

ka′bel: ~**kanaal**, cable duct; ~**klem**, cable thimble (clip); ~**koste**, cable expenses; ~**las, (-se)**, cable joint; ~**lasser**, cable jointer; ~**lêer**, cable layer; ~**legging**, cable-laying; ~**leiding**, cable line; ~**lengte**, cable's length; range; ~**mof**, cable sleeve; ~**net**, electric mains; ~**onderhoud**, cable mainten‑ ance; ~**ontspanner**, cable release; ~**pale**, bitts (ship); ~**roete**, cable route; ~**rol**, cable reel; ~**ruimte**, capacity of conduits; ~**skip**, cable ship; ~**skoen**, cable-end connector; ~**spoor**, cableway, funicular railway; ~**spoorweg**, cable (funicular)

railway; ~**steek,** cable stitch; ~**string,** cable strand; core; ~**tou,** cable; ~**trommel,** cable drum; ~**vervoer,** cable haulage; ~**wa, (-ens),** cable wagon; ~**weg,** cable route; ~**wissel,** telegraphic transfer.
kabie', (-s), arum-lily.
kabinet', (-te), cabinet; ministry; closet; ~**formaat,** cabinet-size; ~**hout,** *Philippia chamisonis;* ~**jie, (-s),** small cabinet (closet); ~**maker,** cabinet-maker, joiner; ~**poeding,** cabinet pudding; ~**portret, (-te),** cabinet photograph; ~**s'besluit,** decision of the cabinet; ~**seël,** government seal; ~**s'hervorming,** reshuffle of cabinet; ~**s'krisis, (-se),** cabinet crisis; ~**s'kwessie,** cabinet question; ~**s'raad,** cabinet council; ~**stuk,** cabinet painting; ~**vergadering,** cabinet meeting; ~**werk,** cabinet work.
kabob', cabob.
kaboe'del, lot, caboodle.
kaboe'mielie, (-s), (unbroken) boiled mealie.
kaboes', (-e), caboose.
kabou'ter, (-s), gnome, elf, imp, brownie; pug-dog; pixy, pooka, goblin; ~**mannetjie,** hobgoblin, elf, puck.
kabriolet', (-te), cabriolet.
kabriool', (..riole), cabriole.
kadans', (-e), cadence; lilt.
kadas'ter, (-s), cadastre; land registry.
kadastraal', (..strale), cadastral.
kada'wer, (-s), corpse, cadaver; ~**eus', (-e),** cadaverous.
Kad'disj, Kaddish.
ka'de, (-s), quay, wharf.
ka'der, frame, skeleton; limits, scope; framework; *in sy* ~ *PAS,* suit someone's purpose; *dit PAS nie in die* ~ *nie,* it is irrelevant (unsuitable); it does not fit into the scheme; ~**kaart,** skeleton map; ~**personeel,** skeleton staff.
kadet', (-te), cadet; ~**korps,** cadet corps; ~**offisier,** cadet officer; ~**skap,** cadetship.
ka'di, (-'s), kadi.
ka'die, African beer.
kad'mium, cadmium.
kado', (-'s), cadeau, present; *nie iets* ~ *wil hê nie,* not have it as a gift.
kado''tjie, (-s), small present.
kadot', (-te), hat.
kadriel', (-e), quadrille.
kaduks', dilapidated, decrepit, decayed; ill; exhausted, worn-out; ~ *voel,* feel worn-out; ~**heid,** caducity, decay.
kaf¹, (s) **(-te),** paper cover, wrapper, book-jacket.
kaf², (s) chaff; glume; nonsense, bilge, eyewash, punk, poppycock; bunk, tommy-rot; *dis ALLES* ~, it's all nonsense; *daar is baie* ~ *onder die koring,* there is much that is draff (dross); *die* ~ *van die KORING skei,* separate the wheat from the chaff; *die* ~ *kan jy op 'n ander MARK gaan verkoop,* tell that to the marines; *iem.* ~ *in die ORE blaas,* spin someone a yarn; *dis PURE* ~, it's utter (sheer) nonsense; *iem. met* ~ *VANG,* impose upon a person easily; ~ *VERKOOP,* talk nonsense; talk through one's hat; *soos* ~ *voor die WIND,* like chaff before the wind; (b, bw) to pieces, in tatters, pulverized; *klere* ~ *DRA,* wear clothes to pieces; *geslaan deur die HAEL,* smashed to shreds by hail; ~ ~ **agtig, (-e),** chaffy; ~**baal,** bale (bag) of chaff; *'n* ~ *baal,* a man of straw; ~**blaartjie,** glume; ~**draf, (-ge-),** overcome completely; beat easily; finish off (work); devour, polish off, consume (eatables).
kafee', (-s), café; ~**bediende,** waitress (in café); ~**houer,** café-proprietor; ~**-restourant,** café-restaurant; ~**tjie,** small café.
kafeïen', kafeï'ne, caffeine.
kafete'ria, cafeteria.
kaf'fer: ~**bessie,** *Grewia cana (flava);* ~**blits,** (vero.), cheap sweets; ~**boom,** coral tree *(Erythrina);* ~**broodboom,** kaffir-bread tree *(Encephalartos altensteinii);* ~**druiwe,** dwarf shrub *(Pollichia campestris);* ~**slangwortel;** root of *Polygala serpentaria;* ~**tee,** scented plant *(Helichrysum nudifolium);* ~**tjie, (-s),** brownish-black plant *(Wurmbea spicata);* ~**vink,** kaffir finch, red bishop-bird *(Ploceidae);* ~**-wag-'n-bietjie,** cat-thorn *(Acacia caffra);* ~**wortel,** medicinal plant *(Sansevieria thrysiflora),* pileroot.
kaf'hok, chaff barn.
kaf'loop, (-ge-), beat, overcome; finish easily; pip, polish off (food); make mince-meat of; *iem.* ~, knock spots off someone.
kafoe'fel, (ge-), woo, flirt, spoon.
kaf: ~ **praatjies,** nonsense, trash, blether, small (idle) talk, old wives' tales, piffle; ~**sak,** bag filled with chaff; ~**snyer,** chaff-cutter.
kaf'tan, (-s), caftan.
kag'gel, (-s), fireplace; chimney-piece; range; ~**besempie,** fire-brush; ~**pyp,** stove-pipe; chimney-pot hat; ~**steen,** hearthstone; ~**stel, (-le),** fire-irons.
kai'a, (-s), African dwelling; hut.
kai'ing, (-s), greave(s), browsel(s); cacklings; screeds; *jou* ~ *s sal BRAAI,* you'll pay for it; *hy is HARDE* ~, he is cheeky (cocky); *daar sal* ~ *s van KOM,* nothing will come of that; *dit sal* ~ *s KOS,* it will take some doing; *dit was KOUE* ~ *s,* it was worthless; it was of no earthly use; *sy* ~ *s TEËKOM,* meet one's match; ~**klip,** pudding-stone, flint.
Ka'insmerk, Ka'insteken, brand (mark) of Cain; *'n* ~ *dra,* bear the mark of Cain.
Kaï'ro, (s) Cairo; (b) **(-se),** Cairene.
ka'jak, (-s, -ke), kayak.
kajapoet'olie, cajaput-oil.
kajuit', (-e), cabin; cab; ~**bed,** bunk-bed; ~**jonge,** cabin boy; ~**koffer,** cabin-trunk; ~**raad,** council of war; ~ *raad hou,* deliberate, hold council of war; lay heads together; ~**koepel,** cockpit canopy; ~**trap, (-pe),** companion-way, campanion-ladder; ~**venster,** porthole.
kak, (plat), (s) shit; (w) **(ge-),** pass faeces, shit; ~ *(bars) of betaal, is die wet van Transvaal,* pay up and look pleasant.
kaka'o, cocoa; ~**boontjie,** cocoa bean; ~**botter,** cocoa butter; ~**saad,** cocoa bean.
ka'kebeen, jaw, jowl, jaw-bone; ~**ontsteking,** phossy jaw; ~**wa,** ox-wagon.
ka'kelaar, (-s), wood-hoopoe, babbler, monkey-bird *(Phoeniculus purpureus);* chatterbox.
ka'kelbont, motley, variegated, gaudy.
kaketoe'a, (-s), kaketoe', (-s), cockatoo.
ka'kie, (-s), khaki; British soldier, tommy; Englishman; *jy is* ~ *laat,* you've got a hope; ~**bos,** khaki weed *(Alternanthera achyrantha);* stink ~**bos,** Mexican marigold *(Tagetes minuta);* ~**bosolie,** khaki-bush oil; ~**draf,** post (pace of horse); ~**hemp,** khaki shirt; ~**klere,** khaki clothes; ~**kombers,** military blanket; ~**kweek,** *Alternanthera repens;* ~**pak,** khaki suit.
kak'kerlak, (-ke), cockroach *(Blattidae).*
kakofonie', (-ë), cacophony.
kakofo'nies, (-e), cacophonous.
kakografie', (-ë), cacography.
kak'tus, (-se), cactus; ~**kewer,** cactus beetle *(Cactophagus spinolae).*
ka'labarboon, Calabar bean *(Physostigma venenosum).*
Kalaha'ri, Kalahari.
kalamiteit', (-e), calamity.
kalamyn', (-e), calamine.
kalan'der¹, (s) **(-s),** weevil; calender.
kalan'der², (s) **(-s),** calender (machine); (w) **(ge-),** calender.
kalan'der³, (s) yellowwood *(Podocarpus falcatus).*
kalan'derhout = **kalander³.**
kalan'dermeul, calendry.
kalandery', calendry.
kalant', (-e), rogue, scamp; (old) hand, sly fox, shrewd person; *ou* ~, *lank in die land,* a shrewd fellow, an old hand; an old fox.
kalbas', (-se), calabash, gourd; cucurbit; *so HOL soos 'n* ~, quite hollow; *iem. 'n* ~ *vir 'n KOMKOMMER gee,* sell someone a pup; take someone in; *in die* ~ *KYK,* ply the bottle; ~**blaar,** variety of sweet potato; ~**dop,** calabash rind; gourd; ~**melk,** yoghurt; ~**patat,** variety of marrow; ~**peer,** kind of winter pear; ~**pyp,** calabash pipe.

kalbas'sies, mumps; orchitis; small gourds (calabashes).
kaleidoskoop', (..skope), kaleidoscope.
kaleidosko'pies, (-e), kaleidoscopic.
kalen'der, (-s), calendar, almanac; ~**jaar**, calendar year; ~**maand**, calendar month; ~**meisie**, pin-up girl.
ka'lerig, (-e), rather bare; somewhat bald.
kales', (-se), calash.
kalf, (s) **(kalwers)**, calf; transom; *aan sy kalwers ken jy die BOER*, such carpenters, such chips; *die put DEMP as die* ~ *verdrink het*, lock the stabledoor after the steed has been stolen; *die GEMESTE* ~ *slag*, kill the fatted calf; *die GOUE* ~ *aanbid*, worship the golden calf; *nie al jou kalwers in die HOK hê nie*, have a screw loose; *jong kalwers IN= SPAN*, to cat; shoot the cat; vomit; *kalwers van een JAAR wees*, be of the same age; *vir jou 'n goue* ~ *MAAK*, make a golden calf of something; *die* ~ *in die OOG slaan*, tread on someone's corns; *met 'n ander se* ~ *PLOEG*, plough with another's heifer; *die* ~ *is in die PUT*, necessity knows no law (as an excuse for working on Sunday); needs must (when the devil drives); *die* ~ *is VERDRINK*, the die is cast; *as die* ~ *verdrink het, word die PUT gedemp*, when the steed is stolen the stabledoor is locked; *'n* ~ *in die wingerd*, a bull in a china shop; (w) **(ge-)**, calve, drop calf.
kalfaat', (w) **(ge-)** = **kalfater**; ~**dok**, graving-dock; ~**pluis**, oakum; ~**sel**, (-s), caulking compound; ~**yster**, caulking-iron.
kalf'agtig, (-e), calf-like, vitular.
kalfak'ter, (s) (-s), tool; good-for-nothing, loafer, idler, toady; drudge; cringer; (w) **(ge-)**, drudge; toady; gossip; tinker at.
kalfa'ter, (ge-), caulk, repair (ship), patch up; ~**aar**, (-s), patcher, caulker.
kal'fie, (-s, **kalwertjies**), young calf.
kalfs: ~**bors**, breast of veal; ~**boud**, leg of veal; ~**fi= let**, fillet of veal; ~**karmenaadjie**, veal chop; ~**kop**, calf's head; blockhead; ~**kotelet**, veal cutlet.
kalf'skyf, (..**skywe**), veal steak.
kalfs: ~**leer**, calfskin, calf(-leather); kip; ~**lewer**, calf's liver; ~**long**, calf's lights; ~**nier**, calf's kid= ney; ~**oog**, poached egg; ~**perkament**, vellum; ~**poot**, calf's foot; ~**ribbetjie**, veal rib; ~**tand**, calf's tooth; dentil; ~**vel**, calfskin; kip; ~**vleis**, veal; ~**vleisbrood**, veal loaf; ~**voet**, calf's foot (plant).
ka'li, potash, potassium.
kali'ber, calibre, bore (gun); *'n man van hoë geestelike* ~, a man of high intellectual calibre; · **boor**, bit; ~**maat**, hole-gauge; · **passer**, compass-calipers.
kalibreer', (ge-), calibrate; ~**silinder**, standard plug; ~**staf**, caliper rule.
kalibre'ring, calibration, graduation.
ka'lief, (-s), **kalief'**, (-e), caliph.
kalifaat', caliphate.
Kalifor'nië, California.
Kalifor'nies, (-e), Californian.
ka'liko, (-'s), calico.
ka'lisout, potassium salt.
ka'lium, potassium; ~**permanganaat**, permanganate of potash; ~**sulfaat**, sulphate of potash.
kalk, (s) lime; plaster; roughcast; *ONGEBLUSTE* ~, anhydrous (dehydrated) lime; *GEBLUSTE* ~, slaked lime; ~ *maak ryk VADERS maar arm seuns*, lime makes rich fathers but poor sons; (w) **(ge-)**, lime, limewash; ~**aanpaksel**, lime deposit; ~**aarde**, calcareous earth; ~**agtig**, (-e), lime-like, limy, calcareous; ~**bak**, hod; ~**bank**, lime-stone layer; ~**bedekking**, limecast; ~**brander**, lime-burner; ~**brandery**, limekiln; ~**bry**, lime paste.
kalkeer', (ge-), transfer, trace; ~**linne**, tracing-cloth; ~**papier**, tracing-paper, transfer-paper.
kalk: ~**eier**, waterglass egg; ~**erig (-e) = kalkagtig**; ~**gat**, pot-hole; lime-pit; ~**gras**, *Fingerhuthia afri= cana, Sporobolus acinifolius*; ~**houdend**, (-e), cal= careous, calciferous; ~**klip**, limestone; ~**laag**, chalk-bed; coating of plaster (whitewash); ~**lig**, limelight; *in die* ~*lig*, in the limelight; ~**ligverto=**

ning, limelight show; ~**melk**, milk of lime; ~**mer= gel**, calcareous marl; ~**meule**, mortar mill.
kalkoen', (-e), turkey; *so ROOI soos 'n* ~, as red as a turkey-cock; *nie onder 'n* ~ *UITGEBROEI nie*, be not as green as one looks; ~**belle**, turkey wattles; medicinal herb *(Sutherlandia frutescens)*; ~**eier**, turkey's egg; ~**eiergesig**, freckled face; ~**gif**, shrub *(Physalis angulata)*; ~**kuiken**, poult; ~**mannetjie**, turkey-cock, gobbler, bubbly-jock; *so parmantig soos 'n* ~*mannetjie*, as cheeky as a cock sparrow; ~**tjie**, small turkey; wild bulb *(Gladiolus alatus)*; *Tritonia; Sparaxis grandiflora, Brachystelma*; or= ange-throated longclaw *(Macronyx capensis)*; *wilde* ~ *tjie*, bald ibis; ~**wyfie**, turkey-hen.
kalk: ~**oond**, limekiln; ~**rots**, limestone-rock; ~**sal= peter**, nitrate of lime; ~**spaat**, calcareous spar; car= bonate of lime; ~**steen**, limestone; tufa; ~**verf**, dis= temper; ~**vis**, ribbon fish *(Lepidopus caudatus)*; ~**water**, lime-water.
kalligraaf', (..**grawe**), calligrapher; ~**grafie'**, cal= ligraphy; ..**gra'fies**, (-e), calligraphic(al).
kallistenie', callisthenics; ..**ste'nies**, callisthenic(al).
kallositeit', (-e), callosity.
kal'lus, (-se), callus.
kalm, ([-e]; -er, -ste), calm, quiet, composed, quies= cent, placid; cool; eventless; self-possessed; canny; even (temper); halcyon; ~ *BLY, jou* ~ *HOU*, keep calm and collected; *dit* ~ *OPNEEM*, take it calm= ly; ~ *WORD*, calm (cool) down.
kalmeer', (ge-), calm down, soothe, allay, pacify, tranquillize, quiet, compose, lull, appease; ~**mid= del**, paregoric, sedative, calmative, tranquillizer; ~**pil**, tranquillizer; placebo; ~**stroop**, soothing syrup.
kalme'rend, (-e), calming, soothing, paregoric; ~*e middel*, sedative, tranquillizer.
kalme'ring, calming-down, soothing; sedation.
kalmink', calamanco.
kalmoe'graolie, chaulmoogra oil.
kal'moes, calamus, medicinal herb *(Alepidea uma= tymbica)*; sweet flag; ~**wortel**, orris root.
kalm'pies, calmly, quietly; coolly.
kalm'te, quiescence, composedness, composure, quiet(ness), peace, calm, calmness, self-possession; *jou* ~ *herwin*, regain one's composure.
Kalmuk', (-ke), Kalmuck.
kalm'weg, calmly, coolly.
kalmyn', calamine (zinc ore).
kalomel', calomel.
ka'long, (-s), kalong, fruit-bat, flying fox *(Pteropus vampyrus)*.
kalorie', (-ë), heat unit, calory.
kalo'ries, (-e), caloric; thermal.
kalo'ri = ~**meter**, ~**me'ter**, calorimeter; ~**metrie'**, calorimetry; ~**me'tries**, (-e), calorimetric, caloric.
kalos'sie, (-s), ixia.
kalot'jie, (-s), cap, skull-cap, calotte; brimless woman's hat.
kalpat', (-te), penguin-tick *(Argas talaje)*.
kalsiet', calcite.
kalsina'sie, calcination.
kalsineer', (ge-), calcine, calcinate; ·**oond**, calciner, ..**ne'ring**, calcining.
kal'sium, calcium; ~**houdend**, (-e), calcic; ~**sulfaat**, calcium sulphate; ~**verbinding**, calcium com= pound.
kalumet', (-te, -s), calumet, pipe of peace.
Kalva'rie(berg), (ong.), (Mt.) Calvary.
kal'we, (ge-), *see* **kalf**, (w).
kal'wer: ~**bossie**, calf-bush *(Pelargonium sidoides)*; ~**diarree**, white scours; ~**hok**, calvepen; ~**kop**, mullet (fish); ~**liefde**, calflove; puppy-love; ~**meel**, calf meal; ~**tifus**, calf paratyphoid; ~**vel**, calfskin; ~**vleis**, veal.
kam, (s) (-me), comb; pecten, crest; ridge (of moun= tain); bridge (of violin); cam, cog (of wheel); teas= ing (wool); caruncle (of cock); *GROWWE* ~, rake comb; *sy* ~ *word ROOI*, he sees red; he is begin= ning to notice the girls; *almal oor dieselfde* ~ *SKEER*, treat all alike; lump all together; (w) **(ge-)**, comb; card; ~-**as**, thrust-shaft.
kamas', (-te), gaiter, legging; ~**band**, puttee.

kamas'siehout, boxwood *(Gonioma kamassi)*.
kam'been, sphenoid bone.
kam'bene, chine.
kam'bium, cambium (metal).
Kambod'ja, Cambodia.
Kambodjaan', (..jane), Cambodian; ~s', (-e), Cambodian.
kam'bolwol, tops.
Kam'bries, (-e), Cambrian; ..brium, Cambrian.
kambro', (-'s), edible fleshy bulb *(Fockea)*.
Kam'deboo, Camdeboo; ~stinkhout, Camdeboo (white) stinkwood *(Celtis africana)*.
kam: ~draad, worsted yarn; ~draend, (-e), crested.
kamee', (-s, kameë), cameo.
kameel', (kamele), camel; giraffe; ~doring, camelthorn; ~haar, camel's-hair; ~haarkwas, camelhair brush; ~haarstof, camlet; ~korps, camelry, camel corps; ~perd, giraffe; ~perdbul, giraffe bull; ~sool, sole of giraffe-hide; ~ruitery, camelry; ~ryer, cameleer; ~sweep, whip of giraffe-hide; ~vel, camel-skin.
kame'leon, (-s), chameleon; ~'ties, (-e), fickle, unstable, changeable.
kame'lia, (-s), camellia.
kamelot', camlet.
kamenier', (-e, -s), chambermaid; lady's-maid.
ka'mer, (-s), room, chamber; ventricle (heart); *DONKER* ~, dark room; *dit HAPER iem. in die boonste* ~, there is something wrong in his top storey; *jou* ~ *moet HOU,* have to keep to one's room; have to be confined to one's room; ~*s te HUUR,* rooms to let; *K*~ *van KOOPHANDEL,* Chamber of Commerce; *K*~ *van MYNWESE,* Chamber of Mines; ~ *met ONTBYT,* room and breakfast; *op* ~*s WOON,* live in rooms.
ka'mera, (-s), camera.
kameraad', (..rade), comrade, companion, fellow, mate; ~skap, companionship, cameraderie, (good-)fellowship, freemasonry, comradeship; ~skaplik, (-e), companionable, chummy, pally; ~skap'likheid, good-fellowship, cameraderie, companionableness.
kameraderie', cameraderie, palliness.
ka'mer: ~arres, confinement (to one's room); ~deur, door of room; ~baadjie, dressing-jacket; ~bediende, valet; chambermaid; ~buks, saloon rifle; ~dienaar, chamberlain, valet; ~doek, cambric; muslin; lawn; ~doeks, (-e), cambric; ~emmer, slop-pail; ~geleerde, closet-scholar; ~gimnastiek, indoor gymnastics; ~heer, gentleman-in-waiting; Master of the Robe; chamberlain; ~huur, chamber-rent, room-rent; ~japon, dressing-gown; ~jas, dressing-gown, morning-gown; ~konsert, chamber concert; ~lading, bursting charge; ~lid, (~lede), member of chamber of deputies; ~ling, (-e), chamberlain; ~meisie, lady's maid; abigail; ~musiek, chamber music; ~mussie, boudoir-cap.
Kameroen', The Cameroons.
ka'mer: ~orkes, chamber orchestra; ~plant, indoor plant; house-plant; ~pot, chamber (pot); ~s, dig(ging)s; rooms; ~sindelik, house-broken; ~skietbaan, miniature rifle-range; ~stel, bedroom suite; ~tennis, fives; ~tjie, (-s), small room; cell; ~toneel, intimate theatre; ~venster, window of a room; ~wag, orderly; ~woning, flat, maisonette.
Ka'meryk, Cambrai.
kam: ~gare, ..garing, worsted yarn; whipcord; ~hare, combings; ~hout, camwood *(Baphia nitida)*.
kamil'le, camomile; ~olie, oil of camomile; ~tee, camomile tea.
kamisool', (..sole), camisole.
kam'ma, kammakas'tig, kammalie'lies, quasi, as if (it were), for pretence, would-be; pseudo; *hy het* ~ *geleer,* he pretended to study.
kam'maland, dreamland, fairyland, Utopia.
kam'masjien, teasel.
kam'merband, (-e), cummerbund.
kam'metjie, (-s), small comb; freesia *(Freezia refracta)*.
kam'mie, (-s), room-mate.

kam'miebos, *Cliffortia strobilifera*.
kam'mossel, scallop, cockle(burr).
kamoefla'ge = camouflage.
kamoefleer', (ge-), camouflage, disguise.
kamp¹, (s) (-e), camp, encampment, cantonment; enclosure (cattle, fowls), paddock; ~ *OPBREEK,* strike camp; ~ *OPSLAAN,* encamp, pitch camp; (w) (ge-), make paddocks; divide into paddocks.
kamp², (s) fight, struggle, combat; (w) (ge-), fight, struggle; *te* ~ *e hê met,* have to contend with.
kampan'je, (-s), campaign; poopdeck; ~trap, companionway (ladder).
kampanologie', campanology.
kamp'diens, camp-meeting.
kampeer', (ge-), encamp, camp out; pitch (camp); bivouac; ~der, (-s), camper.
kampement', (-e), encampment, camp.
kamperfoe'lie, honeysuckle, woodbine.
kampernoe'lie, (-s), edible mushroom.
kamp'hospitaal, camp-hospital.
kam'pie, (-s), small camp; paddock; pen.
kampioen', (-e), champion; ~prys, blue ribbon; ~skap, championship; ~skapbyeenkoms, championship meeting.
kamp: ~kommandant, camp commander; ~leër, camp idler, deserter; ~motor, caravan; camper.
kam'pong, (-s), compound.
kamp: ~plek, camping-site; arena; ~regter, umpire, referee; ~stryd, struggle (for liberty).
kam'pus, (-se), campus.
kamp: ~vegter, fighter, champion; ~vorming, castramentation; ~vuur, camp-fire.
kam'rat, cog-wheel; cam-wheel; rack-wheel, rag-wheel.
kam'stig, kam'tig, quasi-, as if (it were), for pretence, would-be.
kam: ~stof, worsted fabric; ~vormig, (-e), ctenoid, comb-shaped, pectinate; ~wiel, spur-gear; spur-wheel.
kam'wol, comb-wool, combings, top-wool (combings, tops); ~opbrengs, top-yield.
kan¹, (s) (-ne-), can, jug, pot, tankard; *los die* ~ *en vat die BOTTEL,* don't say "can't", say "can"; *alles is in* ~ *ne en KRUIKE,* everything is cut and dried; *in die* ~ *KYK,* ply the bottle; *LIEFHEBBER v.d.* ~, a tippler; *wie die ONDERSTE uit die* ~ *wil hê, kry die deksel op sy neus,* covet all, lose al.
kan², (w) (ge-, het kon, het kan), be able, can, may; *so AL wat jy* ~, for all you are worth; *dit* ~ *nie ANDERS nie,* there is no other choice; *sy* ~ *nie MEER nie,* she is exhausted; she cannot carry on; ~ *jy nou MEER!* well I never! *ek kon hom gerus SKOP,* I felt like kicking him; *sy* ~ *daar nie VOOR nie,* it is not her fault; *dit* ~ *WAAR wees,* it may be true; *mens* ~ *nooit WEET nie,* one can never tell.
kanaal', (kanale), canal, channel; artery (mine); duct; meatus (anat.); avenue; *die K*~, the Channel; ~geld, canal-dues; ~lig, channel-light; ~sluis, canal-lock, lift-lock.
Ka'naän, Canaan; *die LAND* ~, the promised land; *in* ~ *WEES,* be in clover (heaven); ~iet', (-e), Canaanite; ~i'ties, (-e), Canaanitish.
ka'naänsdruiwe, variety of white grape.
Ka'nada, Canada; ~balsem, Canada balsam.
Kanadees', (s, b) (..dese), Canadian.
kanalisa'sie, canalization.
kanaliseer', (ge-), canalize.
kanal'la, please (among Malays).
kanal'lie, (-s), rogue, scamp, rascal.
kanapee', (-s), couch, sofa.
kana'rie, (-s), canary; ~byter, butcherbird, shrike; ~koutjie, canary-cage; ~saad, canary-seed.
Kana'riese Ei'lande, Canary Islands.
kana'rievoël, canary.
kanas'ter, (-s), canaster; rush basket.
kandeel', caudle, posset; mulled wine; ~wyn, negus.
kan'delaar, (-s, ..lare), chandelier; candlestick; agapanthus (lily); ~blom, chandelier-lily; ~lelie, *Lilium dauricum;* ~sbos, *Cotyledon wallichii, Sarcacaulon spinosum*.
kandela'ber, (-s), candelabrum.
kandidaat', (..date), candidate, applicant; nominee;

kandidatuur — **kantien**

postulant; prospect (insurance); examinee; aspirant; *alle PARTYE stel kandidate*, all parties nominate (put forward) candidates; *jou* ~ *STEL*, offer oneself as candidate, stand as candidate; ~ **prokureur**, articled clerk; ~ **skap**, postulancy; candidateship, candidature; ~ **stelling**, nomination (of a candidate).

kandidatuur', (..ture), candidature.
kandideer', (ge-), stand, be a candidate for.
kandy', candy; ~ **suiker** sugar candy.
kaneel', cinnamon; *wilde* ~, cassia; ~ **blom**, Hesperantha spicata; ~ **bol**, medicinal herb *(Pelargonium triste)*; ~ **boom**, cinnamon tree; ~ **bruin**, cinnamon-coloured; ~ **duif**, cinnamon dove; ~ **kleurig**, (-e), cinnamon (-coloured); ~ **olie**, oil of cinnamon; ~ **steen**, garnet; essonite; ~ **stokkie**, cinnamon stick; ~ **suiker**, sugar of cinnamon; ~ **tjie**, (-s), see **kaneelblom**.
kanet', (-te), *Restio fructicosus, R. triticeus*.
kan'fer, camphor; ~ **agtig**, (-e), camphoric; ~ **bal**, camphor ball; ~ **boom**, camphor tree *(Cinnamomum camphora)*; ~ **brandewyn**, camphor brandy; ~ **foe'lie**, honeysuckle, woodbine; ~ **houdend**, (-e), camphoric; ~ **hout**, camphor wood; ~ **olie**, camphorated oil; ~ **reuk**, camphory smell; ~ **spiritus**, camphorated spirits; ~ **suur**, camphoric acid.
kangaroe', (-s), kangaroo, joey.
ka'nis, (-se), dirty (scruffy) fellow.
kan'ker, (s) cancer; canker; troublesome person; (w) (ge-), annoy; pester, be troublesome; nag; ~ **agtig**, (-e), cancerous; ~ **bestryding**, fight against cancer; ~ **blaar**, medicinal herb *(Ranunculus multifidus)*; ~ **bossie**, cancer bush *(Sutherlandia frutescens)*; ~ **geswel**, cancerous tumour; carcinoma; ~ **lip**, cancer in lip; ~ **lyer**, cancer patient; ~ **ondersoek**, cancer research; ~ **pasiënt**, cancer patient; ~ **pleister**, cancer poultice; ~ **plek**, cancerous spot; ~ **roos**, cockle-burr *(Xanthium occidentale)*.
kan'na, (-s), canna; see **ganna**; ~ **bossie**, lye bush.
kan'nabas(stinkhout), *Passerina filiformis; Dais cotinifolia*.
kan'nasuier, (-s), water sucker.
kanneleer', (ge-), groove, cannel, chamfer.
kannelu're, (-s), groove, flute, chamfer.
kan'netjie, (-s), small can, cannikin; container (gasmask); nipper, kid; waxlike creeper *(Microloma tenuifolium)*; *by die* ~ *kuier*, ply the bottle.
kannibaal', (..bale), cannibal; ~ **s'**, (-e), cannibalistic.
kannibalis'me, cannibalism.
kan'nie: ~ *is dood*, nothing is impossible; there is no such word as cannot.
kan'niedood, (s) (-s), variegated aloe, partridge-breast *(Aloe variegata)*; corkwood *(Commiphora)*; die-hard; (b) indestructible; hardy, tough.
kan'nie-koe'nie, (gew.), jealous; envious; spiteful; *dit is* ~, it is a matter of sour grapes.
kan'nip, (-s) = **jakkalskos**.
kano', **ka'no**, (-'s), canoe; dory; piragua, pirogue.
kanol', (-le), *Watsonia margineta, W. angusta, W. pyramidata*; ~ **pypie** = **kanol**.
ka'non[1], (-s), canon (music, church).
kanon'[2], (-ne), cannon, field-piece, big gun, barker; *die* ~ *ne sal BESLIS*, the guns will settle the matter; *die groot* ~ *ne van die PARTY*, the big guns of the party; *die* ~ *ne sal PRAAT*, the guns will speak; ~ **brons**, cannon brass; ~ **gebulder**, roar (booming) of guns; ~ **gietery**, gunsmithery.
kanoniek', (-e), canonical; ~ *e reg*, canon law.
kanoniseer', (ge-), canonize.
kanon'koeël, (cannon) shell, cannon-ball.
kanonna'de, (-s), cannonade, shelling.
kanonneer', (ge-), cannonade, bombard, shell; ~ **boot**, gunboat.
kanonnier', (-s), gunner, artillerist.
kanon': ~ **pyp**, big pipe; ~ **ring**, chase-girdle; ~ **skoot**, cannon-shot; report of a cannon; ~ **skootafstand**, gunshot range; ~ **vleis**, cannon fodder; ~ **voer**, cannon fodder; food for powder; ~ **vuur**, gunfire, gunnery, cannonade; ~ **wa**, gun-carriage, caisson; ~ **yster**, gun-pig.
kanot'gras, kanot-grass *(Flagellaria guineensis)*.

kans, (-e), chance, opportunity, prospect; adventure; scope; turn; fortune; opening; odds; *jou* ~ *AFWAG*, await one's chance; *iem. 'n* ~ *GEE*, give someone a chance; *die* ~ *e staan GELYK*, the odds are even; ~ *HÊ*, have a chance; *geen* ~ *HÊ nie*, not have a chance, be out of the running; *die* ~ *kan KEER*, the luck may turn; *MIN* ~ *hê*, stand little chance; ~ *SIEN om*, see one's way clear to, see a chance to; *die* ~ *e is maar SKRAAL*, the chances are slight; *die* ~ *e STAAN goed*, the chances are good; *daar is nie VEEL* ~ *nie*, the odds are against; *jou* ~ *laat VERBYGAAN*, miss one's opportunity; *die* ~ *is VERKYK*, the opportunity has been lost; *die* ~ *VERSPEEL*, waste one's chances; *die* ~ *WAAG*, take a chance, chance one's luck; *die* ~ *WAARNEEM (aangryp)*, seize the opportunity.
kan'sel, (-s), pulpit; ~ **ary'**, chancery, chancellery; ~ **ary'hof**, court of chancery; ~ **ary'styl**, officialese; ~ **bybel**, pulpit Bible.
kan'selier', (-s), chancellor.
kansella'sie, cancellation.
kanselleer', (ge-), cancel; ..**selle'ring**, cancellation.
kan'sel: ~ **rede**, sermon; homily; ~ **redenaar**, pulpit orator; homilist; ~ **stem**, pulpit (loud) voice; ~ **styl**, pulpit style (manner); ~ **taal**, pulpit language; ~ **welsprekendheid**, pulpit eloquence, homiletics.
kansonet', (-te), canzonet.
kans: ~ **ooreenkoms**, aleatory contract; ~ **perd**, favourite; ~ **rekening**, theory of chances; ~ **spel**, game of chance, hazard, gamble.
kant'[1], (s) lace; *GEKLOSTE* ~, bobbin lace; *NAGE MAAKTE* ~, imitation lace; *met* ~ *VERSIER*, trim with lace.
kant'[2], (-e), side, edge, brink, border, margin; limb (of a fold); flank (of army); face; hand; rim (of rock); direction; aspect; *na ALLE* ~ *e*, in every direction; from all sides, from all over; *aan die ANDER* ~, on the other hand; *die BLINK* ~ *bo hou*, look on the bright side, keep the sunny side up; *iets v.d. BLINK* ~ *bekyk*, see the bright side of something; *aan die EEN* ~, on the one hand; *alles het 'n GOEIE* ~, every cloud has a silver lining; *iem. van geen* ~ *af KEN nie*, not know someone from Adam; ~ *KIES*, choose sides; ~ *en KLAAR wees*, have everything cut and dried; *geen* ~ *aan iem. KRY nie*, not to know what to make of someone; *vir* ~ *e LOOT*, toss for sides; *aan* ~ *MAAK*, tidy up; *jouself van* ~ *MAAK*, commit suicide; *van* ~ *MAAK*, do away with; *aan die een* ~ *v.d. MOND lag*, laugh on the wrong side of one's mouth; *die een* ~ *OP, die ander* ~ *af*, up and down; *so OP die* ~ *jie af*, a close shave; *close to the wind*, near indecency; *na die OU* ~ *toe*, well on in years; *aan die* ~ *STAAN van*, side with; *op jou* ~ *gaan STAAN*, lie down; take a nap; *dié* ~ *toe STAAN*, taste good; *van VERSKILLENDE* ~ *e*, from various quarters; ~ *en WAL lê*, be full to overflowing; ~ *nòg WAL raak*, be quite beside the point; be wide of the mark; be neither here nor there; *nie WEET watter* ~ *toe nie*, not to know which way to turn; (w) (ge-), side; face; *jou TEEN iets* ~, oppose something, set one's face against something; *dit* ~ *SUID*, it faces south.
kantaan'tekening, marginal note; gloss.
kantari'de, (-s), Spanish fly, cantharides.
kanta'te, (-s), cantata.
kant'beitel, gouge; mortise, chisel; cross-cut chisel.
kant'belegsel, lace trimming.
kant'bewys, counterfoil.
kant: ~ **borduurwerk**, lace embroidery; ~ **draad**, gimp.
kanteel', (s) (..tele), crenelle, battlement, machicolation; (w) (ge-), crenellate, embattle, machicolate; ~ **keep**, embrasure.
kantekleer', chanticleer, cock.
kan'tel, (ge-), topple, cant, tip, tilt, fall, capsize, careen.
kan'telaar, (-s), tilter, tipping-gear.
kan'teldempers, anti-roll cars.
kan'teloond, tipping-furnace.
kan'telwa, (-ens), side-tip lorry.
kant'gare, **kant'garing**, lace thread.
kantien', (-e), tin can; bar, canteen, pub, public

house, pot house, buffet; wet canteen; grog-shop; ~**houer**, (-s), barkeeper; ~**juf**, barmaid; ~**man**, barman, barkeeper, publican.

kan'tig, (-e), angular, sharp-edged; rugged; ~**heid**, angularity.

kant'insetsel, lace insertion.

kant'jie, (-s), side, margin, edge; *dit was so op die* ~ *AF*, that was touch and go, a near thing; *GRAPPE so op die* ~ *af*, jokes bordering on indecency, close to the wind.

kant'klos, (-se), lace bobbin; ~**ster**, female lace= maker.

kant: ~**kraag**, lace collar; ~**kussing**, lace cushion (pillow).

kant'leuning, side railing.

kant'lyn, margin; margin-line; touch-line; side-line (tennis-court, sports field); *'n* ~ *trek*, rule a mar= gin.

kant'nommer, marginal number.

kan'to, (-'s), canto.

kanton', (-s), canton; ~**nement'**, (-e), cantonment.

kantoor', (..tore), office, cabinet; magistrate's court; ~ *van AFSENDING*, office of despatch; ~ *toe GAAN*, go to office; institute legal action; ~ *van ONTVANGS*, receiving office; *OP* ~ *wees*, be at the office; *aan die REGTE* ~, at the right address; *êrens aan die VERKEERDE* ~ *wees*, be barking up the wrong tree; be knocking at the wrong door; ~**adres**, office (business) address; ~**baadjie**, office coat; ~**bediende**, office clerk; ~**bedryf**, office prac= tice; ~**behoeftes**, office requirements; ~**boek**, of= fice book; ~**geriewe**, office accommodation; ~**huur**, office rent(al); ~**jong**, (-e, -ens), office-boy; ~**klerk**, office clerk; ~**kruk**, (-ke), office stool; ~**personeel**, office staff; ~**ruimte**, office accommo= dation; ~**saak**, lawsuit; ~**stoel**, office chair; ~**tyd**, ~**ure**, office hours, business hours; ~**werk**, office work; ~**werker**, office worker.

kan'tor, (-s), cantor.

kant'papier, lace-paper.

kant: ~**reg**, (-te), (b), square (wood); ~**reling**, side railing; ~**ruimte**, margin; ~**ryer**, postil(l)ion; ~**skaaf**, dovetail plane; ~**skeur**, edge fracture; ~**slytasie**, side wear; side cutting (rails).

kant'steek, lace stitch.

kant: ~**steen**, curb; ~**strokie**, counterfoil.

kant'strook, lace strip.

kant'tekening, marginal note, gloss; postil; apostil.

kant: ~**tussensetsel**, lace insertion; ~**verkoopster**, lace woman; ~**verkoper**, lace man.

kant: ~**voorspeler**, wing forward, flanker; ~**vyl**, cant, barette-file.

kant: ~**werk**, lace-work, lace; ~**werker**, lace-maker; lace man; ~**werkster**, (female) lace-maker; ~**win= kel**, lace shop.

kan(n)u'le, (-s), cannula.

kanun'nik, (-e), canon, prebendary; ~**es'**, (-se), can= oness.

kaoet'sjoek, India-rubber, caoutchouc.

kaolien', kaolin (clay).

kap¹, (s) (-pe), shade (lamp); top (of boot); coping (wall); cap, cover; head (of vehicle); capuchin; cart-hood; bonnet (motor); hood, cowl; wimple (of nun); hatch (cabin); pelmet; truss, principal (of roof); *akademiese* ~, academic hood.

kap², (s) cut, chop, chip; *agter die* ~ *van die BYL kom*, find out the ins and outs; get the hang of the matter; *GROOT, klein* ~, grand, small slam (cards); *'n* ~ *VLEIS*, cut of meat; (w) (ge-), fell, cut (wood); chop; chip (gold); paw (horse); bully (hockey); *in stukke* ~, hew to pieces; ~ *dit uit*, give it stick; enjoy it.

kap³, (w) (ge-), dress (hair); cover with hood.

kapa'bel, (-e), capable, in a fit state; *hy is* ~ *en slaan sy pa*, he might well hit his father.

kapar'rang, (-s), wooden sandal, sabot, (Malay) clog, mule.

kapasitan'sie, capacitance.

kapasiteit', (-e), capacity.

kapa'sitor, (-s), capacitor.

kapa'ter, (s) (-s), castrated goat; ~ *ry*, become a Freemason; (w) (ge-), castrate; ~**by**, drone.

kap'baar, (..bare), fit for felling.

kap: ~**bed**, canopy bed; ~**been**, hip-rafter, principal.

kap: ~**beitel**, cutting-chisel; ~**blok**, chopping-block, hack-log.

kap'byl, hatchet; ~**tjie**, (-s), chip-axe.

kapel'¹, (-le), butterfly.

kapel'², (-le), cobra; *bruin* ~, Cape cobra.

kapel'³, (-le), chapel; refectory; orchestra; ~**aan'**, (-s, ..lane), chaplain; ~**meester**, bandmaster; conduc= tor.

kapel'slang, hooded snake.

Ka'penaar¹, (-s, ..nare), Capetonian; inhabitant of the Western Province, of Cape Town, of the Cape Province.

ka'penaar², (-s), silver-fish *(Argyrozona)*.

ka'per, (-s), privateer, pirate, freebooter; hijacker; ~**ag'tig**, (-e), rakish; ~**brief**, letter of reprisal, let= ter of marque.

kaperjol', (-le) = **kapriol**.

ka'perskip, (..skepe), privateer, marque, corsair.

ka'pery, privateering; hijacking.

kap'gebint, chair.

kap'handskoen, gauntlet.

kap'hek, lich-gate.

kap'hou, chop-stroke, cut (tennis); chip (golf).

kapillariteit', capillarity.

kapillêr', (-e), capillary.

kapitaal', (s) (..tale), capital; fund; *DOOIE* ~, dead capital; *GESTORTE* ~, paid-up capital; (b) (..tale), capital; splendid; serious; *'n kapitale IDEE*, capital (excellent) idea; *kapitale LETTERS*, capital letters; ~ *en RENTE*, principal and interest; ~ *SLAAN uit*, make capital out of; ~**af= skrywing**, writing down (reduction) of capital; ~**afvloei**, capital drain; ~**arm**, lacking capital; ~**behoefte**, demand for capital; ~**belegging**, in= vestment of capital; ~**besteding**, capital expendi= ture; ~**dekking**, capital cover; ~**gebrek**, shortage (lack) of capital; ~**heffing**, capital levy; ~**krag**, financial capacity (strength); ~**krag'tig**, (-e), moneyed; ~**nood**, stringency of capital; ~**reke= ning**, capital account; ~**uitgawe**, capital expendi= ture; ~**vlug**, flight of capital; ~**voorsiening**, raising of capital; supplying of capital; ~**wins**, capital gain.

kapitalis', (-te), capitalist; plutocrat; ~**a'sie**, capital= ization; ~**eer'**, (ge-), capitalize; ~**e'ring**, (-e, -s), commutation (of pension); capitalization, realiz= ation; ~**me**, capitalism; ~**ties**, (-e), capitalistic(al).

kapiteel', (..tele), capital (of a column); drum; chap= ter.

kapitonneer', (ge-), pad, upholster; ~**knoop**, tufting button.

Kapitool', Capitol.

kapit'tel¹, (s) (-s), chapter.

kapit'tel², (w) (ge-), lecture, rebuke.

kapit'tel: ~**huis**, chapter-house; ~**kerk**, minster; ~**saal**, chapter-room.

kapitula'sie, capitulation.

kapituleer', (ge-), capitulate.

kap: ~**kap'pie**, (-s), *Eriocephalus racemosus*; ~**kar**, hooded cart; ~**waentjie**, bassinet; ~**knip**, bonnet catch; ~**laars**, top-boot.

kaplaks'! splash, flop!

kap: ~**lamp**, dome-lamp (motor-car); ~**lig**, (-te), dome-light; ~**luik**, companion hatch; ~**mantel**, hooded cloak.

kap'mes, billhook, chopper, hack, chipper, hacking-knife.

kap'mou, cap sleeve.

kapoen', (s) (-e), capon; (w) (ge-), caponize.

kapok', (s) snow; wadding; kapok; (w) (ge-), snow; ~**aartappels**, mashed potatoes; ~**blom**, *Lanaria plumosa*; ~**boom**, kapok-tree; ~**bossie**, *Eriocepha= lus umbellatus*; ~**gewig**, bantam weight; ~**haan= tjie**, bantam cock; cock-sparrow; ~**hennetjie**, ban= tam hen; ~**hoender**, bantam fowl; ~**kie**, (-s), *Erica peziza*; ~**kussing**, kapok cushion; ~**ploeg**, snow-plough; ~**voël**, penduline tit; kapok bird *(Anthos= copus)*; ~**wolk**, snow-cloud.

kapot', (-, -te; -ter, -ste), broken; out of order; defec= tive; exhausted; tired; crocked; ~ *slaan*, knock to

Kappadosië 253 *karig*

pieces; smash; ~ **tjie,** French letter; *Schizodium inflexum.*
Kappado'sië, Cappadocia; ~ **r, (-s),** Cappadocian; ..**do'sies, (-e),** Cappadocian.
kap'pel = kabbel.
kap'per¹, (-s), hairdresser, barber; coiffeur; friseur.
kap'per², billhook; cutter (of wood); chopper; hewer; picker.
kap'per³, (-s), caper *(Capparis spinosa).*
kap'perig, (-e), choppy (sea).
kap'perswinkel, barber's shop.
kap'pertjie, (-s), nasturtium; caper; ~ **sous,** caper sauce.
kap'pie, (-s), sun-bonnet; hood; circumflex (over vowel); coif, capsule; chip-shot (golf); ~ **kommando,** petticoat army; ~ **tjie, (-s),** small bonnet.
kap: ~ **plank,** chopping-board; ~ **ploeg,** rotary plough, rotavator; ~ **reg,** felling rights.
kaprien'suur, kapri'nesuur, capric acid.
kapriol', (-le), caper; capriole; ~ *le maak,* cut capers, gambol.
kapri'se, (-s) = caprice.
kaprisieus', (-e), capricious, whimsical, freakish.
kap'sel¹, capsule, theca (biol.).
kap'sel², cut (meat); divot (golf).
kap'sel³, (-s), head-dress; coiffure; ~ **parade,** hair-style parade.
kap'sie: ~ *maak op,* raise (captious) objections to; take exception to.
kap'skaarploeg, rotavator.
kap'skootjie, click-shot, chip-shot.
kap'skuur, Dutch barn.
kap'spieël, toilet glass.
kap'spit, (ge-), dig (by forcing spade in with the hand).
kap'stewel, top-boot, jackboot, wellington; ~ *s in die lug lê,* come a cropper.
kap'stok, hall stand, hat-rack (peg), hat-stand; *iets as* ~ *gebruik,* use as a peg on which to hang something; *'n saak aan die* ~ *HANG,* leave the matter there; drop the subject; *so MAER soos 'n kapstok,* as thin as a rake; ~ **pen,** hat (coat) peg.
kap'styl, roof-truss.
kapsu'le, (-s), capsule, cap; ..**lêr', (-e),** capsular.
kap'tafel, (ong.), dressing-table.
kaptein', (-s), captain, chief; headman; ~ **skap,** cap-taincy, captainship; ~ **s'rang,** rank of captain; ~ **s'vrou,** captain's wife; chief's wife; ~ **vis,** *Blennophis anguillaris.*
kap'tol, (-le), peg-top.
Kapusy'ner, (-s), Capuchin, Franciscan.
kapusy'neraap, capuchin.
Kapusy'ner: ~ **monnik,** Franciscan friar; ~ **orde,** Franciscan order.
kap'verbod, felling prohibition (trees).
kap: ~ **wa,** hooded waggon; ~ **wieg,** bassinet.
kar, (-re), cart; motor-car.
karaat', (karate), carat.
karabinier', (-s), carabineer.
karabyn', (-e), carbine.
karaf', (-fe), jug, carafe.
karakal', (-s), caracal *(Felis caracal).*
karakoel', (-e), karakul; ~ **mat,** karakul mat (carpet); ~ **skaap,** karakul sheep, ~ **vel,** karakul skin, astra-khan; Swakara; ~ **wol,** karakul wol, astrakhan.
karak'ter, (-s), character, nature; personage; cast; ethos; *in iem. se* ~ *(IN)KLIM,* cast a slur upon someone; damage someone's good name; *SUN-DER eie* ~, without individuality; *iem. met 'n STERK* ~, someone with a great strength of character; ~ **adel,** nobility of character; ~ **beskry-wing,** characterization; ~ **eienskap,** quality of character; characteristic; ~ **iseer', (ge-),** character-ize; ~ **ise'ring, (-e, -s),** characterization; ~ **istiek', (s) (-e),** characteristic; (b) **(-e),** characteristic; ~ **is-'ties, (-e),** characteristic; ~ **kennis,** knowledge of character; ~ **kunde,** knowledge of character; etho-logy; ~ **loos,** (..**lose),** unprincipled, depraved; characterless; ~ **loosheid,** depravity; ~ **ontleding,** analysis of character; ~ **ontwikkeling,** character de-velopment; ~ **skets,** character sketch; ~ **skildering,** portrayal of character, characterization; ~ **studie,** character-study; ~ **stuk,** character-drama; ~ **teke-ning,** character-drawing; portrayal of character; characterization; ~ **trek,** characteristic, trait; ~ **uit-beelding,** portrayal of character; characterization; ~ **vas, (-te),** morally strong; of firm character; ~ **vastheid,** strength of character; ~ **vol, (-le),** (mor-ally) strong, full of character; characteristic; ~ **vor-ming,** character-building.
karamboleer', (ge-), cannon (billiards).
karambool', (..**bole),** cannon (billiards).
karamel', (-le, -s), caramel; ~ **liseer', (ge-),** carmelize; ~ **versiersel,** caramel frosting; ~ **vla,** caramel cus-tard.
karapaks',.(-e), carapace.
kar'as, (-se), cart (motor) axle.
kara'te, karate.
karavaan', (..**vane),** caravan (of camels); ~ **herberg,** caravanserai; ~ **weg, (**..**weë),** caravan route.
karavan'serai, (-s), caravanserai.
karba', (-'s), wicker bottle, demijohn, carboy; osier-bottle.
karbeel', (karbele), corbel.
kar'bekleër, cart-trimmer.
karbi'de, karbied', carbide.
karbinol', carbinol.
karbol', carbolic; **karbo'lies, (-e),** carbolic; ~ **iseer', (ge-),** carbolize; ~ **olie,** carbolic oil; ~ **seep,** carbol-ic soap; ~ **suur,** carbolic acid, phenol.
karbonaad'jie, (-s) = karmenaadjie.
karbonaat', (..**nate),** carbonate.
karbonjseer', (ge-), carbonize.
karbon'kel, (-s), carbuncle; ~ **neus,** ruby-nose.
karburateur', (-s), carburettor.
karbureer', (ge-), carburet; ..**re'ring,** carburation.
kardamom'saad, cardamom.
kardan'as, cardan shaft.
kardan'koppeling, universal joint.
kardemom', cardamom *(Elettaria cardamomum).*
kardiaal', (kardiale), cardinal, cardiac.
kardinaal', (s) (-s, ..**nale),** cardinal; (b) (..**nale),** car-dinal, chief; vital; *'n saak van kardinale belang,* a matter of utmost importance; ~ **getal,** cardinal number; ~ **s'hoed,** cardinal's hat; red hat; ~ **skap, (-pe),** cardinalship; ~ **s'kleed,** cardinal's (purple) robes; ~ **s'kollege,** college of cardinals; ~ **s'verga-dering,** consistory, conclave.
kardinalaat', (..**late),** cardinalate.
kardiograaf', (..**grawe),** cardiograph.
kardiografie', cardiography.
kardiogram', (-me), cardiogram.
kardioï'de, (-s), cardioid.
kardiovaskulêr', (-e), cardiovascular.
kardoen', (-s), cardoon *(Cynara cardunculus).*
Kardoes'¹: *'n BENDE van* ~, gang of robbers; a mis-erable crowd.
kardoes'², (-e), paper-bag; cornet; cartridge; *ou (groot)* ~ *en klein* ~, said of a mother and daugh-ter who resemble each other closely; ~ **broek,** plus-fours; ~ **huls,** cartridge-case; ~ **papier,** cartridge paper.
karee'boom, karee tree *(Rhus lancea).*
karee'bos, shrub *(Rhus tridactyla, R. ciliata).*
karee'-ogie = glaasogie.
Ka'rel, Charles; ~ *die EERSTE,* Charles the First; ~ *die GROTE,* Charlemagne, Charles the Great; *die TYD v.d.* ~ *s,* the Caroline Age.
karelgroot'oog, *Boopsoidea inornata* (fish).
karet', (-te), tortoise-shell; carrier; caret; luggage-rack; ~ **jie, (-s),** luggage-carrier; ~ **skilpad,** turtle *(Chelonidae).*
kargadoor', (-s), shipbroker.
kariati'de, (-s), kariatied', (-e), caryatid.
Kari'bies, (-e), Caribbean; ~ *e EILANDE,* Carib-bees; ~ *e SEE,* Caribbean Sea.
kariboe', (-s), caribou.
karie', honey-beer, mead; k(a)rie; ~ **moer,** k(a)rie-yeast.
ka'riës, caries.
karieus', (-e), carious.
ka'rig, (-e), sparing, niggardly, scanty; frugal (meal); penurious, meagre, slender; ~ *GEMEUBILEER,* scantily furnished; *'n* ~ *e GEBRUIK maak van,* use

sparingly; ~ met *LOF*, chary of praise; ~ **heid**, frugality, scantiness, niggardliness.
karikatuur', (..**ture**), caricature; ~ **aal'**, (..**rale**), ~ **agtig**, (**-e**), caricaturish, exaggerated; ~ **tekenaar**, caricaturist; ~ **tekening**, cartoon, caricature (picture).
kariljon', (**-s**), carillon, chimes.
karkaar', a variety of heath *(Erica imbricata)*; ~ **blom**, *Anapalina revoluta*.
kar'kap, cart-tent, cart-hood.
karkas', (**-se**), carcase, carcass.
karkat'jie, (**-s**), sty(e) (on eye).
karkei', (**-s**), Karoo plant *(Cotyledon, Crassula)*.
karkiet', (**-e**), reed-warbler.
kar'kis, (**-te**), box in seat of cart.
karkoe'hotnot, (**-s, -te**), scaly lizard *(Cordylus giganteus)*.
karkoer', (**-e**), bitter melon, wild coloquint, gourd *(Citrullus vulgaris)*.
kar'kussing, cushion in cart or car.
karlien'blom, poinsettia.
kar'ma, karma, fate, destiny (Buddhism).
kar'maker, (**-s**), cart-builder, coach-maker.
karmedik', medicinal herb *(Cnicus lanceolatus)*.
karmeliet', (**-e**), Carmelite (friar), White Friar.
karmenaad'jie, (**-s**), chop.
karmonk'pitjie, scented pip.
karmosyn', crimson, carmine; ~ **bos**, *Phytolacca americana* (bush yielding red dye); ~ **bruin**, crimson lake.
karmyn', carmine; ~ **rooi**, crimson, carmine.
karnal'lie, (**-s**), rogue, scamp, rascal; '*N* ~, a rascal; *'n UITGESLAPE* ~, a cunning rascal.
karnaval', (**-s**), carnival.
karneool', (**karneole**), cornelian.
karnivoor', (..**vore**), carnivore.
karnuf'fel, (**ge-**), hug, fondle, cuddle; bully, manhandle.
Karoo', Karoo; ~ **agtig**, (**-e**), Karoo-like; **k** ~ **bossie**, Karoo, Karoo-bush *(Pentzia incana, P. globosa)*; **k** ~ **ruspe(r)**, Karoo caterpillar; ~ **tentruspe(r)**, Karoo tent caterpillar; ~ **veld**, Karoo-veld, herbage peculiar to the Karoo; country where Karoo-bush grows; ~ **wêreld**, Karoo district.
karos'[1], (**-se**), skin rug, kaross.
karos'[2], (**-se**), state carriage.
karosserie', (**-e**), coach-work.
karoteen', carotene.
karp, (**-e**), carp (fish); ~ **rug**, roach-back.
Karpa'te, Carpathian Mountains.
kar'perd, cart-horse, coach-horse; *hulle is twee goeie* ~ *e*, they make a good pair.
karpet', (**-te**), floor-rug, carpet.
kar'retjie, (**-s**), trap, light cart, chaise.
kar'ring, (s) (**-s**), churn; (w) (**ge-**), churn; nag (fig.); *aan iem.* ~, pester someone; nag; ~ **melk**, buttermilk; *in* ~ *melk geval*, be dressed all in white; ~ **melkpap**, buttermilk porridge; ~ **melkspaan**, butterscoop; ~ **sel**, churning; ~ **staf**, churn-staff; ~ **stok**, churn-staff; ~ **vaatjie**, churn.
karsaai', kersey (cloth).
kar'siek, car-sick; ~ **te**, car-sickness.
karsinoom', (..**nome**), carcinoma.
kar'spore, wheel-marks (-tracks).
karteer', (**ge-**), plot (out); map, chart; ~ **der**, (**-s**), plotter.
kartel'[1], (**-e**), cartel, combine; trust, consortium.
kar'tel'[2], (s) (**-s**), notch, incision; wave, curl (in hair); crimp (wool); (w) (**ge-**), notch; wave (hair); mill (coins); engrail; deckle; ~ **band**, zigzag braid; ~ **derm**, colon; ~ **formasie**, crimp-formation; ~ **ig**, (**-e**), notched; wavy; milled; ~ **ing**, (**-e, -s**), waviness, notching, milling; crimp; ~ **leer'**, (**ge-**), cartelize; ~ **le'ring**, cartelization; ~ **middel**, hair-setting lotion; ~ **moer**, castellated nut; ~ **rand**, milled edge; deckle-edge; ~ **skêr**, pinking shears; ~ **steek**, wave stitch; knurl; ~ **wurm**, zigzag worm.
karte'ring, (**-e, -s**), mapping, charting.
kartets', (**-e**), grape-shot, case-shot, cannister-shot; ~ **koeël**, grape-shot cartridge; ~ **lading**, case-shot; ~ **vuur**, grape-shot (fire); ~ **vuurpyl**, case-rocket.
kartograaf', (..**grawe**), cartographer.

kartografie', cartography; ..**gra'fies**, (**-e**), cartographic(al).
karton', cardboard, pasteboard; carton; ~ **agtig**, (**-e**), boardy; ~ **band**, boards; ~ **dikpapier**, double-weighted paper; ~ **fabriek**, cardboard factory; ~ **houer**, carton; ~ **mes**, cardboard knife; ~ **neer'**, (**ge-**), put between boards; ~ **plank**, hardboard; ~ **verpakking**, (packing in) cartons; ~ **werk**, cardboard work (modelling).
kar'tuig, cart-harness.
Kartui'ser(monnik), Carthusian (friar).
karveel', (**karvele**), carvel.
kar'vrag, (**-te**), cart-load.
karwats', (s) (**-e**), riding-whip, hunting-crop; quirt; cow-hide; short driving-whip; (w) (**ge-**), horsewhip.
karwei', (s) job, piece of work; (w) (**ge-**), ride, transport; ~ **bus**, station-wag(g)on; ~ **diens**, carrier-service; ~ **er**, (**-s**), transport-rider; carman; carrier, carter; ~ **ery**, cartage; ~ **geld**, cartage; ~ **koste**, cartage charge; ~ **tjie**, (**-s**), odd job.
kar'wiel, cart-wheel.
karwy', caraway-seed.
kas'[1], (**-te**), box, case (watch, printing); cupboard, chest, locker; bookcase; cabinet; *iets uit die* ~ *HAAL*, dig something up; *in iem. se* ~ *KLIM*, tell someone what you think of him.
kas'[2], (**-se**), treasury, treausure-chest, cash-box; coffer; bezel (of ring); socket (of eye); hothouse; *goed BY* ~ *wees*, be in funds; *die TOESTAND van die* ~, the state of the finances; (w) (**ge-**), deposit, bank (money); set (diamond).
kasarm', (**-s**), ramshackle building, rambling house; *die hele* ~, the whole lot (caboodle).
kasa'terwater, wish-wash, dishwater, slops, cat-lap.
kas'ba, kasbah.
kas'bekleding, box-lining.
kas'boek, cashbook.
kas'boom, box-bottom.
kaseïen', **kaseï'ne**, casein.
kasemat', (**-te**), casemate.
kaser'ne, (**-s**), barracks; ~ **arres**, confinement to barracks.
kaserneer', (**ge-**), barrack, house in barracks.
kaser'nekommandant, barracks officer.
kas'geld, cash in hand.
ka'sie, (**-s**), small cheese.
ka'sig, (**-e**), cheesy; ~ *e botter*, curdy butter.
kasjet', (**-te**), cachet.
kasjmier', cashmere (cloth); kerseymere.
kasjoe', cashew; ~ **neut**, cashew nut.
kaska'de, (**-s**), cascade.
kaska'ra, cascara; ~ **pil**, cascara tablet.
kaskena'de, (**-s**), prank, mischievous trick; ~ **s**, antics.
kasmier' = **kasjmier**.
kas'pers, box-press (for wool).
Kas'piese See, Caspian Sea.
kas'plant, hothouse plant.
kas: ~ **register**, cash register, (check-)till; ~ **rekening**, cash-account.
kas'sa: *per* ~, by cash.
kas'saldo, cash balance.
kas'samasjien, (ong.), cash register.
kassa'sie, cassation, appeal, reversal of judgment (on appeal); striking (a barrister) off the rolls.
kassa'we, cassava; tapioca; manioc; ~ **meel**, tapioca, cassava-meal.
kasseer', (**ge-**), cash; cancel; cashier.
kassemier' = **kasjmier**.
kasse'ring, cancellation; cashiering, reversal.
kas'serol, (**-le**), casserole.
kas'sia, cassia; ~ **boom**, locust-tree *(Cinnamomum cassia)*.
kas'sie'[1], cassia.
kas'sie'[2], (**-s**), little box, case; casket; *iem. van die* ~ *na die muur stuur*, send someone from pillar to post.
kassier', (**-s**), cashier; teller (bank); purse-bearer.
kassiteriet', cassiterite.
kas: ~ **slot**, cupboard-lock, padlock; ~ **stuk**, box-leg; hit play; ~ **swaelstertvoeg**, box dovetail-joint.
kastai'ing, (**-s**), chestnut; *vir iem. die* ~ *s uit die VUUR haal*, pull someone's chestnuts out of the

fire; *WILDE* ~, horse-chestnut; ~**boom**, chestnut-tree; ~**bruin**, chestnut, auburn; nut-brown; ~**hout**, chestnut-wood.

kastanjet', (-te), castanet.

kas'te, (-s), caste.

kasteel', (**kastele**), castle, chateau; rook (chess); ~**toring**, keep (of castle).

kas'tegees, caste-feeling.

kas'tekort, cash deficit.

kastelein', (-s), innkeeper, licensee, publican.

kas'temaker, cabinet-maker.

kas'terolie, castor oil; blue-bottle; *iem. so lief soos ~ hê*, loathe someone; ~**boom**, castor-oil plant.

kas'te: ~**stelsel**, caste system; ~**vooroordeel**, class prejudice.

kas'tig, (-e), quasi-, as if it were, make-believe, feigned, pretended, simulated; forsooth; *met ~ e BEWONDERING*, with feigned admiration; *hulle DURF dit ~ nie doen nie*, they make out that they dare not do it; *hy het ~ GESTUDEER*, he made a pretence of studying.

kastiga'sie, (-s), castigation; expurgation.

kastigeer', (ge-), castigate; expurgate.

Kastiliaans', (-e), Castilian.

Kasti'lië, Castile.

kastoor'hoed, beaver (hat).

kastraat', (..**trate**), castrated person, eunuch.

kastra'sie, castration.

kastreer', (ge-), castrate, geld (males and females); spay (females); emasculate (males); ~**der**, (-s), gelder.

kastrol', (-le), saucepan; ~**borsel**, pot-brush.

kasty', (ge-), castigate, chastise, punish, mortify; discipline; *'n mens ~ die een wat jy liefhet*, we chastise those we love; ~**dend**, (-e), flagellant; ~**der**, (-s), castigator, chastiser; ~**ding**, chastisement, punishment; discipline.

ka'suar, (-s), casuarina.

kasua'ris, (-se), cassowary.

kasueel', (**kasuele**), casual, accidental.

kasui'fel, (-s), chasuble; planet.

kasuïs', (-te), casuist; ~**tiek'**, casuistry; ~**ties**, (-e), casuistic.

kasuur', (**kasure**), pittosporum.

kas'voorraad, cash in hand.

kat, (-te), cat; pussy; *te laat vir die ~ se AFVAL kom*, arrive too late even for the scraps; *die ~ die BEL aanbind*, bell the cat; ~ *se BLAD!*, fiddlesticks!; *die ~ uit die BOOM kyk*, sit on the fence; see which way the cat jumps, adopt a waiting policy; *kerm soos 'n ~ oor 'n DERM*, whine; wail; moon; *die ~ in die DONKER knyp*, do things on the sly; do things in an underhand way; *daar is meer as een manier om 'n ~ DOOD te maak*, there are more ways of killing a cat than drowning it in butter; *'n ~ in die DUIWEHOK gooi*, flutter the dovecotes; set a cat among the pigeons; ~ *se GEDAGTES kry*, begin to have ones doubts; *die GELAARSDE ~*, Puss in Boots; *snags is alle ~ te GROU*, in the dark all cats are grey; *g'n ~ om sonder HANDSKOEN aan te pak nie*, not to be tackled without gloves; a difficult person to handle; *soos ~ en HOND lewe*, live like cat and dog; *geen ~ of HOND nie*, not a soul; *vir die ~ kwaad wees en die HOND skop*, take it out on somebody else; *geen ~ se KANS nie*, not to have a snowball's hope; *'n ~ in die KELDER toemessel*, plaster over the cracks; *'n ~ kan ook na 'n KONING kyk*, a cat may look at a king; *hy lyk of die ~ te sy KOS afgeneem het*, he is looking blue (glum); *die ~ sal nie met sy leë MAAG wegloop nie*, he won't go empty; *so welkom as 'n ~ in 'n MELKKAMER*, as welcome as water in a ship; *elke ~ kry sy MIDDAG*, every dog has his day; *as die ~ vol is*, *smaak die MUIS bitter*, plenty is not dainty; *van iem. hou soos 'n ~ van MUISE*, to be as fond of someone as a cat is of mice; *as die ~ weg is, is die MUIS baas*, when the cat is away the mice will play; *so NAT soos 'n ~*, sopping wet; *soos 'n ~ in 'n vreemde PAKHUIS*, like a fish out of water; *om iets draai soos 'n ~ om warm PAP*, behave like a cat that loves fish but fears to wet his paws; *'n ~ val altyd op sy POTE*, he always falls on his feet; *'n REGTE ou ~*, a regular cat (spiteful woman); *hy ROU vir die ~ te*, his fingernails are dirty; *hy weet daar soveel van as 'n ~ van SAFFRAAN*, know as much as the man in the moon; *'n ~ in die SAK koop*, buy a pig in a poke; *soos 'n ~ SING*, to caterwaul; *'n ou ~ lus ook nog SOETMELK*, an old cat laps as much as a young kitten; *wie met 'n ~ SPEEL, word gekrap*, he that handles thorns will prick his fingers; *'n benoude ~ maak benoude SPRONGE*, a drowning man will clutch at a straw; *die ~ kom TERUG*, a bad penny always comes back; *as die ~ te VERGADERING hou*, at the Greek Kalends; *so VRIENDELIK soos 'n ~*, as amicable as a tiger.

katabolie', catabolism; ..**bo'lies**, (-e), catabolic.

katabolis'me, catabolism.

katachre'se, (-s), catachresis.

katafalk', (-e), catafalque.

kat'agtig, (-e), catlike, feline.

katakoe'roe, (-s), cuckoo-shrike *(Campephagidae)*.

katakom'be, (-s), catacomb.

katalek'ties, (-e), catalectic.

katalep'sie, catalepsy, trance.

katalep'ties, (-e), cataleptic.

katalisa'tor, (-e, -s), catalyst.

katali'se, catalysis.

kataliseer', (ge-), catalyze; ..**lise'ring**, catalysis.

katali'ties, (-e), catalytic.

katalogiseer', (ge-), catalogue, list; ~**der**, (-s), cataloguer; ..**se'ring**, cataloguing.

kata'logus, (..**se**, ..**gi**), catalogue, cartulary, ~**prys**, catalogue-price.

Katalo'nië, Catalonia.

katamaran', (-s), catamaran.

katamorfis'me, katamorphism.

kat'anker, backing-anchor.

katapult', (-e), catapult.

katar', (-re), catarrh, coryza.

katarak', (-te), cataract; pearl-eye.

katarraal', (..**rale**), catarrhal.

katar'sis, catharsis.

katastrofaal', (..**fale**), catastrophic.

katastro'fe, (-s), catastrophe.

katastro'fies, (-e), catastrophic.

kata'ter, (-s), scoundrel, blighter.

kat: ~**bakkies**, catface (tomatoes); ~**derm**, catgut; ~**doring**, wild asparagus; thorny shrub; cat-thorn *(Acacia cafra, A. capensis)*.

kate'der, (-s), cathedra; professor's desk; cathedral pulpit.

katedraal', (..**drale**), cathedral, minster.

kategeet', (..**gete**), catechist.

katege'se, catechesis.

kategetiek', catechetics.

katege'ties, (-e), catechetic(al).

kategis', (-te), catechist.

kategis'mus, catechism.

kategorie', (-ë), category; ..**go'ries**, (-e), categorical.

kategu'men, catechumen.

ka'tel, (-s), bedstead; ~**poot**, bed-leg; ~**styl**, bedpost.

ka'ter, (-s), tomcat; chippiness, hangover.

katern', (-s), quire; quaternion.

katesjoe', catechu.

katesjol', catechol.

kate'ter, (-s) catheter.

kate'tometer, katetome'ter, cathetometer.

kat'halstrek, kind of tug of war.

katioon', (**katione**), cation.

katjang'(boontjie), monkey-nut; bean *(Vigna catjang)*.

kat'jie, (-s), kitten, pussy cat, small cat, kit; catkin, lamb's tail (trees); *~ s deur die water dra*, pull the chestnuts out of the fire; ~**drie'blaar**, Knowltonia *hirsuta*; ~**pie'ring**, (-s), gardenia; ~**tee**, painted lady *(Gladiolus blandus; Tritonia pallida)*.

katkisant', (-e), candidate for confirmation, catechumen, confirmand, confirmee.

katkisa'sie, catechism (class); ~**boek**, catechism book; ~**klas**, confirmation class; ~**meester**, catechist.

katkiseer', (ge-), catechise; rebuke; ~**meester**, catechist.

kat: ~ **kop**, (s) cat's head; (gew.) rye-bread; muddle=head; (b) confused, muddled; ~ **lagter**, (-s), babbler *(Turdoides jardineii);* maxim (gun); ~ **musiek**, caterwauling; ~ **nael**, cat's claw; cat-thorn *(Hypobanche sanguinea);* belt lacing, belt fastener.
kato'de, (-s), cathode; ~ **straal**, cathode-ray.
katoen', cotton; ~ **afval**, cotton waste; ~ **agtig, (-e)**, cotton-like; ~ **baal**, bale of cotton; ~ **batis**, percale; ~ **bedryf**, cotton industry; ~ **boom**, cotton-tree; ~ **bos**, *Asclepia*-species, e.g. *A. fruticosa, A. burchellii;* ~ **bou**, cotton-growing (culture); ~ **drukker**, calico-printer; ~ **drukkery**, calico-printing; ~ **dryfriem**, cotton belt; ~ **fabriek**, cotton factory; ~ **fabrikant**, cotton manufacturer; ~ **fluweel**, mock velvet, velveteen; ~ **gaas**, leno; ~ **gare**, ~ **garing**, twist; cotton thread; ~ **goed**, Manchester goods; ~ **handel**, cotton trade; ~ **handelaar**, cotton merchant; ~ **industrie**, cotton industry; ~ **mark, (-te)**, cotton market; ~ **myt**, cotton mite; ~ **nywerheid**, cotton industry; ~ **oes**, cotton harvest (crop); ~ **olie**, cotton oil; ~ **pit**, cotton seed; ~ **plantasie**, cotton plantation; ~ **planter**, cotton planter; ~ **plantluis**, cotton aphid; ~ **pluis**, linters; ~ **pluismeul**, cotton gin; ~ **saad**, cotton seed; ~ **spinnery**, cotton mill; ~ **teelt**, cotton farming; ~ **tjie, (-s)**, print dress; ~ **verwer**, cotton dryer; ~ **vesel**, cotton lint; ~ **watte**, cotton waste; ~ **wewer**, cotton weaver; ~ **wewery**, cotton mill; ~ **wol**, wincey.
katoe'ter, (-s), gadget.
katoliek', (-e), catholic, universal, all-embracing.
Katoliek', (s) (-e), Roman Catholic; (b) (-e), Roman Catholic.
katoliseer', (ge-), catholicize.
Katolisis'me, (Roman) Catholicism.
katolisiteit', catholicity, comprehensiveness, wide prevalence, universality.
katon'kel, (-s), katonkel, barracuda *(Thynnus pelamys);* bonito *(Sarda sarda).*
kat'oog, cat's eye; cat's-eye (gem); cat's eye (small reflector on roads); child's marble; grey eye; sharp eye; periwinkle; *katoë hê*, see well in the dark; ~ **agtig, (-e)**, chatoyant.
katools', (-e), on heat, ruttish; silly; objectionable; boring.
kat'oor, type of weed *(Hypochoeris radicata).*
katoptriek', **katop'trika**, catoptric(s).
katop'tries, (-e), catoptric(al).
katot', (-te), home-made pail.
kat'pootjie, cat's paw; ~ *maak*, bring fingertips together.
katrol', (s) (-le), pulley; gin; block; sheaf; jeers (naut.); (w) (ge-), pulley; ~ **as**, pulley axle; ~ **balk**, cathead; ~ **beuel**, pulley fork; ~ **blok**, tackle (pulley) block; ~ **boom**, derrick; ~ **koppeling**, pulley system; ~ **naaf**, pulley; ~ **rand**, pulley rim; ~ **skyf**, (pulley) sheaf; ~ **spier**, ear muscle *(Musculus trochlearis);* ~ **stel**, block and tackle; ~ **stok**, casting (reel) rod; ~ **tou**, pulley rope.
kats, (s) (-e), cat-o'-nine-tails; (w) (ge-), thrash, lash, whip.
kat'spoegie, short distance; little bit.
kat'stert, cat's tail; willow-herb *(Lachenalia);* prince's-feather; *Asparagus consanguineus.*
kat'swink, unconscious, dazed, in a swoon; *iem.* ~ *slaan*, knock someone out.
kat'te: ~ **bak**, dickey (seat); rumble seat; ~ **belletjie**, cat bell; (hasty) scribble; scrawl; scrawled note; ~ **geslag**, cat tribe, felines; ~ **gespin**, cat's purr; ~ **getjank**, catcall; caterwauling; ~ **goud**, cat's-gold; ~ **kloue**, cat's claws; ~ **kop**, anencephalus; throttle-pipe; regulator valve; ~ **kroeg**, milk-bar; ~ **kruie**, calamint, cat-mint *(Ballota africana, Stachys thunbergii);* ~ **kwaad**, mischief, naughtiness, tricks; ~ **kwaad doen**, be up to mischief; ~ **maai**, (w) (ge-), gallivant, rollick, carry on (with a girl); ~ **maaiery**, gallivanting, rollicking; ~ **moord**, felicide; ~ **musiek**, caterwauling.
kat'terig, (-e), cattish; quarrelsome; chippy; seedy; ~ **heid**, quarrelsomeness; chippiness; hot-coppers, hangover.
kat'teskeer, (ge-), attend classes for confirmation (jocular).

katte: ~ **vrees**, ailurophobia; ~ **vriend**, cat-lover.
kat'tie, (-s), kitty.
kat'tig, (-e), cattish; ~ **heid**, cattishness.
kat: ~ **uil**, wood-owl, brown owl; ~ **vel**, catskin; ~ **vis**, catfish; ~ **voet**, noiselessly; ~ **wilger**, velvet osier *(Salix viminalis, S. discolor).*
Kauka'sië, Caucasus; ~ **r, (-s)**, Caucasian.
Kauka'sies, (-e), Caucasian.
kau'ri[1], (-'s), *Agathis australis.*
kauri[2], (-'s), cowrie (shell).
kau'rieboom, *Heeria concolor.*
kavalier', (-s), cavalier, gallant, lover.
kavalka'de, (-s), cavalcade.
kavallerie', cavalry; ~ **aanval**, cavalry attack; ~ **geveg**, cavalry engagement; ~ **perd**, trooper; ~ **soldaat**, trooper; ..**leris', (-te)**, cavalryman, horse-soldier, trooper.
kaveer', (ge-), raise objections, protest; argue; nag, complain; romp, caper.
kaviaar', caviar(e).
ka'wa, kava.
ke'ël, (-s), cone; ninepin, skittle, bowl.
keel[1], (s) gules (her.).
keel[2], (s) (**kele**), throat; gorge; gullet; *iets by iem. se* ~ *AFDRUK*, ram something down someone's throat; *jou eie* ~ *AFSNY*, cut one's own throat; be one's own undoing; *in iem. se* ~ *AFSPRING*, jump down someone's throat; *iem. se* ~ *laat weet hoe swaar sy AGTERLYF (agterent) is*, string someone up; make someone dance on air; *sy* ~ *is met BLIK uitgelê*, his throat is made of tin; *'n DROË* ~ *hê*, have a parched throat; *DWARS in die* ~ *(krop) bly steek*, stick in one's gizzard, cause resentment; *alles deur die* ~ *laat GAAN*, pour everything down one's throat; *dit GAAN bo jou* ~ , it's more than you can manage; *aan die* ~ *GRYP*, grab someone by the throat; *dit HANG al by my* ~ *uit*, I am already fed up with it; *iem. by die* ~ *HÊ*, have someone by the throat; *alles deur jou* ~ *JAAG*, pour everything down one's throat; *agter in sy* ~ *LAG*, laugh heartily; *die* ~ *NATMAAK*, wet one's whistle; *'n* ~ *OPSIT*, scream (howl, yell); *die* ~ *SMEER*, wet one's whistle; *na iem. se* ~ *SPRING*, go for someone's throat; *in die* ~ *bly STEEK*, stick in one's gizzard; *jou* ~ *laat TOETREK*, take one's breath away; *die woord bly in my* ~ *VASSTEEK*, the word sticks in my throat; *iem. na die* ~ *VLIEG*, fly at a person's throat; (w) (ge-), cut the throat off, kill; ~ **aandoening**, throat trouble; ~ **aar**, jugular vein; ~ **-af**, with a cut-throat; *'n skaap* ~ *-af sny*, cut a sheep's throat; ~ **arts**, throat specialist; ~ **balk**, collar beam; ~ **band**, cap-string; neck-strap; gullet-piece (of headstall); ~ **borsel**, larynx brush.
keël: ~ **draend, (-e)**, coniferous; ~ **draende boom**, cone-bearing tree, conifer; ~ **draer**, conebearer.
keel: ~ **gang**, jowl (horse); ~ **gat**, gullet; *in die verkeerde* ~ *gat*, down the wrong way; ~ **geluid**, guttural sound; ~ **geswel**, tumour in throat; ~ **groef**, jugular groove (horse); ~ **holte**, pharynx; ~ **kanker**, cancer of the throat; ~ **klank**, guttural (sound); ~ **klep(pie)**, epiglottis; ~ **klier**, jugular gland; ~ **knop**, Adam's apple; ~ **kop**, larynx.
ke'ëlkoppie, sugarloaf hill.
keel'letter, guttural (letter).
ke'ëlmantel, cone.
keel: ~ **ontsteking**, inflammation of the throat; pharyngitis, laryngitis; garget (cattle); ~ **operasie**, laryngotomy; ~ **pyn**, sore throat.
ke'ël ~ **rat**, bevel-gear wheel; mitre gear; conical wheel; ~ **regulateur**, cone governor.
keel: ~ **sak**, vocal sac; ~ **seer**, sore throat; ~ **siekte**, throat disease; prunella; angina, garget.
ke'ël: ~ **skyf**, cone pulley; ~ **snee**, parabola; conic section; ~ **spel**, ninepins; tenpins; bowling; skittles; ~ **speler**, skittle player; bowler.
keel: ~ **spieël**, laryngoscope; ~ **stem**, guttural voice; falsetto; ~ **stuk**, jowl; ~ **sweer**, quinsy; ~ **tering**, laryngeal phthisis; ~ **tjie, (-s)**, small throat; ~ **vel**, dewlap, jowl.
ke'ëlvlak, conical surface.
keel'vlek, gorget (birds).

keël: ~ **vorm,** taper; ~ **vormig, (-e),** conical; conoid, cone-shaped, coniform; ~ **wedstryd,** skittles match; bowling match; ~ **wiel,** conic(al) wheel.

keep, (s) (kepe) notch, jag, indentation, nick, tally; cut; hack; (w) **(ge-),** notch, nick, jag; indent; dap; ~ **beitel,** jagger; ~ **las,** dap-joint; ~ **masjien,** jaggle machine; ~ **snyer,** dado-cutter; ~ **stelsel,** notch sys= tem (of ear-marking); ~ **werk,** jagging.

keer, (s) (kere), turn; time; *DRIE* ~, three times; *net hierdie EEN* ~, just this once; *'n ENKELE* ~, once; *te* ~ *(kere) GAAN,* make a fuss; cause a rumpus; *te kere GAAN teen iem.,* oppose someone strongly; rail at someone; *daar was GEEN* ~ *aan hom nie,* he could not be stopped; *betyds* ~ *is 'n goeie GEWEER,* prevention is better than cure; a stitch in time saves nine; *HIERDIE* ~, this time; *die LAASTE* ~, the last time; *'n goeie* ~ *NEEM,* take a favourable turn (illness); ~ *OP* ~, time and again; *gedane SAKE het geen* ~ *nie,* what is done, cannot be undone; *jou nie TWEE* ~ *laat nooi nie,* accept an invitation immediately; (w) **(ge-),** stem (tide); turn; prevent, check, stop; oppose; ~ *vir jou GESIG,* protect your face; *beter ten HALWE ge= keer as ten volle gedwaal,* it is better to be checked half-way than to go completely astray; *IN jouself gekeer wees,* be wrapped up in thought; be self-centred; *NA jou vriend* ~, turn to one's friend; *iets ONDERSTEBO* ~, turn upside down; cause a great confusion; ~ *VOOR!* stop him (it)! ~ **balk,** chock-baulk (bridge), stop-rack; ~ **band,** check-strap; ~ **beitel,** cover-, back-, cap-iron; ~ **blok,** chock (aero.); scotch block; ~ **dag,** return day (jur.); ~ **dam,** barrage, weir; ~ **der, (s),** defender; check; ~ **dig,** rondeau; ~ **klep (-pe),** check-valve; non-return valve; ~ **kring,** tropic (line); ~ **krings= lande,** the tropics; ~ **kringson,** tropical sun; ~ **kringsplant,** tropical plant; ~ **kringsvoël,** tropical bird; ~ **masjien,** tedder; ~ **muur,** retaining wall; ~ **plaat,** baffle-plate; ~ **punt,** turning-point; acme; apsis; cusp; ~ **reël,** burden (of song); ~ **ring,** retain= ing ring; ~ **room,** barrier cream; ~ **staat,** checkrail; ~ **strook,** backing-strip (welding); ~ **strop,** check-strap; ~ **sy,** other side, reverse, obverse, tail (of coin); *ALLES het 'n* ~ *sy,* every metal hath its re= verse; *die* ~ *sy v.d. MEDALJE,* the reverse side of the medal.

keer'swenk, (ge-), wheel about; ~ **ing,** about wheel; ..**wending,** about turn.

keer: ~ **vers,** antiphon; ~ **wal,** weir; ~ **weer,** cul-de-sac; ~ **werk,** defence (rugby); clearance (soccer); fielding.

kees, (kese), monkey; *dis klaar met K* ~, it is all over; *K* ~ **hond,** Dutch barge-dog.

kef, (ge-), yelp, yap, bark; squabble; ~ **fer, (-s),** yap= per, barker; ~ **fertjie, (-s),** worthless boaster; yapper.

ke'gel, (vero.) (-s), cone; skittle; ninepin; **baan, (..bane),** skittle ground; (skittle) alley; ~ **bal, (-le),** skittleball; ~ **spel,** skittles.

kei, (-e), pebble, cobblestone; ~ **appel,** Kei apple *(Dovyalis caffra).*

keil¹, (s) (-e), top hat, chimney-pot hat.

keil², (s) (-e), wedge; splitting-wedge; shim; quoin; (w) **(ge-),** drive in a wedge; fling, pitch.

keil³, (w) (ge-), coil, roll up (fishing line).

keil'skrif, cuneiform writing.

kei'ser, (-s), emperor; *vir die* ~ *se BAARD speel,* play for love; play for the fun of it, *BETAAL aan die* ~ *wat die* ~ *toekom, GEE die* ~ *wat die* ~ *s'n is,* render unto Caesar the things which are Caesar's; *die* ~ *gaan BETAAL,* relieve oneself; *hom verbeel hy is die* ~ *se HOND se oom,* he thinks he is just it; he is full of himself; ~ **geel,** imperial yellow; ~ **in', (-ne),** empress; ~ **in'-weduwee,** empress dowager; ~ **lik, (-e),** imperial; ~ **ryk,** empire; ~ **skap,** empe= rorship; ~ **skroon,** imperial crown; agapanthus; fritillary; ~ **snee,** ~ **sny,** Caesarian (operation); ~ **stad,** city of the emperor; ~ **tyd,** time of the em= perors; imperium.

kei'steen, pebble, cobble-stone.

ke'ker(tjie), dwarf pea *(Cicer arietinum).*

kek'kel, (ge-), cackle, clack; jaw; gaggle; gab(ble); patter; ~ **aar, (-s),** cackler; chatterer; ~ **(a)ry', cackling;** gossip; slander; ~ **bek,** chatterbox, gos= sip; tattler; flibbertigibbet; slanderer, scandalmon= ger, cackler; ~ **end, (-e),** prating, prattling; ~ **praat= jie, (-s),** gossip, slander, tittle-tattle; ~ **vars,** new-laid (egg).

kel'der, (s) (-s), cellar; *hy was by die BAAS se* ~, he has been at the bottle; *na die* ~ *GAAN,* go to Davy Jones's locker; *hy RUIK na die* ~, he reeks of the bottle; *na die* ~ *STUUR,* send to the bottom; (w) **(ge-),** sink; store in a cellar; *'n skip* ~, sink a ship; ~ **bel,** areabell; ~ **deur,** cellar door; ~ **gat,** air-hole; ~ **huur,** cellarage; ~ **ing, (-e, -s)** sinking; ~ **kamer,** basement room; ~ **koors,** cellar fever; ~ **lug,** cellar smell; fusty smell; ~ **luik,** cellar-flap, trapdoor; ~ **man,** cellarman; ~ **meester,** cellarman; ~ **raam,** cellar window; ~ **ruimte,** cellarage; ~ **sleutel,** cellar key; ~ **tjie, (-s),** cellaret, bottle-case; ~ **trap,** cellar stairs; ~ **venster,** cellar window; ~ **verdieping,** base= ment; ~ **woning,** basement dwelling; ~ **wyn,** cellar wine.

kelk, (-e), chalice; calyx; cup (flower); goblet; *'n BIT= TER* ~, a bitter cup; *'n bitter* ~ *DRINK,* have to drain the cup of misery; *die* ~ *van sy GELUK is vol,* he is in ecstasy; he is supremely happy; ~ **blaar,** calyx leaf, sepal; ~ **bloemig, (-e),** calycifloral; ~ **blom,** calyx; ~ **doekie,** purificator; ~ **ie, (-s),** wineglass; moonflower; calicle (of flower); ~ **iewyn, (-e, -s),** Namaqua sandgrouse *(Pterocles namaqua);* ~ **kelkig, (-e),** Iridaceae; ~ **kaffie,** glume; ~ **kleedjie,** chalice veil; **vormig, (-e),** cup= shaped, calciform, chaliced.

kel'ner, (-s), waiter, steward; potboy, ~ **in', (-ne),** waitress.

Kelt, (-e), Celt; ~ **ies, (-e),** Celtic, Gaelic.

Keltoloog', (..loë), Celtologist.

kemp'haan, game-cock, fighting cock; ~ **strandloper,** ruff.

ken¹, (s) (-ne), chin.

ken², (w) (ge-), know; recognize, understand; cognize; *BLY u te* ~ *(ne),* pleased to meet you; *net van BUITE* ~, know the outside only; *VAN BUITE* ~, know by heart; *te* ~ *ne GEE,* give to under= stand; allege; *iem. IN 'n saak nie* ~ *nie,* act without someone's knowledge; *JOUSELF nie meer* ~ *nie,* be above oneself; ~ *en KAN is twee,* theoretical knowledge is no guarantee of practical ability; *jou LAAT* ~, show oneself in one's true colours; prove oneself to be; *iem. LEER* ~, meet someone; get to know someone; *jy sal jou MOET* ~, you will have to know your stuff; *iem van NABY* ~, to be a close acquaintance of someone; *hy laat hom NOOIT* ~ *nie,* he always comes down handsomely; *ek* ~ *hom SLEG,* I hardly know him at all; *UIT mekaar uit* ~, tell (them) apart; *sy WÊRELD* ~, know how to behave; ~ **baar, (..bare),** knowable, recognizable; cognizable, cognoscible; ~ **baarheid,** cognoscibil= ity.

ken'band, curb strap.

ken'bron, source of knowledge.

ken: ~ **holte,** chin-groove; ~ **houer,** chin-rest.

Ke'nia, Kenya; ~ **an', (Keniane),** ~ **'ner, (-s),** inhabit= ant of Kenya, Kenyan; ~ **ans', (-e),** Kenyan.

ken'kaartjie, tag.

ken'ketting, chin-chain, curb; ~ **holte,** chin-groove.

ken'merk, (s) characteristic, attribute, mark, distinc= tive feature; point; cognizance, determinative; cri= terion; (w) **(ge-),** characterize, be typical of, stamp; ~ **end, (-e),** characteristic, salient, distinctive, out= standing, discriminative, diagnostic; ~ *end wees vir,* be characteristic of.

ken'nelik, (-e), recognizable, apparent, evident, manifest, obvious.

ken'ner, (-s), connoisseur, good judge, authority; ~ **sblik,** look (eye) of a connoisseur.

ken'netjie¹, tipcat (game).

ken'netjie², (-s), little chin.

ken'nis, knowledge (of a thing); acquirement; lore; cognizance, cognition; acquaintance, acquaint= anceship (with persons and things); friend; *BAIE* ~ *se hê,* have many acquaintances; *BUITE* ~ *wees,* have lost one's senses; ~ *DRA van,* have know=

ledge of; *GANGBARE* ~, working knowledge; ~ *GEE,* inform; give notice of; *(geen)* ~ *HÊ (dra) van iets,* have (no) knowledge of something; *by* ~ *KOM,* come round; recover one's senses; *met die polisie* ~ *KRY,* receive notice; *met die gereg* ~ *MAAK,* run foul of the police; ~ *MAAK met iets,* become acquainted with a thing; *nader* ~ *MAAK met iem.,* make closer acquaintance with; ~ *is MAG,* knowledge is power; ~ *NEEM van,* take note (cognizance) of; *met* ~ *van SAKE praat,* speak as an expert (authority); *iem. in* ~ *STEL van iets,* inform someone about something; *al ons* ~ *is STUKWERK,* all our knowledge is fragmentary; ~ **dors,** thirst for knowledge.
ken'nisgewing, (-e, -s), notice, announcement; notification, intimation; *vir* ~ *AANNEEM,* note; ~ *van VERSKYNING,* notice of appearance.
ken'nis: ~ **leer,** epistemology, ~ **making,** getting acquainted; acquaintance; ~ **neming,** (taking) cognizance; perusal, inspection; *ter* ~ *neming,* for information.
keno'sis, kenosis.
ken'skets, (ge-), characterize, depict, typify, describe, mark, delineate; ~ **end,** (-e), typical, characteristic; ~ **ing,** characterization, delineation.
ken'skyf, identification disc.
ken'spreuk, motto.
ken'strokie, tag.
ken'ta(g), ken'tang, afraid, unwilling to play (games); ~ *SPEEL,* stretch the rules; ~ *WEES,* afraid to take chances.
ken'teken, (s) characteristic, distinctive mark; badge; cognizance; (w) (ge-), characterize.
ken'teorie, epistemology.
ken'ter, (ge-), change; turn upside down; careen (ship); *die openbare mening begin te* ~, the tide of public opinion is turning; ~ **haak,** cant-hook; ~ **ing,** change; turning (of the tide); *'n* ~ *ing in die oorlog,* a change of fortune during the war.
kentour', (-e), centaur.
ken: ~ **vermoë,** perceptive faculty, cognition; ~ **waarde,** characteristic value; ~ **wysie,** signature tune.
ke'per, (s) twill; chevron; *op die* ~ *beskou,* on close examination (inspection); (w) (ge-), twill; ~ **ig,** (-e), hackly; ~ **kopmoer,** milled nut; ~ **weefkatoen,** jean; ~ **weefsel,** twill weave.
ke'pi, (-'s), kepi.
ke'pie, (-s) small indentation, notch, nick, tally; ~ **smasjien,** flanging-machine.
kep'pierog, spotted ray *(Stoasodon narinari).*
keramiek', ceramics, potter's art.
kera'mies, (-e), ceramic.
keratien', kerati'ne, keratin.
kerati'tis, keratitis.
keratoom', (. .tome), keratoma.
kêrel, (-s), fellow, chap; beau; *'n GAWE* ~, a fine fellow; *HAAR* ~, her fiancé (lover); ~, *MAN!* old boy! ~ **tjie,** (-s), little fellow, stripling; *die* ~ *tjie met die kurkhoed soen,* ply the bottle; ~ **mal,** boy chaser, flirt.
ke'rende: *per* ~ *pos,* by return of post.
kerf, (s) (kerwe), notch, incision, dent, jag; gear (motor); *in die BOONSTE* ~, in top gear; at full pitch; *dit GAAN bo sy* ~, that has him beat; that is too much for him; *boonste* ~ *TREK,* be in top gear; (w) (ge-), carve, notch; cut (tobacco, ball); dent; hackle; jag; scarify (bark); shred, slice; ~ **bank,** cutting frame; ~ **beitel,** jagger; ~ **blok,** cutting-block; ~ **els,** scouring-awl; ~ **hoek,** skive angle; ~ **ie,** (-s), little notch; ~ **masjien,** tobacco-cutting machine; chaff-cutter; ~ **mes,** (-se), cutting knife (tobacco); ~ **plank,** cutting (-up) board (tobacco); ~ **rand,** milled edge; ~ **rat,** (-te), jagging-iron; ~ **sny,** chipcarving; ~ **stelsel,** notching; ~ **stok,** (-ke), nickstick; cutting-block (tobacco); tally; *baie op sy* ~ *stok hê,* have (a tobacco) tally; have a great deal to answer for; ~ **stokstelsel,** tally system; ~ **tabak,** shag; ~ **werk,** chip-carving, carving.
ke'ring, (-e, -s), turning; check.
kerjak'ker, (ge-), romp, play, run about, career.
kerk, (-e), church, congregation; chapel; service; *hy is in die* ~ *GEBORE,* he never shuts a door behind him; ~ *HOU,* conduct a service; *met hom is geen* ~ *te HOU nie,* one can do nothing with him; *die* ~ *KOM uit,* the (church) service is over; *die SEË= PRALENDE* ~, the church triumphant; *SKEI= DING van* ~ *en staat,* disestablishment; ~ *en STAAT,* church and state; *die STRYDENDE* ~, the church militant; *sy* ~ *is UIT,* he has had his time; his days are over; (w) (ge-), solemnize a marriage in church; *getroud maar nie ge* ~ *nie,* living together without being legally married; ~ **amp,** church office; ~ **ban,** excommunication; ~ **bank,** pew; ~ **besoek,** attendance at church; ~ **besoeker,** church-goer, worshipper; ~ **bestuur,** church management; ~ **blad,** church book, service book; church register; ~ **bou,** ~ **kuns,** ecclesiology; ~ **bus,** poor-box; ~ **bybel,** church Bible; pulpit Bible; ~ **deur,** church door; *jy is by die* ~ *deur omgeruil,* where did your parents find you? ~ **diens,** divine service; ~ **dorp,** township (not officially proclaimed) used only for church services.
ker'ker, (s) (-s), prison, dungeon, gaol; (w) (ge-), throw into prison, imprison, incarcerate; ~ **deur,** prison door; ~ **hol,** dungeon; ~ **ing,** imprisonment.
kerk: ~ **fees,** church festival; ~ **gaan,** (-ge-), attend church; ~ **gang,** attendance at church; ~ **ganger,** (-s), worshipper, church-goer; ~ **gebou,** church, chapel; ~ **gebruik,** church usage; ~ **geld,** change (for collection); church funds; ~ **genootskap,** church, denomination; ~ **gesag,** church authority; ~ **gesang,** church hymn, chant; ~ **geskiedenis,** ecclesiastical history; ~ **gewaad,** vestment; ~ **goed,** church property; ~ **hervormer,** (religious) reformer; ~ **hervorming,** reformation; ~ **hof,** churchyard, God's-acre, burial-ground, cemetery; *by die* ~ *hof fluit,* whistle in the dark; ~ **hofblomme,** graveyard flowers; grey hairs; ~ **hofhoes,** sepulchral cough; ~ **hofkapel,** mortuary chapel; ~ **horlosie,** church clock; ~ **huis,** church house; farmer's town house; ~ **inwyding,** church dedication (consecration); ~ **is'me,** ecclesiasticism; ~ **is'ties,** (-e), intolerant in church matters; ~ **kantoor,** church office; ~ **kas,** church funds; ~ **klere,** Sunday best; ~ **klok,** church bell; ~ **kraai,** jackdaw; ~ **leer,** (church) doctrine; ~ **lied,** church hymn, hymnology; ~ **lig,** light (luminary) of the church; ~ **lik,** (-e), ecclesiastic(al), church, religious, clerical, canonical; ~ **loos,** not belonging to a church; ~ **los,** having drifted away from a church; ~ **losheid,** indifference to the church; ~ **muis,** church mouse; *so arm soos 'n* ~ *muis,* as poor as a church mouse; ~ **musiek,** church music; ~ **orde,** church law (regulations); ~ **orgaan,** church magazine; ~ **orrel,** church organ; ~ **pak,** Sunday-suit; ~ **plein,** church square; ~ **portaal,** church porch; ~ **raad,** church council, consistory; presbytery; ~ **raadslid,** member of the consistory; ~ **raam,** church window; ~ **reël,** church rule; ~ **reg,** church (canon) law; ~ **regering,** hierarchy, church government; ~ **register,** church (parish) register; ~ **regsgeleerde,** canonist; ~ **reg'telik,** (-e), canonical, in accordance with church law; ~ **roof,** church-robbery, sacrilege.
kerks, (-e), devout, pious, churchy.
kerk: ~ **saak,** church affair, matter; lawsuit; ~ **sak,** church (offertory) bag; ~ **sang,** church singing.
kerks'gesind, (-e), religious, churchy.
kerks'heid, churchiness, attachment to the church, churchism.
kerk: ~ **sieraad,** church ornament; ~ **skender,** (-s), sacrilegious person; ~ **skennis,** sacrilege; ~ **skeuring,** (church) schism; ~ **skool,** church school; ~ **stoel,** church chair; ~ **styl,** church style; ~ **swael,** church-martin; ~ **sweë:** *van* ~ *sweë,* by the church; ~ **toring,** church tower, steeple; ~ **toringspits,** church spire; ~ **tug,** church discipline; ~ **tyd,** time for church; church time; ~ **uil,** barn-owl, lich-owl *(Tyto alba);* ~ **vader,** church father; patriarch; *van die* ~ *vaders,* patristic; ~ **vaderlik,** (-e), patristic; ~ **vas,** (-te), attached, devoted to the church; ~ **verband,** religious denomination; ~ **vergadering,** church meeting; ~ **verordening,** church ordinance;

~vervolger, persecutor of the church; ~vervolging, persecution of the church; ~versuim, failure to attend church; ~voog, (-de), church warden; hierarch; provisor (R.C.); ~vors (-te), prelate; ~vorstelik, (-e), prelatic(al); ~waarts, churchward(s); ~wet, canonical law; ~winkel, repository; ~wyding, consecration (dedication) of a church.
kerm, (ge-), lament, whine, groan, moan; ~er, (-s), grouser.
ker'mes, kermes; ~eik, *Quercus coccifera*; ~skildluis, *Kermes ilicis*; ~suur, kermesic acid.
ker'mis, (-se), fair, fête; *dis nie elke DAG ~ nie*, Christmas comes but once a year; ~ *HOU*, make hay; *van 'n KOUE ~ tuis kom*, to be given a dressing down (telling off); ~bed, shakedown; ~bed maak, prepare a shakedown; ~koek, gingerbread (bought at a fair); ~kraam, fair booth; ~pret, fun at the fair; ~tent, (fair) booth; fair tent; ~terrein, fair ground; ~vermaak, fair-time fun; ~wa, caravan; ~week, week of the fair; ~wiel, big wheel, fun-fair wheel, ferris wheel.
kerm: ~kous, grouser, moaner; ~sanger, crooner.
kern, (-e, -s), kernel (nut); body; core; pith (of tree); gist (of the matter); essential; quintessence; crux; gravamen; nucleus (of comet); centre; heart; *die ~ van die SAAK*, the pith (gist) of the matter; *daar is 'n ~ van WAARHEID in*, there is a grain of truth in it; ~ *van WEEKYSTER*, kernel of soft iron; ~aandrywing, nuclear power; ~aangedrewe, nuclear-powered; ~aanval, attack by nuclear weapons; ~afval, atomic (nuclear) waste; nuclear fall-out; ~ag'tig, (-e), pithy, terse, concise; ~ag'tigheid, pithiness, terseness, ~-as, nuclear fall-out; ~bars, heartshake; ~besetting, nucleus garrison; ~bom, nuclear (atomic) bomb; A-bomb; H-bomb; ~bou, nuclear structure ~brandstof, nuclear fuel; ~chemie, nuclear chemistry; ~deling, nuclear division; ~draad, core of a rope; ~ei'wit, nucleoprotein; ~energie, nuclear energy; ~fisika, nuclear physics; ~fout, basic error; ~fusie, nuclear fusion; ~gedagte, central (basic) idea, thought; ~gesond, (-e), fundamentally sound, sound to the core; ~hout, hardwood; duramen; ~krag, nuclear power; *deur ~ krag aangedrewe*, nuclear-powered; ~kragsentrale, nuclear power station; ~liggaampie, nucleole, nucleolus; ~lis, (-se), chromosome; ~loos, (..lose), enucleate; ~makery, coremaking (foundry); ~masjien, core-machine; ~moere, foundation seed; ~oond, nuclear reactor; ~oorlog, nuclear war; ~personeel, skeleton (nucleus) staff; ~reaksie, nuclear reaction; ~reaktor, nuclear reactor; ~saak, essential; ~sillabus, core syllabus; ~skaduwee, umbra; ~skede, endodermis; ~skoot, pointblank shot; ~sperverdrag, strategic arms limitation treaty (SALT); ~spil, core bar; ~splitsing, ~splyting, nuclear fission; ~spreuk, pithy saying, aphorism, apophthegm; maxim; ~stuk, core bar; ~transformator, core transformer; ~verbruining, core flush (apple); ~vorming, nucleation; ~vrug, kernel fruit; ~vuur, pointblank fire; ~wapen, nuclear weapon; ~wetenskap, nucleonics.
keroseen', kerosene.
kerplaks'! blast!
ker'rie, curry; *dis ALLES ~*, it is rubbish; ~ *MAAK van iem.*, make mincemeat of someone; ~-eiers, curried eggs; ~kos, curried food; ~kruie: *dis sommer alles ~ kruie*, it is all nonsense; ~rys, curry and rice; ~so(e)p, curry soup; mulligatawny; ~vis, curried fish.
kers[1], (-e), candle; ~ *AANSTEEK*, be courting; *jou ~ te vinnig BRAND*, burn oneself out; *sy ~ is DOOD*, he is out like a candle; *die ~ brand 'n DOODSKLEED*, the candle is wearing a shroud; *'n ~ aan twee KANTE brand*, burn the candle at both ends; *'n ~ waaroor die MOTTE draai*, the centre of attraction; ~ *OPSTEEK by iem.*, seek someone's advice; *so REGOP soos 'n ~*, as straight as a dart (ramrod); *soos 'n ~ UITGAAN*, go out like a candle in a snuff; *nie ~ vir iem. kan VASHOU nie*, not be able to hold a candle to someone; *om die ~ VLIEG tot jy daarin val*, the pitcher goes to the well once too often; play with fire until one burns one's fingers.
kers[2], *see* kersie.
Kers'aand, Christmas Eve.
kers'bessieboom, candleberry tree (*Aleuritis moluccana*).
kers'blok, Yule-log.
kers'blusser, *see* kersdomper.
Kers'boodskap, Christmas message.
kers'boom[1], Christmas tree; *soos 'n ~ lyk*, look like a Christmas tree.
kers'boom[2], long-tail cassia (*Cassia abbreviata*).
kers'boom[3] = kersieboom.
kers'bossie, candle-bush (*Sarcocaulon burmannii*); *see* aapsekos.
Kers'dag, Christmas Day; *Tweede ~*, (Gesinsdag), Boxing Day; ~aand, Christmas-night.
kers: ~domper, candle-extinguisher; ~draer, candle-bearer, acolyte, altar-boy; ~(e)bos, candle-bush (*Euclea tomentosa*); ~ehout, indigenous tree (*Pterocelastrus variabilis*); ~fabriek, candle factory.
Kers'fees, Christmas; ~nommer, *see* Kersmisnommer.
kers'filter, bougie.
Kers: ~fonds, Christmas fund; ~gedig, nativity poem; ~geskenk, Christmas box (present); ~tyd, Christmas time; ~groet, Christmas greeting.
kers'hout, candlewood (*Gardenia rothmannia*).
ker'sie[1], (-s), small candle.
ker'sie[2], (-s), cherry, ~bloeisel, cherry blossom; ~boom, cherry tree; ~hout, cherry-wood; ~kleur, cherry-red; ~kleurig (-e), cerise; ~pit, cherry stone; ~plukker, cherry-picker; ~tyd, cherry time.
kers'kaartjie, Christmas card.
kers'kleurig, (-e), cherry (-coloured).
Kers'koek, Christmas cake.
kers'lelie, agapanthus.
Kers'lied, Christmas carol.
kers'lig, candlelight; ~sterkte, candle-power.
Kers'maal(tyd), Christmas dinner.
kers'maker, chandler; ~y, chandlery.
kers'mandjie, Christmas hamper.
Kers'mis, Christmas; ~nommer, Christmas number; ~roos, hydrangea.
Kers: ~nag, Christmas Eve; ~nommer, Christmas number.
kers'ogie, (-s), white-eye (*Zosterops capensis*).
kers: ~opsteektyd, candle-lighting time, (Malay) calipha; ~pit, candle-wick.
Kers'poeding, Christmas-pudding, plum-pudding.
kers'regop, bolt upright, straight as a ramrod.
kers'rooi, cerise.
Kers: ~roos, Christmas rose, white-flowered hellebore; hydrangea; ~seël, Christmas stamp.
kers: ~snuiter, (-s), pair of snuffers; ~snuitsel, wick end (of candle); ~steek, pricket; ~sterkte, candle-power.
Kers'ten, (ge-), christianize; ~ing, christianization.
Kers: ~tyd, Christmas time; Yule-tide; ~uitgawe, Christmas edition; ~vakansie, Christmas holidays.
kers'vers, fresh, quite new.
kers: ~vet, tallow, candle grease; ~vlam, candle flame; ~vorm, candle mould.
Kers: ~vreugde, Christmas mirth; ~vulsel, mincemeat.
kers'was, candle wax.
Kers: ~week, Christmas week; ~wens, Christmas wish.
ker'we, (ge-) = kerf.
ker'wel, (ge-), chervil; *DOL(LE), GIFTIGE ~*, hemlock; *KAAPSE ~*, blackjacks; *WILDE ~*, hemlock, chervil.
ker'wer, (-s), carver, cutter.
ker'wery, carving, carvery.
ker'wing, notching, scarification.
kês, sour milk, lopperd (milk); curd; *iem. sy ~ gee*, dare someone; challenge someone.
ke'sieblaar = kiesieblaar.
kêskuiken, milksop; youngster.
ke'tel, (-s), kettle; boiler (engine); still; cauldron; cop=

per; *die* ~ *aan die TUIT beethê*, get hold of the wrong end of the stick; *sy* ~ *(tjie) by 'n ander se VUUR sit*, take advantage of another; ~**bekleding**, boiler-coating; ~**buis**, boiler-tube; ~**druk**, boiler-pressure; ~**huis**, boiler-house; ~**inhoud**, boiler-capacity; ~**inspeksie**, boiler-survey; ~**inspekteur**, boiler-inspector; ~**kamer**, boiler-room; ~**klep**, chuck; ~**klou**, boiler-bracket; ~**koek**, plum duff; ~**konstruksie**, boiler-design; ~**lapper, (-s)**, tinker; ~**maker**, boiler-maker; ~**montering**, boiler-fittings; ~**musiek**, rough music; charivari; ~**ontploffings**, boiler-explosions; ~**pak**, boiler-suit; ~**plank**, boiler-plate; ~**pomp**, boiler-pump; ~**pyp**, boiler-tube; ~**sitting**, boiler-seating; ~**stang**, boiler-stay; ~**steen**, scale, fur, boiler-incrustation; fur(stone); ~**stoel**, boiler-bearer; boiler-cradle; ~**trom(mel)**, kettle-drum; ~**tromslaner**, kettle-drummer; ~**tuit**, kettle spout; ~**vermoë**, boiler-capacity; ~**vormig, (-e)**, kettle-shaped.

ke'ten, (ge-), (fig.), chain; ~**ing**, chaining.

ket'jap, ketchup.

ketogene'se, ketogenesis.

ketoge'nies, (-e), ketogenic; ~*e dieet,* ketogenic diet (for epilepsy).

ketoon', (ketone), ketone.

kets, (s) misfire; **(w) (ge-),** miss fire, misfire, hang fire (gun); clatter; ~**gat**, misfire (mining); ~**ing**, misfiring; ~**skoot**, misfire; flash; ~**stoot**, mis-cue.

ket'ter, (s) (-s), heretic; *erger as 'n* ~ *DRINK,* drink like a fish; *elke* ~ *het sy LETTER,* everybody thinks he has grounds for his belief; every heretic knows his text; *VLOEK soos 'n* ~, swear like a trooper; **(w) (ge-),** rage, rant, storm, crackle, crack; ~**afswering**, abjuration of heresy; ~**hoof**, heresiarch; ~**jaer**, persecutor of heretics (heresy); ~**jag**, persecution of heretics; ~**s (-e),** heretical; ~**verbranding**, auto-da-fé; ~**vervolging**, persecution of heretics; ~**y, (-e),** heresy.

ket'ting, (s) (-s), chain; warp (weaving); gyve; *'n* ~ *om die BEEN hê*, be hamstrung; *op die* ~ *BLAAS,* goad, shout to (whip up) the team; *aan 'n* ~ *LÊ*, be chained up; *dis 'n* ~ *om sy NEK,* it is a millstone round his neck; *'n* ~ *is so sterk soos die swakste SKAKEL*, the strength of the chain is in the weakest link; *in* ~ *s SLAAN*, put (cast) into chains; clasp in irons; *iem. onder die* ~ *UITHELP,* help someone out of a jam; *die* ~ *s VERBREEK*, throw off the chains; **(w) (ge-),** chain up; ~**aandrywing**, chain-drive; ~**blits**, globe lightning; ~**boewe**, chain-gang; ~**bout**, link-pin; ~**breuk**, continued fraction; ~**brief**, chain letter; ~**brug**, chain bridge; suspension bridge; ~**domkrag**, chain jack; ~**draad**, warp; warp yarn; ~**draer**, chainman; ~**ent**, inarch; ~**fakture**, continuous stationery invoices; ~**ganger**, chained convict; ~**gedig**, chain poem (last line in verse rhymes with first line next); ~**handel**, chainstores; ~**hond**, bandog, chained dog; ~**hyswerk**, chain haulage; ~**kabel**, chain cable; ~**kas**, gear case; ~**katrol**, chain pulley; ~**koeël**, chain shot; angle-shot; ~**koppeling**, chain coupling; ~**loos**, (..**lose)**, chainless; ~**lyn**, catenary; ~**maat**, ~**meting**, chainage; ~**naat**, chain riveting; ~**oorbringing**, chain drive; ~**organisasie**, chain organization; ~**plaat**, dress-guard (cycle); ~**pomp**, Persian wheel; chain pump; ~**rat**, chain wheel; ~**reaksie**, chain reaction; ~**reken(e)**, double rule of three, chain rule; ~**rekeninge**, continuous stationery accounts; ~**rem**, chain brake; ~**roker**, chain smoker; ~**rol**, chain drum; ~**rooster**, chain grate; ~**ry**, chain riveting; ~**saag**, chain saw; ~**skakel**, chain link; ~**skerm**, chain guard; ~**skryfmasjien**, continuous stationery machine; ~**skryfwerk** (~**tikwerk**), continuous stationery; ~**sleep, (-gesleep),** survey; ~**sleutel**, chain wrench; ~**sluitrede**, chain syllogism, sorites; ~**spanning**, chain adjustment; ~**spil**, fusee; ~**steek**, chain stitch; lock-stitch; ~**sy**, thrown silk; ~**takel**, block chain tackle; ~**trommel**, chain drum; chain barrel; ~**verband**, chain bond; ~**wand**, barrel (of boiler); ~**wiel**, chain wheel, gear (wheel); ~**winkel**, chain store.

ket'tinkie, (-s), small chain, chainlet.

keu, (-e, -s), (billiard) cue.

keu'ken, (-s), cuisine; kitchen; *'n goeie* ~, an excellent cuisine, a good kitchen; ~**meester**, chef.

Keu'len, Cologne; ~**aar, (-s, ..nare),** inhabitant of Cologne.

Keuls, (-e), of Cologne; ~*e water,* eau-de-Cologne.

keur, (s) choice, selection; pick, elite, flower (of army); plate-mark; **(-e)** statute, by(e)-law; charter; *'n* ~ *van artikels,* a wide selection of articles; **(w) (ge-)**, test, judge; assay (metals); seed (sport); sample; pyx; inspect (meat, etc.); *iem. geen BLIK waardig* ~ *nie,* not deign to look at a person; *ge=de SPELER,* seeded player; ~**bende**, picked men; ~**boom**, *Virgilia capensis; van* ~ *boompie na treurboompie,* go through a wood and pick up a crooked stick; ~**bundel**, volume of selected poems (essays); selection, selected volume; ~**der, (-s),** selector; examiner; essayer, assayer; publisher's reader; ~**hout**, best timber.

keu'rig, (-e), fine, elegant, exquisite, nice, choice, select, natty, dapper, dandy, spick-and-span; chaste; ~ *AFGEWERK,* highly-finished; *'n ROK wat* ~ *pas,* a dress which fits like a glove; *daar* ~ *UIT= SIEN,* look very trim and neat; ~**heid**, nicety, exquisiteness, elegance, fineness, choiceness, delicacy, nattiness; chastity.

keu'ring, (-e, -s), selection; assaying (gold); inspection, testing; examination (medical); ~ *van films,* film censorship; ~**skommissie**, examining body.

keur: ~**komitee**, selection committee; ~**korps**, picked (crack) unit, crack regiment; ~**lys**, seeded list; selection list; ~**meester**, assayer; (food) inspector; ~**merk**, hallmark; ~**nael**, centre punch; ~**prins(es)**, electoral prince(ss); ~**raad**, selection board.

keurs'lyf, bodice, corset; corsage; shackles (of convention); *in 'n* ~ *DWING,* put into a strait-jacket; *die* ~ *van die MODE,* the swaddling bands of fashion.

keur: ~**soldaat**, picked soldier; ~**spel**, selection (music); ~**steen**, touchstone; ~**teken**, hallmark; ~**tjie, (-s),** cancer-bush *(Sutherlandia frutescens); Podalyria;* ~**troepe**, picked troops; ~**versameling**, choice selection; ~**verwantskap**, elective affinity.

keur'vors, electoral prince, elector; ~**tedom**, electorate; ~**telik, (-e),** electoral; ~**tin'**, electress.

keur'winkel, supermarket.

keu'se, (-s), choice, selection, option, alternative; election; pick, range (of choice); *'n* ~ *DOEN,* make a selection; take one's choice; *daar is vir my geen* ~ *GELAAT nie,* it is a case of Hobson's choice; *die* ~ *HÊ,* have the option (choice); *vakke NA* ~, optional subjects; *voor die* ~ *STEL,* faced with the choice between; left with the alternative of; *eiers VOLGENS* ~, eggs to order (menu); *uit VRYE* ~, of one's own free will.

keu'sevak, optional subject.

keus'teelt, selective breeding.

keu'tel, (-s), turd; ~**s**, droppings.

keu'wel, (ge-), chat, gossip, natter, babble.

ke'wer, (-s), beetle, bug, dor, chafter; ~**gif**, beetle-poison.

kgot'la, (-s), kgotla.

khan, (-s), khan; ~**aat', (khanate),** khanate.

khedi've, (-s), khedive (in Egypt).

kiaat'(hout), teak (wood).

kib'bel, (ge-), quarrel, squabble, bicker, altercate, wrangle; ~**aar, (-s),** bickerer, wrangler; ~**(a)ry', (-e),** bickering(s), squabbling, wrangling.

kib'boets, (-e), kibbutz.

kief, (kiewe) = **kieu.**

kiek, (ge-), snap, snapshot.

kie'keboe, bo-peep, peek-a-boo.

kie'kie, (-s), snap(shot); *'n* ~ *neem,* take a snap.

kieks, allowance (marble game); *nieks* ~, no allowance.

kiek'toestel, camera.

kiel^1, (s) (-e), overall, smock.

kiel^2, (s) (-e), keel (of a ship); corner (between two outside walls of a building); gully, creek; valley, wedge (of roof); carina (biol.); **(w) (ge-),** keel, careen; heave down; ~**blok**, keel-block; ~**boot**, keel-

boat; ~ **dak**, valley roof; ~ **geld**, keelage; ~ **haal**, (ge-), keel-haul, careen.
kiel'houer, (-s), pickaxe.
kie'lie, (ge-), tickle; ~ **bak**, arm-pit; axil; *met* ~ *bakke in die wind staan*, stand with arms akimbo; ~ **been= tjie**, funnybone; ~ **-kielie**, tickle-tickle; ~ **rig, (-e)**, ticklish; ~ **righeid**, ticklishness; ~ **ry**, tickling.
kiel: ~ **ing**, careenage; ~ **pik**, pickaxe; ~ **reg**, keelage.
kiel'sog, wake; *in iem. se* ~ *vaar*, follow in someone's wake.
kiel'tjie¹, (-s), (boy's) blouse.
kiel'tjie², small keel; corner (between two outside walls).
kiel: ~ **vlak**, fin (aero.); ~ **vormig, (-e)**, carinate; ~ **water**, track, wake, wash, dead water.
kiem, (s) (-e), germ; embryo; bacterium; gemmule; origin; *in die* ~ *smoor*, nip in the bud; (w) (ge-), germ, germinate; sprout; ~ **blaar**, ~ **blad**, seed-leaf; cotyledon, germinal layer; ~ **blaas**, blastocyst; ~ **bladig**, ~ **blarig, (-e)**, cotyledonous; ~ **dodend, (-e)**, germ-destroying; germicidal, antiseptic; ~ *do= dende middel*, germicide; ~ **doder**, germicide; ~ **draer**, (germ-)carrier; ~ **etjie, (-s)**, germule; ~ **ing**, germination; ~ **krag**, germinative power; ~ **krag'tig, (-e)**, germinative; ~ **lob**, cotyledon; ~ **meel**, germ-meal; ~ **(oor)draer**, germ-carrier; ~ **pie, (-s)**, germule; ~ **plantjie**, seedling; ~ **sak**, em= bryo sac; ~ **sel**, germ cell; ovule; ~ **skyf**, blasto= derm; ~ **vernieler**, germicide; ~ **vlek**, nucleolus; ~ **vlies**, hymenium; ~ **vorming**, germination; ~ **vratjie**, caruncle; ~ **vry, (-e)**, germ-free, sterilized; ~ *vry maak*, degerm; ~ **werend, (-e)**, antiseptic; ~ **wit**, endosperm; albumen; ~ **wortel**, radicle.
kien'speletjie, lotto.
kiep, (s) (-e), fowl; (w) (ge-), come! here! (to fowls).
kiepersol'(boom), kiepersol, umbrella-tree (*Cussonia thyrsiflora*), cabbage-tree.
kie'pie, (-s), chicken; ~ **mielie**, popcorn.
kiep-kiep'! chick! chick! (come! come!) (to fowls); *jy moenie sommer* ~ *ROEP nie*, do not judge all by the same yardstick; do not generalize; *hier* ~ , *daar* ~ , *WOERTS in die hoekie*, act hastily; have too many irons in the fire; try to do too many things at once.
kiepkie'pie(s), *Gladiolus alatus, Sutherlandia frutes= cens, Nymania capensis*; ant-lion.
kier, (-e), chink; *op 'n* ~ *tjie OPEN*, open (the door) slightly; *op 'n* ~ *STAAN*, slightly ajar.
kie'rang, (-s) cheating (in games); ~ *het (uit)gebraai*, the deception has been proved; the truth will out; (w) (ge-), cheat, play false; *MOENIE so* ~ *nie*, don't cheat; ~ *SPEEL*, play false, cheat.
kie'rie, (-s), (s) stick, walking-stick, kerrie; gear lever; *loop of jy 'n* ~ *ingesluk het*, walk up straight as a ramrod; (w) (ge-), hit with a stick; throw a stick at; ~ **been**, very thin leg; ~ **hout**, *Rhus laevigata*; ~ **klapper**, russet bushwillow; ~ **slang**, poisonous (S.A.) snake.
kier'tjie, (-s), chink; *die deur staan op 'n* ~ , the door is slightly ajar.
kierts'regop, bolt upright.
kies¹, (s) pyrites.
kies², (-s) (-e, -te), cavity between gum and cheek; jaw, molar (tooth), grinder (tooth); ~ *en KEUR*, pick and choose; *iem. 'n* ~ *UITTREK*, make someone pay through the nose.
kies³, (w) (ge-), choose, make a choice, select, elect; pick; vote; ~ *of DEEL*, take it or leave it; *NIKS te* ~ *hê nie*, have no option; ~ *TUSSEN*, choose be= tween; ~ *UIT*, select from, pick out (from); *tot VOORSITTER* ~ , elect (as) chairman.
kies⁴, (b, bw) (-e; -er, -ste), delicate, dainty; consider= ate; ~ *optree*, act considerately.
kies: ~ **afdeling**, constituency, electoral division; bor= ough; ~ **baar**, (..bare), eligible for election; ~ **baarheid**, eligibility; ~ **beampte**, electoral officer; ~ **bevoegdheid**, qualification for voting; ~ **deler**, electoral quota; ~ **distrik, (-te)**, constituency.
kie'sel, (-s), gravel, silicon; ~ **aarde**, silica; ~ **agtig, (-e)**, flinty, siliceous, gravelly; ~ **goer**, kieselguhr; ~ **houdend, (-e)**, siliceous; ~ **laag**, gravel layer; ~ **steen**, pebble, cobble-stone; ~ **suur**, silicic acid.

kie'ser, (-s), voter, constituent; *jou op die* ~ *s beroep*, go to the country; ~ **es', (-se)**, female voter.
kie'sers: ~ **korps**, electorate; ~ **lys**, voters' roll.
kies'geregtig, (-de), entitled to vote, enfranchised.
kies'heid, delicacy, refinement, considerateness; de= cency; ~ **shalwe**, for the sake of decency.
kies'houdend, (-e), pyritical.
kie'sieblaar, mallow(s) (*Malva parviflora*).
kie'sing, (-e, -s), election.
kieskeu'rig, (-e), particular, fastidious, choosy; per= nickety, picksome, finical; dainty; ~ **heid**, fastidi= ousness, delicacy, daintiness.
kies'kollege, college of electors.
kies'kou, (ge-), nag; *kerm en* ~ , bother, jaw.
kies: ~ **liggaam**, electoral body; ~ **plek**, polling-station (booth); ~ **plig**, compulsory voting.
kies'pyn, toothache.
kies: ~ **reg**, franchise; right of voting; ~ **reghervor= ming**, electoral reform; ~ **sirkel**, electoral circuit; ~ **skakelaar**, selector switch; ~ **skyf**, disc (teleph.); ~ **spel**, eclectic, greensome (golf); ~ **stelsel**, elec= toral system.
kies: ~ **tand**, molar (tooth), cheek-tooth, grinder; ~ **tang**, dental forceps.
kies: ~ **vergadering**, elective assembly; ~ **wet**, election (electoral) law; ballot act; ~ **wyk**, electoral ward.
kiet(s), quits, even, equal; *ons is* ~ , we are quits.
kiet'sie, (-s), pussy, kitten.
kieu, (-e, kuwe), gill; ~ **boog**, gill-arch, branchial arch; ~ **deksel**, gill-flap; operculum; ~ **holte**, gill-open= ing, peribranchial cavity; ~ **-opening**, gill-slit (cleft); ~ **potig, (-e)**, branchiopodous, branchio= pod; ~ **potige, (-s)**, branchiopod(an); ~ **spleet**, gill-slit (-cleft); ~ **vlies**, gill membrane.
kie'wiet, (-e, -s), kie'wietjie, (-s), plover (*Vanellus coron= atus*); ~ **blom**, *Fritillaria meleagris*; ~ **eier**, plover's egg.
kik, (s) (-ke), scarcely audible sound; *geen – GEE nie, nie utter a sound*; *g'n* ~ *NIE*, mum's the word; *jy moet net* ~ *SÊ*, you need only say the word; (w) (ge-), utter a feeble sound; *nie* ~ *of MIK nie*, with= out a sound or movement.
kik'ker, (-s), frog; ~ **konsert**, croaking concert.
Kikoe'joe, (-s), Kikuyu.
kikoe'joegras, kikuyu-grass.
kik'vors, (-e), frog; ~ **vanger**, (variety of) falcon (*Cir= cus ranivorus*).
kil, (-le; -ler, -ste), chilly, cold, bleak; frigid; ~ **hael**, chilled shot; ~ **heid**, chilliness, bleakness, chill.
ki'lo, (-'s), kilo; ~ **gram, (-me)**, kilogram; ~ **liter**, kilo-litre; ~ **meter**, kilometre; ~ **watt**, kilowatt.
kil'te = kilheid.
kim¹, (s) mould; *daar is* ~ *op die konfyt*, the jam is getting mouldy; (w) (ge-), become mouldy; *die kon= fyt het ge* ~ , the jam has become mouldy.
kim², (s) (-me), horizon; bilge (of ship); chire; planing-fin (aero.).
kimberliet', kimberlite, blue ground.
kim: ~ **diepte**, ~ **duiking**, dip of horizon; ~ **dieptekiel**, bilge-keel; ~ **hoek**, angle with the horizon.
kimo'no, (-'s), kimono.
kin, (-ne) = ken, (s).
ki'na, quinine; ~ **bas**, Peruvian bark; ~ **boom**, cin= chona tree; ~ **bossie**, quinine bush (*Leucadendron concinnum*); ~ **druppels**, quinine drops; ~ **pil**, quin= ine pill; ~ **poeier**, quinine powder; ~ **suur**, quinic acid; ~ **vergiftiging**, quinine poisoning, cinchon= ism.
kin'baard, imperial, goatee, chin-beard.
kind, (-ers), child; infant, baby; chicken, chit, bairn, kid; piccaninny; ~ *ers is die ARM man se rykdom*, children are poor men's riches; *die* ~ *met die BAD= WATER uitgooi*, throw out the baby with the bath-water; ~ *ers BLY maar* ~ *ers*, children are children; *'n* ~ *op 'n BOODSKAP stuur*, make a child do a man's work; send a child on an errand; *'n* ~ *des DOODS*, a doomed (dead) man; heaven help you! *'n* ~ *vir die GALG grootmaak*, rear a child for the gallows; ~ *ers moet GESIEN, maar nie gehoor word nie*, children should be seen and not heard; *as 'n* ~ *nie wil HOOR nie, moet hy voel*, who will not listen, must be made to feel; *soos 'n* ~ *by iem. in die HUIS*

wees, be treated like one of the family; **KLEIN** ~ *ers, klein sorge, groot* ~ *ers, groot sorge*, children when they are little make parents fools; when they are great they make them mad; *'n* ~ *op die KNIE hê*, be rearing a child; *al jou* ~*ers onder een KOM= BERS kan toemaak*, have all one's children under one roof; ~ *nòg KRAAI hê*, have neither kith nor kin; *wie sy* ~ *LIEFHET, kasty hom*, spare the rod and spoil the child; *soos die* ~ *is, so is die MAN*, the child is father to the man; *sy is nie MEER 'n* ~ *nie*, she is no longer a chicken; *die – by sy NAAM noem*, call a spade a spade; *die* ~ *se NAAM is Kaatjie (Adoons)*, that's that; it's all over and done with; *NES 'n* ~, like a child; *'n mens is 'n* ~ *van sy OM= GEWING*, one is a product of one's environment; ~ *ers soos ORRELPYPE*, children by the dozen; *so onskuldig soos 'n PASGEBORE* ~, as innocent as a new-born babe; *met 'n* ~ *en steeks PERD moet jy nooit spog nie*, a child and a horse that jibs should not be relied on; *'n* ~ *(en 'n dronk man) PRAAT die waarheid*, out of the mouths of babes and suck= lings (comes the truth); *die* ~ *van die REKENING word*, pay the piper; one who foots the bill; ~ *ers is 'n SEEN van die Here, maar hulle hou die mot uit die klere*, he that has children can call nothing his own; *hou tot die* ~*ers v.d. SKOOL kom*, we'll have to hold out until the next meal; *jy SLAAN jou* ~*ers weg*, you even begrudge your children a share; *SÓ die* ~, *só die man*, the child is father to the man; *gaan jy met* ~*ers uit, kom jy met* ~*ers TUIS*, children, when little, make parents fools; *'n* ~ *van sy TYD*, a product of the times; *eers* ~ *sien, dan VADER (pa) staan*, when you chris= ten the bairn you should know what to call it; *hy is nie VANDAG se* ~ *nie*, no chicken; ~*ers praat die WAARHEID*, children and fools speak the truth.
kin'deke, (vero., Ndl.), (-s), infant; *die K* ~ *Jesus*, the Infant Jesus.
kin'der: ~ **aard**, child nature; ~ **aftrek**, deduction (re= bate) in respect of each child (income-tax).
kinderag'tig, (-e), childish, silly, puerile; frivolous; futile; puppy-headed; ~ **heid**, childishness, silliness, puerility; desipience, frivolity, folly.
kin'der: ~ **arbeid**, child-labour; ~ **arts**, *see* **kinder= dokter**; ~ **bal**, children's ball; ~ **balk**, boarding- (bridle-)joist; ~ **bed**, child's bed, cot; childbed; crib; ~ **bedkoors**, puerperal fever; ~ **beskerming**, child-protection (welfare); **K** ~ **beskermingswet**, Children Protection Act; ~ **bessie**, *Halleria lucida*; ~ **beul**, bully; ~ **bewaarplek**, day-nursery, nursery-school, créche; ~ **bewys**, bond to secure property of chil= dren; ~ **boek**, book for children; ~ **bottel**, nursing bottle; feeder; ~ **breukband**, child's truss; ~ **bybel**, children's Bible; ~ **dae**, childhood; *van sy* ~ *dae af*, since his infancy; ~ **dief**, kidnapper, child-stealer; ~ **diefstal**, kidnapping; ~ **diens**, children's service; ~ **digter**, children's poet; ~ **dokter**, children's spe= cialist, paediatrist; ~ **doop**, infant-baptism; infant-christening; ~ **drag**, children's clothes; ~ **fees**, chil= dren's festival; ~ **gebabbel**, prattle; ~ **geboorte**, childbirth; *pynlose* ~ *geboorte*, painless birth, twi= light sleep; ~ **gees**, childmind; ~ **gek**, lover of chil= dren; ~ **geneeskunde**, paediatrics; ~ **gestamel**, bab= ble, prattle, childish chatter; ~ **goed**, children's clothing; ~ **hand**, child's hand; pud; *'n* ~ *hand is gou gevul*, a child is easily satisfied; ~ **harp**, child's harp; Sunday-school hymn-book; ~ **hart**, child's heart; ~ **hawe**, créche; ~ **hof**, juvenile court; ~ **huis**, children's home; ~ **jare**, childhood; ~ **juffrou**, nursery governess, mother's help; ~ **kaartjie**, child's ticket; ~ **kamer**, nursery; ~ **katel**, cot; ~ **kerk**, children's service; ~ **klere**, baby (chil= dren's) clothes; ~ **kliniek**, child-clinic; ~ **kolonie**, children's camp; ~ **koor**, juvenile choir; ~ **korting**, rebate (deduction) in respect of children; ~ **kos**, children's food; ~ **kuns**, child art; ~ **kwaal**, chil= dren's ailment; ~ **leed**, childish grief; ~ **leidinginsti= tuut**, ~ **leidingkliniek**, child guidance institute (clinic); ~ **lektuur**, juvenile literature; ~ **lewe**, child= hood; child's life; ~ **liefde**, love of one's children; filial affection.

kin'derlik, (-e), childlike, innocent, filial; ~ **heid**, naïvety, artlessness, simplicity.
kin'derloos, (..lose), childless; issueless; ~ **heid**, childlessness.
kin'der; ~ **mandjie**, baby-basket; ~ **maniere**, childish manners; ~ **meel**, infants' food; ~ **meisie**, nursegirl; mother's-help; ~ **mishandeling**, child battering; ~ **moord**, infanticide, child-murder; prolicide; ~ **moord**, infanticide; ~ **oog**, child's eye; ~ **party= tjie**, children's party; ~ **plig**, filial duty; ~ **pokke**, ~ **pokkies**, smallpox; ~ **praatjies**, childish prattle; silly talk; ~ **preek**, sermon for children; ~ **roof**, *see* **kinderdiefstal**; ~ **rympie**, nursery rhyme; ~ **seën**, blessings of parenthood; ~ **siekte**, disease of chil= dren; ~ **skeurbuik**, Barlow's disease, infantile scurvy; ~ **skoen**, child's shoe; *in* ~ *SKOENE wees*, be a mere infant; *die* ~ *skoene ONTWASSE wees*, a child no longer; *die* ~ *skoene UITTREK*, behave like a grown-up; ~ **skool**, school (for children); ~ **skrywer**, writer of juvenile stories; ~ **sorg**, child-welfare; ~ **speelgoed**, toys; ~ **spel(etjies)**, child's play; children's game(s); *dis nie* ~ *speletjies nie*, it is no child's play; ~ **sprokie**, nursery tale; ~ **stem**, child's voice; ~ **sterfte**, infant mortality; ~ **stoel**, baby-chair; ~ **storie**, child's tale; nursery tale; *dis sommer* ~ *stories*, it is all talk; ~ **studie**, child-study; ~ **taal**, child's language; childish talk; ~ **te= huis**, children's home; ~ **toelae**, allowance for chil= dren; ~ **tuin**, kindergarten; ~ **tuinstelsel**, Froebe= lism; ~ **tyd**, childhood; *van sy* ~ *tyd af*, since his childhood; ~ **uitrusting**, ~ **uitset**, layette; ~ **ver= haal**, children's story; nursery tale; ~ **verlamming**, infantile paralysis; poliomyelitis; ~ **versie**, nursery rhyme; ~ **versorger**, baby farmer; ~ **verstand**, child's intelligence; ~ **voeding**, infant feeding; ~ **voedsel**, infants' food; ~ **voorskootjie**, pinny, child's pinafore; ~ **vriend**, lover of children; ~ **wa(entjie)**, perambulator; pram; ~ **wagter**, baby-sitter; ~ **weegskaal**, nursery-scales; ~ **welsyn**, ~ **welvaart**, child welfare; ~ **wêreld**, childland; land of children; ~ **werk**, child's work.
kind'jie, (kindertjies), little child, baby; dear; *eers* ~ *sien, dan vader staan*, look before you leap; commit yourself only after a thorough investigation.
kind'lief, dear child, dear, darling.
kinds, (-e), childish; in one's dotage, senile, anile, dot= ing; ~ **been**: *van* ~ *been af*, since childhood; ~ **deel**, ~ **gedeelte**, child's portion; ~ **heid**, childishness; anility, dotage; childhood, infancy.
kind'skap, filiation.
kinds'kind, grandchild.
kind'-vroutjie, child-wife.
kineas', (-te), filmist.
ki'nema, (-s), cinema, bioscope; ~ **skoop'**, (..**skope**) cinemascope; ~ **'ties**, (-e), cinematic; ~ **tika**, cine= matics.
kinematograaf', (..**grawe**), cinematograph; cinema= tographer.
kinematografie', cinematography.
kinematogra'fies, (-e), cinematographic(al).
kinetiek', kinetics.
kine'ties, (-e), kinetic.
kine'tika, kinetics.
kinien', kini'ne, *see* **kina**.
kink, (s) (-e), twist, knot, hitch; kink; (w) (ge-), twist, rebound; knock.
kin'kel, (-s), knot, twist; hitch; fake (cable); kink; *daar is 'n* ~ *in die kabel*, there is a hitch (snag) somewhere; ~ **bos**, shrub (*Tetragonia fruticosa*); ~ **keperlinne**, twill; ~ **rig**, (-e), kinky.
kin'ketting, curb-chain.
kink'hoes, (w) (w)hooping cough; pertussis.
kin'nebak, (-ke), jaw-bone, mandible; ~ **slag**, box on the jaw.
kin'netjie, (-s), little chin.
kinoloog', (..**loë**), quinologist.
kin'riem, chin strap.
kin'ta, kin'tie, (dear) child; *o nee, ou* ~*!* oh no, my dear!
kiosk', (-e), kiosk.
kip: ~ **kar**, tip-cart; ~ **rooster**, dump-grate; ~ **wa**, tip= ping truck, tip-lorry.

kir, (ge-), coo.
kis, (s) (-te), box, case, trunk, coffer, chest; coffin; hutch (for ore); (w) **(ge-),** coffin; (bw) thoroughly; *jou ~ LAG,* split one's sides with laughter; *iem. ~ LOOP, (speel),* beat thoroughly; outdo; **~dam,** coffer dam; **~deksel,** coffin lid; box (trunk) lid; **~hou,** crack (first-rate) shot (in sport); **~klere,** best clothes, go-to-meeting clothes, one's Sunday best; glad rags; **~sie, (-s),** (small) box; tray (for fruit); casket; pyxis; **~hout,** wood for fruit trays; **~plankie,** shook.
kist, (-e), cyst.
kis'temaker, coffin-maker.
kit, bond (geol.); bonding agent, cement.
kitaar', (-s, kitare), guitar; **~snaar,** guitar string; **~speler,** guitarist.
kit: ~massa, cement; **~middel,** bonding agent, cement, lute.
kits¹, (-e), ketch.
kits², instant; moment; trifle; *IN 'n ~,* in the twinkling of an eye; in a trice; *vir hom is dit SOMMER 'n ~,* for him it is a mere trifle; **~gaar,** ready in a minute; **~inligting,** instant information; **~klaar,** ready for use in a jiffy; **~koffie,** instant coffee; **~kontant,** cash dispenser; **~rekenaar,** ready reckoner; **~rol,** flick-roll; **~vakature,** snap-vacancy.
kit'tel, (ge-), tickle; **~aar, (-s),** clitoris.
kittelo'rig, (-e), ticklish; touchy, short-tempered; **~heid,** ticklishness; touchiness.
Ki'wi, ki'wi, (-'s), Kiwi, kiwi.
kla, (ge-), complain, lament, wail; grumble; grouse; *dit is GOD ge~,* it cries to heaven; *ek KAN nie ~ nie,* I cannot complain; things are not too bad; **~OOR,** complain of.
klaag: ~huis, house of mourning; **~lied,** lamentation, dirge; plaint; *DIE K~liedere,* the Lamentations; *OU ~lied(ere),* grouser, grumbler; **~lik, (-e),** plaintive, doleful; **~muur,** wailing wall (in Jerusalem); **~psalm,** penitential psalm; **~sang,** elegy, elegiac poem, dirge; **~siek, (-e),** querulous; **~skrif, (-te),** plaint; petition; **~stem,** plaintive voice; **~ster, (-s),** female plaintiff; **~toon,** plaintive tone.
klaar, (klare; -der, -ste), ready, finished, done, done for; foredone; game; clear; *die ETE staan ~,* dinner is served; *~ HÊ,* have ready; have done; *so ~ soos 'n KLONTJIE,* as plain as the nose on you face; *~ MAAK,* prepare; finish; get ready; get you down; *dit is ~ MET hom,* he is finished, bankrupt, etc.; *his days are numbered; dis NOU maar ~,* that is a fact, no doubt about that; *klare ONSIN,* sheer nonsense; *gou ~ SPEEL met iem. of iets,* polish someone or something off quickly; *~ STAAN (sit) vir iets,* have a rod in pickle for someone; *~ WAKKER,* already wide awake; *~ WEES met iem.,* have nothing further to do with someone; *~ WEES vir iem.,* be ready for someone; **~blyk'lik, (-e),** clear, evident, obvious, apparent, manifest(ly), plainly; patently, palpably; **~blyk'likheid,** obviousness, clearness; **~gaar,** ready-to-eat; **~gekoop, (-te), ~gemaak, (-te),** ready-made; **~heid,** clarity, clearness; *'n saak tot ~heid bring,* clear a matter up.
klaar'kom, (-ge-), get finished; manage; *ek sal DAREM ~,* I'll be able to manage; *GOED met iem. ~,* get on well with somebody; *~ MET,* make do with; *SONDER iets ~,* do without something.
klaar: ~kry, (-ge-), finish, get ready; **~ligte:** *op ~ ligte dag,* in broad daylight; **~maak, (-ge-),** get (make) ready, finish; prepare (food); dress; dispense (medicine); *hy maak HOM ~,* he is getting ready; *JOU vir iets ~maak,* you can prepare yourself for something; **~middel,** finishing agent; **~pan,** clearing pan; **~praat, (b)** finished, settled; *dis ~praat met hom,* his number is up; he is done for; **~sein,** clearing signal; **~siende,** clear-sighted, shrewd; **~speel, (-ge-),** manage, contrive; polish off; finish off; *ons sal gou met hom ~speel,* we'll fix him up quickly; **~staan, (-ge-),** be ready, stand ready; *vir almal ~staan,* be at everybody's beck and call; **~te,** clarity, clearness.
Klaas¹, Nick; *~ VAAK (Vakie),* Willie Winkie, the dustman, the sandman.

klaas², (klase), servant, subordinate, stick-in-the-mud; *~ is soos BAAS,* like master, like man; *OU ~,* a stick-in-the-mud; *~ WEES,* be a Jack (lackey); be at another's beck and call.
klaaslouw'bossie, weed *(Athanasia trifurcata).*
klad, (s) (-de), blot, slur, stain; rough draft (copy); stigma; *'n ~ op iem. se EER werp,* blacken someone's character; *in ~ OPSTEL,* make a rough draft (of); (w) **(ge-),** blot, stain; daub; **~aanteke= ninge,** rough notes; **~blok,** blotter; **~boek,** scrib= bler, scribbling-book, rough-book; **~derig, (-e),** dauby; full of blots; **~notule,** rough draft of mi= nutes; **~papier,** blotting-paper; scribbling-paper; **~skilder,** dauber; **~skrif,** scribbling; rough-work; scribbling-book; **~werk,** rough copy.
kla'e, (ge-) = kla.
kla'end, (-e), sick, ill, ailing; complaining, plaintive; querimonious; lacrimoso (music).
kla'er, (-s), grumbler; plaintiff, complainant; *waar daar geen ~ is nie, is daar geen gereg nie,* where there is no plaintiff justice cannot be done; **~ig, (-e),** peevish; ill, seedy; complaining, querulous; **~igheid,** querulousness.
klag, (-te), complaint; charge; **~brief,** letter of com= plaint; **~skrif, (-te),** petition; **~staat,** charge-sheet.
klag'te, (-s), complaint; charge; **~boek,** complaint-book; **~kantoor,** charge-office.
klak'keloos, (..lose), unawares; offhand, uncere= moniously, without more ado; without any motive, groundless.
klak'son, (-s), klaxon, electric hooter.
klam, ([e]] mer, -ste), damp, moist, clammy; **~ser= vet,** damp finger napkin; **~heid,** dampness; **~ma= ker,** damper; **~merig, (-e),** rather damp, moist; **~merigheid,** slight moistness; **~migheid,** moist= ness, dampness.
klamp, (s) (-e), clamp, cramp, cleat, bracket; batten; chock; fish(plate); brace; (w) **(ge-),** clamp, fasten with clamps; *hom aan iem. ~,* buttonhole (accost) someone; **~anker,** palm-stay; **~deur,** batten-door; **~laag,** diagonal course; **~spyker,** clamp-nail.
klam'te, dampness; **~tjie,** drizzle; moistness.
klandestien', (-e), clandestine.
klandi'sie, custom, customers, patrons, patronage, clientele; **~waarde,** goodwill (of a business).
klank, (s) (-e), sound, ring, tone; breath; acoustics; *HOL ~e,* empty sounds; *sy NAAM het 'n goeie ~,* he has a good name; *YDELE ~e,* idle words; (w) **(ge-),** sound, articulate; **~baan,** sound-track; film stripe; **~beeld,** sound (illustrated) feature pro= gramme; **~bodem,** sound box; **~boei,** sound buoy; **~bord,** sound(ing)-board; **~demper,** sordine, silencer; **~dig, (-te),** sound-proof; **~digting,** sound-proofing; **~figuur,** acoustic figure; **~film,** talkie, sound film; **~gat,** sound hole; **~getrou,** high-fidelity (hi-fi); **~getrouheid,** high fidelity; **~gevoelig, (-e),** sensitive to sounds; **~golf, (..golwe),** sound (acoustic) wave; **~grens,** sound barrier; **~kas,** belly (of violin); resonance box; **~kleur,** timbre, **~leer,** phonetics; **~lint,** recording tape; **~loos, (..lose),** toneless, silent; **~maat,** prosody; **~meter,** sonometer; **~metode,** phon(et)= ic method; **~nabootsend, (-e),** onomatopoeic; **~nabootsing,** onomatopoeia; echoism; **~(rol)= prent,** sound film, talkie (film); **~ryk, (-e),** sono= rous, rich (voice); **~rykheid,** sonorousness; sonori= ty; **~skrif,** phonetic writing, transcription; **~stel= sel,** phonetic system; **~teken,** phonetic symbol; sound sign; **~toestel,** sounder; **~trou, (-e),** high-fidelity, hi-fi; **~verandering,** change of sound; **~verdower,** damper, mute, sordine; **~verplasing,** metathesis; **~verskuiwing,** shifting of sounds; per= mutation of consonants; Grimm's Law ; **~ver= sterker,** amplifier; **~verwisseling,** mutation; **~ver= wysing,** vowel mutation; **~vol, (-le),** sonorous; **~volume,** sound-volume; **~voorstelling,** phone= tism; **~vorming,** formation of sound; **~wet,** pho= netic (sound) law; **~wysiging,** sound mutation (change).
klant, (-e), customer, client, patron; purchaser; *RARE ~,* queer customer; *TOEKOMSTIGE ~,*

prospect(ive customer); ~e, clientage, clientele; ~elokker, barker, tout; ~emaal, gristing.

klap, (s) (-pe), slap, blow, crack, biff, cuff; facer; flap= per; drop (telephone); side curtain (motor-car); flap; peak (of cap); *in EEN* ~, at one and the same time; *iem. 'n taai* ~ *GEE*, smack someone hard; *'n* ~ *in die GESIG*, a slap in the face; *'n kwaai (taai)* ~ *KRY*, suffer a severe check; receive a hard knock; *hy ken die* ~ *van die SWEEP*, he knows the ropes; *'n TAAI* ~, a slap in the face; ~ *pe UIT= DEEL*, cuff all and sundry; ~ *pe VAL*, slaps are being dealt out; *nie 'n* ~ *WERD nie*, no good at all; quite worthless; *'n* ~ *van die WINDMEULE weg hê*, have a tile loose; have bats in the belfry; (w) (ge-), smack, clap, pop, crack; beat, biff, buffet; flicker (wings); flick; click (with tongue); *HANDE* ~, clap hands; *met die LIPPE* ~, smack the lips; *met die TONG* ~, click with the tongue; ~bank, folding seat; ~bed, convertible bed; ~broek, old-fashioned flap-trousers; ~deur, swing door; ~ek= ster, gray shrike; ~hoed, gibus; ~houtjies, casta= nets, rattlebones, clacks; ~keil, opera-hat; ~klank, explosive (sound) click.

klapklap'pertjie, (-s), variety of lark *(Megalophonus apiatus)*; type of plant.

klap'knip(pie), curtain fastener.

klap'kop, drop-end.

klap'loop, (ge-), sponge, cadge; ..loper, sponger, parasite, cadger, bum; ..lopery, sponging, cadging.

klap'mus, hood-cap; ear-bonnet.

klap'per¹, (s) (-s), tell-tale, tattler; index, register; cracker, explosive (sound).

klap'per², (s) (-s), coco(a)nut; wild orange *(Stry= chnos)*.

klap'per³, (w) (ge-), rattle; flap; chatter (teeth).

klap'per: ~boom, coco(a)nut(-tree); ~dop, coco(a)= nut shell; pate, nob, head (of person); ~haar, coir; ~haarmatras, coir mattress.

klap'permanspoësie, doggerel.

klap'perolie, coco(a)nut oil.

klap'pers, poisonous shrub *(Crotalaria burkeana)*.

klap'persteen, eagle-stone.

klap'pertand, (ge-), make the teeth chatter; *hy* ~ *van die koue*, his teeth are chattering with cold; ~end, (-e), with chattering teeth.

klap'pertert, coco(a)nut tart.

klap'pertjie, (-s), delicate rambler *(Cysticapnos afri= cana)*; clapper lark.

klap'per: ~vesel, coco(a)nut fibre, coir; ~vulsel, co= co(a)nut filling; ~water, coco(a)nut milk; ~ys, co= co(a)nut ice.

klap: ~plaat, fall-plate (loco); ~rib, short rib, thin flank; ~roos, corn-poppy; ~skarnier, flap-hinge; ~skyf, collapsible target; ~slot, slam-lock; ~soen, resounding kiss, smack; ~stoel, folding chair, tip-up seat; ~sy, drop-side; ~tafel, gate-leg table, folding table; turn-over table; Pembroke table; ~visier, leaf-sight; ~vliegtuig, ornithopter; ~vlies, valve, valvule; ~wa, folding (baby) car= riage; ~wiek, (ge-), flap (clap) the wings.

klaret', claret, light-bodied red wine; ~bole, claret cup.

kla'righeid, clearness; readiness; ~ *maak om*, get ready to.

klarinet', (-te), clari(o)net; ~tis', (-te), clarinettist.

kla'ring, clearing, clarification; clearance (customs); ~sbewys, clearance certificate; ~skoste, clearance fee; ~stukke, in-clearing certificates.

klaroen', (-e), clarion; ~geskal, clarion call.

klas (s) (-se), form, grade, standard; class; category; description; genus; ilk; rating; rate; *(in die) EERSTE* ~ *reis*, travel first class; *cf.* eersteklas; *INDEEL by 'n* ~, place in (assign to) a class; ~ *LOOP*, be taking classes; *VERDEEL in* ~*se*, di= vide into classes, classify; (w) (ge-), *see* klasseer; ~bewus, (-te), class conscious; ~boek, class book; ~kamer, class room; ~leier, monitor, prefect; ~lys, (-te), class list; ~maat, class mate; ~onder= wyser, class-teacher, form master.

klas'sebewussyn, class-consciousness.

klasseer', (ge-), class, classify (wool); ~der, (-s), grader; classer.

klas'se: ~gees, class-feeling; ~haat, class hatred; ~- indeling, class grouping; ~loos, (..lose), classless; ~oorheersing, class domination; ~regering, class government; ~'ring, classing, classification; ~stryd, class war(fare); ~vooroordeel, class preju= dice.

klassiek', (-e), classic(al); ~ *e musiek*, classical music; *die* ~ *e*, the classics.

klassifika'sie, (-s), classification.

klassifiseer', (ge-), classify; ~der, (-s), classifier.

klassikaal', (..kale), class; ..*kale onderwys*, class-teaching.

klas'sikus, (-se, ..sici), classicist.

klas'sis, (-se), classis (of church), presbytery.

klassisis', (-te), classicist; ~me, classisism; ~ties, (-e), classicistic(al).

klas'ties, (-e), clastic.

klas'voog, (class) prefect; prepositor.

kla'ter, (ge-), rattle, splash, clatter, patter; ~goud, tinsel; German gold, gaud, Dutch metal; leaf-brass; imitation gold, brass-foil; glare.

klavesim'bel, (-s), harpsichord, clavecin.

klavesinis', (-te), harpsichordist.

klaviatuur', (..ture), clavier, claviature.

klavichord', (-e), clavichord.

klavier', (-e), piano; ~ *speel*, play the piano; ~bege= leiding, piano accompaniment; ~les, piano lesson; ~noot, piano note; ~onderwyser(es), piano teacher; ~simbaal, clavichord; ~skarnier, piano hinge; ~spel, piano-playing; ~speler, pianist; piano player; ~stemmer, piano tuner; ~stoel, mu= sic (piano) stool; ~uitvoering, piano recital.

kla'wer¹, key (piano); *sy* ~ *is DROOG*, he has no voice; *iem. se* ~ *s is VALS*, he hasn't all his wits about him.

kla'wer², (-s), clover, shamrock; club (cards); ~aas, ace of clubs; *die diere loop op* ~ *aas*, the cattle are grazing on bare ground; ~blaar, clover-leaf; ~boer, knave of clubs, pam.

kla'werbord, keyboard.

kla'wer: ~dame, queen of clubs; ~heer, king of clubs; ~jas', jas (card game); ~patroon, trefoil pattern; ~s, clubs (cards); ~saad, clover seed; ~ses', six of clubs; ~slot, lever lock; ~suring, wood sorrel; ~vier', four-leaved clover; four of clubs; ~vrou, queen of clubs.

kle'ding, clothes, clothing, apparel, raiment, gar= ment, garb, dress; habiliments, accoutrement; fig; guise; ~stof, cloth, material; ~stowwe, drapery; ~stuk, garment, article of dress.

kledy', apparel, array, raiment.

kleed, (s) (klede), garment, garb; cloth, frock, dress; apparel.

klee(d), (w) (ge-), clothe, dress; garb; *dit* ~ *haar GOED*, it suits her; *sy* ~ *haar GOED*, she dresses well.

kleed: ~geld, dress allowance; ~hokkie, dressing-box; ~jie, (-s), cloth, tablecloth; saddlecloth; doily; ~kamer, dressing-room; clockroom; vestiary, sac= risty; robing-room; green-room; ~repetisie, full-dress rehearsal; ~stof, fabric; ~tafel, dressing-table.

kleef, (ge-), cling, cleave, stick, adhere; *daar* ~ *bloed aan sy hande*, he is a murderer; ~band, adhesive tape; ~blad, mount (photo); ~deeg, lutin(g); ~deegvulsel, lutin(g) pad; ~krag, adhesive force (power); ~kruid, goose-grass, cleavers; ~middel, adhesive substance; ~myn, limpet mine; ~papier, gummed paper; ~pasta, gloy; ~pleister, sticking-plaster, adhesive plaster; ~stof, gluten, adherent, adhesive, agglutinant; ~vastheid, adhesive strength; ~verband, adhesive bandage.

kleer'tjies, (child's) clothes.

klei, clay; mortar (for building); lute; ~ *AANMAAK*, pug; *IN die* ~ *wees*, be in a fix; ~ *TRAP*, be at a loss; *VOL* ~ *wees*, put on airs; *VUURVASTE* ~, fire-clay; ~aarde, clay; ~agtig, (-e), clayey; dough-baked; bolar(y); ~bewerking, pugging; ~draend, (-e), petitic; ~duif, clay pigeon; ~erig, (-e), clayey; dough-baked; bolar(y); ~gat, clay-hole; ~gruis, hoggin; ~grond, clayey soil; ~hou= dend, (-e), clayey; ~hut, mud hut; ~laag, layer of

kleim

clay; ~ **lat,** clay stick; ~ **latgooi, (-gegooi),** play clay-stick shooting (boys' game).
kleim, (-s), claim (diggings); *'n* ~ *afpen,* peg a claim.
klei'meul(e), pug-mill.
kleim'inspekteur, claim-inspector.
klei'muur, mud wall, clay wall.
klein, (s): ~ *en GROOT was daar,* everybody, big and small, was there; *IN die* ~, in a small way; (b) **(-er, -ste),** small, little; petty; petit(e), puny, pimping, microcosmic, diminutive; exiguous; *van* ~ *s AF,* from an early age; *'n* ~ *BIETJIE,* a tiny bit; ~ *ste gemene DELER,* lowest common factor: ~ *DRUK,* small print; *LOOP dat jy* ~ *word,* run like mad; *jou* ~ *MAAK,* draw oneself in; *iem.* ~ *MAAK,* bring someone to his knees; ~ *van PERSOON, maar groot van patroon,* of small physical but large intellectual proportions; *die* ~ *er SKRYWERS,* the minor writers; ~ *SLAAN,* smash (break) to pieces; ~ *ste gemene VEELVOUD,* lowest common multiple; *by die* ~ *maat VERKOOP,* sell by retail; *hom* ~ *VOEL,* feel small.
Klein'-Asië, Asia Minor.
klein: ~ **blaar,** little leaf; ~ **boer,** smallholder, peasant; ~ **boet,** little brother; ~ **burgerlikheid,** parochialism, narrow-mindedness; ~ **ding,** child, infant; ~ **dogter,** granddaughter.
Klein Duim'pie, Tom Thumb; small boy; a hop-o'-my-thumb.
klei'ne, small things (matters); *wie die* ~ *nie EER nie, is die grote nie werd nie,* he who will not keep a penny shall never have many; *wie die* ~ *VERAG, sal nie die grote vermag,* who scorns small things will never achieve big things.
kleineer', (ge-), belittle, minimize, cheapen, disparage; . . **ne'rend, (-e),** detracting, detractive, disparaging.
klei'nerig, (-e), rather small, smallish.
kleine'ring, belittlement, disparagement.
kleingees'tig, (-e), narrow-minded, petty, small-minded, pettifogging, parochial; ~ **heid,** narrow-mindedness, pettiness, parochialism.
klein'geld, small change, cash; *van iem.* ~ *MAAK,* make mincemeat of someone; *vir iem.* ~ *UITKEER,* let someone have something back with interest; *hy WAG nie vir sy* ~ *nie,* he is quick-tempered; ~ **bewys,** cash voucher.
kleingelo'wig, (-e), of little faith; ~ **heid,** little faith.
klein: ~ **getye,** little office (R.C.); ~ **geweervuur,** small-arms fire; ~ **gewere,** small arms; ~ **goed,** little ones (things), children, kids, youngsters, small fry.
klein'handel, retail trade; ~ **aar,** retail dealer, retailer; ~ **onderneming,** retail concern, retailer; ~ **prys,** retail price.
klein'harsings, cerebellum.
kleinhar'tig, (-e), faint-hearted, pusillanimous; ~ **heid,** faint-heartedness, pusillanimity.
klein: ~ **heid,** smallness, minuteness; diminutiveness; littleness, pettiness, exiguity; ~ **hoewe, (-s),** small holding, plot; ~ **hoof'dig, (-e),** microcephalic, microcephalous; ~ **hout,** scantling; ~ **huisie,** closet, W.C., privy.
klei'nigheid, (..hede), trifle, small thing, bagatelle, drib(b)let, jot, (k)nick-(k)nack; ace; chicken-feed (money); mite, flea-bite; . . **hede,** minutiae.
klein'kas, petty cash; ~ **rekening,** petty-cash account.
klein'kind, grandchild; ~ **erhospitaal,** infant hospital; ~ **erskool,** infant-school; ~ **ertyd,** babyhood.
klein: ~ **kommandowurm,** lesser army worm; ~ **koningriethaan,** gallinule; ~ **kopspyker,** brad; ~ **kombuisie,** scullery; ~ **koring,** *Triticum aestivum.*
klein'kry, (ge-), understand, grasp, master, get the hang of; break in, subdue; *ek sal HOM* ~, I'll break him in (subdue him); *IETS nie* ~ *nie,* not to be able to understand something; *ek kan sy ONDANKBAARHEID nie* ~ *nie,* I fail to understand his ingratitude; *'n VRAAGSTUK* ~, solve a problem.
klein'letter, small letter.
klein'lik, (-e), petty, narrow-minded; ~ **heid,** pettiness.
klein'maak, (-ge-), change (money); break up.

klep

kleinmoe'dig, (-e), faint-hearted, despondent; pusillanimous; ~ **heid,** despondency, pusillanimity.
klein: ~ **neef,** (male) second cousin; ~ **niggie,** (female) second cousin; ~ **nôi,** ~ **nooi,** young lady; young mistress.
klein'ood, (..node), jewel, treasure, gem.
klein: ~ **pensie, (-s),** reticulum; ~ **rat,** pinion; ~ **rygsteek,** running (stitch).
kleinse'rig, (-e), delicate; touchy, sensitive, easily hurt, babyish.
kleinse'righeid, touchiness, sensitiveness; delicacy; ~ *is die voorkant van seer kleinigheid,* touchiness is the characteristic of a small mind.
klein'seun, grandson.
kleinsie'lig, (-e), narrow-minded, small-minded, pusillanimous, petty; ~ **heid,** narrow-mindedness; pettiness; pusillanimity.
klein: ~ **ske'delig, (-e) = kleinhoofdig;** ~ **span,** little ones, youngsters, kids; ~ **ste, (-s),** the smallest; minimus; ~ **ste kwadraat,** least square (math.).
klein'steeds, (-e), provincial, parochial, suburban; ~ **heid,** provincialism, parochialism, suburbanism.
klein: ~ **sus,** little sister; ~ **te,** smallness, littleness.
klein'tjie, (-s), little one, child, kiddy; little animal; *BAIE* ~ *s maak 'n grote,* many a little makes a mickle; *BUITEN die* ~ *s,* not taking petty expenses into account; *ek het amper 'n* ~ *GEKRY,* I almost threw a fit; ~ *s KRY,* bring forth young (animal); *hy LAG hom 'n* ~, he roars with laughter; *PAS die* ~ *s op,* take care of the pence; *'n* ~ *MAAK,* have a spot; *vir geen* ~ *VERVAARD wees nie,* not easily frightened.
klein'tongetjie, uvula; *my* ~ *hang,* my uvula is swollen.
klein: ~ **toontjie,** small toe; ~ **trommel,** side-drum; ~ **tyd,** early youth, babyhood; ~ **vannag,** last night in the small hours; ~ **vee,** small livestock; ~ **verlof,** short leave; ~ **vlerkie,** alula; ~ **wild,** small game.
klei: ~ **os,** clay ox; ~ **pad,** clayey (muddy) road; ~ **perd,** clay horse; ~ **prop,** clay plug; ~ **pyp,** clay pipe; ~ **skoot,** mud blast; ~ **stopsel,** clay plug; ~ **trap, (-ge-),** flounder, vacillate, make excuses; beat about the bush; ~ **trapper,** clodhopper; ~ **trog,** hod; ~ **vloer,** mud floor; ~ **werk,** clay-modelling; ~ **-ystererts,** clay iron-ore.
klem, (s) (-me), stress, accent, emphasis; lock (wrestling); cramp, (bench)clamp; binding-screw; terminal (elect.); fit (forestry); ~ *in die KAAK,* lock-jaw, tetanus; ~ *LÊ op,* (lay) stress (on); *MET* ~ *praat,* speak emphatically; *letik in die* ~ *WEES (raak),* be in a fix; (w) **(ge-),** clench (the teeth); pinch, clasp, jam; bind; *aan die BORS* ~, clasp to one's breast; *die DEUR* ~, the door jams, the door is sticking; *die SKOENE* ~, the shoes are pinching; *die TANDE op mekaar* ~, clench the teeth; *'n VINGER in die deur* ~, jam one's finger in the door.
klema'tis, clematis (flower).
klem: ~ **beuel,** clamp; ~ **binder,** spring binder, spring-file; ~ **binding,** spring-binding; ~ **blok,** terminal block; ~ **bord,** terminal board; ~ **bout,** clamp-bolt; ~ **bus,** chuck; drill-socket.
klemen'sie, clemency, mercy.
klem'haak, dog, clamp-hook, cramp-iron; chamfer-clamp; holdfast.
klem'kaak, lock-jaw, tetanus.
klem'mend, (-e), cogent, forcible; *'n* ~ *e betoog,* a conclusive argument.
klem: ~ **moer,** clamping-nut, locking-nut; clip, clip-plate; ~ **ring,** clamp, circlip; ~ **skroef,** clamping-screw, locking-screw; set-screw; retaining-pin; ~ **stuk,** horse; ~ **teken,** accent, stress mark; ~ **toon,** accent, emphasis, stress, ictus; ~ **veer,** circlip.
klem'weerserum, anti-tetanic serum.
klep, (s) (-pe), flap (pocket); clack; piston; poke (cap); valve; stopper (machinery); curtain; key (horn); (w) **(ge-),** clapper, clang, toll; ~ **as,** cam-shaft; ~ **bedding,** valve-seat; ~ **beuel,** key-bugle; ~ **borg,** valve-guard; ~ **deksel,** valve-cover; ~ **deur,** clack-door; ~ **dop,** valve-cap; ~ **drukstuk,** valve-gland.

kle'pel, (-s), tongue (of a bell), clapper.
klep: ~ **geleiding**, valve-gear; ~ **houer**, valve-holder; ~ **inrigting**, valve-assembly; mechanism of valve; ~ **kas**, valve-chest; ~ **kop**, valve-head; ~ **lighoogte**, valve-lift; ~ **ligter**, (-s), tappet; valve-lifter; ~ **loos**, (..lose), valveless; ~ **opening**, valve-opening; ~ **pakking**, valve-gasket.
klep'pekas, valve box.
klep'per, (s) (-s), rattle; castanet(s); (w) (**ge-**), chatter (teeth); rattle, clack.
klep: ~ **pie**, (-s), valvule; ~ **pote**, valve-wings; ~ **ratwerk**, valve-gearing; ~ **reëling**, valve-timing; ~ **skerm** valve-guard; ~ **sluiting**, valve-closing; ~ **speling**, tappet-clearance; ~ **stand**, valve-position; ~ **steel**, valve-stem; ~ **steelgeleier**, valve-stem guide; ~ **stelling**, valve-adjustment; ~ **stif**, valve-stem; ~ **stoter**, tappet, valve-pushrod; ~ **toestel**, clack-gear.
kleptomaan', (..**mane**), kleptomaniac; ..**manie'**, kleptomania; ..**ma'nies**, (-e), kleptomaniacal.
klep: ~ **veer**, valve-spring; ~ **visier**, leaf-sight; ~ **werk**, valve gear.
klera'sie, clothing; drapery; ~ **handel**, drapery; ~ **handelaar**, draper; outfitter; ~ **stof**, material; ~ **vervaardiging**, manufacture of clothing; ~ **winkel**, outfitter's (draper's) store.
kle're, clothes; clothing; dresses; *uit jou* ~ *KLIM*, be beside oneself with anger; *dit raak sy KOUE* ~ *nie*, it leaves him stone-cold; *die* ~ *maak die MAN*, fine feathers make fine birds; *die* ~ *maak nie die MAN nie*, handsome is as handsome does; *dit gaan nie in 'n mens se* ~ *SIT nie*, it touches one deeply; it does not leave one unmoved; *iem. in die* ~ *STEEK*, clothe a person; *baie geld in* ~ *STEEK*, spend every penny on clothes; ~ **bedryf**, clothing industry; ~ **borsel**, clothes-brush; ~ **drag**, fashion dress, clothing, costume, garb; ~ **fabriek**, clothing factory; ~ **haak**, clothes-hook; ~ **handelaar**, outfitter, clothier; ~ **hanger**, (-s), clothes-hanger; ~ **kas**, wardrobe; clothes-press; chest of drawers; ~ **koffer**, (clothes-)trunk; ~ **koper**, buyer of (old) clothes; old-clothes-man; ~ **maakster**, dressmaker; ~ **maker**, tailor; ~ **makersbaas**, master tailor; ~ **makerskryt**, tailor's chalk; French chalk; ~ **makery**, dressmaking; tailoring; ~ **mot**, clothes-moth; ~ **pers**, clothes-press; ~ **prag**, rich attire; ~ **skeur**: *nie sonder* ~ *skeur nie*, not achieved without scars; not at all easily; ~ **stander**, clothes-horse; ~ **stof**, dress material; cloth; ~ **werker**, clothing worker; ~ **winkel**, outfitter's shop, draper('s store).
klerikaal', (..**kale**), of clergy, clerical; ..*kale drag*, clerical garb.
klerikalis'me, clericalism.
klerk, (-e), clerk; apprentice; white-collar worker; quill-driver (coll.); ~ **ewerk**, clerical work; ~ **lik**, (-e), clerical; ~ *like hulp*, clerical assistance; ~ **opsigter**, shopwalker.
klets, (s) (-e), drivel, twaddle, tommy-rot; (w) (**ge-**), chatter, rattle, natter, talk, gossip, jaw, yap; splash; ~ **er**, (-s), chatterer, talker of tommy-rot, bladder; ~ **erig**, (-e), gossipy, talkative, noisy; ~ **ery**, twaddle, piffle, tommy-rot, gossip, scandal-mongering; ~ **kous**, chatterer, gossip, chatterbox; gossip-monger; ~ **nat**, wet through, dripping wet; ~ **praatjies**, trash, prattle, bosh, gossip, small talk.
klet'ter, (**ge-**), clatter, patter (rain); brawl; hurtle; clash (arms); clang (bell); ~ **end**, (-e), clangorous, pattering.
kleur, (s) (-e), colour, dye, pigment, hue, complexion; flush (of cheeks); suit (cards); timbre (music); ~ *BEKEN*, follow suit (cards); show one's true colours; *BLOU van* ~, blue in colour; *in DIE-SELFDE* ~ *as*, in the same shade as; ~ *GEE aan*, lend colour to; ~ *HOU*, keep its colour; *'n* ~ *KRY*, change colour, blush; *'n* ~ *LOSSPEEL*, establish a hand (at cards); *NIE 'n* ~ *nie*, not diamond-bearing; *te STERK* ~, make too much of something; *van* ~ *VERANDER*, change sides; undergo a change of heart; ~ *VERLOOR*, lose its colour; ~ *VERSAAK*, not to follow suit; *van* ~ *VERSKIET*, not to follow suit; lose (change) colour; *sy* ~ *e WYS*, show his true colours; *die* ~ *e VLOEK met (teen) mekaar*, the colours clash; (w) (**ge-**), colour, stain, dye, tone; blush; *van SKAAMTE* ~, blush with shame; *'n sterk ge* ~ *de VERSLAG*, a highly coloured report; ~ **baadjie**, blazer; ~ **bad**, toning-bath; ~ **balle**, colours (snooker); ~ **beleid**, colour policy; ~ **bewus**, (-te), colour-conscious; ~ **blind**, (-e), colour-blind; ~ **blindheid**, colour-blindness; daltonism, achromatosis; ~ **der**, (-s), dyer; ~ **diepte**, tone (photo); ~ **draer**, chromatophore; ~ **ebeeld**, spectrum; ~ **edruk**, colour-printing; chromatography; ~ **effek**, colour effect; ~ **eg**, (-te), fast-coloured, fadeless; ~ **eharmonie**, colour harmony; ~ **ekombinasie**, combination of colours; ~ **ekontras**, colour contrast; ~ **emengeling**, blending of colours; iridescence; ~ **eprag**, splendour of colours; ~ **erykdom**, riot (blaze, wealth) of colours; ~ **espektrum**, chromatic spectrum; ~ **espel**, play of colours; ~ **espeling**, iridescence; ~ **fikseerbad**, toning- and fixing-bath; ~ **film**, colour film; ~ **filter**, colour filter; ~ **foto**, colour photo; heliochrome; ~ **fotografie**, colour photography; heliochromy, chromatrope, photochromy; ~ **gevoel**, colour sense; ~ **gevoelig**, (-e), orthochromatic, sensitive to colours; ~ **gewend**, (-e), colorific; ~ **houdend**, (-e), fast(-dyed), washable; fadeless; ~ **ig**, (-e), full of colour, colourful; flamboyant, florid; ~ **igheid**, colourfulness; ~ **ing**, coloration; ~ **kryt**, coloured chalk; ~ **leer**, chromatology, chromatics; ~ **ling**, (-e), (neerh.), coloured person; ~ **litografie**, chromolithography; ~ **loos**, (..lose), colourless, achromatic, achromatous, drab; ~ **loosheid**, colourlessness, achromatism; ~ **menging**, colour blending; ~ **meter**, chromatometer, colorimeter; ~ **middel**, (-s), colouring agent; pigment; ~ **plaat**, colour plate; ~ **potlood**, colour pencil; ~ **rolprent**, colour-film; ~ **ryk**, (-e), colourful; ~ **sel**, (-s), colouring; distemper; flash (on helmet); coloration; pigment-cell, chromatophore; ~ **serp**, (ong.), (academic) hood; ~ **sin**, sense of colour; ~ **skaal**, chromatic scale; ~ **skakering**, variation of colours, colour shade; differential toning; ~ **skema**, colour scheme; ~ **skifting**, colour dispersion; ~ **skyf**, colour disk; ~ **skyfie**, colour slide; ~ **slagboom**, colour bar; ~ **span**, team of one colour only; ~ **speling**, play of colours; ~ **steendruk**, chromolithography; ~ **stof**, pigment; dye, colouring matter; ~ **syfer**, colour index; ~ **teken**, badge; ~ **vas**, (-te), fast-dyed, fadeless, sunproof; ~ **vastheid**, colour fastness; ~ **vegie**, touch of colour; ~ **venster**, stained-glass window; ~ **verandering**, change of colour; change of politics; ~ **vol**, (-le), picturesque; colorific; ~ **waarde**, colour value; ~ **wisselaar**, chromatrope; ~ **wisselend**, (-e), versicoloured.
kleu'ter, (-s), toddler, infant, kid; elf; ~ **onderwyseres**, nursery-school teacher; ~ **skool**, nursery school; kindergarten; ~ **taal**, baby-language.
kle'we, (**ge-**), cling, stick, adhere, cleave; *'n smet* ~ *op sy naam*, his reputation is tarnished; ~ **r**, (-s), sticker.
kle'werig, (-e), sticky, adhesive, viscous, glutinous, cloggy, gummy, gluey; grumous; clammy; ~ **heid**, stickiness, adhesiveness, viscosity, lubricity (of oil); gumminess, clamminess, glueyness.
klief, (**ge-**), cleave (waves), plough (the seas); divide; ~ **lyn**, cleavage.
kliek, (s) (-e), clique, set, coterie; cabal; clan; junta; gang; circle; (w) (**ge-**), form a clique (set); ~ **erig**, (-e), cliquey, cliquish, factious; clannish; ~ **erigheid**, cliquishness, clannishness; ~ **gees**, cliquishness, cliquism.
kliënt', (-e), client (of professional person); ~ **ebus**, courtesy bus; ~ **e'le**, (-s), clientele; ~ **skap**, clientship.
klier, (-e), gland; follicle; ~ **agtig**, (-e), glandular, glandiform; scrofulous; ~ **buis**, glandular duct; ~ **derig**, (-e) = **klieragtig**; ~ **geswel**, scrofulous tumour; glandular swelling; bubo; ~ **koors**, glandular fever; ~ **kunde**, adenology; ~ **loos**, (..lose), eglandulous; ~ **lyer**, scrofulous patient; ~ **ontsteking**, inflammation of the glands; ~ **siekte**, scrofulous disease, scrofula; the king's evil; ~ **verswering**, sup-

kliewe — **klits**

puration of the glands; ~**vormig**, (-e), glandiform; ~**weefsel**, glandular tissue.
klie'we, (ge-), see **klief**.
kle'wing, cleavage; fission.
klik¹, (s) (-ke), (vero.); cleek (golf).
klik², (s) (-ke), click (with tongue); click sound; (w) (ge-), click.
klik³, (w) (ge-), tell tales (out of school), peach, blow the gaff; ~**apparaat**, bugging device; ~**bek**, ~**ker**, (-s), tell-tale, blabber; bugging device; ~**kerig**, (-e), tell-tale; ~**kerigheid**, ~**kery**, tale-bearing.
klik'klak, (s) click-clack; (w) (ge-), clack.
klik'klank, click (sound).
klik'lamp, pilot lamp.
klik'spaan, tell-tale, tale-bearer.
klim, (s) climb; (w) (ge-), climb, rise, ascend; creep (belting); *in jou AMP* ~, rise in one's profession; *in die BOOM* ~, climb up (into) a tree; *die JARE* ~, the years are advancing; *die NOOD* ~, the need becomes pressing; *op sy SKOOT* ~, climb onto his lap (knee); *die SON* ~, the sun is climbing.
klimaat', (**klimate**), climate; dampness; ~**beskrywend**, (-e), climatographical; ~**beskrywing**, climatography; ~**gordel**, climatic zone; ~**kenner**, climatologist; ~**kunde**, climatology; ~**reëling**, air-conditioning; ~**s'toestand**, climatic condition; ~**verandering**, change of climate.
kli'maks, (-e), climax; ..**makte'ries**, (-e), climacteric; ..**makte'rium**, climacteric.
klima'ties, (-e), climatic.
klimatologie', climatology; ..**lo'gies**, (-e), climatic; climatologic; ..**loog'**, (..**loë**), climatologist.
klim: - **baan**, climbing lane; - **boon**, runner bean; ~**draai**, climbing turn; ~**duiking**, dip; ~**haak**, holdfast; ~**hoek**, angle of ascent; climbing angle; ~**mend**, (-e), rising, increasing; climbing; rampant, saltant (coat of arms); scandent (botany); ~**mende jare**, advancing age; ~**mer**, (-s), climber; ~**ming**, climbing; ramp; ~**mingsmeter**, climbing indicator; ~**op**, (-**pe**), ivy, creeper, climber (plant), runner, bindweed, traveller's joy, wild clematis; ~**plant**, climber, rambler, bindweed, creeper, climbing plant, runner (plant); ~**pote**, scansorial feet; ~**roos**, rambler (rose); ~**snelheid**, rate of climb; ~**stand**, climbing position; ~**toets**, (hill-) climbing test; ~**tol**, yo-yo; ~**vermoë**, climbing ability; ascentional powers; ~**voël**, scansor, zygodactyle, climber; social climber; ~**yster**, climbing-iron, step-iron.
kling, (-e), blade (sword); *oor die* ~ *ja*, put to the sword.
klin'gel, (ge-), jingle, tinkle, ting; ring (bell); ~**end**, (-e), tintinnabulous; ~**ing**, ting-a-ling, ting-ting, jingling.
kliniek', (-e), clinic.
kli'nies, (-e), clinical.
klink¹, (s) (-e), jack (telephone); catch, latch; pin; detent; dowel; *op die* ~ *sit*, latch.
klink², (w) (ge-), sound, ring, clink, clank, click; rivet; shrink; hob-nob, touch glasses (toasting); chink; bicker; *dit* ~ *BEKEND*, it has a familiar ring; *dit* ~ *BETER*, that sounds better; *DAAROP* ~ *ons*, we touch glasses on this; *dit* ~ *GOED*, that sounds well (good); *IEM.* ~, hit (strike) someone; *aan die KRUIS* ~, nail to the cross; *OPREG* ~, ring true; ~**bout**, dowel, rivet; clinch-bolt; ~**dig**, (-te), sonnet.
klin'kend, (-e), ringing, jingling, resounding, sonorific; ~*e munt*, hard cash.
klin'ker, (-s), vowel; army biscuit; (Dutch) hard brick, clinker; riveter; ~**graaf**, clinker shovel; ~**rym**, assonance; ~**s**, hard tack; ~**steen**, Dutch brick, clinker (brick); ~**vurk**, clinker-fork; ~**wisseling**, vowel gradation.
klink: ~**gat**, pin-hole; ~**hamer**, riveting-hammer, riveter.
klink'klaar, (..**klare**), pure, sheer, mere; ..*klare onsin*, blatant, unadulterated nonsense.
klink: ~**klank**, stilted language; jingle of words, jingle-jangle; ~**las**, (-se), riveted joint; ~**ligter**, disengaging-gear; ~**masjien**, riveter; ~**naat**, riveted flange, clench-joint.

klink'nael, rivet; clench, clinching-nail; ~**broek**, jeans; ~**deurslag**, rivet-punch; ~**gat**, rivet-hole; ~**kop**, (-pe), rivet-head.
klink: ~**ring**, clench-ring; ~**sleutel**, latch key; ~**slot**, latch (lock); ~**stang**, pawl rod; ~**stiebeuel**: *dit gaan* ~ *stiebeuel*, all is going well; ~**tang**, riveting-clamp.
klink'werk, riveting (work); clincher-work; ~**er**, riveter.
kli'nometer, klinome'ter, clinometer.
klip, (-pe, -pers), stone, rock, pebble; cliff, crag; *hy is van sy* ~ *pe AF*, he is off the rails; *'n* ~ *in die BOS gooi*, be provocative; cause a stir; *so DOM soos 'n* ~, abysmally stupid; *oor die EERSTE* ~ *pe wees*, have taken the first hurdle; *iem. oor die* ~ *pe HELP*, help someone over a stile; *dis 'n* ~ *aan sy NEK*, it is like a millstone round his neck; *vir iem. 'n* ~ *uit die PAD rol*, do someone a favour (good turn); *'n* ~ *aan die ROL sit*, set the ball rolling; *soos 'n* ~ *SLAAP*, sleep like a top; *STADIG oor die* ~*pe(rs)*, go slowly and carefully; don't exaggerate; *tussen die* ~ *pe deur STUUR*, steer a safe course; *TEEN die* ~ *pe op*, ignoring all restraints; pressing on regardless; *hy is VAN sy* ~ *af*, he is no longer so cocksure; *baie* ~ *pe VERSIT*, achieve much; move mountains; ~**agtig**, (-e) = **klipperig**; ~**baken**, stone beacon, cairn; ~**ballas**, ballast-stone ~**bank**, reef, stone stratum; ~**beer**, counterfort; ~**beitel**, tooler; stone-chisel; boaster; ~**beitelaar**, stone-cutter; ~**bekleding**, pitching; ~**belletjie**, *Lachenalia tricolor*; ~**blom**, *Liparia comantha*; red crassula; ~**boegoe**, rock-buchu (*Barosma serratifolium*); ~**bok**, chamois; (Cape) klipspringer; ~**boor**, rock (jumper) drill; ~**breker**, saxifrage (plant); quarryman; stone-breaker; ~**brekershamer**, spalling hammer; ~**das**, rock-rabbit; ~**doring**, *Scolopia mundtii*; ~**els**, rock-alder; ~**gat**, quarry; ~**gooier**, stone-thrower; ~**gooiery**, stone-throwing; ~**gruis**, grit; ~**hamer**, stone-breaker's hammer; ~**hard**, (-e), very hard; difficult; *dit reën* ~ *hard*, it's pouring; ~**hout**, hard kind of wood (e.g. *Rhus thunbergii*); ~**huis**, stone house; ~**kapper**, (-s), stone-dresser, stone-breaker; mason; ~**kappery**, stone-cutting; ~-**klip'**, five-stone (game); ~-~ *speel*, play (at) five-stone; ~**klossie**, *Lachenalia tricolor*; ~**koester**, petticoat heath (*Erica glanea*); ~**kop**, rocky hill; obstinate person; ~**kous**, ear shell, sea-ear (a species of *Haliotis*); ~**kraal**, kraal made of stones; ~**krans**, ledge of rock, krantz; ~**lelie**, kind of lily (*Gladinus hyalinus*); ~**maler**, ~**meul**, stone-crusher; ~**mos**, lichen; ~**mossel**, limpet; ~**mossie**, rock bunting; ~**muur**, stone wall; ~**neuker**, (gew.) kind of lizard; (nickname for) geologist; ~-**op-die-hand**, five-stone (game).
klip'per, clipper (ship).
klip: ~**perig**, (-e), stony, rocky; cliffy; flinty; cragged, craggy; ~**perigheid**, stoniness; ~**pie**, (-s, -**pertjies**), small stone, pebble; ~**pie-skop**, hopscotch; ~**plaat**, rocky flats; rocky face; ~**plaveisel**, stone pavement; ~**pyp**, stone pipe; ~**rand**, stone edging; ~**rant**, rocky ridge; ~**rlf**, (..**rlwwe**), rocky ledge; ~**rots**, large rock; ~**rug**, (-ge), rocky ridge, cliff; ~**saag**, stone-saw; ~**sal(a)mander**, rock-lizard; ~**skerm**, stone guard; ~**sorbet**, Edinburgh rock; ~**sout**, rock-salt; ~**springer**, klipspringer; ~**stapel**, cairn; ~**stapeling**, rock-stowing, rock-packing; ~**stapelwerk**, stone-packing; ~**steen**, rock stone; idiot, fool; ~**steenhard**, hard as stone; most difficult, adamantine; cast-iron; ~**steenhard van die geld**, rolling in wealth; ~**storting**, rock-fall; ~**stut**, davit (in mine); ~**suier**, sucker-fish; ~**sweet**, secretion of the rock-rabbit, hyraceum; ~**trap**, stone stairs; ~**tydperk**, stone age; ~**uintjie**, bulbous plant (*Babiana*); ~**vis**, coral fish; ~**vleis**, meat roasted on stones; ~**wagter**, rock-thrush; ~**werk**, stone-work; ~**werker**, stone worker; ~**werktuig**, stone implement.
klis'ma, (-s), clysma, enema.
klisteer', (s) (**klistere**), clyster, enema; (w) (ge-), administer an enema; ~**spuit**, enema (syringe).
klits¹, (s) (-e), bur(r), burdock, dock, cocklebur; tan-

gle (hair); servant; *so 'n KLEIN ~*, the little rascal; *soos 'n ~ aan iem. KLOU*, stick like a burr to someone; *soos 'n ~ VASSIT*, stick like a bur.

klits², (w) (ge-), beat, whip (eggs); thrash; become entangled; kill, pot (with rifle); *iem. ~*, give someone a hiding.

klits: ~**gras**, burdock, bur; ~**klawersaad**, bur; ~**plant**, bur-clover; ~**wol**, wool tangled with burs.

kloaak', (kloake), cloaca.

klod'der, (s) (-s), clot; dab; (w) (ge-), clot, coagulate; ~**ig**, (-e), clotted.

kloek¹, (w) (ge-), cluck.

kloek², (b) (-e), strong, brave, bold, stout, lusty; ~**har'tig**, (-e), bold, fearless; ~**heid**, bravery, boldness, pluck, courage; doughtiness.

kloek'hen, clucking (broody) hen.

kloek: ~**moedig**, (-e), brave, valiant, courageous; ~**moe'digheid**, valour; ~**sin'nig**, (-e), wise; prudent; ~**sin'nigheid**, wisdom, prudence.

klo'fie, (-s), little ravine.

klok¹, (s) (-ke), clock, bell; *alles GAAN volgens die ~*, everything is done by the clock; *aan die groot ~ HANG*, bruit something abroad; proclaim something from the housetops; *dit KLINK soos 'n ~*, that rings true; *op die ~ kan KYK*, be able to tell the time; *hy het die ~ hoor LUI, maar weet nie waar die klepel (bel) hang nie*, have only a vague idea of what it's all about; *die ~ sal agter hom LUI*, he will go under; *'n MAN v.d. ~*, someone who does everything by the clock; *MET die ~*, clockwise; *OP die ~ af*, to the second; *TEEN die ~*, counter-clockwise, anti-clockwise; *dit is alles WERK wat die ~ slaan*, work is the order of the day.

klok², (w) (ge-), chuckle; gobble (turkey-cock), cluck; gurgle.

klok: ~**anker**, bell armature; ~**blom**, bell-flower; columbine; bluebell; ~**boei**, bell-buoy; ~**fles**, bell-jar; ~**gelui**, pealing (booming, tolling) of bells; ~**gietery**, bell-foundry; ~**hamer**, bell-hammer; ~**helder**, clear as a bell.

klok'hen, clucking hen.

klok: ~**huis**, core (of fruit); bell-chamber; ~**hulsel**, bell-housing; ~**kamer**, belfry; ~**kas**, clock-case; ~**kenis'**, (-te), carillonneur, chimer; ~**kespel**, chimes, carillon; peal; ~**kespeler**, chimer; ~**kie**, (-s), little bell (clock); *Erodium moschatum;* harebell, bluebell; Canterbury bell; ~**kiesblom**, campanula; ~**kiesgras**, lady's heart grass; ~**kiesheide**, bell-heath; ~**knoppie**, bellpush; ~**koord**, bell-pull; ~**lied**, chimes; ~**luier**, (-s), bell-ringer; ~**luiery**, bell-ringing; ~**maker**, clockmaker; ~**ojief**, *cyma recta;* ~**rok**, (-ke), flared skirt; ~**sein**, ~**sinjaal**, bell-signal, bell-alarm; ring; ~**slag**, stroke of the clock; ~**slag eenuur**, on the stroke of one, at one o'clock sharp; ~**slot**, time-lock; ~**speelkuns**, campanology; ~**speler**, campanologist; ~**spys**, clock metal; ~**stoel**, bell cage; ~**stuk**, godet (of dress); ~**toring**, bell-tower, campanile, steeple, belfry; ~**tou**, bell-rope; ~**val**, flounce, dress flare; ~**vormig**, (-e), bell-shaped.

klomp¹, (-e), crowd, number, lot, dump, clump, deal, group, heap, chunk, dollop; bulk.

klomp², (-e), wooden shoe, clog, sabot; ~**edans**, clog-dance; ~**emaker**, clog-maker.

klomp: ~**pie**, (-s), a few, a small number, handful, covey; ~**s'gewys(e)**, in drips and drabs.

klomp'vis, head-fish, mole-bat.

klomp'voet, club-foot.

klont, (s) (-e), lump; clot (of blood); clod (of earth); nodule; nugget; ~ *in die BLOED*, thrombosis; *'n ~ op die HARSINGS*, a clot on the brain; (w) (ge-), clot; curdle; become lumpy; coagulate.

klon'ter, (s) (-s), clot, clod, dab; (w) (ge-), become lumpy; clot (blood); form a lump; clog.

klon'terig, (-e), lumpy, clod-like, clotted, grumous, nodular.

klon'tering, clogging; clumping; clotting.

klon'tjie, (-s), *verkleinwoord van* **klont**; ~**s**, (acid) drops; ~**suiker**, loaf-sugar, lump-sugar, cube-sugar.

klont'vorming, clotting.

kloof, (s) (klowe), ravine, cleft, chasm, gulf, gap, gorge, gully, chink, fissure; (w) (ge-), cleave, split, divide; chop (wood); rip (timber); ~**baar**, (..bare), cleavable, fissile; ~**beitel**, cleaving-chisel; ~**byl**, cleaver; ~**mes**, cleaver; ~**nek**, V-neck; ~**saag**, rip-saw, rift-saw, board-saw; ~**sel**, (-s), cleavage; ~**yster**, riving-knife.

kloos'ter, (-s), monastery, abbey, nunnery; cloister, convent; *in 'n ~ gaan*, take holy orders; ~**agtig**, (-e), cloistral, monastic; claustral; ~**balsem**, friar's balsam; ~**broe(de)r**, friar, lay brother; ~**gang**, cloister; ~**gelofte**, monastic vow; ~**gewaad**, monastic dress; ~**gewelf**, cloister vault; ~**herberg**, hospice; ~**kapel**, cloister chapel; ~**kerk**, minster; convent church; ~**latyn**, monk's Latin; ~**lewe**, convent (monastic) life, claustral life, monachism; ~**lik**, (-e), conventual; monastic; ~**ling**, (-e), monk; nun; cenobite; K~**moeder**, Mother Superior; ~**muur**, cloister wall; ~**orde**, monastic order; ~**reël**, monastic rule; ~**sel**, (cloister) cell; ~**skool**, convent school; ~**spreekkamer**, auditorium; ~**tug**, monastic discipline; ~**tuin**, monastery garden; ~**voog**, (-de), prior, abbot; ~**voogdes'**, (-se), prioress, abbess; ~**wese**, monasticism; ~**wet**, monastic law.

kloot, (klote), testicle; ball, globe, sphere.

klop, (s) (-pe), knock, beat; tap; throb; rap; palpitation (of heart); ~ *kry*, be beaten; (w) (ge-), chuck (under chin); knock (at door); tap (on shoulder); flutter, beat, pulsate, throb, palpitate, pulse (heart); balance, tally (figures); defeat, lick; clap; pink (motor); whip (cream); percuss; *dit ~ met sy GEDRAG*, it is in keeping with his behaviour; *iem. onnodig GELD uit die sak ~*, put a person to unnecessary expense; *dit ~ met sy GEWOONTES*, it is of a piece with his habits; *dit ~ NIE*, it does not tally; *die SYFERS ~*, the figures agree; *dit ~ nie met sy VERKLARING nie*, it does not tally with his statement; *daar WORD ge~*, there's a knock (at the door); ~**boor**, pneumatic drill; jack-hammer; air-drill; ~**dans**, tap-dancing; ~**disselboom**: *dit gaan ~ disselboom*, it is plain sailing; everything is in top gear; ~**gees**, rapping spirit; ~**hamer**, mallet, saddler's hammer; ~**hings**, ridgel; cryptorchid; ~**jag**, police drive, round-up, raid; ~**kewer**, death-watch beetle; ~**massering**, tapotement; ~**medium**, spirit-rapper; ~**party**, fighting, scrap; ~**pend** (-e), knocking; throbbing; pulsatile, pulsatory; ~**per**, (-s), knocker, tapper; mallet; ~**pertjie**, (-s), terrestrial grass-warbler; ~**pery**, beating, knocking; ~**pie**, dab; tap (on door); ~**pik**, beater; ~**ping**, (-e, -s), knocking, beat(ing), throb(bing), palpitation, pulsation; ~**plank**, wash-board; ~**ram**, ridgel, cryptorchid; ~**s**, (-e), Malay choir; coon band; ~**steen**, lapstone (of shoemaker); ~**vry** (-e), ~**werend**, (-e), anti-knock.

klos, (s) (-se), bobbin, spool, spindle, reel; tassel, (electric) coil; lock (wool); (w) (ge-), form locks; ~**besem**, mop.

kloset', (-te), closet.

klos: ~**kant**, pillow-lace; bobbin-lace; ~**se**, locks and pieces; ~**sie**, (-s), bobbin; aglet; fringe (of wool); sixia; ~**siesgras**, *Chloris virgata*.

klots, (ge-), beat, dash, lop (of water); kiss (billiards); ~**end**, (-e), plangent; ~**ing**, beating, dashing, lapping (of waves); ~**kanon**, kiss-canon (billiards).

klou, (s) (-e), claw, talon, paw, pounce; clamp, clip (spring); clutch (motor); palm (anchor); fang; jaw, chuck, grip (lathe); grasp; dog; ~ *e AF!*, hands off!; *in die ~e van die GEREG val*, fall into the clutches of the law; ~ *in die GROND slaan*, dig in one's heels; take to one's heels; *as die ~ uitsteek, is die LEEU daaragter*, by his claws you may know the lion; (w) (ge-), stick, cling, claw, cleave; ~**bout**, jigger-bolt; ~**dief**, (..diewe), cat-burglar; ~**doring**, grapple-plant; ~**ent**, claw-end; ~**erig**, (-e), flirtatious; sticky; pawing; ~**gewrig**, (-te), pastern joint (sheep); ~**hamer**, claw-hammer; ~**koevoet**, claw-bar; ~**koppeling**, claw-coupling (clutch); ~**moer**, dog nut; ~**padda**, tree-frog *(Zenopus laevus);* ~**plaat**, face-plate, jaw-chuck; lathe-chuck; ~**plaatring**, chuck-ring; ~**plaatsleutel**, chuck-key; ~**plaatspil**, chuck-spindle; ~**pleister**,

sticking-plaster; ~**seer,** ~**siekte,** foot disease (cattle); claw sickness.
kloustrofobie´, claustrophobia.
klousu´le, (-s), clause, article, paragraph; ~ *reservatoor,* reservatory clause (in will).
klou´tang, locking pliers; claw-tongs, clip-tongs.
klou´ter, (ge-), climb, clamber; ramp; ~**aar, (-s),** climber, clamberer; ~**dief,** cat burglar; ~**vis,** climbing-fish.
klou´tjie, (-s), hoof (animal); small claw; *sy* ~ *tjies het GEKLAP,* he came off second best; *die* ~ *tjie by die OOR kry,* try to make two things tally; ~**solie,** neat's-foot oil.
klou´yster, claw-bar, ripper.
klo´we, (ge-), *see* **kloof,** (w).
klo´wing, cleavage.
klub, (-s), club; ~**baadjie,** club blazer; ~**gebou,** club-house (building); ~**kamer,** club-room; ~**lid,** club-member; ~**lidmaatskap,** club-membership.
klug, (-te), farce, joke, mockery, burlesque; ~**skrywer,** writer of farces; ~**spel,** farce, low comedy.
klug´tig, (-e), farcical, comical, droll, funny; ~**heid,** drollery, farcicalness, oddness, oddity.
kluif, (s) (kluiwe), bone (to pick); *dis 'n hele* ~ , that is a tough job; (w) **(ge-),** pick, gnaw; ~**hout,** jib-boom.
kluis, (-e), hermitage, cell, hut; safe deposit, strong-room; ~**breker,** yegg.
klui´senaar, (-s), hermit, recluse, eremite, ascetic; ~**shut,** hermitage, hermit's cell; ~**skrap,** hermit-crab; ~**slewe,** life of a hermit.
kluis´gat, hawse-hole.
kluis´ter, (s) (-s), chain, fetter; (w) **(ge-), (en)**fetter, shackle, confine; *aan haar bed ge* ~ , confined to her bed, bedridden.
kluit, (-e), clod, lump; ball; divot; *ONDER die* ~ *e,* under the sod; *'n* ~ *SLAAN,* strike a bargain; ~**breker,** land-roller; ~**erig, (-e),** cloddish, cloggy.
klui´tjie, (-s), dumpling, dough-boy; fib, lie; small clod (lump); nub(ble) (coal); ~*s BAK,* tell stories; *iem. met 'n* ~ *in die RIET stuur,* put someone off with fair words; ~**brood,** sodden (doughy) bread; ~**korrel,** Cape bulbul; ~**so(e)p,** dumpling soup; ~**svleis,** meat dumpling.
klui´we, (ge-), *see* **kluif,** (w).
klui´wer, (-s), standing jib.
klun´gel, (s) (-s), idler, loafer; bungler; (w) **(ge-),** idle, loaf; bungle.
kluts: *die* ~ *kwyt raak,* be at sea; lose the thread of discourse); be disconcerted (bewildered).
klu´we, (ns), clew (yarn); ball (string).
knaag, (ge-), gnaw; nag; rankle; prick (conscience); champ; gripe; ~**dier,** rodent (animal), gnawer.
knaap, (knape), lad, boy; chap; lectern; ~**styl,** garçon style.
knab´bel, (ge-), nibble, munch; ~**aar, (-s),** muncher, nibbler.
kna´c, (ge-), *see* **knaag.**
kna´end, (-e), gnawing; troublesome; boring, nagging; ceaseless(ly); griping (pain); ~*e PYN,* unabaiting pain; *dit REEN* ~ , it rains ceaselessly; ~*e SORG,* carking care; ~*e VERDRIET,* poignant grief; *jy is* ~ *VERVELEND,* you are boring to a degree.
kna´er, (-s), gnawer.
kna´ery, kna´ging, gnawing; prick(ing)s (of conscience); stings; pangs; gripe.
knak, (s) (-ke), crack, injury; set-back; *'n* ~ *gee aan,* be a setback to; deal a blow to; (w) **(ge-),** crack, break, snap; impair (health); *sy gesondheid is ge* ~ , his health is impaired; ~**las,** knuckle joint; ~**lont,** spit-fuse; ~**punt,** knick point.
knaks, unfriendly, angry; at loggerheads; *hulle is* ~ *met mekaar,* they are at loggerheads.
knak´skiet, knak´vuur, snap-shooting.
knak´wors, Cambridge sausage.
knal, (s) (-le), report (gun); clap (thunder); pop, bang, crack; detonation, fulmination; peal; (w) **(ge-),** clap, crack, explode, go off (gun), fulminate; ~**bonbon,** Christmas-cracker; ~**buis,** detonating-fuse; ~**demper,** exhaust-box, muffler, silencer; ~**demping,** silencing; ~**doppie,** detonator; fulminating-cap; ~**effek,** clap-trap; stage-effect; ~**gas,** oxyhydrogen; fulminating (detonating, explosive) gas; ~**goud,** fulminate of gold; ~**groen,** glaring green; ~**kwik,** fulminate of mercury; ~**opening,** cut-out; ~**patroon,** detonator; ~**pistool,** cap-gun; ~**poeier,** fulminating-powder; ~**pot,** exhaust-box; muffler, silencer; ~**sas,** detonating-composition; ~**sein,** detonating-signal; ~**silwer,** fulminating-silver; ~**sout,** fulminate; ~**suur,** fulminic acid.
knap¹, (w) **(ge-),** snap, crack; *die GLAS sal* ~ , the glass will crack.
knap², (b) **(-per, -ste),** clever, able, smart, brainy, clear-headed, adroit, a good hand at, proficient; high-spirited; deft; handsome, comely, good-looking; close-fitting; short, scanty, tight; hardly; ~ *van KLEINGELD,* short of change; *die SKOEN sit 'n bietjie* ~ , the shoe fits rather tightly; *'n* ~ *STUDENT,* a clever (brainy) student; *'n* ~ *UITERLIK,* smart looks; (bw) hardly, just; ably; *die son was* ~ *op toe . . . ,* the sun had hardly risen when . . . ; ~**broekie,** panty; scanties; briefs; ~**duik,** trick dive; ~**han´dig,** (b) **(-e),** dexterous, handy; (bw) deftly, expertly; ~**han´digheid,** dexterity; ~**heid,** cleverness, smartness, ability, skillfulness, comeliness, handsomeness.
kna´pie, (-s), little fellow; lectern, small pulpit.
knap´koekie, crunchie.
knap´per, (ge-), crackle; ~**tjie,** crunchie (sweet).
knap´pies, only just; cleverly, skilfully; tightly.
knap´sak, knapsack, wallet; haversack; kitbag; ~**boer,** farmer on small scale.
knap´sakkerwel, knap´sekêrel, knap´sekerwel, (-s), black-jack, beggartick, sweetheart.
knap´sie, (-s), hot pants.
knars, *see* **kners;** ~**been,** gristle, cartilage; ~**end, (-e),** grating; ~**etand, (ge-),** gnash (grind) one's teeth.
knater, (-s), testicle.
knee, (ge-), knead, mould; ~**(d)´baar, (..bare),** mouldable, plastic, pliable; kneadable; ~**emmer,** kneading-machine (-bucket); ~**masjien,** pugg mill.
kneep, (knepe), pinch; *al die knepe ken,* know the ins and outs; know the trick of the trade.
kne´ër, (-s), kneader; ~**y,** kneading.
kneg, (s) (-s, -te), servant; foreman (on farm); slave; (w) **(ge-),** enslave; ~**s, (-e),** servile; ~**skap,** slavery, servitude, bondage; ~**telik, (-e):** ~ *telike berou,* servile regret.
kne´kelhuis, charnel-house, ossuary.
knel, (s) (-le), pinch, difficulty; *in die* ~ *sit,* be in a scrape, predicament; be in a tight corner; (w) **(ge-),** pinch, squeeze, press tightly, get jammed, *'n skoen wat* ~ , a shoe that pinches; ~**lend, (-e),** oppressive; ~**ling, (-e, -s),** oppression; pinch(ing); ~**punt,** bottle-neck.
knel´ter, (ge-) = **kniehalter.**
knel´verband, tourniquet, garrot.
knerp, (ge-), crunch.
kners, (ge-), gnash, grind; creak, gride, grate, jar; grit; crepitate; *op die tande* ~ , gnash teeth; ~**end, (-e),** grating; ~**geluid,** jarring noise; ~**ing,** gnashing, grinding; crepitus.
knet´ter, (ge-), crackle (fire); crepitate; decrepitate (minerals); ~**ing,** crackling; crepitation; decrepitation.
kneu´kel, (-s), knuckle; ~**gewrig, (-te),** knuckle-joint.
kneus, (s) (-e), bruise, contusion; (w) **(ge-),** bruise, contuse; ~**ing, (-e, -s),** ~**plek,** bruise, contusion, lesion; ~**wond,** bruise, contusion, contused wound.
kne´wel, (s) (-s), moustache; anything exceptionally large; whopper, stunner; tommybar; (w) **(ge-),** gag, oppress; extort; ~**(a)ry,** oppression, extortion; ~**skroef,** tommy screw; ~**stang,** gag-bit.
knib´bel, (ge-), haggle, higgle, dicker, bargain, chaffer; ~**aar, (-s),** haggler, bargainer, chafferer; ~**(a)ry,** quibbling, haggling; ~**rig, (-e),** haggling, stingy; ~**spel,** spillikins.
knie¹, (s) (-ë), knee; *tot AAN die* ~ *ë,* up to the knees; *die* ~ *ë voor BAAL buig,* worship Baal; *iem. op die* ~ *ë BRING,* bring someone to his knees; ~ *ë in 'n BROEK,* baggy trousers; *die* ~ *BUIG vir,* bend the

knee to; *sy ~ë DRA,* hurry away; *op die ~ë voor iem. GAAN,* go down on one's knees before someone; *onder die ~ HÊ,* be master of; have a thorough grasp of; *iets onder die ~ KRY,* master something; *'n kind oor die ~ë TREK,* put a child across one's knee; *~ë in die WIND slaan,* take to one's heels.

knie², (w) (ge-), knead; **~bak,** kneading-trough.

knie: **~beskermer,** kneecap; **~boog,** hollow of knee, ham; **~boogband,** hamstring, hough; **~broek,** knickerbocker; knee-breeches; knickers, bloomers; **~buiging,** curtsey; genuflexion; **~diep,** knee-deep; *~diep voor dag,* long before dawn.

knie: **~emmer,** kneading-machine; **~ër, (-s),** kneader; **~ëry,** kneading.

knie: **~gat,** knee-hole; **~gewrig,** knee-joint (man); stifle-joint (horse); **~halter, (ge-),** trammel; knee-halter, hamshackle, handicap; **~halterslag,** builder's knot, hog-tie, clove hitch; **~halterspan, (ge-),** knee-halter and hobble (at the same time); hog-tie; *iem. ~halterspan,* hamstring someone; **~hoog,** (..hoë), knee-high; **~jig,** gout in the knee; **~knik,** curtsey; *'n ~knik maak voor iem.,* curtsey to someone; **~kop,** kneecap; **~kous,** kneecap; **~kuil = knieboog;** **~kussing,** knee puff (on saddle).

kniel, (ge-), kneel; **~bank,** priedieu; **~bankie,** footstool; **~ing,** genuflexion; **~kussing,** hassock, kneeler; **~mat,** prayer rug.

knie: **~plooi,** knee-fold; **~refleks,** knee-reflex.

knies, (ge-), fret, pine, mope, sulk; **~erig, (-e),** fretful, moping, sulky; ill, off-colour.

knie'sening, hamstring.

knie'skottel, kneading-trough.

knie: **~skut,** knee-guard, knee-cap; **~skyf,** knee-cap, patella; **~steun,** knee-rest; **~stuk,** elbow (joint); half-length; **~val,** prostration; knee-tribute; genuflexion; *'n ~val doen voor,* go down on one's knees before someone; **~verband,** toggle-joint; **~vere,** knee-action; **~vering,** knee-springing; knee-action; **~viool,** gamba; **~vormig, (-e),** geniculate(d); **~water,** housemaid's knee(s); water on the knee.

knik, (s) (-ke), nod; rut (in a road); knuckle-joint; (w) (ge-), nod, bob; beckon; *JA ~,* nod assent; *my KNIEË ~,* my knees shake; **~belasting,** collapsing-load.

knik'kebeen, (ge-), give at the knees; be over at the knee (horse).

knik'kebol, (ge-), nod; niddle-noddle; doze.

knik'ker, (-s), marble (toy); **~tjie,** come-sit-by-me (game); **~tjies,** wild plant *(Caesalpina bondu= cella); frutang (Romulea).*

knik'kie, (-s), slight nod; small rut (in road).

knik: **~las,** collapsing load; **~pyp,** cross-over (pipe); **~spanning,** buckling stress; **~spoor,** transverse rut (in a road).

knip, (s) (-pe), bolt, clasp; cut; catch (door); pinch (salt); latch (door); wink; clip (fountain-pen); punch; fastener; hasp; fillip; clip; *nie 'n ~ voor sy neus werd nie,* not worth a pinch of snuff; (w) (ge-), snip, cut (with scissors), clip; wink (eye); flick; shear; *dit is vir HOM ge ~,* it suits him down to the ground; **~beuel,** snap-frame clasp, snap.

knipho'fia, red-hot poker *(Aloides).*

knip'kontak, (-te), catch-contact.

knip'masjien, shearing-machine, shears (mech.).

knip'mes, pocket-knife, clasp-knife, pen-knife; *BUIG soos 'n ~,* fawn, scrape, kotow; *sy LYF ~ hou,* court a girl; *so gou as jy ~ kan SÊ,* before you can say Jack Robinson; **~ry, (-ge-),** swank (it) on horseback.

knip: **~mier,** ant *(Hodotermes mossambicus);* **~model,** cut-out; **~mussie, (-s),** Californian poppy; eschscholtzia; **~ogie,** wink, glad eye; **~oog, (s)** cock (of the eye); flasher (signal); (w) (ge-), wink, blink, give the glad eye; **~patroon,** paper pattern; **~per, (s) (-s),** clipper; (pair of) clippers; cropper; punch; nippers; perforator; (w) (ge-), wink, blink; *met die oë ~ per,* flicker the eyelids; **~pie, (-s),** a little pinch; *'n ~pie sout,* a pinch of salt; **~portret,** pin-up; **~raam,** casement window; **~sel, (-s),** cutting, clip(ping); **~selboek,** scrap-book; **~seldiens,** cutting service; **~sleutel,** latch key; **~slot,** clasp-

lock; latch lock; **~speld,** safety-pin; **~tor,** skipjack; **~veer,** latch spring; **~vlies,** nict(it)ating membrane, third (inner) eyelid, haw.

knob'bel, (-s), bump, knob, swelling, cusp; tuberosity; button; **~rig, (-e),** bumpy, knotty, knobbly.

knoei, (ge-), botch, blunder, mess, bungle, cook (accounts), falsify, tamper with; wangle, intrigue; potter; footle, foozle; graft; manipulate; *AAN iets ~,* meddle with something; *MET iem. ~,* conspire with someone; *SAAM ~,* conspire with; **~bou,** jerry-building; **~bouer,** jerry-builder; **~er, (-s),** bungler; intriguer; dabbler, grafter; tinker; jobber; manipulator; shyster; pettifogger; botcher; adulterator; cobbler; gerrymanderer; fumbler; foozle(r) (golf); **~erig, (-e),** inclined to blunder; **~ery, (-e),** muddle, mess; intrigue; spoliation; graft; hash job; corrupt practices; manipulation; pettifoggery; **~gebou,** jerry-building; **~hou,** foozle(r); **~koper,** auction buyer; **~spel,** bumble-puppy; foul play; **~vendusie,** knock-out sale; **~werk,** patchy work, bad work, botch(ing); bungling, daub; jobbery.

knoes, (-te), knot (in wood); node; knag; knar; knur(r); **~terig, (-e),** knotty, gnarled, nodose, nodular; **~terigheid, ~tigheid,** nodosity, knottiness.

knoet, (-e), knout.

knoets = knoes.

knof'fel, garlic; *wilde ~,* wild garlic *(Tulbaghia allia= cea);* **~agtig, (-e),** garlicky; **~huisie,** clove of garlic; **~polonie,** garlic polony.

knok, (-ke), knuckle, bone.

knok'kelkoors, dengue fever.

knok'kel(toon), bunion.

knol, (-le), hack, nag, jade (horse); tuber, bulb; nodule; *'n OU ~,* a jade; a hack; *iem. ~le vir SI= TROENE verkoop,* make a person believe that the moon is made of green cheese; **~agtig, (-e),** bulbous, tuberous; **~gewas, (-se),** tuberous plant; **~hoef,** chronic laminitis (horse); **~kool,** turnip-cabbage; kohlrabi; **~lerig, (-e),** nodular; **~letjie, (-s),** nodule; tubercle; **~raap,** rutabaga, swede; **~seldery,** celeriac; **~vormig, (-e),** nodular, tuberous.

knoop, (s) (knope), button; knot, tangle, burl, tie; node (music); bend (nautical); curse, oath; junction (railway); hitch, rub, crux, difficulty; jam (traffic); plot (drama); *die Gordiaanse ~ DEURHAK,* cut the Gordian knot; *daar is 'n ~ in die DRAAD,* there is a rift in the lute; there's a hitch; *die ~ is aan die END v.d. riem,* the sting is in the tail; *'n ~ GEE,* swear; *die ~ is GELÊ,* the knot has been tied; *die ~ ONTWAR,* unravel the tangle; *'n ~ in die SAK= DOEK maak,* tie a knot in one's handkerchief; *daar SIT die ~,* there is the rub; *12 knope per UUR aflê,* have a speed of 12 knots per hour; (w) (ge-), tie, knot, button; mesh; ravel; swear, curse; *~ soos 'n MATROOS,* swear like a trooper; *in jou OOR ~,* make a mental note; **~das,** neck-tie; **~derm,** volvulus, ileus, intussusception; gut-tie; **~fabriek,** button factory; **~haak (..hake), ~hakie, (-s),** buttonhook; **~lus, (-se),** frog (uniform); **~lyn,** nodal line; **~naald,** netting-needle; **~plaat,** gusset plate (bridge); **~punt,** nodal point; (railway) junction; **~s'gat,** buttonhole; **~s'gatskêr,** buttonhole scissors; **~s'gatsteek,** buttonhole twist (-stitch); **~skoen,** button-shoe; **~skrif,** quipu; **~steek,** knot-stitch; **~trui,** cardigan; **~werk,** tatting, network, macramé, knotting; netting.

knop, (s) (-pe), knob, head (stick); pommel (saddle); lump (in throat); bulge; protuberance; handle (of door); peg (for hats); bud; boss; burl; bump; newel (staircase); node; gall (on trees); burgeon; knoll; tuberosity; (push)button; oaf, churl, blockhead, bumpkin, clod; *'n DIGTER in die ~,* a budding poet; *iem. 'n ~ DRAAI (steek),* play a trick on a person; score a point off someone; confound someone; *HY is 'n ~,* he is an uncouth person; *'n ~ INHÊ,* have been taken in; *'n ~ in die KEEL hê,* have a lump in the throat, be moved to tears; *in die ~ KOM,* be budding; (w) (ge-), bud; **~draend, (-e),** gemmiferous.

kno'pie, (-s), little button; **~spinnekop,** black widow (spider), button-spider *(Latrodectus indistinctus).*

knop: ~ **ing,** knotting; ~ **kierie,** knobkerrie, club, bludgeon; throwing stick; ~ **neus,** knob-nose, conk, conky; ~ **pe,** galls (on trees); ~ **perig, (-e),** full of knobs, knobbly; nodose, lumpy, gibbous; ~ **pie, (-s),** switch (elec.) gemmule; bead (foresight); nod= ule; little knob.

knop'pies: ~ **blaar,** erinose; ~ **dopskilpad,** tent (geo= metric) tortoise; ~ **doring,** knob-thorn *(Acacia nigrescens)*; ~ **doringbos,** Protea shrub *(Leuca= dendron)*; ~ **hout,** buttonwood; ~ **kool,** Brussels sprouts; ~ **wurm,** intestinal parasite, nodular worm.

knop: ~ **skakelaar,** button-switch; ~ **(vel)siekte,** lumpy skin disease; ~ **vinger,** clubbed finger; ~ **vorming,** budding, germination; ~ **wortel,** root= knot; club-root; ~ **wortelaalwurm,** rootknot nematode.

knor, (s) (-re), grunt, growl; scolding; ~ *kry,* to be growled at, get a scolding; (w) **(ge-),** grumble, growl, grunt; scold, chide; fret; ~ **der, (-s),** grunter; ~ **haan,** gurnet, gurnard; ~ **os,** yak; ~ **pot, (-te),** grumbler, grouser, grouse-pot, croaker.

knor'rig, (-e), grumbling, peevish, testy, choleric, pet= tish, crusty; surly, cross, moody, grumpy, cranky, huffy; ~ **heid,** peevishness, huffiness, bile, choler.

knor: ~ **tjor, (-re),** go-kart; ~ **vis,** grunter.

knot¹, (s) (-te), hank (wool), skein; *'n* ~ *wol,* a hank of wool.

knot², (w) **(ge-),** top, prune, pollard, truncate, curtail; head (down); curtail; ~ **boom,** pollard; ~ **hout,** pollards.

knots, (-e), bludgeon, (Indian) club, cudgel; baffy (golf); ~ **vormig, (-e),** club-shaped, clavate, claviform.

knot'wilg, pollard-willow.

knou, (s) (-e), snap, bite; injury, set-back, damage; *'n* ~ *gee,* cause a set-back; impair (health); (w) **(ge-),** hurt, injure; gnaw, maul.

knul, (-le), dunce, dolt, booby; ~ **lig, (-e),** loutish, doltish, awkward.

knup'pel, (s) **(-s),** club, cudgel, bludgeon; bat; joy= stick; baton, truncheon; cosh; niblick (golf); *'n* ~ *in die hoenderhok gooi,* cause a flutter in the dove= cotes; (w) **(ge-),** cudgel; club; ~ **aanval,** baton charge; ~ **dik,** quite satisfied, gorged; ~ **pad,** cor= duroy road; ~ **vers,** doggerel (rhyme).

knus, (-se; -ser, -ste), snug, cosy, comfy.

knut'sel, (ge-), trifle, tinker at, potter about; ~ **aar, (-s),** trifler, potterer; ~ **kamer,** hobby room; ~ **(a)ry,** ~ **werk,** pottering, trifling, botch, scrimshaw.

knyp, (s) (-e), pinch, nip, fix; *in die* ~ *sit,* be in a fix; (w) **(ge-),** pinch, squeeze, nip; be on tenterhooks; be nipping straws; *ge* ~ *wees,* be hard put to it; ~ **bril,** pince-nez; nippers, barnacle; ~ **er, (-s),** pincher (crab); claw, clasper (insect); pincers, jaws (pliers); clip (for papers); (clothes-)peg; pinchcock; nipper; ~ **erig, (-e),** fond of pinching; stingy, parsimonious; ~ **gangetjie,** bottle-neck; ~ **horing,** ingrowing horn; ~ **ie, (-s),** pinch, nip; *'n* ~ *ie sout,* a pinch of salt; ~ **steek,** rolling hitch; ~ **tang,** (pair of) pinchers (pliers); punch; (small) nippers.

koagula'sie, coagulation.

koaguleer', (ge-), coagulate; . . **le'ring,** coagulation.

koa'la, (-s), koala.

koali'sie, (-s), coalition; ~ **regering,** coalition government.

koalisionis', (te), coalitionist.

ko'balt, cobalt; ~ **blom,** cobalt bloom; ~ **blou,** cobalt blue; ~ **bom,** cobalt bomb; ~ **erts,** zaffer; ~ **glans,** cobalt sheen; ~ **glas,** cobalt glass; smalt; ~ **swart,** cobalt black; ~ **verbinding,** cobalt compound.

ko'bold, (-e), kobold, brownie, goblin.

ko'bra, (-s), cobra.

ko'da, (-s), coda.

kod'dig, (-e), funny, comic, droll, odd; Gilbertian; burlesque; antic; grotesque; ~ **heid,** fun, drol= lery.

ko'de, (-s), code.

kodeer', (ge-), write in code.

kodeïen', kodeï'ne, codeine.

ko'deks, (-e), codex.

ko'de: ~ **slot,** combination lock; ~ **telegram,** code wire; ~ **woord,** code word.

kodifika'sie, codification.

kodifiseer', (ge-), codify.

kodisil', (-le), codicil.

kod'lingmot, (-te), codling moth.

koe'boebessie, cherry-like berry *(Mystroxylon sphaerophyllum)*.

koe'doe, (-s), kudu *(Tragelaphus strepsiceros)*; ~ **bul,** kudu bull.

ko'edukasie, co-education.

koe'ël (s) **(-s),** bullet; ball; pellet; pill; bead (foresight); *elke* ~ *het sy BESTEMMING,* every bullet has its billet; *hy het die* ~ *GEKRY,* he was hit by a bullet; *'n* ~ *is te GOED vir hom,* he is a scoundrel; he is not worth powder and shot; *die* ~ *is deur die KERK,* the die is cast; it is all over; (w) **(ge-),** shoot at, fire upon; throw, pelt; ~ **afstand,** range; ~ **as,** ball-piv= ot; ~ **baan,** trajectory; ballrace; ~ **bui,** rain of bul= lets; ~ **gat,** bullet-hole; ~ **gewrig, (-te),** ball-and- socket joint; enarthrosis; ~ **gieter,** ball-founder; ~ **klep,** pea-valve; glove-valve, ball-valve; ~ **laer,** ball-bearing; ~ **loop,** bullet barrel (of combination gun); ~ **mantel,** bullet-jacket; ~ **meul(e),** ball-mill; ~ **patroon,** ball-cartridge; ~ **reën,** shower of bul= lets; ~ **ring,** ballrace; ~ **rond, (-e),** globular, spheri= cal; ~ **skarnier,** ball-and-socket joint; ~ **skerm,** mantlet; ~ **tang,** crow-bill; ~ **tap,** ball-pivot; ~ **tas, (-se),** cartridge bag; ~ **tjie, (-s),** pellet; globule; ~ **trekker,** worm-screw; wadhook; ~ **vanger,** prac= tice butt, stop butt; vas, (te), bullet-proof; ~ **vorm,** bullet mould; ~ **vormig, (-e),** bullet- shaped; globular; ~ **vry, (-e),** bullet-proof; ~ **vuur,** small-arms fire; ~ **wond,** bullet wound.

koëffisiënt', (-e), coefficient.

koei, (-e), cow; *'n mens noem nie 'n* ~ *BONT as daar nie 'n vlekkie aan is nie,* there is no smoke without fire; *'n* ~ *kan moontlik in 'n BOOM klim,* pigs might fly, but they are very unlikely birds; *die* ~ *e loop in die BRAND,* we have run out of milk; *dis nie die* ~ *wat die hardste BULK wat die meeste melk gee nie,* it is not the hen that cackles (the) most that lays the biggest egg; the greatest talkers are always the least doers; *'n mens kan 'n* ~ *die BULK nie belet nie,* one cannot fly in the face of nature; *die* ~ *by die HORINGS pak,* take the bull by the horns; *'n* ~ *kan moontlik 'n HAAS vang,* one never can tell; *oor* ~ *tjies en KALFIES praat,* chat about this and that, talk commonplaces; *ou* ~ *e uit die SLOOT haal,* rake up old stories; revive an old dispute; *nie so groen dat 'n* ~ *hom sal VREET nie,* not as green as he is cabbage looking; ~ **brug,** orlop; ~ **kamp,** cow-camp, cow-paddock; ~ **kop,** cow's head; ~ **kraal,** cow-pen; ~ **melk,** cow's milk; ~ **mis,** cow- dung; ~ **oog,** cow's eye; ceratoglobus (of the eye); ~ **paal,** post (for fastening cows); *soos 'n* ~ *paal op 'n plaas staan,* idle; ~ **pokke,** cow-pox; ~ **pokstof,** vaccine, lymph; ~ **riempie,** wild edible plant; ~ **stal,** cow-shed; byre; ~ **stert,** cow's tail; ~ **tjie, (-s),** (little) cow; *oor* ~ *tjies en kalfies praat,* indulge in small talk; ~ **vanger,** cow-catcher; ~ **wagter,** cow-herd.

koeja'wel, (-s), guava; *'n harde* ~ , a hard nut, a tough customer; ~ **boom,** guava (tree).

koek, (s) (-e), cake; *die* ~ *te dik AANMAAK,* overdo the friendship; *die* ~ *het in die as geval,* it has fallen flat; it was a wash-out; (w) **(ge-),** cake, clot; knot; swarm (bees), cling together; mat (hair, thread); glomerate; ~ **afdrukker,** cake-cutter.

koek: ~ **bakker,** confectioner; ~ **beslag,** cake batter; ~ **blik,** cake-tin; ~ **bordjie,** cake-plate; ~ **deeg,** cake mixture (dough).

koekeloer', (ge-), peep, peer, spy, pry; ~ **styl,** peek-a- boo.

koek(e)makran'ka, (-s), *Gethyllis spiralis,* kukuma- kranka.

koe'kepan, cocopan; ~ **opsigter,** trammer; ~ **vervoer,** tramming; ~ **werker,** trammer.

koek: ~ **hael,** silver cachon; ~ **heuning,** comb-honey.

koe'kie, (-s), small cake, biscuit; fritter; *'n* ~ *seep, a tablet (cake) of soap;* ~ **sverkoper,** pieman.

koek'kraam, cake-stall.

koekoek', (-e), cuckoo; Plymouth Rock; gowk; *dit is altyd ~ een sang by hom*, he is always harping on the same string; ~**hen**, Plymouth Rock hen, speckled hen; ~**hoender**, Plymouth Rock; ~**klok**, cuckoo-clock; Dutch clock; ~**s'blom**, ragged robin; red campion.

koek: ~**pan**, baking-pan; ~**plaat**, griddle; ~**poeding**, trifle; ~**saad**, aniseed, caraway seed; ~**sister**, (-s), cruller, sugared doughnut; ~**skoppie**, cake-lifter; ~**soda**, sodium bicarbonate, baking-soda; ~**stander**, cake stand; ~**tabak**, cavendish; ~**trommel**, biscuit-tin; cake-tin; ~**vaatjie**, biscuit-barrel; ~**versiering**, cake-decoration, icing; ~**vorm**, cakemould; ~**vurkie**, cake-fork; ~**winkel**, confectioner's shop.

koel, (w) (ge-), cool (down); vent (one's anger); *sy haat ~ aan*, vent his hatred on; (b) ([-e]; -er, -ste), cool, chill, frigid, mild, fresh; reserved, distant (behaviour); phlegmatic; *in ~en BLOEDE*, in cold blood; ~ *BLY in gevaar*, keep one's head in danger; ~ *KLERE*, light clothes; *iem. ~ ONTVANG*, give someone a chilly reception; ~**bak(kie)**, cooler; ~**bewaring**, cold storage; ~**bloe'dig**, (-e), cold-blooded, in cold blood; calculated; ~**bloe'digheid**, cold-bloodedness; impassiveness; ~**buis**, cooling-pipe; ~**drank**, soft drink, cool drink; ~**dranktoonbank**, soda fountain; ~**eier**, chilled egg; ~**emmer**, cooling pail; wine-cooler; ~**er**, (-s), condenser, cooler; ~**erig**, (-e), rather cool; coldish; ~**gat**, cooling-hole (metallurgy); ~**heid**, coolness, coldness, chilliness; frigidity; ~**huis**, cold store.

koel: ~**ing**, cooling; refrigeration; ~**inrigting**, cold-storage, cooling-plant; ~**installasie**, cold-storage plant; refrigerating plant; ~**kamer**, walk-in refrigerator; cool-chamber; ~**kan**, (-ne), goglet; ~**kas**, (-te), refrigerator; ice-box; ~**kelder**, refrigerating cellar; ~**kieu**, cooling-gill (aero.); ~**lamp**, cold-valve; ~**mantel**, water-jacket; cooling-jacket; ~**middel**, refrigerant; cooling-agent; ~**oond**, cooling-oven, annealing-oven; leer (for glass); ~**pakhuis**, cold-storage, warehouse; ~**pan**, (-ne), cooler; ~**pommade**, cold cream; ~**pommadeseep**, cold-cream soap; ~**pyp**, cooling pipe; ~**rooster**, cooling tray; ~**ruim**, refrigerating hold; ~**ruimte**, cold storage space; ~**seil**, wind-sail; ~**skip**, refrigerated ship; ~**slang**, worm; cooling-coil; ~**stelsel**, cooling system; ~**te**, (-s), light breeze; shade; cool; ~**teboom**, shade tree; ~**tegniek**, refrigeration; ~**tetjie**, (-s), shady place; light breeze; ~**tjies**, coolly; *ewe ~ tjies weier hy*, quite coolly he refused; ~**toring**, cooling tower, ~**trok**, refrigerator-truck; ~**vat**, cooling vat, refrigerator, wine-cooler; ~**vleis**, chilled meat; ~**wa**, refrigerator-truck; ~**water**, cooling-water.

koe'mis, ko(u)miss.
koem'kwat, (-s), kumquat.
koen, (ong., digt.), (-e), brave, bold, daring; ~**heid**, boldness, daring, courage.
koe'nie, (-s), shrub *(Rhus mucronata)*.
koe'nie-kannie, see **kannie-koenie**.
koepee', (-s), coupé; compartment.
koepeer', (ge-), cut (cards); dock.
koe'pel, (-s), dome; cupola; kiosk; ~**dak**, dome (-shaped) roof; ~**fort**, cupola-fort; ~**kerk**, domed-church; ~**lering**, cupellation; ~**oond**, cupola-furnace; ~**pan**, cupel-pan; ~**venster**, bow window; ~**vormig**, (-e), dome-shaped.
koeplet', (-te), verse, stanza, couplet.
koepon', (-s), coupon; ~**boekie**, book of coupons; ~**stelsel**, chit-system.
koer, (ge-), coo; make love.
koerant', (-e), newspaper, journal; gazette; *in die ~ KOM*, get into the papers; *LIEG soos 'n ~*, lie like a gasmeter; ~**artikel**, newspaper article ~**berig**, (-te), newspaper report; ~**draer**, newspaper-boy; ~**drukker**, newspaper-printer; ~**drukkery**, (newspaper) printing-works; ~**etaal**, newspaper language; journalese; ~**handelaar**, newspaper vendor, newsagent; ~**knipsel**, press-cutting, newspaper-clipping; ~**krabbelaar**, inkslinger; ~**lêer**, (newspaper) file; ~**leser**, newspaper-reader; ~**oorlog**,

paper war; ~**papier**, printing-paper; ~**seun**, newsboy; ~**skrywer**, journalist; pressman, paragraphist; newspaper contributor (correspondent); ~**skrywery**, practice of sending letters to the press; journalism; ~**styl**, journalistic style, journalese; ~**tjie**, small newspaper; rag; ~**uitknipsel**, press-cutting; newspaper-clipping; ~**verkoper**, newspaper seller (vendor).

koera'sie, courage; *'n man van ~*, a plucky man; a man of mettle.
koerier', (-s), courier, messenger.
Koer'land, Courland; *van ~ se VLEIS eet*, be very lazy; *hy het van ~ se VLEIS geëet*, he is a lotuseater; he has eaten the bread of idleness.
koers, (s) (-e), course, direction; track; exchange rate, currency; quotation (stocks); determination; *skoon van die ~ AF RAAK*, lose one's bearings completely; ~ *HOU*, keep on the right track; steer a steady course; *'n nuwe ~ INSLAAN*, make a new departure; follow a new line of action; *op ~ KOM*, make steady headway; *met iem. ~ KRY*, get along with someone; *met iets nie ~ kan KRY nie*, be unable to get the hang of something; *die ~ KWYTRAAK*, go astray; ~ *RIG op*, set course for; *TEEN watter ~?* at what rate? *van ~ VERANDER*, change one's course; (w) (ge-), steer (one's course), head for; ~**(aan)wyser**, course-indicator; ~**afwyking**, deviation; ~**agio**, (exchange) premium; ~**baken**, landmark; ~**bepaling**, direction finding; ~**berekening**, calculation of exchange; ~**berig**, exchange news; ~**daling**, fall in the exchange; ~**gewer**, course setting device; ~**lamp**, directional lamp; ~**lig**, course-light; ~**loos**, (..lose), irresolute, undecided; ~**loosheid**, lack of direction; ~**lys**, list of quotations; stocklist; ~**notering**, market quotation; ~**peiler**, navigator (aeroplane); ~**skommeling**, fluctuation (in prices); ~**skyf**, direction-disk; ~**tol**, directional gyroscope; ~**vas**, (-te), firm, unswerving; ~**vastheid**, firmness, resolution; directional stability; ~**verandering**, change of course; change of rate; ~**verhoging**, rise in (bank) rate; rise in the exchange; ~**verlaging**, drop in the exchange; ~**verlies**, loss on exchange; ~**verskil**, difference in the rate of exchange, agio; ~**waarde**, exchange value.

koes, (ge-) = **koets**.
koesis'ter = **koeksister**.
koes'koes[1], (s) millet porridge, cuscus.
koes'-koes[2], (s) aromatic grass *(Andropogon zizamoides)*.
koes'-koes[3], (s) (-e), phalanger.
koes'-koes[4], (bw): ~ *beweeg*, frequently dodging while moving forward.
koesnaat'jie, edible wild fruit *(Crassula columnaris)*.
koes'ter, (ge-), cherish, pamper, foster, nurse (children); bask (in sun); entertain, harbour (an idea); foment; hug; *die HOOP ~*, cherish the hope; *hom ~ IN*, bask in; *'n WROK ~*, bear a grudge; ~**ing**, cherishing, nursing; fomentation.
koes'ter(tjie), (-s), pipit (bird).
koes'toeter, siren (air-alarm).
koe'terwaals, jargon, gibberish, double Dutch, lingo, slang.
koets[1], (-e), coach, carriage, charriot; sedan (motor).
koe(t)s[2], (w) (ge-), dodge, duck down, crouch, stop, cower.
koetsier', (-s), coachman; cabby; driver (of carriage); drayman; charioteer.
koets'-koets' = **koes-koes**[4].
koets'perd, coach-horse.
koevert', (-e), envelope; cover; ~**klap**, back flap of envelope.
koe'voet, (-e), crow-bar, handspike; lever; *kort ~*, jemmy.
Koeweit', Kuwait.
kof'fer, (-s), trunk, travelling-box, suitcase; chest, coffer (for money); ~**dam**, coffer dam; ~**deksel**, trunk lid; ~**maker**, trunk manufacturer; ~**sleutel**, trunk key; ~**tjie**, (-s), small trunk, box; handbag, case; ~**vis**, trunk-fish.
kof'fie, coffee; ~ *soos die KAN dit skink*, take things as they come; ~ *met of sonder MELK*, white or

black coffee; ~ **baal**, bale of coffee; ~ **bakkie**, basin of coffee-mill; ~ **bessie**, coffee-berry; ~ **bitter**, caffeine; ~ **blik**, coffee-tin; ~ **boom**, coffee plant; ~ **boon**, coffee-bean; ~ **bou**, coffee culture; ~ **brander**, coffee-roaster; ~ **brandery**, coffee-roasting mill; ~ **bruin**, (-ke), (fur) busby, bearskin. coffee-drinker; ~-**ekstrak**, coffee essence; ~ **geur**, aroma of coffee; ~ **handel**, coffee trade; ~ **huis**, café, tearoom; ~ **ïen**, ~ **ïne** = **kaffeïen, kaffeïne**; ~ **kamer**, refreshment room; ~ **kan**, coffee-pot; coffee-urn; ~ **ketel**, coffee-pot, coffee-kettle; ~ **kleur**, coffee-colour; ~ **koppie**, ~ **kommetjie**, coffee-cup; ~ **kraam**, coffee-stall; ~ **luis**, coffee-bug; ~ **melk**, milk for coffee; ~ **meul(e)**, coffee-mill; ~ **moer**, coffee grounds; ~ **oes**, coffee crop; ~ **pens**, coffee-bibber; ~ **pit**, coffee-bean; ~ **plantasie**, coffee-plantation; ~ **planter**, coffee-planter, coffee-grower; ~ **pot**, coffee-pot; '*n regte ou* ~ *pot*, a coffee addict; ~ **sak**, coffee-bag; ~ **servies**, coffee-set (-service); ~ **siffie**, coffee-strainer; ~ **spaan**, coffee-ladle; ~ **stalletjie**, coffee-stall; ~ **surrogaat**, coffee-substitute; ~ **tafel**, coffee-table; ~ **tjies**, a little coffee; *hoe lyk dit met die* ~ *tjies?* what about some coffee? ~ **trommel**, coffee-tin; ~ **tyd**, time for coffee; ~ **veiling**, coffee auction; ~ **water**, water for coffee.
kofi'a, (-s), fez.
kog'gel, (ge-), mimic, tease, imitate, mock; ~ **aar**, (-s), ape, mimicker; mocking-bird, capped wheatear *(Oenanthe pileate);* ~ **(a)ry'**, mocking, mimicking, teasing; ~ **dans**, strip-tease; ~ **man'der**, (-s), ~ **mannetjie**, black agama, lizard; ~ **ooi**, see **konkelooi**; ~ **ram**, teaser; ~ **stok**, tie rod (between two animals in a team to prevent fighting).
kohe'sie, cohesion, coherence.
ko'hort, (-e), cohort.
koïnsiden'sie coincidence.
ko'ïtus, coitus.
kok, (-ke, -s), cook; *te veel* ~ *s bederwe die BRY*, too many cooks spoil the broth; *EERSTE* ~, chef, head-cook; *as* ~ *en KOKSMAAT rusie kry, kom dit uit waar die sopvleis bly,* when thieves fall out honest men come by their own; *dis nie algar* ~ *s wat lang MESSE dra nie,* every cowl does not hide a friar.
kokaïen', kokaï'ne, cocaine.
Kokan'je: *die land van* ~, the land of Cockaigne; the land of the lotus-eaters.
kokar'de, (-s), cockade, rosette.
kokeleko', (-'s), Brazil nut.
ko'kend, (-e), boiling; furious.
ko'ker, (-s), boiler; case, casing, sheath, quiver, frog; holder, bucket (for whip); socket; etui; well (of life); phallus; plunger (ship); container; *dit het nooit uit jou* ~ *GEKOM nie,* that bolt never came from your quiver; ~ **balk**, box-beam; ~ **boom**, *Aloe dichotoma;* ~ **gat**, box frame; ~ **juffer**, caddis-fly; mayfly; ~ **tjie**, (-s), small case; ocrea; ~ **vrug**, follicle; ~ **wurm**, caddis, case-worm.
ko'kery, cookery; cooking, boiling.
koket', (s) (-te), flirt, coquette; (b) (-te), coquettish; ~ **krulletjie**, kiss curl; ~ **teer'**, (ge-), flirt, coquet(te), philander; ~ **terie'**, coquetry.
kok'hals, (ge-), retch, keck, heave up.
ko'king, boiling, ebullition, coction.
kokkedoor', (..dore), bigwig; *groot* ~, bigwig.
kok'kelkorrels, India berries.
kokkerot', (tc) = **kakkerlak**.
kokketiel', cockatiel *(Nymphicus hollandicus).*
kokkewiet', (-e), bush-shrike; gnome.
kok'kie, (-s), small cook.
kok'kus, (-se, kokki) coccus.
kok'meeu, sea-crow.
kokon', (-s), cocoon.
ko'kos: ~ **boom**, cocoa-nut tree; ~ **mat**, cocoa-nut mat; ~ **melk**, cocoa-nut milk; ~ **neut**, cocoa-nut, ~ **olie**, cocoa-nut oil; ~ **palm**, cocoa-nut palm; ~ **seep**, cocoa-nut soap.
koksidio'se, coccidiosis (diarrhoea).
koks: ~ **maat**, cook's mate; ~ **mus**, cook's cap.
kol, (s) (-le), star (of horse); bull's-eye (of target); butt; patch; cock-shy; spot; stain; *OP 'n* ~, at a certain time; at (in) a certain place; some time; some place; *die* ~ *RAAK, 'n* ~ *SKIET*, hit the mark; score a bull's eye; ~ (w), (ge-), stain, mark with spots.
ko'laboom, cola-tree *(Acuminata).*
kol'bak, (-ke), (fur) busby, bearskin.
Kol'broek, Colebrooke (pig).
kol'chos, (-se), kolkhoz.
ko'le: ~ **bak**, coal-shuttle; ~ **damp**, carbon monoxide; ~ **draer**, coal-heaver; ~ **gas**, coal-gas; ~ **gruis**, coal-dross; ~ **hok**, coal-bunker; coal-shed; ~ **skip**, collier; ~ **skop**, coal-shovel; ~ **stasie**, coaling-station; ~ **tjie**, cinder; ~ **verbruik**, coal-consumption; ~ **wa**, tender (loco.); coal-truck.
kolf, (s) (kolwe), butt-end (rifle); bat (cricket); spadix (botany); receiver (distilling); (w) (ge-), bat; ~ **baan**, mall; ~ **beurt**, innings; ~ **blad**, wicket; ~ **fles**, retort; ~ **glas**, matrass; ~ **hiel**, butt-heel; ~ **ie**, (-s), small bat; ~ **lyn**, batting-crease; ~ **mos**, club-moss; ~ **perk**, batsman's crease, ~ **plaat**, butt-plate; heel-plate; ~ **vormig**, (-e), club-shaped; ~ **vyl**, stub-file.
kol: ~ **gans**, Egyptian goose; ~ **haas**, mountain hare.
kolibrie', (-s), colibri, humming-bird.
koliek', colic; ~ **agtig**, (-e), colicky; ~ **pyn**, gripes.
ko'lie(waar): *so by my* ~! upon my word (soul)!
koli'tis, colitis.
koljan'der, coriander.
kolk, (s) (-e), abyss; whirlpool; eddy; lock-chamber (canal); air-pocket; (w) (ge-), whirl, eddy; ~ **gat**, pot hole (geol.), ~ **ing**, eddying.
kol'-kol', in patches, here and there, sporadically.
kol'lampe, spots (theatre).
kolla'sie, collation; ~ **reg**, advowson.
kollasioneer', (ge-), collate; repeat.
kollateraal', (..rale), collateral.
kolla'tor, (-e), collator.
kolle'ga, (-s), colleague, confrère.
kolle'ge, council; lecture; college; ~ *s LOOP,* attend lectures; *OP* ~, at college; ~ **biblioteek**, college library; ~ **gebou**, college building; ~ **gelde**, tuition fees (college); ~ **lid**, collegian; ~ **student**, collegian; ~ **tehuis**, college hostel.
kollegiaal', (..giale), fraternal, collegial, collegiate, as a colleague; ..**gialiteit'**, fraternal feeling, fellowship.
kollek'sie, (-s), collection (of stamps, etc.).
kollektant', (-e), collector.
kollek'te, (-s), collection; offertory; *'n* ~ *van huis tot huis,* a door-to-door collection; ~ **bord**, collection plate; ~ **bus(sie)**, offertory box, collection box; ~ **dag**, collection (flag) day.
kollekteer', (ge-), collect; send (pass) round the hat; ~ **kampanje**, drive (to collect funds).
kollekte: ~ **lys**, subscription list; whip-round; ~ **sakkie**, offertory bag.
kollektief', (..tiewe), collective.
kollektivis'me, collectivism.
kollektivis'ties, (-e), collectivist.
kollektiwiteit', collectivity.
kollenchiem', collenchyme.
kol: ~ **lerig**, (-e), patchy; spotted; ~ **letjie**, (-s), small spot, dot.
Kol'lie, Kol'liehond, (-e), Collie (dog).
kollima'sielyn, collimation.
kollima'tor, (-s), collimator.
kolli'sie, collision.
kollo'dium, collodion.
kolloïdaal', (..dale), colloidal.
kolloï'de, kolloïed', colloid.
kollu'sie, collusion; covin.
kol'mol, star sand-mole.
kolofon', (-s), colophon (printing); ~ **ium**, colophony, resin of turpentine.
kolokwint', (-e), bitter apple, colocynth.
kolom', (-me), column, pillar; ~ **hoof**, headline; ~ **titel**, headline.
ko'lon, (-s), colon.
kolonel', (-s), colonel; ~-**generaal**, (~s-generaal), colonel-general; ~ **skap**, colonelcy; ~ **s'rang**, colonel's rank; ~ **s'vrou**, colonel's wife.
koloniaal', (..niale), colonial.

Kolonia'ler, (-s), inhabitant of the Cape Province.
kolonialis', (-te), colonialist; ~'me, colonialism; ~ties, (-e), colonialist.
kolo'nie, (-s), colony, settlement; plantation.
kolonis', (-te), colonist; settler; ~a'sie, colonization; ~eer', (ge-), colonize, settle; ~eer'der, (-s), colonizer.
kolonna'de, (-s), colonnade.
kolon'ne, (-s), column (army); *'n vyfde* ~, a fifth column.
koloratuur', colorature, variations (music); coloratura.
koloriet', colouring, colouration.
koloris', (-te), colourist.
kolos', (-se), colossus; ~saal', (..sale), colossal, gigantic, stupendous, prodigious, pyramidal, egregious, whacking, huge, bouncing; ~saal'heid, hugeness.
Kolossen'se, Colossians.
kol'perd, horse with a star.
kolporta'sie, colportage.
kolporteer', (ge-), canvass; hawk books; peddle (newspapers).
kolporteur', (-s), colporteur, salesman (of religious books).
kol'sem, (-s), kelson.
kol: ~ **skietoefening,** application practice; ~**skoot,** bull's-eye.
kol'wer, (-s), batsman, bat.
kolwyn'tjie, (-s), cupcake; ~**pan,** muffin-pan, patty-pan.
kom¹, (s) (-me), basin, bowl, jorum; hollow, vale, dale.
kom², (w) (ge-), come, arrive; *AAN iets* ~, get (come by) something; *AGTER iets* ~, find something out; *AL wat* ~, *is hy,* everybody is here but he; *iets te BOWE* ~, get the better of something; *niks* ~ *DAARBY nie,* there is nothing quite like it; *dit* ~ *DAARVAN,* that's the result; *EERSTE* ~, *eerste maal,* first come, first served; ~ *of jy GEROEP is,* come in the nick of time; *tot HOMSELF* ~, come to his senses; *te KORT* ~, be deficient, fail, fall short; *toe ek my* ~ *KRY,* when I came to my senses; the next thing I knew; *LAAT* ~ *wat wil,* come what may; *LAAT* ~, send for (doctor); order (goods); *oor 'n MOEILIKHEID* ~, get out of a difficulty; *iem. te NA* ~, offend a person; *ek kan nie op sy NAAM* ~ *nie,* I cannot think of his name; *daar sal NIKS van* ~ *nie,* nothing will come of it; *dit* ~ *OP 5c per persoon,* it comes to 5c a head; *te PAS* ~, come in handy; *as ek te STERWE* ~, in the event of my death; *agter die WAARHEID* ~, get to the bottom of something; find out the truth.
ko'ma¹, (-s), coma, stupor, lethargy.
ko'ma², (-s), coma (bot.; astron.).
komaan'! come on! come along!
kom'af, descent, birth.
kombattant', (-e), combatant.
kombers', (-e), blanket; *hulle* ~ *is GESKEUR,* they have come to the parting of the ways; *onder een* ~ *SLAAP,* be hand in glove with someone; ~**blom,** gaillardia, blanket-flower; ~**goed,** blanketing; ~**rebel,** quasi-rebel; ~**sak,** holdall; ~**steek,** blanket-stitch; ~**stem,** the blanket vote.
kom'bi, (-'s), kom'bimotor, kombi, combi.
kombina'sie, (-s), combination; combine; ~**mof,** combination-coupling; ~**slot,** combination-lock; ~**vermoë,** power of combination.
kombineer', (ge-), combine, pool.
kombuis', (-e), kitchen; cuisine; *iem. het in die* ~ *GROOTGEWORD,* he has grown up in a sty; *hy is by die* ~ *LANGS,* he has a touch of the tar-brush; *in die* ~ *OPGROEI,* be ill-mannered; ~**aangeleenthede,** cuisine; ~**afval,** garbage; ~**deur,** kitchen door; ~**gereedskap,** kitchen utensils; ~**hulp,** kitchen servant; ~**kas, (-te),** kitchen dresser; ~**lamp,** kitchen lamp; ~**rak,** kitchen dresser; ~**sout,** common (coarse) salt; ~**stoel,** kitchen chair; ~**taal,** vulgar speech, patois; kitchen language; ~**tafel,** kitchen table; ~**vloer,** kitchen floor; ~**ware,** kitchenware; ~**werk,** kitchen work.
komediant', (-e), comedian, actor; ~**e, (-s),** comedienne.
kome'die, (-s), comedy, farce; *dit is alles LOUTER* ~, it is all put-on; *hy SPEEL maar 'n bietjie* ~, he is putting on an act; ~**spel,** comedy; (mere) make-believe; ~**speler,** comedian actor.
komeet', (komete), comet; ~**stert,** comet's tail.
komforta'bel, (-e), comfortable.
kom'halertjie, (-s), Adam's apple.
komiek', (s) (-e), clown, comic, funny fellow; (b) (-e), comic(al), funny, droll; odd, queer; ~**lik, (-e),** comic(al); queer; oddish, odd-looking; ~**likheid,** comicality, drollery; queerness.
ko'mies, (-e), comic(al), funny; ~-**heroïes,** heroic.
Kominform', (hist.), Cominform.
Komintern', Comintern.
komitee', (-s), committee; *in 'n* ~ *BENOEM,* appoint on a committee; *in 'n* ~ *DIEN,* serve on a committee; *in* ~ *GAAN,* go into committee; *UITVOERENDE* ~, executive committee; ~**kamer,** committee room; ~**lid,** committee member; ~**vergadering,** committee meeting.
komkom'mer, (-s), cucumber; gourd; *so koel soos 'n* ~, as cool as a cucumber; ~**berig,** Balaam; ~**rank,** cucumber tendril; ~**slaai,** cucumber salad; ~**tyd,** dull (slack, flat, dead) season; salad-days; silly (gooseberry) season.
kom'ma, (-s), comma; ~**basil,** comma bacillus *(Vibrio comma)*.
kommandant', (-e), commandant, commander; ~-**generaal,** (~e-**generaal),** commandant-general; ~**skap,** commandantcy; ~**s'rang,** rank of commandant.
kommandeer', (ge-), command, commandeer; requisition; *ek laat my nie* ~ *nie,* I won't be dictated to; ~**brief,** commandeer letter, requisition.
kommandement', command (military district).
kommandeur', (-s), commander; ~**skap,** commandership; ~**s'rang,** rank of commander.
komman'do, (-'s), commando; *op* ~ *gaan,* go on commando; ~**brug,** (captain's) bridge; ~**kastrol,** dixie, dixy; ~**pos,** control post; ~**'tjie, (-s),** small commando; ~**toring,** conningtower; ~**voël,** Cape dikkop *(Burhinus capensis capensis);* ~**wurm,** army-worm, mystery worm.
kom'mapunt, semicolon.
kommensaal', (..sale), commensal; boarder.
kommensalis'me, commensalism.
kommentaar', (..tare), commentary, comment; *postil;* ~ *lewer op,* comment upon.
kommentarieer', (ge-), comment (up)on.
kommenta'tor, (-e, -s), commentator; scholiast, glossarist, glossator.
kom'mer, trouble, distress, care, anxiety sorrow, grief, pain; solicitude; ~**lik, (-e),** distressed, miserable, needy, pitiful; ~**loos, (..lose),** free from care, untroubled; ~**nis,** worry, care, trouble, anxiety.
kommersialiseer', (ge-), commercialize.
kommersialise'ring, commercialization.
kommersieel', (..siële), commercial; ..**siële bron,** commercial source.
kom'mervol, (-le), care-worn, anxious, distressful, wretched.
kom'metjie, (-s), mug, bowl, cup, porringer; basin (around trees); ~**gatmuishond,** water-mongoose; ~**saag,** crown-saw; ~-**tee'water,** wild flower *(Adenandra uniflora).*
kommissariaat', commissariat.
kommissa'ris, (-se), commissioner; *K*~ *van Ede,* Commissioner of Oaths.
kommis'sie, (-s), commission; committee; board; ~ *van ADVIES,* advisory commission; *LID wees van 'n* ~, serve (sit) on a commission; *vir* ~ *VERKOOP,* sell on commission; ~**agent,** commission agent; ~**koste,** commission fees (charges); ~**lid,** committee member; commissioner; ~**loon,** commission; ~**vergadering,** committee meeting; ~**verkoping,** commission sale.
kommitteer', (ge-), commit (child); ..**te'ring, (-e, -s),** committal.
kommunaal', (..nale), communal.
kommunalis'me, communalism.
kommu'ne, (-s), commune.
kommu'nie, Holy Communion; ~**bank,** altar-rail;

~kleed, ~laken, communion-cloth; ~pateen, communion-plate; ~vers, communion-verse.
kommunikant', (-e), communicant.
kommunika'sie, (-s), communication; ~middel, means of communication.
Kommunis', (-te), Communist; ~me, Communism; ~ties, (-e), communistic.
kommuta'sie, commutation.
kommuta'tor, (-e, -s), commutator; ~voetstuk, commutator-base.
kommuteer', (ge-), commute.
kompak', (-te), compact; ~t'heid, compactness.
kompanie', (-ë, -s), company (mil.).
kompanjie', (-s), company, partnership; K~(s)dienaar, servant of the Company; ~skap, partnership; ~(s)'tyd, time (règime) of the East India Company.
komparant', (-e), party (to a suit); appearer (in legal suit).
komparatief', (s) (..tiewe), comparative; (b) (..tiewe), comparative.
kompareer', (ge-), appear (in court).
kompari'sie, appearance (in court).
kompartement', (-e), compartment.
kompas', (-se), compass; *sy* ~ *staan stil*, he is in a fix; he is at sea; he is at a loss; ~aanwysing, compass-reading; ~afwyking, compass deflection; ~beuel, gimbal; ~doos, compass-box; ~huisie, compass-box, binnacle; ~naald, needle of the compass; ~noorde, magnetic north; ~peiling, compass-bearing; ~roos, rhumb card, compass card.
kompas'sie, compassion.
kompas': ~skyf, compass-bowl; ~stand, compass-reading; ~streek, point of the compass, rhumb point; course; ~-uitslag, compass deflection.
kompen'dium, (-s, ..dia), compendium.
kompensa'sie, compensation; ~balans, equalizer; ~slinger, compensation pendulum.
kompensa'tor, (-e, -s), compensator.
kompenseer', (ge-), compensate; counterbalance, set off; make good; adjust (compass); redeem.
kompeteer', (ge-), compete.
kompeten'sie, competence, competency.
kompetent', (-e), competent (jur.).
kompeti'sie, (-s), competition; ~spel, competitive game; ~wedstryd, league match.
kompila'sie, compilation; ~werk, cento; compilation.
kompila'tor, (-e, -s), compiler.
kompileer', (ge-), compile.
kompleet', (..plete) (..pleter, -ste), complete; just as; utter (failure); positive (scandal), bodily; *sy is ~ haar MA*, she is just like her mother; ~ *of hy kon SIEN*, just as if he could see; ~heid, perfection.
kompleks', (-e), complex, complicated.
komplek'sie, complexion.
komplement', (-e), complement; ~êr', (-e), complementary.
kompleteer', (ge-), complete.
komplika'sie, (-s), complication.
kompliment', (-e), compliment; *met die ~e vir die DAG*, with the compliments on this day; *iem. 'n MAAK*, pay someone a compliment; *baie ~e MAAK*, let the compliments fly; *MET my ~e*, with my compliments; *SONDER ~e*, unceremoniously; without frills; ~*e TUIS*, regards to all at home; *hy is VOL ~e*, he is full of fads and fancies; ~eer', (ge-), compliment (someone on); return the compliment; ~êr', (-e), complimentary; ~ere kaartjie, complimentary ticket; ~eus', (-e), complimentary; ~jies, flattery, flummery; ~maker, complimenter.
kompliseer', (ge-), complicate.
komplisiteit', complicity.
komplot', (-te), plot, intrigue, conspiracy; *'n ~ smee*, hatch a plot; ~teer', (ge-), plot, intrigue, conspire.
komponeer', (ge-), compose.
komponent', (-e), component.
komponis', (-te), composer.
kom'pos, compost.
Komposie'te, Compositae.
komposi'sie, (-s), composition; design; ~ *van misdaad*, compounding of crime.

kompo'situm, (-s, ..ta), compound (word).
kompres', (-se), compress, fomentation; cataplasm; bolster.
kompres'sie, (-s), compression; cushioning (of steam); ~kraan, compression-tap; ~slag, compression stroke.
kompres'sor, (-e, -s), compressor.
komprimeer', (ge-), compress.
kompromie', (-ë), **kompromis'**, (-se), compromise; *'n ~ aangaan (tref)*, (make a) compromise.
kompromittant', (-e), compromising.
kompromitteer', (ge-), compromise, commit oneself.
koms, arrival, coming, advent; *op ~ wees*, be coming, be drawing near.
kom'venster, bay window, bow window.
kom'vormig, (-e), bowl-shaped, basined, cotyloid.
komyn', cumin; ~kaas, cumin cheese.
kond: *iets ~ doen*, make something known.
kondee', (-s), cushion (for hair); chignon, bun.
kondensaat', (..sate), condensate.
kondensa'sie, condensation.
kondensa'tor, (-e, -s), condenser.
kondenseer', (ge-), condense; ~'baar (..bare), condensable; ~'pot, steam-trap.
kondense'ring, condensation.
kondens'melk, condensed milk.
konden'sor, (-e, -s), condenser.
kondi'sie, (-s), condition; finish (of stall-fed animal); state; *in GOEIE ~*, in good condition; fit; *OP ~ dat*, on condition that.
kondisioneel', (..nele), conditional.
kondisioneer', (ge-), (make a) condition, stipulate; accustom.
kondolean'sie, (-s), condolence; ~brief, letter of condolence.
kondoleer', (ge-), condole.
kondoneer', (ge-), condone.
kondoom', (kondome), condom, French letter (collo.).
kon'dor, (-s), condor.
konduk'sie, conduction.
kondukteur', (-s), conductor, guard; ~s'wa, guard's van.
konduktri'se, (-s), conductress.
konfedera'sie, (-s), confederacy, confederation.
konfedereer', (ge-), confederate.
konfek'sie, (-s), ready-made clothing; ~pak, ready-made suit.
konfereer', (ge-), confer, hold a conference.
konferen'sie, (-s), conference.
konfes'sie, (-s), confession; ..sioneel', (..nele), confessional; denominational.
konfidensieel', (..siële), confidential.
konfigura'sie, (-s), configuration.
konfirma'sie, (-s), confirmation.
konfirmeer', (ge-), confirm.
konfiska'sie, confiscation.
konfiskeer', (ge-), confiscate.
konfitu're, preserves.
konflik', (-te), conflict; *in ~ kom met*, come in conflict with.
konfoes', (ge-), unsettle, muddle up, turn topsy-turvy; spoil, bungle.
konfoor', (konfore), chafing-dish, brazier, fire-pan; chauffer.
konform', (-e), conformable to; ~a'sie, conformation; ~eer', (ge-), conform to; ~is', (-te), conformist; ~iteit', conformity.
konfra'ter, (-s), confrère, colleague, fellow-member.
konfronta'sie, (-s), confrontation.
konfronteer', (ge-), confront.
konfu'sie, confusion.
konfuta'sie, confutation.
konfuus', abashed, bewildered; broken, spoilt.
konfyt', (-e), jam; preserve; (w) (ge-), preserve; *ge~ wees in iets*, be an expert at something; ~tert, jam tart.
konges'tie, congestion; engorgement.
konglomeraat', (..rate), conglomerate.
Kon'go, The Congo; ~lees', (..lese), Congolese.
kongrega'sie, congregation.
kongregeer', (ge-), congregate.

kongres', (-se), congress; ~**besluit**, decision of (the) congress; ~**ganger**, (-s), ~**lid**, (..**lede**), conferee; member of congress; conference-goer.
kongrueer', (ge-), be congruent.
kongruen'sie, congruency.
kongruent', (-e), congruent.
kong'si, (-'s), combine, trust; clique.
ko'nies, (-e), conical; ~*e DRAAITOESTEL*, taper-attachment; ~*e KLEP*, cup-valve; ~*e RAT*, cone-wheel; ~*e SKYF*, cone-pulley; ~*e TANDRAT*, mitre-wheel, bevel-wheel; ~*e WIEL*, bevel-wheel.
konifeer', (..**fere**), conifer.
ko'ning, (-s), king; *hy verbeel hom hy is die ~ se HOND se (peet)oom*, he is very conceited; he is full of himself; ~ *KRAAI*, be cock of the walk; *soos 'n ~ LEWE*, live like a lord; *die ~ van die POON*, red mullet, surmullet; *die ~ te RYK wees*, as pleased as Punch; ~ *v.d. VERSKRIKKING*, the King of Ter= rors; ~**aasvoël**, black vulture; ~**blousysie**, violet-eared waxbill; ~**in'**, (-**ne**), queen; ~**injellie**, royal jelly; ~**in'-moeder**, queen mother; ~**in'skap**, queenhood; ~**ins'verjaardag**, Queen's Birthday; ~**in'-weduwee**, queen dowager; ~**klipvis**, kingklip *(Epinephelus gigas)*; ~**makriel**, kingfish; ~**riet= haan**, gallinule; ~**rooibekkie**, pintailed widow-bird *(Vidua macroura)*; ~**sadvokaat**, king's counsel; ~**sappel**, pomeroy, king-apple; ~**sarend**, royal eagle; ~**sblou**, royal blue; ~**sdogter**, king's daugh-ter, princess; ~**seer**, king's evil; ~**seun**, king's son, prince; ~**sgeel**, orpiment, king's yellow.
Koningin Maudland, Queen Maud Land.
ko'ningsgesind, (-e), royalist; ~**e**, (-s), royalist.
ko'nings: ~**getuie**, king's evidence; ~**huis**, royal house, dynasty.
ko'ningskap, (-pe), kingship.
ko'nings: ~**kind**, child of royal birth; ~**kleur**, purple; ~**kroon**, royal crown; ~**kruid**, golden rod; mul= lein; ~**mag**, regal (royal) power; ~**moord**, regicide; ~**moorder**, regicide; ~**paar**, royal couple; ~**palm**, royal palm; ~**reg**, royalty; ~**ruiter**, equerry; ~**ti= tel**, title of king; ~**troon**, royal throne; ~**verjaars= dag**, king's birthday; ~**vink**, *see* **bontrokkie**; ~**vis**, kingfish; ~**water**, aqua regia.
ko'ninkie, (-s), petty king, kinglet.
ko'ninklik, (-e), royal, regal, kingly, kinglike; *van ~ e AFKOMS*, of royal descent; *'n ~e ONTHAAL*, a royal feast.
ko'ninkryk, (-e), kingdom, realm.
konjak', cognac.
konjekturaal', (..**rale**), conjectural.
konjektuur', (..**ture**), conjecture.
konjuga'sie, conjugation.
konjugeer', (ge-), conjugate.
konjunk'sie, conjunction.
konjunktief', (..**tiewe**), conjunctive, subjunctive.
konjunktivi'tis, conjunctivitis.
konjunktuur', (..**ture**), conjuncture; economic cycle (situation); ~**leer**, doctrine of economic cycles; ~**styging**, beginning of a boom.
kon'ka, (-s), (petrol) tin, drum, fire-tin, brazier.
konkaaf', (**konkawe**), concave; ~-**konveks'**, concavo-convex.
konkawiteit', concavity.
kon'kel, (ge-), plot, scheme, intrigue, wangle; machi-nate; cabal; botch (bungle); ~**aar**, (-s), intriguer, shyster, botcher, plotter; ~**aarster**, (-s), in= trig(u)ante; ~**(a)ry**, (-e), intriguing, wangling, machination, plotting, underhand work; ~**ooi**, ewe suckling the lamb of another; ~**werk**, muddling, botching; bad work.
konklaaf', (..**klawe**), conclave.
konkludeer', (ge-), conclude.
konklu'sie, (-s), conclusion; ratiocination; ~*s trek uit*, draw conclusions from; ~**f'**, (..**siewe**), con= clusive.
konkordaat', (..**date**), concordat.
konkordan'sie, (-s), concordance.
konkordant', (-e), concordant; ~*e KUS*, longitudi-nal coast; ~*e LAE*, conformable strata.
konkreet', (s) concrete; (b) (..**krete**; ..**kreter**, -**ste**), concrete; ~**heid**, concreteness; ~**menger**, concrete mixer.

konkre'sie, concretion.
konkretiseer', (ge-), concretize.
konkubinaat', concubinage.
konkubi'ne, (-s), concubine.
konkurreer', (ge-), compete.
konkurren'sie, competition, rivalry.
konkurrent', (-e), competitor, rival.
konkus'sie, (-s), concussion.
konnek'sie, (-s), connection.
konnekteer', (ge-), connect.
konnossement', (-e), bill of lading.
konsekra'sie, consecration.
konsekreer', (ge-), consecrate.
konsekutief', (..**tiewe**), consecutive.
konsekwen'sie, (-s), consequence; consistency.
konsekwent', (-e), consistent; consequent.
konsen'sie, conscience.
konsensieus', (-e), conscientious.
konsen'sus, consensus.
konsent', (-e), consent; ~**eer'**, (ge-), consent.
konsentra'sie, concentration; ~**kamp**, concentration (refugee) camp.
konsentreer', (ge-), concentrate.
konsen'tries, (-e), concentric.
konsentrisiteit', concentricity.
konsep', (-te), draft, concept; ~**kontrak**, draft con= tract; ~**ordonnansie**, draft ordinance.
konsep'sie, (-s), conception.
konsep'wet, draft act, bill.
konserf', (**konserwe**), conserve; preserve.
konsert', (-e), concert; ~**ganger**, concert-goer; ~**ge= bou**, concert hall.
konserti'na, (-s), concertina; ~**deur**, folding door; ~**hek**, folding wire gate; ~**plooi**, accordion pleat.
konsert': ~**kaartjie**, concert ticket; ~**reis**, concert tour; ~**saal**, concert hall; ~**sanger**, concert singer; ~**sangeres**, prima donna; ~**stuk**, concert piece; ~**vleuel**, grand piano.
konserva'sie, conservation.
konserva'tor, (-e, -s), conservator, keeper, curator.
konservato'rium, (-s, ..**toria**), academy of music.
konserveer', (ge-), preserve; tin, can.
konserve'ringsmiddel, preservative.
konserwatief', (..**tiewe**), conservative.
konserwatis'me, conservatism.
konses'sie, (-s), concession; ~**kaartjie**, concession-ticket.
konsessiona'ris, (-se), grantee, concessionnaire.
konsiderans', (-e), preamble (law).
konsidera'sie, consideration; *GEEN ~ ken nie*, be re-lentless, have no consideration (for); ~ *TOON teenoor*, show consideration to; *UIT ~ vir*, in de-fence to.
konsidereer', (ge-), consider.
konsilia'sie, conciliation.
konsi'lie, council (of prelates).
konsilieer', (ge-), conciliate.
konsipieer', (ge-), conceive; draft (document).
konsisten'sie, consistency.
konsisto'rie, (-s), consistory, vestry; ~ *hou*, have a private talk; talk about this and that; ~**kamer**, vestry.
konskrip'sie, conscription.
konso'le, (-s), console.
konsolida'sie, consolidation.
konsolideer', (ge-), consolidate; (..**de'ring**), consoli-dation.
konsonan'sie, consonance, harmony.
konsonant', (-e), consonant.
konsor'te, associates, followers, confederates.
konsor'tium, (-s), consortium, combine.
konspira'sie, (-s), conspiracy.
konsta'bel, (-s), constable, policeman, copper; peace-officer.
konstant', (-e), constant, firm; stationary; invariable (maths.); ~**e**, (-s), constant.
Konstantino'pel, Constantinople.
konstateer', (ge-), state, declare, prove, ascertain; es-tablish (a fact); place on record; observe, notice.
konstate'ring, establishment; statement.
konstella'sie, (-s), constellation.
konsterna'sie, consternation.

konstipa′sie, constipation, costiveness.
konstipeer′, (ge-), constipate, bind (the bowels).
konstituant′, (-e), constituent.
konstitueer′, (ge-), constitute.
konstitu′sie, (-s), constitution.
konstitusioneel′, (..nele), constitutional.
konstitutief′, (..tiewe), constitutive.
konstrik′sie, constriction.
konstrueer′, (ge-), construe; construct.
konstruk′sie, (-s), construction; composition; ~ **fout**, structural defect; ~ **tekening**, working drawing.
konstrukteer′, (ge-), construct.
konstrukteur′, (-s), constructor.
konstruktief′, (..tiewe), constructive.
konsuis′, quasi-, as if (it were), ostensibly, forsooth, feignedly.
kon′sul, (-s), consul; ~ **aat′**, (..late), consulate; ~ **ent′**, (-e), relieving minister, substitute clergy= man; consulting expert; ~ **êr′**, (-e), consular; ~ **= generaal′**, (konsuls-generaal), consul-general.
konsult′, (-e), consultation; *'n* ~ *hou*, hold a consulta= tion; ~ **ant**, (-e), consultant; ~ **a′sie**, (-s), consulta= tion; ~ **eer′**, (ge-), consult; ~ **ingenieur**, consulting engineer.
konsu′meer, (ge-), consume.
konsument′, (-e), consumer.
konsump′sie, consumption.
konsumptief′, (s) (..tiewe), consumptive; (b) (..tiewe), consumptive.
kontak′, (-te), contact; ~ *KRY met*, make contact with; *in* ~ *bly MET*, keep in touch with; ~ **besmet= ting**, contagion; ~ **dôder**, ~ **gif**, contact poison (killer); ~ **hoek**, angle of contact; ~ **kussing**, con= tact pad; ~ **lens**, contact lens; ~ **myn**, contact mine; ~ **persoon**, contact; ~ **prop**, (-pe), plug (electr.); ~ **punt**, point of contact; ~ **rol**, trolley-head; ~ **sleutel**, ignition key; ~ **sok**, plug (electr.); ~ **vlak**, (-ke), contact area.
kontamina′sie, contamination.
kontamineer′, (ge-), contaminate.
kontant′, (s) (-e), cash, hard cash; ready cash (pay= ment); ready money; *TEEN* ~, for cash; (b, bw) (-e), cash; forward; pert; ~ *by AFLEWERING*, cash on delivery; *BAIE* ~, over-familiar; very for= ward; ~ *BETAAL*, pay cash (down); ~ *BETAAL, self kom haal*, cash and carry; *hy is baie* ~ *met sy GELD*, he is much too ready with his money; ~ **be= taling**, cash payment; ~ **-en-afhaalstelsel**, cash and carry; ~ **beweging**, cash flow; ~ **geld**, ready cash; ~ **korting**, cash discount; ~ **outomaat**, cash dis= penser; ~ **prys**, cash price; ~ **rekening**, cash ac= count; ~ **uitbetaling**, cash disbursement; ~ **uit= gawes**, out-of-pocket expenses; ~ **uitreikings**, cash issues; ~ **vereffeninge**, cash clearances; ~ **verkoop**, cash sale; ~ **vloei**, cash flow; ~ **waarde**, cash value, present value.
konteks′, context; ~ **gevoelig**, context-sensitive; ~ **vry**, context-free.
kontempla′sie, contemplation.
kontemplatief′, (..tiewe), contemplative.
kontemporêr′, (-e), contemporary.
konten′sie, (-s), contention; ..**sieus′**, (-e), conten= tious.
kontent′, (-e), content.
kon′terfeit, (geselst., gew.) (ge-), portray, picture; ~ **sel**, (-s), portrait, picture.
kontesteer′, (ge-), contest.
kontinen′sie, continence.
kontinent′, (-e), continent; ~ **aal′**, (..tale), continen= tal.
kontingent′, (-e), contingent; ~ **eer′**, (ge-), apply the quota system; ..**te′ring**, application of the quota system.
kontinu′, (-e), continuous.
kontinua′sie, continuation.
kontinueer′, (ge-), continue.
kontinuïteit′, continuity.
konti′nuum, (-s), continuum.
kontoer′, (s) (-e), contour; (w) (ge-), contour; ~ **kaart**, contour map; ~ **plan**, contour plan; ~ **ploeëry**, contour ploughing; ~ **walle**, contour banks (walls).

kontor′sie, (-s), contortion.
kon′tra, contra-, versus, against, counter-; ~ **-aan= treklikheid**, counter-attraction.
kontraban′de, contraband.
kon′trabas, double-bass, contrabass; bass fiddle.
kon′tra: ~ **beleefdheid**, return of civilities; ~ **besoek**, return call; ~ **bewys**, counterfoil; ~ **biljet**, counter= foil; countercheck; checkticket; ~ **boog**, counter= arch; ~ **dans**, contre-danse.
kontradik′sie, (-s), contradiction.
kon′tragewig, counterweight.
kontraheer′, (ge-), contract, shrink.
kontrak′, (-te), contract; agreement; *'n* ~ *AAN= GAAN (sluit)*, make (enter into) a contract; *EEN= SYDIGE, tweesydige, wederkerige* ~, unilateral, bilateral, synallagmatic contract; *hy VERBIND hom by* ~ *om*, he contracts to; ~ **arbeider**, inden= tured labourer; ~ **bepaling**, provision of the con= tract; ~ **breuk**, violation (breach) of contract; ~ *breuk pleeg*, break one's contract; ~ **brug**, con= tract bridge; ~ **prys**, contract price.
kon′trakruk, return crank.
kontrak′: ~ **sie**, contraction; ~ **tant′**, (-e), contracting party, contractor; ~ **teer′**, (ge-), contract, make a contract, enter upon a contract; ~ **tereg**, law of contract; ~ **termyn**, contractual period; ~ **teur′**, (-s), contractor; ~ **tueel′**, (..tuele), contractual; ~ **voorwaardes**, terms of the contract.
kon′tramerk, countermark.
kontrami′ne: *in die* ~ *wees*, be contrary; be contradictious.
kon′tramoer, check-nut, lock-nut.
kon′trapos, counter-entry.
kon′traprestasie, consideration; quid pro quo; equi= valent compensation.
kon′trapunt, counterpoint; ~ **aal′**, (..tale), contra= puntal; ~ **eer′**, (ge-), counterpoint.
kon′traregte, countervailing duties.
kon′trarevolusie, counter-revolution.
kontra′rie, contrary, contradictious.
kontras, (-te), contrast; *'n sterk* ~ *vorm met*, contrast strongly with; ~ **arm**, not strongly contrasted, uni= form (colour); soft (light).
kon′tra: ~ **sein**, counter-signal; ~ **sepsie**, contracep= tion; ~ **staaf**, check-rail.
kontrasteer′, (ge-), contrast.
kon′trateken, counter-signal.
kontrei′, (-e), region, country.
kontrêr′, (-e), contrary.
kontribuant′, (-e), contributor.
kontribueer′, (ge-), contribute.
kontribu′sie, (-s), contribution, subscription.
kontro′le, control, check; supervision; ~ *HOU op*, keep control of (over); ~ *UITOEFEN op die uit= gawes*, exercise control over the expenses; ~ **-as**, control-shaft; ~ **boek**, checkbook; ~ **bord**, tally- board.
kontroleer′, (ge-), control; check, audit; verify; ~ **baar**, (..bare), controllable; verifiable.
kontro′le: ~ **groep**, check group; ~ **handvatsel**, con= trol-handle; ~ **knip**, (-pe), control catch; ~ **kompas**, (-se), master compass; ~ **monster**, check sample; ~ **rekening**, control account; ~ **stelsel**, check (con= trol) system.
kontrole′ring, verification, checking.
kontroleur′, (-s), controller, supervisor, examiner, checker.
kontroleu′se, woman controller.
kontro′le: ~ **veer**, control spring; ~ **woord**, check- word.
kontrovers′, (-e), **kontrover′se** (-s), controversy.
ko′nus, (-se), cone.
konveks′, (-e), convex; ~ **ie**, convection; ~ **iestroom**, convection current; ~ **iteit′**, convexity; ~ **-konkaaf**, convexo-concave.
konvektief′, (..tiewe), convective.
konve′ner, (-s), convener.
konven′sie, (-s), convention; *EIS in* ~, claim in con= vention; *EISER in* ~, plaintiff in the principal ac= tion (convention).
konvensioneel′, (..nele), conventional.
konvent′, (-e), convent.

konventi'kel, (-s), conventicle.
konvergeer', (ge-), converge.
konvergen'sie, convergence.
konverge'rend, (-e), convergent.
konversa'sie, (-s), conversation.
konverseer', (ge-), converse.
konver'sie, conversion; ~ **lening,** conversion loan.
konverteer', (ge-), convert; ~**baar,** (..**bare**), convertible.
konvoka'sie, convocation.
konvooi', (-e), convoy; *onder* ~ *vaar,* sail in convoy; ~ **eer, (ge-),** convoy, escort.
konvooie'ring, convoying.
konvooi'vaarder, (-s), convoy ship.
konyn', (-e), rabbit, cony; ~**hok,** rabbit-hutch; ~ **kamp,** warren; ~ **tjie, (-s),** bun(ny); ~ **tjievel,** rabbit-skin.
kooi, (-e), bed; cage; bunk, berth; cote; ~ *toe GAAN,* go to bed; *dit SIT hom in die* ~, this is too much for him, it has him beat(en); ~-**eend,** decoy-duck; ~**goed,** bed-clothes, bedding, stable bedding; litter; ~ **lig,** bunk-light; ~ **tjie, (-s),** cot; cage.
kook, (s) boiling; *aan die* ~ *bly,* continue to boil; **(w) (ge-),** boil (milk); cook (food); do the cooking; fret, fume (with rage), chafe; *my BLOED* ~, my blood is up, my blood boils; *STADIG* ~, simmer; ~ **appel,** stewing (cooking) apple; ~ **beitel,** blunt chisel; ~**blik,** billy (can); ~**boek,** cookery-book; ~ **bron,** geyser; ~ **demonstrasie,** cookery demonstration; ~ **gas,** gas for cooking; ~ **gereedskap,** cookery utensils; ~ **groente,** vegetables; ~ **hitte,** boiling heat; ~**hoender,** boiler (fowl); ~ **huis,** cook-house; ~ **kuns,** cookery; gastrology; culinary art; ~ **kursus,** cookery course; ~ **lekkers,** boiled sweets; ~**melk,** boiled milk; ~ **plaat,** hotplate; ~ **plek,** place where things are boiled (cooked); range; kitchen; ~ **pot,** (cooking) pot; boiler; ~ **punt,** boiling-point.
kooks, (gas-)coke; breeze.
kook: ~ **sel, (-s),** batch; decoction; enough for one meal; boiling; *'n* ~ *sel BOONTJIES,* enough beans for one meal; *die HELE* ~*sel,* the hole batch.
kooks'gruis, (coke-)breeze.
kook: ~**skerm,** cooking-screen; ~ **skool,** cookery-school; ~**s'oond,** coke oven; ~ **ster (-s),** female cook; ~ **toestel,** cooking apparatus; ~ **vet,** cooking fat; ~ **water,** boiling water; ~ **wyse,** cuisine.
kool¹, (kole), cabbage, cole; *BY my* ~, upon my word of honour; *OOM* ~, the culprit; *daar SIT oom K* ~, there is the very man; there is the culprit; *die* ~ *is die SOUS nie werd nie,* the game is not worth the candle; ~ *sonder SPEK,* stag party; hen-party; *iem. 'n* ~ *STOOF,* do someone a bad turn.
kool²,(kole), coal, ember, carbon; *op die kole BRAAI,* grill; *iem. oor die kole HAAL,* haul someone over the coals; *vurige kole op iem. se HOOF hoop,* heap coals of fire on someone's head; *op hete kole SIT,* be on pins and needles.
kool³: *so by my* ~, upon my soul.
kool: ~ **aanpaksel,** ~ **aanslag,** carbon deposit; ~ **aar,** coal-vein; ~ **afval,** coal debris.
kool'akker, cabbage-patch.
kool: ~ **bak,** coalbox; ~ **bedding,** coalbed.
kool'blaar, cabbage leaf.
kool'borsel, carbon-brush.
kool'bredie, cabbage stew.
kool: ~ **damp,** carbon monoxide; ~ **deurslag,** carbon copy; ~ **draad,** carbon filament; ~ **druk,** carbon print (process); ~ **drukpapier,** carbon paper; ~ **elektrode,** carbon electrode; ~ **gruis,** coal dust; slack coal; ~ **hidraat,** carbohydrate; ~ **hoop,** tupple; ~ **kamer,** coal cellar; ~ **klop,** carbon knock.
kool'kop, head of cabbage.
kool: ~ **laag,** coal layer; ~ **laaier,** coal-whipper; ~ **loos,** (..**lose),** coalless; ~ **myn,** coal mine, colliery; ~ **okside,** ~ **oksied,** carbon oxide; ~ **papier,** carbon-paper.
kool'pister, variety of beetle (*Anthia*).
kool'plantjie, young cabbage plant.
kool: ~ **puin,** goaf; ~ **punt,** carbon point.
kool'raap, swede, cole-rape, kohlrabi; rape.
kool'roet, coom.

kool'saad, cabbage seed; colza, coleseed.
Kool'sak, Coal Sack (in Milky Way).
kool'sif, coal screen; ~ **skop,** coal shovel.
kool'so(e)p, Scotch kale (broth).
kool: ~ **spits,** carbon point (tip); crayon (lamp); ~ **stof,** carbon; grime; duff; ~ **stofdioksiede,** ~ **stofdioksied,** carbon dioxide; ~ **stofhoudend, (-e),** carbonaceous; carboniferous; ~ **stofmonokside,** ~ **stofmonoksied,** carbon monoxide; ~ **stofverbinding,** carbon compound; ~ **stoof,** coal stove.
kool'stronk, cabbage stalk (stump).
kool'suur, carbonic acid; ~ **gas,** carbonic acid gas; ~ **kalk,** carbonate of lime; ~ **sneeu,** solidified carbon dioxide.
kool: ~ **swart,** coal-black; ~ **teer,** coal tar; gas tar.
kool'tjie¹, (-s), coal of fire, cinder; carbon paper; *'n* ~ *vuur kom haal,* look in for a moment.
kool'tjie², small cabbage.
kool: ~ **trok,** coal truck; ~ **valslandmeter,** noctuid moth; ~ **vis,** lythe; ~ **vorming,** carbon formation; ~ **vuur,** coal-fire; ~ **wa,** tender (train); ~ **waterstof,** carburetted hydrogen, hydrocarbon; ~ **waterstofgas,** hydrocarbon gas.
koop, (s) (kope), purchase; bargain; buying; *'n slegte* ~ *DOEN,* make a bad bargain; *met iets te* ~ *LOOP,* bruit something abroad; make common talk of something; *'n* ~ *te (tot) NIET doen,* annul a sale; *OP die* ~ *toe,* into the bargain; to boot; *'n* ~ *SLUIT,* conclude a sale; strike a bargain; *TE* ~ *wees,* be for (on) sale; *TE* ~ *sit,* expose for sale; **(w) (ge-),** buy, purchase; *hom uit die DIENS* ~, buy himself out (of the service); *by 'n FIRMA* ~, deal with a firm; *uit die HAND* ~, buy by private treaty; ~ *en VERKOOP,* buy and sell; ~**akte,** deed of sale; ~ **al, (-le),** one who buys everything; ~ **baar,** (..**bare),** buyable; ~ **brief,** deed of sale and purchase; ~ **briefie,** bought-note (buyer); sold-note (seller); ~ **dag,** day of sale; ~-**en-loop,** cash and carry; ~ -**en-loophappies,** take-away snacks.
koöpera'sie, (-s), co-operation.
koöperatief', (..tiewe), co-operative.
koöpereer', (ge-), co-operate.
koop: ~ **graag,** fond of buying; ~ **handel,** trade, commerce; *Kamer van K* ~ *handel,* Chamber of Commerce; ~ **kontrak,** contract of sale, purchase deed; ~ **krag,** purchasing power; ~ **krag'tig, (-e),** able to buy (spend); ~ **lus,** inclination to buy; ~ **lus'tig, (-e),** fond of buying, in the mood to buy; ~ **lustige, (-s),** prospective buyer.
koop'man, (koopliede, kooplui, -ne, -s), merchant, dealer; ~ *in die GROOT,* wholesale dealer; ~ *in die KLEIN,* retail dealer.
koopmans: ~ **beurs,** produce exchange; ~ **eer,** mercantile honour; commercial honesty; ~ **gebruik,** commercial usage; ~ **gees,** commercial spirit.
koop'man: ~ **skap,** business capacity; ~ **stand,** merchant class.
koop: ~ **monster,** (purchase) sample; ~ **prys,** purchase price, costprice; ~ **seel,** deed of sale; ~ **siek, (-e),** overfond of buying; ~ **skat,** purchase money; ~ **som,** purchase price, cost price; ~ **ster, (-s),** buyer (female); ~ **sug,** overfondness of buying.
koöp'sie, koöpta'sie, co-option.
koöpteer, (ge-), co-opt.
koop'vaarder, (-s), merchantman.
koopvaardy', commercial navigation, mercantile marine; ~ **skip,** merchantman, trading vessel; ~ **vloot,** merchant fleet, mercantile marine.
koop'vaart, mercantile transport; ~ **kruiser,** merchant cruiser; ~ **skip,** merchantman.
koop: ~ **vereniging,** buying association; buy-aid society; ~ **waarde,** buying value; ~ **ware,** merchandise, commodities, ware(s).
koor, (kore), choir (of singers); chorus (of song); chancel; *IN die* ~, in the choir; *IN* ~, in chorus; ~ **afsluiting,** rood-screen; ~ **bank,** choir stall.
koord, (-e), chord; rope, cord, string; flex (electr.); lanyard; piping (dress); ~ **band,** petersham; ~ **danser,** rope-dancer, tight-rope walker, funambulist, equilibrist; ~ **dansersdraai,** pirouette; ~ **dansery,** rope-dancing, funambulism; ~ **drukvoet,** cording foot.

koor'de, (-s), chord, subtense; *gemene* ~ *s*, common chords.
koord: ~**ferweel**, corduroy; ~**fluweel**, ribbed velvet; ~**gordyn**, cord curtain.
koördinaat', (..nate), co-ordinate.
koördina'sie, co-ordination; ~**steuring**, ataxy.
koördineer', (ge-), co-ordinate.
koor'dirigent, choir conductor.
koord'jie, (-s), bit (piece) of string (cord).
koord: ~**spyker**, gimp pin; ~**sy**, grosgrain silk.
koor'leier, precentor, choir master.
koord'lint, cord ribbon.
koord'lys, rope-moulding.
koor: ~**galery**, choir loft; ~**gesang**, choral (songs); choral singing; ~**hek**, rood-screen; ~**hemp**, (..hemde), surplice; ~**kapel**, chantry; ~**kleed**, surplice; ~**knaap**, boy chorister; ~**leier**, choir master (conductor); coryphaeus; ~**lessenaar**, lectern; ~**lid**, chorister, choir member; ~**meisie**, chorus-girl; ~**musiek**, choir music; ~**nis**, apse.
koors, (-e), fever; *ALLEDAAGSE* ~, quotidian fever; *ANDERDAAGSE* ~, intermittent fever; *DRIEDAE* ~, tertian fever; *iem. se* ~ *is HOOG*, he is smitten; he is all on fire; *die* ~ *KRY*, be taken with the fever; *'n pasiënt se* ~ *MEET*, take a patient's temperature; ~**aanval**, attack of fever; ~**ag'tig**, (-e), feverish; hectic, frenzied; pyrexial; ~**ag'tigheid**, feverishness.
koor'sang, choral song; anthem; choral singing; ~**er**, chorister; choralist; choir singer; ~**eres**, female chorister.
koors: ~**blaar**, fever blister; ~**blare**, herpes; ~**boom**, fever-tree (*Acacia xanthophloea*); ~**drank**, febrifuge; ~**erig**, (-e), (rather) feverish; ~**hitte**, fever heat; ~**hol**, fever-trap; ~**ig**, (-e), feverish, febrile, pyretic, hectic; ~**igheid**, feverishness.
koor'singer, chorister, choralist, chanter.
koor'skerm, rood-screen.
koors: ~**kiem**, fever germ; ~**lyer**, fever patient; ~**meter**, clinical thermometer; ~**middel**, antifebrile; pyretic, febrifuge; ~**nes**, fever trap; ~**pennetjie**, clinical thermometer; ~**poeier**, fever powder.
koor'spraak, choral speech.
koors: ~**rilling**, shivering fit, rigor; ~**siekte**, fever; malaria; ~**stillend**, (-e), febrifugal; ~**termometer**, clinical thermometer.
koor'stoel, choir stall.
koors: ~**toestand**, pyrexia; ~**verdrywend**, (-e), febrifugal, antiphlogistic, antifebrile; ~**verwekkend**, (-e),febrogene; ~**vlek**, fever spot; ~**vry**, (-e), fever-free, free from fever; ~**wekkend**, (-e), pyretic; ~**werend**, (-e), antipyretic; ~**woeling**, jactitation; ~**wortel**, valerian.
koor'vereniging, choral society.
koos, (kose), chamber(-pot), jerry.
koot, (kote), knuckle-bone; fetlock, pastern; ~**been**, knuckle-bone; ~**holte**, heel-hollow; ~**jie**, (-s), phalanx (anat).
kop¹, (s) (-pe), head; hill; koppie, peak, summit; cob; ear (of maize); crest (of wave); forehead (of drill); pointing (abscess); nucleus (comet); loaf (of cabbage); head (bowls); bowl (pipe); caption, headline, heading; ~ *AAN (en)* ~, neck and neck; *iem. 'n* ~ *AANSIT*, take someone in; make an ass of someone; *dan laat ek my* ~ *AFKAP*, I'll eat my hat first; ~ *tussen die BENE steek*, buck (horse); *ek kan my* ~ *op 'n BLOK sit*, I'd lay one's head on a block; I'll go bail for that; ~ *voor die BORS*, crestfallen; with a hangdog look; ~ *teen* ~ *BOTS*, collide head on; *jou* ~ *oor iets BREEK*, rack one's brains over something; ~ *BYMEKAARHOU*, keep one's wits together; ~*pe BYMEKAARSTEEK*, lay heads together; *jou* ~ *in 'n BYNES steek*, bring a hornet's nest about one's ears; *sy* ~ *is DEUR*, he has succeeded; he has made it; *sy eie* ~ *DRA*, have a mind of one's own; ~ *EN* ~, neck and neck; ~ *GEE*, yield, give way; submit; *as jy nie daar is nie, word jou* ~ *nie GEWAS nie*, he who comes first to the mill may sit where he will; *hy het 'n GOEIE* ~, he has a sound head; *iem. iets voor die* ~ *GOOI*, cast something in a person's teeth; *die* ~ *laat HANG*, lose heart; *'n HARDE* ~ *hê*, be headstrong; *mekaar aan die* ~ *HÊ*, beat odds; *'n* ~ *daarvoor HÊ*, have a head for something; *sy* ~ *is HOL*, he can't put his thoughts together; *sy* ~ *is op HOL oor*, he has become fanatic about; *iem. se* ~ *op HOL maak*, muddle someone; have someone in two minds; ~ *HOU*, keep cool; *iets die* ~ *INDRUK*, nip something in the bud, suppress, stamp out something; *nie weet waar jy jou* ~ *moet INSTEEK nie*, not to know where to hide one's head; ~ *INTREK*, draw in one's horns; *uit die* ~ *KEN*, know by heart; *'n* ~ *KLEINER maak*, run someone's head from his shoulders; *die* ~ *KOEL hou*, keep a cool head; *jou* ~ *KRAP oor iets*, scratch one's brains; *iem. sy* ~ *laat KRAP*, make him rack his brains; *iem. voor die* ~, *maar nie in die KROP sien nie*, one cannot judge another by appearances; *iets in die* ~ *KRY*, get something into one's head; *op sy* ~ *KRY*, get in the neck; *iem. oor die* ~ *KYK*, cut someone dead; *'n LANG* ~ *hê*, have a long head; *uit die* ~ *LEER*, learn by heart; *'n* ~ *op jou LYF hê*, have a good head on one's shoulders; *aan iem. se* ~ *MAAL oor iets*, pester someone; *dit MAAL in my* ~, something keeps running through my mind; *sy* ~ *MAAL*, his head is spinning; *die* ~ *vol MUISNESTE hê*, be wool-gathering; ~ *of MUNT*, head or tails; ~ *in een MUS wees met iem.*, be hand in glove with someone; *met die* ~ *teen 'n MUUR loop*, run one's head against a stone wall; *jou* ~ *NEERLÊ*, lay down one's head; ~ *ONDERSTEBO*, crestfallen, ashamed; *OP die* ~, precisely, exactly; *OP die* ~ *vyfuur*, on the stroke of five; *iem. se* ~ *tussen sy ORE sit*, put someone in his place; *PER* ~, per head; *met* ~ *en POOTJIES*, neck and crop; boots and all; *ons is* ~ *en POOTJIES daarin*, we are in it boots and all; *iem. iets uit die* ~ *PRAAT*, talk someone out of something; ~ *en PUNT slaap*, sleep head to feet; *van sy* ~ *af RAAK*, become insane; become foolish; *die* ~ *v.d. ROMP raas*, drive someone mad with the noise; *die* ~ *v.d. ROMP SLAAN*, knock someone's block off; *iets uit jou* ~ *SIT*, put something out of one's mind; *nie op jou* ~ *laat SIT nie*, not to allow oneself to be set upon; *op iem. se* ~ *SIT*, sit on a person; *twee* ~ *pe is beter as een, al is een maar 'n SKAAPKOP*, two heads are better than one; *jou* ~ *in die SKOOT lê*, lose courage, submit oneself to one's fate; ~ *en SKOUERS bo iem. uitsteek*, stand head and shoulders above someone; *sy* ~ *staan nie daarna nie*, I don't feel so inclined; *al staan jy op jou* ~, come what may; *sy* ~ *STAAN soontoe*, he has his mind set on that; *jou* ~ *STAMP*, bump one's head; *die* ~ *pe bymekaar STEEK*, lay heads together; *geen* ~ *of STERT van iets uitmaak nie*, be unable to make head or tail of something; *sonder* ~ *of STERT*, with no head or tail to it; *met* ~ *en STERT*, neck and crop; *iem. voor die* ~ *STOOT*, hurt someone's feelings; *jou* ~ *in die STRIK steek*, put one's head into a noose; *jou* ~ *in 'n STROP steek*, run one's head into a noose; *iets op die* ~ *TIK*, hit upon something; have the good fortune to find something; *van* ~ *tot TONE*, from head to foot; from top to toe; *die* ~ *UITSTEEK*, crop up, show itself; come into the open; ~ *UITTREK*, withdraw; back out of something; *jou* ~ *VERLOOR*, lose one's head; *iem van* ~ *tot VOETE opneem*, look someone over from top to toe; *jou eie* ~ *VOLG*, refuse advice; do as one thinks right; *iem. se* ~ *WAS*, give someone a bit of your mind; ~ *bo WATER hou*, keep one's head above water.
kop², (w) (ge-), form a cob (mealie); form a head (cabbage); head (a ball).
kop³, (w) (ge-), cup (a patient).
kop'-af, head off; *doller as* ~ *kan dit nie*, worse it cannot become; anything worse just is not possible.
ko'pal, copal.
kop: ~**bal**, header; ~**band**, fillet; headband; frontal; ~**been**, skull, cranium; ~**beenvleis**, pericranium; ~**bemesting**, top-dressing; ~**doek**, headcloth, kerchief, turban; ~**duik**, header.
kopek', (-ke), copeck.
Ko'penhagen, Copenhagen.
ko'per¹, copper; brass.

ko'per², (-s), buyer, purchaser, customer.
ko'per: ~**aar**, copper vein; ~**agtig**, (-e), coppery, brassy, cupreous; ~**as**, copperas, blue ashes; ~**asuur**, azurite; ~**blad**, copper plate; ~**blasers**, brass (in orchestra); ~**bruilof**, brass wedding; ~**diepdruk**, intaglio printing; ~**draad**, copper wire; ~**druk**, copperplate printing; ~**eend**, shelduck; ~**erts**, copper ore; ~**foelie**, copper foil; ~**gaas**, copper gauze; ~**geld**, copper money; ~**gieter**, brass founder; ~**gietery**, brass works, copper foundry; ~**glans**, coppery lustre; ~**goed**, copper (brass) ware; ~**graveerkuns**, chalcography; ~**gravure**, copperplate; ~**groen**, verdigris, acetate of copper; ~**houdend**, (-e), cupriferous; cupric; ~**kapel**, cobra; ~**karbonaat**, carbonate of copper; ~**kies**, copper pyrites; ~**kleur**, copper colour; ~**kleurig**, (-e), copper-coloured; brazen (sky); cuprine; ~**laag**, heading-course; ~**legering**, copper alloy; ~**meridiaan**, meridian of the globe; ~**myn**, copper mine; ~**okside**, ~**oksied**, cupric oxide; ~**oplossing**, copper solution; ~**plaat**, copper (sheet) plate; ~**plettery**, copper mill; ~**pyp**, copper pipe; ~**roes**, verdigris; ~**rooi**, cupreous red, copperas; ~**slaer**, (-s), ~**smid**, (-s, ..smede), copper smith; ~**snyer**, copper-engraver; ~**soldeersel**, hard solder; ~**staaf**, bar copper; ~**sulfaat**, copper sulphate; ~**suur**, cupric acid.
ko'persweerstand, buyers' resistance.
ko'per: ~**verbinding**, copper compound; ~**waar**, ~**ware**, ~**werk**, brassware, copperware; ~**wiek**, redwing.
kop'glas, cupping-glass.
kop'hou, (ong.) topped shot (golf).
ko'pie¹, (-s), bargain, deal; *dis regtig 'n* ~, that's really a bargain.
kopie'², (-ë), copy, duplicate; manuscript; matter; ~**blaaie**, duplicate folios; ~**boek**, copy-book.
kopieer', (ge-), copy, transcribe; ~**geld**, copying fee; ~**ink**, copying ink; ~**masjien**, copying machine; ~**papier**, copying paper; ~**pers**, letterpress; printing frame; ~**potlood**, copying pencil; ~**werk**, copy-work.
kopie'reg, copyright.
kopië'ring, (-e, -s), copying.
ko'piesoeker, bargain-hunter.
kopiis', (-te), copyist.
kopi'va, copaiba; *wilde* ~, medicinal wild plant (*Bulbine aspodeloides*)
kop: ~**kant**, head (on coin); top side; ~**klep**, overhead valve; ~**klip**, head stone; ~**kool**, cabbage; ~**krap**: *dit het* ~ *krap gekos*, it led to a racking of brains; ~**kussing**, pillow; ~**laag**, protruding layer of bricks; top (heading) course; header-layer; ~**laagsteen**, header (brick); ~**lading**, end-loading; ~**lamp**, head-lamp; ~**las**, heading-joint; headline; ~**lengte**, head (races); ~**lig** (-te), headlight; ~**loos**, (..lose), acephalous, headless; ~**luis**, head-louse; ~**maat**, head measurement; ~**massering**, scalp massage.
kop'pel, (s) (-s), couple (eggs); brace (partridges); belt (sword); leash (dogs); clutch (motor); double (races); (w) (ge-), couple, marry; copulate; tie; put in gear (motor); join (trucks); connect, link.
kop'pelaar, (-s), coupler, procurer; pimp, pander, bawd; matchmaker; clutch (motorcar); ~**flens**, clutch flange; ~**hefboom**, clutch lever; ~**huls**, clutch sleeve; ~**pedaal**, clutch pedal; ~**plaat**, clutch plate; ~**rem**, clutch brake; ~**stang**, clutch rod, ~**ster** (-s), matchmaker; procuress; ~**veer**, clutch spring.
koppelary', matchmaking; panderage, pimping, procuration.
kop'pel: ~**as**, coupling-shaft; ~**balk**, bridging-beam, straining-piece; ~**bord**, traverse board; ~**bout**, draw-bolt; ~**haak**, coupling-hook; ~**huis**, semi-detached house; ~**huls**, coupling-box; ~**ing**, (-e, -s), clutch; gear(ing); coupler (mus.); coupling shackle; panderism; ~**ketting**, coupler; ~**koers**, traverse; ~**letter**, ligature; ~**moer**, coupling-nut; ~**paal**, hitching-post; ~**pen**, coupling-pin; ~**rat**, ratchet-wheel; clutch gear; ~**riem**, coupling-strap (bar); leash; ~**skakel**, safety link; ~**skyf**, flange-coupling; ~**stang**, tie-bar; coupling-rod; pitman; ~**stok**, tie-rod; ~**stuk**, drag-line; cap-piece; ~**teken**, hyphen; ligature (music); ~**toto**, (-'s), double tote; ~**werkwoord**, copula, copulative verb; ~**woord**, copulative, copula.
kop'penent, (-e), head (of a bed).
kop'pesnel, (w) (ge-), go head-hunting; ~**ler**, scalp-hunter, head-hunter; ~**lery**, scalp-hunting, head-hunting.
kop'pie, (-s), cup; small hill, hillock, koppie; small head; cupule; ~**s-en-pierings**, Canterbury bells.
kop'pig, (-e), obstinate, stubborn, headstrong; pig-headed, contumacious; dogged; selfwilled; asinine; contrary, contrariwise; mulish, obdurate, pertinaceous; heady (liquors); ~**heid**, obstinacy, stubbornness, self-will; headiness (liquors); obduracy, pertinacity.
kop'potig, (-e), cephalopod; ~**e**, (-s), cephalopod.
ko'pra, copra; ~**kewer**, copra beetle.
koproliet', coprolite.
kop: ~**ruimte**, head-room; overhead clearance; bulk-head; ~**seer**, headache; ~**skild**, clypeus; ~**skoot**, shot in the head; effective reply, powerful argument; *'n* ~ *skoot gee*, give an apt reply; deliver a telling blow; ~**skroef**, cap-screw; ~**sku**, bridle-shy; shy; wary; evasive; ~**skud**, headshake; *met 'n* ~ *skud antwoord*, answer with a shake of the head; ~**skudding**, headshake; ~**slaai**, lettuce; ~**slagaar**, carotid artery; ~**snee**, top edge (of book); ~**speel**, (-ge-), move the head up and down, prance (horse), niddle-noddle; ~**speld**, pin; ~**spyker**, tack; ~**stasie**, terminal station, dead end; railhead; ~**steen**, header(brick); bond-stone; cope-stone; ~**steun**, head-rest; ~**stem**, head voice; ~**stronk**, cob (maize); ~**stuk**, head; head stall (bridle); headpiece; heading; leader; *die* ~ *stukke v.d. BEWEGING*, the big guns of the movement; *daar is* ~ *stukke GESELS*, we talked the hind leg off a donkey; ~**stut**, head-rest.
kop'telefoon, headphone, ear-phone
Kopt, (-e), Copt.
kop'-teen-kopbotsing, head-on collision.
Kop'ties, (-e), Coptic.
kop'uitlaat, front-head release.
ko'pula, (-s), copula, copulative.
kopula'sie, (-s), copulation; graft.
kopuleer', (ge-), copulate.
kop'vel, scalp; ~**salf**, scalp ointment.
kop: ~**vormig**, (-e), capitate(d); ~**vrot**, ear-rot; ~**wassing**, shampoo; ~**werk**, intellectual work; ~**wond**, head wound; ~**wurm**, cobworm (maize).
koraal'¹, (korale), chorale; choral (song).
koraal'², (korale), coral; ~**agtig**, (-e), coralline, coralloid, corallaceous; ~**bank**, coral-reef, barrier-reef.
koraal'boek, church tune-book, chorale.
koraal': ~**dier**, coral-polyp; ~**eiland**, coral-island.
koraal'gesang, choral song, plain chant.
koraal': ~**kleur**, coral (colour); ~**mos**, coralline, coral-moss.
koraal'musiek, choral music.
koraal': ~**poliep**, coral-polyp; ~**rif**, coral-reef; ~**steen**, corallite; ~**visser**, coral-diver; ~**vormend**, (-e), coralliferous; ~**vormig**, (-e), coralliform.
koraliet', corallite.
koralyn', (s) coralline; (b) (-e), coral-like, coralline.
Ko'ran, **Koran'**, Koran.
Kora'na, (-s), Korana; ~**taal**, Korana language.
kordaat', (..date; ..dater, -ste), brave, undaunted, bold, stout-hearted; ~**heid**, braveness, boldness, stout-heartedness; ~**stuk**, brave (bold) deed, feat, exploit.
kordiet', cordite.
kordon', (-ne, -s), cordon.
Kore'a, Korea; ~**an'**, (Koreane), Korean; ~**ans'**, (s) Korean (language); (b) (-e), Korean.
koren'te, currants; ~**koek**, currant cake.
korf, (korwe), hive; basket; net; corf; ~**bal**, basket-ball; ~**balbaan**, basket-ball field; ~**balspan**, basket-ball team; ~**balspeelster**, female basket-ball player; ~**balspeler**, basket-ball player; ~**behuising**, cluster-housing; ~**fles**, carboy; wicker bottle.
kor'haan, **korhaan'**, (korhane), bustard, heath-cock.

kor'hoender, grouse, moorcock, moorhen (*Lagopus scoticus*).
korifee', (..feë), coryphaeus, dance-leader; leader, chief.
ko'ring, corn, wheat; grist; *daar is nog ~ in EGIPTE*, there is still corn in Egypt; *daar is geen ~ sonder KAF nie*, there is no wheat without chaff; *ook groen ~ op die LAND hê*, have fledglings of one's own; *dit is ~ op sy MEUL(E)*, that is grist to his mill; ~**aar,** ear of corn; ~**afval,** wheatings; ~**akker,** cornfield; ~**beurs,** corn-exchange; ~**blom,** cornflower, bluebottle; cockle; ~**blou,** azure; ~**bou,** corn-cultivation, wheat-cultivation; ~**brood,** wheat bread; ~**dorser,** thresher; ~**gerf,** cornsheaf; ~**halm,** corn-stalk; ~**handel,** corn-trade, wheat-trade; ~**handelaar,** corn-merchant, wheat-merchant, corn-chandler; ~**jaar,** year for corn; ~**kewer,** corn-beetle; ~**koffie,** corn-coffee; ~**koper,** corn-chandler; ~**korrel,** grain of wheat; ~**kriek,** green grass-hopper; corn-crake; ~**land,** cornfield; ~**landkraai,** corn-land crow (*Corvus segetum*), ~**maat,** corn measure; ~**mark, (-te),** corn-market; ~**meel,** flour; ~**meul(e),** corn-mill, flour-mill; ~**mied,** corn-stack; ~**mot,** corn-fly; ~**oes,** wheat-harvest (crop); ~**pap,** frumenty; ~**planter,** wheat-drill; ~**roes,** bunt, smut-ball; ~**roos,** red poppy; ~**sak, (-ke),** grain-bag, corn-sack; ~**semels,** wheaten bran; ~**skurf,** wheat-scab; ~**skuur, (skure),** granary; ~**stoppels,** (corn-)stubble; ~**streek,** corn-belt; ~**veld,** wheat-field; ~**vlieg,** (..vlieë), frit-fly; ~**vlokkie,** corn-flake; ~**voël,** white-browed weaver-bird; ~**wan,** winnow; ~**wet,** corn-law.
korin'te, *see* **korente.**
Korin'thiër, (-s), Corinthian.
Korin'thies, (-e), Corinthian.
koris'te, (-s), chorus-girl.
kor'morant, cormorant.
kor'nael, centre-punch.
kornalyn', (-e), cornelian.
kornet', (-te), cornet.
kornis', (-te), cornice.
kornoe'lie, dogwood.
kornuit', (-e), comrade, mate, crony.
ko'rog, triticale.
koroman'delhout, coromandel wood.
koro'na, (-s), corona.
koronêr', (-e), coronary; ~**e hartsiekte,** coronary heart disease. ~ *e trombose*, coronary thrombosis.
korporaal', (-s), corporal; ~**skap,** ~**s'rang,** corporal's rank; ~**strepe,** corporal's stripes.
korpora'sie, (-s), corporation, body corporate.
korporeel', (..rele), corporal.
korps, (-e), corps; ~**gees,** esprit de corps.
korpulen'sie, corpulency.
korpulent', (-e), corpulent, fat.
kor'pus = **corpus.**
korrek', (-te), correct, right; proper; ~**sie, (-s),** correction; allowance (shooting); ~**siewerk,** correction work; ~**sioneel',** (..nele), correctional; ~**t'heid,** correctness; rectitude; ~**tief',** (..tiewe), corrective; ~**tor, (-e, -s),** corrector.
kor'rel, (s) (-s), grain; sight; foresight; bead (on rifle barrel); pellet; curly tuft of hair; (w) **(ge-),** aim; point a gun at; pick off grapes (from a bunch); granulate.
korrelaat', (..late), correlate.
kor'relagtig, (-e), granular, granulous.
kor'relas, foresight axis.
korrela'sie, (-s), correlation; ~**lyngrafieke,** alignment graphs.
kor'relasskroef, foresight axis locking-screw.
korrelatief', (..tiewe), correlative.
kor'relbeskermer, foresight protector.
kor'relblad, foresight blade; ~**skroef,** foresight blade-screw.
kor'reldraend, (-e), graniferous.
korreleer', (ge-), correlate.
kor'rel: ~**graniet,** disintegrated granite; ~**hou, (-ge-),** aim at, take aim; ~**ig, (-e),** granular, grainy; ~**igheid,** granularity; ~**ing,** granulation; aiming; picking; ~**koeël,** foresight; head (barley, corn);

~**konfyt,** grape jam; ~**kop,** touchy person; crusty fellow, grouser, cross-patch; cantankerous person; head with woolly tufts of hair; ~**kruit,** grained gunpowder; ~**lêmeel,** laying-meal pellets; ~**papier,** torchon paper; ~**rig, (-e),** gritty, granulous, granulate, granular; crumbling; nutty (soil); grumpy, quarrelsome, crusty; grainy; ~*rige grondstruktuur*, granular soil structure; ~**righeid,** granularity; ~**skroef,** foresight screw; ~**steenkool,** coal-beans; ~**suiker,** granulated sugar; ~**tjie, (-s),** grain, granule; grape; *met 'n ~ tjie sout neem*, take with a grain of salt; ~**tjieskop,** head with woolly tufts of hair; ~**vat, (-ge-),** (take) aim; address the ball (golf); ~**voer,** pellet feed.
kor'relvoetstuk, foresight lock; ~**wig,** key foresight lock; ~**dwarspen,** cross-pin, foresight lock.
kor'relvorm, granulated form; ~**ig, (-e),** granular, granulated.
korrespondeer', (ge-), correspond.
korresponden'sie, correspondence; *'n ~ onderhou*, keep up a regular correspondence; ~**kursus,** correspondence course; ~**skool,** correspondence school.
korrespondent', (-e), correspondent; ~**e, (-s),** female correspondent.
kor'ridor, (-s), corridor; *die Poolse K~*, the Polish Corridor.
korrigeer', (ge-), correct; ~**werk,** correction work.
korro'sie, corrosion; ~**bestand,** corrosion-resistant; ~**vry, (-e),** non-corrodible; ~**werend, (-e),** anti-corrosive.
korrup', (-te), corrupt; ~**sie,** corruption.
kors, (s) (-te), crust, incrustation; scab, exuviae (on wound); cortex; encrustment; (w) **(ge-),** form a crust, be crusted with a crust; ~**aanpaksel,** encrustment; ~**bars,** check (in timber); ~**blok,** crust block; ~**breker,** ripper, tiller, scarifier.
korselet', (-te), cors(e)let.
kor'selig, (-e), grumpy, crusty.
kor'serig, (-e), crusty; ~**heid,** crustiness.
korset', (-te), corset, stays, foundation garment; ~**band,** stay-binding; ~**maker,** corseteer; ~**veter,** stay-lace.
kors'glans, bloom (bread).
kor'sie, (-s), crust (of bread); *hy het al harde ~s gekou*, he has known hard times.
Korsikaan', (..kane), Corsican; ~**s', (-e),** Corsican.
kors'mos, lichen.
korsterig, (-e), crusty.
kors'vormig, (-e), crustiform.
kors'vorming, (-s), encrustation.
kors'wel, (3) jest, fun, banter, play, joke, hoax; *uit ~*, in jest; (w) **(ge-),** jest, joke, banter, frolic.
kort, (w) (ge-), shorten; lack; crop (hair); clip (wings); *die TYD ~*, while away the time; *WABANDE ~*, shorten the hoops of wheels; (b, bw) **(-e; -er, -ste),** short, brief, concise, compendious; down (in cards); *op ~ AFSTAND*, at close range, at short distance, ~ *ANTWOORD*, answer briefly (curtly); ~ *AS*, minor axis; ~ *en BONDIG*, short and pithy; ~ *BY*, close by; ~ *DAARNA*, shortly afterwards; ~ *van DRAAD*, short-tempered; *iem. te ~ DOEN*, do someone short; *om ~ te GAAN*, to cut a long story short; ~ *van GEDAGTE*, have a short memory; ~ *GELEDE*, only recently; ~ *GESPAN (vas, gekniehalter, gebaker) wees*, be short-tempered; ~ *en GOED*, short and sweet; *iem. ~ HOU*, keep a tight rein upon a person; keep someone short (of money); *alles ~ en KLEIN slaan*, smash everything to atoms; *te ~ KOM*, fall short; lack; ~ *en KRAGTIG*, short and sweet; ~ *KURSUS*, short course; *te ~ LAND (binnekom)*, undershoot (aero.); *hier te ~ en daar te LANK*, have petty (paltry) objections (excuses); ~ *voor LANK*, before long; *die tyd ~ MAAK*, beguile the time; *te ~ SKIET*, fall short of the mark; *alles wil ~ en klein SLAAN*, want to smash everything to bits; *TOT voor ~*, until recently; ~**aangebonde,** short-tempered; ~**af,** abrupt, blunt, straight; summary, curt, brusque, off-hand; ~**as,** minor axis, stop-axle; ~**asem,** short of breath, pursy, broken-winded; ~**asemig, (-e),** short of breath, asthmatic; ~**asemigheid,** short-winded=

ness; crochet; ~**beenskaap**, sheep with short legs; ~**beensteek**, double crochet; ~**begrip**, summary (of the catechism); ~**broek**, shorts; ~**by**, nearby; short leg (cricket); short stop (baseball); ~**dienstermyn**, short service; ~**elas**, (-se), cutlass; ~**eling**, putlog; ~**elinggat**, putlog hole; ~**gebaker**, (-de), touchy, hot-headed, irritable, quick-tempered; ~**gebonde**, easily offended, touchy, pettish, short-tempered; ~**gebondenheid**, touchiness, short temper; combustibility; ~**geknip**, (-te), close-cropped; ~**gevat**, (-te), touchy; combustible; ~**golf(sender)**, short-wave (transmitter); ~**golfstasie**, short-wave station; ~**haarkam**, shingled-hair comb; ~**harig**, (-e), short-haired; ~**heid**, curtness, shortness, brevity, abruptness, conciseness; ~**heidshalwe**, for the sake of brevity; K~**horingbees**, Shorthorn; ~**horingvee**, short-horned cattle; Shorthorns; ~**ing**, (-e, -s), deduction, discount, reduction, rebate; ~**ingsbewys**, rebate-voucher.

kortisoon', cortisone.

kort: ~**kom**, (-ge-), fall short, lack, be missing; ~**kop**, bobbed head; ~**kop'pig**, (-e), brachycephalic; ~**kort**, frequently, every now and again; ~**kuns**, short prose; short stories and sketches; ~**lewering**, short delivery; ~ **liks**, in short, briefly; ~**ling**, (-e), putlog, swingle-tree; ~**lings**, a short time ago, lately, recently; ~**mourok**, short-sleeved dress; ~**om**, in a word, in fine, in a few words, briefly; ~*om spring*, on one's heels; make a volte face; ~**oor**, crop-ear; ~**pad**, short-cut; ~**papier**, short bills; ~**potig**, (-e), breviped; ~**prosa**, short prose; ~**puntig**, (-e), apiculate; ~**rib**, short-rib (beef).

Kort'ryk, Courtray.

kortsig'tig, (-e), short-sighted, myopic; blear-eyed; purblind; ~**heid**, short-sightedness.

kort: ~**sigwissel**, short-dated bill; ~**sinjaal**, doll-signal; ~**ske'delig**, (-e) = **kortkoppig**; ~**skote**, short game (golf).

kort'sluit, (-ge-), short-circuit; ~**ing**, short circuit(ing).

kort: ~**steelpyp**, pipe with short stem; ~**stert**=, short tail; bobtailed.

kortston'dig, (-e), short, short-lived, evanescent, momentary, ephemeral, fugitive, transitory; ~**heid**, transitoriness, transience, fugacity, fugaciousness, evanescence.

kort: ~**teken**, breve; ~**termynhuur**, short lease.

kort'tyd, short time; ~**sure**, short time (working hours).

kort: ~**vat**, (-ge-), be strict, take stern measures; treat firmly; *iem.* ~ *vat,* keep someone in check; ~**verhaal**, short story; ~**verhaalskrywer**, short-story writer; ~**vlerkig**, (-e), brevipennate, short-winged; ~**weg**, curtly, summarily, briefly; ~**wiek**, (ge-), hamper; clip the wings, pinion, handicap.

korund', corundum.

korvee', (-s), fatigue (party) (mil.); corvée; unpleasant task; statute labour; ~**soldaat**, fatigue-man.

korvet', (-te), corvette.

kos[1], (s) food, victuals, fare, commons, board; provender; living, livelihood; ~ *en INWONING*, board and lodging; *aan die ~ KOM*, earn a livelihood; ~ *BEDIEN*, serve with food; *as die ~ KOUD word, word die vrou warm*, the housewife's temper rises as the dinner cools; as the food grows cold the housewife becomes heated; *iem. die ~ uit die MOND kyk*, stare at someone who is eating; watch someone at his food; *ou ~ OPWARM*, dish up old fare; *dit is OU ~*, that is stale news, that is an old story; *sy ~ verdien*, earn a living; *sy ~ WERD*, worth one's salt (keep).

kos[2], (w) (ge-), cost; *dit ~ BAIE*, it costs a lot of money; it takes much energy (trouble, time); *dit sal twee DAE ~*, it will take two days; *dit ~ GELD*, it has to be paid for; *dit ~ NIKS*, there is no charge for this; *laat dit ~ wat WIL*, whatever the cost may be.

Kô'sa, (-s), Xhosa.

Kosak', (-ke), Cossack.

kos'baar, (..bare), precious (gems); dear, expensive, costly; cherished, valuable (time); sumptuous (banquets); ~**heid**, expensiveness, costliness; sumptuousness; ~**hede**, valuables.

kos: ~ **bal**, bolus; ~**blik**, lunch box; ~**deurtjie**, buttery-hatch; ~**diens**, commissariat.

ko'sekans, (-e, ..kante), cosecant.

kos: ~**emmertjie**, billy(can); ~**ganger**, (-s), boarder; commensal; ~*gangers hou*, take in boarders; ~**geld**, board, boarding-fee; ~**huis**, boarding-house; Good Hope home; hostel; ~**huisgees**, hostel spirit; ~**huiskamer**, hostel room; ~**huiskinders**, school-boarders; children from a Good Hope home; ~**huisreëls**, hostel rules; ~**hyser**, dumbwaiter.

ko'sinus, (-se), cosine.

kos'jer, kosher, ritually clean.

kos: ~**juffrou**, (-e, -ens), landlady; ~**kas**, safe; ~**kommandant**, commissary; ~**leerling**, (school-)boarder, day-boarder.

kosmetiek', (-e), cosmetic; ~**bedryf**, cosmetics industry.

kosme'ties, (-e), cosmetic.

kos'mies, (-e), cosmic; ~*e strale*, cosmic rays.

kosmogonie', cosmogony.

kosmograaf', (..grawe), cosmographer.

kosmografie', cosmography; ..**gra'fies**, (-e), cosmographic(al).

kosmologie', cosmology.

kosmopoliet', (-e), cosmopolitan; ..**li'ties**, (-e), cosmopolitan; ..**litis'me**, cosmopolitanism.

kos'mos, cosmos.

kosnaat'jie, (-s) = **koesnaatjie**.

kos'pap, chyme.

kos'prys, cost price; ~**berekening**, costing.

kos'skool, boarding-school; ~**lewe**, boarding-school life.

kos'soort, kind of food.

kostaal', (kostale), costal.

kos'te, expenses, costs, expenditure, charges; ~ *AANGAAN (maak)*, incur expense(s); *ALGEMENE ~*, overheads; ~ *ASSURANSIE, vrag*, cost, insurance, freight; *die ~ BESTRY uit*, meet (defray) the expense out of; *dit DEK die ~*, this covers expenses; *op my EIE ~*, at my own expense; ~ *v.d. GEDING*, costs of suit; *met GROOT ~*, at great expense; *LOPENDE ~*, running costs; ~ *MEEBRING*, entail expense; *op ~ van 'n ONGELYK*, a loser's risk; *TEN ~ van*, at the cost (expense, risk) of; *tot ~ VEROORDEEL*, condemn to pay costs; *iem. ~ VEROORSAAK*, put a person to expense; ~**beheer**, cost control; ~**berekenaar**, cost accountant; ~**berekening**, calculation of costs, costing; ~**grootboek**, cost-ledger.

kos'telik, (-e), precious, costly, fine, excellent, grand, exquisite; gorgeous; *'n ~e grap*, a priceless joke; ~**heid**, costliness, preciousness, exquisiteness.

kos'teloos, (..lose), free (of charge), gratis, gratuitous, pro deo, costless.

kos'ter, (-s), churchwarden, beadle, sexton; sacristan; verger; clerk, ~**es'**, (-se), lady sexton.

kos'te: ~**raming**, estimate of costs; ~**rekening**, bill of costs; expense account; ~**rekenmeester**, cost accountant.

kos'terskap, sextonship.

kos'tetarief, scale of charges.

kostumeer', (ge-), dress up; *'n ge~de bal*, a fancy-dress ball; ..**me'ring**, dressing (a play).

kostumier', costumier.

kostuum', (-s), costume; frock; ~**bal**, fancy-dress ball; ~**juwele**, costume jewels; ~**juweliersware**, costume jewellery; ~**pop**, dress stand; ~**repetisie**, dress-rehearsal; ~**toneelstuk**, costume piece.

kos: ~**vrou**, landlady; ~**vry**, (-e), free of charge; ~**weieraar**, hunger-striker; ~**winner**, (-s), bread-winner; ~**winning**, livelihood.

kosyn', (-e), frame; sash; still; door-post; ~**skaaf**, sash-plane.

ko'tangens, (-e, kotangente), cotangent.

kotelet', (-te), cutlet; ~**tooisel**, cutlet frill.

koterie', (-ë), coterie, clique.

kotiel', (-e), cotyledon, seed-pod.

kotiljon', (-s), **kotiljons'**, (-e), cotillion.

kots, (ge-), vomit.

kot'ter, (-s), cutter; ~**pen**, key-bolt.

koturn', (-e), cothurnus, buskin.

kou¹, (s) (-e), cage.
kou², (s) cold, chill, algidity, frostiness; ~ *vat*, catch a cold.
kou³, (w) (ge-), chew, masticate, champ, manducate; ~**baar**, (..**bare**), manducatory.
kou: ~ **beitel**, cold-chisel; cold-set; ~**bros**, cold-short.
koud, (kou(e); kouer, -ste), cold, chilly, frigid, frosty; *ek het daar ~ van GEWORD*, it made my blood run cold; ~ *KRY*, feel cold; *dit LAAT my* ~, it leaves me cold; *kou(e) LUGSTREEK*, frigid zone; *koue OORLOG*, cold war; ~ *en WARM (uit een mond) blaas*, blow hot and cold; ~ *WORD van iets*, have cold shivers; ~**bloedig**, (-e), cold-blooded; ~**bros**, cold-short; ~**gesmee**, (..**smede**), chilled; ~**getrokke**, cold-drawn; ~**heid**, coldness, chill; frostiness, frigidity, algidity; rawness (weather); ~**lei**, (-ge-), walk a horse to cool it down; hoodwink, lead astray, gull (person); ~**sit**, (-ge-), surpass, excel; get the better of; oust (in courting).
kou'e, cold chill, frostiness; ~ *vat*, catch a cold; ~**koors**, ague, shivers, rigors, shivering fit; ~**lik** = **koulik**.
kou'er, chewer.
kou'e: ~**front**, cold front; ~**rig**, (-e), chilly, cool, coldish; ~**vuur**, gangrene, mortification, necrosis.
kou'ery, chewing.
kou'(e)water, cold water; ~**inrigting**, hydropathic establishment; ~**kompres**, cold compress; ~**kuur**, cold-water cure; ~**pomp**, cold-water pump.
kou'goed, something to chew: a plant (*Mesembryanthemum tortuosum*).
kou: ~**gom**, chewing-gum, ~**ing**, chewing.
kou'kluim, (-s), one very sensitive to cold.
kou'kus, (-se), caucus.
kou'lekker, chewing-sweet.
kou'lik, (-e), sensitive to cold; chilly; ~**heid**, sensitiveness to cold.
kou'maag, ventricle; crop, gizzard (birds); proventiculus (insects).
kou'middel, masticatory.
kous, (-e), stocking, sock; gaiter (springs); wick (gaslamp); (my)hose, socks, stockings; *haar ~ e is vol ERTAPPELS*, her stockings are full of holes; *die ~ op die KOP kry*, come away with a flea in one's ear (empty-handed); *met die ~ oor die KOP terugkom*, return with empty hands.
kou'saag, cold-saw.
kousaal', (**kousale**), causal.
kousaliteit', causality; ~**s'leer**, doctrine of causation.
kousatief', (..**tiewe**) causative.
kous'band, garter, suspender; *Orde van die K~*, Order of the Garter; ~**slang**, garter-snake.
kous: ~**broek**, panty-stocking, pantyhose; ~**draad**, binding-wire.
kou'sel, (-s), that which is chewed, cud.
kous'handelaar, hosier.
kou'sie, (-s), small sock (stocking); (incandescent) mantle.
kous'ophouer, suspender.
kou'spier, cheek (masticatory) muscle.
kous: ~**steek**, stocking stitch; ~**stopster**, (-s), darning-woman; ~**voet**: *op ~ voete*, in one's stockinged feet; ~**ware**, hosiery; ~**wewer**, stocking-weaver; ~**winkel**, hosier's shop, haberdasher's shop.
kout, (ge-), talk, converse, chat.
kou'ter, (-s), co(u)lter; ~**bos**, *Athanasia trifurcata*.
kou'tjie¹, (-s), little cage; *eers die ~, dan die vroutjie*; be sure before you marry of a house wherein to tarry.
kou'tjie², (-s), cud.
kou'vlak, occlusal surface (of tooth).
kou'voël, kô'voël, tawny eagle (*Aquila rapax*).
kraag, (krae), collar (of a coat, shirt, etc.); frill; collect; apron (of green); flange (of a rail); yoke (of dress); cape; ruff (birds); garland; *baie deur die ~ jaag*, be a heavy drinker; ~**as**, thrust-shaft; ~**blok**, collar-bearing; ~**jas**, fur-collared coat; cape-coat; ~**mannetjie**, lion with mane; ~**omslag**, lapel; ~**steen**, corbel truss; ~**stel**, collar-set; ~**vrot**, collar-rot.
kraai, (s) (-e), crow, daw, corbie; raven; *deur die ~ e*

BESPREEK, as lean as a rake; *elke swart ~ dink sy EIER is die witste*, every one thinks his geese are swans; *so warm dat die ~ e GAAP*, swelteringly hot; *soveel van iets weet soos 'n ~ van GODSDIENS*, know as much as the man in the moon; *geen ~ kan dit HOU nie*, it is swelteringly hot; *lyk of die ~ e sy KOS afgeneem het*, look down in the dumps; *staan of die ~ e sy KOS opgeëet het*, be dejected, be down in the dumps; *so MAER soos 'n ~*, as thin as a lath; *~ e PIK nie mekaar se oë uit nie*, dog does not eat dog; *voel soos 'n ~ met POUVERE*, feel out of place; *een bont ~ maak nie SOMER nie*, one swallow does not make a summer; *moenie dink die ~ e sal vir jou 'n UINTJIE bring nie*, you cannot expect things to be served to you on a platter; *al moet die ~ e dit UITBRING*, murder will out; *'n VLIEËNDE ~ het altyd wat*, jackals seldom go hungry; (w) (ge-), crow; *jy kan GAAN ~*, go and boil your head; *VIKTORIE ~*, shout victory; ~**agtig**, (-e), corvine; ~**bek**, parrot-fish; (monkey-)wrench; shifting-spanner; crocodile-jaw; ~**bekvormig**, (-e), coracoid; ~**bessie**, rub-rub berry, (e.g. *Rhus crenata*); ~**mars**, *die ~ mars blaas*, go west, die; ~**nes**, crow's-nest; look-out; knot in angler's line; ~**poot**, crow's foot; ~**pootjies**, wrinkles at eye-corners; ~**uintjie**, kind of crocus.
kraak, (s) (**krake**), crack; chap; chink; ~ (w) (ge-), crack, crackle, creak, squeak; crunch, grate; *DAT dit so ~*, with might and main; *hy HET 'n krakie*, he has a screw loose; *daar is 'n ~ in sy STEM*, there is a catch in his voice; ~**been**, cartilage, gristle; ~**beenagtig** = ~**benig**; ~**beenstof**, chondrin; ~**beenweefsel**, cartilaginous tissue; ~**benig**, (-e), cartilaginous; gristly; ~**beskuitjie**, cracker; ~**brood**, toast; ~**geluid**, crepitation; ~**nuut**, (..**nuwe**), brand-new; ~**sindelik**, (-e), scrupulously clean; ~**skoen**, creaking shoe; ~**skoon**, spotlessly clean; ~**stem**, creaking voice; ~**vars**, crisp.
kraal¹, (**krale**), bead; beading
kraal², (**krale**), pen, kraal, corral, fold, bawn; village; *dis so IN sy ~*, that is right up his street; *in iem. anders se ~ KOM*, poach on another's preserves; (w) (ge-), drive into kraal.
kraal: ~**agtig**, (-e), beady; ~**boontjie**, love-bean; ~**borduurwerk**, beadwork, beading embroidery; ~**bossie**, one several plants (e.g. *Galenia africana*).
kraal: ~**hek**, kraal gate; ~**hoof**, headman (of village).
kraal'lys, beading; bead-moulding.
kraal: ~**mis**, dung in kraal, kraal manure; ~**muur**, kraal wall.
kraal: ~**ogie**, beady eye; ~**portretjys**, picture-beading; ~**skaaf**, beading-plane; ogee plane; mouldingplane.
kraal'tjie¹, (-s), small kraal.
kraal'tjie², (-s), little bead.
kraam¹, (**krame**), booth, stall; *dit kom in sy ~ te pas*, that suits his purpose.
kraam², childbed, lying-in; *In die ~ kom*, be confined; ~**bed**, childbed; ~**been**, white-leg, milk-leg; ~**drag**, maternity wear; ~**druppels**, Dutch (folk) medicine; ~**gordel**, maternity belt; ~**inrigting**, maternity home; lying-in hospital; ~**kaart**, maternity chart; ~**kamer**, lying-in-room.
kraam'klep, valve-cock.
kraam: ~**koors**, puerperal fever; ~**koste**, lying-in expenses; ~**nasorg**, post-natal care; ~**rok**, maternity gown; ~**toelae**, maternity grant; ~**tyd**, lying-in; ~**verpleegster**, midwife; maternity nurse; ~**verpleging**, midwifery, obstetrics; ~**vrou**, woman in childbed; ~**(vrou)koors**, childbed fever; puerperal fever.
kraan, (**krane**), tap, (stop)cock, faucet; hydrant; derrick, crane; ~**arm**, crane-jib; ~**baan**, cranegantry; ~**baanspoor**, crane-gantry rail; ~**balk**, cathead; crane-jib; davit; girder; ~**bek**, crane's beak; crane-bill (tool); ~**geld**, cranage; ~**oog**, seed of *Nux vomica*; ~**saag**, pit-saw; ~**spil**, crane-post; ~**stellasie**, gantry; ~**voël**, crane; ~**voëlblom**, strelitzia.
krab'bel, (s) scribble, scrawl, scratch, scrabble; doodle; (w) (ge-), scratch, scrawl, scribble; ~**aar**,

krabbertjie (-s), scribbler, scrawler, doodler; ~**poot**, ~**skrif**, crabbed writing, scrawl.

krab'bertjie, (-s), earring.

kraf'fie, (-s), water-bottle, decanter, carafe, kraf.

kraft'papier, kraft (paper).

krag, (-te), strength, power, force, vigour, energy; body; potency, powerfulness; goodness (cookery); efficacy, virtue (medicines); essence; forte; heart; kick; lustiness; effect; rating (motor); met *ALLE* ~, with might and main; *BO iem. se* ~, beyond his strength; *ERVARE* ~*te*, experienced men (work= ers); *jou* ~*te aan iets GEE,* throw oneself into something; *al jou* ~*te inspan,* exert one's utmost strength; *op* ~ *KOM,* recover one's strength; *God gee* ~ *na KRUIS,* God tempers the wind to the shorn lamb; *in die* ~ *van sy LEWE,* in the prime of his life; ~*te MEET met,* pit one's strength against; *met TERUGWERKENDE* ~, retrospectively; *UIT* ~ *van,* by virtue of; *ou* ~*te UITHAAL,* do one's utmost; fall back on reserve strength; *van* ~ *WEES,* be in force; *op volle* ~ *WERK,* work at full capacity; ~ *van WET hê,* have the force of law; *van* ~ *WORD,* come into force; *jou* ~*te WY aan,* de= vote one's energies to; ~**besparing,** conservation of energy; ~**boor,** power-drill; ~**bron,** power-plant; source of power; ~**da'dig,** (-e), effective, effica= cious, vigorous, energetic; ~**da'digheid,** efficacy, efficiency; vigour, energy; forcefulness; ~**draad,** power line; ~**eenheid,** unit of force; power unit; ~**fiets,** moped; ~**gewend,** (-e), invigorating, strength-giving; ~**gies!,** well, I never!; ~**hou,** forc= ing stroke.

kra'gie, (-s), fichu, collar(ette).

krag: ~**installasie,** (electric) power-plant; ~**koekie,** dairy-nut; ~**kop,** power head; ~**leiding,** power-transmission line; ~**lyn,** line of force; ~**man,** bul= bous plant *(Pachypodium bispinosum);* ~**mens,** strong man; ~**mes,** mower; ~**meter,** dynamome= ter; ~**meting,** trail of strength; ~**onderbreking,** power failure; ~**oorbringing,** power-transmission; ~**paraffien,** power-paraffin; ~**persing,** dumping (of wool); ~**perswol,** dumped wool; ~**proef,** trial of strength; ~**prop,** plug; ~**punt,** monad; electric plug; ~**rem,** power brake; ~**saag,** power-saw; ~**sentrale,** (electric) power-station, generating-station, power-house; ~**sentrum,** centre of force.

krags'inspanning, exertion, effort, push.

krag: ~**skrop,** power-scraper; power-operator; ~**slag,** firing stroke; ~**sop,** broth; bisk; ~**span= ning,** stress; ~**steen,** bossage; perpend(er); ~**stroom,** flux; electric current.

krags'uiting, energy; display of strength.

krag'teleer, dynamics, kinetics.

krag'teloos, (..lose), powerless, weak, impotent; pithless; null and void; feckless, effete, invalid; ~ *maak,* nullify, invalidate; ~**heid,** debility, weak= ness, powerlessness, invalidity; inanition.

krag'tens, by virtue of, in consequence of, by right of; ~ *die ordonnansie,* under the ordinance.

krag'term, strong term, expletive, oath.

krag'tie! well, I never!

krag'tig, (-e), powerful, strong, potent, masculine; pithy, forcible, efficacious, energetic, dynamic, co= gent, vigorous, robust, able-bodied; high; inten= sive; drastic (measures); stout (resistance); rich, body-building (food); ~**heid,** powerfulness; inten= sity; ~**lik,** powerfully, strongly, firmly, lustily, forcibly, vigorously.

krag: ~**toer,** (power-)stunt; tour de force; ~**verbruik,** power-consumption; consumption of energy; ~**verlies,** loss of strength (power); ~**verspilling,** waste of energy; ~**vertoon,** display of power (strength); ~**voedsel,** forcing food, concentrated food.

krag'voer, concentrates; ~**koekies,** nuts (dairy).

krag'vol, (-le), powerful, forcible.

krakeel', (s) **(krakele),** wrangle, altercation; (w) **(ge-),** wrangle, quarrel.

kra'keling, (-e), cracknel (pastry).

kra'ker, (-s), cracker.

kra'kie, (-s), *verkleinwoord* van **kraak;** *hy het 'n* ~, he has bats in the belfry; *vgl.* **kraak.**

kra'letjie, (-s), small bead.

kram, (s) (-me), clamp, cramp, staple; clasp; clam; clincher; cramp-iron; crampon; fastener; ~ *en oorslag,* hasp and staple; (w) **(ge-),** clamp, cramp.

kra'mat, kramat', (-te), holy grave (Mohammedan).

kram: ~**bout,** U-bolt; ~**drukker,** stapler.

kra'mer, (-s), pedlar, hawker; mercer; ~**slatyn,** dog-Latin; ~**y,** (-e), hawking; small (pedlar's) wares; haberdashery; mercery; pettifoggery.

kram: ~**masjientjie,** stapler; ~**mer,** (-s), stapler; ~**metjie,** (-s), (wire) staple.

kramp, (-e), cramp, spasm, convulsion; *ek wens jy kry 'n* ~, I wish you'll have a pain where it hurts most; ~**aanval,** cramp attack; ~**aarbreuk,** varicocele; ~**ag'tig,** (-e), convulsive, spasmodic; convulsion= ary; crampy; *jou* ~*agtig vasklem aan,* cling desper= ately to; ~**druppels,** cramp drops (a patent Dutch medicine); ~**hoes,** spasmodic cough; ~**middel,** an= tispasmodic; ~**siekte,** Molteno disease; ~**stillend,** (-e), antispasmodic; ~**vis,** cramp-fish, electric ray (fish); ~**water,** gripe-water.

kram'skieter, stapler.

kra'nig, (-e), brave, bold, smart, clever, fine, crack, dashing, gallant, excellent; ~**heid,** boldness, dash, spirit, gallantry.

krank, (-e), sick, unwell, ill; *'n* ~ *e troos,* poor com= fort; ~**bed,** sick-bed; ~**e,** (-s), patient; ~**heid,** ill= ness, disease; ~**lik,** (-e), sickly.

kranksin'nig, (-e), insane, mad, crazy, demented; dis= tracted, distraught, phrenetic; lunatic; ~**e,** (-s), lu= natic, madman; ~**egestig,** mental hospital, lunatic (insane) asylum; ~**everpleging,** mental nursing; ~**heid,** madness, lunacy, insanity; mental derange= ment, dementia; craze; distraction; frenzy.

krans, (s) (-e), wreath, garland; (children's) circle; chaplet; corona; cincture; rocky ridge; cliff, krantz; *'n* ~ *op iem. se graf lê,* pay someone a final tribute; (w) **(ge-),** garland, wreathe; ~**aasvoël,** Cape vul= ture; ~**bal,** ringball (game); ~**duif,** speckled pigeon; ~**ie,** (-s), small wreath; ~**-krans,** ringball (game); ~**klep,** coronary valve; ~**legging,** wreath-laying (ceremony); ~**lysie,** rock-ledge; chaplet; ~**valk,** rock kestrel.

krap¹, (s) **(-pe),** crab; *Die K*~, Cancer.

krap², (s) madder.

krap³, (s) scratch; (w) **(ge-),** claw, paw; scribble, scrawl; ~ *waar dit nie jeuk nie,* meddle in other people's affairs.

krap⁴, (bw), with difficulty; *dit het* ~ *gegaan,* it was a battle.

krap'agtig, (-e), cancroid, cancrene.

krap'borsel, scrubber.

krap'knypers, crab's pincers.

krap: ~**per,** (-s), rasper, scraper; ~**perig,** (-e), scratchy; hurtful, nasty; ~**pertjie,** (-s), plectrum; ~**sel,** (-s), scrapings.

krap'vormig, (-e), cancrene.

krap'wortel, madder.

krap'yster, scraping iron, scraper, raker (smithy).

kras, (s) **(-se),** scrape, caw, scratch, screech; (w) **(ge-),** croak, screech; creak; rasp; scrape (with a pen, etc.), grate; stridulate; (b) **(-se),** brisk, vigorous (person); drastic (measure); stiff, strong (allega= tion); ~ *optree teen,* take a strong line with; take drastic steps against; ~**blok,** surface-gauge; ~**bor= sel,** scratch-brush; ~**heid,** strength; strictness, severity; ~**send,** (-e), strident, grating, ready, raspy; ~**ser,** (-s), scraper, scratcher.

krat, (-te), crate, skeleton case; tail-board (of wag= (g)on); frame.

kra'ter, (-s), crater; ~**meer,** crater-lake; ~**pyp,** volca= nic pipe; ~**rand,** crater-lip; ~**vormig,** (-e), crater-shaped.

krawat', (-te), cravat.

kraw'wetjie, (-s) = **krabbetjie.**

krea'sie, (-s), creation.

kreatuur', (..ture), creature, being.

krediet', credit; vote of credit; sum at someone's dis= posal (e.g. at a bank); (record of) credit side (of account); sum to the good (on account); belief, trust; (good) reputation; trust in someone (to pay); *iem.* ~ *GEE vir iets,* give a person credit for some=

thing; *sy* ~ *is GOED*, his credit is good; he is fairly rich; *op* ~ *KOOP*, buy on credit; *meer SÊ as waar jy* ~ *voor het*, say more than you can account for; ~**balans**, credit balance; ~**bank**, credit-bank; ~**beperking**, credit, restriction; ~**bewys**, credit voucher; ~**boek**, credit book; ~**boeking**, credit entry; ~**brief**, letter of credit; ~**kaart**, credit card; ~**oordrag**, credit transfer; ~**saldo**, credit balance; ~**stelsel**, credit system; ~**verkoping**, credit sale; ~**waardig**, (-e), solvent; ~**waardigheid**, credit-worthiness; credit rating; solvency.

kre'dit, (-s, -te), (ong., rek.), credit; (sum on) credit side (of account).

krediteer', (ge-), credit; *iem.* ~ *met*, credit a person's account with.

kredite'ring, crediting.

krediteur', (-e, -s), creditor.

kreëer', (ge-), create.

kreef, (-te, krewe), lobster, Cape (rock-)lobster; crayfish, crawfish; ~**agtig**, (-e), cancroid; ~**kelkie**, crayfish cocktail; ~**mandjie**, lobster-pot; ~**meel**, crayferine; **K**~**s'keerkring**, Tropic of Cancer; ~**slaai**, lobster salad; ~**so(e)p**, lobster soup; ~**tegang**, backward march; *die* ~ *tegang gaan*, go downhill; go from bad to worse; ~**tekuit**, coral.

kreet, (krete), cry, scream, shriek; slogan.

kreits, (-e), circle.

krema'sie, cremation.

kremato'rium, (-s, ..toria), crematorium.

kremeer', (ge-), cremate.

kremetart', cream of tartar; ~**boom**, baobab tree

krenelleer', (ge-), crenellate.

kreng¹, (s) (-e), carrion, scoundrel.

kreng², (w) (ge-), careen (ship).

krenk, (ge-), offend, hurt, mortify; (ag)grieve; derange, craze; *gekrenkte GEESVERMOËNS*, unsound mind; *iem. se goeie NAAM* ~, besmirch someone's reputation; *ge* ~ *VOEL*, feel hurt, feel offended; ~**end**, (-e), injurious, mortifying, offensive; ~**ing**, offence, insult, wounding (feelings), mortification, grief.

kren'terig, (-e), mean, niggardly, miserly, stingy; ~**heid**, meanness, stinginess.

kreolien', **kreoli'ne**, creolin(e).

kreoliseer', (ge-), creolize; ..**lise'ring**, act of creolizing, creolization.

kreolis'me, creolism.

Kreool', (Kreole), Creole; ~**s'**, (-e), Creole.

kreosol', creosol.

kreosoot', creosote.

kreosoteer', (ge-), creosote.

krep, crêpe.

krepeer', (ge-), die; ~ *van honger*, die of hunger.

kresol', cresol.

Kre'ta, Crete.

Kreten'ser, (-s), Cretan.

Kreten'sies, (-e), Cretan.

Kre'tie en Ple'tie, ragtag and bob-tail, riff-raff.

kretin', (s), cretin; - **is'me**, cretinism.

kreton', (-s), cretonne.

kreu'kel, (s) (-s) (-e), crease, fold, ruck; pique, pucker; (w) (ge-), crease, fold, crumple, crinkle, rumple; pucker; ~**ing**, (-e, -s), wrinkling, creasing, crumpling; plication; ~**papier**, crinkled paper; ~**rig**, (-e), crinkly; creased, rumpled, crumpled, wrinkled; ~**traag**, (..trae), crease-resistant; ~**vas**, (-te), uncreasable; ~**vry**, (-e), creaseless, noncreasing.

kreun, (s) (-e), moan, groan, pule; (w) (ge-), groan, moan.

kreu'pel, lame, crippled, limping; *hy is baie* ~, he limps badly; ~**bos**, thicket, underwood.

kreu'pele, (-s), cripple; *die* ~ *wil altyd voordans*, fools rush in where angels fear to tread; ~**sorg**, care of cripples.

kreu'pelheid, lameness, crippleness.

kreu'pelhout, brushwood, copse, coppice, scrub, covert; thicket; shrub *(Leucospermum conocarpum)*.

kreu'pelrym, doggerel.

kre'wefuik, lobster pot.

kre'wel, (-s), prawn.

krib'be, (-s), crib.

krie'bel, (ge-) = **kriewel**.

krie'bos, *Lycium*.

kriek, (s) (-e), cricket (insect), grig; *'n langasem* ~, a long-winded speaker; (w) (ge-), chirp.

krie'ket, cricket (game); ~**baan**, cricket pitch; ~**bal**, cricket ball; ~**kolf**, (cricket) bat; ~**paaltjie**, wicket; ~**span**, cricket team; ~**spel**, cricket; ~**speler**, cricketer; ~**veld**, cricket field, oval; ~**wedstryd**, cricket match.

krie'kie, (-s), (house) cricket.

kriek'telefoon, cricket telephone.

kriel, (s) whip-stitch; (w) (ge-), whip-stitch.

kriel'haantjie, bantam cock; cocky little fellow.

kriel: ~**soom**, whipped seam; ~**steek**, whip stitch.

krie'sel, (-s), bit, particle; ~**tjie**, (-s), particle, grain, atom; *nie 'n* ~ *tjie om in 'n mens se OOG te steek nie*, not even the merest iota; *geen* ~ *tjie WAARHEID nie*, not a grain of truth.

krie'wel, (ge-), trickle, itch; fidget; creep; ~**ing**, (-e, -s), formication; tickling; itching; ~**hoes**, tickling cough; ~**kop**, fussy person; crosspatch; ~**krappers**, whims, caprices; ~**muggies**, simulidae; ~**rig**, (-e), ticklish; itchy; fussy; cross-grained (person); crawly; peevish; petulant; ~**siekte**, itch.

kri'ging, kriging (math.); *universele* ~, universal kriging.

krik, (-ke), lifting-jack, jack, jack-screw.

kril, krill.

Krim: *die* ~, the Crimea; *die* ~ *oorlog*, the Crimean War.

kriminalis', (-te), criminalist.

kriminaliteit', criminality, crime.

krimineel', (..nele), criminal, outrageous; *dit het* ~ *gegaan*, it was uphill work.

kriminologie', criminology; ..**nolo'gies**, (-e), criminological.

kriminoloog', (..loë), criminologist.

krimp, (ge-), shrink, contract, diminish; pinch (in reef); ~ *van die pyn*, writhe with pain; ~**baar**, (..bare), contractile; ~**gat**, shrink-hole; ~**ing**, (-e, -s), shrinkage; contraction; ~**maat**, shrinkage; measure of contraction; ~**maatstaf**, contraction-rule; ~**passing**, shrink fit; ~**siekte**, cattle disease caused by eating the **krimpsiektebos** *(Cotyledon wallichii ventricosa)*; ~**skaal**, contraction rule; ~**skeur**, contraction-fissure; ~**traag**, (..trae), shrink-resistant; ~**vas**, (-te), unshrinkable; ~**voeg**, contraction joint; ~**vry**, (-e), unshrinkable; shrink-proof; ~**(yster)varkie**, South African hedgehog.

kring¹, (s) (-e), carrion, carcase, (fig.) scoundrel, rotter.

kring², (s) (-e), circle, district, area; ring, orbit; halo; walk of life; coterie, set; radius; circuit; *die BESTE* ~ *e*, the best circles; *in hoë* ~ *e BEWEEG*, move in the best circles; *BLOU* ~ *e onder die oë*, livid rings (dark circles) under the eyes, 'n e *MAAK oor die water*, circle over the water; *in 'n* ~ *REDENEER*, argue in a circle; *in SEKERE* ~ *e*, in certain quarters; (w) (ge-), circle; mark with a circle; leave a round stain; ~**duikel**, loop the loop; ~**duikeling**, looping the loop.

krin'gel, (ge-), curl (smoke).

kring: ~**end**, (-e), circumambient; ~**etjie**, (-s), small circle (ring); circlet; ~**etjies rook blaas**, blow smoke-rings; ~**gat(bok)**, waterbuck; ~**gatpampoen**, Turkish cap (pumpkin); ~**loop**, circular course/cycle (years); circulation; gyration; rotation (crops); circuit (electric); *BOSE* ~ *loop*, vicious circle; *GESLOTE* ~ *loop*, closed circle; ~**rit**, circle (riding-school); ~**ry**, circle (riding-school); ~**spier**, constrictor; ~**storm**, cyclone; ~**stroom**, circular circuit; ~**vlek**, ring blotch (cabbages); ~**vlug**, circular flight; circuit; ~**vlugreëls**, circuit rules; ~**vormig**, (-e), circular, gyrate, gyrous, rotatory.

krink, (s) (-e), swivel-plate; swivel, swing; (w) (ge-), turn (pole of wagon); swivel; heel; ~**arm**, steering arm; ~**as**, stub-axle; swivel-arm (motor).

krin'kel, (s) (-s), crinkle; (w) (ge-), crinkle.

krink'spil, kingpin (motor).

krinolet', crinolette.

krinolien', (-e), **krinoli'ne**, (-s), crinoline; ~**band**, crinoline-band (loco).
krioel', (ge-), swarm, abound (teem) with; crawl; bristle with (errors); *dit* ~ *hier van muise*, the place is overrun with mice.
krioliet', cryolite.
krip[1], crêpe, crape.
krip[2], (-pe), manger; crib; *aan die* ~ *staan*, have a plush job (especially in the civil service).
krip[3], (-te), **kript**, (-e), **krip'ta**, (-s), crypt.
krip'ties, (-e), cryptic(al).
kriptogaam', (..game), cryptogam (e.g. fern); (b) (..game), cryptogamous.
kriptogram', (-me), cryptogram.
krip'ton, crypton.
krip: ~**verband**, crêpe bandage; ~**vreter**, government official; ~**werk**, crib-work; false work.
kris, (-se), creese, kris.
krisant', (-e), chrysanthemum.
kri'sis, (-se), crisis, critical point, turning point; slump; climacteric; acme, juncture; *'n* ~ *deurmaak*, pass through a crisis (critical stage); ~**jaar**, year of crisis; ~**periode**, period of crisis.
kris'kras, (s) grating, scratching; (bw) crisscross, in all directions.
Kris'misie, Christmas; *hy DINK hy's* ~, he is full of himself; ~ *kom net eenmaal in die JAAR*, Christmas comes but once a year.
kris'misroos, Christmas rose; hydrangea; Syrian hibiscus.
kristal', (-le), crystal; ~**agtig**, (-e), crystalline; ~**beskrywing**, crystallography; ~**buis**, transistor; ~**druiwe**, crystal grapes; ~**helder**, as clear as crystal, crystalline; hyaline; ~**holte**, geode, vug; ~**klip**, crystal; ~**kunde**, crystallography; ~**kyker**, crystal gazer; ~**kykery**, crystal-gazing; ~**leer**, crystallography; ~**lens**, crystalline lens.
kristallisa'sie, crystallization.
kristalliseer', (ge-), crystallice; effloresce.
kristallise'ring, crystallizing; efflorescence.
kristallograaf', (..grawe), crystallographer.
kristallografie', crystallography; ..**gra'fies**, (-e), crystallographic(al).
kristallyn', (-e), crystalline.
kristal': ~**ontvanger**, crystal receiver; ~**stel**, crystal set; ~**stelsel**, system of crystallization; ~**ster**, stellate crystal; ~**voorspelling**, crystal-gazing; ~**vorm**, crystalline form; ~**vormig**, (-e), crystal-shaped; crystalloid; ~**vorming**, crystallization; ~**water**, water of crystallization; ~**werk**, crystal ware.
krite'rium (-s, ..ria), criterion, test, norm.
kritiek', (s) criticism, review, critique, censure; animadversion; comment; (-e), review; *BENEDE alle* ~, beneath contempt, abominable; ~ *UITOE= FEN op*, criticize; *dit sal* ~ *UITLOK*, it will call forth adverse criticism; (b) **(-e)**, crucial, critical; climacteric; *die* ~*e toets*, the crucial (acid) test.
kri'ties, (-e), critical; *iets* ~ *BEKYK*, regard something with a critical eye; *'n* ~*e BESKOUING*, a (book) review; a critical examination; ~*e SNEL= HEID*, critical velocity (depth).
kritikas'ter, (-s), criticaster.
kri'tikus, (-se, ..tici), critic; reviewer.
kritiseer', (ge-), criticize; review (book); cavil, censure, find fault with, disapprove of, animadvert, comment.
Kroaat', (**Kroate**), Croat.
Kroa'sië, Croatia.
kroa'ties, (-e), Croatian.
kroeg, (**kroeë**), public house, pub, bar, buffet, tavern, dram-shop; ~**bediende**, wine steward; ~**houer**, barkeeper; publican; ~**juffrou**, barmaid; ~**krui= per**, pub-crawler; ~**loper**, tippler, boozer, pub-crawler; ~**man**, barman; ~**sitkamer**, bar lounge; ~**stoeltjie**, bar stool; ~**taal**, pot-house talk; ~**vlieg**, bar fly.
kroek', (-e), slum; hovel; location.
kroep, croup; ~**agtig**, (-e), croupy; ~**hoes**, croup cough; ~**ketel**, (bronchitis) steam-kettle.
kroes[1], (s) (-e), mug, noggin, crucible.
kroes[2], (w) (ge-), frizz; (b) curly, frizzy, crisp; crêpe; *ge*~*te hare*, frizzy hair.

kroes[3], (b, bw) ill; ~ *voel*, feel seedy; ~**erig**, (-e), fuzzy; out-of-sorts.
kroe'sestaal, crucible steel.
kroes: ~**hare**, frizzy hair; staring (ruffled) hair; ~**harig**, (-e), woolly-haired.
kroes'heid, crispness; seediness.
kroes'kop, curly-head.
kroes'tang, crucible-tongs.
krokant', (-e), crisp.
kroket', (-te), croquette.
krokodil', (-le), crocodile; ~**trane**, crocodile tears, hypocrisy; ~**wagter**, crocodile bird *(Cursarius aegyptus)*.
kro'kus, (-se), crocus; ~**blom** crocus(-flower).
krom, (w) (ge-), bow, bend; *jou onder die vyand se juk* ~, submit to the enemy; (b) crooked, curved, bent; awry; aquiline, hooked (nose); broken, incorrect (language); ~ *BENE*, bandy legs; ~ *van die LAG*, bent double with laughter; ~ *Afrikaans PRAAT*, speak faulty (broken) Afrikaans; ~ *TREK*, warp, buckle; ~ *VAN*, bent down by; *jou* ~ *WERK*, work oneself to death; ~**balk**, cantilever; ~**been**, bandy-legged person; baker-legged; ~**bek**, pipe-wrench; ~**bekstrandloper**, curlew sandpiper.
kro'meskie, (-s), kromeski.
krom: ~**guts**, bent gouge; ~**hals**, retort; ~**heid**, crookedness; ~**hout**, vine; camber; knee (techn.); ~*houtsop gedrink hê*, be tipsy; ~**knie**, calf-knees; ~**lynig**, (-e), curvilinial; curvilinear; ~**lynmeter**, opisometer; ~**me**, (-s), curve (graphs); ~**ming**, (-e, -s), curve, turn, bend; sinuosity; curvature; elbow; camber; flexion; crook; ~**mingshoek**, angle of curvature; ~**mingslyn**, line of curvature; ~**nek**, retort; ~**nekkaatjie:** *hy het K*~*nekkaatjie gesoen*, he has been at the bottle; ~**neksleutel**, bent wrench; ~**neus**, hawk-nose; hooked nose; beak; ~**passer**, (outside) callipers; ~**pokkeltjie**, kind of insect; ~**praat**, (-ge-), speak haltingly, mutilate a language, speak (a language) imperfectly; talk the language of children; lisp; ~**prater**, mutilator of a language; ~**saag**, circular saw; curved saw; bow saw, frame saw; ~**spoor**, curved track; ~**staf**, crosier; ~**swaard**, scimitar; ~**taal**, gibberish; faulty language; ~**te**, crookedness; crook; flexure; ~**trek**, (-ge-), cast (timber), warp, buckle, distort; lift (floor); hunch; ~**trekking**, warp, casting, buckling, distortion.
kroniek', (-e), chronicle; *iem. die* ~*e voorlees*, give someone a talking to; read someone a lesson; ~**skrywer**, chronicler.
kro'ning, (-e, -s), coronation, crowning.
kro'nings: ~**dag**, coronation day; ~**eed**, coronation oath; ~**fees**, coronation festivities; ~**plegtigheid**, coronation ceremony.
kron'kel, (s) (-s), twist, crinkle, coil, kink; gyrus (of cerebrum); (w) (ge-), wind, twist, twirl, coil; meander; crinkle; ~**derm**, ileum; ~**dermontste= king**, ileitis; ~**end**, (-e), twisting, winding, coiling; devious; serpentine; meandrous; creeky; peristaltic; ~**gang**, maze; meandering, winding course; ~**ig**, (-e), winding, sinuous, meandering, ~**igheid**, winding (meandering) formation; ~**ing**, (-e, -s), winding, coil, twist; fold; sinuosity; meandering; anfractuosity; curl; convolution; circumvolution; insinuation; ~**loop**, winding (meandering) course; torsion; ~**pad**, (..**paaie**), ~**weg**, (..**weë**), winding path (road); serpentine.
kroon, (s) (**krone**), crown, coronet; corona, corolla (flower); coronal (gems); chandelier, gaselier, lustre (light); circle; *iem. die* ~ *v.d. hoof NEEM*, put someone to shame; *die* ~ *NEERLÊ*, give up the crown, abdicate (the throne); *die* ~ *op die werk SIT*, crown it all; *die* ~ *SPAN*, bear away the palm, cap everything; *iem. na die* ~ *STEEK*, vie with a person; (w) (ge-), crown; *dit* ~ *ALLES*, that caps everything; *tot KONING* ~, crown as king; ~**arend**, crowned eagle; ~**been**, lower pastern; ~**blaar**, petal; ~**draer**, bearer of a crown; ~**duif**, victoria; ~**-ertjie**, imperial pea; ~**formaat**, crown size; ~**gal**, crown-gall; ~**getuie**, crown witness; ~**gewrig**, pastern joint; ~**glas**, crown-glass; ~**grond**, crown-land ; ~**grondbrief**, crown(-land)

grant; ~**hare**, hair on crown of head; ~**juwele**, crown jewels; ~**kandelaar**, girandole; ~**kolonie**, crown colony; ~**lamp**, (elektr.), electrolier; ~**land**, crown-land; ~**lig**, chandelier; ~**lote**, leading shoots; ~**lugter**, candelabrum, chandelier; ~**lys**, cornice; pediment; corona; ~**moer**, castle-nut; ~**naat**, cranial suture; ~**papier**, crown papier; ~**prins**, crown prince; dauphin; ~**prinses**, dauphiness; crown princess; princess royal; ~**rat**, crown-wheel; ~**roes**, crown-rust (in corn); ~**saag**, drum-saw; ~**sierade**, regalia; ~**slagaar**, coronary artery; ~**slagaartrombose**, coronary thrombosis; ~**takke**, leading branches; ~**tjie**, (-s), crown (in hair); cowlick; small crown; coronet; ~**toelae**, civil list; ~**vervolger**, public prosecutor; ~**vormig**, (-e), crown-shaped; ~**vrot**, crown-rot (in lucern); ~**wiel**, crown-wheel.

kroos[1], duckweed.

kroos[2], offspring, progeny, issue, descendants; ~**trooster**, baby-sitter.

krop, (s) (-pe), crop (of fowl); jowl (of bird); maw (of ruminant); gizzard, craw; goitre; head (lettuce); pouch; *DWARS in die ~ steek*, go against the grain (stick in the gizzard); ~ *v.d. MAAG*, solar plexus; (w) (ge-), cram, bottle up; *iets nie kan ~ nie*, be unable to swallow (put up with, stomach) something; ~**aargras**, cocksfoot; ~**duif**, cropper, pouter (pigeon); ~**gans**, pelican; ~**geswel**, goitre, Derbyshire neck, bronchocele, struma; ~**mens**, cretin; ~**slaai**, (cabbage) lettuce, cos.

krosidoliet, orocidolite, blue asbestos.

krot, (-te), hovel, den, hut, shanty; ~**bewoner**, slum-dweller; ~**opruiming**, slum-clearance; ~**stad**, shanty-town, slum-area; ~**-te**, ~**tebuurt**, slums; ~**woning**, slum-dwelling.

kro'ton, (-s), croton.

krou'kie, (-s), croquet; ~**speler**, croquet-player.

kru, crude; ~**diteit**, ~**heid**, crudity.

Kru'gerdag, Kruger Day (Oct. 10).

Kru'gerrand, Kruger rand.

krui[1], (ge-), trundle (in wheelbarrow); go at a slow pace, crawl along.

krui[2], (ge-), spice, season; lend piquancy to; *'n sterk ge~ de verhaal*, a spicy (improper) story.

kruid, (kruie), herb; spice(s); *daar het geen ~ voor GEGROEI nie, daarteen is geen ~ GEWASSE nie*, there is no remedy for it; *sy kruie was te STERK*, he has had a drop too much; ~**agtig**, (-e), herbaceous; ~**boek**, herbal.

kruidenier', (-s), grocer; chandler; ~**s'artikels**, grocery lines; ~**s'ware**, groceries; ~**s'winkel**, grocery shop.

krui'(d)erig, (-e), spicy, spiced.

krui'dery, (-e), condiment, spice.

kruidjie-roer'-my-nie, (-s), touch-me-not, sensitive plant; touchy fellow.

kruid koek, seed-cake.

krui'e, (w) (ge-) = **krui**[1] en **krui**[2].

krui'e: ~**bier**, herb-beer, ~**boek**, herbal, ~**brandewyn**, spiced brandy; ~**dokter**, ~**kenner**, herbalist; ~**kennis**, herbalism; ~**middel**, herbal remedy.

krui'er, (-s), porter, barrowman.

krui'erig, (-e), herby.

krui'ersloon, porterage.

krui'eruik, spicy smell.

krui'ery[1], (-e), porterage.

kru'iery[2], condiment.

krui'eryskyf, monkey-gland steak.

krui'e: ~**salf**, herbal ointment; ~**sous**, ketchup, condiment; ~**versameling**, herbarium; ~**wyn**, spiced wine, sangaree, hippocras.

kruik, (-e), pitcher, jug, urn, crock; *die ~ gaan te water tot dit breek*, the pitcher goes so often to the well that it is broken at last.

krui'middel, seasoning.

kruin, (-e), top crown, head; summit; crest (wave).

krui'naeltjie, (-s), clove; ~**-olie**, oil of cloves.

kruin: ~**lyn**, crest-line; ~**plaat**, crown-plate (loco.); ~**ryer**, crown driver; ~**skering**, tonsure; ~**waarde**, amplitude.

kruip, (ge-), creep, crawl, glide; trail; cringe, grovel, play the toady, fawn; crouch; *eers ~, dan LOOP*, begin in a small way; *VOOR iem. ~*, cringe before someone; ~**bal**, daisy-cutter; creeper (cricket); ~**band**, half-track; ~**broekie**, crawler; ~**distel**, creeping-thistle; ~**end**, (-e), creeping abject; insidious; cringing; procumbent; ~ *ende dier*, reptile; ~**er**, (-s), creeper, crawler; cringer, toady, lick-spittle, fawner, bootlicker, groveller, sycophant.

krui'perig, (-e), cringing, fawning, servile, adulatory, sneaking, obsequious, grovelling; ~**heid**, cringing, obsequiousness, servility, toadyism, sycophancy, abjection.

krui'perlaaigraaf, crawler loader.

krui'pery, fawning, toadyism, cringing.

kruip: ~**gangetjie**, cat-walk; ~**gat**, toady; ~**houding**, position for crawling; ~**knie**, housemaid's knee; ~**lig**, (-te), dip-light; ~**loopgraaf**, (..grawe), crawl-trench; ~**mol**, (-le), golden mole; ~**pak**, (-ke), (child's) crawler; ~**plant**, creeper (plant); groundling; ~**ronding**, camber (road); ~**ruspe**, geometer; ~**sand**, shifting sand; ~**slag**, crawl stroke; ~**s(w)eer**, (spreading) ulcer; ringworm; ~**swem**, crawl (swimming stroke); ~**trekker**, caterpillar tractor, crawler tractor; ~**waster**, creep-washer; ~**werend**, (-e), anti-creep.

kruis, (s) (-e), cross; crucifix; sharp (music); croup (animal); rump (of beef); crux, quarters, crupper (horse); trial, affliction; chine, loin, small of the back, fork, crotch (of trousers); *die BLOU K ~*, the Blue Cross; *elkeen moet sy ~ DRA*, each must bear his own burden; ~ *na KRAG en krag na ~*, God shapes the back for the burden; *'s en MOLLE*, sharps and flats; ~ *of MUNT*, heads or tails; cross or pile; *die ROOI K ~*, the Red Cross; *'n hele paar ~e agter die RUG hê*, be well advanced in years; have seen many summers; *'n ~ SLAAN*, make the sign of the cross; *aan die ~ SLAAN*, nail to the cross; *met 'n ~ TEKEN*, sign by making a mark (a cross); (w) (ge-), cross, intersect; interbreed, cross-breed; nail to the cross, crucify; cruise; *BEESTE ~*, cross(-breed) cattle; ~ *HOM*, crucify him; *'n gekruiste TJEK*, a crossed cheque; (bw); ~ *en DWARS*, crisscross; ~ *en dwars BESPREEK*, thrash out a matter; ~**afneming**, deposition; descent from the Cross; ~**arm**, limb (of cross); ~**arsering**, cross-hatching; ~**baar**, (..bare), compatible (biol.); ~**balans**, cross-balance; ~**balanseer**, cross-balancing; ~**balk**, cross-beam; T-piece; ~**band**, crucial ligament; (pair of) braces; ~**bank**, cross-bench; ~**beeld**, crucifix; ~**been**, sacrum; ~**been=**, with crossed legs; ~**beitel**, firmer-chisel; ~**bek**, crosbill (bird); ~**bereik**, cruising range; ~**bessie**, four corners (*Grewia occidentalis*); ~**bestuiwing**, cross-pollination, xenogamy; allogamy; ~**beuk**, transept; ~**bevrugting**, cross-fertilization; ~**blom**, passion-flower, star of Bethlehem; finial; ~**blommig**, (-e), cruciferous; ~**bolletjie**, hot-cross bun; ~**boog**, crossbow; diagonal arch; ogive; ~**dag**, Rogation day; ~**dood**, death on the cross; ~**draad**, reticle; spider-line, cross-wire; hair-line (lens); ~**draagbalk**, top-rest; ~**draend**, (-e), cruciferous; ~**draer**, cross-bearer.

krui'sel, seasoning.

krui's(e)lings, crosswise, crossways; decussate.

kruisement', mint; ~ *en staalpille*, penny-royal and steel pills; ~**sous**, mint sauce; ~**tablette**, mint tablets.

krui'ser, (-s), cruiser; ~**gewig**, cruiserweight.

kruis: ~**galery**, rood-loft; ~**gang**, way of the cross, Calvary; ~**geding**, cross-action; ~**gewelf**, cross-vault, groined vault; ~**gewys(e)**, crosswise, cross-ways; ~**grafiek**, cruising chart; ~**gras**, Bermuda grass.

Kruis'heer, Crosier Father; ~**aflaat**, Crosier Indulgence.

kruis'hoogte, cruising level.

kruis'hout, (the) cross; marking (carpenter's) gauge; ~**saag**, cross-cut saw.

krui'sie, (-s), small cross, crucifix, crosslet; dagger; mark (instead of signature); *'n ~ aan die BALK maak*, chalk up a date; *sy ~ gaan MAAK*, register one's vote; make one's cross.

krui'sig, (ge-), crucify; ~**ing**, crucifixion.

krui'sing, (-e, -s), cross-breed(ing); chiasma; decussation; grade; crossing, intersection; junction (railway); hybrid, hybridization, hybridism; ~**shoek**, angle of intersection; ~**sproduk**, cross.

kruis'inlating: ~ *op halwe hout*, cross-lapping.

kruis: ~**juk**, cross head; ~**karmenaadjie**, chump chop; ~**kerk**, cruciform church; ~**klamp**, bevel; ~**klets**, cross talk (tel.); ~**knoop**, reef knot; ~**kop**, cross head; ~**koppelaar**, universal joint; ~**kruid**, ragwort; ~**laag**, broken course (masonry); ~**lings**, (-e) = kruiselings; ~**loper**, crab (mech.); ~**maat**, cross; ~**nok**, fly-hip; ~**offer**, sacrifice on the cross; ~**ondervraging**, cross examination; ~**optelling**, cross-cast; ~**pad**, (..paaie), cross-road; ~**peiling**, cross-bearing; ~**pen**, gudgeon; ~**prosessie**, rogation procession; ~**punt**, point of intersection; junction, crossing (railway); ~**raam**, Gothic window; ~**ras**, cross, cross-breed; ~**rib**, diagonal rib; ~**ridder**, crusader; ~**riem**, lion-strap; ~**skoot**, cross-shot; ~**skuif**, cross-slide; ~**skyf**, rump steak; ~**snarig**, (-e), overstrung; ~**snelheid**, cruising speed; ~**stang**, crosshead; ~**stangpen**, crosshead gudgeon; ~**steek**, cross-stitch; ~**straat**, cross-street; ~**streep**, cross-line; ~**stuk**, rump; chump (of sheep); crossing (rails); ~**teelt**, cross-breeding; hybridization; ~**teken**, sign of the cross; ~**tog**, (-te), crusade; cruise; ~**uitwykspoor**, crossing-loop; ~**vaarder**, (-s), crusader; ~**vaart**, crusade; ~**val**, mizzen topsail, halyard; ~**verband**, cross-bandage; ~**verering**, adoration of the cross; ~**verheffing**, exaltation of the cross; ~**verhoor**, cross-examination; cross-questioning; ~**vermoë**, cruising power; ~**vervoer**, cross-haulage; ~**verwysing**, cross-reference; ~**vinding**, finding of the cross; ~**vlug**, cruise; ~**vormig**, (-e), cruciform; crucial; ~**vra**, (ge-), cross-examine, cross-question; catechize; ~**vraag**, cross-question; ~**vuur**, cross-fire; ~**weg**, the way of the Cross; cross-way; ~**werk**, crading(ceiling); ~**wissel**, diamond (crossing) points (railway); ~**woorde**, words spoken on the Cross; ~**woordraaisel**, *see* blokkiesraaisel.

kruit, (gun)powder; *sonder ~ 'n BOK skiet*, drop a brick; *sy ~ DROOG hou*, keep his powder dry; *hy het nog nie ~ GERUIK nie*, he has not yet smelt powder; *sy ~ is NAT*, he is out of the running; his cake is dough; he hasn't a hope; *nie 'n SKOOT ~ werd nie*, not worth powder and shot; *jou ~ VERSPIL*, waste one's powder and shot; *soos ~ en VUUR wees*, be like fire and tow; be at loggerheads; *al sy ~ WEGSKIET (verskiet)*, shoot his bolt; ~**bladjie**, flake of gunpowder; ~**bom**, petard; ~**bus**, powder-flask; ~**damp**, gunpowder smoke; ~**fabriek**, powder-factory (mill); ~**horing**, powder-horn; flask; ~**huis**, powder-magazine; ~**kamer**, magazine, powder-room, gunpowder chamber; ~**kis**, powder-chest; ~**koek**, gunpowder press-cake; ~**kolom**, powder-train; ~**korrel**, grain of gunpowder; ~**lading**, gunpowder charge; powder; ~**maat**, powder-measure; ~**magasyn**, powder-magazine; ~**meul**, gunpowder mill; ~**myn**, powder mine; ~**pan**, touchpan; ~**pers**, gunpowder cake-press; ~**poeier**, powder-dust; ~**sas**, gunpowder composition; ~**slym**, beads of gunpowder; ~**springlading**, gunpowder bursting-charge; ~**stof**, powder-dust; ~**vaatjie**, powder-barrel; ~**wa**, powder-cart; ~**water**, water containing sulphuretted hydrogen.

krui'wa, wheelbarrow; *'n ~ hê*, have a friend at court; ~**vol**, (wheel)barrow-load; ~**vrag**, wheelbarrow-load.

kruk, (-ke), crutch; stool; crank; door-handle; *MET ~ke loop*, walk with crutches; *'n OU ~*, an old crock; ~**arm**, crank-lever; ~**as**, crank-shaft; ~**aslaer**, crank-shaft bearing; ~**boor**, belly-brace; ~**kas**, crank-case; ~**kassteun**, cranking-case stay; ~**ker**, (-s), crock; ~**kerig**, (-e), seedy; crocky; ~**kerlys**, casualty list (sport); ~**liggaam**, body of crank; ~**pen**, gudgeon-pin, crank-pin; ~**riemskyf**, crank-pulley; ~**skyf**, disc-crank; ~**stang**, crank-rod, connecting-rod; ~**wang**, crank-web.

krul, (s) (-le), curl; shaving (of wood); scroll; spin, screw (tennis); flourish, quirk; *uit die ~ RAAK*, come out of curl; *VOL ~le wees*, be full of frills (whims); (w) (ge-), curl, frizz(le), wave (hair); screw (ball); cockle; crimp; ~**andyvie**, chicory, curly endive; ~**bal**, curly (cricket); ~**blaar**, curl (leaf-disease); ~**golf**, comber; ~**hakie**, bracket, braces (printing); ~**hare**, curly hair, frizz; ~**hou**, screw, curly ball; cut-shot (tennis); ~**kool**, kale; ~**kop**, frizz, curly-head; ~**kopklonkie**, little curly-head; ~**lebol**, curly-head; ~**lerig**, (-e), curly; crisp; ~**letjie**, (-s), little curl, ringlet; ~**letter**, flourish; ~**ling**, (-e, -s), curling, curl; ~**lyn**, spiral line; ~**lys**, scroll; ~**papier**, curling-paper; ~**pen**, curling-pen; ~**slag**, cut-shot (tennis); ~**tang**, curling tongs; crisping-iron; ~**veer**, coil-spring; ~**werk**, cartouch(e); ~**yster**, curling tongs.

krum'mel, (s) (-s), crumb; bit; something worthless; (pl) inferior cattle (animals); ~*s is ook brood*, half a loaf is better than no bread; (w) (ge-), crumble; ~**biefstuk**, crumbed steak; ~**deeg**, plain pastry; ~**koek**, shortbread; ~**ig**, (-e), crumbly, loose, mealy; pulverous, pulverulent; ~**karmenaadjie**, crumbed chop; ~**kors**, crumb crust; ~**vleis**, crumbed meat.

krup'pel, lame, cripple(d), limping; ~ *loop*, walk with a limp; ~**heid**, lameness.

krup'sies: *vol ~ wees*, be full of affectation; put on airs.

Krustase'ë, Crustaceans.

kry, (ge-), get, obtain, acquire; receive; gather; catch (cold); hit on; *BLARE ~*, put forth leaves, break into leaf; *ek kan hom nie DAARTOE ~ nie*, I cannot get him to do it; *die DIEF het drie maande ge ~*, the thief was sentenced to three months' imprisonment; *ek sal jou ~!* I'll get you! I'll make you pay for it; *GELYK ~*, be put (in the) right; *van iets GENOEG ~*, have (get) enough of something; *HET jy dit of ~ jy dit?* what is amusing (tickling) you? *HONGER ~*, become hungry; *IETS ~*, come in for something; *JY sal ~*, you'll get a hiding; *iem. onder die KLIPPE ~*, throw stones at someone; *toe ek my KOM ~*, the next thing I knew; when I began to notice; *KOUD (warm) ~*, begin to feel cold (warm); *iem. LEKKER ~*, take someone in; catch someone out; *iem. sover ~ OM*, manage to get someone to; *'n ONGELUK ~*, meet with an accident; *ons ~ REËN*, it looks as if we will have rain; *jy SAL ~*, you'll pay for it; *nie meer TE ~ nie*, no longer obtainable (to be had); *'n TOEVAL ~*, have an attack (a fit); *VERKOUE ~*, catch a cold; *g'n WOORD uit hom ~ nie*, not get a word out of him.

kryg, war, fight; ~ *voer*, wage war; ~**er**, (-s), warrior.

krygs: ~**banier**, banner of war; ~**basuin**, war trumpet; ~**bedryf**, feat of arms; military organization; ~**behoefte-afdeling**, stores section; ~**behoefte-offisier**, stores officer; ~**behoeftes**, munitions of war; ~**beleid**, military skill; ~**bende**, troop of soldiers; cohort; ~**bevelhebber**, military commander; ~**daad**, warlike action; ~**diens**, military service; ~**eer**, honours of war; military glory; ~**gebruik**, custom of war; ~**gedruis**, tumult of war; ~**geroep**, war-cry; ~**gevangene**, prisoner of war; ~**gevange(n)skap**, captivity (as prisoner of war); ~**geweld**, force of arms; ~**god**, god of war; ~**haf'tig**, (-e), warlike, martial, bellicose; ~**haf'tigheid**, martial spirit; ~**heer**, war-lord; ~**held**, military hero; ~**heldin**, military heroine; ~**kans**, chance of war; ~**kas**, war-chest; ~**kneg**, (-te), soldier.

kryg'skool, military college.

krygs: ~**kunde**, strategy; tactics; military science; art of war; ~**kun'dig**, (-e), military; strategical; ~**kun'dige**, (-s), tactician; military expert; strategist; ~**kuns**, soldiership; generalship; ~**leuse**, slogan; ~**lewe**, military life; ~**lied**, war-song; ~**liede**, soldiers, warriors; ~**lis**, strategy, stratagem; ruse; ~**mag**, military force; armament; ~**man**, (-ne, krygsliede), soldier, warrior; ~**managtig**, (-e), warlike; ~**manseer**, military honour; ~**masjinerie**, ordnance machinery; ~**musiek**, military music; ~**oefening**, manoeuvre; ~**owerste**, military leader; ~**plan**, plan of campaign; ~**plig**, military duty; ~**raad**, court martial; council of war; ~**reg**, martial law; ~ **roem**, military glory; ~ **rumoer**, bustle of war; ~ **taal**, military terminology; ~ **toerusting**, military equipment; armament; ~ **tog**, military expedition (campaign); ~ **toneel**, theatre of war; ~ **trompet**, trumpet of war; ~ **tug**, military discipline; ~ **tuig**, implements of war.

krygsug'tig, (-e), bellicose, warlike; ~ **heid**, warlikeness; pugnacity.

krygs: ~ **verrigting, (-e, -s)**, military operations; ~ **vliegtuig**, military aeroplane; ~ **volk**, soldiers; ~ **voorraad**, military stores; munitions; ~ **wese**, military system; ~ **wet**, martial law; ~ **wetenskap**, military science.

kryg'voerend, (-e), belligerent; ~ *e moondhede*, belligerent powers.

krys, (s) scream, cry, shriek, craw; **(w) (ge-)**, crock, scream, cry, squawk, croak; screech.

kryt¹, (s) ring (for boxing), arena; *in die* ~ *TREE*, enter the list; *in die* ~ *TREE vir*, take up (the) cudgels for.

kryt², (s) chalk, crayon; *in die* ~ *staan by iem.*, be indebted to someone.

kryt³, (w) (ge-), cry.

kryt: ~ **agtig, (-e)**, chalky; cretaceous; ~ **bakkie**, chalk-box; ~ **blom**, gypsophila; ~ **gebergte**, chalk hills; ~ **groef**, chalk-pit; ~ **houdend, (-e)**, chalky.

kryt'kennis, ring-craft.

kryt'laag, chalk-bed; layer of chalk.

kryt'meester, arena steward.

kryt: ~ **rots**, chalk cliff; ~ **streep**, chalk line; ~ **tekening**, crayon drawing; ~ **vernuf**, ring-craft; boxing craft (know-how); ~ **wit**, as white as chalk.

k''tjie, (-s), small k

Ku'ba, Cuba; ~ **an', (Kubane)**, Cuban; ~ **ans', (-e)**, Cuban.

kubeer', (ge-), cube.

kuberne'tika, cybernetics.

kubiek', (-e), cubic; ~ *e INHOUD*, cubic content; ~ *e MAAT*, cubic measure; ~ **getal**, cube measure; ~ **wortel**, cubic (cube) root; ~ *wortel trek*, find the cube root.

ku'bies, (-e), cubic(al).

kubis', (-te), cubist.

kubis'me, cubism; **kubis'ties, (-e)**, cubistic.

ku'bus, (-se), cube; ~ **vormig, (-e)**, cubiform, cubeshaped.

kud'de, (-s), flock, herd; troop, drove, fold (sheep); ~ **dier**, gregarious animal; ~ **gees**, ~ **gevoel**, ~ **-instink**, herd instinct, gregariousness.

kug, (s) (-ge), dry cough; **(w) (ge-)**, give a dry cough, hem; clear one's throat, hack; ~ **gie, (-s)**, dry cough.

kui'er, (s) outing, visit, call; **(w) (ge-)**, visit, call; walk; *BY iem.* ~, stay with someone; *IEWERS* ~, to be calling on someone; *ek KOM vir jou* ~, I intend to visit you; *OP en neer* ~ *van pyn*, walk up and down because of pain; ~ **gas**, guest; ~ **koop**, windowshopping; ~ **mense**, visitors; ~ **plek**, visiting-place; holiday resort; ~ **tjie, (-s)**, short visit; walk; ~ **y**, visiting.

kuif, (kuiwe), crest (of bird); aigrette; tuft (of hair); forelock (of horse); cowlick; ~ **aap**, macaque; ~ **akkedis**, basilisk; ~ **bal**, shuttlecock; ~ **eend**, tufted duck; ~ **fisant**, crested pheasant; ~ **kop**, person with a curl; fowl with tuft; tiptol, topknot, blackhead (bird); ~ **kopduiker**, crested grebe; ~ **kophoender**, tufted fowl; ~ **koptarentaal**, crested guinea-fowl; ~ **kopvalk**, black hawk; ~ **kopvisvanger**, malachite kingfisher; ~ **kopvoël**, blackcap, bulbul, topknot; ~ **reier**, aigrette; ~ **wol**, topknot.

kui'ken, (-s), chicken; poult; *nog SOMMER 'n* ~, a mere chicken; ~ *s TEL voor hulle gepik het*, count one's chickens before they are hatched; ~ **dief**, kite (*Mulvus aegypticus*), harrier, hen-harrier; cradle snatcher; ~ **kos**, chicken-feed.

kui'kenmoord, bullying (of children); *iem. vir* ~ *OPBRING*, pick on those who are smaller or weaker; ~ *PLEEG*, bully (children).

kuil, (s) (-s), pool, dam; dimple (in cheek); bunker (golf); pit, hole; *graaf jy 'n* ~ *vir ander, dan val jy daar self in*, be hoist with one's own petard; harm watch, harm catch; **(w) (ge-)**, put in a silo, ensile; ~ **saag**, pitsaw; ~ **tjie, (-s)**, dimple; pool; *met* ~ *tjies in die wange*, with dimpled cheeks; ~ **toring**, silo; ~ **voer**, silo-fodder; (en)silage; ~ **voerbunker**, bunker silo; ~ **vuur**, pot-fire.

kuip¹, (s) (-e), tub, vat, barrel, cistern; kit; pit; **(w) (ge-)**, cooper.

kuip², (w) (ge-), intrigue, scheme, plot.

kuip: ~ **bad**, bathtub; ~ **balie**, tub.

kui'per¹, cooper.

kui'per², intriguer, caballer.

kui'pers: ~ **ambag**, cooper's work; ~ **beitel**, adze; ~ **dissel**, cooper's adze; ~ **loon**, ~ **werk**, ~ **winkel**, cooperage.

kui'pery¹, (-e), intriguing, machination, cabal, graft.

kui'pery², cooper's trade, cooperage.

kui'perhout, staves.

kuis, (w) (ge-), expurgate; *ge* ~ *te taal*, purified language; **(b) (|-e|; -er, -ste)**, chaste, pure, innocent, virtuous, continent; ~ **heid**, chastity, purity, innocence, chasteness, continence, pudicity.

kuit¹, (-e), calf (of leg).

kuit², (-e), roe, spat, spawn, milt (fish).

kuit: ~ **been**, fibula, splint-bone, brooch-bone; ~ **beenbroek**, knee-breeches, plus-fours; ~ **broek**, knee-breeches; ~ **kouse**, half-hose; ~ **kramp**, sural spasm; ~ **parade**, display of legs.

kuit'skiet, (-e-), spawn.

kuit'spier, sural muscle.

kuit'steen, oolite.

kuit'vis, spawner.

kuit'vlies, fleshy part of leg

kul, (ge-), cheat, deceive, (be)fool, mystify, outwit, hoax, diddle, lead up the garden path, do out of; gag; ~ **kunstenaar**, conjurer, prestidigitator; ~ **ler, (-s)**, cheater, hoaxer; ~ **lery**, cheating, deceit; mystification, hocuspocus, bunkum, hoaxing; bilking; humbug(gery).

kulmina'sie, culmination; ~ **punt**, culminating point.

kulmineer', (ge-), culminate.

kul'ties, (-e), cultic.

kul'tivar, (-s), cultivar.

kultiveer', (ge-), cultivate.

kultive'ring, cultivation.

kul'toertjie, trick.

kultureel', (..rele), cultural.

kul'tus, cult, creed.

kultuur', (..ture), culture, civilization; cultivation; *suiwer* ~, pure culture; ~ **geskiedenis**, social (cultural) history; ~ **histories, (-e)**, socio-historical; ~ **medium**, culture medium; ~ **plant**, cultivated plant; ~ **stelsel**, culture system; ~ **stryd**, struggle for maintenance of culture; ~ **vereniging**, cultural society; ~ **volk**, (highly-)cultured nation.

kul'werk, deceit; cheating.

kum'mel, kummel.

kumula'sie, cumulation; ~ **reg**, cumulative right.

kumulatief', (..tiewe), cumulative.

kumuleer', (ge-), cumulate.

kun'de, knowledge, art, lore; know-how.

kun'dig, (-e), able, competent, skilful, knowing; ~ **heid**, skill, accomplishment, ability, attainment, proficiency, know-how, technology.

kun'ne, sex; *van beiderlei* ~, of both sexes.

kuns, (-te, -e), art; skill, knack, trick, sleight (of hand); *iem. die* ~ *AFKYK*, catch (learn) the trick from a person; *die BEELDENDE* ~ *te*, the plastic arts; *DIT is die* ~, that's the point; *dit is G'N* ~ *nie*, that is easy enough; it is child's play; *die SKONE* ~ *te*, the fine arts; *die SWART(E)* ~, necromancy, black art; *die* ~ *VERSTAAN om*, know the art of; *met* ~ *en VLIEGWERK*, by artificial means; by strange devices; ~ *te en WETENSKAPPE*, arts and sciences; ~ *afdruk*, artprint.

kuns'arm¹, (s) artificial arm, prosthesis.

kuns'arm², (b) (-e), deficient in art.

kuns: ~ **baan**, metal (road); ~ **been**, artificial leg, prosthesis; ~ **beertjie**, teddybear; ~ **beskermer**, art patron; ~ **beskouing**, aesthetic view, conception of art; ~ **bevrugting**, artificial insemination; ~ **blom**, artificial flower; ~ **botter**, artificial butter; margarine; oleomargarine; ~ **broe(de)r**, fellow artist; ~ **diamant**, artificial diamond; ~ **draaier**, (ivory) turner; ~draaiery, turnery; ~galery, art museum, picture-gallery, art gallery; ~gebit, denture, (set of) artificial teeth; ~genootskap, society of arts; ~genot, artistic pleasure; ~geskiedenis, history of art; ~gevoel, sense of art; ~gewrog, work of art; ~gom, dextrine; ~goud, oroide; oreide; ~greep, artifice, device; doubling, trick, contrivance, sleight; ~handelaar, dealer in works of art, art dealer; ~handwerk, manual arts, craft-work; ~handwerker, craftsman, craftworker; ~hars, artificial (synthetic) resin, plastics; ~histories, (-e), art-historical; ~historikus, (..rici, -se), art historian; ~ideaal, artistic ideal; ~ie, (-s), trick, knack, dodge; hanky-panky; *die ~ies KEN*, know the tricks of the trade; *hondeafrig om ~ies te VERTOON*, train dogs to perform; ~kenner, art connoisseur; ~kleur, technicolour; ~klei, plasticine (reg. trade name); ~koffie, coffee substitute; ~kooktoestel, fireless cooker; ~koper, dealer in works of art, art dealer; ~kring, society of artists; art circle, art club; ~kritiek, art criticism; ~kritikus, art critic; ~ledemate, artificial limbs, prostheses; ~leer, artificial leather, pegamoid, leatherette; ~lewe, life of artists; ~lied, art song; ~liefde, love of arts; ~liefhebber, art-lover; lover of art; ~lie'wend, (-e), art-loving; philotechnic; ~lig, artificial light; ~ligpapier, gaslight paper; ~maan, artificial moon, satellite.

kunsma'tig, (-e), artificial, factitious, made; *~e ASEMHALING*, artificial respiration; *~e DRINKRIETJIE*, artificial drinking-straw; *~e DROGING*, artificial seasoning; *~e GLANS*, glamour; *~e INSEMINASIE*, artificial insemination; *~e REËNBESPROEIING*, overhead irrigation; *~e VERJONGING*, assisted regeneration; ~heid, artificiality.

kuns: ~middel, artificial means; expedient; ~minnaar, lover of art; ~mis, fertiliser, artificial manure; ~moeder, foster-mother; artificial breeder; hover, brooder; ~museum, art museum (gallery); ~naaldwerk, art needlework; ~newel, screening smoke; ~nywerheid, industrial arts, arts and crafts; ~onderrig, art education; ~oog, artificial eye; ~opvattings, aesthetic views; ~papier, art paper; ~plaat, engraving; ~plank, beaver-board; ~produk, (-te), product of art; ~redenaar, elocutionist; ~reël, rule of arts; ~regter, art critic; ~reis, professional tour; ~room, synthetic cream; ~rubber, artificial (synthetic) rubber; ~ruiter, ~ryer, trick rider; ~ryk, (-e), artistic; ~saal, picture-gallery; ~sentrum, art centre; ~sin, artistic taste (judgment, talent); artistry; ~sin'nig, (-e), artistic, art-loving; ~sin'nigheid, artisticity; love of art; ~skaats, figure (fancy) skating; ~skaatser, figureskater; fancy skater; ~skatte, art treasures; ~skepping, work of art; ~skilder, artist, painter; ~skool, school of art; ~smaak, artistic taste; ~smeedwerk, ornamental ironwork; ~smid, maker of ornamental ironwork; ~steen, paste; ~stop, invisible mending; ~stuk, work of art; clever feat; ~sy, artificial silk, rayon; ~taal, artificial language (e.g. Esperanto); language of art; ~tand, artificial tooth; ~tande, artificial teeth; dental plate; ~teloos, (..lose), artless, naïve; ~temaker, acrobat; juggler; ~temakery, acrobatics; ~tempel, temple of art; ~tenaar, (-s, ..nare), artist; artificer; ~tenares', (-se), artist(e); ~tentoonstelling, art exhibition; ~term, art term; ~tig, (-e), ingenious, clever, artful; artistic(al); ~tigheid, ingeniousness, ingenuity; artfulness.

kunsvaar'dig, (-e), clever, skilful; ~heid, artistry, cleverness; skill, adroitness, art.

kuns: ~vereniging, art society; ~versameling, art collection; ~vesel, artificial (synthetic) fibre; ~vlieër, aerobat; stunt flier; ~vlieëry, aerobatics, stunt (trick) flying; ~vlieg, badger; doctor; hackle, artificial fly (for fishing); ~vlug, air trick (stunt); flying-trick; ~vlugvertoning, aerobatic display; ~vlyt, arts and crafts; art work; ~vol, (-le), artistic; ~voorwerp, object of art; ~vorm, artistic form; ~vriend, (amateur) lover of art; ~waarde, artistic value; ~wedstryd, eisteddfod; ~wêreld, world of art; ~werk, work of art, creation; ~winkel, art store; ~wol, artificial wool; devil's wool; ~woord, art term; ~woordeboek, art dictionary; ~ys, artificial ice.

ku'pel, (-s), cupel; ~leer', cupellate; ~leer'oond, cupel furnace.

Ku'pido, Cupido; ~'tjie, kewpie.

ku'pie, (-s), kewpie.

ku'rang: *~sal braai*, it will all come out.

kuras', (-se), cuirass; ~sier', (-s), cuirassier.

kurate'le, guardianship, curatorship; *onder ~ stel*, appoint a guardian over; place under curatorship.

kura'tor, (-e, -s), curator, guardian, assignee, trustee; ..to'rium, (-s, ..ria), governing body (council); ~skap, guardianship.

kuratri'se, (-s), curatrix.

kuret', (-te), curette; ~teer', (ge-), curette.

kuriaal', (kuriale), curial.

ku'rie, curia; Holy See.

kurieus', (-e), curious, peculiar, odd.

kuriositeit', (-e), curiosity, relic, curio; ~ehandelaar, curio dealer.

kurio'sum, (-s, ..riosa), curiosity; curious article.

kurk, (s) (-e), cork; handle (spade); (w) (ge-), cork, close (bottle); ~agtig, (-e), corky, corked; ~asemhalingtoestel, cork respirator; ~binnesole, cork soles; cork cocks; ~boom, cork tree *(Erythrina tomentosa)*; ~droog, (..droë), as dry as a bone; ~(e)trekker, cork-screw; bottle-screw; ~geld, corkage; ~meel, powdered cork; ~mes, cork-cutter; ~pakking, cork-packing; ~smaak, corky taste; ~suur, suberic acid.

kurku'ma, (-s), curcuma.

kurk'wasser, kurk'waster, cork washer.

kur'per, (-s), *Tilapia*, kurper.

kurri'kulum, (-s), curriculum.

kursief', (kursiewe), italic, in italics; ~druk, italics.

kursiveer', (ge-), print in italics, italicize, underline; *ek ~*, the italics are mine.

kursive'ring, italics.

kurso'ries, (-s), cursory.

kur'sus, (-se), course (of study); class; *'n ~ volg*, take a course; ~geld, course fee; ~ganger, course-goer.

kurwatuur', (..ture), curvature.

kur'we, (-s), curve (mathematics); graph; ~saag, coping saw.

kus¹, (s) (-se), kiss; ~, (w) (ge-), kiss.

kus², (s): *te ~ en te KEUR*, for the picking and choosing; in abundance; *jy kan te ~ en te KEUR gaan*, you can pick and choose.

kus³, (s) (-te), coast, shore; *naby die ~ BLY*, hug the shore; *K~ van die Dood*, Skeleton Coast; ~affuit, coastal defence mounting; ~artillerie, coastal artillery; ~artilleriebrigade, coast-artillery brigade; ~battery, coastal battery; ~besetting, coast garrison; ~bewoner, coast-dweller; ~boot, coaster, coasting-vessel; ~deining, land-swell.

ku'sek (-s), cusec.

kus: ~fort, martello; ~garnisoen, coastal garrison; ~gebied, coastal area, littoral; ~geskut, coastal artillery; ~gordel, coastal belt; ~handel, coasting-trade; cabotage; ~handjie, hand-blown kiss; *'n ~handjie gee*, blow a kiss; ~klimaat, coastal climate; ~lig, coast light; ~loodsdiens, coast pilotage; ~lugmag, coastal air force; ~lyn, coast-line; ~pad, marine drive; coast road; ~plek, seaside place; ~rif, coastal reef; ~ryweg, marine drive.

kus'sing, (-s), pillow, cushion, bolster; *op die ~ s BLY*, remain in office; *op die ~ KOM*, come into office; *op die ~ SIT*, hold office; ~band, balloon tyre; ~blok, journal; bearing; wall-plate; ~els, panel-awl; ~geveg, (-te), pillow-fight; ~hamer, cushion-hammer; ~kleedjie, pillow sham; ~klep, (-pe), cushion-valve; ~lawa, pillow-lava; ~oortrek(sel), cushion-cover; ~plaat, pintle-plate; ~sloop, pillow, case, pillow-slip, bolster, cover; ~tuig, (..tuie), hovercraft; ~veer, (..vere), cushion-spring; ~verband, dressing; ~vormig, (-e), pulvinate.

kus'sinkie, (-s), little cushion; pad (harness).

kus: ~sloep, shore boat; ~soom, seaboard; ~stad,

kusting coast(al) town; ~**streek,** coastal region; ~**strook,** coastal strip, littoral; ~**terras,** coastal platform.

kus'ting, mortgage, bond, hypothec; ~**sbrief,** seller's (mortgage) bond.

kus: ~**vaarder, (-s),** coaster; coasting-vessel; ~**vaart,** coasting(-trade); ~**vaartuig,** *see* **kusvaarder;** ~**verdediging,** coastal defence; seaward defence; ~**verdedigingskorps,** coastal defence corps; ~**verdedigingswerke,** coastal defences; ~**verligting,** coast lights; ~**vlakte,** coastal plain; ~**vuur,** coast fire (light); ~**wag(ter),** coastguard; ~**weg,** beach road; ~**wind,** shore wind.

kuur[1]**, (kure),** whim, freak, caprice; *vol kure,* full of whims.

kuur[2]**, (kure),** cure, treatment.

kwaad, (s) (kwade), evil, mischief, harm, wrong; *geen ~ sonder BAAT,* it is an ill wind that blows nobody any good; every cloud has a silver lining; *geen ~ BEDOEL nie,* mean no harm; *~ DOEN,* do harm, be up to mischief; *dit kan geen ~ DOEN nie,* it can do no harm; *goed en ~,* good and evil; *dit KAN geen ~ nie,* it can do no harm; *die ~ loon sy MEESTER,* every sin brings its punishment with it; *'n NOODSAAKLIKE ~,* a necessary evil; *daar STEEK geen ~ in nie,* there is no harm in it; *~ STIG (steek, stook),* brew mischief; cause trouble; *die ~ STRAF homself,* every sin brings its punishment with it; *van TWEE kwade die minste kies,* choose the lesser evil; *moenie ~ met ~ VERGELD nie,* do not return evil for evil; *~ met goed VERGELD,* return good for evil; *die VERHELP,* put right what is wrong; *van iem. geen ~ WEET nie,* not to allow anything to be said against another; *van geen ~ WEET nie,* be quite innocent; *daar het ~ in die WOND gekom,* the wound is festering; **(b, bw), (kwade; kwaaier, kwater, -ste; erger, ergste),** evil; angry, cross, displeased, annoyed, vexed; *~ BLOED sit,* cause bad blood; *van ~ na ERGER,* from bad to worse, *hy HET dit nie so ~ nie,* he is not badly off; *iem ~ MAAK,* make someone angry; *dit nie ~ MEEN nie,* mean well; *~ PRAAT van iem.,* speak evil of someone; *nog nie SO ~ nie,* not bad by half; *kwade TROU,* bad faith; *~ WEES vir,* be angry with, *~ WORD,* become angry.

kwaadaar'dig, (-e), malignant, virulent (tumour); malicious, vicious, rancorous, ill-natured; pernicious; haggish; ~**heid,** malice, malignancy, viciousness, haggishness, maleficence; virulence.

kwaadden'kend, (-e), suspicious, evil-minded; ~**heid,** suspicion; evil-mindedness.

kwaad'doener, (-s), evil doer, malefactor, rascal; -**ig, (-e),** mischievous; ~**y,** mischief, wrongdoing.

kwaad'geld: *vir ~ rondloop,* loaf about, play the vagabond; *op skylarking.*

kwand: ~gesind, (-e), malevolent, evilly-disposed, ill-disposed; ~**gesindheid,** ill will, malevolence; ~**heid,** anger, ire; chagrin.

kwaad'-kwaad', annoyed, *~-~ wegloop,* walk away annoyed.

kwaad: ~**praat, (-ge-)** = **kwaadspreek:** ~**pratery,** slander; ~**sappig, (-e),** cachectic; ~**sappigheid,** cachexy; ~**skiks,** unwillingly; ~**spreek, (-ge-),** slander, defame, speak ill of, malign, backbite, revile; ~**spreker,** backbiter, maligner, slanderer, scandalmonger; ~**sprekery,** maligning, scandalmongering; ~**steker, (-s),** mischief-maker; ~**stigtery,** mischief-making; ~**stoker, (-s),** mischief-maker, busybody, mischief-monger; ~**stekery, (-e),** mischief-making; ~**stook, (-ge-),** brew mischief, cause trouble.

kwaadwil'lig, (-e), malevolent, malicious, ill-disposed; ~**e (-s),** maligner; ~**heid,** malevolence, malice, despite, ill will.

kwaai, (-er, -ste), vicious, bad-tempered; severe, harsh; tough formidable; *'n ~ BUL,* a vicious bull; *~e DAG,* evil day; *hy DRINK ~,* he drinks heavily; *die GRIEP is net ~,* the flu is very prevalent; *'n ~ HOOFPYN,* a splitting headache; *'n ~ MEESTER,* a strict teacher; ~**erig, (-e),** rather strict; rather bad-tempered; ~**heid,** viciousness; strictness; hot-temperedness, ~**kop,** quick-tempered person; ~**vri(e)n'de,** bad friends; ~**vri(e)nd'skap,** enmity, state of being bad friends.

kwaak, (ge-), croak, quack.

kwaal, (kwale), ailment, complaint, disease, malady; *sy ou ~,* his old complaint.

kwab, (-be), lobe.

kwa'de: *die ~ DAG uitstel,* put off the evil day; *iem. iets ten ~ DUI,* take something ill (amiss); *~r TROU,* in bad faith, mala fide; *te ~r URE,* in an evil hour.

kwadraat', (. .drate), square, quadrate; quadratic; *tot die ~ verhef,* square; ~**getal,** square number; ~**s'vergelyking,** quadratic equation; ~**teël,** quarry tile; ~**wortel,** square root.

kwadrant', (-e), quadrant; ~**pyp,** quarter-bend.

kwadrateer', (ge-), quadrate.

kwadra'ties, (-e), quadratic.

kwadratuur', quadrature.

kwadreer', (ge-) = **kwadrateer.**

kwadriljoen', (-e), quadrillion.

kwadroon', (kwadrone), quadron.

kwa'drupleeg, (. .pleë), quadruplegic.

kwag'ga, (-s), quagga; zebra; *egte ~,* true quagga; ~**politiek,** short-sighted politics; ostrich policies; ~**streep,** zebra crossing.

kwa'jong, (-ens), mischievous (naughty) boy, urchin; ~**ensagtig, (-e),** impish, childish, silly; ~**streek,** monkey-trick, boyish prank.

kwak[1]**, (s) (-ke),** thud, bump; **(w) (ge-),** fall (throw) down with a thud; hurl, pitch.

kwak[2]**, (s) (ke),** quack.

kwa'ker[1]**, (-s),** croaker.

Kwa'ker[2]**, (-s),** Quaker; ~**agtig,** Quakerish; ~**y,** Quakerism.

kwak'kel, (-s) = **kwartel.**

kwak'salwer, (-s), quack, charlatan, mountebank, medicaster, empiricist; quack doctor; ~**ag'tig,** quackish; ~**middel,** quack medicine; nostrum; ~**y,** quackery, empiricism, charlatanism.

kwal, (-le), slobber; jellyfish; medusa.

kwalifika'sie, (-s), qualification.

kwalifiseer', (ge-), qualify; *. .se'rend, (-e),* qualifying; ~**baar, (. .bare),** qualifiable.

kwa'lik, ill, amiss; hardly, scarcely; *~ deur 'n EKSAMEN kom,* pass an examination with difficulty; *~ verkrygde GOED gedy nie,* ill-gotten gains never prosper; *~ NEEM,* take amiss, take offence at; *NEEM my nie ~ nie,* please don't take me amiss; *iem. ~ NEEM,* blame someone; *iem. iets ~ NEEM,* take exception to something someone has done; ~**gesind, (-e),** evilly-disposed.

kwalitatief', (. .tiewe), qualitative.

kwaliteit', (-e), quality; capacity; alloy; grade; *in sy ~ as amptenaar,* in his official capacity; ~**s'artikel,** article of quality; ~**s'wyn,** vintage wine.

kwan'sel, (ge-), barter, haggle, exchange, bargain; ~**aar, (-s),** barterer, bargainer; ~**(a)ry',** bartering, bargaining, haggling; ~**sug,** desire to barter (exchange).

kwansuis', as if (it were); quasi-, ostensibly; *hy is ~ 'n deskundige* he pretends to be an expert.

kwantitatief', (. .tiewe), quantitative.

kwantiteit', (-e), quantity.

kwan'tum, (-s), quantum, amount.

kwarantyn', quarantine; *onder ~ sit,* put in quarantine.

kwart, (-e), quart; quarter; fourth part; crotchet (music); fourth, *~ OOR agt,* a quarter past eight; *~ VOOR agt,* a quarter to eight.

kwartaal', (. .tale), quarter (of a year), (school) term; ~**blad, (. .blaaie),** quarterly; ~**geld,** quarterage; ~**liks, (-e),** quarterly; ~**rekening,** quarterly account; ~**s'gewys,** quarterly, every three months; ~**staat,** quarterly (statement) return(s); ~**toets,** quarterly test.

kwart'draai, quarter turn.

kwart'duim, quarter of an inch.

kwarteer', (ge-), quarter.

kwart'eeu, quarter of a century; ~**fees,** quarter-century celebration.

kwart'eindronde, quarter-final round.

kwar'tel, (-s), quail *(Coturnix africana); so doof soos*

'n ~, as deaf as a post; stonedeaf; ~**koning**, crake, corn-crake, landrail; ~**slag**, quail-call.
kwartêr', (-e) quarternary.
kwarte'ring, quartering.
kwartet', (-te), quartet(te).
kwartier', (-e), quarter (of an hour, of the moon); quarter (in battle); district; *EERSTE* ~, first quarter; *geen* ~ *GEE nie*, give no quarter; *die KLOK slaan die* ~ *e*, the clock strikes the quarter-hours; ~**arres**, confinement to quarters; ~**e**, quarters; depot; ~**meester**, quartermaster; ~**mus**, ~**pet**, forage cap; ~**stand**, quarter (of moon).
kwart'lyn, 25 yard line (22,85 metres).
kwart'myl, quarter mile; ~**loper**, quarter-miler.
kwart: ~**naatjie**, quadroon; ~**noot**, crotchet (music).
kwar'to, (-'s), quarto; ~**formaat**, quarto size.
kwart'pint, gill.
kwarts, quartz; ~**aar**, quartz vein; ~**agtig**, (-e), quartzy, quartz-like; ~**bevattend**, (-e), quartzose, quartzous; ~**houdend**, (-e), quartziferous; ~**iet'**, quartzite; ~**lamp**, quartz-lamp.
kwart'sirkel, quadrant.
kwarts: ~**porfier**, quartz porphyry; ~**stamper**, quartz-crusher; ~**swelling**, quartz-blow.
kwart: ~**swenking**, quarter-wheel; ~**toon**, quartertone; ~**wending**, quarter-turn.
kwartyn', (-e), quarto.
kwas¹, (lemon) squash.
kwas², (-te), brush; tuft; switch (tail); tassel (on cord); node, knot, knar (in wood); *dis R1 AAN sy* ~, he'll have to pay R1; *dis BAIE aan sy* ~, he will feel it; *dit aan sy* ~ *KRY*, bear the brunt; have to shoulder the blame; *na sy* ~ *SKOP*, be hale and hearty; be in high spirits.
kwa'sar, (-s), quasar.
kwa'sie, quasi-, as if, make-believe, mock, in a manner; ~**geleerd**, quasi-learned.
kwasjior'kor, kwashiorkor.
kwas'serig, (-e) = **kwasterig**.
kwas'sie, (-s), small brush, tuft; pompom.
kwas'siehout, quassia.
kwas'terig, (-e), knotty, nodular, gnarled, nodose; irritable, bad-tempered; crusty; ~**heid**, nodosity; irritability; crustiness.
kwa'ter, *see* **kwaad**.
kwaternêr', (-e), quarternary.
kwater'nion, (-e), quaternion.
kwatryn', (-e), quatrain.
kwedien', (-e), Black lad.
kweek¹, (s) couch (quick) grass; *van die* ~ *af raak*, kick the bucket; hop the twig.
kweek², (w) cultivate, grow, raise (plants); train; breed, rear; engender; foster, nourish; *dit sal AG= TERDOG* ~, this will breed suspicion; *ge* ~ *te RENTE*, accrued interest; *VRUGTEBOME* ~, grow (cultivate) fruit trees; ~**bedding**, seed-bed; ~**boom**, nurse-tree; ~**dam**, nursery.
kweek'gras, couch grass; furrow-weed.
kweek: ~**groep**, colony; ~**huis**, greenhouse; hothouse; ~**periodes**, incubation intervals (organisms); ~**plek**, nursery; hotbed (of sedition); ~**skool**, seminary (for theological students), training college; ~**tuin**, nursery (garden); ~**tydperke**, incubation intervals (organisms).
kweel, (ge-), warble, chirrup.
kween, (kwene), barren animal (e.g. cow); slut.
kwee'passer, odd-leg callipers.
kwe'keling, (-e), pupil-teacher, teacher-student; trainee, probationer; ~**onderwyser**, pupil-teacher.
kwe'ker, (-s), grower, breeder, fancier; raiser; nurseryman; ~**y**, ~**e**, nursery(-garden); cultivation; hatchery; ~**ywerk**, nursery-work.
kwe'king, (-e, -s), culture; training; cultivation.
kwê-kwê', (-'s), tailor-bird.
kwel, (ge-), worry, torment, agonize, harrow, harass, plague, trouble, vex, annoy, afflict, fash, fret, grind, haunt (conscience), mortify, persecute; *ek* ~ *MY daaroor*, I worry about it; ~*lende SORGE*, carking cares; *ge* ~ *WORD deur*, be tortured with (worried by).
kwê'la, (ge-), kwela; ~**fluit**, penny whistle.
kwel: ~**duiwel**, ~**gees**, tormentor, pest, pesterer; ~**lend**, (-e), harrowing, harassing; ~**ler**, (-s), tormentor, pest, plaguer; ~**ling**, (-e, -s), vexation, trouble, care, anxiety, agony, botheration, mortification, pest, harassment, gall, chagrin; *'n* ~ *ling des GEESTES*, a load on one's mind; ~*lings van die GEWETE*, prickings (qualms) of conscience; *dis 'n WARE* ~ *ling vir my*, it is a sore trial to me; ~**siek**, vexatious; ~**sug**, vexatiousness; ~**sugtig**, (-e), vexatious; ~**vraag**, heckling question.
kwe'per, (-s), quince; ~**heining**, quince hedge; ~**konfyt**, quince jam; ~**laning**, quince hedge; ~**lat**, quince stick; cane; *onder die* ~ *lat deurloop*, be given a birching; ~**vreter**, fruit eater (bird).
kwes, (ge-), wound, injure; bite; ~**baar**, (..**bare**), vulnerable; ~**baarheid**, vulnerability.
kwe'sel, (ge-), play the bigot; ~**aar**, (-s), bigot; pietist; ~**agtig**, (-e), bigoted; pietistic; ~**ary'**, bigotry; pietism, religionism.
kwes'plek, wound; scar.
kwes'sie, (-s), question, point, matter; dispute; *BUITE* ~, without doubt, beyond dispute; *BUITE die* ~, it is out of the question; *GEEN* ~ *van nie*, there is no question about it; *hulle het 'n* ~ *GE= HAD*, they had a difference; ~*s KRY met*, be at odds with; be at cross purposes with; *die SAAK in* ~, the point at issue; *'n* ~ *van TYD*, a matter of time.
kwestieus', (-e), dubious, doubtful; contentious.
kwes'tor, (-s), quaestor.
kwestuur', quaestorship.
kwets, (ge-), grieve, offend; *iem. se gevoelens* ~, hurt someone's feelings; ~**baar**, (..**bare**), vulnerable; ~**end**, (-e), offensive, hurtful; ~**ing**, injury, hurt, offence.
kwetsuur', (kwetsure), wound, injury.
kwet'ter, (ge-), chirrup, twitter, chatter, chirp.
kwê'voël, go-away bird, grey lourie *(Corythaixoides concolor)*.
kwiek, (ge-), croak; *of jy nou* ~ *(kwik) en of jy nou KWAK*, whatever you may (choose to) do; *sonder te* ~ *of te KWAK*, without a murmur.
kwiëtis', (-te), quietist; ~**me**, quietism.
kwik¹, (s) mercury, quicksilver; *die* ~ *sak*, the barometer is falling.
kwik², (w) (ge-), croak; *jy kan* ~ *of kwak*, it's no use, whether you want to or not, you can do what you like.
kwik: ~**bad**, mercurial bath; ~**barometer**, mercury barometer; ~**buis**, mercury tube; ~**damp**, mercurial vapour.
kwik'kie¹, (-s), wagtail.
kwik'kie²: ~*s en strikkies*, frills and fancies.
kwik: ~**kolom**, mercury column; ~**kuur**, mercury cure; ~**middel**, mercurial; ~**myn**, quicksilver mine; ~**okside**, ~**oksied**, mercurial preparation; mercuric oxide; ~**salf**, blue (mercury) ointment; ~**sand**, quicksand.
kwik'silwer, mercury, quicksilver; ~**agtig**, (-e), mercurial; ~**erts**, mercurial ore.
kwik'sout, mercuric salt.
kwik'stertjie, (-s), wagtail.
kwik: ~**termometer**, mercury thermometer; ~**verf**, foil; ~**vergiftiging**, mercury poisoning; ~**waterpas**, mercury level.
kwinêr', (-e), quinary.
kwing'kwang, zig-zag.
kwinkeleer', (ge-), twitter, warble, carol.
kwink'slag, witticism, funny saying, bonmot, quirk, wisecrack, jest, sally, flash of wit, quip.
kwint, (s) (-e), whim, freak, prank, trick; fifth, quint (music); *vol* ~ *e wees*, be full of frills and fancies (whims); (w), (ge-), beat; *iem. (iets)* ~, give someone (something) a beating.
kwintaal', (kwintale), quintal.
kwint'appel, bitter apple.
kwin'tessens, quintessence.
kwintet', (-te), quintet(te).
kwintiljoen', quintillion.
kwint'snaar, E-string.
kwispedoor', (-s, ..**dore**), spittoon, cuspidor.
kwis'pel, (ge-), wag, frisk.
kwis'pelstert, (ge-), wag the tail.

kwis'tig, (-e), lavish, wasteful, prodigal; effusive; profuse; ~ *wees met lof oor,* be unsparing in one's praise of; ~**heid,** lavishness, liberality, prodigality, profuseness.
kwitan'sie, (-s), receipt; quittance; ~**boekie,** book of receipts; ~**seël,** receipt stamp; ~**strook,** receipt slip.
kwiteer', (ge-), receipt; quit.
kwo'rum, (-s), quorum.
kwosiënt', (-e), quotient.
kwo'ta, (-s), quota; ~**'sie, (-s),** quotation.
kwoteer', (ge-), quote; estimate; list (shares); **kwote'ring, (-s),** quotation.
kwyl, (s) slaver, drivel; **(w) (ge-),** slaver, drivel, dribble, salivate; ~**baard, (-e),** ~**er, (-s),** driveller, slobberer; ~**erig, (-e),** slobbery; ~**ing,** slavering, salivation; ~**wortel,** pyrethrum.
kwyn, (ge-), languish, linger, pine (away); wilt, flag (interest); droop (flower); ~**end, (-e),** flagging; languishing; ~**ing,** drooping, wilting; decline.
kwyt, (w) (ge-): *jou* ~ *van,* acquit oneself of (a duty); **(bw),** *jy is DIT* ~ , you have lost it; *sy VERSTAND* ~ *wees,* be out of his mind; ~**brief,** acquittance; receipt; ~**ing,** payment; discharge; ~**raak, (-ge-),** lose, be delivered of, dispose of, get rid of.
kwyt'skel(d), (-ge-), remit, forgive, pardon, acquit, quit, condone, absolve, let off.
kwyt'skelding, remission, pardon, forgiveness, condonation, acquittance, discharge, absolution; quittance; quietus; ~**sregister,** remission book.
kyf, (s). *DUITE* ~ , without doubt, *DUITE ulle* ~ , without a shadow of doubt.

kyf, (w) (ge-), quarrel, dispute; ~**agtig, (-e),** quarrelsome; ~**agtigheid,** quarrelsomeness; ~**siek, (-e),** quarrelsome.
kyk, (s) view, look, aspect; outlook; *'n BREË* ~ *hê op,* have a broad outlook on; *'n juiste* ~ *GEE op,* give a correct view of; *'n* ~ *op iets KRY,* acquire an insight into something; *jou* ~ *op die SAAK,* one's views about the matter; *te* ~ *STAAN,* be on view; *sy* ~ *op die LEWE,* his outlook on life; *te* ~ *STEL voor,* expose to the gaze of; **(w) (ge-),** look, see, view; pry; peer; ~ *op BLADSY 5,* see page 5; ~ *'n BIETJIE,* just have a look; *OP die klok* ~ , tell the time; *VLUGTIG* ~ , glance at; ~**dag,** viewing day; ~**er, (-s),** looker-on, spectator; (television) viewer; eye, pupil (of eye); operaglass(es); ~**gat,** peep-hole; loop-hole; eye-hole; judas; ~**geld,** television licence; ~**gleuf,** observation slit; vizor; ~**graag,** curious person; ~**ie, (-s),** peep, look; *'n* ~ *ie agter die skerms,* a peep behind the scenes; ~**-in-die-pot,** Paul Pry; snooper; ~**kas,** peep-show; show-box; raree-show; ~**koper,** window-shopper; ~**lus,** curiosity, inquisitiveness; ~**lus'tig, (-e),** curious, inquisitive, eager to see; ~**rit,** sight-seeing tour; ~**spel,** peep-show; diorama; cosmorama; ~**spelagtig, (-e),** cosmoramic; ~**spleet,** diopter; observation slit; aperture; ~**stuk,** spectacular play; ~**tyd,** viewing time; ~**uit',** peep-hole; look-out; ~**venster,** peep-window.
kys, (s) (studentetaal), **(-e),** regular sweetheart, steady; **(w) (ge-),** go steady with; *ge* ~ *wees,* have a regular sweetheart.
ky'wery, (-e), wrangling, quarrel(ling).

L

l, (-'e, -'s), l.
la, la.
laaf, (ge-), refresh, bathe; help one to recover from a swoon; try to restore consciousness; ~**drank,** refreshing drink, restorative, pick-me-up.
laaf'nis, refreshment, relief.
laag¹, (s) (lae), layer, stratum; coat, coating (paint); vein (of coal); seam, bed (of coal); cloak (snow); course (bricks); facing; ply (wood); *die BREË lae van die volk,* the great mass of the people; *in al die lae van die VOLK,* among all classes of people, **(w) (ge-),** course, *'n dik* ~ *VUILGOED,* a thick coating of filth.
laag², (s) (lae), round, broadside; *die vyand die VOLLE* ~ *gee,* give the enemy a broadside.
laag³, (s) (lae), snare, ambush; *iem. lae lê,* lay snares (set traps) for a person.
laag³, (b) (lae; laer, -ste), low, base, mean, vulgar, plebeian, rascal, gross, despicable, abject, caitiff, dirty, grovelling; *rok met lae HALS,* low-necked dress; *teen 'n lae PRYS,* at a low price; **(bw)** low; basely, meanly, lowly; ~ *NEERSIEN op,* look down upon; *VAT* ~ *!* tackle low! ~**betaal, (-de),** low-paid; ~**-by-die-gronds, (-e),** commonplace, trite, ordinary; ~**-by-die-grondsheid,** triteness, pedestrianism; ~**dekker,** low-wing monoplane; ~**-drukgebied,** depression; low-pressure area; cyclone; ~**gebore,** lowly-born; ~**geleë,** low-lying; ~**geprys, (-de),** low-priced; ~**gestem, (-de),** low-pitched; ~**gety,** ebb; neap-tide; ~**har'tig, (-e),** base, vile, mean; ~**har'tigheid,** baseness, meanness; ~**heid,** meanness, baseness, scurrility, despicableness, abjection, villainy; vulgarity; turpitude.
laag: ~**helling,** dip (of stratum); ~**hout,** plywood; ~**koek,** layer-cake.
laag: ~**land,** low-lying land; ~**liggend, (-e),** low-lying; ~**reliëf,** bas-relief, low-relief.
laag: ~**s'gewys(e),** in layers.
laag: ~**slag,** run-up (golf); ~**spanning,** low tension; low voltage; ~**spanningsdraad,** low-tension wire; ~**stammig, (-e),** short-stemmed, low-stocked (plant); ~**ste,** lowest; ~**ste in rang,** most junior;

~**te, (-s),** valley, dale, glen, dip; ~**tepunt,** low point (level); nadir; ~**tetjie, (-s),** slight dip; ~**ty,** ebb-tide; ~**vat, (-te),** low tackle; ~**vlak,** bedding-plane; ~**vlakte,** low-lying plain.
laag: ~**vormig, (-e),** stratified, in seams; ~**vorming,** lamination, stratification.
laag: ~**water,** low tide, ebb-tide; ~**waterbrug,** causeway, low-level bridge.
laag'wolke, strati.
laai¹, (s) (-e), drawer (table); till; stock (gun).
laai², (s) (-e), trick, dodge, stunt, *BAIE* ~ *e hê,* play fast and loose; be up to many pranks; *dis sy OU* ~ , that's his old trick.
laai³, (w) load; charge (battery); prime; freight; pack; *te VEEL op jou* ~ , undertake too much; *'n ge* ~ *de WA,* a loaded wagon; ~**bak,** loading bin.
laai'besteling, till-lifting.
laai: ~**beweging,** loading movement; ~**blad,** loading-strip; ~**bok,** derrick; ~**boom,** derrick; ~**brief,** way-bill, consignment note; ~**brug,** ramp; gantry-crane; ~**buis,** tube; ~**datum,** loading date.
laai'dief, till-robber.
laai: ~**er, (-s),** charger (elect.); ~**gat,** loading hole, touch-hole.
laai: ~**geld,** loading charges; ~**geriewe,** loading facilities; ~**graaf,** loader; ~**groewe,** loading groove; ~**hark,** sweep rake, buck rake; ~**hawe,** port of loading; ~**hingsel,** drop-handle; ~**hoof,** cargo hatchway.
laai'kas¹, chest of drawers; tallboy; box (mine).
laai'kas², container.
laai'kis, container.
laai: ~**koste,** loading charges; ~**kraal,** loading pen; ~**lepel,** gun ladle.
laai'ligter, till-sneak, shoplifter.
laai: ~**luik,** loading hatch; ~**meester,** load-checker; tally clerk (in harbour); ~**plaatjie,** clip; charger; ~**plank,** skid, loading board; pallet; ~**platform,** loading platform; ~**plek,** loading place; berth (ship); entraining point.
laai'ruim, (cargo-)hold; ~**te,** cargo-capacity, stowage, tonnage, loading space, holding capacity.

laai'spanning, charging voltage.
laai'steier, loading stage.
laai'sterkte, charge rate (of battery).
laai'stok, ramrod; gun-rod, rammer, gun-stick; cheesa (charging) stick; tamping-rod; *dit lyk of hy 'n ~ ingesluk het*, it looks as if he has swallowed a ramrod (poker).
laai'stroom, charging-current.
laai: ~ **swaelstertvoeg**, drawer-dovetail; ~ **tafel**, chest of drawers; ~ **tjie, (-s)**, little drawer, till; locker.
laai: ~ **tregter**, feed hopper; ~ **vermoë**, carrying capacity, load-capacity; charging rate (of battery); stowage.
laak, (ge-), blame, censure, find fault with, decry, dispraise.
laak'baar, (..bare), blamable, objectionable, condemnable, censurable, exceptionable, reprehensible; rebukable; ~ **heid**, reprehensibleness, blameworthiness.
laan, (lane), avenue, lane, alley.
laars, (-e), boot; ~ **ekap**, top of boot; ~ **ie, (-s)**, small boot.
laas, last; lastly; lately; *na LANGE* ~, at long last; *LANK* ~, long ago; *hy was ~ nog in die LEER*, he was still in the army (when we last heard of him); *die ~ OORGEBLEWE getuie*, the last surviving witness; *OP* ~, at last; *vir OU* ~, for the last time; *VIR ~ nog 'n bietjie gesels*, have a last chat; ~ **gebore**, last-born, last; ~ **genoemde, (-s)**, last-named, the latter; ~ **lede**, last, ultimo; ~ *lede Maandag*, Monday last.
laas'te, (s) (-s), (every) last one; *DIE* ~, the latter, the last one; *van hierdie DORPE is die* ~ ..., of these villages the last named is ...; *baie ~s sal EERSTES wees*, many that are last shall be first, and many that are first shall be last; *die ~ maar nie die MINSTE nie*, last but not least; *OP sy* ~, at death's door; *tot OP die* ~, until the last moment; *TEN* ~, at last; lastly; (b) last, latest (letter); last-named; latter; back; final; extreme; *in die ~ DEEL v.d. boek*, in the latter part of the book; *leer v.d.* ~ *DINGE*, the doctrine of the last things; *die ~ EEN*, every man jack; every single one; *die ~ EEN van julle*, every one of you; *die ~ MAAL*, the last time; *die ~ MENS was daar*, there wasn't a soul missing; *die ~ OORDEEL*, the last judgment; *op die ~ OOMBLIK*, at the last moment; *die ~ RYE*, the back rows; *in die ~ TYD*, of late, lately; *nog 'n ~ WOORDJIE*, just a final word; (bw) last; *wie ~ lag, lag die lekkerste*, he laughs best who laughs last; ~ **lik**, lastly, finally; lately; ultimately.
laat, (w) (ge-), let, allow; refrain from (doing); make (one) do; leave (letter); *ver AGTER* ~, leave far behind; *ek ~ dit DAARBY*, I leave it at that; *~ haar dit DOEN*, let her do it! *iets ~ DOEN*, have (get) something done; ~ *HAAL*, send for; ~ *maar LOOP*, let (him her, it) go; ~ *MAAR*, leave it! *hy kan dit NIE ~ nie*, he cannot refrain from doing it; *~ jou RAAI*, be advised; ~ *SIEN*, show; ~ *ek SIEN*, let me see; ~ *haar STAAN*, leave her alone; ~ *STAAN dit!* leave it alone! ~ *WAG*, keep waiting; ~ *WEET*, inform, send word; *'n WIND* ~, fart; (b, bw) ((late:) later, -ste), late; ~ *in die AAND*, late at night; *HOE* ~ *is dit?* what is the time? ~ *IN die dag*, late in the day; *JY'S* ~ ! I don't think! you've got a hope! *LIEWER ~ as nooit*, better late than never; *is dit SO ~ met hom?* is that how things are with him? *TOT ~ in die nag*, until a late hour; *die late VERSKYNING*, the belated appearance; *is dit al WEER so* ~? are you at it again? *hy WEET hoe ~ dit is*, he knows what's what; ~ **bloeiend, (-e)**, late-flowering.
laat'kommer, (-s), late-comer.
laat-maar-loop'-houding, laissez-faire attitude.
laat: ~ **opstaner**, late riser; ~ **port**, late fee (letters); ~ **roes**, late blight; Irish blight; ~ **slaper**, late riser, sleepy-head, lie-abed.
laat'ste, latest; *op sy ~*, at the very latest.
laat'te, lateness; *teen die* ~, at a late hour.
laat'vy, (-e), donkey.
lab'berlot, (-te), clumsy fellow; ~ **'tig, (-e)**, clumsy.

labiaal', (labiale), labial; *labiale klank*, labial (lip) sound.
labialisa'sie, labialization.
labialiseer', (ge-), labialize.
labiel', (-e; -er, -ste), labile, unstable; ~ *e ewewig*, neutral equilibrium; ..**biliteit'**, lability.
labiodentaal', labiodental.
labirint', (-e), labyrinth; ~ **ies, (-e)**, labyrinthine; ~ **vormig, (-e)**, labyrinthiform.
laborato'rium, (..ria, -s), laboratory.
Lacedemo'nië, Lacedaemonia; ..**mo'nies, (-e)**, Lacedaemonian.
lad'der, (-s), scale (mus.).
la'ding, (-e, -s), cargo, freight, load, stowage, bulk, shipment; charge (of electricity); blast (dynamite); ~ **bestuurder**, supercargo; ~ **kamer**, explosive chamber; ~ **meester**, checker; ~ **sbrief**, bill of lading; ~ **skoste**, shipping charges; ~ **staat**, load-sheet; ~ **svermoë**, load-capacity; ~ **wyser**, librascope.
la'e, courses (in stone and brickwork); strata; *see* **laag**; ~ **drukband**, low-pressure tyre; ~ **graads, (-e)**, low grade; ~ **druksilinder**, low-pressure cylinder.
la'er¹, (s) (-s), camp, lager; corral; ~ *trek*, pitch camp, form a laager; (w) (ge-), go into camp, laager.
la'er², (s) (-s), bearing (of machine).
la'er³, (b) vgl. **laag**; lower, inferior; primary; ~ *ONDERWYS*, primary education; ~ *WAL*, lee shore.
la'er: ~ **baan**, bearing race; ~ **bus**, bearing bush; ~ **dop**, bearing cap.
la'erhof, lower court, inferior court.
La'erhuis, House of Assembly, Lower House, House of Commons.
la'erhulsel, bearing-housing.
la'er: ~ **kamp**, perimeter camp; ~ **kommandant**, laager commandant; ~ **koors**, camp-fever.
la'er: ~ **kraag**, bearing collar; ~ **metaal**, bearing metal; anti-friction metal.
la'er: ~ **naloper**, camp-follower; ~ **plek**, site of laager.
la'erskool, primary school; ~ **leerling**, primary pupil.
la'ervuur, camp-fire.
La'eveld, Low Country; Lowveld.
lae'veld, low country; low veld.
laf, (lawwe), insipid, silly, flat; cowardly; tasteless (food); *'n lawwe grap*, a silly joke; ~ **aard, (-s)**, coward, funk, pudding-heart, poltroon, craven, cur; caitiff, dastard; ~ **bek**, fool.
la'fenis, *see* **laafnis**
lafhar'tig, (-e), cowardly, chicken-hearted, dastard, lily-livered; heartless; craven, poor-spirited, recreant, having cold feet; currish, mean-spirited, white-livered; ~ **heid**, cowardice, poltroonery, pusillanimity.
laf'heid, insipidity, flatness, mawkishness.
lag, (s) laugh, laughter; *DIK v.d.* ~ **wees**, ready to burst out laughing; *ek kon my ~ nie HOU nie*, I could not help laughing; *SKATER v.d.* ~, shake with laughter; *STIK v.d.* ~, be convulsed with laughter; *UITBARS v.d.* ~, burst out laughing; *VOL ~ wees*, be bursting with laughter; (w) (ge-), laugh; ~ *of hy BETAAL word*, he is rocking with laughter; ~ *soos 'n BOER wat tandpyn het*, laugh on the wrong side of one's face; *ek moet DAAROOR* ~, it makes me laugh; *van ~ (ge) kom HUIL(E)*, laugh before breakfast, you'll cry before supper; *wie die LAASTE ~, ~ die lekkerste*, he laughs best, who laughs last; *iem. LAAT ~*, make someone laugh; ~ *soos 'n kind wat MAAGPYN het*, laugh on the wrong side of one's face; ~ *OM*, laugh at; *OOR iets ~*, laugh at (over) something; *dis nie iets om OOR te ~ nie*, it is no laughing matter; *jou SIEK ~*, split one's sides with laughter; *jou SLAP ~*, be limp with laughter; ~ **bek**, giggler; ~ **bui**, fit of laughter.
la'ger(bier), lager (beer).
lag: ~ **gas**, laughing-gas; **-gend, (-e)**, laughing, smiling; ~ **ger, (-s)**, laugher; ~ **gerig, (-e)**, inclined to laugh; laughter-loving; ~ **gery**, laughing; ~ **gie, (-s)**, smile.
la'gie, (-s), small layer, lamella; film.
lag: ~ **kramp**, convulsion of laughter; cynic spasm; ~ **-lag**, laughing all the while, laughingly; ~ **lus**, in=

clination to laugh, hilarity; *die ~lus opwek,* provoke laughter; **~lus'tig, (-e),** hilarious, laughter-loving; **~plooitjie,** crow's-foot; **~siek,** giggling, given to laughter; **~siekte,** giggles; **~spier,** risorial muscle; *dit prikkel sy ~spiere,* it tickles him.

lagu'ne, (-s), lagoon (lagune); **~rif, (..riwwe),** atoll.

lag'vermoë, laughing faculty, ability to laugh.

lagwek'kend, (-e), ludicrous, laughable, risible; **~heid,** ludicrousness, risibility.

lai'tie, laitie, lanie, young boy.

lak¹, (s) seal, sealing-wax, japan, lacquer; lake (colour); (aeroplane), dope; (w) **(ge-),** seal; japan; cement; dope (aero.).

lak², (s) scoundrel; *jou lae ~!* you rogue!

lak³, (w) (ge-), tackle, bring down (rugby).

lakei', (-e), footman, lackey, flunkey.

la'ken, (-s), cloth; sheet; *die ~s uitdeel,* lay down the law; rule the roost; **~fabriek,** cloth factory; **~fabrikant,** cloth manufacturer; clothier; **~goed,** sheeting; **~handel,** cloth trade; **~handelaar,** cloth merchant; **~linne,** sheeting; **~pers,** hot-press, calender.

la'kense, broadcloth, cloth; **~pak,** broadcloth suit.

la'ken: ~stof, broadcloth; **~verwer,** cloth-dyer; **~wewer,** cloth-weaver; **~winkel,** draper's (shop).

la'ker, (-s), fault-finder.

la'king, blaming, censuring.

lak'ker, (-s), varnisher.

lak'koliet, laccolite.

lak'leer, patent leather.

lak'moes, litmus; **~papier,** litmus paper.

lakoniek', (-e), laconic.

lako'nies, (-s), laconic.

lakonis'me, laconism.

lak'poleer: ~der, French-polisher; **~werk,** French-polishing.

lak'politoer, French polish.

laks, (-e), lax, indolent, slack.

laksatief', (s, b) (..tiewe), laxative, purgative.

lakseer', (s) purging; (w) **(ge-),** purge, open the bowels; **~jas,** good-for-nothing; **~middel,** laxative, purgative, aperient.

lak'sel, vermicelli.

laks'heid, laxity, slackness, looseness, indolence.

lak: ~skilder, doper; **~skoen,** patent-leather shoe, pump.

laks'man, (-s, -ne), hangman, executioner, headsman; butcher-bird, fiscal-shrike, shrike, Jack Ketch.

lak'spuit, doper (tool).

lakta'se, lactase.

lakta'sie, lactation.

lakteaal', (lakteale), lacteal.

lak'tometer, laktome'ter, lactometer.

lakto'se, sugar of milk, lactose.

laktoskoop', (..skope), lactoscope.

laku'ne, (-s), gap, vacancy, lacuna.

lak: ~verf, drop-colour; lake; **~vernis,** lac varnish, lacquer; **~vernisser,** French-polisher; **~werk,** lacquer, japanned goods; lacquered ware.

la'la, (ge-), sleep (nursery term of Zulu origin).

laloen'tjie, (-s), (kind of) small musk-melon.

lam¹, (s) (-mers), lamb; *soos 'n ~ na die SLAGBANK gelei word,* be led like a lamb to the slaughter; *as die ~ geskeer is, sorg God vir 'n warm WINDJIE,* God tempers the wind to the shorn lamb; (w) **(ge-),** lamb, cast young, drop.

lam², (b) (-mer, -ste), paralysed; weary, fatigued; **~geskrik,** paralysed with fright.

la'ma¹, (-s), llama (animal).

la'ma², (-s), lama (priest); **~ïsme,** lamaism; **~klooster,** lamasery.

la'mawol, llama (wool).

lambdavor'mig, (-e), lambdoid(al).

lam'bosluis, paralytic tick.

lambriseer', (ge-), (fit with) wainscot, panel.

lambrise'ring, wainscot(ing); panelling.

lamé', lamé.

lamel', (-le), lamella, lamina.

lamelleer', (ge-), laminate.

lamellêr', (-e), laminated.

lamelle'ring, lamination.

lamenta'sie, (-s), lamentation.

lamenteer', (ge-), lament.

lam'heid, lameness, paralysis, palsy.

lamineer', (ge-), laminate.

lam: ~kruis, sway-back (sheep disease); **~lê, (-ge-),** paralyse.

lamlen'dig, (-e), lazy, indolent; miserable, wretched; weak; **~heid,** slackness, indolence; miserableness; weakness.

lam'me, (-s), paralytic.

lam'meling, (-e), miserable fellow, good-for-nothing.

lam'mer: ~gier, lammergeyer, bearded vulture *(Gypaetus barbatus);* **~hok,** lamb's-pen; **~kraal,** creep; **~oes,** lamb crop, fall; **~ooi,** ewe with lamb at foot; **~skape,** ewes with lambs at foot; **~tyd,** lambing season; **~vanger,** golden eagle, lammergeyer; bearded eagle; school attendance officer; **~vleis = lamsvleis; ~wol,** hoggets, lambs'-wool; **~wolke,** fleecy clouds.

lam'metjie, (-s, lammertjies), (little) lamb, lambkin; *laat ~,* child born a long time after others; an afterthought.

lam'migheid, lameness.

lamp, (-e), lamp; (radio) valve; *teen die ~ LOOP,* bump one's head; *jou ~ onder 'n MAATEMMER sit,* hide one's light under a bushel; *na die ~ RUIK,* smell of the lamp; **~brander,** lamp-burner.

lampet'beker, lampet'kan, ewer, toilet-jug.

lampet'kom, washstand-basin.

lamp: ~fabriek, lamp factory; **~glas,** (lamp) chimney; **~houer,** lamp holder (socket).

lam'pit, (-s), small lamp.

lampion', (-ne, -s), Chinese lantern; lampion; **~vrug,** winter cherry.

lamp: ~kap, lamp-shade; **~kousie,** mantle (gaslamp); **~lig,** lamp-light; **~olie,** paraffin oil; kerosene; **~opsteker,** lamplighter; **~paal,** lamp post; **~pit,** lamp wick; **~sein,** lamp signal; **~sender,** valve transmitter; **~swart,** lampblack.

lam: ~sak, lazy bones, weakling, shirker, milksop, slacker, defeatist; poltroon; **~sakgees,** defeatism; **~sakkerig, (-e),** laggard, spiritless, spunkless.

lams'boud, leg of lamb.

lam'siekte, lameness, paralysis; „lamsiekte" *(Osteomalacia);* botulism.

lams'kotelet, lamb cutlet.

lam'slaan, (-ge-), paralyse, cripple; *dit het my lam geslaan,* it knocked me sideways; I was struck all of a heap.

lam: ~s'leer, lambskin (leather); **~s'ribbetjie,** lambchop; **~s'rug,** saddle of lamb; **~s'vel,** lamb skin; **~(s)velbont,** budge; **~(s)vlees, ~(s)vleis,** lamb (meat); **~s'vlies,** amnion; **~tyd,** lambing season.

land, (s) (-e), land, country; ground, field; *AAN ~,* on land; *lank in die ~, bietjie BAARD, maar klipsteenhard,* an old hand; a past master; *die ~ van BELOFTE,* the promised land; *die ~ aan iets HÊ,* detest something; *aan ~ GAAN,* go ashore; *aan ~ KOM,* land; *êrens te ~e KOM,* land somewhere; *waar sal hy te ~e KOM?* what will become of (happen to) him? *hy is al LANK in die ~,* he knows the world; he is an old hand; *LIEWE ~!* good gracious; *'n ~ wat oorloop van MELK en heuning,* a land flowing with milk and honey; *op sy KOP te ~e kom,* land on one's head; *ONDERONTWIKKELDE ~,* under-developed country; *OOR ~,* by road, over land; *~ en SAND aanmekaar praat,* talk without stopping (incessantly); *hier TE ~e, in this part of the world; strydkragte TE ~ en ter see,* forces on land and at sea; *die ~ VERLAAT,* leave the country; *~ en VOLK,* the country and its people; *te ~ en te WATER,* by land and sea; *~s WYS,* when in Rome do as the Romans do; (w) **(ge-),** land, disembark, arrive, alight; **~aanwas,** alluvion; **~aard,** national character; **~adel,** landed nobility (gentry); **~afsetting,** terrestrial deposit; **~arbeider,** field labourer.

landau'er, (-s), landau.

land: ~bank, farmer's bank, land bank; *L~bank,* Land Bank; **~besit,** ownership of land; landed property; **~besitter,** landed proprietor; **~beskrywing,** description of land; **~bewonend, (-e),** epig(a)eal; **~bewoner,** country-dweller.

land'bou, agriculture; *Departement van L~*, Department of Agriculture; *Minister van L~*, Minister of Agriculture; ~**bedryf**, agriculture; ~**blad**, (..**blaaie**), agricultural journal; ~**departement**, department of agriculture; ~**ekonomie**, agro-economics; ~**er**, farmer, agriculturist; agrarian; peasant; planter; ~**genootskap**, agricultural society; ~**gereedskap**, agricultural implements; ~**grond**, arable land; ~**hoewe**, plot, agricultural smallholding; ~**joernaal**, agricultural journal; ~**kalk**, agricultural lime; ~**kenner**, agricultural expert; ~**ketel**, stationary engine; ~**kollege**, agricultural college; ~**krediet**, agricultural credit; ~**kredietbank**, rural bank, land bank; ~**kunde**, agriculture; agronomy; ~**kun'dig, (-e)**, geoponic, agricultural; ~**kun'dige, (-s)**, agriculturist; ~**kursus**, course in, agriculture; ~**motor**, agrimotor; ~-**onderwys**, rural education, agricultural instruction; ~**opleiding**, agricultural training; ~**produk**, agricultural product, farm produce; ~**proefstasie**, agricultural experimental station; ~**skeikunde**, agricultural chemistry; ~**skool**, school of agriculture; ~**streek**, agricultural district (belt); ~**tentoonstelling**, agricultural show; ~**vereniging**, farmer's association; ~**weerstasie**, crop weather station; ~**werktuig**, agricultural implement; ~**wetenskap**, agricultural science; ~**woordvoerder**, agricultural spokesman.

land: ~**bries**, land breeze; ~**dag**, diet; *die Ierse* ~ *dag*, the Irish diet (parliament); ~**diens**, land-service; ~**dier**, land animal, terrestrial animal; ~**dros, (-te)**, landdros, magistrate; ~**drosdistrik, (-te)**, magisterial district; ~**drossetel**, seat of a magistracy; ~**eienaar**, landowner; ~**eiendom**, landed property.

lan'delik, (-e), rural, rustic, bucolic, countrified; georgic; agrarian, agrestic; ~*e ERF*, rural tenement; ~*e SERVITUUT*, rural servitude; ~**heid**, rusticity, rural charm.

land: ~**engte, (-s)**, isthmus; ~**ery'e**, fields, cultivated land; ~**ewedstryd**, international test match; ~**genoot**, (..**note**), countryman, fellow-countryman, compatriot; ~**goed, (-ere)**, estate, country-seat, manor, demesne; ~**goedwyn**, estate wine; ~**graaf**, landgrave; ~**graafskap**, landgraviate; ~**gravin**, landgravine; ~**grens**, frontier; border; ~**heer**, country gentleman; landowner; ~**heerswoning**, mansion house; ~**honger**, land-hunger; lust for territory; ~**hoof**, abutment (bridge); ~**huis**, country-house; country villa; ~**huishoudkunde**, rural economy; agronomy; ~**huishoudkun'dige, (-s)**, rural economist; ~**huur**, land-rent.

lan'ding, (-e, -s), landing; disembarkation (from ship).

lan'dings: ~**baan**, landing-strip; ~**blad**, (..**blaaie**), landing apron; heliport; ~**boot**, tender; ~**brug**, landing-bridge, gangway; ~**dek**, flight deck; ~**divisie**, landing-party, shore-party; ~**hoof**, pier, jetty, landing-stage; ~**lig**, landing-light; ~**onderneming**, landing-enterprise; ~**plaas**, ~**plek**, landing-place; pier; ~**toestel**, undercarriage; ~**troepe**, landing-forces; ~**vaartuig**, landing-craft, barge; ~**veld**, landing-field; ~**wyser**, librascope.

land: ~**in'waarts**, inland; ~**jeug**, country youth; ~**jie, (-s)**, small country; small field; ~**jonker**, (hist.), country squire; ~**kaart**, map; ~**kant**, land side; ~**ketel**, land-engine; ~**klimaat**, country (continental) climate; ~**krap**, land-crab; ~**leër**, land-forces; ~**lewe**, country life; rustication; ~**loop**, cross-country race; ~**loper, (-s)**, vagrant, hobo, tramp, vagabond; landlubber; ~**lopery**, tramping, vagrancy, vagabondage; ~**lyn**, land-line; ~**maat**, land-measure; ~**mag, (-te)**, land-forces; military force; ~**magvliegtuig**, army co-operation aeroplane; ~**man**, farmer.

land'meet, (-ge-), survey; ~**kunde**, surveying, geodesy; ~**kun'dig, (-e)**, surveying, geodetic.

land'meter, (land) surveyor; ~-**generaal**, (land-meters-generaal), surveyor-general; ~**shulp**, chainman, rod-man; ~**sketting**, surveyor's chain, measuring-chain, gauge-way.

land: ~**metery**, ~**meting**, surveying; ~**myl**, statute mile; ~**myn**, landmine (in war); ~**onteiening**, expropriation of land; ~**ontginner**, tiller of land, farmer.

lan'dou, (-e), pasture, field.

land: ~**paal**, boundary limit; ~**pag**, land-rent; ~**plaag**, see ~**splaag**; ~**pos**, overland mail; ~**punt**, cape; promontory; headland; shore-end (cable); naze; point; L~**raad**, Lands Commission; L~**rasvark**, Landrace pig; ~**reën**, general rains; ~**reis**, journey; ~**roete**, overland route; ~**rot**, land-rat, landlubber; ~**saat**, countryman; ~**sake**, affairs of a country, national affairs.

lands: ~**belang**, national interest; ~**bestuur**, public administration; ~**diens**, country's service; land-labour.

land'seun, son of the soil.

lands: ~**geaardheid**, nature of a country; character of a nation; ~**geld**, public money; ~**grens**, frontier.

land'skap, (-pe), landscape; ~**argitek**, landscape designer; ~**beskrywer**, chorographer; ~**beskrywing**, chorography; ~**skilder**, landscape painter.

land: ~**s'kas**, national treasury, exchequer; ~**skeiding**, boundary; ~**skilpad**, (land) tortoise.

lands: ~**man, (-ne, landsliede, landslui)**, countryman; *watter* ~ *man is hy?* from what country is he? ~**nood**, state of national emergency; ~**pad**, national road; ~**plaag**, public nuisance; epidemic, national pest.

lands: ~**reën**, ~**reent**, general rain, set-in rain; ~**reg**, law of the country; ~**regering**, government of a country; ~**reis**, journey (through the whole country); national tour; ~**taal**, vernacular, language of the country.

land'streek, region, district.

lands: ~**vader** *(plegt.)*, father of the people; member of parliament; ~**veiligheid**, national security; ~**verdediging**, defence of the country; home-defence; ~**vlag**, national flag; ~**vuilis, (-se)**, scoundrel, rotter, good-for-nothing; ~**vyand**, national enemy; ~**weë**: *van* ~ *weë*, on behalf of the country; ~**weerberig**, national weather forecast; ~**wet**, law of the land; ~**wyd**, (..**wye**), nation-wide, country-wide; *'n landswye veldtog*, a nation-wide campaign.

land'sy, landside.

land: ~**teken**, landmark; ~**tong**, spit of land; foreland, ness, naze; ~**troepe**, land-service; ~**verhuiser**, emigrant; immigrant; ~**verhuising**, emigration; immigration; ~**verraad**, high treason; ~**verraaier**, traitor to one's country; ~**verskuiwing**, landslide; ~**vliegtuig**, land-based aircraft; ~**voog, (-de)**, governor; ~**waarts, (-e)**, land-ward(s); ~**weer**, territorial force, militia; ~**weerman**, militiaman, territorial; ~**weerstelsel**, militia system; ~**weg**, country road; overland route; ~**werk**, field labour; ~**wind**, land-wind, off-shore wind; ~**winning**, reclaiming of land; ~**wyn**, wine of the country; ~**ys**, inland ice.

lan'fer, crape (crêpe), mourning.

lang, (attributief), **(-e; -er, -ste)**, long, tall; great; *hoe* ~ *er hoe BETER*, the longer the better; *hoe* ~ *er hoe ERGER*, the longer the worse; *in* ~ *e JARE*, for many years; *hoe* ~ *er hoe MEER*, more and more; *OP* ~ *e na nie*, not by a long chalk; *OP sy* ~ *ste*, at its longest; *'n WEEK op sy* ~ *ste*, a week at the outside; ~**ademig, (-e)**, long-winded, verbose; ~**afstandsbomwerper**, long-range bomber; ~**afstandsverkeer**, long-distance traffic; ~**afstandsvlug**, long-distance flight; ~**armig, (-e)**, long-armed; ~**as**, major axis; ~**asemdans**, non-stop dance; ~**asem(kriek)**, ~**asemsprinkaan**, cricket *(Cicada)*; *'n* ~ *asemkriek*, a long-winded person; ~**balk**, wall-plate (of mine); ~**been**, (s) long-shanks; long legs; treble stitch; ~**been-**, (b) long-legged; ~**beenspinnekop**, daddy-long-legs; ~**beentjie, (-s)**, kind of shrub *(Leucadendron)*; ~**beentregter**, thistle funnel; ~**bekmaande**, the winter months when vegetables are scarce; ~**bekvoël**, long-bill; ~**be'nig, (-e)**, long-legged, long-shanked; ~**be'nigheid**, legginess; ~**by**, long leg (cricket); ~**byvoor**, long on.

langdra'dig, (-e), long(-winded), wordy, lengthy, long-spun, tedious, prolix; diffuse; ~**heid**, long-windedness, prolixity.

langdu'rig, (-e), long, lasting; chronic; lengthy; protracted, prolonged; long-term; ~**heid**, long duration, length, diffuseness.
langelier'boom, medicinal plant *(Polygola myrifolia)*.
lan'gelaas: *op* ~, in the end, ultimately.
lang'eraad, middle finger.
lang'erig, (-e), rather long, longish.
langes, see **langs**.
lan'getjie, (-s), small long one.
lang: ~**gatboor**, slot-borer; ~**gerek, (-te)**, protracted, long drawn-out; ~**golfstasie**, long-wave station; ~**harig; (-e)**, long-haired; pilose; ~**heid**, length; ~**hoofdig, (-e)**, long-headed; dolichocephalic; macrocephalic; ~**horingsprinkaan**, katydid; ~**jarig, (-e)**, long-standing; ~**kop**, jigger; smart person; ~**lewend, (-e)**, long-lived; long-living; ~**lewendheid**, longevity; ~**man**, middle finger; ~**melk**, ropy milk; ~**mourok**, long-sleeved dress; ~**nekerf**, panhandle erf (stand); ~**nekkaatjie**, the bottle; ~**nekkameel**, camelopard; ~**neus**, nosy; busy-body; ~**oog**: ~*oog wees*, be green with envy; ~**oor**, long-ear; ass; ~**oorvlermuis**, long-eared bat; ~**orig, (-e)**, long-eared; ~**poot**, (s) cranefly; daddy-long-legs; ~**poot-**, (b) long-legged; ~**pootmuggie**, long-legged gnat.
langs, along, next to, beside, alongside of; ~ *die GROND*, along the ground; ~ *die PAD*, on the way; next to the road; ~ *my VERBY*, past me.
lang'saam, (..same), slow, tardy, leisurely; slow-moving; ~ *maar seker*, slow but sure; ~**heid**, slowness, tardiness.
langs'aan, next to, next door; alongside.
langs'aar, longitudinal seam (mine).
lang'samerhand, gradually, little by little, by degrees.
langs: ~**balk**, longitudinal member; ~**deursnee**, longitudinal section; ~**hellingmeter**, longitudinal clinometer; ~**hout**, edge grain.
lang'sig, long date; *op* ~ *betaalbaar*, payable after 90 days; ~ *wissel*, long bill.
lang'skedelig, (-e), see **langhoofdig**.
langs'kepe, elongated grooves.
lang'slaper, late riser, sleepy-head.
langs'lewend. (-e), surviving; ~**e, (-s)**, survivor (one who lives longest); *die* ~ *e erf niks*, the estate is in insolvent.
lang'snoetmuis, (-e), dwarf shrew.
lang'skeeps, (-e), fore and aft; along-ships; longitudinal.
langs'snee, (..sneë), longitudinal section.
lang: ~**span**, tandem; ~**speelplaat**, long-playing record; ~**steel-**, long-handled; ~**steelstert**, long-tailed tit; ~**stuk**, top timber.
langs'uitsetting, linear expansion.
lang: ~**tand**, reluctantly, unwillingly; ~**termyndrywing**, long-term shift (drift); ~**termyngemiddelde**, long-term average; ~**termynhuur**, long lease; ~**termynnavorsing**, long-term research; ~**toon**, jacana; ~**verlof**, long leave; ~**verwag, (-te)**, long-expected; ~**vingerig, (-e)**, thievish, light-fingered, sticky-fingered; ~**vintornyn**, germon; ~**vleuelig, (-e)**, macropterous; ~**voc'tig, (-e)**, long-footed, longiped; ~**wa, (-ens)**, long wagon, perch-pole; ~**weg**, long off (cricket).
langwer'pig, (-e), oblong, rectangular; elongate; *die wêreld het toe* ~ *geword*, then the troubles accumulated; ~**heid**, oblongness.
lang'wol, long wool, longs.
langwy'lig, (-e), tedious, prolix; ~**heid**, prolixity.
la'ning, (-s), hedge, avenue, alley.
lank, (b, bw) (predikatief), long, tall; for long; *AL* ~ *gesond*, well for a long time now; *dis so* ~ *as wat dit BREED is*, it is six of one and half a dozen of the other, it is as long as it is broad; ~ *nie so DOM nie*, not at all stupid; ~ *nie GOED nie*, far from good; *JARE* ~, for (many) years; ~ *LAAS*, a long time ago; *haar LEWE* ~, all her life; *hy val so* ~ *SOOS hy was*, he falls full length; ~ *van STOF wees*, be long-winded; *nie te* ~ *nie of hy was TERUG*, before long he was back; *'n TYD* ~, for a time; *'n VOET* ~, a foot long; *jy kan* ~ *WAG*, you can wait until Doomsday; ~**al**, long ago; for a long while now; *hy moes dit* ~ *al gedoen het*, he should have done it a long time ago.
lankmoe'dig, (-e), patient, long-suffering; clement, longanimous; ~**heid**, forebearance, patience; clemency, longanimity.
lank'-uit, at full length.
lanolien', lanoli'ne, lanolin; ~**salf**, lanolin ointment.
lans, (-e), lance, spear; pike; *'n* ~ *(ie) breek MET*, break a lance with; *'n* ~ *(ie) breek VIR*, break a lance for.
lanseer', (ge-), launch (missile, torpedo); float (ship); catapult (aero.); start (theory); lance, pierce, open (tumour); *'n onderneming* ~, start (launch) an undertaking; ~**baan**, launching site (pad); ~**buis**, launching-tube; ~**der, (-s)**, launcher; ~**helling**, launching ramp; ~**mes**, lancet; ~**stelling**, launching platform; ~**toestel**, launching gear.
lanse'ring, (-e, -s), launching.
lanset', (-te), lancet, incision-knife; ~**vormig, (-e)**, lanceolate.
lansier', (-s), lancer; ~**s**, lancers (dance).
lans: ~**peil**, tent-pegging (sport); ~**punt**, lancehead; ~**ruiter**, lancer.
lans'skag¹, spear shaft.
lans'skag², lancewood.
lans: ~**steek**, spear shaft; lancewood; lance-thrust; ~**stok**, pikestaff; ~**vormig, (-e)**, lance-shaped; lanceolate (bot.)
lanterfan'ter, (s) (-s), idler, loafer; (w) (ge-), idle, laze (about), loiter, dawdle, loaf.
lantern', (-s), lantern; *groot* ~, *wainig lig*, someone whose father was no glazier; all brawn but little brain; ~**dak**, deck-roof; ~**draer**, lantern-bearer; ~**glas**, lantern glass; ~**heide**, lantern-heath; ~**kersie**, candle for lantern; ~**opsteker**, lamp-lighter; ~**paal**, lantern post; ~**plaat**, lantern slide; ~**rat**, lantern wheel, trundle-head.
Laodice'a, Laodicea.
Laodice'ër, (-s), Laodicean.
La'os, Laos; ~**iaans', (-e)**, Laotian.
Lap¹, (s) (-pe), Lapp, Laplander.
lap², (s) (-pe), patch; cloth, rag (for wiping); piece, remnant (material); bandage (for wound); clout; gaiter (tyre); *op die* ~ *pe BRING*, bring on the tapis; *met iets op die* ~ *pe KOM*, bring to light; *afvee met 'n NAT* ~, wipe (off) with a damp rag; *soos 'n ROOI* ~ *op 'n bul werk*, have the effect of a red rag on a bull; *'n* ~ *SIT op*, put a patch on; (w) (ge-), mend, patch; *'n ge* ~ *te broek*, patched trousers; ~**bestrating**, crazy paving; ~**boek**, rag book.
laparoskopie', laparoscopy.
lapel', (-le), lapel; ~**kraag**, reverse collar.
lap'hoed, floppy hat.
lapidêr', (-e), lapidary.
lapis lazu'li, *kyk* **lasuursteen**.
Lap'land, Lapland; ~**er, (-s)**, Lapp, Laplander; ~**s, (-e)**, Lappish, Lapponian.
lap: ~**las**, lap-weld; ~**middel**, patchwork; palliative measure, makeshift; ~**opteller**, rag-picker, ~**per, (-s)**, piecer; patcher.
lap'pie, (-s), small rag (cloth); small patch; *'n* ~ *pie GROND*, a small piece of ground, a small farm; ~**vleis**, slice of meat, collop; ~**dag**, remnant day; ~**sak**, rag-bag; ~**sdeken**, crazy quilt, patchwork quilt; ~**smous**, nickname for commercial traveller.
lap: ~**plek**, mend, patch; ~**pop**, rag doll.
Laps, (-e), Lappish, Lapponian.
lap'sus, (-se), slip (of the tongue, pen), lapse.
lap'werk, patchwork, mending, tinkering, patching.
lardeer', (ge-), lard; ~**naald**, larding-needle; ~**sel**, lard; ~**spek**, lard, pork fat.
la're: ~ *en penate*, lares and penates.
la'rie, flapdoodle, stuff and nonsense; *dit is alles* ~, it is all nonsense (poppycock).
la'riksboom, larch.
laringi'tis, laryngitis.
laringoskoop', (..skope), laryngoscope.
la'rinks, (-e), larynx.
larvaal', (larvale), larval.
lar'we, (-s), larva; ~**gif**, larvicide; ~**toestand**, larva stage.
las¹, (s) (-se), seam, join(t), weld; scarf (of leather);

fish (strenghening bar); (w) (ge-), join, weld; pool funds.

las², (s) (-te), burden, load, weight; cargo; nuisance, trouble, annoyance; command, order; *jou ~ te DRA*, bear one's burdens; *~ GEE*, give orders; be a nuisance; *~ HÊ van*, be troubled with, suffer from; *hom van 'n ~ KWYT*, acquit oneself of an obligation; *iem. iets ten ~ te LÊ*, lay it to someone's charge; *OP ~*, by order; *OP ~ van*, by order of; *'n ~ WEES*, be a nuisance.

lasaret', (-te), lazaret(to).

la'sarus, leprosy.

las: *~ baar*, (..bare), weldable; *~ bak*, flush box; *~ bout*, fish bolt.

las'brief, order, warrant, writ, summons; commission; *~ vir huissoeking*, search-warrant.

las: *~ dier*, beast of burden, pack-animal; *~ diervervoer*, pack-transport.

las'draad, tying wire.

las: *~ draend*, (-e), onerary; *~ draer*, burden-bearer, load-carrier; *die ~ draer wees*, be the one who has to bear the responsibility; *~ gewer*, principal, mandator; *~ gewing*, (-e, -s), mandate; commission; *~ hebber*, (-s), mandatory.

la'serstraal, laser ray.

Laskaar', (Laskare), Lascar.

las'lap, patch(ing); gore.

las: *~ lening*, charge loan; *~ lyn*, Plimsoll line, load-line; *~ nemer*, mandatory.

las: *~ plaat*, fish-plate; *~ plek*, joint, weld, (place of) connection.

las'pos, (-te), nuisance, troublesome person; gadfly.

las: *~ riem*, belt-race; *~ ser*, (-s), jointer; *~ sie*, (-s), *kyk las*; *~ skakel*, master-link.

las'so (s), (-'s), lasso, lariat; (w) (ge-), lasso.

las'stoel, joint-chair.

las'ter, (s) slander, calumny, libel; blasphemy; defamation, aspersion, obloquy; (w) (ge-), slander, defame; blaspheme, curse; *~ aar*, (-s), slanderer; blasphemer; defamer, detractor; *~ agtig*, (-e), slanderous, libellous; *~ end*, (-e), abusive, detractive, defamatory, calumniatory, calumnious; *~ ing*, (-e), blasphemy; slander; curse; *~ kampanje*, campaign of calumny; defamation campaign; *~ lik*, (-e), defamatory, slanderous, libellous; blasphemous; detracting, calumnious, calumniatory; *~ praatjies*, scandal, slanderous talk; *~ saak*, libel case; *~ siek*, (-e), slanderous, calumnious; *~ skrif*, libel; *~ sug*, slanderousness; *~ taal*, slander, calumny, defamatory language; blasphemy; *~ tong*, scandalmonger.

las'tig, (-e), troublesome, burdensome, annoying, forward, fractious, bothersome, importunate, pestilent; petulant; knotty, awkward (case); difficult, delicate (matter) cumbersome, cumbrous; *dit vir iem. ~ MAAK*, make things difficult for someone; *~ VAL*, worry, bother, importune, trouble, pester; *'n ~ e VENT*, a troublesome customer; *~ WEES*, be a nuisance; put to inconvenience; *~ heid*, nuisance, troublesomeness, importunity; petulance, petulancy; *~ heidsfaktor*, nuisance value.

lasuur', lapis lazuli; azure; *~ steen*, lapis lazuli, lazulite, Armenian stone.

las: *~ verbinding*, rail-bond; *~ verdeling*, load-distribution.

lat, (-te), lath, stick, cane; birch-rod; slat; strip (of wood); *die ~ INLÊ*, whip someone; *onder die ~ KRY*, cane someone; *~ bekleding*, lagging (mine); *~ bos*, fascine.

latei', (-e), lintel.

la'teks, latex.

latent', (-e), latent; potential; *~ heid*, latency.

la'ter, later; puisne (law); *hoe ~, hoe kwater*, the longer it lasts, the worse it becomes.

lateraal', (..rale), lateral.

Lateraan', Lateran, -s', (-e), Lateran.

lateriet', laterite.

la'terig, (-e), fairly late, latish.

latier'boom, swinging-bail.

Latinis', (-te), Latinist; *~ eer'*, (ge-), Romanize; *~ me*, Latinism.

latitudinêr', (-e), latitudinarian.

lat'jie, (-s), little stick.

la'tjiebeen: *jou ~ hou by 'n nooi*, pay one's attentions to a girl.

latoen', (-e), latten.

latri'ne, (-s), latrine.

lat'te: *~ muur*, battened wall; *~ solder*, grid (theatre).

lat'werk, lattice-work, trellis, espalier, lathing; crating.

Latyn', Latin; *~ s'*, (-e), Latin.

latyn'seil, lateen sail.

lavas', (-se), lovage *(Lavisticum officinale)*.

laveer', (ge-), tack (about), beat against the wind, ply.

laven'tel, lavender, perfume; *~ blom*, lavender flower; *~ bos*, scented shrub *(Heteropyxis natalensis)*; *~ haan*, dandy; *~ heining*, lavender hedge; *~ jantjie*, dandy; *~ olie*, oil of lavender; spike oil; *~ sakkie*, lavender bag; *~ sproeier*, *~ spuitjie*, scent-spray; *~ water*, lavender-water.

lawa, lava.

lawaai', (s) noise, hubbub, pother, racket, tumult, brawl; blare, din; charivari; clatter, clamour, bluster, hullabaloo; hurly-burly, outcry, fuss; *'n ~ v.d. ander WÊRELD*, a noise to rouse the dead; *groot ~, weinig WOL*, much cry and little wool; much ado about nothing; *meer ~ as WOL*, much ado about nothing; (w) (ge-), be rowdy, make a noise; blare; *~ erig*, (-e), noisy, loud, obstreperous, clamant, clamorous, blatant; rackety, fussy; *~ erigheid*, clamorousness, noise; fussiness; *~ maker*, rowdy person, blusterer, roisterer, clamourer, hooligan; *~ makery*, rowdiness, hooliganism; *~ water*, brandy, liquor, booze; *hy het ~ water gedrink*, he is in his cups.

la'wa: *~ -as*, lava-ash, *~ dek*, sheet; *~ glas*, hyalite, obsidian; *~ koepel*, volcanic dome; *~ muur*, dike; *~ stroom*, torrent of lava.

la'we, (ge-), *see* **laaf**.

lawement', (-e), clyster, enema, injection, lavement; *~ spuit*, enema (syringe).

lawi'ne, (-s), avalanche, snow-slip.

la'wing, refreshment.

law'werig, (-e), rather silly.

law'wigheid, silliness, foolishness, tommy-rot; puppyism.

lê, (s) laying; lying, lie; *die HENNE is nou aan die ~*, the hens are beginning to lay; *die gholfspeler kla oor 'n SLEGTE ~*, the golfer complains about a bad lie; *hy SOEK sy ~*, he is trying to find a comfortable position (in which to lie); (w) (ge-), lay (egg, ambush); place, put; lie, be situated; couch; *as dit AAN my ~*, if I have any say in the matter; *dit ~ AAN hom*, it depends (devolves) on him; *dit ~ nie AAN my nie*, it is not my fault (responsibility); *die BAL bly daar ~*, the ball came to rest there; *BLY ~*, remain in bed; *aan die DAG ~*, show; *daar ~ die DING*, there's the rub; that's the snag; *dit ~ voor die HAND*, it goes without saying, it is obvious; *'n HOEKSTEEN ~*, lay a foundation stone; *LAAT ~*, leave (alone); *hulle ~ aan die MASELS*, they are down with measles; *~ ONDER*, lie under, underlie; *ONDER ~*, lie underneath (beneath); *op STERWE ~*, be at death's door; *die WIND het gaan ~*, the wind has abated; *~ aas*, ledger-bait.

leb, rennet; lab; *~ maag*, abomasum, rennet-bag.

lê: *~ boor*, ovipositor; *~ buis*, egg-tube; *~ dae*, days of demurrage.

le'de, *see* **lid** (s): *'n siekte onder ~ hê*, have an illness coming on, be sickening for; (b): *met ~ oë aanskou*, eye with envy; view with regret; *~ braak*, (ge-), break on the wheel; *~ geld*, subscription, membership fee.

ledekant', (-e), bedstead; *~ gordyn*, bed-curtain; *~ hemel*, canopy, tester.

le'delande, member nations.

le'de: *~ lys*, list of members; *~ mate*, limbs; *~ pop*, lay figure, manikin, puppet; *~ staat*, member state; list of members; *~ tal*, number of members; member ship; *~ vergadering*, members' meeting; *~ water*, synovial fluid, synovia, housemaid's knee.

le'dig, (w) (ge-), empty; deplete; (b) (-e), idle, without employment, inactive; *~ sit*, idle; *~ ganger*, idler; *~ heid*, idleness, inactivity; emptiness; *~ heid is die* *duiwel se oorkussing,* Satan finds some mischief for idle hands to do; an idle person is the devil's play=fellow; ~ **ing,** depletion; kenosis.

leed, pain, sorrow, affliction, grief, dolour; harm, in=jury; *iem.* ~ *AANDOEN,* cause someone grief; *dit DOEN my* ~ , I regret, I am sorry; *aan iem. jou* ~ *KLA,* pour out one's grief to someone; ~ **vermaak,** pleasure at another's misfortune, malicious pleasure, schadenfreude; *met* ~ *vermaak aansien,* gloat over; ~ **wese,** sorrow, regret; *tot my* ~ *wese,* to my regret.

leef, (ge-), live; *al wat* ~ *en BEEF,* every living soul; ~ *en LAAT* ~ , live and let live; *hy KAN nie* ~ *nie,* he can wait no longer; *te MIN om van te* ~ *en te veel om van dood te gaan,* live on the ragged edge of nothing; live on the breadline; *van NIKS* ~ *nie,* live on nothing; *volgens jou OORTUIGING* ~ , live up (according) to one's convictions; *lank lewe die RE=PUBLIEK,* three cheers for the Republic; *die TUIN* ~ *van die miere,* the garden is teeming with ants; *wie dan* ~ , *wie dan SORG,* sufficient unto the day is the evil thereof; don't anticipate the evil day; ~ **baar,** (..**bare),** reasonable, bearable, fair, not too bad; ~ **reël,** rule of life, regimen, diet; ~ **ruimte,** living space; ~ **tog,** victuals, provisions, subsist=ence.

leef'tyd, lifetime, time of life, age; date; *mense van GEVORDERDE (hoë)* ~ , people of advanced years; *op MIDDELBARE* ~ , in middle life; *OP dié* ~ , at that age; *iem. OP* ~ , a man of years; ~ **sgrens,** age-limit, ~ **sgroep,** age-group.

leef'wyse, manner of living (life).

leeg, (leë; leër, -ste), empty, inane, void, vacant; addled; blank; *leë BOULBEURT,* maiden over; *my VULPEN is* ~ , my fountain-pen has run dry; ~ **drink, (-ge-),** drain, drink off, empty (by drinking); ~ **eet, (-geëet),** eat all the contents (of); ~ **gewig,** empty weight; ~ **heid,** emptiness; ~ **hoof, (-de),** empty-headed fellow, nitwit; ~ **hoofdig, (-e),** empty-headed; ~ **lê, (-ge-),** loaf, idle, laze; ~ **lêer,** idler, do-nothing, loafer; remittance man; ~ **lêerig, (-e),** otiose, inclined to be lazy; ~ **lêery,** loafing, idling; ~ **loop, (-ge-),** idle, loaf; run out (water from cask), empty; become empty (theatre); *laat* ~ *loop,* drain off, empty; ~ **loper,** idler, loafer, loiterer, do=nothing; ~ **lopery,** loafing, vagabondage; ~ **maak, (-ge-),** empty, gut; clear, evacuate; ~ **plunder, (-ge-),** rifle, loot; ~ **pomp, (-ge-),** pump dry; exhaust; ~ **skep, (-ge-),** scoop dry; ~ **skud, (-ge-),** shake out the contents of; ~ **staan, (-ge-),** be empty, be unoccupied; ~ **steel, (-ge-),** rifle, loot; ~ **te,** emp=tiness, void; inanition, inanity; *see* **laagte.**

leek, (leke), layman, laic, lay person; dilettante.

leem, loam, clay; ~ **agtig, (-e),** loamy; ~ **bank,** layer of loam; loam-pit.

leemet'ford(geweer), Lee-Metford (rifle).

leem'grond, loamy soil.

leem'te, (-s), lack, want, defect, deficiency, gap, blank, hiatus, lacuna; *'n* ~ *aanvul,* fill (up) a gap.

leen, (s) (lene), fief; loan; *te* ~ *(lene) GEE,* lend, give the loan of; *in* ~ *HÊ,* have on loan; *te* ~ *VRA,* ask the loan of, borrow; **(w) (ge-),** lend (to); borrow (from); carry (arith.); ~ *AAN iem.* ~ , lend to some=one; *BY (van) iem.* ~ , borrow from someone; *die OOR* ~ *aan,* lend one's ears to; *jou TOT iets* ~ , lend oneself to; ~ **bank,** loan-bank; ~ **besitter,** feu=dal tenant; ~ **boek,** loan register.

le'end, (-e), lying; couchant.

leen: ~ **bevoegdheid,** borrowing powers; ~ **diens,** feu=dal service; ~ **eed,** oath of allegiance; ~ **geld,** bor=rowed money; ~ **goed,** feoff, feudal estate, fief; things lent (borrowed); ~ **grond,** quitrent land; ~ **heer,** feudal lord, feoffer, liege(lord); ~ **man,** vassal, feudal tenant, feudatory, liegeman; ~ **man=skap,** vassalage; ~ **manstrou,** fealty, allegiance; ~ **plig,** fealty, feudal duty, feudality; ~ **reg,** feudal law (right), feudality; ~ **roe'rig, (-e),** feudal; ~ **roe=righeid,** feudality; ~ **spreuk,** motto, device; apho=rism; ~ **stelsel,** feudal system; ~ **tjie-buur:** ~ *tjie=buur speel,* be an inveterate borrower; ~ **vors,** feudal prince; ~ **vrou,** liege lady; ~ **woord,** loan=word.

leep'oog, blear-eye; ..**ogig, (-e),** blear-eyed.

leer¹, (s) leather; *van ANDERMAN se* ~ *breë rieme sny,* cut out large thongs of another man's leather; ~ *OM* ~ , tit for tat.

leer², (s) (lere), ladder; *'n KOUS met 'n* ~ , a stocking with a ladder; *die MAATSKAPLIKE* ~ , the social ladder; *teen die* ~ *OPKLIM,* climb a ladder; **(w) (ge-),** ladder; *my kous het ge* ~ , there is a ladder in my stocking.

leer³, (s) apprenticeship; **(-stellinge),** doctrine, teach=ing, faith, creed; theory; *die* ~ *van AWERY,* the theory of averages; *die CHRISTELIKE* ~ , the Christian doctrine; *in die* ~ *DOEN,* apprentice to; *in die* ~ *GAAN by iem.,* become apprenticed to someone; learn from another; *SUIWER in die* ~ , according to doctrine; orthodox; *in die* ~ *WEES by 'n apteker,* be apprenticed to a chemist; **(w) (ge-),** learn, study; teach, instruct; train; *'n gedig van BUITE* ~ , learn a poem by heart; *vir DOKTER* ~ , study medicine; *EK sal jou* ~ *!,* I'll teach you! (said as threat); *JUFFROU* ~ *die kind lees,* the teacher is teaching the child to read; *iem.* ~ *KEN,* get to know someone; *die KIND* ~ *lees,* the child is learn=ing to read; *'n jong PERD* ~ , train (break in) a young horse; *VER* ~ , get a sound education; *VIR advokaat* ~ , study law.

le'ër¹, (s) (-s), army; host, multitude.

le'ër², (s) (-s), lair, bed.

le'ër³, (w) (ge-), encamp.

lê'er, (-s), layer (hen); register; file; leaguer (for wine); sleeper (railway), girder.

le'ërafdeling, army division, brigade.

leer: ~ **afval,** scrap (waste) leather; ~ **agtig, (-e),** leathery, coriaceous, alutaceous.

leer'baar, (..bare), learnable.

le'ërbagasie, impedimenta, army baggage.

leer'band, (leather) strap; leather binding.

le'ër: ~ **bed,** camp-stretcher; ~ **begroting,** army esti=mates (budget).

leer'bekleding, leather upholstery.

le'ër: ~ **bende,** troop of soldiers; ~ **beperking,** army reduction.

leer'bereider, currier.

le'ërberig, (-te), army bulletin.

leer'bewerker, leather-dresser.

leer: ~ **boek,** textbook; ~ **dery,** learning; ~ **dig, (-te),** didactic poem; ~ **dwang,** compulsory education; ~ **gang,** course of study, curriculum; ~ **geld,** school (tuition) fees; *duur* ~ *geld betaal,* pay heavily for one's experience; ~ **gie'rig, (-e),** eager to learn, stu=dious; ~ **gle'righeid,** studiousness, eagerness to learn.

leer'goed, leather goods.

leer'graag, (..grage), studious.

leer'handel, leather trade.

le'ërhoof, army commander.

leer'huid, corium.

le'ërig, (-e), fairly (rather) empty.

lë'erig, (-e), prone to lie, lazy.

le'ëring, quartering; billet.

leer: ~ **jaar,** year of study; ~ **jare,** apprenticeship; ~ **jonge, (-ns),** apprentice; ~ **jongskap,** indenture=ship.

lêer: ~ **kas, (-te),** filing cabinet; ~ **klerk,** records clerk.

leerklerk, (-e), articled clerk.

leerkleu'rig, (-e), alutaceous.

leer'kontrak, (-te), articles of apprenticeship, indentures.

le'ërkorps, army corps.

leer'krag, (-te), teacher.

leer'lappie, sampler; leather patch; shammy.

le'ërleweransier, army contractor.

leer'ling, (-e), scholar, pupil; alumnus; beginner; pro=bationer; ~ **apteker,** chemist's apprentice; ~ **ekon=sert,** school concert; ~ **klerk,** indentured (articled) clerk; ~ **lisensie,** learner's licence; ~ **mynwerker,** learner miner; ~ **nedersetter,** trainee-settler; ~ **on=derwyser,** pupil-teacher; ~ **padvinder** (wolf-)cub; ~ **prokureur,** articled clerk; ~ **skap,** apprentice=ship; ~ **stelsel,** apprenticeship system; ~ **telegrafis, (-te),** telegraph-learner; ~ **tegnikus,** learner tech=

nician; ~**tolk**, student-interpreter; ~**verpleegster**, probationer (nurse); ~**vlieër**, student-pilot, pupil-pilot; ~**wamaker**, wagon-builder's apprentice.

leer'looier, (-s), tanner, currier; ~**skuip**, layer; ~**y, (-e)**, tannery; tanning.

leer'lus, eagerness to learn, studiousness.

le'ërmag, army.

leer: ~**meester**, teacher, instructor; ~**meisie**, (girl) apprentice.

leer'mes, (-se), skive.

leer'middele, teaching aids, educational appliances, books, school material.

leer'nywerheid, leather industry.

le'ër: ~**order**, army order; ~**owerste**, army commander; ~**plaas**, army-camp.

leer: ~**plan**, curriculum, syllabus, scheme of work; ~**plig**, compulsory education; ~**plig'tig, (-e)**, subject to compulsory education; of school-going age; ~**politoer**, leather polish, dubbin; ~**rede**, sermon; instruction; ~**reël**, canon.

leer'ring, leather washer.

leer'ryk, (-e), instructive.

leer'saam, (..same), instructive, informative; educable; studious, docile; ~**heid**, instructiveness; docility, studiousness.

le'ërskare, host, army.

leer'skilpad, leather-back tortoise.

leer'skool, practice (demonstration) school; *dis 'n GOEIE* ~ *vir hom*, it will make him worldly-wise; it will give him valuable experience; *die* ~ *van die LEWE*, the school of life.

leer: ~**smeer**, leather polish, dubbin; ~**snippers**, leather parings; ~**soort**, kind of leather.

leer'sport, rung of ladder.

le'ërstede, couch, bed.

leer'steek, faggoting, straight faggoting.

leer: ~**stel'lig, (-e)**, dogmatic; doctrinal, doctrinarian; ~**stel'ligheid**, dogmatism; ~**stelling**, dogma; doctrine, tenet; ~**stelsel**, (religious) system; dogma, tenet (of faith).

le'ërsterkte, strength of the army, manpower.

leer: ~**stoel**, chair (at a university), professorship; ~*stoel vir Plantkunde*, chair of Botany; ~**stof**, subject matter of tuition; ~**stuk**, dogma, tenet.

leer'styl, ladder-post.

leer'tjie¹, (-s), small ladder; step-ladder.

leer'tjie², (-s), strip of leather; tongue (of shoe).

leër: ~**tjie, (-s)**, small army; ~**trein**, military train; ~**tros**, army baggage, impedimenta.

leer: ~**tyd**, time of learning; pupilage; apprenticeship; noviciate; ~**uur**, hour for study; ~**vak**, subject (branch) of study.

leer: ~**vet**, dubbin; ~**vis**, garrick *(Lichia amia)*; ~**voorskoot**, leather apron, dickey.

leer'wa = kakebeenwa.

leer: ~**ware**, leather ware (goods); ~**wasser**, ~**waster, (-s)**, leather washer.

leer'werk¹, leatherwork.

leer'werk², studies; things to be learnt.

le'ërwet, military law.

leer'wyse, method of teaching; method of studying.

lê'ery, lying about.

lees¹, (s) (-te), last; shoe-tree; figure, waist; *op die selfde* ~ *SKOEI*, cast in the same mould; *haar SLANKE* ~, her slender form.

lees², (w) (ge-), read; *die BOEK* ~ *moeilik*, it is a difficult book; *iem. se HART* ~, read a person's heart; *die PERD moet net kan* ~ *en skrywe*, all the horse cannot do is read and write.

lees'baar, (..bare), readable, legible; ~**heid**, legibility, readability.

lees: ~**beurt**, turn to read; lay-preacher's service; ~**blindheid**, alexia; ~**boek**, reader, reading-book; ~**bril**, reading-glasses (spectacles); ~**diens**, church service conducted by an elder; ~**drama**, closet play; ~**gedeelte**, lesson; ~**geselskap**, reading-club; ~**graag**, fond of reading; ~**inrigting**, reading-room (at stationer's); public library; ~**kaart**, reading-chart; ~**kamer**, reading-room; ~**klub**, reading-club; ~**kring**, reading-club, reading-circle; ~**kuns**, art of reading; ~**lamp**, reading lamp; ~**lekker**, motto kiss (sweet); ~**les**, reading-lesson; ~**lint**, bookmark; ~**lus**, eagerness to read, love of reading.

lees: ~**metode**, method of reading; ~**oefening**, reading-exercise (practice); ~**onderwys**, teaching of reading; ~**saal**, reading-room; athenaeum; ~**stof**, reading-matter, literature; ~**stuk**, pericope; passage for reading; ~**tafel**, reading-table; ~**teken**, punctuation mark; ~**toon**, tone of reading; ~**trant**, style of reading; ~**tyd**, reading-time; ~**unie**, reading-club; ~**uur**, reading-hour; ~**woede**, rage for reading; ~**wyse**, manner of reading; ~**wyser**, book-mark.

leeu, (-s), lion; *DIE Leeu*, Leo; *so reg in die* ~ *se BEK*, right into the lion's jaws; *soos 'n BRIESENDE* ~, like a raging lion; *hy en die* ~ *was DEURMEKAAR*, he is half seas over; ~**agtig, (-e)**, lion-like, leonine; ~**bekkie**, antirrhinum, snapdragon; ~**eaandeel**, lion's share; ~**ekuil**; lion's den; ~**emoed**, great (lion's) courage; ~**hok**, lion's cage; ~**in, (-ne)**, lioness; ~**jag**, lion-hunt; ~**jagter**, lion-hunter; ~**mannetjie**, male lion.

leeu'rik, (-e), (sky)lark, laverock.

leeu: ~**temmer**, lion-tamer; ~**tier**, liger; ~**tjie, (-s)**, small lion; (lion) cub; ~**vel**, lion's skin; ~**welp**, lion cub; ~**wêreld**, lion country; ~**wyfie**, lioness.

legaal', (legale), legal.

legaat', (legate), legate; legacy; *Pouslike L* ~, Papal Legate.

legalisa'sie, legalization.

legaliseer', (ge-), legalize.

legaliteit', legality.

lega'sie, (-s), legation, embassy; ~**sekretaris**, secretary of the legation.

legata'ris, (-se), legatee.

legateer', (ge-), bequeath.

leg'boor, *see* lêboor.

legeer'¹, (ge-), bequeath.

legeer'², (ge-), alloy; ~**metaal**, alloy metal.

lê' geld, demurrage; dock-dues, pier-dues, pierage.

legenda'ries, (-e), legendary.

legen'de, (-s), legend; ~**boek**, book of legends.

lege'ring, (-s), alloy; ~**staal**, alloy steel.

le'ges, fees (of church).

le'gio, legion; *die foute is* ~, the number of mistakes is legion.

legioen', (-e), legion; ~**soldaat**, legionary.

legislatief', (..tiewe), legislative.

legitiem', (-e), legitimate.

legitima'sie, legitimation; ~**bewys**, identification certificate.

legitimeer', (ge-), legitimate, legitimize, admit to the ministry.

legitimiteit', legitimacy.

leg: ~**kaart**, jigsaw puzzle; ~**sel, (-s)**, eggs laid; ~**werk**, inlaid work.

lê: ~**hen**, laying-hen, layer; ~**hoender**, laying-hen, layer; ~**huis**, laying-house.

lei¹, (s) (-e), slate; hornblende, schist; *met 'n skoon BEGIN*, start with a clean sheet; *'n skoon* ~ *HÊ*, have a clean record.

lei², (w) (ge-), lead, direct, conduct, guide, conduce; captain; pilot; govern; preside (at meeting); train (plants); *dit sal DAARTOE* ~, this will tend to lead to (give rise to); *jou LAAT* ~ *deur*, be guided by; *'n lekker LEWE* ~, lead a pleasant life; *tot NIKS* ~, serve no purpose; lead nowhere; *dit sal tot RUSIE* ~, this will cause dissension; *na die VERDERF* ~, lead to destruction; *iem. VERKEERD* ~, lead someone astray.

lei: ~**aarde**, shale; slate; ~**agtig, (-e)**, slaty, shaly.

lei: ~**baan**, slide-bar; guide; ~**baar, (..bare)**, leadable; ~**balk**, runner, guide; ~**band**, leading-string(s); ~**beurt**, turn to use water (from common furrow); ~**blok**, guide-block shoe; sliding-die; ~**boom**, runner, guide; espalier; ~**bus**, guide-box.

lei'dak, slate roof; *dit loop alles van 'n* ~, everything is going smoothly; ~**pan**, rag.

lei'dam, irrigation dam.

lei'dekker, slater; ~**sbyl**, slate cutter.

lei'dend, (-e), leading; guiding; directive, directorial; deferent.

lei'ding, direction, lead, management; guidance,

leadership; generalship; conduct; duct; runner, guide; conductorship; line, piping, conduit; ~ *GEE*, guide, give guidance; *die* ~ *NEEM*, take the lead; *ONDER* ~ *van*, under leadership of.
lei'draad, guide, clue, lead, guidance.
Leids, (-e), Leyden; ~ *e fles*, Leyden jar.
leids'man, (-ne, leidsliede), leader, guide.
leid'ster[1], (-re), guiding-star, lodestar, cynosure.
leid'ster[2], (-s), female leader.
leids'vrou, conductress.
lei'er, (-s), leader; mastermind, prime mover; protagonist; conductor; head, dux; director; guide; fugleman; chief; *'n gebore* ~, a born leader; ~ **skap**, leadership; hegemony; ~ **skonferensie**, summit conference; conference of leaders.
lei'groef, slate quarry.
lei: ~ **hond**, guide dog; ~ **kanaal**, conduit; irrigation canal; ~ **katrol**, idler pulley.
lei: ~ **kleurig**, (-e), slate-coloured; ~ **klip**, slate.
lei: ~ **pen**, fence-pin; ~ **pengat**, gauging hole; ~ **plaat**, guide-plate; baffle-plate (aero.); ~ **rat**, guide-wheel; ~ **riem**, commanche bridle, leading-rein; dog-lead; leash; ~ **rol**, roller (aero.).
lei'sel, (-s), rein; (mv) driving-reins; *die* ~ *s in HANDE neem*, take over the reins, assume control (the management); ~ *s HOU*, hold the reins; *die PERDE die* ~ *s gee*, give the horses their heads; ~ **houer**, driver.
lei: ~ **spy**, feather; ~ **stang**, tail-rod; guide-rod.
lei'steen, slate; schist.
lel. ~ **tou**, lead; guy rope; ~ **vermoë**, conductivity; ~ **voor**, irrigation furrow; ~ **water**, water for irrigation; ~ **wiel**, idler; ~ **-yster**, slide-bar; guide-rail.
lek[1], (s) (-ke), leak(age); puncture; (w) (ge-), leak, drip (tap).
lek[2], (s) (-ke), lick (for cattle); (w) (ge-), lick (flame, tongue, etc.); fawn on, toady, adulate; beslaver; *iem. skoon* ~, lick someone's shoes.
lek'bak, drip tray, dripping-pan.
le'ke: ~ **broer**, lay brother; ~ **dom**, laity; ~ **prediker**, lay preacher; ~ **publiek**, lay public; ~ **suster**, lay sister.
lek: ~ **hart**, leaking heart; ~ **kan**, drip-can; ~ **ka'sie**, (-s), leak(age); ~ **kend**, (-e), leaking; lambent.
lek'ker[1], (s) (-s), licker; toady, lickspittle.
lek'ker[2], (s) (-s), sweet.
lek'ker[3], (s) pleasure; ~ *is maar 'n vinger lank*, pleasure does not last long; (b) dainty, nice, sweet, palatable, delectable, savoury, delicate, delicious; pleasant; cosy; tipsy; luscious, exquisite; cushy; merry; *'n* ~ *werkie*, a cushy job; (bw) merrily; ~ *KRY*, get a thrill, experience pleasure; *hy KRY* ~, he likes it; *maak soos jy* ~ *KRY*, do as you please; *iem.* ~ *MAAK*, make someone tipsy (jolly); ~ *RUIK*, smell sweet; *die stoele SIT* ~, the chairs are comfortable; *hy VOEL nie* ~ *daaroor nie*, he is not happy about it; *nie* ~ *VOEL nie*, not feel well; ~ *WARM*, comfortably warm; ~ *WEES*, be in one's cups.
lek'kerbek, epicure, sweet-tooth, gourmand; gourmet; free-liver, gastronome, gastronomist; - **kery**, gourmandism; ~ **'kig**, (-e), fond of dainty dishes, epicurean, fastidious, sweet-toothed, gastronomic(al); ~ **kigheid**, fastidiousness; gastronomy.
lek'ker: ~ **breek**, *Ochna pulchra*; ~ **geloof**, religious sect which does not observe strict rules; ~ **goed**, sweets; bon bons, confection(ery), fudge; - **goedmaker**, confectioner; ~ **goedwinkel**, confectionery shop, sweet-shop; ~ **heid**, niceness, deliciousness, toothsomeness; ~ **jeuk**, ~ **krap**, itch, scabies; ~ **kry**, thrill, pleasurable sensation; ~ **lyf**, jolly, merry, mellow, half tipsy; ~ **wees**, be in one's cups; ~ **ny'**, (-e), ~ **ny'tjie**, (-s), titbit, delicacy; sweet, confectionery; ~ **ruikheide**, scented heath; ~ **s**, sweets; dainties; ~ **fabriek**, sweet factory; ~ **te**, enjoyment; ~ **tjie**, (-s), sweet(y); ~ **winkel**, sweet-shop, tuck-shop.
lek'kery[1], fawning, toadying, licking.
lek'kery[2], (-e), leak(ing).
lek: ~ **klep**, leaky valve; drip-valve; ~ **medisyne**, electuary; ~ **plek**, leakage; puncture; fault; (cattle) lick.
lê'kraag, turned-back collar, soft collar.

lek'sel, (-s), lick; ~ **tjie**, (-s), small quantity, tiny bit.
leksikaal', (..**kale**), lexical.
leksikograaf', (..**grawe**), lexicographer, dictionary-maker.
leksikografie', lexicography; dictionary-making (-writing); ..**gra'fies**, (-e), lexicographic(al).
leksikologie', lexicology.
leksikoloog', (..**loë**), lexicologist.
lek'sikon, (-s, ..**sika**), lexicon; dictionary.
lek: ~ **sout**, salt-lick; ~ **steen**, hood-mould; ~ **sug**, salt-sickness.
lek'tor, (-e, -s), lecturer; prelector; ~ **aat'**, (..**rate**), lectureship; readership; ~ **gids**, lecturer-guide; ~ **skap**, lectureship.
lektri'se, (-s), female lecturer.
lektuur', reading matter.
lek: ~ **vas**, (-te), leak-proof; ~ **vry**, (-e), puncture-proof, leak-proof; ~ **water**, leakage water.
lel, (-le), lobe (of the ear); wattle (bird); gill.
le'lie, (-s), lily; ~ **agtig**, (-e), lily-like, liliaceous, iridaceous; ~ **blank**, (-e), lily-white; ~ **-der-da'le**, lily of the valley; ~ **vormig**, (-e), crinoid; ~ **wit** = **lelieblank**.
le'lik, (-e), ugly, plain, unsightly, ill-favoured, deformed; nasty, horrid; bad (habit); elephantine; ~ *BONTSTAAN*, have a hot time; be hard put to it; ~ *SEERKRY*, be hurt badly; *as* ~ *'n SIEKTE was, dan was hy lankal dood*, he is unspeakably ugly; *so* ~ *SOEBAT*, plead for all one is worth; *jou* ~ *VERGIS*, be sorely mistaken; ~ **erd**, (-s), ugly person (sight); ~ **heid**, ugliness, unsightliness; *huil van* ~ **heid**, be grotesquely ugly.
lel: ~ **kraanvoël**, wattled crane; ~ **letjie**, (-s), flap; lobule; ~ **spreeu**, wattled starling.
lem, (s) (-me), blade (of a knife); (w) (ge-), stab.
lê'meel, laying-meal; ~ **korrels**, laying-meal pellets.
lem'metjie[1], (-s), (razor) blade; small blade.
lem'metjie[2], (-s), lime *(Citrus medica)*; ~ **sap**, lime juice.
lem'ming, (-s), lemming.
lemoen', (-e), orange; ~ **bloeisel**, orange-blossom; ~ **bloeiselolie**, neroli; ~ **bloeisels**, white-paper heath; ~ **boom**, orange tree; ~ **boord**, orange orchard; ~ **botter**, orange curd; ~ **duif**, laughing-dove *(Stigmatopelia senegalensis aequatorialis)*; ~ **essens**, orange essence; ~ **geur**, orange flavour; ~ **gras**, scented grass *(Andropogon schoemanthus)*; ~ **hout**, lemonwood, wild lemon *(Xymalos monospora)*; ~ **huisie**, segment, section (of orange); ~ **kleurig**, (-e), orange-coloured; citron; ~ **klimop**, clematis, traveller's-joy; ~ **konfyt**, orange jam; ~ **kwas**, orange squash; ~ **mot**, false codling-moth; ~ **pampoen**, orange squash; ~ **pampoentjie**, gem squash; ~ **pit**, orange-pip; ~ **room**, orange cream; ~ **sap**, orangeade, orange squash, orange juice (crush); ~ **skil**, orange peel; ~ **spanspek**, vine-peach; ~ **stokkie**, (-s), orange(wood) stick; ~ **stroop**, orange syrup; ~ **uitdrukker**, orange squeezer; ~ **vrug**, citrus; ~ **vulsel**, orange filling.
le'mur[1], (-e), lemur, hostile spirit of an unburied corpse.
le'mur[2], (-s), lemur; ~ **aap**, macaco *(Lemur macaco)*.
lem'vormig, (-e), bladed.
len'de, (-ne, -s), loin, sirloin; *die* ~ *ne omgord*, gird one's loins; ~ **breuk**, rupture of the loin(s); ~ **doek**, loin-cloth; ~ **jig**, lumbago; ~ **karmenaadjie**, loin chop; ~ **kleed**, loin-cloth; ~ **lam**, hip-shot; ramshackle, rickety (chair), shaky, tottering; crank(y); decrepit; ~ **pyn**, lumbago; ~ **skyf**, sirloin (porterhouse) steak; ~ **spier**, lumbar muscle; ~ **streek**, lumbar region; ~ **stuk**, sirloin; tenderloin; saddle (of mutton); ~ **werwel**, lumbar vertebra.
le'ner, (-s), lender; borrower; ~ **y**, borrowing; lending.
leng[1], (s) (-e), ling (fish).
leng[2], (s) ropiness (in bread).
leng[3], (w) (ge-), become longer (day).
leng'te, (-s), length; longitude; fly (of flag); *tot in* ~ *van DAE*, for a long time to come; *IN die* ~, lengthwise; *op die regte* ~ *KNIP*, cut to the exact (correct) length; *'n PORTRET in volle* ~, full-length photo; *TOTALE* ~, overall length; *in sy*

VOLLE ~, (at its) full length; ~ **as**, long(itudinal) axis; ~ **balk**, longitudinal girder; ~ **deursnee**, longi= tudinal section; ~ **draad**, warp, lengthwise thread; ~ **duin**, seif, saif; ~ **-eenheid**, unit of length; ~ **graad**, degree of longitude; ~ **groei**, longitudinal growth; ~ **lys**, size-roll (of soldier); ~ **maat**, linear (lineal) measure; linear dimension; ~ **meting**, cal= culation of longitude; ~ **rigting**, linear; ~ **sirkel**, meridian; circle of longitude; ~ **spier**, longitudinal muscle; ~ **spleet**, longitudinal crevasse; ~ **stabili= teit**, longitudinal stability; ~ **teken**, macron; quan= tity-mark; ~ **trilling**, longitudinal vibration; ~ **-uit= setting**, linear expansion; ~ **veer**, axial spring; ~ **verskil**, meridional distance; difference in length; ~ **voet**, linear foot.

le'nig¹, (w) (ge-), alleviate (pain), relieve, allay, as= suage, abate, mitigate, lessen.

le'nig², (b) (-e), supple, pliant, pliable, lithe, agile, lissome, flexible, limber.

le'nig: ~ **er**, (-s), alleviator, reliever, mitigator, as= suager; ~ **heid**, litheness, pliantness, suppleness, lissomeness, flexibility; ~ **ing**, relief, mitigation, alleviation.

le'ning, (-e, -s), loan; *'n* ~ *AANGAAN (sluit)*, con= tract a loan; *'n* ~ *OMSIT*, convert a loan; *OP= VORDERBARE* ~, call-loan.

le'nings: ~ **bank**, credit bank; loan bank; ~ **begroting**, loan-estimates; ~ **bevoegdheid**, borrowing-powers; ~ **fonds**, loans fund; ~ **kommissie**, raising-fee; ~ **plaas**, quitrent farm; loan-farm; ~ **rekening**, loan account.

Leninis'me, Leninism.

le'no, leno, (cotton) gauze.

lens, (-e), lens; eyepiece, glass; ~ **glas**, lenticular glass.

len'sie¹, (-s), lenticule, small lens.

len'sie², (-s), lentil; ~ **so(e)p**, lentil soup; mess of pottage.

lens: ~ **opening**, diaphragm; setting (camera); ~ **pomp**, bilge-pump; ~ **vormig**, (-e), lens-shaped; lenticular, lentoid.

len'te, (-s), spring; prime; ~ **aand**, spring-evening; ~ **agtig**, (-e), springlike, vernal; ~ **blom**, spring flower; ~ **bode**, harbinger of spring; ~ **dag**, spring day; ~ **fees**, spring festival; ~ **klokkie**, harebell; ~ **lied**, spring song; ~ **lug**, spring air; ~ **maand**, spring month; ~ **maneuwers**, spring manoeuvres; ~ **môre**, ~ **more**, spring morning; ~ **nagewening**, vernal equinox; ~ **sang**, spring song; ~ **skool**, re= fresher course; ~ **son**, spring sun(shine); ~ **teken**, vernal sign; ~ **tyd**, springtime; heyday; ~ **weer**, spring weather.

lentisel', (-le), lenticel.

len'to, lento, slowly (music).

Leo'nies, (-e), Leonine, ~ *e vers*, Leonine verse.

le'pel, (-s), spoon, ladle; ~ *in die DAK steek*, give up the ghost; kick the bucket; *met 'n GOUE* ~ *gebore wees*, be born with a silver spoon in one's mouth; *die* ~ *INTRAP*, depress the accelarator; *v.d.* ~ *na die MOND val die pap op die grond*, there is many a slip 'twixt the cup and the lip; *so lank as die* ~ *in die PAPPOT staan*, as long as there is something in the larder; *die* ~ *te vol SKEP*, drink too much; *'n vrou dra meer uit met 'n* ~ *as 'n man inbring met 'n SKE= PEL*, a thriftless wife can be a husband's undoing; *met die* ~ *VOER (ingee)*, spoonfeed; ~ **aar**, (-s), spoonbill; ~ **bak**, spoon-box; ~ **blad**, bowl of spoon; ~ **beitel**, spoon-chisel; ~ **boor**, spoon-bit, drill-bit, shell-gimlet; shell-auger, nose-bit; ~ **eend**, spoonbill duck; ~ **gans**, spoonbill; ~ **hou**, half-vol= ley (tennis); ~ **hout**, ladle-wood *(Hartogia capen= sis)*; ~ **lê**, (-ge-), lie like spoons, lie bodkin; cuddle; ~ **ruimer**, shell-reamer; ~ **sgewys(e)**, by spoonfuls; ~ **steel**, handle of spoon; ~ **tjie**, (-s), small spoon; ~ **vol**, (lepelsvol), spoonful; ~ **vormig**, (-e), spoon-shaped; ~ **vurk**, runcible spoon.

lê'plek, lair, den; place (room) to lie down; bed; cov= ert; haunt; burrow; recess; form (hare); *'n* ~ *êrens maak*, visit someone's house continually.

lep'oog = **leepoog**.

le'pra, leprosy; ~ **lyer**, leper.

lepreus', (-e), leprous.

leproos', (leprose), leper.

lepro'segestig, (-te), leper-hospital (-asylum).

lepro'sis, nailhead rust, leprosis (in citrus).

le'raar, (s) (-s, lerare), minister (of religion), parson; (w) (ge-), minister, preach; teach; ~ **samp**, ~ **skap**, ministership; ministry.

lê'ras, laying-strain (poultry).

le'rend, (-e), didactic, preceptive.

le'ring, (-e), instruction; precept; doctrine; edifi= cation; ~ *e wek, voorbeelde trek*, example is better than precept.

les¹, (s) (-se), lesson, lecture, instruction; ~ *GEE*, give lessons, teach; *iem. die* ~ *LEES*, give someone a talking to; read someone a lecture; ~ *NEEM by*, take lessons with (from); *ONDER die* ~, during the lesson; ~ *OPSÊ*, say one's lesson; be called to account.

les², (w) (ge-), quench, slake, lay.

les³, (b) last; ~ *bes*, last but not least.

Les'biër, (-s), Lesbian.

Les'bies, (-e), Lesbian.

Lesbinis'me, Lesbianism.

le'se-majesté', crimen laesae majestatis, treason.

le'senaar, (-s), lectern.

lesenswaar'dig, (-e), readable, worth reading.

le'ser, (-s), reader, peruser; lecturer; ~ **es'**, (-se), (woman) reader; ~ **skring**, reading public.

les'geld, tuition fee.

le'sing, (-e, -s), lecture, reading; version; prelection; ~ **saal**, lecture hall.

Leso'tho, Lesotho.

les: ~ **rooster**, timetable (school); ~ **senaar**, (-s), desk, reading-desk; ~ **sie**, (-s), (short) lesson.

les'sing, quenching, slaking.

les: ~ **uur**, period in school, lesson-time; ~ **vliegtuig**, trainer.

Let¹, (-te), Lett, Latvian.

let², (ge-), heed, mind; prevent; *ge* ~ *op die FEITE*, bearing in mind the facts; *sonder om te* ~ *op die GEVAAR*, heedless of the danger; *dit* ~ *MY nie*, it does not concern me; it is none of my business; ~ *WEL!* take notice! ~ *op my WOORDE*, mark my words.

letargie', lethargy; **letar'gies**, (-e), lethargic.

Le'the, Lethe.

l''etjie, (-s), small l.

Let'land, Latvia; ~ **s**, (-e), Lettish, Latvian.

Lets, Lettish, Lettic (language).

let'sel, (-s), hurt, damage, injury; lesion; wound; *sonder* ~, unscathed, unhurt.

let'ter, (s) (-s), letter; type; lettering; character; *die* ~ *maak DOOD, maar die gees maak lewend*, the letter killeth, but the spirit giveth life; *'n DOOIE* ~ *bly*, remain a dead letter; *die FRAAIE* ~ *e*, belles lettres; *baie* ~ *s GEËET hê*, be well-lettered; *na die* ~ *en na die GEES*, in letter and in spirit; *in GOUE* ~ *s skryf*, written in letters of gold; *aan die* ~ *HOU*, stick to the letter; *KURSIEWE* ~ *s*, italics; *NA die* ~, to the letter; *in die* ~ *e STUDEER*, study literature; *VET* ~ *s*, bold type; *na die* ~ *van die WET*, accord= ing to the letter of the law; (w) (ge-), mark, letter; ~ **aanbidding**, letter-worship; ~ **bakkie**, type-box; ~ **beeld**, (letter) face; ~ **dief**, plagiarist; pirate; ~ **diefstal**, ~ **diewery**, plagiarism; piracy; cribbing; ~ **diewery pleeg**, plagiarize; ~ **druk**, letterpress; ~ **e**, literature; arts; *FAKULTEIT van* ~ *e (en wys= begeerte)*, faculty of arts (and philosophy); *die SKONE* ~ *e*, belles lettres; ~ **fout**, literal error; ~ **gieter**, type-founder; ~ **gietery**, type-foundry; ~ **greep**, syllable; ~ **greepverdeling**, syllabification; ~ **haak**, composing-stick; ~ **hout**, letter-wood; ~ **ink**, marking-ink; ~ **kas**, letter-stand, type-case, case-rack; ~ **keer**, anagram; palindrome; ~ **kneg**, slave of the letter; literalist; ~ **knegtery**, slavery of the letter; letter-worship; literalism; verbalism; ~ **krans**, garland; ~ **kunde**, literature; *in die* ~ *kunde studeer*, study literature; ~ **kun'dig**, (-e), literary, pertaining to literature; ~ **kun'dige**, (-s), littérateur, man of letters, literator; ~ **kwas**, sign= writer's brush; ~ **lap**, sampler; ~ **liewend**, (-e), liter= ary; ~ **lik**, (-e), literal(ly) to the letter; *hulle is* ~ *lik afgemaai*, they were literally decimated; ~ **likheid**, literalness; ~ **merk**, letter-mark; ~ **metaal**, type-

metal; ~**proef**, proof-sheet; ~**raaisel**, logogriph, letter riddle (puzzle); ~**rak**, case-rack; ~**rym**, alliteration; ~**setter**, compositor; type-setter; ~**settery**, composing; case-room; ~**sifter**, hair-splitter, caviller; ~**skilder**, signwriter; ~**skrif**, writing in characters; ~**slot**, combination lock; puzzle-lock; wheel-lock; letter-lock; ~**snyer**, letter-cutter; ~**soort**, fount, kind of type; ~**spesie**, type-metal; ~**teken**, character; ~**tipe**, type fount; type face; ~**tjie**, (-s), small letter; *'n paar* ~ *tjies skryf*, drop a line; ~**vas**, (-te), word-perfect; letter-bound; ~**verbinding**, combination of letters; ~**voet**, foot of letter; ~**vreter**, studious person, bookworm; ~**werk**, lettering; ~**wisseling**, transposition cypher; metathesis; ~**woord**, grammalogue; ~**yster**, branding-iron.
Let'ties, (-e), Lettish, Latvian.
lê'tyd, laying-period.
leu'en, (-s), lie, falsehood, untruth, fib; *van* ~ *s AANMEKAARGESIT wees*, tell nothing but lies; *'n* ~ *het maar 'n kort BEEN*, the truth will out; *'n* ~ *tjie om BESWIL*, a white lie; *'n* ~ *in NOOD is so goed soos 'n stukkie brood*, a lie may do one grace; a lie may save one's skin; *'n PUBLIEKE* ~, a blatant lie; *al is die* ~ *nog so snel, die WAARHEID agterhaal hom wel*, truth will out; liars have short wings; ~**aar, (-s),** liar; *iem. tot* ~ *aar maak*, give a person the lie; call someone a liar; ~**ag'tig, (-e),** untruthful, false, lying, emendacious; ~**ag'tigheid,** mendacity, lying, falseness, falsity; ~**ares', (-se),** (woman) liar; ~**klikker,** lie-detector; ~**taal,** mendacity, falsehood, untruth, lie; ~**tjie, (-s),** fib.
leukemie', leukaemia; **leuke'mies,** leukaemic.
leukopatie', leucopathy.
leukosiet', (-e), leucocyte, white blood corpuscle.
leukotomie', leucotomy.
leun, (ge-), lean; recline; ~ *OP iem.*, lean on someone; ~ *TEEN 'n muur*, lean against a wall; ~**end, (-e),** leaning, recumbent; ~**ing, (-s),** support, back (of a chair); rail, balustrade (staircase); banister; railing; guard (vehicle); ~**ingstoel,** arm-chair; ~**muur,** parapet; ~**stoel,** easy-chair; ~**stokkie,** mahlstick (of painter); ~**stut,** raker, raking shore; ~**wa,** semi-trailer.
leus, (-e), leu'se, (-s), motto, device, slogan, watchword, catchword; gnome.
leusiet', leucite.
leu'ter, (ge-), prate, drivel; loiter, dawdle; ~**kous,** dawdler; prater.
Leu'ven, Louvain.
Levant', Levant; ~**s', (-e),** ~**yns', (-e),** Levantine.
levia'tan, (-s), leviathan.
Leviet', (-e), Levite, priest; *iem. die L* ~ *e voorlees*, rebuke a person; take someone to task.
leviraat', levirate.
lê'visier, fixed sight, block-sight.
Levi'ties, (-e), Levitical.
Levi'tikus: ~ *voorlees*, read someone a lesson.
levulo'se, fruit-sugar, levulose.
le'we, (s) (-s, -ns), life; living; heart-blood; quick; bustle, liveliness, pep; *'n nuwe* ~ *BEGIN*, start life anew; begin a new life; *met 'n* ~ *BOET*, pay with one's life; *om die* ~ *BRING*, put to death; ~ *in die BROUERY bring*, make things hum; *tussen* ~ *en DOOD*, between life and death; *sy* ~ *hang aan 'n DRAADJIE*, his life hangs by a thread; *jou* ~ *GEE*, give one's life; *die* ~ *GEE aan*, give birth to; *na die* ~ *GESKILDER*, painted from life; *GROOT* ~, live a life of luxury; *geen* ~ *HÊ nie*, lead no life at all; *sy HELE* ~, all his life; *die HIERNAMAALSE* ~, the life hereafter; *so lank daar* ~ *is*, *is daar HOOP*, while there is life there is hope; *aan die* ~ *HOU*, keep alive; *die* ~ *HOU*, keep going; remain alive; *die* ~ *inboet*, pay with one's life; *die* ~ *INSKIET*, lose one's life; *jou* ~ *LAAT*, lay down (lose) one's life; ~ *en LAAT* ~, live and let live; *sy* ~ *LANK*, all his life; *'n lekker* ~ *LEI*, lead a pleasant life; *iem. die* ~ *MOEILIK maak*, make life difficult for someone; *jou* ~ *NEEM*, take one's life; *in die* ~ *ROEP*, establish, set up, found; *nie jou* ~ *SEKER wees nie*, not be sure of one's life; *die* ~ *SKENK aan*, give birth to; *in die* ~ *SNY*, cut to the quick; *sy* ~ *staan op die SPEL*, his life is at stake; *iem. na die* ~ *STAAN*, make an attempt on someone's life; *hoe STAAN die* ~? how is life? *vir iem. die* ~ *SUUR maak*, make life miserable for someone; *jou* ~ *VEIL hê*, be prepared to pay with one's life; *jou* ~ *duur VERKOOP*, set a high price on one's life; **(w) (ge-),** *see* **leef.**
lê'wedstryd, laying-competition (poultry).
le'we: ~**gewend, (-e),** life-giving; ~**loos, (..lose),** lifeless, dead, inanimate.
le'wend, (-e), living; live; ~ *e HAWE*, livestock; *in* ~ *e LYWE*, in the flesh; ~**e, (-s),** live person; *die* ~ *es en die dooies*, the quick and the dead.
le'wendig, (-e), living, live, alive, quick; dapper, racy; buxom, buoyant, lively, vivacious; graphic, vivid (description); crisp, breezy, gay; keen, peppy, animated, spirited, frisky (horse); bright (eyes); busy, brisk (trade); keen (argument); ~ *e BELANG*, vital interest; ~ *belang in 'n saak STEL*, take a lively interest in a matter; ~ **dood**, more dead than alive; ~**heid,** vivacity, esprit, liveliness, gayness, animation, alacrity; buoyancy (of prices); quickness; animal spirits.
le'wens: ~**aand,** evening of life; ~**aar,** life-artery.
le'wensap, vital juice, sap.
le'wens: ~**asem,** breath (of life); ~**baan,** (course of) life; ~**beginsel,** vital principle; ~**behoeftes,** necessities of life, provisions; ~**behoud,** preservation of life; ~**belang,** vital importance; ~**belangrik,** vital, of utmost (crucial) importance; ~**benodigdhede,** necessities of life, provisions; ~**berig,** obituary; biographical sketch; ~**beskouing,** philosophy of life; ~**beskrywer,** biographer; ~**beskrywing,** biography; life(-history); memoirs; ~**bestaan,** livelihood, subsistence; ~**bloed,** life-blood; ~**blyheid,** joy of living, joie de vivre; ~**boek,** book of life; ~**boom,** tree of life; ~**bron,** source of life; life-spring; ~**dae,** days of life; *al my* ~ *dae*, all my born days; ~**dele,** vitals; ~**doel,** purpose of life, aim in life; ~**draad,** thread of life; *iem. se* ~ *draad is geknip*, his candle has been snuffed; ~**drang,** ~**drif,** vital urge; libido; ~**duur,** duration of life; natural life; durability, life (of machinery); ~**duurte,** cost of living.
le'wensee, ocean of life.
le'wens: ~**eliksir,** elixir of life; ~**energie,** physical energy; ~**ervaring,** experience; ~**essens,** essence of life; ~**filosofie,** philosophy of life; ~**geeste,** vital spirits; ~**genietinge,** amenities of life; ~**geluk,** joy of (in) life; ~**genot,** enjoyment of life; ~**gesel,** helpmate; helpmeet, life-partner; ~**geskiedenis,** life-story; ~**getrou, (-e),** true to life; lifelike; ~**gevaar,** danger (peril) of life; *met* ~ *gevaar*, at the risk of one's life; ~**gevaarlik, (-e),** dangerous to life, very dangerous (perilous); ~**gewoontes,** living-habits; ~**groot,** life-size, full-length; as large as life; ~**grootte,** life-size; ~**houding,** attitude towards life; ~**jaar,** year of life; ~**kans,** expectation of life.
le'wensketts, biography.
le'wens: ~**kiem,** germ of life; ~**koste,** cost of living; ~**kostetoelae,** cost of living allowance; ~**krag,** vital power, vitality; life-force; ~**krag'tig, (-e),** energetic; virile; ~**kring,** life-cycle; ~**kuns,** art of living; ~**kwessie,** vital question, matter of vital importance; ~**kyk,** outlook on life; ~**lang, (-e),** ~**lank,** life-long (friendship); perpetual; indeterminate, life (sentence); *for life*; ~ *lange erelid*, honorary life member; ~**las,** burden of life; ~**leer,** biology; philosophy of life; ~**lid,** life member; ~**lig,** light of life; *die* ~ *lig aanskou*, see the light of day, be born; ~**loop,** career, course of life; ~**loos, (..lose),** dead, lifeless, inanimate; breathless; ~**loosheid,** lifelessness; ~**lot,** lot in life, fate; ~**lus,** zest, energy, vivacity; elation; animal spirits; ~**lus'tig, (-e),** vivacious, full of life; ~**lus'tigheid,** vivacity; ~**lyn,** line of life; ~**middele,** foodstuffs, provisions, supplies, victuals; ~**moed,** courage to live; ~**moeg, (..moeë),** weary of life; ~**omstandighede,** circumstances of life; ~**onderhoud,** maintenance; subsistence, sustenance; livelihood, living; ~**ontvlugting,** escapism; ~**onvatbaar, (..bare),** non-viable; ~**oorgang,** change of life, menopause; ~**opvatting,**

view of life; ~**pad**, path of life; ~**peil**, standard of living; ~**redder**, life-saver; ~**reg**, life interest; ~**reis**, life's journey; ~**ruimte**, living-room; ~**taak**, life-work, mission.
le′**wenstandaard**, standard of life.
le′**wens**: ~**teken**, sign of life; ~**terrein**, sphere of life; ~**toestande**, conditions of living.
le′**wenstreep**, line of life.
le′**wenstryd**, struggle of (for) life.
le′**wens**: ~**tyd**, life-span; ~**uur**, hour of life; ~**vatbaar**, (..**bare**), viable, capable of life; feasible; ~**vatbaarheid**, vitality, viability; feasibility; ~**verandering**, change of life; menopause; ~**verhaal**, life-story; ~**versekering**, life insurance; ~**versekeringsmaatskappy**, life-insurance company; ~**versekeringspolis**, insurance policy; ~**versekeringspremie**, premium on a life policy; ~**verwagting**, life expectancy; ~**voorwaarde**, condition of life; vital condition; ~**vorm**, life-form; ~**vraag**, vital question, question of life and death; ~**vreugde**, joy of life; ~**wandel**, conduct in life; ~**warmte**, vital warmth; ~**weg**, path of life; ~**werk**, life-work; ~**wyse**, manner of life, way of living; ~**wysheid**, knowledge of the world.
le′**wentjie**, (-s), little life.
le′**wer**[1], (s) (-s), liver; ′n DROË ~, a dry liver; wat het oor jou ~ GELOOP? what is eating you? sy ~ is NAT, he likes to keep his throat wet; ′n WIT ~ hê, be much widowed.
le′**wer**[2], (w) (ge-), supply, provide, produce, purvey, deliver, do (good work); furnish (proof); BEWYS ~, give proof, prove; SLAG ~, give battle; goeie WERK ~, turn out good work.
le′**weraandoening**, liver complaint.
le′**weraar**[1], (..**are**), hepatic vein.
le′**weraar**[2], (-s), supplier.
le′**werabses**, liver abscess, hepatic ulcer.
leweran′sie, supply, delivery; purveyance; ~**r′**, (-s), furnisher, purveyor, provider, supplier, caterer.
leweransiers′hek, (-ke), **leweransiers′ingang**, (-e), tradesman's entrance.
le′**werbaar**, (..**bare**), (immediately) deliverable.
le′**werik**, (-e) = **leeurik**.
le′**werikie**, (-s) = **leeurik**.
le′**wering**, (-e, -s), delivery, supply; by ~, on delivery.
le′**werings**: ~**kontrak**, delivery-contract; ~**koste**, delivery-charges; ~**termyn**, time of delivery; ~**tyd**, time of (for) delivery; ~**voorwaardes**, terms of delivery.
le′**werkie**, (-s), (sky)lark.
le′**wer**: ~**kleur**, liver-colour; ~**kleurig**, (-e), liver-coloured; hepatic(al); ~**koekie**, liver rissole; ~**kruid**, liverwort; ~**kwaal**, liver-complaint (disease); ~**mos**, liverwort; ~**ontsteking**, inflammation of the liver, hepatitis; ~**oorplanting**, liver transplant; ~**pastei**, liver pie; ~**pil**, liver pill; ~**siekte**, liver disease; rot (sheep); ~**slagaar**, hepatic artery; ~**slak**, liver-fluke; ~**sout**, liver saline, liver-salts; ~**sug′tig**, (-e), liverish; ~**tablette**, liver lozenges; ~**traan**, codliver oil; ~**vlek**, liver-spot; ~**wors**, liver sausage, liver polony.
le′**wetjie** = le′**wentjie**.
le′**wewekkend**, (-e), life-giving, inspiring, animating.
liaan′, (**liane**), liana (liane).
liai′son, (-s), liaison; illicit love-affair.
lias′, (-se), file (for papers); ~**pen**, file-spike; ~**seer′**, (ge-), file; ~**se′ring**, filing; ~**stelsel**, system of filing.
Li′banon, Lebanon.
libel′[1], (-le), libel.
libel[2], (-le), dragonfly.
liberaal′, (..**rale**), liberal; Liberale Party, Liberal Party.
liberalis′, (-te), liberalist; ~**me**, liberalism; ~**ties**, (-e), liberalistic.
liberaliteit′, liberality.
Libe′riër, (s) (-s), Liberian.
Libe′ries, (b) (-e), Liberian.
libertyn′, (-e), libertine; ~**s′**, (-e), libertine.
li′bido, libido.
Li′bië, Libya; ~**r**, (-s), Libyan.
Li′bies, (-e), Libyan.

librettis′, (-te), librettist.
libret′to, (-′s), libretto; ~**skrywer**, librettist.
lid, (**lede**), member, fellow (society); term (ratio) lid (eye); limb (body); ′n SIEKTE onder lede hê, sicken for something; tot in die VIERDE ~, unto the fourth generation; ~ WORD van, become a member of; see **lede**.
liddiet′, lyddite.
lid′doring, corn; ~**agtig**, (-e), corny; ~**kussinkie**, corn-pad; ~**mes**, corn-razor; ~**salf**, corn-cure; ~**skaaf**, corn-plane; ~**snyer**, pedicure; chiropodist; ~**verwyderingsmiddel**, corn-remover, corn-cure.
Li′dië, Lydia (country); ~**r**, (-s), Lydian.
Li′dies, (-e), Lydian.
lid: ~**kerk**, member church; ~**land**, member country.
lid′maat, (**lidmate**), member (of church); parishioner; fellow; ~**skap**, membership; fellowship; ~**skapskaart**, membership card.
lid′staat, member state.
lid′woord, article.
lie, (ge-), tell lies, lie.
lied, (-**ere**), song, hymn, lay, carol, air, aria, descant (poet); ′n ~ AANHEF, break into song; die ~ te HOOG insit, overdo a friendship; **lieder**, (mus.), lieder; die OU ~, the same old story.
lie′der: ~**bundel**, song-book, book of hymns; ~**aand**, sing-song, evening of singing; ~**komponis**, melodist.
lie′derlik, (-e), filthy, dirty, rakish, bawdy, obscene, dissolute; ~**heid**, debauchery, dissoluteness, filth, obsceneness, obscenity.
lie′derwysie, tune (of a song); modern tune (to replace older chorale in D.R. Church hymnal).
lied′jie, (-s), song, ballad, ditty; dis die OU ~, it is the old, old story; ′n ander ~ SING, sing another tune; altyd dieselfde ~ SING, sing the same old song; ~**sanger**, ballad-singer; singer of a tune; ~**sdigter**, ballad-monger.
lief, (s): in ~ en LEED, for better or for worse; come rain come shine; iets maar vir ~ NEEM, put up with a thing; (b) (**liewe**; **liewer**, **-ste**), dear, beloved, amiable, lovely, affectionate, sweet; pretty; die liewe lange DAG, the livelong day; ′n liewe MEISIE, a sweet (charming) girl; (bw) nicely, sweetly; ek sou net so ~, I would as lief (just as soon).
liefda′dig, (-e), charitable, benevolent.
liefda′digheid, charity, benevolence, charitableness.
liefda′digheids: ~**basaar**, charity bazaar; ~**genootskap**, benevolent society; ~**inrigting**, ~**instelling**, charitable institution; ~**konsert**, charity concert; ~**vereniging**, benevolent society; ~**voorstelling**, charity performance.
lief′de, love, affection, charity, affectionateness, heart; ~ is BLIND, love is blind; ′n HUWELIK uit ~, a love-match; KINDERLIKE ~, filial affection; ~ vir die KUNS, love of art; MET ~, with pleasure; ou ~ ROES nie, first love never dies; UIT ~ vir haar, for love of her; van ~ en kou WATER leef, live on love and fresh air; ~**band**, love-tie; ~**blyk**, love-token; ~**brand**, ardour; ~**daad**, act of love (charity); ~**diens**, act of charity; good turn, kind deed; ~**drank**, love-potion, love-philtre; ~**dronk**, intoxicated with love; ~**gawe**, ~**gif**, alms; (mv) charities; pittance; ~**groete**: met innige ~**groete**, with fondest love; ~**knoop**, love-knot; ~**loos**, (..**lose**), loveless, unkind, uncharitable, hard-hearted; ~**loosheid**, lovelessness, uncharitableness; ~**maal**, love-feast, agape; ~**pand**, pledge of love; love-token; child; ~**roes**, transport of love; ~**ryk**, (-e), loving, affectionate, fond, benign(ant); ~**rykheid**, lovingness, affection, benignancy; ~**saak**, love-affair.
lief′des: ~**avontuur**, amour; love-affair; ~**betrekking**, love-affair; ′n ~ betrekking aanknoop, begin a courtship; ~**betuiging**, profession of love; declaration of love; ~**brief**, love-letter; ~**ervaring**, love-experience; ~**geskiedenis**, love-story, love-affair; ~**god**, god of love; Cupid, Eros; ~**naam**: in ~ naam, in heaven's name; ~**pyl**, love-shaft.
lief′desuster, sister of mercy.

lief'des: ~ **verhaal,** love-story; romance; ~ **verklaring,** declaration of love; proposal (of marriage); ~ **ver= lange,** lovelornness; ~ **werk,** labour of love.

lief'deswil: *om* ~, for goodness sake.

lief'de: ~ **taal,** language of love; ~ **vlam,** love-flame; ~ **vol, (-le),** full of loving, loving; ~ **vuur,** fire of love; ~ **werk,** work of charity; labour of love.

lief'hê, (liefgehad), love, care for, be fond of, cherish.

lief'hebbend, (-e), loving, affectionate.

lief'hebber, (s) (-s), lover; amateur, devotee, dabbler, dilettante, enthusiast, fan, fancier; *'n* ~ *wees van lees,* be fond of reading; (w) **(ge-),** do amateur work, dabble in; ~ **y', (-e),** hobby; delettantism, amateurism, fancy; favourite pursuit; ~ **y'konsert,** amateur concert; ~ **y'toneel,** private (amateur) theatricals; amateur theatre.

lief'heid, sweetness; *see* **lief.**

lie'fie, (-s), dear, darling; mistress, paramour; ~ **s,** nicely, sweetly, charmingly.

lief'koos, (ge-), caress, fondle, stroke, cherish, cosset, hug, pet; *my ge* ~ *de boek,* my favourite book.

lief'kosery, liefkosery', caressing, fondling, petting.

lief'kosing, (-e, -s), caress, endearment, dalliance, mothering.

lief'kry, (-ge-), fall in love with, get to like, grow fond of.

lief'lik, (-e), charming, lovely, beautiful, sweet; ~ **heid,** charm, loveliness, beauty.

lief'ling, (-e), darling, pet, favourite; ~ **sbesigheid,** favourite occupation; ~ **sboek,** favourite book; ~ **sdier,** pet (animal); ~ **sdigter,** favourite poet; ~ **shond,** pet dog; ~ **skrywer,** favourite author; ~ **snaam,** pet name; term of endearment; ~ **studie,** favourite study; ~ **svak,** favourite subject; ~ **swerk,** favourite work, hobby.

liefs, preferably, rather; best; *ek sal* ~ *nie gaan nie,* I'd rather not go.

lief'ste, (s) (-s), sweetheart, darling, beloved, dearest; (b) dearest, favourite.

lieftal'lig, (-e), sweet, attractive, amiable, winsome; ~ **heid,** sweetness, attractiveness, loveliness, win= someness.

lieg, (ge-), lie, tell lies, fib; *hy* ~ *of dit GEDRUK staan,* he is an expert liar; *hy* ~ *dat hy homself GLO,* he is an expert liar; *hy* ~ *'n HOU,* he lies like a trooper; *dit* ~ *JY!* that's a lie!; *hy* ~ *soos tien PERDE skop,* he lies like a gasmeter; ~ *dat 'n mens dit met 'n STOK kan voel,* tell lies by the score; ~ **ery,** lying, mendacity.

lie'maak, (-ge-), whet the appetite without satisfying it, tease; tell a dummy; side-step (football); feint; *iem.* ~, delude someone; raise false hopes; ~ **kuier,** a very short visit, apology for a visit.

liep'lapper, (-s), loafer, ne'er-do-well, vagrant; rotter.

Lier¹, Lierre.

lier², (-e), lyre; winch, windlass; lyra (anat.); *jou* ~ *aan die wilger hang,* hang one's harp on the willow; ~ **dig,** lyric (poem); ~ **digter,** lyric poet; ~ **sang,** lyric poem; lyric; ~ **speler,** lyrist; ~ **stang,** lifting-rod; ~ **trommel,** winding-drum; ~ **voël,** lyre-bird; ~ **vormig, (-e),** lyrate.

lies, (-e, -te), groin; flank; ~ **band,** jock-strap; ~ **breuk,** enterocele; inguinal hernia; ~ **ontsteking,** inflammation in the groin; ~ **skyf,** flank steak (beef); ~ **wol,** flankers.

liet'sjie, (-s), litchi.

lieweheers'besie, (-s), ladybird.

lie'weling, (-e), darling, pet, favourite.

lie'werd, (-s), darling, dear.

lie'werlee: *van* ~, little by little, gradually.

lie'wer(s), lie'werste(r), rather, preferably; afore; *ek wil* ~ *hierdie EEN hê,* I would rather have this one; *hy MOET* ~ *gaan werk,* he had better go to work; *OF nog* ~, or better still.

lie'wigheid, sweetness, amenity, amiability.

lig¹, (s) (-te), light; *in heeltemal 'n ANDER* ~, in a totally different light; *iets aan die* ~ *BRING,* reveal something; bring something to light; *daar GAAN nou vir my 'n* ~ *op,* light dawns on me; I begin to see daylight; *in die* ~ *GEE,* make something see the light, publish; *teen die* ~ *HOU,* hold up to the light; *IN die* ~ *van,* in the light of; ~ *te INSTEL,* focus lights (of car); *aan die* ~ *KOM,* come to light; *jou* ~ *onder 'n KORINGMAAT sit,* hide one's light under a bushel; ~ *OPSTEEK (maak),* turn (switch) on the light; strike a light; *die* ~ *van die REDE,* the light of reason; ~ *SIEN,* see the light; *die* ~ *SIEN,* see the light; *jou* ~ *laat SKYN,* let one's light shine; *sonder* ~ *RY,* ride (travel) with= out lights; *in jou eie* ~ *STAAN,* stand in one's own light; *in die* ~ *STEL,* bring to light; ~ *te VERDOF (domp),* dim the lights; ~ *WERP op,* throw light on; (w) **(ge-),** give light; shine, dawn; lighten (clouds); hold the light; ~ *bietjie met die KERS,* please hold the candle; *dit begin te* ~ *in die OOSTE,* the day is dawning in the east; (b, bw) **(-te; -ter, -ste),** light (colour); bright; not dark; blond, fair (hair); *dit word AL* ~, it is beginning to grow light; *dis* ~ *te MAAN,* there is a moon.

lig², (w) (ge-), lift, raise (hat, weight); weigh, heave (anchor); empty, clear (letterbox); claim (certifi= cate); *'n BAL* ~, lift a ball; *iem. van die GROND* ~, lift someone off the ground.

lig³, (b) (-te; -ter, -ste), light (food, sleep, weight); gentle (touch, wind); not strong (drink); slight (wound); mild (tobacco); *'n* ~ *te ETE,* a light meal; collation; (bw) lightly, easily; *te* ~ *oor iets DINK,* underestimate something; *'n saak baie* ~ *OP= NEEM,* take a matter very lightly; *iem. is TE* ~, someone is too weak financially; someone is un= equal to a task; ~ *soos 'n VEER,* as light as a feather; *'n* ~ *te VROU,* a loose woman; ~ *tei WORD,* lose weight.

li'ga, (-s), league.

ligament', (-e), ligament.

li'gawedstryd, league match.

lig: ~ **baak,** ~ **baken,** beacon-light; ~ **beeld,** lantern-slide; photograph; ~ **behandeling,** phototherapy; ~ **besparing,** saving of light; ~ **blond,** fair, blonde, light; ~ **blou,** pale blue; ~ **boei,** light-buoy; ~ **bom,** flare-bomb; ~ **boog,** electric arc; ~ **boogsweising,** arc welding; ~ **breking,** refraction of light, refrin= gency; ~ **bron,** source of light; ~ **bruin,** light brown, hazel; ~ **bundel,** beam of light, pencil of rays; ~ **dag,** daylight; *net voor* ~ *dag,* just before dawn; ~ **deurlatend, (-e),** translucent, diaphanous; ~ **deurlatingsvermoë,** translucency, diaphaneity; ~ **draer,** light bearer; ~ **druk,** blueprint; phototype; photoprint; ~ **drukbeeld,** ~ **drukkuns,** phototype; ~ **drukpapier,** printing-paper (photo); ~ **eenheid,** candle-power; unit of illumination; ~ **effek,** light effect; ~ **eg, (-te),** sunproof, fast (colour); ~ **egt= heid,** fastness (to light); ~ **en-donker,** chiaroscuro; ~ **fakkel,** flare.

lig'gaam, (liggame), body, form, anatomy, carcass, corpus; flesh; entity; solid; liquid; *GELEIDENDE* ~, conductor (of heat); *met* ~ *en SIEL,* body and soul; *VASTE* ~, solid; ~ **'lik, (-e),** bodily, physical, corporal, corporeal; ~ *like straf,* corporal punish= ment; ~ **likheid,** corporality, corporeality; ~ **loos, (..lose),** discarnate; ~ **pie, (-s),** corpuscle; little body.

lig'gaams: ~ **arbeid,** bodily labour; ~ **beweging,** physical exercise; ~ **bou,** build of body, stature, physique, frame; ~ **deel,** limb; ~ **gebrek,** bodily de= fect; ~ **gestel,** constitution; physique, habit; ~ **ge= steldheid,** physical condition; constitution; ~ **gewig,** body-weight; ~ **grootte,** stature; ~ **hitte,** bodily warmth; ~ **hoek,** solid angle; ~ **holte,** body-cavity; ~ **houding,** attitude, posture, carriage; ~ **krag,** bodily (physical) strength; ~ **kultuur,** phys= ical training; ~ **leer,** somatology; ~ **mate,** body measurements; ~ **oefening,** physical training (exer= cise); ~ **oefeningklas,** exercise class, physical train= ing class; ~ **opbou,** body-building; ~ **opvoeding,** physical culture (training); physical education; ~ **poeier,** dusting-powder.

lig'gaam: ~ **straf,** corporal punishment, ~ **streek,** body region; ~ **swakte,** (bodily) debility.

lig'gaams: ~ **wand,** body wall; ~ **warmte,** body heat; ~ **weerstand,** body resistance.

lig: ~ **gas,** coal gas; ~ **gat,** loophole (ship); dream-hole (tower); ~ **geel,** pale yellow, buff, citron.

liggelo'wig, (-e), gullible, easy of belief, credulous, dupable; ~**heid,** credulity, gullibility.
lig'gend, (-e), recumbent, prone, prostrate, lying, decumbent.
lig'geraak, (-te), touchy, testy, sensitive, huffy; quick to take offence, quick of temper; ratty; ~**theid,** touchiness, huffiness, petulancy.
lig'geroer, (-de) emotional, maudlin.
lig: ~**gestalte,** luminous form; ~**gevoelig (-e),** sensitive to light.
lig'gewapen, (-de), lightly-armed.
lig: ~**gewend, (-e),** luminous, illuminative, luminiferous; ~**gewer,** illuminator.
lig'gewig, lightweight; ~**(boks)kampioen,** lightweight boxing champion.
lig'gie, (-s), small light.
lig'gies, lightly, slightly.
lig'ging, (-e, -s), site; position, situation, aspect, decumbence, location, lie (of land); ~**sbepaling,** orientation; ~**skaart,** plan of site; ~**splan,** location plan; ~**swaarde,** site value.
lig: ~**glans,** gleam of light; light (in the eyes); lustre; ~**golf,** light-wave; ~**granaat,** star(shell); ~**groen,** pale green, glaucous; ~**grys,** light grey, griseous.
lighar'tig, (-e), light-hearted; ~**heid,** light-heartedness.
lighoof'dig, (-e), dizzy, light-headed; ~**heid,** dizziness, light-headedness.
lig: ~**installasie,** (electric) light-plant; ~**jaar,** light-year; ~**kant,** bright side; ~**keël,** cone of light; ~**kewer,** glow-worm; ~**kleurig, (-e),** light-coloured; ~**knip,** ~**knop(pie),** electric-light switch; ~**koeël,** fire-ball; Very light; ~**kol,** spot of light; ~**koperdruk,** heliography; ~**korrel,** luminous foresight; ~**krans,** halo, aureole, aureola (round saint's head); corona (round sun); ~**kring,** circle of light, luminous circle, photosphere; ~**kroon,** chandelier; ~**kunde,** photology; ~**leiding,** electric light wiring; ~**leidraad,** flexible thread; ~**letter,** illuminated sign; ~**lila,** lavender.
lig'matroos, ordinary seaman.
lig: ~**meter,** photometer; ~**meting,** photometry.
lig'mis, (-se), libertine, reveller, débauchee, rake; man about town.
lig'mof, light-socket.
ligniet', lignite, brown coal.
lig: ~**paal,** electric standard; ~**pen,** high-light pen, highlighter; ~**pers,** mauve; ~**pistool,** star-pistol; ~**plek,** spot of light; ~**punt,** bright spot, ray of hope; redeeming feature; luminary; plug; ~**reklame,** illuminated sign (advertisement); ~**rooi,** light red, pink, carnation; ~**roos,** pink; ~**sein,** light-signal, luminous signal.
ligsin'nig, (-e), frivolous, thoughtless; flippant; light-minded, harum-scarum; ~**heid,** frivolity, levity, flippancy, frivolousness; lightness; giddiness.
lig: ~**skakelaar,** lighting-switch; ~**skerm,** light-shade, screen; ~**skip,** light-ship; ~**sku (-we),** shy of the light, lucifugous; ~**skuheid,** photophobia; ~**skynsel,** gleam of light; ~**snelheid,** velocity of light; ~**snoer,** flexible thread; ~**sok,** light-socket; ~**spreiding,** diffused lighting.
lig'spoor, (flame-)tracer; ~**buisie,** (flame-)tracer-tube; ~**koeël,** (flame-)tracer-bullet; ~**patroon,** (flame-)tracer-cartridge; ~**sas,** (flame-)tracer-mixture.
lig'steendrukkuns, photolithography.
lig'sterkte, luminosity, intensity of light; ~**meter,** photometer.
lig: ~**stip,** dot (speck) of light; ~**stof,** luminous matter; ~**steuring,** light failure; ~**straal,** ray of light; glimpse, glint; ~**streep,** streak of light; ~**strooiing,** dispersion of light; ~**stroom,** stream of light.
lig'swaargewig, light heavyweight, cruiser weight.
lig'sy, light (bright) side.
lig'tekooi, (-e), prostitute, harlot, light woman, lady of pleasure, baggage, courtesan, drab, light-o'-love.
lig'tekop, blonde.
lig'telaaie: *in* ~, in flames; ablaze.
lig'telik, lightly, easily; ~ *boos,* mildly angered.
lig'tend, (-e), shining, luminous; *'n* ~ *e voorbeeld,* a shining example.

lig'ter, (-s), lifter, hoist, lever; lift (elevator); (ship's) lighter; heaver; hoy; lofter, mashie (golf).
lig'terapie, phototherapeutics.
lig'ter: ~ **geld,** lighterage; ~**hout,** lever, crowbar; ~**ig, (-e),** lightish; ~**skip,** lighter.
ligt'heid, lightness.
lig'ting, (-e, -s), levy, collection (letters); draft (of an army); raising.
lig: ~**toestel,** easing-gear; lighting apparatus; ~**toets,** light test; ~**uitstraling,** emission of light.
Ligu'rië, Liguria; ~**r, (-s),** Ligurian.
Ligu'ries, (-e), Ligurian.
ligus'ter, (-s), privet.
ligvaar'dig, (-e), heedless, reckless, rash; ~**heid,** thoughtlessness, heedlessness.
lig: ~**verf,** luminous paint; ~**visier,** luminous backsight; ~**voetig, (-e),** light of foot; ~**voet(s),** nimble-footed; ~**voorsiening,** supply of light; ~**vos,** light chestnut; ~**weerkaatsing,** reflection of light; ~**weg,** lightly; ~**werper,** flashlight.
likeur', (-e, -s), liqueur; cordial; ~**brandewyn,** liqueur brandy; ~**glas,** liqueur-glass; ~**keldertjie,** cellaret; ~**sjokolade,** liqueur chocolates; ~**stelletjie,** liqueur frame, liqueur stand; ~**stokery,** liqueur distillery.
likiditeit', liquidity.
likied', (b) (-e), liquid (assets).
lik'kebaard, lik'kebroer, belly-god, gastronome.
likkewaan', (..wane), iguana, leguan; ~ *staan,* go a-wooing.
likopo'dium, lycopodium.
liksens', (-e), licence; *see* **lisensie.**
likwida'sie, winding-up, liquidation; ~**bevel,** winding-up order, liquidation order; ~**koste,** liquidation costs; ~**rekening,** liquidation account; ~**verkoping,** liquidation sale.
likwidateur', (-e, -s), liquidator; ~**s'rekening,** liquidator's account.
likwideer', (ge-), liquidate; wind up; put out of the way; ~**der, (-s),** liquidator.
likwiditeit', liquidity.
likwied', (b) (-e), liquid (assets).
li'la, lilac, mauve.
li lange'ni, li langeni (pl. **emalangeni,** Swaziland note equal to one rand).
Lil'liputter, (-s), Lilliputian; ~**ig, (-e),** Lilliputian.
lim'bus, limbo.
lim'eriek, (-s), limerick.
limf, lymph; ~**a'ties, (-e),** lymphatic; ~**klier,** lymph gland; ~**sel, (-le),** lymphocyte; ~**stelsel,** lymphatic system; ~**vat,** lymphatic (vessel); ~**vog,** chyle; ~**weefsel,** lymphoid tissue.
limiet', (-e), limit; ~**prys,** reserve price.
limita'sie, (-s), limitation.
limitatief', (..tiewe), limitative.
limiteer', (ge-), limit.
limona'de, lemonade.
limousi'ne, (-s), limousine.
lin'de, lime-tree, linden (tree); ~**bas,** linden bark; ~**blaar,** lime-leaf, linden-leaf; ~**boom** = **linde;** ~**hout,** lime-wood; ~**laan,** avenue of lime-trees.
lineêr, (-e), linear.
linguis', (-te), linguist; ~**tiek',** linguistics; ~**ties (-e),** linguistic.
liniaal', (liniale), ruler.
liniatuur', form, manner of ruling; ruling.
li'nie, (-s), line (of ships); fighting-line; equator; *oor die HELE* ~, all along the line; *die* ~ *PASSEER,* cross the line; *erfgename in manlike, REGTE, opgaande* ~, heirs in the male, direct, ascending line.
linieer', (ge-), rule (lines); ~**masjien,** machine-ruler, ruling-machine.
linië'ring, lineation, ruling.
li'nie: ~**kruiser,** (line-of-)battle cruiser; ~**regiment,** battle-regiment; ~**skip,** line-of-battle ship; ~**soldaat,** liner, linesman; ~**troepe,** (line-of-)battle troops.
liniment', (-e), liniment, ointment.
lin'ker, left (arm); near (horse); ~**agterbeen,** left hind-leg; ~**arm,** left arm; ~**been,** left leg; ~**bladsy,** left-hand page, verso; ~**bors,** left breast; ~**haakhou,** left hook; ~**hak,** left heel.

lin'kerhand, left-hand; bridle-hand; *die ~ moet nie weet wat die REGTERHAND doen nie*, let not your left hand know what your right hand doeth; *met die ~ TROU*, marry with the left hand (morganatically); **~s, (-e)**, left, on the left; **~speler**, left-hand player; southpaw.

lin'ker: **~hartklep**, mitral valve; **~hou**, lefthander; left; **~kant, (-se, -ste)**, near-side, left side; **~oog**, left eye; **~oor**, left ear; **~skakel**, left half-back (soccer); **~skouer**, left shoulder; **~stuur**, left-hand drive, left-drive wheel; **~sy**, left side, onside; nearside (oxen); **~vleuel**, left wing; **~voet**, left foot; **~wang**, left cheek; **~winkbrou**, left eyebrow.

links, left-handed; to (on) the left; gauche; *~af*, to the left; *~e DRAAD*, left-hand thread; *iem. ~ laat LÊ*, give someone the cold shoulder; *NA ~*, to the left, leftward(s); *~ OM*, round to the left; *~e PARTY*, left party; *~ en REGS*, left and right; *~ SWENK!* left wheel! *nie ~ WEES nie*, act smartly; make no further ado; **~agter**, left hind; **~draai**, left turn; **~draaiend, (-e)**, rotating towards the left; **L~e (-s)**, supporter of the Left; **~effek**, left side (billiards); **~gesind, (-e)**, leftist, leftish; **~handig, (-e)**, left-handed; **~handigheid**, left-handedness, awkwardness; **~voor**, left front.

lin'ne, linen, holland; cloth (binding); *gekeperde ~*, twill; **~band**, cloth-binding; **~fabriek**, linen factory; **~goed**, linen; **~handel**, linen trade; **~handelaar**, linen-draper; **~juffrou**, linen-keeper; **~kamer**, linen closet; **~kas, (-te)**, linen press; **~koper**, linen-draper; **~lae**, canvas layers; **~mandjie**, (soiled-) linen basket; **~omslag**, cloth boards; **~pers**, linen press; **~wewer**, linen-weaver; **~winkel**, linen-draper's shop; **~wol**, linsey-woolsey.

lino'leum, (-s), linoleum; **~druk**, lino-block print; **~patroon**, linocut.

li'notipe, linotype.

lint, (-e), ribbon, riband (for medal); tape; cordon; **~ag'tig, (-e)**, ribbon-like; **~bebouing**, ribbon (string) development (building); **~belegsel**, ribbon facing; **~blom**, ray floret; **~buisie**, ribbon tube (pipe); **~doos**, bandbox; **~draad**, ribbon wire; **~gras**, ribbon grass; **~jie, (-s)**, ribbon; order of knighthood; *'n ~jie KRY*, obtain a ribbon of honour; **~saag**, belt-saw, band-saw; **~vis**, bandfish; ribbon-fish; **~vormig, (-e)**, ribbon-like; **~werker**, **~wewer**, ribbon-weaver; **~wurm**, tapeworm, taenia, cestoid; **~wurmkop**, scolex.

lip, (-pe), lip; brow (of mine); clip (horseshoe); *sy ~ pe AFLEK*, lick his lips; *op ALMAL se ~ pe*, on everybody's lips; *tussen ~ en BEKER lê 'n groot onseker*, there's many a slip 'twixt the cup and the lip; *aan sy ~ (-e) BRING*, raise to his lips; *op die ~ pe BYT*, bite one's lips; *iem het nog niks oor sy ~ pe GEHAD nie*, nothing has passed his lips; *sy ~ HANG*, he is down-hearted; he is crestfallen; *aan iem. se ~ pe HANG*, hang on someone's lips; *dit sal nooit weer oor my ~ pe KOM nie*, I'll never breathe a word about it; *op die ~ pe LÊ*, have on the tip of one's tongue; *jy LEK verniet jou ~ pe af*, you needn't lick your lips; *hy TRAP sy ~ pe vas*, he is hanging the lip; **~aanbidding**, lip-homage (worship); **~blommig, (-e)**, labiate; **~boor**, nose bit; **~kas**, lip-box (mine); **~las, (-se)**, trap-cut; **~lesery**, lip-reading; speech-reading; **~letter**, labial (letter); **~loos, (..lose)**, achilous; lipless; **~pediens**, lip-homage, lip-service; **~petaal**, lip-language; idle words; *dis alles net ~ petaal*, it's nothing but talk; **~salf**, lip salve; rose liniment; **~stiffie**, lipstick; **~tandletter**, labio-dental; **~versiering**, labret; **~vis**, wrasse; **~vormig, (-e)**, lip-shaped, labial, labiate.

Lippizza'ner, Lippizzaner (breed of white horses from Lippiza near Trieste).

li'ra, li're, (-s), lira.

liriek', lyric poetry, lyrics.

li'ries, (-e), lyric(al).

li'rikus, (..rici, -se), lyric poet, lyricist.

liris'me, lyricism.

lis¹, (-se), noose, loop; frog (on uniform); *see* **lus**.

lis², (-te), trick, device, stratagem, ruse, art, contrivance, fraud, wile, guile, cunning, artifice; **~gebruik**, use guile.

lis'blom, iris.

lisensiaat', (..siate), licenciate.

lisen'sie, (-s), licence; *in ~ vervaardig*, manufacture under licence; **~bewys**, clearance certificate.

lisensieer', (ge-), license.

lisen'sie: **~geld**, licence fee; **~hof**, licensing court; **~houer**, licensee; licence-holder; **~owerheid**, licensing authority; **~raad**, licensing board; **~raampie**, licence-holder; **~verlener**; licenser.

lis'hanger, straphanger.

lis'pel, (ge-), murmur, lisp.

Lis'sabon, Lisbon; **~ner, (-s)**, Lisabonian.

lis'sie, (-s), loop; bow; bight, hitch, noose.

lis'tig, (-e), cunning, artful, wily, subtle; pawky, guileful; **~heid**, cunning, subtlety, slyness, artfulness, craftiness; **~lik**, cunningly; *see* **listig**.

lit, (-te), joint, articulation; internode; *jou uit ~ LAG*, split one's sides (with laughter); *~ te LOSMAAK*, limber up; do physical jerks; *jou uit ~ SKRIK*, have the fright of one's life; *UIT ~*, out of joint.

litanie', (-ë), litany.

Litau'e, Lithuania; **~r, (-s)**, Lithuanian.

Litaus', (s) Lithuanic; (b) (-e), Lithuanian.

li'ter, (-s), litre; **~bottel**, litre bottle.

litera'tor, (-e, -s), literator, man of letters.

literatuur', (..ture), literature; **~geskiedenis**, history of literature; **~lys**, bibliography; **~oorsig**, review of literature.

literêr', (-e), literary.

li'tium, lithium.

lit'jie, (-s), small joint.

lit'jies: **~gras**, variety of couch grass; **~kaktus**, jointed cactus; **~kweek**, coarse quick (grass).

litograaf', (..grawe), lithographer; **..grafeer', (ge-)**, lithograph.

litografie', lithography; ..gra'fies, (-e), lithographic.

litoli'se, litholysis.

litologie', lithology; ..logies, (-e), lithological.

li'tosfeer, lithosphere.

litoskoop', (..skope), lithoscope.

lito'tes, litotes.

litotomie', lithotomy.

lit'roos, Christmas cactus.

lit'teken, scar, cicatrice, ciccatrix; mark; **~weefsel**, scar tissue.

lit'terig, (-e), nodular, nodiform, nodose.

littoraal', (..rale), littoral.

liturg', (-e), liturgist.

liturgie', (-ë), liturgy; **litur'gies, (-e)**, liturgical.

Liv'ius, Livy.

Livor'no, Leghorn.

livrei', (-e), livery; **~baadjie**, livery coat; **~bediende**, livery servant, liveryman; **~kneg**, livery servant, page, lackey, buttons.

LO, physical training; exercise; **~-saal**, exercise hall.

lob, (-be), lobe.

lob'bes, (Ndl.), (-e), huge (hulking) fellow.

lob'big, (-e), lobate; parted.

lobe'lia, (-s), lobelia.

lobo'la, (-s), lobola.

lobotomie', lobotomy.

lob'vormig, (-e), lobate, lobular.

lo'ding, (-s), sounding.

loe'der, (-s), mean (base) person; whore, harlot.

loef, luff, windward (weather) side; *iem. die ~ afsteek*, take the wind out of someone's sails; **~anker**, windward-side (weather-side) anchor; **~balk**, outrigger; **~kant**, luff; **~sy**, windward side; **~waarts**, to windward.

loei, (ge-), low, bellow, moo; roar (wind).

lo'ën, (ge-), deny, disaffirm; **~aar, (-s)**, denier, gainsayer; **~baar, (..bare)**, deniable; **~ing**, denial, disavowal, disaffirmation.

lo'ënstraf, (ge-), belie, disprove, give the lie to (statement); falsify.

loep, (-e), magnifying glass; *iets onder die ~ neem*, scrutinize carefully.

loer: *op die ~ lê*, lie in wait; **(ge-)**, peep, pry, spy, watch, lurk, peek, peer; prey; *wie ~, kry niks*, no

peeping! ~**der**, (-s), lurker, spy, Peeping Tom, peeper; ~**gat**, spy-hole, peep-hole.
loe'rie, (-s), lourie.
loer: ~**koop**, window-shopping; ~**plek**, lurking-hole; ~**skildwag**, observation sentry; ~**stelling**, observation post; watching position; ~**venstertjie**, view-finder (of camera); peephole.
loe'sing, (-s), thrashing, hiding, caning, beating, flogging, spanking, drubbing, walloping; *iem. 'n afgedankste ~ gee,* give someone a severe thrashing.
lof¹, (lowwe), foliage, tops, leaves, leafage.
lof², praise, eulogy, commendation, laudation; *ALLE ~ kom hom toe vir,* all praise to him for; *sy EIE ~ verkondig,* sing his own praises; *vol ~ PRAAT oor,* speak highly of; *met ~ SLAAG,* pass with honours; *eie ~ STINK,* self-praise is no recommendation; *iem. groot ~ TOESWAAI,* praise someone very highly; *iem. se ~ VERKONDIG,* sing the praises of; ~**basuin**, trumpet of praise; *die ~ basuin blaas,* sound the praises of; ~**dig**, (-te), panegyric; ~**digter**, panegyrist; ~**gesang**, song (hymn) of praise; ~**lied**, hymn of praise, paean; ~**lik**, (-e), praiseworthy, commendable; ~**likheid**, praiseworthiness; ~**psalm**, canticle, hymn of praise; ~**rede**, panegyric, eulogy, encomium; ~**redenaar**, panegyrist, eulogist, encomiast; ~**sang**, song of praise, ode; hymn of thanksgiving, canticle; hosanna; doxology; alleluia; carol; anthem; gloria; ~**sing**, (-ge-), praise, laud, extol; ~**spraak**, praise, eulogy, laudation; encomium; ~**trompet**, trumpet of praise; *die ~ trompet steek,* sound the praises of; ~**tuiter**, (-s), panegyrist; ~**tuiting**, (-e, -s), praise, commendation; ~**uiting**, (-e, -s), praise; ~**verkondiging**, blazonment, blazoning; ~**waar'dig**, (-e), praiseworthy, laudable; ~**waar'digheid**, praiseworthiness; ~**werk**, fretwork; leafage.
log¹, (s) (-ge), log (ship).
log², (b) (-ge), unwieldy, clumsy, cumbersome, cumbrous.
lo'ganbessie, loganberry.
logarit'me, (-s), logarithm; ~**tafel**, logarithmic table.
logarit'mies, (-e), logarithmic.
log'boek, log-book.
lo'ge, (-s), box, (in a theatre), loge.
log'ger, (-s), lugger; ~**seil**, lug.
log'gia, (-s), loggia, balcony.
log'heid, unwieldiness, heaviness, cumbersomeness.
lo'gies, (-e), logical, dialectic; discursive.
lo'gika, logic, dialectics.
lo'gikus, (..ci, -se), logician, dialectitian.
logistiek', logistics.
logis'ties, (-e), logistical.
log'lyn, log-line.
logograaf', (..grawe), logographer.
logogram', (-me), logogram.
logogrief', (..griewe), logogriph.
logopedie', **logope'dika**, logopedics.
lojaal', (lojale), loyal.
lojalis', (-te), loyalist; ~**me**, loyalism.
lojaliteit', loyalty.
lok¹, (s) (-ke), curl, lock.
lok², (w) (ge-), decoy, entice, (al)lure; *klante ~,* tout.
lokaal', (lokale), hall, room; (b) **(lokale)**, local.
lok'aas, (lokase), bait, allurement, decoy, gudgeon, lure.
lokalisa'sie, localization.
lokaliseer', (ge-), localize.
lokaliteit', (-e), locality.
loka'sie¹, (-s), location; *hy het by die ~ grootgeword,* he has grown up in a pigsty.
lok'asie², (-s), small bait.
lokatief', (..tiewe), locative.
lok: ~**dans**, strip-tease; ~**duif**, stool-pigeon, call-pigeon; ~**eend**, decoy-duck.
loket', (-te), ticket-window, cash-aperture; box-office; pay-box; pigeon-hole; ~**kluis**, safe deposit; ~**treffer**, box-office hit.
lok: ~**fluitjie**, call; soft whistle; ~**gif**, poison-bait; ~**kertjie**, (-s), decoy; enticing morsel.
lok'kig, (-e), curly.
lok'middel, bait, temptation, lure, allurement, enticement; decoy.

lo'ko, (-'s), loco; ~**kraan**, jenny; ~**mobiel'**, (-e), road locomotive.
lokomotief', (..tiewe), locomotive, railway engine; ~**afdeling**, loco(motive) department; ~**loods**, loco shed; ~**personeel**, engine-men.
lokomoto'ries, (-e), locomotor; ~*e ataksie,* locomotor ataxia.
lok: ~**prent**, trailer (bioscope); ~**roep**, lure, siren-call.
loksodroom', (..drome), rhumb-line (aero.).
lok'stem, enticing (siren) voice, call.
loku'sie, (-s), locution.
lok: ~**val**, trap; ~**valstelsel**, trapping-system; ~**vink**, decoy, trap (I.D.B.), nark (slang); ~**voël**, decoy-bird, decoy, call-bird; trap, bonnet.
lol, (w) (ge-), bother, trouble, nag, carp; ~**ler**, (-s), nagger, bore; ~**lerig**, (-e), troublesome, annoying, fussy; ~**lery**, nagging, teasing, botheration; ~**pot**, troublesome person, nuisance, bore, meddler.
Lombar'diër, Lombard.
Lombar'dies, (-e), Lombard.
Lombardy'e, Lombardy.
lo'merig, (-e), sleepy, drowsy, dozy, heavy with sleep, languid; ~**heid**, languor, sleepiness, drowsiness.
lom'mer, shade, foliage; ~**agtig**, (-e), shady.
lom'merd, (-s), pawnshop, dolly-shop.
lom'merryk, (-e), shady.
lomp, (w) (ge-): *jou nie laat ~ nie,* not to let oneself be taken in.
lomp, (b) (|-e|; -er, -ste), clumsy, awkward, hulking, cumbersome, elephantine, clownish, maladroit, boorish, butter-fingered, bearish, discourteous, coarse, churlish, gauche, gawky, heavy(-footed); gross.
lom'pe, rags; *in ~ gekleed wees,* dressed in rags.
lomp'erd, (-s), clumsy person, boor, hind, gawk, blunderer, bumpkin.
lom'pewol, shoddy (wool).
lomp'heid, clumsiness, maladresse, maladroitness, burliness, awkwardness, cumbersomeness, coarseness, churlishness, gaucherie.
Lon'den, London; ~**aar**, (-s, -are), Londoner; ~**s**, (-e), London.
lo'nend, (-e), paying, rewarding, remunerative, profitable; *'n bedryf ~ maak,* make a business pay; ~**heidsondersoek**, feasibility study.
long, (-e), lung; ~**aandoening**, affection of the lungs; ~**aar**, pulmonary vein; ~**bloeding**, haemorrhage of the lungs; ~**kanker**, cancer of the lung; ~**kruid**, lungwort; ~**kwaal**, pulmonary disease; ~**lyer**, consumptive, pulmonic; ~**middel**, pulmonic; ~**ontsteking**, inflammation of the lungs, pulmonary inflammation, pneumonia; *dubbele ~ ontsteking,* double pneumonia; ~**pes**, pneumonic plague, lung plague; ~**pyp**, windpipe, bronchium, bronchus; ~**pypontsteking**, bronchitis; ~**sakkie**, infundibulum; ~**siekte**, lung sickness; pulmonary disease; contagious bovine pleuro-pneumonia; ~**slagaar**, pulmonary artery; ~**tering**, pulmonary consumption, phthisis; ~**vis**, lungfish.
long'vlies, pleura; ~**ontsteking**, pleurisy.
long'wurm, lungworm; ~**siekte**, hoose, husk.
lonk, (s) (-e), wink, leer, glad eye, blink; (w) (ge-), ogle, cast side-glances at; blink; make eyes at, wink, leer.
lons, (ge-), lunge; ~**riem**, lunge; ~**teul**, lunging-rein.
lont, (-e), fuse, igniter; ~ *RUIK,* smell a rat; *'n ~ STEL,* time a fuse; ~**aansteker**, fuse-lighter; ~**dop**, fuse-head; ~**stok**, linstock; ~**tang**, fuse-pliers.
lood, (s) (-de), lead; plumb, plummet; sinker; *met ~ in sy SKOENE,* leaden-footed; *onder die ~ STEEK,* fire (shoot) at; *UIT die ~,* out of plumb; *dit is ~ om ou YSTER,* six of one and half a dozen of the other; (w) (ge-), sound; lead (panes); shoot, pepper; *mekaar ~,* shoot at each other; (bw): *dit GAAN ~,* things are grim; *dit ~ KRY,* have a gruelling time; ~**aanslag**, lead-fouling; ~**aar**, lead vein; ~**agtig**, (-e), lead-like; plumbeous; ~**asetaat**, lead acetate; ~**asyn**, basic lead acetate; ~**blomme**, flowers of lead; ~**blou**, livid; lead-blue; ~**boom**, arbor saturn; ~**erts**, galena; lead-glance; lead-ore; ~**foelie**,

loods / **lopend**

lead-foil; ~**geel**, lead-ochre, massicot; ~**gieter**, plumber; ~**gieterswerk**, plumbing; ~**gietery**, plumbery; plumbing; ~**gif**, litharge, ~**glans**, galena; silver leaf *(Stereum purpureum)*; lead-glance: blue lead; ~**glasuur**, lead glaze; ~**glit**, litharge; ~**grys**, lead-grey; leaden; ~**houdend** (-e), plumbic; ~**hout**, leadwood; ~**jie**, (-s), small lump of lead; plumb-bob; *die* ~*jie LÊ*, be the least; *die laaste* ~*jies weeg die SWAARSTE*, it is the last straw that breaks the camel's back; ~**kleur**, lead-colour; lividity; ~**kleurig**, (-e), lead-coloured; ~**koeël**, lead bullet; ~**koliek**, lead colic; ~**lat**, rifle; ~**lepel**, lead ladle; ~**lyn**, offset (trigon.); lead-line, perpendicular (line); ~**makerswerk**, lead-work; ~**menie**, red lead; ~**myn**, lead mine; ~**puntkoeël**, soft-nose bullet; ~**pyp**, lead pipe; ~**reg**, (-te), perpendicular, plumb, vertical, sheer; ~**regtheid**, erectness, perpendicularity.
loods¹, (s) (-e), shed; hangar.
loods², (s) (-e), pilot (of ship); (w) (ge-), pilot; steer, direct; *'n mosie deur 'n kongres* ~, pilot a measure through a congress; ~**ballon**, pilot balloon; ~**boot**, pilot boat; ~**diens**, pilotage.
lood'sekering, lead fuse.
loods: ~**geld**, pilotage; hangar fee; ~**kaart**, pilot chart; ~**kotter**, pilot cutter; ~**kunde**, pilotage; ~**man**, sucker-fish *(Naucrates ductor)*.
lood'smeltery, lead-works.
loods'sein, pilot signal.
lood: ~**spons**, spongy lead; ~**suiker**, sugar of lead, plumbic acetate; ~**sulfaat**, lead sulphate; ~**suur**, plumbic acid.
loods: ~**vis**, pilot-fish; ~**vlag**, pilot flag (jack).
lood'swaar, leaden, as heavy as lead.
loods: ~**werktuigkundige**, hangar mechanic; ~**wese**, pilotage.
lood: ~**verbinding**, lead compound; ~**verf**, lead-coloured paint; ~**vergiftiging**, painter's colic, saturnism, lead-poisoning, plumbism; ~**verlamming**, lead-palsy; ~**ware**, ~**werk**, leading; ~**wit**, white lead, flake white; ceruse.
loof¹, (s) foliage, leaves, leafage, greenery.
loof², (w) (ge-), praise, extol, eulogize, speak highly of, glorify, applaud; bless.
loof: ~**boom**, leaf-tree, hardwood tree; ~**houtsoorte**, hardwoods.
Loofhut'tefees, Feast of the Tabernacles.
loof: ~**plant**, thallophyte; ~**ryk**, (-e), leafy; ~**werk**, festoon; tracery; leaf-work, garland.
loog, (s) lye, buck, lixivium, bate; (w) (ge-), bate; steep in lye; ~**agtig**, (-e), alkaline; lixivial; ~**as**, buck ashes; kelp; ~**bak**, bucking-tub; ~**bos**, lye bush *(Mesembryanthemum micranthum)*; ~**kruid**, glasswort; ~**kuip**, bucking-tub, bark-pit, steeper, lye-tub; ~**sout**, alkaline salt, alkali; natron; ~**vat**, leach (tub); lye-tub; ~**water**, lye, buck, lixivium.
looi, (ge-), tan; beat; hide; curry (with whip); thrash; pepper; ~**bas**, tanning-bark; wattle-bark; ~**er**, (-s), tanner; -**ery**, (-e), tannery; tanner's trade; tanning; tan-works; tan-yard; alutation; ~**kuip**, tan vat (pit); bark-pit; *'n* ~ *kuip van sy kies maak*, chew (tobacco); ~**mes**, grainer; ~**stof**, tannin; ~**suur**, tannic acid.
loom, (lome; lomer, -ste), heavy, languid, slow, dull, drowsy; ~**heid**, heaviness, slowness, drowsiness, languor.
loon, (s) (lone), reward; pay, wages, emolument, hire; payment; *met BEHOUD van* ~, on full pay; *die* ~ *van die SONDE is die dood*, the wages of sin is death; *'n karige* ~ *TREK*, earn a scanty wage; *hy kry sy VERDIENDE* ~, it serves him right; ~ *na WERK*, one is rewarded according to one's deserts; (w) (ge-), reward, pay; *dit sal die moeite* ~, it will repay the trouble; it will be worth while; ~**aksie**, agitation for higher wages; ~**arbeider**, wage-earner; ~**bederwer**, blackleg; ~**beslag**, garnishment; ~*beslag neem teen*, garnishee; ~**beslaglegger**, garnisher; ~**eis**, demand for (higher) wages; ~**geskil**, wage dispute; ~**kaart**, clock card; ~**klerk**, pay clerk; ~**lys**, paysheet; ~**ooreenkoms**, wage agreement; L~**raad**, Wage Board; ~**reëling**, regulation of wages; ~**skaal**, scale of wages; ~**slaaf**, wage

slave, hack; ~**staat**, pay-list, pay-sheet; ~**staking**, wage-strike; ~**standaard**, wage-rate; ~**stelsel**, wages system; ~**stryd**, wage-war; ~**s'verhoging**, increase of wages; ~**s'vermindering**, drop in (reduction of) wages; ~**tjie**, (-s), small wage; ~**trekkend**, (-e), wage-earning, paid; ~**trekker**, wage-earner; hireling; ~**vasstelling**, wage determination; ~**vrag**, pay-load; L~**wet**, Wage Act.
loop, (s) (**lope**), course, march, run; current, stream, watercourse; barrel (gun); walk, gait; turn, trend, currency, flow, line (of thought); *in die* ~ *van die DAG*, in the course of the day; *op die* ~ *GAAN*, run for it, run away; *op* ~ *GAAN*, bolt (horse); take to one's heels; *aan die* ~ *HOU*, keep going; *in die* ~ *van die JAAR*, during the course of the year; *'n MINUUT se* ~, a minute's walk; *'n ander* ~ *NEEM*, take a different turn; *die* ~ *NEEM*, take to one's heels; *op* ~ *SIT*, take to one's heels; *die VRYE* ~ *laat gaan*, let matters take their course; (w) (ge-), walk, go; run (nose, eyes); flow (river); discharge (wound); run (lease); *die saak het glad ANDERS ge*~, the matter turned out quite differently; *die BOEK* ~ *goed*, the book is selling well; *iem. DAARIN laat* ~, lead someone into a trap; *ten EINDE (en se kant toe)* ~, draw to a close; *die GEVOELENS* ~ *hoog*, feeling is running high; *HOOG* ~ *met*, be taken up with; *KLAS* ~, follow lectures; ~ *dat hy KLEIN word*, run like mad; *die KLOK* ~ *voor (agter)*, the clock is fast (slow); *iem. daarin LAAT* ~, take someone in; *TEEN iem.* ~, bump into a person; *die TREIN* ~ *nie*, the train is not running; *UITMEKAAR* ~, diverge (roads); *onder WATER* ~, be flooded; ~**baan**, career, orbit, course; race; ~**borsel**, piassaba brush; ~**brug**, foot-bridge; ~**deksel**, muzzle-cover; ~**dop**, stirrup-cup; ~**gang**, ambulatory; ~**geluid**, footfall; ~**geselser**, walkie-talkie.
loop'graaf, trench; entrenchment; ~**bagger**, trench excavator; ~**besetting**, trench garrison; ~**diens**, trench routine; ~**jas**, trench coat; ~**koors**, trench fever; ~**mortier**, trench mortar; ~**net**, trench system; ~**oorlog**, trench warfare; ~**skuiling**, trench shelter; ~**spieël**, trench mirror; ~**wag**, trench picket.
loop: ~**jong(e)**, messenger boy; devil; ~**kat**, trolley; ~**kewer**, carabid; ~**koeël**, anti-friction ball; ~**kraan**, mobile (travelling) crane; overhead traveller; ~**kring**, orbit; ~**lys**, catwalk; ~**mare**, news; ~**pad**, footpath; ~**pas**, double-quick (time); *op die* ~*pas*, at the double; ~**plank**, gangway (ship); gang-plank; footboard (train); running-board (motor); platform (mannequins); ~**plek**, walk, place to walk; haunt; feeding-place; *dis haar* ~*plek*, she is a frequent caller here; ~**prater**, walkie-talkie; ~**rat**, impeller; ~**s**, (-e), ruttish, hot; on heat; ~**sand**, sand-drift; running sand; ~**s'heid**, rut, heat; ~**skoen**, walking-shoe; ~**slag**, trudgeon stroke; ~**sport**, pedestrianism; ~**steier**, travelling stage; -**stoeltjie**, walking chair; ~**stuk**, tread; ~**toer**, walking-tour; ~**tyd**, time to go; currency of a bill; running time; ~**ure**, running hours (railw.); ~**vlak**, tread (tyre); ~**voël**, courser, cursorial bird.
loos¹, (w) (ge-), void (urine); discharge; heave; *'n sug* ~, heave a sigh.
loos², (lose, loser; -ste), sly, cunning, artful; ~**heid**, slyness, cunning, artfulness.
loos'gat, limber, drainage hole.
loot¹, (s) (**lote**), shoot, sucker (tobacco plants); outgrowth; descendant, offspring.
loot², (w) (ge-), draw (cast) lots; raffle; toss; cut (for partners); ballot; ~ *om*, draw lots for; ~**jie**, (-s), lottery (sweepstake) ticket; ~*jies trek*, draw lots; ~**jiestrekkery**, drawing of lots; sortilege; ~**wenner**, winner of the toss.
lo'pend, (-e), current, present; running (water); cursive (writing); cursorial (birds); unexpired (insurance); day-to-day (expenses); ~*e BAND*, assembly line; ~*e BESLAG*, running batter; ~*e KOMMENTAAR*, running commentary; *die vyfde van die* ~*e MAAND*, the fifth instant; ~*e OË*, discharging eyes; ~*e REKENING*, current account;

'n ~ *e SAAK*, a going concern; *die* ~ *e SAKE*, current (routine) affairs; ~ *e SKRIF*, cursive writing.
lo'per, (-s), walker, runner; goer; stair-carpet, carpet-runner; bishop (chess); table-centre; big (buck) shot; master-key, check-key; cursor; ~**ig**, (-e), fluid; ~**y**, walking (to and fro).
lo'pie, (-s), little stream, brook; water-course; run (cricket); *'n* ~ *met iem. neem*, pull someone's leg.
lor, (-re), rag; straw, snap of the fingers; *geen* ~ *daarvoor OMGEE nie*, not to care a rap about something; *dit kan my geen* ~ *SKEEL nie*, it is not of the least concern to me.
lord, (-s), lord; ~**skap**, peerage, lordship.
lordo'se, lordosis.
lork, (-e), larch.
lornjet', (-te), eye-glasses with handle, lorgnette, opera-glass.
lor'rekraam, (ong.), (old-)rag stall.
lor'rie, (-s), lorry, motor trolley.
los¹, (s) (-se), lynx.
los², (w) (ge-), fire (shot); redeem (pledge); ransom (captive); claim (goods); discharge (load); unload (ship), release, free, let go; mention, drop (a hint); disregard; ~ *HOM!* let him go! *LAAT* ~ *!* let go! (b) (**l-se**|; -ser, -ste), loose, free, quit; movable; detachable; detached; unfastened (buttons); unpackaged (tea); disconnected (sentences); casual (work, remark); idle (rumour); dissolute, lax; light; gay; disengaged; glib, fluent; disjointed; fast, immoral (behaviour); odd, spare (copy); ~ *GEDAGTES*, random thoughts; *'n* ~ *GERUG*, a wild rumour; *op* ~ *GROND gebou*, built on insecure foundations; *'n* ~ *HOTNOT*, a casual labourer, a person without definite employment; someone free of responsibility; a freelance; ~ *KRUIT*, blank cartridge; *'n* ~ *LEWE*, a loose life; ~ *van MOND wees*, gossip, be unable to keep a secret; ~ *SIN*, detached sentence; ~ *TAFELTJIE*, occasional table; (bw) loosely; ~ *en vas LIEG*, tell lies by the score; ~ *en vas KOOP*, buy wildly; ~ *en vas PRAAT*, have a loose tongue in one's head; *daarop* ~ *SLAAN*, hit out; ~ *SLAAP*, sleep lightly, ~ *en vas STEEL*, steal everything one can lay hands on; *hy is* ~ *VOOR*, he is streets (miles) ahead; ~ *van die WÊRELD*, dead to the world; ~ **baar**, (. .bare), redeemable.
losban'dig, (-e), dissolute, licentious, dissipated, raffish; rakish; profligate, loose, gay, Bohemian; abandoned, lawless, debauched; ~**e**, (-s), rake, profligate, libertine; ~**heid**, dissoluteness, dissipation, profligacy, abandon(ment), libertinage, libertinism, licence, licentiousness, looseness, debauch(ery), lawlessness, rakishness.
los'bars, (-ge-), burst (break) loose, belch (forth), fly out, explode; ~**ting**, (-e, -s), explosion, outbreak, outburst.
los: ~ **bek**, enfant terrible; chatterbox; ~ **berg**, residual mountain; ~**bind**, (-ge-), unbind, untie, undo; ~**bladdagboek**, loose-leaf diary; ~**bla'dig**, (-e), loose-leaved.
los'bol, (-le), rake, libertine, profligate, roué, city slicker, wild spark, playboy, Don Juan, Cyprian, free-liver; ~**kunstenaar**, Bohemian.
los'boom, false bottom.
los'brand, (v) (-ge-), discharge, open fire, blaze, fire off; ~ *op*, fire upon; ~, (s), loose smut; ~**ing**, discharge, firing.
los'breek, (-ge-), break loose (away); break out (adrift); ~**haak**, detaching-hook.
los'dele, spares (motor).
los'draai, (-ge-), unscrew, untwist; untangle (wool); *die rem* ~, release the brake; take it easy, relax.
loseer', (ge-), lodge, board; ~**der**, (-s), boarder, paying-guest, lodger; ~**gas**, guest; ~**kamer**, room at boarding-house; room for visitor; ~**plaas**, guest-farm.
los: ~ **gaan**, (-ge-), get (become) loose, come undone; ~**geld**, ransom; cost of discharge; ~**gespe(r)**, (-ge-), unbuckle, unstrap.
los'goed, movables, effects, movable property; loose stuff, chattels; ~**verband**, chattel-mortgage.
los: ~ **gooi**, (-ge-), unmoor, loosen; ~ **haak**, (-ge-), unhook, unhitch.

los'hande, (s) loose hands (banana); (b) easily; with hands free; ~ *wen*, win at a canter.
los'hang, (-ge-), hang loose; dangle; ~**end**, (-e), fly-away (hair).
los: ~ **hawe**, port of discharge; ~**hefboom**, release lever; ~**heid**, looseness, laxity, carelessness, abandon; flippancy; laxity, laxness; fastness (way of life); detachment; ~**hoof'dig**, (-e), flippant, frivolous.
lo'sie, (-s), lodge (of Freemasons).
losies', lodging, boarding, board, accommodation; *vry* ~ *hê*, free board and lodging; be in gaol; ~**huis**, boarding-house; ~**plek**, lodgings.
lo'sing, voidance, evacuation; passing (urine).
los: ~ **klep**, release valve; ~**knoop**, (-ge-), untie; unbutton; undo; ~**kom**, (-ge-), get off, get loose, get out (of gaol); be released (discharged); come into circulation, be available (money); ~ **koop**, (-ge-), ransom, redeem, buy off; ~ **kop**, scatter-brain; loosehead (rugby); tailstick (of lathe); relict (geol.); ~ **koppel**, (-ge-), uncouple; throw out of gear; disconnect; ~ **kopstut**, loosehead prop (rugby).
los'kruit, blank; *met* ~ *skiet*, put the wind up someone; ~ **patroon**, blank cartridge; ~ **skoot**, blank round.
los'kry, (-ge-), get loose, untie, unscrew; secure, obtain (acquittal, release of prisoner); extract (an answer); get (money) out of.
los'laat, (-ge-), release, discharge; turn loose; let go; come off, become detached; absolve; liberate, set free; quit; unleash; *die GEDAGTE laat my nie los nie*, the thought haunts me; *hy laat NIKS los nie*, he does not let out any information.
los'lating, release, discharge, detachment.
los'lieg, (-ge-), get off by lying; *die aangeklaagde probeer hom* ~, the accused is trying to get off by lying.
loslip'pig, (-e), loose-tongued, flippant, gossipy; ~**heid**, incontinence (irresponsibility) of speech; ~ **heid kweek verraad (onheil)**, the tongue talks at the head's cost.
los: ~ **littig**, (-e), loose-jointed; ~**loop**, (-ge-), run loose, be at large; free-wheel; idle; ~**lopende persoon**, unmarried person; ~**lootjie**, bye (in games); ~**lopie**, (-s), bye, extra (cricket).
losly'wig, (-e), having loose bowels; ~**heid**, looseness of the bowels.
los'maak, (-ge-), loosen, unfasten, untie, undo, set free; dissociate, disjoin; detach, disattach; scarify; release; disconnect; extricate; disassociate; disentagle; unleash; *ek wil my hiervan* ~, I want to dissociate myself from this.
los: ~ **making**, severance, loosening, laxation; ~ **melkkoei**, cow that need not be tied at milking; ~ **pitperske**, free-stone peach; ~ **plek**, discharging berth; ~ **prys**, ransom.
los'raak, (-ge-), escape, get loose; go adrift; become unfastened; *na 'n sopie raak sy tong los*, after a drink his tongue starts wagging.
los'rafel, (-ge-), unravel; ravel out; become ragged at the edge.
los'roei, (-ge-), paddle; ~**er**, paddler.
los: ~ **ruk**, (-ge-), tear off, break away, wrench oneself free; ~ **rye**, ~ **ryg**, (-ge-), unlace, undo.
los'ser, (-s), unloader; redeemer; heaver; hoppertruck; release device; ~**ig**, (-e), rather loose, loosely.
los: ~ **sies**, loosely, casually, lightly; ~**sigheid**, looseness.
los'sing, unloading, discharge; redemption; ~**skoste**, cost of unloading, landing-charges.
lossin'nig, (-e), frivolous, feather-brained, flighty, thoughtless; ~**heid**, frivolity, thoughtlessness, flightiness.
los'sittend, (-e), loose-fitting.
los'skakel, (s) flyhalf (rugby); (w) (-ge-), uncouple; throw out of gear; disconnect; ~**ing**, disconnection.
los: ~ **skeur**, (-ge-), sever, rend asunder, tear away; ~**skroef**, ~**skroewe**, (-ge-), unscrew; ~**skud**, (-ge-), shake loose; ~**slaan**, (-ge-), free (oneself) by fighting (hitting); wangle; squeeze (money) from;

losstaan — **lug**

break away; ~**sny, (-ge-),** cut loose; ~**spel,** loose (rugby); ~**speld, (-ge-),** unpin; ~**speler,** rover, flank forward (rugby); ~**spring, (-ge-),** fly open; jump (spring) free.
los'staan, (-ge-), stand loose, be detached (unconnected); ~**de huise,** detached dwellings.
los'steek, (-ge-), dig loose; lash out, pitch into, let fly; *op iem.* ~, go for someone; let fly at someone.
los'storm, (-ge-): ~ *op,* rush upon.
los: ~ **strik, (-ge-),** untie (bow); ~**torring, (-ge-),** unpick, undo (sewing); rip loose (free); ~**trek, (-ge-),** unpick, pull loose; ladder (stocking); pull out (knitting); tear loose; let fly; get going; ~**tyd,** time for unloading; ~**vingers,** loose fingers (banana); ~**voorspeler,** loose forward; ~**weg,** loosely, unconcernedly, lightly.
los'werk, (s) odd job(s); unloading; char; chore; (w) **(-ge-),** work (oneself) loose; extricate (free) oneself; ~**er,** casual labourer; ~**ie,** odd job, chore.
los'wikkel, (-ge-), loosen (by moving to and fro), wriggle free; unwrap; dislodge; extricate; ~**ing,** extrication; loosening; dislodgement.
los: ~ **wind, (-ge-),** unwind, untwine; ~**woel, (-ge-)** = **loswikkel.**
lot¹, fate, destiny, fortune, doom; destination; lot; *die* ~ *is vir my BESKORE,* it is my lot; *die* ~ *laat BESLIS,* decide by casting lots; *dieselfde* ~ *DEEL,* meet with the same fate; *jou* ~ *met iem. INGOOI,* throw one's lot in with someone; *dit is my* ~, that is my fate; *hom aan sy* ~ *OORLAAT,* leave him to his fate.
lot², (e), lottery ticket, die ~ *is gewerp,* the die is cast.
lo'tehout, alburn(um).
lo'teling, (-e), conscript; ballotee.
lo'tery, (-e), lottery, raffle; gamble; ~**kaartjie,** lottery ticket; **L**~**wet,** Lottery Act.
lot: ~ **genoot,** (..**note),** fellow-sufferer, comrade in distress; ~**geval,** adventure, misfortune.
Lo'tharinge, Lorraine; ~**r, (-s),** Lorrainer.
lo'ting, (-e, -s), drawing of lots, draw.
lot'jie: *van* ~ *getik wees,* have a screw loose; be moonstruck.
lots: ~ **bestemming,** destiny; ~**verbetering,** betterment (of one's circumstances); ~**wisseling,** vicissitude.
lot'to, lotto.
lo'tus, (-se), lotus; ~**eter,** lotus-eater.
lou, lukewarm, tepid; slow (oven).
louda'num, laudanum.
lou'er, (ge-), laud, honour, crown with laurels; ~**e,** laurels; *op jou* ~ *e rus,* rest on one's laurels.
lou'erig, (-e), (rather) lukewarm.
lou'erkrans, laurel wreath.
lou'heid, tepidness; half-heartedness; indifference (towards religion).
lourier': ~ **boom,** laurel (tree); cherry-bay; bay (-tree); ~**krans,** laurel wreath.
lou'ter, (w) (ge-), purify, refine, depurate; rectify; test; (b, bw) **(-e),** pure; mere; sheer; ~ *GOUD,* pure gold, ~ *LEUENS,* sheer lies; *dit is* ~ *ONSIN,* this is sheer nonsense; ~ *uit SELFVERDEDIGING,* in sheer self-defence; *die* ~ *e WAARHEID,* the naked truth; ~**aar, (-s),** refiner; ~**end, (-e),** depurative, refining; ~**ing,** refining, purification, depuration, refinement; ~**middel,** cleaning agent; ~**proses,** process of purification; ~**staal,** refined steel.
lou'warm, lukewarm, tepid.
lo'we, (ge-) = **loof.**
lo'wend, (-e), laudative, laudatory, praising.
lo'wer¹, lauder.
lo'wer², foliage; ~**groen,** quite (very) green; ~**ryk, (-e),** leafy.
low'we, leaves (of vegetables); foliage, tops.
Lu'cifer, Lucifer.
Lucul'lus: *'n* ~, an epicure; a gourmet.
lu'do, ludo.
luf'fa, luffa, loofah; ~**spons,** loofah, vegetable sponge.
lug, (s) **(-te),** air, sky; atmosphere; smell; *die BLOU* ~, the blue sky; *uit die* ~ *GEGRYP,* fictitious, fanciful; ~ *gee aan jou GEMOED (gevoelens),* give vent to one's feelings; *uit die* ~ *GRYP,* suck some-

thing from one's thumb; *in die* ~ *HANG,* it is all up in the air; *daar HANG 'n* ~ *gie aan,* there is something fishy about it; *die* ~ *KRY van,* get the wind of, scent; *SAAMGEPERSTE* ~, compressed air; *in die* ~ *SIT en kyk,* stare into space; *dit SIT in die* ~, it is in the air; ~ *SKEP,* take a breather; *in die* ~ *SKERM,* beat the air; *in die* ~ *SWEWE,* be exalted; *uit die* ~ *VAL,* drop from the sky; *VARS* ~, fresh air; *die* ~ *VERPES,* poison the air; *in die* ~ *VLIEG,* be blown up; (w) **(ge-),** air, ventilate; vent, disburden; *jou GELEERDHEID* ~, show off, parade one's learning; *jou HART* ~, give vent to one's feelings; *die KAMERS* ~, air the rooms; ~**advertensie,** sky-sign; ~**afdeling,** air compartment (of gas-mask); air department (of army); ~**afkoeling,** air-cooling; ~**afstroming,** air-cataract; ~**afvoer,** air drainage; ~**afweer,** anti-aircraft defence; ~**afweergeskut,** anti-aircraft artillery; ~**alarm,** aircraft alarm; ~**baan,** air trajectory; air passage; ~**bad,** air-bath; ~**baken,** aviation beacon; ~**bal,** lob; ~**ballon,** (air-)balloon; ~**band,** tube, pneumatic tyre; ~**basis,** air-base; ~**bedryf,** flying operations; ~**bel,** air-bubble; bell; ~**belwaterpas,** spirit-level; ~**bemanning,** air crew; ~**beskrywer,** aerographer; ~**beskrywing,** aerography; ~**besoedeling,** air-pollution; ~**bewapening,** air-armament; ~**bewoner,** denizen of the air; ~**bewus, (-te),** air-minded; ~**blasie,** air bubble; ~**bom,** airbomb; ~**bombardement** air raid; ~**boog,** flying buttress; ~**boor,** pneumatic drill; ~**boormasjien,** air-drill; ~**brug,** air-lift; fly-over bridge; ~**buffer,** air buffer; ~**buis,** air-pipe; ~(**buite)band,** tubeless tyre; ~**dig, (-te),** air-tight, hermetic; -**digtheid,** air density; air-tightness; ~**dinamika,** aero-dynamics; ~**doelgeskut,** anti-aircraft gun; ack-ack; ~**doelkanon,** anti-aircraft gun; ~**doelvuur,** flak; ~**doelvuurboot,** flak-ship; ~**draad,** aerial, antenna; overhead wire; ~**droging,** air-curing (of tobacco); ~**drogingskuur,** air-curing barn; ~**droog,** (..**droë**), air-dried; ~**druk,** atmospheric pressure; pneumatic pressure; ~**drukboor,** compressor-drill; ~**drukmeting,** air-pressure measurement; ~**drukpyp,** pneumatic dispatch-tube; ~**drukrem,** pneumatic brake; ~**duik,** sky-diving; ~**duiker,** sky-diver; ~**elektrisiteit,** atmospheric electricity; ~**eskader,** air squadron; ~**filter,** air filter; ~**fles,** air bottle; ~**foto,** aerial photograph; ~**fotografie,** aerial photography; ~**gaatjie,** small air-hole; spiracle; ~**gas,** air-gas; ~**gat,** ventilator, air-hole; vent; air-pocket; blow-hole; spiracle (whale); ~**gees,** sylph; ~**gehaltemeter,** eudiometer; ~**gang,** airway; air-passage; ~**gekoel, (-de),** air-cooled; ~**geleiding,** overhead wires; ~**gesig,** skyscape; ~**gesteldheid,** climate; ~**geswel,** emphysema; ~**geveg, (-te),** (aerial) dogfight; air-fight (battle); ~**gie, (-s),** faint air (of wind), breeze; tang; whiff, scent; ~**golf,** air-wave; ~**hamer,** pneumatic hammer.
lughar'tig, (-e), light-hearted, happy-go-lucky; flippant; ~**heid,** light-heartedness.
lug: ~**hawe,** airport; ~**heerskappy,** mastery of the air; ~**holte,** air-pocket; ~**hou,** lob (tennis); skyer (oriekot); ~**hys,** pneumatic hoist, ~**inlêer,** air-layer; ~**kaartjie,** aeroplane ticket; ~**kabel,** overhead cable; ~**kabellyn,** telpher line; ~**kamer,** air-chamber; ~**kanaal,** air-flue; ~**kaping,** skyjacking; ~**kartering,** aerial survey; ~**kasteel,** castle in the air; day-dream; pipe dream; ~**kastele bou,** build castles in the air, ~**klep,** air (blast, reverse) valve; ~**klere,** aviation kit; ~**knik,** air-pocket; ~**koeler,** air-cooler; ~**koeling,** air-cooling; ~**koker,** ventiduct; ~**kolk,** wind-pocket; ~**kolom,** column of air; ~**kraan,** air-inlet cock; ~**kruising,** air crossing; ~**kryg,** aerial warfare; ~**kunde,** pneumatics; aerology; ~**kussing,** air-cushion; ~**kuur,** air cure; ~**laag,** stratum (layer) of air; ~**landskap,** skyscape; ~**lating,** bleeding; ~**ledig, (-e),** ~**leeg,** (..**leë),** ~**leë RUIMTE,** vacuum; ~**leë TENK,** vacuum tank; ~**leegte,** vacuum; air-pocket; ~**leiding,** overhead line; ~**lyn,** airline; bee-line; ~**maarskalk,** Air Marshall; ~**mag,** air force; ~**magkapelaan,** air-force chaplain; ~**magoffisier,** air officer; ~**magtak,** air com-

ponent; ~**man**, airman; ~**mantel**, air-case; ~**massa**, mass of air; ~**matras**, air mattress; ~**meter**, aerometer; ~**net**, aerials; ~**omloop**, air circulation; ~**ondersoek**, aeroscopy; ~**oorlog**, aerial warfare; ~**opening**, air-hole; spiracle; ~**opmeting**, aerial survey; ~**opname**, aerial photograph; ~**opsigter**, dust sampler; ~**perser**, air compressor; ~**persing**, air-compressing; ~**plant**, air plant, aerophyte, epiphyte; ~**pomp**, air-pump; pneumatic pump; ~**port**, air-mail postage; ~**pos**, airmail; ~**posfotobrief**, airgraph; ~**posvliegtuig**, airmail plane; ~**prop**, airlock; ~**pyp(ie)**, windpipe, trachea, bronchial tube; breather-pipe; ~**pypontsteking**, trachitis; ~**redery**, airline (firm); ~**reëlaar**, air regulator; ~**reëling**, air-conditioning; *met* ~*reëling*, air-conditioned; ~**reg**, air-law; ~**reis**, air-voyage; air-trip; ~**reisiger**, aviator; air-traveller; balloonist; ~**reiskaartjie**, air ticket; ~**reklame**, sky-writing; ~**rem**, pneumatic brake; vacuum brake; ~**roete**, airway; ~**rooster**, air-brick; ventilator; ~**ruim**, atmosphere, space; ether; ~**ruimte**, air-space; ~**sak**, air-pocket, air-hole; ~**sel**, **(-le)**, air-cell; ~**siek**, air-sick; ~**siekte**, air-sickness; ~**sin**, flying-sense; ~**skakeloffisier**, air liaison officer; ~**skeepvaart**, aviation, aeronautics, aerial navigation; ~**skip**, airship, airliner; ~**skipper**, aviator, airman, pilot, aeronaut; ~**skoot**, lofted shot; shot in the air; ~**skop**, punt (rugby); ~**skrif**, sky-writing; ~**skroef**, propeller, airscrew.
lug'slag¹, lob, loft, lofted shot.
lug'slag², air-battle.
lug: ~**sleepteiken**, drogue; ~**sluiting**, air-lock; ~**snelheid**, air speed; ~**spieëling**, mirage; fata morgana; ~**spleet**, air-gap; ~**spoorweg**, elevated (aerial) railway; ~**spuit**, air gun; ~**staf**, air staff; ~**stafhoof**, air chief of staff; ~**stamp**, air bump; ~**steen**, air brick; ~**steunpunt**, air-base; ~**steurings**, ~**storings**, atmospherics; ~**storting**, air-cataract; ~**streek**, zone; climate; ~**stroom**, current of air, atmospheric current; draught; ~**stryd**, aerial warfare; ~**strydkragte**, air-force; ~**suier**, aspirator; ~**suil**, column of air; ~**suiweraar**, air-cleaner; ~**suiwerend**, **(-e)**, (air-)purifying; ~**taxi**, air-taxi, taxiplane.
lug'ter, **(s)**, candelabrum, chandelier; electrolier.
lug'termometer, air thermometer.
lug'tig, **(-e)**, airy, light; light-hearted, gay, jaunty; cool (clothes); afraid, scared; *'n ~e KAMER*, a well ventilated room; ~ *vir die baas WEES*, be afraid of the boss; ~**heid**, airiness, lightness; jauntiness, levity; fear.
lug: ~**ting**, ventilation; aeration (of soil); ~**toevoer**, air-supply, ventilation; ~**tonnel**, air-adit; ~**torpedo**, **(-'s)**, aerial torpedo; ~**tou**, overhead rope.
lugu'ber, **(-e)**, lugubrious, dismal, lurid.
lug: ~**uitlaat**, air-exhaust, air-escape; ~**vaarder**, **(-s)**, airman, aeronaut.
lug'vaart, aviation, aeronautics; ~**afdeling**, air-force; ~**baken**, air-beacon; ~**diens**, aerial service; ~**gesind**, air-minded; ~**kaart**, air-map; ~**kunde**, aeronautics, aviation; ~**kun'dig**, **(-e)**, aeronautic(al); ~**lyn**, airline; ~**maatskappy**, aviation company; ~**skool**, aviation school; ~**skou**, aerial display; ~**versekering**, aviation insurance; **L**~**wet**, Air Navigation Act; ~**wetgewing**, air-legislation.
lug: ~**verdediging**, air-defence; ~**verkeer**, air-traffic; ~**verkoeling**, air-cooling; ~**verontreiniging**, air-pollution; ~**verskynsel**, atmospheric phenomenon; ~**versorging**, air-conditioning; ~**versperring**, aerial barrage; ~**verstopping**, air-lock; ~**vertoning**, air rally; ~**vervarser**, ventilator; ~**vervarsing**, (air-) purification, ventilation; ~**vervarsingskema**, ventilation scheme; ~**vervoer**, aerial transport; ~**vloot**, air force (fleet); ~**vlootbasis**, air-base; ~**vogmeter**, hygroscope; ~**vogtigheid**, humidity, moisture-content; ~**vogtigheidsmeter**, hygrometer, hygroscope; ~**vormig**, **(-e)**, aeriform; ~**vrag**, air freight; ~**vry**, **(-e)**, air-free; ~**waaier**, fan; ~**waar'dig**, **(-e)**, air-worthy; ~**waardigheid**, airworthiness; ~**waardin**, air-hostess; ~**waarneming**, aeroscopy; ~**wagter**, air-warden; ~**wapen**, air-arm; ~**weegkunde**, aerostatics; ~**weerstand**, air-resistance; air-drag;

~**weg**, air-passage; air-way; ~**werktuigkundige**, air-mechanic; ~**werweling**, atmospheric vorticity; ~**wortel**, air-root (plant).
lui¹, (s) people, folk; *die hoë* ~, the élite.
lui², (w) (ge-), sound, peal, ring, toll, clang, chime, go ding; *hoe ~ die brief*, how does the letter run (read)? *soos die GESEGDE* ~, as the saying goes.
lui³, (b) lazy, idle, indolent, slothful; backward; sluggish (motor); ~ *by die VAK (werk)*, *fluks by die bak*, slow at work, quick at meat; a bad worker but a good eater; *hy is ~ VERBY*, he is bone-idle.
lui'aard, **(-s)**, sluggard, lazybones, slacker, laggard, drone, do-nothing; *'n ~ dra hom dood, maar hy loop nie twee maal nie*, lazy folks take the most pains.
lui: ~**bossie**, slow-burning shrub *(Lobostemon fruticosus)*; ~**broek**, sluggard, lazybones.
luid, (s): *na ~ van*, according to; in terms of; **(-e)**, noisy, loud, forte; aloud; full-mouthed.
lui'dens, according to; in terms of.
lui'dier, sloth.
luid'keels, at the top of one's voice, very loudly.
luidrug'tig, **(-e)**, noisy, clamorous, blatant, rumbustious, boisterous, rowdy, hoydenish, loud, rattleheaded, rattlepated, rampageous, obstreperous; ~**heid**, noisiness, rowdiness, clamorousness, loudness, obstreperousness, rampage.
luid'spreker, **(-s)**, loudspeaker, megaphone; ~**wa**, public-address van.
lui'er¹, (s) **(-s)**, swaddling cloth; napkin (baby), diaper.
lui'er², (w) (ge-), be lazy; idle (engine).
lui'er: ~**broekie**, pilch; ~**diens**, napkin service.
lui'erig, **(-e)**, rather lazy (idle).
lui'er: ~**mandjie**, baby-linen basket; ~**speld**, safety-pin, napkin-pin.
lui'er, ~**spoed**, idling speed; ~**stoel**, easy chair, morris chair.
lui: ~**gat**, (plat), lazybones, lazy bastard; ~**haai**, tiger-shark; ~**heid**, laziness, sloth; ~*heid is die duiwel se oorkussing*, idleness is the devil's bolster.
Luik¹, Liège.
luik², (s) **(-e)**, shutter (of window); trap-door, trap-cover, hatch; manhole; flap; (w) (ge-), shut, close, wink; ~**deur**, companion-hatch; ~**gat**, hatchway; scuttle; ~**lys**, coaming; ~**klappe**, hatch-cleats; ~**skarnier**, blind-hinge; shutter butt.
lui'lak, (s) **(-ke)**, sluggard, lazybones, loafer, slacker; (w) (ge-), loaf, idle (about); hibernate.
luilek'ker, **(-s)**, luxurious, comfortable, easeful; **L**~**land**, (land of) Cockaigne, fool's paradise, happy-valley, Lotus-land.
luim, **(-e)**, humour; whim, mood, caprice; crank; megrim; *in 'n goeie* ~, in a good mood; ~**ig**, **(-e)**, capricious; humorous, witty, comic(al); ~**igheid**, humorousness, humour, pleasantry; caprice.
lui'perd, **(-s)**, leopard, catamountain.
luis, **(-e)**, louse; *so ARM soos 'n ~ op 'n kam*, as poor as a church mouse; *jou LAE* ~! you miserable insect! you dirty louse!
lui'sak, lazy-bones, slacker, sluggard.
luis'boom, bug-tree.
luis'hond: *'n kaal* ~, a pauper; a starveling.
lui'sies(bos), shrub with louse-like seeds *(Leucospernum nutans)*; pincushions.
lui'sig, **(-e)**, lousy, pedicular, pediculous.
luis'koors, typhus.
lui'slang, python, boa-constrictor, anaconda; ~**vel**, python-skin.
luis'ter¹, (s) lustre, splendour, glory, éclat, glitter, radiance, magnificence; fulgency, refulgence; ~ *bysit*, add lustre to.
luis'ter², (w) (ge-), listen, hear, hark, heed, hearken; obey; listen-in; *die HOND ~ na sy naam*, the dog answers to its name; *na goeie RAAD* ~, follow good advice; *die kind ~ na sy VADER*, the child obeys his father; ~**aar**, **(-s)**, listener; listener-in; ~**galery**, listening-gallery; ~**geld**, radio licence; ~**frekwensie**, listening-frequency; ~**klink**, listen-in jack; ~**net**, listening-system; ~**plek**, ~**pos**, listening-post; ~**ryk**, **(-e)**, brilliant, glorious, magnific(al); lustrous, fulgent; radiant, pompous,

princely, magnificent; ~**sap,** listening-sap; ~**stroombaan,** listening-system; ~**toestel,** listening-apparatus; ~**trompet,** acoustic telescope; ~**vergunning,** radio licence; ~**vink,** eavesdropper; ~**wa,** listening-tender.
lui'stoel, easy chair.
luis'vlieg, ked.
luit, (-e), lute.
luitenant', (-e, -s), lieutenant; ~**-generaal, (-s),** lieutenant-general; ~**-goewerneur, (-s),** lieutenant-governor; ~**-kolonel, (-s),** lieutenant-colonel; ~**-kommandeur, (-s),** lieutenant-commander; ~**skap,** lieutenancy; ~**-ter-see, (-e-ter-see),** naval lieutenant; ~**vlieër,** flight-lieutenant.
lui'ters, unaware, innocent; *hom (dood)* ~ *hou,* maintain a pose of innocence (ignorance); pretend to be innocent.
luit'speler, lute-player, lutist, lutanist.
luk'raak, (..rake), at random, haphazard, by guess and by God; hit and miss.
lukratief', (..tiewe), lucrative.
lukubra'sie, (-s), lucubration, night-study.
lukwart', (-e), loquat.
lumbaal', (lumbale), lumbar; *lumbale punksie,* lumbar puncture.
lumier', (s) dawn, daybreak; **(w) (ge-),** dawn.
luminessen'sie, luminescence.
lumineus', (-e), luminous.
lum'mel, (s) (-s), simpleton, boor, lout, churl, nincompoop, lubber, stupid fellow, hobbledehoy; **(w) (ge-),** laze about; ~**agtig, (-e),** boorish.
luna'ries, (-e), lunarian.
lunet', (te), lunette; watch-glass.
luns, (-e), linch-pin, axle-pin; ~**gat,** pinhole; ~**riem,** strap to fasten the linch-pin; dirty fellow, cad, swine.
lupien', (-e), lupi'ne, (-s), lupin.
lupino'se, lupinosis.
lu'pus, lupus, eating-tetter; ~**lyer,** lupus sufferer (patient).
lus¹, (s) (-te), desire, appetite, inclination, liking, mind; delight; craving, itching; greed; fancy; *die ~ BEKRUIP hom,* the desire grows within him; *DANS dat dit 'n ~ is,* dance with a will; ~ *HÊ,* have a mind; *dit is sy ~ en sy LEWE,* that is meat and drink to him; *'n ~ vir die OË,* a feast for the eyes; *jou ~ oor MAAK,* satisfy one's desires (appetite); *weinig ~ TOON om,* show little desire to; *VLEESLIKE ~ te,* animal appetites (desires); *met meer ~ WERK,* work with greater zest; **(w) (ge-),** like; feel inclined; *hy ~ geen kos nie,* he has no appetite.
lus², (-se), noose, loop; tab, tag; *see* **lis.**
lusern', lucerne; ~**baal,** bale of lucerne; ~**hooi,** lucerne hay; ~**kamp,** lucerne paddock; ~**land,** field of lucerne; ~**meel,** lucerne meal; ~**oes,** lucerne harvest (crop); **saad,** lucerne seed.
lus'gevoel, sensation of pleasure.
lus: ~**hof,** pleasure garden; ~**huis,** pleasure-house.
lus: ~**makertjie,** aperitif, appetizer, bracer; ~**oord,** pleasure resort; delightful spot.
lus'prieel, bower.
lus'sie, (-s), *see* **lissie.**
lus'slot, château.
lus'stof, loopy fabric.
lus'teloos, (..lose), listless, spiritless, apathetic; dull, languid, flat; ~**heid,** listlessness, dullness, depression of spirits, languor, apathy.
lus'ter, (-s), girandole, chandelier.
lus'tig, (-e), gay, cheerful, merry, blithe, lusty, cheery; ~**heid,** gayness, cheerfulness.
lus'trum, (-s, ..tra), lustrum, quinquennium.
lus'wekkertjie, (-s), appetizer.
Lutheraan', (..rane), Lutheran.
Lutheranis'me, Lutheranism.
Lu'thers, (-e), Lutheran.
lut'tel, (-e), small, little, weak.
lut'terig, (-e), ramshackle, rickety.
luuks, (-e), luxurious.
luuk'se, luxury; ~**artikel,** fancy article; article of luxury; ~**bus,** luxury bus; ~**model,** de luxe model; ~**skryftafel,** executive writing-desk; ~**-uit**gawe, edition de luxe; ~**voorwerp,** object of luxury.
luuksueus', (plegt., ong.**), (-e),** luxurious.
Luzern', Lucerne.
ly¹, (s) lee (side); *aan ~,* leeward.
ly², (w) (ge-), suffer, bear, endure; *DORS ~,* suffer thirst; *te ~ HÊ van,* be afflicted with, have to suffer from; *aan HOOFPYN ~,* suffer from headaches; *~ ONDER iets,* suffer on account of something; *SKIPBREUK ~,* be shipwrecked; fail; *dit ~ geen TWYFEL nie,* there is no question (doubt) about it; *'n VERLIES ~,* sustain a loss; *~ wat daarop VOLG,* suffer the consequences.
ly: ~**anker,** lee anchor; ~**boeilyn,** lee bowline; ~**boord,** lee side; ~**bras,** lee brace.
ly'de, suffering.
ly'delik, (-e), passive, submissive; *~e verset,* passive resistance; ~**heid,** passiveness, (im)passivity, meekness.
ly'dend, (-e), suffering, passive; *die ~e PARTY,* the sufferer, the injured party; *~e VORM,* passive voice.
ly'dens: ~**beker,** cup of bitterness; ~**geskiedenis,** Passion; tale of woe; ~**kelk,** cup of suffering (sorrow); **L~preek,** Passion sermon; **L~tyd,** Passion tide; **L~week,** Passion Week; ~**weg,** via dolorosa, way of the Cross.
ly'ding, suffering; *STERF na 'n lange ~,* die after a long and painful illness; *'n dier uit sy ~ VERLOS,* put an animal out of its suffering.
lyd'saam, (same), meek, patient; passible; ~**heid,** patience, resignation, meekness, endurance.
ly'e, suffering.
ly'er, (-s), sufferer, patient; endurer; ~**es', (-se),** (feminine) sufferer, patient.
lyf, (lywe), body; carcase; *sy ~ AASVOËL hou,* arrive at mealtimes; sponge; *sy ~ ADELAAR hou,* give oneself airs; *van sy ~ AFHOU,* keep at bay; *BEEF oor sy hele ~,* tremble from head to foot; *jou ~ BÊRE,* shirk work; *'n ~ soos 'n BERG en 'n hart soos 'n perskepit,* a giant of a man with the heart of a mouse; *BLY van my ~ af,* leave me alone; *iem. te ~ GAAN,* lay about someone; *GESOND van ~ en lede,* sound in life and limb; *sy ~ GROOTMAN hou,* boast, brag; be cocky; *alles aan haar ~ HANG,* spend all her money on clothes; *nie veel om die ~ HÊ nie,* not be worth much; *jou ~ INGOOI,* throw oneself into; *sy ~ KNIPMES hou,* pay one's court to; set one's cap at; *hy sal dit uit sy ~ LAAT,* he will never dream of doing it; *iets op die ~ LOOP,* come upon something; *iem. op die ~ LOOP,* bump into someone; *hy het 'n MOOI (die regte) ~ daarvoor,* that suits (becomes) him admirably; look the part; *dit het NIKS om die ~ nie,* there isn't much in it; *OM die ~,* round the waist; *jou ~ REG HOU,* prepare oneself for; *sy ~ SPAAR,* shirk work; *jy kan maar jou ~ VEISMEER,* you are in for it; *aan die ~ VOEL,* be made painfully aware; *hoe VOEL jou ~?* how do you feel? *jou ~ WEGSTEEK,* shirk work; *jou ~ WINDMAKER hou,* cut a dash; swagger; ~**arts,** physician-in-ordinary, personal physician, court physician; ~**band,** waist-band, belt, sash; cincture; ~**bediende,** personal (body-) servant; batman, valet; *vroulike ~bediende,* lady's-maid; ~**blad,** favourite newspaper; newspaper espousing a person (cause); house magazine, mouthpiece; ~**borsel,** fleshbrush; ~**eiene, (-s),** serf, villain, bondsman; ~**eienskap,** serfdom, bondage; ~**garde,** bodyguard; ~**hare,** body-hair; ~**hou,** body-blow; ~**ie, (-s),** bodice; little body; basque, corsage; ~**jong,** valet, personal attendant, henchman; ~**kneg,** body servant, valet.
Lyf'land, Livonia; ~**s, (-e),** Livonian.
lyf: ~**lik, (-e),** bodily; ~**likheid,** corporeality; ~**linne,** body-linen; ~**luis,** body louse; ~**orgaan,** mouthpiece; personal paper; ~**rente,** annuity, gratuity; ~**rentenier,** annuitant; ~**s'behoud,** preservation of life; ~**s'gevaar,** danger to life; ~**s'geweld,** personal violence; ~**sieraad,** personal ornament; ~**spreuk,** motto; household word; ~**straf,** corporal punishment; ~*straf oplê (toedien),* impose (inflict) cor-

poral punishment; ~**swaai**, sway; ~**tog**, usufruct; ~**wag**, body-guard; household troops.

lyk¹, (s) (-e), corpse, cadaver; *'n* ~ *AFLÊ*, lay out a corpse; *so WIT soos 'n* ~, as white as a sheet.

lyk², (w) (ge-), resemble, appear, look, seem to be; *jy* ~ *DAARNA*, you look like it; you've got a hope! *dit* ~ *na HAEL*, it looks like hail, *jy* ~ *'n MOOI een*, you've got a hope; *baie NA mekaar* ~, resemble each other very closely; *dit* ~ *na NIKS*, it looks like nothing on earth; *jy* ~ *na jou PA*, you resemble your father; *dit* ~ *SO*, it looks like it; *dit* ~ *SPREKEND*, it is a speaking likeness; *dit* ~ *VIR my*, it seems to me.

lyk'agtig, (-e), cadaverous.

ly'kant, lee side.

lyk: ~**baar,** bier; ~**besorger,** undertaker; layer-out; ~**besorging,** undertaking; ~**bidder,** mute (at funeral); ~**bus,** funeral (cinerary) urn; ~**dief,** body-snatcher; ~**diefstal,** body-snatching; ~**diens,** funeral service; burial service, obsequies; dead-office; ~**draer,** bearer (of the body); ~**gif,** septic virus; ptomaine; ~**huis,** mortuary, morgue; ~**kis,** coffin; ~**klag,** funeral wail; ~**kleed,** shroud; pall; ~**kleur,** livid colour; ~**kleurig, (-e),** livid, cadaverous; ~**koets,** hearse; ~**laken,** shroud; ~**lug,** cadaverous smell; ~**offer,** funeral sacrifice; ~**omhulsel,** shrouding; ~**oond,** cremator; ~**opening,** autopsy; necropsy; ~**rede,** funeral oration (sermon); ~**roof,** body-snatching; ~**rower,** body-snatcher; ~**sang,** dirge; coronach; ~**skouer,** coroner; ~**skouing,** inquest, post-mortem (examination), autopsy; necropsy, necroscopy; (coroner's) inquest; *geregtelike* ~*skouing,* inquest; ~**stapel,** funeral pile; ~**stasie,** ~**stoet,** funeral procession; obsequies; ~**styfheid,** rigor mortis; ~**verassing,** ~**verbranding,** cremation; ~**verslinder,** ghoul; ~**verstywing,** rigor mortis; ~**vet,** adipocere; ~**vretend, (-e),** necrophagous; ~**wa,** hearse, funeral carriage, catafalque; ~**wit,** ghastly white, livid.

lym, (s) glue, paste, colloid, cement, size; **(w) (ge-),** glue, size, glutinate; ~**agtig, (-e),** gluey, colloidal; ~**er, (-s),** gluer; ~**erig, (-e),** gluey, sticky; ~**erigheid,** glueyness; ~**fabriek,** glue-works; ~**grondlaag,** glue-priming; ~**koker,** glue-boiler; ~**kwas,** paste-brush, glue-brush; ~**pot,** glue-pot, gum-pot; untidy beard; ~**skroef,** cramp; ~**vel,** fly-paper; ~**water,** size, glue wash.

lyn, (-e), rope, line, cord, string; track (railway); (mv) lines, strains (genetics); range; leash; *in 'n regte* ~ *AFSTAM*, be a direct lineal descendant; *'n trein op 'n ander* ~ *BRING*, shunt a train; *op een* ~ *BRING*, bring into line; *EWEWYDIGE* ~ *e*, parallel lines; *in GROOT* ~ *e*, in broad outlines; *dit LÊ in sy* ~, that suits him; *'n bok op* ~ *SLAAN*, tether a goat; *'n* ~ *SLAAN*, form a line; *iem.* ~ *SLAAN*, make someone toe the line; *goed vir die SLANKE* ~, good for the figure; *op een* ~ *STAAN*, be on a level; be in line with; *op een* ~ *STEL met*, bring on a level with; **(w) (ge-),** rule, line; ~**baan,** rope-walk; ~**band,** band, netcord; ~**boor, (ge-),** line-bore; ~**boot,** liner.

lynch, (ge-), lynch; ~**wet,** lynch-law.

lyn: ~**cliché,** line-block; ~**draad,** boundary fence; ~**geleier,** line-conductor; ~**gooi,** casting (angling); ~**houtjie,** ruler; ~**inspekteur,** line-inspector; ~**koek,** linseed cake; ~**meel,** linseed meal; ~**oefening,** rope-drill; ~**olie,** linseed oil; *rou* ~ *olie*, raw linseed oil; ~**opsigter,** linesman; ~**perspektief,** linear perspective; ~**reg,** straight, perpendicular; diametrical; *in* ~ *regte teenspraak met*, in direct opposition to; ~**saad** linseed; ~**saadaftreksel,** linseed tea; ~**saadkoek,** oilcake; ~**saadpap,** linseed poultice; ~**skip,** liner; ~**slaer,** rope-maker; ~**staan, (s)** (..**stane**), line-out (rugby); **(w) (-ge-),** line up; queue; line out (rugby); ~**stand,** square stance; ~**tanding,** line-perforation; ~**teelt,** line-breeding; ~**tekene,** linear drawing; ~**tekening,** geometrical drawing; mechanical drawing; ~**tjie, (-s),** piece of string; *iem. aan 'n* ~ *tjie HÊ*, have someone on a string; *iem. aan 'n* ~ *tjie HOU*, keep someone on a string; ~**verdeler,** graduator; ~**vis,** line fish; ~**vissery,** line fishing; ~**waad,** linen; ~**wagter,** ~**werker,** linesman.

lys, (s) (-te), list, catalogue; schedule; file; rail, frame (picture); cornice, moulding, cyma (arch.); skirting-board; ledge (rock); (subscription) list; *van die* ~ *krap*, strike off the roll; *in 'n* ~ *SIT*, frame (picture); *op die* ~ *SIT*, enroll; put on the voters' roll; *op die SWART* ~, on the black list; **(w) (ge-),** frame (picture); list; schedule; *'n gelyste Kommunis*, a listed Communist; ~**beitel,** moulding iron.

ly'seil, stunsail, studding sail.

ly'sie, (-s), small frame; small list; small ledge.

ly'sig, (-e), drawling, slow.

lys: ~**skaaf,** moulding-plane, beading-plane, ogeeplane; ~**temaker,** frame-maker.

ly'ster, (-s) thrush; ~**bes,** mountain ash; ~**skaaf,** badger-plane.

lys'ting, (-e, -s), enrolment; listing.

lys'werk, moulding, framework, astragal, cornice, fret.

ly: ~**sy,** lee side; ~**waarts,** leeward; ~**wal,** lee shore.

ly'we: *in LEWENDE* ~, in the flesh; *in LEWENDE* ~ *teenwoordig wees*, be there as large as life.

ly'wig, (-e), corpulent, fat; thick, bulky, voluminous; full-bodied; ~**heid,** corpulency; voluminousness (book); body, consistency (of milk, wine).

M

m, (-'e, -'s), m.

ma, (-'s), mother, mum, mummy, ma(m)ma; *jy sal jou* ~ *vir 'n EENDVOËL aansien*, you will find yourself in Queer Street; *iem. SLAAN dat hy sy* ~ *vir 'n eendvoël aansien*, beat the daylights out of someone.

maag¹, (mae, mage), stomach; maw (of animal); gizzard (bird); tummy, corporation; *van jou* ~ *'n AF GOD maak*, make a god of one's belly; *dit sit hom DWARS in die* ~, that sticks in his gullet; *aan sy* ~ *LY*, suffer from gastric (stomach) trouble; *op sy NUGTER* ~, on his empty stomach; *met iets in sy* ~ *SIT*, be embarrassed by something; have a flea in one's ear; *jy kan dit op jou* ~ *SKRYF (en met jou hemp afvee)*, you can whistle for it; *jou* ~ *VASHOU v.d. lag*, shake with laughter; *'n* ~ *soos 'n VOLSTRUIS hê*, he has the stomach of an ostrich; *van sy* ~ *'n WOLSAK maak*, make a god of his stomach; guzzle.

maag², (ong.), kin, kinsman, kinswoman.

maag: ~**aandoening,** affection of the stomach; ~**bitter,** bitter tonic; ~**bloeding,** gastric (internal) haemorrhage; ~**bom,** dumpling; ~**bry,** chyme.

maagd, (-e), virgin, maiden.

Maagd: *DIE* ~, Virgo; *die HEILIGE* ~, the Holy Virgin.

maag'de: ~**blom,** periwinkle; ~**goud,** virgin gold; ~**lik, (-e),** maidenly, virginal; ~**likheid,** virginity, maidenliness; ~**melk,** virginal milk; ~**palm,** periwinkle; ~**rei,** (vero.), virgin chorus.

maag: ~**dermkanaal,** gastro-intestinal tract; ~**dermontsteking,** gastro-enteritis.

maagde: ~**roof, (ong.),** rape, ravishment of women; ~**vlies,** hymen; ~**was,** propolis.

maag'dokter, stomach specialist, gastronomist.

maag'dom, virginity, maidenhood.

maag: ~**druppels,** stomachic elixir; ~**geluide,** borborygmus; collywobbles; ~**holte,** pit of stomach, stomach cavity; ~**kanker,** cancer of the stomach; ~**katar,** catarrh of the stomach; ~**klier,** gastric gland; ~**koors**, gastric fever; enteric fever; military fever; ~**kramp**, spasm of the stomach, gripe; straining disease (horse); ~**kwaal**, stomach complaint; ~**lyer**, stomach-sufferer; ~**ontsteking**, gastritis; ~**operasie**, gastrectomy; ~**pomp**, stomach-pump; ~**pyn**, stomach-ache, gripes; *dit gee 'n mens* ~*pyn*, it makes one sick; it turns one's stomach; ~**pynbossie**, *Myrica quercifolia;* ~**pyp**, stomach-tube; ~**sap**, gastric juice, chyle; ~**seer**, stomach ulcer, peptic ulcer; stomach-ache; ~**senuwee**, stomachic nerve; ~**siekte**, stomach disease.

maag'skap, kindred, kinsfolk, kin; kinship; consanguinity.

maag: ~**slot**, pylorus; ~**spieël**, gastroscope; ~**spoeling**, gastrolavage; ~**steen**, gastrolith; ~**streek**, abdominal (gastric) region; ~**suur**, acidity of the stomach, heartburn; ~**uitgang**, pylorus; ~**vergoding**, belly-worship; ~**vlies**, stomach lining; ~**vliesontsteking**, gastritis; ~**vol**, satiated, satisfied; fed up; ~*vol wees vir iets*, be fed up with something; ~**voorraad**, belly-timber; ~**wand**, stomach wall; ~**werking**, diarrhoea; scouring; ~**wind**, flatus; ~**wind(e)**, flatulence; ~**windmiddel**, carminative; ~**wond**, stomach wound; ~**wurm**, stomach worm.

maai¹, (s) mother, dam; *LOOP na jou* ~*!* go to the devil! *NA sy* ~, gone to the devil.

maai², (w), (ge-), mow, reap; *BAIE mense is toe afge* ~, a large number of people were mown down; *hy* ~ *waar hy nie GESAAI het nie*, he reaps the benefit of another's labour; *wat jy GESAAI het*, reap what one has sown; ~ *ONDER*, shoot a large number of; ~ *en PAGAAI*, bustle and fidget; *wie wil* ~, *moet SAAI*, we must sow to reap.

maai'er¹, (-s), mower, reaper, harvester.

maai'er², (-s), maggot, grub; ~**besmet**, fly-blown (meat).

maai'ery, mowing.

maai'foedie, maai'foerie, (-s), rascal, scoundrel, blackguard.

maai: ~**masjien**, reaper, mowing-machine, mower; grass-cutting machine; ~**tyd**, harvest time, reaping time.

maak, (s) make; making; *sy het 'n rok in die* ~, she is having a dress made; (w) (ge-), make, do; shape, fashion; fabricate, produce; render; *alles wil* ~ *en BREEK*, try to have things exactly one's own way; try to force the issue; ramp and rage; *iem. kan* ~ *en BREEK*, he can do as he pleases; *hy* ~ *DAARNA*, he asks for it; he is looking for it; ~ *dat jy dit DOEN*, see that you do it; *iets ERGER* ~, make something worse; *met die HAND ge*~, made by hand; hand-made; *HOE* ~ *jy dit?* how are things with you? *klere LAAT* ~, have clothes made; *dit nie meer LANK sal* ~ *nie*, not to be able to hold out much longer; *jy* ~ *te LANK*, you are taking too long; *jy* ~ *nie MOOI nie*, that isn't nice; *hy kan NIKS* ~ *nie*, he can do nothing; *dit het daar NIKS mee te* ~ *nie*, that is beside the point; *hy het daar NIKS mee te* ~ *(make) nie*, it is none of his business; *dit NOOIT* ~ *nie*, have no hope of success; *dit* ~ *geen SAAK nie*, it does not matter; *ek* ~ *my STERK om te beweer*, I make bold to state; *jou oor iets VROLIK* ~, laugh at something; *nie WEET wat om daarvan te* ~ *nie*, not to know what to make of it; ~ *dat jy WEGKOM*, be off; ~**loon**, charge for making; ~**sel**, (-s), make, making, manufacture; fabric; handiwork; fashion, structure; ~**werk**, literature made to order (lacking inspiration), pot-boiler.

maal¹, (s) (**male**), meal.

maal², (s) (**male**), time; times (multiplied by); *AL drie* ~, three times already; *LENGTE* ~ *breedte*, length multiplied by breadth; *TEN ene male*, once and for all; *'n* ~ *of TWEE, drie*, two or three times; (w) (ge-), multiply; ~ *8 met 2*, multiply 8 by 2.

maal³, (w) (ge-), grind, mill; mince; pulp, pound.

maal⁴, (w) (ge-), mull about, circle round and round (cattle); be dizzy; eddy, whirl; be crazy; *heeldag oor DIESELFDE ding* ~, be harping on the same thing; *nou* ~ *JY*, now you are crazy; you are talking nonsense; *die WYSIE* ~ *deur my kop*, the tune keeps on running through my head.

maal⁵, (w) (ge-), paint, picture.

maal: ~**beweging**, grinding motion; ~**gat**, whirlpool; pothole; ~**geld**, miller's fee; multure; ~**graan**, grist; ~**klip**, muller, grinding-stone; ~**koring**, grist; ~**loon**, miller's fee; ~**stroom**, whirlpool, eddy, maelstrom; ~**tand**, molar; azzle-tooth.

maal'teken, multiplication sign.

maal'toets, mill test.

maal'tyd, meal, repast; *'n* ~ *opdien*, serve a meal; ~**beplanning**, meal planning.

maal'vleis, mince(meat).

maan¹, (s) (**mane**), moon; *vir die* ~ *BLAF*, bark at the moon; cry for the moon; *dis DONKER* ~, there is no moon; *met die* ~ *GEPLA*, mad at intervals (moonstruck); *deur die* ~ *GETIK wees*, be balmy (moonstruck); *die HALWE* ~, the crescent; *glo dat die* ~ *van KAAS gemaak is*, believe that the moon is made of green cheese; *die* ~ *KOM op!* here comes bald-pate! *by LIGTE* ~, on a moonlit night; *LOOP na die* ~, go to blazes; *alles is NA die* ~, everything is lost; it's all gone; *sy vooruitsigte is NA die* ~, all his expectations have been upset; *sy gesondheid is NA die* ~, his health has broken down; *die skool gaan NA die* ~, the school is going to rack and ruin; *aan die* ~ *wil VAT*, ask (reach) for the moon; *VLIEG na die* ~, go to Jericho; *hy kan na die* ~ *VLIEG*, he can go to Hong Kong; *die WASSENDE, afnemende* ~, the waxing, waning moon.

maan², (w) (ge-), warn, urge; dun (for money).

maan: ~**baan**, moon's orbit; ~**besie**, moon buggy; ~**beskrywing**, selenography; ~**bewoner**, inhabitant of the moon, man in the moon; lunarian selenite; ~**bewing**, moon quake; ~**blom**, moon-flower.

maan'brief, letter of demand; monitory.

maand, (-e), month; *die* ~ *Maart*, the month of March; moon (poetic).

Maan'dag, Monday; *BLOU* ~, blue Monday; *ek was maar 'n blou* ~ *daar*, I hardly spent a day there; *elke blou* ~, every now and then; *'n blou* ~ *BLY*, stay a short time; ~ *HOU*, be taking it easy; *hy KOM altoos* ~*s (..dae)*, he always comes on a Monday; ~**aand**, Monday evening; ~**s**, (-e), Monday; *iets wat* ~*s GEBEUR*, something which happens on a Monday; *die* ~*se KOERANT*, Monday's paper; ~**siek**, Mondayish.

maand: ~**blad**, monthly magazine (periodical, publication); ~**doek**, sanitary towel; ~**elange**, lasting for months, for months (on end); ~**eliks**, (-e), monthly, every month; ~**geld**, monthly salary (wage); ~**gemiddelde**, monthly average; ~**kaartjie**, monthly ticket; ~**loon**, monthly wage(s); ~**oud**, (~**oue**), month-old; ~**staat**, monthly return(s); ~**stonde**, (-s), menstruation, period, catamenia, monthly change; ~**stondpille**, amenorrhoea pills; ~**verslag**, monthly report.

maan: ~**eklips**, eclipse of the moon; ~**foto**, moon photo; ~**gesig**, moon-face; ~**gestalte**, phase of the moon; ~**glas**, lunette.

maan'haar, (s) mane; hog's back, central ridge (in farm road); *sy maanhare rys gou*, he is quick to take offence; (b) **maanhaar-**, jubate; ~**jakkals**, maned jackal, aardwolf *(Proteles cristatus);* ~**kam**, mane-comb; ~**leeu**, lion with mane; ~**paadjie**, hog's-back, track (with ridge).

maan: ~**jaar**, lunar year, moon year; ~**kaart**, chart of the moon; ~**kalf**, mooncalf; ~**kenner**, lunarian; ~**kop**, poppy; ~**krans**, lunar corona; ~**kring**, lunar circle; ~**kruid**, moonwort; ~**landing**, moon-landing; ~**lig**, moonlight; ~**ligaand**, moonlit night; ~**ligstraal**, moonbeam; ~**loos**, moonless; ~**maand**, lunar month; ~**missiellansering**, moon probe (shot); ~**reënboog**, lunar rainbow; ~**reis**, moon probe; ~**reisiger**, moon-traveller; ~**(ruim= te)vaart**, moon probe; ~**saad**, poppy-seed; ~**saadolie**, poppy-seed oil; ~**satellietlansering**, moon probe (shot); ~**sekel**, crescent (of the moon); ~**siek**, lunatic, moonstruck, moony; ~**siekte**, lunacy; ~**sirkel**, lunar (metonic) circle; ~**skyf**, disc of the moon; ~**skyn**, moonlight; *dit was alles* ~*skyn en rosegeur*, everything in the garden was

lovely; ~s'omloop, lunation; ~s'ondergang, moonset; ~s'opgang, moonrise; ~steen, moonstone, girasol(e); ~straal, moonbeam; ~s'verduistering, lunar eclipse; ~tjie, (-s), moonlet; ~tuig, moon craft; ~vis, moon-fish; ~vlek, moon spot; ~vlug, moon flight; ~vormig, (-e), lunar; lunate (leaves); moonlike.
maar¹, (s) (mare), crater, lake.
maar², (s) (ong.) tidings, news.
maar³, (s) (mare), but; *daar KOM 'n ~ by*, there is a but (condition) attached; *GEEN ~ nie, hoor*, but me no buts! (vgw) but, merely, only, yet, just; ~ *ALTE graag*, only too gladly; *BEKEN ~*, you may as well admit; *hy staan ~ en LAG*, he just stands laughing; *LOOP nou ~*, you may go now; ~ *'n SNUITER*, only a youngster; *TOE ~!* righto! all right! don't mention it! *dit is ~ VERVELEND*, it is rather boring; *WAG ~*, (you) just wait; *soveel soos jy ~ WIL*, as much as ever you want.
maar'skalk, (-e), marshal; ~skap, marshalship; ~staf, marshal's baton.
Maart, March; ~maand, the month of March.
Maas¹, Meuse.
maas², (s) = amaas.
maas³, (s) (mase), mesh, stitch; eye (net); (w) (ge-), darn; do invisible mending; ~bal, darning-ball; ~kouse, mesh stockings; ~naald, darning-needle; ~steek, basket-stitch; ~werk, network; tracery; ~wydte, size of mesh.
maat¹, (-s, maters), mate, comrade, compeer, companion, fellow, friend, pal, chum, partner; *DIK ~s wees*, be as thick as thieves; *sy maters is klein DOOD*, he has no equal; *hy is nie JOU ~ nie*, he is your superior; *~s MAAK*, make friends; *OU ~*, old chap; *waar is dié SKOEN se ~?*, where is the pair to this shoe?
maat², (mate), measure, dimension, size; metre (poetry): gauge; bar, time (music); *die ~ AANGEE*, beat time; *BO die ~*, oversized; *BO mate*, beyond measure; more than usual; *mate en GEWIGTE*, weights and measures; *by die GROOT ~ verkoop*, sell wholesale; *~ HOU*, keep within limits; *met watter ~ jy MEET, sal jy weer gemeet word*, you will be measured by your own yardstick; with what measure ye mete, it shall be measured to you again; *met twee mate MEET*, be biased; measure by two standards; *op die ~ van die MUSIEK*, in time to the music; *NA ~*, to measure; *iem. se ~ NEEM*, take someone's measure; *sy ~ is VOL*, his cup is full; he has reached the limit; *see* mate.
maat: ~afdeling, bespoke department; ~analise, volumetric analysis; ~band, tape-measure; ~eenheid, unit of measure; ~emmer, bucket-measure; ~fles, measuring-flask; ~gevoel, time-sense; ~glas, measuring-glass, graduated glass; burette; ~grafie, measuring-scoop.
maat'jie¹, (-s, matertjies), little friend (playmate), little pal.
maat'jie², (-s), small measure.
maat: ~kleremaker, bespoke tailor; ~kleremakery, bespoke tailoring; ~koeël, standard bullet; ~lint, tape-measure; ~lont, time-fuse; ~loos: *..lose verse*, free verse; ~lyn, dimension-line; ~lys, size-roll (clothes); ~motief, phrase; ~plaat, templet, template; ~reël, measure, precautionary measure; ~*reëls neem (tref)*, take steps (action); ~rol, full roll (material).
maat'skap, comradeship.
maatskap'lik, (-e), social; ~*e GEREGTIGHEID*, social justice; ~*e KAPITAAL*, joint stock, nominal capital; ~*e WERK*, welfare work; ~*e WERKSTER*, welfare worker (lady).
maatskappy', (-e), society; company; community; ~ *op AANDELE*, joint-stock company; ~ *met BEPERKTE aanspreeklikheid*, limited liability company; ~ewet, companies act; ~hervorming, social reformation; ~leer, sociology; social science; company studies.
maat: ~skets, diagram to scale; ~skoene, bespoke boots; ~slag, beat (music).
maats'makerig, (-e), mat(e)y.
maat'staf, set-rod.

maat'staf, (..stawe, ..stawwe), measuring-stick; measure, gauge; module; criterion, standard; *aan 'n ~ VOLDOEN*, satisfy the standard set; *tot ~ NEEM*, take as a criterion; *~ van VERGELYKING*, standard of comparison.
maat: ~stok, yardstick, rule; size-stick (cobbler); gauge; dip-stick; baton; ~streep, bar (music); ~syfer, dimension figure; ~tabel, time-table (music); ~vas, (-te), perfect in keeping time (music).
maca'dam, macadam.
macadamiseer', (ge-), macadamize.
macaro'ni, macaroni.
Macedo'nië, Macedonia; ~r, (-s), Macedonian.
Machiavellis'me, Machiavellism; ..lis'ties, (-e), machiavellian.
Madagas'karbees, Madagascar ox.
Madagas'sies, (-e), Madagascan, Madagascarian.
madam', (-s), madam, lady.
madapolam', madapollam.
madei'ra: ~koek, Madeira cake; ~stoel, Madeira chair, grass chair; ~wyn, Madeira (wine).
ma'deliefie, (-s), daisy; gowan.
Madon'na, (-s), Madonna; ~beeld, image of the Madonna; ~lelie, Madonna lily.
madrigaal', (..gale), madrigal.
Madrileens', (-e), Madrilenian.
maece'nas, (-se), maecenas, art patron.
ma'er, (-der, -ste), lean, thin; meagre; angular, bony; jejune; attenuated; gaunt; lathlike, lathy; *~ JARE*, lean years; *~ KAAS*, skimmed-milk cheese; *~ KALK*, cold lime; *so ~ soos 'n KRAAI*, as thin as a lath; *~ VLEIS*, lean meat; *~ WORD*, grow thin, loose flesh; ~heid, thinness, leanness; jejuneness, meagreness; ~man, medicinal herb *(Urginea altissima)*; ~merrie, shin; ~te = maerheid.
maes'tro, (-'s), maestro.
mag¹, (s) (-te), power, might, authority, strength, force; grasp, grip, hold; control, command; potency; posse (police); puissance; *uit (met) ALLE ~*, with might and main; *BOKANT my ~*, beyond my power; *BUITE my ~*, beyond my power; *BY ~ te wees om*, be able (empowered) to; *'n ~ van GELD*, a power (mint) of money; *die GESTELDE ~te*, the powers that be; *'n GEWAPENDE ~*, an armed force; *die ~ van die GEWOONTE*, the force of habit; *die ~ in HANDE hê*, be in power; *'n ~ der MENIGTE*, a multitude; a horde; *'n ~ van MENSE*, a great number of people; *~ is REG*, might is right; *uit alle ~ SKREEU*, shout at the top of one's voice; *die UITVOERENDE ~*, the executive authority; *VERDELING van ~*, power-sharing; *x tot die derde ~ VERHEF*, raise x to the third power; *iem. die ~ VERLEEN om*, empower (authorize) someone to; *geen ~ ter WÊRELD*, no power on earth; *WETGEWENDE ~*, legislative power.
mag², (w) (het mag, het gemag; mog), may, be allowed; *~ GOD my help*, may God help me; *MOG hy my daaroor vervolg*, should he want to institute proceedings against me; *dit ~ NIE*, this is not allowed; *~ dit WAAR wees*, may that be true; *WAT ook ~ gebeur*, happen what may.
magasyn', (-e), shop, warehouse, store; magazine (of rifle); arsenal; emporium; promptuary; ~geweer, magazine rifle; ~knip, magazine catch; ~meester, storekeeper; stockkeeper; ~werker, magazine man.
mag: ~brief, warrant, power of attorney; ~dom, lot, heap(s); tons; *daar was 'n ~dom van mense*, there were crowds of people.
magen'ta, magenta.
mag'gewer, principal; person for whom another acts as agent.
mag'gies, good gracious!
mag: ~hebbende, (-s), ruler, one in authority; ~hebber, (-s), ruler, one in authority; authorized representative.
magie'¹, magic art.
ma'gie², (-s), small stomach, tummy.
ma'giër¹, (-s), magician.
ma'giër², (-s), magus, mage.
ma'gies, (-e), magic(al).

magis'ter, (-s), master (of arts); master's degree; ~**graad,** master's degree.
magistraal', (..strale), authoritative, magisterial; imposing.
magistraat', (..strate), magistrate; ~**s'distrik,** magistracy; ~**setel,** seat of magistracy; ~**s'hof,** magistrate's court; ~**s'huis,** residency; ~**s'kantoor,** magistrate's office; ~**skap,** magistracy.
magistratuur', (..ture), magistracy.
Magjaar', (Magjare), Magyar; ~**s', (-e),** Magyar= (ian).
mag'ma, (-s), magma; ~**'ties, (-e),** magmatic.
Mag'na Car'ta, Magna C(h)arta.
magnaat', (magnate), magnate.
magneet¹, (magnete), magnet; loadstone (lodestone); ~**afwyking,** magnetic declination; ~**anker,** magnetic armature; ~**helling,** magnetic inclination; ~**krag,** magnetic force; ~**naald,** magnetic needle; ~**ontsteking,** magneto-ignition; ~**pool,** magnetic pole; ~**steen,** magnetic pyrite; lodestone; ~**veld,** magnetic field; ~**yster,** magnetite; magnetic iron.
magne'sia, magnesia; bitter-earth; ~**melk,** milk of magnesia.
magne'sies, (-e), magnesian.
magnesiet', magnesite.
magne'sium, magnesium; ~**lamp,** flash-light lamp; ~**lig,** flash-light; ~**melk,** milk of magnesia; ~**patroon,** flash-cartridge; ~**sulfaat,** Epsom salts.
magne'ties, (-e), magnetic; ~*e AANTREKKING,* magnetic attraction; ~*e AFWYKING,* magnetic declination; ~*e MYN,* magnetic mine; ~*e NOORDE,* magnetic north; ~*e WEERSTAND,* magnetic resistance, reluctance.
magnetiet', magnetite.
magnetiseer', (ge-), magnetize; ~**der, (-s),** magnet= izer.
magnetise'ring, magnetization.
magnetiseur', (-s), magnetizer; mesmerist.
magnetis'me, magnetism; *dierlike* ~, animal magnet= ism.
magne'to, (-'s), magneto; ~**meter,** magnetometer.
magno'lia, (-s), magnolia.
magou', magou.
mag'punt, power (of lever); radial axis.
mags: ~ **aanwyser,** (algebraic) exponent, index; ~ **argument,** baculine argument; ~ **ewewig,** balance of power; ~ **gebied,** sphere of influence; ~ **misbruik,** abuse of power, misfeasance; ~ **politiek,** power politics; ~ **posisie,** position of power.
mag'spreuk, conclusive argument, clincher; peremp= tory command; catchword.
mags: ~ **uitbreiding,** expansion of power; ~ **verhef= fing,** involution (maths.); ~ **vertoon,** display of power; ~ **wellus,** craving for power.
mag'teloos, (..lose), powerless, helpless, impotent, impuissant; ~ **heid,** powerlessness, impotence; par= alysis; impuissance.
mag'tie, good gracious! heavens!
mag'tig, (w) (ge-), authorize, warrant, accredit, em= power; (b) **(-e),** powerful, mighty; rich (food); (bw) mightily; *IETS* ~ *wees,* have mastered (have full command of) something; *dit is vir my TE* ~, that is (a bit) too steep (rich) for me; (tw): *my* ~! good gracious me! ~**heid,** mightiness.
mag'tiging, (-e,-s), mandate, warrant, authority, fiat, authorization; *INGEVOLGE* ~ *van,* by virtue of the authority conferred by; *MET* ~ *van,* on the authority of; *op SKRIFTELIKE* ~ *van,* on the written authority of; ~**sbrief,** letter of authority; charter; ~ **swet,** enabling act
mags'woord, authoritative word, catchword; clincher.
maharad'ja, (-s), maharaja(h).
mahara'ni, (-'s), maharani.
Maharat'ta, (-s), Maharatta.
mahat'ma, (-s), mahatma.
mah'di, (-'s), mahdi.
mahem'(kraanvoël), wattled crane.
maho'nie, (-s), mahogany; ~**boom,** mahogany (tree); ~**meubels,** mahogany furniture; ~**hout,** mahog= any (wood).

ma'-hulle, mother and the rest (cum suis), mum and co(mpany).
mainteneer', (ge-), maintain, keep (a mistress).
maitres'se, (-s), mistress, kept woman.
maize'na, maizena (registered trade name).
ma'jesteit, (-e), majesty; splendour; ~**skennis,** high treason, lèse-majesté.
majestueus', (-e), majestic, august.
majeur', major; ~**toonladder,** ~**toonleer,** major scale.
majo'lika, majolica.
majoor', (-s), major; ~**skap,** majority; ~**s'rang,** rank of major, majority.
majoraat', (..rate), primogeniture; entailed estate.
majordo'mus, (-se), major-domo.
majus'kel, (-s), majuscule.
mak, (-ker, -ste), tame, docile, gentle, tractable, quiet, domestic (animals); familiar; *AL* ~ *word,* lose one's shyness; *'n* ~ *ENGELSMAN,* an Afrikaner= ised Englishman; *so* ~ *soos 'n LAM,* as meek as a lamb; *iem.* ~ *MAAK,* keep a person in his place; *die perd WORD al* ~, the horse is becoming tame.
makaak'aap, (..ape), macaco.
maka'ber, (-e), macabre.
makada'mia, (-s), macadamia; ~**boord,** macadamia orchard; ~**neut,** macadamia nut.
makas'sar, (-s), Macassar; **m**~**olie,** Macassar oil.
makas'terkop, curly-head; wooly hair.
mataan', (-s, ..tane), wild watermelon.
makeer', (ge-), ail, lack; matter; be wanting, be amiss; *sy* ~ *ALTYD iets,* there is always something wrong with her; *wat* ~ *JOU?* what is the matter with you? *sy* ~ *NOOIT,* she is always present; *daar* ~ *10 SKAPE,* there are 10 sheep missing.
ma'kelaar, (-s), broker; banian, banyan (Hindoo); ~ *in EFFEKTE,* stockbroker; ~ *in vaste EIENDOM,* (real) estate agent.
ma'kelaars: ~**brief(ie),** broker's note; ~**kommissie,** ~**loon,** brokerage; ~**rekening,** broker's account, account at the broker; ~**werk,** jobbing.
makelary', broker's business, brokerage.
ma'ker, (-s), maker, fabricator; creator.
maket', (-te), maquette.
mak'gemaak, (-te), tame; *'n* ~ *te Engelsman,* an Afri= kanerised Englishman.
mak'heid, tameness, docility.
mak'ker, (-s), companion, pal.
mak'lik, (b) (-e), easy, comfortable; (bw) at (with) ease, readily, easily, light; ~**heid,** ease, easiness, comfortableness.
makop'pa, (-s), mamba.
makou', (-e), Muscovy duck; rabbit (cricket); duffer (golf); ~**mannetjie,** Muscovy drake; ~**wyfie,** Mus= covy duck.
makriel', (-e), mackerel.
ma'krokern, macronucleus.
ma'krokosmos, macrocosm.
makrol', (-le), ~**letjie, (-s),** almond cake, macaroon.
makrosko'pies, (-e), macroscopic.
ma'krospoor, macrospore.
ma'krostraler, (-s), jumbo jet.
mak'si, (s) (-'s), maxi; (b) **maksi-,** maxi-.
maksil', (-le), maxilla; ~**lêr', (-e),** maxillary.
maksimaal', (..male), maximum, maximal.
maksimalis', (-te), maximalist.
maksimaliseer', (ge-), maximize.
mak'simum, (s, b) (-s, ..ma), maximum; ~**prys,** maximum (ceiling) price.
maku'basnuif, maccaboy, maccabaw.
mal¹, (s), (-le), mould, gauge, model, shape, templet; stencil plate.
mal², (b) mad; foolish, silly, daft; raving, potty; rabid; phrenetic; *'n* ~ *BOBBEJAAN wees,* be a very fun= ny and lively person; be a real clown; *sy* ~ *le MOER af sukkel,* have an exhausting struggle; *iem. WERK hom* ~ *en moer,* he works himself to the bone.
Ma'labaar, Malabar; ~**s', (-e),** Malabar.
ma'lagawyn, malaga (wine).
malagiet', (-e), malachite.
malai'se, malaise; (trade) depression, slump.
malai'ta = amalaita.

Malak'ka, Malacca.
mala'ria, malaria; ~**aanval**, malarial attack; ~-**agtig, (-e)**, miasmatic; ~**basil**, malaria(l) germ; ~**infeksie**, malarial infection; ~**koors**, malarial fever; ~**lyer**, malaria sufferer; ~**muskiet**, anopheles, malaria(l) mosquito; ~**streek**, malaria region; ~**verskynsel**, malaria(l) symptom(s); ~**vry, (-e)**, free from malaria.
Mala'wi, Malawi; (-'s), inhabitant of Malawi; ~**es, (-e)**, Malawian.
Malbaar'[1], (..**bare**), (native of) Malabar.
malbaar'[2], (..**bare**), chatterbox.
mal'boet, (-e), messenger.
mal'by, solitary bee.
ma'le: *ten ene* ~, entirely, absolutely.
maledik'sie, malediction.
Malea'gi, Malachi.
Malei'er, (-s), Malay.
Malei'a, Malaya.
Maleis', (-e), Malay; ~**ië**, Malaysia.
malen'ger, (s) (-s), malingerer, shirker; (w) **(ge-)**, feign sickness, malinger; ~**ing**, malingering, shirking of duty.
malgas'[1], **(-se)**, gannet.
Malgas'[2], **(-se)**, Malagasy, Madagascan; Madagascar ox; ~**sies, (-e)**, Malagasy.
mal: ~**gif**, poison for arrows; ~**heid**, madness, insanity; nonsense, foolishness, silliness, daftness; ~**huis**, madhouse, lunatic asylum.
ma'lie[1], (s) (geselsel.), money.
ma'lie[2], (s) pall-mall (kind of game); (w) **(ge-)**, play the game of pall-mall.
ma'lie[3], (s) ring (of coat of mail).
ma'liebaan, court on which pall-mall is played; mall.
ma'liehemp, coat of mail.
ma'lieklip, chucker-quoit.
ma'liekolder, coat of mail, hauberk, chain-mail.
ma'ling, milling, whirling; gurgitation; eddy; ~ *aan iets HÊ*, not care two straws about something; *iem. in die* ~ *NEEM*, play the fool with someone.
mal'jan: ~ *onder die hoenders*, a thorn among the roses.
mal'kop, (s) mad person; harum-scarum, madcap, tomboy; (b) silly, mad; ~ *WEES oor iets*, be excited about something; *moenie so* ~ *WEES nie*, don't behave like a madman; ~**by**, mason-bee; ~**kuns**, crazy art; ~**meelkewer**, confused flour-beetle; ~**siekte**, blind staggers (horse); goggles (sheep); ~**streek**, foolish trick, prank, antic.
mal'kuns, ultra-modern art; crazy art.
mal'lemeule, (-s), merry-go-round.
mal'lemok, mallemuck, mollymauk.
mal'lemot, variety of hornet.
mal'lerig, (-e), rather foolish, loony; ~**heid**, foolishness, silliness.
mal: ~**ligheid**, nonsense, foolishness, silliness, tomfoolery; ~**maakmeisie**, glamour girl.
malmok', (-ke), fulmar; ~**albatros**, black-browed albatross; ~**kie, (-s)**, guinea-pig, marmot.
mals, (-e, -er, -ste), soft, juicy, tender (meat); mellow (fruit); lush (grass); ~**heid**, softness, juiciness, tenderness, mellowness.
Mal'ta, Malta; ~**koors**, Malta fever.
malta'se, maltase.
Maltees', (Maltese), Maltese.
Malte'ser, (-s), Maltese.
Malthusiaan', (..siane), Malthusian; ~**s, (-e)**, Malthusian.
Malthusianis'me, Malthusianism.
malto'se, maltose.
mal'trap, (-pe), madcap, silly person, tomboy, harum-scarum.
mal'va, (-s), geranium; crane's bill; ~**lekker**, marshmallow.
malversa'sie, (-s), malversation.
malvesy'(wyn), malmsey.
mal'water, alcohol, strong drink.
mama', (-'s), mam(m)a.
mama'tjie, mam'matjie, (-s), mummy (mother).
mam'ba, (-s), mamba.
Mameluk', (-ke), Mameluke.
mam'mie, (-s), (little) mother, mummy.

mam'moet, (-e), mammoth; ~**boom**, sequoia.
Mam'mon, Mammon; ~ *dien*, serve Mammon; ~**is'me**, Mammonism; ~**verering**, Mammon worship.
mampar'ra, (-s), stupid person; worthless ore.
mampoer', home-distilled brandy.
mam's(ie), mum, mummy.
man, (-s, -ne), man; husband; *'n* ~ *van AANSIEN*, a man of (high) standing; *iets op die* ~ *AF vra*, ask a straight question; *die arm* ~ *se BAADJIE*, the sun; *iets aan die* ~ *BRING*, sell something; *'n* ~ *v.d. DAAD*, a man of action; *'n* ~ *DUISEND*, a man in a million (thousand); *soos EEN* ~, unanimously; *'n* ~ *van EER*, an honourable man; ~*s GENOEG wees om*, be man enough to; *die GEWONE* ~, the man in the street; the common man; *'n* ~ *HONDERD*, a Trojan; a stalwart; *tot die LAASTE* ~, to the last man; *sy* ~ *KRY*, catch a Tartar; ~ *en MAAG*, man, woman and child; *'n* ~ *van iem. MAAK*, make a man out of a person; *net so min as die* ~ *in die MAAN*, no more than the man in the moon; *met* ~ *en MAG*, with might and main; *met* ~ *en MUIS vergaan*, be lost with all aboard; go down with all hands; *ONDER ons* ~*s*, among us; *OP die* ~ *af*, to his face; straight from the shoulder; *'n* ~ *PURE* ~, a man through and through; ~ *en PERD noem*, quote chapter and verse; *jou* ~ *STAAN*, stand one's ground; *ek hou van 'n* ~ *wat sy* ~ *kan STAAN*, I admire a person who can hold his own; *'n geveg van* ~ *TEEN* ~, a hand-to-hand fight; ~ *VIR* ~, man for man; *op die* ~ *af VRA*, ask someone point-blank; *elke* ~ *soen sy VROU op sy eie manier*, everybody does things in his own way; ~ *en VROU*, husband and wife; *'n* ~ *van die WÊRELD*, a man of the world; *'n* ~ *van sy WOORD*, a man of his word; *'n* ~ *se WOORD, 'n* ~ *se eer*, an honest man's word is as good as his bond; ~**ag'tig, (-e)**, mannish, masculine; ~**ag'tigheid**, mannishness; ~**alleen**, without any assistance; all alone; all on his own.
man'baar, (..bare), marriageable; pubescent; ~**heid**, manhood, puberty, marriageableness; ~**wording**, pubescence.
mandaat', (mandate), mandate; warrant; authority; ~**gebied**, mandated territory; mandate; ~**houer, (-s)**, mandatary.
man'dag, man-day.
mandari'n(e), (-s), mandarin(e).
mandaryn', (-e), mandarin; ~**eend**, mandarin duck.
mandata'ris, (-se), mandatary.
mandateer', (ge-), mandate.
mandement', (-e), mandament; ~ *van spolie*, mandament of spoliation.
man'djie, (-s), basket; corf; crate; hamper; panier; *met die hele* ~ *PATATS uitkom*, let the cat out of the bag; ~**bal**, basket-ball; ~**boot**, coracle, basketboat; ~**bottel**, osier bottle; ~**fles**, wicker-bottle; demijohn; carboy (for acids); ~**handel**, basket trade; ~**hut**, wattle-and-daub hut; ~**maker**, basket-maker; ~**smakery**, basket factory; ~**tjie, (-s)**, pottle (for strawberries); small basket; ~**vol, (mandjiesvol)**, basketful; ~**wa**, basket-carriage; wicker-work carriage; ~**werk**, wickerwork, osier-work, basketry; ~**wieg**, wicker cradle.
mandolien', (-e, -s), mandoli'ne, (-s), mandolin(e); ~**speler**, mandolinist.
mandoor', (-s, mandore), foreman.
mandrago'ra, mandragora, mandrake.
mandril', (-le -s), mandrill.
ma'ne, mane (of horse).
Man'eilander, Manxman.
manel', (-le), dress-coat, frock-coat; manille (ombre); ~**letjie, (-s)**, small frock-coat; ~**pak**, morning dress; ~**pant**, coat-tail.
ma'ner, (-s), dunner.
ma'neskyn = maanskyn.
maneu'ver, (-s), manoeuvre, piece of generalship; operation (mil.).
maneuvreer', (ge-), manoeuvre; ~**baar, (..bare)**, manoeuvrable; ~**baarheid**, manoeuvrability.
maneuvre'ring, manoeuvring, handling.
manewa'le(s), antics, capers.

mangaan', manganese; ~**brons**, manganese bronze; ~**chloride**, ~**chloried**, chloride of manganese; ~**erts**, manganese ore; braunite; ~**houdend**, (-e), manganiferous; ~**kool**, pelagite; ~**yster**, ferromanganese, mirror-iron.
manganaat', manganate.
manganiet', manganite.
man'gat, manhole.
man'gel¹, (s) (-s), tonsil.
man'gel², (s) (-s), mangle; (w) (ge-), mangle; calender.
man'gel³, (s) want, lack; *by* ~ *van vertroue*, in the absence of confidence; (w) be lacking; *dit* ~ *hom aan selfvertroue*, he lacks selfconfidence.
man'gelaar, (-s), mangler.
man'gelontsteking, amygdalitis, tonsilitis.
man'gelwortel, mangold (-wurzel), mangel-wurzel.
man'go, (-'s), mango.
man'gostan, mangosteen.
manhaf'tig, (-e), brave, courageous, manly, valorous, valiant, virile, doughty; ~**heid**, bravery, courage; manliness, virility, doughtiness, prowess.
maniak', (-ke), maniac; faddist, crank.
Maniche"is'me, Manicheism.
ma'nie, (-ë, -s), mania; craze, rage, fad.
manier', (-e), manner, fashion, way; *iets so op 'n* ~ *DOEN*, do something after a fashion; *op EEN of ander* ~, in one way or another; *op ELKE moont= like* ~, in every possible way; *GEEN* ~ *e ken nie*, be ill-mannered; *dit is GEEN* ~ *nie*, that is not the way to do things; *OP hierdie* ~, in this way; *OP sy* ~, in his own way.
maniëris', (-te), mannerist, ~**me**, mannerism; ~**ties**, (-e), manneristic.
manier'lik, (-e), polite, well-behaved, mannerly; ~**heid**, politeness, good behaviour, mannerliness, good form, gentlemanliness.
manier'tjie, (-s), trick, mannerism.
ma'nies, (-e), manic; ~**-depressief**, manic-depressive.
manifes', (-te), manifest(o); ~**ta'sie**, manifestation; ~**teer'**, (ge-), manifest; ~**te'ring**, manifesting.
manikuur', (s) (..kure), manicure; (w) (ge-), manicure; ~**stel**, manicure set.
manikuris', (-te), manicurist.
manil'la, (-s), Manilla (cigar); ~**papier**, Manilla paper.
maniok', manioc.
mani'pel, (-le), maniple.
manipula'sie, (-s), manipulation.
manipuleer', (ge-), manipulate; wangle, cook.
manipule'ring, manipulating, manipulation.
manjifiek', (-e), magnificent, splendid.
mank, limping, lame, crippled, halt(ing); ~ *loop*, limp, walk with a limp.
man'ke, (-s), lame person, cripple.
mankement', (-e), fault, defect.
mank'heid, lameness, limpness.
mankoliek'(ig), (-e), ill; ~ *wees*, be ill, be crocked; be rickety (furniture); ~**heid**, illness; ricketiness.
mank'poot, dot-and-go-one (limping gait).
man'lief, hubby.
man'lik, (-e), manly; manlike; masculine; male (offspring); ~**heid**, manliness, valour, courage; masculinity.
manmoe'dig, (-e), brave, manly, courageous; ~**heid**, bravery, courageousness.
man'na, manna; millet; ~**gras**, manna-grass *(Saeteria spp.)* ~**saad**, manna seed; ~**suiker**, mannite.
man'ne: ~**hater**, man-hater; ~**kiesreg**, manhood suffrage; ~**klooster**, monastery; ~**koor**, male choir; **krag**, manly strength, manpower, human resources; labour.
mannekyn', (-e), mannequin.
man'ne: ~**moed**, manly courage; ~**stem**, male voice; man's voice; ~**taal**, forcible (manly) language.
man'netjie, (-s), little man (fellow); jockey (mining); manikin, chappie; male (of animals); ~**(s)kat**, tomcat; ~**sagtig**, (-e), shrewish, termagant; mannish; ~**(s)bobbejaan**, male monkey (baboon); ~**sduif**, cock pigeon; ~**(s)eend**, drake; ~**(s)gans**, gander; ~**sjakkals**, dog-fox; ~**(s)kalkoen**, turkey-cock; ~**skonyn**, buck rabbit; ~**solifant**, bull elephant; ~**volk**, toroeli ovaring, male fern; ~**svolstruis**,

male ostrich; ~**svrou**, virago, shrew, mazon; ~**swaan**, cob.
man'newerk, man's work.
man'nie, hubby.
mannin', (-ne), (ong.) woman; virago.
man'nitol, mannitol.
ma'nometer, manome'ter, (-s), manometer; steam gauge.
manome'tries, (-e), manometric.
man'saal¹, cross-saddle.
man'saal², men's dormitory; men's ward.
mans: ~**afdeling**, men's department (ward); ~**broek**, man's trousers; ~**drag**, men's wear; ~**dubbelspel**, men's doubles; ~**enkelspel**, men's singles; ~**ferweel**, corduroy; ~**frokkie**, singlet; ~**goed**, male clothes; ~**hand**, man's hand; man's handwriting; ~**handskoen**, (gentle)man's glove; ~**hangkas**, man's wardrobe; ~**hemp**, (hemde), man's shirt; ~**hoed**, man's hat; ~**hoogte**, man's height; *die seun is al amper* ~ *hoogte*, the boy is almost as tall as a man.
man'siek, (-e), lovesick, man-mad, yearning for men; ~**te**, nymphomania.
mansjet', (-te), cuff; ~**knoop**, (cuff-)link.
man'skap, (-pe), crew man; soldier, private; rating (in navy).
mans'kleding, mans'klere, male attire (apparel), men's wear.
mans'klerehandelaar, men's outfitter.
man'skoen, man's shoe.
man'slag, manslaughter; homicide; *strafbare* ~, culpable homicide.
mans: ~**lengte**, man's size, man's height; ~**mens**, man, male; ~**moeder**, husband's mother; ~**naam**, man's name; ~**oor**, hazelwort; ~**pak**, men's suit; ~**persoon**, *see* **mansmens**; ~**portret**, portrait of a man; ~**rol**, male role.
man: ~**stem**, male voice; ~**suster**, husband's sister.
man'tel, (-s), mantle, gown, cloak, cape, capote; cope (building); fire-screen; casing; jacket; sheath; *met die* ~ *van LIEFDE bedek*, cover with the cloak of charity; *ONDER die* ~ *van*, under the cloak of; *sy* ~ *het op sy VRIEND geval*, his mantle fell upon his friend's shoulders; *sy* ~ *na die WIND hang*, trim one's sails to the wind; ~**aap**, capuchin monkey; ~**dier**, tunicate; ~**draaier**, turncoat, chameleon, temporizer; ~**kostuum**, coat and skirt (costume); ~**kraag**, cape (of a cloak); ~**meeu**, saddleback; ~**mou** cape sleeve; ~**pak**, coat and skirt (costume); ~**plaat**, wrapper-plate; ~**projektiel**, mantle-projectile; ~**silinder**, jacketed cylinder; ~**tjie**, (-s), mantelet; ~**vlies**, diaphragm; skirting.
mantil'la, (-s), mantilla.
mantis'se, (-s), mantissa.
Mantsjoery'e, Manchuria; ~**r**, Manchurian.
mannaal', **(manuale)**, handbook, manual; keyboard (of organ).
manufaktu're, drapery, piece-goods.
manumis'sie, manumission.
manuskrip', (-te), manuscript; copy.
man'uur, man hour.
Mao'ri, (-'s), Maori.
map, (-pe), folder.
map'stieks! good gracious! my word!
maraboe'ooievaar, (-s), marabou (stork).
maraboet', (-e), marabout, Moslem hermit.
marak'ka, maran'ka, (-s), maraca, calabash marrow.
maraschi'no, maraskyn', maraschino; ~**kersie**, maraschino cherry.
Ma'ratlion, Marathon.
ma'rathon, (-s), marathon; ~**loper**, marathon runner; ~**wedloop**, marathon race.
marco'nigram, (-me), radiogram, marconigram.
marconis', (-te), marconi operator.
ma're, (-s), news, report, tidings; rumour.
ma'retak, mistletoe.
margarien', margari'ne, margarine.
mar'ge, (-s), margin.
marginaal', (..nale), marginal; ..*nale wins*, marginal profit.
margriet'jie, (-s), marguerite, daisy, moonflower; *wilde* wh ~, ox-eyed daisy.

Mari'a, Mary; ~-**aanbidding,** Mariolatry; ~**beeld,** Madonna, statue of Mary; ~**boodskap,** Annunciation Day; ~**ligmis,** Candlemas.
mari'astrane, Mary's-tears (a stoep plant).
Mari'averering, Mariolatry.
marien', (-e), marine; ~*e plantegroei,* sea vegetation.
mariët'teklokkie, Canterbury bell.
marim'ba, (-s), marimba.
mari'na, (-s), marina; ~**woongebied,** marina.
marina'de, (-s), marinade.
mari'ne, navy, seapower; ~**artillerie,** naval artillery; ~**blou,** navy blue.
marineer', (ge-), marinade (marinate), pickle.
mari'ne: ~**hospitaal,** naval hospital; ~-**instituut,** naval college; ~**konstruksie,** naval construction; ~**lugmag,** navy-air component; ~**offisier,** naval officer; ~**soldaat,** marine; ~**staf,** naval staff; ~**stasie,** naval station; ~**verbindingsdiens,** naval communication; ~**vlieër,** naval flyer; ~**vliegtuig,** naval aeroplane; ~**werf,** (naval) dockyard; shipyard; ~**wese,** naval affairs, navy.
marinier', (-s), marine(r).
marinis', (-te), marinist; navalist.
marinis'me, marinism (geol.).
marionet', (-te), puppet; ~**speler,** puppet-man; ~**(te)spel,** puppet-show.
maritaal', (..tale), marital.
maritiem', (-e), maritime.
marjolein', marjoram.
mark¹, (-e), mark (German coin).
mark², (-te), market; emporium; *op die* ~ *BRING,* put on the market; *na die* ~ *GAAN,* go to market; *vir die* ~ *GESKIK,* marketable; *die* ~ *KUNSMATIG beïnvloed,* manipulate the market; *ONDER die* ~ *verkoop,* sell below current prices; *die* ~ *OORSTROOM,* flood (swamp) the market; *op alle* ~ *te TUIS,* an all-round man; a man of many parts.
markant', (-e), salient, outstanding, striking.
markasiet', marcasite.
mark: ~**bederwer,** (-s), spoil-trade; ~**berig,** (-te), market report; ~**dag,** market day.
markeer', (ge-), mark (time); *die pas* ~ , mark time.
markee'tent, marquee (tent).
markeur', (-s), marker (billiards).
mar'ketenter, (-s), vivandier, sutler.
mar'ketentster, (-s), vivandière.
mark: ~**gebou,** market building; ~**geld,** market money; market-dues.
mark'graaf, margrave; ~**skap,** margravate.
markgravin', (-ne), margravine.
markies', (-e), marquis; ~**in',** (-ne), marchioness; ~**tent,** marquee (tent).
mark'inmenging, interfering in the market; market interference.
markisaat', (..sate), marquisate.
markiset', (-te), marquisette.
mark: ~**klaar,** finished (product); ~**meester,** market master; assizer; ~**opname,** market survey; ~**plein,** market square; ~**prys,** market price; ~**sakkie,** pocket (for oranges, potatoes); ~**stad,** market town; ~**stalletjie,** market stall.
Mar'kus, Mark.
mark: ~**verslag,** market report; ~**waarde,** market (current) value; ~**wette,** market regulations.
marl'priem, marl'spyker, marline spike.
marlyn', (-e), marlin(e), spearfish (genus *Makaira*).
marmela'de, marmalade.
mar'mer, (s) marble; (w) (ge-), marble; grain; ~**aar,** vein in marble; ~**agtig,** (-e), marble-like, marmoreal; ~**beeld,** marble statue; ~**blad,** marble top; ~**buuste,** marble bust; ~**groef,** marble quarry; ~**ing,** graining, marbling; ~**iseer',** (ge-), marmorize; ~**kleur,** marble colour; ~**myn,** marble quarry (mine); ~**plaat,** marble slab; ~**rand,** marble edge; ~**saag,** grub saw; ~**skilder,** grainer; ~**slypsel,** marble dust; ~**steen,** marble (stone); ~**struktuur,** marbling (in beef); ~**werker,** marble worker.
marmo'tjie, (-s), guinea-pig, marmot.
maroe'la, (-s), marula *(Sclerocarya caffra).*
Marokkaan', (..kane), Moroccan; ~**s',** (-e), Moroccan.

Marok'ko, Morocco.
marokyn', Morocco (leather); ~**leer,** saffian; *nagemaakte* ~ *leer,* paste-grain.
marqueterie', inlaid work, marquetry.
Mars¹, Mars; *van* ~ , Martian.
mars², (-e), pack (of pedlar); *HEELWAT in sy* ~ *hê,* know a thing or two; *hy het nie VEEL in sy* ~ *nie,* he does not know much.
mars³, top (naval).
mars⁴, (-e), march (of troops); march (music); *op* ~ *gaan,* be on the march.
marsa'la, Marsala (wine).
marsban'ker = masbanker.
mars'bevel, (-e), marching order.
Mars'bewoner, Martian.
Marsei'lle, Marseilles.
Marseillai'se, Marseillaise.
mar'sepein, marchpane, marzipan, almond paste.
marsiaal', (marsia'le), martial.
marsjeer', (ge-), march; move.
mars'kolonne, marching column.
mars'kramer, pedlar, hawker; haggler; cadger; ~**lisensie,** hawker's licence.
mars'leuning, toprail.
mars'linie, line of march; ~**oefening,** routemarch; ~**orde,** order of marching; ~**order,** marching order; ~**roete,** line of march route.
mars: ~**seil,** topsail; ~**steng,** topmast.
mars: ~**tempo,** march time (music); pace; ~**tenue,** marching uniform; ~**tyd,** march time; ~**vaardig,** (-e), mobile; ready to march; ~**weg,** route of march.
mar'tel, (ge-), torment, torture, rack, martyr, excruciate.
mar'telaar, (-s, ..lare), martyr.
mar'telaars: ~**aanbidding,** martyrolatry; ~**bloed,** martyr's blood; baptism of blood: ~**boek,** martyrology; ~**geskiedenis,** martyrology.
mar'telaarskap, martyrdom.
mar'telaars: ~**kerk,** martyry; ~**kroon,** crown of martyrdom.
mar'tel: ~**ares',** (-se), (woman) martyr; ~**(a)ry',** torture; ~**dood,** death by torture, martyr's death; ~**end,** (-e), harrowing; ~**gang,** way of martyrdom; ~**ing,** torture, excruciation, martyrdom; ~**tuig,** instrument of torture.
mar'ter, marten; ~**bont,** marten.
martini-hen'ry, (-'s), Martini-Henry (rifle).
Mar'tjie: ~ *Louw,* Martial Law.
Marxis', (-te), Marxist; ~**me,** Marxism; ~**ties,** (-e), Marxian, Marxist(ic).
mas, (-te), mast, pole; *sien om die* ~ *op te kom,* do one's own work, fend for oneself; ~**band,** hank.
masban'ker, (-s), horse (jack) mackerel; masbanker, maasbanker *(Trachurus trachurus).*
Masbie'ker, (-s), Mozambiquer.
mas: ~**boom,** (Norway) pine; ~**bos,** fir (-wood); forest of masts.
ma'sels, measles, rubeola; *Duitse* ~ , German measles, rubella.
ma'selvarkvleis, measly pork.
mas'hout, pine(-wood).
masjien', (-e), machine; engine; ~**bediener,** machine minder; ~**bou,** engine construction; mechanical engineering; ~**bouer,** mechanical; ~**defek,** engine trouble; ~**domkrag,** mechanical jack; ~**eleer,** science of machinery, mechanics; ~**fabriek,** machine factory, engineering works; ~**garing,** machine cotton; ~**gereedskap,** machine tools; power tools; ~**gestik,** machine-stitched; ~**geweer,** machine-gun; ~**insteller,** (engine) fitter; ~**kamer,** engine-room; ~**kap,** bonnet of engine; ~**krag,** engine-power; ~**loods,** engine-shed; ~**maker,** machinist; ~**monteur,** assembler, machine fitter; ~**olie,** machine oil; lubricating oil; ~**papier,** machine-made paper; ~**proef,** press proof; ~**setter,** machine compositor; ~**skrif,** typewriting; ~**tekenaar,** engineering draughtsman; ~**tekene,** mechanical (engineering) drawing; ~**werk,** machine work, machining; ~**werker,** machinist; ~**werkplaas,** machine shop; ~ **werktuie,** machine tools; ~**winkel,** machine shop.

masjinaal, (..nale), mechanical(ly); ~ *AF=GEWERK*, machine-finished; ~ *BEWERK*, machine-made; (made by) machine; ~*nale BEWERKING*, machining.
masjineer', (ge-), machine.
masjinerie', (-ë), machinery, plant, enginery.
masjine'ring, machining.
masjinis', (-te), machinist; engineer; engine-driver; motor attendant.
Masjo'naland, Mashonaland.
maska'ra, mascara.
mas'kas! by Jove! good gracious!
maskeer', (ge-), mask, screen, camouflage, veil, disguise.
mas'ker, (s) (-s), mask, (dis)guise; veil; *iem. die ~ AFRUK*, unmask a person; *die ~ AFWERP*, throw off the disguise; *onder die ~ van VROOMHEID*, under the clock of piety; (w) (ge-), mask, veil; *ge ~ de bal*, masked ball; ~ **a'de**, (-s), masquerade; ~ **bal**, masked ball; ~ **blom**, monkey-flower; ~ **ing**, camouflage; ~ **kostuum**, fancy dress; ~ **spel**, masque.
maskie', *see* **almaskie**.
mas'korf, **(maskorwe)**, crow's-nest.
mas'kraan, sheers.
masochis', (-te), masochist; ~ **me**, masochism; ~ **ties**, (-e), masochistic.
mas'reg, pannage.
mas'sa, (-s), mass, crowd; lump, bulk, gross, host, a large amount of; body; block; dollop; pile; congeries; *'n ~ GELD*, a large amount of money; *die GROOT ~*, the great majority, the crowd; *IN ~*, (in) bulk; *~ -aanval*, mass attack.
massaal', (massale), in mass, wholesale; massive.
mas'sa: ~ **-artikel**, mass-produced article; ~ **betoging**, mass demonstration.
massa'ge, (-s), massage.
mas'sa: ~ **getal**, mass number; ~ **graf**, mass grave; ~ **historie**, mass hysteria; ~ **kommunikasiemedia**, mass communications media; ~ **media**, ~ **mediums**, mass media; ~ **graf**, (-te), mass grave; ~ **meter**, mass meter; ~ **moord**, genocide; wholesale murder; ~ **produksie**, mass production; ~ **produksie van gewasse**, mass crops; ~ **vergadering**, mass meeting; ~ **vervoer**, transport in bulk; mass transport; public transport; ~ **voorraad**, bulk.
masseer', (ge-), massage; ~ **der**, (-s), masseur; ~ **salon**, massage parlour; ..**se'ring**, massage, massaging; ~ **ster**, (-s), masseuse.
massé'stoot, massé.
masseur', (-s), masseur.
masseu'se, (-s), masseuse.
massief', (massiewe), massive, solid.
massifika'sie, massification.
massiwiteit', massiveness, solidity.
mastiek' = **mastik(boom)**.
mas'tig! gracious!
mas'tik: ~ **(boom)**, mastic (tree), lentiscus; ~ **gom**, mastic.
masti'tis, mastitis.
mastodon', (-s, -te), mastodon.
mastoïde, (s) (-s), **mastoied'**, (-e), mastoid; (b) **mastoïed**, (-e), mastoid.
mas'top, mast-head.
masturba'sie, masturbation.
masturbeer', (ge-), masturbate.
masur'ka, (-s), mazurka.
mas'vis, cachelot.
mas'wang, fish (of mast).
mas'werk, clove hitching; ~ **knoop**, clove hitch, hog-tie.
mat¹, (s) (-te), (door)mat; (chair) bottom, seat; *jou ~ te OPROL*, pack one's things; *deur die ~ VAL*, not succeed; (w), (ge-), mat, bottom, rush (chair).
mat², (s) (-te), piastre.
mat³, (b, bw), checkmate; ~ *sit*, mate.
mat⁴, (b, bw), tired, weary; lifeless, languid; dull; mat(t) (paper); lack-lustre (eye); dim (light), dull (colour).
matabe'lieblom, species of *Striga*.
mat'besempie, (-s), carpet whisk.

ma'tador, (-s), matador; matador (at cards).
mat'druk, faint printing.
ma'te, measure, extent, degree; *BOWE ~*, more than usual; *in HOË ~*, to a great extent; *in 'n GROOT ~*, to a large extent, largely; *in die HOOGSTE ~*, to the highest degree; *IN die ~ dat dit moontlik geword het*, to the extent that it became possible; *doen dit MET ~*, do it moderately; *alles MET ~*, everything in moderation; *in RUIM ~*, in large measure; *in SEKERE ~*, to some extent; *NA die ~ van sy vermoë*, to the extent of his powers; *met TWEE ~ meet*, measure by different standards; be unfair.
Matebe'le, (-s), Matabele; ~ **land**, Matabeleland.
ma'teloos, (..lose), measureless, excessive, immoderate; ~ **heid**, excessiveness, lack of moderation.
matema'ties, (-e), mathematical.
matema'tikus, (..tici, -se), mathematician.
materiaal', (..riale), material; coating; *rollende ~*, rolling stock; ~ **berekenaar**, quantity surveyor; ~ **fout**, faulty material; ~ **gebrek**, shortage of materials; faulty material.
materialis', (-te), materialist; ~ **me**, materialism; hylozoism; ~ **ties**, (-e), materialistic.
mate'rie, matter.
materieel', (..riële), material; ..*riële reg*, substantive law.
ma'ters, companions, chums, friends; *sy ~ is dood*, he has no equal; cf. **maat¹**.
mate'sis, mathematics.
mat'glas, ground (frosted) glass, milk glass, mat glass.
mat'heid, fatigue, exhaustion, weariness; dimness, dullness.
Ma'tie¹, (-s), Matie (Stellenbosch student).
ma'tie², (-s), matey, chummy; ~ **rig**, matey; ~ **righeid**, mateyness.
ma'tig, (w) (ge-), moderate, mitigate, allay, alloy, qualify, temper; curb, restrain; abate; (b, bw) (-e), moderate, abstinent, abstentious, continent, abstemious, gentle, frugal, temperate; slow (oven); ~ *GESNOEI*, moderately pruned; *iets ~ GEBRUIK*, make moderate use of something; use something in moderation; *maar ~ TEVREDE*, not particularly pleased.
ma'tigheid, moderation, moderateness, temperance; abstention, continence, abstemiousness, abstinence; frugality; ~ **sgenootskap**, temperance society.
ma'tiging, moderation, mitigation.
matinee', (-s), matinee.
matineus', (-e), early.
ma'tjie, (-s), small mother, mummy.
mat'jie, (-s), rug, little mat.
mat'jies: ~ **goed**, rush(es), bulrush *(Cyperus sexangularis)*; reed; ~ **huis**, reed hut.
mat'klopper, carpet-beater.
mat'kool, splint-coal.
matras', (-se), mattress, ~ **goed**, ticking, ~ **kop**, mophead; bushy head; ~ **maker**, mattress-maker, upholsterer; ~ **oortreksel**, mattress cover; ~ **steek**, spot-stitch; ~ **tyk**, tick(ing).
matriargaal', (..gale), matriarchal.
matriargaat', matriarchy.
matriek', matric(ulation).
ma'triks, (-e), matrix.
matrikulant', (-e), matriculant.
matrikula'sie, matriculation.
matrikula'sie: ~ **-eksamen**, matriculation examination; M ~ **raad**, Matriculation Board.
matrikuleer', (ge-), matriculate.
matrilineaal', (..lineale), **matrilineêr'**, (-e), matrilinear, in the female line.
matrili'nie, (-s), female line.
matro'ne, (-s), matron, house-mother, dame.
matroos', (matrose), sailor; deck(-hand); *vloek soos 'n ~*, swear like a trooper; ~ **baadjie**, sailor's blouse; monkey-jacket; ~ **bloese**, sailor-blouse; ~ **bredie**, lobscouse; ~ **broek**, sailor's trousers; ~ **dans**, sailor's dance; ~ **drag**, sailor's dress; ~ **hoed**, sailor hat; ~ **kop**, crew-cut; ~ **kraag**, sailor collar; ~ **kuller**, land-shark; ~ **lied**, sailor's song; chanty;

~**pakkie,** sailor suit; ~**sak,** ditty-bag; ~**taal,** billingsgate; ~**werk,** sailor's work.
matro'se: ~**kerk,** bethel; ~**koor,** sailors' chorus; ~**kroeg,** sailor's tavern.
matrys', (-e), matrix, mould, bed-die; proplasm; ~**houer,** matrix-holder; ~**model,** die model; ~**papier,** flong; ~**snyblok,** master die; ~**steen,** matrix stone; ~**stempel,** hub.
mat'springer, trampolinist; ~**y,** trampoline jumping.
matteer', (ge-), mat.
Matthe'üs, Matthew.
matura'sie, maturation, ripening.
mat'verf, flat paint.
mat: ~**vlegter,** mat-plaiter; ~**werk,** matting; frostwork (silver).
mat'wit, dead white.
mat'so, (-'s), matzo(h).
Mau-Mau', Mau-Mau.
Mauritiaan', (..tiane), Mauritian; ~**s',** (-e), Mauritian.
mau'ser, (-s), Mauser; ~**patroon,** Mauser bullet; ~**rewolwer,** Mauser revolver.
mausole'um, (..**lea,** -s), mausoleum.
mau've, mauve.
max'im, (-s), maxim (gun).
mayonnai'se(sous), mayonnaise.
mayonnai'sesmeer, sandwich relish (spread).
mean'der, (-s), meander; ~**meer,** ox-bow lake.
me'bos, dried and sugared apricots, mebos; ~**konfyt,** apricot preserve, mebos jam.
Mech'elen, Malines, Mechlin.
medal'je, (-s), medal; *een KANT v.d.* ~, one side of the matter; *die ander KANT v.d.* ~, the other side of the shield; ~**balk,** (medal) bar; ~**houer,** medallist; ~**snyer,** medallist; ~**wenner,** medallist.
medaljon', (-s), medallion; locket; ~**portret,** medallion portrait.
Me'de[1], *die* ~, the Medes.
me'de[2], to some extent, partly; also.
me'de[3], co-, fellow- (in compounds).
me'deaangeklaagde, (-s), co-accused; co-respondent.
me'deaanspreeklik, (-e), co-responsible; ~**heid,** co-responsibility, joint liability.
me'de: ~**aanwesig,** (-e), likewise present; ~**-Afrikaner,** fellow-Afrikander; ~**amptenaar,** colleague (in public service); ~**arbeider,** fellow labourer, fellow worker; ~**begiftigde,** (-s), co-donee; ~**belanghebbende,** (-s), co-partner; person also interested; ~**beredderaar,** co-administrator; ~**besitter,** joint owner; ~**beskuldigde,** co-respondent; ~**bestaan,** co-existence; ~**bestuurder,** co-manager; ~**bewoner,** co-habitant; ~**borg,** co-surety; ~**broeder,** fellow man, colleague; ~**burger,** fellow citizen; ~**-Christen,** fellow Christian; ~**dader,** (-s), accessory, accomplice.
mededeel'baar, (..**bare),** communicable; ~**heid,** communicability.
me(d)edeel'saam, (..**same),** liberal, generous, charitable; communicative; ~**heid,** liberality, charitableness, generosity; communicativeness.
me'dedeler, (-s), communicant; informer; communicator.
me'(d)edeling, (-e, -s), communication, information, advice; conveyance.
me'dedingend, (-e), competitive, emulous.
me'dedinger, (-s), competitor, rival; emulator.
me'dedinging, competition, rivalry.
me'dedirekteur, joint director; co-director.
me(d)edo'ë, pity, compassion, mercy.
me(d)edo'ënd, (-e), compassionate, merciful; ~**heid,** compassion, sympathy, mercifulness.
me'de: ~**-eienaar,** joint owner, part-owner; ~**-eksekuteur,** co-executor; ~**-eksekutrise,** co-executrix; ~**-erfgenaam,** co-heir, joint heir, co-legatee, fellow-heir, parcener; ~**-erfgename,** co-heiress; ~**-ewig,** (-e), co-eternal; ~**gas,** fellow-guest; ~**gebruik,** joint use; ~**gedaagde,** co-defendant; ~**genoot,** (..**note),** co-partner, consort, associate; ~**geregtigde,** (-s), co-participant; ~**getuie,** fellow witness; ~**gevangene,** fellow prisoner.
me'de: ~**heerser,** joint sovereign; ~**helper,** co-operator, assistant, collaborator, helpmate, coadjutor;

~**hoofbestuurder,** joint general manager; ~**hoofskuldenaar,** co-principal (debtor); ~**huurder,** cotenant; joint tenant; ~**-ingesetene,** (-s), fellow-inhabitant; ~**kieser,** fellow elector; ~**klinker,** consonant; ~**krygsman,** fellow warrior, fellow soldier; ~**leerling,** fellow scholar (pupil); ~**leraar,** joint minister; ~**lid,** fellow member, confrère.
medely'(d)e, compassion, pity, commiseration; altropathy; ~ *HÊ met,* have (take) pity on, sympathize with; *UIT* ~ *met,* from a feeling of pity for.
medely'dend, (-e), compassionate, merciful, clement, pitiful, pitying.
me'demens, fellow man, fellow creature.
me'deminnaar, (-s), rival lover; ..**minnares,** (-se), female rival in love.
me'deondergetekende, (-s), co-undersigned.
me'deonderteken, (~), countersign; ~ **aar,** co-signatory; countersigner; ~**ing,** countersignature, co-signature.
me'deoorlogvoerende, (-s), co-belligerent.
me'deoorsaak, contributory cause.
me'deouteur, joint author.
me'depassasier, fellow passenger.
medeplig'tig, (-e), accessory to, party to, concerned in; ~**e,** (-s), accomplice, abettor, associate, accessory; ~ *e voor (na) die daad,* accessory before (after) the act; ~**heid,** complicity.
me'de: ~**redakteur,** co-editor; ~**regent,** co-regent; ~**regter,** fellow judge; ~**reisiger,** fellow-traveller; ~**seggenskap,** joint authority; a share in the control; ~**seggenskap hê,** control jointly; ~**skenker,** (-s), co-donor; ~**skepsel,** fellow creature; ~**skrywer,** co-author; ~**skuldeiser,** co-obligee; ~**skuldenaar,** co-obligor; ~**skuldige,** fellow culprit; ~**spreker,** interlocutor; ~**stander,** partisan, associate, partner; ~**stigter,** ~**stryder,** fellow fighter; ~**student,** fellow student.
me'de: ~**verbonde,** ally; ~**verweerder,** co-respondent, co-defendant; ~**vlieër,** co-pilot; ~**voog,** (-de), fellow (joint) guardian; co-tutor; co-trustee, co-guardian; ~**werkend,** (-e), co-operating, contributory; ~**werker,** co-operator; contributor (to a paper); fellow worker, collaborator, part-author, coadjutor, co-agent; deuteronomist.
me'(d)ewerking, co-operation, collaboration, assistance, contribution, co-agency, concurrence, instrumentality.
me'dewete, knowledge; privity; *sonder die* ~ *van A.,* without A.'s knowledge; ~**r,** (-s), one privy to something; *die* ~**rs** , those in the know.
me'dia, media; *die* ~, the media.
mediaan', (**mediane),** median (print); pica (type); medium (paper); ~**folio,** demi-folio; ~**formaat,** medium size; ~**kwarto,** median line; ~**letter,** pica; ~**oktaaf,** median-octavo.
me'dia: ~**dekking,** media coverage; ~**konferensie,** media conference; ~**personeel,** media staff.
media'sie, mediation.
mediateur', (-s), mediator, intercessor.
Me'diër, (-s, **Mede),** Mede, Median.
Me'dies[1], (-e), Median.
me'dies[2], (-e), medical; ~*e ARGIEF,* medical archives; ~*e HULPVERENIGING,* medical benefit society; ~*e KEURING (ondersoek),* medical inspection; ~*e REG,* medical jurisprudence.
medikament', (-e), medicine, medicament, drug.
me'dikus, (..**dici,** -se), physician, doctor, medical practitioner.
mediokriteit', mediocrity.
medisinaal', (..**nale),** medicinal; ..*nale GEWIG,* apothecaries' weight; ..*nale WATER,* medicated water.
medisyn'agtig, (-e), like medicine, physicky.
medisy'ne, (-s), medicine; *hy het te veel* ~ *GEDRINK,* he has had a drop too much; ~ *INGEE,* drench (vet.); ~**botteltjie,** medicine bottle; ~**drupper,** medicine dropper; ~**flessie,** medicine bottle; ~**kassie,** medicine chest; ~**moord,** medicine murder; ~**stroop,** julep; ~**trommel,** medicine chest.
medisyn'meester, doctor, physician; ~, *genees jouself,* practise what you preach; physician, heal thyself!

medita'sie,(-s), meditation.
mediteer', **(ge-),** meditate.
Mediterreens', (-e), Mediterranean; ~*e klimaat*, Mediterranean climate, winter-rainfall climate.
me'dium, (..**dia, -s**), medium, means; ~**bouler**, medium bowler; ~**frekwensie,** medium broadcast band; ~**golf,** medium wave.
me'diumiek, (-e), mediumistic.
me'dium: ~**kwessie,** ~**vraagstuk,** language-medium question (problem).
medo'ra, (-s), bridal crown (Malay).
Medu'sa, Medusa; ~**hoof,** Medusa head.
mee¹, (s) honey-beer, mead.
mee², with, together; also, likewise.
mee³-, (in compounds), fellow-; co-.
mee'arbei, (-ge-), co-operate.
mee'bring, (-ge-), cause, entail; involve (in danger); bring (along) with one; *dit sal oponthoud* ~, this will cause delay.
mee'deel, (-ge-), inform (a person); communicate, impart (news); acquaint; notify; record (occurrences); advise; convey.
meedeel'saam = **me(d)edeelsaam.**
mee'deling = **me(d)edeling.**
mee'ding, (-ge-), compete; be a candidate.
mee'doen, (-ge-), participate in; assist; join in.
meedo'ë(n)loos, (..**lose**), pitiless, merciless, unmerciful; ruthless, cut-throat; grim; ~**heid,** pitilessness.
mee'dra, (-ge-), carry along.
mee'-erf, (meeëerf), be joint heir
mee'-eter, guest; blackhead.
mee'gaan, (-ge-), accompany, go along (with), agree, ~ *MET A se voorstel,* agree to A's proposal; ~ *met A IN...,* agree with A about...; ~**de,** accommodating, complaisant; agreeing, concomitant; pliable; ~ *de sekerheid,* collateral security.
mee'gee, (-ge-), send (along) with; yield, give way.
mee'gevoel, sympathy, fellow-feeling.
mee'help, (-ge-), contribute, assist, lend a hand.
mee'kom, (-ge-), come along, accompany.
mee'krap, madder; ~**wortel,** madder root.
mee'kry, (-ge-), receive; carry (an audience).
meel, meal; flour; ~**agtig,** (-e), mealy, farinaceous; ~**blik,** flour-bin; ~**blom,** flour; ~**bol,** flour-ball; cooked flour; ~**dou,** mildew, blight; ~**draad,** stamen; anther; ~**draadblom,** staminate flower; ~**draadkrans,** androecium.
mee'leef, ..**lewe,** (-ge-), enter into the spirit of; ~ *met,* sympathize with.
mee'lewing, sympathy
meel: ~**handel,** flour trade; ~**handelaar,** flour merchant; ~**houdend,** (-e), farinaceous; ~**kalk,** powdered lime; ~**kis,** flour-tin; ~**koek,** (flour) cake; ~**kos,** meal (farinaceous) food; carbohydrates; mash (for poultry).
mee'loop, (-ge-), accompany, walk with one; *vir die gelukkige sal alles* ~, nothing succeeds like success.
mee'loper, (-s), collaborator (with enemy).
mee'lopertjie: *dis nogal 'n* ~, it is a bit (spot) of luck.
mee'luister, (-ge-), monitor; bug; ~**ing,** monitoring; bugging.
mee'lye = **medely(d)e.**
meel: ~**pap,** meal porridge; meal paste; ~**sak,** flour-bag; ~**sif,** flour (meal) sieve; bolter; ~**solder,** flour-loft; ~**strooier,** dredge-box, flour-dredger; ~**trommel,** flour-bin; ~**wurm,** corn-weevil.
mee'maak, (-ge-), go through, be a witness to, experience, take part in.
meen, (ge-), mean, intend; suppose, think, reckon, be of opinion; *hy* ~ *DIT,* he is quite serious; *ek het ge* ~ *om dit vandag te DOEN,* I intended doing it today; ~ *jy dit REGTIG?* do you really mean it? *ek* ~ *te SÊ,* I really mean; indeed, let me tell you, *ons het SO ge* ~, we were under the impression; *SOOS ek* ~, as I suppose (presume).
mee'neem, (-ge-), take with one, take along; ~**skyf,** catch-plate; ~**voedsel,** take-away food.
mee'nemer, catch-plate; driver (lathe).
meent, (-e), commonage, town lands.
mee'praat, (-ge-), have a say in; have experience of.
meer¹, (s) (mere), lake.
meer², (w) (ge-), moor; tie up (ship).

meer³, (b, bw) more; beyond; ~ *AS,* more than; ~ *BIED as,* outbid; *DES te* ~, all the more; so much the more; ~ *as GENOEG,* more than enough, too much; ~ *as 'n HALFUUR,* upwards of half an hour; *IETS* ~, something more; *hy IS nie* ~ *nie,* he is dead; *KAN jy nou* ~! did you ever! *g'n KIND* ~ *nie,* no longer a child; *hoe LANGER hoe* ~, more and more; *NIKS* ~ *as billik nie,* no more than fair; *NIKS* ~ *as sy plig nie,* only his duty; no more than his duty; *NOOIT* ~ *nie,* never again; *ONDER* ~, amongst others; *SONDER* ~, without any further ado; *iets SONDER* ~ *aanneem,* accept something without further comment; *STEEDS* ~, more and more; *wat dies* ~ *SY,* what is more; as the case may be; *TE* ~, the more so; *WAT* ~ *is,* what is more; moreover.
meer'aal, conger eel.
meer'armtrap, stair with several flights; multiflight stairs.
meer'boei, mooring-buoy.
meer'daags, (-e), lasting several days.
meer'dekker, multiplane.
meer'der, (-e), more; more numerous; additional; ~*e ERVARING,* more experience; *in* ~ *e of mindere MATE,* to a greater or lesser extent.
meer'dere, (-s), superior; senior.
meer'derheid, majority, superiority; bulk; body; ascendency; plurality; odds; *met 'n* ~ *AANNEEM,* carry by a majority; *jou* ~ *BEWYS,* prove your superiority; *by* ~ *van STEMME,* by a majority of votes; *STILLE meerderheid,* silent majority; *met 'n VOLSTREKTE* ~, with a clear majority.
meer'derheids: ~**besluit,** majority decision; ~**gevoel,** sense of superiority; ~**party,** majority party; ~**uitspraak,** majority verdict; ~**verslag,** majority report.
meerderja'rig, (-e), major, of age; ~ *word,* come of age, attain majority; ~**heid,** majority, full age; ~**verklaring,** emancipation (from father's jurisdiction).
meer'derman: *as* ~ *kom, moet minderman wyk,* the sun puts all the stars to flight; the lesser must make way for the greater.
meerderwaar'dig, (-e), superior; ~**heid,** superiority; ~**heidsgevoel,** feeling of superiority.
meer'doelig, (-e), multipurpose.
mee'reis, (-ge-), travel with, accompany.
mee'reken, (-ge-), include, count (in).
meer'fasig, (-e), multiphase.
meer'gegoed, (-e), better off, richer.
meer'gemeld, meer'genoemd, (-e), before-mentioned.
meer'gesig, lakescape.
meer'hoewig, (-e), odd-toed, polyungulate.
meer'jarig, (-e), perennial.
meer'kabel, mooring-cable.
meer'kat, (-te), meercat; mongoose; ~**gat,** (-e), hole of meercat.
meer'kleurig, (-e), variegated.
meer'koet, (-e), coot.
meer'kol, (-le), jay.
meer'kool, sea-kale.
meer'kunde, limnology.
meer'lagig, (-e), stratified.
meer'lettergrepig, (-e), polysyllabic; -*e woord,* polysyllabic (word).
meer'maal, meer'male, more than once, often, frequently, repeatedly.
meer'man, (-ne), merman, triton.
meer'mas, mooring-mast.
meer'min, (-ne), mermaid.
meermoto'rig, (-e), multi-engined.
meer: ~**paal,** mooring-post; ~**pen,** mooring-pin, moor-pin.
meer'skuim, meerschaum; ~**pyp,** meerschaum pipe.
meerslag'tig, (-e), heterogeneous, polygenous; ~**heid,** polygeny, heterogeneity.
meerstem'mig, (-e), (to be) sung in unison, polyphonic; ~*e lied,* part-song; ~**heid,** polyphony.
meer'sydig, (-e), multilateral.
meer'tou, mooring-cable; ~**e,** moorings.

meervor'mig, (-e), allotropic; ~heid, allotropy, allotropism.
meer'voud, (-e), plural; ~'ig, (-e), plural; multiple; ~'igheid, plurality.
meer'vouds: ~uitgang, plural ending; ~vorm, plural form; ~vorming, formation of the plural.
meer'waarde, surplus value.
meerwaar'dig, (-e), multivalent; ~heid, multivalence, polyvalence; ~heidsgevoel, feeling of superiority.
mees¹, (s) (mese), titmouse; tomtit, tit(ling).
mees², (b) most; *in die ~ te GEVALLE*, in most cases; (bw) mostly; *die ~ te MENSE*, most people.
mees'al = meestal.
mees'begunstigde, most-favoured.
mee'sleep, (-ge-), carry (drag) along; fascinate; *die musiek sal jou ~,* the music will carry you away.
mee'slepend, (-e), fascinating, compelling.
mees'muil, (ge-), sneer, smirk, grin, simper.
mee'speel, (-ge-), join in (a game); take part (a hand) in a game.
mees'tal, generally, as a rule, mostly, for the most part.
mees'te, most; greatest; *die ~ FOUTE,* (the) most mistakes; *die ~ MENSE,* most people; *hy SKRYF die ~,* he writes most.
mees'tendeels, for the most (greater) part.
mees'ter, (-s), master, teacher; dominie; maestro; preceptor; past-master; *daar is ~ BO ~,* every man may meet his match; diamond cuts diamond; *~ van JOUSELF wees,* keep control of oneself; *hom ~ MAAK van,* become the master of; *verskeie TALE ~ wees,* have (thorough) command of several languages; *~ van die TOESTAND wees,* have the situation well in hand; *hy is ~ van sy VAK,* he knows his trade thoroughly; *jou ~ VIND in,* meet one's match in; *iets ~ WEES,* be master of; ~agtig, (-e), masterful, imperious; formal; magisterial; peremptory; pedantic; ~bouer, master builder; ~es', (-se), mistress; ~goed, medicine; ~hand, master('s) hand; *dit verraai 'n ~ hand,* one can see a master's hand in it; ~kneg, clicker; ~lik, (-e), excellent, masterly; ~likheid, masterliness; ~sanger, master singer; ~sgraad, master's degree; ~skap, authority, mastery, mastership, command, grip; *sy ~ skap oor die taal,* his command of the language; ~stuk, masterpiece; chef-d'oeuvre; ~vel, master sheet; ~werk, classic, masterpiece; master-stroke.
mee'stry, (-ge-), join in argument; compete; join in battle.
meet¹, (s) starting-point; *van ~ af begin,* start from the beginning.
meet², (w) (ge-), measure, gauge, mete, mensurate; *hy het sy lengte op die GROND ge ~,* he measured his length on the ground; *LAND ~,* survey land; *jou MET iem. ~,* match oneself against someone; *hy ~ die STRAAT,* he is tipsy; ~baar, (..bare), measurable; commensurable; gaugeable; ~baarheid, measurability; commensurability; ~band, tape-measure; ~bestek, range; ~bord, plate-table; ~driehoek, plotting-instrument; plotter.
mee'tel, (-ge-), include, count; *sy tel nie meer mee nie,* she is no longer considered.
meet: ~gebied, range; ~geld, measuring-fee; ~glas, measuring-glass; ~grens, range; ~instrument, measuring-instrument; ~ketting, surveyor's chain; measuring-chain; ~*ketting sleep,* be a surveyor; ~koord, measuring-line; ~kunde, geometry; euclid; ~kun'dig (-e), geometrical; ~kun'dige, (-s), geometer, geometrician; ~kuns, mensuration; ~lat, surveyor's rod; ~lint, tape measure; tapeline; ~lood, sounding-lead; plummet; ~loon, meterage; ~lyn, plumb-line; ~net, graticule; ~passer, callipers; ~patroon, key cartridge; ~punt, datum (in building); ~rat, surveyor's wheel.
mee'trek, (-ge-), pull along; move (trek) with; drag with.
mee'treurend, (-e), condolent.
meet'roede, surveyor's rod, bacule.
mee'troon, (-ge-), coax along, entice away.
meet: ~skyf, quadrant, sextant; ~sluis, gauging-weir; ~stok, measuring-rod, dipstick; ~tafel, plane table; planchette; ~wiel, ambulator; odometer, viameter.
meeu, (-e), mew, sea-gull.
mee'val, (-ge-), cause surprise, succeed (beyond expectation); *dit val my mee,* I didn't expect as much; it might have been worse; ~ler, ~lertjie, (-s), piece of good luck, windfall.
mee'voelend, (-e), condolatory.
mee'voer, (-ge-), carry away.
meewa'rig, (-e), compassionate; sympathetic; ~heid, compassion, sympathy.
mee'werk, (-ge-), co-operate, collaborate, assist; concur, contribute; ~ing = medewerking.
mee'wind, rear wind, following wind.
Mefisto'feles, Mephistopheles.
megafoon', (-s, ..fone), megaphone.
megalomanie', megalomania.
meganiek', mechanism; action; assembly; clockwork.
mega'nies, (-e), mechanical; perfunctory.
mega'nika, mechanics.
mega'nikus, (..nici, -se), mechanician.
meganisa'sie, mechanization.
meganiseer', (ge-), mechanize.
meganise'ring, mechanization.
meganis'me, mechanism.
me'gaperiode, megacycle.
megaskoop', (..skope), megascope.
megasko'pies, (-e), megascopic.
me'gaton, megaton.
me'gawatt, megawatt.
me'gohm, megohm.
Mei, May; ~betoging, May demonstration.
mei: ~blom, Mayflower, May-bush; ~boom, maypole.
Mei'dag, May Day.
mei: ~doring, haw(thorn); May-flower, May-bush; ~kewer, cockroach, cockchafer.
Mei: ~koningin, May queen; ~maand, month of May.
meine'dig, (-e), perjured, forsworn, perfidious; perjurious; ~e, (-s), perjurer.
mein'eed, perjury, oath-breaking; *~ pleeg,* commit perjury.
mei'sie, (-s), girl, maiden, maid, miss, damsel; fiancée; *dit BLY tussen ons ~s,* it remains between ourselves; *~s wat FLUIT word die deur uitgesmyt (en hennetjies wat kraai word die nek omgedraai),* a whistling woman and a crowing hen are neither fit for God nor men; *~s is nie GEPLANT nie, maar gesaai, ~s is nie HANDVOL nie, maar landvol,* there are as good fish in the sea as ever come out of it; *ONDER ons ~s,* sub rosa; between ourselves; *so TUSSEN ons ~s gesê,* between us girls (ourselves); *jy sal dit VERGROEI voor jy 'n ~ is,* never mind, you'll soon get over it; ~agtig, (-e), girlish, maidenly, girl-like, silly; ~agtigheid, girlishness, maidenliness, silliness; ~kind, girl; ~mens, wench, girl; female (young) woman; ~naam, maiden name.
mei'sies: ~boek, girls' book; ~drag, girls' wear (clothes); ~dubbelspel, girls' doubles; ~enkelspel, girls' singles; ~gek, dangler after women; flirt; poodle-faker; amorist; ~gesig, girl's face; ~hand, girl's hand; ~hoed, girl's hat; ~inrigting, institution for girls; ~jare, (years of) girlhood; ~klere, girls' attire (clothing).
mei'sieskool, girls' school.
mei'sies: ~koor, girls' choir; ~koshuis, girls' hostel; ~leeftyd, girlhood; ~lewe, girl's life; girlhood; ~naam, girl's name.
mei'siespan, girls' team.
mei'siestem, girlish voice; girl's voice; ~reg, flapper-vote.
mei'sies: ~verhaal, girls' story; ~werk, girls' work.
mei'sievroutjie, child-wife.
Mei'viering, May-Day celebration.
mejuf'frou, (-e), miss; madam; *~ A.,* Miss A.
mekaar', each other, one another; *BY ~,* with each other; *veel met ~ GEMEEN hê,* have much in common; *NA ~ toe,* towards each other; *NA ~,* one after another; *ONDER ~,* between (among) them(selves); *OP ~,* on top of each other.

Mek'ka, Mecca; ~**ganger**, pilgrim to Mecca.
melaats', (-e), leprous; ~ **e**, (-s), leper; ~ **heid**, leprosy.
melancholie', melancholy.
melancholiek', (-e), melancholic; *hy lyk net ~ van=dag*, he is looking thoroughly seedy today.
melancho'lies, (-e), melancholy.
melancho'likus, (-se, ..**lici**), melancholiac.
Melane'sië, Melanesia; ~ **r**, (-s), Melanesian; ..**sies**, (-e), Melanesian.
melaniet', melanite.
melanis'me, melanism.
melanis'ties, (-e), melanistic.
melano'se, melano'sis, melanosis.
melas'se, molasses.
mel'baperske, pêche Melba.
mel'basysie, common melba finch.
meld, (ge-), mention, inform, state, report; *iem. per BRIEF ~*, inform someone by letter; *~ asb. jou NOMMER*, please quote your number; ~**baar**, (..**bare**), reportable.
meldenswaar'dig, (-e), worth mentioning.
mel'der, (-s), informer.
mel'ding, mention; reference; *~ maak van*, make mention of.
mêlée', (-s), mêlée.
me'lerig, (-e), mealy, farinose, farinaceous, floury.
meliliet', melilite.
meliniet', melinite.
melioratief', (..**tiewe**), meliorative.
melioris', (-te), meliorist; ~**me**, meliorism.
melk, (s) milk, *altyd iets in die ~ te BROKKEL hê*, have much to grumble about; *niks in die ~ te BROKKEL hê nie*, have no room to talk; *EERSTE ~*, foremilk, beestings; *~ is GOED vir elk*, milk is a wholesome food; *LAASTE ~*, strippings; (w) (ge-), milk; *iem. ~*, fleece a person; ~**aar**, lacteal vein; ~**afskeidend**, (-e), lactiferous; ~**afskeiding**, lactation; ~**agtig**, (-e), milky, galactic, lactescent; ~**agtigheid**, milkiness; ~**baard**, down (on the chin), soft beard; milksop; ~**bak**, milk container; ~**balie**, milk vat; ~**bees**, milch cow; ~**bek**, white muzzle (vet.); ~**beker**, milk jug; ~**blom**, Karoo shrub; ~**boer**, dairy farmer; ~**boerdery**, dairy farm(ing); ~**bok**, milch goat, Swiss goat; ~**boom**, *Ficus cordata*; ~**bos**, various shrubs with a white resinous sap *(Euphorbia)*; ~**bottel**, milk bottle; ~**bringer**, milkman; ~**brood**, milk loaf; ~**buffet**, milk-bar; ~**buis**, lacteal vein (duct); ~**dieet**, milk diet; ~**dissel**, sow-thistle; ~**doek**, strainer, filter=ing-cloth, butter-muslin; ~**duur**, lactation period; ~**emmer**, milk pail; ~**er**, (-s), milker; ~**erig**, (-e), milky, lacteous; ~**erigheid**, milkiness, lactescence; ~**ery**, (-e), dairy (farm); milking; ~**fabriek**, milk factory; ~**gebit**, milk teeth; ~**gesig**, childish face; ~**gewend**, (-e), in milk; *'n ~ gewende koei*, a cow in milk; ~**gif**, tyrotoxin; ~**glas**, opal glass; milk glass; ~**houdend**, (-e), lactiferous; ~**hout**, milk=wood; ~**huis**, dairy; ~**jong**, milkman; ~**kalf**, sucking calf; ~**kamer**, dairy, creamery (on farm), milk room; ~**kan**, milk jug; milk can; ~**kar**, milk cart; ~**kleur**, milky colour; ~**klier**, mammary gland, lacteal gland; ~**klierontsteking**, mammitis; ~**koei**, milch cow, milker; *'n ~ koeitjie*, a profit=able business; someone on whom one can sponge; ~**koker**, milk boiler; ~**kom**, milk basin; ~**koors**, milk (lacteal, puerperal) fever; ~**kos**, milk food; ~**kroeg**, milk bar; ~**kruid**, milkwort; ~**kudde**, dairy herd; ~**kuur**, milk cure; ~**kwarts**, milky quartz; ~**lappie**, doily; ~**leier**, milk duct; ~**ma=sjien**, milking-machine; ~**meisie**, milkmaid; ~**me=ter**, (ga)lactometer; ~**ooi**, milch ewe; ~**pap**, milk porridge; ~**pens**, abomasum; ~**plaas**, dairy farm; ~**poeier**, powdered milk; ~**salon**, milk-bar; ~**sap**, milky juice; latex; ~**siekte**, milk-sickness; ~**sif**, milk strainer; ~**skinkery**, milk-bar; ~**skurfte**, milk scab; ~**sop**, milk-soup; ~**spieël**, escutcheon; ~**steen**, chalcedony; ~**stoeltjie**, milking-stool; **M**~**straat**, Milky Way; ~**suiker**, sugar of milk, lactose; ~**suur**, lactic acid; ~**suursout**, lactate; ~**tand**, milk-tooth; colt's (calf's) tooth; ~**tert**, milk tart; ~**tyd**, milking-time; ~**uier**, udder con=taining much milk; ~**vat**, milk tub, lacteal vessel,

~**vee**, dairy cattle; ~**verkoper**, dairyman; milk=man; ~**vervalsing**, adulteration of milk; ~**vloeityd=perk**, lactation period; ~**voeding**, milk feeding; ~**voorsiening**, milk supply; ~**vorming**, lactation; ~**wa**, milk cart, milk van; **M**~**weg**, Milky Way, galaxy; ~**wei**, whey; ~**winkel**, dairy shop; ~**wit**, milky white, as white as milk.
melliet', mellite.
melodie', (-ë), melody, air.
melo'dies, (-e), melodic(al).
melodieus', (-e), melodious.
me'lodrama, melodrama; ~ **'ties**, (-e), melodramatic.
melomaan', (..**mane**), melomaniac.
melomanie', melomania.
membraan', (**membrane**), membrane.
mê'me, (-s), (vero.), nurse.
memen'to, (-'s), memento.
memoi'res, memoires.
memoran'dum, (..**da**, -s), memorandum.
memoreer', (ge-), recall to memory, remember.
memorialis', (-te), memorialist.
memo'rie, (-s), petition, document.
memoriseer', (ge-), commit to memory, memorize; ..**se'ring**, memorization.
mena'de, (-s), maenad.
menagerie', (-ë), menagery.
mena'sie, mess (club); ~**boek**, mess book; ~**geld**, mess fees; ~**reglement**, mess rules; ~**rekening**, mess account; ~**soldaat**, mess orderly; ~**tafel**, mess table.
Mendelis'me, Mendelism.
meneer', (s) (**menere**), sir, mister; Mr. (in address); gentleman, master; *die groot ~ UITHANG*, do the grand; pretend to be high and mighty; *JA, ~*, yes, Sir; *MENERE*, messieurs; *dis ~ VOOR en ~ agter*, "mister" one continually; *~ A.*, Mr. A.; *ek ~ en jy ~, wie sal dan die WA gaan smeer?*, I stout (proud) and thou stout, who shall bear the ashes out?; (w) (ge-), mister.
meng, (ge-), mix, shake (drinks); alloy (metals); blend (colours, tea); mingle, commingle (with people); adulterate, dilute (milk); admix; intermix, amal=gamate; mash; interfere in; *hom met politiek ~*, take part in politics.
meng'baar, (..**bare**), miscible, mixable; ~**heid**, mis=cibility, mixability.
meng'bak, mixing-bowl.
men'gel, (ge-), mix, mingle; ~**digte**, miscellaneous poems; ~**drank**, cocktail; ~**ing**, (-e, -s), medley, mingling, mixture; ~**moes**, mixture, jumble, hotch-potch (hodge-podge), mash; pot-pourri; sal=magundi; gallimaufry; podrida; mash; mish-mash; ~**taal**, lingua franca; ~**werk**, miscellany.
meng: ~ **er**, (-s), blender, mixer, compounder; ~**ing**, amalgamation, blending; ~**kristal**, mix-crystal; ~**masjien**, mixer, mixing machine; ~**mis**, com=post.
meng'sel, (-s), mixture, blend, assortment, admix=ture, compound, commixture, mash; intermixture; alloy, alligation; hotch-potch; ~**meter**, mixture-indicator.
meng: ~**stof**, medium; ~**waaier**, mixing-fan.
me'nie, red lead, minium.
me'nige, many, several.
me'nig, ~**een**, many, many a one; ~**erlei**, various, manifold; ~**maal**, often, frequently; ~**te**, (-s), mul=titude, crowd, assemblage, quantity; press; plural=ity; populace; abundance, concourse, cluster, host.
menigvul'dig, (-e), manifold, abundant; ~**heid**, abundance, numerousness, plenty, frequency, multiplicity.
me'nigwerf, (vero., ong.), many times, often.
me'ning, (-e, -s), opinion, belief, view; mind; *by jou ~ BLY*, stick to one's opinion; *iem. se ~ DEEL*, share someone'e opinion; *'n ~ HULDIG*, hold a belief; *MET ~*, in earnest; *NA (volgens) my ~*, to my mind, in my opinion; *die OPENBARE ~*, pub=lic opinion; *vir jou ~ UITKOM*, speak one's mind; *van ~ VERANDER omtrent*, alter one's opinion concerning; *in die ~ VERKEER*, be under the im=pression; *van ~ VERSKIL met*, differ in opinion from; *die ~ VRA van*, ask the opinion of; *van*

dieselfde ~ *WEES,* see eye to eye; be of one mind.
meningi'tis, meningitis.
me'nings: ~**opname,** (opinion) poll; ~**peiler,** pollster; ~**peiling,** (opinion) poll; ~**peiling,** opinion polling; public opinion research; ~**uiting,** expression of opinion; ~**verskil,** difference (clash) of opinion, diversity of opinion; ~**vormer,** opinion former, opinion-shaper.
Menis', (-te), Mennonite.
menis'kus, (-se), meniscus.
men'ner, (-s), driver, charioteer; trainer.
menologie', menology.
menopou'se, menopause; **manlike** ~, male climacteric (menopause).
mens, (s) (-e), human being, man, person; (pl) people; *die ou* ~ *AFLÊ,* turn over a new leaf; *BAIE* ~*e,* many people; *DAAR is* ~*e,* there are visitors; *die* ~ *wik, maar GOD beskik,* man proposes, God disposes; *G'N* ~ *nie,* not a soul; *'n GOEIE* ~, a good soul; ~*e KRY,* expect (receive) visitors; *eers* ~, *dan LANGOOR; eers ou* ~*e dan LANGORE,* grown-ups first; *van iem. 'n* ~ *MAAK,* make a human being of someone; *ek is MAAR 'n* ~, I am only human; *'n* ~ *is MAAR 'n* ~, to err is human; *OOK 'n* ~, a poor sort; a sorry lot; *die* ~*e SÊ,* people say; it is rumoured; *'n SNAAKSE entjie* ~*!,* a queer specimen!; *SO is die* ~, such is human nature; *'n STUKKIE* ~*!,* some specimen of humanity!; *die inwendige* ~ *VERSTERK,* refresh the inner-man; eat or drink something; *by gesonde* ~*e WAAK,* bill and coo; (vnw) one, they, you; *('n)* ~ *kan jou MENING verander,* one can change one's opinion; *'n* ~ *kan nooit WEET wat jou kan oorkom nie,* one never knows what may happen; ~**aap,** man-ape, anthropoid; ~**agtig,** (-e), anthropoid; ~**beelding,** characterization; ~**bloed,** human blood; ~**dief,** kidnapper; ~**dom,** humanity, mankind, humankind; crowd.
men'se: ~**gedaante,** a human figure; ~**geraamte,** human skeleton; ~**geslag,** human race; ~**guns,** favour of men; ~**haat,** misanthropy; ~**hand,** human hand; ~**handel,** slave-trade; ~**hatend,** (-e), misanthropic; ~**hater,** misanthrope; ~**heugenis,** living memory; ~**jag,** man-hunt; ~**kenner,** judge of human nature; ~**kennis,** knowledge of human nature; ~**kind,** child of man, human being; ~**leeftyd,** mortal span, lifetime, generation; ~**lewe,** human life; *verlies aan* ~*lewens,* loss of life; ~**liefde,** humanity, love of mankind, philanthrophy, charity; ~**lot,** fate of man; ~**massa,** crowd, multitude; ~**materiaal,** human resources, human material; ~**menigte,** multitude, crowd, push; ~**offer,** human sacrifice; ~**paar,** human couple; ~**ras,** human race; ~**redder,** life-saver; ~**reg(te),** human right(s); ~**roof,** man-stealing, kidnapping; ~**rower,** kidnapper; ~**stem,** human voice.
mens'eter, cannibal, man-eater, anthropophagus, anthropophagite.
men'se: ~**verhoudings,** human relations; ~**verstand,** human understanding; ~**vrees,** anthropophobia, timidity, shyness; ~**vri(e)nd,** humanitarian, philanthropist; ~**wêreld,** human world; ~**werk,** work of man; ~**wysheid,** human wisdom.
mens: ~**gemaak,** (-te), man-made; ~**hater,** misanthrope; ~**heid,** mankind, humanity; ~**ie,** (-s), diminutive person, midget, homuncule.
men'sig! by Jove! I say!
mens'kunde, knowledge of human nature, anthropology.
menskun'dig, (-e), having knowledge of human nature; anthropologic.
menslie'wend, (-e), philanthropic(al), charitable, humane; ~**heid,** philanthropy, humanity, milk of human kindness, humanitarianism, charitableness.
mens'lik, (-e), human, humane; anthropomorphic; mortal.
mens'likerwys(e): ~ *gesproke,* humanly speaking.
mens'likheid, humanity, human nature; humaneness, humane feeling; ~**sverlof,** compassionate leave.
mens: ~ **meting,** anthropometry; ~**onterend,** (-e), un-

worthy of a human being; ~**siening,** view of humanity; characterization.
mens'sku, (-we), unsociable, shy; ~**heid,** shyness, unsociableness, anthropophobia.
menstruaal', (**menstruale**), menstrual.
menstrua'sie, menstruation.
menstrueer', (ge-), menstruate.
mensuraal', (..**rale**), mensural; mensurable.
mens'vlees, mens'vleis, human flesh.
mens'vreter, *see* **menseter;** ~**haai,** man-eating (killer) shark; man-eater; ~**y,** cannibalism.
menswaar'dig, (-e), worthy of a human being; decent; *'n* ~ *e bestaan hê,* make a decent living; ~**heid,** human dignity.
mens'wording, incarnation.
mentaliteit', mentality.
men'tol, menthol; ~**sigaret,** menthol cigarette; ~**sproeimiddel,** menthol spray.
men'tor, (-s), mentor.
menu', (-'s), menu, bill of fare; dietary.
menuet', (-te), minuet.
merceriseer', (ge-), mercerize.
Mercu'rius, Mercury.
me'rel, (-s), blackbird, ouzel, merle.
me'rendeel, majority, the greater part; ~**s,** mostly, for the greater part.
merg = **murg;** *deur* ~ *en been DRING,* pierce to the very marrow; *Arikaans IN* ~ *en been,* Afrikaans to the core.
meridiaan', (..**diane**), meridian; ~**hoogte,** meridian altitude; ~**sirkel,** meridian circle.
meridionaal', (..**nale**), meridional.
meridionaliteit', meridionality.
merie'te, merits; *die saak op sy* ~ *BESKOU,* judge the case according to its merits; *op die* ~ *van die saak INGAAN,* go into the merits of the case; ~**bevordering,** promotion on merit; ~**komitee,** merit committee.
merin'gue, (-s), meringue.
meri'no, (-'s), merino; ~**skaap,** merino sheep; ~**wol,** merino wool.
merk, (s) (-e), mark; sign, token; brand (goods); marking; impress; tag; hallmark (silver); trademark; line (tennis court); pit (pox); (w) (**ge-**), mark; observe, notice; cicatrize; print; *jy moet niks LAAT* ~ *nie,* don't appear to know anything, don't give yourself away; *iets NIE laat* ~ *nie,* betray no sign of; *ek* ~ *aan sy STEM,* I know by his voice.
merkantiel', (-e), mercantile; ..**tilis'me,** mercantilism, commercialism.
merk: ~ **baar,** (..**bare**), perceptible, noticeable, pronounced, distinct; *'n* ..*bare verbetering,* a pronounced improvement; ~**baarheid,** perceptibility; ~**baken,** marker-beacon; ~**blad,** mark-sheet; ~**er,** (-s), marker; ~**ink,** marking-ink; ~**kryt,** tailor's chalk; ~**mes,** marking-knife.
mer'kolwas, mercolized wax.
merk'teken, sign, mark, scar, token.
merku'chloride, calomel.
merk'yster, marker; branding-iron.
merkwaar'dig, (-e), remarkable, phenomenal, curious, noteworthy, extraordinary, notable; eventful; ~**hede,** sights; notabilia; ~**heid,** remarkableness; curiuisity.
merloen', (-e), merlon.
merlyn', (-e), merlin; ~**boot,** merlin boat; ~**vangs,** merlin catch.
Merowin'ger, (-s), Merovingian.
Merowin'gies, (-e), Merovingian.
mer'rel, marl.
mer'rie, (-s), mare; ~**perd,** mare; ~**vul,** (-lens), filly.
mes^1, (s) (-se), knife; blade (lawn mower); *sy* ~ *sny aan albei KANTE,* he and his wife are both earning money; his bread is buttered on both sides; *die* ~ *sny albei KANTE toe,* it cuts both ways; *hy hou die* ~ *op sy vriend se KEEL,* he is continually threatening his friend; *onder die* ~ *KRY,* operate on; *voor jy "mes" kon SÊ,* before you could say "Jack Robinson"; *sy* ~ *is STOMP,* he won't get far; he hasn't a hope; ~ *se en VURKE,* cutlery.
mes^2, (w) (**ge-**), fatten; *die ge*~*te kalf slag,* kill the fatted calf.

mesallian'ce, (-s), misalliance.
mes'dood, knife death; knife killing.
mesente'ries, (-e), mesenteric.
mes: ~**handel,** cutlery (trade); ~**hef,** (~**hewwe),** knife-handle.
mesket, (-e), mesquite *(Nahuati mizquiti).*
mes: ~**lêer,** knife-rest; ~**lem,** knife-blade; ~**maker,** cutler; ~**makery,** cutlery.
mesme'ries, (-e), mesmeric.
mesmeriseer', (ge-), mesmerize.
mesmeris'me, mesmerism, animal magnetism.
mes'moord, knife killing (murder); ~**enaar,** knife killer (murderer).
me'sofiet, mesophyte.
mesoli'ties, (-e), mesolithic.
Mesopota'mië, Mesopotamia.
Mesoso'ïes, (-e), Mesozoic.
Mesoso'ïkum, Mesozoic.
mes'plank, *see* **mes(se)plank.**
mes'se: ~**bak,** knife-tray; *hy het in die* ~ *bak geslaap,* he is as sharp as a needle; ~**goed,** cutlery.
mes'sel, (ge-), lay bricks; build; ~**aar, (-s),** bricklayer, mason; ~**aarsbak,** hod; ~**aarsbeitel,** drove; ~**by,** mason bee; ~**dagha,** mortar; ~**kalk,** building lime; ~**klei,** mortar; ~**werk,** brickwork, masonry.
mes'se: ~**maker,** cutler; ~**makery,** cutlery; ~**plank,** knife-board; ~**skede,** knife-sheath; ~**slyper,** knife-grinder.
Messiaans', (-e), Messianic.
Messi'as, Messiah.
mes'sing, (yellow) brass; maslin; brazing-solder; ~**band,** brass tape; ~**soldeersel,** brazing-solder.
mes: ~**snee,** knife-edge; ~**steek,** stab with knife; stab-wound.
mesties', (-e), mestizo.
mes: ~**vormig, (-e),** cultrate, cultriform; ~**ware,** cutlery.
met, with; along; by, at; ~ *dit AL,* in spite of this; for all that; ~ *'n BOOT,* by boat; ~ *die DAG verbeter,* improve daily; ~ *GEWELD,* by force; ~ *INK,* in ink; ~ *die KAR,* by car(t); *iem.* ~ *'n sterk KA= RAKTER,* a person of strong character; ~ *KERS= FEES,* at Christmas; *een KISSIE* ~ *100 appels;* one box containing 100 apples; ~ *10 PERSENT toeneem,* increase by 10 per cent; ~ *die eerste SLAG,* at the first stroke (attempt); *reisigers* ~ *hierdie TREIN,* passengers by this train; *huis toe gaan* ~ *die VAKANSIE,* go home for the holidays; *iem.* ~ *VREDE LAAT,* leave someone in peace.
metaal', (metale), metal; ~**aar,** metallic vein, lode; ~**afdruk,** cliché; ~**afknipsel,** scissel; ~**afval,** scrap metal; ~**agtig, (-e),** metallic; brazen; metalline; ~**barometer,** metallic barometer; ~**beskrywing,** metallography; ~**bewerker,** metal-worker; ~**bou,** metal construction; ~**dekking,** bullion (bank); ~**draad,** metal wire; coil; ~**draadlamp,** metal-filament lamp; ~**duimstok,** straight edge; metal rule; ~**gaas,** expanded metal; wire gauze; ~**gieter,** (brass) founder; ~**gietery,** (brass) foundry; ~**glans,** metallic lustre; ~**houdend, (-e),** metalliferous; ~**industrie,** metallurgic industry; ~**kenner,** metallurgist; ~**kennis,** metallurgy; ~**klank,** metallic sound (ring); ~**korrel,** regulus; ~**krulle,** turnings; ~**kunde,** metallurgy; ~**kun'dig, (-e),** metallurgic(al); ~**kun'dige, (-s),** metallurgist; ~**laag,** metal coating; ~**legering,** metallic alloy; ~**mengsel,** alloy, amalgam; ~**-metaalbinding,** metal-metal bond; ~**pakking,** metallic packing; ~**plaat,** metal sheet; ~**plettery,** metal-rolling mill; ~**poeier,** plate-powder; ~**punt,** tag; ~**saag,** hack-saw; ~**skuim,** dross, slack, clinker; ~**slak,** slag, scoria; ~**spieël,** metal mirror; ~**staaf,** ingot; ~**strook,** lamina; ~**suiwering,** scorification; ~**uitputting,** metal fatigue; ~**voorraad,** bullion; ~**vuil,** metallic fouling; ~**ware,** metal wares; ~**werk,** metalwork; ~**werker,** metalworker.
metaan', methane; ~**gas,** methane.
metabo'lies, (-e), metabolic.
metabolis'me, metabolism.
metafi'sies, (-e), metaphysical.
metafi'sika, metaphysics, mental philosophy.
metafi'sikus, (..sici, -se), metaphysician.

metafoor', (..fore), metaphor.
metafo'ries, (-e), metaphorical.
metagene'se, metagenesis.
meta'le, (b), metallic (sound).
me'talinguisties, (-e), metalinguistic.
metalliek', (-e), metallic.
metallisa'sie, metallization.
metalliseer', (ge-), metallize; ..se'ring, metallization.
metallis'me, metallism.
metal'lofoon, (..fone), metallophone.
metallografie', metallography.
metalloï'de, (-s), metalloïed', (-e), metalloid.
metallurg', (-e), metallurgist; ~**ie',** metallurgy.
metallur'gies, (-e), metallurgic(al); ~**e ingenieurs= wese,** metallurgical engineering.
me'tameer, (..mere), metamere.
metamorf', metamor'fies, (-e), metamorphic.
metamorfis'me, metamorphism.
metamorfo'se, metamorphosis.
metamorfoseer', (ge-), metamorphose.
metaplasie', metaplasia.
metaplas'me, metaplasm.
metasta'se, metastasis.
me'tataal, metalanguage.
metatar'sus, (-se), metatarsus.
meta'tesis, metathesis.
met'dat, just when; at the moment when; with that.
meteen', at the same time; ~**s',** all of a sudden; outright; at once, suddenly.
metempsigo'se, metempsychosis, transmigration of the soul.
meteoor', (meteore), meteor; ~**reën,** meteoric shower; ~**steen,** aerolite, meteorite, falling stone.
meteoroï'de, (-s), meteoroïed', (-e), meteoroid.
meteo'ries, (-e), meteoric.
meteoriet', (-e), meteorite.
meteorograaf', (..grawe), meteorograph.
meteoroliet', (-e), meteorolite.
meteorologie', meteorology.
meteorolo'gies, (-e), meteorological.
meteoroloog', (..loë), meteorologist.
me'ter¹, (-s), metre (measure of length).
me'ter², (-s), meter (gas), gauge; indicator; measurer; ~**huur,** meter-rent; ~**opnemer,** meter-reader; ~**skyf,** gauge-disc; ~**stand,** reading of the meter; ~**tjie, (-s),** tape-measure; ~**wyser,** gauge-pointer.
met'gesel, (-le), companion, mate; concomitant; conjunct; ~**lin', (-ne),** (lady) companion.
metiel', methyl; ~**alkohol,** methyl alcohol; spirits.
metier', métier, trade, occupation, profession, line.
me'ting, (-e, -s), measuring, mensuration; testing.
m''etjie, (-s), small **m.**
meto'de, (-s), method, manner; procedure; ~ *BRING in,* introduce method into; *te werk gaan VOLGENS 'n* ~, follow a method (plan); ~**leer,** methodology.
metodiek', methodology, methodics, science of method.
meto'dies, (-e), methodical.
Metodis', (-te), Methodist; ~**me,** Methodism; ~**te= kerk,** Methodist church; ~**ties, (-e),** Methodistic(al).
metodologie', methodology.
metodolo'gies, (-e), methodological.
me'tol, methol.
meto'nies, (-e), metonic; ~**e siklus,** metonic cycle.
metoni'mia, metonymy.
metoni'mies, (-e), metonymical.
metriek¹, (s) prosody.
metriek², (b) (-e), metric; ~**e stelsel,** metric system.
me'tries, (-e), metrical; metric; ~**e vers,** metric(al) verse (poem).
metriseer', (w) (ge-), metricize; ..se'ring, metricizing, metrification.
metrograaf', (..grawe), metrograph.
metrologie', metrology.
metrolo'gies, (-e), metrologic.
metroloog', (..loë), metrologist.
metronomie', metronomy.
metronoom', (..nome), metronome.
metropoliet', (-e), metropolitan.
metro'polis, (-se), metropolis, capital (town).

metropolitaan', (..tane), metropolitan; ~s', (-e), metropolitan; ~ se gebied, metropolitan area.
metropool' = metropolis.
me'trum, (-s, ..tra), metre (in poetry).
met'te, matins; *DONKERE* ~, tenebrae; *KORTE* ~ *maak*, give someone (something) short shrift; *iem. die* ~ *LEES*, have someone on the carpet; read someone a lesson.
metterdaad', indeed, in fact.
mettertyd', in (the) course of time, in due course.
metterwoon': *jou êrens* ~ *vestig*, make one's home somewhere; take up residence.
Metu'salem, Methuselah; *'n OU Metusalem*, a Methuselah; *so OUD soos* ~, as old as the hills; as old as Methuselah.
met'wors, German pork sausage.
meu'bel, (-s), piece of furniture; ~ **bedryf**, furniture trade; ~ **fabriek**, furniture factory; ~ **handel**, furniture trade; ~ **lak**, cabinet varnish; ~ **magasyn**, furniture store; pantechnicon; ~ **maker**, cabinet-maker, furniture-maker; ~ **makery**, cabinet-making; furniture factory; ~ **ontwerp**, furniture design; ~ **politoer**, furniture polish; ~ **s**, furniture; ~ **saak**, furniture firm; ~ **sis**, furniture chintz, cretonne; ~ **stuk**, piece of furniture; ~ **toelae**, furniture allowance; ~ **vernis**, liquid veneer; ~ **vervoer**, furniture-re=moval; ~ **wa**, furniture (removal) van, pan=technicon; ~ **waks**, furniture wax; French polish; ~ **winkel**, furniture store.
meubileer', (ge-), furnish; ~ **der, (-s)**, (house) furnisher.
meubilêr', (-e), furniture.
meubile'ring, furnishing.
meublement', furniture, furnishings.
meug, liking.
meul, (-e), mill; noughts and crosses; *eerste by die* ~, *eerste MAAL*, first come, first served; *Gods* ~ *MAAL langsaam*, the mills of God grind slowly, but they grind exceeding small; ~ **afval**, mill-sweepings; ~ **as**, sail-axle; ~ **bouer**, millwright; ~ **dam**, mill-dam, mill-pond; ~ **e, (-s, -ns)** = **meul**; ~ **eienaar**, mill-owner; ~ **enaar, (-s)**, miller; ~ **klip**, millstone; ~ **maker**, millwright; ~ **rat**, mill-wheel; ~ **roede**, sail-arm; ~ **sloot**, mill-race; ~ **sluis**, mill-sluice; ~ **spel**, nine man's morris; ~ **spruitjie**, mill-brook; ~ **steen**, millstone; ~ **stof**, mill-dust; ~ **stroom**, mill-stream; leat; raceway; ~ **tregter**, mill-hopper; ~ **vliegtuig**, autogyro; ~ **werker**, mill-hand; ~ **wiel**, mill-wheel.
mevrou', (-e), madam; my lady; mistress; ~ *A.*, Mrs. A.; *JA,* ~, yes, Madam; *is* ~ *TUIS?* is the mistress (madam) (the lady of the house) at home?
Mexikaan', (..kane), Mexican; ~ s', (-e), Mexican.
Me'xiko, Mexico.
mez'zosopraan, mezzo-soprano.
mez'zotint, mezzotint.
mia(a)u', (ge-), mew, miaow.
mias'ma, (-s, ..ta), miasma.
Mi'das: *'n* ~, a Midas.
mid'dag, midday, noon; afternoon; *NA die* ~, in the afternoon; *VOOR die* ~, before noon; *'n VRY* ~, an afternoon off; a half-holiday; ~ **beurt**, afternoon service; ~ **breedte**, latitude at noon; ~ **diens**, afternoon service; ~ **dutjie**, afternoon nap, siesta; ~ **ete**, luncheon, lunch; (midday) dinner; ~ **etens=uur**, lunch hour; ~ **hoogte**, meridian altitude; ~ **kring**, meridian; ~ **lyn**, meridian; ~ **maal**, midday meal, dinner; ~ **pouse**, midday (lunch) interval; lunch break; ~ **rok**, afternoon frock; ~ **rus**, afternoon rest; ~ **sirkel**, meridian; ~ **sitting**, afternoon session; ~ **slapie**, afternoon sleep, siesta; ~ **son**, afternoon sun; ~ **tee**, afternoon tea; ~ **trein**, afternoon train; ~ **uur**, noon(tide); lunch-hour; ~ **ver=toning**, ~ **voorstelling**, matinée, afternoon per=formance.
mid'dae, in the afternoon.
mid'de, middle, midst; *in die* ~ *BRING*, raise a point; *te* ~ *van GEVAAR*, in the midst of danger; *IN ons* ~, in our midst; *iets in die* ~ *LAAT*, leave something undecided (in mid-air); **M~-Afrika**, Central Africa; ~ **-in**, in the middle of.
mid'del¹, (-e), means, resources; medium, contriv=ance, help; money; instrument, agent; remedy; (mv) wherewithal; *'n* ~ *AANWEND*, employ means; *'n BEDERFWERENDE* ~, a preservative; *eie* ~ *e van BESTAAN hê*, have private means; ~ *e van BESTAAN*, means of subsistence; *DEUR* ~ *van*, by means of; *die* ~ *is erger as die KWAAL*, the remedy is worse than the disease; *'n* ~ *teen TAND=PYN*, a remedy for toothache; *'n* ~ *TOT 'n doel*, a means to an end; *iem. VAN* ~ *e*, a man of means.
mid'del², (-s), centre, middle; waist; *IN die* ~ *van die wêreld wees*, be on the horns of a dilemma; *'n MEI=SIE met 'n slanke* ~ *tjie*, a girl with a slender waist.
mid'delaar, (-s), mediator; ~ **skap**, mediatorship; ~ **swerk**, mediation, intercession.
mid'del: ~ **afstand**, centre distance; ~ **agter**, centre back; ~ **agternek**, nape; ~ **baadjie**, cardigan; ~ **baan**, centre court; midwicket; middle stripe (flag); ~ **baar, (..bare)**, secondary (education); av=erage, moderate; middle; mean (time); ~ *bare GROOTTE*, medium size; *VAN* ~ *bare grootte*, medium-sized; *VAN* ~ *bare leeftyd*, middle-aged; ~ **borssegment**, mesothorax; ~ **deel**, middle part; ~ **dek**, waist; middle deck.
mid'deldeur¹, (s) middle door.
mid'deldeur², (b) in two, asunder, in half.
mid'deldriekwart, (ong.), centre three-quarter.
Mid'deleeue, Middle Ages.
Mid'deleeus¹, (-e), mediaeval.
mid'deleeus², (-e), passé, old-hat; old-fashioned.
Mid'delengels, Middle English.
mid'delerwyl, meanwhile.
mid'deletoets, means test.
Mid'de(l)-Europa, Central Europe.
mid'deleweredige, mean proportional.
mid'del: ~ **gehalte**, medium quality (standard value); ~ **gewig**, middleweight; ~ **groot**, medium(-sized); ~ **grootte**, medium size.
mid'delhand, metacarpus; ~ **beentjies**, metacarpal bones.
mid'delharsings, midbrain.
Mid'delhoogduits, Middle High German.
mid'delhuid, dermis, corium.
middelja'rig, (-e), middle-aged; ~ **heid**, middle age.
mid'del: ~ **kerk**, intermediate service half-way be=tween two Holy Communions; ~ **klas**, middle class; gentry; ~ **kleur**, intermediate colour; ~ **koers**, middle rate; ~ **korrelrig, (-e)**, medium-grained.
mid'delkring, magpie (in target); ~ **skoot**, magpie.
mid'del: ~ **laer**, middle bearing; ~ **land**, midland.
Mid'dellandse See, Mediterranean Sea.
mid'del: ~ **lik, (-e)**, indirect; mediate; ~ *like dader*, innocent agent; ~ **loop**, middle course; ~ **lyf**, middle, waist; ~ **lyn**, diameter, centre line, equator, half-way line, axial line, median (line); waistline; ~ **lynmeter**, eriometer; ~ **maat**, medium, mean, av=erage; waist measure; *die gulde* ~ *maat*, the golden mean; ~ **man**, middleman; ~ **mannetjie**, hog's-back, ridge (in road).
middelma'tig, (-e), mediocre, indifferent; moderate; middle-rate; mean; betwixt and between, medium, so-so, middling; ~ **heid**, mediocrity.
mid'del: ~ **moot**, middle slice; centre section; ~ **muur**, partition; (inside) wall.
Mid'delnederlands, Middle Dutch.
mid'delnerf, nervure; midrib.
mid'deloor, middle ear, tympanum; ~ **ontsteking**, tympanitis.
Mid'de(l)-Ooste, Middle East.
mid'del: ~ **paadjie**, parting (in hair); central aisle; ~ **pad**, central path.
mid'delpunt, centre; pivot, ganglion, hub; ~ **ig, (-e)**, centric; ~ **soe'kend, (-e)**, centripetal; ~ **soe'ker**, centre-finder; ~ **vlie'dend, (-e)**, centrifugal; ~ **vuur**, converging fire.
mid'del: ~ **rib**, web (of beam); midrib; ~ **rif**, midriff, diaphragm; ~ **ring**, eternity ring; ~ **ry**, centre row; ~ **skip**, midship(s); ~ **skorting**, partition (room); septum (nose); ~ **skot**, centre partition; intermedi=ate payment; ~ **slag**, medium; middling; ~ **soet**, medium sweet (wine); ~ **soort**, medium sort; ~ **speler**, centre-jumper (basketball); ~ **stand**,

middeltjie 329 *milligram*

middle class gentry; middle position; ~ **stang,** king=
bolt; ~ **ste,** middle, central, middlemost; ~*ste
dwarsaar*, medial cross-vein; ~ **stuk,** die (arch.);
epergne; middle (central) piece; mesosoma; ~ **styl,**
kingpost; monial (window); munnion; mullion;
~ **syfer,** average figure; ~ **term,** mean.
mid′deltjie¹, (-s), slender waist.
mid′deltjie², (-s), trick, device, expedient, makeshift;
remedy.
mid′deltoon, mediant.
Mid′delveld, Middle Veld.
mid′delveld, mid field; mid wicket.
mid′del: ~ **vinger,** middle finger; ~ **vlies,** mediasti=
num; ~ **voet,** metatarsus; instep; ~ **voor,** centre for=
ward; ~ **waarde,** median.
mid′delweg, middle course; the golden mean; *die* ~
BEWANDEL, follow a middle course; *die GULDE
(GOUE)* ~ , the golden mean; *'n* ~ *VIND*, strike
the happy medium, adopt a middle course.
Mid′de-Ooste, Middle East.
mid′dernag, midnight; *lank NA* ~ , long past mid=
night; in the small hours; *TEEN* ~ , towards mid=
night; ~ **fees,** midnight feast; ~ **sending,** midnight
mission; ~ **son,** midnight sun; ~ **′telik, (-e),** (at)
midnight.
mid′deweg, *see* **middelweg.**
mi′di, (s) (-'s), midi; (b) midi-, midi.
mid: ~ **skeeps, (-e),** amidship(s); ~ **somer,** midsum=
mer; ~ **winter,** midwinter.
mied, (-e, -ens), pile, heap, rick, stack; ~ **brand,** stack=
burn; ~ **pakker,** stacker.
mie′lie, (-s), mealie, maize; Indian corn; *GE=
BREEKTE* ~ *s*, crushed maize; *GEMAALDE* ~ *s
en hawer*, provender; *GESTAMPTE* ~ *s*, samp; *'n
mens kan* ~ *s in sy ORE plant*, his ears need wash=
ing; ~ **afmaker,** maize-sheller; ~ **atjar,** pickled
mealies; ~ **baard,** mealie beard; ~ **blaar,** mealie
leaf; ~ **blom,** corn-flour; ~ **boer,** mealie farmer;
~ **breker,** corn-cracker; ~ **brood,** mealie bread;
pone; ~ **geel,** maize; ~ **gruis,** mealie-rice, broken
mealies, maize grits; ~ **heide,** mealie-heath;
~ **kiemmeel,** germ-meal; ~ **kop,** mealie ear; cob;
~ **land,** mealie field; ~ **meel,** mealie meal; ~ **-oes,**
mealie harvest; ~ **pap,** mealie porridge; ~ **pit,** ker=
nel (on cob); mealie grain, ~ **planter,** mealie plant=
er; **M ~ raad,** Maize Board; ~ **ruspe(r),** mealie bor=
er; ~ **rys,** mealie rice; ~ **s,** maize (kernels); mealies;
~ **saad,** mealie seed; ~ **semels,** mealie (maize) bran;
fyn ~ *semels*, hominy chop; ~ **stamruspe(r),** maize-
stalk borer; ~ **streek,** mealie belt; ~ **stronk,** mealie
stalk; ~ **stronke,** stower; ~ **stronkpyp,** corn-cob
pipe, ~ **strooi,** maize stover; ~ **stroop,** maize syrup;
~ **suurtjies,** pickled mealies; ~ **vloer,** mealie thresh=
ing-floor; ~ **vlokkie,** cornflake; ~ **vrug,** delicious
monster (plant); ~ **wêreld,** maize world; ~ **wurm,**
mealie-worm; mealie-cob worm.
mieli′tis, myelitis.
mie′nie-mie′nie, lucky bean, love bean.
mier, (-e), ant; emmet; pismire; ~ *e HÊ*, be fidgety; be
on pins and needles; *LOOP (gaan) na die* ~ *e, jou
luiaard*, go to the ant, thou sluggard; ~ **broodjies,**
Beltian (Belt's) body; ~ **eiers,** ant-eggs, ~ **eter,** ant-
eater; ~ **gif,** ant-poison; ~ **kat,** meercat; ~ **klein,** as
small as an ant; ~ **koningin,** ant-queen; ~ **leeu,** ant-
lion; ~ **nes,** ant-hill, ant's nest.
mier: ~ **(s)′hoop,** antheap, anthill; ~ **suur,** formic
acid; ~ **vreter,** ant-eater, ant-bear.
mie′sies, (-e), missis, missus.
miet¹, (-e), meal moth, fig moth *(Ephestia)*; larva of
certain moths and beetles; mite, tuber-worm; skip=
per (cheese).
miet², (-e) = **mied.**
mie′ta, (-s), namesake; comrade.
migma′ties, (-e), migmatic.
migrai′ne, migraine, megrim.
migra′sie, migration.
migreer′, (ge-), migrate.
mik¹, (s), (-ke), fork (of tree); forked stick, gibbet.
mik², (w) (ge-), aim, point; *HOOG* ~ , aim high; ~
NA, aim at; ~ *OP*, aim for.
mi′ka, mica; ~ **-agtig,** micaceous.
mika′do, (-'s), mikado.

mikaniet′, micanite.
mi′kaplaat, mica plate.
mik: ~ **bal,** object ball, jack; ~ **hout,** forked stick.
mikologie′, mycology.
mikolo′gies, (-e), mycologic(al).
mikoloog′, (. . **loë),** mycologist.
mik′punt, aim; mark, butt, target; cock-shy; objec=
tive; *die* ~ *van hulle grappe*, their laughing-stock,
the butt of their jokes.
mi′kro: ~ **-analise,** micro-analysis; ~ **-artropode,** mi=
cro-arthropod; ~ **balans,** microbalance; ~ **barome=
ter,** microbarometer.
mikro′be, (-s), microbe.
mikro′bies, (-e), microbial, microbic.
mi′kro: ~ **chemie,** microchemistry; ~ **-elektronies,**
micro-electronic; ~ **-elektronika,** micro-electron=
ics; ~ **-element,** micro element; ~ **flora,** micro-flo=
ra; ~ **film,** microfilm; ~ **fiche,** microfiche; ~ **foon′,**
(. . **fone),** microphone, mike; ~ **fotografeer′, (ge-),**
microphotograph; ~ **fotografie′,** microphoto=
graphy; ~ **galvanometer,** microgalvanometer;
~ **golf,** microwave; ~ **golfoond,** microwave oven;
~ **graaf,** micrograph; ~ **graniet,** microgranite;
~ **klimaat,** microclimate; ~ **kos′mies, (-e),** micro=
cosmic; ~ **kos′mos,** microcosm; ~ **kristallyn,**
microcrystalline.
mikroliet′, microlite; microlith.
mi′kromanipulasie, micromanipulation.
mi′krometer, mikrome′ter, micrometer.
mi′krometode, micromethod.
mikrometrio′, micrometry.
mikrome′tries, (-e), micrometric.
mi′kron, (-e), micron.
mikroörganis′me, micro-organism.
mikroskoop′, (. . **skope),** microscope.
mikroskopie′, microscopy.
mikrosko′pies, (-e), microscopic(al).
mikroskopis′, (-te), microscopist.
mik′rotoom, (-s), microtome.
mikrotomie′, microtomy.
mi′krotoon, microtone.
mi′krovliegtuig, microlite.
mik: ~ **skeer,** (s) crutching (sheep); (w) **(ge-),** crutch;
~ **stertbyevanger,** fork-tailed drongo; ~ **stok,**
forked stick; ~ **stuk,** crutch.
mikstuur′, (miksture), (ong.), mixture, blend.
mik′wol, crutchings.
Milaan′, Milan.
Milanees′, (. . **nese),** Milanese.
mild, (-e), generous, liberal, open-handed; lenient;
profuse; flush; *'n* ~ *e BYDRAE*, a generous contri=
bution; *met* ~ *e HAND*, freely, lavishly; *'n* ~ *e
REËN*, a good downpour.
mildda′dig, (-e), liberal, generous, bounteous, muni=
ficent, bountiful; ~ **heid,** generosity, liberality,
bounty, munificence.
mil′delik, generous(ly); liberal(ly).
mild′heid, liberality, generosity, open-handedness;
bounty, largesse.
miliêr′, (-e), miliary.
milieu′, (-'s), milieu, environment, atmosphere,
surroundings.
mili′sie, militia; ~ **mag,** militia force; . . **lisiën′, (-s),**
militiaman; ~ **pligtig, (-e),** liable to military service;
~ **stelsel,** militia system.
militant′, (-e), militant, pugnacious.
militaris′, (-te), militarist; ~ **eer′, (ge-),** militarize;
~ **me,** militarism; ~ **ties, (-e),** militarist(ic).
militêr′, (s) **(-e),** military man, soldier; (b) **(-e),** mili=
tary, warlike; ~ *e ATTACHÉ*, military attaché;
DIE ~ *e*, the soldiery, the military; ~ *e DIENS*,
military service; ~ *e DOKTER*, army doctor; *met*
~ *e EER*, with military honours; ~ *e MAG*, mili=
tary force.
miljard′, (-e), milliard; ~ **êr′, (-s),** milliardaire.
miljoen′, (-e), million; ~ **êr′, (-s),** millionaire; ~ **erede,**
budget speech; ~ **ste,** millionth.
miljui′sende, (geselst.), thousands, very many.
millen′nium, (-s, . . **nia),** millennium.
milleriet′, millerite.
mil′libar, (-s), millibar.
mil′ligram, milligram.

mil'liliter, millilitre.
mil'limeter, millimetre.
mil'livolt, millivolt.
miloriet', mylorite.
mil'reis, milreis.
milt, (-e), spleen, milt; ~ **aar,** splenic vein; ~ **koors,** splenic fever; ~ **kruid,** spleenwort; ~ **ontsteking,** splenitis; ~ **siekte,** anthrax; splenic fever; ~ **steek,** splenalgia; ~ **sug,** spleen; ~ **sug'tig, (-e),** splenetic; ~ **syfer,** spleen index; ~ **vergroting,** ague-cake; ~ **vuur,** anthrax; braxy.
mimeograaf', (..grawe), mimeograph.
mime'ties, (-e), mimetic.
mimiek', mimicry.
mi'mies, (-e), mimic.
mi'mikus, (..mici, -se), mimic.
mimi'tafeltjies, nest of tables.
mimo'sa, (-s), mimosa.
min[1], (s) love; *see* **minne; (-ne),** (wet-) nurse; **(w) (ge-),** love.
min[2], (b) little, few; (bw) minus, less; ~ *of MEER,* more or less; *te* ~ *om van RYK te word, te veel om van dood te gaan,* a mere pittance; not much to speak of; *drie SENT te* ~, three cents short; ~ *WORD,* become less.
mi'na, (-s), mina.
min'ag, (ge-), hold in contempt, despise, disdain, slight, undervalue, disesteem, contemn, disregard; misesteem; ~ **tend, (-e),** disdainful, contemptuous, slighting, disrespectful, depreciatory, disparaging; ~ **ting,** disdain, slight, contempt, disesteem, disparagement, decrial, despite, disrespect, misesteem, depreciation; ~ *ting v.d. hof,* contempt of court.
minaret', (-te), minaret.
min'der, (w) (ge-), decrease; lessen; take in (sails); narrow (knitting); (b, bw) less, fewer; inferior; *niem.* ~ *nie AS,* no less a person than; *van* ~ *BELANG,* of secondary importance; *DIS nou* ~, that is a minor (of minor importance); *die* ~ *e GODE,* the lesser lights; ~ *MAAK,* reduce; *die* ~ *e STAND,* the lower orders; *vir* ~ *VERKOOP,* sell for less; ~ *WORD,* decrease, diminish, become smaller, decline, fall off; grow worse.
Min'derbroeder, Friar Minor; Minorite.
min'der: ~ **e, (-s),** inferior; rating(s) (naval); junior; *die* ~ *e van sy broer,* inferior to his brother; ~ **es,** other ranks; rank and file; ~ **heid,** minority; inferiority; ~ **heidsrapport,** ~ **heidsverslag,** minority report; ~ **ing,** diminishing, narrowing (on knitting); discount; *in* ~ *ing van die hoofsom,* to be deducted from the principal.
minderja'rig, (-e), under age, minor; pupilary; ~ **e, (-s),** minor, one under age; ~ **heid,** minority, nonage; pupilage.
min'derman, see **meerderman.**
min'derterm, minor term.
minderwaar'dig, (-e), inferior; base; low-grade, poor, of poor quality; *geestelik* ~, mentally deficient; ~ **heid,** inferiority; baseness; ~ **heidsgevoel,** feeling (sense) of inferiority; ~ **heidskompleks,** inferiority complex.
mineer', (ge-), mine (mil.); ~ **werk,** mine work.
mineraal', (s, b), (..rale), mineral; *minerale BRON,* mineral spring; *minerale REGTE,* mineral rights; ~ **aar,** mineral vein; ~ **afsetting,** mineral deposit; ~ **bron,** mineral spring; ~ **gebrek,** mineral deficiency; ~ **grond,** placer; ~ **olie,** mineral oil; ~ **ryk, (-e),** rich in minerals; ~ **sout,** mineral salt; ~ **tekort,** mineral deficiency; ~ **verbindings,** mineral compounds; ~ **voeding,** mineral nutrition; ~ **water,** mineral water; ~ **waterfabriek,** mineral-water factory.
minera'le: ~ **regte,** mineral rights; ~ **ryk,** mineral kingdom.
mineraliseer', (ge-), mineralize.
mineralise'ring, mineralization.
mineralogie', mineralogy.
mineralo'gies, (-e), mineralogical.
mineraloog', (..loë), mineralogist.
minestro'ne, minestrone, Italian vegetable soup.
mineur'[1], minor, flat (music).
mineur'[2], (-s), soldier who lays mines; miner (mil.).

min'genot, venery, sexual indulgence; love.
min'gerhout, *Adina microcephala.*
mi'ni, (s) (-'s), mini; mini-skirt; (b) **mini-,** mini-.
miniatuur', (..ture), miniature; ~ **geweer,** miniature rifle; ~ **gholf,** midget-golf; ~ **portret,** miniature (portrait); ~ **seël,** miniature stamp; ~ **skilder,** miniaturist; ~ **skildery,** miniature (painting).
mi'nie = **menie.**
miniem', (s) minim; (b) **(-e),** extremely small, slight, trifling, diminutive.
minimaal' (..male), minimal.
minimaliseer', (ge-), minimize.
mi'nimotor, midget (car), minicar.
mi'nimum, (..nima, -s), minimum; *tot 'n* ~ *bring,* reduce to a minimum; ~ **loon,** minimum pay; ~-**maksimumfout,** minimum-maximum deviation; ~ **prys,** lowest (minimum) price, floor price; preserve price; ~ **tarief,** flat rate; ~ **termometer,** minimum thermometer.
mi'ni: ~ **rok,** miniskirt; ~ **skyf, (..skywe),** ministeak; ~ **staat,** ministate.
minis'ter, (-s), minister; *M* ~ *van BINNELANDSE Sake,* Minister of the Interior; ~ *van BOSBOU,* Minister of Forestry; ~ *van BUITELANDSE Sake,* Minister of Foreign Affairs; *EERSTE M* ~, Prime Minister; *M* ~ *van FINANSIES,* Minister of Finance; *M* ~ *van GEMEENSKAPSBOU,* Minister of Community Development; ~ *van LANDBOU,* Minister of Agriculture; *M* ~ *van MYNWESE,* Minister of Mines; *M* ~ *van ONDERWYS, Kuns en Wetenskap,* Minister of Education, Arts and Science; *M* ~ *van SPORT en Ontspanning,* Minister of Sport and Recreation; *M* ~ *van TOERISME,* Minister of Tourism; *M* ~ *van VERVOER,* Minister of Transport; *M* ~ *van VOLKSWELSYN,* Minister of Social Welfare; *M* ~ *van WATERWESE,* Minister of Water Affairs.
ministe'rie, (-s), ministry, cabinet.
minis'ter: ~ **ieel', (..riële),** ministerial; ~-**president,** prime minister, premier; ~ **raad,** cabinet council.
minis'ters: ~ **pos,** portfolio; ~ **vrou,** minister's wife; ~ **woning,** minister's residence.
minjonet', (-te), mignonette.
min'lik, (-e), lovable, sweet, amicable, friendly; ~ **heid,** sweetness, amicableness, friendliness, affability.
min'naar, (-s), lover, beau, suitor; cherisher, gallant, fancy-man, paramour.
minnares', (-se), lady-love; fancy-girl, paramour; mistress.
minnary'(tjie), (-s), love-affair, amouret(te).
min'ne: *in der* ~ *skik,* settle amicably; ~ **band,** love-tie; ~ **brand,** flame of love; ~ **brief,** love-letter; ~ **dig,** erotic (love) poem; ~ **digter,** amatory (erotic) poet; ~ **drank,** love-potion; philtre; ~ **drif,** amorous passion; ~ **gloed,** ardour of love; ~ **god,** god of love; ~ **godin,** goddess of love; ~ **klag,** love's lament; ~ **koors,** flame of love; ~ **koos, (ge-),** bill and coo, make love; ~ **kosery,** love-making; ~ **kout,** lovers' talk; ~ **lekkers,** valentines (sweets); ~ **lied,** love-song; ~ **lok,** lovelock.
min'nenswaardig, (-e), lovable.
min'ne: ~ **pand,** love-pledge; illegitimate child; ~ **pyl,** love-shaft; ~ **pyn,** pangs of love; ~ **sanger,** minstrel; ~ **sangerskuns,** minstrelsy; ~ **taal,** language of love; ~ **vlam,** flame of love; ~ **vuur,** fire of love; ~ **waansin,** erotomania.
mi'nor, subsumption.
minoraat', ultimogeniture.
Minoriet', (-e), Minorite.
Minor'ka, Minorca; ~ **hoender,** Minorca (fowl).
minotau'rus, (..ri), minotaur.
min'saam, (..same), kind, affable; bland, suave, debonair; gentle; benign; ~ **heid,** affability, kindness, condescension, amiability; suavity, blandness; amenity, gentleness.
min'siek, (-e), amorous, love-sick, erotic.
min'ste, least, fewest, smallest; *by die* ~ *BEWEGING,* at the slightest movement; *nie die* ~ *IDEE van iets hê nie,* not have the faintest notion of something; *nie IN die* ~ *nie,* not in the least; *OP sy* ~,

minstens 331 *misluk*

(at) the least; *TEN* ~, at least; *VIR die* ~, at least; *die* ~ *WEES*, give in, yield.
min'stens, at least; not less than; *sy is* ~ *VEERTIG*, she is forty if she is a day; she is at least forty years old; *dit WEEG* ~ *tien kilogram*, it weighs at least ten kilogram.
minstreel', **(minstrele)**, minstrel, gleeman.
min'teken, minus sign.
min'tig!, goodness!
mi'nus, minus.
minusieus', **(-e)**, close, scrupulous; minute (attention); ~**heid**, minuteness.
minus'kel, **(-s)**, small letter.
minuskuul', **(..kule)**, very small, miniscule.
mi'nusteken, minus sign, negative sign.
minu'te, **(-s)**, minute, memorandum.
minuut', **(minute)**, minute; *op die* ~, to the minute; ~**glas**, sand-glass; ~**s'gewys(e)**, occurring every minute; ~**skote**, minute-guns; ~**wys(t)er**, minute-hand.
min'vermoënd, **(-e)**, poor, indigent.
miologie', myology; **..lo'gies**, **(-e)**, myological.
mioloog', **(..loë)**, myologist.
miopie', myopia.
Mioseen', Miocene.
mioso'tis, myosotis.
mira'kel, **(-s)**, miracle, wonder; ~**land**, land of mystery; ~**spel**, miracle play.
mirakuleus', (ong.), **(-e)**, miraculous.
mir'liton, **(-s)**, mirliton.
mir're, myrrh.
mirt, **(-e)**, myrtle; ~**bos**, myrtle grove; ~**krans**, myrtle-wreath.
mis¹, (s) manure, dung, droppings, faeces; *wie met* ~ *omgaan, word daarmee besmet*, evil communications corrupt good manners; play with pitch and you'll be defiled; (w) **(ge-)**, mute, void the faeces; dung; ~ *op*, befoul.
mis², (s) **(-se)**, mass (R. Catholic); *die* ~ *hoor*, hear mass.
mis³, (s) mist, fog; haze; *deur 'n dik* ~ *vertraag*, delayed by a thick fog; (w) **(ge-)**, be foggy (misty).
mis⁴, (w) **(ge-)**, miss (train); do without (drink); lose (boat); lack (experience); *sy DOEL* ~, miss the mark; be ineffective; *kan jy die GELD* ~, can you spare the money?; *dit* ~ *NIE*, it never fails; *ek* ~ *twee STOELE*, two chairs are missing; (b, bw) wrong, amiss; *dit* ~ *HÊ*, be mistaken; ~ *IS* ~, a miss is as good as a mile; ~ *of RAAK*, hit or miss; *die SKOOT was* ~, the shot went wide.
misantroop', **(..trope)**, misanthrope.
misantropie', misanthropy.
misantro'pies, **(-e)**, misanthropic.
misbaar'¹, (s) **(..bare)**, noise, clamour.
mis'baar², (b) **(..bare)**, dispensable; non-essential.
mis'baksel, monstrosity, monster, deformity; churl; abortion; wastrel.
mis'bank, fog-bank.
mis: ~**bel**, sacring-bell; ~**boek**, missal, massbook.
mis'bredie, pigweed *(Portulaca oleracea)*.
mis'bruik, (s) **(-e)**, abuse, misuse; misapplication; misemployment; ~ *MAAK van, abuse, take advantage of*; ~ *van VERTROUE*, breach of trust.
misbruik', (w) **(~)**, abuse, misuse, misapply; misappropriate, misemploy; pervert; prostitute, profane; ~**er**, **(-s)**, perverter; profaner.
mis'daad, crime, offence, misdeed; delict; delinquency; felony; *'n* ~ *BEGAAN*, commit a crime; *geen* ~ *word VERMOED nie*, foul play is not suspected; ~**dossier**, crime docket; ~**situasie**, crime situation; ~**syfer**, crime rate; ~**toneel**, crime site (spot); criminal scene.
misda'dig, **(-e)**, criminal, felonious, maleficent; ~**er**, **(-s)**, criminal, evil-doer, delinquent, felon, malefactor; ~**ersbende**, gang of criminals; ~**heid**, criminality, felony, flagitiousness, feloniousness.
misdeel', **(~)**, misdeal.
misdeeld', **(-e)**, unprovided, deprived of; destitute, stupid; ~ *van verstand*, feeble-minded.
misdeel'de, **(-s)**, destitute.
mis: ~**dienaar**, server, acolyte; ~**diens**, celebration of mass; ~**doek**, corporas, corporal.

misdoen', **(~)**, do wrong, act wrongly, sin.
misdra', **(~)**, behave badly, misbehave; *hy het hom skandelik* ~, he has misbehaved shockingly.
mis: ~**drag**, miscarriage, abortion; ~**druk**, misprint, mackle.
mis'drup, fog-drip.
mis'dryf, (s) **(misdrywe)**, crime, offence, misdemeanour.
misdryf', **misdry'we**, (w) **(~)**, sin, do wrong, misbehave.
misdui'ding, misinterpretation.
mise en scè'ne, stage setting.
misera'bel, **(-e; -er, -ste)**, miserable, rotten, wretched, paltry, measly.
misè're, **(-s)**, misery, wretchedness.
misgaan', **(~)**, misbehave.
mis'geboorte, deformity; miscarriage, abortion.
mis'gewade, mass vestments.
mis'gewas, failure of crops; abortion; *hy is sommer 'n* ~, he is just a good-for-nothing.
misgis', **(~)**, be mistaken; err, miscalculate; *ek het my deerlik* ~, I made a big mistake; ~**sing**, mistake, error.
mis'gooi, **(-ge-)**, mis gooi (mis ge-), miss, fail to hit.
mis'gordel, fog-belt.
mis: ~**greep**, **(..grepe)**, mistake, blunder, slip; ~**gryp**, **(-ge-)**, miss (in catching), fail to catch; misbehave; ~**gun'**, **(~)**, (be)grudge, envy; ~**haag'**, **(~)**, displease, dissatisfy; ~**ha'e**, (s) displeasure, annoyance.
mishan'del, **(~)**, ill-use, ill-treat, maltreat, abuse, misuse, ~**ing**, ill-treatment, maltreatment, abuse, ill-usage, misusage.
mis'hark, muck-rake.
mis'hemp, alb.
mis'hoop, dunghill, muck-heap; dumping-ground.
mis'horing, fog-horn, siren.
mis'hou, miss, mishit.
mis'kar, dung-cart; tumbrel.
mis'kelk(ie), chalice.
misken', **(~)**, misjudge, slight, undervalue, ignore, fail to appreciate, misprize; *'n* ~ *de genie*, a neglected genius; ~**ning**, misappreciation, slight, disregard, misprision.
miskien', perhaps, perchance, maybe.
mis'kleed¹, vestment worn at mass.
mis'kleed², covering of mist (fog).
mis: ~**klos**, **(-se)**, dag, dung lock (in wool); ~**koek**, hard piece of dung; wretch, miserable fellow.
mis'koop, (s) bad bargain; (w) **(~)**, *jou* ~, buy a pig in a poke.
mis'kraal, kraal made of (full of) dung.
mis'kraam, miscarriage, abortion, slip.
mis'kruier, **(-s)**, scarab; tumble-bug, dung-beetle *(Scarabaeus sacer)*; sexton beetle; scavenger; miserable fellow.
mis'kyk, **(-ge-)**, miss (in looking), overlook, err; ignore, cut (a person).
mis'laag¹, fog-layer.
mis'laag², layer of manure.
mislei', **(~)**, deceive, lead up the garden path, dupe, fool; decoy; hoodwink, mislead; beguile, delude, circumvent; ~**baar**, **(..bare)**, deceivable; ~**dend**, **(-e)**, deceptive; misleading, guileful, elusive, elusory, delusive; fallacious; ~**ding**, **(-e)**, deception, deceit, delusion, circumvention; fallacy, guile; ~**er**, deceiver, impostor, deluder, misleader.
mis'lik, **(-e)**, sick, squeamish, queasy, bilious; crapulent, crapulous; disgusting, nasty; ~**heid**, sickness, vomiturition; crapulence, morning sickness, nausea, squeamishness, queasiness, biliousness.
mis'loop, **(-ge-)**, miss the way; be unsuccessful, miscarry; fail, go wrong; *hulle het MEKAAR misgeloop*, they missed each other; *SAKE loop mis*, things are going wrong.
misluk', **(~)**, fail, miscarry (plan), fall through, come to nothing, fall flat, come to grief, collapse; *DIT het hom* ~, he did not succeed; ~*te GRAPPIES*, jokes that fell flat; ~*te POGING*, vain (unsuccessful, abortive) attempt; ~**keling**, **(-e)**, misfit, failure; ~**king**, **(-e, -s)**, failure, miscarriage, wash-out, débâcle, fiasco, frost, collapse; *op 'n* ~*king UIT*-

mismaak 332 *model*

LOOP, end in failure, prove a fiasco; *'n VOLSLAE ~king*, an utter failure.
mismaak', (w) (~), deform, disfigure; (b) (-te), deformed, disfigured, misshapen; ~**t'heid**, deformity, disfigurement, abnormity.
mis: ~**ma'ker**, deformer; ~**ma'king**, deformation, disfiguration.
mismoe'dig, (-e), discouraged, dejected, despondent, down-hearted; *iem.* ~ *maak*, discourage someone; ~**heid**, dejection, discouragement.
misnoe'ë, discontent, displeasure, dissatisfaction.
misnoeg', (-de), dissatisfied, displeased, discontented, ill-pleased; ~**d'heid**, displeasure, dissatisfaction.
mis'oes, failure of crops (harvest); failure; *SO 'n* ~, the wretch; *dit WAS 'n* ~, it was a failure (washout).
misogamie', misogamy.
misogamis', (-te), misogamist.
mis'pel, (-s), medlar (tree).
misplaas', (w) (~), misplace; (b) (-te), misplaced, ill-placed; ~*te SKERTS*, ill-timed joke; ~ *WEES*, be out of place.
mispla'sing, misplacing, misplacement.
misprys', (~), disapprove of, dispraise, discommend; ~**ing**, dispraise, disapprobation.
mis'punt, rotter, blighter.
mis'reën, drizzle.
mis'reken,[1], (-ge-), miscalculate.
misre'ken[2], (~), be mistaken, meet with disappointment; *ek het my lelik* ~, I made a bad mistake (miscalculation).
mis'ryblom, mis'rybol, variety of *Haemanthus*.
missaal', (missale), missal.
mis'sein, fog-signal.
mis'sie, (-s), mission.
missiel', (-e), missile.
mis'sinjaal, fog-signal.
mis'sit, (-ge-), miss one's seat.
missi've, (-s), (vero., ong.), missive, (official) letter.
misska'pe, misshapen.
misskat'ting, (-s), error of judgment; wrong estimate.
mis'skiet, (-ge-), **mis skiet, (mis ge-)**, miss (when shooting), shoot wide of the mark.
mis'skoot, miss, wide shot.
mis'skop, miskick.
mis' slaan, (-ge-), miss (when hitting); mishit.
mis'slag, error, fault; accident; mishit; miscarriage; *'n* ~ *van die tong*, a slip of the tongue.
mis: ~**sluier**, film; fog-veil; ~**smelter**, demister.
mis'stand, (-e), abuse, evil.
mis'stap, false step, wrong step; fault, faux-pas, misstep; error; aberration; *'n* ~ *BEGAAN*, do something wrong; *'n* ~ *DOEN*, make a false step.
mis'steek, (-ge-), **mis steek, (mis ge-)**, miss (in stabbing).
mis'stof, manure, fertilizer.
mis'stoot, miss, miscue.
mis'strooier, manure-spreader.
mis'tas, (-ge-), make a mistake (blunder); ~**ting**, error (of judgment).
mis'tel[1], (s) (-s), mistletoe.
mis'tel[2], (w) (-ge-), count wrongly, miscount; ~**ling**, miscount(ing).
miste'rie, (-ë, -s), mystery; ~**spel**, mystery play; ~**vertolker**, mystagogue.
misterieus', (-e), mysterious.
mistiek', (s) mysticism; (b) (-e), mystic(al); ~*e ligsgaam*, mystical body.
mistifika'sie, mystification.
mistifiseer', (ge-), mystify.
mis'tig, (-e), foggy, misty, drizzly, hazy, brumal; ~**heid**, fogginess, mistiness.
mis'tikus, (-se, ..tici), mystic, gymnosophist.
mistisis'me, mysticism.
mistral', (-s), mistral.
mis'trap, (s) = **misstap**; (w) (-ge-), miss (a step) in walking, take the wrong step.
mistroos'tig, (-e), dejected, disconsolate; ~**heid**, dejection, sadness.
mistrou', (~), mistrust, distrust; ~**e**, distrust, suspicion.
mistrou'ig, (-e), distrustful; ~**heid**, distrustfulness.

mis'vat, (-ge-), misunderstand, take amiss; miss, fumble (in catching); ~**ting**, misunderstanding, misconception, wrong impression.
mis'verstaan, (~), misunderstand, misconstrue, mistake, misapprehend; ~**baar**, (..**bare**), mistakable.
mis'verstand, misunderstanding, error, misapprehension; misconception.
misvloer, floor smeared with cow-dung, dungfloor.
misvorm', (w) (~), disfigure, defeature, shape wrongly; (b) (-de), deformed, disfigured, abnormal, misshapen, miscreated; ~**d'heid**, malformation, deformity; ~**ig**, (-e), deformed; ~**igheid**, deformity; ~**ing**, deformation, disfigurement, deformity.
mis'vurk, dung-fork.
mis'vuur[1], (s) dungfire.
mis'vuur[2], (w) (-ge-), miss (when shooting).
mis'water, liquid manure.
mis'weer, foggy weather; ~**vlieëry**, fog-flying.
mis'wurm, cutworm, white grub, caterpillar, dungworm, muck-worm.
mi'te, (-s), myth; ~**digter**, mythopoet; ~**skrywer**, mythographer.
mi'ties, (-e), mythical.
mitiga'sie, mitigation.
mitologie', mythology.
mitolo'gies, (-e), mythological.
mitologiseer', (ge-), mythologize.
mitoloog', (..loë), mythologist.
mito'se, mitosis.
mitrailleur', (ong., Ndl.), (-s), machine-gun; machine-gunner.
mits, provided (that), providing, on the understanding that; *DAAR is 'n* ~ *by*, it contains a proviso; ~ *DESE*, hereby, by this; *ek sal jou HELP* ~ *jy my vertrou*, I will help you if you trust me.
mitsdien', therefore, consequently.
mitsga'ders, together with, as well as.
mnemoniek', mnemonics.
mnemotegniek', mnemotechnique, mnemotechnics.
mnemoteg'nies, (-e), mnemotechnic(al).
Moabiet', (-e), Moabite.
Moabi'ties, (-e), Moabite.
mobiel', (-e), mobile.
mobilisa'sie, mobilization; ~**bevel**, mobilization order; ~**plan**, mobilization plan.
mobiliseer', (ge-), mobilize.
mobiliteit', mobility.
modaal', (modale), modal.
modaliteit', modality.
mod'der, mud, mire, sludge, ooze, dirt; *met* ~ *GOOI*, throw mud at; *iem. uit die* ~ *(uit) HELP*, help someone out of a ditch; *iem. deur die* ~ *SLEEP*, drag someone's name through the mud; ~**agtig**, (-e), muddy, miry, oozy; ~**agtigheid**, muddiness; ~**as**, mud, mire; ~**bad**, mud-bath; ~**bank**, mudflat; ~**gat**, mud hole; ~**gooier**, mud-slinger; ~**gooiery**, mud-slinging; ~**ig**, (-e), muddy, miry; feculent, puddly; oozy; ~**igheid**, muddiness; feculence; ~**koekie**, mud-pie; ~**kruiper**, ground-gudgeon; ~**meul**, dredge(r), dredging-machine; ~**plas**, puddle; ~**poel**, slough, quagmire; ~**skerm**, mudguard; ~**sloot**, muddy ditch; ~**steen**, mud-stone; ~**vet**, as fat as butter; ~**vloed**, mud-rush.
mo'de, (-s), fashion, mode, vogue; rage; *die* ~ *AANGEE*, set the fashion; *liewer DOOD as uit die* ~, be in (the) fashion at any price; *IN die* ~, in vogue; *uit die* ~ *RAAK*, go out of fashion; *met die* ~ *SAAMGAAN*, follow the fashion; ~ *WORD*, become the fashion; ~**artikel**, fashionable (fancy) article; novelty; article on fashions; ~**blad**, fashion paper; ~**boek**, book of fashions; ~**drag**, fashionable wear; ~**gek**, dandy, fop, fashion-monger, nut, beau, buck; ~**gril**, whim of fashion; ~**heertjie**, dandy, swell; ~**huis**, fashion house; ~**juffer**, mannequin; ~**kleur**, fashionable colour; ~**kwaal**, fashionable complaint.
model', (-le), pattern, example, model; exemplar; paragon; manikin; ~**boerdery**, model farm(ing); ~**eggenoot**, model husband; ~**eggenote**, ideal wife; ~**kamer**, model-room; specimen-room; ~**klei**, plastic clay; ~**maker**, model-maker; fashion-maker; ~**leer'**, (ge-), model, fashion;

mould, pattern; ~**leer'der**, (-s), modeller; ~**klei**, plastic clay; ~**leer'kuns**, modelling; ~**leer'plank**, modelling-board; ~**werk**, modelling; ~**le'ring**, modelling, shaping; patterning; ~**staat**, model state; ~**stewel**, regulation boot; ~**tekening**, model-drawing; academy figure.

mo'de: ~**maakster**, dressmaker; ~**makery**, dress-making; ~**parade**, mannequin-parade; fashion-parade; ~**plaat**, fashion-plate; ~**pop**, fop, dandy; doll, show-girl, mannequin; exquisite (male); ~**prent**, fashion-plate.

modera'men = **moderatuur**.

modera'sie, moderation.

moderateur', (-s), moderator; ~**lamp**, moderator lamp.

modera'tor, (-e, -s), moderator; ~**skap**, moderatorship.

moderatuur', (..ture), moderamen; executive council of a synod.

modereer', (ge-), moderate.

modern', (-e), modern, fashionable; advanced; ~**isa'sie**, modernization; ~**iseer'**, (ge-), modernize; ~**is'me**, modernism; ~**is'ties**, (-e), modernist(ic); ~**iteit'**, modernity, modernness.

mo'de: ~**skou**, mannequin-parade, fashion parade; ~**sug**, modishness; ~**tydskrif**, fashion magazine; ~**vertoonster**, (-s), mannequin; ~**winkel**, fashion shop; ~**woord**, vogue-word.

modieus', (-e), fashionable, chic, modish.

modifika'sie, (-s), modification.

modifiseer', (ge), modify.

modis'te, (-s), milliner, modiste, dressmaker, costumier.

modula'sie, (-s), modulation; *ultrahoë* ~, high frequency transmission.

moduleer', (ge-), modulate.

modulêr', (-e), modular.

mo'dulus, (-se), modulus.

mo'dus, (-se, ..di), mode; mood (of verb); ~ *operandi*, modus operandi (way a person goes to work, way a thing operates).

moed, courage, heart, fortitude, gallantry, manliness, prowess, mettle, spirit, audaciousness; *sy* ~ *het hom BEGEWE*, he lost heart; ~ *BYMEKAARSKRAAP*, muster (summon) courage; *iem.* ~ *GEE*, put heart into someone; *hou GOEIE* ~, die slegte kom vanself, never say die; ~ *HOU*, keep a good heart; ~ *INBOESEM (inspreek)*, inspire with courage; *die* ~ *van jou OORTUIGING hê*, have the courage of one's convictions; ~ *SKEP*, take courage; *sy* ~ *het in sy SKOENE gesink*, his courage failed him; his heart sank into his boots; *die* ~ *VERLOOR*, lose heart (courage).

moe'de: *BLY te* ~, with a happy heart; *DROEF te* ~, with a heavy heart; *TE* ~, in spirit; *jy begryp hoe ek te* ~ *VOEL*, you understand how I feel.

moe'deloos, (..lose), dejected, spiritless, cheerless, dispirited, out of heart, faint-hearted, dull, broken, cast-down, down in the dumps, disheartened, discouraged, despondent; ~**heid**, dejectedness, despondency, faint-heartedness, dispiritedness.

moe'der, (-s), mother, mater; mother (of institution); dam (of animals); *M* ~ *GANS*, Mother Hubbard; Mother Goose; ~ *NATUUR*, mother nature; ~**aarde**, mother earth; ~**agtig**, motherly; ~**boom**, mother tree; ~**bors**, mother's breast; ~**by**, queen bee; **M**~**sdag**, Mother's Day; ~**dier**, mother animal; ~**gek**, mother-sick; ~**gesteente**, mother (parent) rock; ~**hart**, mother's heart; ~**huis**, parental home; mother institution; ~**kappie**, various wild orchids (e.g. *Pterygodium catholicum*); ~**eschscholtzia**; ~**kerk**, Mother Church; ~**klok**, master clock; ~**koek**, placenta; ~**kompas**, master compass; ~**koring**, ergot; ~**krans**, pessary; ~**kruid**, majoram; feverfew; ~**kultuur**, mother culture (in cheese-making); ~**kunde**, mother-craft; ~**land**, mother country, native land; ~**lief**, dear mother; ~**liefde**, maternal (mother-)love; ~**liggaam**, parent body; ~**lik**, (-e), motherly, maternal; ~**likheid**, motherliness, maternal nature; ~**loog**, mother lye, mother liquor; bittern; ~**loos**, (..lose), motherless; **M**~**maagd**, Holy Virgin; ~**maat**-

skappy, holding company; ~**melk**, mother's milk; *met die* ~ *melk iets indrink*, imbibe something with the mother's milk; ~**-met-die-kindertjies**, hydrangea; ~**moord**, ~**moordenaar**, matricide; ~**naak**, (-te), ~**nakend**, (-e), stark naked; ~**oog**, maternal eye; ~**-owerste**, Mother Superior; ~**plant**, parent plant; ~**reg**, matriarchy; mother-right; ~**sdeel**, maternal portion; ~**sel**, parent cell; ~**sielalleen**, quite alone; ~**skant**: *van* ~ *skant*, on the mother's side; on the distaff side; ~**skap**, motherhood; maternity; mother-craft; ~**-skep-oppies**, mother-lay-the-table (plant); ~**skindjie**, milksop; ~**skip**, depot ship; tender (for aeroplanes); aircraft carrier; ~**sknie**: *aan* ~ *sknie*, at mother's knee; as a child; ~**skoentjies**, nemesia; ~**skoot**, womb; mother's lap; ~**smart**, mother's sorrow; ~**sorg**, maternal care; maternity welfare; mothering; ~**sporsie**, maternal portion; ~**stad**, metropolis; mother city; ~**sterfte**, maternal mortality; ~**sy**, mother's side; ~**taal**, mother tongue; vernacular; native language; ~**tjie**, (-s), mother dear; little mother; ~**vlek**, birthmark, mole, mother-spot, strawberry-mark; ~**vorm**, matrix; ~**vreugde**, mother's joy; ~**weelde**, maternal bliss.

moed'gewend, (-e), hopeful.

moe'dig, (-e), brave, courageous, audacious, valiant, plucky, dauntless, game, manful; ~**heid**, courage(ousness), spirit, manfulness, dauntlessness, valour.

moeds'wil, mischievousness; petulance; wilfulness; *MET* , on purpose; *UIT* ~, wantonly, wilfully; ~**'lig**, (-e), wilful, mischievous, refractory; purposely; petulant; intentional; prepense; ~**'ligheid**, petulance, wantonness, wilfulness.

moed'verloor, despondency, dejection; *op* ~ *se vlakte wees*, be in the Slough of Despond, have lost all hope.

moeg, (**moeë**; **moeër**, -ste), tired, fatigued, weary; *hy is* ~ *GEBORE*, he is extremely lazy; ~ *GEWERK*, tired from working; ~ *vir WERK*, tired (weary) of work; *jou* ~ *WERK*, work oneself to a standstill; ~**heid**, fatigue, weariness.

moei'lik, (-e), difficult, hard, arduous, hard to handle; involved; embarrassing; *iem. IS* ~, touchy (crusty); *iem.* ~ *MAAK*, irritate a person; ~ *e MENSE*, kittle cattle; ~ *WORD*, cut up rough; bristle up.

moei'likheid, difficulty, trouble; pickle, scrape, fix, snag; involvement, hardship; puzzle; push; *uit die* ~ *RAAK*, get out of the difficulty; *jy SOEK* ~, you are looking for trouble; *op 'n* ~ *STUIT*, encounter a difficulty; *die VRAAGSTUK is vol ..hede*, the problem bristles with difficulties.

moei'saam, (..same), tiresome, wearisome, laborious, fatiguing, arduous; ~**heid**, tiresomeness, laboriousness.

moei'te, trouble, difficulty, pains; labour; ~ *DOEN (neem)*, take pains; ~ *GEE*, give trouble; *hom die* ~ *GEE*, trouble him; *jou bale* ~ *GETROOS*, go to a great deal of trouble, take pains; ~ *nòg KOSTE spaar*, spare neither trouble nor expense; *g'n* ~ *ONTSIEN nie*, go to no end of trouble; *SONDER* ~ *kry 'n mens niks*, no gains without pains; *as dit nie te VEEL* ~ *is nie*, if it is not too much trouble; *nie die* ~ *WERD nie*, not worth the trouble; ~**vol**, (-le), hard, difficult, wearisome, laboured.

moel, (-e), bank (of dam); ~**voor**, raised furrow.

moe'nie!, don't!; ~ *dat hy OPSTAAN nie*, don't let him get up; ~ *so SÊ nie*, don't say that.

moe'pel, (-s), milkwood (*Mimusops zeyheri*); fruit of the tree.

moer[1], grounds, sediment, dregs, draff; lees (wine); faeces.

moer[2], (-e), (plat), womb; matrix; dam (animal); *jou malle* ~ *AFWAG*, wait an age; *die* ~ *IN wees*, have one's hackles up; *LOOP na jou* ~*!*, go to the devil!; *NA sy* ~, a goner, gone west.

moer[3], (-e), seed-potato.

moer[4], (-e), nut (on bolt); female screw.

moeras', (-se), marsh, morass, bog, swamp, fen; quag; plash; ~**agtig**, (-e), marshy, boggy; ~**agtigheid**, marshiness, bogginess; ~**bewer**, coypu, tria; ~erts, bog-ore; ~gas, marsh gas, methane; ~koors, marsh fever; malaria; jungle fever; ~land, swampy land; ~plant, marsh plant; helophyte; ~siekte, impaludism; ~sig, (-e), fenny, quaggy, marshy; uliginose; waterlogged; ~sigheid, marshiness, swampiness; ~turf, peat; ~voël, marsh bird.

moer'balk, binding-beam, sleeper.

moer'bei, (-e), mulberry; *vir die swartste ~ klim mens die hoogste in die boom*, if a thing is worth having, it is worth the trouble; ~**boom**, mulberry tree; ~**drank**, morat; ~**kleurig**, (-e), murrey.

moer'derig, (-e), dreggish, dreggy.

moer: ~**draad**, female thread; ~**hamer**, adjustable spanner.

moer'koffie, filter coffee.

moer: ~**koppeling**, union joint; ~**plaat**, washer; ~**skroef**, female screw; ~**sleutel**, screw-wrench; spanner; key-spanner.

moer'tjie[1], (-s), small nut.

moer'tjie[2], seed-potato.

moer'wortel, umbelliferous plant *(Anacampseros ustulata)*.

moes[1], (s) pulp, mash, purée.

moes[2], (w) *verlede tyd van* **moet**, (w).

moeselien', moeseli'ne, muslin.

moe'selwyn, moselle.

moe'sie, (-s), mole, birthmark; beauty-spot.

moesjiek', (-s), moujik.

moes'kruid, vegetables, greens.

moe'soek, moe'soep, match, superior; ~ *EET*, gormandize; *iem. SE ~*, a person's superior.

moeson', (-s), monsoon.

moestas', (-se), moustache.

moes'tuin, vegetable garden.

moet[1], (s) (-e), dent, mark, scar; weal.

moet[2], (w) (**moes**), must, should, ought, be obliged, have to; *DIT ~*, it must, it is obligatory; *~ is DWANG en huil is kindergesang*, "must" is a king's word; *hy moes jou GESÊ het*, he should have told you; *my vriend ~ om tienuur KOM*, my friend should arrive at ten; *ek moes LAG*, I couldn't help laughing; *hy ~ MAAR bly*, he had better stay; *dit ~ MOS verkeerd loop*, it is bound to go wrong; *ons ~ 'n NUWE hê*, we need (want) a new one; *daar ~ 'n POSSEËL op*, it requires a stamp; *sy ~ dit SIEN*, she is bound (ought) to see it; *so iets ~ UITLEK*, such a thing is bound to become known; *WAAR ~ dit na toe?*, what are things coming to?; *WAAR ~ ek dit kry?*, where am I to find it?; *die trein wat om sesuur hier ~ WEES*, the train which is due here at six o'clock.

Mof[1], (**Mowwe**), (Ndl.), German, Boche, Hun, Jerry.

mof[2], (s) (**mowwe**), merino (sheep); hybrid head of cattle.

mof[3], (s) (**mowwe**), muff, sleeve, socket; coupling (for machinery).

mof[4], (s) mitten (for hands).

mof[5], (b) drunk, dazed.

mof: ~**bees**, Friesland (bull, cow, ox); cross-bred head of cattle; ~**bul**, Friesland bull.

mof'fel, (ge-), muffle; ~**oond**, muffle furnace.

mof'fie[1], (-s) mitten.

mof'fie[2], (-s), nancy-boy, queer, male homosexual.

mof'klep, sleeve valve.

mof'koei, (-s), cross-bred cow.

mof'koppeling, sleeve-coupling.

mof'skaap, merino sheep.

mof'verbinding, box-coupling.

mog'gel, (-s), barbel *(Barbus capensis)*.

mo'gol, (-s), mogul.

Moham'med, Mohammed; ~**aan'**, (..**dane**), Mohammedan; ~**aans'**, (-e), Mohammedan; ~**anis'me**, Mohammedanism.

mo'hur, mohur (coin).

moiré', (s) moiré, watered silk; (b) moiré.

mok[1], (s) mud-fever; grease (on horse's hoof), greasy heel.

mok[2], (w) (ge-), pout, sulk; fret.

mo'kassin, (-s), moccasin.

mo'ker, (s) (-s), maul; (w) (ge-), strike, beat, hit, maul, hammer, punch, pound, smash, baste, bash, pummel; slog, crump; ~**aar**, slogger, hard-hitter;

~**hamer**, club-hammer; ~**hou**, slog; smash, stunner (tennis); crippling blow, smasher (boxing); crump.

moket', moquette.

mok'ka: ~**koffie**, Mocha (coffee); ~**steen**, Mocha (stone).

mok'kig, (-e), greasy (horse).

mo'ko, moko, bacterial wilt.

mol[1], (-le), mole; wen; *so BLIND soos 'n ~*, as blind as a bat; *die ~ STOOT*, be pregnant.

mol[2], gram-molecule, mol.

mol[3], (-le), flat; minor key (mus.); ~**akkoord**, minor chord.

mol: ~**afspraak**, ~**datum**, blind date.

Molda'wië, Moldavia; ~**r**, (-s), Moldavian.

Molda'wies, (-e), Moldavian.

moleku'le, (-s), molecule.

molekulêr', (-e), molecular; ~*e biologie*, molecular biology.

molekuul', (..**kule**), molecule.

moles', (-te), trouble, harm; fuss, commotion; *dit het 'n groot ~ AFGEGEE*, it caused a rumpus; *~ maak*, stir up trouble; create a scene.

molesta'sie, molestation.

molesteer', (ge-), molest; ~**der**, (-s), molester.

mol: ~**gang**, mole-track; ~**gans**, Cape gannet; ~**gif**, mole-poison.

molibdeen'glans, molibdeniet', molybdenite.

molibdiet', molybdite.

Molinis'me, Molinism.

mol: ~**kriek**, mole-cricket; ~**letjie**, (-s), small mole (animal).

mol'lig, (-e), soft, chubby, plump, fleshy; mellow (brandy); crumby; ~**heid**, softness, plumpness, chubbiness.

mollusk', (-e), mollusc.

molm, (s) mull; dry rot; (w) (**ge-**), moulder away, decay; ~**agtig**, (-e), worm-eaten, mouldy.

Mo'log, Moloch.

mol: ~**ploeg**, subsoil plough; ~**rot**, kind of rat *(Georychus hottentotus)*; ~**s'gat**, mole-hole; ~**s'hoop**, molehill, mole-cast; *van 'n ~shoop 'n berg maak*, make mountains out of molehills; ~**skyn**, moleskin; ~**slaai**, dandelion; ~**slang**, mole-snake *(Pseudaspis cana)*.

mol'teken, flat (music).

molte'nosiekte, black gall-sickness (in cattle).

mol'trein, underground train, tube.

Moluk'ke, Moluccas.

mol: ~**val**, mole-trap; ~**vel**, moleskin; ~**wa**, small low wagon; trolley.

mom, (-**me**), mask; *onder die ~ van*, under the guise (cloak) of; ~**bakkies**, (-e), mask.

moment', (-e), moment; ~**aan'**, (..**tane**), momentary; ~**afsluiter**, instantaneous shutter; ~**eel'**, (..**tele**), momentary; just now, for the moment; ~**opname**, instantaneous exposure, snapshot; ~**sluiter**, ~**sluiting**, instantaneous shutting.

mom'net, camouflage net.

mom'pel, (ge-), mutter, mumble, maunder, murmur, hum, grumble; ~**aar**, (-s), mumbler, mutterer; ~**ing**, (-e, -s), muttering, mumbling.

mom: ~**skerm**, camouflage screen; ~**skilder**, camouflage artist.

mona'de, monad.

mona'dies, (-e), monadic.

monandrie', monandry.

monarg', (-e), monarch; ~**aal'**, (..**gale**), monarchic(al); ~**ie'**, (-ë), monarchy.

monar'gies, (-e), monarchic(al).

monargis', (-te), monarchist; ~**me**, monarchism; ~**ties**, (-e), monarchic(al).

monato'mies, (-e), monatomic.

mond, (-e), mouth; estuary (river); muzzle (gun); *BITTER in die ~ maak die maag gesond*, bitter pills have blessed effects; *BY ~ e van*, through (by) the mouth of; *die ~ van 'n DRONK man praat die waarheid*, drunkards and fools cannot lie; *ek het dit uit sy EIE ~*, I had it from his own mouth; *uit EEN ~*, with one voice; *van ~ tot ~ GAAN*, pass from mouth to mouth; *iem. iets in die ~ GEE (lê)*, give someone his cue; *het jy GEEN ~ nie?*, have you lost

your tongue?; *nie op sy* ~ *GEVAL wees nie*, have a ready tongue; *'n GROOT* ~ *hê*, have a big mouth; indulge in big talk; *HOU jou* ~ *!*, shut up!; *jou* ~ *oral INSTEEK*, poke one's nose into everything; *so 'n* ~ *verdien JAM*, that's the way to talk!; *uit die* ~ *v.d. KINDERS*, out of the mouths of babes and sucklings; *KONTANT wees met sy* ~, have too much lip; *sy* ~ *nie verniet KOS gee nie*, have a ready tongue; *KOUD en warm uit een* ~ *blaas*, blow hot and cold; *as jy nie daardie* ~ *gehad het nie, het die KRAAIE al jou oë uitgepik*, what would have become of you if you hadn't a mouth?; *in die* ~ *LÊ*, put words into someone's mouth; *LOS in die* ~ *wees*, be foul-mouthed; *met oop* ~ *LUISTER*, listen very attentively (open-mouthed); *sy* ~ *het OOPGEHANG*, he was open-mouthed; *hy het sy* ~ *nie OOPGEMAAK nie*, he did not open his mouth; *iem. na die* ~ *PRAAT*, soft-soap someone; *met twee* ~*e PRAAT*, be double-faced, blow hot and cold; *so moet 'n* ~ *PRAAT!*, that's the way to talk!, that's telling me!, you've said it!; *nie jou* ~ *aan iets SIT nie*, not to touch food; *van sy* ~ *'n SKOORSTEEN maak*, smoke like a chimney; *iem. die* ~ *SNOER*, silence (muzzle) someone; *iets uit jou* ~ *SPAAR*, save the left-overs; *dit SPREEK sonder* ~, it is self-evident; *haar* ~ *is nooit STIL nie*, her tongue is never still; *met die* ~ *vol TANDE staan*, be tongue-tied; *met TWEE* ~*e praat*, blow hot and cold; speak with two voices; *UIT een* ~ *uit*, unanimously; *jy moet jou* ~ *gaan UITSPOEL*, you should wash your mouth; *ek het my* ~ *VER BRAND*, *ek het my* ~ *VERBYGEPRAAT*, I said too much, I put my foot in it; *die* ~ *VUL hê van*, talk a lot about; *iem. se* ~ *laat WATER*, make someone's mouth water; *'n* ~ *soos 'n WAWIEL hê*, have a mouth like a barn-door; a mouth like a furnace.
mondain', (-e), fashionable, chic.
mond: ~**behoeftes**, provisions; victuals, supplies; food(-supplies), belly-timber; ~**deksel**, nose-cap; muzzle-plug; ~**dele**, mouth parts.
mon'delik = **mondeling**.
mondeling(s), (b, bw) (-e), oral(ly), verbal(ly); nuncupative, nuncupatory; *'n* ~*e EKSAMEN*, an oral examination; *'n* ~*e OOREENKOMS*, a verbal agreement.
mond'-en-klouseer, foot-and-mouth disease.
monde'ring, (-e, -s), equipment; fig; caparison; kit; paraphernalia; accoutrement; ~**s**, regimentals.
mond: ~**fluitjie**, mouth-organ, harmonica; ~**gat**, orifice; ~**gesprek**, conversation, parley; ~**glas**, mouth-glass; ~**harmonika**, mouth-organ; ~**hoek**, corner of the mouth; ~**holte**, mouth cavity.
mon'dig, (-e), of age, full age, major; precocious; ~**word**, come of age; ~**e**, (-s), major; ~**heid**, majority; ~**heidsfees**, coming-of-age party; ~**wording**, coming of age.
mon'ding, (-e, -s), mouth (river), estuary; ~**svlam**, flash (gun); outfall.
mond'jie, (-s), (little) mouth; *nie op haar* ~ *GEVAL nie*, she has a ready tongue; *haar* ~ *op 'n PLOOI trek*, purse her lips; ~**vol**, **(mondjiesvol)**, mouthful, sip; tiny bit; smattering; *hy ken 'n* ~ *vol Engels*, he knows a little English.
mond: ~**klem**, gag; lockjaw; trismus; ~**kyker**, stomatoscope; ~**loos**, (..lose), astomatous; ~**middel**, oral medicine; ~**opening**, mouth-opening; stoma, orifice; ~**prop**, gag; ~**provisie**, victuals, food, provisions, supplies; ~**seer**, canker; ~**slag**: *'n goeie* ~ *slag doen*, know how to put it away; ~**slymvlies**, buccal mucosa; ~**spieël**, mouth-mirror, stomatoscope; ~**spleet**, mouth fissure; ~**spoeling**, mouthwash; ~**spons**, mouth-sponge; ~**stand**, position of the mouth; ~**stuk**, mouthpiece; embouchure (flute); muzzle (gun); nozzle; tip; ~**vlies**, buccal mucosa; ~**vol**, **(mondevol)**, mouthful; ~**voorraad**, see **mondbehoeftes**; ~**water**, mouth-wash.
mond'werk: *'n goeie* ~ *hê*, have the gift of the gab.
monetêr', (-e), monetary.
Mongo'lië, Mongolia.
mongolis'me, Down syndrome, mongolism.
Mongool', **(Mongole)**, Mongol(ian); ~**s'**, (-e),

Mongolian; ~*se plooi*, Mongolian (epicanthic) fold.
monis', (-te), monist; ~**me**, monism; ~**ties**, (-e), monistic.
moniteer', (ge-), (ong.), monitor.
mo'nitor¹, (s) (-s), monitor; prefect.
mo'nitor², (ge-), monitor.
mon'nik: (-e), monk, friar, monastic, cenobite, frater; ~**agtig**, (-e), monkish, monastic; ~**ag'tigheid**, monkishness.
mon'nike: ~**balsem**, friar's balm (balsam); ~**dom**, monkdom; ~**gees**, monachism; ~**klooster**, monastery, friary; ~**latyn**, monk's Latin; ~**lewe**, monastic life; ~**monkery**; ~**orde**, monastic order; ~**stand**, monachism, monastic state; monkery; ~**werk**, monkish (useless) work; ~**wese**, monasticism.
mon'niks: ~**kap**, cowl; monk's-hood (flower); capouch; monkhood; ~**kleed**, monk's frock, monastic frock, cowl; ~**py**, monastic frock.
monochor'dium, (-s), monochord.
monochromasie', **monochromatis'me**, monochromatism.
monochromie', monochromy.
monochroom', (..chrome), monochrome.
monodaktiel', monodactylous.
monodie', (-ë), monody.
mo'nodrama, monodrama.
mo'nofiets, monocycle.
monoftong', (-e), monophthong.
monogaam', (..game), monogamous.
monogamie', monogamy.
monogamis', (-te), monogamist; ~**ties**, (-e), monogamous.
monogene'se, monogenesis.
monografie', (-ë), monograph; ..**gra'fies**, (-e), monographic; ..**grafis'**, (-te), ~**skrywer**, monographer.
monogram', (-me), monogram, printer's mark.
mo'nokarp, (s), monocarp; (b) -**e**, ~**ies**, (-e), monocarpal.
mono'kel, (-s), monocle, quizzing-glass.
monoklinaal', (..nale), monoclinal.
monokotiel', (s) (-e), monocotyledon; (b) (-e), monocotyledonous.
monokotile'don, (-s), monocotyledon.
monokrasie', (-ë), monocracy.
monoksi'de, (-s), **monoksied'**, (-e), monoxide.
monoliet', (-e), monolith.
mo'nokultuur, monoculture.
monoloog', (..loë), monologue, soliloquy.
monomaan', (..mane), (s) monomaniac; (b) monomaniacal.
monomanie', monomania.
monometallis', (-te), monometallist; ~**me**, monometallism.
monomiaal', (..miale), monomial.
monomorf', (-e), monomorphic.
monopatie', monopathy.
monoplaan', (..plane), monoplane.
monopo'lie, **monopolie'**, (-ë, -s), monopoly.
monopolis', (-te), monopolist.
monopolisa'sie, monopolization.
monopoliseer', (ge-), monopolize.
monopolis'ties, (-e), monopolistic.
monorga'nies, (-e), monorganic.
monosilla'be, monosyllable.
monosilla'bies, (-e), monosyllabic; ~ **c woord**, monosyllabic word.
monoteïs', (-te), monotheist; ~**me**, monotheism; ~**ties**, (-e), monotheistic.
mo'notipe, monotype.
monotonie', monotony.
monotoon', (..tone), monotonous.
Mon'roeleer, Monroe doctrine.
mon'ster¹, (s) (-s), sample, specimen, example; pattern, trade sample; *'n volledige STEL* ~ *s*, a complete range of samples; ~*s sonder WAARDE*, samples not for sale.
mon'ster², (-s), freak (of nature); monster, monstrous creature, abortion; gorgon.
mon'ster³, (w) (ge-), compare; muster (soldiers), (pass in) review, marshal.

mon'steragtig, (-e), monstrous; ~**heid**, monstrosity; monstrousness.
mon'ster: ~**blik**, sample-tin; ~**boek**, sample-book; ~**briefie**, sampling-order.
mon'sterdier, monster.
mon'stereksemplaar, specimen copy.
mon'stering, (-e, -s), review, muster; perlustration; ~**sparade**, muster-parade.
mon'ster: ~**kaart**, sample-card; ~**kamer**, sample-room; ~**kis**, sample-case; ~**lap**, sampler.
mon'sterlik, (-e), monstrous.
mon'ster: ~**nemer**, sampler; ~**neming**, sampling; ~**perseel**, sample plot; ~**petisie**, mass (monster) petition.
mon'sterplek, muster-place.
mon'sterpos, sample-post.
mon'ster: ~**rol**, muster-roll; ship's company; ~**vergadering**, mass meeting.
monstrans', (-e), monstrance, ostensory, pyx.
monstruositeit', (-e), monstrosity.
monta'sie, setting, mounting (jewels); erection, fitting (machine); assemblage, assembly (machine); ~**bou**, prefabricated building; ~**werk**, fitting-work, assembling-work; ~**woning**, prefabricated house.
montbre'tia, montbretia.
monteer', (ge-), set, mount (jewel); fit out; stage (play); assemble, adjust, fit up (machine); ~**fabriek**, fitting-shop; assembling-plant; ~**huis**, prefabricated house; ~**werk**, assembling-work (motor-car); ~**winkel**, see **monteerfabriek.**
Montene'gro, Montenegro.
Montenegryn', (-e), Montenegrin; ~**s'**, (-e), Montenegrin.
mon'ter, merry, happy, game, lively, brisk, cheerful.
monte'ring, mounting (picture); erection, adjusting (machinery); assembly, assembling (motor); staging (play); uniform (military); (-s), fittings.
Montesso'rimetode, Montessori method.
monteur', (-s), mounter, stager, fitter, erector, assembler.
montuur', (monture), frame, setting, mounting.
monument', (-e), monument; ~**aal'**, (..**tale**), monumental; ~**ekommissie**, monuments committee; ~**esorg**, care of monuments.
mooi, (s): ~ *doen SEER*, beauty knows no pain; ~ *VERGAAN, maar deug bly staan*, beauty without bounty avails not; (b, bw) handsome, beautiful, nice, fine, pretty, fair, gallant, grand, choice; *die* ~ *ste van ALLES was dat . . .*, to crown all, the best of all was; ~ *BROODJIES bak*, curry favour; *dis 'n* ~ *GRAP!* well, I never! I like that! *JY'S 'n* ~ *e! JY is 'n* ~ *een!* you are a fine fellow! *die* ~ *ste moet nog KOM*, the best part is still coming; *iem.* ~ *KRY*, take someone in; *oor* ~ *en LELIK kan mens nie stry nie*, tastes differ; ~ *LUISTER na*, listen closely to; *jy LYK 'n* ~ *een om dit te doen*, you look like doing that! *jy MAAK nie* ~ *nie*, you are not doing the right thing; *nou NOG* ~ *er!* did you ever? well, I never! ~ *SKOOT!* shot! ~ *SO!* well done! *iets* ~ *VIND*, like something; *die weer is* ~ *VIR reën*, the weather portends rain, the weather is promising (for rain); *die WEER is* ~, the weather is fine; ~**doenery**, mere show, swank; ~**e**, (-s): *die* ~*e daarvan*, the beauty of it; ~**erig**, (-e), rather pretty, prettyish.
mooi'heid, beauty, fineness, prettiness, pulchritude; ~ *vergaan, maar deug bly staan*, beauty is but skin-deep; beauty is but a blossom.
mooi'igheid, prettiness; gentleness, gentle persuasion; *in ALLE* ~, in all friendliness; *'n geskil met* ~ *OPLOS*, settle a dispute amicably.
mooi: ~**maak**, (-ge-), make up; prink; titivate; ~**maakgoed**, cosmetics; ~**makery**, titivation, prinking; ~**meisiekoekoek**, emerald cuckoo; ~**nôientjie**, ~**nooi(e)ntjie**, bamboo fish; ~**praat**, (ge-), flatter, coax, beg; try to persuade.
mooi'praatjies, flattery, coaxing, cajolery, blarney, soft-soaping; ~ *met iem. hê*, wheedle someone; butter someone up.
mooi: ~ **prater**, coaxer, flatterer; ~**pratery**, coaxing, smooth words; ~**s:** *iets* ~ *s*, something fine;

~**skrywery**, flashy style; style with purple patches; ~**tjies**, finely; prettily; *ek moes* ~ *tjies betaal*, I had jolly well to pay.
mooi'weer: *met iem. se GOED* ~ *speel*, play ducks and drakes with a person's things; *met iem.* ~ *SPEEL*, fawn on a person; play up to someone.
moond'heid, (..**hede**), power, state; *die groot moondhede*, the great powers.
moont'lik, (b, bw) (-e), possible; possibly; eventual; potential; maybe; *al die* ~ *e DOEN om*, do one's utmost to, do everything possible to; ~ *DOEN hy dit nog*, it is possible that he will still do it; *so GOED* ~, as well as possible; *alle* ~ *e HULP*, all the assistance possible; ~ *e KOPERS*, potential buyers; *iets vir iem.* ~ *MAAK*, enable someone to; *OP alle* ~ *e maniere*, in every possible way; *by* ~ *e MOEILIKHEDE*, in case any difficulties should arise; ~**es**, possibles; ~**heid**, (..**hede**), possibility, feasibility, practicability, potentiality, contingency, chance, off chance.
Moor[1], **(More)**, Moor.
moor[2], (w) (ge-), murder; treat badly, maltreat; overwork (animal); *dié werk* ~ *'n man*, this work kills a person.
moord, (-e), murder; slaughter; ~ *en BRAND skree*, scream blue murder; make a great fuss; raise a hue and cry; *dis nie* ~ *en DOODSLAG nie*, it is not a matter of life and death; *die* ~ *STEEK*, give up the ghost; *van die hele* ~ *niks WEET nie*, be quite ignorant of the whole affair; know nothing at all about the matter; ~**aanslag**, murderous assault, attempted murder.
moordda'dig, (-e), murderous, bloody-minded, butcherly, internecine, bloodthirsty, homicidal; galling; ~**heid**, murderousness, bloodthirstiness.
moor'denaar, (-s, ..**nare**), murderer, manslayer, cut-throat, homicide; ~**sbende**, gang of murderers; ..**nares'**, (-se), murderess.
moor'dend, (-e), gruelling; homicidal.
moord-en-roof'eenheid, murder and robbery squad (unit).
moor'dery, massacre; maltreatment (of animals); butchery.
moord: ~**geroep**, cry of murder; ~**geskiedenis**, murder story; ~**geskreeu**, see **moordgeroep**; ~**gie'rig**, (-e), sanguinary, bloodthirsty; ~**gie'righeid**, blood-lust; ~**klok**, alarm bell; ~**kuil**, murderer's den; *ek maak geen* ~ *kuil van my hart nie*, I speak my mind without fear or favour; ~**lus**, blood-lust; ~**lus'tig**, (-e), bloodthirsty; ~**saak**, murder case; ~**toneel**, scene of a murder; ~**tuig**, murderous (murderer's) implement (weapon); ~**vis**, killer whale; ~**wapen**, murderous (murderer's) weapon.
Moors, (-e), Moorish, Moresque.
moot, (**mote**), slice; fillet; flitch (of halibut); valley between two ridges; stead (fish); ~**jie**, (-s), slice, small piece; ~**saag**, jack-saw; whip-saw; cross-cut saw.
mop[1], (-pe), pug(-dog).
mop[2], greasy heel, grease (horse-sickness).
mopa'nie, mopani (*Copaifera mopane*); ~**wurm**, mopani worm.
mop'per, (ge-), grumble, grouse; boggle; ~**aar**, (-s), grumbler; ~**ig**, (-e), grumbling, disgruntled.
mop'pie, (-s), coon song.
mops'hondjie, pug(-dog), mops.
mops'neus, pug-nose.
mop'tapper, spinner of yarns.
mor, (ge-), grumble, murmur.
moraal', moral (of a story); morals.
moralis', (-te), moralist; ~**a'sie**, (-s), moralization; ~**eer'**, (ge-), moralize, preachify, point a moral.
moraliteit', morality, (-e), morality play
morato'rium, (-s), moratorium.
Mora'wië, Moravia.
Mora'wies, (-e), Moravian; ~*e Broeders*, Moravian Brotherhood.
morbied', (-e), morbid.
mô're, mo're, (-s), morning, morrow; tomorrow; *die DAG van* ~, the morrow; *so nugter soos* ~ *die hele DAG*, perfectly sober; ~ *is nog 'n DAG*, tomorrow will do just as well; *op 'n GOEIE* ~, one fine morn=

ing; *KOM ek daar nie vandag nie, dan kom ek daar* ~, why hurry? ~ *SÊ!* good morning! *in die VROEË* ~, early in the morning; ~ *oor 'n WEEK*, tomorrow week; ~**aand,** tomorrow evening; ~**besoek,** morning call; ~**beurs,** high change; ~**blad,** morning paper; ~**diens,** morning service (church); ~**dou,** morning dew; ~**drag,** morning dress; ~**drank,** morning drink; ~**-edisie,** morning edition.
moreel', (s), morale (of troops); (b) **(morele),** moral .. ~ *rele standaarde,* moral standards.
moreen', **(morene),** moreen (fabric).
mô're, mo're: ~**gebed,** morning prayer; ~**groet,** aubade, morning salutation; ~**hulde,** aubade; ~**japon,** morning gown; ~**koelte,** morning coolness.
morel', (-le), morello.
Mô'reland, the Orient (East); ~**er,** (-s), Oriental.
mô're, mo're: ~**lied,** morning song; ~**lig,** dawn; ~**lug,** morning air; ~**maal,** breakfast.
more'ne, (-s), moraine.
mô're, mo're: ~**oggend,** tomorrow morning; ~**oormôre,** within the next day or two, soon; ~**pak,** morning suit; ~**pos,** morning post; ~**praatjies:** *sy* ~ *praatjies en aandpraatjies kom nie ooreen nie,* you cannot rely (up)on his word; ~**rok,** négligé; ~**rooi,** flush of dawn.
mo'res: *iem.* ~ *leer,* tell someone a thing or two; read someone a lesson.
mô're, mo're: ~**sang,** morning song; ~**sinjaal,** reveille; ~**sitting,** morning session; ~**skemering,** dawn; ~**skoot,** morning shot; ~**son,** morning sun; ~**ster,** morning star; day-star; daffodil; ~**stond,** morning hour; *die* ~ *stond het goud in die mond,* the early bird catches the worm; ~**taak,** morning task; ~**uur,** morning hour, ~**vroeg,** tomorrow morning (early); ~**wag,** morning watch.
morfeem', **(morfeme),** morpheme.
morfien', morfi'ne, morphia, morphine; ~**spuitjie,** morphine syringe.
morfinis', (-te), morphinist, morphinomaniac; ~**me,** morphinism.
morfografie', morphography.
morfologie', morphology.
morfolo'gies, (-e), morphologic(al).
morfonologie', morphonology.
morfonomie', morphonomy.
morfo'se, morphosis.
morg, (-e), morgen.
morgana'ties, (-e), morganatic, left-handed (marriage).
morg'-voet, morgen foot.
Mormonis', (-te), Mormonist; ~**me,** Mormonism.
Mormoon', **(Mormone),** Mormon; Latter-day Saint; ~**s',** (-e), Mormon.
mo'ron, (-e), moron.
Mor'pheus, Morpheus; *in die arms van* ~, in the arms of Morpheus.
mor'rie, (-s), sheila, moll.
mors, (ge-), dirty, make a mess, soil; idle away (time); waste (money); spill (ink); puddle; *met 'n TAAL* ~, mutilate a language; *die WATER loop* ~, the water is running to waste; ~**af,** clean off, broken right off; ~**dood,** stone-dead; as dead as a doornail.
morse: ~**alfabet,** Morse (alphabet); ~**kode,** Morse code; ~**lamp,** Morse lamp.
mor'sel: (ong.) *iets te* ~ *slaan,* smash something up.
mors: ~**er,** dabbler; waster; ~**ery,** mess, waste, wastage.
morse'skrif, Morse code.
mor'sig, (-e), dirty, filthy, squalid, grimy, messy; puddly; dingy; ~**heid,** dirtiness, filthiness, filth; dinginess.
mors: ~**jors,** (-e), litterbug; ~**jurkie,** overall (of child); ~**kleedjie,** crumb-cloth; ~**klep,** overflow valve; ~**mou,** loose sleeve; ~**pak,** crawler; ~**pot,** dirty person, messer, litterbug; ~**pyp,** overflow pipe.
mortaliteit', (-e), mortality.
mor'tel, mortar.
mortier', (-e), mortar (cannon); ~**battery,** mortar-battery; ~**is',** (-te), mortar-gunner; ~**kar,** mortar-carrier; ~**stamper,** pestle; ~**stand,** mortar-emplacement.
mortifika'sie, mortification.
mos¹, (s) new wine, must (grape); *die* ~ *begin werk,* matters are developing; things are beginning to hum.
mos², (s) lichen.
mos³, (bw) indeed, at least; *jy het hom* ~ *gesien,* you have seen him, haven't you?
mosag'tig, (-e), mossy, lichenous, muscoid.
mosaïek', mosaic; ~**goud,** ormolu; ~**siekte,** mosaic disease; ~**vloer,** mosaic floor, tessellated floor, diaper pavement; ~**werk,** mosaic; tessellation.
Mosaïes, (-e), Mosaic.
Mosambiek', Mozambique; ~**er,** (-s), Mozambican; ~**s,** (-e), Mozambican.
mosasou'rus, mosasaurus.
mos: ~**balie,** must-vat; ~**beskuit,** must-rusk.
mos'blommetjie, stone crop.
mos: ~**bolletjie,** must bun; ~**doppie,** billycock, derby.
Mo'ses¹, Moses; *die vyf BOEKE van* ~, the Pentateuch; *iem. met die vyf fingers van* ~ *gee,* give someone a smack.
mo'ses², match, superior; *sy* ~ *is DOOD,* he has no equal; *sy* ~ *TEËKOM,* meet his match.
mo'sie, (-s), motion, resolution, vote; *'n* ~ *van DANK,* a vote of thanks; *'n* ~ *INDIEN (voorstel),* introduce (propose) a motion; *'n* ~ *van VERTROUE,* a vote of confidence; *'n* ~ *VERWERP,* reject a motion; *'n* ~ *van WANTROUE,* a motion of no-confidence.
moskee', (..keë, -s), mosque.
mos'konfyt, moskonfyt, grape syrup, must syrup.
Mos'kou, Moscow.
Moskowiet', (-e), Muscovite.
mos'kunde, lichenology, muscology, bryology.
Mos'lem, (-s), Moslem; -**s,** (-e), Moslem.
mos'roos, moss-rose.
mos'sel, (-s), mussel; lamellibranch; ~**agtig,** (-e), mytiloid; ~**bank,** mussel bed; ~**skulp,** mussel shell; ~**vangs,** mussel-fishing.
mos'sie, (-s), (hedge)sparrow; *so DOOD soos 'n* ~, as dead as a doornail; *hom oor 'n DOOIE* ~ *verheug,* rejoice at some imaginary good; make a fuss about nothing; ~ *maar MAN,* small, but as tough as nails; ~**nes,** sparrow's nest; cubby-hole.
mos'sigheid, mossiness.
mos'steek, moss-stitch.
mos'suurdeeg, must yeast.
mos'terd, mustard; ~ *na die MAAL,* after meat mustard; *iem. deur die* ~ *TREK,* haul someone over the coals; choke someone off; ~**atjar,** mustard pickles; ~**bad,** (-baaie), mustard bath; ~**gas,** mustard gas; ~**lepeltjie,** mustard spoon; ~**pap,** ~**pleister,** mustard poultice (plaster); sinapism; mustard blister; ~**pot,** mustard-pot; ~**saad,** mustard seed; ~**sous,** mustard sauce; ~**suur,** mustard pickles.
mot¹, (s) (-te-), moth.
mot², (w) (ge-), drizzle.
mot: ~**balletjie,** moth ball; ~**bestand,** moth-proof; ~**by,** death's-head moth; bee-moth.
motel', (-s, -le), motel.
motet', (-te), motet; ~**tekoor,** motet choir.
mot: ~**gaatjie,** moth(-eaten) hole; ~**gevreet,** (..vrete), moth-eaten.
motief', **(motiewe),** motive, reason, ground, motive force; motif (sculpture).
motiel', (-e), motile; **motiliteit',** motility.
motiveer', (ge-), give reasons for, motivate.
motive'ring, giving reasons for, motivation; *die* ~ *van sy DAAD,* the motive given for his act; *SONDER behoorlike* ~, without stating proper grounds.
mot'jie¹ (-s), old woman.
mot'jie², (-s), small moth.
mo'tor, (s) (-e), motor; (-s), engine; motor car; automobile; (w) (ge-), motor; ~**afdak,** carport; ~**anker,** motor-armature; ~**barkas,** motor launch; ~**bestuurder,** motor driver, chauffeur; ~**boot,** motor boat; ~**bril,** goggles; ~**bus,** motor (omni)bus; ~**defek,** engine trouble, breakdown of

motor; ~**diefstal**, car theft; ~**diens**, mechanical transport; ~**fiets**, motorcycle; ~**fliek**, drive-in theatre; ~**gondel**, engine-car; ~**handel**, motor trade; ~**handelaar**, motor trader; ~**handskoen**, gauntlet; ~**hawe**, garage; ~**hek**, motor gate (grid); ~**herstelwinkel**, engine repair park; ~**huis**, (private) garage; ~**huur**, car rent; car leasing; ~**hysbak**, motor skip.
moto'ries, (-e), motor; ~*e krag*, motor power.
motoriseer', (ge-), motorize.
motorise'ring, motorization.
mo'tor: ~**jaer**, (-s), racing driver; ~**jag**, (-te), motor yacht; ~**jas**, (-se), dust-coat; ~**kap**, bonnet (of car); ~**kar**, motor car; ~**kas**, motor casing; ~**konstabel**; speedcop; ~**krag**, engine power; ~**lisensie**, motor licence; ~**loos**, (..lose) motorless; ~**monteur**, engine-fitter; ~**olie**, motor oil; ~**onderdele**, motor spares; ~**onderhoud**, motor maintenance; ~**ongeluk**, car accident; ~**oordak**, car port; ~**optog**, motorcade; ~**pad**, motor road; ~**park**, car park; ~**patrollie**, motor patrol; ~**pomp**, motor pump; ~**resiesbaan**, motordrome; ~**rit**, motor ride (spin); ~**ry**, motoring; ~**ryer**, motorist; ~**ryskool**, school of motor driving; ~**rytuig**, motorvehicle (car); ~**siek**, motor sick; ~**skuiling**, car-port; ~**stoet**, motorcade; ~**tjie**, (-s), small car; ~**vaartuig**, motor vessel; ~**verkeer**, ~**vervoer**, mechanical transport; ~**vlug**, power-flight; ~**voertuig**, motor vehicle; ~**voertuigwerkplaas**, ~**voertuigwerkplek**, ~**voertuigwerkwinkel**, mechanical workshop; ~**vragwa**, motor lorry (truck); ~**wa**, (motor) van (truck); ~**wedren**, car (automobile) race; ~**weiering**, motor breakdown; ~**wese**, motoring; ~**woonskuit**, cabin cruiser.
mot'reën, (s) drizzle, Scotch mist; dribble; (w) (ge-), drizzle.
mot'reënerig, (-e), drizzly.
mot'reent = motreën; ~**jie**, slight drizzle.
mot'te: ~**doder**, moth-killer; ~**gif**, naphthaline, moth-poison; ~**kruid**, cuscus (*Cymbopogon marginatus*).
mot'tig, (-e), pitted, pock-marked.
mot'to, (-'s), motto, device, impress.
mot: ~**vry**, (-e), moth-proof; ~**werend**, (-e), moth-resisting; ~**worteltjies** = mottekruid.
mou, (-e), sleeve; *iets in die* ~ *HÊ (voer)*, have something up one's sleeve; *iets in die* ~ *HOU*, have something up one's sleeve; *die* ~*e OPROL*, get ready for action; roll up one's sleeves; *daar nie 'n* ~ *aan kan PAS nie*, not find a peg to fit the hole; unable to make head or tail of something; *iets uit die* ~ *SKUD*, do a thing without effort; conjure up something; *iem. iets op die* ~ *SPELD*, impose upon (delude) a person; put something into someone's mind; ~**beskermer**, plastic cuff; ~**boordjie**, cuff; ~**ophouer**, sleeve holder; ~**plank**, sleeve board.
mous'gat, arm-hole.
mou: ~**skakels**, cufflinks; ~**streep**, chevron.
mout, malt; ~**afval**, malt dust; ~**agtig**, (-e), malty; ~**asyn**, malt vinegar; ~**beskuitjie**, malted rusk; ~**drank**, malt liquor; ~**ekstrak**, malt extract; ~**er**, (-s), maltster; ~**ery**, (-e), malt-house; malting; ~**gars**, malting barley; ~**melk**, malted milk; ~**meul(e)**, malt-mill; ~**oond**, malt-kiln; ~**poeier**, powdered malt; ~**suiker**, maltose; ~**vloer**, malt floor; ~**voedsel**, malted food; ~**werker**, maltster; ~**wyn**, malt spirits.
moveer', (ge-), vex, pester, tease, badger, attack, trouble, molest; actuate; *iem* ~, badger (pester) someone.
mud, (s) (-de, -dens), muid, (three-bushel) bag; (w) (ge-), bag (grain); ~**sak**, muid, muid-bag.
mues'li, muesli.
muez'zin, (-s), muezzin.
muf, (s) mildew, mould(iness); (b) (**muwwe; muwwer**, **-ste**), musty, fusty, stuffy; stale; ~**ferig**, (-e), rather musty; ~**heid**, mustiness, fustiness.
muf'ti, (-'s), mufti.
mug'gesifter, (-s), hair-splitter, hypercritic, gnat-strainer; ~**y**, hair-splitting.
mug'gie, (-s), gnat, midge; *die* ~ *uitsif, maar die KA=*

MEEL insluk, strain at a gnat and swallow a camel; *van 'n* ~ *'n OLIFANT maak*, make a mountain out of a molehill; ~**gewig**, gnat-weight; ~**motor**, midget car, minicar; ~**vliegtuig**, microlite.
muil[1], (-e), mule; half-caste.
muil[2], (-e), mouth (of animal), muzzle.
muil'band, (s) muzzle; (w) (ge-), muzzle, gag; *iem.* ~, stop a person's mouth.
muil: ~**drywer**, mule-driver, muleteer; ~**esel**, mule; hinny; ~**skop**, mule-kick; ~**span**, mule team; ~**wa**, mule waggon.
muis, (-e), mouse; ball (of thumb); butt (of hand); mouse-piece (beef); frog (on horse's hoof); fetlock; *so vas soos 'n* ~ *in 'n KALBAS*, caught like a rat in a trap; *klein* ~ *ies het groot ORE*, little pitchers have long ears; *die* ~*ie sal 'n STERTJIE hê*, this will have serious consequences; the last word has not yet been heard about the matter; *so STIL soos 'n* ~, as quiet as a mouse; *as die* ~ *VOL (dik) is, is die meel bitter*, plenty is not dainty; when the mouse has had enough the meal is bitter; ~**agtig**, (-e), mousy; ~**gat**, mousehole; ~**gif**, ratsbane; ~**grou**, dun (colour); ~**hare**, fetlock; mouse-hairs; ~**hond**, polecat; mongoose (*Ictonyx*); chestnut (e.g. on a horse's leg); ~**hondkruie**, (evil-smelling) shrub; ~**ie**, (-s), small mouse; ~**kleur**, mouse-colour; ~**nes**, mouse-nest; ~**oor**, small ear; ~**stert**, mouse tail; ~**stil**, quiet as a mouse; ~**tandjie**, milk-tooth; ~**vaal**, dun, mouse-grey; ~**val**, mousetrap; ~**valk**, buzzard; ~**vanger**, mouser; ratter; ~**vangery**, mousing; ~**voël**, mouse-bird.
muit, (ge-), mutiny, revolt, rebel; ~**agtig**, (-e), mutinous; ~**eling**, (-e), ~**er**, (-s), mutineer; rebel; ~**ery**, (-e), insurrection, mutiny, revolt, sedition, rebellion; ~**siek**, (-e), mutinous, seditious; ~**sug**, rebellious spirit; ~**sug'tig**, (-e), mutinous.
mul[1], (s) (-le), mullet.
mul[2], (b) (-le), fine, loose, shifting (sand).
mulat', (-te), mulatto; ~**tin'**, (-ne), mulatto woman.
Mu'le-operasie, Mule operation (on sheep).
mul'tilateraal, (..rale), multilateral.
mul'timiljoenêr', multimillionaire.
multimiljoenrandonderne'ming, multimillion rands undertaking.
multi'pel, (-e), multiple.
multiplika'tor, (-e, -s), multiplier.
mum'mel, (ge-), munch; mumble.
mum'mie, (-s), mummy.
mummifika'sie, mummification.
mummifiseer', (ge-), mummify.
Mün'chen, Munich.
muni'sie, munition; ~**-aanmaak**, munition-making; ~**fabriek**, munition-works; ~**fabrikant**, munitioneer; munition manufacturer; ~**handel**, munition trade; ~**magasyn**, ammunition magazine; ~**maker**, munition worker, munitioneer; ~**trein**, munition train; ~**wa**, munition wagon, caisson; ~**werker**, munitioneer, munition worker.
munisipaal', (..pale), municipal; *..pale gebou*, municipal buildings.
munisipaliteit', (-e), municipality.
mun'ster, (-s), minster.
munt, (s) (-e), mint, coin, piece, coinage, currency, money; *alles vir goeie* ~ *AANNEEM*, take for gospel; take everything in good part; *met dieselfde (gelyke)* ~ *BETAAL*, pay back in his own coin; *vir GOEIE* ~ *aanneem*, accept in good faith; *KLINKENDE* ~, hard cash; *dit was OP jou ge* ~, it was aimed at you; *hy SLAAN daar* ~ *uit*, he profits by (makes capital out of) this; (w) (ge-), mint, coin; ~**eenheid**, monetary unit; ~**er**, coiner, minter; ~**gehalte**, alloy of coins; ~**geld**, ~**goud**, standard gold; ~**hervorming**, currency reform; ~**ing**, coinage, minting; ~**kabinet**, numismatic cabinet; ~**kamer**, mint hall (room); ~**kenner**, numismatist; ~**kissie**, pyx; ~**kunde**, numismatics; ~**land**, currency country; ~**loon**, mintage; ~**matrys**, coinage-die; ~**meester**, mintmaster; Master of the Mint; ~**metaal**, bullion; ~**omloop**, coin circulation; ~**outomaat**, vending machine; ~**pariteit**, parity (of exchange); ~**pers**, coining-press; ~**plaat(jie)**, coin-plate; planchet; blank; ~**politiek**, monetary

policy; ~rand, coin edge; ~reg, right of coinage; seigniorage; mintage; ~ring, coinage-collar; ~skulp, cowrie, cowry; ~slag, minting, coinage; ~slagkuns, coinage; ~snoeier, coin clipper; ~soort, currency; ~spesie, coin, cash, specie; ~spesie smelt, melt down coin; ~stelsel, monetary system; coinage; ~stempel, coinage-stamp, coinage-die, die-stamp; ~stuk, coin; ~teken, mintmark; ~versamelaar, coin-collector, numismatist; ~versameling, coin collection; ~vervalser, forger of coins; ~vervalsing, false coining, forging of coins; ~voet, standard of coinage; ~vorm, coin mould; ~vraagstuk, currency problem; ~wese, coinage; currency; ~wet, coinage act.
mura'sie, (-s), old walls, ruins (of house).
murg, marrow; pulp (of tooth); pith; *deur ~ en BEEN gaan*, pierce to the marrow of one's bones; *in ~ en BEEN*, to the quick; *~ in sy PYPE hê*, be all muscle and bone; be all thews and sinews; *SONDER ~ wees*, be spineless; ~**agtig**, (-e), myeloid; ~**been**, marrowbone; ~**holte**, pulp cavity; ~**kern**, medulla; ~**pampoen**, vegetable marrow; ~**peer**, avocado; ~**pommade**, marrow-pommade; ~**pyp**, marrowbone; ~**ryk**, (-e), marrowy; ~**stof**, medullin; ~**straal**, medullary ray.
murg'-van-groente, vegetable marrow, squash.
murg'vet, marrow-fat.
mur'mel, (ge-), murmur, babble, purl, gurgle; ~**end**, (-e), murmuring; humming; ~**ing**, purling, murmur, babbling, gurgling.
murmureer', (ge-), murmur, grouse, grumble; der, (-s), murmurer.
murmure'ring, murmur, grumbling, grousing.
mus, (-se), cap, beret; headpiece; nightcap; comforter: tea-cosy; ~**band**, cap string (ribbon).
mu'se, (-s), muse.
Mu'selman, Mohammedan, Mussulman.
muse'um, (..sea, -s), museum; ~**stuk**, museumpiece.
musiek', music; harmonium; *~ MAAK*, play music; *~ van die MEESTERS*, classical music; *MET ~*, to the sound of music; *op ~ SIT*, set to music; *STILLE ~*, the conversation has stopped completely; *met VOLLE ~*, with the band playing; ~**aand**, musical evening, musical(e), recital; ~**beoordelaar**, music(al) critic; ~**blad**, sheet of music; ~**blyspel**, musical comedy; ~**boek**, music book; ~**doos**, musical box; ~**drama**, musical drama; ~**fees**, musical festival; ~**geselskap**, musical party (troupe); ~**geskiedenis**, history of music; ~**handel**, music shop; ~**handelaar**, music seller; ~**instrument**, musical instrument; ~**kamer**, music-room; ~**kassie**, music cabinet, canterbury; ~**kenner**, connoisseur of music; ~**korps**, band; ~**kritikus**, music critic; ~**kuns**, art of music, musical art; ~**leer**, theory of music; ~**les**, music lesson; ~**liefhebber**, music lover; philharmonic; ~**liewend**, (-e), philharmonic; ~**meester**, music teacher; ~**nommer**, musical item; ~**noot**, (musical) note; ~**onderwys**, musical teaching, ~**onderwys**, music teacher; ~**onderwyseres**, music teacher (lady); ~**outomaat**, musical box; ~**papier**, music paper; ~**partituur**, musical score; ~**sak**, music case; ~**skaal**, gamut; ~**skool**, school of music, conservatorium, conservatoire; ~**sleutel**, clef; ~**stander**, music stand; ~**stoel**, piano stool; ~**stuk**, piece of music, musical composition; ~**tas**, music case; musical composition; ~**tent**, bandstand; ~**uitvoering**, musical performance; ~**vereniging**, musical society; ~**wêreld**, musical world; world of music; ~**winkel**, music store (shop).
musikaal', (..kale), musical; *'n ..kale gehoor hê*, have an ear for music; ..**kaliteit'**, musicality.
musikant', (-e), musician, member of a band, player.
musikologie', musicology; ..**lo'gies** (-e), musicological.
musikoloog', (..loë), musicologist.
mu'sikus, (..sici, -se), musician, harmonist.
musiseer', (ge-), make music.
muskaat', nutmeg; ~**blom**, mace; ~**boom**, nutmeg-tree; ~**neut**, nutmeg; ~**olie**, nutmegoil.
muskadel', muscadel; ~**appel**, musk-apple; ~**druiwe**, muscadel (grapes); ~**pruim**, musk-plum; ~**wyn**, muscadel wine.
muskeljaat', musk; ~**kat**, musk cat, genet.
musket', (-te), fusil, musket.
musketier', (-s), musketeer.
muskiet'¹, (-e), mesquite (*Nahauti mizquiti*).
muskiet'², (-e), mosquito; mesquite (tree); ~**byt**, mosquito-bite; ~**gaas**, mosquito-proof gauze; ~**gewig**, mosquito-weight; ~**larwe**, wriggler; ~**muggie**, midge; ~**net**, mosquito-net; ~**olie**, mosquito-lotion; ~**vry**, (-e), mosquito-proof.
muskoviet'mika, muscovite.
muskulatuur', musculature.
mus'kus, musk; ~**agtig**, (-e), musky; ~**dier**, musk; ~**geur**, muskiness; ~**hert**, musk-deer; ~**kat**, civet (*Viverra civetta*); ~**kruid**, fodder plant (*Erodium muscatum*); ~**os**, musk-ox; ~**plant**, musk-plant; moschatel; ~**reuk**, smell of musk; ~**roos**, musk-rose; ~**rot**, musk-rat, musquash; ~**vark**, peccary.
musseljaat'kat = **muskeljaatkat**.
mus'sie, (-s), small cap; tea-cosy; bonnet.
mus'tang, mustang.
muta'sie, (-s), mutation.
mutila'sie, mutilation.
mutileer', (ge-), mutilate.
mutograaf', (..grawe), mutograph.
mutograveer', (ge-), mutograph.
mutoskoop', (..skope), mutoscope.
mutosko'pies, (-e), mutoscopic.
mutueel', (mutuele), mutual(ly).
muur, (mure), wall, *oor 'n wh ~ KYK*, wear a stiff collar; *OOR die ~ wees*, be done for; *die mure het ore*, walls have ears; *'n SJINESE ~*, a Chinese wall; an insuperable obstacle; *soos 'n ~ STAAN*, stand as firm as a rock; *TUSSEN vier mure sit*, behind bars; ~**anker**, brace, tie-iron; ~**bal**, squash (rackets); ~**balbaan**, squash court; ~**band**, copestone, coping; ~**behangsel**, tapestry; ~**belasting**, murage; ~**blaker**, sconcer; ~**blom**, gillyflower, bleeding-heart; wall-flower (at a dance); ~**breker**, battering ram; ~**haak**, wall-hook, ~**kaart**, wall-map; ~**kalender**, sheet almanac; ~**kalk**, distemper; ~**kap**, coping; ~**kas**, wall-cupboard; cuddy; ~**klem**, wall clip; ~**klok**, wall clock; ~**kontak**, wall plug; ~**kram**, wall cramp; ~**krans**, cordon; ~**kruid**, chickweed; *rooi ~ kruid*, scarlet pimpernel (*Nagallis arvensis*); ~**lamp**, wall lamp; ~**lym**, size; ~**papier**, wallpaper; ~**plaat**, wall-plate; ~**prop**, wall plug; ~**reklame**, wall advertisements; ~**ruimte**, wall space; ~**skildering**, ~**skildery**, mural painting, fresco; ~**sok**, wall socket; ~**stut**, shore; ~**swaeltjie**, martlet; ~**tapyt**, tapestry; arras; hangings; gobelin; ~**teël**, wall tile; ~**versiering**, mural decoration; ~**vors**, cap(ping) (wall); ~**werk**, walling, brickwork, masonry.
muw'werig, (-e), rather musty; ~**heid**, mustiness.
my¹, (w) (ge-), avoid, shun, fight shy of, keep aloof from.
my², (vnw) me, my, mine; *~ DUNK*, methinks; *dis vir ~ te DUUR*, it is too expensive for me; *~ is OPGEDRA, I have been instructed; *dit SPYT ~*, I am sorry; *ek vra ~ af*, I ask myself; *ek WAS ~*, I am washing myself.
myl, (-e), mile; *baie ~ e lê tussen doen en sê*, actions speak louder than words; more easily said than done; ~**afstand**, mileage; ~**geld**, mileage; ~**hardloper**, miler; ~**meter**, speedometer; ~**paal**, mile-stone; landmark; ~**skaal**, mileage scale; ~**toelae**, mileage allowance; ~**vreter**, speed maniac; mile-hunter, road hog; ~**wyser**, see **mylmeter**.
my'mer, (ge-), ponder, meditate, muse; ~**aar**, (-s), muser, day-dreamer; ~**ing**, (-e, -s), meditation, musing; ~**y**, (-e), meditation, daydreaming.
myn¹, (s) (-e), mine; (w) (ge-), mine.
myn², (vnw); *die ~ en die DYN*, mine and thine; *geen besef van ~ en DYN hê nie*, not to know the difference between mine and thine.
myn: ~**aandeel**, mining share; ~**aandelemark**, market for mining shares; ~**aar**, lode, load; ~**amptenaar**, mine official; ~**arbeid**, mining, mine work; ~**baas**, mine owner; mine captain; (mining) magnate; ~**bedryf**, mining industry; ~**bek**, pithead,

~ **bestuurder**, mine manager; ~ **bou**, mining (industry); ~ **boukunde**, science of mining; ~ **boukundige**, (-s), mining engineer; ~ **byter**, paravane; ~ **distrik**, mining district.
my'ne, mine; *gee* ~ *hier*, give me mine.
myn'eienaar, mine-owner.
my'nentweë, as for me; on my part.
my'ner, (vnw): *gedenk* ~, remember me.
myn: ~ **galery**, working level, mine gallery; ~ **gang**, passage in a mine, head(ing), drive; ~ **gas**, firedamp, methane; ~ **gebied**, mining area; ~ **gees**, kobold; ~ **granaat**, elongated shell; ~ **grawer**, sapper; ~ **hoop**, mine dump; ~ **hout**, mine timber; ~ **huur**, mining lease; ~ **hyser**, skip; ~ **ingang**, pit, pithead; ~ **ingenieur**, mining engineer; ~ **installasie**, mine plant; ~ **kaart**, mine plan; ~ **kamer**, mine chamber; ~ **kamp**, mining camp/compound; ~ **kaptein**, mine captain; ~ **klikker**, mine detector; ~ **kommissaris**, mining commissioner; ~ **kompas**, miner's dial; ~ **krater**, mine crater; ~ **kruit**, blasting-powder; ~ **lamp**, safety lamp; ~ **lêer**, minelayer; ~ **lont**, monk; ~ **maatskappy**, mining company; ~ **magnaat**, mine owner, mining magnate; ~ **masjinerie**, mine plant; ~ **opmeter**, mine surveyor; ~ **opsigter**, mine overseer; ~ **pag**, mining lease (mynpacht); ~ **pomp**, mining pump; ~ **portaal**, mine entrance;
~ **proposisie**, prospect; ~ **put**, sump; ~ **reg**, mining rights.
myns: ~ *insiens*, in my opinion, to my mind.
myn: ~ **skag**, shaft; pit; ~ **staking**, miner's strike; ~ **stut**, mine timber; ~ **tering**, miner's phthisis; silicosis; M ~ **teringraad**, Phthisis Board; ~ **tregter**, mine crater; ~ **veër**, minesweeper; ~ **veëry**, minedragging; ~ **veld**, minefield; ~ **versperring**, mine blockade; ~ **waentjie**, miner's truck; ~ **water**, pit water; ~ **werk**, pit-work; mining; ~ **werker**, miner; pitman; ~ **werkersbond**, miners' union; ~ **werksaamhede**, mining activities; ~ **werper**, minethrower; ~ **wese**, mining, mines; *DEPARTEMENT van M* ~ *wese*, Department of Mines; *KAMER van M* ~ *wese*, Chamber of Mines; *SKOOL vir M* ~ *wese*, School of Mines; ~ **wurm**, hook-worm; ~ **wurmsiekte**, hook-worm disease; miners' anaemia.
myself', myself; *ek BAD* ~, I bath myself; *ek PRAAT net vir* ~, I speak only for myself.
myt, (-e), mite (*Acarina*); ~ **doder**, acaricide, miticide.
my'ter, (-s), mitre; ~ **doos**, mitre-box; ~ **draer**, (-s), mitred person; ~ **klep**, mitral valve; ~ **stad**, episcopal town; ~ **vormig**, (-e), mitre-shaped, mitral, mitriform.

N

n, (-'s, -'e), n.
'n, a, an; ~ *mens*, one, you.
na¹, (b, bw), (-der, naaste), near, close; *ons is* ~ *FAMILIE*, we are near relatives; *twee bediendes daarop* ~ *HOU*, have two servants; *iem. te* ~ *KOM*, offend someone, injure someone's reputation; *almal op een* ~, all except one; *op VERRE* ~ *nie*, not by a long way; *te* ~ *aan die VUUR sit*, sit too close to the fire.
na², (vs) according to; to; in; after; at; of; ~ *DESE*, hereafter, from now on; ~ *KEUSE*, to choice; ~ *MEKAAR*, one after the other; ~ *NEGE*, after nine; ~ *die SKOOL gaan*, go to school; ~ *SKOOL*, after school; *dit smaak* ~ *TEER*, the sample was very good; ~ *URE*, after hours; ~ *iem. VERNEEM*, inquire after someone; ~ *VORE kom*, come forward; ~ *WYN ruik*, smell of wine.
na³, (vgw) as; *AL* ~ *dit val*, as the case may be; ~ *ons VERNEEM*, according to our information.
na'-aap, (-ge-), ape, imitate, mimic; monkey; ~ **ster**, (-s), *vroulik* van **na-aper**.
naaf, (nawe), nave, hub; hollow rod; boss (of wheel); ~ **band**, nave-ring; hub-band; ~ **bout**, boss-bolt; ~ **bus**, nave-box, bush; ~ **buskop**, hub-cap; ~ **dop**, axle-cap, hub-cap, dust-cap; ~ **drukstuk**, hubgland; ~ **kap**, spinner, airscrew; ~ **skroef**, hubbolt; ~ **voering**, hub-lining.
naai, (ge-), stitch, sew; have sexual intercourse; ~ **bank**, sewing-press; ~ **bos**, spiny shrub (*Azima tetracantha*); ~ **doos**, work-box; ~ **els**, sewing-awl; ~ **garing**, sewing-cotton; ~ **goed**, sewing; needlework; ~ **kissie**, work-box; sewing-box; ~ **mandjie**, work-basket; ~ **masjien**, sewing-machine; ~ **naald**, sewing-needle; ~ **riempie**, sewing-riempie; ~ **sakkie**, housewife; ditty-bag; ~ **skool**, sewing-school; ~ **ster**, needlewoman, dressmaker, seamstress; machinist; ~ **werk**, needlework, sewing, needlecraft.
naak¹, (w) (ge-), approach.
naak², (b) (-te), naked, nude, bare; *vertel my nou die* ~ *te waarheid*, tell me the whole (plain) truth; ~ **figuur**, nude figure; ~ **loper**, nudist; Adamite; ~ **lopery**, nudism; ~ **sadig**, (-e), gymnospermous; ~ **slak**, slug; ~ **studie**, study in the nude.
naakt'heid, nudity, nakedness, bareness.
naald, (-e), needle; striker (gun); spire; obelisk; tongue (balance); pointer; spicule (bot.); *'n* ~ *in 'n HOOIMIED soek*, hunt for a needle in a haystack; *'n* ~ *INSTEEK*, thread a needle; *van 'n* ~ *tot 'n KOEVOET*, from a needle to an anchor; *'n* ~ *in die Here se OOG steek*, do one's sewing on Sundays; *op* ~ *e en SPELDE sit*, be on pins and needles; *'n mens kan hom deur 'n* ~ *TREK*, he is as neat as a pin; he is very smartly dressed; ~ **afwyking**, deviation of the needle; ~ **boom**, pine-tree, conifer; coniferous tree; ~ **bossie**, dysentery herb.
naal'de: ~ **boekie**, needle-book; ~ **koker**, (-s), needlecase; dragon-fly; ~ **kussing**, pincushion.
naal'derig, (-e), acicular.
naald: ~ **fabriek**, needle-factory; ~ **geweer**, needlegun; ~ **hout**, softwood; ~ **jie**, (-s), little needle; ~ **kant**, point-lace; ~ **klep**, needle-valve; ~ **laer**, needle-bearing; ~ **prikking**, acupuncture; ~ **steek**, (-ge-), throw out a feeler, sound a person; ~ **telegraaf**, needle-instrument; ~ **vis**, needle-fish (*Hemiramphus calabareus*); pipe-fish; ~ **vormig**, (-e), tapering, needle-shaped; acerose, acicular, aciform; ~ **(e)werk**, needlework, sewing; ~ **wurm**, pinworm; ~ **ys**, needle ice.
naam, (name), name, appellation, appellative, designation; credit; image; *'n AANGENOME* ~, an assumed name, an alias; *BEKEND staan onder die* ~ *van*, be known by the name of; *nie jou* ~ *laat BESOEDEL nie*, not to allow one's name to be sullied; *die goeie* ~ *BESOEDEL van*, tarnish the good name of; *as ek dit doen, is my* ~ *BLES*, I'm blowed if I'll do such a thing; *iets vir die* ~ *DOEN*, do something for show; *die* ~ *DRA*, have the name of; *die* ~ *DRA dat jy iets gedoen het*, have a deed ascribed to you; *'n GOEIE* ~ *hê*, enjoy a good reputation; *jou* ~ *HOOG hou*, keep one's good name (reputation); *'n Christen IN* ~, a Christian in name only; *IN (uit)* ~ *van*, in the name of; *net van* ~ *KEN*, know only by name; *op iem. anders se* ~ *KOOP*, buy in someone else's name; ~ *MAAK*, make a name for oneself; *iets by die NAAM noem*, call a spade a spade; *by sy* ~ *NOEM*, address a person by name; *geen name NOEM nie*, mention no names; no names, no pack-drill; *'n SKRYWER van* ~, an author of note; *jou* ~ *is op die SPEL*, your good name is at stake; *op* ~ *van iem. STAAN*, be entered under someone's name; *hy kan maar sy* ~ *TEKEN*, his number is up; *UIT* ~ *van my vader*, on behalf of my father; *'n man VAN* ~, a man of mark; *hy doen dit net VIR die* ~, he does it merely for show; *onder die* ~ *van VRIENDSKAP*, in the name of friendship; ~ **blok**, imprint block; mast-

head; ~boek, nominal roll (book); ~bord(jie), name-plate; door-plate; brass plate; plant-marker; ~christen, lip-Christian; ~dig, acrostic; ~draer, name-child; ~fout, misnomer; ~gedig, acrostic; ~genoot, (..note), namesake; ~gewend, (-e), eponymous; appellative; ~gewer, nomenclator, eponum; ~gewing, naming; nomenclature; name-giving, nomenclature; ~kaartjie, visiting-card; ~kunde, onomastics; onomatology; ~kun'dig, (-e), onomastic; onomatologist; ~lik, namely, to wit, viz; *jy moet ~lik weet,* for you must know; ~loos, (..lose), nameless, anonymous; *see* name-loos; ~*lose oproep,* nameless (phone)call; ~*lose vennootskap,* joint-stock company; limited-liability company; ~lys, list of names; nomenclature; index, catalogue; panel (of jury); ~pie, (-s), little name; ~plaat(jie), door-plate, name-plate; ~rol, list of names; panel; ~siek, (-e), very fond of one's name; ~skilder, signwriter; ~stempel, signature stamp; ~s'verandering, change of name; ~s'verwisseling, antonomasia; ~syfer, cipher, initials; monogram; ~tekening, signature; ~val, case (grammar); ~valsuitgang, case-ending (grammar); ~vers, acrostic; ~verwarring, confusion of names; ~wisseling, metonymy; ~woord, noun, substantive, nomen; *selfstandige* ~*woord,* noun, substantive; ~woordelik, nominal; ~wyser, index of names.

naand! good evening!

na'-aper, (-s), imitator, mimic, copier; ~y, imitation, mimicry, aping.

naar, (b, bw) (nare; -der, -ste), sick, giddy, bilious; dreary, sad, dark, faint, queer; dismal; bad (smell); miserable; awkward; nasty, unpleasant, disagreeable (day); horrible (book); odious (behaviour); gaunt; horrid; *hulle het* ~ *GERAAS,* they made a very great noise; *die wêreld LYK* ~ *van die droogte,* the country looks dreary (dismal) on account of the drought; ~ *om te SIEN,* sad to see, *'n nure SMAAK,* a nasty taste; *ek VOEL* ~, I feel unwell (queer).

naargees'tig, (-e), melancholic, dismal, sad, funereal, sombre, gloomy; ~heid, melancholy, dreariness, gloom.

naar'heid, sadness, misery; awkwardness; sickness, biliousness, nausea; *dis 'n GEKROONDE* ~, it is an appalling state of affairs; *hy lieg dat dit 'n* ~ *IS,* he tells the most dreadful lies; *die* ~ *daarvan IS,* what is so sad is; *JOU* ~! you wretch! *dit was 'n* ~ *soos hy SPOOK,* he fought like mad; *WAT 'n* ~! how terrible!

naars'tig, (-e), industrious, diligent, assiduous; ~heid, diligence, assiduity; sedulity ~lik, diligently, industriously.

naas[1], (w) (ge-), expropriate, nationalize, take over.

naas[2], (vs) next to, beside, by the side of, alongside of; *ons woon* ~ *MEKAAR,* we live next door to each other; ~ *mekaar SIT,* sit side by side, sit next to each other; ~aan, next to; ~agter, second from rear (in a team); ~bestaan, co-existence; *vreedsame* ~ *bestaan,* peaceful co-existence; ~bestaande, (-s), next of kin, nearest relative; ~beste, second-best; *die* ~*beste,* runner-up; ~eergister, three days ago, the day before yesterday; ~geleë, adjacent, contiguous; ~mekaarstelling, juxtaposition; ~oormôre, three days hence, the day after the day after tomorrow.

naas'te, (s) (-s), neighbour, fellow man; (b) nearest; immediate (vicinity); lowest (price); proximate; *my* ~ *BUURMAN,* my next-door (nearest) neighbour; *die* ~ *PAD,* the shortest route; *in die* ~ *TOEKOMS,* in the near future; (bw) nearest; *wat die* ~ *LÊ moet die swaarste weeg,* charity begins at home; *hy STAAN my die* ~, he is my best friend; ~by, approximately, more or less; ~liefde, love of one's neighbour, altruism.

naas'ting, (-e), expropriation, nationalization; seizure.

naas: ~volgende, following, next; ~voor, second from the front (in a team); ~wenner, runner-up; ~wit, off-white.

naat, (nate), seam; join(t); suture; fissure, chink; commissure; scarf (weld); juncture; *deur sy nate*

GROEI, burst out of his clothes; *OORHANDSE* ~, sew-and-fell seam; *op die* ~ *van jou RUG lê,* lie flat on your back; ~jie, little seam; *die* ~*jie v.d. kous wil weet,* want to know all the ins and outs; ~loos, (..lose), seamless; ~los, burst in the seams; silly, crack-brained; ~stelsel, joint-system; ~vorming, jointing.

na'babbel, (-ge-), repeat, parrot, echo.

na'bank, rocky bed; ridge.

na'beeld, after-image.

na'behandel, (~), follow up; give after-care; ~ing, after-care (treatment); curing (of cement).

na'berig, postscript, epilogue.

na'berou, repentance, remorse; ~ *is galberout (galgberou),* remorse is the poison of life; remorse comes too late.

na'bestaande, (-s), close relative, relation, kinsman, connection.

na'bestel, (~), repeat an order, re-order; ~ling, (-e,-s), repeat-order, additional order.

na'betaal, (~), pay afterwards; pay an additional sum.

na'betaling, deferred payment; supplementary payment.

na'betragting, meditation, reflection; ~ *hou oor 'n vergadering,* discuss what has happened at a meeting; hold a post-mortem (fig.); ~sdiens, service after Holy Communion (in D.R. Church).

na'bewing, after-shock.

na'blaf, (-ge-), bark after; imitate.

na'bloeding, secondary haemorrhage.

na'bloei[1] – nabloeding.

na'bloei[2], second (late) bloom; *die werk v.d. digter se* ~, work of the poet's old age; ~er, (-s), late flowerer.

na'bly, (-ge-), remain behind; be kept in, be detained (in school).

na'bob, (-s), nabob; wealthy (affluent) person.

na'boom, species of *Euphorbia.*

na'boor, (-ge-), rebore.

na'boots, (-ge-), imitate, copy, mimic; simulate; mock; echo; ~end, (-e), imitative, mimetic, mimic; ~er, (-s), simulant; imitator, reproducer, copyist; mimic; ~ing, (-e, -s), imitation, mimicry; reproduction; echo; simulacrum; mockery; ~ingstalent, imitative power (talent).

na'boring, reboring.

Na'bot: ~ *se wingerd,* Naboth's vineyard.

na'brom, (-ge-), grumble after.

na'brul, (-ge-), roar after.

nabu'rig, (-e), neighbouring, adjacent, contiguous; ~heid, contiguity, nearness.

na'buur, neighbour; ~skap, neighbourhood, vicinity.

na'by, (b) (-e; nader, naaste), near (by); *die N* ~ *e OOSTE,* the Near East; *die Verre OOSTE,* the Far East; *in die* ~ *e TOEKOMS,* in the near future; (bw) near, close to, anigh, contiguous, hard on (by); imminent; *vc.* ~ *BEKYK,* inspect at close quarters; ~ *die DOOD omdraai,* have been at death's door; *van* ~ *KEN,* know intimately; *nie* ~ *sy broer KOM nie,* not be a patch on his brother, *VAN* ~, from close by, at close quarters; ~beeld, close-up; ~geleë, adjacent, neighbouring; ~'heid, neighbourhood, vicinity, proximity; propinquity; imminence, nearness; ~synde, nearby; approaching.

na'damp, afterdamp.

na'dat, after, when; ~ *hy dit gesê het, het hy vertrek,* after having said this, he departed.

na'dateer, (~), postdate.

na'deel, (nadele), loss, injury; prejudice, detriment, disadvantage, disfavour, disability, drawback; harm, damage; ~ *BEROKKEN aan,* do damage to; *IN jou* ~, to your disadvantage; *geen* ~ *van iets ONDERVIND nie,* be none the worse for it; *TEN nadele van,* to the prejudice (detriment) of; *TOT sy eie* ~, at loss to himself; to his own disadvantage.

nade'lig, (-e), detrimental, injurious, prejudicial, disadvantageous, disserviceable, harmful, adverse, deleterious; ~*e SALDO,* debit balance; ~ *VIR,* detrimental (harmful, disadvantageous) to; ~heid, harmfulness, injuriousness; ~heidstoelae, disability allowance.

na'demaal, whereas, forasmuch as.
na'denke, reflection, meditation, consideration; thought; *STOF tot* ~ *hê*, have food for thought; *in diep* ~ *VERSINK*, absorbed in deep thought.
naden'kend, (-e), thoughtful, reflective, pensive, meditative; ~**heid**, pensiveness.
nadenk'lik, (-e), deliberate.
na'der, (w) (ge-), approach, come nearer, advance towards; approximate; (b, bw) **(-e)**, nearer; more closely; specific (instructions); further; ~ *AANDUI*, indicate more precisely; *HOE* ~ , *hoe doller*, the nearer the event, the greater the excitement; ~ *op iets INGAAN*, enter into greater detail; go more closely into something (a matter); *by* ~ *INSIEN*, on second thoughts; ~ *KENNIS maak*, make closer acquaintance; ~ *KOM*, approach; ~ *ONDERSOEK*, closer investigation; *tot* ~ *ORDER*, until further notice; ~ *VERWANT*, more closely related; ~**by**, nearer; ~**end, (-e)**, coming (nearer), approaching, oncoming, impending; ~**hand**, afterwards, later (on), at length, subsequently; ~**hou**, approach (shot) (golf); ~**ing**, approach; ~**ingshoek**, angle of approach.
na'dessert, dessert.
na'diens, extension of service.
na'dink, (-ge-), reflect, consider, meditate, ponder; make a pause; *ek moet EERS daaroor* ~ , I must think about it first; *SONDER* ~ , thoughtlessly, without thinking, mechanically.
na'dir, nadir (opposite *zenith*).
na'dis, (-se), dessert.
na'doen, (-ge-), imitate, copy, mimic; *jy kan hom dit nie* ~ *nie*, you can't beat that.
na'doods, (-e): ~*e ondersoek*, post mortem.
na'dors, thirst after a drinking-bout, after-thirst.
na'dra, (-ge-), carry after.
na'draai, after-effects, sequel, aftermath.
na'draf, (-ge-), trot after; follow, imitate.
na'drag, after-crop.
na'drentel, (-ge-), trot (jog) after.
na'droejakkals, maned jackal *(Proteles cristatus)*.
na'druiwe, after-vintage.
na'druk¹, (s) emphasis, accent, stress; energy; ~ *lê op*, emphasize, lay stress on.
na'druk², (-ke), pirate edition, spurious edition; piracy; ~ *verbode*, copyright, all rights reserved; (w) **(-ge-)**, pirate, reprint spuriously; ~**ker**, pirate.
nadruk'lik, (-e), emphatic(ally); energetic; decidedly; with meaning; ~**heid**, impressiveness, force, emphasis, stress.
na'drukvorm, emphatic form.
na'duik, (-ge-), plunge (dive) after.
na'el¹, (s) (-s), nail (of finger); claw; nail, rivet; funicle, hilum; *sy* ~ *s is in die rou*, his fingernails need cleaning; ~**s**, species of *Lachenalia;* (w) **(ge-)**, nail, secure (fasten) with nails; catch, get hold of; *aan die grond ge*~ , rooted to the ground.
na'el², (-s) = **nawel.**
na'el³, (w) (ge-), sprint, tear along, race, hurry along; *hy het laat* ~ , he took to his heels.
na'elband, umbilical (belly-) bandage.
na'el: ~**blom**, gillyflower; ~**bol**, allspice.
na'elborsel, nailbrush.
na'elbreuk, rupture of the navel; omphalocele.
na'elbyter, nail-biter.
na'elgordel, umbilical belt.
na'elklinker, riveter.
na'el: ~ **knipper**, nail-cutter, nail-trimmer; ~ **knyper**, nail-nipper.
na'elkruid, navelwort; hare's-foot.
na'ellak, nail polish.
na'el: ~ **loop**, sprint; ~ **loper, (-s)**, sprinter.
na'el: ~ **maantjie**, lunula; ~ **poets**, manicure; nail polish; ~ **poetser**, manicurist; ~ **politoer**, nail polish, nail varnish; ~ **potlood**, nail-crayon; ~ **riem**, cuticle (of the nail).
na'el: ~ **rit**, sprint (cycling); ~ **ryer**, sprinter (cycling).
na'el: ~ **skêrtjie**, nail-scissors; ~ **skoen**, spiked shoe; ~ **skoonmaakmiddel**, nail-cleaner.
na'elskraap, by the skin of the teeth; *dit het so* ~ *GEGAAN*, it was a close shave; *die WERK* ~ *klaar kry*, finish the work just in time.

na'el: ~ **smeer**, nail polish; ~**stel**, manicure set; ~**stokkie**, nail-stick, orange stick.
na'elstring, umbilical cord, navel-string.
na'elsweer, agnail.
na'eltjie¹, (-s), navel.
na'eltjie², (-s), hyacinth; rivet; clove; small nail; ~**bol**, hyacinth bulb; ~**boom**, clove-tree.
na'eltjies, cloves; Lachenalia; ~**brandewyn**, clove-brandy; ~ **olie**, oil of cloves.
na'el: ~ **trekker**, nail-puller; ~ **vas, (-te)**, fixed with rivets; *dinge wat* ~ *vas is*, fixtures.
na'el: ~ **velletjie**, cuticle; ~ **velskêr**, cuticle-scissors; ~ **vernis**, nail polish; ~ **versorging**, manicure; ~ **vlies**, web-eye; ~**vyltjie**, nail-file.
na'elwedloop, flat race.
na'elwortel, root of the nail.
na'elyster, heading-tool.
na'fladder, (-ge-), flutter after.
na'fluit, (-ge-), whistle after; hoot, boo.
naf'ta, naphtha; ~**leen'**, naphthalene, naphthaline; ~ **leen'bal**, naphthalene ball; ~ **leen'skilfers**, naphthalene flakes; ~ **leen'stuk**, naphthalene lump; ~ **leen'vlokkie**, naphthalene flake (shell).
nag, (-te), night; *BY* ~ , in the night-time; by (at) night; *van die* ~ *DAG maak*, turn night into day; *DIEP in die* ~ , at dead of night; *so DONKER soos die* ~ , pitch-dark; *die HELE* ~ , all night; *so LELIK soos die* ~ , as ugly as sin; *so SWART soos die* ~ , as black as soot; ~! good night!
na'gaan, (-ge-), trace, follow; check, control, inspect, verify; supervise (work); review, retrace (mentally); overhaul (motor); run over (with the eye); watch; deduce; feel; *BOEKE* ~ , check books; *iets in GEDAGTE* ~ , run something over in one's mind; *jy kan SELF* ~ , you may imagine; *VIR sover as ek kan* ~ , as far as I can ascertain; ~ '**de**, critical, suspicious; spiteful; ~**d'heid**, suspicion; spite.
nag'aanval, night-attack.
na'gaap, (-ge-), gape after.
nag'adder, night-adder.
na'galm, (s) resounding, reverberation, echo; (w) **(-ge-)**, resound, echo, reverberate.
naga'na, nagana.
nag: ~ **apie**, bushbaby; ~ **arbeid**, night-work; ~ **bel**, night-bell; ~ **besoek**, nocturnal visit; ~ **blind, (-e)** night-blind, nyctalopic; ~ **blinde, (-s)**, nyctalope; ~ **blindheid**, night-blindness, nyctalopia; ~ **blom**, nocturnal flower; ~ **bomwerper**, night-bomber; ~ **boot**, night-boat; ~ **braak, (ge-)**, lucubrate, burn the midnight oil; ~ **broek**, pyjama trousers; ~ **diens**, night-duty; ~ **dier**, nocturnal animal.
na'geboorte, afterbith, placenta.
na'gedagte, afterthought; ~ **nis**, memory, remembrance; *ter* ~ *nis aan (van)*, in commemoration (memory) of.
na'gedruk, (-te), piratic (in printing).
na'gee, (-ge-), charge with, blame for; relate about; *ek moet hom dit ter ere* ~ , I must say this to his credit.
na'gekome: ~ *berigte*, stop-press news.
na'gelaat, (..late), left behind; posthumous; omitted, left undone.
na'gemaak, (-te), forged, false, counterfeit, imitated, artificial, faked; bad; mock.
na'genoeg, almost, just about, practically.
na'gereg, (-te), dessert, pudding.
na'gesang, hymn after the sermon.
na'geslag, posterity, descendants; issue; progeny; ~ **toets**, progeny-test.
na'gewas, after-growth.
nag: ~ **ewening**, equinox; ~ **eweningspunt**, equinoctial point; ~ **gesig**, nocturnal vision; ~ **gewaad**, night-dress (attire); ~ **glas**, nightglass; ~ **goed**, night-clothes; ~ **hemp**, nightdress, night-shirt; ~ **herberg**, night-accommodation; ~ **huisie**, binnacle.
na'giet, (nage-), pour after.
na'gis, (-ge-), ferment again; ~ **ting**, after-fermentation.
nag: ~ **jagter**, night fighter; night-hunter; ~ **jak**, night-jacket; ~ **japon**, night-gown, nighty; ~ **kabaai**, night-shirt; night-gown; ~ **kafee**, night-café; ~ **kar**, night-soil cart; ~ **kassie**, bedside cabinet;

~ kers, rushlight; night-light; ~ klere, night-clothes; ~ klok, curfew; ~ klub, nightclub; ~ koelte, coolness of the night; ~ kroeg, all-night pub; ~ kwartier, night-quarters; ~ lampie, night-lamp; ~ landing, night-landing; ~ lewe, night-life; ~ lied, nocturne; ~ lig, night-light.
na'gloed, afterglow.
na'gloei, (-ge-), glow after the extinction of the flame, anneal.
nag: ~ loper, reveller, night-bird, fly-by-night; ~ lug, night-air.
na'gluur, (-ge-), ogle (after).
na'gly, (-ge-), slide after.
Nag'maal, Holy Communion; Eucharist.
nag'maals: ~ beker, chalice, communion-cup; ~ brood, communion-bread; ~ ganger, communicant; ~ kelkie, communion-cup; ~ tafel, communion-table; credence (R.C.); ~ viering, communion; ~ wyn, communion-wine.
nag: ~ mars, night-march; ~ merrie, nightmare; bugbear; incubus; ~ motte, noctuidae; ~ mus, nightcap; ~ opname, night-time photography; ~ oproep, night-call; ~ pak, pyjamas; ~ personeel, nightstaff; ~ pitjie, rushlight, floating wick; ~ ploeg, night-team; ~ pommade, night-cream; ~ portier, night-porter; ~ pos, nightwatch.
na'graads, (-e), postgraduate.
nag'raaf, (..rawe), common owl.
na'gras, aftermath-grazing, aftermath, after-grass, fog.
nag; ~ redakteur, night editor; ~ reier, night heron; ~ reis, ~ rit, night-journey.
na'groei, aftermath.
nag: ~ rok, night-dress, night-gown; bedgown; ~ rondte, night-round (patrol); ~ rus, sleep, night's rest; ~ sê, (-ge-), say goodnight; ~ siende, day-blind; ~ siendheid, day-blindness; ~ sig, night visibility; ~ sinjaal, flare; ~ skade, nightshade; bittersweet; banewort; ~ skel, night-bell; ~ skof, night-shift; ~ skoot, evening-gun; ~ skuiling, night-shelter; ~ skuit, night-boat; met die ~ skuit gekom, be quite in the dark; ~ slang, night-snake; snake-flower; ~ slot, double lock; ~ slotsleutel, passkey; ~ soen, goodnight kiss; ~ sopie, nightcap; ~ stilte, silence of the night; ~ stoel, commode; ~ studie, lucubration; ~ stuk, night-scene, nocturne; ~ suster, night-nurse (sister); ~ swael, nightjar; ~ swaeltjie, goatsucker; ~ sweet, night-sweats; ~ tafeltjie, bedside table; ~ tarief, night-tariff.
nag'tegaal, (..gale), nightingale; Philomela; ~ stem, voice of a nightingale.
nag'telik, (-e), nocturnal, nightly; ~ e duister, darkness of night.
nag'trein, night-train; lyk soos een wat met die ~ gekom het, look very slovenly (ill-kept); look like one who has slept in his clothes.
nag: ~ tyd, night-time, ~ ull, nightjar; chamber-pot; ~ valkie, night-hawk; ~ verblyf, night-accommodation; ~ verkeer, night traffic; ~ verligting, night-lighting; ~ verpleegster, night-nurse; ~ vliegend, (-e), night-flying; ~ vliegende motte, noctuidae; ~ vlinder, night-hawk; ~ vlug, night-flight; ~ voël, night-bird; ~ vrees, nyctophobia; ~ vuil, night-soil; ~ wa, see nagkar; ~ waak, night-watch; pernoctation; vigil; ~ wag, ~ wagter, night-watch, night-watchman; ~ waker, night-watchman, ~ wandelaar, somnambulist, sleep-walker; ~ werk, night-work; lucubration; ~ werker, night-worker; lucubrator; ~ wind, night-wind; ~ wolf, night-bird.
na'hardloop, (-ge-), run after.
na'hol, (-ge-), run (rush) after.
na'hou, (-ge-), keep, detain (in school); iets daarop ~, keep in store; stock; hold (opinion).
na'huppel, (-ge-), hop (jump, skip) after.
na'huweliks, (-e), post-nuptial; ~ e skulde, post-nuptial debts.
naïef', (naïewe; naïewer, -ste), naïve, simple, ingenuous, artless; ~ heid, ingenuousness, artlessness.
naïwiteit', artlessness, simplicity, naïvety (naïveté).
na'ja(ag), (-ge-), pursue, chase, course; grasp at; hunt after; covet, aim at.
na'jaar, autumn; ~ sopruiming, autumn sale; ~ storm, autumn gale; ~ sverkoping, see najaarsopruiming; ~ sweer, autumnal weather.
naja'de, (-s), naiad.
na'jaer, pursuer.
na'jaging, pursuit, quest.
na'kend, (-e), naked, nude, bare; imminent (danger); ~ LOOP, go nude; jou ~ UITTREK, strip naked.
na'kind, posthumous child; child from a later marriage.
na'klank, echo, resonance; cipher (organ).
na'klink, (-ge-), resound, (re-)echo, continue to sound; cipher (organ).
na'klip, bright-coloured (disintegrated) rock.
na'kom, (-ge-), fulfil, carry out, do, perform, meet (obligation); redeem (duty); keep, comply; come later; iem. te na kom, run someone down; die REËLS nie ~ nie, infringe (fail to observe) the rules.
na'komeling, (-e), descendant; ~ skap, posterity; offspring, progeny, issue, progeniture; descent; generation.
na'komer, (-s), late arrival.
na'koming, fulfilment, compliance, performance, pursuance, discharge.
na'kommertjie, (-s), late-comer, child born long after the others.
na'kroos, progeny, offspring, issue.
na'kruip, (-ge-), creep (crawl) after.
na'kyk, (-ge-), look after; examine, revise, check, correct, mark (examination papers); eye.
na'laat, (ge-), bequeath, leave (as inheritance); forbear; leave off (smoking); omit; neglect (warning); fail (in duty); refrain; ek kan nie ~ om op te MERK dat, I cannot refrain from observing that; jy moet veral NIE ~ nie om, you should make a special point of; jou PLIG ~, neglect your duty.
na'lam, late lamb.
na'latenskap, (-pe), inheritance, heritage, bequeathment, assets, dower, legacy.
nala'tig, (-e), negligent, careless, neglectful; remiss, defaulting; ~ e, (-s), defaulter; ~ heid, negligence, carelessness, misprision, default, failure; lashes (law).
na'lating, (-e, -s), omission; neglect.
na'leef, (-ge-), observe, live up to (a principle); follow (rules); honour, keep (a promise).
na'lees, (-ge-), read over (up), peruse; glean.
na'leser, collator.
na'lesing, perusal.
na'lewe, (-ge-) = naleef.
na'lewer, (-ge-), deliver subsequently; ~ ing, subsequent delivery.
na'lewing, observance, living up to.
na'loer, (-ge-), peer after, watch, dog.
na'loop, (s) second runnings, faints (distilling brandy); (w) (-ge-), run after, follow, haunt: 'n MEISIF ~, dangle after a girl; die WERKERS ~, supervise the workers.
na'loper, follower; imitator; dangler; ~ tjie, tag, tagtail.
Na'ma, Nama.
na'maak, (s) imitation, counterfeit, fake(ment), forgery; pas op vir ~, beware of imitations; (w) (-ge-), forge (signature); imitate, fake, copy, pattern after, mimic, falsify, counterfeit; ~ sel, imitation, counterfeit, fake, copy, simulacrum; pinchbeck; ~ silwer, argentine; ~ sy, mercerized cotton.
na'maker, imitator, counterfeiter, forger.
na'making, forgery.
Nama'kwa, (-s), Namaqua.
nama'kwadiuf, Namaqua dove.
Nama'kwaland, Namaqualand; ~ er, (-s), inhabitant of Namaqualand.
nama'kwapatrys, Namaqua sand-grouse, coast-partridge.
nama'te, as, in proportion to.
na'me: BY ~ aandui, designate by name; MET (by) ~, namely, viz.
na'meet, (-ge-), measure again; check.
na'meloos, (..lose), inexpressible, unspeakable; nameless.
Na'men, Namur.

na'mens, in the name of, on behalf of, for.
na'meting, checking of measurement; remeasurement.
Nami'bië, Namibia.
namid'dag, na'middag, afternoon; ~diens, afternoon service; ~slapie, afternoon sleep; ~wag, afternoon watch.
nam'mies, nams, sweets (nursery term).
namptissement', (-e), provisional sentence.
na'nag, latter part of the night, small hours.
nan'king, nankeen; ~se broek, nankeens, nankeen trousers.
nan'soek, nainsook.
na'oes, (s) after-crop, second crop; (w) (-ge-), gather in the after-crop.
na'oog, (-ge-), look (stare) after, follow with the eyes.
na'oorlogs, (-e), post-war.
na'palm, napalm.
Na'pels, Naples.
na'pelsgeel, Naples yellow.
na'pleit, (-ge-), go on pleading (after judgment has been given).
na'ploeg, (-ge-), plough again.
na'pluis, (-ge-), scrutinize, investigate, ferret out anew, pry.
na'pluk, (s) aftercrop; (w) (-ge-), reap the aftercrop.
napo'leon, (-s), napoleon (20 franc piece); nap (card game).
Napoleon'ties, (-e), Napoleonic.
Napolitaan', (..tane), Neapolitan; ~s', (-e), Neapolitan.
na'port, late fee.
na'pos, late letters.
na'praat, (-ge-), repeat (another's words), chime, echo; gossip; remain chatting; ~ster, vroulik van naprater.
na'prater, (-s), repeater of another's words, parrot; ~y, echoing, gossiping, parrot-talk.
na'pret, after-feast, fun after the event.
nap'slak, patella.
na'pyn, afterpains.
Nar, (-re), fool, jester, buffoon, clown, pierrot; ~agtig, (-e), clownish.
narcis'me, narcissis'me, narcissism.
Nar'cissus, Narcissus.
narcis'ties, (-e), narcissistic.
nar'dus, nard, spikenard; ~gras, matweed.
na'rede, epilogue.
na'reken, (-ge-), reckon again, verify, check; ~baar, (..bare), controllable.
na'rig, (-te), information, intelligence, report.
na'righeid, dizziness, biliousness; nastiness; misery, bad plight; *ek wou die ~ na die ongeluk nie aanskou nie*, I did not want to see the misery (suffering) after the accident.
narkolep'sie, narcolepsy.
narkomanie', drug habit.
narko'se, narcosis, anaesthesia; *onder ~ bring*, anaesthetize.
narko'ties, (-e), narcotic.
narko'tikum, (-s, ..tika), narcotic.
narkotiseer', (ge-), narcotize, anaesthetize.
narkotiseur', (-s), anaesthetist, narcotist.
na'roei, (-ge-), row after.
na'roep, (-ge-), call after; call names.
na'rol, (-ge-), roll after.
nar'ra, (-s), butter pits *(Acanthosicyos horrida)*.
nar're: ~bel, fool's bell; ~kap, fool's cap; ~maat, fool's mate; ~pak, motley; ~septer; bauble; ~spel, harlequinade; ~streke, clownery.
nar'sing, (-s), narcissus; ~lelie, amaryllis.
nar'tjie, (-s), naartjie, mandarin, tangerine; ~kleur, tangerine.
nar'wal, (-le, -s), narwhal, unicorn-fish.
na'ry, (-ge-), ride after.
nasaal', (nasale), nasal.
na'saat, (nasate), descendant.
nasaleer', (ge-), nasalize.
nasale'ring, nasalization.
nasaliteit', nasality.
na'sang, concluding hymn.
Nasare'ner, (-s), Nazarene.

Na'saret, Nazareth; *kan daar iets goed uit ~ kom?* can any good thing come out of Nazareth?
na'sê, (-ge-), repeat (another's words), say after; concur with.
na'seil, (-ge-), sail after.
na'send, (-ge-), redirect (letter); send after.
na'sie, (-s), nation, people, tribe, clan; creatures; *hy is VAN die ~*, he is one of the chosen race, he is a Jew; *VROUMENSE? dis 'n moeilike ~*, women are troublesome creatures; ~bou, nation-building; ~eer, national honour; ~gees, national spirit; ~heil, national welfare.
na'sien, (-ge-), correct, mark (exercise); overhaul, examine, verify, check, look over, revise (a manuscript); audit; ~er, (-s), checker.
na'sie: ~skap, nationhood; ~trots, national pride; ~vlag, national flag.
na'sing, (-ge-), sing after.
nasionaal', (..nale), national; *..nale PAD*, national road; *die Nasionale PARTY*, the National Party; *..nale POEDING*, roly-poly (pudding); *..nale VRYWILLIGER*, national volunteer.
Nasionaal'-Sosialis'me, National Socialism.
Nasionalis', (-te), Nationalist.
nasionalis', nationalist; ~a'sie, nationalization; ~eer', (ge-), nationalize.
nasionalis'me, nationalism.
nasionalis'ties, (-e), nationalist(ic).
nasionaliteit', (-e), nationality; ~s'gevoel, sense of nationhood, national feeling; ~s'kenmerk, mark of nationality.
Nasire'ër, (-s), Nazarite.
na'sit, (s): *sy naam is ~*, he is a real stickler; (w) (-ge-), pursue, chase, follow, run after, chevy.
na'skets, (-ge-), copy (a sketch).
na'skiet, (-ge-), send a bullet after.
na'skilder, (-ge-), copy, reproduce (painting).
na'skreeu, (-ge-), cry (bawl) after.
na'skrif, postscript.
na'skryf, na'skrywe, (-ge-), copy; plagiarize.
na'slaan, (-ge-), look up, consult (a book); read up; *maklik om na te slaan*, easy to refer to; ~biblioteek, reference library; ~boek, reference book, book of reference.
na'sleep, (s) consequence, result, aftermath, sequel, after-effects, train; *die ~ van die oorlog*, the aftermath of the war; (w) (-ge-), drag (after).
na'smaak, after-taste.
na'snuffel, (-ge-), search, scrutinize, investigate; ferret out; pry into.
na'sny, (-ge-), chase (metal work).
na'somer, Martinmas summer; latter part of the summer; Indian summer.
na'sorg, after-care.
na'spanning, residual stress.
na'speel, (-ge-), play after, imitate in playing.
na'spel¹, (s) after-play, afterpiece; postlude; sequel; aftermath.
na'spel², (w) (-ge-), spell after.
na'speur, (-ge-), trace, investigate; ~'baar, (..bare), ascertainable; ~der, (-s), inquisitor; ~ing, investigation, tracing; ~'lik, (-e), traceable.
na'spoor = naspeur.
na'sporing, investigation, quest; caster.
na'spreek, (-ge-), repeat after.
na'spring, (-ge-), jump after.
nassen'sie, nascency.
nas'sent, (-e), nascent.
na'staar, (-ge-), gaze (stare) after.
nas'tergal, garden nightshade, banewort *(Solanum nigrum)*; *swart ~*, morel.
na'stoot, next stroke (billiards); last push.
na'streef, (-ge-), strive after, pursue (wealth); emulate (person); ~baar, (..bare), pursuable.
nastrewe, (-ge-) = nastreef.
na'strewer, emulator.
na'strewing, emulation; pursuance.
na'stuk, afterpiece.
na'stuur, (-ge-), send after, redirect (letter).
na'sukkel, (-ge-), trudge (struggle) after.
na'sweef, (-ge-), float (hover, glide) after.
na'swem, (-ge-), swim after.

na'swewe, (-ge-) = nasweef.
na'syfer, (-ge-), check, verify.
nat, (s): *die stille* ~, the deep; the main; (b) wet, moist, clammy, dank; *HY is* ~, he is tipsy; *so ~ soos 'n KAT*, wet through; soaked to the skin; like a drowned rat; ~ *van die SWEET*, wet with perspiration.
Nat, (-tes), Nationalist.
Natal', Natal; ~**ler, (-s),** Natalian; ~**s, (-e),** Natalian.
na'teken, (-ge-), copy, draw (from a model); ~**ing,** copy, tracing.
na'tel, (-ge-), re-count, count over; count after; check; ~**ler, (-s),** checker, scrutineer; ~**ling,** re-count, checking.
nat: ~**gooi, (-ge-),** water; wet; ~**hals,** toper, tippler, soaker; ~**heid,** moistness, wetness, dampness; ~**laken,** drip-sheet; ~**lei, (-ge-),** irrigate; ~**maak, (-ge-),** wet; water (garden).
na'tou, tree-killer.
nat'reën, nat'reent, (-ge-), be caught in the rain, become drenched with rain.
na'trek, (s) tracing; double-action (gun); **(w) (-ge-),** go after, follow; trace, copy; calk; ~**linne,** tracing-cloth; ~**papier,** tracing-paper; ~**ster,** lady tracer; ~**tekening,** ~**werk,** tracing.
na'tril, (-ge-), continue vibrating; vibrate in unison.
na'trium, sodium; ~**arseniet,** arsenite of soda; ~**bikarbonaat,** sodium bicarbonate, baking soda.
na'troliet, natrolite.
na'tron, natron, sodium carbonate; ~**loog,** caustic-soda solution.
na'tros, bunch of late grapes.
nat'spat, (-ge-), sprinkle, perfuse.
Nat'te, (-s) = Nat.
nat'terig, (-e), slightly moist (damp, wet); chilly; dankish; slightly tipsy; ~**heid,** moistness, dampness.
nat'tigheid, dampness, moisture.
natu'ra: *in* ~, in kind.
natura'lieë, produce.
naturalis', (-te), naturalist; ~**a'sie,** naturalization; ~**a'siewet,** naturalization law (act); ~**eer', (ge-),** naturalize; *jou laat ~ eer*, take out letters of naturalization; ~**me,** naturalism; ~**ties, (-e),** naturalistic.
natuur'¹, nature; scenery; (..ture), temper; character, temperament, disposition; grain; *die ~ is sterker as die LEER*, nature passes nurture; *die ~ is daar baie MOOI*, the scenery is very beautiful there; *NA die ~*, from nature; *'n TWEEDE ~*, a second nature; *VAN nature*, by nature, naturally; *in die VRYE ~*, in the open.
na'tuur², (-ge-), peer after.
natuur': ~**aanbidder,** nature worshipper; ~**aanbidding,** nature worship; ~**beskerming,** protection of nature; ~**beskouing,** attitude towards nature; ~**beskrywing,** physiography, description of nature; natural history; ~**bewaring,** conservation of nature; ~**bos,** indigenous forest; ~**diens,** worship of nature; ~**drif,** instinct; sexual desire; ~**frats,** freak of nature; ~**geneeswyse,** nature cure; physiatrics; ~**geneser,** naturopath; ~**genoot,** (..note), fellow creature; fellow being; ~**genot,** enjoyment of nature; ~**geskiedenis,** natural history; ~**getrou, (-e),** true to nature; ~**godsdiens,** natural religion; ~**gril,** freak of nature; ~**historie,** (ong.), natural history; ~**histories, (-e),** natural-historical; ~**historikus,** ~**kenner,** naturalist; ~**kennis,** natural history; nature study; ~**keuse,** natural selection; ~**kind,** child of nature; ~**krag,** force of nature, natural power; ~**kunde,** physical science; physics; ~**kun'dig, (-e),** physical; ~**kun'dige, (-s),** physicist; naturalist; ~**leer,** natural philosophy; physiology; ~**lewe,** wild life; life in nature; ~**liefde,** love of nature; ~**liefhebber,** lover of nature.
natuur'lik, (b) (-e), natural; unaffected; effortless; genuine; matter-of-course; *'n ~e AANLEG*, a natural bent; ~*e BATES*, natural resources; ~*e DOOD*, natural death; ~*e HISTORIE*, natural history; *'n ~e KIND*, a child born out of wedlock; an artless child; (bw) of course; naturally; *hy sal ~ kom*, of course he will come; ~**erwys(e),** naturally; ~**heid,** simplicity, naturalness, artlessness, unaffectedness.
natuur': ~**magte,** powers of nature; act of God; ~**mens,** man in his natural state; ~**minnaar,** lover of nature; ~**monument,** place of natural beauty; ~**ondersoeker,** naturalist; ~**opname,** nature photograph; ~**park,** nature reserve; ~**prag,** beautiful scenery; ~**produk,** natural product; ~**ramp,** act of God; catastrophe in nature; ~**reg,** natural right; law of nature; ~**reservaat,** nature reserve; ~**skoon,** (beautiful) scenery, beauty of nature; ~**speling,** freak of nature; ~**staat,** natural state; ~**steen,** natural stone; ~**studie,** nature study; ~**tafereel,** scene of natural beauty; natural scene; ~**verskynsel,** natural phenomenon; ~**vesting,** natural fortification; ~**volk,** primitive race; ~**voortbrengsel,** natural product; ~**vorser,** naturalist; ~**vriend,** nature-lover; ~**werking,** operation of nature; ~**wet,** law of nature.
natuur'wetenskap, (natural) science; physical science; natural philosophy; ~'**lik, (-e),** pertaining to natural science, scientific; ~ *like vakke*, natural sciences.
natuur': ~**wol,** natural wool; ~**wonder,** prodigy of nature; ~**woud,** primeval forest; ~**wyn,** natural wine.
na'uurs, (-e), part-time; after hours.
na'vertel, (~), repeat; adapt from (stories).
na'verwant, (s) (-e), kinsman, close relation; (b) (-e), closely related; ~**skap,** relationship, propinquity.
naviga'sie, navigation.
na'vlieg, (-ge-), fly after.
na'volg, (-ge-), follow; imitate; *vry nagevolg uit die Frans*, freely adapted from the French; ~'**baar,** (..bare), imitable; ~'**baarheid,** imitability; ~**enswaar'dig, (-e),** worthy of imitation; worth following; ~**er, (-s),** follower, imitator; ~**ing,** imitation; *in ~ing van*, in imitation of; on the model of.
na'vors, (-ge-), examine closely, investigate, do research work; explore; ~**er, (-s),** research worker, investigator; scientist; explorer; diver; ~**ing,** investigation, inquiry, research; exploration; ~**ingsdoelwit,** research aim (goal); ~**ingsingenieur,** research engineer; ~**ingsrigting,** aspect of research; ~**ingswerk,** work connected with any investigation, research work.
na'vra, (-ge-), inquire.
na'vraag, inquiry; demand; ~ *DOEN (na 'n persoon)*, seek information (about a person); *daar is GROOT ~ na iets*, something is in great demand; ~**kantoor,** ..**vraekantoor,** inquiry office.
na'waarde, unexpired value.
na'was, backwash.
na'weë, unpleasant consequences; afterpains; aftermath; hangover.
na'weeg, (-ge-), reweigh.
na'week, week-end; ~ *hou,* spend a week-end; ~**ekskursie,** week-end excursion.
na'wei, after-grass.
na'wel, (-s), navel; umbilicus; ~**band,** navel bandage; binder; ~**besmetting,** umbilical pyaemia; ~**breuk,** navel rupture; ~**lemoen,** navel orange; ~**siekte,** navel-ill; ~**string,** navel-string, umbilical cord; ~**stringbesmetting,** navel-ill, joint-ill.
na'werk, (-ge-), continue (to work), linger on; do overtime; *die oorlede man se invloed het nog nagewerk*, the deceased man's influence continued after his death; ~**end,** persistent; ~*e spuitmiddel,* residual spray; ~**ing, (-e, -s),** after-effect(s); persistence (gas); residual effect.
na'winner, reclaimer.
na'winning, reclaiming.
na'winter, latter part of the winter.
na'wys, (-ge-), point at.
na'yl, (-ge-), rush after; lag (instruments); ~**ingsfout,** lag error.
na'ywer, envy, jealousy; rivalry; emulation.
nay'werig, (-e), envious, jealous; emulous.
Na'zi, (-'s), Nazi; ~**is'me,** Nazi-ism, Hitlerism; ~**isties, (-e),** Nazi.

nè? is it not? isn't it? yes? *dink 'n bietjie*, ~! just imagine (fancy)!
Nean'derdalmens, Neanderthal man.
ne'bula, (-s), nebula.
nebulis', (-te), nebulist.
Ne'derduits, (-e), Dutch; Low German; ~ *(e) GE=REFORMEERDE Kerk*, Dutch Reformed Church.
ne'derig, (-e), humble, modest, diffident, cap-in-hand, meek; low (birth); ~ **heid**, modesty, humility, descension, diffidence, lowliness, meekness.
ne'derlaag = **neerlaag.**
Ne'derland, the Netherlands; ~ **er**, (-s), Dutchman; ~ **erskap**, Dutch nationality; ~ **s**, (s) Dutch (language); (b) (-e), belonging to the Netherlands, Netherlandic; ~ **s-Indië**, (hist.), the Netherlands East Indies.
Ne'der: ~ **-Ryn,** Lower Rhine; ~ **-Sakse,** Lower Saxony.
ne'dersetter, (-s), settler, colonist.
ne'dersetting, (-e, -s), settlement, colony; establishment.
ne'derwaarts, (-e), downward(s).
nee, no; *AG* ~! well I never! oh, no! ~ *ANT=WOORD*, answer in the negative; *O,* ~! oh, no! ~ *SÊ*, say no; refuse; ~ *WAT!* no! don't!
neef, (-s), nephew, (male) cousin; young man; *volle* ~, first cousin; ~ **skap**, cousinship; nephewship.
neem, (ge-), take, receive, accept; engage (room); capture; *'n EINDE* ~, come to an end; *'n FORT* ~, capture a fort; ~ *soos dit KOM*, take things as they come; *uit die MOND* ~, remove from one's mouth; ~ *NOG enetjie*, have another one; *OP hom* ~, take upon himself, undertake; *haar tot VROU* ~, marry her, take her to wife; ~ **baar,** (..**bare**), liable to capture.
ne'ënde = **negende.**
ne'ëntig = **negentig.**
ne'ënuur, nine o'clock.
neer, down, downwards; *op en* ~, up and down.
neer'biggel, (-ge-), trickle down.
neer'blik, (-ge-), look down.
neer'buig, (-ge-), bend down, kneel, stoop; condescend.
neerbui'gend, (-e), condescending, patronizing; ~ **heid**, condescension.
neer'buiging, kneeling; stooping; condescension; prostration.
neer'buk, (-ge-), stoop (down); ~ **king**, kneeling, stooping.
neer'daal, (-ge-), descend, dismount; fall (snow).
neer'daling, descent; fall.
neer'druk, (-ge-), press down, depress; couch; chill; ~ **'kend**, (-e), depressing; ~ **ker**, depressor; ~ **king**, depression.
neer'drup, (-ge-), drip (trickle) down.
neer'gaan, (-ge-), go down, descend; ~ *de beweging*, downward movement.
neer'gebuig, (-de), bent down; reclinate (bot.).
neer'gedruk, (-te), cast-down, depressed.
neer'geslaan, (-de), sad (bread), heavy; doughy, clammy (cake).
neer'gly, (-ge-), slip (slide, glide) down.
neer'gooi, (-ge-), throw down, cast down, down, floor.
neer'haal, (s) (**neerhale**), downstroke (in writing); (w) (-ge-), lower, fetch (haul) down, pull down; shoot down; *iem.* ~, run someone down, disparage someone.
neer'hak, (-ge-), fell, cut down.
neerha'lend, (-e), derogatory, insulting.
neer'hang, (-ge-), hang down; droop, sag; ~ **end**, (-e), pendant, drooping, hanging.
neer'hou, (-ge-), keep down; cut down; put to the sword.
neer'hurk, (-ge-), squat down; ~ **end**, (-e), couchant.
neer'ja(ag), (-ge-), hunt down, chase.
neer'kap, (-ge-), fell, cut down.
neer'klater, (-ge-), cascade (down).
neer'kletter, (-ge-), pelt down; ~ **ing**, pelting; cascading.
neer'klim, (-ge-), climb down.

neer'kniel, (-ge-), kneel down; ~ **ing**, prostration.
neer'kom, (-ge-), come down, alight; fall on; come to; devolve; descend; land (plane); *ALLES sal op hom* ~, he will have to bear the brunt; *dit sal feitlik HIEROP* ~, actually it will come to this; *dit kom alles OP dieselfde neer*, it comes (works out) to the same thing; ~ *OP*, be tantamount to; *WAAR ek op wil* ~, the point I want to make; ~ **s**, descension, descent.
neer'krabbel, (-ge-), scribble down.
neer'kyk, (-ge-), look down; ~ *op iem.*, look down upon someone, hold someone in contempt.
neer'laag, (**neerlae**), defeat, reverse, check, foil, discomfiture; *die* ~ *ly*, suffer a defeat, be defeated (worsted).
neer'laat, (-ge-), let down, lower, let fall; douse.
Neerlan'dikus, (..**dici, -se**), student of Dutch literature and language, Netherlandicist.
Neerlandis'me, (-s), Netherlandism.
Neerlandistiek', Dutch linguistics.
neer'lê¹, (-ge-), lie down.
neer'lê², (-ge-), lay down, abdicate, resign; abide by; relinquish (post); put; deposit; embody, incorporate; express; down; demit; provide; *sy AMP* ~, resign from office; *hom BY iets* ~, acquiesce in; resign oneself to; *die WERK* ~, cease work, strike work, down tools.
neer'legging, laying down, resignation.
neer'liggend, (-e), prostrate, prone, procumbent.
neer'maai, (-ge-), mow down.
neer'pen, (-ge-), pen, write down.
neer'plof, (-ge-), fall down with a thud, plump down, flop down; douse.
neer'rol, (-ge-), roll down.
neer'ruk, (-ge-), pull (jerk) down.
neer'sabel, (-ge-), cut down, put to the sword.
neer'sak, (-ge-), sink down; *geleidelik laat* ~, lower gradually.
neer'sien, (-ge-), look down (upon); *minagtend* ~ *op*, hold in contempt, look down (up)on.
neer'sink, (-ge-), sink down.
neer'sit, (-ge-), put down.
neer'skiet, (-ge-), shoot down, pot, bring down, fetch down; pounce.
neer'skryf, neer'skrywe, (-ge-), write down, set (put) down in writing.
neer'skud, (-ge-), shake down.
neer'skyn, (-ge-), shine down.
neer'slaan, (-ge-), strike down, knock down, cast down; settle (deposit); lodge (wheat); precipitate, deposit (chemistry); dim (motor-car lights); lower (eyes); *die BLIK* ~, lower one's gaze; *met neergeslaande KAP*, drop-head car; *die KOEK sal* ~, the cake will sink; the cake will become doughy (sad, heavy); ~ **middel**, precipitant.
neer'slag, downpour, downfall; deposition; (..**slae**), settlings; precipitate (chemistry); precipitation; down-beat (music); ~ **gebied**, catchment area; area of precipitation; ~ **middel**, precipitant; ~ **put**, sedimentation pit; ~ **snelheid**, rate of deposition.
neerslag'tig, (-e), dejected, despondent, melancholy, downcast, down-hearted, blue, in a blue mood, cheerless, depressed, dull, down in the mouth, low-spirited, low, gloomy, down; damp; ~ **heid**, dejection, despondency, depression, the doldrums, the dismals.
neer'slagtempo, precipitation rate.
neer'slagtoestel, damper.
neer'smyt, (-ge-), chuck (fling) down, dump.
neer'stamp, (-ge-), ram (push) down.
neer'stoot, (-ge-), thrust down.
neer'stort, (-ge-), fall down; crash (aeroplane); collapse; come down in torrents; ~ **ing**, falling down; crash; precipitation.
neer'straal, (-ge-), beat (stream) down.
neer'stroom, (-ge-), stream (pour) down.
neer'stryk, (-ge-), alight, descend; land (aeroplane); perch (bird); ~ **ing**, landing.
neer'sweef, (-ge-), float down.
neer'syg, (-ge-), collapse; sink down.
neer'tel¹, (-ge-), put down; lift off; lift down.
neer'tel², (-ge-), count down (money).

neer'trap, (-ge-), tread (trample) down.
neer'trek, (-ge-), pull down, drag down; drop (bird); grass, collar, tackle (rugby); *jou ~ op die bed*, lie down.
neer'tuimel, (-ge-), tumble down.
neer'val, (-ge-), fall down, drop, dump; prolapse.
neer'vel, (-ge-), fell; lay out (boxing), strike down, cut down.
neer'vlieg, (-ge-), fly down.
neer'vloei, (-ge-), flow down.
neer'vly, (-ge-), lay down; *hom ~*, lie down.
neer'waai, (-ge-), blow down; be blown down.
neer'waarts, downward(s).
neer'werp, (-ge-), throw down, prostrate; *jou ~*, throw oneself down.
neet, (nete), nit; *KALE ~*, an impecunious fellow; tatterdemalion; ragamuffin; *KLOU (sit) soos 'n ~*, cling like a leech; *vir die nete nog moet SORG*, have to provide for one's grandchildren too.
nee'woord, refusal; *die ~ kry*, be refused (by a girl); be turned down.
nef'fens, next to, alongside of, beside.
ne'fie, (-s), little nephew (cousin); young man.
nefriet', kidney-stone, nephrite.
nefri'ties, (-e), nephritic.
nefri'tis, nephritis, inflammation of the kidneys.
nega'sie, (-s), negation.
negatief', (s) (..tiewe), negative; (b) (..tiewe), negative.
negativis'me, negativism.
ne'ge, nine; *~ maal*, nine times, *~ daags*, (-e), of nine days, nine-day; *~ delig*, (-e), of nine parts.
ne'gedubbel(d), (-de), ninefold.
negeer', (ge-), disregard, ignore, cut (person); give the go-by.
ne'gehoek, nonagon; *~ig*, (-e), nonagonal.
ne'gejarig, (-e), nine years old, of nine years.
ne'gelettergrepig, (-e), of nine syllables.
ne'gende, (s) (-s), ninth (part); (b) ninth; *ten ~*, in the ninth place.
ne'gentien, nineteen; *~de*, nineteenth; *~de-eeus*, (-e), nineteenth century.
ne'gentig, ninety; *in die jare ~*, in the nineties; *~er*, (-s), person in the nineties, of the nineties; *~erjare*, nineties; *~jarig*, (-e), ninety years old, of ninety years; *~jarige*, (-s), nonagenarian; *~ste*, ninetieth.
ne'ge: *~oog*, carbuncle, furuncle; lamprey; anthrax; *~ponder*, ninepounder; *~proef*, casting out the nines.
Ne'ger, (-s), Negro; *~aap*, Negro monkey; *~agtig*, (-e), Negroid; *~bevolking*, Negro population; *~bloed*, Negro blood; *~dans*, Negro dance; cakewalk; *~handel*, Negro traffic; *~in'*, (-ne), Negress; *~lied*, Negro song, Negro spiritual; *~ras*, Negro race; *~sangers*, Negro (Christy) minstrels; *~tipe*, Negro type, Negroid.
ne'getal, nine; ennead; nonary; *~lig*, (-e), nonary.
ne'geuur, nine o'clock.
ne'gevoud, multiple of nine; *~ig*, (-e), ninefold.
néglígé', (-s), undies, négligé.
negosiant', (-e), trader.
nego'sie, trade goods.
nego'sie: *~goed*, merchandise, wares; *~kas*, packing-case; *as 'n ~kas 'n stoel word*, when nobody becomes somebody; *~ware*, merchandise, wares; *~winkel*, shop (groceries and drapery), general store.
negroïde', (-s), negroïed', (-e), negroid.
Ne'gus[1], Negus, Emperor of Abyssinia.
ne'gus[2], negus (kind of drink).
neig, (ge-), bend, incline; gravitate; *ten EINDE ~*, draw to a close; *mense is ge~ OM*, people are apt to; *die SON ~ ter kimme*, the sun is declining; *ten VAL ~*, totter to its ruin; *~hoek*, angle of inclination.
nei'ging, (-e, -s), inclination; drive, bearing, addiction, leaning, fancy, hang; determination; tendency, proneness, propensity, bent, bias; proclivity; penchant; habit; drift; ply (fig.); *~ TOT*, leaning towards; *'n ~ VERTOON*, be apt (inclined) to; show an inclination.
nek, (s) (-ke), neck; socket (golf); mountain pass; col;

cervix; *iem. met die ~ AANKYK*, give a person the cold shoulder; *deur jou ~ BETAAL*, pay through your nose; *'n DIK ~ hê*, have a lofty air; be conceited; *iem. DRAAI sy ~ om*, he is being contrary; *die droogte het sy ~ GEBREEK*, the drought has ruined him; *iem. in die ~ KYK*, deceive someone; do someone a shot in the eye; *op iem. anders se ~ LÊ*, inconvenience people by staying with them; outstay one's welcome; *iem. se ~ vol LIEG*, pump a person full of lies; *sy ~ OMDRAAI*, wring a man's neck; *deur sy ~ PRAAT*, talk through his hat, talk nonsense; *jou ~ in die STROP steek*, run one's head into a noose; *sy ~ is in die STROP*, he is in a fix; he has the noose around his neck; *iets deur die ~ TREK (ruk)*, eat or drink something; (w) (ge-), break the neck of; *~aar*, jugular (neck) vein; *~-af*, with broken neck; *~been*, neckbone; *~brekerrewolwer*, break-action revolver; *~doek*, neckerchief; *~haar*, hair of the nape; *~hanger(tjie)*, locket; *~houtjie*, cang(ue); cross-bar (of a cart); forked yoke (to prevent animals from passing through fences); *sy ~hare het gerys*, his hair stood on end; *~ketting*, neck-chain; guard-chain; *~kramp*, cerebrospinal meningitis; cramp in the neck; *~kuil*, nape of the neck, nucha; *~lengte*, neck-length; *~plank*, cang(ue); *~riem*, neck-strap.
nekrologie', necrology.
nekroloog', (..loë), necrologist.
nekromansie', necromancy.
nekroman'ties, (-e), necromantic.
nekro'polis, (-se), necropolis.
nekro'se, necrosis.
nekro'ties, (-e), necrotic.
nek: *~rug*, nape; *~slag*, finishing stroke, death-blow; *iem. 'n ~slag gee*, deal someone a death-blow; *~slagaar*, carotid; *~spier*, neck-muscle.
nek'tar, nectar.
nek: *~vel*, scruff of the neck; *iem. aan die ~vel vat*, take someone by the scruff of his neck; *~vere*, hackle (of fowls); *~vrot*, neck-rot (in onions); *~werwel*, cervical vertebra.
nel, (-e), nine of trumps; manille (cards).
nematisied', (-e), ..i'de, (-s), nematicide; *~toediening*, nematicide application.
nemato'de, (-s), nematode, round worm.
nematologie', nematology.
nematoloog', nematologist.
ne'mer, (-s), taker; capturer; payee.
Ne'mesis, Nemesis, retribution.
ne'ming, taking.
ne'-ne, (-s), ne-ne *(Nesochen sandvicensis)*.
nê'ne, (-s), nanny.
nen'ta, nenta shrub *(Cotyledon)*.
neofiet', (-e), neophyte.
neogeen', neogene.
ne'oklassiek, (-e), neo-classical.
neologie', neology.
neologis'me, (-s), neologism, new-coined word.
neoloog', (..loë), neologist.
ne'on, neon; *~buis*, neon tube; *~lig*, (-te), neon light; *~verligting*, neon lighting.
nepotis'me, nepotism.
Neptu'nus, Neptune.
nê'rens, nowhere; *~ voor DEUG nie*, serve no earthly purpose; *~ voor OMGEE nie*, care for nothing.
nerf, (-s) (nerwe), outer skin, cuticle; nervature, nervure, grain (leather); *FYN (dun) van ~*, very sensitive, thin-skinned; *die ~ het GESKEEL, OP die ~ na*, within an ace of; very sensitive; thin-skinned; (w) (ge-), peel off the outer skin, grain; *~-af*, abraded; with cuticle gone; *~kant*, hair-side; *~skeel: dit was so ~skeel*, it was touch and go.
neri'na, (-s), nerina, nerine.
ne'ring, (-e, -s), trade, occupation, custom; *~doende*, (-s), shopkeeper, tradesman; *~loos*, (..lose), without a trade.
Ne'ro: *'n regte ~*, a Nero.
ners, anus, arse; *~derm*, rectum; *~dermklier*, rectal gland.
nerts, (-e), mink; *~mantel*, mink coat.
nerveus', (-e), nervous; *~heid*, nervousness.
nervositeit', nervousness.

nerwatuur', nervature, nervure, venation.
nes¹, (s) (-te), nest; nidus (insect); eyrie (of bird of prey); haunt, hole (of fox; of a place); hotbed (of crime); litter (of pups); *jou eie ~ BEVUIL (vuil maak)*, foul one's own nest; *hulle SKOP al ~*, they are thinking of getting married; (w) **(ge-)**, (make a) nest.
nes², (bw) as soon as; whenever; just as; just like; *~ hy AANKOM*, as soon as he arrives; *~ sy PA lyk*, look exactly like his father.
nes: ~ **bouery**, nidification; ~ **dons**, nest-down; ~ **eier**, nest-egg; *hulle het al 'n mooi ~eier*, they have a nice nest-egg; ~ **kassie**, nest-box; ~ **kuiken**, nestling; ~ **sie**, little nest; pigeon hole; nidulus; ~ **sitters**, nidicolae; ~ **skop**, **(-ge-)**, make a nest; prepare a home (for marriage); settle down.
nes'tel, (ge-), settle; nestle, snuggle.
nes'tor, Nestor, father; doyen.
nes: ~ **vere**, first feathers, down; ~ **voël**, nestling.
net¹, (s) (-te), net; rack (in railway carriage); parcel-net (in motor-car); network (of railways); *in iem. se ~ VAL*, fall into someone's snare; *agter die ~ VIS*, come too late, come a day after the fair.
net², (s): *'n stuk in die ~ skrywe*, make a fair copy of a document.
net³, (b) (-ter, -ste), neat, fair, clean; *see* **netjies**.
net⁴, (bw) just, only; alone; exactly; accurately; *ek het hom ~ AANGERAAK*, I only touched him; *~ EEN*, only one; *~ GENOEG*, just enough; *dis ~ IETS vir hom*, it is just like him; it will suit him to a T; *hy kan daar ~ IN*, it just fits him; *~ soos hy hier KOM*, whenever he comes here; *hy is ~ KWAAD*, he is really angry; *dit is ~ SESUUR*, it is just six (o'clock); *~ SOOS hy kom*, the minute he arrives; *~ VIR lede*, members only.
net: ~ **agtig**, **(-e)**, retiform; ~ **bal**, netball; ~ **breuk**, omental hernia, omentocele.
ne'tel, (-s), nettle; ~ **bos**, nettle bush, nettles.
ne'tel: ~ **doek**, muslin; cheese-cloth, book muslin; ~ **doeks**, **(-e)**, muslin.
ne'telhaar, stinging hair.
ne'telig, **(-e)**, knotty (problem); critical, thorny; ticklish (situation); tricky; delicate; ~ **heid**, critical state, thorniness.
ne'telroos, nettle-rash, urticaria.
net'heid, tidiness, neatness, precision.
n'etjie, **(-s)**, small n.
net'jies, (b) (-e), neat, spruce, tidy, prim, clean, dapper; becoming; correct; well-groomed; dinky, trim; (bw) neatly, nicely; properly, respectably; prettily; *alles KEURIG en ~ agterlaat*, leave everything nice and tidy; *dis NIE ~ om met jou mes te eet nie*, it is bad form to put a knife into your mouth.
net: ~ **katoen**, net-cotton; ~ **maag**, reticulum; honeycomb.
net'maker, net-maker; ~ **y**, **(-e)**, fishing-net factory.
net'nerwig, **(-e)**, reticulated.
net-net', just; in the nick of time; *iets ~ BYKOM*, only just be able to reach something; *~ die trein HAAL*, catch the train at the last minute.
net'nou, net'noumaar(tjies), just now, presently, before long, in a moment, anon; *ek KOM ~*, I'll be there in a moment; *hy WAS ~ nog hier*, a minute ago he was still here.
net: ~ **paal**, net-pole (post); ~ **papier**, mesh paper; ~ **skêr**, torpedo scissors.
net'skrif, fair copy; fair-copy book.
net'to, net; *~ GEWIG*, net weight; *~ OPBRENGS*, net proceeds; *~ WINS*, net profit.
net: ~ **vet**, caul, omentum; ~ **vlegnaald**, netting-needle; ~ **vler'kig**, **(-e)**, lace-winged, neuropterous.
net'vlies, retina; ~ **loslating**, detachment of retina; ~ **ontsteking**, retinitis; ~ **pigment**, retinal pigment.
net'vormig, **(-e)**, reticulate, net-like; *~e are*, net-veined.
net'vorming, reticulation.
net'werk¹, network, meshwork, netting; gridiron; plexus; *'n ~ van leuens*, a tissue of lies.
net'werk², neat copy.
neuk, (geselst.), **(ge-)**, hit, whack, thrash, trounce; bother, trouble, annoy; *MOENIE met my ~ nie*,

don't pester me; *NOU ~ dit*, now we're in for trouble; ~ **ery**, botheration, annoyance, nuisance.
neul, **(ge-)**, grumble, bother, pester, nag; be troublesome, grizzle, maunder, trouble, annoy; ~ **erig**, **(-e)**, grumbling, troublesome, annoying; ~ **ery**, nagging; grumbling, bother; ~ **kous**, grumbler, bore, troublesome fellow, nagger.
neuralgie', neuralgia; ..**ral'gies**, **(-e)**, neuralgic.
neurastenie', neurasthenia; ..**te'nies**, **(-e)**, neurasthenic.
neuraste'nikus, **(-se**, ..**nici)**, neurasthenic.
neu'rie, **(ge-)**, hum, croon; ~ **sanger**, crooner, hummer; ~ **toon**, croon.
neuri'ties, **(-e)**, neuritic.
neuri'tis, neuritis.
neu'rochirurg, neurosurgeon; ~ **ie**, neurosurgery.
neurologie', neurology; ..**lo'gies**, **(-e)**, neorological; ..**loog'**, neurologist.
neu'ron, **(-e)**, neuron, nerve.
neuropaat', (..**pate**), neuropath.
neuropa'ties, **(-e)**, neuropathic.
neuro'se, neurosis.
neuro'ties, **(-e)**, neurotic.
neuro'tikus, **(-se**, ..**tici)**, neurotic.
neus, (s) **(-e)**, nose; beak; nozzle (hose); point, cape, shoulder (of mountain); toe-cap (shoe); prow (ship); proboscis; *agter jou ~ AANLOOP*, follow one's nose; *hy sit met sy ~ in die BOEKE*, have one's nose in one's books; *met sy ~ in die BOTTER val*, strike oil; be very fortunate; *eers ~, dan BRIL*, grown-ups first; *'n fyn ~ HÊ vir*, have a flair (keen scent) for; *jou ~ oral INSTEEK*, poke one's nose into everything; *iets in die ~ KRY*, get wind of something; *op sy ~ staan en KYK*, be embarrassed (disappointed); feel a fool; *LANGS die ~ weg iets sê*, pass a shy remark; *nie verder sien as jou ~ LANK is nie*, not see further than one's nose; *onder sy ~ LÊ*, lie under his very nose; *iem. aan die ~ LEI*, lead a person by the nose; *sy ~ LOOP*, he is running at the nose; *met die ~ in die LUG loop*, walk with one's nose in the air; *sy ~ daarvoor OPTREK*, sneer at a thing; turn up one's nose at something; *deur die ~ PRAAT*, speak through one's nose; *die ~ie v.d. SALM*, a delicacy; a titbit; *wie sy ~ sny, SKEND sy aangesig*, he who cuts off his nose spites his face; *~ UITSNUIT*, blow the nose; *teen jou ~ VASKYK*, wear blinkers; not to see further than one's nose; *dis sy ~ VERBY*, *dis ~ ie VERBY*, he has missed the boat; *jou ~ VERBYPRAAT*, let something slip; *tussen ~ en VINGER verdwyn*, take French leave; *VLAK voor sy ~*, under his very nose; *iets voor iem. se ~ WEGNEEM*, take something from under a person's very nose; *iem. iets onder die ~ VRYWE*, cast something in someone's teeth; rub it in; *jou ~ in die WIND steek*, have a haughty air; (w) **(ge-)**, nose; *in 'n boek ~*, glance at a book.
neus: ~ **aap**, nose-monkey; ~ **arts**, nose (and throat) specialist; ~ **bad**, nasal douche; ~ **been**, cartilage of the nose; ~ **beer**, coati; ~ **bloeding**, bleeding of the nose; epitaxis; ~ **brug**, bridge of nose; ~ **dokter**, *see* **neusarts;** ~ **duikvlug**, nosedive; ~ **gang**, nasal tract; ~ **gat**, **(-e)**, nostril; ~ **geluid**, nasal sound (twang); ~ **geswel**, nasal tumour; ~ **hare**, hair in the nostril, vibrissa; ~ **heelkunde**, rhinology; ~ **holte**, nasal cavity; ~ **horing**, rhinoceros; ~ **horingvoël**, hornbill; ~ **ie**, **(-s)**, little nose; ~ *ie en oorslag*, hasp and staple; ~ **instekerig**, **(-e)**, meddlesome; ~ **katar**, nasal catarrh; ~, **keel- en oor'arts**, nose, ear and throat surgeon; ~ **klank**, nasal sound; ~ **knyper**, barnacles (horse); nose-ring; pince-nez; ~ **lengte**, nose length; ~ **letter**, nasal (letter); ~ **loop**, rhinorrhoea; ~ **lys**, cyma recta; ~ **mangel**, **(-s)**, adenoid; ~ **optrekkerig**, **(-e)**, offish, disdainful; ~ **plankie**, nose-board; ~ **poliep**, polypus (tumour) of the nose; ~ **punt**, nasal peak; ~ **riem**, musrol(e), noseband; ~ **ring**, nose-ring, cattle-leader; ~ **skild**, nose-guard, nasal guard; ~ **slymvlies**, mucous membrane; ~ **spieël**, rhinoscope; ~ **spuit**, atomizer, nasal syringe; ~ **ster**, gab-string; ~ **stuk**, nose-piece; ~ **verband**, nasal attachments; ~ **verkoue**, snivels, cold in the nose; coryza; ~ **verstopping**,

snuffles; ~ **vleuel**, wing of the nose; ~ **warmmaker**, (-s), nosewarmer, pipe with a short stem; ~ **wortel**, root of nose; ~ **wys**, conceited, cocky; ~ **wysheid**, conceit, cockiness.

neut, (-e), nut; nutmeg; die (arch.); *nie om DOWE ~ e iets doen nie*, do something for a particular reason; *'n HARDE ~ om te kraak*, a tough nut to crack; ~ **agtig**, (-e), nutty; ~ **boom**, nutmeg-tree; ~ **edop**, nutshell; cockle-boat; *in 'n ~ dop*, in a nutshell; ~ **ekoek**, nut cake; ~ **hout**, hickory; ~ **kool**, nut-coal; nuts; ~ **kraker**, (-s), nutcracker; ~ **kraker= werking**, nutcracker action; ~ **muskaat'**, nutmeg; ~ **olie**, nut-oil; ~ **plukker**, nutter.

neutraal', (**neutrale**), neutral; bland; ~ *BLY*, remain neutral; *..trale DIEET*, bland diet; *'n ..trale HOUDING aanneem*, adopt a neutral attitude.

neutralisa'sie, neutralization.

neutraliseer', (ge-), neutralize.

neutraliteit', neutrality; ~ **s'reg**, right of neutrality.

neutri'no, neutrino.

neu'tron, (-e), neutron.

neut: ~ **skraper**, nutmeg-grater; ~ **vars**, quite fresh; sweet as a nut.

newcas'tlesiekte, Newcastle disease.

ne'we: ~ **artikel**, side line; ~ **as**, minor axis; ~ **bedoel= ing**, ulterior motive; ~ **bedryf**, auxiliary business, subsidiary industry; ~ **-effek**, side-effect; ~ **gaande** = **newensgaande**; ~ **geskik**, (-te) = **neweskikkend**; ~ **hoek**, adjacent angle; ~ **krater**, lateral crater.

ne'wel, (-s), mist, fog haze, brume; ~ **agtig**, (-e), mis= ty, foggy; aeriform; nebulous; ~ **agtigheid**, hazi= ness, nebulosity, mistiness, nebulousness, foggi= ness; ~ **hank**, fog-bank; ~ **beeld**, airy vision, phantom, mirage; ~ **ig**, (-e), misty, foggy, hazy; ~ **kern**, fog nucleus; ~ **kring**, coma (of comet); burr (round moon); ~ **laag**, layer of fog; ~ **sirene**, fog-horn; ~ **ster**, nebulous star, nebula; ~ **streek**, mist belt; ~ **teorie**, nebular theory; ~ **vlek**, nebulous spot, nebula; ~ **wolk**, fog, cloud.

ne'wens, next to; besides; ~ **gaande**, accompanying, enclosed.

ne'we: ~ **persoon**, minor character (novel); ~ **produk**, by-product; ~ **skikkend**, (-e), co-ordinate; ~ **skik= king**, co-ordination, parataxis, parathesis; ~ **ver= trek**, side-room; ~ **vraagstuk**, side issue.

Nicara'gua, Nicaragua; ~ **an'**, (..**guane**), Nicara= guan; ~ **ans'**, (-e), Nicaraguan.

nie, not; *bespreek of dit AL of ~ raadsaam is ~*, dis= cuss the advisability or otherwise; ~ *EERS dit ~*, not even this; ~ *so GOED ~*, not too well (good); ~ *MEER as die begin ~*, no more than the begin= ning; *dis ~ SO ~*, that is not so; ~ *SY ~*, not she at all; ~ **-aflewering**, non-delivery; ~ **-Afrikaans= sprekend**, (-e), non-Afrikaans-speaking; ~ **-alkoho= lies**, (-e), non-alcoholic, soft (drink); ~ **-amptelik**, (-e), unofficial; ~ **-bedleend**, (-e), ambulant; ~ **-be= dwelmend**, (-e), non-intoxicant; ~ **belasbaar**, non-taxable; ~ **-belasbare inkomste**, non-taxable in= come; ~ **-beskikbaar**, (..**bare**), not available; ~ **-bestaan**, non-existence; ~ **-bestaande**, non-exist= ent; ~ **-betaling**, non-payment; ~ **-Blanke**, Non-White; ~ **-brandstigtend**, (-e), non-incendiary; ~ **-bytend**, (-e), non-corrosive; ~ **-dragtig**, empty (cow); ~ **-elektries**, (-e), non-electric; ~ **-Europees**, (..**pese**), non-European; ~ **gebruiker**, non-user; ~ **-geestelik**, (-e), lay; ~ **-geleier**, non-conductor; ~ **-gelowige**, non-believer, agnostic; ~ **-intekenaar**, non-subscriber; ~ **-inwonersbelang**, non-residents' interest; ~ **-lewering**, non-delivery; ~ **-lid**, non-member; ~ **-lonend**, (-e), unremunerative; ~ **-mag= neties**, (-e), non-magnetic.

nie'mand, nobody, none, no one; ~ *ANDERS as*, none other than; ~ *minder AS ...*, no less a person than ..; ~ *MEER?* no further offer? ~ **sland**, no-man's-land.

nie'mendal, nothing at all, absolutely nothing.

nie'-metaal, non-metal.

nie'-nakoming, non-fulfilment, non-observance; *die ~ van voorskrifte*, the non-observance of regu= lations.

nie'-ontplofbaar, (..**bare**), non-explosive; *..bare stof*, non-explosive.

nie'-ontvanklik, (-e), inadmissible.

nie'-ontvlambaar, (..**bare**), non-inflammable.

nie'-openbaar, (..**bare**), non-public.

nie'-oordragbaar, (..**bare**), not transferable.

nie'-oorlogvoerend, (-e), non-belligerent.

nie'-pensioendraend, (-e), non-pensionable.

nier, (-e), kidney; *wandelende ~*, floating kidney; ~ **aandoening**, kidney disease (trouble); ~ **bekken**, pelvis; ~ **bekkenontsteking**, pyelitis; ~ **beskrywing**, nephrology; ~ **boontjie**, kidney bean; ~ **dialise**, kidney dialysis; ~ **dialisemasjien**, kidney dialysis machine; ~ **erts**, kidney ore; ~ **hou**, kidney-punch; ~ **knyper**, home-made Boer saddle; ~ **koliek**, renal colic; ~ **kwaal**, kidney disease, nephritis; ~ **lyer**, nephritic sufferer; ~ **middel**, nephritic.

nie'-roker, non-smoker.

nier: ~ **ontsteking**, nephritis; ~ **operasie**, nephro= tomy; ~ **pille**, kidney pills; ~ **pyn**, nephritis; ~ **siekte**, renal (nephritic) disease; ~ **steen**, jade, nephrolith; renal calculus, stone in the kidney; ~ **stuk**, loin, sirloin; ~ **tjie**, (-s), (small) kidney; ~ **tjiesop**, kidney soup; ~ **tjiesaal**, *see* **nierknyper**; ~ **vet**, kidney suet; ~ **vormig**, (-e), kidney-shaped, reniform.

nies, (s) (-e), sneeze; sternutation; (w) (ge-), sneeze; ~ **bui**, attack of sneezing; ~ **erig**, (-e), sneezy; ~ **ery**, sneezing; ~ **gas**, sneeze-gas; ~ **hout**, sneeze-wood; ~ **kruid**, hellebore; Christmas rose; ~ **mid= del**, sternutative, sneezing-powder, snuff; ~ **poeier**, sneezing-powder.

niet, nothing, nought; nothingness, (-e), blank (in lot= tery); *ALLES is tot ~*, all is lost (gone); *te ~ DOEN*, nullify; *te ~ GAAN*, perish, be lost; cease to exist; become void, lapse; fall to pieces; *as ~ kom tot IET, ken iet sigselwe niet*, set a beggar on horseback and he'll ride at a gallop to the devil; *tot ~ MAAK*, do away with; *alles is TOT ~*, every-thing is lost; *twee ~ e TREK*, draw two blanks; *tot ~ VERKLAAR*, declare null and void; *in die ~ VERSINK*, sink into nothingness (oblivion).

nie'teenstaande, (vgw) notwithstanding; although; ~ *hy so hard gewerk het*, although he worked so hard; (vs) in spite of, despite; ~ *al sy pogings*, in spite of all his efforts.

nie'teling, (-e), nonentity.

nie'temin, none the less, nevertheless.

nie'tig, (-e), insignificant, futile, paltry, trifling, petty, null, negligible, minute, frivolous; cheap; nugatory, void; potty; pimping; ~ *MAAK*, render void, invalidate; ~ *VERKLAAR*, nullify, declare null and void; ~ **heid**, insignificance, nothingness, nullity, trifle, pettiness, paltriness; ~ **heid van huwelik**, nullity of marriage; ~ **verklaring**, nullifi= cation, annulment, defeasance; setting aside (judg= ment).

niets'beduidend, (-e), insignificant.

nie'-tussenkoms, non-interference.

Nieu-Bruns'wyk, New Brunswick.

Nieu' Engels, modern English.

nieu'gebore, new-born.

Nieu'-Hoogduits, modern High German.

nieu'ligter, (ong.), modernist; ~ **y**, modernism.

nieumo'dies, (-e), new-fashioned, modern, stylish.

Nieu'-Nederlands, modern Dutch.

Nieu-See'land, New Zealand; ~ **er**, New Zealander; ~ **s**, (-e), New Zealand.

nieu'silwer, German silver, F.P.N.S.

Nieu'-Testamenties, (-e), New Testament.

Nieu'-Testamentikus, (-se, ..**tici**), New Testament scholar (authority).

nicu'vorming, new formation, neologism.

nie'-verhandelbaar, (..**bare**), not negotiable.

nie'-verskyner, defaulter.

nie'-verskyning, non-appearance.

nie'-verwant, (-e), unrelated.

nie'-vlugtig, (-e), non-volatile, fixed.

nie'-voeging, non-joinder.

nie'-vretend, (-e), non-corrosive.

nie'wers, nowhere.

nie-winsge'wend, non-profitable; unprofitable; ~ *e dienste*, non-profitable services.

nie'-ysterhoudend, (-e), non-ferrous.

nig, (-te), niece, (female) cousin; ~ *Maria*, cousin Mary.
Nige'rië, Nigeria; ~**r**, (-s), Nigerian.
Nige'ries, (-e), Nigerian.
nig'gie, (-s) = **nig**.
nigromansie', necromancy, black art.
ni'hil, nil; ~ **is'**, (-te), nihilist; ~ **is'me**, nihilism; ~ **is'ties**, (-e), nihilistic.
nik'kel, nickel; ~ **iet'**, niccolite; ~ **kies**, nickel pyrites; ~ **legering**, nickel alloy; ~ **munt**, nickel coin; ~ **silwer**, nickel silver; ~ **spons**, spongy nickel; ~ **staal**, nickel steel, invar.
nik'ker, (-s), imp, fiend, nix; ~ **bol**, niggerball; ~ **pop**, golliwog.
nikotien', **nikoti'ne**, nicotine; ~ **vergiftiging**, nicotine poisoning, nicotinism.
niks, nothing; *DIS* ~ *!* that's nothing! never mind! it doesn't matter; *daar sal* ~ *van KOM nie*, nothing will come of it; ~ *vir* ~ *en baie MIN vir 'n sikspens*, nothing for nothing, and very little for a halfpenny; *dis* ~ *MOOI nie*, it isn't pretty at all; ~ *anders te doen staan as* . . ., have no option but to . . .; *dis* ~ *as SPOG nie*, it's mere boasting; *vir* ~ *SPEEL nie*, play for love; *dit het op* ~ *UITGELOOP (uitgedraai) nie*, it came to nought; *dit maak* ~ *(g'n) VERSKIL nie*, it makes no difference at all; *nie VIR* ~ *nie*, to some purpose; *jy WEET* ~ *nie*, you know nothing; ~ **beduidend**, (-e), good-for-nothing; insignificant; worthless; futile, nugatory; ~ **beduidendheid**, worthlessness, insignificance; flimsiness; ~ **betekenend**, (-e), insignificant; valueless, flimsy; ~ **doen**, idleness; *salige* ~ *doen*, dolce far niente; ~ **doende**, idle; ~ **doener**, (-s), idler, loafer; ~ **doenery**, idling, loafing.
ni'kse, (-s), nixie, female watersprite.
niks: ~ **gewend'**, (-e), unrefined, boorish; ~ **nut**, (te), ~ **nuts**, (-e), good-for-nothing, rotter; ~ **nut'sig**, (-e), good-for-nothing, worthless; ~ **seggend**, (-e), meaningless; expressionless; non-committal; ~ **vermoedend**, (-e), unaware, unsuspecting, aware of nothing; ~ **werd**, worth nothing, worthless, futile.
nim'bus, (-se), nimbus, halo.
nimf, (-e), nymph; ~ **agtig**, (-e), nymphlike.
nimfolep'sie, nympholepsy.
nimfomanie', nymphomania.
nim'lik, (-e), identical, very same; *die* ~ *e hy*, the very man.
nim'mer, never; *so* ~ *as te NOOIT*, never at all; ~ *of NOU*, now or never; ~ **meer**, never again, nevermore; ~ **sat**, wood stork.
nim'rod, (-s), Nimrod, great hunter.
ni'non, ninon.
nip, (s) (-pe), nip; (w) (ge-), sip (liqueur).
nip'pel, (-s), nipple; adaptor (bomb); ~ **draad**, thread of nipple; ~ **sleutel**, spoke-key.
nip'pertjie: *op die* ~, in the very nick of time, touch-and-go.
Nip'pon, Nippon: ~ **'ies**, (-e), Nipponese.
nirwa'na, nirvana.
nis, (-se), niche, recess.
ni'si, order, rule; *bevel* ~, decree (order) nisi.
nitraat', (nitrate), nitrate.
nitreer', (ge-), nitrate, nitrify.
nitre'ring, nitration.
nitrifise'ring, nitrification.
nitrogeen', nitrogen.
ni'trogelatien, **ni'trogelatine**, nitro-gelatine.
ni'trogliserien, **ni'trogliserine**, nitro-glycerine.
ni'trosellulose, nitro-cellulose.
niveau', (-s), level, plane.
nivelleer', (ge-), level; take a level; ~ **der**, (dumpy) level; ~ **skroef**, levelling-screw; ~ **stelsel**, levelling system; ~ **werktuig**, levelling-instrument.
nivelle'ring, levelling.
nja'la, (-s), nyala (antelope) *(Tragelaphus angasii)*; ~ **bul**, nyala bull; ~ **ooi**, nyala ewe.
No'ag, Noah; *dit was saam met* ~ *in die ARK*, it is as old as the hills; it is antediluvian; *van* ~ *se SAP gedrink*, have been at the bottle; **n**~**- en veteraanmotors**, vintage and veteran cars; **n**~**model**, vintage car.
no'bel, (-e), noble; ~ **heid**, nobility.

Nobel'prys, Nobel prize.
nodaal', (nodale), nodal.
no'de, reluctantly; *iets* ~ *DOEN*, do something reluctantly; *van* ~ *HÊ*, need; ~ **loos**, (. . lose), needless, unnecessary, gratuitous; ~ **loosheid**, needlessness.
no'dig, (-e), necessary, required, requisite, wanted; *as jy dit* ~ *AG*, if you think (deem) it necessary; *DIE* ~ *e*, what is necessary; *met die* ~ *e EERBEWYSE*, with all due honour; ~ *HÊ*, be in want of, need; *dit* ~ *MAAK*, necessitate; *met die* ~ *e SORG*, with proper care; ~ *WEES*, be necessary; ~ **heid**, need, necessity.
no'dus, (-se), node.
noe'del, (-s), noodle.
noem, (s): *net by die* ~ *van die NAAM*, at the mere mention of the name; **(ge-)**, call, name, mention, denominate, dub; *FEITE* ~, state facts; *ek* ~ *sy NAAM nooit*, I never mention his name; *haar op haar NAAM* ~, address her by name; ~ **baar** (. . bare), mentionable; nameable.
noemenswaar'dig, (-e), worth mentioning, important; *niks* ~ *s nie*, nothing to speak of.
noe'mer, (-s), denominator.
noem'naam, name by which one is known.
noem-noem', num-num *(Carissa arduina)*.
noen, noon; ~ **maal**, lunch(eon); *die* ~ *maal gebruik by*, have lunch with; ~ **stel**, luncheon set.
noes'te, diligent, industrious, unwearying; *sy* ~ *vlyt*, his unflagging industry.
noest'heid, diligence, laboriousness, indefatigability.
nòg: (vgw): ~ . . .~, neither . . . nor; ~ *A* ~ *B*, neither A nor B.
nog¹, (bw) now; *tot* ~ *toe*, up till now.
nog², (b, bw), still, again; further; as yet; *AL is hy* ~ *so goed*, be he ever so good; ~ *'n BIETJIE*, some more; ~ *DRIE jaar gelede*, as recently as (only) three years ago; ~ *EENS*, once more, again; ~ *IETS?* anything else? ~ *'n KEER*, once more; ~ *10 KISSIES bestel*, order a further 10 boxes, order 10 more cases; ~ *'n MAAL soveel*, as much again; *toe hy* ~ *MAAR 'n kind was*, when he was a mere child; ~ *'n MAN*, another man; ~ *NIE*, not yet; *OF* ~ *beter*, or better still; ~ *TE meer omdat*, the more so because; *is daar* ~ *TEE?* is there any tea left? ~ *TEN minste 5 jaar*, for at least 5 years more; *ek moet dit* ~ *VANDAG hê*, I must have it this very day; *ek begin VANDAG* ~, I start this very day; ~ *VOORDAT hy praat*, even before he spoke; ~ *'n bietjie VROEG*, still rather early; *hy sal* ~ *WEL kom*, he is sure to turn up yet.
no'ga, nougat.
nog: ~ **al**, rather, quite, fairly; ~ *al mooi*, rather pretty; ~ **maals**, once more; ~ **tans**, however, yet, nevertheless, even so.
nôi, (-ens) = **nooi**, (s).
nôi'ens: ~ **boom**, umbrella-tree; ~ **haar**, maidenhair (fern); ~ **lok**, love-lies-bleeding; ~ **uil**, Cape barn-owl; ~ **van**, maiden name.
nôi'entjie, (-s) = **nooientjie**.
nok, (-ke), ridge, top (of roof); cam; gab; ~ **as**, cam-shaft; ~ **asbus**, cam-bush; ~ **balk**, hip rafter, roof-tree, ridge purlin; ~ **kas**, cam-box; ~ **paal**, ridge-pole; ~ **pan**, ridge tile; ~ **skyf**, cam-disc; ~ **sleutel**, jaw-spanner; ~ **spar**, hip purlin; ~ **spil**, cam-spindle; ~ **trommel**, cam-drum.
noktur'ne, (-s), nocturne.
no'lens vo'lens, willy-nilly, nolens volens.
noma'de, (-s), nomad; ~ **volk**, nomad tribe.
noma'dies, (-e), nomadic.
nomenklatuur', (. . ture), nomenclature.
nominaal', (. . nale), nominal.
nominalis', (-te), nominalist; ~ **me**, nominalism.
nomina'sie, (-s), nomination; ~ **dag**, nomination day; ~ **vergadering**, nomination meeting.
nominatief', (. . tiewe), nominative.
nomineer', (ge-), nominate.
nom'mer, (s) (-s), number; copy, issue (of paper); event (sports); size (shoe); item (of programme); impression; *DINK aan* ~ *een*, have an eye on the main chance; *op iem. se* ~ *DRUK*, give someone a reminder; give someone a nudge; ~ *EEN*, first;

number one; top (of class); *die klere is* ~ *PAS*, the clothes fit to a T; *iem. op sy* ~ *SIT*, rebuke a person; put someone in his place; *'n* ~ *VRA*, put through a call; (w) (ge-), number; ~**bord**, throw-indicator; number board; ~**ing**, numbering; ~**plaat**, number-plate; ~**reeks**, series of numbers; ~**skyf**, dial (telephone); ~**stempel**, numbering stamp.
non, (-ne), nun; ~**agtig**, (-e), nunnish, nunlike.
non-aktief', (..tiewe), not in active service; transferred to the supernumerary list; inactive.
non-aktiwiteit', state of being unattached (mil.); non-activity; *op* ~, not in active service; place on the unattached (supernumerary) list; not in use.
non-alkoho'lies, (-e), non-alcoholic.
nonchalan'ce, nonchalance.
nonchalant', (-e), nonchalant.
no'ne, (-s), none; ninth (music).
nonentiteit', (-e), nonentity; pigmy (fig.).
non-interven'sie, non-intervention.
no'nius, (-se), vernier (scale); nonius.
non-kombattant', (-e), non-combatant.
nonkonformis', (-te), nonconformist; ~**me**, nonconformism; ~**ties**, (-e), nonconformist.
nonkonformiteit', nonconformity.
non'na, (vero.), (-s), young mistress, miss(ie).
non'ne: ~**kleed**, nun's dress; ~**klooster**, nunnery, convent; ~**koor**, nuns' choir; ~**orde**, order of nuns; ~**sluier**, nun's veil; ~**tjie**, (-s), little nun; ~**tjie-eend**, white-faced duck; ~**tjieuil**, barn-owl.
non'nie, (-s), *see* **nonna**.
non-sekta'ries, (-e), unsectarian, undenominational.
non'sens, **non'sies**, nonsense.
nood, need, distress, want, necessity, destitution; famine; exigence, exigency; danger; emergency; pinch; push; ~ *leer BID*, necessity is the mother of invention; *van die* ~ *'n DEUG maak*, make a virtue of necessity; *deur die* ~ *GEDWING*, compelled by necessity; *daar is GEEN* ~ *nie*, there is no hurry; *in GEVAL van* ~, in case of emergency; *iem. uit die* ~ *HELP*, help someone in need; *die* ~ *is HOOG*, there is great distress; *as die* ~ *die HOOGSTE is, is die uitkoms die naaste*, the darkest hour is just before dawn; *IN* ~, in great peril; *sy* ~ *KLA*, unbosom oneself; unburden one's mind; *LELIK in die* ~, very much troubled; in great anxiety; *as die* ~ *aan die MAN kom*, when the worst comes to the worst; *in die UITERSTE* ~, in a dire emergency; *in die* ~ *leer 'n mens jou VRIENDE ken*, a friend in need is a friend indeed; ~ *breek WET*, necessity knows no law; ~**adres**, address in case of need (emergency); ~**anker**, spare anchor; sheet-anchor; ~**band**, spare tyre; ~**berig**, distress communication; ~**brug**, temporary bridge; ~**deur**, emergency (escape) door, fire-escape; ~**doop**, lay baptism; ~**drang**, urgent need, compulsion.
nood'druf, want, distress, destitution; provisions; ~**'tig**, (-e), needy, destitute, indigent; ~**'tigheid**, indigence, destitution, neediness.
nood: ~**dryfvlak**, hydrovane; ~**dwang**, compulsion; acute distress; ~**gedwonge**, perforce, from sheer necessity; ~**geld**, emergency money; ~**geroep**, ~**geskreeu**, cry (cries) of distress, shout for help; ~**geval**, emergency; ~**hawe**, port of distress; ~**helper**, emergency man; ~**helpers**, breakdown gang.
nood'hulp, first aid; emergency man; makeshift; ~**fonds**, emergency fund; ~**kissie**, first-aid box; ~**liga**, first-aid league; ~**man**, first-aider; first-aid member; ~**toerusting**, first-aid outfit; ~**voertuig**, emergency transport.
nood: ~**jaar**, year of distress; ~**kennis**, working knowledge; ~**ketting**, chain-check (coupling); side chain; safety (auxiliary) chain; ~**klok**, alarm-bell; ~**koppeling**, emergency coupling; ~**kreet**, cry of distress; ~**landing**, emergency (forced) landing; ~**leer**, emergency (accommodation, escape) ladder; ~**lenigend**, (-e), ameliorative; ~**leniging**, relief of distress; ~**lening**, emergency loan; ~**leningsfonds**, relief fund; ~**leuen**, white lie.
nood'lot, fate, destiny, doom, fatality, kismet; ~**swanger**, fateful.

noodlot'tig, (-e), fatal (accident); ill-fated, disastrous (decision); fated, fateful; ~**heid**, fatality.
nood: ~**lughawe**, emergency airport; ~**luik**, escape-hatch.
noodly'dend, (-e), destitute, indigent, necessitous, distressed; *die* ~*es*, those in distress.
nood: ~**maatreëls**, emergency measures; ~**mars**, forced march; ~**mas**, jury-mast; ~**oproep**, distress call; ~**ploeg**, emergency squad; ~**rantsoen**, emergency (iron) rations; ~**regulasies**, emergency regulations; ~**rem**, safety (emergency) brake; communication cord; ~**remhouer**, safety-guard; ~**ring**, ferrule; ~**roep**, distress call; ~**roer**, jury-rudder.
nood'saak, (s) need, necessity; *SONDER* ~, unnecessarily; *UIT* ~, from necessity; (w) (ge-), compel, necessitate; oblige; *iem. tot 'n stap* ~, force someone to take a step.
noodsaak'lik, (b) (-e), necessary, essential, imperative, needful; prerequisite; *gebiedend* ~, imperative, essential; (bw) necessarily, of necessity; very urgently; ~**erwys(e)**, of necessity, perforce; ~**heid**, necessity, need(fulness), urgency.
nood: ~**sein**, signal of distress, SOS; ~**skag**, escape-shaft; ~**skakelaar**, emergency switch; ~**skoot**, distress-gun, signal-gun; ~**skop**, fly-kick; ~**sloot**, flood-ditch; ~**stok**, niblick; ~**stuk**, bird-caging (railw.); ~**tenk**, emergency tank; ~**toestand**, state of emergency; ~**trap**, fire-escape; emergency stair(s); ~**uitgang**, emergency exit; ~**verband**, first-aid bandage; ~**verpleging**, emergency nursing; ~**vlag**, flag of distress; ~**voor**, storm water ditch; ~**voorraad**, emergency stock; stockpile; reserve; ~**wal**, emergency embankment; ~**weer**, stormy weather; self-defence (law); *uit* ~ *weer optree*, act in self-defence; ~**weg**, road of necessity.
noodwen'dig, (-e), necessary; inevitable, ultimate; fatal; (bw) inevitably; ~**heid**, necessity, inevitability.
noodwet, emergency act; ~**wiel**, spare wheel; ~**woning**, emergency dwelling.
nooi[1], (s) (-ens), mistress; young lady, girl, miss, maiden; sweetheart; *sy* ~ *is JONK dood*, the love of his life died young; *'n* ~ *STOMPOOR sny*, lay claim to a girl; *sy WAS 'n* ~ *Brink*, her maiden name was Brink.
nooi[2], (w) (ge-), invite; bid; *hy laat hom nooit* ~ *nie*, he does not wait to be asked (invited).
nooi'ens: ~**boom**, umbrella-tree *(Cussonia thyrsiflora)*; ~**borsie**, variety of pear; ~**lok**, love-lies-bleeding (plant); ~**perske**, variety of peach; ~**uil**, barn-owl; ~**van**, maiden name.
nooi'entjie, (-s), girl, lass(ie), young lady; sweetheart.
nooit, never; *dis* ~ *ANDERS nie*, that must be the reason; *so* ~ *AS te nimmer!* never! ~ *is te LANK*, never is too long; ~ *OFTE nimmer!* never!
noop, (ge-), urge, compel; *ge*~ *voel om*, feel obliged to.
Noor, (Nore), Norwegian.
noord, north; ~ *VAN*, north of; *die WIND is* ~, the wind is north.
Noord: ~**-Afrika**, North Africa; ~**-Amerika**, North America; ~**-Amerikaner**, North American; ~**-Duitsland**, North Germany.
noor'de, north; *TEN* ~ *van*, to the north of; *na die* ~ *VERTREK*, leave for the north; ~**kant**, north (side); ~**lik**, (-e), northern, northerly; ~*lik van*, north of.
noor'der: ~**breedte**, north latitude; ~**deklinasie**, northing; N~**halfrond**, Northern Hemisphere, N~**keerkring**, Tropic of Cancer; N~**land**, Norland; ~**lig**, aurora borealis; pole light; ~**ling**, hyperborean; northerner; ~**meting**, northing; ~**son**: *met die* ~*son vertrek*, take French leave; slip away.
Noord'-Europa, Northern Europe.
noor'dewind, north wind.
noord'grens, northern border.
noor(d)'kapper, (-s), common (Greenland) whale; grampus.
noord: ~**kus**, north coast; ~**lyn**, north line; ~**oos**, north-east; ~**oos'passaat**, north-east tradewind.

noordoos'te, north-east; ~**lik, (-e),** north-easterly, north-eastern; ~**wind,** north-east wind.
Noord-pool, North Pole; ~**gebied,** ~**lande,** Arctic regions; ~**reisiger,** Polar (Arctic) explorer; ~**sirkel,** northern (Arctic) circle; ~**streke,** Arctic regions; ~**tog,** Arctic expedition; ~**vaarder,** Arctic navigator.
noord'punt, north(ern) point.
Noord'see, North Sea.
noord: N~ster, North star, pole-star, lodestar; ~**sy,** north side; ~**waarts, (-e),** northward(s); ~**wes',** north-west.
noordwes'te, north-west; ~**lik, (-e),** north-westerly, north-western; *die N~like Deurvaart,* the North-West Passage; ~**r,** ~**wind,** north-west wind.
noor'kapper, *see* **noor(d)kapper.**
Noor'man, (-ne), Norman, Norseman.
Noors¹, (b) (-e), Norwegian, Norse.
noors², (s) (-e), species of *Euphorbia.*
noors³, (b) (-e), surly, cross, ill-tempered.
noors'doring = noors².
noors'heid, surliness, ill-temper.
Noor'weë, Norway; ..**weegs', (-e),** Norwegian; ~**r, (-s),** Norwegian.
noot, (note), note; *AGTSTE ~,* quaver; *HALWE ~,* minim; *HELE ~,* semibreve; *'n te HOË ~,* too high a note; *werk dat jy die KROMME note haal,* work oneself to a standstill; *iem. slaan dat die KROMME note hom haal,* give someone a thrashing; *jy is 'n ou ~ in die PSALM,* you must always shove in your oar; *'n ~ in die PSALM hê,* have something to say; *baie note op sy SANG hê,* have much to say; *'n ~ laer SING,* change one's tune; climb down; *SESTIENDE ~,* semiquaver; *TWEE-EN-DERTIGSTE ~,* demisemiquaver; *VIERDE ~,* crotchet; *'n rek soos 'n VOORSLAGRIEMPIE,* stretch a note out interminably; ~**vas, (-te),** able to sing in tune.
nop, (-pe), nap; pile, burl; *die ~ van 'n setperk,* the nap of a green (golf).
no'pal, nopal (plant).
no'pens, with regard to, regarding, concerning, anent.
nop'pies: *in sy ~,* highly delighted; as pleased as Punch.
Nor'dies, (-e), Nordic.
noriet', norite.
nori'ties, (-e), noritic.
norm, (-e), rule, standard, norm.
normaal', (..male), normal; *BO die normale,* above normal; *normale DRUK,* normal pressure; ~**afwyking,** aberration; ~**profiel,** geological column, columnar section; ~**draad,** standard wire gauge; ~**inrigting,** ~**skool,** normal (training) college; ~**spoor,** standard gauge; ~**weg,** normally.
normalisa'sie, normalization.
normaliseer', (ge-), regulate, normalize.
normalise'ring, regulation, normalization.
normaliteit', normality.
norma'liter, normally.
Norman'dië, Normandy; ~**r, (-s),** Norman; ..**dies, (-e),** Norman.
normatief', (..tiewe), normative.
nor'ra, (-s), nape, nucha.
nor'ring, crowd, mob, swarm; *'n ~ van mense,* an enormous crowd.
nors, (-e), surly, crusty, gruff, cantankerous, morose, peevish, grumpy, harsh, crabbed, cross, dour, grim-faced; ~**erig, (-e),** gruffish, grumpy; ~**heid,** grimness, gruffness, peevishness, surliness, crustiness, crabbedness.
no'sem, (-s), ducktail, Teddy boy.
no'sie, (-s), notion, idea.
nosografie', nosography.
nosologie', nosology; ..**lo'gies, (-e),** nosological.
nosologis', (-te), nosologist.
nosonomie', nosonomy.
nosotaksie', nosotaxy.
nostalgie', nostalgia; ..**tal'gies, (-e),** nostalgic.
no'ta, (-s), note; account; ~ *BENE,* nota bene, please note; *goeie ~ NEEM van,* take due note of.
nota'bel, (-e), notable, prominent; ~**e, (-s),** leading resident, notability.

no'taboekie, notebook, jotter.
notariaat', notaryship.
notarieel', (..riële), notarial.
nota'ris, (-se), notary; ~**amp,** notary's profession; ~**kantoor,** notary's office; ~**klerk,** notary's clerk; ~**skap** notaryship.
nota'sie, (-s), notation.
no'tawisseling, exchange of notes.
no'te, *see* **noot;** ~**balk,** staff, stave; ~**beurs,** notecase, wallet; ~**dop,** (vero.), nutshell; cockle-shell, cockleboat; *in 'n ~ dop,* in a nutshell, briefly.
noteer', (ge-), jot down; book, note down; quote (prices).
no'tepapier, music-paper.
note'ring, (-e, -s), taking down; quoting, quotation (on Stock Exchange).
no'teskrif, staff notation.
notifika'sie, (-s), notification.
noti'sie, notice; **(-s),** note, jotting; ~ *neem van,* take notice of; ~**boek,** notice-book, pocket-book.
notu'le, no'tule, minutes; *die ~ LEES en goedkeur,* read and confirm the minutes; *in die ~ AANTEKEN (opneem),* enter in the minutes; ~**boek,** minute-book.
notuleer', (ge-), record, minute, take down (proposal, minutes).
notu'lehouer, recorder, minuting secretary.
notule'ring, minuting.
nou¹, (s) narrows, strait(s); *in die ~ BRING (jaag),* drive into a tight corner; *in die ~ WEES,* be in a fix.
nou², (b, bw) ([-e]; -er, -ste), narrow (bridge); tight (clothes); cramped; *die KLERE is te ~,* the clothes are too tight; ~ *VERWANT,* closely related.
nou³, (bw) now, at present; ~ *AL,* now, already; ~ *die DAG,* a few days ago; ~ *en DAN,* now and then; ~ *EERS,* only now; ~ *GOED,* very well; ~ *NET,* a minute ago; ~ *NOG,* even now; ~ *of NOOIT,* now or never; *TOT ~ toe,* until now, hitherto; *VAN ~ af,* from this moment.
nou⁴, (tw) well; ~, *HOE dink jy?* well, what do you think? ~ *JA,* well? ~ *TOE ~!* well I never!
nou'dat, now that.
nou'erig, (-e), rather narrow.
nou'geset, (-te), conscientious, careful, precise, painstaking; accurate; narrow-minded; ~**heid,** conscientiousness; exactitude, preciseness; narrow-mindedness.
nou'heid, narrowness, tightness.
noukeu'rig, (b) (-e), exact, accurate, minute, definite, correct, elaborate, precise, careful; close; (bw) exactly, accurately, precisely; duly; closely; ~**heid,** accuracy, exactness, justness, exactitude, precision, preciseness; closeness; nicety.
noulet'tend, (-e), watchful, scrupulous, strict, attentive; ~**heid,** scrupulousness, strictness, exactness, close attention.
nou'liks, scarcely, hardly, barely.
nou'-nou, just now, in a moment, presently; *ek KOM ~,* I'll be there in a minute; *sy WAS ~ nog hier,* a moment ago she was still here.
nou'passend, (-e), tight-fitting.
nou'pypbroek, stove-pipe trousers.
nousien'de, particular, fastidious.
nousiend'heid, fastidiousness.
nou'sluitend, (-e), close-fitting, tight, tight-fitting; ~*e rok,* tight dress, close-fitting dress.
nou'strop: ~ *trek,* be hard pressed, feel the pinch.
nou'te, (-s), narrowness; narrow pass; *in die ~,* in a tight corner.
no'va, (-s), nova, new star.
novel'le, (-s), short novel, novelette; ~**bundel,** volume of short novels.
novellis', (-te), writer of novelettes; novelist.
Novem'ber, November; ~**peer,** November pear.
noviet', (-e), freshman; novice.
novi'se, (-s), novice.
novisiaat', noviciate.
nuan'se, (-s), shade of colour, tint, nuance.
nuanseer', (ge-), give a delicate shade of difference, nuance, shade.

nuanse'ring, (-e, -s), shading, shade-effect, fine shades.
Nu'bië, Nubia; ~ **r, (-s),** Nubian; ..**bies, (-e),** Nubian.
nudis', (-te), nudist; ~ **me,** nudism, skinny dipping; ~ **ties, (-e),** nudist.
nuditeit', nudity.
nuf'fie, (-s), conceited girl; prude.
nuf'fig, (-e), conceited; prudish.
nug'ter, ([-e]; -e; -der, -ste), sober (not drunk); sober-minded, matter-of-fact, clear-headed; hard-headed; *'n SAAK* ~ *beskou,* examine a matter calmly (dispassionately); ~ *WAKKER,* wide awake; ~ *WEET,* goodness knows; ~ **derm,** jejunum; ~ **heid,** soberness, sobriety.
nuk, (-ke), freak, whim, caprice, mood, fancy; ~ **kebol, (-le),** crusty fellow, curmudgeon, cross-patch.
nuk'kerig, (-e), moody, capricious, angry, whimsical, freakish; ~ **heid,** moodiness, peevishness.
nuk'kie, (-s), rest (billiards).
nukleaat', (nukleate), nucleate.
nukleêr', (-e), nuclear.
nu'kleon, (-e), nucleon.
nukleool', (nukleole), nucleolus.
nu'kleus, (nukleï, -se), nucleus.
nul, (-le), nil, zero, nought; cipher, blob, blank; duck (cricket); scratch (golf); love (tennis); pip-squeak, nonentity; nothing; *van* ~ *en GENER waarde,* utterly useless; null and void; *hy is maar 'n GROOT* ~ , he is a nonentity; *in die JAAR* ~ , in the year dot; never; on the Greek calends; *'n* ~ *op 'n KONTRAK (rekwes),* not worth a straw; *hy WEET dat* ~ ~ *is,* he knows a thing or two; ~ **las,** no-load; ~ **lltelt', (-e),** nullity; nonentity; ~ **lyn,** zero line, datum line; ~ **man,** scratch man; ~ **meridiaan,** prime meridian; ~ **merk,** scratch mark; ~ **opgawe,** nil return; ~ **passer,** spring-bows; ~ **pot,** love game; ~ **punt,** zero, freezing-point; ~ **spel,** pointless draw; ~ **speler,** scratch player; ~ **stand,** neutral (gear); ~ **stel,** love set (tennis); ~ **streep,** zero mark.
numereer', (ge-), number.
Nu'meri, Numbers.
numeriek', (-e), numerical(ly).
Numi'dië, Numidia; ~ **r, (-s),** Numidian; ..**dies, (-e),** Numidian.
numismatiek', numismatics.
numisma'ties, (-e), numismatic.
numisma'tikus, (-se, ..tici), numismatist.
numismatografie', numismatography.
numismatologie', numismatology.
num'mer, (ong.), *see* **nommer.**
nunsiatuur', nunciature.
nun'tius, (-se), nuncio, papal legate.
nurks, (vero.) (-e), peevish, pettish, grumpish; ~ **heid,** grumpiness.
nu'sie, (-s), small news-item.
nut, use, benefit, avail; usefulness, utility, profit, advantage; *is dit van ENIGE* ~ ? is this any good? *van GEEN* ~ *nie,* of no use; *iets tot* ~ *MAAK, iets ten* - *te MAAK,* put to good use, make the most of; ~ *OPLEWER,* serve a useful purpose; *TEN* ~ *te van,* for the benefit of; *TOT* ~ *van,* to the advantage of; ~ *TREK uit,* derive profit from; *VAN* ~ *wees,* be serviceable, serve a useful purpose, be useful.
nuta'sie, nutation.
nu'terig, (-e), somewhat new.
nuts: ~ **bedryf,** public utility; ~ **man,** handyman.
nut'teloos, (..lose), useless, vain, fruitless, inutile; profitless; ~ **heid,** uselessness, futility, inutility.
nut'tig¹, (w) (ge-), partake (of a meal), eat, take (food).
nut'tig² (s): *eers die* ~ *e, dan die aangename,* business before pleasure; **(b, bw) (-e),** handy, useful, advantageous; helpful, available; conducible, serviceable, profitable; ~ *e ARBEID,* effective work; ~ *e BELASTING,* payload; *jou GELD* ~ *bestee,* spend your money profitably; ~ *e INLIGTING,* useful information; ~ *e VRAG,* payload, useful load; ~ **heid,** utility, usefulness; ~ **heidsgraad,** efficiency; ~ **heidsfaktor,** mechanical advantage; ~ **heidskoëffisiënt,** mechanical advantage; ~ **heidskromme,** efficiency-curve; ~ **heidsleer,** utilitarianism, doctrine of utility; ~ **heidsoogpunt,** utilitarian viewpoint; ~ **ing,** partaking (of meal); eating; drinking.
nuus, news, tidings, intelligence, *die* ~ *van die DAG,* the news of the day; *GEEN* ~ , *goeie* ~ , no news is good news; *die JONGSTE* ~ , the latest intelligence; *dis OU* ~ , I've heard that before; that is stale news; it's ancient history; ~ **aanbringer,** informant; bringer of news, intelligencer; ~ **agent,** press agent; ~ **agentskap,** news-agency; ~ **berig,** news-item; ~ **blad, (** ~ **blaaie),** newspaper, gazette; ~ **brief,** newsletter; ~ **draer,** tell-tale, gossip, news-monger; quidnunc; *hy is 'n* ~ *draer,* he is a tell-tale; ~ **draery,** gossip; ~ **film,** newsreel; ~ **honger,** newshunger.
nuuskie'rig, (-e), curious, inquisitive; prying; ~ *e agie,* inquisitive person, quidnunc, Paul Pry; ~ **heid,** inquisitiveness, curiosity.
nuus: ~ **kommentator,** news commentator; ~ **konferensie,** news conference; ~ **leser,** newscaster, news reader; ~ **man,** journalist; ~ **redakteur,** news editor; ~ **(rol)prent,** news-reel; ~ **uitsending,** news broadcast; ~ **verspreier,** newsmonger; ~ **waarde,** news value; ~ **waar'dig, (-e),** newsworthy; ~ **waar'digheid,** newsworthiness.
nuut, (nuwe; nuwer, -ste), new, recent, novel; further, additional (supplies); renewed (hope); modern (language); *DIE* ~ *ste op die gebied van,* the last word in; *in die nuwe JAAR,* in the new year; *nuwe KAAS,* green (new) cheese; *daar is niks* ~ *s onder die SON nie,* there is nothing new under the sun, *nuwe STAAT,* mint condition (of book); *die Nuwe TESTAMENT,* the New Testament; *VAN* ~ *s af,* anew, from the beginning again; *nuwe WOL,* virgin wool; ~ **heid,** newness, novelty; recency; ~ **jie, (-s),** piece of news; something new; ~ **ste,** latest; ~ **wording** neogenesis.
Nuwejaar', New Year.
Nuwejaars': ~ **appel,** apple ripening early in January; ~ **dag,** New-Year's day; ~ **(dag)aand,** New-Year's eve; ~ **fees,** New Year celebration; ~ **geskenk,** New-Year's gift; ~ **present,** New-Year's present; han(d)sel; ~ **voël,** black-crested cuckoo *(Melanophus serratus);* ~ **voorneme,** New Year resolution; ~ **wens,** New-Year's wish.
Nu'weland, Newlands.
nu'weling, (-e), novice, newcomer, greenhorn, fresher; intrant; apprentice, beginner, neophyte, griff(in), colt, greener; recruit; ~ **stoespraak,** maiden speech.
nu'wemaan, new moon.
nu'werig, (-e), rather new, fairly new; ~ **heid,** newishness.
nuwerwets', (-e), modern, new-fangled; neoteric; up-to-date; ~ **heid,** modernity, modernness.
nu'wesiekte, strangles (horse-disease).
nu'wigheid, (..hede), novelty; innovation.
nyd, envy, jealousy.
ny'dig, (-e), angry; jealous; vicious, despiteful; ~ *WEES op iem.,* detest (hate) someone; ~ *WORD,* fly into a rage; ~ **heid,** anger; jealousy.
nyg, (ge-), bow, bend, incline (the head); ~ **ing, (-e, -s),** bow, curtsy, dip (of head).
Nyl, Nile.
ny'lon, (-s), nylon; ~ **kouse,** nylon stockings.
Nyl: ~ **reier,** sacred ibis; ~ **streekbewoner,** Nilot.
Ny'megen, Nimwegen, Nimeguen.
ny'pend, (-e), grinding; nipping, biting; pressing, urgent; ~ *e KOUE,* piercing cold; *in* ~ *e NOOD,* in time of great distress; ~ *e tekort aan VOEDSEL,* acute shortage of food.
ny'wer, (-e), industrious, diligent; ~ **aar, (-s),** manufacturer, producer, industrialist; entrepreneur.
ny'werheid, (..hede), industry.
ny'werheids: ~ **dermatitis,** industrial dermatitis; ~ **diamant,** industrial diamond; ~ **gebied,** industrial area; domain of industry.
ny'werheidskool, industrial school.
ny'werheids: ~ **raad,** industrial council; ~ **raadgewer,** industrial consultant; ~ **tentoonstelling,** industrial exhibition (show); ~ **wese,** industrialism; industry.

o, (-'s), o.
o, O, oh, ah; ~ *HEDE!* oh my! ~ *SO!* aha! ~ *liewe TYD!* O dear me!
oa'se, (-s), oasis.
Obad'ja, Obadiah.
obelisk', (-e), obelisk, needle.
o'-bene, bandy legs.
o'bi, (-'s), obi.
ob'iit, (L), obiit (he/she has died).
o'biter dic'tum, incidental remark, obiter dictum.
objek', (-te), object; ~ **glas,** slide; ~ **lens,** object glass; ~**sie, (-s),** objection; ~**teer', (ge-),** object; ~**tief',** (s) (..**tiewe**), focussing-lens; (b) (..**tiewe**), objective, detached.
objektiveer', (ge-), objectify.
objektive'ring, objectivation.
objektiwiteit', objectivity, objectiveness.
oblaat', (oblate), host, consecrated wafer; oblate.
oblie'tjie, (-s), (rolled) wafer; ~**pan,** ~**yster,** wafer-iron.
obligaat', (..gate), obligato (music).
obliga'sie, (-s), debenture (obligation), bond; ~**beleggingspolis,** bond-investment policy; ~**houer,** debenture holder, bondholder; obligee; ~**lening,** debenture loan; ~**rente,** interest on debentures (bonds); ~**-uitgifte,** issue of debentures (bonds).
obligato'ries, (-e), obligatory.
obool', (obole), obol (ancient Greek coin).
obsedeer', (ge-), obsess; *ge*~ *deur*, obsessed by.
obseen', (obsene), obscene, repulsive, filthy.
obseniteit', obscenity, repulsiveness, filthiness.
observa'sie, (-s), observation; ~**pos,** observation-post.
observa'tor, (-e, -s), observer.
observato'rium, (..ria, -s), observatory.
observeer', (ge-), observe, keep, adhere to; perceive, watch.
obses'sie, (-s), obsession; *dis 'n* ~ , it is an obsession.
obsidiaan', obsidian.
obskurant', (-e), obscurantist; ~**is'me,** obscurantism.
obskuriteit', obscurity, indistinctness; humbleness.
obskuur', (obskure; -der, -ste), obscure, indistinct; unknown to fame, humble.
obsoleet', (..lete), obsolete, disused, discarded.
obstetrie', obstetrics, midwifery.
obste'tries, (-e), obstetric(al).
obste'trikus, (-se, ..trici), obstetrician.
obstinaat', (..nate), obstinate, stubborn; ~**heid,** obstinacy, stubbornness.
obstipa'sie, constipation.
obstruk'sie, (-s), obstruction, hindering; ~ *voer*, practise obstruction; ~**voerder, (-s),** obstructionist.
obstruksionis', (-te), obstructionist; ~**me,** obstructionism (talking to waste time esp. in Parliament).
odalisk', (-e), odalisque.
o'de, (-s), ode; ~**digter, (-s),** maker of odes, odist.
ode'on, (-s), odeon.
odeur', (-e), scent, odour; ~**flessie,** scent-bottle.
o'dium, hatred, odium.
o'dometer, odome'ter, (-s), speedometer, hadometer.
Odysse'a, Odyssee', Odyssey (of Homer).
o'ë: ~**bank,** eye-bank; ~**dienaar,** eye-servant; flatterer; ~**diens,** time serving; flattery.
oef! ugh!
oe'fen, (ge-), exercise, practise, train, drill, coach; *invloed op iem.* ~ , exercise influence on someone; ~**aar,** lay preacher; ~**bal,** practice-ball; ~**berig,** training-message; ~**bof,** practice tee (golf); ~**bom,** practice-bomb; ~**granaat,** practice-shell; ~**ing, (-e),** exercise, practice, training; discipline; ~*ing baar KUNS,* ~*ing maak die MEESTER*, practice makes perfect; ~**ingboek,** exercise book; ~**kamp,** training-camp; ~**kryt,** training ring; ~**maat,** sparring partner; ~**meester,** coach; ~**skip,** training-ship; ~**skool,** training-school; ~**skrif,** exercise book; ~**spring,** practice-jump; ~**terrein,** training-ground; ~**tyd,** time for practising; ~**veld,** practice-ground; ~**vlug,** practice-flight.
Oegan'da, Uganda.

oeka'se, (-s), ukase (Russian ordinance).
Oekraï'ne, Ukraine.
oela'ma, (-s), oelema', (-'s), ulema.
oemaram'ba, (-s), dry watercourse.
oemfaan', (-s), umfaan.
o'ënskou: *in* ~ *neem*, inspect, examine, look at, survey.
oënskyn'lik, (b) **(-e),** apparent, ostensible; (bw) apparently, seemingly, on the face of it; professedly; ~**heid,** ostensibility.
oe'pasboom, upas (-tree).
oer¹, ore.
oer-², primitive, primordial, primeval.
Oe'ralgebergte, Ural Mountains.
oer'bos, *see* **oerwoud**.
oer'christelik, (b), **(-e),** early Christian; proto-Christian; primitive Christian.
oer'dier, protozoon.
oer'dom, dunderheaded.
Oer'germaans, (-e), Proto-Germanic.
oer: ~**gesteente,** primitive rock; ~**inwoners,** aborigines; ~**mens,** first (primeval) man; protoplast; ~**os,** aurochs; *Amerikaanse* ~*os*, bison; ~**oud, (..oue),** primeval, primitive; ~*oue kwessie*, age-old question; ~**sel,** primordial cell; ~**slymdiertjie,** protozoon; ~**sted, (-s),** oersted; ~**taal,** original language; protolanguage; ~**teks,** original text; ~**tipe,** archetype, prototype; ~**tyd,** primeval (prehistoric) times; ~**volk,** primeval race; ~**woud,** virgin forest; primeval forest; jungle.
oes¹, (s) (-te), harvest, crop; gathering, reaping; output; (w) **(ge-),** harvest, reap, gather, crop; produce; *'n teenstander* ~ , beat an opponent.
oes², (b) bad, feeble, off-colour, seedy, out of sorts; *'n* ~ *AFFÊRE*, a feeble affair; *'n* ~ *VENT*, a seedy fellow; ~ VOEL, feel indisposed; ~**dorsmasjien,** ~**dorster,** combine; ~**erig, (-e),** rather bad, feeble; indisposed.
oes: ~**fees,** harvest (home) festival; ~**lied,** harvest song; ~**masjien,** harvester; ~**skatting,** crop estimates, estimate of yield.
oes'ter¹, (-s), harvester, reaper.
oes'ter², (-s), oyster, bivalve; ~**bank,** oyster-bank; layer; planting-ground; ~**bed,** oyster-bed; ~**eter,** ostreophagist; ~**kweker,** oyster-culturist; ~**kwekery,** oyster-culture; ~**mandjie,** oyster-basket; ~**mes,** oyster-knife; ~**park,** oyster-preserve; ~**pastei,** oyster-patty; ~**plant,** oyster-bank; ~**skuit,** oyster-boat; ~**skulp,** oyster shell; ~**teelt,** oyster-culture; ostreiculture; ~**vanger,** oyster-catcher; ~**vergiftiging,** oyster-poisoning; ~**visser,** oyster-fisher; ~**vissery,** oyster-fishery.
oes: ~**tery,** reaping, harvesting; ~**tyd,** harvest time, reaping-time; ~**volk,** harvesters, reapers.
o'ë: ~**toets,** sight-test; ~**troos,** eye-bright, euphrasy (plant); poor consolation.
oeuv're, oeuvre, works.
o'ëverblindery, hallucination, pretence, optic delusion, make-believe, ruse, blind.
oe'wer, (-s), shore (of sea); river-bank; ~**bewoner,** riparian, riverain; ~**eienaar,** riparian owner; ~**einde,** shore end (of bridge); ~**grond,** riparian land; ~**ondersteuning,** abutment; ~**regte,** riparian rights.
of, or; but; if, whether; either; *'n stuk* ~ *DRIE*, about three; *ons het GESELS* ~ *ons ou vriende was*, we chatted as if we were old friends; *òf JY òf ek*, either you or I; *ek KAN daar nie aan dink nie* ~ *ek moet lag*, I cannot think about it without laughing; *dit was nie te LANK nie* ~ , it was not long before; *MIN* ~ *meer*, more or less; *NIEM.* ~ *hy weet dit*, no one but he knows it; *ek weet nie* ~ *dit WAAR is nie*, I don't know whether it is true.
offensief', (s) (..siewe), offensive, push; (b) **(..siewe),** offensive, aggressive; ~ *optree*, take the offensive.
of'fer, (s) (-s), sacrifice, offering, oblation, immolation; victim; *ten* ~ *BRING*, sacrifice; *die* ~ *van sy DRIFTE*, the victim of his passions; (w) **(ge-),** devote, sacrifice, offer, immolate; ~**aar,** offerer, sacrificer, immolator; ~**altaar,** sacrificial altar;

~ande, (-s), offering, sacrifice, oblation, immolation; **~bus,** poor-box, alms-box; **~diens,** sacrificial service; **~dier,** victim, sacrificial animal; **~fees,** sacrificial feast; **~gawe,** oblation; offering; **~gebed,** offertory; **~ing, (-e, -s),** offering; **~kelk,** sacrificial cup; **~kleed,** sacrificial dress; **~lam,** sacrificial lamb; **~maal,** sacrificial banquet; **~mes,** sacrificial knife; **~pannetjie,** patella; **~plegtigheid,** sacrificial ceremony; **~plek,** place of sacrifice; **~skaal,** collection plate; votive bowl; offertory plate; **~stokkie,** joss-stick.

offer'te, (-s), offer, tender.

offervaar'dig, (-e), willing to sacrifice; generous, open-handed, charitable; **~heid,** willingness to make sacrifices; generosity, liberality.

offi'sie, office, function (R.C.).

offisieel', (..siële), official.

offisier', (-e, -s), (military or naval) officer; **~-geneeskundige,** military surgeon.

offisiers': **~aanstelling,** commission (in the army or navy); **~eksamen,** officers' examination; **~klub,** officers' club; **~kwartier,** officers' quarters; **~lys,** navy list; **~menasie,** officers' mess; **~pos,** commission; **~rang,** rank of officer.

offisier'skap, commission.

offisiers': **~tafel,** officers' mess; **~vrou,** officer's wife.

offisier'vlieënier, flight officer.

offisieus', (ong.), (-e), officious; obliging; semi-official.

offreer', (ong.), (ge-), offer.

ofiologie', ophiology (study of snakes).

ofskoon', although, though.

oftalmie', ophthalmia; **..tal'mies,** ophthalmic.

oftalmoskoop', (..skope), ophthalmoscope.

of'te: *nooit* **~** *NIMMER*, never, on no condition; *REËN* **~** *nie, ek gaan*, whether it rains or not, I'm going; **~** *WEL*, or.

og! oh! alas! **~** *kom*, oh come! you don't mean to say so! indeed!

og'gend, (-e), morning; **~blad,** morning paper; **~diens,** morning service; **~drankie,** morning draught; **~ete,** morning meal, breakfast; **~gebed,** morning prayer; **~godsdiens,** morning prayers; **~japon,** morning gown; **~mark,** morning market; **~parade,** stand-to; **~resepsie,** levee; **~rok,** morning dress; **~siekte,** morning sickness; **~sinjaal,** reveille; **~stond,** dawn, morning hour; **~vertoning,** morning performance.

o'gie, (-s), little eye; bud (tree); eyelet (potato); *'n ~ op iem. HÊ*, pay attentions to someone; be sweet on someone; *~s MAAK*, wink, give the glad eye, cast a sheep's eye at; *'n ~ in die SEIL hou*, keep one's weather-eye open.

ogief', (ogiewe), ogive.

o giesdraad, wire netting.

ogivaal', (..vale), ogival.

oglokraat', (..krate), ochlocrat.

oglokrasie', ochlocracy.

Og'poe, Ogpu.

ohm, (-s), ohm; **~meter,** ohm meter.

oho'! aha!

oï'dium, oidium (vine-disease).

ojief', (ojiewe), ogee; cyma; *OMGEKEERDE* **~**, cyma reversa; *REGTE* **~**, cyma recta; **~boog,** ogee-arch; **~skaaf,** ogee-plane.

oka'pi, (-'s), okapi *(Okapia johnstoni).*

okari'na, (-s), ocarina.

o'ker, ochre, red clay; **~agtig, (-e),** ochreous; **~geel,** ochreous yellow; **~kleurig, (-e),** ochreous.

okka'sie, (-s), occasion.

okkerneut', walnut; **~boom,** walnut-tree; **~hout,** walnut.

okkludeer', (ge-), occlude.

okklu'sie, (-s), occlusion; **~f', (..siewe),** occlusive.

okkult', (-e), occult; **~is', (-te),** occultist; **~is'me,** occultism.

okkupa'sie, (-s), occupation; **~reg,** right of occupation.

okkupeer', (ge-), occupy.

oksaal', (oksale), choir loft.

oksaal'suur, oxalic acid.

ok'sel, (-s), armpit; axil, axilla; **~blaar,** axillary leaf; **~holte,** armpit; **~slagaar,** axillary artery; **~stuk,** gusset.

oks'hoof, (-de), hogshead, large wine-vat.

ok'si-asetileen', oxy-acetylene.

oksida'sie, oxidation.

oksi'de, (-s), oksied', (-e), oxide.

oksideer', (ge-), oxidize; **~middel,** oxidizing agent; **~vlam,** oxidizing flame.

oksigeen', oxygen.

oksigeneer', (ge-), oxygenate; **..gene'ring,** oxygenation.

oksimo'ron, (-s), oxymoron.

oktaaf', (oktawe), octave; **~fluit,** octave flute, piccolo.

oktaan', octane; **~waarde,** octane number.

oktaë'der, (-s), octahedron.

oktaë'dries, (-e), octahedral.

oktant', (-e), octant.

okta'vo, (-'s), octavo (8vo); **~formaat,** octavo (size).

Okto'ber, October; **~maand,** month of October.

oktogoon', (..gone), octagon.

ok'topus, (-se), octopus.

oktrooi', (-e), charter; patent; privilege, octroi; **~brief,** letters patent, charter; **~eer', (ge-),** charter, patent; **~houer,** patentee.

okula'sie, inoculation, grafting, budding.

okuleer', (ge-), bud, inoculate; **~hout,** budwood; **~mes,** budding-knife.

okulêr', (s) (-e), eyepiece; ocular; (b) (-e), ocular.

okulë ring, budding.

okulis', (-te), oculist, eye-specialist.

olan'na, (-s), big bug; master.

olean'der, (-s), oleander.

olel': *jy GEE my die* **~** , you irritate me beyond measure; you make me sick; *die* **~** *KRY*, a fit (fig.).

oleografie', oleography.

o'leometer, oleome'ter, (-s), oleometer.

o'lie, (s) (-s), oil; grease; **~** *op die VUUR gooi*, add fuel to the fire; **~** *op die WATER gooi*, pour oil on troubled waters, **~** *in die WONDE giet*, pour balm on the wounds; (w) **(ge-),** oil, lubricate; *ge~ wees*, be well oiled; **~aanwyser,** oil-gauge; **~agtigheid,** oiliness; **~baadjie,** oil-coat; **~bad,** oilbath; **~bak,** sump (motor-car); **~bestand, (-e),** oilproof; **~bol,** doughnut; **~boom,** castor-oil plant *(Ricinus);* **~boortoring,** oil-drilling rig (platform); **~boot,** oilsteamer, oiltanker, oiler; **~brandbom,** oil canister (type of incendiary bomb); **~bron,** oil well; **~dig, (-te),** oilproof; **~druk,** oil pressure; **~drukrem,** oil brake; **~-en-asyn'stel,** cruet-stand; **-fabriek,** oil factory; **~fakkel,** oil flare; **~filter,** oil-filter; **~gas,** oil gas; **~gat,** oil hole, oil way; **~gehalte,** oil content; **~handel,** oil trade; **~handelaar,** oil dealer; **~houdend, (-e),** containing oil, oil-bearing; **~jan,** oilskin, **~kannetjie,** oil can; oil container; preen gland, uropygial gland (birds); **~kantas,** oil-can case; **~kleed,** waxcloth, oilskin (material); **~kleedjie,** oilskin cover; **~klere,** oilskins; **~klip,** oilstone/oilshale; **~koek,** doughnut; **~koeke,** good-for-nothing, nincompoop; **~koker,** oil-container (bottle); **~kol,** oil stain; **~kolonie,** (geselst.), eau-de-cologne; **~konka,** oildrum; **~kop,** oilcup, lubricator; **~kraan,** oilcock; **~kruik,** oil jar; **~laag,** film of oil; **~lamp,** oil lamp; **~leiding,** oil feed; **~leiklip,** oilshale; **~maat,** oil measure; **~maatskappy,** oil company; **~man,** greaser; **~masjien,** oil engine; **~meter,** oil gauge; oleometer; **~meul(e),** oil mill.

olien'hout, wild olive *(Olea).*

o'lie: **~pak,** oilskins; **~palm,** oil palm; **~papier,** oil paper; **~peil,** oil level; **~pen,** dipstick; **~pers,** oil press; **~pomp,** oilpump, paraffin-pump; **~pot,** oil box; preen gland (birds); **~pyplyn,** oil pipeline; **~rig, (-e),** oily, greasy; **~ring,** oil ring; doughnut; **~saad,** oilseed; **Oliesaadbeheerraad,** Oilseed Control Board; **~sel,** extreme unction (R.C.); **~skalie,** oilshale; **~smaak,** oily taste; **~smering,** lubrication; **~soektog,** search for oil, oil search; **~spuitbron,** gush; **~spuit(jie),** oil squirt (gun); **~stand,** oil level; **~steen,** oilstone; whetstone; hone; **~stoof,** oil cooking stove; paraffin-stove; **~suiweraar,** oil

filter; ~ **suur**, oleic acid; ~ **tenk**, reservoir; oil tank; ~ **toevoer**, oilfeed; ~ **vanger**, oil trap; ~ **vas, (-te)**, oilproof; ~ **veld**, oil field; ~ **verbruik**, oil consumption.
o'lieverf, oil paint, oil colours; ~ **verfskilder**, oil painter; ~ **skildery**, oil painting.
o'lie: ~ **verstuiwer**, oil-atomizer; ~ **verwarmer**, oil-heater; ~ **vlek**, oil stain; ~ **vlies**, oil film.
olie'wenhout = olienhout.
o'lie: ~ **vonds, (-te)**, oil strike; ~ **wyser**, oil-level indicator.
o'lifant, (-e), elephant; *WIT* ~, white elephant (useless building, article); ~ **agtig, (-e)**, elephantine; ~ **drywer**, mahout; ~ **jag**, elephant hunt; ~ **jagter**, elephant hunter; ~ **jie, (-s)**, little elephant; sphinx-moth; ~ **jong**, mahout; ~ **kalf**, elephant calf; ~ **koei**, elephant cow; ~ **koord**, corduroy, whipcord; ~ **roer**, old-fashioned muzzle-loading gun; ~ **saal**, howdah; ~ **sgras** elephant grass *(Danthonia elephantina)*; Napier grass; ~ **siekte**, elephantiasis; ~ **sklip**, dolomite; ~ **skraper**, ~ **skrop**, bulldozer; ~ **spoot**, Hottentot's-bread *(Testudinaria elephantipes)*; ~ **sriet**, rope-grass; ~ **stand**, ivory; elephant's tusk; ~ **steek**, jumping-stitch; ~ **svel**, elephant's skin.
oligarg', (-e), oligarch; ~ **ie', (-ë, -s)**, oligarchy; ..gar'gies, (-e), oligarchic(al).
oligopolie', oligopoly.
oligopolis', (-te), oligopolist.
Oligoseen', Oligocene.
o'lik, (-e), bad, unwell, seedy, out of sorts; ~ **heid**, indisposition, seediness.
o'lim: *in die dae van* ~, in days of yore.
olimpia'de, olympiad.
Olim'pies, Olympic; ~ *e Spele*, Olympic Games.
Olim'pus, Olympus.
oliveniet', olivenite.
olivien', olivine; peridot; ~ **basalt**, olivine basalt.
olm, (-s, -e), olm'boom, elm (tree).
olyf' (olywe), olive; ~ **agtig, (-e)**, olivaceous.
Olyf'berg, Mount of Olives.
olyf': ~ **boom**, olive-tree; ~ **bos**, olive-grove; ~ **erts**, olivenite; ~ **groen**, olive-green; olivaceous; ~ **kleur**, olive-colour; ~ **kleurig, (-e)**, olive-coloured; olivaceous; ~ **krans**, olive wreath; ~ **olie**, olive-oil; ~ **pers**, olive-press; ~ **tak**, olive-branch; ~ **vormig, (-e)**, olivary, olive-shaped.
om¹, (bw), round; up, over; out; expired; *voor die DAG* ~ *is*, before the end of the day; ~ *EN* ~, over and over, round and round; *die JAAR is* ~, the year is out (is over, has passed); *buite MY* ~, over my head, without consulting me; *my VERLOF is* ~, my leave is up (has expired).
om², (vs) round, at, about; for; *AL* ~ *die tweede dag*, every second day; *BEROEMD* ~, famous for; ~ *die BEURT*, in turn; ~ *en BY vyftig*, about fifty; ~ *die HOEK*, round the corner; ~ *die NEK*, round the neck; ~ *hierdie REDE*, for this reason; *die TYD is* ~, time is up; ~ *die twee UUR*, every two hours; ~ *WERK vra*, ask for work.
om³, (met te) in order to, to; *'n huis* ~ *te HUUR*, a house to let; ~ *KORT te gaan*, briefly, to make a long story short; *mooi* ~ *te SIEN*, beautiful to look at; ~ *die TYD* ~ *te kry*, to pass the time.
om⁴, (vgw), because, as, since, seeing that; ~ *sy my so liefhet, sal ek by haar bly*, because she loves me so much, I shall not leave her.
omarm', (~), embrace, hug; clip; clasp; ~ **ing, (-e, -s)**, embrace, hug.
om'ber¹, ombre.
om'ber², umber (pigment).
om'berkleurig, (-e), umber.
om'berspel, game of ombre.
om'bind, (-ge-), tie round (up), gird, wrap round; fillet; ~ **sel, (-s)**, bandages.
om'blaai, (-ge-), turn over (leaves of a book); ~ *asb.*, please turn over.
om'blaas, (-ge-), blow over, blow down.
om'boor, (-ge-), hem, edge, pipe, border; braid, mull, face (material); purl; purfle; ~ **sel, (-s)**, edging, hemming, bordering; piping, binding, galloon, braid.

om'bou, (-ge-), reconstruct; alter structurally; convert; ~ **ing**, conversion, rebuilding.
om'braak, (-ge-), plough up.
om'bring, (-ge-), pass (time); kill, slay.
om'budsman, ombudsman.
om'buig, ..buie, (-ge-), bend (round, down); turn (up).
om'buitel, (-ge-), tumble down; topple over.
om'dans, (-ge-), overturn (by dancing), upset; pass the time (by dancing).
om'dat, because, since, as, seeing that; ~ *ek oud is, word ek oor die hoof gesien*, because I am old, I am ignored.
om'dool, (-ge-), wander, roam, ramble about; ..**doling, (-e)**, roaming.
om'dop, (-ge-), turn inside out; collapse, faint, fall down; evaginate; evert; ~ **ping**, eversion; evagination; turning inside out.
om'dra, (-ge-), carry about; harbour, entertain (thought, idea).
om'draai, (-ge-), turn round; turn back, reverse; slew; twist, revolve, rotate, circumvolve; wrap in; *JOU* ~, turn round, face about; *iem. die NEK* ~, twist a person's neck (kill someone); *'n SLEUTEL* ~, turn a key; ~ **ing, (-e, -s)**, (circum)rotation, revolution; turn(ing).
om'drentel, (-ge-), lounge about; idle away (the time).
o'mega, ome'ga, (-s), omega.
omelet', (-te), omelet(te).
omfloers', (~), muffle; shroud, envelop, cover; *'n* ~ *te trom*, a muffled drum.
om'gaan, (-ge-), go round; call at; mix with, associate; pass (time); pass through (mind); manage, control; *wat in sy GEMOED* ~, what is passing through his mind; what his feelings are; *om 'n HOEK* ~, turn a corner; *by die HUIS* ~, call at the house; *ek kan nie met KINDERS* ~ *nie*, I cannot get on with children; *met LEUENS* ~, deal in lies; *per* ~ *de POS*, by return of post; *die TYD gaan om*, time passes; *VERTROULIK* ~, be familiar; be on intimate terms.
om'gang, intercourse; association, company; rotation, circuit; gallery, battlement; communication; commerce; *in die* ~ *BEKEND as A*, generally known as A; *GESLAGTELIKE* ~ *hê met*, have sexual intercourse with; *die SWART O* ~, the Black Circuit Court (Assize).
om'gangstaal, colloquial language, vernacular; familiar (informal) language.
om'geboor, (-de), braided, bound.
om'gebuig, (-de), bent, turned down, doubled.
om'gee, (-ge-), care, mind; give round, distribute; reck; *nie* ~ *nie*, not care.
omgeef', (~) = omgewe.
om'gekeerd, (b) (-e), turned upside down, reversed, inverted; inverse (proportion); (bw) inversely, vice versa; conversely, otherwise; contrariwise; ~ *e BEELD*, inverted image; ~ *e BOOG*, inverted arch; *DIE* ~ *e*, the reverse, opposite; *in die* ~ *e GEVAL*, in the opposite case; on the other hand; *in* ~ *e ORDE*, in inverted order; *die* ~ *e van 'n STELLING*, the converse of a proposition; *in* ~ *e VERHOUDING*, in inverse proportion.
om'gekrap, (-te), untidy; unruly; irritable; *'n* ~ *te HUIS*, an untidy home; ~ *SPEEL*, play exceedingly well; *baie* ~ *VOEL oor iets*, feel very upset about a matter; *'n* ~ *te VENT*, a difficult customer.
om'geleë, surrounding, neighbouring.
om'geslaan, (-de, ..geslane), turned over (page); overturned (vehicle); turn-down (collar).
om'gewaai, (-de), overblown; ~ *de hout*, windfall timber.
omge'we, (~), surround, encircle; cover; edge; girth, gird; lap; fence (in); environ; *van gevare* ~, beset with dangers.
om'gewerk, (-te), remade, recast; rewritten; ~ *te botter*, remade butter.
omge'wing, (-s), surroundings, environs, environment, neighbourhood, vicinity, precincts; ambit; setting; *aanpassing by die* ~, adaptation to the environment; ~ **sleer**, study of the environment; environmental studies.

om'giet, (-ge-), circumfuse; recast.
om'gooi, (-ge-), upset, cant(le); bowl over; fling down; throw round (overcoat); toss (pancake); overturn (car); ~ **er**, (-s), tilter.
omgord', (~), cincture, begird, engirdle, gird up; *die lendene* ~, gird up one's loins.
om'gord, (-ge-), bind, buckle.
om'gordel, (~), cincture.
om'graaf, om'grawe, (-ge-), dig (up).
omgrens', (w), (~), bound; limit, circumscribe, confine; (b) **(-de)**, bounded.
om'haal¹, (s) fuss, ado; circumstance; *GROOT* ~ *van woorde*, verbosity, wordiness; *SONDER baie* ~, without much ado.
om'haal², (w) (-ge-), persuade.
om'hang, (-ge-), put on, wrap round (the shoulders), drape; hood.
om'hê, (..gehad), have on (round); wear.
omheen', round about, around; *jy praat daar* ~, you beat about the bush.
omhein', (~), fence in, enclose, hedge in, palisade; ~**ing**, (-s), fence, enclosure, close; hoarding; ~**ingsdraad**, fencing-wire; ~**ingsmateriaal**, fencing material; ~**ingswet**, fencing act.
omhels', (w) (~), embrace, hug, cuddle, (en)clasp; adopt (theory); espouse; embosom; (b) **(-de)**, embraced; ~ **er**, (-s), embracer; ~**ing**, (-e, -s), embrace, hug, cuddle, clasp; espousal; embracement.
omhoog', aloft, on high; upwards; above; ~ *HOU*, hold up; ~ *SPRING*, jump up, leap into the air; ~ *STYG*, ascend, rise.
om'hou, (-ge-), cut down, fell (trees).
omhul', (~), envelop, enwrap, enfold, hood, curtain, lap, enshroud; ~**ling**, (-e, -s), envelopment; ~ **sel**, (-s), cover, envelope, outer covering, husk, casing, capsule, housing; mantle, hull; envelopment; involucre (bot.); *die stoflike* ~ *sel*, the mortal remains.
o'mie, (-s), *verkleinwoord van* **oom**; male adult.
omineus', (ong., lit.), (-e), ominous, inauspicious.
omis'sie, (-s), omission.
om'kantel, (-ge-), fall over, topple over, be upset, capsize, overturn.
om'kap, (-ge-), fell, cut down; pot; faint; seduce, have intercourse with; overcast (dressmaker); ~ **steek**, overcast stitch.
om'keer, (s) sudden change; about-turn, volte-face, reversal, revolution; *'n hele* ~, quite a big change; (w) (-ge-), turn (round, over, upside down, inside out); turn back (running sheep); reverse; subvert; invert; pervert; obvert; *jou sakke* ~, turn out your pockets; ~ **as**, reversing-shaft; ~ **baar**, (..bare), reversible; ~ **beweging**, reversing motion; ~ **hefboom**, reversing-lever; ~ **inrigting**, reversing-gear; ~ **suier**, reversing-piston.
om'kering, (-e, -s), conversion, inversion (order of words); reversal; obversion.
omkip'pelaar, (-s), tippling-gear, tippler.
om'kleding, (-s), change.
omkleed', (~), clothe in; enshroud; *met redene* ~, motivated; armed with a multitude of reasons.
omklem', (~), clench, clasp, grasp (sword); embrace, clip; grapple.
om'klink, (-ge-), rivet; edge (a tool); die; clench; ~ **spyker**, clench, clinching-nail.
omknel', (~), clench, clasp, grip.
om'kom, (-ge-), die, perish; come round, turn; *toe ek die HOEK* ~, when I turned the corner; ~ *van KOUE*, perish with cold.
om'kook, (-ge-), dissuade, divert, win over, cajole; *iem. het hom laat* ~, he has let himself be talked into it.
om'koop, (-ge-), bribe, corrupt, suborn, buy, grease someone's palm; gratify; *'n getuie* ~, bribe a witness.
omkoop'baar, (..bare), venal, corruptible, open to bribery, mercenary; ~**heid**, corruptibility.
om'koopgeld, hush-money, bribe, palm-oil.
om'koper, briber, suborner, corrupter; ~**y**, bribery, corruption, palm-greasing.
om'koping, bribery, corruption, subornation.
omkors', (w) (~), incrustate, (en)crust; (b) **(-te)**, encrusted, encysted; ~ **ting**, (en)crustation.

omkraal', (~), cover with beadwork.
omkra'ling, beading.
omkrans', (~), (en)wreath, (en)garland.
om'krap, (-ge-), throw into disorder, upset, disarrange; litter; *IEM.* ~, vex (irritate) someone; *omgekrap VOEL*, be upset.
om'kristallisasie, recrystallization.
omkristalliseer', (~), recrystallize.
om'kronkel, (-ge-), wind, twirl round.
om'kruip, (-ge-), pass slowly, drag (time); creep round.
om'krul, (-ge-), curl up (round); buckle up.
om'kry, (-ge-), get round; pass (time); fell (tree).
om'kyk, (-ge-), look back, look round; attend to, look after.
omlaag', down below; *NA* ~, down; *VAN* ~, from the bottom; ~**drukker**, depressor (muscle).
om'lê, (-ge-), be upset, be blown down, be overthrown; place (lay) round; put on (bandage); *AL die plante lê om*, all the plants are flattened; *LAAT* ~, turn the edge of.
om'legging, turning over (down); putting on (bandage).
om'legsel, edging, binding.
om'lei, (-ge-), lead round (about); ~ **ding**, bypass.
omlig'gende, neighbouring, surrounding, circumjacent; adjacent.
om'loop, (s) circulation; circumvolution; currency; circuit; (..lope), tinea, cutaneous disease, ringworm; dew-worm; *in* ~ *BRING*, spread about; bring into circulation; *die GERUG is in* ~, the rumour is abroad; *buite* ~ *STEL*, withdraw from circulation; *in* ~ *WEES*, be in circulation (money); (w) ~ (-ge-), walk (go) round; make a detour; circulate, rotate; run down, knock down; ~ **klep**, bypass-valve; ~ **leiding**, bypass; ~ **snelheid**, velocity; ~ **spoor**, run-round loop; ~ **tyd**, time of revolution; currency (of bill).
omlyn', (~), outline, sketch, define; *'n duidelik* ~ *de voorstel*, a clearly-defined proposal; ~ **ing**, outline, defining; outlining.
omlys', (w) (~), frame; fillet; (b) **(-te)**, framed, set; ~ **ting**, (-e, -s), framing, frame; framework, setting, background (novel).
om'mekeer = **omkeer**, (s).
om'mesientjie: *in 'n* ~, in a moment's time, in a trice (jiffy).
om'meswaai, *see* **omswaai**.
om'mesy, overleaf; *kyk (sien)* ~, please turn over.
om'munt, (-ge-), recoin; ~ **ing**, recoining.
ommuur', (~), wall in; mure, immure.
om'nibus, (-se), omnibus; ~ **diens**, (omni)bus service.
omnipoten'sie, omnipotence.
omnipotent', (-e), omnipotent.
omnivoor', (s) (..vore), omnivorous animal; (b) omnivoor.
ompaal', (~), fence in with stakes, palisade.
om'pad, round-about way, detour.
om'pak, (-ge-), repack.
om'plant, (-ge-), plant round; transplant.
om'ploeg, ..ploeë, (-ge-), plough up.
om'plooi, (-ge-), fold down (in).
om'praat, (-ge-), persuade, dissuade, prevail upon, talk round, cajole.
om'prating, persuasion.
omrand', (~), border, edge.
omras'ter, (~), rail in; ~ **ing**, railing (fence).
omre'de, because; ~ *een of ander gebeurtenis*, because of some or other event.
om'reis, (-ge-), travel round.
om'reken, (-ge-), convert; reduce; *'n bedrag in rande* ~, convert an amount into rands; ~ **aar**, converter; ~ **baar**, (..bare), convertible; ~ **ing**, conversion.
omring', (~), surround, encircle, encompass, ensphere, beset, begird, hedge; ~ **end**, (-e), surrounding, ambient.
om'roep, (s) broadcasting-station; (w) (-ge-), broadcast, announce; ~ **band**, broadcast-band; ~ **er**, (-s), (town-)crier; announcer (radio).
om'roer, (-ge-), stir (tea).
om'rol, (-ge-), roll over, cant(le).

om'ruil, (-ge-), exchange; change; ~ **baar**, (..bare), exchangeable, interchangeable; ~ **ing**, exchange.
om'ruk, (-ge-), jerk down (round), upset by jerking, pull down.
om'ry, (-ge-), drive (ride) down; drive (ride) round; knock down, run over (down); make a detour; *'n KIND is omgery*, a child was knocked down; *by die STASIE* ~, touch at the station.
omseil'¹, (~), steer (keep) clear of, obviate, avoid; *moeilikhede* ~, steer clear of difficulties; ~**ing**, avoidance.
om'seil², (-ge-), double (cape), sail round; ~**ing**, (-e, -s), circumnavigation.
om'send, (-ge-), send round; ~ **brief**, circular (letter); encyclical (R.C. Church).
om'set, (s) turnover; volume of business; return; takings; (w) (-ge-), turn over, change (money); commute; ~ **as**, reversing-shaft; ~ **baar**, (..bare), convertible; ~ **baarheid**, convertibility; ~ **belasting**, turnover tax; ~ **masjien**, reversing-engine; ~ **olie**, transformer oil; ~ **ter**, (-s), transformer (elect.); converter; ~ **ting**, transposition, change; reverse; commutation; conversion; permutation, inversion; ~ **tingskoers**, conversion rate; ~ **tingslening**, conversion loan.
om'sien, (-ge-), look round (back, after); *na sy moeder* ~, look after his mother.
om'sientjiestyd: (ong.) *in 'n* ~, in a moment, in a trice (jiffy).
omsig'tig, (-e), cautious, circumspect, discreet; precautious; ~ **heid**, circumspection, caution.
omsin'gel, (~), surround, enclose, encircle, circle, hem in, envelop; besiege, invest (city); ~ **ing**, enclosing, encircling; investment (city); ~ **ingsbeweging**, enveloping movement.
omsir'kel, (~), encircle; ~ **ing**, encirclement.
om'sit, (-ge-), put (turn) around; transpose; convert, reverse; invert; *'n DAS* ~, put on a tie; *in GELD* ~, convert into money; ~ **pomp**, converter pump.
om'skakel, (-ge-), switch over; reverse; convert; ~ **aar**, (-s), reverser, commutator; change-over switch; ~ **ing**, commutation; conversion; change-over.
omskans', (~), fortify, erect fortifications; ~ **ing**, (-s), circumvallation, entrenchment, fortification.
om'skep¹, (-ge-), transfer, ladle.
om'skep², (-ge-), transfigure, transform; recreate; metamorphose; *die tennisbaan word in 'n tuin omgeskep*, the tennis-court is being turned into a garden; ~ **ping**, transfiguration, transformation; total change.
om'skiet, (-ge-), shoot down.
om'skik, (-ge-), arrange differently, rearrange; ~ **king**, rearrangement.
om'skommel, (-ge-), shake about; reshuffle; ~ **ing**, shaking about; reshuffle (cards).
om'skop, (-ge-), kick over.
om'skrif, (-te-), inscription (on medal), legend.
omskryf', **omskry'we**, (~), describe, define (word); formulate; paraphrase; set out, set forth; specify; circumscribe (geometry).
omskryf'baar, (..bare), qualifiable, definable.
omskry'wend, (-e), periphrastic, paraphrastic, circumlocutory, circumscriptive.
omskry'wer, (-s), circumscriber.
omskry'wing, (-e, -s), description, definition, circumscription, periphrasis, circumlocution; specification, paraphrase.
om'slaan, (-ge-), knock down; overthrow, topple over; put around; turn up (collar); turn over (page); capsize (boat); overturn (vehicle); veer (round); *LIEFDE wat* ~ *in haat*, love which turns to hate; *die WEER kan skielik* ~, the weather may change suddenly; *die WIND het omgeslaan*, the wind has veered round; ~ **kraag**, reverse, turn-down collar; ~ **steek**, whipping (needlework).
om'slag¹, (..slae), hem, border, cuff (of sleeve); turn-up (of trousers); fold-over; binder; envelope, file; dust-cover, wrapper, cover, jacket (book); brace; cataplasm; compress; facing; *KOUE* ~, cold compress; *WARM* ~, fomentation; ~ **advertensie**, blurb; ~ **blad**, flap; ~ **boor**, hand-brace; belly-brace; ~ **klembus**, brace-chuck; ~ **las**, grooved joint; ~ **naat**, grooved seam; ~ **ploeg**, breast-plough; ~ **swikboor**, gimlet bit; ~ **tekening**, cover-drawing.
om'slag², fuss, ado, bustle; *GROOT* ~ *maak*, make a great fuss; be very ceremonious; *vir iem.* ~ *MAAK*, put oneself out to entertain a person; *met WEINIG* ~, without much ado.
omslag'tig, (-e), wordy, circumstantial, lengthy, roundabout, discursive (account); cumbrous (method); ponderous, fussy; diffuse, digressive, prolix.
omslag'tigheid¹, wordiness, prolixity, long-windedness, departmentalism, discursiveness, circumlocution, circumbendibus.
omslag'tigheid², fussiness; red tape.
om'sleep, (-ge-), drag about (round).
om'slenter, (-ge-), loiter about; *die tyd* ~, idle away the time.
om'slinger¹, (-ge-), overturn, knock over; stagger round.
omslin'ger², (~), twine round.
omslui'er, (~), cover with a veil; ~**ing**, veiling, disguise.
om'sluip, (-ge-), prowl round.
omsluit', (~), encircle, include, embrace, compass, enfold, embosom, envelop; girdle; fold about; begird; enclasp; invest (city); ~**ing**, (-e, -s), encircling, envelopment; clasp; fence.
om'smelt, (-ge-), remelt; ~**ing**, remelting; melting-down.
om'smyt, (-ge-), throw over, upset, knock down.
om'snel, (-ge-), rush round; fly (time).
omsnoer'¹, (~), entwine.
om'snoer², (-ge-), tie round.
om'sny, (-e), (whole) slice (of bread).
omsons', useless, vain; unprovoked.
om'soom¹, (-ge-), hem; edge.
omsoom'², (~), fringe, border, purfle.
omspan'¹, (~), span, encircle, comprise.
om'span'², (-ge-), change (horses).
omspat', (~), splash round.
omspin', (~), spin round; ~**ning**, roving; ~**sel**, rove.
om'spoel, (-ge-), rinse, wash; wash over; wash away; *die gebou is omgespoel*, the building has been washed away.
omspoel', (~), wash (round), lave.
omspon'ne, covered (wire); roved.
om'spring, (-ge-), jump round; handle, manage (a person or thing); change colour (politically); *weet hoe om met kinders om te spring*, know how to manage children.
om'staan, (-ge-), stand about (round); move up (away).
om'stamp, (-ge-), push over, upset.
om'stander, (-s), bystander, witness, onlooker.
omstan'dig, (b) (-e), detailed, circumstantial; (bw) minute(ly), in detail; ~ *vertel*, give a detailed account; ~ **heid**, (..hede) circumstance; minuteness, detail; circumstantiality; adjunct; case; *BESWARENDE* ~*hede*, incriminating circumstances; *DEUR* ~*hede*, owing to special (unforeseen) circumstances; *sy GELDELIKE* ~*hede*, his financial position; *in GESEËNDE* ~*hede*, in the family way; *ONDER geen* ~ *hede nie*, under no circumstances; *'n SAMELOOP van* ~*hede*, juncture, coincidence.
omstan'digheidsgetuienis, circumstantial evidence.
om'stap, (-ge-), walk round (about).
om'stedelik, (-e), peri-urban.
om'stel, (-ge-), reverse; change over; ~ **ler**, (-s), reversing gear (ship); ~ **ling**, reversing; reversal.
om'stik, (-ge-), hem; ~ **sel**, (-s), hem, stitching.
om'stoot, (-ge-), push down, upset, overthrow, overturn.
om'stort, (-ge-), overturn, cause to fall down.
omstraal', (~), shine around, surround with rays; halo.
omstre'de, contentious, controversial; *'n* ~ *vraagstuk*, a controversial (vexed) question.
om'streeks, **omstreeks'**, more or less, in the vicinity of, about.

om'streke, vicinity, neighbourhood, surrounding country, environs.
omstren'gel, (~), entwine; embrace.
om'strik, (-ge-), tie round.
omstro'mend, (-e), circumfluent.
omstro'ming, circumfluence.
om'stulp, (-ge-), invert, evert; ~ing, inversion, eversion.
om'stuur, (-ge-), send round, circulate.
om'sukkel, (-ge-), struggle round (golf-course); pass laboriously (time).
om'swaai, (s) swing, swinging round; volte-face; change radically, about-face; turn (of events); (w) (-ge-), swing round; change (political opinion).
omswag'tel, (~), swathe, swaddle, bandage.
om'swem, (-ge-), swim round.
om'swenk, (-ge-), wheel round.
om'swerf, om'swerwe, (-ge-), wander (roam) about, nomadize.
om'swerm, (-ge-), swarm round; ramble.
om'swerwing, (-e, -s), wandering, roaming about, rambling; errantry.
om'swoeg, (-ge-), labour, toil, drudge.
om'tak, (-ge-), shunt (mech.); ~spoel, shunt coil.
om'tas, (-ge-), grope about.
om'tower, (-ge-), change as if by magic; transfigure, transform.
om'trap, (-ge-), kick down (over); trample on.
om'trek, (s) (-ke), outline, circle; compass; girth; periphery; circumference; perimeter; circumscription; neighbourhood, vicinity; ambit; purlieu; circuit; contour; girdle; locality; *IN* ~, in circumference; in circuit; *IN die* ~, in the neighbourhood; *in* ~ *SKETS*, sketch in outline; (w) (-ge-), march round, outflank; circumvent; compass; pull down; ~king, encirclement; ~lyn, contour line; ~spanning, circumferential stress.
omtrent', about, concerning, with regard to; in the region (neighbourhood) of, almost, nearly; *dis* ~ *KOUD*, it is extremely cold; ~ *5 KM*, about 5 kilometer; *dis vir jou* ~ *'n NOOI!*, there's a girl for you!; ~ *jou VERSOEK*, with regard to your request.
om'tuimel, (-ge-), tumble down, topple over.
omtuin', (ong.), (~), enclose, hedge in, fence in.
om'vaar¹, (-ge-), sail round; sail down.
omvaar'², (~), circumnavigate, sail about, double (cape); ~der, (-s), circumnagivator.
om'val, (-ge-), fall over (down), topple over, capsize; ~ *van die LAG*, split one's sides with laughter; ~ *van die SLAAP*, so sleepy that one is ready to drop.
om'vang, (s) extent; circumference, size, girth (of tree); dimensions, volume, amount, measure; gamut; girdle; extension; capaciousness; reach; purview; radius (of action); amplitude; consuetude; perimeter (camp); latitude (of idea); scope; compass, ambit (of meaning); range (of voice); *die ~ van OPERASIES*, the radius of action (battle); *TOENEEM in* ~, grow in volume; *beperk VAN* ~, limited in extent.
omvang', (w) (~), encompass, embrace.
omvang'ryk, (-e), extensive, comprehensive, voluminous, vast, massive; bulky; ~heid, extent, comprehensiveness, extensiveness, magnitude.
om'vangsbepaling, denotation.
omva'ring, circumnavigation.
omvat'¹, (~), embrace, enclose, include; fathom; purport, comprise; girth; comprehend; clutch, enclasp; enlace; cover, encompass; embody; *juwele deur goud* ~, jewels set in gold.
om'vat², (-ge-), take around.
omvat'tend, (-e), embracing, comprehensive, catholic; expansive.
omvat'ting, encompassment.
omver', down, upside-down, over; ~gooi, (-ge-), overturn, upset, throw down; subvert (system); shatter (hopes); ~loop, (-ge-), run (knock) down; ~ry, (-ge-), knock down, run down; ~stoot, (-ge-), push over; ~waai, (-ge-), blow down; be blown over; ~werp, (-ge-), overturn, overthrow, upset; frustrate; ~werping, upsetting, overthrow, defeat.
om'vleg, (-ge-), plait round, twine round; *omgevlegte draad*, braided wire.

omvleu'el, (~), encircle, outflank.
om'vlie(g), (-ge-), fly round; upset by flying; rush by, go quickly, fly; *die tyd vlieg om*, time flies.
om'vloei, (-ge-), flow round, circulate; ~end, (-e), circumfluent.
om'vorm, (-ge-), transform, remodel; ~er, (-s), converter; ~ing, transformation, conversion.
om'vou, (-ge-), fold down (over), turn (down or up); fold back, dog's-ear (a page).
om'vroetel, (-ge-), root (dig) up, burrow, rootle, rummage, grub.
om'swaai, (-ge-), blow down; be blown down; blow over.
om'waai, (-ge-), blow down; blow off one's feet; be blown over.
om'wal', (~), wall in, rampart, circumvallate; ~ling, circumvallation.
om'wandel, (-ge-), walk about, stroll about; ~ing, sojourn(ing); *die ~ing van Jesus*, Christ's sojourn on earth.
om'weg, roundabout way, detour, compass; *sonder omweë verklaar*, declare straight out.
omwelf', (~), enclose.
om'wend, (-ge-), turn round; *toe ek my* ~, when I turned round.
om'wentel, (-ge-), turn round, revolve, rotate, circumvolve.
omwen'teling, (-e, -s), revolution; circumvolution; cataclysm; (circum)gyration, rotation; *'n ~ TEWEEGBRING*, revolutionize; *die SPAANSE O*~, the Spanish Revolution.
omwen'telings: ~as, axis of rotation; ~tyd, time of rotation; ~vlak, plane of rotation.
om'werk, (-ge-), dig up; recast, revise; hem, border; refashion; rewrite (book); cultivate (soil); ~ing, (-e, -s), recasting, revision; rewriting; border; cultivation; preparation.
om'werp, (-ge-), cast down, overthrow, upset; ~ing, overthrow.
om'wikkel¹, (-ge-), wrap round; envelop.
omwik'kel², (~), wrap up, envelop; ~*de beton*, bound concrete.
om'wind, (-ge-), enwind, entwine.
omwind'sel, (-s), wrapper, bandage; involucre (bot.).
om'wissel, (-ge-), alternate; change; convert, re-exchange, exchange (money); ~baar, (..bare), interchangeable; ~ing, change, changing; exchange.
om'woel¹, (-ge-), dig up, root up, rootle; churn.
om'woel², (~), wind round (wire).
omwolk', (~), envelop (in clouds).
onaandag'tig, (-e), inattentive; ~heid, inattentiveness.
onaandoen'lik, (-e), impassive, cold, apathetic, unemotional; ~heid, impassiveness, apathy, solidity.
onaan'gedaan, unaffected, unmoved, untouched.
onaan'gedien, (-de), unannounced.
onaan'gekleed, (..klede), undressed, in dishabille.
onaan'gemeld, (-e), unannounced, not ushered in.
onaan'genaam, (..name), unpleasant, displeasing, harsh, disagreeable, forbidding, offensive (smell); distateful (conduct, behaviour); uncongenial (company); *..name REUK*, offensive smell; *..name WAARHEID*, unpalatable truth.
onaan'genaamheid, (..hede), unpleasantness, disagreeableness; discomfort; ~*KRY*, have unpleasantness (trouble); ~ *kry MET iem.*, fall out with someone.
onaan'genome, rejected, unaccepted.
onaan'geraak, (-te), untouched.
onaan'geroer(d), (-de), untouched, intact; unmoved.
onaan'getas, (-te), untouched, intact, unaffected.
onaan'geteken, (-de), unregistered.
on'aangetrek, en déshabillé, in dishabille, undressed.
onaan'gevul, (-de), unreplenished.
onaanlok'lik, (-e), uninviting, unattractive.
onaanneem'lik, (-e), unacceptable; inadmissible; implausible; ~heid, unacceptableness, inadmissibility.
onaansien'lik, (-e), insignificant, inconsiderable, little, homely, humble; ~heid, insignificance, inconsiderableness, homeliness.

onaanspreek'lik, (-e), irresponsible, not answerable.
onaanstoot'lik, (-e), inoffensive, unobjectionable; ~**heid**, inoffensiveness, unobjectionableness.
onaantas'baar, (..bare), invoilable, unassailable, unimpeachable; ~**heid**, unassailability.
onaantrek'lik, (-e), unattractive, uninviting, unalluring.
onaanvaar'baar, (..bare), unacceptable; ~**heid**, unacceptability.
onaanveg'baar, (..bare), indisputable, beyond challenge, indefeasible; ~**heid**, indefeasibility.
onaanwend'baar, (..bare), inapplicable; ~**heid**, inapplicability.
onaar'dig, (-e), unpleasant, nasty; *nie* ~ *nie*, not unattractive; not too bad; ~**heid**, unpleasantness, rudeness.
onaf', incomplete, unfinished.
onaf'gebroke, unexpired, continuous, incessant, without interruption, without intermission, uninterrupted, unbroken; ~ *vlug,* non-stop flight; ~**nheid**, incessantness, continuousness.
onaf'gedaan, (..dane), unfinished, unsettled, outstanding.
onaf'gedank, (-te), undisbanded.
onaf'gehaal, (-de), unclaimed, not called for.
onaf'gehandel, (-de), pending, unsettled.
onaf'gelaai, (-de), not unloaded, undischarged (load).
onaf'gelewer, (-de), undelivered.
onaf'gelos, (-te), unrelieved (soldiers); outstanding (debts); unredeemed (pledges); perpetual.
onaf'gemaak, -te), unfinished; unshelled (peas).
onaf'gerond, (-e), unfinished, uncompleted; ~**heid**, unfinishedness, uncompleteness.
on'afgesny, (-de), uncut; deckle-edged.
onaf'gewerk, (-te), unfinished, rough.
onafhank'lik, (-e), independent; autocephalous; ~ *VAN alle ander oorwegings*, apart from all other considerations; ~ *WEES van*, be independent of; ~**e**, (-s), independent person; freelance; ~**heid**, independence.
onafhank'lik: ~**heidsoorlog**, war of independence; ~**verklaring**, declaration of independence; ~**wording**, attainment of independence.
onaflos'baar, (..bare), irredeemable; ~**heid**, irredeemability.
onafneem'baar, (..bare), undetachable.
onafrikaans', (-e), foreign to Afrikaans, not Afrikaans; foreign to the Afrikaner.
onafsien'baar, (..bare), innumerable (people); limitless, endless, vast.
onafskei(d)'baar, (..bare), inseparable.
onafskei'delik, (-e), inseparable; ~ *verbonde*, indissolubly connected; ~**heid**, inseparability.
onafwend'baar, (..bare), unavoidable; inevitable; ~**heid**, inevitability, unavoidableness.
onafwys'baar, (..bare), what must be accepted, imperative; (that which) cannot be evaded; irrecusable.
onag'saam, (..same), inattentive, careless, negligent, inadvertent, heedless; ~**heid**, inattentiveness, carelessness, negligence, inadvertence.
onaktief', (..tiewe), inactive, inert.
onanie', onanism.
onanis', (-te), onanist.
onartistiek', (-e), inartistic.
onbaatsug'tig, (-e), disinterested, selfless, unselfish; ~**heid**, disinterestedness, unselfishness.
onbarmhar'tig, (-e), merciless, unmerciful; pitiless; ~**heid**, mercilessness, pitilessness.
onbeangs', (-te), fearless.
onbeant'woord, (-e), unanswered; unrequited (love).
onbebou', (-de), untilled, uncultivated; not built on, vacant (stand); ~ *de grond*, virgin soil.
onbedaard', (-e), uncontrollable, violent.
onbedaar'lik, (-e), unrestrainable, violent, intense, uncontrollable; ~ *lag*, laugh helplessly.
onbedag', (-te), thoughtless, incautious, imprudent, ill-considered.
onbedag'saam, (..same), thoughtless, careless, rash, inconsiderate; ~**heid**, thoughtlessness, rashness.
onbedeel(d)', (-de), not possessing, dowerless; without, devoid of; ~ *met wêreldse rykdom*, unendowed with worldly goods.
onbedek', (-te), uncovered, bare; plain; ~**t'heid**, bareness.
onbederf'lik, (-e), imperishable, incorruptible.
onbedoeld', (b) (-e), not meant, unintentional; (bw) unwittingly, inadvertently.
onbedor'we, innocent, pure, unspoiled; uncorrupted; ~**nheid**, innocence, purity.
onbedre'we, inexperienced, unskilled; raw; ~**nheid**, inexperience, clumsiness.
onbedrieg'lik, (-e), unmistakable, infallible (sign).
onbedruk', (-te), unprinted, blank.
onbedui'dend, (-e), insignificant, trivial, of no consequence, petty, negligible, exiguous, inane, pointless, puny; meaningless; ~**heid**, insignificance, inanity, platitude, triviality.
onbedwing'baar, (..bare), unrestrainable, unruly, indomitable; irrepressible; ~**heid**, unrestrainableness, unruliness.
onbedwon'ge, unrestrained, unsubdued.
onbe'ëdig, (-de), unsworn.
onbegaaf', (-de), untalented; *nie* ~ *nie*, not untalented.
onbegaan'baar, (..bare), impassable, untraversable; ~**heid**, impassability.
onbegeer(d)', (-de), uncoveted, undesired.
onbegeer'lik, (-e), undesirable.
onbegon'ne, unavailing, hopeless; *'n* ~ *taak*, an impossible task.
onbegra'we, unburied.
onbegrens', (-de), unlimited, endless, unrestricted, without limit, illimitable, boundless; ~**d'heid**, immensity, endlessness.
onbegre'pe, not understood.
onbegryp'lik, (-e), inconceivable, incomprehensible; ~**heid**, inconceivableness, incomprehensibility; acatalepsy.
onbehaag'lik, (-e), ill at ease, out of sorts, unpleasant, uncomfortable, uneasy, charmless; ~**heid**, unpleasantness, discomfort.
onbehaar', (-de), hairless; glabrous (plant).
onbehan'del(d), (-de), not treated, untreated; undiscussed; not dealt with.
onbehan'ge, unpapered.
onbeheer(d)', (-de), ownerless, unclaimed, derelict, unadministered; stray (animal).
onbeheers', (-te), uncontrolled, unrestrained.
onbeheers'baar, (..bare), uncontrollable, ungovernable.
onbeheerst'heid, lack of restraint.
onbehen'dig, (-e), clumsy, awkward.
onbehoed', (-e), unprotected; ~**saam**, rash, reckless.
onbehol'pe, awkward, clumsy; helpless; crude, unpolished; ~**nheid**, awkwardness, clumsiness.
onbehoor'lik, (-e), improper, indecent, coarse, unseemly; ~**heid**, impropriety, indecency, unseemliness.
onbehou'e, clumsy, uncouth, rude; ~**nheid**, rudeness, clumsiness.
onbehulp'saam, (..same), disobliging, unwilling to help.
onbeïn'vloed, (-e), uninfluenced.
onbekeer'baar, (..bare), that cannot be converted; impervious.
onbekeerd', (-e), unconverted.
onbekend', (-e), unknown, obscure, unacquainted, unfamiliar; dark (horse); new; *'n* ~*e BEROEMD= HEID*, an obscure person, a (mere) nobody; *die skenker wil* ~ *BLY*, the donor wishes to remain anonymous; *ek is HIER* ~, I am a stranger here; ~ *MAAK onbemind*, unknown, unloved; ~ *MET*, ignorant of, unacquainted with; ~**e**, (-s), stranger; *die* ~*e*, the unknown; ~**heid**, unfamiliarity; obscurity; ignorance.
onbeklaag', (-de), unlamented, unpitied, unwept.
onbeklad', (-de), unsullied, unstained.
onbekleed', (..klede), unupholstered; vacant (billet).
onbeklem(d)', (-e), cheerful; light-hearted; unaccented (vowel); *'n* ~*de gemoed*, a cheerful heart (spirit).
onbeklem'toon, (-de), unstressed.

onbeklim'baar, (..bare), inaccessible; unclimbable, unscalable; ~**heid**, inaccessibility; unclimbableness.
onbekom'baar, (..bare), not obtainable, sold out, out of print.
onbekom'merd, (-e), unconcerned, careless, happy-go-lucky; ~**heid**, carelessness, unconcern, lightheartedness.
onbekook', (-te), ill-considered; inconsiderate; thoughtless, careless, rash, superficial; crude; raw, half-baked; ~**t'heid**, crudeness, crudity; carelessness.
onbekrom'pe, liberal, generous; broadminded; ~**nheid**, broadmindedness, liberality.
onbekwaam', (..kwame), incapable, unable, incompetent, unfit; feckless; *die vrugte is nog* ~, the fruit is still immature; ~**heid**, inability, incompetence; insufficiency; immaturity (of fruit); disability; ~**making**, disablement.
onbelang'rik, (-e), unimportant, immaterial, of no consequence, insignificant; ~**heid**, insignificance, unimportance.
onbelas', (-te), unburdened, unencumbered; untaxed, not mortgaged (property); ~**baar**, (..bare), free (exempt) from taxes; ~**baarheid**, exemption from taxation.
onbeleef', (-de), impolite, uncouth, uncivil, disrespectful, discourteous, disobliging, off-hand; ill-mannered; ~**d'heid**, (..hede), incivility, impoliteness, discourtesy, disobligingness, disrespectfulness.
onbeleg, (-de), not invested (money).
onbelem'merd, (-e), unhindered, unhampered, unimpeded, free, uninterrupted (view); free(-footed); ~**heid**, unimpededness, freedom.
onbele'se, unread, illiterate; ~**nheid**, lack of extensive reading.
onbeloon', (-de), unrewarded, unrequited; *dit sal nie* ~ *bly nie*, it will not go unrewarded.
onbeman', (-de), unmanned, without a crew; pilotless (aeroplane).
onbemark'baar, (..bare), unmarketable.
onbemerk', (-te), unperceived, unnoticed; ~**baar**, (..bare), imperceptible.
onbemes', (-te), unmanured.
onbemid'del(d), (-de), impecunious, without means; ~**heid**, impecuniosity.
onbemin(d)', (-de), unloved, unpopular.
onbemin'lik, (-e), unamiable, unlovable.
onbene'pe, large; frank, candid; uncramped.
onbene'wel(d), (-de), unclouded.
onbenoem', (-de), unnamed; *'n* ~ *de getal*, an abstract number; ~**baar**, (..bare), ineligible.
onbenul'lig, (-e), fatuous, stupid, dull-witted, lumpish, trifling, paltry, fiddling; ~**heid**, fatuity, fatuousness, stupidity.
onbenut', (-te), unused.
onbenut'tig, (-de), unused.
onbeny', (-de), unenvied; ~**baar**, (..bare), unenviable (task); ~**denswaar'dig**, (-e), unenviable.
onbeoog', (-de), not aimed at.
onbepaal'baar, (..bare), indeterminable.
on'bepaal(d), (-de), indefinite, unlimited; unfixed; vague; ~ *de MAG*, unlimited power; *vir 'n* ~ *de TYD*, for an unlimited period, indefinitely; ~ *de VONNIS*, indeterminate (sentence); ~ *de WYS*, infinitive mood; ~**dheid**, vagueness, indefiniteness.
onbepa'lend, (-e), indefinite.
onbeperk', (-te), unlimited, boundless, limitless; absolute; plenary; ~**t'heid**, unlimitedness; absoluteness.
onbeplant', (-e), unplanted.
onbeproef', (-de), untried, untested; *niks* ~ *laat nie*, leave no stone unturned.
onbera'de, ill-advised, rash, reckless; ~**nheid**, rashness, recklessness.
onbere'de, unmounted, dismounted.
onberedeneer(d)', (-de), unreasoned, without argumentary proof; ~**d'heid**, thoughtlessness.
onbereid', (-e), unprepared.
onbereik'baar, (..bare), unattainable, inaccessible; ~**heid**, unattainableness, inaccessibleness.

onbereis', (-de), untravelled (country, people); unfrequented (place).
onbere'kenbaar, (..bare), incalculable; unpredictable; ~**heid**, incalculability, capriciousness.
onberis'pelik, (-e), faultless, blameless, unimpeachable; flawless, irreproachable; immaculate; ~**heid**, faultlessness, blamelessness, irreproachableness, immaculateness.
onberoep'baar, (..bare), not capable of being called (clergyman); not free.
onbery'baar, (..bare), impassable, untraversable (road).
onberym(d)', (-e), unrhymed.
onbesa'dig, (-de), impetuous, hot-headed, rash; ~**dheid**, rashness, impetuosity.
onbeseer(d)', (-de), unhurt, uninjured.
onbeset', (-te), vacant, unoccupied, unarmed; disengaged; ~**heid**, disengagement.
onbesiel(d)', (-de), inanimate; lifeless; uninspired; insentient; ~**heid**, inanimation.
onbesien', (-e), unseen, uninspected.
onbesiens', unseen, uninspected; *iets* ~ *koop*, buy something without having seen it.
onbeskaaf', (-de), rude, uncivilized, uncultured, unrefined, barbaric, uncouth, ill-bred; ~**d'heid**, lack of civility, rudeness, want of refinement, barbarism, barbarity.
onbeskaamd', (-e), impudent, impertinent, shameless, audacious, contumelious, cheeky, cool, unabashed, brazen-faced, insolent; (mala)pert; ~**heid**, impudence, shamelessness, presumption, assurance, audaciousness, audacity, boldness, cheek, face, brazenness, contumely, hardihood, insolence, pertness, effrontery.
onbeska'dig, (-de), undamaged, intact, entire, unimpaired, unharmed; scot-free; ~**dheid**, undamaged condition, intactness.
onbeskei'denheid, indiscretion; immodesty.
onbeskei'e, indiscreet, immodest, forward.
onbeskerm(d)', (-de), unprotected, undefended, unguarded.
onbeskof', (-te), insolent, impudent, ill-mannered, in bad form, boarish, boorish, rude, agrestic, impertinent; ~**t'heid**, impertinence, insolence, rudeness, grossness.
onbeskre'we, blank, not written on; unrecorded; unwritten; ~**nheid**, blankness.
onbeskroomd', (-e), fearless, bold, undaunted, intrepid, outspoken; ~**heid**, boldness.
onbeskryf'lik, (-e), indescribable, beyond description (expression).
onbeskut', (-te), unprotected, unsheltered, bleak, fenceless; naked.
onbeslaan', (..slane, -de), unshod (horse).
onbesleg', (-te), undecided; not settled (dispute); drawn (game).
onbeslis', (-te), undecided, uncertain, indecisive; vacillating, irresolute; sub judice, pending; ~ *te SPEL*, drawn game, tie; ~ *te WEDLOOP*, dead heat; ~**baar**, (..bare), indeterminable; ~**t'heid**, indecision, hesitation.
onbeslis'te, not decided; undecided.
onbesmet', (-te), spotless, stainless, uninfected, uncontaminated, unsullied, undefiled; ~**lik**, (-e), non-infectious.
onbesne'de, uncircumcised, gentile; ~**ne**, (-s), gentile.
onbesoe'del(d), (-de), uncontaminated, unsullied, undefiled, stainless.
onbesoldig, (-de), unsalaried, unpaid.
onbeson'ge, unsung.
onbeson'ne, thoughtless, inconsiderate, rash, precipitate, rattleheaded, foolish, headlong, rattle-(hare-)brained, ill-judged, imprudent; ~**nheid**, thoughtlessness, inconsiderateness, flippancy, precipitance, recklessness.
onbesorg', (-de), light-hearted, cheerful, carefree, happy-go-lucky; undelivered (letter); ~**d'heid**, light-heartedness, cheerfulness, freedom from care.
onbespied', (-e), unespied; unwatched.
onbespreek', (-te), unbooked, unreserved (seats); undiscussed.
onbespro'ke, irreproachable, blameless; ~ *gedrag*, ir-

reproachable conduct; ~**nheid,** irreproachableness, blamelessness.

onbestaan'baar, (..bare), not existing; incompatible, inconsistent, absurd, imaginary; ~ *met mekaar,* contradictory to each other; inconsistent with each other; ~**heid,** incompatability; absurdity; nihility.

onbestand', not proof (against).

onbesteed', (..stede), unused, unspent.

onbestel'baar, (..bare), undeliverable; *'n onbestelbare brief,* a dead letter.

onbestemd', (-e), undetermined, uncertain, vague, unfixed, objectless; ~**heid,** vagueness.

onbesten'dig, (-e), unstable, inconstant; fickle (person); impermanent; unsteady (market); unsettled (weather); astatic; ~**heid,** unstableness, inconstancy, instability; impermanence; unsettled state (weather); desultoriness.

onbestor'we, fresh; temporary; ~ *VLEIS,* fresh meat; ~ *WEDUWEE,* grass widow.

onbestraf'baar, (..bare), unpunishable.

onbestraf'lik, (-e), immaculate, blameless.

onbestre'de, undisputed, unopposed; ~ *voorstel,* unopposed motion.

onbestre'ke, defiladed.

onbestryk'baar, (..bare), defiladed.

onbestuur'baar, (..bare), unsteerable, undirigible, uncontrollable, unmanageable.

onbesuis', (-de), rash, reckless, hot-headed; harum-scarum; hare-brained; *'n ~ de vent,* a reckless fellow; ~**d'heid,** rashness, recklessness.

onbeswaard', (-e), unencumbered (estate); clear, free (conscience).

onbeswe'ke, unyielding, unshaken, unflinching.

onbetaal'baar, (..bare), priceless, invaluable; beyond price; prohibitive (prices); *'n ..bare grap,* a priceless (capital) joke; ~**heid,** pricelessness.

onbetaal(d)', (-de), unpaid, outstanding; ~ *de rekeninge,* outstanding debts, unpaid accounts.

onbetaam'lik, (-e), unbecoming, improper, unseemly, indecent; ~**heid,** impropriety, unbecomingness, unseemliness, indecency.

onbete'kenend, (-e), insignificant, negligible, blank, petty; ~**heid,** insignificance.

onbeteu'el, (-de), unbridled, unrestrained.

onbetoom'baar, (..bare), ungovernable, uncontrollable.

onbetrap', (-te), uncaught.

onbetre'de, untrodden.

onbetreur(d), (-de), unwept, unmourned, unlamented.

onbetrou'baar, (..bare), unreliable, untrustworthy, faithless; ~**heid,** untrustworthiness, unreliableness, unreliability.

onbetuig', (-de), unattested; *hy laat hom nie ~ nie,* he gives a good account of himself.

onbetwis', (-te), undisputed, unchallenged, uncontested (election); ~ **baar, (..bare),** indisputable, beyond all dispute, beyond debate, irrefragable; *..bare reg,* clear right; ~**baarheid,** indisputableness.

onbetwy'felbaar, (..bare), indubitable, unquestionable.

onbevaar'baar, (..bare), innavigable; ~**heid,** innavigability.

onbeval'lig, (-e), ungraceful, uncomely; graceless, inelegant; ~**heid,** ungracefulness, inelegance.

onbevan'ge, with an air of detachment, open-minded, unbiased, free, impartial, unconcerned, detached; ~**nheid,** unconcern, detachment, impartiality, candour.

onbevat'lik, (-e), dull, slow of comprehension; ~**heid,** dullness, stupidity.

onbeves'tig, (-de), unconfirmed.

onbevlek', (-te), undefiled, untainted, immaculate, unsullied, innocent, unstained, pure; ~**t'heid,** spotlessness, purity.

onbevoeg', (-de), incompetent, unqualified, unfit; unauthorized; ~ **de,** incompetent person, chancer; ~**d'heid,** incompetence; disablement; ~**making,** incapacitation.

onbevolk', (-te), unpopulated, unpeopled.

onbevooroor'deel(d), (-de), unprejudiced, unbiased, open-minded, liberal, detached; catholic; ~**dheid,** freedom from prejudice, impartiality.

onbevoor'reg, (-te), unprivileged.

onbevre'dig, (-de), unsatisfied, unappeased; ~**baar, (..bare),** inappeasable; ~**end, (-e),** unsatisfactory, dissatisfactory.

onbevrees', (-de), undaunted, dauntless, fearless; ~**d'heid,** fearlessness, intrepidity.

onbevrug', (-te), unimpregnated, sterile; unfertilized (plant).

onbevry', (-de), not liberated, unreleased.

onbewaak', (-te), ungaurded, unprotected.

onbeweeg'baar, (..bare), immovable; ~**heid,** immovableness.

onbeweeg'lik, (-e), motionless, immovable, fixed, immobile; ~**heid,** immobility; deadness (of water); immovability; firmness.

onbeween', (-de), unwept, unlamented.

onbewerk', (-te), unmanufactured, raw (products); unworked (mine); untilled (land); unwrought (gold); raw (hide).

onbewe'se, not proved, unproved.

onbewim'peld, (-e), frank, candid, outspoken, open, undisguised; flat, plain, declaredly; *iem. ~ die waarheid sê,* tell someone the plain truth.

onbewo'ë, unmoved, undisturbed, placid; ~**nheid,** placidity.

onbewolk', (-te), unclouded, bright, cloudless.

onbewoon', (-de), uninhabited, desolate, deserted, disinhabited; ~**baar, (..bare),** uninhabitable.

onbewus', (-te), ignorant, unaware, unwitting, inadvertent, by inadvertence; unconscious; *die ~ te,* the unconscious; ~**t'heid,** ignorance, unawareness, unwittingness; unconsciousness.

onbewys'baar, (..bare), unprovable.

onbil'lik, (-e), unfair, unjust, unreasonable; ~**heid,** injustice, unreasonableness.

onbloe'dig, (-e), bloodless (victory).

onblus'baar, (..bare), unquenchable, quenchless, inextinguishable; ~**heid,** quenchlessness.

onboetvaar'dig, (-e), impenitent, unrepentant, unrepenting; ~**heid,** impenitence.

onbrand'baar, (..bare), incombustible, non-inflammable, fire-proof; asbestine; ~**heid,** incombustibility.

onbreek'baar, (..bare), unbreakable, infrangible; adamantine; cast-iron; foolproof; ~**heid,** infrangibility, unbreakableness.

onbroe'derlik, (-e), unbrotherly, not brotherlike.

on'bruik, disuse, desuetude; *in ~ raak,* fall into desuetude.

onbruik'baar, (..bare), useless, not fit for use, unserviceable, inadaptable; castaway; naughty; ~ *maak,* render unfit for use; cancel (stamp); ~**heid,** uselessness; naughtiness; ~**making,** incapacitation.

onbuig'baar, (..bare), inflexible, rigid, unbending; cast-iron; inexorable (law); indeclinable (grammar); ~**heid,** inflexibility, rigidity, unbendableness.

onbuig'saam, (..same), unbending, unyielding, obstinate, stubborn; ~**heid,** inflexibility, obstinacy.

onbur'gerlik, (-e), uncivic.

onby'bels, (-e), unbiblical, not according to Holy Writ, antiscriptural.

onchris'telik, (-e), unchristian, not christianlike; ~**heid,** unchristianliness.

on'dank, ingratitude, thanklessness; ~ *is wêreldsloon,* the world pays with ingratitude.

ondank'baar, (..bare), ungrateful, thankless; unrewarding; *'n ..bare werk,* a thankless task; ~**heid,** ingratitude, thanklessness.

on'danks, in spite of, notwithstanding, despite; *des ~,* in spite of this.

ondeeg'lik, (-e), superficial; unsound; ~**heid,** superficiality; shallowness.

ondeel'baar, (..bare), indivisible; *..bare GETALLE,* prime numbers; ~ *KLEIN,* inconceivably small; ~**heid,** indivisibility.

ondefinieer'baar, (..bare), indefinable; ~**heid,** indefinableness.

ondemokra'ties, (-e), undemocratic.

ondenk'baar, (..bare), inconceivable, unthinkable.

on'der, (bw) below, down; *ten ~ BRING*, bring into subjection; *~ IN die bottel*, at the bottom of the bottle; *NA ~*, downstairs; *~ OP die bladsy*, at the foot of the page; *die SON is ~*, the sun has set; *VAN ~ af*, from below, from the bottom; *ons WOON ~*, we live on the ground floor; (vs) below, under(neath); amid(st); *~ AL die skrywers*, of all the writers; *~ ANDERE*, inter alia, among other things; *~ EDE bevestig*, confirm (corroborate) under oath; *~ tien JAAR*, under ten years old; *~ die LEES*, while reading; *~ MEKAAR deel*, share between themselves; *~ vier OË*, in private; *~ ONS*, between us; *~ PARI*, below par; *~ die PREEK*, during the sermon; *~ die REGERING van koningin Victoria*, during the reign of Queen Victoria; *~ die TAFEL deur kruip*, pass under the table; *~ TRANE*, in tears; *~ VRIENDE*, among friends; *~ die WAPENS*, under arms.
on'deraan, at the foot of, at the bottom of.
on'deraandeel, (..dele), subshare.
on'deraannemer, subcontractor.
on'deraansig, bottom view.
onderaards', (-e), subterranean, underground.
on'deradjudant, orderly sergeant.
on'deradmiraal, vice-admiral.
on'der: *~ afdeling*, subdivision, subsection; *~agent*, subagent; *~ arm*, forearm; *~ armmaat*, underarm measurement; *~baadjie*, waistcoat; *~baas*, foreman, chargeman, chargehand; *~balju*, deputy sheriff; *~balk*, purlin, epistyle, architrave; *~been*, lower part of leg; ankle.
on'derbeklemtoon, (~), underemphasize; ..toning, under emphasis.
on'derbelig, (-te), underexposed (photo); *~ting*, under-exposure.
on'derbestuurder, submanager.
on'derbetaling, underpayment.
on'derbevelhebber, (-s), second in command.
on'derbevolk, (-te), underpopulated.
on'derbewel, (-de), understocked (farm).
on'derbewus, (-te), subconscious; subliminal; *~syn*, subconsciousness.
on'derbibliotekaris, sublibrarian.
on'derbind, (-ge-), bind under, tie on; ligate; *~ing*, ligature.
on'derbos, underbush, undergrowth.
on'derbly, (-ge-), remain below, stay under (water).
on'derbootsman, boatswain's mate.
on'derbou, substructure, groundwork, foundation.
onderbreek', (~), interrupt; disturb; punctuate; break (journey).
onderbre'ker, (-s), interrupter.
onderbre'king, (-e, -s), interruption; break (in ladderway); pause; check; intermittence; fault; *sonder ~*, without a break, uninterruptedly; *~snok*, contactbreaker, interrupter.
on'derbring, (-ge-), shelter, quarter, house; store (goods); classify, place; *'n woord by 'n groep ~*, put a word in a group.
on'derbroek, underpants, drawers.
onderbro'ke, interrupted, discontinuous, intermittent, *~ rels*, broken journey.
on'derbuik, abdomen; *~streek*, hypogastric (abdominal) region.
on'derburgemeester, deputy mayor.
on'derdaan, (..dane), subject; *~skap*, citizenship, nationality.
on'derdak, house, shelter, lodgement, housing; *geen ~ HÊ nie*, not to have a roof over one's head; *~ VRA*, ask for shelter.
onderda'nig, (-e), submissive, obedient, humble, deferent(ial), dutiful; *~heid*, submissiveness, humility; dutifulness; allegiance.
on'derdeel, subdivision; spare part, accessory; member; fraction; component, sub-unit; ..dele, fittings; mountings; accessories; spare parts (of motor-car); *~tjie*, (-s), fractional part.
on'derdek, lower deck.
on'derdeur[1], (s) lower (half of a divided) door; hatch, half-door; *oor die ~ loer*, take notice of the boys.
onderdeur'[2], (bw) through at the bottom; underneath; *by die DRAAD is hy ~*, he crept through the fence; *~ LOER*, steal sidelong glances; look slyly at; *~ LOOP*, walk underneath (a ladder); *~ WEES*, fail in an examination; have ploughed.
onderdeur': *~loop*, (-ge-), be reprimanded; be caned; *~spring*, (-ge-), deceive, cheat; *iem. ~spring*, take someone in.
on'derdirekteur, assistant- director.
on'derdoen, (-ge-), be inferior; be no match (for); *vir niem. ~ nie*, be second to none.
on'derdompel, (-ge-), immerse, submerge, duck; baptize by immersion; plunge; *~ing*, immersion; ducking.
on'derdop, plastron (tortoise).
onderdruk'[1], (~), oppress (a nation); suppress (feelings); repress, stifle, quench; grind (down), keep under; quell (riot).
on'derdruk[2], (-ge-), press down or under; put (hold) down, crush, quell; choke; dip.
onderdruk': *~kend*, (-e), oppressive; *~ker*, (-s), oppressor, depressor, suppressor; queller; *~king*, oppression, suppression; dragonade.
on'derduik, (-ge-), dive under; go into hiding, go underground (during war); *~er*, (-s), person in hiding.
onderduims', (-e), underhand, cunning, hole-and-corner; furtive; *~ wees*, be underhanded; *~heid*, underhandedness, cunning, furtiveness, slyness.
on'derdypees, hamstring.
ondereen', together, pell-mell.
on'dereen, bottom (lower) end, foot of (page).
on'derfamilie, subfamily.
ondergaan'[1], (~), undergo, suffer, endure, go through; *BEHANDELING ~*, receive treatment; *sy LOT ~*, submit to his fate.
on'dergaan[2], (-ge-), set (sun), go under, go down; perish, be ruined; *~ in die stryd*, perish in the struggle.
on'dergang, setting (sun); ruin, downfall; decline; doom, fate; extinction; fall; bane; *dit beteken sy ~*, this means his undoing (downfall).
on'dergeskik, (-te), subordinate, minor, inferior, menial; ancillary; adjective; accidental; *~ MAAK aan*, subordinate to; *~ te REGTER*, puisne judge; *~te SIN*, subordinate clause; *~te*, (-s), inferior (person), menial; stooge; *SY ~tes*, his inferiors (subordinates); *~t'heid*, subordination, inferiority.
ondergete'kende, (-s), undersigned; self (cheque); *ek, die ~, verklaar*, I, the undersigned, declare.
on'dergewig, short weight, underweight.
on'dergod, demiurge.
on'dergoed, underwear, lingerie.
on'dergoewerneur, vice-governor.
on'dergooi, (-ge-), throw under (in wrestling), floor.
on'dergordyntjie, short blind.
on'dergraads, (~), reject-grade; *~e ware*, rejects.
ondergraaf', ..gra'we, (~), undermine, sap, countermine.
ondergra'wing, undermining, subversion.
on'dergrond, underground, subsoil; groundwork; basis; *~s*, (-e), underground, subterranean; phreatic; *~se spoorweg*, underground railway, tube.
onderhan'del, (~), negotiate, bargain, parley, discuss terms; palaver; *~aar*, (-s), negotiator; parlementaire; *~ing*, (-e, -s), negotiation, parley; *~inge aanknoop*, enter into (open) negotiations; *~ingspolitiek*, politics of negotiation.
on'derhands, (-e), underhand, private, collusive; *'n ~e verkoop*, a sale out of hand (by private treaty).
onderha'wig, (-e), in question; present; *in die ~e geval*, in the case in hand (under consideration).
on'derhemp, (..hemde), vest, undershirt; singlet, chemise; *~materiaal*, vesting.
onderhe'wig, liable to, subject to, open to; *~ aan BELASTING*, liable to duty (taxation); *~ aan baie SIEKTES*, subject (prone) to many diseases; *~ aan TWYFEL*, open to doubt; *~heid*, liability.
onderho'rig, (-e), dependent, inferior; *sy ~es*, his subordinates; *~heid*, dependence, subordination.
onderhou'[1], (~), support, maintain, preserve; keep (commandments); keep in repair (roads, houses); keep one's hand in; keep up (studies); entertain,

feed; *iem. aangenaam* ~, have a pleasant interview with someone.
on'derhou², (-ge-), hold down (under); repress.
on'derhoud¹, maintenance, support, upkeep, keep, alimony; alimentation, subsistence, sustenance; *BEVEL tot* ~, maintenance order; ~ *EIS*, sue for alimony.
on'derhoud², (-e), conversation, discourse; interview; conference; *'n* ~ *hê met iem.*, (have an) interview (with) someone.
onderhou'dend, (-e), entertaining, interesting, amusing, conversable.
onderhou'ding, observance, keeping.
onderhoudplig'tig, (-e), bound to keep in good repair.
on'derhoudskoste, cost of upkeep, maintenance costs; maintaining-expense; ~ **toelae,** subsistence allowance.
onderhou'er, (-s), maintainer, supporter.
on'derhuid, cutis, hypodermis; ~**s,** (-e), subcutaneous, hypodermic; ~ *se spuit,* hypodermic syringe; ~ **weefsel,** subcutaneous tissue.
on'derhuis, ground floor; lower part of house.
on'derhuur, (s), subletting, sublease, subtenancy; (w) (-ge-), subrent; ~ **der,** subtenant, sublessee.
on'derin, in below, in at the bottom.
on'derinspekteur, subinspector.
on'derkaak, . . **kakebeen,** lower jaw; maxilla (insect); mandible.
on'derkamp, subcamp.
on'derkanselier, vice-chancellor.
on'derkant, (s) bottom, lower side; (bw) below.
on'derkaptein, vice-captain; subchief.
on'derkas, lower case (printing).
on'derken¹, (s) (-ne), double chin.
onderken'², (w) (~), distinguish (between), recognize; identify; ~ **baar,** (. . **bare**), distinguishable.
on'derkerk, lower church; crypt.
on'derkin = **onderken¹**.
on'derklas, subclass.
on'derkleed, undergarment; doublet; ~ **jie,** undercloth.
on'derklere, underclothing, underwear, lingerie.
on'derklerk, junior clerk.
on'derkok, assistant cook.
on'derkombers, underblanket.
on'derkome, shelter, lodging; *geen* ~ *hê nie,* not have a roof over one's head.
on'derkoning, viceroy; ~ **in,** vicereine; ~ **skap,** viceroyalty.
on'derkorporaal, lance-corporal.
on'derkruip¹, (-ge-), creep under.
onderkruip'², (~), undersell, undercut; interlope; supplant; blackleg; ~ **er,** (-s), blackleg, strikebreaker, scab; rat; interloper; ~ **ery,** ~ **ing,** underselling, undercutting; playing the blackleg, blacklegging.
on'derkry, (-ge-), master, overpower, floor.
on'derkussing, underpillow, bolster.
on'derlaag, bottom layer, substratum; base-coat, undercoat (of paint); ~ **room,** foundation cream.
on'derlaken, undersheet.
on'derlangs, along the bottom; covertly, furtively; ~ *na iem. KYK*, not look a person straight in the eye; peer slyly at someone; ~ *wees,* be furtive.
on'derlêer, (-s), ground-plate (railw.); underlay.
onderleg', (-de), prepared, well-grounded; *goed* ~ *in matesis*, with a sound knowledge of the first principles of mathematics, well-grounded in mathematics; ~ **dheid,** grounding.
on'derlendestuk, fillet, undercut.
onderlig'gend, (~), underlying; subjacent.
on'derling, mutual; relative; *die* ~ *e LIGGING,* the relative position; ~ *RAADPLEEG,* consult together; ~ *VERDEELD*, divided among themselves; ~ **heid,** mutualness.
on'derlinne, underlinen.
on'derlip, underlip, lower lip; *sy* ~ *HANG, 'n mens kan van sy* ~ *SKOENSOLE maak,* he is in a sulky frame of mind; he hangs the nether lip.
on'derloop, (-ge-), be flooded; *laat* ~, inundate.
on'derlosser, hopper.
on'derluitenant, sub-lieutenant, subaltern.

on'derlyf, body below the hips; ~ **ie,** (-s), camisole, bodice, chemisette.
ondermaans', (-e), earthly, mundane, sublunary; *die* ~ *e,* life on earth.
on'dermaat, undersize.
ondermekaar'trouery, intermarriage.
on'dermelk, skimmed milk, separated milk.
on'dermou, undersleeve.
ondermyn', (~), undermine, sap; ~ **end,** (-e), subversive; ~ **ing,** undermining, sapping.
onderneem', (~), undertake, attempt, venture, assay.
onderne'gentien, (-s), under-nineteen; ~ **span,** undernineteen team.
on'dernek, clod, sticking-piece (of beef).
onderne'mend, (-e), enterprising, pushful, daring, adventurous; pushing; ~ **heid,** enterprising spirit, daring, pluck.
onderne'mer, undertaker; entrepreneur; ~ **skapitaal,** risk-capital.
onderne'ming, (-e, -s), enterprise, undertaking, project, concern, attempt, venture; *'n gewaagde* ~, a perilous (risky) undertaking; ~ **sgees,** spirit of enterprise, gumption.
on'dernormaal, (. . **male**), subnormal.
on'deroffisier, non-commissioned officer; warrant-officer, petty officer.
on'derom, round the bottom.
onderon'sie, (-s), private affair; small family-social; intimate party.
on'derooglid, lower eyelid.
on'derorde, suborder.
on'derpag, sublease; ~ **ter,** sublessee.
on'derpand, pledge, guarantee, collateral security.
on'derpastoor, curate (R.C.)
on'derploeg, (-ge-), plough under (weeds); plough down.
on'derproduksie, underproduction.
on'derredakteur, assistant-editor; sub-editor.
on'derregent, vice-regent.
on'derrig¹, (s) instruction, tuition, lessons.
onderrig'², (w) (~), instruct, teach, inform; pupilize; prime; ~ **ter,** (-s), edifier, instructor; ~ **ting,** instruction; information.
on'derrok, underskirt, petticoat, slip.
on'dersaal, bottom die.
ondersee'boot, onderse'ër, (-s), submarine.
ondersees', (. . **sese**), submarine; *'n ondersese kabel,* a submarine cable.
on'dersekretaris, under-secretary.
on'dersersant, lance-sergeant.
on'dersit, (-ge-), put underneath; knock down, lay low, overpower, subdue.
onderskat', (~), undervalue, underestimate, depreciate, underrate, minimize, disparage, misappreciate, misprize; ~ **ting,** undervaluation, underestimation, understatement, misappreciation, misesteem.
on'derskedel, base of skull.
onderskei', (~), distinguish, differentiate, discriminate; discern; contradistinguish; *hy kan nie wyn van ASYN* ~ *nie,* he cannot tell wine from vinegar; *hom* ~ *in die OORLOG,* distinguish himself during the war; ~ **baar,** (. . **bare**), distinguishable.
on'derskeid, difference, distinction, discrimination; *JARE van* ~, years of discretion; ~ *MAAK tussen,* distinguish between; *almal SONDER* ~, all without exception.
onderskei'delik, respectively; severally.
onderskei'dend, (-e), distinctive; honorific; diacritical; discriminative, discriminating, percipient.
onderskei'ding, (-e, -s), distinction; discrimination, discernment; eminence; differentiation; prominence; honour(s); *met* ~ *SLAAG*, pass cum laude, pass with distinction; *TER* ~ *van,* in distinction from.
onderskei'dings: ~ **lys,** honours list; ~ **teken,** mark of distinction; distinguishing mark; differentia; insignia; ensign; ~ **vermoë,** discretionary power, judgement, discernment, discretion.
onderskei'e, various, different, distinct, divers.
onderskep', (~), intercept; ~ **per,** (-s), interceptor; ~ **ping,** interception.

on'derskik, (-ge-), subordinate; ~ kend, (-e), subordinate; ~kende voegwoord, subordinating conjunction; ~ king, subordination.
on'derskout, deputy-sheriff.
onderskraag', (~), support; prop (up).
onderskra'ging, support, assistance.
on'derskrif, signature; inscription, legend, caption; motto.
onderskryf', onderskry'we, (~), endorse (a statement); sign; approve; underwrite (shares).
onderskry'wing, endorsement, approval; underwriting.
onderskuif', onderskui'we, (~), substitute fraudulently, foist in(to).
onderskui'wing, surreptitious substitution (of a child).
on'derslag, shot-woof; ~ rat, undershot wheel.
ondersny', (~), undercut.
on'dersoek[1], (s) examination, inspection, scrutiny; test; survey; inquiry; investigation; research; quest; perusal; ~ DOEN, make inquiry; ~ INSTEL, inquire into; by NADER ~, on closer examination.
ondersoek'[2], (w) (~), examine, investigate, explore, feel, scrutinize, inquire, probe, assay, search; prospect; bolt; canvass; peruse, look into; die OË ~, test the eyes; 'n WOND ~, probe a wound.
on'dersoek: ~ 'baar, (..bare), explorable; ~ boor, sounding-borer (-drill, -pipe); ~ 'end, (-e), explorative, searching, inquiring, inquisitive.
ondersoe'ker, (-s), investigator, research-worker explorer, examiner, examinant, inquirer; peruser, probator, querist.
ondersoe'king, (-e, -s), research, investigation, exploration.
ondersoe'kings: ~ gebied, field of research; ~ reg, right of search; ~ reis, journey of exploration; expedition; ~ tog, exploratory expedition; ~ werk, investigations.
on'dersoort, subspecies.
on'derspit[1] (s): die ~ delf, be worsted, come off second best.
on'derspit, (-ge-), dig (into the ground).
on'derstaande, subjoined, following, undermentioned.
on'derstam, root-stock.
on'derstand, relief, assistance, aid; ~ verleen, lend assistance; afford relief; ~ ig, (-e), hypogenous, inferior; ~ igheid, hypogyny.
on'derstands: ~ geld, subsidy, dole; ~ raad, board of aid; ~ werke, relief-works.
on'derste, (s) bottom; heel (of tumbler); (b) lowermost, lowest; die ~ BLARE afbreek, prime (tobacco); ~ ROOKKANAAL, bottom flue; ~ VERDIEPING, ground floor.
onderstebo', upside-down, higgledy-piggledy, upset, untidy, topsy-turvy; ~ GOOI, knock (throw) down, upset; KOP ~ loop, be crestfallen; ~ LOOP, knock down; ~ koek, upside-down cake.
on'dersteek, (s) (..steke), bedpan; (w) (-ge-), shove (push) under.
on'derstel[1], (s) (le), chassis, undercarriage, bogie; running-gear, underframe; landing-gear (of aeroplane).
onderstel'[2], (w) (~), suppose, presume, assume; presuppose; ~ ling, (-e, -s), supposition, hypothesis, assumption; presupposition; uitgaande van die ~ ling dat, on the assumption that.
ondersteun', (~), support, succour, assist, befriend, bolster, help, patronize, buoy; follow up (rugby); further, back up, sponsor; ~ de besluit, supporting resolution; ~ er, (-s), supporter; prop; paranymph (university).
ondersteu'ning, support, relief, assistance, help; aliment; patronage; ter ~ van, in support of; ~ sfonds, benevolent fund, relief fund, sustentation fund, provident fund.
on'derstok, rhizome, root-stock.
on'derstopmasjien, tamping machine.
onderstreep', (~), underline; dash; emphasize, stress; punctuate; ek ~, the italics are mine; ..stre'ping, underlining, stressing.
on'derstroom, undercurrent.

on'derstuk, lower end, bottom piece, base; seat (of valve).
onderstut', (~), prop, support, buttress (up).
on'derstuurman, second mate.
on'dersuur, hypoacid.
on'dertand, lower(-jaw) tooth.
onderte'ken, (~), sign, affix one's signature, undersign; ~ aar, (-s), signatory (power); subscriber; wie is die ~ aar? who is the signatory? ~ ing, signature; signing.
on'dertitel, subtitle, subheading.
on'dertoe, lower down, to the bottom; downstairs, downwards; ~ gaan, go down(wards).
on'dertoon, undertone.
on'dertrou, (s) betrothal, notice of marriage.
ondertrou', (w) (~), intermarry; (b) (-de), betrothed; ~ de, (-s), the betrothed (bride, bridegroom); ~ ery, intermarriage.
ondertus'sen, meanwhile, in the meantime.
on'deruit, out at the bottom.
ondervang', (~), intercept; discount, meet (obligations); ~ ing, interception, obviating.
On'derveld, interior, up-country (districts), back-country, hinterland; ~ er, (-s), inlander; ~ s, (-e), from up-country.
on'derverdeel, (~), subdivide.
on'derverdeling, subdivision.
on'derverdieping, ground floor; stalls (in theatre).
on'derverhuring, subletting; sublease.
on'derverhuur, (~), sublet; sublease, ~ der, sublessor.
on'dervermeld, (-e), mentioned below.
on'derversadig, (-de), undersaturated; ~ ing, undersaturation.
on'derverseker, (~), underinsure; ~ ing, underinsurance.
ondervind', (~), experience; teenstand ~, meet with opposition.
ondervin'ding, (-e, -s), experience; BY (uit) ~, from experience; ~ is die beste LEERMEESTER, experience makes fools wise; experience is the mother (father) of wisdom (knowledge); 'n MAN van ~, a man of experience.
on'dervlak, ground-surface, base, bottom.
ondervoed', (w) (~), underfeed; (b) (-e), underfed; ~ ing, underfeeding, malnutrition.
on'dervoorman, chargeman.
on'dervoorsitter, vice-president, deputy-chairman.
ondervra', (~), interrogate, question, examine, cross-question; catechize; interview; ~ er, (-s), interrogator, questioner; examiner, catechist, heckler; interviewer, examinant; interpellant; ~ ging, interrogation, examination; interrogatory.
onderwa'terplant, submersed plant, natant plant.
onderwa'tersetting, inundation, flooding.
onderweg', on the way, in transit; ~ NA, bound for; ~ WEES, be on the way.
on'derwêreld, lower world, underworld; infernal regions, Hades.
on'derwerp[1], (s) (-e), subject, topic, argument, point, matter, theme.
onderwerp'[2], (w) (~), subdue, subject, subjugate, reduce, conquer; submit; hy ~ HOM, he submits; hom aan 'n ONDERSOEK ~, undergo an examination; jou aan Gods WIL ~, resign oneself to God's will.
onderwer'ping, submission, resignation, subjection, reducement; quietism; reduction; deference, duty; ~ sbepaling, submission clause.
on'derwerpsin, subject (noun) clause.
onderwor'pe, subject (to), submissive, obsequious, resigned (to); liable (to); ~ aan die volgende BEPALINGS, subject to the following stipulations; ~ aan die minister se GOEDKEURING, subject to the minister's approval; 'n ~ VOLK, a subjected nation; ~ nheid, submissiveness, obsequiousness, resignation, mansuetude.
onderwyl', meanwhile, while.
on'derwys[1], (s) education, tuition, teaching, instruction; DEPARTEMENT van O ~, Education Department; ~ GEE, teach; HOËR ~, higher (university, academic) education; KLASSIEKE ~,

classical education; *KLASSIKALE* ~, class-teaching; *LAER (primêre)* ~, primary (elementary) education; *MIDDELBARE (sekondêre)* ~, secondary education; *MINISTER van O* ~, Minister of Education; *TEGNIESE* ~, technical education; ~ *aan (vir) VOLWASSENES*, adult education.
onderwys'², (w) (~), teach, instruct, inform, educate; *die* ~ *ende personeel*, the teaching staff.
on'derwys: ~ **baar**, (..bare), educable; ~ **baarheid**, educability; ~ **beroep**, teaching profession; ~ **betrekking**, teaching post; ~ **bevoegdheid**, teaching certificate; qualification to teach; ~ **blad**, educational paper; ~ **department**, department of education.
onderwy'ser, (-s), teacher, instructor, educator; dominie; master, preceptor; ~ **es'**, **(-se)**, (lady) teacher, mistress; ~ **salaris**, teacher's salary.
onderwy'sers: ~ **amp**, teaching profession; ~ **eksamen**, teacher's examination.
onderwy'sersertifikaat, teacher's certificate.
onderwy'sers: ~ **kollege**, training college; ~ **nood**, dearth of teachers; ~ **opleiding**, training of teachers; ~ **pos**, teaching post, mastership; ~ **vereniging**, teachers' association.
on'derwyservaring, teaching experience.
onderwy'sing, instruction, lesson.
on'derwys: ~ **inrigting**, educational institution; ~ **konferensie**, education conference; ~ **kragte**, (teaching) staff, teachers; ~ **kunde**, didactics; ~ **metode**, method of teaching; ~ **peil**, standard of education (teaching); ~ **personeel**, teaching staff; ~ **sake**, educational matters; ~ **stelsel**, system of education; ~ **talent**, teaching capacity; ~ **vraagstuk**, problem of education; ~ **wet**, education act.
ondeskun'dig, (-e), inexpert, lay; ~ **heid**, inexpertness.
on'deug, (-de), vice, mischief, depravity; bounder, imp; *'n klein* ~, a little bounder; ~ **'delik**, **(-e)**, unsound, defective, imperfect; ~ *delike poging*, impossible attempt; ~ **'saam**, **(..same)**, without virtue.
ondeund', (-e), mischievous, naughty, roguish, puckish, impish, elfish; ~ **heid**, naughtiness, mischievousness, archness; mischief.
ondeurdag', (-te), ill-considered, shallow, rash, unstudied; ~ **t'heid**, lack of sound consideration.
ondeurdring'baar, (..bare), impenetrable, impermeable, impervious; proof (against); ~ **heid**, impenetrability, imperviousness; ~ *heid vir warmte*, adiathermancy.
ondeurgrond'baar, (..bare), unfathomable, inscrutable; ~ **heid**, inscrutability.
ondeurgron'delik, (-e), unfathomable, inscrutable, unsearchable; ~ **heid**, inscrutability, impenetrability.
ondeurla'tend, (-e), impermeable, impervious; ~ **heid**, impermeability.
ondeursig'tig, (-e), not transparent, opaque; obscure; ~ **heid**, opacity, intransparency; obscurity.
ondeursky'nend, (-e), not translucent, opaque; ~ **heid**, opacity.
ondeurtrek'baar, (..bare), impermeable.
ondeurwaad'baar, (..bare), unfordable, impassable; ~ **heid**, impassability.
ondien'lik, (-e), unserviceable, useless.
on'diens, disservice; *iem. 'n* ~ *bewys*, do someone a bad turn (ill service).
ondiens'tig, (-e), unserviceable; hurtful; inexpedient; *dit sou* ~ *wees*, it would serve no useful purpose; ~ **heid**, unserviceableness, inexpediency.
ondiensvaar'dig, (-e), disobliging, unhelpful.
on'diep, shallow; ~ **te**, shallows, shallowness.
on'dier, monster, brute.
on'dig¹, (s) prose.
on'dig², (b) (-te), leaky; not tight, loose;
ondig'terlik, (-e), unpoetic(al), prosaic.
on'digtheid, leaky (loose) condition.
on'ding, absurdity, nonsense; monstrosity.
ondoelma'tig, (-e), ineffectual, unsuitable, inappropriate; ~ **heid**, inappropriateness, unsuitability.
ondoeltref'fend, (-e), ineffective; ~ **heid**, ineffectiveness, inefficiency.

ondoen'lik, (-e), impracticable, unfeasible; ~ **heid**, impracticability.
ondraag'baar, (..bare), too heavy (to carry); not portable; unwearable.
ondraag'lik, (-e), intolerable, unendurable, insufferable, beyond bearing, excruciating; abhorrent; insupportable; ~ *e pyne*, excruciating pains; ~ **heid**, intolerableness, unendurableness, insufferableness.
ondrink'baar, (..bare), undrinkable.
ondruk'baar, (..bare), unprintable.
ondubbelsin'nig, (-e), unambiguous, unequivocal, clear, direct; ~ **heid**, directness, clarity.
ondui'delik, (-e), indistinct, faint, dim, cloudy, ambiguous, crabbed, imperfect(ly), blurred, obscure; *'n* ~ *e BEELD*, a blurred image; ~ *e SKRIF*, illegible writing; ~ **heid**, indistinctness, obscurity, faintness, haze.
ondula'sie, undulation.
onduld'baar, (..bare), unbearable, intolerable.
onduleer', (ge-), undulate; wave (hair).
one'del, (-e), ignoble, mean; illiberal; ~ *e metale*, base metals; ~ **moe'dig**, (-e), ungenerous; ~ **moe'digheid**, ungenerousness; illiberality.
on'eens, at variance, disagreeing; *hulle is dit* ~ *met mekaar*, they are at odds with one another.
oneens'gesind, (-e), at variance, differing, disunited, divided; ~ **heid**, disharmony, dissension.
on'eer, dishonour, disgrace, discredit, obloquy; *dit strek hom nie tot* ~ *nie*, it is no disparagement of him.
oneer'baar, (..bare), indecent, improper; dishonourable; ~ **heid**, indecency, impropriety; dishonourableness.
oneerbie'dig, (-e), disrespectful, irreverent, flippant, impious; ~ **heid**, disrespect, disrespectfulness, irreverence, impiety.
oneer'lik, (-e), dishonest, unfair, fraudulent, crooked, dishonourable; disingenuous; foul; ~ *e praktyke*, sharp practices; ~ **heid**, dishonesty, bad faith, improbity, crookedness.
oneersug'tig, (-e), unambitious.
oneer'vol, (-le), dishonourable; ignominious.
oneet'baar, (..bare), inedible, uneatable; ~ **heid**, inedibility.
on'effe, (-ner, -nste), uneven, rugged; bumpy; ~ **nheid**, unevenness, ruggedness.
oneg', (-te), illegitimate, adulterine, baseborn, misbegotten (child); spurious (document); counterfeit (coin); falsified, unauthentic, dummy, pseudo-, false, fictitious, mock, bogus (trial); pasty (jewels); ~ *te BREUK*, improper fraction; ~ *te DIAMANT*, imitation diamond; ~ *te KIND*, natural (illegitimate) child; bastard; ~ *te PÊRELS*, artificial pearls; ~ *te TIPE*, off-type.
onegaal', (..gale), **onega'lig**, (-e), uneven, unequal; changeable, fickle.
oneg'telik, (-e), out of wedlock, illegitimate.
onegt'heid, spuriousness; illegitimacy, bastardy; baseness; fictitiousness.
onein'dig, (-e), infinite, endless, interminable; ~ *DANKBAAR*, everlastingly grateful; ~ *KLEIN*, infinitesimally small; ~ *veel MOEITE*, no end of trouble.
onein'dige, infinity, infinite; *tot in die* ~, ad infinitum.
onein'digheid, infinity.
oneint'lik, (-e), improper (fraction); figurative, metaphorical; ~ *e vruggebruik*, quasi-usufruct.
on'ekonomies, (-e), uneconomic(al), wasteful.
oneksak', (-te), inexact; ~ **t'heid**, inexactitude.
onelas'ties, (-e), rigid, inelastic.
onelegant', (-e), inelegant, dowdy.
one'nig, at variance; discordant, disagreeing, divided; ~ **heid**, disagreement, discord, embroilment, difference, disunion, dissension, quarrel, dissidence, division, faction; ~ *heid kry*, fall out, quarrel.
onergden'kend, (-e), unsuspicious, innocent; ~ **heid**, unsuspiciousness.
onerkent'lik, (-e), ungrateful; ~ **heid**, ingratitude.
onerva're, (-ner, -nste), inexperienced, green, fresh, callow; ~ **ne**, (-s), tyro; ~ **nheid**, inexperience.

one'ties, (-e), unethical.
one'we, unequal, odd, uneven; ~ *getal,* odd number.
onewere'dig, (-e), disproportionate, disproportional, disproportioned; inadequate; proportionless; ~ **heid**, disproportion, asymmetry.
onewewig'tig, (-e), unbalanced, unpoised, ill-balanced, lop-sided; ~ **heid**, lack of balance.
onfatsoen'lik, (-e), indecent, improper, unmannerly, rude; ~ **heid**, indecency, impropriety.
onfeil'baar, (..bare), infallible, unerring, never-failing, foolproof; ~ **heid**, infallibility.
onfortuin'lik, (-e), unfortunate, unlucky.
onfris', (-se), stuffy (room); unwell (person); ~ **heid**, lack of freshness; indisposition.
onfyn', vulgar, unrefined.
ongaar', underdone; undercooked; slack-baked; (fig.) stupid.
ongaar'ne, (Ndl.), unwillingly, reluctantly, grudgingly, hesitatingly.
ongang'baar, (..bare), not current.
on'gans, (s) impurity in the blood; (bw) too much; ~ *gevreet,* overeaten.
ongas'vry, (-e), inhospitable.
ongeaard', (-e), ill-mannered, rude, low-class.
ongeadresseer(d)', (-de), without address, unaddressed (letter).
ongeag', (-te), unesteemed, unnoticed; (vs) irrespective of, apart from, notwithstanding.
ongebaan', (-de), unbeaten, untrodden, unpaved, pathless.
ongebleek', ..**bleik'**, (-te), unbleached
ongeblus', (-te), unslaked (lime); unextinguished (fire); unquenched (ardour).
ongebo'ë, straight, erect.
ongeboei', (-de), unfettered, unchained; without handcuffs.
ongebon'de, unbound (book); unfettered, free; licentious; *'n ~ BOEK,* book with paper cover; *~ STYL,* loose (prose) style; ~ **nheid**, unfettered condition, licentiousness, dissoluteness.
ongeborduur(d)', (-de), unembroidered.
ongebo're, unborn.
ongebrand', (-e), unroasted (coffee); unbranded (cattle); unburnt (brick).
ongebrei'del, (-de), unbridled, unchecked.
ongebro'ke, unbroken.
ongebruik', (-te), unused, unemployed, idle (capital); mint (stamp); ~ **lik**, (-e), unusual, uncommon.
ongedaan', (..dane), undone; *~ MAAK,* undo, cancel; *geen POGING ~ laat nie,* spare no effort.
ongedag'teken, (-de), undated.
ongedateer(d)', (-de), undated.
ongedeerd', (-e), unhurt, uninjured, safe, unscathed; *daar ~ van afkom,* escape unhurt.
ongedek', (-te), uncovered (animal); uninsured; not laid (table); unthatched.
ongediens'tig, (-e), disobliging, inofficious; ~ **heid**, disobligingness.
ongedier'te, vermin; (-s), wild animals (beasts).
ongedissiplineer(d)', (-de), undisciplined.
ongedoop', (-te), unbaptized, unchristened.
ongedop', (-te), unshelled (peas).
ongedors', (-te), unthreshed.
ongedroog', (-de), undried.
ongedroom', (-de), undreamt of.
ongedruk', (-te), unprinted.
on'geduld, impatience; ~ **'ig**, (-e), impatient; ~ **'igheid**, impatience.
ongedu'rig, (-e), fickle, inconstant, fidgety, restless, variable, erratic; ~ **heid**, fickleness, inconstancy; restlessness.
ongedwon'ge, unconstrained, natural, free, familiar, effortless, easy; *op 'n ~ toon,* in a natural voice; ~ **nheid**, naturalness, ease, unconstraint, familiarity.
ongeëer', (-de), unhonoured.
ongeërg', (-de), without creating a fuss; undesignedly, with no evil intention; nonchalant, calm, unperturbed, dry, offhand, casual; ~ **dheid**, coolness, unconcern, nonchalance.
ongeëwenaar(d)', (-de), unequalled, unsurpassed, unparalleled, unrivalled, peerless.

ongefrankeer(d)', (-de), with postage unpaid, unstamped.
ongegeneer(d)', (-de), unceremonious, free and easy, informal, offhand.
ongegis', (-te), unfermented, unleavened, azymous.
ongegoed', (-de), without means, moneyless.
ongegom', (-de), ungummed.
ongegradueer'de, (-s), undergraduate.
ongegren'del, (-de), unbolted.
ongegrond', (-e), false, unfounded, baseless, gratuitous, groundless, causeless; *heeltemal ~,* without any foundation; ~ **heid**, falseness, baselessness, groundlessness.
ongehard', (-e), unhardened; untempered.
ongeha'wend, (-e), undamaged, in good condition.
ongehei'lig, (-de), unhallowed, unsanctified.
ongehin'derd, (-e), unhindered, unobstructed, free.
ongehoop', (-te), not hoped for, unexpected.
ongehoor(d)', (-de), unheard of, unprecedented.
ongehoor'saam, (..same), disobedient, insubordinate; ~ **heid**, disobedience.
ongehuud', (..hude) unmarried; *ongehude staat,* state of celibacy; unmarried state.
ongeïsoleer', (-de), naked, not isolated.
ongekam', (-de), uncombed, unkempt.
ongekap', (-te), uncut (wood), unchopped.
ongekend', (-e), unknown; matchless; unprecedented.
ongekerf', (-de), uncut.
ongekers'ten, (-de), unchristened.
ongeklee', (..klede), undressed, unclothed, in undress.
ongeknak', (-te), whole, unimpaired.
ongekneus', (-de), unbruised.
ongeknip', (-te), uncut; unclipped (ticket).
ongekook', (-te), unboiled, raw, not cooked.
ongekou', (-de), unchewed.
ongekreuk', (-te), uncreased; unblemished.
ongekroon', (-de), uncrowned.
ongekruis', (-te), uncrossed.
ongekrul', (-de), uncurled.
ongekuis', (-te), unchastened; *~ te taal,* impure language.
ongekuns'teld, (-e), simple, artless, naïve, natural; ~ **heid**, artlessness, naturalness, simplicity, rusticity, naïveté, naïvety.
ongekwes', (-te), unwounded, unhurt.
ongelaag', (-de), unstratified; massive.
ongelaai', (-de), unloaded, unladen; undercharged (battery).
ongel'dig, (-e), invalid, null and void; ~ *verklaar,* nullify, declare null and void; ~ **heid**, invalidity; nullity; ~ **making**, vitiation; ~ **verklaring**, nullification, annulment, invalidation.
ongele'ë, inconvenient, inopportune, ill-timed.
ongeleed', (..lede), inarticulate, anarthrous.
ongeleent'heid, inconvenience, inopportuneness; *In ~ BRING,* inconvenience; *in GELDELIKE ~,* in pecuniary (financial) difficulties; *in ~ WEES,* be embarrassed.
ongeleer(d)', (-de), uneducated, illiterate; untrained, untamed, not broken-in (horse), rude, uncouth; ~ **d'heid**, illiterateness, illiteracy.
ongelees', (..lese), unread.
ongelek', (-te), unlicked; unmannered.
ongeles', (-te), unquenched.
ongelet'ter(d), (-de), illiterate, uneducated; abecedarian; not marked (washing); ~ **dheid**, illiteracy; ~ **de**, (-s), analphabete, illiterate person.
ongelief', (-de), unloved.
ongelik', (-te), unlicked; unmannerly.
ongelinieer', (-de), unruled, plain (paper).
on'geloof, unbelief, disbelief, misbelief; ~ **'baar**, (..bare), ~ **'lik**, (-e), incredible, beyond belief, fabulous, past all belief; ~ **'baarheid**, ~ **'likheid**, incredibility; ~ **waar'dig**, (-e), incredible; ~ **waar'digheid**, inveracity, unreliability.
ongelooi', (-de), untanned.
ongelou'ter, (-de), unpurified.
ongelo'wig, (-e), unbelieving, sceptical, incredulous; gentile; hard of belief, faithless; ~ **e**, (-s), unbeliever, disbeliever, heathen, misbeliever, infidel; ~ **heid**, incredulity, faithlessness, scepticism.

on'geluk, (-ke), accident, mishap, mischance, disaster, casualty, misfortune, ill fortune, misadventure; break-down (machine); *'n ~ BEGAAN*, cause someone hurt; *vir die ~ GEBORE wees*, have been born under an evil star; *die ~ het hom GETREF*, he has had some bad luck; *vir die ~ GEBORE wees*, be born under an unlucky star; *die ~ sal jou HAAL*, evil will befall you; *soos die ~ dit wou HÊ*, as ill luck would have it; you are looking for trouble; *die ~ IN wees*, be in a rage; *'n ~ KOM nooit alleen nie*, it never rains but it pours; *'n ~ KRY*, come to harm, meet with an accident; *jou 'n ~ LAG*, be convulsed with laughter; *PER ~*, accidentally, by accident; *iem. in die ~ STORT*, bring about someone's ruin; *dis SY ~*, that is his misfortune; *WAT die ~ wil jy hê?* what the dickens do you want?

ongeluk'kig, (-e), unhappy; hapless, unfortunate, unlucky; miserable, distressful; *~ in die LIEFDE*, unlucky in love; *~ in die SPEL*, having no luck in games; **~erwys(e)**, unfortunately; **~heid**, unluckiness.

on'geluks: ~bode, bringer of bad tidings (news); **~dag**, ill-fated day; **~jaar**, ill-fated year; **~kind**, unlucky person; bird of ill omen; a person born under an evil star; **~profeet**, prophet of doom; croaker; **~toneel**, scene of an accident; **~voël**, bird of ill omen.

on'gelukvry, (-e), accident-free.

on'gelyk¹, (s) wrong; *~ HÊ*, be in the wrong; *iem. in die ~ STEL*, put someone in the wrong.

ongelyk'², (b) (-e), unequal, uneven; dissimilar; disproportional; odd; disparate; one-legged; ragged; **~be'nig, (-e)**, scalene (triangle); **~heid**, inequality; unevenness; burr; odds; imparity, disparity; **~ma'tig, (-e)**, disproportionate, unequal, uneven, asymmetric(al); **~ma'tigheid**, disproportionateness; **~na'mig, (-e)**, (fractions) with different denominators; **~soor'tig, (-e)**, dissimilar, heterogeneous, disparate; **~soor'tigheid**, dissimilarity, heterogeneity; **~sy'dig, (-e)**, with unequal sides, scalene; **~vor'mig, (-e)**, dissimilar (triangles); **~vor'migheid**, dissimilarity; inconformity.

ongelym', (-de), unglued.

ongelyn', (-de), unlined, unruled (paper).

ongemaak', (-te), unmade; artless, natural.

ongemaal', (-de), not ground, unground.

ongemag'tig, (-de), unauthorized.

on'gemak, (-ke), inconvenience, hardship, discomfort; **~'lik, (-e)**, uncomfortable, uneasy, inconvenient; difficult to please; *iem. met 'n ~ like humeur*, somebody with a capricious temper; **~'lik'heid**, inconvenience, discomfort.

ongemanierd', (-e), rude, uncivil, misbehaved, bearish, discourteous, ill-mannered, mannerless, hoydenish; **~heid**, lack of manners (good breeding), rudeness, incivility, ill breeding, awkwardness, discourtesy.

ongemas'ker, (-de), unmasked.

ongema'tig, (-de), intemperate; immoderate; **~dheid**, intemperance; extremeness.

ongemeen', (..mene), uncommon, out of the common; unusual; **~heid**, uncommonness.

ongemeld', (-e), unmentioned.

ongemeng', (-de), unmixed; neat, pure (drink).

ongemerk', (b) (-te), unmarked (sheep); unperceived (approach); (bw) unnoticed, unperceived, imperceptibly.

ongemeubileer(d)', (-de), unfurnished.

ongemoei(d)', (-de), unmolested.

ongemotiveer(d)', (-de), unwarranted, groundless, not motivated, gratuitous; unsupported by evidence, unsupported by reasons.

ongemunt', (-e), uncoined, unminted.

ongenaak'baar, (..bare), inaccessible; stand-offish; unapproachable (person); **~heid**, inaccessibility.

on'genade, disfavour; disgrace; displeasure; *by iem. in ~ VAL*, incur someone's displeasure; *in ~ WEES*, be in disfavour (out of favour).

ongena'dig, (-e), merciless, cruel; violent, like hell.

ongene'ë, disinclined, unwilling, loath, chary; *sy is hom nie ~ nie*, she rather likes him.

ongeneent'heid, disinclination.

ongenees', (..nese), uncured; **~baar, (..bare)**, cureless, incurable, past recovery; confirmed, inveterate (criminal); **~lik, (-e)**, incurable, cureless, irremediable; beyond (past) recovery; **~like, (-s)**, incurable; **~likheid**, incurableness, incurability.

ongeneig', (-de), disinclined, unwilling; **~d'heid**, disinclination.

ongeniet'baar, (..bare), unenjoyable, unpalatable.

on'genoeë, displeasure; *~ HÊ*, be at loggerheads; *sy ~ te KENNE gee oor*, express his displeasure at; *in ~ LEWE*, be at odds with life.

ongenoeg'lik, (-e), unpleasant.

ongenoeg'saam, (..same), insufficient, inadequate; **~heid**, insufficiency.

ongenoem', (-de), unnamed, anonymous.

ongenom'mer(d), (-de), unnumbered.

ongenooi', (-de), uninvited, unbidden.

ongeoe'fen(d), (-de), unpractised, untrained, undrilled; **~dheid**, want of practice, inexperience.

ongeoor'loof, (-de), not allowed, unpermitted, forbidden, unlawful, illegal, illicit; illegitimate; clandestine; **~dheid**, unlawfulness, illegality; illegitimacy.

ongeo'pen, (-de), unopened.

ongeopenbaar', (-de), unrevealed.

ongeor'den, (-de), unordained; unarranged, disorderly, disordered, confused.

ongeorganiseer(d)', (-de), unorganized.

ongepaard', (-e), unpaired, not in pairs.

ongepas', (-te), unsuitable, unseemly, improper, misbecoming, inappropriate; **~t'heid**, unsuitability, unsuitableness, unseemliness, impropriety, inappropriateness.

ongepermiteer(d)', (ong.), (-de), unpermitted, not allowed.

ongeplaas', (-te), unplaced, unissued (shares).

ongeplak', (-te), unpapered (walls); unpasted (stamps).

ongeplavei', (-de), unpaved.

ongeplei'ster, (-de), unplastered.

ongeploeg', (-de), unploughed.

ongepoets', (-te), uncouth, ill-mannered, rude; uncleaned (shoes); **~t'heid**, uncouthness.

ongepolitoer', (-de), unpolished.

ongepolys', (-te), unpolished; rough-hewn.

ongeprys'¹, (-de), unpraised.

ongeprys'², (-de), unpriced.

ongera'de, inadvisable, inexpedient; **~nheid**, inadvisability.

ongered', (-de), unsaved.

on'gereed, unprepared.

ongere'ël, (-de), unsettled (matter); unorganized; unarranged (gathering).

ongereeld', (-e), irregular, disorderly, erratic; intercurrent; casual (customers); odd (job); fitful; *~e LEËR*, irregular army; mercenary army; *~e TROEPE*, irregulars; mercenaries; *op ~e TYE*, at odd times; **~heid, (..hede)**, irregularity, disorder(liness); (pl) riots.

ongeregistreer(d)', (-de), unregistered.

ongereg'tig¹, (-de), not entitled to, without any claim to; *~ tot die titel*, without a claim to the title.

ongereg'tig², (-e), unrighteous, wicked; **~heid**, unrighteousness, injustice; *ons ongeregtighede*, our iniquities (trespasses).

ongeregver'dig, (-de), unwarranted, unjustified.

ongere'kend, (-e), not counted, exclusive of; not taken notice of; casual; reckless, careless; *'n ~e houding*, a careless attitude.

ongerep', (-te), untouched, intact, inviolate, unmentioned; *~ te woud*, virgin forest; **~t'heid**, virginity; spotlessness, purity.

on'gerief, (..riewe), inconvenience, discomfort; *groot ~ ONDERVIND van*, suffer great inconvenience; **~'lik, (-e)**, inconvenient, uncomfortable; comfortless; **~'likheid**, inconvenience, uncomfortableness.

ongerig', (-te), undirected.

ongerim'peld, (-e), unlined, unwrinkled.

ongeroe'pe, uncalled for, unbidden.

ongeroer', (-de), unstirred, untouched.

ongerond', (-e), not rounded (vowel).

ongerook', (-te), unsmoked.
ongerus', (-te), uneasy, anxious; ~ *oor iem.*, anxious about a person; ~ **t'heid**, uneasiness, anxiety, care, disquiet.
ongerymd', (-e), absurd, preposterous, incongruous; ~ **heid**, absurdity, extravagance, preposterousness.
ongeryp', (-te), immature; unmatured.
ongerys', (-de), unleavened.
ongesaag', (-de), unsawn.
ongesalarieer', (-de), unpaid, unsalaried.
ongesalf', (-de), unanointed.
ongesê', (..segde), unsaid; *dit is beter om sulke dinge ~ te laat*, it is better to leave such things unsaid.
ongese'ël, (-de), unsealed, unstamped.
ongeseg'lik, (-e), indocile, intractable, wilful, disobedient; ~ **heid**, intractability, indocility.
ongesel'lig, (-e), unsociable, uncompanionable (person); cheerless, dull, gloomy, dreary (place); ~ **heid**, unsociableness, cheerlessness.
ongesertifiseer(d)', (-de), uncertified.
ongesien', unseen; ~ **s**: *goedere ~ s betaal*, pay for goods without having examined (seen) them.
ongesif', (-te), unsifted.
ongeskaaf', (-de), unplaned.
ongeskeer', (-de), unshorn (sheep); unshaven (chin).
ongeskei'e, unparted, unseparated.
ongeskend', (-e), uninjured, unviolated, undamaged.
ongeskeur', (-de), untorn.
ongeskik', (-te), unsuitable, unfit, inapt; improper, uncouth, ill mannered, rude, inadaptable, malapropos; disabled; inconvenient; ~ *te GEDRAG*, rude behaviour; ~ *MAAK*, render unfit; ~ **t'heid**, unsuitability, unfitness; uncouthness, bad manners, rudeness; incapacitation, disablement, infirmity, disability; inadaptability; inaptitude; disqualification; ~ **verklaring**, disqualification.
ongeskil', (-de), unpeeled.
ongeskil'der, (-de), unpainted.
ongeskoei', (-de), bootless, unshod.
ongeskok', (-te), unshaken (credit); unshocked.
ongeskon'de, uninjured, undamaged, intact; inviolate, unprofaned; integrate; ~ **nheid**, inviolateness, integrity.
ongeskool', (-de), untrained, unskilled; ~ *de arbeid*, unskilled labour.
ongeskre'we, unwritten; ~ *reg*, customary law.
ongeslag'telik, (-e), asexual.
ongeslyp', (-te), not sharpened, not whetted (knife); unpolished (diamond).
ongesmelt', (-e), unmelted, unfused.
ongesny', (-de), uncut, not castrated, entire.
ongesog', (-te), unsought; natural, spontaneous; convenient; ~ **t'heid**, naturalness.
ongesond', (-e), unhealthy, injurious to health, unwholesome, unsound (food); sickly (complexion); morbid, cachectic; insanitary; *'n ~ e toestand van sake*, an unhealthy state of affairs, ~ **heid**, unhealthiness, unsoundness, ill health; morbidity.
ongesorteer(d)', (-de), unsorted; unassorted.
ongesout', (-e), unsalted, fresh; not hardened; uninitiated; ~ *e perd*, horse not immune to horse-sick'ness.
ongespan'ne, lax (vowel).
ongespesifiseer(d)', (-de), unspecified.
ongesta'dig, (-e), inconstant, unstable, unsettled, changeable, fickle; fluent, fluxional; desultory, fitful; ~ *e weer*, unsettled weather; ~ **heid**, inconstancy, instability, fickleness; desultoriness; ~ **heid** *van die weer*, unsettled state of the weather.
ongesteel', (-de), sessile (bot).
ongesteld', (-de), unwell, indisposed, off colour; diseased; ~ **heid**, indisposition, ailment, illness, disorder, distemper, complaint.
ongestem', (-de), untuned.
ongestem'pel, (-de), unstamped; uncancelled (stamp).
ongesterk', (-te), unstrengthened.
ongesteur(d)', (-de), undisturbed, uninterrupted.
ongestig', (-te), unedified.
ongestil', (-de), unappeased, unquenched.
ongestoor(d)', (-de), uninterrupted, undisturbed.
ongestort', (-e), unpaid, uncalled (capital).

ongestraf', (b) (-te), unpunished; (bw) with impunity.
ongestryk', (-te), unironed.
ongestudeer', (-de), unstudied.
ongestyf', (-de), unstarched.
ongesubsidieer', (-de), unsubsidized.
ongesui'ker, (-de), unsweetened.
ongesui'wer(d), (-de), unpurified, unrefined, crude.
ongesuur', (-de), unleavened.
on'getand, (-e), imperforate.
ongete'ken(d), (-de), unsigned, anonymous.
ongetel', (-de), uncounted, untold, countless.
ongetem', (-de), untamed.
ongetem'per, (-de), untempered.
ongetoom', (-de), unbridled.
ongetroos', (-te), uncomforted, disconsolate, unconsoled.
ongetrou', (-e), unfaithful, disloyal.
ongetroud', (-e), unmarried, single, celibate; ~ *e tante*, maiden aunt.
ongetrou'heid, unfaithfulness, infidelity, disloyalty.
ongetwy'feld, undoubted(ly), doubtless, no doubt; beyond a doubt, certainly, questionless.
ongetwyn', (-de), untwined.
ongeuit', (-e), unuttered.
ongevaar'lik, (-e), harmless, non-hazardous, undangerous.
on'geval, (-le), accident, mishap; casualty; *dood deur 'n ~*, accidental death; ~ **leafdeling**, casualty ward; ~ **lelys**, list of casualties; ~ **lesaal**, casualty ward; ~ **leversekering**, insurance against accidents, accident insurance; **O ~ lewet**, Workmen's Compensation Act.
ongevee(g)', (-de), unswept.
on'geveer, almost, about, approximately, round about, in the neighbourhood of; some; *wat sal ~ die waarde wees?* what will the approximate value be?
ongeveer(d)'¹, (-de), without springs.
ongeveer(d)'², (-de), unfeathered.
ongeveins', (-de), sincere, unfeigned, undissembling; ~ **d'heid**, unfeignedness, sincerity.
ongeverf', (-de), unpainted; undyed.
ongevlek', (-te), unspotted, unstained; mint condition.
ongevoeg', (-de), unpointed.
ongevoeg'lik, (-e), indecent, unbecoming.
ongevoe'lig, (-e), insensitive, unfeeling, apathetic, phlegmatic, cynical, insensate, insensible, callous, chilly, cold-hearted, impassive; cruel; anaesthetic; dull, insusceptible, impassible; impercipient; *MAAK*, desensitize; ~ *VIR*, insensitive to; ~ **heid**, insensitiveness, lethargy, impassivity; analgesia; anaesthesia; apathy; callousness, hardness, insensibility, impassibility.
ongevoer'¹, (-de), unfed.
ongevoer'² (-de), unlined.
ongevon'nis, (-te), unsentenced.
ongevorm(d), (-de), unformed, not moulded, unshaped.
ongevou', (-de), unfolded.
ongevraag', (-de), unasked, uninvited, uncalled for; *iets ~ vertel*, volunteer the information.
ongewaardeer', (-de), unvalued, unappreciated.
ongewaar'sku, (-de), unwarned.
ongewa'pen(d), (-de), unarmed, unprepared.
ongewas', (-te), unwashed.
ongewend', (-de), unaccustomed.
ongewens', (-te), undesired; undesirable; ~ *te besoeker*, undesirable (undesired) visitor; ~ **te**, (-s), undesirable; ~ **t'heid**, undesirability.
ongewer'wel(d), (-de), invertebrate; ~ *de diere*, invertebrates.
ongewet'tig, (-de), unwarranted, unauthorized; unlawful (marriage); unfounded, groundless.
ongewild', (-e), unintentional; not in demand, unpopular; ~ **heid**, unpopularity.
ongewil'lig, (-e), unwilling, ~ **heid**, unwillingness.
ongewis', (-se), uncertain; ~ **heid**, uncertainty.
ongewis'sel(d), (-de), unchanged; unshed, uncut (teeth).
ongewit', (-te), not whitewashed; not whitened.
ongewond', (-e), unwounded.

ongewoon', (..wone), unusual, bizarre, uncommon, rare, extraordinary; *iets* ~ *s,* something out of the common (ordinary).
ongewoond', (-e), unaccustomed, unused to; ~ **heid**, unaccustomedness, unusualness.
ongewoon'heid, unusualness, uncommonness, extraordinariness.
on'gewoonte, strangeness, unaccustomedness, unfamiliarity; disuse.
ongewraak', (-te), undisputed, unchallenged.
ongewreek', (-te), unavenged.
ongewyd', (-e), unhallowed, profane, unconsecrated; secular (music).
ongewy'sig, (-de), unmodified, unaltered.
ongod'delik, (-e), ungodly.
ongodis', (-te), atheist.
ongodsdiens'tig, (-e), irreligious; ~ **heid**, irreligion, ungodliness.
ongodvrug'tig, (-e), impious, ungodly.
ongraag', unwillingly, reluctantly.
ongrammatikaal', (..kale), ungrammatical.
ongrondwet'lik, (-e), **ongrondwet'tig**, (-e), unconstitutional; ~ **heid**, unconstitutionality.
ongryp'baar, (..bare), unseizable, elusive.
on guns, disfavour; disgrace; *IN* ~ *by,* out of favour with; *in* ~ *RAAK,* fall into disfavour; ~ **'tig**, (-e), unfavourable, inauspicious, bad, disadvantageous; foul (weather); ~ **'tigheid**, inauspiciousness, unfavourableness.
onguur', (ongure), inclement, horrible, repulsive; *ongure BESONDERHEDE,* unsavory details; *ongure WEER,* inclement weather; ~ **heid**, inclemency; horribleness.
onhan'delbaar, (..bare), unmanageable, intractable; refractory; perverse, unruly; impracticable; ~ **heid**, intractability.
onhan'dig, (-e), awkward, clumsy, butter-fingered, maladroit, clownish, gauche (person); unwieldy (weapon); ~ **heid**, awkwardness, clumsiness, maladresse, maladroitness, gaucherie.
onhanteer'baar, (..bare), difficult to handle, unwieldy, clumsy; ~ **heid**, unmanageableness, clumsiness.
onharmo'nies, (-e), inharmonious.
onhart'lik, (-e), unfriendly, cold, frigid; ~ **heid**, unfriendliness, coolness.
onheb'belik, (-e), rude, ill-mannered (child); huge (piece); ~ **heid**, rudeness, unmannerliness.
onheel'baar, (..bare), incurable; ~ **heid**, incurableness.
on'heil, (-e), calamity, disaster; ~ *stig,* brew evil; ~ **'ig**, (-e), unholy; ~ **'igheid**, profanity; ~ **'saam**, (..same), unwholesome (influence); evil.
on'heils: ~ **bode**, messenger of ill luck; ~ **dag**, fatal day; unlucky day.
onheilspel'lend, (-e), ominous, inauspicious, baleful, bodeful, dark, portentous, eerie, ill-omened, ill-starred, menacing; ~ **heid**, portentousness; eeriness.
on'heilsprofeet, prophet of doom.
on'heil: ~ **stigter**, mischief-maker, ~ **swanger**, (-e), pregnant with disaster, fatal.
onhel'der, unclear, indistinct.
onherberg'saam, (..same), inhospitable; barren; ~ **heid**, inhospitability.
onherken'baar, (..bare), unrecognizable.
onherkryg'baar, (..bare), irrecoverable.
onherlei'baar, (..bare), irreducible; ~ **heid**, irreducibility.
onherroep'baar, (..bare), **onherroep'lik**, (-e), irrevocable, unrepealable, unalterable, final; ~ **heid**, irrevocability.
onherstel'baar, (..bare), irreparable; irretrieveable, irrecoverable; beyond (past) recovery; ~ *BESKADIG,* damaged beyond repair; ..*bare VERLIES,* irreparable loss; ~ **heid**, irreparableness; irretrievability.
onheug'lik, (-e), immemorial; ~ *e GEBRUIK,* immemorial use; *sedert* ~ *e TYE,* from time immemorial.
onhigië'nies, (-e), unhygienic, insanitary.
onhisto'ries, (-e), unhistorical.

onhof'lik, (-e), impolite, discourteous, inurbane; ~ **heid**, impoliteness, discourtesy, inurbanity.
onhoor'baar, (..bare), inaudible; catlike.
onhou(d)'baar, (..bare), untenable; unbearable; ~ **heid**, untenableness; unbearableness.
onhu'baar, (..bare), unmarriagable.
onhuis'lik, (-e), undomestic; unsociable, unhomely.
o'niks, (-e), onyx.
onin'baar, (..bare), irrecoverable; ..*bare vorderinge (skulde),* bad debts.
onin'gebonde, unbound.
onin'geënt, (-e), unvaccinated.
onin'gelig, (-te), unenlightened, uninformed.
onin'genaai, (-de), unstitched, in sheets (book).
onin'gevul, (-de), not filled up; blank.
onin'gewy, (-de), uninitiated; not consecrated (church); profane; *die* ~ *des,* the uninitiated, the outsiders.
oninskik'lik, (-e), uncomplying, unaccommodating.
oninteressant', (-e), uninteresting.
oninvor'derbaar, irrecoverable; ~ **heid**, irrecoverability.
oninwis'selbaar, inexchangeable, inconvertible.
onjuis', (-te), incorrect, erroneous, inaccurate; improper; ~ *te redenering,* faulty reasoning; ~ **t'heid**, incorrectness, error, erroneousness, inaccuracy; impropriety.
on'kant, offside (rugby).
onkapa'bel, (-e), incapable; incapacitated.
onkeer'baar, (..bare), irrepressible, not to be stopped; determined.
onken'baar, (..bare), unrecognizable, undistinguishable; unknowable; ~ **heid**, incognisance, unrecognizability; unknowableness.
onkerk'lik, (-e), secular, worldly.
onkerks', (-e), not church-going; indifferent to the church; ~ **heid**, indifference to the church.
onkies', (-e), indelicate, indecent, improper, immodest; ~ **heid**, indelicacy, bad taste, immodesty, indecency.
onkin'derlik, unchildlike; unfilial.
on'klaar, unfinished; out of order; unprepared, not ready; foul; pregnant; ~ *RAAK,* break down; ~ *TRAP,* get into trouble; get out of hand, kick over the traces; become confused; ~ **'heid**, malfunction; indistinctness, vagueness.
onklassifiseer'baar, (..bare), nondescript, unclassifiable.
on'kleur, odd colour; defective eye colour (in fowls); ~ **span**, team (of oxen) of varying colours.
onknap': *nie* ~ *nie,* no fool; rather clever; not at all bad-looking; good-looking.
onkoop'baar, (..bare), unpurchasable.
onkonstitusioneel', (..nele), unconstitutional.
onkontroleer'baar, (..bare), unverifiable.
on'koste, expense(s), charges, cost; damages, outlay; *na AFTREK van* ~, after deduction of expenses; *KLEIN* ~, petty expenses; ~ **besparing**, saving of expense; ~ **nota**, note of charges; ~ **rekening**, bill of charges.
onkreuk'baar, (..bare), unimpeachable; ~ **heid**, tried integrity, inflexible honesty, probity, rectitude, uprightness.
onkri'ties, (-e), uncritical.
on'kruid, (-e), weeds; *jy moet altyd* ~ *SAAI,* sow discord; you are always causing trouble; ~ *VERGAAN nie,* ill weeds grow apace; ~ **doder**, weedkiller, weedicide, herbicide; ~ **middel**, weed-killer.
onkrygshaf'tig, (-e), unwarlike, unmartial.
onkuis', (-e), unchaste, impure, immoral, obscene; ~ **heid**, unchastity, impurity; obscenity.
on'kunde, ignorance.
onkun'dig, (-e), ignorant; *iem.* ~ *LAAT van,* keep someone in the dark about (it); ~ *VAN,* ignorant of; ~ **heid**, ignorance.
onkwe(t)s'baar, (..bare), invulnerable; ~ **heid**, invulnerability.
on'langs, (b) (-e), recent; *u brief van* ~, your letter of recent date; (bw) recently, lately, freshly, newly; ~ **heid**, recency.
onle'dig, busy, occupied; *jou* ~ *hou met,* busy oneself with.

onleef'baar, (..bare), unbearable.
onleer'saam, (..same), indocile; ~heid, indocility.
onlees'baar, (..bare), unreadable, illegible; ~heid, illegibility.
onles'baar, (..bare), unquenchable; quenchless; ~heid, quenchlessness.
onliggaam'lik, (-e), incorporeal, bodiless; ~heid, incorporeity.
onlo'ënbaar, (..bare), undeniable, indisputable; demonstrable; ~heid, indisputability; demonstrability.
onlo'gies, (-e), illogical, inconsequent, alogical.
onlos'baar, (..bare), unredeemable, incommutable.
onlosmaak'lik, (-e), indissoluble, inseparable.
onlugwaar'dig, (-e), air-unworthy.
on'lus, dislike, listlessness; (pl) (-te), disorder, disturbances, riots; ~te-eenheid, riot squad; ~'tig, (-e), listless, dull; ~'tigheid, listlessness, dullness.
onmaatskap'lik, (-e), antisocial, unsocial.
on'mag, impotence, powerlessness; faintness, weakness; GESLAGTELIKE ~, sexual impotence; in ~ VAL, swoon, (become) faint; ~'tig, (-e), unable; impotent.
onmanier'lik, (-e), ill-bred, rude, ill-mannered; ~heid, lack of good breeding, rudeness, bad form.
onman'lik, (-e), unmanly.
onma'tig, (-e), intemperate, immoderate, extravagant, excessive; huge; crapulent, crapulous; ~heid, immoderateness, intemperance, insobriety, excess; crapulence.
onme(d)edeel'saam, (..same), uncommunicative; sparing, stingy.
onmc(d)cdo'ënd, ..do'gend, (-e), merciless, pitiless; ~heid, pitilessness, mercilessness, ruthlessness.
onmeet'baar, (..bare),immeasurable, incommensurable; irrational (maths.); ..bare getalle, surds; ~heid, immeasurableness, immeasurability, irrationality.
onmeet'lik, (-e), immense, vast, limitless, immeasurable; ~heid, immensity, vastness, immeasurability.
onmeng'baar, (..bare), immiscible; ~heid, immiscibility.
on'mens, monster, miscreant, brute.
onmens'lik, (-e), inhuman, cruel, brutal; ~heid, lack of humane feeling, cruelty, brutality.
onmerk'baar, (..bare), imperceptible, unnoticeable, insensible; ~heid, insensibility.
onmeto'dies, (-e), unmethodical.
onmid'dellik, (-e), immediate(ly), at once, direct(ly), prompt(ly), without delay; ~ AGTER my, directly behind me; EK kom ~, I am coming directly; GAAN ~, go at once; ~ WEG, off like a shot; ~e lewering, immediate delivery; ~heid, immediateness, immediacy.
on'min, disagreement, discord; in ~ GERAAK, to have fallen out; be at loggerheads; a cat-and-dog life, a life of discord.
onmis'baar, (..bare), indispensable, essential, vital; ~heid, indispensableness.
onmisken'baar, (..bare), undeniable, unmistakable.
onmoe'derlik, (-e), unmotherly.
onmon'dig, (-e), minor, under age; ~e, (-s), minor; pupil; ~heid, minority; nonage, pupilage.
onmoont'lik, (-e), impossible; ~e DINGE eis, demand impossibilities; cry for the moon; die ~e EIS, demand the impossible; ek kan ~ KOM, I cannot possibly come; in 'n ~e POSISIE raak, get oneself into an impossible situation; op 'n ~e UUR, at an unearthly hour; ~heid, impossibility.
onmusikaal', (..kale), unmusical.
onnaden'kend, (-e), thoughtless, inconsiderate, inadvertent, unreflecting, giddy, blundering; ~heid, thoughtlessness, inadvertence.
onnaspeur'lik, (-e), inscrutable, unsearchable; ~heid, inscrutability.
on'natuur, unnaturalness.
onnatuur'lik, (-e), unnatural, forced, affected; constrained; ~heid, unnaturalness, artificiality, affectedness.
onnavolg'baar, (..bare), inimitable; ~heid, inimitability.

onneem'baar, (..bare), impregnable; inexpugnable; ~heid, impregnability.
onnet', (-te; -ter, -ste), untidy, slovenly, slipshod; ~heid, untidiness.
on'nie, (omgangst.), teacher.
onno'dig, (-e), unnecessary, needless, useless; iets ~ maak, do away with something; ~heid, needlessness.
onnoem'baar, (..bare), onnoem'lik, (-e), countless; inexpressible, unmentionable; innominate.
onno'sel, (-e; -er, -ste), stupid, silly, dull-brained, blockheaded, anserine, fat-headed, dotty, dull, feather-brained, goofy, idiotic; innocent; ~e VENT, simpleton, booby, Simple Simon; 'n ~e BIETJIE, a mere trifle; JOU ~! you silly! ~heid, stupidity, silliness, idiocy; innocence, hebetude, doltishness.
onnoukeu'rig, (-e), inaccurate, careless; loose; ~heid, inaccuracy, inexactitude.
on'nut, (s), (-te), naughty child; good-for-nothing; (b) (-te), useless.
onnut'sig, (-e), mischievous, naughty; ~heid, mischievousness; disobedience.
onnut'tig, (-e), useless.
onoffisieel', (..siële), unofficial; informal.
onomastiek', onomastics.
onomas'ties, (-e), onomastic.
onomatopee', (..peë), onomatopoeia.
onomatope'ïes, (-e), onomatopoe(t)ic.
onomkeer'baar, (..bare), irreversible.
onomkoop'baar, (..bare), incorruptible, unbribable, money-proof; die politikus is ~, the politician is incorruptible; ~heid, incorruptibility.
onomskryf'baar, (..bare), indefinable.
onomstel'baar, (..bare), irreversible.
onomstoot'lik, (-e), irrefutable, incontestable, unshakable; axiomatic; cast-iron; irreversible.
onomstre'de, undisputed.
onomwon'de, in plain words, blunt, frank, outspoken, without mincing matters, outright, plump.
ononderbro'ke, uninterrupted, continuous, unbroken; non-stop (journey).
onontbeer'lik, (-e), indispensable; ~heid, indispensableness.
onontbind'baar, (..bare), indissoluble.
onontgin', (-de), onontgon'ne, not opened up; undeveloped, uncultivated.
onontkom'baar, (..bare), unescapable, inevitable.
on'ontplof, (-te), live, unexploded (shell).
onontplof'baar, (..bare), inexplosive, non-explosive.
onontsy'ferbaar, (..bare), indecipherable.
onontvank'lik, (-e), not receptive, irresponsive (to), not teachable; insusceptible; ~e pleit, bad plea.
onontvlam'baar, (..bare), non-inflammable.
onontvreem'baar, (..bare), inalienable.
onontwar'baar, (..bare), inextricable; ~heid, inextricableness.
onontwik'keld, (-e), undeveloped; illiterate, uneducated.
onontwyk'baar, (..bare), not to be evaded, inescapable, inevitable; irrecusable.
onoog'lik, (-e), unsightly; unlovely; ~heid, unsightliness.
onoop'gesny, (-de), uncut, unopened.
onoorbrug'baar, (..bare), unbridgeable.
onoordag', (-te), thoughtless.
onoordeelkun'dig, (-e), injudicious, ill-considered, impolitic; ill-contrived; ~heid, injudiciousness.
onoordraag'baar, (..bare), intransmissible, not transferable.
onoorgank'lik, (-e), intransitive.
onoorko(o)m'baar, (..bare), insurmountable.
onoorko'melik, onoorkoom'lik, (-e), insuperable, insurmountable; ~heid, insuperability.
onoorreed'baar, (..bare), not to be persuaded.
onoorsien'baar, (..bare), immense, interminable.
onoortref'baar, (..bare), onoortref'lik, (-e), unsurpassable.
onoortrof'fe, unsurpassed, unrivalled.
onoortuig'baar, (..bare), inconvincible, pig-headed.
onoortui'gend, (-e), inconclusive, unconvincing.

onoorwin'lik, (-e), unconquerable, invincible; ~ heid, invincibility.
onoorwon'ne, unconquered.
onopereer'baar, (..bare), inoperable.
onop'geëis, (-te), unclaimed; abandoned.
onop'gehelder, (-de), not cleared up, unexplained.
onop'gelos, (-te), unsolved (riddle); undissolved (powder); in abeyance.
onop'gemaak, (-te), not made (bed); untrimmed (hat); without make-up (face).
onop'gemerk, (-te), unobserved, unnoticed.
onop'geplak, (-te), unmounted; not glued on.
onop'geroep, (-te), uncalled; ~ te kapitaal, uncalled capital.
onop'gesmuk, (-te), unadorned; unvarnished (truth); unembellished, plain, bald.
onop'gevoed, (-e), uneducated, rude, ill-bred; ~ heid, lack of good breeding, rudeness.
onop'gevoer¹, (-de), not stall-fed; ~ de beeste, unfinished cattle.
onop'gevoer², (-de), unstaged (play).
onop'gevra, (~ agde), unclaimed; dormant; uncalled (money).
onophou'delik, (-e), incessant, continuous, ceaseless, perpetual, continual, never-ceasing.
onoplet'tend, (-e), inattentive, heedless, inadvertent, inobservant; ~ heid, inattentiveness, inattention, inadvertence.
onoplos'baar, (..bare), insoluble (salt); unsolvable, irresolvable (problem); ~ heid, insolubility.
onopmerk'saam, (..same), unobservant; ~ heid, incuriosity; inattention.
onopreg', (-te), insincere, disingenuous, false; ~ t'heid, insincerity, falseness, disingenuousness.
onopset'lik, (-e), unintentional, inadvertent; ~ heid, fortuity.
onopsig'telik, onopsig'tig, (-e), unobtrusive, inconspicuous.
onopval'lend, (-e), inconspicuous, unobtrusive, unpretentious.
onop'voedbaar, (..bare), uneducable.
onop'voerbaar, (..bare), unsuitable for the stage.
onor'delik, (-e), disorderly, dishevelled; rowdy; ~ heid, disorderliness, dishevelment.
onordent'lik, (-e), unbecoming, unseemly, improper, indecent.
on'paar, odd, unmatched; ~ kouse, odd stockings.
onpadwaar'dig, (-e), unroadworthy.
onparlementêr', (-e), unparliamentary.
onparty'dig, (-e), impartial, unbiased; even, evenhanded; disinterested; dispassionate; without fear or favour, just; neutral; ~ heid, impartiality, equity; disinterestedness.
on'pas: NOMMER ~ wees, be a square peg in a round hole; inopportune; inept; inappropriate.
onpas'lik, (-e), unbecoming, improper; ill, sick; ~ heid, impropriety.
onpas'send, (-e), unsuitable, inappropriate, out of place.
on'pedagogies, (-e), unpedagogic(al).
onpeil'baar, (..bare), unfathomable, abysmal; ~ heid, unfathomableness.
onpersoon'lik, (-e), impersonal; ~ heid, impersonality.
onplesie'rig, (-e), unpleasant, disagreeable; ~ heid, unpleasantness.
onpoë'ties, (-e), unpoetic(al).
onpopulariteit', unpopularity.
onpopulêr', (-e), unpopular.
onprak'ties, (-e), unpractical, academic.
onpresies', (-e), careless, inexact.
onproduktief', (..tiewe), unproductive, non-revenue-producing.
onproduktiwiteit', unproductiveness.
onpubliseer'baar, (..bare), unprintable, unpublishable.
on'raad, danger, trouble; DAAR is ~, there is something wrong; ~ MERK, smell a rat, scent danger.
onraad'saam, (..same), inadvisable; ~ heid, inadvisability.
onrealis'ties, (-e), unrealistic.

onred'baar, (..bare), past saving, irretrievable, irredeemable; beyond hope.
onre'delik, (-e), unreasonable, unfair, irrational, perverse; ~ heid, unreasonableness, irrationality.
onreëlma'tig, (-e), irregular, anomalous; abnormal; diffuse; unlawful; ataxic; ~ heid, irregularity, anomaly; abnormity; ataxy.
on'reg, wrong, injustice; iem. ~ AANDOEN, wrong a person; ~ DOEN, do wrong; act wrongly; 'n SKREIENDE ~, a glaring injustice; TEN ~ te, wrongly, erroneously.
onregeer'baar, (..bare), rebellious, unmanageable.
onregma'tig, (-e), unfair, unjust; tortuous; illegal, unlawful; actionable wrong, delict; ~ e BESIT, improper possession; ~ e DAAD, wrongful act; ~ e HOUER, unlawful holder; jou ~ TOE-EIEN, appropriate illegally (dishonestly); ~ heid, unfairness, injustice.
onregsin'nig, (-e), heterodox; ~ heid, heterodoxy.
on'regstreeks, (-e), indirect(ly), circuitous.
onregver'dig, (-e), unjust, unfair, inequitable; ~ heid, injustice, inequity.
on'rein, unclean (beast); impure; unchaste, foul; ~ heid, lack of purity, want of chastity, unchastity; impurity (speech).
onrek'baar, (..bare), inelastic; inductile.
onrid'derlik, (-e), unchivalrous; ~ heid, lack of chivalry.
onroe'rend, (-e), immovable; ~ e goed(ere), immovable property, real estate, landed property.
onrook'baar, (..bare), unsmokable.
onroman'ties, (-e), unromantic.
on'rus, unrest, anxiety, disquiet, disturbance, perturbation, commotion, trouble, flutter; fly (of watch); ~ BAAR, create alarm; wie ~ saai, sal MOEITE maai, who sows the wind will reap the whirlwind; in ~ VERKEER oor, be anxious about; ~ ba'rend, (-e), disquieting, alarming; ~ saaier, ~ stoker, (-s), mischief-maker, factionist, fire-brand; flag-waver, scaremonger, agitator; ~ 'tig, (-e), restless, uneasy, concerned (about); anxious; turbulent; ~ tig slaap, sleep uneasily (fitfully); ~ 'tigheid, restlessness, distraction, anxiety; turbulence; inquietude; ~ veer, hairspring.
onry'baar, (..bare), untraversable, impassable (road); unridable (horse).
on'rym, prose.
on'ryp, unripe, immature; crude; ~ heid, immaturity, unripeness, greenness.
ons¹, (s) (-e), ounce; 'n ~ GELUK is meer as 'n pond verstand, an ounce of fortune is worth a pound of forecast; HOEVEEL ~ e is daar in jou pond, who are "we"? 'n ~ PRAKTYK is beter as 'n pond teorie, practice is better than precept; TWEE ~, two ounces; VLOEIBARE ~, fluid ounce.
ons², (vnw), we, us; our; ~ E! heavens! EEN van ~, one of us (our party); ~ es INSIENS, to our mind, in our opinion; dit moet ONDER ~ bly, this must remain a secret; ~ SELF, we ourselves; ~ S'N, ours.
onsaakkun'dig, (-e), unbusinesslike, inexpert.
onsaak'lik, (-e), irrelevant; ~ heid, irrelevancy.
on'sag, (-te), ungentle, rude, violent, hard.
onsa'lig, (-e), unholy, unblest; unhappy; wicked.
onsamedruk'baar, (..bare), incompressible; ~ heid, incompressibility.
onsamehan'gend, (-e), disconnected, scrappy, rambling, discontinuous, loose, incoherent, desultory, disjointed; ~ heid, incoherency, disjointedness, discontinuity.
onse'delik, (-e), immoral; obscene; ~ heid, immorality; obscenity, depravity.
onse'dig, (-e), immodest; ~ heid, immodesty.
onseewaar'dig, (-e), unseaworthy.
onseg'baar, (..bare), unutterable.
onse'ker, ([-e]; -der,-ste), uncertain, unsafe, insecure, hazardous, chancy, casual, dubious, unsteady, precarious, unstable, doubtful, contingent, equivocal; ~ (e), doubt; uncertainty; iem. in die ~ e laat, leave someone in doubt; keep someone guessing; in die ~ WEES, be in doubt; ~ heid, uncertainty, doubt, precariousness, hazardousness, doubtfulness; aca=

talepsy; insecurity; toss-up; *in* ~ *heid verkeer,* be in doubt.
onsekta'ries, (-e), unsectarian, undenominational.
onselfstan'dig, (-e), dependent (on others); ~ **heid,** dependence.
onselfsug'tig, (-e), unselfish, generous, altruistic; ~ **heid,** unselfishness, altruism.
ons(e)lieweheers'besie, ladybird
Onse Va'der, the Lord's Prayer; Our Father.
onsien'lik, (-e), invisible.
onsier'lik, (-e), inelegant, ungainly; ungraceful; ~ **heid,** inelegance.
onsig'baar, (..bare), invisible, unseen; ~ **heid,** invisibility.
onsimme'tries, (-e), unsymmetrical, dissymmetrical.
onsimpatiek', (-e), unsympathetic; uncongenial (company); irresponsive.
on'sin, nonsense, bilge, bunkum, boloney, moonshine, persiflage, balderdash, rot, bosh, trash, claptrap; *dis LOUTERE* ~, it is pure nonsense; ~ *UITKRAAM,* talk rubbish.
onsin'delik, (-e), unclean(ly), dirty; ~ **heid,** uncleanliness, dirtiness.
onsink'baar, (..bare), unsinkable.
onsin'nig, (-e), absurd, nonsensical, inept, fatuous; preposterous; ~ **heid,** absurdity, nonsense, fatuousness.
on'sinrympie, nonsense verse, clerihew.
onska'delik, (-e), harmless, inoffensive, innocuous; ~ *maak,* render harmless; put out of the way; ~ **lucid,** harmlessness, innocuity, inoffensiveness.
onskap'lik, (-e), unreasonable, disobliging.
onskat'baar, (..bare), invaluable, priceless; beyond price, inestimable; ~ **heid,** pricelessness, invaluableness.
onskei(d)'baar, (..bare), inseparable; ~ **heid,** inseparability.
onskend'baar, (..bare), inviolable, irrefrangible; ~ **heid,** inviolability, immunity, inviolacy.
on'skerp, (-e), out of focus (photo).
onskeur'baar, (..bare), untearable.
onskoon', (onskone), unbeautiful, ugly, not pretty.
onskriftuur'lik, (-e), contrary to Holy Writ, antiscriptural.
on'skuld, innocence, guiltlessness; *sy* ~ *BETUIG,* protest his innocence; *IN my* ~, in my innocence; *die VERDRUKTE* ~, injured innocence.
onskul'dig, (-e), innocent, artless, guiltless, guileless; harmless; clean, clean-handed, clear; inoffensive, unoffending; with clean hands, not guilty; *'n* ~ *e GRAPPIE,* an inoffensive joke; ~ *PLEIT,* plead not guilty; *SO* ~ *soos 'n lam,* as innocent as a lamb; *'n* ~ *e VERMAAK,* a harmless amusement; ~ **bevinding,** acquittal; ~ **heid,** innocence.
onslyt'baar, (..bare), hard-wearing, not easily worn out; indestructible.
onsmaak'lik, (-e), unpalatable, unappetising, unsavoury; gross; distasteful; ~ **heid,** unsavouriness.
onsmeed'baar, (..bare), inductile.
onsmelt'baar, (..bare), infusible; ~ **heid,** infusibility.
onsolied', unsteady, unsound, not solid, flimsy.
onspeel'baar, (..bare), unplayable, unactable.
onsplin'terbaar, (..bare), unsplinterable.
onsplits'baar, (..bare), indivisible.
on'spoed, adversity.
onsportief', (..tiewe), unsportsmanlike, unsporting.
onsportiwiteit', unsporting behaviour.
onsself', ourselves.
onstaatkun'dig, (-e), impolitic.
onstabiel', (-e), unstable; **..biliteit',** instability.
on'stade: *te* ~, inconveniently; at an inopportune moment.
onstandvas'tig, (-e), inconstant, fickle, unstable; light; ~ **heid,** inconstancy, instability; disequilibrium.
onstelselma'tig, (-e), unsystematic.
onsterf'lik, (-e), immortal, undying; ~ **heid,** immortality; athanasia.
onstig'telik, (-e), unedifying; offensive; ~ **heid,** lack of spiritual benefit; offensiveness.
onstil'baar, (..bare), inappeasable.

onstof'lik, (-e), immaterial, incorporeal, spiritual, disembodied; ~ **heid,** immateriality, incorporeity.
onstraf'baar, (..bare), unpunishable.
onstrafwaar'dig, (-e), inculpable.
onstui'mig, (-e), impetuous; tempestuous, gusty; eager; rabid; turbulent, wild, boisterous; ~ **heid,** turbulence, boisterousness; impetuosity.
on'suiwer, (s) insects (in produce); vermin (on head); maggots (in sheep); *daar is* ~ *onder die skape,* the sheep have maggots; **(b) (-e),** false, flat (note), inexact; impure; faulty; ~ *e LEER,* unsound doctrine; ~ *LOOP,* run untrue; ~ **heid,** impurity.
onsy'dig, (-e), neuter (gender); neutral (state); impartial (judgement); ~ **heid,** neutrality; impartiality.
ontaalkun'dig, (-e), unlinguistic.
ontaard', (w) (~), deteriorate, degenerate; **(b) (-e),** degenerate; ~ **heid,** degeneracy; ~ **ing,** degeneration, depravation.
ontak'ties, (-e), ontakt'vol, (-le), tactless.
ontas'baar, (..bare), impalpable, intangible; ~ **heid,** impalpability, intangibility.
ontbas', (~), decorticate.
ontbeen', (~), bone, fillet.
ontbeer', (~), miss, lack, do without, forego, be destitute of; *iets nie kan* ~ *nie,* be unable to do without something; ~ **lik, (-e),** dispensable; *dit is* ~ *lik,* it can be dispensed with.
ontbe'ning, boning.
ontbe'ring, (-e, -s), hardship, privation, want; endurance.
ontbied', (~), send for, summon; ~ **ing,** summoning.
ontbind', (~), dissolve (partnership, marriage), annul, cancel; decay (matter); untie, undo, disattach, loosen (knot); demobilize, disband (forces); dismount (guards); resolve; decompose (body); disembody; disestablish; dismiss (meeting); *in FAKTORE* ~, factorize; *die PARLEMENT* ~, dissolve parliament; ~ *ende VOORWAARDE,* subsequent (resolutive) condition; ~ **baar, (..bare),** dissolvable; dissoluble; decomposable; analysable; ~ **baarheid,** dissolubility; ~ **end, (-e),** dissolvent; ~ **ing,** untying; decay, decomposition; separation; demobilization, disbandment; resolution (into component parts); analysis; disestablishment; dismissal; dissolution; *in* ~ *ing,* in a state of decomposition.
ontblaar', (~), defoliate, strip off (leaves).
ontbla'ring, defoliation.
ontbloot', (w) (~), strip, deprive, uncover, lay bare; disclose (fact); expose (body); divest; **(b) (..blote),** deprived, devoid; uncovered, naked, exposed; *van alle GROND* ~, utterly unfounded; *MET ontblote hoof,* bare-headed; ~ *VAN,* denuded of; destitute of; devoid of.
ontblo'ting, denunciation; divestment; (indecent) exposure, baring, uncovering, stripping; nudation.
ontboei', (~), unchain, unfetter.
ontboe'sem, (~), unbosom, unburden, pour out one's heart; ~ **ing, (-e, -s),** effusion; confession, outpouring.
ontbon'de, dissolved; decomposed.
ontbos', (~), deforest; ~ **sing,** deforestation, bush clearance.
ontbrand', (~), take fire, ignite; break out (war); *liefde laat* ~ *vir,* kindle love for; ~ **baar, (..bare),** inflammable, ignitable; ~ **baarheid,** combustibility; ~ **er, (-s),** igniter; ~ **ing,** ignition, conflagration; ~ **ingspunt,** flash-point.
ontbreek', (~), be wanting, be missing, be in want of, be lacking; *dit* ~ *hom aan GELD,* he is in need of money; *dit* ~ *hom aan MOED,* he is lacking in courage; *die ontbrekende SKAKEL,* the missing link.
ontbrei'del, (~), unbridle.
ontbur'ger, (~), disfranchise; deprive of civil rights; ~ **ing,** attainder; disfranchisement.
ontbyt', (s) (-e), breakfast; **(w) (~),** have breakfast; ~ **graan,** breakfast cereal; ~ **rit,** breakfast run (motorbikes); ~ **tafel,** breakfast table.
ontdaan', upset; ~ *van,* divested of, stripped of, devoid of.
ontdek', (~), discover, find out; uncover, detect; dis-

close; ~baar, (..bare), discoverable; ~kend, (-e), detecting; ~ker, (-s), discoverer, explorer; detector.
ontdek'king, (-e, -s), discovery; ~sreis, expedition, exploration, journey of discovery; exploratory trip; ~sreisiger, explorer.
ontdoen', (~), divest, strip (off); disrobe; *jou van jou jas* ~, take off one's overcoat.
ontdons'proses, delinting (cotton).
ontdooi', (~), thaw, melt; unbend; defrost (food).
ontduik', (~), shirk, dodge, evade, elude, escape defeat; ~end, (-e), evasive; elusive; ~ing, evasion; elusion, eluding; fake; jink (aero.); ~*ing v.d. wet,* evasion of the law.
onteenseg'lik, (b) (-e), unquestionable, incontestable; (bw) confessedly; beyond debate; unquestionably, undoubtedly, undeniably.
onteer', (~), dishonour, disgrace, defame, deflower; brand; ravish, violate, rape, defile (a woman); ~der, (-s), defiler, violator
onteg'nies, (-e), untechnical.
ontei'en, (~), dispossess; expropriate; disseize; nationalize; ~aar, (-s), dispossessor; expropriator; ~ing, (-e, -s), dispossession; expropriation; nationalization; ~ingsreg, law (right) of expropriation; ~ingswet, expropriation act.
ontel'baar, (..bare), countless, innumerable, uncountable; ~heid, countlessness, innumerability.
ontem'baar, (..bare), untamable, indomitable; wild, violent; ~heid, untamableness, indomitability.
onte'rend, (-e), dishonourable, ignominious, base, menial, discreditable.
onterf', (~), disinherit.
onte'ring, desecration; rape, violation, defloration; prostitution.
onter'we, (w) (~) = onterf.
onter'wing, disinheritance, disherison.
ontevre'de, (-ner, -nste), discontented, dissatisfied; disaffected, displeased, disgruntled; out of conceit; *DIE* ~*nes,* the malcontents; ~ *OOR,* discontented (dissatisfied) with; ~nheid, discontent(ment); displeasure, dissatisfaction, disaffection, disaffectedness.
ontferm', (~), take pity (on), have mercy (on), commiserate; *HEER,* ~ *U,* Lord, have mercy; *jou* ~ *OOR,* take pity on; ~ing, pity, mercy, commiseration.
ontfut'sel, (~), pilfer, filch, wheedle out of, purloin; abstract (from); prig.
ontgaan', (~), escape, evade, dodge, elude; *dit het my* ~, it slipped my mind, I forgot.
ontgas', (~), degas, decontaminate; ~sing, decontamination.
ontgel'd(e), (~): *dit moet* ~, have to pay (suffer) for it.
ontges'pe, (~), unbuckle.
ontgin', (~), prepare for cultivation; develop, reclaim, exploit; work (mine); ~ner, (-s), exploiter; ~ning, clearing, developing; exploitation; working; reclamation, cultivation.
ontglaas', (~), devitrify; ..gla'sing, devitrification.
ontglip', (~), slip out (away), escape; *HY het my* ~, he gave me the slip; *'n KANS laat* ~, let a chance slip; *die WOORD het my* ~, the word escaped me.
ontgloei', (~), grow red-hot, take fire; be roused (to).
ontgo'ding, debunking.
ontgo'ël, ontgo'gel, (~), disillusion, disenchant; undeceive; ~ing, disillusionment, disenchantment, dishallucination.
ontgom', (~), degum.
ontgon'ne, cultivated, developed.
ontgraat', (~), bone (fish).
ontgren'del, (~), unbolt, unbar.
ontgroei', (~), outgrow; *die plak* ~, outgrow the rod.
ontgroen', (~), initiate; ~ing, initiation; ~ingsdag, day of initiation; ~ingsfees, initiation feast.
onthaak', (~), unhook.
onthaal', (s) (..hale), reception, treat, entertainment, feast; (w) (~), entertain; cheer; treat, regale, feast; *iem. op lekkernye* ~, treat someone to delicacies; ~toelae, entertainment allowance.
onthaar', (~), strip (hair off dog); depilate; ~middel, depilatory.

ontha'ler, (-s), entertainer.
onthals', (~), decapitate, behead.
onthal'we, for the sake of; *om sy* ~, for his sake, on his account.
onthard', (~), soften (water); ~ing, softening.
ontha'rend, (-e), depilatory.
ontha'ring, depilation; ~smiddel, depilatory.
ontheem'de, (-s), homeless (displaced) person.
onthef', (~), exempt, exonerate (from blame); discharge (from office); release; dispense; *van sorg* ~, free from care; ~fing, exemption, exoneration; discharge; dispensation; disencumbrance.
onthei'lig, (~), desecrate, profane; deconsecrate; ~er, (-s), desecrator; ~end, (-e), profane; ~er, (-s), profaner; ~ing, desecration, profanation.
onthe'we, freed from.
onthoof', (~), behead, decapitate, execute, guillotine; decollate; ~ding, (-e, -s), decapitation, beheading; decollation.
ontho'ring, (~), dishorn, dehorn.
onthou', (s) remembering; *goed van* ~ *wees,* have a retentive memory; (w) (~), remember, bear in mind; retain; abstain, withhold, refrain; *hom van GEWELD* ~, abstain from violence; *HELP my* ~, remind me, please; *hom* ~ *VAN,* refrain from (doing something); ~dend, (-e), abstemious, abstinent; ~ding, denial, abstinence, abstinency; forbearance; ~dingsdag, abstinence day; ~er, (-s), abstainer, teetotaler.
onthul', (~), unveil (statue); lay bare (one's heart); reveal, unfold, disclose (a secret); betray; divulge; ~ling, (-e, -s), disclosure, revelation, divulgation; exposure; unveiling; ~lingsplegtigheid, unveiling ceremony.
onthuts', (w) (~), confuse, discomfit, disconcert, consternate, discompose, perplex; (b) (-te), confused, perplexed, discomfited, upset, bewildered, disconcerted; ~ing, dismay, bewilderment.
ontkalk', (~), decalcify; ~ing, decalcification.
ontken', (~), deny, disclaim, repudiate, disown, disavow, negate; abnegate; gainsay; controvert; ~nend, (-e), negative; privative; ~*nend antwoord,* reply in the negative; ~ner, (-s), denier, gainsayer; ~ning, (-e, -s), denial, negation, repudiation; traverse (facts in pleadings); disclaimer; disavowal; abnegation; negative; *die dubbele* ~*ning,* the double negative.
ontkern', (~), degerminate; enucleate.
ontkers'ten, (~), dechristianize; ~ing, dechristianizing.
ontke'ten, (~), unchain, unfetter, let loose; create, provoke; ~ing, unchaining.
ont'kiem¹, (~), degerminate.
ontkiem'², (~), germinate; germ; ~baar, (..bare), live; ..*bare perskepitte,* live peach-stones; ~ing, germination; ~ingskrag, germinating power; ~ingstyd, incubation period.
ontkie'ser, (~), disfranchise; ~ing, disfranchisement.
ontkle'ding, undressing; divestment, divestiture.
ontklee', (~), undress, disrobe; disarrange; divest; *jy moet jou* ~, you must undress; ~danseres, striptease dancer.
ontkleur', (~), decolour, discolour, blanch, loose colour, fade; ~ing, discoloration, decoloration.
ontklits', (~), deburr.
ontkluis'ter, (~), unfetter, unshackle.
ontknoop', (~), unbutton; undo, unravel.
ontkno'ping, unravelling; event; denouement, catastrophe (in drama); unbuttoning.
ontko'ling, decarbonization.
ontkom', (~), escape, get away; *aan iets* ~, escape from something.
ontko'ming, (-e, -s), escape, let-off.
ontkom'kans, chance of escape.
ontkool', (~), decarbonize.
ontkop'pel, (w) (~), declutch; uncouple, disconnect, disengage (gears); unleash (dogs); (b) (de-), out of gear; uncoupled; ~ing, declutching, throwing out of gear; ~ingstoestel, disengaging-gear (-hook).
ontkors'ting, decrustation.

ontkrag', (~), enfeeble, weaken; ~ **tig**, (~), invalidate; ~ **tiging**, invalidation.
ontkroon', (~), depose (king); head (tree).
ontkurk', (~), uncork.
ontlaai', (~), discharge; *'n geweer* ~, unload a gun; ~ **er**, unloader; ~ **stok**, cleaning-rod; ~ **tang**, discharger.
ontla'ding, discharge, discharging; détente.
ontlas', (~), unburden, discharge; disencumber; deplete; disburden; defecate, empty, evacuate (the bowels); ~ **klep**, escape- (relief-, discharge-) valve; ~ **kraan**, cylinder-cock, drain-cock; ~ **pyp**, delivery-pipe; ~ **ting**, (-e, -s), discharge; disencumbrance; defecation, stool, excrement, bowel action, evacuation, movement (of the bowels); ~ *ting hê*, go to stool; ~ **tingsiektes**, excremental diseases.
ontle'dend, (-e), analytic.
ontle'der, (-s), dissector, anatomist; analyst.
ontle'ding, (-e, -s), analysis, parsing (of words); dissection; resolution (into parts); anatomy.
ontleed', (~), analyse, parse; dissect, anatomize; prosect; ~ **baar**, (..bare), analysable; ~ **kamer**, dissecting-room; ~ **kunde**, anatomy; analytics; ~ **kun'dig**, (-e), anatomical; analytic; ~ **kun'dige**, (-s), anatomist; ~ **mes**, dissecting-knife; scalpel; ~ **tafel**, dissecting-table.
ontleen', (w) (~), borrow (from); derive (from); (b) (-de), derived, adscititious; ~ *aan ENGELS*, borrowed from English.
onle'ning, (-e, -s), borrowing, derivation; loanword.
ontlig'gaam, (w) (~), disembody; (b) (-de), disembodied (spirit).
ontlok', (~), elicit; *iem. 'n geheim* ~, worm a secret out of someone.
ontloop', (~), evade, escape, slip away.
ontlug', (~), de-aerate; vent; ~ **ter**, de-aerator; vent; ~ **ting**, de-aeration; venting.
ontluik', (~), open, unfold; bud; burst (into flower); ~ **end**, (-e), opening, unfolding; evolving; budding; ~ *ende LIEFDE*, nascent love; ~ *ende TALENT*, budding talent; ~ **ing**, opening, unfolding.
ontluis', (~), delouse, deverminize; ~ **ing**, delousing; ~ **ingstent**, delousing-tent.
ontlui'ster, (~), dim, tarnish; debunk; ~ **ing**, debunking.
ontlym', (~), deglutinate.
ontmaagd', (~), ravish, defile, deflower (a woman); ~ **ing**, defloration.
ontmagnetiseer', (~), demagnetize, degauss.
ontman', (~), castrate, emasculate, evirate, geld; weaken; ~ **de**, (-s), eunuch, castrate; ~ **ning**, castration, emasculation.
ontman'tel, (~), dismantle (a fortress); ~ **ing**, dismantling.
ontmas', (~), demast, dismast.
ontmas'ker, (~), expose, unmask, debunk, dismask; ~ **ing**, unmasking, exposure, debunking.
ontmens', (~), dehumanize.
ontmoe'dig, (w) (~), discourage, dishearten, damp the spirits (of), depress, deject, demoralize, dispirit, disanimate, discountenance, dismay; (b) crestfallen, disheartened; ~ **end**, (-e), discouraging, disheartening, chilling, demoralizing; deterring; ~ **ing**, discouragement, dismay, disheartening, disanimation, disheartenment.
ontmoet', (~), meet, encounter, come across; *ons het mekaar daar* ~, we met each other there; ~ **ing**, meeting, encounter, experience; ~ **ingsgeveg**, encounter, skirmish.
ontmunt', (~), demonetize; ~ **ing**, demonetization.
ontneem', (~), deprive (of), take away; bereave; detract; *iem. alle HOOP* ~, deprive a person of all hope; *iem. die LEWE* ~, kill someone; *'n kind 'n MES* ~, take away a knife from a child; *dit* ~ *my MOED om weer te probeer*, that deprives me of the desire to try again.
ontne'ming, deprivation; dispossession.
ontnug'ter, (~), make sober; disillusion, disenchant, disabuse; ~ **ing**, disillusion(ment), rude awakening; dishallucination; disenchantment.
ontoegank'lik, (-e), inaccessible; unapproachable;

impassable; impervious; ~ **heid**, inaccessibility; impassableness.
ontoegeef'lik, ontoege'wend, (-e), uncomplying, unaccommodating, unyielding; ~ **heid**, unwillingness to comply, disobligingness.
ontoelaat'baar, (..bare), inadmissible; impermissible; ~ **heid**, impermissibility; inadmissibility.
ontoepas'lik, (-e), inapplicable; irrelevant; ~ **heid**, inapplicability; irrelevancy.
ontoerei'kend, (-e), inadequate (forces); deficient; insufficient (strength); ~ **heid**, inadequacy, insufficiency.
ontoere'kenbaar, (..bare), not chargeable; not answerable; irresponsible; of unsound mind; not imputable; ~ *wees*, not to be responsible for one's actions; ~ **heid**, irresponsibility.
ontoeskiet'lik, (-e), disobliging, unaccommodating, uncompromising; irresponsive.
ontogene'se, ontogenesis.
ontogene'ties, (-e), ontogenetic.
ontogenie', ontogeny.
ontologie', ontology; ..**lo'gies**, (-e), ontological.
ontoom'baar, (..bare), uncontrollable; indomitable.
ontoon'baar, (..bare), not fit to be shown, unpresentable.
ontpak', (~), unpack.
ontpers', (~), wring from, extort from; draw (tears).
ontpit', (~), remove seeds (pips) from; ~ *te rosyntjies*, seeded raisins; ~ **ting**, stoning.
ontplof', (~), explode, detonate, pop, go off, discharge; fulminate; ~ **baar**, (..bare), explosive; ~ **baarheid**, explosiveness; ~ **fer**, (-s), detonator; ~ **fing**, (-e, -s), explosion, detonation; fulmination; blow-out; ~ **fingsdoos**, box-trap; ~ **fingsgeluid**, explosive (consonant); ~ **fingsgelatien**, blasting-gelatine; ~ **fingskamer**, ignition-chamber (motor); ~ **fingsmiddel**, explosive; blasting-material; ~ **stof**, explosives, blasting-agent.
ontplooi', (~), unfold, unfurl (flag); put forth, display, develop, expand; deploy (troops); evolve; unravel; ~ **ing**, unfolding; development; deployment; evolution.
ontpop', (~), leave the pupal case; turn out to be, unveil as, blossom out into, emerge as; *jou* ~ *as digter*, turn out to be a poet.
ontraad'sel, (~), unravel.
ontraai', (~), dissuade, advise against.
ontra'dend, (-e), dissuasive.
ontra'ding, dissuasion, dehortation.
onra'fel, (~), unravel, unweave; unscramble.
ontred'der, (~), dislocate, disorganize, cripple, disable, impair; dismantle (ship); ~ (**d**), (-**de**), damaged, disabled, out of order; ~ **ing**, disorganization, collapse, breakdown, ruin.
ontref'baar, (..bare), invulnerable.
ontrei'nig, (~), pollute, defile, sully.
ontreuk', (~), deodorize.
ontrief', ..**rie'we**, (~), inconvenience, deprive (of); *as dit jou nie sal* ~ *nie*, if it will not inconvenience you.
ontrim'peling, face-lifting.
ontroer', (~), move, touch, affect; commove; impassion; ~ (**d**), (-**de**), touched, moved; ~ **ing**, emotion.
ontroes', (~), free from rust.
ontrol', (~), unfurl, unroll, roll out; ~ **ling**, evolution.
ontrond', (~), unround; delabialize; ~ **ing**, unrounding, lack of rounding; delabialization.
ontroof', (~), bereave, deprive, rob of, defraud, ravish; *iem. sy geld* ~, rob someone of his money.
ontroom', skim cream off, separate (cream from milk), cream.
ontroos'baar, (..bare), inconsolable, heartbroken, disconsolate; ~ **heid**, disconsolateness.
ontrou', (b) (-**e**), untrue, disloyal, faithless, unfaithful; disaffected; false.
on'trou, ontrou'heid, (s) unfaithfulness, disloyalty, infidelity, disaffection, perfidy, faithlessness, defection.
ontro'we, (w) (~) = ontroof.
ontro'wing, robbing; ravishment; bereavement.
ontruim', (~), evacuate, vacate, clear; deplenish; ~ **eling**, (-e), evacuee; ~ **elingskamp**, evacuee camp;

~ing, evacuation, clearing; ~ingsbevel, ejectment order.
ontruk', (~), snatch away, wrench from; *aan die vergetelheid* ~, save from oblivion.
ontrus', (~), disturb, worry, alarm.
ontsag', awe, respect, deference; prestige; ~ *INBOESEM*, inspire with awe; *SONDER* ~ *vir die regte van ander*, without regard for the rights of others; ~lik, (-e), awful; formidable; enormous, imposing; prodigious; ~likheid, awfulness; immensity, enormousness; enormity; ~wek'kend, (-e), awe-inspiring, imposing.
ontsê', (~), deny, refuse, forbid; abnegate, forgo; *jou die GENOT* ~ *van*, deny oneself the joy of; *hom GENOT* ~, forgo pleasure.
ontse'ël, (~), unseal; uncap (honeycombs).
ontseg', (~) = ontsê.
ontseg'ging, denial, refusal; abnegation.
ontseil', (~), steer clear of, avoid.
ontse'nu, (~), unnerve; refute (allegations); enervate; emasculate; invalidate; ~wing, enervation; refutation; invalidation.
ontset', (s) relief; (w) (~), relieve; perplex, appal; remove, expel (from office); ~ *uit sy POS*, removed from his post; ~ *STAAN oor*, stand aghast at; *'n STAD* ~, relieve a town; (b) (-te), appalled, aghast.
ontse'tel, (~), unseat, disseat.
ontset': ~tend, (-e), terrible, awful, appalling, dreadful; ~ting, fright, terror, consternation, horror, astonishment, dread; eviction; relief (siege); ~tingstroepe, relief, relieving force.
ontsiel', (~), deprive of life, disanimate; ~ing, disanimation.
ontsien', (~), respect, stand in awe of; spare; ~ *sy grys HARE*, have respect for his grey hairs; *geen MOEITE* ~ *nie*, spare no pains; *hy* ~ *NIKS*, he has no scruples.
ontsier', (~), deface, disfigure, deform, disfeature, mar (beauty); ~der, (-s), defacer; ~ing, disfigurement, defacement.
ontsil'wer, (~), desilverize.
ontsink', (~), fail, sink away; *die moed* ~ *my*, my courage fails me.
ontskaak', (~), carry away (off); kidnap.
ontskeep', (~), disembark; discharge; debark.
ontske'per, (-s), discharger (of ship's cargo).
ontske'ping, disembarkation, debarkation.
ontskiet', (~), slip from; *sy naam het my* ~, I have forgotten his name.
ontskui'mer, (-s), defoamer, antifoaming agent.
ontslaan', (~), dismiss, discharge, depose; acquit; free; release (military duties), cashier; exempt; exonerate; *iem. van 'n BELOFTE* ~, absolve someone from a promise; *iem. uit sy BETREKKING* ~, relieve someone of his office, dismiss someone.
ontslaap', (~), die, pass away.
ontsla'e, discharged; rid; ~ *raak van*, get rid of.
ontslag', release, discharge, acquittal, dismissal; resignation; walking-ticket, walking-orders, congé, firing; ~ *AANVRA*, tender one's resignation; ~ *GEE*, dismiss, discharge; ~ *NEEM*, resign; ~bewys, clearance-certificate; ~brief, discharge certificate; dismissal notice; ~depot, dispersal depot; ~neming, resignation.
ontsla'pe, dead, deceased; ~ne, (-s), the deceased, the departed.
ontslui'er, (~), reveal, unveil, disclose; ~ing, revelation; unveiling.
ontsluit', (~), open, unlock; flux (chem.); develop (mining); ~er, developer; ~ing, unlocking; exposure; development (mining); ~ingspunt, development end.
ontsmet', (~), disinfect; fumigate; degas; ~middel, ~stof, disinfectant, antiseptic; ~tend, (-e), aseptic, antiseptic; ~ter, fumigator; disinfector.
ontsmet'ting, antiseptic, disinfection; fumigation.
ontsmet'tings: ~inrigting, disinfecting establishment; ~linne, antiseptic lint; ~middel, disinfectant,, aseptic, antiseptic; deodorant; ~naelkussing, antiseptic umbilical pad; ~oond, disinfection-stove, fumigator, disinfector; ~pleister, antiseptic plaster; ~verband, antiseptic dressing.

ontsnaar', (~), unstring.
ontsnap', (~), escape, evade, elude; ~ *aan*, escape from; ~per, (-s), escaper; ~ping, escape; ~te, (-s), escaped person, escapee.
ontson'dig, (~), cleanse, purge, shrive; ~ing, shriving, absolution.
ontsout', (~), freshen, edulcorate, desalt, desalinate; ~ing, desalting, desalination.
ontspan', (~), relax, recreate; divert; release (spring); unbend; emolliate; ~ne, relaxed; ~nend, (-e), recreative.
ontspan'ning, rest, recreation, relaxation; détente; disportment; diversion; ~ *neem*, take exercise; rest from work, indulge in recreation.
ontspannings: ~drag, leisure wear; ~lektuur, light reading; ~lokaal, recreation hall; ~oord, public resort; ~politiek, détente; ~terrein, recreation ground.
ontspoor', (~), derail, run off the line, leave the rails; ~der, (-s), derailer.
ontspo'ring, (-e, -s), derailment.
ontspring', (~), escape; rise (river); originate; *die Vaalrivier* ~ *naby Breyten*, the Vaal River has its source near Breyten.
ontspruit', (~), sprout forth, germinate; originate, arise; ~ *uit*, arise from; be descended from.
ontstaan', (s) origin; beginning; birth, genesis; nascency; origination; ~ *van 'n DORP*, establishment of a town; ~ *van SOORTE*, origin of species; (w) (~), begin, originate, arise; come into being; grow; *skade* ~ *de DEUR*, damage arising from; *HAAT laat* ~, arouse hatred; ~s'geskiedenis, history of origin(s); ~s'tyd, time of origin.
ontstam', (~), detribalize; *'n* ~ *de Swarte*, a detribalized Black; ~ming, detribalization.
ontstank', (~), deodorize; ~ing, deodorization.
ontsteek', (~), kindle, light, fire; ignite; inflame (wound); prime (a gun); enkindle; rankle; *in toorn* ~, fly into a rage.
ontsteel', (~), rob, steal from.
ontste'ker, primer; exploder; *die* ~ *aanbring*, prime (a gun).
ontste'king, sparking, kindling, firing; ignition; inflammation.
ontste'kings: ~geklop, pink (of engine); ~inrigting, firing-gear; ~kas, ignition chamber; ~klep, ignition valve; ~klos, ignition coil; ~magneet, magneto; ~middel, primer; ~pen, striker-stud (torpedo); ~prop, spark plug; ~reëling, ignition control; ~temperatuur, flash-point.
ontstel', (~), startle, upset, disconcert, appal, consternate, confuse; *ek het my* ~, I became upset; ~d, (-e), alarmed, dismayed, aghast, affrighted, upset, disconcerted, bewildered; discoloured; ~lend, (-e), disturbing, upsetting, unsettling; ~tenis, alarm, dismay, consternation, discomposure.
ontstem', (~), put out of tune; ruffle, get into a temper; mistune; jangle (nerves); ~d, (-e), displeased, ruffled, cross; ~ming, ill humour, discomposure, heart-burning.
ontsten'tenis, default; non-appearance; *by* ~ *van*, in default of, failing.
ontstig', (~), annoy, offend; shock, scandalize; ~ting, annoyance, offence.
ontstin'gel, (~), stem (raisins).
ontsto'ke, swollen, inflamed (wound); *sy toorn was* ~, his wrath was kindled.
ontstry', (~), dispute; *hy laat hom dit nie* ~ *nie*, he won't be reasoned out of it.
ontstyg', (~), rise up from.
ontsty'sel, (~), destarch.
ontsui'ering, desuckering.
ontsuur', (~), edulcorate; ..su'ring, edulcoration.
ontswag'tel, (~), undress (wound), unbandage.
ontsy'fer, (~), decipher, decode; puzzle out; ~aar, (-s), decipherer; ~baar, (..bare), decipherable; ~ing, deciphering, decipherment.
ontta'kel, (~), strip, dismantle, disable, disarm (ship); ~ing, dismantling, dismantlement, stripping (of ship).
onttrein', (~), detrain.

onttrek', (~), withdraw, recuse (legal); wriggle out of; divert; draft; *HOM* ~ *aan*, withdraw from; *die REGTER het hom aan die saak* ~, the judge recused himself; ~**king**, withdrawal, abstraction; recusation.
onttro'ner, (-s), dethroner.
onttro'ning, (-e, -s), dethronement, deposition.
onttroon', (~), dethrone.
on'tug, lewdness, unchastity; prostitution; fornication; harlotry; concupiscence; immorality; *huise van* ~, houses of ill fame; ~'**tig**, (-e), lascivious, lewd; meretricious; concupiscent, bawdy; ~'**tige**, (-s), fornicator; ~'**tigheid**, lewdness, lasciviousness; meretriciousness; bawdiness.
on'tuig, rabble, riff-raff; weeds; vermin.
ontuis', not at ease; ~ *voel*, be ill at ease.
ontval', (~), slip out, escape; lose by death; *die MOEDER het die kinders* ~, the children lost their mother; *die WOORD het my* ~, the word escaped me.
ontvang', (~), receive; conceive; *hulle* ~ *BAIE*, they entertain a great deal; *HARTLIK* ~, welcome cordially; *SALARIS* ~, draw pay; *sy* ~ *nie VANDAG nie*, she is not at home today; ~**baar**, (..**bare**), receivable, receptible; ~**baarheid**, receptibility; ~**end**, (-e), recipient; ~**enis**, conception; ~**er**, (-s), recipient, receiver, acceptor, remittee, donee, payee, grantee, consignee; tax gatherer, tax receiver; lander (of kibble); receptacle; ~**er van inkomste**, receiver of revenue; ~**erskantoor**, office of the receiver of revenue.
ontvangs', (-te), receipt; acceptance; reception; at-home; takings, returns; receiving; perception (law); *NA (by)* ~ *van*, on the receipt of; *in* ~ *NEEM*, take delivery of; *ek kry 'n goeie* ~ *met my TOESTEL*, I get a good reception on my set; *'n WARM* ~ *kry*, be given a warm reception.
ontvang'saal, reception room; reception hall.
ontvangs': ~**aand**, at-home (visiting) night; ~**afdeling**, receiving depot; intake section; reception; ~**bak**, receiver; ~**berig**, return message; ~**bewys**, receipt; ~**buis**, receiving tube; ~**dag**, at-home (visiting) day; ~**dame**, receptionist; ~**kamer**, reception room, parlour; ~**kantoor**, reception room; reception (office); ~**klerk**, receptionist; reception clerk.
ontvang': ~**stasie**, receiving station; ~**stoestel**, receiver, receiving set.
ontvank'lik, (-e), receptive, susceptible; accessible; open-minded, impressionable; ~**heid**, receptivity; accessibility; predisposition; receptiveness; receptibility.
ontvars', (~), season (with condiments); ~**ing**, seasoning.
ontveer', (~), displume, defeather.
ontveins', (~), dissimulate, dissemble; disguise; *ek kan my nie* ~ *nie*, I must admit, I cannot disguise the fact.
ontvel', (~), skin, graze; excoriate.
ontve'sel, (~), decorticate; ~**ing**, decortication; delinting.
ontvet', (~), cleanse, remove grease (fat) from.
ontvlam', (~), inflame, burst into flame; kindle; flash; *in woede* ~, burst into a rage; ~**baar**, (..**bare**), inflammable, flammable, (easily) combustible; fiery; ~**baarheid**, inflammability, combustibility; ~**ming**, bursting into flame; inflammation; ~**mingspunt**, flash-point.
ontvlees', (w) (~), strip off (flesh); deflesh; (b) (-de), unfleshed; excarnate.
ontvlek', (~), remove stains from; ~**king**, removal of stains; ~**kingsmiddel**, stain-remover.
ontvlieg', (~), fly away from; escape.
ontvlok', (~), deflocculate.
ontvlug', (~), escape; flee, fly; ~**baar**, (..**bare**), escapable; ~**ter**, (-s), escaper; ~**ting**, escape, flight, escapement; ~**tingskag**, escape-shaft.
ontvoer', (~), abduct; elope with; kidnap; ravish; ~**der**, (-s), abductor; ravisher; kidnapper; ~**ing**, abduction; kidnapping; elopement; ravishing.
ontvog'(tig), dehumidify; ..**tiger**, (-s), dehumidifier; ~**ting**, dehumidification.

ontvolk', (w) (~), depopulate, dispeople, unpeople; (b) (-te), depopulated; desolate; ~**ing**, depopulation; desolation.
ontvonk', (~), kindle, set on fire.
ontvoog', (~), emancipate; remove from guardianship; ~**ding**, emancipation.
ontvou', (~), unfold, evolve, develop, set out, explain; ~**ing**, evolution, unfolding, development.
ontvreem', (w) (~), abstract; misappropriate; steal; (b) (-de), dispossessed; stolen, embezzled; ~**ding**, embezzlement; abstraction, misappropriation; alienation; dispossession; peculation.
ontvries', (~), defrost; unfreeze; ~ *de vleis*, defrosted meat; ~**ing**, defrosting; ~**toestel**, defroster.
ontwaak', (~), awake, waken; ~ *uit 'n droom*, awake from a dream.
ontwaar', (~), perceive, descry, discern.
ontwaar'ding, devaluation.
ontwa'king, awakening.
ontwa'pen, (~), disarm; ~**ing**, disarmament; ~**ingskonferensie**, disarmament conference.
ontwar', (~), unravel, ravel out, disentangle; enucleate; disinvolve; disembroil; extricate; ~**baar**, (..**bare**), extricable; ~**ring**, unravelling, disentanglement, extrication.
ontwa'sem, (~), demist; ~**er**, (-s), demister.
ontwas'se, outgrown.
ontwa'ter, (w) (~), unwater; dehydrate; (b) (-de), dehydrated; ~**ing**, dehydration.
ontwei', (~), disembowel, viscerate, eviscerate, gut, exenterate.
ontwel', (~), well up, spring from.
ontwel'dig, (~), wrest from, seize.
ontwen', (~), disaccustom, unlearn (habit); dishabituate; *iem. aan 'n gewoonte* ~, get a person out of a habit; ~**ning**, disuse, unlearning.
ontwerp', (s) (-e), draft, sketch, project, design, concept, device, drawing; projection, planning, plotting, forecast; mould; scheme, bill (in parliament); (w) (~), project, plan, draft, frame; delineate; devise; plot (cartography); lay-out; forecast; model; design; ~**afdeling**, planning section; ~**belasting**, rated load; ~**end**, (-e), designing; ~**er**, (-s), framer, creator, designer, projector, draughtsman; drafter; originator; planner; plotter; ~**kuns**, art of design; ~**model**, dummy; maquette; ~**reglement**, draft regulation; ~**stroom**, current rating; rated current; ~**tekening**, architect's sketch; ~**vermoë**, rated capacity, rated current; ~**wet**, draft bill (law).
ontwik'kel, (~), develop, set out, evolve; expose; generate (current), raise (steam); pullulate; *'n FILM* ~, develop a film; *SAKE laat* ~, allow matters to develop; ~**aar**, generator; developer; ~**aaraansluiter**, generator terminal; ~**aaranker**, generator armature; ~**beker**, solution-cup; ~**d**, (-e), developed; educated, cultured; ~**end**, (-e), developing, nascent; ~**ing**, (-e, -s), development, evolution; culture, cultivation; education; growth; generation; *algemene* ~**ing**, general education.
ontwik'kelings: ~**bad**, developing bath; ~**gang**, course of development, evolution; progress; ~**geskiedenis**, ontogeny, history of development; ~**leer**, theory of evolution; embryology; transformism; ~**moontlikheid**, possibility of development, potentiality; ~**peil**, standard of education; ~**plan**, development plan; ~**tydperk**, period of development; ~**uitgawe**, expenditure on development; ~**vermoë**, power to develop; generating power.
ontwil', sake; *om my* ~, for my sake.
ontwoe'ker, (~), reclaim, wrest from.
ontwol', (~), dewool.
ontwors'tel, (~), disengage, wrest from, force from.
ontwor'tel, (~), uproot, eradicate, deracinate, grub; ~**de**, (-s), displaced person; ~**ing**, uprooting, eradication; displacement.
ontwrig', (w) (~), dislocate, put out of joint (limb); disrupt; depolarize; disjoint; luxate; (b) (-te), disjointed; disorganised; out of gear; ~**tend**, (-e), disjunctive; ~**ting**, dislocation; unsettlement; disruption; disintegration; disjunction; luxation.
ontwring', (~), wrest from, extort from; rectify (pho-

to); ~ing, extortion (confession); rectification (photo).
ontwy', (~), desecrate, profane; defile; deconsecrate; ~der, (-s), desecrator, profaner; ~ding, desecration, profanation; defloration; prostitution.
ontwy'felbaar, (..bare), indubitable, undoubted; ~heid, indubitableness, certainty.
ontwyk', (~), evade, shun, escape, dodge, flee, fly, elude; funk; keep clear of; *'n vraag* ~, evade a question; ~end, (-e), evasive, elusive; circumlocutory; elusory; ~er, eschewer; ~ing, evasion, avoidance, elusion; quibble.
on'tyd, unseasonable, inconvenient time; *ten* ~ *e*, at an inconvenient hour; at an inopportune moment.
onty'dig, (-e), untimely, unseasonable, premature, ill-timed, inopportune; ~ *e bevalling*, premature confinement; ~heid, unseasonableness, prematureness, inopportuneness.
ontys', (w) (~), defrost, de-ice; (b) (-de), defrosted; ~er, defroster.
onuitblus'baar, (..bare), ..blus'lik, (-e), inextinguishable.
onuit'gedruk, (-te), unexpressed.
onuit'gegee, unpublished.
onuit'gekeer, (-de), undistributed, unpaid.
onuit'geloot, (..lote), non-drawn (bonds); unraffled.
onuit'gelok, (-te), unprovoked.
onuit'gemaak, (-te), not settled, debatable, doubtful, problematic, undecided, in abeyance; *dit is nog* ~, it is still sub judice (an open question).
onuit'geput, (-te), unexhausted.
onuit'gesoek, (-te), unsorted; taken at random.
onuit'gesproke, unspoken, unexpressed.
onuit'gevoer¹, (-de), unlined (coat).
onuit'gevoer², (-de), unexecuted (command); unexported.
onuit'gewerk, (-te), not worked out; ~ *te rifdeel*, back (mining).
onuithou(d)'baar, (..bare), ..hou'delik, (-e), unbearable, intolerable.
onuitleg'baar, (..bare), inexplicable.
onuitput'lik, (-e), inexhaustible; never-failing; ~heid, inexhaustibility.
onuitroei'baar, (..bare), inexterminable, ineradicable.
onuitspreek'baar, (..bare), unpronounceable.
onuitspreek'lik, (-e), inexpressible, unutterable, beyond description, not to be expressed, unspeakable.
onuitstaan'baar, (..bare), intolerable, unbearable; insufferable; impossible (person); ~heid, intolerableness.
onuitvoer'baar, (..bare), impracticable, unfeasible, unenforceable; not fit for export; ~heid, impracticability, unfeasibility.
onuitwis'baar, (..bare), indelible, ineffaceable; ~heid, ineffaceability, indelibility.
o'nus, onus, burden, duty, responsibility; ~ *probandi*, burden of proof resting on maker of assertion, onus probandi.
onva'derlands, (-e), unpatriotic.
on'vanpas, out of place, unsuitable; inconvenient, inopportune; inappropriate, malapropos, tactless; amiss.
onvas', (-te), unstable, unsteady, shaky (gait); uncertain (state of things); astatic; fugitive, non-fast, fading (colour); afloat; ~t'heid, instability, unsteadiness; uncertainty; astaticism.
onvat'baar, (..bare), insusceptible (to pity); immune (to disease); impervious to, deaf to; ~ *vir verbetering*, incapable of improvement; ~heid, insusceptibility; immunity; ~making, immunization.
onvei'lig, (-e), unsafe; insecure; ~ *maak*, make unsafe; infest (the roads); ~heid, unsafety, unsafeness; insecurity.
onveran'derbaar, (..bare), unchangeable.
onveran'der(d), (-de), unchanged, unaltered.
onveran'derlik, (-e), invariable, constant, uniform (behaviour); immutable, unalterable (decision); cast-iron; ~e, (-s), invariant; ~heid, immutability, invariableness, invariability, unalterability.
on'verantwoord, (-e), unaccounted for; unjustified.

onverantwoor'delik, (-e), irresponsible; unaccountable; unjustifiable, inexcusable; ~heid, irresponsibility, unwarrantableness, unaccountableness.
onverbas'ter(d), (-de), undegenerate(d); pure-blooded; not cross-fertilised.
onverbe'ter(d), (-de,), uncorrected (scripts); unreformed (convicts).
onverbe'ter: ~ *baar*, (..bare), incorrigible; cannot be improved upon; inimitable; irremediable; ~baarheid, incorrigibility; ~lik, (-e) = onverbeterbaar.
onverbid'delik, (-e), inexorable, relentless; grim; implacable; ~heid, inexorability, implacability.
onverbind', (-e), unbandaged; uncommitted.
onverbleek'baar, onverbleik'baar, (..bare), fadeless, fast (colour).
onverbloem(d)', (-de), plain, naked, honest, undisguised, unvarnished; *die* ~ *de waarheid*, the unvarnished truth.
onverbo'ë, undeclined, uninflected.
onverbon'de, undressed (wounds); unattached, free; uncommitted.
onverbrand', (-e), unburnt, unconsumed (by fire); ~baar, (..bare), incombustible; ~baarheid, incombustibility.
onverbreek'baar, (..bare), ..breek'lik, (-e), unbreakable, inviolable; indissoluble; ~heid, indissolubility.
onverbruik'baar, (..bare), inconsumable.
onverbuig'baar, (..bare), indeclinable, flexionless.
onverdag', (-te), unsuspected, above suspicion, undoubted.
onverde'dig, (-de), undefended; ~baar, (..bare), indefensible, unjustifiable.
onverdeel'baar, (..bare), indivisible; impartible; ~heid, indivisibility; ~*heid van die kroon*, indivisibility of the crown.
onverdeeld', (-de), undivided (attention); unanimous (vote); united (party); unqualified (praise); whole-hearted (support); unipartite.
onverdelg'baar, (..bare), indestructible.
onverderf'lik, (-e), imperishable, incorruptible; ~heid, imperishability, incorruptibility.
onverdien(d)', (-de), undeserved, unmerited (praise); unearned (money).
onverdiens'telik, (-e), undeserving, demeritorious; *nie* ~ *nie*, not without merit.
onverdig', (-te), uncondensed; true, not fictitious; ~baar, (..bare), uncondensable.
onverdoof', (-de), not rendered insensible.
onverdor'we, uncorrupted, undepraved; ~nheid, undepraved character, purity.
onverdraag'baar, (..bare), unbearable.
onverdraag'lik = ondraaglik.
onverdraag'saam, (..same), intolerant; ~heid, intolerance.
onverdro'te, untiring, unflagging.
onverduis'ter(d), (-de), unobscured, undarkened, not eclipsed.
onverdun', (-de), unadiluted, neat; not thinned.
onveref'fen, (-de), unsettled, outstanding (debts).
onvere'nigbaar, (..bare), not to be united, inconsistent, irreconcilable, incompatible; mutually exclusive; ~heid, incompatibility.
onverflou', (-de), unabated (energy); unrelaxing, unremitting (care); unflagging (attention).
onvergank'lik, (-e), imperishable, undying, everlasting; ~heid, imperishability, indefectibility.
onvergeef'lik, (-e), unpardonable; irremissible; ~heid, unpardonableness.
onvergeet'lik, (-e), never to be forgotten, ever memorable, unforgettable.
onvergelyk'baar, (..bare), non-comparable.
onvergelyk'lik, (-e), incomparable, unparalleled, matchless, nonpareil.
onvergenoeg', (-de), discontented, dissatisfied; ~d'heid, discontent.
onvergesel', (-de), unaccompanied, companionless.
onverge'te, unforgotten.
onverge'we, unpardoned, unforgiven; ~nsgesind, (-e), unforgiving.
onverglaas', (-de), unglazed; ~ *de erdewerk*, unglazed porcelain.

onvergroot', not enlarged, not exaggerated.
onverhaal'baar, (..**bare**), irrecoverable (debts).
onverhan'delbaar, (..**bare**), unnegotiable, not transferable.
onverhelp'baar, (..**bare**), that cannot be helped.
onverhin'derd, (-e), unhindered, unimpeded.
onverhoeds', (-e), unexpectedly, unawares; surprise (attack).
onverho'le, (b) unconcealed, undisguised (contempt); (bw) frankly.
onverhoop', (-te), unhoped for, unexpected.
onverhoor(d)', (-de), unheard; unanswered (prayer); unexamined; untried (case).
onverhuur(d)', (-de), unlet, untenanted; ..**huurbaar**, (..**bare**), unlettable.
onverjaar', (-de), unforfeited, not prescribed; ~**baar**, (..**bare**) imprescriptible.
onverkies'baar, (..**bare**), ineligible.
onverkies'lik, (-e), not preferable, undesirable.
onverklaar', (-de), unexplained; undeclared.
onverklaar'baar, (..**bare**), inexplicable, unaccountable; ~**heid**, inexplicability.
onverklein'baar, (..**bare**), irreducible.
onverkleur'baar, (..**bare**), fadeless, fast (colour).
onverkoop', (-te), unsold; ~**baar**, (..**bare**), unsaleable.
onverkort', (-e), unabridged.
onverkry(g)baar, (..**bare**), unobtainable, unprocurable.
onverkwik'lik, (-e), disagreeable, unsavoury, unpleasant.
onverlaat, (..**late**), wretch, miscreant, villain, brute.
onverlief', (-de), heart free, fancy-free.
onverlig', (-te), not lighted up, dark (room); unenlightened (person); unrelieved (pain).
onverloof', (-de), not engaged, unbetrothed, free.
onverlos', (-te), unsaved; unrescued; undelivered.
onvermaak'lik, (-e), unpleasant; *nie* ~ *nie*, rather amusing; not unpleasant.
onvermaard', (-e), without fame.
onvermeld', (-e), unmentioned, unrecorded.
onvermeng', (-de), unmixed, pure, unblended; elemental; unalloyed; raw (spirits).
onvermin'der(d), (-de), undiminished, unabated.
onvermink', (-te), unmaimed, unmutilated.
on'vermoë, impotence, impuissance; inability, disability; indigence; *sy* ~ *om*, his inability to.
onvermoed', (-e), unsuspected.
onvermoei'baar, (..**bare**), indefatigable, tireless; ~**heid**, indefatigability.
onvermoeid', (-e), untiring, tireless, patient; ~**heid**, tireless patience.
onvermo'end, (-e), impotent, unable; indigent, impecunious, poor.
onvermom', (-de), unmasked, undisguised.
onvermurf'baar, (..**bare**), unrelenting, inexorable, inflexible, adamant; immitigable.
onvermy(d)'baar, (..**bare**), unavoidable, inevitable.
onvermy'delik, (-e), unavoidable, inevitable; necessary; fateful, fatal; ~**heid**, unavoidableness, inevitability; fatality; necessity.
onvernicl'baar, (..**bare**), undestroyable, indestructible, foolproof.
onvernie'tigbaar, (..**bare**), indestructible.
onvernieu', (-de), **onvernu'de**, unrenewed (subscription).
onvernis', (-te), unvarnished.
onvernuf'tig, (-e), not ingenious.
onveroor'deeld, (-e), unconvicted, unsentenced.
onverou'der(d), (-de), youthful, not aged; not obsolete.
onvero'wer, (-de), unconquered.
onverpag', (-te), unlet, untenanted.
onverpak', (-te), unpacked, unwrapped.
onverplaas', (-te), unremoved; ~**baar**, (..**bare**), immovable; not transferable, irremovable.
onverpoos', (-de), continuous, uninterrupted; ceaseless, incessant.
onverrig', (-te), undone; ~ *ter sake*, without having effected a purpose, unsuccessfully.
onverruil'baar, (..**bare**), inconvertible; not exchangeable; ~**heid**, inconvertibility.

onversaag', (-de), undaunted, intrepid, bold; ~**d'heid**, undauntedness, dauntlessness, intrepidity, hardihood, hardiness.
onversa'delik, (-e), insatiable; ~**heid**, insatiability.
onversa'dig, (-de), insatiated, unsatisfied; unsaturated (solution); ~**baar**, (..**bare**), insatiable.
onversag', (-te), unmitigated.
onverse'ël, (-de), unsealed.
on'verseker(d), (-de), uninsured, uncovered (by insurance).
on'versekerbaar, (..**bare**), uninsurable.
onverset'lik, (-e), obstinate, stubborn; immovable; unyielding; ~**heid**, stubbornness, obstinacy.
onversier(d)', (-de), unadorned, undecorated, inornate, plain.
onversig'tig, (-e), imprudent, incautious, reckless, improvident; ~**heid**, imprudence, rashness.
onverskil'lig, (-e), indifferent; in cold blood, cold-blooded; apathetic, phlegmatic; devil-may-care; cool; listless; casual; cold; insensible; nonchalant; careless; half-hearted; frosty; rash, reckless, heedless; *vir MY is dit* ~, it is all the same (immaterial) to me; ~ *RY*, drive recklessly; ~ *WIE dit gesê het*, no matter who said so; ~**e**, (-s), indifferentist; pococurante; ~**heid**, indifference, carelessness; coolness, coldness; apathy; casualness; rashness, recklessness, abandon; insensibility; inappetence; phlegm.
onverskoon'baar, (..**bare**), inexcusable, unpardonable; ~**heid**, inexcusableness, unpardonableness.
onverskrok'ke, intrepid, bold, undaunted, dauntless, doughty, fearless; ~**nheid**, intrepidity, boldness, dauntlessness, doughtiness, fearlessness.
onverslaan', (..**slane**), unbeaten; not gone flat (beer).
onversla'e, undismayed.
onverslap', (-te), unflagging, unabated.
onverslyt', (-e), not worn out; ~**baar**, (..**bare**), not easily worn out, lasting, durable.
onversoen', (-de), unreconciled.
onversoen'lik, (-e), irreconcilable, implacable; intransigent; ~**e**, (-s), die-hard, irreconcilable; ~**heid**, irreconcilability, implacability.
onversoet', (-e), unsweetened.
onversorg', (-de), unprovided for, not attended to, uncared for; untidy; ~*de taal*, slipshod language; ~**d'heid**, slovenliness, untidiness.
onverstaan'baar, (..**bare**), incomprehensible, unintelligible; indistinct; ~**heid**, incomprehensibility, unintelligibility.
on'verstand, unwisdom, stupidity, ignorance; ~'**ig**, (-e), unwise, foolish, stupid; impolitic; ~'**igheid**, imprudence, folly, insipience.
onversterk', (-te), unstrengthened; unfortified.
onversteur(d)', (-de), ..**stoor(d)'**, (-de), undisturbed; imperturbable.
onversteur'baar, (,,**bare**), imperturbable; indisturbable; ~**heid**, imperturbability.
overstre'ke, unexpired (period).
onverswak', (-te), not enfeebled; unimpaired.
onvertaal(d)', (-de), untranslated.
onvertaal'baar, (..**bare**), untranslatable.
onvertak', (-te), unramified, simple (bot.).
onverteer(d)', (-de), undigested; unconsumed; crude (knowledge).
onverteer'baar, (..**bare**), indigestible; ~**heid**, indigestibility.
onvertel'baar, (..**bare**), not fit to be related.
onvertin', (-de), untinned.
onvertraag', (-de), undelayed; unremitting.
onvervaard', (-e), undaunted, fearless; ~**heid**, dauntlessness, fearlessness.
onvervals', (-te), genuine; unadulterated (milk); pure, heart-whole; arrant (nonsense); honest; ~**t'heid**, genuineness, purity.
onvervang'baar, (..**bare**), irreplaceable; ~**heid**, irreplaceability.
onvervolg', (-de), unprosecuted.
onvervreem(d)'baar, (..**bare**), inalienable; imprescriptible; ~**heid**, inalienability.
onvervul', (-de), unfulfilled, unperformed, unexecuted (task); ~**baar**, (..**bare**), unrealisable.
onvervyf', (-de), unconverted (try).

onverwag', (-te), unexpected; abrupt, sudden; ~ s', unexpectedly, unawares, suddenly; ~ t'heid, unexpectedness.
onverwarm(d)', (-de), unheated, unwarmed.
onverwelk', (-te), unfaded; ~ baar, (..bare), fadeless, unfading; imperishable (glory); amaranthine; ~ lik, (-e), everlasting, imperishable.
onverwerk', (-te), not worked up; unprocessed; unassimilated (knowledge).
onverwin'lik, (-e), unconquerable, invincible; impregnable; ~ heid, invincibility.
onverwis'sel, (-de), uncharged; ~ baar, (..bare), inconvertible; non-interchangeable; not exchangeable; ~ baarheid, incommutableness, inconvertibility; inexchangeability.
onverwoes'baar, (..bare), indestructible; ~ heid, indestructibility.
onverwyld', (-e), immediate(ly), direct(ly), forthwith.
onvind'baar, (..bare), not to be found.
onvlei'end, (-e), unflattering.
onvoed'saam, (..same), innutritious.
onvoeg'saam, (..same), indecent, unbecoming, unfitting, unseemly; ~ heid, indecency, unseemliness.
onvoel'baar, (..bare), intangible, impalpable; ~ heid, impalpability.
onvolbrag', (-te), unperformed.
onvoldaan', (..dane), unpaid (bills); dissatisfied (people); ~ heid, dissatisfaction.
onvoldoen'de, insufficient, inadequate; deficient; 'n BLOTE kennisgewing is ~, a mere notification will not meet the case; ~ ONTWIKKEL(D), underdeveloped.
onvoldoend'heid, inadequacy.
onvoldra'e, premature; unripe; undeveloped.
onvolgroei', (-de), immature; ~ d'heid, immaturity.
onvolko'me, imperfect, incomplete; defective; ~ nheid, imperfection, incompleteness; defect, deficiency.
onvolle'dig, (-e), incomplete, fragmentary; catalectic; ~ heid, incompleteness, defectiveness, fragmentariness.
onvolmaak', (-te), imperfect, defective; ~ t'heid, imperfection, deficiency.
onvolpre'se, beyond praise, unsurpassed.
onvoltal'lig, (-e), incomplete.
onvoltooi(d)', (-de), imperfect; incomplete; ~ de tyd, imperfect (progressive) tense.
onvoltrok'ke, not executed; not solemnized (marriage).
onvolvoer', (-de), unperformed, unfulfilled.
onvolwaar'dig, (-e), inefficient; inadequate, deficient.
onvolwas'se, not full-grown, immature; ~ nheid, immaturity.
onvoor'bedag, (-te), unpremeditated, unintentional; ~ 'telik, without premeditation.
onvoor'berei(d), (-de), unprepared, extempore, offhand, impromptu, improvised; 'n ~ de toespraak, an extempore speech.
onvoorde'lig, (-e), disadvantageous; unprofitable; profitless; ~ e besuiniging, false economy; ~ heid, unprofitableness.
onvoorsien', (-e), unforeseen, unexpected, unprovided; ~ e omstandighede, unforeseen circumstances; ~ s', unawares; unexpectedly.
onvoorspel'baar, (..bare), unpredictable.
onvoorspoe'dig, (-e), unpropitious; unthriving.
onvoorstel'baar, (..bare), unimaginable.
onvoorwaar'delik, (-e), unconditional; iem. ~ glo, believe a person implicitly.
onvors'telik, (-e), unprincely, unkingly.
on'vrede, discord; feud; in ~ lewe, lead a cat-and-dog life, be at odds with life.
onvri(e)n'delik, (-e), unkind, unfriendly, disagreeable, cold, discourteous; ~ heid, unkindness, coldness, unfriendliness.
onvri(e)ndskap'lik, (-e), unfriendly, in an unfriendly way.
onvrou'lik, (-e), unfeminine, unwomanly.
onvrug'baar, (..bare), sterile, barren, dead, arid, infertile; ~ heid, sterility, barrenness,. unproductiveness, infecundity; besmetlike ~ heid, infectious sterility; ~ making, sterilization.

on'vry, (-e), lacking freedom; not private; ~ e, (-s), serf; ~ heid, bondage; lack of freedom; ~ moe'dig, (-e), diffident; ~ sin'nig, (-e), illiberal.
onvrywil'lig, (-e), involuntary, compulsory.
on'waar, (..ware), untrue, false, untruthful; ~ ag'tig, (-e), untruthful.
on'waarde, voidness, invalidity, worthlessness.
onwaardeer'baar, (..bare), invaluable, inestimable.
onwaarde'rend, (-e), inappreciative, unappreciative.
onwaar'dig, (-e), unworthy; undignified; ~ heid, unworthiness.
on'waarheid, (..hede), untruth, falsehood.
onwaarneem'baar, (..bare), imperceptible; ~ heid, imperceptibleness; imperceptibility.
onwaarskyn'lik, (-e), improbable, unlikely; ~ heid, improbability.
onwan'kelbaar, (..bare), unshakable, unfaltering, unwavering.
onweeg'baar, (..bare), unweighable, imponderable; ~ heid, imponderability.
on'weer, (s) thunderstorm; bad weather; daar is ~ in die lug, there is a storm brewing; (w) (ge-), thunder, storm.
onweer'baar, (..bare), not able-bodied.
onweerhou'baar, (..bare), irrepressible.
onweerleg'baar, (..bare), irrefutable, indisputable, incontestable; apodictic; irrefragable; ~ heid, irrefutability.
on'weersbui, thunderstorm.
onweerspreek'baar, (..bare), indisputable, undeniable.
onweerspro'ke, uncontradicted.
onweerstaan'baar, (..bare), irresistible; overpowering; ~ heid, irresistibility.
on'weersvoël, stormy petrel, bird of ill omen.
on'weerswolk, thunder-cloud, storm-cloud.
on'wel, unwell, indisposed.
onwelgeval'lig, (-e), displeasing, unpleasant.
onwel'kom, (-e), unwelcome.
onwelle'wend, (-e), impolite, ill-mannered, discourteous, inurbane; ~ heid, impoliteness.
onwellui'dend, (-e), discordant, harsh, cacophonous, inharmonious; ~ heid, want of harmony, cacophony.
onwelrie'kend, (-e), evil-smelling, malodorous; nidorous; rammish, rammy.
onwelvoeg'lik, (-e), indecent, unseemly, improper, unmannerly; ~ heid, indecency, unseemliness, indecorum.
onwelwil'lend, (-e), disobliging, unsympathetic, unkind, discourteous; ~ heid, unkindness.
onwen'nig, (-e), strange, unaccustomed; ~ heid, strangeness.
onwens'lik, (-e), undesirable; ~ heid, undesirability.
onwerk'lik, (-e), unreal.
onwerk'saam, (..same), inactive.
onwe'senlik, (-e), unreal; non-essential; ~ heid, unreality.
onwe'tend, (-e), ignorant; nescient; uninformed; empty-headed; ~ heid, ignorance; nescience.
onwe'tens, unknowingly.
onwetenskap'lik, (-e), unscientific.
onwet'tig, (-e), unlawful, illegal; adulterine, illegitimate (child); naughty, mischievous; ~ e DIAMANTHANDEL, I(llicit) D(iamond) B(uying); ~ e DRANKHANDEL, illicit liquor trade; ~ MAAK, invalidate; ~ heid, unlawfulness, illegality; naughtiness, mischievousness; illegitimacy, bastardy.
on'wil, unwillingness; dis pure ~, it is sheer obstinacy.
onwillekeu'rig, (b) (-e), involuntary; instinctive; (bw) involuntarily; ek moes ~ lag, I could not help laughing; ~ heid, involuntariness; automatism.
onwil'lig, (-e), unwilling, loth, reluctant, averse; ~ heid, unwillingness, reluctance, averseness.
on'wis, uncertain.
onwraak'baar, (..bare), unimpeachable.
onwraaksug'tig, (-e), not vindictive.
onwrik'baar, (..bare), immovable, adamant, firm, rocklike, unshakeable, unflinching, steadfast; ~ heid, immovabilty.

onwys', (-e), unwise, foolish.
onwysge'rig, (-e), unphilosophical.
onwys'heid, folly, madness, foolishness.
oog, (oë), eye; fountain, source (river); lash (whip); loop (string); bar, pub; spot (on dice); mesh; hilum (bean); gudgeon; *oë van AGTER en van voor hê*, have eyes on both sides of one's head; *sy oë BEDERF*, ruin one's eyesight; *met die BLOTE ~*, with the naked eye; *'n BLOU ~*, a black eye (after receiving a blow); *onder die ~ BRING*, direct one's attention to; *in sy EIE oë*, in his own eyes; *aldag na die ~ toe GAAN*, frequent the tavern; *met geen ~ GESIEN nie*, not to have laid eyes on; *GEBROKE oë*, glazed eyes; *sy oë nie GLO nie*, not believe one's eyes; *GROEN en geel voor jou oë word*, see spots before one's eyes; *met GROOT oë*, wide-eyed; *GROOT oë maak*, glare at; be surprised; *uit die ~*, *uit die HART*, out of sight, out of mind; *jou ~ op iem. HÊ*, mistrust someone; have one's eye on someone (a girl); *op die ~ HÊ*, have in view (mind); *die ~ wil ook iets HÊ*, looks also count; *'n ~ vir iets HÊ*, have an eye for something; *iets voor oë HOU*, bear something in mind; *die ~ HOU op*, keep an eye on; *in die ~ HOU*, not to lose sight of; *IN my oë*, in my opinion; *sy oë KNIP*, blink; *moenie onder my oë KOM nie*, keep out of my sight; *die oë uit die KOP skaam*, be deeply ashamed; *in die ~ KRY*, catch sight of; *jou oë goed KOS gee*, feast one's eyes; *iem. vierkant in die oë KYK*, look someone squarely in the face; *iem. na die oë KYK*, be beholden to someone; *met LEDE oë aanskou*, view with sorrow; eye with envy; *GEEN ~ vir kuns hê nie*, have no eye for art, *sy oë is groter as sy MAAG*, he has taken more than he can eat; *ogies MAAK*, give the glad eye, look amorously at, make eyes; *die ~ van die MEESTER (baas) maak die perd vet*, the master's eye makes the cattle thrive; *MET die ~ op*, with a view (an eye) to; *NET vir die ~*, just for show; *ONDER die oë kry*, set eyes on; *hulle oë gaan OOP*, their eyes are being opened; *sy oë OOPHOU*, tread warily; *jy moet jou oë OOPMAAK*, you must keep your eyes peeled; *net vir een ding ~ en OOR hê*, have eyes and ears for one thing only; *~ en OOR hê vir iets*, be all eyes and ears; *met die ~ OP*, with a view to; *OP die ~*, superficially; *een ~ op die POT en die ander op die skoorsteen*, squint; *'n ~ in die SEIL hou*, be on the alert; keep one's weather eye open; *iem. na die oë SIEN*, depend upon someone; *iets onder die oë SIEN*, face the music; *niem. na die oë hoef te SIEN nie*, not to be beholden to another; *iem in die oë SIEN*, look someone in the eyes; *wat die ~ nie SIEN nie, deer die hart nie*, what the eye does not see, the heart does not grieve over; *iem. se oë vol SAND skop*, deceive someone; *die oë SLAAN op*, set eyes on; *die oë SLUIT vir iets*, shut one's eyes to something; *die oë SLUIT*, connive at; *iem. op die oë SPEEL*, punch someone in the eye; *in die ~ SPRING*, spring to view; *dit STEEK my in die ~*, it is an eyesore; *dit STEEK hom in die ~*, he regards it with envy; *~ om ~ en TAND om tand*, an eye for an eye and a tooth for a tooth; *g'n ~ TOEMAAK nie*, not catch a wink of sleep; *sy oë swem in TRANE*, his eyes are swimming with tears; *iem. se oë wil UITSTEEK*, be very jealous of someone; *dit VAL in die ~*, it catches the eye; *iem. se ~ VANG*, catch someone's eyes; *jou oë van VERBASING uitvryf*, rub one's eyes in amazement; *uit die ~ VERLOOR*, lose sight of; *onder VIER oë sien*, have someone in for a talking to; *net VIR die ~*, just for show; *een en al ~ WEES*, be all eyes; *die oë laat WEI oor*, run one's eyes over; **~aandoening**, (-e, -s), eye-trouble; **~ appel**, eyeball, pupil, the apple of one's eye, darling; **~ arts**, ophthalmologist, eye-specialist, ophthalmic surgeon; **~ badjie**, eye-cup; **~ bal**, eyeball; globe; **~ bank**, eye-brow ridge; eye-bank; *teen jou ~ banke vaskyk*, be wearing blinkers; **~ beslag**, pintle-plate; **~ bindvlies**, conjunctiva; **~ bol**, eyeball; **~ bout**, eye-bolt, ring-bolt; **~ deksel**, (ong.), eyelid; **~ dokter**, eye doctor; ophthalmologist, eye-specialist; **~ druppels**, eye-drops, eye-lotion; **~ geheue**, visual memory; **~ getuie**, eyewitness; **~ glas**, eye-glass (monocle); quizzing-glass;

eyepiece; **~ haar**, eyelash; **~ hare**, eyelashes; cilia; **~ heelkunde**, ophthalmology; **~ heelkun'dig**, (-e), ophthalmological; **~ heelkun'dige**, (-s), ophthalmologist; **~ hoek**, corner of the eye; **~ holte**, orbit; eye-socket; **~ hoogte**, eye-level; **~ kamer**, chamber of the eye; **~ kas**, (-se), eye-socket; **~ kelkie**, eye-cap; **~ klap**, blinker; eye-flap, winker (harness); blind(er); lunette; goggle; eye-shield; *iem. ~ klappe aansit*, hoodwink a person.
oog: **~ klier**, lachrymal gland; **~ kliniek**, eye clinic; **~ knip**, wink; *in 'n ~ knip*, in the twinkling of an eye; **~ kun'dige**, (-s), ophthalmic surgeon, ophthalmologist; **~ kwaal**, eye-disease; **~ lens**, eye-lens; **~ lid**, (..lede), eyelid; *teen jou ~ lede vaskyk*, be wearing blinkers; **~ lidklier**, tarsal gland; **~ lidontsteking**, blepharitis; **~ lo'pend**, (-e), conspicuous, striking; *dis ~ lopend*, it is obvious; **~ lo'pendheid**, conspicuousness.
ooglui'kend, (-e), stealthily, on the sly; *iets ~ toelaat*, connive at something; *~ e TOELATING*, connivance.
oog'luiking, connivance.
oog: **~ lyer**, eye-sufferer; **~ lyn**, line of vision; loopline; **~ maat**, accuracy of eye, rule of thumb; **~ maatskets**, eye-sketching; **~ merk**, aim, intention, design; device; purpose, end (in view); intent; object; **~ middel**, ophthalmic remedy; **~ ontsteking**, inflammation of the eye; ophthalmia; **~ opleiding**, eye-training; **~ opslag**, glance; *met 'n ~ opslag*, at a glance; **~ pêrel**, cataract; **~ pistertjie**, variety of beetle *(Anthia)*; **~ plaat**, ring plate.
oog'punt, point of view; viewpoint; aspect; *uit daardie ~ BESKOU*, viewed from that angle; *UIT 'n ~ van*, with a view to.
oog: **~ rand**, edge of eye; **~ rimpel**, crow's-foot; **~ ring**, thimble, protector of cable eye; **~ rok**, sclerotic, sclera; **~ salf**, eye-ointment, eye-salve; collyrium; **~ senuwee**, optic nerve; **~ siekte**, eye-trouble; **~ skatting**, ocular estimate; **~ skerm**, eye-guard (-shield); face-piece; **~ skepping**, visual training; **~ spanning**, eye-strain; **~ spieël**, ophthalmoscope; **~ spier**, eye-muscle; **~ splits(ing)**, eye-splicing; **~ stuk**, eyepiece; loop (bridle); **~ tand**, eye-tooth, dog-tooth, canine; **~ uitpuiling**, exophthalmia; **~ vel**, eyelid; *teen jou ~ velle vaskyk*, wear blinkers; **~ verblin'dend**, (-e), blinding, dazzling; **~ verblinding**, delusion; **~ vermoeidheid**, eye-strain; **~ vlek**, spot on the eye; ocellus; **~ vlies**, tunicle (of the eye); **~ vormig**, (-e), ocellate; **~ water**, eye wash; **~ wenk** = oogwink; **~ wimper**, (-s), eyelash.
oog'wink, moment; wink, blink; *in 'n ~*, in the twinkling of an eye.
oog'wit, white of the eye; purpose.
ooi, (-e), ewe; *nie-dragtige ~*, maiden ewe (which has not yet lambed); **~ bok**, she-goat.
ooi'evaar, (-s, ..vare), stork.
ooi'evaars: **~ bek**, stork's bill; **~ bene**, spindleshanks; **~ drag**, maternity wear; **~ nes**, stork's nest.
ooi'lam, ewe lamb; *ons enigste ~*, our only ewe lamb.
ooit, ever, at any time; *die mooiste wat ~ GESIEN is*, the most beautiful ever seen; *HET jy ~!* well, I never!
ook, also, too; even, as well, likewise; *ek is DOM en jy ~*, I am stupid and so are you; *dis vir my ~ GOED*, that will suit me just as well; *HOE ~ al*, be that as it may; *dit kan ~ NIE anders nie*, it cannot be otherwise; *hy weet ~ NIKS*, he never knows a thing; *al is dit ~ NOG so klein*, be it ever so small; *dis WAAR ~*, and so it is; *WAAR ~ al*, wheresoever; *WAT ~ al*, whatsoever; *wat het hy ~ WEER gesê?* whatever did he say? *WIE ~ al*, whosoever.
ööliet', oolite; **~ korrel**, oolith.
oölogie', oology; **oölo'gies**, (-e), oologic(al).
oöloog', (oöloë), oologist.
oom, (-s), uncle; *~ KOOL*, ace (cards); a funny person; a butt; also applied to animals, especially the lion; *daar SIT ~ Kool!* there we have our friend!
oom'blik, (-ke), moment, instant; jiffy; *die gunstige ~ AFWAG*, bide one's time, await a favourable opportunity; *hy kan ELKE ~ kom*, he may come at any moment; *IN 'n ~*, in the twinkling of an eye; *'n ~ LATER*, a moment later; the next moment; *NET*

'n ~, just a moment, half a minute; *OP die* ~, on the spur of the moment; just at present; *op die REGTE* ~, at the right moment; in the very nick of time; *SONDER om 'n* ~ *na te dink*, without a moment's reflection; *VIR die* ~, for the present.

oomblik'lik, (-e), instantaneous(ly), immediate(ly), direct(ly), instantly; actual; momentary; this moment; ~ *e GEVAAR*, immediate danger; ~ *e VERHITTINGSMETODE*, flash-system.

oom'pie, (-s), *verkleinwoord van* **oom.**

ooms'kind, cousin.

oond, (-e), oven, furnace; kiln; flue; scrum (rugby); ~ **bos,** *Conyza ivaefolia;* ~ **braad,** oven roast; ~ **brood,** oven(-baked) bread; ~ **deksel,** door of the oven; ~ **droging,** kiln-drying; firing (tea); ~ **droog,** (..droë), oven-dry; ~ **gedroog,** (-de), oven-dried; ~ **hark,** rabble; ~ **jie,** (-s), small oven; ~ **klaar,** oven-ready; ~ **koek,** (oven-)cake; ~ **skop,** oven-rake, rabble; ~ **vas,** (-te), ovenproof (dish); ~ **vurk,** oven-fork.

oop, (ope; oper, -ste), open; uncovered; vacant (seat); clear; fenceless; blank (form); naked (wire); *met* ~ *ARMS ontvang*, receive with open arms; ~ *en BLOOT*, quite open; *'n* ~ *GEHEIM*, a public secret; *in die ope (oop) LUG*, in the open (air).

oop'bars, (-ge-), burst open; dehisce (pods); ~ **ting,** splitting, cracking, dehiscence (bot.).

oop'battery, open battery.

oop'blaas, (-ge-), blow open.

oop'bly, (-ge-), remain open.

oop'breek, (-ge-), break (force, burst, prise) open.

oop'broodjie, open sandwich.

oop'byt, (-ge-), bite open.

oop'draai, (-ge-), screw open; turn on (tap).

oop'druk, (-ge-), push (press) open.

oop'-en-toe: ~ *êrens AANKOM*, come rushing in; ~ *HARDLOOP*, run for all you are worth.

oop'gaan, (-ge-), open; burst; come to a head.

oop'gesit, (-te), **oop'getrek,** (-te), abroach (of barrels); opened.

oop'gewerk, (-te), open-work.

oop'gooi, (s) throwing (wool); (w) (-ge-), throw (fling) open; spread out (blanket).

oop'groefmyn, open-pit mine.

oop'hand, dummy hand (cards).

oop'hang, (-ge-), hang open (mouth).

oop'heid, clearness.

oop'hou, (-ge-), keep open; keep vacant; reserve.

oop'kap, (-ge-), cut open, clear.

oop'kar, hoodless cart.

oop'kloof, (-ge-), wedge; cut open.

oop'knoop, (-ge-), unbutton, unfasten.

oop'krap, (-ge-), scratch open.

oop'kry, (-ge-), get open (lock).

oop'laat, (-ge-), leave open; leave running (tap); leave blank (page); leave vacant (seat).

oop'lê, (-ge-), lay open; lie open; expose; disclose (plan); lay out (materials); *die KAARTE* ~, expose the cards; *LOOP dat jy so* ~, run at breakneck speed; run flat out.

oop'legging, exposure (facts); exposition; discovery (of documents); ~ **sbevel,** discovery-order (law).

oop'maak, (-ge-), open, prise open, unlock, undo; expose.

oop'mond, open-mouthed; surprised, nonplussed.

oop'nekhemp, open-necked shirt.

oop'oë, open-eyed.

oop'prik, (-ge-), prick open.

oop'ruk, (-ge-), jerk open, rip open.

oop'sit, (-ge-), open (door).

oop'skeur, (-ge-), tear open, rip open.

oop'skoen, slipper.

oop'skop, (-ge-), kick open (door).

oop'skuif, oop'skuiwe, (-ge-), shove open, slide open.

oop'slaan, (-ge-), open (book); beat open; broach; ~ *de venster*, casement window; ~ **venster,** French window.

oop'sluit, (-ge-), unlock.

oop'smyt, (-ge-), fling open.

oop'sny, (-ge-), cut open; *'n boek* ~, cut the pages of a book.

oop'spalk, (-ge-), dilate; stretch out; *met oopgespalkte KAKE*, with distended jaws; *met oopgespalkte OË*, with dilated eyes.

oop'sper, (-ge-), distend, open wide; flare (pipes).

oop'splits, (-ge-), split asunder.

oop'spring, (-ge-), open suddenly; burst open; crack open; dehisce (pod).

oop'staan, (-ge-), be open (door); be vacant (post); *'n* ~ *de REKENING*, an unpaid account.

oop'stamp, (-ge-), knock open.

oop'steek, (-ge-), prick open; pick (a lock); broach (cask).

oop'steker, pricker.

oop'stel, (-ge-), throw open; ~ **ling,** opening; *die* ~ *ling v.d. diamantvelde*, the opening-up of the diamond fields.

oop'stoot, (-ge-), push open.

oop'te, (-s), open space (e.g. in a wood).

oop'torring, (-ge-), rip open; unstitch.

oop'trap, (-ge-), kick (trample) open; *oopgetrapte pad*, beaten track.

oop'trek, (-ge-), draw open; give a hiding; clear up (cloudy sky); uncork (bottle).

oop'val, (-ge-), fall open; become vacant.

oop'veg, (-ge-), fight open (through).

oop'visier, open sight (rifle).

oop'vlek, (-ge-), cut open; throw open; gut (fish).

oop'vlieg, (-ge-), fly open.

oop'vou, (-ge-), unfold.

oop'waai, (-ge-), be blown open, fly open (door).

oop'werk, open-work.

oor¹, (s) (ore), ear; handle (of a jug); *iem. iets in die* ~ *BLAAS*, whisper something into someone's ear; *BLOOS tot agter haar ore*, blush to the roots of her hair; *nog nie DROOG agter die ore nie*, not dry behind the ears; *EEN en al* ~ *wees*, be all ears; *iem. om die ore GEE*, box someone's ears; *dit het my ter ore GEKOM*, it has come to my ears; *'n GEOEFENDE* ~, a good (trained) ear; *het jou ore nie GETUIT nie?* weren't your ears burning? *met 'n HALWE* ~ *luister*, listen with half an ear; *sy ore HANG*, be downcast; be crestfallen; *geen ore vir iets HÊ nie*, be deaf to; *HET jy ore?* where are your ears? *wie ore het om te HOOR, laat hom hoor*, he that hath ears to hear, let him hear; *die een* ~ *IN, die ander* ~ *uit*, it goes in at one ear and out at the other; *in die* ~ *KNOOP*, make a point of remembering; *ter ore KOM*, come to one's ears; *iem. se ore van sy KOP af eet*, eat someone out of house and home; *iem. se ore van sy KOP af praat*, talk the hind leg off a donkey; *geen ore aan sy KOP hê nie*, not to listen to what one is told; *KOPPIE sonder* ~, handleless cup; *LANG ore hê*, have long ears; *die* ~ *LEEN*, give (lend an) ear to; *iem. aan die ore LOL*, buzz around someone's ears; *ek het daar wel ore NA*, I rather like the idea; *nog NAT agter die ore*, not dry behind the ears; *die* ~ *NEIG*, incline the ear; *NET* ~ *wees*, be all ears; *'n OPE* ~ *hê*, lend a ready ear; *tot oor sy ore in die SKULD*, over one's ears (up to one's neck) in debt; *sy ore SLUIT vir*, turn a deaf ear to; *die ore SPITS*, prick up one's ears; *dit STREEL die* ~, it charms (delights) the ear; *my ore het TOEGESLAAN*, my ears are blocked; *sy ore TUIT*, his ears hum; *sy ore UITLEEN*, lend one's ears to all sorts of talk; *tot oor die ore VERLIEF*, head over heels in love; *loop WAS jou ore*, you should wash out your ears; *tot oor die ore in die WERK wees*, be up to one's ears in work.

oor², (vgw) because; ~ *ek so LANK is*, lag hulle my uit, because I am so tall, they laugh at me; *dit kom* ~ *jy so TROTS is*, it happens because you are so proud.

oor³, (bw) over, past; ~ *EN* ~, again and again, repeatedly; ~ *GROOT genoeg om iets self te doen*, quite old enough to do it alone; *dit is MY* ~, that beats me; *ek het NIKS* ~ *nie*, I have nothing left; *die reën is* ~, the weather is clearing up; *die RUSIE is* ~, the quarrel is at an end; *die STORM is* ~, the storm has spent itself; ~ *en WEER*, to and fro; mutually; *iem.* ~ *WEES*, excel over someone.

oor⁴, (vs) over, via; beyond, across; ~ *die ALGEMEEN*, in general; ~ *'n DAG of wat*, in a day or two; *die DOKTER gaan* ~ *my*, the doctor is treat-

ing me; ~ *die GEHEEL*, on the whole; ~ *die GRENSE*, across the frontiers; ~ *die HONDERD*, more than a hundred; ~ *'n JAAR*, a year hence; ~ *LAND en see*, by land and sea; ~ *TAFEL bid (dank)*, say grace at table; *hy is ver* ~ *sy TYD*, he is very much overdue; *vandag* ~ *'n WEEK*, today week; ~ *'n WEEK*, in a week's time; *goed* ~ *die WEG kom met iem.*, get on well with a person.
oor: ~ **aandoening**, ear-trouble; ~ **aap**, galago.
oor'angsvallig, (-e), meticulous.
oor'arts, ear-specialist, aurist.
oor'baar, (..bare), (vero.) becoming, seemly, proper; allowable; ~ **heid**, seemliness, decency.
oor'bagasie, excess luggage.
oor'bak, (-ge-), bake again, rebake.
oor'bekend, (-e), very well known; widely known; notorious.
oor'beklemtoon, (w) (~), overemphasize.
oor'bel, (-le), ear-ring; ear-lobe.
oor'belas, (w), (~), overtax; overcharge; overload; (b) **(-te)**, overtaxed; overweight; overloaded; ~ **ting**, overcharging; overloading; overtaxation.
oor'beleef, (-de), too polite, over-polite, officious; ~ **dheid**, ultra-politeness, officiousness.
oor'belig, (~), over-expose; ~ **ting**, over-exposure.
oor'beset, (~), overstaff.
oor'beskaaf, (-de), over-civilized; over-educated.
oor'beskawing, over-civilization.
oor'beskeidenheid, excessive modesty.
oor'beskeie, too diffident, too modest.
oor'besorgdheid, over anxiety.
oor'besteding, overpayment.
oor'betaal, (~), overpay; pay someone, pay into someone's account.
oor'betaling, surcharge; excess payment; transfer to an account; overpayment.
oor'bevolk, (-te), over-populated, over-peopled, crowded, congested; ~ **ing**, surplus population, overpopulation.
oor'bewei, (w) (~), overstock; overgraze; (b) **(-de)**, overgrazed; overstocked; ~ **ding**, overgrazing.
oorbie', (~), bid too much; bid more; overcall (cards).
oor'bieg, auricular (oral) confession.
oorbie'tjie, (-s), ourebi antelope *(Ourebia scoparia)*, oribi.
oor'bind, (-ge-), tie, bind over (again); rebind (books).
oor'blaas, (-ge-), gild; plate.
oor'blaser, (-s), tale-bearer; slanderer, gossiper.
oor'blocs, (-e), ..blocse, (s), jumper, overblouse.
oor'bluf, (w) (~), disconcert, strike dumb, put out of countenance, overawe, nonplus; browbeat; (b) **(-te)**, overawed, dumbfounded; *heeltemal* ~ *wees*, be flabbergasted; be completely dumbfounded.
oor'bly¹, (w) (-ge-), remain (over); pass the night; *daar het vir ons niks anders oorgebly as om in die veld te slaap nie*, the only thing we could do was to sleep in the veld.
oor'bly², (b), overjoyed.
oor'blyfsel, (-s), remains, remainder, remnant, residue, leavings; vestige; survival, relic; exuviae; pickings.
oorbly'wend, (-e), remaining; *die* ~ *es*, the survivors; ~ *e LUG*, residual air; ~ *e PLANTE*, perennial plants.
oorbo'dig, (-e), superfluous, excessive, redundant; needless; unnecessary; uncalled for (remark); ~ *MAAK*, do away with, make unnecessary; *dis byna* ~ *om te SÊ*, I need hardly say; ~ **heid**, superfluity, redundance.
oor'boek, (-ge-), transfer an entry; post into another book; ~ **ing**, transfer(ence).
oorboord', overboard; ~ *GOOI*, throw overboard, jettison; scrap, discard; *alles IS* ~, everything is at sixes and sevens; ~ **werping**, jettisoning.
oor'borrel, (-ge-), bubble over, gush.
oor'brand, (-ge-), duff (cattle).
oor'brei, (-ge-), knit over again.
oor'brief, (-ge-), inform by letter; tell tales, repeat (to others), blab.
oor'brenging = **oorbringing**.

oor'bring, (-ge-), convey, deliver, transmit, carry forward, transfer, transport; convey (sounds); translate (languages); transpose (algebraic terms); repeat, pass on (news); ~ **as**, transmission shaft; ~ **er, (-s)**, carrier, informer, telltale; communicator; translator; conveyor; conductor; ~ **ing**, transportation, transfer, transmission; conveyance.
oor'broek, overall, work-garment, dungarees.
oor'brug, (s) fly-over bridge.
oorbrug', (w) (~), bridge (over); ~ **ging**, bridging.
oor'buig, (-ge-), bend over.
oord, (-e), place, locality, region, bower; *na beter* ~ *e verhuis*, die.
oor'daad, excess, extravagance; profusion, superabundance, copiousness; intemperance; luxury; redundance, redundancy; *in* ~ *lewe*, live extravagantly.
oorda'dig, (-e), excessive, extravagant; in excess; profuse; intemperate; ~ **heid**, excess, extravagance.
oordag', during the day, by day.
oor'dans, (-ge-), dance again.
oordans', (~), dance too much; *jou* ~, exhaust oneself by dancing.
oor'dat, because.
oor'deel, (s) (..dele), judgment, verdict, doom, sentence; opinion; account; adjudgment; discretion; discernment; *GESONDE* ~, sound judgment; *die LAASTE O* ~, last judgment; *'n OPGESKORTE* ~, a suspended sentence; ~ *UITSPREEK (vel)*, pass judgment; give an opinion; ~ *VEL oor*, sit in judgment on; *van* ~ *WEES*, hold the opinion; (w) **(-ge-)**, judge; consider; be of opinion; deem; adjudicate; *moenie jou NAASTE* ~ *nle*, don't judge your fellow man; *iets nie RAADSAAM* ~ *nie*, deem something inadvisable; *TE* ~ *na wat jy sê*, judging from what you say; ~ **kun'dig, (-e)**, discerning, judicial, discreet, judicious; ~ **kun'dige, (-s)**, competent judge; ~ **sdag**, judgment-day; doomsday; ~ **sfout**, error of judgment; ~ **vaardigheid**, readiness of judgment; ~ **velling, (-e, -s)**, judgment; ~ **vermoë**, discernment, judicative faculty.
oordek'¹, (~), cover; overlap; overspread; ~ *te tennisbaan*, covered (roofed) tennis-court.
oor'dek², (-ge-), lay (table) over again; rethatch (house); cover again (mare); cap.
oordek'king, cover(ing); overlap.
oor'delaar, (-s), judge.
oorden'kend, (-e), contemplative.
oorden'king, (-e, -s), reflection, meditation, contemplation, thinking over, consideration.
oordink', (~), reflect on, meditate upon, ruminate, premeditate, turn over in one's mind, cogitate; *'n saak goed* ~, consider a matter well.
oor'doen, (-ge-), do over again.
oor'dokter, ear-specialist, aural surgeon.
oordon'der, (~), browbeat, put off completely (by shouting angrily), overawe.
oor'doop, (-ge-), rebaptize.
oor'dra, (-ge-), carry (bring) forward; carry over; make over, delegate, cede, assign, transfer (property); convey (meaning); transmit (disease); assign, attorn; devolute, devolve; consign; enfeoff; endorse; grant (right).
oordraag'baar, (..bare), transferable; communicable; conveyable.
oor'draer, transferor, transferer; tell-tale; assignor.
oor'drag, transfer, cession, assignment, assignation, attornment, consignation, conveyance; devolution; delivery; grant; ~ *van bevoegdhede*, delegation of powers; ~ **bewys**, transfer voucher; ~ **boek**, transfer book; ~ **ing**, transfer(ence), conveyance; ~ **koste**, transfer-fee.
oor'drags: ~ **akte**, deed of transfer; ~ **brief**, deed of assignment; ~ **erkenning**, attornment.
oordrag'telik, (-e), metaphorical, figurative, tropological.
oordre'we, exaggerated, overdone, excessive, extreme; fancy; inordinate, extravagant; fabulous; ~ *beleefdheid*, exaggerated politeness; ~ **nheid**, exaggeration, excessiveness; extravagance.
oor'druk¹, (s) (-ke), offprint; overprint (on stamp); reprint; surcharge (on stamp); overpressure; (w)

(-ge-), reprint; transfer; press over; print too many copies.
oor'druk², (b) too busy, over-busy.
oor'druk: ~ **papier,** transfer-paper; ~ **plaatjie,** transfer, transfer-picture.
oor'druppels, ear-drops.
oor'dryf, oor'drywe¹, (-ge-), drive over; float across (river); blow over (clouds); *die storm het oorgedryf,* the storm has blown over.
oordryf', oordry'we², (~), exaggerate, overdo, magnify, carry to excess; overstate; overact (drama); *jy* ~, you are going to extremes.
oordry'wend, (-e), exaggerative.
oordry'wer, (-s), faddist.
oordry'wing, (-e, -s), exaggeration, overstatement; hyperbole, hyperbolism; aggravation.
oor'duidelik, amply clear, manifest.
oordui'wel, (~), bedevil, overawe, bluff.
oordwars', crosswise, athwart, transverse.
ooreen'bring, (-ge-), reconcile, cause to agree; conciliate (with facts); quadrate; ~ **ing,** reconciliation.
ooreen'gekome, agreed; *op 'n* ~ *datum,* on a date agreed upon.
ooreen'kom, (-ge-), agree, harmonize, tally; be equal to, resemble, correspond; collude; coincide; bargain; arrange; article; concur; close (with); *'n AMP wat daarmee* ~, a post which corresponds to that; *nie met sy BEGINSELS* ~ *nie,* militate against his principles; *die KLEURE moet* ~, the colours must match; *nie MET die beskrywing* ~ *nie,* not answer (correspond) to the description; *die twee PARTYE kom ooreen,* the two parties agree.
ooreen'koms, (-te), resemblance, conformity, congruity; agreement, contract, treaty, concurrence; correspondence; bargain, arrangement; article; compact; cartel; concordat, entente; congruence; affinity; concordance; parallelism; propinquity; *'n* ~ *AANGAAN (sluit, tref),* conclude (effect) an agreement; *tot 'n* ~ *KOM,* come to (arrive at) an agreement; ~ *VERTOON met,* bear a resemblance to; *VOLGENS* ~, as per agreement.
ooreenkoms'tig, (-e), corresponding, similar; analogical, analogous; correspondent; congruous; pursuant; consonant; (bw) accordingly, according (to); in conformity with; conformable; in accordance with; ~ *GESTELD,* similarly situated; ~ *e HOEKE,* corresponding angles; *hy is* ~ *sy RANG behandel,* the treatment was in keeping with his rank; ~ *sy WENSE,* in compliance with his wishes; ~ *die WET,* in accordance with the law; ~ **heid,** conformity, similarity, conformability.
ooreen'liggend, (-e), superimposed.
ooreen'slaan, (-ge-), agree, tally; lap.
ooreen'stem, (-ge-), agree, concur, correspond, coincide, accord, be in keeping (with), tally; quadrate; consort; harmonize; ~ **mend,** (-e), accordant; corresponding; coincident(al); concordant; consentaneous; consentient; congruent; ~ **ming,** agreement, harmony, concurrence; sequence; coincidence; analogy; resemblance, correspondence; keeping; congruence; consentaneity; accord(ance); concord(ance); concert; compliance, constancy; consonance; conformation; *in* ~ *ming BRING met,* bring into accord (line) with, harmonize with; *tot* ~ *ming KOM,* come to an agreement.
ooreen'val, (-ge-), overlap.
ooreet', (~), overeat.
ooreis', (~), strain, overstrain; overdrive; overtax; *hy het hom* ~, he has overtaxed himself; ~ **ing,** overstrain, overtaxing.
oor'-en-oor, again and again, repeatedly, over and over.
oor'ent, (oorgeënt), revaccinate; regraft; implant (bot.); reinoculate; ~ **ing,** revaccination; reinoculation; regrafting, implantation (bot.).
oor'entsel, (-s), graft.
oor'erf, (..geërf), inherit; be heritable; pass to (farm); ~ **baar,** (..**bare**), descendable.
oorerf'lik, (-e), hereditary; inheritable; transmissible; ~ **heid,** heredity; hereditability; ~ **heidsleer,** (doctrine of) heredity.
oor'erwe, (..geërwe), inherit.

oor'erwing, heredity; inheritance; ~ **sleer,** heredity.
oor'gaan, (-ge-), go over (across), proceed; stop, pass off (headache); move up, be moved up; pass over, cross (river); get across; *voordat ons DAARTOE* ~, before we pass on to that; *tot DADE* ~, turn to action; *IN iets anders* ~, change into something else; *tot 'n hoër STANDERD* ~, pass (be moved up) to a higher standard; *tot STEMMING* ~, put to the vote; *tot die VYAND* ~, join the enemy; ~ **baar,** (..**bare**), fordable; ~ **plek,** crossing, ford.
oor'gaar, overdone.
oor'gang, (-e), transition (music); transit (of Venus); passing across; passage, crossing; change; descent; devolution; landing (stairs); gradation.
oor'gangs: ~ **akkoord,** transient chord; ~ **bepaling,** interim regulation; transition (transitory) clause; ~ **brug,** cross-over bridge; ~ **eksamen,** promotion examination; ~ **hoogte,** clearance; ~ **jare,** menopausal years; change of life; menopause; ~ **kamp,** transit-camp, ~ **klank,** glide; ~ **leeftyd,** change of life; menopause; ~ **noot,** passing note; ~ **punt,** transition point; ~ **reg,** right of transfer; right of way; ~ **toestand,** state of transition, transitional state; ~ **tydperk,** climacteric; transition stage (period); ~ **vorm,** transition form; ~ **werking,** transitory operation.
oorgank'lik, (-e), transitive (verb).
oor'gat, ear-hole.
oor'gawe, (-s), surrender, capitulation; transfer, cession (of rights); abandon(ment); goodwill.
oor'geblaas, (-de), plated, rolled (gold).
oor'geblewe, remaining, residual.
oor'gedienstig, (-e), (over)officious, obsequious.
oor'gee, (-ge-), surrender, give up, capitulate, yield, hand over, cede, deliver up; abandon; fork out; *hom* ~ *aan,* surrender himself to; become a slave (addicted) to.
oor'geër, (-s), one who capitulates.
oor'geërf, (-de), congenital; inherited, hereditary.
oor'gehaal, (-de), cocked (gun); ready, on the point of; *ek was* ~ *vir hom,* I was ready to fight (oppose) him.
oor'gelukkig, (-e), most happy, overjoyed.
oor'genoeg, more than enough.
oor'gerus, (-te), over-confident; ~ **theid,** over-confidence.
oor'geswel, swelling (tumour) in the ear.
oor'getuie, ear-witness.
oor'gevoelig, (-e), over-sensitive, hyperaesthetic, highly-strung, irritable, maudlin, hypersensitive; sentimental; ~ **heid,** over-sensitiveness, hypersensitiveness; hyperaesthesia; sentimentality; irritability.
oor'gewig, overweight, excess weight; ~ **bagasie,** excess-weight luggage; ~ **koste,** surcharge.
oor'giet¹, (-ge-), pour over (into), decant.
oor'giet², (~), transfuse, suffuse; ~ *met,* drench (suffuse) with.
oorgie'ting, suffusion.
oor'glip, (-ge-), slip over, pay a short visit; ~ **pad,** fly-over.
oor'goed, (..**goeie**), too kind, too good.
oor'gooi, (-ge-), throw over; decant (wine).
oor'gord, surcingle.
oor'gretig, (-e), over-eager.
oor'groot, (..**grote**), too big; vast; *die* ~ *meerderheid,* the great majority.
oor'grootmoeder, great-grandmother.
oor'grootouers, great-grandparents.
oor'grootvader, great-grandfather.
oor'grote, major; largest, greatest; ~ *deel,* major part; largest part; *die* ~ *meerderheid,* the largest majority.
oor'haal, (-ge-), fetch across; win over, persuade; prevail on; draw in; debauch; cock (rifle); refine, clarify; ferry; *ek het HOM oorgehaal,* I have prevailed upon (persuaded) him; *vir iem. oorgehaal SIT,* be ready to give someone a bit of one's mind; *jou VIR iem.* ~, get ready to give someone a bit of one's mind; ..**haler,** rectifier; ~ **skuit,** ferry-boat.
oorhaas', (~), hurry too much, fluster, precipitate; *ek wil my nie* ~ *nie,* I don't want to hurry unduly.

oorhaas'tig, (-e), too hurried; rash, headlong, overhasty, precipitate; premature; precipitous; ~**heid**, too great hurry; precipitance, rashness, precipitousness.
oorhaas'ting, fluster, precipitation, precipitance; flat spin.
oor'haler, (-s), persuader.
oor'haling, persuasion.
oor'hand, supremacy, mastery, upper hand, predominance, prevalence, prevalency, preponderance, better; *die* ~ *HÊ*, have the upper hand, be superior, be uppermost, predominate; *die* ~ *KRY*, gain the mastery, get the better of.
oorhan'dig, (~), hand over, deliver; ~**ing**, handing-over, delivery.
oorhan(d)s', overhand; ~ *naai*, do top-sewing, overcast; ~**naat**, top-sewn seam.
oorhand'steek, oorhands'werk, top-sewing.
oor'hang, (-ge-), hang over, lean over, bend over; rake; list (ship); flare (skirt); *kos* ~, cook; put food on the stove.
oor'hangend, (-e), beetling, declivitous, declivous, pendant.
oor'hanger, (-s), ear-drop.
oorhans' = **oorhan(d)s**.
oor'hê, (..gehad), have left; have a surplus; be willing to sacrifice; *ALLES vir jou volk* ~, ready to sacrifice everything for one's people; *iem. vra of hy 'n PAAR oorhet*, ask someone whether he has a few to spare.
oor'heelkunde, otiatrics, otology.
oorheelkun'dig, (-e), otological; ~**e**, (-s), otologist.
oorheen', over, across; *pale wat agter* ~ *HANG*, poles protruding at the back; *êrens* ~ *KOM*, recover from something; *êrens* ~ *LEES*, not notice when reading; *êrens* ~ *PRAAT*, talk about something else to divert attention; ~ *SKIET*, overshoot; *êrens* ~ *STAP*, ignore a difficulty, objection, etc.; ~**skoot**, shot beyond the target.
oor'heerlik, (-e), very delicious, exquisite.
oorheers', (~), dominate, domineer, play the tyrant, predominate; preponderate; ~**end**, (-e), (pre)dominant; domineering; *die alles* ~ *ende vraag*, the all-important question; ~**er**, (-s), tyrant; dominator; ~**ing**, domination, domineering; predominance.
oor'hel, (-ge-), incline (to), lean (hang) over (towards), careene, rake; bank (aero.); gravitate (towards); heel, list (ship); ~ *na*, have a leaning towards; ~**lend**, (-e), proclivious, leaning; ~**ling**, inclination, proclivity, leaning, gravitation; heel, list (ship); cant; tilt.
oor'help, (-ge-), help across.
oor'hemp, (..hemde), (day) shirt; dress shirt; ~**s-knopie**, (-s), stud.
oor'hewel, (-ge-), siphon over.
oorhooks', (-e), diagonally, cornerwise; at loggerheads; ~*e ANKER*, diagonal stay; *jou* ~ *WERK*, work oneself to a frazzle; ~**hout**, diagonal grain (wood).
oor'holte, cavity of the ear.
oorhoof's, overhead; ~*e koste* (bokoste), overhead expenses, overheads.
oorhoop', in confusion, at variance, pell-mell, in a heap, in a mess; *met iem.* ~ *lê*, be at loggerheads with someone.
oor'hou, (-ge-), save; have left; carry; *iets van 'n siekte* ~, have as the result of an illness.
oor'hys, (-ge-), hoist over; ~**ing**, hoisting over.
oorhys', (~), overwind; ~**ing**, overwind.
oorjaag'¹, (~), overdrive, jade.
oor'jaag², (-ge-), drive over (again); rerun (race).
oorja'rig, (-e), perennial (plant).
oor'jas, (-se), overcoat, dust-coat; paletot, gaberdine.
oor'jurk, smock.
oor'kant, (s) other (opposite) side; beyond; *aan die* ~ *van die straat*, on the opposite side of the street; on the far side of the street; (bw, vs) across, on the opposite side; beyond.
oor'kantel, (-ge-), topple over; tilt over.
oor'kantse, ..**kantste**, opposite.
oor'kapitaliseer, (-ge-), over-capitalize.
oor'klap, ear-flap.

oorklee', (w) (~), cover, clothe, upholster.
oor'kleed, (s) (..**klede**), upper garment, overdress.
oor'klep, ear-cap.
oor'klere, overall, work-garment.
oor'klier, parotid (gland).
oor'klik, (-ge-), let out (secret).
oor'klim, (-ge-), climb over, scale (wall); change (trains); ~**trap**, stile.
oor'knoopbaadjie, double-breasted coat.
oorkoe'pel, (~), overarch, cover.
oorkom'¹, (~), surmount, get over, recover from, overcome; *iem. se besware* ~, remove someone's objections.
oor'kom², (-ge-), come over; befall, happen to; visit; *so BOOS dat ek iets kan* ~, be in a terrible rage; *sy sal daar NIKS van* ~ *nie*, she will suffer no ill effects; *iets SNAAKS het my oorgekom*, I experienced something queer; ~**s**, call, visit; arrival.
oor'konde, (-s), record, deed, charter; protocol; munimento; bull (papal); address; ~**boek**, cartulary; ~**leer**, diplomatics.
oor'konkel¹, (s) (-s), box on the ear; *iem. 'n* ~ *gee*, box someone's ear.
oor'konkel², (w) (-ge-), persuade by improper methods.
oor'kook, (-ge-), reboil; boil again; boil over; vomit.
oorkoom'lik, (-e), surmountable.
oorkors'ting, incrustation.
oor'kous, gaiter.
oor'krabbetjie, oor'krawwetjie, (-s), ear-ring, ear-drop.
oorkrop', (-te), overburdened.
oor'kruip, (-ge-), crawl over.
oor'kruiper, (-s), earwig; centipede, galleyworm.
oorkruis', crosswise; across; ~ *span*, tie crosswise (the legs of an animal); ~**rygsteek**, catch-stitch.
oor'krulletjie, kiss-curl.
oor'kry, (-ge-), get over; *vriende* ~, receive (a visit from) friends.
oor'kunde, otology.
oor'kussing, pillow.
oor'kyk, (-ge-), peruse, look over; correct, mark (papers); scrutinize; look beyond.
oor'kyker, otoscope.
oorlaai'¹, (~), overload, overcharge (battery); overcrowd (map); overburden, flood, glut (market); cloy; overstock; ply; deluge (with); overwhelm (with kindness); shower; bestow; *die MAAG* ~, eat too much; *hy is met PRESENTE* ~, presents were heaped upon him; *iem.* ~ *met WERK*, overburden someone with work; (b) (**de**), overcharged (battery); surfeited (stomach); overcrowded (map); overloaded (wagon); glutted (market); congested (curriculum); gorgeous; luscious; plethoric.
oor'laai², (-ge-), reload, load over again, trans-ship; ~**ery**, reloading, transfer; ~**koste**, trans-shipment charges; ~**loods**, trans-shipping shed.
oor'laat, (-ge-), leave (over), leave (to others); *iem. aan HOMSELF* ~, leave to his own devices; *aan sy LOT* ~, leave to his fate.
oorla'de, ornate.
oorla'ding¹, overcharging; overburdening; overcrowding; congestion; deluge; gorgeousness; hoarding.
oor'lading², trans-shipment.
oorlams', (-e), clever, handy, shrewd, sharp, fly; ~ *WEES*, be shrewd; ~**heid**, cleverness, shrewdness, wiliness.
oorland', by land, overland; ~**reis**, overland journey; ~**vlug**, cross-country flight.
oorlangs', (-e), lengthwise, longitudinal; endways.
oor'lap, (-ge-), patch again, repatch.
oor'las, nuisance, trouble; molestation; *iem.* ~ *AANDOEN*, inconvenience a person; incommode; molest; importune; *jy IS 'n* ~, you are a nuisance; *tot 'n* ~ *WEES*, make a nuisance of oneself.
oorlê'¹, (~), consider, turn over in one's mind; plan out; *'n saak met iem.* ~, consult a person about a matter.
oor'lê², (-ge-), lie over, wait (for); put over; submit; file (in law); exhibit (documents); save, put away; ~**dae**, days of demurrage

oor'le, oorle'de, oorlee', deceased, late, departed; defunct; ~ *JAN*, the late John; *sag en KALM oorlede*, passed away peacefully; *oorle OUPA*, my late grandfather.

oorle'dene, (-s), the deceased, the defunct, the departed, dead person.

oorleë', = oorlede.

oorleef'[1] (~) = oorlewe[1].

oor'leef[2] = oorlewe[2].

oor'leer[1], (s) upper-leather (boots), uppers, vamp.

oor'leer[2], (w) (-ge-), learn over again.

oorleer'[3], (w) (~), study too much.

oor'lêery, delay; waiting (for a train); demurrage.

oor'lees, (-ge-), read through, peruse.

oorleg', (s) deliberation, consideration, judgement, thought; gumption; foresight; discretion; policy; *IN ~ met*, in consultation with; *MET ~*, with deliberation, after due consideration; *~ PLEEG (met)*, take council with someone; consult.

oor'lêgeld, demurrage.

oorleg'ging[1], (-e), consideration, deliberation.

oor'legging[2], exhibition, production (of document).

oor'lel, (-le), lobe of the ear, lappet.

oor'lepel, ear-pick.

oor'leun, (-ge-), lean to(wards); lean over.

oorle'we[1], (~), outlive, survive, outlast.

oor'lewe[2], (-ge-), live over again, relive.

oorle'wende, (-s), survivor.

oor'lewer, (-ge-), deliver, transmit, hand over (down); consign (to); devote; *jou aan jou VYAND ~*, deliver oneself into the hands of one's enemy; *oorgelewer WEES aan*, be at the mercy of; ~ **ing, (-e, -s)**, tradition; legend; surrender; deliverance, delivery.

oorle'wing; ~ *(van die sterkste)*, survival (of the fittest).

oor'log, (..loë), war, warfare; *DRIEJARIGE ~, ENGELSE ~*, Anglo-Boer War; *IN ~ met*, at war with; *IN (gedurende, tydens) die ~*, during the war; *KOUE ~*, cold war; *NA die ~*, after the war; *SEWEJARIGE ~*, Seven Years' War; *in die ~ STORT*, plunge into war; *TAGTIGJARIGE ~*, Eighty Years' War; *~ TUSSEN Boer en Brit*, Anglo-Boer War; *~ VERKLAAR*, declare war; *~ VOER*, wage war; ~ **gie, (-s)**, small war.

oor'logs: ~ **aanblaser**, warmonger; ~ **artikel**, war-store (requirement); article manufactured in time of war; ~ **banier**, war-banner; ~ **basuin**, trumpet of war; ~ **beginsel**, principle of war; ~ **begroting**, war-time budget; army estimates; ~ **behoeftes**, necessaries of war, armament, war-supplies; ~ **belasting**, war-tax; ~ **beriggewer**, war-correspondent; ~ **bonus, (-se)**, war-bonus; ~ **brand**, conflagration; ~ **buit**, spoils of war; ~ **daad**, martial achievement; ~ **dans**, war-dance; ~ **deug**, warlike virtue; ~ **diens**, war service; ~ **dok**, Mulberry dock; ~ **fakkel**, war-torch; ~ **gebied**, theatre of war (operations); ~ **gedenkskrifte**, war-records; ~ **gees**, war spirit; ~ **gerug**, rumour of war; ~ **gesind, (-e)**, warlike, bellicose; ~ **gevaar**, danger of war; ~ **geweld**, force of arms; ~ **god**, war-god; ~ **graf**, war grave; ~ **hawe**, military port; ~ **held**, war hero; ~ **kaart**, war map (chart); ~ **kabinet**, war cabinet; ~ **kans**, fortune of war; ~ **kas**, war-chest.

oor'log: ~ **skatting**, war-levy, war contribution; ~ **skip**, (..**skepe**), man-of-war.

oor'logs: ~ **kontraband(e)**, contraband of war; ~ **korrespondent**, war-correspondent; ~ **koste**, war expenses; ~ **kreet**, war-cry.

oor'logskuld, war-debt; war-guilt.

oor'logs: ~ **kunde**, art of war(fare); ~ **laste**, war-debts; ~ **lening**, war-loan; ~ **lis**, strategy; stratagem; ~ **mag**, war-forces; ~ **masjien**, engine of war; ~ **materiaal**, war-material; ~ **medalje**, war-medal; ~ **misdadiger**, war criminal; ~ **moed**, heroism; ~ **moegheid**, war-weariness; ~ **obligasie**, war-bond; ~ **opstoker**, warmonger; ~ **pad**, warpath; *op die ~ pad*, on the warpath; ~ **party**, war-party; ~ **perd**, war-horse; ~ **poging**; war-effort; ~ **prys**, war-price; ~ **raad**, war council; ~ **ramp**, war catastrophe; ~ **reg**, laws of war; rights of war; ~ **risiko**, war-risk(s); ~ **roem**, military glory.

oor'logsterkte, fighting strength.

oor'logs: ~ **terrein**, theatre of war; ~ **toeslag**, war-bonus; war-levy; ~ **toestand**, state of war; ~ **toneel**, theatre of war; ~ **toorts**, torch of war; ~ **tuig**, machinery (implements) of war; ~ **tyd**, time of war, wartime.

oor'logsug, lust for war.

oorlogsug'tig, (-e), warlike, belligerent, bellicose; ~ **heid**, warlikeness, bellicosity, belligerence.

oor'logs: ~ **uitgawes**, war expenses; ~ **veld**, battle-field; ~ **verklaring**, declaration of war; ~ **verslaggewer**, war-correspondent; ~ **vlag**, war ensign; ~ **vliegtuig**, war-plane; ~ **vloot**, war-fleet; ~ **voet**: *op ~ voet*, on a war footing; ~ **vuur**, flame of war; ~ **wapen**, implement of war; ~ **wet**, law of war; ~ **wins**, war profit; ~ **winsmaker**, war-profiteer; ~ **woede**, war fury; ~ **wolk**, war-cloud.

oor'logvoerend, (-e), belligerent, waging war, at war; ~ **e, (-s)**, belligerent.

oor'logvoering, conduct of war, warfare.

oor'lok[1], (s) lovelock.

oor'lok[2], (w) (-ge-), entice over.

oor'loop, (s) overflow, lasher, spillway; catch-drain; weir; spillage; ridge, cross, crossing; landing (stair); (w) (-ge-), walk (come) over; defect, desert, rat; turn one's coat; overbrim, overflow, overspill; ~ *van VRIENDELIKHEID*, be all kindness; ~ *na die VYAND*, desert to the enemy; ~ **dek**, orlop; ~ **pyp**, overflow pipe.

oor'lopend, (-e), overflowing; effusive, gushing.

oor'lopens: *tot ~ toe*, to the brim.

oor'loper, (-s), deserter, renegade, backslider, turncoat, rat.

oorlo'sie, (-s), (ook **horlosie**), watch, clock; *my ~ is AGTER*, my watch is slow; *op die ~ KYK*, tell the time; *soos 'n goedkoop ~ LIEG*, lie like a cheap watch; *kyk waar STAAN die ~ al*, look at the time; *soos die ~ TUIS tik, tik hy nêrens*, the smoke of a man's house is better than the fire of another's; *my ~ is VOOR*, my watch is fast; ~ **armband**, watch-bracelet; ~ **blom**, passion-flower; ~ **glas**, watch-glass; ~ **kas**, watch-case; ~ **ketting**, watch-chain; ~ **maker**, watch-maker; ~ **sakkie**, watch-case, fob; watch-pocket; ~ **skut**, watch-guard; ~ **sleutel**, watch-key; ~ **veer**, watch-spring.

oorly', (~, **oorlede**), die, pass away.

oorly'de, oorly'ding, oorly'e, death, demise.

oor'maak, (-ge-), do over again; assign, cede, transfer (property); transmit (money).

oor'maat, excess, surplus; overmeasure; *tot ~ van ramp*, to make matters worse, to crown all, on top of it all.

oor'mag, superior power, greater numbers; act of God; supremacy, superior force; predominance, prepotence, prepotency; *vir die ~ beswyk*, succumb to superior numbers; ~ **'tig, (-e)**, superior (force).

oorma'ki, (-'s), galago.

oor'making, (-e, -s), transfer; remittance.

oorman', (~), overpower, overwhelm; *deur die slaap ~*, overcome by sleep.

oorma'tig[1], (-e), excessive; undue; prepotent; *~e BESPROEIING*, over-irrigation; *~ EET*, overeat, eat to excess.

oor'matig[2], (-e), too temperate, too moderate.

oorma'tigheid, intemperance; excess.

oormees'ter, (~), overpower; master; subdue; overmaster; seize (a country); overcome (by feelings); ~ **ing**, overpowering, mastering; seizure.

oor'meet, (-ge-), measure again.

oormekaar', the one over (across) the other; *~ KYK*, be cross-eyed; *~ SIT*, cross the legs; *~ SLAAN*, put across; overlap; *~ VAL*, fall one over the other; overlap; ~ **oë**, asquint.

oor'merk[1], (s) (-e), earmark; (w) (ge-), earmark (sheep).

oor'merk[2], (w) (-ge-), re-mark, mark over again.

oor'moed, boldness; presumption; audacity, recklessness; arrogance.

oormoe'dig, (-e), daring; presumptuous, overweening, arrogant; over-confident; reckless; ~ **heid**, overconfidence, rashness.

oor'môre, oor'more, the day after tomorrow; *more*,

~, one of these days; ~ **aand**, the evening of the day after tomorrow, two nights hence.
oor'mou, sham sleeve, oversleeve.
oor'munt, (-ge-), recoin.
oor'naai, (-ge-), sew (over) again; overcast.
oor'naat, over-seam; ~ **s**, (-e), clinker-built.
oornag', (w) (~), stay overnight, pass the night; (b, bw), overnight; ~ *ryk word*, grow rich overnight; ~ **ting**, (-s, -e), overnight stay.
oor'name, (-s), taking over, purchase; adoption.
oor'neem, (-ge-), take over, buy, acquire (business); assume (command); adopt (foreign word); copy, borrow (from author); *ander koerante geliewe oor te neem*, other papers please copy.
oor'neming, taking over, acquisition; borrowing; adoption.
oor'netjies, finical.
oor'noeming, metonymy.
oor'nommer¹, (s) (-s), ear number.
oor'nommer², (w) (-ge-), number anew, number over again.
oor'ontsteking, inflamation of the ear; otitis.
oor'ontwikkel, (~), overdevelop.
oor'oop, overblown.
oor'oorgrootvader, great-great-grandfather
oor'opbrengs, overrun (in dairying).
oor'opgewondenheid, over-excitement.
oor'opwinding, overwind (of cable).
oor'oud, (..oue), very old.
oor'pad: *reg van* ~ right of way.
oor'pak¹, (s) overall(s); smock.
oor'pak², (w) (-ge-), pack from one container into another; pack over again, repack.
oorpeins', (~), meditate, reflect, contemplate, muse, chew the cud; ~ **ing**, (-e, -s), meditation, cogitation, musing, contemplation.
oor'plaas, (-ge-), transfer, shift, remove; ~ **kaart**, transfer (-card).
oor'plaatjie, ear-tag.
oor'plak, (-ge-), paste over again; repaper.
oor'plant, (-ge-), transplant; replant; ~ **ing**, (-e, -s), transplanting; replanting.
oor'plasing, (-e, -s), transfer, removal.
oor'pleister, (-ge-), plaster over again.
oor'ploeg, (-ge-), plough over again.
oor'pluisie, (-s), ear-plug.
oor'pomp¹, (s) ear-syringe.
oor'pomp², (w) (-ge-), pump over (again).
oorprik'kel, (w) (~), over-exite, over-stimulate; (b) (-d), overstring; ~ *de senuwees*, overstring nerves; ~ **baar**, (..bare), hyperaesthetic; ~ **ing**, (-e, -s), over-excitement; over-stimulation.
oor'produksie, over-production, surplus production.
oor'produseer, (~), over-produce.
oor: ~ **pyn**, ear-ache, otalgia, otalgy; ~ **rand**, helix.
oorre'dend, (-e), persuasive.
oorre'der, (-s), persuader.
oorre'ding, persuasion.
oorre'dings: ~ **krag**, persuasiveness; power of per= suasion; ~ **kuns**, art of persuasion; ~ **middel**, per= suasive argument; inducement.
oorreed', (~), persuade, prevail on; overpersuade; *iem*. ~ *om te gaan*, persuade someone to go; ~ **baar**, (..bare), open to persuasion, persuadable, persuasible.
oor'reik, (-ge-), hand over, pass.
oorrek', (~), overstretch, overreach oneself; stretch over.
oor'reken, (-ge-), reckon again, recalculate.
oor'ring, car-ring.
oor'roei, (-ge-), row across.
oor'rok, overskirt; overall (for a woman).
oorrom'pel, (~), surprise, catch unawares, take by surprise, fall upon, overwhelm; ~ **ing**, surprise (attack).
oorry'¹, (~), run over, knock (ride) down; override (a horse).
oor'ry², (-ge-), ride over again; drive over.
oor'ryp, overripe.
oor'saai, (-ge-), resow, sow over (again).
oor'saak, (..sake), cause, reason, factor, origin; birth; breeder; occasion; ~ *en GEVOLG*, cause and effect; *KLEIN oorsake het groot gevolge*, little strokes fell great oaks; *NAASTE* ~, proximate cause; *TER oorsake van*, for reason of; *VERWY= DERDE* ~, remote cause.
oorsaak'lik, (-e), causal, causative; ~ *e verband*, causal nexus; ~ **heid**, causation, causality; ~ **heids= leer**, causality, causation.
oor'saaksleer, etiology.
oor'sê, (-ge-), repeat, say again.
oorsee', oversea(s), transmarine, transoceanic; *van* ~, from oversea; ~ **s'**, (..**seese**), oversea, trans= marine; ..*seese vakansie*, holiday abroad.
oor'seil, (-ge-), sail across; sail again.
oor'sein, (-ge-), signal over (again); telegraph, wire, cable; ~ **ing**, transmission.
oor'send, (-ge-), send over, remit, transmit; ~ **ing**, re= mittal, transmission, despatch.
oor'senuwee, auricular nerve.
oor'set, (-ge-), reset, set up again; putt again.
oor'setting, (-e, -s), translation, transference; reset= ting; crossing; reputting; ~ *van skuld*, delegation of debt.
oor'siekte, ear-disease.
oor'sien¹, (-ge-), look over, correct; excuse, pardon.
oorsien'², (~), survey, overlook; *die gevolge is nie te* ~ *nie*, the results cannot be visualized; ~ **baar**, (..**bare**), surveyable, calculable.
oor'sieraad, ear-jewel, girandole.
oor'sig, (-te), view; survey; review; summary; analy= sis; précis, digest; conspectus; ~ **kaart**, survey map; site map.
oor'sigs: ~ **jaar**, year under review; ~ **tabel**, synoptic table.
oorsig'telik, (-e), (easily) surveyable; synoptic; ~ **heid**, state of being easily surveyable; *ter wille van die* ~ *heid*, for ease of survey.
oorsil'wer, (~), silver, silver-plate.
oor'sing, (-ge-), sing again.
oor'sit, (-ge-), put over; translate; promote (pupils); ferry over, convey across.
oorska'du, (~), overshadow, eclipse, outshine, ef= face; adumbrate; darken; ~ **wing**, overshadowing; darkening.
oor'skakel, (-ge-), change (gears); switch over; con= nect with; ~ **baar**, convertible; ~ **ing**, switch(ing)= over; gear-changing.
oor'skat¹, (-ge-), revalue, estimate again.
oorskat'², (~), over-estimate, overrate; ~ **ting**, over= estimation, overrating.
oor'skeep, (-ge-), trans-ship.
oor'skeer, (-ge-), shave over again; shear again.
oor'skep, (-ge-), ladle from one receptacle into another.
oor'skeping, trans-shipment.
oor: ~ **skerm**, ear-guard, ear-cap; ~ **skerping**, aural training.
oor'skiet¹, (s) remains, rest, remnant; pickings; draff; offal; orts; left-overs, leavings; (w) (-ge-), remain; be left over.
oor'skiet², (w) (-ge-), shoot over again.
oor'sklet: ~ **gereg**, made-up dish; ~ **koolgereg**, bubble-and-squeak; ~ **kos**, left-overs, left-over food, scraps; ~ **sel**, remains, rest, remnant; ~ **stuk= kies**, scraps; ~ **vleis**, left-over meat.
oor'skilder, (-ge-), paint over again; recoat; *drie maal* ~, give three coats of paint.
oor'skink, (-ge-), pour over, decant.
oor'skoen, galosh, gumboot, overshoe, patten.
oor'skop, (-ge-), rekick, kick over; convert (a try).
oor'skot, (-te), remainder, residue, balance, excess; remnant; surplus; overplus; factory-reject; debris; *die stoflike* ~, the mortal remains; ~ **bates**, surplus assets; ~ **waarde**, scrap value; ~ **winkel**, factory-rejects store.
oorskreeu', (~), outcry, shout down.
oorskry', (~), exceed (debts); surpass; violate; in= fringe; overstep; *jou bevoegdheid* ~, overstep the limits of one's authority; ~ **ding**, transgression (of law); overstepping (bounds); violation.
oorskryf', **oorskry'we¹**, (~), oversubscribe; *die le= ning is* ~, the loan is oversubscribed.

oor'skryf, oor'skrywe², (-ge-), transcribe, copy, rewrite.
oor'skrywer, (-s), copyist.
oor'skrywing, (-e, -s), transfer; rewriting; copying; ~**skoste,** transfer dues.
oor'skuiwe, (-ge-), shift across.
oor'skuiwing, overthrust; thrust-fault; ~**svlak,** thrust-plane.
oor'skulp, external ear, auricle; ear-lobe; ~**rand,** helix.
oor'skut, ear-guard, ear-cap.
oor'slaan, (-ge-), omit, pass over, miss out, skip, jump (some pages); turn head over heels; pretermit; misfire (gun); spread to (fire); hit over (ball); not consider; *'n AMPTENAAR* ~, not consider an official (for promotion); ~ *in (na) ENGELS,* change to English; *die SKAAL laat* ~, turn the scale (the balance); *sy STEM slaan oor,* his voice is breaking; ~**ooi,** skip (ewe).
oor'slag, (..slae), turn-up; flap; hasp (and staple); clasp; overslaugh (mil.); ~**greep,** overlapping grip (golf); ~**las,** lap joint; flashing.
oor'sleep, (-ge-), drag over (across).
oor'smeer¹, (s) ear-wax, cerumen.
oor'smeer², (w) (-ge-), smear (rub) over; spread over.
oor'smyt, (-ge-), throw (fling) over (across).
oor'soet, more than sweet, luscious, over-sweet, cloying.
oorso'mer, (~), (spend the) summer.
oor'span¹, (-ge-), stretch across (over); change (horses in) a team.
oorspan'², (~), overstrain, over-exert; *hy het hom* ~, he overstrained himself; ~**ne,** overspent, strained; overstrung; ~*ne senuwees,* overwrought nerves.
oorspan'ning¹, (-e, -s), span (of bridge).
oorspan'ning², over-exertion, overstrain.
oor'speekselklier, parotid gland; ..**ontste'king,** parotitis.
oor'spel = owerspel.
oorspe'lig, (-e), adulterous; adulterine.
oor'spieël, otoscope, auriscope.
oor'sprei, (s) coverlet; **(w) (-ge-),** spread over.
oor'spring, (-ge-), jump over (across), clear, leap over; miss out, omit, skip; pound.
oor'sproei, (s), earspray; **(w) (-ge-),** respray, spray again.
oor'sprong, (-e), origin, cause, root, head, source, germ, nascency, origination.
oorspronk'lik, (-e), original, primary, elemental, aboriginal, primogenital, pristine, primordial; primeval; primitive; radical; *die* ~ *e,* the original; ~**heid,** originality; raciness, freshness.
oor'spuitjie, ear-syringe.
oor'staan, (-ge-), stand over; be postponed; hold over; *ten* ~ *van,* in the hearing of; ~**d, (-e),** opposite; ~*de hoeke,* opposite angles; ~**katoen,** satoon cotton.
oorstag', bw: ~ *gooi,* stay, tack (boat).
oorstal'lig, (-e), overabundant (rain).
oor'stap, (-ge-), walk (step) across; change (trains); disregard; ~**kaartjie,** transfer-ticket.
oor'steek¹, (s) (..steke), eave; skirt (of roof).
oor'steek², (s) ear-pain.
oor'steek³, (w) (-ge-), cross (river).
oor'steek⁴, (w) (-ge-), prick again.
oor'steentjie, otolith.
oorstelp', (w) (~), overwhelm; overpower; heap upon; inundate, swamp with, deluge; ~ *met AANSOEKE,* swamped with applications; ~ *van VREUGDE,* overcome with joy; (b) **(-te),** overcome; ~**end, (-e),** baffling, overwhelming; ~**ing,** overwhelming; inundation.
oorstem'¹, (~), outvote, overrule; deafen; drown (sound); overtone.
oor'stem², (-ge-), vote again; retune, tune again; ~**ming,** retuning.
oor'stewel, overboot.
oor'stook, (-ge-), redistil.
oor'stoot, (-ge-), push over.
oor'stop, (-ge-), darn again; fill again (pipe).
oor'stort, (-ge-), spill (fall) over.
oor'streng, (-e), too strict.

oorstro'ming, (-e, -s), inundation, flood(ing), cataclysm, deluge; freshet; overflow; ~**skade,** flood damage.
oor'stroom¹, (-ge-), flow over.
oorstroom'², (~), overflow, inundate, flood, deluge; (en)gulf; overrun; overstock (market).
oor'stuur¹, (w) (-ge-), send over (across); consign.
oorstuur'², (b) in disorder, out of order, bewildered, upset; *sy was heeltemal* ~, she was completely bewildered, she was thoroughly upset.
oorsui'ker¹, (~), (sprinkle) sugar (over).
oor'suiker², (~), sugar again.
oor'suising, (-e, -s), ringing (tingling) in the ears, tinnitus.
oor'suur, peracid.
oor'swem, (-ge-), swim over (across); swim again.
oor'swering, ear-canker.
oor'sy, opposite side.
oortal'lig, (-e), supernumerary.
oor'tap, (-ge-), rack (wine); pour from one vessel into another; transfuse (blood); ~**ping,** transfusion.
oor'teken¹, (-ge-), redraw, draw over again; sign again.
oorte'ken², (~), oversubscribe (loan).
oor'tel, (-ge-), recount, count over; lift over (across); ~**ling,** recount.
oor'tik, (-ge-), retype.
oor'tip, tip (lobe) of the ear.
oor'tjie¹, (-s), farthing.
oor'tjie², (-s), little ear; ~**suil,** horned owl.
oor'tog, (-te), passage, crossing berth; ~**geld,** pass-age-money.
oortol'lig, (-e), superfluous, redundant; excessive; surplus; ~**heid,** superfluity, redundance; surplus-age (in pleadings).
oortre'der, (-s), trespasser, transgressor, offender, culprit, misdoer, delinquent, lawbreaker; *JEUGDIGE* ~ *s,* juvenile delinquents; ~*s sal VERVOLG word,* trespassers will be prosecuted.
oortre'ding, (-e, -s), transgression, trespass; error, offence, infringement, encroachment, misfeasance, delinquency, violation, contravention, defiance.
oortree'¹, (~), transgress, trespass, infringe, encroach, contravene.
oor'tree², (-ge-), pace over again; step across (over).
oortref', (~), surpass, excel, better; foil; outvie; outreach; exceed; outclass, preponderate, outstrip, outrival; outbid; outdo; outweigh; go one better; go beyond; head; *in GETAL* ~, outnumber; *JOUSELF* ~, surpass oneself; *'n TEENSTANDER* ~, outclass an opponent; ~**fend, (-e),** superlative.
oor'trek¹, (s) (-ke), cover, case, casing; coat; **(w) (-ge-),** cover; recover; pull over; encase; redraw; cross; move across; trace over; upholster; drape; deck; *'n KUSSING* ~, put on a cushion-cover; ~ *NA 'n nuwe huis,* move into a new house.
oortrek'², (w) (~), cover; overdraw (banking account); ~ *met ONKRUID,* covered with weeds; ~ *WEES,* be in the red, in debt; ~**king,** overdraft.
oor'trek: ~ **papier,** tracing-paper; ~**sel, (-s),** cover(ing), casing, coating, slip, case; ~**trui,** pullover, jersey, sweater.
oortroef', (~), overtrump, outbid, outtrump.
oortrok'ke, overdrawn (account); ~ *rekening,* overdraft, overdrawn account.
oor'trommel, ear-drum.
oor'trou, (-e-), remarry (same couple).
oortuig', (~), convince, satisfy (oneself); carry conviction; convict (of guilt); persuade; *ek HOU my* ~ *dat...,* I feel quite sure that ..; *'n* ~ *de SOSIALIS,* a confirmed socialist; *vas* ~ *wees VAN iets,* be firmly convinced of something.
oortuig'baar, (..bare), convincible.
oortui'gend, (-e), convincing, cogent, convictive.
oortui'ging, (-e, -s), conviction; belief; persuasion; *IN die* ~ *dat,* in the belief that; *alle* ~ *MIS,* be utterly unconvincing; *tot die* ~ *KOM,* come to the conclusion; *'n* ~ *TOEGEDAAN wees,* hold the conviction; *nie VATBAAR vir* ~ *nie,* not open to persuasion; ~**skrag,** convincingness, cogency, force.
oor'tuiting, tingling of the ears, tinnitus.
oor'tyd, overtime; ~**s, (-e),** overtime (work).

oor'uil, eagle owl.
oor'ure, overtime.
oor'vaar¹, **(-ge-)**, cross over, ferry across; punt.
oorvaar'², (~), run down (a vessel).
oor'vaart, passage, crossing.
oor'val¹, (s) **(-le)**, fit; surprise attack, hold-up; coup-de-main; descent; (w) **(-ge-)**, fall over, capsize.
oorval'², (~), surprise; overtake (darkness); overcome (sleep); swoop (down on), waylay; burst upon; invade; *die reën het ons* ~, we were caught in the rain; ~**ling**, invasion.
oor'veeg, (..veë), box on the ear; *iem. 'n* ~ *gee*, give someone a clip on the ear.
oor'verdowend, **(-e)**, deafening, ear-splitting.
oor'vereenvoudig, (~), oversimplify; ~**ing**, oversimplification.
oor'verf, **(-ge-)**, repaint; redye.
oor'verfyn, **(-d)**, over-refined.
oor'verhit, (w) (~), overheat; reheat; (b) **(-te)**, overheated; superheated (steam); ~**ter**, **(-s)**, superheater (steam); ~**ting**, overheating, superheating; reheating.
oor'vermoei, (~), overtire.
oor'vermoeid, **(-e)**, overtired, over-fatigued; ~**heid**, over-fatigue.
oor'versadig, (w) (~), supersaturate; cloy, surfeit, satiate; drug; (b) **(-de)**, supersaturated; ~**ing**, supersaturation; surfeit, satiation; glut.
oor'verseker, (~), over-insure.
oor'versier, **(-de)**, ornate.
oor'versigtig, **(-e)**, overcautious.
oor'vertel, (~), tell over again, repeat, tell others; ~**ling**, retelling.
oor'vet, too fat (meat, people); too fatty (soup).
oor'vleg, **(-ge-)**, replait.
oorvleu'el, (~), surpass, outstrip; outflank; overlap; ~**ing**, overlapping; overlap (ground); outflanking; outdoing; surpassing.
oor'vlieg, **(-ge-)**, fly again; fly across.
oor'vlies, ear-membrane, ear-drum, tympanum.
oor'vloed, abundance, plenty, superabundance, glut, plentitude, plethora; affluence; exuberance; profuseness; redundance, redundancy; plenteousness; ~ *van BOME*, abounding in trees; ~ *van HARE*, profusion of hair; *HORING van* ~, cornucopia, horn of plenty; *IN* ~, in profusion, galore; *TEN* ~ *e*, moreover.
oorvloe'dig, **(-e)**, plentiful, abundant, plenteous, gushing, full; bounteous, bountiful; free, liberal; bumper, ample; affluent, lavish, exuberant; copious, profuse, redundant, plethoric; ~**heid**, abundance, copiousness, plenty, profusion, amplitude; ampleness.
oorvloei'¹, (~), flood; exuberate.
oor'vloei², **(-ge-)**, flow over, brim over.
oor'vlug, **(-te)**, overflight (with plane).
oorvoed', (w) (~), overfeed (human beings); (b) **(-e)**, overfed.
oorvoe'ding, overfeeding, supernutrition.
oor'voer¹, **(-ge-)**, carry over, lead across, convey across.
oorvoer'², (~), feed too much, overfeed (animals); glut (market).
oor'voering¹, conveyance, transport.
oorvoe'ring², glutting; overfeeding.
oor'vol, **(-le)**, brimful; overfull, overfilled, overcrowded, crammed, crowded (room); congested; ~**heid**, glut; plethora; ~ **op**, superabundant.
oor'volteken, oversubscribe.
oor'vordering, overcharge.
oorvor'mig, **(-e)**, auriculate, auriform.
oorvra'¹, (~), overcharge, surcharge.
oor'vra², **(-ge-)**, ask again; invite (over).
oor'vrag, excess load; excess luggage.
oorvra'ging, **(-s)**, overcharging; overcharge.
oor'vriendelik, **(-e)**, overkind.
oor'waai, **(-ge-)**, blow over; blow off; drop in (visitor).
oor: ~ *waks*, **(-e)**, box on the ear; ~ *was*, ear-wax, cerumen; ~ *watte*, ear-wool.
oor'weeg¹, **(-ge-)**, reweigh.
oorweeg'², (~), consider, think over, cogitate, reason, reflect, ponder, bethink, weigh (fig.), contemplate, meditate, prepend, deliberate; preponderate; decide the issue.
oor'weg¹, level crossing; overhead crossing; crossroad.
oorweg'²: *goed met iem.* ~ *kom*, get on well with somebody.
oorwe'gend, **(-e)**, preponderating; for the most part, predominant, preponderant, principal.
oorwe'ging, **(-e, -s)**, consideration, deliberation, contemplation, cogitation; *by NADERE* ~, on second thoughts; after further reflection (consideration); *IN* ~, under consideration; *in* ~ *NEEM*, take into consideration; *TER* ~, for consideration; *UIT* ~ *dat*, on the ground that, considering that.
oor'wegwagter, gateman (at a level crossing).
oorwel'dig, (~), overpower, overwhelm; force; ~**end**, **(-e)**, overpowering, overwhelming; ~**er**, **(-s)**, usurper; ~**ing**, overpowering, usurpation.
oorwelf', (~), overarch, vault; cope; ~**sel**, **(-s)**, vault.
oorwel'wing, **(-e, -s)**, vault.
oor'werk¹, (s) overwork; overtime; overlabour; (w) **(-ge-)**, (do) work over again; ~ *van bome*, reworking (top-working) of trees.
oorwerk'², (~), overwork, over-exert; overdrive; ~**t'heid**, overwork.
oor'werp, **(-ge-)**, throw over.
oor'wig, preponderance; supremacy; ascendancy; prepotence, prepotency; prevalence; prevalency; paramountcy; *dit HET die* ~, this preponderates; ~ *in die LUG*, air supremacy.
oor'wikkel, **(-ge-)**, overwind, ~**ing**, overwinding.
oorwin', (~), conquer, overcome, gain the victory, vanquish, subdue (the enemy), get the better (best) of, overmaster, surmount (difficulties); foil; pill; ~**lik**, **(-e)**, conquerable; ~**naar**, **(-s)**, conqueror, victor; champion; ~**ning**, **(-e, -s)**, victory; conquest; *die* ~ *ning behaal*, gain the victory; ~**ningsfees**, victory celebration; ~**ningsroes**, flush of victory.
oor'wins, surplus profit, excess profit; ~ **belasting**, excess-profit duty; supertax; ~ **maker**, profiteer.
oorwin'ter, (~), (spend the) winter, hibernate; ~**end**, **(-e)**, hibernating; ~**ing**, wintering, hibernation.
oor'wip, **(-ge-)**, jump over (across); make a hasty visit, drop in, pop over; hop over.
oor'wit, **(-ge-)**, rewhitewash.
oorwo'ë, contemplated; considered (opinion).
oorwon'ne, conquered, defeated; ~**ling**, **(-e)**, ~ **ne**, **(-s)**, vanquished (person), loser.
oor'wurm, earwig.
ooryld', **(-e)**, hurried, rash, precipitate.
oory'ling, undue haste, precipitance, rashness.
oor'yster, casque.
oory'werig, **(-e)**, over-zealous, over-eager.
oos, east; orient; ~ *WES, tuis bes*, east or west, home's best; there is no place like home; *die WIND is* ~, the wind is east.
Oos'-Afrika, East Africa; ~ **ans'**, **(-e)**, East African.
Oos'-Duitsland, East Germany.
oos'end, eastern end.
Oos'-Europa, Eastern Europe.
Oos'-Europees, (..pese), East European.
oösfeer, (oösfere), oosphere.
Oos'-Gote, Ostrogoths.
Oos'-Goties, **(-e)**, Ostrogothic.
oos'grens, eastern frontier.
Oos-In'dië, East India; ~ **r**, **(-s)**, East Indian.
Oos-In'dies, **(-e)**, East Indian; ~ *doof wees*, pretend not to hear, feign deafness; ~ *e kerriesop*, mulligatawny soup.
Oos-In'diëvaarder, **(-s)**, East Indiaman.
oos'kus, east coast; ~ **koors**, east-coast fever.
oos'moeson, (north-)east monsoon, dry monsoon.
oos'noordoos, east-north-east.
oos'passaat, east tradewind.
oösperm', **(-e)**, oosperm.
oos'pier, east pier.
oöspoor', (oöspore), oospore.
Oos'-Pruise, Eastern Prussia.
Oos'see, Baltic Sea.
oos'suidoos, east-south-east.

oos'sy, east(ern) side.
oos'te = oos.
Oos'te, Orient, East; *die NABYE* ~, the Near East; *die VERRE* ~, the Far East.
oos'tekant, east (side).
oos'telik, (-e), eastern, easterly; *die O~e Halfrond,* the Eastern Hemisphere; ~ **ste,** easternmost.
Oost'ende, Ostend.
Oos'tenryk, Austria; ~**er, (-s),** Austrian; ~-**Hongarye,** Austria-Hungary; ~**s, (-e),** Austrian.
oos'ter: ~ **front,** eastern front; ~**grens,** eastern border (frontier); ~**kim,** eastern horizon; ~**lengte,** eastern longitude.
Oos'terling, (-e), Oriental, Easterling.
oos'termeting, easting.
Oos'ters, (-e), Oriental; *die ~e kwessie,* the Oriental question.
oos'tewind, eastwind; *van die ~ lewe,* live on fresh air.
oos'waarts, (-e), eastward.
oot'moed, humility, submission, meekness.
ootmoe'dig, (-e), humble, submissive, meek; ~**heid,** meekness, humility.
op, (vs), on, upon, in, at; ~ *AFRIKAANS,* in Afrikaans; ~ *'n AFSTAND,* at a distance; *ALMAL ~ een na,* all but one; ~ *BLOEMFONTEIN,* at Bloemfontein; *BRIEF ~ brief,* letter after letter; ~ *'n sekere DAG,* on a certain day; one day; ~ *sy ou DAG,* in his old age; ~ *die DAK,* on the roof; ~ *iem. DRINK,* drink to the health of; *algar ~ EEN na,* all but one; ~ *die ou END,* eventually, in the long run; ~ *GROND van,* by virtue of; *een ~ HONDERD,* one per hundred; ~ *sy HOOGSTE,* at its highest; ~ *JAG gaan,* go hunting; ~ *die KOOP toe,* into the bargain; ~ *LANGELAAS,* at (long) last, finally; ~ *die LAASTE,* at the latest; ~ *LAND,* on land; ~ *'n MANIER,* in a manner, after a fashion; ~ *PAD,* on the way; ~ *die PLATTELAND,* in the country; ~ *REIS,* on tour; ~ *SEE,* at sea; ~ *SIG,* on appro(val); ~ *SKOOL,* at school; ~ *SKOOL bly,* be detained at school; ~ *STERWE,* dying; ~ *STRAAT,* in the street; *dis TE ~ Sondag,* it is too near Sunday; ~ *TYD,* in time; ~ *die VEL dra,* wear next to the skin; ~ *WAG,* on guard; (b, bw), used-up, exhausted, finished; upon; *hy is AL ~,* he is already out of bed; ~ *en AF (~ en NEER),* up and down; *sy GELD is ~,* he has no more money; ~ *of ONDER,* all (neck) or nothing; *die SON is ~,* the sun has risen; *die STRAAT ~,* up the street; *die SUIKER is ~,* the sugar is finished; *sy is WEER ~,* she is out of bed (after her illness).
opaak', (opake), opaque.
opaal', (opale), opal; ~**agtig, (-e),** opaline; ~**blou,** opalescent, milk-blue; ~**glans,** opalescence; ~**glansend, (-e),** opalescent; ~**steen,** opal.
opalessen'sie, opalescence.
opasiteit', opacity.
op'baar, (-ge-), place on a bier.
op'bagger, (-ge-), dredge (up).
op'bak, (-ge-), use up in baking.
op'baker, (-ge-), muffle up.
op'bel, (-ge-), ring up, call up (on phone), phone.
op'bêre, op'berg, (-ge-), put away, store; file.
op'berging, storage; ~**sduikplek,** storage-pit (apples).
op'berg: ~**kamer,** record room; ~**kas,** filing cabinet.
op'betaal, (~), pay up fully; ~**d, (-e),** (fully) paid-up.
op'beur, (-ge-), lift up, prop; cheer up, comfort, console, liven, hearten; ~**end, (-e),** cheering, heartening; ~**ing,** cheering, heartening, consolation.
op'bied, (-ge-), bid; ~ *teen,* bid against.
op'bieg, (-ge-), confess, own up; *alles ~,* make a clean breast of it.
op'bind, (-ge-), tie up, bind up; truss; ~**naald,** trussing-needle.
op'blaas, (-ge-), inflate, blow up, balloon; mine (mil.); bloat, puff up; blast; ~**siekte,** tympanites, hoove.
op'blasing, hoven, bloat.
op'bloei, (s) flourishing condition; revival; (w) (-ge-), flourish; revive.
op'blokking, blockage, block(ing).
op'bly, (-ge-), remain up, sit up.

op'bod, higher bid; *by ~ verkoop,* sell by auction.
op'bol, (-ge-), bulge.
op'bondel, (-ge-), make into a bundle.
op'borrel, (-ge-), bubble up, effervesce; ~**end, (-e),** effervescent; ~**ing,** bubbling up, ebullition; gurgitation.
op'borsel, (-ge-), brush up.
op'bou, (s) building-up; construction; edification; (w) (-ge-), edify; build up.
op'bouend, (-e), constructive; edifying; ~*e kritiek,* constructive criticism.
op'bouer, edifier.
op'bouing, building-up; erection, construction; edification.
op'bou: ~**proses,** build up; ~**sentrum,** outbreakcentre; ~**swerms,** incipient swarms (locusts); ~**voetgangerswerms,** incipient hopper-outbreaks (locusts).
op'braaksel, eructation, belching.
op'brand, (-ge-), burn completely, consume (by fire); be burnt completely; press for payment, dun.
op'brander, (-s), scolding, dun, demand (for payment).
op'breek, (-ge-), break up, tear up, split up; cut; disjoint; belch; *'n BELEG ~,* raise a siege; *die KAMP ~,* strike camp, strike one's tents; *WIND ~,* belch, emit wind, eructate.
op'brei, (-ge-), use up by knitting.
op'breking, dissociation (chem.); breaking up.
op'brengs = **opbrings.**
op'bring, (-ge-), bring in, realize, yield (crop); carry up; rear (child); arrest; vomit; ~**neut,** nux vomica; ~**s,** output, yield, proceeds, amount, gettings, haul; harvest, crop (wheat); produce, product, production; *aanhoudende ~s,* sustained yield; ~**svermoë,** rentability.
op'brokkel, (-ge-), crumble up, disintegrate; ~**ing,** crumbling-up, disintegration.
op'bruis, (-ge-), effervesce, bubble up; ~**end, (-e),** effervescent; hot-tempered; ebullient; ~**ing,** effervescence; ebullience, ebullition.
op'bult, (-ge-), bulge.
op'daag, (-ge-), turn up, arrive, put in an appearance.
op'dam, (-ge-), dam up, stem, embank; pond; block up; ~**ming, (-s),** embankment, damming (-up); pondage.
op'damp, (-ge-), evaporate.
op'damwater, back water.
op'dans, (-ge-), wear out (by dancing).
op'dat, (form.), that, in order that; ~ *dit nie,* lest.
op'delf, ..**delwe, (-ge-),** dig up, quarry.
op'dien, (-ge-), serve up, dish up.
op'diep, (-ge-), disentomb, unearth, fish out, fork out, trace, hunt up.
op'dirk, (-ge-), dress up most gorgeously; doll up.
op'dis, (-ge-), dish up, serve up; *'n verhaal ~,* invent a yarn.
op'doek, (-ge-), furl, gather up (flag); discard, do away with; shut up (shop).
op'doem, (-ge-), loom (up), heave in sight; ~**ing,** looming (-up).
op'doen, (-ge-), get, gain; acquire, obtain; contract (disease); recondition (engine); *kennis ~,* acquire knowledge.
op'dok, (-ge-), pay, foot the bill, cash up, fork out, plank down, pay up.
op'domkrag, (-ge-), jack up.
op'donder, (-ge-), (plat), lambaste, attack violently, give (someone) hell.
op'dons, (-ge-), do carelessly, bungle, foozle, spoil; pommel, treat severely, knock about; let a person have it; *IEM. ~,* give someone a drubbing; *iem. dons maar OP,* he does things in his own sweet way; ~**ery,** slapdash; bungled work; knocking-about.
op'dra, (-ge-), wear to shreds; carry up; commission, charge; lay under a command; entrust; enjoin; dedicate (a book to); commend; confer; *MY is opgedra,* I am instructed (directed); *KOS ~,* set food on the table; *ek dra dit aan jou SORG op,* I leave it in your care.
op'draai, (-ge-), turn higher; wind up; coil, reel.
op'draand, (s) **(-e, -es, -s),** rise, slope; ramp; ascent;

opdraande — *opfris*

rising ground; gradient, incline; upgrade; acclivity; (b, bw) **(-e)**, uphill, ascending; ascendent, acclivous; difficult, arduous; *hy KRY dit maar* ~, he is having a hard time of it; *hoe STEILER die* ~, *hoe nader die end*, it is darkest just before dawn.
op'draande, (-s, opdraans) = **opdraand**, (s).
op'draer, (-s), dedicator.
op'drag, (-te), instruction, order; mandate; injunction; commission; behest; brief; charge (jury); delegation; inscription, dedication (in book); terms of reference (committee); mission; errand; assignment; *met die BESONDERE* ~ *om*, with the special duty of; ~ *GEE om*, instruct, assign, give an order to; *in* ~ *van*, by order of, instructed by; *my* ~ *LUI om*, my instructions are to; *MET* ~ *om*, with orders to; ~ **gewer**, principal, employer.
op'dreun, (-ge-), recite monotonously, rattle (reel) off; make it hot for, treat severely; drive a worker on.
op'drifsel, (-s), washings-up, floatage, driftwood, debris, affluvion.
op'dring, (-ge-), thrust upon, enforce on, obtrude; intrude; *EK wil my nie* ~ *nie*, I don't want to be obtrusive; I don't want to thrust myself forward; *iem. 'n PRESENT* ~, force a present upon someone; ~ **er**, (-s), obtruder; intruder; pusher; ~ **'erig**, (-e), obtrusive; clamant; insistent; intrusive; protrusive, flaunting(ly); fresh; ~ **'erigheid**, obtrusiveness; ~ **ing**, obtrusion; intrusion.
op'drink, (-ge-), empty, toss off, finish (a drink), imbibe.
op'droë, (-ge-), dry up, desiccate, parch, exsiccate.
op'droënd, (-e), desiccant, desiccative.
op'droging, drying-up, (de)siccation, exsiccation.
op'droog, (-ge-) = **op'droë**.
op'druk, (s) **(-ke)**, overprint; (w) **(-ge-)**, imprint upon; print with raised letters; push up; bustle, hurry along (to finish in time); overprint (photography); surcharge; ~ *vir betaling*, press (dun) for payment.
op'dryf, op'drywe, (-ge-), drive (force) up, inflate (price); key (machine).
op'drywing, forcing-up.
op'duik, (-ge-), turn up, crop up; emerge; 'surface (submarine); ~ **ing**, emergence.
op'duiwel, (-ge-), rush up; go for a person.
op'dweil, (-ge-), mop up.
op'dwing, (-ge-), force (up)on; enforce; *iem 'n taak* ~, force a task on someone.
o'pe, open; vacant; uncovered, blank (line); public (secret); ~ *KAMPIOEN*, open champion; *'n* ~ *REKENING*, a current account; *dis nog 'n* ~ *VRAAG*, it remains a moot point; *see* **oop**.
op'êe, (opgeêe) = **opeg**.
opeen', in a heap, one upon another.
opeen'dring, (-ge-), crowd together, huddle.
opeen'gehoop, (-te), accumulated, accumulative, agglomerate, cumulate, piled up.
opeen'hoop, (-gehoop), heap (pile) up, accumulate, agglomerate, bunch.
opeen'hoping, piling-up, heaping-up, accumulation, agglomeration, (con)glomeration; congestion (traffic).
opeen'ja(ag), (-ge-), drive together.
opeen'klem, (-ge-), clench (teeth).
opeen'pak, (-ge-), pack together.
opeen'plak, (-ge-), glue together.
opeens', all of a sudden, suddenly, all at once.
opeen'stapel, (-ge-), heap up, pile up, accumulate; ~ **ing**, piling-up, accumulation.
opeen'volg, (-gevolg), follow each other; ~ **'end**, (-e), successive, consecutive; *vir tien* ~ *ende dae*, for ten consecutive days; ~ **ing**, succession, sequence, course.
op'eet, (-geëet), eat up, finish.
op'eg, (-geëg), harrow.
o pehartoperasie, open-heart operation.
op'eis, (-geëis), demand, claim; ~ **'baar**, (. . bare), reclaimable, claimable; due for payment; exigible; ~ **ing**, (-e, -s), claim, demand.
o'pelug: ~ skool, open-air school; ~ **spel**, outdoor game; ~ **teater**, open-air theatre.

o'pelyf, evacuation (motion) of the bowels; *gereelde* ~ *hê*, have regular movement of the bowels.
o'pen, (ge-), open; ~ *met GEBED*, open with prayer; *iem. se OË* ~, undeceive a person.
op-en-af'spel, snakes and ladders.
openbaar', (w) (ge-), make public, disclose, reveal, divulge, expose, betray; evince; (b) (. . bare), public; common; overt; patent; exoteric; manifest; *IN die* ~, in public; ~ *MAAK*, make public, publish; reveal, divulge; *die . . bare AANDAG*, public attention; public eye; *die . . bare MENING*, public opinion; *. . bare SKOOL*, public school; *. . bare VYANDSKAP*, open enmity; ~ **der**, (-s), detector; ~ **heid**, publicity; ~ **maker**, exposer, promulgator; ~ **making**, publication, disclosure, divulgation; release.
openba'rend, (-e), revealing.
openba'ring, (-e, -s), eye-opener, revelation; disclosure; manifestation; *die Openbaring van JOHANNES*, the Apocalypse, the Revelation of St. John; *dit WAS vir my 'n* ~, it was an eye-opener for me; ~ **sleer**, doctrine of revelation.
o'penend, (-e), opening; aperient.
openhar'tig, (-e), open-hearted, frank, direct, outspoken, candid; ~ **heid**, frankness, open-heartedness, candour, freeness, candidness, outspokenness, plain speaking.
o'penheid, openness, candour.
o'pening, (-e, -s), opening, beginning; gap, hiatus; chink, aperture; cloaca, hole, orifice; outlet; foramen; inauguration, opening ceremony.
o'penings: ~ **dag**, opening-day; first day, ~ **plegtigheid**, opening ceremony; ~ **rede**, inaugural address; ~ **woord**, inaugural speech.
o'peninkie, (-s), small opening, gap, aperture, slit.
o'penlik, (-e), open(ly); public(ly); barely; declaredly; frank(ly); avowed(ly).
op'-en-top, out-and-out, every inch; tops; *'n* ~ *sportman*, every inch a sportsman.
o'pera, (-s), opera; ~ **gebou**, opera house; ~ **geselskap**, opera company; ~ **hoed**, gibus; ~ **koor**, operatic chorus; ~ **musiek**, operatic music, grand opera; ~ **regisseur**, opera director; ~ **sanger**, opera singer; ~ **sangeres**, (-se), diva, prima donna; ~ **seisoen**, opera season.
opera'sie, (-s), operation; ~ *aan die KEEL*, operation of the throat; *'n* ~ *ONDERGAAN*, undergo an operation; ~ **basis**, base of operations; ~ **bereik**, radius of action (battle); ~ **kamer**, operating-room, operating-theatre; ~ **mes**, surgeon's knife; ~ **plan**, plan of campaign; ~ **saal**, operating-theatre; ~ **sentrale**, operation centre (mil.); ~ **suster**, theatre sister, theatre-nurse; ~ **tafel**, operating-table; ~ **tjie**, (-s), minor operation.
o'pera: ~ **ster**, operatic star; ~ **teks**, libretto.
operateur', (-s), operator.
operatief', (. . tiewe), (ong.), operative.
operatri'se, (-s), lady operator.
op'erd, (s) ridging of potatoes; (w) **(-ge-)**, list (maize); ridge, bank, earth (up) (potatoes), hill; ~ **ploeg**, lister-plough, ridger.
opereer', (ge-), operate (on), perform an operation; *vir blindederm* ~, operate on for appendicitis; ~ **baar**, (. . bare), operable; ~ **mes**, surgeon's knife, bistoury, catling.
operet', (-te), **operet'te**, (-s), operetta; ~ **geselskap**, operetta company; ~ **komponis**, operetta composer; ~ **sanger**, operetta singer.
oper'kulum, (-s), operculum.
operment', orpiment.
op'feil, (-ge-), scrub.
op'fleur, (-ge-), cheer up, brighten up, hearten, give a fillip.
op'flikker, (-ge-), flicker up; flare up; ~ **ing**, (-e, -s), flickering; flicker (hope); fillip; flashing; flash-in-the-pan; flare-up.
op'foeter, (-ge-), *see* **opdons**.
op'fris, (-ge-), refresh, freshen, revive; fillip; brush up; *iem. se geheue* ~, refresh someone's memory; ~ **send**, (-e), bracing, refreshing; ~ **sertjie**, (-s), pick-me-up, refresher; ~ **sing**, refreshing, refreshment; brushing up; ~ **singkursus**, refresher course.

op'frommel, (-ge-), crumple up.
op'gaaf, (..gawe), (poll-) tax, hut-tax.
op'gaan, (-ge-), go up, ascend, rise; mount; *die ARGUMENT gaan nie op nie*, the argument does not hold water; *vir 'n EKSAMEN* ~, enter (go up) for an examination; ~ *IN die menigte*, be lost in the crowd; *dit gaan nie OP nie*, that doesn't hold good; *die verkeerde PAD* ~, fall into bad habits; ride for a fall; *in VLAMME* ~, go up in flames; ~ *in sy WERK*, be absorbed in his work; ~**de**, rising, ascending, aliquot; ~*de trein*, up-train.
op'gaar, (-ge-), collect, save, amass, accumulate; hoard; ~**battery**, accumulator; ~**dam**, storage dam; ~**der**, (-s), gatherer; hoarder; ~**program**, stockpiling; ~**tenk**, storage tank, reservoir.
op'gang, (-e), rise, ascent; success; furore; growth, development; ~ *MAAK*, become popular (a success); *geen* ~ *MAAK nie*, not become popular; not catch on; *die STUK maak groot* ~, that piece is a great hit.
op'garing, hoarding; storing.
op'gawe, (-s), list, return; statement, report; task; problem; exercise (set to pupils), examination question; statement (facts); (official) returns; *KWARTAALLIKSE* ~*s*, quarterly returns; *met* ~ *van REDES*, stating the grounds.
op'geblaas, (-de), blown up, inflated; hoven; bloated (cattle); ~**dheid**, inflated condition; flatulence; hoove; bloatedness.
op'geblase, puffed up, swollen, inflated, bloated; puffy; elated; flatulent; ~**nheid**, conceit, arrogance; swelled head; elation; pomposity.
op'gebruik, (~), use up, consume.
op gebuig, (-de), bent upward; ascendant (bot.).
op'gedronge, **op'gedwonge**, forced.
op'gedruk, (-te), pushed up; ~*te vloer*, pushed-up footwall.
op'gee, (-ge-), give up (hope); state (reasons); propound; return (statistics); record, set (task); give out (text); specify (details); abandon, stop (smoking); give up (post); lose (courage); drop (work), leave off; quit; discharge (phlegm); vomit; forgo; *BREED (hoog)* ~ *van*, make a boast of; take great pride in; *MOENIE* ~ *nie*, never say die; *jou NAAM* ~ *vir*, enter (one's name) for; *ROOK* ~, give up (stop) smoking.
op'geefsel, (-s), mirage, fata morgana.
op gegroei, (-de), grown-up.
op'gehewe, swollen; erect; *'n* ~ *GESIG*, a swollen face; *met* ~ *HOOF*, with head erect.
op'gehoop, (-te), heaped up; ~ *te BEDRAE*, accruals; ~ *te TEELEPEL*, heaped teaspoon.
op'gehys, (-te), hoisted, atrip (anchor).
op geknap, (-te), renewed, reconditioned.
op'gekommandeer, (-de), conscript.
op'gekrop, (-te), pent-up (feelings).
op'geld, agio, surplus; *dit doen* ~, be in demand (popular); meet with success.
op'gelê, (..legde), laid up (ship); imposed (taxes); (ship) in ordinary, not in commission; superimposed; laminated.
op'gelei, (-de), trained.
op'geloop, (-te), accumulated, accumulative.
op'gemaak, (-te), trimmed, dressed, powdered and painted, made-up (face); made (bed); invented (story); instigated, put-up.
op'gemonter, (-de), bucked, heartened, cheerful.
op'geplak, (-te), mounted (photo).
op'geprop, (-te), crammed (with).
op'gerol, (-de), collared, rolled (meat); furled (umbrella).
op'geruimd, (-e), cheerful, bright, jovial, lively, merry, mirthful, gay, blithe, buoyant, good-humoured, bobbish, hilarious; ~**heid**, cheerfulness, good humour, blitheness, hilarity, brightness, merriment, mirth.
op'geskeep, (-te), saddled (with a person); at a loss; *met JOUSELF* ~, at a loose end, not know what to do with oneself; ~ *SIT met iets of iem.*, be saddled with something (someone).
op'geskik, (-te), decorated.
op'geskort, (-e), suspended (sentence); deferred (payment); in abeyance.

op'geskote, young, nearly full-grown, in the teens, adolescent.
op'geskroef, (-de), screwed up; pent up; bombastic, stilted (language).
op'gesluit, (-e), locked; pent.
op'gesmuk, (-te), gaudy, showy, overdecorated; ~**theid**, gaudiness.
op'gestel, (-de), mounted (guards, gun-carriage).
op'gestik, (-te), stitched on.
op'gestop, (-te), stuffed (animal); padded (shoulders); upholstered (furniture).
op'geswel, (-de), swollen, bloated, blown.
op'getoë, delighted, elated, enraptured, exultant, rapturous, overjoyed, ecstatic; ~**nheid**, delight, rapture, elation, ecstasy, exultancy, exultation.
op'gevoedheid, gentlemanliness; culture; education.
op'gewarm, (-de), warmed up; ~ *de kos*, warmed-up food, rechauffé.
op'gewasse, equal (to); *hulle is teen MEKAAR* ~, they are evenly matched, they are equal in strength; *nie* ~ *TEEN*, no match for; unequal to.
op'gewek, (-te), cheerful, lively, animated, good-humoured, gay, light-spirited, light-hearted, bright; wide awake, brisk; ~ *te musiek*, bright (light) music; ~**theid**, cheerfulness, liveliness, brightness, briskness, cheeriness, gladness, exhilaration, glowing spirits, joviality.
op'gewip, (-te), tipped up; turned up (nose).
op'gewonde, excited, agitated, ablaze, agog, astir, flurried; ~**nheid**, excitement, agitation, excitability, fever, excitation, flurry, razzle-dazzle.
op'giet, (-ge-), pour on.
op'gooi, (s) toss; *die* ~ *wen*, win the toss; (w) (-ge-), throw up; pitch; chuck up; puke, vomit; toss up; *laat ons* ~, let us toss.
op'graaf, **op'grawe**, (-ge-), dig up; disinter, disentomb, exhume; excavate; grub.
op'gradeer, (-ge-), upgrade; ..**gradering**, upgrading.
op'grawer, (-s), excavator.
op'grawing, (-e, -s), exhumation; excavation; disinterment.
op'groei, (-ge-), grow up; ~**end**, (-e), adolescent; *die* ~ *ende geslag*, the rising generation.
op'haal, (s) (..hale), upstroke; hairline; (w) (-ge-), draw up, hoist (flag), pull up; weigh (anchor); refer to, mention, recall; *moenie OU stories* ~ *nie*, let bygones be bygones; *die SKOUERS* ~, shrug the shoulders; ~**brug**, drawbridge; leaf-bridge; lift-bridge; ~**gordyn**, blind; ~**lyn**, hairline (writing); ~**net**, purse-net; ~**sluis**, lift-lock.
op'haler, (-s), collector, gatherer.
ophan'de, approaching, at hand, near.
op'hang, (-ge-), gibbet, halter, hang (person); suspend, hang up (clothes); *die telefoon weer* ~, replace the receiver; ~**band**, suspensory ligament; ~**draad**, suspension wire; ~**ing**, suspension; ~**punt**, suspension-point.
op'hap, (-ge-), snap up.
op'hark, (-ge-), rake up, rake together.
op'hê, (..gehad), have on (hat); have eaten (food); *veel* ~ *met iem.*, be taken up with a person.
op'hef[1], (s) fuss; ado; *'n groot* ~ *maak van*, make a great song about, make much fuss about.
op'hef[2], (w) (-ge-), lift, raise, elevate (the eyes); do away with, discontinue, abolish, abrogate (law); neutralize, cancel (effect); disannul; depauperize; *die BELEG* ~, raise the siege; *MEKAAR* ~, neutralize (counterbalance) each other (forces); ~**fing**, raising; upheaval; elevation, uplifting (the poor); abolition, annulment, repeal, abrogation, derestriction; disannulment; defeasance.
op'helder, (-ge-), clear up, explain, account for, clarify, elucidate, illustrate; brighten (face); gloss; ~**end**, (-e), elucidative, elucidatory, explanatory; illustrative; ~**ing**, (-e, -s), explanation, elucidation, illustration, clarification; clearance; exemplification; brightening, gloss.
op'help, (-ge-), help up, assist in rising, raise.
op'hemel, (-ge-), extol, (be)laud, panegyrize, praise highly, glorify, eulogize, exalt, puff, emblazon, sing the praises of; ~**ing**, exaltation, excessive praise, eulogy.

op'hits, (-ge-), incite, instigate, egg on; commove; heat, ferment; ~**er**, (-s), inciter, instigator, agitator; ~**ing**, inciting, instigation, incitement.
op'hoepel, (-ge-), skedaddle, hop it.
op'hoes, (-ge-), cough up.
op'hoging, (-e, -s), raised soil, embankment.
op'hoog, (-ge-), heighten; raise.
op'hoop, (-ge-), pile up, accumulate, mount up, heap up, drift; amass, hoard; cumulate; ~**baar**, (..**bare**), accumulative (leave).
op'hopend, (-e), cumulative.
op'hoping, (-e, -s), congestion; accumulation, agglomeration, cumulation.
op'hou, (s) stopping; discontinuance; *sonder* ~, continuously, without stopping; (w) (-ge-), support, hold up; discontinue; check; detain, keep back, retain (urine); delay (train); take time (work); leave off; keep on (hat); keep up (position); uphold; hold (breath); stop, cease; frequent; make a pause; intermit (fever); drop (wind); ~ *om te BESTAAN*, cease to exist; *ek hou my nie DAARMEE op nie*, I refuse to have anything to do with it; *hom ÊRENS* ~, frequent (stay in) a certain place; *hom* ~ *met slegte GESELSKAP*, associate with bad company; *HOU op!* stop it! *dit sal my LANK* ~, this will delay me very much; *ek sal u NIE* ~ *nie*, I won't detain you; *die REËN sal nou* ~, it will cease raining now; *sy REPUTASIE* ~, keep up one's reputation; ~ *met WERK*, stop working; ~**ding**, cessation, stopping; ~**tyd**, time to stop, knocking-off time.
op'hys, (-ge-), hoist, haul up.
oplaat', (**oplate**), opiate.
opi'nie, (-s), opinion; *van DIESELFDE* ~ *wees*, hold the same opinion; *van* ~ *VERANDER*, change one's mind; *VOLGENS (na) my* ~, in my opinion; *'n* ~ *toegedaan WEES*, hold an opinion; ~**ondersoek**, questionnaire; ~**peiling**, opinion poll, public opinion research; ~**vormer**, opinion former, opinion shaper.
o'pium, opium; ~**ekstrak**, opium extract; ~**handel**, opium trade (traffic); ~**handelaar**, opium dealer; ~**hol**, opium den; ~**pag**, opium farm; ~**pyp**, opium pipe; ~**regie**, state control of opium production and distribution; ~**roker**, ~**skuiwer**, (-s), opium-smoker; ~**smokkelaar**, opium-smuggler; opium-running vessel; ~**tinktuur**, tincture of opium; laudanum; ~**verbruik**, consumption of opium.
op'ja(ag), (-ge-), drive up; speed up; beat up, hunt up, rouse, dislodge; unkennel; run up (auction); raise (dust); flutter; flush (birds); frighten (drive) away (game); inflate, force up (prices).
op'jaer, (-s), puffer; booster; ~**y**, running-up (prices, bids).
op'kalfater, (-ge-), do up, refurbish.
op'kam, (-ge-), comb up.
op'keil, (-ge-), wedge up; reprimand, make it hot (for someone); urge on, drive on; make things difficult; *IEM.* ~, give someone a dressing down; *my TAND keil my op*, my tooth is troubling me.
op'kikker, (-ge-), ginger up, rouse; dope (racehorse); ~**ing**, rousing, enlivening.
op'klaar, (-ge-), brighten (face); clear up (weather); lift (clouds); clarify, elucidate (problem).
op'klap, (-ge-), raise (back-sight); tip up, turn up; ~**baar**, (..**bare**), folding; ~**bed**, turn-up bed.
op'klaring, clearing-up; clarification.
op'kleur, (-ge-), liven up (heighten) the colour.
op'klim, (-ge-), climb, mount, ascend; *van onder af* ~, rise from the ranks, ~**mend**, (-e), progressive; ~**mende oefeninge**, graded (graduated) exercises; ~**ming**, ascent, gradation, progression; ~**plek**, ~**punt**, boarding-point.
op'klink[1], (s) taking-up; (w) (-ge-), tighten (take) up (machinery); rivet.
op'klink[2], (w) (-ge-), resound.
op'klop, (-ge-), knock up; rouse; beat up (eggs).
op'klouter, (-ge-), clamber up, scramble up.
op'knabbel, (-ge-), munch (up).
op'knap, (-ge-), tidy up, clean up, smarten up, mend, furbish up, patch (touch) up; renovate; make fit (health); recuperate; put right; overhaul, recondition (engine); brush up; recruit; *ek GAAN my 'n bietjie* ~, I am going to titivate myself; *ek sal die SAKIE vir jou* ~, I'll put the matter right for you; ~**kamer**, powder room; ~**pertjie**, (-s), tonic; refresher course; ~**ping**, overhaul; renovation; ~**pingskursus**, refresher course.

op'knoop, (-ge-), tie (button) up; string up; hang (a person).
op'koking, ebullition, priming.
op'kom, (-ge-), come up, rise; germinate; surface (submarine); get up; emerge, appear; set in, brew (storm); arise, crop up (out); occur; object, take exception to; enter (on stage); spring up (wind); flow (tide); heave; attend (meeting); *die GEDAGTE kom by my op*, the thought occurs to me; *vir sy REGTE* ~, stand up for one's rights; ~ *TEEN*, object to; ~ *VIR*, stand up for; take the part of; ~**end**, (-e), rising, nascent; budding (writer); *die* ~ *ende geslag*, the rising generation.
op'kommandeer, (-ge-), commandeer; conscribe, conscript.
op'kommandering, conscription.
op'koms, rise (of a barrister); rising (of sun); attendance (at meeting).
op'kook, (-ge-), boil up; prime (boiler).
op'koop, (s) buying-up; forestalling; (w) (-ge-), forestall; buy up; corner (market); ~**spekulasie**, cornering.
op'koper, buyer; wholesale (speculative) buyer; engrosser; forestaller; ~**sgroep**, corner-combine.
op'koping, buying; engrossment.
op'koste, overhead expenses.
op'kreukel, (-ge-), crease.
op'krimp, (-ge-), shrink, shrivel up.
op'krop, (-ge-), endure, pocket, bottle up; *opgekropte woede*, pent-up wrath.
op'kruip, (-ge-), creep up; ride up (of garment).
op'krul, (-ge-), curl up; buckle up.
op'kry, (-ge-), get up; get on (hat); get finished; finish; *dit nie alles kan* ~ *nie*, be unable to eat everything.
op'kweek, (-ge-), rear (plants); bring up, educate (children), foster.
op'kweking, rearing, educating, fosterage.
op'kyk, (-ge-), look up; *NA iem.* ~, look up to someone; *daar VREEMD van* ~, be surprised about something; look up in surprise.
op'laag, (..**lae**), edition; impression; circulation; *'n nuwe* ~ *druk*, print a new impression; ~**syfer**, circulation figure.
op'laai[1], (-ge-), blaze up, flame, flare up; *die haat sal* ~, hatred will flare up.
op'laai[2], (-ge-), load; give a lift; *hulle het my opgelaai*, they gave me a lift; ~**ery**, loading.
op'laaiing, recrudescence; flare-up.
oplaas', at last, finally.
op'langer, (-s), futtock.
op'lap, (-ge-), patch up, piece up, vamp up; tinker up; fake.
op'lê, (-ge-), apply, impose, enforce (duty) upon; set (task); charge, lay on, enjoin; lay (colours); levy (rates); *BOETE* ~, (inflict a) fine; *STRAF* ~, inflict punishment; *iem. die SWYE* ~, muzzle; impose silence upon; ~**baar**, (..**bare**), imposable.
op'leef, (-ge-) = **oplewe**.
op'lêer, (-s), imponent.
op'legging, imposition, laying on (of hands).
op'legsel, (-s), trimming (gown); veneer (furniture).
op'legslot, rimlock.
op'lei, (-ge-), instruct, educate, train; rear; prepare; *vir 'n eksamen* ~, coach for an examination; ~**baar**, (..**bare**), educable; ~**baarheid**, educability; ~**deling**, trainee; ~**er**, trainer, coach.
op'leiding, education, training; ~**sdepot**, training-depot; ~**sentrum**, training-centre; ~**sgebied**, training-area; ~**sinrigting**, training-establishment; ~**skip**, training-ship; ~**skool**, training-school.
op'leidings: ~**kursus**, training-course; ~**offisier**, training-officer; ~**program**, training-programme.
op'leidingstelsel, training-system.
op'leidingsvoorskrif, training-regulation.
op'leier, trainer (of soldiers).
op'leiwingerd, trellised vines.

op'lek, (-ge-), lick up, lap up.
op'lepel, (-ge-), dish up, spoon up.
op'let, (-ge-), pay (give) attention, attend, observe, take note, give heed, mark.
oplet'tend, (-e), attentive, mindful, heedful; ~ **heid**, attentiveness, attention, heed, mindfulness.
op'lewe, (-ge-), revive; spend (capital); *jou hele salaris* ~, spend one's whole salary.
op'lewer, (-ge-), yield, produce, realize, fetch; present (difficulties); afford; ~ **ing**, (-e, -s), delivery; yield= (ing); ~ **ingstermyn**, period of delivery.
op'lewing, revival; boom; reviviscence; recrud= escence; ~ **speriode**, boom period.
op'lig¹, (-ge-), brighten (face); become lighter.
op'lig², (-ge-), raise, lift up; cheat; kidnap; ~ **klep**, level valve, lifting valve; ~ **ter**, (-s), cheat, swindler; lifter; ~ **tery**, cheating, swindling; confidence trick; ~ **ting**, fraud, swindle.
op'loop¹, (s) crowd, tumult; riot; affray.
op'loop², (w) (-ge-), accumulate, accrue, increase; walk up; sustain (wound); suffer (damage); catch, come in for (punishment); mount up (debt); as= cend, slope up; *'n REKENING laat* ~, run up an account; *opgeloopte RENTE*, accrued interest; *'n SIEKTE* ~, contract a disease; *STRAF* ~, incur punishment.
op'lopend¹, (-e), sloping upwards; cumulative (interest); ~ *e verlof*, accumulative leave.
oplo'pend², (-e), hot-tempered, irascible; ~ **heid**, iras= cibility, quickness of temper.
op'loping, accruement.
op'los, (-ge-), dissolve (in water); solve, puzzle out (problem); decompose; disintegrate; analyse; ~ **'baar**, (..bare), (dis)soluble; (dis)solvable; de= composable; analysable; ~ **'baarheid**, (dis)solu= bility; solvability; ~ **middel**, solvent; dissolvent; re= solutive vehicle; ~ **send**, (-e), dissolvent; ~ **sing**, (-e, -s), (dis)solution; explanation; decomposition; ~ **singsmiddel**, solvent.
op'lug, (-ge-), relieve; *ek voel opgelug*, I feel relieved; ~ **ting**, relief.
op'lui, (-ge-), phone, ring up, put through a call (on phone).
op'luister, (-ge-), illustrate; add lustre; grace, adorn; ~ **ing**, illustration, adornment.
op'maak, (s), make-up, get-up; drawing-up, making out, doing up; lay-out (printing); (w) (-ge-), dress, make up (face); trim (hats); do up (hair); make up (list, bed); shape (bread); draw up, frame (plan); cast up (accounts); spend, squander; concoct (story); instigate, incite (the mob); deduce; justify (printing); gather, conclude; *al sy geld* ~, spend all his money; *die KOSTE* ~, calculate the cost; *WOORDE waaruit ek* ~, words from which I gather (infer); ~ **sel**, (-s), fib, fiction; trimming.
op'maat, up-beat.
op'maker, (-s), clicker, lay-out man (printing); insti= gator; framer; preparer; spendthrift.
op'mars, march forward, advance; ~ **jeer**, (-ge-), march forward, advance.
op'meet, (-ge-), survey, measure.
opmekaar', clustered; close together; ~ **volgend**, (-e), successive.
op'merk, (-ge-), notice, observe, remark, discern, espy.
opmerk'baar, (..bare), noticeable, noteworthy.
opmer'kend, (-e), observant.
opmerkenswaar'dig, (-e), noteworthy, remarkable.
op'merker, (-s), observer.
op'merking, (-e, -s), remark, observation; anno= tation; animadversion; *dit verdien* ~ *dat*, it is worth noting that; ~ **sgawe**, gift of observation; ~ **sver= moë**, powers of observation.
op'merkinkie, (-s), little remark.
opmerk'lik, (-e), remarkable, marked, prominent; strange, salient, signal; ~ **heid**, noteworthiness.
opmerk'saam, (..same), attentive, observant, per= ceptive; ~ **heid**, attentiveness; advertency, advert= ence, notice.
op'messel, (-ge-), wall up, run (build) up (a wall).
op'meting, (-e, -s), survey(ing); mensuration.
op'metings: ~ **afdeling**, survey department; ~ **diens**, surveying-service; ~ **groep**, survey group; ~ **ka= mera**, survey camera.
op'metingskip, surveying-vessel.
op'metings: ~ **kompanjie**, survey company; ~ **koste**, surveying-expenses.
op'meting: ~ **sloep**, surveying-sloop; ~ **span**, survey detachment.
op'metings: ~ **pos**, survey post; ~ **vlug**, survey flight.
op'monter, (-ge-), (ong.), cheer up, hearten, give a fil= lip; ~ **ing**, cheering, heartening.
op'naai, (-ge-), sew on; take in a tuck; ~ **sel**, (-s), tuck; ~ **selmaat**, tucked seam.
op'name, taking up, assimilation, adoption (into a family); admission (to an association); occlusion; insertion (in a paper); survey (land, population); recording (broadcast); snap(shot); filming; *'n foto= grafiese* ~, a photo (snap, picture).
op'neem, (-ge-), take up; receive; shelter, pick up; in= sert (in paper); admit (as member); size up; list, take stock; survey; assimilate (immigrants); bor= row (money); film; digest; adopt; assume; occlude; absorb (heat); count (votes); *DIT vir iem.* ~, take up the cudgels for someone; *GELD* ~, borrow money; *iets GOED* ~, take something in good part; *'n LID* ~, admit a member; *'n METER* ~, read a meter; *NAME* ~, take down names; *PAS= SASIERS* ~, pick up passengers; *op 'n PLAAT* ~, (make a) record(ing); *die SKADE* ~, size up the damage; *iem. van TOP tot toon* ~, size someone up, take stock of a person; *die TYD* ~, time (a race); *iets verkeerd* ~, take something ill (amiss); *die VOORRAAD* ~, take stock; ~ **baar**, (..bare), assimilable; ~ **toestel**, recording apparatus.
op'nemer, (-s), counter (of votes); registration officer; reader (meter).
op'neming, admission (to an association); survey; borrowing (money); insertion (in newspaper); in= clusion; stock taking; aggregation; examination; intussusception (physiol.); ~ *van warmte*, absorp= tion of heat.
op'nemings: ~ **bevel**, reception-order; ~ **brigade**, sur= veying-party; ~ **vaartuig**, surveying-vessel; ~ **ver= moë**, receptive faculty, receptivity.
op'neuk, (-ge-), thrash; bungle along; ~ **er**, (-s), blow, punch; *iem. 'n* ~ *er gee*, fetch someone a wallop.
op'noem, (-ge-), name, enumerate; *te veel om op te noem*, too many (numerous) to mention; ~ **ing**, enumeration, naming.
opnuut', anew, again, once more, afresh, freshly.
opodel'dok, opodeldoc.
op'offer, (-ge-), sacrifice; devote; ~ **ing**, (-e, -s), sacri= fice; *jou* ~ *inge GETROOS*, make sacrifices; *MET* ~ *ing van*, at the sacrifice of; ~ **baar**, (..bare), ex= pendable.
op'onthoud, delay, stoppage; breakdown; wait; de= tention.
opos'sum, (-s), opossum.
op'pak, (-ge-), pack up; gather up; stack (hay).
op'pas, (-ge-), be careful; care for, have a care, guard, take heed, beware; mind (dog); wait on, nurse, at= tend to, care for (invalid); try on (hat); herd (sheep); groom (horse); invigilate (exam); foster; *pas op!* be careful! look out! fore! (golf).
oppas'send, (-e), well-behaved, careful, neat; ~ **heid**, good behaviour, carefulness.
op'passer, (-s), orderly; nurse, attendant, caretaker; guardian; peon.
op'passing, tending, nursing, looking after; attend= ance.
op'passter, (-s), nurse (of infant).
op'per¹, (s) (-s), haycock, haystack.
op'per², (w) (ge-), suggest, moot; raise (objection); advance (opinion); offer; *'n nuwe plan* ~, put for= ward a new plan.
op'perarmbeen, humerus.
op'perbes, most excellent.
op'perbestuur, supreme direction.
op'perbevel, supreme (high) command; ~ **hebber**, (-s), commander-in-chief; generalissimo.
op'perbewind, supreme direction (rule).
op'perdek, upper deck.

op'pergesag, supreme authority, supremacy, paramountcy.
op'perheer, sovereign, lord paramount, overlord; ~ser, (-s), overlord; sovereign; ~skappy, sovereignty; supremacy; mastery.
op'perhoof, chief, headman, paramount chief; ~skap, chieftaincy.
op'per: ~huid, epidermis, cuticle, scarf-skin; ~kerkvoog, primate; ~kerkvoogdy, primacy; ~kleed, upper garment; ~kok, chief cook; ~koopman, senior merchant; ~krygsheer, chief war-lord; ~landvoog, governor, viceroy.
op'perleen, high chief; ~heer, overlord; ~man, tenant-in-chief.
op'per: ~mag, supreme power, supremacy; imperium; ~mag'tig, (-e), all-powerful, supreme; ~majesteit, supreme majesty; ~man, hodman, hod-carrier; ~mens, superman; ~offisier, superior officer; ~priester, high priest; hierophant; ~priesterlik, (-e), hierophantic; pontificate; ~rabbi, (-'s), chief rabbi.
op'pers, (-ge-), force up.
op'persaal, upper room.
op'perskinker, chief cup-bearer.
op'perstalmeester, chief equerry; Master of the Horse.
op'perste, (s) chief; (b) uppermost, highest; paramount; 'n ~ vabond, an arch-scoundrel.
op'perstuurman, (..stuurlui, -ne), first mate.
op'pervlak, surface; bedding surface; face; 'n gladde (ruwe) ~, a smooth (rough) surface.
oppervlak'kig, (-e), superficial, shallow; frothy; desultory; cursory; frivolous; ~ BESKOU, taken at face value; ~e BYSMAAK, surface taint (in butter); 'n ~e KENNIS, a superficial knowledge; a nodding acquaintance; 'n ~e KENNIS van Grieks, a smattering of Greek; ~heid, superficiality; frivolousness; perfunctoriness; cursoriness; outwardness.
op'pervlakte, area; 'n ~ van 10 vierkante sentimeter, an area of 10 square centimetres; ~maat, square measure; ~meter, planimeter; ~reg, surface right; ~water, surface water.
Op'perwese, Supreme Being, God.
op'peusel, (-ge-), munch (nibble) up.
op'piep, (-ge-), coddle, pet, pamper, cosset.
op'pies, (kindert.) upsy-daisy.
op'pik, (-ge-), peck up (bird); pick up (drowning person); iets goedkoop ~, pick up something cheaply.
op'plak, (-ge-), paste on; mount (photo); post up; affix; ~kwas, mounting-brush.
op'poets, (-ge-), polish, rub on; furbish; clean up.
op'pomp, (-ge-), pump up (water); inflate (tyre).
opponeer', (ge-), oppose.
opponent', (-e), opponent, adversary.
op'pook, (-ge-), poke up, stir (fire).
op'por, (-ge-), poke (fire); stir up.
opportunis', (-te), opportunist; ~me, opportunism; ~ties, (-e), opportunistic.
opposi'sie, (-s), opposition; ~aanval, attack by the opposition; -blad, opposition paper; ~gees, spirit of opposition; ~groep, opposition group; ~leier, leader of the opposition; ~kant, the opposition; opposing side; ~party, opposition (party); ~stem, opposition vote.
op'pot, (-ge-), save (money); hoard (wealth); be miserly; pot; ~ter, (-s), accumulator; miser; hoarder; ~ting, hoard(ing).
op'pik, (-ge-), pin up; stick.
op'prop, (-ge-), cram, fill up (to excess), plug, ~ping, cramming, gorging.
op'raak, (-ge-), become consumed, run short, become exhausted, give out.
op'raap, (-ge-), pick up, snatch up, take up; gather; ~sel, (-s), pickings, scraps; guttersnipe; mongrel.
op'rakel, (-ge-), stir up (fire); rake up; moenie dit nou weer ~ nie, let bygones be bygones; keep the hatchet buried.
op'raper, (-s), picker, gatherer.
opreg', (-te; -ter, -ste), sincere, genuine, honest; authentic; candid, direct; devout; pure (bred); thoroughbred, fair(-minded), heartfelt; ~t'heid, sincerity, genuineness, honesty, integrity; authenticity; candidness; rectitude, fair-dealing; bona fides; candour; in alle ~theid, in all honesty.
op'rig, (-ge-), erect (statue); found (college); raise (person); establish (business); set on foot (movement), form (society); rear; promote (company); 'n maatskappy ~, float a company; ~baar, (..bare), erectile; ~spier, erector muscle; ~ter, (-s), founder; promoter; raiser; constructor; erector; ~tersaandele, founders' (promoters') shares; ~ting, erection, founding, inception; flotation; installation (of machinery); establishment; ~tingskoste, costs of erection; preliminary expenses.
op'risp, (-ge-), belch, emit wind noisily from throat; ~ing, belch(ing).
op'rit, drive; ramp (in garage); onramp (traffic); approach.
op'roei, (-ge-), row up (a stream).
op'roep, (s) (-e), summons, call (to arms, telephone); appeal; (w) (-ge-), convene, convoke, call up; raise (spirit); conjure up; muster; evocate; evoke; rouse; BY ~, by call; on demand; 'n VERGADERING ~, convene a meeting; ~end, (-e), evocative; ~er, (-s), convener; ~ing, (-e, -s), summons, convocation, evocation; foreclosure (mortgage); ~klap, call-drop (telephone); ~klokkie, call-bell; ~sein, call-signal (telephone); ~ster, female convener.
op'roer, (-e), revolt, insurrection, riot, disorder; hullabaloo; mutiny; ~ KRAAI, preach sedition; ~ MAAK, cause a riot; ~eenheid, riot squad.
oproe'rig, (-e), rebellious, riotous, insurgent, factious, mutinous; ~heid, rebelliousness, seditiousness, factiousness.
op'roer: ~leier, anarch, leader of revolt; ~ling, (-e), seditionist, insurgent, rioter, insurrectionist, mutineer, rebel; ~maker, (-s), rioter, insurgent; anarchist; agitator, inciter, seditionary; ~vlag, flag of revolt, red flag; ~wet, riot act.
op'rol, (-ge-), roll up, furl; wind up; clew; coil; collar (meat); convolve; fake; reel.
op'rook, (-ge-), finish smoking (cigarette); al die tabak ~, smoke all the tobacco.
op'rui, (-ge-), incite, instigate; ~end, (-e), instigating, inciting; inflammatory (speech); ~er, (-s), inciter, instigator; agitator, alarmist; ~ing, instigation, inciting.
op'ruim, (-ge-), clear away, tidy, clean, clean up; sell out, clear off (stock); do away with, discard, get rid of, scrap; ~beitel, mortise-cleaner; ~er, (-s), scavenger; ~ing, clearance (sale), clearing; mopping up (enemy, remnants); disposal; ~ingsprys, sale price; ~ingsuitverkoping, clearance sale; ~ingswerk, removal of wreckage (debris); salvage work.
op'ruk, (-ge-), advance, march (against) (army); jerk up; hitch up; ~ teen die vyand, advance on the enemy; ~king, advance.
op'ry, (-ge-), drive up (hill).
op'ryg, (-ge-), tack (sewing); lace up; ~sel, (-s), tuck; ~stewel, laced boot.
op'rylaan, carriage-drive, driveway.
op'rys, (-ge-), rise, emerge; ~end, (-e), emergent; ~ing, emergency.
op'saal, (-ge-), saddle; iem. met werk ~, give a person more work than he can conveniently do; ~! to horse!
op'samel, (-ge-), hoard, hive.
op'sê, (-ge-), recite (poetry); say (prayers); call in (money); dismiss (from service); give notice; terminate (lease); die huur ~, give notice (of vacating rented property).
opseg'baar, (..bare), terminable at will; ..bare geld, money on demand, call money.
op'segging, notice of termination; call; denunciation; met ~ van 'n maand, at a month's notice; ~stermyn, term of notice.
op'seil, (-ge-), sail up.
opsent' = **absent.**
op'set, plan, ground-plan, framework, design; premeditation; purpose, intention; MET ~, on purpose, purposely, intentionally; SONDER ~, unintentionally; die ~ van die VERHAAL, the setting of the story.

opset'lik, (-e), on purpose, intentional(ly), deliberate=(ly); purposely; express(ly); prepense; malicious (injury to property); in cold blood, wilfully; design=edly; knowingly; ~*e HANDELING*, deliberate act; ~*e VERSUIM*, wilful default; ~**heid**, deliber=ateness; wilfulness.
op'setting, swelling.
op'sie, (-s), option; refusal; put; *'n DUBBELE* ~, put-and-call; *'n* ~ *GEE*, give the (first) refusal, give an option.
op'sien, (s), surprise; ~ *baar*, create a sensation, make a splash; (w) **(-ge-)**, look up; *NA iem.* ~, look up to a person; respect a person; *TEEN iets* ~, jib at a task; ~**ba'rend, (-e)**, sensational; ~**er, (-s)**, overseer, supervisor, inspector; invigilator, com=missioner (at examinations); conservator; elder (in church); ~**ersamp**, commissionership; eldership.
op'sier, (-ge-), trim, decorate, embellish, beautify, or=nament; prink; ~**ing**, decoration, embellishment; ~**sel, (-s)**, trimming, ornament.
op'sig, (-te), supervision; respect; *in ALLE* ~ *te*, in all respects; *TEN* ~ *te van*, with respect to; in respect of.
opsigself'staande, isolated, separate.
op'sigster, (-s), forewoman.
opsig'telik, (-e), showy, flashy, gaudy, loud (colours, clothes); conspicuous, obtrusive; ~**heid**, showi=ness, ostentation.
op'sigter, (-s), custodian, caretaker; overseer; clerk of works; conservator; checker; green-ranger; keeper; groundsman; banksman; gaffer; ganger.
opsigteres', (-se), op'sigster, (-s), female caretaker.
opsig'tig, (-e), showy, gaudy, loud (colours), tawdry, ostentatious; meretricious; gay, flashy, flamboy=ant, garish; flaunting; conspicuous, obtrusive; ~**heid**, showiness, gaudiness, flashiness; meretri=ciousness, conspicuousness.
opsioneel', (..nele), optional.
op'sit, (-ge-), clap on, put on, don (hat); set up, start (a business); remain sitting up, wait up; court, spoon, woo; cast on (knitting); swell up; stake (money); inlay; *'n keel* ~, start crying, set up a wail; ~**kers**, courting-candle; ~**prys**, upset price.
op'skaaf, (-ge-), plane, smooth.
op'skakel, (-ge-), change up (gears).
op'skarrel, (-ge-), hunt up, rummage up, ferret round (up, out).
op'skeep, (-ge-), saddle with, foist upon; have on one's hands; *opgeskeep sit met iets*, have something on one's hands; be bothered (saddled) with something.
op'skep, (-ge-), serve up, dish up, ladle out; boast; rant; undercut (golf); ~**blad**, serving-top; ~**lepel**, serving spoon; ~**loer, (s)**: *met 'n* ~*loer aankyk*, give someone an imploring look; (w) **(opskepge=loer)**, arrive conveniently at mealtimes; sponge on, cadge; ~**loerder**, cadger, sponger; ~**per, (-s)**, ladle; boaster, braggart; ~**pery**, bluff, swank; ~**skoot**, undercut; ~**skottel**, meat-dish; serving-dish; ~**troffel**, fish-slice.
op'skerp, (-ge-), sharpen, whet; refresh (memory); ~**ing**, sharpening, whetting.
op'skeur, (-ge-), tear up.
op'skiet, (-ge-), shoot up; make headway, get busy, make progress; spend, use up (ammunition); shoot (spring) up (plants); fake (cable); *MET mekaar* ~ get along with each other; *julle MOET nou* ~, you must hurry up now.
op'skik, (s) finery; accoutrement; garniture; attire; adornment, display, frippery; prink; (w) **(-ge-)**, dress-up, trick out, titivate, array, attire, adonize, bedeck, bedizen.
op'skilder, (-ge-), paint anew.
op'skilfer, (-ge-), peel off, flake off (paint).
op'skoffel, (-ge-), hoe.
op'skommel, (-ge-), shake up.
op'skop, (-ge-), kick up; *'n bombarie* ~, make a fuss, kick up a dust.
op'skort, (-ge-), suspend, defer, reserve (judgment); stay; withdraw; leave in abeyance; adjourn, post=pone; delay; prorogue; *drie JAAR* ~, suspend for three years; ~*ende PLEIT*, plea in abatement; *op=geskorte VONNIS*, suspended sentence; ~*ende VOORWAARDE*, suspensive condition; condition precedent; ~**ing, (-e, -s)**, suspension (judgment); prorogation; postponement, delay; abeyance.
op'skraap, (-ge-), scrape up; force to pay; ~**sel, (-s)**, scraping.
op'skrif, (-te), inscription, caption, legend, title, let=tering, superscription; address; headline (newspa=per); epigraph; heading (chapter); *van 'n* ~ *voor=sien*, supply a heading; ~**skilder**, sign-writer.
op'skrik, (-ge-), give a start; be startled.
op'skroef, op'skroewe, (-ge-), screw up; press, urge (for payment); key (machine).
op'skryf, op'skrywe, (-ge-), write down; chalk up; put to one's account; make a list of; log; note; pen=cil; *hy LAAT maar* ~, he runs (up) an account; *skryf my MAAR op*, put my name down.
op'skud, (-ge-), shake up; stir; hurry up; ~ *nou!* hurry up, now! ~**ding**, agitation, sensation, disturbance, hurly-burly, alarm, fracas, combustion; commo=tion, fuss; cataclysm; *'n hele* ~*ding verwek*, create a commotion, flutter the dovecotes.
op'skuif, op'skuiwe, (-ge-), move up, shove up; get married.
op'skuifraam, sash-window.
op'skuiwing, shifting up; thrust, (reversed) fault (in mines); upthrow (mineralogy); ~**skrag**, thrust.
op'skuur, (-ge-), scour, polish.
op'slaan, (-ge-), raise, put up (hood of car); lift, ele=vate (eyes); turn up (collar); cock (hat); turn up (page); raise (price); put (a cent) on (the price); pitch (tent); put into (a warehouse); ratoon (sugar-cane); rebound; ricochet (bullet); prefabricate (building); knock up; ~**bou**, prefabrication; ~**huis**, prefabricated house.
op'slag, (..slae), upstroke; structure; advance, incre=ment, rise; glance; self-set plants, volunteer plants, voluntary plants; cuff (jacket); storage; bounce; re=growth (wheat); ratoon (tobacco); ricochet; *iem.* ~ *GEE*, give someone a rise in salary; *iem. slaan dat hy opslae MAAK*, give someone a severe hiding; *'n SAAK wat opslae sal maak*, a matter that will cause repercussions (a stir); *by* ~ *VERKOOP*, sell at auc=tion; ~**bak**, storage bin; ~**bal**, bouncer; ~**bewys**, warehouse receipt; ~**depot**, shed, store, dump; ~**fontein**, ephemeral spring; ~**gewas**, ratoon crop; ~**hou**, bumper, bump-ball; ~**kamer**, storage room; ~**koeël**, ricochet shot; ~**plantjie**, self-sown seedling; ~**plek**, storage building; depot, supply dump; ~**ruimte**, storage space, warehouse room; ~**skoot**, rebounding shot; ricochet; ~**somertjie**, Indian summer; ~**tabak**, ratoon tobacco; ~**ter=rein**, storage yard.
op'slaner, (-s), bounder (in warehouse).
op'sleep, (-ge-), drag up.
op'slobber, (-ge-), slobber (lap) up.
op'sluit¹, (w), (-ge-), lock up, confine, imprison; crib; closet; coop, encage, fold; impound, lock in; pen; cloister; *dit lê opgesluit in*, it is implied by, it is im=plicit in.
opsluit'², (bw) absolutely; *hy wou* ~ *binnekom*, he in=sisted on entering.
op'sluiting, (-e, -s), confinement, incarceration; de=tention; occlusion (of gas); *eensame* ~, solitary confinement; ~**moer**, locknut; ~**pen**, steady-pin, mortise bolt; ~**vrees**, claustrophobia.
op'sluk, (-ge-), gulp down, swallow, engorge, engulf, absorb; pouch, raven.
op'slurp, (-ge-), drink noisily, lap (up), bib; ~**end, (-e)**, bibulous; absorbent; ~**ing**, absorption; lap=ping up.
op'smuk, (s) finery, trimmings, trappings; (w) **(-ge-)**, trim, deck out, embellish, adonize; *opgesmukte styl*, ornate style.
op'smyt, (-ge-), fling (chuck) up.
op'snap, (-ge-), snap up.
op'snuffel, (-ge-), ferret out, search out.
op'snuif, (-ge-), sniff up, inhale.
op'sny, (-ge-), cut up; draw the long bow, brag, bluff.
op'snyer, (-s), braggart, boaster; ~**ig, (-e)**, boastful; ~**y**, boasting, bragging, bounce, swank(ing).

op'soek, (-ge-), search for, look for; call on, look up; spot (aeroplane, target).
op'som, (-ge-), summarize, sum up, numerate, enumerate; detail; digest; ~'**mend**, (-e), enumerative; ~**mer**, (-s), précis-writer; summer-up; enumerator; ~**ming**, (-e, -s), summary, résumé, (e)numeration; recapitulation; recital, recitation; digest; précis; summing-up (by judge); conspectus; pemmican (fig.).
op'spaar, (-ge-), save up, lay by.
op'speld, (-ge-), pin up, pin on.
op'spoor, (-ge-), track, trace, find out, track down, ferret out, locate, detect; lodge (game); ~**der**, (-s), detector.
op'sporing, (-e, -s), tracing, tracking, seeking-out, finding-out, detection; ~**sdiens**, investigation department; ~**swerk**, tracking-down; tracing; exploratory work.
op'spraak, sensation, commotion; scandal; *in* ~ *BRING*, set people's tongues wagging; *in* ~ *KOM*, become the talk of the town; ~ *VERWEK*, create a commotion, flutter the dovecote; ~**wek'kend**, (-e), notorious.
op'spring, (-ge-), jump up, bounce, bump, hop; *van vreugde* ~, leap for joy.
op'staan, (-ge-), stand up, rise, arise, get up; get on one's legs; rebel, revolt; *uit die BED* ~, get out of bed; *van TAFEL* ~, rise from the table; *teen 'n VERDRUKKER* ~, resist the oppressor; *as jy hom wil fop, moet jy VROEG* ~, if you wish to catch him, you must be wide awake; ~**boordjie**, stand-up collar.
op'stal, (-le), farmstead, premises, homestead, buildings (with surrounding land), grange.
op'stand, (-e), revolt, insurrection, rebellion; commotion; elevation (in architecture); stand (of wood), standing timber; *in* ~ *kom teen*, revolt against.
opstan'deling, (-e), insurgent, rebel, revolutionary, reactionary.
opstan'dig, (-e), insurgent, mutinous, rebellious, obstreperous, insurrectionary; reactionary; ~**heid**, rebelliousness, ferment.
op'standing, resurrection; ~**sdag**, resurrection day.
op'stap, (-ge-), walk up (on).
op'stapel, (-ge-), pile up, stack up, heap up, hoard, bank, accumulate, store; ~**ing**, stacking, piling, accumulation; coacervation.
op'steek, (s): *deur* ~ *van hande*, by a show of hands; (w) (-ge-), raise, put up, lift (hands); light (candle); incite (to mischief); prick up (the ears); work up (for rain); set in, freshen, spring up (wind, storm).
op'steker, (-s), lighter; inciter; ~**y**, lighting; incitation, incitement.
op'stel, (s) (-le), essay, composition; (w) (-ge-), plan, compose, draft (parliamentary bill); compile; marshal, arrange (facts); mount (tripod); draw up (soldiers, document); set up (hypothesis); fit up; run (candidate); mount (gun); range; plant; array; station (police); *'n REKENING* ~, make out an account; *SORGVULDIG opgestel*, carefully worded; ~**ler**, (-s), composer, compiler, editor, framer; compère; ~**ling**, drawing-up, putting in position, assembling, installation (of machine); disposition (troops); ~**lingsterrein**, ~**lingswerf**, marshalling yard; ~**plaas**, ~**plek**, waiting-place; ~**skrywer**, essayist.
op'stoker, (-s), inciter, instigator, setter-on, agitator; abettor; ~**y**, instigation, incitement; intriguing.
op'stoking, instigation, stirring up strife.
op'stoof, (-ge-), stew (up).
op'stook, (-ge-), stir up, poke up; egg on; incite; instigate; abet; brew.
op'stoot, (-ge-), push up; increase, raise.
op'stootjie, (-s), riot, disturbance.
op'stop, (-ge-), fill up, stuff; mount; tamp; *opgestopte diere*, stuffed animals; ~**per**, (-s), blow, smack, upper-cut, cuff, punch; stuffer, mounter, taxidermist; ~**ping**, stuffing, mounting; tamping; jam (in street); congestion; ~**sel**, padding, stuffing.
op'storm, (-ge-), rush up.
op'stroop, (-ge-), turn up (trousers); roll up (sleeves); tuck up (skirts).

op'stry, (-ge-), argue with; deny; contradict.
op'stryk, (-ge-), twirl up, turn up; rake in, pocket (money).
op'stuif, (-ge-), fly up; flame up, flare up.
op'stuit, (-ge-), rise (water).
op'stuiwe, (-ge-) = **opstuif**.
op'stuur, (-ge-), send on (up).
op'styg, (-ge-), rise, ascend; take off (aero.); mount (horse); arise from; ~**end**, (-e), ascending, assurgent; ~**ing**, take-off, ascent, rising; start (aero.); ~**plek**, take-off point, starting-point; ~**snelheid**, take-off speed.
op'suie, **op'suig**, (-ge-), absorb, suck in, imbibe, take up.
op'suig: ~**baar**, (..**bare**), absorbable; ~**baarheid**, absorbability; ~**end**, (-e), absorptive; absorbent; ~**ing**, absorption; resorption; aspiration; ~**middel**, absorbent.
op'suip, (-ge-), guzzle; drink (up), spend money on liquor.
op'swaai, (-ge-), swing up.
op'sweep, (-ge-), whip up, drive up, incite; *die gemoedere* ~, rouse the feelings, inflame the passions; ~**baar**, (..**bare**), fomentable.
op'swel, (-ge-), swell, inflate; become bloated; ~ *van trots*, swell with pride.
op'swelg, (-ge-), gulp down, swallow up.
op'swelling, inflation; tumefaction, swelling.
op'swepend, (-e), rabble-rousing.
op'sweper, (-s), agitator; ~**y**, incitement, agitation.
opsy', aside, aloof, apart; ~ *GAAN*, step aside; ~ *GOOI*, fling aside; *VAN* ~, from one side.
opsy'sit, (-gesit), set aside; waive (a claim).
op'takel, (-ge-), rig up; trick up, deck out.
optatief', (..**tiewe**), optative.
optati'vus, optative mood.
opteer'[1], (ge-), choose, opt.
op'teer[2], (-ge-), spend, use up.
op'teken, (-ge-), note, write down, jot down, enter in, minute, chronicle, record; ~**aar**, recorder; calendarer; ~**ing**, noting-down, recording.
op'tel[1], (-ge-), lift, elevate, pick up; worry, give a hard time; purchase; raise; *die rugpyn tel my vreeslik op*, backache makes my life a misery.
op'tel[2], (-ge-), add, enumerate, count up, cast up, check.
op'tel: ~**fout**, mistake in adding; ~**goed**, findings; rubbish; ~*goed is HOUGOED*, findings keepings; ~*goed is JAKKALSPIS*, finding is not keeping; ~**kind**, illegitimate child; foundling.
op'telkolom, addition column.
op'teller[1], (s) (-s), picker.
op'teller[2], (s) (-s), adder; enumerator.
op'tel: ~**ling**, (-e, -s) addition, enumeration; ~**masjien**, adding-machine; ~**som**, addition sum.
optiek', optics; optical instruments.
op'ties, (-e), optic(al); ~*e AANPEILTOESTEL*, visual homing-device; ~*e ANOMALIE*, optical anomaly; ~*e DRAAIVERMOË*, optical rotary power.
op'tika, optics.
op'tikus, (-se, ..**tici**), optician.
optimaal', (..**male**), optimal, optimum; *optimale dieet*, optimal diet.
optimis', (-te), optimist; ~**me**, optimism; ~**ties**, (-e), optimistic.
op'timmer, (-ge-), build up; repair; erect.
op'timum, (-s, ..**tima**), optimum.
optisiën', (-e), optician.
op'tog, (-te), procession, march, parade; *HISTORIESE* ~, historical pageant; ~ *te PERD*, cavalcade.
op'tometer, **optome'ter**, (-s), optometer.
optometriek', optometry.
optometris', (-te), optometrist.
op'tooi, (-ge-), dress up, decorate, adorn, attire, perk up, embellish, bedizen; prank; prink; ~**ing**, adornment, decoration; ~**sel**, (-s), finery, decoration, adornment.
op'toom, (-ge-), bridle (a horse).
op'torring, (-ge-), rip up, rip open.
optou'setting, flo(a)tation.

op'trede, action, proceeding; appearance, conduct, behaviour, comportment, address; *EERSTE* ~, first appearance; début; *GESAMENTLIKE* ~, joint action; *sy HELE* ~, his whole manner.

op'tree¹, (s) (..treë), stair-rise, step, riser.

op'tree², (w) (-ge-), appear, occur, set in, come into play; act on stage, play, perform; preach; take steps, take action; *STRENGER* ~, take more rigorous action; ~ *TEEN*, take action against; ~ *VIR iem.*, deputize for someone; ~ *as VOORSIT= TER*, act as chairman.

op'trek, (-ge-), move forward (army), take the field, march against; hoist; pull up (blind); gather, draw up; raise, erect (building); cock (head); purchase; (w)hoop (whooping cough); *die NEUS* ~ *vir die kos*, turn up one's nose at the food; *die SKOUERS* ~, shrug one's shoulders; ~**king**, erection; advance; ~**spier**, retractor muscle.

op'tuig, (-ge-), harness; caparison; rig (ship).

opulen'sie, opulence.

opulent', (-e), opulent.

o'pus, (-se, **opera**), opus, work; *magnum* ~, writer's (artist's) chief work.

op'vaar, (-ge-), ascend; sail up; ~**t**, ascension.

op'val, (-ge-), strike, arrest attention, catch the eye, be conspicuous; *in 'n HOEK waar dit nie* ~ *nie*, in a corner where it is not conspicuous; *dit SAL jou* ~, it will strike you; you will notice it; *SONDER dat dit* ~, unostentatiously.

opval'lend, (-e), striking, conspicuous, noticeable, bold, marked(ly), glaring, flagrant, outstanding; ~**heid**, flagrancy; conspicuousness.

op'vang, (-ge-), intercept; catch up; overhear; check, receive (blow); absorb (shock); pick up (signal); collect (water); ~**dam**, catch dam; ~**draad**, aerial; ~**gebied**, catchment-area; drainage-basin; ~**pan**, dripping pan; ~**plek**, point of intake; ~**riool**, catch drain; ~**toestel**, recorder, receiver.

op'varende, (-s), one on board (crew, passenger).

op'varing, ascension; sailing-up.

op'vat, (-ge-), understand, take up (in), conceive; construe; *as 'n BELEDIGING* ~, take as an insult; *iets ERNSTIG* ~, regard (take) something seriously; *sy taak LIG* ~, take his task lightly; *jy moet dit nie VERKEERD* ~ *nie*, you must not take it up in the wrong way; ~**ting** (-e, -s), idea, opinion, conception, view, interpretation.

op'vee, op'veeg, (-ge-), sweep up, wipe up.

op'veegsels, sweepings.

op'veil, (-ge-), sell by auction, auctioneer; ~**ing**, auction.

op'vis, (-ge-), fish out (up); recover.

op'vlam, (-ge-), flare up, blaze up; deflagrate, flash; ~**ming**, flare-up, blaze.

op'vlie, (-ge-), fly up.

opvlie'ënd, (-e), quick-tempered, irascible, choleric, peppery, hot-tempered, explosive, fiery; ~**heid**, irascibility, choler, hastiness of temper.

op'vlieg, (-ge-), fly up; flare up.

op'voed, (-ge-), educate, rear, bring up, foster; ~**'baar**, (..**bare**), educable; ~**end**, (-e), educative; ~**er**, (-s), educator, educationist; ~**ing**, education, schooling, upbringing, fosterage; ~**ingsinrigting**, educational institution; protectory (R.C.); ~**kunde**, pedagogy; ~**kun'dig**, (-e), educational, educative, pedagogic; ~**kun'dige**, (-s), educationist, pedagogue.

op'voer¹, (-ge-), fatten, finish for the market.

op'voer², (-ge-), lead up to; perform, stage, produce, act; ~**'baar**, (..**bare**), performable; ~**der**, (-s), producer.

op'voering¹, (-e, -s), performance, production (play).

op'voering², feeding.

op'voer: ~**ingsreg**, ~**reg**, acting rights, right of performance, dramatic copyright.

op'volg, (-ge-), follow, succeed; observe, comply with (rules); follow on (cricket); ~**beurt**, follow-on; ~**end**, (-e), incoming, following; ~**er**, (-s), successor; ~**ing**, succession, sequence, consecution.

op'vorder, (-ge-), demand, claim, call up; ~**baar**, (..**bare**), claimable, demandable; ~**ing**, (-e, -s), demand, claim.

op'vou, (-ge-), fold up; furl (sail); ~**'baar**, (..**bare**), collapsible; ..*bare buisie*, collapsible tube.

op'vra, (-ge-), call in, withdraw, demand (money); ~**'baar**, (..**bare**), witdrawable; claimable.

op'vraging, (-e, -s), withdrawal; *by* ~, on demand.

op'vreet, (-ge-), devour, (by animals); eat voraciously, raven; *ek het al baie van jou opgevreet*, I have already swallowed a lot (of nonsense) from you.

op'vrolik, (-ge-), brighten, gladden, cheer (up), (en)liven, comfort, exhilarate.

op'vryf, op'vrywe, (-ge-), polish, rub up, furbish.

op'vryf: ~**doek**, polishing cloth; ~**stok**, mop.

op'vul, (-ge-), fill (up), stuff; tamp; pad; ~**ling**, (-s), stuffing; padding; aggradition; tamping; packing; ~**sel**, (-s), wadding; stuffing, padding; anaplerosis; ~**werk**, fill(ing).

op'vysel, (-ge-), extol, sing the praises of, puff; ~**ing**, (-e, -s), write-up; excessive praise.

op'waai, (-ge-), blow up; be blown up.

op'waarts, (-e), upward(s); ~*e druk*, upward pressure, buoyancy.

op'wag, (-ge-), wait for, expect; ~**ting**, ceremonious visit; *sy* ~**ting maak**, pay his respects, call.

op'walling, banking.

op'warm, (-ge-), warm up (food); rake up (old story), rehash; *opgewarmde kos*, reheated food; rechauffé, rehash; ~**ing**, rehash; warming-up.

op'was¹, (-ge-), grow up; *see* **opgewasse**.

op'was², (-ge-), wash up; ~**bak**, (wash-up) sink; ~**masjien**, dish washer; ~**plek**, scullery; ~**tafel**, wash-up table.

op'weeg, (-ge-), counterbalance, set off, compensate for, counteract; equalize; *jy kan nie teen hom* ~ *nie*, you are not equal to him; you do not weigh up to him.

op'wegend, (-e), equiponderant.

op'wek, (-ge-), awake, stimulate, (a)rouse, animate, elate, ginger up; cheer up; generate, excite, create (doubt); exhilarate; enkindle; ~**'kend**, (-e), exciting, excitative, excitatory, rousing, stirring, stimulating, exhilarating, exhilarant, cheery, encouraging; recreative; ~**ker**, (-s), reviver, stimulant; dynamo; generator (elec.); ~**king**, (-e, -s), resuscitation, stimulation, awak(en)ing, arousal; generation (elec.); raising; resurrection; quickening; *die* ~*king van Lasarus*, the raising of Lazarus; ~**kingsdiens**, revival meeting; ~**kingsmiddel**, stimulant; ~**kingsprediker**, revivalist.

op'wel, (-ge-), well up, bubble up, spring up.

op'welling, ebullition, flush, impulse; *'n* ~ *van DRIF*, an outburst of temper; *die EERSTE* ~, one's first impulse.

op'wen, (-ge-), wind up; get excited; ~**ding**, winding.

op'werk, (-ge-), work up, embellish; work one's way up; ~**plank**, embossing board.

op'werp, (-ge-), throw up, raise (objection); *hom* ~ *as leier*, set himself up as leader, imagine that he can be the leader.

op'wig, (-ge-), wedge up; key.

op'wikkel, (-ge-), wind.

op'win, (-ge-) = **opwen**.

op'windend, opwin'dend, (-e), exciting.

op'winding, (-e, -s), coil; excitement, agitation; orgasm; winding; ~**sinstallasie**, winding plant.

op'wip, (-ge-), jump up (lightly); tilt up; skip up; ~**neus**, tip-tilted (retroussé) nose.

ora'gie, (-s), noise.

ora'kel, (-s), oracle; ~**agtig**, (-e), oracular; ~**spreuk**, oracle; ~**taal**, oracular language.

o'ral(s), everywhere; ~ *oor*, about this and that; miscellaneous (writings).

orangea'de, orangeade.

orang-oe'tang, (-s), orang-outang.

oran'je, orange (colour); ~ *blanje blou*, orange, white and blue; ~**agtig**, (-e), orange-like; ~**bitter**, orange bitters; ~**bloeisel**, orange-blossom; ~**geel**, orange, fulvous, luteous; ~**kleur**, orange (colour); ~**rie'**, (-ë), orangery.

Oran'jerivier, Orange River.

oran'jestrikkie, orange favour.

Oran'je-Vrystaat, Orange Free State; ~**s**, (-e), of the Orange Free State.

ora'sie, (-s), oration; tumult, row.
ora'tor, (-e, -s), orator; **..to'ries**, (-e), oratorical; **..to'rium**, (..ria, -s), oratorio; oratory.
or'de, order, arrangement; class; *in* ~ *BRING*, adjust, put in(to) order; *BUITE* ~ *wees*, be out of order; *die* ~ *van die DAG*, the order of the day; *GEESTELIKE* ~, religious order; *in GOEIE* ~, in good order; *die* ~ *HERSTEL*, restore order; *goed kan* ~ *HOU*, be a good disciplinarian; ~ *HOU*, keep order; *aan die* ~ *KOM*, come up for discussion; *die O* ~ *van die KOUSBAND*, the Order of the Garter; *buite* ~ *REËL*, rule out of order; *iem. tot* ~ *ROEP*, call a person to order; *aan die* ~ *STEL*, allow discussion on; *in VERSPREIDE* ~, in extended (loose) order; *in VOLMAAKTE* ~, in apple-pie order; ~**band**, cordon; ~**broe(de)r**, brother; fellow; friar; ~**grootte**, order, extent; size; ~**houer**, (-s), disciplinarian; ~**ketting**, chain, collar (of an order); ~**kleed**, habit; ~**kruis**, cross of an order); ~**lie'wend**, (-e), fond of order, orderly; law-abiding; ~**lie'wendheid**, love of order; ~**lik**, (-e), orderly; ~**likheid**, orderliness; ~**loos**, (..lose), disorderly; anarchic(al); ~**loosheid**, disorderliness; anarchy; ~**lys**, order paper; ~**merk**, order-mark, black mark.
or'den, (ge-), ordain (minister of religion); arrange, put in order, regulate, dispose, classify, marshall; ~**ing**, (-e, -s), ordination; arrangement.
ordent'lik, (-e), decent, proper, respectable, behaved; reasonable; fair; fair-sized; ~ *groot*, fairly big; ~**heid**, decency; fairness; respectability; ~**heidshalwe**, for decency's sake.
or'der, (s) (-s), command; order; *AAN die* ~ *van A.*, by order of A.; *tot NADER* ~, till further orders; *OP* ~ *van A.*, at the command of A.; ~**boek**, order book; ~**briefie**, note (of hand); order form; ~**tjek**, cheque to order.
or'deteken, ribbon (of an order), badge; (-s), insignia.
or'devoorstel, motion on a point of order.
ordinaat', (..nate), ordinate.
ordinan'sie, (-ë, -s), ordinance (of God).
ordina'ris, (-se), ordinary (R.C. Church).
ordineer', (ge-), ordain.
ordinêr', (-e), ordinary, common; vulgar; ~**heid**, commonness; vulgarity.
ordine'ring, ordaining.
ordonnans', (-e), orderly.
ordonnan'sie, (-s), ordinance.
ordonnans'offisier, orderly officer.
ordonneer', (ge-), decree, order.
o're: *ter* ~ *kom*, come to one's ears.
oreer', (ge-), orate, declaim, harangue.
orent', upright, straight, endways, erect, on end; ~ *KOM*, stand up; ~ *SIT*, place straight (upright); sit up; ~ *STAAN*, stand up straight.
Or'feus, Orpheus.
Or'fies Orphic.
orgaan' (..gane), organ; apparatus; ~**bank**, organ-bank.
organdie', organdie.
orga'nies, (-e), organic; ~ *e stowwe*, organic matter.
organisa'sie, (-s), organization; set-up; ~**talent**, organizing ability; ~**vorm**, form of organization.
organisa'tor, (-e, -s), organizer; **..to'ries**, (-e), organizing.
organiseer', (ge-), organize; promote; arrange (meeting); ~**der**, (-s), organizer; promoter; ~**ster**, (-s), woman organizer.
organis'me, (-s), organism.
organologie', organology.
organsyn'sy, organzine.
organ'za, organza.
orgas'me, (-s), orgasm.
orgidee', (..deë), orchid; ~**agtig**, (-e), orchidaceous.
orgie', (-ë), orgy, debauching.
ori'bie, (-s), oribi antelope (*Ourebia scoparia*); *see* oorbietjie.
O'rient, Orient; ~**aal'**, (..tale); Oriental; ~**alis'**, (-te), Orientalist.
oriënta'sie, orientation; ~**knobbel**, bump of locality; ~**vermoë**, sense of locality.

oriënteer', (ge-), become acquainted with, find one's bearings, find out how one stands, orientate.
oriënte'ring, orientation, fixing of position, position-finding; ~**spunt**, check-point (navig.); fix (aero.).
o'rig¹, (-e), silly, meddlesome, intrusive; flirtatious; *moenie jou* ~ *HOU nie*, stop meddling; *jy IS* ~, you are silly.
o'rig², (-e), left, remaining; *DIE* ~ *es*, the rest (remainder); *VIR die* ~ *e*, for the rest; ~**ens**, for the rest; otherwise.
o'righeid, intrusiveness, silliness.
originaliteit', originality.
origineel', (..nele), original.
oril'lonpasser, bow compasses.
O'rion, Orion.
orkaan', (orkane), hurricane; ~**agtig**, (-e), cyclonic; ~**sterkte**, hurricane force.
orkes', (-te), orchestra, band; ~**begeleiding**, orchestral accompaniment; ~**dirigent**, conductor; ~**leidster**, ~**leier**, orchestra leader; ~**meester**, conductor, bandmaster; orchestra leader; ~**musiek**, orchestral music; ~**nommer**, orchestral item; ~**opname**, orchestral recording; ~**partituur**, orchestral score; ~**party**, orchestral part; ~**ruim**, orchestra pit; ~**toon**, concert pitch; ~**traal'**, (..trale), orchestral; ~**tra'sie**, orchestration; ~**treer'**, (ge-), orchestrate, score.
orkes'trion, (-s), orchestrina, orchestrion.
orkes'verhoog, bandstand.
ornaat', official robes (vestments), canonicals; *in volle* ~, in full vestments.
ornament', (-e), ornament; enrichment; ~**a'sic**, ornamentation; ~**eel'**, (..tele), ornamental; ~**eer'**, (ge-), ornament; ~**iek'**, ornamental art.
ornitologie', ornithology; **..lo'gies**, (-e), ornithological.
ornitoloog', (..loë), ornithologist.
orogeen', (orogene), orogenic.
orografie', orography; **..gra'fies**, (-e), orographic.
Or'pington, Orpington.
or'rel, (-s), organ; ~**blaasbalk**, organ bellows; ~**draaier**, organ-grinder; ~**fries**, linenfold moulding; ~**galery**, organ-loft; ~**is'**, (-te), organist; ~**is'te**, (-s), lady organist; ~**kanon**, multiple-barrel gun; ~**kas**, organ-case; ~**klank**, organ sound; ~**konsert**, organ recital; organ concerto; ~**maker**, organ builder; ~**musiek**, organ music; ~**punt**, pedal; ~**pyp**, organ-pipe; flue; pause; *kinders soos* ~**pype**, children by the dozen; ~**register**, organ-stop; gamba; register; ~**spel**, organ-playing; ~**speler**, organist; organ-player; ~**stemmer**, organ-tuner; ~**stryk**: *alles het* ~ *stryk gegaan*, things went off without a hitch; ~**toon**, organ tone; ~**trapper**, organ-treader; bellows-blower; ~**uitvoering**, organ recital.
ortodoks', (-e), orthodox; **io'**, orthodoxy.
ortoëpie', orthoepy.
ortografie', (-ë), orthography; **..gra'fies**, (-e), orthographic(al).
ortoklaas', orthoclase.
ortolaan', (..lane), ortolan (bird).
ortopedie', orthopaedy; **..pe'dies**, (-e), orthopaedic; -*e chirurg*, orthopaedic surgeon.
ortopedis', (-te), orthopaedic surgeon.
ortosen'tries, (-e), orthocentric.
os, (-se), ox; bullock; *v.d.* ~ *op die ESEL (jas)*, stray from one subject to another; *JONG* ~ *se inspan*, vomit; shoot the cat; *all sy* ~ *sies is nie in die KRAAL nie*, he is not all there; he hasn't all his wits about him; *soos 'n* ~ *NEERSLAAN*, fall down heavily; fall as if pole-axed; *PLOEË met die* ~ *se wat ons het*, exploit what we have; *SLAAP soos 'n* ~, sleep like a log; *eers sy* ~ *sies goed agtermekaar SPAN*, wait and see which way the cat jumps; *uit die* ~ *UIT wees*, be rather odd; ~**bloed**, blood of oxen.
oseaan', (oseane), ocean; *die* ~ *probeer leeg drink*, try to drink the ocean dry.
Osea'nië, Oceania.
osea'nies, (-e), oceanic.
oseanograaf', (..grawe), oceanographer.
oseanografie', oceanography.

**oseanologie', ** oceanology.
**oselot', (-te), ** ocelot.
**Osi'ris, ** Osiris.
os: ** ~kop** ox-head; ~**koper, ** cattle-dealer; ~**kraal, ** ox-kraal.
**osmiri'dium, ** osmiridium.
**os'mium, ** osmium.
**osmologie', ** osmology.
**os'mometer, osmome'ter, (-s), ** osmometer.
**osmo'se, ** osmosis.
**osmo'ties, (-e), ** osmotic.
**osoniseer', (ge-), ** ozonize.
osoon', ** ozone; ~apparaat, ** ozonizer.
os: ** ~riem, ** ox-riem; ~**sewa, ** ox-wagon.
**ossifika'sie, ** ossification.
**ossifiseer', (ge-), ** ossify.
**ossilla'sie, ** oscillation.
**ossilla'tor, (-s), ** oscillator.
**ossilleer', (ge-), ** oscillate.
**ossillograaf', (..grawe), ** oscillograph.
**osteofagie', ** osteophagy.
os'stert, ** oxtail; ~sop, ** oxtail soup.
**ossua'rium, (-s, ..ria), ** ossuary.
**ostenta'sie, ** ostentation.
**osteologie', ** osteology.
**osteopaat', (..pate), ** osteopath.
**os'tong, ** ox-tongue; bugloss (plant).
**ostraseer', (ge-), ** ostracize, banish.
**ostrasis'me, ** ostracism.
**os'vel, ** oxhide.
**ot'jie, (-s), ** pig; chor-chor, grunter (fish).
**o''tjie, (-s), ** small o.
ot'ter, (-s), ** otter; ~blom, ** otter-flower.
**Ottomaans', (-e), ** Ottoman, Turkish.
**ot'toman, (-s), ** ottoman.
**Ottoma'nies, (-e), ** Ottoman, Turkish.
**ou¹, (s) (-es, -ens), ** (old) chap, fellow; *'n GAWE* ~, a fine fellow, a good chap; *jy's 'n MOOI* ~*! * you're a fine fellow! (b) (attributively used), **(-er, oudste), ** old, aged; dear; pristine; ~ *BROOD, * stale bread; *op die* ~ *END, * finally; in the long run; *'n* ~ *HOU, * a terrific blow (shot); ~ *KANT toe staan, * getting on in years; *die* ~ *SKRYWERS, * the old writers, the classics; *die* ~ *TALE, * the classical languages; *die* ~ *TYE, * the (good) old times; *my* ~ *VRIEND, * my dear friend.
**ou², (w) (ge-), ** give; ~ *vir Mamma, * give to Mother.
**ou'baas, ** old gentleman; old master (boss); gaffer; *die* ~, the old man, dad.
**oubak'ke, oud'bakke, ** (ong., Ndl.), stale; old-fashioned, out of date.
**ou'boet, (-e), ou'boeta, (-s), ** eldest brother; chum.
**ou'bos, ** Leucosidea sericea.
**oud¹, ** (predicatively used), **(ouer, -ste), ** old; aged; *hoe ouer hoe GEKKER, * no fool like an old fool; ~ *maar nog nie KOUD nie, * plenty of life in the old dog yet; *'n mens word nooit te* ~ *om te LEER nie, * one is never too old to learn; *so* ~ *soos METUSALEM, * as old as the hills; *vir* ~ *en NUUT straf, * punish for all sins, past and present; *ouer as TWAALF, * not born yesterday; no greenhorn; ~ *voor jou TYD, * old before one's time; ~ *WORD, * grow old(er).
**oud-², ** former, ex-, retired.
**ou'dag, ** old age; *OP sy* ~, in his old age; *SPAAR vir die* ~, save for old age.
**ou'dak, (-ke), ** frog.
oud-: ** ~amptenaar, ** ex-official; ~**burgemeester, ** ex-mayor.
**Oud'-Duits, (s) ** Old German; (b) **(-e), ** Old German.
**ou'de: ** old folks; *soos die* ~ *songe, so piepe de jonge, * as the old cock crows, the young one learns.
**Oud'-Engels, (s) ** Old English; (b) **(-e), ** Old English.
**ou'der: ** ~ *gewoonte, * as is the custom.
**ou'derdom, (-me), ** age; *'n hoë* ~ *BEREIK, * attain a great age; *die* ~ *kom met GEBREKE, * age has its disabilities; *op TIENJARIGE* ~, at ten years old.
ou'derdoms: ** ~grens, ** age-limit; ~**kwaal, ** old-age ailment; ~**pensioen, ** old-age pension; ~**versekering, ** old-age insurance; ~**verswakking, ** senile decay; ~**verval, ** consenescence.
**ou'derdomswakte, ** senility.

ou'derling, (-e, -s), ** elder; presbyter; ~sbank, ** elders' pew; ~**skap, ** eldership.
**oudertous', (-e), ** old-fashioned.
ouderwets', (-e), ** old-fashioned, quaint, ancient, antiquated, out-of-date; precocious (child); cute, knowing; forward; ~heid, ** old-fashionedness; precociousness; ancientry.
**Oud'-Frans, (s) ** Old French; (b) **(-e), ** Old French.
**oud-'gediende, (-s), ** veteran, ex-serviceman.
**Oud'-Germaans, (s) ** Old Germanic; (b) Old Germanic.
**oud'hede, ** antiquities.
oud'heid, ** antiquity; ancientry; oldness, old age; ~kenner, ** antiquarian; ~**kunde, ** archaeology; antiquarian science; ~**kun'dig, (-e), ** antiquarian; archaeologic; ~**kun'dige, (-s), ** antiquarian; archaeologist.
**Oud'-Hollands, ** Old Dutch.
**Oud'-Hoogduits, ** Old High German.
oudiën'sie, (-s), ** audience; *in* ~ *ONTVANG, * receive (someone) in audience; ~ *VERLEEN, * grant an audience; ~saal, ** presence-room, presence-chamber, audience-hall.
**ou'diometer, oudiome'ter, (-s), ** audiometer.
**oudiometrie', ** audiometry.
**oudiovisueel', (..suele), ** audio-visual.
**oudi'sie, (-s), ** audition.
**ou'dit, (-s), ** audit; (w), audit.
ouditeer', (ge-), ** audit; ~opgawe, ** audit return.
**oudite'ring, ** auditing.
ouditeur', (-e, -s), ** auditor; ~-generaal, (-s-generaal), ** auditor-general; ~**s'navraag, ** ~**s'vraag, ** audit query; ~**sverslag, ** auditor's report.
**ouditief', (..tiewe), ** auditive.
**ou'ditkunde, ** (science of) auditing.
**oudito'rium, (..ria, -s), ** auditory; audience.
**ou'ditspan, ** auditing team.
**ou'ditverslag, (..verslae), ** auditors' report.
**oud'-leerling, ** ex-scholar; old pupil, old scholar.
oud'-modies = oumodies.
**Oud'-Noors, (s) ** Old Norse; (b) **(-e), ** Old Norse.
**oud'-oom, ** grand-uncle.
**oud'-ouderling, ** ex-elder.
**ouds: ** *VAN* ~, of yore, formerly; *VAN* ~ *af, * from olden days.
**Oud'-Saksies, (s) ** Old Saxon; (b) **(-e), ** Old Saxon.
**ouds'her: ** *van* ~, from time immemorial, from long ago.
**oud'-soldaat, ** ex-soldier, ex-serviceman, veteran.
**oud'ste, (-s), ** eldest; elder (of two); doyen; *die* ~ *word onterf, * someone is done out of his due.
oud'-stryder, (-s), ** veteran; ex-warrior (-burgher); ~sbond, ** league of ex-burghers.
oud'-student, ** ex-student, alumnus; ~e-unie, ** old students' union; alumni union; ~**evereniging, ** old students' association; alumni association.
**oud'tante, ** grand-aunt.
**oud'tyds, ** in olden times, of old.
**ou'e, (-s), ** old one; chap; *die* ~ *s van DAE, * the aged; ~*s DOOD en kleintjies eet groot, * stuff oneself; *HAAI julle* ~*s! * I say, you chaps!
**ou'el, (-s), ** consecrated wafer, altar-bread, host; cachet.
**ou'er, (s) (-s), ** parent; ~*s vra, * ask parents' consent to get married.
**ou'erhuis, ** parental (maternal) home.
**ou'erig, (-e), ** rather old, oldish.
ou'er: ** ~liefde, ** parental love; ~**lik, (-e), ** parental; ~**loos, (..lose), ** without parents, orphan(ed); ~**loosheid, ** orphanhood; ~**vereniging, ** parents' association; ~**vreugde, ** parental joy (bliss).
**ou'etehuis, ** old people's home.
**ou'etjie, (-s), ** old man, old woman.
**ougment, (-e), ** augment.
**ou'gras, ** grass of the previous season; *DUBBELE* ~, grass of the previous two seasons; *jy is IN die* ~, you are on the wrong track.
**ou'hout, ** *Cordia caffra.*
**Ou'jaar, ** Old Year.
Ou'jaars: ** ~aand, ** New-Year's Eve; ~**dag, ** last day of the year; New-Year's Eve; ~**dagaand, ** ~**dagnag, ** ~**nag, ** New-Year's Eve, Old-Year's Night.

ou'jongkêrel, bachelor; celibate; *'n verstokte ~*, a confirmed bachelor; ~**skap**, bachelorhood.
ou'jongmeisie, (ong.), spinster, old maid; ~**skap**, spinsterhood.
ou'jongnôi, ou'jongnooi, spinster, old maid; ~**agtig**, (-e), old-maidish.
ou'klerekoper, old-clothesman.
ou'klip, pudding-stone, gravel-stone, laterite; ferricrete.
ou'koei, old cow; *~ kom ook in die kraal*, slow but sure wins the race.
ouksiliër', (-e), auxiliary.
ou'laas, the very last; *iets vir ~ doen*, do something for the very last time (before parting).
ou'land, fallow land; *~gras*, love-grass (*Eragrostis curvula*).
ou'lap, (-pe), (vero.) penny; *vir 'n ~ en 'n BOK=STERT*, for a mere song, dirt cheap; *'n ~ twee maal OMKEER*, turn every coin over twice; *'n ~ se ROOI maak mooi*, a dash of red works wonders.
ou'lik, (-e), precocious; arch(ly); tricky; nice; sophisti= cated, clever; fancy; diplomatic; cute, forward, fly, pawky, canny, sharp, smart; *'n ~e kêreltjie*, a smart little chap; ~**heid**, precocity; dexterity, smartness, trickiness, cuteness.
ou'ma, (-s), grandmother; granny; *jy sal jou ~ vir 'n EENDVOËL aansien*, you will get much more than you bargained for; I'll knock spots out of you; *sy ~ die PAPLEPEL leer vashou*, teach one's grand= mother to suck eggs; ~**grootjie**, great-grandmoth= er, ~**kappie**, ~**kappertjie**, (-s), various orchids (e.g. *Pterygodium catholicum*).
ouman', hubby.
ouman'nehuis, home for aged men, almshouse.
ou'matjie, (-s), little grandmother, granny.
ou'menspeer, bon chretien pear.
ou'modies, (-e), old-fashioned, outmoded, out-of-date.
ou'nôi, ou'nooi, (-ens), old mistress (missus).
ou'ooi, ewe that has stopped lambing, old ewe.
ou'pa, (-s), grandfather; *my ~ se hond en sy pa s'n het saam aas weggesleep*, we are very distantly related; we are distant cousins twice removed.
ou'pad: *in die ~ wees*, be on the wrong track altogether.
ou'pagrootjie, great-grandfather.
oupa-pyp'-in-die-bek, begging-hand (*Disa spa= thulata*).
ou'patjie, (-s), little grandfather.
oureool', (oureole), aureole.
ou'rikel, (-s), auricle.
ousan'na, (-s), flint-lock gun, firelock.
ou'sie, (-s), eldest sister.
ouskulta'sie, auscultation, stethoscopy.
ouskulteer', (ge-), auscultate.
ouspi'sieë, auspices.
oustraal', (oustrale), austral, southern.
ou'sus, eldest sister.
ou'tannie, grannie.
outargie', autarchy.
outentiek', (-e), authentic, authenticated.
outentisiteit', authenticity.
Ou-Testamen'ties, (-e), pertaining to the Old Testament.
Ou-Testamentikus, (-se, ..tici), Old Testament scholar.
outeur', (-s), author; ~**s'aandeel**, royalty; ~**skap**, au= thorship; ~**s'reg**, copyright.
outis'me, autism.
outis'ties, (-e), autistic.
ou'tjie, (-s), (old) fellow, chap; *die klein ~s*, the tiny tots.
ou'to, (-'s), motor-car.
outobiograaf', (..grawe), autobiographer.
outobiografie', (-ë), autobiography; ..**gra'fies**, (-e), autobiographic(al).
outochtoon', (..tone), autochthon (aborigine).
outodidak', (-te), autodidact; ~**'ties**, (-e), self-taught, autodidactic.

outograaf', (..grawe), autograph.
outografeer', (ge-), autograph.
outografie', (-ë), autography; ..**gra'fies**, (-e), autographic(al).
outogram', (-me), autograph
outokraat', (..krate), autocrat, Great Cham.
outokrasie', autocracy, Ceasarism.
outokra'ties, (-e), autocratic.
outoliet', autolith; connate (cognate) inclusion.
outomaat', (..mate), automaton; slot-machine.
outoma'ties, (-e), automatic; self-acting; *~e RAT= STELSEL*, automatic gear-change; *~e TELE= FOON*, automatic telephone; *~ WERKEND*, self-acting.
outomatisa'sie, automation.
outomatiseer', (ge-), automatize.
outomatise'ring, automation.
outomatis'me, automatism.
outomobiel', (-e), automobile, motor-car; ~**vereni= ging**, automobile association.
outomobilis', (-te), motorist; ~**me**, automobilism.
outomorf', (-e), automorphic.
outonomie', autonomy, self-government; ..**no'mies**, (-e), autonomous.
outonoom', (..nome), autonomous.
outopsie', (-s), autopsy, post-mortem examination.
outorisa'sie, authorization.
outoriseer', (ge-), authorize.
outoriteit', (-e), authority; *die ~e*, those in authority, the government.
outoriter', (-e), authoritative.
outosuggestie, autosuggestion.
outoterapie', autotherapy.
ou'totipe, (-s), autotype.
ou'to'tjie, (-s), small motor-car, minicar
ou'tyds, (-e), old-fashioned, old-fangled, ancient.
ouvertu're, (-s), overture.
ou'volk, (-e), spiny-tailed lizard.
ou'vrou, (-e, -ens), old woman; gammer; midwife; ~**agtig**, (-e), anile; old-womanish; ~**ehuis**, home for aged women.
ou'vrouenskoop, granny knot.
ou'vrou-onder-die-kombers, toad-in-the-hole.
ou'wyf, (ouwywe), iris (flower); *~se verhale*, idle gos= sip, tittle-tattle, old wives' tales.
ou'-yster, scrap-iron; ~**werf**, scrap-yard.
ouwy'wepraatjies, old wives' tales.
ovaal', (ovale), oval; ~**vormig**, (-e), oval-shaped.
Ovam'bo, (-'s), Ovambo.
ovariotomie', ovariotomy.
ovaris'me, ovarism.
ovari'tis, ovaritis.
ova'rium, (..ria, -s), ovary.
ova'sie, (-s), ovation; *'n ~ kry*, receive an ova= tion.
O'verberg: *die ~*, South Western Districts, C.P.
Ovi'dius, Ovid.
ovipaar', (..pare), oviparous.
ovula'sie, (-s), ovulation; ~**-induksie**, ovulation in= duction; ~**tegniek**, ovulation technique.
ovuleer', (ge-), ovulate.
o'vum, (ova), ovum, egg.
o'werheid, (..hede), government, authorities; *PLAASLIKE ~*, local authority; ~**sbesteding**, government expenditure; ~**sdaad**, act of state; *~ skant*, on the part of the authorities; ~**spersoon**, government official, authority; praetor (Rome); *~ sweë: van ~ sweë*, by the state (authorities).
o'werigens, for the rest.
o'wermoed, (vero.), boldness, recklessness; ~**moe'= dig**, (-e), bold, reckless.
o'werpriester, high priest; chief priest.
o'werspeelster, (-s), adulteress.
o'werspel, adultery, fornication, misconduct, crimi= nal connection; ~**er**, (-s), adulterer, fornicator; ..**spe'lig**, (-e), adulterous; ..**spelige kind(ers)**, adulterine child(ren).
o'werstaan: *ten ~ van*, in the hearing of.
o'werste, (-s), chief, head.

P

p, (-'s), p.
pa, (-'s), pa, father, dad, daddy; *nie ~ vir die kindjie wil staan nie*, not wish to be answerable for something.
paad'jie, (-s), foot-path, small path; aisle; parting (hair); *met iem. 'n ~ loop*, punish (rebuke) someone.
paai¹, (s) (-e), gaffer; stick-in-the-mud; dad; *ou ~ en ou maai*, gaffer and gammer.
paai²,(w) (ge-), appease, coax, placate, disarm, propitiate, conciliate, soothe; *~beleid*, policy of appeasement.
paai'boelie, (-s), hobgoblin, bugbear, bog(e)y; golliwog; ogre, chimera; *~agtig, (-e)*, ogrish.
paai'diggie, (-s), nursery rhyme.
paai'e: *~afdeling*, roads department; *~-ingenieur*, (ong.), road engineer.
paaiement', (-e), instalment; *~s'gewys(e)*, in instalments.
paai'enet(werk), road network.
paai'er, (-s), appeaser, coaxer; *~ig, (-e)*, placatory; *~y*, appeasement, placation.
paai'middel, sop.
paal, (pale), pole, post, stake, mast; spile, pile (in mines); picket; prop; pale; pillar (of gate); *GE= KLOOFDE pale*, split poles; *die ~ nie HAAL nie*, be unable to attain the goal; *die ~ HAAL*, make the grade; get there; *aan iets ~ en PERK stel*, set bounds to something; *so STYF soos 'n ~*, as stiff as a poker; *soos 'n ~ bo WATER staan*, be as plain as a pikestaff; *~bewoner*, lake-dweller; *~brug*, pile-bridge; *~dorp*, lake-settlement; *~fundering*, pile-work foundation; *~heining, paling*; *~huis*, pile-house; *~sitter*, pole-sitter; *~skerm*, palisade, paling; *~spring*, (s) pole-vault, pole-jump; (w) (ge-), do the pole-vault; *~springer*, pole-vaulter; *~sprong*, pole-vault; *~tjie, (s)*, small pole; stump, wicket (cricket); *'n ~ vat*, take a wicket; *die ~s omboul*, bowl the wickets; *~tjiesheining*, split-pole fence; *~tjiewagter*, wicket-keeper; *~vas, (-te)*, immovable, firm; *~werk*, palisade; spiling; pile-work; *~woning*, pile-dwelling; lake-dwelling; *~woningtydperk*, lacustrine age; *~wurm*, ship-worm *(Toledo)*, teredo, pile-worm.
paap, (pape), papist; *~s, (-e)*, papal; popish; *~s'ge= sind, (-e)*, papist, popish; *~s'gesinde, (-s)*, papist.
paar, (s) (pare), couple, pair; a few; dyad; duet; double; *'n ~ DAE*, a few days; *die GELUKKIGE ~*, the happy couple; *by PARE*, in pairs; *die SKOENE is nie 'n ~ nie*, the shoes do not match; *by die ~ VERKOOP*, sell in pairs; *VIER pare spelers*, four couples of players; *VIER ~ skoene*, four pairs of shoes; (w) (ge-), pair, mate, copulate; pair off; cast (hawks); geminate; conjugate; *die diere BEGIN te ~*, the animals begin to mate; *die DANSERS moet nou ~*, the dancers must now form couples; *moed ~ aan DEUG*, combine courage with virtue; *gepaard GAAN met*, be coupled with, go hand in hand with; (b) even; *~ of onpaar*, odd or even.
Paarl, Paarl; *in die ~ woon*, live at Paarl; *~iet', (-e)*, Paarlite, inhabitant of Paarl; *~s, (-e)*, of Paarl, Paarl; *~se druiwe*, Paarl grapes.
paar: *~s'gewys(e)*, in pairs; binate; *~tjie, (-s)*, couple (of lovers); pair; *~tyd*, mating-season, rutting-season.
Paas: *~aand*, Easter Eve; *~blom*, moonwort, primrose; *~bolletjie*, hot cross bun; *~boodskap*, Easter message; *~brood*, Easter loaf; Passover cake; azyme; *~dag*, Easter Day; *~eier*, Easter egg; *~fees*, Easter; Passover; *~kers*, paschal candle; *~lam*, paschal lamb, Passover lamb; *~lelie*, daffodil; *~maal*, paschal repast; *~maandag*, Easter (Black) Monday; *~naweek*, Easter weekend; *~preek*, Easter sermon; *~skou*, Easter show; *~sondag*, Easter Sunday; *~tentoonstelling*, Easter show; *~tyd*, Easter time, Eastertide; paschal time; *~vakansie*, Easter holidays; *~week*, Easter week; Passover.
pad, (paaie), path, road, way, drive; *jou op ~ BE=* *GEWE*, take the road; *BESTRATE ~*, paved road; *uit iem. se ~ BLY*, avoid someone; steer clear of someone; *die BREË ~*, the primrose path; *die ~ van DEUG bewandel*, be on the straight and narrow path; *uit jou ~ GAAN*, go out of your way; *op die GLADDE ~ wees*, be on the road to ruin; *die GROOT ~*, the main road; *HARDE ~ kry*, be given hard labour; *die ~ na die HEL is met mooi planne geplavei*, the road to hell is paved with good intentions; *die HELE ~ is syne*, he is reeling; *KROM paaie loop*, be devious; *LANGS die ~*, next to (along) the road; on the way; *'n ~ LOOP deur*, run rings round, overcome easily; *met iem. 'n paadjie LOOP*, have a set-to with someone; *~ MAAK vir*, clear the way for; *OORDEKTE ~*, covered way; *OP ~*, on the way; on the road; *die OU paaie verlaat*, foresake the old ways; *PRIVAAT ~*, private road; *die REGTE ~ gaan (hou)*, go straight; be on the right road; *iem. op die REGTE ~ bring*, help someone to go straight; *alle paaie gaan na ROME*, all roads lead to Rome; *so oud soos die ~ na ROME*, as old as the hills; *sy ~ gaan op ROSE*, it is roses, roses all the way; *die SMAL ~ bewandel*, follow the straight (and narrow) path; *in die ~ STAAN*, hinder, obstruct; *iem. in die ~ STEEK*, give somebody the sack; send someone packing; *in die ~ VAL*, take to the road, begin a journey; *die VERKEERDE ~ gaan*, go astray; *na die ~ VRA*, ask the way; *die ~ WYS*, lead the way; *~aanleg*, *~bou*, road-construction; road-building; road engineering; *~aansluiting*, road-junction; *~bouer*, road-builder; road-maker, road engineer; *~bou= kun'dige*, road engineer; *~breker*, road-breaker; *~buffel*, (road) hog.
pad'da, (-s), frog, toad; *'n ~ in die KEEL hê*, have a frog in the throat; *so waar as ~ MANEL dra*, as true as faith; honour bright; *soos 'n OPGEBLAAS= DE ~ lyk*, be in a huff; angry; *so SKURF soos 'n ~*, as horny as a toad; *van 'n ~ VERE probeer pluk*, make a silk purse out of a sow's ear; *~agtig, (-e)*, ranine; *~eiers*, frog-spawn; sago pudding; *~klou*, *Teucrium africanum*; *~man*, frogman; *~olimpia= de*, frog olympiad; *~skuim*, toadspit; *~slagter*, blunt knife; *~slyk*, *~slym*, fine filaments of fresh-water algae *(Spirogyra)*; duckweed; *~springkom= petisie*, frog-jumping competition; *~steen*, toad-stone; *~stoel*, toadstool (poisonous); mushroom (edible); agaric; fungus; paddock-stool; *soos ~ stoele verrys*, spring up like mushrooms; *~stoel= agtig, (-e)*, fungous; *~vanger*, hammerhead (bird); *~vis*, tadpole; newt.
pad: *~dekmateriaal*, road-surfacing; *~diens*, road-service; *~eg*, scarifier; *~gee, (-ge-)*, go out of the way, give way, make room; cave in, collapse; *~ge= bruiker*, road-user; *~geld*, conduct-money; *~gids*, road-book; *~gogga*, road louse; *~gruis*, road-metal; *~helling*, gradient of road; *~hoof*, road-head; *~houvermoë*, road-holding ability; *~inge= nieur*, road engineer; *~ingenieurswese*, road engineering; road-building; *~instink*, road-sense; *~kaart*, road map; *~knoop*, road-junction; *~kode*, traffic code; *~kos*, provisions (food) for a journey; prog; *~krater*, road-crater.
pad'langs, (fig.), straight; categorical; *~ LOOP*, be straightforward, act in an honest way; *~ PRAAT*, speak out (straight), be outspoken; *iem. ~ die WAARHEID vertel*, tell someone the plain truth.
pad'loper, (-s), vagabond, tramp; tortoise; *~tjie, (-s)*, (kind of tufted) bird.
pad: *~maker, (-s)*, road-worker; road-builder; road-maker; *~makery*, road-construction; *~mik*, bifurcation; *~motordiens*, road-motor service; *~net*, road system; *~ogie*, cat's eye; *~onderhoud*, road-maintenance; *~ongeluk*, road accident; *~ploeg*, road-plough; *~rand*, (road) shoulder; *~reg*, right of way; *~roller*, road-roller; *~rower*, knight of the road; *~serwituut*, right of way; *~sin*, road-sense; *~(skild)wag*, road-sentry; *~skouer*, (road) shoulder; *~skraper*, road-grader; *~teken*, road sign, traffic sign; *~vaar'dig, (-e)*, ready for the road;

~**vark**, road hog; ~**vas, (-te)**, holding the road (motor); ~**veiligheid**, road safety; ~**verharding**, road-metal; ~**verkeer**, road-traffic; ~**verkeersteken**, road traffic sign; ~**verkenning**, road-reconnaissance; ~**verlegging**, road-deviation; ~**vernuf**, road-sense; ~**verslag**, road-report; ~**versperring**, road-barrier; ~**verstand**, road-sense; ~**vervoer**, road-transport.
pad'vinder, (-s), pathfinder; Boy Scout; ~**beweging**, Boy-Scout Movement; ~**y**, scouting, guiding.
pad'vindster, (-s), Girl Guide.
pad'vurk, fork, bifurcation.
padwaar'dig, (-e), roadworthy; ~**heid**, roadworthiness.
pad: ~**wals**, road-roller; ~**wedloop**, road race; ~**werker, (-s)**, road-worker; ~**wyser**, handpost, signpost, road-indicator, directing-post, guide(-post).
paf! bang! ~**ferd, (-s)**, weak exploder; ~**gat**, pophole; ~**granaat**, weak-exploding grenade; ~**lading**, weak charge.
pag, (s) (-te), lease, quitrent; *in* ~ *GEE*, let out, hire out.
pagai', (s) (-e), paddle; (w) **(ge-)**, paddle; ~**er, (-s)**, paddler.
paganis', (-te), pagan; ~**me**, paganism; ~**ties, (-e)**, pagan(ish).
pag: ~**boer**, tenant farmer; ~**brief**, (deed of) lease; ~**eiendom**, quitrent property; ~**geld**, farm rent, rental; ~**ger, (-s)**, palisade, fence; ~**goed**, leasehold; ~**grond, (-e)**, leaseholding.
pa'gina, (-s), page; ~**proef**, page proof.
pagineer', (ge-), page, paginate, leaf.
pagine'ring, paging, pagination.
pag'land, leased land, leaseholding.
pago'de, (-s), pagoda.
pag: ~**reg**, right of lease (quitrent); ~**som**, rental; ~**stelsel**, leasehold system, land tenure, quitrent; ~**ter, (-s)**, tenant farmer, leaseholder, farmer, crofter; ~**tyd**, period of lease; ~**vry, (-e)**, rent-free.
pa'-hulle, father and the rest (cum suis); dad and co(mpany).
pais, (vero.), peace; *in* ~ *en vree*, in peace.
paja'ma, (-s), pyjamas; ~**pak**, pyjamas.
pak, (s) (-ke), suit (of clothes); costume; pack, packet, parcel, bundle; load, burden; thrashing, beating, hiding, caning, licking; *'n* ~ *op sy tyd is soos BROOD en konfyt*, timely chastisement is (of) the essence of wisdom; *in* ~ *ke GEBIND*, tied up into bundles; *dis 'n* ~ *van my HART af*, that is a load off one's shoulders; *'n* ~ *KLERE*, a suit of clothes; *'n* ~ *KRY*, get a thrashing (spanking); *met* ~ *en SAK*, with bag and baggage; *by die* ~ *ke gaan SIT*, give up in despair; *moenie by die* ~ *ke gaan SIT nie*, don't give up; don't throw in the towel; *'n* ~ *slae is jou naam*, you're in for a hiding; *'n* ~ *SLAE*, a thrashing; (w) **(ge-)**, pack up; seize, grasp; grab; cuddle; grip; thrill, catch on; get at; *'n INBREKER* ~, catch a burglar; *sy KOFFER* ~, pack one's trunk; *die SKULD op iem.* ~, lay the blame on someone.
paka'ters, capers; ~ *maak*, cut capers.
pak: ~**bedding**, gasket seat; ~**dier**, pack-animal; ~**doek**, packing-sheet; ~**draer, (-s)**, porter, carrier; ~**els**, packing-awl; ~**esel**, pack-mule, sumpter-mule; drudge; ~**garing**, packing-thread, twine; ~**goed**, packing-material; ~**hout**, dunnage; ~**huis**, warehouse; magazine; bond; packinghouse; garner, entrepôt; promptuary; ~**huisbewaring**, warehousing; ~**huisgeld**, storage; ~**huisruimte**, storage capacity; storage area.
Pa'kistan, Pakistan; ~**i, (-'s)**, Pakistani.
pakkaas', the whole caboodle; riff-raff.
pak: ~**kamer**, store-room; ~**kas**, packing-case; ~**ka'sie, (-s)**, package, luggage; riff-raff; ~**kelder**, packing-cellar; ~**kend, (-e)**, gripping, stirring, thrilling; striking; catchy (tune); ~**ker, (-s)**, packer; ~**kery, (-e)**, packing; packing-yard.
pakket', (-e), parcel, packet; package; *ons bied u 'n volle* ~ *aan*, we offer a complete package; *ons* ~ *sluit salaris, behuising en versekering in*, our package includes salary, housing and insurance; ~**-ak=**

koord, package deal; ~**boot**, packet(-boat); ~**pos**, parcel post; ~**tekantoor**, parcels office; ~**transaksie**, package deal.
pak: ~**kie, (-s)**, packet; small parcel; *ELKEEN moet sy eie* ~ *kie dra*, each must bear his own burden; ~**kiesdraer**, porter; ~**kieskamer**, ~**kieskantoor**, parcel office; ~**king**, packing, gasket; ~**kingbusring**, gland-sleeve; ~**kingplaat**, cylinder-head gasket; ~**kingring**, packing-washer; ~**kis**, packing-case; ~**linne**, packing-cloth, canvas; ~**loon**, package-money; storage fees; ~**mandjie**, hamper; ~**muil**, pack-mule; ~**naald**, packing-needle; corking-pin; ~**os**, pack-ox; ~**papier**, packing-paper, wrapping-pa=per, brown paper; cap; ~**perd**, packhorse, bat-horse, led-horse, sumpter-horse; ~**plaat**, gasket; ~**plek**, storage; storage room (space); ~**ring**, gasket-ring; ~**ruimte**, storage room; storage area; ~**saal**, pack-saddle; ~**sak**, kitbag; ~**sel**, packing; ~**skip**, hulk; ~**skuur**, packstore; warehouse; ~**solder**, warehouse-loft; ~**stuk**, gasket.
pakt, (-e), pact, agreement.
pak: ~**toestel**, pack-set; ~**tou**, packing-twine.
pakt'regering, pact government.
pak'ys, pack-ice.
pal¹, (s) (-le), click; catch, pawl, ratchet(-wheel); stay-peg, pin-peg.
pal², (bw) firm, immovable; continuous; ~ *STAAN*, stand firm; ~ *TUIS bly*, be a stay-at-home.
paladyn', (-e), paladin.
palankyn', (-s), palanquin.
pal'as, ratchet-pawl spindle.
palataal', (..tale), palatal; *..tale klank*, palatal sound.
palatalisa'sie, palatalization.
palataliseer', (ge-), palatalize.
palatalise'ring, palatalization.
palatografie', palatography.
palatogram', (-me), palatogram.
paleis', (-e), palace; ~**agtig, (-e)**, palatial; ~**rewolusie**, palace revolution (upheaval); internal change of power.
paleograaf', (..grawe), palaeographer.
paleografie', palaeography; ..gra'fies, (-e), palaeographical(ly).
paleoliet', palaeolith; *..li'ties*, palaeolithic.
paleologie', palaeology.
paleontologie', palaeontology; *..lo'gies, (-e)*, palaeontologic(al).
paleontoloog, (..loë), palaeontologist.
Palcoso'ies, (-e), Palaeozoic.
Palesti'na, Palestine.
Palestyns', (-e), Palestinian; ~ *e Bevrydingsorganisasie* **(PBO)**, Palestinian Liberation Organization (PLO).
palet', (-te), palette; ~**mes**, palette-knife, amasette.
palfrenier', (-s), groom.
palimpses', (tc), palimpsest.
palindroom', palindrome.
pa'ling, (-s), eel; *so glad soos 'n* ~, as slippery as an eel; ~**agtig, (-e)**, eel-like.
palingene'se, palingenesis.
pa'ling: ~**fuik**, eel-trap; ~**pastei**, eel-pie; ~**steker, (-s)**, eel-catcher; ~**vel**, eelskin; ~**vormig, (-e)**, eel-shaped.
pa'linkie, (-s), grig, small eel.
palino'de, palinode.
palissa'de, (-s), palisade, stockade.
palissadeer', (ge-), palisade.
palissade'ring, palisading, palisades.
palissan'derhout, black boxwood; rosewood.
paljas'¹, charm; spell; philtre; ~ *dra*, practise magic; (w) **(ge-)**, bewitch, cast a spell on.
paljas'², (-se), clown, buffoon; ~**agtig, (-e)**, clownish.
palla'dium, (-s, ..dia), palladium.
palm, (-s), palm (of hand); palm(-tree); *die* ~ *wegdra*, gain the victory, bear the palm; ~**agtig, (-e)**, palmaceous, palmy; ~**blaar**, palm-leaf; ~**boom**, palm(-tree); ~**bos**, palm-grove; ~**botter**, palmbutter; ~**draend, (-e)**, palmiferous; ~**hout**, boxwood; ~**huis**, palm-house.
palmiet', (-e), bulrush *(Prionum serratum)*; ~**bos**,

clump of (bul)rushes; ~**manna**, bulrush-millet; ~**sop**, unfermented (young) wine; ~**vlei**, valley overgrown with bulrushes.
palmitien', palmiti'ne, palmitine.
palm'olie, palm-oil; palm-grease, tip (to porter).
Palm'sondag, Palm Sunday.
palm'sop, unfermented wine.
palm: ~**stander**, palm-stand, ~**struik**, box-shrub; ~**suiker**, jaggery; ~**tak**, palm-branch; ~**tuin**, palm garden; ~**wyn**, palm-wine.
Palomi'no, (-'s), Palomino (horse).
palpa'sie, (-s), palpation.
palpeer', (ge-), palpate.
palpita'sie, palpitation.
palpiteer', (ge-), palpitate.
pal: ~**rand**, capstan-rim; ~**rat**, click-wheel; ratchet-wheel; ~**stang**, catch-rod; ~**trekker**, trigger (for ratchet).
Palts, Palatinate; ~**graaf**, Count Palatine; ~**graafskap**, palatinate; ~**gravin**, Countess Palatine.
pal'werk, ratch(et).
pamflet', (-te), pamphlet; bulletin; ~**kassie**, box-file; ~**skrywer**, (-s), ~**tis'**, (-te), pamphleteer.
pam'pa, (-s), pampa.
pam'pasgras, pampas-grass.
pampelmoes', (-e), shaddock; pampelmouse; bluefish, butter-bream.
pampelmoe'sie, (-s), gooseberry.
pamperlang', (ge-) flatter, cajole, adulate, coax, fawn.
pampoen', (-e), pumpkin; blockhead, bumpkin; *vir kou(e)* ~ *skrik*, take fright easily; ~**blaar**, pumpkin leaf; ~**bril**: *'n* ~ *bril ophê*, not to see what's in front of your nose; be wearing blinkers; ~**koekie**, pumpkin fritter; ~**kop**, blockhead, dunce, fathead; ~**land**, pumpkin field; ~**moes**, breaded pumpkin; pumpkin mash; ~**oes**, pumpkin crop; *na die* ~ *oes betaal*, pay later; ~**pit**, pumpkin pip; ~**rank**, pumpkin tendril; ~**skil**, pumpkin skin; ~**spook**, spookish head made of a hollowed pumpkin; *vir* ~ *spoke bang word*, take fright easily; ~**stoel**, pumpkin plant (stool).
pampoen'tjies, mumps.
pan, (-ne), pan; tile; priming-pan; tray; small lake; *in die* ~ *HAK*, cut to pieces, butcher to the last man; *'n VEEG uit die* ~ *kry*, be reprimanded.
panache', panache.
Pan'-Afrikaans, Pan-African.
Pan'-Afrikanisme, Pan-Africanism.
pa'namahoed, Panama hat.
Pa'namakanaal, Panama Canal.
Panamees', (..mese), Panamanian.
Pan'-Amerikaans, Pan-American.
Pan'-Amerikanisme, Pan-Americanism.
panasee', (-s), panacea, cure-all, catholicon.
pan: ~**bakker**, tile-maker; ~**bakkersoond**, tile-kiln; ~**bakkery**, tile-works; ~**boor**, trepan; ~**breker**, subsoiler, subplough.
pan'chromaties, (-e), panchromatic.
pand, (-e), pledge, pawn; forfeit; security; flap; *in* ~ *GEE*, leave as security; *die* ~ *van ons liefde*, the child (pledge) of our love; *'n* ~ *LOS*, redeem a pledge; *'n* ~ *VERBEUR*, forfeit a pledge.
pan'dak, tiled roof; ~**huis**, house with a tiled roof.
pand: ~**akte**, deed of pledge; ~**bewys**, pawn-ticket; ~**brief**, mortgage bond; contract of pledge.
pandek', (-te), pandect.
pan: ~**dekker**, tiler; ~**deksel**, apron (plumbing).
pandemie', pandemic; ..de'mies, (-e), pandemic.
pandemo'nium, pandemonium.
pand: ~**geër**, (-s), pawner; pledger; ~**genot**, use of the thing pledged, antichresis.
pand'houer, (-s), pawnbroker, pledgee, pawnee; ~**y**, pawnbroking.
pand'huishouer, pawnbroker.
Pand'jab, Punjab.
pand'jies: ~**baas**, pawnbroker, uncle; ~**houer**, pawnbroker; ~**huis**, pawnshop.
pand'nemer, (-s), pawnee.
pandoer', (-e, -s), pawnour (originally (1741) rapacious and brutal soldier in the Balkans), armed guard.

pandoor', pandora, pandore.
Pando'ra, Pandora; ~ *se doos*, Pandora's box.
pand: ~**reg**, lien, right of pledge; ~**speel**, (-ge-), play forfeits; ~**speletjie**, (game of) forfeits.
paneel', (**panele**), panel; ~**bord**, dashboard; ~**deur**, panelled door; ~**gewelf**, panel-vault; ~**inspeksie**, corporate inspection (school); ~**kassie**, cubbyhole; glove compartment; ~**oorlosie**, dashboard clock; ~**saag**, panel-saw; ~**tjie**, (-s), easel-piece; panel-picture; ~**wa**, panel-van; ~**werk**, panelling, wainscoting.
paneer', (ge-), coat with breadcrumbs, crumb; ~**meel**, breadcrumbs (used in cooking).
pan'ga¹, (-s), pangar *(Pargrus laniarius)*.
pan'ga², (-s), panga; ~**moordenaar**, panga-killer (-murderer).
Pan'-Germanisme, Pan-Germanism.
pan'geweer, flint-lock gun.
paniek', panic, scare, stampede; ~**bevange**, panic-stricken; ~**erig**, (-e), panic-stricken, panicky; ~**erigheid**, state of being easily panic-stricken, nervousness.
pa'nies, (-e): ~ *e angs*, panic fear; great (uncontrollable) fear; *met* ~ *e skrik vervul*, throw into a panic.
pan: ~**klaar**, ready for the pan; ~**kop**, (-pe), bald head.
pan'kreas, pancreas; sweetbread; ~**operasie**, pancreas operation.
pankrea'ties, (-e), pancreatic.
pan'kruit, priming.
pan'lekker, (-s), sponger.
pan'na, panna.
pan'nebakker, tile-maker.
pan'nekoek, pancake; *so plat soos 'n* ~, as flat as a pancake; ~**weer**, rainy weather.
pan'netjie, (-s), pannikin, small pan; lakelet.
panop'tikum, (-s), panopticon.
panora'ma, (-s), panorama.
panora'mies, (-e), panoramic.
Pan'-Russies, Pan-Russian.
Pan'-Slavisme, Pan-Slavism.
pan'spoelings, pannings.
pant, (-e), tail (of a coat); gore, width (of a dress); ~**baadjie**, tailcoat, morning coat.
panteïs', (-te), pantheist; ~**me**, pantheism; ~**ties**, (-e), pantheistic(al).
pan'ter, (-s), panther; ~**kat**, ocelot; ~**wyfie**, pantheress.
Pan'theon, (-s), Pantheon.
pantisokrasie', pantisocracy.
pantof'fel, (-s), slipper; *onder die* ~ *staan*, be henpecked; be under petticoat government; ~**blom**, calceolaria; ~**diertjie**, slipper animalcule; ~**held**, henpecked husband; ~**plant**, slipper plant; ~**regering**, petticoat government; *onder die* ~*regering staan*, be henpecked; be under petticoat government; ~**vormig**, (-e), calceolate.
pantograaf', (..grawe), pantograph.
pantomi'me, (-s), pantomime, dumb show.
pantomimiek', pantomimicry.
pantomi'mies, (-e), pantomimic.
pantomimis', (-te), pantomimist.
pant'sak, pocket in tail of coat.
pant'ser, (s) mail; (-s), armour-plating; plate; armature; coat of mail; cuirass; carapace (zool.); (w) (ge-), armour; *jou TEEN iets* ~, steel oneself against something; *die gepantserde VUIS*, the mailed fist; ~**affuit**, armoured mounting; ~**afweer**, anti-tank protection; ~**afweermyn**, anti-tank mine; ~**bedekking**, plating; ~**dek**, armoured deck; ~**dier**, armadillo; ~**fort**, armoured fort; ~**glas**, armoured glass; ~**handskoen**, gauntlet; ~**hemp**, mail-shirt; lorica; ~**ing**, armouring; ~**kabel**, armoured cable; ~**klere**, armour; ~**koeël**, armour-piercing bullet; ~**korps**, armoured corps; ~**motor**, pantzer, armoured car; ~**plaat**, armour-plate; ~**skip**, ironclad; ~**soldaat**, trooper; ~**toring**, armoured turret; ~**trein**, armoured train; ~**vuis**, mailed fist; ~**wa**, armoured car.
pan'was, (-se), panning (mine).
pap¹, (s) porridge; poultice (on wound); cataplasm; gruel; paste; mush; pulp; mash; *as die* ~ *te dik is*,

BRAND *dit aan*, familiarity breeds contempt; *praat of jy warm ~ in jou MOND het*, speak as if one had a marble in one's mouth; *as dit ~ REËN, moet jy skep*, one must strike while the iron is hot; *~ word altyd WARMER gekook as wat dit geëet word*, things are always exaggerated; people always lay it on thick; (w) **(ge-)**, poultice; paste (paper).

pap², (b, bw), **(-per, -ste)**, soft, feeble, flabby; flaccid, weak; flat, deflated; *'n ~ BAND*, a deflated (flat) tyre; *'n ~ KÊREL*, a milksop; a softy; *~ SLAAN*, knock into a cocked hat; *~ VOEL*, feel worn out; feel limp.

papa', (-'s), papa.
papa'ja, (-s), papaw, pawpaw.
papa'tjie, daddy dear.
papat'so, (-'s), papatso.
papa'wer, (-s), poppy; red weed; *Yslandse ~* , Iceland poppy; *~ agtig*, (-e), papaverous; *~ bol*, poppyhead; *~ olie*, poppy-oil; *~ saad*, poppy-seed; mawseed; *~ suur*, meconic acid.
pap'bord, porridge plate.
pap'broek, milksop, coward, poltroon, funk, mollycoddle, defeatist, cissy, softy.
papbroe'kerig, (-e), cowardly, funky, milksoppy; spineless; poor-spirited, lily-livered; *~ heid*, cowardice, pusillanimity, poltroonery, spinelessness.
papegaai', (-e), parrot, polly; poll; popinjay; *soos 'n ~*, parrot-like; *~ agtig*, (-e), parrot-like; psittaceous, psittacine; *~ bek*, pipe-wrench, hawk-bill (wrench); *~ duif*, green pigeon; *~ duiker*, auk; puffin; sea-parrot; *~ lys*, beak-moulding; *~ nes*, parrot nest; parrot cage; *~ neus*, crooked nose; *~ siekte*, psittacosis; *~ stok*, outrigger; *~ vis*, parrot-fish, scarus.
papelel'lekoors, fit of the blues; sham fever; trembling fit; malingering; *~ kry*, sham Abraham; swing the lead.
papelel'lie, sticky mass.
paperas'se, papers, waste papers, bumf.
pa'pery, popery.
pap'heid, weakness, feebleness.
pa'pie, (-s), chrysalis, cocoon, nymph; pupa; *ek lag my 'n ~*, I can laugh my head off; *~ dop*, puparium.
papier', (-e), paper; *op ~ BRING*, put on paper; *~ is GEDULDIG*, pens may blot but they cannot blush; *GELDWAARDIGE ~ e*, valuable securities; *GOEIE ~ e hê*, have good testimonials (certificates); *OP ~*, on paper; *~ afval*, waste paper; *~ agtig*, (-e), papery; papyracious; *~ band*, paper cover; paperback; *~ binder*, paper-fastener; *~ blom*, artificial flower; statice; paper-flower; *~ boerdery*, farming on paper; *~ boom*, paper-tree; *~ boordjie*, paper collar; *~ bord*, paper plate; *~ deeg*, papier mâché; *~ doekie*, tissue; *~ drukker*, paper-weight; *~ fabriek*, paper-mill; *~ fabrikant*, paper manufacturer; *~ formaat*, crown (size of paper); *~ geld*, paper money; notes; assignat; *~ gewig*, paper-weight; *~ goud*, paper gold; *~ haak*, paper-hook; file; *~ handel*, paper trade; stationery; *~ huls*, paper-case; *~ kind*, book; piece of writing; *~ klem*, paper-fastener; *~ knip*, paperclip; file; *~ knyper*, paper-clip, paper-fastener; *~ lêer*, (paper-) file; *~ lint*, streamer; *~ mandjie*, waste-paper basket; *~ masjien*, guillotine; *~ merk*, watermark; *~ mes*, paper-knife; paper-cutter; cutter; *~ meul(e)*, paper-mill; *~ oorlog*, paper warfare; *~ opteller*, kennel-raker; *~ pap*, papier mâché, paper pulp; *~ plant*, paper plant; *~ prop(pie)*, paper pellet; *~ riet*, papyrus; *~ rolletjie*, fidibus; *~ sakkie*, paper-bag; *~ servet*, paper serviette; *~ skêr*, paper-cutter; *~ strook*, fillet of paper; *~ tjie*, (-s), bit (scrap) of paper; *~ wol*, paper shavings (wool).
pa'pies, the botts (horse-sickness).
pa'piestadium, pupal stage.
pa'pievlieg, bot-fly.
papil', (-le), papilla.
papiljot', (-te), curling-paper.
papillêr', (-e), papillary.
papil'vormig, (-e), papillate.
Papiniaan'se pot, Papin's digester.

papi'rus, (-se, ..piri), papyrus; *~ plant*, papyrus (plant).
papis', (-te), papist; *~ me*, papism; *~ tery*, papistry; *~ ties*, (-e), papist, popish.
pap: *~ klaas* (..klase), milksop, nincompoop; *~ kuil*, bulrush *(Typha capensis)*; *~ kwas*, paste-brush.
pap'lepel, table-spoon, porridge-spoon; *iem. met die ~ INGEE*, spoon-feed someone; *met die ~ VOER*, spoon-feed someone.
pap: *~ maak*, (-ge-), pulp; soften; *~ meul(e)*, pulpmill; *~ nat*, dripping wet, soppy, sopping.
Papoe'a, (-s), Papuan.
pap'pa, (-s), papa.
pap'patjie, (-s), daddy dear.
pappera'sie, slush.
pap'perig, (-e), pappy, soft, pulpy, mashy, mushy, soggy, pasty, pultaceous, doughy, flabby; *~ heid*, flabbiness, flaccidity.
pappery', slush, mash.
pap'pie, (-s), daddy, dad, da, poppa, pop.
pap'pot, porridge-pot; *by die ~ BLY*, stay at home; be a homebird; *algar moenie uit een ~ wil EET nie*, the same families should not always be intermarrying.
pa'prika, Hungarian red pepper, paprika.
paps, da, dad, pop.
pap: *~ saf*, *~ sag*, (-te), very soft, mushy; *~ sak*, spineless person, softy; *~ slaan*, (-ge-), crush; lambaste, pound, beat to a pulp.
paraaf', (parawe), paraph, initials.
paraat', (parate), ready, prepared; *parate EKSEKU= SIE*, summary execution; *parate KENNIS*, ready knowledge; *~ heid*, readiness, preparedness.
pa'rabasis, parabasis.
para'bel, (-s), parable.
parabo'lies, (-e), parabolic(al).
parabool', (..bole), parabola, parobole.
parachronis'me, parachronism.
para'de, (-s), review, parade; *op ~*, on parade; *~ bed*, state bed.
paradeer', (ge-), parade, show off.
para'de: *~ pas*, parade-step, goose-step; *~ perd*, state horse; *~ plek*, review-ground; *~ terrein*, paradeground; *~ vry*, (-e), off parade.
paradig'ma, (-s), paradigm, example.
paradigma'ties, (-e), paradigmatic.
paradoks', (-e), paradox; *~ aal'*, (..sale), paradoxical.
parados', parados.
paradys', (-e), paradise; *~ agtig*, (-e), heavenly; paradisical, paradisiaс(al), paradisian, *~ appel*, paradise apple; love-apple; *~ blom*, strelitzia; *~ geskie= denis*, history of man's fall; *~ kleed*, nature's garb, buff; *~ voël*, bird of paradise.
parafeer', (ge-), initial, sign with initials.
parafe'ring, initialling.
paraferna'lia, paraphernalia.
paraffien', paraffin oil; kerosene; *~ blik*, paraffin tin; *~ gaas*, paraffin gauze; *~ koelkas*, oil refrigerator; *~ lamp*, paraffin lamp; *~ olie*, paraffin oil; *~ stoof*, paraffin stove, paraffin heater; *~ was*, paraffin wax.
parafi'se, (-s), paraphysis.
parafra'se, (-s), paraphrase.
parafraseer', (ge-), paraphrase.
paragene'se, paragenesis.
paragesteen'te, pararock.
parago'ge, paragoge (addition of letter or syllable to a word); *..go'gies*, (-e), paragogic.
paragon', (-s), paragon.
paragraaf', (..grawe), paragraph; clause; *~ teken*, section mark.
paragrafeer', (ge-), divide into paragraphs, paragraph.
paragrafe'ring, paragraphing.
Paraguaan', (..guane), Paraguayan; *~ s'*, (-e), Paraguayan.
Parakleet', (..klete), Paraclete, the Holy Spirit.
pa'ralans, paralance.
paraldehi'de, paraldehied', paraldehyde.
parali'se, paralysis.
parali'ties, (-e), paralytic.

parallaks', (-e), parallax.
parallak'ties, (-e), parallactic.
parallel', (-le), parallel; collateral; analogue; line (parallel) of latitude; ~**epi'pedum**, (-s), parallelepiped; ~**is'me**, parallelism; ~**klas**, parallel class; ~**mediumskool**, parallel medium school; ~**ogram**, (-me), parallelogram; ~**skakelaar**, multiple (parallel) switch; ~**skool**, parallel school; ~**vyl**, blunt-file.
parame'dies, (-e), paramedical; ~*e behandeling*, paramedical treatment.
parame'dikus, (-se, ..dici), paramedic.
pa'rameter, parame'ter, parameter.
paramnesie', paramnesia.
pa'raneut, Brazil nut, Para nut.
paranimf', (-e), paranymph, assistant.
paranoi'a, paranoia.
parano'ies, (-e), paranoiac.
parano'ïkus, (-se, ..ici), paranoiac.
parapet', (-s), parapet.
parapleeg', (..pleë), paraplegic.
paraplegie', paraplegia.
paraplek'ties, (-e), paraplegic, paraplectic.
paraplu', (-'s), umbrella.
parapsigologie', parapsychology.
parapsigoloog', (..loë), parapsychologist.
parasiet', (-e), parasite; ~**agtig**, (-e), parasitic(al); ~**besmetting**, infestation; ~**gif**, parasiticide; ~**plant**, parasite (plant); ~**wurm**, parasite (worm).
parasinte'se, parasynthesis.
parasiteer', (ge-), play the parasite, sponge upon someone.
parasitêr', parasi'ties, (-e), parasitic(al).
parasitis'me, parasitism.
parasitologie', parasitology; ..**lo'gies**, (-e), parasitological.
parasjutis', (-te), parachutist.
parasjuut', (..sjute), parachute; ~**kommando**, parachute commando; ~**opleiding**, parachute training.
parasol', (-s), sunshade; parasol (monoplane).
paratak'se, paratak'sis, parataxis.
parati'fus, paratyphoid.
paravaan', (..vane), paravane.
pardoems'!, bang! flop! slap-bang! plop!
pardoen', (-e), backstays (ship).
pardon', (s) pardon; *geen ~ gee nie*, show no mercy; (tw) so sorry! excuse me! ~**neer'**, (ge-), pardon.
pareer', (ge-), parry, ward off; make a show, show off; counter; limp, walk with a limp.
parenchiem', parenchyma.
parenchima'ties, (-e), parenchymatic, parenchymal.
parente'se, (-s), parenthesis.
parente'ties, (-e), parenthetic(al).
pare'se, paresis.
parfait', parfait.
parfumeer', (ge-), perfume, scent.
parfumerie', (-ë), perfumery, scent.
parfumeur', (-s), perfumer.
parfuum', (-s), perfume, scent; ~**blom**, perfumed flower; sweet-smelling flower; ~**spuitjie**, scent-spray; ~**ware**, perfumery.
parhe'lium, parhelion.
pa'ri, par; *A ~*, at par; *BO ~*, above par, at a premium; *ONDER ~*, below par, at a discount; *TEEN ~*, at par.
pa'ria, (-s), pariah, outcast.
pariëtaal', (..tale), parietal.
pa'rikoers, par value.
pa'ring, mating, pairing, copulation, coition; ~**sdaad**, coitus; ~**svlug**, nuptial flight.
Parisien'ne, (-s), Parisienne.
parisilla'bies, (-e), parisyllabic.
pariteit', parity; ~**s'koers**, parity price, parrate (of exchange).
park, (-e), park, ground; ~**argitek**, landscape architect; ~**e en ontspanning**, parks and recreation.
parkeer', (ge-), park (vehicle); ~**beampte**; parking-attendant; ~**garage**, parking-garage; ~**geld**, parking-fee; ~**inham**, parking-bay; ~**ligte**, parking-lights; ~**meter**, parking-meter; ~**oortreding**, parking-offence; ~**plek**, parking-place; ~**regulasie**, parking-regulation; ~**ruimte**, parking-accommodation; parking-area; ~**streep**, parking line; ~**terrein**, parking-site, carpark; ~**wagter**, parking-attendant.
parke'ring, parking.
parket', (-te), parquet; *iem. in 'n moeilike ~ BRING*, put someone in an awkward hole (predicament); *in 'n moeilike (lastige) ~ WEES*, be on the horns of a dilemma; be in a quandary; ~**teer'**, (ge-), parquet; ~**vloer**, parquet floor; inlaid floor, parquetry.
parkiet', (-e), parakeet; ~**jie**, (-s), budgerigar, budgie.
park'opsigter, park-keeper.
parlement', (-e), parliament; ~**a'riër**, (-s), parliamentarian; ~**aris'me**, parliamentarism; ~**eer'**, (ge-), parley; ~**êr'**, (-e), parliamentary; ~**s'gebou**, ~**s'huis**, house(s) of parliament; ~**sitting**, session of parliament; ~**s'lid**, member of parliament; ~**s'verkiesing**, parliamentary election; ~**s'verslag**, Hansard.
parmant', (-e), impudent (cheeky) person, saucebox.
parman'tig, (-e), impudent, saucy, impertinent, pert, perky, cheeky, forward; aggressive; *ewe ~*, very cocky; ~**heid**, impudence, insolence, cheek, cheekiness; aplomb, face.
Parnas'sus, Parnassus; *die ~ bestyg*, aspire to Parnassus.
parodie', (-ë), parody, travesty, squib; ..**dieer'**, (ge-), parody, burlesque; ..**dis'**, parodist; ~**skrywer**, parodist.
parogiaal', (..giale), parochial.
parogiaan', (..giane), parishioner.
parogie', (-ë), parish; ~**kerk**, parish church.
paroksis'me, (-s), paroxism.
paroniem', (-e), paronym.
paroni'mies, (-e), paronymous.
paronoma'sia, paronomasia.
parool', (**parole**), parole, watchword; *op ~*, on parole.
pars, (ge-), press; ~**balie**, winepress.
par'sek, parsec.
par'sie, (bloody) diarrhoea.
parsieel', (**parsiële**), partial.
pars: ~**kuip**, winepress; ~**tyd**, vintage time; grape-harvesting; ~**yster**, sad-iron, flat-iron; press-iron.
part[1], (-e), part, portion, share; ~ *nòg DEEL hê aan*, have neither part nor lot in; *vir my ~ GAAN*, go instead of me; *vir MY ~*, as far as I am concerned.
part[2], (-e), trick; *my GEHEUE begin my ~ e speel*, my memory is playing me false; *iem. ~ e SPEEL*, play tricks on a person.
partenogene'se, parthenogenesis.
Parth, (-e), **Parther**, (-s), Parthian.
Par'thies, (-e), Parthian; ~*e pyl*, Parthian shot.
parti'kel, (-s), particle; ~**gewys(e)**, particulate.
partikularis', (-te), particularist; ~**eer'**, (ge-), particularize; ~**me**, sectionalism, particularism; ~**ties**, (-e), particularistic.
partikulier', (s), private person; (b) (-e), particular, private, special.
partisaan', (..sane), partisan (fighter).
parti'sie, (-s), partition.
partisipieel', (..piële), participial.
partisi'pium, (-s, ..pia), participle.
partitief', (..tiewe), partitive; ..*tiewe genitief*, partitive genitive.
partituur', (..ture), music score.
party', (s) (-e), party, faction, group; parcel (of diamonds); *'n ~ GEE*, give a party; ~ *KIES*, take sides; *vir iem. ~ KIES*, side with someone; espouse someone's cause; *die LYDENDE ~*, the loser; *van die omstandighede ~ TREK*, take advantage of the circumstances; *vir iem. ~ TREK*, favour someone; ~ *TREK uit*, be making something out of it; (b) some, a few; ~ *KERE*, sometimes; ~ *MENSE dink*, some people think; ~**aanhanger**, party man; ~**belang**, party interest; ~**benoeming**, party nomination; ~**dig**, (-e), partial, biased; ~**digheid**, partiality, prejudice, bias; partisanship; favour; predilection; ~**dissipline**, party discipline; ~**ganger**, (-s), partisan; ~**gees**, party spirit; ~**kas**, party funds; ~**keer**, sometimes; ~**kongres**, party congress; ~**kwessie**, party issue; ~**leier**, party leader; ~**leus(e)**, party cry (slogan); catchword; ~**loos**,

(..**lose**), non-party; ~**maal**, sometimes, occasionally; ~**man**, party man; factionist; ~**manifes**, party manifesto; ~**orgaan**, party organ; ~**organisasie**, party organization; ~**organiseerder**, party organizer; ~**pers**, party press; ~**politiek**, party politics; ~**program**, party platform (programme); ~**regering**, party government; ~**saak**, party matter; ~**skap**, partisanship; faction; ~**stemming**, party vote; *'n suiwere* ~ *stemming*, a vote strictly on party lines; ~**stryd**, party struggle; ~**sug**, party spirit; faction spirit; ~**sug'tig, (-e)**, factious, factionist; ~**sug'tigheid**, factiousness; ~**tak**, party branch; ~**tjie, (-s)**, small party; game (of chess); ~**tug**, party discipline; ~**verband**, party allegiance; ~**verkiesing**, party election.
parvenu', (-'s), upstart, new-rich, parvenu; ~**agtig, (-e)**, parvenu, shoddy.
Parys', (s) Paris (France); Parys (O.F.S.): (b) **(-e)**, Parisian..
parys'blou, Paris blue.
Pary'senaar, (-s), Parisian.
pas¹, (s) (-se), pass; permit; ticket; pace, step, gait; gap, neck, defile; amble, rack (horse); *die* ~ *AANGEE*, set the pace; *iem. die* ~ *AFSNY*, forestall someone; *die BLOU* ~ *gee (kry)*, be sent packing; ~ *DRA*, carry a pass; *IN die* ~, in step; *in die* ~ *LOOP*, keep in step; *uit die* ~ *RAAK*, fall out of step.
pas², (s), (correct) time, place; fit, fitting; *die GELD het nie mooi te* ~ *gekom*, the money came in very handy; *van* ~ *KOM*, come in the nick of time; *NOMMER* ~, a perfect fit; *te* ~ *en te ONPAS*, in season and out of season, (w) **(ge-)**, fit, fit on, try on (dress); be proper, behove, beseem, become; suit, be convenient; *die twee KLEURE* ~ *nie by mekaar nie*, the two colours do not match; *sal dit jou* ~ *as ek sewe-uur KOM?*, will it suit you if I come at seven o'clock?; *die PAK* ~ *my goed*, the suit fits me well; *iets wat 'n PREDIKANT nie* ~ *nie*, something which does not become a minister.
pas³, (bw) only, just; hardly, scarcely; *ek is nog maar* ~ *BY bl. 2*, I have only read as far as page 2; ~ *GELEDE*, just recently; ~ *was die seun weg OF sy pa sterf*, the son had hardly left when his father died; ~*-UITGETREDE PRESIDENT*, immediate past-president; ~ *VERLEDE maand*, only last month.
pas: ~**aangeër**, pace-maker; pace-setter; ~**bekeerde**, neophyte; ~**benoemde**, designated (person), elected (person).
pas'bout, fitted bolt.
Pa'se, Easter.
pasel'la, (-s), gift.
pas'foto, (-'s), pass(port) photograph.
Pas'ga, Passover.
pas'gang, amble; ~**er, (-s)**, ambling horse, ambler, pacer.
pas'gebore, new-born; ~**ne, (-s)**, new(-born) arrival.
pas'gelê, (..legde), new laid.
pasiënt', (-e), patient, case.
pasifika'sie, pacification.
pasifis', (-te), pacifist; ~**eer', (ge-)**, pacify; ~**me**, pacifism; ~**ties, (-e)**, pacifist.
pa'sja, (-s), pasha.
pas'kamer, fitting-room.
paskewil', (-le), fuss, bustle, ado.
pas'klaar, ready for fitting on; cut to size; readymade; ready-to-wear; cut-and-dried; *iets* ~ *maak vir*, fashion something for.
paskwil', (-le), farce, lampoon.
pas'lik, (-e), fitting, suitable, appropriate, becoming; *so iets is nie* ~ *vir 'n DAME nie*, a thing like that does not become a lady; *iem. met* ~*e WOORDE bedank*, express thanks in appropriate terms; ~**heid**, suitability; eligibility.
pas'lood, plummet, sounding lead, plumb (-rule).
pas'maak, (s) truing; (w) **(-ge-)**, rectify (bullet); fit.
pas'meter, pedometer.
pas'munt, change; currency, circulating medium.
pasop', (ge-), mind, take care; *jy moet* ~, you must be careful

pasop'pens: *in sy* ~ *bly*, mind one's P's and Q's; watch one's step.
pas'poort, (-e), passport; *iem. sy* ~ *GEE*, give someone his ticket of leave; send someone packing; *dink dat jy 'n* ~ *HEMEL toe het*, think yourself far superior to other people.
pas: ~**prop**, adaptor; ~**ring**, adaptor ring.
passaat', (passate), trade wind; passage (on boat); ~**gordel**, trades; ~**wind**, trade wind.
passa'bel, (-e), passable, tolerable; fordable; ~**heid**, passableness.
passa'sie, (-s), passage; ~ *BESPREEK na Europa*, book passage to Europe; ~ *uit 'n ROMAN*, passage (fragment) from a novel; ~**geld**, fare, passage-money; ~**peiling**, transit (in astronomy).
passasier', (-s), passenger; *blinde* ~, stowaway.
passasiers': ~**boot**, passenger-steamer; ~**kar**, coach, passenger cart; ~**lys**, passenger-list; ~**trein**, passenger train; mail (train); ~**verkeer**, passenger-traffic; ~**vliegtuig**, passenger plane; ~**wa**, passenger-coach, saloon-coach.
passeer', (ge-), pass, cross; occur, happen; overtake, go past; pass by (over); *in hierdie jaar het baie gepasseer*, in this year much has happened.
passement', (-e), braid, trimming; ~**werker**, lacemaker; ~**winkel**, lace shop.
pas'send, (-e), fitting, suitable, appropriate, proper, beseeming, apposite, befitting, fit, conformable, congenial; congruent; *'n* ~*e antwoord*, a suitable reply.
pas'se-partout, passe-partout; skeleton-key; general pass.
pas'ser, (-s), pair of compasses; fitter; ~**doos**, box of mathematical instruments; ~**punt**, compass-point; ~**steek**, (b), exactly.
pas'sie¹, (-s), small step; ~*s MAAK*, cut capers; *hy MAAK sy* ~*s daar*, he is calling there.
pas'sie², passion, craze; *die P* ~ *van Christus*, the Passion of Christ; ~**blom**, passion-flower, passiflora (*Passiflora caerulea*).
passief', (passiewe), passive; ~**heid**, passivity.
pas'sie: ~**spel**, passion-play; ~**vol, (-le)**, passionate.
Pas'sieweek, Passion Week, Holy Week (R.C.)
pas'sim, passim.
pas'simeter, passimeter.
pas'sing, (-e, -s), fitting (of shoe); fit.
passioneer', (ge-): *jou* ~, devote oneself to something.
passi'va, liabilities; *activa en* ~, assets and liabilities.
passiwiteit', passivity.
pas'steen, bat (pottery).
pas'stelsel, pass system.
pas'stuk, adaptor.
pas'ta, (-s), paste (toothpaste).
pastei', (-e), pie, pastry; ~**bakker**, pastrycook; ~**deeg**, paste; ~**korsie**, piecrust; ~**tjie, (e), patty**; small pie; ~**vulsel**, mincemeat.
pastel', (-le, -s), crayon, pastel; ~**leer', (ge-)**, pastelling (of tobacco); ~**tekenaar**, pastel(l)ist; ~**tekening**, crayon drawing.
pas'tersteek, (bw) accurately; *dit GAAN* ~, things are going smoothly; ~ *SKIET*, hit the bull's eye.
pasteurisa'sie, pasteurization.
pasteuriseer', (ge-), pasteurize, sterilize; ..**rise'ring**, pasteurization.
pasti'che, pastiche.
pastil', (-le), pastille.
pas'toestel, truing tool.
pastoor', (-s, ..tore), pastor, priest, parish priest.
pas'tor, (-s), clergyman; ~ *loci*, local clergyman.
pastoraal', (..rale), pastoral.
pastora'le, (-s), pastorale, pastoral play.
pastorie', (-ë), parsonage, presbytery, vicarage, rectory, manse; ~**paar**, minister and wife.
pat, stalemate (chess).
Pata'go'nië, Patagonia; ~**r, (-s)**, Patagonian.
Patago'nies, (-e), Patagonian.
patat', patat'ta, (-s), sweet potato; *soos 'n WARM* ~ *laat val*, drop like a hot potato; ~**rank**, sweet-potato slip (runner).
patchou'li, patchouli.
patee', (s), paste (fishpaste), pâté.

pateen', paten.
patent', (s) **(-e),** patent; licence; letters patent; ~ *AANVRA,* apply for a patent; *'n* ~ *UITNEEM op,* take out a patent for; (b) **(-e),** excellent, capital, prime; patent; ~ *e KOS,* patent food; ~ *e MEDI= SYNE,* patent medicine(s); ~ *e MIDDEL,* patent remedy; ~ **agent,** patent agent; ~ **belasting,** patent-right tax; ~ **brief,** letters patent.
patenteer', (ge-), patent, register.
patent': ~ **houer,** patentee; ~ **kantoor,** patent office; ~ **knoop,** bachelor's buttons; ~ **olie,** patent oil; ~ **reg,** patent right; ~ **register,** patent roll; ~ **regi= strasie,** patent registration; P ~ **wet,** Patents' Act.
pa'ter, (-s), priest, father; ~ **familias,** father of the family; ~ **nos'ter,** (-s), paternoster; ~ **nos'tertjie,** love-bean.
pate'ties, (-e), pathetic.
pa'tina, patina.
patineer', (ge-), patinate.
patine'ring, patination.
pa''tjie, (-s), small father.
patogeen'[1], (..**gene**), pathogenic.
patogeen'[2], (..**gene**), pathogen(e).
patogene'se, pathogenesis.
pa'tois, dialect, patois.
patologie', pathology; ..**lo'gies, (-e),** pathologic(al).
patoloog', (..**loë**), pathologist.
pa'tos, pathos.
pa'tria, fatherland, mother country; *pro* ~ , for the fatherland, pro patria.
patriarg', (-te), patriarch; ~ **aal',** (..**gale**), patriarchal; ~ **aat',** patriarchate; ~ **is'me,** patriarchism.
patrilineaal', (..**neale**), **patrilineêr',** (-e), patrilinear, in the male line.
patrili'nie, (-s), male line.
patrimoniaal', (..**niale**), patrimonial.
patrimo'nium, patrimony.
patriot', (-te), patriot; partisan; ..**rio'ties, (-e),** patri= otic; ..**riotis'me,** patriotism.
Patriots', language of *Die Patriot.*
patri'siër, (-s), patrician.
patri'sies, (-e), patrician.
patristiek', patristics.
patris'ties, (-e), patristic, patrician.
patrolleer', (ge-), patrol.
patrol'lie, (-s), patrol, beat; foraging-party; *vlieënde* ~ , flying squad, mobile patrol; ~ **boot,** patrol boat; ~ **vliegtuig,** patrol plane; ~ **wa,** pick-up van.
patrologie', patrology.
patronaat', patronage; ~ **fees,** patronal festival.
patro'ne, ammunition.
patrones', (-se), patroness, (female) patron saint.
patroni'mies, (-e), patronymic; ~ **e naam,** patro= nymic.
patroon', (**patrone**), round (shooting); cartridge; tem= plate (mech.); patron; model, design, pattern; patron saint; master employer; *'n oulike* ~ *tjie,* charming little person; ~ **band,** bandoleer, feed-band (machine-gun); ~ **dop,** cartridge-case; ~ **dop= pie,** cartridge-cap; ~ **houer,** clip (rifle); feed-band (machine-gun); magazine; ~ **huls,** cartridge-case; ~ **maker,** pattern-maker; ~ **ontwerper,** designer; ~ **sak,** cartridge-case; cartridge-bag; ~ **tekenaar,** pattern-drawer; ~ **tekening,** designing; ~ **toets= baan,** proof-range; ~ **trekker,** cartridge-extractor.
patrys'[1], (-e), partridge; sand-grouse.
patrys'[2], (-e), patrix (printing).
patrys': ~ **eier,** partridge egg; ~ **hael,** fine shot; ~ **hond,** pointer (-dog); spaniel; ~ **jag,** partridge-shooting; ~ **kos,** bulbous plant *(Watsonia spp.);* ~ **net,** tunnel-net; ~ **poort,** scuttle-port; porthole; cabin window; port; ~ **roer,** fowling-piece; ~ **valk,** goshawk.
pats, (-e), smack, sap.
patyn', patina.
Pauli'nies, (-e), Pauline, of St. Paul.
Pau'lus, Paul.
paviljoen' = **pawiljoen.**
pawee'perske, pawie'perske, white clingstone peach.
paviljoen', (-e), **pawiljoen',** (-e), pavilion, (grand) stand.
pê'[1], (s): *sy* ~ *is uit,* he is done for; he is all-in; (bw) tired out, worn out; boo! *hy kan nie* ~ *SÊ nie,* he can't say "boo" to a goose; ~ *VOEL,* feel fagged out; feel seedy.
pê[2]! (tw) boo! yah!
pedaal', (**pedale**), pedal; ~ **harp,** pedal harp.
pedagogiek', pedagogics, education.
pedago'gies, (-e), pedagogic(al), educational.
pedagogis'me, pedagogism.
pedagoog', (..**goë**), pedagogue, educationist.
pedant', (s) **(-e),** pedant, prig, priggish person; (b) **(-e),** pedantic, priggish, donnish; ~ **erie',** (-ë), ped= antry, priggishness; ~ **heid,** pedantry, priggery; ~ **ies,** (-e), pedantic, priggish.
ped'die, (-s), rice-corn still in its husk.
pedel', (-le), janitor, beadle, bumble.
pederas', (-te), paederast; ~ **tie',** paederasty.
pedia'ter, (-s), paediatrist.
pediatrie', paediatry.
pedia'tries, (-e), paediatric.
pedikuur', pedicure.
pe'dometer, pedome'ter, pedometer.
peer, (pere), pear; testicle; bulb (of thermometer); *met die gebakte pere bly sit,* be saddled with something; be left with the baby; ~ **boom,** pear-tree; ~ **brand,** pear-scab; ~ **oes,** pear crop; ~ **slak,** pear-slug; ~ **vormig,** (-e), pear-shaped; pyriform; ~ **vormige** *slakwurm,* conical fluke; ~ **wyn,** perry.
pees, (pese), tendon, sinew; *hy het baie pese op sy boog,* he has many strings to his bow; ~ **agtig,** (-e), tendon-like; full of tendons; stringy, sinewy, ten= dinous; ~ **knobbel,** tendinous knot; ~ **knoop,** ganglion; ~ **skede,** tendon sheath.
pees'ter, (plat), (-s), penis; pizzle (of animal).
peet, (pete), sponsor, godparent; *sy ou* ~ *AFWAG,* have to wait ages; *LOOP na jou* ~ *jie!* go to the devil! ~ *STAAN,* stand godparent; *na jou* ~ *jie WEES,* have gone west; ~ **dogter,** goddaughter; ~ **kind,** godchild; ~ **ma,** ~ **moeder,** godmother; ~ **oom,** godfather; ~ **ouers,** godparents; ~ **pa,** god= father; ~ **seun,** godson; ~ **skap,** sponsorship; ~ **tante,** godmother; ~ **vader,** godfather.
Pe'gasus, Pegasus.
pegmatiet', pegmatite.
pegmati'ties, pegmatoïed', (-e), pegmatoid.
peil, (s) mark, gauge (water); level; standard; *BE= NEDE* ~ , below the mark; *op* ~ *HOU,* keep up to the mark; *op 'n lae* ~ *STAAN,* be on a low moral plane; *op iem.* ~ *TREK,* depend upon someone; count on someone; *die* ~ *VERHOOG,* raise the standard (level); (w), (ge-), sound, fathom (the sea); take one's bearings; gauge, plumb; probe; colli= mate; *die diepte van sy HAAT* ~ , fathom the depth of his hatred; *iem. se KENNIS* ~ , sound a man's knowledge; *die* ~ *VERHOOG,* raise the level; ~ **baar,** (..**bare**), fathomable; ~ **bom,** pilot-bomb; ~ **blok,** sighting block; ~ **er,** (-s), gauger, sounder; ~ **glas,** gauge-glass; ~ **ing,** (-s), bearings; sounding; gauging; ~ **ketting,** gauging-chain; ~ **koers,** head= ing; ~ **kraan,** gauge-cock; ~ **lood,** (..**lode**), plum= met; plumb; plumb-bob; ~ **loos,** (..**lose**), fathom= less; unfathomable; ~ **lyn,** collimation; ~ **merk,** water mark; ~ **skaal,** gauge; ~ **skoot,** sighting-shot; sighter; ~ **skyf,** pelorus, azimuth instrument; ~ **stok,** gauging-rod; gauge, dipstick; ~ **toestel,** sea-gauge; waterlevel indicator; sounding-device; ~ **vlag,** gauging-flag; ~ **yster,** probing bar.
peins, (ge-), meditate, muse, ponder; ~ **end,** (-e), re= flective, cogitative, meditative, pensive; ~ **er,** (-s), muse, meditator; thinker; ~ **ing,** meditation, musing.
peits, (-e), whip.
pejoratief', (s, b) (..**tiewe**), pejorative.
pe'kanneut, pecan-nut.
peka'ri, (-'s), peccary.
pe'kel, (s) brine; pickle; difficulty; *in die* ~ *sit,* be in a pickle; get into hot water; (w) (ge-), salt, souse, brine; pickle; ~ **aar,** (-s), salt herring; ~ **agtig,** (-e), briny, saltish; ~ **haring,** pickled herring; ~ **pomp,** pickle-pump; ~ **sonde,** old sin, closet-sin, pecca= dillo; ~ **sout,** briny, very salt (food); ~ **vleis,** salted meat; souse; ~ **vleisvaatjie,** harness-cask; ~ **water,** pickle-liquor, brine.

Pekinees', (..nese), Pekin(g)ese.
Pe'king, Peking; **p~(-sy)**, peking.
pek'kotee, pekoe.
pektien', **pekti'ne**, pectin; ~**suur**, pectic acid.
pektoraal', (..rale), pectoral.
pekto'se, pectose.
pel, (ge-), peel, shell, husk; hull (rice); blanch (nuts); *gepelde rys*, hulled rice.
pelageen', (..gene), pelagic.
pela'gies, (-e), pelagic; ~*e vis*, pelagic fish.
pelagiet', pelagite.
pelargo'nium, pelargonium.
pelerien', (-e), **peleri'ne**, (-s), pelerine; ~**mantel**, pelerine.
pel'grim, (-s), pilgrim; ~**sgewaad**, ~**skleed**, pilgrim's garment (dress); ~**sreis**, pilgrimage; ~**staf**, pilgrim's staff; Jacob's staff; ~**stog**, pilgrimage; ~**svader**, pilgrim father.
pelie'le, (Zoeloe), finished, used up.
pelikaan', (..kane), pelican.
pella'gra, pellagra.
pel'lery, shelling, peeling, husking.
pellies', (-e), pelisse.
Peloponne'sies, (-e), Peloponnesian; ..**ne'sus**, Peloponnesus.
peloton', (-s), squad, platoon; ~**opstelling**, platoon formation; ~**skietery**, platoon firing; ~**vuur**, platoon firing.
pels, (-e), fur, skin; coat (animals), pelage; pelt; ~**dier**, furred animal.
pel'ser, (-s), pilchard.
pels: ~**handel**, fur trade; ~**handelaar**, fur trader; furrier; ~**jagter**, fur trapper; ~**jas**, fur coat; ~**kraag**, pelerine, fur necklet, tippet; ~**mantel**, fur cloak; ~**mof**, muff; ~**mus**, fur cap; ~**stola**, fur stole; ~**vreters**, mallophaga; ~**werk**, furriery; ~**werker**, furrier.
pel'tery, (-e), furriery, peltry.
pe'lu, (ong.), (-'s), pillow, bolster.
pem'mikan, (-s), pemmican.
pen[1], (s) (-ne), pen, nib, quill; tee (quoits); hob; *in die ~ BLY*, remain unwritten; *sy ~ in GAL doop*, dip one's pen in gall; *in die ~ GEE*, dictate; inspire; *GOU met die ~ wees*, be an able penman; *na die ~ GRYP*, take up one's pen; rush into print; *van sy ~ LEWE*, live by one's pen; *die ~ VOER*, wield the pen; *'n WELVERSNEDE ~ hê*, be an expert penman; (w) **(ge-)**, write, pen.
pen[2], (-ne), pin, spike; peg; tee (golf); peen, pane (of hammer); stump (cricket); gudgeon; dowel; pintle (in mineo); *aan die ~ RY*, be called to account; be brought to book, *VOOR die ~ne*, at the wickets.
penaal', (penale), penal.
pen'afveër, (-s), penwiper.
penaliseer', (ge-), penalize.
penant': ~**spieël**, pier-glass; ~**tafel**, pier-table.
pena'rie, trouble, fix; *in die ~ wees*, be in a fix (hole); be in misery.
pena'te, penates, household gods.
pen'bakkie, pentray.
pendant', (-e), pendant; companion.
pen'delaar, commuter.
pen'doring, long thorn, spike-thorn.
pendu'le, (-s), ornamental clock.
pen'els, peg-awl.
penetra'sie, penetration.
penetreer', (ge-), penetrate.
pen'hamer, peening tool.
pen'holto, **kryming**, **krywaat**.
pen'houer, (-s), penholder.
pe'nis, (-se), penis.
penisillien', **penisilli'ne**, penicillin.
peniten'sie, penitence, sorrow.
pen'koker, pen-case.
pen'kop, young fellow, stripling, hobbledehoy, inexperienced youth; youngest (male) member of the Voortrekker movement; ~**ag'tig**, (-e), hobbledehoyish.
pen'krabbel, thumb-nail sketch.
pen'lekker, (-s), clerk, pen-driver, quill-driver, hodman (fig.); ~**y**, pen driving.

pen'maat, pen-friend.
pen'ne: ~**bak**, pen-tray; ~**lekker** = **penlekker**; ~**mes**, penknife; ~**naam**, pseudonym, pen-name; ~**skroef**, pin-vice; ~**streep**, stroke, dash (of the pen); *met een ~ streep*, with one stroke of the pen; ~**stryd**, polemics, controversy; ~**tjie**, small pen; tee (golf); ~**veër**, pen-wiper; ~**vrug**, writings; book; ~**wisser**, (-s), pen-wiper.
pen'nie, (-s), penny; *suinig met die ~s, rojaal met die ponde*, penny wise, pound foolish.
pen'ning, (-e, -s), medal; penny, mite; ~**graveerkuns**, medallurgy; ~**kruid**, moneywort; ~**kunde**, numismatics; ~**kun'dig**, (-e), numismatic; ~**kun'dige**, (-s), numismatist; ~**leer**, numismatology; ~**meester**, treasurer; purse-bearer; bursar; ~**meesteres**, (lady) treasurer.
Penni'niese Alpe, Pennine Alps.
Pennsilva'nië, Pennsylvania; ~**r**, Pennsylvanian; ..**nies**, (-e), Pennsylvanian.
pen'nyweight, (-s), pennyweight.
penologie', penology.
penolo'gies, (-e), penologic(al).
penoloog', (..loë), penologist.
pen'orent, erect, straight up, upright.
pen'punt, nib, pen-point.
pen'regop, erect, perpendicular; bolt upright.
pens, (-e), belly, stomach, paunch (animal); tripe; maw; ~ *en POOTJIES*, neck and crop; boots and all; *jy kan dit maar op jou ~ SKRYF*, you can whistle for it.
penseel', (s) (..sele), brush; (w) **(ge-)**, paint; ~**skimmel**, penicillin; ~**streek**, stroke of the brush; ~**voering**, brushwork; ~**vormig**, (-e), penciliform, penicillate; ~**werk**, brushwork.
pensioen', (-e), retiring pay, pension; *MET ~ aftree*, be pensioned off; ~ *VERLEEN*, grant a pension: ~**bydrae**, contribution (to a pension fund); pension contribution; ~**draend**, (-e), pensionable; ~**eer'**, (ge-), pension.
pensione'ring, superannuation, retirement.
pensioen': ~**fonds**, pension fund; ~**geld**, pension money; ~**geregtig**, (-de), entitled to a pension; ~**leeftyd**, pensionable age; **P~raad**, Pension Board; ~**trekkend**, (-e), having (drawing) a pension; ~**trekker**, pensioner; ~**versekering**, pension insurance; **P~wet**, Pensions Act.
pension', (-s), boarding house; ~**aat'**, (..nate), hostel, boarding house.
pensiona'ris, (-se), pensioner.
pen'skets, pen-portrait; pen-and-ink sketch.
pens'klavier, (geselst.), accordeon.
pen'steek, **pen'stekery**, tent-pegging.
pens: ~**winkeltjie**, (-s), pedlar's wallet (tray); ~**wol**, bellies, broke (wool).
pentaë'der, (-s), pentahedron; ~**taë'dries**, (-e), pentahedral.
pentagonaal', (..nale), pentagonal.
pentagoon', (..gone), pentagon.
pentagram', (-me), pentacle, pentagram.
penta'meter, (-s), pentameter.
Pentateug', Pentateuch (the five books of Moses).
pentat'lon, pentathlon.
pen: ~**tekenaar**, black-and-white (pen-and-ink) artist; ~**tekening**, pen-painting; black-and-white drawing; pen-and-ink drawing.
pento'de, (-s), pentode.
penum'bra, (-s), penumbra.
pen: ~**vis**, porcupine fish; ~**voerder**, (-s) wielder of the pen; ~**vormig**, (-e), fusiform; ~**vriend**, pen-friend; ~**wortel**, tap-root.
pe'per, (s) pepper; *iem. ~ GEE*, give someone a thrashing; ~ *en KOLJANDER, die een is soos die ander*, there is little to choose between them; they are like Tweedledum and Tweedledee; *dit is ~ en SOUT*, it is six of the one and half a dozen of the other; (w) **(ge-)**, pepper; criticize; give a hiding; *ge~de styl*, pungent style; ~**agtig**, (-e), peppery; ~**boom**, pepper-tree; ~**bos(sie)**, pepperbush; ~**bus(sie)**, pepperbox, pepper-castor; ~**duur**, sinfully dear; excessively expensive; ~**-en-soutkleur**, pepper-and-salt (colour); ~**-en-soutstelletjie**, cruet-stand; ~**koek**, gingerbread; peppercake; ~**kop**,

peperment, woolly-head; ~**korrel**, peppercorn; ~**korreltjies**, woolly hair; ~**krulle**, tight curls (in karakul skins).
peperment', peppermint; ~**likeur**, crème de menthe; ~**olie**, peppermint-oil.
pe'permeul, pepper-mill.
pe'perwortel, pepperwort; horse-radish.
pep'lum, (-s), peplum.
pepsien', **pepsi'ne**, pepsin.
pep'ties, (-e), peptic.
peptisa'sie, peptization.
pep'ton, peptone; ~**iseer'**, (ge-), peptonize.
per, by, via, per; ~ *ABUIS*, by mistake; ~ *ADRES*, care of; ~ *GELUK*, luckily; ~ *KONTRA*, per contra; ~ *POND*, by the pound; ~ *POS*, by post; ~ *kerende POS*, by return of post.
perd, (-e), horse; vaulting-horse; knight (chess); *'n gegewe ~ moet jy nie in die BEK kyk nie*, don't look a gift-horse in the mouth; *'n ou ~ kry ook lus vir GROENVOER*, he stil has a tooth for green stuff; *die HINKENDE ~ kom agterna*, the sting is in the tail; *as die ~ e HORINGS kry*, when pigs fly; *'n ~ KNIPMES ry*, make a horse arch its neck; *die ~ wat die KORRELS (hawer) verdien, kry die strooi*, one beats the bush but the other catches the bird; *die gewillige ~ moet die LAS dra*, all lay load on the willing horse; *die ~ e die LEISELS gee*, let the horses have their heads; *OU ~!* stout fellow! *PURE ~*, feel tip-top; *die maerste ~ SKOP die seerste*, it is the unforeseen that always happens; *die ~ die SPORE gee*, spur the horse on; *die ~ ruik sy STAL*, he is making a final effort; *soos 'n STEEKS ~*, like a jibbing horse; *die ~ se STERT af praat*, talk the hind leg off a donkey; *'n ~ met vier bene STRUIKEL ook*, a horse stumbles that has four legs; *TE ~*, on horseback; *iem. oor die ~ TEL*, make too much of someone; *die TROJAANSE ~ inbring*, bring in the Trojan horse; *'n VERKEERDE ~ opklim (opsaal)*, back the wrong horse; *jy kan 'n ~ na die WATER bring, maar kan hom nie dwing om te suip nie*, you may take a horse to the water, but can't make him drink; *daar sal ~ e WEES*, there will be trouble; ~**ag'tig**, (-e), horsy, equine.
per'de: ~**afrigter**, horse-breaker; ~**bloed**, horse's blood; liquorice; ~**blom**, dandelion; ~**blomsaad**, blowball; ~**boer**, horse-farmer (-breeder); ~**borsel**, dandy-brush; ~**by**, wasp; hornet; ~**bylyfie**, wasp-waist; ~**bynes**, wasps' nest, vespiary; ~**dam**, horse-pond; ~**dief**, horse-thief; ~**deken**, body-cloth; housing; ~**dokter**, horse-doctor; ~**doktery**, farriery; ~**drol**, ball of horse-dung; *iem. ~ drolle vir sitroene (vye) verkoop*, sell someone a pup; ~**duiwel**, rough-rider; ~**familie**, equines; ~**froetang**, horse-frutang; ~**griep**, equine influenza; ~**haar**, horsehair; ~**hoef**, horse's hoof; horseshoe; ~**hok**, horse-box (on ships); ~**houer**, horse-holder; ~**-influensa**, pink-eye; ~**jong**, groom; ~**kamp**, horse-paddock; ~**kar**, horse-cart; ~**kenner**, judge of horses; ~**keurraad**, horse-casting board; ~**kneg**, groom; ~**kombers**, horse-rug, horse-blanket; ~**koper**, horse-dealer; horse-coper; *oneerlike ~ koper*, horse-chanter; ~**krag**, horsepower; ~**leerder**, horse-breaker; ~**mark**, horse-market; ~**medisyne**, horse-drench; ~**mis**, horse-dung; ~**patrollie**, mounted patrol; ~**pis**, horse-urine; *Clausena inaequalis;* ~**pleuropneumonie**, equine pleuropneumonia; ~**poot**, horse's hoof; ~**pootjie**, limpet; ~**pram**, mare's teat; knobwood *(Fogara capensis);* ~**ras**, breed of horses; ~**reisies**, ~**wedren**, horse-race; ~**ruiter**, horseman, rider, equestrian; mounted trooper; ~**siekte**, horse-sickness; ~**skuit**, horse-boat; ~**slagter**, horse/ knacker; ~**slagtery**, knackery; ~**smous**, horse-trader; ~**spoor**, horse's track (spoor); ~**sport**, horse-racing; hippic sport; ~**sportbyeenkoms**, gymkhana; ~**staanplek**, horse-standing; ~**stal**, stable; ~**stamboek**, stud-book; ~**stapel**, stock of horses; ~**steler**, horse-thief; ~**stert**, horse's tail; ~**stoetery**, stud; ~**stert**, bottle-brush (plant); ~**teelt**, horse-breeding; ~**teler**, (-s), horse-breeder; ~**temmer**, rough-rider; horse-breaker; ~**trekkrag**, horse-draught; ~**trem**, horse-tram; ~**trok**, horse-box (railw.); ~**tuig**,

horse-appointments, trappings; horse harness; ~**vleis**, horse-flesh; ~**vlieg**, horse-fly, cleg, bot-fly, breeze; ~**voer**, grain; ~**voertuig**, horse-drawn vehicle; ~**voetjie**, limpet; ~**vy**, sour fig; horse-apple; ~**wa**, horse-waggon; ~**wagter**, horse-boy; ~**wedren**, horse-race; ~**-yster**, horseshoe.
perd: ~**fris**, hale and hearty, in the pink (of condition); vigorous, healthy; ~**gerus**, (-te), unsuspecting, perfectly calm, unconcerned(ly).
perd'jie, (-s), small horse, pony; *die ~ het maar net gespring*, never mind, it is only a little dust; *oor sy ~ GETEL*, full of himself; *gou op sy ~ WEES*, be touchy; be quick to take offence.
perd'mens, centaur.
perd'ry, (s) horse-riding; (w) (-ge-), ride on horseback; ~**kuns**, horsemanship.
pe're: ~**boom** = **peerboom**; ~**drank**, perry.
Pê'rel, Paarl.
pê'rel, (s) (-s), pearl; cataract (on the eye); bead (perspiration); *'n ~ van 'n MEISIE*, a jewel of a girl; *~ s voor die SWYNE gooi*, cast pearls before swine; (w) (ge-), form beads of perspiration; pearl; ~**agtig**, (-e), pearly, pearl-like; ~**as**, pearl ash; ~**bank**, pearl-bed; ~**duiker**, pearl-diver; ~**gort**, pearl barley; ~**gruis**, seed-pearls; ~**grys**, pearl-grey; griseous; ~**hoender**, guinea-fowl; ~**kleurig**, (-e), pearl-coloured; ~**mossel**, pearl-mussel; ~**oester**, pearloyster; ~**siekte**, pearl-disease; ~**skulp**, pearl-shell; ~**snoer**, string of pearls; ~**visser**, pearl-fisher; pearl-diver; ~**vissery**, pearl-fishery; ~**vormig**, (-e), pearl-shaped; ~**wit**, pearl-white.
peremto'ries, (ong.), (-e), peremptory; *~ e pleit*, plea in abatement.
pe'rewyn, perry.
perfek', (-te), perfect; ~**sie**, perfection; ~**sioneer'**, (ge-), perfect, make perfect; ~**sionis'**, (-te), perfectionist; ~**sionis'me**, perfectionism; ~**sionis'ties**, (-e), perfectionist(ic); ~**tief'**, (..tiewe), perfective; ~**tiwiteit'**, perfection, perfectness; ~**tum**, (-s, ..fekta), perfect (tense).
perfora'sie, (-s), perforation.
perforeer', (ge-), perforate; punch; ~**werk**, punched work.
perfore'ring, (-s), perforation.
pergo'la, (-s), pergola.
pe'ri (-'s), peri.
peridoot', (..dote), peridot.
perifeer', (..fere), peripheral.
periferie', (-ë), periphery.
perifra'se, (-s), periphrasis.
perifras'ties, (-e), periphrastic.
perige'um, perigee.
perihe'lium, perihelion.
perikard', (-e), **perikar'dium**, (-s), pericardium.
perikardi'tis, pericarditis.
peri'kel, (-s), peril.
perikoop', (..kope), pericope.
perime'ter, (-s), perimeter.
perio'de, (-s), period; cycle.
periodiek', **perio'dies**, (-e), periodic(al).
periodisiteit', periodicity.
peripate'ties, (-e), peripatetic.
peripate'tikus, (-se, ..tici), peripatetic.
peripetie', (-ë), dénouement, peripeteia.
periskoop', (..skope), periscope.
perisko'pies, (-e), periscopic.
peristaltiek', peristalsis.
perital'ties, (-e), peristaltic.
pe'ristyl, (-e), peristyle.
peritoneaal', (..neale), peritoneal.
perk, (-e), limit; flower-bed; arena; green (golf, bowls); *BINNE die ~ e bly*, remain within bounds (the limits); *BUITE ~*, out of bounds; *alle ~ e te BUITE gaan*, go beyond all limits; *die ~ e OORSKRY*, exceed the bounds; *in die ~ TREE teen*, enter the lists against.
perkal', percale.
perkament', (-e), parchment; ~**agtig**, (-e), parchment-like; pergameneous; ~**papier**, parchment paper, vellum paper; ~**rol**, scroll.
perk: ~**baas**, green-ranger (-keeper); ~**opsigter**, green-keeper, green-warden; ~**tyd**, deadline.

perkus'sie, percussion; ~**doppie**, percussion cap; ~**slot**, percussion lock.
perkutaan', (..tane), percutaneous.
perkuteer', (ge-), percuss.
perlemoen', **perlmoer'**, mother of pearl; abalone; nacre; ~**agtig**, (-e), nacreous; ~**knoppie**, mother-of-pearl button; pearl button; ~**vlinder**, fritillary; ~**wolk**, mother-of-pearl cloud; nacreous (iridescent) cloud.
perliet', perlite.
Perm, Permian.
permanen'sie, permanence.
permanent', (-e), permanent; standing; perennial; ~**heid**, permanence.
permanganaat', permanganate.
permea'bel, (-e), permeable.
permeabiliteit', permeability.
permis'sie, permission; allowance; met ~, with your permission, with (by) your leave; with apologies.
permissief', (..siewe), permissive; ..*siewe gemeenskap*, permissive society.
permissiwiteit', permissiveness.
permit', (-te), permit, pass; ~**teer'**, (ge-), allow, permit.
permuta'sie, permutation; ~**leer**, permutation theory.
permuteer', (ge-), permute.
pernisieus', (-e), pernicious.
peroksied', (-e), **peroksi'de**, (-s), peroxide.
perora'sie, peroration.
peroreer', (ge-), perorate.
perron', (-s), platform, perron; ~**kaartjie**, platform ticket.
pers¹, (s) purple.
pers², (s) (-e), printing-press; *ter ~e GAAN*, go to press; *die GEEL ~*, the yellow press; *IN (op) die ~*, in the press; *TER ~e*, in the press.
pers³, (w) (ge-), press (suit); dump (wool in bales); squeeze; *trane in die oë ~*, force tears to the eyes.
pers: ~**bank**, press gallery; ~**beampte**, pressman; ~**berig**, press report.
pers'blok, pressing-block.
pers'bruin, puce.
pers'buro, (-'s), press bureau; press agency.
perseel', (persele), lot, plot; premises; allotment; ~**s'gewys(e)**, in lots.
persent', per cent; ~**a'sie**, (-s), percentage; ~**s'gewys(e)**, proportionally; by percentages.
persep'sie, perception.
perseptueel', (..tuele), perceptual.
per'ser, (-s), presser.
pers: ~**fotograaf**, press photographer; ~**galery**, press gallery.
pers'gas, high-pressure gas.
pers: ~**gesprek**, interview; ~**groep**, press-group; press-gang; ~**huisie**, press-box.
per'sie, diarrhoea.
Per'sië, Persia, ~**r**, Persian, ..sies, (b) Persian.
persifla'ge, persiflage, banter.
persifleer', (ge-), banter, rail.
per'sing, pressing, pressure.
persipieer', (ge-), perceive, apperceive.
pers: ~**kaart**, press pass; ~**kampanje**, press campaign.
pers'kas, press.
per'ske, (-s), peach; *dis oor met jou ~s*, it is no use asking; you are wasting your breath; ~**agtig**, (-e), peachy; ~**bloeisel**, peach blossom; ~**boom**, peach-tree; ~**brandewyn**, peach brandy; ~**hare**, peach down; ~**kleurig**, (-e), peachy, peach-coloured; ~**konfyt**, peach jam; ~**krulbaar**, peachleaf curl; ~**likeur**, persico; ~**luis**, peach aphis, ~**oor**, cauliflower ear; ~**pit**, peach-stone; ~**pitvloer**, floor inlaid with peach-stones; ~**roos**, flowering peach; ~**smeer**, dried peach-pulp; ~**sop**, peach juice; peach brandy; ~**tjie**, (-s), small peach.
pers: ~**klaar**, ready for the press; ~**klaarmaker**, sub-editor, redactor; publisher's reader; ~**kommentaar**, press comment(s); ~**kopie**, press copy; ~**leser**, reader; ~**man**, pressman, journalist.
persona'lia, personalia, personal details (news).
personaliteit', personality.
persona'sie, personage, person; impersonation.

personeel', (..nele), staff, personnel; domestics (hotel); *in die ~ DIEN*, serve on the staff; *die DIENSDOENDE ~*, the staff on duty; *te VEEL ~ hê*, be overstaffed; ~**gebrek**, shortage of staff; ~**kamer**, common-room, staff room; ~**klerk**, staff clerk; ~**uitbreiding**, increase of staff; ~**vermindering**, reduction of staff; ~**winkel**, canteen.
personeer', (ge-), impersonate.
perso'ne: ~**hysbak**, cage, skip; ~**hyser**, passenger-lift; ~**kolom**, personal column.
personifieer', (ge-), personify.
personifika'sie, (-s), personification.
persoon', (..sone), person, individual; personage; body; (mv) people; *die AANGEWESE ~*, the right (proper) person; *in EIE ~*, in person; *die deug IN ~*, virtue personified; *IN ~*, personally, in his own person; *klein van ~, maar groot van PATROON*, don't judge a person's mental abilities by his size; *KLEIN van ~*, of small stature; *'n rand PER ~*, a rand a head; ~**lik**, (-e), personal, personally, individual, peculiar(ly); private; *moenie ~ lik word nie*, don't indulge in personalities; ~**like vete**, personal feud; ~**likheid**, individuality; presence; (..hede), personality, person of importance.
persoons': ~**bedrog**, (im)personation; ~**belasting**, personal tax; ~**berig**, personals; ~**bewys**, ~**kaart**, identity card; ~**verbeelding**, personification, prosopopoeia; ~**vergissing**, mistaken identity; ~**vorm**, finite form.
pers: ~**oorsig**, press review; ~**orgaan**, press organ; paper, newspaper; ~**pas**, press pass.
perspektief', (..tiewe), perspective; ~**tekening**, scenography.
perspekti'wies, (-e), in perspective, perspectively.
perspira'sie, perspiration.
perspirato'ries, (-e), perspiratory, perspirative.
perspireer', (ge-), perspire.
pers: ~**plank**, pressing-board; ~**pomp**, force-pump; feed-pump.
pers'propaganda, press propaganda.
pers: ~**pyp**, delivery pipe; ~**raam**, tympan.
pers'revisie, final proof.
pers'rooi, magenta; solferino.
pers: ~**sensor**, press censor; ~**sensuur**, press censorship.
pers'staal, pressed steel.
pers: ~**tafel**, press table; ~**telegram**, press telegram.
pers'toets, dumping-test.
pers: ~**tribune**, press gallery; ~**verslag**, press report; ~**verteenwoordiger**, press representative; ~**vryheid**, liberty of the press; ~**wet**, press law.
pers'yster, smoothing-iron, goose (tailor), seam-press.
pertinen'sie, relevance, pertinence.
pertinent', (-e), pertinent, relevant; positive, downright, categorical, assured; *'n ~e leuen*, a downright lie.
pertjoe'ma, for love (games), nothing doing!
Peru', Peru; ~**aan'**, (Peruane), Peruvian; ~**aans'**, (-e), Peruvian; ~**balsem**, Peru balsam.
pervers', (-e), perverse; ~**iteit'**, perversity; depravity.
pes, (s) (-te), pest; plague, Black Death; bane; lues; *iem. soos die ~ haat*, hate someone like the plague; (w) (ge-), plague, pester; ~**agtig**, (-e), pestilent, pestilential; ~**basil**, plague bacillus; ~**bestryding**, plague-fighting; ~**blaar**, plague-blotch; ~**buil**, plague-spot, sore spot; ~**epidemie**, plague-epidemic.
pese'ta, (-s), peseta.
pes: ~**geval**, plague case; ~**haard**, plague centre; ~**hospitaal**, plague hospital; ~**huis**, pest-house, plague house; ~**kiem**, plague germ; ~**lug**, pestilential air; ~**lyer**, plague patient.
pe'so, (-'s), peso.
pes: ~**pokke**, pestilential pox; ~**regulasie**, plague regulation; ~**serum**, plague serum; ~**sickte**, plague, pestilence.
pessimis', (-te), pessimist; ~**me**, pessimism; ~**ties**, (-e), pessimistic.
pes'stof, plague virus.
pes'tery, annoyance, botheration.
pestilen'sie, (-s), pestilence.

pestologie', pestology.
pes: ~ **tyd**, plague time; ~ **virus**, plague virus; ~ **vlek**, plague-spot.
pet, (-te), cap, kepi.
petal'je, petal'lie, (-s), affair, ado; prank; trick.
petie'terig, (-e), small, tiny, petite.
peti'sie, (-s), petition.
petisiona'ris, (-se), petitioner; memorialist.
petisioneer', (ge-), petition, memorialize.
petrefak', (-te), petrefact.
petrifak'sie, petrification.
petrifieer', petrifiseer', (ge-), petrify.
petrogene'se, petrogenesis.
petroglief', (..gliewe), petroglyph.
petrografie', petrography; **..gra'fies, (-e),** petrographic(al).
pe'trol, petrol, motor spirit, gas(oline); ~ **aangedrewe,** petrol-driven; ~ **aanvoer,** petrol supply.
petrola'tum, petroleum jelly.
pe'trolbom, petrol bomb; Molotov cocktail.
petro'leum, petroleum; ~ **ontdek,** strike oil; ~ **bron,** oil-well; ~ **lamp,** oil-lamp; ~ **maatskappy,** oil company; ~ **motor,** petrol-motor; ~ **skip,** oil-ship; ~ **veld,** oilfield.
pe'trol: ~ **kontroleur,** petrol-controller; ~ **lewering,** petrol supply; ~ **leiding,** petrol system; ~ **ogie',** petrology; ~ **o'gies, (-e),** petrological; ~ **oog', (..loë),** petrologist; ~ **pomp,** petrol pump; boser; ~ **stasie,** pit (races); ~ **tenk,** petrol tank; ~ **toevoer,** petrol feed; ~ **verbruik,** petrol consumption, gas consumption; ~ **voorraad,** petrol supply.
pet'to: *in* ~ , up one's sleeve, in reserve.
pet'tuit, peak of cap.
petu'nia, (-s), petunia.
peul¹, (s) (-e), pod, husk, shell.
peul², (s) (-e), (long) cushion, bolster; pillow; hull.
peul³, (w) (ge-) = **puil.**
peul: ~ **draend, (-e),** leguminous; ~ **gewas,** legume; ~ **groente,** legume vegetable; ~ **vrug,** legume, pulse, leguminous plant, pod-plant, gram.
peu'sel, (ge-), niggle; nibble, pick; peck (at food); potter; ~ **goed,** ~ **happies,** snacks; ~ **kroeg,** snack-bar; ~ **werkie,** odd job; pottering.
peu'ter, (ge-), tamper, fiddle; worry, fumble, piffle; potter; piddle (archaic); nobble (race-horses); ~ **aar, (-s),** potterer, fiddler, fuss-pot; ~ **ig, (-e),** niggling, finical, piffling, pernickety, pettifogging, poky; ~ **igheid,** finicalness; ~ **vry, (-e),** foolproof; ~ **werkie,** piffling (odd) job; ~ **y,** fiddling, tinkering.
pê'voël = **kwêvoël.**
pi, pi (math.).
pianet', (-te), pianette.
piani'no, (-'s), pianino.
pianis', (-te), pianist; ~ **te, (-s),** female pianist.
pia'no, (-'s), piano; ~ **begeleiding,** piano accompaniment; ~ **-eksamen,** examination for piano(forte); ~ **forte,** pianoforte; ~ **konsert,** piano concerto; piano recital.
pianola', (-s), pianola, player-piano.
pia'no: ~ **les,** piano lesson; ~ **musiek,** piano music; ~ **-onderwyser,** piano teacher; ~ **-onderwyseres, (-se),** (lady) piano teacher; ~ **party,** piano part; ~ **speelster,** (lady) pianist; ~ **spel,** piano playing; ~ **speler,** piano player; ~ **stemmer,** piano tuner; ~ **stoel,** piano stool; ~ **uitvoering,** piano concert (recital).
pias'ter, piaster, piastre.
pi'cador, (-s), picador.
pic'colo, (-'s), piccolo; button; ~ **speler,** piccolo player.
picot'randwerk, picot edging.
pie'dewiet, (-s), pilawit.
piek, (-e), peak; pike; ~ **draer,** pikeman.
piekanien', (-s), piccanin.
pie'kel, (ge-), carry (go) with difficulty, drag.
piekenier', (-s), pikeman.
pie'ker, (ge-), worry, fret, puzzle, brood.
pie'keval, peak-halyard.
piek'fyn, spick-and-span; grand, smart.
piek'niek, (s) (-s), picnic; (w) **(ge-),** picnic; ~ **agtig, (-e),** picnicky; ~ **dans,** picnic dance; ~ **er, (-s),**

~ **ganger, (-s),** picnicker; ~ **mandjie,** picnic basket; ~ **plek,** picnic-place, picnic-spot.
piek'waarde, peak value, top value.
piel, (plat), (-e), penis, male member.
pie'lie-pie'lie! ducky-ducky!
piëli'tis, pyelitis.
piëmie', pyaemia.
pie'nang: ~ **bossie,** quinine-bush; ~ **neut,** areca nut, penang nut; ~ **vleis,** curried meat.
pienk, pink (colour); ~ **erig, (-e),** pinkish, pinky, rosy; ~ **wange,** rosy cheeks..
piep, (s) pip (chicken disease); *hy HET die* ~ , he imagines himself to be ill; he has the pip; *die* ~ *KRY van iets,* be irritated by; be given the pip; (w) **(ge-),** chirp, cheep, squeak, peep (chicken); molly-coddle, pamper; pule; (tw) peep!
pie'perig, (-e), sickly, weak, puny, thin; squeaky; puling; ~ **heid,** sickliness; squeakiness; thinness.
pie'pie, (nursery term) (s), **(-s),** pee; (w), **(ge-),** make water, piddle, wee-wee.
piep: ~ **jong,** ~ **jonk,** very young; tender, soft; ~ **klein,** tiny.
piep'kuiken, spring chicken; *sy is nie (meer) 'n* ~ *nie,* she is no spring chicken.
piep'stemmetjie, squeaky (high, thin) voice.
pier¹, (s) (-e), pier, jetty, groyne, mole.
pier², (s) (-e), worm; *so dood soos 'n* ~ , as dead as a doornail.
pier³, (w) (ge-), cheat, deceive; fool, take in.
pie'rewaai, (ge-), (be on the) spree, have a fling; ~ **er, (-s),** rake, reveller, merrymaker, playboy, roué.
pie'rewiet, (-e, -s) = **piedewiet.**
pier'geld, pierage.
pie'ring, (-s), saucer; ~ **skiet,** skeet-shooting; ~ **vaarder,** saucerian.
pie'rinkie, (-s), small saucer.
pierret'te, (-s), pierrette.
pierrot', (-s), pierrot.
pie'sang, (-s), banana; ~ **aspaai,** banana split; ~ **blaaspootjie,** banana thrips; ~ **boer,** banana farmer; person from Natal; ~ **brood,** banana loaf; ~ **hand,** banana hand; **P** ~ **land,** Natal; ~ **roomys,** banana split; ~ **skil,** banana peel (skin); ~ **vulsel,** banana filling.
pie'sankie, (-s), small banana.
Piet¹, Peter; *hy is 'n HELE* ~ , he is a big shot (noise); ~ , *PAUL en Klaas,* Tom, Dick and Harry; *die* ~ *e van die PLEK,* the bigwigs; the big noises; *'n SAAI* ~ , a dull dog; ~ *VERDRIET,* a wailing Willy.
piet², (-e), joker (cards).
piëta', (-'s), pieta.
piëteit', piety, reverence; ~ **loos, (..lose),** irreverent; ~ **s'gevoel,** feeling of piety, religious feeling.
pie'terman, weever (fish).
pieterse'lie, pietersie'lie, parsley.
Pie'terskerk, St. Peter's Church.
piëtis', (s) (-te), pietist; ~ **me,** pietism; ~ **ties, (-e),** pietist.
pie'tjiekanarie, brown canary, chee-chee.
piet'-my-vrou, (-e), red-chested cuckoo *(Cuculus solitarius).*
piets, (ge-), whip lightly, flick.
piet'sie, (-s), small quantity; *'n* ~ *wyn,* a spot of wine.
pietsnot', (-te), fool, idiot, simpleton.
piet'-tjou-tjou, (-s), (Cape) grey tit.
pigmee', (pigmeë), pygmy, dwarf.
pigment', pigment; ~ **a'sie,** pigmentation.
pik¹, (s) pitch; *wie met* ~ *omgaan, word daarmee besmeer,* he that toucheth pitch shall be defiled.
pik², (s) (-ke), peck, pickaxe; (w) **(ge-),** peck, bite; pick; find fault; nag at; *GEPIK wees,* be dotty, not all there; *LAAT* ~ , take to one's heels; *OP iem.* ~ , find fault with somebody; single someone out for criticism.
pi'ka, pica.
pik'agtig, (-e), pitch-like.
pikant', (-e), piquant, spicy, racy, seasoned; pungent; high; ~ *e sous,* piquant sauce; ~ **erie',** ~ **heid,** piquancy, spiciness.
Pikar'dië, Picardy.
pikaresk', (-e), picaresque.
pik: ~ **blende,** pitchblende; ~ **broek,** blue-jacket,

Jack Tar; ~**den**, pitch-pine; ~**donker**, pitch dark; ~**draad**, shoe (pitch-) thread.
pikee', piqué.
pikeer', (ong.), (ge-), pique, irritate.
piket', (-te), piquet (cards); picket; peg.
pikeur', (-s), riding-master (circus).
pik'gitswart, pitch-black.
pik'hamer, scutch.
pikkedil', (-le), trifle, peccadillo.
pik'ker, (-s), pecker; picker.
pikkewyn', (-e), penguin; ~**eier**, penguin-egg.
pik'kie, (-s), little fellow.
pik'nies, (-e), pyknic.
pik'ploeg, subsoiler.
pikrien'suur, pikri'nesuur, picric acid.
pikriet', picrite.
pik'steel, pickaxe handle.
pik'steen, pitchstone.
pik'swart, pitch-black, black as jet, atrous, raven.
pikturaal', (..rale), pictorial.
pil, (-le), pill; *'n BITTER* ~ *sluk*, swallow a bitter pill; *iem. 'n* ~ *DRAAI*, play a nasty joke on someone; *die* ~ *VERGULD*, gild the pill.
pilaar', (pilare), pillar, column, bearer, pier, post; prop; staunch supporter, stalwart; *regop* ~, upright (pillar, post); ~**bou**, pillar and stall; ~**byter**, (-s), hypocrite, dissimulator; ~**heilige**, (-s), pillar saint; ~**kop**, capital, cornice (of pillar); ~**skag**, pillar shaft; ~**tjie**, (-s), banister; ~**voet**, base (of pillar), pedestal.
pilnf', pilaff, pilau.
pilas'ter, (-s), pilaster.
Pila'tus, Pilate.
pil: ~**dosie**, pillbox.
pil'le: ~**dokter**, pill-monger; ~**dosie**, pillbox; ~**draaier**, (-s), pill-roller, apothecary; ~**tjie**, (-s), small pill, tabloid, pilule, globule.
piloon', (pilone), pylon.
piloot' (pilote), pilot, air pilot
pils, pil'sener, Pilsener beer.
pil'vormig, (-e), pilular.
piment', allspice, pimento.
pim'pel: ~ *en pers*, black and blue.
pimpernel', pimpernel, burnet.
pim'perneut, pistachio (nut).
pinakoï'de, (-s), **pinakoïed**, (-e), pinacoid.
pinakoteek', (ong.) (..teke), art gallery.
pinas', (-se), pinnace.
Pinda'ries, Pindaric; ~*e ode*, Pindaric ode.
pineaal', (pineale), pineal.
ping'pong, ping-pong.
pink, (ge-), blink; wipe (tear from eye).
pin'kie, (-s), little finger; *iem. om jou* ~ *DRAAI*, twist someone round one's (little) finger; *GEE hom die* ~ *en hy vat die hele hand*, give him an inch, and he will take an ell; *iets op sy* ~ *KEN*, have at one's fingertips.
Pink'ster, Whitsuntide, Pentecost; ~**biduur**, prayer-meeting during Whitsuntide; ~**dag**, Whit Sunday; ~**fees**, Whitsuntide, Pentecost; ~**maandag**, Whit Monday; ~**roos**, peony; ~**sondag**, Whit Sunday; ~**tyd**, Whitsuntide; ~**vakansie**, Whitsun(tide) holiday(s); ~**week**, Whit(sun) week.
pino'tiebossie, burweed *(Xanthium spinosum)*.
pins'bek, pinchbeck, Bath metal.
pinset', (-te), forceps, tweezers.
pint, (-e), pint; ~**bottel**, pint bottle; ~**maat**, pint measure; ~**pot**, pint pot.
Pinz'gauer, (-s), Pinzgauer.
pioen', (-e), peony.
pion', (-ne), pawn (chess).
pionier', (-e, -s), pioneer.
pioniers': ~**arbeid**, pioneer work; ~**gees**, pioneer spirit; ~**gereedskap**, pioneer's tools; ~**werk**, pioneer work.
piorree', pyorrhoea.
piou'ter, pewter; ~**beker**, pewter mug; ~**werk**, pewter work.
pipet', (-te), pipette; ~**teer'**, (ge-), pipette.
piramidaal', (..dale), pyramidal; enormous; *..dale struktuur*, pyramid(al) structure.
pirami'de, (-s), pyramid.

pirek'sie, pyrexia.
Pirene'ë, Pyrenees.
pire'trum, pyrethrum.
pir'heliometer, pyrheliometer.
piriet', pyrites.
pirogeen', (..gene), pyrogeneous.
pirogene'ties, (-e), pyrogenetic.
piromagne'ties, pyromagnetic.
piromanie', pyromania.
pi'rometer, pirome'ter, (-s), pyrometer.
piroskoop', (..skope), pyroscope.
pirotegniek', pyrotechnics, fireworks.
piroteg'nies, (-e), pyrotechnic(al).
pis, (plat), (s) piss, urine; (w) (ge-), pass water, urinate; ~**blaas**, (urinary) bladder; ~**buis**, urethra; ~**drywer**, diuretic; ~**glas**, urinal; ~**leier**, ureter; ~**lou**, lukewarm; ~**pot**, chamber-pot, po; ~**ser**, (-s), piddler; ~**sery**, urination; ~**siekte**, micturition.
pis'ton, (-s), piston; cornet.
pistool'¹, pistole (coin).
pistool'², (..tole), pistol; barker; detonator; ~**bossie**, pistol bush; ~**houer**, pistol-holster; ~**sak**, pistol-case, holster; ~**skoot**, pistol-shot; ~**tjie**, (-s), small pistol, pocket-pistol.
pis'wol, (plat), wool stained by urine.
pit, (-te), kernel (nut); core (of tree); stone (peach); pip (orange); marrow; medulla, pith (tree); wick (lamp); pep, grit, gumption, ginger, heart, push; *BAIE* ~ *te hê*, have pots of money; *GEEN* ~ *hê nie*, have no grit, ~**bert**, monadnock; ~**boom**, seedling (tree), tree raised from the stone (pip); ~**helm**, pith helmet; ~**jie**, (-s), small kernel (pip); ~**tjies**, pig-measles; ~**kos**, concentrates (grain); (fig.) something having substance and pithiness; ~**loos**, seed-less; ~*lose rosyntjies*, seedless raisin.
Pit(h)ago'ries, (-e), Pythagorean.
pi'ton, (-s), python.
pit'seer, (pitsere), furuncle, boil.
pit'so, (-'s), pitso, gathering, assembly.
pit'sweer = **pitseer**.
pit'te, dibs, spondulicks, money.
pit'tig, (-e), pithy; terse, concise; crisp; gritty; ~*e wyn*, wine with body; ~**heid**, pith, pithiness; terseness; body (wine).
pittoresk', (-e), picturesque.
pituïtêr', (-e), pituitary.
pit: ~**voer**, corn ration; ~**vrug**, stone-fruit, drupe.
pla, (ge-), tease, annoy, vex, nag, disturb, fret, plague, harass, molest, pester, persecute, worry; twit, banter; *moenie die DIERE* ~ *nie*, don't pester the animals; *met HOOFPYN ge*~, troubled with headaches; *ek het boetie SOMMER ge*~, I was only chaffing my brother.
plaag, (plae), plague, blight, infestation, pest, lues, affliction; vexation; *die plae van Egipte*, the plagues of Egypt; ~**beheer**, pest control; ~**gees**, tease, tormenting fiend, pesterer; ~**siek**, (-e), fond of teasing; ~**sug**, fondness of teasing.
plaak, plaque (of teeth) ~**borsel**, plaque brush; ~**middel**, ~**verwyderaar**, plaque remover.
plaas, (s) (plase), farm; place, local; *in die EERSTE* ~, in the first place; *IN* ~ *van*, instead of, in lieu of; *'n* ~ *deur jou KEEL trek*, pour a fortune down one's throat; ~ *NEEM*, take a seat; *TER aangehaalde* ~, at the cited place, loco citato; (w) (ge-), put, place (an order); locate; station (troops), remember (person); insert; collocate; lodge (power); plant; negotiate (loan); ~**baron**, land-baron; ~**bekleër**, (-s), substitute, deputy, locum tenens; ~**bepaling**, localization; ~**beskrywer**, topographer; ~**beskrywing**, topography; ~**bespreking**, booking, reservation (of seats); ~**bestemming**, destination; ~**boer**, farmer; country-dweller; ~**boere**, farmers, farming community; ~**botter**, farm butter; ~**gebrek**, want of space; ~**hou**, well-paced shot (tennis); ~**huis**, farm-house; ~**hulp**, farm hand; ~**japie**, yokel, country cousin (bumpkin); ~**jong**, farm hand; ~**kaartjie**, ticket; ~**kiosk**, farm stall; ~**lewe**, farm life; ~**lik**, (-e), local; ~*like KEUSE*, local option; ~*like VERDOWING*, local anaesthetic; ~**naam**, place-name; name of a farm;

~ **pad**, track; farm road; ~ **produk**, farm (agricultural) product; ~ **produkte**, farm (agricultural) produce; ~ **ruimte**, room, space; accommodation; ~ **skool**, farm school; ~ **tronk**, farm gaol; ~ **vervangend**, (-e), acting, taking the place of, deputizing; ~ **vervanger**, (-s), substitute, deputy; understudy; locum tenens; alternate; ~ **vervanging**, substitution; locum-tenency; ~ **vind**, (-ge-), take place, occur, happen; ~ **voorman**, farm foreman; ~ **werf**, farmyard; ~ **werk**, farm work; ~ **werker**, farm worker.

plaat, (plate), plate (name, dental photography); pan (bread); slab (granite); sheet (iron); dial; flat (country); picture; plateau; stretch (bush); record (gramophone); sill (geol.); plaque; tablet (mural); *BOEK met plate*, illustrated book; *die ~ POETS*, take oneself off; take French leave; ~ **anker**, gusset-plate (loco.); ~ **buiging**, plate-bending; ~ **draaier**, disc jockey; ~ **druk**, plate-printing, copperplate; ~ **drukker**, copperplate printer; ~ **drukkery**, copperplate printing-office; ~ **fout**, plate-error; ~ **gaas**, expanded metal; ~ **gelatien**, sheet gelatine; ~ **glas**, flat glassware; ~ **tjie**, (-s), little plate; picture; slide; disc; ~ **klem**, cramp, adjustable clamp; ~ **klip**, slab-stone; ~ **koek**, crumpet; drop-scone; flapjack; ~ **koper**, sheet copper; ~ **metaal**, sheet metal; ~ **metaalwerker**, sheet-metal worker; ~ **meule**, sheet-works; ~ **pantser**, plate armour; ~ **rooster**, (fry-top) griller.

plaat'se: *ter AANGEHAALDE ~*, loco citato; *TER ~*, locally, on the spot.

plaat: ~ **skêr**, block-shears; ~ **snykuns**, chalcography; ~ **speler**, record-player; disc jockey; ~ **staal**, sheet steel; ~ **steun**, gusset; ~ **werk**, copperplate work, illustration; ~ **yster**, sheet iron, plate iron.

place'bo, placebo.

pla'er, (-s), tease(r), nagger, molester, harrier; plaguer; ~ **ig**, (-e), fond of teasing; nagging; ~ **y**, teasing, raillery, chaff, banter; molestation.

plafon', (-ne, -s), ceiling; ~ **lamp**, ceiling-lamp; ~ **lys**, ceiling-cornice; ~ **neer'**, (ge-), put in a ceiling; ~ **plank**, ceiling-board; ~ **prys**, ceiling price; ~ **venster**, ceiling-light (window); ~ **waaier**, ceiling-fan.

plagiaat', plagiarism, (literary) piracy; ~ *pleeg*, plagiarize.

plagiaris', (-te), **plagia'tor**, (-e, -s), plagiarist.

plagieer', (ge-), plagiarize.

plak¹, (s) (-ke), ferule, cane; whip, strap; swatter; slice, slab; *onder die ~ DEURLOOP*, be given a hiding; *onder die ~ SIT*, be henpecked.

plak², (w) (ge-), paste (paper), hang (paper), stick; squat (on vacant land); *êrens bly ~*, settle down somewhere; remain seated; ~ **advertensie**, sticker; ~ **album**, scrap album; ~ **band**, gummed tape; ~ **boek**, scrapbook.

plaket', (-te), plaque, plaquette.

plak'hout, plywood.

plakkaat', (..kate), placard, poster; edict; ~ **boek**, collection of edicts; ~ **draer**, sandwich-man; placard carrier; ~ **plakker**, billsticker.

plak'ker, (-s), paster, decorator, paper-hanger; bill-sticker; sticker; squatter; ~ **sdorp**, squatters' settlement; ~ **skamp**, squatters' camp.

plak'kie, (-s), slab; slip-on; tacky; *Crassula portulacea*.

plak: ~ **krul**, spit-curl; ~ **kwas**, paste-brush; ~ **middel**, paste, adhesive; ~ **model**, paste-up; ~ **okulering**, patch-budding; ~ **pap**, wallpaper paste; ~ **papier**, wallpaper; ~ **pleister**, sticking-plaster; ~ **poppie**, pin-up girl; ~ **seël**, (-s), adhesive stamp; ~ **strokie**, (stamp-)hinge; stamp-mount.

plak'sel, plak'stysel, paste.

plak'sool, adhesive sole.

plan, (-ne), plan, scheme, project, game; draft; purpose, design; forecast; aim, intention; contrivance; *'n ~ BERAAM*, devise a plan; *'n ~ is 'n BOERDERY*, ideas are worth money; *BREË (algemene) ~*, broad (=ly-outlined) plan; *dit GAAN so op 'n ~*, things are quite fair, so-so; *GROOT ~ne*, great schemes; *hy het HONDERD ~ne en nog 'n sakkie vol*, there is no end to his schemes; he is full of ideas; *'n ~ MAAK*, contrive means; *met die ~ OM*, with the intention of; *van ~ VERANDER*, change one's mind; *WAT is jou ~?* what are you going to do? *van ~ WEES*, intend.

plandoe'ka, (-s), type of frog.

planeer', (ge-), plane, glide; smooth; planish; size (paper); ~ **boot**, hydroplane.

planeet', (..nete), planet; ~ **baan**, orbit of a planet; ~ **rat**, planet wheel; ~ **stelsel**, planetary system.

planeta'ries, planetary.

planeta'rium, (-s, ..ria), planetarium, orrery.

planetêr', (-e), planetary.

plane'testand, configuration.

planetoï'de, (-s), **planetoïed'**, (-e), planetoid.

pla'nimeter, planime'ter, (-s), planimeter.

planimetrie', planimetry, plane geometry; ~ **me'tries**, planimetric.

planisfeer', planisphere.

plank, (-e), plank, board; deal; shelf; *van die BOONSTE ~ (rak)*, first-rate, of the highest order; *so DUN soos 'n ~ wees*, famished; *DUN ~*, scantling; *op die ~ e KOM*, be brought to the stage; *~ e SAAG*, be driving hogs to market; ~ **dun**, as thin as a rake; very hungry; ~ **evrees**, stage fright; ~ **ie**, (-s), small plank; planchette (spiritism); ~ **skutting**, (wooden) partition; hoarding; ~ **skyf**, planked stead; ~ **swaai**, plank swings.

plank'ton, plankton.

plank: ~ **vloer**, wooden (boarded) floor; ~ **werk**, boarding, planking.

plan: ~ **loos**, (..lose), planless, haphazard; ~ **maker**, (-s), schemer, planner; drawer of a plan; contriver, deviser; projector.

planma'tig, (-e), systematical, methodical; ~ **heid**, system, method.

plan: ~ **neraad**, planning council; ~ **netjie**, (-s), little plan (scheme).

planolitografie', off-set lithography, planolithography.

pla'nometer, planome'ter, planometer.

plansjet', (-te), planchette.

plant, (s) (-e), plant; (w) (ge-), plant; implant; *IEM. ~*, bring someone down, grass someone (rugby); *'n ~ TEEL*, breed a plant; ~ **aan'**, plantain; ~ **aarde**, mould; ~ **aar'dig**, (-e), vegetable; ~ **aardige stof**, vegetable matter; ~ **anatomie**, phytotomy; ~ **a'sie**, (-s), plantation; ~ **beskrywing**, phytography; ~ **blik**, botanical case; ~ **dier**, zoophyte; ~ **egordel**, floral zone; ~ **egroei**, vegetation, flora; ~ **ekologie**, plant ecology; ~ **er**, (-s), planter; seed-drill; ~ **erplaat**, drill plate; ~ **eryk**, vegetable kingdom; ~ **eteelt**, phytogeny, phytogenesis; plant-breeding; ~ **eteeltstasie**, plant-breeding station; ~ **etend**, (-e), herbivorous; phytophagous; ~ **eter**, herbivore; ~ **(e)vet**, vegetable fat; ~ **ing**, planting; implantation: ~ **jellie**, pectin; ~ **jie**, (-s), small plant; seedling, transplant; ~ **jiesuurdeeg**, leavened dough preserved for yeast; ~ **kenner**, botanist; ~ **kunde**, botany; ~ **kun'dig**, (-e), botanical; ~ **kun'dige**, (-s), botanist; ~ **kweker**, nursery-gardener; ~ **kwekery**, nursery; ~ **lewe**, plant life; ~ **luis**, plant-louse, blight, garden-bug, aphis; green fly; ~ **naam**, plant name; ~ **parasiet**, plant parasite; ~ **parasities**, plant-parasitic; ~ **seisoen**, planting-season (-time); ~ **siekte**, plant-disease; ~ **siekteleer**, phytopathology.

plantsoen', (-e), park, pleasure-garden, plantation.

plant: ~ **soort**, (plant) species; ~ **stelsel**, vegetable system; ~ **stok**, bibbing-stick, dibble; ~ **suier**, plant-bug; ~ **tyd**, planting season; ~ **vet**, vegetable tallow; ~ **vesel**, plant fibre; ~ **virus**, plant-virus; ~ **was**, vegetable wax; ~ **yster**, dibber.

plas, (s) (-se), pool, puddle, paddling-pond; *'n ~ sie maak*, pee, piddle; (w) (ge-), paddle, splash, dabble, plash; pour down; ~ **dammetjie**, paddling pool.

plasen'ta, (-s), placenta.

pla'sie, (-s), small farm, plot.

pla'sing, (-s), placing, collocation; emplacement; insertion (in press); investment; flotation; deposition; arrangement.

plas'ma, plasm; ~ **ägtig**, plasmatic.

plasma'ties, plas'mies, (-e), plasmatic, plasmic.

plas'reën, plas'reent, (s) heavy, rain, downpour; (w) **(ge-),** pour with rain, rain heavily.
plas'ser, (-s), paddler; ~**y,** paddling.
plastiek', plastic art; plastic (material); ~ **asblik,** plastic refuse bin; ~ **bal,** plastic ball; ~ **blik,** plastic container; ~ **speelgoed,** plastic toys; ~ **stof,** plastic fabric.
plas'ties, (-e), plastic; pliable; ~ *e CHIRURG,* plastic surgeon; ~ *e KUNSTE,* plastic arts; *'n* ~ *e TEKENING,* a vivid description.
plastiseer', (ge-), plasticize; ~ **middel,** plasticizer.
plastisien', plastisi'ne, plasticine (registered trade name).
plastisiteit', plasticity.
plas'tron, (-ne), plastron, fencing-pad.
plat, (s) flat (of sword); shelf (geol.); *vastelandse* ~, continental shelf; (b) flat, level, even, procumbent; plain; prostrate; flatwise, horizontal; gross; low, coarse, slangy, vulgar (language); *my BEURS is* ~, I am hard up; *om dit* ~ *uit te DRUK,* to put it vulgarly; *'n* ~ *GRAP,* a coarse joke; ~ *KANTE,* flats (motor); *so* ~ *soos 'n PANNEKOEK,* as flat as a pancake; ~ *TAAL,* slang, vulgar language; lingo.
plataan', (platane), plane-tree.
platan'na, (-s), spur-toed frog; clawed toad *(Xenopus laevis).*
plat: ~ **bak,** flat-deck body (motor); ~ **beitel,** flat chisel; ~ **bektang,** flat-nose pliers; ~ **bol,** plano-convex; ~ **boomvaartuig,** flat-bottomed vessel, flat, scow; punt; bark; ~ **boot,** pram; ~ **bord,** platter, flat plate; meat plate; ~ **dak,** flat roof, ~ **dakhuis,** flat-roofed house; ~ **druk,** (-ge-), flatten out, crush, squash.
Plat'duits, Low German.
plateel', faience, art pottery.
pla'te: ~ **kabinet,** record cabinet; ~ **liefhebber,** record collector; ~ **speler,** record-player; ~ **versameling,** collection of records.
plat'form, (-s), platform; landing-place; ~ **ingang,** platform entrance; ~ **kaartjie,** platform ticket; ~ **spreker,** platform speaker; politician.
plat: ~ **gooi,** (-ge-), throw down; run away; bring down, grass (rugby); ~ **hakskoen,** low-heeled shoe; ~ **heid,** flatness, evenness; broadness (speech); platitude; vulgarism, coarseness; ~ **hoed,** flat hat; ~ **hoef,** flat hoof; ~ **hol,** plano-concave.
pla'tina, platinum ore; ~ **blond,** platinum blonde; ~ **draad,** platinum wire; ~ **erts,** dunite; ~ **houdend,** (-e), platinum-bearing.
platineer', (ge-), platinize.
platinoï'de, platenoïed', platinoid.
pla'tinum, platinum (chemical element, Pt).
plat'jie, (-s), rogue, scamp; imp; ~ **rig,** (-e), impish, roguish.
plat: ~ **kissie,** tray (for packing fruit); ~ **knoop,** reef-knot; ~ **koekie,** muffin, flapjack; ~ **kop,** (-pe), octopus; flat-headed person; catfish; ~ **duif,** turbit; ~ **kopspyker,** tack, clout nail; ~ **krul,** spit-curl; ~ **kryt,** tailor's chalk, ~ **lê,** (-ge-), lie flat, be prostrate; lie upon, crush; ~ **liggend,** (-e), prostrate.
plat'loop, (-ge-), overrun; overcome; *die hele PLEK* ~, go everywhere; *'n WERK* ~, finish a task quickly.
plat: ~ **luis,** crab-louse, morpion; ~ **maak,** (s) flattening; (w) **(ge-),** flatten; ~ **naat,** run-and-fell seam; flat seam; ~ **neus,** flat nose, pug-nose.
plato', (-'s), plateau.
plato'nies, (-e), Platonic; ~ *e liefde,* Platonic love; ~ *e vriendskap,* Platonic friendship.
plato'rand, escarpment, plateau.
Pla'tostaat, city-state.
plat'pens, hungry.
plat'plooi, box-pleat; ~ **romp,** pleated skirt.
plat'rib, flat rib (beef).
plat'riem, ferule, strap; *iem. met die* ~ *gee,* give someone a hiding.
plat: ~ **ring,** quoit; ~ **ry,** (-ge-), travel in all directions; ride over, crush.
plat'sak, hard up, penniless, "broke", impecunious; *EK is* ~, I'm hard up (broke); *TOTAAL* ~, stony-broke.

plat'skiet, (-ge-), shoot down, fusillade; ~ **er,** pot-hunter.
plat: ~ **slaan,** (-ge-), knock down, floor; laminate; raze (building); flatten; beat out; ~ **snyer,** swather; ~ **stryk,** (-ge-), iron flat (out); ~ **stuk,** slab.
plat'te, flat part; *heeldag op die* ~ *van sy voete staan,* be on his feet the whole day.
platteer', (ge-), plate; ~ **werk,** plated ware.
plat'tegrond, ground-plan, sketch; map; ~ **tekening,** ichnography.
plat'teland, country (districts), rural districts; backveld; ~ **er,** (-s), country-dweller, backvelder, one from the country; provincial; ~ **s,** (-e), rural, country; ~ **sgemeente,** rural congregation.
plat'terig, (-e), flattish, rather flat; vulgar.
plat'trap, (-ge-), trample down; crush; *die platgetrapte paadjie,* the beaten path.
plat: ~ **trek,** (-ge-), shoot down, pull down, lay low; ~ **val,** (-ge-), fall flat; ~ **veer,** plate-spring; ~ **vis,** butt, dab, flat-fish; ~ **visier,** fixed sight; lowered (block-) sight.
plat'vloers, (-e), banal, common; ~ **heid,** banality.
plat'voet, flat-foot, fallen arch; ~ **loper,** plantigrade; ~ **wag,** second dogwatch.
plat: ~ **vyl,** barette, flat file; ~ **waai,** (-ge-), blow down; lodge (corn); lay flat (by wind).
plat'weg, straight away; bluntly; unassumingly; ~ **weier,** refuse flatly.
plat: ~ **wurm,** flatworm; ~ **yster,** flat-iron.
plavei', (ge-), pave; ~ **blok,** paving-block; ~ **klinker,** adamant clinker; ~ **sel,** (-s), pavement, paving, pavage, flagging; ~ **steen,** paving-stone, flagstone.
plebe'jer, (-s), plebeian.
plebe'jies, (-e), plebeian.
plebissiet', (-e), plebiscite.
plebs, rabble, populace, plebs.
pleeg, (ge-), commit, perpetrate; be in the habit of; *OORLEG* ~ *met,* consult with; *SELFMOORD* ~, commit suicide; *VERSET* ~ *teen,* offer resistance to; ~ **baar,** (..bare), commitable; ~ **boom,** nurse-tree; ~ **broer,** foster-brother; ~ **dogter,** foster-daughter; ~ **kind,** foster-child; pupil, charge; nurse-child; ~ **moeder,** foster-mother; ~ **ouers,** foster-parents; ~ **seun,** foster-son; ~ **vader,** foster-father, adoptive parent.
pleet, plate, plated ware; ~ **poeier,** plate powder; ~ **silwer,** German silver, silver plate; ~ **werk,** electroplate, German silver.
pleg'anker, sheet-anchor; palladium.
ple'ger, (-s), perpetrator.
pleg'gewaad, ceremonial dress.
ple'ging, commitment, perpetration, commission.
plegsta'tig, (-e), stately, ceremonious, ceremonial, solemn; ~ **heid,** stateliness, ceremoniousness, pomp.
pleg'tig, (-e), solemn, ceremonious, formal, grave; stately, impressive; devout; ~ *open,* openly, formally; ~ **heid,** (..hede), ceremony, rite, function; gravity.
pleidooi', (-e), plea, argument, pleading, defence; *'n* ~ *hou vir,* make a plea for.
plein, (-e), square; esplanade, piazza; ~ **vrees,** agoraphobia.
pleis'ter, (s) (-s), plaster; poultice, cataplasm; stucco (on wall); *dit was 'n* ~ *op sy wond,* that soothed his feelings; (w) **(ge-),** plaster, stucco; parget; ~ **aar,** (-s), plasterer; ~ **bak,** poultice bowl; ~ **beeld,** plaster-cast; ~ **bord,** plaster-board; hand-hawk; ~ **ing,** gunite; plastering; ~ **kalk,** lime plaster, grout, parget; ~ **laag,** plaster coat; ~ **plank,** hawk; plastering-plank; ~ **troffel,** plastering-trowel; ~ **werk,** plaster-work, plastering, stucco.
Pleistoseen', Pleistocene.
pleit, (s) plea, dispute; pleading; *die* ~ *is BESLEG,* the matter is settled; their fate is sealed: *die* ~ *is GEWIN,* they have carried the day; (w) **(ge-),** plead; intercede; ~ *vir,* plead in favour of, advocate; ~ **besorger,** advocate, attorney, lawyer, pleader; advocator; ~ **er,** (-s), pleader; barrister; ~ **rede,** (-s), pleading(s), plea; ~ **siek,** litigious; ~ **skrifte,** ~ **stukke,** pleadings.
Pleja'de, Pleiades.
plek, (-ke), place, spot; point; room, space; seat; pew

ition; location (mil.); passage (from book); scene; post (in an office); ~ **BESPREEK**, book a seat; *'n ~ DEK*, set a cover; lay a place; *in die EERSTE ~*, in the first place; *IN die ~ van*, instead (in place) of; *~ INRUIM vir*, make room for; *~ MAAK*, make room; *OOP ~*, vacancy; vacant seat; *OP die ~*, there and then, immediately; *'n ~ PLATLOOP*, walk all over the place; *op die ~ RUS!*, stand at ease! *iem. op sy ~ SIT*, put someone in his place, rebuke someone; *iem. se ~ toe STAAN, 'n ~ vol STAAN*, take someone's place; *in die ~ TREE van*, step into (take) the place of; *uit jou ~ VOEL*, feel out of place, not feel at home (at ease); ~ **aanduidend, (-e)**, locative; ~ **aanwyser**, usher; ~ **aanwysing**, ushering; allocation; ~ **bepaling**, fixing of position; orientation; location; position-finding; ~ **bespreking**, booking (reservation) of seat; ~ **bestemming**, destination; ~ **geheue**, sense of locality; ~ **geld**, cover charge, convert; ~ **loting**, draw (horses); ~ **melding**, position-report; ~ **naam**, place-name; ~ **naamkunde**, toponymics; ~ **naamkun'dig, (-e)**, toponymic(al).
plek'-plek, here and there, in places.
pleks, instead; *~ van (om) dit te DOEN*, instead of doing this; *~ VAN*, instead of.
plek'sin, sense of locality.
plek'trum, (-s, ..tra), plectrum.
pleng, (ge-), shed (blood); spill (liquor); offer (libation); ~ **ing**, shedding; ~ **offer**, libation.
pleonas'me, pleonasm.
pleonas'ties, (-e), pleonastic.
plesier', (s) pleasure, enjoyment, merriment, fun, frolic; favour; *iem. 'n ~ DOEN*, do a person a favour; *met die GROOTSTE ~*, with the greatest pleasure; *~ HÊ in iets*, enjoy a thing; *~ is nes 'n jong KOMKOMMER, as jy hom pluk, verlep hy sommer*, pleasures are like poppies spread; you seize the flower, its bloom is shed (Burns); *~ MAAK*, make merry, go on a jaunt; *MET ~!* with pleasure! *VEEL ~!* enjoy yourself! *~ VIND in iets*, find pleasure in something; *VIR sy ~*, to amuse himself; (w) **(ge-)**, please, oblige; ~ **boot(jie)**, pleasure-boat, launch; ~ **ig**, (b) **(-e)**, pleasant, happy, merry, jovial, mirthful; *'n ~ ige ou*, a jolly fellow; (tw) cheerio! ~ **igheid**, pleasantness, mirthfulness, happiness, merriment; ~ **jag**, hunting for pleasure; pleasure-seeking; pleasure-launch (-yacht); ~ **maker**, holiday-maker, merrymaker, reveller, playboy; ~ **oord**, pleasure-resort; ~ **reis**, pleasure-trip, pleasure-cruise; ~ **reisiger**, tourist, tripper, excursionist; ~ **rit**, pleasure-drive, jaunt, joy-ride; ~ **ryer**, joy-rider; ~ **rytuig** chaise; ~ **soeker**, pleasure-seeker; ~ **stap**, hike; ~ **stapper**, hiker; ~ **tog**, pleasure-trip, excursion; ~ **trein**, pleasure-train; ~ **vluggie**, flip (in plane).
plet, (ge-), flatten, hammer, roll out, planish, laminate; foliate; ~ **baar, (..bare)**, malleable, capable of being flattened (rolled out); ~ **baarheid**, malleability; ~ **hammer**, flatter.
Ple'tie: *die Kretie en ~ was daar*, the riff-raff was there.
plet: ~ **metaal**, sheet metal; ~ **meule**, rolling-mill; roller mill; ~ **rol**, flatting-roller.
plet'ter, planisher; roller; *hom te ~ LOOP*, be smashed (to a pulp); *sy kop te ~ loop TEEN*, dash one's head against.
plet: ~ **tery, (-e)**, rolling-mill; ~ **werk**, flattening.
pleu'ra, pleura.
pleuraal', (pleurale), pleural.
pleu'ris, pleuri'tis, pleurisy, pleuritis.
plig, (-te), duty, obligation; devoir; part; office; *iem. tot sy ~ BRING*, teach a person his duty; *sy ~ DOEN (nakom)*, do one's duty; *die LAASTE ~ te vervul*, perform the last (mournful) offices; *sy ~ VERSUIM*, neglect one's duty; ~ **getrou, (-e)**, conscientious, dutiful; ~ **getrouheid**, conscientiousness; duteousness; ~ **ma'tig, (-e)**, conformable to one's duty, dutiful, duteous; ~ **matigheid**, dutifulness; ~ **pleging, (-e, -s)**, ceremony, courtesy, form, ceremonial; compliment.
pligs: ~ **besef**, sense of duty; ~ **betragting**, devotion to duty; grace; ~ **getrou = pliggetrou;** ~ **gevoel**,

sense of duty; grace; ~ **halwe**, dutifully, as in duty bound.
plig'staat, duty sheet.
pligs: ~ **versaking**, neglect of duty; ~ **versuim**, neglect (breach, dereliction) of duty; ~ **versuimer**, shirker; ~ **vervulling**, performance of duty.
pligvaar'dig, (-e), dutiful, duteous.
plim'sollmerk, Plimsoll line.
plint, (-e), plinth, skirting-board.
Plioseen', Pliocene.
plisseer', (ge-), make fine pleats.
ploe'ë, (ge-), plough; furrow; *in die grond ~*, have a fall; plough through the ground.
ploe'ër, (-s), ploughman; ~ **y**, ploughing.
ploeg, (ge-) = ploeë.
ploeg, (ploeë), plough; fang (of workers); shift; duff, sclaff (golf); *in ploeë WERK*, work in relays; *die P ~*, Charles's Wain; ~ **baar, (..bare)**, arable, tillable, ploughable, cultivable, cultivatable; ~ **baas**, ganger, foreman; gang boss; ~ **balk**, plough-beam (-tree); ~ **bank**, plough-sole; ~ **hou**, sclaff (golf); ~ **kouter**, coulter; ~ **land**, ploughland, land under cultivation; arable land; ~ **os**, plough-ox; ~ **reën**, early rain; ~ **skaaf**, match-plane; fay; grooving-plane; ~ **skaar**, ploughshare; ~ **sool**, plough-sole; hardpan; ~ **stelsel**, relay system; ~ **stert**, plough-tail, plough-handle(s); *~ stert hou*, hold the plough-handles; ~ **tyd**, ploughing-season; ~ **voor**, furrow; ~ **walletjie**, furrow-slice; ~ **werker**, plate-layer; ~ **yster**, coulter.
ploems, plop.
ploert, (-e), cad, low fellow; snob, flunkey; ~ **agtig, (-e)**, caddish; ~ **(er)ig, (-e)**, caddish; snobbish; ~ **ery**, meanness, caddish action; ~ **estreek**, mean (scurvy) trick; ~ **igheid**, meanness; snobbishness, snobbism.
ploe'ter, (ge-), drudge, toil, plod, peg away at; grub; ~ **aar, (-s)**, plodder, drudge.
plof, (s) (plowwe), thud, thump, flump, flop; plump, plunk; (w) **(ge-)**, flop down, fall with a thud; pop; ~ **fer, (-s)**, plosive; ~ **gas**, explosive gas; ~ **kop**, warhead; ~ **mengsel**, explosive mixture; ~ **stof**, explosive; giant-powder; ~ **toestel**, explosive device; ~ **vas, (-te)**, ~ **vry, (-e)**, non-explosive.
plombeer', (ge-), fill (tooth); fill with lead, plug, seal; ~ **sel**, filling, plug.
plomp, (-er, -ste), stout, gross, blunt, clumsy; ~ **heid**, stoutness, grossness; clumsiness; ~ **weg**, bluntly, curtly.
plons, (s) **(-e)**, splash, plunge, plop; plump; (w) **(ge-)**, splash, plunge, plop.
plooi, (s) **(-e)**, fold, furl; wrinkle (face); crease (trousers); pleat, gathering (skirt); collop; kilt; pucker; plait; flute; plication; *'n goeie ~ aan iets GEE, iets in die regte ~ e GOOI*, present something in a favourable light; *jou gesig in die ~ HOU*, keep a straight face; *in die beste ~ e LÊ*, present in the best light; (w) **(ge-)**, fold; crease; pleat; pucker; purse (lips); enfold; ruff, ruffle; flute; gof(f)er; arrange; crimp; frill; gauge; gather; kilt; *'n saak so ~ dat dit aanneemlik lyk*, present something in the best light; ~ **as**, axis of fold; ~ **baar, (..bare)**, pliable, flexible, pliant; conformable; ~ **baarheid**, pliability, flexibility; conformity; ~ **bakkies**, wrinkled face; ~ **dal**, syncline; ~ **e**, pleats; ~ **er**, plaiter; ~ **erig, (-e)**, creased, wrinkled; ~ **ing, (-e, -s)**, anticline; folding; raising; ~ **kamer**, creasing-room; ~ **kraag**, ruff; ~ **paneel**, linenfold, linen scroll; ~ **rok**, pleated skirt; ~ **rug**, anticline; ~ **sel, (-s)**, fold(ing), pleat(ing), frill(ing), pucker(ing), tuck, jabot; ~ **tang**, crimping-iron; ~ **yster**, gof(f)er, creasing-iron.
plosief', (..siewe), stop, explosive.
plot'seling, (b) (-e), sudden, abrupt; (bw) suddenly, all of a sudden, abruptly.
plousi'bel, (-e), plausible; ..**biliteit'**, plausibility.
pluche, plush.
plui'ens, plui'sings, rags, tatters, cast-off clothing.
pluim, (-e), plume, feather; aigrette; panicle (of oats); ~ **agtig, (-e)**, plumose, feathery; ~ **aluin**, plume alum; ~ **a'sie**, plumage; ~ **bal**, badminton; shuttle-cock; ~ **bereider**, plumassier; ~ **bos**, plume, crest;

~**den**, cluster pine; ~**loos**, (..**lose**), featherless, plumeless.
pluim'pie, (-s), compliment; plumelet; *iem. 'n ~ GEE*, compliment a person; *'n ~ KRY*, be paid a compliment; *dis 'n ~ VIR hom*, that is a feather in his cap.
pluim'stryk, (ge-), adulate, flatter, butter up (a person), toady; ~**er**, (-s), mean flatterer, toady, adulator, wheedler; ~**ery**, wheedling, adulation, toadyism, flunkeyism.
pluim'vee, poultry; ~**afval**, giblets; ~**boerdery**, poultry-farm(ing); ~**handelaar**, poulterer; ~**hok**, poultry house; ~**houer**, poultry-keeper; ~**kamp**, poultry run; ~**teelt**, poultry-rearing; ~**tentoonstelling**, poultry-show; ~**voer**, poultry food.
pluis[1], (s) ginning (cotton); oakum; nap; (w) (ge-), gin (cotton); tease (wool); flue; make fluffy, pick, fluff; flake (fish); fiberise (minerals).
pluis[2], (b) all right, in order, clear; *die saak is nie ~ nie*, there is something fishy about the business (affair); *hy IS nie ~ nie*, he hasn't all his wits about him.
pluis: ~**er**, ginner; ~**erig**, (-e), fuzzy; nappy; ~**ery**, ginning; ~**hoed**, silk top hat; chimney-pot hat; ~**ie**, (-s), plug; fluff; plush; wad; flue; fug; piece of cotton wool; swab; ~**kam**, (ge-), tease (hair); ~**katoen**, ginning; ~**keil**, top hat, topper; ~**leer**, willow calf; ~**masjien**, willow-machine; ~**mat**, tufted rug; ~**meul(e)**, ginning-machine, ginnery; ~**stof**, napped fabric; ~**wol**, mungo, fluffy wool.
pluk, (s) picking (of fruit); plucking (of feathers); (w) (ge-), pick, gather; fleece, pluck, deplume; reap; *iem. ~*, fleece someone; ~**blom**, cut flower; ~**haar**, (ge-), tousle, tussle, scuffle; ~**ker**, (-s), harvester, picker, gatherer; puller; ~**kis**, lug-box; ~**masjien**, picker(-machine); ~**sel**, (-s), lint (bandage); crop (ostrich-feathers); picking; ~**selfverband**, pledget, lint bandage; ~**tyd**, plucking time; picking season; ~**wol**, plucked wool.
plun'der, (ge-), plunder, ransack, loot, maraud, foray, forage, harry, depredate, rifle, pillage (town); prey; picaroon; ravage; raid; rob (man); despoil; ~**aar**, (-s), plunderer, pillager, marauder, harrier, depredator, ravager; raider; ravener; ~**end**, (-e), depredatory; ravaging; ~**ing**, pillage, looting, depredation, despoliation, ransacking, plundering; ~**tog**, plundering-raid, marauding-expedition; depredation, despoliation, sackage, rapine.
plun'jer, (-s), plunger; ~**slot**, plunger-lock.
pluraal', plural.
plura'lis, (-se), plural.
pluralis', (-te), pluralist; ~**me**, pluralism.
pluraliteit', plurality.
pluriformiteit', pluriformity.
plus, plus; ~**faktor**, plus factor; ~**-minus**, about, more or less; ~**punt**, advantage; ~**speler**, plus player; ~**teken**, plus sign.
plutokraat', (..**krate**), plutocrat.
plutokrasie', plutocracy.
plutokra'ties, (-e), plutocratic.
pluto'nies, plutonic.
Plutonis', (-te), Plutonist; ~**me**, Plutonism.
pluto'nium, plutonium.
plu'viometer, **pluviome'ter**, (-s), pluviometer.
pneumatiek', pneumatics.
pneuma'ties, (-e), pneumatic.
pneuma'tika, pneumatics.
pneumatoli'se, pneumatolysis.
pneumokonio'se, pneumoconiosis.
pneumonie', pneumonia.
po'dagra, podagra, gout.
podagreus', (-e), podagric, gouty.
podagris', (-te), gouty person.
po'dium, (-s), podium, platform.
pod'zol, podzol.
poe! phew! ugh!
poe'del, (-s), poodle; ~**hond**, poodle.
poe'del: ~**naak**, (-te), ~**nakend**, (-e), stark naked.
poe'delprys, booby prize.
poe'ding, (-s), pudding; ~**bord**, pudding-plate; ~**vorm**, pudding-mould.
poe'dinkie, (-s), small pudding.

poëem', (**poëme**), poem.
poëet, (**poëte**), poet.
poef[1], (s) (-e), pouffe.
poef[2]! (tw) bang! pop!
poe'gaai, dog-tired; drunk.
poei'er, (s) (-s), powder; (w) (ge-), powder; ~**agtig**, (-e), powdery; farinaceous; pulverous; pulverulent; ~**asbes**, asbestos powder; ~**bevatter**, powder-compact; ~**doos**, powder-box; flapjack; ~**ig**, (-e), powdery; ~**ing**, pulverization; ~**kwas**, powder-puff; ~**melk**, powdered milk; ~**meule**, pulverizer; ~**mis**, poudrette; ~**onderlaag**, powder base; ~**steen**, blanco; ~**suiker**, powdered sugar; ~**vormig**, (-e), powdery, pulverized.
poel, (-e), pool, puddle; ~**etjie**, (-s), small pool.
poelier', (-s), poulterer.
poelpetaan', (..**tane**), **poelpetaat'**, (..**tate**), **poelpeta'ter**, (-s), guinea-fowl; pintado bird.
poel'snip, snipe.
poe'ma, (-s), puma, cougar.
poe'na, (-s), old-fashioned musket; poll, pollard.
poens'kop, hornless ox or cow, poll, pollard.
poep, (plat), (s) (-e), fart; (w) (ge-), fart.
poesa'ka, (gew.), (-s), heirloom.
poe'selig, (-e), chubby; ~**heid**, chubbiness.
poësie', poetry.
poes'pas, (ong.), hodge-podge, jumble.
poë'ties, (-e), poetic(al).
poë'tika, poetics.
poëtiseer', (ge-), poetize.
poe'toe, putu (porridge).
poets[1], (s) (-e), trick, prank, quiz; *iem. 'n ~ bak*, play a trick on someone.
poets[2], (s) polish; (w) (ge-), polish, shine; ~**besem**, mop; ~**borsel**, polishing brush; ~**doek**, polishing-cloth; ~**er**, (-s), polisher, cleaner; ~**goed**, polishing-material, polish; ~**katoen**, cotton waste; ~**lap**, cleaning cloth; ~**leer**, buff leather; ~**middel**, polisher; ~**plank**, glossing board; ~**skaaf**, smoothing-plane; ~**trommel**, rumbler; ~**werk**, rubbing, elbow-grease; ~**yster**, glossing iron.
poewa'sa, Mohammedan fast.
pof, (s) (**powwe**), puff; (w) (ge-), puff; *ge ~ te rys*, puffed rice; ~**adder**, (-s), puff-adder; ~**broek**, plus-fours; knickerbockers; ~**eiers**, fluffy eggs; ~**fertjie**, (-s), fritter, puff-cake, puff; ~**koring**, puffed wheat; ~**mou**, puff(ed) sleeves, balloon sleeve, gigot sleeve; ~**opnaaisel**, air tuck.
pog, (ge-), brag, swagger; ~**ger**, (-s), braggart; ~**gery**, bragging, boasting; ~**hans**, (-e), swaggerer, braggadocio.
po'ging, (-e, -s), effort, attempt, endeavour, essay; exertion; *'n ~ AANWEND*, make an effort; *~ tot MOORD*, attempted murder; *nog 'n ~ WAAG*, try once more, make another attempt.
pogrom', (-s), pogrom, massacre.
poinset'tia, (-s), poinsettia.
pointillis'me, pointillism; ..**listies**, pointillistic.
pok, (-ke), pock; peck (in wood); *die ~ke*, smallpox; ~**agtig**, (-e), pocky; ~**da'lig**, (-e), pock-marked, pitted (by pox), pocky; ~**epidemic**, smallpox epidemic.
po'ker(spel), poker.
pok'hout, lignum vitae, pockwood, guaicum.
pok'ke, smallpox, variola; pox; ~**entstof**, vaccine.
pok'kel, (-s), lump, corpus; fatty (person).
pok: ~**kies**, smallpox, pox (animals); ~**merk**, pock-mark; ~**steen**, variolite; ~**stof**, variola vaccine.
pol, (-le), tuft of grass, tussock.
pola'rimeter, **polarime'ter**, polarimeter, polariscope.
polarisa'sie, polarization; ~**vlak**, plane of polarization.
polarisa'tor, (-s), polarizer.
polariseer', (ge-), polarize.
polariskoop', (..**skope**), polariscope.
polariteit', polarity.
pol'der, (-s), polder, drained land; ~**bestuur**, polder board; ~**dyk**, dike of a polder; ~**land**, polder land.
Po'le, Poland.
poleer', (ge-), polish, burnish; ~**der**, (-s), furbisher, polisher, planisher; ~**skyf**, polishing wheel; ~**steen**, polishing stone.

polemiek', (-e), controversy, polemics.
pole'mies, (-e), controversial, argumentative; eristic, agonistic.
polemis', (-te), controversialist, polemic writer.
polemiseer', (ge-), carry on a controversy, polemize.
polêr', (-e), polar.
pole'ring, polishing.
polfyn'tjie, (-s), forfeit (in games); keepsake.
pol'gras, tuft(ed) grass.
poliandrie', polyandry.
polian'dries, (-e), polyandrous.
polichromie', polychromy.
polichroom', polychrome.
poliep', (-e), polyp(e) (animal); polypus (growth); ~ **agtig**, (-e), polypous.
poliës'ter, polyester.
poliets', (-e; -er, -ste), artful, sly, cunning, clever, polite, diplomatic; ~ **heid**, artfulness, cleverness, cunning; politeness, diplomacy.
polifonie', polyphony.
polifoon', (*. fone), polyphonic.
poligaam', (..game), polygamous.
poligamie', polygamy.
poligamis', (-te), polygamist.
poliglot', (-te), polyglot; ~ **ties**, (-e), polyglot.
poligoon', (..gone), polygon.
polikliniek', policlinic, polyclinic.
polimeer', (..mere), polymer (chem.); polymere (geol.).
polimerie', polymerism.
polimerisa'sie, polymerization.
polimorf', (-e), polymorphous.
Poline'sië, Polynesia; ~ **r**, (-s), Polynesian.
Poline'sies, (-e), Polynesian.
po'lio, **poliomiëli'tis**, polio(myelitis), infantile paralysis.
po'lis, (-se), insurance policy; ~ **houer**, (-s), policyholder.
poli'sie, police; *'n saak by die* ~ *aangee*, report a matter to the police; ~ **agent**, policeman, constable; ~ **beampte**, policeman, police-constable; ~ **blad**, police-gazette; ~ **buro**, (-'s), charge-office; ~ **dienaar**, policeman, bobby, cop, peon; ~ **geleide**, police escort; ~ **hond**, police dog; ~ **kantoor**, charge-office, police station; ~ **klok**, curfew; ~ **kommissaris**, commissioner of police; ~ **kwartiere**, police barracks; ~ **mag**, police force; posse; police authority; ~ **man**, policeman; ~ **ondersoek**, police investigation; ~ **pos**, police post; ~ **soldaat**, gendarme; ~ **spioen**, police spy (-trap); ~ **staat**, police state; ~ **toesig**, police supervision, policing; ~ **val**, police-trap; ~ **verordening**, police regulation; ~ **wa**, police van, black Maria; ~ **wag**, police watch; ~ **wese**, the police; ~ **wet**, police law.
polisilla'be, polysyllable.
polisilla'bies, (-e), polysyllabic.
polisin'deton, polysyndeton.
polisinte'ties, (-e), polysynthetic.
polisioneel', (..nele), police.
polis'lening, policy loan.
politeen', (..tene), polythene.
politegniek', polytechnic(s).
politeg'nies, (-e), polytechnic.
politeïs', (-te), polytheist; ~ **me**, polytheism; ~ **ties**, (-e), polytheistic.
politiek', (s) politics; policy; *met* ~ *te werk gaan*, set about something diplomatically; (b) (-e), political, politic; wily; ~ **ery**, politicizing.
poli'ties, (-e), political.
politikas'ter, (-s), incompetent (insignificant) politician; ~ **y**, politicizing.
poli'tikus, (..tici, -se), politician.
politiseer', (ge-), take to politics, be a politician, politicize, talk politics.
politoer', (s) (-e), polish; (w) (ge-), polish, furbish; ~ **der**, (-s), polisher; ~ **hout**, glazing-sticks; ~ **sel**, (-s), French polish.
pol'ka, (s) (-s), polka; (w) (ge-), dance the polka; ~ **haarkam**, bobbed-hair comb; ~ **hare**, bobbed hair; ~ **masur'ka**, polka-mazurka; ~ **styl**, bob (hair).
pollak', (neerh.), pollack.

po'lo, polo.
polonai'se, (-s), polonaise.
polo'nie, (-s), polony.
polo'nium, polonium.
polonys', (-e), polonaise.
pols, (s) (-e), pulse; wrist; (w) (ge-), feel the pulse; sound; *IEM.* ~, *iem. se* ~ *VOEL, VOEL hoe iem, se* ~ *klop*, sound someone; throw out a feeler; ~ **aar**, radial artery; ~ **band**, wrist-strap; ~ **beentjie**, carpal bone; ~ **gewrig**, wrist; carpal joint; ~ **horlosie**, wrist-watch; ~ **meter**, pulsimeter; sphygmograph; ~ **mof**, muffetee; ~ **oorlosie**, wristwatch; ~ **skut**, wrist-guard; ~ **slag**, pulsation, beat (of the pulse); ~ **slagaar**, radial artery; ~ **snelheid**, frequency of the pulse; pulse rate; ~ **stok**, leaping-pole; ~ **stokspring**, pole-jumping; ~ **werk**, wrist action.
pol'tergees, poltergeist.
pol'vormig, (-e), tufted.
polvy', (-e), heel (of a shoe); ~ **spoor**, box-spur; ~ **stalletjie**, heel bar; ~ **stuk**, heel-piece.
polys', (ge-), polish, burnish, furbish, planish, buff; lap; civilize; ~ **hout**, emery stick; ~ **papier**, emery-paper; ~ **poeier**, polishing-powder; ~ **rooi**, crocus; ~ **skyf**, polishing-wheel; lap; ~ **steen**, polishing-stone, sleek-stone; ~ **ter**, (-s), glazer, polisher; lapper; ~ **ting**, polishing; ~ **werk**, polishing; ~ **yster**, paring-chisel.
pome'lo, **po'melo**, (-'s), grapefruit, pomelo; ~ **kelkie**, grapefruit cocktail; ~ **nartjie**, tangelo.
pomerans', (-e), cue-tip.
pomma'de, (-s), pomade; ..**madeer'**, (ge-), pomade.
Pom'mer, Pomeranian; ~ **e**, Pomerania; ~ **s**, (-e), Pomeranian.
pomologie', pomology; ..**lo'gies**, (-e), pomological.
pomoloog', (..**loë**), pomologist.
pomp, (s) (-e), pump, inflator; (w) (ge-), pump, draw (water).
pompadoer', (-s), pompadour.
pomp'bak, pump cistern.
pomp: ~ **buisie**, pump connection; ~ **buiteband**, tubeless tyre; ~ **dompelaar**, pump plunger.
Pompe'ji, Pompeii; ~ **es**, (-e), Pompeian.
Pompe'jus, Pompey.
pompe(l)moer', (Cape) gooseberry.
pom'pelmoes = **pampelmoes.**
pom'per, (-s), pumper.
pompernik'kel, (-s), pumpernickel (Westphalian rye bread).
pompeus', (ong., lit.), (-e), pompous; ~ **heid**, pomposity.
pom'pie, (-s), little pump; *eerste geruik, het* ~ *gebruik*, he who smells it first is the guilty one.
pomp: ~ **joggie**, petrol attendant; ~ **kamer**, pump-room; ~ **klep**, pump valve; ~ **man**, pumpman; ~ **masjinis**, pump-station man.
pom-pom', (-s), pom-pom.
pompon', (-s), pompon.
pomp: ~ **pakking**, pump gasket; ~ **silinder**, pump barrel; ~ **slinger**, swing, handle (of a pump); ~ **stang**, pump rod; ~ **stasie**, pumping-station; ~ **stofie**, (-s), pressure-stove; etna; ~ **suier**, (-s), sucker of a pump, piston; ~ **swingel**, pump brake; ~ **toestel**, pump gear; ~ **trollie**, pump trolley; ~ **water**, pump-water; ~ **werk**, pumping-gear; ~ **werker**, (-s), pumpman.
pond, (-e), pound, sovereign; quid (coll.); *PER* ~, per lb.; ~ *STERLING*, pound sterling; ~ *VIR* ~, pound for pound.
pond: ~ **geld**, poundage; ~ **noot**, pound note.
Pon'do, (-'s), Pondo.
pondok', (-ke), hovel, hut, shanty, shack; wigwam.
Pon'doland, Pondoland.
poneer', (ge-), put forward, advance, propound.
pongee', pongee (silk).
po'nie, (-s), pony, cob; fringe (hair); ~ **slagskip**, pocket battleship; ~ **stert**, pony-tail.
pon'jaard, (-e), poniard, dagger.
pons¹, punch; jorum.
pons², (-e), punch (tool); (w) punch, perforate; ~ **er**, (-s), puncher; ~ **kaart**, punched card.
pons'kom, punch-bowl.

pons 419 *portuur*

pons: ~ **masjien,** punching machine; ~ **stelsel,** punch system; ~ **werk,** punching.
pont, (-e), ferry-boat, pontoon, punt.
pontak', pontak'wyn, dark wine, pontac.
pont: ~ **boot,** ferry-boat; ~ **geld,** fordage.
pontifikaal', (..**kale),** pontifical.
pontifikaat', pontificate.
Pon'tius, Pontius; *iem. van* ~ *na Pilatus stuur,* send a person from pillar to post.
pont'man, ferryman.
ponton', (-s), pontoon; ~ **brug,** pontoon (bridge); ~ *brugge bou,* pontoon; ~ **dok,** pontoon (-dock); ~ **nier', (-s),** pontoneer; ~ **wa,** pontoon-wag(g)on.
pont: ~ **skuit,** punt; ~ **trein,** bridge-train; pontoon train; ~ **wagter,** ferryman; ~ **werker,** pontoneer.
poog, (ge-), try, attempt, endeavour.
pooi'er, (Ndl.), **(-s),** pimp.
pook, (s) (poke), poker, pricker-bar; (w) **(ge-),** poke; ~ **yster,** poker.
Pool¹, (Pole), Pole.
pool², pile (of carpet).
pool³, (pole), pole; terminal; tension, stress; *NEGA=TIEWE* ~, cathode; *POSITIEWE* ~, anode; ~ **afstand,** distance between poles; ~ **beer,** polar bear; ~ **boog,** polar curve.
pool'draad, pole-thread.
pool: ~ **ekspedisie,** polar expedition; **P** ~ **hond,** husky (dog); ~ **klem,** battery terminal; ~ **lande,** polar countries; ~ **lig,** northern lights, aurora; ~ **lug,** polar air; ~ **reisiger,** Arctic explorer, polar explorer.
Pools, (-e), Polish.
pool: P ~ **see,** Arctic sea; ~ **s'hoogte,** elevation of the pole; latitude; ~ *shoogte neem,* find one's bearings; see how the land lies; sound the feelings; ~ **sirkel,** polar circle; ~ **skip,** polar ship; ~ **ster,** polar star, pole-(lode-)star; cynosure; ~ **streek,** polar region, frigid zone; ~ **stuk,** armature (magnet); ~ **tog,** Arctic expedition.
pool'vas, (-te), pile-proof.
pool: ~ **vos,** Arctic fox; ~ **ys,** polar ice.
poon, (pone), pony, cob; ~ *maar perd,* stocky but sturdy.
poort, (-e), gate, doorway; narrow pass between precipitous mountains; defile; gateway; port; portal; porch; pylon (of temple); *geen* ~ *na KENNIS,* the gateway to knowledge; *die ENG* ~, the strait gate; ~ **aar,** portal vein; ~ **jie, (-s),** small gate; small pass; ~ **laken,** baize; ~ **spier,** sphincter; ~ **wagter,** gatekeeper.
poos, (pose), pose, **(-s),** while, pause, interval; *by pose, at intervals.*
poot, (pote), foot, leg, paw; claw; fist (handwriting); pad (hare); *op jou AGTERSTE pote gaan staan,* get up on one's hind legs; *iem. op sy pote HELP,* set someone on his feet; *geen* ~ *ROER nie,* not to lift a finger; *'n* ~ *SKRYF,* write an awful scrawl; *op eie pote STAAN,* stand on one's own feet; *sy redenering STAAN op pote,* his reasoning is sound (foursquare); *op pote STAAN,* make sense; *op jou pote TEREGKOM,* land on one's feet; *hou jou pote TUIS,* hands off, keep your hands to yourself; *geen* ~ *wil VERSIT nie,* not willing to lift a finger; *dat so 'n* ~ *moet VROT!* what a pity that the writer of such an excellent hand must die! ~ **jie, (s)** gout, podagra; **(-s),** little paw (hand); *'n* ~ *tjie gee,* give a paw (dog); offer someone a limp hand; ~ **jies,** trotters; ~ **tjieslang,** snake-lizard; ~ **jieswol,** shankings; ~ **loos,** (..**lose),** apod(al); ~ **rollertjie,** caster (furniture); ~ **seer,** footsore(ness).
poot'-uit, down, done for; dog-tired, exhausted; ~ *raak,* become dead-tired; go bankrupt.
pop¹, (s) (-pe), doll; effigy, dummy; marionette, puppet; *die* ~ *pe is aan die DANS,* the fat is in the fire; *'n MOOI* ~, a beautiful girl.
pop=², (b) afk. van **populêr.**
pop: ~ **agtig, (-e),** doll like; ~ **baadjie,** doll's jacket; ~ **bedjie,** doll's bed.
po'pe, (-s), Russian priest, pope.
po'pel, (ge-), quiver, throb, flutter; *'n* ~ *ende hart,* a quivering heart.
popelien', popeli'ne, poplin.
po'peling, quivering, throbbing.

pop: ~ **gesig,** doll's face; ~ **geweertjie,** popgun; ~ **goed,** toys, playthings; doll's clothes; ~ **hoed,** doll's hat; ~ **huis,** doll's house; ~ **kateltjie,** doll's bed; ~ **kombuis,** kitchenette; ~ **kuns,** pop art.
pop'lied, pop song.
pop'mooi, as pretty as a doll.
pop'musiek, pop music.
pop: ~ **oë,** doll's eyes; ~ **orkes,** pop orchestra; ~ **pekas,** puppet-show; doll's houe; ~ **pekastery,** puppetry; ~ **perig, (-e),** doll-like, dollish; ~ **perigheid,** dollishness; ~ **pespel,** puppet-play; playing with dolls; ~ **petentoonstelling,** doll-show; ~ **pie, (-s),** little doll; ~ **rok,** doll's dress.
pop'sanger, pop singer.
pop: ~ **skyf,** figure target; ~ **speel, (-ge-),** play with dolls; *hy wil* ~ *speel,* he wants to indulge in cradle-snatching; ~ **staat,** puppet-state; ~ **ster,** pop star.
popularisa'sie, popularization.
populariseer', (ge-), make popular, popularize.
populariteit', popularity.
popula'sie, population.
populêr', (-e), popular; esoteric; emotic; ~ **-wetenskaplik, (-e),** semi-scientific; popular.
populier', (-e), poplar; ~ **boom,** poplar; ~ **bos,** poplar-grove; ~ **hout,** poplar (-wood); ~ **tak,** poplar-branch.
pop: ~ **waentjie,** doll's cart, toy pram; ~ **winkel,** toy-shop, doll-shop.
por, (s) (-re), thrust, dig, poke, jab; (w) **(ge-),** poke, nudge, jab; urge, incite, encourage, spur on, egg on; *see* **aanpor.**
poreus', (-e), porous; ~ **heid,** porosity.
porfier', porphyry, ..**fi'ries, (-e),** porphyritic; ..**firiet',** porphyrite.
porie', (-ë), pore.
pornograaf', (..**grawe),** pornographer.
pornografie', pornography.
pornogra'fies, (-e), pornographic.
porselein', (real) china, porcelain; purslane, purslain; spode; ~ **aarde,** china (porcelain) clay; ~ **agtig, (-e),** porcellaneous; ~ **bak,** porcelain basin; ~ **blommetjie,** London pride; ~ **eier,** china egg; ~ **fabriek,** porcelain factory; ~ **goed,** chinaware; ~ **grond,** kaolin; ~ **kas,** display cabinet; china-chest; ~ **klei,** kaolin; china clay; ~ **lak,** porcelain lacquer; ~ **skottel,** porcelain dish; ~ **skulp,** porcelain-shell; ~ **slak,** cypraea, cowrie; ~ **ware,** china-ware; crockery; ~ **winkel,** china shop.
por'sie, (-s), portion, share; helping (food), serving.
por'stok, prodder.
port¹, port (wine).
port², postage.
portaal', (..**tale),** porch, lobby, hall, entrance hall; landing (stairs); portal; narthex; ~ **kraan,** gantry-crane.
portofoul'jo, (-o), portfolio; wallet, *die* ~ *AANVAAR,* accept office; *MINISTER sonder* ~, minister without portfolio; *'n STEWIGE* ~ *hê,* have good shares.
portfisie'deur, folding doors.
port'glasie, (-s), (port) wineglass.
portiek', (-e), portico, porch, prostyle.
portier', (-e, -s), porter (hotel); commissionare; door-keeper; hall-porter; gate-keeper; carriage door; ~ **klier,** pyloric gland; ~ **s'woning,** porter's lodge.
port'landsement, Portland cement.
portnatal': ~ **boontjie,** variety of bean; ~ **patat,** ~ **patatta,** sweet potato.
por'to, postage.
Portorikaan', (..kane), Porto (Puerto) Rican; ~ **s', (-e),** Porto (Puerto) Rican.
Por'to Ri'co, Porto (Puerto) Rico.
portret', (-te), portrait, photo(graph), likeness; portraiture; ~ **album,** portrait-album; ~ **hakie,** picture hook; ~ **kuns,** portraiture; ~ **lys,** picture-rail; ~ **lysie,** photoframe; ~ **raam,** picture-frame; ~ **skilder,** portrait painter; ~ **teer', (ge-),** portray, paint.
port'seël, due-stamp.
Por'tugal, Portugal.
Portugees', (s, b) (..**gese),** Portuguese.
portulak', (-ke), portulaca.
portuur', (..**ture),** match, equal; peer; *baklei met jou*

portvry   420   *pot*

eie ~, fight someone your own size; ~ **groep**, peer group.
port'vry, post-free.
port'wyn, port wine.
pos, (s) (-te), mail; post-office; picket; post, situation, job, billet; entry, item (book); posting; place; func= tion; *OOR die* ~, through the post; by post; *OP sy* ~ *wees*, be at one's post; *PER* ~, through the post, by post; *op* ~ *STAAN*, stand sentry; *STUKKE vir die* ~, postal matter; ~ *te UITSIT*, post sentries; *'n* ~ *van VERTROUE*, a position of confidence (trust); (w) (ge-), post, mail (a letter); enter (bookk.); picket; *'n BRIEF* ~, post a letter; *in die GROOTBOEK* ~, enter in ledger; *'n bedrag VER= KEERD* ~, make a wrong entry; ~ **administrasie**, postal administration; ~ **agent**, postal agent; ~ **amptenaar**, mail clerk; ~ **beampte**, postal of= ficial; ~ **beskrywing**, job description; ~ **bestelling**, mail order; ~ **beuel**, post-horn; ~ **bewys**, postal note; ~ **bode**, post-boy; postal messenger; post= man; ~ **boot**, mail boat; ~ **bus**, post-box; letter-box; ~ **dag**, mail day.
pos: ~ **diens**, postal (mail) service; ~ **duif**, homer, homing pigeon, carrier-pigeon; ~ **duiweversorger**, pigeoneer.
po'se^1, (-s), pose, attitude; *dis pure* ~, it's a mere pose.
po'se^2 = **poos.**
pos'eenheid, postal unit.
poseer', (ge-), pose, sit for, give a sitting; assume an attitude, attitudinize; posture.
poseur', (-s), poser, affected person, one striking an attitude, attitudinizer, attitudinarian.
pos: ~ **geld**, postage; ~ **gids**, postal guide.
po'sie, (-s), little while.
posi'sie, (-s), position, post, place, situation, status; posture; *'n hoë* ~ *BEREIK*, achieve eminence (a high position); *soldate STAAN in* ~, soldiers stand at attention; *in 'n moeilike (onhoudbare)* ~ *VER= KEER*, be in an awkward (untenable) position; ~ **oorlog**, trench warfare.
positief', (..tiewe), positive, definite; cocksure; *posi= tiewe BEWYS*, positive proof; *positiewe POOL*, anode; ~ *SEKER*, absolutely certain; ..*tiewe SERWITUUT*, affirmative servitude.
positie'we, senses; consciousness; *sy* ~ *BYME= KAARHOU*, keep one's wits about one; *NIE by sy* ~ *nie*, not in his right mind; *sy* ~ *VERLOOR*, lose his head.
positivis', (-te), positivist; ~ **me**, positivism; ~ **ties**, (-e), positivistic.
po'sitron, (-e), positron.
posjeer', (ge-), poach; *'n ge* ~ *de eier*, a poached egg: ~ **pan**, egg poacher.
pos: ~ **jong**, postman; ~ **kaart**, postcard; ~ **kantoor**, post-office; ~ **kar**, mail-coach, post-cart; ~ **kode**, postcode; ~ **koets**, mail-coach; ~ **lys**, mailing list; ~ **meester**, postmaster; ~ **meesteres**, postmistress; ~ **meester-generaal**, (posmeesters-generaal), Post= master-General; ~ **meesterskap**, postmastership; ~ **merk**, postmark; ~ **motor**, mail-van; ~ **ontle= ding**, job analysis; ~ **order**, postal order; ~ **pakket**, postal parcel; ~ **papier**, writing-paper; note-paper; ~ **perd**, post-horse; ~ **personeel**, postal staff; ~ **ryer**, post-cart driver; courier; ~ **sak**, post-bag, mail bag; *private* ~ *sak*, private bag; ~ **seël**, post= age stamp; ~ **seëlalbum**, stamp-album; ~ **seëlboe= kie**, stamp-booklet; ~ **seëlhandelaar**, stamp-dealer; ~ **seëlkleefpapier**, stamp-hinge; ~ **seëlkunde**, phi= lately; ~ **seëlplakstrokie**, stamp-hinge; ~ **seëlvas= houer**, stamp-hinge; ~ **seëlversamelaar**, philatelist; stamp-collector; ~ **seëlversameling**, stamp-collec= tion; ~ **seun**, post-boy; ~ **sie**, (-s), small job; ~ **spaarbank**, post-office savings bank; ~ **stempel**, postmark; ~ **stoomboot**, mail packet; ~ **stuk**, post= al article (matter); ~ **tarief**, postal tariff, rates of postage.
post'dateer, (ge-), postdate.
posteer', (ong.), (ge-), post (soldiers), station, picket.
postelein', purslane, purslain.
pos'te restan'te, poste restante, to be called for.
poste'ring, posting, picketing.
postery'e, postal affairs, posts.

postiljon', (-s), postil(l)ion.
pos'trein, postal train, mail train.
post'scriptum, (-s, ..ta), postscript.
postulaat', (..late), postulate.
postuleer', (ge-), postulate, posit.
postuum', (..tume), posthumous.
postuur', (..ture), posture, figure, pose; *'n nooi met 'n MOOI* ~, a girl with a trim figure; *jou in* ~ *STEL*, take up your attitude; ~ **drag**, foundation-garment.
pos'unie, postal union.
pos: ~ **vat**, (-ge-), take root; take up one's position (stand); *'n mening wat begin* ~ *vat*, an opinion which is gaining ground; ~ **verbinding**, postal con= nection; ~ **verdrag**, postal convention (treaty); ~ **vereniging**, postal union; ~ **verkeer**, postal traf= fic; ~ **vliegtuig**, mail plane; ~ **vry**, post-free; ~ **wese**, postal system, posts; *MINISTER van POS= en Telegraafwese*, Minister of Posts and Tele= graphs; *P* ~ **wet**, Post-Office Act; ~ **wissel**, money order.
pot, (s) (-te), pot; jar; saucepan; stakes, kitty, pool; bank; chamber(-pot), jordan; cauldron; game; *elke* ~ *kry sy DEKSEL*, every Jack has his Jill; *so DIG soos 'n* ~, as close as an oyster; *al is 'n* ~ *nog so skeef, dit kry darem 'n DEKSEL*, every Jack shall have his Jill; *in EEN* ~ *gooi*, pool, throw into a common fund; *hy het* ~ *te GELEK*, there is a dirty mark on his face; *die* ~ *verwyt die KETEL dat hy swart is*, the pot calls the kettle black; *die* ~ *aan die KOOK hou*, be able to make both ends meet; *die* ~ *MIS sit*, miss the mark (bus); ~ *te en PANNE*, pots and pans; *vir die* ~ *SKIET*, shoot for the pot; *die* ~ *was VERSPEEL*, the chance was lost; *die* ~ *VER= TEER*, pay the piper; (w) (ge-), save up, hoard; *see* **oppot**.
potamografie', potamography.
potamologie', potamology.
pot'as, potash.
pot: ~ **blou**, bright blue; livid; ~ **braai**, (-ge-), pot-roast; ~ **brood**, pot-bread; ~ **deksel**, pot lid; ~ **dig**, (-te), airtight, perfectly closed; very reserved; ~ **doof**, (..dowe), stone-deaf.
potensiaal', (s) (..siale), potential.
potensialiteit', potentiality.
poten'sie, (-s), potency, power.
potensieel', (..siële), potential.
potentaat', (..tate), potentate.
pot: ~ **geld**, pool, collective stakes (in game); ~ **hing= sel**, pot-handle (-hook); ~ **jagter**, pot-hunter.
pot'jie, (-s), small pot; socket; game; *sy eie* ~ *KRAP*, provide for oneself; *met iem. 'n* ~ *LOOP*, fall out with someone; *'n* ~ *MAAK*, have a game; *klein* ~ *s het groot ORE*, little pitchers have long ears; *'n* ~ *SPEEL*, play a round; *in die kleinste* ~ *s bewaar mens die beste SALF*, the best things are often wrapped up in the smallest parcels; *arm UIT die* ~, arm out of the socket; ~ **rol**, (-le), fatty, podge; ~ **slatyn**, kitchen-Latin, apothecary's Latin, dog Latin, jargon; ~ **svleis**, potted meat.
pot'klaar, dressed.
pot'klei, pipeclay, potter's clay, argil; pot-clay, plas= tic clay; ~ **bank**, layer of pipeclay.
pot: ~ **lap**, pot-holder; ~ **klep**, pot-valve; ~ **lepel**, kitchen ladle, dipper, pot ladle.
pot'lood, (..lode), (lead) pencil; *skryf met* ~, write in pencil; ~ **doos**, pencil-case, pencil-box; ~ **koker**, pencil-case; ~ **masjien**, pencil-sharpener; ~ **passer**, pencil-compasses; ~ **skerpmaker**, (-s), pencil-sharpener; ~ **skets**, pencil-sketch; ~ **slyper**, pencil-sharpener; ~ **streep**, pencil mark (line); ~ **tekening**, pencil-drawing.
potnat': *dit is een* ~, it is Hobson's choice.
pot'plant, potplant.
potpourri', (-'s), potpourri, medley.
potsier'lik, (-e), queer, odd, droll, comic(al); ~ **heid**, queerness, oddity, comicalness.
pot: ~ **skerf**, (..skerwe), potsherd; ~ **skoot**, pot-shot; ~ **skraper**, pot-scraper; ~ **skuurder**, pot-scourer; ~ **spel**, pool; snooker; ~ **stander**, saucepan stand; ~ **stelsel**, pool system; ~ **swartsel**, pot-black, lampblack.

pot'te: ~**bakker,** potter, ceramist; ~**bakkersklei,** potter's clay, argil; ~**bakkerskuns,** ceramics; pottery; fictile art; ~**bakkerskyf,** ~**bakkerswiel,** potter's wheel; pallet; ~**bakkerswinkel,** pottery; ~**bakkery,** pottery; ~**bank,** (ong.), (kitchen) dresser; ~**krapper,** miser; ~**rak,** pot rack.

pot'toe, tightly closed; *my ore het ~ geslaan,* my ears were blocked.

pot: ~**vis,** cachalot, sperm-whale *(Physeter cotodon);* ~**yster,** cast-iron.

pou, (-e), peacock, peafowl; *so trots soos 'n ~,* as proud as a peacock; ~**agtig, (-e),** peacockish, peacocky, pavonine; ~**blou,** peacock blue; ~**bors,** peacock's breast; ~**bors maak,** puff oneself up; ~**eier,** peahen's egg.

pouk, (-e), kettle-drum; ~**enis, (-te),** ~**slaner,** kettledrummer.

pou: ~**kuiken,** pea-chick; ~**oogmot,** Christmas moth, emperor moth, peacock-moth; ~**oog(vis),** peacock-fish.

pou'per, (-s), pauper; ~**is'me,** pauperism.

pous, (-e), pope; ~**dom,** papacy.

pou'se, (-s), interval, pause, break, recess.

pouseer', (ge-), pause, make a pause, have an interval.

pouse'ring, pausing, pause, stop, break, interval.

pous'gesind, (-e), papist, popish; ~**e, (-s),** papist, papalist; ~**heid,** popery, papistry, papalism.

pous'lik, (-e), papal; popish; pontific(al); ~*e GESANT,* papal nuncio; ~*e ONFEILBAARHEID,* papal infallibility; ~*e STOEL,* papal seat.

pous'skap, pontificate

pou: ~**stert,** peacock's tail; ~**veer,** peacock's feather; ~**wyfie,** peahen.

po'wer, (-e; -der, -ste), poor, lamentable, miserable; *'n ~ e ekskuus,* a miserable excuse; ~**heid,** poverty; lamentableness, miserableness.

Praag, Prague.

praai, (ge-), hail (ship).

praal, (s) pomp, magnificence, emblazonry, bravery, gaud, ostentation; **(w) (ge-),** boast, make a display of, shine, be resplendent, blazon, flaunt, flourish; ~**bed,** bed of state; ~**boog,** triumphal arch; ~**gewaad,** robes of state; ~**graf,** mausoleum, cenotaph; ~**koets,** state coach; ~**siek, (-e),** fond of display, ostentatious; ~**sug,** ostentation; ~**sug'tig, (-e),** ostentatious; ~**vertoon,** pomposity; pomp, pageantry; ~**wa,** float (procession); ~**wet,** sumptuary law.

praat, (s) talk; confab(ulation); *aan die ~ BLY,* continue talking; *aan die ~ HOU,* keep someone talking; *aan die ~ KRY,* get someone talking; *sy ~ was seker OP,* apparently he had nothing more to say; *aan die ~ RAAK,* begin talking; **(w) (ge-),** talk, chat, converse; confabulate; ~ *v.d. DING!* well, I never! you don't say! *soetjies ~, is DUIWELSRAAD,* it is rude to whisper in company; ~ *GOU, want ek woon ver,* please come to the point; *om iets HEEN ~,* beat around the bush; *LOS en vas ~,* indulge in loose talk; *jy kan MAKLIK ~,* more easily said than done; talk is cheap; *laat die MENSE maar ~,* let them talk; *ek MOET met hom ~,* I must have a talk with him; *REGUIT ~,* talk straight; *daar VAL met hom nie te ~ nie,* he will not listen to reason; ~**agtig, (-e),** talkative, loquacious; ~**agtigheid,** loquacity, garrulity; ~**al,** chatterbox; ~**graag,** talkative person; ~**horing,** auricular tube; ~**huis,** gabble-shop; Parliament.

praat'jie, (-s), talk; rumour; gossip, confabulation; chat; hearsay; *DIS ~ s,* it is a piece of hearsay; ~*s vul g'n GAATJIES nie,* fair words butter no parsnips; talk is cheap; ~*s LOOP rond,* there are stories doing the rounds; *'n ~ MAAK,* have a chat; *MAAK daar nou maar geen ~ s oor nie,* say nothing more about the matter; *dis SOMMER ~ s,* it is idle talk; *STEUR jou nie aan ~ s nie,* you shouldn't take notice of gossip; ~*s vir die VAAK,* tittle-tattle; *hy het te VEEL ~ s,* he talks too much; ~**smaker, (-s),** tattler, babbler, phrase-monger, windbag; ~**strooier,** gobemouche, rumour-monger.

praat: ~**kous,** (incessant) talker, gasbag; ~**lus'tig, (-e),** loquacious; ~**masjien,** gramophone; ~**rol-**

prent, talkie, phonofilm; ~**sel,** silence box; ~**siek, (-e),** talkative, loquacious, garrulous.

praat'stoel: *op sy ~ sit,* be in a talkative mood.

praat'sug, loquacity, garrulity; anecdotage; ~**'tig, (-e),** loquacious, garrulous.

praat'werk: *die ~ doen,* do the talking.

prag, splendour, magnificence; emblazonry; array; gorgeousness, grandeur; amplitude; *'n ~ van 'n PERD,* a beauty of a horse; ~ *en PRAAL,* pomp and splendour; ~**band,** ornamental binding; ~**eksemplaar,** de luxe copy (of a book); fine specimen (of something); ~**-en-praal'wet,** sumptuary law; ~**kêrel,** fine fellow; ~**kewer,** buprestid; ~**lelie,** gloriosa; ~**lie'wend, (-e),** fond of splendour, ostentatious.

pragmatiek', (-e), pragmatic.

pragma'ties, (-e), pragmatic; ~*e sanksie,* pragmatic sanction.

pragmatis', (-te), pragmatist; ~**me,** pragmatism.

prag: ~**ras,** fancy breed; ~**stuk,** beauty, masterpiece; ~**tig, (b) (-e),** beautiful, magnificent, gorgeous, grand, glorious; (bw) beautifully; ~**uitgaaf,** ~**uitgawe,** edition de luxe; ~**vertoon,** fine display; ~**werk,** thing of beauty, masterpiece; drawing-room book.

praksa'sie, (-s), scheme, argument, contrivance; meditation, devising.

prakseer', (ge-), think, consider, plan, contrive, devise.

prak'ties, (h) (-e), practical, workable, feasible, hard-headed; (bw) practically, virtually; ~ *DOENLIK,* practical, workable; ~ *ONAFHANKLIK,* virtually independent; ~ *ONMOONTLIK,* practically impossible; *'n ~ e PLAN,* a workable plan; ~**heid,** practicality.

prak'tikum, (..ka, -s), laboratory (class) work; practical examination.

prak'tikus, (..tici, -se), practical person, practised hand; practician.

praktiseer', (ge-), practise; ..**tise'rend,** practising.

praktisyn', (-s), practitioner; *mediese ~,* medical practitioner.

praktyk', practice (of doctor); *in die ~ BRING,* bring into practice; *daardie dokter het 'n GOEIE ~,* that doctor has a large practice; *IN die ~,* in practice; *VERKEERDE ~ e,* evil practices; ~**waarde,** goodwill.

pra'lend, (-e), boasting, flaunting(ly).

pra'ler, (-s), showy fellow, braggart; ~**ig, (-e),** showy, ostentatious, swaggering, swanky; ~**y,** boasting, swaggering, ostentation, swank.

pralien', (-e), prali'ne, (-s), praline.

pram, (-me), woman's breast, mamma; bulb, teat; pap; ~**doring,** wild cardamom; ~**kop,** butte.

prang, (ge-), pinch, squeeze, press; trouble, worry; *die ge~ de gemoed,* the troubled mind.

prat, proud; *hulle gaan ~ op hulle geld,* they pride themselves on their wealth.

pra'ter, (-s), talker, conversationalist; ~**ig, (-e),** talkative, garrulous; prattling; ~**igheid,** talkativeness, garrulity; ~**y,** talk, gossip, tattle.

pre'advies, report; recommendation.

preben'de, (-s), prebend.

predel'la, predella.

predestina'sie, predestination; ~**leer,** predestination doctrine.

predestineer', (ge-), predestine, predestinate; define precisely (beforehand); predeterminate.

pre'dik, (ge-), preach.

predikaat', (..kate), predicate; (class) mark; ~**trein,** (gew.), train for students who have failed.

predikament', (-e), predicament.

pre'dikamp, ministry.

predikant', (-e), minister, parson, clergyman; preacher; guidepost, signpost; ~**agtig, (-e),** parsonic; ~**e,** clergy; ~**skap,** ministry; curacy.

predikants': ~**pos,** incumbency; ~**vrou,** minister's wife; clergywoman; ~**woning,** parsonage, vicarage.

predika'sie, (-s), sermon, homily; ~**boek,** book of sermons.

predikatief', (..tiewe), predicative.

Pre'diker, Ecclesiastes.

prediker

pre'diker, (-s), preacher.
pre'diking, preaching.
predilek'sie, predilection.
pre'disposisie, predisposition.
preek, (s) (**preke**), sermon, homily; (w) (**ge-**), preach; officiate; sermonize; reprove; ~ **ag'tig**, (-e), preachy; ~ **amp**, preachership; ~ **beurt**, turn to officiate (preach); ~ **stoel**, pulpit; ~ **styl**, manner of preaching, pulpit style; ~ **toon**, preacher's tone; drawl; ~ **trant**, see **preekstyl**.
pre'fek, (-te), prefect; prepositor; ~ **tuur'**, (..**ture**), prefecture; prefectship.
prefereer', (**ge-**), prefer.
preferen'sie, (-s), preference; ~ *hê op*, have (the first) refusal of.
preferent', (-e), preferent; preferential; ~ *e AAN= DELE*, preference shares; ~ *e SKULDE*, preferred debts.
prefigura'sie, (-s), prefiguration.
prefigureer', (**ge-**), prefigure.
prefiks', (-e), prefix.
pregnan'sie, (fig.) pregnancy.
pregnant', (-e), (fig.) pregnant.
pre'histories, (-e), prehistoric(al).
prei, (-e), leek, chive.
prejudiseer', **prejudisieer'**, (**ge-**), prejudice.
prekêr', (-e), precarious.
pre'ker, (-s), preachifier; preacher.
pre'kerig, (-e), preachy; drawling; predicatory; ~ **heid**, preachiness.
pre'kery, preaching.
prelaat', (..**late**), prelate; ~ **amp**, prelature; ~ **skap**, prelacy.
preliminêr', (b) (-e), preliminary.
preliminê're, (s, mv) preliminaries.
prelu'de, (-s), **prelu'dium**, (..**ia**, -s), prelude.
preludeer', (**ge-**), preludize; foreshadow.
prematuur', (..**tu're**), premature.
premedita'sie, premeditation.
pre'mie, (-s), premium; bounty; bonus; *'n* ~ *stel op*, put a premium on; ~ **-eksemplaar**, thirteenth copy; ~ **lening**, lottery loan; ~ **lot**, premium bond; ~ **plaat**, presentation plate.
premier', (-s), premier, prime minister.
premiè're, (-s), first night (of a play), première; ~ **ganger**, first-nighter.
premier'skap, premiership, prime-ministership.
pre'miestelsel, premium (bonus) system.
pre'mieverlaging, rebate of premium.
pre'mievry, (-e), non-contributory; ~ *e polis*, fully paid-up policy.
premis', (-se), premise; *van foutiewe* ~ *se uitgaan*, make wrong inferences.
prenataal', (..**tale**), prenatal.
prent, (s) (-e), picture, illustration; engraving; print; (w) (**ge-**), imprint, impress on; ~ **briefkaart**, picture postcard; ~ **ebeeld**, pictorial view; ~ **eboek**, picturebook; ~ **ebybel**, pictorial Bible; ~ **handelaar**, print-seller; ~ **jie**, (-s), little picture; ~ **jiemooi**, pretty; picturesque; ~ **kaart**, face-card; court-card; picture-card; ~ **lys**, picture-rail; ~ **optooier**, print-trimmer; ~ **plakkaat**, illustrated poster; ~ **poskaart**, picture postcard; ~ **raam**, picture-frame; ~ **strokies**, ~ **verhale**, comic strips; ~ **winkel**, print-shop.
preokkupa'sie, preoccupation.
preokkupeer', (**ge-**), preoccupy.
preordina'sie, preordination.
preordineer', (**ge-**), preordain.
preparaat', (..**rate**), preparation (the prepared thing); slide, mount.
prepara'sie, (-s), (the process of) preparation.
prepareer', (**ge-**), prepare; dress (hides).
preposi'sie, preposition.
prê'rie, (-s), prairie; ~ **brand**, prairie fire; ~ **gras**, prairie grass; ~ **hoender**, prairie chicken; ~ **hond**, prairie dog; ~ **wolf**, prairie wolf, coyote.
prerogatief', (..**tiewe**), prerogative, sovereign right; ~ *van die koning*, royal prerogative.
pres, (**ge-**), press, crimp (recruits), force.
presbioop', (..**biope**), (s) presbyope; (b) presbyopic.
presbiopie', presbyopia.

pretloop

presbi'ter, (-s), presbyter.
Presbiteriaan', (s) (..**riane**), Presbyterian; ~**s'**, (-e), Presbyterian.
Presbiterianis'me, Presbyterianism.
presedeer', (**ge-**), precede; ~ **saak**, leading case.
preseden'sie, precedence.
presedent', (-e), precedent; ~ **reg**, case-law.
presen'sie, (-s), presence, attendance; ~ **geld**, attendance-allowance; ~ **lys**, list of those present, attendance-roll.
present', (s) (-e), present, gift; ~ *gee*, give as a present; (bw) as a present; ~ **a'bel**, (-e), presentable; ~ **a'sie**, (-s), presentation; ~ **boek**, presentation book, gift-book; ~ **eer'**, (**ge-**), offer, hand round, present; *jou self* ~ *eer*, apply in person; ~ **eer'blad**, tray, salver; ~ **eksemplaar**, presentation copy; ~ **kaartjie**, complimentary ticket; ~ **perd**, gift-horse.
preserva'sie, preservation.
preserveer', (**ge-**), preserve; *ge* ~ *de voedsel*, preserves; ~ **middel**, preservative.
preserve'ring, preservation.
preserwatief', (..**tiewe**), preservative.
preses'sie, precession.
presideer', (**ge-**), preside.
presiden'sie, residence of the president; presidency.
presidensieel', (..**siële**), presidential.
president', (-e), president; chairman; commodore; ~ **e**, (-s), (lady) president, chairwoman; ~ **s'huis**, presidency; **P** ~ **sraad**, President's Council; ~ **skap**, presidency; ~ **s'verkiesing**, election of president; ~ **s'vrou**, president's wife; ~ **s'woning**, presidency.
presidiaal', (..**diale**), presidial.
presi'dium, (-s, ..**dia**), presidium, chairmanship.
presies', (b) (-e), exact, precise; definite; just; particular; regular; neat, clean(ly); tidy; prim; formal; (bw) exactly, precisely; punctual; plumb; for all the world; to a hair; *OM tienuur* ~, at ten o'clock precisely; ~ *op TYD*, just on time; *om* ~ *te WEES*, to be exact; ~ **heid**, precision, preciseness, exactness, punctuality, minuteness, accuracy; tidiness, neatness.
presieus', (-e), precious; finicky; affected; ~ **heid**, preciosity; affectation.
presipitaat', (..**tate**), precipitate.
presipitant', (-e), precipitant.
presipita'tor, (-s), precipitator.
presipiteer', (**ge-**), precipitate; ~ **der**, (-s), precipitator; ~ **middel**, precipitant.
presipite'ring, precipitation.
presiseer', (**ge-**), define (describe) precisely, specify.
presise'ring, specification, precise statement (definition).
presi'sie, precision; high fidelity, accuracy; ~ **appa= raat**, precision instrument; ~ **gereedskap**, precision tools.
preskrip'sie, (-s), prescription.
pres'sie, pressure; ~ *uitoefen op*, bring pressure to bear upon; ~ **groep**, pressure group.
presta'sie, (-s), performance, exploit, achievement, accomplishment, attainment; ~ **meting**, achievement rating; ~ **vermoë**, capacity; performance.
presteer', (**ge-**), achieve, perform, be worth.
presti'ge, prestige, influence; ~ *verloor*, loose prestige (face); ~ **verlies**, loss of face.
presuma'sie, presumption, suspicion.
presumeer', (**ge-**), presume.
presump'sie, presumption.
pret, pleasure, fun, merriment, gaiety, jollification; ~ *MAAK*, make fun, enjoy oneself; *VIR die* ~, for fun; ~ **bederwer**, spoil-sport, killjoy; ~ **draf**, jog; ~ **drawwer**, jogger.
pretendeer', (**ge-**), pretend; claim.
pretendent', (-e), pretender, claimant.
preten'sie, (-s), pretence, claim, pretension; ~ **loos**, (..**lose**), unpretentious, unassuming; ~ **loosheid**, unpretentiousness.
pretensieus', (-e), assuming, pretentious; ambitious.
prete'ritum, (-s, ..**ta**), past (tense), preterite.
pret'jie, (-s), bit of fun.
pret'loop, jog; ~ **vereniging**, jogging association; **pretloper**, jogger.

pretlustig 423 **proef**

pretlus'tig, (-e), fun-loving.
pret'maker, reveller, merry-maker; jester, joker; ~y, merry-making, revelry.
pre'tor, (-e, -s), praetor.
Pretoriaan', (..riane), Pretoria'ner; (-s), Pretorian.
pretoriaans', (-e), praetorian.
Preto'riase, Pretorian.
pret'park, amusement park, fun-fair.
pret'tig, (-e), nice, pleasant, agreeable, pleasing; *iets* ~ *vind,* enjoy something; ~**heid,** pleasantness, agreeableness.
pret'wiel, joy-wheel.
preuts, (-e), coy, prudish; pert; ~**heid,** coyness, prud= ishness; prudery, primness, Grundyism.
preventief', (..tiewe), preventive, preventative.
pre'wel, (ge-), mutter; maunder; ~**aar, (-s),** mutterer; ~**gebed,** muttered prayer.
Pri'amus, Priam.
prieel', (priële), summer-house, arbour, pergola, trel= lised vine, alcove, bower.
priem, (s) (-e), bodkin, awl, piercer, pricker; bradawl, spike; broach; prod; (w) **(ge-),** pierce, prick; prod; ~**getal,** prime number; ~**vormig, (-e),** styloid.
pries'ter, (-s), priest, presbyter; ~**amp,** priestly office; ~**-digter,** priest-poet; ~**dom,** priesthood; ~**es', (-se),** priestess; ~**fees,** priestly festival; ~**gewaad,** sacerdotal dress; ~**heerskappy,** sacerdotalism, hierarchy; ~**kaste,** priestly caste; ~**kleed,** priestly dress, surplice; pluvial; cassock; ~**lik, (-e),** priestly; ~**lis,** priestcraft; ~**mantel,** cope; ~**orde,** monastic (priestly) order; ~**skap,** priesthood; ~**woning,** presbytery; ~**wyding,** ordination.
prie'wie, (omgangst.), **(-s),** privy, (water-)closet, latrine.
prik, (s) (-ke), prick, sting, stab; puncture; *op 'n* ~ *KEN,* know to the minutest detail; (w) **(ge-),** prick, sting; pink.
prik'kel, (s) (-s) spur, pricker, prod, prickle, prick, barb, goad, stimulus; stimulant, impulse, incentive; inducement; excitant; *dit het hom 'n* ~ *GEGEE,* this gave him an incentive; (w) **(ge-),** prick; vex, irritate; excite, provoke, goad, prod, prickle, stimu= late; incite; tickle (the appetite); fillip (one's mem= ory); exacerbate; ~**baar, (..bare),** peevish, petu= lant, provocative, ratty, cantankerous, irritable, touchy, fretful, crabbed; excitable; ~**baard,** barb (of fish); ~**baarheid,** irritability, choler, petulancy, excitability; ~**draad,** barbed wire; ~**draadversper= ring,** wire entanglement; ~**end, (-e),** prickly, titil= lating, piquant, stimulating; irritant, pungent, irri= tating, excitant, excitative, excitatory; peppery; ~**gas,** irritant; ~**gif,** irritant poison; ~**ig, (-e),** irri= tating, barbed; echinate(d); ~**ing, (-e, -s),** irrita= tion; excitement, excitation, stimulation, titillation; ~**lektuur,** penny dreadful; sensational literature; ~**middel,** irritant; ~**pop,** glamour-girl; ~**pos,** teaser mail; ~**stof,** irritant; ~**stok,** prodder.
prik: ~**tanding,** pin-perforation; ~**tol,** pegtop; ~**vis,** lamprey; ~**werk,** pointing (stonework).
pril, (-le), early; prime; *in sy* ~ *le jeug,* in early youth.
pri'ma, prime, first rate; prima; ~**donna,** prima don= na; ~ *effekte (sekuriteite),* gilt-edged securities.
primaat', (..mate), primate; ~**skap,** primacy.
prima'ria, (-s), chief delegate (lady); head student (girl).
pri'marib, prime rib.
prima'rius, (-se, ..rii), head student; chief delegate.
pri'mawissel, first of exchange.
primêr', (-e), primary; protogenic; ~*e ONDERWYS,* primary education; ~*e SKOOL,* primary school.
primitief', (..tiewe), primitive, crude.
primitiwiteit', primitiveness.
pri'mo, firstly, in the first place; ~**genituur',** primo= geniture.
primordiaal', (..diale), primordial.
pri'mula, (-s)!, primrose.
primus, (-se), primus, first deputy; head boy, dux.
prins, (-e), prince; *van die* ~ *geen KWAAD weet nie,* be blissfully unaware; *soos 'n* ~ *LEEF,* lead a princely life; ~**dom,** principality; princedom; ~**es', (-se),** princess; ~**es'styl,** princess style; ~**-gemaal, (-s, ..male),** prince consort; ~**gesinde,** royalist.

prinsiep' = prinsipe.
prinsipaal', (..pale), principal, head(master); ~**skap, (-pe),** principalship.
prinsipa'le, (-s), (female) principal.
prinsi'pe, (-s), principle; *dit in* ~ *EENS wees,* agree in principle; *UIT* ~, on principle.
prinsipieel', (..piële), fundamental, basic, radical.
prins'lik, (-e), princely.
prins'metaal, prince's metal.
prins'-regent, prince regent.
pri'or, (-s), prior; ~**aat', (..rate),** priorate; priority; priorship; ~**es', (-se),** prioress; ~**iteit',** priority; ~**skap,** priorate, priorship; priory; ~**y', (-e),** priory.
pris'ma, (-s), prism; ~**kyker,** prismatic glasses.
prisma'ties, (-e), prismatic.
prisonier', (-s), prisoner, convict; ~**s'kamp,** prison= ers' camp.
privaat'¹, (s) (..vate), lavatory, (water-)closet.
privaat'², (b) (~, ..vate), private; *private (~) BE= SIT,* private property; *vir* ~ *(private) GEBRUIK,* for private use; *private PAD,* private road; *private POSSAK,* private post-bag; *private SEKRETA= RIS,* private secretary; *private SKOOL,* private school; *private SYLYN,* private siding; ~**dosent,** private university-teacher; ~**heid,** privacy; ~**reg,** private law.
privatief', (..tiewe), privative.
privile'gie, (-s), privilege; charter; prerogative.
privilegieer', (ge-), give priority to, privilege.
pro, pro; *die* ~ *en CONTRA,* for and against, the pros and cons; ~ *DEO,* pro Deo; ~ *FORMA,* for the form; ~ *RATA,* proportionally.
pro-Afrikaans', pro-Afrikaans.
probaat', (..bate), efficacious, approved, tested, ex= cellent, sovereign (remedy); *'n probate middel teen tandpyn,* a proved remedy for toothache.
probeer', (ge-), try, attempt, make an effort, endea= vour, have a try, essay, assay, sample (drink); test (gun); try out (motor-car); prove; ~ *is die beste GEWEER,* there is nothing like trying; ~ *dit nou NET met my,* just try that with me; ~ *vroeg KOM,* try to come early; *dis wat hy* ~ *SÊ het,* that is what he tried to say; *jy moet SEKER* ~, you must make a special effort; ~**-en-trefmetode,** trial-and-error method; ~**sel, (-s),** ~**slag,** trial, attempt, effort.
probleem', (probleme), problem; proposition; ~**kind,** problem child.
problematiek', study of problems.
problema'ties, (-e), problematic(al), doubtful.
pro-Boer', pro-Boer.
pro-Duits', (-e), pro-German.
produk', (-te), product (of brain); produce (of the earth); outcome, result (of an attempt).
produk'sie, production, produce, output, yield; ~**baan,** production line; ~**kapasiteit,** capacity of production; ~**koste,** cost of production; ~**leier,** producer (of film); ~**middel,** means of production; ~**oorskot,** excess of production; ~**vermoë,** pro= ductivity.
produk'te, produce, ~**agent,** goods agent; ~**handel,** produce trade; ~**handelaar,** produce dealer; ~**mark,** produce market.
produktief', (..tiewe), productive; *..tiewe skulde,* productive debts.
produktiwiteit', productiveness, productive capacity, productivity.
produseer', (ge-), produce, manufacture, make; ~**baar, (..bare),** producible.
produsent', (-e), producer; ~**eprys,** producer's price.
produse'ring, production, producing.
proe, (w) **(ge-),** taste, sample.
proef, (s) (proewe), experiment, test, trial; example, specimen, sample, assay, proof; *die* ~ *DEUR= STAAN,* stand the test; *iem. se GEDULD op die* ~ *stel,* tax one's patience; *'n* ~ *NEEM,* make a trial experiment; *OP* ~, on trial, on approbation; *dit is die* ~ *op die SOM,* that settles the matter; *iem. op die* ~ *STEL,* put someone to the test; *proewe TREK,* pull proofs; *by WYSE van* ~, by way of trial; (w) **(ge-),** test, try; assay; ~**aanleg,** experi= mental plant; ~**afdruk,** sample-print; ~**akker,** ex=

perimental plot; ~**balans**, trial balance; ~**ballon**, trial balloon (kite); feeler; *'n* ~*ballon oplaat*, put out a feeler; fly a kite; ~**bank**, testing bench; ~**beampte**, welfare officer; probation officer; ~**beligting**, test-exposure, trial exposure; ~**berig**, test-message; ~**bestelling**, trial order; ~**blad**, specimen page; proof-sheet; ~**brief**, test-letter; ~**buis**, test-tube; ~**buisbaba**, test-tube baby; ~**druk**, proof (first) impression; ~**eksemplaar**, specimen copy; ~**geweer**, key-rifle; ~**gewig**, standard weight; ~**goud**, assay-gold; ~**houdend**, (-e), proof; standard; ~**huwelik**, trial marriage; companionate marriage, companionship marriage; ~**ie**, (-s), small experiment; small sample; ~**instrument**, testing instrument; ~**jaar**, year of probation; ~**kantoor**, assay office; ~**konyn**, experimental (laboratory) animal (rabbit); test object; guinea-pig; *as* ~*konyn dien*, be a guinea-pig; ~**kraan**, gaugecock; ~**leerling**, probationer, apprentice; ~**leesletters**, optotype; ~**les**, test-lesson, criticism-lesson; ~**leser**, proof-reader; corrector of the press; ~**lesery**, proof-reading; ~**loop**, trial run; ~**maand**, trial month; ~**monster**, sample; ~**munt**, sample coin; ~**naald**, touch-needle; ~**nemer**, (-s), experimenter, experimentalist; ~**neming**, (-e, -s), experiment; experimentation; ~**nommer**, specimen copy; ~**ondervin'delik**, (-e), empirical, experimental; ~**onderwys**, practice teaching, student teaching; ~**oond**, assay-furnace; ~**plaas**, experimental farm; ~**plaat**, proof; ~**preek**, probation sermon; ~**projek**, pilot project; ~**punt**, test point; ~**rit**, trial ride, trial run; ~**sending**, trial consignment (shipment); ~**sensus**, pilot census; ~**skietbaan**, testing range; ~**skoot**, trial shot, sighting shot, sighter; ~**skrif**, dissertation, thesis; ~**stadium**, experimental stage; ~**stasie**, experimental station; ~**steen**, touchstone; model brick; ~**stuk**, sample piece, specimen; ~**tekening**, cartoon; ~**terrein**, proving ground; ~**toestel**, test-set (teleph.); ~**tog**, trial trip; ~**tyd**, period of probation; apprenticeship; noviciate; ~**vaart**, shakedown cruise; ~**vel**, proof-sheet; ~**vlieër**, test-pilot; ~**vlug**, trial flight; trial ascent; ~**voordrag**, audition; ~**wedstryd**, trial match; ~**werk**, test work.
pro-En'gels, (-e), pro-English.
proes, (ge-), sneeze aloud, snort; ~ *van die lag*, burst out laughing; ~**terig**, (-e), snorting; inclined to giggling.
proe'we, (-s), specimen, sample.
proe'weling, (-e), probationer.
proe'wer, (-s), taster.
proe'wing, tasting, gustation.
profaan', **(profane)**, profane.
profana'sie, profanation.
profaneer', (ge-), profane.
profaniteit', profanity.
profeet', **(profete)**, prophet; prognosticator, prophesier; *'n* ~ *wat BROOD eet*, a false prophet; *die GROOT en klein profete*, the major and minor prophets; *'n* ~ *word nie in sy eie LAND geëer nie*, a prophet is not without honour save in his own country; *die OU profete is dood (en die jonges eet brood)*, the days of the prophets are long past.
profesie', (-ë), prophecy.
profes'sie, (-s), profession.
professionalis'me, professionalism.
pofessioneel', (..nele), professional.
profes'sor, (-e, -s), professor; ~**aal'**, (..rale), professorial; ~**aat'**, (..rate), ~**skap**, professorship, chair.
profeteer', (ge-), prophesy, foretell.
profe'temantel, prophet's mantle; *die* ~ *omhang*, don the mantle of a prophet.
profetes', (-se), prophetess.
profe'ties, (-e), prophetic, fatidical; pythonic.
profiel', (-e), profile, side-face; *in* ~, from the side, in profile; ~**maker**, face moulder; ~**patroon**, face-mould; ~**ruimer**, broach; ~**saag**, scribe saw; ~**skaaf**, moulding plane; ~**tekening**, profile drawing, side view; ~**yster**, section.
profilak'se, prophylaxis.
profilak'ties, (-e), prophylactic.

profileer', (ge-), profile.
profiteer', (ge-), profit, share in, have advantage of; *van iets* ~, profit by something, make the most of.
progno'se, (-s), forecast, prognosis.
profyt', (-e), profit, gain; ~ *trek van*, derive benefit from; ~**lik**, (-e), profitable; ~**makery**, profiteering.
progno'se, (-s), forecast, prognosis.
prognostiseer', (ge-), prognosticate.
program', (-me), programme; card; playbill; *'n punt in die politieke* ~, a plank in the political platform; ~**materiaal**, ~**matuur**, software (computer); ~**meer'**, (ge-), program(me); ~**meer'der**, (-s), programmist; programmer; ~**me'ring**, programming; ~**musiek**, programme music.
progres'sie, progression.
progressief', (s) (..siewe), progressionist; (b) (..siewe), progressive; (bw), progressively.
progressiwiteit', progressiveness.
prohibi'sie, (-s), prohibition.
prohibisionis', (-te), prohibitionist.
prohibitief', (..tiewe), prohibitive.
projek', (-te), project, design, scheme; ~**sie**, (-s), projection; forecast; ~**sielamp**, projecting lantern; ~**sieskerm**, screen; ~**sietekening**, projection-drawing; ~**sietoestel**, projector; ~**sievlak**, projection-level; ~**skool**, project-school; ~**teer'**, (ge-), project, plan; forecast; cast (image on screen).
projektiel', (-e), projectile, missile; *gerigte* ~, guided missile.
projek'tor, (-s), projector.
proklama'sie, (-s), proclamation.
proklameer', (ge-), proclaim, make known.
proklame'ring, proclamation; proclaiming.
prokli'se, (-s), proclisis.
prokli'ties, (-e), proclitic.
pro'konsul, proconsul; ~**aat'**, proconsulate; ~**skap**, proconsulship.
prokopee', aphaeresis.
prokreëer', (ge-), procreate.
Prokrus'tesbed, bed of Procrustes.
prokura'sie, (-s), procuration, proxy, power of attorney; ~**houer**, (-s), holder of a power of attorney; proxy, assignee; ~**skap**, attorneyship.
prokura'tor, (-e, -s), procurator.
prokureur', (-s), solicitor, attorney; *'n* ~ *toelaat*, admit as attorney; ~**generaal**, solicitor-general, attorney-general; ~**s'eksamen**, law examination; ~**s'firma**, firm of attorneys; ~**s'kantoor**, solicitor's office; ~**skap**, attorneyship; ~**s'leerling**, articled clerk; P~**s'orde**, (Incorporated) Law Society; ~**s'praktyk**, attorney's practice.
proleet', (..lete), proletarian; plebeian, vulgarian.
prolego'mena, prolegomena (introductory discourse).
prolep'sis, prolepsis.
proletariaat', proletariat.
proleta'riër, (-s), proletarian.
proleta'ries, (-e), proletarian.
prole'tedom, plebs; proletariat.
prolonga'sie, prolongation, carry(ing)-over; renewal.
prolongeer', (ge-), renew, prolongate, extend.
proloog', (..loë), prologue, proem.
promena'de, (-s), promenade; ~**dek**, promenade deck; ~**konsert**, promenade concert.
promes'se, (-s), promissory note, note of hand, IOU, due bill.
prominen'sie, prominence.
prominent', (-e), prominent, outstanding.
promisku', (-e), promiscuous; ~**ïteit'**, promiscuity.
promo'sie, (-s), promotion, rise, advance, advancement; graduation; ~**dag**, degree day; graduation day; ~**dinee**, promotion dinner; ~**lys**, promotion list; ~**plegtigheid**, promotion (graduation) ceremony.
promo'tor, (-s), promoter (of company); presenter (of a candidate for a degree).
promoveer', (ge-), graduate, take one's (doctor's) degree; promote; *cum LAUDE* ~, *met LOF* ~, graduate with honours (cum laude).
promoven'dus, (-se, ..di), candidate for a doctor's degree.

promp   425   *proviand*

promp, (-te), prompt, quick, immediate; ~ *te BEDIENING,* quick service; ~ *op tyd BETAAL,* pay punctually.
promulga′sie, promulgation.
promulgeer′, (ge-), promulgate.
pronk, (s) show; pride, ostentation, display, coxcombry; ridge (on back of animal); *te* ~ *loop met,* show off, parade; **(w) (ge-),** show off, display, strut, flash, prank, plume, flaunt, crow, prance; *die BLOMME* ~ *in my tuin,* the flowers make a proud show in my garden; *hy* ~ *DAAR,* that is where he is calling; ~ *met geleende VERE,* strut in borrowed plumes; ~**bed,** bed of state; ~**bok,** show-goat; ~**boontjie,** scarlet runner; ~**dril,** swagger parade; ~**duif,** fantail pigeon; ~**end, (-e),** bragging, prancing, flaunting; ~**er, (-s),** coxcomb, dandy, fop, beau; ~**erig, (-e),** foppish, gaudy, ostentatious, flashy, garish; pretentious; dandyish; ~**erigheid,** ostentation, dandyism; pretentiousness; ~**-ertjie,** sweet pea; ~**ery,** show, parade, ostentation; bravery, foppery, coxcombry, fanfaronade; ~**gewaad,** state dress; ~**hamel,** show-wether; ~**jonker,** playboy; ~**juweel,** jewel, gem; ~**kamer,** stateroom, best room; ~**ridderspoor,** delphinium; P~**rughond,** Rhodesian ridgeback (dog); ~**siek, (-e),** showy, ostentatious; ~**speler,** crack player; ~**stuk,** show-piece, ornament; ~**sug,** ostentation, ostentatiousness; ~**swaard,** dress sword.
prono′men, (..nomina), pronoun.
pronominaal′, (..nale), pronominal.
prononseer′, (ge-), accentuate, cause to stand out prominently.
pronsaal′boontjie, Provence bean.
pront, ready, exact, pure, prompt; pronto (slang); ~ *BETAAL,* pay promptly; ~ *KEN,* know off pat; ~**heid,** readiness, accuracy, promptness; ~**-uit,** straight out, flatly; ~**-uit weier,** refuse flatly.
prooi, (-e), prey, quarry, game; *ten* ~ *aan,* a prey to, at the mercy of.
proos, (-te), dean; provost.
proosdy′, (-e), deanery.
prop, (s) (-pe) stopper (bottle); plug (wound); cork, bung (barrel); fid (cannon); wad (rifle); gag (in the mouth); lump (in the throat); tubby person; tampon; dottle (in pipe); *op die* ~ *pe KOM,* come to light; come on the tapsis; ~ *UITTREK,* unplug; **(w) (ge-),** cram (the mouth); plug (a wound); dump.
propaan′, propane.
propagan′da, propaganda; ~ *maak vir,* agitate for; propagate; ~ **stuk,** propagandist play; ~**werk,** propaganda.
propagandis′, (-te), propagandist; ~**ties, (-e),** propagandist(ic).
propageer′, (ge-), propagate; ~**baar, (..bare),** propagable; ~**der, (-s),** propagator.
propedeu′ties, (-e), propaedeutic (examination).
propedeu′tika, propaedeutics.
pro′per, tidy, neat.
prop′gat, plug-hole.
prop′geweer, *see* **propskieter.**
proponeer′, (ge-), propose.
proponent′, (-e), candidate for the ministry; ~**s′eksamen,** final examination for the ministry.
propor′sie, (-s), proportion.
proporsioneel′, (..nele), proportional, proportionate.
proposi′sie, (-s), proposition; prospect.
prop: ~**perig, (-e),** dumpy; ~**pers,** really, properly; ~**pie, (-s),** small work pellet, short person; ~**skieter, (-s),** popgun; ~**stoof,** plug-in stove; ~**trekker,** wad-hook; ~**vol,** chock-full, cropful, filled to capacity, full to the brim, stuffed with, brimful, brimming, jam-packed; ~**vorming,** embolism.
prorogeer′, (ge-), prorogue; ..**gering,** prorogation.
pro′sa, (-s) ~**gedig,** prose poem; ~**′ies, (-e),** prosaic, prosy; pedestrian; ~**′is′, (-te),** prose writer; prosaist; ~**mens,** prosaic person; ~**skrywer,** prose writer; story writer; proser, prosaist; ~**styl,** prose style; ~**werk,** prose work.
prosce′nium, (-s), proscenium.
prosedeer′, (ge-), litigate, go to law, be at law; *as iem.*

jou ~ *vir jou KOEI, gee die kalf daarby,* agree, for the law is costly; ~**der, (-s),** litigant.
prosedu′re, (-s), procedure.
prosek′tor, prosector.
proseku′sie, (ong.) (-s), prosecution.
proseliet′, (-e), proselyte, follower; ~**maker,** proselytizer; ~**makery,** proselytism.
proses′, (-se), process; course; method; legal proceedings, lawsuit; litigation; *kort* ~ *maak,* give short shrift; ~**akte** (siviel), civil process; ~**koste,** costs of a lawsuit, legal costs; ~**reg,** law of procedure; ~**sie, (-s),** procession; ~**siegesang,** processional; ~**stuk,** document of a lawsuit, process, docket.
pro′sit! your health! (when drinking).
prosodie′, prosody; ..**so′dies, (-e),** prosodic.
prosodis′, (-te), prosodist.
prosopopee′, prosopopoeia.
prospekteer′, (ge-), prospect; ~ *na diamante,* prospect for diamonds; ~**der, (-s),** prospector; ~**dery,** prospecting; ~**gat,** prospect pit; ~**lisensie,** prospector's licence; ~**skag,** prospect shaft; ~**sloot,** prospect trench; ~**tonnel,** prospect adit.
prospekte′ring, prospecting.
prospek′tor, (-s), prospector.
prospek′tus, (-se), prospectus.
prostaat′, prostate; ~**klier,** prostate gland.
prostituee′, (-s), prostitute.
prostitueer′, (ge-), prostitute.
prostitu′sie, prostitution.
prostituut′, (..tute) = **prostituee.**
protagonis′, (-te), protagonist.
pro′tasis, (-se), protasis.
pro′tea, (-s), protea.
protégé, (-′s), protégé, fosterling; ~**e, (-s),** protégée.
protegeer′, (ge-), protect, take up as charge, patronize.
proteï′de, (-s), proteïed′, (-e), proteid.
proteï′en, (-e), proteï′ne, (-s), protein; ~**arm,** lowprotein; ~**gehalte,** protein quality; ~**inhoud,** protein content; ~**ryk,** protein-rich; ~**voedsel,** protein food.
protek′sie, protection; ~**handel,** protected trade, protectionism.
proteksionis′, (-te), protectionist; ~**me,** protectionism; ~**ties, (-e),** protectionist(ic).
protektoraat′, (..rate), protectorate; protectorship.
protes′, (-te), protest; challenge; outcry; caveat; reclamation; ~ *AANTEKEN teen,* register a protest against; enter a caveat; *ONDER* ~, under protest; *SONDER* ~, without demur; ~**akte,** deed of protest.
prote′se, artificial limb, prothesis.
pro′tesis, prothesis.
protes′nota, note of protest.
Protestant′, (-e), Protestant; ~**is′me,** Protestantism; ~**s′, (-e),** Protestant.
protesta′sie, protestation.
protesteer′, (ge-), protest, object; ~**der, ..te′rende, (-s),** protestor.
protes′veldtog, campaign of protest.
protes′vergadering, protest meeting.
prote′ties, (-e), prothetic.
pro′teusagtig, protean.
protokol′, (-le), record, report, protocol; ~**lêr′, (-e),** protocolar.
pro′totaal, protolanguage.
pro′toman, (-e), protoman.
protoplas′ma, protoplasm.
protoplasma′ties, protoplas′mies, (-e), protoplasmic.
protosoön, (..soa, ..soë), protozoon.
pro′tospan, prototeam.
prototi′pe, prototype.
provenier′, (-s), beadsman, inmate of an almshouse.
Provensaals′, (-e), Provencal.
proviand′, provisions, victuals; supplies; ~**eer′, (ge-),** provide with food, provision, victual; cater; ~**e′ring,** purveyance, victualling; catering; provisionment; ~**ier′, (-s),** caterer; ~**meester,** storekeeper (of commissariat); purveyor; ~**skip,** provision (store-), ship.

provinsiaal', (..siale), provincial; *Provinsiale Sekretaris*, Provincial Secretary.
provinsialis', (-te), provincialist; ~ **me**, provincialism; ~ **ties**, (-e), provincialistic.
provin'sie, (-s), province, canton, country; ~ **bewoner**, provincial.
provi'sie, (-s), provision; ~ **handelaar**, provision merchant; ~ **kamer**, larder, pantry; ~ **kas**, pantry cupboard.
provisioneel', (..nele), provisional, provisory.
provoka'sie, (-s), provocation; ~ **middel**, provocative.
provokeer', **provoseer'**, (ge-), provoke.
provoos', (-te), provost.
pruik, (-e), wig, peruke, (peri)wig, bob(-wig); ~ **bol**, wig block; ~ **etyd**, periwig period; ~ **maker**, wigmaker; ~ **stert**, pigtail.
pruil, (ge-), pout, sulk, be sulky; ~ **er**, (-s), pouter; ~ **erig**, (-e), sulky, pouting.
pruim¹, (s) (-e), plum; prune (dried); *hy kan nie ~ sê nie*, he can't say "boo" to a goose.
pruim², (w) (ge-), chew (tobacco); *hoe ~ daardie twak vir jou?*, how do you like that?
pruim: ~ **agtig**, plummy; ~ **appelkoos**, plumcot; ~ **bas**, sumach; ~ **bessie**, edible berry; ~ **boom**, plum-tree; ~ **edant'**, (-e), prune; prunello.
prui'mer, (-s), chewer, quiddist.
pruim'konfyt, plum-jam.
pruim: ~ **pie**, (-s), quid, chew (tobacco); chaw-bacon; fid; plug.
pruim: ~ **pit**, plum-stone (-pip); ~ **sap**, plum-juice.
pruim: ~ **sop**, tobacco-juice; ~ **tabak**, chewing-tobacco.
Pruis, (-e), Prussian; ~ **e**, Prussia; ~ **ies**, (-e), Prussian.
prui'sies: ~ **blou**, Prussian blue; ~ **suur**, prussic acid.
prul, (s) (-le), trifle, trash, rubbish, gimcrack, gewgaw, fal-lal; (w) (ge-), cull; ~ **beeste**, scrub cattle; ~ **digter**, poetaster, rhymer; ~ **lerig**, (-e), trashy, scrubby; punk; shoddy, knicknackish; ~ **poëet**, poetaster, rhymer; ~ **roman**, trashy novel; ~ **skrywer**, paltry writer, hedge-writer, literary hack; ~ **werk**, trash, rubbish, sloppy work.
prunel'la, prunella.
prunel'sout, prunella salt.
prut, (ge-), simmer, bubble; ~ **kissie**, hay-box.
pruts'ding, trifle, trash.
prut'sel, (ge-), tinker, fiddle, potter; ~ **aar**, (-s), tinkerer, potterer; ~ **werk**, bungled work; pottering, trifling job.
prut'sery, (-e), tinkering, pottering.
prut'tel, (ge-), grumble, grouse; bubble, simmer (boiling water; food); ~ **aar**, (-s), ~ **kous**, (-e), grumbler, grouser; ~ **rig**, (-e), grumbling, grumpy; ~ **righeid**, grumpiness.
pry, (-e), carrion; hag, shrew.
pryk, (ge-), shine, look fine, stand forth; parade, show off; appear, figure, grace; *sy naam ~ in die koerant*, his name appears in the paper.
prys, (-e), (s) price, value, cost, charge; award, premium, prize; praise; expense; plate (races); *die eerste ~ BEHAAL*, win the first prize; *die BEPAAL (vasstel) op R1*, fix the price at R1; *tot ELKE ~*, at all costs; *GOED op ~ wees*, maintain good prices; *'n ~ op iem. se HOOF (kop) sit*, set a price on someone's head; *die HOOGSTE ~ betaal*, pay top price; *op ~ HOU*, keep up to market value; *ONDER die ~ verkoop*, sell at a loss; *'n ~ OPGEE vir*, submit an estimate for; *op ~ STEL*, value something highly; *TEEN die ~ van*, at the price of; *'n ~ TOEKEN*, award a prize; *'n ~ UITLOOF*, offer a prize; *iets vir dieselfde ~ VERKOOP*, tell (the news) for what it is worth; *die ~ WEGDRA*, carry off the prize; (w) (ge-), extol, commend, eulogize, laud, praise, applaud, exalt; price; *iem. GELUKKIG ~*, call someone happy; *iem. HEMELHOOG ~*, laud someone to the skies; ~ **aanvraag**, enquiry (regarding price); ~ **bederwer**, price-spoiler, spoil-trade, underseller; ~ **bepaling**, fixing of prices; ~ **bepalingsrekening**, costing account; ~ **berekening**, estimate of cost; ~ **besnoeiing**, price-cutting; ~ **binding**, price maintenance; ~ **daling**, drop (fall) in prices; ~ **end**, (-e), lauditive, laudatory, plauditory, encomiastic; ~ **enswaar'dig**, (-e), praiseworthy, commendable, laudable; ~ **enswaar'digheid**, praiseworthiness; ~ **er**, lauder; ~ **fees**, sale.
prys'gee, (-ge-), abandon, give up; *AAN die verwaarlosing ~*, allow to go to rack and ruin; *'n WEDSTRYD ~*, not play a match.
prys: ~ **gegee**, walk-over (sport); ~ **geld**, prize-money; jackpot; ~ **gerig**, prize-court; ~ **gewing**, abandonment; walk-over; ~ **grens**, price-limit; ~ **herstel**, recovery in prices; ~ **hof**, prize court; ~ **hoogte**, price level; ~ **houdend**, (-e), firm (in market value); ~ **jagter**, pot-hunter; ~ **kaartjie**, price-ticket; price-mark; ~ **klas**, price-class; ~ **koerant**, catalogue; ~ **kontroleur**, price-controller; ~ **lys**, price-list, catalogue; prize-list; ~ **maak**, (-ge-), prize (a ship); ~ **making**, capture, seizure; ~ **notering**, quotation (of prices); ~ **opdrywing**, forcing up prices; inflation of prices; ~ **opgaaf**, ~ **opgawe**, quotation of prices, estimate; ~ **opjaer**, puffer; ~ **opslag**, increase in price; ~ **peil**, price level; ~ **raaisel**, prize competition; ~ **reëling**, regulation of prices; ~ **regter**, prize judge; ~ **skiet**, bisley; prize-meeting; ~ **skip**, prize-ship; ~ **skommeling**, fluctuation of prices; ~ **styging**, rise in price(s); *skielike (plotselinge) ~ styging*, boom; ~ **uitdeling**, speech-day, distribution of prizes, presentation of prizes; ~ **vasstelling**, price determination; ~ **verbetering**, advance (in price); ~ **verhandeling**, prize essay; ~ **verhoging**, advance (in price), increase, rise; ~ **verlaging**, price-reduction, cut, abatement (of price); ~ **vermindering**, price-reduction; ~ **verskil**, difference in price; ~ **vraag**, prize subject; competition; ~ **weerstand**, buyers' resistance; ~ **wenner**, ~ **winner**, prize-winner; ~ **wisseling**, fluctuation in price.
psalm, (-s), psalm; ~ **beryming**, rhymed version of the Psalms; ~ **boek**, psalm-book, psalter; ~ **digter**, psalmist; ~ **gesang**, psalmody; ~ **is'**, (-te), psalmist.
psalmodieer', (ge-), psalmodize.
psalm'sing, (-ge-), psalmodize.
psal'ter, (-s), psalter; psaltery.
pseu'do-, pseudo-, pretended, bogus.
pseudomorf', (-e), pseudomorphous; ~ **is'me**, pseudomorphism.
pseudoniem', (s) (-e), pseudonym; (b) (-e), pseudonymous.
psi'ge, psyche, mind, soul.
psigede'lies, (-e), psychedelic; ~ *e kleure*, psychedelic colours.
psigia'ter, (-s), psychiatrist.
psigiatrie', psychiatry.
psigia'tries, (-e), psychiatric(al).
psi'gies, (-e), psychic.
psigoanalis', (-te), psychoanalyst; ~ **eer'**, (ge-), psychoanalyse; ~ **e**, psychoanalysis.
psigoanali'ties, (-e), psycho-analytic(al).
psigogene'se, psychogenesis.
psigologie', psychology; ..**lo'gies**, (-e), psychological; ..**loog'**, (..loë), psychologist.
psigoma'ties, (-e), psychomatic.
psi'gometer, psychometer.
psigometrie', psychometry.
psigome'tries, (-e), psychometric(al).
psigoot', (psigote), psychotic.
psigopaat', (..pate), psychopath.
psigopatie', psychopathy.
psigopa'ties, (-e), psychopathic.
psigopatologie', psychopathology.
psigo'se, (-s), psychosis; mental derangement.
psigosoma'ties, (-e), psychosomatic.
psigotegniek', psychotechnics.
psigoteg'nies, (-e), psychotechnic(al).
psigoterapie', psychotherapy.
psigoterapeu'ties, psychotherapeutic.
psigo'ties, (-e), psychotic.
psi'grometer, **psigrome'ter**, psychrometer.
psil'la, psylla (citrus-lice).
psil'liumsaad, psyllium seed.
psittako'se, psittacosis.
pst!, st! hush!

Psy'che, Psyche.
p'tjie, (-s), small **p.**
Ptoleme'ies, Ptolemaic.
Ptoleme'us, Ptolemy.
ptomaïen', ptomaï'ne, ptomaine; ~**vergiftiging,** ptomaine poisoning.
pu'ber, (-s), adolescent.
puberteit', puberty; ~**s'jare,** age of puberty, adolescence; ~**s'leeftyd,** age of puberty.
publiek', (s) public; audience; *die GROOT* ~, the public at large, the general public; *IN die* ~, in public, publicly; (b, bw) **(-e),** public; ~*e HUIS*, brothel; *'n* ~*e LEUEN*, a barefaced lie; ~ *MAAK*, give publicity to; *dit voel* ~ *OF*, it feels exactly as though; ~*e REG*, public law; ~ *VERKOOP*, sell by auction; *dit VOEL* ~, it seems just as if; *'n* ~*e VROU*, prostitute; ~ *WORD*, become known.
publiekreg'telik, (-e), according to public law.
publika'sie, (-s), publication.
publiseer', (ge-), publish; print; ~**der, (-s),** publisher.
publisis', (-te), publicist, publisher.
publisiteit', publicity; ~ *gee*, make public, give publicity to; ~**s'agent,** publicity agent; ~**s'buro, (-'s),** publicity bureau (office).
pud'del, (ge-), puddle.
pueriel', (-e), puerile, childish.
puerilis'me, puerilism.
puerilisiteit', (-e), puerility.
puf, (s) grit, go; *hy het nie* ~ *nie,* he has no grit (gumption); (w) **(ge-),** puff.
puik, (s) pick, choice, *die* ~ *v.d. oes,* the pick of the harvest; (b) **(-er, -ste),** excellent, choice, high quality; *die konsert was sommer* ~, the concert was really excellent.
puil, (ge-), protrude, bulge; ~**oog,** goggle-eye.
puim'steen, pumice (-stone), bathing-stone; ~**agtig, (-e),** pumiceous.
puin, ruins; debris, rubble; talus; dirt; detritus; *in* ~ *val,* fall into decay; ~**gesteente,** fragmental rock, ~**helling,** talus slope; ~**hoop,** heap of ruins, rubbish-heap; ~**keël,** talus cone.
pui'sie, (-s), pimple, pustule; acne; papula, papule; ~**agtig, (-e),** full of pimples, pimply; ~**byter,** crane-fly; ~**middel,** acne remedy; ~**rig, (-e),** pimply; pustular; ~**siekte,** acne.
pul, (-le), amphora, pot-bellied jug.
pulp, pulp; ~**meul,** pulp-mill.
pulsa'sie, (-s), beating, beat, pulsation.
pulsa'tor, (-s), pulsator.
pulseer', (ge-), pulse, beat; *..se'ring,* pulsation.
pul'someter, pulsome'ter, (-s), pulsometer.
pul'wer, dust, powder; ~**iseer', (ge-),** pulverize.
Pu'nies, (-e), Punic.
punk'sie, (-s), (med.) puncture.
punktualiteit', punctuality.
punktua'sie, (-s), punctuation; pointing; ~**stelsel,** punctuation system; ~**teken,** punctuation mark.
punktueel', (..tuele), punctual.
punkteer', (ge-), punctuate.
punktuur', (..ture), (med.) puncture; puncturing.
punt, (s) **(-e),** point (of pin); tip (of tongue); nose (of torpedo); horn (of anvil); peak; hook; apex; end (of sail); chapter; dot, stop; full stop, period; question, item, matter (under discussion); mark (examination); mucro (bot.); projection; ~*e AANTEKEN*, score points; *'n* ~ *van BELANG*, a matter of importance; *op 'n DOOIE* ~, at a deadlock; *iets na 'n* ~ *DRYF*, bring something to a head; *hoë* ~*e in die EKSAMEN*, good (high) marks in the examination; *5* ~*e MAAK*, score 5 points; *iem, van* ~*tjie na PAALTJIE stuur,* send someone from pillar to post; *hoe STAAN die* ~*e*, what is the score?; *op die* ~ *STAAN om te vertrek,* be on the point of departure; *'n* ~ *STEL,* make a point; ~*e en STREPIES,* dots and dashes; *'n SWAK* ~, a weak point; *'n TEER* ~, a sore point; *in 'n* ~ *UITLOOP,* taper off; *op die* ~ *e v.d. VINGERS ken,* have something at one's fingertips; ~ *VIR* ~, point by point; *met* ~*e WEN,* win on points; (w) **(ge-),** point, sharpen into a point; *'n baard* ~, trim a beard; ~**baard,** pointed beard (French-cut); ~**boei,** nun-buoy; ~**dig, (te),** epigram; ~**digter,** epigrammatist;

~**eboek,** mark-book; ~**eer', (ge-),** stipple; ~**eer'der,** stippler; ~**ekaart,** score-card; ~**elys,** log; mark-sheet; score-sheet.
puntene'rig, punteneu'rig, (-e), touchy, easily offended; particular, fastidious, pernickety; punctilious; ~**heid,** fastidiousness; touchiness.
pun'te: ~**spel,** (gholf), stableford; ~**stand,** score, log; ~**stelsel,** points system; ~**telling,** score; ~**totaal,** total points.
punt: ~**gewel,** pointed gable; ~**granaat,** elongated shell; ~**hamer,** pointed hammer; ~**helm,** spiked helmet; ~**hoed,** sugarloaf hat.
pun'tig, (-e), pointed, sharp, jagged, edged; angular; awl-shaped; pithy (saying); peaked; ~**heid,** pointedness, sharpness, point.
pun'tjie, (-s), tip, dot, point; picot; end; spicule; *alles mooi IN die* ~*s*, everything in applepie order; *tot in die* ~*s KEN,* have at one's fingertips; *iem. van* ~ *na PAALTJIE stuur,* send someone from pillar to post; *as* ~ *by PAALTJIE kom,* when it comes to the push; *die* ~ *op die i's SIT,* dot one's i's and cross one's t's; *'n STOMP* ~, a dimwit; ~**soom,** picot-edging.
punt: ~**lading,** nose-bursting charge; ~**landing,** spot-landing; ~**lyn,** dotted line; ~**naald,** stippler; ~**oog,** ocellus; ~**penseel,** stippler; ~**s'gewys(e),** seriatim, point by point; ~**skoen,** pointed shoe; ~**sweis,(ge-),** spot-weld; ~**sweising,** spot welding; ~**wissels,** facing points (loco.).
pupil', (-le), pupil (of eye); ward, minor.
puree', puree, mash.
purga'sie, (s), purgative, laxative, aperient; purging; ~**middel,** purgative; laxative.
purgatief', (..tiewe), purgative.
purgeer', (ge-), purge; ~**middel,** purgative, laxative, cathartic, evacuant; ~**neut,** purging-nut.
purge'rend, (-e), laxative, evacuant.
purge'ring, catharsis, purgation.
Pu'rim, Purim (Jewish feast).
puris', (-te), purist; ~**me,** purism; ~**ties, (-e),** puristic.
puritanis'me, puritanism.
Puriteins', (-e), Puritan; ~**s', (-e),** Puritan; ~**s'gesind, (-e),** Puritan.
pur'per, purple, amethyst; amaranth; *met die* ~ *BEKLEE(D) word,* be raised to the purple; *in die* ~ *GEBORE wees,* be cradled in the purple; ~**agtig, (-e),** purplish; ~**blou,** indigo-blue; ~**kleurig, (-e),** purple; ~**kol,** purple patch; ~**koors,** purple fever; ~**rooi,** purple, murrey; ~**slak,** purple-fish, murex; purpura; ~**suur,** purpuric acid; ~**vlinder,** purple emperor; ~**winde,** morning glory.
put, (s) **(-te),** well, draw-well, pit; cesspool; *die* ~ *DEMP wanneer die kalf verdrink is,* lock the stable-door after the steed is stolen; *wie 'n* ~ *vir 'n ander GRAAF, val daar self in,* be hoist with one's own petard; harm watch, harm catch; *'n* ~ *GRAWE,* sink a well; (w) **(ge-),** draw (water); *uit die BRONNE self* ~, get information from the original source; *HOOP* ~ *uit,* derive hope from; *TROOS* ~ *uit,* derive comfort from; *sy kennis* ~ *UIT, borrow* one's knowledge from; ~**domkrag,** drop-pit jack; ~**emmer,** well-bucket; ~**grawer, (-s),** well-digger, well-sinker.
put'haak, bucket-hook; *oor die* ~ *trou,* marry over the broomstick.
put'jie, (-s), hole (golf); ~ *in een (*~ *-een) maak,* hole out in one (golf); ~**spel,** match-play (golf); *wen met 2 putjies voor en 1 om te speel,* win by 2 up and 1 to go.
putrefak'sie, putrefaction.
put'riool, French drain.
puts, (-e), tar-bucket; well.
put'ter, (-s), water-drawer.
put'tingyster, channel-plate.
put'water, well-water.
puur, (pure), pure, sheer, mere; nothing but; excellent; plumb; *sy gesig was pure BLOED,* his face was covered with blood (bleeding all over); *'n pure MAN,* every inch a man; *pure ONSIN (kaf),* sheer (absolute, rank) nonsense; *'n koejawel is pure PITTE,* a guava is nothing but pips.
py, (-e), cowl; habit, jacket, sailor's smock.

pyl, (s) (-e), arrow, dart; clock (on socks); *soos 'n ~ uit die BOOG*, as swift as an arrow; *meer as een ~ op sy BOOG hê*, have two strings to one's bow; *nog 'n ~ in sy KOKER hê*, have another shot in his locker; *al sy ~ e VERSKIET (wegskiet)*, all his bullets are spent; shoot all his bolts; (w) **(ge-)**, dart, go straight, make for, go swiftly; *na die deur ~*, make straight for the door; **~ bondel**, bundle of arrows; **~ bord**, dart-board; **~ er**, (-s), column, pillar; pile bridge; pier; **~ geweer**, dart gun; **~ gif**, arrow-poison; **~ gooi**, darts (game); **~ koker**, quiver; **~ kruid**, arrowhead; **~ naat**, dart; **~ punt**, arrow-head; **~ puntvormig**; (-e), sagittate; **~ reguit**, straight as an arrow (a die); **~ skoot**, arrowshot; **~ skrif**, cuneiform characters; **~ skyf**, dart-board; **~ snel**, very swift; **~ spits**, fork-head; **~ stert**, (-e), sting-ray, eagle-ray; pintail; jumping ray; widow-bird; **~ stertmot**, hawk-moth; **~ stertrog**, **~ stertvis** = **pylstert**; **~ stok**, arrow shaft; **~ tand**, herring-bone tooth; **~ tjie**, small arrow, dart; direction light; **~ tjies**, **~ tjiesgooi**, darts; **~ vak**, home stretch, straight (athl.); **~ vlerk**, swept-back wing; **~ vor'mig**, (-e), arrow-shaped, sagittal; **~ wortel**, arrowroot; **~ wortelmeel**, arrowroot.

pyn, (s) (-e), pain, ache, anguish; *FOLTERENDE ~ e*, excruciating pains; *INEENKRIMP van ~*, writhe with pain; *dit gee 'n mens ~ op jou NAARHEID*, it makes one sick; (w) **(ge-)**, ache, smart, pain.

pyn'appel, pineapple, pine, ananas; **~ klier**, pineal gland; **~ konfyt**, pineapple preserve; **~ plaas**, pinery; **~ vulsel**, pineapple filling.

pyn'bank, rack; *iem. op die ~ lê*, put a person to the rack.

pyn: ~ boom, pine-tree, fir-tree; **~ hars**, pine-resin.

py'nig, (ge-), torture, torment, harrow; pinch; **~ er**, (-s), tormentor, torturer; **~ ing**, (-e, -s), torture, excruciation, pang.

pyn'kamer, torture-chamber.

pyn'lik, (-e), painful; distressing, dolorous; poignant; embarrassing; **~ heid**, painfulness, poignancy.

pyn: ~ loos, (..lose), painless; *lose BEVALLING*, twilight sleep; *lose DOOD*, euthanasia; *lose SEER*, indolent ulcer; **~ loosheid**, painlessness; **~ stillend**, (-e), pain-killing, soothing, analgesic;
anodyne; **~ stiller**, (-s), pain-killer, analgesic; **~ verdrywer**, pain-expeller.

pyp, (s) (-e), pipe; briar; tube; leg (of trousers); flue (chimney); barrel; fife; flute; butt; quill; conduit; stick (of cinnamon); *nie 'n ~ DAGGA werd nie*, not worth a pinch of snuff; *na iem. se ~ e DANS*, dance to someone's tune; *'n lelike ~ ROOK*, come in for something unpleasant; *die ~ ROOK*, pull a thing off; *'n ~ STOP*, fill a pipe; (w) **(ge-)**, pipe; fife, flute, goffer; **~ aarde**, pipeclay; **~ been**, shank, shin-bone; **~ borsel**, tube-brush (-cleaner); **~ deursteker**, pipe-cleaner; **~ doppie**, pipe-cover; **~ draad**, pipe-thread; **~ elmboog**, pipe elbow; **~ er**, (-s), piper, fifer; **~ fabriek**, pipe-factory; **~ gat**, tube hole; **~ grond**, pipeclay; **~ hamer**, pipe-hammer; **~ hek**, tubular gate.

py'pie, (-s), small pipe; little tube; pipette; "painted lady" and several (other) plants with tubular flowers e.g. *Watsonia gladiolus*; blue-bells.

pyp: ~ kalbas, pipe-gourd; **~ kan**, (s) feeding-bottle, feeder; (w) **(ge-)** cheat, fool; (sell a) dummy (rugby); **~ kaneel**, cinnamon (in sticks); **~ ketel**, tubular boiler; **~ klem**, pipe-clip; **~ klip**, pipestone; **~ kop**, pipe-bowl; **~ koppeling**, pipe-union; **~ kraag**, ruff; **~ kruit**, cylinder gunpowder, powder in tubes; **~ las**, (-se), pipe joint; **~ lêer**, (-s), pipe-fitter; pipe-layer; **~ leiding**, pipe-line; pipage; piping; **~ lyn**, pipe-line; **~ moer**, dottle; **~ mossel**, pencil-bait; **~ olie**, pipe-oil, nicotine; **~ orrel**, pipe-organ; **~ passer**, pipe-fitter; **~ plooie**, goffer; **~ plooi-yster**, goffering-iron; **~ rak**, pipe-rack; **~ roker**, pipe-smoker; **~ rook**, pipe-smoke; pipe-smoking; **~ roller**, expander; **~ skêr**, goffering-irons; **~ skoonmaker**, pipe-cleaner; **~ skroefdraad**, pipe thread; **~ sleutel**, monkey wrench; alligator-wrench, box-spanner; **~ snyer**, pipe-cutter; **~ sok**, pipe-socket; **~ stadium**, pipe stage (grass); **~ stander**, (-s), pipe-rack; **~ steel**, pipe-stem; **~ steelerf**, panhandle stand; **~ steier**, tubular scaffolding; **~ swa(w)el**, roll-sulphur; **~ tabak**, pipe-tobacco; **~ versiering**, piping; **~ vorm**, pipe-bending machine; **~ vormig**, (-e), tubular; **~ werker**, pipe-fitter; **~ wig**, fish-back; **~ wydte**, pipe width; **~ yster**, goffering-iron.

Pyr'rhusoorwinning, Pyrrhic victory.

Q

q, (-'s), q.
q'tjie, (-s), small q.
quaes'tor, (-s), quaestor; *Q ~ Synodi*, Treasurer of the Synod.
questionnai're, (-s), questionnaire.
quid' pro quo, (-'s), quid pro quo, compensation.

Quirinaal': *die ~*, the Quirinal.
quis'ling, (-s), the quisling.
qui-vi've, who goes there? *op jou ~ wees*, be on the alert.
quod'libet, quod libet, as you like it; potpourri.

R

r, (-'s, -'e), r.
ra, (-'s), yard (of sail); *groot ~*, mainyard.
raad[1], (**~ gewinge, ~ gewings**), advice, counsel; help; admonishment; *BUITE ~ wees*, be at a loss; *iem. met ~ en DAAD bystaan*, assist someone by word and deed; *van ~ DIEN*, assist with advice; *ten EINDE ~ wees*, be at one's wits' end; *te rade GAAN met*, consult with; *~ GEE*, advise, give advice; *GOEIE ~ is nou duur*, sound advice is a rare commodity; *~ INWIN*, ask advice; *nie ~ met iem. WEET nie*, be at a loss about what to do with a person; *OP ~ van*, on the advice of; *as ek jou ~ VERSKULDIG is*, if I may offer a word of advice; *iem. se ~ VOLG*, follow someone's advice; *iem. om ~ VRA*, seek a person's advice; *g'n ~ WEET nie*,
be at a loss; *altyd ~ WEET*, always find a way out; *~ in die WIND slaan*, disregard advice.

raad[2], (rade), council, board; *GEHEIME ~*, Privy Council; *IN 'n ~ dien (sit)*, be on a council.

raad: ~ gewend, (-e), advisory (capacity); consulting (engineer); **~ gewer**, (-s), adviser, counsellor, counsel; mentor; consultee; **~ gewing**, (-e, -s), advice, counsel.

raad: ~ huis, council-hall; city hall; **~ kamer**, council-chamber.

raad'-op, at one's wits' end; be at a loss.

raad'pleeg, (ge-), consult, take counsel with; see; commune with; *'n ADVOKAAT ~*, consult a lawyer; *met iem. OOR 'n saak ~*, take counsel with someone about a matter.

raad: ~ plegend, (-e), consultative; consulting; consultatory; ~ pleger, (-s), consulter, consultant; ~ pleging, (-e, -s), consultation; reference; *na* ~ *pleging met,* after (in) consultation with.

raad'saal, council-chamber; board-room; Volksraad chamber (in former republics).

raad'saam, (..same), advisable, expedient; ~ heid, advisability.

raads: ~ besluit, decision (resolution) of the council; ~ heer, councillor; alderman; bishop (in chess).

raad'sitting, council meeting.

raads: ~ kamer, council-chamber; cabinet; ~ lid, (..lede), councillor; member of council; ~ man, (-ne, ..liede), adviser, counsellor; ~ vergadering, council meeting; ~ verkiesing, council election; ~ verslag, records (minutes) of council meeting; council's report.

raaf, (rawe), raven; *so SWART soos 'n* ~, as black as a crow; *die rawe sal dit UITBRING,* murder will out; the stones will proclaim the truth; *'n WIT* ~, a black swan, a white crow; ~ agtig, (-e), corvine.

raag'bol, ceiling-mop.

raai, (ge-), guess, make a guess, conjecture; advise; spot (a question); *ek GEE jou te* ~ *(e) wie hier is,* guess who is here; *iem. IETS laat* ~, let a person guess something; ~, ~ *RIEPA,* here's a riddle for you; riddle-me-ree; ~ *WAT!* just fancy! ~ baar, (..bare), conjecturable; ~ er, (-s), guesser; ~ ery, (-e), guessing, guesswork, guess, conjecture.

raai'sel, (-s), riddle, puzzle; enigma, conundrum, problem; charade; *DIS vir my 'n* ~, it is a mystery to me; *'n* ~ *OPGEE,* ask a riddle; *'n* ~ *OPLOS,* clear up a mystery; *in* ~ *s PRAAT,* talk in riddles; ~ ag'tig, (-e), enigmatic(al), ambiguous, mysterious, puzzling, baffling; oracular, Delphic; ~ ag'tigheid, incomprehensibility, mystery, ambiguity; ~ tert, mystery tart.

raai'skatting, guesstimate, guess-estimate.

raai'skoot, raai'slag, guess.

raak, (w) (ge-), hit (target); touch (wall); catch; affect, concern (person); *byna aan IETS* ~, barely miss something; almost touch something; *uit die MODE* ~, go out of fashion; *dit* ~ *MY nie,* it is no concern of mine; *aan die PRAAT* ~, get (start) talking; *SKRAMS* ~, graze, touch lightly; *SLAAGS* ~, come to blows; *van sy VERSTAND* ~, go out of his mind (become insane); (b, bw), hit, touched; effective, telling, to the point; *'n* ~ *ANTWOORD,* a home thrust; *DIT is* ~, that hits the mark; that went home; *'n* ~ *HOU,* a hit; a telling blow; *sy VAT alles* ~, she is very handy; ~ bal, toucher (bowls); ~ gooi, (-ge-), hit (by throwing), strike.

raak'dag, see **skietdag.**

raak'-en-ry-ongeluk, hit-and-run accident.

raak'lings, very close to; ~ *verbygaan,* graze past, brush past.

raak: ~ loop, (-ge-), meet, come across; ~ lyn, tangent; ~ oppervlak, contact surface; ~ punt, tangent point, point of contact; ~ ry, (-ge-), drive (ride) up against; collide with, hit; ~ sien, (-ge-), notice, see; spot; ~ skiet, (-ge-), hit; ~ skoot, hit; homeshot; ~ slaan, (-ge-), hit; ~ stoot, cannon (billiards); ~ vlak, tangent plane; contact surface; interface.

raal, (rale), stony ridge, ledge (in river); corrugation (in road).

raam, (s) (rame), window-frame; frame (of picture); casing; grid; chase; (w) (ge-), estimate, assess; budget; crib; (en)frame; ~ antenne, frame aerial; ~ baar, (..bare), framable; ~ brug, frame bridge; ~ draagtap, frame-trunnion; ~ haak, sash-fastener; ~ koord, sash-cord; ~ kosyn, window-frame; ~ ligter, window pull, window lift; ~ lood, sash-lead; ~ lyn, sash-cord; ~ lys, framebead; ~ maker, framer, frame-maker; ~ monteur, rigger; ~ saag, gang-saw, frame-saw; ~ spanstuk, frame-stretcher; ~ styl, mullion; ~ takke, scaffold-branches; ~ tou, sash-line (cord); ~ visier, frame-sight; ~ werk, chassis, frame; cadre; plan, outline, sketch; fuselage (aeroplane); framework (of model); cradling (ceiling); frame-assembly.

raap¹, (s) (rape), rape, turnip.

raap², (w) (ge-), gather, pick up; ~ *en skraap,* collect indiscriminately (haphazardly); scrape together.

raap: ~ koek, rape-cake; ~ kool, kohlrabi; turnip cabbage; ~ olie, rape(seed)-oil; colza-oil; ~ saad, rape-seed; cole-seed; ~ stele, turnip-tops; ~ tol, edible corn *(Cyanella capensis);* ~ vormig, (-e), rapaceous.

raar, (rare; -der, -ste), funny, strange, odd, queer, quaint; *'n rare vent,* a queer fellow.

raas, (s) scolding; ~ *kry,* get a scolding; (ge-), make a noise, clank; scold, rave, bluster, kick up a row, rage; ~ bek, rowdy (noisy) fellow; ~ bessie, guarri; ~ blaar, Zeyher's bush willow *(Combretum zeyheri);* ~ kal, (ge-), talk nonsense; ~ water, brandy, booze; a rowdy.

raat, (rate), remedy; (honey)comb.

ra'band, head-line (ship).

rabar'ber, rhubarb; ~ konfyt, rhubarb preserve (jam); ~ plant, rhubarb plant; ~ poeding, rhubarb pudding; ~ poeier, gregory-powder; ~ stoel, rhubarb plant; ~ stroop, rhubarb syrup.

rabat', (-te), allowance, trade discount, rebate; rabbet; cavity wall; border (in garden); ~ teer', (ge-), deduct, give discount.

rabbedoe', (-ë, -s), rough (careless) person, tomboy, hoyden, a happy-go-lucky.

rab'bi, (-'s), rabbi; ~ naat', (..nate), rabbinate; ~ nis'me, rabbinism.

rabbyn', (-e), rabbi, Jewish divine.

rabbyns', (-e), rabbinical.

ra'bol = **raagbol.**

ra'dar, radar; radio-location; ~ operateur, radar operator.

rad'braak, (ge-), break upon the wheel, mutilate (a person, a language).

rad'draaier, (-s), ringleader.

radeer', (ge-), erase; etch; trace; ~ der, (-s), rubber, eraser; ~ kuns, etching; ~ mes, erasing knife; ~ naald, graver, burin, cradle; ~ wiel, tracing-wheel.

ra'deloos, (..lose), desperate, helpless; distracted; ~ heid, desperation, distraction, despair.

ra'derepubliek, soviet republic.

ra'derwerk, machinery.

radiaal', (s) (radiale), radian; (b) radial.

radia'sie, radiation.

radia'tor, (-e, -s), radiator.

radikaal', (..kale), radical, drastic, sweeping.

radikalis'me, radicalism.

radikalis'ties, (-e), radicalistic.

ra'dio, (-'s), radio, wireless (obs.); ~ aanwysing, radio-location; ~ afdeling, wireless department; ~ aktief', (..tiewe), radioactive; ~ aktiewe neerslag, radioactive fall-out; ~ aktiwiteit', radioactivity; ~ ateljee, radio studio; ~ berig, radio message; *geheimhouding van* ~ *berigte,* radio security; ~ besturing, radio control; ~ buis, radio valve; ~ diens, broadcasting (radio) service, ~ drama, radio drama, radio play; ~ fonie', radiophony; ~ fotografie', radiophotography; ~ frekwensie, radio frequency; ~ frekwensiestemming, radio-frequency interference; ~ gesprek, radio conversation; ~ graaf', (..grawe), radiograph; ~ grafie', radiography; ~ gra'fies, (-e), radiographic; ~ grafis', (-te), radiographer; ~ gram', radiogram; ~ hersteller, radio repairer; ~ isotoop, radio-isotope; ~ koerslyn, radio beam; ~ kommentator, (radio) commentator; ~ lamp, (radio) valve.

radiola'rieë, radiolaria.

ra'dio: ~ logie', radiology; ~ lo'gies, (-e), radiologic(al); ~ lokasie, radar; radio-location; ~ loog, (..loë), radiologist; ~ me'ter, (-s), radiometer; ~ musiek, radio music; ~ nasporing, radio-location; radar; ~ -omroep, radio station; ~ ontdekking, radio-location; ~ peiler, radio direction-finder; ~ peiling, radio bearing (sounding); ~ program, radio programme; ~ rede, broadcast (radio) speech; ~ rigtingsbaken, radio direction-beacon; ~ sender, radio transmitter; ~ sending, radio transmission; ~ sendstasie, transmitting (broadcasting) station; ~ skoop, (..skope), radioscope; ~ skrywer, radio script-writer; ~ stasie, radio station;

~stel, radio set; ~steurings, atmospherics; ~stilte, radio silence; ~tegniek, radio-technics; ~telefonie', radio telephony; ~telefonis', radio telephonist; ~telegrafie', radio telegraphy; ~telegrafis', radio telegraphist; ~telegram', radio telegram; ~teleskoop', radio-telescope; ~terapie', radiotherapy; ~'tjie, (-s), small radio set; ~toestel, radio (set); ~-uitsending, broadcast; ~vasvraprogram, radio quiz programme; ~vas'vrawedstryd, radio quiz; ~verbinding, radio communication; ~wa, radio tender; ~werktuigkundige, radio mechanic (technician).
ra'dium, radium; ~behandeling, radium treatment; ~terapie', radium therapy.
ra'dius, (-se), radius.
rad'ja, (-s), rajah.
ra'don, radon.
radys', (-e), radish.
rafel, (s) (-s), fray, ravel; (w) (ge-), ravel, fray out; ~draad, loose thread; ~kant, fag-end; ~rig, (-e), frayed; ~sy, ravelled silk; ~werk, drawn-work.
raf'fia, raffia; ~mat, raffia mat; ~vesel, raffia; ~werk, raffia work.
raffinadery', raffina'dery, (-e), (sugar-)refinery.
raffinadeur', (-s), (sugar-)refiner.
raffineer', (ge-), refine (sugar); 'n ge=de skurk, a crafty rogue; ~der, (-s), refiner; ~dery, (-e), (sugar-)refinery.
raffinement', (ong.), (over-)refinement; cunning; slyness.
rag'fyn, (-e), gossamer-like, cobwebby, flimsy.
ragi'ties, (-e), rachitic.
ragi'tis, rickets, rachitis.
rag'lan, raglan; ~mou, raglan sleeve; ~patroon, raglan-sleeve pattern.
ragout', (-s), ragout.
raisin-blanc', raisin-blanc.
rak, (-ke), rack, shelf; web; carrier (bomb); uit die boonste ~ke PRAAT, talk on learned topics; op die ~ SIT, be an old maid; ~bediende, stack attendant (in library).
ra'kel, (ge-), rake, poke.
ra'kelings = raaklings.
ra'kelyster, (baker's) raker.
ra'kend, (-e), touching, contiguous; affecting; ~e, (vs) concerning, regarding.
raket', (-te), racket (racquet); battledore; rocket; ~bal, shuttlecock; ~pers, racket-press; ~spel, battledore and shuttlecock; rackets.
ra'king, tangency; contact; ~shoek, angle of contact.
rak: ~kas, cupboard; ~ke, shelving.
rak'ker, (-s), little bounder, rascal, blighter; gipsy.
rak: ~klamp, clamp; ~lewe, shelf life; ~planke, shelving.
ram¹, (s) (-me), ram; die Ram, Aries.
ram², (s) rammer (siege-works); (w) (ge-), ram.
Ra'manspektroskopie, Raman spectroscopy.
ram'blok, (-ke), monkey.
ramenas', (-se), horse-radish, black (wild) radish.
ram'hok, rams' shed, rams' pen; mens' hostel.
ra'mie, ramie.
ra'ming, (-e, -s), estimate, assessment, calculation; ~som, estimated cost.
ram: ~kamp, rams' paddock; men's quarters; ~kat, stunner, topper, ripper, first-rater, out-and-outer.
ramkie', (-s, -ë), primitive guitar, ramkie; ~tjie, (-s), small ramkie.
rammei', (-e), battering-ram; beetle (tool).
ram'mel, (ge-), rattle, clatter, clank, jingle, peal, patter, chink; op 'n piano ~, drum on a piano; ~aar, rattler, jingler; ~ing, rattling, shaking; ~kas, rattletrap, crock, Tin Lizzie, ramshackle old vehicle; jalop(p)y; old piano.
ram'metjie, (-s), little ram; ~-uit'nek, (s) swaggerer; (bw) swaggering, arrogantly, boastfully.
ramp, (-e), disaster, calamity, catastrophe, blow; plague, affliction; tot oormaat van ~, to crown all, on top of it, to make matters worse.
ram'party, stag-party.
rampat'sjaan, (-s), tyre (rubber) sandal.
ramp'fonds, disaster fund.
rampok', (s) (-ke), gang; (w) (ge-), plunder.

rampok'ker, (-s), gangster; ~bende, criminal gang; ~y, gangsterism.
ram'pomp, ram.
rampsa'lig, (-e), wretched, miserable; forlorn; ~heid, wretchedness, miserableness, doom.
ramp'spoed, adversity, calamity; ~'ig, (-e), calamitous, disastrous, catastrophic, fatal.
rams: ~horing, ram's-horn; Aponogeton natalensis; ~kop, ram's head.
ram'wol, ram's wool, bucks.
Rand¹, (s) (-e), Rand; op die ~, on the Rand.
rand², (s) (-e), rand (monetary unit); BETAAL my in ~e, pay me in rands; dit KOS twee ~, the price is two rand.
rand³, (s) (-e), brim (hat); brink (of abyss); edge, curbing, edging, kerb, border; margin (paper); rim (spectacles); verge (disaster); ledge (in mine); lip (cup); balk, baulk (between furrows); chime (barrel); flange; selvedge (of cloth); fringe, fringing; welt (of shoe); aan die ~ van die GRAF, with one foot in the grave; on the verge of death; die ~ van die STAD, the outskirts of the city; (w) (ge-), border; ~akker, herbaceous border; ~-dollarwisselkoers, rand-dollar exhange rate; ~dorp, peri-urban area; ~eier, outer (outside) egg (in clutch); outsider; wallflower; 'n ~eier broei nooit 'n gesonde kuiken uit nie, a wild goose never laid a tame egg; ~gebergte, border mountains; ~gebied, border area; peripheral area; ~hoekyster, flange-angle; ~jie, (-s), small edge; ~kant, lace edging; ~koek, flan; ~koord, tracing-cord (cloth); ~moreen, lateral moraine; ~naat, welt, seam (of shoe).
rand'noot, rand note.
rand: ~omboorsel, mulling; ~plaat, edge-plate; ~skaaf, chamfer-plane; ~skrif, legend (of coin); circumscription; ~snyer, edging-tool; ~spanning, edge stress; ~staat, border state; ~stan'dig, (-e), marginal, peripheral; ~steek, outline stitch; ~steen, kerb, kerbstone; curb; ~stiksel, edgestitching; ~strook, beading; ~stuk, edging; ~versiering, border-flourish (ornament), cartouch(e).
rang, (-e), rank, class, grade; estate; position; rating; van die EERSTE ~, first-rate, of the first order; in ~ GELYKSTAAN, dieselfde ~ HÊ, hold the same rank, be equal in rank; ~ en STAND, rank and station.
rangeer', (ge-), shunt; ~der, (-s), shunter; ~lokomotief, shunting-engine; ~lokomotiefie, pug; ~lyn, shunting-line; ~masjien, shunting-engine; ~meester, yard-master; ~skyf, turntable; ~terrein, ~werf, shunting-yard; ~werk, shunting; ~wissel, shunting-switch.
range'ring, shunting.
rang: ~getal, ordinal number; ~lys, seniority list; army (navy) list; list of candidates; ~nommer, number on the list; ~orde, order (of preference, precedence).
rang'skik, (ge-), arrange, tabulate, classify, class, marshal, calendar, collocate, size, grade; range; rank; ~kend, (-e), ordinate; ~kende telwoord, ordinal; ~ker, (-s), classifier, marshaller; ~king, (-e, -s), arrangement, classification, collocation, composition, grouping, marshalling, ranking.
rang'streep, chevron, epaulette.
rang'telwoord, ordinal number.
rank¹, (s) (-e), tendril, runner; coil, clasper; twig, shoot, sprout; (w) (ge-), sprout, put forth shoots, trail, shoot tendrils, twine round.
rank², (b) (-e), frail, slender, slim; 'n ~e BOOTJIE, a cranky boat; 'n ~e RIET, a slender reed.
rank: ~boontjie, runner bean; ~doring, grappleplant; ~end, (-e), rambling; ~parasiet, twining parasite; ~plant, creeper, climber; ~roos, rambler (rose).
ranku'ne, rancour, spite.
ranon'kel, (-s), ranunculus, crow-foot; ~agtig, (-e), ranunculaceous.
ran'sel¹, (-s), holdall, rucksack, kitbag.
ran'sel², (s) thrashing, flogging; (w) (ge-), thrash, flog; fustigate; ~ing, (-e, -s), thrashing, flogging.
ran'sig, (-e), rancid; ~heid, rancidity.
rant, (-e), hill, ridge, reef.

rant'jie, (-s), small hill, ridge; ~*s se kant toe staan,* seek cover, take refuge, run away; ~**sveld,** broken country.
rantsoen', (-e), ration, allowance; ransom; *op* ~ *stel,* (place on) ration; ~**boek,** ration book; ~**eer', (ge-),** ration, give allowance; ~**e'ring,** rationing; ~**kaart(jie),** ration card.
rapal'lie, rabble, hooligans, mob.
rapat', (-ter, -ste), rapid, alert, agile, nimble; ~ *wees,* be alert (agile); ~**heid,** quickness, alertness, agility.
rapé', rappee.
rapier', (-e), rapier, foil.
rappel', (-s), recall (of a representative).
rapport', (-e), report, statement, account, dispatch; ~ *LEWER,* give account of; ~ *UITBRING oor,* issue a report on; ~**eer', (ge-),** report; cover (news story); ~**eer'baar,** notifiable; reportable; ~**eur',** (ong.), **(-s),** reporter; ~**ryer, (-s),** dispatch-rider.
raps, (s), (-e), stroke, flick, blow, lash, hit, flip, cut (with whip); *hy het 'n goeie* ~ *weg,* he has had a drop too much; **(w) (ge-),** strike, flip, cut, hit, flick; ~**ie, (-s),** a little, small quantity; slight blow; *'n* ~ *ie te GOU,* just a little too soon (quick); *net 'n* ~*ie GROTER,* slightly larger.
rapsodie', (-ë), rhapsody.
rapso'dies, (-e), rhapsodical.
rapsodis', (-te), rhapsodist.
raps'skoot, near shot.
rarefak'sie, rarefaction.
ra'righeid, (..hede), strangeness, strange thing, oddity.
rariteit', (-e), curiosity, rarity; (mv) curios, bric-a-brac.
ras¹, (s) (-se), race; breed; strain, stock; *GEKRUISTE* ~, crossbreed; *van SUIWER* ~, thoroughbred.
ras², (b, bw) (-se; -ser, -ste), swift(ly), quick; *met* ~ *se skrede,* swiftly.
ras'bewus, (-te), race-conscious; ~**theid,** race-consciousness.
ras'dier, pedigree animal.
raseer', (ge-), raze.
ras'eg, (-te), pure-bred, thoroughbred, true to type; ~**t'heid,** pure-bloodedness.
ras'eie, characteristic; ~**nskap,** racial characteristic.
ra'seil, square sail.
ra'send, (-e), furious, raving, fuming, delirious, frenzied, phrenetic, savage; like fury, in a fury; *'n* ~ *e HONGER,* a ravenous appetite; *dit MAAK hom* ~, it makes him furious.
ra'serig, (-e), noisy, rowdy, clamorous; scolding; ~**heid,** noisiness, clamorousness; shrewishness.
raserny', (-e), madness, rage, fury, frenzy; mania; *tot* ~ *bring,* drive mad.
ras'genoot, (..note), member of the same race; ~**skap,** breeders' society.
ras: ~groep, race group; ~**hoender,** pedigree fowl, pure-bred fowl; ~**hond,** pedigree dog, pure-bred dog.
raslonaal', (..nale), rational (maths).
rasionalis', (-te), rationalist; ~**a'sie,** rationalization; ~**eer', (ge-),** rationalize; ~**me,** rationalism; ~**ties, (-e),** rationalist(ic).
rasioneel', (..nele), rational.
ras'pe(r), (s) (-s), rasp, grater; rasper; **(w) (ge-),** rasp, grate.
ras'perd, thoroughbred (horse).
ras'per: ~ **kaas,** grated cheese, ~**tong,** radula; ~**vyl,** rasping file.
ras'se: ~aangeleenthede, racial affairs; ~**beleid,** racial policy; ~**betrekkinge,** race relations; ~**haat,** race hatred, racialism; ~**hater, (-s),** racialist; ~**leer,** racial theory; ~**stryd,** racial struggle; ~**verhoudings,** racial relations; ~**vermenging,** mixture of races; miscegenation; ~**vooroordeel,** racial prejudice; ~**vraagstuk,** racial problem; ~**waan,** racial mania.
ras: ~sis'me, racism; ~**suiwer,** pure-bred; ~**suiwerheid,** racial purity.
ras'ter, (-s), screen; raster; ~**werk,** lathing, latticework; paling.
ras: ~vee, pedigree cattle; ~**verbeteringsleer,** eugenics, euthenics; ~**vermenging,** mixture of races; miscegenation; ~**verskil,** racial difference; ~**verspreidingsleer,** anthropography; ~**vooroordeel,** racial prejudice.
rat, (-te), cog wheel, wheel; gear; *die* ~ *van die fortuin,* the wheel of fortune; *iem. 'n* ~ *voor die OË draai,* pull the wool over one's eyes; ~ *te WISSEL,* change gears.
rata'fia, ratafia.
ra'taplan, rataplan; *die hele* ~, the whole caboodle.
rat'arm, gear lever.
rat: ~boot, paddle-boat; ~**bus,** gearbox; ~**diertjie,** rotifer; ~**draaier,** ringleader.
ra'tel¹, (s) (-s), Cape badger, honey-badger.
ra'tel², (s) (-s), rattle; **(w) (ge-),** rattle; hurtle; peal; patter; clank; chatter; ~**aar,** flapper; clapper; ~**bek,** chatterbox; ~**boor,** single-cutting drill; ratch(et); ~**handvatsel,** ratchet handle; ~**kous,** chatterbox; rattle-box, bag-box; ~**moersleutel,** ratchet wrench; ~**omslag,** ratch(et) brace; ~**slag,** rattling peal; ~**slang,** rattler, rattlesnake.
rat: ~hefboom, gear lever; ~**hulsel,** gear-housing.
ratifika'sie, ratification.
ratifiseer', (ge-), ratify, confirm.
ra'tio, (-'s), ratio.
ra'tjie, (-s), little (cog) wheel.
ratjietoe', hotchpotch; medley; ratatouille.
rat: ~kas, gear-casing; paddle-box; gear-box; ~**lyn,** cycloid; ~**omhulsel,** gear case.
rats, (-er, -ste), nimble, swift, quick, agile, lissome, rapid, light of foot, dexterous; lucid, nimbleness, agility, fleetness.
rat: ~stoomboot, paddle-steamer; paddler; ~**tand,** cog; ~**werk,** machinery, gearing; clockwork; enginery; ~**wissel,** gearshift.
ratyn', ratteen, ratine.
ravelyn', (-e), ravelin.
ravot', (ge-), romp; ~**ter, (-s),** romper.
ravyn', (-e), ravine, gorge, gullet.
ra'we: ~bek, raven's bill; ~**gekras,** raven's croaking; ~**swart,** raven, pitch-black.
ray'on, rayon.
raz'zia, raid, razzia.
re, in the matter of, concerning.
reaal', (reale), real (coin).
reageer', (ge-), react; respond; ~**buis,** test-tube; ~**middel,** reagent; ~**papier,** litmus paper, test paper.
reagens', (..gentia), reagent, test agent.
reage'rend, (-e), reactive.
reak'sie, (-s), reaction.
reaksionêr', (-e), reactionary.
reak'tor, (-e, -s), reactor; ~**stelsel,** reactor system.
real'gar, realgar.
realis', (-te), realist; ~**a'sie,** realization; ~**eer', (ge-),** realize; convert into money; ~**eer'baar, (..bare),** realizable; convertible; ~**eer'baarheid,** realizability, convertibility; ~**e ring,** realization; ~**me,** realism; ~**ties, (-e),** realistic.
realiteit', (e), reality.
rebel', (-le), rebel; insurgent, insurrectionist; ~**leer', (ge-),** rebel; ~**lie, (-s),** rebellion; ~**s', (-e),** ~**s'gesind, (-e),** rebellious; *rebels wees,* feel rebellious; ~**s'heid,** rebelliousness.
re'bus, rebus, puzzle.
red, (ge-), save, rescue; salve, salvage; *LAAT hy homself* ~, let him fend for himself; *iem. uit die NOOD* ~, help someone out of distress; *die SEUN v.d. mens het gekom om te* ~ *wat verlore was,* the Son of Man came to save that which was lost; *SIELE* ~, save souls; *ek sal my WEL hou*, I'll be able to manage.
redak'sie, (-s), editorial staff; wording; redaction; *onder* ~ *van,* edited by; ~**buro,** editorial office; ~**kamer,** editor's room; ~**kommissie,** editorial committee; ~**koste,** editorial expenses; ~**werk,** editing; journalistic work; ~**wysiging,** change in the wording.
redaksioneel', (..nele), editorial.
redakteur', (-s), editor; ~**skap,** editorship.
redak'tor, (-e, -s), redactor, reviser.
redaktri'se, (-s), lady editor, editress.
red'deloos, (..lose), past recovery, irretrievable, irrecoverable; ~**verlore,** past redemption.

red'der, (-s), rescuer, deliverer, saver, saviour, re= coverer.
red'ding, (-e, -s), rescue, salvation; salvage; preservation.
.red'dings: ~**baadjie,** life-jacket, cork jacket; ~**boei,** life-buoy; ~**boot,** lifeboat; ~**geselskap,** rescue par= ty; ~**gordel,** lifebelt; ~**huis,** Magdalene's Home; rescue home; ~**medalje,** medal for saving (human) life; ~**maatskappy,** life-saving society; ~**middel,** means of rescue; ~**toestel,** life-saving apparatus; fire-escape; ~**tou,** lifeline; ~**vlot,** life-raft; ~**vlug,** mercy flight; ~**werk,** salvage (rescue) work.
rede¹, (-s), roadstead, roads (for ships).
re'de², (-s), sense; reason, cause; account; speech, ad= dress, oration; *daar BESTAAN alle* ~ *om te dink dat,* there is every reason to believe that; ~ *van BESTAAN,* reason for existence; *iem. tot* ~ *BRING,* bring someone to his senses; *DIREKTE* ~, direct speech; *GEGRONDE* ~ *hê om,* have sound cause to; ~ *HÊ om,* have reason to; *'n* ~ *HOU,* make a speech; *INDIREKTE* ~, indirect speech; *na* ~ *LUISTER,* listen to reason; *OM een of ander* ~, for some reason or other; *sonder OP= GAAF van* ~ *s,* without stating any reasons; *SKULDIG op* ~, guilty under provocation; *SONDER enige* ~, without any reason; *iem in die* ~ *VAL,* chip in; ~ *VERSTAAN,* be open to reason; ~**deel,** part of speech; ~**gewend, (-e),** causal.
re'dekawel, (ge-), argue, reason, chop logic; ~**ing, (-e, -s),** argument, reasoning.
redekun'dig, (-e), rhetorical; logical.
re'dekuns, rhetoric; ~**tenaar,** rhetorician; ~**tig, (-e),** rhetorical.
re'delik, (-e), tolerable, fair, rational, reasonable; middling, moderately good; equitable, con= scionable; ~**erwys(e),** reasonably, in justice; ~**heid,** reasonableness, reason, rationality.
re'deloos, (..lose), devoid of reason, irrational; reasonless; *'n redelose dier,* an unreasoning (brute) beast; ~**heid,** irrationality.
re'denaar, (-s, ..nare), orator; ~**sgawe,** oratorical talent; ~**skuns,** oratory; public speaking; ~**sta= lent,** oratorical talent.
redena'sie, reasoning.
redeneer', (ge-), reason, argue; ~**der, (-s),** reasoner; ~**kunde,** logic; ~**kun'dig, (-e),** logical; ~**kuns,** logic, art of reasoning; eristic; ~**siek,** disputatious, disputative; ~**trant,** manner of reasoning; ~**ver= moë,** power of reasoning.
redene'ring, (-e, -s), reasoning, argument, argumen= tation; discourse.
re'der, (-s), shipowner; ~**y', (-e),** freighting, equip= ment (of ship); shipping line.
re'deryker, (hist.), **(-s),** member of a guild of rhetoric, rhetorician; ~**skamer,** society of rhetoricians; ~**s= kuns,** rhetoric.
re'desiftery, hair-splitting.
re'detwis, (s) dispute, disputation; debate; (w) **(ge-),** dispute, wrangle, argue; pettifog; ~**ter, (-s),** dis= puter, controversialist, disputant.
re'devoerder, (-s), orator, public speaker.
re'devoering, (-e, -s), discourse, address, speech, dec= lamation, oration; descant; allocution; *'n* ~ *hou,* deliver an address.
re'dewisseling, conversation.
redigeer', (ge-), edit (newspaper); redact; conduct (magazine); compose, draw up (document).
redingo'te, (-s), redingote, edge-to-edge coat.
re'distribusie, redistribution.
red'middel, remedy, contrivance, means of rescue; makeshift, expedient.
redoebleer', (ge-), redouble (bridge).
redres', **redress; ~seer', (ge-),** redress, rectify.
reduk'sie, (-s), reduction; ~**deling,** meiosis; ~**inrig= ting,** reduction-works; ~**middel,** reducing agent; ~**passer,** reducing compass; ~**prys,** reduced price; ~**tafel,** plotting scale; ~**trap,** reduced grade; ~**vo= kaal,** reduced vowel.
reduplika'sie, (-s), reduplication; ~**woord,** reiterative (word).
redupliseer', (ge-), reduplicate.

reduseer', (ge-), reduce; ~**baar, (..bare),** reducible; ~**der, (-s),** reducer; ~**vlam,** reducing flame.
ree, (reë), roe, hind; doe; ~**bok,** reebuck, roe (deer); ~**bruin,** fawn.
reeds, already; ~ *jare GELEDE,* many years ago; *ek doen dit* ~ *OM . . .,* I am doing this on purpose to . . .
reëel, (reële; reëler, -ste), real, genuine; *reële KEN= NIS,* practical knowledge; *in reële TERME,* in real terms; *reële bruto binnelandse PRODUK,* real gross domestic product.
reef, (s) (rewe), reef, hand (sail); (w) **(ge-),** reef (sail).
ree'kalf, fawn.
reeks, (-e), progression (arithmetical); chain, cycle, course, series, row, sequence; range; procession; *'n* ~ *BERGE,* a chain of mountains; *'n* ~ *GEBEUR= TENISSE,* a train of events; *'n* ~ *VOOR= BEELDE,* a series of examples; ~**letter,** serial let= ter; ~**nommer,** serial number; ~**skakeling,** series connection.
re'ël, (s) (-s), rule; line; custom; order; *die* ~ *van DRIE,* the rule of three; *daar is GEEN* ~ *in die huishouding nie,* there is no order in the housekeep= ing; *'n GULDE* ~, a golden rule; *jou aan die* ~ *s HOU,* observe the rules; *IN die* ~, as a rule; *teen alle* ~ *s IN,* contrary to all rules; *tussen die* ~ *s LEES,* read between the lines; *'n* ~ *OORSLAAN,* skip a line; *dis TEEN die* ~ *s,* it is against the rules; *'n UITSONDERING op die* ~, an exception to the rule; (w) **(ge-),** regulate, arrange, organize, adjust, dispose; set (grenade); fashion; settle; *DIT kan ge* ~ *word,* it can be arranged; *die VERKEER* ~, regu= late the traffic; ~**aar,** adjuster, regulator, governor; ~**baar, (..bare),** capable of regulation, adjustable.
re'ëling, (-e, -s), regulation, adjustment, disposal, get= up, organization, arrangement; setting (grenade); timing (of fuse); constitution; *'n* ~ *tref,* make an arrangement; lay down a plan; come to an agree= ment; ~**sdompelaar,** control-plunger; ~**skomitee,** ~**skommissie,** organizing committee.
re'ël: ~**lengte,** length of line; ~**loos, (..lose),** without rule, irregular, disorderly; ~**loosheid,** irregularity; ~**maat,** regularity, order.
reëlma'tig, (-e), regular; ~**heid,** regularity.
re'ëlreg, (b) (-te), perfectly straight; downright; (bw) straight away; diametrically; ~ *op jou DOEL af= stuur,* make straight for one's goal; ~ *in STRYD met,* in direct conflict with.
re'ën, (s) (-s), rain; *na* ~ *kom SONSKYN,* sunshine after rain; *net voor die* ~ *TUISKOM,* arrive in the nick of time; (w) **(ge-),** rain; *as dit op die een* ~, *DRUP dit op die ander,* fortune to one is mother, to another stepmother; *v.d.* ~ *in die DRUP kom,* from the frying-pan into the fire; *dit GAAN* ~, it's going to rain; well I never! look who is here; *dit* ~ *KLAGTES,* complaints are pouring in; ~**agtig, (-e),** rainy; pluvial; ~**arm,** arid; ~**bak,** cistern, tank; ~**besweerder,** rainmaker.
re'ënboog, rainbow; iris; ~**kleurig, (-e),** iridescent; ~**vlies,** iris (of the eye); ~**vliesontsteking,** iritis; ~**voël,** hornbill, toucan.
re'ën: ~**bui,** shower (of rain); downfall; rainstorm; ~**dag,** rainy day; ~**dig, (-te),** rainproof, raintight; watertight; ~**druppel,** raindrop; ~**erig, (-e),** rainy; ~**erigheid,** raininess; ~**gordel,** rainbelt; ~**jas,** mackintosh, raincoat; ~**kaart,** rain-chart; ~**loos, (..lose),** rainless; ~**loosheid,** rainlessness; ~**lug,** rainy sky; ~**maand,** rainy month; ~**maker,** rain= maker; ~**mantel,** rain-cloak; ~**meter,** rain-gauge; pluviometer, ombrometer; ~**meting,** rainfall re= cording; ~**mis,** rain-fog; ~**padda,** rain-frog; ~**sei= soen,** rainy season; ~**skade,** rain-damage; ~**skerm,** umbrella; ~**skoen,** wellington; ~**storm,** rain-storm, thunderstorm.
reent, (s) (reëns), rain; (w) **(ge-),** rain.
re'ën: ~**tjie, (-s),** small shower; ~**tyd,** rainy season; ~**val,** rainfall; ~**vas, (-te),** all-weather; ~**veër,** windscreen-wiper; ~**vlaag,** shower, gust (of rain); ~**vloed,** torrent (of rain); ~**voël,** rain-bird; ~**waarnemings,** rainfall observations; ~**water,** rain-water; ~**waterpyp,** downpipe; ~**weer,** wet

reep 433 **regisseer**

weather; ~**wind,** rain-wind; ~**wolk,** nimbus; thunder cloud, rain-cloud; ~**woud,** rain forest; ~**wurm,** earthworm, ground-worm.
reep, (repe), string, strip; stoppered rope; slab (of chocolate); *aan repe SNY,* cut to shreds; *'n* ~ *SPEK,* a rasher of bacon; ~**koekie,** bar cookie; ~**snyer,** shredder.
reet, (rete), crevice, cleft, split, fissure.
refak'sie, (-s), allowance for damaged goods; tret.
referaat', (..rate), report, lecture, paper.
refereer', (ge-), refer.
referenda'ris, (-se), referendary.
referen'dum, (-s), referendum; ~**uitslag,** referendum result.
referen'sie, (-s), reference.
referent', (-e), reporter, informer; lecturer, speaker.
refer'te, (vero., form.), reference; *met* ~ *tot,* with reference to.
refleks', (-e), reflex; ~**beweging,** reflex action; ~**boog,** reflex arc.
reflek'sie, (-s), reflection; ~**f', (..siewe),** reflective; reflexive.
refleks'verligting, indirect lighting.
reflekteer', (ge-), reflect.
reflek'tor, (-s), reflector.
reflektoskoop', (..skope), reflectoscope.
reforma'sie, (-s), reformation; *die R*~, the Reformation.
reforma'tor, (-e, -s), reformer; (~), **mato'ries, (-e),** reforming, reformatory.
roformccr', (gt-), reform.
refrak'sie, refraction; ~**vermoë,** refringence.
refraktêr', (-e), refractory.
refraktief', (..tiewe), refractive.
refrak'tor, (-s), refractor.
refrein', (-e), chorus, refrain; burden (of song).
ref'ter, (-s), refectory; ~**meester,** refectioner.
refrak'tometer, refractometer.
reg¹, (s) (-te), right, title, claim; law, justice; duty, due; ~ *van APPEL,* right of appeal; ~ *van BESTAAN,* right to existence; *BINNE sy* ~ *wees,* be within his rights; *die BURGERLIKE* ~, civil law; ~ *DOEN aan,* do justice to; *die* ~ *van EERSGEBOORTE,* the right of primogeniture; *EIE* ~ *gebruik,* take the law into one's own hands; *sy* ~ *laat GELD,* assert one's rights; *die* ~ *van GRASIE,* the prerogative of pardon; ~ *HE op,* have a right to; *IN* ~ *te geldig,* valid in law; *KERKLIKE* ~, canon law; *tot sy* ~ *KOM,* show to better advantage; *die* ~ *moet sy LOOP neem,* the law must run its course; *MET* ~, justly, rightly, *NA* ~ *te,* by right; really; *die ON= GESKREWE* ~, the unwritten law; *dit is ONS* ~, we have this right; *die* ~ *van OPVOERING,* the stage right; ~ *te en PLIGTE,* rights and duties; *RO= MEINS-HOLLANDSE* ~, Roman-Dutch law; *op sy* ~ *STAAN,* stand on his rights; ~ *v.d. STERKSTE,* right of the strongest; club-law; *in die* ~ *te STUDEER,* study law; *homself* ~ *VERSKAF,* be one's own pledge; ~ *van VETO,* veto power, right of veto; *met die VOLSTE* ~, with perfect justice; ~ *van VOORKEUR geniet,* enjoy priority; ~ *van VRUGGEBRUIK,* usufruct; *ons* ~ *te en VRY= HEDE,* our rights and privileges; *iedereen* ~ *laat WEDERVAAR,* do justice to everyone.
reg², (b, bw), right, correct, proper; ready, straight, true; all right; ~ *AAN,* straight on; ~ *AGTER,* right at the back (behind); ~ *BO,* right at the top; ~ *DEUR,* straight through; *'n* ~ *te DOMKOP,* a real blockhead; ~ *GENOEG!* quite so! true! granted! ~ *HANDEL,* deal justly; *hy is nie HEELTE= MAL* ~ *nie,* he is not all there; he is not quite right; ~ *te HOEK,* right angel; ~ *HOU,* keep in position; keep in order; *IS hy* ~? does he belong to our political party? *in* ~ *te LYN,* as the crow flies; *die* ~ *te MAN op die* ~ *te plek,* the right man in the right place; *die* ~ *te REDE,* the true reason; ~ *SLAAN,* hit into shape; ~ *STAAN vir,* be ready for; ~ *STEL,* adjust; *TER* ~ *ter tyd,* in due time; ~ *van VOOR,* head-on; ~ *VOOR,* right in front; facing; ~ *VORENTOE,* straight on; *nie* ~ *WEET nie,* not quite know; ~**aan,** straight on (forward); ~**af,** straight down; **agter,** long-stop (cricket).

rega'lia, regalia.
regat'ta, (-s), regatta.
reg'bank, court of justice; tribunal, judicature; areopagus; bench; *buite die* ~ *om reël,* settle out of court.
reg: ~**bo,** right at the top; ~**bokant,** right on top, right above; ~**by,** square leg (cricket); ~**deur,** straight through; ~**draads, (-e),** with the grain.
regeer', (ge-), rule, govern, reign; handle, manage, control; rage (disease); *die KINDERS het vreeslik ge* ~, the children kicked up an awful shindy; *die regerende PARTY,* the party in power; ~**baar, (..bare),** governable, manageable; manoeuvrable; ~**der, (-s),** ruler; ~**kuns,** kingcraft; art of governing, statecraft; ~**mag,** power of government.
regenera'sie, regeneration.
regenereer', (ge-), regenerate.
regent', (-e), regent; ~**es', (-se),** (lady) regent; ~**skap,** regency, guardianship; ~**skapraad,** council of regency.
rege'ring, (-e, -s), government; reign, rule; *die* ~ *AANVAAR,* take up the reins of government; *op die* ~ *se koste LOSEER,* be behind bars; *die* ~ *OMVERGOOI,* overthrow the government; *ON= DER die* ~ *van,* during the reign of.
rege'ringloos, (..lose), anarchic(al); without a government; ~**heid,** anarchy.
rege'ringsaak, government affair (matter).
rege'rings: ~**almanak,** government chronicle and directory; ~**amn.** government post; ~**amptonaar,** government official; ~**banke,** government benches; ~**beleid,** policy of the government; ~**besluit,** resolution of the cabinet; ~**blad,** government newspaper; ~**brood,** standard bread; ~**gebou,** government building; ~**hoof,** head of government; ~**inmenging,** state intervention; ~**kant,** government's side; ~**koste:** *op* ~ *koste loseer,* to be detained at the state's pleasure; ~**kringe,** government circles; ~**maatreël,** government measure; ~**man, (-ne),** government supporter; ~**masjien,** governmental machine; ~**party,** government party; ~**persoon,** government official; ~**pos,** post under the government; ~**reglement,** constitution ordinance.
rege'ring: ~**statistiek,** government statistics; ~**stelsel,** system of government.
rege'rings: ~**troepe,** government troops; ~**tussenkoms,** government intervention; ~**vorm,** polity, form (frame) of government; ~**weë:** *van* ~ *weë,* officially.
reg'geaard, (-e), good-natured; right minded; ~**heid,** good-naturedness; right-mindedness.
reg'gesind, (-e), right-minded.
reg'hebbende, (-s), rightful claimant (owner), person (party) entitled.
reg'help, (-ge-), correct, rectify, show someone the correct method, disabuse, put a person wise.
reg'hoek, rectangle; orthogon; ~**'ig, (-e),** rectangular; right-angled; orthogonal; ~**ige driehoek,** rectangular triangle; ~**ig op,** at right angles to; ~**sy,** rectangle side.
reg'hou, (-ge-), keep in order, keep right; poise; ~**!** on guard!
regie', producing; stage management; state monopoly; *spel onder* ~ *van,* play produced by.
regi'me, (-s), régime.
re'gimen, regimen; economy.
regiment', (-e), regiment.
regiments': ~**bevelvoerder,** regimental commander; ~**front,** regimental front; ~**hoofkwartier,** regimental headquarters; ~**kleremaker,** regimental tailor; ~**kok,** regimental cook; ~**kolonne,** regimental column; ~**menasie,** regimental mess; ~**orders,** regimental orders; ~**poste,** regimental duties; ~**vaandel,** regimental colours; ~**vak,** regimental sector; ~**wagte,** regimental duties; ~**wapen,** regimental crest.
re'gio, (-ne), region; ~**naal', (..nale),** regional; *..nale dialek,* regional dialect; ~**nalis', (-te),** regionalist; ~**nalis'me,** regionalism; ~**nalis'ties, (-e),** regionalistic.
regisseer', (ge-), produce (a play).

regisseur', (-s), producer.
regisseu'se, (-s), female producer.
regis'ter, (-s), register, record, index; stop (organ); *'n ~ AANLÊ*, open a register; *'n ~ BYHOU*, keep a register of; *~ ton*, register ton; registered tonnage.
registra'sie, registration; recording; *~ akte*, certificate of incorporation; *~ bewys*, registration certificate; *~ kantoor*, registry; registrar's office; *~ koste*, registration fees.
registrateur', (-s), registrar; *~s'kantoor*, registrar's office.
registreer', (ge-), register, record; *~ toestel*, recording instrument, recorder.
reg'kant, (ge-), list (wood); *~ ing*, listing.
reg'kom, (-ge-), come right; manage; find one's feet; recover; become converted (adjusted, settled); turn out all right; *ALLES sal ~ (sê Jan Brand)*, all will be well; *EK kom mooi ~*, I am managing quite well; *die saak sal LATER ~*, the matter will adjust itself later; *hy sal NOG ~*, he will still come round to our way of thinking.
reg'kry, (-ge-), manage, contrive, compass.
reglement', (-e), rules, regulations; by-laws *~ van orde*, standing orders; *~ eer'*, (ge-), regulate, provide rules for; regiment; *~ êr'*, (-e), prescribed, regular; *~ e'ring*, regimentation.
reglet', (-te), reglet.
regly'nig, (-e), rectilinear, rectilineal; *~ e lens*, rectilinear lens.
reg'maak, (-ge-), correct, put right, fix up; defray, settle; redress, repair; mend; doctor; true up (tools); castrate (animal).
reg'makertjie, (-s), pick-me-up, tot, nip.
regma'tig, (-e), rightful, lawful, fair; *~ heid*, rightfulness, lawfulness.
reg: *~ ONDER*, right at the bottom; *~ ONDERKANT*, right underneath.
reg'merkie, (-s), tick; correction mark.
reg'oor, right opposite, facing.
reg'op, erect, vertical, perpendicular, upright, on edge, endwise, endways, on end, straight (up); plumb; horrent; *~ paal*, upright post; *~ groeiend*, (-e), (growing) erect; *~ staande*, erect, upright; orthotropic, orthotropous; *~ standigheid*, erectness; orthotropy, orthotropism.
reg'-reg', truly, quite so, really; terribly.
regres', recourse; *~ reg*, right of recourse, *~ sie*, regression (return to former psychic state); *~ sief'*, (..siewe), regressive.
reg'ruk, (-ge-), put in order, pull right (straight); spruce oneself up; dress quickly; *jy moet jou ~*, you must pull yourself together; *~ ker*, pick-me-up.
regs, (b) (-e), right-handed; dextrous; right; (bw) to the right; *~ AF*, (away, down) to the right; *~ en AWEREGS*, plain and purl; *~ en LINKS*, right and left; *~ OM*, to the right! right about! *~ SWENK*, right wheel!
reg: *~ saak*, lawsuit, case; *~ saal*, court-room.
regs: *~ advies*, legal advice; *~ adviseur*, law-adviser, legal adviser; *~ bedeling*, administration of law; *~ beginsel*, legal principle; *~ begrip*, notion of justice; legal notion; *~ belang*, legal interest; *~ bepaling*, legal provision; *~ beroep*, legal profession; *~ bevoeg*, (-de), (legally) competent; *~ bevoegdheid*, (legal) competence; jurisdiction; *~ bewussyn*, sense of justice; *~ bron*, source of law; *~ bystand*, legal aid; *~ dienaar*, law-officer; *~ draad*, straight thread.
regs'draaiend, (-e), dextrorotatory.
regs: *~ dwaling*, mistake of law; miscarriage of justice; *~ dwang*, legal compulsion; *~ filosofie*, philosophy of law; *~ formaliteit*, legal formality; *~ gebied*, jurisdiction; *~ gebruik*, legal practice; *~ geding*, lawsuit, legal proceedings, litigation process.
regsgel'dig, (-e), valid in law, legal; *~ heid*, validity, legality, force of law.
regs'geleerd, (-e), learned in the law, legal; jurisprudent; juristic; *~ e*, (-s), jurist, lawyer; legist; jurisprudent; jurisconsult; *~ heid*, jurisprudence, law.
regs: *~ gelykheid*, equality before the law; *~ geneeskunde*, forensic medicine; medical jurisprudence; *~ geneeskundig*, (-e), forensic; medicolegal.

regs'gesind, (-e), conservative, rightist; *~ e*, (-s), conservative, rightist; *~ heid*, conservatism.
regs: *~ geskiedenis*, history of law; *~ geskil*, legal dispute; *~ gevoel*, sense of justice; *~ gevolge*, legal consequences; *~ grond*, legal ground; *~ handeling*, juristic act.
regs: *~ han'dig*, (-e), right-handed; *~ han'digheid*, right-handedness; *~ heid*, dexterity; right-handedness.
regs'hulp, legal aid.
reg'sien, (-ge-), put right, arrange properly; put someone in his place, cure someone of a bad habit.
regsin'nig, (-e), orthodox; *~ heid*, orthodoxy.
reg'sit, (-ge-), correct; place in correct position, adjust.
regska'pe, honest, righteous; *~ nheid*, honesty, probity, integrity, rectitude.
regs'koste, cost of suit, legal expenses.
regs'krag, legal force; *~ 'tig*, (-e), enforceable (by law).
regskun'dig, (-e), legal; *~ e advies*, legal advice.
regs'kwessie, legal question.
reg'slaan, (-ge-), hit into position.
regs: *~ leer*, jurisprudence; *~ mag*, legal authority, jurisdiction; *~ middel*, legal remedy; *~ misbruik*, abuse of justice.
reg'sny, (-ge-), cut right, trim.
regsoewereiniteit', rule of law.
regs'offisier, legal officer (army).
regs'omkeer, rightabout turn; volte-face; *~ maak*, do a rightabout turn.
regs: *~ onbevoegdheid*, legal disability; *~ ongeldig*, legally invalid; void in law; *~ onsekerheid*, insecurity of justice; *~ opvatting*, legal opinion; *~ opvolger*, successor in title; *~ orde*, rule of law.
regs'persoon, artificial (juristic) person, body corporate, incorporated society; legal entity; *~ likheid*, incorporation, body corporate; legal individuality; *~ likheid verkry*, be incorporated.
regs: *~ pleging*, administration of justice, judicature; *~ plig*, legal duty; *~ posisie*, legal position.
reg'spraak, judicature; judgment, administration of justice; verdict.
regs: *~ praktisyn*, lawyer, legal practitioner; *~ praktyk*, legal practice.
reg: *~ spreek*, (-ge-), administer justice; give a verdict; *~ spreker*, justiciary; *~ spreuk*, (legal) adage, maxim.
regs: *~ prosedure*, legal procedure; *~ proses*, legal process; *~ punt*, legal point, point of law; *~ reël*, rule of law; *~ taal*, legal terms, legal terminology.
regstan'dig, (-e), vertical, perpendicular.
reg'stel, (-ge-), adjust, put right, rectify; correct (impression); *~ ling*, correction, rectification.
reg'stelsel, legal system.
regs: *~ term*, legal term; *~ titel*, legal title; *~ toestand*, legal position.
reg'streeks, (b) (-e), direct; straight; (bw) directly; *~ e BEWYS*, direct evidence; *~ e VERHOUDING*, direct proportion.
reg'student, law-student.
regs: *~ vaktaal*, legal terminology; legal language; *~ verband*, legal connection; *~ verdraaier*, pettifogger; *~ verdraaiing*, chicane, chicanery, pettifoggery; *~ verhouding*, legal relationship; *~ verkragter*, (-s), violater of the law; *~ verkragting*, violation of the law (justice); *~ vermoede*, legal presumption; presumption of law; *~ verordeninge*, judicial regulations; *~ verpligtings*, legal duties; *~ versuim*, legal oversight; failure to appear in court; *~ verteenwoordiger*, legal representative; *~ vervolging*, legal prosecution; *~ voorganger*, predecessor in title; *~ vordering*, legal action, legal claim; *~ vorm*, form of judicature; *~ vraag*, question of law.
regs'weë: *van ~*, by law, according to law.
regs: *~ wese*, judicature, justice; *~ wetenskap*, jurisprudence; *~ wetenskaplike*, jurist.
reg'te[1], (s) rights; law; duties (on imports); *student in die ~*, law-student.
reg'te[2], (bw) really; *~ bly wees*, be really glad, very glad indeed.

reg'telik, (-e), legal; ~*e beskerming*, legal protection.
reg'teloos, (..lose), without rights; lawless; ~**heid**, rightlessness; lawlessness.
reg'tens, in (at, by) law; *hy kan dit* ~ *DOEN*, he is lawfully entitled to do so; ~ *ONGEGROND*, bad in law.
reg'ter¹, (s) (-s), judge, justice; *AS* ~ *optree oor*, sit in judgment on; *hom as* ~ *OPWERP*, constitute oneself a judge; ~ *in jou eie SAAK wees*, judge one's own cause.
reg'ter², (-s), (s) right, righthander (boxing); (b) right; ~**agterpoot**, right hind leg; ~**arm**, right arm, sword-arm; ~**been**, right leg; ~**bors**, right breast; ~**haak'hou**, right hook; ~**hak**, right heel; ~**hand**, right hand; factotum; whip hand; *iem. se* ~*hand*, someone's right hand; ~**hou**, right (boxing); ~**kant**, (-se, -ste), right side; off-side (vehicle).
reg'terlik, (-e), judicial; ~*e dwaling*, miscarriage of justice.
reg'teroewer, right bank.
reg'ter-president, (-s-president), judge president.
reg'terskakel, right half-back (soccer).
reg'ter: ~**skap**, judgeship; ~**stoel**, judgment seat; tribunal.
regter: ~**stuur**, right-hand drive; ~**sy**, right side; ~**vleuel**, right wing; ~**voet**, right foot; ~**voorpoot**, right (off-) front leg; ~**voorwiel**, right (off-) front wheel.
reg'tig, (b) (-e), real, true; (bw) really, truly; indeed, upon my conscience! faith! actually; ~ *BLY wees, be really glad, very glad indeed*; *WAAR*, truly, honestly!
reg'trek, (-ge-), straighten; pull straight (tie).
reg'uit, (b) straight, honest, candid, blunt, frank, point-blank; forthright, fair and square; point-to-point (race); straight, outspokenly, openly, candidly; ~ *BUIG*, force out straight; straighten by bending; ~ *MAAK*, straighten; ~ *PRAAT*, not mince matters, be outspoken.
regularisa'sie, regularization.
regulariseer', (ge-), regularize.
regula'sie, (-s), regulation.
regulateur', (-s), governor; throttle (of engine).
regulatief', (..tiewe), regulative.
regula'tor, (-e, -s), regulator.
reguleer', (ge-), regulate, modulate, adjust; time; ~**baar**, (..**bare**), adjustable; ~**der**, (-s), adjuster; ~**klep**, regulating valve; ~**rat**, timing-gear; ~**toestel**, timing-gear; ~**wiel**, balance wheel.
regulêr', (-e), regular.
regule'rend, (-e), regulating, regulative.
regule'ring, adjustment, regulation, timing.
re'gulus, regulus.
regver'dig, (w) (ge-), justify; (b) (-e), just, righteous, fair; conscionable; equal; ~**e, (-s)**, righteous one; ~**end, (-e)**, justificative, justificatory; ~**heid**, righteousness, justice, fairness; ~**ing**, justification; ~**making**, justification; sanctification.
reg'verkrygende, (s), assignee (in law), cessionary.
reg'verkryger, assign, cessionary.
rehabilita'sie, rehabilitation; discharge; ~**bevel**, rehabilitation order.
rehabiliteer', (ge-), rehabilitate; discharge.
rei¹, (-e), straight-edge (carpentry).
rei², (hist.), (-e), chorus, choir song; ~**dans**, choric dance.
rei'er, (-s), heron; egret; ~**nek**, heron-neck, long neck; ~**nes**, heron's nest.
rei'hout, straight-edge (mason's tool).
reik, (ge-), reach extend to stretch; pass; hand; *iem die hand* ~ , lend someone a helping hand, shake hands with someone.
reik'hals, (ge-), yearn for, long for; ~**end**, (bw) yearningly, longingly; ~**ing**, yearning, longing.
rein, (-e; -er, -ste), pure, clean, chaste; *die* ~ *ste DWAASHEID*, the sheerest folly; *alles vir die* ~ *e WAARHEID vertel*, tell everything as gospel truth; *in die* ~ *e BRING*, clear up, put right, thrash out; *in die* ~ *e KOM*, come right.
rei'ne, (-s), pure one; what is pure; *vir die* ~ *is ALLES rein*, to the pure all things are pure; *SALIG is die* ~*s van hart*, blessed are the pure in heart.

rein'heid, purity, pureness, chastity, chasteness.
rei'nig, (ge-), purify, cleanse; edulcorate; lustrate; purge; chasten; clarify; ~**end, (-e)**, purifying, abstergent, purgative; abstersive; detergent; ~**er, (-s)**, purifier; purger; cleaner, cleanser; ~**ing**, purification, purge, cleaning, cleansing; ablution; abstersion; lustration; catharsis (in drama); *chemiese* ~*ing*, dry-cleaning; ~**ingsdiens**, sewerage; street-cleaning; sanitary service; ~**ingsmiddel**, cleanser, purifier; detergent; ~**ingsroom**, cleaning-cream; ~**ingsweg**, purgative way; purgation.
reïnkarna'sie, reincarnation.
reïnkarneer', (ge-), reincarnate.
rein'kultuur, pure culture.
reis, (s) (-e), journey, trip, voyage, peregrination, tour; reis (coin); *ENKELE* ~ , single journey; *op* ~ *GAAN*, go on a journey; *GOEIE* ~! pleasant journey! *die* ~ *HEEN en terug*, the journey there and back; '*n* ~ *MAAK*, make a journey; *NIE vir die* ~ *nie*, not wanted during the voyage; '*n* ~ *ONDERBREEK*, break a journey; *ONDERBROKE* ~ , broken journey; *OP* ~ , on a journey; travelling; *die* ~ *UIT en tuis*, the outward and homeward journey; '*n* ~ *om die WÊRELD*, a trip round the world; (w) (ge-), travel, journey, tour; ~**agent**, travel agent; ~**agentskap**, tourist agency.
rei'sang, chorus.
reis: ~**artikel**, article required on a journey; ~**avontuur**, adventure on a journey; ~**benodigdhede**, travelling-requisites; ~**beskrywing**, account of a journey; book of travel, itinerary, ~**beurs**, travelling-scholarship; ~**biblioteek**, travelling-library; ~**boek**, route-book; book of travel; ~**buro**, tourist agency; ~**deken**, (travelling-)rug; ~**duur**, duration of a journey (voyage); ~**end, (-e)**, travelling; itinerant; mobile (workshop); ~**-en-verblyfkoste**, hotel and travelling expenses; ~**geld**, travel(ling) expenses, fare; passage(-money); ~**geleentheid**, means of travelling; lift; ~**geleide**, travel-escort; ~**genoot**, (..**note**), ~**gesel, (-le)**, fellow-traveller; ~**geselskap**, travelling-party; tourist party; ~**gids**, traveller's guide; timetable, itinerary; ~**herinneringe**, travel reminiscences; ~**ie, (-s)**, short trip (journey).
rei'sies, races; race-meeting; ~ **jaag**, race; ~**baan**, racecourse; speedway; race-track; ~**jaagster**, jockette; ~**jaery**, racing; ~**perd**, racehorse, racer.
rei'siger, (-s), traveller, tourist; passenger; ~**stjek**, traveller's cheque.
reis: ~**indrukke**, impressions of travel; ~**joernaal**, travel diary, logbook.
rei'skaaf, trying-plane, jack-plane.
reis: ~**kaartjie**, (travel-)ticket; ~**koffer**, travelling-trunk, box; ~**kombers**, travelling-rug; ~**konsessie**, travelling-concession; ~**koste**, travelling-expenses; ~**kostuum**, travelling-costume; going-away dress; ~**lektuur**, travel-reading; ~**lus**, love of travel(ling); ~**makker**, fellow-traveller; ~**moeder**, chaperon (on a journey); lady in charge of a travelling party; ~**ouers**, pair of travelling chaperons; ~**pas**, passport; ~**plan**, plan of tour; intention to travel; itinerary; ~**roete**, route, itinerary; ~**rok**, travelling-costume; ~**rol**, holdall; ~**sak**, suitcase; holdall; portmanteau, carpet-bag; gladstone (bag); ~**skets**, travelling-sketch; ~**tabberd**, going-away dress; ~**tas**, suitcase; ~**tjek**, traveller's cheque; ~**toelae**, travelling-allowance; ~**vaar'dig, (-e)**, ready to set out (to depart); ~**vader**, gentleman in charge of touring party; ~**verhaal**, account of one's travels; **wa**, *diligence*; travelling wagon, caravan; ~**waardin**, travel hostess; purserette; ~**wissel**, letter of credit, circular note; ~**wyser**, road sign; route-book; *van* ~*wysers voorsien*, route, furnish with road signs.
reïtera'sie, reiteration.
reïtereer', (ge-), reiterate.
rek, (s) tension (of wire); elasticity; elastic; **(-ke)**, catapult; (w) (ge-), stretch, extend, spin out; distend; draw; protract (agony); prolong (visit); *jou BENE* ~ , stretch one's legs; *jou NEK* ~ , crane one's neck; *jou OË* ~ , open one's eyes wide.
rekapitula'sie, recapitulation.

rekapituleer', (ge-), recapitulate; ..le'rend, (-e), recapitulatory.
rek'as, axis of elasticity.
rek'baar, (..bare), elastic, ductile (metals); protractile; distensible; tensile; extensible; ~heid, elasticity, extensibility; malleability, ductility; distensibility, tensibility.
re'kel, (-s), rascal.
re'ken, (ge-), calculate, count, account, cipher, rate, compute, reckon, do sums; consider, regard; *DEURMEKAAR gereken*, on an average; ~ *OP*, depend (up)on; *RENTE ge~ teen 5%*, interest calculated at 5%; *iem. onder jou VRIENDE ~*, consider someone as a friend; ~**boek**, arithmetic book; ready reckoner; ~**bord**, abacus; ~**e**, arithmetic; ~**fout**, miscalculation, error in calculation.
re'kenaar, (-s), arithmetician; reckoner; computer; calculator; ~**hulp**, computer aid; ~**kommunikasie**, computer communications; ~**stelsel**, computer system; ~**tyd**, computer time; ~**wetenskap**, computer science.
re'kening, (-e, -s), bill of costs, count, statement, account; calculation; calculus; *in ~ BRING*, charge to somebody's account; *vir EIE ~ begin*, launch out on one's own account; *~ HOU met*, take into account, allow for; *op ~ KOOP*, buy on credit; *buite ~ LAAT*, not to take into account; *LOPENDE ~*, current account; *ek NEEM dit vir my ~*, I take the responsibility; *'n ~ OPEN*, open an account; *~e OPMAAK*, cast accounts; *per SLOT van ~*, ultimately, after all; *'n ~ SLUIT*, close an account; *'n ~ VEREFFEN*, settle an account; *dit is VIR sy ~*, I lay that at his door; ~**afdeling**, accounting department; ~**boek**, account book; ~**koerant'**, current account; ~**kontrole**, audit; ~**kontroleur**, accountant; ~**kunde**, accounting, accountancy; ~**kun'dige**, (-s), accountant; ~**meester**, accountant.
re'keninkie, (-s), small account
re'ken: ~**kunde**, arithmetic; ~**kun'dig**, (-e), arithmetical; ~*kundige reeks*, arithmetical progression; ~**kun'dige**, (-s), arithmetician; ~**lat**, slide-rule; ~**les**, arithmetic lesson; ~**liniaal**, sliding rule, slide-rule; ~**masjien**, calculating-machine, comptometer; arithmometer; ~**meester**, accountant, calculator; ~**meesterskap**, accountancy; ~**munt**, money of account; ~**onderwys**, teaching of arithmetic; ~**outomaat**, computer; ~**penning**, counter; ~**plig'tig**, (-e), accountable; ~*pligtige amptenaar*, accounting official; ~**plig'tigheid**, accountability; ~**raam**, abacus, ball-frame.
re'kenskap, account; ~ *GEE van*, account for; *hom ~ GEE van*, account for; form an idea of; ~ *VRA van 'n saak*, demand an account of a matter.
re'kensom, sum (in arithmetic).
rek'-en-trekgordel, two-way girdle.
re'ken: ~**tafel**, calculator, numeration table; ready reckoner; ~**werk**, calculations, figurework; ~**wyse**, method of calculation; calculus.
rek'getal, elasticity coefficient.
rek'grens, elastic limit.
rek'ker, (-s), elastic; catapult; garter; stretcher (of gloves).
rek'king, (-e, -s), stretching, lengthening; prolongation; tension.
reklamant', (-e), claimant.
rekla'me, advertisement; puffing; reclame; boosting; sales promotion; ~ *maak*, boom, boost (Amer.); advertise very widely; ~**afdeling**, advertising department; ~**artikel**, article merely for advertisement; ~**beampte**, publicity officer; ~**bord**, billboard; ~**buro**, publicity office; ~**doeleindes**, purposes of advertisement.
reklameer', (ge-), put in a claim; protest.
rekla'me: ~**kaart**, show-card; ~**lig**, electric sign; ~**maker**, boomer, puffer, booster (Amer.); publicity agent; ~**makery**, puffing; puffery; ~**plaat**, pictorial advertisement, picture-poster; ~**seël**, advertising sticker; ~**tekenaar**, commercial artist; ~**tekenwerk**, commercial art.
reklasse'ringsbeampte, probation officer.
rek'lik, (-e), elastic, yielding, ductile.

rekogni'sie(geld), *see* **rekonie**.
rekommanda'sie, (-s), recommendation.
rekommandeer', (ge-), recommend.
rekonie', quitrent.
rekonsilia'sie, reconciliation.
rekonsilieer', (ge-), reconcile.
rekonstitueer', (ge-), reconstitute.
rekonstrueer', (ge-), reconstruct.
rekonstruk'sie, (-s), reconstruction.
re'kord, (-s), record; *'n ~ OPSTEL*, set up a record; *die ~ SLAAN*, beat (break) the record; ~**houding**, keeping of records; ~**syfer**, record number; ~**vlug**, record flight.
rek'proef, tensile test.
rekrea'sie, recreation.
rekreëer', (ge-), recreate.
rekruteer', (ge-), recruit.
rekrute'ring, recruiting, recruitment.
rekruut', (..krute), recruit; *rou (baar) ~*, raw recruit.
rek: ~**siekte**, gut-tie; ~**spier**, dilator; dilatator; ~**steek**, plain knitting; garter stitch; ~**stok**, swingbar, horizontal bar; catapult's handle.
rektaal', (rektale), rectal.
rektifika'sie, (-s), rectification.
rektifiseer', (ge-), rectify.
rek'tor, (-e, -s), rector; ~**aal'**, (..rale), rectoral; ~**aat'**, (..rate), rectorate, rectorship; ~**skap**, rectorship, rectorate; ~**swoning**, rectory.
rek'tum, (-s), rectum; ~**pyp**, ~**spuit**, rectal pipe.
rekuseer', (ge-), recuse.
rek'verband, elastic bandage.
rek'weefsel, elastic tissue.
rekwes', (-te), memorial petition.
rekwireer', (ong.), (ge-), requisition.
rekwisiet', (-e), prop, property (theatrical); ~**ekamer**, property room; ~**emeester**, property man.
rekwisi'sie, (-s), requisition.
relaas', (relase), story, tale, report, account.
rela'sie, (-s), relation.
relatief', (..tiewe), relative.
relatiwiteit', relativity; ~**s'teorie**, theory of relativity.
relê', (-s), relais (electr.)
relega'sie, (-s), relegation.
relegeer', (ge-), relegate, exile.
relevan'sie, relevance, relevancy.
relevant', (-e), relevant.
releveer', (ge-), relevate, refer to; note.
reliëf', (-s), relief; *meer ~ gee aan*, bring out into greater relief; ~**bord**, embossing board; ~**kaart**, relief map; ~**letters**, raised (embossed) letters; ~**werk**, embossment.
reliek', (-e), relic; ~**skryn**, reliquary.
reli'gie, (-ë, -s), religion.
religieus', (-e), religious.
relik', (-te), relic.
relikwie', (-ë), holy relic (R.C. Church); ~**kissie**, reliquary, shrine, feretory, phylactery.
re'ling, (-s), railing, balustrade; handrail; guardrail; rave, rail (wagon); ~**paal**, baluster.
rel'letjie, (-s), scandal, row, squabble, affray, brawl, fracas.
rem, (s) (-me), brake; counter, check; (w) (ge-), apply a brake, brake; restrain, curb; drag; ~**as**, brake shaft; ~**band**, brake-band; ~**blok**, brake-block, drag-block, friction-block; sprag; ~**druk**, brake-pressure.
reme'die, (-s), remedy.
remedieer', (ge-), remedy; *remediërende onderwys*, remedial education.
rem'hefboom, brake-lever.
rem'hoogte, steep hill.
remi'se, (-s), remittance; tram-shed, car-shed; drawn game, stalemate (chess).
remitteer', (ge-), remit, transmit.
remittent', (-e), remitter.
rem'ketting, brake-chain; lock-chain, drag-chain.
rem'krag, brake-pressure.
rem'mend, (-e), restraining; inhibitory.
rem'mer, (-s), brakesman.
rem'ming, (-e, -s), braking, check-action; inhibition.

remonstran'sie, (-s), remonstration.
Remonstrant', (-e), Remonstrant.
remonstrasie', remonstration.
remonstreer', (ge-), remonstrate.
remon'te, (-s), army remount; ~**perd**, remount (army).
rem: ~**pedaal**, brake-pedal; ~**perdekrag**, brake-horsepower.
remplacant', (-e), substitute.
rem'skoen, skid, lock-shoe, brakeshoe; (slipper)drag; drag-shoe; old fog(e)y, stick-in-the-mud; conserva≠ tive; obscurant, obscurantist; pull-back; ~**agtig= heid**, conservatism, fogyism; ~**party**, conservative party; ~**politiek**, conservatism; obscurantism.
rem: ~**skyf**, brake-pulley; ~**stang**, brake-rod; ~**toe= stel**, brake; ~**toets**, brake-test; ~**trommel**, brake-drum.
remunera'sie, remuneration.
rem: ~**vlak**, braking-surface; ~**vloeistof**, brake-fluid; ~**voering**, brake-lining (facing).
ren, (s) (-ne), race; (w) (ge-), race, run.
Renaissan'ce, Renaissance, revival.
Renaissancis', (-te), Renaissance writer (painter); Renaissancist; ~**ties**, (-e), Renaissance.
ren: ~**baan**, racecourse; ~**bode**, courier, express messenger, estafette.
renda'bel, (-e), payable, paying; remunerative.
rendabiliteit', remunerativeness.
rendeer', (ge-), pay, show a profit.
rendement', efficiency (of machine); yield, return, profit.
rendezvous', rendezvous.
ren'dier, reindeer, caribou.
ren'duif, homer; racing pigeon.
renegaat', (..gate), renegade, apostate, pervert.
ren'motor, racer.
renons', aversion; discard (at cards); *in iem. (iets) 'n ~ hê*, have a dislike for someone (something); ~**eer'**, (ge-), revoke, not follow suit.
renos'ter, (-s), rhinoceros; ~**bossie**, rhinoceros bush *(Elytropappus rhinocerotis)*; ~**pad**, game track; ~**voël**, oxpecker, rhino-bird.
renova'sie, (-s), renovation.
renoveer', (ge-), renovate, renew.
ren'perd, racehorse, courser; ~**estal**, racing-stable.
rens, sour (milk); rancid; rank; ~**erig**, (-e), rather rancid, sourish; ~**heid**, rancidity.
ren'sport, racing.
ren'te, (-s), interest; ~ *DRA*, bear interest; *van sy ~ lewe*, live on the interest on one's capital (on private means); *OP* ~, at interest; *OPGELOOPTE* ~, ac= crued interest; *SAMEGESTELDE* ~, compound interest; *op ~ SIT*, put out at interest; *TEEN 'n lae* ~, at a low rate of interest; ~ *TREK van*, draw interest on; ~**bedrag**, amount of interest; ~**bere= kening**, calculation of interest; ~**brief**, exchequer bill, obligation; **daling**, fall in the rate of interest; ~**datum**, interest date; ~**draend**, ~**gewend**, (-e), bearing interest; ~**koers**, rate of interest; ~**las**, burden of interest; ~**loos**, (..lose), without interest, free of interest, bearing no interest; unpro= ductive; ~**nier**, (s) (-e, -s), (retired) person of inde= pendent means; (w) (ge-), live on one's interest; lead a carefree life; ~**skuld**, interest owing; ~**stan= daard**, rate of interest; ~**tabel**, ~**tafel**, interest table; ~**vergoeding**, payment of interest; ~**verla= ging**, lowering of the rate of interest; ~**verlies**, loss of interest; ~**versekering**, annuity insurance; ~**verskil**, difference in the rate of interest; ~**voet**, rate of interest.
rent'meester, manager, steward, agent; ~**skap**, stew-ardship.
reorganisa'sie, reorganization.
reoriënta'sie, reorientation.
reoriënteer', (ge-), reorient.
reostaat', (reostate), rheostat.
rep, (s) commotion; *in ~ en roer*, astir, all hustle and bustle; (w) (ge-), hurry up; mention; ~ *JOU!* make haste! bestir yourself! *NIKS van iets ~ nie*, not breathe a word about something.
repara'sie, (-s), repair, mending; reparation; refit; *in ~*, under repair; ~**doos**, repair outfit; ~**koste**, cost of repairs; ~**-uitrusting**, repair outfit; ~**werk**, re= pair work.
reparateur', (-s), repairer, mender.
repareer', (ge-), repair, mend, overhaul, refit, recon= dition.
repatria'sie, repatriation; ~**skema**, repatriation scheme; ~**skuld**, repatriation debt.
repatrieer' (ge-), repatriate.
re'pel, (s) (-s), ripple (flax); (w) (ge-), ripple.
reperkus'sie, repercussion.
repertoi're, (-s), programme of plays, repertory, rep= ertoire; ~**stuk**, stock play, stock piece.
reperto'rium, (-s, ..ria), repertory; index.
repeteer', (ge-), repeat, recur; rehearse; *repeterende breuk*, recurring decimal; ~**geweer**, repeating rifle; repeater; ~**pistool**, automatic.
repeti'sie, (-s), repetition; rehearsal; *geklede ~*, dress rehearsal; ~**werk**, revision.
re'pie, (-s), chip; shred, strip; ~**smarmelade**, shred= ded marmelade.
repliek', (-e), reply; counterplea, replication, rebuttal.
re'plika, (-s), replica.
repliseer', (ge-), reply.
representant' (-e), representative.
representa'sie, (-s), representation; ~**gelde**, (pecuni= ary) allowance for representation.
representatief', (..tiewe), representative, represen= tational.
representeer', (ge-), represent.
repres'sie, repression; ~**f'**, (..siewe), repressive.
reproduk'sie, (-s), reproduction.
reproduktief', (..tiewe), reproductive.
reproduktiwiteit', reproductiveness.
reproduseer', (ge-), reproduce; process; ~**baar**, (..bare), reproducible.
reprodusent', (-e), reproducer.
reptiel', (-e), reptile; ~**versameling**, collection of rep= tiles.
republiek', (s) (-e), republic; commonwealth; *die R ~ van Suid-Afrika*, The Republic of South Africa; *R ~ dag*, Republic Day; ~**wording**, attainment of republican status.
republikanis'me, republicanism.
republikein', (-e), republican.
republikeins', (-e), republican; ~**gesind**, (-e), republi= can; ~**gesinde**, (-s), republican; ~**gesindheid**, re= publicanism.
repudia'sie, repudiation.
repudieer', (ge-), repudiate.
reputasie', reputation; *'n FIRMA met 'n gevestigde ~*, a firm of established reputation; *'n slegte ~ HÊ*, stand in bad repute; have a bad reputation.
re'quiem, (-s), requiem.
rê'rig, really, truly, actual.
res, (s) (-te), rest, remainder; balance, scraps, leav= ings; (w) (ge-), remain; *dit ~ my alleen om* . . ., it only remains for me to . . ..
re'seda, (-s), reseda (colour); mignonette.
resek'sie, resection.
resenseer', (ge-), review (book).
resensent', (-e), reviewer, critic.
resen'sie, (-s), review, criticism; ~**-eksemplaar**, re= view copy.
resent', (-e; -er, -ste), recent.
resep', (-te), recipe; prescription; formula; *'n ~ op= maak*, dispense a prescription.
resep'sie, (-s), reception.
resep'teboek, recipe-book, cookery-book.
resepteer', (ge-), dispense.
resepteur', (-s), dispenser.
reseptuur', dispensing.
reseptiwiteit', receptivity.
reservaat', (..vate), reserve; sanctuary (for animals).
reserva'sie, (-s), reservation.
reserveer', (ge-), reserve, book, set aside.
reserve'ring, reserving, reservation.
reservis', (-te), reservist.
reservoir', (-s), reservoir, tank.
reser'we, (-s), reserve; reservation, qualification; ar= rearage; *IN ~ hou*, hold in reserve; *SONDER ~*, without reserve, frankly; ~**band**, spare tyre; ~**bank**, reserve bank; ~**bout**, spare bolt; ~**dele**,

spare parts; ~**fonds,** reserve fund; ~**kapitaal,** reserve capital; ~**krag,** reserve of strength; ~**mag,** reserve force; ~**manskappe,** reserves, reserve troops; ~**moer,** spare nut; ~**prys,** upset (reserve) price; ~**rekening,** reserve account; ~**ring,** spare ring; ~**tenk,** emergency tank; ~**troepe,** reserve forces; ~**voorraad,** reserve stock; ~**wa,** emergency wagon; ~**wiel,** spare wheel.
reses', (-se), interval, recess; *op* ~ *gaan,* go into recess.
reses'sie, (..siewe), recessive; *resessiewe eienskappe,* recessive characteristics.
res'getal, remainder.
residen'sie, (-s), residence; residency.
residensieel', (..siële), residential.
resident', (-e), resident; ~**-landdros,** resident magistrate.
residivis', (-te), recidivist, old offender, old lag; ~**me,** recidivism.
residu', (-'s), residue.
re'sies = **reisies.**
resipieer', (ge-), receive (law).
resiprook', (..proke), reciprocal.
resiproseer', (ge-), reciprocate.
resiprositeit', reciprocity.
resita'sie, (-s), recitation.
resitatief', (..tiewe), recitative.
resiteer', (ge-), recite.
res'lap, remnant (of material).
resoen', (-e), ration, allowance.
resolu'sie, (-s), resolution.
resoluut', (..lute), resolute, determined.
resonan'sie, resonance; ~**bodem,** sounding-board; ~**ruimte,** resonance space.
resona'tor, (-s), resonator.
resoneer', (ge-), resound, reverberate.
resorbeer', (ge-), resorb.
resorp'sie, resorption.
respek', respect, esteem, regard; ~ *AFDWING,* command respect; *UIT* ~ *vir,* out of respect for; *hy het* ~ *vir sy VADER,* he honours (respects) his father; ~**ta'bel,** (-e), respectable; ~**te,** respect, esteem; ~**teer',** (ge-), respect, hold in respect, honour.
respektief', (..tiewe), respective, several; ~**lik,** respectively, relatively.
respektie'welik = **respektieflik.**
respira'sie, respiration.
respira'tor, (-s), respirator; ..**to'ries,** (-e), respiratory.
respireer', (ge-), respire.
respi'rometer, respirome'ter, respirometer.
respondeer', (ge-), answer, respond.
respondent', (-e), respondent.
respon'sie, response, answer; ~**kollege,** practical class.
respyt', respite, delay, grace; ~**dae,** days of grace.
ressort', (-e), resort; area; jurisdiction; *in laaste* ~, in the last resort; ~ **eer',** (ge-), come within the jurisdiction of; belong to; ~ *eer onder,* fall under.
restant', (-e), remainder, remains; oddment; ~**verkoping,** remnant sale.
restaurant' = **restourant.**
resteer', (ge-), remain, be left.
res'testelling, remainder theorem.
restitueer', (ge-), make restitution, restore, repay.
restitu'sie, restitution, refund, repayment.
restourant', (-e, -s), restaurant; ~**houer,** restaurateur.
restoura'sie, (-s), restoration.
restoureer', (ge-), restore, renovate, refresh.
restrik'sie, (-s), restriction.
resultaat', (..tate), result, outcome, consequence; corollary; produce, product; *resultate KRY,* get results; *SONDER* ~, in vain, to no purpose.
resultan'te, (-s), resultant.
resumé', (-s), summary, synopsis, resumé.
resumeer', (ge-), sum up, summarize.
re'sus(aap), rhesus (monkey).
re'susfaktor, rhesus (Rh) factor.
reta'bel, (-s), retable.
reten'sie, retention; ~**geld,** ~**honorarium,** retaining fee; ~**reg,** lien, right of retention.
retiku'le, (-s), reticule.

reti'kulum, reticulum; honeycomb tripe.
re'tina, (-s), retina.
retira'de, (-s), water-closet, lavatory, loo.
retireer', (ge-), retire, retreat.
r''etjie, (-s), small r.
retoer', (-e), return; ~**gedeelte,** return portion; ~**kaartjie,** return ticket; ~**lyn,** return crease; ~**reis,** return journey; ~**vloot,** return fleet; ~**vrag,** home freight; ~**wissel,** redraft.
retoesjeer', (ge-), retouch.
re'tor, (-e, -s), rhetorician.
retoriek', rhetoric.
reto'ries, (-e), rhetorical, ornate, declamatory.
reto'rika, rhetoric.
reto'rikus, (-se, ..rici), rhetorician.
retort', (-e), retort, still.
retrogressief', (..siewe), retrogressive.
retrospektief', (..tiewe), retrospective, in retrospect.
retziaan', retzian.
reuk, (-e), scent, smell, odour; perfume; *daar KLEEF 'n* ~ *ie aan,* there is something fishy about it; *in 'n slegte* ~ *STAAN,* be in ill repute (bad odour); be badly thought of; ~**altaar,** incense altar; ~**bal,** pomander; ~**dosie,** scent-box; pouncet-box; ~**flessie,** (-s), scent-bottle; ~**goed,** perfumery; essence; ~**klier,** scent-gland; ~**lob,** olfactory lobe; ~**loos,** (..lose), scentless, odourless; inodorous; ~*loos maak,* deodorize; ~**offer,** incense offering; ~**orgaan,** organ of scent; olfactory organ; ~**sakkie,** (-s), scent-bag: sachet; ~**senuwee,** olfactory nerve; ~**sin,** olfaction, sense of smell; ~**sout,** smelling-salts; ~**vat,** incenser; censer; ~**verdrywer,** deodorant, deodorizer; ~**verlies,** arosmia; ~**verwydering,** deodorization; ~**water,** scent, perfumed water; perfumes; ~**waterspuit,** perfume-spray; ~**weerder,** deodorizer; ~**weermiddel,** deodorant; ~**werk,** scents, perfume, perfumery.
reun, (-e, -s), gelding; male dog; ~**hond,** male dog.
reü'nie, (-s), reunion; ~**fees,** reunion feast; gaudy (English schools).
reun'perd, gelding.
reus, (-e), giant; colossus.
reusag'tig, (-e), gigantic, huge, colossal, giant(-like); leviathan, mammoth; ~**heid,** gigantic size (stature), hugeness, vastness.
reu'se: ~**arbeid,** gigantic task; ~**beeld,** colossal statue; ~**geslag,** giant race; ~**gestalte,** gigantic figure; ~**groei,** giantism; ~**haai,** basking-shark; ~**krag,** gigantic (Herculean) strength; ~**taak,** Herculean task.
reu'sel, (-s), lard, suet, flare (leaf) lard.
reu'se: ~**letters,** mammoth type; ~**oorwinning,** runaway victory; ~**skilpad,** green turtle; ~**skip,** giant ship, mammoth vessel.
reu'seskrede, giant stride; *met* ~*s vooruitgaan,* go forward by leaps and bounds.
reu'se: ~**stad,** huge city; metropolis; megalopolis; ~**sterk,** as strong as a giant; ~**stormvoël,** giant petrel; ~**stryd,** gigantic struggle; gigantomachy; ~**suikerbos,** giant protea; ~**sukses,** gigantic success; ~**taak,** gigantic task; ~**treë,** giant strides; ~**vliegtuig,** giant aeroplane; ~**werk,** gigantic work, Herculean task; ~**wynkruik,** jeroboam.
revalua'sie, revaluation.
revalueer', (ge-), revalue.
revalue'ring, revaluation.
revan'che, (ong., lit.), revenge.
reveil', revival (religious).
reveil'le, reveille; morning-call.
reverbereer'oond, reverberating furnace.
revers', (-e), revers.
reviseer', (ge-), revise.
reviseur', (-s), reviser, reader.
revi'sie, revision; review.
revisionis', (-te), revisionist; ~**me,** revisionism; ~**ties,** (-e), revisionist.
revoka'sie, revocation, repeal.
revolu'sie, ens. = **rewolusie,** ens.
revue', (-s), review; revue; *die* ~ *passeer,* file past.
re'wer, (-s), reefer.
rewolu'sie, (-s), revolution; ~**gees,** revolutionary spirit; ~**jaar,** year of revolution.

rewolusionêr', (-e), revolutionary.
rewolusionis', (-te), revolutionist; ~**me**, revolutionism.
rewol'wer, (-s), revolver, Colt; ~**kanon**, Gatling gun; ~**koeël**, revolver bullet; ~**patroon**, revolver cartridge; ~**skoot**, revolver shot.
rhizo'pusvrot, rhizopus rot.
Rhode'sië, (hist.), Rhodesia; ~**r**, (-s), Rhodesian; ..**sies**, (-e), Rhodesian.
rib, (-be(s)), rib; web (of rail); joist; spline; *'n mens kan sy ~ be tel*, he is only skin and bone; ~**arig**, (-e), costal-veined; ~**bebeen**, rib; *sy ~ bebeen kry*, get his life's partner; ~**beboog**, costal arch.
rib'bekas, thoracic skeleton; *iem. op sy ~ gee*, punch someone in the ribs.
rib'bel, (-s), ripple; (w) (ge-), ripple; ~**ing**, (-e, -s), ~**merk**, ripple; ~**stof**, ripple cloth.
rib'betjie, (-s), rib; rafter (ship); cutlet; *sy ~ is SEER*, he is in love; *jy kan sy ~s TEL*, you can count his ribs.
rib'bok, rheebok; *soos 'n ~ HARDLOOP*, run like a hare; *ROOI ~*, mountain rheebok; *VAAL ~*, grey reebok; ~**blom**, large brown Afrikaner (flower).
rib: ~**filet**, sirloin steak, rib steak; ~**karmenaadjie**, rib-chop; ~**koord**, whipcord; ~**rol**, rolled rib; ~**skaaf**, reeding-plane; ~**stof**, ribbed material; ~**skoot**, dig in the ribs; ~**stuk**, rib of beef, mutton; ~**werk**, ribbing.
rid'der, (-s), knight, chevalier; companion (of an order); *DOLENDE ~*, knight errant; *~ van die DROEWIGE figuur*, knight of the rueful countenance; *~ v.d. EL*, knight of the yardstick (tailor); *R~ v.d. KOUSBAND*, Knight of the Garter; *tot ~ SLAAN*, (confer) knight(hood on); dub knight; ~**diens**, knightly service; ~**eer**, honour of a knight; ~**eeu**, age of chivalry; ~**gees**, spirit of chivalry; ~**geskiedenis**, tale of chivalry; ~**goed**, baronial (manorial) estate; ~**kruis**, cross of knighthood; ~**leen**, knight's fief; ~**lik**, (-e), knightly, chivalrous, noble; ~**likheid**, chivalrousness, chivalry; ~**lint**, ribbon of a knightly order; ~**orde**, order of knighthood; ~**poësie**, poetry of the age of chivalry; ~**roman**, romance of chivalry; ~**saal**, knights' hall; ~**skap**, knighthood; chivalry; ~**slag**, accolade, dubb(ing); *iem. die ~slag gee*, knight someone; ~**slot**, manor house; ~**spel**, tournament; ~**spoor**, larkspur; ~**stand**, knighthood; ~**tyd**, age of chivalry; ~**verhaal**, tale of chivalry; ~**wese**, chivalry.
ridikuul', (ong.), ridicule.
riel, (-e), reel, dance.
riem¹, (-e), strap, thong; belt (machine); lanyard (pistol); leash; *iem. se ~ AFSNY*, deceive someone; *die ~ e BÊRE (neersit)*, take to one's heels; *iem. 'n ~ onder die HART steek ('n hart onder die ~ steek)*, put fresh heart into someone; encourage someone; *sy ~ e is LOS*, he is in love; *'n ROU ~*, a rough diamond; *~ e SNY na die vel*, cut the coat according to the cloth; *hy het sy ~ e STYFGELOOP*, he has come to the end of his tether; he has met his Waterloo; *iem. in die ~ laat TRAP*, deceive (cheat) someone, *UIT jou ~ uit wees*, be in a bad temper; *breë ~ e uit 'n ander se VEL sny*, cut large thongs from other men's leather.
riem², (-e), ream (of paper).
riem³, (-e), oar; *die ~ e BINNEHAAL*, ship the oars; give up a plan; *ROEI met die ~ e wat jy het*, make shift with what one has.
riem'aandrywing, belt-driving.
Riem'land, the North-Eastern Free State.
riem: ~**leer**, belt leather; ~**loos**, strapless.
riem'mik, rowlock.
riem'pie, (-s), leather thong; *'n ~ van die ou vel*, a chip of the old block; ~**smat**, chairseat made of riempies; ~**svel**, cured buckskin from which to cut riempies.
riem: ~**skyf**, belt-pulley, drum; ~**spanning**, belt tension.
riem'spring, (ge-), skip; *iem. laat ~*, give someone a hiding.
riem: ~**tang**, belt-shifter; ~**telegram**, unverified report, mere rumour; canard; grapevine (fig.); ~**ver**

binder, belt-fastener; ~**verbinding**, belt joint; ~**vurk**, belt fork.
riet, (-e), reed, rush, cane, thatch; *'n GEKNAKTE ~*, a broken reed; *ROER jou ~ e*, hurry up, stir your stumps! ~**agtig**, (-e), reedy; ~**beentjie**, match-stick (fig.); ~**bok**, reedbuck; ~**bos**, clump of weeds; ~**dak**, thatched roof; ~**dakhuis**, house with thatched roof; ~**dekker**, thatcher; ~**erig**, (-e), reedy; ~**fluit**, reedpipe; ~**gans**, bean-goose; ~**gras**, sword-grass, flag, reed-grass, bent; ~**haan**, water-hen; Cape rail; ~**jie**, (-s), small reed; straw (for drinking); ~**kooi**, bed of rushes (reeds); ~**kwartel**, button-quail; ~**lelie**, bluebell; ~**mat**, cane-seat of chair; reed mat; ~**mes**, cane-knife; ~**meubels**, cane furniture; ~**perd**, cane horse; ~**pypie**, bluebell; ~**reismandjie**, pilgrim basket; ~**rot**, cane-rat; ~**sanger**, reed-warbler; ~**sap**, sling, cane-juice; ~**skerm**, reed screen; ~**skraal**, very thin; as thin as a rake; ~**spiritus**, cane-spirit; ~**stoel**, wicker chair, cane chair; ~**suiker**, cane-sugar, sucrose; ~**vink**, reed-finch, reed-warbler, reed-babbler, masked weaver-bird; ~**vlei**, valley (marsh) with reeds and rushes.
rie'was-rie'was, knick-knacks; trifles.
rif¹, (riwwe), reef (of sail).
rif², (riwwe), reef, ledge; ridge, edge; ~**dikte**, channel width; ~**saag**, ~**snyer**, reef-cutter.
rif'fel, (s) (-s), ripple, wrinkle, ridge, crinkle, ruffle; corrugation (road); rib, ribbing (knitting); (w) (ge-), wrinkle; corrugate; crimp (paper); *'n ge~ de pad*, a corrugated road; ~**ferweel**, corduroy; ~**ing**, (-e, -s), ripple, wrinkle; corrugation (road); ~**karton**, corrugated cardboard; ~**pad**, corrugated road; ~**papier**, corrugated paper; ~**plaat**, channel-plate; ~**rig**, (-e), full of ripples, wrinkled; corrugated; ~**sink**, corrugated iron; ~**skaaf**, reed-plane; ~**steek**, ribbing; ~**stof**, ribbed material; ~**strook**, ribbing, ~**tang**, crimping-pliers; ~**yster**, corrugated iron.
rif: ~**gang**, drive; ~**goud**, reef-gold; ~**opvulling**, reef-packing; ~**rigting**, strike.
Rif'rughond, Rhodesian Ridgeback (dog).
Rif'stam, Riff tribe.
rif'steen, veinstone, gangue.
rig¹, (s) sighting; (w) (ge-), direct, address; set (chart); aim; make out; level, lay aim, point (weapon); dress; collimate; *'n vraag ~ AAN*, put a question to; *sy skredes ~ NA*, direct one's steps towards; *'n GEWEER ~*, aim a gun; *die oog ~ OP*, fix the eye on; *die woord ~ TOT*, address (one's words to).
rig², (ge-), judge, act as judge.
rig: ~**bok**, sighting-frame; ~**boog**, elevating arc; ~**diens**, direction-finding service.
rig'gel, (-s), edge, ridge, border, rail; frame, chamfer; ~**s**, flanges.
rig: ~**hamer**, peening tool; ~**hoek**, angle of sight.
rigied', (form.), rigid.
rig: ~**juistheid**, accuracy (of aim); ~**lyn**, guideline, guiding line; plumbline, directive; directrix (maths.); *die ~ lyne aangee*, indicate the lines; ~**magneet**, controlling magnet; ~**mas**, direction-finding mast; ~**middel**, gun-sight; ~**muur**, lead.
rigoris', (-te), rigorist; ~**me**, rigorism.
rig: ~**plank**, jointing-rule; ~**punt**, point aimed at; fixed point; ~**skoot**, trial (sighting) shot; ~**skuifie**, focusing slide (rifle); ~**skutter**, layer (shooting).
rig'snoer, rule of conduct; guiding principle; *tot ~ DIEN*, serve as a guide; *'n VASLÊ*, lay down rules.
rig: ~**spaak**, handspike; ~**straal**, beam-track; ~**straaldiens**, beam service; ~**straalradio**, beam radio; ~**streep**, direction-mark (on compass); ray; ~**tend**, (-e), directive.
rig'ter¹, (-s), judge, justice; *Rigters*, Book of Judges.
rig'ter², (-s), layer; launcher (of rocket).
rig'ting, (-e, -s), direction; setting (map); range; strike (geol.); collimation; trend, tenor; creed; *mense van ALLE ~ e*, people of all opinions; *die GOEIE ~*, the right direction; *ONS ~*, our school of thought, our persuasion; *VAN ~ verander*, change one's opinions (politics); ~**armpie**, indicator; ~**flits**, indicator; ~**flitser**, flash indicator; ~**gewend**, (-e),

directorial; directive; ~**loos**, (..**lose**), irresolute, undecided; ~**sbepaling**, direction-finding; ~**sgang**, driftway; ~**skyf**, arrow-disc; ~**slyn**, plumb-line; alignment; ~**smerk**, direction-mark; ~**soeker**, direction-finder; ~**speiling**, direction-finding, bearing; ~**sroer**, rudder; ~**sverandering**, change of direction; ~**sverskuiwing**, strike-fault; ~**wyser**, direction-indicator (-signal).

rigvaar'dig, (-e), flexible; ~**heid**, flexibility (gun).

rik'ketik, pit-a-pat, pitter-patter.

riks'daalder, (-s), rix-dollar; *'n bietjie dik vir 'n* ~, that's rather thick.

rik'sja, (-s), rickshaw.

ril, (ge-), shiver, shudder, tremble, quake; freeze; ~ *van die KOUE*, shiver with cold; *dis iets om VAN te* ~, something which gives one the creeps; ~**boek**, ~**ler**, thriller; ~**lerig**, (-e), shivery; ~**ling**, (-e, -s), shudder, shiver, ague; ~**prent**, thriller (film); ~**stuk**, thriller (play).

rim'pel, (s) (-s), wrinkle, fold, crease, furrow, rumple, ruffle; pucker; cockle; gather; (w) (ge-), wrinkle, ripple, rumple, ruffle; crimp, crinkle; fret; purse (lips); gauge; enfold; *die voorhoof* ~, knit the brow; ~**ig**, (-e), wrinkled, furrowed, puckered; ropy (paint); ~**ing**, (-e, -s), wrinkling, rippling, ruffling, puckering, ripple (on water); ~**masjien**, corrugating machine; gatherer; ~**papier**, crinkled paper; ~**plooie**, shirring; ~**rig**, (-e) = **rimpelig**; ~**stof**, puckered cloth; ~**werk**, shirring.

ring, (s) (-e), ring; circle; hoop; halo; girdle-joint; sleeve; eye (of rope); collet; church district, presbytery; cartel; cringle (rope); *hy kan deur 'n* ~ *SPRING, jy kan hom deur 'n* ~ *TREK*, he is as neat as a pin; (w) (ge-), ring (bird, tree); cincture; ~**as**, collet; ~**baan**, circular track (railway); ~**bandstelsel**, loose-leaf system; ~**bars**, ring shake; ~**been**, ringbone; ~**duif**, ring-dove; ~**eiland**, atoll.

ringeleer', (ge-), ring-bark; ..**le'ring**, ringbarking.

rin'geloor, (ge-), order about, bully.

ring: ~**er**, (-s), ringer; ~**etjie**, (-s), small ring, ringlet; eyelet; annulet; collar (coin); circlet; ~**gebergte**, circular mountain range; ~**geut**, ring (in shaft); ~**gooi**, (s), quoits; (w) (ge-), play quoits; ~**haak**, gudgeon; ~**kanaal**, circular canal; ~**kabel**, concentric cable; ~**kop**, (Zulu) veteran; ~**korrel**, ring-sight; ~**kraakbeen**, cricoid cartilage; ~**kreef**, isopod; ~**lyn**, loop-line; ~**mes**, guillotine (med.); ~**muur**, circular wall; enceinte (of fort); ~**naat**, circumferential seam; ~**nekkiewiet**, ringed sloven; ~**oond**, annular kiln; ~**sitting**, meeting of the presbytery; ~**skeur**, cup(ring)-shake; ~**s'kommissie**, presbyterial committee; ~**skroef**, double screw; ~**skroefsleutel**, ring-spanner; ~**slang**, grass snake; ~**sloot**, circular ditch; ~**smeerder**, ring-oiler; ~**smering**, ring-lubrication; ~**snyer**, stock and dies; ~**spier**, sphincter; ~**s'ressort**, presbytery; ~**steek**, (s) tilting at the ring; (w) (ge-), tilt at the ring; ~**tennis**, tenniquoits, deck tennis; ~**vat**, annular vessel; ~**vinger**, ring-finger; third finger; ~**visier**, ring-sight; ~**vormig**, (-e), annular, circular; ring-shaped; cyclic; ~**vorming**, annulation; ~**vrot**, ring rot; ~**wurm**, ringworm.

rin'kel, (ge-), jingle, tinkle, clatter.

rink'hals, (-e), ring-neck(ed animal); twist (dance); ~**duif**, ring-neck pigeon; ~**slang**, ring-necked cobra.

rinkink', (ge-), tinkle, jingle, rattle, row; gambol, make merry, gallivant, gad about.

rinnewa'sie = **ruïnasie**.

rinneweer', (ge-) = **ruïneer**.

rinoskoop', (..**skope**), rhinoscope.

rioel', (-e), *see* **riool**.

rioleer', (ge-), sewer, drain, gutter.

riole'ring, sewerage, drainage.

riool', (riole), drain, sewer, gutter; grip; cloaca; ~**buis**, drainage-pipe; ~**gas**, sewer-gas; ~**gat**, gulley; ~**lêer**, drain-layer; ~**put**, gulley; ~**plaas**, sewage farm; ~**put**, sewage sump; gulley; ~**pyp**, sewer-pipe; ~**sluis**, gulley-trap; ~**slyk**, sewage; ~**slykwerke**, sewage disposal works; ~**stelsel**, sewerage system; ~**vuil**, sewage; ~**water**, sewage; diluted sewerage; ~**werker**, sewer-cleaner.

rips, rep.

ri'siko, (-'s), risk; hazard; *'n* ~ *AANGAAN*, take a risk; *jou aan* ~ *BLOOTSTEL*, take chances; *vir EIE* ~, at owner's risk; *OP jou* ~, at your risk; ~**kapitaal**, risk capital.

riskant', (-e), hazardous, risky; ~**heid**, riskiness.

riskeer', (ge-), risk, venture.

risoom', (**risome**), rhizome.

ris'sie, (-s), cayenne pepper, chilli, capsicum; minx; *sy IS 'n* ~, she is a shrew (vixen); ~*s bo PEPER*, diamond cuts diamond; ~**agtig**, (-e), peppery; shrewish, vixenish; ~**pit**, chilli-seed; shrew.

rit, (-te), ride, drive, spin; ~**boek**, log-book.

ri'te, (-s), rite.

rit'jie, (-s), drive, spin; *'n* ~ *maak*, go for a spin.

rit'me, (-s), rhythm; beat, cadence, lift.

rit: ~**meester**, cavalry captain; ~**meter**, trip meter.

ritmiek', rhythm; rhythmics.

rit'mies, (-e), rhythmic(al).

ritornel', (-le), ritornel; ritornello.

rits, (-e), string, series; zip-fastener; bunch; sound of tearing (material); queue; ~**baadjie**, lumber-jacket; ~**beitel**, bolt-chisel, cross-cut (cape) chisel.

rit'sel, (ge-), rustle, crackle; quiver; ~**ing**, (-e, -s), rustling, rustle, quivering.

rits'hamer, fuller.

rits'hout, marking-gauge.

rit'sig, (-e), ruttish; ~**heid**, ruttishness, rut.

rits: ~**mat**, trampoline; ~**sluiter**, zip-fastener; ~**sluiting**, zip fastening; ~**tuig**, jolly jumper.

rit'tel, (ge-), shake, shiver, tremble, quiver; ~ *van vrees*, shake with fear.

rit'teldans, (s) (-e), jive session; jitterbugging; (w) (ge-), jive, jitterbug.

ritteltit(s)', jitters, shivers; *die* ~ *kry*, become hysterical.

rituaal', (**rituale**), ritual.

ritualis', (-te), ritualist; ~**me**, ritualism; ~**ties**, (-e), ritualistic.

ritueel', (**rituele**), ritual.

ri'tus, (-se), rite; ritual.

rivier', (-e), river; *die* ~ *AF*, down the river; *die* ~ *OP*, up the river; ~**arm**, branch of a river; ~**bedding**, river-bed; ~**beskrywing**, potamography; ~**bewoner**, riverain; ~**boot**, river-boat; ~**dam**, dam on (across) river; ~**eilandjie**, ait; holm; ~**god**, river-god; ~**grond**, river soil; ~**kant**, riverside; ~**klei**, river mud; ~**kreef**, crayfish; ~**kunde**, potamology; ~**loop**, course of a river; ~**mond**, estuary, river mouth, firth, frith; ~**nimf**, water-nymph; ~**oewer**, riverside; river-bank; ~**skilpad**, marsh tortoise; ~**stelsel**, river system; ~**vis**, freshwater fish; ~**wal**, river-bank; ~**water**, river-water.

rob, (-be), seal, phoca; Cape sea-lion.

robbedoe', (-ë, -s) = **rabbedoe**.

rob'be: ~**jag**, seal-hunt; ~**jagter**, seal-hunter; ~**kolonie**, seal-rookery; ~**skip**, sealer; ~**spek**, seal-blubber; ~**traan**, seal-oil; ~**vaarder**, sealing-vessel; ~**vangs**, seal-hunting; seal-fishery; ~**vel**, seal-skin.

robinsona'de, (-s), robinsonade.

ro'bot, (-s, -te), robot, mechanical man; ~ *voor*, robot ahead; ~**vliegtuig**, pilotless aeroplane.

robuus', (-te; -ter, -ste), robust, stalwart; ~**t'heid**, robustness.

robyn', (-e), ruby; ~**rooi**, ruby(-red); ~**silver**, red silver.

ro'del, (ge-), toboggan; ~**slee**, toboggan.

ro'dium, rhodium.

rododen'dron, (-s), rhododendron.

roe'bel, (-s), rouble.

roe'de, (-s), rod, birch; verge; rood, perch (measure); mace; switch; *KAAPSE* ~, (Cape) rood; *MANLIKE* ~, penis; *wie die* ~ *SPAAR, bederf die kind*, spare the rod and spoil the child; ~**draer**, mace-bearer.

roef, (**roewe**), slanting top of a coffin; deck-house; notch.

roei[1], (s) (-e), tail of a comet; lattice; mullion.

roei[2], (w) (ge-), row; pull (oars); ~**bank**, rowing-bench; thwart; ~**boot**, rowing-boat; ~**dol**, row-lock; ~**er**, (-s), rower; oarsman, waterman; sculler;

oar; ~**klamp**, rowlock; ~**klub**, boating (rowing) club; ~**kuns**, oarsmanship; watermanship; ~**mik**, rowlock; ~**pen**, thole; ~**riem**, oar; ~**spaan**, (..**spane**), oar, scull; paddle; ~**sport**, rowing.
roei'ster, comet.
roei: ~**stok**, gauging rod; ~**tog**, row; pull; ~**vereniging**, rowing club; ~**wedstryd**, boat-race, regatta.
roek, (-e), rook.
roe'keloos, (..lose), rash, reckless, careless; cockbrained, devil-may-care, dare-devilish; adventurous; blindly, blindfold; foolhardy; wicked, profane; prodigal; profligate; *roekelose bestuurder*, reckless driver; ~**heid**, rashness, recklessness, foolhardiness; diablerie, devilry, prodigality.
roekoek', **(ge-)**, coo (dove).
roem, (s) glory, fame, renown, repute; boast; praise; lustre; ~ *BEHAAL*, earn fame; *EIE* ~ *stink*, self-praise is no recommendation; *op jou* ~ *TEER*, rest on one's laurels; *TOT* ~ *van*, for the glory of; (w) **(ge-)**, praise, extol, laud; boast; *IN God* ~ *ons die hele dag*, in God we boast all the day long; *dis NIKS om oor te* ~ *nie*, nothing to boast about; *hy* ~ *op sy RYKDOM*, he boasts of his wealth.
Roemeen', (..**mene**), Roumanian; ~**s'**, (-e), Roumanian.
Roeme'nië, Roumania; ~**r**, (-s), Roumanian.
roe'mer, (-s), rummer, large wineglass; braggart.
roemgie'rig, (-e), thirsting for glory; ambitious.
roem'loos, (..**lose**), inglorious.
roemrug'tig, (-e), renowned.
roem'ryk, (e), glorious, famous, splendid, magnificent, lustrous.
roem'sug, vainglory; desire for fame; ~'**tig**, (-e), vainglorious.
roem'vol, (-le), illustrious, renowned.
roep, (s) call, cry; (w) **(ge-)**, call, cry, shout, halloo; declare (cards); *'n GENEESHEER* ~, call (send for) a doctor; *hom HEES* ~, shout oneself hoarse; *LAAT* ~, send for; *iets in die LEWE* ~, call something into being; *OM hulp* ~, cry (shout) for help; *ek VOEL my nie geroepe nie*, I do not feel called upon; ~**afstand**, hailing distance.
roepee', (-s), rupee.
roep: ~**ende**, (-es), one who calls; ~**er**, (-s), crier, one who calls; megaphone; bleeper.
roe'ping, (-e, -s), calling, vocation, avocation, mission, purpose; *hy het sy* ~ *gemis*, he has missed his vocation.
roep'naam, call-sign; pet name.
roep'radio, bleeper.
roep'stem, call, voice, summons, cry.
rocr¹, (s) (-s), gun, rifle; *HOU jou* ~ *reg*, keep your powder dry; *so REG soos 'n* ~, as right as rain; as straight as a die.
roer², (s) (-e, -s), rudder, helm; *die* ~ *in HANDE hê*, be at the helm; *aan die* ~ *KOM*, assume control; *die* ~ *OMGOOI*, change one's course; *aan die* ~ *van SAKE wees (staan)*, be at the helm.
roer³ (s). *in rep en* ~, in turmoil; all agog; all hustle and bustle.
roer⁴, (w) **(ge-)**, stir, move, agitate; touch; ~ *jou ANGEL (riete)*, get a move on; ~ *(vir) JOU*, make haste; *sy PREKE* ~ *my altyd*, I am always moved by his sermons; *tot TRANE* ~, move to tears; *aan 'n ou TWIS* ~, rake up an old quarrel.
roer: ~**baar**, (..**bare**), movable (property); ~**bak**, pulp-engine; ~**der**, (-s), stirrer; agitator (mining).
roer'domp, (-e), bittern.
roer'eiers, scrambled eggs.
roe'rend, (b) (e), touching, moving, pathetic; movable; ~*e GOEDERE*, movables; goods and chattels; *'n* ~*e VERHAAL*, a touching (pathetic) story; (bw) quite; *hulle is dit* ~ *EENS*, they agree (heartily) in all respects.
roer'ganger, (-s), helmsman.
roer'haak, pintle (in mines).
roe'rig, (-e), active, stirring, lively; ~**heid**, activity, liveliness.
roe'ring, commotion, stir; emotion.
roer'koning, rudder-head.
roer: ~**lepel**, stirrer; ~**loos**, (..**lose**), motionless; rudderless.

roer: ~**meter**, telltale (hoisting-engine); ~**oog**, gudgeon; ~**pen**, tiller, helmstock; pintle (in mines).
roer'sel, (-e, -s), impulse, motive; ~*e v.d. hart*, the stirring of the heart.
roer'spaan, stirrer, spatula; stirring rod.
roer'stang, rabbler.
roer'stok, stirrer, whip-staff; agitator (mine); ~**toestel**, stirring-gear; agitator (in mines).
roer'tou, tiller-rope.
roes¹, (s), rust, blight, brand (in corn); *hy IS 'n* ~, he is a wastrel; *'n* ~ *in iem. se SAK*, a drain on one's pocket; (w) **(ge-)**, rust, corrode; get rusty; *ou LIEFDE* ~ *nie*, true love never grows old; *my REKENKUNDE is al 'n bietjie ge* ~, my arithmetic is a bit rusty.
roes², (s) intoxication bout, drunken fit; ecstasy, frenzy; flush (of victory); *sy* ~ *UITSLAAP*, sleep off the effects of one's debauch; *in die* ~ *van VRYHEID*, in the intoxication of liberty.
roes: ~**agtig**, (-e), rusty; ~**bruin**, rust-brown; ~**dopluis**, rusty scale.
roe'semoes, confusion, disorder, tumult, bustle.
roe'serig, (-e), rusty; ~**heid**, rustiness.
roes: ~**hoop**, scrap-heap; ~**kleur**, rust colour; ~**kleurig**, (-e), rust-coloured, foxy; ~**laag**, patina; ~**oplosmiddel**, rust solvent; ~**rooi**, rust-red; ~**terig**, (-e), rusty; ~**terigheid**, rustiness; ~**vlek**, rust stain; ~**vry**, rust-proof, stainless; ~**werend**, (-e), anti-rust, anti-corrosion, rust-proof.
roet, soot; (lamp-)black; *met* ~ *GOOI*, besmirch the good name of others; *dit was* ~ *in sy KOS*, that spoiled his game; that was a spot of bother to him; ~ *in iem. se KOS gooi*, be a spoilsport; *as jy met* ~ *SPEEL*, *word jy swart*, he who touches pitch shall be defiled; ~**aankorsting**, carbon deposit; ~**agtig**, (-e), sooty; fuliginous; ~**blaser**, soot-blower; tubecleaner; ~**bruin**, bistre.
roe'te, (-s), route, road; ~**aanwyser**, route-indicator; ~**kaart**, route-map, traverse-map.
roe'terig, (-e), sooty; ~**heid**, sootiness.
roeti'ne, routine; groove.
roet'kleur, sooty colour; ~**ig**, (-e), of a sooty colour, soot-coloured.
roet: ~**kol**, smut; ~**korreltjie**, soot-flake; ~**lug**, sooty smell.
roets'baan, switchback (railway).
roet: ~**swart**, carbon black, black as soot; ~**vanger**, chimney trap; ~**vlek**, smut.
rof, (**rowwe**), rough, rude, coarse, rugged; *see* **ru**.
rof'fel¹, (s) ruffle, roll (of drum); (w) **(ge-)**, beat a ruffle (on drum).
rof'fel², (s) (-s), plane; (w) **(ge-)**, rough-hew; plane; ~**skaaf**, trying-plane.
rof'felvuur, roll-fire, drum-fire.
ro'fie, (-s), bit of scab, slough.
rof'kas, (s) roughcast; (w) **(ge-)**, roughcast.
rof'stoei, all-in wrestling.
rog¹, (ge, rôc), skate, spotted ray.
rog², rye; ~**(ge)brood**, rye bread; pumpernickel.
rog'gel, (s) phlegm, ruckle; (w) **(ge-)**, rattle (in the throat), ruckle.
Rog'geveld, Roggeveld.
rog'meel, rye meal.
rojaal', (**rojale**), royal; generous, liberal, lavish; handsome; ~ *lewe*, live extravagantly.
rojalis', (-te), royalist; ~**me**, royalism; ~**ties**, (-e), royalistic.
rojaliteit', generosity, liberality.
rojeer', (ong.), **(ge-)**, cancel, delete, annul; strike off as member, disbar (lawyer); ~**masjien**, (stamps) cancelling machine.
roje'ring, (ong.), cancellation.
rok¹, roc (bird).
rok², (-ke), skirt, dress, costume; petticoat; *hy dra die* ~, his wife wears the breeches; he is henpecked; ~**band**, skirt-tape, waist-band; petticoat string; *hy is nog aan sy ma se* ~*band vas*, he is a mother's darling; ~**beskermer**, dress protector; ~**broek**, divided skirt, tennis shorts, harem-skirt, bloomers.
rokeer', **(ge-)**, castle (chess).
ro'ker, (-s), smoker; ~**ig**, (-e), smoky; fumy; reeky;

dingy; ~**igheid**, smokiness; ~**shart**, tobacco heart; ~**y**, smoking.
rok: ~**goed**, skirting; dress material; ~**hanger**, dress-hanger; ~**hoepel**, dress (skirt) hoop.
ro'kie, (-s), wisp of smoke; *daar trek nooit 'n ~ nie of daar brand 'n vuurtjie*, there is never smoke without fire.
rok'kie, (-s), little skirt (dress); *Skotse ~*, kilt.
roko'ko, rococo (style).
rok: ~**ophouer**, (-s), dress-supporter, dress-clip; page; ~**pant**, (-e), panel, gore, width (of skirt); ~**slip**, skirt placket; ~**soldaat**, kiltie; ~**soom**, hemline; ~**stof**, dress material; ~**voorskoot**, overall.
rol, (s) (-le), roll, list; calendar; coil; reel; piece; part, rôle; personage; character; scroll; cylinder, roller; *aan die ~ BRING*, set going; *die ~ le OMKEER*, reverse the parts; *aan die ~ SIT*, set the ball rolling; *van die ~ SKRAP*, strike off the roll; *'n ~ SPEEL*, play (act) a part; *uit die ~ VAL*, act out of character; *die ~ le VERDEEL*, assign (cast) the parts; (w) (ge-), roll; tumble; *die GELD laat ~*, spend much money; ~*lende MATERIAAL*, rolling-stock; *met die OË ~*, roll one's eyes; *iem. se SAKKE ~*, pick someone's pockets; ~**aap**, cebus; capuchin; ~**as**, rolling axis; ~**baan**, runway; ~**bal**, bowls (game); ~**balspan**, rink; ~**balspeler**, bowls-player, bowler; ~**balveld**, bowling green; ~**bed**, trundle-bed; truckle-bed; ~**besetting**, cast (of a play); ~**blinding**, roller blind; ~**deksel**, roll-top; ~**demper**, stabilizer; ~**domkrag**, trolley jack; ~**druk**, rolling-pressure; ~**eg**, disc-harrow; ~**filmkamera**, roll-film camera; ~**gordyn**, roller blind; ~**haak**, cant-hook; ~**hals**, poloneck; ~**ham**, rolled ham; ~**handdoek**, roller towel; jack-towel; ~**kas**, chain-box (road-bridge); ~**kewer**, eumolpus beetle, tumble-bug; ~**koek**, Swiss roll; ~**kontak**, trolley; ~**kraag**, roll collar; ~**kraan**, travelling-crane; ~**laag**, upright course (of masonry); ~**la'de**, (-s), rolled meat; ~**laer**, roller-bearing; ~**len'de**, rolled beef; ~**ler**, (-s), roller platen (typewriter); ~**lesing**, call-over; play-reading.
rol'letjie, (-s), small roll, reel (cotton); castor (under table-leg); rouleau; *alles gaan op ~s*, everything is running smoothly; ~**stang**, roller-bit.
rol: ~**luik**, roller shutter; ~**luiklessenaar**, rolltop desk; ~**maat**, tape-measure; ~**merk**, (s) roller-mark; (w) (ge-), roller-mark; ~**naat**, run-and-fell seam, trend-seam, French seam; ~**passer**, traveller; ~**pens**, minced meat in tripe; ~**pers**, rolling-press; ~**plek**, place where animals roll; place where a young man courts; *sy ~ plek is daar*, that is where he is calling; ~**poeding**, roly-poly; ~**prent**, cinema film; moving picture; ~**prentster**, film star; movie star; ~**prentwerk**, screen work; ~**punt**, ball-point; ~**puntpen**, ball-point (pen); ~**rib**, rolled rib; ~**roer**, aileron; ~**skaats**, roller skate; roller-skating; ~**skaatser**, roller-skater, rinker; ~**skoffel**, rotovator; ~**soom**, roll hem; ~**steen**, pebble; ~**stoel**, Bath chair, wheel chair; invalid's chair; ~**stok**, rolling-pin; ~**tabak**, twist, rolled tobacco; ~**tanding**, interrupted perforation; ~**tong**, rolled tongue; proboscis; ~**tou**, parbuckle; ~**trap**, escalator; moving staircase; ~**varkie**, hedgehog; ~**vas**, (-te), letter-perfect; word-perfect; ~**verband**, roller bandage; ~**verdeling**, cast (of a play); ~**vervulling**, personation; ~**wa**, truck, trundle; ~**waentjie**, (-s), trolley; dinner-waggon; ~**ystervark**, hedgehog.
Romaans', (-e), Romanic.
ro'man[1], (-ne, -s), red (roman), fish; large red spider, solifuge *(Solifuga)*.
roman'[2], (-s), novel; ~**esk'**, (-e), romanesque.
roman'held, book hero, novel hero; ~**in**, (-ne), heroine of fiction.
Romanis', (-te), Romanist.
romaniseer', (ge-), romanize; ..**se'ring**, romanizing.
roman': ~**leser**, novel reader; ~**literatuur**, fiction, novels; ~**netjie**, (-s), novelette; ~**reeks**, series of novels; ~**se**, (-s), romance; ~**sier'**, (-s), novelist, romancer; ~**skryfster**, (lady) novelist; ~**skrywer**, novelist, fiction writer.
ro'manspinnekop, large red (roman) spider, solifuge.
Romantiek'[1], Romanticism; Romantic period.

romantiek'[2], romance, romanticism; ~**erig**, (-e), sentimentally romantic, over-romantic; ~**erigheid**, sentimentality.
roman'ties, (-e), romantic.
roman'tikus, (..**tici**, -se), romantic novelist, romanticist.
romantiseer', (ge-), romanticize.
romantisis'me, romanticism.
roman'werke, fiction.
rom'bies, (-e), rhombic.
romboë'der, (-s), rhombohedron.
romboë'dries, (-e), rhombohedral.
romboïdaal', (..**dale**), rhomboid(al).
romboï'de, (-s), **romboïed'**, (-e), rhomboid.
rom'bus, (-se), rhombus.
Ro'me, Rome; *hoe nader aan ~, hoe slegter CHRISTEN*, the nearer the church, the farther from God; *~ is nie in een DAG gebou nie*, Rome was not built in a day; *as 'n mens in ~ is, moet jy maak soos die ROMEINE*, when in Rome do as the Romans do.
romein'[1], roman type.
Romein'[2], (-e), Roman; ~**s'**, (-e), Roman; ~*se LETTERS*, Roman letters, uncials; ~*s Hollandse REG*, (vero.), Roman-Dutch Law; ~*se SYFERS*, Roman numerals.
ro'merig, (-e), creamy.
ro'mery, (-e), creamery.
ro'mig, (-e), creamy.
rom'mel, (s) lumber, litter, mess, refuse, garbage, rubbish, frippery, trash, paraphernalia, junk; confusion; flotsam and jetsam; (w) (ge-), rumble (of thunder); rummage; ~**(a)ry**, lumber, rubbish; ~**hoop**, scrap-heap, ~**ig**, (-e) = **rommelrig**; ~**ing**, (-e), rumbling; ~**kamer**, lumber-room; ~**kas**, lumber-box; soldier's box; ~**kaswet**, omnibus act; ~**plek**, glory-hole; ~**pot**, rumbler; ~**raper**, kennel-raker; ~**rig**, (-e), untidy, littery, disorderly; ~**sakkie**, tidy; ~**solder**, lumber-room, loft; ~**spul**, job lot; ~**strooiing**, littering, ~**terrein**, scrap-yard; ~**verkoping**, rummage sale, jumble sale; ~**werf**, scrap-yard; ~**wetsontwerp**, omnibus bill; ~**winkel**, jumble-shop, clobbertique.
romp, (-e), trunk (of person), torso; barrel; hull (ship); carcase; skirt; fuselage; ~ *en stomp*, lock, stock and barrel; ~**slomp**, bother, ado; red tape; *administratiewe ~*, administrative red tape.
rond, (-e), round; rotund; orbicular, orbed; *'n ~e GETAL*, a round number; *'n ~e JAAR*, a full year; *hy gaan die LAND ~*, he goes all over the country; *'n ~e SOM*, a round sum; *in ~e SYFERS*, in round figures; *die ~e WAARHEID vertel*, tell the plain truth; *~e WASVAT*, round buddle; ~**agtig**, (-e), roundish; ~**agtigheid**, roundishness.
rondas', (-se), buckler, shield.
ronda'wel, (-s), round hut, rondavel; ~**huis**, cottage in rondavel style.
rond'basuin, (-ge-), trumpet abroad, spread the news, blaze forth.
rond'boog, round arch, Roman arch.
rondbor'stig, (-e), candid, frank, outspoken, plainly, outright; declaredly; ~**heid**, candour, frankness, straightforwardness, outspokenness.
rond'breimasjien, circular knitting machine.
rond'brief, (-ge-), spread, announce (by circular).
rond'bring, (-ge-), carry round; serve round; deliver (to the customer); ~**er**, roundsman.
rond'dans, (-ge-), dance about.
rond'deel, (-ge-), deal round, distribute, hand round; serve.
rond'dien, (-ge-), serve round, hang round.
rond'dobber, (-ge-), drift about.
rond'doling, wandering.
rond'dool, (-ge-), wander about, rove, roam, ramble (about); ..**doler**, (-s), rambler.
rond'dra, (-ge-), carry about (around).
rond'draai, (-ge-), rotate, turn round, spin round, eddy, gyrate, circumgyrate, circle; linger, loiter; ~**end**, (-e), rotary, turning, gyratory, peristrephic; ~**ing**, eddying, gyration, circumgyration.
rond'draf, (-ge-), trot about.
rond'drentel, (-ge-), lounge about, loiter about, gad about.

rond'dryf, rond'drywe, (-ge-), drift (float) about.
rond'dwaal, (-ge-), roam, wander about, range.
rond'dwarrel, (-ge-), whirl about.
ron'de, (-s), round, tour; beat (of sentry); patrol; lap (of race); *'n ~ DRANKIES,* a round of drinks; *~ s UITDEEL,* let fly with the fists; deal out punches right and left.
ron'dedans, ring-dance, roundel(ay).
rondeel', (rondele), rondeau, rondel; roundel (tower).
ron'de: *~* **hoek,** radius corner (mech.); *~* **hout,** spar; *~* **kop,** cup-headed; button-head (bolt); *~* **kopbout,** round-headed bolt; *~* **kophamer,** ball-peen hammer; *~* **lied,** round; *~* **rig, (-e),** roundish; *~* **roei,** cot-bar; *~* **saag,** buzz-saw; *~* **skaaf,** circular plane; *~* **skag,** circular shaft; *~* **sny,** (whole) slice of bread; *~* **wurm,** nematode.
rond'fladder, (-ge-), flutter about.
rond'flenter, (-ge-), flutter about, knock about the streets, gallivant.
rond'gaan, (-ge-), go about, go round, circulate; get about; *iets LAAT ~,* pass something round; *PRAATJIES gaan rond,* it is rumoured.
rond'gaande, rotary; travelling; ambulatory; encyclical; circular; *~ BRIEF,* circular letter; *~ HOF,* circuit court; eyre.
rond'gang, perambulation, beat, circuit, round; tour; *~ in sy KIESAFDELING,* tour of his constituency; *OP ~,* on circuit.
rond'gee, (-ge-), hand round, pass round.
rond'giet, (-ge-), circumfuse.
rond'gooi, (-ge-), fling about.
rondhang, (go), idle, hang about.
rond'heid, roundness, rotundity, circularity.
rond'hol, (-ge-), run about, roam about, frisk about, rush about.
ron'ding, (-e, -s), rounding, curve; *~ boontoe,* camber (of road); *~* **smeter,** spherometer.
rond'jakker, (-ge-), career about.
rond'jie, (-s), round of drinks; *'n ~ trakteer,* stand a round.
rond'jol, (-ge-), gallivant.
rond'kom, (-ge-), come round; manage, make ends meet; *met 'n klein pensioentjie ~,* manage on a small pension.
rond'koppig, (-e), bullet-headed.
rond'kruip, (-ge-), crawl about.
rond'kuier, (-ge-), stroll about; visit friends.
rond'kyk, (-ge-), look about; *~* **toer,** sight-seeing tour.
rond'lê, (-ge-), lie about; laze; *gerugte wat ~,* rumours which are going round; *~* **er, (-s),** lounger, loafer.
rond'lei, (-ge-), lead about; *iem. oral ~,* show a person over a place.
rond'loop, (-ge-), stroll, loaf, walk (gad) about; ramble; (per)ambulate, circumambulate; *met 'n LYS ~,* make a house-to-house collection; *met 'n PLAN ~,* have a scheme in mind.
rond'loper, (-s), loafer, tramp, vagrant, gadabout, ranger, vagabond, hobo, *~* **hond,** pariah dog.
rond'luier, (-ge-), lounge about, laze.
rond'maal, (-ge-), mill around.
rond'neem, (-ge-), take round, show round.
ron'do, (-'s), rondeau, rondel.
rond'om, all round, on every side, around; *~ toe,* ring-fenced; closed on every side; *~* **heen,** on all sides; *~* **sny,** whole slice.
rondomta'lie, (s) pug-mill; (b) round about, in a circle; whirling (platform); *~ draai,* turn round quickly (completely), spin round.
rond'peuter, (-ge-), mess (potter) about; *~* **ing,** pottering.
rond'reis, (s) (circular) tour; wayfaring; itinerancy; (w) **(-ge-),** travel about, tour; peregrinate; *~* **end, (-e),** ambulant, itinerant; *~* **kaartjie,** circular ticket; *~* **pos,** itinerant post.
rond'rits, (-ge-), gallivant, gad about.
rond'rol, (-ge-), roll around, toss.
rond'ry, (-ge-), ride (drive) about.
rond'saag, jigsaw.
rond'sel, (-s), pinion; *~* **as,** pinion-shaft; *~* **huis,** pinion-case.
rond'skaaf, rounding plane, fluting plane.
rond'skarrel, (-ge-), scramble about, potter about, mess about.
rond'skink, (-ge-), pour out (drinks, tea) all round.
rond'skommel, (-ge-), shake; swing about.
rond'skrif, round hand(writing).
rond'skryf, rond'skrywe, (-ge-), write (send letters) to different places (people).
rond'skrywe, (-s), circular (letter); questionnaire.
rond'sleep, (-ge-), drag around (about).
rond'slenter, (-ge-), lounge about, loaf about, idle about, gad about.
rond'slinger, (-ge-), fling about; loaf about.
rond'sluip, (-ge-), steal (prowl) about; *~* **er,** prowler.
rond'smous, (-ge-), hawk round, cadge, huckster.
rond'smyt, (-ge-), fling about, chuck round.
rond'snuffel, (-ge-), nose round, poke about, sniff about (around); fossick.
rond'soek, (-ge-), look around, search all over; grope; *~* **er, (-s),** groper.
rond'spartel, (-ge-), jumble; flounder.
rond'spook, (-ge-), wrestle; be busy; haunt.
rond'spring, (-ge-), jump about, romp; prevaricate; chop and change; *hy het lelik rondgespring,* he had all kinds of excuses; *~* **erig, (-e),** desultory, disconnected; evasive.
rond'staan, (-ge-), stand about; loiter; bulge.
rond'stapper, (-s), itinerant, peripatetic.
rond'strooi, (-ge-), strew about, scatter about; circulate, spread (news), rumour; intersperse; litter; *~* **er,** circulator; *~* **ing,** interspersion.
rond'stuur, (-ge-), send about (round).
rond'swalk, (-ge-), toss about; drift about.
rond'swerf, rond'swerwe, (-ge-), roam about, wander about.
rond'swier, (-ge-), glide about; stroll about.
rond'tas, (-ge-), feel about, grope about; *in die donker ~,* grope about in the dark.
rond'te, (-s), round; circle; circumference; roundness; beat; lap (of track); round (of golf); *AL in die ~,* in a circle; *die ~ van Vader CLOETE doen,* call on everybody in turn; *die ~ DOEN,* make one's rounds.
rond'tol, (-ge-), whirl round.
rond'trap, (-ge-), tread about; be restless (horse).
rond'trek, (-ge-), move (journey) about; (per)ambulate; itinerate; pull about; *~* **kend, (-e),** vagrant, nomadic, itinerant, peripatetic, perambulatory.
rond'uit, outspokenly, frankly, roundly, outright, flatly; *~ GESÊ,* frankly, candidly; *om dit MAAR ~ te sê,* to put it bluntly; *~ PRAAT,* speak out freely, speak one's mind, *iem. ~ die WAARHEID sê,* tell someone some hometruths; *~ WEIER,* refuse flatly.
rond'vaar, (-ge-), sail about, cruise; *~* **t,** circular trip; cruise.
rond'val, (-ge-), beat about, rush around; cast about; *~ vir,* cast about for.
rond'vat, (-ge-), fumble (about); take round.
rond'vent, (-ge-), hawk about, peddle.
rond'vertel, (~), spread round (news), blab, blaze abroad; let out (secret); circulate (scandal).
rond'vlieg, (-ge-), fly about (round).
rond'vlug, (s) circuitous flight, round-flight; (w) **(-ge-),** flee from place to place.
rond'voer, (-ge-), lead about.
rond'vra, (-ge-), inquire (all over).
rond'vraag, inquiry by circular letter; question-time; general (on agenda); *iets in ~ BRING,* put the question; *die ~ DOEN,* inquire of those present.
rond'waar, (-ge-), haunt, wander about.
rond'wandel, (-ge-), walk about, perambulate; expatiate; *~* **ing,** perambulation.
rond'weg, roundly, frankly, outspokenly, fairly and squarely.
rond'wentel, (-ge-), revolve, rotate.
ro'neo, (ge-), duplicate, roneo (registered trade name); *~* **masjien,** duplicating (roneo) machine.
rong, (-e), standard, stanchion (wagon); rung (of ladder).
ronk, (ge-), snore; snort; throb, purr (of engine).
ron'kedoor, (..dore), rogue elephant.

ron'sel, (ge-), impress, crimp (soldiers); ~**aar, (-s),** crimp.
rönt'gen, röntgen; ~**apparaat,** Röntgen (X-ray) apparatus; ~**foto,** ~**gram,** X-ray photo(graph); ~**fotograaf, (..grawe),** radiographer; ~**fotografie',** radiography; ~**ologie',** radiology; ~**oloog, (..loë),** radiologist, X-ray specialist; ~**ondersoek,** X-ray examination; ~**strale,** Röntgen rays, X-rays; ~**toestel,** Röntgen (X-ray) apparatus.
roof¹, (s) (rowe), scab; scurf; exuvial, slough (wound).
roof², (s) plunder, booty, swag, loot; prey, ravin (poet.); rapine, depredation, raid, foray; **(w) (ge-),** rob, loot, plunder, pillage, pirate, raven; rape; capture; filch, foray, filibuster; ~**aanval,** robbery; ~**agtig, (-e),** rapacious, plunderous; ~**arend,** tawny-eagle; ~**bou,** exhaustion of arable land, exploitational cropping, overcropping, continuous cropping; ~**dier,** beast of prey; ~**duiker,** frigate-bird; ~**ekspedisie,** marauding (looting) expedition; ~**gie'rig, (-e),** rapacious, plunderous; ravenous; ~**kewer,** rove-beetle; ~**meeu,** great skua; *bruin* ~*meeu,* Antarctic skua; ~**moord,** murder with intent to rob; ~**oorval,** hold-up, robbery; ~**politiek,** policy of spoliation; ~**ridder,** robber-knight; ~**siek, (-e),** rapacious; ~**skip,** pirate ship; ~**sug,** rapacity; ~**sug'tig, (-e),** rapacious; vulturous, predatory; predacious; ~**tog,** marauding (looting) expedition; razzia; prowl, raid; ~**vis,** fish of prey; ~**vlieg,** hornet, ~**voël,** bird of prey; raptorial.
roof'vorming, incrustation.
roof'vyand, predator.
Rooi¹, Communistic; *die* ~ *leër,* the Red (Russian) army.
rooi², Pro-English; *die R~es,* the English.
rooi³, red; ruddy; damask; gules (her.); ~ *BLOEDLIGGAAMPIE,* red corpuscle; *hoe* ~*er hoe MOOIER,* a dash (pennyworth) of red works wonders; ~ *WORD,* grow red; blush; ~**aarde,** red ochre, ruddle; ~**aas,** red-bait (ascidian used as bait); ~**agtig, (-e),** reddish; ~**assie,** orange-breasted waxbill; ~**baadjie, (-s),** red-coat (British soldier); hopper (locust); ~**beet,** beet; ~**bekeend,** red-bill teal; ~**bekkakelaar,** red-billed hoopoe; ~**bekkie, (-s),** robin redbreast, common waxbill; *grys* ~*bekkie,* lavender finch; ~**bekvink,** red-billed finch, quelea; ~**bessie,** hard-pear; ~**blaar,** bush-willow; ~**blom,** witchweed; Matabele flower *(Striga lutea);* ~**bok,** redbuck, impala (antelope); ~**bolus,** red bolus; ~**bont,** red-speckled; roan (cattle), skewbald (horse); ~**borsduifie,** laughing dove; ~**bors, (-s),** robin redbreast; ~**borslaksman,** crimson-breasted shrike; ~**bos,** red bush *(Borbonia spp.);* ~**bostee,** redbush tea; ~**breukig, (-e),** red short (iron); ~**bruin,** reddish brown; sorrel (horse), rubiginous, puce; foxy (paint); ~**dag,** dawn, daybreak, aurora; ~**dagwag,** morning watch; ~**derm,** oesophagus; ~**doek,** Turkey twill; ~**dopluis,** red scale; ~**doring,** red-thorn *(Acacia gerrardi);* ~**duiker,** red (Natal) duiker; R~**e, (-s),** Communist; Britisher; ~**e,** red one; jingo; ~**-els,** red alder; ~**erig, (-e),** reddish; rubicund; ~**erigheid,** reddishness; ~**esse(n)houtboom,** thunder tree; Natal mahogany; ~**geel,** fulvous; ~**gloeiend, (-e),** red-hot; ~**gom,** red gum; ~**gras,** red-grass; ~**greinhout,** redwood; ~**grond,** red keel; ~**haar-,** red-haired; ~**haartjie,** red erica; ~**haas,** rock-hare; ~**harig, (-e),** red-haired; ~**heid,** redness; rubicundity; heat; ~**hitte,** red heat; ~'**hond,** German measles; prickly heat; rubeola, rubella; ~**hout,** redwood, Cape plane; red ivory *(Rhamnus zeyheri);* ~**houtjies,** logwood; R~**huid,** Red Indian, Redskin; ~**jakkals,** red jackal; R~**kappie,** Red Riding-Hood; ~**kat,** serval (cerval) cat; lynx, caracal; ~**keelfisant,** rednecked frankolin; ~**klei,** red clay; raddle; ~**kleurig, (-e),** ruddy, red-coloured; ~**kool,** red cabbage; ~**kop,** red-head; "carrots", "ginger"; ~**koper,** red copper; ~**kopibis,** bald ibis; ~**krans(boom),** *Acacia cyclops;* ~**kwas,** April fool (flower); ~**looderts,** crocoite; ~**maakmiddel,** rubefacient; ~**manna,** red millet; ~**meerkat,** bushy-tailed meerkat; ~**melkhout,** red milkwood; ~**menie,** red lead; minium; ~**mier,** red ant; ~**muur,** scarlet pimpernel.
Rooi'nek, pommy, limey, Englishman.
rooi: ~**nekduiker,** loom (bird); ~**oker,** raddle; ~**padda,** bull frog; ~**pensskilpad,** angulate tortoise; ~**peper,** cayenne pepper; R~**poenskop,** Red-Poll; ~**pootelsie,** black-winged stilt; ~**pootjie,** Cape hare; ~**pypie,** watsonia; red africander; ~**ribbok,** mountain reedbuck; ~**roes,** brown rust; ~**sel,** rouge; ~**skimmel(perd),** (strawberry) roan, red roan (horse); ~**smeer, (-ge-),** ruddle, reddle; ~**steenbras,** red steenbras; ~**stompneus,** red stumpnose; ~**tjie, (-s),** silver-fish.
Rooi'taal, English; *hy gooi die* ~ *goed,* he speaks English like a native.
rooi: ~**valk,** kestrel; ~**vink,** redpoll, red finch (bishopbird); ~**vlagdraer,** danger-man; ~**vleis,** red meat; ~**vlerkpatrys,** red-wing partridge; ~**vlerkspreeu,** red-winged starling; ~**vonk,** scarlatina, scarlet fever; ~**vrot,** pink rot; ~**wangig, (-e),** red-cheeked; ~**wangparkiet,** rosy-faced lovebird; ~**water,** Texas fever; redwater (cattle); bilharziosis (humans); ~**ysterklip,** red-granite; norite.
rook, (s) smoke; fume; *hulle het al* ~ *GEMAAK,* they have already obtained their parents' consent to their marriage; *in* ~ *OPGAAN,* go up in smoke; *g'n* ~ *sonder VUUR nie,* there is no smoke without fire; **(w) (ge-),** smoke; reek; cure (meat); gammon (ham); smoke-dry; fume; *hy* ~ *soos 'n skoorsteen,* he smokes like a chimney; ~**afdeling,** smoking-compartment; ~**agtig, (-e),** smoky; ~**ammunisie,** smoke; ~**baadjie,** smoking-jacket; ~**baar, (..bare),** smokable; ~**bom,** smoke-bomb; ~**dig, (-te),** smoke-tight; ~**gang,** flue; ~**gas,** fuel-gas; ~**gat,** fumarole (volcano); ~**gewend, (-e),** smoke-producing; ~**glas,** smoked glass; ~**goed,** smoking-requisites; smokables; ~**gordyn,** smoke-screen; ~**granaat,** smoke grenade; ~**haring,** kippered herring; ~**kamer,** smoking-room; ~**kanaal,** smoke-tube; boiler-flue; ~**kas,** smoke-box; ~**kers,** smoke-candle; ~**koeël,** smoke-ball; ~**kolom,** pillar of smoke; ~**kompartement,** smokers' compartment; ~**konsert,** smoking-concert; ~**loos, (..lose),** smokeless; ~**lug,** smell of smoke; ~**masker,** smoke-mask; ~**mis,** smog; ~**mortier,** smoke-mortar; ~**pot,** smoke-pot; ~**pyp,** flue; ~**salon,** smoking-room; ~**sas,** smoke-producing composition; ~**skerm,** smoke-screen; camouflage; ~**skrif,** smoke-writing; sky-writing; ~**skuif,** smoke-damper; ~**sluier,** smoke-sceen; ~**smaak,** smoky flavour; ~**spek,** smoked bacon; ~**suil,** smoke-pillar; ~**swak, (-ke),** smokeless; ~**tabak,** smoking-tobacco; ~**tafeltjie,** smoking-table; ~**topaas,** cairngorm; ~**tregter,** smoke-pillar; ~**trommel,** smoke-drum; ~**vanger,** smoke-jack; ~**verbrander,** smoke-consumer; ~**verdrywer, (-s),** smoke-expeller; ~**vleis,** smoked meat; ~**vry, (-e),** smokeless; ~**wolk,** cloud (gust) of smoke; pother; ~**wors,** smoked sausage.
room, cream; head (milk); *die* ~ *AFSKEP,* skim the cream from; *BESKERMENDE* ~, barrier cream; *DOOIE* ~, sleepy cream; ~**afskeier,** (cream-)separator; ~**agtig, (-e),** creamy; ~**bewerking,** processing (cream); ~**gehalte,** cream content; ~**horinkie,** cream horn; ~**huis,** creamery; ~**kaas,** cream cheese; ~**kan,** cream can; ~**kleur,** cream colour; ~**kleurig, (-e),** cream(-coloured); ~**klopper,** whisk; ~**koekie,** cream cake; ~**laag, (..lae),** cream layer; ~**peperment,** peppermint cream; ~**poeier,** cream powder; ~**poffertjie,** cream puff.
Rooms, (-e), Roman Catholic; popish; ~**gesind, (-e),** Roman Catholic; ~**-Katoliek, (-e),** Roman Catholic.
room: ~**soesie, (-s),** cream puff; ~**tert,** cream tart, éclair.
room'ys, ice-cream; hokey-pokey (street); ~**karretjie,** ice-cream cart; ~**melk,** milkshake; ~**piesang,** banana split.
roos¹, erysipelas; eczema; roseola, rose-rash.
roos², (rose), rose; *'n* ~ *tussen die DORINGS,* a rose among thorns; *geen* ~ *sonder DORINGS,* no rose without a thorn; *ONDER die* ~, under the rose; in confidence; *rose op iem. se PAD strooi,* strew roses

on someone's path; *SLAAP soos 'n* ~, sleep like a top; *rose op die WANGE hê*, have rosy cheeks.
roos'agtig¹, (-e), erysipelatous.
roos'agtig², (-e), rosy.
roos: ~ **boom**, rose-tree; ~ **bottel**, rose-hip; ~ **geur**, *see* **rosegeur**; ~ **hout**, rosewood; ~ **kleur**, rose-colour; ~ **kleurig**, (-e), rose-coloured, rosy, pink; healthy; ~ **knop**, rose-bud; hip; ~ **kweker**, (-s), rose-grower, rosarian; ~ **laning**, rose hedge; ~ **maryn'**, rosemary; ~ **olie**, oil of roses; otto; attar; ~ **rooi**, rose-coloured, pink; ~ **steek**, bullion stitch; ~ **steggie**, ~ **stiggie**, rose-cutting; ~ **struik**, rose-bush.
roos'ter, (s) (-s), gridiron, grate, grill, griller; griddle; grating; rack (for luggage); timetable; *volgens* ~ *AFTREE*, retire in rotation; *'n* ~ *van WERK= SAAMHEDE*, a timetable; (w) (-ge-), roast, grill; broil; toast (bread); ~ **brood**, toast; ~ **gereg**, grill; ~ **hek**, motor-gate, grid; ~ **kaas**, rarebit; Welsh rabbit; ~ **koek**, girdle-cake; bannock; muffin; griddle-cake; ~ **kuiken**, broiler; ~ **oond**, griller, grilling furnace; ~ **oppervlakte**, grate-area; ~ **pan**, broiler pan; grilling-pan; ~ **raam**, bar frame; ~ **sif**, grizzly (mining); ~ **standertjie**, toast-rack; ~ **struk= tuur**, cross-hatching; ~ **vleis**, grill; ~ **vurk**, toasting-fork; ~ **wapening**, two-way reinforcement; ~ **werk**, grate, grating; grillage, grill(e); ~ **yster**, fire-bar.
roos: ~ **tuin**, rose-garden; rosarium, rosary; ~ **uitslag**, roseola, rose-rash; ~ **venster**, rose-window; Catherine-wheel; ~ **vingerig**, (-e), rosy-fingered; ~ **water**, rose-water.
root, retting-place (for flax).
ropy', (-e) = **roepee**.
ros¹, (vero.), (s) (-se), steed, horse.
ros², (b) (-se), reddish-brown, ruddy.
rosa'ki, rosaki (grape).
rô'se¹, pink.
rosé'², rosé (wine).
ro'segeur, scent of roses; *nie alles* ~ *en maneskyn nie*, life is not moonlight and roses; not all beer and skittles.
ro'sekrans, garland of roses; rosary, beads; chaplet; ~ **vormig**, (-e), moniliform.
Ro'sekruiser, (-s), Rosicrucian.
ro'serooi, rose-coloured.
roset', (-te), rosette; ~ **steen**, rose diamond.
ro'setentoonstelling, rose-show.
roset': ~ **venster**, marigold window, rosace, rose win= dow; ~ **vormig**, (-e), rosaceous.
ro'sie, (-s), small rose.
ro'sig, (-e), rosy; ~ **heid**, rosiness.
ros'kam, (s) curry-comb, (w) (ge-), curry(-comb), groom, dress (horse); criticize severely; *lem.* ~, take someone to task; give someone a dressing down.
Ross'-see, Ross Sea.
ros'sig, (-e), ruddy.
ros'trum, (-s), platform, rostrum.
rosyn', (-e), raisin.
rosyn'tjie, (-s), raisin; ~ **bos**, raisin bush; ~ **brood**, raisin bread; ~ **koek**, plum cake; ~ **ontpitter**, rai= sin-seeder; ~ **poeding**, plum pudding; ~ **rys**, rice with raisins.
rot¹, (s) (-te), rat; *jou oor 'n DOOIE* ~ *verheug*, find a mare's nest; *so KAAL soos 'n* ~, as poor as a church mouse; *hy is 'n OU* ~, an old hand; an old fox.
rot², (w) (-ge-), rot; ~ *tende blare*, rotting leaves; (b) rotten, putrid.
rot³, (bw): *iem.* ~ *en kaal STEEL*, strip someone bare.
Rotarie', Rotary (organisation); International, Rotary International.
Rota'riër, (-s), Rotarian; ~ **klub**, Rotary Club.
rota'sie, rotation; ~ **hoek**, angle of rotation; ~ **pers**, rotary press; ~ **pomp**, rotary pump.
rot'dig, (-te), vermin-proof; ~ **ting**, vermin-proofing.
roteer', (ge-), rotate.
rot'heid, rottenness, putrescence.
ro'ting, retting; ~ **sbak**, retting-tank.
rot'koors, *see* **rottekoors**.
ro'togravure, rotogravure.
roton'de, (-s), rotunda.

ro'tor, (-s), rotor; ~ **boot**, rotor-boat.
rots, (-e), rock, cliff; crag; *'n* ~ *van struikeling*, a rock of offence; ~ **afstorting**, fall of rock; ~ **agtig**, (-e), rocky; petrous; cliffy; rock-bound (coast); ~ **ag= tigheid**, craggedness, cragginess; rockiness; ~ **bank**, bank (layer) of rock; ~ **barsting**, rock-burst; ~ **blok**, lump of rock, boulder; ~ **bodem**, rock-bed; ~ **boor**, rock-drill; jumper; ~ **breker**, rock-breaker; ~ **eiland**, rock-island; ~ **fosfaat**, rock-phosphate; ~ **gevaarte**, rocky mass; ~ **gravering**, petroglyph; ~ **gruis**, detritus; ~ **holte**, pothole; ~ **ig**, (-e), rocky; ~ **kleur**, rock-colour; ~ **klimmer**, cragsman; ~ **koe= kie**, rock-cake; ~ **kristal**, rock-crystal; ~ **kus**, rocky coast; ~ **laag**, shelf; reef; ~ **lys**, ledge; ~ **massa**, rocky mass; ~ **mossel**, limpet; ~ **opvulling**, pack= (ing), stowing; ~ **plant**, rock-plant; ~ **punt**, crag; ~ **rand**, rocky ledge; ~ **skeur**, rock-burst; ~ **skil= dering**, ~ **skildery**, rock-painting; ~ **skuiling**, rock-shelter; ~ **skulp**, limpet; ~ **spelonk**, rocky cave, grotto; ~ **spleet**, rock-crevice; ~ **steen**, rock (also fig.); ~ **storting**, fall of rock, rock-fall; ~ **tekening**, rock-engraving; ~ **tonnel**, tunnel through rock; ~ **tuin**, rockery; ~ **vas**, (-te), firm as a rock; ~ **wand**, rock-face, precipice; ~ **wol**, rock-wool; ~ **woning**, cave-dwelling.
rot'tang, (-s), cane, rattan; calamus; ~ **agtig**, (-e), cane-like; ~ **kierie**, cane walking-stick; ~ **mandjie**, cane-basket; ~ **mat**, cane-seat; ~ **meubels**, cane furniture; ~ **olie**, strap-oil; ~ *olie gee*, cane; ~ **werk**, cane-work.
rot'tankie, (-s), little cane.
rot'te, ~ **gat**, rat-burrow, ~ **gif**, rat-poison; ~ **jag**, rat-hunting; ~ **koors**, putrid fever; ~ **kruid**, ar= senic, ratsbane; ~ **nes**, rat's nest; ~ **neus**, glanders; ~ **pes**, bubonic plague; ~ **plaag**, rat pest; ~ **val**, rat-trap; ~ **vanger**, (-s), rat-catcher; ~ **verdelging**, rat-extermination.
rot'ting, putrefaction, decay, putrescence; ~ **sput**, septic tank.
rou¹, (s), mourning; ~ *BEDRYF oor*, mourn for; ~ *DRA*, mourn; *in die* ~ *WEES*, be in mourning; (w) (ge-), mourn, go into mourning; *hy* ~ *vir die katte*, his nails have not been cleaned.
rou², (b) (-er, -ste), raw, uncooked; hoarse; inexperi= enced; ~ *GROND*, virgin soil; *hy is HEELTE= MAL* ~, he is quite inexperienced; ~ *LEER*, raw (untreated) hide; ~ *LYNOLIE*, raw linseed oil; ~ *STYSEL*, coldwater starch.
rou: ~ **band**, mourning-band; crêpe; ~ **bedryf**, mourning; ~ **beklag**, condolence; ~ **brief**, death-circular; letter on mourning-paper; ~ **dag**, day of mourning; ~ **diens**, memorial service; ~ **dig**, (-te), elegy; ~ **draer**, (-s), mourner.
rou'erig, (-e), half-raw, underdone.
rou: ~ **floers**, crape; ~ **gewaad**, mourning garb.
rou'heid, rawness.
rou: ~ **kaart**, in memoriam card; ~ **kamer**, funeral parlour; ~ **klaag**, (ge-), lament, bewail, mourn for; ~ **klag**, lamentation; ~ **kleed**, mourning-dress; black; ~ **koevert**, black-edged (mourning-) envel= ope; ~ **koop**, forfeit-money; rue-bargain; ~ **krans**, funeral wreath
roulette', roulette.
rou: ~ **lint**, mourning-ribbon; ~ **papier**, mourning-paper; ~ **rand**, black border.
rou'riem, tenderfoot, newcomer, novice; uncouth person.
rou'sluier, widow's veil, weeper.
rou: ~ **sool**, untanned leather; ~ **soolveldskoen**, shoe made of untanned leather; ~ **span**, awkward squad.
rou'stasie, funeral procession; cortège.
rou'steen, clay brick, unbaked brick.
rou'tyd, period of mourning.
rou'vel, raw hide.
rou'vlag, flag of mourning, flag flying half-mast.
roux, roux.
ro'we, (ge-), rob, plunder, loot, pillage; *see* **roof**.
ro'wer, (-s), robber, pirate, brigand, filibuster, ravisher; pillager; picaroon; highwayman; ~ **bende**, band of robbers; ~ **hoofman**, robber chief.
ro'wershol, robbers' den.

rower: ~skip, pirate ship; ~y, (-e), robbery.

ru, (ruwe; -wer, ruuste), rough (treatment); rude, coarse, discourteous (remarks); harsh, hard, foul (language); raw, uncouth (person); agrestic; craggy, jagged (rocks); hard-mouthed; gross; braky; crude (oil); rugged (hills); *'n ruwe HANDDOEK*, a coarse towel; *'n ruwe SEE*, a rough sea; *ruwe SKATTING*, rough estimate, guesstimate.

rubar'ber, rhubarb; *see* **rabarber.**

rub'ber¹, (-s), rubber (in bridge).

rub'ber², rubber; ~**aanplanting,** rubber plantation; ~**boom,** rubber tree; ~**bootjie,** (rubber) dinghy; ~**kloupleister,** rubber adhesive plaster; ~**lym,** rubber solution; ~**maatskappy,** rubber company; ~**plantasie,** rubber plantation; ~**pyp,** hose; ~**skyf,** puck; ~**stempel,** rubber stamp; ~**stewel,** rubber (gum-)boot.

ru'beitel, broach.

rubel'la = **rooihond.**

rubeo'la, *see* **masels.**

Ru'bicon: *die* ~ *oortrek,* cross the Rubicon.

ru'blaar(tert)deeg, rough puff pastry.

ru'borduurwerk, collage.

rubriek', (-e), rubric, category, head, column (newspaper); feature (show); ~**letter,** rubric letter; ~**skrywer,** columnist.

rubriseer', (ge-), rubricate; class.

rubrise'ring, classification.

rudiment', (-e), rudiment; ~**êr',** (-e), rudimentary.

rû'ensagteroor, straight back.

rû'ensveld, ridgy country (with many low ridges).

rug¹, (-ge, rûe, rûens), back; bridge (of nose); spine (of book); *in die* ~ *AANVAL*, attack in the rear; *AGTER die* ~, behind the back; *hy het al baie AGTER die* ~, he has been through much; *dis gelukkig AGTER die* ~, fortunately that is over and done with; *AGTER iem. se* ~, behind someone's back; *hy het 'n BREË* ~, he has broad shoulders; he can bear responsibility; *agter sy* ~ *iets DOEN*, do something behind someone's back; *die* ~ *op iem. DRAAI*, turn one's back on someone; *dis GELUKKIG agter die* ~, fortunately that is over; *baie JARE agter die* ~ *hê*, be old; *KRAP my* ~, *dan krap ek joue*, you roll my log, and I'll roll yours; *met die* ~ *teen die MUUR staan*, have one's back to the wall; *agter iem. se* ~ *PRAAT*, talk behind someone's back; *op iem. se* ~ *RY*, sponge on someone; *op die* ~ *gaan STAAN*, lie down; *iem. in die* ~ *STEEK*, stab someone in the back; *'n STOEL met 'n hoë* ~, high-backed chair; *iem. die* ~ *TOEKEER*, turn one's back on someone; *jou* ~ *VET smeer*, prepare oneself for a hiding.

rug², (-gens, rûens), ridge, hill.

ru'-gare, ru'-garing, cotton (linen) thread.

rug'baar, notorious, well-known; ~ *MAAK*, make (publicly) known; ~ *WORD*, get (noised) abroad, become known; ~**heid,** notoriety, publicity.

rug'by, rugby; ~**administrateur,** rugby administrator; ~**baas,** rugby boss; ~**speler,** rugby player; ~**unie,** rugby union; ~**veld,** rugby field; ~**voetbal,** rugby football; ~**wedstryd,** rugby match.

rug'dop, carapace.

ru'-gekap, (-te), rough-hewn, rough-axed; ~ *te klip*, hammer-faced stone.

ru'-gewals, (-te), roughcast.

rug: ~**graat,** backbone, spine, chine; ~**graatkoors,** meningitis; ~**graatvekromming,** curvature of the spine; ~**haal,** backstroke (swimming); ~**hou,** backhand shot (tennis); ~**kant,** back; blunt side (knife); ~**klopper,** back-slapper; ~**krapper,** back-scratcher (lit. and fig.), toady; **krappery,** back-scratching; ~**lat,** spit; ~**leuning,** back (of chair); back-rest, backboard; ~**materiaal,** backing (books); ~**murg,** spinal (-cord) marrow; ~**murgontsteking,** meningitis; myelitis; ~**murgtering,** spinal consumption; locomotor ataxy; ~**plank,** backboard; ~**plooi,** anticline; ~**pyn,** backache; ~**ryer,** parasite; ~**saag,** tenon-saw, back-saw; ~**sak,** rucksack; ~**sening,** dorsal nerve; ~**skerm,** parados; ~**skild,** carapace, elytron; ~**slag,** back-stroke (tennis); ~**spier,** dorsal muscle; ~**spraak,** consultation; ~**spraak hou met,** confer with, take counsel with someone; ~**spuitpomp,** knapsack sprayer; ~**steun,** (s) back, bolster, support; (w) (ge-), support; ~**streep,** line (on animal's body); ~**string,** spinal cord, vertebral column, chine; ~**stuk,** saddle (of beef, mutton); chine (pork); ~**stut,** bed-rest; support (for back); ~**stutkruisbande,** spinal brace; ~**stutwerk,** ashlaring; ~**teken,** (ge-), endorse; ~**tekening,** endorsement; ~**tering,** spinal caries; ~**veer,** scapular; ~**verf,** backing (photo); ~**vin,** dorsal fin; ~**vinwalvis,** rorqual, razor-back whale; ~**vlug,** inverted flight; ~**voeg,** saddle-joint; ~**vuur,** reverse fire; ~**waarts,** (b) (-e), backward; (bw) backward(s); ~**weer,** parados; ~**werwel,** (-s), dorsal vertebra; ~**wind,** rear wind; ~**wol,** backs (wool); rig wool.

ru'harig, (-e), shaggy, rough-coated; wire-haired (dog).

ru'heid, roughness; rudeness, coarseness; ruggedness; asperity, harshness; cragginess.

Ruhr, Ruhr; ~**gebied,** Ruhr area.

rui, (ge-), moult.

ruig, (ruie; -er, -ste), bushy, shrubby, dense, brushy; hirsute, hispid, shaggy, hairy; ~**heid,** bushiness, shrubbiness; hairiness; ~**te,** undergrowth, copse, jungle, bosk, bosket, coppice, bosquet, covert; rough (golf).

ruik, (s) (-e), scent, smell, odour; perfume; *van iets* ~ *KRY*, smell a rat; *in SLEGTE* ~ *staan*, be in bad repute (odour); (w) (ge-), smell, scent; sniff; ~ *AAN*, smell, have a sniff at; *ek KON dit nie* ~ *nie*, how could I possibly know it; *jy sal daar NOOIT aan* ~ *nie*, you'll never see it; *STERK* ~ *na drank*, smell strongly of liquor; *WATER* ~ *nie*, water has no smell; ~**er,** (-s), nosegay, buttonhole; bouquet, posy; smeller; ~**ertjie,** (-s), nosegay, buttonhole; ~**ie,** (-s), whiff, slight smell; *daar is 'n* ~*ie aan*, there is something unsavoury (fishy) about it; ~**klier,** scent-gland.

ruil, (s) exchange, barter; *'n goeie* ~ *aangaan*, make a good bargain; (w) (ge-), barter, exchange; dicker; *nie GRAAG met iem. wil* ~ *nie*, not like to be in someone's shoes; *as twee* ~, *moet een HUIL*, someone always has the worst of a bargain; ~**artikel,** article of barter; ~**baar,** (..bare), exchangeable; interchangeable; ~**eksemplaar,** exchange copy; ~**geld,** token money; ~**handel,** barter; truck; ~**ing,** exchange; ~**middel,** medium of exchange; circulation (coin); ~**nommer,** exchange copy; ~**ooreenkoms,** barter agreement; ~**professor,** exchange professor; ~**stelsel,** system of exchange; ~**tog,** bartering expedition; ~**verdrag,** treaty of barter; ~**verkeer,** traffic trade (in kind); barter; ~**waarde,** exchange value.

ruim, (s) hold, bulge (of a ship); nave (of church); firmament; (w) (ge-), make room, empty, evacuate; plug; rectify; ream; widen; *vir iem. die VELD* ~, yield ground to an opponent; *uit die WEG* ~, remove (misunderstanding); (b, bw) ((-e), -er, -ste), ample, wide, spacious, expansive; full (dress); plentiful; commodious, roomy; broadminded, liberal (outlook); accommodating (conscience); in every way; generous, handsome; *'n* ~ *BLIK*, a broad outlook; *mense wat* ~ *DINK*, broadminded people; *DIT nie* ~ *hê nie*, be in straitened circumstances; ~ *GEDRUK*, loosely printed; *'n* ~ *GEWETE*, an elastic conscience; *dit* ~ *HÊ*, be in affluent circumstances; *'n JAAR gelede*, more than a year ago; *'n* ~ *e KEUSE*, a wide choice; *'n* ~ *KRING*, a wide circle; ~ *MEET*, measure liberally; *in die* ~ *ste SIN v.d. woord*, in the fullest sense of the word; ~ *VYFTIG jaar*, over fifty years; ~**boor,** reamer bit (iron); ~**er,** (-s), cesspool-emptier; fraise rectifier (drill), reamer, broach; ~**har'tig,** (-e), broadminded; ~**heid,** spaciousness, roominess, width, ampleness; ~**ing,** plugging; evacuation (of house); ~**naald,** priming-needle, primer; reamer; ~**pomp,** bilge-pump; ~**skoots,** plentiful, copiously, amply, generously.

ruim'te, (-s), room, space, commodiousness; expanse; scope, compass; clearance (in mines); interval, distance; fullness (needlew.); ~ *van BEWEGING*, elbow-room; ~ *BIED vir*, have accommodation for;

~ *van BLIK*, breadth of outlook (vision); *GE=BREK aan* ~, cramped for room; *skepe KIES die* ~, ships put out to sea; *die ONEINDIGE* ~, infinite space; *in die* ~ *PRAAT*, indulge in empty talk; *WEENS gebrek aan* ~, owing to lack of space; ~**beperking**, limitation of space; ~**gebrek**, lack of space; ~**-inhoud**, cubic capacity; ~**kunde**, space science; ~**kundige**, space scientist; ~**lading**, space-charge; ~**lik, (-e)**, spatial; ~**maat**, measure of capacity, cubic measure; ~**man**, astronaut, cosmonaut; ~**meetkunde**, solid geometry; ~**merk**, clearance-indicator; ~**reisiger**, astronaut; ~**skip**, spaceship; ~**tyd**, space time; ~**vaarder**, astronaut, cosmonaut; ~**vaart**, astronautics; space travel; ~**vlug**, space travel (flight); ~**vrees**, agoraphobia.

ruim'water, bilge water.

ruim'yster, tapping-bar.

ruïna'sie, ruination.

ruï'ne, (-s), ruin.

ruïneer', (ge-), ruin, damage, play havoc among (with); ~**der**, devastator, destroyer.

ruis, (ge-), rustle, murmur; ~**ing**, rustle, rustling, murmur(ing).

ruit, (s) (-e), (window-)pane; glass; rhombus; facet (of diamond); lozenge; check (material); square (chess); chequer; (w) (ge-), chequer.

rui'te = ruitens, diamonds (cards).

rui'tekaart, grid map.

rui'te(n): ~**aas**, ace of diamonds; ~**boer**, jack of diamonds.

rui'tenet, grid

rui'te(n)heer, king of diamonds.

rui'tens, diamonds (in cards); ~ *is troef*, diamonds are trumps.

rui'te(n): ~**tien**, ten of diamonds; ~**vrou**, queen of diamonds.

rui'ter, (-s), horseman, horse-rider, chevalier, equestrian; ~**aanval**, cavalry (mounted) attack; ~**afdeling**, riding squad; ~**bal**, horseback rounders; ~**balk**, ridge rafter; ~**bende**, troop of horses; ~**geveg**, cavalry engagement; ~**in', (-ne)**, horsewoman; ~**jas**, redingote; ~**kuns**, horsemanship; ~**liedjie**, cowboy song; ~**lik, (-e)**, frank, straight out; chivalrous, cavalier; ~**likheid**, chivalrousness; frankness; ~**paadjie**, mule-track, bridle-path; ~**patrollie**, mounted patrol; ~**pistool**, horse-pistol, petronel; ~**regiment**, horse, mounted regiment; ~**salf**, mercurial ointment; ~**skap**, equitation; ~**standbeeld**, equestrian statue; ~**stoet**, cavalcade; ~**stof**, habit cloth; ~**taktiek**, mounted tactics; ~**wag**, horse-guard; mounted-rifleman guard; ~**wissel**, accommodation bill; ~**y**, cavalry, horse; ~**yskool**, cavalry school.

rui'te: ~**stelsel**, grid system; ~**wasser**, window-cleaner.

ruit'gebied, grid zone.

ruit'glas, pane-glass; ~**ring**, window bezel.

ruit'insitter, glazier.

rui'tjie, (-s), small pane; check; facet.

ruit'jies: ~**goed**, check (material); ~**papier**, squared paper; ~**pens**, honeycomb-stomach, reticulum.

ruit: ~**klem**, sprig; ~**spykertjie**, sprig; ~**koevert**, window envelope; ~**maker**, glazier; ~**papier**, quadrille paper; ~**patroon**, check pattern; ~**rubber**, glazing rubber; ~**veër**, wind-screen wiper; ~**vormig, (-e)**, rhomboidal, rhombic; diamond-shaped, lozenge-shaped; ~**werker**, glazier.

rui'tyd, moulting-time.

ruk, (s) (-ke), pull, tug, jerk, wrench; gush (of wind); while, time; *vir 'n KORT* ~, for a short while; *met* ~*ke en STOTE*, by fits and starts; (w) (ge-), pull, tug, jerk, job (of horse); overcharge; *HAND-UIT* ~, get out of hand; *iem. LELIK* ~, rook (fleece) someone; ~ *en PLUK*, pull and tug; *WOORDE uit hulle verband* ~, quote words out of their context.

ruk'-en-pluk, rock and roll (dance).

ruk'kerig, (-e), jerky, spasmodic; ~*e wind*, a gusty wind; ~**heid**, jerkiness.

ruk: ~**kie, (-s)**, moment, little time, little while; ~**king, (-s)**, convulsion; ~**kramp**, tetanic spasm, tetany.

ru'klawer, hare's foot.

ru: ~**klip**, rubble; ~**koper**, blister-copper; ~**-kos**, roughage.

ruk'skêr, jar(s).

ruk'wind, squall, gust (of wind); puff of wind.

ru'lood, pig-lead.

rum, rum.

rumatiek', rheumatism; ~druppels, rheumatism drops; ~**koors**, rheumatic fever; ~**kuur**, rheumatism cure; ~**lyer, (-s)**, rheumatic patient.

ruma'ties, (-e), rheumatic.

rum: ~**fles**, rum bottle; ~**grok**, rum toddy.

rumoer', (s) (-e), uproar, noise, rumpus, hubbub, pother, racket, fuss, boisterousness, bustle; (w) (ge-), make a noise, be rowdy; ~**ig, (-e)**, noisy, boisterous, uproarious; ~**igheid**, noisiness, rowdiness.

rum'pons, rum-punch.

rund, (-ere), bovine animal; ~**eragtig, (-e)**, bovine.

run'derpes, rinderpest.

ru'ne, (-s), rune; ~**alfabet**, runic alphabet, futhorc; ~**-inskripsie**, runic (inscription); ~**skrif**, runic (writing), rune.

ru'nies, (-e), runic.

run'nik, (ge-), neigh, whinny, hinny; ~**lag**, horselaugh.

ru'-olie, crude oil.

Rus¹, (-se), Russian.

rus², (s) rest, repose; tranquillity, peace; pause (elocution); break, leisure; dormancy; safety-catch (rifle); rest (mus.); caesura (poetry); *jou ter* ~ *e BEGEEF*, seek one's rest; *tot* ~ *BRING*, set at rest; *in DIEPE* ~, in a deep sleep; *DOOIE* ~ *skiet*, shoot at dead rest; *geen* ~ *of DUUR hê nie*, not have a moment's peace; *die EWIGE* ~ *ingaan*, pass into one's eternal rest; *ter* ~ *te GAAN*, retire, go to bed; *geen* ~ *vir die HOLTE van jou voet hê nie*, have no rest for the hollow of one's foot; *hy kan nie sy* ~ *HOU nie*, he cannot keep the peace; *IN* ~, in neutral (gear); in the safety-catch; *tot* ~ *KOM*, settle down; *met* ~ *LAAT*, leave someone in peace; *ter* ~ *te LÊ*, bury, lay to rest; ~ *ROES*, rest breeds rust; ~ *en VREDE*, peace and quiet; *volkome* ~ *VOORSKRYF*, order absolute rest; (w) **(ge-)**, rest, repose; *HIER* ~, here lies . . .; *'n saak LAAT* ~, let a matter rest; *op die PLEK* ~!, stand at ease! *die VERANTWOORDELIKHEID* ~ *op hom*, the responsibility rests on him; *WEL te* ~ *te*, good night; sleep well; ~**bank**, couch, sofa, setee, chesterfield, divan; ~**bed**, couch; ~**dag**, day of rest, Sabbath; ~**gewas**, ley crop; ~**golf**, compensating wave; spacing wave.

rus: ~**hoek**, angle of repose; ~**huis**, rest-home.

ru'sie, (-s), quarrel, dispute, brawl, bicker, breach of the peace, embroilment, wrangle, feud, altercation, fight, fracas, fray; jangle; ~ *KRY*, have a quarrel; ~ *MAAK*, quarrel, altercate; ~ *SOEK*, seek a quarrel; ~**agtig, (-e)**, quarrelsome; litigious; ~**maker, (-s)**, brawler, quarrelsome person, wrangler, bully; ~**makerig, (-e)**, quarrelsome, cantankerous, aggressive; ~**soeker, (-s)**, bully, meddler, quarreler.

rus: ~**kamer**, rest-room; ~**kamp**, rest-camp; ~**kuur**, rest-cure; ~**laer**, rest-camp; ~**land**, ley (land).

Rus'land, Russia.

ru'-sleutel, blank key.

rus: ~**oes**, ley (crop); ~**oord**, place of rest.

rus'pe(r), (-s), caterpillar; ~**band**, track (tractor); ~**bandtrekker**, caterpillar tractor; ~**graaf**, traxcavator; ~**tenk**, caterpillar tank; ~**trekker**, crawler tractor.

rus: ~**plaas**, ~**plek**, resting-place; ~**poos**, interval, half-time; pause; ~**pouse**, pause for rest; ~**punt**, (point of) rest, pause.

Russeliet', (vero.), (-e), Russellite; ~**e**, Jehovah's Witnesses.

Rus'sies, (s) Russian; (b) **(-e)**, Russian; ~**gesinde**, Russophil(e).

russifika'sie, Russification.

russifiseer', (ge-), Russianize.

rus: ~**soldy**, retired pay; ~**stand**, natural position; ~**stoel**, easy chair, Morris chair; ~**stroombaan**, closed circuit.

ru: ~-staal, blister-steel; ~-steenkoper, matte.
rus'teken, rest (music).
rus'teloos, (..lose), restless, fidgety; indefatigable; ~heid, restlessness; tirelessness, fidgetiness.
rus'tend, (-e), retired (farmer), emeritus (parson); dormant (biol.); quiescent (volcano); recumbent; latent (disease); dead (load); ~*e OUDERLING*, retired elder; ~*e TOESTAND*, dormant condition.
rustiek', (-e), rustic (seat); rural (country).
rus'tig, (-e), calm, quiet, tranquil, still, restful, peaceful; ~heid, quietness, tranquillity, placidity, restfulness, peacefulness.
ru'stuk, blank.
rus: ~tyd, holiday, time of rest; interval, half-time (games); pause; dormancy, latent period (biol.); ~uur, hour of rest; ~versteurder, ~verstoorder, (-s), stormy petrel, disturber of the peace; ~versteuring, ~verstoring, (-e, -s), disturbance, breach of the peace, disorder.
rutiel', rutile.
ruts'baan, switchback (railway).
ru: ~veld, rough (golf); ~voer, roughage; ~waster, service-washer; ~werker, navvy.
ru'-yster, pig-iron; ~klont, sow; ~staaf, pig.
ry¹, (s) (-e), row, series; file, queue; drill (for vegetables, etc.); *ALMAL in 'n* ~, all in a row; *OP 'n* ~, in a row; *VIER in 'n* ~, four abreast; four in a row.
ry², (s) driving; riding; *IN die* ~ *afklim*, dismount while the vehicle is in motion; *KRY jou* ~! get going! off with you! (w) (ge-), ride, drive, taxi (aero.); convey; *wat het jou gery om dit te DOEN?* what possessed you to do such a thing? *die trein* ~ *ELKE halfuur*, the train departs every half hour; *'n entjie GAAN* ~, go for a (spin) drive; *'n perd LAM* ~, override a horse; *iem. (bloots) LELIK* ~, we gave them a drubbing; make it unpleasant for someone; *MIS* ~, cart manure; miss something when driving; *SKAATS* ~, skate; *met die TREIN moet* ~, have to travel by train; ~baan, taxiway (aero.); track; ~baar, (..bare), ridable (horse); passable (road); ~bereik, radius of action (vehicles); ~bewys, driver's licence; ~bewysraampie, licence-holder; ~broek, pair of riding-breeches; ~dier, riding-animal, mount; ~ding, conveyance; mount.
ry'e, (w) (ge-) = ryg.
ry'er, (-s), rider; driver (of vehicle); ~y, riding, driving; *versigtige* ~*y*, careful driving.
ryg, (ge-), lace (shoe); string (beads); gather, run, tack, baste; ~draad, (tacking-)thread; ~gaatjie, eyelet.
ry'geld, fare.
ryg: ~gaatjie, eyelet; ~hakie, threading-hook; ~lyfie, bodice; stays; ~lyntjie, knittle; ~naald, bodkin; ~naat, tacked seam; ~penomslag, apron file; ~plooi, gather; ~plooitjies, gathers, gathering; ~skoen, laced shoe; ~steek, tack, tacking stitch, running stitch; ~veter, (boot-)lace; ~werk, stringing (beads); lashing; lacing.
ry: ~handskoen, riding-glove; ~instrukteur, riding-master.
ryk¹, (s) (-e), empire, kingdom, realm, domain; *die DUISENDJARIGE* ~, the millennium; *sy* ~ *is UIT*, his reign is at an end; *die* ~ *v.d. VERBEELDING*, the realm of fancy.
ryk², (b, bw) (-e; -er, -ste), rich, wealthy, well-to-do, opulent, affluent; copious (language); abundant, fertile, fat (ground); ~ *en ARM*, rich and poor; ~ *gesaai, BANKROT gemaai*, easy come, easy go; ~ *GEÏLLUSTREER(D)*, copiously illustrated; *hoe* ~*er, hoe GIERIGER*, the more one has, the more one wants; ~ *MAAK*, enrich; ~ *SIT*, spread oneself; lean back comfortably; ~ *TROU*, marry money; ~aard, (-s), rich man; Croesus; ~dom, (-me), wealth, riches, affluence, fortune, money, opulence; abundance, profusion; ~e, (-s), rich person; ~heid, richness, opulence; ~lik, abundant, plentiful; ~*lik beloon*, handsomely rewarded; ~manskind, child of rich people.
ry: ~koste, running costs; ~kostuum, riding-habit, riding-dress.

ryks: ~adelaar, imperial eagle; ~advokaat, king's (queen's) counsel; ~argief, public archives; ~argivaris, keeper of the public archives; ~dag, diet (parliamentary assembly); ~gebied, territory of the state; ~gesag, sovereignty, supreme power of the state; ~kanselier, imperial chancellor; ~konferensie, imperial conference; ~munt, coin of the realm; ~museum, national museum; ~regering, imperial government.
ryk'stad, imperial city; free city.
ryks: ~tentoonstelling, empire exhibition; ~universiteit, state university; ~verdediging, defence of empire; ~voorkeur, imperial preference; ~weë: *van* ~ *weë*, on behalf of the state.
ry: ~kuns, horsemanship, equitation; jockeyism; ~laan, drive, carriage-road; ~les, riding-lesson, driving-lesson; ~loon, cartage; fare.
ry'loop, (ge-), hitch-hike; ..loper, hitch-hiker; ..lopery, hitch-hiking.
rym, (s), (-e), rhyme; *SLEPENDE* ~, feminine rhyme; *STAANDE* ~, masculine rhyme; (w) (ge-), rhyme; chime; tally; *die twee ANTWOORDE is nie met mekaar te* ~ *nie*, these two answers are irreconcilable; *dit* ~ *nie met die FEITE nie*, this does not tally with the facts; ~aar, poetic vein;` ~bybel, rhymed Bible.
ry'mel (ge-), write doggerel, clink; ~aar, (-s), poetaster, rhymester, verser, verse-monger; ~ary', doggerel, jingel, verse-mongering.
rym: ~er, (-s), rhymester; ~klank, rhyme; ~kuns, art of rhyming; ~loos, (..lose), blank (verse).
rym'pie, (-s), short rhyme; verse; *ek KEN daardie* ~, that is an old story; *op 'n* ~ *kan LIEG*, tell lies pat.
rym: ~speletjie, crambo; ~woord, rhyming word.
Ryn, Rhine; ~s, (-e), Rhenish; ~land, Rhineland; ~lander, (-s), Rhinelander; ~lands, (-e), Rhenish.
ryn: ~steen, rhinestone; ~wyn, Rhine wine, hock.
ryp¹, (s) frost, rime; (w) (ge-), frost; *die witge* ~ *te TUIN*, the garden covered with frost; *vannag sal dit TUSSEN man en vrou* ~, there will be a severe frost to-night.
ryp², (w) (ge-), ripen, mature; *sy ge* ~ *te KUNS*, his mature art; (bw, w), ripe, mature, mellow; *na* ~ *e BERAAD*, after due consideration; ~ *vir die GALG*, gallows-ripe; ~ *en GROEN*, the ripe and the green; *dit het by my die PLAN laat* ~, this made me decide; *VROEG* ~, *vroeg vrot*, soon ripe, soon rotten; ~ *WORD*, ripen; ~ *WYN*, matured wine.
ry'pad, roadway, drive.
rypag'tig, (-e), frosty.
ry: ~pak, riding-habit; ~perd (s) riding-horse, saddle-horse; ~perd!, well done! splendid! hot-stuff! attaboy!
ryp: ~erigheid, frostiness; ~grens, frost line.
ryp'heid, maturity, ripeness, mellowness.
ry: ~plank, scooter; surf-board; ~plek, riding-place.
ryp: ~lik, maturely, fully, duly; ~maak, ripen; ~maaksentrale, ripening depot (plant); ~making, ripening.
rypskade, damage by frost.
ryp: ~vrot, ripe-rot.
ryp'vry, (-e), frost-free.
ryp'weer, frosty weather.
ryp'wording, ripening, maturing, fruition.
ry: ~reg, right of way; ~rok, riding-dress (-habit).
rys¹, (s) rice; *'n hele tydjie in die vaal* ~ *wees*, have been on the road a long time.
rys², (w) (ge-), (a)rise, ascend; ferment; ~ *en DAAL*, rise and fall; *iets wat voor die GEES* ~, something that occurs to the mind.
rys: ~akker, rice field; ~bier, saké; ~bou, cultivation of rice; ~brandewyn, arrack; ~brensie, rice with turmeric; ~bry, rice milk; ~dop, rice husk.
rys'gang, rise.
rys'handelaar, rice-dealer.
ry'skaaf, trying-plane.
rys'kluitjie, rice-dumpling.
ry'skool, riding-school, manège.
rys: ~korrel, grain of rice; ~kultuur, rice-culture; ~land, rice field, paddy; ~meel, rice-meal.

rysmiddel, leavening agent.
rys'mier, (s) white ant (termite); (w) **(ge-)**, undermine, sap, sabbotage; ~**ing**, undermining.
rys: ~ **oes**, rice-crop; ~ **papier**, rice-paper; ~**planta= sie**, rice-plantation; ~ **poeding**, rice-pudding; ~**so(e)p**, rice-soup; ~ **soort**, kind of rice; ~**stysel**, rice-starch; ~ **tafel**, rice-table.
ry'stang, riding-bit.
rys'tebry, rice-porridge.
rys'terplaat, rys'terplank, mould-board.
rys'terplaatploeg, mouldboard-plough.
ry: ~ **stewel**, riding-boot; ~ **stoel**, rocking-chair, in= valid chair, wheel(ed) chair.
rys: ~ **veld**, rice field; ~ **voël**, rice-bird; reed bird; ~ **water**, rice-water; ~ *water kry*, be put on spare diet.
ry'sweep, riding-whip; quirt; horsewhip.
rys'wyn, rice-wine, saké.
ryt, (ge-), tear, rip.
ry'toer, drive, run, spin.
ry'tuig, (. . **tuie**), coach, vehicle, conveyance, carriage; hansom; ~ **fabriek**, coachbuilder's workshop; ~ **maker**, (-s), coach-builder; ~ **veer**, carriage spring; ~ **verkeer**, vehicular traffic.
ry: ~ **tyd**, driving time; ~ **vaar'digheid**, driving skill; ~ **voorrang**, right of way; ~ **weg**, drive; road(way).
ry'wiel, (bi)cycle; ~ **maker**, (-s), cycle repairer; ~ **pomp**, bicycle pump; ~ **winkel**, bicycle shop.

S

s, (-'e), s; *'n ~ gooi*, make a sharp turn; show off.
sa! catch him! tally-ho!
saad, (**sade**), seed; seedling; semen, (human) sperm; inflorescence; tassel; progeny, offspring; *ABRA= HAM en sy* ~, Abraham and his seed; ~ **met DONS**, undelinted seed; ~ *sonder DONS*, delinted seed; *in die* ~ *KOM*, come into tassel; *kwade* ~ *SAAI*, sow seeds of discord; ~ *SKIET*, run to seed; *die ~ van TWEEDRAG*, the seed of discord; ~**aartappel**, seed potato; ~ **akker**, acre sown for seed; seed-plot; ~ **bak(kie)**, seed-tray; hopper; ~ **bal**, testicle; ~ **bed(ding)**, seed-bed; ~ **blom**, seed-head; ~ **bolletjie**, boll (flax); ~ **buis**, seminal duct, ejaculatory duct; ~ **diertjie**, spermatozoon; ~ **doos**, capsule; ~ **dop**, testa; seed-pod; ~ **draend**, (-e), seed-bearing; ~ **draer**, placenta (bot.); ~ **eiwit**, perisperm; ~ **eter**, seed-eater; ~ **gedraagde siekte**, seedborne disease; ~ **gras**, dropseed (*Sporobolus indicus*); ~ **handel**, seed-trade; ~ **handelaar**, seed-man; ~ **hawer**, seed-oats; ~ **houer**, seminal vesicle; ~**huid**, seed-coat, episperm; ~ **huisie**, capsule, seed-pod; follicle; lobule; ~ **jie**, (-s), small grain of seed; ~ **kiem**, germ; embryo; ~ **knop**, ovule (bot.); ~ **koek**, placenta (bot.); ~ **kool**, seedy cabbage; ~ **kop**, seed-head; ~ **koper**, seedsman; ~ **koring**, seed-corn; ~ **korrel**, grain of seed; ~ **kwekery**, seed-nursery; ~ **lob**, seed-lobe; cotyledon; ~ **lobbig**, (-e), cotyledonous; ~ **loos**, (. . **lose**), seedless; ~ **losing**, seminal emission; ~ **lys**, placenta (bot.); ~ **maga= syn**, seed store; ~ **mantel**, integument; ~ **mielies**, seed-maize; ~ **olie**, seed-oil; ~ **omhulsel**, seed-coat; ~ **plant**, seed-plant; flowering plant; ~ **pluim**, coma; egret; ~ **pluis**, pappus; ~ **sak(kie)**, sperma= theca, seminal vesicle; ~ **sel**, sperm cell, spermato= zoön; ~ **skiet**, (-ge-), run to seed, go to seed; ejacu= late (seed); ~ **skieting**, running to seed; ejaculation; ~ **uitbarsting**, semination; ~ **storting**, ejaculation, seminal discharge; ~ **vat**, seed-vessel, pericarp; ~ **verkoper**, seedsman; ~ **verspreiding**, seed-dis= persal; ~ **vlies**, seed-coat, pericarp; ~ **vloeistof**, spermatic fluid, seminal fluid; ~ **vorming**, semina= tion; ~ **winkel**, seed-shop; ~ **winning**, seed-getting; ~ **wol**, pappus, seedy wool.
saag, (s) (**sae**); (w) (ge-), saw, cut; scrape (on violin); *aanhou ~ oor iets*, harp on the same string; ~ **bak**, saw-horse; ~ **bek**, goosander; saw-shark; ~ **blad**, blade (of saw); ~ **bladhouer**, blade-holder; ~ **bok**, jack saw-trestle; ~ **kerf**, saw-notch saw-cut; ~ **kuil**, saw-pit; ~ **masjien**, sawing machine; ~ **meel**, sawdust; ~ **meul(e)**, lumber-mill, sawmill; ~ **raam**, saw-frame, deal-frame; ~ **sel**, sawdust; scobs; ~ **setter**, saw-die; saw-setter (person); ~ **steller**, saw-set; ~ **tand**, tooth of a saw; ~ **tandig**, (-e), sawtoothed, serrated; ~ **vis**, sawfish; ~ **vormig**, (-e), serrated; saw-shaped; ~ **vyl**, triangular file; ~ **werk**, sawing; indentation; fret; ~ **wesp**, saw-fly.
saai¹, (s) shalloon; serge.
saai², (b) (-e; -er, -ste), dull, tedious, drab, featureless.
saai³, (w) (ge-), sow, scatter, intersperse; *iets wat maar DUN ge~ is*, something not easily come by; *jy moes die KLOMP sien* ~, you should have seen the crowd scatter; *iem. LAAT* ~, put someone to flight; *ge~ LÊ*, be widespread; *die een* ~, *'n ander MAAI*, some do the sowing, others the mowing; *wat jy* ~, *sal jy MAAI*, you must reap what you have sown; *wie nie ~ nie, SAL nie maai nie*, he who does not sow shall not reap; ~ **baar**, (. . **bare**), sow= able; ~ **boer**, grain farmer; ~ **boerdery**, crop-farm= ing; ~ **boontjie**, seed-bean; ~ **dam**, wheat-field in bed of river; ~ **er**, (-s), sower; ~ **grond**, arable land.
saai'heid, dullness, tedium.
saai: ~ **ing**, sowing; ~ **korting**, seed-corn; ~ **land**, ar= able land; croft; ~ **ling**, (-e), seedling; ~ **masjien**, seeding machine, saving machine; ~ **plaas**, agricul= tural farm; ~ **ploeg**, drill-plough; ~ **saad**, seed for sowing; ~ **sak**, sower's bag; ~ **sel**, (-s), sowing; ~ **toestel**, drill (for sowing crops); ~ **tyd**, sowing season.
saak, (**sake**), affair, thing, matter; (court) case, action (at law), (law)suit; business, undertaking, shop, concern; cause; *'n ~ BEGIN*, set up a business; *in sake van BELANG*, in important matters; *BE= MOEI jou met jou eie sake*, mind your own busi= ness; *elke ~ het sy BLINK kant*, there is a bright side to everything; *ter sake DIENENDE*, relevant; *goeie sake DOEN*, do good business; *GEDANE sake het geen keer nie*, it is no use crying over spilt milk; *GEMENE ~ maak*, make common cause with; *vir 'n GOEIE* ~, for a good cause; *dis die HELE* ~, that is the matter in a nutshell; *sake IS sake*, business is business; *'n ~ na 'n KANT toe drywe (voer)*, force a decision; bring a matter to a point; *tot die ~ KOM*, come to the point; *LO= PENDE sake*, current affairs; *tot die ~ KOM*, come to the point; *'n ~ MAAK*, take proceedings; *dit MAAK g'n ~ nie*, it does not matter; *dis MY* ~, that is my concern; *ONVERRIGTER sake*, labour lost; *'n ~ OPPER*, raise a matter; *'n ~ laat RUS*, drop a matter; *so STAAN sake*, that is how matters stand; *soos sake nou STAAN*, as things are now; *vir sake na die STAD gaan*, go to town on business; *op STUK van sake*, after all; as a matter of fact; *dis sy* ~, that's his business; *TER sake*, to the point; *nie TER sake nie*, beside the question, irrelevant; *'n UITGEMAAKTE* ~, a foregone conclusion; *dis nie VEEL ~s nie*, it is not up to much; it is of in= ferior quality; ~ **beskadiging**, property damage; ~ **gelastigde**, (-s), commissioned agent, representa= tive; commissioner (D.R. Church); charge d'af= faires; procurator; proctor; ~ **kennis**, practical (professional) knowledge; business experience; ~ **kun'dig**, (-e), conversant with the subject, expert, efficient; ~ **kun'dige**, (-s), expert, authority.
saak'lik, (-e), matter-of-fact, succinct, precise; rel= evant, apposite, ad rem; businesslike; objective, compendious, essential; hardheaded; pertinent; concise; ~ *e REG*, right in rem; ~ *e SEKERHEID*, real security; ~ **heid**, succinctness, essence, rel= evancy, pertinence, appositeness; vital point; con= ciseness; efficiency; compendiousness.

saak: ~ma'kend, (-e), material; ~naam, name of a thing; noun; ~register, index of subjects.
saak'ryk, (-e), full of substance, important; ~heid, importance.
saak'waarnemer, (-s), agent, proctor; ~skap, proctorship.
saal¹, (s) (sale), hall, house, saloon; ward (hospital); *vol sale trek,* draw crowded houses.
saal², (-s), saddle; *in die ~ BLY,* remain in power; *iem. in die ~ HELP,* put someone back on his feet; *iem. uit die ~ LIG,* unsaddle (oust) someone; *VAS in die ~ sit,* enjoy full confidence; have the reins firmly in hand; (w) **(ge-),** saddle.
saal'aar, saddle vein.
saal: ~bediende, ward maid (orderly); **~bekooievaar,** saddlebill stork.
saal: ~bok, saddle-tree; **~boog,** cantle; **~boom,** saddle-tree; ~ *boom RY,* ride holding to the saddle; trot; ~ *boom STEEK,* post; **~boomknop,** pommel.
saal'dak, saddle-roof, double-pitch roof, ridge roof, saddleback-roof.
saal'droes, burr.
saal'gord, saddle-girth.
saal'huur, hire of a hall.
saal: ~klap, saddle-flap; skirt; **~kleedjie, (-s),** saddle-cloth; shabrack; **~knop,** pommel; saddle-bow; **~kram,** dee; **~kussing,** saddle-cushion; panel; **~leer,** saddle-leather; **~maker,** saddler; **~makersels,** drawing-awl; **~makershamer,** saddler's hammer; **~makery, (-e),** saddlery; **~pak,** pack-drill; **~perd,** saddle-horse; **~rug,** saddleback; **~sak,** saddle (bicycle); **~seep,** saddle-soap; **~seer,** saddle-sore; **~stang,** saddle-pillar; **~stuk,** saddle (mech.).
saal'suster, wardsister.
saal: ~tjie, (-s), little saddle; **~vas (-te),** firm in the saddle; **~veer,** saddle-spring; **~vlerk,** jockey saddle; **~vormig, (-e),** saddle-shaped.
saal'wagter, hall-attendant; caretaker.
saam, together, (con)jointly; between them; *almal ~,* all together.
saam'bind, (-ge-), tie together, connect, colligate, bundle.
saam'blaf, (-ge-), bark at the same time; agree noisily with others, argue with everybody.
saam'bly, (-ge-), live together, cohabit.
saam'boer, (-ge-), farm together; herd with; live with.
saam'bring, (-ge-), bring together, bring with (one); focus.
saam'doen, (-ge-), act together, do with others.
saam'dra, (-ge-), carry (with one), bring along.
saam'dring, (-ge-), crowd together, congest, jam.
saam'drink, (-ge-), drink together, hob-nob.
saam'drom, (-ge-), flock together, congregate.
saam'druk¹, (-ge-), print together.
saam'druk², (-ge-), press together, compress; **~'baar, (..bare),** compressible; **~'baarheid,** compressibility; **~'kend, (-e),** compressive; **~king,** compression.
saam'dryf, saam'drywe, (-ge-), drive together, round up (cattle); float together.
saam'eet, (-ge-), eat together, eat (mess) with, join in meal; *MET iem. ~,* break bread with someone; *VLEIS met mosterd ~,* take mustard with meat.
saam'flans, (-ge-), patch up, botch up, piece up, cobble, concoct (story), fudge.
saam'frommel, (-ge-), crumple up (together).
saam'gaan (-ge-), go together, go with, accompany; agree; match; hang together; *GAAN jy saam?* are you coming (with me)? ~ *KERK toe,* accompany a person to church; *die KLEURE sal goed ~,* the colours will match well.
saam'gedrongenheid, compactness; congestion.
saam'geflans, (-te), patched up.
saam'gegroei, (-de), fasciated, intertwined.
saam'gepak, (-te), conglomerated; piled up.
saam'gepers, (-te), compressed; ~ *te lug,* compressed air.
saam'gestel(d), (-de), compound, complex; composite; **~dheid,** complexity.
saam'geswornes, conspirators.
saam'getrokke, contracted, concentrated.

saam'gevoeg, (-de), joined; ~ *de rots,* jointed rock.
saam'gooi, (-ge-), throw together, pool, mix.
saam'groei, (-ge-), grow together; heal; **~ing,** growing together, concrescence, concretion, fasciation.
saam'hang, (-ge-), be united, hang together, cohere.
saam'heg, (-ge-), connect, fasten together; sew up.
saam'hok, (-ge-), herd (huddle) together; pig it together.
saam'hoop, (-ge-), accumulate, heap up, pile up.
saam'hoort, (-ge-), belong together.
saam'hoping, accumulation, heaping up, piling up.
saamho'rig, (-e), belonging together, related.
saamho'righeid, solidarity, coherence; **~sgevoel,** feeling of coherence, solidarity, esprit de corps.
saam'hou, (-ge-), keep together.
saam'huis, (-ge-), cohabit (as husband and wife).
saam'kleef, (-ge-), stick (adhere) together, cohere.
saam'klewing, conglutination.
saam'kliek, (-ge-), become a clique.
saam'klink¹, (-ge-), harmonize, chime together.
saam'klink², (-ge-), rivet together.
saam'klonter, (-ge-), agglutinate; **~ing,** agglutination.
saam'knoei, (-ge-), collude.
saam'knoop, (-ge-), tie together, knot together; correlate.
saam'knyp, (-ge-), press together, compress.
saam'koek, (-ge-), mat together; huddle together; *saamgekoekte hare,* matted hair.
saam'kom, (-ge-), come together, meet, assemble, flock; accompany; unite; **~plek,** rendezvous.
saam'kook, (-ge-), cook together; concoct.
saam'koppel, (-ge-), couple, link.
saam'lag, (-ge-), join in the laughter, laugh together.
saam'lap, (-ge-), piece together, patch up.
saam'leef, saam'lewe, (-ge-), live together, cohabit; consort.
saamle'wend, (-e), cohabiting; symbiotic (bot.).
saam'lewing, cohabitation; symbiosis (bot.).
saam'loop, (-ge-), walk together; accompany; meet (in a point), converge.
saam'lopend, (-e), concurrent (lines).
saam'lym, (-ge-), glue together, conglutinate.
saam'maak, (-ge-), co-operate; pool.
saam'meng, (-ge-), mix together.
saam'neem, (-ge-), take along (with one); consider together; **~diens,** take away service.
saam'neigend, (-e), connivent (bot.).
saam'pak, (-ge-), pack (crowd) together, pile up, gather; **~king,** conglomeration.
saam'pers, (-ge-), press together, compress; condense; crush; stem (explosives); **~'baar, (..bare),** compressible; **~ing,** compression, pressing together.
saam'plak, (-ge-), glue together.
saam'praat, (-ge-), join in the conversation; have a say in the matter; **..prater,** colloquist.
saam'raap, (-ge-), gather, collect, pick up, scrape together.
saam'reis, (-ge-), travel together (with).
saam'roep, (-ge-), call together, convoke, convene; **~er, (-s),** convener; **~ster,** lady convener.
saam'rol, (-ge-), roll together; convolve.
saam'rot, (-ge-), conspire.
saam'ry, (-ge-), accompany (on a drive or ride); *vra om te mag ~,* ask for a lift, thumb a lift.
saam'skik, (-ge-), arrange together.
saam'skool, (-ge-), flock (band) together, mob, crowd together.
saam'skraap, (-ge-), scrape together.
saam'sleep, (-ge-), drag along; force to go along with.
saam'smee, (-ge-), forge together.
saam'smelt, (-ge-), unite, fuse, merge, melt together, amalgamate, coalesce; **~end, (-e),** coalescent; **~ing,** merger, fusion.
saam'snoer, (-ge-), string together (beads).
saam'span, (-ge-), conspire, plot together, collude; collogue; co-operate, unite, club together.
saam'speel, (-ge-), play together; combine (in playing); act together (on stage); join in (game, play); play ball (fig.); *ons speel NIE saam nie,* we won't have anything to do with it; *die WEER wou*

nie ~ *nie*, the weather was unkind (uncooperative).
saam'staan, (-ge-), stand (act) together, stand by each other.
saam'stel, (-ge-), put together, assemble, constitute; make up (train); frame, compose; compound; compile, fabricate; ~ **lend, (-e);** ~ *lende dele,* component parts; ~ **ler, (-s),** composer (of address); compiler (of anthology); constructor.
saam'stem, (-ge-), agree, concur, be in agreement; harmonize; ~ **mend, (-e),** consonant, concordant.
saam'stroom, (-ge-), flow together; flock together, mob.
saam'sweer, (-ge-), conspire, plot, cabal.
saam'tel, (-ge-), add up; include; be of some account.
saam'tref, (-ge-), meet; coincide.
saam'trek, (s) (-ke), rally, meeting; assembly, gathering; concentration; (w) **(-ge-),** contract (muscles); knit (eyebrows); focus; concentrate, assemble, adduct (forces); work together; astringe; constrict; constringe; ~ **kend, (-e),** astringent; astrictive; constringent; ~ **ker,** fellow-trekker; contractor; constrictor; ~ **king,** astriction; adduction; constriction; ~ **kingsfase,** systole; ~ **middel,** astringent; ~ **spier,** contractor (muscle).
saam'treur, (-ge-), condole (mourn) with.
saam'trop, (-ge-), herd together.
saam'val, (-ge-), fall together; coincide, be congruent; concur, synchronize; clash; ~ **lend, (-e),** concurrent.
saam'vat, (-ge-), take with (together), sum up, condense, summarize; compress.
saam'vleg, (-ge-), interlace, plait together.
saam'vloei, (-ge-), flow together; blend, coalesce, merge; ~ **end, (-e),** confluent; ~ **ing,** conflux, coalescence.
saam'voeg, (-ge-), join, unite; bracket; couple; aggregate; assort; frame; compound; conjoin; piece together; ~ **ing,** fagot(ing) (of iron); aggregation.
saam'vou, (-ge-), fold (together); fold up; ~ **baar,** (..bare), foldable, collapsible.
saam'werk, (s) co-operation; (w) **(-ge-),** co-operate, join hands, collaborate, coact, act together, work in concert, collude; ~ **end, (-e),** co-operative; ~ **er,** co-operator.
saam: ~ **wonery,** sharing living quarters; ~ **woning,** sharing of house; cohabitation (man and wife); ~ **woon, (-ge-),** cohabit; live together, share (a house).
saans, in the evening, at night, of an evening.
Saar'tjie, Sally; *ou* ~ *soen,* ply the bottle.
saat, (sate) = **saad.**
saban'der, (ge-), run away, flee, scoot.
Sab'bat, (-te), Sabbath; ~ **a'riër (-s),** Sabbatarian; ~ **a'ries, (-e),** Sabbatarian; ~ **dag,** Sabbath day, Holy Sabbath.
Sab'bats: ~ **heiligheid,** observance of the Sabbath; ~ **jaar,** sabbatic(al) year.
Sab'bat: ~ **skender, (-s),** Sabbath-breaker; ~ **skennis,** Sabbath-breaking.
sab'bats: ~ **reis,** Sabbath day's journey; *dis net 'n* ~ *reis daarheen,* it is but a Sabbath day's journey; **S** ~ **rus,** Sabbath rest.
Sab'batstilte, silence (quiet) of the Sabbath.
sab'bel, (ge-), suck.
sa'bel¹, (-s), sword, sabre.
sa'bel², (-s), sable (fur).
sa'bel: ~ **bajonet,** sword bayonet; ~ **band,** swordsling; ~ **bek,** avocet (a wading bird); ~ **bene,** sicklehocks.
sa'bel: ~ **bont,** sable fur; ~ **dier,** sable.
sa'bel: ~ **dril,** sword-drill; ~ **gekletter,** sabre-rattling; ~ **hou,** sabre-thrust, sword-cut; ~ **kap,** sword-cut; ~ **koppel,** sword-belt; ~ **kwas,** sword-knot; ~ **lem,** sword-blade; ~ **reg,** sword-law; ~ **riem,** sword-belt; ~ **sak,** sabretache; ~ **skede,** sword-sheath, sabre-sheath; ~ **stoot,** sword-thrust.
sa'belvel, sable skin.
sa'belvormig, (-e), sword-shaped.
Sa'biër, (-s), Sabian.
sabota'sie, sabotage, rattening.
saboteer', (ge-), commit sabotage, ratten.

saboteur', (-s), saboteur, rattener.
sachet', (-s), sachet.
Sadduse'ër, (-s), Sadducee.
Saddusees', (..sese), Sadducean.
sadis', (-te), sadist; ~ **me,** sadism (sexual perversion); ~ **ties, (-e),** sadistic.
sa'e = **saag,** (w).
sa'er, (-s), sawyer.
saf, (-te; -ter, -ste), soft, pappy; intoxicated; tipsy; *iem. is* ~, he is muzzy (squiffy).
safa'ri, (-'s), safari.
saffiaan', morocco (leather).
saffier', (-e), sapphire; ~ **blou,** sapphire (blue); sapphirine; ~ **kwarts,** blue quartz; ~ **steen,** sapphire (stone).
saffraan', saffron; ~ **agtig, (-e),** saffron-like; ~ **blom,** crocus; ~ **boom,** saffron-wood; ~ **geel,** saffron yellow; ~ **kleurig, (-e),** croceate; ~ **peer,** saffron pear.
saf'terig = **sawwerig.**
sag, (b, bw), (-te; -ter, -ste), soft, mellow; downy; lenient, gentle, clement (treatment), mild (punishment, climate); smooth (skin); low (voice); easy (punishment); meek; tender (meat); pulpy; pultacious; plumpy; ~ *te BAND,* limp cover (book); ~ *te BRAND,* soft scald (apples); ~ *te DOPLUIS,* soft scale; ~ *gekookte EIER,* soft-boiled egg; *op sy* ~ *ste GESÊ,* putting it (very) mildly; ~ *te HUMEUR,* sweet temper; ~ *soos 'n LAM,* gentle as a lamb; ~ *MAAK,* tenderize (meat); soften up; macerate; ~ *te OLIE,* bland oil; ~ *(gies) PRAAT,* speak softly, ~ *te SOLDEERSEL,* soft solder; ~ *te STAAL,* mild steel; ~ *te VRUGTE,* deciduous fruit; ~ *te WATER,* soft water; ~ *te WYN,* smooth wine.
sa'ga, (-s), saga.
sagaar'dig, (-e), gentle, sweet, dove-like, mild-spirited; ~ **heid,** gentleness, sweetness.
sa'ge, (-s), legend, myth, fairy-tale; saga.
saggarien', saggari'ne, saccharin.
sag'gerig = **sagterig.**
sag'gies, gently, softly, quietly, lightly; ~ *praat,* speak softly.
sag'harig, (-e), soft-haired, fluffy, pubescent.
sagittaal', (..tale), sagittate.
sag'kens, gentle, softly; ~ *handel met,* deal gently with.
sagmoe'dig, (-e), sweet, benign, gentle; ~ **heid,** sweetness, benignity, gentleness, kindness.
sa'go, sago; ~ **meel,** sago flour; ~ **palm,** sago palm; ~ **poeding,** sago pudding.
sagryn'leer, shagreen.
sagsin'nig, (-e), gentle, friendly; lenient, mild; meek; ~ **heid,** gentleness, friendliness; meekness.
sag: ~ **tebal,** softball; ~ **tehout,** softwood; ~ **terig (-e),** rather soft; ~ **teseep,** soft soap.
sagt'heid, softness, smoothness, gentleness; balminess; clemency, leniency.
sag'werkend, (-e), mild (medicine).
Saha'ra, Sahara; ~ **woestyn,** Sahara desert.
sajet', sayette; woollen yarn; ~ **seil,** half worsted web; ~ **stowwe,** half-worsted tissues.
sak¹, (s) (-ke), bag (of wheat); pocket (of sugar; in coat); sack (of flour); poke; portfolio; pouch (of animals; for tobacco); cyst; *in* ~ *en AS sit,* be in sackcloth and ashes; *iets in die* ~ *BRING,* profit by something; ~ *ke vol GELD,* bags (pots) of money; *iem. in die* ~ *HÊ,* have a person in one's pocket; *met* ~ *en PAK,* with bag and baggage; *iem. uit jou* ~ *SKUD,* keep down an overweening person; tell someone where he gets off; *in sy* ~ *STEEK,* take to heart; *STEEK dit in jou* ~, put that in your pipe and smoke it; *dit VAT aan 'n man se* ~, it is rather expensive.
sak², (ge-), sink, subside; fail (examination); fall, go down, gravitate, go flat; sag; drop; dip; *in 'n EKSAMEN* ~, fail in an examination; *die GORDYN laat* ~, let down the curtain, let the curtain fall; *die KOEI* ~, the cow is giving her milk down, the cow is letting her milk flow; *sy KOP laat* ~, bow (drop) his head; *die MOED laat* ~, lose courage.
sak: ~ **almanak,** pocket calendar; ~ **beenpasser,** drop-compasses; ~ **boek,** notebook, pocket-book,

pay-book; ~**boog**, drop-arch; ~**broek**, Oxford bags; plus-fours; ~**bybeltjie**, pocket Bible; ~**doek**, handkerchief, hanky; ~**doekpoeierkwas**, puff-handkerchief.
sa′ke, saki, sake, rice beer (Jap.).
sa′ke: *ter* ~, to the point, relevant, ad rem; ~**adres**, business address; ~**besoek**, business call; ~**brief**, business letter; ~**buurt**, business centre; ~**geheim**, business secret; ~**kamer**, chamber of commerce; ~**kennis**, business knowledge; trade craft; ~**kringloop**, business cycle; ~**lys**, agenda; ~**man**, businessman; ~**ondernemer**, entrepreneur; ~**onderneming**, business undertaking; ~**oogpunt**: *uit 'n* ~, from a business point of view; ~**reis**, business trip; ~**rol**, cause-list; ~**vernuf**, business acumen; ~**vrou**, business woman; ~**wêreld**, business circle.
sak: ~**filterkamer**, baghouse (metallurgy); ~**formaat**, pocket-size; ~**geld**, pocket money; pin-money; ~**goed**, sacking, gunny; ~**horlosie**, (pocket) watch; ~**kamera**, vest-pocket camera; ~**kammetjie**, pocket comb.
sakkarien′, sakkari′ne = saggarien, saggarine.
sakkerloot′, by Jove!
sak′keroller, (-s), pickpocket, cutpurse; ~**y**, pocket picking.
sak′kie, (-s), small bag; cod; fob; pocket (of sugar); sac, sachet; follicle (biol.).
sak′king, (-e, -s), subsidence, sinking, settlement; drop (of door); slump; down-throw (of fault).
sak: ~**klap**, pocket flap; ~**linne**, sackcloth, dowlas; ~**loop**, sack-race; ~**materiaal**, sacking; ~**mes**, pocket-knife, penknife; ~**net**, purse-seine; purse-net; ~**oorlosie**, (pocket) watch; ~**opening**, pocket-opening; ~**pistool**, derringer; pocket-pistol.
sak′plek, subsidence; slack in line (railw.).
sak′portefeulje, pocket-book, wallet.
sak′pyp, downcomer (steam-engine).
sakraal′, (..**krale**), sacral; *sakrale streek*, sacral region (anat.).
sakrament′, (-e), sacrament; *die HEILIGE* ~*e*, the holy sacraments; *die heilige* ~*e TOEDIEN (R.C.)*, administer extreme unction; ~**eel′**, (..**tele**), sacramental; ~**huisie**, tabernacle.
sak′reisies, sack-race.
sak′rekenaar, (-s), (portable) calculator.
sakristie′, (-ë), sacristy.
sakristyn′, (-e), sacristan.
sak′rok, sack (dress).
Sak′se, Saxony; ~**r**, (-s), Saxon.
Sak′sies, (-e), Saxon; ~*e PORSELEIN*, Dresden china; ~*e VENSTER*, gabled window.
sak′siesblou, saxe (blue).
sak: ~**spieël**, pocket mirror; ~**uitgawe**, pocket edition.
sak′vet, cod (beef).
sak: ~**vol** (**sakkevol**), pocketful, bagful; ~**vorming**, (-e), bag-like, sack-shaped, sacciform; ~**vorming**, bagging; ~**water**, subterranean water; water from (canvas) cooler; ~**woordeboek**, pocket dictionary.
sal, (sou), shall, will; *hy sou dit AGTERLAAT*, he was to have left it behind; *VOLGENS 'n gerug sou hy gesê het*, according to a report he is alleged to have said; *ek (hy) sou bly WEES*, I should (he would) have been glad.
sal(a)man′der, (-s), salamander, eft.
sala′mi, salami.
salammo′niak, sal ammoniac, ammonium chloride.
salarieer′, (ge-), pay (a salary), salary; ..**rië′ring**, (rate of) pay.
sala′ris, (-se), salary, emoluments; *met volle* ~, on full pay; ~**aanpassing**, salary adjustment; ~**aksie**, agitation for increase of salary; ~**hersiening**, revision of salary; ~**reëling**, salary arrangement, fixing of salary scales; ~**skaal**, salary scale; ~**trekkers**, salariat; ~**verhoging**, rise in (increase of) salary; increment; ~**vermindering**, reduction in salary, Irish rise.
Saldan′habaai, Saldanha Bay.
sal′do, (-'s), balance; residue; *BATIGE* ~, credit balance; *NADELIGE* ~, debit balance; *VOORDELIGE* ~, credit balance.
salep′, salep.

salet′jonker, (-s), beau, carpet-knight.
salf, (s) (salwe), ointment, salve, unguent; *iem.* ~ *om die OË smeer*, try to hoodwink someone; *aan hom is g'n* ~ *te SMEER nie*, he is past redemption; *dit is* ~ *op sy WOND*, this is balm to his wounds; (w) (ge-), anoint, salve; ~**agtig**, (-e), unctuous, greasy; ~**doos**, salve-box; ~**olie**, unction oil, chrism; ~**pot**, ointment pot, gallipot; ~**spuit**, ointment injector.
sa′lie, salvia, sage; ~**hout**, sage wood; ~**kaas**, sage cheese; ~**uiesous**, sage-and-onion sauce.
Sa′lies, (-e), Salic, Salian (Frankish); *die* ~*e wet*, the Salic law.
sa′lig, (-e), blessed; blissful, happy; glorious; ~ *is die BESITTERS*, possession is nine points of the law; ~ *MAAK*, save (a sinner); ~ *SPREEK (verklaar)*, beatify; *'n* ~*e VAKANSIE*, a glorious holiday; ~ *WORD*, be saved.
sa′liger, late, sainted; (more) blessed; *dis* ~ *om te GEE as om te ontvang*, it is more blessed to give than to receive; *GROOTVADER* ~, grandfather of blessed memory; ~ *NAGEDAGTENIS*, blessed memory.
sa′ligheid, salvation; beatitude; bliss(fulness), blessedness (of soul); glory, heavenliness; *sy* ~ *hang daarvan af*, his fate depends upon it.
sa′ligmakend, (-e), saving, sanctifying, beatific; ~*e genade*, saving grace.
Sa′ligmaker, Saviour, Redeemer.
sa′lig: ~**making**, salvation, redemption; beatification; ~**spreking**, beatification; (-e, -s), beatitude(s); ~**verklaring**, beatification.
sali′ne, saline.
salisiel′, salicyl; ~**suur**, salicylic acid.
salisien′, salisi′ne, salicine.
salisilaat′, (..**late**), salicylate.
salm, (-s), salmon; ~**agtig**, (-e), salmon-like; ~**forel**, bulltrout, salmon trout.
sal′mi, salmi.
salmiak′, sal-ammoniac; ~**gees**, liquid ammonia.
salm: ~**kleur**, salmon pink; ~**kleurig**, (-e), salmon-coloured; ~**moot**, slice (fillet) of salmon; ~**net**, salmon net.
salmonel′la, salmonella.
salmoniak′, sal-ammoniac.
salm: ~**teelt**, salmon-rearing; ~**vangs**, salmon-fishing; ~**vissery**, salmon-fishing.
Sa′lomo, Solomon; ~ *'s wysheid*, the wisdom of Solomon; ..**mo′nies**, (-e), Solomonic.
salon′, (-ne, -s), drawing-room, salon, saloon; ~**held**, carpet-knight; drawing-room knight; ~**rytuig**, ~**wa**, saloon-carriage (on train).
salot′, (-te), shallot; ~**ui**, shallot, spring onion.
salpe′ter, saltpetre, nitre; ~**agtig**, (-e), saltpetrous, nitrous; ~**gees**, spirit of saltpetre; ~**papier**, touch-paper; ~**suur**, nitric acid; ~**suursout**, nitrate; ~**uitslag**, saltpetre rot; ~**vorming**, nitrification; ~**water**, nitrous solution.
salueer′, (ge-), salute; ~**lyn**, saluting-base.
saluta′sie, salutation.
saluut′, (s) (**salute**), salute; *'n* ~ *BEANTWOORD*, return a salute; *'n* ~ *WAARNEEM*, take the salute; hail (interj); ~**skoot**, gun-salute.
salvarsan′, salvarsan (registered trade name).
sal′vo, (-'s), salute, volley, fusillade; ~**vuur**, volley-firing.
sal′we (ge-), anoint; salve.
sal′wend, (-e), unctuous; soothing.
sal′wing, anointment, unction.
samaar′, (-s), cymar.
samajou′ = sammejoa.
Samari′a, Samaria.
Samaritaan′, (..**tane**), Samaritan; *die barmhartige* ~, the good Samaritan; ~**s′**, (-e), Samaritan.
sambal′, sambal (condiment); grated quince; ~**broek**, pair of wide trousers, (Oxford) bags, galligaskins; ~**slaai**, spiced salad.
sambok′, (-ke), sjambok, cowhide whip; ~**inlê**, apply the whip; ~**bosplant**, sanseviera; ~**wurm**, whip-worm.
sambreel′, (-s, ..**brele**), umbrella, parasol; gingham, spider (in camouflage); *hulle BOER onder een* ~,

they agree in everything; they are hand in glove with each other; *'n ~ OPHÉ*, wear a broad-brimmed hat; *TERUG onder die ou ~* , back in the fold; **~ bak**, umbrella-stand; **~ boom**, umbrella-tree *(Cussonia spp.)*; **~ dak**, umbrella roof; **~ den= (neboom)**, umbrella-pine; **~ stander**, umbrella-stand; **~ vormig, (-e)**, umbrella-shaped, umbelliform.

sa'**me**, together, (con)jointly, between them; *see* **saam**.

sa'**mebestaan**, coexistence.

sa'**medromming, (-e, -s)**, flocking together.

sa'**medrukking**, compression.

sameet', samite.

sa'**meflansing**, patching (piecing) together; conglomeration (of lies).

sa'**megesteld, (-e)**, compound; *~ e BLOM*, composite flower; *~ e BREUK*, complex fraction (arith.); *~ e OLIE*, compound oil; *~ e RENTE*, compound interest; *~ e SIN*, compound sentence; *~ e VRUG*, collective fruit; *~ e WOORD*, compound word; **~ blommig, (-e)**, composite; **~ heid**, complexity.

sa'**megesworenes**, conspirators.

sa'**megroeiing**, concrescence, coalescence; growing together.

sa'**mehang, (s)** connection (articles); context (words); order, coherence (speech); dependence; cohesion; consecution (mus.); continuity; (w) **(-ge-)**, hang together; be linked, bound up; cohere; **~ end, (-e)**, connected, coherent; *~ ende krag*, cohesion.

sa'**mehegting**, fastening together.

sa'**mehoping**, accumulation; congeries; coacervation.

sa'**meklank**, concord, harmony, consonance.

sa'**meklewend, (-e)**, conglutinative.

sa'**meklewing**, conglutination.

sa'**meklontering**, conglomeration.

sa'**mekoms, (-te)**, gathering, meeting.

sa'**mekoppeling**, joining, linking, coupling; word combination.

sa'**melewing**, society, community; co-habitation.

sa'**meloop**, concourse (of people); junction; coincidence; confluence (of rivers); *'n ongelukkige ~ van omstandighede*, an unfortunate combination of circumstances, an unfortunate coincidence.

sa'**melopende**, concurrent; convergent, converging; *~ strawwe*, concurrent punishment (sentences).

sa'**meloping**, convergence, convergency.

sa'**mepakking**, conglomeration; piling-up.

sa'**mepersing**, compression, pressing together.

sa'**meraapsel, (-s)**, rabble; jumble, medley, hotchpotch; *'n ~ van leuens*, a pack (tissue) of lies.

sa'**meroeper**, convener.

sa'**meroeping**, calling together, convocation; convening.

sa'**meroepster**, lady convener.

sa'**merot, (-ge-)**, conspire; **~ ting**, conspiracy, riot.

sa'**meskoling**, riotous assemblage.

sa'**meskraapsel**, scrapings, rabble.

sa'**mesluit, (-ge-)**, combine, merge, **~ ing**, combination, merger (companies).

sa'**mesmelting**, massing (estate); fusion, coalition, union, amalgamation; merger, merging; coalescence, fluxion.

sa'**mesnoering**, stringing together; combination.

sa'**mespannend, (-e)**, collusive.

sa'**mespanning, (-e, -s)**, conspiracy, plot, collusion.

sa'**mespel**, combination (rugby); teamwork; ensemble (playing)

sa'**mespraak, (..sprake)**, dialogue; conference; colloquy.

sa'**mespreking, (-e, -s)**, interview; conference; discussion; symposium; *kwade ~ e bederf goeie sedes*, evil communications corrupt good manners.

sa'**mestel, (s)** system; apparatus; structure; arrangement; construction; (w) **(-ge-)**, make up (train); prepare; devise; frame; draft, arrange, compile; **~ lend, (-e)**, component; compositive; constitutive; constructive; **~ ler, (-s)**, composer; collector; compiler; constructor; constituter; **~ ling, (-e, -s)**, composition, combination, constitution; compilation;

structure (rock); texture (of material); make-up, assembly (of trains); *~ ling van kleure*, combination of colours; **~ lingsvermoë**, constructiveness.

sa'**mestemming**, concord, agreement.

sa'**mestroming**, concourse; concentration, flocking together.

sa'**mesweerder, (-s)**, conspirator, machinator, plotter.

sa'**meswering, (-e, -s)**, conspiracy, plot, frame-up, plotting, machination; *'n ~ smee*, lay a plot.

sa'**mesyn**, gathering; *die ~* , the being together.

sa'**metrekbaar, (..bare)**, contractile, contractible; **~ heid**, contractility, contractibility.

sa'**metrekking, (-e, -s)**, contraction (of muscles); concentration (of troops); astringency, constringency (of medicine); syncopation (music); **~ sfase**, systole.

sa'**metrekkingsteken**, circumflex.

sa'**mevat, (-ge-)** = **saamvat**; **~ ting, (-e, -s)**, résumé, summary; compendium, précis, recapitulation; compilation.

sa'**mevloeiing, (-e, -s)**, confluence (of rivers); junction.

sa'**mevoeging, (-e, -s)**, union, junction, bond; compound (word); *~ van aanklagte (aksies)*, joinder of counts (actions).

sa'**meweefsel**, contexture, tissue.

sa'**mewerking**, co-operation, collaboration, co-action; concurrency; concert.

sa'**mewoning**, living together, cohabitation.

sammejo'a, its all the same, it doesn't matter.

samoem', (s), samoom.

Samojeed', (..jede), Samoyed; **~ s', (s)** Samoyed; (b) **(-e)**, Samoyed(ic).

sa'**mowar, (-s)**, samovar.

sam'**pan, (-s)**, sampan.

sampioen', **(-e)**, champignon, mushroom; **~ sop**, mushroom soup.

samsonlet', samsonite.

San Alleman, everywoman.

sanato'rium, **(-s, ..ria)**, sanatorium.

sand, sand, grit; *soos droë ~ AANMEKAAR HANG*, lack coherence; *op ~ BOU*, build on sand; *in die ~ BYT*, bite the dust; *op ~ KOU*, eat dirt; *~ in die OË strooi*, throw dust into someone's eyes; *so talryk soos die ~ van die SEE*, numberless as the sands (on the seashore); *SKULD soos ~ hê*, be over one's ears in debt; *~ VREET*, bite the dust; come a cropper.

sandaal'[1], **(sandale)**, sandal.

sand'aal[2], (..ale), sand-eel.

sand: **~ agtig, (-e)**, sandy; **~ appel**, dwarf shrub *(Parinarium capense)*; **~ bad**, sand-bath; **~ bak**, sand-box; **~ bank**, sand-bar, sandbank; hurst; shoal; tie-box; **~ bedding**, bed of sand; **~ berg**, sand hill; **~ bestraling**, sand-blasting; **~ blaastoc= stel**, sand-blasting machine; **~ blad**, sand-leaf (of tobacco); **~ blaser**, sand-blaster; **~ bloue**, mussel-cracker; **~ bom**, sand-bomb; **~ duin**, sand-dune.

san'**delhout**, sandalwood; *rooi ~* , red sandalwood, rubywood.

san'**derig, (-e)**, sandy; loamy; arenaceous, arenose; gritty; *~ e grond*, loam; **~ heid**, sandiness; grit; grittiness.

sand: **~ geelhoutboom**, silver terminalia; **~ glas**, hour-glass; **~ groef**, (..groewe), sand-pit; **~ grond**, sandy soil; **~ haai**, dogfish, sand shark; **~ haas**, foot-slogger, mud-crusher; **~ hawer**, lyme grass *(Elymus arenarius)*; **~ heuwel**, sand-hill, sand-drift.

sand'**hi**, sandhi; **~ reël**, sandhi-rule.

sand: **~ hoop**, heap of sand; **~ hoos**, dust devil; **~ hou= dend, (-e)**, sandy; **~ jie, (-s)**, grain of sand; piece of grit; **~ kar**, sand-cart; **~ kis**, sand-box; tie-box; **~ klip**, sandstone; **~ koekie**, sand-cake; **~ korrel**, grain of sand; **~ kruiper**, spotted sand-shark; fiddle-fish; shovel-nose; **~ kuil**, sand-pit; bunker (golf); **~ laag**, layer of sand; **~ lelie**, mauve african= der; **~ loper(tjie), (-s)**, hour-glass, egg-glass; egg-timer; **~ mannetjie, (-s)**, the dustman; **~ opvulling**, sand-fill; **~ pad**, sandy path; **~ patrys**, sand-grouse; **~ plaat**, sandy stretch; **~ pypie**, mauve afri=

cander; ~ riffel, ribble-mark; ~ ruiter, unhorsed rider; ~ *ruiter word*, come a cropper; ~ sak, sandbag; ~ rif, riddle; screen; ~ slang, sand-snake; ~ spuit, sand-spray; ~ steen, sandstone, gritstone; ~ storm, sand-storm; ~ straal, sandblast; ~ strooier, sander (loco.); pounce-box; ~ strook, garboard, ~ stuiwing, sand-drift; ~ suier, (-s), suction-dredger; ~ suiker, crystallized sugar; ~ trapper, country cousin; Free Stater; navvy; one in (monetary) difficulties; ~ vanger, sand-trap; ~ veld, sand veld; sandy country.

Sand'veldhaakwurm, Sandveld hook-worm *(Gaigeria pachyscelis)*.

sand: ~ vlakte, sandy plain; ~ vlieg, sand-fly; ~ vlooi, jigger-flea, chigoe, sandflea; sand beetle; ~ wal, sand-bar; sowback; ~ wiek, hairy vetch; ~ woestyn, sandy desert; ~ wol, sandy wool; ~ wurm, sand-worm.

saneer', (ge-), sanify; put in a sound condition; reconstruct, reorganize.

sane'ring, reorganization, rationalization; restoring to health.

sang, (-e), song, tune, singing; poetry; verse, canto; ~ *studeer*, study singing; ~ aand, evening devoted to song; ~ album, song album.

Sang'berg, Parnassus; Helicon, *die* ~ *bestyg*, climb Parnassus.

san'ger, (-s), singer, vocalist; bard, poet; gleeman; melodist; vocal performer; *ons geveerde* ~ *s*, our feathered songsters; ~ es', (-se), (lady) singer, vocalist, songstress.

san'gerig, (-e), melodious, tuneful; lilting; ~ heid, melodiousness.

sang: ~ fees, song festival; ~ geselskap, choral society.

sang'god, god of song; ~ in', (-ne), muse.

sang: ~ kleur, coloratura; ~ koor, choir; ~ kuns, art of singing; ~ kursus, singing-course; ~ les, singing-lesson; ~ lus, love of singing; ~ lyster, song-thrush, mavis; ~ meester, singing-master; singing-teacher; ~ metode, method of singing; ~ musiek, vocal music; ~ nommer, vocal item; ~ oefening, singing-exercise (-practice); ~ onderwys, instruction in singing, singing-lesson; ~ onderwyser, ~ onderwyseres, singing-teacher; ~ party, voice part; ~ ryk, (-e), melodious, tuneful; ~ rykheid, melodiousness; ~ skool, school of singing; ~ sleutel, clef; ~ spel, operette; musical comedy; ~ speletjie, action-song; ~ -ster, singing star; ~ ster, songstress; ~ stuk, song.

sangui'nies, (-e), sanguine.

sang: ~ uitvoering, choral concert; ~ vereniging, choral society; ~ voël, songster, songbird; ~ wedstryd, singing-competition; ~ wyse, method of singing; ~ wysie, tune.

San'hedrin, Sanhedrin, Sanhedrim.

sa'nik, (ge-), worry, nag, be a bore, maunder, bother; ~ er, (-s), bore, nuisance, nagger; ~ ery, bothering, nagging.

sanita'sie, sanitation.

sanitêr', (-e), sanitary; ~ *e ingenieur*, sanitary engineer.

sank'sie, (-s), sanction; ~ *s toepas*, apply sanctions.

sanksioneer', (ge-), sanction, approve, ratify.

san'na, (-s), blunderbus, flint-lock.

San'skrit, Sanskrit.

Sanskritis', (-te), Sanskritist.

Sanskri'ties, (-e), Sanskrit(ic).

sant, (-e), (ong.), saint.

san'tekraam, lot, concern; caboodle; *die hele* ~, the whole caboodle.

santepetiek', san'tepiek, (whole) lot, the whole caboodle.

Sap¹, (-pe), (vero., hist.), S(outh) A(frican) P(arty) man.

sap², (-pe), juice, sap; ~ groen, sap-green; ~ loos, (..lose), sapless, juiceless.

saponiet', saponite, soapstone.

Sap'party, (vero.), South African Party.

sappeer', (ge-), sap (mil.).

sap perig, (-e), juicy, succulent; ~ heid, juiciness, succulence.

sappeur', (-s), sapper (mil.).

sap'pies, juice; drinks.

sap'pig, (-e), juicy; lush; mellow; ~ *e voer*, succulent feed; ~ heid, juiciness, succulence.

sapree', (-s), mountain cypress.

saprofiet', (-e), saphrophyte.

sap'ryk, (-e), juicy, succulent, sappy; ~ heid, juiciness, succulence, sappiness.

sap'verf, sap-colour.

sar, (ge-), vex, provoke, tease, nag, badger.

saraban'de, (-s), saraband.

sara'nie, (-s), Christian Malay; half-caste.

Saraseen', (..sene), Saracen; ~ s', (-e), Saracenic.

sardiens', sardines.

sardiens'blik, sardine tin.

sardien'tjie, (-s), sardine.

Sardi'nië, Sardinia; ~ r, (-s), Sardinian; ..nies, (-e), Sardinian.

sar'dis, sard.

sardo'nies, (-e), sardonic.

sardo'niks, (-e), sardonyx.

sardyn', (-e), sardyn'tjie, (-s), pilchard.

Sa'rel, Charles; *sak Sarel!* that's a tall story.

sa'ri, (-'s), sari.

sarkas'me, sarcasm, causticity; ..kas'ties, (-e), sarcastic, cynical, caustic.

sarkofaag', (..fae), sarcophagus.

sarkoom', (sarkome), sarcoma.

sa'rong, (-s), sarong.

sar'rend, (-e), nagging, vexing, teasing.

sarsaparil'la, sarsaparilla.

sar'sie, (-s), volley; sally; peal; rally (tennis); charge; *'n* ~ *maak*, fire a volley; charge; ~ wapen, automatic.

sas¹, (s) composition (explosive).

sas², (s) (-se), sluice, lock-chamber.

sas'safras, sassafras; ~ olie, oil of sassafras.

sat, sick; tired; satiated; blasé; ~ *van DAE*, old and decrepit; *hom* ~ *EET*, eat one's fill; *ek is NOU* ~ *daarvan*, I am fed up with it; ~ *WEES vir iets*, be sick of an affair.

sa'tan(as), sa'tang, (geselst.), Satan; *die* ~ *en sy moer*, the devil and his dam.

Sa'tan(g)bos, Sa'tansbos, silverleaf bitter apple *(Solanum elaeagnifolium)*.

sata'nies, (-e), satanic(al), diabolic(al); ..nis'me, satanism.

sa'tans, (-e), satanic; ~ kind, limb of the devil, wicked person; ~ werk, diabolical deed.

satelliet', (-e), satellite; ~ dorp, satellite town; ~ land, satellite country; ~ staat, satellite state.

sa'ter, (-s), satyr.

Sa'terdae, on Saturdays, of a Saturday.

Sa'terdag, Saturday; *klein* ~, Wednesday; *jou* ~ *is langer as jou Sondag*, your slip is showing; ~ aand, Saturday evening; *hy het* ~ *aand klaargekom*, he is too slow to catch a snail; he is a slowcoach; ~ middag, Saturday afternoon; ~ môre, Saturday morning; ~ nag, Saturday night; ~ s, (-e), on Saturdays.

Sa'terdagskind, illegitimate child.

sat'heid, satiety, weariness.

satineer', (ge-), hot-press, satinize; ~ der, (-s), hot-presser.

satinet', (-te), sateen.

sati're, (-s), satire.

satiriek', (-e), satiric(al).

sati'ries, (-e), satirical.

sati'rikus, (..tirici, -se), satirist.

satiriseer', (ge-), satirize.

satisfak'sie, satisfaction.

satraap', (satrape), satrap.

satrapie', (-ë), satrapy.

satureer', (ge-), saturate.

Saturna'lieë, Saturnalia.

saturnis'me, lead-poisoning, saturnism.

Satur'nus, Saturn.

satyn', satin; *geblomde* ~, figured satin; ~ agtig, (-e), satinlike, satin; ~ fabriek, satin factory; ~ glans, satiny finish; ~ hout, satinwood; ~ papier, satin paper; cambric paper; ~ skoen, satin shoe; ~ sy, sateen; ~ wewer, satin weaver.

Saul, Saul; *is* ~ *ook onder die profete?* is Saul among the prophets?
sau'na, (-s), sauna.
savan'ne, (-s), savannah.
savo'jekool, savoy cabbage.
saw'werig, (-e), rather soft.
sax'ofoon, (..fone), saxophone.
sca'la, (-s), scale, gamut; tone scale.
scena'rio, (-'s), scenario.
scê'ne, (-s), scene; *'n* ~ *maak*, cause a scene.
scenografie', scenography.
Scri'ba Syno'di, secretary of the synod.
Scyl'la: *tussen* ~ *en CHARYBDIS*, between Scylla and Charybdis, between the devil and the deep (blue) sea; *van* ~ *in CHARYBDIS verval*, fall from the frying-pan into the fire.
s'-draai, hairpin bend.
se, 's, of; belonging to; *pa* ~ *hoed*, father's hat.
sê, (s) say; ~ *en DOEN is twee*, promising is one thing, performing another; fine words butter no parsnips; *sy* ~ *SÊ*, have his say; (w) (ge-), say, speak, tell, order; state; *daar is BAIE voor te* ~, it has much to commend it; *DIS te* ~ *!* well, I never; *DIT* ~ *nie*, it does not matter; *EK* ~ *niks*, no comment; *so ge* ~, *so GEDAAN*, no sooner said than done; *GOUER ge* ~ *as gedaan*, sooner said than done; *hy HET niks te* ~ *nie*, he has no authority; he is tongue-tied; *HULLE* ~ *hy is...*, he is said to be...; *wat* ~ *JY?* what do you say? *hy LAAT hom niks* ~ *nie*, you can tell him nothing; *hy LAAT hom niks ge* ~ *nie*, he won't be told anything; ~ *MAAR*, granted, supposing; *wat MEER* ~, and what is more; *MOENIE* ~ *nie*, mum's the word; *ek het jou MOS ge* ~, I told you so; ~ *nou NET*, just suppose; *dit* ~ *NIE*, it doesn't follow; *daar is NIKS voor te* ~ *nie*, there is nothing to be said for it; *dit* ~ *NIKS*, that means nothing; *hy het NIKS te* ~ *nie*, he has nothing to say; *ek* ~ *jou NIKS!* take a look at that! ~ *NOU*, supposing; *ONDER ons ge* ~, between ourselves; ~ *maar SO*, agreed; *SO te* ~, so to speak, practically; *SONDER om iets te* ~, without saying a word; *jy* ~ *te VEEL*, you talk too much; you are overdoing it; *ek* ~ *nie te VEEL nie*, I am not overdoing it; *om die WAARHEID te* ~, to tell the truth; *WAT* ~ *jy daarvan?* what do you say to that? *WAT nog te* ~, not to speak of; *WAT het ek jou ge* ~ *?* didn't I tell you? *dis nou WEER te* ~ *!* well, I never! *die feite* ~ *WEINIG*, the facts convey (very) little; *dit WIL* ~, that is to say.
sean'ce, (-s), seance.
se'boe, (-s), zebu.
seborree', seborrhoea.
se'bra, (-s), zebra; ~ *merrie*, zebra mare; ~ **oorgang**, zebra crossing.
secun'da(wissel), second of exchange.
sedan'(motor), sedan (car).
se'de, (-s), habit, custom; (mv) morals, manners; ethos; ~ **bederf**, corruption of morals, demoralization; ~ **bederwend**, (-e), corruptive, demoralizing; ~ **deugde**, moral virtues.
sedeer', (ge-), cede, give.
se'de: ~ **kunde**, ethics, moral philosophy; ~ **kun'dig**, (-e), ethical; ~ **leer**, ethics, morality; deontology; ~ **les**, moral (of a fable).
se'delik, (-e), moral, ethical; ~ **heid**, morality; ~ **heidsgevoel**, moral sense; ~ **heidswet**, moral law; Public Morality Act.
se'deloos, (..lose), immoral; profligate; ~ **heid**, immorality, profligacy, depravity.
se'ne: ~ **meester**, moralizer, moralist; censor; ~ **misdryf**, offence against public morals.
sedentêr, (-e), sedentary.
se'de: ~ **preek**, moral lecture; ~ **preker**, moralizer, moralist; ~ **prekery**, moralization, preachment.
se'der, (-s), cedar; ~ **agtig**, (-e), cedrine; ~ **boom**, cedar (tree); ~ **hout**, cedar-wood.
se'dert, since; ~ *drie DAE*, for the last three days; ~ *verlede MAAND*, ever since last month; ~ **dien'**, since then.
se'de: ~ **skandaal**, moral scandal; ~ **spreuk**, maxim; ~ **verbastering**, moral depravity; ~ **wet**, moral law.

se'dig, (-e), modest; coy, prim, demure; ~ **heid**, modesty; primness, coyness, demureness; discretion.
sediment', sediment; ~ **a'sie**, sedimentation; ~ **êr'**, (-e), sedimentary; ~ **gesteente**, sedimentary rock.
sê'ding, witticism, wisecrack; saying.
sedi'sie, (-s), sedition, rebellion.
sedisieus', (-e), seditious, rebellious.
seduk'sie, seduction.
see, (seë), sea, ocean, the deep, main; multitude; *die* ~ *kan dit nie AFWAS nie*, the sea can't cleanse him; *'n* ~ *van BLOED*, a sea of blood; *BY die* ~, at the seaside; *reg deur* ~ *GAAN*, steer a straight course; not mince matters; *oor* ~ *GAAN*, go by sea; go abroad; *in* ~ *GAAN*, launch out on an undertaking; *die* ~ *KIES*, put out to sea; *ter* ~ *en te LAND*, by sea and (by) land; *'n* ~ *van LIGTE*, a multitude of lights; *'n* ~ *van RAMPE*, a pack of troubles; *in* ~ *STEEK*, put out to sea, launch out, set forth; *'n* ~ *van TRANE*, a flood of tears; *in VOLLE* ~, on the high seas; *die* ~ *kan hom nie skoon WAS nie*, the sea can't cleanse him.
see: ~ **aanval**, sea-attack; ~ **ajuin**, squill; ~ **anemoon**, sea anemone; ~ **anker**, sea-anchor; ~ **arend**, osprey; sea-eagle; ~ **arm**, estuary; ~ **assuransie**, marine insurance; ~ **atlas**, marine (nautical) atlas; ~ **baars**, bass; ~ **bad**, (..**baaie**), sea bath; ~ **badplek**, bathing place (resort); ~ **baken**, sea-mark; ~ **bamboes**, sea bamboo; tang; ~ **bank**, bar; ~ **banket**, herring; ~ **barbeel**, red mullet; ~ **bedding**, seabed; ~ **beer**, ursine seal; ~ **bene**, sea-legs; ~ **bene HE**, have found one's sea legs; *jou* ~ *bene KRY*, find one's sea-legs; ~ **berig**, maritime intelligence; ~ **beril**, aquamarine; ~ **beskrywer**, hydrographer; oceanographer; ~ **beskrywing**, seaquake; ~ **bewoner**, inhabitant of the sea; pelagian; ~ **blom**, sea-flower; ~ **blou**, (-e), marine blue; ~ **bodem**, bottom of the sea; ~ **bodemafsetting**, marine deposit; ~ **boei**, marine buoy; ~ **bog**, bight, bay; ~ **bonk**, (-e), Jack Tar; ~ **boot**, sea-boat; ~ **brasem**, sea-bream, grobman; ~ **breker**, pier, breakwater, mole; ~ **brief**, ocean letter; sea-letter; ~ **bries**, sea-breeze; ~ **buitreg**, prize-law; ~ **dadel**, date-shell; ~ **den**, pinaster; ~ **diens**, naval service; ~ **diepte**, depth of the sea; ~ **dier**, marine animal; ~ **dorp**, village on the coast; ~ **drif(sel)**, flotsam, floatage; ~ **duif**, Cape pigeon; ~ **duiker**, diver, cormorant; shag; garrot; ~ **duiwel**, sea-toad, frog-fish, toad-fish; devil-fish; angler; ~ **dyk**, sea-wall; ~ **eend**, sea-duck; yellow-bill; garrot; ~ **eier**, echinoid; ~ **engel**, angel-fish; ~ **engte**, strait; ~ **fauna**, marine fauna; ~ **gans**, gannet; ~ **gat**, sea-inlet, estuary; *die* ~ *gat uitvaar*, put out to sea; ~ **gedrog**, sea-monster; ~ **gesig**, seascape; sea-view; ~ **geskut**, naval ordnance; ~ **gevaar**, peril of the sea; ~ **geveg**, naval battle; sea-fight; ~ **gewes**, maritime province; ~ **god**, sea-god; ~ **godin**, sea-goddess; ~ **golf**, sea-wave; ~ **gras**, seaweed; fucus; alga; ~ **groen**, (-e), sea-green, glaucous; ~ **groensteen**, aquamarine; ~ **handel**, maritime ((over)sea) trade; ~ **handelaar**, overseas trader; ~ **hawe**, port, harbour; ~ **hawer**, lyme grass; ~ **heerskappy**, naval supremacy; ~ **held**, naval hero; ~ **hiasint**, squill; ~ **hond**, seal, sea-dog; phoca; ~ **hoof**, pier, jetty; ~ **joernaal**, log-book, ship's log; ~ **kaart**, sea chart; hydrographical map; ~ **kaartboek**, chart-book; ~ **kabel**, marine cable; ~ **kadet**, naval (sea-) cadet; ~ **kanaal**, channel.
see'kant, seaside; *na die* ~ *toe*, seaward; *van die* ~, from seaward.
see: ~ **kaptein**, sea-captain; ~ **kastaiing**, echinoid; sea urchin; ~ **kasteel**, ocean castle; ~ **kat**, cuttle-fish, sepia, poulp(e), catfish, squid, octopus.
see'koegat = **seekoeigat**.
see'koei, hippopotamus; manatee; ~ **bul**, hippopotamus bull; ~ **gat**, deep pool in a river; hippo pool; ~ **kalf**, baby hippo; ~ **koei**, hippopotamus cow; ~ **spek**, hippopotamus fat.
see: ~ **koelte**, sea-breeze; ~ **komkommer**, sea-cucumber; holothurian; ~ **kompas**, mariner's compass; ~ **koning**, sea-king; ~ **kool**, sea-cabbage; ~ **kos**, seafood; ~ **krap**, sea-crab; ~ **kreef**, lobster; ~ **kus**, coast, seashore, seaside; ~ **kwal**, jellyfish, acaleph(e).

seel¹, (sele), strap, trace.
seel², (-s), (birth) certificate; *sy ~ lig*, enquire into a person's past.
se'ēl, (s) (-s), seal, stamp; *sy ~ op iets DRUK (sit)*, set his seal to something; sanction something; *onder die ~ van GEHEIMHOUDING*, under the seal of secrecy; (w) (ge-), seal; stamp (a letter); ~**afdruk**, seal.
See'land, Zeeland.
seël: ~**belasting**, stamp-duty; ~**bewaarder**, keeper of the seal.
see: ~**leeu**, seal, sea-lion; ~**lewe**, life at sea; marine life.
se'ëlgelde, stamp duties.
see'liede, seamen, mariners.
se'ēl: ~**klammaker**, stamp-moistener; ~**koste**, stamp-charges; ~**lak**, sealing-wax; ~**lakker**, stamp-hinge; ~**lood**, lead-seal; ~**merk**, impression of a seal; ~**reg**, stamp-duty; ~**ring**, seal-ring, signet-ring; ~**snyer**, seal-engraver; ~**stempel**, stamp.
seelt, tench.
see'lug, sea-air; ~**hawe**, seadrome.
see'mag, sea (naval) power, fleet, navy.
see'man, (-ne, seeliede, seelui), sailor, marine(r); ~**sak**, kitbag.
see'mans: ~**almanak**, nautical almanac; ~**graad**, rating (naut.); ~**huis**, sailors' home; ~**jekker**, pea jacket, seaman's jacket.
see'manskap, seamanship.
see'mans: ~**kis**, sea chest; ~**knoop**, running knot; ~**kuns**, art of navigation; ~**lewe**, sailor's life; ~**taal**, sailor's language; ~**tehuis**, seamen's home; ~**term**, sea term; ~**woordeboek**, nautical dictionary.
see: ~**meermin**, mermaid; ~**meeu**, sea-gull; gannet; ~**mis**, sea mist, sea fog; ~**monster**, sea-monster; ~**moondheid**, naval (maritime) power; ~**mos**, sea moss.
seems'leer, shammy, chamois-leather, cheverel, white leather.
see: ~**myl**, nautical mile; ~**myn**, sea mine, naval mine, drifting mine.
se'ën¹, (s) (-s), seine, net.
se'ën², (s) (-inge, -ings), benediction, blessing; boon; *sy ~ daaraan GEE*, give one's blessing to; *sy is in geseënde OMSTANDIGHEDE*, she is enceinte, in the family way; *daar sal geen ~ op RUS nie*, no good will come of it; *die ~ UITSPREEK*, pronounce the benediction; (w) (ge-), bless; ~**bede**, blessing, benediction.
see: ~**netel**, acaleph(e); ~**newel**, sea mist, sea haze.
see'nimf, Oceanid, sea-nymph.
se'ën: ~**ing**, (-e, -s), blessing, benediction; ~**ryk**, beneficial; ~**wens**, blessing, good wishes.
see: ~**offisier**, naval officer; ~**olifant**, sea elephant; ~**oorlog**, naval war; ~**opleiding**, naval (sea) training; ~**otter**, sea otter.
seep, (s) (sepe), soap; *so GLAD soos ~* , as slippery as an eel; *GROEN ~*, soft soap; *'n KOEKIE ~*, a piece (tablet) of soap; *'n STEEN ~*, a bar of soap; (w) (ge-), soap; lather; ~**agtig**, (-e), soapy.
see'paling, conger eel.
seep: ~**bakkie**, soap-dish; ~**bel**, soap bubble; ~**bossie**, soap-bush.
see'perdjie, hippocampus, sea-horse.
seep: ~**fabriek**, soap works; ~**fabrikant**, soap-boiler; ~**glad**, (b) (-de), smooth; (bw) smoothly.
see'pier, lug-worm.
seep: ~**ketel**, soap-copper; ~**kis**, soap box; ~**kispolitikus**, tub-thumper; soap-box politician; ~**klip**, saponite, soap-stone; ~**kokery**, soapery, soap-house; ~**koper**, soap-merchant.
see: ~**plant**, sea (marine) plant; ~**poliep**, sea polyp; ~**polis**, marine policy.
seep'opera, soap opera.
see pos, ocean (overseas) mail; sea-post; ~**diens**, ocean mail service; ~**kontrak**, ocean (overseas) mail contract.
seep: ~**poeier**, soap powder; ~**pot**, soap cauldron.
se'ëpraal, (s) triumph; (w) (ge-), triumph.
se'ëpralend, (-e), victorious, triumphant.
see'prik, sea lamprey.

seep: ~**sieder**, soap-boiler; ~**siedery**, soap-works; ~**skuim**, lather, froth; ~**smeergoed**, opodeldoc; ~**soda**, caustic soda; ~**sop**, lather, soapsuds; ~**steen**, saponite, soapstone; ~**verhaal**, soap opera; ~**vlokkies**, soap-flakes; ~**vlokkiespoeier**, soap-flakes powder; ~**water**, soapy water.
seer¹, (s) (sere), sore, wound; *LOPENDE ~*, running sore; fester; *iem. in sy ~ TAS*, touch someone on the raw; (b) painful, sore; raw; *'n ~ plek*, a sore place.
seer², (bw) very much, extremely, highly; *ALTE ~*, only too much; *~ GEAGTE*, dear; *~ SEKER*, certainly; *TEN ~ste*, greatly, highly, very much indeed.
see: ~**raad**, naval board, admiralty; ~**raaf**, cormorant; ~**ramp**, naval (shipping) disaster.
seer'derig, (-e), rather sore.
see: ~**reënboog**, marine rainbow; ~**reg**, maritime (marine) law.
see'reis, voyage; ~**iger**, voyager, sea-traveller.
seer'heid, painfulness, soreness.
see'risiko, sea-risk.
seer: ~**keel**, sore throat; ~**kry**, (-ge-), get hurt; ~**maak**, (-ge-), hurt, damage; crock.
see'rob, sea-dog, seal.
seer'oë, sore eyes; ophthalmia.
see'roete, sea-route.
see'roof, piracy; ~ *pleeg*, commit piracy.
seer'oogblom, sore-eye flower.
see: ~**rook**, sea-smoke; ~**roos**, sea-anemone; ~**rowend**, (-e), piratic; ~**rower**, pirate; buccaneer, picaroon, corsair; ~**rowersnes**, pirates' lair; ~**rowersvlag**, Jolly Roger, pirate flag; ~**rowery**, piracy, buccaneering.
seer'rug, sore back, scalded back (of a horse); *'n onderwerp ~ ry*, harp on the same string continually; hackney a topic.
seer: ~**tjie**, (-s), small sore; ~**voet**, footsore (human); ~**vorming**, ulceration.
see'sand, sea-sand.
see'siek, seasick; ~**te**, seasickness, mal de mer.
see: ~**skade**, sea damage; ~**skap**, seascape; ~**skilder**, seascape painter; ~**skilpad**, sea turtle.
see'skuim, sea-foam; ~**er**, (-s), pirate, corsair, rover; ~**ery**, piracy.
see: ~**skulp**, sea-shell; ~**slag**, naval battle; ~**slak**, sea-slug; ~**slang**, sea-serpent; ~**sog**, trough, wake (of ship); ~**soldaat**, marine; ~**spieël**, sea level; *bo ~ spieël*, above sea level; ~**spinnekop**, spider-crab; ~**stad**, town on the coast; sea-city, coastal city; ~**ster**, starfish, sea-pad; finger-fish; ~**stewel**, sea-boot; ~**stilte**, calm at sea; ~**storm**, storm at sea; ~**straat**, strait; gut; ~**strand**, beach, foreshore; seashore; plage; ~**stroom**, ocean current; ~**strydmag**, naval force; ~**stuk**, seascape, seapiece; ~**swael**, scray; ~**tak**, coral branch; ~**teken**, seamark; ~**term**, sea term; ~**tog**, voyage; ~**tong**, sole; ~**tonnel**, submarine tunnel; ~**transport**, ocean (overseas) transport (freight); ~**trompet**, speaking-trumpet.
Seeu', Zealander; ~**s'**, (-e), of Zealand.
see'vaarder, (-s), navigator, mariner.
see'vaart, navigation; ~**kunde**, art of navigation; ~**kun'dig**, (-e), nautical; ~**lig**, marine light; ~**skool**, school of navigation.
see: ~**vaartuig**, sea(-going) vessel; ~**varend**, (-e), seafaring (nation); ocean-going (vessel); ~**vark**, porpoise, sea-hog; ~**verbinding(sdiens)**, sea communication; ~**versekeraar**, (marine) underwriter; ~**versekering**, marine insurance; ~**vesting**, coastal fortress.
se'ëvier, (ge-), triumph, carry the day, conquer; gain the victory; prevail; ~**end**, (-e), triumphant, victorious.
see'vinkel, sea fennel.
see'vis, sea-fish; ~**sery**, deep-sea fishing.
see: ~**vlak**, sea-level; ~**vlakmeting**, sea-level measurement; ~**vlakstasie**, sea-level station; ~**vliegtuig**, seaplane; ~**vliegtuigmoederskip**, sea-plane-carrier; ~**vlooi**, sea-flea; ~**voël**, sea-bird; ~**vrag**, freight; ~**vrou**, mermaid; ~**waar'dig**, (-e), seaworthy; ~**waar'digheid**, seaworthiness;

sefalopode / *sekretaresse*

~waarts, (b) (-e), seaward; (bw) seawards, towards the sea; ~water, sea-water; *al die ~water kan hom nie skoon was nie,* the sea can't cleanse him; ~watersteen, beryl; ~weer, seaward defence; ~weerboot, seaward defence vessel; ~weg, sea-route; ~wering, breakwater; ~wese, naval affairs; ~wette, maritime (marine) laws; ~wier, seaweed; alga; ~wind, sea-breeze, sea-wind; ~wolf, wolffish; ~wurm, sea worm, marine worm, lug.
sefalopo'de, (-s), cephalopod.
se'fier¹, (-e, -s), zephyr.
se'fier², (-e, -s), zephyr (cloth); ~stof, zephyr (cloth).
seg, (ge-) = sê.
se'ge, victory, triumph; ~krans, triumphal wreath; ~kroon, crown of victory; ~lied, paean, song (of victory); ~poort, triumphal arch; ~praal, (s) (..prale), triumph, victory; (w) (ge-), gain the victory, triumph (over); ~teken, trophy; ~tog, triumphal march; ~vuur, bonfire; ~wa, chariot.
seg'genskap, say, authority, voice; ~ *in 'n saak hê,* have a say (voice) in a matter.
seg'gingskrag, expressiveness, power of expression.
segment', (-e), segment; ~a'sie, segmentation; ~vormig, (-e), segmentary.
sê'goed, sayings, idiom(s); arguments; witticisms.
segrega'sie, segregation; ~beleid, segregation policy; ~skema, segregation scheme.
segregasionis', (-te), segregationist.
segregeer', (ge-), segregate.
segryns'leer, shagreen.
segs'man, (-ne, segeliede, eegolui), informant, authority, communicant, spokesman.
segs'wyse, (-s), standing phrase, set expression, saying; diction, manner of speech; idiom.
sei'dissel, (-s), milky thistle *(Sonchus oleraceus).*
seil, (s) (-e), tarpaulin, awning, sheet, sail, canvas; *alle ~e BYSIT,* hoist all sails; leave no stone unturned; *onder ~ GAAN,* set sail; *~e HYS,* hoist sail(s); *~e INNEEM,* take in (reef) sail(s); *~e ONTPLOOI,* unfurl sail(s); *die ~ vir iem. STRYK,* lower one's flag for someone; *die ~ in TOP voer,* live lavishly; *~e STRYK,* strike sail(s); *die ~ na die WIND hang,* trim one's sails to suit the wind; (w) (ge-), sail; slither (snake); ~balk, mast, beam; ~boot, sailing-boat; ~buikgord, wide girth; ~doek, sail-cloth, canvas, duck; ~doekse broek, ducks (trousers of sail-cloth); ~emmer, canvas bucket; ~er, (-s), sailing-ship; ~gare, ~garing, sail-yarn, thread, packthread, twine, string; ~jag, sailing-yacht; ~kamaste, canvas leggings; ~maker, sailmaker; ~makery, sail-works, sail yard; sail loft; ~mat, canvas bed (stretcher); ~naald, sail-needle, ~sak, canvas bag (pocket); ~skip, sailing-vessel; windjammer; brig; ~skoen, tacky; canvas shoe; ~slak, nautilus; ~sport, yachting; ~stoel, deckchair; hammock-chair; ~stof, canvas cloth; ~tog, sailing-excursion, ~vaartuig, sailing-vessel; ~vereniging, sailing club; ~vermoë, sailing power; ~vliegtuig, glider; ~wedstryd, regatta, yacht-race.
sein, (s) (-e), signal, sign; bell; *~e gee,* make signals; (w) (ge-), telegraph, wire; signal; flag (train); flash; *die nuus word na die hele wêreld ge~,* the news is flashed all over the world; ~afdeling, signalling-section; ~antenne, transmitting aerial; ~arm, signal-arm; ~behoeftes, signalling-stores; ~boek, signal-book; ~bord, signboard, signal board; ~brug, gantry; ~diens, signal service; ~dienseenheid, signal unit; ~diensoffisier, signal officer; ~dissipline, signal discipline; ~er, (-s), signaller, signal-man; ~fluit, signal-whistle; ~fout, telegraphic error; ~gewer, (-s), signalman (railways); banksman; starter (race); transmitter (telegram); manipulator; ~gleuf, signal-slit; ~granaat, signal grenade; ~huis(ie), ~kamer, signal cabin; ~kanon, signal-gun; ~kantoor, signal office; ~klok, signal-bell; ~kode, signalling-code; ~koste, telegraph charges; ~kramp, telegraph cramp; ~lamp, signalling-lamp; ~lantern, signal(ling)-lantern; ~lap, code-strip; ~letter, signal letter; ~lig, signal-light; ~man, signalman; ~mas, signal-post; ~meester, signal-master; ~middels, signal resources; ~ontvanger, (telephone) receiver; signal receiver; ~paal, signal-post; semaphore; ~pistool, signal-pistol; ~pos, signalling-post; ~register, signal code; ~skool, signalling-school; ~skoot, signal-gun (shot); ~skyf, signalling-disc; ~sleutel, transmitting key; ~spieël, heliograph; ~stasie, signalling-station; ~strook, signalling-panel; ~toestel, signalling apparatus.
seintuur', (..ture), belt (lady's); cincture (archit.); ~band, belting; ~koordband, petersham belting.
sein: ~verkeer, signal traffic; ~vlag, signal flag; jack; semaphore; ~vuur, signal fire; beacon; ~vuurpyl, signal rocket; ~wagter, signaller, signal-man; ~weg, signal route; ~werk, signalling.
seis, (-e), scythe.
sei'sing, gasket.
seis'mies, (-e), seismic.
seismograaf', (..grawe), seismograph (instrument); seismographer (person); ..mogram', (-me), seismogram; ..mologie', seismology; ..molo'gies, (-e), seismological; ..moloog', (..loë, ..loge), seismologist.
seis'mometer, **seismome'ter**, (-s), seismometer.
seismoskoop, (..skope), seismoscope.
seisoen', (-e), season; *BUITE die ~,* out of season; *VRUGTE volgens (na) die ~,* fruit in season.
seisoens': ~behoeftes, seasonal requirements; ~kaartjie, season-ticket; ~opruiming, end-of-season clearance (sale); ~verandering, change of season; seasonal variation; ~winde, periodical winds; ~wisseling, change of season.
se'kans, (sekante), secant (of circle).
sê'kans, opportunity of saying something; *ek het geen ~ gekry nie,* I couldn't get a word in edgeways.
se'kel, (-s), sickle; hook; reaping-hook; ~bos, sickle-bush *(Dichrostachys nutans);* ~duin, barchan; ~maan, sickle moon; ~nek, arched neck; ~stert, sickle tail; ~veer, sickle-feather; ~vormig, (-e), sickle-shaped, falcate, falciform.
se'ker, (b) [(-e)]; ~der, -ste, certain, sure; assured, positive, fiducial; *'n ~e IEM.,* a certain person; *'n ~e IETS,* something; *IETS ~s,* something positive; *van 'n ~e LEEFTYD,* of a certain age; *'n ~e MNR. X,* a certain Mr. X; *hy is altyd ~ van sy SAAK,* he is always so cocksure; *in ~e SIN,* in a sense.
se'ker, (bw) certainly, surely, assuredly, without fail; *ALTE ~,* precisely; *ek weet DIT ~,* I know it for a fact; *jy GAAN ~ dorp toe,* I suppose you are going to town; *ek IS nie so ~ nie,* I have my doubts; *daar was ~ 500 MENSE,* there were at least 500 people; *ek hoef ~ nie te SÊ nie,* I need scarcely say; *SO ~ as twee maal twee vier is,* as sure as fate; *jy SPEEL ~,* surely you don't mean that.
se'kere: *die ~ voor die onsekere neem,* take no chances.
se'kerheid, certainty, assurance, positiveness, caution; confidence; cert; certitude; safety; *vir ALLE ~,* to make doubly sure; *~ van AMPSBEHOUD,* security of tenure (of office); *BYKOMENDE (aanvullende) ~,* collateral security; *die ~ HÊ,* be satisfied (sure); *MET ~,* certainly, for sure.
se'kerheids: ~halwe, for safety sake; ~klep, safety-valve; ~koëffisiënt, degree of safety, safety factor; ~maatreël, security measure.
se'kerheidstelling, guarantee; security (loan); caution.
se'kering, (-e, -s), safety (cut-out) fuse; *die ~ het uitgebrand,* the fuse has blown.
se'kerings: ~bord, fuse board; ~doos, fuse box; ~draad, fuse-wire; ~kas, fuse-box; ~patroon, fuse-cartridge.
se'kerlik, certainly, decidedly, assuredly.
sekondant', (-e), second(er) (of motion); bottle-holder (prize ring); second (in duel).
sekon'de, (-s), second.
sekondeer', (ge-), second.
sekondêr', (-e), secondary; *~e skool,* secondary (high) school.
sekon'dewyser, second hand (watch).
sekreet', (sekrete), water-closet, privy.
sekre'sie, secretion.
sekretares'se, (-s), lady secretary.

sekretariaat', (..riate), secretaryship, secretariat(e).
sekretarieel', (..riële), secretarial.
sekreta'ris, (-se), secretary; amanuensis; clerk; ~**bene**, legs like broomsticks; ~**-tesourier**, secretary-treasurer; ~**voël**, secretary-bird.
seks, (s) sex, sexuality; (w) (ge-), sex.
sek'se, (-s), (ong.), sex; *die skone* ~, the fair sex; ~**r**, (-s), sexer.
sek'sie, (-s), section; platoon (mil.); ~**aanvoerder**, section-leader; ~**kamer**, dissecting room; ~**kolonne**, column of platoons; ~**vergadering**, group meeting.
seksis'me, sexism.
seksisties',(-e), sexistic.
seks'lewe, sex life.
seks'stimuleermiddel, aphrodisiac(s).
sekstant', (-e), sextant.
sekstet', (-te), sextet.
seksualiteit', sexuality.
seksueel', (seksuele), sexual; *..ele aantrekkingskrag*, sexual attraction.
seksuologie', sexology; ..**lo'gies**, sexological; ..**loog'**, (..loë), sexologist.
sekta'riër, (-s), sectarian.
sekta'ries, (-e), sectarian; denominational.
sektaris', (-se), sectarian.
sek'te, (-s), sect; denomination; ~**gees**, sectarianism; ~**-onderwys**, denominational education; ~**skool**, denominational school; ~**wese**, sectarianism, sectarism.
sek'tor, (-e, -s), sector.
sekularisa'sie, secularization, impropriation.
sekulariseer', (ge-), secularize, impropriate.
sekularis'me, secularism.
sekulêr', (-e), secular.
sekun'dawissel, second of exchange.
sekun'de, (-s), secunde.
sekun'dus, (..di, -se), secundus, second deputy; proxy.
sekureer', (ge-), secure; safeguard.
sekuriteit', (-e), security; safety; *prima* ~, gilt-edged security; ~**sheining**, security (safety) fence; ~**stroepe**, security troops; ~**swag**, security guard.
sekuur', ([..kure]; -der, -ste), exact, precise, accurate; *'n ding* ~ *weet*, know something positively; ~**heid**, precision, accuracy.
sekwen'sie, (-s), sequence.
sekwes'ter, (-s), sequestrator.
sekwestra'sie, sequestration; ~**bevel**, sequestration order.
sekwestreer', (ge-), sequestrate.
sel, (-le), cell; ~**agtig**, (-e), celluloid.
seladon', celadon (green).
seladoniet', celadonite.
selakant', (-e), coelacanth.
sel'beton, cellular concrete.
sel'de, seldom, rarely; ~ *of NOOIT*, ~ *indien OOIT*, seldom if ever, hardly ever.
sel'deling, cell division.
sel(d)ery', celery; *wilde* ~, smallage; ~**sout**, celery salt.
seld'saam, (..same), rare, scarce; peculiar; few and far between; ~**heid**, rarity, scarcity, fewness; peculiarity; curiosity, prodigy.
selebreer', (ge-), celebrate.
selebriteit', (-e), celebrity.
seleen', silenium.
selei' = **sjelei**.
selek'sie, (-s), selection.
selekteer', (ge-), select.
selektief', (..tiewe), selective.
selektiwiteit', selectivity.
seleniet', selenite.
sele'nium, selenium.
self, (s) self; ego, own individuality; (vnw) self; *die BELEEFDHEID* ~, the essence of politeness; *sy DOEN dit* ~, she does it in person; *EK* ~, I myself; *hy moet* ~ *GAAN*, he must go himself; *ek het dit* ~ *GESIEN*, I saw it with my own eyes; *ek het* ~ *VYF*, I have five of my own.
self: ~ **aanbidding**, self-worship; narcissism; ~**aansitter**, (-s), self-starter.

self'aanvullend, (-e), self-renewing; ~*e krediet*, revolving credit.
self: ~**afsluiter**, (-s), automatic shutter; ~**agting**, self-respect; ~**analise**, self-analysis.
self'bediening, self-service; ~**swinkel**, self-service shop.
self: ~**bedrog**, self-deception; self-deceit; ~**bedwang**, restraint, self-control; ~**begogeling**, self-delusion; ~**behaag'lik**, (-e), self-complacent; ~**behae**, self-complacency.
self'beheersing, self-control, self-possession, collectedness; *jou* ~ *bewaar*, keep one's self-control.
self: ~**behoud**, self-preservation; self-defence; ~**bejammering**, self-pity; ~**beklag**, self-pity; ~**beperking**, self-restraint; ~**besinning**, introspection; ~**beskerming**, self-protection; ~**beskikking**, self-determination; ~**beskikkingsreg**, right of self-determination; ~**beskimping**, self-abuse.
self: ~**beskuldiging**, self-accusation; ~**bespieëlend**, (-e), introspective; ~**bespieëling**, introspection; ~**bestemming**, self-determination; ~**bestuiwing**, self-pollination; ~**besturend (-e)**, autonomous; ~**bestuur**, self-government, home-rule, autonomy; ~**bevlekking**, onanism, self-pollution, masturbation; ~**bevrediging**, self-indulgence; ~**bewegend**, (-e), automatic, self-propelling, self-acting; automotive.
self'bewus, (-te), self-assured; self-conscious; assertive; ~**syn**, self-assertion; self-consciousness; ~**theid**, self-consciousness; aplomb.
self'binder, (-s), self-binder.
self'de, same, identical; ~ *wat*, it does not matter what; ~ *wie*, it does not matter who.
self: ~**dienwinkel**, self-service shop; ~**digtend**, (-e), self-sealing; ~**gedrewe**, self-propelled; ~**gekose**, self-elected; ~**gemaak**, (-te), self-made; home-brewed, home-made.
self'genoegsaam, (..same), self-sufficient; smug; ~**heid**, self-sufficiency; egotism, smugness.
self: ~**gevoel**, self-consciousness; ~**geweefde**, ~**gewewe**, homespun; ~**handhawing**, self-assertion; ~**heid**, personality, selfhood.
self'ingenome, self-complacent, smug; ~**heid**, self-complacency.
self'kant, selvedge (selvage); *die* ~ *v.d. samelewing*, the dregs of society; ~**garing**, list yarn.
self: ~**kastyding**, self-chastisement, self-torture; ~**kennis**, self-knowledge; ~**kritiek**, self-criticism; ~**kweller**, self-tormentor; ~**kwelling**, self-torture; ~**laaier**, self-loading gun (rifle); ~**liefde**, self-love, narcissism; ~**meting**, autometry.
self'moord, suicide; felo de se; *met* ~ *GELYK*= *STAAN*, be suicidal; ~ *PLEEG*, commit suicide; ~**enaar**, suicide; felo de se; ~**enares**, female suicide; ~**end**, (-e), suicidal; ~**gedagtes**, suicide thoughts; ~**neigings**, suicidal tendencies.
self: ~**offering**, self-immolation; ~**onderhoudend**, (-e), self-supporting; ~**onderrig**, self-tuition.
self'ondersoek, self-examination; heart-searching, introspection; ~**end**, (-e), introspective.
self: ~**ontbrandend**, (-e), self-igniting; ~**ontbranding**, auto-ignition, spontaneous (self-) ignition (combustion); ~**onthouding**, self-denial; ~**ontleding**, self-analysis; ~**ontplooiing**, self-expression, self-realization; ~**ontstaan**, spontaneous generation.
self'ontsteking = **selfontbranding**.
self: ~**ontwikkeling**, self-education, self-development; ~**oorgawe**, self-surrender; ~**oorskatting**, self-conceit; ~**oorwinning**, self-conquest; ~**opgeleg**, (-de), self-imposed; ~**opofferend**, (-e), self-sacrificing; ~**opoffering**, self-sacrifice, self-devotion; ~**opvoeding**, self-education; ~**portret**, self-portrait.
self'pyniging, self-mortification, self-torture.
self'reëlend, (-e), self-regulating, self-adjusting.
self: ~**reëling**, autoregulation; ~**regerend**, (-e), self-governing, autonomous; ~**regering**, self-government, autonomy, homerule; ~**registrerend**, (-e), self-recording, self-registering.
self'respek, self-respect, self-esteem; ~**terend**, (-e), self-respecting.
self'rigtend, (-e), self-aligning.

selfrysend, (-e), self-raising (flour).
selfs, even; ~ *AS dit waar was,* even if it were true; ~ *JAN was laat,* even John was late; ~ *30 km ver kan 'n mens die bergtop sien,* even at a distance of 30 km one can see the mountain-top.
self'sentrerend, (-e), self-centring; ~ *e klouplaat,* scroll-chuck.
self'sluitend, (-e), self-closing; ~ *e DEUR,* self-closing door; ~ *e KLEP,* automatic-closing valve.
self: ~ **sluitmoer,** self-locking nut; ~ **smerend, (-e),** self-lubricating; ~ **spot,** self-ridicule.
selfstan'dig, (-e), independent, self-reliant, self-supporting, unaided; ~ *e NAAMWOORD,* noun, substantive; ~ *WEES,* be one's own master; ~ **heid,** independence, autonomy; individuality; identity; self-reliance; ~ **heidsverandering,** transubstantiation.
self'steller, self-adjuster.
self'stryd, internal struggle.
self'sug, egoism, selfishness; ~ **'tig, (-e),** selfish, egoistic; ~ **'tigheid,** selfishness.
self'tevrede, self-contented, self-satisfied; complacent; ~ **nheid,** complacency.
self: ~ **tug,** self-discipline; ~ **uiting,** self-expression; ~ **veragting,** self-contempt; ~ **verblinding,** self-deception; ~ **verbranding,** spontaneous combustion; ~ **verdediging,** self-defence; ~ **verduidelikend,** self-explanatory.
self'vergenoeg, (-de), self-complacent; ~ **dheid,** self-sufficiency; complacency.
self: ~ **vergiftiging,** auto-intoxication, self-poisoning; ~ **vergoding,** self-idolization, self-worship; ~ **verheerliking,** self-glorification; ~ **verheffing,** self-exaltation; ~ **verklarend, (-e),** self-explanatory; ~ **verloënend, (-e),** self-denying; ~ **verloëning,** self-denial, abnegation, mortification; ~ **vernedering,** self-abasement; ~ **vernietiging,** self-destruction; ~ **veroordeling,** self-condemnation; ~ **verryking,** self-enrichment; ~ **versaking,** self-denial, abnegation; ~ **versekerdheid,** aplomb, self-possession.
self'versorgend, (-e), self-supplying; self-supporting.
self'versorging, self-sufficiency.
self'vertroue, self-reliance, self-confidence, morale, assurance; ~ **nd, (-e),** cocksure; self-confident, self-reliant.
self: ~ **verwesenliking,** self-realization; ~ **verwyt,** self-reproach; ~ **voerder,** automatic feeder.
self'voldaan, (..dane), self-complacent; smug; ~ **heid,** self-sufficiency, complacency, smugness.
self: ~ **voldoening,** self-complacency, self-satisfaction; ~ **voorsiening,** self-sufficiency; ~ **waardering,** autometry
self'weerspreking, contradicting oneself; contradiction in terms.
self'werkend, (-e), automatic, self-acting; autodynamic; ~ *e ONTKOPPELING,* automatic disconnecting-coupling; ~ *e SMEERTOESTEL,* automatic lubricator; ~ *e SMERING,* automatic oiling.
self'werksaamheid, self activity.
sel'holte, cell lumen.
selibaat', (-bate), celibacy; **..batêr', (-e),** celibate, celibatarian.
sel: ~ **kern,** nucleus of the cell; ~ **leer,** cytology; ~ **letjie, (-s),** cellule.
sellofaan', cellophane (registered trade name).
sellulêr', (-e), cellular; ~ *e opsluiting,* solitary confinement.
sellulo'ïde, selluloïed', celluloid.
sellulo'se, cellulose.
se'loglas, celoglass (registered trade name).
selons': ~ **pampoen,** hook-necked pumpkin, ~ **roos,** Ceylon rose, oleander.
sel'ontwikkeling, cytogenesis.
seloom', (selome), coelom.
seloot', (selote), zealot.
sel: ~ **oplossing,** cytolysis; ~ **orgaan,** organelle; ~ **protoplasma,** cytoplasm; ~ **sisteem,** solitary-confinement system; ~ **stof,** cellulose; ~ **straf,** solitary confinement; ~ **teorie,** cell theory; ~ **verdeling,** mitosis; ~ **vergif,** cytotoxin; ~ **vormig, (-e),** cellular; cellulate; ~ **vorming,** cellulation; ~ **wand,** cell wall; ~ **weefsel, (-s),** cellular tissue, parenchyma.

semafoor', (..fore), semaphore, signal-post; ~ **berig,** semaphore message; ~ **kode,** semaphore code; ~ **seiner,** semaphore signaller; ~ **vlag,** semaphore flag.
semantiek', semantics.
seman'ties, (-e), semantic.
semasiologie', semasiology; **..lo'gies, (-e),** semasiologic(al).
se'mel: ~ **agtig, (-e),** full of bran, branny; ~ **broek,** shy fellow; ~ **brood,** bran bread (loaf); ~ **knoper,** hair-splitter; ~ **meel,** pollard; ~ **s,** bran; *meng jou met ~ s, dan vreet die varke jou,* he that toucheth pitch shall be defiled; ~ **sakkie,** bustle; ~ **water,** bran-gruel.
se'men, semen; ~ **telling,** semen count.
sement', (-e), cement; ~ **agtig, (-e),** cementitious; ~ **a'sie,** cementation; ~ **bekleding,** cement lining; ~ **beton,** cement concrete; ~ **blok,** cement block; ~ **eer', (ge-),** cement; ~ **eer'oond,** cementing furnace; ~ **e'ring,** cementation; ~ **fabriek,** cement factory; ~ **gips,** cement stucco; ~ **klip,** cement-rock, ~ **koper,** cement buyer; cement copper; ~ **laag, (..lae),** cement gunning; ~ **plaat,** ~ **platstuk,** cement slab; ~ **spuit,** cement-gun; ~ **staal,** blister (converted) steel; ~ **steen,** cement brick; ~ **stryksel,** cement wash; ~ **verf,** concrete paint; ~ **vloer,** cement floor; ~ **yster,** cement iron.
semes'ter, (-s), semester, half-year.
Semiet', (-e), Semite.
se'mifinale, (-s), semifinal (game).
seminaar', (..nare), seminar.
semina'rie, (-s), seminary.
semiotiek', semiotics.
semio'ties, (-e), semiotic.
Semi'ties, (-e), Semitic.
Semitis'me, Semitism; **..tis'ties, (-e),** Semitic.
senaat', (senate), senate; ~ **sitting,** session of the senate; ~ **s'vergadering,** senate meeting.
sena'tor, (-e, -s), senator.
senatri'se, (-s), senatrix, senatress.
send, (ge-), send; ~ **antenne,** transmitting aerial; ~ **brief,** epistle, letter, missive.
sen'deling, (-e), missionary; emissary; propagandist; ~ **genootskap,** missionary society.
sen'der, (-s), sender, consignor; transmitter (radio).
send'golf, transmitting-wave.
sen'ding, consignment; mission; *die binnelandse ~,* home mission; ~ **fees,** mission festival; ~ **genootskap,** missionary society; ~ **kerk,** mission church; ~ **pos,** mission station; ~ **skool,** mission(ary) school; ~ **stasie,** mission station; ~ **veld,** mission field; ~ **werk,** mission(ary) work; ~ **werkster,** female mission worker.
send: ~ **sleutel,** sending-key, transmission key; ~ **stasie,** transmitting station; sending-station; ~ **toestel,** transmitting set.
se'neblare, senna leaves *(Cassia senna obovata).*
Se'negal, Senegal; ~ **ees', (..lese),** Senegalese.
se'negroen, bugle-weed.
se'nepeule, senna pods.
seng, (ge-), singe, scorch, burn; ~ **ing,** singeing, scorching.
seniel', (-e), senile.
seniliteit', senility.
se'ning, (-s), sinew; ~ **agtig, (-e),** tendinous; ~ **blare,** *see* **seneblare;** ~ **gare,** ~ **garing,** sinewy cords along the spine; ~ **knoop,** ganglion; ~ **rig, (-e),** sinewy, leathery.
se'nior, (-s), senior; ~ **teit',** seniority; ~ **sertifikaat,** senior certificate (examination).
se'nit, zenith, summit.
sen'na, senna (leaves) = **seneblare.**
senobiet', (-e), cenobite.
senotaaf', (-e), cenotaph.
sens, (-e), scythe, reaping-hook.
sensa'sie, (-s), sensation; thrill; stir; ~ **berig,** sensational news; ~ **jag,** sensationalism; ~ **nuus,** sensational news; ~ **pers,** yellow press; gutter press; ~ **roman,** thriller, penny horrible, penny dreadful, shocker; ~ **soeker,** sensation-hunter; ~ **stuk,** thriller, sensation play; shock play; ~ **sug,** sen-

sationalism; ~**verhaal**, thriller, hair-raising story; ~**wekkend**, **(-e)**, sensational.
sensasioneel', (..**nele**), sensational, hair-raising.
sensibilisa'sie, sensitization.
sensibiliseer', **(ge-)**, sensitize.
sensitief', (..**tiewe**), sensitive.
sensitivis', **(-te)**, sensitivist; ~**me**, sensitivism.
sensitiwiteit', sensitiveness, sensitivity; ~**sopleiding**, sensitivity training.
sen'sor, **(-s)**, censor; ~**sen'sor**, **(ge-)**, ~**eer'**, **(ge-)**, censor.
senso'ries, **(-e)**, sensorial, sensory.
sensualis', **(-te)**, sensualist; ~**me**, sensualism; ~**ties**, **(-e)**, sensualistic.
senso'ries, **(-e)**, sensorial, sensory.
sensualis', **(-te)**, sensualist; ~**me**, sensualism; ~**ties**, **(-e)**, sensualistic.
sensualiteit', sensuality.
sensueel', (**sensuele**), sensual.
sensureer', **(ge-)**, censure.
sen'sus, **(-se)**, census; ~**kantoor**, census office; ~**opgaaf**, ~**opgawe**, census return; ~**opnemer**, census taker.
sensuur', censure; censorship; excommunication; *MOSIE van* ~ , motion of censure; *ONDER* ~ *sit*, forbid someone the use of the sacraments; ~**raad**, board of censors.
sent, **(-e)**, cent; *REKEN dit om in* ~*e*, convert it to cents; *g'n* ~ *WERD nie*, not worth a button.
sen'tenaar, **(-s)**, hundredweight, cental, quintal.
sen'ter, **(-s)**, centre; ~**boor**, centre bit; ~**driekwart**, centre three-quarter; ~**pons**, centre punch; ~**-speler**, centre player; centre forward.
sentesimaal', (..**male**), centesimal.
sen'ti: ~**aar**, sentaire; ~**gram**, centigramme; ~**liter**, centilitre.
sentiment', sentiment; ~**alis'**, **(-te)**, sentimentalist; ~**aliteit'**, sentimentality; mawkishness; ~**eel'**, (..**tele**), sentimental; lackadaisical; maudlin, mawkish.
sen'timeter, centimeter.
sen'tour, **(-s)** centaur.
sentraal', (..**trale**), central; ..*trale ERUPSIE*, central eruption; ..*trale SMERING*, central lubrication; ..*trale VERWARMING*, central heating.
sentra'le, **(-s)**, power-station, power-house, generating-plant; (telephone) exchange.
sentralisa'sie, centralization.
sentraliseer', **(ge-)**, centralize.
sentraliteit', centrality.
sentreer', **(ge-)**, centre; ~**haak**, centre-square; ~**skroef**, centring-screw.
sentrifugaal', (..**gale**), centrifugal.
sentripetaal', (..**tale**), centripetal, afferent.
sen'trum, (..**tra**, **-s**), centre; ~**party**, centre (middle) party.
se'nu: *see* **senuwee**; ~**aandoening**, nervous affection; ~**aanval**, nervous attack, hysterics; ~**ag'tig**, **(-e)**, nervous; ~**ag'tigheid**, nervousness; ~**arts**, neuropathist, nerve specialist; ~**as**, neuron; ~**baan**, nerve track; ~**beroerte**, apoplexy; ~**bundel**, nervebundle; ~**dokter**, neuropathist, nerve specialist; ~**gestel**, nervous system; ~**hoofpyn**, nervous headache; ~**-insinking**; ~**-instorting**, nervous break-down (collapse); ~**knoop**, ganglion; ~**kwaal**, nervous disease; neurotic disease; ~**loos**, (..**lose**), nerveless; ~**lyer**, nervous sufferer, neurotic; ~**middel**, neurotic; ~**ontsteking**, neuritis; ~**oorlog**, war of nerves; ~**pasiënt**, neurotic, nerve patient; ~**prikkeling**, stimulation (excitation) of the nerves; ~**pyn**, nerve pain; neuralgia; ~**ring**, nerve-ring; ~**sel**, nerve cell; ~**sentrum**, ganglion; ~**siek**, **(-e)**, neurotic; ~**siekte**, nerve disease, neurosis; ~**skok**, nervous shock; ~**spanning**, nervous tension; ~**stelsel**, nervous system; ~**sterkend**, **(-e)**, nerve-strengthening; ~**stillend**, **(-e)**, soothing for the nerves; ~**storing**, nervous disturbance; ~**swak**, neurasthenic; ~**swakte**, neurasthenia; ~**tergend**, **(-e)**, nerve-racking; ~**toeval**, nervous breakdown; ~**trekking**, nervous twitch; ~**verslappend**, **(-e)**, enervating; ~**versterker**, nerve tonic; ~**vesel**, nerve fibre.

se'nuwee, **(-s)**, nerve; *AFFERENTE* ~ , afferent nerve; *EFFERENTE* ~ , efferent nerve; *dit op sy* ~*s KRY*, become hysterical (wrought-up); *aan die* ~*s LY*, suffer from nerves; *MOTORIESE* ~ , motor nerve; *SIMPATIESE* ~ , sympathetic nerve; ~**aandoening**, affection of the nerves; ~**aanval**, hysterics; ~**ag'tig**, **(-e)**, nervous, neurotic; jumpy, flurried; *dit maak my* ~ *agtig*, it gets on my nerves; it makes me nervous; ~**ag'tigheid**, nervousness; jumpiness; ~**draad**, nerve fibre.
se'nuweefsel, nerve tissue.
se'nuwee: ~**hoofpyn**, migraine; ~**knoop**, ganglion, nerve-knot; ~**kwellend**, **(-e)**, nerve-racking; ~**middel**, nerve specific; ~**ontsteking**, neuritis; ~**oorlog**, war of nerves; ~**orrel**, excitable (nervous) person; bundle of nerves; ~**pasiënt**, neurotic; ~**prikkeling**, excitation of the nerves; innervation; ~**pyn**, neuralgia; ~**sel**, nerve cell; ~**siekte**, neurosis; ~**siekteleer**, neurology; ~**stelsel**, nervous system; ~**swakte**, neurasthenia; ~**toeval**, nervous prostration; ~**trekking**, jactitation, jerk; chorea; ~**vleg**, plexus; ~**weefsel**, nerve tissue; ~**wrak**, nervous wreck.
se'nu: ~**werking**, nervous action; ~**wortel**, nerveroot.
separa'sie, separation.
separatis', **(-te)**, separatist; ~**me**, separatism; ~**ties**, **(-e)**, separatist(ic).
separeer', (ong.), **(ge-)**, separate.
se'perig, **(-e)**, soapy; ~**heid**, soapiness.
se'pia, sepia; brown pigment from cuttle-fish.
sep'sis, sepsis, putrefaction.
Septem'ber, September; ~**blom** chinkerinchee; ~**vakansie**, Michaelmas.
sep'ter, **(-s)**, sceptre; *die* ~ *swaai*, wield the sceptre.
septet', **(-te)**, septet.
sep'ties, **(-e)**, septic.
septisemie', septicaemia.
Septuagint', Septuagint.
se'raf, **(-im, -s)**, seraph.
se'rafslied, song of angels.
serafyn'orrel, melodeon, melodion, seraphine.
serail', **(-s)**, seraglio.
seramiek', ceramics.
sera'mies, **(-e)**, ceramic.
serasi'ne, cerasin (cherry-gum).
se're, sere (bot.).
serebel'lum, **(-s)**, cerebellum.
serebraal', (..**brale**), cerebral; *serebrale gestremdheid*, cerebral palsy.
se'rebrum, **(-s)**, cerebrum.
sereen', (**serene**; **serener**, **-ste**), serene.
seremo'nie, **(-s)**, ceremony; function; ..**nieel'**, (..**niële**), ceremonial, formal; ~**meester**, master of ceremonies; ~**meesteres**, mistress of ceremonies; ..**nieus'**, **(-e)**, ceremonial, formal.
serena'de, **(-s)**, serenade.
sereniteit', serenity.
se'rerig, **(-e)**, rather sore.
sereus', **(-e)**, serous.
serfyn', **(-e)**, harmonium.
ser'ge, serge.
se'rie, **(-ë, -s)**, series; break (billiards); ~**beeld**, serial photograph; ~**beeldkamera**, serial camera; ~**skakeling**, series connection; ~**gewyse**, serially.
serieus', **(-e)**, serious; ~**heid**, seriousness.
sering', **(-e)**, lilac; ~**bessie**, chinaberry; ~**bloeisel**, lilac-blossom; ~**boom**, lilac-tree, pipe-tree; ~**suur**, syringaic acid.
serk', **(-e)**, tombstone.
sermein'peer, St. Germain pear; *so suur soos 'n* ~ , as sour as a lemon.
sermoen', **(-e)**, sermon, lecture.
se'ro, **(-'s)**, naught, zero.
seroet'¹, **(-e)**, cheroot, cigar.
seroet'², **(-e)**, Native basket.
serologie', serology; ..**lo'gies**, serological.
seroloog', (..**loë**), serologist.
serp, **(-e)**, muffler, scarf, sash.
serpent', **(-e)**, serpent; shrew.
serpentyn', serpentine; ~**klip**, ~**steen**, serpentine stone.

ser're, (-s), conservatory, closed (glass) verandah.
serru'ria, blushing brides (sweets).
sersant', (-e), sergeant; ~-**majoor**, (-s), sergeant-major; ~ **s'menasie**, sergeants' mess; ~ **strepe**, sergeant's stripes.
ser'sje, serge.
sersjet', sergette.
sertifikaat', (..**kate**), certificate; diploma; licence.
sertifiseer', (ge-), certify.
se'rum, (-s), serum.
serval', (-s), serval, tiger-cat.
servet', (-te), serviette, (table-)napkin; *te groot vir 'n ~ en te klein vir 'n tafeldoek (-laken)*, between hay and grass; ~ **goed**, diaper; napery; ~ **ring**, serviette-ring.
servies', (-e), dinner-service, set (of crockery, glass-ware).
servikaal', (..**kale**), cervical.
serviliteit', servility.
servituut' = **serwituut**.
ser'vomotor, (-e), servomotor.
Ser'wië, Serbia; ~ **r**, (-s), Serbian; ..**wies**, (-e), Serbian.
serwituut', (..**tute**), claim, servitude, easement; burden (on landed property); *met 'n ~ BESWAAR, 'n ~ LÊ op*, subject to an easement; impose a servitude on.
ses, (-se), six; *'n man van ~ se KLAAR*, a man of many parts; *'n ~ SLAAN*, hit a (six) boundary; ~ **ag(t)ste**, six-eighths.
se'sam, sesame; ~, *gaan oop!* open sesame!
ses: ~ **benig**, (-e), six-legged; ~ **daags**, (-e), sextan (fever); six-day (week); ~ **de**, (-s), sixth; ~ **delig**, (-e), consisting of six parts; ~ **dubbel(d)**, (-de), sixfold.
seses'sie, secession.
sesessionis', (-te), secessionist; ~ **me**, secessionism.
ses'hoek, hexagon; ~ **ig**, (-e), hexagonal.
ses'honderd, six hundred.
ses: ~ **jarig**, (-e), of six years, six years old; ~ **jarige**, (-s), six-year-old (child); ~ **kantig**, (-e), six-sided, hexagonal; ~ **kantkoppeling**, hexagon connection; ~ **lettergrepig**, (-e), of six syllables; ~ **ling**, sextuplet; ~ **loopsrewolwer**, six-shooter; ~ **maandeliks**, (-e), half-yearly.
Seso'tho, Sesotho.
ses: ~ **pantbal**, six-panel ball; ~ **ponder**, (-s), six-pounder; ~ **poot**, hexapod; ~ **potig**, (-e), hexapodal.
ses'reëlig, (-e), of six lines; ~ *e versie*, sextain, sextina.
ses'sie¹, (-s), session, sitting.
ses'sie², (-s), cession.
ses'sie³, (-s), little six.
sessiel', sessile.
sessiona'ris, (-se), cessionary, assignee, transferee.
ses'snarig, (-e), six-stringed.
ses'stemmig, (-e), six-voiced.
ses'sydig, (-e), six-sided, hexagonal.
ses'tal, six; hexad; ~ **lig**, (-e), six in number, senary.
ses'tien, sixteen; ~ **de**, (-s), sixteenth; ~ **de-eeus**, (-e), of the 16th century.
ses'tig, sixty; *jy is ~!* you are silly; ~ **er**, (-s), sexagenarian; *in die ~ erjare*, in the years between 60 and 70 (the sixties); ~ **jarig**, (-e), of sixty years, sixty years old; ~ **ste**, (-s), sixtieth; ~ **tal**, (about) sixty; ~ **voud**, multiple of sixty.
ses'urig, (-e), of six hours; six-hour(ly).
ses'uur¹, six o'clock.
sesuur², (..**sure**), caesura.
ses'vlak, hexahedron; ~ **kig**, (-e), hexahedral.
ses'voet, hexameter; ~ **ig**, (-e), hexametric.
ses'voud, multiple of six, ~ **ig**, (-e), sextuple, sixfold.
set, (s) (-te), move, push, trick; crank (plates); putt (golf); mount (diamonds); set; *'n GEESTIGE ~*, a witty saying (bon mot); *'n GEMENE ~*, a dirty trick; *'n SLIM ~*, a clever move; *'n VERKEERDE ~*, a wrong move; (w) (ge-), set, compose, set up (in type); *'n BEEN ~*, set a leg; *HARE ~*, set hair; *LETTERS ~*, compose type; *SAAGTANDE ~*, set a saw; *in SILWER ge~*, mounted in silver.
Seta'seë, Cetaceans (whales).
se'tel, (s) (-s), seat (in parliament); see (papal); throne; headquarters (of company); chair; bench; residence; (w) (ge-), reside, live in (at); sit.
set: ~ **fout**, printer's error; ~ **gereedskap**, setting-tool; ~ **haak**, boat-hook; composing stick (printing); ~ **hamer**, set-hammer, fuller, dolly; ~ **hou**, putt.
seties', (-e), schottische.
set'laar, (-s), settler.
Set'laarsdag, Settlers' Day.
set'lyn¹, paternoster line (fishing).
set'lyn², composing-rule.
set: ~ **maat**, jig (gauge); ~ **masjien**, linotype, monotype, composing-machine, typograph.
set'meel, amylum, amyloid, starch, farina; ~ **agtig**, (-e), amylaceous, starchy; ~ **skede**, endoderm.
set: ~ **perk**, (putting-)green (golf); ~ **pil**, suppository, collyrium.
set: ~ **plank**, (printer's) galley; ~ **raam**, composing-frame; ~ **sel**, (-s), composed lines, type.
set-set', putt-putt.
set: ~ **spel**, putting; ~ **spieël**, type-page (-area); ~ **stok**, putter.
set'ter¹, (-s), putter (golf).
set'ter², (-s), compositor; ~ **drukker**, twicer; ~ **y**, (-e), compositor's room; composition.
set'ting, (-e, -s), setting, mounting, mount, reduction (surgery).
set: ~ **werk**, type-setting; putting (golf); ~ **yster**, saw-die; putter (golf).
seun, (-s), son, lad, boy, gossoon; *die Seun van die MENS*, the Son of Man; *die VERLORE ~*, the prodigal son; ~ **kind**, boy.
seuns: ~ **agtig**, (-e), boyish; ~ **boek**, boy's book; ~ **dubbelspel**, boys' doubles; ~ **enkelspel**, boys' singles; ~ **jare**, boyhood (in years).
seun'skap, sonship.
seuns: ~ **kind**, boy; ~ **klas**, boys' class.
seun'skoen, boy's shoe; *sy ~ e ontgroei*, grow up.
seun'skool, boys' school.
seuns'koshuis, boys' hostel.
seun'tjie, (-s), small boy; boy baby.
seur¹, (vero.), (s) (-s), sir, boss.
seur², (w) (ge-), worry, nag, bother; ~ **der**, (-s), dawdler; ~ **derig**, (-e), bothersome, tedious; ~ **kous**, tedious person, bore, pest, nuisance; ~ **stem**, tedious voice.
se'vraag, leading question.
se'we, (-(n)s), seven; ~ *MAAL*, seven times; ~ *UUR*, seven hours; ~ **armig**, (-e), seven-armed; seven-branched; ~ **daags**, (-e), seven-day, seven days'; ~ **delig**, (-e), consisting of seven parts; ~ **dubbeld**, (-e), seven-fold.
Se'wegesternte, Pleiades.
se'wehoek, heptagon; ~ **ig**, (-e), heptagonal, septangular.
se'we: ~ **jaarliks**, (-e), septennial; ~ **jaartjie**, (-s), immortelle, everlasting.
se'wejarig, (-e), of seven years; seven years old, septennial; ~ **e**, (-s), a seven-year-old.
se'we: ~ **lettergrepig**, (-e), heptasyllabic; ~ **maands**, (-e), of seven months, seven months old.
se'wemylslaarse, seven league boots; *met ~ oor jou moeilikheid heenstap*, take one's troubles in one's stride.
se'wende, (-s), seventh.
Se'wendedagadventiste, Seventh Day Adventists.
se'wentien, seventeen; ~ **de**, (-s), seventeenth; ~ **de-eeus**, (-e), of the seventeenth century.
se'wentig, seventy; ~ **er**, (-s), septuagenarian; *in die ~ erjare*, in the seventies; ~ **jarig**, (-e), seventy years old, septuagenary, septuagenarian; ~ **jarig**, (-s), septuagenarian; ~ **ste**, seventieth; ~ **voud**, (-e), ~ **voudig**, (-e), seventyfold.
se'wenuur, seven o'clock.
Se'wester, Pleiades.
se'wetal, seven; heptad; ~ **lig**, (-e), seven in number, septenary.
se'wetjie, (-s), small seven; ~ **s**, sevens (card game).
se'we-uur, seven o'clock.
se'wevlak, heptahedron; ~ **ig**, (-e), heptahedral.
se'wevoetig, (-e), with seven feet.
se'wevoud, multiple of seven; ~ **ig**, (-e), sevenfold, septuple.

se'we: ~weeksvaring, thirty day fern, seven week fern, hare's-foot; ~yster, no. 7 iron, mashie niblick.
Seychel'le: die ~, the Seychelles.
sfeer, (sfere), sphere; region; domain; walk (of life) range.
sfe'ries, (-e), spherical.
sferoïdaal', (..dale), spheroidal.
sferoï'de, (-s), sferoïed', (-e), spheroid.
sfinks, (-e), sphinx; ~agtig, (-e), sphinx-like.
siaan', cyanogen; ~kali, potassium cyanide; ~suur, cyanic acid; ~waterstofgas, hydrocyanic acid gas, prussic acid.
Si'am, Siam; ~ees', (..mese), Siamese.
siani'de, sianied', cyanide.
sibariet', (-e), sybarite.
sibari'ties, (-e), sybaritic.
sib'be, (-s), sib; ~toets, sib-test.
Sibe'rië, Siberia; ~r, (-s), Siberian; ..ries, (-e), Siberian.
sibil'le, (-s), sibyl.
sibillyns', (-e), sibylline.
sibo'rie, ciborium.
Siciliaan', (..liane), Sicilian; ~s', (-e), Sicilian.
Sici'lië, Sicily.
sid'der, (ge-), shudder, shake, tremble; quiver; ~aal, electric eel; ~ing, trembling, shudder, quake, quaking; ~rog, electric ray.
si'der, cider.
side'ries, (-e), sidereal.
s''ie, (-s) small s.
sie = sie(s)!
sie'al, inauspicious; unfortunate; dis ~ om onder 'n LEER deur te loop, it's unfortunate to pass underneath a ladder; moenie ~ PRAAT nie, don't tempt fortune.
sie'bie, (s) (-s), little dog, pup; (w) (ge-), wee-wee; drizzle.
sied, (ge-), boil, seethe.
siedaar'! see! behold!
sie'dat: nie ~ nie, not even as little as this.
sie'dend, (-e), seething, boiling; ~ BOOS, ~ van WOEDE, exceedingly angry, seething with rage.
sieg'lem, scraper (woodwork).
sie'jy! get out! go away! scram! (to a dog).
siek, ill, sick, indisposed; distempered; invalid; so ~ soos 'n HOND, as sick as a dog; hy HOU hom ~, he feigns illness, he is malingering; jou ~ LAG, split one's sides with laughing; laugh oneself sick; jy is SKOON ~! you don't know what you are talking about; ~ WEES vir, be sick of something; ~ WORD, fall ill; ~bed, sick-bed; dit was sy laaste ~bed, it was his death-bed.
sie'ke, (-s), patient, sick person, invalid; die ~ dra die gesonde, the less privileged helps the more privileged; ~afdeling, sick (infirmary) ward; ~appèl, sick-parade; ~besoek, sick-call, visit to the sick; ~besorger, infirmarion; ~boeg, sick-berth; sickbay; ~dieet, invalid diet; ~draer, stretcher-bearer; ~fonds, sick-fund; ~geld, sick-pay; ~huis, hospital, infirmary; ~-inrigting, infirmary; ~kamer, sick-room; ~kamermaniere, bedside manner; ~kookkuns, invalid cookery; ~kos, invalid fare; ~lokaal, sick-bay (hospital); ~loon, sick pay; ~lys, sick-list; ~parade, sick-parade; ~rapport, sick-report; ~rig, (-e), unwell, indisposed; ~righeid, indisposition; ~saal, ward; ~saaldiens, ward-duty; ~saaloppasser, ward-orderly; ~sinjaal, sick-call; ~stoel, invalid-chair; ~troos, comfort for the sick; ~trooster, sick-visitor (-comforter), curate; ~verpleegster, nurse; ~verpleging, nursing.
siek'lik, (-e), ailing, sickly; in bad health; morbid; abnormal; pimping; peccant; peaky; ~heid, ill-health, sickliness; morbidity.
siek'makend, (-e), pathogenic.
siek'te, (-s), illness, malady, sickness, affection; ailment, disease, distemper; 'n AANSTEEKLIKE ~, an infectious disease; 'n BESMETLIKE ~, a contagious disease; 'n ~ KRY, contract a disease; 'n ~ onder LEDE hê, be sickening for something (a disease); moenie met ~ SPOT nie, it is ill jesting with the sooth; met ~ TUIS, off sick; ~ VEINS (voorwend), malinger; ~beeld, clinical picture, syndrome; ~bepaling, diagnosis; ~beskrywing, pathography, nosography; ~bestryding, fighting (against) disease; ~draer, disease-carrier, germ-carrier; ~geskiedenis, clinical history; ~geval, case (of sickness); ~kenner, pathologist; ~kiem, disease germ; ~leer, pathology; nosology; ~loon, sick pay; ~ontstaan, pathogenesis; ~oorbringer, disease carrier; ~proses, process of disease; ~soldy, sick-pay; ~stof, morbid matter; ~syfer, sick-rate; ~tekens, symptoms; ~toelae, sick-benefit; ~toestand, state of disease; ~verlof, sick-leave; met ~ verlof, on sick-leave; ~verloop, course of a disease; ~versekering, insurance against sickness; ~verskynsel, symptom; ~verwekkend, (-e), disease-producing, pathogenic; ~verwekker, pathogen; ~werend, (-e), antibiotic; ~wet, diseases' act.
siel, (-e), soul, mind, psyche, spirit, heart; met sy ~ onder die ARM rondloop, be mooning around; BY my ~! upon my soul! dit DOEN my ~ goed, it does my heart good; 'n DORP van 5 000 ~e, a town of 5 000 inhabitants; 'n GOEIE ou ~, a good soul; geen LEWENDE ~ nie, not a living soul; ~ en LIGGAAM aan mekaar hou, keep body and soul together; jou ~ in LYDSAAMHEID besit, possess one's soul in patience; die ~ van 'n ONDERNEMING, the life and soul of an undertaking; 'n ~ van POTKLEI, a dull dog; a worthless scamp; by sy ~ en SALIGHEID sweer, swear by what's holy; sy ~ en SALIGHEID vir iets verkoop, sell one's soul; TER ~e wees, be dead and gone; iem. se ~ UITTREK, tease the life out of someone; hoe meer ~e hoe meer VREUGDE, the more the merrier; ~dodend, (-e), soul-deadening, monotonous.
sie'le: ~adel, nobility of soul; ~grootheid, magnanimity; ~heil, salvation; ~herder, pastor; ~leed, mental suffering, grief; ~lewe, spiritual (mental) life; ~pyn, anguish, mental agony; ~sorg, cure of souls; ~stryd, see sielstryd; ~tal, number (of souls); ~troos, comfort for the soul, spiritual comfort; ~vrede, peace of mind; ~vreugde, soul's delight.
sie'lig, (-e), pitiful, miserable.
sie'ling, (-s), (vero.), shilling.
siel: ~kunde, psychology; ~kun'dig, (-e), psychological; ~kun'dige, (-s), psychologist; ~loos, (..lose), soulless; lifeless, exanimate; ~loosheid, soullessness; lifelessness; ~mis, requiem (mass) for the soul; ~pynigend, (-e), agonizing; ~roe'rend, (-e), pathetic, touching, soul-stirring.
siels: ~aandoening, very strong emotion; ~angs, (mental) agony; ~bedroef, (-de), deeply afflicted; ~begeerte, fervent desire; ~beminde, dearly beloved; ~bly, heartily delighted; ~ervaring, mental experience; ~gebrek, defect, infirmity of the mind; ~genot, heart's delight; ~gesteldheid, state of mind.
siel'siek, (-e), soul-sick; psychopathic, mentally deranged; ~e, (-s), mental patient, psychopath; ~ehospitaal, ~e-inrigting, mental hospital; ~te, mental derangement, disorder of the mind, psychopathy, psychosis.
siels: ~krag, strength of soul; fortitude; ~kwelling, anguish, mental agony.
siel'smart, grief, sorrow, heartache, agony.
siels: ~mis, mass for the dead; ~oog, mind's eye; ~rus, equanimity, tranquillity, peace of mind; ~toestand, state of mind.
siel: ~strelend, (-e), satisfying to the mind, soul-satisfying; ~stryd, spiritual struggle.
siels: ~verdriet, deep-felt sorrow, mental distress; ~verheug, (-de), overjoyed; ~verhuising, death; transmigration of souls, metempsychosis; ~verlange, fervent desire; ~verrukking, rapture, ecstasy, trance; ~vervoering, ecstasy, trance.
siels'verwant, congenial; ~skap, affinity of soul.
siels'vriend, lifelong (intimate) friend, soulmate.
siel'tergend, (-e), soul-searing.

siel'tjie, (-s), little soul; *'n ~ sonder sorg*, a happy-go-lucky fellow.
sielto'gend, (-e), dying, struggling with death, moribund.
siel: *~ toging*, agony of death, death-struggle; *~ toog, (ge-)*, lie in agony of death; *~ verheffend, (-e)*, soulful, inspiring, uplifting; *~ verkoper*, white-slave trafficker, crimp, bawd; *~ verkwikkend, (-e)*, uplifting; *~ versorger, (-s)*, spiritual adviser; *~ vol, (-le)*, soulful.
siem'bamba, simbamba (picnic-dance).
sien, (ge-), see, look, view, observe, perceive, clap eyes on; *jy moet hom ~ BEWEEG*, you must try to urge him; *om BETER te kan ~*, to get a better view of; *EK sal ~*, I'll think about it; *dis ELKE dag te ~*, it is on view every day; *die wêreld GAAN ~*, go to see the world; *ek ~ hom liewer GAAN as kom*, I like his room better than his company; *~ is GLO*, seeing is believing; *hy ~ GOED*, his eyesight is good; *dit ~ ek nie GRAAG nie*, that is something I don't like; *~ kom KLAAR*, have to do without; *te ~ KRY*, get a view of; *dis LAASTE ~ van die blikkantien*, we'll never see it again; *LAAT ~*, show; *niks te ~ kry nie*, not get a glimpse of anything; *~ jy NOU*, there; see! I told you so! *laat ONS ~*, let us see; *toe ek WEER ~*, the next thing I knew; *~ de*, seeing; sighted; *~ de blind*, have eyes and no eyes; *~ deroë*, visibly; *hy word ~ deroë maerder*, he is growing visibly thinner; *~ er, (-s)*, seer, prophet; *~ ersblik*, prophetic eye; *~ ersoog*, prophetic eye.
siëniet', syenite (rock).
sie'ning, vision, view.
sien'lik, (-e), visible.
siën'na, sienna.
siens: *tot ~*, so long! good-bye!
siens'wyse, (-s), opinion, view, attitude of mind; *'n ~ DEEL*, share an opinion; *'n ~ TOEGEDAAN wees*, hold a view; be of the opinion; *van ~ VERSKIL met*, dissent (differ in opinion) from.
siëntologie', scientology.
sieps(op)-en-braai'boud, thrashing, whipping.
sier¹, (ong.), (s) whit, atom, bit; *GEEN ~ tjie nie*, not a whit; not the least bit; *geen ~ OMGEE nie*, not to care a rap.
sier², (s) cheer; *goeie ~ maak*, make good cheer.
sier³, (w) (ge-), adorn, decorate, grace.
sie'raad, (..rade), ornament, trinket, charm.
sier: *~ band*, braid; *~ belegsel*, trimming, facing; *~ boom*, ornamental tree; *~ boontjie*, scarlet runner bean; *~ diamant*, gem diamond; *~ duif*, fancy pigeon; *~ groef*, flute, *~ hout*, ornamental wood; *~ ertjie*, sweet pea; *~ gewas*, ornamental shrub.
sie'rie, (-s), wild canary.
sie'riehout, camphor-wood, wild sage *(Iarchonanthus camphoratus)*.
sier'insetsel, decorative insertion.
sier: *~ kam*, ornamental comb; *~ kers*, decorative candle; *~ krans*, garland.
sier'kuns, decorative art; *~ tenaar*, decorative artist.
sier: *~ kweper*, flowering quince; *~ lamp*, fairy (ornamental) lamp; *~ lassteek*, faggoting; *~ letter*, ornamental letter.
sier'lik, (-e), ornamental; ornate; elegant, neat, beautiful, graceful; *~ heid*, gracefulness, elegance; ornateness.
sier: *~ lissie*, *~ lussie*, frog-fastener; *~ lys*, decorative moulding; *~ metaal*, art metal; *~ perske*, flowering peach; *~ plant*, ornamental plant; *~ pleister*, (s) parget; (w) (ge-), parget, parge; *~ pruim*, flowering plum.
siër'ra, (-s), sierra.
sier'rand, ornamental border, purfle.
sier'sel, (-s), ornament, decoration.
sier: *~ skaatser*, figure-skater; *~ skrif*, ornamental writing; *~ snoeikuns*, topiaria, topiary art; *~ soomsteek*, hemstitch; *~ steek*, decorative stitch; *~ steen*, face-brick; semiprecious stone; *~ steenkunde*, gemmology; *~ stof*, fancy cloth.
sier: *~ voël*, bird with beautifully-coloured plumage, fancy bird; *~ wa*, (decorated) float.
sies, fie! for shame! sis! siss! foof! foofie! pooh! phew! pshaw! bah! *~ tog!* for shame! hard lines!

sie'so! that's that! *~, dis nou klaar*, well, that's finished!
sies'ta, (-s), nap, siesta.
sif, (s) (siwwe), sieve, strainer (for liquid); screen, colander (solids); bolter, grid (mines); cradle (diggings); *my geheue is soos 'n ~*, my memory is like a sieve; (w) (ge-), sift (solids, evidence); strain (liquids); screen (coal, people); *~ agtig, (-e)*, cribiform, ethmoid; *~ been*, ethmoid bone; *~ deur*, screen door; *~ doek*, tammy; *~ draad*, gauze; wire netting; *~ druk*, silk-screening; *~ fie, (-s)*, strainer.
si'filis, syphilis, venereal disease.
sifili'ties, (-e), syphilitic.
sif'masjinerie, screening-plant.
sifon', (-s), siphon; *~ speld*, piercing-pin (-syphon).
sif: *~ plaat*, perforated plate; *~ porie*, sieve pore; *~ rol*, perforated roller.
sif'sel¹, (-s), siftings, screenings.
sif'sel², sieve-cell.
sif: *~ tery*, cavilling, criticism; *~ ting, (-e, -s)*, sifting; *~ vat*, bast-vessel; *~ vormig, (-e)*, cribiform, sievelike.
sig¹, (s) sight; visibility; *BETAALBAAR op ~*, payable at sight (on demand); *IN ~*, in sight; *NA ~*, after sight; *OP ~*, at sight; *op ~ STUUR*, send on appro(val); *die ~ uit die TREIN was moeilik*, it was difficult to see from the train.
sig², (vnw) (vero., ong.), himself, herself, itself, oneself, themselves.
sigaar', (..gare), cigar; *~ as*, cigar ash; *~ handversameraar*, vitolphilist; *~ doos*, cigar-box; *~ endvrot*, cigar-end rot; *~ fabriek*, cigar factory, *~ handel*, cigar trade; *~ handelaar*, dealer in cigars, tobacconist; *~ kissie*, cigar-box; *~ knipper*, cigar-cutter; *~ koker*, cigar-case; *~ pypie*, cigar-holder; *~ rook*, cigar smoke; *~ stompie*, cigar butt; *~ vor'mig, (-e)*, cigar-shaped, fusiform; *~ winkel*, cigar-shop, tobacco-shop; tobacconist; *divan* (oriental).
sigaret', (-s, -te), cigarette; *~ aansteker*, cigarette-lighter; *~ as*, cigarette ash; *~ beentjies*, very thin legs, legs like pipe-stems, spindle-shanks; *~ dosie*, cigarette-box; *~ fabriek*, cigarette-factory; *~ houer*, cigarette-holder; *~ koker*, cigarette case; *~ papier*, cigarette paper; *~ pypie*, cigarette-holder; *~ stompie*, cigarette-butt (-end); *~ tabak*, cigarette tobacco.
sigato'ka, sigatoka.
sig'baar, (b) (..bare), visible; discernible; *sigbare gebrek*, patent defect; (bw) visibly, clearly, manifestly; *die SEUN was ~ uitgeput*, the boy was visibly exhausted; *die VROU was ~ aangedaan*, the woman was visibly moved; *~ heid*, visibility, conspicuity.
sig'baarheidsveld, field of visibility.
sig'baarwording, emergence.
sigeu'ner, (-s), gipsy; Tzigane; *~ ag'tig, (-e)*, gipsylsh; *~ dom*, gipsydom; *~ in', (-ne)*, gipsy woman; *~ kamp*, gipsy camp; *~ lied*, gipsy song; *~ musiek*, gipsy music; *~ taal*, Romany; *~ volk*, gipsies.
Sigeuns', (-e), Tzigane.
sig: *~ kant*, facing, *~ koers*, sight-exchange; *~ laag*, ground course (building); *~ lyn*, line of vision; *~ meter*, visibility meter.
sigmoï'de, sigmoïed', sigmoid (anat.).
sigomorf', (-e), zygomorphic; *~ ie'*, zygomorphism.
sigoot', (sigote) zygote.
sigorei', chicory.
sig'sag, zigzag; *~ blits*, forked lightning; *~ pad*, zigzag road; *~ steek*, zigzag stitch; *~ vormig, (-e)*, in a zigzag line.
sigself', sigsel'wers, itself, oneself; *op ~ beskou*, judged on its own merits, as such.
sig: *~ vlak*, exposed face; *~ waarde*, face value; *~ wissel*, sight-draft.
sika'de, (-s), cicada.
sikadee', (..deë), cycad.
sik'kel, (-s), shekel.
sik'katief, (..tiewe), drier, siccative.
sikkeneu'rig, (-e), testy, peevish.
sik'kepit, little bit; *geen ~ werd nie*, not worth a straw.
si'klies, (-e), cyclic.

sikloïde *sikloï'de*, (-s), sikloïed', (-e), cycloid.
siklonaal', (..nale), cyclonic.
sikloon', (siklone), cyclone.
sikloop', (siklope), cyclop(s); **siklo'pies**, (-e), cyclopean.
siklora'ma, (-s), cyclorama.
siklotron', (-s), cyclotron.
si'klus, (-se), cycle.
siks: *by my ~!* upon my word! truly!
siks'pens, (vero.), (-e), sixpence; *so BLINK soos 'n nuwe ~, soos 'n splinternuwe ~ LYK,* be as neat as a new pin; *nie eers 'n ~ WERD nie,* not worth a brass farthing.
Sile'sië, Silesia; ~**r**, (-s), Silesian; ..**sies**, (-e), Silesian.
silhoeët', (-te), silhouette; ~**teer'**, (ge-), silhouette; ~**tekenaar**, profilist.
siliêr', (-e), ciliary.
si'lika, silica.
silikaat', silicate; ~**houdend**, (-e), silicious.
silika'sie, silication.
si'likon, silicon.
siliko'se, silicosis.
silin'der, (-s), cylinder; sleeve (grenade); ~**blok**, cylinder-block; ~**boring**, cylinder-bore; ~**deksel**, cylinder-cover; ~**deursnee**, cylinder-bore; ~**inhoud**, cylinder capacity; ~**kop**, cylinder-head; ~**mantel**, cylinder-jacket; ~**meul(e)**, tubemill; ~**pers**, cylinder-press; ~**rol**, drum-roller; ~**voering**, cylinder-lining; ~**vormig**, (-e), cylinder-shaped, cylindriform; ~**wand**, cylinder-wall (skirt).
silin'dries, (-e), cylindrical; ~*e ketel,* cylinder-boiler.
sili'sium, silicon.
silla'be, (-s), syllable.
silla'bies, (-e), syllabic.
silla'bus, (-se), syllabus.
sillogis'me, syllogism.
sillogis'ties, (-e), syllogistic.
si'lo, (-'s), silo.
silt, (-e), salt, saltish, briny; *die ~e nat,* the ocean; ~**ig**, (-e), briny, salty; ~**igheid**, saltiness, brininess.
Siluur', Silurian (geol.).
sil'wer, (s) silver; plate; (b) (-e), argent, silver, (colour); silvery; ~**aar**, silver vein; ~**agtig**, (-e), silvery; argentic, argentous; ~**bad**, silver-bath; ~**beker**, silver cup; ~**beslag**, silver mounting; ~**blaar**, silver leaf; ~**blaarbitterappel**, silverleaf bitter apple *(Solanum elaeagnifolium);* ~**blad**, silver foil; ~**boom**, silver-tree; pipe-tree; pipe-poplar; ~**brokaat**, silver brocade; ~**bruilof**, silver wedding; ~**den**, silver fir; ~**doek**, silver (cinema) screen; ~**draad**, silver thread (wire); ~**draadwerk**, silver filigree; ~**duiker**, grebe; ~**ertjie**, silver pea; ~**erts**, silver ore; ~**gehalte**, silver content, percentage of pure silver; ~**geld**, silver money; ~**gerei**, silver plate; ~**glans**, silvery lustre; ~**goed**, silver plate; ~**grys**, (-e), silvery grey; ~**houdend**, (-e), argentic; containing silver; argentiferous; ~**jakkals**, silver jackal; ~**kleur**, silvery colour; ~**kleurig**, (-e), silver-coloured; ~**kollekte**, silver collection; ~**legering**, silver alloy; ~**lepel**, silver spoon; *met 'n ~lepel in die mond gebore,* born with a silver spoon in the mouth; ~**ling**, (-e), piece of silver; ~**mot**, silver moth; ~**munt**, silver coin; ~**myn**, silver mine; ~**nitraat**, silver nitrate; ~**oplossing**, solution of silver; ~**papier**, silver paper, silver foil; ~**pleet**, plated silver; ~**pletter**, silver-beater; ~**poeier**, silver dust; plate-powder; ~**populier**, white poplar; ~**servies**, silver service; ~**skoon**, spotlessly (meticulously) clean; ~**smid**, silversmith; ~**spons**, spongy silver; ~**staaf**, bar (ingot) of silver; ~**standaard**, silver standard; ~**stuk**, silver coin; ~**suikerbrood**, angel food (cake); ~**vis**, silverfish; ~**vloot**, (Spanish) treasure-fleet; ~**werk**, silver plate; silverware; ~**wit**, argent, silver-white.
sima'se, zymase.
simbaal', (simbale), cymbal.
simbio'se, symbiosis.
simbio'ties, (-e), symbiotic.
simboliek', symbolism.
simbo'lies, (-e), symbolic(al).
simbolis', (-te), symbolist.
simboliseer', (ge-), symbolize.
simbolis'me, symbolism.
simbool', (simbole), symbol, emblem; ~**staat**, statement of symbols.
simfonie', (-ë), symphony; ~**konsert**, symphony concert; ~**orkes**, symphony orchestra.
simfo'nies, (-e), symphonic.
simmetrie', symmetry; ..'**tries**, (-e), symmetric(al); ~**vlak**, plane of symmetry.
simonie', simony.
simo'se, zymosis.
simpate'ties, (-e), sympathetic (pain, ink).
simpatie', (-ë), sympathy; altropathy; ~ *met jou verlies,* sincere sympathy; ~, hard lines! hard luck!
simpatiek', (-e), sympathetic (person); condolatory (card); congenial; ~**gesind**, (-e), sympathetic.
simpa'ties, (-e), sympathetic; ~*e senuwee,* sympathetic nerve, sympatheticus.
simpatie'staking, sympathetic strike.
simpatiseer', (ge-), sympathize; ..**se'rend**, (-e), sympathetic.
sim'pel, (-e; -er, -ste), silly, foolish; barmy, half-witted; batty, dotty; mere; simple; plain (dress); ~**heid**, simplicity; silliness; plainness.
sim'pleks, (-e), simplex.
simplifika'sie, simplification.
simplifiseer', (ge-), simplify.
simplisiteit', simplicity.
simplis'ties, (-e), simplistic, superficial, facile.
simpo'dium, (-s, ..dia), sympodium (bot.)
sim'posium, (-s, ..sia), symposium.
simptoma'ties, (-e), symptomatic.
simpto'megroep, syndrome.
simptoom', (..tome), symptom; diagnostic; ~**leer**, symptomatology.
Sim'son, Samson.
simulant', (-e), simulator; malingerer.
simula'sie, simulation; malingering.
simuleer', (ge-), simulate; malinger; ..**le'rend**, (-e), simulating; ..**le'ring**, simulation; mimesis.
simultaan', (..tane), simultaneous.
sin¹, (s) (-ne), sentence.
sin², (s) (-ne), sense, mind; liking, inclination; purport, meaning; taste; fancy; (pl) senses; *van sy ~ne BEROOF wees,* be bereft of one's senses; *nie heeltemal BY sy ~ne nie,* not (be) quite all there; *sy ~ne BYMEKAARHOU,* keep one's wits together; *iem. se ~ DOEN,* please another; *EEN van ~ wees,* be of one mind; *in ENGER ~,* in a more restricted sense; *in FIGUURLIKE ~,* in a figurative sense; *iem. sy ~ GEE,* let someone have his way; *dit het GEEN ~ nie,* there is no sense in it; *daarin het ek GEEN ~ nie,* I don't fancy it; *dit het my in die ~ GESKIET,* it struck me; it suddenly occurred to me; *nie GOED by sy ~ne wees nie,* be out of his senses; *iets in die ~ HÊ,* have in mind; be up to something; ~ *in iets HÊ,* have a liking for something; *dit HET geen ~ nie,* there is no sense in it; ~ *vir HUMOR,* sense of humour; *hy het ~ IN haar,* he fancies her; *by jou ~ne KOM,* regain consciousness; come to one's senses; *geen ~ vir KOS hê nie,* have no desire for food; *sy ~ KRY,* get his way; *hy kon nie iets na sy ~ KRY nie,* he could not get what he fancied; *hy het geen KWAAD in die ~ nie,* he intends no harm; *iem. na die ~ MAAK,* please a person; *NA my ~,* to my liking; *in SEKERE ~,* in a certain sense; *jou ~ne op iets SIT,* set your mind on something; *TEEN sy ~,* against his will; *WATTER ~ het dit?* what is the sense of it? *na sy ~ WEES,* be to his liking; *van ~ WEES,* intend, have a mind to; *in die volle ~ v.d. WOORD,* in the full sense of the word.
sin³, (w) (ge-), ponder, muse, brood; *op wraak ~,* brood (intent) on revenge.
sinagogaal', (..gale), synagogical.
sinago'ge, (-s), synagogue; *uit die ~ werp,* cast out of the synagogue.
sinchroniseer', (ge-), synchronize; ~**der**, (-s), synchronizer.
sinchronis'me, synchronism.
sinchronis'ties, (-e), synchronistic.
sin'chroskakelend, (-e), syncromesh.

sinchroskoop', (..skope), synchroscope.
sin'chrotron, (-s), synchrotron.
sin'delik, (-e), clean, tidy, neat; *die HONDJIE is al* ~, the puppy is already house-broken; *die KIND is* ~, the baby knows its numbers properly already; *'n* ~ *e KLEUR*, a practical colour; ~ **heid**, cleanliness, tidiness, cleanness, neatness.
sindikaat', (..kate), syndicate, combine; pool, ring.
sindikalis', (-te), syndicalist; ~ **me**, syndicalism.
sindikalis'ties, (-e), syndicalist(ic).
sindikeer', (ge-), syndicate.
sindroom', (sindrome), syndrome.
sinds, since; ~ **dien**, since then.
sinek'dogee, (-s), synecdoche.
sineku're, (-s), **sinekuur'**, (..kure), sinecure.
sinergis'me, synergism.
sinestesie', synaesthesia.
sing, (ge-), sing, chant; warble; twitter; pipe; *die KETEL* ~, the kettle is singing; *iem. aan die SLAAP* ~, sing someone to sleep; *jy* ~ *TOE nie!* surely you did not get annoyed! you are not even annoyed! *VALS* ~, sing out of tune.
Singalees', (..lese), Singhalese.
sin'gel, (-s), crescent; moat; rampart.
singene'ties, (-e), syngenetic.
sing'baar, (..bare), singable; ~ **heid**, singableness.
sin'genot, (..genietinge), sensual pleasure.
sin'ger, (-s), singer, vocalist; warbler (bird); ~ **y**, singing.
sing'-sing', singing all the while.
singulier', (-e), (ong.), strange, odd, singular
si'nies, (-e), cynic(al).
si'nikus, (..nici, se), cynic.
sinis'me, cynicism.
sinis'ter, (-e), sinister.
sinjaal', (sinjale), signal; call-sign(al); ~ **arm**, signal-arm; ~ **fluit**, signal-whistle; ~ **huis(ie)**, signal-cabin; ~ **klok**, signal-bell; ~ **man**, signalman; ~ **pyl**, signal arrow; ~ **skyf**, blinder; ~ **toestel**, signalling apparatus; ~ **vuur**, bale-fire.
sinjaleer', (ge-), signal (a ship); signalize; point out.
sinjalement', (-e), (ong.), personal description.
sinjatuur', (..ture), catch line; section-mark (printing).
sinjeur', (-s), fellow, odd fish; sir.
sink¹, (s) zinc, sheet-iron, galvanized (corrugated) iron; spelter.
sink², (s) sinking, foundering; sink; go down, founder (ship); fall; flag; *'n skip self LAAT* ~, scuttle a ship; *sy MOED* ~, his courage ebbs.
sink: ~ **bad**, zinc bath; ~ **bedekking**, zinc covering; ~ **blende**, zinc blende.
sink'boor, countersink, rose-bit.
sink'dak, galvanized (corrugated) iron roof.
Sink'dal, *kyk* **Slenkdal**.
sin'ker, (-s), lead sinker; sink.
sink: ~ **erts**, zinc ore; ~ **gat**, pump-well, sinkhole; ~ **gebou**, iron building; ~ **graveur**, zincographer; ~ **houdend**, (-e), containing zinc, zinciferous.
sin'kings, rheumatic pains, neuralgia; aches and pains; aching bones; ~ **koors**, rheumatic fever; ~ **kuur**, neuralgia cure; ~ **mengsel**, neuralgia mixture.
sink: ~ **laag**, zinc coat; ~ **legering**, zinc alloy.
sinkline, (-s), syncline.
sinkli'nies, (-e), synclinal.
sink: ~ **lood**, sinker; ~ **lugdruk**, zincograph.
sinkografie', zincograph, process engraving.
sink'okside, **sink'oksied**, zinc oxide.
sinkopee', syncope.
sinkopeer', (ge-), syncopate.
sinkope'ring, syncopation.
sink: ~ **plaat**, sheet of galvanized (corrugated) iron; corrugations (in road); ~ **plaatpad**, corrugated road; ~ **pondok**, tin shanty.
sink'put, cesspool, drainage-well; sink(hole); draintap; cloaca; soakage-pit, gully.
sinkre'ties, (-e), syncretic.
sinkretis'me, syncretism.
sinkretis'ties, (-e), syncretistic.
sink'salf, zinc ointment.
sinkseep', superfatted soap.

sink: ~ **spaat**, zinc spar; smithsonite; ~ **staaf**, zinc rod; ~ **sulfaat**, sulphate of zinc; ~ **vitrioel**, white vitriol; ~ **wit**, zinc oxide.
sin'ledig, (-e), devoid of sense, empty, meaningless; ~ **heid**, lack of sense, meaninglessness.
sin'lik, (-e), sensual, carnal, lustful, animal, bestial; ~ **heid**, sensuality, lust, animalism, carnalism, carnality.
sin'loos, (..lose), meaningless, senseless, inane; ~ **heid**, meaninglessness, inanity.
sinna'ber, cinnabar.
sin'nebeeld, symbol, emblem, allegory.
sinnebeel'dig, (-e), emblematic(al), symbolic(al), figurative, allegorical.
sin'nelik, (-e), sensory, sensuous, of the senses.
sin'neloos, (..lose), senseless, mad; ~ **heid**, senselessness, madness.
sin'nespel, (-e), allegorical play, morality play.
sin'nigheid, liking, inclination, fancy; *ek het daar geen* ~ *in nie*, I have no liking (inclination) for it.
sinodaal', (..dale), synodic(al), synodal.
sino'de, (-s), synod; ~ **sitting**, session of the synod.
Sinologie', Sinology.
Sinoloog', (..loë), Sinologue.
sinoniem', (s) (-e), synonym; (b) (-e), synonymous.
sinonimie', synonymy.
sinop'sis, (-se), synopsis.
sinop'ties, (-e), synoptic; ~ *e weerkaart*, synoptic weather-chart.
sin'ryk, (-e), ingenious; significant, meaningful; witty; sententious, ~ **heid**, ingenuity, wittiness; significance.
sins: ~ **bedrog**, delusion, illusion, hallucination; ~ **begogeling**, hallucination, illusion; ~ **bou**, construction of a sentence; ~ **deel**, part of a sentence; phrase, clause; ~ **indruk**, sensorial impression.
sin'snede, (-s), clause; phrase.
sins'ontleding, analysis (sentence).
sin'speel, (ge-), allude, hint; ..**spelend**, (-e), allusive; ..**speling**, (-e, -s), allusion, hint, reference.
sin'spreuk, motto, device, maxim, gnome, apophthegm.
sinsteu'rend, **sinsto'rend**, (-e), confusing.
sins: ~ **verband**, context; ~ **verbetering**, correction of sentences.
sins: ~ **verbystering**, mental derangement; bewilderment, daze, confusion of mind; ~ **verrukking**, transport, trance.
sins'verwantskap, synonymy.
sins'verwarring, (sensory) derangement.
sins'wending, turn (of phrase), phrasing, phraseology.
sint, (-e), saint (St.).
sintak'sis, syntax.
sintak'ties, (-e), syntactic(al); ~ *e struktuur*, syntactic structure.
Sint Ber'nardhond, Saint Bernard.
sintek'sis, syntexis (geol.).
sintek'ties, (-e), syntectic.
sin'tel, (-s), cinder, breeze; ~ **baan**, cinder-track, dirt-track; ~ **beton**, clinker concrete; ~ **ing**, clinkering; ~ **sif**, cinder-sifter; ~ **steen**, breeze brick, cinder-stone; ~ **valpyp**, cinder-chute.
Sinterklaas', Santa Claus; Father Christmas.
sinte'se, synthesis.
sinte'ties, (-e), synthetic(al); ~ *e BRANDSTOF*, synthetic fuel; ~ *e RUBBER*, synthetic rubber.
sin'tuig, (..tuie), sense organ; ~ **lik**, (-e), sensory, sensorial; ~ *like waarneming*, sense perception.
Sint Vi'tusdans, St. Vitus's dance.
si'nus, (-se), sinus (anat.); sine (math.); ~ **itis**, sinusitis; ~ **lyn**, harmonic curve; ~ **ontsteking**, sinusitis; ~ **operasie**, sinus operation; ~ **vormig**, (-e), sine-wave form.
sin'verwant, (-e), synonymous, related in meaning; ~ **skap**, synonymity.
sin'vol, (-le) = **sinryk**.
Si'on, Zion.
Sionis', (-te), Zionist; ~ **me**, Zionism; ~ **ties**, (-e), Zionistic.
sipier', (-e, -s), gaoler, turnkey, keeper, prison warder

sipres', (-se), cypress; ~**boom**, cypress-tree.
sir, (-s), sir; knight, baronet.
Si're, (hist.), Your Majesty, Sire.
sire'ne, (-s), siren; ~**sang**, siren's song.
Si'rië, Syria; ~**r**, (-s), Syrian.
Si'ries, (s) Syriac (language); (b) (-e), Syrian.
sir'kel, (s) (-s), circle; (w) (ge-), circle, circle round; ~**boog**, arc of a circle; ~**gang**, circular course, circuit; ~**omtrek**, circumference of a circle; ~**oppervlakte**, area of a circle; ~**redenering**, begging the question; ~**rok**, circular skirt; ~**rond**, (-e), circular; ~**saag**, circular saw; compass saw; ~**saagbank**, circular bench; ~**segment**, segment of a circle; ~**sektor**, sector of a circle; ~**straal**, radius; ~**tjie**, (-s), circlet; ~**vlak**, circle plane; ~**vorm**, form of a circle; ~**vormig**, (-e), circular, in the form of a circle; **gyrate**; ~**vormigheid**, circulatory.
sirkoon', zircon.
sirkula'sie, circulation; *in* ~ *bring*, bring (put) into circulation; ~**bank**, bank of circulation (issue); ~**middel**, circulating medium; ~**pomp**, circulation pump.
sirkuleer', (ge-), circulate.
sirkulê're, (-s), circular (letter).
sir'kumfleks, (-e), circumflex.
sirkumpolêr', (-e), circumpolar; ~*e stroom*, circumpolar current.
sir'kus, (-se), circus; hippodrome; ~**baas**, showman.
sirok'ko, (-'s), sirocco.
sirro'se, cirrhosis.
sirro'ties, (-e), cirrhotic.
sir'sakar, seersucker.
sir'skap, (-pe), baronetcy, knighthood.
sis¹, (s) chintz, print; *Duitse* ~, German print.
sis², (ge-), hiss; sizzle; assibilate; ~*send warm*, piping hot.
si'sal, sisal; ~**hennep**, sisal hemp *(Agave rigida sisalana)*.
siseleer', (ge-), chase, emboss.
sis: ~**geluid**, sibilation; hiss; ~**klank**, hissing sound; sibilant.
sis'ser, (-s), squib, cracker; *met 'n* ~ *afloop*, fizzle out.
sis'sewinkel, *see* **sitsewinkel.**
sis'sing, sibilance, hissing.
sist, (-e), cyst; ~**aalwurm**, cist nematode.
sisteem', (sisteme), system, plan.
sistematiek', systematics, taxonomy.
sistema'ties, (-e), systematic.
sistema'tikus, (-se, ..tici), systematicist.
sistematiseer', (ge-), systematize.
sis'ties, (-e), cystic.
sisti'tis, cystitis.
sistool', **(sistole)**, systole.
Sisufosarbeid, Sisyphean labour.
sit, (s) sitting position; seat; *hy het nog nie sy* ~ *gekry nie*, he has not yet found a comfortable sitting position; (w) **(ge-)**, sit; put, place; *daar* ~ *iets AGTER*, there is something behind it; *AGTER iem.* ~, egg someone on; *die BAADJIE* ~ *goed*, the coat fits well; *dit* ~ *in sy BLOED*, it runs in his blood; *BLY* ~, remain seated; not be promoted; flunk, fail; *met iets BLY* ~, be left with something on one's hands; *die komitee* ~ *vandag DAAROOR*, the committee will decide about it today; *hy* ~ *daar DIEP in*, he is up to his ears in it; *GAAN* ~! sit down! take a seat; *daar GOED in* ~, be well-to-do; *daar* ~ *iets IN*, there is something in that; *dit* ~ *nie IN hom nie*, he hasn't got it in him; *kyk, die ding* ~ *so INMEKAAR*, look, it is like this; *dit moet jy in die KOERANT* ~, you must have it put in the paper; *LAAT* ~, leave in the lurch; *die stoel* ~ *LEKKER*, this chair is comfortable; *op LOOP* ~, take to flight; run away; bolt (horse); *in die MOEILIKHEID* ~, be in trouble; *'n gedig op MUSIEK* ~, set a poem to music; *daar* ~ *NIKS in hom nie*, he is not up to much; *op PAPIER* ~, put down on paper; commit to paper; *van* ~ *en STAAN, kom niks gedaan*, standing around won't finish the job; *vir 'n SKILDER* ~, sit to a painter; *uit die SKOOL* ~, expel from school; *die STADSRAAD* ~ *nou*, the town (city) council is holding its meeting now; *aan TAFEL* ~, sit (be) at table; *in die TRONK* ~, put into prison; be in prison; *UIT die huis* ~, evict from the house; *VASGELAK* ~, be glued to one's seat; *die VOLKSRAAD* ~ *nog nie*, Parliament is not in session yet; *hy het sy VROU laat* ~, he deserted his wife.
sitaat', **(sitate)**, citation, quotation.
sitadel', (-le), citadel, fortress.
sita'sie, (-s), citation.
sit: ~**bad**, hip-bath, sitz-bath; ~**bank**, bench; settee; ~**been**, ischium; ~**betoging**, sit-in (protest); ~**dag**, day of sitting.
siteer', (ge-), cite (law); quote.
si'ter¹, (-s), citron.
si'ter², (-s), zither; ~**spel**, zither-playing; ~**speler**, zither-player, zitherist.
sitiologie', sitiology.
sit'kamer, drawing-room, sitting-room, parlour, lounge (room); ~**held**, carpet-knight; ~**stel**, drawing-room suite.
sit: ~**kierie**, shooting-stick; ~**kussing**, pouffe.
sitologie', sitology; cytology.
sitoplas'ma, cytoplasm.
si'to-si'to, quickly, hurriedly, in the twinkling of an eye.
sit'plaas, **sit'plek**, seat, place; seating accommodation; perch; ~**bespreking**, booking of seats.
si'traat, **(sitrate)**, citrate.
si'treen, citrene.
sitreer', (ge-), citrate; **sitre'ring**, citration.
sitrien'¹, (-e), citrine (geol.).
sitrien'², **sitri'ne**, citrin (chem.).
sitroen', (-e), citron, lemon; ~**boom**, lemon-tree; ~**geel**, citron-yellow, citreous, citrine; lemon-coloured; ~**hout**, citron-wood; ~**kleur**, lemon colour; ~**olie**, oil of citron; ~**pers**, lemon-squeezer; ~**sap**, lemon juice; ~**skil**, lemon peel; ~**suur**, citric acid.
sitronel'la, citronella; ~**olie**, citronella oil.
si'trus, citrus; ~**blaaspootjie**, citrus thrips; ~**boerdery**, citrus farming; ~**bou**, citriculture; ~**kanker**, citrus cancer; ~**nematode**, citrus nematode; ~**uitvoer**, citrus export; ~**vrug**, citrus fruit; ~**witluis**, citrus bug *(Planococcus citri)*.
sit'sewinkel: *die hele* ~, the whole lot, whole caboodle, box and dice.
sit'-sit', sitting; sitting for a while; ~ *LOOP*, walk, but sit down occasionally; ~ *SLAAP*, sleep in a sitting posture.
sit: ~**-slaapkamer**, bed-sitting-room, bedsitter; ~**staker**, sit-down striker; ~**staking**, sitdown strike; ~**stok**, shooting-stick, rest-stick.
sit'tend, (-e), sitting; sedentary; sessile (bot.); *'n* ~*e LEWE*, a sedentary life; *die* ~*e LID*, the sitting member.
sit'ter, (-s), sitter.
sit'ting, (-e, -s), seat, bottom; session, sitting; *GEHEIME* ~, secret session; *twee maal per jaar* ~ *HOU*, meet (sit) twice a year; ~ *hê in 'n KOMMISSIE*, be a member of (sit on) a committee; ~ *NEEM in die bestuur*, become a member of the executive (directorate).
sit'tings: ~**dag**, court day; session day; ~**termyn**, law term; ~**tyd**, session time.
sit'tyd, session time; term of imprisonment.
situa'sie, (-s), situation; ~**beskrywing**, description of the situation; ~**tekening**, plan of site.
situeer', (ge-), situate.
sit'vlak, seat, buttocks, bum, nates.
sivet', civet; ~**kat**, civet-cat.
siviel'¹, (s) mufti; *in* ~, in mufti.
siviel'², (b) (-e), civil; ~*e AMPTENAAR*, civil servant; ~*e DIENS*, civil service; ~*e GYSELING*, civil imprisonment; *'n* ~*e HOFSAAK*, a civil suit; ~*e INGENIEUR*, civil engineer.
siviliteit', (ong.), civility.
Sixtyns': *die* ~*e Kapel*, the Sistine Chapel.
sjaal, (-s), shawl; ~**kraag**, shawl collar.
sjabloneer', (ge-), stencil.
sjabloon', (..blone), stencil; ~**plaat**, stencil-sheet; ~**tekening**, stencil; ~**werk**, stencilling.
sjag'gel, **sjag'ger**, (ge-), bargain, haggle; ~**aar**, (-s), bargainer, haggler.
sjagryn', chagrin, mortification.

sjah, (-s), shah.
sjako', (-'s), shako.
sjampan'je, champagne, fizz.
sjampoe', (-s), shampoo.
Sjangaan', (-s), Shangaan.
sjan'ker, (-s), chancre.
sjantoeng', shantung.
sjarmant', (-e), charming; ~**heid**, charm.
sjar'me, charm, allure.
sjarmeer', (ge-), charm.
sjef, (-s), chief; chef; ~**kok**, chef.
sjeg, (-te), sheik (religious).
sjeik, (-s), sheik (political).
sjelei', jelly; ~**agtig**, (-e), gelatinous; jelly-like.
sjer'rie, sherry.
sjevron', chevron, sleeve-bar (N.C.O.).
sjib'bolet, (-te), shibboleth.
sjiek, (-e; -er, -ste), chic, fashionable, smart; ~**heid**, smartness, chic.
sjie'ling, (vero.), (-s), shilling.
sji'maan, isi-shimeyana.
sjimpansee', (-s), chimpanzee, jocko.
Sji'na, China; ..**nees'**, (..**nese**), Chinese; ..*nese krip*, crêpe de Chine.
Sjintoïs'me, Shintoism.
sjoe! brr! phew! (referring to cold); ~**broekie**, (-s), hotpants.
sjoel'bak, (ong.), shovelboard.
sjo'fel, (-e), (Ndl.), poor; worn; shabby; ~**heid**, poverty; shabbiness.
sjokoor', (ge-), (ong.), shook.
sjokola'de, chocolate; cocoa (drink); ~**bruin**, chocolate brown; ~**klapper**, chocolate coconut; ~**kleurig**, (-e), chocolate-coloured; ~**koek**, chocolate cake; ~**pepermen**t, peppermint crisp.
Sjo'na, (-s), Shona.
sjor, (ge-), strap, fasten, pull tight; ~**sluiting**, zip-fastener.
sjou, (ge-), (Ndl.), carry heavy burdens, toil, lug; ~**er**, (-s), stevedore; longshoreman; ~**erman**, stevedore, docker.
sjt! sjuut! hush!
skaad, (ge-), damage, harm, injure, hurt.
skaaf, (s) (**skawe**), plane; (w) (**ge-**), plane; chafe, abrade; graze (skin); fray (clothes); brush (skin); ~**bank**, carpenter's bench; planing-bench; ~**beitel**, planing-cutter; bit; planer-tool; ~**blok**, apron (of plane); ~**krul**, shaving; ~**masjien**, planer, planing-machine; ~**mes**, plane-iron; fleshing-iron; ~**middel**, abrasive, abradant; ~**plank**, shooting-board; ~**plek**, place to plane; abrasion, gall, chafe, saddle-sore; burr; graze, cause of friction; ~**rusblok**, cradle (wood); ~**sel**, (-s), shaving; turning; ~**strook**, chafer-strip; ~**werk**, planing; ~**wond**, gall; abrasion; ~**yster**, plane blade (pit).
skaai, (geselst.), (ge-), steal, pinch; ~**er**, (-s), poacher.
skaak¹, (w) (ge-), kidnap, abduct; elope with; rob.
skaak², (s) chess; *'n POTJIE* ~, a game of chess; ~ *SIT*, check, ~! check! ~ *SPEEL*, play chess; (w) (ge-), (Ndl.) play chess; check; ~**bord**, chess-board; ~**figuur**, chessman; ~**geselskap**, chess club; ~**kampioen**, chess champion; ~**klok**, chess clock; ~**klub**, chess club; ~**mat**, checkmate; *hy is* ~ *mat gesit*, he is checkmated; ~**party**, (Ndl.), chess evening (party); ~**set**, chess move; ~**spel**, (game of) chess; set of chessmen; ~**speler**, chess-player; ~**stuk**, (chess)man, piece; ~**wedstryd**, chess tournament; ~**wêreld**, world of chess.
skaal¹, (**skale**), scale, balance; *op GROOT* ~, on a large scale; *die ~ laat OORSLAAN*, tip the scale; *op* ~ *TEKEN*, draw to scale; *volgens n VASTE of glydende* ~, on a fixed or sliding scale.
skaal², (s) shell (of crustacean).
skaal'breuk, representative fraction.
skaal: ~**dier**, crustaceous animal; ~**insek**, scale insect.
skaal: ~**passer**, scale callipers; ~**plank**, slab, flitch.
skaal'tjie¹, (-s), small scale.
skaal'tjie², (-s), capsule.
skaal: ~**verdeling**, scale division; graduated scale; ~**wydte**, range.
skaam, (w) (ge-), be (feel) ashamed; *~ JOU!* fie! for shame! you should be ashamed! *die oë uit die KOP* ~, be terribly ashamed; (b) shy, bashful, abashed, coy, diffident, timid; ashamed; ~**agtigheid**, bashfulness, shyness, coyness; ~**been**, pubic bone, pubis; ~**blom**, mountain rose; ~**boompie**, *Mimosa pudica;* ~**dele**, genitals, private parts, pudenda; ~**doek**, towel bandage; ~**haai**, lazy shark; ~**hare**, pubic hair, pubes; ~**heid**, shyness; timidity; coyness; ~**heuwel**, mountain of Venus, mons pubis (anat.); ~**kwaad**, angry and full of shame; ~**lip**, labium; ~**rooi**, flushed with shame; ~**spleet**, vulva; ~**streek**, pubic region.
skaam'te, shame; shyness, modesty; prudence; prudency; private parts, genitals; *geen klere om haar* ~ *te BEDEK nie*, no clothes to cover her body; *met* ~ *ERKEN*, admit with a sense of shame; *hy het GEEN* ~ *nie*, he has no sense of shame; *MAAGDELIKE* ~, virginal modesty; *jy moet jou* ~ *OORKOM*, you must overcome your bashfulness; *SONDER* ~, without shame, unashamedly; *geen VALS* ~ *hê nie*, have no false pride; ~**blos**, blush of shame; ~**gevoel**, sense of shame.
skaam'teloos, (..**lose**), shameless, impudent, barefaced, devoid of shame, flagrant; ~**heid**, shamelessness, impudence, brass, impudicity.
skaam'testreek, pubes.
skaap, (**skape**), sheep; *skape AANJA*, be reeling; *die skape van die BOKKE skei*, separate the sheep from the goats; *sy skapies op die DROË hê*, be well-to-do; *as een* ~ *deur die HEK is*, volg al die ander, if one sheep leaps over the dyke all the rest will follow; *so SKEEL soos 'n* ~, cross-eyed; cockeyed; *hulle het hul skapies in een KRAAL*, they are married; *daar gaan baie mak skape in een KRAAL*, a patient crowd can be packed into a very small space; *een SKURWE* ~ *kan die hele trop aansteek*, one scabbed sheep infects the whole lot; *elke trop het sy SWART* ~, there is a black sheep in every flock; *die SWART* ~ *wees*, be the black sheep; *een brandsiek* ~ *steek die hele TROP aan*, one sickly sheep infects the flock; *soos VERDWAALDE skape*, like lost sheep; *die VERLORE* ~, the lost sheep; ~**afval**, offal, tripe and trotters; ~**agtig**, (-e), sheepish, sheep-like; ovine; ~**blad**, shoulder of mutton; ~**boer**, sheep-farmer; flockmaster; ~**boerdery**, sheep-farming; ~**bos**, sheep-bush; ~**boud**, leg of mutton; ~**dip**, sheep-wash; ~**dipvloeistof**, sheep-dip (fluid); ~**drol**, (plat), sheep's dung; ~**harslag**, lamb's-fry; ~**herder**, shepherd; S~**hond**, Collie; ~**hutspot**, (Lancashire) hotpot; (Irish) stew; ~**kameel**, llama; alpaca; ~**karmenaadjie**, mutton chop; ~**kloutjie**, sheep's trotter; ~**kop**, sheep's head; blockhead; ~**kotelet**, mutton cutlet; ~**kraal**, sheep kraal; sheep fold, sheep-pen; ~**lam**, lamb; ~**leer**, sheepskin, roan; ~**lende**, loin of mutton; ~**lewer**, lamb's fry; ~**luis**, sheep-tick, ked; ~**melk**, sheep milk; ~**mis**, sheep-dung, kraal-manure; ~**ogie:** *ogies gooi*, cast a sheep's eye at; ~**ooi**, ewe; ~**pens**, sheep's tripe; ~**plaas**, sheep-farm; ~**pokke**, scab-rot; ~**pootjies**, sheep's trotters; ~**ram**, ram; ~**ras**, breed of sheep; ~**rib**, sheep's rib; ~**ribbetjie**, (-s), mutton rib; ~**saal**, saddle of mutton; ~**skeerder**, sheep-shearer; ~**skêr**, pair of shears.
skaaps'klere, sheep's clothing; *in* ~, in sheep's clothing.
skaap: ~**stert**, sheep's tail; gauntlet; *onder die* ~ *stert deurloop*, run the gauntlet; ~**sult**, sheep's brawn; ~**suring**, (sheep) sorrel; ~**vag**, sheep's fleece; ~**vel**, sheepskin; ~**veld**, sheep pasturage, ~**vet**, mutton fat; ~**vetderm**, mutton chitterling(s); ~**vleis**, mutton; ~**vleisbredie**, mutton bredie; ~**vrug**, Mexican hawthorn; ~**wagter**, shepherd; ~**wagtertjie**, capped wheatear; hooded chat; ~**wol**, sheep's wool; ~**wolk**, wool pack; ~**wolkies**, cirro-cumulus.
skaar¹, (ong.), (s) (**skare**), crowd, multitude, host.
skaar², (s) (**skare**), plough-share.
skaar³, (s) (**skare**), chip, notch, gap; *vol skare*, chipped.
skaar⁴, (w) (ge-), range, array; *hom aan iem. se sy* ~, take someone's side, join someone's ranks.

skaars, (b) scarce, rare; scanty; tight (money); (bw) hardly, barely, scarcely; *hom baie* ~ *HOU, hy hou sy LYF* ~, be making oneself a stranger; ~**heid**, scarcity; scantiness; ~**te**, dearth, shortage, paucity; want; *daar is 'n* ~ *te aan vleis*, there is a shortage of meat.
skaats, (s) (-e), skate; (w) (ge-), skate; ~**baan**, skating-rink; ~**plank**, skate-board; ~**ry**, (-ge-), skate, ~**ryer**, (-s), skater.
skabel', (-le), footstool.
skabrak', (-ke), ornamented saddle-cloth.
skabreus', (-e), scabrous, scurvy.
ska'de¹, (s) shadow, shade.
ska'de², (s) damage, loss, detriment, harm, cost; disadvantage; ~ *AANRIG (berokken)*, cause damage (calamity); *dis 'n* ~ *in die BOEDEL*, that is a great loss; *EIE doen eie geen* ~ *aan*, one does not harm one's own; ~ *INHAAL*, make good one's losses; ~ *LY*, suffer damage (loss); *deur* ~ *en SKANDE wys word*, experience makes fools wise; *deur* ~ *en SKANDE van iets afkom*, come out of something with loss and shame; *die* ~ *TAKSEER*, estimate the damage(s); *TOT* ~ *van*, to the detriment of; *die* ~ *VASSTEL*, assess the damage; *die* ~ *VERHAAL op*, recover the damage(s) from; ~**bepaling**, assessment of damage; ~**-eis**, claim for damages.
ska'delik, (-e), harmful, injurious, detrimental, noxious, hurtful, disadvantageous, prejudicial; deleterious; pestilent, pestiferous; pathogenic; ~ *vir die skool se BELANGE*, detrimental to the school's interests; ~ *vir die GESONDHEID*, injurious to health; ~*e KRINGLOOP*, vicious circle; ~*e ONKRUID*, noxious weeds; ~**heid**, harmfulness; noxiousness, hurtfulness, disadvantageousness; destructiveness, perniciousness.
ska'deloos, (..lose), harmless; without damage(s); *'n skadelose MIDDEL*, a harmless remedy; ~ *STEL*, indemnify; recoup, recompense; *jou* ~ *STEL*, reimburse oneself; ~**stel'lend**, (-e), compensatory; ~**steller**, compensator; ~**stelling**, compensation, recompense, recoupment, indemnification, solatium; S~**stellingswet**, Workmen's Compensation Act.
skadeplig'tig, (-e), liable for damages; ~**heid**, liability for damages.
ska'depos, (-te), loss, debit entry.
ska'detjie¹, (-s), small damage.
ska'detjie², (-s), small shadow (shade).
ska'devergoeding, compensation, damages, indemnification; ~ *eis vir*, claim compensation for; sue for damages; ~**sfonds**, caution-money.
ska'du, (-'s), shadow, shade; ~**agtig**, (-e), shadowy; ~**beeld**, silhouette; ~**kant**, shady side; ~**loos**, (..lose), shadeless; ~**ryk**, (s) realm of shades; (b) (-e), shady, shadowy; ~**sy**, dark (shadowy) side, unpleasant part.
ska'duwee, (-s), shade, shadow; *BANG vir sy eie* ~, afraid of his own shadow, very nervous; *daar groei niks in die* ~ *van 'n groot BOOM nie*, nothing can grow in the shade of a huge tree; *die* ~ *v.d. DOOD*, the shadow of death; *in die* ~ *LAAT*, keep dark; *nie in iem. se* ~ *kan STAAN nie*, not be able to hold a candle to somebody; not to be in the same street as another; *iem. in die* ~ *STEL*, outrival someone, overshadow (eclipse) someone; *soos 'n* ~ *VERBYGAAN*, pass like a shadow; *iem. soos 'n* ~ *VOLG*, follow someone like his shadow; *net 'n* ~ *van wat hy VROEËR was*, a shadow of his former self; *iem. se* ~ *WEES*, be someone's shadow; dog someone's footsteps; *'n* ~ *WERP oor*, throw a shadow (gloom) upon; ~**agtig**, (-e) = skaduagtig; ~**kant**, shady side; ~**projeksie**, sciagraphy; ~**verdraend**, (-e), tolerant (of shade); ~**verdraende boom**, shade-tolerant tree; ~**tjie**, little shadow (shade).
ska'duwerk, shadow-work.
skaf, (ge-), furnish, supply.
ska'fie, (-s), small plane.
skaf'lik, (-e), fair, tolerable, passable; middling, moderate; so-so; *dit gaan* ~, it goes fairly well; ~**heid**, fairness, tolerableness.
skaf'tyd, knocking-off time; interval for meals, dinner-hour.

skag, (-te), shaft (of arrow); stem (of bolt); shank (of drill); quill (of feather); leg (of boot); pit (of mine); *blinde* ~, blind shaft; ~**bek**, pithead; ~**bodem**, shaft bottom; ~**bok**, headgear (mine); shaft-head; ~**boktoestel**, pithead gear; ~**delwer**; ~**grawer**, shaft-sinker; ~**delwing**, shaft-sinking; ~**kas**, shaft-box; ~**mond**, pitmouth; ~**opening**, eye (of mine); ~**sein**, call-bell; ~**sluiting**, barrier; ~**toring**, headgear.
skag'wagter, banksman; *BOGRONDSE* ~, banksman; *ONDERGRONDSE* ~, onsetter.
skakeer', (ge-), tint, shade, chequer, variegate; gradate.
ska'kel, (s) (-s), link; liaison; shackle; half-back (rugby); mesh (cog-wheel); switch (elec.); pivot (water polo); (w) (ge-), link, concatenate; connect, couple; get into touch with; dial (teleph.); mesh (gears).
ska'kelaar, (-s), switch; ~**kontak**, switch contact; ~**skild**, switch-shutter; ~**slot**, switch lock; ~**wyserplaat**, switch-indicator dial.
ska'kel: ~**armband**, chain bracelet; ~**beampte**, liaison officer; public relations officer, P.R.O.; ~**bord**, keyboard, switchboard; ~**brief**, liaison letter; ~**diagram**, wiring diagram; ~**diens**, liaison duties; ~**funksie**, liaison function; ~**hefboom**, switch-lever; ~**huis**, semi-detached house; townhouse; ~**huisie**, switch-box; ~**huispaar**, pair of semi-detached houses; ~**huisry**, row of semi-detached houses; ~**ing**, linking, concatenation; meshing; ~**ketting**, link-chain; ~**komitee**, link (liaison) committee; ~**man**, contact man; ~**net**, trammel-net; ~**offisier**, liaison officer; ~**organisasie**, chain-organization; ~**patrollie**, liaison patrol; ~**peer**, pear-switch; ~**plaat**, link-plate; ~**pos**, liaison post; ~**rat**, balance-wheel (of watch); escapement-wheel; ~**sein**, dial-tone; ~**skema**, wiring diagram; ~**skyf**, telephone dial; ~**sleutel**, switch-key; ~**toon**, dial(ing) tone; ~**tuig**, switch-gear; ~**verbinding**, link-plate; ~**vuur**, liaison fire; ~**werk**, liaison work; public relations.
ska'ker¹, (ong.), (-s), chess-player.
ska'ker², (-s), abductor, kidnapper.
skake'ring, (-e, -s), tint, shade (of meaning); variegation, gradation, nuance.
ska'king, (-e, -s), elopement; abduction; kidnapping.
skal, (ge-), (re)sound, clang.
skalaar', (skalare), scalar (math.).
skald, (-e), skald, bard.
skal'depoësie, skaldic poetry.
skalêr', (-e), scalar (math.).
ska'lie, shale; ~**agtig**, (-e), shaly.
skalks, (-e), quizzical, roguish, sly, waggish; ~**heid**, roguery, waggery, archness.
skalm, (-s), links (of chain).
skalpeer', (ge-), scalp; ~**mes**, scalpel.
skalpel', (-s), scalpel.
ska'mel¹, (s) (-s), upper portion of the "onderstel" (chassis) of ox-wagon or cart; baseplate (director); pivot-plate; transom; bolster; turntable (on the bogie).
ska'mel³, (b) (e-; -er, -ste), meagre, poor, shabby.
ska'mel: ~**bout**, kingpin (kingbolt) of oxwagon; ~**haak**, gambrel; ~**hanger**, swing-link (bogie).
ska'melheid, poverty, meagreness, shabbiness.
ska'mel: ~**kar**, cart without springs, bogie-cart; ~**plaat**, pivot plate (ox-wagon); ~**trok**, bolster-truck; ~**wa**, bogie truck, springless waggon.
ska'merig, (-e), bashful, timid, coy; ashamed; rather shy; ~**heid**, shyness, bashfulness, timidity.
skam'per, (-e; -der, -ste), bitter, scornful, sarcastic; ~ *lag*, laugh scornfully; ~**heid**, scorn, bitterness, asperity of tone.
skamp'paal, rubbing-post (cattle).
skamp'skeut, (-e), cutting remark.
skandaal', (..dale), scandal, disgrace.
skandaleus', (-e), scandalous.
skanda'lig, (-e), scandalous, disgraceful; outrageous; ~**heid**, scandalousness.
skandaliseer', (ge-), scandalize.
skand'daad, scandalous act, deed of infamy, outrage.
skan'de, (-s), shame, disgrace, ignominy, disrepute,

discredit, dishonour; degradation; scorn, contumely, obloquy; *in die* ~ *KOM*, disgrace oneself; *te* ~ *MAAK*, bring disgrace upon; bring to shame; *tot* ~ *REKEN*, consider a disgrace; *in die* ~ *STEEK*, disgrace, put to shame; *dit sal jou tot* ~ *STREK*, it will bring disgrace upon you.

skandeer', **(ge-)**, scan.

skan'dekwaad, furious, wild, mad with anger.

skan'delik, (b) **(-e)**, shameful, discreditable, disreputable; glaring, disgraceful, dishonourable, flagitious, ignominious, infamous; ~ **heid**, shamefulness, ignominy, infamy, foulness, flagitiousness.

skande'ring, scansion.

skand'geld, dishonest(ly earned) money.

Skandina'wië, Scandinavia; ~ **r**, **(-s)**, Scandinavian; **..wies**, **(-e)**, Scandinavian.

skand'jonge, **(-ns)**, catamite.

skand'merk, (s) mark of infamy, stigma; (w) **(ge-)**, stigmatize.

skand: ~ **paal**, pillory; *aan die* ~ *paal bind*, put in the pillory; ~ **skrif**, libel; lampoon; ~ **teken**, stigma, disgrace.

skand'vlek, (s) disgrace, blot, stigma; *die* ~ *v.d. familie*, a disgrace to the family; the black sheep of the family; (w) **(ge-)**, disgrace, brand, dishonour.

skans, **(-e)**, bulwark, ditch, redoubt, trench, fort, earthwork, entrenchment; ~ **grawer**, trench-digger; sapper.

skan'sie¹, **(-s)**, small trench.

skan'sie², scansion.

skans; ~ **korf**, gabion; ~ **loper**, soldier's greatcoat; ~ **mandjie**, basket, gabion; ~ **pale**, palisade.

ska'pic, **(-s)**, little sheep; lamb; (little) dear; ~ *s DEURMEKAARJAAG*, about to get married; *hy het sy* ~ *s op die DROË*, he has made his pile; *hulle het hulle* ~ *s in een KLOMP*, they have become one.

skap'lik = **skaflik**.

skapulier', **(-e)**, scapular(y).

skarabee', **(..beë)**, scarab.

ska're, **(-s)**, crowd, multitude, host.

ska'rerig, **(-e)**, chipped.

skarifika'sie, scarification.

skarla'ken, scarlet; ~ **koors**, scarlatina; scarlet fever; ~ **luis**, cochineal (insect); ~ **rooi**, scarlet; ~ **s**, **(-e)**, scarlet.

skarmin'kel, **(-s)**, spindle-shanks.

skarnier', (s) **(-e)**, hinge; knuckle (arch.); (w) **(ge-)**, hinge; ~ **as**, hinge stud; ~ **band**, hinge ligament; ~ **blad**, hinge; ~ **bout**, waist-pin, hinge bolt; ~ **deksel**, hinged cover; ~ **gewrig**, hinge joint, ginglymus; ~ **hefboom**, toggle; ~ **ketting**, sprocket chain; ~ **klep**, hinged valve, clack-valve; ~ **koppeling**, cyejoint; joint-coupling; ~ **oog**, gudgeon; ~ **pen**, hinge pin, hinge stud; ~ **skroef**, hinge screw; ~ **stif**, hinge stud; ~ **verbinding**, knuckle-joint; ~ **vyl**, joint-file; ~ **werking**, toggle action; ~ **wissel**, hinged switch.

skar'rel, **(ge-)**, rummage, scrabble, rootle; crawl; philander; ~ **aar**, **(-s)**, scimitar-bill (*Rhinopomastus cyanomelas*); petty dealer; philanderer; ~ **been**, crawling foot, straddle-leg.

skar'tel, **(ge-)**, (ong.), rummage, rootle.

skat¹, (s) **(-te)**, treasure, wealth; argosy; precious one, dearest; *'n mens waardeer die* ~ *eers as dit VERLORE is*, you never miss the water until the well runs dry; ~ *te VERSAMEL*, lay up (gather) treasures.

skat², (w) **(ge-)**, estimate (numbers); value, assess (property); deem, guess; *ek* ~ *hy sal LATER kom*, I think (I hazard a guess) that he will come later; *WAARDE te hoog* ~ overestimate the value; ~ **baar**, (**..bare**), taxable, ratable, computable, assessable; appreciable; ~ **bewaarder**, purse-bearer, treasurer.

ska'ter, **(ge-)**, burst out laughing, roar (with laughter); cachinnate, chortle; ~ **lag**, (s) loud laugh, guffaw, peal of laughter, cachinnation; (w) **(ge-)**, laugh heartily.

skat: ~ **grawer**, treasure-hunter; ~ **jie**, **(-s)**, small treasure; darling, dearest, precious one; ~ **kamer**, public treasury; storehouse, treasure-house.

skat'kis, treasury, exchequer; purse, coffer; ~ **bewys**, treasury warrant; ~ **biljet**, bill of credit, warrant, voucher; treasury note; ~ **magbrief**, treasury warrant; ~ **noot**, currency note, treasury note; ~ **obligasie**, treasury bond; ~ **order**, *see* **skatkisbiljet**; ~ **rekening**, exchequer account; ~ **wissel**, treasury bill.

skat: ~ **lam**, sweetheart, darling; popsy-wopsy; ~ **lik**, **(-e)**, beautiful; lovable, sweet; ~ **likheid**, sweetness, dearness; ~ **meester**, fiscal treasurer; ~ **plig'tig**, **(-e)**, tributary, ratable, taxable; ~ *pligtig maak*, lay under contribution; ~ **ryk**, very rich; ~ **skip**, argosy; ~ **tebol**, darling (child); ~ **teboud**, darling (term of endearment for children); ~ **tejag**, treasure hunt; ~ **ter**, **(-s)**, appraiser, valuator, computer, assessor; ~ **tie**, **(-s)**, sweetheart; ~ **tig**, **(-e)**, dear, lovely, sweet.

skat'ting, **(-e, -s)**, tax, estimate, valuation, appraisal, appraisement; estimation; appreciation; ratal, assessment; contribution; extent (law); judgment; esteem; cess, computation; ~ *BETAAL*, pay tribute; *'n GLOBALE* ~, a rough estimate; *VOLGENS* ~, roughly, approximately.

skat'tings: ~ **hof**, valuation court; ~ **koste**, valuation expenses; ~ **lys**, valuation roll.

skavot', **(-te)**, scaffold; tailor's table; ~ **kleurig**, **(-e)**, dark red, crimson; ~ **paal**, whipping-post.

skavuit', **(-te)**, rascal, rogue, knave; ~ **(e)streek**, rascality, roguery, knavery.

ska'we, **(ge-)**, plane; graze; raw; chafe, gall; ~ **r**, **(-s)**, planer.

ska'wing, chafe; attrition.

ske'de, **(-s)**, sheath, scabbard; vagina (anat.); ~ **gespe(r)**, chape.

ske'del, **(-s)**, skull, cranium; ~ **beskrywing**, craniography; ~ **bodem**, base of skull; ~ **boor**, trepan, trephine; ~ **boring**, trepanation, trepanning; ~ **breuk**, cranial fracture, fracture of the skull; ~ **holte**, cranial cavity; ~ **huid**, pericranium; ~ **indeks**, cranial index; ~ **kunde**, craniology, phrenology; ~ **kun'dige**, (s), craniologist, phrenologist; ~ **leer**, craniology, phrenology; ~ **meter**, craniometer; ~ **meting**, craniometry; ~ **naat**, cranial suture; ~ **pet**, skull-cap; ~ **punt**, apex, summit; ~ **saag**, trephine; ~ **vlies**, pericranium; ~ **vormig**, **(-e)**, skull-shaped.

ske'de: ~ **mes**, case-knife; ~ **ontsteking**, vaginitis; ~ **rok**, ~ **tabberd**, sheath dress.

skeef, (b) **(skewe)**, crooked, awry, slanting, lopsided; squinting, asquint (eyes); oblique (angle); distorted (account); down-trodden (heels); skew; (bw), crookedly, awry, wrongly, amiss; askance, askew; *iem.* ~ *AANKYK*, look askance at a person; *jou HOED sit* ~, your hat is askew; ~ *OPKYK*, be (unpleasantly) surprised; *die SAKE loop* ~, matters are going wrong; *iets* ~ *VOORSTEL*, distort something; ~ **bek**, *see* **skewebek**; ~ **blommetjie**, candytuft; ~ **heid**, wryness, crookedness; ~ **hoek**, oblique angle; ~ **kyk**, **(-ge-)**, squint; be taken aback; ~ **oop**, **(-ge-)**, go wrong, be unsuccessful; ~ **nek**, wryneck; ~ **te**, crookedness, lopsidedness; ~ **trek**, **(-ge-)**, warp.

skeel, (w) **(ge-)**, matter; lack, ail, want; differ; *dit* ~ *BAIE*, it makes a great difference; *daar* ~ *hom altyd IETS*, there is always something wrong with him; *wat KAN dit my* ~? what does it matter to me? I don't care; *dit het MIN ge* ~ *of hy het 'n ongeluk gehad*, he very nearly had an accident; *hulle* ~ *net 'n WEEK*, they differ only a week in age, (b) **(skeler, -ste)**, squinting, cockeyed, squint-eyed; *so* ~ *soos 'n skaap*, squint badly; ~ **garing**, slip fibre; ~ **heid**, strabismus, squint; ~ **hoofpyn**, megrim, migraine; ~ **kant**, blind side (rugby); ~ **kyker**, squinter; ~ **oog**, (**..oë**), squint-eyed person, squinter, cockeyed person.

skeen, **(skene)**, shin; *'n BLOU* ~ *kry*, be turned down (by girl); *sy skene word ROOI*, he has reached the courting stage; ~ **been**, shin-bone, tibia; heel-bone; ~ **beenslagaar**, tibial artery; ~ **dekker**, shin-guard; ~ **plaat**, greave; ~ **skut**, shin-guard; ~ **slagaar**, tibial artery.

skeep'gaan, **(-ge-)**, go on board, embark.

skeeps: ~ **affuit**, naval gun-carriage; ~ **agent**, shipping-agent; ~ **behoeftes**, naval stores; ~ **beman-**

skeefskaaf 470 **skema**

ning, crew; ~**berigte**, shipping-news; ~**beskuit**, ship's biscuits; pilot bread; ~**bevragting** affreightment; ~**bou**, shipbuilding; ~**boukun'dig**, (-e), belonging to naval architecture; ~**boukun'dige**, (-s), naval architect; ~**boumeester**, shipbuilder; ~**bouwerf**, shipyard; ~**dokter**, ship's surgeon; ~**eienaar**, shipowner; ~**geleentheid**, shipping facility; ~**geskut**, sea-service ordnance; metal; ~**halter**, ship's halter; ~**helling**, slipway; ~**horlosie**, chronometer; ~**huur**, affreightment; freight; ~**ingenieur**, marine engineer; ~**joernaal**, daily journal of a navigator, logbook; ~**jonge**, (-ns), cabin-boy; boy seaman.

skeef'skaaf, drawing-knife.

skeeps: ~**kameraad**, shipmate; ~**kanon**, naval gun; ~**kaptein**, skipper, ship's captain; ~**ketel**, ship's boiler; ~**koffer**, cabin trunk; ~**kok**, ship's cook; ~**kole**, bunker-coal; ~**kombuis**, caboose, gallery; ~**kompas**, mariner's compass; ~**kontrak**, shipping-articles, ship's articles; ~**lading**, shipment, cargo; ~**lantern**, ship's lantern; bull's-eye; ~**lengte**, ship's length; ~**leweransier**, ship's chandler; ~**maat**, shipmate; ~**mag**, naval force, navy; ~**magnetisme**, ship's inductional magnetism; ~**makelaar**, ship-broker; ~**masjinis**, marine engineer; ~**monteur**, marine fitter; ~**motor**, marine motor; ~**offisier**, ship's officer; ~**onkoste**, ship's charges; ~**oorlosie** = skeepshorlosie; ~**papiere**, ship's papers; ~**provoos**, master-at-arms; ~**raad**, marine board; shipping-board; ~**ramp**, shipping disaster; ~**redery**, shipping-firm; ~**reg**, maritime law; *drie maal is* ~*reg*, thrice done is well done; third time lucky; ~**register**, registry of shipping; ~**roeper**, (-s), megaphone, speaking-trumpet; ~**rol**, ship's roll (-call); ~**romp**, hull; hulk; ~**ruim**, ship's hold; ~**ruimte**, tonnage, carrying-capacity; ~**takel**, ship's tackle; ~**term**, naval (marine) term; ~**terminus**, marine terminal; ~**timmerhout**, ship's timber; ~**timmerman**, shipwright; ~**timmerwerf**, shipbuilding yard; ~**ton**, register ton (of ship); ~**tyding**, shipping intelligence; ~**versekering**, marine insurance; ~**volk**, ship's company, crew; ~**vrag**, shipload, cargo, freight; ~**waardin**, ship's hostess, purserette; ~**werf**, dockyard, shipyard; ~**winkel**, dolly-shop; ~**wurm**, ship-borer.

skeep'vaart, navigation, shipping; ~**berigte**, shipping news; ~**kunde**, nautical science; ~**lyn**, shipping-line; ~**maatskappy**, shipping-company; ~**raad**, shipping board; ~**term**, nautical term.

skeer, (ge-), shave (beard); clip, shear (sheep); cut, trim (hair); crop; warp; poodle (dog); skim (writer); *HARE laat* ~, have one's hair cut; *ek* ~ *my elke MÔRE*, I shave every morning; *OOR die huise* ~, graze the housetops; *die boer* ~ *sy SKAPE*, the farmer is shearing; ~**afval**, cropping waste; ~**bakkie**, (-s), shaving-bowl; ~**bekmuis**, dwarf shrew; ~**borsel**, shaving-brush; ~**der**, (-s), shearer; barber; ~**dery**, shaving; shearing; ~**geld**, shearing-money (-wages, -expenses); ~**gereedskap**, shaving-kit; ~**goed**, shaving-set; ~**goedtas**, wet pack; ~**hok**, shearing-pen; ~**hou**, daisy-cutter (sport); ~**huis**, shearing-shed; ~**kant**, butt end (of fleece); ~**kraal**, shearing-pen; ~**kuns**, tonsorial art; ~**kwas**, shaving-brush; ~**lem(metjie)**, (razor) blade; ~**masjien**, clipper, warping-machine; ~**mes**, razor; razor-blade; *elektriese* ~, electric razor; ~**meslem**, razor-blade; ~**paper**, shaving-paper; ~**poeier**, shaving-powder; ~**pommade**, shaving-cream; ~**riem**, strop; razor-strop; ~**room**, shaving-cream; ~**salon**, shaving-saloon; ~**seep**, shaving-soap; shaving-stick; ~**seisoen**, shearing-season; ~**sel**, (-s), shearings; clipping, clip fleece; ~**skuur**, shearing-shed; ~**messlyper**, razor-grinder; ~**spieël**, shaving-mirror; ~**staaf**, shaving-stick; ~**tuig**, hovercraft; ~**tyd**, shearing-time; ~**vliegtuig**, ground-attack aeroplane; ~**vlug**, ground-attack flight; hedge-hopping; ~**vlugaanval**, ground-attack, low-level attack; ~**wasmiddel**, shaving-lotion; ~**water**, shaving-water; ~**winkel**, barber's shop; ~**wol**, fleece-wool; ~**wond**, razor-cut.

skeet, (skete), fart (vulgar); imaginary ailment, hypochondria; whim, caprice; *van 'n* ~ *'n donderslag (kanonskoot) MAAK*, make a mountain out of a molehill; *VOL skete*, full of imaginary complaints.

skeg'beeld, figurehead, fiddle-head.

skei¹, (s) (-e), yoke-pin, skey.

skei², (w) (ge-), part, separate, divide, disconnect, disjoin, sever; divorce; *hy LAAT hom van haar* ~, he is divorcing her; *van TAFEL en bed* ~, be divorced from bed and board; *ons WEË moet hier* ~, here our roads must part; ~**brief**, bill of divorce.

skei(d)'baar, (..bare), separable; discerptible; dissociable; ..**bare werkwoord**, particle verb; ~**heid**, separableness, separability; discerptibility; detachment.

skei'dend, (-e), dividing, disjunctive.

skei'ding, (-e, -s), parting; boundary; separation, divorce; ~ *in die HARE*, parting in the hair; ~ *van TAFEL en bed*, divorce from bed and board; ~ *van die WEË*, parting of the ways.

skei'dings: ~**bevel**, separation order; ~**lyn**, line of demarcation; line(s) of cleavage; dividing line; ~**toelae**, separation allowance; ~**wand**, partition; dividing wall (biol).

skeids: ~**brief**, *see* **skeibrief**; ~**gereg**, court of arbitration; ~**lyn**, dividing (boundary) line; line of demarcation; ~**man**, arbiter, arbitrator, sequester; ~**muur**, partition wall, party (dividing) wall; barrier (fig.); ~**regter**, judge, arbitrator, umpire (games), referee (rugby), adjudicator; ~**regterlik**, (-e), by arbitration, arbitral; ~*regterlike uitsprake*, arbitral awards.

skeids'weg, crossroad(s); *by die* ~ *staan*, be at the crossroad(s).

skei'e, (ge-), = **skei²**; ~**r**, divider, spacer.

skei'gat, skey-hole.

skei'kunde, chemistry; *ANORGANIESE* ~, inorganic chemistry; *ORGANIESE* ~, organic chemistry.

skeikun'dig, (-e), chemical; ~**e**, (-s), chemist, analyst.

skeil, (-e), membrane, mesenterium.

skei: ~**lyn**, *see* **skeidslyn**; ~**lys**, list, fillet (of columns); ~**muur**, dividing wall; ~**plaat**, parting-plate; ~**skakelaar**, isolating-switch; ~**teken**, diaeresis; ~**tregter**, separating funnel; ~**waster**, (-s), parting-washer; ~**weg**, crossroad(s).

skel¹, (s) (-le), bell; (w) (ge-), ring (bell).

skel², (w) (ge-), abuse, scold, rave, call names.

skel³, (b) (-ler, -ste), harsh, shrill; glaring (light).

skel(d): ~**naam**, abusive (nick)name; ~**taal**, abuse, abusive language; ~**woord**, invective, expletive, abusive word.

skel'eend, golden-eye, garrot.

skelet', (-te), skeleton, carcass; atomy; ~**gebou**, framed building; ~**teer**, (ge-), skeletonize.

Skelf'see, Red Sea.

skel: ~**heid**, shrillness, harshness; ~**klinkend**, (-e), high-sounding, shrill; ~**koord**, bell-string, bell-pull; ~**kruid**, swallow-wort.

skellak', shellac; ~**politoer**, French polish.

skel'le, (vero.), (mv) scales; *die* ~ *(skille) het van sy oë geval*, the scales fell from his eyes; cf. **skil**.

skel'ling, (-s), (hist.), twopence-farthing; *vier* ~, ninepence.

skel'linkie, (ong.), (-s), seat in the gods (theatre).

skelm, (s) (-s), rogue, crook, rapscallion, swindler, scamp, rascal; (b) knavish, dishonest, cunning, furtive; ~ *wegraak*, disappear on the sly; ~**ag'tig**, (-e), roguish, knavish; ~**ag'tigheid**, roguery, knavery, dishonesty.

skelm: ~**ery'**, (-e), dishonest work, piece of knavery; ~**eryversekering**, fidelity-guarantee insurance; ~**heid**, dishonesty; furtiveness.

skelm'pies, unobserved, furtively stealthily.

skelm: ~**roman**, picaresque novel; ~-~, slily, on the sly; ~**streek**, dishonest trick; ~**stuk**, knavery, roguish trick, dodge, plant, sharp dealing.

skel'naam = **skel(d)naam**.

skel'trompet, clarion.

skel'vis, haddock; ~**sop**, bisque.

skel'woord = **skel(d)woord**.

skel'wortel, *see* **skelkruid**.

ske'ma, (-s), scheme, sketch, project, outline.

skema'ties, (-e), schematic, in diagram, diagrammatic, in outline.

ske'mer, (s) twilight, dusk, gloaming; dimness; (w) (ge-), grow dusk; dawn; glimmer, gleam, shine feebly; *die HUISE* ~ *tussen die bome*, the houses can be seen dimly between the trees; *daar* ~ *my so iets voor die GEES*, I have a faint recollection of such a matter; *dit* ~ *voor my OË*, my head reels; *ons SIT lekker en* ~, we are enjoying the twilight; (b) dusky, dim; ~ **aand**, dusk, twilight, gloaming.

ske'meragtig, (-e), dusky; crepuscular; ~ **heid**, duskiness.

ske'mer: ~ **dag**, dawn; ~ **donker**, dusk; ~ **ig**, (-e), dim; crepuscular; ~ **ing**, twilight; dusk; glimmer; gloom; owl-light; dawn; ~ **kelkie**, sundowner, cocktail; ~ **kelkieparty**, cocktail party; ~ **kelkierondte**, cocktail circuit; ~ **lamp**, twilight lamp; ~ **lig**, dawn; twilight; gleam; ~ **oggend**, at early dawn; morning twilight; ~ **party(tjie)**, cocktail party; ~ **skakelaar**, dimswitch; ~ **tabberd**, cocktail frock; ~ **te**, ~ **tyd**, dawn; twilight; ~ **uur**, twilight hour.

skend, (ge-), violate (word); desecrate (something sacred); mutilate, deface, spoil (book); betray (secret); deform, blemish, disfigure; disfeature; abuse; flaw; infringe (regulations); transgress, break (the law); defile (honour); *sy goeie NAAM* ~, sully his fair name; *die NEUTRALITEIT* ~, abuse neutrality; ~ **blad**, defamatory paper; ~ **brief**, defamatory letter; ~ **er**, (-s), violator, profaner, transgressor; defacer; defiler *(see **skinder**)*; ~ **ig**, (-e), defamatory; sacrilegious; ~ **ing**, (-e, -s), violation; desecration; breach, disfiguration, defloration; ~ *ing v.d. lugruim*, violation of the airspace; ~ **skrif**, libel; lampoon; ~ **taal**, libellous (defamatory) language.

skenk, (ge-), give, donate (money); bestow (favour), endow (an institution); remit, waive (penalty); *die rente* ~ *ek jou*, you may keep the interest.

sken'kel, (-s), femur, thigh-bone (of human); gaskin (of horse); shank (of pork, veal, mutton); shin (of beef); *iem.* ~ *in die heup slaan*, smite hip and thigh; ~ **been**, femur, shin, shank; ~ **sening**, hamstring.

sken'ker, (-s), donor, giver, grantor, endower, presenter.

sken'king, (-e, -s), grant, endowment, bestowal, donation, gift, benefaction.

sken'kings: ~ **akte**, deed of gift; ~ **fonds**, endowment fund; ~ **polis**, endowment policy.

skenk'ster, (-s), donatress.

sken'nis, violation, desecration, profanation; *see* **skend**.

skep¹, (w) (ge-, geskape), create, call into existence, form; establish; bring about (state of affairs); *'n pos* ~, establish a post.

skep², (s) (-pe), ladle, shovel, scoop; spoonful; ladleful, helping; (w) (ge-), dip out, scoop, ladle (soup); dish (into plate); *ASEM* ~, take breath; have a breathing space; *BAIE* ~, drink heavily; *BEHAE* ~ *in*, take pleasure (delight) in; *LUG* ~, draw breath; *MOED* ~, take courage, *te VEEL* ~, drink too much (alcohol); *VOL* ~, fill; ~ **bak**, ladle (of water-wheel); paddle; scoop; ~ **ding**, scoop, scooping-utensil, bailer, dipper; ~ **doel**, drop-goal (rugby).

ske'pekennis, (-se), (hist.), mortgage bond.

ske'pel, (-s), bushel.

ske'peling, (-e), sailor, seafarer.

ske'pelmandjie, (-s), bushel-basket.

skep'emmer, (well-)bucket.

ske'pen, (-e), (hist.), judge, sheriff, alderman, councillor; ~ **domsreg**, Schependoms Law (of succession).

skep'hou, (-e), half-volley (tennis, cricket).

ske'pie, (-s), small boat (vessel).

skep: ~ **lepel**, ladle; bailer; ~ **lig**, skylight; ~ **mes**, teller-knife; ~ **net**, dip-net, landing-net, scoop-net, spoon-net.

skep'pend, (-e), creative; fictive; ~ *e vermoë*, creative power.

Skep'per, Creator.

skep'per¹, (-s), author, creator.

skep'per², (-s), scooper, dipper.

skep'pie, (-s), small helping; spoonful; *'n tweede* ~, a second helping.

skep'ping, (-e, -s), creation, genesis.

skep'pings: ~ **daad**, creative deed; ~ **dag**, day of creation; ~ **drang**, creative impulse; ~ **geskiedenis**, story of creation; ~ **krag**, creative energy; ~ **teorie**, cosmogony; ~ **verhaal**, story of creation; ~ **vermoë**, creative power; ~ **werk** (work of) creation.

skep: ~ **plaat**, shovel-plate; ~ **pyp**, bailer; ~ **rat**, paddle (-wheel); water-wheel; bucket-wheel, scoop, breast-wheel, (gravity-)wheel.

skep'sel, (-e, -s), creature, human being, man; *hy is 'n snaakse* ~, he is a funny chap.

skep'sis, scepsis.

skep: ~ **skoot**, *see* **skephou**; ~ **skop**, (s) drop-kick; (w) (ge-), drop-kick; ~ **spaan**, paddle.

skep'ties, (-e), sceptical.

skep'tikus, (-se, .. tici), sceptic; pyrrhonist.

skeptisis'me, scepticism.

skep'wiel, paddle-wheel.

skêr, (-e), pair of scissors (for nails); clipper, pair of shears (for trees, sheep); *gaan koop 'n* ~, go and buy a pair of scissor; ~ **bek**, scissor-bill; ~ **beweging**, scissors movement (rugby).

skerf, (skerwe), shard; bit, morsel, fragment; *die skerwe het gewaai*, the chips flew; ~ **bom**, splinter-bomb; ~ **breking**, fragmentation; ~ **ie**, (-s), chip, splinter; ~ **vry**, (-e), splinter-proof; ~ **vryglas**, splinter-proof glass.

ske'ring, warp; ~ *en INSLAG*, warp and woof; *dit VORM* ~ *en inslag*, this is the order of the day; ~ **draad**, warp.

skêr: ~ **kap**, scissors truss; ~ **klem**, scissors lock.

skerm¹, (s) (-s), screen; curtain; awning; shelter; shield; guard; flat (theatre); umbel (bot.); *AGTER die* ~ *s*, behind the scenes; *'n KYKIE agter die* ~ *s*, a peep behind the scenes; *agter die* ~ *s SIEN*, see what is behind it all; *agter die* ~ *s SIT*, pull the wires; *WIE sit agter die* ~ *s?* who is pulling the strings?

skerm², (w) (ge-), fence, parry; spar (boxing); flourish; defend.

skerm'blom, umbellifer; ~ **mig**, umbelliferous; ~ **mige**, (-s), umbellifer.

skerm: ~ **bril**, goggles; ~ **dak**, penthouse; ~ **degen**, foil, fencing sabre; ~ **den**, stone-pine; ~ **draend**, (-e), umbelliferous; ~ **draer**, umbellifer; ~ **handskoen**, fencing glove; ~ **hulsel**, protective cover; ~ **er**, (-s), fencer; ~ **kuns**, swordmanship, art of fencing; ~ **les**, fencing lesson; ~ **maat**, sparring partner; ~ **masker**, fencing mask; ~ **meester**, fencing master; ~ **muur**, enclosure wall; ~ **plaat**, screen plate; baffle; ~ **rooster**, screen grid, grating; ~ **skool**, fencing skool; ~ **steier**, fan scaffold; ~ **stoot**, pass, thrust; ~ **uitvoering**, assault-at-arms.

skermut'sel, (ge-), skirmish; ~ *met woorde*, spar with words; ~ **ing**, (-e, -s), skirmish, mêlée, brush, verbal duel.

skerm'veër, windscreen wiper.

skerm'vereniging, fencing club.

skerm: ~ **vormig**, (-e), umbelliform; umbrella-shaped; ~ **werking**, screening effect.

skerp, sharp, edged, edgy; keen (intelligence, competition), eager; clear (outline); acute, severe, biting, bitter (pain); cynical, cutting (words); poignant (grief), pungent (odour); hard, harsh (words); acrid (taste), caustic (wit); *'n* ~ *ANTWOORD*, a cutting reply; *'n* ~ *BERISPING*, a severe reproof; ~ *van GEHOOR wees*, have a quick ear; ~ **GELAATSTREKKE**, clear-cut (sharp) features; ~ **HOEK**, acute angle; ~ **KONSONANT**, voiceless consonant; ~ **LEPEL**, curette; ~ **LUISTER**, listen attentively; ~ *MAAK*, sharpen; *'n* ~ *STEM*, a piercing voice; *dit kom* ~ *UIT*, it stands out boldly; ~ **by**, fine leg (cricket); ~ **gereedskap**, edged tool; ~ **glip**, fine slip (cricket); ~ **heid**, sharpness, acuity; acerbity, harshness; asperity, poignancy; pungency; ~ **hoe'kig**, (-e), acute-angled; ~ **hoekkruising**, acute-angle crossing.

skerpioen', (-e), scorpion; *die S~*, Scorpio(n); ~ **ang-**

skerp

tig, (-e), scorpion-like; ~**kruid,** furze; ~**spinnekop,** pedipalp; ~**vis,** rock-fish.
skerp: ~**kan'tig, (-e),** sharp-edged; ~**regter,** executioner, hangman, headsman; ~**rug,** hogback; ~**siende,** discerning, sharp-sighted, hawk-eyed, eagle-eyed, penetrating, accipitral, perceiving; ~**siend'heid,** sharp-sightedness, quick-sightedness, penetration, perspicacity.
skerpsin'nig, (-e), perspicacious, sagacious, acute, quick-witted, keen, perceiving, astute; penetrating; ~**heid,** discrimination, perspicacity, acuteness, sagacity, acumen, ingenuity, astuteness, penetration.
skerp'skutter, (-s), sniper, sharpshooter; marksman.
skerp'skutterkuns, marksmanship.
skerp'snydend, (-e), sharp, keen; ~*e swaard,* sharp sword.
skerp'te, sharpness, keenness, edge; definition (of image); acerbity, poignancy (grief); severeness (fig.); *met die ~ v.d. swaard slaan,* smite with the edge of the sword.
skêr: ~**slyper,** scissors-grinder; ~**sprong,** scissors-jump.
skerts, (s) (-e), chaff, pleasantry, fun, joke, jest, frolic, raillery; quip; game; *die ~ te ver DRYF,* carry a joke too far; *~ of ERNS,* jest or earnest; *hy LAAT nie met hom ~ nie,* he is not to be fooled with; *iets in ~ SÊ,* say something in jest; *hy kan geen ~ VERDRA nie,* he cannot stand a joke; (w) **(ge-),** jest, joke; quip.
skert'send, (-e), joking, jesting; facetious; *~ bedoel,* by way of a joke; ~**erwys(e),** jestingly, jokingly, in fun.
skert'ser, (-s), joker, jester; ~**y, (-e),** jesting, joking, raillery, fun.
skets, (s) (-e), sketch; outline; draft; (rough) plan; plotting, diagram; (w) **(ge-),** sketch, plot (graphs); delineate, design, draw roughly; *in breë trekke ~,* sketch in broad outline; ~**boek,** sketch-book; ~**er, (-s),** delineator, sketcher; ~**kaart,** sketch-map; skeleton-map; ~**ma'tig, (-e),** sketchy, in outline (drawing); ~**plan,** rough plan; ~**tekening,** sketch (drawing).
sket'ter, (ge-), blare, bray, flourish; brag, bluster; blow (bugle); ~**aar, (-s),** ~**bek, (-ke),** boaster, bluffer; ~**stem, (-me),** harsh (piercing) voice.
skeur, (s) (-e), tear, rent (in clothes); crack (in glass); crevice, fissure (in rock); (w) **(ge-),** tear, rend; cleave, split, lacerate; *'n DOKUMENT stukkend ~,* tear up a document; *die WÊRELD ~,* run away very quickly; ~**almanak,** block calendar; tear-off calendar.
skeur'buik, scurvy; ~**lyer,** scorbutic; ~**middel,** antiscorbutic.
skeur: ~**dal,** rift valley; ~**der, (-s),** schismatic; ~**effusie,** fissure eruption; ~**end, (-e),** disruptive; ~**ing, (-e, -s),** division, rupture; sheaving (geol.); scissure, schism, split; (dis)ruption; ~**kalender,** tear-off (block) calendar; ~**makend, (-e),** schismatic; ~**maker, (-s),** schismatic; disrupter, ~**nael,** lagnail, hang-nail; ~**papier,** waste paper; ~**ploeg,** subsoiler, ripper; ~**sterkte,** tearing strength; ~**tand,** fang, laniary, sectorial (tooth); ~**tjie, (-s),** small tear; ~**wond,** laceration.
skeut, (-e), shoot, sprig; dash, draught (wine, water); lacing (liquor); ~**ig, (-e),** liberal, open-handed; ~**igheid,** liberality, openhandedness.
ske'webek, wry face; grimace; *~trek,* pull faces, mop and mow.
ske'weboog, skew arch.
ski, (s) (-'s), ski; (w) **(ge-),** ski.
skie'lik, (-e), sudden(ly), quick(ly), unexpected(ly); fast, expeditious; abrupt; ~**heid,** suddenness, unexpectedness; abruptness.
skie'mansgaring, spun yarn.
ski'ër, (-s), skier.
skier, nearly, almost.
skier'eiland, peninsula, chersonese.
skier'lik = skielik.
skier'vlakte, peneplain.
skiet¹, (s): *~ GEE,* let go, give rope, pay out, ease; *iem. ~ GEE,* give someone a freer rein; give someone more rope.

skiet², (s) (-e), (stud.), invitation; *die nooi het twee ~ e vir die konsert,* the girl has two invitations for the concert; (w) **(ge-),** invite; *is jy al ge~ vir vanaand?,* have you been invited for tonight?
skiet³, (w) (ge-), shoot, fire, snipe; blast (with dynamite); bag (game); apply (for post); put forth (buds); eject (semen); advance (money); (stud.), take out (a girl); *dit ~ deur my GEDAGTE,* it flashes through my mind; *GELD ~,* lend money; *te KORT ~,* shoot short of the mark; not come up to expectations; *LAAT ~,* give rope, slack; *OP iem. ~,* shoot at a person; *SAAD ~,* run to seed; *TEIKEN ~,* shoot at a target; *TRANE ~ haar in die oë,* tears welled up in(to) her eyes; ~**afdeling,** detail; ~**baan,** butts, rifle-range; ~**beitel,** channeler, cross-cut chisel; ~**dag,** shooting-day; *dit is aldag ~ dag, maar nie aldag raakdag nie,* a hunter is not always lucky; one has one's off-days; ~**dampe,** (blasting) fumes; ~**doppie,** percussion cap; ~**draad,** woof thread; ~**er, (-s),** shooter; fireman; blaster; plunger (in lock); ~**ery,** firing, shooting, fire; gunning; ~**gat,** loophole; crenel; embrasure; ~**gebed,** ejaculatory prayer; ejaculation, hurried prayer; ~**gelatien,** blasting gelatine; ~**goed,** ammunition; arguments; ~**hael,** shot; ~**katoen,** gun-cotton; ~**kommando,** rifle commando; ~**kuns,** musketry; marksmanship; ~**lading,** blasting charge; ~**lamp,** shooting-lamp; spot-lamp; ~**leer,** gunnery.
skiet'lig, spotlight; ~**koker,** spotlight-projector; barrel (of gun); ~**toestel,** spotlight-apparatus; ~**visier,** spotlight-sight.
skiet: ~**lood, (..lode),** plummet; plumb-bob, plumb-line; balance-bob; ~**lus'tig,** trigger-happy; fond of hunting (shooting); ~**mielies,** pop corn; ~**moot,** avenue of fire; ~**oefening,** target-shooting, rifle-practice; ~**oorlog,** shooting war; ~**party,** hunting party; shooting affair; ~**perd,** hunter (horse); ~**plaas,** farm with game; ~**plek,** firing-point; ~**pouse,** firing-interval; ~**prop,** plug; ~**register,** practice-records; ~**sertifikaat,** blasting certificate; ~**-skop-en-donder(boek),** detective story, whodunit, thriller; ~**-skop-en-donderprent,** blood and thunder film; ~**staking,** cease-fire; ~**stand,** range; ~**stilstand,** cease-fire; ~**stoel,** ejection chair; ~**stowwe,** explosives; ~**stroom,** rapid; ~**tent,** shooting-gal-lery; ~**terrein** practice-ground, shooting-range; ~**tog,** shooting expedition; ~**vak,** bay; ~**veld,** game-district; ~**vereniging,** rifle-club; ~**voorraad,** ammunition; ~**voorval,** shooting incident; ~**vrug,** catapult-fruit; ~**wedstryd,** shooting competition; ~**werk,** blasting operations; ~**werker,** blaster; ~**wet,** game-law; ~**wond,** gun-shot wound.
skif¹, (w) (ge-), run, coagulate, curdle (milk); become worn out, become threadbare (clothes); sift, divide, sort out.
skif², (s) (-fe), skiff; ~**roei,** skiffing.
skif'ting, (-e, -s), curdling, sifting, dividing, sorting, screening.
skig, (-te), arrow, bolt; flash (lightning).
skig'tig, (-e), shy, skittish (horse); ~**heid,** shyness, skittishness.
skik¹, (s) liking, pleasure, *in sy ~ wees,* be delighted.
skik², (w) (ge-), arrange, order; settle, patch up (peace); conform oneself to; *jou ~ na OMSTANDIGHEDE,* adapt oneself to circumstances; *hom ~ in die ONVERMYDELIKE,* resign oneself to the inevitable; *'n SAAK in der minne ~,* settle a matter (dispute) amicably; *blomme in 'n VAAS ~,* arrange flowers; *WANNEER dit jou ~,* when it suits you; ~**plan,** settlement plan.
Skik'godinne, goddesses of destiny, the Fates, Parcae.
skik'king, (-e, -s), arrangement, agreement, settlement; adjustment, compromise, accommodation, disposition, disposal; composition (debts); *tot 'n ~ KOM,* come to an agreement; *'n MINLIKE ~,* an amicable settlement; *'n ~ TREF met sy skuldeisers,* make a composition (compound) with your creditors; ~**svoorwaardes,** terms of settlement.
skik'lik, (-e), reasonable, accommodative, accommo-

dating; ~**heid**, willingness to accommodate, reasonableness, complaisance, accommodation.

skik'tyd, (..**tye**), flex-time; flexitime.

skil, (s) (-**le**), peel, skin, shell, coat, rind, husk, hull; cf. **skelle**; *ertappels met ~ en al kook*, boil potatoes in their jackets; (w) (**ge-**), peel, skin (tomato); pare (away); ~**beitel**, bevelled-edge (pacing) chisel; ~**brand**, superficial burn (scald).

skild, (-**e**), shield; aegis, buckler, badge, escutcheon; *iets in die ~ voer*, have something up one's sleeve; ~**agtig**, (-**e**), shield-like; ~**battery**, shield-battery; ~**been**, shoulder-blade (of ox); ~**dak**, hip-roof; ~**draer**, shield-bearer.

skil'der, (s) (-**s**), painter, artist; house-painter; (w) (**ge-**), paint, portray; depict; limn, delineate; *'n muur drie lae ~*, give a wall three coats of paint; (b) speckled, roan (ox).

skilderag'tig, (-**e**), picturesque; ~**heid**, picturesqueness.

skil'derboontjie, speckled bean.

skil'der: ~**doek**, canvas; ~**doos**, paintbox; ~**end**, (-**e**), graphic; ~**es'**, (-**se**), (woman) painter; ~**gerei**, artist's materials; ~**ing**, (-**e**, -**s**), depiction; portrayal, portraiture; ~**kuns**, (art of) painting; ~**kwas**, paint-brush; ~**les**, painting-lesson.

skil'ders: ~**esel**, painter's easel; ~**gerei**, artist's materials; ~**kneg**, journeyman-painter.

skil'der: ~**skool**, school of painting; school of painters; ~**skrif**, signwriting.

skil'ders: ~**linne**, painter's canvas; ~**mes**, palette knife; ~**palet**, painter's palette; ~**penseel**, paint-brush.

skil'der: ~**stok**, guiding stick (of painters); mahlstick, maulstick; ~**stuk**, painting.

skil'dersverf, artist's colour(s).

skil'derwerk, painting; paintwork, brushwork.

skildery', (-**e**), picture; canvas; painting; ~**kabinet**, picture-gallery; ~**lys**, picture-rail; ~**museum**, picture-gallery; ~**raam**, picture-frame; ~**tentoonstelling**, exhibition of paintings; ~**tou**, picture-cord; ~**versameling**, collection of paintings; ~**winkel**, paint-shop.

skild: ~**hoek**, canton (herald.); ~**hoof**, chief (herald.); ~**jie**, (-**s**), small shield; scutellum; ~**kewer**, helmet-beetle; ~**klier**, thyroid gland; ~**klierag'tig**, (-**e**), goitrous; ~**kliervergroting**, goitre; ~**knaap**, esquire, shield-bearer; ~**knop**, mushroom-head (bolt); shield-boss; umbo; ~**kraakbeen**, thyroid cartilage; ~**luis**, scale insect *(Coccida)*; ~**vel**, rawhide shield; ~**vlerkig**, ~**vleuelig**, (-**e**), sheath-winged (insects); ~**vormig**, (-**e**), shieldlike, clypeate; peltate (bot.); scutate (zool.); ~*vormige kraakbeen*, thyroid cartilage.

skild'wag, (-**te**), sentry, sentinel, guard; *op ~ staan*, stand sentry; do sentry-duty; ~**diens**, sentry-go; ~**huisie**, sentry-box; ~**lyn**, sentry-line; ~**pos**, sentry's post; ~**ronde**, sentry's beat.

skil'fer, (s) (-**s**), flake, blister (rocks); furfur; lamella; scale, ~**s**, dandruff; (w) (**ge-**), scale, flake, chip (varnish), peel off; ~**agtig**, (-**e**), dandruffy, scaly; flaky; laminose, laminate; ~**agtigheid**, scaliness; ~**ig**, (-**e**), full of dandruff; flaky; ~**igheid**, flakiness; ~**ing**, lamination, flaking; ~**kool**, coal-slate; ~**kors**, puff pastry; ~**lak**, shellac; ~**rys**, flaky rice; ~**steen**, schist; ~**tertdeeg**, puff paste, puff pastry; ~**wasmiddel**, dandruff-lotion (-shampoo).

skil: ~**ler**, (-**s**), peeler; parer; ~**masjien**, peeling-machine, parer; ~**mes**, paring-knife.

ski'loper, ski-runner, skier.

skil'pad, (..**paaie**), tortoise (land); turtle (water); slow coach; derailer; *die ~ KRUIP gou in sy dop*, he soon crept into his shell; *soos 'n ~ LOOP*, go at a snail's pace; ~ *TREK*, tortoise tug of war; *van 'n ~ VERE probeer pluk*, make a silk purse out of a sow's ear; ~**bessie**, dune berry *(Mundtia spinosa)*; ~**blom**, ink-plant *(Hyobanche sanquinea)*; ~**bossie**, wild tea(bush) *(Grubbia rosmarinifolia)*; ~**dop**, tortoise-shell, carapace; ~**draffie**, shuffle, shuffling gait, jog-trot; ~**jie**, (-**s**), small tortoise; ladybird; ~**so(e)p**, turtle soup; *nagemaakte ~so(e)p*, mock turtle soup; ~**vere**, pigeon's milk.

skim, (-**me**), apparition, ghost, spectre, shadow; eidolon; *'n ~ NAJAAG*, chase shadows; *'n ~ van wat hy WAS*, a shadow of his former self; ~**agtig**, (-**e**), shadowy, ghost-like; ~**kabinet**, shadow cabinet.

skim'mel¹, (s) (-**s**), grey (dapple, roan) horse; *blou ~*, grey horse; roan (horse, ox); (b) grey, dapple-grey; roan.

skim'mel², (s) mildew, mould, mustiness; fungus; efflorescence (on wall); (w) (**ge-**), moulder, grow mouldy (mildewy); (b) mouldy, musty, mildewy; bashful.

skim'melagtig¹, (-**e**), greyish; dapple(d).

skim'melagtig², (-**e**), mouldy, musty; *~e uitslag*, mould-like efflorescence; ~**heid**, mouldiness.

skim'mel: ~**brood**, mouldy bread; bashful person; ~**dag**, dawn; ~**draad**, hypha; ~**ig**, (-**e**), mouldy; ~**kultuur**, mould-culture.

skim'melperd, grey, dapple-grey horse; roan.

skim'melplant, filamentous fungus, mould.

skim'melrig¹, (-**e**), mouldy.

skim'melrig², (-**e**), dapple(d).

skim'mel: ~**siekte**, mycosis; ~**swam**, mould; ~**vergiftiging**, fungus-poisoning; ~**vlek**, mouldy stain.

skim'me: ~**ryk**, land of shades, Hades; ~**spel**, galanty-show, shadow-show.

skimp, (s) (-**e**), taunt, mockery, gibe, jeer, contumely, scoff; innuendo, allusion; hurried glance; *iem. net MET 'n ~ sien*, catch a fleeting glimpse of someone; *met ~e OORLAAI*, heap abuse on; (w) (**ge-**), hint, make covert references; mock, taunt, gibe, jeer, scoff, revile, rail at; ~**agtig**, (-**e**), contumelious, scoffing; ~**dig**, (-**te**), satiric; **digter**, satirist; ~**enderwys(e)**, mockingly, gibingly, jeeringly; ~**er**, (-**s**), mocker, railer, scoffer; ~**ery**, derision, mockery, gibing, scoffing; ~**lag**, derisive (jeering, mocking) laugh; ~**naam**, abusive name; ~**rede**, taunt; invective; diatribe; ~**skeut**, ~**skoot**, gibe, taunt, quip, sly hit; ~**skrif**, lampoon; libel; ~**taal**, mockery, mocking language, scoffing, jeers; invective; ~**woord**, abusive term, gibe.

skin'der, (**ge-**), slander, backbite, libel; gossip, ~**aar**, (-**s**), ~**bek**, slanderer, detractor, detractress, rumour-monger, quidnunc, gobemouche, gossip; (news-)pedlar; ~**praatjies**, slander(ous talk); gossip; ~**siek**, (-**e**), slanderous; ~**taal**, slanderous (calumnious) language; ~**tong**, slanderous tongue; slanderer; ~**y**, backbiting.

skink, (**ge-**), pour (out), serve; *'n glas half vol ~*, pour (out) half a glass; ~**bord**, tray, salver, platter.

skin'kel, (-**s**) = **skenkel**.

skink: ~**er**, (-**s**), cup-bearer, butler, Ganymede; ~**juffrou**, (-**e**), barmaid; ~**kan**, tankard; flagon; ~**ster**, (-**s**), (female) server, pourer; ~**tafel**, sideboard, tea-table, coffee-table.

ski'onderstel, ski-undercarriage.

skip, (**skepe**), ship, vessel, boat; auditory, nave (of church); *daar KOM nog altyd beter skepe in as wat daar uitgaan*, there are as good fish in the sea as ever came out of it; *wag tot my ~ KOM*, wait till my ship comes home; *SKOON ~ maak*, make a clean sweep, sweep the boards; *die ~ van die STAAT*, the ship of state; *sy skepe agter hom VERBRAND*, burn one's boats (behind one); *'n ~ te WATER laat*, launch a ship; *die ~ v.d. WOESTYN*, ship of the desert (camel).

skip'breuk, shipwreck; ~ *ly*, be (ship)wrecked; *sy PLANNE het ~ gely*, his plans have miscarried; ~**eling**, (-**e**), shipwrecked person, castaway.

skip: ~**brug**, bridge of boats, pontoon bridge; ~**haak**, grappling-iron; ~**net**, landing-net.

skip'per¹, (s) (-**s**), captain; bargee, bargeman, master (mariner), skipper.

skip'per², (w) (**ge-**), temporize, be a time-server, trim, compromise; ~**aard**, (-**s**), trimmer; time-server.

Skip'perke, Skipperkie ~, Schipperke.

skip'pers: ~**haak**, boat-hook; ~**kind**, bargeman's child; ~**kneg**, bargeman's mate; ~**taal**, nautical language; ~**woord**, mariner's term.

skip'pie, (-**s**), small boat (vessel).

skis, (-**te**), schist; ~**agtig**, (-**e**), schistose.

skis'ma, (-**s**), schism; ~**tiek'**, (-**e**), schismatic; ~**'ties**, (-**e**), schismatic(al); ~**'tikus**, (..**tici**, -**se**), schismaticist.

skisofreen', (..frene), schizophrenic.
skisofrenie', schizophrenia.
ski'sport, skiing.
skist, (-e), = skis.
Skith, (-e), Scythian.
Ski'thië, Scythia.
ski'troepe, ski-troops.
skit'ter, (ge-), glitter, shine, scintillate, blaze, sparkle, flash; ~ *deur afwesigheid*, be conspicuous by one's absence; ~ **blink**, (ge-), sparkle, flash, scintillate; ~ **end**, (-e), glittering, brilliant, sparkling, bright, gorgeous, effulgent, splendid, lustrous; ~ **resultate**, magnificent (splendid) results; ~ **glans**, lustre; ~ **ing**, glittering, sparkling, radiance, splendour, lustre, brilliance, effulgence, flash, glare, brightness, flashing; ~ **lig**, glittering (dazzling) light; flashlight; ~ **stof**, brilliant dust.
skittery', (s) diarrhoea (animals); scours; (w) (ge-), have diarrhoea; ~ **siekte**, Molteno (cattle) disease.
skiw'werig, (-e), curdy.
skle'ra, sclera.
skleri'tis, scleritis.
sklero'se, sclerosis.
sklero'ties, (-e), sclerotic.
skob, (-be), scale; *see* **skub**.
skob'bejak, (-ke), rascal, scamp, rogue, cur, blackguard, blighter, scoundrel, rapscallion, ragamuffin, vagabond, bad egg.
skob'vormig, (-e), squamiform.
skoei, (ge-), shoe; tread (tyre); *op dieselfde lees* ~, cast in the same mould; ~ **sel**, (-s), footwear, footgear.
skoe'lapper, (-s), butterfly; ~ **agtig**, (-e), papilionaceous.
skoen, (-e), shoe, boot; (mv) footwear; *elkeen weet die beste waar die* ~ *hom DRUK*, each one knows best where the shoe pinches; *te GROOT wees vir sy* ~ *e*, too big for his boots; *wie die* ~ *PAS, kan dit aantrek*, whom the cap fits, let him wear it; *iem. iets in die* ~ *e SKUIF*, lay something at someone's door; *nie in sy* ~ *e wil STAAN nie*, not want to stand in his shoes; *die STOUTE* ~ *e aantrek*, muster up courage; take the bull by the horns; *VAS in jou* ~ *e staan*, stand firm; *moenie ou* ~ *e WEGGOOI voordat jy nuwes het nie*, don't be off with the old love before you are on with the new; do not drop the substance for the shadow; ~ **band**, shoe-strap; ~ **borsel**, blacking-brush, shoe-brush; ~ **doos**, shoe-box.
skoe'ner, (-s), schooner.
skoe'nerak, shoe-rack, boot-rack.
skoe'nerbrik, brigantine.
skoen: ~ **fabriek**, footwear factory; ~ **fabrikant**, footwear manufacturer; ~ **gespe**, shoe-buckle; ~ **handel**, boot-trade; ~ **horing**, (-s), shoehorn, shoe-lift; ~ **lapper**, (-s), cobbler; *see* **skoelapper**; ~ **leer**, shoe-leather, boot-leather; ~ **leertjie**, tongue of shoe (boot); ~ **lees**, (-te), (boot-)last; ~ **lepel**, shoehorn.
skoen'maker, cobbler, shoemaker; ~ *se KINDERS loop kaalvoet*, who is worse shod than a shoemaker's wife?; *ek sal my* ~ *aan jou KLEREMAKER voorstel*, you'll get a taste of my boot; ~ , *hou jou by jou LEES*, cobbler, stick to your last; ~ **sels**, bradawl; ~ **y**, shoe-factory; shoemaking.
skoen: ~ **poetser**, (-s), shoeblack, boots; ~ **riem**, shoe-lace, shoe-string; latchet; *nie werd om sy* ~ *rieme los te maak (te ontbind) nie*, not fit to tie someone else's shoelaces; ~ **smeer**, boot-polish; ~ **sool**, sole of a shoe; ~ **spyker**, shoe-nail; hobnail; ~ **tjie**, (-s), little shoe; shuttle (sewing machine); ~ **veter**, shoe-lace; ~ **vorm**, shoe tree; ~ **waks**, boot-polish; ~ **ware**, footwear; ~ **winkel**, boot-store.
skoerie'kel, (ge-), beat, thrash.
skoert, (ge-), scoot, go away, be gone, avaunt, skedaddle.
skof¹, (skowwe), shoulder (ox), hump, withers (horse).
skof², (-te), distance covered in one trek; hop (aero.); lap, stage; shift; relief (at work); task; *die laaste* ~ *gery het*, to have gone on one's last journey.
skof³, (-te), blackguard.
skof'baas, shift boss.
skoffeer', (ge-), ravish, devastate.

skof'fel, (s) (-s), hoe; cultivator; (ge-), clear (of weeds), hoe; dance; *die nag deur* ~ , dance (through) the whole night; ~ **aar**, (-s), cultivator; one who hoes; ~ **pik**, (weed-)hoe; ~ **ploeg**, cultivator; ~ **werktuig**, cultivator.
skof'werk, work in shifts, shift-work.
skok, (s) (-ke), shock, fright; dash, jerk, jolt, jar; concussion; impact; percussion (blasting); (w) (ge-), shock, horrify, frighten, shake; concuss; jar, jolt; *my vertroue in hom is ge* ~ , I have lost faith in him; ~ **behandeling**, shock-treatment; ~ **bom**, percussion bomb; ~ **breker**, shock-breaker, snubber, shock-absorber (motor-car); recoil-reducer; ~ **breking**, shock-absorption; ~ **buis**, percussion fuse (tube); ~ **demper**, (-s), shock-absorber.
skokiaan', skokiaan.
skok'kend, (-e), shocking, frightful, terrible.
skok: ~ **koord**, shock-cord; ~ **myn**, contact-mine; ~ **naald**, percussion needle; ~ **nederlaag**, shock defeat; ~ **ontsteker**, percussion igniter; ~ **taktiek**, shock tactics; ~ **toets**, scragg (springs); ~ **troepe**, shock-troops; ~ **vas**, (-te), shockproof; ~ **vuur**, percussion fire; ~ **werking**, shock-action; ~ **wiel**, pilot wheel.
skol¹, (-le), plaice (fish).
skol², (-le), floe (ice).
skolastiek', scholasticism.
skolas'ties, (-e), scholastic.
skolas'tikus, (-se, ..tici), scholastic.
sko'le: ~ rugby, schools' rugby; ~ **span**, schools' team; ~ **wedstryd**, inter-school competition.
skolias', (-te), scholiast.
skolier', (-e), scholar; pupil; ~ **kaartjie**, scholar's ticket; ~ **patrollie**, scholar patrol.
sko'ling, schooling, training; skill.
skol'lie, (-s), ragamuffin, street arab, hooligan.
skom'mel, (s) (-s), swing; (w) (ge-), rock, swing, oscillate, roll, wobble; shuffle, make (cards); fluctuate (market prices); ~ **aar**, rocker (slime-washer); ~ **drank**, cocktail; ~ **ing**, oscillation; fluctuation; swinging; ~ **klip**, logan(-stone); ~ **musiek**, swing music; ~ **perd**, hobby-horse, rocking-horse; ~ **perdbeweging**, rocking-horse motion; ~ **rig**, (-e), rocking, wobbly; ~ **rooster**, rocking-grate; ~ **sif**, swinging-screen, baby (diamond-fields); ~ **sifter**, continuous jigger (in mines); ~ **stoel**, rocking-chair; ~ **stuk**, shackle; ~ **wiel**, balance.
skon, (-s), scone.
sko'ne, beauty (of nature); (-s), beautiful woman, beauty.
skoof, (skowe), sheaf.
skooi, (ge-), (ong.), tramp, roam aimlessly; beg; ~ **er**, (-s), tramp, beggar, ragamuffin; ~ **eragtig**, (-e), like a wastrel, raffish; ~ **erdom**, beggardom; street arabs as a class; ~ **ery**, vagrancy, vagabondage.
skool¹, (s) (**skole**), shoal (of fish); (w) (ge-), shoal (fish); flock together.
skool², (s) (**skole**), school; *op* ~ *BLY*, be kept in at school; *HOËR* ~ , high (secondary) school; *INDUSTRIËLE* ~ , industrial school; *INTERMEDIËRE* ~ , intermediate school; *uit die* ~ *KLAP (praat)*, tell tales out of school; *LAER* ~ , primary (elementary) school; *MIDDELBARE* ~ , secondary school; *NA* ~ *gaan*, go to school; ~ *vir voortgesette ONDERWYS*, continuation school; *OP* ~ , at school; *OPENBARE* ~ , public school; *PRIVAAT* ~ , private school; *in die* ~ *SIT*, put to school; *die* ~ *SLUIT vandag*, school breaks up today; *TEGNIESE* ~ , technical school; *VOORBEREIDENDE* ~ , preparatory school; (w) (ge-), school, train, teach; *ge* ~ *de werkers*, skilled workers; ~ **arts**, school medical officer; ~ **bank**, desk, form; ~ **behoeftes**, school requisites; ~ **besoek**, attendance (at school); ~ **besoekbeampte**, attendance-officer; ~ **biblioteek**, school library; ~ **blad**, school magazine; ~ **bly**, (-ge-), be kept in, stay after school; ~ **boek**, school-book; ~ **bord**, blackboard; ~ **bus**, school bus; ~ **dag**, school day; ~ **dogter**, schoolgirl; ~ **dokter**, school doctor, medical inspector of schools; ~ **dwang**, compulsory attendance.
skooleindsertifikaat', school-leaving certificate;

~eksamen, school-leaving certificate examination.
skool: ~eksamen, school examination; ~ekskursie, school excursion; ~fees, school function (festival); ~fonds, school fund; ~gaan, (-ge-), go to (attend) school; ~gebou, school building; ~gebruik, use in schools; ~geld, school fees; *baie ~geld moet BETAAL*, have to learn by experience (in a hard school); *jy moet jou ~geld gaan TERUGVRA*, your education has been sadly neglected; ~geleerdheid, book-learning; ~higiëne, school hygiene; ~hoof, principal, headmaster; ~hou, (-ge-), give lessons, teach; ~inspeksie, school-inspection; ~inspekteur, school-inspector, inspector of education; ~jaar, school year; ~jeug, school children; ~joernaal, school journal; ~jong, school servant; ~jonge, (-ns), school boy; ~juffrou, school mistress, lady teacher; ~kamer, school room; classroom; ~kameraad, schoolmate, schoolfellow; ~kind, pupil, school-going child; *iem. soos 'n ~kind behandel*, treat someone like a schoolchild; ~klere, school clothes; ~kleure, school colours; ~kommissie, school committee; ~kwartaal, school term; ~lied, school song; ~lokaal, school room, classroom; ~maat, school friend, schoolmate.
skool'meester, schoolmaster, teacher; pedagogue; pedant; ~ag'tig, (-e), pedantic, conceited; ~ag'tigheid, pedantry, pedagogism.
skool: ~meisie, school girl; ~meubels, school furniture; ~onderrig, school-instruction; ~onderwys, school-teaching; schooling, school education; ~opsiener, school caretaker, ~orde, school discipline; ~plaas, school farm; ~plig, compulsory education; ~raad, school board; ~rapport, school report; ~regulasies, school regulations, The Code; ~reis, school journey; tour of scholars; ~ryp, ready for schooling.
skools, (-e), scholastic; *~e geleerdheid*, book-learning, school-knowledge.
skool: ~sak, school bag, school case; ~seun, school boy; ~siek, malingering, shamming; ~siekte, sham illness, malingering; ~sit, (-ge-), be kept in; ~span, school team; ~taal, school language; ~tas, school bag; ~terrein, school grounds; ~tug, school discipline; ~tuin, school garden; ~tyd, school hours; school days; ~ure, school hours; ~vak, school subject; ~vakansie, school holidays; ~versuim, truancy; ~vertrek, school room; ~voeding, feeding children at school; ~vos, pedant; gerund-grinder; ~vossery, pedantry; ~werk, school work; ~wese, education; ~wet, school regulation; education act; ~wysheid, pedantry; book-learning.
skoon, (s) the beautiful; *~ vergaan, maar DEUG bly staan*, beauty without bounty avails not; *uiterlike ~ is slegs VERTOON*, beauty is but skin-deep; (skone, -ste) (b), clean; pure; beautiful, handsome; clear, bright (sky); neat (drink); net (profit); *jou GEDAGTES ~ hou*, keep your thoughts pure; *die skone GESLAG*, the fair sex; *jou KAMER ~ hou*, keep your room clean; *'n ~ paar KOUSE*, a clean pair of socks; *die skone KUNSTE*, the fine arts; *'n ~ STEL*, a straight set (tennis); (bw) clean, quite, altogether; absolutely, completely; *my geld is ~ OP*, my money is all gone (spent); *iets ~ VERGEET*, completely forget something.
skoon: ~brand, (-ge-), grave (ship); burn clean; ~broer, brother-in-law; ~byt, (-ge-), pickle metals (with acids); ~dogter, daughter-in-law; ~familie, relatives by marriage, in laws; ~gewig, dressed weight.
skoon'heid, (..hede), cleanliness; beauty, beautifulness; *'n BEROEMDE ~*, a famous beauty; *~ (mooi) vergaan, maar DEUG bly staan*, beauty is only skin-deep; *~ word uit SMART gebore*, beauty is gained with pain; ~salon, beauty parlour.
skoonheids: ~behandeling, beauty treatment; ~dweper, aesthete; ~gevoel, sense of beauty; ~hulpmiddels, aids to beauty.
skoon'heidsin, sense of beauty.
skoon'heids: ~koningin, beauty queen; ~kunde, beauty culture; ~kundige, beauty specialist, cosmetician; ~leer, aesthetics; ~liefhebber, philocalist; ~merkie, beauty spot; ~middel, cosmetic; beautifier; ~moesie, beauty spot.
skoon'heidspesialis, beautician, beauty specialist, cosmetician.
skoon'heids: ~pleistertjie, beauty spot; ~water, beauty wash; ~wedstryd, beauty competition.
skoon: ~hou, (-ge-), keep clean; ~klinkend, (-e), melodious; plausible, specious (excuse); ~ma, (-'s), mother-in-law; ~maak, (s) cleaning, clean-up; clearing; *die groot ~maak*, spring-cleaning; (w) (-ge-), clean (up, out); char; dress (animals); weed (flower-beds); gut, gill (fish); pick (a bone); purify; polish up; clear (land); groom (animals); trim (lamp).
skoon'maak: ~dag, house-cleaning; ~middel, cleansing agent; detergent; ~span, scavenging-squad; ~ster, char(woman); ~tyd, cleaning time; ~woede, cleaning frenzy.
skoon'maker, cleaner; purifier.
skoon'moeder, mother-in-law; *al is 'n ~ hoe gesuiker, sy bly maar suur*, a mother-in-law is never a true mother.
skoon'opbrengs, clean content (of wool); scoured yield.
skoon: ~ouers, parents-in-law; ~pa, (-'s), father-in-law.
skoon: ~praat, (-ge-), exculpate; ~semels, all-bran.
skoon'seun, son-in-law.
skoon'skip: ~ maak, make a clean sweep; win (clear out) everything; sweep the boards.
skoon: ~skrif, calligraphy; copybook writing; penmanship; ~skrifte, copybooks; ~skryfkuns, calligraphy, penmanship; ~skrywer, calligraphist, penman.
skoon'skynend, (-e), fair on the surface; specious, meretricious, plausible; ~heid, speciousness; plausibility.
skoon: ~steen, facing brick; ~suster, sister-in-law; ~teer, coal-tar; ~tjies, nicely, cleanly; ~vader, father-in-law; ~vang, mark (rugby); ~veld, (s) fairway (golf); (b) clean gone, vanished out of sight; *~ veld wees*, be clean gone; have vanished without a trace; ~werk, (s) face-work; (w) (-ge-), dress down (masonry).
skoor¹, (s): *~ soek*, look for trouble, pick a quarrel.
skoor², (s) (skore), support, prop, shore; (w) (ge-), support, shore up; ~balk, lattice truss; ~muur, buttress; ~paal, strut (in mines); ~plaat, wall piece.
skoor'soeker, quarrelsome fellow; ~ig, (e), quarrelsome; ~y, looking for trouble.
skoor'steen, (..stene), chimney (house); stack (foundry); funnel (ship); flue; *daar KAN die ~ nie van rook nie*, that won't keep the pot boiling; *hy ROOK soos 'n ~*, he smokes like a chimney; ~anker, chimney-tie; ~besem, flue-brush; ~gat, flue hole; ~kap, cowl; chimney (funnel) hood; ~klep, chimney-trap; ~kraag, chimney-bonnet (locomotive); ~mantel, chimney-mantel, mantelpiece, overmantel; ~plaat, hearth-plate; ~pot, chimney-pot; ~pyp, chimney-flue, stack, shank, shaft (of chimney); funnel (boat); ~rak, ~rand, mantelshelf; ~roet, soot (from chimney); ~skag, chimney-shaft; ~skuif, damper; ~sluk, chimney-petticoat; ~spieël, (over)mantel-mirror; ~veër, (-s), chimney-sweep; sacred ibis; ~verband, chimney-bond; ~voet, chimney base; ~werker, steeplejack; ~wissel, kite.
skoor'voetend, reluctant(ly), hesitating(ly), with lagging steps.
skoor'wal, (-le), sand-bar, bay-bar.
skoot¹, (s) (skote), shot, report; blast; time, turn; fold; sheet (ship); *BINNE (onder) ~ kom*, come within range; *BUITE ~ wees*, out of range; *die ~ HOOG deur hê*, be intoxicated, the worse for liquor; *onder ~ KRY*, have within range; fire upon; *MOOI ~!*, well done! shot!; *ONDER ~*, under fire; *ONDER ~ wees*, be within range; be under fire; *goed ONDER ~ wees*, be open to attack; be in a vulnerable position; *skote PRETOORS!*, well done!

shot! *'n RAAK ~*, a bull's-eye; *SO ~ vir ~*, every time.
skoot², (s) **(skote)**, lap; womb; bosom; *in die ~ van die AARDE*, in the bowels of the earth; *in die ~ v.d. GODE*, in the lap of the gods; *in die ~ v.d. KERK*, in the bosom of the church; *die ~ van MOEDER= AARDE*, the lap of mother earth; *OP die ~*, on the lap; *in die ~ v.d. TYD*, in the lap of the future; *in die ~ VAL*, fall into the lap of; *iem. iets in die ~ WERP*, lay something in someone's lap.
skoot'afstand, gun-range.
skoot: ~ **ete**, lap supper; ~ **hondjie**, lap-dog; pet dog; ~ **kindjie**, pet (favourite) child; infant in arms; ~ **riem**, lap-strap.
skoots'afstand, skoots'bereik, gunshot, (shot-)range; *binne ~*, within gunshot, within range.
skoot'sku, (-we), gun-shy; ~ **heid**, gun-shyness.
skoot'vry, (-e), bullet-proof, bomb-proof.
skop¹, (s) (-pe), shovel.
skop², (s) (-pe), kick, recoil (of rifle); (w) (ge-), kick, recoil (rifle); lunge out (horse); *ek kan my ~*, I could kick myself; ~ **fiets**, motor scooter.
skop'graaf, shovel.
skop'peaas = **skoppenaas**.
skoppelmaai', (-e), ~ **er**, (-s), swing; ~ *ry*, swing.
skop, pe(n)aas, ace of spades.
skop'pens¹, kicks (marble games); *ni(e)ks ~*, nix kicks.
skop'pens², spades; ~ **boer**, knave of spades; ~ **heer**, king of spades; ~ **tien**, ten of spades; ~ **vrou**, queen of spades.
skop'per, (-s), kicker.
skoppermaai' = **skoppelmaai**.
skop'pie¹, (-s), little kick; *kort ~*, short punt.
skop'pie², (-s), small shovel; dust pan.
skop'vry, (-e), without recoil.
skor, ([-re]; -der, -ste), hoarse, husky, raucous, throaty; ~ **heid**, hoarseness, huskiness, raucity.
skorbutiek', skorbu'ties, (-e), scorbutic.
skorbuut', scurvy.
skor'heid, hoarseness.
sko'ring, shoring.
skor'rie, ducktail, Teddy boy.
skorrie-mor'rie, rabble, ragtag and bobtail, riff-raff, hooligans, plebs.
skors¹, (s) (-e), bark; cortex.
skors², (w) (ge-), suspend (person); adjourn (meeting).
skors: ~ **ag'tig**, (-e), corticate; ~ **bundel**, cortical bundle.
skorsenier'wortel, salsify, snake-weed *(Schorzonera hispanica)*.
skor'sie, (-s), squash (vegetable).
skor'sing, suspension; adjournment; interdict; ~ *van vonnis*, arrest of judgment.
skor'sings: ~ **besluit**, suspension decree; ~ **reg**, suspensive power.
skors'weefsel, cortical tissue.
skort¹, (s) (-e), pinafore, apron.
skort², (w) (ge-), ail, lack, be wanting; *wat ~ daar?*, what is the matter there?; ~ **ing**, thing wanting; lack; *wat is die ~ ing?*, what is the matter (trouble)?
skort: ~ **muur**, apron wall; ~ **plaat**, apron plate.
skot¹, (-te), bulkhead (ship); screen; partition; brattice (mining); baffle-plate; ~ *GEE*, veer; let go; ~ *en LOT betaal*, pay scot and lot.
Skot², (-te), Scotchman, Scot.
skot³, (e) = **skoot¹**.
skot'balk, divider.
sko'tig, (-e), gradually sloping; *'n ~ e afdraand*, a gradual declivity (decline), a gentle slope.
Skot'land, Scotland.
skot'plaat, baffle plate.
Skots¹, (-e), Scottish; ~ *e GERUIT*, tartan, plaid; ~ *e ROKKIE*, kilt.
skots², (s) (-e), lump (flake) of ice.
skots³, (bw) skew; ~ *en skeef*, all in a muddle, jumbled up, topsyturvy.
skots'kar, Scotch-cart, tip-cart.
skot'skrif, lampoon, squib, pasquinade.
skot'spyker, sprig (nail).
skot'tel, (-s), dish basin; ~ **doek**, dish cloth; ~ **eg**,

disc-harrow, ~ **goed**, dishes, crockery; *iem. moet ~ goed was*, somebody will have to wash the dishes; ~ **goeddroograk**, dish drainer; ~ **goedkamer**, scullery; ~ **goedwasser**, dishwasher; ~ **goedwater**, slops; dishwater, pig wash; ~ **ploeg**, disc plough; ~ **skaar**, disk, disc; ~ **wiel**, disc wheel.
skot'tipe, bulkhead type.
skot'venster, hopper (hospital) window.
skot'vers, heifer in milk.
skot'vry, (-e), sheltered, untouched, scot-free.
skou, (s) (-e), review, inspection, exhibition, show; (w) (ge-), look at, view, inspect, put on show.
skou'burg, (-e), theatre, cinema, picture-house; ~ **besoek**, play-going; ~ **besoeker**, theatre-goer; ~ **direkteur**, theatre manager; ~ **geselskap**, theatrical company; ~ **mal**, theatre-mad; ~ **publiek**, theatre-going public; ~ **wêreld**, theatrical world.
skou'er, (s) (-s), shoulder; *iem. oor die ~ AANSIEN*, give someone the cold shoulder; *BREË ~ s hê*, have broad shoulders; *op die ~ s DRA*, carry shoulder-high; *op die ~ GEWEER!*, shoulder arms!; *iem. op die ~ KLOP*, pat someone on the shoulder; *sy KYK al oor haar ~*, she is beginning to take notice of boys; *die ~ s OPHAAL*, shrug the shoulders; *die ~ s onder iets sit*, put one's shoulder to the wheel; ~ *aan ~ STAAN*, stand shoulder to shoulder; ~ *teen die WIEL sit*, put the shoulder to the wheel; (w) (ge-), shoulder (rifle); ~ **balk**, haunched beam; ~ **band**, shoulder-strap; ~ **been**, collar bone; ~ **belegsel**, shoulder-trimming; ~ **blad**, shoulder-blade, scapula, omoplate; ~ **breedte**, shoulder-width; ~ **breuk**, rupture of the shoulder; ~ **doek**, amice (R.C.); ~ **gat**, (-e), shoulder-hole; ~ **gewrig**, shoulder-joint; ~ **haak**, clothes-hanger; ~ **hoog**, shoulder-high; ~ **kleed**, scapular; ~ **klep**, shoulder-scale; ~ **koord**, lanyard; ~ **kussing**, shoulder-pad; ~ **kwas**, shoulder-knot; ~ **lap(pie)**, shoulder-strap (on uniform); ~ **letters**, shoulder-titles; ~ **loos**, (..lose), strapless (dress); ~ **mantel**, cape, pallium, pelerine; ~ **ontwrigting**, dislocation of the shoulder; ~ **pels**, fur cape; ~ **riem**, baldric; shoulder-strap; ~ **rok**, dungaree skirt; ~ **ruiker**, shoulder-spray; ~ **skaaf**, shoulder-plane; ~ **ster**, pip, shoulder-star (officer's rank); ~ **stuk**, shoulder-strap (mil.); shoulder (meat); pip, shoulder-piece (mil.); ~ **tjie**, (-s), clothes-hanger; ~ **trog**, hod.
skou'put, (ong.), manhole.
skou'spel, spectacle, scene, sight; ~ **agtig**, (-e), spectacular.
skout, (-e), gaoler; bailiff; (hist.) spy; ~ **-admiraal**, (-s), rear-admiral (S.A.); ~ **-by-nag**, (skoute-by-nag), rear-admiral.
skraag, (s) (skrae), support; stay; bracket; trestle; (w) (ge-), prop, support, buttress (up); ~ **balk**, supporting beam; ~ **brug**, trestle-bridge; ~ **werk**, trestle-work.
skraal, meagre, thin, slender, lank, gaunt, lean, reedy (person); scanty (returns); hungry, poor (soil); bleak (wind); *'n ~ BEURS*, an empty purse; ~ *DIEET*, spare diet; *'n ~ OES*, a poor harvest; ~ *in die SKRIF wees*, be uneducated; *'n skrale TROOS*, a poor consolation; *'n ~ WIND*, a bleak wind; ~ **draer**, shy bearer (tree).
skraal'hans, (-e), niggard, miser; *dit IS by hom maar ~*, he is having a lean time of it; ~ *is vandag KEUKENMEESTER*, (ong.), the fare is meagre today.
skraal: ~ **heid**, meagreness, lankness, leanness, slenderness; scantiness; poorness (soil); ~ **te**, thinness, slenderness; poverty, poorness (soil); ~ **tjies**, scantily, niggardly, meanly.
skraap, (s) (skrape), scratch; stria(tion); (w) (ge-), grab; scrape, scratch; chase, run after; rasp; *'n DAM ~*, excavate a dam; *die KEEL ~*, clear the throat; *WORTELS ~*, scrape carrots; ~ **agtig**, (-e), scraping, stingy, miserly; ~ **blok**, dam-scraper; ~ **mes**, scraper; scarifier (med.); ~ **sel**, (-s), scraping; ~ **sug**, avarice, covetousness; rapacity; stinginess; ~ **sug'tig**, (-e), avaricious, covetous; stingy, miserly; ~ **trekker**, tractor-scraper; ~ **wol**, rubbings; ~ **wond**, superficial wound; ~ **yster**, scraper.
skra'gie, (-s), bracket.
skra'lerig, (-e), rather thin, lean, poor.

skram, (s) (-me), scratch, scar; (w) (ge-), skim, graze, scratch; hook (cricket); ~**hou**, snick, glance; ~**kap**, deflector.

skrams, grazingly; from the corner of one's eye; *hy is ~ GERAAK*, he received a graze (glancing wound); *ek het hom net so ~ GESIEN*, I only caught a glimpse of him; ~**hou**, glancing blow.

skram'skoot, skram'skot, graze (slight wound), grazing shot.

skran'der, intelligent, sagacious, acute, ingenious, shrewd, discerning, clever; brilliant; ~**heid**, intelligence, brilliance, perspicacity, shrewdness, discernment, sagacity, ingenuity, acuteness.

skrap, (ge-), erase, strike off, scratch out, delete, cross out, cancel, expunge; *as LID ~*, remove from the list of members; *van die LYS ~*, remove from the register; ~ *waar NODIG*, delete whichever is not applicable.

skra'per, (-s), scraper; grader (road); money-grubber; ~**ig**, (-e), scraping; covetous, stringy, greedy; ~**igheid**, covetousness, greed; ~**lem**, blade terracer.

skra'pie, (-s), scratch, graze.

skra'ping, (-e, -s), scraping; curettage (med.).

skrapnel', (-le, -s), shrapnel; ~**wond**, shrapnel wound.

skrap'pies, poorly; scarcely, narrowly.

skrap'ping, (-e, -s), striking off (out), deletion, cancellation.

skraps, poorly, scarcely, narrowly; bare, scanty (weight); skimpy.

skrap'sie, hot pants.

skrap'sies, poorly, scarcely, narrowly.

skre'de, (-s), step, tread, stride, pace; *die EERSTE ~*, the first step; *met RASSE ~*, with rapid strides.

skree, (skreë), *see* **skreeu**.

skre'ër, (-s), screamer, boisterous talker, bawler, shrill-voiced person.

skre'ërig, (-e), crying, clamorous, screaming, shouting, ranting, shrill.

skre'ëry, shouting, crying, screaming, bawling, ranting, clamouring.

skreeu, (s) (-e), shout, scream, cry; shriek (of woman); bawl; croak (of frogs); bray (of donkey); squeal (of pigs); (w) (ge-), scream, cry, give a cry, halloo, yell, shout, bawl, clamour, shriek; squeal (pig); bray (donkey); *om HULP ~*, cry for help; ~*ende KLEURE*, loud colours; *uit alle MAG ~*, shout at the top of one's voice; *~ SOOS 'n maer vark*, squeal like a stuck pig; ~**balie**, (-s), cry-baby; ~**bek**, brat; cry-baby; ~**end**, (-e), bawling, loud, blatant; glaring; puling; ~**er**, (-s), *see* **skreër**; ~**erig**, (-e), inclined to scream, to cry; blaring (music); blatant, loud-mouthed, bawling; ~**erigheid**, blatancy; ~**ery**, *see* **skreëry**.

skreeu'lelik, (s) (-s), bawler, cry-baby, mewler; (b) (e), very ugly.

skreeu'snaaks, (-e), screamingly funny.

skre'tie, (-s), little opening, slit; *die deur staan op 'n ~*, the door stands ajar.

skrei, (vero., plegt.), (ge-), weep, cry; ~*ende LEUEN*, blatant lie; *'n ~ ende ONREG*, a glaring injustice; *'n ~ende SKANDE*, a crying shame.

skri'ba, (-s), secretary of a church council.

skribent', (-e), (ong.), penny-a-liner, hack-writer.

skriel, (e; -er, -ste), thin, slender, gaunt, scanty; stingy; ~**heid**, scantiness, meanness.

Skrif[1]: *die Heilige ~*, the Scriptures, Holy Writ.

skrif[2], handwriting, script, writing, print, character; (-te), exercise book; *SKRAAL in die ~ wees*, be poorly read; *LOPENDE ~*, cursive handwriting; *NETJIESE ~*, copperplate writing; *OP ~*, in writing; S~**gedeelte**, lesson (in church); ~**geleerd**, (-e), well-versed in the Scriptures; educated; cunning; ~*geleerd wees*, be shrewd (sly, cunning); ~**geleerde**, (-s), scribe; ~**graniet**, graphic granite; ~**kenner**, student of the Scriptures; palaeographer; ~**kun'dige**, (-s), handwriting expert, graphologist; ~**lesing**, reading of the lesson; prayers; ~**ma'tig**, (-e), scriptural; ~**stuk**, document, record; ~**telik**, (-e), in writing; epistolary; ~ *telike eksamen*, written examination.

skriftuur', (..**ture**), scripture; document; ~**lik**, (-e), scriptural; ~**plaas**, text (from the Bible); ~**woorde**, words from the Scriptures.

skrif: ~**uitleer**, exegete, interpreter; ~**uitlegging**, exegesis; ~**verklaarder**, exegete, exegetist; ~**verklaring**, exegesis, hermeneutics.

skrif'vervalser, (-s), scriptural interpolator (tamperer); forger; ..**valsing**, interpolation of the Scriptures; forgery.

skrik, (s) fright, terror, dread, alarm start; *iem. ~ AANJA*, strike fear into someone's heart; *met die ~ daarvan AFKOM*, escape with a shock; *v.d. ~ BEKOM*, get over the shock; *die ~ v.d. BUURT*, the terror of the neighbourhood; *iem. die ~ op die LYF ja*, frighten someone out of his wits; *die ~ is nog in sy LYF*, he is still suffering from shock; *met ~ VERVUL*, strike terror into; (w) (ge-), be startled, be frightened, take fright; shy (horse); *hy het hom LAM ge~*, he was paralysed with fright; *WAKKER ~*, awake (with a start); ~**aanjaer**, panic-monger, intimidator, terrorist; ~**aanja(g)end**, (-e), frightening, terrifying; ~**aanjaging**, terrorization; frightfulness.

skrikag'tig, (-e), timorous, shy; ~**heid**, timidity, shyness.

skrik: ~**ba'rend**, (-e), terrible, alarming, terrifying, horrific, fearful, frightful; ~**beeld**, gorgon; chimera; bugbear, ogre, bogey; ~**bewind**, terrorism, reign of terror.

skrik'keldag, intercalary (leap-year's) day.

skrik'keljaar, leap-year, bissextile; *die nie ALJAAR ~ nie*, Christmas comes but once a year; *so ELKE ~*, once in a blue moon.

skrik'kelmaand, February.

skrik'kerig, (-e), nervous, jumpy; skittish, shy, balky (horse), pigeon-hearted, rather afraid; ~**heid**, nervousness, jumpiness.

skrik'lik, (-e), dreadful, terrible, frightful; ~**heid**, dreadfulness, terribleness.

skrik: ~**maak**, (-ge-), frighten, startle, give a fright, scare; ~**makertjie**, pick-me-up, tot, appetiser; ~**partytjie**, (-s), surprise party; ~**wek'kend**, (-e), alarming, terrifying.

skril, (-le; -ler, -ste), shrill, sharp, piercing, glaring; *in ~ le teëstelling*, in glaring (sharp) contrast.

skrip'sie, (-s), essay, paper.

skrobbeer', (ge-), slate, scold, reprimand, rebuke, caution.

skrob'bel, (ge-), scribble (wool)

skrobbe'rend, admonitory.

skrobbe'ring, (e, -s), scolding, dressing-down, telling-off, lecture, reprimand, rating, slating, talking to.

skroef, (s) (skroewe), vice, clamp; pin (instrument); chuck, screw (boat); propeller (aeroplane); peg; *daar is 'n ~ LOS by hom*, he has a screw loose; *daar is 'n ~ LOS*, there is something wrong; *alles STAAN op los skroewe*, everything is at sixes and sevens; (w) (ge-), screw; ~**anker**, screw anchor, screwed stay; ~**as**, propeller shaft; ~**bakterie**, screw bacterium, spirillum; ~**band**, screw-binding; ~**bank**, vice-bench; ~**bek**, vice jaws (paws); ~**blad**, propeller-blade; fan; ~**boor**, auger, worm-bit; ~**bout**, through-bolt, screw-bolt; ~**bus**, screwed bush; ~**deksel**, screw-top; ~**domkrag**, screw-jack; jack-screw; ~**draad**, worm (of screw); screw-thread; bit; ~**draadmaat**, gauge of thread; ~**draaier** = **skroewedraaier**; ~**draaikaliber**, thread-gauge; ~**ent**, screw-end; ~**haak**, screw-hook; dresser hook; ~**hamer**, shifting-spanner; adjustable wrench; ~**koppeling**, screw-coupling; ~**las**, (se), screw joint; ~**loos**, (..**lose**): ..*lose vliegtuig*, jet(-propelled) plane; ~**lyn**, helix, helicoid; helical curve; ~**mikrometer**, micrometer screw; ~**moer**, nut, female screw; ~**naaf**, airscrew hub; propeller hub; stern-boss (ship); ~**nael**, screw-rivet; ~**palm**, screw-palm; ~**pen**, screw-picket; ~**pers**, screw-press; ~**pomp**, hydraulic screw; ~**prop**, screwed plug; ~**pyp**, screwed conduit; ~**rat**, spiral gear; screw-gearing; ~**sirkel**, air-screw disc; ~**slag**, turn of the screw; ~**sleutel**, (screw-)wrench, monkey-wrench; ~**slinger**, vice lever; ~**slot**, turn-buckle; ~**snyersgereedskap**, stocks and dies; ~**sny-yster**, die; ~**staal**, comb (steel); chasing tool, chaser; ~**steek**, screw-pitch; ~**stewe**, propeller-post; ~**stoomboot**, screw-steamer; ~**turbine**, turboprop; ~**veer**, volute-spring; ~**verband**, tourniquet; ~**voortstuwing**, propeller propulsion; ~**vormig, (-e)**, screw-shaped, helical, cochleary, spiral; ~**waaier**, propeller fan.

skroei, (ge-), scorch, burn, singe (hair); sear (leaves); cauterize (wounds); scald, char; *ge~de AARDE* scorched earth; *~end WARM*, searingly hot; ~**merk**, scorch mark; ~**siekte**, blight; ~**wond**, scald; ~**yster**, cauterizing iron.

skroe'we, (ge-), screw; ~**draaier, (-s)**, screw-driver.

skrofuleus', (-e), scrofulous.

skrofulo'se, scrofulosis.

skrok, (ong.), (s) (-ke), glutton; (w) **(ge-)**, eat gluttonously, gormandize, gulp (bolt) down, guzzle; ~**ker, (-s)**, glutton; ~**kig, (-e)**, gluttonous.

skro'melik = skroomlik.

skrom'pel, (ge-), wither, shrivel; ~**lewer**, cirrhotic liver.

skrooi'tou, parbuckle.

skroom, (s) timidity, diffidence; modesty, fear, scruple; (w) **(ge-)**, hesitate, be shy, fear, scruple, dread; ~**ag'tig, (-e)**, timorous, bashful; ~**ag'tigheid**, timorousness, timidity, bashfulness; ~**har'tig, (-e)**, pusillanimous, faint-hearted; ~**lik**, terribly, sorely, badly; *jou~lik vergis*, be sorely mistaken.

skroomval'lig, (-e), timid, diffident, timorous; ~**heid**, timidity, timorousness.

skroot, grapeshot, hail-shot, small shot; scrap(-iron) shot; case-shot; ~**beitel**, anvil chisel; ~**boor**, short drill; ~**hamer**, spalling-hammer; ~**sak**, grape shot bag; ~**stuk**, grapeshot (gun), cannon; ~**vuur**, canister-shot (fire).

skrop, (s) (-pe), dam-dredge; scraper; (w) **(ge-)**, scrub, scour, scrape (dam); scratch (poultry); doing odd-jobs; ~**borsel**, scrubbing brush; ~**goed**, litter; ~**dag**, scrubbing day; ~**knieë**, housemaid's knee; ~**per, (-s)**, scrubber; ~**saag**, keyhole-saw; ~**skaaf**, German jackplane; scrub-plane; ~**vrou**, charwoman; ~**vyl**, coarse file.

skrum, (s) (-s), scrum, scrummage; (w) **(ge-)**, scrum; ~**mer, (-s)**, scrummager; ~**oor**, cauliflower-ear; ~**skakel**, scrumhalf.

skru'pel, (-s), scruple (weight).

skrupu'le, (-s), (ong.), objection, scruple.

skrupuleus', (-e), (ong.), scrupulous, conscientious.

skry, (ge-), stride, step.

skryf, (ge-), write, drive the pen, pen; *met INK ~*, write in ink; *LEESBAAR ~*, write legibly; *~ OM 'n katalogus*, write for a catalogue; ~**behoeftes**, writing-materials; stationery; ~**blok**, writing-pad; scratch-gauze (mines); ~**boek**, exercise book; writing-pad; ~**bord**, blackboard; ~**buro**, writing-desk; ~**fout**, mistake in writing, slip of the pen, clerical error; lapsus calami; ~**gereedskap**, writing-materials; ~**ink**, writing-ink; ~**kramp**, writer's cramp; ~**kuns**, art of writing; penmanship; ~**lessenaar**, writing-desk; ~**letter**, written letter; script letter (typ.); ~**lus**, passion for writing; ~**masjien**, typewriter; ~**naam**, pen-name, nom de plume; ~**papier**, writing-paper; note-paper; ~**pen**, pen; quill; ~**rol**, roller, platen; ~**salon**, writing-saloon; ~**sel, (-s)**, screed; ~**ster, (-s)**, authoress, woman writer; ~**stif**, stylus; ~**taal**, written language; ~**tafel**, bureau, davenport, writing-table, escritoire, desk; ~**talent**, literary talent; ~**teken**, letter; grapheme; ~**toestel**, recorder (teleg.); ~**trant**, style of writing; phraseology; ~**ware**, stationery; ~**werk**, writing, copy-work, clerical work, desk-work; ~**woede**, mania for writing; ~**wyse**, manner (style) of writing; notation; spelling.

skry'lings, astride, astraddle.

skryn¹, (s) (-e), cabinet.

skryn², (w) (ge-), abrade, graze; fret; cause pain; *~ende pyn*, smarting pain; ~**erig, (-e)**, painful; ~**erigheid**, painfulness.

skryn'werk, joinery; ~**er**, joiner; ~**ery**, joinery, joiner's shop.

skry'we, (s) letter; minute; favour; *u ~ van die 3e deser*, your letter (minute, favour) of the 3rd; (w) **(ge-)**, write; *daar staan ge~*, it is written.

skry'wer, (-s), writer, author, amanuensis; *van die ~*, with the compliments of the author; ~**saandeel**, royalty; ~**snaam**, name of an author; pen-name, nom de plume; ~**y**, writing, scribbling.

sku, (w) (ge-), shun, eschew, flee; (b) **(skuwer, skuuste)**, shy, unsociable, timid, bashful; skittish (of horses).

skub, (-be) = skob; ~ **agtig, (-e)**, scaly; ~**b(er)ig, (-e)**, scaly; furfuracious (bot.); ~**b(er)igheid**, scaliness; ~**dier**, armadillo; crustacean.

sku'bliesroos, pride of India.

skub'patroon, imbrication.

skubs'gewyse, in scales; imbricate.

skub: ~**vlerkig, (-e)**, scaly-winged, lepidopteral; ~**vleuelig, (-e)**, lepidopterous; ~**vleueliges**, lepidoptera; ~**vormig, (-e)**, squamose.

skud, (ge-), shake, rock; shuffle (cards); tremble, quake (from fear); jog (memory); jolt, concuss (brains); *hy ~ soos hy lag*, he is convulsed with laughter; ~**beton**, vibrated concrete; ~**debol**, nid-nod, niddle-noddle; ~**der, (-s)**, shaker; vibrator; ~**ding**, shaking, concussion; quaking, quake, tremor; vibration; ~**dingsgolwe**, vibration waves; ~**geut**, shaker; ~**rooster**, rocking-grate; ~**sif**, vibrating screen; ~**tafel**, reciprocating table.

skug'ter, shy, timid, coy; ~**heid**, coyness, bashfulness.

sku'heid, timidity, shyness; skittishness.

skuif, (s) (skuiwe), slide, lock-paddle; bolt, fastener (of door); move (chess); shove; damper (chimney); puff (pipe); *groot skuiwe trek*, puff away vigorously; (w) **(ge-)**, shove, slip, push, shift; move (chess); *die skuld op 'n ander ~*, lay the blame on someone else; ~**as**, shift shaft; ~**balk**, grouser; ~**beurt**, move (games); ~**beweging**, sliding movement; ~**blad**, sliding board; leaf (of table); ~**blinding**, Venetian blind; ~**bok**, extension trestle; ~**bout**, sliding bolt; ~**dak**, sunshine roof; sliding hood; ~**deur**, sliding door; ~**dop**, slip-on cap.

skui'fel, (ge-), shuffle; slide; ~**aar, (-s)**, shuffler; ~**beentjie**, splint.

skuif: ~**gordyn**, (sliding) curtain; ~**grendel**, barrel-bolt, tower-bolt; ~**hek**, sliding gate; ~**ie, (-s)**, barrel-bolt; draw (on cigarette); casing (needlew.); ~**kap**, sunshine roof (motor-car); ~**kas**, steam chest (locomotive); ~**klep**, slide-valve; ~**klepmotor**, sleeve-valve engine; ~**knoop**, running knot, slip-knot, slide-knot; ~**krag**, shear force; ~**laai**, drawer; ~**las**, slip-joint; ~**leer**, extension ladder; ~**ligte**, concealed lights; ~**liniaal**, slide-rule; ~**luik**, booby-hatch (naut.); sliding shutter; ~**maat**, sliding gauge; ~**meul(e)**, children's game (noughts and crosses); pretext, excuse; *hy het altyd 'n ~meul(e)*, he always has an excuse; ~**mikroskoop**, travelling microscope; ~**naald**, bodkin; ~**passer**, sliding (vernier) gauge, callipers; ~**plank**, slip-board; ~**potlood**, propeller pencil; ~**raam**, sash-window; ~**ring**, umbrella-runner; ~**sitplekke**, adjustable seats; ~**skeur**, shear; ~**sok**, slip-socket; ~**spanning**, shear stress; ~**speld**, paper-clip; gem-clip; ~**tafel**, sliding table; extension table; ~**trompet**, trombone, sliding trumpet; ~**vastheid**, shearing strength; ~**venster**, sash-window; ~**visier**, sliding sight; ~**weerstand**, shear resistance; ~**wind**, shear wind; ~**wrywing**, sliding friction.

skuil, (ge-), hide, take shelter; *daar ~ iets AGTER*, there is more to it than meets the eye; there is something mysterious about it; *die een ~ AGTER die ander*, one shelters behind the other; *~ vir die REËN*, take shelter from the rain; ~**beligting**, concealed lighting; ~**gaan, (-ge-)**, hide, lurk; ~**gat**, foxhole; ~**hoek**, hiding-place; cover; ~**hou, (-ge-)**, hide oneself, lie low; ~**ing**, shelter; cover; hiding (-place); *granaatvrye ~ing*, shell-proof shelter; ~**kelder**, air-raid shelter; ~**naam**, pen-name, pseudonym; ~**plaas**, ~**plek**, hiding-place, cover, hide-out, harbour(age), lurking-place, retreat, refuge; rifle-pit (target); covert (for game); funk-hole; ~**sloot**, slit trench; ~**te, (-s)**, sheltered nook, shelter; ~**verligting**, concealed lighting; ~**verwarming**, concealed heating.

skuim, (s) foam (of liquids); scum, froth, lather; spray; dross (of metals); refuse, dregs; head (beer); *die SAAK is* ~ *van bo en van onder*, the business is froth above and dregs below; *die* ~ *STAAN om sy mond*, he is foaming at the mouth; *die* ~ *van die VOLK*, the rabble, the dregs of the nation; (w) **(ge-)**, foam, froth; lather; spume, sparkle, bead (wine); sponge; ~*ende drank*, sparkling drink; ~**aarde**, skimmings; ~**agtig, (-e)**, foamy, frothy, spumy; ~**agtigheid**, foaminess, frothiness, spuminess; ~**bek, (ge-)**, foam at the mouth; fume with rage; ~**besie**, frog-hopper; spittle-bug; ~**beton**, foam concrete; ~**bier**, foaming beer; ~**brandblusser**, foam fire-extinguisher; ~**breker**, defoamer; ~**end, (-e)**, foaming, foamy, frothy, nappy; ~**er, (-s)**, cadger, sponger; ~**erig, (-e)**, barmy, frothy, foamy, drossy; ~**erigheid**, frothiness; ~**ing**, frothing; ~**koekie**, meringue; ~**kop**, meringue top; ~**kraan**, scumcock; ~**lepel**, skimming ladle; ~**loos**, (..lose), foamless; ~**melk**, milk shake; ~**middel**, foaming agent; ~**nagereg**, whip; ~**omelet**, soufflé, omelet(te); ~**pie, (-s)**, meringue, kiss (cake); ~**rubber**, foam rubber; ~**spaan**, (..spane), basting-ladle; skimmer; ~**tert**, chiffon tart; ~**wyn**, sparkling wine.

skuin, (ong.), obscene, smutty (jokes).

skuins, sloping, slanting, oblique; crank (boat); on the cross, edgewise; italic (printing); scarf-wise, slantwise; bevel (edge); askance; ~ *AANGEE*, oblique pass (rugby); *iem*. ~ *AANSIEN (aankyk)*, look askance at a person; ~ *DAK*, inclined roof; ~ *GEDRUK*, (printed) in italics; ~ *HOU*, tilt; ~ *HOUT*, canted timber; ~ *KANT*, bevelled edge, chamfer; *gaan* ~ *LÊ*, take a nap; ~ *MAAK*, bevel, chamfer, slant off; ~ *MUUR*, canted wall; ~ *OORSTEEK*, cross diagonally; ~ *OPKYK van iets*, look up in surprise; ~ *PARKERING*, angle parking; ~ *STEEK*, diagonal stitch; ~*draadse STOF*, croswoven material; ~ *SY (van 'n driehoek)*, hypotenuse; ~ *VOOR twaalf*, shortly before twelve; ~**balk**, bar sinister (her.); ~**band**, bias (binding); ~**beitel** skew chisel; ~**hamer**, taperingtool (blacksmith); ~**heid**, slant, obliquity, inclination; ~**hoogte**, slant height; ~**kant**, bevelled edge, bevel, bezel; feather-edge; chamfer; ~**lyne**, oblique lines; ~**maak**, (-ge-), bevel; ~**omboorsel**, bias binding; ~**oor**, (b) slope-eared; (bw) obliquely (slantwise) opposite; *'n NOOI* ~ *oor sny*, lay claim to a girl's affection; *die WINKEL* ~ *oor ons*, the shop nearly opposite (diagonally across from) us; ~**opname**, oblique photograph; ~**seilend, (-e)**, loxodromic; ~**skaal**, diagonal scale; ~**skag, (-te)**, incline(d) shaft; ~**skrif**, sloping writing; ~**sny**, shearing-cut; ~**strook**, bias binding; ~**te, (-s)**, slant, slope; bevel, pitch (roof); bias; loft (of a club); *op die* ~ *te sny*, cut on the bias; ~**vlak**, inclined plane; ~**verskuiwing**, oblique fault; ~**weg**, aslant; on bevel; ~**werk**, splayed work (carpentry).

skuit, (-e), boat; *in EEN* ~ *wees*, be in the same boat; be of the same opinion; *ons SIT algar in dieselfde* ~, we are all in the same boat; *ons SIT in die* ~ *en moet meevaar*, we are all in the same boat; ~**jie, (-s)**, small boat, dinghy; shuttle (of sewing machine); ~**jiebeen**, navicular bone; ~**passer**, calliper square (carpentry); ~**voerder**, boatman, lighterman; ~**vormig, (-e)**, boat-shaped.

skui'we, (ge-), *see* **skuif**, (w), shore, move, push; ~**r, (-s)**, creeper; plunger, shifter.

skul'wergat, drain-hole (in kraal); scaffolding-hole; scupper (ship); back door (fig.); loophole.

skuld, (s) **(-e)**, debt; fault; guilt; culpability; embarrassment; arrearage; *AGTERSTALLIGE* ~*e*, arrears; ~ *BELY*, confess one's guilt; *ek kan nie my* ~*e BETAAL nie*, I cannot meet my obligations; *BUITE my* ~, through no fault of mine; *DIEP in die* ~ *raak*, run heavily into debt; *die slegte weer DRA die* ~, the bad weather is to blame; *dis jou EIE* ~, you have only yourself to blame; *soveel* ~ *as HARE op jou kop*, up to one's ears in debt; ~ *MAAK*, incur a debt; *ONINVORDERBARE* ~*e*, irrecoverable debts; *die* ~ *op iem. anders SKUIF*, lay the blame on someone else; *jou in die* ~ *STEEK*, get oneself into debt; *VERGEEF ons ons* ~*e*, forgive us our trespasses; *VROT v.d.* ~ *wees*, be deeply in debt; (w) **(ge-)**, owe, be indebted; ~**aanvaarding**, acceptance of guilt; ~**afbetaling**, repayment of debt; ~**bekentenis**, confession of guilt; IOU; peccavi; recognizance; ~**belydenis**, confession of guilt; ~**besef**, consciousness (sense) of guilt; ~**beslagorder**, garnishee order; ~**bewus, (-te)**, conscious of guilt; ~**bewys**, ~**bekentenis**, confession of guilt; IOU; ~**boek**, accoun00book; ~**brief**, debenture, bond, obligation; ~**delging**, debt redemption; amortization; ~**delgingsfonds**, amortization fund, sinking-fund; ~**e**, liabilities; ~**eiser, (-s)**, creditor, obligee; ~**elas**, burden (of debt), encumbrance; ~**eloos, (..lose)**, innocent, guiltless, blameless, faultless; ~**eloosheid**, innocence, guiltlessness; ~**enaar, (-s, ..nare)**, debtor, obligator; ~**erkenning**, admission of guilt; ~**gevoel**, sense of guilt.

skul'dig, (-e), guilty, culpable; due; condemned; owing; bound; indebted; *die ANTWOORD* ~ *bly*, fail to reply; *GELD* ~ *wees*, owe money; ~ *MAAK aan*, render guilty of; ~ *aan 'n MISDAAD*, guilty of a crime; ~ *PLEIT*, plead guilty; ~*e PLIG*, bounden duty; ~ *VERKLAAR*, find guilty, convict; *die dood* ~ *WEES*, be bound to die; ~**bevinding**, verdict of guilty; conviction; ~**e, (-s)**, culprit, offender, delinquent; perpetrator; ~**heid**, culpability, guilt; ~**verklaring**, a verdict of guild, conviction.

skuld: ~**invorderaar**, debt-collector; ~**invordering**, collection of debt; ~**kwytskelding**, remission of debt; ~**las**, load (burden) of debt; ~**oorsaak**, cause of debt; ~**pos**, debit entry; ~**reëling**, debt-settlement; ~**verbintenis**, debt-obligation; ~**vereffening**, liquidation of debt; ~**vergelyking**, set-off; ~**vergif(fe)nis**, remission, pardon; ~**vermoeding**, presumption of guilt; ~**vernuwing**, renewal of debt; ~**vordering**, claim, demand; ~**wissel**, bill payable.

skulp, (s) (-e), shell, conch; *uit jou* ~ *KOM*, creep out of one's shell; *in sy* ~ *kruip*, creep into one's shell; (w) **(ge-)**, scallop; ornament (adorn) with shells; ~**boor**, shell-bit; ~**dier**, bivalve, crustacean; ~**kalk**, shell-lime; ~**krale**, wampum; ~**krul**, pincurl; ~**kunde**, conchology; ~**kundige**, conchologist; ~**rand**, scalloped edge; ~**saag**, jack-saw; ripping-saw; ~**slak**, snail; ~**steek**, scallop stitch.

skulp'tuur, sculpture.

skulp'vis, shellfish; ~**ser**, shell-gatherer.

skulp'vormig, (-e), shell-shaped, helicoid, conchoidal.

skulp'werk, scalloping; ornamenting with shells.

skun'nig, (-e), shabby, dirty, mean; ~**heid**, shabbiness, meanness; ribaldry.

sku'rend, (-e), fricative.

skurf, (skurwe), scabby, mangy (animals); rough, chapped (hands); obscene (joke); ~**ag'tig (-e)**, mangy, scabby; ~**ag'tigheid**, manginess; ~**heid**, scabbiness, manginess, scaliness, roughness; ~**kruid**, gipsy rose; pincushion; ~**middel**, psoric; ~**myt**, itch-mite; scab-mite; ~**siekte**, scab, mange (animals); scabies, itch, psora (human beings); fusicladium (orchard); ~**te**, scab, scurf, mange (animals), scabies; psora (humans); roughness, chappiness; ~**tig, (-e)**, scurfy.

sku'ring, scouring; friction, rubbing, fret; ~**sgeluid**, sound of friction; ~**sklank**, fricative, spirant.

skurk, (-e), rascal, rogue, scoundrel, rapscallion, blackguard, thug, huckster, hooligan, hoodlum, knave, miscreant; ~**agtig, (-e)**, roguish, knavish, rascally, villainous; ~**agtigheid**, villainy, knavishness, foul play, roguery; ~**ery**, villainy, roguishness; ~**estreek**, villainy, roguery, rascality.

skur'webas, scaly bark (citrus disease).

skur'webeen, scaly leg.

skur'wejantjie, (-s), rough-scaled lizard.

skur'wepadda, toad.

skur'werig, (-e), slightly chapped; rough-scaled; scabby.

skut¹, (s) (-s), shot, marksman.
skut², (s) (-te), protection; guard, pad, aegis; screen; (w) (ge-), protect.
skut³, (s) pound, pinfold (for stray animals); lost-property office; excess depot; (w) (ge-), pound, impound, pinfold.
skut: ~ **balk**, fender; ~ **band**, masking tape; ~ **bekleding**, sheathing.
skut'berig, (-te), pound notice.
skut: ~ **blaar**, bract (of plant); ~ **blaartjie**, bracteole; ~ **blad**, flyleaf (of book); ~ **boom**, nurse-tree; ~ **bord**, fender; dashboard (cart); ~ **bus**, grummet; ~ **dak**, pent-roof.
skut'geld, poundage; pound-money.
skut: ~ **glas**, globe; ~ **huls**, protecting sleeve; ~ **kleur**, camouflage; ~ **kleur(ing)**, camouflage-painting.
skut: ~ **kraal**, pound; ~ **loods**, excess depot; ~ **meester**, pound-master; pound-keeper; ~ **merk**, pound mark.
skut: ~ **paal**, fender; ~ **papier**, protective paper; ~ **patroon**, patron saint; ~ **plank**, weather-board; fender-board; ~ **raam**, cradle (on hospital bed).
skut'reg, right to impound.
skuts: ~ **engel**, guardian angel; ~ **heer**, patron; ~ **heilige**, patron saint.
skut'sluis, lock (in canal).
skuts'patroon, patron (saint).
skut: ~ **spel**, pad-play (cricket); ~ **spoor**, side-line.
skut'vrou, patroness, protectress.
Skut'ter, die, Sagittarius (constellation).
skut'ter¹, (-s), rifleman, marksman; firer.
skut'ter², (-s), impounder.
skut: ~ **tersnes**, sniper's nest; ~ **tery**, civic (national) guard, militia.
skut'ting¹, (-e, -s), fence, palisade, paling; hoarding; billboard; bail.
skut'ting², impoundage.
skut'tingsreklame, hoarding (advertisement-) display.
skut: ~ **vee**, impounded cattle; ~ **verkoping**, pound sale.
skuur¹, (s) (**skure**), barn, cote, shed; garner, grange; depot; hangar.
skuur², (w) (ge-), polish, rub, sandpaper, burnish, scour; graze, chafe (skin); ~ **borsel**, scrubbing-brush.
skuur'deur, shed-door, barn-door.
skuur: ~ **klank**, fricative; ~ **klip**, rubbing stone (for washing); ~ **kurk**, cork rubber; ~ **lap**, scouring-cloth; emery-cloth; ~ **linne**, emery-cloth; ~ **masjien**, sanding-machine; ~ **middel**, abrasive, abradant; ~ **paal**, rubbing-post (for animals); ~ **papier**, sandpaper; glass-paper, emery-paper; ~ **plaat**, chafing-plate; rubbing-plate; ~ **plek**, abrasion (-mark); ~ **poeier**, plate-powder; abrasive (powder); ~ **sand**, scouring-sand; ~ **sel**, (-s), scourings; ~ **steen**, emery; bath-brick; hearthstone; ~ **trommel**, sanding drum; ~ **wol**, scouring-wool; ~ **yster**, chafing-beam.
sku'(w)erig, (-e), rather coy, rather shy; ~ **heid**, coyness, shyness.
skyf, (**skywe**), slice (fruit); disc, quoit; dial; puff (of smoke); segment (section) of an orange; target; dead-eye (naut.); flitch (of bacon); *in skywe sny*, slice; ~ **boor**, disc-drill; ~ **breker**, disc-crusher; ~ **draers**, butt-party; ~ **gooier**, discobolus; discus thrower; ~ **ie**, (-s), clove; quarter (of an orange); pig(iron); slice; slide; section (for microscope); fritter; ~ **ieskonfyt**, sliced jam; ~ **iespel**, tiddly-winks; ~ **ievertoning**, slide show; ~ **klep**, disc valve; ~ **koppelaar**, disc clutch; ~ **letsel**, slipped disc; ~ **ploeg**, disc-plough; ~ **skiet**, (-ge-), shoot at targets; have rifle-practice; ~ **skietery**, target-shooting; bisley; ~ **skietoefening**, range-practice; ~ **snyer**, slicer; ~ **vormig**, (-e), disc-shaped, discoid; ~ **werper**, discobolus, discus-thrower; ~ **wiel**, disc-wheel, solid wheel.
skyn, (s) light, glow; appearance, show, pretence, semblance; *die* ~ *AANNEEM*, take on the appearance of; *op die* ~ *AFGAAN*, judge by appearances; *dis ALLES* ~ , it is all show; ~ *BEDRIEG*, appearances are deceptive; *die* ~ *BEWAAR*, keep up appearances; *nie 'n* ~ *tjie BEWYS nie*, not a shred of evidence; *IN* ~ , to all appearances; on the surface; *NA alle* ~ , to all appearances; *ONDER die* ~ *van*, in the guise of; *die* ~ *RED*, save appearances; ~ *nòg SKADUWEE van bewys*, without a shred of evidence; *die* ~ *VERMY van*, avoid creating the impression; *VIR die* ~ , for the sake of appearances; *onder die* ~ *van VRIENDSKAP*, under the cloak of friendship; *die* ~ *WEK van*, create the impression of; ~ *en WESE*, substance and shadow; *tussen* ~ *en WESE onderskei*, distinguish the substance from the shadow; (w) (ge-), shine, glimmer; seem, appear; *hy* ~ *nie te BESEF dat . . .*, he does not appear to realize that . . . ; ~ **aanval**, feigned attack; diversion; ~ **as**, false axis; ~ **baar**, (. . bare), apparent, ostensible; *sonder* ~ *bare rede*, for no apparent reason; ~ **bas**, false bark; ~ **beeld**, phantom; simulacrum; ~ **belasting**, dummy load; ~ **beweging**, feint; ~ **deug**, feigned virtue; ~ **dood**, (s) apparent death, suspended animation, trance; asphyxia, asphyxy; (b) seemingly dead; ~ **geleerde**, smatterer, sciolist; ~ **geleerdheid**, sciolism; ~ **geluk**, false happiness; ~ **gestalte**, phase (of the moon); ~ **geveg**, sham (mock) fight.
skynhei'lig, (-e), sanctimonious, hypocritical, pharisaic, goody-goody; false; ~ **e**, (-s), hypocrite, goody-goody; ~ **heid**, sanctimony, hypocrisy, pharisaism, goody-goodiness.
skyn: ~ **hofsaak**, mock trial; ~ **hoof**, figurehead; ~ **huwelik**, fictitious marriage; ~ **koop**, bogus purchase; ~ **maatskappy**, dummy company; ~ **parlement**, mock parliament; ~ **regering**, puppet government.
skyn'sedig, (-e), prudish; ~ **heid**, prudishness.
skyn'sel, (-s), light, glow, shine, glimmer, gleam; glance; ~ **werend**, (-e), glare-proof.
skyn'siek, pretending to be sick; ~ **wees**, be malingering; ~ **e**, malingerer; ~ **te**, malingering.
skyn: ~ **skoon**, tinsel, trumpery; ~ **stam**, pseudostem; ~ **struktuur**, pseudomorph.
skyn'tjie, (-s), trifle; *geen* ~ *KANS nie*, not a ghost of a chance; *daar is geen* ~ *van WAAR nie*, there is no sign of truth in it.
skyn: ~ **uitval**, diversionary sally; ~ **verdrag**, bogus treaty; ~ **verhoor**, mock trial; ~ **vermaak**, false pleasure; ~ **vertoon**, sham, make-believe; puppetry; ~ **vrede**, false peace; ~ **vriend**, fair-weather friend; ~ **vroom**, (. . vrome), sanctimonious, hypocritical; ~ **vroomheid**, prudery, lip-service; ~ **waarheid**, verisimilitude; ~ **werper**, reflector, projector, search-light.
skyt, (ge-), (plat) shit.
sla = **slae**.
Slaaf¹, (**Slawe**), Slav, Slavonian.
slaaf², (s) (**slawe**), slave, blackbird; bond(s)man, drudge, helot; *'n* ~ *van die GEWOONTE wees*, be the slave of habit; *'n* ~ *v.d. MODE*, a slave of fashion; *gy 'n* ~ *van sy WOORD nie*, no slave to his word (promises); (w) (ge-), slave, drudge, toil; ~ *en swoeg*, toil and moil.
slaafs, (-e), slavish, servile, menial, obsequious, sequacious; ~ **heid**, servility, slavishness.
slaag, (ge-), succeed, be successful; pass, get through (an examination), make the grade, do; *ek het DAARIN ge* ~ , I succeeded in . . . ; *in 'n EKSAMEN* ~ , pass an examination.
slaags: ~ *RAAK*, go into action, come to blows, join issue; ~ *WEES*, be engaged in fighting.
slaag'vereistes, requirements for a pass.
slaai, salad; lettuce; *in iem. se* ~ *krap*, poke one's nose into someone's affairs; court someone else's girl; ~ **-akkertjie**, lettuce bed; ~ **bak**, salad-bowl; ~ **boontjie**, haricot bean; ~ **bos**, ice-plant; ~ **gereg**, salad dish; ~ **kop**, head of salad; ~ **lepel-en-vurk**, salad-serves; ~ **olie**, salad-oil; ~ **saad**, lettuce-seed; ~ **sous**, salad-dressing, mayonnaise; ~ **tjie**, (-s), small lettuce; tobacco-chew, quid.
slaak, (ge-), heave, breathe; *'n sug* ~ , heave a sigh.
slaan, (ge-), beat, birch, thrash, flog, spank, bash, clout, pommel, pound, punch, buffet, cuff, hammer, whack, strike; mint (coin); pulsate; flap (sails); build (bridge); *'n BLIK* ~ *op*, cast a glance; *'n*

slaap | 481 | *slagtyd*

DEUR ~, bang a door; ~ *kom van twee KANTE*, it takes two to start a fight; *jy* ~ *jou KINDERS weg*, you even begrudge your children a share; *die KLOK* ~, the clock strikes; ~ *is niks nie, maar die OOR-EN-WEER-slanery*, it's not the hitting back that matters but the hitting back; *die ROOITAAL* ~, speak English; *die TROMMEL* ~, beat the drum; ~ *is TWEE man se werk*, it takes two to start a fight; *dit* ~ *op 'n VORIGE hoofstuk*, this refers to a previous chapter; ~**bal**, object-ball (billiards); ~**beurt**, innings; ~**de**, striking; ~**ding**, cane, something to hit with; goad; colt (naut.); ~**hamer**, maul; ~**kant**, trip (-hammer); ~**krag**, hitting power; ~**lyn**, batsman's crease (cricket); ~**sak**, punching-bag; ~**vlak**, (hammer-)face.

slaap¹, (s) sleep; *DEUR die* ~ *wees*, be half asleep; too fatigued to sleep; *die EWIGE* ~, one's last sleep; eternal sleep (rest); *die* ~ *v.d. REGVER= DIGES*, the sleep of the just; *in (aan)* ~ *SING*, sing to sleep; *in (aan)* ~ *SUS*, lull to sleep; *UIT die* ~ *hou*, keep away (keep from) sleep(ing); *in (aan)* ~ *VAL*, fall asleep; *in (aan)* ~ *WIEG*, rock to sleep; (w) (ge-), sleep, be asleep; *my BEEN* ~, I have pins and needles in my leg, my leg has gone to sleep; ~ *soos 'n BEES*, sleep like a log; *EERS 'n bietjie oor iets* ~, take counsel with one's pillow; *GAAN* ~, go to bed; ~ *GERUS!* good night; *jy KAN maar gaan* ~, you can forget about it; *LOOP* ~, buzz off!
slaap², (s) (**slape**), temple (of head).
slaap: ~**baadjie**, pyjama jacket; ~**bank**, couch; ~**bankraam**, bed-frame (train).
slaap'been, temporal bone.
slaap: ~**broek**, pyjama trousers; ~**deuntjie**, (-s), lul= laby; ~**drank**, narcotic, hypnotic, sleeping-draught; ~**dronk**, drowsy; ~**geleentheid**, sleeping accommodation; ~**goed**, nightwear; ~**huis**, doss-house; lodgings for travellers; ~**jakkie**, bedjacket; ~**kamer**, bedroom; ~**kamerstel**, bedroom suite; ~**klere**, pyjamas; ~**kop**, ~**kous**, drowsy-head, sleepyhead; ~**liedjie**, lullaby; ~**loos** = **slapeloos**; ~**maat**, bedfellow (lit. and fig.); ~**middel**, sopor= ific, narcotic, opiate, sleeping-draught; ~**mus**, nightcap; ~**pak**, pyjamas; ~**plek**, sleeping accom= modation; berth (on ship); night-quarters; roost (fowls); ~**pop**, sleeping doll; ~**prater**, somnil= oquist; ~**pratery**, somniloquism; ~**rusbank**, bed-settee; ~**rytuig**, sleeper, pullman (car); ~**saal**, dor= mitory; ~**sak**, sleeping-bag; ~**siekte**, slee= ping-sickness; lethargy.
slaap'slagaar, temporal artery.
slaap: ~**sokkie**, bedsock; ~**sopie**, nightcap; ~**stee**, (..**steë**), bedstead; ~**ster**, (-s), sleeper; *die Skone S*~*ster*, the Sleeping Beauty; ~**stoep**, sleeping porch; ~**stok**, perch, roost (for fowls); ~**sug**, nar= cotism; coma; ~**sug'tig**, (-e), comatose; ~**tjek**, post-dated cheque; ~**tyd**, bedtime; ~**vertrek**, bed-room; ~**vliegtuig**, sleeper (aeroplane); ~**wa**, sleep= ing-car, sleeper; ~**wandelaar**, sleepwalker, som= nambulist; noctambulist; ~**wandelend**, (-e), somnambulistic; noctambulant; ~**wandelary**, somnambulism; noctambulism; ~**wekkend**, (-e), narcotic, soporiferous, somniferous, somnolent; hypnotic; ~**werend**, (-e), sleep-dispelling.
slabak', (ge-), slack, loaf, idle.
sla'e, thrashing, hiding, lashes, dressing-down, drub= bing; *'n pak* ~, a thrashing.
slag¹, (s) kind, sort, ilk; *mense van allerlei* ~, all sorts and conditions of men.
slag², (s) (**slae**), battle; blow, clout, buffet, slap (with hand); box (on ears); stroke (clock, swimmer); clap (thunder); beat (pulse); impulse (heart); sweep (of brace); impact; trick (cards); twist (rope); knack, art (of doing something); time, turn; percussion (music); *van* ~ *AF wees*, be out of form; have lost one's touch; *'n* ~ *AFWEER*, parry a blow; *'n* ~ *om die ARM hou*, keep something in reserve; be non-committal; *in die* ~ *BLY*, fall in battle; *iem. van* ~ *BRING*, upset someone; become a victim; *met EEN* ~, at one blow; *die EERSTE* ~, the first time; *ELKE* ~, every time; *op* ~ *GEDOOD*, killed in= stantaneously; *die* ~ *is GELEWER*, the battle is over; *'n* ~ *in die GESIG*, a slap in the face; *GOED op* ~ *wees*, be in good form; *GROOT* ~, grand slam; *die* ~ *HÊ*, have tact; have the knack; *KLEIN* ~, small slam; *die KLOK is van* ~ *af*, the clock is out of strike; *op* ~ *KOM*, begin to understand; get into form; ~ *LEWER*, fight a battle; *hy het 'n* ~ *v.d. MEULE weg*, he has a bee in his bonnet; ~ *OP* ~, time and again; blow upon blow; stroke by stroke; *sy* ~ *SLAAN*, take advantage of; make a bargain; *sonder* ~ *of STOOT*, without striking a blow; *'n SWAAR* ~, a severe blow.
slag³, (w) (ge-), slaughter, kill; *onder die vyand* ~, kill a great number of the enemy.
slag'aar, artery; ~**bloed**, arterial blood; ~**bloeding**, arterial haemorrhage; ~**breuk**, rupture of an artery; ~**geswel**, aneurism; ~**verkalking**, arterio= sclerosis; ~**verwyding**, arterial dilatation.
slag: ~**bank**, shambles; ~**bees**, slaughter-ox (-cow); ~**blok**, slaughtering-block.
slag: ~**bodem**, (-s), man-of-war, battleship; ~**boom**, bar, barrier, turnpike; ~**boor**, jumper-drill, per= cussion-drill.
slag'byl, butcher's axe; pole-axe; battle-axe.
slag'demper, (-s), dashpot, silencer.
slag'dier, ..**ding**, slaughter-animal.
slag'doppie, percussion cap; detonator.
slag'gat, pothole (in road).
slag'geld, abattoir fees.
slag'gereed, ready for action.
slag: ~**gewig**, dressed weight; ~**goed**, slaughter-animals.
slag: ~**hamer**, mallet; ~**hamerontsteking**, percussion ignition; ~**hoedjie**, percussion cap; detonator.
slag'hoender, table fowl (chicken); broiler, griller.
slag'horlosie, striking clock.
slag'huis, butchery, butcher's shop.
slag'instrument, instrument of percussion.
slag'kreet, battle-cry; slogan.
slag: ~**kruit**, priming powder, gunpowder, ~**kwik**, fulminate of mercury.
slag: ~**lengte**, stroke (of engine); ~**linie**, line of battle.
slag: ~**masker**, humane killer; ~**merk**, slaughter-mark; ~**mes**, butcher's knife.
slag'net, clap-net.
slag: ~**offer**, victim; prey; *'n* ~ *word van*, fall a victim to; ~**orde**, battle-array.
slag'orkes, percussion band.
slag: ~**os**, slaughter-ox; ~**pale**, slaughtering-place; abattoir.
slag'pen, quill-feather, pen-feather; flight-feather; striking pin (of bolt machine); *iem. se* ~ *uittrek*, limit someone's power; handicap.
slag'plaas, see **slagplek**.
slag'plaatjie, keeper-plate (of lock).
slag: ~**plek**, slaughtering-place; abattoir; shambles; ~**pluimvee**, table-poultry.
slag: ~**pomp**, ram; ~**pypie**, percussion tube; ~**rat**, ratchet, toothed wheel.
slag'reën, ..**reent**, heavy shower of rain, down= pour.
slag: ~**riem**, stroke (oar); ~**roeier**, stroke (oarsman).
slag'room, whipped cream; ~**buisie**, cream-tube.
slag'skaap, slaughter-sheep.
slag: ~**skaduwee**, cast (central) shadow, umbra.
slag'skip, battleship, man-of-war.
slag: ~**spel**, medal play (golf); ~**spreuk**, slogan.
slag: ~**swaard**, broadsword; ~**tand**, tusk (of el= ephant); fang, (canine) tooth.
slag'ter, (-s), butcher; blockman; ~**saak**, butchery, butcher's business.
slag'ters: ~**blok**, chopping-block; ~**byl**, butcher's axe; chopper; pole-axe; ~**hond**, mastiff; ~**kneg**, butcher's man; ~**mes**, gully; ~**rekening**, butcher's bill; ~**winkel**, butcher's shop, butchery.
slag'tery, slagtery', (-e), butcher's shop, butchery; butchering, slaughtering.
slag'ting, slaughter, massacre; *'n* ~ *AANRIG*, cause (commit) wholesale slaughter; *daar was 'n* ~ *onder die KANDIDATE*, it was a slaughter; *PYNLOSE* ~, humane killing.
slag'tyd, slaughtering-time.

slagvaar'dig, (-e), ready for battle; quick-witted; ~**heid**, preparedness, readiness (for battle), concert pitch; quickness at repartee.

slag: ~**vark**, porker; ~**vee**, slaughter-animals, slaughter-stock; ~**veeboer**, grazier.

slag'veer, mainspring, striking spring; flight-feather.

slag'vel, batter-head (of drum).

slag'veld, battlefield; field of battle (death); *die ~ behou*, be victorious; hold the field.

slag'werk, strike-mechanism (of clock); percussives; ~**er**, percussionist.

slag: ~**woord**, keyword, slogan, catchword; ~**wydte**, sparking-distance; explosive distance; spark gap.

slag'yster, spring-trap; mousetrap; *vir iem. 'n ~ STEL*, set a trap for someone; *in 'n ~ TRAP*, fall into a trap.

slak¹, (s) slag (mining), clinker, dross, scoria.

slak², (s) (-ke), snail, slug, fluke (liver); ~**agtig**, (-e), snail-like, scoriaceous; ~**blom** koester, (*Drosera spp.*); ~**huisie**, snail's shell; cochlea (of ear); ~**kegang**, snail's pace; *die ~kegang gaan*, move at a snail's pace.

slak'ke: ~**meel**, basic slag; ~**wol**, slag-wool.

Slamai'er, (-s), Malay; Moslem, Mohammedan.

slampam'per, (s) (-s), reveller, tippler, toper, scallywag; idler; (w) **(ge-)**, revel, carouse, make merry; ~**liedjie**, ditty, short simple song (poem); carousal-song, drinking-song.

Slams, (-e), Malay; Mohammedan, Moslem.

sla'ner, (-s), beater, hitter; batsman, compiler (of runs).

slang, (-e), snake, serpent; (rubber) tube, hosepipe; culverine; *'n ~ in jou BOESEM koester*, cherish a snake in one's bosom; *as dit 'n ~ was, dan het hy jou lankal GEBYT*, if it were a bear it would bite you; *daar is 'n ~ in die GRAS*, there is a snake in the grass; *die OU ~*, the serpent; *hy kon ~e VANG toe hy dit hoor*, he could murder when he heard that; ~**aal**, snake-eel; ~**aanbidder**, snake-worshipper, ophite; ~**aanbidding**, ophiolatry; ~**agtig**, (-e), snaky, colubrine, ophidian, serpentine; ~**besweerder**, snake-charmer; ~**bossie**, soft velvety shrub (*Elytropappus glandulosus*); ~**byt**, snake-bite; ~**dans**, snake-dance; ~**diens**, snake-worship; ~**eier**, snake's egg; ~**etjie**, small snake; snake-fish; ~**(e)tuin**, snake-park; ~**gif**, snake-poison; ~**halsvoël**, darter; ~**houtjies**, snakeroot; ~**klem**, hose clip; ~**kop**, snake's head; blue weed (*Ornithoglossum spp.*); ~**koppelaar**, ~**koppeling**, hose connection; ~**kos**, deathcup, mushroom, toadstool; ~**kruid**, viper's bugloss; snake-root; ~**leer**, snake-skin (leather); ~**mens**, contortionist, posture-maker, distortionist, serpent-man; ~**muishond**, weasel, mongoose; ~**park**, snake-park; ~**spoeg**, snake's spit; ~**staf**, Mercury's rod, caduceus; ~**steen**, snake-stone, ammonite; ~**stert**, serpent's tail; ~**tol**, hose-reel; ~**tong**, adder's (serpent's) tongue; ~**tuin**, snake-park, ~**vanger**, snake-catcher; secretary-bird; ~**vel**, snakeskin, slough; ~**verklikker**, ground-robin; ~**vis**, ophidiom; ~**vormig**, (-e), serpentine; ~**vreter**, secretary-bird; ~**wortel**, snakeroot (*Polygaea senega*); adder's wort.

slank, (-e), slender, fragile, slight, willowy, slim; *GOED vir die ~e lyn*, good for the figure (for slimming); *die ~e LYN*, the slim line; ~**heid**, slenderness, slimness; span-cord ratio.

slap, loose (adjustment); slack (rope); dull (trade); enervate; flaccid; flimsy; flexible, supple (limbs); soft (collar); limp (figure); weak (tea); faded; flabby; ~ *BESLAG*, slack batter; ~ *BETON*, wet concrete; ~ *HANG*, droop; *nie laat ~ HANG nie*, keep up courage and perservere; *jou ~ LAG*, laugh till you cry; *so ~ as 'n LAP*, as limp as a rag; *'n ~ TYD*, a dull time; a slack season.

sla'peloos, (..lose), sleepless; ~**heid**, sleeplessness, insomnia, wakefulness.

sla'pend, (-e), sleeping; dormant, latent; *die S~e Skone*, the Sleeping Beauty.

sla'penstyd, bedtime.

sla'per, (-s), sleeper; dreamer.

sla'perig, (-e), sleepy, drowsy, comatose; ~**heid**, sleepiness, drowsiness; lethargy.

slap: ~**hakskeentjies**, cooked onion salad; ~**heid**, slackness; weakness; looseness; dullness; flabbiness.

sla'pie, (-s), snooze, nap.

slap: ~**lemmes**, egg-lifter; spatula; ~**lit'tig**, (-e), double-jointed; ~**peling**, (-e), weak-kneed fellow, slacker.

slap'perig, (-e), rather slack, loose, weak, flabby; ~**heid**, flabbiness, slackness, limpness.

slap: ~**pies**, poorly, slackly; ~**randhoed**, slouch hat; ~**saag**, unset saw; ~**siekte**, dourine; ~**te**, dullness (market), slump, depression; flaccidity, languor.

slavin', (-ne), female slave, slave-woman, bondmaid.

sla'we, (ge-), slave, drudge, toil; ~**arbeid**, slave-labour, slavery, drudgery; ~**band**, slave-bangle; ~**diens**, bond-service; ~**drywer**, slave-driver; ~**handel**, slave-trade, blackbirding; ~**handelaar**, slave-trader; ~**jag**, slave-hunt; ~**juk**, yoke of slavery, thraldom, bondage; ~**ketting**, slave-chain; ~**kind**, slave-child; ~**lewe**, slavery, life of toil; ~**mark**, slave-market; ~**opstand**, revolt of slaves.

slawerny', slavery, servitude, bondage, helotism, helotry.

slaweskip, slave-ship, slaver.

sla'wetyd: *in ~ se dae*, in the days of slavery.

Sla'wies, (s) Slavic, Slavonian (people); (b) (-e), Slav, Slavonic.

Slawo'nië, Slavonia; ~**r**, (-s), Slavonian.

Slawo'nies, (-e), Slavonian.

slee, (sleë), sledge, sleigh (for persons), sled (for goods); cradle (lathe); launching-cradle; ~**baan**, ice-run; ~**hond**, sledge-dog.

sleep, (s) (slepe), retinue, train; tow (ship); *die BRUID se ~*, the bride's train; *'n ~ KLEINGOED*, a trail of children; *OP ~*, in tow; *die slymerige ~ van 'n SLAK*, the slimy trail of a slug; (w) **(ge-)**, drag, draw, haul, trail, tow (car); lug; *'n boot in die HAWE ~*, tow a boat into harbour; *LELIKE gevolge na hom ~*, bring dire consequences in its train; *die SAAK bly ~*, the matter drags on; ~**anker**, drag-anchor; ~**antenne**, trailing aerial; ~**boot**, tug, tugboat; ~**diens**, breakdown (towing) service; ~**draer**, train-bearer; ~**eg**, smoothing harrow; ~**gewaad**, flowing garments; ~**gewig**, curb-weight; ~**haak**, hauling-iron (wa(g)gon); ~**helling**, slipway; ~**japon**, gown with a train; ~**kabel**, guide-rope (of balloon); towing-cable; hawser; ~**kar**, trailer; ~**ketting**, drag-chain; ~**kontak**, sliding-contact; collector; ~**koste**, towage (charges); ~**loon**, towage; haulage; ~**lugdraad**, trailing aerial; ~**lus**, towing-loop; ~**net**, dragnet; drag; trailing net; sweep-net; ~**ring**, collector ring; slip-ring (aeroplane); ~**rok**, dress with train; trailing skirt; ~**sabel**, cavalry sword; ~**sel**, (-s), trail, drag; ~**swingel**: *dit gaan ~swingel*, things are going badly; ~**teiken**, tow(ed)-target; ~**tong**: *~ tong praat*, have a heavy tongue.

sleep'tou, towing-rope; drag-rope; guest-rope; painter; *op ~ HE*, have in tow; *'n HELE ~*, a whole train; *op ~ HOU*, keep in tow; keep one on a string; *op ~ NEEM*, take in tow; ~**vlug**, towing-flight.

sleep: ~**trekker**, haulage tractor; ~**tros**, tow-line, towing-hawser; ~**vak**, subject that has to be repeated; ~**vliegtuig**, towing-aeroplane; ~**vlug**, towed flight; ~**voetend**, (-e), shuffling (gait); ~**wa**, trailer; ~**werk**, haulage.

Slees'wyk, Schleswig; ~**er**, (-s), Schleswig-man.

Slees'wyk-Holstein, Schleswig-Holstein.

Slees'wyks, (-e), of Schleswig.

slee'tjie, (-s), small sled, sleigh; ~ *ry*, toboggan.

slee'tog, sledge-ride (-expedition).

sleg¹, (s): *jou ~*, you rotter!

sleg², (w) **(ge-)**, (vero.), demolish, raze, level.

sleg³, (b) (-te), bad, evil; poor, indifferent (health); graceless; foul; *die ~ste daarvan AFKOM*, have the worst of it; come off second-best; ~ *te ASEM*, halitosis; ~ *DAARAAN toe wees*, be in a sorry plight; ~ *van GESIG wees*, have weak eyesight; ~ *te GESONDHEID*, ill-health; ~ *van GOEIIGHEID*, kind to a fault; ~ *te HUIS*, house of ill fame; ~ *te SMAAK*, bad taste; *daar* ~ *aan TOE wees*, be in a bad way; *jy is* ~ *VERBY*, you are past redemption; ~ *ter WORD*, grow worse, deteriorate; (bw) badly, ill, poorly; *dit GAAN* ~ *met die sieke*, the patient is in a poor way; *dit baie* ~ *TREF*, have very bad luck; ~ **befaam, (-de)**, of evil repute; ~ **geaard, (-e)**, ill-natured; ~ **gemanier(d), (-e)**, ill-mannered; ~ **gerig, (-e)**, rather bad; ~ **gesind, (-e)**, hostile; ~ **maak, (-ge-)**, disparage (slander) someone; blacken someone's name; malign; ~ **makery, (-e)**, disparagement; ~ **ruikend, (-e)**, evil-smelling, malodorous.

slegs, only, but, merely.

sleg'sê, (-ge-), scold, reprimand, rebuke; run down; *iem.* ~, tell someone what you think of him; ~ *is geen KUNS nie*, there is no art in calling names; ~ **ery**, abuse.

sleg: ~ **ste**, worst; *op sy* ~ *ste*, at its worst; ~ **te**, (s) the bad; *die goeie met die* ~ *te neem*, take the good with the bad; ~ **terig, (-e)**, rather bad, poor; ~ **t'heid**, badness, evil, wickedness, devilry, peccancy, pravity, perversity, depravity.

sleg'tigheid, weakness, badness, rottenness; carelessness; *dis sommer van skone* ~, it is due to sheer carelessness.

sleg'ting, levelling, razing, demolition.

sleg'vang, (s) fumble; (w) (-ge-), fumble.

slemp¹, (s) saffron milk.

slemp², (w) (ge-), carouse, feast; ~ **maal**, carousal; **party**, carousal.

Slenk'dal, Rift Valley; ~ **koors**, Rift Valley fever.

slen'ter¹, (s) (-s), knavery, dodge, trick, excuse; *met 'n* ~ *vang*, trick into.

slen'ter², (w) (ge-), saunter, stroll, slouch, gad, loiter; ~ **aar, (-s)**, jay-walker, gadabout, loiterer, saunterer, lounger; ~ **broek**, jeans; slacks.

slen'terdraai, dodge; *met 'n nuwe* ~ *kom*, come up with a new dodge.

slen'ter: ~ **drag**, casual wear; ~ **gang**, sauntering gait, saunter; *die ou* ~ *gang gaan*, carry on in the same old way; ~ **ing**, sauntering; ~ **loper**, jay-walker.

slen'terslag, (..slae), fake, dodge, trick, roguery.

slen'tery, strolling, sauntering.

sle'pend, (-e), dragging; decumbent; ~ *e RYM*, female rhyme; ~ *e SIEKTE*, lingering disease; ~ *e STEM*, drawling voice.

sle'per, (-s), sleeper, tug; hauler; ~ **wa**, dray; ~ **y**, haulage, towage.

slet, (-te), slut, prostitute, harlot, drab, jade; queen.

sleuf, (sleuwe), groove, slit, slot.

sleur, (s) (-e), habit, humdrum way, rut, rote, drudgery, routine; *met die* ~ *BREEK*, get out of the rut; *IN 'n* ~, in a rut, in a groove; *die OU* ~, the old humdrum way; *die ou* ~ *VOLG*, carry on in the same old way; (w) (ge-), drag, ~ **agtig, (-e)**, groovy; ~ **diens**, perfunctoriness; ~ **gang**, jogtrot; routine course; ~ **mens**, creature of habit, man of routine, routinist; ~ **werk**, routine work.

sleu'tel, (-s), key, clef (music); communicator (elec.); spanner; cotter (nut); *die* ~ *besit van*, hold the key to; ~ **baard**, key-bit; ~ **bedryf**, key industry; ~ **been**, collar-bone, clavicle; ~ **bek**, spanner jaw; ~ **blom**, primula, polyanthus, primrose, cowslip; ~ **bord**, key-rack; ~ **bos**, bunch of keys; ~ **draer**, key-keeper, key-bearer; ~ **figuur**, keyman; ~ **gat**, keyhole; ~ **gatplaat**, keyhole-cover; escutcheon; ~ **geld**, key money; ~ **haak**, key-hook; ~ **houer**, key container; ~ **industrie**, pivotal industry, key industry; ~ **kaart**, index map, key map; ~ **kepies**, ward (in lock); ~ **ketting**, chatelaine; ~ **man**, key man; ~ **mandjie**, key-basket; ~ **nywerheid**, key industry; ~ **posisie**, key position; ~ **pyp**, spanner pipe; ~ **ring**, key-ring; ~ **skild**, escutcheon; ~ **steel**, key-shank; ~ **stelling**, key position; ~ **teken**, clef; ~ **vonnis**, leading case; ~ **vormig, (-e)**, claviform; ~ **vrug**, key-fruit, samara; ~ **vyl**, blade-file; ~ **woord**, keyword.

slib, mud, mire, silt, ooze, slime; silt; ~ **agtig, (-e)**, slimy, miry; ~ **berig, (-e)**, miry, slimy; ~ **berigheid**, sliminess, muddiness; ~ **besinksel**, silt deposit; ~ **kus**, alluvial coast.

slier, (-e), streak, smear, dab; string; ~ **aspersie**, asparagus stalk; ~ **ig, (-e)**, streaky.

sliert, (-e), string, line, streak; *'n* ~ *HARE*, a wisp of hair; *'n* ~ *jie WEGHÊ*, be tipsy; have had a drop or two; ~ **ig, (-e)**, streakily; lineal.

slik, *see* **slyk;** ~ **gat**, mud hole; ~ **grond**, silt; ~ **put**, silt-pit; ~ **steen**, siltstone.

slim, clever, intelligent, clear-headed, astute; crafty, sly, cunning, shifty, fly; ~ *vang sy BAAS*, one can be too clever by half; *wie nie STERK is nie, moet* ~ *wees*, one must either be brainy or brawny; ~ **heid**, cleverness, astuteness; cunning, cuteness, slyness; ~ **jan**, cunning fox; know-all; ~ **kop**, egg-head; ~ **merd, (-s)**, cunning fox, sly boots; coon; ~ **merig, (-e)**, cleverish; ~ **migheid**, cuteness; sly trick; cunning; ~ **praatjies**, ~ **stories**, stories, prevarications, glib talk, claptrap, evasive talk; ~ *praatjies verkoop*, talk together; chatter.

slin'ger, (s) (-s), pendulum (clock); (starting-) crank, handle; sling (for missile; bandage); festoon, garland; (w) (ge-), sling; oscillate, swing, sway; rock, roll, pitch (ship); reel, stagger (drunkard); lurch; meander, wind (path); fling, hurl; *DRONK deur die strate* ~, stagger drunkenly through the streets; *'n VERWYT* ~ *na*, fling a reproach at; ~ **aap**, spider-monkey; ~ **aar, (-s)**, slinger; ~ **anker**, sling-stay (loco); ~ **as**, axis of oscillation; ~ **beweging**, oscillating movement; reel, lurch; ~ **end, (-e)**, zigzag; flipperty-flopperty; meandering; oscillating; ~ **gewig**, bob, pendulum weight; ~ **heuning**, pure honey; ~ **ing, (-e, -s)**, swing(ing); oscillation; fling; hunting (machine); ~ **klip**, sling-stone, ~ **laan**, winding alley; ~ **lat**, table-rack; ~ **lyn**, meandering line; ~ **magneet**, pendulum magnet; ~ **myn**, fougade, fougasse; ~ **-om-die-smoel**, milk soup; ~ **pad**, winding path; ~ **periode**, period of oscillation; ~ **plant**, creeper; liana; ~ **proef**, (Foucault's) pendulum proof (physics); ~ **punt**, centre of oscillation; ~ **roos**, hedgebell; ~ **skag**, starting-handle, shaft (motor); ~ **stang**, pendulum rod; ~ **steen**, sling-stone; ~ **steun**, crank support; ~ **trap**, helical stairs; ~ **tyd**, period of swing (oscillation); ~ **uurwerk**, pendulum clock; ~ **vel**, catapult; ~ **verband**, sling bandage; ~ **wette**, laws of pendulum motion (oscillation); ~ **wydte**, amplitude.

slink, (ge-), shrink, diminish; boil down; decline, fall off; ~ *tot op*, dwindle down to; ~ **ing**, shrinkage, decrease.

slinks, (-e), clandestine, treacherous, cunning, artful, fraudulent; crooked; *op* ~ *e wyse*, in an underhand way; ~ **heid**, cunning, artfulness, treacherousness, guile.

slip, (s) (-pe), slit (earmark; in coat); tail (of shirt); flap, placket (of skirt); lappet (head-dress); opening; edge; (w) (ge-), slip; ~ **baadjie**, coat with a slit; ~ **draer, (-s)**, pallbearer; ~ **gat**, placket-hole; ~ **haak**, quick release; ~ **knoop**, slip-knot; ~ **strook**, gusset; ~ **stroom**, slip-stream; ~ **vry, (-e)**, non-skid (tyre).

slob'ber, (ge-), sip audibly, slobber, lap; ~ **ig, (-e)**, sloppy, slobbery.

slob'berbroek, baggy trousers.

slob'kous, gaiter; spat, spattee; untidy person.

slod'der, (ge-), hang loosely (clothes); ~ **ig, (-e)**, slovenly, slatternly; ill-fitting; ~ **igheid**, slovenliness, slatternliness; ~ **joggem**, untidy person; ~ **kous**, untidy girl, draggle-tail, slattern.

sloep¹, (-e), gully, creak.

sloep², (-e), sloop, shallop, barge; pinnace; cockboat; gig; galley; ~ **dek**, boat-deck.

sloer, (ge-), loiter, linger, dawdle, drag (on), procrastinate, keep putting off, go slow; *lank met 'n saak* ~, keep on postponing a matter; ~ **dery**, dawdling, procrastination.

sloe'rie, (-s), slovenly woman, hussy, dowdy, slut, drab, slattern.

sloer'staking, go-slow (strike).

slof, (s) **(slowwe)**, slipper, worn-out shoe; slut, slovenly woman; (w) (ge-), shuffle along, drag one's feet; ~ **fie, (-s)**, slipper; *OP sy* ~ *fies*, slowly, at his ease; *uit sy* ~ *fies SKIET*, get a move on; ~ **gang**, shamble, shambling (gait).

slöjd, manual training, sloid.

slok, (-ke), mouthful, gulp; ~-op, (-pe), glutton, gobbler.

slons, (-e), dowd(y), frump, slut, draggle-tail; ~ **agtig**, (-e), slovenly, draggle-tailed; frumphish, frumpy, dowdy.

slon′s(er)ig, (-e), slovenly, untidy; ~**heid**, slovenliness, untidiness.

sloof, (s) **(slowe)**, drudge; (w) **(ge-)**, drudge, toil; ~**werk**, drudgery.

sloop¹, (s) **(slope)**, pillow-case, pillow-slip.

sloop², (w) **(ge-)**, demolish, level, raze (building); undermine (health); break up, scrap (ship); sap, drain (strength); dismantle (fort).

sloop′rok, shift dress.

sloops′gewyse, like a pillow-slip.

sloop: ~ **waarde**, breaking-up value; ~**werk**, demolition work.

sloot, **(slote)**, ditch, fosse, donga, dike, furrow, channel, drain, gutter, trench; *hy kan 'n* ~ *EET*, he eats like a horse; *'n* ~ *in die dag SLAAP*, sleep far into the day; ~**grawer**, (-s), ditcher; excavator; ~**grawery**, ditching; ~**kant**, side of a ditch; ~**water**, ditch-water.

slop, slum; blind alley; ~**eend**, Cape shoveller (bird).

slo′per, (-s), wrecker, housebreaker, demolisher; ship-breaker; ~**y**, ship-breaking yard.

slo′pie, (-s), small pillow-case.

slo′ping, demolition, undermining, dismantling.

slo′pings: ~**koste**, cost of demolition; ~**werk**, demolition work.

slor′dig, (-e), careless, slovenly, untidy; sloppy, sluttish, dowdy, dishevelled (hair); draggle-tail, down-at-heel, baggy (trousers), slipshod (style); ~*e vrou*, frump; ~**heid**, untidiness, slovenliness, slatternliness, carelessness.

slot¹, end(ing), conclusion; peroration; *per* ~ *van REKENING*, after all, ultimately; *die* ~ *v.d. SAAK*, the end of the matter; *TEN* ~ *te*, finally, in the end, lastly; *TOT* ~, in conclusion; ~ *VOLG*, to be concluded.

slot², (-te), lock (of door); clasp (of book); key (of gun); *AGTER* ~, under lock and key; locked up; *'n FIETS op* ~ *sit*, lock a bicycle; *agter* ~ *en GRENDEL sit*, be in prison; put in prison; *iets agter* ~ *HOU*, keep under lock and key; *'n* ~ *voor die MOND sit*, seal someone's mouth; *'n* ~ *OOPSLUIT*, unlock something; *OP* ~, locked up.

slot³, (-te), castle, citadel; *'n adellike* ~, the castle of a nobleman.

slot: ~**akkoord**, final chord; ~**alinea**, last paragraph; ~**artikel**, concluding article (newspaper); last section (law).

slot′as, lock-shaft.

slot: ~**balans**, final balance; ~**bedryf**, last act; ~**bepaling**, final provision.

slot′bewaarder, castle-keeper.

slot′byeenkoms, final session.

slot′brug, lock-bridge.

slo′terig, (-e), furrowy.

slot′gesang, recessional (closing) hymn.

slot: ~**grendel**, lock bolt; ~**haak**, picklock.

slot: ~**hoofstuk**, concluding chapter; ~**klinker**, final vowel.

slot′knip, lock(ing)-catch.

slot′koers, closing price (quotation).

slot′lem, safety razor.

slot′letter, final letter.

slot′maker, locksmith.

slot: ~**medeklinker**, final consonant; ~**nommer**, last item; closing number; ~**notering**, closing price.

slot: ~**oopsteker**, picklock; ~**opening**, lock-cavity (railway).

slot′opmerking, concluding remark.

slot′plaatjie, lappet.

slot: ~**pleidooi**, closing argument; ~**rede**, closing remark; peroration; ~**reël**, final line; ~**repetisie**, final rehearsal; ~**rym**, final rhyme; ~**sang**, final song (hymn); epode, last canto; ~**sin**, closing sentence; ~**som**, result, conclusion; *tot die* ~*som kom*, come to the conclusion.

slot′steek, lock-stitch.

slot: ~**toespraak**, epilogue; ~**toneel**, closing scene.

slot′toring, donjon, keep.

slot′uitkering, final payment; final dividend (shares).

slot: ~**vas**, (-te), locked; ~**veer**, catch spring.

slot′vers, final verse, final hymn.

slot′voog, castellan; governor of a castle.

slot′voorraad, closing stock.

slot′vyl, warding-file.

slot′woord, last word, concluding remark, peroration.

slot′wys(t)er, lock indicator.

Slowaak′, **(Slowake)**, Slovak; ~**s′**, (-e), **Slowa′kies**, (-e), Slovak(ian).

Slowaky′e, Slovakia.

slo′we, (ge-), drudge, slave, toil; ~**r**, (-s), plodder.

Sloween′, (..**wene**), Slovene; ~**s′**, (-e), Slovenian.

slu, (-we, -wer, **sluuste**), sly, foxy, cunning, artful, astute, designing, furtive, insidious, shrewd, wily, crafty; ~**heid**, cunning, shrewdness, slyness, astuteness, artfulness, wiliness.

slui′er, (s) (-s), veil, mask; film; mantilla; fog; *die* ~ *AANNEEM*, take the veil; *onder die* ~ *van die NAG*, under cover of night; *die* ~ *OPLIG*, lift the veil; explain something; *die* ~ *laat VAL oor*, draw a veil over; (w) **(ge-)**, veil; cover, conceal; fog (phot.); ~**dans**, veil-dance; ~**ing**, fading (radio); ~**stof**, veiling; ~**wolk**, cirro-stratus.

sluik, lank, straight (hair).

sluik: ~**goedere**, smuggled goods, contraband; ~**handel**, smuggling; contraband; black market; ~**handelaar**, smuggler; illicit trader; ~**kroeg**, shebeen.

sluik′harig, (-e), lank-haired.

slui′mer, (s) slumber; (w) **(ge-)**, slumber, nap, doze; lie dormant, be latent (feelings); ~**aar**, slumberer; ~**end**, (-e), slumbering, delitescent; latent; ~**ig**, (-e), sleepy; ~**ing**, slumber, nap, doze.

sluip, **(ge-)**, steal along (away), slink (sneak) away, prowl; slip away; crawl, glide; *'n fout het in my brief ge* ~, an error has crept into my letter; ~**dief**, cat burglar, sneak-thief; ~**end**, (-e), prowling; insidious; ~**er**, prowler, sneaker; ~**gat**, bolt-hole; ~**hawe**, lee shore; pirate's nest; ~**hoek**, hiding-place; ~**jag**, game-stalking; ~**jagter**, stalker; ~**koors**, remittent fever; ~**luister**, (ge-), bug; ~**luistering**, bugging; ~**moord**, assassination; ~**moordenaar**, assassin, thug; ~**patrollie**, spy patrol, reconnoitring party; ~**skiet**, (ge-), snipe; ~**skietery**, sniping; ~**skutter**, sniper; ~**slaper**, yard-sneaker, yard-snoozer, sly lodger; ~**slapery**, yard sneaking; ~**vlieg**, tachinid; ~**weg**, secret road; trick; ~**wesp**, ichneumon fly.

sluis, (-e), sluice; lock, flood-gate; apron; *die* ~ *e v.d. HEMEL was oop*, the flood-gates of the heavens were opened; *die* ~ *e OOPTREK*, open the flood-gates; *die* ~ *e van WELSPREKENDHEID*, the flood-gates of eloquence; ~**balk**, lock-beam; ~**dam**, barrage; ~**deur**, lock-gate, penstock, flood-gate; ~**geld**, lock-dues; lockage; ~**kamer**, coffer; sluice-chamber; ~**kanaal**, sluice-way, lock-canal; ~**klep**, sluice-valve; ~**kolk**, lock-chamber; ~**trog**, sluice-box; ~**wagter**, (-s), lock-master, lock-keeper, locksman.

sluit, **(ge-)**, lock (with key); shut, close, fasten (window); hasp; turn off (tap); break up (school); balance (budget); close down (business); clasp (in arms); conclude, enter into (contract); effect (insurance); prorogue (parliament); *'n kind in sy ARMS* ~, clasp a child in one's arms; *die BEGROTING* ~ *nie*, the budget does not balance; *'n HUWELIK* ~, contract a marriage; *in MEKAAR* ~, dovetail into one another; *iem. die MOND* ~, shut someone's mouth; *die REDENERING* ~ *nie*, the argument does not hold water; *die SKOLE* ~ *vandag*, the schools are breaking up to-day; *VRIENDSKAP* ~, form a friendship; ~**arm**, locking lever; ~**band**, belly-band, bandage; locket (mil.); ~**blok**, slipper (axle-box); ~**boom**, swing-gate, boom; ~**bout**, locking-bolt; ~**buis**, locking-tube (elec.); ~**datum**, closing date; ~**draad**, rip-cord (aeroplane); ~**end**, (-e), balanced; *'n rekening* ~*end maak*, balance an account; ~**er**, (-s), shutter (camera); fastener, fas=

tening; ~ **gatboor**, tap-borer; ~**haak**, cabin-hook; clasp.
slui'ting, closing, breaking-up (schools); closure (of debate); prorogation (of parliament); closing-down (of a business); conclusion; fastening (of clothes); seal; *die* ~ *toepas*, apply the closure (guillotine).
slui'tings: ~**datum**, closing date; ~ **plegtigheid**, closing ceremony; ~ **prys**, closing price; final price; ~ **reg**, closure; ~ **tyd**, closing time; ~ **uitverkoping**, closing-down sale; ~ **uur**, hour of closing.
sluit: ~ **kas**, locker, ~ **keep**, notch; ~ **klem**, binding-clamp; ~ **knip**, keeper; locking catch; ~ **laken**, binder; ~ **letter**, final letter; ~ **lig**, tail-light; ~ **mandjie**, hamper; ~ **moer**, lock-nut, check-nut, back-nut; ~ **naat**, lapped seam; ~ **nota**, covering note; ~ **paal**, boom; ~ **pan**, flap tile; ~ **pen**, cotter-pin; locking-peg (motor); retainer; ~ **plaat**, locking-plate; ~ **rede**, syllogism; ~ **reël**, last line; ~ **rib**, rib-band; ~ **ring**, washer; ~ **seël**, poster-stamp; ~ **sein**, clearing-signal(s); ~ **skroef**, check-screw, retaining pin; ~ **skuif**, lock-hatch; ~ **soom**, wrapped hem, counter-hem; ~ **spie**, key pin; ~ **spier**, sphincter, constrictor, obturator; ~ **spy**, forelock; key pin; ~ **steek**, lock stitch; ~ **steen**, keystone, arch-stone; cope-stone; closer; top-stone; perpend(er); ~ **stuk**, breech-piece (of gun); ~ **tand**, tab; ~ **term**, consequent (maths.); ~ **veer**, locking-spring; ~ **waster**, tab, lock(ing)-washer.
sluk, (s) (-ke), gulp, draught, swallow, mouthful; gullet (of saw); throat (of chimney); epiglottis; *als 'n hele* ~ *op die BOTTEL*, it is a considerable part; that is a great help; *dit skeel 'n* ~ *op 'n BOTTEL*, it makes quite a difference; *in EEN* ~, at one gulp; (w) (ge-), swallow, gulp; endure, put up with, stomach; *hy* ~ *ALLES wat hy hoor*, he believes everything he hears; *ek moes die VERWYT* ~, I had to pocket the reproach; ~ **derm**, gullet, oesophagus; ~ **entstof**, oral vaccine; ~ **ker**, swallower; *ARME* ~ *ker*, poor devil (wretch); *GULSIGE* ~ *ker*, glutton, guzzler; ~ **kie**, (-s), mouthful, draught, sip; ~ **op**, (-pe), giant petrel; ~ **pyp**, back vent, puff pipe; ~ **skoot**, gobble (golf); ~ **toestel**, gullet.
slun'gel, (-s), lubber, lout, hobbledehoy, booby; ~ **agtig**, (-e), clumsy, awkward, gawky.
slurf, (ong.), (slurwe), trunk, proboscis; spout.
slurp, (s) (-e), trunk, proboscis; haustellum; appendix (balloon); (w) (ge-), swill, gulp, guzzle, gobble; ~ **dier**, proboscidean; ~ **knoop**, lanyard knot; ~ **tenk**, parachute tank.
slyk, mud, mire, slime (mining); ooze; silt; slush, sludge (sewerage); dirt; *AARDSE* ~, filthy lucre, dross; *iem. deur die* ~ *HAAL*, drag someone through the mire; *in* ~ *WENTEL*, wallow in the muck; ~ **agtig**, (-e), muddy; ~ **bad**, mud-bath; ~ **dam**, slimes dam; ~ **erig**, (-e), slimy, muddy; ~ **erigheid**, muddiness; ~ **gat**, sludge hole, ~ **olie**, sludge oil; ~ **put**, sludge sump.
slym, slime, phlegm, mucus, mucilage; ~ **afdrywend**, (-e), phlegm-expelling, mucific; ~ **afskeidend**, (-e), pituitous, pituitary; ~ **afskeiding**, rheum, mucous secretion.
slym'agtig, (-e), slimy, mucous, phlegmatic; pituitary; ~ **heid**, sliminess, mucousness, phlegm.
slym: ~ **appel**, Bengal quince, wood-apple; ~ **beroerte**, pituitous apoplexy; ~ **beurs**, bursa; ~ **beursontsteking**, bursitis; ~ **bol**, gob; ~ **diertjie**, (-s), amoeba.
sly'merig, (-e), slimy, mucoid, phlegmy; ~ **heid**, sliminess, mucosity.
slym: ~ **gom**, mucilage; ~ **hoes**, catarrhal cough; ~ **klier**, pituitary gland, slime gland; ~ **koors**, pituitous fever, pituitary fever; ~ **prik**, hagfish *(Heptatretus)*; ~ **stof**, mucin; ~ **suur**, mucic acid; ~ **swam**, slime fungus (mould); ~ **uintjie**, soldier-in-the-box; ~ **vis**, shanny, blenny; ~ **vlies**, mucous membrane; ~ **vliesontsteking**, catarrh; ~ **vliesweefsel**, mucous tissue.
slyp, (ge-), sharpen, set (saw), whet, grind, set on edge (teeth); hone (razor); polish (diamond); *sy tande vir iets* ~, lick one's chops; ~ **bank**, grinding-lathe;

~ **er**, (-s), grinder; polisher, cutter (of diamonds); ~ **ery**, (-e), grinding; grinding-shop; (diamond-)cutting (polishing) works; ~ **masjien**, grinding-machine, grinder; ~ **meul(e)**, grinding-mill; polishing-mill; ~ **middel**, abrasive; ~ **pasta**, grinding-paste; ~ **plank**, knife-board; ~ **poeier**, grinding-powder, polishing-powder; ~ **rat**, emery-wheel; ~ **riem**, razor strop; ~ **sel**, (-s), grindings; ~ **skyf**, lap; emery-wheel; grinding-wheel; ~ **staal**, steel; ~ **steen**, whetstone, grindstone, hone; ~ **vlak**, facet; ~ **werk**, grinding; ~ **wiel**, emery-wheel.
slyt, (ge-), wear; wear away (out) (clothes); spend, pass (life, days); ~ **a'sie**, wear (and tear); wastage; ~ **band**, binding; ~ **dele**, wearing parts; ~ **end**, (-e), wearing; wasting; ~ *ende bate*, wasting asset; ~ **erig**, (-e), well-worn (clothes); ~ **ing**, wear; erosion; ~ **laag**, overlay (bearings); ~ **pasta**, grinding-paste; ~ **ring**, wearing-ring; ~ **vlak**, wearing surface.
smaad, (s) insult, scorn, disdain, abuse, gibe, contumely, opprobrium, obloquy; *iem.* ~ *aandoen*, insult someone; (w) (ge-), insult, malign, gibe, abuse, scorn, revile; ~ **rede**, invective, diatribe; ~ **skrif**, libel, lampoon; ~ **woord**, opprobrious word.
smaak, (s) taste, flavour, gustation, sapor, savour, relish; appetite; fancy, gusto, liking; *AANGENAAM van* ~, pleasant to the taste; *'n FYN* ~ *hê*, taste delicious; have a fine palate; *GOEIE* ~ *hê*, have good taste, be discriminating; ~ *KRY vir*, develop a liking for; *take a fancy to*; *'n MAN van* ~, a man of taste; *MET* ~, with relish; *NA my* ~, to my liking; *'n slegte* ~ *NALAAT*, leave a bad taste in the mouth; *oor (die)* ~ *val nie te REDENEER nie*, there is no accounting for taste; *SONDER* ~, without flavour; without relish; *oor die* ~ *val nie te TWIS nie*, tastes differ; *in die* ~ *VAL*, find favour with; hit the popular fancy; (w) (ge-), taste, savour, enjoy; appear, seem; *die DOOD* ~, taste of death; *dit* ~ *na MEER*, it tastes good; I'd like some more; *dit* ~ *MY asof hy iets wegsteek*, it seems to me that he is concealing something; ~ **gewend**, (-e), saporific; ~ **lik**, (-e), palatable, savoury, toothsome, juicy, delicious, appetizing, flavourous, flavoursome; *EET* ~ *lik*, enjoy your food; *daar* ~ *lik UITSIEN*, look attractive; ~ **likheid**, tastefulness, palatability; sapidity; ~ **loos**, (..lose), tasteless, insipid, savourless, flat; graceless, in bad taste; ~ **loosheid**, tastelessness, flatness, insipidity; ~ **middel**, seasoning, flavouring, condiment; ~ **orgaan**, organ of taste; ~ **senuwee**, gustatory nerve; ~ **sin**, sense of taste; ~ **tepel**, taste bud (on tongue); ~ **vol**, (-le), tasteful, elegant, dressy, pleasing.
smaal, (ge-), sneer, rail at, abuse; scoff; ~ **dig**, (-te), lampoon; ~ **skrif**, lampoon, libel.
sma'delik, (-e), opprobrious, insulting, contumelious, scornful, derisive, disdainful; ignominious; ~ **heid**, ignominy, scorn, contumely, disdain.
sma'dend, (-e), contumelious.
sma'der, (-s), reviler, maligner.
smag, (ge-), long for, yearn, languish, pine for; ~ *na reën*, long for rain; ~ **tend**, (-e), pining, longing, languishing, melting, wistful; ~ **ting**, pining.
smak, (s) (-ke), thud, crash; smack (lips); (w) (ge-), smack (lips); cast down; fall down.
sma'keloos = **smaakloos**.
smal, narrow, thin; *die smalle WEG*, the strait and narrow way; *die WÊRELD word te* ~, be in dire straits; ~ **blad**, spoonwood *(Hartogia capensis)*; ~ **bladig**, (-e), narrow-leaved; ~ **deel**, (-s), squadron
sma'lend, (-e), sneering, railing, opprobrious, abusive.
sma'ler, (-s), sneerer, railer.
smal: ~ **heid**, narrowness; ~ **kant**, edgeways; ~ **lerig**, (-e), rather narrow; ~ **letjies**, thin; lean; sparingly, poorly; ~ **ligheid**, narrowness; ~ **spoor**, narrow gauge (railway).
smalt, smalt, vitreous sand; ~ **blou**, powder blue.
smal'te, narrowness.
smarag', (-de), emerald; ~ **groen**, emerald green.
smart, (s) (-e), pain, distress, ache; pang, dolour; grief, sorrow, affliction, anguish; *gedeelde* ~ *is*

HALWE ~, company in distress makes sorrow less; sorrow shared is sorrow halved; *MET* ~ *verwag*, expect anxiously; (w) (ge-), (ong.), pain, afflict; grieve; *dit* ~ *my*, it grieves me; ~ **eloos**, (..**lose**), painless; ~ **kreet**, cry of pain.
smart'lik, (-e), grievous, dolorous, painful, poignant, distressful; ~ **heid**, painfulness; grief.
smart'ryk, smart'vol = **smartlik**
sme'der, (-s), blacksmith, forgeman.
sme'dery, (-e), blacksmith's shop, smithy, forge.
sme'dig, (-e), flexible, pliable, pliant.
sme'ding, forging.
smee, (ge-), weld, forge, hammer; malleate; coin (word); contrive; devise; invent, hatch, concoct (plot); *'n KOMPLOT* ~, hatch a plot; *nuwe WOORDE* ~, coin new words; ~ *die YSTER solank dit warm is*, strike the iron while it is hot; ~ **baar**, (..**bare**), malleable, weldable, ductile; ~ **baarheid**, malleability, ductility; ~ **dsel**, forging; ~ **-eendjie**, red-bill (duck); ~ **hamer**, forging-hammer; tip-hammer; tilt (hammer); ~ **stuk**, forged piece; ~ **werk**, forging, smith's work; ~ **yster**, wrought iron.
smeek, (ge-), pray, beg, beseech, entreat, plead, supplicate, implore; *iem. om hulp* ~, implore a person's help; ~ **bede**, entreaty, plea, supplication; ~ **gebed**, humble prayer, supplication.
smee: ~ **kole**, forge-coal; ~ **koper**, wrought copper.
smeek: ~ **skrif**, petition; ~ **taal**, supplicatory language; imploring terms; supplication.
smee'oond, forge furnace.
smeer, (s) (**smere**), grease; stain, smear (of blood); beeswax; shortening; spread (meat); pomate; *om die* ~, for the sake of gain; (w) (ge-), smear, oil, grease, lubricate; dab, daub; rub (with embrocation); brush (with egg); dub; spread (butter); *botter op die BROOD* ~, spread butter on bread; ~ **apparaat**, lubricator; ~ **appelkose**, apricot leather; ~ **bladjie**, libellous rag, gutter paper; ~ **boel**, horrible mess; ~ **brief**, defamatory letter; ~ **buik**, pot belly; ~ **bus**, grease cup, lubricator; ~ **der**, (-s), greaser, oiler; ~ **dery**, greasing, oiling; ~ **gaatjie**, (-s), oil-hole; ~ **goed**, liniment, embrocation, balsam; ointment; ~ **kaas**, cottage cheese; ~ **kalk**, parget, rough plaster; ~ **kanis**, dirty (dishonest) person; ~ **kwassie**, pastry brush; ~ **kers**, tallow candle; ~ **klier**, sebaceous gland; ~ **lap**, (-pe), oil-rag; ragamuffin; dirty person, hog, debauchee, loafer, rotter, blackguard, swine, skunk, cad; ~ **lappery**, filth; meanness; ~ **middel**, lubricant; liniment; ~ **olie**, lubricating oil; ~ **poets**, (-e), dirty fellow, cad, blackguard; ~ **pot**, grease-pot; lubricator; ~ **prop**, shot-plug; ~ **salf**, ointment; lotion; smear; ~ **sel**, (-s), liniment; grease; rubbing; ~ **stelsel**, lubricating system; ~ **vlek**, grease spot; ~ **wortel**, or-pin(e); *Russiese* ~ *wortel*, comfrey.
smee: ~ **staal**, forged steel; ~ **stuk**, forged piece; ~ **tang**, smith's tongs; ~ **werk**, forging, smith's work; ~ **yster**, wrought iron.
sme'keling, (-e), petitioner, suppliant.
sme'kend, (-e), beseeching, appealing, entreating; pleading (look), imploring.
sme'ker, (-s), craver, suppliant; ~ **y**, beseeching, begging.
sme'king, (-e), supplication, entreaty, prayer.
smelt, (ge-), melt, liquefy, dissolve; fuse (wire); blow (fuse); smelt (ore); render, melt down (fat); merge, combine (in a coalition of parties); ~ **baar**, (..**bare**), fusible; soluble; liquefiable; ~ **baarheid**, fusibility; solubility; ~ **bom**, fusion bomb; ~ **deel**, fuse element; ~ **draad**, fuse-wire; ~ **end**, (-e), (de)liquescent; ~ **er**, (-s), melter, founder, smelter; (political) fusionist; ~ **erig**, (-e), soft (butter); ~ **erskassie**, glove-box (in car); ~ **ery**, (-e), foundry, smelting-works; fusion (of political parties); ~ **glas**, enamel; frisk; ~ **hitte**, melting-point heat; ~ **ing**, fusion; rendering; melting; ~ **ingswarmte**, latent heat of fusion; ~ **koekie**, melting moment; ~ **kroes**, crucible, melting-pot (fig.); furnace; *deur die* ~ *kroes gaan*, pass through the melting pot; ~ **lepel**, melting-ladle; ~ **middel**, fusing agent; flux; ~ **oond**, forge, melting-furnace; reduction-works;

~ **pommade**, vanishing cream; ~ **pot**, melting pot; ~ **prop**, fusing-plug; safety lead; ~ **punt**, melting-point; ~ **sekering**, safety fuse; ~ **sel**, melt; ~ **sous**, hard sauce; ~ **sweising**, fusion-welding; ~ **vas**, (-te), infusible; ~ **vastheid**, infusibility.
sme'rig, (-e), dirty, filthy, foul, obscene, messy; ~ *behandel*, treat shabbily; ~ **heid**, dirt, filth, muckiness, meanness.
sme'ring, lubrication, greasing.
smet, (-te), blot, blur, stain, blemish, slur (on character); *sonder* ~ *of BLAAM*, without blame or blemish; *geen* ~ *of VLEK nie*, no flaw or blemish; *van VREEMDE* ~ *te vry*, free of extraneous matter; ~ **ham**, sour ham; ~ **stof**, miasma, virus; ~ (**te**)**loos**, (..**lose**), blameless, spotless, immaculate, stainless, flawless, speckless, unblemished; ~ (**te**)**loosheid**, blamelessness, spotlessness, stainlessness.
smet'terig, (-e), putrid, decomposed; moist, inflamed (wound); ~ *e vleis*, tainted meat; ~ **heid**, putridity, putridness; inflamed condition.
smeul, (ge-), smoulder, glow; ~ **end**, (-e), smouldering; ~ **kole**, anthracite; ~ **stoof**, slow-combustion stove; ~ **vuur**, smudge (fire), smouldering fire.
smid, (-s, **smede**), (black)smith, knight of the hammer.
smid'dae, smid'dags, in the afternoon; of an afternoon; at noon.
smids: ~ **aambeeld**, blacksmith's anvil; ~ **ambag**, smith's trade; ~ **blaasbalk**, forge-bellows; ~ **gereedskap**, smith's tools; ~ **hamer**, blacksmith's hammer; forge-hammer; sledge-hammer; ~ **kole**, forge coal, breeze (coal); ~ **oond**, forge; ~ **tang**, fire-tongs; ~ **wa**, field forge; ~ **werk**, smith's work; ~ **winkel**, smithy, blacksmith's shop, forge.
smit, (-te) = **smid**.
smoel, (-e), mouth, snout, mug (vulgarism); *HOU jou* ~ !, shut up!; ~ *op iets HÊ*, fancy something; have a liking for something; ~ **pleen**, (..**plene**), smoothing-plane.
smoe'sie, (-s), pretext, eyewash, make-believe, excuse.
smok, (s) (-ke), smock; (w) (ge-), smock.
smok'kel, (s) smuggling; (w) (ge-), smuggle, run (liquor); cheat; ~ **aar**, (-s), smuggler, bootlegger; ~ (**a**)**ry**, smuggling; ~ **bende**, gang of smugglers; ~ **goed**, contraband; ~ **handel**, black market, smuggling trade; contraband; ~ **kroeg**, shebeen; ~ **skip**, smuggler (ship); ~ **ware**, contraband (goods).
smok: ~ **steek**, smocking; ~ **werk**, smocking.
smoor, (s); *hoog die* ~ *in*, be in a towering rage; (w) (ge-), suffocate, smother; choke, throttle (car engine); jugulate (med.); hush up (scandal); stifle (conscience); braise (meat); sweat (vegetables in fat); drown (sound); *gesmoorde BIEFSTUK*, braised steak; *in die GEBOORTE* ~, nip in the bud; *ge* ~ *de HAAS*, jugged hare; *ge* ~ *de HOENDER*, sauté of chicken; (bw), exceedingly; with difficulty; *dit het* ~ *GEGAAN*, it was heavy going; *dit* ~ *KRY*, have a very hard time; ~ **buis**, choke tube; ~ **der**, throttle, choke, stifler; ~ **dronk**, dead drunk; as drunk as a lord.
smoor'gewas, smother-crop.
smoor: ~ **heet**, (..**hete**), sultry, stiflingly hot; ~ **hitte**, sweltering heat; ~ **klep**, choke-valve, throttle-valve; ~ **kwaad**, furious, mad with anger.
smoor'lik, very much, exceedingly; ~ *verlief*, head over heels in love, madly in love.
smoor: ~ **pan**, stew-pan; ~ **plaat**, baffle-plate; ~ **pyp**, choke-tube (motor); ~ **skroef**, choke-screw; ~ **spoel**, choking-coil.
smoor'verlief, (-de), love-lorn, head over heels in love.
smoor: ~ **vis**, braised fish; ~ **vleis**, braised meat.
smoor'warm, sultry, suffocatingly hot.
smô'rens, smo'rens, in the (of a) morning.
smous, (s) (-e), hawker, pedlar, itinerant trader; Cheap Jack, cadger, huckster; differ; (w) (ge-), barter, hawk; peddle; huckster; *ERENS* ~, go courting someone; *met GODSDIENS* ~, trade on (take unscrupulous advantage of) a person's religious feelings; ~ **ery**, bargaining; pedlary, hawk-

smout — **snel**

ing; ~**goed**, ~**vraggie**, hawker's ware, mixed merchandise; ~**vrou**, hucksteress; ~**wa**, hawker's wagon; ~**ware**, truck, pedlary; ~**winkel**, hawker's shop; second-hand shop.

smout, grease, fat, lard; ~**drukker**, jobber; job-printer; ~**drukkery**, job-printing business; ~**setter**, display or table(work) compositor; ~**werk**, tabular work, jobbing, job-printing, table-work.

smuk, finery, decoration, ornament; ~**dosie**, vanity box; ~**spieëltjie**, vanity mirror; ~**tassie**, vanity case.

smul, (ge-), feast, banquet, tuck in, junket; ~ *van*, feast on; relish; gloat over; ~**broer**, ~**paap**, epicure, gastronome, gourmand; ~**party**, carousal, feast.

smy'dig, (-e), pliant, supple; ~**heid**, suppleness, pliancy, litheness.

smyt, (ge-), throw, fling, hurl, pitch, cast; hurtle; *met geld* ~, squander money; ~**er**, (-s), thrower, pitcher; ~**erig**, (-e), inclined to fling or hurl.

s'n, 's, of; *HULLE* ~, theirs; *MA* ~, mother's; *PA* ~, father's; *WIE* ~, whose?

snaaks, (-e), droll, funny, queer, strange, quaint, comical; eccentric; amusing, jocose, jocular; odd(ly), odd-looking; *hy probeer hom* ~ *hou*, he tries to be funny (nasty); ~**erig**, (-e), rather funny; queerish; ~**heid**, queerness, comicality, drollness, drollery, quaintness, oddity; jocularity.

snaar, (snare), (s) string, cord; chord; gut (racquet); queer fellow; lover; (mv) whims; *'n gevoelige* ~ *AANRAAK*, touch upon a sore spot; *hy is 'n* ~ *van HAAR*, he is a lover of hers; *'n OU* ~, a queer bird; *die REGTE* ~ *aanraak*, strike the right note; *altyd op dieselfde* ~ *SPEEL*, harp on the same string; *met* ~ *en ST(R)AMBOEL*, on Shanks's pony; *die snare te styf SPAN*, keep the bow bent too long; *iem. is VOL snare*, someone is full of whims; (w) (ge-), string (violin); *ek moet my raket laat* ~, I must have my racquet restrung; ~**gesang**, song accompanied by stringed instruments; ~**instrument**, stringed instrument; ~**werk**, stringing (racquet).

snags, in the (of a) night, during the night.

snak, (ge-), long for, yearn, pine for; gasp (for air), pant; *na ASEM* ~, gasp for breath; ~ *na LUG*, gasp for air; ~ *na die UUR*, long for the hour.

snap, (ge-), understand, comprehend, twig, catch; *die BETEKENIS* ~ *van*, grasp the meaning of; *hy* ~ *DIT*, he grasps it; *hy* ~ *dit GOU*, he is quick on the uptake; *het JY dit ge* ~, got it? do you catch on (twig it)?

snap: ~**haan**, flintlock, musket, firelock, matchlock; ~**per**, (-s), prattler, tattler; snap-tool; ~**perkop**, snap-head (tool).

snaps, (-e), drop, drink, tot, appetiser, nip; *'n* ~ *maak*, take a spot; ~**ie**, (-s), drop, drink, tot, nip; schnap(p)s.

sna'respel, music of stringed instruments, string music.

snar'ig, (-e), quick-tempered, tart, acrimonious.

snars, whit, atom, bit; *hy GEE g'n* ~ *om nie*, he doesn't care a straw; *hy VERSTAAN daar geen* ~ *van nie*, he does not understand one thing about it.

sna'ter, (s) jaw, snout, mug; beak (of bird); *hou jou* ~!, shut up!, hold your jaw!; (w) (ge-), jabber (persons); chatter (birds); ~**bek**, chatterbox.

sna'wel, (-s) beak, bill; rostrum (of flower); ~**agtig**, (-e), rostral, rostriform; ~**vormig**, (-e), beak-shaped.

sne'de, (-s), edge, cutting side (knife), bit (chisel).

sne'dig, (-e), cutting, sharp, vicious, bitter, virulent, malignant; witty, smart, neat (answer), shrewd; ~**heid**, smartness, ready wit, shrewdness, quickness at repartee.

snee, (sneë) edge; caesura (in verse); section (for microscope); bit (in drill); *verguld op* ~, gilt-edged (book); *see* **snede**.

snees'doekie, tissue.

snees'papier, tissue paper; ~**tjie**, tissue (paper).

snees'vis, oarfish.

snees'vraggie, (-s), mixed merchandise, (load of) trade goods.

sneeu, (s) snow; *nat* ~ *sleet*, slush; (w) (ge-), snow;

~**agtig**, (-e), snowy, niveous; ~**baan**, beaten path on snow; ~**bal**, snowball; guelder rose; ~**bank**, snow-drift; ~**berg**, snow-capped mountain; ~**blind**, (-e), snow-blind; ~**blindheid**, snow-blindness; ~**blom**, *Protea cryophila;* ~**bril**, snow-goggles; ~**bui**, fall (shower) of snow; ~**gans**, snow-goose, wav(e)y; ~**grens**, snow-line; ~**hoender**, snow-grouse, ptarmigan; ~**hoop**, snow-drift; ~**jag**, snow-drift; blizzard; ~**klokkie**, (-s), snow-drop; ~**klomp**, heap of snow; ~**laag**, snow-layer; ~**linie**, snow-line; ~**lug**, snowy sky; ~**man**, (-ne), snow man; ~**mens**, snowman, yeti; ~**ploeg**, snow-plough, track-sweeper; ~**pop**, snowman; ~**roos**, snowball (plant); guelder rose; ~**skaats**, (ge-), ski; ~**skoen**, snow-shoe; pattern; ~**skop**, snow-shovel; ~**spoor**, crampon; ~**storm**, snowstorm, blizzard; ~**storting**, snow-slip, avalanche; ~**val**, snow-fall; ~**versiersel**, seven-minute frosting; ~**verskuiwing**, avalanche; ~**vink**, snow-bird; ~**vlaag**, snow-shower; ~**vlokkie**, (-s), snow-flake; ~**water**, snow-water; ~**weer**, snowy weather; ~**werking**, nivation; ~**wit**, snow-white; S~**witjie**, Snowdrop; (Little) Snow White; ~**wolk**, snow-cloud.

smee'werk, carved work.

snek'rat, (-te), fusee (of watch); snail(-wheel).

snel, (w) (ge-), rush, hurry, hasten, career; *iem. te hulp* ~, rush to the assistance of somebody; (b) -[le], fast, rapid, quick, speedy; ~**besteldiens**, express-delivery service; ~**blusser**, (-s), fire-extinguisher; ~**bomwerper**, high speed bomber; ~**boor**, sensitive drill; ~**boormasjien**, sensitive drillingmachine; ~**boot**, speedboat; ~**bouler**, fast bowler; ~**briewediens**, express-letter service; ~**buffet**, snack-bar; ~**diens**, express service; ~**dig**, (-te), epigram; ~**draaistaal**, high-speed steel; ~**duif**, racing-pigeon; ~**droogskoonmaker**, walk-in dry-cleaner; ~**duik**, crash dive; ~**fiets**, racer; ~**gang**, overdrive.

snel'heid, (..hede), velocity, speed (of bullet); rapidity, swiftness; promptness, quickness (of action); momentum; frequency; *MEER* ~ *kry*, gather speed; get an increase in velocity; *die maksimum* ~ *OORSKRY*, exceed the speed-limit; *TEEN (met) 'n* ~ *van*, at a speed of.

snel'heids: ~**beperking**, speed restriction; ~**duiwel**, road-hog; ~**grens**, speed-limit; ~**manie**, speed craze; ~**meter**, chronoscope, speedometer, tachometer; ~**perk**, speed-limit; ~**reëlaar**, speeder, governor (of speed); ~**rekord**, speed-record; ~**rit**, speed-trial; ~**toename**, increase in velocity, acceleration; ~**tocts**, speed-trial; ~**veld**, speed range (aero.).

snel: ~**herstel**, quick (fast) recovery; ~**kafee**, snack-bar; ~**klep**, quick-acting valve; ~**knip**, instantaneous grip; ~**koker**, pressure- (lightning-)cooker; ~**laaler**, (-s), rapid loader; ~**laaigeskut**, quick-firing guns; ~**ler**, (-s), trigger, sprinter; three-quarter (rugby); ~**lerbeuel**, trigger-guard; ~**lermal**, trigger-happy; ~**lerwerking**, triggering; ~**lont**, runner-fuse; ~**losser**, quick-release handle; ~**oorgang**, fly-over (bridge); ~**pad**, expressway, freeway, motorway; ~**perk**, speed-limit; ~**pers**, fast steam-press, fly-press; ~**rat**, overdrive (gear); ~**reg**, summary jurisdiction; ~**rekenaar**, lightning-calculator; ready reckoner; ~**rem**, rapid brake; ~**restourant**, lunch-room; ~**seër**, tongue-twister; ~**seiler**, fast sailer; ~**sement**, quick-hardening cement; ~**skrif**, shorthand, stenography; ~**skriftikster**, shorthand typist; ~**skrywer**, stenographer; ~**span**, flying gang; ~**staal**, high-speed steel; ~**stomer**, ocean greyhound; ~**strik**, speed-trap; ~**trein**, express train, fast train; ~**vaarder**, speedboat; ~**varend**, (-e), fast-sailing; rakish (of ship); ~**verbranding**, instantaneous combustion; ~**verkeer**, high-speed traffic; ~**(verkeers)weg**, freeway, motorway, expressway; ~**vis**, doree, dory; ~**voetig**, (-e), nimble-footed; ~**vrag**, express freight; ~**vries**, quick-freeze.

snel'vuur, quick-fire; rapid fire; ~**geskut**, quick-firing guns; ~**kanon**, quick-firing gun.

snel: ~**vyl**, rough file; ~**wa**, express van, ~**weg**, expressway, speedway; ~**werkend**, (-e), rapid,

speedy, quick-acting (poison); ~**werking**, quick action.
snerp, (ge-), bite, cut; ~**end**, (-e), painful, biting; smarting; piercing (wind); shrill (sound); ~*ende koue*, biting cold.
sners = **snars**.
snert, rubbish, nonsense, rot, trash; ~**aandele**, worthless shares; ~**roman**, trashy novel; ~**saak**, third-rate business.
snesie, (-s), tissue.
sneu'wel, (ge-), be killed, perish, be slain, fall (in battle).
snik, (s) (-ke), sob, gasp, sniffle; *die laaste* ~, the last gasp; (w) (ge-), sob, gasp; ~**heet**, (..**hete**), stifling, suffocatingly hot; ~**kend**, (-e), sobbing; ~**sanger**, crooner; ~ **warm** = **snikheet**.
snip, (-pe), snipe; saucy (perky) girl; *'n* ~ *van 'n meisie*, a sharp-tongued girl, a minx; ~**hond**, cocker spaniel; ~**(pe)jag**, snipe-shooting.
snip'per, (s) (-s), chip, slice, piece, scrap, cutting, snippet, shred; fritter; (w) (ge-), chip, shred, cut into small pieces; ~**ig**, (-e), perky, precocious, forward, sharp-tongued; ~**jag**, paper-chase, hare-and-hounds; ~**konfyt**, shredded jam; ~**mandjie**, waste-paper basket; ~**tjie**, (-s), shred, scrap; ~**toestel**, slicer; ~**uurtjie**, spare hour, leisure hour; ~**vleis**, shredded meat, chipped meat.
snip'pie, (-s), minx, perky girl (person).
snip'vis, sea snipe; trumpet-fish.
snit, (-te), cut, fit; edge (knife); *die laaste (nuutste)* ~, the latest fashion (cut).
snob, (-s), snob; ~**berig**, (-e), snobbish; ~**bery**, ~**is'me**, snobbery, snobbishness; *cf.* **ploert**.
snoef, (ge-), brag, boast, bluster; ~**taal**, boastful language.
snoei, (ge-), prune (trees), clip, trim (hedge); lop, cut (branches), economize; ~**er**, (-s), pruner, clipper; parer; ~**ery**, pruning; ~**ing**, pruning, cutting; ~**kuns**, art of pruning, topiary art; ~**kunstenaar**, topiarist; ~**mes**, pruning-knife, hedge-knife; hedge-bill; ~**saag**, pruning-saw; ~**sel**, (-s), clipping, lopping; ~**skêr**, garden-shears, sécateur, hedge-clipper; ~**tyd**, pruning-season; ~**werk**, pruning, cutting.
snoek, sea-pike; barracuda; snoek *(Thyrsites atun);* ~**boot**, snoeker, snoek boat.
snoe'ker, snooker (game); ~**toernooi**, snooker competition.
snoek: ~**galjoen**, parrot-fish; ~**kop**, snoek's head; dished face; ~**mootjie**, slice of salted snoek; ~**vangs**, snoek-fishing; snoek catch.
snoep, (w) (ge-), eat dainties secretly; sneak; (b) greedy, miserly; ~**wees**, not willing to share; ~**doos**, tuck box; ~**er**, (-s), greedy person; sweet tooth; ~**erig**, (-e), greedy; fond of eating sweets; ~**ery**, (-e), sweets, dainties; thieving of dainties; ~**gereg**, savoury course; hors d'oeuvres; snacks; ~**goed**, dainties, sweets; ~**happie**, cocktail snack; ~**heid**, fondness for dainty foods; greediness; ~**lus**, fondness for sweets; ~**lustig**, (-e), fond of sweets; ~**stokkie**, cocktail-stick; ~**winkeltjie**, tuck-shop.
snoer, (s) (-e), string, chaplet (beads); line (fish); cordon; cord; flex; file, lace; *'n* ~ *pêrels*, a string (rope, band) of pearls; (w) (ge-), tie, string, file; close (mouth); ~**steun**, flex support; ~**wurm**, ribbon-worm, nemertean.
snoes'haan, queer fellow, odd fish; windbag, braggart; dandy, exquisite.
snoe'sig, (-e), nice, pretty, ducky, sweet, dainty.
snoet, (-e), snout (of pig); muzzle (of dog); mug (contemptuously for humans); face; *'n aardige* ~*jie*, a pretty face; ~**walvis**, beaked whale.
snoe'wend, (-e), blustering.
snoe'wer, (-s), boaster, braggart; ~**y**, boasting, bragging, bravado.
snol, (ong.), (-le), harlot, tart.
snood, (**snode**), bad, evil, base (plans); heinous (crime); *'n snode misdaad*, a heinous crime; ~**aard**, (-s), miscreant, wretch, villain; ~**heid**, baseness, meanness; atrocity; felony; foulness.
snor¹, (s) (-re), moustache.

snor², (w) (ge-), whizz (bullet); whir (propeller); drone (dynamo); purr.
snor: ~**baard**, moustache; whiskers; ~**koppie**, moustache-cup.
snork, (s) (-e), snore (human); snort (horse); (w) (ge-), snore; snort.
snor'kel, (-s), snort, schnorkel (submarine).
snork: ~**er**, (-s), snorer; braggart; ~**ery**, snoring; bragging.
snor'retjie, (-s), tooth-brush moustache.
snot, mucus, snot; ~**blom**, sundew *(Drosera spp.);* ~**koker**, snotty nose (vulgarism); ~**neus**, snotty nose; brat; little horror; ~**psalm**: *die* ~ *psalm aanhef*, start blubbering; ~**siekte**, malignant catarrhal fever.
snot'ter, (ge-), snivel, blubber; ~**bel**, *Polygonum spp.;* ~**ig**, (-e), snotty, snivelly, having a running nose.
snot: ~**vis**, hagfish *(Heptatretus);* ~**wortel**, *Mesembrianthemum pugioniforme*.
snou, (s) (-e), snarl; rebuke; (w) (ge-), snarl; snap; rebuke; ~**erig**, (-e), snarling, unkind, fond of scolding; ~**erigheid**, unkindness, carping, captiousness, grumpiness.
snuf, smell, inkling, wind; *'n* ~ *in die neus kry*, get wind of something.
snuf'fel, (ge-), sniff, nose, sniffle, smell (out), dig (out), ferret (out), pry, rummage; search; investigate; muzzle; grub; ~ *AAN*, sniff at, rummage in; ~ *IN*, pry in(to); ~**aar**, (-s), ferreter, Paul Pry; prier; ~**graag**, ferreter, Paul Pry.
snuf'fie, (-s), whiff, smell; *die nuutste* ~, the latest novelty.
snug'ger, bright, shrewd, smart, sharp; ~**heid**, brightness, cleverness, shrewdness.
snuif, (s) (**snuiwe**), snuff; ~ *in iem. se oë blaas*, do someone a shot in the eye; (w) (ge-), take snuff; sniff, inhale; snort (horse); ~**doos**, mull, snuff-box; ~**ie**, (-s), pinch of snuff; ~**klep**, snifting valve; ~**knippie**: *in 'n* ~*knippie*, in a jiffy; ~**kraan**, petcock; ~**meul(e)**, snuff-mill; ~**siekte**, snuffles; ~**tabak**, snuff-tobacco.
snuis'tery, (-e), trinket, toy, bric-a-brac, knick-knack, gewgaw, kickshaw, frippery, charm, bauble, curio, falderal; ~**e**, fancy goods, fancy articles, pretty-pretties; gewgaws; ~**winkel**, trinket-shop.
snuit, (s) (-e), snout (pig); nose, muzzle (dog); trunk (elephant); proboscis (insect); (w) (ge-), blow (the nose); trim, snuff (candle); ~**er**, (-s), snuffer; little fellow, youngster, mere chit, puppy (fig.); kiddy, fledgeling, blood brat, chicken, johnny, coxcomb; jockey; pair of snuffers; ~**erbakkie**, snuffer-tray; ~**kewer**, snout-beetle; ~**papier**, tissue; ~**sels**, candle-snuff.
snui'we, (ge-), take snuff; snort, sniff; ~**r**, (-s), snuff-taker; snort, schnorkel.
sny, (s) (-e), slice; cut; incision, gash; emasculation; (w) (ge-), cut, slice (ham); castrate, geld, emasculate, caponize (cock); gash; operate on; carve; shred; engrave; sprint; finesse (at cards); *met (teen) die DRAAD* ~, cut along (against) the grain; *die LYNE* ~ *mekaar*, the lines intersect; *in REPIES* ~, shred; *SPOOR* ~, track, follow the track (spoor); *dit* ~ *na TWEE kante*, it cuts both ways; ~**baar**, (..**bare**), sectile; ready for cutting; ~**bank**, chopping-bench; ~**beet**, spinach-beet; ~**beitel**, knife-tool (lathe); cutter (blacksmith); cutting chisel; ~**blok**, die; ~**blokontwerp**, die design; ~**blom**, cut flower; ~**boontjie**, French bean, haricot, case-knife bean; kidney-bean; ~**brander**, (-s), fusing burner; ~**dend**, (-e), biting, stinging (reply); cutting, sharp; sectorial; ~**diamant**, glass diamond.
sny'ding¹, (-e), cutting instrument, cutter.
sny'ding², (-e, -s), cutting, incision; intersection (of lines); caesura (in poetry); ~**shoek**, angle of intersection.
sny: ~**dokter**, surgeon; ~**er**, (-s), tailor; cutter; carver; mower.
sny'ers: ~**ambag**, tailoring; ~**bene**, bandy legs; ~**gaas**, tailor's canvas; ~**kryt**, tailor's chalk; ~**naat**, tailored seam; ~**pak**, tailor-made suit; ~**tafel**, tailor's board; ~**werk**, tailoring; ~**winkel**, tailor's shop.

sny'ervoël, tailor-bird.

sny: ~ **gereedskap**, edged tools; ~ **gras**, sedge; ~ **hoek**, cutting angle (tools); ~ **hou**, cut (in games); ~ **kamer**, dissecting-room; cutting-room (tailor); operating-theatre; ~ **kant**, cutting edge (tools); knife-edge; arris (on wood); *die* ~ *kant invoeg*, tip tools; ~ **kruishout**, cutting-gauge; ~ **kuns**, surgery; ~ **kussing**, screw-die; ~ **lyn**, secant, intersecting line; ~ **masjien**, reaper, mower; cutting machine; harvester; plough (printing); ~ **mes**, addice, drawknife; spoke-shave; ~ **model**, cut-out; ~ **moer**, die(-nut); ~ **plaat**, screw-plate; die-plate; ~ **plank**, chopping-board; ~ **punt**, point of intersection; check-point; ~ **sel**, (-s), off-cut, cut-off piece; ~ **selkonfyt**, sliced jam; ~ **sels**, ~ **seltjies**, flakes; doughcuttings, home-made noodles; ~ **slag**, finesse; ~ **stuk**, bit (of drill); ~ **tafel**, operating-table; dissecting-table; ~ **tand**, incisor, foretooth, chiseltooth; nipper (of horse); ~ **tang**, cutting-tongs; ~ **tap**, tap; ~ **tjie**, (-s), collop (of meat); small slice, cut; notch; ~ **tuig**, stocks and dies; ~ **vlak**, cutting plane; ~ **werk**, carving, graving; fretwork; carved work; ~ **werktuig**, edged tool; edger; ~ **wiel**, milling-cutter; ~ **wond**, incised wound; ~ **wurm**, cutworm; ~ **wydte**, swath.

so, (bw), so, thus, in this way, like this; (tw.) enough! *AG* ~ *?*, oh, really?; ~ *ARM as hy is*, poor as he is; ~ *BESKOU*, looked at in this manner; looked at this way; *ek DINK* ~ *by myself*, I thought to myself; ~ *nie, dan GAAN jy*, if not, then you go; *GOED* ~ *!*, well done!, serves you right!; ~ *HEER* ~ *kneg*, like master, like man; *HOE* ~ *?*, how is that (possible)?; ~ *IETS*, some such thing; *dit IS* ~, it is like this; *LAAT dit* ~, leave the matter there; leave it as it is; ~ *is die LEWE*, such is life; ~ *NOU*, that will do!; that's enough; ~ *PAS*, only just, recently; *op* ~ *en* ~ *'n PLEK*, at such and such a place; ~ *te SÊ*, practically; ~ *is SEUNS nou maar*, boys will be boys; ~ *groot SOOS sy broer*, as tall as his brother; *dit SY* ~, so be it; *VAT* ~ *!*, shake!; ~ *VER as sy loop, mors sy*, all along the way she is making a mess; ~ *'n VERMOEDE*, I have a shrewd suspicion; ~ *'n VOORGEVOEL*, a kind of presentiment; ~, *en WAAR is Jan?*, and where is John?; ~ *WAT van vloek het ek nog nooit gehoor nie*, such terrible cursing I have never heard before; *WEES* ~ *goed om*, be so kind as to; (vgw) if; ~ *GOD wil*, God willing; ~ *NIE*, if not.

so'as = **soos**.

so'ber, (|-e|; -der, -ste), sober, temperate, frugal; ~ **heid**, sobriety, temperance, frugality.

So'crates = **Sokrates**.

so'da, soda; ~ **arseniet**, arsenite of soda; ~ **-as**, sodaash; ~ **fabriek**, soda-works.

so'danig, (-e), such, such like, in such a way, so as; *AS* ~, as such, in that capacity; *op* ~ *e DATUM as*, on such date as; *die TOESTAND is* ~ *dat*, the position is such that; ~ **e**, (-s), such a person; *die* ~ *es*, such people.

so'dapomp, soda fountain.

so'dat, so that, in order that.

so'dawater, soda-water.

so'diak, zodiac; ~ **aal'**, (..**kale**), zodiacal; ~ *ale lig*, zodiacal light.

so'dium, sodium; ~ **nitraat**, nitrate of soda.

so'doende, thus, in that manner, and so, consequently.

sodomie', sodomy.

sodomiet', (-e), sodomite, bugger; ~ **erskraap**, catamite.

so'domsappel, Sodom apple.

sodra', as soon as, the moment that, once.

soe!, ugh! brr! (referring to heat).

soe'bat, (ge-), beg, entreat, coax, implore, plead; ~ *om*, beg for; ~ **ry**, (ge-), hitch-hike; ~ **tery**, entreating, pleading, begging.

soe'broekie, (-s), hot pants.

Soedan', S(o)udan.

soedan'gras, S(o)udan grass *(Sorghum sudanense)*.

Soedannees', (..**nese**), S(o)udanese.

soef, (ge-), rustle (wind), sough.

so-ef'fe = **so-ewe**.

soek, (s); *op* ~ *NA*, in search of; ~ *RAAK*, be mislaid; be missing; *op* ~ *WEES*, be lost; (w), (ge-), seek (help); look for (trouble); hunt for, search; prospect (for minerals); *daar iets AGTER* ~, look for an ulterior motive; *dit het ek nie AGTER hom gesoek nie*, I did not expect that from him; *die BAAS* ~ *jou*, the master wants you; *BAIE gesog*, very much in demand; *GAAN* ~, go in search of; *ek het my GEK ge* ~, I searched like mad; ~ *my HOED*, find my hat; *HOMSELF* ~, seek one's own advantage; *jy kan LANK* ~ *voor jy iets beters kry*, you will have to go a long way to find something better; *jy* ~ *MY, nè?* you are asking for trouble! ~ *NA*, look (search) for; *dis NET wat ons* ~, this is the very thing we are looking for; *ORAL(S)* ~, hunt high and low; *RUSIE, SKOOR* ~, look for trouble; *voorbeelde is nie VER te* ~ *nie*, examples are not far to seek; *ek* ~ *nie wat ek nie VERLOOR het nie*, I do not poke my nose into other people's business; I am not just wandering around aimlessly; *iets* ~ *wat jy VERLOOR het*, potter about; ~ *en jy sal VIND*, seek and ye shall find; *WERK* ~, look for work; *WOORDE* ~, grope for words; (bw) lost; ~ **er**, (-s), seeker; viewfinder (camera); ~ **ertjie**, (-s), little seeker; ~ **ertjies**, smalls; *persoonlike* ~ *ertjies*, agony column; ~ **ery**, (-e), search; ~ **geld**, search-fee; ~ **geselskap**, searchparty; ~ **glas**, view-finder; ~ **lamp**, inspection-lamp; ~ **lig**, searchlight; spotlight; projector, *in die* ~ *lig KOM*, come under the searchlight; *die* ~ *lig WERP op*, throw the searchlight on; ~ **prentjie**, puzzle-picture; ~ **sloot**, prospect trench; ~ **tog**, search; *'n* ~ *tog op tou sit na*, begin a search for; ~ **yster**, probing-bar.

soel¹, (b) balmy, mild; sultry.

soel², (b) dark-skinned, sallow.

soel'heid'¹, balminess.

soel'heid², sallowness.

soel'te, balminess; sultriness.

soem'pie, (-s), blue-buck.

soen¹, (b) atonement, expiation; peace.

soen², (s) (-e), kiss; (w) (ge-), kiss, osculate; *elke man* ~ *sy vrou op sy eie manier*, each man to his own taste; ~ **altaar**, altar of atonement; ~ **bloed**, blood of atonement, redeeming blood.

Soen'daeilande, Sunda Islands.

Soendanees', (..**nese**), Sundanese.

soen'dood, redeeming death, death of atonement.

soen: ~ **er**, (-s), kisser; ~ **erig**, (-e), given to kissing; ~ **ery**, kissing.

soen'geld, blood-money, ransom.

soen'groet, (ge-), greet (say good-bye) with a kiss.

soen'offer, atonement, expiatory offering, sin-offering; peace-offering.

soen'vas, (-te), kiss-proof.

so'-en-so, so-and-so.

soep, soup; *see* **sop**.

soepee', (-s), supper; ~ **r'**, (ge-), take (have) supper, sup.

soe'pel, supple, pliable, pliant, flexible, lithe; ~ **heid**, suppleness.

soe'perig, wishy-washy, watery, sloppy.

soes, (s) drowsiness; (w) (ge-), doze, drowse, be woolgathering.

soe'serig, (-e), drowsy, dreamy; ~ **heid**, drowsiness.

soe'sie, (-s), cream puff.

soe'soe, (-s), sou-sou, chou-chou, chayote.

soet, sweet (to taste); dulcet (tones); well-behaved, good (child); fresh (water); *'n* ~ *KIND*, a good (well-behaved) child; *die* ~ *en SUUR van die lewe*, the ups and downs of life; the rough and the smooth; ~ *WATER*, fresh water; ~ **agtig**, (-e), sweetish; ~ **doring**, Karoo thorntree *(Acacia karroo)*; ~ **ema'ling**, tuberose; ~ **erig**, (-e), sweetish; namby-pamby; ~ **erigheid**, sweetishness; (weak) sentimentality; ~ **gebak**, pastry, confectionery; ~ **gras**, sweet grass *(Chloris virgata, Panicum laevifolium)*; ~ **happies**, friandises; ~ **heid**, sweetness; ~ **hout**, (stick of) liquorice; ~ **houtbossie**, sweet root bush *(Rafnia amplexicaulis)*; ~ **igheid**, sweet-

ness; sweets; ~**jies**, gently, softly, unnoticed, noiselessly; ~**klinkend, (-e)**, euphonic, euphonious.
soet'koek, sweet cake; *more BAK ons* ~, I've heard it all before; *seuns soos* ~*ies GROOTMAAK*, not to let one's sons dirty their hands; *dit GAAN soos* ~, it sells like hot cakes; *alles vir* ~ *OPEET*, take everything for gospel truth; *dit VERKOOP soos* ~, it sells like hot cakes.
soet: ~ **kop**, ink-plant; ~ **land**: ~ *land sit*, go courting; ~ **lemoen**, orange; ~ **lief**, sweetheart; ~ **lik, (-e)**, mawkish, cloying, namby-pamby; ~ **luidend, (-e)**, melodious; ~ **maakmiddel**, sweetener; ~ **melk**, fresh milk; ~ **melkkaas**, fresh-milk cheese; ~ **noorsdoring**, *Euphorbia coerulescens*; ~ **olie**, salad oil; sweet oil; ~ **peul**, honey-locust *(Gleditsia triacanthos)*; ~ **riet**, sugar-cane; ~ **rissie**, bell-pepper, green pepper *(Capsicum annuum)*; ~ **roombotter**, sweet butter.
soetsap'pig, (-e), insipid, goody-goody, namby-pamby, meek, mealy-mouthed, honeyed; ~ **heid**, insipidity, meekness, wish-wash.
soet'skaaf, smoothing plane.
soet: ~ **skeel**, slightly squint-eyed; ~ **sopie**, liqueur.
soet'suur, bitter-sweet; sour-sweet; ~ **deeg**, salt-rising yeast.
soet'vleis, sweetbread.
soetvloei'end, (-e), melodious, mellifluous, fluent; ~ **heid**, fluency, melodiousness, mellifluence.
soet'vyl, smooth file.
soet'water, fresh water; ~ **vis**, freshwater fish.
soet'wolfsboontjie, yellow lupin.
so-e'we, just now, a moment ago.
soewenier', (-s), souvenir, keepsake, remembrance; ~ **jagter**, souvenir hunter; ~ **winkel**, souvenir shop.
soewerein', (s) (-e), sovereign; (b) (-e), sovereign, supreme; ~ **iteit'**, sovereignty.
so'fa, (-s), sofa, coach.
soffiet', (-e), soffit.
sofis', (-te), sophist; ~ **me**, sophism; ~ **tery**, sophistry; ~ **ties, (-e)**, sophistic(al); ~ **tika'sie**, sophistication; falsifying (of metals).
sog¹, (s) (sôe, -ge), sow.
sog², (s) wake of a ship; *in iem. se* ~ *vaar*, follow in someone's wake.
so'genaamd, (b) (-e), so-called, bogus, pretended, pseudo=, would-be; (bw) in name, ostensibly; *'n* ~ *e OPSTEL*, an apology for an essay; *hy het VERTREK*, ~ *om dit te gaan soek*, he departed on the pretext of searching for it.
so'genoemde, (b) so called.
sog'gens, in the (of a) morning.
so'ging, lactation.
sog'water, wake (of a ship).
so'heen, there, thither; ~ **toe**, thither, that way, there.
soiree', (-s), evening party, soirée.
so'ja: ~ **boontjie**, soy(a)-bean, oil-bean; ~ **brood**, soy(a) bread; ~ **olie**, bean-oil, soya oil; ~ **sous**, soya sauce.
sok, (-ke), sock; socket, sleeve (mech.); ~ **beitel**, socket chisel; ~ **deel**, socket portion; ~ **gat**, plug outlet.
sok'ker, association football, soccer; ~ **spel**, association (soccer) game; ~ **voetbal**, association (soccer) football.
sok'kie, (-s), sock; ~ **houer**, ~ **ophouer, (-s)**, suspender(s).
sok'ophouer, (-s), suspender(s).
sok'pyp, socket pipe.
So'krates, Socrates.
Sokra'ties, (-e), Socratic.
sok'sleutel, box spanner.
sol, sol (music).
so'la, (-s) = solawissel.
so'langs, (along) this way; that way.
solanien', solani'ne, solanine.
solank', as long as, while, for the time being, meanwhile; *ek sal* ~ *GAAN*, I shall go meanwhile; ~ *ek LEEF*, as long as I live.
sola'ri: ~ **graaf**, (..grawe), solarigraph; ~ **meter**, solarimeter, (-s); ~ **sa'sie**, solarization; ~ **seer, (ge-)**, solarize.
sola'rium, (..ria, -s), solarium.
so'lawissel, sole bill of exchange, sola.

soldaat', (..date), soldier, dragoon, campaigner, man-at-arms; torch-lily; red-hot poker; ~ *jie SPEEL*, play (at) soldiers; ~ *WORD*, turn soldier, enlist; ~ **skoen**, ammunition boot; ~ **skrywer**, military clerk.
solda'te: ~ **beroep**, soldiering; ~ **brood**, ammunition bread; ~ **kind**, soldier's child; ~ **lewe**, soldier's life; ~ **lied**, soldiers' song; ~ **nommer**, regimental number; ~ **regering**, stratocracy; ~ **rok**: *die* ~ *rok uittrek*, return to civvy street; ~ **ry**, soldiering; ~ **kamp**, military camp; ~ **sak**, kitbag.
soldatesk', (-e), (ong.), soldierly.
solda'te: ~ **stand**, military profession; ~ **uniform**, military uniform; ~ **volk**, soldiery, soldiers.
soldeer', (ge-), solder; ~ **bout**, soldering-iron; ~ **brander**, bellows-blowpipe; ~ **der, (-s)**, solderer, plumber; ~ **lamp**, soldering-lamp, blowlamp; brazing-lamp; ceiling-lamp; ~ **las**, soldered joint; ~ **lood**, lead solder; ~ **roet**, smudge; ~ **sel**, solder, soldering; ~ **suur**, killed spirits; ~ **tang**, soldering-tongs; ~ **tin**, tin solder; ~ **toestel**, soldering apparatus; ~ **vlam**, blow-flame; ~ **vuur**, pot-fire; ~ **werk**, soldering work, plumbing.
sol'der, (-s), ceiling; garret, (cock-)loft; *op* ~, in the loft; ~ **balk**, loft beam; ~ **bewoner**, garreteer; ~ **deur**, loft-door; ~ **ing**, ceiling; ~ **kamertjie**, attic, garret; ~ **leer**, loft-ladder; ~ **lig**, skylight; ~ **luik**, trapdoor; ~ **raam**, loft-window, dormer-window; ~ **rib**, ceiling-joist; ~ **styl**, ashlar; ~ **trap**, loftstairs, garret staircase; ~ **venster**, garret (loft-) window, attic window; ~ **verdieping**, half-storey; ~ **vloer**, loft-floor.
soldy', (soldier's) pay, wages.
solemneel', (..nele), solemn, serious, devout, formal.
solenoïde, (-s), solenoid.
solesis'me, (-s), solecism.
sol'fa: ~ **metode**, ~ **musiek**, tonic solfa; ~ **skrif**, tonic-solfa notation.
solfata'ra, solfatara.
solfè'ge, solfeggio.
solidariseer', (ge-), solidify; consolidate.
solidariteit', solidarity.
solidariteits'gevoel, feeling of solidarity.
solidariteit'staking, sympathetic strike.
solidêr', (-e), solidary; jointly and severally.
soliditeit', solidity (of matter); respectability (of character); solvency (of firm).
solied', (-e), solid, reliable; gilt-edged; bona fide; solvent; reputable, well-established; *'n* ~ *e firma*, a substantial firm; *see* **soliditeit**.
solipsis', (-te), solipsist; ~ **me**, solipsism.
solis', (-te), soloist, solo vocalist; ~ **te, (-s)**, female soloist.
solitêr, solitaire.
sollisitant', (-e), candidate, applicant.
sollisita'sie, application.
sollisiteer', (ge-), apply; ~ *om 'n betrekking*, apply for a post.
so'lo, (-'s), solo; ~ **sang**, solo singing; vocal solo; ~ **sanger**, soloist; ~ **spel**, solo performance; ~ **vlug**, solo flight.
sol'sleutel, treble clef, G clef.
solsti'tium, (ong.), solstice.
solu'sie, (-s), solution.
solven'sie, solvency.
solvent', (-e), solvent; ~ **skap**, solvency.
som, (-me), sum, total; count, amount; problem; *hy is GOED in* ~ *me*, he is good at sums; *'n GROOT* ~ *geld*, a large sum of money; *VIR die* ~ *van R50*, for the sum of R50.
so'ma¹, (-s, -ta), soma, body.
so'ma², soma (Indian plant).
so'maar = **sommer**.
so'maar(so) = **sommer(so)**.
Soma'li, (-'s), Somali; ~ **ër, (-s)**, Somali; ~ **es, (-e)**, Somali.
Soma'liland, Somaliland, Somalia.
soma'ties, (-e), somatic.
somatologie', somatology.
somato'se, somatose.
som'ber, sombre, gloomy, melancholy, dreary, dull,

sombrero / **sonder**

funereal, cheerless; ~**heid**, gloom, gloominess, dreariness, melancholy; ~**te**, gloom, melancholy.
sombre′ro, (-'s), sombrero.
so′mer, (-s), summer; *die* ~ *DEURBRING*, spend the summer, aestivate; *hy is in die* ~ *GEBORE*, he is hot-tempered; *IN die* ~, in (during) summer; *in die* ~ *v.d. LEWE*, in the prime of his life; ~**aand**, summer evening; ~**aster**, China aster; ~**bed**, summer level (of river); ~**besie**, Christmas beetle, cicada; ~**blom**, summer flower; ~**broek**, summer trousers; ~**dag**, summer's day; ~**diens**, summer service; ~**drag**, summer wear; ~**gewas**, (-se), summer growth; ~**goed**, summer clothes; ~**hitte**, summer heat; ~**hoed**, summer hat; ~**huis(ie)**, alcove, arbour, bower, summer-house; ~**jas**, (-se), covert coat; ~**jurk(ie)**, summer frock; ~**kleed**, summer dress; summer plumage; ~**klere**, summer attire (wear); ~**koelte**, summer breeze; ~**kwartaal**, summer term; ~**lug**, summer air; ~**maand**, summer month; ~**middag**, summer afternoon; ~**môre**, ~**oggend**, summer morning; ~**nag**, summer night; ~**onderklere**, summer underwear; ~**opruiming**, summer clearance (sale); ~**pak**, summer suit; ~**paleis**, summer palace; ~**rok**, summer dress; ~**s**, (-e), summer(y); ~*se weer*, summery weather; ~**seisoen**, summer season; ~**slaap**, summer sleep, aestivation; ~**snoei**, summer pruning; ~**son**, summer sun; ~**sonstilstand**, summer solstice; ~**sproet**, summer freckle; heat-spot; ~**stof**, summer materials (wear); ~**tabberd**, summer frock (dress); ~**tyd**, summer time; ~**uitverkoping**, summer sale(s); ~**vakansie**, summer holiday(s), ~**verblyf**, summer residence; ~**vrugte**, summer fruit(s); deciduous fruit; ~**warmte**, summer heat; ~**weer**, summer weather.
somiet′, (-e), somite.
som′ma, (ong.), (-s), sum total, total.
somma′sie, (-s), summons, writ.
sommeer′, (ge-), summon(s); call up; notify.
som′mer, just, for no reason; at a glance; immediately, straight off, merely, without further ado; *hoekom dan? AG* ~, why then? oh, just because! *hy kry ALLES* ~ *reg*, he manages everything without any difficulty; ~ *BAIE*, quite a number; ~ *so BLOU van die koue*, absolutely blue with cold; *ek DOEN dit maar* ~, I do it for no particular reason; *ek laat my nie* ~ *FOP nie*, I am not to be fooled so easily; ~ *HUIL*, cry for no reason; *ek KAN dit nie* ~ *sê nie*, I can't say off-hand; *hy is nie* ~ *so 'n KÊREL nie*, he is not just an ordinary fellow; he rather fancies himself; *hy is* ~ *MAN*, he is a real brick; *sy is* ~ *'n lekker NOOI*, she is a real good sport; ~ *NABY*, quite near; *dis* ~ *ONSIN*, it is just nonsense; *dis nie* ~ *se PERDE nie*, these are not ordinary horses; ~ *het geen REDE nie*, Y is a crooked letter and you can't make it straight, "because" is a woman's reason; *jy SÊ* ~ *so*, you're just saying that; *ek het* ~ *aan die SLAAP geraak*, I fell asleep immediately; *VAT* ~ *een*, just take any one at random.
som′merso, in a way, anyhow, after a fashion, simply, without further ado; *jy sal my nie* ~ *BETRAP nie*, you won't catch me so easily; *hy het al sy BOEKE* ~ *laat lê*, he left all his books lying about; *hy BOER* ~, he farms after a fashion; *LAAT dit* ~, just leave it as it is; *hy WIP* ~ *v.d. skrik*, he got such a fright that he jumped up, he got the fright of his life.
som′metjie, (-s), small sum; *dit is 'n mooi (aardige)* ~, it makes a tidy little sum.
som′mige, some; ~ *SEUNS vorder mooi*, some boys are making good progress; ~ *STEM saam*, some agree.
somnambu′le, (-s), somnambulist.
somnambulis′me somnambulism.
soms, **som′tyds**, sometimes, at times, now and then, occasionally; *hy gaan* ~ *KERK toe*, now and then he attends church; *'n mens kan nie RAAI wat* ~ *nog kan gebeur nie*, one cannot guess what may perhaps occur.
som′wyle, (vero.) verhewe; sometimes.
son, (-ne), sun; *die opkomende* ~ *AANBID*, worship the rising sun; *laat die* ~ *nie ondergaan oor jou BOOSHEID nie*, let not the sun go down upon your wrath; *in die* ~ *GEDROOG*, sun-dried; *die* ~ *KOM op (gaan onder)*, the sun rises (sets); *sy* ~ *het ONDERGEGAAN terwyl dit nog dag was*, his sun set while it was still day; *die OPGAANDE* ~, the rising sun; *in iem. se* ~ *STAAN*, be a nuisance to somebody; stand in someone's light; *in jou eie* ~ *STAAN*, stand in your own light; *die* ~ *STAAN stil*, the sun beats down; *die* ~ *TREK water*, the sun is declining; it is going to rain; *hy kan nie sien dat die* ~ *in 'n ander se WATER skyn nie*, there is nothing that he does not begrudge another; *hy is nie WERD dat die* ~ *op hom skyn nie*, he is beneath contempt; *as die* ~ *aan die WESTE is*, *is die luiaard op sy beste*, the sluggard is at his best when the sun sinks in the west; ~**aanbidder**, sun-worshipper; ~**aanbidding**, sun-worship.
so′nar, asdic, sonar.
sona′te, (-s), sonata.
sonati′ne, (-s), sonatina.
son: ~**baan**, ecliptic; ~**bad**, (..**baaie**), sun-bath; insolation; ~**badkamer**, solarium; ~**behandeling**, heliotherapy; ~**beligting**, solarisation; ~**besie**, (-s), cricket, cicada; ~**beskrywing**, heliography; ~**bestraling**, insolation; ~**blinding**, sun-blind, jalousie; ~**brand**, sunburn; ~**bril**, sun-goggles; ~**bruin**, sun-tanned; ~**bruinolie**, sun-tan oil.
son′daar, (-s, ..**dare**), sinner, offender; *'n verstokte* ~, a hardened sinner.
son′daarsbankie, penitents' form, stool of repentance; *op die* ~ *plek neem*, sit on the stool of repentance.
Son′dae, on Sundays; ~ *gaan ons kerk toe*, on Sundays we go to church.
Son′dag, Sunday; the Lord's Day; *dis nie ALDAG (elke dag)* ~ *nie*, Christmas comes but once a year; everyday is not a holiday; ~ *oor agt DAE*, next Sunday week; ~ *is langer as MAANDAG*, her petticoat (slip) is showing; *VERLEDE* ~, last Sunday; ~**aand**, Sunday night (evening); ~**blad**, Sunday paper; ~**diens**, Sunday service; ~**nag**, Sunday night.
Son′dags, (b) (-e), Sunday; ~ *(..dae) gaan ons KERK toe*, on Sunday we go to church; *in* ~ *e KLERE*, in his Sunday best; ~**gesig**, sanctimonious mien; ~**heiliging**, Sunday observance; ~**kind**, Sunday's child; one born with a silver spoon in his mouth; ~**klere**, Sunday clothes; Sunday best.
Son′dagskool, Sunday-school; ~**onderwyser**, Sunday-school teacher; ~**onderwyseres**, female Sunday-school teacher.
Son′dags: ~**pak**, Sunday suit; ~**publiek**, Sunday public; ~**rus**, sabbath rest, observance of the sabbath; ~**viering**, sabbath observance; ~**weer**, beautiful weather; ~**wet**, Sunday Closing Act, Sunday Observance Act.
son′dak, awning, sun roof.
sondares′, (-se), sinner (woman).
son′de[1], (-s), sin, trespass; evil; trouble; peccancy; *iem.* ~ *AANDOEN*, cause someone much trouble; be a nuisance to someone; *vir sy* ~ *BOET*, atone for his sin(s); ~ *DOEN*, commit sin; *dis* ~ *van so 'n mooi GEBOU*, it is a pity about such a beautiful building; *dis* ~ *en JAMMER*, it is a great pity; ~ *SOEK*, look for trouble; *'n* ~ *TEEN die Heilige Gees*, a sin against the Holy Ghost; *VERGEEFLIKE* ~, venial offence, peccadillo.
son′de[2], (s) probe, explorer (med.); sonde.
son′debok, scapegoat (lit. & fig.), whipping-boy; *die* ~ *wees*, be the scapegoat.
sondeer′, (ge-), probe, sound, plumb; ~**naald**, searcher; ~**yster**, probe, sound.
son′dek, sun-deck.
son′de: ~**las**, burden of sins; ~**loos**, (..**lose**), sinless; ~**loosheid**, sinlessness; ~**lys**, list of offences.
son′der, without; ~ *BELANGSTELLING*, devoid of interest; ~ *DATUM*, undated; ~ *sy HULP*, but for his help; without his assistance; ~ *iets KLAARKOM*, do without something; ~ *MEDELYE*, without pity; ~ *MEER*, merely, without more ado; at will; ~ *REGSKENDING*, without prejudice

(law); ~ *TUISTE*, of no fixed abode; ~ *VERHAAL*, without recourse (law); ~ *twyfel WAAR*, no doubt true; ~ *WERK*, out of work, unemployed; ~**baar**, (..**bare**), strange, queer, singular; ~**baarheid**, singularity, strangeness, queerness.
son'deregister, register (list) of sins.
sonde'ring, probing, plumbing, sounding.
son'derling, (s) (**-e**), eccentric (person), crank; (b) (**-e**), singular, eccentric, odd, peculiar, quaint, queer, curious; ~ **heid**, singularity, peculiarity, queerness, oddity, eccentricity, curiosity.
son'de: ~ **skuld**, burden of sins; ~**soeker**, (**-s**), vexatious person, trouble-seeker; ~ **tjie**, (**-s**), peccadillo; ~**val**, fall of man, the Fall; ~**vergewing**, remission of sins.
son'diens, sun-worship.
son'dig, (w) (**ge-**), trespass, sin, offend against; *onwetend* ~ *nie*, who sins unwittingly sins not at all; (b) (**-e**), sinful, evil; ~**heid**, sinfulness.
son: ~**doek**, havelock; ~**dou(tjie)**, sundew *(Drosera cistifolia)*.
sond'offer, (**-s**), sin-offer, expiatory sacrifice.
son'droog, sun-dry.
sond'vloed, deluge, great flood; cataclysm; *van NA die* ~, post-diluvian; *van VOOR die* ~, antediluvian.
so'ne, (**-s**), zone; ~**-indeling**, zoning.
son: ~ **eklips**, eclipse of the sun; ~ **gebruin**, (**-de**), suntanned; ~**gedroog**, (**-de**), sun-cured; ~**glans**, splendour of the sun; ~**gloed**, blaze (glare) of the sun; ~**god**, sun-god; ~**helm**, sun-helmet; ~**hitte**, heat of the sun; ~**hoed**, sun-hat; ~**hoogte**, solar altitude; ~**hortjies**, Venetian blind.
so'nie, sonny, my boy.
so'nies, (**-e**), sonic.
son: ~**jaar**, natural year, solar year; ~**kamer**, sun room; ~ **kant**, sunny side; ~**kap**, awning; ~**kappie**, sun-bonnet; ~**keerkring**, tropic; ~**kiel'tjie**, (**-s**), jonquil *(Narcissus jonquilla)*; ~ **koors**, dengue (fever); ~**krag**, solar power; ~ **krans**, solar corona.
son'kwasriet, Sonqua reeds.
son: ~**kyker**, (**-s**), helioscope; giant zonure; ~ **lig**, sunlight; ~**ligbehandeling**, heliotherapy; ~**loop**, course of the sun; ~ **loos**, (..**lose**), sunless; ~**lyn**, equator; ~**maand**, solar month; ~**meter**, heliometer; ~**mite**, sun-myth.
son'ne: ~**blom**, sunflower, helianthus; ~**blomolie**, sunflower-seed oil; ~**blomsaad**, sunflower seed; ~**dag**, solar day; ~**diens**, sun-worship; ~**klaar**, quite clear; irrefutable; ~**kyker**, helioscope; ~**priester**, Baal priest; ~**ring**, astronomical ring; ~**sirkel**, solar cycle; ~**stand**, sun's altitude; ~**stelsel**, solar system; ~**stilstand**, solstice.
sonnet', (**-te**), sonnet; ~**digter**, sonneteer; ~**jie**, (**-s**), sonnet.
son'netjie, (**-s**), little sun; *sy was die* ~ *in ons HUIS*, she was a ray of sunshine in our home; *die* ~ *is lekker WARM*, the sun is nice and warm.
sonnet'te: ~**krans**, sonnet cycle; ~**skrywer**, sonneteer.
son'ne: ~**vleg**, solar plexus; ~**wa**, chariot of the sun; ~**warmte**, heat of the sun; ~**weg**, ecliptic; ~**wende**, heliotrope; solstice.
son'newyser, (**-s**), sun dial; ~**pen**, gnomon.
son'nig, (**-e**), sunny, bright; *'n* ~*e geaardheid*, a bright disposition; ~**heid**, sunniness.
so'nometer, sonome'ter, (**-s**), sonometer.
sonome'tries, (**-e**), sonometric; melodious; clear.
son'onder, (s) sunset; *teen* ~, at sunset, in the gloaming.
sonoor', (**sonore**), sonorous.
son'op, (s) sunrise; *teen (met)* ~, at sunrise; ~**rigting**, direction of the rising sun.
sonoriteit', sonority.
son: ~**pak**, sun suit; ~**plant**, heliophyte.
sons: ~**afstand**, perihelion; ~**hoogte**, sun's altitude.
son: ~**sirkel**, solar cycle; ~**skerm**, awning, sunshade; sun-visor (motor); ~**skyf**, disc of the sun; ~**skyn**, sunshine; ~**soekertjie**, cherry-pie; heliotrope.
sons: ~**ondergang**, sunset; ~**opgang**, sunrise.
son: ~**spektrum**, solar spectrum; ~**spieël**, helioscope; ~**stand**, sun's altitude; ~**steek**, sunstroke; heliosis; heat-stroke; ~**stelsel**, solar system; ~**stilstand**, solstice; ~**straal**, sunbeam; sunstroke; ~**straalplooie**, sun-ray pleats; ~**straling**, solar radiation.
sons'verduistering, solar eclipse.
son: ~**tent**, sun-canopy, howdah; ~**tyd**, solar time; ~**uit**, at dawn; ~**vas**, (**-te**), sunfirm; ~**verhitting**, solar heating; ~**verwarmer**, solar heater; ~**vis**, John Dory; ~**vlek**, sun-spot, solar spot; ~**voël**, bird of paradise; ~**wa**, chariot of the sun; ~**weg**, ecliptic, sun's orbit; ~**wyser**, sun-dial; ~**wyserpen**, gnomon.
soöfiet', (**-e**), zoophyte.
soog, (**ge-**), suckle, give suck, nurse; ~**dier**, mammal; ~**dierkunde**, mammalogy; ~**moeder**, nursing mother.
soögrafie', zoography.
soog: ~**tyd**, period of lactation; ~**vrou**, wet-nurse.
sooi, (**-e**), sod; turf; divot (golf); *ONDER die* ~*e*, beneath the sod, buried; *sit alle* ~ *tjies TERUG*, replace all divots; ~**bank**, turf seat; ~**bekleding**, sodding; ~**brand**, heartburn, pyrosis, flatulence; ~**tjie**, (**-s**), divot.
sool, (**sole**), sole; *sole uit iem. se lippe kan sny*, be in a huff; have the sulks; ~**afwerker**, knifer; ~**beslag**, boot-protectors; ~**ganger**, plantigrade (animal); ~**leer**, sole-leather; bend-leather; ~**loper**, plantigrade; ~**naaier**, fair stitcher.
soölogie', zoology.
soölo'gies, (**-e**), zoological.
soöloog', (..**loë**), zoological.
sool: ~**tjie**, (**-s**), little sole; crackling; ~**vrat**, plantar wart.
soom, (s) (**some**), seam, hem; edge, border, fringe, fringing; (w) (**ge-**), hem, border; ~**masjien**, hemmer; ~**naat**, hem; ~**steek**, hemstitch; ~**voetjie**, (foot) hemmer; ~**werk**, hemming.
soon'toe, thither, that way, there.
soort, (**-e**), kind, sort, species, variety, type, breed, genre; kidney, caliber; description; genus; brand; *ENIG in sy* ~, the only one of its kind; unique of its kind; *GOED in sy* ~, good in its way, good of its kind; *MENSE van die* ~, people of that type; *ONS* ~ *mense*, people like us; ~ *SOEK* ~, birds of a feather flock together; ~**beskrywing**, generic description; ~**eg**, (**-te**), true to type; ~**gelyk**, (**-e**), similar, of the same kind, suchlike; ~**genoot**, (..**note**), fellow; congener.
soort'lik, (**-e**), specific; ~*e GEWIG*, specific gravity, density; ~*e WARMTE*, specific heat; ~*e WEERSTAND*, specific resistance.
soort'naam, common name, generic name; appellative.
soos, as, like, such as, just as; *NET* ~, just as; *VRIENDE* ~ *julle*, friends like you.
so'öspoor, swarm-spore, zoospore.
soöterapie', zootherapy.
soötomie', zootomy.
sop, soup, juice (fruit); *iem. in sy eie* ~ *laat GAARKOOK*, let a person stew in his own juice; *die* ~ *is die KOOL nie werd nie*, the game is not worth the candle; *hy SIT in die* ~, he is in the soup; ~**aftreksel**, soup stock; ~**been**, soup-bone; ~**bord**, soup-plate; ~**groente**, soup greens.
so'pie, (**-s**), glass of liquor, drink, tot, dram, drop (liquor), quencher; pick-me-up; appetizer, aperitif; ~**maat**, tot measure.
sop: ~**inrigting**, soup kitchen; ~**kaartjie**, soup-ticket; ~**ketel**, soup-kettle; ~**kluitjie**, soup-dumpling; ~**kom**, soup-bowl; ~**kombuis**, soup-kitchen; ~**lepel**, soup-spoon; soup-ladle; ~**nat**, drenched, dropping wet.
soporatief', (..**tiewe**), soporative.
sop'pies, juice.
sop'pot, soup-pot.
sopraan', (**soprane**), soprano; ~**party**, soprano part; ~**sangeres**, soprano; ~**stem**, soprano, treble.
sop: ~**skottel**, tureen; ~**tablet**, soup-tablet; ~**uitdeling**, distribution of soup; ~**vleis**, soup-meat.
sorbet', sorbet; sherbet.
sô're = **sorg** (w).
sorg, (s) (**-e**), care, charge; trouble; worry, grief, anxiety, concern, solicitude; ~ *BAAR*, cause

sorgbarend 493 **sout**

anxiety; ~ **aan iets BESTEE**, take pains over; ~ **DRA**, take care of; **GELDELIKE** ~**e**, financial worries; *die* ~ *vir sy HUISGESIN*, the care of his family; *'n LEWE vol* ~*e*, a life full of anxiety; *dit is van LATER* ~, there is no hurry; *MAAK jou daar geen* ~ *e oor nie*, don't trouble yourself about that; don't let that worry you; *ONDER die* ~ *van*, in the care of; *in die* ~ *SIT*, have much to worry about; *SONDER* ~, careless(ly); *aan iem. se* ~ *TOEVERTROU*, leave in someone's charge, entrust to someone's care; *VRY van* ~*e*, carefree; (w) (ge-), care for, take care, mind, look after; provide for, make provision for; ~ *dat jy DAAR is*, see that you are there; ~ *vir die GELD*, provide the money; take charge of the money; *hy* ~ *vir HOMSELF*, he fends for himself; *die vrou* ~ *vir die KOKERY*, the wife attends to the cooking; ~ *vir die OUDAG*, provide for one's old age.
sorgba'rend, (-e), alarming, critical.
sorg'behoewend, (-e), in need of care.
sorg'eenheid, (..hede), intensive care unit.
sor'g(e)loos, (..lose), careless, improvident, happy-go-lucky, reckless, easy-going, carefree; ~**heid**, carelessness, improvidence, recklessness.
sor'ghum, sorghum.
sorg'saam, (..same), provident, attentive, careful, painstaking; ~**heid**, carefulness; considerateness, solicitude.
sorg'lik, (-e), alarming, causing anxiety.
sorgvul'dig, (-e), careful, thorough; ~**heid**, carefulness, thoroughness.
sorgwek'kend, (-e), alarming, full of anxiety, critical, *'n* ~*e toename*, an alarming increase; ~**heid**, alarming nature.
sororaat', sorority.
sorteer', (ge-), sort, assort, select, pick out; grade; ~**band**, sorting belt; ~**der**, (-s), sorter; grader; ~**kamer**, sorting room; ~**mandjie**, skep; ~**masjien**, grading machine, grader, sizer; sorting machine; ~**nommer**, sorting number; ~**ster**, (-s), (woman) sorter; grader; ~**tafel**, sorting-table; ~**wa**, sorting-van.
sorte'ring, (-e, -s), assortment, selection; sorting; grading.
sor'tie¹, (-s), opera-cloak.
sor'tie², (-s), (mil.) sally.
sosa'tie, (-s), sosatie, kabob, grilled curried-meat.
soseer'¹, so much, in the first place; *nie* ~ *vir myself nie*, not in the first place for myself.
so'seer², to such an extent; *sy het my* ~ *teleurgestel dat*, she has disappointed me to such an extent that.
sosiaal', (sosiale), social; ~**-demokraat'**, social democrat; ~**-demokrasie'**, social democracy; ~**-demokra'ties**, (-e), social-democratic; ~**-ekono'mies**, (-e), social and economic, socio-economic.
Sosialis', (-te), member of Socialist Party.
sosialis', (-te), socialist; ~**me**, socialism; ~**ties**, (-e), socialist(ic).
sosiëteit', (ong.), club.
sosiologie', sociology.
sosiolo'gies, (-e), sociological.
sosioloog', (..loë), sociologist.
so-so', **so'-so**, only middling, tolerably, so-so, fairly well (good), not too good (well).
sosys', (ong.), (-e), sausage; ~**broodjie**, sausage roll.
sot, (s) (-te), fool, coxcomb; first-year student; (b) (-ter, -ste), foolish, mad, fond.
soteer', (ge-), sauté; *ge* ~ *de lamsvleis*, sauté of lamb.
soteriologie', soteriology.
soteriolo'gies, (-e), soteriological.
sot'heid, folly, madness.
So'tho, Sotho.
sots: ~**kap**, cap and bells; fool's cap; fool; ~**kolf**, bauble.
sot: ~**tepraatjies**, nonsense; ~**ternie'**, (-ë), mediaeval farce; ~**terny'**, (-e), foolishness; ~**tin'**, (-ne), fool (woman); freshette.
sou¹, (s) sou (French coin).
sou², (w) *(verlede tyd* van **sal**); should, would; *ek* ~ *so DINK*, of course; *hy* ~ *dit ONDERNEEM*, he was (supposed) to undertake this; *hy* ~ *dit ONDERNEEM het*, he was to have undertaken this.
sou'erig, (-e), modest; timid.
soufflé', soufflé.
souffleer', (ge-), prompt.
souffleur', (-s), prompter.
souffleurs'hok, prompt-box.
souffleu'se, female prompter.
sourdi'ne, (-s), sordine, damper, mute (violin).
sou'riër, (-s), saurian.
Souriski'ër, (-s), Saurischian.
sous, (s) (-e), sauce; gravy (meat); dressing; whole caboodle; *die HELE* ~, the whole lot (box and dice); *van die hele* ~ *niks WEET nie*, know nothing about it at all; (w) (ge-), pour (of rain); sauce (tobacco); ~**bekertjie**, gravy-boat; ~**boontjies**, haricot beans; bean salad; ~**erig**, (-e), juicy; with plenty of gravy; ~**kleursel**, gravy colouring; ~**kluitjies**, cinnamon dumplings; ~**kom**, sauce-boat, butter-boat, gravy-boat; ~**lepel**, sauce-ladle; ~**potjie**, (sauce-) boat, gravy-boat; ~**stowevleis**, fricassee; ~**tannie**, (-s), stout (corpulent) lady; ~**vet**, dripping; ~**vleis**, gravy beef.
sout, (s) salt; *die* ~ *van die AARDE*, the salt of the earth; *ATTIESE* ~, Attic salt (wit); *so* ~ *soos BREM*, as salt as Lot's wife; *ENGELSE* ~, Epsom salt(s); *'n* ~*-en-peper KLEUR*, a spotted grey colour; ~ *NODIG hê*, be insipid; require salt; ~ *op 'n voël se STERT gooi*, put salt on a bird's tail; *sy* ~ *VERDIEN (werd wees)*, be worth one's salt; *van geen* ~ *of WATER weet nie*, be completely in the dark; (w) (ge-), salt, season (with salt), cure; plant (mine); initiate (scholars); immunize; *IEM.* ~, initiate a fresher; *'n MYN* ~, salt (plant) a mine; *'n gesoute PERD*, salted (immune) horse; (b) briny, salt; ~**aanmaak**, salt manufacture; ~**agtig**, (-e), saltish, briny, haloid; ~**aksyns**, salt-duty, gabelle.
souta'ne, (-s), soutane, cassock.
sout: ~**bak**, salt-box; ~**beesbors**, corned brisket of beef; ~**beesvleis**, corned beef; ~**bos**, saltbush *(Atriplex sp.)*; ~**briket'**, salt-briquette; ~**bron**, saline spring, salt-well; ~**eloos** = **soutloos**; ~**-enpeperstel**, cruet(-stand); ~**er**, salter, curer; ~**erig**, (-e), saltish, brackish; ~**erigheid**, salinity; ~**ery**, salt-works; ~**ganna**, *Salsola aphylla*; ~**gees**, spirits of salt; ~**gehalte**, salinity, salt content; ~**gereg**, savoury dish; ~**handel**, salt-trade; ~**handelaar**, salter; ~**happies**, salty snacks, savouries; ~**heid**, saltiness, brininess; ~**houdend**, (-e), saline, saliferous.
sou'tig, (e), savoury; ~*e omelet*, savoury omelette; ~**heid**, saltiness; something salt; ~**heidjie**, savoury.
sout: ~**ing**, salting; immunity; ~**korrel**, grain of salt; ~**kors**, crust of salt; ~**krakeling**, pretzel; ~**kuip**, salting-tub; ~**laag**, salt stratum (layer); ~**liewend**, (-e), halophile.
sout'loos, (..lose), saltless, flat; insipid; silly; ~**heid**, saltlessness; silliness; insipidity.
sout: ~**maker**, salt-maker; ~**makery**, salt-works; saltern; ~**meer**, salt lake; ~**meter**, salinometer; ~**moeras**, salt marsh; ~**monopolie**, salt monopoly; ~**myn**, salt-pit, salt-mine; ~**neerslag**, saline deposit; ~**oplossing**, saline solution; ~**pag**, farming of salt-works; ~**pakhuis**, salt storehouse; ~**pan**, small lake with salt crust, salt-pan; saltern; ~**pilaar**, pillar of salt; *staan soos 'n* ~ *pilaar*, stand stock-still; ~**plant**, halophyte; ~**plek**, spot for salt-lick (animals); *'n groot* ~ *plek hê*, be bald; ~**potjie**, salt-cellar; ~**raffinadery**, salt refinery; ~**regte**, salt monopoly (control); ~**ribbetjie**, salted (corned) rib (of mutton); ~**sak**, salt-bag.
Sout'see, Dead Sea.
sout: ~**siedery**, saltern, salt-works; ~**slaai**, ice-plant; ~**smaak**, salty taste; ~**smokkelaar**, salt-smuggler; ~**steenskuim**, (purified) saltpetre; ~**stingeltjie**, savoury twig; ~**strooier**, salt-dredge; ~**suur**, hydrochloric (muriatic) acid; ~**vaatjie**, (-s), salt-cellar; stone-chat; ~**vervanger**, salt substitute; ~**vleis**, salted meat; corned meat; ~**water**, brine; ~**waterseep**, marine soap; ~**watervis**, sea-fish; ~**wette**, salt laws; ~**winning**, salt-making.

so'veel, so much, so many; ~ *te BETER*, so much the better; ~ *te MEER*, all the more; *NOG eens* ~, as much again, twice as much; ~ *is SEKER*, that much is certain.

so'veelste, umpteenth; *dis nou vir die* ~ *maal*, this is now for the umpteenth time.

so'ver, sover', so far, thus far; *in* ~ *DAT*, in so far that; *ons het nou* ~ *GEKOM*, we have now come to such a pass that; *as dit* ~ *KOM*, if it does happen; if it comes to that; when the time comes; *TOT* ~, thus far; as far as this; *VIR* ~, in so far as; inasmuch as; ~ *ek WEET*, as far as I know.

sowaar'! truly! indeed! really! forsooth! (ironically); *hy het* ~ *my hoed gevat*, he actually took my hat.

so'wat, about, roughly; ~ *vyftig rand*, fifty rands odd; *cf.* **so**.

sowel', both . . . and; as well (as); ~ *AS*, as well as; ~ *die EEN as die ander*, both the one and the other, both this and that; *HY* ~ *as sy*, ~ *HY as sy*, both he and she; *NET* ~, just as well.

Sow'jet, Soviet; S~**iseer, (ge-)**, sovietize; ~ **regering**, Soviet Government; ~ **republiek**, Soviet Republic.

spa = **spade**.

spaak: ~ *loop*, go wrong; ~ **been**, radial bone, radius (forearm).

spaan, (spane), scoop, skimmer; spatula (artist; doctor); oar; shingle (roof); bat (table-tennis); ~ **dak**, shingle roof.

spaan'der, (s) (-s), chip (of wood), splinter; (mv) chippings; (w) **(ge-)**, run away, skedadle, scoot; *laat* ~, take to one's heels; ~ **bord**, chipboard.

Spaans, (-e), Spanish; ~ *e GRIEP*, Spanish flu; ~ *e LEER*, cordovan; ~ *e PEPER*, red pepper, chilli.

spaansriet', Spanish (common) reed; rat(t)an; *Arundo donax*.

spaans'vlieg, Spanish fly, blister-beetle, smeller (*Cantharides*).

spaar, (ge-), save, lay by (money), economize; husband (strength); spare (life); *GELD* ~, save money; *jou KRAG* ~, reserve one's strength; *jy kan jou die MOEITE* ~, you may save yourself the trouble.

spaar'bank, savings bank; ~ **boekie**, deposit book; ~ **rekening**, savings bank account.

spaar: ~ **beweging**, thrift movement; ~ **der, (-s)**, saver, depositor; economizer; ~ **duitjies**, savings; ~ **fonds**, provident fund; ~ **geld**, savings, nest-egg; ~ **kapitaal**, saved-up capital; ~ **kas**, provident bank; ~ **klub**, thrift club; ~ **penninge**, savings; ~ **pot**, money-box; ~ **rekening**, savings (bank) account.

spaar'saam, (..same), thrifty, provident, frugal, chary (of praise); economic(al); ~ *wees met*, use sparingly; ~ **heid**, thrift, economy, frugality.

spaar: ~ **sente**, savings; ~ **sertifikaat**, savings certificate; ~ **sin**, thrift; ~ **veld**, rested veld; ~ **vereniging**, thrift society.

spaat, spar; ~ **agtig, (-e)**, sparry; spathic.

spa'de, late; ~ *reën*, late rain (Bib.).

spaghet'ti, spaghetti.

spalk, (s) (-e), splint; cradle; (w) **(ge-)**, splint, put in splints; set (leg or arm); fish (mech.); ~ **bout**, fish bolt; ~ **ing**, splinting; ~ **las**, splice; ~ **plaat**, fish plate.

span, (s) (-ne), span (oxen); team (of horses, players); gang (of workmen); fleet (buses); *uit die* ~ *SPRING*, change one's political opinion; leave the fold; *die SWART* ~, the brethren in black; *'n* ~ *TABAK*, a span of tobacco; (w) **(ge-)**, stretch (rope); strain (eyes); cock (gun); bend (bow); strap (cow); hobble (horse); tenter (textiles); spread (sail); *DRAAD* ~, put up wire; *die LYN* ~, string the line; *ge~ne SENUWEES*, highly strung nerves; *'n STRIK* ~, lay a snare; set a trap; *TENTLYNE* ~, guy a tent; *ge~ne VERHOUDINGS*, strained relations; *in ge~ne VERWAGTING*, on tenterhooks, on tiptoe with expectation; ~ **baas**, (team) foreman, squad ganger; ~ **balk**, strainingbeam; ~ **beton**, pre-stressed concrete; ~ **broek**, (pair of) tights.

spanda'bel, (-e), spendthrift, wasteful, extravagant, prodigal; ~ **heid**, extravagance.

spandeer', (ge-), spend; ~ *aan boeke*, spend on books.

span: ~ **doek**, banner-streamer; banner (stretched across street); ~ **draad**, spanning wire.

spang, (-e), hook, clasp.

span: ~ **gees**, team spirit, esprit de corps; ~ **haak**, tenterhook; ~ **hout**, dropper.

Spanjaard', (-e), Spaniard.

Span'je, Spain.

spanjool'(siekte), venereal disease.

span'klem, end clip.

span: ~ **kleur**, team colour; ~ **klos**, box clamp; ~ **klou**, gripping jaw; ~ **krag**, tension, tensile force; elasticity; expansive force; ~ **laken**, draw-sheet; ~ **leier**, patrol (troop) leader; ~ **maat**, partner (games); team-mate; ~ **mas**, pylon (electrical); ~ **masjien**, tenter; ~ **moer**, thumb nut (of compasses); turn-buckle.

span'nend, (-e), tight; thrilling, exciting; ~ *e oomblikke*, tense seconds (moments).

span'ner, tightener; tensioner.

span'ning, tension, suspense, excitement; pressure; stress, strain; voltage (elec.); spread; span (of bridge); tone (med.); tightness (market); turgor, turgidity (biol.); *in ANGSTIGE* ~, in great anxiety; *daar HEERS* ~, tension prevails; *HOË* ~, high tension; *iem. in* ~ *HOU*, keep someone on tenterhooks; *ONDER* ~, live (elec.).

span'nings: ~ **breuk**, strain burst; ~ **meter**, voltameter; tensometer; tonometer; ~ **reëlaar**, voltage regulator; ~ **val**, voltage drop; ~ **verklikker**, voltage indicator; ~ **verskil**, potential difference.

span: ~ **nommer**, team event; ~ **ooi** = **vasmaakooi**; ~ **paal**, straining-pole; dropper; ~ **pak**, tights; ~ **passer**, wing-compasses; ~ **plaat**, stretcher plate; ~ **plooi**, scrimp; ~ **punt**, reef-point; ~ **raam**, stretcher frame, tenter frame; ~ **randkernhulsel**, flipper (tyre); ~ **rib**, rafter; ~ **riem**, hobble, hobbling riem; ~ **ring**, snap-ring; ~ **saag**, frame-saw, bow-saw; bent saw; ~ **skêr**, frame shears; ~ **skroef**, tightening-screw; ~ **skyf**, hanging-roller.

spanspek', (-ke), musk-melon, honey-sweet melon, cantaloup(e).

span: ~ **spier**, tensor muscle; ~ **staaf**, compressing rod; binding stay; ~ **stang**, tie rod; ~ **stuk**, web; brace; stretcher.

spant, (-e), joist.

span: ~ **toring**, pylon; ~ **tou, (-e)**, knee-strap, milking-strap, hobble; ~ **veer**, tension-spring; ~ **vlak**, helical plane; ~ **wedloop**, relay-race, team-race; ~ **werk**, team-work; ~ **wiel**, draught-wheel (train-signals); ~ **wurm**, inch-worm; ~ **wydte**, span.

spar, (-re), pole; rafter (of roof); dropper (wire fence); spruce fir; *Kanadese* ~, Canadian spruce; ~ **boom**, spruce fir; ~ **bout**, dropper-bolt; ~ **dek**, spar-deck.

Spar'ta, Sparta.

Spartaan' (..tane), Spartan; ~ **s', (-e)**, Spartan.

spartaans', spartan.

spar'tel, (ge-), sprawl, flounder; struggle; ~ *om te bestaan*, struggle to make a livelihood (to make ends meet); ~ **ing, (-e, -s)**, sprawling, floundering; struggle.

spa'sie, (-s), space, opening, room; ~ **-anker**, space stay (engine); ~ **balk**, space bar.

spasieer', (ge-), space; ..**sië'ring**, spacing.

spasmo'dies, (-e), spasmodic.

spas'ties, (-e), spastic.

spas'tikus, (-se, ..tici), spastic.

spat¹, (s) (-te), splash, spatter; spot, stain; *die* ~ *neem*, take to one's heels; (w) **(ge-)**, splash, spatter, splutter; spurt; *laat* ~, take to one's heels.

spat², (s) spavin; ~ **aar**, varicose vein; ~ **aarbreuk**, varicocele; ~ **aarkous**, varicose stocking.

spat: ~ **bord**, splash-board, mudguard, fender; ~ **dig, (-te)**, splash-proof.

spa'tel, (-s), spatula, depressor (med.); palette-knife.

spat'lys, base-board, skirting-board.

spat'sel, (-s), drop, spatter, splash.

spat: ~ **skerm**, splash-board, mudguard, fender; ~ **smering**, splash-feed (lubrication).

Spea'ker, (-s), Speaker (of parliament).

speek, (speke), spoke; *iem. met 'n ou* ~ *kan DOOD*

speeksel   495   *spelkuns*

SLAAN, like to wring someone's neck; *daar is 'n ~ LOS*, all is not well; *die ONDERSTE ~ kom ook bo*, every dog has his day; *jou speke ROER*, bestir one's stumps; *iem. 'n ~ in die WIEL steek*, put a spoke in someone's wheel; ~**been**, radial bone, radius; ~**beentjies**, spindle-shanks; ~**hout**, spokewood; ~**los**, with loose spokes; mad, not all there; ill; ~**maat**, spoke-gauge.

speek'sel, spittle, saliva, sputum; ~**afskeiding**, salivation, flow of saliva; ~**klier**, salivary gland.

speek: ~**skaaf**, spokeshave; drawing-knife; ~**wiel**, artillery-wheel.

speel, (ge-), play, have a game; trifle with; perform, (en)act; chime; gamble; *hy ~ AMPIE*, he plays the part of Ampie; *om groot BEDRAE ~*, play for heavy (high) stakes; *met sy GELUK ~*, gamble with his happiness; *GOU ~*, be quick about it; *GROOTMAN ~*, play the big man; *ek LAAT nie met my ~ nie*, I won't be trifled with; *ek ~ MAAR*, I am only joking; *jy ~ MET my*, you are joking; *ons ~ nie SAAM nie*, we'll have no part in it; *SOMMER ~*, be only joking; *die STUK ~ in*, the scene is laid in; ~**aand**, play-night; ~**baar**, (..**bare**), fit to be played or acted, performable; playable; ~**bal**, plaything; puppet; cue-ball; playing-ball; *'n politieke ~ bal*, a political football; ~**bank**, gamingtable; ~**beertjie**, teddy bear; ~**beurt**, innings; ~**broekie**, romper(s); ~**dag**, play-day; ~**ding**, plaything, toy; ~**doos**, musical box; ~**duiwel**, demon of gambling; *hy is van die ~ duiwel besete*, he is an inveterate gambler; ~**geld**, pool, stakes, gaming-money; ~**genoot**, (..**note**), playfellow, playmate; ~**geweertjie**, popgun.

speel'goed, toys, playthings; ~**winkel**, toyshop.

speel: ~**grond**, playground; ~**hok**, playing-pen; ~**hol**, gambling-den; ~**huis**, gambling-house; ~**kaart**, playing-card; ~**kaarte**, playing-cards, the devil's books; ~**kamer**, playroom, nursery (room); card-room, ~**kant**, on side, all on side (football); ~**kas**, jukebox; ~**maat**, playmate, playfellow; partner; ~**man**, minstrel, fiddler; ~**munt**, counter; ~**pak**, playsuit; ~**pistool**, toy pistol; ~**plek**, playground; ~**pop**, doll, puppet; stooge; ~**prent**, dramatic film; ~**reël**, rule(s) of the game; ~**ruimte**, playground; play, scope, range, latitude, allowance, margin, elbow-room, free play; clearance; backlash (machine).

speels, (-e; -er, -ste), playful, kittenish, gamesome; on heat.

speel: ~**saal**, gambling-room; ~**seisoen**, season (for theatrical performances).

speels: ~**gewyse**, playfully, in play; ~**heid**, playfulness; desipience; ruttishness.

speel: ~**siek**, gamesome, frolicsome; addicted to gambling; ~**skuld**, gambling-debt; play-debt; ~**speel**, playing (all the while); easily, without exertion; *iets ~ -~ doen*, do something with the greatest ease; ~**ster**, (-s), player, actress; gambler (woman); ~**styl**, style of play; ~**sug**, passion for gambling; ~**tafel**, card-table; gaming-table, green cloth, green table, gambling-table; console (organ); ~**terrein**, recreation ground; enclosure, close; ~**toneel**, stage; ~**tuig**, musical instrument; ~**tuin**, children's park; ~**tyd**, playtime, recess, interval; ~**uur**, recess, play-hour; ~**uurwerk**, chimes; ~**veld**, playing-field; ~**wyse**, playing-method.

speen, (s) (**spene**), teat, nipple; (w) (ge-), wean; ablactate; *ge ~ wees van*, be weaned from; be lacking in; ~**kalf**, weaner; weanling (calf); ~**kruid**, figwort; ~**oud**, weaned; ~**vark**, sucking-pig, porkling; baby pork.

speer, (**spere**), spear, javelin; ~**draer**, spearman; ~**haak**, bickern; beak-iron; ~**kruid**, Jacob's ladder (plant); ~**maat**, calliper measure; ~**punt**, spearhead, fluke; ~**ruiter**, spearman, lancer; ~**staak**, beak-iron, bick-iron; ~**vis**, spearfish; ~**vormig**, (-e), spear-shaped, hastate.

speet'jiespaling, spitchcock eel.

speg, (-te), woodpecker.

spek, bacon, pork; blubber (whale); *vir ~ en BOONTJIES*, for no rhyme or reason; for the fun of it; *met ~ SKIET*, draw the long-bow; ~**agtig**, (-e), bacony; lardaceous (med.); ~**bokkem**, fat-bloater; ~**boom**, elephant's food (*Portulacaria afra*); ~**buik**, paunch; ~**gomlastiek**, crêpe rubber; ~**hout**, porkwood; ~**jood**, unorthodox Jew; ~**kerig**, (-e), lardy; ~**kewer**, bacon-beetle; ~**repie**, lardon; ~**rol**, bacon roll; ~**skiet**, (-ge-), tell a lie; exaggerate; ~**skieter**, fibber, liar; ~**skietery**, exaggeration; fibbing; ~**slaer**, pork-butcher; ~**sool**, crêpe sole; ~**steen**, steatite, soapstone; French chalk.

spekta'kel, (-s), scene, row, sight, spectacle, uproar, rumpus, racket, hubbub, tumult; scarecrow; ~**stuk**, melodrama, slapstick comedy.

spektatoriaal', (..**riale**), spectatorial.

spek'tor, bacon-beetle.

spektraal', (..**trale**), spectral; ~**analise**, spectral analysis.

spektrografie', spectrography.

spektrogra'fies, (-e), spectrographic.

spektrogram', (-me), spectrogram.

spek'trometer, spektrome'ter, (-s), spectrometer.

spektroskoop', (..**skope**), spectroscope.

spektroskopie', spectroscopy.

spektrosko'pies, (-e), spectroscopic.

spek'trum, (-s, ..**tra**), spectrum; ~**lyn**, spectral line.

spekulant', (-e), speculator; plunger; ~-*op-DALING*, bear; ~-*op-STYGING*, bull (stock exchange).

spekula'sie, (-s), speculation, agiotage; flutter (on stock exchange), venture, gamble, stagging; *op ~*, on spec(ulation).

spekulatief', (..**tiewe**), speculative.

spekuleer', (ge-), speculate; plunge; stag; *~ op iem. se goedheid*, trade on someone's kindness.

spek: ~**vark**, baconer; ~**vet**, (b) very fat, as plump as a partridge.

spek'vleis, bacon; ~**rol**, bacon roll; ~**sy**, flitch.

spek'vreter, (-s), pork-eater; (familiar) chat.

spel¹, (-e) (ge-), game; play; performance, acting (theatre); playing, execution (music); pack (cards); rubber (cards); recreation, pastime; *ALLES op die ~ sit*, stake one's all upon a throw; *daar is BAIE op die ~*, there is much at stake; *BUITE die ~ bly*, leave out (exclude); *daar is 'n DAME in die ~*, there is a woman in it; *die ~ staan GELYK*, the score is even; the scores are level; *die ~ GEWONNE gee*, admit defeat; *ONEERLIKE ~*, foul play; *ONGELUKKIG in die ~, gelukkig in die liefde*, lucky in love, unlucky at cards; *'n SKANDALIGE (skandelike) ~ met iem. speel*, play a dirty game with someone; *op die ~ STAAN*, be at stake; *hoe STAAN die ~?* what is the score? *STIL ~*, byplay, silent action; *VRYE ~ hê*, enjoy a free hand; *VUIL ~*, foul play.

spel², (ge-), spell; portend, foretell.

spel'bederwer, (-s), killjoy, wet blanket, spoilsport.

spel'boek, spelling-book, speller.

spel'breker — spelbederwer.

speld, (s) (-e), pin; *op ~ e SIT*, be on pins and needles; *'n mens kon 'n ~ hoor VAL*, one could have heard a pin drop; *soos 'n groot ~ VERDWYN*, take French leave, clear off on the sly; (w) (ge-), pin, fasten.

spel'de: ~**bakkie**, ~**doos**, pin-box; ~**gaatjie**, pin-hole; ~**geld**, pin-money; ~**koker**, needle-case; pin-case; ~**kop**, pin's head; pin-head; ~**kussing**, pin-cushion; ~**kussings**, pincushions (*Leucospermum sp.*); ~**prik**, pinprick; ~**prikkamera**, pin-hole camera; ~**punt**, pin-point.

speld'strepie, pin stripe.

spe'lenderwys(e), in play, playfully, jocularly.

speleologie', spel(a)eology; ..**lo'gies**, (-e), spel(a)eological; ..**loog'**, (..**loë**), spel(a)eologist.

spe'ler, (-s), player; actor; performer, musician, executant; gamester, gambler; ~**ig**, (-e), playful, merry; ~**igheid**, playfulness; ~**s**, field (cricket).

spe'letjie, (-s), game, fun; *sonder ~ s*, joking apart.

spel'fout, spelling mistake.

spel'gehalte, standard (quality) of play.

spe'ling, play, scope, latitude, margin, range, elbow-room, clearance; *~ van die natuur*, freak of nature.

spel'kuns, orthography.

spel'le = spel² (w).
spel: ~ **leiding**, direction; ~ **leier**, producer (of a play); leader (of a game).
spel'ler, (-s), speller.
spel'lesing, play-reading.
spel'letjie, (-s), game; *'n ~ kaart*, a game of cards.
spel'ling, (-e, -s), spelling, orthography; ~ **hervorming**, spelling reform; ~ **sisteem**, orthography; ~ **uitspraak**, spelling pronunciation; ~ **verandering**, change of spelling.
spel'lys, (-te), spelling list.
spel'maat, partner (in games).
spel'metode, method of spelling; spelling method.
spelonk', (-e), cave, cavern, grotto; ~ **agtig**, (-e), cavernous; ~ **bewoner**, troglodyte, cave-dweller; ~ **kunde**, spel(a)eology; ~ **kun'dig**, (-e), spel(a)eological; ~ **kun'dige**, (-s), spel(a)eologist; ~ **tee**, Bushman's tea.
spel'reël, spelling rule, orthographic rule; rule of play; playing rule.
spelt, spelt, German wheat.
spel'ter, spelter (copper for soldering).
spel'verwisseling, exchanges (sport).
spel: ~ **vorm**, spelling; ~ **wedstryd**, spelling-bee; ~ **wyse**, method (system) of spelling.
spe'ning, weaning, ablactation.
spens, (-e), pantry, larder, buttery, cook's store; ~ **bak**, (pantry-)bin; ~ **bediende**, pantryman; ~ **kas**, provision cupboard; ~ **rak**, pantry shelf.
sper, (ge-), block up, bar, jam; open very wide, distend (eyes); ~ **boom**, bar, barrier; ~ **der**, trap; ~ **fort**, barrier-fort.
sper'ma, sperm, semen.
spermace'ti, spermaceti; ~ **kers**, spermaceti candle; ~ **-olie**, sperm-oil, spermaceti oil.
spermatofiet', (-e), seedplant.
spermatoso'ön, (..soa, ..soë), spermatozoon.
sper: ~ **streep**, barrier line; ~ **rat**, ratchet; ~ **ring**, blocker ring; ~ **tyd**, deadline; ~ **vlak**, barrier level; ~ **vuur**, barrage, (curtain-) fire.
sper'wel, (-s), **sper'wer**, (-s), goshawk.
spesery', (-e), spice; ~ **agtig**, (-e), spicy; ~ **e**, condiments; ~ **handel**, spice trade; ~ **handelaar**, spice dealer; ~ **kas**, spice-box; ~ **koek**, spice cake.
spesiaal', (..siale), special; particular (friend); exceptional (case).
spesialis', (-te), specialist; ~ **a'sie**, specialization; ~ **eer'**, (ge-), specialize; ~ **e'ring**, specialization.
spesialiteit', (-e), speciality.
spe'sie¹, (-s), species, kind.
spe'sie², (-s), specie, ready money, cash; species; ~ **bewakers**, specie escorts; ~ **handel**, trade in bullion; ~ **onderskeiding**, species discrimination; species description; ~ **voorraad**, bullion.
spesifiek', (-e), specific.
spesifika'sie, (-s), specification.
spesifiseer', (ge-), specify, itemize, set out in detail.
spe'simen, (-s), specimen (biol.).
spesmaas', idea, notion, inkling, suspicion; *ek het 'n ~ dat . . .*, I have an idea that . . .
spet'ter, (ge-), splutter, spatter; sizzle.
speur, (ge-), track, trace, spy, ferret out; discover, detect; ~ **der**, (-s), detective; dick (coll.); S ~ **diens**, Criminal Investigation Department (C.I.D.); ~ **gas**, tracer gas; ~ **hond**, sleuth-hound, police-dog; bloodhound; ~ **sin**, detecting talent; penetration, acumen; ~ **verhaal**, detective story; ~ **werk**, detective work.
spicca'to, spiccato.
spie, (-e), pin, peg, wedge, plug, cotter; ~ **bout**, cotter bolt.
spie'ël, (s) (-s), mirror, looking-glass; level (of the sea); stern; speculum; *hulle sit onder die ~*, they are about to take the plunge; their banns are being published; (w) (ge-), mirror; reflect; *hom ~ AAN*, take warning from; *wie hom aan 'n ander ~, ~ hom sag*, one man's fault is another man's lesson; it is good to learn at another's cost; ~ **beeld**, reflected image, reflection; illusion; phantom; ~ **buffet**, mirrored sideboard; ~ **druk**, mirror-print; ~ **eier**, fried egg; ~ **erts**, iron ore; ~ **geveg**, sham (mock) fight, mimic warfare; exhibition battle; ~ **glad**, smooth as a mirror; ~ **glas**, plate glass; ~ **harpuis**, ~ **hars**, colophony, resin (fiddler's); ~ **ing**, reflection; ~ **karp**, mirror-carp; ~ **kas**, wardrobe with mirrors; ~ **lamp**, lamp (with reflector); ~ **lys**, looking-glass frame; ~ **mikroskoop**, reflecting microscope; ~ **pou**, peacock-pheasant; ~ **ruit**, plateglass window; ~ **saal**, hall of mirrors; ~ **skrif**, mirror-writing; ~ **tafel**, dressing-table; chest of drawers; ~ **teleskoop**, reflecting telescope; ~ **vlak**, mirror surface; ~ **yster**, specular iron.
spie'gleuf, spie'groef, keyway.
spie'pen, cotter pin.
spier, (-e), muscle, thew; *geen ~ VERTREK nie*, keep a straight face; without turning a hair, without flinching; *WILLEKEURIGE ~*, voluntary muscle; ~ **afmatting**, muscular fatigue; ~ **beheersing**, muscle-control; ~ **beskrywing**, myography; ~ **beweging**, muscular movement; ~ **bundel**, muscular fascicle; ~ **haai**, grey shark; sweet-william.
spie'ring, (-s), smelt (fish); sprat; *'n ~ uitgooi om 'n kabeljou te vang*, throw a sprat to catch a whale.
spie'rinkie, (-s), whitebait.
spier: ~ **krag**, muscular strength, brawniness, muscularity; ~ **kramp**, muscular spasm (cramp), crick; ~ **kunde**, myology; ~ **kun'dig**, (-e), myological; ~ **kun'dige**, (-s), myologist; ~ **loos**, (..lose), muscleless; ~ **maag**, muscular stomach, gizzard; ~ **naak**, (-te), stark naked; ~ **ontsteking**, myositis; ~ **pyn**, muscular pains, myalgia; ~ **rumatiek**, muscular rheumatism; ~ **skede**, sheath of muscle; ~ **slapte**, atony; ~ **spanning**, muscular tension; ~ **stelsel**, musculature, muscular system; ~ **styfheid**, muscular stiffness; ~ **suiker**, muscle-sugar; ~ **trekking**, muscular twitch, jactitation; ~ **uitputting**, muscular fatigue; ~ **verlamming**, paresis, muscular paralysis; ~ **verrekking**, strain; ~ **vesel**, muscle fibre; ~ **wand**, muscular wall; ~ **weefsel**, muscular tissue; ~ **werking**, muscular activity.
spier'wit, snow-white, milk-white, lily-white.
spies, (s) (-e), spear, pike, javelin, lance; (w) (ge-), gaff; ~ **bok**, pricket, brocket; ~ **draer**, pikeman, spearman, javelin man; ~ **glans**, native antimony; ~ **gooi**, javelin throw(ing); ~ **gooier**, javelin thrower; ~ **hert**, pricket, brocket; ~ **punt**, spear point; ~ **visser**, spear fisherman; ~ **vissery**, spear-fishing; ~ **vormig**, (-e), spear-shaped, hastate.
spie'tapbout, cotter stud.
spiets, (s) (-e), (geselst.), speech; comical incident, joke; *dit was vir jou 'n ~*, that was quite a to-do; (w) (ge-), make a speech, address a meeting.
spie'waster, cotter washer.
spig'tig, (-e), lank, spiky, spindly, ~ **heid**, spindliness.
spik'kel, (s) (-s), spot, speck, fleck; (w) (ge-), speckle, spot; ~ **angelier**, picotee; ~ **binding**, spot weave; ~ **formasie**, artillery formation; ~ **(r)ig**, (-e), speckled; ~ **seep**, mottled soap.
spik'splinternuut, (..nuwe), brand-new, spick-and-span.
spil¹, (s) (-le), pivot, axis, newel, axle, hinge, arbor, hub; gudgeon; centre pin, centre, (lathe) mandril, swivel; spindle; *die ~ waarom alles draai*, the keyman; the crux of the matter.
spil², (w) (ge-), waste, spill.
spil: ~ **as**, privotal axis; ~ **bed**, capstan socket; ~ **bene**, spindly legs; ~ **breuk**, pivotal fault; ~ **gare**, ~ **garing**, spindle-drawn thread; ~ **gewrig**, pivot joint; ~ **haak**, cam; ~ **kop**, capstan head; headstock (lathe); spindle head; ~ **laer**, spindle bearing; ~ **las**, swivel joint; ~ **maat**, gauge; ~ **pen**, pivot pin; pintle; ~ **plaat**, pivot plate; ~ **siek**, (-e), prodigal, lavish, extravagant; ~ **spoel**, swivel (shuttle); ~ **sug**, extravagance, prodigality, squander mania; ~ **sy**, spindle side; distaff side; ~ **tap**, pivot pin, collar-key; ~ **vor'mig**, (-e), fusiform.
spin¹, (s) leaf-miner, split-worm.
spin², (w) (ge-), spin; purr (cat).
spinaal', (spinale), (spinal) (cord).
spin'agtig, (-e), arachnid.
spina'sie, spinach; ~ **beet**, sea-kale beet; ~ **suring**, patience-dock.
spin'draad, spinning-thread.
spinel', (-le), spinel.

spinet', (-te), spinet, virginal.
spin: ~**glas**, spun glass; ~**hout**, sapwood.
spin'huis, spinning-house; house of correction; ~**boef**, gaol-bird.
spin: ~**klier**, spinneret, silk-gland; ~**koring**, shredded wheat; ~**masjien**, spinning-jenny, spinning-mill, spinning-mule.
spin'nekop, (-pe), spider; ~**blom**, spider-flower; ~**bos**, spider-bush.
spin'ner, (-s), spinner.
spin'nerak, (-ke), cobweb; gossamer; ~**agtig**, (-e), cobweblike, arachnoid; ~**draad**, spider-thread; ~**wol**, webby wool.
spin'nery, (-e), spinning-mill; spinning.
spin'ne: ~**web**, cobweb; ~**wiel**, (ong.), spinning-wheel.
spin'orgaan, spinneret.
spin'rag, gossamer; ~**fyn**, as fine as gossamer.
spin'rok, (-ke), distaff.
spins'bek, pinchbeck.
spin: ~**spil**, spindle; ~**ster**, (-s), spinner (woman); ~**stok**, distaff; ~**suiker**, spun sugar; ~**sy**, spinning-silk; ~**tepel**, spinneret.
spint: ~**hout**, sapwood; ~**streep**, sap-streak.
spin: ~**vermoë**, spinning ability; ~**wol**, spinning-wool.
spioen', (s) (-e), agent, spy; scout; prier; (w) **(ge-)**, spy; scout.
spioena'sie, espionage, spying; ~**diens**, secret service; ~**ring**, spy-ring; ~**stelsel**, spy system.
spioeneer', **(ge-)**, spy, pry.
spiraal', (spirale), spiral, coil; helix; **boor**, twist-drill; auger bit; spiral drill; ~**daling**, spiral dive; ~**draadlamp**, spiral-filament lamp; ~**draai**, volution; ~**duik**, spiral dive; ~**klep**, spiral valve; ~**lyn**, spiral line, helix; ~**rat**, spiral-gear wheel; ~**rol**, barrel-roll; ~**s'gewys(e)**, spirally; ~**veer**, coil-spring; hairspring, helical spring; ~**vormig**, (-e), voluted, spiral, helical, corkscrew; ~**wurm**, spiral nematode.
spirant', (-e), spirant, fricative; ~**ies**, (-e), (as a) spirant, fricative.
spiril', (-le), spirillum; ~**lekoors**, relapsing fever; ~**lo'se**, relapsing fever.
spiritis', (-te), spiritist; spirit-rapper; ~**me**, spiritism; animism; ~**ties**, (-e), spiritistic.
spiritua'lieë, spirits (alcoholic), spirituous liquors.
spiritualis', (-te), spiritualist; ~**me**, spiritualism; ~**ties**, (-e), spiritualistic.
spiritueel', (..tuele), spiritual.
spi'ritus, spirit(s), alcohol; ~**lamp**, spirit-lamp; ~**stoof**, spirit-stove.
spirocheet', (..chete), spiroch(a)ete.
spiroche'tekoors, tick fever, relapsing fever.
spi'rometer, spirome'ter, (-s), spirometer.
spit¹, (s) (-te), spadeful; spade-depth; *die ~ afbyt*, bear the brunt; (w) **(ge-)**, dig, delve.
spit², (s) (-te), split (for roasting).
spit³, (s) crick (in the back), lumbago.
spit: ~**braad**, spit roasted meat, ~**draaier**, (-s), turn-spit, roasting jack.
spits, (s) (-e), point; top, tip, pinnacle, spire, vertex, peak, summit; forefront; cusp (bot.); *iets op die ~ DRYF*, bring to a head; *aan die ~ van die LEËR*, at the head of the army; (w) **(ge-)**, point; *jou OP iets ~*, set one's heart on; *die ORE ~*, prick up (cock) the ears; (b, bw), pointed, fine, sharp (features); peaked; cuspate(d); *~ DAK*, steep roof; *~ GESIG*, peaky face; *~ TOELOOP*, taper; *~ TORINKIE*, pinnacle.
spits: ~**baard**, pointed beard, torpedo-beard; ~**bekmuis**, shrew(-mouse); ~**belasting**, peak load; ~**beraad**, summit talks; ~**boef**, blackguard, scoundrel; ~**boog**, pointed arch, lancet arch; ogive; ~**boogvenster**, oriel (window); lancet window; ~**boogvormig**, (-e), ogival; ~**boor**, common bit; ~**borstig**, (-e), chicken-breasted; ~**bout**, pointed bolt, taper-bolt; ~**broer**, comrade, brother-in-arms; ~**hamer**, pointed hammer; ~**heid**, sharpness, pointedness; S~**hond**, Spitz, Pomeranian; ~**koeël**, conical bullet, pointed bullet; ~**kool**, cabbage with pointed head; ~**kop**, conical hill; ~**kruis**, cross-pointed (her.); ~**lading**, peak load; ~**man**, point (patrol);

~**muis**, shrew, shrew-mouse; ~**neus**, pointed nose; ~**prop**, taper plug.
spits'roede, gauntlet; *onder die ~ deurloop*, run the gauntlet.
spits: ~**rugwalvis**, razor-back whale; ~**saag**, compass-saw, keyhole-saw, lock-saw; ~**spoorstaaf**, point-rail; ~**uur**, rush hour, peak hour; ~**voet**, drop-foot.
spitsvon'dig, (-e), witty; subtle; quibbling, captious, far-fetched, fine-spun; ~**heid**, wit; subtlety; trifling distinction, quibble, cavil, quip, quiddity.
spits: ~**vor'mig**, (-e), fine-drawn; tapered; ~**vyl**, taper file; ~**werk**, pointing.
spit: ~**ter**, (-s), digger; grubber; ~**vark**, sucking-pig roasted on spit; ~**vleis**, meat roasted on spit; ~**vurk**, digging-fork, garden-fork; ~**werk**, digging.
spleet, (splete), crevice, slit, fissure, cleft, aperture, scissure, chink; ~**ent**, cleft-grafting; ~**hoewig**, (-e), fissiped, cloven-footed; ~**klei**, gouge; ~**klap**, slotted flap (aero.); ~**rok**, slit skirt; ~**rolroer**, slotted aileron; ~**sak**, slit pocket; ~**skroef**, slotted propeller; ~**sluiter**, focal plane-shutter, economical shutter; ~**veer**, splinter; ~**visier**, peep-hole sight; ~**vlerk**, slotted wing (aero.); ~**voet**, cloven foot.
sple'tig, (-e), full of cracks (fissures).
splint, (-e), splinter, chip; splint (in horses).
splin'ter, (s) (-s), splinter, shiver(s), sliver, chip; *die ~ in 'n ander se oog sien en nie die balk in sy eie nie*, see the mote in another's eye and not the beam in one's own; (w) **(ge-)**, splinter, shiver; ~**bom**, disintegration-bomb; ~**breuk**, comminuted fracture; ~**groep**, splinter group; ~**hamer**, spalling hammer; ~**ig**, (-e), splintery, inclined to chip; ~**keerder**, chip-guard; ~**nakend**, (-e), stark naked; ~**nuut**, (..nuwe), brand-new; mint (coins); ~**party**, splinter party; ~**skerm**, ship-shield; ~**vry**, (-e), splinter-proof, shatter-proof.
splint'hout, sapwood.
split, (s) (-te), slit, vent, placket-hole; mixture of two different liquors; (w) **(ge-)**, split, divide; ~**erte**, split peas; ~**kraag**, collet, split collar; ~**las**, splicer (elec.); ~**moer**, split nut; ~**nael**, split rivet; ~**oog**, split link; ~**pen**, cotter pin, split pin; ~**ring**, split ring; ~**rok**, split (divided) skirt.
splits, **(ge-)**, split, divide, cleave; splice (rope); bisect; ~**baar** (..bare), divisible; ~**baarheid**, divisibility; ~**end**, (-e), disjunctive; ~**er**, (-s), splitter, splicer; chink; ~**horing**, splicing-fid; ~**ing**, splitting-up; splicing, split, rupture; disruption; fission, segmentation (biol.); cleavage (geol.); resolution (maths.); ~**las**, (-se), splice; ~**mof**, distribution box; ~**priem**, fid (naut.); ~**ring**, key-ring; split ring.
split'vrug, dehiscent fruit.
splyt, **(ge-, gesplete)**, cleave, slit, split; *gesplete HOEF*, cloven hoof; *gesplete LIP*, harelip, split lip; ~**baar**, (..bare), cleavable, fissible; ~**haarheid**, fissibility; ~**ing**, cleavage, fission; ~**pen**, split pin; ~**swam**, fission fungus, schizomycete; ~**vlak**, cleavage plane; ~**wig**, (ge, ..wie), splitting wedge.
spoed, (s) speed; progress; expedition, haste; pitch (airscrew); *met BEKWAME ~*, as fast as possible; *HAASTIGE ~ is selde goed*, haste makes waste; *jou met alle ~ en KRAG versit*, oppose vigorously; (w) **(ge-)**, speed, despatch; hurry, hasten, make haste; ~**beperking**, speed restriction; ~**bestelling**, express order; express delivery; rush order; ~**breker**, speed-hump; ~**brief**, express letter; ~**eisend**, (-e), urgent; ~**geval**, emergency case; ~**grens**, speed limit; ~**ig**, (-e), soon, speedy, speedily, quick(ly); early; ~**meter**, speedometer; ~**operasie**, emergency operation; ~**perk**, speed limit; ~**pos**, express post; ~**program**, crash programme; ~**reëlaar**, governor; ~**sertifikaat**, medical certificate of urgency; ~**stuk**, express letter; ~**vergadering**, emergency meeting; ~**wal**, speed hump.
spoeg, (s) spittle, spit, sputum, saliva, expectoration; (w) **(ge-)**, spit, gob, expectorate; *~ VERBODE*, expectorating prohibited; *VUUR en vlam ~*, be in a violent temper; ~**bak**, spittoon, cuspidor; ~**besie**, foam beetle; ~**klier**, salivary gland; ~**lok**, kiss-

curl; ~**middel**, expectorant; ~**sel**, spittle; ~**slang**, ringed cobra, spitting snake.

spoel[1], (s) (-e), spool, reel, bobbin, shuttle; quill; coil (magneto).

spoel[2], (w) (ge-), wash, rinse, flush; flow; *die keel~*, wet one's whistle; ~**bak**, wash-tub; cistern (W.C.); ~**brug**, causeway; ~**dek**, wash deck; ~**delwerye**, alluvial diggings; ~**diamant**, alluvial diamond; placer-diamond; ~**drank**, gargle; chaser; ~**er, (-s)**, irrigator (med.); wash, diluvium; ~**ertsafsetter**, placer (deposit); ~**gemak**, flush lavatory; ~**geut**, launder; ~**goud**, alluvial gold; ~**grond**, alluvial soil; alluvium; ~**gruis**, shingle; ~**ing, (-e, -s)**, rinsing, washing; pigwash, swill; ~**kamer**, sluice-room; ~**kliplaag**, pebble-bed; ~**klippie**, pebble; ~**kom**, slop-basin; bowl; ~**kombuis**, scullery; ~**masjien**, rinsing machine; ~**pyp**, flush pipe; ~**riolering**, flush sanitation; ~**sel, (-s)**, tailings, rinse, wash; washing water; ~**silinder**, bobbin cylinder; ~**stelsel**, water-closet system; ~**tinerts**, steam-tin.

spoel: ~**tol**, coil-bobbin (elect.); ~**vormig, (-e)**, fusiform.

spoel: ~**wassery**, placer-mining; ~**water**, slops, dishwater; flood-water; casual water (golf); ~**werk**, tatting; ~**wurm**, maw-worm *(Ascaris);* nematode; ~**wyn**, wine-drippings.

spoet'nik, sputnik.

spog, (ge-), boast, crow, show off, brag, rant, prank, gasconade; ~**broodpoeding**, green's pudding; ~**ding**, swell thing; show-article; ~**ger, (-s)**, *see* **spogter;** ~**gerig, (-e)**, grand, boastful showy, swell, fancy; fond of bragging; ~**gerigheid**, showiness, boastfulness, ostentation; ~**gery**, *see* **spogtery;** ~**hings**, best (prize-) stallion; ~**hou**, fancy shot; ~**kantien**, gin-palace; ~**perd**, show horse; ~**spel**, gallery-play, play for the stand.

spog'ter, (-s), braggart, boaster; ~**y**, bragging, boasting, gasconade.

spog'verkoper, bestseller.

spo'kerig, (-e), spookish, haunted.

spo'kery, fighting, row; haunting apparition.

spon, (-ne), bung.

spon'de, (-s), bed(stead), couch.

spondee', (. .deë), spondee.

spon'gat, bung-hole.

spongiet', spongite.

spon'ning, (-s), groove, slit, rabbet, channelling, ledge; ~**skaaf**, rabbet-plane, rebate-plane.

spons, (s) (-e), sponge; spigot; (w) (ge-), sponge.

sponsag'tig, (-e), spongey; fungoid, fungous; bibulous; ~**heid**, sponginess.

spons: ~**beenweefsel**, cancellous tissue; ~**beton**, aeroconcrete; ~**dweil**, squeegee; ~**doek**, sponge cloth; ~**gat**, bung-hole; ~**goud**, sponge gold; ~**hanger**, sponge-hanger (-basket); ~**koek**, sponge-cake; ~**lap**, sponge cloth; ~**lekker(goed)**, marshmallow; ~**naald**, sponge spicule; ~**papier**, absorbent paper; ~**pen**, sponge flagellum; ~**poeding**, sponge pudding; ~**rubber**, foam rubber; ~**siekte**, black quarter, quarter-evil (cattle-disease); ~**siekte-entstof**, black-legine; ~**steen**, pumice, spongite; ~**wol**, spongy wool.

spontaan', (. .tane; . .**taner, -ste)**, spontaneous; . .*tane GENERASIE*, spontaneous generation; . .*tane VARIASIE*, mutation.

spontaneïteit', spontaneity.

spook, (s) (spoke), ghost, apparition, spectre, bog(e)y, phantom, goblin; *so MAER soos 'n ~*, as lean as a rake; *spoke SIEN*, see ghosts; (w) (ge-), be very active, work hard, struggle; fight; be haunted; haunt; *dit ~ DAAR*, that place is haunted; *ons sal MOET ~*, we shall have to exert ourselves; ~**ag'tig, (-e)**, ghostlike, apparitional, spooky, eerie; ~**ag'tigheid**, ghostliness, ghastliness; ~**asem**, candyfloss; white bread; ~**beeld**, phantom, spectre; ~**dier**, spectral tarsier; ~**geskiedenis**, ghost story; ~**gestalte**, phantom, apparition, spectre; ~**huis**, haunted house; ~**personeel**, skeleton staff; ~**pop**, golliwog; ~**sel, (-s)**, goblin, phantom, ghostly apparition; ~**skip**, phantom ship, spectre ship; ~**skrywer**, ghost writer; ~**sprinkaan**, stick insect; ~**storie**,

ghost story; ~**uur**, witching hour; ~**verskyning**, apparition, phantom; ~**voël**, grey-headed bushshrike; ~**wag**, middle watch.

spoo'nerisme, spoonerism.

spoor[1], (s) (**spore**), footprint, footmark, hoof-mark, print, trail, scent; line, rail, railway; sign, trace, clue; track, rut (of vehicle); slot (of deer); spur; foil (of game); *op die ~ BRING*, give someone a clue; *die ~ BYSTER raak*, go quite astray; off the track; *DUBBELE ~*, double track; *ENKELE ~*, single track; *op die ~ KOM*, get on the right track; *die ~ KWYTRAAK*, go off the track, lose the way; *in sy spore bly LÊ*, drop in one's tracks; *spore MAAK*, run away; walk quickly; *geen ~ NALAAT nie*, leave no trace; *OP iem. se ~ wees*, be on someone's track; *PER ~*, by rail; *v.d. ~ RAAK*, go off the rails; go astray; *twee RYE spore loop*, be intoxicated; *SMAL ~*, narrow gauge; *in sy ~ TRAP*, mind his p's and q's; *diep spore TRAP*, make one's mark; *die ~ VAT (vind)*, pick up the scent; get a clue; *uit die VIER spore*, from the very beginning; *in sy VIER spore vassteek*, stop in one's tracks; pull up suddenly; *geen ~ meer VIND nie*, find no further trace of; *iem. se ~ VOLG*, follow in someone's footsteps; (w) (ge-), travel by rail; align, put in alignment (vehicle).

spoor[2], (s) (**spore**), spur; *iem. met spore RY*, ride someone hard; *sy spore VERDIEN*, win his spurs; (w) (ge-), spur.

spoor[3], (s) (**spore**), spore (bot.).

spoor: ~**baan**, railroad, railway track, permanent way; ~**beampte**, railwayman, railway official, railway employee; ~**boek**, railway guide; ~**boom**, level-crossing barrier; ~**bou**, railway construction; ~**breedte**, gauge, tread (of vehicle); ~**brug**, railway bridge; ~**buier**, Jim Crow (implement); ~**bus**, rail-bus; rail-car; railway bus.

spoor'der, aligner (of wheels).

spoor'draend, (-e), spur-bearing.

spoor'element, trace-element.

spoor: ~**hamer**, dogging-hammer; ~**hek**, level-crossing gate; ~**hoogte**, rail level; ~**hou, (-ge-)**, keep to the trail; ~**lêer**, platelayer; railway sleeper; ~**legging**, platelaying, laying of rails.

spoor'leier, ribband.

spoor'loos, (b) (. .lose), trackless; (bw) completely; ~**verdwyn**, vanish into space; disappear without a trace.

spoor: ~**lyn**, railway line; ~**maat**, rail gauge; ~**maker**, trail blazer; ~**man, (-ne)**, railworker.

spoor'maker, spurrier.

spoor: ~**motor**, rail-motor; rail-trolley; ~**oorweg**, level crossing, railway crossing.

spoor'plant, spore-bearing plant; cryptogam.

spoor: ~**ratjie, (-s)**, rowel; ~**reis**, railway journey.

spoor'riem, spur-strap.

spoor'skroef, coach-screw.

spoor'slag, incentive, urge, stimulus; *tot ~ dien*, serve as an incentive, urge on.

spoor'sny, (-ge-), take the scent, track; ~**er**, tracker.

spoor'spyker, dog-spike; ~**hamer**, spike-hammer.

spoor: ~**staaf**, rail: ~**staaflens**, rail-flange; ~**stawe**, metals (railway); ~**tang**, rail-tongs.

spoor'tjie[1], **(-s)**, small footprint.

spoor'tjie[2], **(-s)**, small spur.

spoor'tjie[3], **(-s)**, sporule (bot.).

spoor'toestel, aligner.

spoor: ~**trein**, railway train; ~**verbinding**, railway connection; ~**vervoer**, carriage (transport) by rail; railway transport; ~**vrag**, railway charges, railage.

spoor'vorm, (-e), spore form; ~**ing**, sporation.

spoor: ~**wa**, railway carriage (car); saloon; truck; ~**wagter**, signalman; pointsman; flagman; ~**wal**, bank; (railway) embankment.

spoor'weg, (. .weë), railway, railroad; ~**aandeel**, railway share; ~**aanleg**, railway construction; ~**aansluiting**, railway junction; ~**administrasie**, railway administration; ~**beampte**, railway official; ~**boekhandel**, station bookstall; ~**bou**, railway construction; ~**brug**, railway bridge; ~**dienaar**, railway servant; ~**diens**, railway service; ~**dokter**, railway doctor; ~**eiendom**, railway property; S~-

spoor en Haweraad, Railways and Harbours Board; ~gids, railway guide; ~halte, railway halt (siding); ~hek, level-crossing gate; ~huis, railway house; ~inkomste, railway revenue, railway earnings; ~inrigting, railway plant; ~kaart, railway map; ~kaartjie, rail(way) ticket; ~knoop, railway junction; ~kommissaris, railway commissioner; ~koste, railage; ~lektuur, railway (light) reading matter; ~lyn, railway line; ~maatskappy, railway company; ~man, railwayman; ~mandaat, rail(way) warrant; ~materiaal, railway stock; ~motor, rail-car; ~motordiens, rail-motor service; ~net, network of railways; railway system; ~ongeluk, railway accident; ~oorgang, level (railway) crossing; ~order, rail-warrant; ~personeel, railway staff; ~ramp, railway disaster; ~rytuig, railway carriage; ~stasie, railway station; ~stelsel, railway system; ~tarief, railway rate; ~terminus, railhead; ~tonnel, railway tunnel; ~uitbreiding, railway extension; ~verbinding, railway connection; ~verkeer, railway traffic; ~verversingskamer, railway refreshment-room; ~werf, railway yard; ~werker, platelayer; railworker; S~wet, Railway Act; ~werkswinkel, railway workshop.

spoor: ~wiel, (-e), rail wheel; ~wieletjie, (-s), rowel; ~wissel, railway switch, points; ~wydte, rail gauge, wheel-track.

spora'dies, (-e), sporadic.

sporan'gium, (-s, ..gieë), sporangium.

spo're: ~blaas, ascus; ~dosie, sporogonium.

spo're: ~draend, (-e), spur-bearing; ~draer, sporophore; ~hopie, sorus; ~houer, sporangium; ~loos, (..lose), sporeless; ~sak(kie), spore-case.

Spo'reslag, Battle of the Spurs.

spo're: ~vorming, spore-formation, sporogenesis; ~vrug, spore-fruit, sporocarp.

spo'ring, alignment (of wheels); tracking.

spo'restang, track-rod (railway); tie-rod (motor).

spor'ling, (-s), trouble; ~ maak, cause trouble.

sporokarp', (-e), sporocarp.

spor'rie, spurr(e)y (Heliophila sp.).

spo'rofiet, sporophyte.

spo'rofil, sporophyll.

sporofi'ties, (-e), sporophytic.

sporofoor', (..fore), sporophore.

sport[1], (s) (-e), rung, step (of ladder); rail (of chair); *sy het die hoogste ~ BEREIK*, she has got to the top of the tree; *tot die HOOGSTE ~ in die maatskappy opklim*, climb to the top of the social ladder.

sport[2], (s) (-e, -soorte), sport; ~afdeling, sports department; ~baadjie, sports coat; ~benodigdhede, sport(ing) requisites; ~berigte, sporting news; ~blad, sports paper; ~bloes(e), sports blouse; ~broek, (sports) shorts; ~byeenkoms, sports (athletic) meeting; ~doeleindes, sporting purposes; ~drag, sports wear; ~fees, sports meeting; gymkhana; ~gees, sportsmanship, sporting spirit; ~hemp, sports shirt; ~ief', (..tiewe), sporting, sportsmanlike; fond of sport; ~iwiteit, sportsmanship; sporting spirit; ~klub, sports club; ~kostuum, sports dress; ~kringe, sporting circles; ~liefhebber, sportsman, sporting man; ~lie'wend, (-e), keen on sports; sporting; ~mal, mad on sport; ~man, sportsman; ~manskap, sportsmanship; ~motor, sports car; ~nommer, (sports) event; ~nuus, sporting news; ~oor, cauliflower-ear; ~pak, sports suit; ~redakteur, sports editor; ~rubriek, sports column; ~skrywer, sports writer; ~term, sporting term; ~terrein, sports ground(s); playing field; athletic field; recreation grounds; ~uitrusting, sports outfit; ~uitslae, sports results, ~vereniging, sports (athletic) association; ~vis, game fish; ~vliegtuig, sportster; ~wêreld, sporting world (community); ~winkel, sports shop.

spot, (s) ridicule, derision, scorn, mockery; banter; raillery, persiflage; *die ~ DRYWE met*, mock at; make a fool of; (w) (ge-), jest, joke; deride, mock, jeer; quiz; *met ALLES ~* , poke fun at everything; *met GODSDIENS ~* , blaspheme; *hy LAAT nie met hom ~ nie*, he stands no nonsense; ~agtig (-e), mocking, jeering, derisive; ~dig, (-te), satire, parody; ~digter, satirist; ~goedkoop, dirt cheap; ~lag, jeer, sneer, derisive laughter, fleer; ~lus, love of satire (joking); ~lyster, catbird; ~naam, nickname, sobriquet; byword; ~prent, caricature, cartoon; ~prenttekenaar, caricaturist, cartoonist; ~prys, bargain price, ridiculously low price; booby prize; ~rede, diatribe; ~siek, (-e), fond of banter, satirical, sarcastic; ~skrif, (-te), skit, lampoon; ~sug, love of sarcasm, mockery, scoffing; ~tend, (-e), derisive, jeering, mocking, ironical, contumelious; ~tenderwys(e), jokingly; gibingly, mockingly, in derision.

spot'ter, (-s), scoffer, mocker; *~ se huis BRAND ook af, ~ kry sy LOON*, mocking is catching; ~ig, (-e), full of mockery, sarcastic.

spotterny', (-e), mockery; badinage, raillery.

spot'tery, jesting, chaffing, banter.

spot'voël, mocking-bird; joker, mocker, teaser.

spraak, speech; *jou ~ maak jou openbaar*, your words give you away; ~belemmering, impediment in one's speech; ~gebrek, speech defect, impediment in speech; ~gebruik, idiom, parlance; *die gewone ~gebruik*, colloquial speech; ~klank, speech sound; phoneme; ~kuns, grammar; ~kuns'tig, (-e), grammatical; ~loos = sprakeloos; ~leer, speech training; grammar; ~makende, (-e), language-forming; *die ~makende gemeenskap*, those who speak the language; language community; ~motoriek, speech mechanism; ~onderwyser, elocutionist; ~opleiding, speach training; ~orgaan, organ of speech.

spraak'saam, (..same), talkative, garrulous, conversational, loquacious, chatty; ~heid, talkativeness, loquacity, garrulity.

spraak: ~verlies, aphasia; ~vermoë, power of speech; ~verwarring, confusion of tongues; *die Babiloniese ~verwarring*, the Confusion of Tongues; babel; ~wending, idiom, turn of speech, phrase; ~werktuig = spraakorgaan.

spra'ke, talk, rumour; *ter ~ BRING*, broach a subject; *DAAR is ~ van . . .,* it is said that . . .; *GEEN ~ van nie*, no question about it; *daar IS ~ dat*, there is talk of; *TER ~ kom*, be raised, crop up; ~loos, (..lose), speechless, inarticulate; dumb, mute; ~loosheid, speechlessness, aphonia, muteness.

sprank, (-e), spark; particle; *g'n ~ie menslike gevoel nie*, without a spark of human feeling.

spran'kel, (ge-), spark, sparkle; scintillate; ~ing, sparkle, scintillation.

spreek, (ge-), speak, talk, converse, discourse; *dit ~ BOEKDELE*, it speaks volumes; *mag ek die HOOF ~?* may I see the principal? *ons sal mekaar NADER ~* , I intend to have a word with you; *NIE te ~ wees nie*, not available for consultation; *hy is daar SLEG oor te ~*, he does not wish to discuss the matter; *dit ~ VANSELF*, it stands to reason; it goes without saying; *dit ~ tot die VERBEELDING*, it appeals to the imagination; ~beurt, lecture, engagement (to speak); turn to speak; ~buis, speaking-tube; mouthpiece; *iem. se ~buis wees*, be somebody's mouthpiece; ~film, (vero.), talkie, sound film; ~fout, slip of the tongue; ~gestoelte, platform, rostrum, desk; ~horing, speaking-trumpet; ~kamer, consulting room; locutary; ~kanaal, channel of speech; ~koor, speech chorus; ~kuns, art of speech; public speaking; ~les, conversation exercise; ~onderwys, conversation lesson(s); elocution, speech-training; ~rolprent, sound-film; ~stem, speaking voice; ~ster, (-s), speaker (woman); ~taal, spoken language, colloquial speech; vernacular; ~taaluitdrukking, colloquialism; ~trant, manner of speech; ~trompet, speaking-trumpet; mouthpiece; ~tyd, speaking time; ~uur, consulting hour(s).

spreek'woord, proverb, saying, adage; idiom; ~eboek, dictionary of proverbs.

spreekwoor'delik, (-e), proverbial.

spreek: ~woordemaker, proverbialist; ~wyse, manner of speaking; idiom; expression; address.

spreeu, (-s), starling; *Indiese ~*, mina; ~eier, starling's egg; ~nes, starling's nest; dug-out.

sprei[1], (s) (-e), counterpane, bedspread, coverlet.

sprei², (w) (ge-), scatter, spread out; stagger; open out (football); ~ **ding**, spread(ing), dispersion, staggering (of holidays, hours, etc.); fall-out (radioactivity); ~**-ent**, splayed end; ~ **er**, spreader, rose (watering-can); vane (machinery); ~ **kop**, rose; ~ **lig**, floodlight; ~ **verf**, duco; ~ **verligting**, floodlighting; ~ **wydte**, spread.

spre'kend, (-e), speaking, lifelike, living (image); *'n ~ e BEWYS*, a telling proof; *'n ~ e GELYKENIS*, a speaking likeness; *hy lyk ~ op sy VADER*, he is the very image of his father.

spre'ker, (-s), speaker, orator, lecturer.

spre'kerstalent, gift of speech.

spreuk, (-e), proverb, aphorism, adage, maxim; motto, device; *S ~ e van Salomo*, Book of Proverbs; ~ **digter**, maker of aphorisms; ~ **vormig**, (-e), gnomic.

spriet, (-e), blade (of grass); feeler, antenna (of insect); sprit (ship); ~ **seil**, sprit-sail.

sprik'kel, (s) (-s), spot, speck; (w) (ge-), speckle, spot.

spring, (s) (-e), jump, leap, bound; caper, gambol; hop; *met groot ~ e*, by leaps and bounds; (w) (ge-), jump, leap, bound; buck; prance (horse); hop, skip; explode; ~ **aar**, spring, fountain-head; ~ **bok**, springbok, springbuck; *S ~ bok*, Springbok (sport); ~ **boontjie**, jumping-bean; ~ **bron**, fountain; ~ **bus**, detonator; petard; ~ **er**, (-s), jumper, hopper, springer, leaper; bumper (cricket); ~ **fontein**, fountain; ~ **haas**, Cape kangaroo, jumping-hare, jerboa *(Pedetis capensis)*; ~ **haaslamp**, bull's-eye lamp; ~ **haasmuis**, gerbille; ~ **jurk**, gym, gymnastic costume; ~ **kewer**, skipjack; flea-beetle; ~ **koring**, puffed wheat; ~ **lading**, bursting charge, explosive charge; filling (bomb); burster; ~ **laken**, jumping-sheet; ~ **lewendig**, (-e), very much alive, sprightly, alive and kicking, as fresh as paint; ~ **mat**, trampoline; ~ **matras**, spring mattress; gymnastic mattress; ~ **middel**, explosive, blasting agent; ~ **mielies**, popcorn; ~ **nommers**, jumping events; ~ **oefening**, vaulting exercise; ~ **paal**, fen-pole; vaulting pole; ~ **patroon**, blasting-cartridge; ~ **perd**, vaulting-horse (gymnast.); ~ **plank**, diving-board; jumping-board; ~ **plooi**, inverted pleat; ~ **punt**, burst; ~ **riem**, skipping-rope; martingale; ~ **rok**, gym, gymnastic costume; ~ **rys**, puffed rice; ~ **slot**, snap-lock; ~ **spinnekop**, saltigrade; ~ **steek**, gobble-stitch; ~ **stok**, vaulting-pole; ~ **teuel**, martingale; bearing-rein; *iem. met ~ teuels ry*, keep a firm hand on someone; ~ **tou**, skipping-rope; ~ **ty**, spring tide; ~ **veer**, snap-spring; spiral metallic spring; ~ **veermatras**, box-mattress; inner-spring mattress; ~ **vloed**, spring tide; high water; ~ **werk**, blasting.

sprin'kaan, (..kane), locust, grasshopper; *so maer soos 'n ~*, as lean as a rake; ~ **beampte**, locust-officer; ~ **boom**, honey-locust (tree) *(Gleditsia triacanthos)*; ~ **bos**, locust-wood *(Senecio ilicifolius)*; ~ **bosvergiftiging**, senecio poisoning; ~ **gif**, locust-poison; ~ **jaar**: *die ~ jare*, the years that the locusts have eaten; ~ **plaag**, locust menace; ~ **swerm**, swarm of locusts; ~ **voël**, stork; locust-bird *(Ciconia ciconia)*; (black-winged) pratincole *(Glareola nordmanni)*.

sprin'kel, (s) (-s), speck, spot; (w) (ge-), sprinkle; dabble; damp (laundry); sparge; ~ **aar**, sprinkler; sparger; ~ **besproeiing**, overhead irrigation, spray-irrigation; ~ **blusser**, sprinkler; ~ **blusstelsel**, sprinkler installation; ~ **poeier**, pounce; ~ **spuit**, sprinkler; ~ **wa**, water-sprinkler.

sprits, (Ndl.), shortbread.

sproei¹, (s) = **spru**

sproei², (w) (ge-), spray (with insecticide); sprinkle (water); ~ **aanval**, spray-attack; ~ **er**, (-s), sprinkler, spray-nozzle, sprayer, jet, vaporizer, rose; ~ **ery**, spraying, sprinkling; ~ **klep**, sprayer-valve; ~ **kop**, rose, spraying nozzle; ~ **masjien**, spraying machine; ~ **middel**, insect-spray; ~ **reën**, spray; ~ **spuit**, spray-gun; ~ **toestel**, spraying apparatus; ~ **verf**, duco; ~ **vlug**, spraying-flight; ~ **wa**, street-sprinkler, water-cart; ~ **water**, spray.

sproet, (-e), freckle, macula; fleck; ~ **agtig**, (-e), freckled; ~ **erig**, (-e), freckled, full of freckles; lentiginous; ~ **erigheid**, lentigo; ~ **gesig**, freckled face; ~ **room**, freckle-cream (med.).

spro'kie, (-s), fable, fairytale; fiction.

spro'kies: ~ **agtig**, (-e), fairylike; *S ~ land*, Fairyland; ~ **verhaal**, fairytale, fairy story; ~ **verteller**, storyteller.

sprok'kel, (ge-), gather, pick (wood); ~ **ing**, wood-picking; gleaning; ~ **wurm**, caddis-worm.

sprong, (-e), jump, leap, bounce, bound, caper, hop; *'n ~ in die DUISTER doen*, take a leap in the dark; *met EEN ~*, at a bound, with a leap; *met GROOT ~ e*, by leaps and bounds; *KROM ~ e maak*, resort to devious devices; *op ~ STAAN*, be on the point of; *met 'n ~ VOORUITGAAN*, take a great leap forward; *'n ~ WAAG*, take the plunge; ~ **been**, astragalus; ~ **beweging**, saltation; ~ **gewrig**, hock, hough; ~ **hoogte**, throw.

sprongs'gewys(e), by leaps and bounds.

sprong'stuk, spring-bend.

sprook, (sproke), tale, story; *hy sprak g'n ~*, he was tongue-tied; he ne'er said a word.

sprot, (-te), sprat.

spru, thrush, sprue; aphtha; red gum.

spruit, (s) (-e), shoot, sprout, sprig, ratoon, offshoot; watercourse, sidestream, creek, affluent, brook, rivulet; scion, descendant; *'n ADELLIKE ~*, sprig of the nobility; *MY ~ e*, my olive-branches (children); (w) (ge-), sprout, shoot; arise; descend from.

spruit: ~ **jie**, (-s), brooklet; small sprout; *Brusselse ~ jies* Brussels sprouts; ~ **kool**, broccoli; *Brusselse ~ kool*, Brussels sprouts; ~ **pyp**, ~ **stuk**, manifold.

spu, (w) (ge-) = **spoeg**; ~ **middel**, expectorant.

spui'er, (-s), spout, gargoyle, gutter spout.

spui'gat, (-e), scupper; cleaning aperture; *dit loop die ~ e uit*, it passes all bounds, that is the limit.

spuit, (s) (-e), syringe, douche, enema, squirt; jet, hose, spout (fire-engine); (w) (ge-), inject; spout, spray, squirt; syringe; blow (whale); ~ **aandrywing**, jet-propulsion; ~ **aartappels**, duchess potatoes; ~ **bron**, geyser; ~ **buisie**, forcing tube; ~ **druk**, spray-painting; ~ **er**, (-s), spouter, (oil) gusher; ~ **fles**, siphon; scent-spray; ~ **fontein**, playing fountain; ~ **gat**, blowhole (of cetaceans); spiracle; ~ **jie**, (-s), syringe; injection; ~ **middel**, spray; ~ **neus**, hose nozzle; sprinkler; ~ **pomp**, spray-pump; ~ **sement**, gunite; ~ **skilder**, spray-painter; ~ **slang**, (garden) hose; ~ **stof**, spray; ~ **toestel**, spraying apparatus; ~ **verf**, duco; cellulose paint; (w) (ge-), spray-paint; ~ **verwer**, spray-painter; ~ **vis**, cuttle-fish; ~ **vliegtuig**, spray-plane; ~ **water**, aerated water; soda-water, mineral water; ~ **waterbottel**, ~ **waterfles**, soda-water bottle, siphon; ~ **watertoestel**, gazogene.

spul, affair, case; lot, caboodle; *'n DEURMEKAAR ~*, a chaotic affair; mix-up; *hulle het ~ gehad met mekaar*, they have fallen out; *die HELE ~*, the whole lot; *dit sal 'n LELIKE ~ afgee*, that will be a nasty affair; *met SO 'n ~ wil ek niks uit te waaie hê nie*, I will have no truck with such a lot; ~ **letjie**, (-s), affair, thing, business; ~ *letjies AANVANG*, be up to mischief; *geen ~ letjies DULD (verdra) nie*, stand no nonsense.

spur'rie, see **sporrie**

sput'ter, (ge-), grumble; sputter; fizz; sizzle.

spu(ug) = **spoeg**; (s) spittle, expectoration, saliva; (w) (ge-), spit, expectorate; ~ **afskeiding**, ptyalism; ~ **bak**, spittoon; spitting-mug; ~ **lok**, kiss-curl, cow-lick; ~ **sel**, spittle; ~ **slang**, ringed cobra, spitting snake.

spu'wing, (-e, -s), spitting, expectoration; *'n ~ hê*, give up blood.

spy, (-e) = **spie**.

spy'ker, (s) (-s), nail, brad, tack; *'n ~ in die DOODKIS*, a nail in one's coffin; *die ~ op die KOP slaan*, hit the nail on the head; *~ s met KOPPE slaan*, not spare one's punches; not to mince matters; *~ s op LAAGWATER soek*, cavil; try to find something to quibble about; (w) (ge-), nail; ~ **bak**, nail-box; ~ **balsem**, "Spijker" salve; ~ **beentjies**, spindly legs; ~ **boor**, gimlet; wimble; ~ **broek**, jeans; ~ **draad**, nail-shank; ~ **drywer**, nail-punch; ~ **els**, bradawl; ~ **fabriek**, nailery; ~ **gat**, nail-hole; ~ **groef**, fuller-

spypen 501 **staan-staan**

ing; ~**haak**, ripper; ~**hak**, stiletto heel; ~**hard**, nail-proof; ~**kop**, nail-head; ~**klou**, nail-claw; ~**maker**, nailer; ~**makery**, (-e), nailery; ~**pons**, nail-punch; ~**skoene**, (shoes with) spikes; ~**skrif**, cuneiform characters (writing); ~**smid**, nailer, nailsmith; ~**tafel**, pintable; ~**trekker**, claw-hammer, nail extractor; puller; ~**vas**, (-te), fixed; *wat* ~ *vas is*, the fixtures; ~**vormig**, (-e), cuneiform, nail-shaped; ~**wurm**, screw-worm.

spy'pen, cotter pin.

spys, (-e), **spy'se**, food, viands, cheer, victuals; mess; ~ *en DRANK*, meat and drink; *VERANDERING van* ~ *laat eet*, change of food whets the appetite; ~**beampte**, catering officer; ~**bry**, chyme.

spysenier', (s) (-s), caterer; (w) (ge-), cater; ~**ing**, catering.

spyseniers': ~**bedryf**, catering trade; ~**diens**, catering service; ~**pak**, catering pack.

spy'sig, (ge-), feed, give to eat; ~**ing**, feeding, nourishing.

spys: ~**kaart**, menu, bill of fare; ~**kamer**, pantry; ~**kanaal**, digestive tract, alimentary canal; ~**lys**, menu, bill of fare; ~**offer**, meat-offering; ~**sap**, chyle; ~**verterend**, (-e), peptic; ~**vertering**, digestion; *slegte* ~ *vertering*, indigestion, dyspepsia; ~**verteringskanaal**, alimentary (digestive) canal; ~**verteringsorgane**, digestive organs; the peptics; ~**verteringstelsel**, digestive system; ~**verteringsteuring**, dyspepsia.

spyt, (s) compunction, regret, sorrow; ~ *is 'n goeie DING, maar dit is altyd te laat*, ~ *kom altyd te LAAT*, it is no use crying over spilt milk; remorse always comes too late; *meer* ~ *as HARE op die kop hê*, have many regrets; *TEN* ~ *e van*, in spite of, notwithstanding; *TOT my* ~ *merk ek*, I notice with regret; ~ *VOEL oor*, feel sorry about; (w) (ge-), regret, be sorry; *dit* ~ *my*, I am sorry; ~**betuiging**, expression of regret.

spy'tig, (-e), envious, cross; regrettable, disappointing; ~**heid**, regrettableness, pique; envy.

Sri' Lanka, Sri Lanka (Ceylon).

st! hush!

staaf¹, (s) (stawe), bar, staff, rod; stave; ingot (of gold); pig (of iron); brick (of copper); *'n* ~ *goud*, an ingot of gold.

staaf², (w) (ge-), confirm, prove, bear out; substantiate (a charge); *deur GETUIE ge* ~, duly attested; *stawende GETUIENIS*, supporting evidence.

staaf: ~**battery**, battery; ~**bundel**, fasces; ~**diertjie**, bacillus; ~**gewig**, bar bell; ~**goud**, bar gold; gold bullion; ~**ketting**, sprocket chain; ~**klamp**, barclamp; ~**koper**, bar copper; copper bar; ~**koppeling**, rod coupling; ~**magneet**, bar magnet; ~**silwer**, bar silver; bullion; ~**tin**, bar tin; ~**vorm**, ingot mould; ~**vormig**, (-e), in bar form; bacillary; ~**yster**, bar-iron; puddle-bar.

staak¹, (w) (ge-), strike, cease work; discontinue, stop, suspend; stall; *die ARBEIDERS* ~, the workmen down tools (strike work); *sy RESOEKE* ~, discontinue his visits; *die MASJIEN* ~, the engine stalls; *die STEMME* ~, the votes are equally divided.

staak², (s) (stake), stake, pole; ~**heining**, palisade; ~**houer**, (-s), stake-horse; ~**net**, stake-net.

staal¹, (stale), sample, pattern.

staal², (s) steel; *sagte* ~, mild steel; (w) (ge-), steel; ~**agtig**, (-e), steel-like; ~**bad**, steel bath; ~**balk**, steel girder; ~**band**, steel tape; ~**bedryf**, steel industry; ~**bekleding**, steel facing (cladding); ~**blou**, (-e), steel blue.

staal'boek, sampler, pattern-book.

staal: ~**borsel**, wire brush; ~**bron**, chalybeate spring; ~**dekking**, steel facing; ~**draad**, steel wire; ~**draadtou**, wire rope (cable); ~**druppels**, chalybeate drops; ~**dwarslêer**, steel sleeper (railway); ~**fabriek**, steelworks; ~**gietery**, steel-foundry; ~**graveerkuns**, siderography, steel engraving; ~**graveur**, steel-engraver; ~**gravure**, steel engraving; ~**grys**, (-e), steel grey; ~**hamer**, steel hammer; ~**hard**, (-e), hard as steel; ~**helm**, steel helmet; ~**houdend**, (-e), steely (water), chalybeate.

staal'kaart, sample-card, pattern-book.

staal: ~**kabel**, wire rope, cable-wire; ~**kis**, steel cabinet; steel box; steel coffin; ~**kleurig**, (-e), steel-coloured.

staal'meester, syndic (of clothier's guild); *Die Staalmeesters*, The Syndics (by Rembrandt).

staal: ~**middel**, steel medicine; ~**pen**, steel pin; ~**pil**, chalybeate pill; bullet; ~**plaat**, steel plate, steel engraving; ~**rei**, straight edge; ~**smedery**, steel factory.

staal'tjie, (-s), yarn, joke; cast; sample, pattern; instance (of behaviour); anecdote.

staal: ~**tou**, wire rope; ~**vlot**, float; ~**water**, chalybeate water; ~**werk**, steelwork; ~**wig**, gad; ~**wol**, steel wool; ~**wyn**, steel wine, wine of iron.

staan, (ge-), stand; stop; be erect, remain upright; *dit* ~ *my nie AAN nie*, it does not appeal to me; *AGTER iem.* ~, stand behind someone; back someone up; egg someone on; *dit* ~ *nog te BESIEN*, that remains to be seen; *BLY* ~, remain standing; stop; come to a halt; be stuck; *BO-AAN* ~, head the list; *die vyand tot* ~ *BRING*, check (the progress of) the enemy; *daar* ~ *ek BUITE*, that is no concern of mine; *BY iem.* ~, stand by someone; *in die BYBEL* ~, it says in the Bible; *ek* ~ *DAAROP*, I insist upon it; *in DIENS* ~ *van*, be in the employ of; *ek weet wat my te DOEN* ~, I know my duty; *DUUR te* ~ *kom*, pay dearly for; *voor die FEIT* ~, have to face the fact; *GAAN* ~, come to a standstill; *sulke GEDRAG* ~ *jou nie*, such behaviour does not become you; *dit* ~ *nêrens GESKRYWE nie*, there is no proof of it; *dit* ~ *GESKRYWE*, it is written; *dit kom iem. GOED te* ~, something stands someone in good stead; *GOED* ~ *vir iem.*, vouch for someone; *HOE* ~ *die lewe?* how is life? ~ *de HOU*, keep someone on his legs; stop someone (e.g. in the street); *sy KANSE* ~ *goed*, he stands a good chance; *dit KOM te* ~ *op*, it (the price) amounts to; *voor iets te* ~ *KOM*, be confronted with something; *al sy KOS het bly* ~, his food remained untouched; *hy weet niks, LAAT* ~ *haar*, he knows nothing, nor to mention her; *LAAT* ~, leave it at that; leave it alone; ~ *de LEËR*, regular (standing) army; ~ *de MAG*, permanent force; *dit* ~ *jou nie MOOI nie*, it does not become you; *ONDER iem.* ~, be under the authority of someone; *OPSY* ~, stand aside; *die ROK* ~ *jou goed*, the dress suits you; *ROND en bont* ~, be hard put to it; *ROOK laat* ~, stop (give up) smoking; ~ *of ek SKIET*, stand or I shoot; *alles het net SO bly* ~, everything remained untouched; *STERK* ~, be in a strong position; *hy* ~ *STERK*, he is well-to-do; *SWAK* ~, be poorly off; *TOT* ~ *kom*, come to a standstill; ~ *of VAL by iets*, stand or fall by something; *op VERTREK* ~, be on the point of leaving; *VIR niks* ~ *nie*, stop at nothing; *VOOR 'n feit* ~, be faced with a fact; *sy VROU het hom laat* ~, his wife left him; *dit* ~ *jou VRY*, you are at liberty; ~ **as**, tower-shaft; ~**balk**, principal rafter, ~**bord**, footplate; ~**dak**, pitched roof, inclined roof.

staan'de, (b) standing; stationary; stand up; masculine (rhyme); perpendicular; permanent; ~ *HOU dat . . .*, maintain that . . .; *jou* ~ *HOU*, hold one's own; ~ *RYM*, masculine rhyme; ~ *SKRIF*, perpendicular writing; ~ *die vergadering*, during (at) the meeting; ~ *WATER*, stagnant water.

staan: ~**der**, (-s), standard; · geld, demurrage, stallage, grazing-fee; ~**klavier**, upright piano; ~**klok**, mantelpiece clock; grandfather's clock; ~**kraag**, stand up collar; ~**kruin**, pillar-tap, ~**kroeg**, stand-up bar; ~**laer**, bearing block; ~**lamp**, table-lamp; pedestal lamp; ~**leer**, step-ladder; ~**lig**, parking light; ~**oorlosie**, grandfather's clock; ~**plank**, duck-board; footboard; ~**plek**, standing room; stand; pitch; parking-area, parking-place; taxi-rank; encampment; halting-place; *geen* ~ *plek*, no parking; ~**pyp**, stand-pipe; ~**ruimte**, standing-room.

staan'spoor, start, beginning; base; *UIT die* ~ *uit*, *VAN die* ~ *af*, from the very beginning.

staan'-staan', given to standing around, loitering; in an upright position; ~ *loop*, walk slowly, stopping every now and then.

staan: ~ **steen**, brick on end, soldier; ~ **stut**, vertical shore.
staar, (s) pearl-eye, cataract; *GROEN* ~, glaucoma; *GROU* ~, cataract; *SWART* ~, amaurosis; (w) (**ge-**), gaze, stare, glower, glare at; *jou BLIND* ~ *op*, be blind to everything but; *VOOR jou uit* ~, stare into vacancy.
staar'ligting, couching (a cataract).
staat, (state), state; condition; return, list, statement, record, form; rank, position, status; ~ *van BELEG*, state of siege; *DIE* ~, the body politic; the State (jur.); *EGTELIKE (huwelike)* ~, matrimony; *FINANSIËLE* ~, financial statement; *in* ~ *van OORLOG verkeer*, be in a state of war; *in* ~ *van ONTBINDING*, in a state of decomposition; *die* ~ *van SAKE*, the state of affairs; *in* ~ *STEL*, enable; *TOT alles in* ~, capable of anything; *in* ~ *WEES*, be capable of; ~ **huis'houdkunde**, political economy; economics; plutonomy; the dismal science; ~ **huishoudkun'dig**, (-e), pertaining to political economy; ~ **huishoudkun'dige**, (-s), political economist; ~ **kunde**, politics, statecraft, statemanship; policy; political science.
staatkun'dig, (-e), political; ~ **e**, (-s), politician, statesman; political scientist.
staat'lik, (-e), grand, stately; ~ **heid**, stateliness, grandeur.
staat'loos, (..**lose**), stateless; ~ **heid**, statelessness.
staat'maak, (-ge-): ~ *op*, rely (count, depend) on.
staat'maker, (-s), mainstay, stalwart, reliable person, prop, brick.
staat'saak, state affair; state's case; public affair.
staats: ~ **aangeleentheid**, affair of state; ~ **aanklaer**, public prosecutor; ~ **almanak**, red book.
staats'amp, government office, post in the civil service; ~ **tenaar**, government official, civil servant, public servant.
staats: ~ **bank**, state (national) bank; ~ **bankrotskap**, national bankruptcy; ~ **bedryf**, government enterprise; ~ **begrafnis**, state funeral; ~ **begroting**, budget; ~ **belang**, interest of the state; ~ **beleid**, policy of the state; national policy; ~ **bemoeiing**, state interference; ~ **besit**, government property; ~ **besluit**, government decree; ~ **besoek**, state visit; ~ **bestuur**, government; ~ **betrekking**, government post; ~ **bewind**, polity, government; ~ **biblioteek**, state library; ~ **bibliotekaris**, state librarian; ~ **blad**, government (press) organ, government gazette; ~ **burger**, citizen; ~ **bydrae**, government contribution; ~ **dienaar**, civil (public) servant; ~ **diens**, civil service; ~ **dokument**, state paper; ~ **drukkery**, government printing-works (printer); ~ **eenheid**, state unity; ~ **eiendom**, public property, state property.
staat'sekretaris, secretary of state; chief secretary (for colonies).
staats: ~ **eksamen**, government (civil service) examination; ~ **eksploitasie**, state exploitation; ~ **entrepot**, government warehouse; ~ **fondse**, government securities; ~ **geheim**, state secret, secret of state; ~ **gelde**, state money, government funds; ~ **geleentheid**, state occasion; ~ **gesag**, authority of the state; ~ **gesinde**, (-s), loyalist; ~ **gevaarlik**, (-e), dangerous to the state; ~ **gevangene**, prisoner of state; political prisoner; ~ **gevangenis**, state prison; ~ **godsdiens**, state religion; ~ **greep**, coup d'état; ~ **grond**, public lands; ~ **hoof**, head of (the) state; ~ **hulp**, government help, state aid.
staat'sie, ceremony, state, pomp; procession; *met groot* ~, with great pomp; ~ **bed**, state bed; *op 'n* ~ *bed lê*, lie in state; ~ **kleed**, state robes; ~ **koets**, state coach; ~ **saal**, stateroom.
staats: ~ **inkomste**, public revenue; ~ **inmenging**, government interference; ~ **inrigting**, government institution; frame of government; ~ **instelling**, public institution; ~ **kas**, public treasury, exchequer; ~ **kerk**, state church; established church; establishment; ~ **koerant**, government gazette.
staat'skool, government school.
staats'korting, (-s), government rebate.
staats'koste: *op* ~ *LOSEER*, be lodged at the state's pleasure; *OP* ~, at public expense.

staat'skuld, national debt, public debt.
staats: ~ **leer**, political science; ~ **lening**, state loan; ~ **liggaam**, body politic; ~ **lotery**, state lottery; ~ **man**, (-ne, **staatsliede**), statesman, diplomatist, diplomat, politician; ~ **mansblik**, political insight; ~ **masjinerie**, machinery of state; ~ **manswysheid**, statesmanship; ~ **minister**, minister of state; ~ **misdaad**, political offence; ~ **misdadiger**, political offender; ~ **monopolie**, state monopoly; ~ **myningenieur**, government mining engineer; ~ **omwenteling**, revolution; ~ **onderneming**, government enterprise; ~ **ondersteuning**, government aid; ~ **ontvangste**, national revenue; ~ **opvattinge**, political philosophy; ~ **order**, government order (warrant).
staat'sorg, government care; ~ **e**, cares of state.
staats'papiere, public securities, public funds, the funds, stocks; state documents.
staats'pensioen, government pension.
staat'spoorweg, government railways.
staats: ~ **president**, state president; ~ **prokureur**, attorney-general; ~ **reëling**, constitution (of a state); polity; ~ **reg**, constitutional law; ~ **rekeninge**, public accounts.
staat'steun, government assistance.
staats: ~ **televisiediens**, state (government) television service; ~ **toelae**, government subsidy; ~ **toesig**, government supervision.
staat'stuk, state document.
staats: ~ **uitgawe**, public expenditure; ~ **veiligheid**, state security; ~ **verband**, political allegiance; ~ **verhoor**, state trial; ~ **verkeer**, government traffic; ~ **verraad**, high treason; ~ **vertaler**, government translator; ~ **verwisseling**, change of state (status); ~ **vliegveld**, state-owned aerodrome; ~ **vorm**, form of government.
staats'weë: *van* ~, on behalf of the government, by authority.
staats: ~ **wet**, public law; ~ **wetenskap**, political science.
stabiel', (-e), solid, firm, stable, steady.
stabilisa'sie, stabilization.
stabilisa'tor, (-s), stabilizer.
stabiliseer', (ge-), stabilize; ~ **der**, (-s), stabilizer.
stabiliteit', stability.
stacca'to, staccato (music).
stad, (**stede**), town, city; *die Ewige S* ~, the Eternal City; *die* ~ *INGAAN*, go down town; ~ *en OMGEWING*, town and environs; ~ **agtig**, (-e), town-like; ~ **bewoner**, city-dweller.
sta'de : *te* ~ *kom*, come in handy; suit one well.
stad'genoot, (..**note**), fellow townsman, fellow citizen.
stad'huis, town hall, city hall; ~ **styl**, formal style; officialese; ~ **taal**, committee language (style); ~ **woord**, official term; pompous word.
sta'dig, (-e), slow; slow-moving; adagio (music); leisurely, at a snail's pace; ~ *maar seker*, slow but sure; ~ **aan**, gradually; ~ **heid**, slowness; ~ **ies**, gradually; slowly.
sta'dion, (-s), stadium.
sta'dium, (-s, ..**dia**), stage, phase, period; stadium (length); *in (op) hierdie* ~, at this stage.
stad'jie, (-s), small city.
stad'saal, town hall, city hall.
stads: ~ **aanleg**, town planning; ~ **amptenaar**, town official; ~ **argief**, town archives; ~ **beeld**, aspect of the town; ~ **belasting**, municipal tax; ~ **beplanning**, town planning; ~ **bestuur**, municipality, municipal government, city (town) council (corporation); ~ **bewoner**, townsman, city-dweller; ~ **biblioteek**, city library; ~ **bode**, beadle; ~ **bou**, town planning; ~ **gebied**, jurisdiction of a town; town area; ~ **gebou**, municipal building; ~ **geneesheer**, medical officer of health of a city; ~ **gesig**, town view; townscape; ~ **gesondheidsdiens**, municipal health department; ~ **gevangenis**, city prison; ~ **grens**, city boundary; ~ **huis**, house in town; city residence; ~ **ingenieur**, city engineer; ~ **kern**, city core; ~ **kind**, city-bred child; ~ **klerk**, town clerk; ~ **klok**, town clock.
stad'skool, town (city) school.

stad'skouburg, city theatre.
stads: ~**lewe,** city life, urban life; ~**mense,** townspeople, townsfolk, city-dwellers; ~**muur,** city wall; ~**juffie, (-s),** town miss; ~**nuus,** city news; ~**omroeper,** town crier; ~**orkes,** city orchestra; ~**park,** city park; ~**pomp,** parish pump; ~**poort,** city gate; ~**raad,** town (city) council, municipality; ~**raadslid,** city councillor; ~**reiniging,** municipal sewerage, street-cleaning; ~**reisiger,** town traveller; ~**seël,** town seal; ~**tesourier,** city (town) treasurer; ~**toring,** steeple of a town; ~**uitbreidingsplan,** town planning; ~**verkeer,** urban traffic; ~**vryheid,** freedom of a city; ~**wal,** city rampart; ~**wapen,** city coat of arms; ~**weë:** *van* ~ *weë,* on behalf of the city; by the authority of the city; ~**woning,** town house; city residence (dwelling); ~**wyk,** municipal ward; town quarter.
stad'waarts, (-e), towards the town, townward(s).
staf¹, (stawe), staff (sign of office); mace (parliament); baton (marshall); crozier; support, prop; sceptre; *die* ~ *BREEK oor iem.,* pass judgment on someone; *die GENERALE* ~, the general staff; *die v.d. LEWE,* the staff of life; *die REDAKTEUR en sy* ~, the editor and his staff; *iem. se* ~ *en STEUN,* someone's chief support; *die* ~ *SWAAI oor,* reign over; wield the rod; *met 'n* ~ *van YSTER heers,* rule with an iron rod; ~**bal,** staff ball; ~**draer,** mace-bearer.
staf², staff, personnel.
staf'fel, calculation on the decimals; ~**metode,** system of working on the decimals.
staf'fie, small staff, baton.
staf: ~**hoof,** chief of staff; ~**houer,** staff receptacle
sta'fie, (-s), small rod.
sta'fies, (-e), bacillary; ~**vormig, (-e),** bacilliform.
staf: ~**kaart,** ordnance map; ~**kaptein,** staff captain; ~**kwartier,** divisional headquarters; ~**musiek,** regimental music; ~**noodstok,** mashie-niblick; ~**offisier,** staff officer; ~**rym,** alliteration; ~**suster,** staff nurse; ~**vergadering,** staff (personnel) meeting; ~**vormig, (-e),** staff-like.
stag, (-ge, stae), stay (nautical).
stagnant', (-e), stagnant.
stagna'sie, stagnation.
stagneer', (ge-), stagnate.
stag'seil, staysail.
sta'ker, (-s), striker.
sta'kerswag, picket.
staket'sel, (-s), palisade, enclosure, trellis-fence; bail.
sta'king, (-e, -s), strike, suspension (of payment); cessation (of work); discontinuity, discontinuance; *die* ~ *AF(GE)LAS,* countermand the strike; *die* ~ *OPHEF,* call off the strike, *by* ~ *van STEMME,* in the case of an equal vote.
sta'kings: ~**fonds,** strike fund; ~**kas,** strike fund; ~**komitee,** strike committee; ~**leier,** strike leader; ~**reg,** right to strike; ~**toelaag,** strike pay; ~**uitkering,** strike pay.
stak'ker, (-s), poor devil, poor creature.
stal, (s) (-le), stable (for horses); cowshed; stall; *die KONINKLIKE* ~ *le,* the royal mews; *op* ~ *SIT,* put in the stable, stable; (w) **(ge-),** stable.
stalagmiet', (-e), stalagmite; **..mi'ties, (-e),** stalagmitic.
stalaktiet', (-e), stalactite; **..ti'ties, (-e),** stalactitic.
sta'le, (fig.), steel; *'n* ~ *wil,* an iron will.
stal: ~**besem,** stable-broom, bass broom; ~**boom,** stable-bar; ~**deur,** stable door; *jou - deur staan oop,* your fly (office door) is open; ~**emmer,** stable-pail; ~**geld,** stabling-money; ~**geleentheid,** stabling; ~**hings,** stallion; ~**houer,** liveryman; ~**houery,** livery stable; ~**huur,** stable rent; ~**jong, (-ens),** groom, stable-boy; ~**kneg,** (h)ostler, groom; ~**lantern,** stable-lantern.
stal'les, stalls (theatre).
stal'letjie, (-s), bookstall; booth, stall; small stable bar.
stal: ~**ling,** mews; lairage, stabling (of horses); garaging, garage accommodation; ~**lug,** stable odour; ~**maat,** stable-companion; ~**meester,** equerry; ~**mis,** stable manure; ~**perd,** stable-horse; ~**vurk,** stable-prong(-fork), pitchfork.

stam, (s) (-me), trunk, bole (tree); ha(u)lm (of peas); family, tribe, clan, race (of people); stock, strain (of stock); stem, root (of word); *die TWAALF S* ~ *me,* the Twelve Tribes; *UIT dieselfde* ~, from the same stock; (w) **(ge-),** form a stem; descend, come (from); ~ *uit die TYD van,* date from the time of; *WOORDE* ~ *uit,* words are derived from; ~**boek,** stud-book; herd-book; pedigree (genealogical) register; ~**boekperd,** pedigree horse; ~**nommer,** stud-number; ~**perd,** stud-horse, thoroughbred horse; ~**vee,** stud cattle, pedigree cattle.
stamboel', *see* **snaar**
Stamboel', Constantinople, Istanbul.
stam: ~**boom,** genealogical tree, family tree, pedigree; ~**boontjie,** dwarf bean, field-bean; ~**boorder,** stalk-borer; ~**brand,** stem smut (rye); ~**eenheid,** parent unit; unity of the tribe; ~**eiendom,** tribal property.
sta'mel, (ge-), stutter, stammer; falter; ~**aar, (-s),** stammerer; ~**end, (-e),** faltering; ~**ing, (-e),** faltering prayer; stammering.
stam: ~**ent,** butt-end; ~**gas,** habitué, regular customer; ~**genoot, (..note),** clansman, tribesman; ~**genootskap,** clanship; ~**geskiedenis,** phylogeny; ~**gesteente,** mother rock; ~**geveg,** tribal fight (clash); ~**god,** tribal god; ~**goed,** hereditary property; ~**hoof,** tribal chief; ~**houer, (-s),** son and heir; male heir; ~**hout,** trunk wood; ~**huis,** dynasty house; ~**huwelik,** endogamy.
sta'mina, stamina, staying-power, endurance, power of endurance.
stam: ~**kapitaal,** original capital; ~**klinker,** stem-vowel, radical vowel; ~**land,** mother country, country of origin; ~**lid,** tribesman; ~**loot,** coppice; ~**lys,** genealogical register; ~**metjie, (-s),** little stem; small tribe; shank (of button); ~**moeder,** first mother (Eve); fundatrix; ~**naam,** family name; name of tribe; ~**organisasie,** tribal organization; ~**ouers,** ancestors, progenitors; ~**owerheid,** tribal authority.
stamp, (s) (-e), knock, stamp (of foot); blow, punch; jolt (of cart); *met* ~ *e en STOTE gaan,* go by fits and starts; ~ *e en STOTE kry,* have to put up with rebuffs; *deur* ~ *e en STOTE word mens wys,* adversity makes a man wise, not rich; *met* ~ *e en STOTE,* with considerable difficulty; by fits and starts; (w) **(ge-),** pound, stamp, knock; jolt; push, jostle; dig (in the ribs); elbow (out of the way); crush (ore); pitch (ship); stump (cricket); ram (down throat); bump (one's foot); *FYN* ~, pound; bray; *iets in die KOP* ~, drum something into someone's head; *ge* ~ *te MIELIES,* pounded mealies, samp; *tot POEIER* ~, crush to powder, pulverize; ~**aarde,** pisé, rammed clay (earth); ~**balk,** fender-beam; ~**battery,** stamp-battery; ~**beton,** rammed concrete; ~**blok,** pounding-block, woodin mortar; ~**boor,** jumper; ~**bout,** fender; ~**er, (-s),** pounder, rammer, buffer, bumper; beater, crusher; pestle; tamper; pavio(u)r; pistil (of flower); stamp (in mill); (mv) thick legs; *met* ~ *er en stoter reis,* go by foot; ~**erblom,** female flower; ~**erdraend, (-e),** pistilliferous; ~**erig, (-e),** jolting, bumpy; ~**erigheid,** bumpiness; ~**plakker,** bumper sticker; ~**ery,** pushing, jostling; stamp-battery; ~**hamer,** mash-hammer; ~**hou,** push-shot, jab; ~**hout,** Cape lilac; ~**kar,** springless cart; stock car; ~**kop,** shoe (mining); ~**koring,** crushed wheat; ~**kussing,** buffer.
stamp: ~**meul,** stamping-mill, crushing-mill; ~**mielies,** pounded mealies, samp; ~**motor,** stock car; ~**motorjaery,** ~**motorwedren,** stock-car race; ~**plaat,** key-plate; ~**plek,** bruise; bumpy place (in road); ~**pomp,** ram-pump; ~**pot,** hotchpotch; ~**see,** pitching sea; ~**skoot,** push-shot; ~**stok,** tamping rod; ~**tou,** fender; ~**veer,** bumper; ~**voet, (ge-),** stamp with the feet; paw the ground (animals); ~**vol, (-le),** chock-full, overfull, crammed; ~**yster,** butting-bar (foundry).
stam: ~**register,** genealogical register; ~**roes,** black rust (in cereals); ~**roos,** standard rose; ~**ruspe(r),** stalk-borer; ~**salaris,** basic salary; ~**snyblok,** master die; ~**steek,** stem stitch; ~**stempel,** master die;

~ **taal,** parent language; ~ **tafel,** habitué's table; ~ **vader,** ancestor, progenitor; ~ **vee,** foundation stock; ~ **verband,** tribal relationship.
stam'verwant, (s) (-e), kinsman, blood-relation; (b) (-e), akin, cognate; consanguineous; ~ **skap,** affinity, (racial or tribal) kinship; consanguinity.
stam'volk, parent people, aboriginal race.
stam'vrot, foot rot.
stam'vrug, (-te), wild plum; ~ **teboom,** wild-plum tree *(Chrysophyllum magalismontanum).*
stam'woord, root-word, radical (word), stem, etymon.
stand, (-e), position, attitude, posture; rank, caste, birth; gentility; quality, place, standing, station (in society); circle; phase (of the moon); reading (thermometer); stance (golf); score (in a game); level, height (water, thermometer); *BENEDE sy* ~, below his social status; *in* ~ *BLY,* prevail; endure; *iets tot* ~ *BRING,* achieve something; bring about something; *dit HOU g'n* ~ *nie,* it does not last; *in* ~ *HOU,* keep up, maintain, preserve; *tot* ~ *KOM,* come into being; come about; *bo sy* ~ *LEWE,* live beyond his means; *die* ~*e van die MAAN,* the phases of the moon; *jou* ~ *OPHOU,* keep up one's position; *die* ~ *van SAKE,* the state of affairs; *iem. VAN* ~, someone of rank; *die VIERDE* ~, the fourth estate.
standaard', (-e), standard, criterion; archetype; gauge; ~ **formaat,** standard size; ~ **gewig,** standard weight; ~ **goud,** standard gold; ~ **grootte,** standard size.
standaardisa'sie, standardization.
standaardiseer', (ge-), standardize; ..**se'ring,** standardization.
standaard': ~ **kaliber,** standard gauge; ~ **ketel,** standard boiler; ~ **kompas,** landing-compass; ~ **loon,** standard wage; ~ **maat,** standard gauge; ~ **motor,** stock car; ~ **patroon,** standard (stock) pattern; ~ **peiling,** swing-bearing (aero.); ~ **prys,** standard price; ~ **tyd,** standard time; ~ **uitgawe,** standard publication; ~ **uitspraak,** standard pronunciation; ~ **werk,** standard work.
stand'beeld, (-e), statue.
stan'der, (-s), stand (for coats); upright (of bed); vertical stay, post, pedestal; cruet-stand.
stan'derd, (-s), standard, class, form (in school); ~ **sesser,** (-s), pupil in Std VI; ~ **twee,** (-s), standard two pupil.
stand: ~ **ertjie,** (-s), small stand; cruet-stand; lectern; ~ **genoot,** (..**note),** peer, social equal, one of the same social standing; ~ **hoek,** dihedral angle; ~ **hou,** (-ge-), hold out, stand firm; last, endure; ~ **hou'dend,** (-e), lasting, continuous; permanent; perennial (stream); ~ **jie,** (-s), reproof; quarrel, row, affray, tiff; *iem. 'n* ~ *jie gee,* give someone a talking-to; ~ **plaas,** official post; ~ **plek,** cab stand, cab rank; parking space.
stand'punt, standpoint, point of view, attitude of mind; *van 'n breë* ~ *BEKYK,* take a broad view; *'n* ~ *INNEEM,* take a view; *jou op 'n* ~ *STEL,* take a stand.
stand: ~ **pyp,** hydrant, stand-pipe; ~ **reg,** summary justice; ~ **regterlike krygsraad,** drumhead court martial.
stands: ~ **gees,** class-feeling; ~ **herstel,** recovery (after dive) (aero.); ~ **verheffing,** raising in rank; ~ **verskil,** class distinction; social inequality; ~ **verwisseling,** change of rank; ~ **vooroordeel,** class prejudice.
standvas'tig, (-e), firm, steadfast, constant; persevering; fast (colours); ~ **heid,** firmness, constancy, steadfastness.
stand: ~ **veer,** locating spring; ~ **verandering,** change in position (state level); ~ **voël,** non-migratory bird, resident bird.
sta'ner, (-s), stander, one who stands.
stang, (-e), bit (of bridle); bar, branch; barbit; rod; gag; *iem. 'n* ~ *in die BEK sit,* curb someone; keep someone in control; *iem. op* ~ *JAAG,* make someone see red; *IEM. op die* ~ *RY,* keep a tight rein on someone, treat someone harshly; *stywe* ~ *e RY,* be having a hard time; *die* ~ *VASBYT,* be unmanageable; take the bit between the teeth; *teen die* ~ *WERK,* be up against it; ~ **etjie,** (-s), small bar (rod); ~ **koeël,** barshot; ~ **koppeling,** bar-coupling; ~ **passer,** beam compasses, calliper-gauge; ~ **toom,** gab-string.
sta'ning, (-s), (place for) grazing; outspan.
stank, (-e), stench, malodour, stink, bad smell, reek, fetor; ~ *vir dank,* small thanks; the world pays with ingratitude; ~ **afsluiter,** stench-trap, air-trap, gully trap, stink trap; ~ **klier,** stink-gland; ~ **loos,** (..lose), inodorous; ~ **verdrywend,** (-e), stench-expelling; ~ **werend,** (-e), stench-preventing.
stanniet', stannite.
stanniool', tin foil, stanniol.
stan'sa, (-s), stanza.
stap, (s) (-pe), step, pace, stride, footstep; move; *met AFGEMETE* ~, with measured tread; ~ *pe DOEN,* take steps; take action; *die EERSTE* ~ *doen,* take the first step; *by ELKE* ~, at every step; *op* ~ *GAAN,* set out; *dit GAAN op 'n* ~ *pie,* it is soso; *daarmee is ons geen* ~ *NADER nie,* that brings us no farther; *die NODIGE* ~ *pe,* the necessary measures; *so OP 'n* ~ *pie,* so-so; fairly well; ~ *VIR* ~, step by step; *'n* ~ *VOORUIT,* a step forward; a progressive movement; *'n* ~ *WAAG,* take the plunge; (w) (ge-), walk, step, go on foot, stride, move, pace, march, stalk; hike; *'n ENDJIE gaan* ~, go for a walk; *op die TREIN* ~, board the train; ~ **dans,** two-step; one-step (dance).
sta'pel[1], (s) (-s), staple (wool).
sta'pel[2], (s) (-s), pile, heap, stack; stock (of cattle); stocks (shipbuilding): accumulation; cumulus; *goed van* ~ *LOOP,* pass off without a hitch; *op* ~ *LÊ,* arrange in a pile; *OP* ~, on the stocks; *op* ~ *SIT,* put on the stocks; launch something; *van* ~ *STUUR (laat loop),* launch; get going; (w) (ge-), heap up, pile, stack; ~ **artikel,** stock (staple) commodity; ~ **benodigdhede,** stock-pile; ~ **blok,** keel block; ~ **boor,** pile-drill; ~ **gek,** mad as a hatter, raving mad, stark mad; ~ **goed,** (-ere), staple commodities; ~ **ing,** (-e, -s), (stock-)piling; palletization; ~ **muur,** dry-wall(ing); ~ **plaas,** depot, emporium, mart; dumping-place; ~ **riool,** French drain; ~ **wolk,** stack-cloud, cumulus.
stap: ~ **geluid,** footfall; footsteps; ~ **klip,** stepping-stone.
stap'per, (-s), hiker, walker; pacer.
stap: ~ **plooi,** kick-pleat; ~ **snelheid,** footpace.
staps'gewys(e), step by step.
stap: ~ **skoen,** walking-shoe; ~ **steen,** stepping-stone; ~ **stewel,** hiking boot; ~ **toer,** walking-tour, hiking-tour; ~ **tog,** ramble, walking-tour; ~ **voets,** at a walking-pace, step by step; ~ **wedstryd,** walking-race.
star, (-re; -der, -ste), fixed, stiff; glassy (look); rigid, inelastic (system); ~ **heid,** glassiness (of eye); rigidity; ~ **oog,** (ge-), stare, gaze (at); ~ **sug,** catalepsy; ~ **sug'tig,** cataleptic.
sta'sie, (-s), station; ~ **boekwinkel,** station bookstall; ~ **gebou,** railway station, station building; ~ **kleed,** hammer-cloth; ~ **meester,** station-master; ~ **naambord,** station name-board; ~ **pad,** station road; ~ **wa,** station-wag(g)on; ~ **weg,** station road.
stasioneer', (ge-), station; picket, post.
stasionêr', (-e), stationary.
stat, (-te), tribal village.
sta'tebond, federation of states; **S**~, League of Nations; Commonwealth.
State: ~ **bybel,** State Bible (the authorized version of the States General); ~ **-Generaal,** States General.
sta'ter, (-s), stater.
sta'tery, comity of nations; *plek in die* ~, position among nations.
Sta'te: ~ **vergadering,** meeting of the States General; ~ **vertaling,** Dutch Authorized Version (of the Bible of 1637).
statief', (statiewe), tripod (for a camera or theodolite).
sta'ties, (-e), static; ~ *e HEFKRAG,* buoyancy, static lift; ~ *SWEEF,* soar.
sta'tig, (-e), elegant, dignified, stately, majestic; courtly, gallant; portly; ~ **heid,** stateliness, elegance; gravity; portliness; dignity.

sta'tika, statics.
statistiek', (-e), statistics, figures.
statis'ties, (-e), statistical.
statis'tikus, (..tici, -se), statistician.
sta'tor, (-s), stator.
statoskoop', (..skope), statoscope.
sta'tus, position, status; ~ *quo*, status quo.
statu'teboek, (-e), book containing the articles of constitution; statute-book.
statutêr', (-e), statutory; ~ *e kapitaal*, authorized capital; ~ *e meineed*, statutory perjory.
statuur', (**stature**), stature; status.
statuut', (**statute**), statute, articles, regulation (of a constitution).
sta'wing, proof, confirmation, substantiation; *bewys ter* ~ *aanvoer*, adduce proof in support of.
stearien', **steari'ne**, stearine; ~ **kers**, stearine (dropless) candle.
steatiet', steatite, soapstone.
steatopigie', steatopygy.
ste'de: *in* ~ *van*, instead of; ~ **aanleg**, town planning; ~ **bond**, league of cities; ~ **bou**, ~ **boukunde**, town planning; ~ **boukun'dig**, (-e), town planning; ~ **houer**, viceroy, substitute; ~ *houer van Christus*, Vicar of Christ, the Pope; ~ **lik**, (-e), urban, civic, municipal; ~ **ling**, (-e), townsman, city-dweller.
steeds[1], (b) (-e), municipal, urban, town; ~ *e gewoontes*, city customs.
steeds[2], (bw) constantly, always, ever, continually; ~ *KOUER*, colder and colder; ~ *MEER*, more and more; *NOG* ~, still; ~ *die UWE*, ever yours.
steeg, (**stege**, **steë**), lane, alley, passage, bar (saddle), *blinde* ~, blind alley.
steek, (s) (**steke**), prick (pin); stitch (needle); prong; poke, jab; sting (bee); bite (mosquito); stab (dagger); thrust (sword); twinge (pain); point (fencing); *g'n* ~ *AFWYK nie*, not to budge an inch; *g'n* ~ *GEDOEN nie*, not a stroke of work done; *die redenering HOU nie* ~ *nie*, it does not apply to all cases; it is not entirely valid; *iem. in die* ~ *LAAT*, leave someone in the lurch, fail someone; *daar is 'n* ~ *aan LOS*, there is something wrong with it; *iem. 'n* ~ *in die RUG gee*, give someone a stab in the back; *g'n* ~ *kan SIEN nie*, be unable to see a thing; *'n* ~ *op tyd SPAAR nege uit*, a stitch in time saves nine; *'n* ~ *laat VAL*, drop a stitch; *'n* ~ *onder WATER*, a blow below the belt; *geen* ~ *WERK verrig nie*, not to do a stroke of work; (w) (**ge-**), prick; jab (with dagger); thrust (with sword); gore (with horns); prod (with stick); scorch (sun); *daar* ~ *iets AGTER*, there is a catch in it; there is a hidden motive; *daar* ~ *BAIE in hom*, he is brilliant (talented); *BLY* ~ *in*, lodge (bullet); stick (fast) in; *daar* ~ *IETS agter*, there is something behind it; *daar* ~ *baie IN*, there is much in it; *daar* ~ *iets IN*, there is something in it; *geld in 'n ONDERNEMING* ~, put (sink) money in an undertaking; *hom in SKULD* ~, run into debt; ~ **appel**, thorn-apple; ~ **baard**, hard, (straight) whiskers; (type of) dog; ~ **balk**, hammer-beam; ~ **bank**, slotting-machine; ~ **beitel**, ripping-chisel; mortice chisel; firmer chisel; jagger; ~ **blaker**, pricket; ~ **bossie**, burweed, Mexican poppy; ~ **brem**, gorse; ~ **deel**, plug portion; ~ **ding**, pricker; ~ **draad**, barbed wire; ~ **draadversperring**, barbed-wire entanglement; ~ **els**, stab-awl; ~ **graaf**, cutting spade; ~ **gras**, stick grass *(Aristida barbicollis)*; ~ **guts**, scribing-gouge; ~ **haar**, kemp; ~ **haarskaap**, hairy sheep; *S* ~ **haarterriër**, wire-haired terrier; ~ **haarwol**, kemp; ~ **hare**, bristles.
steek'(hoed), three-cornered hat, cocked hat.
steek'hock, angle of pitch.
steek'houdend, (-e), valid, sound, consistent; ~ *e argumente*, sound arguments.
steek: ~ **kontak**, electric plug; ~ **lyn**, pitch-line; ~ **masjien**, paring-machine; ~ **mindering**, decreasing; ~ **palm**, holly (fern); holly-oak; ~ **pan**, bedpan, slipper-pan.
steek'pas, goose-step.
steek: ~ **passer**, dividers, dividing compasses; ~ **pen**, skewer; ~ **pil**, suppository, pessary; ~ **priem**, bodkin; ~ **proef**, test-check, random sample (test);

sample taken at random, test sample; ~ **pyn**, twinge, shooting pain; ~ **riet**, *Eragrostis cyperoides*.
steeks, (-e), obstinate; balky, restive, jibbing (horse); ~ *WEES*, be recalcitrant; be like a jibbing horse; *die arbeider is* ~ *by die WERK*, the labourer jibs at his work.
steek'saad, bur-clover.
steek'saag, compass-saw; lock-saw; keyhole-saw; piercing-saw.
steeks'heid, obstinacy; restiveness, jibbing (horse).
steek: ~ **sirkel**, pitch-circle (of rivets); ~ **skoor**, diagonal stay; ~ **skop**, grubber-kick; ~ **sleutel**, box-wrench; picklock; ~ **sok**, socket-outlet; ~ **spel**, tourney, tilt, joust; ~ **vas**, (-te), hole-proof; non-laddering; ~ **vlam**, blowpipe-flame; ~ **vlieg**, gadfly; breeze; fruit-fly; tabanid; ~ **vry**, (-e), invulnerable; ~ **wapen**, thrust-weapon; ~ **wond**, stab- wound; ~ **yster**, graver.
steel[1], (s) (**stele**), handle; stalk (of flower); stem (pipe); helve, haft (of axe); ~ *van 'n roeispaan*, loom of an oar.
steel[2], (w) (**ge-**), steal, purloin, filch; poach; *dit* ~ *'n mens se hart*, that wins (steals) one's heart; ~ **baar**, (..**bare**), that which can be stolen.
steel: ~ **blaar**, bracteole; ~ **deurslag**, rod-punch (tool); ~ **gat**, eye (of hammer); borrow-pit; ~ **kant**, blind side (rugby); ~ **lig**, borrowed light; ~ **loos**, (..**lose**), stalkless; sessile.
steel: ~ **manie**, kleptomania; ~ **s**, (-e), stealthy, furtive, surreptitious; ~ **s'gewys(e)**, stealthily furtively, on the sly; ~ **sieke**, kleptomaniac; ~ **steek**, crewel stitch; ~ **sug**, kleptomania; ~ **sug'tige**, (-s), kleptomaniac.
steel'tjie, (-s), little handle; pedicle; peduncle (anat.).
steel'vry, (-e), burglar-proof.
steen, (**stene**), brick; stone; calculus; bar (of soap); *'n* ~ *des AANSTOOTS*, a cause of annoyance; a stumbling-block; ~ *en BEEN kla*, complain bitterly; *stene vir BRODE gee*, give someone stones for bread; *sy* ~ *tjie BYDRA*, contribute one's mite; *die EERSTE* ~ *lê*, lay the foundation; *die eerste* ~ *GOOI*, cast the first stone; *twee HARDE stene maal nie*, hard with hard does not make the stone wall; *geen* ~ *op die ander LAAT nie*, leave no stone standing; *geen* ~ *ONAANGEROER laat nie*, leave no stone unturned; *jou nie twee maal aan dieselfde* ~ *STOOT nie*, not to make the same mistake twice; *in* ~ *VERANDER*, turn into stone, petrify; *die* ~ *van die WYSE*, the philsopher's stone; ~ **aar**, rocky vein; ~ **agtig**, (-e), stony, rocky, petrous; lithic, calculous; ~ **agtigheid**, stoniness; ~ **aluin**, rock-alum; ~ **arend**, golden eagle; ~ **bakker**, brick-maker; ~ **bakkery**, brick-yard, brick-field, brick-kiln; brickmaking; ~ **beitel**, bolster.
steen'bok, steenbok (small antelope); *die S* ~, Capricornus; ~ **lopers**, buck shot.
Steen'bokskeerkring, Tropic of Capricorn.
steen'boksuring, dock, sheep sorrel *(Rumex acetosella)*.
steen'bout, rag-bolt.
steen'bras, (-se), steenbras (fish) *(Spurus salpa)*.
steen'brasem, mussel-cracker *(Sparus salpa)*, porgy.
steen: ~ **breker**, (-s), stone-breaker; ~ **druiwe**, stone-grapes.
steen'druk, lithography; lithograph; ~ **ker**, lithographer; ~ **kery**, lithographic printing-press; ~ **kuns**, lithography; ~ **plaat**, lithograph.
steen: ~ **eik**, holm-oak, ilex; ~ **es**, wild ash; ~ **gal**, wind-gall; ~ **goed**, crockery, stoneware; ~ **groef**, stonepit, quarry; ~ **groefwerker**, quarryman; ~ **grond**, stony ground; ~ **gruis**, brick-dust, broken bricks, metal; road gravel; ~ **hamer**, bricklayer's hammer; ~ **hoop**, heap of stones (bricks); ~ **houer**, stone-cutter; ~ **kern**, drupe; ~ **klawer**, white clover; ~ **klei**, pug; ~ **kleuredruk**, lithochromy; ~ **kleurig**, (-e), brick-coloured; ~ **klipvis**, steenfish; butter-fish.
steen'kool, coal; black diamond; ~ **aar**, coal-vein; ~ **afval**, gob; ~ **agtig**, (-e), coaly; ~ **as**, coal-slack; coaldust; coal-ashes; ~ **bak**, coal-scuttle; ~ **bed**, coal-layer, stratum of coal; ~ **damp**, coal-smoke;

~**formasie,** carbonaceous system; ~**gas,** coal-gas; ~**groef,** coal channel; ~**gruis,** slack; debris; coaldross; culm; ~**handel,** coal-trade; ~**hawehoof,** collier jetty; ~**hok,** coal-shed; bunker (ship); ~**kreosoot,** creosote; ~**laag,** coal-layer; coal-bed; coal-seam; ~**loods,** coal-shed; ~**myn,** coal-mine, colliery; ~**periode,** coal(-forming) age; ~**produksie,** coal-production (-output); ~**ring,** coal-ring; ~**ruim,** coal-bunker; ~**saag,** coal cutter; ~**steier,** coaling-stage; ~**stof,** culm, coal dust; ~**tang,** coaltongs; ~**teer,** coal-tar; ~**veld,** coal-field; ~**verbruik,** coal-consumption; ~**voorraad,** coal-supply; ~**wa,** coal-tender; ~**werker,** collier.

steen: ~**kunde,** petrology; lithology; ~**laag,** layer of bricks; ~**legging,** stone-laying; laying of foundation; ~**lym,** stone cement; mastic; ~**maker,** brickmaker; ~**makery,** brick-yard; ~**mos,** rock lichen; ~**olie,** petroleum; ~**oond,** brick-kiln; ~**periode,** stone age; ~**puisie,** boil; furuncle; ~**rooi,** brickred; ~**sel,** stone cell, grit cell; ~**setwerk,** jewelling; ~**siekte,** lithiasis; ~**skrif,** lapidary writing; ~**slot,** flint-lock; ~**slyper,** lapidary; ~**snyer,** lapidary; lithotomist; ~**snykuns,** glyptography, glyptics, lithotomy; ~**suur,** lithic acid; ~**tjie,** small brick; pebble; *Cantharus emarginatus;* steentjie (fish); ~**tjieskweek,** nutgrass; S~**tydperk,** Stone Age; ~**uil,** barn-owl, screech-owl; ~**valk,** stone-falcon, merlin; ~**vink,** sandpiper; ~**vis,** nigger-fish; ~**vlas,** earth flax, asbestos; ~**vloer,** brick (stone) floor; ~**vorm,** brick-mould; ~**vormery,** brickmaking; ~**vorming,** lithiasis (med.); ~**vrug,** stonefruit, drupe; ~**worp,** a stone's throw; ~**wyn,** stonegrape wine.

steg¹, (s) (-ge), foot-bridge; stile.

steg², (s) (-ge), cutting, slip; (w) (ge-), make slips (cuttings).

steg'gie¹, (-s), cutting, slip.

steg'gie², (-s), little foot-bridge; little stile.

ste'gie, (-s), alley, little lane.

ste'ier¹, (s) (-s), scaffold, building-platform; gantry; jetty, landing-stage; stage.

ste'ier², (w) (ge-), prance, rear (horse); stagger, lurch, reel, walk unsteadily, rock from side to side; *hy KLAP my dat ek ~,* he slapped me with such force that I staggered; *'n ~ende LEEU,* lion rampant (her.); *'n ~ende PERD,* a prancing horse.

stei'er: ~**balk,** putlog, scaffolding-beam, ledger; ~**bok,** scaffold trestle; ~**gat,** putlog-hole, scaffold hole; ~**paal,** scaffold pole; ~**paaltjie,** ricker; ~**plank,** scaffold board, ledger-board; ~**tou,** putlog rope; ~**werk,** scaffolding, staging; ~**werker,** scaffolder.

steil, steep, precipitous; bluff; straight (hair); highpitched (roof); ~**heid,** bluffness; steepness; lankness (of hair); ~**rem,** hill-holder (brake); ~**skrif,** perpendicular writing; ~**te,** (-s), steepness, acclivity, precipitousness, precipice, cliff.

ste'keblind, stone-blind.

ste'kel, (-s), prickle, spine, sting; barbule.

ste'kelagtig, (-e), prickly; stinging; ~**heid,** prickliness; sharpness, sarcasm.

ste'kelap, sampler.

ste'kelbaars, minnow, stickleback.

ste'kelhuidig, (-e), echinate; ~**e,** (-s), echinoderm.

ste'kelig, (-e), prickly, spinous, aculeate; caustic, sarcastic; ~**heid,** prickliness, spinosity; acrimony.

ste'kelrig, (-e), spiny; ~**heid,** spininess.

ste'ker, (-s), sampler (cheese); plug; sticker, stabber, pricker; ~**ig,** (-e), inclined to sting; prickly; waspish, irritable, tart, sharp in retort; ~**igheid,** inclination to sting, waspishness.

ste'kie, (-s), dab; small stitch.

stek'ker, (-s), plug.

stel¹, (s) (-le), set (tennis); (dinner-, tea-) service; suite (of rooms); lot; trap; fount (of type); flush (cards); *'n ~ AFTRAP,* have an unpleasant experience; *'n ~ KLOKKE,* a ring (peal) of bells; *op ~ en SPRONG,* then and there, like a shot; *'n ~ TENNIS,* a set at tennis.

stel², (w) (ge-), fix, put; adjust; draw up (documents); focus (camera); make (demands); set (standard); write; state; prescribe, lay down (conditions); *ek ~ dit AAN jou,* I put it to you; *BINNE die ge~ de tyd,* within the time specified; *ge~ DAT,* supposing that; *buite DIENS ~,* lay off; *ter HAND ~,* hand over to; *niks met iem. te ~ wil HÊ nie,* refuse to have anything to do with someone; *KANDIDATE ~,* nominate candidates; *'n KANON ~,* train a gun; *in die LIG ~,* bring to light; *die ge~ de MAGTE,* the powers that be; *NIKS met hom te ~ wil hê nie,* refuse to have anything to do with him; refuse to have any truck with him; *'n OORLOSIE ~,* adjust a watch; *jou in iem. anders se PLEK ~,* put oneself in someone else's place; *SLEG ge~,* badly worded; ill written; *onder die SORG ~,* place under the care of; *iets ter SYDE ~,* set something aside; *'n VAL ~,* set a trap; *'n VERGASSER ~,* adjust a carburettor; *alle middele in die WERK ~,* leave no stone unturned, employ every means; ~**arm,** (gear-)lever; ~**armgeleiding,** lever-guide; ~**baar,** (..bare), adjustable; ~**baarheid,** adjustability; ~**blad,** adjusting board; ~**bout,** checkbolt; ~**driehoek,** adjustable triangle.

ste'le, (-s), stele.

stelêr', (-e), stellar.

ste'ler, (-s), thief, stealer, pilferer, purloiner, poacher (game); ~**y,** pilfering, thieving.

stel: ~**geweer,** gun trap; ~**hefboom,** trimming-lever; ~**hoek,** ledger-hook; ~**inrigting,** adjusting gear.

stel'kunde, algebra; ..**kun'dig,** (-e), algebraic.

stella'sie, (-s), scaffolding; framework, structure, reed platform (for drying fruit, etc.); stillage; gantry (for barrels); *vroeg op die ~ klim,* turn in early.

Stellenbos'se, of Stellenbosch; ~**r,** (-s), inhabitant of Stellenbosch.

stel'ler, (-s), writer; adjuster; trainer.

stel'les, composition lesson.

stel'letjie¹, (s) small set (e.g. cruet-stand).

stel'letjie², (-s), commode, chamber-stool.

stel'lig, (-e), certain, surely, positive (assertion); explicit (answer); definite (promise); doubtless, most probable; assured; categorical (denial); *ek kan jou ten ~ ste verseker,* I can positively assure you; ~**heid,** positiveness, certainty; explicitness.

stel'ling, (-e, -s), view; statement; thesis, hypothesis; theorem, proposition (maths.); doctrine (of church); emplacement (guns); position (mil.); stance; *in ~ BRING,* bring in position (guns); *'n ~ ONTWIKKEL,* develop a proposition (theorem); *'n STERK ~ inneem,* take a firm stand against; ~**oorlog,** positional warfare, trench-warfare.

stellionaat', stellionatus (law).

stel: ~**lyn,** boulter; ledger-line; ~**maat,** setting gauge; ~**moer,** adjusting nut; ~**oefening,** composition exercise; praxis.

stelp, (ge-), sta(u)nch, stop, check (the flow of blood).

stel'pen, dowel; setting-pin.

stelp: ~**end,** (-e), astrictive; astringent; styptic; ~**ping,** sta(u)nching (of blood), astriction; ~**middel,** styptic.

stel: ~**prop,** adjusting plug; ~**rat,** adjusting gear; ~**reël,** maxim, precept, rule; ~**ring,** adjusting ring; ~**saag,** gauge saw.

stel'sel, (-s), system; form; frame; *metrieke ~,* metric system.

stel'selloos, (..lose), unsystematic(al); ~**heid,** want of system.

stelselma'tig, (-e), systematic(al); formal; ~**heid,** systematicalness, orderliness.

stel'skaaf, adjusting-plane.

stel'skop, place-kick (rugby); ~**per,** place-kicker.

stel: ~**skroef,** adjusting screw; regulating screw; bench-vice; ~**sleutel,** adjusting-spanner; ~**stang,** adjusting rod.

stelt, (-e), stilt; *op ~e LOOP,* be high-faluting; *alles op ~e SIT,* turn everything topsy-turvy; cause a hubbub (commotion).

stel'tang, combination pliers.

stelt: ~**boog,** stilted arch; ~**loper,** (-s), stilt-bird, long-legged (wading-)bird; stilt-walker; ~**poot,** stilt (bird); ~**potig,** (-e), grallatorial (zool.); ~**voël,** stilt-bird; ~**wortel,** prop root.

stel: ~**vlak,** trimming-plane; ~**waster,** (-s), adjusting washer; ~**wiel,** gauge-wheel; ~**wig,** quoin; ~**win**=

kelhaak, adjustable square; ~**yster,** adjusting tool.

stem, (s) (-me), voice; vote (at election); *ADVISERENDE* ~, advisory vote; *met ALGEMENE* ~*me*, unanimously; with one voice; *die* ~ *v.d. BLOED*, the call of the blood; *die EERSTE (tweede)* ~, the first (second) part (music); *die* ~*me het GESTAAK*, there was a tie in the voting; *die* ~ *v.d. GEWETE*, the voice of one's conscience; *met LUIDER* ~ *(me)*, in a loud voice; *met MEERDERHEID van* ~*me aanneem*, carry (pass, agree to) by a majority of votes; *die* ~ *van die NATUUR*, the call of nature; ~*me OPNEEM*, count (scrutinize) votes; *die* ~ *v.d. ROEPENDE in die woestyn*, a voice crying in the wilderness; ~*me UITBRING*, cast votes, poll; *die* ~ *VERHEF*, raise the voice; *jou* ~ *teen iets VERHEF*, raise one's voice against; *die seun se* ~ *begin te WISSEL*, the boy's voice is breaking; (w) (**ge-**), tune (piano); pitch (instrument); voice (organ); cast one's vote, vote, go to the poll; *GUNSTIG* ~, predispose in favour of; *LAAT* ~ *oor*, put to the vote; *dit* ~ *tot NADENKE*, it provides food for thought; *TREURIG* ~, sadden, make sad; ~ *VIR*, cast one's vote for; ~ *VOOR*, vote in favour; ~**balletjie,** ballot; ~**band,** vocal cord; ~**bandeksplosief,** ~**bandklapper,** ~**bandkonsonant,** glottal stop; ~**beampte,** polling officer; ~**biljet,** ~**briefie,** ballot-paper; *'n ongeldige* ~*briefie*, a spoilt vote; ~**buiging,** modulation, intonation, cadence, accent; ~**buro,** (-'s), polling station, polling booth; ~**bus,** ballot-box; poll; ~**dag,** election (polling) day; ~**distrik,** electoral division; ~**dwang,** compulsory voting; ~**fluitjie,** pitch-pipe; ~**geluid,** sound of the voice.
stem'geregtig, (-de), entitled to vote, enfranchised; ~**de,** (-s), registered voter; ~**dheid,** right to vote, enfranchisement.
stem'hamer, tuning-key; tuning-hammer.
stem'hebbend, stemheb'bend, (-e), voiced; ~*e medeklinker*, voiced consonant; ~**heid,** voicedness.
stem: ~ **horing,** tuning-cone; ~**hokkie,** polling booth; ~**krag,** voting power; ~**kunstenaar,** voice artist; ~**lokaal,** polling booth.
stem'loos, (..lose), voiceless; mute, dumb; unvoiced, surd; without a vote; ..*lose medekliner*, mute, surd; ~**heid,** voicelessness; muteness; disenfranchisement.
stem'meaantal, number of votes; ballot.
stem'mer, (-s), tuner; voter; ~**y,** polling; tuning.
stem'me: ~**tal,** number of votes; ~**tjie,** (-s), small voice; ~**totaal,** total vote; ~**vangery,** vote-catching; ~**verhouding,** proportion of votes; ~**werwer,** canvasser for votes; ~**werwery,** canvassing for votes.
stem'mig, (-e), serious, sedate, modest, quiet, demure, grave, staid, sober; subdued; conservative (of dress); ~**heid,** sedateness, gravity; modesty, quietness, sobriety, conservativeness (in dress); demureness (in manner).
stem'ming, (-e, -s), ballot, election, voting, poll, polling; mood, frame of mind, disposition; feeling; division (parliament); tuning (of piano), *alle* ~ *BEDERF*, damp the spirits; *in die BESTE* ~ *wees*, be in the best possible mood; *buite* ~ *BLY*, abstain from voting; *iets tot* ~ *BRING*, put something to the vote; *BY* ~, after voting; *GEHEIME* ~, secret ballot; *in 'n GOEIE* ~ *bring*, put in a good mood; *HOOFDELIKE* ~, division; ~ *MAAK*, create an atmosphere; *tot* ~ *OORGAAN*, proceed to vote; *'n* ~ *SKEP*, create an atmosphere; *SONDER* ~, without a division (in parliament); *in feestelike* ~ *VERKEER*, be in a festive mood; ~**maker,** propagandist, lobbyist.
stem'mings: ~**beeld,** impression; ~**poësie,** poetry expressing a mood; ~**vol,** (-le), full of atmosphere.
stem: ~**oefening,** voice-training; ~**omvang,** compass (range) of the voice; ~**opnemer,** (-s), polling officer, returning officer, scrutineer; teller (parliament); ~**opneming,** counting of votes; ~**orgaan,** vocal organ; syrinx (of bird).
stem'pel, (s) (-s), seal (on wax); stamp, postmark; hallmark, impress; die (for embossing); impression; imprint; stigma (botany); tool (book); *sy* ~ *op iets AFDRUK*, put one's stamp on something, leave the impress of one's individuality on something; *'n man v.d. EGTE* ~, a sterling fellow; *die* ~ *van GOUD*, the hallmark of gold; *'n man van die OU* ~, a man of the old stamp; ~ *en SNYPLAAT*, punch and die; *die* ~ *v.d. WAARHEID dra*, bear the hallmark of truth; (w) (**ge-**), stamp, imprint, impress, hallmark; pressmark; print; brand, mark; strike (coins); ~**aar,** (-s), stamper; marker; ~**afdruk,** imprint; stamp, seal, mark; ~**band,** cloth-binding; ~**blok,** die-stamp; ~**datum,** postmark date; ~**ing,** stamping; ~**ink,** ink for stamping; ~**kussing,** stamp-pad; ~**maker,** engraver; die-sinker; ~**masjien,** franking-machine; stamping-machine; ~**merk,** hallmark; ~**pers,** stamping-press; ~**skroef,** stamp-screw; ~**snyer,** (-s), stamp-cutter, die-sinker; ~**versiering,** tooling.
stem: ~ **plek,** polling station (booth); ~**plig,** compulsory voting; ~**reg,** franchise; right to vote; *ALGEMENE* ~**reg,** universal suffrage; *die* ~**reg** *UITOEFEN*, exercise the vote; ~**reg** *VERLEEN*, give the vote, enfranchise; ~**register,** voter's list; vocal register; ~**regvrou,** suffragette; ~**skroef,** tuning-peg, tuning-pin; ~**sleutel,** tuning-key, wrest; ~**spleet,** glottis; ~**uitbrenging,** voting; ~**val,** cadence; ~**vangery,** *see* **stemmevangery;** ~**vee,** the unthinking mass; electoral mob; ~**verandering,** change of voice; ~**verheffing,** raising of the voice; ~**vorming,** voice-production; ~**vurk,** tuning-fork; ~**werwer,** canvasser (for votes); **wermery,** ~**werwing,** canvass(ing); ~**wisseling,** breaking (change) of volce.
steng'el, *see* **sting'el**
sten'geweer, sten gun.
ste'nig, (**ge-**), stone (to death), lapidate; *iem. kan* ~, want to murder someone; ~**ing,** lapidation, stoning.
stenochromie', stenochromy.
stenograaf', (..grawe), stenographer, shorthand-writer; ~**grafeer',** (**ge-**), take down in shorthand; write shorthand; ..**grafie',** stenography, shorthand; ..**gra'fies,** (-e), stenographic.
stenogram', (-me), stenogram.
stenotelegrafie', stenotelegraphy.
stenotipis', (-te), shorthand typist; ~**te,** (-s), female shorthand typist.
sten'tor, (-s), stentor; ~**stem,** stentorian voice.
step'pe, (-s), steppe; ~**bewoner,** inhabitant of the steppes; ~**streek,** steppe region.
ster, (-re), star; officer's pip; luminary; cataract (eye); *met* ~*re BESAAI*, star strewn, starry; *sy* ~*re DANK*, thank one's lucky stars; *sy* ~ *GAAN op*, his star is rising; *iem. tot die* ~*re OPHEMEL*, land someone to the skies; *iem.* ~*retjies laat SIEN*, give someone a severe blow; ~*re en STREPE*, stars and stripes; *VALLENDE* ~, meteor, shooting star; *VASTE* ~, fixed star; *sy* ~ *VERBLEIK*, his star is on the wane; ~**anys,** star-aniseed, badian; ~**band,** ornamented headstrop (on bridle); ~**besetting,** all-star cast; ~**distel,** caltrop, star-thistle.
ste're, (geselst.), (mv) buttocks; *see* **stert.**
stereo, (-'s), stereo.
stereochemie', stereochemistry; ..**chromie',** stereochromy; ..**fo'nies,** (-e), stereophonic.
ste'reofoto, (-'s), stereophotograph.
stereognos'ties, (-e), stereognostic.
stereografie', stereography.
stereogra'fies, (-e), stereographic.
ste'reometer, stereome'ter, stereometer.
stereometrie', solid geometry, stereometry.
stereome'tries, (-e), stereometric(al).
stereoskoop', (..skope), stereoscope; ..**sko'pies,** (-e), stereoscopic(al).
stereotiep', (-e), stereotyped.
stereoti'pe, (-s), stereotype.
stereotipeer', (**ge-**), stereotype.
stereotipeur', (-s), stereotyper.
stereotipie', stereotypy.
stereotropie', stereotropism.
sterf, (**ge-**), die, depart this life, pass away; *AAN siekte, van honger* ~, die of a disease, of hunger; ~

op die BRANDSTAPEL, die at the stake; *op sterwe na DOOD*, all but dead; *van DORS* ~, die of thirst; *DUISEND dode* ~, die a thousand deaths; *op sterwe LÊ*, be at death's door; ~ *op die SKAVOT*, die on the scaffold; *see* **sterwe**; ~**bed**, dying bed, deathbed; ~**bewys**, death certificate; ~**dag**, dying day; day of death; ~**eis**, death claim; ~**geval**, death; ~**huis**, house of mourning; house in which someone has just died; ~**jaar**, year of someone's death; ~**kamer**, death-room; ~**kans**, expectation of death; ~**kennis**, death notice.
sterf'lik, (-e), mortal; ~**heid**, mortality.
sterf'ling, (-e), mortal (being), earthling; *geen* ~ *nie*, not a living soul.
sterf: ~**lys**, mortality list; ~**reg**, death duty; ~**register**, death-register; register of deaths; ~**regte**, succession duties.
sterf'te, mortality, death-rate; ~**sertifikaat**, death certificate; ~**statistiek**, mortality returns; ~**syfer**, death-rate, rate of mortality; ~**tabel**, mortality table, life-table.
sterf'uur, dying hour, hour of death.
ster: ~**gewelf**, firmament, starry vault; ~**gras**, stunted sedge.
steriel', (-e), sterile, barren, unproductive.
sterilisa'sie, sterilization.
sterilisa'tor, (-s), sterilizer.
steriliseer', (ge-), sterilize.
steriliteit', sterility, barrenness.
sterk, (w) (ge-), strengthen, invigorate; *iem. in sy kwaad* ~, encourage a person in his wrong-doing; (b, bw) strong, powerful, vigorous, hardy, hefty, virile; hot (favourite); able-bodied, able, athletic, robust; hard (liquor); high (meat); hot; ~ *BOTTER*, rancid butter; ~ *DRANK*, spirituous (alcoholic) liquor, strong drink, ardent spirits; ~ *GEHEUE*, retentive memory; ~ *van iets OORTUIG wees*, be firmly convinced of something; *'n* ~ *ROKER*, a heavy smoker; *wie nie* ~ *is nie, moet SLIM wees*, where force fails one must use guile; ~ *STAAN*, have a strong case; ~ *in TALE*, well-up in languages; *iets TEN* ~ *ste ontken*, deny something emphatically; *jou* ~ *UITDRUK*, express oneself forcibly; ~ *WERKWOORD*, strong verb; ~**gebou**, well-built; ~**gekleur, (-de)**, highly coloured (exaggerated); ~**gespierd, (-e)**, muscular; ~**heid**, strength, strongness.
sterk: ~**igheidjie**, spot, tot, dram, drink; ~**ing**, strengthening; ~**kos**, Cape cress.
ster: ~**klits**, star-burr; ~**koraal**, madrepore, starcoral.
sterk: ~**peper**, cubeb; ~**stroom**, high-tension current (power).
sterk'te, strength, potency; courage; power (lens); rating (motor); loudness, volume (of sound); intensity (of light); penetration (of lens); complement (of officers); fort, stronghold; *op* ~ *hou*, keep up to strength; ~**graad**, proof (of spirits); ~**leer**, strength (of materials); ~**punt**, strong point (mil.); ~**reëlaar**, ~**reëling**, volume control; ~**staat**, table of effectives, strength return.
sterk'water, spirits of wine, aqua fortis; *iets op* ~ *sit*, lay in lavender.
ster'lig, starlight; ~**meter**, astrometer.
ster'ling, sterling; ~**gebied**, sterling area; ~**koers**, exchange rate for sterling; ~**silver**, sterling silver.
ster'motor, radial engine.
ster're, (geselst.), buttocks; *op sy* ~ *kry*, have one's bottom tanned; *see* **stert**.
ster're: ~**aanbidder**, worshipper of stars; ~**baan**, orbit of a star; ~**beeld**, constellation; ~**dag**, sidereal day; ~**diens**, star-worship; ~**gewelf**, starry vault; ~**heer**, starry host; ~**hemel**, starry heavens; ~**hoogtemeter**, astrolabe; ~**jaar**, sidereal year; ~**kaart**, celestial map; ~**kunde**, astronomy; uranology; ~**kun'dig, (-e)**, asterial; astronomical; ~**kun'dige, (-s)**, astronomer; ~**kyker, (-s)**, telescope; star-gazer; ~**kykery**, star-gazing; ~**ligmeter**, astrometer; ~**loop**, course (motion) of the stars; ~**muur**, chickweed; ~**prag**, starry splendour; ~**reën**, meteoric shower; ~**stelsel**, galaxy; ~**tjie, (-s)**, little star; starlet (actress); asterisk (in printing); tern (bird); ~**verering**, Sabaism; starworship; ~**waarsêery**, horoscopy; ~**wag, (-te)**, observatory; ~**wiggelaar, (-s)**, astrologer; ~**wigge-lary**, astrology, horoscopy.
ster'saag, rift-saw.
ster'saffier, star-stone, sapphire.
stert, (-e, stêre), buttocks; tail; pigtail, queue; brush (of fox); rear, train; remnant, fag-end; trail (comet); handle (plough); *'n* ~ *AANLAS*, add a story of one's own; *by die* ~ *AF*, touch and go; *die* ~ *AFSNY*, dock; *iets by die* ~ *BEET hê*, get hold of the wrong end of the stick; *met die* ~ *tussen die BENE*, hangdog, ashamed; with one's tail between one's legs; *'n* ~ *jie HÊ*, have a repercussion; *met die* ~ *KWISPEL*, wag the tail; *jou* ~ *teen iem. OPLIG (optel)*, to be cheeky (saucy); *die* ~ *WIP*, be roused to anger; have one's back up; ~**as**, tail-end shaft; ~**balk**, tail-boom (aero.); ~**been**, coccyx, tail-bone; ~**hamer**, tilt hammer; ~**holte**, dock; ~**inrigting**, empennage; ~**jie, (-s)**, tail, scut (of hare); ending (of word); ~**klavier**, grand piano; ~**kwas**, switch; ~**loos, (..lose)**, tailless, anourous; ~**pen**, tail-feather; ~**pit**, dock; ~**riem**, crupper (harness); G-string; jock-belt (of wrestler); abbreviated (bathing-)trunks; ~**riemlis(sie)**, dock (harness); ~**skroef**, breech-pin; leg-vice; ~**skutter**, rear-gunner; ~**ster**, comet; ~**steun**, (tail-)skid (aero.); ~**stomp**, dock (of tail); ~**stuk**, tailpiece, aitchbone; rump-piece; edge-bone; body (of weapon); ~**swaai**, tail-swishing; ~**veer**, tail-feather; *iem. se* ~ *vere UITTREK*, bring someone down a peg or two; ~**vet**, tail-fat; ~**vlegsel**, pigtail; ~**vin**, tail-fin; ~**vlak**, tail-plane; tail-surface (aero.); ~**werwel**, caudal vertebra; ~**wiel**, tailwheel; ~**wol**, dodds wool, say-cast; ~**wortel**, tailhead, dock.
ster: ~**vormig, (-e)**, star-shaped, stellate, asteroid; ~**vuurwerk**, asteroids.
ster'we, (ge-), die, pass away, depart this life; *op* ~ *na DOOD*, on one's last legs; more dead than alive; *te* ~ *KOM*, pass away; die.
ster'wend, (-e), dying, expiring, moribund.
ster'wens: ~**nood**, death-struggle; ~**uur**, hour of death, dying hour; ~**wens**, dying wish.
stet, stet, leave.
stetoskoop', (..skope), stethoscope; **..ko'pies, (-e)**, stethoscopic.
steun¹, (s) (-e), moan, groan; (w) (ge-), moan, groan; ~ *van pyn*, groan with pain.
steun², (s) support, benefit, assistance, help; **(-e)**, stand-by, aid, prop, anchor; ~ *BIED aan*, offer support to; *GELDELIKE* ~, financial aid; ~ *GENIET van*, have the support of; *MET die* ~ *van*, with the backing of; ~ *SOEK*, look for support; *TOT* ~ *van*, in support of; ~ *TREK*, receive relief (the dole); ~ *VERLEEN aan*, render assistance; (w) (ge-), support (a motion); aid, assist, favour (cause); stay, buttress, prop (a wall); countenance (an action); *die BALKE* ~ *op die muur*, the beams rest on (are supported by) the wall; *GELDELIK* ~, assist financially; ~**arm**, suspension arm; ~**balk**, supporting beam, girder; ~**beeld**, caryatid (arch.); ~**beer**, buttress.
steun'blaar, ..blad, stipule; ~**draend, (-e)**, stipulate(d); ~**loos, (..lose)**, exstipulate.
steun: ~**boog**, arch-buttress; ~**fonds**, relief fund; ~**lat**, fillet; ~**muur**, retaining wall; counterfort, buttress; ~**paal**, stanchion; ~**pilaar**, support, supporting column (pillar), buttress; abutment; mainstay; supporter, stalwart (of society); ~**plaat**, backing plate; ~**punt**, fulcrum, pivot; point d'appui, base, locality (mil.); foothold; strong point; beam centre; ~**raam**, racketing; abutment; ~**sel, (-s)**, prop, stay, support; bar (of horse's foot); ~**sool**, arch-support; ~**stang**, stay rod; ~**stuk**, pier; console (bracket); ~**trekker**, dolesman; ~**troepe**, supporting forces; ~**vlak**, supporting surface; ~**wal**, buttress; ~**weefsel**, stroma; ~**wiel**, dolly (wheel).
steur¹, (s) (-e), sturgeon.
steur², (w) (ge-), disturb, trouble, interfere with, interrupt, intrude, inconvenience; *MOENIE jou daar*

aan ~ nie, don't mind that; hom nie ~ aan 'n REËL nie, ignore all rules; ~ der, (-s), interrupter; ~ end, (-e), disturbing, upsetting, inconvenient.
steur'garnaal, prawn.
steur: ~ ing, disturbance, interruption; derangement; intrusion; interference, nuisance, failure (of machine); fault (teleg.); atmosferiese ~ ings, atmospherics; ~ ingvry, (-e), troublefree; ~ nis, (-se), disturbance, confusion; interference; intrusion; ~ sender, jamming-station.
ste'we, (-ns), prow, stem, bow; die ~ wend, veer round, put the ship about; ~ beeld, figurehead (on ship), fiddlehead.
ste'wel, (-s), boot; vier ~ s in die lug lê, lie flat on the back; lie stiff and stark; ~ kneg, bootboy, boots; bootjack.
ste'wig, (-e), firm; thorough; sturdy, strapping, burly; compact, solid; sound, substantial; ~ AANSTAP, walk at a good pace; ~ DRINK, drink hard; 'n ~ e MAAL, a substantial meal; 'n ~ e NOOI, a strapping (buxom) girl; ~ STAAN, stand firm; ~ VASHOU, grip frimly, hold tightly; ~ VERPAK, strongly-packed; ~ heid, firmness; solidity.
stiebeuel', (-s), stirrup; stapes (anat.); ~ klappe, skirts; ~ knip, stirrup-bar; ~ pomp, stirrup-pump.
stief, nominally related; harsh, hard-hearted; niggardly; iem. ~ behandel, treat someone badly; ~ broer, stepbrother; ~ dogter, stepdaughter; ~ kind, stepchild; ~ ma, ~ moeder, stepmother.
stiefmoe'derlik, (-e), stepmotherly, niggardly; ons is maar altyd ~ BEHANDEL, we have always been treated like poor relations (orphans), die NATUUR het hom maar ~ bedeel, nature has not been kind to him.
stief: ~ ouer, stepparent; ~ seun, stepson; ~ suster, stepsister; ~ vader, stepfather.
stieg'riem, stirrup-strap; ~ klappe, skirts.
stie'kem, (Ndl.), hom ~ hou, keep out of sight; lie low.
stier, (-e), bull; die S~, Taurus, the Bull; ~ geveg, bullfight; tauromachy.
Stier'marke, Styria.
stier: ~ mens, minotaur; ~ vegter, matador, bullfighter, toreador.
stif, (-te), pen; pin, tack; style, stiletto, point; shank (of tool); stick; burin; pricker; ~ fie, small pin; rod; stick; ~ vormig, (-e), styliform.
stig, (ge-), found, establish (a business); institute (a society); stir up, cause; erect (a monument); raise, start (a fund); edify (by preaching) BRAND ~, set fire to (building, etc.); KWAAD ~, do harm; OPROER ~, stir up mutiny; nie oor iets ge~ WEES nie, not at all pleased about something.
stig'gie, (-s) = **steggie¹**.
stig'ma, (-s, -ta), stigma, mark, brand; ~ tisa'sie, stigmatization; ~ tiseer', (ge-), stigmatize, brand.
stig'telik, (-e), edifying, ennobling; ~ e boeke, books of a religious nature; ~ heid, edification; devoutness.
stig'ter, (-s), founder, institutor; eponym; beginner; raiser; ~ es', (-se), foundress; ~ lid, founder member.
stig'ters: ~ aandeel, promoter's share; ~ dag, founders' day; ~ lid, founder (foundation) member.
stig'ting, (-e, -s), erection; foundation; founding; home, institution; institute; edification, uplift, improvement.
stig'tings: ~ akte, deed of foundation; ~ dag, founding day; ~ lid, foundation member; ~ vergadering, inaugural meeting.
stik¹, (ge-), stitch (with machine).
stik², (ge-), choke, suffocate; be suffocated, stifle, moulder, rot; LAAT hom ~, leave someone to stew in his own juice; let him choke; die MIELIES ~ in die grond, the mealies rot in the ground; ~ van WOEDE, choke with rage; ~ bom, asphyxiating bomb; ~ damp, choke-damp; ~ donker, pitch dark; ~ gas, choke damp, asphyxiant, asphyxiating gas, mustard gas; ~ gat, wine-pit; ~ kend, (-e), stifling; ~ kend warm, stiflingly hot.
stik'ker, (-s), stitcher.
stik'lug, choke-damp, suffocating air, mephitic air.

stik: ~ masjien, stitching machine; ~ naald, stitching-needle; ~ sel, stitching.
stik'sienig, stiksie'nig, (-e), short-sighted, myopic; ~ heid, myopia.
stik'stof, nitrogen, azote; ~ bakterie, nitrobacter; ~ bemesting, nitrogenous manure; ~ binding, nitrogen fixation; ~ ewewig, nitrogenous equilibrium; ~ houdend, (-e), nitrogenous; ~ verbinding, nitrogen compound; ~ voeding, nitrogen fixation; ~ voorraad, supply of nitrogen.
stik'sweis, spot-welding.
stik: ~ vol, (-le), chock-full, cram-full; ~ warm, stiflingly hot.
stik'werk, stitching, quilting; machine-work.
stil, (w) (ge-), calm, soothe (a child); quiet, hush, alleviate, allay (pain); satisfy, appease (hunger); quench (thirst); (b) (-le), quiet, calm, peaceful, eventless, silent; met die ~ le HOOP, with the secret hope; iets ~ HOU, keep something secret; ~ LEWE, live quietly; ~ MENSE, quiet-living people, S~ le OSEAAN, Pacific Ocean; 'n ~ ROLPRENT, a silent film; ~ TYD, a slack season; quiet time; 'n ~ (le) VENNOOT, a sleeping partner; (tw) be quiet! shut-up! hold your tongue!
stilb, (-e), stilb (unit of brightness).
stil'bestrol, stilbestrol.
stil'bly, (-ge-), remain silent, hold one's peace, quiesce; keep quiet; pause; ~ is ook 'n ANTWOORD, silence often speaks volumes; no answer is also an answer; ~, KINDERS, not a word from you children!
stileer', (ge-), compose; stylize, formalize; .. le'ring, styling.
stilet', (-te), stiletto.
stil: ~ foto, still; ~ fotografie, still(s) photography; ~ hang, (-ge-), hover (aeroplane); ~ heid, silence, stillness; calmness.
stil'hou, (-ge-), keep quiet, be silent; come to a stop, pull up, stop; hush up; iets ~, keep something dark, ~ plek, stop, stopping place.
stilis', (-te), stylist; ~ tiek', stylistics; ~ ties, (-e), stylistic.
stil: ~ lê, (-ge-), lie still, lie idle; put a stop to; lay up; ~ lees, silent reading; ~ legging, closing down; laying up (off); ~ lerig, (-e), rather quiet, rather still.
stil'letjie, (-s) = **stelletjie**
stil'letjies, softly, quietly, on the sly, secretly.
stil'lewe, (-ns), still life (painting).
stil'ligheid, quiet, secrecy; in die ~, on the quiet; in secret.
stil'ling, quenching; allaying, alleviation.
stil'loop, smooth running; die ~ van die motor, the smooth running of the engine.
stil'maak, (-ge-), calm; hush, silence, shout down (a speaker), shut up.
stil'middel, sedative.
stilograaf', (grawe), stylograph; ~ pen, stylograph pen; .. grafie', stylography; .. gra'fies, (-e), stylographic.
stil'sit, (-ge-), sit still, be quiet; remain inactive.
stil'staan, (-ge-), stand still, stop, halt, come to a standstill, pause; ~ by 'n GEDAGTE, dwell on a thought; ~ de, stagnant (water); static; parked; stationary.
stil'stand, truce, cessation, standstill, stoppage, lull, inactivity, stagnation; solstice; tot ~ KOM, come to a standstill (stop); ~ van WAPENS, armistice.
stil'swye, silence, die ~ BEWAAR, keep silent; die ~ OPLÊ, enjoin silence.
stilswy'end, stil'swyend, (-e), quiet, silent, taciturn; tacit; implicit; iets ~ aanneem, take something for granted; .. swy'gendheid, silence, taciturnity, reticence.
stil'te, (-s), quietness, calm, noiselessness, lull, peace, silence, privacy; IN die ~, secretly, on the sly; in private; IN ~, in silence; die ~ voor die STORM, the lull (calm) before the storm; ~ gordel, doldrums, belt of calms; ~ tyd, quiet time (for prayer).
sti'lus, (-se), stylus.
stil'veld: ~ wees, have taken French leave.
stil: ~ vertoning, dumb show; ~ water, dead water (aero.); ~ weg, quietly.

sti'mulans, (-e), stimulant; stimulus.
stimulant', (-e), stimulant.
stimula'sie, (-s), stimulation.
stimuleer', (ge-), stimulate; ~**middel**, stimulant.
sti'mulus, (-se, ..li), stimulus; stimulant.
stin'gel, (-s), stalk, stem (of plant); ha(u)lm (of beans); ~**blad**, stem leaf; ~**blom**, pedunculate flower; ~**knol**, corm; ~**knoop**, node; ~**knop**, stem-bud; ~**lit**, internode; ~**loos**, (..lose), stalkless, stemless; ~**plant**, cormophyte; ~**rank**, stemtendril; ~**rig, (-e)**, stalky; ~**rosyntjies**, stalk-raisins; ~**tros**, corymb; ~**steek**, stem stitch; ~**voet**, corm; ~**vormig, (-e)**, stalklike, cauliform; ~**vrot**, stem rot.
stink, (w) (ge-), stink, reek, have a bad smell; (b) stinking, fetid, foul, olid; rotten, disgusting; ~**afrikaner**, African marigold; ~**akkedis**, skunk; ~**besie**, stink-bug, twig-wilter; ~**blaar**, thorn-apple *(Datura stramonium)*, datura; ~**blom**, stinking camomile; ~**bol**, stink-ball; ~**bom**, stink-bomb; ~**boontjie**, Australian blackwood; ~**bos**, stinkbush; ~**brand**, bunt (of wheat); stinking smut; ~**das**, stinking badger; ~**dier**, polecat, skunk; ~**end, (-e)**, fetid, malodorous, mephetic, stinking; *jou* ~ *end maak by*, become most unpopular with; ~**erd, (-s)**, scoundrel, stinker, skunk, rogue; ~**erig, (-e)**, rather stinking, smelly; ~**gogga**, stink-bug, garden-bug; ~**granaat**, stink-shell; ~**gras**, stinkgrass *(Eragrostis major);* ~**hout**, stinkwood, Cape laurel; *Kamdeboo*~*hout*, white stinkwood; ~**kakiebos**, Mexican marigold; ~**klawer**, melitot; ~**klier**, scent-gland; ~**koeël**, stink-ball; ~**muishond**, Cape polecat; ~**olie(boom)**, *see* **stinkblaar**; ~**peulboom**, red-heart; ~**poel**, cesspool; ~**pot**, Cape hen *(Majaques aequinoctialis);* black albatross; ~**sprinkaan**, elegant grasshopper *(Zonoserus elegance);* ~**stok**, bad cigar, penny-stinker, weed; ~**swam**, stink-horn; ~**vis**, bamboo-fish *(Box salpha);* ~**vlieg**, garden-bug, cluster-stinkfly (-bug); antesia bug.
stip¹, (s) (-pe), spot, point, dot, speckle, stipple.
stip², (b) (-te), strict; prompt; punctual; exact, accurate, precise; *iem.* ~ *AANKYK*, stare at a person; ~ *te BETALING*, prompt payment; ~ *BETYDS (op tyd) wees*, be punctual; *jou* ~ *aan 'n REËL hou*, adhere strictly to a rule.
stipendiaat', (..dia'te), stipendiary.
stipen'dium, (-s, ..dia), stipend; bursary, scholarship.
stip'pel, (s) (-s), spot, dot, point, speckle, stipple; (w) (ge-), spot, dot, speckle, stipple; ~ **aar**, roan horse; ~**druk**, stipple-printing; ~**kanaal**, spore canal; ~**kwas**, stippling-brush; ~**lig**, spotlight (signals); ~**lyn**, dotted line; ~**streep**, dotted line (traffic); ~**tjie, (-s)**, mote; ~**wiel**, dotted wheel.
stip'pie, (-s), spot, dot, point, speckle.
stip'seltjie, (-s), mote.
stip'telik, promptly, precisely, strictly, scrupulously.
stipt'heid, precision, accuracy; punctuality, promptness.
stipula'sie, (-s), stipulation, condition, proviso.
stipuleer', (ge-), stipulate, demand.
stoei, (ge-), wrestle; romp; jostle; mill; ~**er, (-s)**, wrestler; forward (player) (in rugby); ~**erig, (-e)**, romping; ~**ery**, wrestling; scrimmage; romping; fray; ~**geveg**, *see* **stoeiwedstryd**; ~**kryt**, wrestling-ring; ~**siek, (-e)**, romping, wanton; ~**wedstryd**, wrestling-match.
stoel, (s) (-e), chair, seat, stool; see (of bishop); pedestal; stool (plant); *vir* ~*e en BANKE praat*, talk to empty seats; *nie onder* ~*e en BANKE wegsteek nie*, make no secret of; *nie op DIESELFDE* ~ *sit nie*, not to see eye to eye; *die ELEKTRIESE* ~, the electric chair; *as jy op twee* ~*e tegelyk wil sit, kom jy op die GROND te lande*, between two stools one falls to the ground; *die HEILIGE S*~, the Holy See; *op TWEE* ~*e sit*, run with the hare and hunt with the hounds; *iem. 'n LELIKE* ~ *sit*, do someone a bad turn; *op twee* ~*e SIT*, sit on the fence; keep in with both sides; (w) (ge-), stool, form a stool (plant); ~**bed**, chair (for tenon); ~**bekleedsel**, chair covering; ~**dans**, musical chairs; ~**gang**, motion of bowels, stool, defecation; ~**geld**, chair rent; ~**gras**, tussock-grass; ~**jare**, old age; ~**kleedjie**, chair cover; ~**kussing**, chair-cushion; ~**leuning**, chair back; ~**mat**, chair-bottom; ~**matter, (-s)**, chair-bottomer; ~**poot**, chair leg; ~**rug**, chair back; ~**sitting**, seat, chair-bottom; ~**tjie, (-s)**, small stool; small chair.
stoep, (-e), stoep, veranda; perron; *voor sy eie* ~ *vee*, mind one's own business; sweep before your own door; ~**bank**, stoep-bench; ~**ie, (-s)**, little stoep; ~**kamer**, stoep-room, room opening on to the veranda; ~**plant**, stoep-plant, pot plant; ~**sitter, (-s)**, lazy fellow, sluggard; ~**trap**, veranda steps.
stoer, (-e), powerful, brave, sturdy, hardy; staunch; ~**heid**, sturdiness, staunchness, bravery.
stoet, (-e), procession; retinue, train, cortége; stud (animals); ~**boerdery**, stud farming; ~**dier**, stud animal.
stoe'tery, (-e), stud; stud-farm.
stoet'haspel, (-s), duffer, simpleton, juggins.
stoet: ~**hings**, stud stallion; ~**merrie**, brood mare; ~**ooi**, stud ewe; ~**perd**, stud horse; ~**ram**, stud ram.
stoets, obtuse; blunt, stumpy, stubby; surly, gruff; ~ *HOEK*, obtuse angle; ~ *NEUS*, stumpy nose; ~**heid**, obtuseness; stubbiness; gruffness.
stoet: ~**skaap**, stud sheep; ~**vee**, stud stock.
stof¹, (s) stowwe, material, fabric; coating; matter, theme, subject-matter; *KORT van* ~, short-spoken; of but a few words; *LANK van* ~, be long-winded; ~ *tot NADENKE*, food for thought; ~ *VERSAMEL vir 'n roman*, collect material for a novel.
stof², (s) (stowwe), dust; powder; grit; *iem. die* ~ *laat BYT*, make someone bite the dust; *nie by 'n ander se* ~ *KOM nie*, be far surpassed by someone; not be in the same street as another; *in die* ~ *KRUIP*, lick the dust; *iem. onder* ~ *LOOP*, send someone flying; knock someone over; ~ *OPJAAG*, make (raise) the dust; *jou* ~ *nie laat SIEN nie*, not put in an appearance; *die* ~ *van sy voete SKUD*, shake the dust from one's feet; *TOE onder die* ~, covered with dust; *loop dat die* ~ *so TREK*, run like the wind; *tot* ~ *VERGAAN*, turn to dust; *in die* ~ *VERNEDER*, humble to the dust; *in die* ~ *VERTRAP*, trample in the dust; (w) (ge-), dust, remove dust; *see* **afstof**; ~**aanbidding**, materialism; ~**bakkie**, dustpan; ~**besem**, duster, broom; ~**bestryding**, dust-prevention; ~**blik**, dustpan; ~**borsel**, dust-brush; ~**breedte**, width of cloth; ~**bril**, goggles; ~**deeltjie**, particle of dust; mote, molecule, atom; ~**deksel**, dust-cover; ~**dig, (-te)**, dustproof; ~**digting**, dustproofing; ~**doek**, duster, dust-cloth; ~**dop**, dust-cap; ~**dweil**, mop.
stoffa'sie, (-s), material, stuff; *'n man van ANDER* ~, a man of different calibre; *sy* ~ *WYS*, show his mettle.
stoffeer', (ge-), furnish; garnish; upholster; ~**der, (-s)**, upholsterer; ~**dery**, upholstery; ~**kant**, broad lace; ~**stof**, upholstery fabric; ~**werk**, upholstery.
stof'feloos, (..lose), immaterial, spiritual.
stof'fer, (-s), duster; ~**ig, (-e)**, dusty; ~**igheid**, dustiness.
stoffe'ring, (-e, -s), furnishing; upholstering, upholstery.
stof'fie, (-s), particle (atom) of dust, mote, speck of dust; *'n* ~ *aan die weegskaal*, a mere speck.
stof'fig = stoww(er)ig.
stof: ~**gehalte**, dust-content; percentage of dust; ~**goud**, gold-dust; ~**hael**, fine shot, dust-shot; ~**hoop**, dust-heap.
sto'fie, (-s), small stove; footstool.
stof: ~**inaseming**, coniosis; ~**inhoud**, fabric composition; ~**jas**, dust-coat; ~**keerder**, dust-excluder; ~**kleur**, dust-colour; ~**kleu'rig, (-e)**, dust-coloured; dusty; ~**kole**, dross coal; ~**kom**, dust-bowl; ~**laag**, layer (coating) of dust; ~**laken**, dust-sheet; ~**lap**, duster; ~**leer**, coniology.
stof'lik, (-e), mortal; material; carnal; earthly; tangible; ~*e oorskot*, mortal remains; ~**heid**, materiality.
stof: ~**loos, (..lose)**, immaterial; dustless; ~**loosheid**,

immaterialness; ~ **luis,** psocid, book-louse; ~ **man= tel,** dust-cloak; ~ **meel,** flour dust; ~ **meter,** koni= meter, coniscope; ~ **naam,** name of material; ~ **nat,** wet on top; *dis net ~ nat,* it was a very light shower of rain (only a few drops); ~ **nes,** dust-trap; ~ **om= slag,** dust-cover (of books); ~ **plaag,** plague of dust.

stof'reën, stof'reent, (s) fine rain, drizzle; (w) **(ge-),** drizzle.

stof: ~ **siekte,** coniosis; ~ **skerm,** dust-shield; dust- board; ~ **steenkool,** dross-coal; ~ **storm,** dust- storm; ~ **suier, (-s),** vacuum cleaner; ~ **trapper= (tjie), (-s),** very short person; ~ **vry, (-e),** dustfree, dustless, dustproof; ~ **werend, (-e),** dust-prevent= ing; ~ **wering,** dust-prevention; ~ **wisselend, (-e),** metabolic; ~ **wisseling,** metabolism; ~ **wisselings= produk,** metabolite; ~ **wol,** dusty wool.

stof'wolk, cloud of dust; pother; *'n ~ opskop,* make much ado about nothing.

Stoï'es, (-e), Stoic(al).

Stoïsis'me, Stoicism.

Stoïsyn', (-e), Stoic; ~ **s', (-e),** Stoic(al).

stok¹, (s) **(-ke),** stick, cane, staff, pole, (broom) handle; (golf-)club; pointer, vine; crop (whip); (mv) sticks (hockey); stock (timber frame with holes) (hist.); ~ *ALLEEN,* quite alone; *hy is nie met 'n ~ te BEWEEG nie,* wild horses will not drag him away; *'n ~ in 'n BYENES steek,* stir up a hornet's nest; *met die ~ GEE,* give someone a caning; *dit met iem. aan die ~ HÊ,* be at odds with someone; *die hoenders GAAN op ~,* the fowls go to roost; *iem. voor ~ KRY,* give someone a talking to; *dit aan die ~ KRY met iem.,* fall out with someone; *onder die ~ KRY,* give someone a caning; *moenie verder SPRING as wat jou ~ lank is nie,* don't bite off more than you can chew; *iem. in die ~ SLUIT,* confine someone in the stocks; *hy is nie met ~ ke en SWAARDE weg te kry nie,* he is not to be moved by any manner of means; *iets met 'n ~ kan VOEL,* be as plain as a pikestaff; *iem. 'n ~ in die WIEL steek,* throw a spanner into the works; put a spoke in the wheel.

stok², (w) **(ge-),** stop, gasp (for breath); flag; *haar stem het ge~,* her voice broke down; there was a catch in her voice.

stok: ~ **alleen,** all alone, quite alone; ~ **beitel,** clear= ing-chisel; ~ **bewaarder,** gaoler; ~ **blind, (-e),** stone= blind; ~ **boon,** runner-bean; ~ **doof, (..dowe),** stone-deaf; ~ **draer,** caddy (golf); ~ **dweil,** mop.

sto'kebrand, firebrand, mischief-maker.

sto'ker, (-s), stoker, fireman; distiller (spirits); fire- brand; ~ **y,** distillery; mischief-making.

stok'flou, finished, dead tired.

sto'king, distillation.

stok'insek, stick insect.

stok'kerig, (-e), stringy, wooden (fig.); stiff, clumsy; ~ **heid,** woodiness; woodenness; clumsiness.

stok'kie, (-s), little stick; *na dieselfde ~ MIK,* have the same thing in view; *'n ~ voor iets STEEK,* put a stop to something, forestall (something); ~ **lekker,** sucker.

stok'kiesdraai, (-ge-), play truant; ~ **er, (-s),** truant; delinquent; ~ **ery,** truancy.

stok'kiesdraer, harvester ant *(Hodotermus mosam= bicus).*

stok'kiesduiwel, stick insect.

stokkinet', stockinette.

stok: ~ **lam, (-me),** completely lame; ~ **lengte,** club- length; ~ **mes,** drawing-knife; ~ **oud, (..oue),** very old, hoary with age; ~ **passer,** beam compasses.

stok'perdjie, (-s), hobby-horse; pet notion, hobby; fad; *op sy ~ sit,* ride one's hobby-horse.

stok'roos, hollyhock.

stok'siel(salig)alleen, all alone.

stok: ~ **skêr,** block-shears; ~ **stertmeerkat,** suricate; ~ **stil,** stock-still, motionless; ~ **styf,** as stiff as a poker; ~ **vis,** stockfish, split (dried) cod, hake.

stol, (ge-), congeal, coagulate, set; clot, curdle, curd; concrete, inspissate; freeze; *dit het my bloed laat ~,* it made my blood run cold.

sto'la, (-s), stole; stola (Roman).

stol: ~ **ling, (-e, -s),** congealing, solidification; con- gealment, fixation, concretion, coagulation; ~ **lingstyd,** setting time; ~ **lingsgesteente,** igneous rock; ~ **middel,** coagulator.

stolp, (-e), glass cover, bell-glass; case; ~ **plooi,** box- pleat.

stol: ~ **punt,** setting point; point of solidification; ~ **room,** clotted cream; ~ **sel,** clot.

stom, (-me), dumb, mute, inarticulate, speechless; dense, crass, stupid; wretched, pitiable; *die ~ me DIERE,* the poor animals (brutes); *dit was ~ me GELUK,* that was sheer luck; *'n ~ LETTER,* a mute (consonant); ~ *van VERBASING,* in blank amazement.

sto'ma, (-s, -ta), stoma.

stom'dronk, dead drunk, blind drunk, drunk as a lord.

sto'mery, (-e), dry-cleaning; dry-cleaning works.

stom'geluk: *dit was ~,* that was sheer luck.

stom'heid, dumbness, muteness, mutism; crassness, density, denseness, stupidity.

sto'ming, steaming; dry-cleaning.

stom'mel, (ge-), bustle, clutter, fumble.

stom'meling¹, (-e), bustle, cluttering.

stom'meling², (-e), stupid fool, dullard, dolt, blockhead.

stom: ~ **merik, (-e),** stupid fool, dullard, ignoramus, blockhead, dunce, ass; ~ **migheid,** stupidity; ~ **mi= teit', (-e),** stupid thing, howler, blunder, bloomer, stupidness, folly; *'n ~ miteit begaan,* make a blunder.

stomp, (s) (-e), snag, chump, stump, stub, stem, trunk (of tree); (b) blunt, pointless, dull; bluff; obtuse (angle); stumpy; cropped; ~ *MAAK,* make dull; *REGTEROOR ~,* right ear cropped; ~ **as,** stub- axle; ~ **doring,** wild gardenia; ~ **heid,** bluntness; dullness; obtuseness; ~ **hoekig,** obtuse-angled; ~ **ie, (-s),** cigarette end (butt), fag-end; stub; (small) stump; tubby (stocky) person; shorty; ~ **ieag'tig, (-e),** cobby; ~ **ie-enting,** stub grafting; - **icsocker, (-s),** cobby; ~ **kant,** butt; ~ **kop,** crew-cut, cropped head, croppy; ~ **las,** butt-joint; ~ **neus,** flat nose; ~ **neusdolfyn,** bottlenose dolphin; ~ **neusskaaf,** bullnose; ~ **oor,** crew-cropped (-cut); crop-eared sheep; ~ *oor GEMERK,* be an old maid; be on the shelf; *'n nooi ~ oor SNY,* monopolize (single out) a girl.

stompsin'nig, (-e), dull, stupid, feeble-minded, dense; ~ **heid,** dullness, stupidity, feeble-mindedness.

stomp'stert, tailless, dock-tail; ~ **arend,** bateleur eagle; ~ **baadjie,** dinner jacket; ~ **hond,** dog with stumpy tail, -y, (-s), crombec; ~ **kat,** Manx cat.

stomp'sweis, (s) butt-welding; (w) **(ge-),** butt-weld.

stomp'weg, flatly, bluntly.

stom'vervelend, (-e), deadly boring (dull), dull as ditchwater.

ston'de, (-s), hour, time; ~ **s,** menses, (menstrual) periods.

stonk, (ge-), stump (cricket); approach (in marble- games); ~ **streep,** (popping) crease (cricket); taw (in marbles).

stont'(h)ol, (-le), Zulu musical instrument (with one string).

stoof, (s) (stowe), stove, range; footwarmer; (w) **(ge-),** stew; *ge~ de haasvleis,* jugged hare; ~ **appel,** stew= ing apple; ~ **blad,** cooking top, hob; ~ **borsel,** stove brush; ~ **deksel,** stove lid; ~ **kap,** stove hood; ~ **kussing,** stove-dabber; - **pan,** stew pan; - **pa= tats,** glazed sweet potatoes; ~ **peer,** stewing pear; ~ **plaat,** stove plate; ~ **politoer,** stove polish; ~ **ring,** stove ring; ~ **steen,** firebrick; ~ **swartsel,** stove polish (-blacking); ~ **vleis,** stew; stewing meat; ragout; fricassee; ~ **vrug,** cooker (fruit); ~ **waks,** stove polish.

stook, (ge-), fire, stoke, fuel; burn; distil (spirits); make a fire; pick (teeth); *KWAAD ~,* stir up trouble (strife); *hy ~ KWAAI,* he drinks (smokes) a great deal; ~ **gas,** fuel-gas; ~ **gat, (-e),** firehole; stokehole; ~ **kas, (-te),** stove; hothouse; ~ **ketel,** still; ~ **olie,** oil-fuel; ~ **oond,** furnace; ~ **plek, (-ke),** fire- place; stokehole; ~ **ruim,** stokehold (ship); ~ **wyn,** distilling wine; ~ **yster,** poker (of fireman).

stool, (stole), stole (of woman).

stoom, (s) steam; ~ *AFBLAAS*, blow off steam; *ONDER* ~, with steam up; *met VOLLE* ~, at full steam; (w) **(ge-)**, steam; *ge~de vis*, steamed fish; ~**bad**, steam bath; ~**baggermasjien**, steam-dredger; ~**barkas**, steam launch; ~**boor**, steam-drill; ~**boot**, steamship, ~**dig**, **(-te)**, steam-proof; ~**druk**, steam-pressure; head (of steam); ~**drukketel**, pressure-boiler; ~**drukmeter**, steam-gauge; ~**drukpers**, power-press; ~**fluit**, steam whistle; buzzer; ~**gaatjie**, vesicle; ~**grawer**, steam-shovel; ~**hamer**, steam hammer; pile-driver; ~**hitte**, steam-heat; ~**jag**, steam yacht; ~**kas**, **(-te)**, steam-chest; ~**kastrol**, waterless cooker; steamer; ~**ketel**, boiler; ~**klep**, steam-valve; ~**koker**, pressure-boiler (-cooker); ~**kole**, steamcoal; ~**kraan**, steam crane; steam-cock; ~**krag**, steam-power; ~**kursus**, refresher course; ~**leiding**, steam-line; ~**mantel**, steam-jacket; ~**masjien**, steam-engine; ~**meter**, steam-pressure gauge; ~**meul(e)**, steam-mill; power mill; ~**middel**, inhalant; ~**opwekking**, steam-generation; ~**pers**, steam-press; ~**ploeg**, steam plough; ~**pomp**, steam-pump; ~**pyp**, steam-pipe; ~**rem**, steam-brake; ~**roller**, (s) steamroller; *see* **stoomwals**; (w) **(ge-)**, steamroller; ~**silinder**, steam-cylinder; ~**skip**, steamship; steamer; ~**sleper**, steam tug; ~**sloep**, steam launch; ~**suier**, steam-piston; ~**trekker**, steam-tractor.

stoom'vaart, steam navigation; ~**lyn**, steamship line; ~**maatskappy**, liner company, steamship company; ~**verbinding**, steamship communication (link); ~**verbruik**, steam-consumption; ~**verwarming**, heating by steam, central heating; ~**wals**, steam-roller; ~**wassery**, steam laundry; ~**werktuig**, steam engine.

stoor[1], **(ge-)**, disturb, interrupt (conversation); interfere with, trouble, inconvenience (a person); ~**nis**, **(-se)**, disturbance, confusion; ~**sender**, jamming-station.

stoor[2], (w) store; (n), store, packing store.

stoot, (s) **(stote)**, push; stab, blow, thrust (with dagger); gore, poke (with horns); move (chess); impulse, stroke (in billiards); *die EERSTE ~ gee*, set the ball rolling; be the prime mover; *iem. 'n ~ vorentoe GEE*, give someone a push; *'n KWAAI ~*, uphill work; *'n ~ VORENTOE*, a forward move; a leg up; (w) push, bump, knock; toss, butt; jostle (in a crowd); *jou AAN iem. se gedrag ~*, take offence at someone's behaviour; *'n BILJARTBAL ~*, play a billiard ball; *~ TEEN*, abut; *v.d. TROON ~*, dethrone; *hy ~ VANDAG*, he is in a bad mood today; he is grumpy today; ~**bal**, pushball; ~**balk**, buffer beam; ~**band**, skirt-binding, braid; cushion (billiards); ~**block**, chock, buffer; ~**demper**, **(-s)**, shock-reducer; ~**kant**, binding, hem, border, welt; false hem; ~**karretjie**, pushcart; handcart; ~**klep**, poppet valve; ~**koevoet**, pinch bar, ripping bar; ~**krag**, push, thrust; ~**kussing**, buffer; ~**las**, butt-scarf, butt-joint; ~**lat**, bead (woodwork); ~**naat**, butt-joint; ~**plaat**, buffer plate; guard (of rifle); ~**ring**, abutment ring; ~**saag**, compass saw; ~**serie**, break (billiards); ~**skraap**, **(ge-)**, bulldoze; ~**skraper**, bulldozer; ~**stang**, push-rod; ~**stoel**, invalid's chair; push chair; wheel chair; ~**stok**, cue; barge-pole; ~**stuk**, toe-piece (steps); ~**trollie**, push trolley; ~**veer**, buffing-spring; ~**waentjie**, handcart, go-cart, pushcart; perambulator.

stop[1], (s) **(-pe)**, fill (of tobacco); darn; plug; (w) **(ge-)**, darn (sock); fill up (holes), plug; stuff (poultry, food, cushion); pack, bundle into; slip (into pocket); *iem. 'n FOOITJIE in die hand ~*, slip a tip into someone's hand; *KOUSE ~*, darn stockings; *al die kinders in die MOTOR ~*, bundle all the children into the car; *~ van MYNE*, fill your pipe with my tobacco; *'n PYP ~*, fill a pipe; *TANDE laat ~*, have teeth filled.

stop[2], (w) **(ge-)**, stop, halt, pull up; come to a standstill; *BLOEDING (buikloop) ~*, put a stop to bleeding (diarrhoea); *iem. se MOND ~*, silence someone; *TREINE ~ hier*, trains stop here; *~!*, halt!

stop: ~**alarm**, stop-alarm; ~**bal**, hazard (billiards); darner; ~**blok**, stop-block.

stop: ~**fles**, stoppered bottle; ~**garing**, darning-cotton; ~**gat**, electric socket; ~**hamer**, caulking-hammer; ~**hars**, joiner's putty; ~**katoen**, darning-cotton, mending-wool; ~**klei**, puddle; ~**klip**, filler (stone); ~**kontak**, plug, connection, power plug, wall plug (elec.); ~**lap**, stopgap; fill-up; expletive; ~**lig**, stop light; ~**-maar-in**, hold-all; ~**mandjie**, darning-basket; ~**mengsel**, glazing compound; ~**mes**, putty knife.

stop'middel, astringent; stopgap.
stop'naald, darning-needle; larding-pin (-needle).
stop'oorlosie, stop watch.
stop'pel, **(-s)**, stubble; *op iem. se ~s oes*, catch a girl on the rebound; ~**baard**, stubbly beard; ~**bewerking**, mulching; ~**gans**, stubble-goose; ~**hare**, stubbly hair; ~**ig**, **(-e)**, stubbly; ~**land**, stubble-field; *iets op die ~ land JAAG*, allow something to go to rack and ruin; *op die ~ land SIT*, have been left on the shelf; ~**ploeg**, trash plough; ~**rig**, **(-e)**, stubbly; ~**veld**, stubble-field; ~**vere**, pin-feathers.
stop'per, **(-s)**, darner.
stop'plek[1], stopping-place, halt, stop.
stop'plek[2], darn.
stop'sein, stop signal.
stop'sel, **(-s)**, padding, filling (of tooth); fill (of tobacco); wad, plug; darn.
stop: ~**setting**, stoppage, closing down; ~**sit**, **(-ge-)**, put a stop to, shut, close down; stanch; ~**skakelaar**, plug switch.
stop'spek, lardo(o)n.
stop: ~**steek**, darning-stitch; ~**ster**, **(-s)**, darner.
stop: ~**straat**, stop street; ~**streep**, halt line; ~**stuk**, filler (in newspaper); chock (mining).
stop'sy, darning silk.
stop'teken, stop sign, halt sign.
stop: ~**touwerk**, gasket (for sails); ~**trein**, slow train (stopping along route).
stop'verf, putty.
stop'vet, larding fat.
stop'vry, **(-e)**, hole-proof.
stop'was, propolis.
stop: ~**werk**, darning; ~**wol**, darning (mending) wool.
stop'woord, expletive, stopgap, filler.
sto'raks, storax.
sto'rend, **(-e)**, disturbing, upsetting; *dit werk ~*, it has a disturbing influence.
sto'rie, **(-s)**, story, tale; fib; *~s vertel*, tell stories; gossip; lie; ~**boek**, storybook; ~**tyd**, story-telling time.
sto'ring, **(-e, -s)**, disturbance, interruption; discontinuance; trouble; derangement; perturbation; fault; *atmosferiese ~*, atmospherics.
sto'ringsvryheid, selectivity.
storm, (s) **(-s)**, storm, tempest, gale, blast; *'n ~ in 'n GLAS water*, a storm in a teacup; (w) **(ge-)**, attack, charge, storm, assault; *BUITE ~ dit*, outside a gale is blowing; *'n FORT ~*, storm a fort; *uit 'n KAMER ~*, rush out of a room; ~**aanval**, close attack, assault; ~**afdeling**, assault party; ~**afstand**, close range.
stormag'tig, **(-e)**, stormy, tempestuous, inclement, tumultuous, boisterous, gusty; ~**heid**, storminess, inclemency.
storm: ~**baan**, storm-path; ~**bal**, black ball; ~**band**, chinstrap; ~**bok**, battering-ram; ~**bui**, squall; ~**dak**, testudo, mantlet; ~**dek**, hurricane-deck; ~**deur**, storm-door; ~**enderhand**, by storm; ~**-en-drang**: *die ~-en-drang-periode*, the time of fret and fury; ~**fok**, forestay sail; ~**gebied**, storm-area; ~**geteister**, **(-de)**, storm-torn; ~**gety**, storm-tide; ~**hoed**, headpiece; morion; ~**hoek**, storm-quarter; ~**ja(ag)**, **(-ge-)**, storm, charge; attack; ~**jaer**, assailant, stormer; dumpling cooked in fat, doughnut, vetkoek.
Storm'kaap, Cape of Storms.
storm: ~**klok**, alarm bell, tocsin; ~**kraag**, storm-collar; ~**lamp**, hurricane-lamp; ~**leer**, scaling-ladder; ~**loop**, (s) (..**lope**), rush, onslaught, assault, on-rush, run (on a bank); (w) **(ge-)**, attack, rush at, assault, storm; ~**lyn**, guy(-rope); ~**paal**, fraise; ~**party**, assault party; ~**pas**, double-quick march; ~**ram**, battering-ram; ~**rand**, welt (of boot);

~sein, ~sinjaal, storm-signal; ~sentrum, storm-centre; ~skade, storm-damage; ~soldaat, storm-trooper; ~sterkte, gale force; ~tou, weather-line; ~troepe, shock-troops; ~vis, grampus, orc; ~vloed, storm-water flood; ~voël, stormy petrel, fulmar, albatross, Mother Carey's chicken, hurricane-bird; ~voorspelling, gale forecast; ~waarskuwing, gale warning; ~weer, tempestuous weather; ~wind, gale, hurricane, tempest.

storneer', (ge-), make a counter-entry, adjust an account.

storno', (-'s), counter-entry, adjustment of account.

stort, (ge-), pour, spill (milk); shed (tears, blood); deposit, pay in (in bank); throw, dump (rubbish); plunge; *jou in iem. se ARMS* ~, throw oneself in someone's arms; *BUITE begin dit te* ~, outside it is beginning to pour; *in DUIE* ~, miscarry; *GELD op aandele* ~, pay up shares; *GELD op 'n rekening* ~, pay into account; *gestorte KAPITAAL*, paid-up capital; *in OORLOG* ~, plunge into war; *die RIVIER* ~ *hom uit in die see*, the river disembogues (debouches) into the sea; *in die VERDERF* ~, dash to ruin; ~bad, shower-bath; douche; ~baaie neem, take showers; ~bak, dump body; hopper; ~bestand, (-e), spillproof; ~bui, heavy downpour; drenching (soaking) rain, deluge; ~deur, dump-door; ~er, (-s), depositor; dumper; ~gat, chute-hole; ~geut, chute; ~goedere, bulk stores; ~gordyn, shower curtain; ~graan, grain in bulk; ~hokkie, shower-cubicle; ~hoop, tip-mound.

stor'ting, (-e, -s), payment, contribution, paying in (bank), instalment, deposit; tipping; dumping; effusion; spillage; receipt; ~ *verbode*, no dumping.

stor'tings: ~bedrag, (amount of) deposit; ~bewys, deposit receipt (slip); ~vorm, paying-in slip, deposit slip.

stort: ~kar, dump-cart; tipcart; ~kas, hopper; ~klep, jettison valve (aero.); return valve; ~klip, rip-rap; ~koker, chute, shoot; ~lading, cargo in bulk; ~plek, dump; dumping-ground; depositing site; ~reën, ~reent, (s) deluge, heavy downpour; (w) (ge-), come down in torrents, come pouring down; ~see, head sea; ~sel, spillage; cast (concrete); ~tafel, casting table; ~terrein, tipping-site; ~toestel, tipping-plant; ~trok, hopper-truck; ~vas, (-te), spillproof; ~vloed, flood, deluge, cataract; *'n* ~ *vloed van woorde*, a torrent of words; ~wa, tip-truck, dump-wagon, hopper-truck.

sto'tend, (-e), offensive; pushing.

sto'ter, (¹s), girdle strap; bumper (car); pusher; butter; poker.

sto'terig, (-e), not fluent, stumbling, stuttering; given to butting (bull).

sto'tertenk, tankdozer.

stot'ter, (ge-), stammer, stutter, falter, hum and ha; ~aar, (-s), stammerer, stutterer.

stou, (ge-), stow, trim; ~er, stower, stevedore, trimmer; ~plek, stowage.

stout, (-e; -er, -ste), naughty; bold, daring; *die ste verwagtings oortref*, exceed the boldest (wildest) expectations.

stou'terd, (-s), naughty child.

stout'heid, naughtiness, boldness, daring.

stout'igheid, naughtiness, mischievousness.

stoutmoe'dig, (-e), bold, undaunted, daring; ~heid, boldness, daring, assurance.

stou'werk, stowage.

sto'we, (ge-), warm; stew (meat); smother; bask (in sun); *iem. 'n kool* ~, play a trick upon someone; ~vleis, stewing meat.

stow'w(er)ig, (-e), dusty; fuggy; ~heid, dustiness.

straal, (s) (strale), beam, ray; frog (of horse's hoof); flash (of lightning); jet, spout, spurt (water); radius (of circle); gleam (of hope); (w) (ge-), radiate, beam; glitter, ray, shine, gleam; ~ *van geluk*, beam with happiness; ~aandrywing, jet propulsion; ~bad, needle bath; ~bars, radial shake; ~behandeling, ray treatment; ~blom, ray flower; ~brekend, (-e), dioptric(al); refractive; ~breking, refraction; diffraction; ~brekingsleer, dioptrics, anaclastics; ~buiging, diffraction; ~buis, jet; ~bundel, pencil of rays; ~dier, radiate (animal);

~eeu, jet age; ~floute, jet lag; ~hoek, radian; ~jaer, jet fighter; ~jakkeraars, jet set; ~kaatser, reflex reflector; ~kaggel, reflector fire; ~kanker, cancer of the hoof; ~koud, stonecold; *dit laat my* ~ *koud*, it leaves me quite unmoved; ~lig, radiated light; ~lyn, radial line; ~motor, jet engine; ~pomp, jet pump; ~pyp, jet pipe; nozzle; ~radio, beam radio.

straals'gewys(e), radically, actiniform.

straal: ~skroef, jet; ~steen, actinolite; ~stelsel, beam-directing system; ~stuk, jet; ~tjie, (-s), gleam, flicker, weak ray; trickle; squirt; ~verspreider, ~verwarmer, radiator; ~visier, radial backsight; ~vliegtuig, jet aeroplane; ~vormig, (-e), radial, actiniform; ~werper, spotlight; ~wyser, radius post (railway).

straat, (s) (strate), street; channel, strait (of the sea); *'n BLINDE* ~, a blind alley; a dead-end; *die* ~ *MEET*, stagger along drunkenly; be reeling; *OP* ~, in the street; *op* ~ *SIT*, turn someone out into the street; *op* ~ *STAAN*, be out on the street; (w) (ge-), pave; ~arm, poor as a church mouse; ~belasting, pavage; ~betoging, street demonstration; ~boef, hooligan; ~boewery, hooliganism, gangsterism; ~bordjie, nameplate; ~briewebus, pillar box; ~deuntjie, street tune, vulgar ditty; ~deur, street door; ~gans, jay-walker; ~geroep, street cry; ~gerug, noise in the street; ~gespuis, mob, rabble, hooligans; ~geut, street gutter; ~geveg, street fight; ~handelaar, street trader; ~hoek, ~hoekie, street corner; jeug, juggles, scamps, street arabs, guttersnipes; ~kei, (-e), cobble; ~kind, street arab, street child, guttersnipe; ~klip, pitcher; ~knop, road stud; ~kollekte, street collection; ~kunstenaar, street performer; ~lamp, street lamp; ~lawaai, street noise; ~liedjie, street song; vulgar ditty; ~lig, street light; ~lokomotief, steam-traction engine; ~loper, vagabond, tramp; streetwalker; corner boy; gadabout; ~maker, road maker; paver, paviour; ~meisie, streetwalker, prostitute; ~musiek, street music; ~musikant, street musician; ~naam, street name; ~orrel, barrel organ; ~predikant, street preacher; ~privaat, chalet; public convenience; ~rand, kerb(ing); ~reiniger, street orderly; ~reiniging, street-cleansing; ~roep, street cry; ~roof, street-robbery; ~roomys, hokey-pokey; ~rower, street robber; ~rumoer, tumult in the street; ~sanger, street singer; ~skender, (-s), hooligan; ~skendery, hooliganism; ~skreeuer, ranter; ~skurk, apache; ~slet, woman of the streets, prostitute; ~sloot, gutter, kennel; ~slyper, guttersnipe, loafer; ~smous, gutter-merchant, costermonger, hawker; ~stamper, ram, paver's monkey; paving beetle; ~steen, paving-stone; cobble; paving-brick; ~taal, vulgar language, billingsgate; ~toneel, street scene; ~veër, (-s), crossing-sweeper, street sweeper; ~venter, pedlar, hawker, costermonger; ~verkeer, street traffic; ~verkoper, hawker; ~verligting, street lighting; ~voor, gutter; ~vrou, prostitute; ~weg, highway, highroad; ~werker, street paver; road-maker; ~wysie, street tune.

strabis'me, strabismus.

straf, (s) (strawwe), punishment, penalty, chastisement; affliction; penance; *sy GERIGTE* ~ *ondergaan*, undergo his condign punishment; *OP* ~ *van*, under penalty of; ~ *UITDEEL*, mete out punishment; *VIR sy* ~, as his punishment; (w) (ge-), punish, castigate, penalize, chastise; correct; (bw) (strawwe), severe (winter); rigid (attitude); sharp (reprimand); hard (task); *hy rook* ~, he is a heavy smoker; ~baar, (..bare), punishable; chastisable, actionable; culpable; penal; guilty; ..*bare manslag*, culpable homicide; ~baarheid, punishableness; culpability; ~baarmaking, penalization; ~bediening, ~bepaling, penalty clause; ~bevoegdheid, disciplinary powers; ~boek, punishment-book; ~doel, ~drie, penalty goal; ~ekspedisie, punitive expedition; ~fe: *op* ~ *fe*, upon penalty of; in peril of; ~(fe)loos, (..lose), with impunity; non-punishable; ~(fe)loosheid, impunity; ~fend, (-e), punitive; ~gebied, penalty area; geding, criminal

trial; ~ **geld**, surcharge; ~ **gerig**, judg(e)ment upon criminals, fine; ~ *gerig van GOD*, the justice of God; ~ **gevangenis**, convict prison, penitentiary.
straf'heid, severity, austerity.
straf: ~ **hervorming**, penal reform; ~ **hoek**, penalty corner (soccer); ~ **hof**, criminal court; ~ **hou**, free hit; penalty stroke; ~ **inrigting**, penal establishment; ~ **klousule**, penalty clause; ~ **kolonie**, convict colony, penal settlement; ~ **kommando**, punitive commando; ~ **maatreël**, punitive measure; ~ **middel**, means of punishment; ~ **oefening**, penalty drill; execution (of a sentence); ~ **oplegging**, imposition (of punishment); ~ **peloton**, punishment squad; ~ **plaas**, place of execution; ~ **pleging**, execution of punishment; ~ **port**, excess postage, surcharge; additional postage; ~ **portseël**, postage-due stamp; ~ **predikasie**, lecture, reproof; ~ **prediker**, reprover, moralist; ~ **proses**, criminal procedure; ~ **prosesreg**, law of criminal procedure; ~ **punt**, point (as penalty); ~ **reëls**, punishment lines; ~ **reg**, criminal law, penal law; ~ **regadvokaat**, criminal lawyer; ~ **register**, record, dossier (of criminal), punishment-book.
strafreg'telik, (-e), penal; of criminal law.
straf: ~ **regter**, criminal judge; ~ **saak**, criminal case; ~ **sitting**, session (of the criminal court); *iem. ter* ~ *sitting verwys*, commit a person for trial; ~ **skepskop**, penalty drop(-kick) (rugby); ~ **skerm**, penalty bully; ~ **skop**, free kick, penalty kick; ~ **skul'dig, (-e)**, guilty, culpable; ~ **skul'digheid**, guilt, culpability; ~ **stelsel**, penal system; system of punishment; ~ **tyd**, term (period) of imprisonment; ~ **vermindering**, mitigation of punishment; ~ **verordening**, police regulation; ~ **voltrekking**, execution of judgment, penalty, punishment; ~ **vordering**, criminal procedure; ~ **waar'dig, (-e)**, culpable, guilty, deserving punishment; ~ **werk**, punishment, detention work (at school); imposition; criminal work (legal).
straf'wet, penal law; ~ **boek**, penal code; ~ **gewing**, criminal legislation.
straf'worp, penalty throw.
strak, (-ke), taut, tight, tense, stiff, set, fixed, severe; *iem.* ~ *aankyk*, look fixedly (stare) at a person; ~ **heid**, tautness, tightness, stiffness, tenseness.
strak'kies, perhaps; presently, by and by, anon; just now; *hy KOM* ~, he'll be here in a moment; *TOT* ~, so long!
straks, perhaps; presently; possibly.
stra'le: ~ **behandeling**, radiotherapy; ~ **bundel**, pencil of rays; ~ **krans**, halo, aureole, gloriole, glory, nimbus.
stra'lend, (-e), radiant, beaming; gleaming; ~ *van geluk*, radiant with happiness.
stra'ler, jet plane; ~ **kliek**, jet set.
stra'ling, (-e, -s), radiation, beaming.
stra'lings: ~ **energie**, radiant energy; ~ **gesteente**, actinolite; ~ **gordel**, radiation belt; ~ **meter**, radiometer.
stra'lingsterkte, intensity of radiation.
stra'lings: ~ **termometer**, black-bulb thermometer; ~ **veld**, light angle (aero.); ~ **vermoë**, radiating power; ~ **verwarmer**, radiant heater; ~ **warmte**, radiant heat.
stram, stiff, hard, rigid; ~ *v.d. KOUE*, stiff with cold; *'n* ~ *SKARNIER*, a stiff hinge.
stramboel': *met snaar en* ~ *(stamboel)*, on foot.
stram'heid, stiffness, rigidity.
stramien', canvas (as framework for embroidery); framework (of novel).
stram'm(er)ig, (-e), somewhat stiff, rather rigid; ~ **heid**, stiffness, rigidity.
stramo'nium, stramonium.
strand (s) (-e), beach, shore, seaside resort, coast, foreshore, strand; *AAN die* ~, on the beach, at the seaside; *op die* ~ *LOOP*, be cast ashore; *OP die* ~, on the beach; *S* ~, Strand; *hy WOON in die S* ~, he lives at the Strand; (w) **(ge-)**, strand, run ashore, ground (ships); come to grief; ~ **battery**, shore-battery; ~ **bewoner**, coast-dweller; ~ **dief**, beachcomber; strand robber; ~ **drag**, seaside wear; ~ **gas**, guest at seaside resort; ~ **gebied**, foreshore;

~ **gedeelte**, sea front; ~ **goed**, wrecked goods, jetsam, flotsam; ~ **gruis**, shingle; ~ **hoed**, beach hat; ~ **hoof**, beachhead; ~ **huis**, beach cottage; ~ **ing**, stranding; shipwreck; ~ **jut, (-te)**, brown hyena; beachcomber (fig.); ~ **kommandant**, beach master; ~ **leuning**, beach rest.
Strand'loper, (-s), Beachranger, Strandloper.
strand: ~ **loper, (-s)**, dott(e)rel; sandpiper; ~ **lopertjie, (-s)**, three-banded plover, sand plover; ~ **lyn**, beach-line; hand (fishing-) line; ~ **meer**, lagoon; ~ **mes**, whaling-knife; ~ **muur**, sea wall; ~ **myn**, beach mine; ~ **oord**, ~ **plek**, seaside resort; ~ **pruim**, sand plum; ~ **reg**, right of salvage, law regarding wrecked goods; ~ **rok**, beach dress; ~ **roof**, beachcombing; ~ **roos**, statice *(Limonium)*; ~ **sandale**, beach sandals; ~ **skoen**, sand shoe; ~ **stoel**, beach chair; ~ **vlooi**, sand flea; ~ **vonder**, receiver of wreck; ~ **voog**, wreck master; ~ **wag(ter)**, coastguard; ~ **weg**, marine drive; esplanade; beach road; ~ **wolf**, brown hyena.
strangula'sie, strangulation.
stranguleer', (ge-), strangulate.
strateeg', (..teë), strategist.
strategie', strategy.
strate'gies, (-e), strategic(al).
stratifika'sie, stratification.
stratifiseer', (ge-), stratify.
stratigrafie', stratigraphy.
stratografie', stratography.
stratosfeer', stratosphere; ..fe'ries, (-e), stratospheric(al).
stra'tum, (..ta), stratum.
strawa'sie, difficulty; fuss; hubbub; ~ *maak*, make a fuss.
straw'wer, (s) (-s), chastiser, punisher; (b), more severe, severer.
streef, (ge-), *see* **strewe**.
streek, (streke), district, area, country, region, zone, tract; point (compass); artifice, trick, prank, dodge; joke; *iem. sy streke AFLEER*, cure a person of his tricks; wean someone from his bad habits; *iem. van* ~ *BRING*, put someone off his stroke; *een* ~ *DEUR*, at at stretch; *IN die* ~ *van*, in the region of; *op* ~ *KOM*, get under way; *'n mal* ~ *UITHAAL*, do a foolish thing; *vol streke WEES*, be full of mischief; ~ **beplanning**, regional planning; ~ **bou**, zoning; ~ **hof**, regional court; ~ **indeling**, zoning; ~ **kantoor**, regional office; ~ **komitee**, regional committee; ~ **landdros**, regional magistrate; ~ **lyn**, loxodromic curve; ~ **magistraat**, regional magistrate; ~ **naam**, name of a region; ~ **nuus**, regional news; ~ **ontwikkeling**, regional development; ~ **roman**, regional novel; ~ **seël**, local stamp.
streeks'gewys(e), on a regional basis, regionally.
streek: ~ **spraak**, ~ **taal**, dialect; regional speech; ~ **tyd**, zonal time; ~ **verteenwoordiger**, regional representative; ~ **wind**, zonal wind.
streel, (ge-), caress, stroke, pet, fondle; flatter; tickle (one's fancy); ~ **naam**, pet name.
streep, (s) (strepe), line, stroke, stripe (on cloth); dash (punctuation mark); streak (of lightning); quirk (in character); striation (in science); crease (cricket); tabby (material); *een* ~ *DEUR*, without a break; *'n* ~ *HÊ*, be daft, have a screw loose; *dis 'n* ~ *deur sy REKENING*, that upsets his applecart; *die vaal* ~ *SKEP*, take the road; *'n* ~ *v.d. TEERKWAS weg hê*, have a touch of the tarbrush; *iem. 'n* ~ *TREK*, play a trick (up)on someone; *'n* ~ *TREK deur*, pull a stroke through; rule something out; (w) **(ge-)**, stripe, streak, line, hit, cane; ~ **bliksem**, forked lightning; ~ **bou**, ribbon development; ~ **broek**, morning trousers; ~ **das**, striped tie; ~ **dassie**, zebra (fish); ~ **gravering**, line-engraving; ~ **koppie**, bunting; ~ **lig**, strip light; ~ **muis**, striped fieldmouse; ~ **muishond**, striped polecat; ~ **sak**, grainbag; ~ **siekte**, streak (in sugar cane, maize); ~ **spekvleis**, streaky bacon; ~ **stof**, striped material; ~ **suiker**, thrashing, hiding, strap oil; *iem.* ~ *suiker gee*, give someone oil of whip; ~ **vis**, seventy-four (kind of fish); ~ **vy**, tiger fig.
strek, (ge-), stretch, extend; reach; *dit* ~ *jou tot EER*, it does you credit; *so ver sy GENADE* ~, as far as

his mercy extends; *jou op die GRAS ~ (uitstrek)*, extend oneself on the grass; *~ TOT*, be conducive to; *solank ons VOORRAAD ~*, as long as our supply lasts; ~**baar, (..bare)**, protrusile; ~**dam**, barrage, breakwater; ~**grens**, yield point; ~**king, (-e, -s)**, tendency, bent, tenor, purport, drift, object; purpose (of deed); scope (of law); purview; *woorde van dieselfde ~king*, words of the same effect; ~**kingsroman**, novel with a purpose; ~**laag**, course of stretchers; ~**las**, running joint; ~**maat**, running measurement; ~**pees**, ~**sening**, ~**spier**, protractor, (ex)tensor tendon; ~**steen**, stretcher (brick); ~**verband**, stretcher bond; ~**vermoë**, coverage, covering capacity.
stre'lend, (-e), pleasant, flattering, caressing, gratifying; grateful; *~e klanke*, sweet (soothing) sounds.
stre'ling, caress, fondling, stroking; endearment; flattery.
strem, (ge-), congeal, coagulate, curdle (milk); retard; congest; hinder, hold up (traffic); obstruct; *oorlog ~ die handel, oorlog werk ~mend op die handel*, war brings trade to a standstill; ~**melk**, junket; ~**mend**, retarding; ~**middel**, goagulant; ~**ming**, coagulation, congelation, congealment, curdling; retardation; hindrance; congestion, traffic jam; ~**sel**, curds; rennet; coagulator; ~**selkoek**, cheesecake; ~**seltablet**, junket tablet; ~**stof**, rennet; coagulant.
streng, (-e), astringent; austere (life); strict (diet); stern (master); severe (winter); rigorous (climate); *deur (manners), ~ LOGIES*, strictly logical; *n reël ~ TOEPAS*, enforce a rule rigorously; *~ VERBODE*, strictly prohibited.
stren'gel, (ge-), plait, twine, twist; *krale ~*, string beads; ~**ing**, plaiting, twining, twisting.
streng'heid, austerity, asperity, strictness, severity, harshness, rigour; astringency.
stre'perig, (-e), streaky (paint); striped; *~e kors*, streaky crust; ~**heid**, streakiness, stripiness.
stre'pie, (-s), hyphen, dash; little streak; stripe, line; *'n ~ voor hê*, be a favourite.
stre'pieskode, bar code; ..**kodering**, bar coding.
stre'piesgoed, striped material.
streptokok'kus, (..kokke), streptococcus.
streptomisien', ..misi'ne, streptomycin.
streu'kel = struikel.
stre'we, (s) striving, aspiration, aim, endeavour; conation; (w) **(ge-)**, strive, endeavour, aspire to, strain after; struggle; *~ na EER*, strive after honour; *iem. OPSY ~*, outrival someone; ~**r**, one who strives, trier, go-ahead person.
stre'wing, (-e) = strewe, (s)
strib'bel, (ge-), struggle, oppose, kick against the pricks; haggle; ~**ing**, dispute, wrangle, row.
striem, (s) (-e), stripe; weal, wale; (w) **(ge-)**, flog, beat, lash, weal; *~ende ironie*, biting irony
strignien', strigni'ne, strychnine.
strik[1]**, (s) (-ke)**, bow, knot, noose, ambush; gin, trap, snare; mesh; *in eie ~ GEVANG wees*, be caught in one's own snares; be hoist with one's own petard; *in die ~ LOOP*, be caught in a trap; *in die ~ SIT*, be caught; be ensnared; *vir iem. 'n ~ SPAN*, set a trap for someone; (w) **(ge-)**, tie, knot (with a bow); ~**das**, bowtie; ~**kie, (-s)**, rosette, bow, knot; ~**knoop**, looped knot.
strik[2]**, (b) (-te)**, strict; precise, accurate, exact; severe.
strik'rede, sophism.
strikt'heid, strictness; precision, accuracy.
striktuur', constriction.
strik'vraag, catchy question, twister, poser.
string, (s) (-e), string (of pearls); trace (of harness); strand (of rope); skein (of yarn); cord (of testicle); hank; head (of silk); *sy ~e STYF loop*, be called to account; meet one's Waterloo; *~ UIE*, rope of onions; (w) **(ge-)**, string; *tabak ~*, hang tobacco; ~**draad**, stranded wire; ~**etjie, (-s)**, small skein; *see* **string**; ~**gare**, ~**garing**, skin yarn; ~**giet**, continuous casting; ~**kabel**, stranded cable.
stroboskoop', **(..skope)**, stroboscope.
stroef, (stroewe), gruffy, surly, harsh (manners); rigid, grim, hidebound (outlook); stiff (hinge); **heid**, stiffness; gruffness, coolness.

stro'fe, (-s), strophe.
stro'fies, (-e), strophic.
stro'kie (-s), slip (paper); comic strip; strip; counterfoil
stro'kies, comics, comic strips; ~**film**, film strip; ~**verhaal**, comic (strip).
stro'ming, (-e, -s), stream, current, tendency, trend, drift; flux.
strom'pel, (ge-), stumble along, hobble, limp along, totter, dodder; ~**aar, (-s)**, hobbler, stumbler; ~**ig, (-e)**, stumbling, hobbling; limping; ~**rig, (-e) = strompelig**; ~**rok**, hobble skirt.
stronk, (-e), stalk; stump (tree); cob (mealie); (mv) stover; ~**boorder, (-s)**, stalk-borer; ~**meel**, cobmeal.
stronsiaan', strontia.
stron'sium, strontium (chem.).
stront, (plat), shit, dung; blackguard; nonsense; ~**erig, (-e)**, befouled; caddish.
strooi, (s) straw; litter (in stable); *g'n ~ BREEK nie*, not lift a finger; *so DROOG soos ~*, as dry as dust; *niemand 'n ~ in die WEG lê nie*, give offence to no one; do nobody a bad turn; *soos ~ in die WIND*, like chaff in the wind; (w) **(ge-)**, distribute, scatter; strew, spread (manure); act as bestman or bridesmaid; sprinkle, dredge (sugar, meal); ~**biljet**, handbill, leaflet.
strooi: ~**blom**, immortelle, everlasting; ~**bos**, bundle of straw.
strooi'dak, thatched roof; ~**huis**, house with a thatched roof.
strooi'dekker, (-s), thatcher.
strooi'er, (-s), strewer; sprinkler, castor, dredger.
strooi: ~**halm**, blade of straw; ~**hoed**, straw hat, boater, basher, chip-hat; leghorn (hat).
strooi'huis, straw hut.
strooi'ing, (-e, -s), strewing, scattering.
strooi'jonker, (-s), best man; groomsman.
strooi: ~**karton**, cardboard; ~**klei**, cob; ~**kleur**, straw-colour; ~**kleurig, (-e)**, straw-coloured; ~**lig**, diffused light; ~**man**, stooge, man of straw; ~**mandjie**, flower basket; ~**matras**, chaff mattress; paillasse, pallet.
strooi'meisie, bridesmaid.
strooi: ~**myn**, loose-floating mine; ~**poeier**, lycopodium; ~**pop**, straw doll; figurehead, man of straw; puppet, stooge.
strooi, (-e) = strooihuis.
strooi: ~**sand**, fine sand, pounce; ~**sel**, something used for strewing, e.g. litter, sawdust.
strooi: ~**snyer**, straw-cutter; ~**steen**, cob brick; ~**suiker**, caster sugar.
strooi'tjie, (-s), little straw; *aan 'n ~ vasklou*, catch at a straw.
strook, (s) (stroke), strip; frill, flounce, panel (of skirt), fillet (needlework); band, stroke; run (in mining); counterfoil, belt (maize); (w) **(ge-)**, agree, tally, be in accordance, accord; *dit ~ met my belange*, this suits my own interests; ~**bou**, long-wall; ~**film**, film strip; ~**filmbiblioteek**, film-strip library; ~**lat, batten**; ~**mynbou**, long-wall mining; ~**pad**, strip road; ~**proef**, galley proof; ~**yster**, strip-iron; ~**vloer**, strip flooring; ~**weerlig**, ribbon lightning.
stroom, (s) (strome), stream (of water); current (in sea or electricity); flow, torrent (of words); ~ *AF*, down stream; *'n ~ van GASTE*, a stream of guests; *teen die ~ INGAAN*, try to stem the tide; *as die ~ LOOP, moet jy skep*, make hay while the sun shines; *~ OP*, up stream; *~ OPWEK*, generate current; *strome REËN*, torrents of rain; *met die ~ SAAMGAAN*, drift with the stream; *TEEN die ~ in*, against the stream (current); *die ~ VOLG*, go with the stream; (w) **(ge-)**, stream, flow, pour, rush; *al die mense ~ daarheen*, all the people flock there; ~**aanwyser**, galvanometer; ~**af'waarts**, down stream; ~**baan**, circuit; ~**bed**, river-bed; runway; ~**belyn**, streamlined; ~**belyning**, streamlining; ~**breker, (-s)** weir, breakwater; cut-off; contactbreaker, circuit-breaker; interrupter, oscillator; make-and-break (motor); starling (of bridge); ~**draad**, contact wire, live wire; ~**draend, (-e)**, cur-

rent-carrying; ~**dravermoë**, current rating; ~**eenheid**, unit of current; ~**gebied**, river basin; catchment area; ~**gebruiker**, consumer of current; ~**geleiding**, conduction (of current); ~**geleier**, conductor; ~**god**, river-god; ~**godin**, naiad; ~**kaart**, current-chart; ~**kontak**, power plug; ~**kring**, circuit; ~**lewering**, supply of electricity; ~**loop**, flow of current; ~**lyn**, (s) streamline; (w) (ge-), streamline; *ge~lynde motor*, streamlined car; ~**meter**, flow-meter; amperemeter; ammeter; rheometer; ~**nimf**, water nymph; ~**onderbreker**, current-breaker; ~**oorbrenging**, transmission of current; ~**-op**, (fig.) perverse, contrary; *altyd ~-op gaan*, swim against the stream; ~**op'waarts**, up stream; ~**pie**, (-s), rivulet, beck, burn, streamlet; ~**punt**, power point; ~**reëlaar**, graduator; ~**sluiter**, (-s), circuit-closer; ~**snelheid**, rate of flow; ~**spanning**, voltage; ~**sterkte**, strength of current; amperage; intensity of current; ~**toevoer**, current supply; ~**verbreker**, circuit-breaker; cutout; ~**verbruik**, consumption of current; ~**verdeler**, distributor of current; ~**verdeling**, distribution of current; ~**versnelling**, shoot, chute; rapid (in river); ~**(ver)wisselaar**, (-s), reversing-switch; permutator, switch-commutator; ~**vloei**, current flow; ~**voerend**, (-e), current-carrying; ~**voorsiening**, electricity supply; ~**wender**, (-s), permutator, commutator; ~**wisselaar**, commutator.

stroop[1], (s) **(strope)**, syrup, treacle, molasses; ~ *om die MOND smeer*, cajole, soft-soap; *'n OU ~*, an old namby-pamby.

stroop[2], (s) love (tennis); *dertig ~*, thirty love.

stroop[3], (w) **(ge-)**, pillage, plunder, maraud, forage; strip (plant); poach (in games).

stroop: ~**agtig**, (-e), syrupy; ~**balletjie**, lollipop.

stroop: ~**beitel**, stripping-chisel; ~**bende**, troop of marauders; ~**hamer**, stripping-tool.

stroop: ~**kwas**: *met die ~kwas rondloop*, go about buttering up (soft-soaping) people; ~**lekker**, (-s), toady, flatterer; ~**lepel**, syrup-spoon; ~**mengsel**, electuary (med.).

stroop'party, party of marauders; raid.

stroop: ~**poeding**, golden pudding.

stroop'pot[1], treacle-pot.

stroop'pot[2], love game (tennis).

stroop'soet, very sweet; very good (of child).

stroop: ~**spel**, love game (tennis); ~**stel**, love set (tennis).

stroop: ~**sug**, love of pillage; ~**tog**, raid, marauding expedition.

strop, (s) **(-pe)**, strap, halter, rope, noose; luck; *onder die ~ laat DEURLOOP*, flog; *hy sal nog ~pe DRAAI*, he is in for a hard time; he is in for a rude awakening; *met die ~ GEE*, flog; *vir die ~ GROOTWORD*, grow up for the gallows; *die ~ KRY weens moord*, swing for murder; *die ~ om iem. se NEK sit*, put the halter round someone's neck; have put the halter round someone's neck; *die ~ om die NEK hê*, have one's neck in the noose; *dit VERDIEN die ~*, that ought to be punished by the gallows; *tot die ~ VEROORDEEL word*, be condemned to the gallows; (w) **(ge-)**, flog, beat; ~**das**, bow-tie, choker.

stro'per, (-s), poacher, plunderer, prowler; raider; combine, combination harvester (agric.).

stro'perig, (-e), syrupy, sweet, cloying; maudlin; mealy-mouthed, namby-pamby; ~**heid**, syrupiness, sentimentality.

strop: ~**gespe**, stock-buckle; ~**(hals)snoer**, choker; ~**naaiwerk**, thonging; ~**skarnier**, strap-hinge.

strot, (-te), throat; weasand, throttle; ~**aar**, jugular vein; ~**klep**, throttle; epiglottis; ~**tehoof**, larynx; ~**tehoofontsteking**, laryngitis; ~**teklep**, epiglottis.

struif, (struiwe), omelette.

struik, (-e), bush, shrub; frutex; ~**agtig**, (-e), bushy, shrubby; frutescent, fruticose; ~**boontjie**, bushbean, field-bean.

strui'kel, **(ge-)**, stumble, trip; blunder; ~**blok**, stumbling-block, obstacle; pull-back; ~**ing**, (-e), stumbling.

struik: ~**gewas**, shrubs; brushwood, chaparral, shrubbery; ~**roos**, bush-rose.

struik'rower, highwayman, robber; bandit, brigand; ~**y**, (-e), highway robbery; brigandage.

struik'vormig, **(-e)**, shrublike, frutescent.

struis[1], (s) (-e), straw hut.

struis[2], (b), sturdy, buxom.

struktureel', (..**rele**), structural.

struktuur', (..**ture**), structure; texture (min.); fabric; ~**formule**, structural formula.

stru'ma, struma, scrofula

stru'weling, (-e, -s), dispute, wrangle, trouble, row.

stry, (s): ~ *kry met 'n vriend*, fall out with a friend; (w) **(ge-)**, dispute, argue, contend, clash, bandy words, contradict; combat, fight; *jy KAN tog nie daarteen ~ nie*, you can't deny that; ~ *teen die VYAND*, fight (struggle) against the enemy.

stryd, fight, strife, struggle, contest, conflict, combat, action, war; *die ~ AANBIND met*, join issue with; *die ~ BESLIS*, win the battle; *die ~ om die BESTAAN*, the struggle for existence; *die ~ GEWONNE gee*, admit defeat; *IN ~ met*, in conflict with, contrary to; *die INWENDIGE ~*, the inward struggle; *'n ~ op LEWE en dood*, a life-and-death struggle; *die PUNT waaroor die ~ gaan*, the point at issue; *die goeie ~ STRY*, fight the good fight; *'n SWAAR ~*, a hard fight; *ten ~e TREK teen*, go to war against; ~ *VOER teen*, be at war against; *in 'n ~ WEES (verkeer)*, experience a religious crisis (spiritual conflict).

stryd'baar, (..**bare**), warlike, combative, martial, capable of bearing arms; Amazonian; ~**heid**, militancy, warlikeness; valour; fitness for war.

stryd: ~**byl**, battle-axe; pole-axe; *die ~byl begrawe*, bury the hatchet; ~**dag**, (political) party rally; day of combat.

stry'dend, (-e), conflicting, contrary; combative, militant; contending; ~*e BELANGE*, conflicting interests; *die ~e KERK*, the church militant.

stryd: ~**er**, (-s), warrior, fighter, combatant; ~**fonds**, party fund; fighting-fund; ~**genoot**, (..**note**), brother-in-arms, fellow soldier; ~**gereed**, fit, ready (for action).

stry'dig, (-e), conflicting (interests); contrary, dissonant, incompatible with (views); antagonistic, hostile; ~ *MET*, contrary to; incompatible with; ~ *met die WET*, against the law; ~**heid**, difference, disparity, discordance, incompatibility.

stryd: ~**kas**, fighting-fund; war-chest; ~**knots**, mace; club; ~**krag**, fighting power; ~**kragte**, (military) forces; manpower; ~**kreet**, battle-cry, war-cry; slogan; ~**leus(e)**, slogan, battle-cry; ~**lied**, song of battle; ~**lus**, warlike spirit, militancy, pugnacity; ~**lus'tig**, (-e), militant, bellicose, pugnacious; agonistic; eristic; eager to fight, aggressive; ~**lus'tigheid**, pugnacity, aggressiveness; ~**mag**, (military) force; ~**makker**, brother-in-arms; ~**middel**, weapon; ~**perk**, arena; lists; amphitheatre; *in die ~perk tree*, enter the lists (arena); ~**punt**, see ~**vraag**; ~**ros**, war-horse; ~**skrif**, controversial pamphlet; ~**toneel**, scene of battle; ~**vaar'dig**, (-e), ready for battle, game; ~**vaar'digheid**, readiness for battle (war); ~**voerder**, fighter; controversialist; ~**vraag**, question at issue, point in dispute, moot point; controversy; ~**wa**, war-chariot; ~**wek'kend**, (-e), contentious, causing strife.

stry'er, (-s), disputer, arguer, contender; ~**ig**, (-e), argumentative; ~**igheid**, contentiousness; ~**y**, (-e), bickering, quarrelling, wrangling.

stryk[1], (s) stroke, pace (of horse); *iem. van ~ BRING*, put someone off; *een ~ DEUR*, without a break; *nog ~ HOU*, keep it up; *op ~ KOM*, to strike form; *dit gaan nog maar (op die) OU ~*, things are jogging along in the same old way; *van ~ WEES*, be out of form (off-colour); (w) **(ge-)**, go, walk, march, stride; *HOE ~ dit?* how are things going? *HUIS toe ~*, go home; *hulle kan nie met MEKAAR ~ nie*, they could not hit it off; *SAKE wil nie ~ nie*, matters aren't running smoothly.

stryk[2], (w) **(ge-)**, iron (clothes); smooth (hair); stroke (one's chin); strike (flag); float (plaster); *GELD v.d. toonbank ~*, sweep up money from the counter; *die HAND oor die voorkop ~*, pass one's hand over

one's forehead; *'n VOU uit 'n rok* ~, iron a crease out of a dress; *oor die WATER* ~, skim the water.
stryk: ~ **bord,** ironing-board; smoothing-board, mould-board; breast (of plough); ~ **bout,** iron-heater.
stryk'deur¹, (s) jib door.
stryk'deur², (bw) continuously.
strykelings, closely, skimmingly
stry'ker¹, (-s), ironer.
stry'ker², (-s), fiddler; *die* ~ *s,* the strings.
stryk'geld, charge for ironing; premium (to highest bidder).
stryk'goed, things to be ironed, ironing.
stryk: ~ **instrument,** stringed instrument; ~ **konsert,** concert for strings; ~ **kwartet,** string quartette.
stryk'laag, stretching course (bricks).
stryk: ~ **laken,** ironing sheet; ~ **lap,** ironing cloth.
stryk'loper, pacer (horse).
stryk'meisie, laundrywoman, ironer.
stryk'mes, spatula.
stryk: ~ **musiek,** string music; ~ **orkes,** string band (orchestra).
stryk'plaat, landside (of plough).
stryk'plank, ironing-board; float(er) (plasterwork).
stryk'riem, razor-strop.
stryks: ~ *van vieruur,* about four o'clock.
stryk'sel, filler; ~ **laag,** filler coat.
stryk'snelheid, cruising speed.
stryk'steen, whet-stone; stretcher (brick).
stryk'ster, (-s), ironer, laundry-woman.
stryk'stok, fiddlestick, fiddle-bow; *daar bly heelwat aan die* ~ *hang,* a great deal sticks to the fingers (of the officials).
stryk: ~ **tafel,** ironing-table; ~ **tang,** gof(f)er; ~ **troffel,** darby float; ~ **verband,** stretching-bond; ~ **vernis,** liquid veneer; ~ **voeg,** horizontal joint.
stryk'voor, dead furrow.
stryk'vry, (-e), not to be ironed (fabric); non-iron.
stryk: ~ **vuur,** raking fire; ~ **werk,** ironing, bowing (violin); ~ **yster,** flat-iron, sad-iron.
stu, (ge-), push, propel; prop; stow; dam up; *die* ~ *wende krag,* the driving power; ~ **dam,** barrage, weir.
studeer', (ge-), study, read for; ~ *vir ONDERWYSER,* study to become a teacher; ~ *vir PREDIKANT* ~, study for the ministry; *in die REGTE* ~, study law; ~ **kamer,** study; ~ **kamerkommunis,** arm-chair Communist; ~ **lamp,** reading-lamp; ~ **slaapkamer,** bedroom-study; ~ **tyd,** time for study; ~ **vertrek,** study.
student', (-e), student; ~ **e,** (-s), woman student.
studen'te: ~ **almanak,** students' almanac; ~ **beweging,** student movement; ~ **blad,** students' magazine; ~ **bond,** students' union; ~ **grap,** students' prank; ~ **hawer,** (Ndl.), nuts and raisins; ~ **jare, college years;** ~ **jool,** students' rag; ~ **lewe,** college life; ~ **lied,** students' song; ~ **parlement,** students' parliament; ~ **pret,** student fun; ~ **raad,** students' (representative) council; ~ **streek,** students' prank; ~ **taal,** students' jargon; ~ **vereniging,** students' society
studentikoos', (..kose), student-like, collegian-like.
stu'die, (-s), study; ~ *MAAK van,* make a study of; investigate; *sy* ~ *VOORTSIT,* continue his studies; ~ **aanspoorfonds,** educational advancement fund; ~ **beurs,** scholarship, bursary, exhibition; ~ **boek,** book of study; textbook, ~ **fonds,** scholarship-fund; ~ **gebied,** field of study; ~ **geld,** tuition-fee; ~ **gids,** teaching guide; ~ **jaar,** year of study; ~ **komitee,** studies-committee; ~ **kop,** close student; ~ **koste,** college expenses; ~ **kring,** study-circle; ~ **kursus,** course of studies; ~ **leier,** tutor; ~ **planne,** plans for reading; ~ **reis,** study tour; educational tour; ~ **saal,** study room; ~ **toesig,** supervision of study; ~ **tyd,** time as a student; time for studying.
studieus', (-e), studious.
stu'die: ~ **vak,** branch of study; ~ **veld,** field of study; ~ **verlof,** study-leave.
stu'dio, (-'s), studio.
studio'sus, (..si), (form.), student.
stug, (ge), stubborn, obstinate, unfriendly, harsh,

morose, surly, sullen; ~ **heid,** stubbornness, surliness, curtness.
stu'goed, dunnage.
stu'hout, billet, thick piece of firewood.
stuif, *see* **stuiwe;** ~ **aarde,** mould; ~ **bal,** puffball (*Lycoperdaceae*); ~ **brand,** smut (*Ustilago*).
stuif'meel, pollen (bot.); starch (chem.); mill-dust; ~ **buis,** pollen-tube; ~ **draer,** pollen-carrier; ~ **korrel,** pollen-grain; ~ **sel,** (-le), pollen cell; ~ **vormend,** (-e), polliniferous.
stuif: ~ **poeier,** nebulizer, lycopodium dust; dusting-powder; ~ **pomp,** spray-pump; ~ **reën,** drizzle; ~ **sand,** drift-sand; ~ **swam,** puffball, fuzz-ball (*Lycoperdaceae*).
stuik, (-e), shock, butt; ~ **las,** butt-joint, end-joint; ~ **naat,** butt-seam; ~ **sweis,** (ge-), butt-weld; ~ **sweising,** butt-welding; ~ **voeg,** butt-joint.
stuip'agtig, (-e), convulsive, paroxysmal.
stui'pe, convulsions; fit(s); *die* ~ *KRY,* be livid with anger; throw a fit; *iem. die* ~ *op die LYF jaag,* frighten someone out of his wits; ~ **bossie,** Chinese lantern (*Nymania capensis*).
stuip'gif, convulsant.
stuip'trek, (ge-), be convulsed, convulse, twitch; ~ **kend,** (-e), in convulsion; ~ **kerig,** (-e), convulsive.
stuip'trekking, (-e, -s), convulsion, twitching; *die laaste* ~ *s,* the last agonies.
stuit, (ge-), stop, check, bar, arrest; dam; shock, offend, disgust, give offence; *dit* ~ *my teen die BORS,* it goes against the grain with me; *iets in sy LOOP* ~, stay (check) something in its course; *op MOEILIKHEDE* ~, meet with difficulties; *teen 'n MUUR* ~, strike against a wall; *die VLOED* ~, stem the tide; ~ **baar,** (..**bare**), stoppable; ~ **been,** coccyx, tail-bone.
stui'tend, (-e), offensive, obnoxious, objectionable, shocking.
stui'ter, (-s), check, bumper, stop.
stui'tig, (-e), foolish; insipid; objectionable, inept, repellent; ~ **heid,** foolishness; insipidity; outrageousness, ineptitude.
stui'ting, (counter)check.
stuit'jie, (-s), rump, tail-bone (of animals); pope's nose (fowl); coccyx (of man).
stuit'laai, lock-stop drawer.
stuit'lik, (-e) = **stuitig**
stuit: ~ **pen,** stop pin; ~ **plaat,** limiting plate; ~ **skroef,** check screw; ~ **streek,** coccygeal region.
stuit'stuk, rump-piece, aitchbone; pope's (parson's) nose (poultry)
stui'we, (ge-), make dust; be dusty; drizzle; fly, rush.
stui'wer, (-s), halfpenny; bawbee; *'n AARDIGE* ~ *met iets verdien,* earn a pretty penny with something; *'n* ~ *in die ARMBEURS gooi,* throw in a remark; put in an oar; *'n OU LAP en 'n* ~, a penny halfpenny.
stuk, (-ke), piece (of bread); fragment, chip (of glass); chunk (of lead); play (stage); part; piece, man (chess); plot (of ground); length (material); article (of clothing); paper, document; counter (chess); *iem. van sy* ~ *BRING,* upset (put off) someone; take someone aback; *by* ~ *ke en BROKKE,* piece-meal; *een* ~ *DEUR,* without a break; at a stretch; *'n man uit EEN* ~, a man of sterling character; *van EEN* ~, without a break; *GEEN* ~ *nie,* not a scrap; *hy het* ~ *ke beter GESPEEL,* he played a great deal better; *ek glo G'N* ~ *wat hy sê nie,* I don't believe a word he says; *op die* ~ *van GODSDIENS,* on a point of religion; *'n INGESONDE* ~, a contribution (of editor); *OP* ~ *van,* on the score of; *sy is 'n OU* ~ *van hom,* she is an old flame of his; *PER* ~, per piece, each; *van jou* ~ *RAAK,* be thrown off one's stride; *een RAND* ~, one rand each; *op* ~ *van SAKE,* after all; when it comes to the push; *'n* ~ *(kie) SEEP,* a piece of soap; *aan* ~ *ke SKEUR,* tear to pieces; *op sy* ~ *ke bly STAAN,* stick to his guns; *'n* ~ *of TWAALF,* about twelve; *twintig* ~ *s VEE,* twenty head of cattle; ~ *VIR* ~, one by one, bit by bit; *'n* ~ *of WAT,* a few or more; *op sy* ~ *ke WEES,* be in form.

stukadoor 518 *styl*

stukadoor', (s) **(-s, ..dore)**, plasterer, stucco-worker; (w) **(ge-)**, plaster, cover with stucco.
stukadoors': ~**gips**, stucco; ~**pleisters**, stucco; ~**werk**, stucco-work.
stuk'goed(ere), piece-goods; general cargo.
stuk'kend, (-e), broken, in pieces; torn; out of order; ~ *BREEK*, smash, break to pieces; ~ *GAAN*, break, come to pieces; ~ *GOOI*, smash, break (by throwing); *iem. IS* ~, someone is intoxicated; *iem.* ~ *KYK*, look daggers at someone; ~ *LEES*, read to tatters; *iem.* ~ *LOOP*, overcome (beat) someone easily; ~ *MAAK*, break, smash; ~ *SKEUR*, disrupt; tear to pieces; *SKOENE* ~ *LOOP*, wear out shoes, ~ *TRAP*, trample to pieces; ~ *VAL*, fall to pieces; ~**(e)rig, (-e)**, rather broken, rather worn or torn.
stuk'kie, (-s), *verkleinwoord van* **stuk**; (small) piece, morsel, bit; pat (butter); (mv) chips; *van* ~ *tot BROKKIE*, in the finest detail; ~*s en BROKKIES*, odds and ends; *'n* ~ *BROOD*, a morsel of bread; *'n* ~ *gaan EET*, go and eat something; *wat 'n* ~ *MENS*! what a specimen of humanity! *'n SNAAKSE* ~ *mens*, a queer specimen; *SY* ~, his lady-love.
stuk: ~**kiesvleis**, meat pieces; dog's meat; ~**konfyt**, conserve, preserve; ~**kool**, round coal; ~**lengte**, bolt (of cloth), cloth length; ~**loon**, piece-wages.
stu'krag, driving power, push, propulsive force, propulsion; impulsion; moving spirit.
stuks, number, piece; *hoeveel* ~ *is daar?* how many (articles) are there? ~**gewys(e)**, bit by bit, one by one, piecemeal, singly, separately; per piece.
stuk: ~**steenkool**, round coal, rounds; ~**suiker**, loaf sugar; ~**swa(w)el**, rock sulphur; ~**vat, (-e)**, butt vat.
stuk'werk, piecework; tut (work); task-work; job work; ~**er**, pieceworker, jobbing-hand.
stuk'wol, pieces (wool).
stulp¹, (s) (-e), hut, hovel; cover, bell-glass; lamp-shade; (w) **(ge-)**, cover with bell-glass; swell out, balloon.
stulp², (w) **(ge-)**, coagulate, congeal, curdle.
stulp'vormig, (-e), bell-shaped.
stu'materiaal, dunnage.
stum'per(d), (ong.) **(-s)**, bungler, pitiful creature, dullard, poor fellow, wretch.
stum'peragtig, (-e), bungling, miserable, wretched.
stut, (s) (-te), support, prop; strut; crutch; cantilever; buttress (roof); truss (bridge); shore, stanchion, sprag, stay; puncheon, post, pillar; (w) **(ge-)**, support, prop, brace, bolster up, shore, buttress up; ~**bak**, cockpit; ~**balk**, joist; collar beam; strut beam; truss; ~**hok**, crib (in mining); ~**muur**, buttress; ~**paal**, dropper, prop, stay, shore; ~**sel, (-s)**, prop, support, stay; ~**skoen**, patten (shoe); ~**stapel**, pack (mining); ~**tap**, pivot journal; ~**ting**, bridging (floors); propping; ~**werk**, lagging; trestle-work; false work, propping; ~**wortel**, buttress root.
stuur, (s) (sture), rudder, helm (ship); handle, handles, handlebars (bicycle); steering wheel, steering gear; *agter die* ~ *sit*, be at the wheel (motor); (w) **(ge-)**, send, dispatch, forward; steer, direct, guide, manage (horse); *om die DOKTER* ~, send for the doctor; *GOEDERE* ~ *na*, send goods to; ~**arm**, joystick; drop-arm; steering lever; ~**as**, steering axle; steering shaft; ~**bak**, cockpit; ~**ballon**, dirigible (balloon); ~**beheer**, steering control; ~**boord**, starboard; *iem. van* ~*boord na bakboord stuur*, send someone from pillar to post; ~**der, (-s)**, sender; steersman; ~**draad**, control wire; ~**hefboom**, control lever; ~**huis**, cockpit, control cabin (aeroplane); wheelhouse (ship); ~**hut**, cockpit; ~**inrigting**, controls, steering gear; ~**kajuit**, (pilot's) cockpit; ~**kas**, steering box; ~**ketting**, tiller-chain; ~**klep**, control valve; ~**knuppel**, joystick; ~**kolom**, control column; steering column; ~**kuip**, cockpit; ~**kuns**, driving skill, steermanship; ~**las**, trim.
stuurliede = **stuurman**
stuur'loos, (..lose), out of control; without steering gear, rudderless.

stuur'man, (-ne, stuurliede, stuurlui), helmsman, chief mate; cox(swain); pilot (sea); *EERSTE* ~, chief mate; *die beste stuurlui staan aan WAL*, bachelors' wives and old maids' children are the best trained; ~**skap**, seamanship, navigation.
stuur: ~**manskuns**, art of navigation; ~**masjien**, steering engine (on ship); ~**outomaat**, automatic pilot; ~**pen**, rectrix (of bird); steering pin; ~**rat**, steering wheel, steering gear, helm; ~**reep**, tiller-rope, wheel rope; ~**riem**, steering oar.
stuurs, (-e), surly, sulky, sullen, crusty, morose, gruff, sour, peevish, cross-grained, crabbled; ~**heid**, surliness, sulkiness, crustiness, sullenness, sourness, peevishness, gruffness, crabbedness; ~**erig, (-e)**, rather peevish; ~**heid**, curtness; *see also* **stuurs**.
stuur: ~**sok**, steering socket; ~**stang**, steering rod; control lever; handle bar; drag link (motor); ~**stoel**, cockpit; stern sheets; ~**stok**, joystick, control lever; tiller, handle; ~**streep**, lubber's line (compass); ~**toestel**, steering gear; controls; ~**tou**, tiller-rope, guy(-rope); ~**weerstand**, control drag (aero.); ~**wiel**, steering wheel; driving wheel; ~**wurm**, steering worm.
stuwadoor', (-s, ..dore), stevedore.
stuwa'sie, stowage; ~**geld**, stowage expenses; ~**hout**, stow wood.
stu'water, backwater.
stu'wend, (-e), propulsive.
stu'wing, (-e, -s) congestion; propulsion.
styf, (w) *see* **stywe**; (b) **(stywe)**, stiff, tight, taut; starched; rigid; proud, prim, formal; firm (market); frozen; fresh (wind); *stywe BOORDJIE*, stiff collar; ~ *van die KOUE*, stiff with cold; *stywe NEK*, stiff neck; crick in the neck; *so* ~ *soos 'n PAAL*, as stiff as a poker; ~ *VAS*, very tight; ~ *WORD*, set (jelly); become stiff (solid); ~**band**, belting; ~**gaas**, foundation muslin; buckram, stiffening; ~**heid**, stiffness, tightness; crick; rigidity; torpor, torpidity.
styfhoof'dig, (-e), obstinate, headstrong, opinionated; ~**heid**, obstinacy, pigheadedness.
styf'kop, headstrong person; ~'**pig, (-e)**, headstrong, obstinate; ~'**pigheid**, obstinacy, contumacy.
styf: ~**kramp**, lockjaw, tetanus; ~**linne**, (dressmaker's) stiffening, buckram, petersham.
styf'loop, (w) **(-ge-)**, stretch.
styf'siekte, stiff sickness (caused by the rattle-bush or lack of phosphates); crotalism; ~**bossie**, rattle-bush (*Crotalaria burkeana*).
styf'te, stiffness, rigidity.
styg, (ge-), ascend, mount, climb up; rise, tend upwards; increase; advance; appreciate, soar (price); *AANDELE* ~ *vinnig*, shares are booming; *te PERD* ~, mount a horse; *die SPANNING* ~, the tension mounts; ~**baan**, runway, landing strip; ~**draai**, climbing turn; ~**end, (-e)**, rising, ascending, mounting; ~**gang**, raise, rise (mining); ~**hoek**, angle of ascent; ~**hoogte**, rise.
sty'ging, (-e, -s), rise; increase; upthrow (mine); jump, boom, advance (in price); grade, gradient.
sty'gingsvermoë, climbing power, buoyancy; lifting power.
styg'koper, bull (stock exchange).
styg: ~**krag**, lifting power, lift; ~**meter**, variometer; ~**plek**, jumping-off place; ~**slag**, upstroke; ~**snelheid**, rate of climb; ~**stand**, climbing position; ~**stroom**, upwash; ~**stuk**, riser (of stairs); ~**vermoë**, climb (aero.); ~**wind**, up-current.
styl¹, (-e), doorpost, support; bedpost; style (bot.).
styl², style, manner; diction (poetry); *in verhewe* ~, in elevated style.
styl'band, astragal.
styl: ~**blommetjie**, purple patch (style); flower (of speech); ~**figuur**, figure of speech; ~**fout**, stylistic error; ~**gebrek**, fault of style; ~**leer**, art of composition; stylistics; ~**loos, (..lose)**, styleless; ~**loosheid**, stylelessness; ~**meubels**, period furniture; ~**oefening**, composition exercise; ~**suiwerheid**, purity of style; ~**vaardigheid**, skill in style; ~**vol**, in elegant style, stylish.
styl: ~**vormig, (-e)**, styliform; ~**vorming**, style-formation.

sty'sel, starch; farina, amylum; ~ **agtig, (-e)**, starchy; ~ **dieet**, farinaceous diet; ~ **ensiem**, amylase; ~ **fabriek**, starch factory; ~ **glans**, mixture of starch and borax; ~ **houdend, (-e)**, starchy, farinaceous; ~ **korrel**, starch grain; ~ **kos**, starchy food; ~ **kwas**, paste brush; ~ **pap**, paste; ~ **sel**, starch cell; ~ **water**, starch water.
sty'we, (ge-), starch, clear starch, stiffen; strengthen, increase; *om die KAS te* ~, to increase the funds; *iem. in sy KWAAD* ~, encourage someone in his wrongdoing.
sty'werig, (-e), rather stiff, rather rigid, stiffish; ~ **heid**, stiffishness.
sty'wesiekte, stiffsickness.
sty'wigheid, stiffness; buckram.
sty'wing, stiffening; strengthening (of funds); *tot* ~ *van*, in support of.
sub, sub, under; ~ *JUDICE*, sub judice; ~ *ROSA*, sub rosa, secretly.
sub'agent, subagent; ~ **skap**, subagency.
sub'artikel, subleader (in a paper), leaderette.
sub'baan, subcircuit.
sub'ekonomies, (-e), subeconomic; ~ *e behuising*, subeconomic housing.
subiet', suddenly, immediately.
subjek', (-te), subject; ~ **tief', (..tiewe)**, subjective; ~ **tivis'me**, subjectivism; ~ **tiwis'ties, (-e)**, subjectivistic(ally); ~ **tiwiteit'**, subjectivity.
subjunktief', (..tiewe), subjunctive.
sub'komitee, subcommittee.
sub'kommissie, subcommission.
sub'kontinent, subcontinent.
sub'kring, subcircuit.
subliem', (-e), sublime.
sublimaat', (..mate), sublimate.
sublima'sie, sublimation.
sublimeer', (ge-), sublimate.
sublime'ring, sublimation.
sublimiteit', sublimity.
subluna'ries, (-e), (ong.), sublunary; *die* ~ *e dal*, the earth.
sub'masjiengeweer, sub-machine-gun.
submis'sie, submission.
sub'normaal, (..male), subnormal.
subordina'sie, subordination.
subordineer', (ge-), subordinate.
suborna'sie, subornation.
suborneer', (ge-), suborn.
subpoe'na, subpoena.
sub'redaksie, subediting; subeditors.
sub'redakteur, subeditor.
subrep'sie, subreption; *by* ~, by deceit; by stealth; ~ **f', (..siewe)**, deceitful.
subroga'sie, subrogation.
subsi'die, (-s), subsidy, grant-in-aid.
subsidieer', (ge-), subsidize.
subsidiêr', (-e), subsidiary.
subsidië'ring, subsidizing.
subskrip'sie, (-s), subscription.
sub'standerd, substandard.
substan'sie, (-s), substance, matter.
substansieel', (..siële), substantial.
substantief', (..tiewe), substantive, noun.
substantiveer', (ge-), use as substantive, substantivize.
substanti'wies, (-e), as substantive, substantival.
sub'stasie, substation.
substitueer', (ge-), substitute.
substitu'sie, substitution.
substituut', (..tute), deputy, substitute.
sub'straat, (..strate), subtratum.
subsumeer', (ge-), subsume.
subsump'sie, subsumption.
subtiel', (-e), subtle.
subtiliteit', subtlety.
subtro'pies, (-e), subtropical.
sukku'ba, (-e), succuba.
suè'de, suede; ~ **baadjie**, suede jacket; ~ **jas**, suede coat; ~ **skoen**, suede shoe.
Su'ezkanaal, Suez canal.
suf, (w) (ge-), dote; be inattentive; *wat sit jy daar en* ~? are your wits woolgathering? **(b) (suwwe)**, dull,
dim, stupid, dazed, dotty, dense, muzzy, doting (from old age); musty (smell).
suf'fer(d), (-s), dotard; dullard, duffer.
suf'ferig, (-e), dull, sleepy, lethargic; doting; ~ **heid**, dullness, sleepiness; dotage.
suf'fery, daze, dose, drowse; dotage.
suf'fiks, (-e), suffix.
suffisant', (-e), sufficient.
suffragaan', suffragan.
suffrajet', (-s, -te), suffragette.
suf'heid, dullness, stupidity, anility, mustiness.
sug¹, (s) (-te), sigh; groan(ing); passion, lust, craving, desire, mania; *die* ~ *tot NAVOLGING*, the desire to imitate; *'n* ~ *SLAAK*, heave a sigh; **(w) (ge-)**, sigh, fetch a sigh; groan, moan; ~ *onder die juk van*, groan under the yoke of.
sug², (s) pus, matter (from wounds); dropsy.
suggereer', (ge-), suggest; ~ **baar, (..bare)**, suggestible.
sugges'tie, (-s), suggestion.
suggestief', (..tiewe), suggestive, equivocal.
suggestiwiteit', suggestiveness.
sug: ~ **geut**, gutter; ~ **gie, (-s)**, small sigh; ~ **riolering**, underground drainage; ~ **sloot**, drainage ditch, drain; ~ **ting, (-e)**, sighing, wail; ~ **voor**, agricultural drain.
suid, south.
Suid-Afrika, South Africa.
Suid-Afrikaans', (-e), South African.
Suid-Afrika'ner, (-s), South African.
Suid-Ame'rika, South America.
Suid-Amerikaans', (-e), South American.
Suid-Amerika'ner, South American.
Suid'-Asië, Southern Asia.
Suid'-Asies, (-e), South Asiatic.
Suid-Australië, South Australia.
Suid'-Brabant, South Brabant.
Suid'-Duitsland, South Germany.
sui'de, south; *op die* ~ *GELEE*, having a southern aspect; *NA die* ~, to(wards) the south.
sui'de: ~ **kant**, south side; ~ **lik, (-e)**, southern, southerly; meridional; austral; *S* ~ *like Halfrond*, Southern Hemisphere.
suid'end, south(ern) end.
Sui'der-Afrika, Southern Africa.
sui'der: ~ **breedte**, south latitude; ~ **halfrond**, southern hemisphere; ~ **keerkring**, southern tropic, Tropic of Capricorn.
Sui'derkruis, Southern Cross.
sui'derlig, aurora australis, southern lights.
Sui'derling, Meridional.
Sui'dersee, Zuider Sea.
sui'der: ~ **son**, south sun, ~ **storm**, storm from the south; ~ **strand**, southern coast.
Suid'-Europa, Southern Europe.
Suid-Europees', (..pese), South European.
sui'dewind, south wind.
suid: ~ **grens**, southern boundary; ~ **hoek**, southern corner.
Suid'-Holland, South Holland; ~ **s (-e)**, South Dutch.
sui'dissel, milky thistle, sow-thistle.
suid'kus, south coast.
suidoos', (s) south-east; south-east wind, southeaster; **(b)** south-east; ~ **te**, south-east; ~ **telik, (-e)**, south-easterly; ~ **ter**, ~ **tewind**, south-east wind, south-easter; *swart* ~ *ter*, black southeaster.
Suid'pool, South Pole; ~ **ekspedisie**, South Pole (Antarctic) expedition; ~ **lande**, Antarctic regions; ~ **reisiger**, Antarctic explorer; ~ **see**, Antarctic Ocean; ~ **sirkel**, Antarctic Circle; ~ **tog**, Antarctic expedition; ~ **vaarder**, Antarctic navigator.
suid'punt, southern point.
Suid'see, South Sea; *Stille* ~, Pacific Ocean; ~ **-eilande**, South Sea Islands; ~ **-eilander**, South Sea Islander; ~ **vaarder, (-s)**, South Sea navigator.
Suid'-Sotho, South Sotho.
suid: ~ **suidoos**, south-south-east; ~ **suidwes**, south-south-west; ~ **vrugte**, semi-tropical fruit; ~ **waarts (-e)**, southwards; ~ **wes', (s, b)** south-west.
Suidwes'-Afrika, South West Africa, Namibia.
suidwes'te, the south west.

Suidwes'telik, (-e), south-westerly.
suidwes'ter, south-western (wind); **(-s)**, south-wester (waterproof hat with broad brim).
Suidwes'ter, (-s), South Wester, person from South West Africa, Namibian.
suidwes'tewind, southwester (wind).
sui'e, (ge-) = suig.
sui'er, (s) (-s), piston; plunger (pump); sucker, off-shoot, sprout (of plant); (w) **(ge-)**, remove suckers; ~**deksel**, piston-cover; ~**klap**, piston-slap; ~**klep**, piston-valve (of engine); suction valve (of pump); ~**klop**, piston-knock; ~**kop**, piston-head; ~**moer**, piston-nut; ~**oppervlakte**, piston-area; ~**pen**, piston-pin, gudgeon-pin; ~**pomp**, reciprocating pump; suction pump; ~**ring**, piston-ring; ~**slag**, piston-stroke; ~**spanveer**, piston-spring; ~**stang**, piston-rod, connecting rod; ~**stangkop**, big end; ~**stoot**, piston-lift; ~**tjie, (-s)**, cupule (zool.); ~**veer**, piston-spring; ~**waggel**, piston-slap; ~**wand**, piston-wall; ~**wikkeling**, piston-slap.
suig, (ge-), absorb; suck, suckle; ~ *aan*, suck at.
suig: ~**bagger**, suction dredger; ~**bal**, sucker (golf); ~**besem**, suction sweeper; ~**bottel**, feeding-bottle; suction glass; ~**buis**, tail-pipe; suction pipe; aspirator; ~**dop**, suction-cup.
sui'geling = suigling.
suig: ~**fles**, feeding-bottle, suction-flask; ~**gas**, suction-gas; ~**gat**, vent; ~**glas**, sucking-glass; suction-cup; ~**ing**, suction; ~**kind**, suckling; ~**klank**, click; ~**klep**, suction-valve; foot-valve; ~**krag**, suction-power; ~**lap**, swab; ~**leer**, sucking-disc; sucker; ~**leiding**, suction-piping; ~**ling, (-e)**, baby, infant, suckling; ~**lingkliniek**, baby clinic; ~**lingsterfte**, infant mortality; ~**lingsterftesyfer**, infant-mortality rate; ~**mond**, suctorial mouth; proboscis; ~**nappie**, sucker (zool.); cupule, sucking disc; ~**olie**, suction-oil; ~**orgaan**, sucking-disc; suctorial organ; ~**papier**, blotting-paper; ~**perspomp**, double-action pump; ~**pil**, lozenge; ~**plant**, parasitic plant; ~**ploeg**, suction-plough; ~**pomp**, suction-pump; ~**pootjie**, tube-foot; ~**pyp**, sucking-pipe; sucker; ~**slag**, intake-stroke; ~**slang**, suction-hose; ~**snawel**, proboscis, trunk (of insect); ~**snuit**, suctorial mouth; ~**spriet**, suctorial antenna; ~**stokkie**, sucker; ~**strooitjie**, drinking-straw; ~**tenk**, vacuum tank; ~**tong**, proboscis; ~**ventilator**; exhaust-fan; ~**vis**, sucking-fish, remora; ~**waaier**, suction-fan, extraction fan; ~**werking**, aspirating action; ~**wortel**, sucking-root; ~**wurm**, fluke(-worm), trematode.
sui'ker, (s) sugar; *vir jou* ~ *uitkruip*, earn one's own living; (w) **(ge-)**, sugar, sweeten; ~**agtig, (-e)**, sugary; ~**aksyns**, duty on sugar; sugar excise; ~**appel**, custard-apple; ~**bakker**, confectioner; ~**bakkery**, confectionery; ~**beet**, sugar beet; ~**bekkie, (-s)**, sugarbird, sunbird; ~**belasting**, duty on sugar; ~**bier**, sherbet; ~**boontjie**, sugar-bean; ~**bos**, protea, sugarbush; ~**bosblom**, protea; ~**bosvoël**, Cape sugarbird; ~**brood**, sugar-loaf; spongecake; ~**dennehout**, sugar-pine; ~**dons**, candy floss; ~**ertjie**, sugar pea; ~**fabriek**, sugar-mill; ~**fabrikant**, sugar-refiner; ~**gebak**, confectionery; ~**gehalte**, sugar content; ~**glasuur**, (sugar) icing; ~**goed**, sweetmeats, comfit, confectionery; ~**handel**, sugar trade; ~**houdend, (-e)**, sacchariferous; ~**huis**, brothel, house of ill fame; ~**ig, (-e)**, sugary, sweet; ~**industrie**, sugar industry; ~**kan**, red afrikander; protea; ~**kis**, sugar-cask, sugar-bin; ~**klontjie**, lump of sugar; sugar candy; darling; ~**koekie**, sugar lozenge; sugar cake; ~**kokery**, sugar-boiling; ~**kultuur**, ~**kwekery**, sugar-growing; ~**laagpil**, sugar-coated pill; ~**land**, field of sugar cane; ~**lepeltjie**, sugar spoon; ~**meter**, saccharimeter; ~**meul(e)**, sugar-mill; ~**mielies**, dent mealies; sweetcorn; ~**nywerheid**, sugar industry; ~**oes**, sugar crop; ~**oom**, sugar daddy; gold (rich) uncle; ~**peul**, sugar peas in pod; ~**pitte**, dent mealies; ~**plantasie**, sugar plantation; ~**planter**, sugar-planter; ~**pop**, lollipop, sugar doll; ~**pot**, sugar basin; ~**produksie**, sugar production; ~**raffinadery**, sugar refinery; ~**raffinadeur**, sugar-refiner; ~**riet**, sugar cane; ~*riet PLANT*, hole; *UIT=GEPERSTE* ~*riet*, megass(e); ~**sak**, sugar pocket; ~**siekte**, diabetes; ~**siektelyer**, diabetic; ~**skeppie**, sugar spoon; ~**skil**, candied peel; ~**skoppie**, sugar scoop; ~**smaak**, sugary taste; ~**soet**, sweet as sugar; honeyed (words); ~**span-spek**, sugar melon; ~**stok**, sugarstick; ~**strooibus**, sugar dredger; ~**strooier, (-s)**, sugar castor; ~**stroop**, molasses; sugar syrup; ~**suur**, saccharic acid; ~**tand**, sweet tooth; *die* ~ *tande uittrek*, have to deny one's sweet tooth; have to go without sweets; ~**tangetjie**, sugar tongs; ~**tante**, gold (rich) aunt; ~**verbinding**, saccharine combination; ~**voël**, sugarbird (*Promerops caffer*); ~**vrugte**, crystallized fruit; ~**water**, sugar water; ~**wortel**, skirret; ~**wurm**, sugar mite; entozoon.
suil, (-e), column, pillar, obelisk; pile; bole; *DO-RIESE* ~, Doric column; *IONIESE* ~, Ionian column; *KORINTIESE* ~, Corinthian column; *die S~e van HERCULES*, the Pillars of Hercules; ~ *van VOLTA*, Voltaic pile, galvanic pile.
suil'draer, stylobate.
sui'le: ~**boog**, archway; ~**bundel**, clustered column; ~**galery**, colonnade, row of columns; ~**gang**, portico, peristyle, prostyle, cloister, colonnade; ~**ry**, colonnade, peristyle; ~**saal**, hall of columns.
suil: ~**groef**, flute, channel, chamfer; ~**hoof**, capital (of a column); ~**struktuur**, columnar structure; ~**tjie**, columella; ~**voet**, column-base; ~**vormig, (-e)**, columnar.
sui'nig, (-e), stingy, cheeseparing, mean, tight-fisted, parsimonious, close-fisted, niggardly; sparing, chary, thrifty, frugal, economical; ~ *met iets werk*, use something sparingly; economize; ~**aard**, niggard, skinflint.
sui'nigheid, stinginess, cheeseparing; chariness; costiveness (fig.); thrift, frugality, economy; parsimony.
sui'nigheids: ~**brander**, economical burner; ~**halwe**, for the sake of economy; ~**maatreël**, measure to ensure economy, economy-measure; ~**redes**: *om* ~*redes*, for the sake of economy.
sui'nigies, sparingly, economically.
suip, (s), booze, drinking; *aan die* ~, on the booze; (w) **(ge-)**, drink (animals); soak, tope, carouse, alcoholize, fuddle, guzzle, tipple, booze; ~**er, (-s)**, toper, boozer, tippler, drinker; ~**emmer**, watering-bucket.
sui'pery, drinking, toping, boozing, potation.
sui'ping, (-e, -s), drinking-place, watering-place (of animals).
suip: ~**kalf**, calf at foot; ~**lam**, sucking lamb; ~**lap, (-pe)**, toper, tippler, boozer, carouser, Bacchanalian, soaker, swiller, confirmed drunkard; ~**ooi**, foster-ewe; ~**party**, toping-party, spree, orgy, drinking-bout, drunken revelry, carousal; ~**plek**, drinking-place (persons, animals); watering-place (of animals); ~**trog**, watering-trough.
suis, (ge-), rustle, sigh; sough (of wind); whiz (bullet); buzz, sing (in ears).
sui'sel, (ge-), rustle, buzz, sough; be giddy; ~**ig, (-e)**, giddy, dizzy; ~**ing, (-e, -s)**, buzzing, singing, tingling; giddiness.
sui'serig, (-e), buzzing.
sui'sing, (-e, -s), buzzing, rustling, singing, tingling; ~ *in die ore*, tinnitus.
sui'te, (-s), suite.
sui'wel, milk, dairy product, butter and cheese; ~**bedryf**, dairy industry; ~**bereiding**, dairying; ~**boer**, dairy farmer; ~**boerdery**, dairy-farming; ~**bond**, dairy-farmers' union; ~**fabriek**, butter-and-cheese factory, creamery, dairy factory; ~**industrie**, ~**nywerheid**, dairy(ing) industry; ~**produkte**, dairy products.
sui'wer[1], (s) (-s), shoot, sprout (tobacco); (w) **(ge-)**, remove suckers.
sui'wer[2], (w) (ge-), purify (air); refine; cleanse, clarify (oil); rectify (spirits); clear (one's name); fumigate, disinfect (room); try (metal); purge, expurgate, bowdlerise (book); filter (oil); exonerate (from blame); gin (cotton); (b, bw) pure (gold); clean (hands); unadulterated, sheer (nonsense); genuine, pure (delight); clear (conscience); correct

suiwerings 521 *suur*

(language); ~ *en ALLEEN om*, purely and simply to; *'n ~ GEWETE*, a clear conscience; *nie ~ in die LEER nie*, not orthodox; *dis NIE alles ~ nie*, there is something fishy going on; ~ *ONSIN*, sheer nonsense; *'n ~ UITSPRAAK*, a correct pronunciation; *die ~ WAARHEID*, the plain (whole) truth; ~ *WATER*, pure water; ~ **aar**, (-s), refiner, expurgator; purifier; filter; ~ **end**, (-e), purifying; purging; cathartic, purgative (med.); ~ *ende middel*, detergent; cathartic; ~ **heid**, purity, cleanness; ~ **ing**, (-e, -s), purification, purging; refinement; clarification (of liquids); exoneration (from blame); fumigation (of room); ablution (of sin).
sui'werings: ~ **eed**, oath of purgation; ~ **fabriek**, refinery; ~ **middel**, purifier; aperient, purgative, cathartic (med.); detergent (of wound); clarifier (of liquid); ~ **proses**, purifying process; ~ **tenk**, settling-tank; ~ **toestel**, purification plant.
sui'wer-uit, indeed, truly; *hy is ~ slim*, he is really clever.
sui'werwit, pure white.
sujet', (-te), scamp, rapscallion, rogue.
suka'de, candy, candied peel, succades, lemon peel.
suk'kel, (ge-), progress poorly, toil, cope with many difficulties and have little success; plod (trudge) along, drudge; *hy ~ met sy gesondheid*, he is in indifferent health; ~ **aar**, (-s), struggler, plodder, stick-in-the-mud, bungler, dolt, ninny; crock.
sukkelary', plodding, toiling and moiling.
suk'kel: ~ **bestaan**, precarious existence; ~ **draf**, (ge-), proceed laboriously, trudge; ~ **draffie**, (-s), dog-trot, jogtrot, slow trot; *dit gaan op 'n ~ draffie*, things are jogging along; ~ **gang**, jogtrot; crawl; ~ **poging**, laborious attempt; ~ **rig**, (-e), ailing; slow; bungling, plodding; ~ **ry** = **sukkelary**; ~ **spel**, puzzle; ~ **trein**, slow train; ~ **veld**, rough (golf); ~ **vers**, prentice poetry, tiro verse; ~ **wedloop**, obstacle race; ~ **werk**, laborious work unsuccessfully done.
sukkulent', succulent.
sukro'se, sucrose, cane-sugar.
sukses', (-se), success; ~ *BEHAAL*, achieve success; be successful, succeed; ~ *HÊ*, catch on, be a decided hit; be successful; *MET ~*, successfully, with success; *ek WENS jou ~!* good luck to you; I wish you every success; ~ **boek**, best seller; ~ **roman**, bestseller (novel).
sukses'sie, (-s), succession; ~ **belasting**, inheritance tax, death-duties.
suksessief', (..siewe), successive; ..**siewelik**, successively.
sukses'sie: ~ **oorlog**, war of succession; ~ **regte**, death duties, estate duty, probate duties.
suksessie'welik, successively.
sukses'siewet, law of settlement; succession act.
sukses'stuk, draw, hit, box-office success.
sukses'vol, (-le), successful.
sul, (-le), softy, goody-goody.
sulfaat', (sulfate), sulphate.
sul'fa: ~ **middel**, sulpha drug; ~ **preparaat**, sulpha preparation.
sulfeer', (ge-), sulphate.
sul'fer, (s) sulphur; (w) sulphate; ~ **ing**, sulphating.
sulfereus', (-e), sulphurous.
sulfi'de, **sulfied'**, sulphide.
sulfiet' (-e), sulphite.
sul'ke, such; *MORE ~ tyd*, this time tomorrow; *is dit ~ TYD*, is that how matters stand? *is dit al WEER ~ tyd?* has it happened again? ~ **s**, such people.
sulks, such, this, that.
sult¹, brawn; calves-foot jelly; cow-heel.
sult², (-e), simpleton, softy; *'n ~ van 'n mens*, a softy.
sul'tan, (-s), sultan.
sulta'na, (-s), sultana.
sultanaat', (..nate), sultanate.
sulta'nadruiwe, sultanas, sultana grapes.
sulta'narosyne, sultana raisins.
sulta'ne, (-s), sultana, sultan's wife.
sulta'nies, (-e), sultan-like.
sult: ~ **bone**, pickled beans; ~ **brood**, brawn loaf.
Suma'tra, Sumatra.
Sumatraan', ..**trane**, Sumatran; ~ **s'**, (-e), Sumatran.

summier', (-e), summary; summarily.
sum'mum, height, acme.
sumptueus', (-e), sumptuous.
sun'der(tjie), (-s), fuse; igniter, primer.
sund'gat, vent, touch-hole.
sunn'hennep, sunn hemp.
su'per: ~ **belasting**, supertax; ~ **dividend**, (-e), superdividend; ~ **fosfaat'**, superphosphate; ~ **fyn**, superfine.
superieur', (-e), superior.
superintendent', (-e), superintendent; ~ -**generaal**, (~ e-generaal), superintendent-general.
superioriteit', superiority.
superlatief', (..tiewe), superlative.
su'permark, (-te), supermarket.
supernaturalis'me, supernaturalism.
supernumerêr', (-s), supernumerary.
su'perposisie, superposition.
superso'nies, (-e), supersonic.
su'perverhitting, superheating.
su'perverkoeling, supercooling.
supplement', (-e), supplement; ~ **êr'**, (-e), supplementary.
supplements'hoek, supplementary angle.
supplikant', (-e), supplicant.
suppliseer', (ge-), supplicate.
supposi'sie, (-s), supposition.
supremasie', supremacy.
su'rerig = **suurderig**
su'righeid, sourness, something sour.
su'ring, *corrol, ootbare*, dock, ~ **sout**, salt of sorrel; ~ **suiker**, saccharine; ~ **suur**, oxalic acid.
sur'plus, (-se), surplus, excess; cover.
surrealis', (-te), surrealist; ~ **me**, surrealism; ~ **ties**, (-e), surrealist.
surrogaat', (..gate), substitute; makeshift, surrogate.
sus¹, (s) (-se), sis(ter).
sus², (w) (ge-), hush, quiet (child); pacify, calm (person); soothe (one's conscience); *sy GEWETE ~*, silence his conscience; *'n SKANDAAL ~*, hush up a scandal.
sus³, (bw) thus; ~ *of SO*, either one way or another, this way or that; *meneer Sus en meneer SO*, Mr. This and Mr. That.
suserein', (-e), suzerain; ~ **iteit'**, suzerainty.
suspendeer', (ge-), suspend.
suspen'sie, suspension.
suspensoï'de, **suspensoïed'**, suspensoid.
suspi'sie, (-s), suspicion.
suspisieus', (o), suspicious.
sus'sie, (s), little sister; shad (fish).
sustenta'sie, sustentation; ~ **fonds**, sustentation fund.
sus'ter: (-s), sister; nurse, (nursing) sister; *roep ~ A.*, call nurse A.; ~ **blad**, contemporary (newspaper); ~ **gemeente**, sister church (congregation); ~ **huis**, nunnery; affiliated house; ~ **kerk**, sister church; ~ **liefde**, sisterly love, ~ **lik**, (-e), sisterly; ~ **loos**, (..lose), sisterless; ~ **moord**, sororicide; ~ **moordenaar**, sororicide.
Sustero'werste, Mother Superior.
sus'ter: ~ **paar**, couple of sisters; ~ **skap**, sisterhood.
sus'terskind, nephew, niece, sister's child.
sus'tertjie, (-s), little sister; nursey.
sus'tervereniging, society of parish ladies; women's guild; affiliated society.
sus'terwinkel, chain store.
sutuur', (suture), suture.
suur, (s) heartburn, acidity (of stomach); (sure), acid (chem.), *nu ~ kom soet*, sunshine follows rain; after a storm comes a calm; (b, bw) **(sure)**, sour, acid, acrid; hard (beer); peevish, cantankerous, unpleasant; *dit sal jou ~ BEKOM*, you will rue it; ~ *KYK*, be surly (churlish); *vir iem. die LEWE ~ maak*, make life unpleasant for someone; *'n sure ONDERVINDING*, an unpleasant experience; ~ *VERDIEN*, earned the hard way; ~ *VRUGTE*, sour fruit; ~ *WEES*, be peevish; ~ *WORD*, grow (turn) sour; ~ **agtig**, (-e), sourish, acidulous; ~ **bad**, pickle; acid bath; *in 'n ~ bad steek*, put into pickle; ~ **bessie**, barberry; Cape cranberry; ~ **bestand**, (-e),

suurlemoen 522 **swaer**

acid-proof; ~**bier**, alegar; ~**braak**, pyrosis; ~**deeg**, yeast, ferment, leaven; 'n koekie ~**deeg**, cake of yeast; ~**deegkoek**, yeast cake; ~**deegplantjie**, yeast starter; ~**derig**, (-e), sourish, acescent, acidulous; ~**desem** = **suurdeeg**; ~**doring**, barberry; Karoo thorntree *(Acacia karroo)*; ~**gehalte**, acid content, acidity; ~**gesig**, sourface; ~**gras**, sour grass *(Enneapogon scaber)*; ~**heid**, sourness, acidity; acerbity; ~**kanol**, several species of *Watsonia* and *Antholyza*; ~**karee**, tree *(Rhus tridactyla)*; ~**klontjie**, (-s), acid drop; ~**knol**, crab, surly fellow; *see* **suurkanol**; ~**kool**, sauerkraut.

suur'lemoen, lemon; *'n gesig soos 'n ~ hê*, be surly, have a wry face; ~**botter**, lemon curd; ~**drank**, lemon squash; ~**essens**, lemon essence; ~**geur**, lemon flavouring; ~**geursel**, lemon essence; ~**koekie**, lemon jumble; ~**konfyt**, lemon marmalade; ~**kwas**, lemon squash; ~**sap**, lemon juice; *daar loop ~sap deur*, there is something dishonest (fishy) about it; ~**skil**, lemon peel; ~**smeer**, lemon curd; ~**sop**, lemon juice; ~**stroop**, lemon syrup; ~**vulsel**, lemon filling.

suur: ~**ling**, (-e), sourface; ~**melk**, sour milk; ~**melkkaas**, cottage cheese, skim-milk cheese; ~**meter**, acidimeter; ~**muil**, sourface, crabbed person; ~**pap**, (unfermented) mealiemeal drink; sour porridge; ~**pol**, lemon grass *(Elionurus argenteus)*; ~**pomp**, acid pump; ~**pootjie**, small tortoise *(Testudo geometrica)*; ~**pruim**, wild plum *(Ximenia caffra)*; surly person, curmudgeon, spoilsport, killjoy; ~**smeer**, lemon curd; ~**soet**, soursweet; ~**sous**, vinegar-and-egg sauce.

suur'stof, oxygen; ~**atoom**, oxygen atom; ~**draer**, oxygen-carrier; ~**gas**, oxygen; ~**houdend**, (-e), oxygenous; ~**masker**, oxygen mask; ~**opname**, oxidation; ~**silinder**, oxygen cylinder; ~**snypyp**, oxygen lance (welding); ~**tent**, oxygen tent; ~**toestel**, oxygen apparatus; ~**verbinding**, oxide; ~**water**, hydrogen peroxide.

suur: ~**suiker**, sherbet; ~**suurdeeg**, sour-dough yeast; ~**tjie**, (-s), acid drop; (mv) pickles, pickled vegetables; ~**uie**, pickled onions; ~**vas**, (-te), acid-proof; ~**veld**, sour veld (pasture of poor quality); ~**verdien**, (-de), hard-earned; ~**vormend**, (-e), acidific; ~**vorming**, acidification; ~**vry**, (-e), free of acid; ~**vurk**, (-e), pickle-fork; ~**vy**, sour fig *(Mesembryanthemum spp.)*; ~**werend**, (-e), acid-resisting.

suut'jies, gently, softly, unnoticed, noiseless.

Swaab, (Swabe), Swabian.

swaai, (s) (-e), swing, caracol(e) (of horse); cant (of ship); sweep (of the arm); wave, flutter (flag); *met draaie en ~e loop*, dawdle by the way, follow a circuitous way; (w) **(ge-)**, swing, sway, reel; flourish, brandish, wield; flirt; caracol(e); wheel (rugby); ~**arm**, swing beam; ~**armkraan**, jib crane; ~**bal**, swerver, swinger; ~**brug**, suspension bridge; ~**deur**, swing door; ~**-ent**, off-set end; ~**haak**, bevel gauge; sliding square; ~**hoek**, angle of traverse; ~**holte**, gap-bed; ~**hou**, swing (cricket); ~**ing**, swinging, brandishing, waving; ~**koevoet**, slewing bar; ~**lemsnyer**, rotary cutter; ~**musiek**, swing music; ~**raam**, casement (window); ~**slag**, swinging blow, swing; ~**wiel**, joy-wheel.

swaan, (swane), swan; *jong ~*, cygnet; ~**boerdery**, swannery; ~**nek**, swan's neck; swan-neck (fig.).

Swaan'ridder, Knight of the Swan.

swaap, (swape), blockhead, chuckle-head, boob(y), guy, nitwit, dunce, idiot; ~**streek**, foolish act (prank).

swaar, (sware), heavy, ponderous, weighty (goods); hard, difficult, severe, arduous, toilsome (task); strong (drink); deep, laboured (breathing); rich (diet); grave (illness); ~ *BELAS*, heavily burdened (taxed); ~ *BEPROEWING*, sore trial; ~ *DRA*, carry a heavy burden; ~ *GESKUT*, heavy artillery; ~ *JARE*, difficult years; ~ *in die KOP wees*, be thick-headed; ~ *KRY*, suffer hardship; ~ *MISDAAD*, grave offence; ~ *in die ROU*, in deep mourning; ~ *VERKOUE wees*, have a bad cold; *wat die ~ste is, moet die ~ste WEEG*, first things first; *te ~ WEES*, be overweight; ~ *WERK*, drudgery, toil; ~*der WORD*, gain (put on) weight; ~ *WYN*, full-bodied (heavy-bodied) wine; ~**belaai**, (-de), heavy-laden.

swaard, (-e), sword, brand, rapier; leeboard (of boat); *die ~ AANGORD*, buckle one's sword; *die ~ van DAMOKLES*, the sword of Damocles; *die ~ van GEREGTIGHEID*, the sword of justice; *na die ~ GRYP*, take up arms; draw the sword; *die ~ in die SKEDE steek*, sheathe the sword; *die ~ uit die SKEDE trek*, draw the sword; *met ~e en STOKKE*, armed to the teeth; *dis 'n TWEESNYDENDE ~*, a two-edged sword; *met die ~ in die VUIS*, sword in hand; ~**blom**, sword-lily, gladiolus; ~**dans**, sword-dance; ~**draer**, sword-bearer; ~**gekletter**, rattling of swords; ~**geveg**, sword-fight; ~**knop**, pommel; ~**lelie**, gladiolus; ~**lem**, sword-blade; ~**reg**, right (rule) of the sword; ~**skede**, (sword) sheath; ~**slag**, stroke of the sword; ~**sy**, male branch (of family); ~**veër**, (-s), sword-cutler; ~**vegter**, gladiator, sword-player; ~**vis**, sword-fish; rapier-fish; ~**vormig**, (-e), sword-shaped, ziphoid, ensiform.

swaar: ~**gebou(d)**, (-de), stalwart, heavily built; ~**geskut**, heavy ordnance; ~**gewig**, heavyweight; ~**gewonde**, (-s), transport (stretcher-) case; ~**heid**, heaviness, weight, grossness; massiveness.

swaarhoof'dig, (-e), despondent, pessimistic, morose, gloomy; ~**heid**, despondency, gloom, pessimism.

swaarklink'end, (-e), full-mouthed, sonorous.

swaar'kry, hardship, adversity.

swaarly'wig, (-e), corpulent, stout, obese, puffy, burly, portly; ~**heid**, corpulence, obesity, portliness, puffiness.

swaarmoe'dig, (-e), melancholic, heavy-hearted, dejected, moody, pensive, depressed; ~**e**, (-s), melancholiac; hypochondriac; ~**heid**, melancholy, dejection, depression, moodiness, melancholia, pessimism, gloom, heavy-heartedness; hypochondria.

swaar'spaat, heavy spar, barite, barytes.

swaar'te, weight, heaviness; worry; gravity, ~**krag**, gravitation, (force of) gravity; ~**kragveld**, gravitational field; ~**kragwerking**, gravitation; ~**lyn**, median; ~**meter**, baroscope; gravimeter; ~**punt**, centre of gravity; gravamen; main point (of argument); ~**veld**, gravity field.

swaartil'lend, (-e), pessimistic, morose; ~**heid**, pessimism, moroseness.

swaar'water, heavy water; ~**stof**, heavy hydrogen, deuterium.

swaar'weer, thunderstorm; thunder(y) weather.

swaarwig'tig, (-e), ponderous; important; ~**heid**, weightiness, ponderousness.

swab'ber, (s) (-s), mop, swab; (w) **(ge-)**, mop, swab; start boozing.

Swa'be, Swabia.

Swa'bies, (s) (-e), Swabian.

swa'el¹, (s) (-s), swallow.

swa'el², (s) sulphur (*see* **swawel**); (w) **(ge-)**, sulphur(ize); drink, booze, tope; *hy ~ BAIE*, he plies the bottle; *geswael WEES*, be tipsy; ~**aar**, sulphur-spring (-vein); ~**agtig**, (-e), sulphurous; ~**bad**, sulphur bath; ~**blom**, flowers of sulphur; ~**erts**, sulphur ore; ~**houdend**, (-e), sulphurous; ~**houtjie**, (sulphur-) match; ~**kies**, iron pyrites; ~**kruid**, great celandine.

swa'elnes, swallow's nest.

swa'elstert, (s) swallow's tail; dovetail (joint); V-shaped earmark (on sheep); swallow-tail(ed) coat; dress suit; (w) **(ge-)**, dovetail; ~**baadjie**, cut-away evening coat, tails; ~**beitel**, corner-chisel; ~**inlating**, dovetail-housing; ~**pak**, tails; ~**saag**, dovetail-saw; ~**skaaf**, dovetail-plane; ~**tap**, dovetail-tenon; ~**voeg**, dovetail-joint; ~**vyl**, dovetail-file.

swa'elsuur, sulphuric acid.

swa'eltjie, swallow; *een ~ maak nie 'n SOMER nie, een ~ maak nog geen SOMER nie, een ~ kan nie SOMER maak nie*, one swallow does not make a summer.

swaer, (-s), brother-in-law; ~**s'huwelik**, levirate;

~skap, affinity by marriage; relationship of brother-in-law.
swag'tel, (s) (-s), bandage, ligature; swathing-cloth; ligament; sling; (w) (ge-), bandage.
Swahi'li, Swahili (language); (-'s), Swahili.
swak, (s) weakness, weak side, soft spot, failing, foible; *iem. in sy ~ AANTAS*, touch someone on the raw; *'n ~ vir iets HÊ*, have a weakness for something; *iem. in sy ~ TAS*, attack someone on his weak side; (b, bw) weak (child); feeble (attempt); delicate, frail (health); slender (means); faint (noise); poor, bad (show); *'n ~ GEHEUE*, a poor memory; *die ~ GESLAG*, the weaker sex; *iem. se ~ KANT ken*, know a person's soft spot; *hy is ~ van KARAKTER*, he has a weak character; *'n ~ LIGGAAM*, a frail body; *~ MENGSEL*, lean mixture; *in 'n ~ OOMBLIK*, in a weak moment; *~ PLEK*, flaw; *'n ~ POGING*, a feeble attempt; *'n ~ POLS*, a weak pulse; *~ STAAN*, be rickety (unsteady); be financially weak; *die ~ VERBUIGING*, the weak declension; *'n ~ WERKWOORD*, a weak verb.
Swaka'ra, Swakara (trade name of South African Karakul pelts).
swak: ~**gelowig**, having little faith; ~**heid**, (..hede), weakness, feebleness, debility, invalidity; flimsiness; delicacy; shortcoming, frailty, foible (of character); ~**hoof'dig**, (-e), weak-brained, feebleminded; ~**hoof'digheid**, feeble-mindedness; ~**keling**, (-e), weakling; ~**kerig**, (-e), rather weak, poor; ~**kies**, weakly, feebly, faintly, poorly; ~**siende**, weak-sighted.
swaksin'nig, (-e), feeble minded, mentally deficient, imbecile; ~**e**, (-s), mentally deficient person, imbecile; ~**heid**, mental deficiency, feeble-mindedness, imbecility.
swak'stroom, low voltage, weak current; ~**kabel**, low-voltage cable; ~**net**, low-voltage system.
swak'te, weakness, feebleness, infirmity, shortcoming, debility.
swalk, (ge-), rove, drift about; be tossed hither and thither (ship); ~**er**, (-s), drifter, rover, vagabond.
swalp, (ge-), splash, pour, surge.
swam, (-me), fungus, agaric, punk; spavin (of horses); ~**agtig**, (-e), spongy; fungous, fungoid; ~**dodend**, (-e), fungicidal; ~**doder**, fungicide; ~**draad**, hypha; ~**etend**, (-e), fungivorous; ~**kenner**, mycologist; ~**kunde**, mycology; ~**kundige**, (-s), mycologist; ~**meleer** = **swamkunde**; ~**mig**, (-e), spumous, punky; ~**papil**, fungiform papilla; ~**siekte**, fungous disease; wet-rot; mycosis; ~**spoor**, fungus spore; ~**steen**, mushroom stone; ~**suur**, fungic acid; ~**vlokke**, mycelium; ~**vor'mig**, (-e), fungiform.
swa'ne: ~**blom**, flowering rush; ~**brood**, calamus; ~**dons**, swan's down; swansdown (material); ~**hals**, swan's neck; arched neck; **sang**, swansong, death-song.
swang, vogue, fashion; *in ~ BRING*, bring into vogue; *in ~ KOM*, become the fashion; *in ~ WEES*, be in fashion.
swan'ger, pregnant, gravid, (gone) with child, enceinte, expecting; ~**heid**, ~**skap**, pregnancy, gestation, child-bearing; ~**skapsduur**, period of pregnancy; gestation.
swa'pestreek = **swaapstreek**
swareweer', see **swaarweer**
swa'righeid, (..hede), objection, difficulty, hitch; scruple; ~ *MAAK*, raise an objection; *daar geen ~ in SIEN nie om*, not scruple to.
Swart¹: *die ~ DOOD*, the Black Death; *DRAER van die ~ ROEDE*, Bearer of the Black Rod; *~ POENSKOP (bees)*, Black Poll; *die ~ SEE*, the Black Sea; *die ~ WOUD*, the Black Wood.
Swart²: ~**arbeid**, Black (African) labour; ~**bewussyn**, Black Consciousness; ~**mag**, Black Power; ~**man**, Black man, African; ~**mense**, Black people, Blacks, Africans; ~**vrou**, Black woman.
swart³, (s) black; *in ~ gekleed*, dressed in black; (b) black, ebony, sable; swarthy (person); *die ~ HANDEL (mark)*, the black market; *~ lyk van die HONGER*, be gaunt with hunger; *die ~ KUNS*, the black art; ~ *KYK*, look black; *die ~ LYS*, blacklist; ~ *v.d. MENSE*, swarming with people; *so min soos die ~ van jou NAEL*, a wee bit; next to nothing; ~ *STINKHOUT*, black stinkwood; *iets ~ op WIT kry*, get something in black and white; ~**aasvoël**, black vulture; ~**agtig**, (-e), blackish, nigrescent; ~**baars**, black bass; ~**bas**, black bark; ~**beer**, black bear; ~**beits**, (ge-), ebonize; ~**bekboontjie**, Black-eyed Susan; ~**bessie**, black currant; ~**bier**, stout; ~**blou**, blue-black; ~**bont**, black and white; piebald (horse); ~**brand**, charred stubble; anthracnose; ~**bruin**, black-brown; ~**damp**, black damp (mining); ~**druk**, black letter (type); ~**e**, (-s), black one, darky; S~**e**, Black; ~**erig**, (-e), blackish; ~**etjie**, (-s), little black one.
swartgal'lig, (-e), melancholy, morose, splenetic, atrabilious; ~**heid**, melancholy, spleen.
swart'gerand, (-e), black-bordered (-edged).
swart: ~**goed**, black material; ~**haak**, hookthorn *(Acacia detinens);* ~**harig**, (-e), black-haired; ~**heid**, blackness, negritude.
Swart'hemp, Blackshirt.
swart: ~**hout**, blackwood; ~**houtboom**, black stinkwood tree; ~**houtjies**, logwood; ~**jie**, (-s), black(e)y, blackamoor; ~**koors**, black fever; ~**kop**, black-haired child; Persian sheep; ~**koper**, black copper.
swart'kop: ~**geelgat**, black-fronted bulbul *(Pyenonotus capensis);* ~**mees**, marsh tit; ~**meeu**, black-headed gull; S~**-Persie**, (s), black-headed Persian (sheep); ~**pie**, black head canary; *Wambeu capensis* (flower); blackhead; ~**reier**, black-headed heron.
swart: ~**kraai**, black crow; ~**kruit**, black (gun-)powder; ~**kuns**, black art (magic), necromancy; ~**kunstenaar**, necromancer; ~**laken**, broadcloth; ~**lakens**, (-e), of broadcloth; ~**lap**, piebald (horse); ~**maak**, (-ge-), blacken; defame, slander; S~**man**, Black; S~**mense**, Black people, Africans; ~**merrie**, locomotive; ~**muf**, black spot; ~**oog**, black-eyed person; gipsy; ~**oor**, lynx; ~**piek**, ant-eating chat; ~**roes**, anthracnose; ~**ryp**, black frost; ~**sel**, blacking; ~**skaap**, black sheep (of the family).
swart'skimmel¹, (-s), black mould.
swart'skimmel², (-s), iron-grey horse.
swart: ~**slang**, black cobra; ~**smeer**, (-ge-), blacken, denigrate; defame, slander; ~**smeerdery**, defamation, vilification, slandering; blackening; ~**span**, black team; church council; *voor die ~ span kom*, appear before the church council; ~**sperwer**, black goshawk; ~**stroop**, treacle; ~**sug**, melanosis; ~**tee**, bohea; ~**vrot**, black rot; ~**waterkoors**, black-water fever; ~**wildebees**, black wildebeest, white-tailed gnu; ~**witpens(bok)**, sable antelope; ~**wittekening**, black and white drawing; ~**wording**, melanosis; ~**wou**, black kite.
swasti'ka, (-s), swastika, fylfot, gammadion.
swa'wel¹, (s) (-s), swallow.
swa'wel² = (**swael**); (s) sulphur, (w) (ge-), sulphur(ize); see **swael**; *hy is ge~*, he is intoxicated; ~**aar**, sulphur vein; ~**agtig**, (-e), sulphurous; hirundine; ~**bad**, sulphur bath; ~**blom**, flowers of sulphur; ~**bron**, sulphur spring; ~**damp**, sulphurous vapour; ~**diokside**, ~**dioksied**, sulphur dioxide; ~**erts**, brimstone ore; iron pyrites; ~**eter**, sulphuric ether; ~**geel**, sulphur-yellow; ~**houdend**, (-e), sulphurous; ~**kies**, pyrites; marcasite; ~**koolstof**, carbon bisulphide; ~**lood**, galena; ~**lug**, sulphurous odour; ~**melk**, milk of sulphur; ~**reën**, sulphur rain; ~**silwer**, sulphide of silver; ~**sink**, zinc sulphide; ~**suur**, sulphuric acid; ~**suursout**, (-e), sulphate; ~**swart**, sulphur-black; ~**verbinding**, sulphide; ~**waterstof**, sulphuretted hydrogen; ~**waterstofgas**, hydrogen sulphide; ~**waterstofwater**, hepatic water; ~**wortel**, sulphur-wort.
Swa'zi, (-'s), Swazi; ~**land**, Swaziland.
Swe'de, Sweden.
Sweed, (Swede), Swede; ~**s**, (s) Swedish; (b) (-e), Swedish; ~**se vuurhoutjies**, Swedish safety matches.
sweef, (ge-), see **swewe**; ~**baan**, cableway, aerial railway; telpher-way; ~**brug**, suspension bridge;

~**klub**, gliding club; ~**krag**, floating power; ~**kuns**, gliding; ~**mengsel**, solution in suspension; ~**meule**, giant's stride; ~**rek**, trapeze; ~**rib**, floating rib; ~**spoor**, cableway, aerial railway; ~**sport**, gliding; ~**ster**, (-s), female glider pilot; ~**stok**, trapeze; ~**tuig**, glider; ~**veld**, gliding site; ~**vermoë**, suspensibility; power of levitation; ~**vervoer**, aerial haulage; ~**vlieër**, glider(-pilot), volplanist; soarer; ~**vlieg**, (ge-), volplane, glide; hover-fly; ~**vliegtuig**, glider; sail-plane; ~**vlug**, volplane, gliding flight, glide.

sweem, (s) semblance; shadow; hint, shade, touch, dash, trace; *sonder 'n* ~ *van ANGS*, without the least trace of anxiety; *g'n* ~ *van HOOP nie*, without a flicker of hope; (w) (ge-), bear a likeness to, look like; *dit* ~ *na*, it looks like, it borders upon.

sweem'pie, (-s), slight trace.

sweep, (swepe), whip, lash; *onder die* ~ *kry*, give someone a whipping; ~**diertjie**, flagellate; ~**haar**, flagellum; ~**koker**, whip-holder; whip-socket; ~**slag**, whip-lash; racer; ~**slang**, whip-snake; racer; ~**stok**, whip-stick; ~**stoksiekte**, frenching; ~**tenk**, flail-tank; ~**tol**, whipping-top.

sweer[1], (s) (swere), abscess, ulcer, boil, core, fester, blain; (w) (ge-), fester, ulcerate, putrefy; *'n swerende toon*, a festering toe.

sweer[2], (w) (ge-), swear, vow, take an oath; *BY iem.* ~, swear by someone; *HOOG en laag* ~, swear by all that is holy; *LAAT* ~, administer an oath (to a person), put (someone) on (his) oath; *'n MENS sou* ~, one would swear; *TROU* ~, swear fidelity; take the oath of allegiance; *VALS* ~, commit perjury; *ek kan daar nie VOOR* ~ *nie*, I cannot swear to it.

sweer'klou, foot-rot.

sweer'lik, surely, without a doubt, actually; *hy het dit* ~ *weer gedoen*, he has actually done it again.

sweet, (s) perspiration, sudation, sweat; *in die* ~ *van sy AANSKYN (aangesig)*, in the sweat of one's brow; *koue* ~ *BREEK by hom uit*, break out in a cold sweat; *PAPNAT van die* ~, streaming with perspiration; (w) (ge-), perspire, sweat, get into a lather; cure (tobacco); ~**afskeiding**, hidrosis; ~**bad**, sweating-bath, sudatory; ~**doek**, sweat-cloth; ~**drank**, sudorific; ~**druppel**, drop (bead) of perspiration; ~**drywend**, (-e), sudorific; ~**gat**, pore; ~**hande**, sweating (sweaty) hands; ~**kamer**, sweating-room, estufa; ~**kanaaltjie**, sweat-duct; ~**kliertjie**, sweat-gland; ~**klosse**, sweat-locks; ~**koors**, miliary fever, sweating-fever; ~**kraal**, sweating pen; ~**kruie**, diaphoretic herbs; ~**kuur**, sudorific cure; ~**lappie**, dress-shield; ~**lug**, sweaty smell; ~**middel**, sudorific, perspirative, diaphoretic; ~**neus**, sweat nose (dog, ox); ~**pak**, track suit; ~**pêrels**, beads of perspiration; ~**porie**, sweat-pore; ~**siekte**, sweating-sickness; ~**trui**, sweater; ~**uitdrywend**, (-e), sudorific, diaphoretic; ~**vlek**, perspiration mark; ~**voete**, sweating (sweaty) feet; ~**vos**, sorrel, bright bay horse, (dark) chestnut; ~**wol**, greasy wool.

swei, (-e), bevel square, angle bevel.

sweis, (ge-), forge; weld; ~**baar**, (..bare), weldable; ~**bril**, goggles (welding); ~**er**, (-s), welder; ~**ing**, welding; ~**las**, welded joint; ~**naat**, welded seam; ~**pyp**, welding torch; ~**soldeer**, (ge-), braze; ~**soldeersel**, brazing solder; ~**werk**, welding; ~**winkel**, welding-shop.

swel, (ge-), swell, expand, distend, dilate, belly out, protuberate; ~*lende KNOPPE*, swelling buds; ~ *v.d. LAG*, be bursting with laughter.

swelg, (w) (ge-), swallow, gormandize, gorge, swill, glut, carouse; ~ *in*, revel in; ~**end**, (-e), Bacchanalian; ~**er**, (-s), gormandizer, glutton, quaffer; ~**ery**, gormandizing, gluttony, gorge; (s) (-e), revelry, orgy; ~**party**, bacchanal, orgy, revelry.

swel'ling, (-e, -s), swelling, intumescence.

swel: ~**register**, swell-organ; ~**water**, water of imbibition.

swel'sel, (-s), swelling, tumour.

swel'vrat(jie), ergot.

swem, (ge-), swim; *GAAN* ~, go for a swim; *sy OË* ~ *in trane*, his eyes are swimming with tears; ~**bad**, (-de, -dens), swimming-bath; ~**bal**, cistern float;

~**blaas**, swimming-bladder, natatory bladder; ~**broek**, bathing-trousers (-trunks); ~**duiker**, skin diver; ~**duikery**, skin diving; ~**gala**, swimming gala; ~**gat**, swimming-pool; ~**gordel**, swimming-belt, lifebelt; ~**inrigting**, bathing-establishment; ~**klere**, ~**kostuum**, swimming-costume, bathing-costume; ~**kuns**, art of swimming, natation; ~**matrassie**, air mattress; ~**mer**, (-s), swimmer; ~**oefening**, swimming-practice (-exercise); ~**onderwyser**, swimming-teacher; ~**pak**, swimming-costume; ~**piepatrys**, coqui partridge; ~**plank**, surf-board; ~**plek**, swimming-place; ~**poot**, web-foot, flipper; ~**potig**, (-e), web-footed; ~**skool**, swimming-school; ~**spaan**, swimming paddle; ~**sport**, swimming, natation; ~**ster**, (-s), (female) swimmer; ~**toestel**, swimming-apparatus; ~**vlies**, web; ~**voël**, swimming bird; palmiped(e); ~**voet**, web-foot (of birds); flipper; ~**wedstryd**, swimming-competition.

swen'del, (s) (-s), gross fraud, fakement, swindle; (w) (ge-), swindle; ~**aar**, (-s), chevalier of industry, swindler, sharper; ~**(a)ry**, fraud, ramp, swindling; plant; ~**firma**, long-firm; ~**maatskappy**, bogus company, bubble company, mushroom company.

swenk, (s) swerve, turn, side-step (rugby); (w) (ge-), swing round, swerve, wheel about; *regs* ~! right wheel! ~**gras**, fescue; Kentucky grass; ~**hoek**, angle of wheeling; ~**ing**, swerve, swing, volte face, change of front; caracol(e); ~**pas**, side-step.

swerf, (ge-), *see* **swerwe**; ~**blok**, erratic block; perched block (geol.); ~**geld**: *erfgeld is* ~ *geld*, easy come, easy go; ~**hart**, wandering heart; ~**ling**, (-e), wanderer, tramp; ~**lus**, roving disposition; ~**nier**, floating kidney; ~**rot**, migrant rat; ~**sand**, drift-sand; ~**senu(wee)**, vagus nerve; ~**siek**, of a roving disposition; ~**skrywer**, roving journalist; ~**spinnekop**, hunting spider; ~**ster**, (-s), wanderer (woman); ~**tog**, roaming expedition, travels, ramble, peregrination; ~**valk**, peregrine falcon; ~**voël**, nomadic bird; gipsy, migrant, straggler.

swe'ring, asseveration; ulceration.

swerk, sky, firmament, welkin.

swerm, (s) (-s), swarm (bees); flock, covey (birds); flight (wasps); cluster; throng, host, horde; *saam met die* ~ *vlieg*, side with the majority; espouse the popular cause; (w) (ge-), swarm; cluster; crowd; ~**korf**, swarmer (hive); ~**sel**, swarm-spore; ~**tyd**, swarming-season.

swer'kater, (-s), **swer'noot**, (..note), **swer'noter**, (-s), rascal, rogue, bounder, vile beast, devil.

swer'nootjie, (-s), little rascal; funny-bone.

swer'we, (ge-), roam, wander, rove, ramble, peregrinate, tramp; ~**ing** = **swerfling**; ~**nd**, (-e), wandering, fugitive, nomadic, errant, erratic; rambling; *'n* ~*nde lewe lei*, lead a nomadic life.

swer'wer, (-s), wanderer, vagabond, rambler, nomad, drifter, rover, tramp, hobo; *'n* ~ *bly 'n derwer*, a rolling stone gathers no moss; ~**slewe**, roving life.

swe'serik, (-e), sweetbread, thymus.

swe'terig, (-e), sweaty; ~**heid**, sweatiness.

swe'ting, sweating, diaphoresis (med.).

swets, (ge-), swear, curse.

swet'ser, (-s), swearer, curser; ~**y**, swearing, cursing, profanity.

swetterjoel', (-s), host, crowd, lot, multitude.

swe'we, (ge-), hover, float, soar, be suspended (in air); flit, glide (by); levitate (spiritualism); *voor die GEES* ~, be present to the mind; *tussen LEWE en dood* ~, hover between life and death; ~*nde NIER*, floating kidney; ~*nde RIB*, floating rib.

swe'wing, floating, suspension; levitation.

swe'wingstoestel, heterodyne (radio).

swiep, (ge-), bend (of mast); swish (with cane).

swier, (s) elegance, gracefulness, grace; dash, elan, jauntiness; *iets met* ~ *DOEN*, do things in style, with a swagger; *aan die* ~ *GAAN*, go on the spree; (w) (ge-), gad about, be on the spree; carry oneself gracefully; whirl about, reel; ~**bol**, (-le), rake, dandy, gad-about, gay blade, playboy, wild spark; ~**ig**, (-e), elegant, stylish; gay; jaunty, dashing, gallant; grand; ~**igheid**, dandyism, elegance, stylishness, jauntiness.

swig, (ge-), give in, give way, succumb to temptation; yield (to opposition).
swik¹, (ge-), sprain (ankle); stumble.
swik², (s) (-ke), bung, spigot, vent-peg; ~ **boor,** gimlet auger; ~ **gat,** bung-hole, vent.
swil'vrat, chestnut (e.g. on horse's leg).
swingel, (-s), swingle, whipple-tree, gangrel (of cart); handle (of pump); ~ **boor,** crank-brace; ~ **hout,** splinter-bar, whipple-tree, swingle-tree; ~ **riem,** swingle-strap.
swink, (ong.), glimpse; *ek het haar net so met 'n ~ gesien,* I merely caught a glimpse of her.
Swit'ser, (-s) Swiss; ~ **land,** Switzerland; ~ **s, (-e),** Swiss; ~ *se rolkoek,* Swiss roll.
swoe'ë, (ge-), drudge, slave, toil and moil, slog away, plod, plug.
swoe'ër, (-s), toiler, drudge; ~ **y,** drudgery.
swoeg, (ge-) = swoeë.
swoel, sultry, close, oppressive; ~ **heid,** ~ **te,** sultriness, closeness, oppressiveness.
swoer(d), bacon rind, crackling.
swy'e, (s) silence; *'n BATTERY tot ~ bring,* silence a battery; *iem. die ~ OPLÊ,* impose silence on someone; *spreek is SILWER, ~ is goud,* speech is silver, silence is golden.
swyg, (w) (ge-), be silent; keep quiet, keep secret; *om NOG te ~ van,* to say nothing of; not to mention; *wie ~, STEM toe,* silence gives consent.
swy'gend, (-e), silent, taciturn, mute, in silence.
swy'ger, (-s), silent person; *Willem die S~,* William the Silent.
swyg'agtig, (-e), taciturn, silent.
swyg'saam, (..same), silent, taciturn, reticent, incommunicative; ~ **heid,** incommunicativeness.
swym, faint, swoon, coma; *in ~ val,* swoon, faint away.
swy'mel, (s) giddiness, daze; (w) (ge-), become dizzy.
swyn, (-e) hog, pig, swine.
swyn'agtig, (-e), swinish, piggish; ~ **heid,** swinishness.
swy'ne: ~ **aard,** swinish nature; ~ **boel,** filthy pigsty, dirty hovel (fig.); piggery; ~ **hoeder,** swineherd; ~ **hond,** dirty swine; scoundrel; ~ **jag,** boar hunt; ~ **kos,** hog's meat; ~ **oppasser,** swineherd; ~ **stal,** pigsty; ~ **trog,** hog's trough; ~ **vleis,** pork.
swyn'hond, Schwein(e)hund, dirty swine.
swyns'kop, boar's head.
sy¹, (s) silk.
sy², (s) (-e), side; flank (of army); ~ *AAN ~,* side by side; *met HANDE in die ~ e,* with arms akimbo; *op~ SIT,* put aside; waive (claim); earmark (funds).
sy³, (w) (only subjunctive) be; *DIT ~ so,* so be it; *HOE dit ook ~,* whatever the case may be; *dit ~ VERRE,* perish the thought.
sy⁴, (pers vnw) she.
sy⁵, (bes vnw), his, its.
sy: ~ **aansig,** side view; side elevation, end elevation; ~ **aanval,** flank attack; ~ **aap,** lion (silky) monkey; ~ **agtig, (-e),** silky; ~ **altaar,** side altar; ~ **anker,** side-stay; ~ **balie,** side bar; ~ **band,** side-band; ~ **bank,** side bench; ~ '**bas,** silk-bark; ~ **beuk,** side-aisle; ~ **beweging,** flank movement; S ~ **bok,** Angora (goat); S ~ **bokhaar,** mohair; ~ **boom,** silk tree; ~ **broek,** silk trousers (men); silk drawers (women); ~ **damas,** damask silk.
sy'de: *ter ~ LAAT,* leave on one side; *iem. ter ~ NEEM,* take a person aside; *iem. ter ~ STAAN,* assist someone; stand by someone; *ter ~ STEL,* set aside; ~ **lings, (-e),** sideways, sidelong; (col)lateral; glancing; indirectly; ~ *lingse BLIK,* sidelong glance; ~ *lingse SEKURITEIT,* (col)lateral security.
sy: ~ **deur,** side-door; pestern; ~ **druk,** side thrust; ~ **draad,** gimp; ~ **erig, (-e),** silky; ~ **fabriek,** silk factory, silk-mill; ~ **fabrikant,** silk-manufacturer.
sy'fer¹, (s) (-s), digit, figure, number; bogey (golf); *HOE ~ s behaal,* obtain high marks; *in RONDE ~ s,* in round figures; (w) (ge-), calculate, figure, cipher.
sy'fer², (w) (ge-), ooze (through), filter, percolate; ~ **dig, (-te),** impermeable; ~ **digtheid,** impermeability; ~ **filter,** percolator; ~ **fontein,** sluggish spring; ~ **gat,** seep-hole; weep-hole; ~ **grond,** spongy ground, sponges.
sy'fering¹, ciphering.
sy'fering², seepage.
sy'ferklok, digit clock.
syfer: ~ **laag,** percolation bed; bleeder well, percolating pit; ~ **pyp,** weep pipe; bleeder pipe; ~ **riool,** weep drain; ~ **skrif,** cipher; code-writing; ~ **skrifoffisier,** cipher operator; ~ **sleutel,** cipher key; ~ **water,** seepage water.
syg, (ge-), strain, percolate, ooze, filter; sink down; tammy.
sy'gaas, silk gauze, tiffany.
sy: ~ **galery,** side-gallery; ~ **gang,** side-corridor; *op 'n ~ gang gaan,* stray from the straight and narrow path; ~ **gare,** spun silk.
syg'doek, cloth strainer, butter muslin; tammy.
sy: ~ **gebou,** annexe, wing; ~ **gedeelte,** quarter (beef); ~ **geweer,** side-arm; ~ **gewel,** side-gable; ~ **glans,** silky lustre; ~ **handel,** silk trade; ~ **handelaar,** silk-trader, mercer; ~ **ig, (-e),** silky; ~ **hemp,** silk shirt; ~ **hoek,** face angle; ~ **industrie,** silk industry; ~ **ingang,** side entrance; ~ **kamer,** side anteroom; ~ **kammetjie,** side comb; ~ **kanaal,** side canal; *iets deur 'n ~ kanaal hoor,* hear something at second hand.
sy'kant¹, side; *aan die ~ kant,* on the side.
sy'kant², silk lace.
sy: ~ **klap,** side flap; ~ **klep,** side valve; ~ **knol,** lateral tuber; ~ **knop,** lateral bud; ~ **kous,** silk stocking; ~ **kultuur,** silk-culture; ~ **laan,** side avenue; ~ **lamp,** side-lamp; ~ **leuning,** handrail; arm-rest (chair); ~ **lig,** side-light; ~ **linie,** branch-line; collateral line; ~ **loge,** side-box (in theatre); ~ **lyn,** margin; feeder, branch-line; touch-line; lateral line; ~ **muur,** side wall.
syn¹, (s) being, existence.
syn², (vnw) (ong.), his; *see* **s'n.**
sy'naat, side-seam.
syn'de: *dit so ~,* as this is so, this being so.
sy'ne, (s): *hy en die ~ (s),* he and those with him; (bes. vnw), 's, his; *DIS ~,* that is his; *die hele PAD is ~,* he is intoxicated; he is reeling.
sy'ner: *ter ~ tyd,* in due course.
sy'nersyds, on his part, from his side; as far as he is concerned.
sy'net, silk net.
syns¹, (s) (-e), rate; tribute.
syns², (pers. vnw) his; ~ *GELYKE,* his equal (peer); ~ *INSIENS,* according to his opinion.
syns'baar, (..bare), taxable, excisable, tributary.
syns'leer, ontology.
sy: ~ **nywerheid,** silk industry; ~ **opening,** lateral opening; ~ **opstand,** side elevation; ~ **paadjie, (-s),** sidewalk, pavement; footpath, footway, sidepath; backway; ~ **pad,** sidepath, bypath; deviation; lateral road; ~ **padtekenaar,** pavement artist; ~ **papier,** silk paper.
sy'pel, (ge-), ooze, trickle; percolate, filter, seep; ~ **aar,** filter percolator; ~ **dig, (-te),** impermeable; ~ **ing,** seepage; ~ **kan,** drip (filter), coffee pot; percolator; ~ **meter,** lysimeter; ~ **riool,** weep drain; ~ **water,** seepage water.
sy: ~ **plank,** running-board; foot-board; side board; ~ **pyp,** side-pipe; ~ **rivier,** tributary; feeder, branch; effluent; ~ **rok,** silk dress; ~ **ruspe,** silkworm; ~ **sakdoek,** silk handkerchief; ~ **satyn,** atlas, rich satin.
sy'sie, (-s), waxbill.
sy: ~ **skerm,** side-screen; coulisse; ~ **skip,** side-aisle; ~ **slip,** side-slip (aviation); ~ **spanning,** lateral stress; ~ **span(wa),** sidecar; ~ **spek,** flitch; ~ **spel,** byplay; ~ **speling,** sideplay; ~ **spoor,** side-track; siding; deviation; ~ **spraak,** aside; ~ **sprong,** side-jump, side-leap, side-step; ~ **standig, (-e),** lateral; ~ **stappie,** side-step; ~ **stoep,** side-stoep; ~ **stof,** silk; ~ **straat,** side street; off-street; bystreet; ~ **stuk,** side-piece; check (of hammer); ~ **tabberd,** silk dress; ~ **tak,** side-branch; effluent, tributary (of river); offshoot, collateral branch (of family); ~ **teelt,** silk-culture; ~ **uitgang,** side-exit; ~ **uitsig,** side-view; ~ **venster,** side window; ~ **vlak,** lateral

T

t, (-'s), t.
't: *AAN ~ speel*, playing; *AS ~ ware*, as it were; *dis om ~ EWE*, it is all the same.
ta¹, (-'s), papa, dad.
ta², (-'s), fellow; animal; baboon; *~ loer vir my uit die BOS*, the animal (lion) was watching me from the bush; *'n REGTE ~*, an oaf; a boor.
ta³, (w) (ge-), give; thanks.
Taag, Tagus.
taai, (-e), tough, hardy, wiry, stringy, leathery; dogged; sizy, cloggy, adhesive, gummy, sticky; *~ in die BEK*, hard-bitten; *~e GEDULD*, untiring patience; *'n ~ GEHEUE*, a long memory; *HOU jou ~*, keep your pecker up; don't lose heart; *iem. 'n ~ KLAP gee*, give someone a hard smack; *so ~ soos 'n RATEL*, as tough as nails; *iem. ~ SÊ*, give someone a bit of one's mind; *'n ~ TAMELETJIE*, something unpleasant, e.g. a big account; a sound thrashing; **~bekkig, (-e),** hard-mouthed; **~bos,** *Rhus sp.*; **~erig, (-e),** sticky, rather tough; **~erigheid,** stickiness, toughness; **~heid,** toughness; doggedness, tenacity; hardiness; gumminess, stickiness, viscosity; **~pitappelkoos,** clingstone apricot; **~pitperske,** clingstone peach; **~polgras,** dropseed (grass); **~vloeibaar,** (..bare), viscous, viscid; **~vloeibaarheid,** viscosity.
taak, (take), task, job, duty, assignment; office; *iem. 'n ~ OPLÊ*, impose a task upon someone; *hom tot ~ STEL*, set oneself the task; **~gewer,** taskmaster; **~loon,** piece-work wage; **~mag,** task force; **~stelling,** definition of assignment.
taal, (tale), language, speech, tongue; *in die ALLEDAAGSE ~*, in common parlance; *SWAAR ter tale wees*, be slow of speech; *GEKRUIDE ~*, spicy language; *'n ~ maklik GOOI*, speak a language like a native; *die ~ van Kanaän*, pious talk; *'n ~ MORS*, mangle a language; *SWAAR ter tale wees*, be slow of speech; *~ nòg TEKEN gee*, show no sign of life; *~ nòg TYDING ontvang*, receive no news; *die ~ v.d. VEROWERAAR in die mond v.d. veroweerde is die ~ van slawe*, the language of the conqueror in the mouths of the conquered is the language of slaves; *VUIL ~*, foul language; *WEL ter tale wees*, have the gift of the gab; **~aangeleentheid,** language matter; **~armoede,** poverty of language; **~bederf,** corruption of a language; **~bederwer,** corrupter of a language; **~begrip,** knowledge of a language; **~beheersing,** mastery (command) of a language; **~beskawing,** language refinement; **~beskouing,** view of (a) language; **~beweging,** language movement; **~boek,** grammar-book, language manual; **~eie,** idiom; **~eienaardigheid,** idiom(atic peculiarity); **~eksamen,** language examination; **~familie,** language family (group); **~figuur,** figure of speech; **~fout,** grammatical (linguistic) error; **~gebied,** sphere (zone) of a language; *op ~ gebied*, in the linguistic sphere; **~gebruik,** (language) usage, language use; colloquial usage; **~geleerde,** linguist, grammarian, philologist; **~gelykheid,** equal language rights; **~gemeenskap,** language (linguistic) community; **~geografie,** linguistic geography, dialect geography; **~geskiedenis,** history of a language; **~geslag,** grammatical gender; **~gevoel,** language sense; **~gids,** guide to a language; **~grens,** language boundary; **~groei,** growth of language; **~groep,** linguistic group; **~hervormer,** speech (language) reformer; **~hervorming,** language reform; **~indoena,** language pundit; **~kaart,** language chart; **~kenner,** linguist; **~kennis,** linguistic knowledge; **~kongres,** language (linguistic) congress; **~kunde,** linguistics; philology; grammar; **~kun'dig, (-e),** philological; grammatical; linguistic; **~kun'dige, (-s),** linguist, philologist; grammatist, grammarian; **~kwessie,** language problem; **~les,** language lesson; **~man,** master of languages; **~navorsing,** language (linguistic) research; **~oefening,** grammatical exercise; **~onderwys,** language-teaching, instruction in a language; **~onderwyser,** language-teacher; **~ontwikkeling,** development of a language; **~partikularis, ~puris,** purist; **~reël,** linguistic (grammatical) rule; **~skat,** vocabulary (of a language); **~sous:** *~ sous brou*, mangle a language; **~stryd,** language struggle; **~studie,** study of language(s); **~suiweraar,** purist; **~suiwerend, (-e),** puristic(al); **~suiwerheid,** linguistic purity; **~suiwering,** purism; **~tipe,** type of language; **~universeel, ~universalium,** language universal; **~verarming,** impoverishment of a language; **~vereenvoudiging,** simplification of a language; **~vermenging,** blending (mixture) of languages; **~verryking,** enrichment of a language; **~verskynsel,** linguistic phenomenon; **~verwantskap,** linguistic affinity; **~verwarring,** confusion of tongues; **~verwildering,** degeneration of a language; **~vitter,** language censor (caviller); **~vorm,** grammatical form; **~vorser,** language researcher, linguist; philologist; **~wet,** linguistic law; **~wetenskap,** linguistics; **~wetenskaplik, (-e),** linguistic.
taam'lik, (b) (-e), fair, passable, tolerable, goodish; (bw) rather, tolerably, fairly; pretty, middling; *~ GOED*, fairly good; *~ VEEL geld*, a fairly large amount of money.
taan, (ge-), grow dim, fade, diminish, wane; *sy invloed is aan die ~*, his influence is on the wane; **~kleur,** tawny colour; tan; **~kleu'rig, (-e),** tan-coloured, fulvous, tawny.
tabak', tobacco; *see* **twak;** *~ DRAAI*, twist tobacco; *~ KERF*, cut tobacco; *hoe ROOK daardie ~ vir jou?* what have you to say about that? **~as,** tobacco ashes; **~belasting,** tobacco tax; **~blaar,** tobacco leaf; **~boerdery,** tobacco-farming; **~bos,** *Senecio halimifolius*; **~bou,** tobacco-culture; **~chlorose,** tobacco chlorosis; **~damp,** fume of tobacco; **~doos,** tobacco-box; **~draaier,** tobacco-twister; **~fabriek,** tobacco factory; **~geur,** tobacco odour; **~handel,** tobacco trade; **~handelaar,** tobacconist; **~hart,** smoker's heart; **~keel,** smoker's throat; **~kerwer, (-s),** tobacco-cutter; **~koper,** buyer of tobacco; **~land,** tobacco field; **~maatskappy,** tobacco company; **~mandjie,** canaster; **~nywerheid,** tobacco industry; **~oes,** tobacco crop; **~papier,** tobacco paper; **~plant,** tobacco plant; **~plantasie,** tobacco plantation; **~planter,** tobacco grower; **~pot,** tobacco-pot; tobacco-jar; **~pruimpie, (-s),** tobacco-chew, quid; **~pyp,** (tobacco-) pipe; **~reuk,** tobacco smell; **~rol,** tobacco roll; **~rook,** tobacco smoke; **~ruik,** tobacco smell; **~saad,** tobacco seed; **~sak,** tobacco-pouch; **~skuur,** tobacco shed; **~snuif,** (tobacco) snuff; **~soort,** kind of tobacco; **~sop,** tobacco juice; **~steel,** tobacco stalk; **~stoel,** tobacco-plant; **~stof,** tobacco dust; **~stronk,** tobacco stalk; **~walm,** tobacco smoke; **~water,** tobacco extract; **~winkel,** tobacconist's shop.
tab'berd, (-s), gown, frock, dress; **~goed,** dress material; **~slip,** frock placket; **~stof,** dress material.
tabeet'jies, (gew., vero.), greetings; presents.
tabel', (-le), table, list, tabular statement; index;

tabernakel 527 *talk*

~**la'ries**, (-e), tabular, tabulated; ~**leer'**, (ge-), tabulate; ~**le'ring**, tabulation.
taberna'kel, (-s), tabernacle; *die AARDSE* ~, the fleshly tabernacle; *ons GAAN hier g'n* ~ *bou nie*, we are not going to set up our home here; *iem. op sy* ~ *GEE*, give someone a spanking.
tablatuur', tablature.
tableau', (-x) = **tablo**; ~-**vivant'**, living picture.
tablet', (-te), tablet, pastil, tabloid, lozenge; ~**vorm**, tablet-form.
tablo', (-'s), tableau.
taboe', (s, b) taboo.
taboeret', (-te), tabouret, footstool.
ta'boes, (-e), short driving-whip.
tabuleer', (ge-), tabulate.
tabyn', tabby cat.
taf, taffeta.
ta'fel, (s) (-s), table; index; ~ *AFDEK*, clear the table; *tussen* ~ *en BED geskei*, judicially separated between bed and board; *aan* ~ *BID*, say grace; *BOAAN (onderaan) die* ~, at the head (foot) of the table; *iets ter* ~ *BRING*, raise a matter; ~ *DEK*, lay the table; *die* ~ *oor iem. DEK*, speak ill of someone; *iem. onder die* ~ *DRINK*, drink someone under the table; *'n GOEIE* ~ *hou*, keep a good table; *die GROEN* ~, the conference table; *oop* ~ *HOU*, keep open house; *jy dek* ~ *vir KATTE en honde*, your shirt is hanging out; *aan* ~ *SIT*, sit at table; ~ *van VERMENIGVULDIGING*, multiplication table; *die* ~ *s van die WET*, the tables of the Law, (w) (ge-), sit at table, ~**afval**, table-scraps; ~**almanak**, desk-calendar; ~**appel**, dessert-apple.
Ta'felbaai, Table Bay.
ta'fel: ~**basalt**, tabular basalt; ~**bediende**, waiter (at table), steward; ~**bediening**, waiting (serving) at table; ~**bel**, table-bell.
Ta'felberg, Table Mountain; *toe* ~ *nog 'n vulletjie was*, very long ago, in the days of yore; in the year one.
ta'fel: ~**blad**, tabletop; (loose) table-leaf; ~**borsel**, crumb-brush; ~**botter**, table-butter; ~**dans**, table-rapping, table-lifting; ~**dek**, table setting; ~**doek**, table-cloth; ~**drank**, table-drink; ~**druiwe**, table-grapes; ~**fles**, flagon; ~**gebed**, blessing, grace before (after) meat (meals); ~**geld**, messing, messing allowance; ~**geleentheid**, messing; ~**genoot**, table-companion, commensal, messmate; ~**gereedskap**, tableware, cutlery; ~**gesprek**, table-talk; ~**glas**, plate glass; ~**goed**, table-linen, napery; ~**kleedjie**, tablecloth, overlay; ~**klokkie**, table-bell; ~**klop(pery)**, table-rapping; ~**kop**, flat-topped hill; ~**koste**, messing-charges; ~**laai**, table-drawer; ~**laken**, tablecloth; ~**lamp**, table-lamp; ~**land**, plateau; ~**linne**, napery, table-linen; ~**loper**, table-centre; ~**loseerder**, table boarder; ~**maat**, table companion; messmate; ~**maniere**, table manners; ~**matjie**, table-mat; ~**mes**, table-knife; ~**middelstuk**, epergne; ~**piano**, grand piano; ~**poot**, table-leg; ~**rede**, after-dinner speech; post-prandial speech; T~**ronde**, Round Table; ~**ronde**, round-table conference; ~**servies**, dinner service; ~**silwer**, plate, silverware; ~**skoppie**, crumb-tray; ~**skuimer**, (-s), sponger, parasite; ~**sout**, table-salt; ~**stoof**, table cooker; ~**telefoon**, desk-telephone; ~**tennis**, ping-pong, table tennis; ~**toelae**, table-money, messing allowance; ~**ui**, spring-onion; ~**veër**, crumb-brush; ~**versiering**, table decoration; ~**vormig**, (-e), tabular; ~**vreugde**, pleasures of the table; ~**vriend**, table-friend; ~**vurk**, dinner fork; ~**werker**, table-hand; ~**wyn**, table wine.
tafereel', (..rele), scene, picture, description.
taf'sy, jaconet, silk taffeta.
tag! good gracious!
tag'gentig, *see* **tagtig**.
tagiblas'ties, (-e), tachyblastic.
tagigraaf', (tagigrawe), tachygraph.
tagikardie', tachycardy.
ta'gimeter, **tagime'ter**, (-s), tachymeter, tacheometer.
tagistoskoop', (..skope), tachistoscope.
ta'gometer, **tagome'ter**, (-s), tachometer.

tag'tig, eighty; ~**er**, octogenarian; *T~er*, writer in Holland of the eighteen-eighties; *die* ~*erjare*, *die jare* ~, the eighties; ~**jarig**, (-e), eighty years old, of eighty years; *T~jarige Oorlog*, Eighty Years' War; ~**jarige**, (-s), octogenarian; ~**ste**, eightieth.
taille, (-s), waist.
tailleer', (ge-), cut in (at the waist).
tak, (s) (-ke), branch (of tree, river, business); limb; bough (of tree); tine (of antler); antlers (of stag); affluent, tributary (of river); ~**ke**, greenery; *DEUR die* ~*ke wees*, be half seas over; *HOOG in die* ~*ke wees*, be three sheets in the wind; *IEM. se* ~, someone's sweetheart; *die* ~*ke INSIT*, take to one's heels; (w) (ge-), branch off (out).
takamahak', tacamahac.
tak: ~**baan**, branch circuit; ~**bestuur**, branch management; branch committee; ~**bestuurder**, branch manager; ~**bok**, stag, deer, hart; ~**bos**, faggot, facsine; ~**bout**, rag-bolt.
ta'kel, (s) (-s), tackle, pulley-block, system of pulleys; (w) (ge-), rig, tackle; fall upon, grapple with, knock about; ~**aar**, rigger; ~**a'sie**, tackling, rigging; ~**blok**, tackle; hoist-block; ~**stel**, block and tackle; ~**toue**, cordage, tackle-fall, tackle-ropes; ~**werk**, tackling, rigging.
tak'haar, (..hare), backvelder, farmer of the old stamp, country cousin, bumpkin, lout; ~**agtig**, (-e), uncouth, agrestic; ~**maniere**, unpolished manners.
tak: ~**kantoor**, branch office; ~**kie**, (-s), twig, small branch; ~**kraal**, zareba; ~**kring**, branch circuit; ~**laer**, abat(t)is; ~**las**, (se), branch joint; ~**loos**, (..lose), branchless; ~**lyn**, branch-line.
tak: ~**meter**, metronome; ~**meting**, metronomy.
tak'rivier, tributary.
taks, (s) estimate, rate, share, portion; *dis my GEWONE* ~, this is my usual share; (bw), repeatedly, regularly; ~ *OM* ~, every time; *so* ~ *elke WEEK kom*, come regularly every week.
taksa'sie, (-s), taxation; valuation; estimation.
taksateur', (-s), appraiser, valuator.
takseer', (w) (ge-), estimate, value, appraise, assess, rate, size; ~**baar**, (..bare), appraisable; ~**meester**, taxing-officer.
takse'ring, (-e), valuation, appraisement (of damages); taxation; taxing (of court costs).
taksidermis', (-te), taxidermist.
tak'sis[1], (-se), yew-tree.
tak'sis[2], taxis (med.).
tak'spoorweg, branch railway.
taksonomie', classification, taxonomy; ..**no'mies**, (-e), taxonomic; ..**noom'**, (..**nome**), taxonomist.
tak'sus, *see* **tak'sis**[1].
takt, tact; adroitness; generalship; ~ *gebruik*, exercise tact.
taktiek', (e), tactics.
taktiel', (-e), tactile.
tak'ties, (-e), tactical.
tak'tikus, (..tici, -se), tactician.
takt'loos, (..lose), tactless, gauche; ~**heid**, tactlessness.
takt'vol, (-le), tactful, discreet, judicious.
tak: ~**vergadering**, branch meeting; ~**vormig**, (-e), branch-shaped, ramiform.
tal, (-le), number; *SONDER* ~, numberless; ~*le (VAN mense)*, a number of, numerous people.
talaar', (**talare**), gown (jurist).
talent', (-e), talent, natural gift, endowment, ability, accomplishment; genius; talent (weight, money); *met sy* ~ *e woeker*, make the most of one's talents; ~**e**, acquirements, talents, ability; ~**loos**, (..lose), untalented, ungifted; ~**verlies**, brain drain; ~**vol**, (-le), talented, gifted.
ta'lespraak, gift of tongues, glossolalia.
talg, tallow; ~**klier**, sebaceous gland.
ta'lie, (-s), tackle, pulley; ~**reep**, lanyard.
ta'ling, teal.
ta'lisman, (-s), talisman, charm, amulet.
tal'je, *see* **taille**.
talk, tallow; talc; ~**aarde**, French chalk; ~**agtig**, (-e), tallowy; talcose; ~**houdend**, (-e), talcose; ~**kers**, tallow-candle; ~**lei**, talcose slate; ~**olie**, oil of talc;

~ **pan**, tallow-tray; ~ **poeier**, talc powder, French chalk; ~ **steen**, talc, soapstone; ~ **stof**, stearine; ~ **vet**, tallow-grease.
tal'loos, (..lose), innumerable, numberless, countless.
tal'lus, (-se), thallus.
talm, (ge-), linger, delay, loiter, dawdle, dally, procrastinate, lag; ~ **er, (-s)**, loiterer, lingerer; ~ **(e)rig, (-e)**, inclined to dawdle, slow, dilatory; ~ **(e)righeid**, dilatoriness; ~ **(e)ry**, delay, lingering, loitering; ~ **lont, (-e)**, delayed-action fuse.
Tal'moed, Talmud; ~ **geleerde**, ~ **is'**, Talmudist.
tal'ryk, (-e), numerous, multitudinous; plentiful; ~ **heid**, numerousness, multitude, plurality.
tal'stelsel, scale of notation, numeral system.
ta'lus, (-se), talus, ankle-bone; knuckle-bone.
tam, tired, exhausted, weary.
tamaai', very large, enormous, whopping, almighty, great, huge, colossal; *'n ~ groot stuk*, a very large piece indeed.
tamara'ka, (-s), tamarack *(Albuca major)*.
tamarin'de, (-s), tamarind.
tamarisk', (-e), tamarisk *(Tamarix articulata)*.
tamaryn¹, tamarind (fruit); ~ **stroop**, tamarind-syrup.
tamaryn'², navy cut, cavendish (tobacco); ~ **tabak**, tamarind-tobacco.
tama'tie, (-s), tomato; ~ **blatjang**, tomato chutney; ~ **bredie**, tomato bredie; ~ **kultivar**, tomato cultivar; ~ **kelkie**, tomato cocktail; ~ **konfyt**, tomato jam; ~ **pruim**, persimmon; ~ **roomsop**, tomato cream soup; ~ **slaai**, tomato salad; ~ **so(e)p**, tomato soup; ~ **sous**, tomato sauce.
tama'tiestraat: *hy is in ~*, he has no hope, he is in difficulties, he is in Queer Street.
tamboe'kie: ~ **doring**, tambookie-thorn; ~ **gras**, tambookie-grass *(Cymbopogon validus)*.
tamboer', (-e), drum; tambour (archit.); drummer, frustum, drum (of column); ~ **slaan**, beat the drum; ~ **eer', (ge-)**, do tambour-work; tambour; ~ **majoor**, drum major; ~ **nooi(entjie)**, drum majorette; ~ **slaan, (-ge-)**, (beat the) drum; ~ **slaner, (-s)**, drummer.
tamboeryn', (-e), tambourine, timbrel.
tambo'tie, tambotie *(Excoecaria africana)*; ~ **gras**, *Andropogon marginatus*.
tamelet'jie, (-s), "tameletjie", toffee; unexpected account; *iem. ~ s GEE*, give a person a hiding; give someone a dressing down; *~ KRY*, be given a dressing down.
tam'heid, exhaustion, tiredness, fatigue, weariness.
tamp, (ge-), toll (of bell).
tam'pan, (-s), tampan (tick).
tam'pa(s), compensation (in games); *ni(e)ks ~*, no damages; I am not going to pay back anything.
tampon', (-s), tampon, (cotton) plug; ~ **neer' (ge-)**, plug with a tampon.
tam-tam', (-s), tom-tom.
tand, (s) (-e), tooth; cog, cam (wheel); prong, tine (harrow); *op jou ~ e BYT*, clench one's teeth; *tot die ~ e GEWAPEN*, armed to the teeth; *nie genoeg vir 'n HOL ~ nie*, hardly a mouthful; *~ e KRY*, cut one's teeth; *met LANG ~ e eet*, eat without relish; *die ~ e laat SIEN*, bare (show) one's teeth; *die ~ e SLYP*, look forward with keen anticipation; *ou mense se ~ te TEL*, take in all that grown-ups say; *die ~ van die TYD*, the ravages (wear and tear) of time; *'n ~ UITTREK*, extract a tooth; *iem. aan die ~ VOEL*, test someone's knowledge; size someone up; *WIT ~ e lag*, laugh with joy; *die ~ e WYS*, show one's teeth; (w) **(ge-)**, perforate (stamps); ~ **aanpaksel**, tartar deposit; ~ **afstand**, pitch (of gear); ~ **arts**, dentist; ~ **been**, dentine; ~ **bederf**, tooth-decay; ~ **beitel**, jagger, jagging-iron; ~ **beskrywing**, odontography; ~ **boog**, sector; quadrant; ~ **boor**, dental drill; ~ **deeg**, toothpaste.
tan'de: ~ **beker**, tooth-mug; ~ **borsel**, tooth-brush; ~ **dokter**, dentist; dental surgeon.
tand'eg, spike harrow.
tan'de: ~ **geknars**, gnashing of the teeth; ~ **kliniek**, dental clinic; ~ **knersend, (-e)**, teeth-gnashing; ~ **loos, (..lose)**, edentate, toothless.

tan'dem, (-s), tandem.
tan'de: ~ **maker**, dental mechanic; ~ **pasta**, toothpaste; ~ **poeier**, dental powder, dentifrice; ~ **ring**, teething ring; ~ **stokkie, (-s)**, toothpick; quill; ~ **tang**, dental forceps; ~ **trekker**, tooth-extractor, dental forceps; *lieg soos 'n ~ trekker*, lie like a trooper; tell barefaced lies.
tand: ~ **formule**, dental formula; ~ **glasuur**, enamel (of tooth); ~ **heelkunde**, dentistry, dental science.
tandheelkun'dig, (-e), dental; ~ **e, (-s)**, dentist, dental surgeon.
tand: ~ **hoek**, pitch (of tooth of saw); ~ **holte**, cavity in a tooth; alveolus.
tan'ding, cogging (carpentry); perforation.
tand: ~ **ivoor**, dentine; ~ **kas, (-se)**, socket, alveolus; ~ **kiem**, dental pulp; ~ **knobbel**, cusp (of tooth); ~ **kroon**, crown of a tooth; ~ **kunde**, odontology; ~ **las**, tusk-tenon; cogged joint; ~ **leer**, odontology; ~ **merk**, tooth-mark; ~ **letter**, dental (letter); ~ **lys**, dental moulding; ~ **meter**, perforation gauge; ~ **middel**, dentifrice; odontic; ~ **murg**, tooth-pulp, dental pulp; ~ **mol**, mole-rat; ~ **pasta**, toothpaste; ~ **plaat**, dental plate; ~ **priem**, broach; ~ **pyn**, toothache; ~ **pynmiddel**, toothache remedy; ~ **pynwortel**, *Sium thunbergii*; ~ **rat**, cog wheel; sprocket, pinion; *koniese ~ rat*, bevel wheel; ~ **ratbaan**, rack-railway; ~ **ratdryfwerk**, race and pinion; ~ **ratspoor**, rack-railway; ~ **ruitpatroon**, dog's-tooth design; ~ **ruitstof**, dog's tooth check; ~ **saag**, double saw; ~ **senuwee**, tooth-nerve; ~ **setter**, saw-set, sawsetter; ~ **skaaf**, toothed plane; ~ **skyf**, ratch(et); ~ **stang**, rack; ~ **stangmoer**, rack nut; ~ **steek**, tooth pitch; ~ **steen**, scale (tartar) on the teeth; ~ **steller**, swage; ~ **stelsel**, dentition; ~ **stopsel**, stopping, filling (of a tooth); ~ **tang**, dental forceps; ~ **tap**, tusk-tenon; ~ **tegnikus**, dental mechanic; ~ **verrotting**, tooth-decay; ~ **vleis**, gum(s); ~ **vleisontsteking**, gingivitis; lampas (in horse); ~ **vleissiekte**, pyorrhoea; ~ **vleissweer**, gumboil; ~ **vormig, (-e)**, tooth-shaped, serrated, dentate, dentiform; ~ **vulling**, stopping, filling, plugging (of a tooth); ~ **walvis**, toothed whale.
tand'werk, tooth-work; cogging, gear; denture; ~ **tuigkundige, (-s)**, dental mechanic.
tand: ~ **wiel**, toothed wheel; cog wheel; ~ **wisseling**, change (shedding) of teeth; ~ **wortel**, root (fang) of a tooth.
tang, (-e), pair of tongs (for coal); pincers (for nails); forceps (doctor's); pliers (for wire); *iem. met g'n ~ kan AANRAAK nie*, someone not fit to be touched with a barge-pole; *'n ~ van 'n VROUMENS*, a hell-cat, vixen, shrew; ~ **arm**, handle (of pliers).
Tanganji'ka, (hist.), Tanganyika.
tan'gens, (..gente), tangent; ~ **iaal', (..siale)**, tangential.
tangent', (-e), tangent.
tan'getjie, (-s), small tongs; pincers, tweezers.
tang'mes, nipper knife.
tan'go, (-'s), tango.
tang'sleutel, vice-grip wrench.
tang'vorm, mould (for bullets); ~ **ig, (-e)**, shaped like a pair of tongs (pinchers).
ta'nig, (-e), tawny.
tanjel'lo, (-'s), tangello (citrus-fruit).
tan'nie, (-s), aunt, auntie; adult lady, woman.
tannien', tanni'ne, tannin; ~ **suur**, tannic acid.
tans, now, at present, nowadays.
tant, aunt (when followed by proper name); *~ Annie*, Aunt Annie.
tantalisa'sie, (-s), tantalization.
tantaliseer', (ge-), tantalize.
tanta'lium, tantalium.
Tan'talus, Tantalus; **t~ beker**, Tantalus-cup; **t~ kwelling**, torture of Tantalus.
tan'te, (-s), aunt; adult; ~ **tjie, (-s)**, auntie.
tantiè'me, (-s), royalty.
Tanza'nië, Tanzania.
Taoïs'me, Taoism.
Taoïs'ties, (-e), Taoist.
tap, (s) (-pe), tap (for barrel); tenon (for mortise); bung, spigot; plug (for hole in barrel); trunnion (of cannon); (w) **(ge-)**, tap, draw; mortise; dowel;

~ **beitel**, mortise-chisel; socket-chisel; ~ **boor**, tap-borer, tap-drill; ~ **boormasjien**, mortise machine; ~ **bout**, stud; ~ **-en-gatvoeg**, mortise and tenon (joint); ~ **gat**, tap-hole, mortise; bung-hole (in cask); ~ **gatboor**, mortise machine; ~ **huis**, (ong.), alehouse, tavern.
tapio'ka, tapioca.
ta'pir, (-s), tapir.
tapisserie', (-ë), tapestry.
tap: ~ **kamer**, (ong.), tap-room; bar-room; ~ **kraan**, bib-cock; faucet.
tap: ~ **kruishout**, mortise gauge; ~ **masjien**, mortise machine.
tap: ~ **pen**, dowel, tenon pin; ~ **pyp**, draw-off pipe.
taps, (-e), tapering, cone-shaped; ~ *(e) ENT*, feather edge; ~ *(e) GAT*, taper hole; ~ *TOELOOP*, taper.
tap: ~ **saag**, tenon-saw; back-saw; ~ **slot**, mortise lock.
taps'heid, taper(ing).
tap'toe, tattoo; last post; *LAASTE* ~, last post; *die* ~ *SLAAN*, beat the tattoo.
tap: ~ **verbinding**, dowelling; ~ **voeg**, mortise (and tenon) joint; ~ **yster**, tapping-bar (foundry).
tapyt', (s) (-e), carpet, floor-rug, mat; *met iets op die* ~ *kom*, bring up something for discussion; ~ **band**, carpet binding; ~ **behangsel**, wall-tapestry; ~ **borsel**, carpet-broom; ~ **fabriek**, carpet factory; ~ **goed**, carpeting; ~ **klopper**, carpet-beater; ~ **loper**, carpet runner; ~ **maker**, carpet-weaver; ~ **sak**, carpet-bag; ~ **skoen**, slipper; ~ **skroef**, carpet-stud; ~ **spyker**, carpet-tack, tin tack; ~ **stafie**, stair-rod; ~ **stof**, carpeting; ~ **werk**, carpeting; ~ **werker**, carpet weaver; ~ **wewery**, carpet-weaving.
tarantel', (-le), wolf-spider, tarantula.
tarantel'la, (-s), tarantella.
tarantis'me, tarantism.
taran'tula, (-s), tarantula, wolf-spider.
tar'bot, (-te), turbot (fish).
tarentaal', (..tale), guinea-fowl; pintado; ~ **wyfie**, guinea-hen.
tarief', (..riewe), tariff, regulation fare, scale of charges, terms, rate; ~ **hersiening**, tariff reform; ~ **meter**, taximeter; ~ **premie**, tariff premium; ~ **vasstelling**, fixing the tariff; ~ **wysiging**, change of tariff.
tarie'we: ~ **kantoor**, rates office ; ~ **oorlog**, tariff war, war of rates
tar'latan, tarlatan.
tar'ra, tare!
tar'sus, (-se), tarsus.
tart, (ge-), taunt, provoke, dare, challenge, defy, set at defiance, brave, outdare; *dit* ~ *ALLE beskrywing*, it beggars description; *GEVARE* ~, defy dangers.
tartaan', (tartane), tartan(e) (boat).
Tartaar', (Tartare), Tartar; ~ **s'**, (-e), Tartar(ian).
tartan, (-s), tartan; ~ **baan**, tartan track (athletics); ~ **klere**, tartan dress (clothes).
Tartary'e, Tartary.
tar'tend, (-e), defiant, provoking, provocative; ~ *e optrede*, provocative action.
tar'ting, (-e, -s), defiance, provocation.
tartraat', (tartrate), tartrate.
tas¹, (s) (-se), bag, handbag, case, pouch, pocket, satchel; wallet; *aan 'n mens se* ~ *vat*, make a hole in one's pocket.
tas², (s): *op die* ~ *sy pad vind*, grope his way; plod along; (w) (ge-), feel, touch, grope.
tasal', pickled meat, tasal.
tasa'terwater = **kasaterwater**.
tas'baar, (..bare), tangible, tactual, palpable, concrete; *'n tasbare BEWYS*, a tangible proof; *tasbare DUISTERNIS*, palpable darkness; ~ **heid**, tangibility, palpability.
tas'dief, (ong.), bag-snatcher.
tas'liggaampie, tactile corpuscle.
Tasma'nië, Tasmania; ~ **r**, (-s), Tasmanian.
Tasma'nies, (-e), Tasmanian.
tas'orgaan, tentacle, organ of touch.
tas'sie, (-s), handbag.
tas: ~ **sin**, sense of touch, tactile sense; ~ **telik**, (-e), tangible, palpable; ~ **ter**, (-s), feeler, palp; ~ **ting**, feeling, touching.

ta'ta, ta-ta, cheerio, goodbye.
ta'te, (-s), *see* **ta**.
ta'ter, (-s), scoundrel, rascal, villain, blackamoor.
tatgaai', dwarf shrub *(Staavia radiata)*.
tatoeëer', (ge-), tattoo.
tatoeë'ring, tattooing.
taver'ne, (-s), tavern.
taw'werd = **tabberd**.
tax'i, (-'s), taxi; ~ **bestuurder**, taxi-man.
T'-bout, T bolt.
te, (bw) too; *jou* ~ *BUITE gaan*, indulge too freely; go to excess; ~ *KLEIN*, too small; *(des)* ~ *MEER*, moreover; (so much) the more; ~ *MIN*, insufficient; not enough, too little; ~ *SLEG*, too bad; (vs) to, at, on, in; ~ *gronde GAAN*, perish; ~ *HUUR*, to let; ~ *KENNE gee*, make known; ~ *bo(we) KOM*, surmount; ~ *KOOP*, for sale; ~ *PERD*, on horseback; ~ *PRETORIA*, in Pretoria; ~ *goeder TROU*, bona fide; ~ *alle TYE*, at all times, always; ~ *VOET*, on foot; ~ *WETE*, namely, to wit, viz.
tea'ter, (-s), theatre; ~ **besoeker**, playgoer; ~ **held**, stage hero; ~ **heldin**, stage heroine.
teatraal', (..trale), theatrical (in manner), emotional, stagy, histrionic.
tebeurt'valing, devolution; falling to one's lot.
teboek'stelling, committing to writing; registration.
ted'diebeer, teddy bear.
te'der, (-e), tender, delicate; ~ **heid**, tenderness, delicacy.
tee, tea; *iem. se BITTER maak, in iem. se* ~ *BLAAS*, *iem. se* ~ *ROER*, cut out a rival suitor; put someone's nose out of joint; *sy* ~ *was te STERK*, he has had a drop too much.
te'ë, against; tired of; *ek is DAAROP* ~, I am against it; *hy is* ~ *vir VIS*, he is tired of fish; *see also* **teen** *for compounds*.
te'ë: ~ **aanval**, counter-attack; ~ **beeld**, counterpart; ~ **beklag**, counter-plea; ~ **belemmering**, countercheck; ~ **belofte**, counter-promise; ~ **berig**, counter-report; ~ **beskuldiging**, countercharge, recrimination; ~ **besoek**, return visit; ~ **betoog**, counter-expostulation; ~ **bevel**, counter-order, countermand, contrary order; ~ **beweging**, counter-movement, counter-motion; ~ **bewys**, counter-proof, proof of the contrary; counter-evidence; counterfoil.
tee'blaar, tea-leaf.
te'ëblad, counterfoil.
tee'blik, tea canister.
te'ë: ~ **blink**, (ge), flash at; ~ **bod**, counterbid
tee: ~ **bossie**, tea-plant, ~ **bus**, tea-canister, tea-caddy; ~ **doek**, tea-cloth, tray-cloth; ~ **doeke**, tea shower.
te'ëdriehoek, antipodal triangle
te'ëdrink, (-ge-), cloy (surfeit, satiate) with drink.
tee-eet, (-geëet), eat to nauseous satiety, revolt against food because of overeating.
teef, (tewe), bitch.
te'ëgaan, (-ge-), oppose; prevent, check, thwart; repress.
tee'gerei, tea ware.
te'ëgesteld, (-e), opposite, contrary.
te'ëgetuienis, counter-evidence.
te'ëgif, antidote, mithridate.
tee'goed, tea-things, cups and saucers; ~ **balie**, tub for washing tea-things; ~ **doek**, tea-towel.
te'ëgraaf, ..**grawe**, (-ge-), countermine.
te'ëgreep, counter-grip.
te'ëgroet, (ge), return a salute.
te'ëgrond, counter-argument.
tee'handel, tea-trade; ~ **aar**, tea-merchant.
te'ëhanger, (-s), contrast; match, counterpart.
te'ëhoek, angle opposite.
te'ëhou, (-ge-), arrest, check, impede, hold back, restrain, cohibit, obstruct (progress); press against; ~ **ers**, very dry variety of sweet potatoes; *see* **wurgpatat**.
tee'kan, tea-urn.
te'ëkandidaat, opposition (rival) candidate.
te'ëkant, (-ge-), oppose; ~ **ing**, opposition.
tee'ketel, tea-kettle.

teëklag, countercharge.
tee'kleedjie, tea-cloth.
te'ëklink, (-ge-), resound.
tee'koek, pikelet.
te'ëkom, (-ge-), meet, encounter, come across, hit upon, chance on, light on; ~**s**, meeting.
tee'koppie, tea-cup.
teel, (ge-), breed, rear, raise (cattle); grow, cultivate (crop); engender, generate; sire, beget, procreate (offspring).
te'ël, (s) (-s), tile; (w) **(ge-)**, tile.
teel'aarde, vegetable earth, humus, garden-mould; black earth.
te'ëlag, (-ge-), smile upon.
te'ëlbad, tiled bath.
te'ëlbakker, tile-maker; ~**y**, tile-fields.
teel'bal, testicle.
te'ëlbekleding, tiling.
teel'buis, generative duct.
teël: ~ **dak**, tiled roof; ~ **dekker, (-s)**, tiler.
teel: ~ **dele**, genital organs; ~ **drif**, generative (sexual) instinct.
teel'eendjie, Cape teal.
tee'lepel, teaspoon; ~ **vol**, teaspoonful.
teel: ~ **gewas**, cultivated plant; ~ **grond**, vegetable mould; ~ **hings**, stud-stallion.
te'ëlis, counterplot, counter-stratagem.
teel: ~ **keuse**, natural selection; ~ **krag**, generative faculty, procreative power, virility, procreativeness; ~ **kuns**, selection.
te'ëllaag, tile-layer.
teel'laag, cambium; tilth, top-layer soil.
te'ëllêer, tiler.
tee'lood, lead foil; tea lead.
teel'ooi, breeding ewe.
te'ëloop, (-ge-), fail, go wrong, be unsuccessful; go to meet; *alles het my teëgeloop*, everything went against me.
te'ël: ~ **muur**, tiled wall; ~ **pan**, roof-tile, tegula.
teel'sak, scrotum, cod.
teelt, culture, cultivation; breeding; ~ **keus(e)**, selective breeding, natural (sexual) selection.
teel'toom, breeding-pen.
teel'tyd, rutting season.
te'ëlvloer, tiled floor.
teem, (ge-), drawl.
te'ëmaak, (-ge-), cause a loathing for a thing, nauseate.
tee'maaltyd, high tea.
te'ëmaatreël, countermeasure.
te'ëmars, countermarch.
te'ëmiddel, antidote, remedy.
Teems, Thames.
tee'mus, tea-cosy.
teen, (vs) against, in contravention of, contrary to (law); towards; ~ *die AAND*, towards evening; *GELD* ~ *6 persent*, money at 6 per cent; *iets* ~ *die LIG hou*, keep something up against the light; ~ *MIDDERNAG*, about midnight; ~ *die MUUR*, against the wall; ~ *'n RAND 'n kilo*, at a rand a kilogram; *SPRINGBOKKE* ~ *All Blacks*, Springboks against All Blacks; ~ *my WENS*, contrary to (against) my wish; ~ *WIL en dank*, in spite of everything; (bw) against; *daar was 5 stemme* ~, there were 5 votes against; *see also* **teë** *for compounds*.
teen'aan, against; *teen die muur aan*, ~ *die muur*, against the wall.
teen: ~ **aanbod**, (..**aanbiedinge**), counter-offer; ~ **aangestel(d), (-de)**, contraposed; ~ **aanligging**, juxtaposition; ~ **beeld**, antitype; ~ **beskuldiger**, recriminator; ~ **beskuldiging**, recrimination; ~ **beswaar**, counter-objection.
teen'bevel = **teëbevel**.
teen'beweging = **teëbeweging**.
teen: ~ **bewys**, refutation, disproof; ~ **blad**, (..**blaaie**), counterfoil, stub; voucher; ~ **buiging**, contrary flexure (railway).
teen'bod, counter-bid.
teen'boeking, cross entry.
teen'boor, (s) counter-bore; (w) **(-ge-)**, counter-drill.

teen: ~ **boring**, counter-boring; ~ **brand**, counter-fire.
teen'deel, contrary; reverse, opposite; *die* ~ *is waar*, the contrary is true.
teen'draads, (-e), against the grain.
teen'druk, counter-pressure, back-pressure.
teen'eis, counter-claim, counter-bill; ~ **er**, plaintiff in reconvention.
teen'gestel(d), (-de), opposite; adverse; antipodal; ..**stelde, (-s)**, antonym; reverse.
teen'gewig, balance weight, counterweight.
teen: ~ **gif**, antidote, counter-poison, antitoxin, antivenene; ~ **hang**, counter-slope; ~ **hanger**, counterpart, pendant; ~ **helling**, counter-slope; ~ **hou, (-ge-)**, retard, arrest (progress); hold up (traffic); stop, delay, check; foreclose; ~ **insurgensie**, counter-insurgence.
teen'kant = **teëkant**.
teen'kap, **(-ge-)**, retort sharply.
teen'klag, counter-complaint, recrimination.
teen'klink = **teëklink**.
teen'kom = **teëkom**.
teen: ~ **krag**, counter-force; ~ **krediet**, paid-on; ~ **liggaam**, antibody; ~ **lis**, counter-plot; ~ **maatreël**, counter measure; ~ **mekaar**, close together; ~ **moer**, counter-nut; ~ **myn**, counter mine.
teen: ~ **natuurlik, (-e)**, unnatural, contrary to nature; ~ **offensief**, counter-offensive; ~ **omwenteling**, counter-revolution.
teen'oor, teenoor', over against, facing; in the face of; compared with; opposite to; as opposed to; *sy GEDRAG* ~ *my*, his behaviour towards me; ~ *HIERDIE feite*, in the face of these facts, as opposed to these facts; *MAN* ~ *man*, man to man; *SKUINS* ~ *my*, diagonally opposite to me.
teenoor'geleë, opposite.
teenoor'gesteld, (-e), opposite, contrary, converse; *LYNREG* ~ *aan*, diametrically opposed to; *PRESIES die* ~ *e*, exactly the opposite, quite the reverse.
teen'oormekaarstaande, opposite, contrary.
teen'oorstelling, placing opposite each other, confrontation, contraposition.
teen'party, adversary, opponent, reclaimant, rival, antagonist, counter-party; opposition.
teen: ~ **passaat**, anti-trade wind; ~ **plaat**, caul; ~ **plan**, counter-scheme; ~ **petisie**, cross-petition; ~ **pleit**, plea in reconvention; ~ **pos**, cross entry; ~ **praat, (-ge-)**, contradict; answer back, argue; ~ **prater**, contradictor; ~ **prestasie**, (valuable) consideration (law); quid pro quo, counter-performance; ~ **proses**, counter-suit; ~ **pruttel, (-ge-)**, mutter objections, grumble (murmur) against; ~ **reaksie**, backlash; ~ **rekening**, contra account; offset; ~ **rewolusie**, counter-revolution; ~ **rewolusionêr, (-e)**, counter-revolutionary.
teen'rigting-, offset; ~ **skotteleg**, offset disc harrow.
teen'sang, antiphony, responsory; palinode; ~ **digter**, palinodist.
teen'see, backwash.
teen'set, countermove.
teen'sin = **teësin**.
teen'sit, (-ge-), offer opposition; *jou* ~, protest, resist; bear up (in misfortune).
teen'slag, setback, reverse, counterstroke.
teen'span, opposition team.
teen'spartel, (-ge-), struggle against, kick against, resent strongly; recalcitrate; ~ **ing**, opposition; resentment.
teen: ~ **speler**, opposite number (player); ~ **spervuur**, counter-barrage; ~ **spier**, antagonist (muscle); ~ **spioenasie**, counter-espionage.
teen'spoed, adversity, ill fortune, ill luck; ambs-ace; check, misadventure; disadventure; hard lines; ~ **diens**, breakdown service.
teenspoe'dig, (-e), unfortunate, ill-fated, disastrous; adverse.
teen'spraak = **teëspraak**.
teen'spreek = **teëspreek**.
teen'staan, (-ge-), resist, withstand; nauseate.
teen'stand, resistance, opposition; antagonism; contravention; ~ *bied*, offer resistance; ~ **er, (-s)**, adversary, opponent, antagonist, enemy, foe.

teen'stel, (-ge-), contrast, oppose; ..*gestelde pool*, antipole; ~**lend,** adversative; antithetic.
teen'stelling, (-e, -s), contrast, set-off; *in* ~ *met sy BROER*, unlike his brother; *in* ~ *MET*, as contrasted with, as against.
teen'stem = **teëstem.**
teen: ~**stof,** antibody; ~**stoot,** counterstroke; counter-action; ~**strewend, (-e),** recalcitrant.
teen'stribbel = **teëstribbel.**
teen'stroom, back-current, backset, counter-current.
teen'stryd: *in* ~ *met,* in conflict with; ~**er,** antagonist.
teenstry'dig, (-e), contradictory, conflicting (opinions), adverse; antagonistic, opposed; ~**heid,** (..**hede**), contradiction; discrepancy; contrariety (law); contrariness (of character).
teen'suur, antacid.
teenswoor'dig, (-e), nowadays, present-day, at present; *vir die* ~ *e,* for the present.
teen'val, (Ndl.), (-ge-), be disappointing; *die klein winsie het teengeval,* the small profit was disappointing.
teen'verkeer, opposite traffic.
teen'verklaring, counter-statement, protest.
teen'verskansing, contravallation.
teen'voeter = **teëvoeter.**
teen'voorstel = **teëvoorstel.**
teen'wal, counterscarp.
teen'wedstryd, return match; return fight.
teen'werp = **teëwerp.**
teen'wig = **teëwig**
teen'wind = **teëwind.**
teenwoor'dig, (-e), present; ~*e TYD,* present tense; ~ *WEES,* be present; ~**heid,** presence; attendance; ~*heid van gees,* presence of mind.
te'ëoffensief, counter-offensive.
te'ëparty, opponent, adversary, rival.
tee'party, tea-party.
tee'pot, teapot; ~**vatlappie,** teapot holder.
tee'pouse, tea-break.
te'ëpraat, (-ge-), contradict, voice objections.
te'ëprater, (-s), contradictor.
te'ëprikkel, counter-irritant.
tee'proewer, tea-taster.
te'ëpruttel, (-ge-), grumble, mutter objections.
teer¹, (s) tar; *dit smaak na* ~ *(ek lus nog meer),* this is delicious, may I have some more? **(w) (ge-),** tar; *iem.* ~ *en veer,* tar and feather someone.
teer², (w) (ge-), consume, live on; *op sy roem* ~, rest on his laurels.
teer³, (b) (tere), tender, slender; gentle; delicate; fine, *'n* ~ *PUNT,* a sore point; *'n tere SAAK,* a delicate matter.
teer'agtig, (-e), tarry.
teer'bemind, (-e), dearly beloved.
teergevoe'lig, (-e), tender, sensitive; susceptible; ~**held,** tenderness, sensitiveness.
teer'gieter, (-s), tar-spreading can.
teerhar'tig, (-e), tender-hearted, soft-hearted; ~**held,** tender-heartedness, fondness.
teerheid, tenderness; delicacy.
teer'houtboom, loxostylis.
teer: ~**ketel,** tar-melter; ~**kleedjie,** tarpaulin; ~**kokery,** tar-works.
teer'kos, provisions (for a journey).
teer'kwas, tar-brush; *'n streep van die* ~ *weghê,* be of mixed blood, have a touch of the tar-brush.
teer'ling, (-e), die, cube; *die* ~ *is gewerp,* the die is cast.
teer'olie, tar-oil.
tee'roos, tea-rose.
teer: ~**paal,** tarred pole; ~**pad,** tarred (asphalt) road; ~**pot,** tar-pot; ~**puts,** tar-bucket; grub; dirty fellow; ~**seep,** tar-soap; ~**seil,** tarpaulin; ~**straat,** tarred (asphalt) street; ~**tou,** dirty (greasy) fellow; ~**vat,** tar-barrel; ~**vernis,** black varnish; ~**vlek,** tar-stain; ~**water,** tar-water; ~**werk,** tarring.
tee'sakkie, tea-bag; *toutjielose* ~, stringless tea-bag.
te'ësang, refrain, antistrophe; palinode.
tee: ~**servet,** tea-napkin; ~**servies,** tea-service.
te'ëset, countermove.
tee'sif, tea-strainer.

te'ësin, aversion, dislike; reluctance, disinclination; antipathy; distaste; ~ *HÊ in,* have an aversion to; *MET* ~, unwillingly; against one's will; *iets met* ~ *TOEGEE,* admit something grudgingly (with a bad grace); ~'**nig, (-e),** averse, chary, reluctant; disinclined.
te'ësit = **teensit.**
te'ëskans, contravallation.
te'ëslag, reverse, set-back; rebuff.
tee: ~**sluier,** tea shower; ~**soort,** kind of tea.
te'ëspartel = **teenspartel.**
te'ëspoed = **teenspoed.**
te'ëspraak, contradiction; disclaimer, denial; protest; contrariety; *in* ~ *KOM met homself,* contradict oneself; *SONDER* ~, without contradiction.
te'ëspreek, (-ge-), contradict, deny, gainsay, disaffirm, counter.
te'ëspreker, (-s), contradictor, gainsayer.
te'ëstaan = **teenstaan.**
te'ëstand = **teenstand.**
tee'stel (-le), tea-set.
te'ëstel = **teenstel.**
te'ëstem, (s) negative vote, dissentient vote; countervote; counterpart (music); **(w) (-ge-),** vote against, vote in the negative, ~**mers,** noes, those who vote in the negative.
te'ëstreef, (-ge-), resist, oppose.
te'ëstribbel, (-ge-), resent, kick against the pricks, demur, recalcitrate.
tee: ~**struik,** tea-bush, tea-shrub; ~**suiker,** sugar candy; ~**tafel,** tea-table; ~**tuin,** tea-garden; ~**tyd,** tea-time.
te'ëval, (-ge-) = **teenval;** ~**ler, (-s),** disappointment.
te'ëvoeter, (-s), antipode.
tee'voorraad, tea-supply.
te'ëvoorstel, counter-proposal, counter-motion.
te'ëwaarde, countervalue.
tee: ~**waentjie,** tea trolley (wagon); ~**water,** tea-water.
te'ëweer, resistance, defence.
te'ëwerk, (-ge-), oppose, thwart; work against, counteract, cross, counterplot, counter, countermine; ~*ende krag,* counter-agent; ~**ing,** opposition; reaction, counterwork, counteraction.
te'ëwerp, (-ge-), object, refute; ~**ing,** exception, objection, refutation, retort; discouragement.
te'ëwig, counterpoise, counterweight; (counter)balance; makeweight; set-off; balance, equiponderance; equipoise; *'n* ~ *vorm teen,* counterbalance.
te'ëwind, adverse (contrary) wind, head wind; noser; ~**e,** baffling winds.
tef, tef'gras, teff.
tegel'demaking, realization, sale.
tegelyk', together, at the same time; *ALMAL* ~, all together; *EEN* ~ *asseblief,* one at a time, please.
tegely'kertyd, simultaneously, at the same time.
tegemoet'gaan, (-gegaan), go to meet; *sy ongeluk* ~, ride for a fall.
tegemoet'kom, (-gekom), meet (someone) half-way; compensate, meet (demand); ~**end, (-e),** obliging, accommodating; ~**endheid,** courtesy, willingness to oblige, complaisance; ~**ing, (-e, -s),** meeting half-way, compensation; obligingness, willingness to accommodate; ~**ingskaal,** relief scale.
tegemoet'loop, (-geloop), go (walk) to meet.
tegemoet'ry, (-gery), ride (drive) out to meet.
tegemoet'sien, (-gesien), look forward to, await.
tegemoet'snel, (-gesnel), rush to meet.
tegemoet'tree, (-getree), advance towards, come forward to meet.
tegniek', technique; technical science, technics.
teg'nies, (-e), technical; ~*e TERME,* technical terms; ~*e UITDRUKKING,* technical phrase; ~*e VAARDIGHEID,* know-how.
teg'nikus, (-se, ..nici), technician.
tegnokraat', (..krate), technocrat.
tegnokrasie', technocracy.
tegnokra'ties, (-e), technocratic.
tegnologie', technology; ..**lo'gies, (-e),** technological; ..**loog', (..loë),** technologist.
tegoed', credit balance.
tehuis', (-e), hostel, home, hospice.

teïen', theine.
tei'ken, (-s), target; objective; ~**gehoor,** target audience; ~**groep,** target group; ~**skiet, (-ge-),** shoot at a target, have rifle-practice.
tei'lings, tailings (diggings).
teï'ne = teïen.
teïs, (-te), theist; ~**me,** theism.
teis'ter, (ge-), afflict, ravage, devastate, scourge; *die ge~de gebiede,* the distressed (stricken) areas; ~**ing, (-e, -s),** affliction, ravaging, devastation, harassment.
teïs'ties, (-e), theistic(al).
te'ken, (s) (-s), token; signal (of distress); mark; symbol; sign; symptom (of disease); indication; *'n ~ van AGTING,* a mark of esteem; *'n ~ GEE,* give a signal; *'n ~ van LEWE,* evidence of life; *OP 'n ~ van,* at a sign of; *as ~ van TOESTEMMING,* as a sign of assent; *'n ~ v.d. TYD,* a sign of the times; *die ~s WYS op,* the indications point to; (w) **(ge-),** sign (a document); draw, sketch (a curve); sketch, pencil, paint (a landscape); autograph (a collector's book); *dit ~ HOM,* that's just like him; *MOOI ge~,* beautifully marked (animal); *na die NATUUR ~,* draw from nature; *~ VIR,* sign for (on behalf of) someone; ~**aap,** pantograph; ~**aar, (-s),** drawer; designer, draughtsman; cartoonist, caricaturist; ~**agtig, (-e),** picturesque, graphic, vivid; ~**bank,** drawing-bench; ~**behoeftes,** drawing-materials; ~**blok,** drawing-block, sketch-block; ~**boek,** drawing-book; sketch-book; ~**bord,** drawing-board; ~**buro,** drawing-office; ~**doos,** drawing-case; ~**driehoek,** set square; ~**end, (-e),** figurative; characteristic; ~**geld,** token money; ~**haak,** T-square, drawing-square; ~**ing, (-e, -s),** signing; signature; design, diagram, drawing, sketch; marking; plotting; plan; ~**ink,** drawing-ink; ~**instrument,** pantograph; ~**kantoor,** drawing-office; ~**karton,** millboard; ~**kryt,** crayon, drawing-chalk; ~**kuns,** art of drawing, draughtsmanship; designing; ~**les,** drawing-lesson; ~**meester,** drawing-master; ~**metode,** method of drawing; ~**munt,** token coin; ~**onderwys,** teaching of drawing; ~**onderwyser,** drawing-teacher; ~**papier,** drawing-paper; ~**passer,** drawing-compasses; , ~**pen,** crayon-holder; drawing-pen; ~**plank,** drawing-board; ~**potlood,** drawing-pencil; ~**prent,** cartoon; ~**skool,** drawing-school; ~**skrif,** hieroglyphics; cuneiform characters (writing); ~**spruit,** aerograph; ~**storie,** comic strip; ~**taal,** sign language; ~**tafel,** drawing-table; plane-table; ~**voorbeeld,** drawing-copy; ~**werk,** drawing(s).
tekort', (s) (-e), deficit, deficiency, shortage; *'n ~ DEK,* cover a deficit; *'n ~ aan MIELIES,* a shortage of maize; *te kort KOM (skiet), see kort;* ~**koming, (-e, -s),** shortcoming, failing, fault, failure, imperfection.
teks, (-te), text (of book); letterpress; words (music); copy; reading-matter (in book); *by die ~ BLY,* stick to one's text; *v.d. ~ RAAK,* stray from the point; *~ en uitleg gee,* quote chapter and verse; ~**boek,** libretto; textbook; handbook; ~**hakie,** square bracket; ~**ie, (-s),** short text; ~**kritiek,** textual criticism; ~**ontleding,** textual analysis.
tekstiel', (-e), textile; ~**bedryf,** textile industry; ~**fabriek,** textile factory; ~**goedere,** soft goods; ~**nywerheid,** textile industry; ~**stof,** textile fabric; ~**vesel,** textile fibre; ~**ware,** textiles, soft (dry) goods.
tekstueel', (..tuele), literal, textual.
tekstuur', (..ture), texture.
teks: ~uitgaaf, ~**uitgawe,** text edition; ~**uitleer, (-s),** exegete, interpreter (of a text); ~**uitlegging,** exegesis; ~**verbeteraar,** castigator; ~**verbetering,** text improvement, castigation; ~**verdraaiing,** false interpretation of texts; ~**verklaarder,** exegete; ~**verklaring,** explication of text, exegesis; ~**vervalsing,** falsification of text; ~**woord,** text.
tektologie', tectology.
tektolo'gies, (-e), tectological.
tektomor'fies, (-e), tectomorphic.
tektoniek', tectonics.
tekto'nies, (-e), tectonic, structural.

tektoniet', tectonite.
tel, (s) count; *die ~ KWYT wees,* lose count; *in 'n PAAR ~le,* in a jiffy, in a moment or two; *op sy ~le PAS,* mind his P's and Q's; *nie in ~ WEES nie,* be unpopular; (w) **(ge-),** count, cast up, (e)numerate; number; keep count; reckon; *sy DAE is ge~,* his days are numbered; *ons ~ nie meer MEE nie,* we don't count anymore; *getelde OPROEPE,* metered calls; *~ vir 3 PUNTE,* this counts (as) 3 points; *hy STAAN daar of hy nie drie kan ~ nie,* he stands there like a dummy; *ek ~ hom onder my VRIENDE,* I regard him as a friend.
telas'telegging, (-e, -s), accusation, imputation.
tel'baar, (..bare), numerable, countable; ~**heid,** numerability.
tel: ~bord, scoring-board, scoreboard; ~**buis,** counter (in games).
te'ledrukker, teletype setter.
telefoneer', (ge-), telephone, phone.
telefonie', telephony; **..fo'nies, (-e),** telephonic, over the phone; *in ..foniese verbinding wees,* be connected by telephone.
telefonis', (-te), telephone operator, telephonist; ~**te, (-s),** (female) telephone operator.
telefoon', (..fone), telephone; *daar is iem. AAN die ~,* there is someone (speaking) on the phone; *'n ~ AANLÊ (insit),* install a telephone; *die ~ BEDIEN,* attend to the telephone; *aan die ~ BLY,* hold the line; *PER ~,* by phone; ~**aanleg,** installation of a phone; ~**aansluiting,** telephone connection; ~**berig,** telephone message; ~**boek,** telephone directory; ~**buro,** telephone exchange (office); ~**diens,** telephone service; ~**draad,** telephone wire; ~**gebruiker,** telephone user; ~**gesprek,** telephone conversation; telephone call; ~**gids,** telephone directory; ~**hokkie,** telephone booth, call-box; ~**horing,** telephone receiver; ~**huisie,** call-box; ~**huur,** telephone subscription; ~**juffrou,** telephonist, exchange-girl, hello-girl; ~**kabel,** telephone cable; ~**kantoor,** telephone exchange; ~**liefie,** call-girl; ~**meisie,** exchange girl, hello-girl; ~**net,** telephone system; ~**nommer,** telephone number; ~**oproep,** telephone call; ~**paal,** telephone pole; ~**personeel,** telephone staff; ~**roete,** telephone route; ~**sel,** call-office; ~**sentrale,** central exchange; ~**snol,** call-girl; ~**toestel,** telephone set; ~**verbinding,** telephone connection.
telefo'to, (-'s), telephoto.
telegraaf', (..grawe), telegraph; ~**beampte,** telegraph official; ~**diens,** telegraph service; ~**draad,** telegraph-wire; ~**kabel,** telegraph-cable; ~**kantoor,** telegraph office; ~**klerk,** telegraph clerk; ~**koste,** telegraph charges; ~**lyn,** telegraph-line; ~**paal,** telegraph-pole; *'n ~paal,* a daddy-long-legs, a red broomstick; ~**roete,** telegraph-route; ~**strokie,** ticker tape; ~**tarief,** telegraph rates; ~**toestel,** telegraphic apparatus, ticker; ~**wese,** telegraph system.
telegrafeer', (ge-), wire, telegraph.
telegrafie', telegraphy; **..gra'fies, (-e),** telegraphic, by wire; **..grafis', (-te),** telegraphist, telegraph operator.
telegram', (-me), telegram, wire; *~ met antwoord betaal,* reply-paid telegram; ~**adres,** telegraphic address; ~**besteller,** telegram-carrier; messenger boy; ~**strook,** telegraphic tape; ~**styl,** telegraphese; ~**vorm,** telegram form; ~**wisseling,** exchange of telegrams.
te'leks, telex, ticker.
telekommunika'sie, telecommunication.
te'lemeter, teleme'ter, (-s), telemeter.
te'lend, (-e), generative; genial.
teleologie', teleology, finality; **..lo'gies, (-e),** teleologic(al).
telepaat', (..pate), telepathist; **..patie',** telepathy, mind-projection; **..pa'ties, (-e),** telepathic.
te'ler, (-s), breeder; grower, cultivator (of grain); raiser; begetter (of children).
te'lersvereniging, breeders' society.
teleskoop', (..skope), telescope; ~**hek,** telescopic gate; **..skopeer', (ge-),** telescope; **..sko'pies, (-e),** telescopic.

teleur'gestel(d), (-de), disappointed; ~ *IN my verwagting*, disappointed of my expectations; ~ *MET die resultaat*, disappointed with the result; ~ *OOR my seun*, disappointed in my son.
teleur'stel, (-ge-), disappoint, fail; frustrate; ~**ling, (-e, -s)**, disappointment, frustration.
televi'sie, television; *draagbare* ~*sender*, portable TV, walkie-lookie; ~**beeld**, television picture; ~**diens**, television service; ~**ontvangs**, television reception; ~**toestel**, television set.
tel'fout, error in counting.
telg, (-e), offshoot, offspring, scion, descendant.
tel'gang, amble, ambling gait (horse); ~**er, (-s)**, ambler, pacer (horse).
te'ling, procreation; breeding; generation, cultivation.
tel'kaart, score-card; honour(s) (card).
tel'kemale, everytime, again and again, time and again.
te'lkens, every time, ever and anon; ~ *as*, whenever.
tel'klerk, tally clerk.
tel'ler, (-s), counter, reckoner, teller; scorer, marker (bisley, golf); numerator (of fraction); ~ *en noemer*, numerator and denominator; ~**y**, counting.
tel'ling, (-e, -s), census; addition; numeration, count; counting; tally, score (games); *in tien* ~*s iets DOEN*, do something in a jiffy; *ELKE tien* ~*s*, every now and then; *geen* ~ *HOU nie*, keep no tally.
tellu'ries, (-e), telluric; tellurian (geol.)
tellu'rium, tellurium; tellurion.
tellu'rometer, tellurome'ter, tellurometer.
tel'masjien, numbering machine.
teloor'gaan, (-ge-), get lost, go by the board.
tel'pas, amble.
tel: ~**raam**, abacus, ball-frame; ~**skaal**, number-chart; scale of notation; ~**werk**, addition (work); ~**woord**, numeral.
tem, (ge-), tame, curb, break in, domesticate, subdue, master.
te'ma, (-s), theme, subject; ~**'ties, (-e)**, thematic; ~**tologie'**, thematology.
tem'baar, (..bare), tamable; ~**heid**, tamability.
Tem'boe, (-s), Tembu; ~**land**, Tembuland.
te'mer, (-s), drawler.
te'merig, (-e), drawling; ~**heid**, drawling manner.
te'mery, drawling.
tem: ~**mer, (-s)**, tamer, trainer; ~**ming**, taming, domestication, training, breaking-in.
tem'pel, (-s), temple; fane; ~**bou**, building of a temple; ~**dienaar**, priest; ~**diens**, temple service; ~**heer**, ~**ier', (-e, -s)**, templar; *Goeie T*~*ier*, Good Templar; ~**ingang**, temple entrance, propylaeum; *T*~**orde**, Order of the Templars; ~**poort**, temple gate; *T*~**ridder**, Knight Templar; ~**skender**, violator of a temple; ~**wyding**, consecration of a temple.
tem'per, (ge-), temper, anneal (steel); moderate, mitigate, allay (pain); tone down (colour, sound); season (iron); damp (ardour); *ge*~*de lig*, subdued light.
tem'pera, distemper; *In* ~ *skilder*, paint in distemper.
temperament', (-e), temperament; temper; ~**vol, (-le)**, spirited; temperamental.
temperatuur', (..ture), temperature; temperament (music); *op* ~ *hou*, maintain the temperature of; ~**afwyking**, difference in temperature; ~**daling**, fall of temperature; ~**meter**, temperature gauge; ~**meting**, thermometry; ~**skommeling**, fluctuation in temperature; ~**staat**, temperature chart; ~**styging**, rise in temperature; ~**verandering**, change of temperature; ~**verhoging**, rise in temperature; ~**verlaging**, lowering of temperature; ~**vermindering**, fall in temperature; ~**verskil**, difference in temperature; ~**wisseling**, variation in temperature.
tem'pering, tempering, moderation; fuse-setting (army).
tem'per: ~**kleur**, tempering colour; ~**mes**, amasette, palette-knife; ~**oond**, tempering furnace; ~**staal**, tempered steel.
tem'pie, (-s), variety of scone.

tem'po, (-'s), tempo (mus.); pace (of horse); rate, speed; *die* ~ *versnel*, quicken the pace.
temporeel', (..rele), temporal; **..porêr', (-e)**, temporary.
temporisa'sie, temporizing; marking time.
temporiseer', (ge-), temporize; mark time.
tempta'sie, (-s), temptation; vexation.
temp'teer, (ge-), vex, tease, annoy.
ten, at, to, in; ~ *AANSIEN van*, with regard to; ~ *AANSKOUE van*, in the sight of; ~ *behoewe van*, for the sake of; ~ *DELE*, partly; ~ *ANTWOORD*, in reply; ~ *DOEL hê*, have as object; ~ *EERSTE*, in the first place; ~ *EINDE*, in order to; ~ *GEVOLGE van*, as a result of; ~ *GOEDE kom*, be of service; ~ *KOSTE van*, at the expense of; ~ *LAASTE*, finally; ~ *LASTE lê*, accuse of; ~ *ene MALE*, in any case; absolutely; ~ *MINSTE*, at least; ~ *NOORDE van*, to the north of; ~ *ONDER gaan*, perish, go under; be brought to ruin; ~ *ONREGTE*, wrongly; ~ *OPSIGTE van*, with respect to; ~ *SLOTTE*, finally; ~ *SPYTE van*, in spite of; ~ *STRYDE trek*, go to war; ~ *TOON stel*, show, exhibit; expose; ~ *TYDE van*, during; ~ *UITVOER bring*, execute; ~ *VOLLE*, completely, fully.
tendens', (-e), tendency, trend; purpose, aim; ~**ie**, tendency; ~**ieus', (-e)**, tendentious, with an underlying purpose; biased; ~**roman**, novel with a moral or purpose; purpose-novel.
ten'der, (s) (-s), tender; (w) (ge-), tender; ~**aar, (-s)**, tenderer; **boot**, tender (vessel), launch; ~**lokomotief**, tank engine; *T*~**raad**, Tender Board; ~**sisteem**, tender system.
ten'do, (-'s), tendon.
ten'ger, (-e) = **tinger;** ~**ig, (-e)** = **tingerig.**
teniet'doen, (-gedoen), annul, countermand, undo; ~**ing**, annulment, cancellation, undoing; *cf.* **niet.**
teniet'gaan, (-gegaan), perish, disappear, come to nought; *cf.* **niet.**
tenk, (-e, -s), tank; cistern; ~**afweerkanon**, anti-tank gun; ~**divisie**, tank division; ~**inhoud**, tankage; ~**kuil**, tank trap; ~**maat**, tankage; ~**motor**, motor tanker; ~**skip**, tanker; ~**versperrings**, dragon's teeth, anti-tank obstacles; ~**wa**, road tanker.
ten'nis, (s) tennis; (w) (ge-), play tennis; ~**arm**, tennis elbow, tennis arm; ~**baan**, tennis court; ~**bal**, tennis ball; ~**klere**, tennis wear; ~**klub**, tennis club; ~**maat**, tennis partner; ~**net**, tennis net; ~**raket**, tennis racquet (racket); ~**speelster**, lady tennis-player; ~**skoen**, tennis shoe; ~**spel**, (game of) tennis; ~**speler**, tennis-player; ~**toernooi**, tennis tournament; ~**wedstryd**, tennis match.
tenoor', (tenore), tenor; ~**party**, tenor part; ~**sanger**, tenor singer; tenor; ~**sleutel**, tenor clef; ~**stem**, tenor (voice).
ten'sie, tension.
ten'simeter, tensimeter.
ten'siometer, tensiometer.
tensy', unless; *ek sal kom* ~ *dit reën*, I shall come unless it rains
tent, (-e), tent, hood (of vehicle); awning (on vessel); pavilion; *sy* ~ *êrens opslaan*, pitch one's tent somewhere; settle somewhere.
tenta'kel, (-s), tentacle.
tenta'men, (-s), preliminary examination.
tentatief', (..tiewe), tentative, experimental.
tent: ~**bewoner**, tent-dweller; ~**dak**, tent-roof; tilt-roof; ~**dek**, sun-deck; ~**doek**, tent-cloth, canvas; ~**hamer**, tent-mallet; ~**kamp**, tent-camp; ~**kar**, hooded cart, tilt-cart; ~**klap**, fly (of tent); ~**maker**, tent-maker.
tentoon'spreiding, display.
ten toon stel, *see* **ten** *and* **toon.**
tentoon'steller, exhibitor; exposer.
tentoon'stelling, (-e, -s), show, exhibition, display, exposure.
tentoon'stellings: ~**gebou**, exhibition building; ~**terrein**, show-grounds.
tent: ~**paal**, tent-pole; ~**pen**, tent-peg; ~**skuit**, tilt-boat; ~**steek**, tent-stitch; ~**wa**, hooded (covered) wagon.

tenue′, uniform, dress; *in GROOT* ~, in full dress, in full uniform; *in KLEIN* ~, in military undress.
tenuit′voerbrenging, execution (of plan); carrying out, implementation.
teodisee′, (..seë), theodicy.
teodoliet′, (-e), theodolite.
teofanie′, theophany.
teogonie′, theogony.
teokrasie′, theocracy.
teokra′ties, (-e), theocratic.
teologie′, theology.
teolo′gies, (-e), theological; ~*e skool*, theological school (seminary).
teoloog′, (..loë), theologian.
teore′ma, (-s), theorem, proposition.
teore′ties, (-e), theoretical, academical; ~*e mening*, arm-chair opinion.
teore′tikus, (..tici, -se), theorist.
teoretiseer′, (ge-), theorize, speculate.
teorie′, (-ë), theory, speculation; *in* ~ *en praktyk*, in theory and in practice.
teosofie′, theosophy; ..**so′fies**, (-e), theosophic(al); ..**soof′**, (..sowe), theosophist.
te′pel, (-s), nipple, teat, dug, papilla, mamilla; ~**beskermer**, nipple-shield; ~**spier**, papillary muscle; ~**vormig**, (-e), mastoid, papillary, papillate, mamilliform.
ter, at to, in; ~ *AARDE bestel*, inter, bury; ~ *BESKIKKING stel*, put at the disposal of; ~ *BESTUDERING*, in order to study; ~ *BETALING van*, in payment of; ~ *DOOD bring*, execute; ~ *ELFDER ure*, at the eleventh hour; ~ *HAND neem*, take in hand; ~ *HARTE neem*, take to heart; ~ *INLIGTING*, for (your) information; *te LAND en* ~ *see*, by land and (by) sea; ~ *LEEN gee*, make a loan of; *iem.* ~ *ORE kom*, reach someone's ear; ~ *PLAATSE*, in loco; at the spot; ~ *RUSTE lê*, lay to rest; ~ *SAKE*, to the point; ~ *hand STEL*, hand over, present; ~ *syner TYD*, in his own (sweet) time; ~ *wille WEES*, be obliging; *waar* ~ *WÊRELD is ons?* where in the world are we? ~ *WILLE van*, for the sake of.
teraar′debestelling, (-e, -s), interment, burial.
terapeut′, (-e), therapeutist; therapist; ~**ies**, (-e), therapeutic(al).
terapie′, therapeutics; therapy.
terde′ë, thoroughly, soundly; duly; *ek BESEF dit* ~, I fully realize that; *iem.* ~ *die WAARHEID sê*, tell someone the plain truth.
terdood′brenging, putting to death, execution.
terdood′veroordeling, condemnation to death.
terdui′wel, rascal, rogue, blackguard; *wie* ~? who the devil?
tê′re = **terg(e)**.
tereg′, rightly, justly, correctly, duly, deservedly, reasonably, aright, with good reason; ~ *BEROEMD wees*, be deservedly famous; *hulle KLA daaroor en* ~, they complain about it and with reason; ~**bring**, (-gebring), put in order, arrange; reclaim (from vice); ~**help**, (-ge-), set right; direct; get out of trouble; ~**kom**, (-ge-), arrive at; come right, land; *sal die brief so* ~*kom?* will the letter reach its destination like this? ~**staan**, (-ge-), stand trial, be tried.
tereg′stel, (-gestel), execute; ~**ling**, (-e, -s), execution.
tereg′wys, (-gewys), show the right way, set right; instruct; rebuke, admonish, reprimand, reprove; ~**end**, (-e), admonitory; ~**ing**, (-e, -s), admonition, correction, reproof, rebuke, rating.
terg, (ge-), tease, annoy, nag, irritate, rally, provoke, harass, exasperate, chaff, torment, bait, gall; ~**ag′tig**, (-e), fond of teasing; annoying; ~**ag′tigheid**, devilment.
ter′ge, (gew.), (ge-), = **terg**.
terg: ~**end**, (-e), harassing, galling, exasperating, annoying, provocative, provoking, vexatious; ~**er**, (-s), teaser, provoker; ~**erig**, (-e), given to teasing; annoying, puckish, quizzical.
ter′gery, teasing, nagging, provoking, baiting, legpulling.
terg′gees, nagging fellow, tormentor, tease(r), legpuller.

ter′ging, provocation; teasing; exasperation.
terg′siek, (-e), fond of teasing.
terhand′stelling, handing over, delivery.
te′ring, consumption, phthisis, tuberculosis, silicosis; expense; *die* ~ *na die NERING sit*, cut one's coat according to one's cloth; *VLIEËNDE* ~, galloping consumption; ~**ag′tig**, (-e), hectic, consumptive, tuberculous, phthisical; ~**ag′tigheid**, consumptiveness; ~**bestryding**, prevention of tuberculosis; ~**blos**, hectic flush; ~**bos**, *Thesium sp.*; ~**hoes**, hectic cough; ~**kleur**, hectic flush; ~**koors**, hectic fever; ~**lyer**, consumptive (patient), hectic.
teriomor′fies, (-e), theriomorphic.
ter′leton, turlington.
terloops′, (b) (-e), casual, incidental (remark); (bw) by the way, incidentally, cursorily, in passing, casually, obiter dictum.
term¹, (-e), term; phrase; *die* ~*e van die BESLUIT*, the terms of the decision; *in KRAGTIGE* ~*e uitgedruk*, expressed in forcible (vigorous) terms, strongly worded; *binne die* ~*e van die WET*, within the terms (provisions) of the law.
term², (-e), therm (unit of heat).
termaal′, (termale), thermal.
termiek′, (-e), thermic convection current.
ter′mies, (-e), thermal; ~*e vermoë*, thermal capacity.
termiet′, (-e), white ant; termite; thermite.
termina′sie, termination.
termineer′, (ge-), terminate, end.
terminologie′, nomenclature, terminology; ..**lo′gies**, (-e), terminological; ..**loog′**, (..loë), terminologist.
ter′minus, (-se, ..ni), terminus.
termio′nies, (-e), thermionic.
termochemie′, thermochemistry; ..**che′mies**, (-e), thermochemical.
termodina′mies, (-e), thermodynamic.
termodina′mika, thermodynamics.
termoëlektrisiteit′, thermo-electricity.
ter′mofiel, (-e), thermophilic.
termogeen′, (..gene), thermogene.
termograaf′, (..grawe), thermograph.
ter′mokoppel, thermocouple.
ter′mokrag, thermo-electrical power.
ter′mometer, (-s), thermometer; ~**bol**, thermometer bulb; ~**lesing**, ~**stand**, thermometer reading.
termometrie′, thermometry.
termome′tries, (-e), thermometric(al).
termonukleêr′, (-e), thermonuclear.
ter′moplasties, (-e), thermoplastic.
termoskoop′, (..skope), thermoscope.
termostaat′, (..state), thermostat.
termosta′ties, (-e), thermostatic.
termoterapie′, thermotherapy.
termyn′, (-e), term, time; period; time-limit; instalment; currency (of a bill); *in* ~*e BETAAL*, pay by instalment(s); *BINNE die vasgestelde* ~, within the appointed time; *op KORT* ~, at short date; *op LANG* ~, at long date; *OP* ~, for account; ~**afdoening**, part-payment; ~**betaling**, time-payment; ~**handel**, forward trade; dealing in futures; ~**huur**, periodic lease; ~**mark**, futures market; ~**obligasie**, debenture; ~**polis**, endowment policy; ~**prys**, price of futures; ~**saak**, time-bargain; ~**valuta**, forward exchange.
terneer′druk, (-ge-), weigh down, make despondent.
terneer′gebuig, (-de), prostrate.
terneer′gedruk, (-te), despondent, depressed; ~**theid**, despondency, dejection.
terneer′geslae, dejected, down-hearted, cast-down, crestfallen, dispirited; ~**nheid**, dejection.
ternêr′, (-e), ternary.
ternou′ernood, scarcely, barely, hardly; ~ *GENOEG vir een*, barely sufficient for one; ~ *ONTKOM*, have a hairbreadth escape.
terpentyn′, turpentine, oil of terebinth; ~**agtig**, (-e), like turpentine; ~**boom**, turpentine-tree, mopane (*Copaifera*), terebinth; ~**gras**, turpentine-grass (*Cymbopogon excavatus*); ~**olie**, (oil of) turpentine, turps.
terpi′neol, terpineol.
terra-cot′ta, terracotta.
terra′rium, (..ria, -s), terrarium.

terras', (-se), terrace; ~ **bou,** terrace cultivation; ~ **gooier,** terracing-grader; ~ **land,** terrace country; ~ **sebou,** rows of houses along the face of a slope; ~ **seer'**, (ge-), terrace; ~ **tuin,** terraced garden; ~ **vormig,** (-e), terraced.

terrein', (-e), building-site, ground; sphere, domain, province (of thought); yard; *die* ~ *v.d. GESKIEDENIS*, the field of history; *op GEVAARLIKE* ~, on dangerous ground; *ONBEBOUDE* ~, a vacant stand (piece of ground); *VERBODE* ~, forbidden ground (area); *die* ~ *VERKEN*, explore the ground; reconnoitre; *VERLORE* ~ *herwin*, regain lost ground; ~ **aanleg,** landscape-gardening; ~ **argitek,** landscape architect; ~ **baken,** landmark (aero.); ~ **beplanner,** landscape designer; ~ **dekking,** plot coverage; building; ~ **gesteldheid,** feature; position of the ground; ~ **hoek,** ground angle; ~ **huur,** site-rent; ~ **insinking,** depression, sunken place; ~ **kaart,** topographical map; ~ **kenmerke,** ground features; ~ **kennis,** field knowledge; knowledge of the ground; ~ **leer,** topography; ~ **meting,** ground survey; ~ **onderhoud,** yard-maintenance; ~ **oneffenhede,** unevenness of the ground; ~ **opname,** ground-survey, sketch; ~ **tekening,** ground-sketch; ~ **verkenning,** reconnaissance; ~ **vorm,** ground features (aero.); ~ **waarde,** site-value; ~ **water,** surface water; ~ **wins,** territorial gain.

terreur', terror, terrorism.
ter'riër, (-s), terrier.
territoriaal', (..riale), territorial.
territo'rium, (-s), territory.
terroris', (-te), terrorist; ~ **a'sie,** terrorisation; ~ **eer'**, (ge-), terrorize; ~ **me,** terrorism.
terself'dertyd, at the same time.
terset', (-te), terzetto.
Tersiêr', (-e), Tertiary (period).
tersi'ne, (-s), tercet, terzina.
tersluiks', on the sly, stealthily, furtively.
terstond', at once, immediately, forthwith.
tersy'de, (s) (-s), aside (stage).
tersy'(de), (bw) aside; ~ *STAAN*, stand by, assist, help; ~ *STEL*, put aside, take no notice of; ~ **lating,** leaving aside; ~ **stelling,** putting aside, neglect, disregard.
tert, (-e), tart; pie; *oop* ~, flan; ~ **bakker,** pastry-cook, confectioner; ~ **deeg,** puff pastry; ~ **dop,** pastry shell; ~ **gebak,** pastry; ~ **jie,** (-s), tartlet; ~ **kors,** tart crust; ~ **pan,** tart-pan; ~ **roller,** pastry-roll.
terts, (ong., mus.), (-e), third (music); tierce; *GROOT* ~, major third; *KLEIN* ~, minor third.
tert'vulsel, tart-filling.
terug', back, backwards; ago; aback; *HEEN en* ~, there and back; ~ *na die KERK*, back to the church; *'n PAAR maande* ~, a few months ago; ~ **aangee,** reverse pass; ~ **aarding,** throw-back; atavism.
terug'besorg, (~), return, cause to be returned; ~ **ing,** return; ~ **ingsbewys,** clearance certificate.
terug'betaal, (~), pay back, reimburse, repay, refund; quit; ~ **baar,** (..bare), repayable.
terug'betaling, repayment, refund, reimbursement; ~ **sboek,** refund-book.
terug'blik, (s) retrospective view; retrospect; (w) (-ge-), look back, cast a glance backward, pass in review.
terug'boek, (-ge-), write back, reverse (entry).
terug'bring, (-ge-), return, bring back, restore; reclaim; *'n boete tot die helfte* ~, reduce a fine by half; ~ **ing,** reduction, bringing back.
terug'buig, (-ge-), bend back, recurve; ~ **ing,** bending back, recurvature.
terug'deins, (-ge-), shrink from, flinch, quail, funk (football), wince, recoil; ~ **ing,** recoil, wincing, flinching.
terug'dink, (-ge-), recall to mind, cast back one's thoughts.
terug'draai, (-ge-), turn back, reverse.
terug'dring, (-ge-), press (push) back.
terug'dryf, terug'drywe, (-ge-), repel, drive back, repulse; drift back.
terug'eis, (-geëis), reclaim, demand back, redemand.

terug'fiets, (-ge-), cycle back.
terug'flits, (-e), flashback.
terug'gaan, (-ge-), go back, retrace one's steps; hark back; *tot die Middeleeue* ~, reach back to the Middle Ages; ~ **de,** recessional; recessive.
terug'gang, going back; decline, retrogression.
terug'gawe, restitution, reddition, return, giving back, redelivery.
terug'gebuig, (-de), recurvate.
terug'gee, (-ge-), return, restore, give back, redeliver.
terug'getrokke, reserved, retiring, distant, reclusive; ~ **nheid,** reserve, aloofness, closeness.
terug'gevorder, (-de), reclaimed.
terug'gevou, (-de), folded back.
terug'gooi, (-ge-), cast back.
terug'groet, (-ge-), return a salutation, acknowledge a greeting.
terug'haal, (-ge-), fetch back.
terug'hê (-gehad), have back.
terug'hou, (-ge-), keep back, retain; refrain (from deed); hold back, withhold; hold at bay (enemy); ~ **'dend,** (-e), distant, incommunicative, reserved, guarded, close; disinclined to buy (shares); ~ **'dendheid,** reticence, reserve(dness), distance; ~ **ding,** keeping back; reserve; detention; *reg van* ~ **ding,** lien; ~ **dingsvermoë,** retentivity.
terug'ja(ag), (-ge-), drive back; race back.
terug'kaats, (-ge-), reflect, throw back (sound); return (ball); re-echo, reverberate; ~ **ing,** (-e, -s), reflection, echo, reverberation; ~ **ingshoek,** angle of reflection.
terug'kabel, (s) return cable; (w) (-ge-), cable back.
terug'kap, (-ge-), retort (sharply).
terug'keer, (s) return; recurrence; (w) (-ge-), return, turn back; head back; revert (to old method); *terugkerende breuk,* recurring decimal; ..**kering,** reversion.
terug'kom, (-ge-), come back (home), return; recur; ~ *na iem.,* come back to someone, contact someone again; ~ *op 'n saak,* revert to a matter; ~ **kaartjie,** (-s), pass-out, return card.
terug'komend, (-e), returning, recurrent.
terug'koms return.
terug'koop, (-ge-), buy back, repurchase, redeem.
terug'koppeling, back-coupling, feedback; retroaction.
terug'krabbel, (-ge-), back out of, go back on one's promise, wriggle out of; ~ **ing,** backing-out, climb-down.
terug'krimp, (-ge-), shrink back, gather.
terug'krul, (-ge-), recoil, backspin.
terug'kry, (-ge-), get back, recover; receive in return; get change; ~ **ging,** recovery.
terug'kyk, (-ge-), look back; ~ **spieël,** rear-view mirror.
terug'lading, return cargo.
terug'lei, (-ge-), lead back; reduce.
terug'lesing, backsight (survey).
terug'loop, (-ge-), walk back; flow back; recoil (cannon).
terug'mars, homeward (return) march; ~ **jeer,** (-ge-), march back.
terug'name, taking back, retraction, withdrawal, recaption.
terug'neem, (-ge-), take back, retract (one's words); reassume (position); recall (dismissed officer); withdraw; reinstate (striker).
terug'plaas, (-ge-), put back, replace; reinstate.
terug'plof, (s) backfire; (w) (-ge-), backfire.
terug'reis, return journey; homeward journey; (w) (-ge-), return, travel back.
terug'reken, (-ge-), reckon back(wards), work back.
terug'rit, drive (ride) back, homeward drive.
terug'roei, (-ge-), row back.
terug'roep, (-ge-), call back, encore (actor); recall (ambassador); hark back (memory); ~ **ing,** recall.
terug'ry, (-ge-), ride back, drive back.
terug'seil, (-ge-), sail back.
terug'sender, returning officer.
terug'sending, return, sending back; reconsignment.
terug'setting, set-back, reverse; putting back; demotion (army); reduction (law).

terug'sien, (-ge-), look back, see back; see again.
terug'sit, (-ge-), put back, replace; demote; reduce (to ranks); handicap.
terug'skakel, (-ge-), switch back; change down (gears); telephone back.
terug'skiet, (-ge-), shoot back.
terug'skop, (-ge-), kick back.
terug'skrik, (-ge-), recoil, shrink from; ~ *vir,* shrink (flinch) from.
terug'skryf, terug'skrywe, (-ge-), answer a letter, reply, write back.
terug'skuif, terug'skuiwe, (-ge-), slide back; push back.
terug'slaan, (-ge-), repulse, repel, beat back (the enemy); hit back (with fist); turn back (leaf); return (ball); rebound; rebut; revert (to type); *op 'n vorige hoofstuk* ~, refer to a previous chapter; ~ **de,** atavistic.
terug'slag, recoil, bounce (spring); rebound; set-back (illness); reverse; counterstroke; backset; back-fire (motor); reversion to type; relapse (invalid); ~ **breker,** recoil-absorber; ~ **plaat,** baffle plate; ~ **veer,** baffle spring (tools);
terug'slaner, one who hits back; receiver (tennis).
terug'snel, (-ge-), hasten back.
terug'sny, (-ge-), cut back.
terug'speel, (-ge-), play back, return (a ball, shot); return lead (cards).
terug'spoed, (-ge-), rush (hasten, hurry) back.
terug'spoeling, backwash.
terug'spring, (-ge-), jump back; recoil, rebound, resile; ~**ing,** resilience.
terug'sprong, backward jump; rebound, recoil.
terug'staan, (-ge-), stand back; retire (from contest); *vir iem.* ~, give precedence to someone, stand down for someone.
terug'steek, riposte.
terug'stel, (-ge-), place back, put back, set back; ~ **ling,** retrogression, set-back.
terug'stoot, (s) rebound; recoil (of gun); counterbluff; (w) **(-ge-),** push back, rebuff, repulse, repel; counter-bluff.
terug'stotend, (-e), repulsive, repellent.
terug'stoting, rebuff, repulse.
terug'stroming, flowing back, flow reflux.
terug'stroom, (-ge-), flow back.
terug'stuit, (-ge-), recoil, rebound; redound; *vir niks* ~ *nie,* dare anything; shrink from nothing; ~**ing,** rebound.
terug'stuur, (-ge-), send back, return; *teruggestuurde leë houers,* empty returns.
terug'swaai, (s) backswing; (w) **(-ge-),** swing back.
terug'swem, (-ge-), swim back.
terug'tog, retreat; *iem. se* ~ *AFSNY,* cut off someone's line of retreat; *die* ~ *BLAAS,* sound the retreat; ~ *slyn,* line of retreat (withdrawal).
terug'trap, (-ge-), tread back; back-pedal; ~ **rem,** back-pedal brake.
terug'tredend, (-e), withdrawing, recessive.
terug'treding, retirement; recession.
terug'tree, (-ge-), step back; withdraw.
terug'trek, (-ge-), retreat; withdraw (one's hand); retract (one's words); recall (envoy); pull back; retire; fall back (army); scratch (sport); *jou* ~, retire from; ~ **king,** withdrawal; retreat; retirement; recantation, retraction; ~ **spier,** retraction muscle; ~ **veer,** release spring.
terug'vaar, (-ge-), sail back, return by sea; ~ **t,** return trip (voyage).
terug'val, (s) (-le), retreat; fall-out; (w) **(-ge-),** fall back, drop back (in right place); relapse; backslide (into wrong-doing); ~ *na,* revest in; ~ **ler,** recidivist.
terug'verlang, (~), wish back, yearn nostalgically for.
terug'verplaas, (~), retransfer; ..**plasing,** retransfer.
terug'vertaal, (~), retranslate.
terug'vervoer, (~), reconvey; convey back.
terug'verwys, (~), refer back; remit, recommit; ~**ing,** recommittal, remittal.
terug'vind, (-ge-), recover.
terug'vlieg, (-ge-), fly back.

terug'vloei, (-ge-), flow back; ~ **end, (-e),** refluent; ~**ing,** reflux.
terug'vlug, return flight.
terug'voer, (-ge-), carry back; lead back; ~**ing,** feedback.
terug'vorder, (-ge-), claim back, reclaim, redemand, demand again, ask back; ~ **baar, (..bare),** recoverable; reclaimable; ~**ing,** withdrawal; demand (money); recovery, reclamation.
terug'vra, (-ge-), ask back, demand the return of.
terug'wen, (-ge-), win back, regain, recover.
terug'werk, (-ge-), work back; retroact; react; *die motor laat* ~, reverse the engine; ~ **end, (-e),** retrospective; *met* ~ *ende krag,* with retrospective force; ~**ing,** reaction; retroaction.
terug'werp, (-ge-), cast (throw) back; return, reflect.
terug'win = terugwen; ~**ning,** recovery, reclamation.
terug'wyk, (-ge-), recede, retreat, fall back; ~**ing,** retreat, retrocession.
terug'wys, (-ge-), point backwards; reject.
terwyl', while, as whilst, whereas, in the meanwhile.
tes, (-se), earthen fire-pot; chafing-dish, fire-pan.
tesaam', tesa'me, together, altogether.
te'sis, (-se), thesis; *M.A.-tesis,* M.A. thesis.
tesourie', treasury; ~ **r, (-e, -s),** treasurer; quaestor (of synod); purse-bearer; ~ **re, (-s),** (lady) treasurer; ~**r-generaal, (tesouriers-generaal),** treasurer-general.
tes'sie, *see* **tes.**
testament', (-e), testament; will; *by* ~ *BEMAAK,* bequeath by will; *sy* ~ *laat MAAK,* admit defeat; throw in the towel; *hy kan maar sy* ~ *MAAK,* he is done for; *iem. in sy* ~ *NOEM,* remember someone in one's will; *die OU en die Nuwe T* ~, the Old and the New Testament; *SONDER* ~, intestate; ~ **bepaling,** term of a will; ~ **êr', (-e),** testamentary; ~ **loosheid,** intestacy; ~ **maakster, (-s),** testatrix; ~ **maker, (-s),** testator.
testateur', (-e, -s), testator.
testatri'se, (-s), testatrix.
testeer', (ge-), bequeath; make a will; test (metal).
tes'tikel, (-s), testicle.
testimo'nium, (-s), testimonial.
tetanie', (-e), tetany; ..**ta'nies, (-e),** tetanic.
tet, (-te), (plat), woman's breast, teat, tit.
tetanis'me, tetanism.
te'tanus, tetanus, lockjaw.
tête-a-tê'te, tête-a-tête; private interview (conversation).
te'ties, (-e), thetical.
tetra'de, (-s), tetrad.
tetraë'der, (-s), tetrahedron.
tetraëdraal', (..drale), tetrahedral.
tetralogie', tetralogy.
tetrarg', (-e), tetrarch.
teu'el, (-s), bridle, rein; check, restrain; *die* ~ *s van BEWIND,* the reins of government; *die* ~ *s KORT (styf) hou,* keep a tight rein; *die* ~ *s laat SKIET,* give more rope; allow more scope; give rein; *die VRYE* ~ *gee,* give a free hand; allow a free hand; ~ **hand,** bridle-hand; ~ **loos, (..lose),** unrestrained, unbridled; excessive; ~ **loosheid,** unrestrainedness; excess.
teug, (teue), draught, mouthful, sip, swig, gulp; *in EEN* ~, at a draught; *met VOLLE teue drink,* drink deep draughts, gulp down; *met VOLLE teue geniet,* enjoy to the full.
Teutoon', (..tone), Teuton; ~ **s', (-e),** Teutonic.
teveel', excess; surplus; ~ **betaling,** overpayment.
tevergeefs', in vain, unsuccessfully, without effect (avail), to no end, to no purpose, with no effect, for nothing.
tevoor'skynkoming, emersion; appearance.
tevo're, before, previously.
tevre'de, (~ -ner, -nste; meer ~, mees ~), satisfied, content(ed); complacent; happy; pleased; ~ **nheid,** contentment, contentedness, satisfaction; ~ **stelling,** satisfaction.
tewa'terlater, launcher.
tewa'terlating, launching.
teweeg'bring, (-gebring), effect, bring about, cause, produce.

te'wens, besides, also, at the same time; *'n saal vir vergaderinge wat* ~ *as kerk dien,* a hall for meetings which also serves as church.
tewerk'stelling, employment.
T'-haak, T square.
Thebaan', (..**bane**), Theban; ~**s'**, (-e), Theban.
The'be, Thebes.
Tho'mas, Thomas; *'n ongelowige* ~, a doubting Thomas; ~**slak,** basic slag; ~**-staal,** basic steel.
Thra'sië, Thrace; ~**r,** (-s), Thracian; **Thrasies,** (-e), Thracian.
Thu'le, Thule.
tia'ra, (-s), tiara.
Ti'ber, Tiber.
Tibe'rias: *Meer van* ~, Lake of Tiberias; Sea of Galilee.
tibet'[1], tibet (material).
Tibet'[2], Tibet; ~ **aan',** (..**tane**), Tibetan; ~ **aans',** (-e), Tibetan.
ti'bia, (-s), tibia, shin-bone.
tie'kie, (-s), tickey, threepenny bit.
tie'kiedraai, (-gedraai), dance; picnic dances, folk-dances.
tie'mie, thyme, basil; ~ **agtig,** (-e), thymy; ~ **gliserine,** glycerin(e) of thymol.
tien, (-e), ten; ~ *teen EEN,* ten to one; *hy lyk of hy nie* ~ *kan TEL nie,* he does not seem too bright; ~ **daags,** (-e), of ten days, every ten days; ~ **de,** (-s), tenth, tithe; ~ *des betaal,* (pay) tithe(s).
tien'de: ~ **heffer,** (-s), tithe-gatherer, tither; ~ **heffing,** tithing.
tiende'lig, (-e), decimal, decennial; ~ *e BREUK,* decimal fraction; ~ *e STELSEL,* decimal (metric) system.
tien'depligtig, (-e), tithable.
tien'der, (-s), teenager.
tien'dereg, right to levy tithes.
tien'derjarig, (-e), teen-aged; ~ **e,** (-s), teenager, bobby-soxer (girl).
tien: ~ **dubbel(d),** (-e), tenfold, decuple; ~ **duisendste,** ten thousandth; ~ **er,** teenager; ~ **hoek,** decagon; ~ **jarig,** (-e), of ten years, ten years old, decennial; ~ **kamp,** decathlon; ~ **lettergrepig,** (-e), decasyllabic; ~ **manskap,** decemvirate; ~ **ponder,** (-s), ten-pounder; ~ **potig,** ~ **po'tig,** (-e), ten-legged; ~ **randnoot,** ten-rand note; ~ **reëlig,** (-e), of ten lines; ~ **sjielingstuk,** half-sovereign; ~ **snarig,** (-e), with ten strings; ~ **tal,** ten; decade; dicker (of hides); ~ **tallig,** (-e), decimal, denary; ~ **uur,** ten o'clock; ~ **vlak,** decahedron; ~ **voud,** (-e), decuple; ~ **vou'dig,** (-e), tenfold.
tier[1], (s) (-e, -s), tiger, S.A. leopard; *die* ~ *het hom GEBYT,* he is worse for drink; *OU* ~! well done! what a man! *sy* ~ *TEËKOM,* have met his match; *iem. se* ~ *WEES,* be someone's superior; be more than a match for someone.
tier[2], (w) rage, rant, bluster, storm; *die* ~ *ende gespuis,* the raging mob.
tier[3], (w) thrive, flourish, prosper; *plante wat orals* ~, plants which thrive everywhere.
tier: ~ **agtig,** (-e), tigrish; tigerlike; ~ **boskat,** serval.
tierelier', (ge-), warble, sing, twitter.
tierentyn', linsey-woolsey.
tier: ~ **haai,** tiger-shark; ~ **hok,** tiger's cage; ~ **jagter,** tiger-hunter; ~ **kat,** tiger-cat.
tierlantyn'tjie, (-s), flourish, trifle, knick-knack, pretty-pretties, frippery, fandangle, gewgaw, bauble, furbelow, ornament.
tier: ~ **leeu,** (-s), tigon; ~ **lelie,** tiger-lily; ~ **mannetjie,** tiger; ~ **melk,** strong drink, fire-water; *hy het* ~ *melk gedrink,* he has had a drop too many; ~ **oog,** tiger's-eye (min.); tiger-eye; ~ **val,** tiger-trap; ~ **vel,** tiger's skin; ~ **wolf,** spotted hyena; ~ **wyfie,** tigress; *so kwaai soos 'n* ~ *wyfie,* as fierce as a tigress.
tiet, (-e), nipple, teat.
tifeus', (-e), typhoid, enteric; ~ *e koors,* typhoid (enteric) fever.
tifoon', (**tifone**), typhoon.
ti'fus, typhus fever, camp-fever; ~ **basil,** typhus bacillus.
tik, (s) (-ke), pat, touch; typing; tap (billiards); flip,

flick, tick (of watch); rap (with stick); (w) **(ge-),** tap, rap, dab, pat; tick (of watch); type; chip (golf); *ge* ~ *wees,* have a screw loose; ~ **hou(tjie),** chip, chip-shot (golf); ~ **kamer,** typing-office; ~ **kantoor,** typing-office; ~ **ker,** typist, ticker; ~ **kie,** little bit; pat, slight touch; hint, tinge; *'n* ~ *kie PEPER,* a dash of pepper; *hy* ~ *kie te VEEL,* a bit too much; ~ **masjien,** typewriter; ~ **poel,** typing pool; ~ **rol,** platen; ~ **skoppie,** tap kick (rugby); ~ **skrif,** typing; ~ **ster,** (-s), (lady) typist.
tik'tak, tick-tack, pit-a-pat; backgammon; ~ **tol',** noughts and crosses.
tik'werk, typing.
til: *daar is iets op* ~, there is something afoot.
tila'pia, (-s), tilapia.
til'da, til'de, tilde (phonetic nasalation sign).
tim'bre, timbre, tone-colour.
timiditeit', timidity.
tim'mer, (ge-), build, construct, carpenter, do carpenter's work; *hy* ~ *nie baie hoog nie,* he won't set the Thames on fire; ~ **a'sie,** (-s), timbering; framework (of a roof), structure; ~ **gereedskap,** carpenter's tools; ~ **hout,** timber lumber; ~ **houtwerf,** timber-yard.
tim'merman, (-ne, -s), carpenter.
tim'mermans: ~ **ambag,** carpenter's trade, carpentry; ~ **baas,** master carpenter; ~ **byl,** half-hatchet; ~ **gereedskap,** carpenter's tools; ~ **waterpas,** plumb-rule; ~ **(werk)winkel,** carpenter's shop.
tim'mer: ~ **werf,** carpenter's yard; timber-yard; ~ **werk,** carpentering, joinery.
timokrasie', timocracy; ..**kra'ties,** (-e), timocratic.
Timo'theüs, Timothy.
timpaan', (timpane), tympan (in printing); tympanum, eardrum.
ti'mus, thymus; ~ **klier,** thymus gland.
tin, tin, pewter; ~ **agtig,** (-e), tin-like, stannic; ~ **as,** tin-ashes, tin-putty; ~ **erts,** tin-ore; ~ **foelie,** tin foil.
tin'gel, (ge-), tinkle, jingle; ~ **ing',** tingling; ~ **ing'eling,** ting-a-ling; ting-ting; ~ **tan'gel,** (-s), café chantant; penny gaff.
tin'ger, slender, delicate, slight, slim; ~ **heid,** slenderness, slimness, fragility, frailness.
tin'gerig, (-e), slender, slim, fragile, frail, tender; reedy; puny; ~ **heid** = **tingerheid.**
tin'gieter, tinman, tinsmith, pewterer; *politieke* ~, armchair politician; a political tinkerer; ~ **y,** tinsmith's workshop.
tin: ~ **groewe,** tin-mine; ~ **houdend,** (-e), tinny, stanniferous.
tin'kel, (ge-), tinkle.
tin'kies, stannite.
tinktin'kie, (-s), cisticola.
tinktuur', (tinkture), tincture.
tin: ~ **myn,** tin-mine; stannery; ~ **oplossing,** solution of tin; ~ **soldeersel,** soft solder; ~ **steen,** cassiterite; ~ **suur,** stannic acid.
tint, (s) (-e), tinge, hue, tint, shade, colour; (w) **(ge-),** tinge, colour, dye.
tin'tel, (s) tingling (of the fingers); twinkle; (w) **(ge-),** twinkle (of star); sparkle, scintillate; tingle; ~ **end,** (-e), sparkling, crisp; ~ **ing,** (-e, -s), twinkling, sparkling; tingling; ~ **oog, (ge-),** sparkle (eyes); ~ **tonnetjie,** funny-bone.
tint: ~ **ing,** tinting; ~ **meter,** tintometer; ~ **wyn,** tinto.
tin'werk, pewter-work.
tip, (s) (-pe), tip, point, extremity.
ti'pe, (-s), type, character.
tipeer', (ge-), typify, characterize.
tipe'rend, (-e), typical.
tip'hou, snick.
ti'pies, (-e), typical.
tipis', (-te), typist; ~ **te,** (-s), (lady) typist.
tipograaf', (..**grawe**), typographer; ..**grafie',** tipography; ..**gra'fies,** (-e), typographic(al).
tipologie', typology; ..**lo'gies,** (-e), typological(ly).
tip'pie, (-s), tip, point, extreme end; *op die* ~, in the very nick of time; *wag tot OP die* ~, wait until the last moment.
tip'tol, (-le), bulbul.
tira'de, (-s), tirade.

tiran', (-ne), tyrant.
tirannie', (-ë), tyranny.
tiranniek', (-e), tyrannical, proscriptive.
tiran'nies, (-e), tyrannical.
tiranniseer', (ge-), tyrannize, bully.
Tirol', Tyrol; ~er, (-s), Tyrolese.
Tirools', (-e), Tyrolese.
titaan', titanium; ~houdend, (-e), titaniferous; ~sement, titan cement.
ti'tan, (-e), titan, giant.
tita'nies, (-e), titanic.
titaniet', titanite.
tita'nium, titanium.
ti'tel, (s) (-s), title, heading; caption (cartoon); (w) (ge-), entitle, style; title; ~blad, title-page; ~geveg, title-fight; ~houer, title-holder; ~plaat, frontispiece; ~prent, headpiece; ~rol, title-role; title-part, name-part; ~stempel, lettering-tool; ~sug, title mania.
titra'sie, titration.
titreer', (ge-), titrate.
tit'seltjie, (-s), bit, particle; 'n ~ *botter*, a dab of butter.
tit'tel, (-s), tittle, jot, iota.
titula'ris, (-se), titular(y), holder of an office, functionary.
titulatuur', titles.
tituleer', (ge-), style, title.
titulêr', (-e), titulary, titular.
tjak'kie-tjak'kie, for pretence, for love (in marble-game).
tja'lie, (-s), shawl.
tjalk, (-e), spritsail barge.
tjank, (ge-), yelp, howl, blub, bleat, whine; ~balie, ~balk, cry-baby; ~end, (-e), yelping, howling; ~er, (-s), howler; ~erig, (-e), inclined to howl; puling; ~ery, yelping, howling.
tjap, (s) (-pe), stamp; mark made by stamp; (w) (ge-), stamp.
tjek, (-s), cheque; *BLANKO* ~, blank cheque; *'n ~ vir R100*, a cheque for R100; *'n GEKRUISTE* ~, a crossed cheque.
tje'ka, cheka.
tjek: ~boek, cheque book; ~boekboer, wealthy farmer; ~kie, (-s), small cheque; ~rekening, drawing account; ~strokie, cheque stub; ~teenblad, cheque stub; ~waarborg, cheque guarantee.
tjellis', (-te), (violin)cellist.
tjel'lo, (-'s), (violon)cello.
tjêr-tjêr'[1], (-s), honey heath.
tjêr-tjêr'[2], (-s), chirper (bird).
tjienkerientjee', (-s), chinkerinchee *(Ornithogalum thyrsoides)*.
tjilp, (ge-), chirp, twitter, cheep.
tjin'gel, (ge-), jingle, tinkle, thrum; ~-tjan'gel, penny gaff; old piano.
tjir, (ge-), chirr.
tjoek, (-e), washer, ring (used in boys' games); chucker.
tjoe'kie, (-s), quod, choky, prison, lock-up, stir.
tjoe'ma, for love (in children's games).
tjoep, quiet, silent; ~stil, very quiet, absolutely silent.
tjok'ka, (-s), cuttle-fish, squid.
tjok'ker(tjie), (-s), youngster, young chap; windbag.
tjok'kerbek-aasvoël, black vulture *(Aquila rapax)*.
tjok'vol, (-le), chock-full.
tjom'mel, (ge-), grouse, grumble; ~aar, grumbler, grouser.
tjor'rie, (-s), flivver, old motor car, ramshackle car.
tjor'-tjor', chor-chor (kind of fish) *(Pristipona benettii)*; grunter *(Pomadasys opercularis)*.
tjorts, (ge-), fart.
tjou'-tjou'[1], (-s), Cape grey titmouse.
tjou-tjou'[2], chow-chow; hotchpotch; ~konfyt, mixed preserves; ~spul, a feeble lot (performance); common crowd.
tjou'voël, (-s), grey titmouse.
T'-las, T-joint.
tnok'ka, (gew.), (-s), nape (of neck).
tob, (ge-), plod, toil, drudge; worry, fidget, fret, brood; *sy ~ oor haar kinders*, she worries about her children; ~ber, (-s), toiler; fretter; ~berig, (-e),

toiling; worrying, fretting; ~bery, toiling, drudging; fretting.
tobog'gan, (-s), toboggan.
toe, (b) closed, shut; *'n ~ BAAN*, a closed circuit; *'n ~ DEUR*, a closed door; *die GROND lê ~ onder die ryp*, the ground is covered with frost; *'n ~ MOTOR*, a saloon car; *met ~ OË*, with eyes shut; ~*bokant die ORE*, very stupid; (bw) in the direction of; up to; forward; then, at that time; *AF en ~*, now and then; *op die KOOP ~*, in addition, as an extra; *~ en NOU*, then and now; *SLEG daaraan ~ wees*, be badly off; *na die STAD ~*, to the city; *TOT die laaste sent ~ betaal*, pay up to the last cent; *VAN ~ af*, since then; (vgw) when, while, as; *~ dit BEGIN reën, moes die spel ophou*, when it started raining, the game had to be stopped; *~ hy van my WEGSTAP, gebeur dit*, as he walked away from me it happened; (tw), do, come on, please; hush! *~ DAN maar*, all right! *EN ~?* what do you want? what next? *~ MAAR, kindjie*, hush, my child! *NOU ~?* what now? *~ dan TOG*, hurry up, please do!
Toe'areg, (-s), Tuareg.
toe'baker, (-ge-), swaddle up.
toe'bedeel, (~), allot, assign, apportion, allocate; ~de, (-s), allottee.
toe'behoorsels, belongings; accessories, fittings; paraphernalia.
toe'behoor(t), (~), belong to, appertain to.
toe'behore(ns), belongings; accessories, fittings, appurtenances; furnishings; *los en vaste ~*, fittings and fixtures.
toe'bek(moer)sleutel, ring spanner.
toe'berei, (~), prepare; season; dispense (medicine); ~der, (-s), dispenser; ~ding, preparation; dressing; seasoning; dispensing.
toe'bereidsels, preparations.
toe'beskik, (~), dispose, arrange for.
toe'betrou, (~), entrust, give in charge, commit.
toe'bid, (-ge-), pray for, invoke upon.
toe'bind, (-ge-), tie up, close, fasten; ~ing, ligation.
toe'blok, (-ge-), block; seal (fig.)
toe'bly, (-ge-), remain closed.
toe'bou, (-ge-), build in (on all sides).
toe'brei, (-ge-), knit up (to close an opening).
toe'bring, (-ge-), give; inflict; cause; *die vyand verliese ~*, cause losses to the enemy.
toe'broek, bloomers.
toe'broodjie, (-s), sandwich.
toe'brul, (-ge-), roar (bellow) at.
toe'buie, toe'buig, (-ge-), close by bending.
toe'byt, (-ge-), snarl; shut by biting; *iem. verwyte ~*, snarl reproaches at someone.
toe'dam, (-ge-), dam in; crowd round.
toe'deel, (-ge-), allot, parcel out, apportion; admeasure.
toe'dek, (-ge-), cover up; tuck in; thatch.
toe'deling, apportionment.
toe'dien, (-ge-), administer to (medicine); mete out (punishment); dose (sheep); plant (a blow); ~ing, administration (of medicine); application (e.g. fertilizer).
toe'dig, (-ge-), ascribe, impute; fasten upon; *iem. onedele motiewe ~*, ascribe dishonourable motives to someone; ~ting, imputation.
toe'ding = **toering**.
toe'doen, (s) assistance, aid; instrumentality; *BUITE my ~*, through no fault of mine; *SONDER my ~, sou dit hom nie geluk het nie*, without my help, he would have failed; (w) (-ge-), shut, close; add; *jy MAG daar niks aan ~ nie*, you may not add anything to it; *dit sal daar NIKS aan ~ nie*, it will make no difference.
toe'dra, (-ge-), bear; *iem. agting ~*, hold someone in esteem.
toe'draai, (-ge-), wrap up (parcel); gange (fish-hook); swaddle (baby); turn off (tap); screw on (to close); *iem. die rug ~*, turn one's back upon someone.
toe'drag, particulars, circumstances; *die ware ~ v.d. saak*, the ins and outs (precise facts) of the affair.
toe'drink, (-ge-), drink to (a person's health.)

toedruk 539 *toenaam*

toe'druk, (-ge-), shut, close, push to; *iem. se keel* ~, strangle a person.
toe'-eien, (-geëien), appropriate, usurp (power); pocket, assume (rights); take; ~ **baar,** (..**bare**), appropriable; ~ **ing,** appropriation, assumption; conversion (law).
toe'ërig, (-e), rather closed in (shut in); cloudy (sky); rather stupid.
toef, (ge-), tarry, linger.
toe'fa, tufa (rock); ~ **ägtig,** tufaceous.
toe'fluister, (-ge-), whisper (in the ear).
toe'gaan, (-ge-), close; heal (wound); *dit sal daar snaaks* ~, strange things are going to happen there.
toe'gang, entrance, admission, admittance, entrée; door-money; gate; access; *VERBODE* ~, no admission; ~ *VERLEEN tot,* give admission (access) to; ~ *VRY,* admission free; *die* ~ *WEIER,* refuse admission.
toe'gangs: ~ **bewys,** admission ticket; ~ **deur,** access door; ~ **geld,** gate-money; entrance fee, admission money; ~ **kaartjie,** admission ticket; ~ **prys,** entrance (gate-, admission) money; ~ **reg,** right of admission; ~ **tonnel,** adit; ~ **weg,** approach.
toe'gangstrook, access strip.
toegank'lik, (-e), accessible, approachable; pervious, penetrable; ~ *MAAK,* open up; ~ *vir NUWE denkbeelde,* be open (amenable) to new ideas; ~ **heid,** accessibility; perviousness.
toe'gedaan, attached to; *die mening* ~ *wees,* hold the opinion.
toe'gee, (-ge-), yield, admit, concede, accede; *GRAAG* ~ *dat* ..., readily concede that ...; *NIKS (g'n duimbreed)* ~ *nie,* be uncompromising, not budge an inch; *'n SOMMETJIE* ~, give (add) an extra amount; *te VEEL* ~, be too indulgent.
toegeef'lik, (-e), indulgent, compliant, lenient; ~ **heid,** indulgence.
toe'geëien, (-de), assumed.
toe'gee: ~ **pad,** yield road; ~ **teken,** yield sign.
toe'gegooi, (-de), covered (up); ~ *onder die werk,* snowed under with work.
toe'gegroei, (-de), overgrown.
toe'gelaat, (..late), accredited; allowed.
toe'geneë, kindly-disposed, affectionate, devoted; *jou* ~ *vriend,* yours affectionately.
toe'geneentheid, inclination; affection, devotedness, devotion; goodwill.
toe'gepas, (-te), applied; ~ *te wiskunde,* applied mathematics.
toe'gerus, (-te), equipped, endowed.
toe'geskrewe, ascribed, imputed.
toe'gesluit, (-e), close-barred, locked.
toe'gespe(r), (-ge-), buckle (up), clasp.
toe'gespits, (-te), tapered (fingers); concentrated (attention).
toe'gestaan, (..stane), granted.
toe'gevoeg, (-de), added, adjunct.
toe'gevou, (-de), folded up.
toege'wend, (-e), compliant, clement, yielding, indulgent, lenient, acquiescent; concessive (clause); ~ **heid** pliancy, indulgence, leniency.
toe'gewer, release wire (signal).
toe'gewing, concession, compliance.
toe'gewy, (-de), devoted, dedicated; destined.
toe'gewydheid, devotedness.
toe'gif, (-te), extra, bonus, additional allowance; encore (concert); addition.
toe'gooi, (-ge-), throw to; bang, slam (a door); fill up; cover up; *toegegooi onder werk,* snowed under (overwhelmed) with work.
toe'grendel, (-ge-), bolt.
toe'groei, (-ge-), close, heal (wound); grow together; knit, conglutinate (wound); overgrow (weeds).
toe'gryns, (-ge-), grin at.
toe'haak, (-ge-), clasp, hook.
toe'hoor, (-ge-), listen to.
toe'hoorder, (-s), hearer; *die* ~ *s,* the audience.
toe'hou, (-ge-), keep closed, keep shut.
toe'juig, (-ge-), cheer, applaud, approve, acclaim, encore; ~ **end,** (-e), acclamatory, plauditory; ~ **ing,** applause, cheers, cheering, plaudits, acclaim, acclamation, ovation.

toe'ka, long ago; already; indeed; *van* ~ *se dae,* from time immemorial.
toe'kamp, (-ge-), hedge about, fence off.
toe'kan, (-s), toucan.
toe'keer, (-ge-), turn to; *iem. die rug* ~, turn one's back upon someone.
toe'ken, (-ge-), award (prize); grant, allocate, confer (degree); allot; assign (meaning); *die kinders is aan die vader toegeken,* the father was granted custody of the children; ~ **ning,** (-e, -s), grant, award; conferment; allotment; ~ **ningsbrief,** letter of allotment.
toe'klap, (-ge-), bang, slam (door); swing to a closed position, become shut.
toe'knik, (-ge-), nod at, nod to.
toe'knip(pie), (-s), press-stud.
toe'knoop, (-ge-), button up, clasp, tie.
toe'knyp, (-ge-), screw up, close tightly (eyes).
toe'kom, (-ge-), have a right to; deserve (honour), be due to; accrue (to); *dit KOM hom toe,* it is his due, he has a right to it.
toeko'mend, (-e), next, future; ~ *e tyd,* future tense; future.
toe'koms, futurity, future; *IN die* ~, in future; *die OOG op die* ~ *hou,* take the long view; ~ **beeld,** picture of things to come; ~ **beleid,** future policy; ~ **droom,** dream of the future; ~ **leerkundige,** futurologist; ~ **musiek,** castles in the air; dreams of the future; ~ **planne,** plans for the future; ~ **'tig,** (-e), future; intended; prospective; ~ **tigheid,** futurity.
toe'kos, dessert; side-dish.
toe'kruid, condiment.
toe'kry, (-ge-), succeed in closing; get something into the bargain.
toe'kurk, (-ge-), cork.
toe'kyk, (-ge-), look on; ~ **er,** (-s), onlooker, spectator.
toe'laag, (..laes), grant, gratuity, bonus, allowance; fellowship; *plaaslike* ~, local allowance.
toe'laat, (-ge-), admit, permit, suffer, allow; recognize; authorize; licence; *as ADVOKAAT* ~, admit as barrister, call to the bar; *OOGLUIKEND* ~, connive at; *dit laat nie die minste TWYFEL toe nie,* it leaves no room for any doubt whatsoever; ~ **'baar,** (..**bare**), allowable, permissible, admissible; ..*bare spanning,* allowable (permissible) stress; ~ **'baarheid,** admissibility.
toe'lae, (-s) = **toelaag.**
toe'lag, (-ge-), smile upon (at).
toe'lagie, (-s), small grant.
toe'lak, (-ge-), seal up.
toe'lating, admission, admittance, permission, entrance, authorization; allowance.
toe'latings: ~ **eksamen,** entrance examination; ~ **vereiste,** entrance requirement.
toe'lê, (-ge-), devote oneself to, apply oneself to, be bent on, aim at, make a point of; *hy lê hom DAAROP toe om my te beledig,* he makes a point of insulting me; *jou op jou STUDIE* ~, apply oneself to one's studies.
toe'leg, plan, design, aim, attempt; *die* ~ *het misluk,* the attempt (plot) failed.
toe'lig, (-ge-), illustrate, elucidate, explain; *iets NADER* ~, explain something more fully; *met VOORBEELDE* ~, illustrate with examples; ~ **tend,** (-e), elucidatory; ~ **ter,** elucidator; ~ **ting,** explanation, interpretation, elucidation, explanatory memorandum.
toe'lonk, (-ge-), ogle, cast sheep's eyes at, look tenderly at.
toe'loop, (s) concourse, crowd, throng, run, (w) (-ge-), run to; *spits* ~, taper.
toe'luister, (-ge-), listen.
toe'maak, (-ge-), shut, close; cover up; ~ **goed,** covering materials, wrapping materials, wraps; ~ **tyd,** closing time.
toe'meet, (-ge-), measure out, allot.
toe'messel, (-ge-), wall up.
toe'mond, with closed mouth; ~ *praat,* mumble.
toe'motor, sedan car (motor).
toe'naai, (-ge-), sew up.
toe'naam, epithet, surname, nickname.

toe'nader, (-ge-), approach, make advances, strive to reconcile; **~ing,** friendly advance, rapprochement; **~ing soek,** make friendly overtures; **~ing(spoging),** détente.
toe'name, increase, accruement.
toen'dra, (-s), tundra.
toe'neem, (-ge-), increase, advance, accrue, grow, progress; become worse.
toene'mend, (-e), increasing, growing, progressive, accumulating; **~e BELANGSTELLING,** growing interest; *in ~e MATE,* progressively.
toe'neming, increase, rise, advance, progress; access; growth.
toen'koe, (-s), tunku.
toen'maals, then, at that time.
toenma'lig, (-e), then, of the time; *die ~e eerste minister,* the then premier.
toen'tertyd, then, at that time.
toe'oog, (s) solid eye (underground spring); (bw) with closed eyes; *iets ~ (..oë) kan doen,* be able to do something very easily, do something with one's eyes shut.
toe'pak, (-ge-), pack in (on all sides), crowd; head upon, load with.
toe'pas, (-ge-), apply to, enforce (rules); put into practice; practise (patience); *verkeerd ~,* misapply; **~'baar, (..bare),** enforceable; **~'baarheid,** enforceability; **~'lik, (-e),** suitable, apposite, relevant, appropriate, fitting, pertinent, applicable; **~'likheid,** suitability, applicability, relevance, relevancy.
toe'passing, (-e, -s), application; administration; enforcement; *in ~ BRING,* put into practice; *van ~ WEES op,* apply to, be applicable to.
toe'plak, (-ge-), paste up (over), glue over; cover (hole); seal (a letter).
toe'pleister, (-ge-), plaster up, grout.
toe'ploeë, toe'ploeg, (-ge-), plough under.
toe'prop, (-ge-), cork, plug, bung.
toer, (s) (-e), tour, trip, excursion, drive, spin, walk; trick, stunt; revolution (of engine); *dit was 'n hele ~ om dit REG te kry,* it took some doing; **~e UITHAAL,** perform tricks (stunts); (w) (ge-), tour, travel; **~bus,** char-a-banc, touring-bus.
toe'reik, (-ge-), hand (to), pass.
toerei'kend, (-e), sufficient, adequate, enough; *~ wees,* suffice; **~heid,** sufficiency, adequacy.
toe'reken, (-ge-), ascribe to, lay at a person's door, impute, attribute, make accountable for.
toere'kenbaar, (..bare), imputable; accountable, responsible; *nie ~ wees nie,* not responsible for one's actions; **~heid,** responsibility, accountability, imputability.
toe'rekening, attribution, imputation.
toe're: *~ tal,* number of revolutions; **~teller, (-s),** tachometer.
toer'gids, tour guide.
toe'ring, (-s), pointed (Malay) hat.
toeris', (-te), tourist; **~me,** tourism, sightseeing; **~te-aantreklikheid,** tourist attraction; **~te-agentskap,** tourist agency; **~tebedryf,** tourist industry; **~teklas,** tourist class; **~te-oord,** tourists' resort; **~tepaspoort,** tourist passport; **~teverkeer,** tourist traffic.
toermalyn', tourmaline.
toer: *~ model,* touring-model, tourer (car); *~ motor,* touring-car.
toerniket', (-te), tourniquet.
toernooi', (-e), tournament, tourney, joust, tilt; **~lans,** tilting-lance.
toe'roep, (-ge-), call to, hail.
toe'roes, (-ge-), become overcrusted with rust.
toe'rol, (-ge-), roll up, wrap up.
toer'tjie, (-s), stunt, trick; trip; *dit was 'n hele ~,* it was a to-do.
toe'ruk, (-ge-), pull to; close with a jerk.
toe'rus, (-ge-), equip (a laboratory); fit out (with clothes); **~ter, (-s),** (out)fitter; **~ting, (-e, -s),** equipment; outfit; plant (of factory).
toe'ryg, (-ge-), lace up.
toe'sak, (-ge-), become overcast (sky); mob; *dit BEGIN ~,* the sky is becoming overcast; *IEM. ~,* rush at someone; *OP iem. ~,* descend upon someone; mob someone; *die SPRINKANE sak die land toe,* the locusts are settling on the field from all sides; *op die VYAND ~,* attack (fall upon) the enemy from all sides.
toe'sang, closing hymn.
toe'sê, (-ge-), promise; allocate.
toe'seël, (-ge-), seal up.
toe'segging, (-e, -s), promise, commitment.
toe'send, (-ge-), consign to, send to; **~ing, (-e, -s),** consignment, forwarding, despatch.
toe'sien, (-ge-), look on; see to, take care of; *die BESTUUR moet ~ dat die geld goed bestee word,* the committee is responsible for the proper administration of the money; *jy sal MAAR moet ~,* that's your busines (affair); *ons moes MAGTELOOS ~ hoe hy verdrink,* we had to look on when he got drowned without being able to save him; **~de,** advisory; *~ de raad,* advisory council, supervising board.
toe'sig, supervision, surveillance, care, control, invigilation; *~ HOU,* supervise, invigilate (at examination); *ONDER ~ van,* under the supervision of; **~houdend, (-e),** supervisory; **~houer,** commissioner; supervisor; floor-walker.
toe'sing, (-ge-), welcome with song; sing to.
toe'sit, (-ge-), cheat, deceive; sit on; close, place in quarantine; *die plaas is toegesit,* the farm is in quarantine.
toe'skiet, (-ge-), rush on, dash at; **~'lik, (-e),** pliant, affable, accommodating, obliging, facile; *nie baie ~ lik nie,* not very obliging; rather distant; **~'likheid,** affability, obligingness.
toe'skou, (-ge-), look on; **~er, (-s),** spectator, onlooker, looker-on, bystander; **~ers,** the gate (spectators); the house (audience).
toe'skree, (-ge-), shout at.
toe'skroef, (-ge-), screw down.
toe'skroei, (-ge-), cauterize, sear; *sy gewete is toegeskroei,* he has no qualms of conscience; **~ing,** cauterization, searing.
toe'skroewe, (-ge-) = **toeskroef.**
toe'skryf, toe'skrywe, (-ge-), ascribe, attribute, impute; **~'baar, (..bare),** assignable, attributable.
toe'skrywing, assignment, attribution, imputation.
toe'skuif, toe'skuiwe, (-ge-), close by pushing; shift to; draw (curtains).
toe'skyn, (-ge-), appear, seem.
toe'slaan, (-ge-), shut, slam, bang; fall (cake); compact, puddle (soil); *toegeslane BROOD,* heavy (sad) bread; *IETS op iem. ~,* knock down something to somebody (at sale); *my ORE het toegeslaan,* my ears were blocked; *~ op die TERRORISTE,* strike at the terrorists.
toe'slag, extra allowance, bonus; surcharge.
toe'slik, (-ge-), silt up; **~king,** silting-up.
toe'sluit, (-ge-), lock up, close, shut; **~kas,** lock-up cupboard.
toe'smeer, (-ge-), smear over, stop up; gloss over, explain away; cover up (a scandal).
toe'smyt, (-ge-), bang (door); fling at.
toe'snel, (-ge-), rush (dash) up.
toe'snoer, (-ge-), lace up; constrict; *hom die mond ~,* stop his mouth.
toe'snou, (-ge-), snarl at, snap at, address harshly.
toe'soldeer, (-ge-), solder.
toe'span, (-ge-), fence in.
toe'speld, (-ge-), pin up.
toe'speling, (-e, -s), allusion, insinuation, hint, innuendo; *'n ~ maak,* make an allusion (insinuation).
toe'spit, (-ge-), close (cover) by digging.
toe'spits, (-ge-), specialize in, apply oneself particularly, become bent on; *hy behoort hom op sy studie toe te spits,* he ought to apply himself to his lessons.
toe'spoel, (-ge-), silt up.
toe'spoor, (-ge-), toe in.
toe'spraak, (..sprake), address, speech, apostrophe, exhortation, harangue; *'n ~ hou,* deliver an address.
toe'spreek, (-ge-), address (meeting); accost, speak to (person); harangue; **..spreking,** addressing.
toe'spring, (-ge-), snap shut.

toe'spyker, (-ge-), nail up.
toe'spys, dessert, side-dish.
toe'staan, (-ge-), allow, permit, grant (request); accede, cede, concede (privilege); assent, accord; be shut (door); be unoccupied (house); cluster round; *'n kantoor ~,* overcrowd an office.
toe'stand, (-e) state, condition (of affairs); position, plight (of person); situation; shape; *in 'n haglike ~,* in a critical state, in a precarious condition.
toe'standsverandering, change of state (condition).
toe'steek, (-ge-), pin up; bung (up) (hole); proffer (one's hand); *die BLOMME ~,* cover the flowers; *'n VOOR ~,* divert a stream.
toe'stel, (-le), apparatus, contrivance, appliance, machine; frame; contraption, device, gadget; set (radio); **~letjie, (-s),** small set; **~saal,** instrument room.
toe'stem, (-ge-), grant (request); assent, consent, accede, comply (with request); **~mend, (-e),** affirmative, permissive; *~mend antwoord,* answer in the affirmative; **~ming,** consent, permission, assent; *met ~ming van,* with the consent of; **~mingsakte,** consent paper.
toe'stop, (-ge-), plug (hole); stop (ears); tuck in (child); slip (into hand); gag (mouth); *iem. 'n FOOITJIE ~,* slip a tip into someone's hand; *die KINDERS word goed toegestop,* the children get numerous presents; **~ping,** occlusion.
toe'storm, (-ge-), swarm round (upon).
toe'stroom, (-ge-), stream (rush) towards; throng; flock in, pour in (of people).
toe'stuur, (-ge-), consign; send, forward, remit.
toe'swaai, (-ge-), swing to; *icm. lof ~,* praise (extol) someone.
toe'swel, (-ge-), become closed by swelling.
toet¹, (s): *uit die JAAR ~,* from the year dot; *'n MANNETJIE van ~,* a nincompoop, a nonentity, a man of straw; *VAN ~,* since the days of yore; *hy WEET nie van ~ of blaas nie,* he does not know chalk from cheese.
toet,² (w) (ge-), blow a horn, sound a hooter, hoot.
toe'takel, (-ge-), mess up one's clothes; knock about, maul, manhandle, belabour, punish; make havoc of.
toe'tas, (-ge-), help oneself (at dinner), begin.
toe'ter, (s) (-s), horn, hooter; (w) **(ge-),** hoot, blow a horn; **~knop,** hooter-button; **~horing,** horn, hooter.
toe'trap, (-ge-), tread down; kick to (door); deceive, cheat; *iem. lelik ~,* take someone in.
toe'trede, toe'treding, (-ge-), entry, joining, acceptance as member; entrance; accession.
toe'tredingsgeld, membership fee, entrance fee.
toe'tree, (-ge-), step up to; become a member of, join (a society); *~ tot die polisie,* join the police.
toe'trek, (-ge-), close, shut, pull to (door); draw (curtains); swindle, cheat; become overcast; *die lug GAAN ~,* the sky is going to be overcast; *IEM. ~,* do someone down; *sy bors WIL ~,* he has a cold on the chest; he is asthmatic; **~baadjie,** lumber-jacket; **~gordyn,** draw-curtain.
toets, (s) (-e), key (of piano); test, ordeal, trial, touch, stroke (painting); assay (metals); *'n ~ deurstaan,* stand a test; (w) **(ge-),** test (a person); check (an engine); assay (metals); sound (lungs); **~aanleg,** pilot plant; **~alkohol,** proof spirit; **~bank,** testing-bench; **~battery,** battery of tests; **~bord,** keyboard, manual; fingerboard, fret (music); **~er, (-s),** assayer, tester, checker; **~geval,** test case; **~glas,** test-glass; **~hamer,** tapping-hammer; **~ing,** testing; **~ingsreg,** right of testing; **~kraan,** petcock; **~las, (-te),** test load; **~latte,** winding-strips; **~loods,** test pilot; **~naald,** touch-needle; **~reeks,** (test) rubber; **~rit,** trial run; **~saak,** test case; **~steen,** touchstone; criterion; **~terrein,** proving-ground; **~wedstryd,** test-match.
toe'val¹, (s) accident, coincidence, random, fortuity, chance; casualty; *dis BLOOT ~,* it is pure chance; *BY ~,* by chance; *soos die ~ dit wou HÊ,* as luck would have it.
toe'val², (s) (-le), fainting fit; epileptic fit; *aan ~ le ly,* be subject to fits.

toe'val³, (w) (-ge-), cave in; become closed by falling; *die MENSE sal my ~ om die huis te huur,* I shall be swamped with offers to rent the house; *my OË wil net ~,* my eyes won't stay open.
toe'val⁴, (w) (-ge-), accrue to; *voordele wat my ~,* benefits which accrue to me.
toeval'lig, (b) (-e), casual, haphazard, random (in statistics); coincidental, accidental, adventitious, chance, fortuitous; (bw) accidentally, by chance; **~erwys(e),** by chance, accidentally; **~heid,** accident, chance, fortuity, casualness.
toe'valling, accrual.
toe'valtoets, random check.
toe'veld, ground under repair (golf).
toe'verlaat, support, refuge, anchor.
toe'vertrou, (~), entrust, deliver in trust, consign, commit (to the care of); *iem. 'n geheim ~,* confide a secret to a person; **~d, (-e),** fiduciary; **~ing,** commitment, entrustment.
toe'vliegtuig, cabin aeroplane.
toe'vloed, affluence, afflux, influx; concourse, throng.
toe'vloei, (-ge-), flow to; accrue to; **~end, (-e),** affluent; **~ing,** concourse; influx.
toe'vlug, refuge, shelter, asylum, recourse, resort, expedient, harbourage; *sy ~ tot 'n vriend neem,* seek a friend's aid.
toe'vlugsoord, refuge, sanctuary, asylum, haven (of rest).
toe'voeg, (-ge-), add, join to; affix, append; *~ AAN,* add to; *iem kwaai WOORDE ~,* give someone a lick with the rough side of one's tongue; **~ing, (-e, -s),** addition, affixture; **~sel, (-s),** supplement, appendix; admixture; addendum; lacing (with liquor).
toe'voer, (s) supply; input (elec.); feed; (w) **(ge-),** supply; feed (press); **~apparaat,** feeder; **~bron,** source of supply; **~buis,** supply-pipe; **~diens,** feeder service; **~end, (-e),** afferent; **~gebied,** intake area; **~kanaal,** feeder; **~klep,** feed-valve; **~lyn,** feeder-line; **~pomp,** feed-pump; **~pyp,** supply-pipe; **~stelsel,** feed-system; **~tenk,** feed-tank; **~vliegtuig,** feeder-plane; **~water,** feed-water.
toe'vou, (-ge-), fold up, fold about; enfold, enwrap.
toe'vra, (-ge-), ask in addition, charge extra.
toe'vries, (-ge-), freeze over.
toe'wa, delivery-van, removal-van.
toe'waai, (-ge-), cover with dust; be blown (shut) to.
toe'we, see **toef.**
toe'wend, turn to.
toe'wens, (-ge-), wish; *iem. die beste ~,* wish a person well.
toe'werk, (-ge-), sew up.
toe'werp, (-ge-), fling to (at).
toe'wikkel, (-ge-), wrap up, enswathe.
toe'wink, (-ge-), beckon to.
toe'wuif, toe'wuiwe, (-ge-), wave to.
toe'wy, (-ge-), dedicate, consecrate, devote; **~dend, (-e),** consecratory, dedicatory; **~der, (-s),** dedicator; **~ding,** dedication, devotion, application; **~dingsplegtigheid,** dedication ceremony.
toe'wys, (-ge-), allot, award, assign, commit, admeasure; allocate; **~baar, (..bare),** assignable; **~ing, (-e, -s),** allotment, disposal, award, allocation, adjudication, assignment; **~ingsbrief,** letter of allotment.
toe'ys, (-ge-), freeze over.
tof'fie, (-s), toffee.
tog¹, (s) (-te), draught, current of air; expedition, journey, cruise, excursion, march, trip.
tog², (bw) yet, still, all the same, for all (in spite of) that, surely; *~ AL genoeg,* enough as it is; *AS ons ~ maar tuis was,* if only we were at home; *as jy ~ DAARLANGS gaan,* if you do go there; *wie kan DIT ~ wees?* whoever can that be? *sy is ~ so GRAPPIG,* she is really so full of fun; *ek sal dit ~ MAAR nie doen nie,* I won't do it after all; *jy loop ~ NOG nie?* surely, you are not going just yet? *hy is ~ nie SIEK nie?* surely, he is not ill? *laat hom ~ STAAN,* please leave him alone; *TOE ~!* do please.

to'ga, (-s), gown, robe, toga; cassock; ~**maker,** robe-maker.

tog: ~**arbeid,** togt (casual) labour; ~**band,** list; ~**deur,** screen door; ~**ganger, (-s),** transport-rider, itinerant trader; ~**gat,** vent-hole; ~**genoot,** fellow-traveller; ~**gie, (-s),** trip, outing, ride.

tog: ~**ryer, (-s),** transport-rider; ~**skerm,** draught-screen; ~**snelheid,** cruising speed; ~**tig, (-e),** draughty; ~**wa,** transport-wagon.

toi'ingrig, (-e), ragged, frayed, tattered; ~ *voel,* feel out of sorts.

toi'ings, rags, tatters; ~**parade,** rag review.

toi'inkies, rags, tatters.

toi'let, toilet; *sy* ~ *maak,* make one's toilet; ~**artikel,** toilet article; ~**benodigdhede,** toilet requisites; ~**doos,** dressing-case; ~**emmer,** slop-pail; ~**kamer,** lavatory; ~**papier,** toilet paper; ~**seep,** toilet soap; ~**spieël,** dressing-glass, toilet mirror; ~**stel,** toilet-set; ~**tafel,** dressing-table.

tok'kel, (ge-), touch (strings of a musical instrument), pluck, plunk; strum, thrum, twang; *die lier* ~, twang the lyre; ~**ing,** twanging, strumming.

tokkelok', (-ke), (student word for) theological student.

tokkelos'sie, (-s), tikoloshe; gremlin, leprechaun.

toksemie', toxaemia.

toksien', (-e), toxin.

tok'sies, (-e), toxic.

toksikologie', toxicology.

toksikolo'gies, (-e), toxicological.

toksikoloog', (..loë), toxicologist.

toksi'ne, (-s) = toksien.

toktok'kie, (-s), tapping-beetle *(Psammodes);* tick-tock (a boys prank); ~ *speel,* play tick-tock.

tol¹, (s) tribute; duty, customs, toll, pike; duties; ~ *BETAAL,* pay duty; pay the price; *die* ~ *aan die NATUUR betaal,* pay one's debt to nature; die.

tol², (s) (-le), top; drum (for winding); bobbin (for winding); reel; *soos 'n* ~ *DRAAI,* spin like a top; *so DRONK soos 'n* ~, as drunk as a lord; **(w) (ge-),** spin (like a top); *my kop* ~ *in die rondte,* my head is reeling.

tol'beampte, customs officer.

tol'beweging, turbination.

tol'boom, toll-bar, turnpike.

tol: ~**bos,** monkey-apple; tumble-weed *(Leucas martiniensis).*

tol'bout, bobbin bolt.

tol: ~**brief,** clearance-note; ~**brug,** toll-bridge.

tol: ~**droër,** spindrier; ~**droog,** spin-dry.

toleran'sie, toleration, tolerance; margin of error.

tolerant', (-e), tolerant.

tolereer', (ge-), tolerate.

tol: ~**gaarder,** tollman, toll collector; ~**geld,** toll, customs; ~*geld betaal,* pay toll; ~**hek,** toll gate; pike; ~**huis,** customs house, clearance house.

tolk, (s) (-e), interpreter; dragoman; mouth-piece; **(w) (ge-),** interpret.

tol: ~**kantoor,** customs house; ~**lenaar, (-s, ..nare),** publican; tax collector.

tol'letjie, (-s), reel, bobbin; small top.

tol'lie, (-s), tolly, young ox.

tol'ling, spinning, turbination, gyration.

tol'man, pikeman.

tol: ~**pad,** toll road; turnpike; ~**plig'tig, (-e),** subject to toll; dutiable; ~**tarief,** customs tariff; ~**unie,** ~**verbond,** tariff (customs) union.

tol: ~**versiersel,** twirling (spinning) decoration; ~**vlieëry,** spinning; ~**vlug,** spin; ~**vormig, (-e),** turbinate, top-shaped.

tol'vry, (-e), duty-free.

tol'wang, bobbin check (elect.).

tol'weg, turnpike road.

to'mahawk, (-s), tomahawk.

tombo'la, (-s), tombola.

tom'be, (-s), (ong.), tomb.

to'meloos = toomloos.

tom'mie, (-s), tommy, British soldier (Tommy Atkins).

tom-tom', (-s), tomtom.

ton, (-ne), cask, tub; ton; *BRITSE* ~, long ton; ~*ne GELD,* tons of money; *KAAPSE* ~, short ton.

tonaal', (tonale), tonal.

tonaliet', tonalite.

tonaliteit', tonality.

ton'dak, barrel roof.

toneel', (..nele), scene, spectacle, sight; stage; *vir die* ~ *BEWERK,* dramatize; *op die* ~ *BRING,* stage, produce; *DERDE bedryf, tweede* ~, third act, second scene; *die* ~ *v.d. OORLOG,* the seat of war; ~ *SPEEL,* act; *van die* ~ *VERDWYN,* disappear (from the stage); make one's exit; *ten tonele VOER,* bring on the stage; ~**aanwysing,** stage direction; ~**agtig, (-e),** theatrical, histrionic; ~**baas,** propertyman; ~**benodigdhede,** stage requisites, stage-props, properties; ~**bestuurder,** stage manager; business manager (of a theatre); ~**bewerking,** dramatization; ~**brief,** property letter; ~**dekor,** (stage) scenery, décor; ~**digter,** playwright; ~**direkteur,** stage manager; ~**effek,** stage effect; ~**geselskap,** theatrical company, troupe; ~**groep,** theatrical group; ~**held,** stage hero; ~**helper,** stage-hand; ~**hulp,** scene-shifter; ~**kneg,** fly-man; ~**koors,** stage fright; ~**kostuum,** stage dress; ~**kritiek,** stage (dramatic) criticism; ~**kritikus,** drama (stage) critic; ~**kuns,** stagecraft; dramatic art, histrionic art, histrionism; ~**kunstenaar,** actor, dramatic artist; ~**kyker,** opera-glass(es), binocle, lorgnette; pair of binoculars; ~**lesing,** play-reading; ~**loopbaan,** stage career; ~**mal,** stage-struck; ~**matig, (-e),** fit for the stage, stagey; ~**meester,** stage manager; ~**naam,** stage name; ~**opvoering,** dramatic performance; ~**regie,** direction; ~**regisseur,** director; ~**reis,** theatrical tour; ~**rekwisiete,** (stage) props, properties; ~**resensent,** dramatic critic; ~**resensie,** dramatic criticism; ~**sensor,** dramatic censor; ~**skerm,** stage curtain; side-scene, coulisse; ~**skikking,** mise en scène, setting (of a scene); ~**skilder,** stage-painter, scene-painter; ~**skoen,** sock, buskin; ~**skool,** drama school; ~**skrywer,** dramatist; playwright; ~**speel, (-ge-),** act; ~**speelster,** actress; ~**spel,** play; acting; play-acting; ~**speler,** player, actor; ~**spelery,** acting; play-acting; dramatics; ~**ster,** stage star; ~**stuk,** play drama; ~**verandering,** scene-shifting; ~**vereniging,** dramatic society; ~**versiering,** stage decoration; ~**voorstelling,** dramatic (theatrical) performance; ~**wêreld,** theatre-land, stage-land, theatrical circles; ~**wese,** the stage.

tong, (-e), tongue; pointer (scales); sole (fish); *die woord BRAND op my* ~, it is on the tip of my tongue; *hy het 'n DUBBELE* ~, he blows hot and cold; *'n FYN* ~ *hê,* be double-tongued; have a delicate palate; *hy is* ~ *GEBONDE,* he is tongue-tied; *'n GLADDE* ~, the gift of the gab; *iem. onder die* ~ *KRY,* give someone a lick with the rough side of one's tongue; *LANK van* ~ *wees,* have a long tongue; *LOS van* ~ *wees,* have a loose tongue; *die wyn maak die* ~*e LOS,* the wine sets the tongues wagging; *dis OP my* ~, it is on the tip of my tongue; *sy* ~ *ROER,* wag his tongue; *'n* ~ *soos 'n SKEERMES,* a very sharp tongue; a tongue like a razor; *haar* ~ *is so SKERP soos 'n naald,* she has a sharp tongue; *sy* ~ *SLAAN dubbel,* he speaks with a heavy tongue; *goed met die* ~ *SLAAN,* have a ready tongue; *sy* ~ *is SWAAR,* he speaks with a heavy tongue; *SWAAR van* ~ *wees,* speak with a thick tongue; *hy het sy* ~ *VERLOOR,* he has lost his tongue; ~**aar,** lingual vein; ~**been,** tongue bone, hyoid; ~**beklemming,** tongue-tie; ~**blaar,** dock *(Rumex);* ~**etjie, (-s),** little tongue; reed (organ); index (scales); lingula; ligula; ~**geswel,** tumour on the tongue; ~**gewelf,** tunnel-vault; ~**kanker,** cancer of the tongue; ~**klier,** lingual gland; ~**knoper,** crack-jaw, jaw-breaker; ~**las, (-se),** tongued joint; ~**letter,** lingual (letter); ~**ontsteking,** glossitis; ~**punt,** tip of the tongue; ~**riem,** fraenum of the tongue; *sy is BREED van die* ~*riem gesny,* she has a glib tongue; *GOED v.d.* ~*riem gesny wees,* be glib; ~**rol,** collared tongue; ~**senuwee,** lingual nerve; ~**skarnier,** strap hinge; ~**skoen,** brogue; ~**slagaar,** lingual artery; ~**spier,** lingual muscle; ~**stand,** position of the tongue; ~**tepeltjie,** papilla (of the tongue); ~**-uit,** with the tongue out; *jou ~-uit hardloop*, run one's legs off; ~**val**, dialect, vernacular; ~**vis**, sole; ~**vormig**, (-e), tongue-shaped, linguiform, lingulate; ~**wortel**, root of the tongue; ~**wurm**, tongue-worm.

to'nies, (-e), tonic.

toniet' tonite.

to'nika, tonic.

to'nikum, (-s, ..ka), tonic; *'n ~ vir die senuwees*, a tonic for the nerves.

ton'ka, (-s), fire-tin; improvised brazier; drum.

ton'ka: ~**boom**, tonka-tree *(Dipteryx odorata)*; ~**boontjie**, tonka bean.

ton'meul, (-e), Archimedean screw.

ton'ne, tonne.

ton'ne-inhoud, burden, tonnage.

ton'nel, (s) (-s), tunnel; adit; (w) (ge-), tunnel, drive, hole; ~**bek**, tunnel shaft; ~**oond**, tunnel-kiln; ~**(werk)front**, heading (mining).

ton'ne: ~**maat**, tonnage; ~**tal**, tonnage.

tonologie', tonology; ..**lo'gies**, (-e), tonological.

ton'rond, (-e), tubby.

tonsili'tis, tonsilitis.

tonsuur', (tonsure), tonsure.

ton'tel, tinder; ~**blaar**, *Hermas gigantea;* ~**bossie**, tinder-shrub *(Asclepias fruticosa);* ~**doek**, tinder; ~**doos**, tinder-box.

to'nus, (-se), tonus (spasm).

ton'verwulf, arched vault.

tonyn', (-e), tunny.

tooi, (s) ornament, finery; attire, array; gear; (w) (ge-), adorn, decorate, array, bedeck; enrich; preen; flower; ~**sel**, ornament, finery; ~*tassie*, vanity case.

toom[1], (-s, **tome**), pen; brood.

toom[2], (-s, **tome**), bridle; *iem. in ~ hou*, keep someone in check; (w) (ge-), bridle, curb, ~**loos**, (..lose), unbridled, unrestrained; ~**loosheid**, unbridled state; uncurbed licentiousness; ~**sluiting**, bridle-lock (points); ~**voeg**, bridle-joint.

toon[1], (s) (**tone**), toe; *tone trap, is RUSIE soek*, be courting trouble; *op iem. se tone TRAP*, tread on someone's corns (toes); *hy laat nie op sy tone TRAP nie*, he stands on his dignity.

toon[2], (s) (**tone**), pitch (of voice); sound, note, strain (of music); *die ~ AANGEE*, strike the keynote; take the lead; set the fashion; *'n hoë ~ AANSLAAN*, ride the high horse; *'n ander ~ AANSLAAN*, adopt a different tone; *op FLUISTERENDE ~*, in an undertone; *'n LAE ~ aanslaan*, sing small; *'n LAER ~ sing*, sing a different tune; *die REGTE ~ tref*, strike the right note; *uit die VAL*, be out of tune with; not be in keeping with.

toon[3], (s): *ten ~ SPREI*, display, show off; *ten ~ STEL*, exhibit, show, place on view; (w) (ge-), show, indicate, prove, demonstrate.

toon'aangewend, (-e), fashionable, leading (the fashion).

toon: ~**aangewing**, intonation; ~**aard**, tonality, mode; key; ~**afstand**, interval; space (music).

toon: ~**baar**, (..**bare**), presentable; ~**bank**, counter; buffet; ~**bankvertoonkaart**, counter display card; ~**bankvoorraad**, counter stock (bank); ~**beeld**, model, example, picture, exampler, pattern, mirror, paragon.

toon'beentjie, phalanx, phalange.

toon'brood, shewbread.

toon'demper, sordine, mute.

toon'der, (-s), bearer (of cheque); ~**opsie**, bearer option; ~**tjek**, bearer cheque.

toon'dig, (-te), musical composition; ~**ter**, musical composer.

toon: ~**gehalte**, quality of tone; ~**gewend**, (-e), leading; ~**heffing**, arsis, ictus; ~**hoogte**, diapason, pitch (of tone).

toon: ~**kabinet**, display cabinet; ~**kamer**, show-room.

toon'kleur, timbre (voice), tone-colour.

toon: ~**knobbel**, bunion; ~**kootjie**, phalanx.

toon'kuns, music; ~**tenaar**, musician.

toon: ~**ladder**, ~**leer**, gamut, scale; diapason; ~**leer**, tone study.

toon'lokaal, showroom.

toon'loos, (..lose), toneless, mute, unstressed, unaccented, atonic (syllable); neutral (phon.); ~**heid**, atony, tonelessness.

toon'loper, (-s), digitigrade.

toon: ~**meter**, tonometer; ~**omvang**, diapason; ~**opnemer**, pick-up; ~**opvolging**, succession of tones.

toon'sertifikaat, bearer certificate.

toon: ~**set**, (**ge-**), compose, put (set) to music; ~**setter**, composer; ~**setting**, (-e, -s), (musical) composition; ~**skaal**, gamut, scale, mode; ~**skakering**, variation of tone; shading of tone colour; ~**skildering**, tone picture; ~**sleutel**, clef; ~**soort**, key; ~**sterkte**, intensity of sound; tone volume.

toon'stuk[1], toe-piece (shoe).

toon'stuk[2], show-piece.

toon: ~**suiwerheid**, purity of tone; ~**teken**, accent.

toon'tjie[1], (-s), small toe; stone-plant.

toon'tjie[2], (-s), tone; *'n ~ laer sing*, climb down.

toon'trapper, pigeon-toed person.

toon: ~**val**, cadence, modulation; ~**vas**, (-te), true in tune (to pitch).

toon'venster, display-window.

toon'waarde[1], present value (bill).

toon'waarde[2], tonal value.

toor, (**ge-**), conjure, practise witchcraft; charm; bedevil; bewitch; put a spell on; ~**balletjie**, bull's-eye (sweets); niggerball; ~**beeld**, magic image; bewitching image; ~**beker**, magic cup; ~**boek**, conjuring book; ~**dery**, magic, witchcraft, sorcery; black art, necromancy, diableric; ~**dokter**, witch-doctor, medicine-man; ~**drank**, magic potion; ~**fee**, fairy, pixy; ~**fluit**, magic flute; ~**formulier**, spell, charm, incantation; ~**goed**, charms, magic articles; ~**heks**, witch, sorceress; ~**houtjie**, (-s), magic stick; ~**klank**, magic sound; ~**knoop**, Davenport knot; ~**krag**, magic power, spell; ~**kring**, magic circle; ~**kruid**, magic herb; ~**kuns**, sorcery, magic, theurgy, necromancy, witchcraft; ~**lantern**, magic lantern; ~**middel**, charm, talisman, amulet.

toorn, (s) anger, ire, wrath, dudgeon; *in ~ ontsteek*, fly into a rage; (w) (ge-), be angry (wrathful).

toor'naar, (**gew.**), (-s), sorcerer, magician.

toor'nig, (b) (-e), angry, wrathful, irate; (bw) angrily; ~**heid**, anger, wrath, rage, ire.

toor: ~**ring**, magic ring; ~**spel**, magic, witchcraft; ~**spreuk**, charm, incantation; ~**staf**, magic wand; ~**teken**, magic sign.

toorts, (-e), torch, (fire-)brand, flambeau; ~**draer**, torch-bearer; ~**lig**, torchlight.

toor'woord, magic word, abracadabra.

top[1], (s) (-**pe**), summit, peak, pinnacle, top, tip (of finger); poll (head); crest, comb (of wave); vertex (of cone); apex (of triangle); *van ~ tot TOON*, from top to toe; *ten ~ VOER*, carry to extremes; (w) (ge-), top, trim; poll (tree); pollard; crop (grass); obtruncate.

top[2]! (tw) game! agreed! that's a deal!

topaas', (**topase**), topaz.

topasoliet', topazolite.

top: ~**bestuur**, top management; ~**boog**, azimuth; ~**hoek**, vertical angle; vertex; ~**lig**, top-light.

topograaf', (..**grawe**), topographer; ..**grafie'**, topography; ..**gra'fies**, (-e), topographic.

toponimie', toponymy; ..**ni'mies**, (-e), toponymic(al)

top'prys, peak price, top price; ceiling.

top'punt, summit, peak; top notch; highest point, azimuth, zenith, limit, culminating point; consummation; crisis; heyday; apex (of triangle); acme, pinnacle; *die ~ BEREIK*, reach the peak (summit, culminating point); *die ~ van ONBESKAAMDHEID*, the height of audacity (shamelessness); *die ~ van VOLMAAKTHEID*, the acme of perfection.

top: ~**ruspe**, mealie-caterpillar; ~**seil**, topsail; ~**sel**, apical cell; ~**snelheid**, maximum speed; ~**steen**, crown (apex) stone; ~**swaar**, top-heavy.

toque, (-s), toque.

tor, (-re), beetle; bumpkin, lout, boor; dor, cockchafer; *'n regte ou ~*, a churl; an uneducated (uncouth)

torakschirurg person, a clodhopper; ~**agtig, (-e)**, uncouth, boorish.
to'rakschirurg, (-s), thorax surgeon.
torbaniet', (-s), torbanite.
toreador', (-s), toreador.
tore'ro, (-'s), torero.
to'ria, thoria.
toriet', thorite.
to'ring, (s) (-s), tower, steeple, belfry, turret; building of a tower; ~**brood**, cottage loaf; ~**geskut**, turret gun; ~**hoog**, (..hoë), as high as a steeple, sky-high, towering; ~**huis**, skyscraper; ~**klok**, tower-bell; tower-clock; ~**naald**, spire of steeple; ~**spits**, spire; ~**swael(tjie)**, swift; ~**top**, steeple-top; ~**uil**, church-owl; ~**valk**, staniel, kestrel, windhover; ~**wagter**, tower-watchman; muezzin; ~**wolk**, altocumulus, castellatus.
to'rinkie, turret.
torment', (-e), torment; trouble; ~**a'sie, (-s)**, torment; annoyance; ~**eer', (ge-)**, torment; trouble, annoy.
torna'do, (-'s), tornado, whirlwind.
tornyn', toothed whale *(Delphinus delphis, Lagenorhynchus obscurus)*; ~**haai**, man-eating shark, blue porpoise-shark.
torpedeer', (ge-), torpedo.
torpe'do, (-'s), torpedo; ~**bomwerper**, torpedo-bomber; ~**boot**, torpedo-boat; ~**buis**, torpedo-tube; ~**front**, cowl (motor); ~**jaer, (-s)**, torpedo-destroyer; ~**kop**, warhead; ~**lanseerbuis**, torpedo-tube; ~**net**, torpedo-net; crinoline; ~**pistool**, warnose (of a torpedo); ~**vis**, torpedo(-fish); ~**vliegtuig**, torpedo carrier.
tor'rerig, (-e), shabby, uncouth, unkept; boorish, countrified, loutish, oafish.
tor'retjie, (-s), little beetle.
tor'ring, (ge-), rip up, unstitch, unpick; pester, bother, nag; meddle with; *MOENIE aan my ~ nie*, stop nagging; *MOENIE daaraan ~ nie*, don't meddle with it; *daar VAL nie aan te ~ nie*, that is final; ~**mes**, ripper-knife (used for unpicking).
tors, (ge-), bear (carry) with difficulty.
tor'sie, torsion; ~**moment**, torsional moment; ~**skaal**, torsion scale; ~**straal**, radius of torsion; ~**veer**, torsion spring.
tor'so, (-'s), torso.
tor'telduif, turtle-dove.
to'rus, torus.
Toskaan', (..kane), Tuscan; ~**s', (-e)**, Tuscan; ~**se boustyl**, Tuscan order.
Toska'ne, Tuscany.
tos'sel, (-s), aglet, tassel.
tot, (vs) to, until, as far as; ~ *AAN*, up to, as far as; ~ *AFSKEID*, in farewell; ~ *ANTWOORD*, in reply; ~ stand *BRING*, bring about, accomplish; *dis ~ DAARNATOE*, so be it, it does not matter; ~ *die DOOD*, unto death; ~ *DUSVER*, thus (so) far; ~ *HIERTOE*, thus far; ~ *aan die KNIEË*, up to the knees, knee-deep; ~ stand *KOM*, come about; be passed (law); be founded (society); ~ *die LAASTE sent*, (down) to the last cent; ~ *niet MAAK*, demolish, nullify, make null and void; ~ *en MET*, up to and including; *hy kom ~ 20 MINUTE laat*, he is sometimes as much as 20 minutes late; ~ *NIET gaan*, perish; ~ *NOG toe*, hitherto, up till now; ~ *elke PRYS*, at any price, at all costs; ~ *SIENS*, goodbye; ~ *STAND bring*, establish; bring about; ~ *TAAK stel*, take as an objective; ~ *VOORSITTER kies*, elect as chairman; (vgw) until; *wag ~ ek jou roep*, wait until I call you; (bw) even; ~ *Jan was laat*, even John came late.
totaal', (s) (totale), total, aggregate; total amount; (b) **(totale)**, gross; complete, whole; quite; ..*tale AFMETING*, overall measure; ..*tale LENGTE*, overall length; ..*tale PRENTJIE*, overall picture; (bw) totally, altogether, entirely, quite, utterly; *iets ~ vergeet*, forget something completely; ~**beeld**, general picture; ~**bedrag**, sum total; ~**effek**, general effect; ~**indruk**, general impression; ~**som**, sum total; ~**syfer**, full sum.
totalisa'tor, (-s), totalisator.
totalitaris', (-te), totalitarian; ~**me**, totalitarianism.
totaliteit', totality.

tot'dat, until, till; *wag ~ ek kom*, wait until I arrive.
to'tem, (-s), totem; ~**dier**, totem animal; ~**is'me**, totemism; ~**paal**, totem pole.
to'to, (-'s), tote, totalisator.
totstand'brenging, accomplishment; establishment, bringing about.
totstand'koming, completion, creation, establishment, realization; passing (of a law).
tou¹, (s) (-e), string, twine, cord, hemp, rope; queue; crocodile (schoolchildren); ~ *in die BEK ry*, ride a horse with a riem instead of a bridle; ~ *in die BEK*, with curbs (checks); *op die ~ BLAAS*, urge oxen on by shouting; ~ *OPGOOI*, lose heart; throw up the sponge; *aan die ~ PRAAT*, talk interminably; *aan die ~ REËN*, be raining incessantly; *iets op ~ SIT*, set the ball rolling; get things going; *die ~ STYF trek*, strain at the rope; tug at the oar; *oor die ~ TRAP*, misbehave oneself, overstep the mark; *onder die ~ UITHELP*, help someone out of his difficulty; *ek kan daar geen ~ aan VASMAAK (vasknoop) nie*, I cannot make head or tail of it; ~ *VAT*, take the lead; (w) **(ge-)**, straggle after; walk in tandem, queue up; beat.
tou², (w) **(ge-)**, taw; dress (leather).
tou: ~**afskorting**, roped arena; ~**agtig, (-e)**, ropy; ~**brug**, rope-bridge; ~**buffel**, queue jumper; ~**doek**, (net) swab; ~**draaier**, ropemaker, roper; ~**draaiery**, ropery; ~**dweil**, rope-mop, swab; ~**gare**, rope yarn; ~**leer**, rope-ladder, Jacob's ladder; ratline(s).
tou'lei, (-ge-), lead the team; ~**er, (-s)**, leader of oxen, leader; plough-boy; *die beste ~ er sit op die voorbok*, bachelors' wives and old maids' children are the best trained.
tou: ~**oog**, grommet; ~**opgooier, (-s)**, coward, quitter; ~**pluiser, (-s)**, oakum-picker; ~**pluksel**, oakum; ~**ring**, grommet.
tourne'dos, tournedos.
tournu're, bustle (pad).
tou'slaer, (-s), rope-maker; ~**y**, rope-yard.
tou'spring, (-ge-), skip; *iem. laat ~*, give a person a hiding.
tou'staan, (-ge-), form a queue, queue (up); file (up), stand in file.
tou'tjie, (-s), cord, piece of string; thin strip of meat; wisp, rat's-tails (hair); *sy klere hang in ~s*, his clothes hang in tatters.
tou'tjiespring, (-gespring), skip.
tou'tjies: ~**rig**, ropy, stringy; ~**vleis**, thin strips of meat; ~**wol**, stringy wool.
toutologie', tautology; ..**lo'gies, (-e)**, tautological.
tou'trek, (s) tug-of-war; (w) **(ge-)**, pull at tug-of-war; tug at a rope; ~**kery**, tug-of-war; pulling strings, scheming, plotting, intrigue.
tou'trommel, winding-drum.
tou'werk, cordage, rigging; ropes, rope-work; ~**er**, ropeman, rigger.
tou'wys, broken-in to a certain extent, partly trained; *iem. ~ maak*, train a person, put someone up to the ropes, show someone the ropes.
to'wenaar, (-s), sorcerer, magician, theurgist, enchanter, wizard; witch-doctor.
to'wer, (ge-), enchant, charm; juggle; conjure; put a spell on; ~**agtig, (-e)**, glamorous; ~**beeld = toorbeeld**; ~**drank**, magic potion, nepenthe; ~**fee**, pixy; ~**fluit**, magic flute; ~**formule**, conjuration; ~**formulier**, spell, charm, incantation; ~**godin**, fairy queen, fairy; ~**goed = toorgoed**; ~**heks**, witch; ~**klank**, magic sound; ~**knoop = toorknoop**; ~**krag**, magic power, spell; ~**kring**, magic circle; ~**kuns = toorkuns**; ~**lamp**, Aladdin's lamp; ~**land**, Fairyland, land of enchantment; ~**lantern**, magic lantern; phantasmagoria; ~**middel = toormiddel**; ~**naar, (-s) = towenaar**; ~**nimf**, nymph; ~**ring**, enchanted ring; ~**slag**, touch of the magic wand; ~**spel**, magic, witchcraft; sorcery; ~**spreuk**, charm, magical formula; ~**staf**, magic wand; ~**wêreld**, world of enchantment; phantasmal world; ~**woord = toorwoord**; ~**y**, witchcraft; *see also* **toor**.
traag, (trae), sluggish, indolent, slow, supine, inactive, lumpish, easeful, inert, dull; languid, slack

(market); ~ **om 'n brief te beantwoord**, a bad correspondent; ~ **heid**, sluggishness, indolence, inertia (phys.); apathy, phlegm, inaction, inactivity, lenitude; backwardness.
traag'heidsmoment, moment of inertia.
traag'heids: ~ **vermoë**, inertia; ~ **werking**, permanency of inertia.
traag'loper, (-s), tardigrade, lazy (sluggish, indolent) person; chameleon.
traak, (ge-), touch, concern; *dit* ~ *MY nie*, I do not care, it is no concern of mine; *ek* ~ *NIE*, I don't care; ~ **-my-nieag'tig, (-e)**, don't-care, happy-go-lucky, nonchalant, irresponsible; ~ **-my-nieag'tig-heid**, nonchalance, carelessness; ~ **-nieag'tig(heid)** = **traak-my-nieagtig(heid)**.
traan[1], (s) fish-oil, blubber; train-oil.
traan[2], (s) **(trane)**, tear; *iem. se trane DROOG*, dry someone's tears; *dit GAAN ou* ~ *(trant)*, it is still as usual; *lang trane HUIL*, repent bitterly; cry tears of remorse; *bitter trane STORT*, shed bitter tears; *in trane SWEM*, bathe in tears; *trane met TUITE huil*, weep bitterly; *in trane UITBARS*, burst into tears; (w) **(ge-)**, water (eyes); bleed (line); fall drop by drop (juices).
traan'afskeiding, lachrymation.
traan'agtig, (-e), like whale-oil.
traan: ~ **bom**, tear-gas; ~ **buis**, lachrymal duct; ~ **flessie**, lachrymals; ~ **gas**, tear-gas.
traan'ketel, oil-kettle.
traan'klier, lachrymal gland.
traan kokery, try works, **koper**, train-oil merchant.
traan: ~ **oog**, bleary-eye, watery eye; ~ **oogkêrel**, bleary-eyed chap; ~ **rook**, tear-gas; ~ **sak**, tear-bag, lachrymal sac; ~ **verwekkend, (-e)**, lachrymatory (gas).
traan'vis, oil-fish.
traan'vol, (-le), tearful.
tradi'sie, (-s), tradition; ~ **vas, (-te)**, tradition-bound.
tradisioneel', (..nele), traditional, time-honoured.
tra'erig, (-e), rather sluggish.
trag, (ge-), try, attempt, endeavour.
tra'gea, (-s), trachea.
trage'die, (-s), tragedy.
tragedien'ne, (-s), tragedienne.
tra'gerig = **traerig**.
tragiek', tragedy; *die* ~ *v.d. lewe*, the tragedy of life.
tra'gies, (-e), tragic.
tragiet', (-e), trachyte.
tra'gikomedie, tragicomedy.
tra'gikomics, (-e), tragicomic.
tra'gikus, (-se, ..gici), tragedian.
tragi'tis, trachitis.
tragoom', trachoma.
trajek', (-te), trajectory; section, stretch, stage.
trak'sie, traction.
traktaat', (..tate), treaty; convention; ~ **jie, (-s)**, (religious) tract; flysheet.
trakta'sie, (-s), treat, feast.
trakteer', (ge-), treat, entertain, regale, stand a treat; *iem. op 'n drankie* ~, stand someone a drink.
traktement', (-e), salary, pay.
traktements'dag, pay-day.
traktement'staat, pay-sheet.
traktements'verhoging, increment of pay.
tra'lie, (-s), bar; grating; trellis, lattice; balustrade; grid; *agter die* ~ *s sit*, behind bars; ~ **balk**, lattice beam; ~ **brug**, lattice(d) bridge; ~ **deur**, grated door; ~ **heining**, trellis fence; ~ **hek**, trellis gate; bars; ~ **ontwerp**, lattice design; ~ **staaf**, grating-bar; ~ **venster**, barred window, lattice window; ~ **werk**, lattice-work, trellis-work, cage-work; grating, lacing, grate, latticing.
tramas'! time! *see* **horreltjies**.
trampolien', (-e, -s), trampoline; ~ **springer**, trampoline jumper.
tra'ne: ~ **brood**, bread of sorrows; ~ **dal**, vale of tears; ~ **rig, (-e)**, full of tears, watery, tearful, lachrymose; ~ **trekker**, tear-jerker; ~ **vloed**, torrent of tears.
trankiel', (ong.), (-e), tranquil, calm; particular; ~ **wees**, be finicky (pernickety).

trans, firmament; **(-e)**, pinnacle, battlement.
transak'sie, (-s), transaction, agreement; ~ **s**, dealings.
Transalpyns', (-e), Transalpine.
Transatlan'ties, (-e), Transatlantic.
transeer', (ge-), carve; ~ **mes**, carving-knife.
transenden'sie, transcendence.
transendentaal', (..tale), transcendental.
transep', (-te), transept.
transfereer', (ge-), transfer.
transfigura'sie, transfiguration.
transforma'sie, (-s), transformation.
transforma'tor, (-s), transformer; ~ **bord**, transformer base-board (elec.); ~ **huisie**, transforming station.
transformeer', (ge-), transform, convert.
transfu'sie, (-s), transfusion.
tran'sie = **trassie**.
Transilva'nië, Transylvania.
transis'tor, (-s), transistor; ~ **radio**, transistor radio.
transitief', (..tiewe), transitive.
transi'to, transit; ~ **handel**, transit trade; ~ **regte**, transit dues; ~ **wissel**, transit bill (of exchange).
Transjorda'nië, Transjordan(ia).
transkontinentaal', (..tale), transcontinental.
transkribeer', (ge-), transcribe.
transkrip'sie, (-s), transcription.
translitera'sie, transliteration.
translitereer', (ge-), transliterate.
transmis'sie, transmission; ~ **-as**, transmission shaft; ~ **-elektronmikroskoop**, transmission electron microscope.
transmitteer', (ge-), transmit.
transmuta'sie, transmutation.
transparant', (s) (-e), transparent; (b) **(-e)**, transparent, diaphanous, pellucid.
transpira'sie, transpiration (plant); perspiration (human).
transpireer', (ge-), transpire (plant); perspire.
transplantaat', (..tate), transplant.
transplanta'sie, transplantation.
transplanteer', (ge-), transplant.
transponeer', (ge-), transpose.
transport'[1], transport; conveyance; amount carried forward; ~ **ry, (-ge)**, ride transport.
transport'[2], **(-e)**, transfer; *loop of hy die* ~ *v.d. plaas in sy sak het*, behave as if the world were his footstool; ~ **akte**, deed of transfer.
transporta'sie, transportation.
tansport'band, conveyor belt.
transport'besorger, conveyancer.
transport': ~ **diens**, transport service; ~ **dler**, transport-animal.
transporteer'[1], **(ge-)**, transport, convey; carry forward (bookkeeping).
transporteer'[2], **(ge-)**, transfer, convey (law).
transporteur', (-s), transporter; protractor.
transport'koste[1], cost of transport.
transport'koste[2], cost of conveyance.
transport'nemer, transferee.
transport': ~ **pad**, main (transport) road; highway, high road; ~ **ryer, (-s)**, transport-rider; ~ **skip**, troop-ship, transport-ship; ~ **trein**, trooptrain.
transport'uitmaker, conveyancer; ~ **y**, conveyancing.
transport': ~ **vlieër**, transport-pilot; ~ **vliegtuig**, transport-aeroplane; ~ **wa**, transport-wa(g)gon.
transport'werk[1], transport (work).
transport'werk[2], conveyancing.
transport'werker, (-s), transport-worker.
transposi'sie, transposition.
transsubstansia'sie, transubstantiation.
Transvaal', Transvaal; ~ **s', (-e)**, Transvaal.
Transva'ler, (-s), Transvaler.
transversaal', (..sale), transversal.
trant, (-e), manner, way, style; *op die ou* ~, in the (same) old way, as usual.
trap[1], (s) **(-pe)**, staircase, flight (of steps); step, stage (of development); degree; pedal, treadle (of machine); *op 'n HOË* ~ *van beskawing*, highly civilized; *OORTREFFENDE* ~, superlative degree; *van* ~ *TOT* ~, by degrees; ~ **pe van VERGELYKING**, degrees of comparison.

trap², (s) stamp (with foot); kick, trample; (w) **(ge-)**, trample, tread; pedal; thresh; ~! scoot off!; *KORING* ~, thresh wheat; *hy LAAT hom nie* ~ *nie*, he does not take things lying down; *ONKLAAR* ~, go wrong; kick over the traces; *die ORREL* ~, blow the organ; *STUKKEND* ~, trample to pieces; *WATER* ~, tread water; ~**aansitter**, kick-starter.
trap: ~**arm**, flight of stairs; ~**as**, pedal shaft.
trap: ~**balie**, winepress; ~**blaasbalk**, foot-blower; ~**blok**, cradle (wood); ~**draaibank**, foot-lathe.
trapees', **(trapese)**, trapeze.
trape'sium, (-s), trapezium; ~**draad**, buttress-thread.
trap: ~**fiets**, push-bike; ~**fout**, foot fault (tennis); ~**getou**, footloom.
trap'gewel, crow-step gable, corbie-gable.
trap'-in-die-water, stick-in-the mud; bungler.
trap'katrol, step pulley.
trap: ~**kleedjie**, stair-carpet; ~**klip**, stepping-stone; ~**kop**, stairhead; ~**leer**, step-ladder, folding steps, set of steps; ~**leuning**, banister, stair-railing; ~**loper**, stair-carpet.
trap'masjien¹, treadle sewing-machine.
trap'masjien², threshing-machine, thresher.
trap: ~**meul(e)**, treadmill; ~**myn**, percussion-mine; ~**pehuis**, well-staircase.
trap'pel, (ge-), trample, stamp the feet, clatter, patter.
trap'per, (-s), pedal; treadle; pedaller; trader.
trap'pie, (-s), small step; estrade; *die gladde* ~ *s af*, on the downgrade.
Trappis', **(-te)**, Trappist (monk).
trap: ~**plank**, treadle; ~**portaal**, landing; ~**rem**, pedal brake; ~**rif**, step reef; ~**roede**, carpet-rod.
trap'sel, (-s), threshing, quantity threshed at one time.
trap'skakelaar, kickdown switch.
trap'gewys(e), (b, bw) gradual(ly), by degrees.
trapsoet'jies, (-e), chameleon; slowcoach; *soos 'n* ~ *LOOP*, walk at a snail's pace; *hy is 'n OU* ~, he is an old slowcoach.
trap'spil, newel.
trap: ~**stang**, treadle-bar; ~**styl**, baluster; ~**suutjies** (-e) = **trapsoetjies**.
trap: ~**tyd**, threshing-time; ~**vloer**, threshing-floor.
trap'vormig, (-e), ladder-shaped, scalariform.
tras, trass; ~**beton**, trass concrete.
traseer', (ge-), mark (trace) out; plot; ~**der**, (s), tracer; ~**werk**, tracery.
Tra'sië, Thrace.
tras'sie, (-s), hermaphrodite; freemartin; ~**bossie**, *Acacia stolonifera*.
trau'ma, (-s, -ta), trauma, wound; ~'**ties**, (-e), traumatic.
travers', (-e), traverse.
travesteer', (ge-), travesty, parody.
travestie', (-ë), travesty; ~**rol**, male part played by female.
trawal', (-le), hard work, great difficulty.
trawant', (-e), hanger-on, satellite, henchman.
tred, **(tredes)**, pace, tread, step; *gelyke* ~ *HOU met*, keep step with; *met VASTE* ~, with a firm step; ~**meul(e)**, treadmill; *in die* ~ *meule loop*, be at the treadmill.
tree, (s) (treë), pace, step; yard; *daar is maar een* ~ *tussen my en die dood*, there is but a step between me and the grave; *50* ~, about 50 yards; (w) **(ge-)**, pace, tread, step; *in BESONDERHEDE* ~, enter into detail; *in DIENS* ~, enter service; *in die HUWELIK* ~, marry; *TUSSENBEI* ~, intervene; *na VORE* ~, come forward; ~**hoogte**, riser (in stairs); ~**lengte**, going (of stairs); ~**meter**, pedometer; ~**plank**, footboard, running-board; foot-plate; ~**teller**, pedometer; ~**tjie**, (-s), little step.
tref, (s) hit; (w) **(ge-)**, hit, strike; affect; fall in with, chance on, come across; overtake, befall (disaster); *MAATREËLS* ~, take steps; *dit* ~ *MY nie*, it does not affect (concern) me; *dit* ~ *ONGELUKKIG*, it comes at an inopportune time; *die SKOOT het ge* ~, that was a hit; *deur die WEERLIG ge* ~, struck by lightning; ~**afstand**, effective range; *binne* ~ *afstand*, within range; ~**baar**, (..**bare**), vulnerable; ~**baarheid**, vulnerability; ~**-en-trap**

voorval, hit and run case; ~**fend**, (-e), striking, stirring, touching, effective, prominent, moving, impressive; salient; ~**fer**, (-s), hit, lucky shot; best seller; ~**ferparade**, hit parade; ~**hoek**, angle of impact; ~**kans**, chance of striking; ~**krag**, effect; appeal; striking-power; force of impact; ~**punt**, point of impact; ~**seker**, (very) accurate; ~**sekerheid**, accuracy, effectiveness; ~**snelheid**, striking velocity; ~**woord**, word-heading; catchword; ~**wydte**, incidence, range, scope, extent.
treg'ter, (-s), funnel, filler; hopper (mill); crater (shell); ~**broek**, bell-bottom trousers; ~**las**, (-se), hopper joint; ~**mond**, estuary; ~**oond**, funnel kiln; ~**spinnekop**, funnel spider; ~**tenk**, parachute tank; ~**vormig**, (-e), funnel-shaped, infundibular.
treil, (s) (-e), tow-line; drag-net; (w) **(ge-)**, tow; trawl; ~**er**, (-s), trawler; ~**lyn**, tow-line, rope; ~**net**, trawl; ~**pad**, track-road; tow-path.
treil'visser, trawler(man); ~**y**, trawling.
trein, (-e), train; retinue, following; *AFGAANDE* ~, down-train; *na die* ~ *BRING*, see off at the station; *DEURGAANDE* ~, through-train; *die* ~ *HAAL*, catch the train; *op die* ~ *KLIM*, board a train; *die* ~ *LOOP op tyd*, the train runs to time; *OPKOMENDE (opgaande)* ~, up-train; *met die STADIGE* ~ *kom*, be late; ~ *STEEL*, travel (on a train) without a ticket; *by die* ~ *gaan WEGSIEN (groet)*, see off at the station; ~**aansluiting**, train-connection; ~**beampte**, railway official; ~**beheer**, control of trains; ~**botsing**, train crash; ~**diens**, train service; ~**geld**, train fare; ~**gids**, railway timetable; ~**kondukteur**, guard, conductor; ~**lading**, train-load; ~**lektuur**, light reading; ~**ongeluk**, railway accident; ~**personeel**, train (running) staff; ~**ramp**, railway disaster; ~**register**, train register; ~**reis**, train journey; ~**roof**, train robbery; ~**rooster**, railway timetable; ~**siek**, train-sick; ~**smid**, wheeltapper; ~**spoor**, railway; ~**tyd**: *dis nog geen* ~ *tyd nie*, there's no hurry; ~**verbinding**, railway connection; ~**wa**, railway carriage.
trei'ter, (ge-), tease, torment, pester, nag, bully; ~**aar**, (-s), pesterer, nagger, tease(r).
trek¹, (s) inclination, desire; appetite; *groot* ~ *HÊ in*, have a strong liking for it; *in* ~ *WEES*, be popular (in vogue).
trek², (s) (-ke), pull; migration; emigration; drift; haul (fish); draught (of air); stroke, flourish (of pen); feature (of face); groove; draw (for competition); puff (of smoke); stage (on bus-route); trick (cards); *in BREË* ~ *ke*, in broad outline; *in EEN* ~, at one go; with a flourish; *die GROOT T* ~, the Great Trek; *in KORT* ~ *ke*, in brief outline; briefly; *'n* ~ *NEEM*, take a whiff (puff); *in die* ~ *SIT*, sit in the draught; (w) **(ge-)**, pull, draw, haul; attract (crowd); cash (cheque); infuse; slur (note); hale (forcibly with rope e.g.); be draughty; migrate (birds); move (in; to new neighbourhood); trek, emigrate; take effect (stimulant); draw (poultice); warp (wood); force (plant); *ons* ~ *MÔRE*, we are moving tomorrow; *iem. se ORE* ~, pull someone's ears; *PROEWE* ~, pull proofs; *'n TAND laat* ~, have a tooth extracted; *in TWYFEL* ~, doubt; *die VIERKANTSWORTEL* ~, extract the square root; ~**arbeid**, migratory labour; ~**bal**, twister (ball); ~**balk**, tie beam; ~**beeste**, draught oxen; cattle on trek; ~**boer**, trek farmer; ~**bout**, draw-bolt; ~**by**, swarming bee; ~**dag**, day of the draw (lottery); moving-day; ~**dier**, yoke-animal, draught animal; ~**dierkrag**, animal power; ~**draad**, drawn thread; ~**duif**, migratory pigeon; ~**duiker**, Cape cormorant; ~**duin**, migrating dune; ~**gat**, vent-hole; ~**gees**, migratory spirit, trekking-spirit, wanderlust; ~**geld**, premium allotment; ~**goed**, gear (of draught animals); draught animals; ~**haak**, turrel, draw-hook; ~**hou**, pull (golf); hook (cricket); ~**kaart**, card of re-entry; ~**kabel**, starting cable; ~**kas**, drag box (mech.); ~**kebek**, (ge-), bill and coo; ~**kend**, (-e), ambulant, ambulatory; emigratory, emigrant, migratory.
trek'ker, (-s), trekker, emigrant; giver, drawer (of bill); recipient (pension); tractor; puller; extractor; hauler; trigger (rifle); ~**beuel**, trigger-guard.

trek'kerig, (-e), draughty; ~**heid**, draughtiness.

trek: ~**kerslewe**, nomadism; ~**kerswee**, woes of the trekker; ~**kery**, moving, drawing, cashing; ~**ketting**, trek chain; ~**king**, drawing, pulling, traction; draught; convulsion; **(-s)**, St. Vitus's dance, fits (med.); twitchings.

trek'kingslys, list of drawings.

trek: ~**klamp**, come-along clamp; ~**klavier**, accordion; ~**koord**, draw chord; ~**krag**, tractive power; thrust (propeller); appeal (to emotions); ~**laai**, drawer; ~**laken**, draw sheet; ~**lewe**, life on trek; ~**lus**, desire to trek about, wanderlust; ~**lyn**, release cord; ~**mes**, draw knife; ~**meter**, tensimeter, manometer; ~**net**, dragnet; trail net, seine; ~**orrel**, concertina; ~**os**, draught ox; ~**paal**, straining post; ~**pad**, trek road; *op die* ~*pad wees*, have taken to the road; ~**pas**, trek permit; *die* ~*pas kry*, be fired; be sent packing; get the sack; ~**pen**, marking-pen; geometrical pen, ruling-pen; ~**perd**, draught horse; ~**pleister**, blister; vesicatory, court plaster; drawing plaster; lover; attraction; draw; ~**pot**, teapot; ~**roete**, migratory route; ~**saag**, jack saw; cross-cut saw; ~**sel, (-s)**, infusion, quantity of coffee, tea, etc. used for one pot, brew(age); ~**skaal**, spring balance; ~**skakelaar**, pull switch; ~**skape**, sheep on trek; ~**skroefvliegtuig**, tractor aeroplane; ~**skuit**, drawboat, hackney boat; ~**sluiter**, zipfastener; ~**spanning**, (tensile) stress, strain; ~**spier**, extensor; erector; abductor; motory muscle; ~**sprinkaan**, migratory (flying) locust; ~**stang**, draw bar, tie beam, radius bar, clevis; pull rod, drag link; connecting-rod; ~**sterkte**, tensile strength; ~**toets**, tension test; ~**tou**, chain; drag rope; plug (W.C.); tow rope, drag rope; draught cable; ~**vas**; ~*vaste staal*, high tensile steel; ~**vastheid**, tensile strength; ~**vee**, livestock on trek; ~**vermoë**, carry (of machine); ~**vervoer**, haulage; ~**vervoerweg**, haulage way; ~**vis**, migratory fish; ~**visser**, seine fisherman; ~**voël**, migratory bird, bird of passage, migrant; ~**voertuig**, towing vehicle; ~**volk**, migratory people; ~**vry, (-e)**, draughtproof; ~**vyl**, draw file; ~**vorming**, tensile strain; ~**weerstand**, tensile strength; ~**werk**, draft gear (of machine).

trem, (-me, -s) tram(-car).

tre'ma, (-s), diaeresis.

tremato'de, (-s), trematode.

trem: ~**bestuurder**, tram-driver; ~**bus**, trackless tram; electric bus; ~**diens**, tram service.

tre'mel, (-s), mill-hopper.

trem: ~**geld**, tram fare; ~**halte**, tram stop; ~**huisie**, tram shelter; ~**kaartjie**, tram ticket; ~**kondukteur**, tram conductor; ~**lyn**, tramline.

trem'mer, (-s), trimmer (ship).

tre'molo, (-'s), tremolo (mus.).

trem: ~**personeel**, tram staff; ~**spoor**, tramline.

tremulant', (-e), tremulant.

trem: ~**verbinding**, tram connection; ~**verkeer**, tramway traffic; ~**wa**, tramcar; ~**weë**, tramways; ~**weëdepartement**, tramway department.

trenodie', (-ë), threnody, threnode.

trens, (-e), snaffle-bit, bridoon; loop (needlework); ~**riem**, thong (for fastening the yoke to the chain), loop strap; ~**toom**, snaffle bridle.

trepaan', (trepane), trepan.

trepaneer', (ge-), trepan; ~**boor**, trepan.

tres, (-se), tress; braid; ~**band**, Prussian binding

tret'ter = treiter.

treur, (ge-), mourn, grieve for; pine; languish; ~ *OM iem.*, mourn for a person; ~ *OOR*, mourn over; ~**dig, (-te)**, elegy, monody, dirge, ~**digter**, elegiac poet.

treu'rig (-e), mournful, sorrowful, sad (at heart), pitiful, doleful, dreary, gloomy, mirthless, lugubrious, dismal; *'n* ~*e vertoning*, a miserable performance (show); ~**heid**, sadness, mournfulness, dreariness, gloom; pitifulness, dolefulness; ~**heid op note**, dear, oh dear!

treur: ~**kleed**, mourning-dress; ~**lied**, elegy, dirge; ~**mare**, sad news; ~**mars**, funeral (dead) march; ~**musiek**, funer(e)al music; ~**nis**, sadness; ~**sang**, elegy, dirge, lament; ~**sangdigter**, elegist

treur'spel, tragedy; ~**digter**, tragedian, tragic poet; ~**speler**, tragedian.

treur: ~**toneel**, tragic scene; ~**toon**, (..**tone**), lamentation, mournful note; ~**tyd**, time of weeping; *annus luctus* (law); ~**wilg, (-e)**, ~**wilgerboom**, ~**wilkerboom**, weeping willow.

treu'sel, (ge-), loiter, dawdle; ~**aar, (-s)**, dawdler.

trew'wa, (-s), trewwa (*Satyrium coriifolium*); bungler, noodle; *'n ou* ~, a stick-in-the-mud; an old stick.

tria'de, (-s), triad.

trian'gel, (-s), triangle (musical instrument).

triangula'sie, triangulation.

trianguleer', (ge-), triangulate.

triargie', (-ë), triumvirate, triarchy.

tribula'sie, (-s), tribulation.

tribunaal', (..nale), tribunal.

tribunaat', (..nate), tribunate, tribuneship.

tribu'ne, (-s), platform, stand.

tribuun', (tribune), (Roman) tribune.

tribuut', tribute, tax.

tri'cot, tricot; tights.

Trier, Treves.

tries'tig, (-e), sad, gloomy, dejected, dreary; ~**heid**, sadness, gloom, dejection.

triet'serig, (-e), weak, feeble, frail; ~**heid**, weakness, frailty.

trifo'lium, trefolium.

trigino'se, trichinosis.

trigologie', trichology.

trigoloog', (..loë), trichologist.

trigonometrie', trigonometry; ..**me'tries, (-e)**, trigonometrical.

trik'trak, backgammon; tick-tack.

tril¹, (s) (plat), **(-le)**, penis.

tril², (w) (ge-), tremble, quiver (voice); vibrate (of sound); flutter, pulsate, pulse, quake, palpitate, quaver, flicker; ~**beeld**, cinematoscopic view; ~**beton**, vibrated concrete; ~**bewing**, vibratory motion; ~**diertjie**, vibrio, ~**gras**, quaking-grass (*Briza maxima*); ~**haar**, vibrissa, cilium; ~**haaragtig, (-e)**, ciliary; ~**haarbeweging**, ciliary movement; cilium; ~**hare**, cilia.

triljoen', (-e), trillion.

tril'ler, (-s), trill, grace-note, shake (mus.); ~**ig, (-e)**, quaky, quavery; ~**veer**, vibrator, trembler.

tril'ling, (-e, -s), vibration, tremor (of voice); flickering; oscillation; palpitation; thrill; trill (music); quaking; chatter (of tool); jarring (of machine); pulsation; quiver.

tril'lings: ~**boog**, arc of vibration; ~**demper**, vibration absorber; ~**duur**, period of vibration; ~**getal**, vibration number, frequency; ~**kring**, oscillatory circuit; ~**meter**, vibroscope; ~**wydte**, amplitude of vibration.

tril'ling: ~**vry, (-e)**, free from vibration; ~**werend, (-e)**, antivibratory.

trilobiet', (-e), trilobite.

trilogie', (-ë), trilogy.

tril: ~**populier**, aspen, mountain ash; ~**register**, tremolant; ~**sif**, vibrating screen; ~**vis**, electric fish; ~**wydte**, amplitude of vibration.

trimes'ter, (-s), term, quarter, three months.

trim'gim, trim gym.

trim'park, trimpark.

tri'o, (-'s), trio.

triolet', (-te), triolet.

triomf', (-e), triumph, victory, ~**ant'lik, (-e)**, triumphant; glorious; ~**a'tor, (-s)**, victor; ~**boog**, triumphal arch; ~**eer', (ge-)**, triumph; ~**kreet**, shout of triumph; ~**lied**, triumphal song, paean; ~**poort**, triumphal arch; ~**suil**, triumphal column; ~**tog**, triumphal procession; ~**wa**, triumphal car (chariot).

triool', (triole), triole.

tri'pang, (-s), trepang.

tripanosoom', (..some), trypanosome.

triparti'sie, (-s), tripartition.

tripleer', (ge-), triplicate.

tri'plekshout, three-ply wood.

**tripliek', **, reply to a reply (e.g. in the press); surrejoinder.

**tripliot', **triplite.

triplikaat', (..**kate**), triplicate.
tripliseer', (ge-), surrejoin.
tri'plo, (-'s), triplicate; *in* ~, in triplicate.
Tri'poli, Tripoli; ~**taans'**, (-e), Tripolitan.
trip'pel, (s) trippling; racking; tripple (of horse); (w) (**ge**-), trip along; pitter-patter; tripple (horse); rack; patter; ~ **aar**, (-s), trippler; racker; ambler; ~**maat**, tripple time (rhythm); ~**pas**, trippling step, trippling gait.
trip'pens, (-e), threepenny bit, tickey.
triptiek', (-e), triptych.
trip'trap, pit-a-pat.
trireem', (trireme), trireme.
tri'ton, (-s), triton.
trits, (-e), trio, triplet, triad.
trium'vir, (-i), triumvir; ~**aat'**, triumvirate.
triviaal', (..**viale**), trivial; trite; petty, insignificant; ..**vialiteit'**, triviality; triteness.
troebadoer', (-s), troubadour.
troe'bel, muddy, turbid, cloudy; *in* ~ *water vis*, fish in troubled waters; ~**agtig**, (-e), muddy; ~**e**, disturbances; ~**heid**, turbidity, muddiness; ~ **rig**, (-e), muddy, unclear, cloudy.
troef, (s), (**troewe**), trump; ~ *BEKEN*, play to trumps; *SONDER troewe*, chicane; *troewe TREK*, draw trumps; ~ *VERSAAK*, renegue; fail to follow suit; ~ *VRA*, lead trumps; trumps; (w) (**ge**-), trump, overtrump; *IEM.* ~, checkmate someone; outwit someone; ~**aas**, ace of trumps; ~ **boer**, knave (jack) of trumps; ~**heer**, king of trumps; ~**kaart**, trump card; *sy* ~**kaart** *speel*, play his trump card; ~**kleur**, trump suit; ~**maker**, declarer (cards); ~**vrou**, queen of trumps.
troei', back! (used to oxen and cows); *vir niemand* ~ *staan nie*, stand back for no one.
troep, (-e), troop; troupe (of actors); bevy (of girls); horde (of ruffians).
troe'pe, troops, forces; array; ~**beweging**, troop movement; ~**kwartier**, cantonment; ~**mag**, military force(s); ~**sametrekking**, concentration of troops; ~**skip**, troopship, trooper; ~**transport**, transportation of troops; ~**verbruik**, wastage of troops; ~**vervoer**, transport of troops; ~**vliegtuig**, troop-carrier.
troep'leier, group-leader, scoutmaster.
troeps'gewys(e), in troops.
troe'tel, (ge-), pet, fondle, caress, coddle, pamper; ~**ary**, pampering; ~**dier**, pet animal; ~**dierskou**, pet show; ~**kind**, spoiled child, darling, favourite; ~*kind v.d. FORTUIN*, fortune's child; *iem. se* ~*kindjie*, one's pet subject; ~**naam**, pet name, term of endearment; ~**woord**, term of endearment.
trofee', (trofeë), trophy, cup (sports).
trof'fel, (-s), trowel; ~**werk**, trowelling.
trog, (trôe, -ge), trough; hod; hutch (for ore).
trogee', (..**geë**, -s), trochee; ..**ge'ïes**, (-e), trochaic.
trog'gel, (ge-), wheedle, coax, cajole.
troglodiet', (-e), cave-dweller, troglodyte.
trog'werk, troughing.
troi'ka, (-s), troika.
Trojaan', (..**jane**), Trojan; *veg soos 'n* ~, fight like a Trojan; ~**s'**, (-e), Trojan; *die* ~ *se perd inhaal*, allow the Trojan horse within one's walls.
Tro'je, Troy; *Helena van* ~, Helen of Troy.
trok, (s) (-**ke**), truck; (w) (ge-), truck; ~**smit**, truck-buster; ~**voorraad**, truckage; ~**vrag**, truckload.
trol, (-**le**), troll.
trol'lie, (-s), trolley.
trom, (-**me**), drum, tomtom; *die groot* ~ *ROER*, beat the big drum; *met stille* ~ *VERTREK*, take French leave.
trombo'ne, (-s), trombone; ..**bonis'**, (-te), trombonist.
trombo'se thrombosis; ~**lyer**, thrombosis patient.
trom'bus, (-se), thrombus.
trom'geroffel, roll of drums.
trom'mel, (s) (-s), drum, trunk; canister; case, box; barrel (watch); tympanum, ear-drum; tummy; ~ *van gangspil*, capstan-barrel; (w) (ge-), drum; (make) rataplan; strum; thrum; ~ **aar**, (-s), drummer; ~**anker**, drum armature; ~ **as**, drum axle; ~**beentjie**, tympanic bone; ~**dik**, quite filled, sated; very satisfied; skinful; ~**holte**, tympanic cavity; ~**saag**, drum saw, cylinder saw; ~**sif**, revolving screen; ~**slag**, drum beat; ~**slaner**, (-s), drummer; ~**spanner**, brace; ~**stok**, drumstick; ~**sug**, hoove, tympanitis; ~**vel**, drumhead; ~ **vis**, drum-fish; ~**vlies**, tympanum, ear-drum; drum-skin; ~**vliesontsteking**, tympanitis; ~**vuur**, drum-fire.
tromp, (-e), toy trumpet; mouth-harp; trunk (of elephant); muzzle (fire-arm); ~**beskermer**, muzzle protector.
trompet', (s) (-te), trumpet; clarion; tromba; horn; *sy eie* ~ *blaas*, blow his own trumpet; (w) (ge-), trumpet; ~**blaser**, (-s), trumpeter; ~**geskal**, fanfare, flourish (blare) of trumpets, trumpetry; *met* ~*geskal uitbasuin*, proclaim with a flourish of trumpets; ~**sinjaal**, trumpet-call; ~**skulp**, sea-trumpet; ~**stoot**, trumpet blast.
trompet'ter, (-s), trumpet; trumpeter; convolvulus; ~ **blom**, convolvulus; bignonia, trumpet-flower.
trompet': ~**vis**, trumpet-fish; ~**voël**, trumpeter (bird); ~**vormig**, (-e), trumpet-shaped.
trom'pie, (-s), mouth-harp, Jew's harp.
tromp'-op, point-blank; directly; close; *iem.* ~ *loop*, let someone have it straight from the shoulder; pitch into someone; ~**skoot**, pot shot.
trom'poppie, (-s), drum majorette.
trom'slaner, kettledrummer.
tro'nie, (-s), face, visage, phiz, mug.
tronk, (-e), prison, goal, lock-up, cooler, bagnio, quod; limbo, calaboose, choky, clink; *in die* ~ *sit*, imprison, incarcerate; ~**bewaarder**, prison warder, gaoler; ~**bewaarster**, wardress; ~**binneplaas**, prison yard; ~**breker**, prison-breaker; ~**deur**, prison door; ~**sel**, prison cell; hold; ~**skip**, hulk; ~**straf**, imprisonment; ~**tralies**, prison bars; ~**voël**, gaol-bird; habitual criminal; ~**wa**, prison van, Black Maria, pick-up van.
troon, (s) (**trone**), throne; *AFSTAND doen v.d.* ~, abdicate; *die* ~ *BEKLIM (bestyg)*, ascend the throne; *van die* ~ *STOOT*, dethrone; drive from the throne; (w) (ge-), reign; be on the throne; *hy* ~ *bokant almal uit*, he excels (surpasses) everybody; ~**hemel**, dais, canopy, baldaquin, baldachin; ~**opvolger**, (-s), heir to the throne; *vermoedelike* ~*opvolger*, heir presumptive; ~**opvolging**, succession to the throne; ~**rede**, king's (queen's) speech; ~**saal**, throne-room.
troons: ~**afstand**, abdication; ~**beklimming**, ~**bestyging**, accession to the throne, ascension, enthronement; ~**verheffing**, enthronement.
troon'verlater, abdicator.
troop, (**trope**), trope, metaphor.
troos, (s) comfort, consolation, solace, relief; *my ENIGSTE* ~, my only consolation; ~ *PUT uit*, derive comfort from; *SKRAAL* ~, cold comfort; poor consolation; Job's comfort; ~ *SOEK by*, seek comfort from; ~ *VIND in*, find comfort in; *iem. tot* ~ *WEES*, be a comfort to someone; (w) (ge-), console, comfort, solace; *jou met die gedagte* ~, console yourself with the thought; ~**brief**, letter of condolence; ~**lied**, consolatory song; ~**medisyne**, placebo; ~**prys**, consolation prize; ~**ryk**, (-e), comforting, consolatory.
troos'teloos, (..**lose**), comfortless, disconsolate; inconsolable; cheerless, drab, bleak, dismal, dreary; ~**heid**, disconsolation; inconsolableness, despair, dreariness, desolateness, desolation; comfortlessness.
troos'tend, (-e), comforting, consoling.
troos'ter, (-s), comforter; dummy; *die T* ~, the Comforter; ~**tjie**, (-s), dummy.
troos: ~**verlof**, compassionate leave; ~**vol**, (-le), consolatory, consoling; ~**woord**, word of comfort.
trop, (-**pe**), flock, fold (sheep); troop (baboons); covey (partridges); gang (workmen); crowd, mass, mob (people); bevy (girls); batch (papers); drove, herd (cattle); pack (dogs); cluster; pride (lions); host (people); crew; flight (birds).
tro'pe, tropics; ~**helm**, tropical helmet; ~ **pak**, tropical suit; ~**vas**, (-te), tropicalized.
tropie', (-**ë**), tropism.

tro'pies, (-e), tropical.
tropis'me, tropism.
tro'posfeer, troposphere.
trop: ~**ram,** flock-ram; ~**sluiter,** professional mourner; ~**sluitertjie, (-s),** youngest child, Benjamin, minimus.
tros, (s) (-se), bunch (of flowers); batch (of children); hand (bananas); cluster (of flowers); fascicle; raceme (bot.); camp-train; (w) **(ge-),** cluster, bunch; ~**behuising,** group building; ~**den,** cluster pine; ~**rosyne,** stalked raisins; ~**topsiekte,** bunchy-top disease; ~**tou,** hawser; ~**vormig, (-e),** racemose; ~**vormigheid,** racemation.
trots, (s) (-se) pride, haughtiness; glory; *met* ~ *op sy PRESTASIE vervul wees,* be filled with pride in his achievement; *hy STEL sy* ~ *daarin,* he takes pride in it; (b, bw) **(-e),** proud, haughty, overbearing, overweening; proud-hearted, prideful, high-minded; high; elated; *niks om oor* ~ *te WEES nie,* nothing to be proud about; ~ *WEES op,* pride oneself on; be proud of; (vs) in spite of, despite, notwithstanding; ~ *dit alles,* in spite of all that; ~**aard, (-s),** proud person; ~**eer', (ge-),** go against, defy, challenge, bid defiance (to), set at defiance, outface, brave, face, fly in the face of; ~**e'rend, (-e),** defiant; ~**e'ring,** defiance, bravado; ~**heid,** pride, haughtiness.
trou¹, (s) fidelity, faith, faithfulness, loyalty, constancy; *te GOEDER* ~, in good faith, bona fide; *GOEIE* ~, good faith, bona fide; *te KWADER* ~, in bad faith; *KWAAIE* ~, bad faith, mala fide; ~ *SWEER aan,* swear allegiance to; (b) **(-e),** faithful; true; loyal (subject); trusty, devoted; regular (reader); accurate (copy); *MEKAAR* ~ *bly,* stand by (be true to) one another; ~ *aan sy WOORD,* true to his word.
trou², (s) marriage; *sy* ~ *hang uit,* he can hardly wait to get married; (w) **(ge-),** marry, wed, get married; *HAASTIG* ~, bring bog berou, marry in haste and repent at leisure; ~ *is niks, maar die lank HOU,* it's not so much getting married as the living together; *onder MEKAAR trou,* intermarry; ~ *MET,* get married to; *uit LIEFDE* ~, marry for love; ~ *is nie PERDE koop nie,* marriage is a serious matter; *met iets getroud WEES,* be tied to something.
trou: ~**akte,** marriage certificate; ~**baar, (..bare),** marriageable, nubile; ~**baarheid,** nubility, marriageableness; ~**belofte,** plighting of troth; promise of marriage, affiance, espousal; ~**bewys,** marriage certificate (lines); ~**breuk,** breach of faith, infidelity, punic faith, betrayal, perfidy; ~**dag,** wedding-day; ~**e,** marriage; *op* ~ *e (staan),* ready to be getting married.
trou'eloos, (..lose), faithless, disloyal, perfidious, false; felonious; ~**heid,** faithlessness, disloyalty, perfidy, perfidiousness.
trou'ens, besides, indeed, really, as a matter of fact, for that matter; *daar is* ~ *nog niks gedoen nie,* nothing, in fact, has yet been done.
trou'elik, faithfully.
trou: ~**ery,** wedding; ~**fees,** wedding feast; ~**gelofte,** marriage vow.
trouhar'tig, (-e), true-hearted, candid, sincere; ~**heid,** true-heartedness, candour, sincerity.
trou: ~**klere,** wedding-clothes; ~**koets,** wedding-coach; ~**koors,** eagerness for marriage; *die* ~ *koors loop hoog,* they are eager for marriage; ~**lus'tig, (-e),** desirous of (keen on) marrying; ~**pak,** wedding-suit; ~**pand,** wedding-ring; marriage-pledge; ~**pant,** roller; ~**party,** wedding-party; ~**planne,** wedding-plans; *hy koester* ~ *planne,* he is planning to get married; ~**plegtigheid,** nuptials, wedding-ceremony; ~**present,** wedding-present; ~**register,** marriage record; ~**ring,** wedding-ring; ~**rok,** wedding-dress; ~**sertifikaat,** marriage certificate.
trous'seau, (-s), trousseau.
troy'gewig, troy weight.
tru, (w) **(ge-),** reverse (car); back (animals); (tw) back! (used to oxen and cows).
truf'fel, (-s), truffle.
trui, (-e), sweater, jersey, pullover; ~**tjie, (-s),** small sweater.

trui'tjie-roer-my-nie = **kruidjie-roer-my-nie.**
tru: ~**kaatser,** reflector; ~**koppelaar,** reverse clutch.
trul, (-le), (plat) prick, cock, penis.
tru: ~**lamp,** back-up lamp; ~**projektor,** overhead projector; ~**rat,** reverse wheel (loco); reverse gear (motor); ~**spanning,** reverse tension; ~**spieëltjie,** rear-view mirror.
trust, (-s), trust; ring, pool; ~**akte,** trust deed; ~**bank,** trust bank; ~**ee', (-s),** trustee; ~**fonds,** trust fund; ~**geld,** trust money; ~**maatskappy,** trust company; ~**rekening,** trust account.
tru'stroom, back stream; reverse current.
truuk, (-s), trick; gimmick.
tru'versnelling, reverse gear.
tryp'ferweel, moquette, mock-velvet.
tsaar, (tsare), czar.
tsam'ma, (-s), wild melon (*Citrullus vulgaris*).
tsa'rewitsj, (-e), czarevitch.
tsari'na, (-s), czarina.
tses'sebe, (-s), tsessebe (*Damaliscus lunatus*).
tset'sevlieg, tsetse(-fly) (*Glossina morsitans*).
Tsjeg, (-ge), Czech; Czech (language); ~**gies, (-e),** Czech.
Tsjeg'go-Slowaky'e, Czechoslovakia.
T'-skarnier, garnet-hinge, cross-garnet.
tsot'si, (-'s), tsotsi.
T'-staaf, T-bar.
T'-stuk, T-piece.
Tswa'na, Tswana.
t'tjie, (-s), small t.
tu'ba, (-s), tuba.
tuber'kel, (-s), tubercle; ~**basil,** tubercle germ.
tuberkuleus', (-e), tubercular, tuberculous.
tuberkulo'se, tuberculosis; ~**bestryding,** fight against tuberculosis; ~**pasiënt,** consumptive; ~**vry, (-e),** free from tuberculosis; ~ *vrye melk,* tuberculin-tested milk.
tuberoos', (..rose), tuberose.
tuf, tuff; ~**agtig, (-e),** tuffaceous; ~**keël,** tuffcone; ~**kryt,** calcareous tufa; ~**steen,** tuff.
tuf-tuf', (-fe, -s), (kindert.), motor-car; train.
tug, (s) discipline; punishment; *hom maklik aan* ~ *ONDERWERP,* be amenable to discipline; *VADERLIKE* ~, paternal discipline; (w) **(ge-),** punish, chastise; discipline; ~**handhawend, (-e),** disciplinary; ~**huis,** house of correction, penitentiary; ~**komitee,** disciplinary committee; ~**maatreël,** disciplinary measure; ~**meester,** disciplinarian; censor; proctor; ~**middel,** disciplinary measure; ~**ordonnansie,** disciplinary regulation; ~**roede,** scourge (fig.); rod of correction, cane; ~**saak,** disciplinary case; ~**skool,** reformatory, truant-school.
tug'teloos, (..lose), undisciplined; insubordinate; dissolute, licentious; ~**heid,** insubordination; want of discipline; dissoluteness.
tug'tig, (ge-), chastise, punish, birch, castigate, correct, discipline, whip; -**ing,** chastisement, punishment, correction, castigation; ~**ingsekspedisie,** punitive expedition.
tui, guy; ~**anker** bow-anchor.
tui'e: ~**beslag,** horse-brasses; ~**kamer,** harness-room; ~**maker,** harness-maker; ~**makersels,** harness-awl; ~**plaatjie,** horse-brass.
tuig, (tuie), harness; rigging; gear; trash; *die* ~ *NEERLE,* retire; *in die* ~ *STERF,* die in harness; ~**huis,** armoury, arsenal; ~**perd,** harness-horse.
tui'kabel, tui'ketting, mooring-cable.
tuil, bunch of flowers; posy; corymb (bot.); ~**vormig, (-e),** corymbous, corymbose.
tui'mel, (ge-), tumble, topple over; ~**aar, (-s),** tumbler (aerobat.; pigeon); rocker (motor), bent lever; porpoise; bell-crank lever; seal (rifle); ~**aarveer,** sear-spring; ~**deur,** turnover door; ~**droër,** tumble-drier; ~**gees,** turbulent spirit; ~**ing,** tumble, fall, somersault; purler; purl; ~**kar,** tip-cart; ~**raam,** bascule window; fanlight; ~**skakel,** tumbler-switch.
tuin, (-e), garden; *iem. om die* ~ *lei,* lead someone by the nose (up the garden path); ~**aanleg,** laying out of garden; ~**angelier,** garden-pink, carnation, gillyflower; ~**argitek,** landscape gardener; ~**baas,** gar-

den-owner; ~**bank,** garden seat; ~**bedding,** garden plot, garden bed; ~**blom,** garden flower; ~**boon,** broad bean.
tuin'bou, horticulture; gardening; ~**kun'dig, (-e),** horticultural; ~**kun'dige (-s),** horticulturist; ~**-onderwys,** horticultural teaching; ~**skool,** horticultural school; ~**tentoonstelling,** horticultural show.
tuin: ~ **deur,** garden gate; ~ **dorp,** garden village; ~**ery, (-e),** garden; ~ **fees,** garden party; ~ **fluiter,** pettichaps; garden-warbler; ~ **gereedskap,** garden(ing) tools; ~ **grafie,** dibble; ~ **groente,** vegetables; ~**grond,** garden plot; garden soil; ~**handskoen,** gardening glove; ~ **hek,** garden gate; ~ **hoed,** garden hat; ~ **huis,** summer-house; town-house; ~ **hulp,** garden help, garden worker.
tuinier', (-e, -s), gardener, horticulturist.
tuiniers': ~**almanak,** gardener's calender; ~**vak,** gardening.
tuin: ~ **kamer,** room facing garden; ~ **kers,** garden cress; ~ **kneg,** gardener's assistant; ~ **maak, (-ge-),** garden; ~ **makery,** gardening; ~ **man, (-ne, ..liede),** gardener; ~ **muur,** garden-wall; ~**ontwerp,** garden design; ~ **ontwerper,** garden-designer; ~ **paadjie,** garden path; ~ **party,** garden party; ~ **skêr,** garden-shears; ~ **slak,** garden snail; ~ **slang,** hose(-pipe); ~ **spinnekop,** diadem-spider; ~ **sproeier, (-s),** garden sprayer; ~ **spruit,** garden hose; ~ **stad,** garden city; ~ **trekker,** garden tractor; ~ **vrug,** garden fruit; ~ **vurk,** weeding-fork; ~ **vygie,** portulaca; ~ **werk,** gardening.
tuis, at home; in; *iem.* ~ *MAAK,* make someone feel at home; ~ *VOEL,* feel at home; ~ *WEES,* be in (at home); ~ *WEES in Latyn,* be at home in Latin; ~**berei, (-de),** home-cooked; ~ **blyer,** stay-at-home.
tuis'bring, (-ge-), bring home, see home; *iets AAN iem.* ~, bring something home to somebody; *ek kan dit NIE* ~ *nie,* I cannot place it; I cannot recall it; ~ *ONDER,* put under; place, classify.
tuis: ~ **dorp,** home town; ~ **front,** home front; ~**gaan, (-ge-),** stay (at), board; ~**gebak, (-te),** home-baked; ~ **hawe,** base port; ~ **hoort, (-ge-),** belong; *die saak hoort nie hier* ~ *nie,* the matter is irrelevant; ~ **hou, (-ge-),** keep at home; ~ **huis,** farmer's town house; ~ **kamer,** farmer's town-room; ~ **karteling,** home-perm; ~ **kom, (-ge-),** arrive (get) home; ~ **koms,** home-coming, return; ~**land,** home country; ~ **lyn,** parent line; ~ **reis,** homeward journey; ~ **sitter,** stay-at-home; ~ **stad,** home town; ~ **stasie,** home (base) station; ~ **te, (-s),** home; abode; ~ **teskepper,** home-maker; ~ **verbruik,** home consumption; ~ **verlof,** home leave; ~ **verpleging,** home-nursing; ~ **wag,** home guard; ~ **weefstof,** homespun.
tuit, (s) (-e), spout, nozzle; poke (hat); mouthpiece; nose-piece; (w) **(ge-),** tingle, sing; pout; *die LIPPE* ~, pout the lips; *my ORE* ~, my ears are tingling (singing); ~**hoed,** poke-bonnet; ~**hoop,** stook (maize).
tui'ting, tingling; tinnitus, ringing of the ears; pouting.
tuit: ~ **kan,** jug with spout, feeding-cup; ~ **kappie,** poke-bonnet; ~ **koppie,** invalid-cup; ~ **miershoop,** conical ants' nest; ~ **plaat,** lip-plate; ~ **vormig, (-e),** nozzle-shaped.
tuk: ~ *op,* bent on, keen on, eager for.
Tuk'kie, (-s), Tukkie, Pretoria University (formerly T.U.C) student.
tul'band, (-e), turban.
tul'le, tulle.
tulp, (-e), tulip; poisonous iris; *GEEL* ~, *Homeria collina; ROOI* ~, *Homeria miniata;* ~ **blom,** magnolia; ~ **bol,** tulip bulb; ~ **boom,** tulip tree; ~ **kweker,** tulip-grower; ~ **kwekery,** tulip-growing; tulip-nursery; ~ **perk,** tulip-bed.
tumult', (-e), tumult, uproar.
tu'na, (-s), tunny.
tung: ~ **boom,** tung-tree; ~ **olie,** tung-oil.
tuniek', (-e), tunic.
Tu'nis, Tunis.
Tuni'siër, (-s), Tunisian.
Tuni'sies, (-e), Tunisian.

turbi'ne, (-s), turbine; ~ **spuitvliegtuig,** turbojet (aeroplane); ~ **stoomboot,** turbine steamer; ~ **straal,** turbojet; ~ **straalvliegtuig,** turbojet.
tur'bodinamo, turbine dynamo.
tureluurs', wild, very angry.
turf, peat, turf; *sy* ~ *SIT,* he is done for; he's in a fix, he's beated; *VASSIT in die* ~, become bogged down; ~**agtig, (-e),** turfy, peaty; ~**grond,** turf, clayey soil; peat-bed (bog); ~**klei,** turfy clay; ~**ryk, (-e),** peaty; ~**steker,** peat-cutter; ~**strooisel,** peat-litter.
Turk, (-e), Turk; ~**ehater,** Turcophobe.
turkoois', (-e), turquoise; ~**blou,** turquoise blue; ~**groen,** turquoise green; ~**kleur,** turquoise (colour).
Turks, (-e), Turkish; ~ *e lekkers,* Turkish delight; ~**gesind, (-e),** Turcophil(e).
turks'naels, *Erodium spp.*
turksvy', prickly pear; "hot potato"; thorny problem; a tricky matter; ~**mot,** cactoblastis; ~**plaag,** prickly-pear menace; ~**ruspe,** cactoblastis cactorium; ~**seep,** prickly-pear soap; ~**stroop,** prickly-pear syrup.
Turky'e, Turkey.
tus'sen, among(st), between, betwixt, amid(st); ~ *die BOME,* among the trees; ~ *HAKIES,* in brackets; by the way; ~ *MAN en vrou,* between husband and wife; *dit bly* ~ *ONS,* that is between you and me.
tus'senafskorting, dissepiment, partition.
tus'senas, countershaft; intermediate shaft; layshaft (motor); jack shaft.
tus'senbalk, intermediate joist.
tus'senbedryf, interlude, entr'acte, interact.
tussenbei'(de), passable, fair, in between; between the two; now and then; ~ *kom,* intervene, interfere.
tus'senblad, interleaf.
tussenbla'rig, (-e), interfoliate.
tus'senboot, intermediate steamer.
tus'sendek, between-decks; steerage.
tus'sendekpassasier, steerage passenger.
tus'sendeur¹, (s) communicating door.
tus'sendeur², (bw) between whiles, in between.
tus'sending, something between the two; mongrel; compromise.
tus'senganger, (-s), go-between, mediator.
tus'sengasheer, intermediate host.
tus'sengebied, buffer state; intervening territory.
tus'sengeleë, interjacent.
tus'sengereg, entrée.
tus'sengesteente, parting (geol.).
tus'sengevoeg, (-de), interpolated, intercalary.
tus'sengewas, catch crop.
tus'senhandel, intermediate trade; ~ **aar,** intermediate agent, middleman.
tus'senhawe, intermediate port.
tus'senin, in between, in amongst.
tus'senjaar, intermedial year.
tus'senkaaks, (-e), intermaxillary.
tus'senkap, cowl (of motor).
tus'senklas, intermediate class.
tus'senkleur, intermediate colour.
tus'senkoms, intervention, intercession, (inter)mediation; agency; ministry; *deur die* ~ *van,* through (by) the good offices of.
tus'senlaag, intermediate layer, intercalation.
tus'senlaer, intermediate bearing.
tus'senlanding, intermediate landing.
tus'senlas, (-ge-), interpolate.
tus'senletter, medial letter.
tus'senlit, medial joint.
tus'senmaaltyd, snack, collation, refection.
tus'senman, intermediary.
tus'senmassa, matrix.
tus'senmedeklinker, medial consonant.
tus'senmeng, (-ge-), intermix.
tus'senmuur, partition wall, mid-wall.
tus'senoes, catch crop.
tus'senpaal, intermediate post.
tus'senpersoon, agent, intermediary, middleman, mediator, go-between; *g'n* ~ *kom in aanmerking nie,* only principals dealt with.
tus'senplaatjie, shim.

tus'senplaneet, intermedial planet.
tus'senplasing, interposition.
tus'senpleitgeding, interpleader.
tus'senpoos, (..pose), ~pose, (-s), interval, pause, intermission.
tus'senproses, mesne process; interlocutory proceedings.
tus'senrat, idler, idle wheel; ~as, idler shaft (motor).
tus'senreël, interlineation.
tus'senregering, interregnum.
tus'senribs, (-e), intercostal.
tus'senrots, parting (geol.).
tus'senruimte, interval, space between, interstice, interspace.
tus'senseisoen, off-season.
tus'sensel, interstitial cell.
tus'sensetsel, insertion.
tus'sensin, parenthetic clause.
tus'senskag, winze.
tus'senskerm, screen; act drop (stage).
tus'senskools, (-e), inter school.
tus'senskoor, intermediate support.
tus'senskot, partition, dissepiment.
tus'senskrywing, interlineation.
tus'sensoort, medium sort.
tus'senspel, interlude, intermezzo, entr'acte, interplay.
tus'senspraak, mediation.
tus'senstasie, intermediate station.
tus'senstedelik, (-e), interurban.
tus'senstyl, mullion, muntin (window).
tus'sensylyn, intermediate siding
tus'sentands, (-e), interdental.
tus'sentyd, meanwhile, interval, interim; *in die* ~, in the meantime; ~s, (-e), meantime, interim; ~*se DIVIDEND*, interim dividend; ~*se RAPPORT*, interim report; ~*se REGERING*, caretaker government; ~*se VERKIESING*, by-election; ~vak, interregnum, interim.
tus'sentys, (-e), intertidal.
tus'senuitwykspoor, interloop.
tus'senveer, intermediate spring.
tus'senverbouing, intercropping.
tus'senverdieping, mezzanine (floor), entresol.
tus'senverhaal, episode.
tus'senverhuring, subletting.
tus'senverhuurder, sublessor.
tus'senverkiesing, by-election.
tus'senvoeg, (-ge-), insert, interpolate; ~ing, insertion, interpolation; ~sel, (-s), insertion, interpolation.
tus'senvoering, interfacing.
tus'senvonnis, interlocutary judgment (order).
tus'senvorm, intermediate form.
tus'senwand, septum.
tus'senweg, middle course.
tus'senwerp, (-ge-), interject; ~er, interjector; ~sel, (-s), interjection.
tus'sor, tussore.
tutu', (-'s), tutu, ballet skirt.
tuur, (ge-), peer, pry; pore; strain one's eyes.
TV, TV, television; ~**akteur**, TV actor; ~-**drama**, TV drama; ~-**onderhoud**, TV interview.
twaalf, (-s, twaalwe), twelve; *hy is ouer as* ~, he knows how many beans make five; ~**daags**, (-e), twelve-day, of twelve days; ~**de**, twelfth; ~**hoek**, dodecagon; ~**hoe'kig**, (-e), dodecagonal; ~**jarig**, (-e), of twelve years, twelve years old; ~**kantig**, ~**kan'tig**, (-e), dodecagonal; ~**ponder**, (-s), twelve-pounder; ~**sy'dig**, (-e), with twelve sides; ~**tal**, twelve, a dozen; ~**tal'lig**, (-e), duodecimal; ~**uur**, twelve o'clock; dinner-hour, dinner time.
twaalf'vingerderm, duodenum.
twaalf'vlak, dodecahedron; ~**'kig**, (-e), dodecahedral.
twaalf'voud, multiple of twelve; ~**'ig**, (-e), twelvefold.
twa'gras, twa grass *(Aristida brevifolia)*.
twak, tobacco, baccy; piffle, nonsense; *laat hom maar sy* ~ *op sy eie manier KERWE*, let him go his own way; *dis pure* ~ *MET hom*, he is full of nonsense; *let him go to pot; sy* ~ *is NAT*, he hasn't a chance;

his powder is damp; *hy is 'n OU* ~, he is a good-for-nothing; *hoe PRUIM daardie* ~ *vir jou?*, how do you like that?; *dis PURE* ~, that is unadulterated nonsense!; *dis PURE* ~ *met hom*, he is full of nonsense; *nie 'n PYP* ~ *werd nie*, not worth one's salt; ~ *VERKOOP*, talk nonsense; ~**kerig**, (-e), nonsensical; ~**praatjies**, nonsense, trash, piffle; ~**sak**, tobacco-pouch; *see* **tabak**.
twee, (**tweë**, -s), two; deuce; ~ *MAAL*, twice; ~ *is PAAR*, *drie is onpaar*, two is company, three is none; ~ *VIR* ~, ~-~, two by two, by two's; ~**ar'mig**, (-e), two-armed; ~**as'sig**, (-e), biaxial; ~**ato'mig**, (-e), diatomic; ~**ba'sies**, (-e), dibasic; ~**be'nig**, (-e), biped, two-legged; ~**bla'rig**, (-e), bifoliate; ~**blom'mig**, (-e), biflorous; ~**daags**, (-e), of two days.
twee'de, second; *T*~ *KERSDAG*, Boxing Day; ~ *RAT*, second gear; ~ *VERDIEPING*, second floor; ~**hands**, (-e), second-hand; ~**jaars**, (-e), second-year (student).
twee'dekker, (-s), biplane, double-decker.
tweedeklas, second-class, inferior.
twee'delesingsdebat, second-reading debate.
twee'delaaste, last but one, penultimate.
tweede'lig, (-e), bipartite; dimerous (bot.); dichotomous (zool.).
twee'deling, bifurcation; binary fission; dichotomy.
twee'de: ~**magswortel**, square root; ~**ns**, in the second place, secondly; ~**rangs**, (-e), second-rate, inferior.
twee'derde, two thirds; ~**meerderheid**, two-third's majority.
twee'dimensionaal, (..nale), two-dimensional.
twee: ~**doe'lig**, (-e), dual purpose; ~**dood**, butcherbird; ~**door(eier)**, double-yolked egg; ~**draads**, (-e), ~**dra'dig**, (-e), two-ply; ~**drag**, discord, dissension; ~*drag saai*, sow the seeds of discord; ~**dubbel(d)**, double; twice two; ~**duim**-, ~**duims**, (-e), two-inch; ~**duimspyp**, two-inch pipe; ~**duisend**, two thousand; ~**duwwel(d)**, *see* **tweedubbel(d)**; ~-**eiig**, (-e), biovular; derived from two ova; ~**-eiige tweeling**, fraternal twins; ~**gatjakkals**, turncoat; double-faced person; hypocrite; ~**gatkontak**, two-way socket; ~**gesprek**, dialogue; ~**geveg**, duel, single combat; ~**geweldak**, double-gable roof, M-roof; ~**handig**, (-e), ambidextrous; bimanal, bimanous; ~**heid**, duality; ~**hoe'kig**, (-e), biangular; ~**hoe'wig**, (-e), cloven-footed; ~**hok'kig**, (-e), bilocular; ~**honderdja'rig**, (-e), two hundred years old, bicentenary; ~**hoof'dig**, (-e), two headed, bicephalous; ~**ho'ringrig**, (-e), bicornous; ~**jaarliks**, (-e), every two years; biennially; ~**jaaroud**, (b) two-year-old (horse); ~**jarig**, (-e), of two years, two-years-old; biennial; ~**juk'kig**, (-e), bijugate; ~**kamerstelsel**, bicameral system (parliament); ~**kamerwoonstel**, two-roomed flat; ~**kar'tig**, (-e), bilateral; ~**kersie**, cherry-bob; ~**kie'wig**, (-e), dibranchiate; ~**klank**, diphthong; ~**klep'pig**, (-e), bivalved; ~**kleu'rig**, (-e), dichroic, dichromatic; ~**kop'pig**, (-e), two-headed; ~**kwartsmaat**, two-four time; ~**laaghout**, two-ply; ~**le'dig**, (-e), double, dual; biarticulate; binary, binomial; ~**lettergre'pig**, (-e), disyllabic.
twee'ling, (-e), twin; *DIE Tweeling*, Gemini; *SIAMESE* ~, Siamese twins; ~**bedde**, twin beds; ~**broer**, twin bother; ~**fiets**, tandem; ~**huis**, semi-detached house; ~**kersie**, cherry-bob; ~**slot**, duplex lock; ~**stel**, twin set; ~**suster**, twin sister; ~**tap**, twin tenon; ~**woord**, doublet.
twee: ~**lip'pig**, (-e), bilabiate; ~**lob'big**, (-e), bilobate, bilobed; ~**loop(geweer)**, double-barrelled gun; ~**luik**, diptych; ~**maan'deliks**, (-e), bimonthly; ~**man'nery**, bigamy; ~**mansaag**, two-handed saw; ~**manskap**, duumvirate; ~**manskool**, two-teacher school; ~**master**, (-s), two-masted ship; ~**moto'rig**, (-e), twin-engined; ~**o'gig**, (-e), binocular; ~**pa'rig**, (-e), bijugate, bijugous; ~**partystelsel**, two-party system.
twee'persoons-, for two, double; ~**bed**, double bed; ~**kar**, two-seater cart; ~**motor**, two-seater car.
twee: ~**pn'lig**, (-e), bipolar; ~**ponder**, (-s), two-pounder.

twee'reëlig, (-e), of two lines; ~*e VERS*, distich, couplet.
twee'rigtingspad, two-way road.
twee'rigtingveldradio, walkie-talkie.
twe'ërlei, of two kinds; ~ *verkoeling*, composite cooling.
twee: ~**ry'ig, (-e),** distichous; ~**'saadlobbig,** ~**saadlob'big, (-e),** dicotyledonous; ~ *saadlobbige plant*, dicotyledon; ~**sa'dig, (-e),** dispermous; ~**sang,** duet; ~**sitplekmotor,** two-seater (motor); ~**skaarploeg,** double-furrow plough; ~**ska'lig, (-e),** bivalve; ~**slagmasjien,** two-stroke engine.
twee: ~**slag'tig, (-e),** amphibious (mil.); amphibian (zool.); androgenous (bot.); hermaphrodite, bisexual; *'n* ~ *slagtige lewe lei*, lead a double life; ~**slag'tigheid,** androgeny; hermaphroditism; ~**slip'pig, (-e),** bicuspid; ~**sna'rig, (-e),** two-stringed; ~**sny'dend, (-e),** two-edged, double-edged; ~**soor'tig, (-e),** of two kinds; ~**spalt,** dissension, discord; ~**span,** two-horse team; ~**spel,** twosome; ~**spraak,** dialogue; ~**sprong,** bifurcation, crossroad, fork (of road); ~**stapdans,** two-step; ~**stem'mig, (-e),** two-part, for two voices; ~**stertjakkals,** turncoat; trimmer; ~**stroompolitiek,** two-stream (race) policy; ~**stryd,** duel; inward struggle; indecision; ~**stukpak,** two-piece suit; ~**sty'lig, (-e),** digynous (bot.); distyle (archit.); ~**sy'dig, (-e),** two-sided, bilateral; distichous (bot.); ~**tak'kig, (-e),** bifurcate; ~**takmotor,** two-stroke motor.
twee'tal, two, pair; semifinalists (in voting).
tweeta'lig, (-e), bilingual; ~**e, (-s),** bilinguist; ~**heid,** bilingualism; ~**heidstoets,** bilingual test.
tweetal'lig, (-e), binary; *die* ~*e stelsel*, the binary scale.
twee'tandskaap, year-old lamb, bident, hogget.
twee'term, binomial; ..**termig, (-e),** binomial.
twee'tjies, two only; *die* ~, the young couple.
twee'toon, ditone (music).
twee'-twee', in twos; two by two.
twee: ~ **uur,** two o'clock; ~**vlak'kig, (-e),** dihedral; ~**vlakshoek,** dihedral angle; ~**vlakwoonstel,** duplex flat; ~**vler'kig,** ~**vleu'elig, (-e),** double-winged, dipterous; ~**voe'tig, (-e),** bipedal, two-footed; ~**voorploeg,** double-furrow plough, gang-plough.
tweevor'mig, (-e), dimorphous, dimorphic; ~**heid,** dimorphism.
twee'voud, multiple of two; double; *in* ~, in duplicate; ~**'ig, (-e),** twofold, double, duplex.
tweewaar'dig, (-e), bivalent; ambivalent; ~**heid,** bivalence; ambivalence.
twee: ~ **weekliks, (-e),** bi-weekly; fortnightly; ~**werf,** twice; ~ **wieler, (-s),** bicycle; two-wheeler; ~**wy'wery,** bigamy; ~**wy'wig, (-e),** bigamous.
twin'tig, twenty; ~**er, (-s),** person in his/her twenties; *in die* ~*erjare*, in the twenties; ~**jarig, (-e),** of twenty years, twenty years old; ~**ponder, (-s),** twenty-pounder; ~**ste,** twentieth; ~**ste-eeus, (-e),** (of the) twentieth century; ~**tal,** twenty, score; ~**vlak,** icosahedron; ~**voud,** multiple of twenty; ~**vou'dig, (-e),** twentyfold; ~**werf,** twentyfold.
twis, (s) (-te), quarrel, dispute, row, strife, fight, feud, fray, squabble, altercation; ~ *soek*, pick a quarrel, look for trouble; (w) **(ge-),** dispute, quarrel, fight, squabble, wrangle, altercate, contend; *oor iets* ~, quarrel about something; ~ **appel,** bone of contention; apple of discord; ~ **geding,** disputation, contentious issue; ~**geskryf,** controversy, polemics; ~**gesprek,** dispute, quarrel; ~**gie'rig, (-e),** quarrelsome, intolerant; ~**graag,** argumentative; quarrelsome; ~ **punt,** point at issue, disputed point; ~**rede,** dispute, disputation; ~**saak,** controversial question; disputed case; ~**siek, (-e),** quarrelsome, disputatious, fractious, fault-finding, contentious, controversial; ~**soeker,** quarrelsome person, barrator, wrangler; ~**soekerig, (-e),** quarrelsome; ~**soekerigheid,** quarrelsomeness, pugnacity; ~**stoker,** mischief-maker, firebrand; ~ **ter, (-s),** quarreller; mischief-maker; ~**terigheid,** fractiousness; ~**vraag,** controversial question, matter at issue; ~**vuur,** fire of discord.

twy'fel, (s) doubt, disbelief, uncertainty, dubitation, misgiving; *dit LY geen* ~ *nie*, there is no doubt about it; *alle* ~ *OPHEF omtrent*, remove all doubt concerning; *SONDER (buite)* ~, without doubt, doubtless, undoubtedly; *in* ~ *TREK*, call in question, query, cast doubt upon; ~ *UITSPREEK*, express doubt; *bo alle* ~ *VERHEWE wees*, be beyond all doubt; (w) **(ge-),** doubt; ~ *AAN*, have doubts about, doubt; *AAN iem. se bedoeling* ~, doubt someone's intention; ~**aar, (-s),** doubter, sceptic; ~**aarbed,** three-quarter bed; ~**ag'tig, (-e),** dubious, ambiguous, equivocal, problematic, doubtful; questionable; ~ **ag'tigheid,** doubtfulness, dubiousness, dubiety; questionableness; ~**ary',** doubt, scepticism; ~**end, (-e),** doubting, dubitative; ~ **geval,** case of doubt; ~**ing,** hesitation; ~**inge,** ~**ings,** doubt.
twyfelmoe'dig, (-e), irresolute, undecided, wavering, vacillating; ~**heid,** irresolution, indecision, vacillation.
twy'felsiek, (-e), prone to scepticism, sceptic.
twy'felsug, strong inclination to doubt, pyrrhonism, scepticism; ~'**tig, (-e)** prone to scepticism, sceptic.
twyg, (twy(g)e), twig, branch; scion; ~**ie, (-s),** small twig, branch.
twyn, twine, twist; ~**der,** twiner, twister; doubler; ~**dery, (-e),** twining mill; ~**garing,** yarn.
ty, (-e), tide; *die* ~ *is verloop*, (ong.), the tables are turned, circumstances have changed.
tyd, (tye), time; tense; season; *sy* ~ *AFWAG*, bide his time; *te ALLE tye*, at all times; *ANDER tye, ander mense*, other times, other manners; *in 'n ANDER* ~ *wees*, be in the family way; *ter BEKWAMER* ~, at a suitable time; at the right time; *BY tye*, at times, occasionally; *te ENIGER* ~, at any time; *die* ~ *met die EWIGHEID verwissel*, put off the mortal to put on the immortal; *ek GEE jou vyf minute* ~, I give you five minutes (grace); *in GEEN* ~, not for some time; *hy het sy* ~ *GEHAD*, he has had his day; ~ *is GELD*, time is money; *'n* ~ *GELEDE*, some time ago; *ter GELEGENER* ~, when it is convenient; at a suitable time; *op GESETTE tye*, at fixed times; *die GOEIE ou* ~, the good old times; *die* ~ *is die beste HEELMEESTER*, time heals all wounds; *alles HET sy* ~, *daar IS 'n* ~ *vir alles*, there is a time for everything; *dis HOOG* ~, it is high time; *op die HOOGTE v.d.* ~, up-to-date; *KOM op* ~, *hoor*, don't be late; *die trein KOM op* ~, the train will arrive on time; *sy* ~ *jie word KORT*, his time is drawing near; *dit sal baie* ~ *KOS*, it will take a long time; *in die LAASTE* ~, of late; *'n* ~ *LANK*, for some time; *die* ~ *sal ons dit LEER*, time will tell; *O, LIEWE* ~!, oh my!; *hy LOOP op sy* ~, he walks leisurely; *MY* ~!, goodness me!; *in die* ~ *van NOOD*, in times of need; *die* ~ *is OM (verstreke)*; time is up; *jou* ~ *OORLEWE*, outlive the times; *OP sy* ~, at his leisure; *OP* ~ *kom*, arrive on time; *in die OU* ~, in olden times; *wie nie PAS op sy* ~ , *is sy maaltyd kwyt*, if you are not in time, you lose your meal; *kom* ~, *kom RAAD*, time solves most problems; time will tell; *te REGTER* ~, in due course; at the right time; *met die* ~ *SAAMGAAN*, keep abreast of times; keep up with the times; *ander tye, ander SEDES*, other times, other manners; *die SLAP* ~, the slack (off-) season; *is dit al weer SULKE* ~?, what, again?; *ter SYNER* ~, at his convenience; *TEEN daardie* ~, by that time; *TEN tyde van*, in the time of; *TEN tye (van)*, during; *TOT* ~ *en wyl*, until such time; *op* ~ *vir die TREIN*, in time for the train; *UIT die* ~ *wees*, be behind the times (old-fashioned); *die* ~ *UITKOOP*, make the most of one's time; use time well; *sy* ~ *UITSIT*, serve one's time; *die* ~ *sal dit UITWYS*, time will tell; *VAN* ~ *tot* ~, from time to time; *sy* ~ *is VERBY*, his time is up; he has had his day; *die* ~ *VERDRYF*, kill time; *VRY(E)* ~, leisure, spare time; ~ *WEN*, gain time; temporize; ~**aangewer,** timekeeper; ~**beeld,** picture of the times; ~**bepaling,** fixing of time; time fixed (appointed); ~**beskrywer,** chronographer; ~**beskrywing,** chronography; ~**besparend, (-e),** time-saving; ~**besparing,** saving of time; ~**bestek,** space

(period) of time; ~**bom**, time bomb; ~**eenheid**, unit of time; ~**elik, (-e)**, temporary; temporal; passing; for the time being; pro tem; *die ~elike met die EWIGE verwissel*, put off the mortal and put on immortality; *~elike MAGNETISME*, temporary magnetism; ~**eloos, (..lose)**, timeless; ~**eloosheid**, timelessness; ~**faktor**, time factor; ~**fout**, parachronism; ~**gebrek**, lack of time; ~**gees**, spirit of the age; ~**gelyk, (-e)**, contemporary; ~**genoot, (..note)**, contemporary; coeval; ~**grens**, time-limit; deadline; ~**houer**, timekeeper.

ty'dig, (-e), seasonable, timely, in time; betimes; ~ *en ontydig*, in season and out (of season); at any time; ~**heid**, timeliness, seasonableness.

ty'ding, (-e, -s), news, tidings; *geen ~, goeie ~*, no news is good news.

tyd: ~**jie, (-s)**, little while, short time; *dit duur 'n ~jie (~ lank)*, it takes some time; ~**kaart**, time card; ~**klok**, time-recording clock; ~**korting**, pastime, kill-time; ~**kring**, period; cycle; ~**lont**, time-fuse; ~**loon**, time-rates; ~**maat**, tempo; ~**meetkunde**, chronometry, horology; ~**merk**, time-mark; ~**meter**, chronometer; chronograph; horometer; ~**ontsteker**, time-fuse; ~**opname**, time exposure; timing; ~**opnemer**, timekeeper; ~**perk**, era, epoch, period; ~**punt**, point of time; ~**reëling**, timing; ~**rekenaar**, chronologist; ~**rekening**, chronology; era; reckoning; ~**ren**, rally; ~**rowend**, ~**ro'wend, (-e)**, taking up much time; ~**ruimte**, space of time; ~**saam, (..same)**, leisurely, deliberately.

tyds: ~**aanwysing**, indication of time; ~**bepaling**, fixture of time, time-limit; ~**besparing**, saving of time; ~**bestek**, space of time; ~**duur**, length of time, duration.

tyd'sein, time-signal.

tyds: ~**gebrek**, lack of time; ~**genoeg**, enough time, time enough; slow, leisurely; ~**gewrig**, conjuncture (juncture) of time.

tyd: ~**skakelaar**, self-timer switch; ~**skrif, (-te)**, periodical, magazine, journal.

tyds: ~**omstandigheid**, circumstance (of the time); ~**orde**, chronological order.

tyd: ~**staat**, time-sheet; ~**stip**, point of time, period, moment, epoch; ~**stroming**, tendency of the age.

tyds: ~**verloop**, lapse (course) of time; ~**verskil**, difference in time.

tyd: ~**tafel**, timetable; chronological tables; roster; ~**teenstrydigheid**, anachronism; ~**vak**, period, epoch; ~**verdryf**, pastime, amusement, fun game, diversion, hobby, recreation, kill-time; ~**verkwisting**, waste of time; ~**verlenging**, extension of time; ~**verlies**, loss of time; ~**verspilling**, waste of time; ~**vorm**, tense form; ~**wenner**, temporizer; ~**wins**, temporizing, gaining time.

ty'hawe, tidal harbour (basin).

tyk, tick(ing); ~**wewer**, ticking-maker (-weaver).

tyl'roos, jonquil.

tym, *see* **tiemie**.

T'-yster, T-bar, T-iron.

U

u¹, (s) (-'s), u.

u², (vnw) you; your; ~ *het ~ hoed vergeet*, you have forgotten your hat.

U'bermensch, (D), superman.

U'-boot, submarine.

U'-buis, U-tube.

U'-balk, U-beam.

u'dometer, (-s), udometer, rain-gauge.

U'-draai, U-turn.

U E'dele, Your Honour.

ui, (-e), onion; joke; *'n ~ tap*, (ong.), crack a joke; ~**(e)agtig, (-e)**, onion-like, oniony.

ui'dak, imperial roof.

ui'e: ~**akkertjie**, ~**bedding**, bed of onions; ~**atjar**, onion pickles; ~**lof, (..lowwe)**, onion leaves; ~**lug**, smell of onions; ~**oes**, onion crop.

ui'er, (s) (-s), udder, bag, dug, mamma; ~**maak**, be with calf; (w) (ge-), be with young (calf); ~**ontsteking**, mastitis; garget; ~**sweer**, ulcer (tumour) of the udder.

ui'e: ~**saad**, onion seed; ~**slaai**, onion salad; ~**smaak**, taste (flavour) of onion; ~**sous**, onion sauce; ~**tjie**, small onion.

uil, (-e), owl; jordan, ~ *e na ATHENE bring*, carry coals to Newcastle; *soos 'n ~ op 'n KLUIT*, all forlorn; *hy is 'n ~ onder die KRAAIE*, he is the laughing-stock of the place; *hy is nie onder 'n ~ UITGEBROEI nie*, he is not as stupid as he looks; he was not born yesterday; *hy dink sy ~ is 'n VALK*, he thinks his geese are swans; every owl thinks her own young the fairest; ~**aap**, macaque; ~**agtig, (-e)**, owlish; stupid; ~**arend**, harrier eagle; ~**bek**, owl-beak; forceps; ~**hortjies**, gambrel, vent; ~**nes**, owl's nest; ~**oog**, owl's eye.

uils'kuiken, goose(y), fathead, duffer, blockhead, oaf, dunce, stupid, noodle, numskull, gaby, gull, dolt; *iem. is 'n ~*, someone is a booby.

Uil'spieël, rogue, clown, wag; *lyk soos ~ in die MAANSKYN*, look like a scarecrow; *'N ~*, a funny (queer) bird.

uil'tjie, (-s), owlet; peacock-flower; *'n ~ knyp (knip)*, take forty winks (a nap).

uin'tjie, (-s), edible bulb(ous) plant (e.g. *Moraea edulis*); ~**kweek**, nut-grass.

uit¹, (w) (ge-), utter, voice, air; emit, pronounce, enunciate; express; *sy mening ~*, voice his opinion.

uit², (bw) out, over, off, on; through; finished; *die BAL is ~*, the ball is out; *dis ~ en GEDAAN*, it is over and done with; *die KERK is ~*, the church service is over; *my PYP is ~*, my pipe is out; *hy SPRING by die venster ~*, he jumps through the window; ~ *en TUIS*, there and back; *dis ~ TUSSEN ons*, I am through with you; *daarop ~ WEES om*, be bent on; make it one's business to; (vs) out (of), from, through; among; ~ *BEGINSEL*, on principle; *een ~ DUISEND*, one in a thousand; ~ *ERVARING*, from (by) experience; ~ *FRANKRYK geboortig*, a native of France; ~ *die HAAK*, out of square; ~ *HOMSELF*, of his own will; ~ *LIEFDE*, out of love; ~ *LIT*, out of joint, dislocated; ~ *NAAM van*, in the name of; ~ *die LOOD*, out of plumb; ~ *NOODWEER*, in self-defence; ~ *VREES dat*, for fear that.

uit'adem, (-ge-) = **uitasem**, (w).

uit'asem¹, (w) (-ge-), exhale, expire, breathe out.

uita'sem², (bw) out of breath, puffy, blown.

uit'aseming, (-e, -s), exhalation, expiration, breathing out.

uit'bagger, (-ge-), dredge.

uit'bak, (-ge-), bake through; fall into disfavour; *uitgebakte BROOD*, well-baked bread; *uitgebak by al sy MAATS*, unpopular with all his pals.

uit'baken, (-ge-), peg out, mark out.

uit'baklei, (-ge-), fight out, settle by fighting.

uit'ban, (-ge-), banish, expel; exorcise (spirits); ~**ning**, banishment, expulsion; exorcism.

uit'bars, (-ge-), burst out, erupt, break out, blaze up, belch (forth), explode; ~ *v.d. lag*, burst out laughing; ~**'tend, (-e)**, eruptive; ~**ting, (-e, -s)**, explosion, eruption, flare-up, outburst, blaze, eructation (volcano), outbreak, ebullition.

uit'basuin, (-ge-), trumpet forth, blaze abroad, (em)blazon, noise abroad; *iets ~*, proclaim something from the house-tops.

uit'beeld, (-ge-), sketch, draw, depict, delineate, personate, represent; ~**er, (-s)**, portrayer, depicter.

uit'beelding, (-e, -s), sketch(ing), delineation, personation, representation.

uit′beeldingsvermoë, ability to delineate or depict.
uit′beitel, (-ge-), chisel out.
uit′besem, (-ge-), expel, bundle out; reprove.
uit′bestee, (~), give out on contract; farm out; place out.
uit′besteding, farming out, contracting.
uit′betaal, (~), disburse, pay out; cash; *iem.* ~, pay someone in full.
uit′betaling, (-e, -s), payment, settlement, disbursement.
uit′betalingsmandaat, warrant (of payment).
uit′blaas, (-ge-), blow out; fuse; *die KERS* ~, blow out the candle; *die LAMP het uitgeblaas,* the light has fused.
uit′blaker, (-ge-), blurt out; *hy sal alles* ~, he wil blurt out (broadcast) everything.
uit′bleik, (-ge-), bleach; fade.
uit′blêr, (-ge-), bawl forth.
uit′blink, (-ge-), outshine, surpass, excel, be conspicuous (outstanding), shine (in conversation), eclipse; *onder die ander* ~, stand out; shine; ~**end, (-e)**, outstanding; pre-eminent; ~**er, (-s)**, one who excels, champion; star turn.
uit′bloei¹, (-ge-), cease flowering (blossoming).
uit′bloei², (-ge-), stop bleeding, exsanguinate.
uit′blus, (-ge-), extinguish, quench, put out (fire).
uit′bly, (-ge-), stay away, tarry, delay, be overdue; be wanting; *oorlog kan nie* ~ *nie,* war is bound to come.
uit′boender, (-ge-), turn out, expel, bundle out.
uit′boer, (-ge-), fail as farmer; become bankrupt, go under, lose everything; fall into disfavour.
uit′boetseer, (-ge-), fashion, model.
uit′bol, (-ge-), bulge, flare.
uit′boor, (-ge-), bore out, drill out; recess; ~**der, (-s)**, pump; ~**masjien**, boring-machine; ~**saag**, fraise.
uit′borrel, (-ge-), bubble up, rush out.
uit′borsel, (-ge-), brush out.
uit′bot, (-ge-), bud, sprout, effloresce, shoot.
uit′bou, (s) wing, annex, projecting room, bay; **(w) (-ge-)**, extend by building, build out; ~**ing**, extending, enlarging; ~**sel**, jut, projection; bay; ~**venster**, bow (bay) window, compass window.
uit′braai, (-ge-), melt down, roast out; fry.
uit′braak¹, (s) gaol-breaking; breaking out.
uit′braak², (w) (-ge-), vomit forth, regurgitate, belch forth; ~**sel**, vomit.
uitbra′king, regurgitation.
uit′brand, (-ge-), burn out, cease burning, become extinct; fuse (elec.); gut; cauterize; *die gloeilampie het uitgebrand,* the bulb has fused; ~**er, (-s)**, rating, telling-off, scolding, reprimand; *iem. 'n* ~ *er gee,* give someone a choking off; ~**ing**, cauterization.
uit′breek, (-ge-), break out, erupt, burst out.
uit′brei¹, (-ge-), knit out.
uit′brei², (-ge-), spread, enlarge, amplify, extend, expand; *die EPIDEMIE brei hom uit,* the epidemic is spreading; *die STEMREG* ~ *tot agtienjariges,* extend the franchise to persons aged 18 years; ~**der, (-s)**, amplifier; ~**ding, (-e, -s)**, extension, expansion, amplification, enlargement, development; accession; ~**dingsbeampte**, extension officer; ~**dingsklas**, extension class; ~**dingskursus**, extension course; ~**dingsplan**, plan for extension.
uit′breking, outbreak, eruption.
uit′bring, (-ge-), bring out; utter; disclose, betray (secret), reveal; cast, record (vote); *'n POS* ~, extend an entry; *'n VERSLAG* ~, report, give (bring out) a report.
uit′broei, (-ge-), hatch (eggs); think out, concoct (plan); ~**gronde**, breeding-grounds; ~**ing, (-s)**, incubation (of eggs); ~**stimulant**, hatching stimulant.
uit′brul, (-ge-), roar out.
uit′buig, (-ge-), bend outwards; ~**end, (-e)**, bulgy; ~**ing**, bulge; flexion (of motor tyre).
uit′buit, (-ge-), exploit, overwork; turn to account, make the most of; fleece (a person); ~**er, (-s)**, exploiter; ~**ing**, exploitation; ~**stelsel**, sweating system.
uit′bulder, (-ge-), vociferate, rave, bellow forth, roar out, bluster out.

uit′bult, (-ge-), bulge; swell (tin); ~**ing**, bulge, swelling.
uitbun′dig, (-e), exceeding, excessive; boisterous, clamorous, exuberant; fey; ~**heid**, excess(iveness); exuberance, clamorousness; friskiness.
uit′byt, (-ge-), bite out; corrode, etch out; loosen (tooth); drive out, expel (from pack, troop).
uit′daag, (-ge-), challenge, brace, dare, defy, provoke, throw down the gauntlet, call out; ~**beker**, challenge cup; ~**ronde**, challenge round.
uitda′gend, (-e), challenging, defying, defiant, provoking, provocative.
uit′dager, (-s), challenger.
uit′daging, (-e, -s), challenge, provocation, defiance; gage.
uit′damp, (-ge-), evaporate; air; exhale; ~**er, (-s)**, vaporizer; ~**ing**, evaporation; airing; exhalation.
uit′deel, (-ge-), distribute, dispense, dole out; portion out, mete out, apportion, parcel out; *KLAPPE* ~, deal out blows; *die LAKENS* ~, boss the show; ~**depot, (-s)**, distributing depot.
uit′deler, (-s), distributor, dispenser.
uit′delf, (-ge-), dig out (up), excavate.
uit′delg, (-ge-), exterminate, extirpate, destroy, root out; *'n skuld* ~, wipe out a debt; ~**er, (-s)**, destroyer, exterminator; ~**ing, (-e, -s)**, extermination, extirpation, destruction.
uit′deling, (-e, -s), distribution, dole; dividend.
uit′dien, (-ge-), serve one's term; last (its time); become obsolete; *dit is al lankal uitgedien,* that has served its time.
uitdiens′treding, retirement (from office, service).
uit′diep, (-ge-), deepen, scoop out; gouge; ~**ing**, gulleting.
uit′dineer, (-ge-), dine out.
uit′dink, (-ge-), contrive, invent; hit on; hatch (plot); hammer out; excogitate, ideate; *'n plan* ~, devise (some) means; ~**′baar, (..bare)**, devisable; ~**er**, deviser, planner.
uit′dolf, (-ge-), dig out, dig up.
uit′donder, (-ge-), swear at; beat; hurl out; stop thundering.
uit′doof, (-ge-), extinguish, quench.
uit′dop, (-ge-), peel, shell, husk (peas); decorticate (orange); ~**per, (-s)**, husker; ~**ping**, decortication.
uit′dor, (-ge-), dry up, shrivel up, wither; ~**ring**, desiccation (of ground).
uit′dors¹, (-ge-), thresh out.
uit′dors², (-ge-), make thirsty.
uit′dos, (-ge-), attire, rig out, prank out, array, bedizen, doll up, enrobe, accoutre, deck out, dress, pink, prink.
uit′dowe, (-ge-) = **uitdoof**.
uit′dowing, extinction; extinguishing.
uit′dra, (-ge-), carry out (furniture); wear out (clothes); propagate (principles).
uit′draai, (-ge-), turn aside; evade; wriggle out; turn out; switch off; *jou ÊRENS* ~, wriggle oneself out of something; *op NIKS* ~, come to naught, fizzle out; ~**pad**, branch (side) road; parting (of the ways); *by die* ~ *pad kom,* come to the parting of the ways.
uit′dring, (-ge-), crowd out, press out, hustle.
uit′drink, (-ge-), empty, drink off (out), drain, quaff.
uit′droë, (-ge-), dry up, become parched, desiccate, wither; dry out (rusks); bake; calcify; wring out (clothes); torrefy; ~**r**, desiccator; wringer.
uit′droging, desiccation, torrefaction.
uit′droog, (-ge-) = **uitdroë**; ~**oond**, baking-oven, drying-oven.
uit′druk, (-ge-), express, enounce, put (into words); squeeze out, press out; *as ek dit so mag* ~, if I may put it like that; ~**′baar (..bare)**, expressible; ~**kend, (-e)**, expressive.
uit′drukking, (-e, -s), expression, enouncement, term, phrase; look (on face); diction; ~ *GEE aan,* give expression to; *tot* ~ *KOM,* find expression; *VOL* ~, expressive; ~**loos, (..lose)**, expressionless, vacant; poker-faced; ~**svermoë**, expressive power; ~**swyse**, mode of expression.
uitdruk′lik, (b) (-e), emphatic, positive, explicit, definite; formal; assertive; categorical; direct; expres=

uitdryf 555 **uitgeloog**

sive; (bw) emphatically; expressly; explicitly, definitely; ~**heid,** expressiveness; explicitness.
uit′dryf, (-ge-), drive out, chase, expel, exorcize; oust; punch out; ~**baar, (..bare),** expellable.
uit′drywe, (-ge-) = **uitdryf;** ~**r, (-s),** expeller.
uit′drywing, expulsion, casting out, exorcism.
uit′dui, (-ge-), point out, show, indicate.
uit′duik, (-ge-), recover by diving; rase (dent).
uit′dun, (s) (-ne), heat (athl.); (w) **(-ge-),** thin out, eliminate; decimate, deplete; ~**ning,** thinning out, decimation; heat (race); ~**wedloop,** heat; ~**wedstryd,** preliminary (knock-out) trial, heat.
uit′dy, (-ge-), expand, fill out, swell, plump; ~**ing,** expansion; ~**werktuig,** prosser-tool.
uit′een, asunder, apart; *see* **uitmekaar.**
uiteen′bars, (-ge-), burst asunder, explode.
uiteen′dryf, uiteen′drywe, (-ge-), disperse, scatter.
uiteen′gaan, (-gegaan), part, separate, disperse; adjourn; *die vergadering het uiteengegaan,* the meeting broke up (adjourned).
uiteen′hou, (-gehou), keep apart; distinguish.
uiteen′jaag, (-gejaag), disperse, scatter.
uiteen′loop, (-geloop), diverge, differ.
uiteenlo′pend, (-e), divergent, different, variegated, diverse; ~**heid,** divergence, difference, diversity.
uiteen′loping, divergence, dissimilarity.
uiteen′setting, (-e, -s), explanation, exposition, disquisition; exposé; brief; detail.
uiteen′sit, (-gesit), explain, state, expound, expose; space.
uiteen′skeur, (-geskeur), rend asunder, tear apart, rip apart; ~**ing,** tearing apart, disruption.
uiteen′slaan, (-geslaan), smash, batter, break up.
uiteen′spat, (-gespat), burst; break up, disrupt, scatter.
uiteen′stuif, uiteen′stuiwe, (-ge-), fly apart, disperse, scatter.
uiteen′val, (-geval), fall to pieces, break up, disintegrate.
uiteen′vlieg, (-gevlieg), fly in different directions, explode.
uit′eet, (-geëet), dine out; *uitgeëet wees,* be sated; have had more than enough.
uit′einde, death; extremity, end, the latter end.
uitein′delik, finally, at last, eventually, ultimately.
uit′ent, (-ge-), vaccinate to the end; stop (spread of disease) by vaccinating.
uitentreu′re, continually, boringly, ad nauseam.
ui′ter, (ge-) = uit, (w).
uiteraard′, naturally, by nature.
ui′terlik, (s) outward appearance, exterior aspect, looks, get-up; *SKOON ~ is slegs vertoon,* beauty is but skin-deep; *VIR die ~ e,* for show; (b) **(-e),** external, outward, exterior; *sy ~ e voorkoms,* his external appearance; (bw) apparently, outwardly, externally; at the utmost, at the latest; *~ môre* tomorrow at the latest; ~**heid,** exterior; superficiality; appearance; formalism.
uiterma′te, exceedingly, excessively, extremely, beyond measure; *~ verheug wees,* be exceedingly glad.
ui′ters, exceedingly, very, most, utterly, excessively, eminently, extremely, to an extreme; at the latest; *dit is ~ JAMMER,* it is a great pity; *~ KLEIN,* extremely small; *~ ONWAARSKYNLIK,* highly improbable.
ui′terste, (s) (-s), death; extremity, extreme, limit; *van die een ~ na die ANDER,* from one extreme to the other; *op sy ~ LÊ,* be (lie) at death's door; *die ~ s RAAK mekaar,* extremes meet; *TOT die ~,* to the utmost; *tot die ~ VEG,* fight to the last ditch; *v.d. een ~ na die ander VERVAL (oorslaan),* go from one extreme to another; *in ~ s VERVAL,* go to extremes; (b) extreme, utmost, last, utter, outermost possible, furthermost, furthest; *'n ~ VABOND,* scoundrel; *sy ~ WILSBESKIKKING,* his last will and testament.
uit′etter, (uitgeëtter), fester out, suppurate out; cease ulcerating.
uit′flap, (-ge-), blurt out; blab out; ~**per,** blabber, telltale.
uit′fluit, (-ge-), boo, hiss out, catcall, hoot.

uit′foeter, (-ge-), beat, overcome, conquer, thrash; throw out.
uit′gaaf, (uit′gawe(s)) = uitgawe.
uit′gaan, (s): *teen die ~ v.d. maand,* towards the end of the month; *~ VAN,* start (originate) from; (w) **(-ge-),** go out; end in; be over (church-service); emanate from (ideas); leave, make one's exit; come out (stains); *die KERK sal nou ~,* the church service will be over presently; *op 'n KLINKER ~,* end in a vowel; *~ met MEISIES,* take out girls; *van 'n STANDPUNT ~,* take the view, proceed from the assumption; *~ v.d. VERONDERSTELLING dat,* proceed on the assumption that; *die VLEK wil nie ~ nie,* the stain won't come out; ~**dag,** day off; ~**de,** outward (-bound); *~ de posboot,* outward-bound mail boat; ~**klere,** Sunday best.
uit′galm, (-ge-), sound forth; bawl out.
uit′gang, (-e), exit, egress(ion), way out, outlet; fall; ending; issue; termination (of a word).
uit′gangs: ~**deur,** exit (door); ~**hawe,** base port; ~**kaartjie,** pass-out; ~**lyn,** position line (aero.); ~**peil,** datum level; ~**punt,** starting-point; premise; base, fixed point, basis, point of reference (aero.).
uit′gas, (-ge-), fumigate.
uit′gawe, (-s), expenditure, expense, costs; impression, edition; issue, publication; *die DERDE ~,* the third edition; *INKOMSTES en ~ s,* revenue (income) and expenditure; *ONVOORSIENE ~ s,* unforeseen expenditure; *VASTE ~,* definitive issue (stamp).
uit′gebak, (-te), well baked; in disfavour; *hy is ~ by die mense,* people have lost all confidence in him; his goose is cooked.
uit′gebeitel, (-de), chiselled.
uit′gebloei, (-de), uit′geblom, (-de), overblown.
uit′geblus, (-te), extinct.
uit′gebraai, (-de): *~ e vet,* dripping.
uit′gebrand, (-e), dead; burnt out.
uit′gebrag: *~ te stemme,* votes cast.
uit′gebrei(d), (-de), extensive, broad, expansive, comprehensive, wide; *'n ~ de reis,* an extended journey; ~**dheid,** extensiveness, comprehensiveness, extent, ambit.
uit′gebuit, (-e), fleeced.
uit′gedien(d), (-de), superannuated; useless, worthless, worn out.
uit′gedoof, (-de), extinct (volcano); put out (fire).
uit′gedos, (-te), in full fig, dressed up.
uit′gedruk, (-te), expressed; exact; squeezed out; *hy is sy pa ~,* he is the very image of his father.
uit′gee, (-ge-), spend (money); give out; distribute; disburse, expend; publish (book); edit (book); deal (cards); pass out (ball); *jou ~ vir,* profess to be, pose as.
uit′geëet, (goöto), well fed.
uit′geër, (-s), dealer (cards); *see* **uitgewer.**
uit′gegiet, (-e, uitgegote), poured out.
uit′gegraaf, (-de, uit′gegrawe), dug up; excavated.
uit′gegroef, (-de), channelled, fluted, chamfered.
uit′gegroei, (-de), full-fledged, adult, full-grown; mature.
uit′gehol, (-de), recessed, hollow.
uit′gehonger(d), (-de), famished, starved; ravenous; ~**dheid,** starvation; ravenousness.
uit′geknip, (-te), cut out; *hy is ~ vir DOKTER,* he is cut out for (to be) a doctor; *hy is ~ sy VADER,* he is the image of his father.
uit′gekuier: *ons is ~ op die plaas,* we have stayed on the farm long enough.
uit′gelate, (-ner, meer ~, -nste, mees ~), exuberant, boisterous, exultant, in high spirits, loud, rampant, cock-a-hoop, wanton.
uit′gelatenheid, exuberance, exultation, elation, boisterousness, loudness; wantonness.
uit′geleef, (-de), worn out, decrepit.
uit′geleer, (-de), cunning.
uit′geleide, escort; send-off, farewell; *iem. ~ doen,* see someone off, give someone a send-off.
uit′gelese, choice, picked; exquisite.
uit′gelesenheid, choiceness, selectness.
uit′geloog, (-de), lixivated.

uit'geloot, (..lote), drawn; *uitgelote obligasies,* drawn bonds.
uit'gemaak, (-te), decided, definite; settled; ascertained; *dit is 'n ~ te saak,* that is a foregone conclusion.
uit'gemergel(d), (-de), emaciated.
uit'genome, except, excluding, save, barring.
uit'gepiets: *fyn ~ wees,* be dressed to the nines.
uit'gepluis, (-de), teased (rope, hair).
uit'geput, (-te), tired, effete, weary, care-worn, exhausted, fagged, (for)spent, run-down, worn out, prostrate; blown (horse).
uit'gerafel, (-de), frayed, worn; fimbriate, unravelled; fringed (bot.).
uit'gerek, (-te), drawn out.
uit'gerus, (-te), equipped, fitted out, appointed; completely rested.
uit'gery, (-de): *die pad is ~,* the road has become rutted.
uit'gesetheid, expansiveness.
uit'geskakel, (-de), eliminated; out of gear, neutral, idle.
uit'geskuins, (-te), splayed.
uit'geskulp, (-te), scalloped.
uit'geslaan, (-de), measled, infected with measles; beaten out; knocked out (boxer).
uit'geslaap, (-te), uit'geslape, sly, cunning, cute, wide awake, shrewd, knowing.
uit'geslapenheid, cunning, shrewdness.
uit'geslote, out of the question, impossible.
uit'geslyt, (-e), worn out.
uit'gesny, (-de), intagliated, cut out.
uit'gesoek, (-te), uit'gesog, (-te), selected, chosen, hand-picked; choice, exquisite.
uit'gesonder(d), except(ing), excluding, save, barring, with the exception of; exempt.
uit'gespoel, (-de), washed out (away); alluvial.
uit'gesponnenheid, circumstantiality, cumbersomeness, circumlocution.
uit'gesprei, (-de), diffuse, patulous.
uit'gesproke, expressed; confirmed; avowed, declared, pronounced; *sy ~ doel,* his avowed object.
uit'gesprokenheid, forthrightness.
uit'gestel, (-de), postponed, deferred.
uit'gestorwe, extinct (species); deserted (city); *'n ~ boedel,* a deceased estate.
uit'gestrek, (-te), extensive, extended, vast, large, outstretched, far-flung.
uit'gestreke, smug(-faced), demure.
uit'gestrektheid, extent, expanse, vastness, amplitude, breadth, extension; extensiveness, range, reach.
uit'getand, (-e), indented.
uit'geteer, (-de), emaciated, tabid.
uit'getrek, (-te), undressed; fleeced.
uit'gevat, (-te), smartly dressed.
uit'gevreet, (..vrete), well-fed, robust; grown-up, full-sized.
uit'geweke, exiled; refugee; **~ne, (-s),** refugee, fugitive, expatriate.
uit'gewer, (-s), publisher, issuer.
uit'gewerk, (-te), elaborated; worked out (mine); detailed; extinct (volcano); figured (cloth); flat (beer).
uit'gewersaak, publishing house.
uit'gewers: ~firma, firm of publishers; **~maatskappy,** publishing company; **~merk,** publisher's imprint.
uit'gewery, (-e), publishing house; distribution; spending.
uit'geworpe, outcast.
uit'geworpene, (-s), pariah.
uit'gewys, (-de), decided (court case).
uit'gier, (-ge-), yell, scream.
uit'giet, (-ge-), pour out, empty, effuse.
uit'gifte, (-s), issue (stamps); flotation (of loan); issuance (mil.); *datum van ~,* date of issue.
uit'gil, (-ge-), scream out, yell.
uit'gleuf, (-ge-), recess.
uit'glip, (-ge-), slip out, prolapse.
uit'gloei, (-ge-), anneal; burn off, temper; **~oond,** annealing furnace.
uit'gly, (-ge-), slip (e.g. on banana skin); skid.
uit'gooi, (-ge-), eject, chuck out, throw out; bleed (bags of grain); reject; cull (sheep); effuse; temper, teem (steel), pour out, empty; spill; *uitgegooide beeste,* culls (animals); **~dier,** cull(ed animal); **~ing,** dumping, ejection.
uit'graaf, uit'grawe, (-ge-), dig up; excavate; pit; quarry; exhume (corpse); cut (railw.).
uit'grawing, (-e, -s), excavation; exhumation; dug-out; cutting (railw.).
uit'groef, (-ge-), flute, channel.
uit'groei, (-ge-), grow; outgrow; protuberate; develop; *'n seun wat uit sy klere ~,* a boy who is growing out of his clothes; **~sel, (-s),** outgrowth, excrescence; development.
uit'haak, (-ge-), hook out, heel (rugby ball); unlimber (cannon); unhook, unhitch.
uit'haal, (-ge-), take out, pull out, draw out; dig up, lift (potatoes); empty; remove (stain); play (joke); unpick; exert oneself; *'n GRAP ~,* play a trick; *jy MOET ~ al wat jy kan,* you must exert yourself to the utmost; *STEKE ~,* unpick stitches; **~voor,** last furrow ploughed.
uit'haler, (s) (-s), adept, dab; lifter; (b) smart, showy; champion, first-rate, crack; **~skut,** crack shot; **~speler,** crack player.
uit'ham, spit (of land).
uit'hamer, (-ge-), draw out (metal); hammer out.
uit'hang, (-ge-), hang out; reside; pose, play a part; make a splash, swank; heave out; *die groot meneer ~,* swagger about; **~bord,** signboard; **~teken,** signboard.
uit'hap, (-ge-), bite out.
uit'hardloop, (-ge-), out-distance; run out (cricket); outpace, outrun.
uit'hark, (-ge-), rake out.
uit'hê, (uitgehad), have finished; get changed.
uitheems', (-e; meer ~, mees ~), foreign, exotic, outlandish; peregrin(e); allophylian (race); **~heid,** foreign characteristics, foreignness, outlandishness.
uit'help, (-ge-), help out; **~er,** helper; rescuer; **~ing,** disembarrassment.
uit'hoek, out-of-the-way place, remote corner.
uit'hoes, (-ge-), cough up (out); expectorate.
uit'hol¹, (-ge-), hollow out, excavate, gouge, gutter, groove, flute, scoop, dig out, gully, pit, hollow, recess.
uit'hol², (-ge-), run out; outrun, outdistance.
uit'holling, cup, excavation; imbrication; recess; hollowing.
uit'holmasjien, recessing machine.
uit'honger, (-ge-), famish, starve; **~ing,** starvation, starving.
uit'hoor, (-ge-), draw, pump (a person); listen to the end, hear (someone) out; *iem ~,* hear someone out.
uit'hou¹, (-ge-), bear, stand, endure, suffer, abide, grin and bear, last, hold out, brave it out.
uit'hou², (-ge-), keep out (from room).
uit'hou³, (-ge-), chop (hack) out, hew, carve (out).
uit'hou: ~(dings)vermoë, stamina, staying-power, endurance, tenacity; **~grens,** endurance limit; **~rekord,** endurance record; **~toets,** endurance test.
uit'huil, (-ge-), weep oneself out, cry away, have a good cry.
uithui'sig, (-e), fond of being away from home, gadabout; **~heid,** fondness of gadding; roving spirit.
uit'huwelik, (-ge-), give in marriage, marry off.
ui'ting, (-e, -s), utterance, expression, saying; enunciation; *~ GEE aan,* give expression to, vent, voice; *tot ~ KOM,* find expression.
uit'jaag, uit'jae, (-ge-), drive out, expel, chase off.
ui'tjie¹, (-s), little onion.
uit'jie², (-s), outing.
uit'jou, (-ge-), boo, hiss at, hoot, catcall, barrack; **~ery,** booing, barracking.
uit'kaf, (-ge-), thresh out (corn); eliminate (weaker elements).
uit'kaffer, (-ge-), (neerh.), abuse, scold, revile.
uit'kalf, uit'kalwe(r), (-ge-), hollow out, wash out, erode (river-bank); fret (by moths).
uit'kalwing, washing out, erosion.

uit'kam, (-ge-), comb out (hair); tease (fibres); ~**sel**, (-s), combing; noil.
uit'kamp, (-ge-), camp out, go under canvas.
uit'kap, (-ge-), chop out, cut out (with axe or pick= axe), thin out, hew out (trees); enjoy; *die jongspan kap dit uit*, the young people are enjoying them= selves.
uit'keep, (-ge-), notch, indent, groove.
uit'keer, (-ge-), pay out; give back (change); pay back; drive aside, head off (cattle); divert (steam); ~**'baar**, (..**bare**), distributable; ~**gang**, drafting race; ~**geld**, change; ~**hok**, drafting-pen; ~**krale**, drafting-yards; ~**polis**, endowment policy.
uit'ken, (-ge-), recognize, identify; ~**merk**, identifi= cation mark; ~**ning**, identification; ~**parade**, identification parade.
uit'keping, (-e, -s), notch, check, recess.
uit'kerf, (-ge-), carve out, notch.
uit'kering, payment, distribution, dole, strike pay; grant, benefit, allowance; dividend.
uit'kerings: ~**fonds**, dole fund; endowment fund.
uit'kies, (-ge-), select, pick out, elect, single out; draw; ~**end**, (-e), eclectic; ~**er**, chooser, selector; ~**wed= stryd**, eclectic (golf).
uit'kla, (-ge-), complain (until nothing remains to be said).
uit'klaar, (-ge-), clear (ship).
uit'klae, (-ge-) = uitkla.
uit'klaring, clearance.
uit'klaringsbrief, clearance certificate.
uit'kleding, undressing, phrasing.
uit'klee, (-ge-), undress, strip.
uit'klim, (-ge-), climb out (down); alight (from ve= hicle); ascend (mountain).
uit'klok, (-ge-), clock out (labourers); flare.
uit'klop, (-ge-), malleate, planish, beat out; knock out, defeat; thrash, cane; ~**beker**, knock-out cup; ~**hou**, knock-out blow; ~**kompetisie**, knock-out competition; ~**per**, (-s), duster; shaker, (panel) beater; ~**reeks**, knock-out series; ~**wedstryd**, knock-out match.
uit'klouter, (-ge-), clamber out (down).
uit'knikker, (-ge-), bowl out, drive out, eject, dismiss.
uit'knip, (-ge-), cut out, clip out; ~**sel**, (-s), cutting, clipping; ~**werk**, cutting-out; cut embroidery.
uit'knop, (-ge-), disbud.
uit'knyp, (-ge-), squeeze out; decamp; take a day off.
uit'koggel, (-ge-), mock, deride, boo, mimic.
uit'kom, (-ge-), come out, effloresce, appear (flowers), turn out, come true (dreams); become known, come to light (facts); suffice, be sufficient; come right (calculations); pullulate (bud); pose (dominoes); hatch (eggs); lead (at card game); de= bouch (river); *EK sal* ~, I'll have enough money; *goed* ~ *op 'n FOTO*, come out clearly in a photo; *laat die KAMER op die stoep* ~, let the room open on to the stoep; *die KUIKENS sal môre* ~, the chicks will hatch tomorrow, *LAAT* ~, disclose; ~ *vir sy OPINIE*, speak one's mind; *SÊ nou dit gaan* ~, what if it comes to light? *die SOM wil nie* ~ *nie*, the sum won't work out correctly; *iets STERK laat* ~, throw something into strong relief; emphasize something; *die VLEK wil nie* ~ *nie*, the stain will not disappear; *die VOORSPELLING kan nog* ~, the prediction may still prove true; ~**end**, (-e), naissant (her.); ~**s(te)**, deliverance, boon, god= send, relief; issue, result, outcome; quotient (arith.).
uit'kook, (-ge-), boil out; scald; try; ~**pot**, (clothes-) boiler; ~**sel**, (-s), decoction.
uit'koop, (ge-), buy off, buy out, ransom; buy (pur= chase) his discharge.
uit'kraai, (-ge-), crow, exult loudly.
uit'kraam, (-ge-), show off, parade, display.
uit'krap, (-ge-), erase, scratch out, cancel, obliterate, expunge; incise, inscribe; ~**ping**, erasion, erasure.
uit'kruip, (-ge-), creep out; *hy sal MOET* ~, he will have to exert himself; ~ *vir sy SUIKER*, become independent; *VROEG* ~, get up early.
uit'kry, (-ge-), get out (receive); come to the end; re= move (efface); utter; get out of; get (work out) the answer (to a sum); dismiss, bowl out (cricket); *kleingeld* ~, get change.

uit'kryt, (-ge-), yell out; belittle, decry, disparage.
uit'kuier, (-ge-), have enough (be tired) of visiting.
uit'kwint, (-ge-), thrash.
uit'kyk, (s) (-e), look-out, view; belvedere, gazebo; (fig.) attitude; *OP die* ~ *na*, on the look-out for; *op die* ~ *WEES*, keep watch; (v) look out, watch for; ~ *op die BERGE*, overlook the mountains; ~ *na 'n KANS*, watch for an opportunity; ~ *op die SUIDE*, face south; ~**er**, (-s), look-out (person); ~**koepel**, rotunda; ~**pos**, observation post; ~**to= ring**, watch- (conning-) tower, bird-watching tower; belvedere, gazebo; ~**venster**, observation window; ~**wa**, observation car.
uit'laai, (-ge-), unload, offload; detrain.
uit'laat, (s) (..**late**), outlet, exhaust (of motor); (v) (-ge-), leave out, omit, skip (word, person); let out; see out (visitors); release; express; exhaust; *die HOND* ~, let the dog out; *jou ONGUNSTIG* ~ *oor*, express oneself unfavourably about; *'n VRIEND per abuis* ~, omit a friend by mistake; ~**buis**, eduction pipe; ~**druk**, exhaust pressure; ~**gas**, exhaust gas; ~**gat**, escape hole; ~**klep**, ex= haust valve; ~**kraan**, discharge cock; ~**nok**, outlet cam; ~**pyp**, exhaust pipe; ~**slag**, exhaust-stroke; ~**stoom**, exhaust steam; ~**teken**, dele; ~**verdeel= klep**, exhaust manifold.
uit'lag, (-ge-), laugh at, deride, be made (make) a guy of; cease laughing.
uit'lander, (-s), outlander, foreigner, alien.
uitlan'dig, (-e), absent (from one's country), abroad; ~**heid**, absence (from one's country).
uit'lands, (-e), foreign, exotic, outlandish.
uit'lap, (-ge-), give away (secret).
uit'lating, (-e, -s), omission; utterance, statement; elimination, elision; letting out; pretermission.
uit'latingsteken, apostrophe; caret.
uit'lê[1], (-ge-), explain, elucidate, expound, clear up, interpret, construe.
uit'lê[2], (-ge-), flag (with stones); lay out; pave; *'n LYK* ~, lay out a corpse; *'n VOORSTAD* ~, plan a suburb.
uit'leef = **uitlewe**.
uit'leefdrang, urge to natural expression.
uit'leen, (-ge-), lend out, make a loan of; put out (money); *jou ore vir skinderpraatjies* ~, listen to gossip; ~**biblioteek**, circulating library.
uit'lêend, (-e), exegetic(al).
uit'lêer, (-s), expositor, explainer, expounder, inter= preter; glossarist; elucidator; commentator; ex= egete; layer-out, planner (of cities).
uit'lees, (-ge-), read out (aloud); read through, finish (a book).
uit'leg[1], (uitlêe), lay-out, plan (township).
uit'leg[2], explanation, interpretation, construction; (-ginge), exegesis; comment, commentary; ~**'baar**, (..**bare**), explicable, explainable; ~**gend**, (-e), ex= positive, expository; ~**ging**, (-e, -s) — **uitleg**[1]; ~**kunde**, exegesis, exegetics, hermeneutics, ~**kun= dig**, (-e), exegetic, hermeneutic; ~**kun'dige**, (-s), exegete.
uit'lei, (-ge-), lead out.
uit'lek[1], (-ge-), lick out (with tongue).
uit'lek[2], (-ge-), leak out, trickle out, ooze out; get out, filter through, become known; ~**king**, leakage, (water, information).
uit'lener, (-s), loaner, lender; ~**y**, lending.
uit'lewe, (-ge-), spend, consume; live one's own free life, have one's fling; *jou beginsels* ~, live up to one's principles.
uit'lewer, (-ge-), deliver, give (hand) over, surrender, extradite; ~**baar**, (..**bare**), extraditable (criminal).
uit'lewering, (-e, -s), surrender, delivery; rendition; extradition; exchange.
uit'lewerings: ~**reg**, law of extradition; ~**traktaat**, extradition treaty; ~**verdrag**, extradition treaty; ~**wet**, law of extradition.
uit'lig[1], (-ge-), lift out; omit, strike out; oust; *iem.* ~, give someone a thrashing; oust someone.
uit'lig[2], (-ge-), light (a guest out); light someone out (on his way).
uit'loging, lye-washing, maceration, lixiviation.
uit'lok, (-ge-), tempt, allure, entice; evoke, draw

forth, elicit (answer); invite, court (trouble); give rise to, provoke (quarrel); solicit (law); *baie kritiek* ~, arouse a great deal of criticism; ~'**kend, (-e)**, inviting, tempting, alluring, provocative; ~**ker, (-s)**, enticer; provoker; ~**king, (-e, -s)**, temptation, allurement; invitation, challenge, provocation; soliciting.
uit'**loods, (-ge-)**, pilot out; show out.
uit'**loof, (-ge-)** = uitlowe.
uit'**loog, (-ge-)**, lixiviate; leach; *uitgeloogde grond*, leached soil.
uit'**looi, (-ge-)**, beat, thrash, drub, dust, (lam)baste; *iem.* ~, give someone a tanning.
uit'**loop, (s) (uitlope)**, drain-pipe; overflow, outflow; out-run, outlet, spillway; landing-run (aero.); effluent; flush; ratoon; (w) **(-ge-)**, walk out; end, result in; grow; germinate; eventuate; drain; debouch (river); outstrip; run out (cricket, fluid); tread (wear) out (shoes); shoot, bud; *op 'n MISLUK= KING* ~, end in failure; ~ *op NIKS*, come to nothing, fizzle out; *in 'n PUNT* ~, end, come to a point; taper; *uitgeloopte UIE*, sprouted onions; ~**sel, (-s)**, shoot, sprout, ratoon, offshoot, bud; small stream, tributary; ~**sloot**, overflow furrow; ~**water**, spillage.
uit'**loot, (-ge-)**, release (bonds by drawings); raffle (a prize); draw; ~'**baar, (..bare)**, redeemable.
uit'**loper, (-s)**, sucker, frond, offshoot; stringer (mining); foothill, spur, salient (of fortification); tongue (geol.); limb (mountain).
uit'**los, (-ge-)**, leave out (alone); *los my maar uit*, don't include me; just leave me alone; let me be.
uit'**loting**, drawing (for prizes), raffle.
uit'**lowe, (-ge-)**, offer, promise, put up (a prize).
uit'**lui, (-ge-)**, ring out, toll out, knell.
uit'**maak, (-ge-)**, make out; determine, settle; constitute, form; discern; denounce; break off; decipher; *DEEL* ~ *van*, form part of; *hy MOET dit self* ~, he must decide that for himself; *deur PROEFNE= MING* ~, determine by experiment; *dis 'n uitge= maakte SAAK*, it is a foregone conclusion; *iem.* ~ *vir al wat SLEG is*, accuse someone of everything that is bad, decry someone; *iets TUSSEN hulleself* ~, settle something between themselves; *'n VER= LOOFSKAP* ~, break off an engagement; *ek kan hierdie WOORD nie* ~ *nie*, I cannot decipher (make out) this word.
uit'**maal, (-ge-)**, erode; mill out (water).
uit'**maling**, erosion; milling out.
uit'**maneuvreer, (-ge-)**, outmanoeuvre.
uit'**mars**, forward march.
uit'**marsjeer, (-ge-)**, march out; outmarch.
uit'**meet, (-ge-)**, mete out, measure off; *iets BREED* ~, lay it on thick; *jou GRIEWE breed* ~, make the most of one's grievances.
uitmekaar', separated, apart, asunder.
uitmekaar'**bars, (-gebars)**, burst asunder, explode.
uitmekaar'**dryf, (-gedryf)**, scatter, disperse; drift apart.
uitmekaar'**gaan, (-gegaan)**, separate (divorce), part; adjourn (meeting).
uitmekaar'**haal, (-gehaal)**, take to pieces, dismantle.
uitmekaar'**jaag, (-gejaag)**, disperse, scatter; drive apart.
uitmekaar'**maak, (-gemaak)**, take to pieces; separate.
uitmekaar'**neem, (-geneem)**, dismantle, take to pieces.
uitmekaar'**spat, (-gespat)**, scatter; explode; be dispersed.
uitmekaar'**vlieg, (-gevlieg)**, fly apart.
uit'**melk, (-gemelk)**, milk dry (a cow); fleece (someone).
uit'**mergel, (-ge-)**, exhaust; grind, impoverish; emaciate; gripe; ~**ing**, exhaustion; impoverishment; emaciation.
uit'**merk, (-ge-)**, mark out.
uit'**meting**, mensuration.
uitmiddelpun'**tig, (-e)**, eccentric; accentric (mech.); ~**heid**, eccentricity (math.).
uit'**mond, (-ge-)**, (dis)embogue into, debouch into, empty into, discharge (river); ~**ing, (-e, -s)**, discharger; disemboguement, issue, debouchment; estuary, outlet.

uit'**monster, (-ge-)**, trim with facings; reject soldiers (after review); ~**ing**, facings; rejection.
uit'**moor, (-ge-)**, massacre, butcher; ~**ding**, massacre.
uit'**munt, (-ge-)**, excel, surpass, outshine.
uitmun'**tend, (-e)**, excellent, eminent, pre-eminent, goodly; ~**heid**, excellence, eminence.
uit'**neem, (-ge-)**, take out; withdraw (from bank); ~**baar, (..bare)**, removable.
uitne'**mend, (-e)**, excellent; distinguished; ~**heid**, excellence; *by* ~ *heid*, par excellence.
uit'**nemer, (-s)**, lifting-screw (moulding).
uit'**nodiging, (-e, -s)**, invitation; call.
uit'**nodigingskaartjie**, invitation card.
uit'**nooi, (-ge-)**, invite, ask out; ~ *na 'n bruilof*, invite to a wedding.
uit'**oefen, (-ge-)**, practise, exercise; exert; carry on; pursue (calling); prosecute (a trade); ply (trade); follow (calling); discharge (duties); wield (power); *DRUK* ~, exert pressure; *KRITIEK* ~, criticize; *REGTE* ~, exercise rights; ~**baar, (..bare)**, exercisable; ~**ing**, practice, exercise; discharge, execution; prosecution; pursuit; exertion; ministration.
uit'**oorlê, (~)**, outmanoeuvre, get the better of, checkmate, out-general, best, outwit, circumvent, jockey out.
uit'**pak, (-ge-)**, unpack; unburden; disclose; *ALLES* ~, unburden oneself; tell everything; spill the beans; *oor IEM.* ~, hold forth about someone; *OOR iets* ~, let oneself go about something; ~ *TEEN*, inveigh against.
uit'**pen, (-ge-)**, peg out; stretch out (by pegging).
uit'**pers, (-ge-)**, squeeze out, press out.
uit'**peul¹, (-ge-)**, shell (peas).
uit'**peul², (-ge-)**, protrude (eyes), bulge, be protuberant: ~**ing**, gibbosity, bulge.
uit'**pieker, (-ge-)**, puzzle out (something).
uit'**piets, (-ge-)**, whip out, thrash; dress up smartly.
uit'**pik, (-ge-)**, peck out; pick out, select, cull, single out.
uit'**plaas, (-ge-)**, place, station.
uit'**plak, (-ge-)**, paper out (house).
uit'**plant, (-ge-)**, bed out, plant out, prick.
uit'**plasing**, stationing, placing.
uit'**ploeë, uit'ploeg, (-ge-)**, plough up.
uit'**pluis, (-ge-)**, pick out; sift out (evidence); ferret out, investigate thoroughly (matter); puzzle out, thrash out, discuss (subject); unravel (puzzle); ~**ing**, discussion.
uit'**pluk, (-ge-)**, snatch out (gun); rip out; pull up (weeds).
uit'**plunder, (-ge-)**, plunder, spoliate, despoil, pillage, ransack; ~**ing**, pillage, spoliation.
uit'**pomp, (-ge-)**, pump out; draw out; exhaust (borehole).
uit'**pons, (-ge-)**, punch out.
uit'**praat, (-ge-)**, say all one wants to say; talk away (out); finish talking; *jou goed* ~, unburden one's heart.
uit'**proes, (-ge-)**, burst out laughing.
uit'**puil, (-ge-)**, protrude, protuberate, be protuberant, bulge (eyes); ~**end, (-e)**, protuberant; ~**ing**, protuberance; ~**oë**, protuberant eyes, goggle-eyes.
uit'**punt, (-ge-)**, scallop.
uit'**put, (-ge-)**, exhaust, drain (resources); impoverish (soil); wear out (one's patience); deplete; ~**'lik, (-e)**, exhaustible; ~**tend, (-e)**, exhausting; exhaustive; gruelling; ~**ting**, exhaustion; distress, prostration; ~**tingsoorlog**, war of attrition.
uit'**raak, (-ge-)**, be broken off (engagement); get out; run short of (food, money); go bankrupt.
uit'**raas, (-ge-)**, rage, let off steam; have one's fling; bluster to the end; spend itself; rave itself out (storm); *die jeug moet* ~, youth will have its fling.
uit'**rafel, (-ge-)**, fray, ravel out; ~**ing**, fraying, ravelling out; pulling (text.).
uit'**rakel, (-ge-)**, rake out, riddle.
uit'**rangeer, (-ge-)**, shunt out (lit.); side-track (fig.).
uit'**ransel, (-ge-)**, thrash, wallop.
uit'**red, (-ge-)**, help out; save, extricate; ~**ding**, deliverance, rescue, extrication, godsend.
uit'**reën, uit'reent, (-ge-)**, rain out, be washed out; stop raining.

uit'reik, (-ge-), hand out; issue (tickets); distribute; deliver; award, present (prizes); ~ 'baar, (..bare), distributable, issuable; ~ bewys, issue voucher; ~ er, (-s), issuer; ~ ing, (-e, - s), distribution, awarding (of prizes); issue; hand-out (money).

uit'reis, (s) (-e), outward journey; *op die* ~, outward-bound; (w) **(-ge-),** set sail, go abroad.

uit'rek, (-ge-), stretch out, elongate; dilate; protract, draw out; crane (neck); ~ 'baar, (..bare), extensible, elastic, protractile.

uit'reken, (-ge-), calculate, compute, reckon out (up), figure out; ~ ing, calculation.

uit'rekking, (-e, -s), stretching out, elongation, protraction; dilation, dilatation; pulling (of flax); extension.

uit'rig, (-ge-), do, perform, accomplish.

uit'roei[1], (-ge-), row out.

uit'roei[2], (-ge-), uproot, exterminate, deracinate, eradicate, stamp out, extirpate; ~ baar, (..bare), eradicable; exterminable; ~ er, (-s), exterminator, extirpator; ~ ing, extermination, eradication, annihilation, extirpation; ~ ingswerk, deed of extermination; ~ middel, exterminator.

uit'roep, (s) (-e), exclamation, cry, interjection, outcry, ejaculation; (w) **(-ge-),** call out, interject, exclaim, shout, ejaculate; herald, proclaim; *iem. tot KONING* ~, proclaim someone king; *'n STAKING* ~, call a strike; ~ end, (-e), exclamatory; ~ er, (-s), exclaimer; proclaimer; ~ ing, proclamation; ~ (ings)teken, exclamation mark.

uit'rol, (-ge-), roll out; unroll.

uit'rook, (-ge-), smoke out; fumigate; fume; ~ middel, fumigant.

uit'ruil, (-ge-), exchange, barter, trade (in kind); ~ ing, (-e, -s), exchange, barter.

uit'ruk, (-ge-), snatch out, rip out, tear out, drag (pull) out; march out (against enemy); get out of hand; ~ king, evulsion.

uit'rus[1], (-ge-), repose, rest.

uit'rus[2], (-ge-), caparison, fit out, equip, apparel; furnish; ~ ter, (-s), outfitter; fitter; ~ ting, (-e, -s), outfit, equipment, accoutrements, caparison; lay-out; kit, turn-out, get-up, apparel; appointment; fitting-out; gear; fittings; ~ tingsak, kitbag; ~ stuk, piece of apparel.

uit'ry, (-ge-), ride out; drive out; go for a drive; carry, convey out (sand); wear out (road).

uit'rys, (-ge-), rise to the full (dough); rise above (mountain).

uit'rywissel, trailing points (railw.).

uit'saag, (-ge-), saw out, fret

uit'saai, (-ge-), sow; scatter; broadcast; disseminate; ~ diens, broadcasting service; ~ er, (-s), commentator; broadcaster; ~ ery, broadcasting; ~ korporasie, broadcasting corporation; ~ maatskappy, broadcasting company; ~ praatjie, broadcast (radio) talk; ~ program, broadcast (radio) programme; ~ stasie, broadcasting station; *sy is 'n* ~ *stasie,* she is a babbler (tattler); ~ toestel, broadcasting apparatus; radio; ~ wese, broadcasting.

uit'sae, (-ge-) = uitsaag.

uit'sak, (-ge-), bulge out, bag out; prolapse; lag behind; begin to rain; ~ king, bulging; sagging, falling; prolapse, prolapsus, procidence (womb); dropping out, lagging behind (in race); downpour (rain).

uit'sê, (-ge-), say (speak) out.

uit'seil, (-ge-), sail out, set sail.

uit'send, (-ge-), send out, dispatch; ~ end, (-e), emissive; ~ ing, dispatch; broadcast; emission; transmission; *gerigte* ~ *ing,* directional transmission.

uit'set, (-te), marriage outfit, trousseau; output, production.

uit'setbaar, (..bare), expansible; dilatable; extensible; ~ heid, expansibility, expansiveness.

uit'settend, (-e), expansive.

uit'setting, (-e, -s), expansion; distension; dilatation; dilation; ejection, expulsion, eviction (house); ousting, expatriation, banishment, deportation; diastole (heart).

uit'settings: ~ bevel, ~ dekreet, writ (order) of expulsion; ~ huis, expansion sleeve; ~ koëffisiënt, coefficient of expansion; ~ ruimte, expansion gap; ~ verhouding, expansion ratio; ~ vermoë, expansive power, expansibility; dilatability.

uit'siek, (-ge-), let an illness run its course.

uit'sien, (-ge-), look out for; long for, look forward to; appear; *daar GOED* ~, be looking well; ~ *NA*, look forward to; ~ *OP 'n tuin,* overlook a garden.

uit'sif, (-ge-), sift (out); ~ sels, screenings.

uit'sig, (-te), view, prospect, vista; perspective; ~ *HÊ op,* command a view, face; *'n ONBELEMMERDE* ~, an unobstructed view; *in* ~ *STEL,* hold out a prospect; *SUIDELIKE* ~, southern aspect; ~ loos, (..lose), viewless; limited; ~ pad, scenic road.

uit'sing, (-ge-), sing out, jubilate; sing to the finish.

uitsin'nig, (-e), mad, demented; rash, foolish; ~ heid, madness; rashness, foolishness.

uit'sit[1], (-ge-), sit out (dance); serve (sentence).

uit'sit[2], (-ge-), invest (money); put outside, post, mount (guard); expel, banish, deport; oust (a rival); eject (from meeting); let out, make bigger (frock), extend; expand, dilate (through heat), bulge; *iem. by sy nooi* ~, cut out someone with his girl; ~ klep, expansion valve; ~ vermoë, expansive power; ~ voeg, expansion joint.

uit'skakel, (-ge-), cut out, switch off, disconnect (current); eliminate (errors); declutch, disengage (gears); leave out; exclude (from competition); disregard (possibility); liberate (elec.); ~ aar, (-s), circuit breaker, cut-out, disjunctor; *outomatiese* ~ aar, automatic cut out; ~ ing, (-e, -s), putting out of circuit; declutching; elimination; liberation (elec.); ~ kas, disconnection box.

uit'skater, (-ge-), burst out laughing, cachinnate.

uit'skei[1], (-ge-), cease, stop; *skei nou uit!* stop it! cut it out!

uit'skei[2], separate; secrete, excrete, discharge

uit'skeiding[1], stoppage.

uit'skeiding[2], separation; excretion

uit'skeidingsproduk, waste product; excretion.

uit'skeipunt, blind spot (engine).

uit'skeityd, knocking-off time; closing-time.

uit'skel, (-ge-), call names, abuse, scold, chide, inveigh (against), revile; ~ woord, term of abuse.

uit'skep, (-ge-), bale out (water); scoop out (earth); ladle out, dish out (food).

uit'skeur, (-ge-), tear out.

uit'skiet, (-ge-), shoot out; beat (win, decide) at target shooting; project (ray); dash away; sprout (plants); ~ sitplek, ~ stoel, ejector seat (aero.).

uit'skilder, (-ge-), depict, portray, paint.

uit'skink, (-ge-), pour out.

uit'skoffel, (-ge-), hoe out; weed out.

uit'skop, (-ge-), kick out; expel, dismiss, fire (clerk); hoof out; find touch (rugby); ~ onderrok, crinoline (stiffened) petticoat; ~ pantoffel, mule.

uit'skot, waste, refuse, offal; tailings (mining); culling; factory reject; garbage; rabble, riff-raff; ~ hoop, refuse dump, ~ sak, poke (dial.); ~ winkel, factory-rejects store; ~ wol, outsorts (wool).

uit'skraap, (-ge-), scratch (scrape) out; curette (med.); ~ sel, scrapings.

uit'skrap, (-ge-), scratch out (with pen), erase, delete; ~ ing, scraping-out; curettage (med.); ~ ping, scratching (out).

uit'skreeu, (-ge-), scream out, cry out; yell; exclaim; ~ end, (-e), exclamatory; ~ er, exclaimer.

uit'skrop, (-ge-), scrub out.

uit'skryf, uit'skrywe, (-ge-), offer (prize); call (meeting); float, issue (loan); copy out, write out, make out (account, cheque); *'n PRYSVRAAG* ~, offer a prize; *'n WEDSTRYD* ~, organize (start) a competition.

uit'skrywing, convocation (meeting); copy; issue (loan); writing out (of cheque etc.).

uit'skud, (-ge-), rob; shake out; strip; *iem.* ~, strip someone bare; take all a P.O.W.'s clothes.

uit'skuif, uit'skuiwe, (-ge-), slide out; shove out; get rid of, eliminate; ~ 'baar, (..bare), extensible; ~ leer, extension ladder; ~ tafel, telescope (extension) table.

uit'skuins, (-ge-), splay, flare; ~ ing, splaying, flanning.

uit'skuiwing, shoving (out), elimination.
uit'skulp, (-ge-), scallop; ~**ing**, scalloping.
uit'skuur, (-ge-), scour out; wear away.
uit'slaan, (-ge-), beat out, drive (hammer) out (nails); become mouldy; appear unexpectedly, drop from the sky; fling out (arms); knock out (boxing); shatter (wheat); spread (wings); smash out (tooth); break out (flames); effloresce; *môre IEWERS* ~, be pitching up somewhere tomorrow; *die KIND is uitgeslaan*, the child has come out in a rash; *'n paar RAND* ~, make a few rands; *iem. se VOETE onder hom* ~, sweep someone off his feet.
uit'slaap, (-ge-), sleep one's fill; sleep away from home; see **uitgeslape**.
uit'slag¹, eruption, (skin) rash; event; efflorescence; decision; drift; exanthem; deflection (springs); (..**slae**), result, issue; *die* ~ *van die verkiesing gee*, declare the poll.
uit'slag², (-ge-), kill off, butcher off (sheep).
uit'slagkoors, dengue (fever).
uit'sleep, (-ge-), drag out.
uit'sloof, uit'slowe, (-ge-), drudge, toil, work oneself to death.
uit'sluip, (-ge-), sneak out, steal out.
uit'sluit, (-ge-), exclude, debar, shut out (a person); rule out (possibility); disqualify (in sport); preclude (doubt).
uitslui'tend, (b) (-e), sole; preclusive; (bw) solely, exclusively; ~**heid**, exclusiveness.
uit'sluiting, exclusion; foreclosure; preclusion; ostracism; lock-out; disqualification; *met* ~ *van*, exclusive of, excluding.
uitsluit'lik, exclusively, solely.
uit'sluitsel, decisive answer; finality.
uit'slyt, (-ge-), wear out; *dis beter om uit te slyt as om vas te roes*, it is better to wear out than to rust out; ~**ing**, wearing hollow.
uit'smee, (-ge-), hammer out; draw out; ~ *volgens grootte*, drawing out to size (blacksmith).
uit'smeer, (-ge-), smear out (e.g. floor with cow-dung).
uit'smelt, (-ge-), smelt (ore); melt down, render, try (fat); ~**ery**, smelting; smelt house; ~**ing**, rendering (fat); smelting (ore).
uit'smyt, (-ge-), eject, fling out, chuck out, kick out, throw out; ~**er, (-s)**, chucker-out, bouncer; ejector; ~**ing**, ejection.
uit'snel, (-ge-), rush out.
uit'snik, (-ge-), sob (one's heart) out.
uit'snuffel, (-ge-), ferret out.
uit'snuit, (-ge-), blow out (nose); snuff out (candle).
uit'sny, (-ge-), cut out, carve out; recess; excise, excide; ~**ding**, excision, cutting; pocket (archit.); recess; ~**saag**, jigsaw; ~**sel, (-s)**, cut-out.
uit'soek, (s) the pick, cream, essence, flower; (w) **(-ge-)**, select, have one's pick, pick, choose, cull, comb out; assort, sort; *sonder* ~, at random.
uit'soek-, selected, hand-picked; ~**appels**, selected apples; ~**buurt**, select quarter (of city); ~**erig, (-e)**, selective, fastidious, cliquish; ~**ery**, selection; ~**jaar**, vintage year; ~**rat**, selection gear.
uit'sonder, (-ge-), except, exempt, exclude.
uit'sondering, (-e, -s), exception; *die* ~ *BEVESTIG die reël*, the exception proves the rule; *BY* ~, by way of exception; *by HOË* ~, hardly (scarcely) ever; seldom if ever; *MET* ~ *van*, with the exception of; *'n* ~ *op die REËL*, an exception to the rule; *SONDER* ~, without exception; one and all; ~**sgeval**, exceptional case.
uitson'derlik, (-e), exceptional.
uit'sorteer, (-ge-), sort out; choose, select.
uit'spaar, (-ge-), save, economise; *nog uitgespaar*, still alive.
uit'span, (-ge-), unharness, outspan; unyoke; stretch out; ~**ning, (-e, -s)**, outspan.
uit'spannings: ~**lokaal**, recreation room (hall); ~**oord**, pleasure (recreation) resort.
uit'spanplek, outspan; halfway house; *dit is anderkant my* ~, that is beyond me.
uit'spansel, firmament, sky.
uit'sparing, saving, economy; recess.
uit'spat, (-ge-), splash out, spurt out; indulge in dissipation.

uitspat'lik, (-e), dissolute, licentious; ~**heid**, licentiousness.
uitspat'tend, (-e), dissipated, dissolute, debauched; loud; ~*e KLEURE*, excessively bright or gaudy colours; *hy is TE* ~, he is too loud.
uit'spatting, (-e, -s), dissipation, debauch(ery), dissoluteness; extravagance; carnival; *hom aan* ~ *oorgee*, lead a dissolute life; indulge in excesses.
uit'speel, (-ge-), play to the end, finish (a game); play, lead (a card); *hulle teen mekaar* ~, play them off against each other.
uit'spel, (-ge-), spell (out).
uit'spin, (-ge-), spin out; draw out (fig.).
uit'spit, (-ge-), dig out.
uit'spoeg, (-ge-), spit out; sputter; ~**sel**, spittle.
uit'spoel, (-ge-), wash away; wash out; rinse; flush; be washed ashore; erode, wear out; gully (channel); irrigate (med.); leach; ~**ing**, douche; erosion; irrigation (med.); ~**sel**, flotsam.
uit'spook, (-ge-), fight out, settle by fighting; obtain by fighting.
uit'spraak, pronunciation, diction, enouncement; sentence, decision, finding, verdict, judgment; pronouncement; award (of arbitrators); deliverance; reference; enunciation; ~ *DOEN*, deliver judgement, pass sentence; ~ *VOORBEHOU*, reserve judgement; ~**fout**, error in pronunciation; ~**kun'dige, (-s)**, orthoepist; ~**leer**, phonetics; orthoepy; ~**register**, docket (law); ~**woordeboek**, pronouncing dictionary.
uit'spreek, (-ge-), pronounce, enounce; deliver (speech); express; *HOM* ~ *vir*, declare oneself for; *'n VONNIS* ~ *oor iem.*, pronounce judgement upon someone; ~**'baar, (..bare)**, pronounceable.
uit'sprei, (-ge-), spread out, unfold, extend, open out, expand; ~**ding**, spreading out, expansion, unfolding.
uit'spring, (-ge-), project, jut out; get busy; jump out; leave home to find work; exert oneself; *iem. sal moet* ~, he will have to look alive; ~**end, (-e)**, projecting (window); salient (angle); protuberant; ~**ing, (-e, -s)**, projection.
uit'spruit, (-ge-), bud, pullulate, sprout out; have its origin in; ~**sel, (-s)**, sprout, shoot, offshoot; result.
uit'spuit, (-ge-), spout out, spurt out, squirt out; syringe (a wound); ejaculate.
uit'spu(ug), (-ge-), = **uitspoeg**.
uit'staan, (-ge-), endure, bear, brook, suffer, withstand; stand out; bulge out, belly; *ek KAN hom nie* ~ *nie*, I cannot bear him; *NIKS met iem. uit te staan hê nie*, be in no way connected with someone; have nothing to do with someone; ~**'baar, (..bare)**, endurable; ~**de**, outstanding (debts); patulous; projecting; ~*de ORE*, prominent ears; ~*de POTE*, splayed feet (of table); ~*de RAND*, projecting edge; ~*de SKULD*, outstanding debt(s).
uit'stal, (-ge-), put out (for sale), display, exhibit; show off (learning); ~**kamer**, sample-room; showroom; ~**kas**, show-case, vitrine; china closet; ~**kuns**, window dressing; ~**ler, (-s)**, window-dresser; exhibitor; ~**ling, (-e, -s)**, display, exhibit, window-dressing; ~**raam**, show-window; ~**venster**, shop-window; show-window.
uit'stamel, (-ge-), stammer (out).
uit'stamp, (-ge-), stamp out; push out violently.
uit'stap, (-ge-), get out, alight, step out, walk out; detrain; ~**pery**, walk-out; ~**pie, (-s)**, excursion, jaunt, trip, outing, ramble, walk.
uitste'dig, (-e), out of town; ~**heid**, absence from town.
uit'steek, (-ge-), put out, pop out, stretch out, hold out (hand), reach out; gouge, stick (dig) out, prick out; jut out, project; stand out above, excel; overhang; *bokant ANDER* ~, tower above others; be much superior to others; *sy uitgesteekte HAND*, his proffered hand; *iem. se OË* ~, put out someone's eyes; *die hand van VRIENDSKAP* ~, make a friendly gesture; extend the hand of friendship; ~**sel, (-s)**, projecting part, jut, protuberance; projection; promontory; prominence; protrusion; ~**tand**, buck-tooth; ~**vorm**, cutter.

uit'stek: *by* ~, par excellence, pre-eminently.
uit'stekend¹, (-e), projecting, protruding, prominent.
uitste'kend², (-e), excellent, first-rate, capital, admirable, eminent, outstanding; gilt-edged (investment); rattling good; ~ heid, excellence, eminence, prominence.
uit'steking, protrusion.
uit'stel, (s) delay, postponement, adjournment, deferment, extension of time; procrastination, prolongation; dalliance; respite; grace; *van* ~ *kom AFSTEL*, procrastination is the thief of time; ~ *is nog nie AFSTEL nie*, all is not lost that is delayed; ~ *van EKSEKUSIE kry*, live on borrowed time; ~ *GEE*, grant an extension of time; ~ *van VONNIS*, reprieve; (w) (-ge-), delay, postpone, put off; prorogue; procrastinate; adjourn (meeting); remand (court case); side-track, defer (payment); *moenie* ~ *tot MÔRE wat jy vandag nog kan besôre*, do not put off till tomorrow what you can do today; *vir onbepaalde TYD* ~, adjourn (postpone) indefinitely (sine die); shelve; ~ dae, days of grace; ~ ler, (-s), procrastinator; ~ 'lerig, (-e), dilatory; ~ lery, postponement, dilly-dallying.
uit'stem, (-ge-), oust (by voting); outvote.
uit'sterf, uit'sterwe (-ge-), become extinct, die out; become deserted (town).
uit'sterwing, extinction.
uit'stippel, (-ge-), indicate with dots; stipple; outline, sketch out, map out.
uit'stoel, (-ge-), form a stool (plant), tiller; ~ ing, tillering, stooling.
uit'stof, (-ge-), dust out; beat (in competition), outdistance, outstrip; *iem.* ~, give someone a dressing down; beat someone hollow.
uit'stoming, dry-cleaning; steam-cleaning.
uit'stoom, (-ge-), steam out; dry-clean (clothes).
uit'stoot, (-ge-), push out, turn out, expel, send to Coventry, extrude, elbow out, thrust out; ejaculate, utter (cry); belch forth (smoke); *die hors* ~, puff up one's chest with pride.
uit'storm, (-ge-), rush out; *by 'n gebou* ~, rush out of a building.
uit'stort, (-ge-), pour out, shed, spill (blood); unbosom; gush, disgorge, disembogue (itself in sea); flood, effuse; *jou hart* ~, unburden one's heart; ~ end, (-e), ejaculatory; effusive; ~ ing, (-e, -s), emission, effusion; diffusion; ejaculation; gush, outpouring, shedding; *die* ~ *ing van die Heilige Gees*, the outpouring of the Holy Ghost.
uit'stoting, (-e, -s), pushing out, expulsion, ejaculation; extrusion.
uit'stotter, (ge), stammer out.
uit'straal, (-ge-), emit; (e)radiate, beam forth, ray, give out (light); emanate from; effuse; diffuse.
uit'straat, (-ge-), pave; line.
uit'stralend (-e), emissive; radioactive.
uit'straler, (-s), radiator.
uit'straling, (-e, -s), (e)radiation; radiating emission; aura; irradiation; diffusion, emanation.
uit'stralings: ~ hitte, radiant heat; ~ punt, radiating point; radiant; ~ teorie, radiation theory; ~ vermoë, radiating power; ~ vlak, radiating surface; ~ warmte, radiant heat.
uit'streep, (-ge-), strike (cross) out.
uit'strek, (-ge-), extend (hands); expand, stretch out, reach out; porrect (zool.); range; ~ king, extension, expansion.
uit'stroming, streaming out, efflux, effluvium, gush, outflow, jetting out (gas), flow, issue, outrush.
uit'strooi, (-ge-), strew, sow, scatter, spread, circulate, disseminate (news); ~ er, disseminator; ~ ing, sowing (seed); spreading, dissemination (news); ~ sel, rumour.
uit'stroom, (-ge-), stream out, gush forth, issue; ~ buis, diffuser.
uit'stry, (-ge-), argue out; fight out.
uit'stryk, (-ge-), iron out, smooth out; *moeilikhede* ~, smooth out difficulties; ~ ing, smoothing out; ~ voor, last furrow ploughed, dead furrow.
uit'studeer, (-ge-), complete one's studies; finish one's study.
uit'stulp, (-ge-), evaginate; ~ ing, evagination.

uit'stuur, (-ge-), steer out (of port); send out (from room); emit (electric waves); *'n omsendbrief* ~, post (send out) a circular.
uit'styg, (-ge-), step down, get off (from vehicle); rise above.
uit'suie, (-ge-) = uitsuig.
uit'suier, (-s), extortioner; extorter, bloodsucker; harpy; ~ y, vampirism; extortion.
uit'suig, (-ge-), suck out; impoverish (country); overcharge; extort (money); sweat, bleed (labourers); *iem.* ~, suck somebody dry.
uit'suiging, extortion.
uit'suinig, (-ge-), save, economize.
uit'suip, (-ge-), suck out (cow); waste on drink; *die kalf het uitgesuip*, the calf has sucked the cow dry.
uit'suiwer, (-ge-), purge, eliminate; ~ ing, (-e, -s), purge.
uit'swaai, (-ge-), swing out (of the way); open outwards (door); centrifuge; ~ bal, outswinger (cricket); ~ deur, outward-opening door; ~ masjien, centrifuge.
uit'swa(w)el, (-ge-), fumigate with sulphur.
uit'sweer, (-ge-), fester out.
uit'sweet, (-ge-), sweat out, exude, perspire; ~ 'baar, (..bare), perspirable.
uit'swel, (-ge-), swell out, expand, dilate.
uit'swem, (-ge-), swim out; outswim; swim the full length.
uit'swenk, (-ge-), turn aside; swerve out (away).
uit'swerm, (-ge-), swarm off (out); disperse.
uit'swelling, exudation, desudation.
uit'syfer, (-ge-), figure out; *see* uitsypel.
uit'sypel, (-ge-), ooze, trickle out; ~ ing, extravasation, oozing.
uit'tand, (s) missing tooth; *'n kind met* ~ *e*, a child with missing teeth; (w) (-ge-), indent; pink (needlework); ~ ing, indentation, jagging; ~ skêr, pinking scissors (shears).
uit'tap, (-ge-), draw off.
uit'tart, (-ge-), provoke, defy, challenge, hurl defiance at; ~ end, provocative; ~ er, (-s), provoker; ~ ing, (-e, -s), provocation, defiance, challenge.
uit'teer¹, (-ge-), pine away, attenuate, macerate, become emaciated; consume.
uit'teer², (-ge-), tar.
uit'teken, (-ge-), delineate, draw, portray; plot (graph).
uit'tel¹, (-ge-), lift out; *'n baba uit 'n motor* ~, lift out a baby from a car.
uit'tel², (-ge-), count out (in boxing); count (sheep as they leave the kraal); ~ ling, count-out (boxing); ~ rympie, counting-out rhyme.
uit'tering, emaciation; tabes, marasmus, wasting away, attenuation, atrophy (of body).
uit'tik, (-ge-), type out.
uit'tog, departure, egression, exodus.
uit'tol, (-ge-), pay out, veer.
uit'torring, (-ge-), unstitch; become unstitched; fray, rip.
uit'trap¹, (-ge-), tread out; step out (sport); stamp out (fire); wear in (shoes); overstock (farm); thresh (grain).
uit'trap², (-ge-), rebuke, berate, scold; thrash; *iem.* ~, give someone a dressing down.
uit'treding, retirement; withdrawal.
uit'tredingshoek, angle of emergence.
uit'tree, (-ge-), retire, withdraw, resign.
uit'tree, (-ge-), step out.
uit'trek, (-ge-), undress, strip off, doff (clothes); pull off (boots); land, grass (fish); educe; arch out; extract (tooth); uproot (weeds), pull out; withdraw (money); *jou vir 'n ANDER* ~, sacrifice oneself for someone else; *iem. se SIEL* ~, tease, plague someone; drive someone to desperation; *'n mens moet jou nie* ~ *voor jy gaan SLAAP nie*, do not put off your doublet (clothes) before you go to bed; who gives away his goods before he is dead, take a beetle and knock him on the head; *'n SOM geld* ~, draw a sum of money; earmark a sum of money; ~ 'baar, (..bare), extractable; extractive; ~ borduurwerk, drawn(-thread) work (embroidery); ~ hek, extension gate; ~ ker, extractor; ~ king, (e)vulsion; ex-

traction; ~**sel, (-s)**, decoction, extract (of herbs); digest, excerpt, précis, brief, abridgement, account, compendium; summary, epitome (of volume); copy (of account); ~**selmaker**, extractor; ~**tafel**, extension (telescope) table; ~**valskerm**, pilot parachute; ~**vlerk**, telescopic wing.

uit'trompet, (-ge-), trumpet forth, blaze abroad.

uit'vaagsel, (-s), scum, scourings, riff-raff, dregs; excrement.

uit'vaar¹, (-ge-), sail out, put to sea.

uit'vaar², (-ge-), inveigh (against), rail (at), rave, rage, rant, declaim, denounce, fulminate.

uit'vaardig, (-ge-), issue (an order); enact, promulgate (a law); emit (paper currency); ~**er**, promulgator, enactor; issuer; ~**ing, (-e, -s)**, decree; enactment; promulgation; issue.

uit'vaart, obsequies, funeral.

uit'val¹, (s) (-le), thrust, lunge, pass (in fencing); sally, sortie, attack; *'n ~ MAAK*, make a sally; (w) **(-ge-)**, hit out, flare up, fly out.

uit'val², (s) (-le), outburst, quarrel.

uit'val³, (w) (-ge-), fall out; come off (hair); drop out; be defeated, lose (an election); stop work, knock off; *dit sal goed ~*, it will turn out well.

uit'valgrond, odd piece (overlap, cantle) of land (ground).

uit'valkompetisie, knock-out competition.

uit'valshoek, angle of reflection.

uit'valspoort, sally-port.

uit'vang, (-ge-), cull (sheep), select; catch (cricket); ~**beampte**, culling officer; ~**dier**, cull(ed animal).

uit'varing, fulmination.

uit'vars, (-ge-), freshen; desalt; ~**ing**, desalination.

uit'vat, (-ge-), take out; dress smartly; *'n fyn uitgevatte dame*, a smartly dressed lady; ~**speletjie**, cat's-cradle (game).

uit'vee, (-ge-), sweep out (room); efface, erase; wipe out (bowl, dish); rub (eyes); expunge (name).

uit'veër, (-s), eraser, rubber.

uit'veg, (-ge-), fight out to a finish.

uit'veging, erasion, erasure.

uit'veil, (-ge-), offer (put up) for sale.

uit'verf, (-ge-), paint (room); paint out.

uit'verkies, (~), elect, single out; predestine; ~**ing**, election; predestination.

uit'verkoop, (s) (clearance) sale; (w) **(~),** sell out, clear; *dit is ~*, it is sold out; it is out of stock; *~*, (the house is) sold out; ~**prys**, bargain price.

uit'verkoping, (-e, -s), clearance sale.

uit'verkore, elect, chosen, select; *die ~ volk*, the chosen people; ~**ne, (-s)**, favourite, elect, chosen one; best girl (boy), sweetheart.

uit'vier¹, (-ge-), celebrate; *die ou jaar ~*, see the old year out.

uit'vier², (-ge-), pay out (rope, cable), veer out, ease out.

uit'vind, (-ge-), invent; find out, ascertain; detect; ~**er, (-s)**, inventor; deviser; coiner; artificer; contriver; ~**ing, (-e, -s)**, invention; gadget, device, coining; contrivance; ~**sel, (-s)**, invention; contrivance, device; coinage; contraption; fabrication.

uit'vis, (-ge-), fish out (lit. and fig.); ferret out, smell out, get to the bottom of (secret).

uit'vlak, (-ge-), erase, wipe out.

uit'vlieg, (-ge-), fly out.

uit'vloei, (-ge-), flow out; emanate (from); result; ~**end, (-e)**, effluvient; ~**ing**, effluvium, effluence, outflow, efflux, emanation, flowing out; ~**sel, (-s)**, result, outcome, consequence; effluent; efflux (of liquid); gleet (med.).

uit'vloek, (-ge-), swear at, curse; bedevil, revile.

uit'vlok, (-ge-), flake out, flocculate; ~**king**, flocculation.

uit'vlug, (s) (-te), excuse, evasion, pretext, subterfuge, chicanery; put-off; loophole, prevarication, doubling; equivocation; ~*te soek*, look for loopholes; prevaricate; (w) **(-ge-)**, escape; ~**soeker**, prevaricator.

uit'voer¹, (s), export, exportation; *ten ~ bring*, carry out, put into effect; (w) **(-ge-)**, export; execute (order); carry out, do, effectuate, carry into execution, accomplish (task); achieve, implement (a contract); commit (a murder); practise, perform (a task); administer, enforce (law); *jy voer NIKS uit nie*, you are accomplishing nothing; *WAT voer jy uit?* what are you up to?

uit'voer², (w) (-ge-), line (a coat).

uit'voerartikel, article of export.

uitvoer'baar, (..bare), feasible, practicable, possible, performable, executable; exportable; ~**heid**, feasibility, practicability; exportability; ~**heidstoets**, ~**heidstudie**, feasibility study.

uit'voer: ~**belasting**, export tax; ~**der, (-s)**, executor; enactor, executant; exporter; ~**druif**, export grape.

uitvoe'rend, (-e), executive; *U ~ e KOMITEE*, Executive Committee; *~ e KUNSTE*, performing arts; *~ e MAG*, executive power.

uit'voer: ~**firma**, shipping-house; ~**handel**, export trade, outward trade; ~**hawe**, export harbour, port of export.

uitvoe'rig, (-e), elaborate, detailed (account); exhaustive (investigation); at length, in extenso, circumstantial, lengthy (consideration); full (particulars); copious (notes); minute (description); ample; ~**heid**, minuteness of detail, ampleness, elaboration, copiousness.

uit'voering, (-e, -s), performance, execution (music); implementation, implementing (of treaty); achievement; effectuation, pursuance; recital (music); entertainment; enforcement (law); get-up (of book); workmanship; *~ geen aan*, execute; give effect to.

uit'voer: ~**land**, exporting country; ~**lisensie**, export licence; ~**mark**, export market; ~**nywerheid**, export industry; ~**premie**, export bounty; ~**produk**, article of export; ~**reg, (-te)**, export duty; ~**verbod**, prohibition of export(ation); ~**ware**, exports, export goods, articles of export.

uit'vors, (-ge-), investigate, ferret out, sift to the bottom; ~**er, (-s)**, investigator.

uit'vra, (-ge-), sound, question, examine, interrogate, pump; invite, ask out (for a meal); *van ~ is die tronke vol*, ask no questions and you will hear no lies; curiosity killed the cat.

uit'vraerig, (-e), inquisitive.

uit'vreet¹, (w) (-ge-), eat away, corrode; eat its fill (an animal).

uit'vreet², (w) (-ge-), take to task, reprimand; revile, abuse; *ek sal hom goed ~*, I shall take him to task severely.

uit'vreting, pitting; corrosion; fretting.

uit'vroetel, (-ge-), burrow up; rummage (ferret) out.

uit'vryf, uit'vrywe, (-ge-), rub out.

uit'waai, (-ge-), blow out, be blown out; rush out; uproot (tree); extinguish (light); flutter (in the wind); *ek het niks met hom uit te waai(e) nie*, I have nothing to to with him; I have no truck with him.

uit'waarts, (b) (-e), outward; *~ e BELEID*, policy of friendship with neighbouring states; *~ e DRAAIING*, supination; (bw) outwards.

uit'wan, (-ge-), winnow.

uit'was¹, (s) (-se), excrescence, protuberance, fungus, outgrowth.

uit'was², (w) (-ge-), wash out, swab out; clean, bathe (wound).

uit'wasem, (-ge-), evaporate, emanate, exude, exhale; give off (smell); perspire; transpire (plants); ~**ing, (-e, -s)**, evaporation, fume, perspiration, emanation, exhalation, exudation, aura (of flowers).

uit'wassend, (-e), excrescent.

uit'wassing, washing out; elutriation (mines).

uit'water, (-ge-), disembogue, debouch, drain into; ~**ing**, debouchment, disemboguement; fall.

uit'weg, outlet, escape, way out, loophole, expedient; alternative.

uit'wei, (-ge-), expatiate, digress, descant, excurse, enlarge, dissert(ate); *~ oor*, enlarge on; ~**dend, (-e)**, digressive, expatiatory; ~**ding, (-e, -s)**, digression, amplification, expatiation, discursion.

uitwen'dig, uit'wendig, (-e), external, exterior, outward, extrinsic; *vir ~ e gebruik*, for external use only, not to be taken (medicine); ~**heid, (..hede)**, exterior, externals; externality.

uit'werk, (-ge-), work out (plan); calculate (a quanti-

ty); develop (scheme, idea); elaborate, belabour (an argument); have its effect (medicine); bring about, effect; wear out (bearings); push out, oust (a person); cease fermenting; work away from home; ~ ing, effect, result; impression; expansion; working out; elaboration.
uit'werkingsafstand, effective range, fighting range.
uit'werp (-ge-), cast out, throw out; eject, expel; excrete; *duiwels* ~, exorcize (drive out) devils; ~eling, (-e), outcast, pariah; ~end, (-e), ejective; projectile; ~er, (-s), ejector, expeller; ~ing, (-e, -s), ejection; excretion; ejaculation; ejectment, expulsion; ~sel, excrement; ~sels, ordure, droppings, frass (larvae), faeces, dejecta; ejecta (geol.).
uit'wied, (-ge-), weed out; ~ing, weeding out.
uit'wikkel, (-ge-), prize out, force up; loosen; *jou uit 'n moeilikheid* ~, wriggle out of a difficulty; ~ing, prizing out, loosening.
uit'wiks, (-ge-), beat (out), thrash.
uit'win, (-ge-), profit (by); save (time); eject (tenant); excuss (debtor); ~'baar, executable; ~ning, saving; excussion.
uit'wip, (-ge-), skip out, jump up; oust (from a post); go (pop) out for a short while.
uit'wis, (-ge-), efface, obliterate, erase, annihilate, delete, blot out, deface, wipe out, expunge; ~'baar, (..bare), effaceable, erasable.
uit'wissel, (-ge-), exchange, cash (cheque); interchange (prisoners); ~baar, (..bare), interchangeable; cashable; ~ing, (-e, -s), exchange; cashing; interchange, reciprocation.
uit'wisser, (-s), defacer; eraser.
uit'wissing, (e, s), effacement, deletion, erasure, expunction, obliteration, erasion; defacement.
uit'woed, (-ge-), spend (itself), cease raging, subside, abate, rave itself out (storm).
uit'woel, (-ge-), burrow up (tree); chase out (rowdy boys); force (turn) out of bed.
uit'wonend, (-e), non-resident.
uit'woon, (-ge-), be non-resident (scholars); cause to be dilapidated (house); ~toelae, living-out allowance.
uit'wring, (-ge-), wring out, squeeze out; extort.
uit'wurm, (-ge-), worm out; screw out.
uit'wyk, (-ge-), turn aside; give way, deviate, dodge, swerve; expatriate, go into exile; emigrate; ~ing, turning aside, deviation, diversion; amplitude, emigration, expatriation; detour, bypass; deviation, loop road; ~ingshoek, angle of deviation; ~pad, by-pass, detour; ~spoor, loop-line, blind siding.
uit'wys, (-ge-), point out, show; prove; pass judgment; banish; expel; *die tyd sal* ~, time will tell.
ui'vormig, (-e), onion-shaped.
ukule'le, (-s), ukulele.
ul'ster, (-s), ulster, (rubber) overcoat.
ultima'tum, (-s), ultimatum; *'n* ~ *stel*, deliver an ultimatum.
ul'timo, ultimo.
ul'tra, ultra, beyond, too excessive(ly).
ultraba'sies, (-e), ultrabasic.
ul'traglad, (-de), ultraplain (sheep).
ul'traklank, ultrasound.
ul'trakortgolf, ultrashortwave.
ultramaryn', (-e), ultramarine, deep (sea-) blue.
ul'tramodern, (-e), ultramodern.
ultramontaan', (..tane), ultramontane; ~s', (-e), ultramontane.
ultraso'nies, (-e), ultrasonic.
ul'trastruktuur, ultrastructure.
ul'traviolet, ultraviolet; ~ *strale*, ultraviolet rays.
Um'brië, Umbria; ~r, (-s), Umbrian.
Um'bries, (-e), Umbrian.
um'laut, umlaut, vowel mutation; ~eer', (ge-), change by umlaut.
unamien', (-e), unanimous.
unanimiteit', unanimity.
undula'sie, undulation; ~punt, point of undulation.
unduleer', (ge-), undulate.
uniaal', (uniale), (pertaining to a) union.
u'nie, (-s), union.
U'nie, Union; ~ *van S.A.*, (hist.), Union of S.A.; ~gebou, Union Buildings.

uniek', (-e), unique, unparalleled.
unifika'sie, (-s), unification.
u'niform, (s) (-s), uniform; (b) (-e), uniform; ~iteit', uniformity.
u'nikum, (-s), unique thing; single copy.
unikursaal', (..sale), unicursal.
u'nilateraal, (..rale), unilateral.
Unionis', (-te), Unionist.
unipetaal¹, (..tale), unipetalous.
u'niseks, unisex.
Unita'riër, (-s), Unitarian.
Unita'ries, (-e), Unitarian.
Unitaris'me, Unitarianism.
unitêr', (-e), unitary.
univariant', (-e), univariant.
universalis', (-te), universalist; ~me, universalism; ~ties, (-e), universalistic.
universaliteit', universality.
universa'lium, (-s), universal.
universeel'¹, (..sele), universal.
universeel'², (..sele), universal, general; (o)ecumenical; sole; ..*sele erfgenaam*, sole heir, residuary legatee; ~passer, universal dividers.
universiteit', (-e), university; ~espan, universities' team.
universiteits': ~biblioteek, university library; ~fonds, university fund; ~geboue, university buildings; ~kollege, university college; ~opleiding, university training.
universiteit'span, university team.
universiteits'; ~professor, university professor; ~terrein, campus; university area.
universitêr', (-e), pertaining to a university.
univer'sum, universe.
un'ster, (-s), steelyard; weigh-beam.
uraan', uranium; *verrykte* ~, enriched uranium; ~pikride, ~pikried, pitchblende; ~suur, uranic acid; ~verryking, uranium enrichment; ~verrykingsaanleg, uranium enrichment plant.
Ura'nia, Urania.
Ura'nies, (-e), Uranian.
uraniet', uranite.
ura'nium, uranium.
uranografie', uranography.
uranologie', uranology.
urbaan', (urbane), (ong.), urbane, suave.
Urbanis', (-te), Urbanist (church).
Urbaniteit', urbanity, suavity.
u're, *see* uur.
u'relange, for hours, lasting for hours.
uremie', ur(a)emia.
uretaan', (uretane), urethane.
ure'ter, (-s), ureter.
ure'tra, (-s), urethra.
ure'um, urea.
urgen'sie, urgency.
urgent', (-e), (ong.), urgent.
Uri'a, Uriah; ~sbrief, letter bearing disastrous news to the recipient (spelling ruin to the recipient).
urien' = urine.
u'rim en tum'mum, urim and thummim
urinaal', (..nale), urinal.
uri'ne, urine; ~blaas, (urine) bladder; ~buis(ie), urethra; urinary tubule; ~drywend, (-e), diuretic; ~eiwit, albuminuria.
urineer', (ge-), urinate, pass water; ~middel, diuretic.
uri'ne: ~glas, urinal; ~kanaal, urinary tract; ~losing, micturition; ~ondersoek, uroscopy, examination of urine; ~suur, uric acid.
urinoir', (-s), (public) urinal.
urn, (-s), urn.
urologie', urology.
urolo'gies, (-e), urological.
uroloog', (..loë), urologist.
uroskopie', uroscopy.
usan'sie, usage, custom.
uself', yourself.
u'so, usance; ~wissel, bill at usance.
U'-staal, channel steel.
usueel', (usuele), customary, usual.
u'sufructus, usufruct, life rent.

usurpa'sie, usurpation.
usurpa'tor, (-s), usurper.
usurpeer', (ge-), usurp.
u'sus, usage, usus.
ut, (ong.), ut, do(h) (music).
u'terus, (..ri), uterus, womb.
utilisa'sie, utilization.
utiliseer', (ge-), utilize.
utilis'me, utilitarianism.
utilitaris', (-te), utilitarian; ~**me,** utilitarianism; ~**ties, (-e),** utilitarian.
utiliteit', utility.
utiliteits'beginsel, utilitarianism.
u''tjie, (-s), small u.
Uto'pia, Utopia.
utopie', (-ë), utopia; dream-image, phantom, phantasm.
uto'pies, (-e), utopian; phantasmal, phantasmic.
utopis', (-te), utopian.
uur, (ure), hour; *ure AANEEN,* for hours; *ter elfder ure,* at the eleventh hour; *op 'n GEGEWE* ~, at a given moment; *sy* ~ *tjie het GESLAAN,* his hour has struck; his time has come; *die KLEIN* ~ *tjies,* the small hours; *te KWADER ure,* in an evil hour; *OM vyfuur,* at five o'clock; *OOR 'n* ~, in an hour; *iets by die* ~ *OPSÊ,* reel something off; *PER* ~, by the (per) hour; *VAN* ~ *tot* ~, from hour to hour; from one hour to another; ~**glas,** hour-glass, sand-glass; ~**hoek,** hour angle; ~**kaart,** time card; ~**loon,** wage per hour, hourly wage; ~**plaat,** dial-plate; ~**sirkel,** hour-circle; ~**staat,** timesheet; ~**vermoë,** hour rating; ~**werk,** timepiece, clock, watch; clockwork; chronometer; ~**wyser, (-s),** hour-hand.
U'-vormig, (-e), U-shaped.
u'vula, (-s), uvula.
uvulaar', (..lare), uvular (sound).
uvulêr, (-e), uvular.
u'we, yours; *DIE* ~, yours faithfully; *GEHEEL die* ~, yours sincerely; *HOOGAGTEND die* ~, yours respectfully.
u'wentwil: *om* ~, for your sake.
U'-yster, U-iron, channel iron.

V

v, (-'s), v.
vaag, (vae, vaer, -ste), vague, undefined, indistinct, hazy, foggy, nebulous (idea); ~**heid,** vagueness, haziness; ~**weg,** vaguely.
vaak, (s), sleepiness; ~ *raak vir BANG baas,* sleep overcomes fear (said about children); ~ *HÊ (kry),* be sleepy; (b) sleepy, dozy, drowsy.
vaak: ~**heid,** doziness; ~**makend, (-e),** somniferous; ~**siekte,** sleepy-sickness, lethargy.
vaal, tawny; sallow, pale, ashen; drab, faded; ~ *v.d. HONGER,* famished; *dit sal nie 'n* ~ *KOL vir my maak nie,* it's all the same to me; ~ *LYK,* look seedy; *vir 'n vale LOOP,* run for all one is worth; *jou* ~ *SKRIK,* have the fright of one's life; *die* ~ *STREEP vat,* take the road; ~ *VERE,* drabs (of ostrich); *die WEDSTRYD het* ~ *kolle gehad,* the game had dull moments; ~**agtig, (-e),** sallowish; greyish; pale; ~**blaarsiekte,** septoria; ~**bleek,** greyish; ~**blou,** blue-dun; ~**bos,** *Tarchonanthus camphoratus;* salt-bush; ~**bossie,** *Stoebe cinerea;* ~**brak,** salt-bush *(Atriplex halimus);* ~**bruin,** straw-coloured, dun, fallow, mealy-bay (horse), greyish-brown, light brown, drab; ~**erts,** grey copper ore; ~**grys,** dun, mouse-grey; ~**haai,** soup-fin (shark); ~**hartbees,** Lichtenstein's hartebeest; ~**heid,** tawniness; drabness; ~**jakkals,** side-striped jackal; ~**japie,** new wine; inferior wine; ~**kameel-(doring),** *Acacia haematoxylon;* ~**karoo(bos),** *Phymaspermum parvifolium;* ~**korhaan,** Karoo korhaan; ~**muishond,** grey mongoose *(Ictonyx striatus).*
Vaal'pens, (-e), Transvaler; Bushman.
vaal'ribbok, grey rhebuck *(Pelea capreolus).*
Vaal'rivier, Vaal River.
vaal: ~**spreeu,** wattled starling; ~**tee,** veldt tea *(Helichrysum serpylligolium; Leysetta tentella);* ~**vrot,** botrytis *(Botrytis cinerea).*
vaal'water = **vaarwater.**
vaam, (vame), fathom; ~**hout,** cordwood; ~**maat,** fathomage.
vaan, (vane), flag, banner, ensign, vane, standard.
vaan'del, (-s), standard, flag, ensign, gonfalon, vane, banner; *met vlieënde* ~ *s,* with flying colours; ~**draer,** gonfalonier, ensign-bearer; standard-bearer; ~**parade,** trooping the colours; ~**skoen,** standard socket; ~**stok,** colour-staff; ~**wag,** colour-party; ~**wyding,** consecration of the colours.
vaan'drig, (-s), standard-bearer, ensign.
vaan'tjie, (-s), weathercock; banderol, pennon.
vaar¹, (s) *(-e),* sire (of animals).
vaar², (w) (ge-), sail, navigate, voyage; *GOED* ~, be successful; *na die HEMEL* ~, ascend to heaven; *LAAT* ~, give up, drop, abandon; *ONDER die S.A. vlag* ~, fly the S.A. flag; ~ *TUSSEN,* ply between; ~**baar, (..bare),** navigable; ~**baarheid,** navigability; ~**bereik,** action radius; ~**der, (-s),** navigator, seafarer, sailor; ~**diepte,** draught (of ship).
vaar'dig, (-e), skilled, handy, clever, proficient, dexterous, deft, ready, prompt; ~ *met die pen,* having a facile pen; ~**heid,** dexterity, skill, skilfulness, proficiency, cleverness, aptitude, know-how, deftness; facility, fluency; expedition, promptitude, readiness; ~**heidstoelae,** proficiency pay; ~**heidstoets,** proficiency test.
vaar'geul, (-e), navigable channel, fairway.
vaar'landsdou, Scotch mist (drizzle).
vaar'landskaap = **vaderlandskaap.**
vaar'landsriet = **vaderlandsriet.**
vaar'landswilg = **vaderlandswilg.**
vaar: ~**lig,** navigation light; ~**plan,** sailing-list; ~**sertifikaat,** navicert; ~**stok,** punt-pole.
vaart, (-e), voyage, navigation; canal; haste, spurt, impetus, leap, speed, pace, momentum, headway, progress; *in DOLLE* ~, at breakneck speed; ~ *KRY,* gather speed; *dit sal so 'n* ~ *nie LOOP nie,* things will not reach such a pass; *MET 'n* ~ *van,* at a speed of; *'n SKIP in die* ~ *bring,* put a ship into commission; *in sy* ~ *STUIT,* stop, check; *in VOLLE* ~, at full speed; ~**belyning,** streamlining; ~**breker,** speed hump.
vaar'tjie, little father.
vaart'krag, momentum.
vaar: ~**tuig, (..tuie),** vessel, boat, ship, craft; ~**vergunning,** navicert.
vaar'water, fairway; navigable water; canal, channel; *BLY maar uit sy* ~ *uit,* give him a wide berth; *in iem. se* ~ *KOM,* thwart someone; fall foul of someone; *in die* ~ *WEES,* be in the soup.
vaar'weg, channel, waterway.
vaarwel', farewell, goodbye; ~ *sê,* say (bid) farewell, take leave, say goodbye; ~**sêery,** parting, leave-taking.
vaas, (vase), vase, flower pot.
vaat'bundel, vascular bundle; ~**skede,** endodermis.
vaat'jie, (-s), barrel, tub, vat, cask, firkin, keg; pudge; potbelly, fatty; *'n* ~ *op sy KANT sit,* tilt a cask; *uit 'n ander* ~ *TAP,* sing a different tune; ~**buik,** podge, potbelly; ~**steek,** bucket tilting.
vaat: ~**kramp,** vasomotor spasm; ~**senuwee,** vascular nerve(s); ~**siekte,** vascular disease; ~**stelsel,** vascular system; ~**vernouing,** vasoconstriction; ~**verwydend, (-e),** vasodilating; ~**verwyder,** vasodilator; ~**verwyding,** vasodilatation; ~**vlies,** choroid membrane; ~**wand,** vascular wall; ~**weefsel,** vascular tissue.

vaat'werk, (Ndl.), casks and tubs; plates and dishes; crockery.
va'bond, (-e), tramp, hobo, vagabond; rogue, rascal; scamp, imp.
va'dem, (s) (-s), fathom; *see* **vaam**; (w) (ge-), fathom.
vademe'kum, (-s), vade mecum.
va'der, (-s), father; sire (of animals); originator; begetter; master, superintendent (hostel); provisor (R.C.); *BESKREWE ~ s*, conscript fathers; *DANKIE ~ bly!* thank the Lord! *die HEMELSE V ~*, the Heavenly Father; *V ~ KRISMIS*, Father Christmas; *ONS V ~ s*, our forefathers (ancestors); *die ONSE V ~*, the Lord's prayer; *van ~ op SEUN*, from father to son; *~ STAAN vir iets*, accept responsibility for something; *tot sy ~ s VERGADER*, gather to his fathers; **~ aard**, nature of a father; **~ agtig**, (-e), fatherly, like a father (uncomplimentary); **~ gek**, doting on father; **~ hand**, father's hand; **~ hart**, paternal heart; **~ huis**, paternal home.
va'derland, native country, fatherland, mother country, home(land); **~ er**, (-s), patriot; **~ s**, (-e), native; national; patriotic.
va'derlandsdou, Scotch mist.
va'derlandskaap, Africander (fat-tailed) sheep.
va'derlands: **~ liefde**, patriotism; **~ lie'wend**, (-e), patriotic; **~ riet**, tall reed *(Pragmites communis)*; **~ rooihout**, wild peach; **~ wilg**, Bushveld tree *(Combretum kraussii, C. salicifolium)*, Cape willow.
va'der: **~ lief**, father dear; daddy; **~ liefde**, paternal love; **~ lik**, (-e), paternal, fatherly; **~ likheid**, fatherliness, **~ loos**, (..lose), fatherless; **~ moord**, parricide; **~ moord-**, parricidal; **~ moordenaar**, **~ moorder**, (-s), parricide; stick-up (stiff) collar; **~ naam**, name of father; **~ -ons**, dear me! **~ plig**, paternal duty; **~ regte**, paternal rights; **~ seën**, paternal blessing.
va'dersgoed, paternal portion.
va'derskant, paternal side, spear side.
va'derskap, fatherhood, paternity; authorship.
va'dersnaam, patronymic; *om V ~*, for God's sake.
va'der: **~ sorg**, fatherly care; **~ stad**, native town; **~ sy = vaderskant**.
vader: **~ tjie**, (-s), little father; *ag ~ tjie!* goodness me! **~ trots**, paternal pride; **~ vreug(de)**, father's joy; **~ weelde**, paternal bliss.
va'doek, dishcloth, washcloth; *iem. GEBRUIK vir 'n ~*, make someone one's lackey; *iem. se ~ WEES*, do another's dirty work; **~ kalbas**, towel-gourd *(Buffa aegyptiaca)*; **~ linne**, huckaback.
vad'sig, (-e), indolent, lazy, slothful; sluggish (motor); **~ heid**, indolence, laziness, sloth; sluggishness (motor).
va'evuur, purgatory.
vag, (-te), fleece, pelt, coat, fell; **~ digtheid**, fleece density.
va'gekierie: *jou ~!* you scamp!
va'gevuur = vaevuur.
va'gina, (-s), vagina.
vaginaal', (..nale), vaginal.
vaginl'tis, vaginitis.
vaginoskoop', (..skope), vaginoscope.
vag'wol, fleece wool.
vak, (-ke), subject; compartment, pigeonhole; craft, trade, vocation, profession; branch; subject (of study); square (draught board); panel; bay (of wall); section (road); *geen ~ KEN nie*, know (have) no trade; *'n MAN van die ~*, a man who knows his job; a professional expert; *dit is nie MY ~ nie*, this is not my line; *'n SMID van ~*, a blacksmith by trade.
vakan'sie, (-s), holiday(s), vacation; recess; *~ HOU*, be on holiday; *IN die ~*, during the holidays; *MET (op) ~*, on holiday; *NA die ~*, after the holiday(s); **~ NEEM**, take a holiday; **~ dag**, holiday; play-day; **~ drukte**, holiday rush; **~ ganger**, holiday-maker; **~ kursus**, vacation course; **~ lektuur**, holiday-reading; **~ oord**, holiday resort; **~ reis**, holiday trip; **~ stemming**, holiday spirits (mood); **~ tyd**, holidays, holiday season; **~ uittog**, holiday exodus; **~ verlof**, vacation leave; **~ werk**, holiday task.

vakant', (-e), vacant; empty; *~ e pos*, vacancy.
vak'arbeid, skilled labour; **~ er**, skilled labourer.
vakatu're, (-s), vacancy, opening; *~ (aan)vul*, fill a vacancy; **~ lys**, list of vacancies.
vak: **~ bekwaamheid**, professional skill; **~ beweging**, trade-unionism; **~ blad**, professional (technical) journal; **~ bond**, trade union, labour union; **~ bondlid**, trade-unionist.
va'kerig, (-e), sleepy, drowsy; **~ heid**, sleepiness, drowsiness.
vak: **~ geheim**, trade secret; **~ geleerde**, expert, specialist; **~ genoot**, (..note), colleague; **~ geselsery**, shop talk; **~ kennis**, technical (expert) knowledge; workmanship; **~ kie**, (-s), compartment, pigeonhole; **~ kun'dig**, (-e), skilled, expert; **~ kun'dige**, (-s), expert; **~ kun'digheid**, expertness, professional skill; **~ leerling**, apprentice; **~ leerlingkontrak**, articles of apprenticeship; **~ leerlingskap**, apprenticeship; **~ man**, (-ne), expert, craftsman, professional man, specialist; artificer; **~ onderwys**, technical (vocational) education (instruction); **~ onderwyser**, special-subject teacher, specialist; **~ opleiding**, vocational training; **~ organisasie**, trade organization; **~ praatjies**, shop talk.
vaksina'sie, vaccination.
vaksi'ne, vaccine; **~ dwang**, compulsory vaccination.
vaksineer', (ge-), vaccinate.
vaksi'nestof, vaccine.
vak: **~ skool**, trade school, technical school, professional school; **~ studie**, subject study; **~ taal**, technical language; terminology; **~ taalburo**, technical terminology bureau.
vak: **~ term**, technical term; **~ terminologie**, technical terminology; **~ tobbery**, shop talk; **~ tydskrif**, technical periodical.
vakuum', (-s), vacuum; **~ fles**, vacuum flask; **~ kamer**, vacuum chamber; **~ pomp**, vacuum pump; **~ rem**, vacuum brake; **~ tenk**, vacuum tank.
vak: **~ vereniging**, trade union; **~ vergadering**, subject meeting; **~ werk**, specialist work; framework; trussing; **~ werkbalk**, truss beam; **~ woordeboek**, dictionary of technical terms; technical dictionary.
val^1, (s) (-le), trap, gin; mantrap; *in 'n ~ LOK*, entice into a trap; *in die ~ LOOP*, be caught in a trap; allow yourself to be cheated; *in 'n ~ SIT*, be caught in a trap; *'n ~ STEL*, set a trap; *in 'n ~ VANG*, catch in a trap.
val^2, (s) (-le), frill, flounce; valance.
val^3, (s) (-le), fall, downfall; slope, drop, gradient; surrender; ruin; *iem. se ~ BEWERK*, bring about someone's ruin; *tot 'n (ten) ~ BRING*, bring to ruin; overthrow, defeat; *die DAK het nie genoeg ~ nie*, the roof does not slope enough; *die ~ v.d. KABINET*, the defeat of the cabinet; *'n MEISIE tot 'n ~ bring*, seduce a girl; *iem. se ~ VEROORSAAK (bewerk)*, cause someone's ruin; (w) (ge-), fall, tumble down, drop, come down; happen; be defeated, succumb (to temptation); *te BEURT ~*, fall to the lot of; *die GORDYN ~*, the curtain falls; *KLAPPE ~*, blows are dealt (out); *LAAG ~*, sink low; *LAAT ~*, let fall, drop; *die regering LAAT ~*, overthrow the government; *dis net NA dit ~*, it just depends on how things turn out; *daar ~ NIKS te sê nie*, there is nothing to be said; *~ ONDER*, come under the jurisdiction of; fall within the scope of; *jy moet eers ~ voordat jy OPSTAAN*, he that falls today may rise tomorrow; *die PRYS laat ~*, lower the price; *in die REDE ~*, interrupt; *dit ~ niks te SÊ nie*, there is nothing to be said; *SKOTE ~*, shots are fired; *in die SMAAK ~*, be popular; *die 9de ~ op SONDAG*, the 9th is a Sunday; *dit ~ my SWAAR*, I find it difficult; I hate doing it; *UIT sy rol ~*, act out of character; *~ WEG!* fall to!
val: **~ boom**, barrier; boom; **~ brug**, drawbridge; **~ byl**, guillotine; **~ bylmasjien**, guillotine (machine); **~ deur**, trapdoor, flap-door, drop-door.
va'le, (-s), something ash-coloured; *loop vir 'n ~*, run for all you are worth; *see* **vaal**.
valen'sie, valence; atomic value.
valeriaan', valerian; **~ suur**, valeric acid.
va'lerig, (-e), tawnish, greyish, grizzly.

va'letjie, (-s), little ash-coloured one.
val: ~gleuf, gravity slot; ~gordyn, drop-curtain; blind; ~hamer, drop-hammer; ~hek, portcullis; boom; ~helm, crash-helmet; ~hoogte, height of lift (drop, throw) (geol.); ~hortjies, drop-shutters; ~hou(tjie), drop-shot (tennis).
valideer', (ge-), validate.
validiteit', validity.
valies', (ong.), (-e), portmanteau, handbag, suitcase, valise.
valk, (-e), falcon, hawk; ~agtig, (-e), hawklike, accipitral; ~eblik, hawk's eye, eagle-eye; ~eier, hawk's egg; ~enier', (-s), falconer; hawker; ~jag, falconry, hawking; ~jagter, falconer.
val: ~klep, trap valve, clack valve; ~knip, gravity catch.
valk'oog: hawk's eye, falcon's eye, keen sight.
val'kruid, arnica.
val'kuil, traphole.
vallei', (-e), valley, dale, vale, dell; bottom.
val'lend, (-e), falling; ~e SIEKTE, epilepsy; ~e STER, shooting star.
val'letjie¹, (-s), frill, furbelow.
val'letjie², (-s), trap.
val'letjie³, (-s), little fall.
val'lig, skylight, drop-light.
val'luik, trapdoor, drop (gallows); drop-shutter; ~spinnekop, trapdoor spider.
val'masjien, Atwood's machine.
val'menger, gravity mixer.
val: ~mes, guillotine; ~nes, trap-nest (fowl); ~net, receiving net.
valorisa'sie, valorization.
val: ~poort, portcullis; ~pyp, chute.
val'reep, manrope; gangway; accommodation ladder, ladder-rope; side-rope; *a glasie op die* ~, a stirrup-cup, a farewell drink, a wee doch-an-doris.
val'reep: ~gas, side-man; ~trap, accommodation ladder.
vals, (b) (-e), false, artificial (teeth); counterfeit, spurious (coin); put on (airs); mendacious, guileful, double-faced, perfidious, treacherous (persons); forged (signature); ~ *BOOM*, false bottom; ~ *BOM*, dummy bomb; ~ *DIAMANT*, imitation diamond; ~ *DOBBELSTENE*, loaded dice; ~ *HANDTEKENING*, a forged signature; ~ *LIG*, deceptive light; ~ *SLEUTEL*, skeleton key; ~ *TANDE*, artificial teeth; (bw) falsely; flat, out of tune; ~ *SING*, sing flat (out of tune); ~ *SWEER*, perjure oneself, commit perjury; ~aard, (-s), treacherous person.
Vals'baai, False Bay.
valshar'tig, (-e), false, deceitful, perfidious; ~heid, falseness, deceit(fulness), perfidy.
vals'heid, falsity, falseness, disingenuousness, hollowness, mendacity, perfidiousness, perfidy, double-dealing, guile, treacherousness, deceit(fulness); ~ *in geskrifte*, forgery.
val'skerm, parachute; ~daling, parachute descent; ~ongeluk, parachute accident; ~sak, parachute bag, parachute pack; ~springer, parachutist; ~sprong, parachute jump (leap); ~troepe, para(chute) troops; ~tuig, parachute harness; ~vlieër, parachute kite, parakite.
val'skerpte, precipitousness; escarpment.
vals: ~klinkend, (-e), discordant; ~kloutjie, dew-claw.
val'skyf, disappearing target.
vals: ~lik, falsely; ~plek, quagmire.
val'sluiter, drop-shutter.
val'smee, (ge-), drop-forge.
vals'munter, (-s), coiner, forger; ~y, forging.
vals'speler, card-sharp(er).
val: ~staaf, crash bar; ~toets, drop test, falling weight test.
val'strik, trap, snare, pitfall, gin.
val: ~stroom, down-draught, down-wash; ~toevoer, gravity feed; ~tregter, funnel, shoot, chute.
valua'sie, (-s), valuation, ratal.
valueer', (ge-), valuate, value.
valu'ta, (-s), value, currency; exchange; ~mark, exchange market.

val: ~venster, drop-light, drop-window; ~wet, law of gravitation; ~wind, sudden squall; down-current.
vampier', (-e, -s), vampire, blood-sucker.
vampiris'me, vampirism.
van¹, (s) (-ne), surname, family name.
van², (vs) of, from, by, with, for; *DIS nou* ~ *hom*, that's a characteristic of him; *'n DRAMA* ~ *Shakespeare*, a play by Shakespeare; *FYN* ~ *vesel*, fine in texture; ~ *HIER*, from here; ~ *JONGS af*, from (since) childhood; *'n KERK* ~ *Moerdyk*, a church (designed) by Moerdyk; ~ *KLEINS af*, from (since) (early) childhood; *iem. ken* ~ *NAAM*, know someone by name; ~ *NUUTS af*, again, anew; ~ *OUDS(HER)*, since (from) olden times; of yore; *'n PALEIS* ~ *'n huis*, a palatial house; ~ *PRETORIA af*, from Pretoria; *iem.* ~ *RAAD dien*, advise someone; ~ *daar is dit SIGBAAR*, it is visible from there; *vaal* ~ *SKRIK*, pale with fright; *die VADER* ~ *Piet*, Peter's father; *huil* ~ *VREUGDE*, weep for joy; *'n VRIEND* ~ *my*, a friend of mine; ~ *WAAR*, from where, whence; (vgw) since, from the time when; ~ *ek hom ken, doen hy dit*, ever since I know him, he has been doing this.
vanaand', this evening, tonight; *kom hy nie* ~ *nie, dan kom hy môreaand*, he'll get here sooner or later.
vana'dium, vanadium; ~suur, vanadic acid.
vanaf', from; ~ *1 MEI*, as from May 1; ~ *die STRAND tot by die straat*, from the beach to the street.
vandaal', (..dale), vandal.
Vandaal', (..dale), Vandal; ~s', (-e), Vandalic.
vandaan', from; *waar kom sy* ~? where does she come from?
vandaar', hence, therefore, that is why, as a result of this; *hier het hy gewoon*; ~ *die monument*, here he lived; hence the monument.
vandag', today; ~ *is nie GISTER nie*, yesterday was yesterday and today is today; *nie* ~ *se KIND nie*, an experienced person; no chicken; *kom ek daar nie* ~ *nie, dan kom ek daar MÔRE*, time is no object; ~ *oor 'n WEEK*, today week.
vandalis'me, vandalism.
vandalis'ties, (-e), vandalistic.
van'dat, since, from the time that.
vandees'jaar, this year; ..maand, this month; ..week, this week.
Van der Hum'likeur, Van der Hum liqueur.
vandermer'we(s)kruie, *Osmites hirsuta*.
vandi'sie, (-s) = vendusie.
vaneen', asunder, apart, to pieces.
vaneen'ruk, (-ge-), tear (wrench) asunder (apart), tear to pieces.
vaneen'skeiding, disseverment.
vaneen'skeur, (-ge-), tear to pieces (asunder, apart).
vanef'fe, a moment ago, just now.
vang, (ge-), catch, seize, capture, take prisoner; secure, cop, arrest, (en)trap, collar, nail, lay by the heels; pinch; land (fish); *HOM laat* ~, allow himself to be caught; *IEM. laat* ~, have a person arrested; *JOU nie maklik laat* ~ *nie*, not to be caught out easily; be wide-awake; ~arm, grab; tentacle; claw; ~bak, catch-basin; ~dam, catch(ment)-dam; catch-dam; ~drade, antennae; ~er, (-s), catcher; ~gat, pitfall; snare, (snare-)pit; ~gebied, catchment area; ~gewas, catch crop; ~haak, grab; ~haar, tentacle; ~hou, catch (in cricket); ~kamp, holding pen; ~kans, chance (cricket); ~lyn, painter (boat); ~punt, fouling point; ~rat, cog wheel; ~riem, lariat, lasso; ~s, (-te), catch, haul; capture, grab, draught (of fishes); draw; ~seil, catch-sail; ~seisoen, capture season; ~slag, catch, act of catching; ~spel, touch (game); ~stok, lasso handle (pole); ~tand, fang; ~toestel, trap; falces (of spider); ~tou, lasso; ~wa, police car, Black Maria.
vaniel'je, vanilla; ~geursel, vanilla essence; ~sjokolade, vanilla chocolate; ~vulsel, vanilla filling; ~ys, vanilla ice.
vanillien', vanilli'ne, vanillin; ~suur, vanillic acid.
vanjaar', this year.
vankrag'wording, coming into force.

vanlie'werlee, gradually, by degrees.
vanmekaar', asunder, separated, to pieces; ~ *AF*, separated, away from each other; ~ *BREEK*, break asunder (apart).
vanmele'we, formerly, in earlier times, in days of yore, before time, long ago; ~ *se dae*, in the days of yore, once upon a time.
vanmid'dag, this afternoon.
vanmô're, vanmo're, this morning.
vannag', tonight; last night; *dit was* ~ *koud*, it was cold last night.
vanog'gend, this morning.
vanouds', of old.
vanpas', opportune, at the right time.
Van Rie'beeckdag, Van Riebeeck Day.
vansle'we = **vanmelewe**.
vanself', of its own accord, by itself, of oneself; automatic(ally); *dit SPREEK* ~, it goes without saying, it stands to reason; *dit VOLG* ~, it follows automatically.
vanselfspre'kend, (-e), as a matter of course; obvious; implicit, implied; ~ **heid**, obviousness; implicitness.
vans'gelyke, the same (to you).
vantevo're, previously, before, beforehand.
vanuit', from, out of.
vanwaar', whence; as a result of which; ~ *al die beswaren*, where do all these objections come from?
vanwe'ë, on account of, because of; ~ *die droogte*, on account of the drought.
vaporisa'sie, vaporization.
vaporisa'tor, (-e, -s), spray, vaporizer, sprinkler.
varaan', (varane), varan.
va'ria, miscellany.
varia'bel, (-e), variable, changeable.
variabiliteit', variability.
va'riakonsert, (-e), variety concert.
variant', (-e), variant; different reading.
varia'sie, (-s), variation, change.
varieer', (ge-), vary, range.
variété', (-s), variety theatre; ~ **arties'**, music hall artist; ~ **geselskap**, variety company.
variëteit', (-e), variety, diversity; ~ **sgeselskap**, variety company.
va'ring, (-s), fern; ~ **agtig, (-e)**, ferny; ~ **blaar**, fern frond; ~ **kun'dige, (-s)**, pteridologist; ~ **huis**, fernery; ~ **mos**, fern-moss.
va'riogram, variogram.
va'riometer, variome'ter, variometer.
vark, (-e, -ens), pig, hog, swine, grunter; ~ *e AANJAAG*, be intoxicated; be reeling; *iem. se BONT* ~ *ie makeer*, someone has a screw loose; he isn't all there; *hy het nie al sy - ies in die HOK nie*, he has a screw loose; *soos 'n MAER* ~ *skreeu*, squeal like a stuck pig; ~ *e skuur hulle MODDER teen pilare af*, bad people slander (the good name of) their betters; *baie* ~ *e maak die SPOELING dun*, where the hogs are many the wash is poor; *soos 'n* ~ *met 'n STROOI in sy bek lyk*, like a baby with a dummy in its mouth; *hy kan geen* ~ *VANG nie*, he has bowlegs; *so VET soos 'n* ~, as fat as a pig; *VIES is 'n woord nie vet nie*, dainty pigs never grow fat; *hy WEET daar soveel van as 'n* ~ *van politiek (godsdiens, borshemp)*, he knows absolutely nothing about it; ~ **agtig, (-e)**, dirty, piggish, hoggish; porky; ~ **bak**, swill-tub; ~ **bek**, pig's mouth; steenbras (fish); ~ **blaas**, hog's bladder; ~ **blom**, arum lily; wake-robin; ~ **boer**, pig farmer, pig breeder; ~ **boerdery**, piggery; ~ **bors**, breast of pork; ~ **borsel**, hog's bristle; ~ **bossie**, goosefoot; ~ **boud**, leg of pork; ~ **brood**, Cyclamen europaeum; ~ **derm**, pig's intestine; ~ **draf**, hogwash, swill; ~ **(ens)gras**, knotweed *(Polygonum aviculare L.)*; ~ **(ens)kos**, pigfeed; unappetizing (bad) food; ~ **(ens)oor**, Cotyledon obiculata; ~ **gooiery**, lying; boasting; ~ **gras**, knotweed; red weed; ~ **hare**, hog's bristles; ~ **hok**, pigsty, piggery, swinery; ~ **ie**, little pig, piggy, pigling; gruntling; *wat sê die* ~ *ie?* what is the wind going to do? ~ **jag**, boar hunt; ~ **karmenaadjie**, pork chop; ~ **kop**, pig's head; ~ **kos**, pannage, hogwash, swill; ~ **kotelet**, pork cutlet; ~ **leer**, pigskin; ~ **lelie**, arum lily; *see* **varkblom**; ~ **maag**, porcine stomach; ~ **masels**, pork measles; ~ **meel**, pig meal;

~ **neus**, pig's nose; ~ **oog**, pig's eye; ~ **oor**, pig's ear; arum lily; ~ **oppasser**, swineherd; ~ **papies**, pig plague; ~ **pastei**, pork pie; ~ **pes**, swine fever, swine plague; ~ **pokke**, swine pox; ~ **pootjies**, pig's trotters, pettitoes; ~ **reusel**, lard; ~ **ribbetjie**, pork rib; ~ **rug**, sow's back; ~ **slagter**, pork butcher; ~ **slagtery**, pork butchery; slaughtering of a pig; ~ **skenkel**, hock; ~ **sog**, sow; ~ **spek**, bacon; ~ **stert**, pig's tail; pigtail (of hair); ~ **swoerd**, pork rind; ~ **tjop**, pork chop; ~ **trog**, hog trough; ~ **vel**, pigskin; crackling; ~ **vet**, pork fat, lard, axunge; ~ **vis**, bay porpoise; ~ **vleis**, pork; pig; ~ **vleispastei**, pork pie; ~ **voer**, pig's fodder; ~ **wang**, jowl; ~ **wors**, pork sausage.
vars, fresh; saltless; recent; ~ *EIERS*, new-laid eggs; ~ *STOOM*, live steam; ~ *WATER*, fresh water; ~ **heid**, freshness; ~ **waterkreef**, crayfish; ~ **waterskilpad**, terrapin; ~ **watersnoek**, pike, luce; ~ **watervis**, freshwater fish.
vas¹, (s) fast(ing); **(w) (ge-)**, abstain from food, fast.
vas², (b, bw) (-te), firm (belief); fixed (abode); permanent (address); standing (committee); stationary (engine); regular (customer); ~ *te ANKER*, rigid stay; ~ *te ARBEIDER*, regular worker (labourer); ~ *te BESTELLING*, standing order; ~ *te BRANDPUNT*, fixed focus; ~ *te BRANDSTOF*, solid fuel; ~ *te DEPOSITO*, fixed deposit; ~ *te EIENDOM*, landed property, real estate; *sy* ~ *te GEWOONTE*, his regular habit (invariable custom); *'n* ~ *te HAND*, a firm (steady) hand; *'n* ~ *te INKOMSTE*, a fixed (regular) income; ~ *te KERN*, hard core; ~ *te KLEURE*, fast colours; ~ *te KOS*, solid food, ~ *te LIGGAME*, solid bodies; ~ *te MASJIEN*, stationary engine; *NOU is jy* ~, now you are cornered; *my* ~ *te OORTUIGING*, my firm conviction; my considered opinion; *ek is* ~ *van PLAN*, I am firmly resolved; ~ *te PUNT*, fixed point; ~ *te REËLS*, hard and fast rules; ~ *op iets REKEN*, depend on something; he quite sure about something; *'n* ~ *te SLAAP*, a sound sleep; *'n* ~ *te STER*, a fixed star; ~ *te STOWWE*, solids; *'n* ~ *te UITDRUKKING*, a standing phrase; ~ *te UITRUSTING*, fixtures; ~ *te VERBETERING*, fixed improvement; ~ *te VOET kry*, get a firm footing; *sy* ~ *te VOORNEME*, his fixed purpose; ~ *te WERK*, regular employment.
vasal', (-le), vassal.
vas'anker, (-ge-), anchor, moor.
vas'berade, resolute, determined, firm.
vas'beradenheid, resoluteness, firmness, determination, doggedness.
vas'beslote, determined; ~ *om te bedank*, determined to resign.
vas: ~ **bind, (-ge-)**, tie up; fasten to; frap, reeve (naut.); gammon; fetter; lash (to); ~ **binding**, fastening; ~ **boei, (-ge-)**, handcuff; ~ **bout, (-ge-)**, bolt (down, together); ~ **brand, (-ge-)**, seize (up) (engine); get into trouble; be unable to cope with; burn (food); *hy sal* ~ *brand*, he'll get himself into a fix; he is going to land in trouble; ~ **branding**, seizing (up).
vas: ~ **dae**, ember days; ~ **dag**, fast-day.
vas: ~ **draai, (-ge-)**, fasten by turning, belay, screw tight; ~ **druk, (-ge-)**, press firmly (tightly); squeeze; cram; ~ **dryf, (-ge-)**, hammer down; get stuck after drifting.
va'sel, (-s), fibre.
vas: ~ **gekeer, (-de)**, cornered; ~ **gelak, (-te)**, glued; ~ *gelak sit*, be glued to one's seat; ~ **geroes:** ~ *geroes in sy gewoontes*, fixed in his habits; ~ **gesneeu, (-de)**, snow-bound; ~ **gespe(r), (-ge-)**, buckle; ~ **gestel, (-de)**, established; fixed (price); appointed; ~ **gewortel, (-de)**, rooted, root-bound; ~ **geys, (-de)**, ice-bound, frost-bound; ~ **goed**, landed (immovable) property; fixtures; ~ **groei, (-ge-)**, grow together; ~ **gryp, (-ge-)**, grasp, catch hold of, grip, clench, gripe; ~ **haak, (-ge-)**, hook on; ~ **haakpaal**, hitching-post; ~ **heg, (-ge-)**, affix, fasten to; ~ **hegting**, fastening, fixing.
vas'hou, (s) adherence; keeping; holding; **(w) (-ge-)**, hold fast, hold in possession, cling, clutch, hang on (on phone); keep hold of, grasp; ~ *aan*, hold on to,

stick to; adhere to; ~ **'dend, (-e)**, tenacious, retentive, close, dogged; ~ **'dendheid**, tenacity, retentiveness, doggedness, adherence; ~ **er, (-s)**, grasper; fastener; fastening; ~ **plek**, grasp; handhold.
va'sie, (-s), small vase.
vas: ~ **keer, (-ge-)**, bring to bay, drive into a corner, trap, hedge in: *iem.* ~ *keer*, drive someone into a corner; ~ **ketting, (-ge-)**, chain up; ~ **klamp, (-ge-)**, cling to, clutch at, fasten upon; ~ **kleef, (-ge-)**, cling to, stick, adhere.
vas'klem, (-ge-), take fast hold of, cling to; jam (in door); clench, grasp; *jou* ~ *aan vooroordele*, cling to prejudices.
vas'klewe = **vaskleef**.
vas'klewend, (-e), adhesive, adherent.
vas'klewing, adhesion, adherence.
vas'klink, (-ge-), rivet.
vas'klop, (-ge-), hammer down.
vas'klou, (-ge-), cling to, clutch, hold on; ~ **ery**, holding (in boxing).
vas'kluister, (-ge-), entomb, fetter, incarcerate.
vas'knel, (-ge-), press close.
vas'knoop, (-ge-), tie (button) up; belay.
vas'koek, (-ge-), become matted (caked) (hair).
vas'koop, (-ge-): *hom* ~ , make a bad purchase.
vas'kop, (-ge-), tight head (rugby); ~ **man**, ~ **speler**, tighthead forward (rugby).
vas'koppel, (-ge-), link together, couple.
vaskulêr, (-e), vascular.
vas'lak, (-ge-), seal.
vas'lê, (-ge-), chain up, tether (an animal); moor, be moored (ship); lie firm; fix, determine, stipulate; pinch, steal; invest (money); record, commit to writing.
vas'legging, fixation; determination.
vas'loop, (-ge-) get into trouble, get stuck; collide (with); run aground; *jou* ~ *teen*, come up against.
vas'lym, (-ge-), glue (together).
vas'maak, (-ge-), fasten, tie, truss, secure; anchor, cable, hand (sails); hitch up (on to); fix, attach, bind, adjust; pinion; picket; ~ **ooi**, ewe that has to be tied up before she will allow her lamb to suck; ~ **paal**, hitching-post; ~ **tou**, tether, picketing rope.
vas'maker, tier, fastener; lashing, fastening.
vas'meer, (-ge-), moor.
vas'naai, (-ge-), sew together, sew up.
vasomoto'ries, (-e), vasomotor.
vas'pak, (-ge-), pack firmly.
vas'pen, (-ge-), peg; spike; pin down, corner; ~ **ning**, pegging down.
vas'plak, (-ge-), paste together, glue, stick, gum.
vas'praat, (-ge-), corner; say too much, let one's tongue run away with one.
vas'raak, (-ge-), get stuck; get into trouble.
vas'reën, vas'reent, (-ge-), be held up by rain, be prevented by rain (from proceeding on one's way).
vas'roes, (-ge-), rust on to; *vasgeroes mees*, be in a rut.
vas'ry, (-ge-), ride (drive) into a dead end (cul-de-sac); collide (with).
vas'ry(e), vas'ryg, (-ge-), tack together; lace.
vas'sak, (-ge-), settle (earth).
vas'setting, entailment.
vas'sit, (-ge-), stick, sit tightly, be jammed; embed, get stuck; fix; settle; make a permanent investment (money); be tied up; seize up; *so* ~ *dat nuwe werk nie onderneem kan word nie*, so tied up that no new work can be undertaken.
vas'sjor, (-ge-), lash up, gammon.
vas'skop, (-ge-), make a stand; offer firm resistance; dig in one's heels.
vas'skroef, vas'skroewe, (-ge-), screw down, screw tight.
vas'slaan, (-ge-), hammer down, nail down; tamp; peg.
vas'sneeu, (-ge-), snow in, be snowed in.
vas'soldeer, (-ge-), solder together.
vas'speld(e), (-ge-), pin on, pin up.
vas'spyker, (-ge-), nail (down, together), tack, spike.
vas'staan, (-ge-), stand firm(ly), stand one's ground, hold one's own, stand fast; be sure; *dit staan by my vas dat*, I am convinced that; ~ **de**, certain, fixed; firmly established.

vas'stamp, (-ge-), ram down, tamp, pun (earth).
vas'steek, (-ge-), pin up, fasten (with pins or pegs); hesitate, stop suddenly, balk, baulk, boggle; get stuck, jam.
vas'stel, (-ge-), appoint, fix, decide (day); establish (truth); ascertain (fact); diagnose (disease); decree, enact; determine, posit, stipulate, lay down (rule); localize, locate.
vas'stelling, establishment, fixation, allocation, fixture, determination, stipulation, proof, provision, declaration.
vas'teland, continent; mainland; ~ **s, (-e)**, continental.
vas'telands: ~ **bewoner**, continentalist; ~ **klimaat**, continental climate; ~ **plat**, continental shelf.
vast'heid, firmness, certainty; density; compactness, solidity; steadiness; fixity.
vas'tigheid, firmness, fixedness, stability; fixture; *'n mens wil graag* ~ *hê*, one likes to have certainty.
vas'trap, (s) popular folk-dance, "vastrap"; (w) **(-ge-)**, tread down firmly; stand firm, persevere; give a hiding; ~ **per, (-s)**, conservative, die-hard; ~ **plek**, footing, foothold; stepping-stone.
vas'trek, (-ge-), pull together (tight); corner; deceive, swindle; frap (naut.).
vas'tyd, time of fasting; Lent.
vas'val, (-ge-), get stuck (in the mud), bog, founder; ~ **gat**, muddy hole (pothole) in the road.
vas'vang, (-ge-), catch, hold firmly.
vas'vat, (-ge-), grip.
vas'vra, (-ge-), corner (by questioning); quiz; ~ **ery**, quizzing; ~ **wedstryd**, quiz (competition).
vas'werk, (-ge-), sew together (on).
vas'wig, (-ge-), wedge.
vas'woel, (-ge-), fasten securely (by winding round); get entangled; frap (naut.); hitch up, belay.
vas'ys, (-ge-), freeze.
vat¹, (s) grip, hold; *jou INVLOED gee jou 'n* ~ *op hom*, your influence gives you a hold on him; ~ *KRY op die massa*, get a hold on the masses; *'n ONHANDIGE* ~ , a clumsy grip; (w) **(ge-)**, grip, take, catch, seize, grasp; understand, take in; mount, set (in gold); start (engine); touch (someone); ~ *jou GOED en trek, Ferreira*, get you gone! pack up and clear off! *edelstene in GOUD ge* ~ , jewels mounted in gold; *KOU(E)* ~ , catch cold; *LAAT* ~ , depart; take to one's heels; ~ *SO!* shake! here is my hand (to greet, to congratulate).
vat², (s) (-e), barrel, cistern, tub; drum, vat, cask; vessel (anat.); *die* ~ *v.d. DANAÏDE vul*, try to square the circle; carry water in a sieve; *op 'n* ~ *GERY het*, be bandy-legged; *HEILIGE vate*, holy vessels; *LEË vate klink die holste (maak die meeste geraas)*, empty vessels make the most noise; *die SWAK* ~ , the weaker vessel; *uit 'n ander vaatjie TAP*, sing a different tune; *bier UIT die* ~ , beer on draught; *'n UITVERKORE* ~ , a chosen vessel, the right choice.
vat'baar, (..bare), subject to, susceptible to (cold); receptive; pervious; liable to, amenable to, open to (persuasion); ~ *MAAK*, predispose; ~ *vir REDE*, amenable to reason; *nie vir VERBETERING* ~ *nie*, incorrigible; ~ **heid**, susceptibility, capacity, impressionability, receptiveness, predisposition, liability; amenability.
vat'bier, draught beer.
Vatikaan', Vatican; ~ **stad**, Vatican City.
vat'jie, (-s), little bit, pinch.
vat'lap, potholder.
vat'maker, cooper.
vat'plek, grip; *'n mens kry geen* ~ *aan hom nie*, he is a slippery customer.
vat'sel, (-s), collet, grip, handle.
vat'terig, (-e), fond of touching; over-free (with women); ~ **heid**, flirtiness.
vat'werk = **vaatwerk**.
vau'deville, vaudeville; ~ **-akteur**, vaudeville actor; ~ **toneel**, vaudeville (stage).
V'-beitel, V tool.
V'-blok, V block.
Ve'da, (-s), Veda.
V'-dak, double lean-to roof.

ve'del, (-s), fiddle; viol; ~ **aar, (-s)**, fiddler.
vee¹, livestock, cattle; *GROOT* ~, large stock (cattle and horses); *KLEIN* ~, small stock (sheep and goats).
vee², (w) (ge-), *see* **veeg**.
vee'aanjaer, drover.
vee'arts, veterinary surgeon, vet; ~ **eny'**, veterinary science; ~ **eny'diens, (-te),** veterinary service; ~ **enykun'dig, (-e),** veterinary; ~ **eny'skool,** veterinary school.
vee'bedryf, stock-farming (industry).
vee'boer, cattle-farmer, sheep-farmer, rancher, stockfarmer; ~ **dery,** stock-farming.
vee'dief, cattle thief, cattle rustler, stock thief; ~ **stal,** cattle-thieving, stock-theft, cattle-lifting.
vee: ~ **dier,** head of cattle; ~ **diewery,** cattle-thieving, stock-theft.
veeg¹, (s) (veë), wipe; whisk; flick; slap, cuff, box (on the ear); *iem. 'n* ~ *uit die pan GEE,* rebuke someone sharply; *'n* ~ *uit die pan KRY,* be given a sharp rebuke; (w) **(ge-),** sweep; wipe; ~ *nou die trane uit jou oë,* now wipe the tears from your eyes.
veeg², (b) (veë), ominous; fey; *'n veë teken,* an ominous sign.
veeg: ~ **hou,** swipe (cricket); ~ **lap,** swab; ~ **las, (-se),** wiped joint; ~ **sel, (-s),** sweepings; ~ **skoot,** cowshot (cricket).
vee'handel, cattle trade; ~ **aar,** cattle-dealer, livestock-dealer.
vee: ~ **-inspekteur,** stock inspector; ~ **kamp,** enclosure, paddock; ~ **keerder,** cattle guard; ~ **koek,** cattle cake; oilcake; ~ **kopor, (s),** cattle-dealer; ~ **kraal,** cattle pen, stockyard, cattle kraal; ~ **kunde,** animal science.
veel¹, (w) (ge-), bear, stand, endure; *ek kan hom nie* ~ *nie,* I cannot bear (the sight of) him.
veel², (b, bw), (-, meer, meeste), much, many, often, frequently; ~ *EERDER,* much sooner; ~ *LIEWER,* much rather; *te* ~ *om te NOEM,* too numerous to mention; *daar is* ~ *voor te SÊ,* a good case may be made out for it; *TE* ~, too much; too many; ~ *s TE* ~, far too many; much too much; *niks was vir hom TE* ~ *nie,* nothing was too much trouble for him.
veel'al, often, as a rule, mostly.
veel'arm, (-s), polypus; octopus; ~ **ig, (-e),** polypous.
veel'barend, (-e), multiparous.
veel'belqwend, (-e), promising, hopeful, auspicious; *'n* ~ *e jong man,* a very promising young man; ~ **heid,** auspiciousness.
veel'besproke, much discussed, celebrated.
veel'betekenend, (-e), significant, expressive, meaning (look).
veel'bewoë, eventful, troublous, chequered (life).
veelbla'rig, (-e), with many leaves, polyphyllous.
veelbloe'mig, (-e), multiflorous.
veel'blombladig, (-e), polypetalous.
veel'blommig, (-e), multiflorous.
veel'broederig, (-e), polyadelphous.
veel'delig, (-e), multipartite.
veel'eer, rather, sooner.
veelei'send, (-e), demanding, exacting; telling, exigent.
veelfa'sig, (-e), multiphase.
veel'gelese, widely read.
veel'geprese, much praised, extolled, boasted, vaunted.
veel'godedom, polytheism.
veel'godery, polytheism.
veelgra'dig, (-e), multigrade.
veel'heid, multiplicity; abundance; multitude, plurality.
veelhel'mig, (-e), polyandrous; ~ **heid,** polyandry.
veel'hoek, polygon.
veelhoe'kig, (-e), polygonal; multiangular.
veelhoe'wig, (-e), multungulate.
veelhok'kig, (-e), multilocular.
veelhoof'dig, (-e), many-headed, multicipital; *'n* ~ *e regering,* a polyarchy.
veelja'rig, (-e), of many years, perennial.
veelklep'pig, (-e), multivalved.
veelkleu'rig, (-e), variegated, polychromatic, many-coloured, multicoloured; ~ **heid,** variegation; polychrome.
veelkno'pig, (-e), polygonaceous.
veelkop'pig, (-e), hydra-headed.
veelkeu'sig, multiple choice.
veelle'dig, (-e), multipartite; multinomial.
veellettergre'pig, (-e), polysyllabic, sesquipedalian.
veel'luik, polyptych.
veel'maals, often, many times.
veelmannery', veel'mannery, polyandry.
veelman'nig, (-e), polyandrous.
veel'meer, rather, much sooner; *hy moet* ~ *bejammer as veroordeel word,* he must rather be pitied than condemned.
veelna'mig, (-e), multinomial.
veelo'gig, (-e), multicular.
veelomvat'tend, (-e), vast; comprehensive, wide, extensive; ~ **heid,** comprehensiveness.
veelpo'tig, (-e), polypous, multiped; *V* ~ *es,* Myriopoda.
veel'prater, chatterbox, loquacious person.
veelras'sig, (-e), multiracial.
veel'rat, cluster gear.
veelre'ëlig, (-e), of many lines.
veels: ~ *GELUK,* hearty congratulations; ~ *te OUD vir jou,* far too old for you; ~ *te VEEL,* altogether too much.
veelsa'dig, (-e), polyspermal.
veelseg'gend, (-e), significant, expressive, meaningful, eloquent (silence); ~ **heid,** pregnancy, significance.
veelsel'lig, (-e), multicellular.
veelsin'nig, (-e), having many meanings.
veel'sins, in many respects.
veel'skrywer, prolific writer, polygraph; ~ **y,** inkslinging, polygraphy.
veelsna'rig, (-e), having many strings.
veelsoor'tig, (-e), manifold, multifarious; multiplex; polygenous; ~ **heid,** variety, multifariousness.
veelstem'mig, (-e), polyphonous, many-voiced; ~ **heid,** polyphony.
veelsy'dig, (-e), many-sided, versatile, encyclopaedic(al) (person); all-round (sportsman); multilateral; ~ **heid,** versatility; many-sidedness.
veelta'lig, (-e), polyglot, multilingual; ~ **heid,** polyglottism, multilinguism.
veeltal'lig, (-e), multitudinous; multiplex.
veel'term, polynomial; multinomial; ~ **'ig, (-e),** polynomial.
veelton'gig, (-e), many-tongued.
veel'tyds, frequently, often.
veelvermo'ënd, (-e), powerful, influential, multipotent, prepotent.
veelver'wig, (-e), multicoloured, variegated.
veelvin'gerig, (-e), many-fingered.
veel'vlak, polyhedron; ~ **'kig, (-e),** polyhedral.
veel'vlakshoek, solid angle, polyhedral angle.
veelvoe'tig, (-e), many-footed, multiped, polypod.
veelvor'mig, (-e), polymorphous, multiform; polyplastic; ~ **heid,** multiformity, polymorphism.
veel'voud, (-e), multiple; *kleinste gemene* ~, least common multiple.
veelvou'dig, (-e), manifold, multiple, multiplex.
veel'voudsteek, multiple stitch.
veel'vraat, (..vrate), glutton; wolverine.
veel'vretend, (-e), polyphygous.
veelvul'dig, (b) (-e), frequent, manifold, multifold; (bw) often; ~ **heid,** frequency, multeity, multifariousness.
veel'weter, (-s), polymath, polyhistor, know-all.
veel'wywery, veelwywery', polygamy, polygyny.
veelwy'wig, (-e), polygamous.
vee'mark, (-te), cattle market, livestock market.
veem'gerig, vehmic court.
veen, (vene), peat, fen, peatbog, peat moor; ~ **agtig, (-e),** peaty, moory, fenny, boggy; ~ **grond,** peatland, fen-land; ~ **land,** peat country; ~ **moeras,** peat bog; peat marsh.
vee: ~ **oorgang,** cattle-crossing; ~ **pes,** cattle plague; rinderpest, murrain; ~ **plaas,** stock farm; ~ **pos,** outlying cattle station.
ve'ër, (-s), sweeper, sweep.

veer¹, (s) **(vere)**, ferry.
veer², (s) **(vere)**, feather; spring (of motor-car, furniture, watch); (w) **(ge-)**, put in springs; be springy; *die nuwe MODEL van hierdie motor is goed ge~*, the new model of this car is well sprung; *met verende STAP loop*, walk with a springy gait; *dis 'n ~ in sy HOED*, it is a feather in his cap; *nie uit die vere kan KOM nie*, unable to drag oneself out of bed; *vere moet LAAT*, have one's feathers plucked; *nog in die vere LÊ*, lie in bed; *so LIG soos 'n ~*, as light as a feather; *met geleende (ander man se) vere PRONK*, strut about in borrowed plumes; *mekaar in die vere SIT*, be at loggerheads; *SKUD jou vere reg*, get ready; *die vere maak die VOËL*, clothes make the man; *VROEG uit die vere*, rise at the crack of dawn; (w) **(ge-)**, feather; **~agtig, (-e)**, feathery; elastic; plumose.
veer: **~anker**, spring anchor; **~bal**, shuttlecock; **~balans**, spring balance; **~balk**, spring beam.
veer: **~bed**, featherbed; **~bekleedsel**, feathering.
veer'blad, spring blade (leaf).
veer'boot, ferry(boat).
veer'bos, panache; plume.
veer'bout, shackle bolt.
veer'dahlia, aster dahlia, cactus dahlia.
veer'diens, ferry service.
veer'drukker, spring compressor.
vee'reier, cattle egret.
veer'geld, ferry rates.
veer'gewig, featherweight.
veer'hak, spring heel.
veer'heide, Prince of Wales heath.
veer: **~karretjie**, dandy-cart; **~klamp**, spring clamp; **~klem**, spring clip; **~klink**, spring latch; **~klou**, spring clamp; **~knip**, spring catch.
veer'kombers, down quilt, eiderdown.
veer: **~kontak**, spring contact; **~kous**, gaiter (on spring); **~krag**, elasticity, springiness, buoyancy, resilience; **~krag'tig, (-e)**, elastic, buoyant, crisp, resilient (fig. and lit.); **~krag'tigheid**, elasticity, buoyancy; resilience; **~loods**, ferry pilot; **~lyn**, hatched line.
veer'man, ferryman.
veer: **~mat**, sprung seat (of chair); **~matras**, spring mattress; **~oog**, spring eye; **~passer**, spring compasses (dividers); bow compasses.
veer'pont, ferry(boat).
veer'poothoender, feather-legged fowl.
veer: **~skaal**, spring balance; **~skakel**, spring shackle.
veer: **~slot**, spring lock; **~staal**, spring steel.
veer: **~steek**, feather stitch; **~stoffer**, feather duster.
veer: **~styl**, compression leg, strut (aero.); **~tandeg**, tiller.
veer'tien, fourteen; ~ *DAE*, a fortnight; *hy is HOOG ~*, he is intoxicated; *ons was MET ons ~*, there were fourteen of us; *vandag OOR ~ dae*, today fortnight; **~daags, (-e)**, lasting a fortnight, fortnightly, biweekly; **~de**, (s) **(-s)**, fourteenth; *drie ~ des*, three fourteenths; (b) fourteenth; **~de-eeus, (-e)**, (of the) fourteenth century; **~jarig, (-e)**, of fourteen years, fourteen years old; **~tal**, fourteen; **~voud, (-e)**, multiple of fourteen; **~vou'dig, (-e)**, fourteenfold.
veer'tig, (-s), forty; **~er**, person of forty years; *die ~ erjare*, the forties; **~daags, (-e)**, quadragesimal; **~jarig, (-e)**, of forty years, forty years old, quadragenarian; **~ponder, (-s)**, forty-pounder; **~ste**, fortieth; **~tal**, forty; **~voud**, multiple of forty; **~vou'dig, (-e)**, fortyfold.
veer'tjie,¹ (-s), little feather; cat's tail *(Struthiola stricta)*.
veer'tjie², small spring.
veer: **~trommel**, spring barrel; **~verdeelpasser**, spring (bow) dividers.
veer'voeg, feather (slip) joint.
veer'vormig, (-e), penniform, plumose.
veer'wa, spring wag(g)on.
veer'wolk, cirrus (cloud).
vee: **~siekte**, cattle disease, stock disease; **~smous**, drover, cattle-dealer; **~stal**, cattle shed; **~stamboek**, stud book; **~stapel**, stock (of cattle); livestock; **~suiping**, watering-place for cattle; **~teelt**, cattle-breeding, stock-breeding; animal husbandry; **~tentoonstelling**, cattle show, livestock show; **~trok**, cattle truck; **~vendusie**, stock fair; **~versekering**, livestock insurance; **~vetmaker**, grazier; **~voer**, forage, fodder; **~wa**, cattle truck; **~wagter**, cattleherd, shepherd, herdsman; **~wagtertjie**, shepherd boy; herdboy.
veg, **(ge-)**, fight, contend; ~ *MET*, fight (with) against; ~ *OM*, fight for; ~ *TEEN*, fight against; **~bui**, fighting mood; **~diens**, combatant duties; **~eskader**, fighter squadron.
vegetaal', (..tale), vegetal.
vegeta'riër, (-s), vegetarian; **..ta'ries**, vegetarian; ~ *tariese dieet*, vegetarian diet; **..taris'me**, vegetarianism.
vegeta'sie, vegetation.
vegetatief', (..tiewe), vegetative.
vegeteer', (ge-), vegetate.
veg: **~formasie**, fighting formation; **~generaal**, field-general, combat-general; **~haan**, game-cock; **~hoender**, game-fowl; **~kuns**, art of war (fighting); **~linie**, front line, line of battle.
veg'lus, pugnacity, fighting spirit; **~'tig, (-e)**, combative, pugnacious, game.
veg: **~party**, fight, scrap, scuffle, affray; **~plek**, cockpit; prize-ring; **~prys**, purse (prize-money); **~ruspe(r)**, carrier (mil.).
vegs'man, combatant.
veg'tenue, battledress.
veg'ter, (-s), fighter, combatant; contender; bruiser; fighter plane; **~beskerming**, fighter cover.
veg'tersbaas, bully, fire-eater.
veg'tery, fight, scrap, scuffle, tussle.
veg: **~troepe**, fighting forces; **~venter**, (box) promotor; **~vermoë**, fighting power; **~vlieër**, fighter pilot; **~vliegtuig**, fighter plane; **~wa**, light armoured vehicle, whippet, caterpillar; tank.
veil¹, (w) **(ge-)**, sell by auction, put up for sale.
veil², (b) venal, mercenary, corruptible; ready to sacrifice; *ALLES ~ hê*, be willing to stake everything; *sy LEWE ~ hê*, be ready to lay down one's life; **~heid**, venality, mercenariness, corruptibility.
vei'lig, (-e), safe, secure, gilt-edged (securities); ~ *SÊ*, say without fear of contradiction; ~ *WEES*, be safe (out of harm's way).
vei'ligheid, safety, security; fuse (elec.); *in ~ BRING*, carry into safety; ~ *EERSTE*, safety first; *die OPENBARE ~*, public safety.
vei'ligheids: **~beweging**, safety-first movement; **~diens**, security service; **~draad**, fuse wire.
vei'ligheidsein, all-clear signal, safety signal.
vei'ligheids: **~glas**, safety glass; **~gordel**, safety belt; **~grens**, margin of safety; **~halwe**, for safety's sake; **~heining**, safety fence; **~hoek**, angle of safety; **~inrigting**, safety device.
vei'ligheidskeermes, safety razor.
vei'ligheids: **~ketting**, safety chain; guard (-chain); **~klep**, safety valve; escape valve, escapement; **~knip**, safety catch; **~koëffisiënt**, factor of safety; **~lamp**, safety lamp, magazine lamp.
vei'ligheidslot, safety lock.
vei'ligheids: **~maatreël**, precautionary (safety) measure; **~meter**, safety gas-meter; **~ooreenkoms**, security pact; **~pal**, safety catch.
vei'ligheidspen, safety pin (mil.).
vei'ligheidspleet, safety slot.
vei'ligheids: **~reëling**, safety measure; **~reling**, guard-rail; **~rem**, safety brake; **~toestel**, safety device; **~wag**, security guard; **~wet**, law concerning public safety.
vei'ligsein, all-clear signal.
vei'ling, (-s), auction.
vei'lings: **~koste**, sale expenses; **~lokaal**, sale room, auction mart; **~verkoping**, auction sale.
veil'voorwaardes, conditions of sale (by auction).
veins, **(ge-)**, feign, sham, pretend (friendship); simulate; **~aard, (-s)**, dissembler, hypocrite; **~er, (-s)**, dissembler, dissimulator; **~ery**, hypocrisy, dissimulation; **~ing**, simulation, shamming, pretence.
vek'tor, (-e), vector.
vel¹, (s) **(-le)**, skin (of humans); integument (biol.);

vel hide; pelt, coat (of animals); sheet (paper); *iem. se ~ AFSTROOP,* fleece someone; *net ~ en BEEN,* just skin and bone; in a very emaciated condition; *beter ~ en BEEN as riem alleen,* better be sure than sorry; *liewer ~ en BEEN as ~ alleen,* rather skin and bone than the skin alone; *die ~ verkoop voordat die BEER geskiet is,* count one's chickens before they are hatched; *iem. het 'n DIK ~,* he is thick-skinned; he does not easily take offence; *jou ~ DUUR verkoop,* fight for dear life; *iem. op sy ~ GEE,* give someone a hiding; *iem. die ~ van die ORE trek,* fleece someone; *'n ~ PAPIER,* a sheet of paper; *dit RAAK aan jou ~,* it touches one deeply; *van 'n ander se ~ breë RIEME sny,* cut large thongs of other men's leather; *'n SAGTE ~ hê,* be thin-skinned; *~ le SLEEP,* drink noisily; *uit sy ~ kan SPRING van vreugde,* be highly delighted; *jou ~ daaraan WAAG,* risk your neck; (w) **(ge-),** flog, beat; *'n stout seun ~,* cane a naughty boy.

vel², (w) **(ge-),** pass (sentence); cut, fell (tree); couch (lance); find (law); *met gevelde BAJONET,* with fixed bayonet; *VONNIS ~,* pass sentence.

velaar,' (s) **(velare),** velar; (b) **(velare),** velar; *velare klank,* velar sound.

vel'-af; bruised; *EK gaan ~,* my skin is peeling off; *~ GAAN,* lose the skin, peel; *~ VAL,* be grazed (in falling).

velariseer', (ge-), velarize; ..**se'ring,** velarization.

vel'bloter, fellmonger, (wool-)puller; **~y,** fellmongery, skin-works; fellmongering, wool-pulling.

vel: ~ bloting, fellmongering, wool-pulling; **~ breier, ourrici, ~ broek,** pair of skin trousers, buckskins.

veld, (-e), veld; grazing, pasture; field (magnet, etc.), plain; territory; ground; *~ AF,* down the field; *die ~ BEHOU,* stand one's ground; *'n groot ~ BESTRYK,* cover a wide field; *'n ruim ~ BIED,* offer a wide scope; *op die ~ van EER sterf,* die on the field of glory; *uit die ~ GESLAAN,* be quite taken aback; *~ IN,* into the field; *die ~ RUIM,* give ground; flee; *iem. uit die ~ SLAAN,* confuse (disconcert) someone; cause someone consternation; *TE ~e,* in the field; *teen iets te ~e TREK,* combat something; *VAN die ~,* off the cuff; off the grass; *in iem. se ~ WEI,* poach on someone's preserves; *~ WEN,* gain ground; **~ ambulans,** field-ambulance; **~ apteek,** field-dispensary; **~ arbeid,** field-work; **~ artillerie,** field artillery; **~ baan,** field-circuit; **~ baro,** *Cyphia volubilis;* **~ basis,** field-base; **~ battery,** field-battery; **~ bed,** camp-bed, pallet, camp-stretcher; **~ beesboerdery,** cattle-ranching; **~ beheer, ~ bestuur,** veld management; **~ binoskoop,** *see* **veldflick; ~ blaasbalk,** portable forge; **~ blom,** wild flower; **~ brand,** veld fire, grass fire; **~ diens,** field-service; **~ eskader,** active-service squadron; **~ eskadron,** field-squadron; **~ fles,** water bottle, canteen; **~ fliek,** drive-in theatre; **~ geskut,** ordnance (guns); **~ gewas,** product of the fields; **~ grou,** (-e), field-grey; **~ heer,** general; **~ heerkuns,** generalship, strategy; **~ heerstaf,** general's baton; **~ heerstalent,** generalship; **~ hospitaal,** field hospital; ambulance; **~ intensiteit,** field strength (phys.); **~ kaart,** field-sheet, **~ kanon,** field-gun; **~ kennis,** bush lore, bushcraft; **~ ketel,** camp kettle, dixie; **~ klere,** field-dress, camp-dress; **~ kombuis,** cooker, canteen, camping-kitchen; **~ kornet,** (-te), field-cornet; **~ kornetskap,** field-cornetcy; **~ kos,** veld food, e.g. berries and wild roots; **~ kring,** field circuit, **~ kuns,** fieldcraft; **~ kyker,** field-glass; **~ leër,** field-army; **~ lens,** field lens; **~ likkewaan,** *see* **ouvolk; ~ loop,** cross-country run.

veld'maarskalk, field marshal; **~ staf,** field marshal's baton.

veld: ~ magneet, field magnet; **~ melkboerdery,** dairy-ranching; **~ meter,** geometer; **~ muis,** fieldmouse; **~ owerste,** general; **~ pad,** country road; **~ party,** picnic; **~ perd,** free-grazing horse; **~ pond,** field sovereign (minted during the Anglo Boer War); **~ pou,** Stanley bustard; **~ prediker,** army chaplain, padre; **~ rantsoen,** field rations; **~ roos,** wild rose; **~ rot,** field-rat; **~ seer,** scaly skin eruption, veld-sore; **~ skans,** field-work; **~ slaai,** field salad, fetticus; **~ slag,** battle; **~ slang,** culverin; **~ smedery,** field-forge; **~ spaat,** felspar; **~ sport,** field sports; **~ sprinkaan,** grasshopper; **~ sterkte,** field strength (of army); intensity of field; **~ stoel,** folding stool, camp-stool, camp-chair; **~ stuk,** field piece; **~ suring,** sour dock; **~ teken,** standard; **~ telefoon,** portable telephone; **~ telegraaf,** field telegraph; **~ tent,** army tent; **~ tenue,** field-service uniform; **~ tog,** campaign; expedition; **~ troepe,** troops on active service; **~ uitrusting,** field kit; **~ verwringing,** field distortion; **~ voertuig,** cross-country vehicle; **~ wagter,** field ranger; **~ wedloop,** cross-country race; **~ werk,** fielding (cricket); field-work; **~ wikkeling,** field winding; **~ winkel,** mobile canteen; **~ wol,** range wool.

ve'lerhande, various; numerous.

ve'lerlei, various, miscellaneous, sundry; many.

vel: ~ handel, furriery; **~ handelaar,** skinner, furrier, dealer in hides and skins; **~ karos,** skin rug; **~ kleur,** skin colour; **~ klier,** cutaneous gland; **~ kombers,** blanket (made of animal skins); skin rug; **~ koper,** buyer (dealer) in skins and hides; peltmonger; **~ letjie,** (-s), sheet (paper); film (on milk); skin (of fruit); cuticle; pellicle; *hulle ~ letjies bymekaargooi,* get married.

vel'ling, (-s), felly, rim, felloe; *los ~,* detachable rim; **~ boom,** rim base; **~ kloutjie,** rim wedge; **~ skaaf,** compass plane; **~ trekker,** rim tool; **~ voering,** rim-lining.

vel'mol, creeping eruption, sandworm.

veloer', velour(e).

ve'lomat, velomat (electronic speedometer).

vel: ~ oorplanting, skin-grafting; **~ sak,** skin pouch (bag); humpty-dumpty.

vel'skoen, homemade shoe, velskoen; **~ blare,** April-fool *(Haemanthus spp.);* **~ draer,** country bumpkin; **~ klap,** (-ge-), kick up one's heels; **~ naat,** seam of velskoen.

vel'steen, dermolith.

velt, couch.

vel'tering, lupus.

ve'lum, (-s), velum.

vel: ~ water, skin lotion; **~ wol,** skinwool.

velyn', vellum, satin paper, wire-wove; **~ papier,** vellum paper.

ven, (-ne), fen.

venaliteit', venality.

Ven'da, Venda (language); (-s), Venda (tribesman).

ven'del, (-s), company (soldiers); **~ swaaier,** (-s), flag-waver.

vendet'ta, (s), vendetta, blood feud.

vendu': ~ afslaer, (-s), auctioneer; **~ kraal,** sale pen; **~ lokaal,** sale room; **~ regte,** auction dues; **~ rol,** auction list.

vendu'sie, (-s), auction, sale; **~ kraal,** auctioneer's stockyard; **~ lokaal,** auction mart.

vene'ries, (-e), venereal.

Venesiaan', (..siane), Venetian, **~ s',** (-e), Venetian; *~ se kant,* Venetian lace.

Vene'sië, Venice; Venetia (province).

Vene'sies, (-e), Venetian; *~e glas,* Venetian glass.

Vene'ters, Veneti.

Vene'ties, (-e), Venetic.

veneus', (-e), venous.

Venezolaan', (..lane), Venezuelan; **~ s',** (-e), Venezuelan.

Venezue'la, Venezuela.

vennoot', (..note), associate, partner, copartner; fellow; *rustende (stille) ~,* sleeping partner; **~ skap,** (-pe), (co)partnership, company; **~ skapsakte,** articles of partnership; **~ skapsreg,** law of partnership.

ven'ster, (-s), window; shelf (in haystack); *BY (voor) die ~,* at the window; *~ MET diefwering,* burglar-proof window; **~ bank,** window sill, window ledge; **~ blinding,** shutter; window blind; **~ boog,** window arch; **~ brief,** window envelope; account; **~ deur,** French window; **~ gewig,** mouse (window); **~ glas,** window pane, window glass, glazing; **~ gordyn,** window curtain; **~ haak,** cabin hook; **~ hoogte,** window level; sill height; **~ kassie,** window box; **~ knip,** window-fastener; **~ koevert,** window envelope; ~ **koord**, sash-cord; ~ **kosyn**, window frame, window sill; ~ **kykery**, window-shopping; ~ **ligter**, window-lift; ~ **lood**, sash-weight, came; ~ **luik**, shutter; ~ **raam**, window frame; ~ **roede**, window rod; ~ **roei**, mullion; window bar; ~ **roset**, rose window; ~ **ruimte**, window space; ~ **ruit**, window pane; ~ **skoonmaker**, window-cleaner; ~ **stof**, casement cloth; ~ **tjie**, small window; peep hole; ~ **tralie**, window grate; ~ **tuin**, window box; ~ **verdeling**, fenestration; ~ **ys**, window ice.

vent[1], (s) (-e), fellow, bloke, chap, cove; churl; cuss; *'n GAWE* ~, a decent chap; *'n SNAAKSE* ~, a funny fellow, an odd sort of chap.

vent[2], (w) (ge-), hawk, peddle, carry about for sale; ~ **er**, (-s), hawker, pedlar, costermonger, huckster, pitcher, street vendor.

ventiel', (-e), valve; ventil (organ); ~ **doppie**, valve cap.

ventila'sie, ventilation; ~ **skag**, upcast, ventilation shaft.

ventileer', (ge-), ventilate.

vent'jie, (-s), little chap, chappie.

ventraal', (ventrale), ventral.

ven'trikel, (-s), ventricle, ventriculus.

ventu'ribuis, choke tube, venturi tube.

Ve'nus, Venus; ~ **berg**, Mountain of Venus.

ve'nusdiens, lasciviousness.

ve'nus: ~ **gordel**, Venus's girdle, cestus; Venus's girdle (mollusc); ~ **haarvaring**, maidenhair fern; ~ **heuwel**, mons pubis, mountain of Venus; ~ **spieël**, flower *(Specuilaria speculum)*.

venyn', venom.

veny'nig, (-e), venomous, vitriolic, virulent, cankerous, vicious; ~ **heid**, viciousness, virulence.

ver, (-re), far, remote; advanced; distant; aloof; ~ *AGTER*, far behind; *dit sal jou nie* ~ *BRING nie*, that won't get you very far; *hy sal dit* ~ *BRING in die lewe*, he will go far in life; ~ *langs FAMILIE*, distantly related; *te* ~ *GAAN*, exceed all bounds; ~ *van HIER*, far from here; ~ *OOR die tagtig*, well over eighty; *die V* ~ *re OOSTE*, the Far East; *OP* ~ *re na nie*, not by a long chalk; not in the least; ~ *van RYK*, far from being rich; ~ *re SY dit van my*, far be it from me; *plekke wat* ~ *UITMEKAAR lê*, places far removed from each other; *in die* ~ *ste VERTE nie*, not at all; ~ *VOOR*, far ahead; *sommer* ~ *WEN*, win hands down.

veraan'genaam, (~), render agreeable, make pleasant.

veraanskou'lik, (~), illustrate, make realistic.

verabsoluteer', (~), absolutize.

vera'deming, breathing-spell, relief, respite.

ver'af, away, remote; ~ **geleë**, remote, distant(ly situated).

veraf'god, (~), idolize, adore; ~ **er**, (-s), idolizer; ~ **ing**, idolization.

veraf'good, (ong.), verafgod.

verafrikaans', (w) (~), make Afrikaans, identify (become identified) with the Afrikaans spirit, Afrikanderize, Afrikaansify; (b) (-te), identified with Afrikaans, Afrikaansified; ~ **ing**, Afrikaansifying, Afrikaansification, Afrikanderization; making South African in character.

veraf'sku, (~), abhor, loathe, abominate, detest, execrate; ~ **wing**, abhorrence, detestation, loathing, abomination, execration.

verag', (~), despise, scorn, hold in contempt, disdain, minimize; ~ **telik**, (-e), despicable, contemptible, despisable, contemptuous, derogatory, ignominious, scornful (glance); disdainful; ~ **telikheid**, despicableness, contemptibility; contemptuousness; ~ **tend**, (-e), despising, scorning, scornful, contemptuous.

verag'ter[1], (s) (-s), despiser.

verag'ter[2], (w) (~), deteriorate, decline, decay; (b) (-de), sunken, poverty-stricken, retrograde, backward; ~ **ing**, decline, retrogression, sinking, deterioration.

verag'ting, contempt, disdain, scorn, minimization, abhorrence.

verag(t)'voudig, (-de), octuple.

veral', especially, particularly, above all things, principally, chiefly; *bring* ~ *die GELD*, be sure (that) you bring the money; ~ *HY*, he especially; *dit* ~ *NIE*, this on no account.

veral'gemeen, (~), generalize.

veral'gemening, generalization.

veramerikaans', (~), Americanize; ~ **ing**, Americanization.

veran'da, (-s), veranda(h).

veran'der, (~), change, alter, modify, convert, vary; rearrange; diversify; *van GODSDIENS* ~, change one's religion; *sy NAAM na (in) Y verander*, change his name to Y; *van PLAN* ~, change one's mind; *dit* ~ *die SAAK*, that alters the case; *WATER in wyn* ~, change water into wine; *die WEER sal* ~, there will be a change in the weather; ~ **baar**, (..bare), variable, modifiable, alterable, convertible; ~ **baarheid**, alterability; convertibility; ~ **end**, (-e), choppy (sea); changing; alterative.

veran'dering, (-e, -s), change, alteration, conversion, rearrangement, change-over, modification, mutation, variation; menstruation; ~ *van SPYSE laat eet*, a change of diet whets the appetite; variety is the spice of life; *alle* ~ *is g'n VERBETERING nie*, let well alone; a change is not always for the better; *VIR (by wyse van) 'n* ~, for a change.

veran'deringstempo, rate of change.

veran'derinkie, (-s), small change, trifling alteration.

veran'derlik, (-e), changeable, unsteady, fickle (person); mutable, fitful, alterable, liable to fluctuation; variable; mercurial (temperament); ~ *e wind*, variable wind; ~ **heid**, changeableness, fickleness, instability, mercuriality; alterability, variability, mobility, mutability.

veran'ker, (~), anchor, moor (mine); picket; ~ **bout**, holding-down bolt; ~ **ing**, anchorage.

verant'woord, (w) (~), answer for, account for; justify; *baie te* ~ *hê*, have a great deal to answer for; (b) (-e), well-founded, justified; ~ **baar**, answerable; justifiable.

verantwoor'delik, (-e), responsible, answerable, accountable; amenable; liable; ~ *e AMPTENAAR*, responsible official, officer-in-charge; *'n* ~ *e POSISIE*, a position of trust; ~ *WEES vir die geld*, be responsible for the money; ~ **heid**, accountability, responsibility; burden; liability, onus; ~ **heidsgevoel**, sense of responsibility.

verant'woording, responsibility; account, justification; ~ *DOEN aan*, be accountable to; *tot (ter)* ~ *ROEP*, call to account.

verarm', (~), become poor; impoverish, depauperate, pauperize.

verarm(d)', (-de), impoverished.

verar'ming, impoverishment, pauperization, depauperation.

veras', (~), cremate; incinerate; (b) (-te), incinerated; cremated; ~ **sing**, cremation; (in)cineration.

verassureer', (~), insure, assure; ~ **de**, (-s), assurer.

verbaal', (..bale), verbal; *..bale sisteem*, verbal system.

verbaas', (w) (~), astonish, surprise, astound, amaze; *hom* ~ *oor*, be astonished (marvel) at; (b, bw) (-de), astonished, surprised, amazed.

verbaasd'heid, astonishment, amazement, surprise.

verbab'bel, (~), chatter (the time) away.

verban', (~), banish, exile, expatriate; dispel; proscribe, expel, eject, dismiss; ostracize; *iets uit jou gemoed* ~, expel something from one's mind.

verband'[1], (-e), bandage, sling, dressing, ligament (med.); ligature (artery); bond (bricks); *die arm in 'n* ~ *DRA*, carry the arm in a sling; *'n* ~ *OMSIT*, apply a bandage.

verband'[2], reference, connection, context; ~ *BRING tussen*, co-ordinate; *in* ~ *BRING met*, relate to; *in HIERDIE* ~, in this connection; *dit HOU* ~ *met*, this is connected with (is relevant to); *in* ~ *MET*, in connection with; *iets uit sy* ~ *RUK*, take something out of its context; *in* ~ *STAAN*, be connected (with); be related to.

verband'[3], (-e), hypothec, mortgage bond; encumbrance bond; *EERSTE* ~, first mortgage bond; *deur 'n* ~ *GEDEK*, secured by a mortgage; *HIPOTEKÊRE* ~, lien; *'n HUIS* ~, *ONDER* ~

verbandgaas / verbleking

PLAAS, mortgage a house; ~**akte,** mortgage deed.
verband'gaas, sterilized gauze.
verband': ~**gewer,** mortgagor, mortgager; ~**gewing,** mortgaging, hypothecation; ~**houdend, (-e),** relevant; ~**houer,** mortgagee.
verband': ~**kamer,** dressing-room; ~**kassie,** ~**kis(sie),** first-aid box; ~**klip,** through stone; bond stone; ~**leer,** bandaging; ~**linne,** (roller) bandages; ~**mandjie,** medical pannier; ~**middele,** surgical appliances (dressings).
verband'nemer, mortgagee.
verband': ~**pakkie,** field dressing (package); ~**plek,** ~**pos,** dressing-station; ~**seksie,** aid-post; ~**staaf,** jointer, bond bar; ~**steen,** bond(ing) brick.
verband'stowwe, dressing, bandages.
verband'stuk, wall clamp.
verband'tang, dressing-forceps.
verband'uitmaker, conveyancer.
verband': ~**wa,** pharmacy wag(g)on; ~**watte,** sterilized cotton wool.
verban': ~**neling, (-e),** exile; ~**nend, (-e),** expulsive, proscriptive; ~**nene, (-s),** deportee, exile; ~**ner, (-s),** dispeller, expeller; ~**ning,** banishment, exile, expatriation; proscription, expulsion; ostracism; excommunication.
verban'nings: ~**besluit,** expulsion order; ~**oord,** place of exile; ~**vonnis,** decree of banishment.
verbarbaars', (~), barbarize.
verba'send, (b) (-e), astonishing, surprising, astounding, marvellous, amazing; (bw) marvellously, astonishingly, surprisingly; ~ *BAIE,* surprisingly many; ~ *SNAAKS,* very funny indeed.
verba'sing, astonishment, amazement, surprise; *EEN en al* ~, blank amazement; lost in wonderment; *MET* ~, in astonishment; *met STOMME* ~, in utter amazement; *TOT my* ~, to my surprise; ~**wekkend, (-e),** astounding, stupendous.
verbas'ter, (~), degenerate, bastardize, corrupt; interbreed, hybridize; ~**ing, (-e, -s),** degeneration, corruption, depravity; miscegenation; hybridization; interbreeding.
verbeel', (~), imagine, fancy; represent; be arrogant; *hy* ~ *hom BAIE,* he is very conceited; ~ *JOU!* just fancy! *ek* ~ *my dis KLAAR,* I think it is finished; *jy* ~ *jou dit MAAR,* that is pure imagination; ~ *jou NET hoe ek gevoel het,* just try to imagine how I felt.
verbeeld', (~), represent; delineate, portray; *die toneel* ~ *'n woestyn,* the scene represents a desert.
verbeel'derig, (-e), conceited; vain, arrogant; ~**heid,** conceit, vanity.
verbeel'ding, (-e, -s), fancy, imagination, imagery; conceit; *dis PURE* ~, that is nothing but imagination; *vol* ~ *s,* full of frills and fancies; ~**siekte,** hypochondria.
verbeel'dingskrag, verbeel'dingsvermoë, imaginative power, imagination, fancifulness.
verbeen', (~), ossify, ~(d)', (-de), ossified.
verbei(d)', (~), await, abide.
verbe'lentheid = **verbeelding.**
verbe'na, (-s), verbena.
verbe'ning, ossification.
verberg', (~), conceal, hide, dissimulate; entomb; hoodwink; obscure; keep dark; *haar ANGS kon sy nie* ~ *nie,* she could not conceal her fear; *die KIND het hom* ~, the child hid himself; ~**baar, (..bare),** concealable; ~**ing,** hiding, concealment, occultation.
verbeson'dering, specialization.
verbe'te, pent up; ~ *teenstand,* obstinate resistance.
verbe'ter, (~), improve, amend, emend (text); correct (essay); rectify (mistake); reform; correct (essay); rectify (mistake), reform (person), better, (a)meliorate, perfect, grade up; mend one's ways; reclaim; redress; *hy het HOM* ~, he has turned over a new leaf; *MISSTANDE* ~, remedy evils, ~**aar, (-s),** corrector, improver; emendator; rectifier; ~**baar, (..bare),** corrigible, mendable, improvable, rectifiable; amendable; ~**baarheid,** improvability, ~**blad,** (page listing) errata, ~**end, (-e),** (a)meliorative, emendatory; reformative; ~**ing, (-e, -s),** improvement, corrigendum, correction, reform, amendment, mending, emendation, betterment, (a)melioration; reclamation; rectification; rally.
verbe'teringsgestig, verbe'teringskool, reformatory, penitentiary; house of correction.
verbe'ter: ~**lik, (-e),** improvable, corrigible; ~**middel,** corrective.
verbeur', (~), forfeit, lose (chance); confiscate; estreat (bail); ~**baar, (..bare),** forfeitable; seizable, confiscable.
verbeurd', (-e), confiscated; forfeited; ~ *verklaarde GELDE,* forfeitures; ~ *VERKLAAR,* declare forfeit; ~**verklaarder,** confiscator; ~**verklaring,** confiscation, forfeiture.
verbeu'ring, forfeit(ure); estreatment (of bail).
verbeur'te, forfeit.
verbeu'sel, (~), trifle away, fritter away, dally away, potter away, dawdle away, idle away.
verbid', (~), mollify; pacify by prayer.
verbied', (~), prohibit, forbid; proscribe, interdict, ban (book); vgl. **verbode;** *ROOK* ~ *(verbode),* no smoking; *ten STRENGSTE* ~, strictly forbidden; ~**end, (-e),** interdictory, prohibitive; ~**er, (-s),** prohibitor.
verbind'¹, (w) (~), mortgage, hypothecate.
verbind², (w) (~), connect, combine; bandage, dress (wound); link up (by telephone); compound (chem.); *in die HUWELIK* ~, unite in marriage; ~ *MET,* connect with, join to; ~ *OM,* undertake to; (b) affined, connected; ~**balk,** tie beam.
verbin'dend, (-e), connective, binding, obligatory, copulative; conjunctive.
verbin'der, dresser (of wounds); connector.
verbin'ding, (-e, -s), connection, junction, union, combination; communication (by telegraph); communion; linkage; compound (chem.); bandaging; *die* ~ *HERSTEL,* restore the communication; *in* ~ *MET,* in conjunction with; in communication with; *in* ~ *STAAN met,* be in communication with; *in* ~ *STEL met,* put into communication (touch) with; *in* ~ *TREE met,* get into touch with.
verbin'dings: ~**balk,** stringer; ~**deur,** connecting door; ~**draad,** connecting wire; ~**eskader,** communication squadron; ~**gang,** communication passage; ~**hakie,** accolade (music); ~**kabel,** canal of communication.
verbin'dingskakel, connecting link.
verbin'dings: ~**kanaal,** junction canal; means of approach; ~**klem,** connecting terminal; ~**leiding,** connecting main; ~**linie,** ~**lyn,** line of communication; join; loop line; ~**middel,** means of communication; ~**net,** communication system; ~**offisier,** liaison officer.
verbin'dingspoor, railway junction.
verbin'dings: ~**pad,** connecting road; ~**pen,** gudgeon (pin); ~**plaat,** junction (connecting) plate; ~**plek,** connecting point, join, joint; ~**punt,** point of junction; ~**pyp,** connecting tube; ~**ratte,** connecting gear.
verbin'dingstang, connecting rod; coupling rod.
verbin'dingsteken, hyphen; slur (music).
verbin'dingstreep, hyphen; vinculum (alg.).
verbin'dingstroepe, communication troops.
verbin'dingstuk, connecting piece, joint.
verbin'dings: ~**vlug,** communication flight; ~**weg,** connection road; ~**woord,** copulative, connective.
verbind'sel, (-s), wound dressing.
verbin'tenis, (-e), union; promise; contract, commitment, engagement; alliance, bond; recognizance; plight; *'n* ~ *aangaan,* make (enter into) a contract.
verbit'ter, (~), embitter (life); exasperate.
verbit'ter(d), (-de), embittered, bitter, acidific, exasperated.
verbit'terdheid, embitterment, exasperation.
verbit'tering, embitterment, exasperation, animosity, exacerbation, irritation.
verbleek', (w) (~), turn (grow) pale, change countenance; fade (fig.); (b) **(-te),** pale, blanched.
verbleik', (~), fade, bleach, etiolate, lose colour, cast (colour), change colour; (b) **(-te),** faded; ~**ing,** fading.
verble'king, fading, etiolation.

verblind', (w) (~), (be)dazzle, blind, purblind; infatuate; (b) (-e), dazzled, purblind, blinded; benighted; ~ end, (-e), glary, dazzling, meteoric; ~ heid, blindness; infatuation; ~ ing, blinding, dazzling.
verbloe'ding, bleeding to death.
verbloei', (~), bleed to death.
verbloem', (~), disguise, cover, hide, conceal, veil (mistakes); blanch over, gloss over, palliate (facts).
verbloem(d)', (-de), disguised, hidden, veiled.
verbloe'mer, (-s), concealer.
verbloe'ming, disguising; euphemism; palliation.
verbluf', (~), dumbfound, nonplus, baffle, abash; startle, stagger; ~ fend, (-e), baffling, staggering, startling.
verbluft'heid, abashment, amazement.
verbly', (~), gladden, please, cheer, delight.
verblyd', (-e), pleased, delighted, glad.
verbly'dend, (-e), joyful, joyous, gladdening, *'n ~ e teken*, a hopeful sign.
verbly'ding, gladdening, joyfulness, cheer, rejoicing, elation.
verblyf', (s) (verblywe), residence, abode, domicile, home, habitat, tenement; sojourn; ~ *HOU*, reside; ~ *ONBEKEND*, address unknown; *sonder VASTE* ~, without fixed abode; (w) (~), reside; remain; ~ koste, expenses for board and lodging; subsistence allowance; ~ plaas, ~ plek, abode, dwelling-place, whereabouts; ~ s'vergunning, visitor's permit, resident's permit, residential permit; ~ toelae, subsistence allowance.
verbod', (..biedinge, ..biedings), prohibition, ban (on books); embargo (on imports); suppression, banning (publication); disallowance; interdict; *'n ~ instel op*, impose a ban on.
verbo'de, prohibited, forbidden; ~ *IMMIGRANT*, prohibited immigrant; ~ *TOEGANG*, no admittance; ~ *VRUGTE smaak die lekkerste*, forbidden fruit taste sweetest; stolen kisses are the sweetest.
verbod'lys, index (exports).
verbods'bepaling, prohibitive regulation.
verbod'teken, prohibitive sign.
verbo'ë, declined, inflected (gram.).
verboe'mel, (~), dissipate, squander.
verboe'mel(d), (-de), dissipated, squandered.
verboep', (-te), stunted, feeble, poor, small; pot-bellied.
verboer', **verboers'**, (~), become countrified (rusticated), go rustic; *verboerste maniere*, countrified manners.
verbol'ge, indignant, wrathful, angry.
verbol'genheid, indignation, wrath, anger.
verbond', (-e), treaty; league; pact; bond; coalition; compact; covenant; alliance; *DRIEVOUDIGE* ~, triple alliance; *die NUWE (ou)* ~, the new (old) dispensation.
verbon'de, connected, combined, (con)joined, linked, united, allied; bound; ~ *KAMERS*, interleading rooms; ~ *MET*, connected with, put through to; *die* ~ *MOONDHEDE*, the allied powers, the allies; ~ *TOT*, committed to; *daar is 'n VOORWAARDE aan* ~, there is a condition attached to it; ~ ne, (-s), convenantee, convenanter.
verbon'denheid, close connection, connectedness.
Verbonds': ~ ark, Ark of the Covenant; ~ beker, chalice (Holy Communion); ~ eed, oath of alliance; ~ god, God of the Covenant; ~ kis, Ark of the Covenant; ~ tafel, (Holy) Communion table; ~ volk, chosen people; ~ wet, Law of the Covenant, the Ten Commandments.
verbor'ge, (-ner, -nste), hidden, concealed; latent (qualities); secret (sin); obscure; occult; cryptic(al); covert; mysterious; *in die* ~ *ne*, in secret; on the quiet.
verbor'genheid, (..hede), secrecy; mystery; abstruseness; latency.
verbou', (~), alter, rebuild (building); cultivate, grow (crops); ~ er, (-s), cultivator, grower; raiser.
verbouereer', (~), perplex, embarrass.
verbouereerd', (-e), flurried, embarrassed, confused, perplexed, nonplussed, bewildered, panic-stricken, flabbergasted; *gou* ~ *word*, lose one's head easily; ~ heid, flurry, consternation, embarrassment, confusion, disconcertment, disconcertation.

verbou'ing, (-e, -s), alteration (to building); cultivation, culture (crops).
verbrak', turn brack(ish).
verbrak'king, salination, salinification.
verbrand', (w) (-ge-), burn, consume; calcine; die by burning; scald; cremate (corpse); incinerate (refuse); (b) (-e), burnt, charred; sunburnt, tanned; confounded; *BRUIN* ~, sun-tanned; *so 'n ~ e DOMKOP*, such a confounded fool; *sy MOND* ~, put one's foot into it, say more than one intends; ~ *e STAAL*, burnt steel; ~ baar, (..bare), combustible; ~ er, (-s), burner; cremator.
verbran'ding, (-e, -s), combustion (chem.); incineration; deflagration, burning; cremation (of corpse).
verbran'dings: ~ dood, death by fire; ~ gas, flue-gas; ~ kamer, combustion chamber; ~ motor, internal combustion engine; ~ oond, incinerator; combustion furnace; ~ produk, product of combustion; ~ proses, process of combustion; ~ waarde, calorific value.
verbrands'!, hang it all! confound it! *dis* ~ *'n GELOL*, it is a confounded nuisance; *dis* ~ *SWAAR*, it is beastly difficult.
verbras', (~), dissipate, squander.
verbre'ding, broadening, widening.
verbree(d)', (w) (~), broaden, widen; (b) (..brede), broadened, widened.
verbreek, (~), break (treaty); sever (relations); burst; run (blockade); violate (oath); alter (building); *die STILTE* ~, break (shatter) the silence; *'n VERLOWING* ~, break off an engagement; ~ baarheid, dissolubility.
verbrei', (~), spread, propagate, disseminate, distribute; ~ (d'), (-e), common, widely spread, disseminated; ~ der, (-s), propagator.
verbreid'heid, distribution, dissemination.
verbrei'ding, spread, propagation, distribution, dissemination.
verbre'ker, (-s), violator, breaker, interrupter.
verbre'king, (-e, -s), breaking, violation; breach (of promise); interruption, severance.
verbrits', (w) (~), Anglify; (b) (-te), Anglified; ~ ing, Anglification.
verbrod'del, (~), mess up.
verbroe'der, (~), fraternize; ~ ing, fraternization.
verbro'ke, broken; *'n ~ gesin*, a broken home.
verbrok'kel, (~), disrupt, break up, disintegrate, crumble to pieces, fritter away.
verbrok'kel(d), (-de), crumbling; broken up.
verbrok'keling, crumbling; disruption, frittering.
verbrons', bronze; ~ *de skoene*, bronzed shoes; ~ ing, bronzing.
verbrou', (~), spoil, muddle, make a mess; queer (slang); misbehave (oneself); *'n ~ de BAL*, burned ball; *dit BY iem.* ~, incur the displeasure of someone; *'n SAAK* ~, make a hash of things.
verbrui', (~), incur (someone's) displeasure.
verbruik', (s) consumption, use; expenditure; (w) (~), use up, consume; expend; ~ baar, (..bare), consumable (by use); ~ er, (-s), consumer; ~ ers(aansluit)punt, consumer's terminal; ~ ersdruk, consumers' pressure; ~ ersgoedere, consumer (consumable) goods; ~ ersprys, consumer's price; ~ erspyp, service pipe; ~ ersvereniging, association of consumers; ~ erslening, loan (for consumption).
verbruiks': ~ aansluiting, service connection; ~ artikel, article of consumption; consumable (expendable) stores; ~ daling, fall in consumption.
verbruik'sekering, service fuse.
verbruiks': ~ goed(ere), consumer goods; ~ leiding, service mains.
verbruik'styging, rise in consumption.
verbruik'syfer, consumption figure.
verbruiks'ware, consumer goods.
verbry'sel, (~), smash, shatter, break to pieces, crush; quash; *'n ~ de hart*, a contrite (broken) heart; ~ ing, smashing, shattering, crushing, disruption.
verbui'e, **verbuig'**, (~), distort, twist, warp, bend; inflect, decline (gram.).
verbuig'baar, (..bare), declinable; flexible; ~ heid, declinability.

verbui'ging, (-e, -s), declension, flexion (gram.); warping (geol.).
verbui'gings: ~ **uitgang,** flexional ending, inflexion; ~ **vorm,** flexional form.
ver'bum, (verba), verb.
verby'[1], (bw) past, beyond, gone by; over, at an end; foregone; *dis ALLES* ~, it is all over; it belongs to the past; *WAT* ~ *is, is* ~, let bygones by bygones; what is done cannot be undone; (vs) past, beyond; *sy is by haar eerste JEUG* ~, she is past her first youth; ~ *die SKOOL,* past the school.
ver'-by[2], long on (cricket).
verby'bring, (-ge-), bring (take) past.
verby'dra, (-ge-), carry past.
verby'dryf, verby'drywe, (-ge-), float past; blow over, drift past.
verby'flits, (w) (-ge-), flash by (past).
verby'gaan, (s): *in die* ~, in passing; (w) (-ge-), pass, go past, go by; leave out; neglect; fore-reach; flit (time); overpass; pretermit; *'n geleentheid LAAT* ~, let an opportunity slip; *STILSWYEND* ~, pass in silence (silently); ~ **de,** passing, fleeting, transitory, fugitive, momentary, transient; *'n* ~ *de gril,* a passing whim.
verby'ganger, (-s), passer-by.
verby'glip, (-ge-), slip past, dodge.
verby'gooi, (-ge-), throw past; overthrow (cricket).
verby'groei, (-ge-), grow past, outgrow.
verby'hardloop, (-ge-), outstrip; run past.
verby'kom, (-ge-), come past, pass by; incur a rebuke or lecture; *jy KAN daar nie* ~ *nie, you cannot ex= plain that away (get past that); iem. LAAT* ~, haul someone over the coals; *ek moes LELIK* ~, I was given a severe scolding.
verby'komkans: *geen* ~ *hê nie,* have no chance to escape; be unable to get away from.
verby'kruip, (-ge-), crawl (creep) past.
verby'laat, (-ge-), let pass.
verby'leer, (-ge-), get ahead (of someone) by studying.
verby'lei, (-ge-), lead past.
verby'loop, (-ge-), walk past; overshoot.
verby'marsjeer, (-ge-), march past.
verby'pad, bypass.
verby'praat, (-ge-): *sy mond* ~, put one's foot in it; commit oneself; let the cat out of the bag.
verby'ratel, (-ge-), clatter by.
verby'rol, (-ge-), roll past.
verby'ry, (-ge-), ride past, drive past.
verby'seil, (-ge-), sail past; outsail.
verby'sien, (-ge-), overlook; look past; ignore.
verby'skiet, (-ge-), shoot past; dash past, overshoot.
verby'skuif, (-ge-), shuffle past.
verby'snel, (-ge-), hurry (rush) past; pass quickly.
verby'spring, (-ge-), sidestep; jump past.
verby'stap, (-ge-), walk past.
verby'steek, (-ge-), pass by, overtake (car); outstrip, surpass, outrival; ~ **sein,** overtake signal.
verby'ster, (-), perplex, fog, daze, bewilder, distract, puzzle, obfuscate, confuse.
verby'sterd, (-de), perplexed, bewildered, puzzled, confused.
verbys'terend, (-e), perplexing, embarrassing.
verbys'tering, perplexity, bewilderment, daze, obfus= cation, embarrassment, confusion, distraction.
verby'streef, verby'strewe, (-ge-), outstrip, outdis= tance, surpass, outrival.
verby'stroom, (-ge-), flow past, stream past.
verby'swem, (-ge-), swim past.
verby'trek, (-ge-), march past; trek past; pass over; pull past; blow over (weather); ~ **king,** passing over.
verby'vlieg, (-ge-), fly past; *die tyd vlieg verby,* time flies.
verby'vloei, (-ge-), flow past.
verby'wandel, (-ge-), walk past, pass.
verchris'telik, (~), Christianize; ~ **ing,** Chris= tianization.
verchro'ming, chromium-plating.
vercrhoom', (w) (~), chromium-plate; (b) **(-de),** chro= mium-plated.
verdaag', (w) (~), adjourn, prorogue, postpone; dis= miss (mil.); (b) **(-de),** adjourned; dismissed.

verdag', **(-te),** suspicious, fishy (happening); queer, suspected (person); equivocal (statement); *iem.* ~ *MAAK,* cast suspicion on someone; *'n* ~ *te PER= SOON,* a suspect(ed person); ~ *VOORKOM,* ap= pear (look) suspicious; *op iets* ~ *WEES,* be wary of something; have one's doubts about something (someone).
verda'ging, (-e, -s), prorogation, adjournment (parliament).
verdag'makery, (-e), **verdag'making,** (-e, -s), rousing of suspicion, insinuation, reflection.
verdag'te, (-s), suspect, person suspected.
verdagt'heid, fishiness, suspiciousness, dubiousness.
verdamp', (w) (~), evaporate; vaporize; ~ **baar,** (..**bare),** evaporable; ~ **end,** (-e), evaporating; ~ **er,** (-s), vaporizer; evaporator.
verdam'ping, (-e, -s), evaporation; gasification.
verdam'pings: ~ **leer,** atmology; ~ **meter,** atmo= meter; evaporimeter; ~ **oppervlak,** surface of evap= oration; ~ **punt,** evaporation point; ~ **toestel,** eva= porator; ~ **vermoë,** evaporation capacity; ~ **warmte,** heat of evaporation.
verde'dig, (~), defend; advocate, plead (cause); stand up for, protect (person); appear for (in court); *die beskuldigde* ~ *in die hof,* appear in court for the accused; ~ **baar,** (..**bare),** defensible, tenable; maintainable; justifiable; ~ **baarheid,** defensibility; ~ **end,** (-e), defensive; apologetic; ~ *end optree,* be on the defensive; ~ **er,** (-s), advocate, counsel for the defence; defender; apologist; maintainer.
verde'diging, defence, justification, vindication; plea; apology; *DEPARTEMENT van V* ~, Department of Defence; *MINISTER van V* ~, Minister of Defence.
verde'digings: ~ **belasting,** defence tax; ~ **linie,** line of defence; ~ **maatreël,** defensive measure; ~ **mag,** de= fence force; ~ **middel,** means of defence; ~ **oorlog,** war of defence; ~ **rede,** speech for the defence.
verde'digingstelsel, system of defence.
verde'digings: ~ **wapen,** defensive weapon; ~ **werke,** defences.
verdeel', (w) (~), divide, separate, disunite; distri= bute, parcel out, apportion (land); trim (load); fur= cate, fork (road); ~ *en heers,* divide and rule; *ONDER mekaar* ~, share between them; ~ **baar,** (..**bare),** divisible; distributable; ~ **baarheid,** di= visibility; ~ **buis,** distributor tube.
verdeel(d)', **(-de),** divided, split up, disunited.
verdeeld'heid, discord, strife, dissension; division; ~ *saai,* sow discord.
verdeel': ~ **kas,** distribution box; ~ **klep,** distribution valve; ~ **kraan,** distributing cock; ~ **passer,** pair of dividers, dividing compasses; ~ **pyp,** distributing pipe; manifold; ~ **rib,** dividing rib; ~ **rondsel,** di= viding pinion; ~ **skyf,** distributor, dividing segment.
verdek', under cover; *jou* ~ *opstel,* lie in ambush.
verdek'seld, (-e), confounded, bally, beastly.
verdek'sels, counfounded(ly).
verde'ler, (-s), divider; distributor (tech.); ~ **sproeier,** distributor jet.
verdelg', (~), destroy, exterminate, annihilate, extir= pate, eradicate; ~ **baar,** (..**bare),** exterminable; ~ **baarheid,** destructibility; ~ **end,** (-e), extermina= tory; ~ **er,** (-s), destroyer, annihilator, extermina= tor, extirpator.
verdel'ging, destruction, extermination, eradication, extirpation; extinction; deletion.
verdel'gingsoorlog, war of extermination; interne= cine war.
verde'ling, (-e, -s), division, distribution, trimming (load), partition.
verde'lings: ~ **koëffisiënt,** distribution coefficient; ~ **klep,** manifold valve; ~ **kolom,** allocation column; ~ **koste,** splitting-fee; ~ **punt,** point of div= ision; ~ **verdrag,** partition treaty.
verden'king, suspicion, mistrust; *BO* ~, above suspi= cion; *in* ~ *BRING,* cast suspicion on; *onder* ~ *KOM,* come (fall) under suspicion.
ver'der, (b) (-e), farther, further; ~ *e vertraging,* further delay; (bw) again; forward; further, also; *from this day on, moreover; DAAR kom nog* ~ *by,*

moreover, in addition to this; *so KOM ons nie* ~ *nie,* this won't get us any further; *ek MOET* ~, I must be getting along; *en SO* ~, and so on.

verderf', (s) ruin, destruction; bane, doom; perdition; *vir die* ~ *GROOTWORD,* grow up for the gallows; *na die* ~ *LEI,* lead to one's ruin; *iem. in die* ~ *STORT,* bring about someone's ruin; (w) (~), ruin, destroy, corrupt, pervert; V ~ **engel,** Angel of Destruction, Angel of Death; ~ **nis,** doom; perdition; ~ **lik, (-e),** pernicious, injurious, baleful, baneful, deleterious, maleficient, perversive; pestiferous, pestilent(ial); ~ **likheid,** perniciousness, banefulness.

verder'we, (~) = **verderf,** (w).

verdien', (~), earn (living); deserve (praise); merit (reward); carry (interest); make money; *jou BROOD* ~, earn a living; *'n PAK slae* ~, deserve a caning.

verdien(d)', **(-de),** deserved; condign; *dis jou* ~ *de LOON,* that serves you right; ~ *de STRAF,* condign punishment.

verdien'ste, desert, merit; wages, earnings, gettings, emolument(s); profit; *BO* ~, beyond one's deserts; *iem. van GROOT* ~, a most deserving person; *NA* ~, according to one's deserts; for what one is worth; *SONDER* ~ *wees,* be without a living; have no saving grace; without merit.

verdien'stelik, (-e), meritorious, deserving; *jou* ~ *maak teenoor,* deserve well of; ~ **heid,** meritoriousness, merit.

verdien'vermoë, earning power.

verdiep', (~), (w) deepen; be absorbed; rout (carpentry); *in 'n BOEK* ~, absorbed in (the perusal of) a book; ~ *in GEDAGTE,* lost in thought; (b) deep; ~ **boor,** router bit; ~ **er, (-s),** router.

verdie'ping, (-e, -s), floor, stor(e)y; deepening; tier (cake); level (mining); *dit skort hom in die BOONSTE* ~, he is a little wrong in the upper stor(e)y; he is not all there; *EERSTE* ~, first floor; *ONDERSTE* ~, ground floor; ~ **huis,** double-stor(e)yed house; ~ **stok,** stor(e)y-rod, stor(e)y-post.

verdiep': ~ **skaaf,** plough-plane, old woman's tooth, routing plane; ~ **t'heid,** engrossment, absorption; ~ **werk,** routing.

verdier'lik, (w) (~), brutalize, debase, dehumanize, imbrute, bestialize; (b) **(-te),** brutalized, debased; ~ **ing,** brutalization, debasement.

verdiet', verdite.

verdiets', (~), Dutchify; ~ **ing,** Dutchification.

verdig'¹, (w) (~), invent, fable, fabricate; (b) **(-te),** fictitious, imaginary.

verdig'², (w) (~), compress, condense (steam); compact (soil); (b) **(-te),** compressed, condensed.

verdig'sel, (-s), fiction, fable, concoction, figment, fabrication.

verdig'ter, (-s), compressor.

verdig'ting¹, fiction, fable, figment (of the imagination).

verdig'ting², condensation, compression; compaction (soil).

verdig'tings: ~ **graad,** degree of compression; ~ **punt,** condensation.

verdik', (~), thicken, condense, coagulate, concentrate; inspissate; incrassate; ~ **baar, (..bare),** condensable; ~ **ker, (-s),** condenser; ~ **king,** thickening, condensation, coagulation, concentration; ~ **kingslaag,** thickening layer; ~ **middel,** thickening agent.

verdink', (~), suspect, distrust.

verdiskonteer', (~), discount, negotiate (bill); ~ **baar, (..bare),** negotiable; ~ **baarheid,** negotiability.

verdiskonteer(d)', (-de), discounted, negotiated; ~ *de waarde,* present value.

verdiskonte'ring, negotiation, discounting.

verdob'bel, (~), gamble away.

verdoem', (w) (~), reject, doom, curse, damn; condemn; (b), **(-de),** doomed, damned.

verdoe'meling, (-e), reprobate, damned creature.

verdoe'menis, doom, perdition, damnation; *na die* ~ *HELP,* send to damnation; *LEERSTUK van* ~, tenet of reprobation (perdition); *aan die ewige* ~ *PRYSGEE,* consign to eternal perdition.

verdoemenswaar'dig, (-e), damnable.

verdoe'ming, damning, damnation.

verdoem'lik, (-e), damnable; ~ **heid,** damnability.

verdoe'sel, (~), stump away; gloss over; ~ **ing,** glossing over.

verdof', (w) (~), dim; blur, tarnish; deaden (sound); fade (radio); (b) **(-te),** dimmed (lights); tarnished; ~ **fing,** dimming (light); deadening (sound); fading (radio); ~ **skakelaar,** dimmer switch.

verdold', (-e), infatuated, demented; ~ *wees op,* be completely infatuated with; ~ **heid,** infatuation.

verdom'¹, (~), make dull, stupefy.

verdom'², (~), damn; *ek* ~ *dit,* I am blowed if I'll do it; **(-de),** damned, blasted.

verdom'ming, stupefaction, brutalization.

verdomp'! dash it! damn it!

verdon'ker, (~), darken, obscure, gloom, (be)dim; becloud; ~ **ing,** black-out.

verdon'kermaan, (~), embezzle, alienate, defalcate; suppress; spirit away.

verdoof', (~) = **verdowe.**

verdool'(d), (-de), stray, astray, strayed; ~ **d'heid,** perversion.

verdoop', (~), rebaptize, rechristen, rename.

verdo'ping, rebaptism, renaming.

verdor', (w) (~), wither, parch, blast, shrivel up; (b) **(-de),** shrivelled up, parched, withered; ~ **d'heid,** withered (parched) condition; ~ **ring,** withering, parching, drying up.

verdor'we, depraved, corrupted; ~ **ne, (-s),** pervert, debauchee, rake; ~ **nheid,** depravity, depravation, corruptiveness, corruption, badness, perversion, perversity.

verdo'we, (~), stun, benumb, deafen, deaden; tarnish (silver); narcotize, drug, anaesthetize (med.); ease, allay (pain); ~ **nd, (-e),** stunning, benumbing; anaesthetic, narcotic (med.); opiate; ~ *nde middels GEBRUIK,* take drugs; *HANDEL in* ~ *nde middels,* drug traffic; ~ *nde MIDDEL,* drug.

verdo'wing, stupor, numbness, stupefaction, narcosis, anaesthesia.

verdo'wings: ~ **hok,** stunning-box (abatoirs); ~ **middel,** drug; narcotic, anaesthetic (med.).

verdow'wing = verdoffing.

verdra', (~), bear, endure, stand, tolerate, forbear, suffer (pain); *ek sal dit nie LANGER* ~ *nie,* I won't stand this any longer; *sulke MENSE kan ek nie* ~ *nie,* I cannot bear such people.

verdraag'lik, (-e), bearable, endurable, sufferable.

verdraag'saam, (..same), tolerant, patient, forbearing; broadminded; ~ **heid,** tolerance, patience, forbearance.

verdraai', (w) (~), twist (arm); distort, contort; pervert, misrepresent, misinterpret (words); (b) **(-de),** distorted, perverted; twisted; whorled; ~ **baar, (..bare),** pervertible; ~ **d'heid,** distortion; anfractuosity; ~ **er, (-s),** distorter, perverter; ~ **ing,** distortion; contortion; perversion, misrepresentation, misstatement.

ver'draend, (-e), long-range (gun); carrying (voice).

verdrag', (..drae), treaty, convention, concordat, cartel, compact, agreement, pact, covenant, accord, contract; *MET* ~, gradually; *'n* ~ *SLUIT,* enter upon a treaty; ~ **bepaling,** treaty provision; ~ **hawe,** treaty port; ~ **staat,** contracting power (country, state); ~ **verpligting,** treaty obligation.

verdrie'dubbel, (~), treble, triple; ~ **ing,** trebling.

verdriet', sorrow, grief, affliction, sadness, dolour; ~ *AANDOEN,* cause sorrow, grieve; *'n regte* ~ *op NOTE,* a real knight of the rueful countenance; a mournful soul; *TOT my* ~, to my sorrow.

verdrie'tig, (-e), sad, grievous, sorrowful; ~ **heid,** sadness, sorrow, distress.

verdriet'lik, (-e), vexatious, irksome; ~ **heid,** vexation, irksomeness.

verdrie'voudig, (~), treble, triple, triplicate; ~ **ing,** triplication.

verdring', (~), push aside; jostle; supplant; oust, crowd out; ~ **er, (-s),** supplanter; ~ **ing,** pushing aside, jostling aside; elimination, ousting, supplanting.

verdrin'gingsmetode, method of elimination.

verdrink', (~), drown, be drowned; drink away, waste on drink; *'n ~ te HOND*, a drowned dog; *sy VERDRIET ~*, drown his sorrows (in drink); ~**ing**, drowning.
verdro'ë, (~), dry up, wither, parch.
verdro'ging, drying up.
verdron'ke, drowned; *die kalf is ~*, it is too late.
verdro(og)', (w) = **verdroë**.
verdroog', (b) (-de), dried up, withered, parched, desiccated.
verdroom', (~), dream away.
verdruk', (w) (~), oppress; *mekaar ~*, jostle each other; (b) (-te), oppressed; ~**kend**, oppressive; ~**ker**, oppressor, tyrant; ~**king**, (-e, -s), oppression; *teen die ~king in groei*, flourish under oppression.
verdryf', **verdry'we**, (~), drive away, expel, banish, chase away; dislodge; while away, pass (time); dissipate (fear); eliminate (alg.).
verdry'wend, (-e), expulsive.
verdry'wing, expulsion, chasing away, dislodgment; whiling away (time); extrusion.
verdub'bel, (~), double, duplicate (quantity); reduplicate, redouble, ~**end**, (-e), reduplicative; ~**ing**, doubling, duplication; reduplication, redoubling; twinning (geol.).
verdui'delik, (~), elucidate, explain; ~**ing**, (-e, -s), elucidation, explanation, amplification, explication.
verdui'kels, confounded.
verdui'sendvoudig, (~), multiply a thousand times.
verduis'ter, (~), eclipse (sun); darken, obscure, becloud, (be)dim, befog, blur, blear, obfuscate (the mind); embezzle, convert (money); peculate, defalcate; ~**aar**, (-s), peculator, embezzler; ~**ing**, (-e, -s), eclipse, obscuration, obfuscation; conversion, embezzlement, defalcation, peculation; ~**ingspapier**, black-out paper; ~**ingsvoorskrifte**, black-out regulations.
verduits', (~), Germanize; become Germanized; ~**ing**, Germanization.
verdui'weld, (-e), confounded, damned, accursed, deuced, darned, bally.
verdui'wels, damn(ed), darned; by George! plaguy; ~**gou**, darned quick(ly).
verdun', (w) (~), thin, attenuate; adulterate; dilute (milk); reduce; rarefy (gas); (b) (-de), adulterated; diluted; ~**nend**, (-e), diluent; ~**ner**, diluent; ~**ning**, thinning, dilution (of liquids); attenuation (of thickness); rarefaction (of air); ~**ningsgraad**, degree of liquifaction; ~**ningskamer**, liquifaction chamber; ~**ningsmiddel**, diluting agent, diluent.
verdu'ring, endurance, enduring.
verdut', (~), pass time sleeping, doze (time) away.
verduur', (~), bear, suffer, endure, put up with; *swaar slae ~*, suffer heavy blows.
verduur'saam, (~), cure (meat); preserve, can; *~ de lewensmiddels*, tinned foods.
verduur'saming, preservation, canning.
verduur'samingsmiddel, preservative.
verdwaal', (w) (~), go astray, lose the way, get lost; (b) (-de), lost, (a)stray, strayed; devious; *~ de KOEËL*, stray bullet; *~ WEES*, have lost one's way; ~**d'heid**, state of being lost.
verdwaas', (w) (~), render foolish; infatuate; (b) (-de), infatuated; stupefied; ~**d'heid**, infatuation.
verdwa'sing, infatuation, stultification.
verdwe'ne, vanished.
verdwerg', (w) miniaturize; dwarf; ~**ing**, miniaturization; dwarfing.
verdwyn' (~), disappear, vanish, fade away; evanish, evanesce, dwindle; go; *LAAT ~*, spirit away; *alle VREES laat ~*, dispel all fear(s); ~**end**, (-e), evanescent.
verdwyn'ing, disappearing, disappearance, (e)vanishment, evanescence; extinction; fading (sound).
verdwyn': ~**pleister**, sticking-plaster (supposed to make boils vanish), *emplastrum plumbi*; ~**punt**, vanishing-point.
ve're: ~**bed**, feather bed; ~**beskrywing**, pterylography.
vere'del, (~), ennoble; refine; humanize; elevate; im-

prove, grade up (cattle); rarefy; *'n ~ de smaak*, a refined taste; ~**ing**, ennoblement, refinement; elevation; (a)melioration; improvement, grading up (cattle); beneficiation (minerals).
vere'delings: ~**bedryf**, finishing industry; ~**proses**, finishing process; process of refinement.
ve'redraend, (-e), penniferous, pennigerous.
vereelt', (w) (~), make callous; become horny; (b) (-e), callous; horny; ~**heid**, callosity; ~**ing**, callus.
vereen'saam, (~), become lonely.
vereen'saming, loneliness.
vereensel'wig, (~), associate; identify (with); ~**ing**, identification; assimilation.
vereenvou'dig, (~), simplify; reduce (fraction); ~**ing**, simplification; reduction.
vereer', (~), honour, respect, venerate, dignify, grace; idolize; adore, worship, revere; ~**der**, (-s), worshipper, admirer, adorer; idolizer.
vereers', for the time being; to begin with, in the first place; *~ nog nie*, not as yet.
vereer'ster, (-s), female admirer; idolatress.
veref'fen, (~), pay (account), settle; even (up), liquidate, wind up (company); adjust, balance, square (business deal); ~**aar**, compounder; liquidator, administrator; ~**ing**, settlement; adjustment; liquidation; *ter ~ ing van*, in settlement of; ~**ingsfonds**, equalization fund; ~**ingsgeld**, adjustment fee; ~**ingskoste**, expense of liquidation.
vereis', (~), require, call for, demand; *die ~ te bedrag*, the necessary amount.
vereis'te, (-s), exigency, desideration, desideratum, requirement, requisite; accessory; qualification, precondition; *'n EERSTE ~*, a prime requisite; *aan alle ~s VOLDOEN*, satisfy all the requirements; *WETLIKE ~*, legal requirements.
ve'rend, (-e), shock-absorbing; elastic, resilient.
vereng', (w) (~), narrow; (b) (-de), narrowed.
veren'gels, (w) (~), Anglicize; become Anglicized; (b), (-te), Anglicised; ~**ing**, Anglicizing process, Anglicization.
veren'ging, narrowing; stricture.
vere'nig, (w) (~), unite; reconcile (opinions); merge, compound, band (together), combine, coalesce, fuse (companies); federate, federalize (states); incorporate (in one body); join (together); *ek kan dit nie met my BEGINSELS ~ nie*, I cannot reconcile this with my principles; (b) (-de), united; federated; connected; combined; conjuctive; associated; *V ~ de State van AMERIKA*, United States of America; *V ~ de KERK*, Dutch Reformed Church; *V ~ de KONINKRYK*, United Kingdom; *V ~ de NASIES*, United Nations; *V ~ de PARTY*, United party; *V ~ de VOLKE(-ORGANISASIE)*, United Nations (Organization); ~**baar**, (..**bare**), unifiable, compatible; consistent; combinable; reconcilable; ~**baarheid**, compatibility, consonance.
vere'niging, (-e, -s), union, joining, junction; association, combine; coalition, coalescence; fraternity, club, g(u)ild, society; combination, conjunction; consolidation.
vere'nigings: ~**jaar**, official year; ~**lewe**, social life; ~**lyn**, commissure; ~**punt**, joint, juncture, point of junction; ~**reg**, right of association.
vererd', (~), enamel; ~**ing**, enamelling.
vere'rend, (-e), flattering; *graag voldoen ek aan u ~ e versoek*, I have much pleasure in acceding to your kind request.
vererf', (~), descend (by inheritance).
vererg', (w) (~), annoy, vex, displease, anger, offend, provoke, make angry; grow angry; *ek ~ my vir hom*, he annoys me; (b) (-de), angry, annoyed.
verergd'heid, vexation, annoyance.
verer'ger, (~), grow worse, worsen, aggravate; deteriorate; ~**end**, (-e), exacerbating, worsening, ingravescent; ~**ing**, aggravation, exacerbation, change for the worse, deterioration; recrudescence.
vererts', (~), mineralize; ~**ing**, mineralization.
verer'wing, descent (by inheritance).
ve'resloop, slip, case (for feathers).
veres'ter, esterize; ~**ing**, esterization.
ve'restoffer, feather duster.
vere'ter, (~), etherify; ~**ing**, etherification.

veretter 578 *vergelyking*

veret'ter, (~), suppurate, fester; ~ing, suppuration, festering.
vereuropees', (~), Europeanize; become Europeanized; (b) (-te), Europeanized; ..pesing, Europeanization.
ve'rewa = veerwa.
vere'wig, (~), immortalize, eternalize; perpetuate; ~ing, immortalization; perpetuation.
verf, (s) (verwe), paint; dye, stain; colour; (w) (ge-), paint; dye; rouge (face); coat (with paint); *ge ~ de goed*, painted articles; ~aarde, dyer's earth; ~bad, dye-bath; ~bord, palette; ~doos, box of paints, paint-box, colour-box; ~fabriek, paint factory; dye factory; ~goud, ormolu; ~handel, oil-and-colour business; ~handelaar, paint-dealer, colourman; ~hout, dye-wood.
verfilm', (~), screen, film; ~ing, filming; film version.
verf: ~koper, colour-man; ~kuip, dyeing-tub; ~kwas, paint-brush; ~laag, coat of paint, couch; ~lap, paint-rag.
verflens', (w) (~), wither, fade; (b) (-te), withered, faded.
verflen'ter, (w) (~), tear; become torn; (b) (-de), in rags, torn, tattered, ragged.
verflou', (~), become faint (of sound); abate, slacken, flag (interest); weaken (energy); dull; cool down; ~ing, abatement, flagging, slackening; weakening.
verf: ~lug, smell of paint; ~merk, paint mark.
verfoei', (~), abhor, detest, loathe, execrate, despise, abominate; ~er, (-s), despiser; ~ing, abhorrence, detestation, loathing, abomination, execration; ~lik, (-e), abominable, detestable, loathsome, despicable, ececrable, abhorrent, accursed, foul, heinous, odious; ~likheid, detestableness, abominableness, loathsomeness; ~sel, abomination.
verfoe'lie, (~), quicksilver, tin foil; ~sel, foil, leaf metal.
verfoes', (w) (~), spoil, bungle, muddle; *iem. het die hele ding ~*, someone has spoilt (bungled, made a hash of) the whole affair; (b) (-de), muddled, bungled, dishevelled.
verfom'faai, (w) (~), crumple, rumple, tousle, dishevel; spoil; (b) (-de), crumpled, rumpled, tousled, dishevelled; spoilt.
verf'poeier, dry paint, paint powder.
verf'pot, paint pot.
verfraai', (~), embellish, beautify, enrich, adorn; decorate; aggrandize; gild; ~er, (-s), beautifier, embellisher; ~ing, (-e, -s), embellishment, decoration, adornment; aggrandizement.
verfrans,' (~), Frenchify, Gallicize; become Gallicized; ~ing, Frenchification.
verf'reuk = verflug.
verfris', (w) (~), refresh; rally; (b) (-te), refreshed; ~send, (-e), refreshing; ~sing, (-e, -s), refreshment.
verfrom'mel, (~), crumple, crush, rumple, tousle.
verfron'sel, (~), crumple, crush, rumple.
verf: ~spatsel, paint-spot; ~spuit, paint-spray(er); ~stof, paints, colours, dyes, dye-stuff, pigment, grain; ~ware, oils and colours, dyes.
verf'werk, paint-work; ~plaas, ~plek, painter's shop, paint-shop.
verfyn', (w) (~), refine, civilize; polish (manners); calcine; rarefy; (b) (-de), refined; elegant, polite.
verfynd'heid, refinement.
verfyn': ~er, refiner; ~ing, refinement, polish.
verg, (ge-), require, exact, demand; *te veel ~*, ask too much.
vergaan', (s) loss, destruction, wreck (of ship); decay (of beauty); passing away; (w) (~), perish; decay, rot, be wrecked, founder (ship); pass away; *van KOU ~*, die of cold; *~ van HOOGMOED*, eaten up with pride; *MOOI ~, maar deug bly staan*, beauty is but skin-deep; (b) (..gane), perished (rubber); decayed, decomposed; wrecked.
ver'gaande = ver'regaande.
vergaap', (~): *JOU ~*, dislocate one's jaw bone by yawning; *JOU ~ aan*, be amazed at.
vergaar', (~), collect, gather, lay up, hoard, amass (money); ~bak, receptacle; cistern, tank, catch-pit; ~der, (-s), gatherer; ~teken, notch (tailor).
verga'der, (~), meet, gather, collect, assemble, congregate, foregather; ~ing, (-e, -s), meeting, gathering, conclave, congress, congregation, assembly; *'n ~ing BELÊ*, call (convene) a meeting; *HUISHOU= DELIKE ~ing*, private meeting; *OPENBARE ~ing*, public meeting; ~plek, rendezvous, rallying point, meeting-place, venue; ~saal, meetingroom, assembly hall.
vergal', (~), embitter (someone's life); gall, envenom; spoil, mar (sport); poison (mind).
vergal'ling, embitterment.
vergaloppeer', (gew.), let one's tongue run away with one; say the wrong thing; commit oneself; *jou ~*, let one's tongue outrun one's discretion.
vergal'ste, confounded, damned.
verga'ne, decomposed, perished, rotten; stranded, wrecked (ship); *~ rubber*, perished rubber.
vergan'ge, (s): *in ~ se DAE*, in bygone days; (b) late, bygone; (bw) lately, lastly; the other day; past; *ek het hom ~ RAAK geloop*, I ran across him recently.
vergank'lik, (-e), transitory, fugitive, perishable, corruptible, evanescent, transient, mortal, fleeting; ~heid, transitoriness, evanescence, frailness, instability.
vergas'¹, (~), treat, regale; *~ op musiek*, regale with a musical treat.
vergas'², (~), gasify, vaporize; ~ser, (-s), carburettor; vaporizer; ~sernaald, caburettor needle; ~serprop, carburettor plug; ~sing, vaporization; gasification; carburation.
vergeef', (~) = vergewe.
vergeef'lik, (-e), pardonable, excusable, venial, forgivable; ~heid, pardonableness, veniality.
vergeefs', (b) (-e), futile, idle, useless, vain, fruitless, unavailing; *~e MOEITE*, vain effort; *'n ~e PO= GING*, an abortive attempt; (bw) in vain, vainly; *alles was ~*, everything was in vain; ~heid, futility, fruitlessness.
vergeel', (~), (become) yellow; *~ de blare*, yellowed leaves.
vergees'telik, (~), etheralize, spiritualize; dematerialize; ~ing, spiritualization; apotheosis, sublimation.
vergeet,' (w) (~), forget, overlook, omit; *ons kan die ding maar ~*, we can forget about it; *ek het SKOON ~*, I quite forgot; (bw): *ek is al klaar ~*, I have finished I don't know how long ago.
vergeet'agtig, (-e), forgetful; oblivious; ~heid, forgetfulness.
vergeet'al, (-le), forgetful person.
vergeet'boek, book of oblivion; *in die ~ raak*, sink into oblivion; be pigeonholed.
vergeet'lik, (-e), forgetable.
vergeet'-my-nietjie, (-s), forget-me-not *(Myosotis)*.
vergeld', (~), requite, reward, recompense; quit; reciprocate; repay, retaliate, pay out; *kwaad met kwaad ~*, render evil for evil; ~er, (-s), avenger.
vergel'ding, requital, return, retaliation, reprisal; reciprocation; recompense; payment; amends; guerdon; *die dag van ~*, the day of reckoning.
vergel'dingsmaatreël, retaliatory measure.
ver'geleë, vergele'ë, remote.
vergele'ke, compared; *~ BY*, compared to; *~ MET*, in comparison with; compared with.
verge'ling, yellowing.
vergelyk', (s) (-e), compromise, arrangement, agreement; *tot 'n ~ KOM*, come to an agreement; *'n ~ SOEK*, seek a compromise; *'n ~ TREF*, negotiate a compromise, arrive at an agreement; (w) (~), compare, check; listen to; confer; confront; *~ met*, compare with; ~baar, (..bare), comparable, comparative; ~baarheid, commensurability.
vergely'kend, (-e), comparative; competitive (examination); *~e taalkunde*, comparative philology; ~erwys(e), comparatively, by comparison.
vergely'ker, (-s), comparer; collator.
vergely'king, (-e, -s), comparison; compare; admeasurement; simile; equation; checking, verification, collation; reconciliation; *BY ~*, in comparison; *die verder DEURTREK*, carry the parallel further; *die*

~ *GAAN nie op nie,* the analogy is at fault; there is no comparison; *'n* ~ *GEBRUIK,* make use of a simile; *daar is GEEN* ~ *moontlik nie,* there is no possible comparison; *'n* ~ *MAAK tussen,* draw a comparison (parallel) between; *in* ~ *MET,* by comparison, in comparison with; ~ *van die TWEEDE graad,* quadratic equation.
vergely'kingsnorm, standard of comparison.
vergely'kingstaat, comparative statement (return).
vergely'kingsweerstand, standard resistance.
vergemak'lik, (~), facilitate, make easier; ease; ~**ing,** facilitation, easing.
vergenoeg', (w) (~), satisfy, content; (b) **(-de),** contented, satisfied; ~**d'heid,** contentment, contentedness, satisfaction.
vergesel', (~), accompany, escort, attend; consort; ~ *DEUR,* attended by; ~ *VAN sy vrou,* accompanied by his wife; ~**lend, (-e),** attendant; concomitant; ~**ling,** accompaniment.
ver'gesig, (-te), view, prospect, vista, perspective.
ver'gesog, vergesog', (-te), far-sought, farfetched.
ver'gesogtheid, vergesogt'heid, farfetchedness.
vergestalt', (~), embody, figure (forth); ~**ing,** figuring forth.
verge'telheid, oblivion; *aan die* ~ *ONTRUK,* save from oblivion; *aan die* ~ *PRYSGEE,* let fall into oblivion; *in die* ~ *RAAK,* sink (fall) into oblivion.
verge'telheidsdrank, nepenthe.
verge'terig, forgetful, absent-minded; ~**heid,** forgetfulness.
ver'gevorder(d), (-de), well-advanced; late; ~**d'heid,** lateness (night); ripeness (age).
verge'we¹, (w) (~), poison; ~ *van,* be teeming (infested) with (fleas).
verge'we², (w) (~), forgive, pardon, absolve; condone; ~ *en vergeet,* forgive and forget.
verge'wensgesind, (-e), forgiving; ~**heid,** forgivingness, willingness to forgive; placability.
verge'wing, pardon, forgiveness, remission; ~ *SKENK,* (grant) pardon, forgive; ~ *van SONDES,* remission of sins.
vergewis' (~), ascertain, make sure of; ~**sing,** ascertainment.
vergiet¹, (s) (Ndl.), strainer, drainer, colander.
vergiet'², (w) (~), shed (tears).
vergiet'bak, (Ndl.), colander.
vergiet': ~**er,** shedder (of blood); ~**ing,** shedding, effusion.
vergiet'tes, (Ndl.) **(-se),** strainer, colander.
vergif', (-te, .. **giwwe),** poison, venom, bane; ~**boom,** poison oak; poison ivy.
vergif'nis, pardon, forgiveness, indulgence, absolution; condonation; amnesty; grace; ~ *SKENK,* grant pardon; *om* ~ *SMEEK,* plead for forgiveness; ~ *van SONDES,* remission of sins; ~ *VRA,* ask for pardon.
vergif', ~**plant,** poisonous plant; ~**stof,** virus; toxin; ~**teleer,** toxicology.
vergif'tig, (~), poison, envenom, embitter; ~**er, (-s),** poisoner, ~**ing,** poisoning.
vergif'ting = **vergiftiging.**
vergif'tigings; ~**geval,** poisoning case; ~**proses,** process of poisoning; ~**verskynsel,** symptom of poisoning.
Vergiliaans', (-e), Virgilian.
Vergi'lius, Virgil.
vergis', (~), mistake; *JOU* ~, be mistaken; *jou in iem,* ~, form a wrong opinion of someone, *SY* ~ *haar,* she is mistaken.
vergis'sing, (-e, -s), mistake, error, slip, lapse, erratum, oversight; *'n* ~ *BEGAAN,* make a mistake; *BY* ~, inadvertently; *'n* ~ *HERSTEL,* rectify a mistake, ~**sein,** error signal.
verglaas' (w) (~), glaze, glass (over); vitrify, enamel; *sy oë het* ~, his eyes (were) glazed (in death); (b) **(-de),** glazed; vitrified; ~**oond,** glaze-kiln, glazing-furnace; ~**sel,** glaze, glazing; enamel, vitrification.
verglans', (w) (~), gloss, glaze; (b) **(-de),** glazed, glossy.
vergla'ser, (-s), glazier, enameller, glazer.
vergla'sing, glazing, vitrification, vitrescence.
verglet'ser, (~), glaciate; ~**ing,** glaciation.

vergly', (~), glide away, slip.
vergod'delik, (~), deify; ~**ing,** deification.
vergo'der, (-s), deifier.
vergo'ding, deification, idolatry, apotheosis.
vergoed', (~), repay, make good (loss); defray, compensate, pay, indemnify, reimburse, refund (costs); redeem; redress; recoup, make amends; gratify; make up for, balance; *skade* ~, compensate; ~**end, (-e),** compensative; ~**er, (-s),** compensator.
vergoe'ding, compensation, indemnity, indemnification, reimbursement; amends, redress, recoupment, consideration; atonement; gratification; fee; ~**spakket,** remuneration package.
vergoei'lik, vergoe'lik, (~), excuse (behaviour); palliate, gloss over, extenuate (conduct); ~**ing,** palliation, glossing over, extenuation; *ter* ~**ing,** in extenuation.
vergooi', (~), throw away; *JOU* ~, demean oneself; *sy KANSE* ~, throw away one's chances.
vergo'te, shed, spilt; ~ *bloed,* shed (spilt) blood.
vergramd', (-e), angry, wrathful; ~**heid,** anger, wrath.
vergrieks', (~), Hellenize, Graecize; ~**ing,** Hellenization.
vergroei', (w) (~), outgrow; grow crooked; grow into one; ~**d',** (b) **(-e),** gnarled, intergrown; coalescent (biol.); ~ *de tong,* tongue-tie; ~**d'heid,** gnarledness; ~**ing, (-e, -s),** intergrowth; growing out of shape; coalescence.
vergrof', (w) (~), coarsen; **(-de),** coarsened.
vergroot', (~), enlarge (portrait); extend, increase, augment (influence); magnify, exaggerate (one's exploits); amplify (sound); *vergrotende trap,* comparative degree; ~**glas,** magnifying glass; *deur 'n* ~ *glas kyk,* see things larger than life.
vergro'ter, (-s), enlarger; magnifier, amplifier.
vergro'ting, (-e, -s), enlargement, increase, augmentation, exaggeration; amplification; ~ *van organe,* enlargement of organs, hypertrophy.
vergro'tingstoestel, enlarging apparatus.
vergro'tingsvermoë, magnifying power.
vergrow'wing, coarsening.
vergruis', (w) (~), pound, crush, pulverize, grind, shatter, comminute; (b) **(-de),** crushed, pulverised, shattered.
vergrui'sing, pulverization, crushing, comminution.
vergryp', (s) **(-e),** transgression (of law); offence, misdemeanour, infringement, outrage, misdeed, delict; (w) (~), commit an offence, infringe, outrage, violate (law); *jou aan IEM.* ~, do violence to someone; *jou aan IETS* ~, lay one's hands on something; filch something.
vergrys', (w) (~), become grey; (b) **(-de),** grown grey.
verguis', (w) (~), revile, libel, abuse; (b) **(-de),** reviled, abused.
vergui'sing, abuse, revilement, libel.
verguld', (w) (~), gild, gold-plate; (b) **(-e),** golden; ~ *de BRONS,* ormolu; ~ *e LYS,* gilt frame; ~ *op SNEE,* gilt-edged (pages).
vergul'der, (s), gilder; gold-plater.
vergul'ders: ~**mes,** gilder's knife; ~**penseel,** gilding tip.
vergul'ding, gilding.
verguld'pers, gilding press.
verguld'sel, (-s), gilding, gilt.
vergun', (~), allow, permit, accord, grant (privilege); license; ~**baar,** (..**bare),** grantable, permissible.
vergun'ning, (-e, -s), permission, allowance, concession, grant, licence, leave; *MET* ~, with (having) permission; licensed; *SONDER* ~, without permission.
verhaal'¹, (s) (..**hale),** story, account, fable, recital, narrative; *ouwyfse verhale,* old wives' tales; (w) (~), narrate, tell, relate; recount.
verhaal², (s) recourse; remedy; redress; *daar is GEEN* ~ *op nie,* there is no recourse; *iets op IEM.* ~, recover something from someone; *tot* ~ *KOM,* recover strength; *SONDER* ~, without redress.
verhaal': ~**baar** (..**bare),** recoverable; ~**kuns,** narrative art, fiction; ~**reg,** right of recovery; ~**op,** right of recovery (remedy, recourse) against; ~**trant,** narrative style.
verhaar', (~), lose hair; change coat (animal).

verhaas', (~), accelerate, precipitate (crisis); hasten, expedite (measure); forward; advance (plan); ~**ting**, acceleration, precipitation, hastening.
verha'lend, (-e), narrative, epic; ~**erwys(e)**, in the form of a story, narratively.
verha'ler, (-s), narrator.
verhalf'sool, (~), half-sole.
verhan'del, (~), discuss, debate (subject); barter, deal, transact; negotiate (bill); ~**aar, (-s)**, essayist; transactor; negotiator; ~**baar, (..bare)**, negotiable, saleable; expendable; ~**ing, (-e, -s)**, essay, treatise; transaction, settlement; act, disquisition; negotiation; dissertation.
verhang', (~), hang differently, rehang.
verhard', (w) (~), (case-)harden; make callous; set (cement); petrify; cauterize (fig.); *jou hart ~*, harden one's heart; (b) **(-e)**, hardened; obdurate; callous; *'n pad met 'n ~ e blad*, a road with a metalled surface; ~**er, (-s)**, hardener; ~**heid**, hardness, obduracy, callousness.
verhar'ding, hardening; setting; obduration; concretion; callosity; sclerosis (of tissue).
verhar'dingsmiddel, (-s), hardening agent.
verha'ring, changing of hair, losing the hair.
verhas'pel, (~), bungle, botch, make a mess of; garble, spell wrongly; pronounce incorrectly; ~**ing**, spoiling, botching, bungling; misspelling; mispronunciation.
verheel', (ong.) (~), conceal, hide; dissemble.
verheer'lik, (~), glorify; aggrandize; celebrate; extol, praise, dignify; deify; emblazon; ~**er, (-s)**, extoller; ~**ing**, glorification; aggrandizement; apotheosis; celebration; extolment, magnification.
verhef', (~), raise, elevate; lift up (heart); pride oneself; dignify; glorify; exalt; elate; extol; prefer; *tot die ADELSTAND ~*, raise to the peerage; *hy ~ hom op sy RYKDOM*, he prides himself on his wealth; *jou STEM ~*, raise your voice, speak more loudly; *jou stem ~ TEEN*, raise your voice (protest) against; *op die TROON ~*, raise to the throne; ~**fend, (-e)**, edifying, ennobling, elevating; ~**fer**, elevator; ~**fing**, elevation, exaltation; raising; elation; glorification, promotion.
ver'heid, distance, remoteness.
verhei'den, (~), heathenize, paganize; ~**ing**, heathenization.
verheim'lik, (~), conceal, keep secret, secrete; ~**ing**, concealment, secretion.
verhel'der, (~), brighten, light up (face); clear up (weather); clarify (liquids); elucidate; enlighten; fix (photo); ~**end, (-e)**, illuminating, ~**ing**, brightening, clarification, elucidation.
verhe'ler, (ong.) (-s), concealer.
verhe'ling, concealment.
verhelp', (~), remedy, redress, rectify, help; *die KWAAD ~*, remedy the evil; *nie MEER te ~ nie*, be past mending; nothing can be done about it; *die TOESTAND ~*, meet the situation; ~**ing**, redress, remedy, recourse, rectification.
verhe'melte, (-s), palate; canopy (bed); *harde (sagte) ~*, hard (soft) palate; ~**klank**, palatal sound; ~**letter**, palatal (letter); ~**ring**, gum-ring.
verheug', (w) (~), rejoice, please, delight, gratify, gladden; enjoy; *ek ~ my OOR (in) jou sukses*, I rejoice with you in your success; I rejoice at your success; *'n ~ ende TEKEN*, a gratifying sign; (b) **(-de)**, delighted, pleased, glad; joyful; *die ~ de skare*, the cheering crowd.
verheu'genis joy.
verheu'ging, joy, rejoicing, gladness, exultation.
verhe'we, raised; exalted, sublime, august, dignified, high, grand, majestic, magnificent, high and mighty, lofty; high-pitched; embossed (letters); swollen; elevated; *bo ONEERLIKHEID ~ wees*, be above dishonesty; *op 'n ~ PLEK*, on a raised spot; *hy ag hom ~ bo sulke WERK*, he considers himself too high and mighty for such work.
verhe'wenheid, elevation (ground); embossment; grandness, exaltedness, augustness, majesty, eminence, loftiness, sublimity; prominence.
verhe'wig, (~), intensify, aggravate; ~**ing**, intensification.

verhin'der, (~), prevent, debar, hinder, preclude; obstruct; forbid; *EK is ~*, I have been held up; *net SIEKTE sal hom ~ om te kom*, only illness will prevent him from coming; ~**end, (-e)**, preventative, preventive, preclusive; ~**ing**, hindering, hindrance, prevention, obstacle, obstruction.
verhipotekeer', (ong.) (~), mortgage.
verhit', (w) (~), heat; fire, inflame (with desire), excite; (b) **(-te)**, heated, hot, aglow; blowzed, blowzy; flushed; *'n ~ te verbeelding*, an inflamed imagination; ~**ting**, heat(ing); calefaction; ~**tingsvermoë**, heating power; ~**tingsvlak**, heating surface.
verhoed', (~), prevent, ward off, forfend; *God ~ e, mag God dit ~*, God forbid! ~**ing**, prevention, preventing.
verho'ging, (-e, -s), elevation; promotion (post); increment, increase, augmentation (salary); preferment; enhancement; intensification (heat); loading; rise (salary).
verho'gingstransformator, step-up transformer.
verho'le, (vero.), hidden, secret, clandestine; ~ *bedoelinge*, secret aims; *cf.* **verheel**.
verhol'lands, (w) (~), Dutchify; become Dutchified; (b) **(-te)**, Dutchified; ~**ing**, Dutchification.
verhol'pe, remedied; vgl. **verhelp**.
verhon'derdvoudig, (~), multiply by a hundred, centuple.
verhon'ger, (~), famish, starve, die of hunger; *laat ~*, starve; ~**ing**, starvation, starving.
verhoog', (s) (..hoë), stage (theatre); platform, estrade, dais; podium; pedestal; (w) **(~)**, raise, heighten; increase (salary); elevate, advance, promote (in post); enhance (qualities); intensify (light); step up; praise, extol; enrich (colour); aggrandize; add to (beauty); *sy BOD ~*, raise his bid; *KRUIE ~ die smaak*, spices enhance the flavour; ~ **MET**, increase by; *in PRYS ~*, advance in price; *in RANG ~*, promote (in rank, status); ~ **TOT**, increase to; *WIE homself ~*, *sal verneder word*, whoever makes himself great will be humbled; (b) **(-de)**, increased; enriched; exalted; intensified; ~**baar (..bare)**, raisable; ~**bestuurder**, stage manager; ~**direkteur**, stage director; ~**kuns**, show business, art of entertaining; ~**kunstenaar**, actor, entertainer (on platform); ~**meisie**, ~**pop**, show-girl; ~**stuk**, stage play; concert; ~**vrees**, stage fever, stage fright.
verhoor', (s) (verhore), hearing, trial, examination; *in ~ NEEM*, interrogate, cross-question; ~ *ONDERGAAN*, be tried; undergo an examination; (w) **(~)**, hear, answer (prayer); try (prisoner); interrogate, examine; ~**afwagtend, (-e)**, awaiting trial; ~**de, (-s)**, person on trial; ~**der**, answerer (of prayer).
verhoorn', (ong.) (~), keratinize; ~**ing**, keratinization.
verho'ring¹, (s) hearing, favourable response, answer (to prayer).
verho'ring², (s) keratiasis; (w) **(~)**, keratinize, become horny.
verhou'ding, (-e, -s), relation; proportion, ratio; (love-) affair; *BUITE ~ hoog*, disproportionately high; *GESPANNE ~*, strained relations; *IN ~ met*, in proportion to; *NA ~*, in proportion, comparatively speaking; *SY ~ tot*, his relationship with; *in ~ TOT*, in proportion to.
verhou'dingsgetal, ratio.
verhou'dingskaal, proportional scale.
verhou'dingspasser, proportional compasses.
verhout', (w) (~), lignify; become woody; (b) **(-e)**, lignified; ~**ing**, lignification.
verhovaar'dig, (~): *hom ~ op*, boast of; take great pride in.
verhuis', (~), move, change lodgings; die, pass away; emigrate (to another country); migrate (birds); ~**dag**, moving day; ~**er, (-s)**, migrant; ~**ing, (-e, -s)**, removal; moving; migration; emigration; flitting; ~**ingskontrakteur**, removal contractor; ~**ingskoste**, removal expenses, expenses (in connection with moving from one house to another); ~**ingswa**, furniture van, removal van, pantechnicon (van).

verhul', (~), conceal, keep secret; ~ *de motiewe*, veiled motives; ~**ling**, veiling; concealment.
verhu'ring, letting, hiring out; leasing.
verhuur', (~), let (house); hire out (animals); lease (farm); *jou* ~, take service with, hire oneself out; ~**baar**, (..**bare**), rentable; lettable; leasable; ~**der**, (-s), landlord; letter, lessor; ~**kantoor**, registry office, employment bureau; ~**voorwaardes**, terms of lease.
verifieer', (ge-), verify; audit; examine (document); prove; adjust (compass); ~**baar**, (..**bare**), verifiable.
verifiëring = **verifikasie**.
verifika'sie, verification; check; audit; ~**vergadering**, first meeting of creditors.
ve'ring, (-e, -s), spring action, springing, suspension; elasticity; ~**koppeling**, suspension joint; ~**stelsel**, suspension system.
verin'nerlik, (~), deepen, intensify, spiritualize; ~**ing**, deepening, spiritualization.
verin'nig, (~), intensify.
veris'me, verism.
veritaliaans', (w) (~), Italianize; (b) (-te), Italianate.
verja(ag)', (~), drive away, chase away, scare away; dislodge (enemy); disperse, dispel (worries).
verjaar¹, (~), celebrate one's birthday; enjoy oneself, revel in, be riotously festive; *OUPA* ~ *môre*, it is grandpa's birthday tomorrow; *die kleingoed* ~ *onder die VRUGTE*, the children are feasting on the fruit.
verjaar², (~), become prescriptive, superannuated; ~ *de SKULD*, prescribed debt; ~ *de TJEK*, stale cheque; ~ *de VONNIS*, superannuated judgement.
verjaar(s)dag, birthday; ~**boekie**, birthday book; ~**fees**, birthday feast; ~**geskenk**, birthday present; ~**maal**, birthday dinner; ~**party**, birthday party; ~**present**, birthday present.
verja'ging, chasing away, driving away, dispelling.
verja'ring¹, anniversary.
verja'ring², superannuation; prescription (of debt); extinction (of rights).
verja'ringsfees, birthday feast; anniversary.
verja'rings: ~**reg**, statute of limitations; law of prescription; ~**termyn**, term of limitation (superannuation); prescriptive period.
verjong', (~), rejuvenate, make young again; ~**ing**, rejuvenation; rejuvenescence; ~**ingskuur**, rejuvenating cure.
verjoods' (w) (~), Judaize; (b) (-te), Judaized; ~**ing**, Judaization.
verkaas', (~), turn into cheese.
verkalk', (~), calcify, calcine; ~ *te are*, calcified arteries.
verkal'king, calcification; ~ *van die are*, arteriosclerosis.
verkan'ker, (~), canker; ~**ing**, cancer formation.
verkap', (w) (~), cut up; (b) (-te), disguised, veiled; *'n* ~ *te dreigement*, a veiled threat; ~**ping**, abat(t)is.
verkas', (~), depart; shift; remove; run away.
verka'sing, caseation; tyrosis (med.).
verkas'sing, departure.
verkeer', (s) traffic; commerce; (inter)communion; dealing; communication; intercourse; *DEURGAANDE* ~, through traffic; *HUISLIKE* ~, home life; ~ *op STRAAT*, street traffic; (w) (~), have intercourse (keep company) with; be in (with, at); labour (under); *waar jy mee* ~, *word jy mee GEËER*, one is judged by the company one keeps; *aan die HOF* ~, move in court circles; *dit KAN* ~, luck may turn; things may change; ~ *MET*, associate with; *in WELSTAND* ~, be in good health.
verkeerd', (-e), wrong, incorrect; inaccurate, mistaken, erroneous; unreasonable; amiss; contrariwise; improper; perverse, perverted, evil; anamorphous (of crystals); ~ *AANHAAL*, misquote; ~ *BEOORDEEL*, misjudge; *iets* ~ *AANPAK*, set about something in the wrong way; *die* ~ *e KEEL*, the wrong way (windpipe); *hy is 'n* ~ *e KÊREL*, he is an unreasonable fellow (a difficult customer); ~ *OPNEEM*, take something up the wrong way; ~ *VERSTAAN*, mistake the sense of, misunderstand;

sommer ~ *WEES*, be unreasonable; be in a bad mood; ~**elik**, mistakenly, wrongly.
verkeerd'deveerhoender, fowl with feathers turned in the wrong direction.
verkeerd'heid, wrongness, perversity, erroneousness, fallaciousness, faultiness.
verkeers': ~**agent**, traffic policeman; ~**baan**, traffic lane; ~**beampte**, traffic officer; ~**belemmering**, obstruction of the traffic; ~**bepaling**, traffic regulation; ~**bestuurder**, traffic manager; ~**brug**, road bridge; ~**diens**, point duty; ~**digtheid**, traffic density; ~**drukte**, traffic rush; ~**eiland**, traffic island.
verkeer'sein, robot.
verkeers'hoof, traffic chief.
verkeer'sirkel, traffic circle, roundabout.
verkeers': ~**kaartjie**, traffic ticket; ~**kamer**, control room; ~**kenmerk**, traffic feature; ~**knoop**, traffic jam; ~**konstabel**, traffic constable; policeman on point duty; ~**lamp**, traffic lamp; ~**lig**, robot, traffic light; ~**lyn**, white (traffic) line; ~**middel**, means of communication; ~**net**, system of communication; ~**ongeval**, road accident; ~**oortreding**, traffic offence; ~**ophoping**, traffic congestion; ~**outomaat**, (..**mate**), robot; ~**polisie**, traffic police; ~**reëling**, regulation of traffic, traffic control; ~**regulasies**, rules of the road; traffic regulations; ~**roete**, traffic route; ~**taal**, common parlance, language of daily intercourse; ~**teken**, traffic sign(al); ~**toring**, control tower.
verkeer'streep, traffic line.
verkeers'tregter, bottleneck.
verkeer'stremming, holding up of traffic, traffic jam.
verkeer'stroom, traffic stream.
verkeers': ~**verordening**, traffic by-law; ~**verslag**, traffic return; ~**versperring**, traffic block; ~**vliegtuig**, passenger plane; ~**voorskrifte**, traffic regulations; ~**vraagstuk**, traffic problem; ~**wagter**, pointsman; ~**weg**, communication road; arterial road; trade route; ~**wese**, traffic and communication, transport; ~**wisselaar**, traffic interchange.
verken', (~), reconnoitre, scout, spy; explore; *die terrein* ~, spy out the land; ~**ner**, (-s), scout.
verken'nerskuns, scoutcraft.
verken'ning, reconnoitring, scouting, spying, reconnaissance; *op* ~ *uitgaan*, go reconnoitring, make a reconnaissance.
verken'ningsdiens, reconnaissance duties, reconnoitring service.
verken'ningskip, look-out ship.
verken'nings: ~**korps**, scout corps; ~**leër**, reconnoitring army; ~**patrollie**, scout patrol; ~**tog**, reconnoitring expedition; ~**troepe**, scouts; reconnaissance troops, recces; ~**vliegtuig**, scouting plane; reconnaissance aircraft; ~**vlug**, scouting flight; ~**werk**, scouting activities.
verkerf', **verker'we**, (~), blunder; *dit by iem.* ~, incur someone's displeasure; fall out with someone.
verkerk'lik, churchify.
verket'ter, (~), charge with heresy, brand as a heretic; decry, disparage; ~**ing**, charge of heresy; disparagement, decrying.
verkies', (~), choose, prefer; elect, return (to parliament); *iem. in die KOMITEE* ~, elect someone to the committee; *NET soos jy* ~, just as you prefer; *tot VOORSITTER* ~, elect as chairman; ~**baar**, (..**bare**), eligible; *jou* ~ *baar stel*, make oneself available for (seek) election; ~**baarheid**, eligibility.
verkie'sel, silicify; ~**ing**, silification.
verkie'sing, (-e, -s), election, poll (by votes); choice; wish; *uit EIE* ~, of one's own free will; *NA* ~, as you please, at pleasure; *'n TUSSENTYDSE* ~, a by-election; *'n* ~ *UITSKRYF*, declare an election.
verkie'sings: ~**agent**, election(eering) agent, canvasser; ~**beampte**, returning officer; ~**buro**, (-'s), election bureau; ~**byeenkoms**, electioneering meeting; ~**dag**, election day, polling day; ~**fonds**, election fund; ~**kantoor**, electoral office, election office; ~**komitee**, election committee; ~**koste**, election expenses; ~**leus(e)**, election cry; platform; ~**maneuver**, electioneering manoeuvre; ~**manifes**, election manifesto; ~**metode**, mode of election; ~**misbruike**, electoral malpractices; ~**pamflet**,

electioneering pamphlet; ~ **plakkaat,** election placard; ~ **program,** election programme; ~ **propaganda,** election propaganda; electioneering speech; ~ **redenaar,** soap-box orator; ~ **toespraak,** election speech.
verkiesing'stryd, election fight (contest).
verkie'sings: ~ **uitslag,** election result; ~ **veldtog,** election campaign; ~ **werk,** electioneering; ~ **wet,** electoral law.
verkies'lik, (-e), preferable, desirable; *geluk is* ~ *bo rykdom,* happiness is preferable to riches; ~ **heid,** preferableness.
verkil', (~), ice, cool off; ~ **ling,** cooling off, chilling.
verkla', (~), accuse, charge with, bring a charge against, inform against; *iem. gaan* ~ , lay a charge against someone.
verklaar', (~), explain (meaning); state; depose, testify, pronounce, declare; interpret, explicate, define, elucidate, clear up, account for; expound; enounce, enunciate; comment; affirm, certify; *onder EED* ~ , swear to, testify (declare) under oath; *OORLOG* ~ , declare war; *PLEGTIG* ~ , declare solemnly; *SKULDIG* ~ , find guilty; *na WAARHEID* ~ , declare truthfully; ~ **baar, (. . bare)** explicable, explainable; interpretable; declarable; *MAKLIK* ~ *baar,* easily explained; *om on* ~ *bare REDES,* for inexplicable reasons; ~ **baarheid,** explicableness; ~ **de,** professed, avowed, declared; ~ **der, (-s),** expositor, exposer, expounder (of Scripture); definer, declarant, commentator; elucidator; annotator; exponent; explainer; attestor; interpreter (of law).
verkla'e = **verklaag.**
verkla'er, (-s), plaintiff; informant.
verklank', (~), voice, phonate; interpret; express in music; ~ **ing,** expression (in music).
verklap', (~), expose, divulge, peach, tell tales, spill the beans, give away, let out a secret, blab; ~ **per, (-s),** telltale, blabber; divulger; ~ **pery,** blabbing.
verkla'rend, (-e), explanatory, expository, glossarial, explicative, explicatory, elucidative; ~ *e woordeboek,* explanatory dictionary.
verkla'ring, (-e, -s) explanation, elucidation, statement, explication, exposition, assertion, evidence, declaration, interpretation, attestation, affirmation, announcement; enunciation; demonstration; manifesto; recognizance; protestation; account, deposition; definition; *'n* ~ *AFLÊ,* make a statement; *'n BEËDIGDE* ~ , an affidavit; ~ *van VOORNEME,* declaration of intent.
verkle'ding, dressing up, changing; disguising.
verklee', (~), change (clothes); disguise, mask; make up; ~ **kamer,** changing-room.
verkleef', (-de), attached; devoted.
verkleefd'heid, attachment, adherence, devotion.
verklein', (~), make smaller, lessen, diminish; dwindle; cancel (fractions); abbreviate (word); belittle, minimize; reduce in size (dress); extenuate (guilt); *'n* ~ *de skaal,* a reduced scale; ~ **baar, (. . bare),** reducible.
verkleineer', (~), minimize, belittle, disparage, detract from; ~ **der, (-s),** minimizer, detractor.
verkleine'ring, disparagement, detraction, minimization.
verklein'glas, diminishing glass.
verklei'ning, (-e, -s), diminution, reduction; disparagement, belittlement, detraction; litotes (figure of speech).
verklei'nings: ~ **element,** reducing (diminishing) part; ~ **uitgang,** diminutive ending; ~ **vorm,** diminutive form.
verklein': ~ **ring,** reducing ring; ~ **woord,** diminutive.
verkleur', (~), fade, lose colour; change colour, discolour; *'n* ~ *de das,* a faded tie; ~ **datum,** date of colour-change; ~ **ing,** fading, discolouring, discoloration; ~ **mannetjie, (-s),** chameleon; turncoat; weather-vane.
verkle'wing, cohesion, cohering, agglutination, cementation (bot.).
verklik', (~), tell tales, split on (a person); peach, squeal, delate; blab, disclose (secret); ~ **ker, (-s),** blabber; rear-view mirror; squealer, telltale, detectograph; detector; ~ **king,** tale-telling; disclosure.
verklomp', (~), aggregate, clump; ~ **ing,** aggregation, clumping.
verkluim', (w) (~), grow stiff (numb) with cold, freeze to death; (b) **(-de),** frost-bitten; frozen to death; ~ *de deeg,* cold dough; ~ **erig, (-e),** chilly.
verkneg', (~), enslave; *'n* ~ *te volk,* an enslaved nation; ~ **ting,** enslavement.
verkneu'kel, verkneu'ter, (~): *hom* ~ *in,* gloat over, chuckle over with delight, feast the mind gleefully on, revel in.
verknies', (~), fret, sit and mope; *jou lewe* ~ , fret (mope) away one's life.
verknip', (~), spoil in cutting, change by cutting.
verknoei', (~), spoil, make a mess of, blunder away, muddle, bungle; corrupt; garble; foozle, fluff (golf); *'n verknoeide foto,* a spoilt photo; ~ **er, (-s),** bungler, muddler; corruption.
verknog', (-te), attached; devoted; ~ *aan sy moeder,* devoted to his mother.
verknogt'heid, great affection, attachment.
verknor'sing, fretting, pining, trouble, distress; *in die* ~ *wees,* be in a dilemma, a sorry plight.
verkoel', (~), cool, refrigerate; grow indifferent; *die LIEFDE het* ~ , they have grown cool towards each other; ~ *de VLEIS,* chilled meat; ~ **end, (-e),** cooling, refreshing; ~ **er, (-s),** cooler; radiator.
verkoe'ler: ~ **beslag,** radiator apron; ~ **buis,** radiator tube; ~ **dop,** radiator cap; ~ **hortjies,** radiator shutters; ~ **hulsel,** radiator shell; ~ **kraan,** radiator cock; ~ **pyp,** radiator hose; ~ **rooster,** radiator grid; ~ **slang,** radiator connection; ~ **tenk,** radiator tank.
verkoe'ling, cooling, chilling; coolness; refrigeration.
verko'ling, carbonization; charring.
verkom'mer, (~), pine away, die of neglect.
verkon'dig, (~), announce, proclaim (the glory), preach (the Gospel); expound (doctrine); enunciate (a theory); promulgate (decree); ~ **er, (-s),** proclaimer, annunciator, promulgator; enunciator; preacher, apostle; ~ **ing,** proclamation; preaching; announcement, publication; annunciation, promulgation.
verkon'kel, (~), mess up, botch.
verkonsumeer', (ong.), **(~),** consume.
verkook', (~), boil away (down), boil to a pulp; evaporate.
verkooks', (~), coke; ~ **ing,** coking.
verkool', (~), carbonize; char; become carbonized; become charred.
verkoop', (~ , . . kope), sale; disposal, merchandizing; *'n* ~ *AFSLUIT,* conclude a sale; *GEREGTELIKE* ~ , judicial sale; *'n* ~ *tot STAND bring,* effect a sale; (w) **(~),** sell, dispose of, huckster, bring under the hammer, merchandize; tell (tales); *by AFSLAG* ~ , sell by (Dutch) auction; *uit die HAND* ~ , sell by private treaty; *by VEILING (op bod)* ~ , sell by auction; *iets* ~ *waarvoor dit WERD is,* retail something for what it is worth; ~ *WORD,* come under the hammer; be sold; ~ **akte,** deed of sale; ~ **baar (. . bare),** saleable, vendible, marketable; ~ **baarheid,** saleability, vendibility; ~ **boek,** sales book; ~ **bord,** notice of sale.
verkoops': ~ **afdeling,** sales department (division); ~ **agent,** selling (sales) agent; ~ **bestuurder,** sales manager; ~ **dag,** sales day, day of sales; ~ **klerk,** sales clerk; shop assistant; ~ **kontrak,** contract of sale; ~ **koste,** selling costs; ~ **kuns,** salesmanship; ~ **lokaal,** sale-room; ~ **nota,** sales note, note of sales; ~ **organisasie,** selling (sales) organization; ~ **ooreenkoms,** sales contract, contract of sales; ~ **prys,** selling price; ~ **rekening,** sales account, account of sales; ~ **plek,** mart; market; location of sales; ~ **prys,** sale (selling) price; ~ **voorwaarde,** condition of sale; ~ **vrag,** carriage on sales; ~ **waarde,** selling (market) value. *NB:* Die bostaande woorde kan ook geskryf word sonder die verbindings *-s.*
verkoop': ~ **ster,** female seller, saleslady; ~ **vlaag,** spate of sales.
verko'per[1], (s) (-s), seller, vendor; salesman; huckster,

verkoper 583 **verlei**

verko'per², (w) (~), copper, copperplate; ~ing, copperplating; *'n ~ de vaas,* a copperplate vase; ~ing, copperplating.
verko'persaandele, vendor's shares.
verko'ping, (-e, -s), sale, auction.
verko're, chosen, elect; *die ~ volk,* the chosen nation.
verkor'rel, (~), granulate; ~ing, granulation.
verkors', (~), crust, crustify; ~ting, incrustation.
verkort', (w) (~), shorten, epitomize, abridge (book); reduce, boil down; abbreviate (word); curtail (visit); condense (story); while away (the time); foreshorten (perspective); (b) (-e), abridged, abbreviated; curtailed; compact; *'n ~e uitgawe,* an abridged edition; ~end, (-e), derogatory; ~enderwys(e), for short; ~er, (-s), epitomist.
verkor'ting, (-e, -s), curtailment, abridgement, shortening, abbreviation; derogation; excerpt.
verkor'tingsteken, apostrophe.
verko'se, returned, elected, chosen; *~ hoofonderwyser,* head master elect.
verkou'e, (s) (-s), cold, chill; *~kry,* catch a cold; (b) having a cold; *~ WEES,* have a cold; *~ WORD,* be in for a cold.
verkou'entheid, cold, chill; catarrh.
verkou'evry, (-e), cold-proof.
verkrag', (~), infringe, violate; ravish; rape, outrage, deflower (woman); ~ter, ravisher, violator; raper; rapist; ~ting, rape, defloration, ravishment (of woman); violation (of law).
verkramp', (b) (-te), reactionary; obscurant; ultra-conservative; narrow minded; te, (s) (-s), obscurantist; rightist, ultra-conservatist, traditionbound person; reactionary; ~t'heid, obscurantism, ultra-conservatism.
verkre'ë, vested (rights), acquired.
verkreu'kel, (~), crumple, crease, crush; ~ing, creasing.
verkrimp', (w) (~), shrink up (away); (b) (-te), shrunken; ~ing, shrinking, shrinkage.
verkrom'ming, curvature.
verkrop', (w) (~), stomach, swallow (one's mortifications); pocket, put up with (an insult); (b) (-te), pent-up; *~ te woede,* pent-up rage; ~ping, pocketing (mortification); swallowing (insults); restraining (feelings).
verkrum'mel, (~), crumble away; ~ing, crumbling.
verkry', (~), obtain; compass; get, gain, procure (a position); acquire (wealth); attain (fame); *nog te ~ van,* still obtainable from; ~(g)'baar, (..bare), gettable, available; attainable, procurable; purchasable; ~(g)er, (-s), procurer, obtainer; ~ging, acquisition, attainment, acquirement, procurement; obtainment, obtaining, getting.
verkul', (~), cheat, trick.
verkurk', (w) (~), suberize; (b) (-te), suberic; ~ing, suberization.
verkwa'lik, (~), take amiss; resent; *jy moet my dit nie ~ nie,* don't take it amiss.
verkwan'sel, (~), waste, barter away; ~ing, wasting, bartering away.
verkwik', (~), refresh; recreate; ~kend, (-e), refreshing; comforting; *'n ~ende buitjie,* a refreshing shower; ~king, (-e, -s), refreshment; comfort; ~lik, (-e), refreshing, strengthening, comforting, edifying.
verkwis', (~), waste (time); squander (money); fritter away, dissipate (energy); ~tend, (-e), prodigal, wasteful, extravagant, improvident; profuse (of promises, of flowers); ~ter, (-s), waster, prodigal, spendthrift; ~terig, (-e), wasteful, prodigal; ~terigheid, prodigality, wastefulness; ~ting, wastage, dissipation, extravagance, squandering, prodigality; lavishing; profuseness, profusion; *organisasie ter bestryding van ~ting,* antiwaste organization.
verkwyn', (~), pine away, languish; ~ing, languishing, pining away.
verkyk', (~), stare in amazement, gape at; *die KANS is ~ (verkeke),* the opportunity is lost; *jou ~ aan die WINKELVENSTERS,* stare at the shop windows.
ver'kyker, (-s), glass, field-glasses, telescope, binocle, binoculars.

verlaag', (~), reduce, lower (price); declass, debase, degrade, abase, disgrace, brutalize, debauch; demean; *jou tot 'n LEUEN ~,* stoop to tell a lie; *PRYSE is ~,* prices have been cut.
verlaat'¹, (~), leave, abandon (ship); desert (wife); forsake (friend); quit, evacuate (town); *jou ~ op,* put your trust in.
verlaat'², (w) (~), (refleks.): *ek het my ~,* it was much later than I thought.
verla'gend, (-e), degrading.
verla'ging, (-e, -s), reduction, lowering (of prices); demission; abasement, degradation, debasement; diminution.
verlak', (w) (~), lacquer, japan, varnish; dope (aero.); (b) (-te), lacquered, japanned, varnished; *~ te skoene,* patent-leather shoes; ~ker, (-s), japanner, varnisher; ~king, varnishing, japanning.
verlam', (w) (~), paralyse (lit. & fig.); lame, cripple (organization); unnerve (person); *'n ~mende uitwerking hê op,* have a paralysing effect on; (b) (-de), palsied; paralytic; lamed; ~de, (-s), paralytic; ~ming, paralysis, crippling, lameness.
verlang', (~), desire, long for, crave, desiderate; aspire (to), want, demand, exact; *vurig ~ NA,* yearn passionately for; *jy ~ te VEEL van my,* you are demanding (expecting) too much from me; ~e, (-ns), eagerness, aspiration, longing, desire, wish, pining; yearning, hankering; *~ e na huis,* homesickness; ~end, (-e), desirous, eager, athirst, anxious, agog, burning, hankering, impatient; ~er, (-s), desirer, ~lys, wanted-list; wish-slip.
verlang'saam, (~), slow down, decelerate.
verlang'ste, (-s), longing, yearning; homesickness.
verla'te, abandoned (ship); lonely (place); forsaken (by friends); forlorn, destitute (person); derelict, deserted (vessel, wife); desolate (place); friendless, lone, defenceless.
verla'tenheid, loneliness, forlorn condition, desolation, abandonment, desertion, forlornness; solitude.
verla'ting, abandonment, desertion, dereliction, forsaking; *kwaadwillige ~,* malicious desertion.
verlê', (w) (~), remove, displace, put in another place, shift, divert (river); mislay, misplace; *'n BRIL ~,* mislay spectacles; *hy het sy NEK ~,* he has a crick in the neck; *die PAD is ~,* the road has been diverted; (b) (..legde), mislaid (documents); crumpled, creased (clothes).
verle'de, (s) past; *die GRYS(E) ~,* the distant past; *in die JONGSTE ~,* in recent times; *MY ~,* my past; (b) past, last; *~ DEELWOORD,* past participle; *~ SONDAG,* last Sunday; *~ TYD,* past tense.
verle'ë, timid, bashful, diffident, abashed; perplexed, disconcerted, embarrassed, at a loss, puzzled, nonplussed; hard-pressed; *~ om GELD,* in want of money; be hard up; *GOU ~,* easily put out; *~ oor IEM.,* be hard up for someone; *~ wees met IETS,* be saddled with something; have something on one's hands; *~ WEES met iets,* be saddled with something.
verleen', (~), grant, give, confer, bestow (favour); render (aid); extend, favour, lend; *HULP ~,* render (lend) assistance; *MAG ~,* delegate power; ~baar, (..bare), grantable.
verleent'heid, embarrassment, confusion, abashment; diffidence, bashfulness, distress, strait, fix, perplexity, quandary, dilemma, pinch; *in ~ bring,* embarrass.
verleer', (~), unlearn (habit); forget.
verleg, (~) = **verlê**.
verleg'ging, shifting, misplacement; displacement; deviation, diversion; *~ v.d. pad,* diversion of the road.
verlei', (~), seduce, betray (woman); ensnare; tempt, allure; deceive; pervert, corrupt (virgin); inveigle; lead astray, mislead; ~baar, (..bare), pervertible; ~delik, (-e), temptable; glamorous, tempting, captivating, enticing, seductive, alluring; ~delikheid, allurement, temptingness, seductiveness, glamour, temptation, fascination; ~ding, (-e, -s), seduction; beguilement, temptation; inveiglement; ~d'ster,

verlekker seductress, temptress; ~**er**, (-s), tempter; deceiver; seducer, corrupter, perverter.
verlek'ker, (~), find pleasure in; anticipate with pleasure; *jou ~ IN*, take delight in; *~ jou daar nie OP nie*, do not bank on that.
verlek'ker(d): *~ op*, keen on, eager for, have a craving for.
verleng', (~), lengthen, prolong, protract (visit); grant extension; produce, continue (line); extend, elongate; renew (bill); *'n LYN ~*, produce a line; *~de RUGMURG*, medulla oblongata; *die vakansie 'n WEEK ~*, extend the vacation by a week; **~baar**, (..**bare**), extensible, protractile; renewable (bill); **~de**, lengthened, extended, elongated, renewed; **~deur**, extension door; **~er**, prolonger; **~ing**, lengthening, prolongation, elongation, protraction; production; extension; **~plaat**, extension plate; **~stuk**, lengthening piece; allonge; extension (piece).
verle'ning, grant(ing), bestowal, conferment, rendering.
verlep', (w) (~), fade, wilt, wither; *~ lyk*, look woebegone (crestfallen); (b) (**-te**), withered; **~siekte**, wilt disease.
verlept'heid, fadedness, witheredness.
verlet', delay.
verle'wendig, (~), revive (hope); enliven (person); freshen, kindle, quicken, stimulate, vivify; **~ing**, enlivenment, vivification, revival (of trade); quickening.
verlief', (**-de**), in love, fond of, sweet on; amorous, amatory; *smoor= (dood) ~ op HAAR*, hopelessly in love with her; *~ RAAK*, fall in love; **~de**, (**-s**), lover; **~derig**, (**-e**), amative, spoony; **~derigheid**, amorousness; amativeness.
verliefd'heid, amorousness; infatuation, fondness.
verlies', (**-e**), loss, bereavement; casualty; cost (of life); disadvantage; decrement; deprivation; *met BAIE ~e*, with many casualties; *'n DROEWIGE ~*, a sad loss (bereavement); *swaar ~e LY*, sustain heavy losses; *met ~ VERKOOP*, sell at a loss; *met ~ WERK*, work at a loss; **~lys**, casualty-list, list of casualties; **~pos**, loss (in balance sheet); **~syfer**, amount of loss; returns of casualties.
verlig'¹, (w) (~), alleviate, relieve, mitigate, palliate, allay, ease (pain); (b) (**-te**), enlightened; lit up; *die ~ te eeu*, the enlightened age.
verlig'², (w) (~), light (lamp); illuminate (a street); irradiate, illumine, beacon, brighten, enkindle, light up; (en)lighten (people); (b) (**-te**), relieved; superenlightened; *met 'n ~ te gevoel*, with a sense of relief.
verliggaam'lik, (**-te**), incarnate.
verlig'te, (**-s**), enlightened person.
verlig': **~tend**, (**-e**), alleviative, alleviatory, relieving; illuminant, illuminative; **~ter**, (**-s**), alleviator.
verlig'ting¹, palliation, mitigation, ease, lightening, alleviation, relief; *medisyne wat ~ gee*, medicine which brings relief.
verlig'ting², lighting, illumination, irradiation.
verlig'tings: **~aanleg**, lighting plant; **~middel**, illuminant.
verlo'ën, (~), deny, disavow, renounce (friendship); forswear; give the lie to, disown (one's son); abjure, repudiate (statement); *jou ~*, practise self-denial; belie one's nature; **~aar**, (**-s**), apostate, denier, renouncer, abjurer; **~ing**, denial, renunciation, repudiation, disavowal, abnegation; apostasy (religion).
verlof', leave; permission, exeat; allowance; furlough, holiday; permittance; permit; licence; *~ AAN= VRA*, apply for leave; *alle ~ INTREK*, cancel all leave; *~ KRY*, obtain leave; *MET u ~*, with your permission; excuse me; *MET ~ wees*, be on leave; *~ NEEM*, take leave; *SONDER ~*, without permission; **~brief**, permit; **~dag**, day off; **~ganger**, soldier on furlough; **~pas**, pass, permit; **~regula= sie**, leave regulation.
verlofs': **~aanvraag**, application for leave; **~bepa= ling**, leave regulation; **~traktement**, furlough pay; **~verlenging**, extension of leave.
verlof'tyd, leave, furlough, vacation.

verlok', (~), allure, entice, lure on, seduce, tempt; lead astray; **~kend**, (**-e**), seductive, alluring, tempting; **~ker**, (**-s**), allurer, enticer, seducer, tempter; **~king**, allurement, enticement, temptation; soliciting, solicitation, inveiglement; **~lik**, (**-e**), seductive, alluring, enticing, tempting; **~likheid**, seductiveness, allurement, enticement.
verlood', (~), cover with lead (lead-plating).
verloof', (w) (~), betroth, become engaged, affiance; *jou AAN mej. A ~*, become engaged to Miss A; *~ WEES*, be engaged; (b) (**-de**), engaged, betrothed, affianced; *twee ~de pare*, two engaged couples; **~de**, (**-s**), betrothed, fiancé(e); **~ring**, engagement ring; **~skap**, (**-pe**), *see* **verlowing**; *'n ~skap uit= maak*, break off an engagement; **~tyd**, (duration of) engagement.
verloop', (s) course, lapse (of time); expiry (of period); progress, passage (of time); *na ~ van 'n MAAND*, after a month had elapsed; *'n gunstige ~ NEEM*, take a favourable turn; *die gewone ~ van SAKE*, the ordinary course of events; *die ~ van 'n SIEKTE*, the course of a disease; (w) (~), elapse, go by; expire, lapse; taper; *na (met) ~ van TYD*, in course of time; *'n KANS laat ~*, let a chance slip; *SODRA 'n week ~ was*, as soon as a week had elapsed; *alles het VLOT ~*, everything went off smoothly; **~sok**, reducer; **~stuk**, adapter, diminisher.
verloop', (**-te**), (b) runaway; dissipated, down-and-out; *'n ~te ADVOKAAT*, an advocate who is down-and-out; *'n ~te MATROOS*, a sailor who has deserted; *'n ~te PERSOON*, a degenerate person.
verloor', (~), lose (caste, life); cast (horseshoe); expend (strength); mislay (letter); *die MOED ~*, lose courage; *die PERD ~ sy lang hare*, the horse is shedding its winter coat; *het jy jou TONG ~?* can't you answer? *TYD ~*, lose time; **~der**, loser; **~derswedloop**, consolation race; **~kant**, losing side; *aan die ~kant wees*, be on the losing side; fight a losing battle.
verloot', (~), raffle (out).
verlo'pe = **verloop**, (b).
verlo're, lost; forlorn; gone; missing; *~ GAAN*, get lost (ship); be wasted (food); *~ MOEITE*, labour lost; vain effort; *'n ~ OOMBLIK*, a spare (odd) moment; *~ RAAK*, get lost; *die ~ SEUN*, the prodigal son; **~ne**, (**-s**), lost one.
verlo'renheid, lostness; solitude.
verlos', (~), deliver, give birth to (a child); release, liberate (from prison); redeem, save (from sin); free, ransom (from imprisonment); ease; *~ ons van die BOSE*, deliver us from evil; *sy is van 'n SEUN ~*, she was delivered of a son; **~kunde**, midwifery; obstetrics, tocology.
verloskun'dig, (**-e**), obstetric(al); ..**kun'dige**, (**-s**), accoucheur, obstetrician; midwife.
verlos'send, (**-e**), redeeming, saving, redemptive.
verlos'ser, (**-s**), deliverer, liberator; saviour; *die V~*, the Redeemer, the Saviour.
verlos': **~sing**, deliverance, redemption, delivery; riddance; accouchement; **~singswerk**, work of redemption; **~tang**, obstetric forceps; **~te**, (**-s**), saved soul; *die ~s*, the saved.
verlo'ting, raffle, raffling; lottery.
verlo'we, (~) = **verloof**, (w).
verlo'wing, (**-e**, **-s**), engagement, espousal, affience, betrothal; *'n ~ verbreek*, break off an engagement.
verlo'wings: **~fees**, engagement festivity; **~kaartjie**, engagement card; **~ring**, engagement ring.
verlug'¹, (w) (~), ventilate.
verlug'², (w) (~), illuminate, illustrate, miniate; (b) (**-te**), historiated; **~ter**, (**-s**), illustrator.
verlug'ting¹, ventilation.
verlug'ting², illustration, illumination.
verlui'¹, (~), become lazy; *in die vakansie ~ 'n mens*, during the holidays one gets lazy.
verlui'², (~), be rumoured.
verluid': *na ~ (van)*, the story goes, according to the rumour.
verlui'er, (~), idle away.

verlustig 585 *vermors*

verlus'tig, (~), amuse; *jou ~ in*, enjoy, delight in, revel in; **~ing**, enjoyment, delight, revelling.
verly', (~), draw up, execute (a deed); **~ding**, execution (of deed).
vermaag'skap, (w) (~), ally by marriage, become related to; (b) **(-te)**, akin.
vermaak¹ (s): *ek is nie V~ se kind nie*, that won't embarrass me; that won't make me envious (jealous); (w) (~), spite, make jealous; *ek laat my nie ~ nie*, you won't spite me.
vermaak², (s) (..make), pleasure, delight, enjoyment, amusement, entertainment, diversion; recreation; *~ SKEP in*, find pleasure in; *~ SOEK*, seek entertainment; *TOT ~ van*, to the delight (amusement) of; (w) (~), enjoy, amuse, divert, recreate.
vermaak'³, (w) (~) = **bemaak**; bequeath.
vermaak'⁴, (w) (~), alter, change (clothes); *'n ou rok ~*, alter an old dress.
vermaak'lik, (-e), enjoyable, pleasurable, amusing, recreative, diverting, good, entertaining; **~heid, (..hede)**, amusement, diversion, entertainment, gaiety; **~heidsbelasting**, amusement (entertainment) tax; **~heidseenheid**, entertainment unit; **~heidsplek**, place of amusement.
vermaak'sug, thirst for pleasure.
vermaal', (~), grind up, crush, triturate, pound.
vermaan', (~), admonish, lecture, exhort, caution expostulate (with), warn; **~brief**, warning letter.
vermaard', (-e), celebrated, famous, illustrious, famed, fabled, renowned; **~heid**, fame, renown, celebrity.
verma'er, (~), grow thin, attenuate, emaciate, lose flesh, reduce (weight); **~ing**, emaciation, attenuation, weight-reduction, slimming; **~ingskuur**, obesity cure, banting, slimming cure, reduction cure.
vermag', (~), have the power to, be able to; *niks teen die vyand ~ nie*, be powerless against the enemy.
verma'ker¹ = **bemaker**, testator.
verma'ker², entertainer, devisor.
verma'kerig, (-e), teasing, spiteful.
verma'king = **bemaking**; bequest.
verma'ledy, (-de), confounded, damned, cursed.
verma'ling, trituration, grinding up; pulverization.
verman', (~): *jou ~*, brace oneself, pull oneself together.
verma'nend (-e), admonitory, (ex)hortative, expostulative, expostulatory.
verma'ner, (-s), admonisher, monitor, expostulator, exhorter.
verma'ning, (-e, -s), admonition, lesson, admonishment, lecture, warning, (ex)hortation, charge.
vermeen'de, alleged, supposed, reputed, fancied; putative (father).
vermeer', (~), vomit; puke; **~bossie**, vomit-bush (*Geigeria passerinoides*).
vermeer'der, (~), increase, enlarge, eke out, augment, add, multiply; redouble; proliferate; *~ de onkoste*, increased expenses; **-end, (-e)**, augmentative; **~ing, (-e, -s)**, increase, multiplication, augmentation, enhancement, growth, accumulation, access, addition, afflux.
vermeer': **~middel**, emetic; **~sel**, vomit; **~siekte**, *Geigeria*-poisoning; **~wortelwyn**, ipecacuanha wine.
vermees'ter, (~), master, capture, conquer, subdue; **~ing**, mastering, capture, subjection, conquest.
vermeet': *jou ~*, presume, dare to.
vermei', (~), amuse oneself, revel in; *jou in iets ~*, take a delight in, enjoy something.
vermeld', (~), mention, state, record, *EERVOL ~*, mentioned in dispatches; *TENSY anders ~*, unless otherwise stated.
vermel'denswaard, vermeldenswaar'dig, (-e), worthy of mention, worth mentioning.
vermel'ding, mention; *eervolle ~*, honourable mention (in examination).
vermeng', (~), mix, (inter)blend, compound, (com)mingle, intermingle, admix; *rasse wat hulle ~ het*, races which have become mixed; **~baar, (..bare)**, miscible; **~er**, mixer, blender; **~ing, (-e, -s)**, blend(ing), (com)mixture; alloy; mixing

vermenigvul'dig, (~), multiply; accumulate; **~baar, (..bare)**, multipliable; **~er, (-s)**, multiplier, multiplicator.
vermenigvul'diging, multiplication; *tafel van ~*, multiplication table.
vermenigvul'digingsfaktor, multiplying factor.
vermenigvul'diging: **~som**, multiplication sum; **~spieël**, multiplying glass.
vermenigvuldigings: **~tafel**, multiplication table; **~tal**, multiplicand; **~teken**, multiplication sign.
vermens'lik, (~), humanize; **~ing**, humanization.
verme'tel, (-e), audacious, bold, daring, rash, reckless, foolhardy; **~heid**, audacity, daring, rashness, foolhardiness, temerity, effrontery.
vermicel'li, vermicelli; **~poeding**, vermicelli pudding; **~so(e)p**, vermicelli soup.
vermikuliet', vermiculite.
vermiljoen', vermilion, cinnabar; **~kleurig, (-e)**, vermilion, cinnabar.
vermin'der, (~), lessen, decrease, cut down (prices); slacken, diminish (speed); abate (violence); decline (population), dwindle; allay; reduce, lower (price); derogate; rebate; *die pryse ~*, reduce the prices; **~ing, (-e, -s)**, diminution, decrease, rebate, reduction, abatement, drop, cut (in price), falling off; reducement.
vermink', (w) (~), mutilate, maim; mangle; deface; garble (a report); dismember, disable; (b) **(-te)**, crippled; mangled; garbled (report); **~er, (-s)**, mutilator; **~ing**, mutilation, dismemberment, concision; defacement, garbling; **~te, (-s)**, mutilated (maimed) person; cripple, invalid.
verminkt'heid, maimedness.
vermis', (w) (~), miss, be missing; *twee soldate word ~*, two soldiers are missing; (b) **(-te)**, missing; *~ te geld*, missing money; **~sing**, loss; **~te, (-s)** missing person; *'n lys v.d. ~ tes*, a list of the missing.
vermits', as, since, whereas; *~ aan die voorwaarde nog nie voldoen is nie . . .*, whereas this condition has not yet been satisfied . . .
vermo'ë, (-ns), fortune, wealth, riches, property, means, estate; ability, capacity; might; power; potency; rating (engineering); *met BEPERKTE ~ns*, with limited capabilities; *na my BESTE ~*, to the best of my ability; *DOEN al wat in jou ~ is*, do everything in your power; *'n MAN van ~*, a man of means; *NA ~*, according to ability; *VERSTAN= DELIKE ~ns*, intellectual faculties.
vermoed', (~), suspect, presume, suppose, expect, surmise, conjecture, divine; *NIKS ~ nie*, have no suspicion; *geen KWAAD ~ nie*, suspect no evil; **~baar, (..bare)**, conjecturable.
vermoe'de, (-ns), suspicion, presumption, inkling, surmise, guess, conjecture, supposition; presumise; *'n STERK ~ hê*, have a strong suspicion; *'n VAE ~ hê*, have a vague suspicion; **~lik**, (b) **(-e)**, probable, apparent, conjectural, presumable, expectant, presumptive; (bw) probably, presumably, apparently; *~ lik dood*, believed killed; presumably dead.
vermoei', (~), tire, weary, fatigue; **~d', (-e)**, fatigued, weary, exhausted, jaded.
vermoeid'heid, weariness, fatigue, lassitude.
vermoeid'heidsweerstand, fatigue resistance.
vermoei': **~end, (-e)**, tiring, fatiguing, wearisome, tedious, tiresome; **~enis, (-se)**, fatigue, lassitude; **~ing**, wearying, fatiguing.
vermo'ënd, (-e), wealthy, rich; influential; powerful.
vermo'ënsbelasting, property tax.
vermoet', vermouth.
vermolm', (~), moulder away; **~ing**, mouldering, dry rot, sap-rot.
vermom', (w) (~), disguise, mask, camouflage; (b) **(-de)**, disguised, masked; *'n ~ de seën*, a blessing in disguise; **~mer, (-s)**, disguiser; **~ming**, disguise, mask, camouflage, masquerade, make-up, get-up.
vermooi', (~), beautify, make pretty; **~ing**, embellishment, beautification.
vermoor', (~), murder, kill, butcher; **~beitel**, former (chisel); **~de, (-s)**, murdered person; **~der, (-s)**, murderer; **~ding, (-e, -s)**, massacre, murder(ing).
vermors', (w) (~), squander, spend, spill, waste,

vermorsel / **verontskuldig**

dawdle away (time), fritter away, trifle away, potter away, fool away; (b) **(-te)**, spilt, wasted, squandered.
vermor'sel, (~), smash, crush to pieces, crunch, pulverize; ~**ing**, pulverization, crushing.
vermor'sing, squandering, waste, dissipation; *vandag* ~, *môre verknorsing*, wilful waste makes woeful want.
vermuf', (w) (~), grow musty; (b) **(-te)**, musty, fusty, mouldy.
vermuft'heid, mustiness.
vermurf', **vermur'we** (~), appease, soften, mollify, assuage.
vermurf'baar, (..bare), mollifiable.
vermur'wing, appeasing, mollification, appeasement, assuagement.
vermy', (~), avoid, eschew, blench, ba(u)lk, forbear, stear clear of, shun, evade, elude; ~**baar**, (..bare), ~**delik**, **(-e)**, avoidable; ~**ding**, avoidance, avoiding, evasion; ~**er**, **(-s)**, eschewer; ~**pad**, bypass; ~**spoor(lyn)**, deviation line, diversion railway.
vernaam', (b) (..name), important, distinctive, grand, great, lordly, distinguished, prominent, of distinction; (bw) especially, particularly; ~**heid**, importance, prominence, style, distinction; gentlehood; lordliness; ~**lik**, especially, chiefly, principally, mainly; primarily; ~**ste**, central, first, cardinal, paramount, prima, prime, primal.
vernael', (~), spike, disable (a gun); ~**ing**, spiking; pricked hoof.
vernag', (~), pass the night.
verne'der, (w) (~), degrade, humble, abase, gall, lower (pride), debase, humiliate; prostrate; *HOM* ~ *voor*, humble oneself before; *iem. se TROTS* ~, humble someone's pride; (b) **(-de)**, debased, humiliated, degraded, diminished; ~**end**, **(-e)**, humiliating, humbling, degrading, derogatory; ~**ing (-e, -s)**, humiliation, degradation; come-down; prostration, debasement, abasement.
verne'derlands, (~) = **verhollands**.
verneem', (~), understand, hear, learn; inquire; *na ons* ~, *KOM hy môre*, we hear (understand) he is coming tomorrow; ~ *NA*, inquire after; ~**baar**, (..bare), audible, perceptible.
verneuk', (~), (plat), cheat, defraud, swindle, take in; *ek het my lekker* ~, I have made a complete ass of myself; ~**beentjie**, funny-bone; ~**by**, silly mid-on (cricket); ~**er**, **(-s)**, cheat, confidence man, fraud; ~**ery**, cheating, swindle, fraud; ~**myn**, booby trap.
verniel', (~), destroy, wreck, demolish, annihilate; overwork; ravage; dilapidate; dissipate; *jy* ~ *die perde*, you are overworking the horses; ~**agtig**, **(-e)**, destructive; ~**al**, destructionist, vandal; ~**baar**, (..bare), destroyable, destructible; ~**baarheid**, destructibility; ~**end**, **(-e)**, destructive; ~**er**, **(-s)**, wrecker, destroyer, demolisher; ~**ery**, destroying, destruction; ~**ing**, destruction, demolition, annihilation; dilapidation; ~**ingslading**, demolition charge; ~**ingswerk**, work of destruction; ~**ingswerktuig**, engine of destruction; ~**siek**, **(-e)**, destructive, vandalistic; ~**sug**, destructiveness, vandalism; ~**sug'tig**, **(-e)**, destructive.
vernier', **(-s)**, vernier; ~**koppeling**, vernier coupling; ~**passer**, vernier callipers.
verniet', in vain; for nothing, free of charge, gratis; unnecessarily; unavailing(ly); *DIS nou net* ~ *of ek dit kan regkry*, I simply can't manage it; *jy is* ~ *so HAASTIG*, you need not be in such a hurry; *hy KLA(E) sommer* ~, he has really no reason to complain; *dit KRY jy* ~, you get this gratis; you need not pay for this; *jy PROBEER* ~, you are trying in vain.
vernie'tig, (~), annihilate, crush, wipe out, destroy, quash, extinguish, blast (one's hopes), blight, confound, cancel, break, abolish, dash (hopes), foil, nullify; pulverize; *alle hoop* ~, destroy all hope; ~**baar**, (..bare), destructible; defeasible; ~**end**, **(-e)**, destructive; crushing, annihilating; scathing (criticism); withering (look); smashing (victory); damning (evidence); ~**er**, **(-s)**, destroyer, annihilator, abolisher; ~**ing**, destruction, annihilation,
ruin; annulment, cancellation; cessation; defeat; eradication; extinction; pulverization; ~**ingsoorlog**, war of extermination.
vernieu', (~), renew; renovate; freshen; redintegrate, recondition; regenerate; (b) **(-de)**, renewed; *met* ~ *de moed*, with renewed courage; ~**baar**, (..bare), renewable.
vernik'kel, (w) (~), nickel, nickel-plate; (b) **(-de)**, nickel-plated; ~**ing**, nickel-plating.
vernis', (s) **(-se)**, varnish, veneer, dope (aero.); (w) (~), varnish; (b) **(-te)**, varnished; ~**laag**, coat of varnish; ~**lak**, lacquer.
vernissa'ge, vernissage, varnishing dry; private view (of art show).
vernis'ser, **(-s)**, varnisher.
vernoem', (~), name after; rename; *die dorp, kleinkind is na die PRESIDENT* ~, the village, grandchild has been named after the president; *die POSKANTOOR is* ~ *tot*, the name of the post office has been changed to; ~**ing**, naming (after); renaming.
vernou', (~), grow narrower, narrow; choke (rifle); take in (clothes); ~**ing**, **(-e, -s)**, narrowing, narrowness, stricture, contraction, constriction, constringency; choke (rifle); gut; ~**spier**, constrictor muscle.
vernuf', **(-te)**, intelligence, talent, ingenuity, acumen; genius, intellect; *Da Vinci is een v.d. GROOTSTE* ~ *te van alle tye*, Da Vinci still remains one of the greatest geniuses of all time; *'n VALS* ~, false brilliancy, affectation; ~**spel**, game of skill; play of wit.
vernuf'tig, **(-e)**, ingenious, bright, intelligent, inventive, clever; *iem. is* ~ *met sy hande*, someone has a ready pair of hands; ~**heid**, ingenuity, intelligence, inventiveness.
vernu'we, (~), = **vernieu**.
vernu'wer, **(-s)**, renewer; renovator, innovator.
vernu'wing, **(-e, -s)**, renewal; renovation, redintegration; refit; regeneration.
vernu'wingsfonds, fund for renewal (renovation).
veronaan'genaam, (~), make (things) unpleasant.
veronag'saam, (~), neglect, slight, ignore, disobey, disregard, leave out in the cold (person); pretermit (fact, custom).
veronag'saming, neglect, slight, disregard; inobservance (of law); negligence; preterition.
veronal', veronal (registered trade name).
veronderstel', (~), suppose, expect, conjecture, presume, opine, believe, assume; *na* ~ *word*, it is assumed, presumably; ~**(d)'**, **(-de)**, suppose, assumed; ~**lend**, **(-e)**, hypothetic.
veronderstel'ling, **(-e, -s)**, supposition, conjecture, hypothesis, assumption, presumption; *IN die* ~, on the assumption; *van 'n* ~ *UITGAAN*, assume that.
veron'geluk, (~), fail, miscarry, knock on the head (plans), come to grief; lose one's life in an accident; be wrecked (ship); crash (aero.); *DIE* ~ *te*, the victim of an accident; *LAAT* ~, cause to miscarry (fail); ~**king**, wrecking, failure; death by accident.
veron'gelyk, (~), wrong, do injustice to; ~**ing**, wrong, injustice, injury, wronging.
vero'nika, **(-s)**, veronica, speedwell.
veron'reg, (~), wrong, do injustice to, aggrieve; ~**ting**, injustice, wrong.
verontag'saam, (~) = **veronagsaam**.
veronthei'lig, (~), profane, desecrate; ~**er**, **(-s)**, desecrator; ~**ing**, profanation, desecration.
verontlig'gaming, disembodiment.
verontrei'nig, (~), soil, pollute, defile, corrupt; ~**ing**, pollution, defilement.
verontrief', (~), inconvenience, incommode.
verontrus', (~), alarm, perturb, disturb, harry, discompose, agitate, disquiet; *jou* ~ *oor 'n gerug*, be alarmed at a rumour; ~**tend**, **(-e)**, disquieting, disturbing, discomposing, alarming; ~**ter**, **(-s)**, agitator, disturber; ~**ting**, alarm, perturbation, disquietude, anxiety, agitation, discomposure.
verontskul'dig, (~), excuse (conduct); exculpate (person); *hy het hom* ~, he excused himself; ~**end**, **(-e)**, exculpatory, apologetic, excusatory; ~**ing**, **(-e,**

-s), excuse, apology, exculpation, justification; plea; ~ *inge aanbied*, offer apologies.

verontwaar'dig, (-de), indignant, grieved; ~ *voel oor*, be indignant about; ~ **ing**, indignation, dudgeon; *van ~ ing kook*, be fuming.

veroor'deel, (~), condemn, denounce, damn, cast (aside); adjudge; sentence, convict, give judgment against; doom; *ter DOOD ~*, condemn to death; *in KOSTE ~*, condemned to pay the costs (of lawsuit); *OPENLIK ~*, denounce openly (publicly); *STRENG ~*, censure severely; *tot TRONKSTRAF ~*, sentence to imprisonment; ~ **de, (-s)**, condemned (person), person under sentence; **..delaar, (-s)**, condemner, denunciator, denouncer.

veroor'delend, (-e), condemnatory, denunciatory, convictive.

veroor'deling, (-e, -s), condemnation, conviction; denunciation, commitment, denouncement.

veroor'loof, veroor'lowe, (w), (~), permit, allow, give leave; ~ *MY om . . .*, I take the liberty to . . .; *hom VRYHEDE ~*, take liberties (b) **(-de)**, permitted, allowed; permissible.

veroor'lowend, (-e), permissive.

veroor'lowing, leave, permission.

veroor'saak, (~), cause, bring about, entail, engender, generate, breed (unrest), occasion; produce, raise; *moeilikheid ~*, give (cause) trouble.

veroor'sakend, (-e), causative.

veroor'saker, (-s), originator, cause.

veroor'saking, causing, causation, breeding (of discontent).

verootmoe'dig, (~), humble, humiliate; ~ **ing**, humiliation; *dag van ~ ing*, day of humiliation.

veror'ber, (~), consume, devour; ~ **ing**, consumption, devouring.

veror'den, (~), order, enact, ordain, decree; ~ **ing, (-e, -s)**, enactment, decree, regulation, ordinance, statute, by(e)-law (municipal).

verordineer', (~), enact, ordain, prescribe, order.

verurdine'ring, ordination, decreeing.

verou'der, (~), grow old, age (person); become obsolete (word); mature (cheese); ~ **d, (-e)**, obsolete, antiquated, fossilized, archaic, old-fashioned; aged; outdated; stale (cheque); discarded (belief); inveterate (ailment); exploded (theory); ~ *de IDEES*, antiquated notions; ~ *de PUBLIKASIE*, obsolete publication; ~ *de VORM*, obsolete form.

verou'derdheid, agedness; obsoleteness; inveteracy.

verou'dering, growing old, ageing, senescence, obsolescence; maturation (wine).

vero'wer, (~), conquer; capture; *'n dame se HART ~*, win a lady's heart; *'n STAD van die vyand ~*, capture a city from the enemy; ~ **aar, (-s)**, conqueror, victor; ~ **baar, (..bare)**, pregnable.

vero'wering, (-e, -s), conquest, capture.

vero'werings: ~ **oorlog**, war of conquest; ~ **politiek**, policy of conquest.

vero'weringsug, greed (lust) for conquest.

verpag', (w) (~), lease, farm out; (b) **(-te)**, leased, farmed out; ~ **ter, (-s)**, lessor; ~ **ting**, letting out, leasing.

verpak', (~), pack up, wrap up; repack; ~ **ker, (-s)**, packer; ~ **king**, packing, casing; ~ **kingsmateriaal**, packing material.

verpand', (w) (~), pawn (watch); pledge, impledge, (en)gage; mortgage, hypothecate (real estate); *ek ~ my woord daarvoor*, I pledge my word (of honour) to that; (b) **(-te)**, pawned; pledged; mortgaged; ~ **baar, (..bare)**, pawnable, pledgeable.

verpan'der, (-s), pawner.

verpan'ding, pledging, pawning; mortgaging, hypothecation.

verpan'dingsreg, right to pledge.

verpas', (~), miss (the train).

verpersoon'lik, (~), personify; incarnate, embody; impersonate; *die ~ te luiheid*, laziness personified; ~ **ing**, personification, impersonation; incarnation.

verpes', (~), infect with plague; contaminate, poison; pester, worry the life out of someone; canker; ~ **telik, (-e)**, pestilential, vexatious; ~ **tend, (-e)**, pestiferous, pestilent, pestilential; pernicious; ~ **ter,** **(-s)**, contaminator, teaser; ~ **ting**, pestilence, plague.

verpiep', (~), spoil by coddling.

verplaas', (w) (~), remove, move, displace (water); offset (geol.); translate (bishop); transfer, shift (to another post); (b) **(-te)**, moved; translated; transferred; ~ **baar, (..bare)**, movable, removable; ~ **baarheid**, movability, removability; ~ **briefie**, notice of transfer.

verplant', (~), transplant, plant out; ~ **baar, (..bare)**, transplantable.

verplan'ting, (-e, -s), transplanting, transplantation.

verpla'sing, (-e, -s), transfer; displacement (water); removal, shifting.

verpleeg', (~), nurse, tend, care for; ~ **de**, inmate, patient; ~ **diens**, nursing service; ~ **inrigting**, nursing home; ~ **kunde**, nursing; ~ **ster, (-s)**, nurse.

verpleeg'sters: ~ **raad**, nursing council; ~ **tehuis**, nurses' home.

verple'ër, verple'ger, (-s), male nurse; hospital attendant.

ver'pleet, (w) (~), electroplate; (b) **(..plete)**, electroplated; *verplete ware*, electroplated ware.

verple'ging, nursing; nursing care.

verple'gings: ~ **artikel**, nursing requisite; ~ **dag**, nursing day; ~ **inrigting**, nursing home; ~ **koste**, hospital charges.

verple'ting, electroplating.

verplet'ter, (~), crush, smash, shatter; squash; bow down; ~ **end, (-e)**, crushing, smashing, shattering; ~ **ing**, crushing, smashing; annihilation.

verplig', (w) (~), oblige, compel, force; *u sal my BAIE ~*, I shall be (very) much obliged to you; (b) **(-te)**, obliged, bound; beholden (to); compulsory; liable; ~ *te ONDERWYS*, compulsory education; ~ *VOEL*, feel obliged; *baie aan iem. ~ WEES*, owe much to somebody; *wetlik ~ WEES om*, be legally bound to; ~ **tend, (-e)**, compulsory, obligatory.

verplig'ting, (-e, -s), obligation; bond; onus; liability; commitment; committal; engagement; *GELDELIKE ~*, monetary (financial) liabilities; *sy ~ NAKOM*, fulfil (meet) his obligations; *'n ~ OPLÊ*, impose an obligation; *SONDER ~*, without any obligation; *onder die UITDRUKLIKE ~*, on the express condition.

verpoei'er, (~), pulverize; triturate (chem.); ~ **baar, (..bare)**, friable.

verpolitiek', (~), politicize; (b) **(-te)**, utterly fascinated, besotted.

verpoos', (~), rest; *'n spel waarmee hy hom ~*, a game for relaxation.

verpop', (~), pupate; ~ **ping**, pupation.

verpo'sing, rest, repose, relaxation; pause, intermission, lull.

verpot', (w) (~), plant in another pot, repot; pot out; (b) **(-te)**, repotted (plant); small, stunted (tree); in poor condition (animal).

verpraat', (~), talk away (time), waste time in gossiping; say more than one intends to, have a slip of the tongue; commit oneself.

verpulp', (~), pulp.

verraad', treason, treachery, betrayal, Punic faith; ~ *pleeg*, commit treason.

verraai', (~), betray, disclose, reveal, give away, divulge, double-cross; *dit ~ slegte smaak*, that shows bad taste; ~ **er, (-s)**, traitor, betrayer, divulger, Judas; ~ **erskus**, Judas kiss; ~ **ery**, treason, treachery.

verra'derlik, (-e), treacherous, treasonable, perfidious (person), insidious (disease); *'n ~ e blos*, a telltale blush; ~ **heid**, treachery, treacherousness, perfidy; insidiousess.

verras', (~), surprise, startle, take (catch) unawares (off one's guard); ~ **send, (-e)**, surprising; ~ **sing, (-e, -s)**, surprise; ~ **singsaanval**, surprise attack, swoop; ~ **singspakkie**, lucky packet; ~ **singsparty**, surprise party; ~ **sinkie, (-s)**, small surprise.

ver're, *see* **ver**.

verre'ën, verreent', (~), be spoiled by rain, be washed out.

ver'regaande, extreme (folly), extraordinary, exorbi-

tant (demands); uncommon, unheard of; down-right, flagrant (mistake).
ver'reikend, (-e), far-reaching.
verreis', (-de), way-worn; travel-strained.
verrek', (~), strain (muscle); twist, disjoint, dislocate (ankle); (w)rick, crick (neck); *jou nek ~ om ('n mooi vrou) te sien*, strain one's neck to see (a pretty woman).
verre'ken, (~), settle, clear, reckon up; misreckon, miscalculate; *jou ~*, miscalculate; *~ bank*, clearing bank; *~ ing*, settlement; clearing; miscalculation; accounting; *~ ingsbewys*, adjustment voucher; *~ ingskoers*, price of settlement; *~ ingsooreenkoms*, clearing agreement; *~ kantoor*, clearing-house.
verrek'king, strain(ing), dislocation, (w)rick, wrenching.
verre'se, risen; *uit die dood ~*, risen from the dead; *cf*. **verrys**.
ver'reweg, by far, far and away; *~ die beste plan*, by far the best plan.
verrig', (~), do, (work); perform (ceremony); execute (order); achieve (wonders); practise (custom); *~ ter, (-s)*, doer; *~ ting, (-e, -s)*, execution, performance, despatch (of business); function, meeting, action, achievement, acquittal (of duty); *~ tinge*, proceedings.
verrim'pel, (w) (~), wrinkle; *~ (d), (b) (-de)*, wrinkled; *~ ing*, wrinkling.
verrinneweer', (~) = verruïneer.
verroer', (~), stir, move, budge.
verroes', (w) (~), rust, get rusty, corrode, rust away; (b) (-te), rusty, rusted, rust-eaten; antiquated; neglected; *~ ting*, rustiness, rust, corrosion.
verrooms', (~), Catholicize; *~ ing*, Catholicization.
verrot', (w) (~), decay, putrefy, decompose; (b) (-te), rotten, decayed, putrid; corrupt; *deur en deur ~*, rotten to the core; *~ tend, (-e)*, putrefactive, putrescent.
verrot'ting, putrefaction, decay, rot; gangrene; putrescence.
verrot'tingsproses, process of decay (decomposition).
verruil', (~), exchange, barter, commute; *~ ing*, exchange, barter, commutation.
verruim', (~), enlarge, widen; broaden (the mind); *jou blik ~*, broaden one's view; *~ ing*, enlargement, widening; *~ ing van blik*, enlargement of one's mental horizon.
verruïneer', (~), spoil, ruin, destroy.
verruk', (w) (~), delight, entrance, charm, ravish, enchant, enrapture; (b) (-te), delighted, enchanted, ecstatic, rapt, overjoyed, enraptured, in raptures; *~ wees oor die goeie nuus*, be in raptures about the good news; *~ king*, delight, entrancement, jubilance, rapture, ecstasy; ravishment; *~ lik, (-e)*, charming, delightful, ecstatic, rapturous, ravishing, enchanting, entrancing; *~ likheid*, delightfulness, rapturousness.
verryk', (~), enrich; *sy kennis ~*, increase one's knowledge; *~ te BROOD*, enriched bread; *~ er, (-s)*, enricher (mixture); *~ ing*, enrichment; aggrandizement; *~ ingsaanspreeklikheid*, enrichment liability.
verrys', ~ rise (from death); spring up, emerge, arise; *soos paddastoele ~*, spring up like mushrooms; *~ enis*, resurrection.
vers¹, (s) (-e), heifer.
vers², (s) (-e), stanza, verse, poem; *iets met ~ en kapittel BEWYS*, quote chapter and verse; prove something up to the hilt; *die ~ e van ons beroemde DIGTER*, the poems by our famous poet; *IN ~ e*, in verse.
versaag', (w) (~), flinch, despair; (b) (-de), fainthearted, pusillanimous.
versaagd'heid, faint-heartedness.
versaak', (w) (~), forsake (friend); renounce, (world); neglect (duty); revoke, not follow suit, disavow; apostatize; (b) (-te), forsaken, neglected; revoked.
versa'dig, (~), satisfy, appease, satiate (appetite); saturate (chem.); *~ baar, (..bare)*, satiable; saturable.

versa'digdheid, satiety; saturation.
versa'dig: *~ ing*, satisfaction, satiety, fill, appeasement; impregnation; saturation; *~ ingspunt*, saturation point.
versag', (~), soften (heart); relieve, mollify, palliate, mitigate, allay (pain); commute (prison sentence); ease, assuage, (a)meliorate, soothe (pain); extenuate; modify (tone), tone down.
versag'tend, (-e), softening, extenuating, alleviating, alleviative, mitigative, (e)mollient, palliative, emulsive, mitigating; *~ e MIDDEL*, palliative, anodyne; *~ e OMSTANDIGHEDE*, extenuating circumstances; *~ e UITDRUKKING*, euphemistic expression, euphemism.
versag': *~ ter, (-s)*, alleviator, mitigator; *~ ting*, alleviation, mitigation, relief, amelioration, modification, extenuation, assuagement, mollification, breathing space; commutation (sentence); palliation; euphemism; *~ tingsmiddel*, palliative, lenitive.
versak', (~), give way, subside, sag.
versa'ker, (-s), renouncer, apostate, neglecter.
versa'king, forsaking, renouncement, neglect, renunciation, forbearance, apostasy, lapse, disvowal; revoke (cards); dereliction (of duty); desertion; exposure.
versak'king, (-e, -s), sinking, subsidence; prolapse, procidence (womb).
versa'mel, (w) (~), collect (stamps); gather (strength); aggregate, congregate, forgather (people); muster (courage); raise (army); compile (book of poems); amass, store up, accumulate (riches); glean (news); (b) (-de), collected; *~ aar, (-s)*, collector, gatherer; compiler; hoarder, accumulator; gleaner; assembler (motor industry); *~ boek*, omnibus book; *~ depot*, collecting depot; *~ end, (-e)*, collective; *~ ing, (-e, -s)*, collection, compilation, anthology; aggregate, aggregation; congregation, gathering, agglomeration; muster; *~ naam*, collective noun; *~ plek*, meeting-place, trysting-place, rendezvous; *~ put*, gully-hole; *~ rekening*, summary account; *~ voël*, sociable weaver; *~ werk*, work of collecting; collective works; *~ woede*, collector's mania; *~ woord*, collective noun.
versand', (w) (~), sand up, silt up; (b) (-e), silted up, sanded; *~ ing*, silting, shallowing.
versap', (~), liquidize, liquefy.
vers'bou, metrical construction, versification.
ver'seboek, book (volume) of poems, anthology.
ver'sebundel, book (volume) of poems.
verse'ël, (w), seal; (b) (-de), sealed; *~ aar, (-s)*, sealer; *~ ing*, sealing.
verseep', (~), saponify, turn to soap.
verseg', (~), refuse point-blank; *ek ~ om dit te doen!* I refuse point-blank to do this; I'm blowed if I will!
verseil': *~ RAAK onder*, get mixed up with, drift into; *niem. weet waar hy ~ GERAAK het nie*, nobody knows what has become of him.
verse'ker, (w) (~), insure, assure; ensure; affirm; profess, avouch, assert, asseverate; ascertain; *JOU ~ van*, make sure of; *WEES daarvan ~*, (you may) rest assured about that; *~ aar, (-s)*, insurer, assurer, underwriter; *~ baar, (..bare)*, assurable, insurable; *~ de, (-s)*, insured, assured, policy-holder, assurer; insurant.
verse'kerdheid, assurance, security.
verse'kering, assurance, insurance; asseveration; protestation; avouchment, averment, affirmation; *~ teen BRAND*, fire-insurance; *ek GEE jou die ~*, I give you the assurance; *~ teen HUISBRAAK*, burglary insurance; *die ~ KRY*, receive the assurance; *~ teen ONGELUKKE*, accident insurance.
verse'kerings: *~ agent*, insurance agent; *~ deskundige*, expert in insurance matters; *~ fonds*, insurance fund; *~ kaartjie*, insurance ticket; *~ kantoor*, insurance office; *~ koste*, cost of insurance; *~ maatskappy*, insurance company; *~ ooreenkoms*, insurance contract; *~ polis*, insurance policy; *~ premie*, insurance premium; *~ reg*, law of insurance; *~ tarief*, insurance rates; *~ voorwaardes*,

conditions of insurance; ~ **wese**, insurance; ~ **wet**, insurance act.
versekureer', (geselst.), (~), secure (against loss).
versend', (~), dispatch, consign (goods); transmit (dispatch); forward (letter); ~ **er**, (-s), consignor, sender, forwarding agent, forwarder.
versen'ding, (-e, -s), dispatch, consignment.
versen'dings: ~ **koste**, transmission charges, forwarding charges; ~ **onderneming**, carrying-agency.
versend'lys, forwarding list.
ver'sene: *die* ~ *teen die prikkels slaan*, kick against the pricks.
verseng', (~), singe, scorch, blast, parch; ~ **end**, (-e), torrid.
verse'ping, saponification.
verses'voudig, (-de), sextuple.
verset', (s) resistance, opposition; revolt, insubordination; recalcitrance; *tot* ~ *AANSPOOR*, excite to resistance; ~ *AANTEKEN*, protest against; *GEWAPENDE* ~, armed resistance; *in* ~ *KOM*, protest; *LYDELIKE* ~, passive resistance; (w) (~), resist; protest; rebel; ~ **beweging**, resistance movement; ~ **pleger**, resister; ~ **pleging**, resistance (to police), resisting arrest.
verse'wevoudig, (-de), septuple.
ver'sie¹, (-s), heifer.
ver'sie², (-s), little verse, verselet.
ver'sie³, (-s), version.
versien', (~), overlook; let slip (opportunity); provide; service (motor-car); renovate; *'n huis* ~, white-wash (paint) a house.
ver'siende, far-seeing; long-sighted, presbyopic.
ver'slendheid, long-sightedness, presbyopia; farsightedness; hypermetropia.
versie'ning, white-washing, painting (building); renovation; servicing, service (motor-car).
versien'stasie, service station.
versier', (w) (~), adorn; frost, ice (cake); array, attire; purfle; prank; fret (woodwork); garland, spangle, deck out, drape, embellish, decorate, pipe (cake); garnish, trim (dress); (b) (-de), adorned, garnished, ornate, decorated; diademed; iced (cake); ~ **end**, (-e), decorative; ~ **der**, (-s), trimmer, decorator.
versie'ring, (-e, -s), decoration, ornament, garniture; frosting, icing (cake); embellishment, ornamentation; figuration; flourish; grace-note; *binnenshuise* ~, interior decorating.
versier'ings: ~ **kuns**, decorative art, ornamental art; ~ **motief**, ornamental motif; ~ **noot**, grace-note (music).
versier'pen, icing needle (nail).
versier'sel, (-s), ornament, decoration; frosting, icing (on cake), garnish; ~ **s**, grace-notes.
ver'siesmaker, (-s), rhymester, poetaster.
verslfika'sle, versification.
versifiseer', (~), versify.
versig'tig, (b) (-e), careful, prudent, chary (with money), cautious, precautionary, provident, wary, discreet, canny; (bw) gingerly; charily; *hy is taamlik* ~, he is not very brave; he is rather wary; ~ **erig**, (-e), rather cautious.
versig'tigheid, caution, prudence, discretion, cautiousness, chariness, carefulness, wariness, circumspection, discreetness; ~ *is die moeder v.d. POR= SELEINKAS*, prudence is the mother of wisdom; safe bind, safe find; let discretion be your tutor; ~ *is die moeder van WYSHEID*, look before you leap.
versig'tigheids: ~ **halwe**, by way of precaution; ~ **maatreël**, precautionary measure, prudentials.
versil'wer, (w) (~), silver, silver-plate (b); (-de), silver-plated; ~ **aar**, plater; ~ **ing**, silver-plating.
versin', (~), invent, devise, contrive (a plan); coin (a word); bethink oneself of; concoct, fabricate, make up (schemes); ~ **baar**, (..**bare**), conceivable.
versink'¹, (~), sink away; be absorbed; *in GE= DAGTE* ~, absorbed (sunk) in thought; *in GE= PEINS* ~, lost in meditation; *in die NIET* ~, pale into insignificance; *in SLAAP* ~, sunk in sleep.
versink², (~), galvanize, coat with zinc.
versink³, (~), countersink, sink (drill); ~ *te kop*,

countersunk head; ~ **beitel**, recessing tool; ~ **boor**, ~ **er**, (-s), countersink bit; ~ **hamer**, raising hammer.
versin'king¹, sinking away.
versin'king², galvanizing, coating with zinc.
versin'lik, (~), render perceptible to the senses; sensualize, carnalize; ~ **ing**, materialization.
versin'nebeeld, (~), symbolize.
versin'ner, (-s), inventor, fabricator.
versin'sel, (-s), invention, fabrication, concoction, made-up story, fiction, fancy, figment, fable; *pure* ~ *s*, pure inventions.
versit'¹, (~), displace, move, shift; *BERGE wil* ~, want to move mountains; *GEEN voet wil* ~ *nie*, unwilling to lift a finger; *hom* ~ *TEEN*, set one's face against, oppose.
versit'², (~), move one's seat, move up; *sy tyd* ~, stay (somewhere) too long.
verskaal', (~), go flat (stale).
verskaf', (~), supply, furnish, purvey, cater, provide with; procure, find; afford (pleasure); ~ **fer**, (-s), provider, purveyor; procurer; caterer; ~ **fing**, furnishing; provision; purveyance, catering.
vers'kalf, (..**kalwers**), heifer (calf).
verskalk', (~), outwit, outmanoeuvre, beguile, hoodwink, circumvent, take in, deceive, ensnare; ~ **er**, (-s), beguiler; ~ **ing**, circumvention, deception, deceit, outwitting.
verskans', (~), fortify, entrench, barricade, palisade; ensconce (oneself); rampart; ~ *te artikels*, entrenched clauses.
verskan'sing, (-e, -s), entrenchment, fortification, bulwarks, barricade, barrier, stockade; *oor die* ~ *HANG*, hang over the rails; ~ *s OPWERP*, throw up entrenchments; ~ **s**, defences.
verskeep', (~), ship, export; trans-ship.
verskei'denheid, (..**hede**), variety, assortment, diversity, diversification, miscellaneousness; range; *groot* ~ *van goedere*, large assortment (diversity, range) of goods.
verskei'denheidskonsert, variety concert.
verskei'e, several; sundry, various, diverse.
verske'ne, published; *'n onlangs* ~ *digbundel*, a recently published book of poems; *cf.* **verskyn**.
verske'ping, (-e, -s), shipment, shipping.
verske'pings: ~ **agent**, shipping agent; ~ **datum**, date of shipment; ~ **diens**, shipping-agency; ~ **koste**, shipping charges.
verskerf', (~), break into fragments.
verskerp', (~), sharpen; increase the severity of, intensify, accentuate; tighten up.; ~ **ing**, accentuation; tightening up.
versker'wing, fragmentation.
verskeur', (~), tear to pieces, rend (asunder); mangle, lacerate; *'n* ~ *de rok*, a torn dress.
verskeurd'heid, dissension, disruption; laceration.
verskeur'end, (-e), savage, ferocious; violent (pain); ~ *e diere*, savage animals, beasts of prey.
verskeu'ring, rending, (di)laceration.
verskiet'¹, (s) future; distance; perspective, vista; *in die* ~, in the distant future.
verskiet'², (w), (~), shoot away (cartridges); shoot (stars); fade, turn pale (colours); shift (pain); ~ *ende ster*, shooting star, meteor; ~ **ing**, shooting (stars); wasteful shooting; fading (colours).
verskik', (~), arrange differently, rearrange.
verskil', (s) (**-le**), difference (of opinion); disparity (in age); discrepancy (of stories); *DEEL die* ~, split the difference; ~ *van GEVOELE (mening)*, difference of opinion; *dit MAAK geen* ~ *nie*, it makes no difference; ~ *maak TUSSEN*, differentiate between; (w) (~), differ, vary; disaccord, disagree; contrast; *ons* ~ *OOR hierdie punt*, we differ on this point; *diere* ~ *VAN mekaar*, animals differ from each other; *ek* ~ *VAN jou*, I differ with you; *VAN mening met iem.* ~, dissent from; hold a different opinion; *dit* ~ *nie VEEL nie*, it does not differ very much.
verskil'fer, (~), peel off; become full of dandruff.
verskil'lend, (-e), different, discrepant, differing, various, unlike, several, diverse, diversified; ~ *van*, different from.

verskil'lerekening, adjustment account.
verskil'punt, point of difference; controversial point.
verskim'mel, (w), (~), become mouldy; (b); **(-de)**, mouldy; shy, timid; *'n ~ de kind*, a shy child.
verskin'der, (~), spoil by cutting (e.g. hair); disfigure, mutilate.
verskoei', (~), retread.
versko'le, hidden; *cf.* **verskuil**.
versko'ning¹, (-s), change of linen.
versko'ning², (-e, -s), excuse, exemption, pardon, apology; TER ~, by way of excuse (apology); ~ *VRA*, make an excuse, beg pardon.
verskoon'¹, (~), put on clean linen.
verskoon'², (~), excuse, pardon, exempt, forgive; ~ *my!* excuse me! ~**baar**, (..**bare**), excusable, pardonable, justifiable.
ver'skoot, long ball.
verskop', (~), kick away; cast out, spurn; ~**peling**, **(-e)**, outcast, pariah.
verskot', cash payment, out-of-pocket expenses.
versko'te, faded (colours); *cf.* **verskiet²**.
verskraal', (~), become thin (attenuated).
verskreeu', (~), scream (yell) at.
verskrik', (w) (~), startle, terrify, frighten, alarm, appal, horrify; (b) **(-te)**, terrified, frightened, awestruck, scared; ~**king**, **(-e, -s)**, horror, terror; *die ~ kinge van 'n aardbewing*, the horrors of an earthquake.
verskrik'lik, (b) **(-e)**, terrible, horrible, awesome, appalling, prodigious, frightful, atrocious, heinous, ghastly, dreadful; (bw) exceedingly; (very) much, awfully; ~**heid**, awfulness, prodigiousness, enormity, dreadfulness, horribleness.
verskroei', (~), scorch, singe, sear, parch; (b) **(-de)**, parched; ~ *de aarde*, scorched earth; ~ **end**, **(-e)**, scorching, singeing; ~**ing**, scorching, singeing, parching.
verskrom'pel, (~), shrivel, shrink, wither, wrinkle; *die ~ de gelaat*, the wrinkled face; ~**ing**, withering, shrivelling.
verskryf', (~), miswrite, make a slip of the pen; use up (ink); *ek het my ~*, I made a slip of the pen.
verskry'wing, **(-e, -s)**, clerical error, slip of the pen.
verskuif', (~), shift, move, slide; disturb; put off, postpone, procrastinate, delay, defer; transfer (to a different position); displace, dislocate; *'n amptenaar ~*, transfer an official; ~**baar**, (..**bare**), movable; postponable.
verskuil', (~), hide, conceal, ensconce (oneself); ~ *de ligte*, concealed lights.
verskui'we, (~) = **verskuif**.
verskui'wing, **(-e, -s)**, shifting, moving, postponement; faulting (geol.); transfer (to another post); reshuffle (of cabinet ministers); ~ *van grond*, landslide.
verskul'dig, **(-de)**, due, bounden (duty); beholden, indebted; owing; *ek is BAIE aan hom ~*, I am greatly indebted to him; *die ~ de BEDRAG betaal*, pay the amount owing (due); *met ~ de EERBIED*, with due respect.
vers'kuns, (art of) poetry; poetics.
verskyn', (~), appear, turn up, put in an appearance; be published (book); *die BOEK sal by Van Schaik ~*, the book will be published by Van Schaik; *voor die LANDDROS ~*, appear before the landdrost; ~ *VIR die beskuldigde*, appear for the accused; ~**dag**, day of appearance (law); ~**ing**, **(-e, -s)**, emergence, appearance; publication; ghost, phantom, phantasm, apparition; ~*ing AANTEKEN*, enter appearance (law); *sy ~ ing MAAK*, put in an appearance.
versky'ningsdag, day of publication; return day (law).
verskyn'sel, **(-s)**, occurrence; phenomenon; appearance, phase.
verslaaf', (w) (~), enslave; (b) **(-de)**, enslaved, addicted; devoted; ~ *RAAK aan*, become addicted to; *aan die drank ~ WEES*, be a slave to drink.
verslaafd'heid, addiction, enslavement; abandonment.
verslaaf'middel, habit-forming drug.
verslaan', (w) (~), defeat, conquer, discomfit; overturn; go flat (beer); *dors ~*, quench thirst; (b) **(-de, ..slane)**, conquered, vanquished; flat, stale.
verslaap', (~), oversleep (oneself); sleep away (time); *ek het my ~*, I overslept.
versla'e, dismayed, disconsolate, cast down; nonplussed, disconcerted, consternated, overcome.
verslae'en(t)heid, dismay, consternation; dejection, prostration.
verslag', (..**slae**), report, account, statement; ~ *DOEN*, give an account; ~ *GEE*, report; ~ *UITBRING*, publish a report; ~**boek**, record book; ~**geefster**, lady reporter; ~**gewer**, **(-s)**, reporter; ~**gewing**, report; ~**jaar**, year under review; ~**klerk**, record clerk; ~**vergadering**, report-back meeting.
verslak', (~), slag.
verslank', (~), slim; reduce (weight); ~**ing**, slimming; ~**ingskuur**, slimming course; ~**ingspil**, slimming pastille (pill).
verslap', (~), relax (muscles); slacken (trade); flag (energy); enfeeble (one's constitution); ~**baar**, (..**bare**), dispensable (law); ~**pend**, **(-e)**, enfeebling; flagging; ~*pende belangstelling*, flagging interest.
versla'ping, oversleeping; death.
verslap'ping, relaxation, slackening; flagging, enervation; ~**sfase**, diastole.
versla'we, (~) = **verslaaf**.
versla'wing, enslavement.
vers'leer, prosody; poetics.
versleg', (~), deteriorate, grow worse, degenerate; degrade; alloy; ~**tering**, ~**ting**, degeneration, deterioration; degradation.
verslen'ter, (~), idle away.
versle'te = **verslyt**, (b).
verslib', **verslik'**, (~), silt up, fill with mud.
verslind', (~), devour, gobble up, gorge, swallow up, consume; absorb; raven; ~**baar**, (..**bare**), absorbable; ~**baarheid**, absorbability.
verslind': ~**end**, **(-e)**, voracious, devouring, ravenous; ~**er**, **(-s)**, absorber; devourer; ~**ing**, devouring, swallowing, engorgement.
verslin'ger, (~), throw oneself away on; get infatuated; *jou ~ aan IETS*, get hooked on something; *hom ~ op (aan) 'n MEISIE benede sy stand*, throw oneself away on a girl beneath one's station; ~ *(d) WEES op*, be completely devoted to; be mad about.
verslons', (w) (~), dress in a slovenly way; ruin, spoil; (b) **(-de)**, slovenly; ~ *de klere*, untidy clothes.
verslonsd'heid, slovenliness, slatternliness.
verslui'er, (~), veil; conceal; fog.
versluk', (~), choke (by swallowing); *ek het my ~*, I swallowed the wrong way.
verslyk', (~), silt up.
verslyt', (w) (~), wear out, become threadbare; spend (time); take as; *vir 'n vriend ~*, (ong.), take as (look upon as) a friend; (b) **(-e)**, worn, threadbare (clothes); trite (expression); commonplace.
versmaad', **versmaai'**, (~), scorn, despise, slight, disdain; treat with contempt; *'n bedrag wat nie te ~ is nie*, an amount not to be despised.
vers'maat, metre; rhythm.
versma'der, **(-s)**, despiser, scorner.
versma'ding, scorn, disdain, contempt; slight.
versmag', (~), be parched; long for, languish, pine for; *van dors ~*, be dying of thirst (for a drink); ~**ting**, longing, pining, languishing.
versmal', (~), narrow, become narrower.
versmelt', (~), melt, smelt (ore), dissolve, liquefy; fuse, blend (colours); *in trane ~*, dissolve in tears; ~**ing**, liquefaction; conjugation; conjunction; fusion, blending.
versmoor', (~), suffocate, stifle, smother, be suffocated, asphyxiate; choke, overlie (piglets); repress (a shout).
versmo'rend, **(-e)**, suffocating, asphyxiant.
versmo'ring, suffocation, smothering, asphyxiation, stifling.
versna'pering, **(-e, -s)**, delicacy, dainty, titbit; light refreshment, snack, choice morsel.
versnel', (~), accelerate, quicken, speed up; *MET*

~de pas, at the double; *die PAS* ~, quicken the pace; *die TEMPO* ~, speed up the rate, increase the tempo; **~klep**, throttle; **~lend, (-e)**, accelerative, acceleratory; **~ler, (-s)**, accelerator; **~lerpedaal**, accelerator; throttle (of diesel engine).

versnel'ling, (-e, -s), acceleration; speed; gear; rapid (in river); *met DRIE* ~s, with three-speed gear; *HOOGSTE* ~, top gear; *LAAGSTE* ~, low gear; *TWEEDE* ~, second gear; *VERANDERLIKE* ~, changeable gear.

versnel'lings: ~bak, gear box; **~hefboom**, gear lever; **~kas**, gear box; **~krag**, accelerating force; **~meter**, accelerometer; **~rat**, speed gear.

versnel'vermoë, pick-up, accelerative power.

versnip'per, (~), cut up, shred; waste, fritter away; *sy tyd ~ met beuselagtighede*, fritter away his time on trivialities; **~ing**, cutting up; waste, frittering away (strength).

versny', (~), cut up; spoil in cutting; recut; blend (wine); **~ding**, offset, set-off (of wall); blending (of wine); cutting (the body) (Bib.).

verso'ber, (~), economize; **~ing**, austerity, economizing.

versoek', (s) (-e), request, petition; bidding; postulation; *'n ~ AFWYS*, refuse a request; *'n ~ om HULP*, a request for aid; *'n ~ INWILLIG*, grant a request; *OP ~*, by (special) request; *aan 'n ~ VOLDOEN*, grant a request; (w) (~), request, ask, demand, invite, desire, beg; pray; tempt; *dit is GOD ~*, this is tempting fate; *hulle het MY ~*, they requested me; *~ OM*, request, ask for; **~end, (-e)**, petitionary; precatory; **~er, (-s)**, petitioner; tempter, Satan.

versoe'king, (-e, -s), temptation; *vir die ~ BESWYK*, yield (succumb) to temptation; *in ~ BRING*, tempt; *in die ~ KOM*, be(come) tempted; *in die ~ LEI*, lead into temptation.

versoek'nommer, item by special request.

versoek'skrif, petition; memorial; *'n ~ INDIEN by*, submit a petition to; *'n ~ RIG aan*, address a petition to.

versoen', (~), reconcile, conciliate, propitiate, placate, atone; accommodate; *sy DAAD met sy beginsels ~*, reconcile his action with his principles; *~ RAAK met 'n vyand*, become reconciled with an enemy; *jou ~ met 'n VERANDERING*, reconcile yourself to a change; **~baar, (..bare)**, reconcilable, placable, atonable, reconciliatory; **~baarheid**, reconcilableness, placability; **V~dag**, Day of Atonement; **~deksel**, mercy-seat.

versoe'nend, (-e), conciliatory, reconciling, propitiatory, placatory, conciliative, expiatory.

versoe'ner, reconciler, conciliator, propitiator.

versoe'ning, (re)conciliation, reconcilement; atonement, propitiation (for sins); expiation.

versoe'nings: ~bloed, blood of atonement; **~bok**, scapegoat; **~dood**, expiatory death; **~gesind, (-e)**, conciliatory; **~offer**, peace-offering, expiatory sacrifice; **~poging**, effort at conciliation; **~politiek**, policy of conciliation; **~raad**, conciliation board; **~werk**, work of redemption.

versoen'lik, (-e), placable, placatory, conciliatory, propitiable; **~heid**, placability.

versoet', (~), sweeten, sugar, edulcorate; **~er**, sweetener; **~ing**, sweetening.

verso'ler, (-s), retreader; resoler.

verso'ling, retreading (tyre); resoling (shoes).

verson'dig, (~), annoy, bother, plague, irritate; *jou in jou siel ~*, be extremely annoyed; **~er**, annoyer, annoying person; **~ing**, annoyance, irritation.

verson'ke, absorbed, lost; sunk; *in GEDAGTE ~*, lost in thought, in a brown study; *~ KLINKNAEL*, sunk rivet; *~ KOP*, countersunk head; *~ SKROEF*, countersunk screw; **~ne, (-s)**, outcast, hobo, derelict, down-and-out.

verson'ne, invented, feigned, concocted, fictitious, fictive; *cf.* versin.

versool', (~), resole; recap (tyre); retread; reseal (road); boot.

versô're, versorg', (~), care for, attend to, provide for, cherish, take care of, look after; service (machine); manicure (nails); edit (manuscript); *goed versorgde TAAL*, polished style; *goed versorgde WEDUWEE*, a widow well provided for.

versorgd'heid, neatness, polish.

versor'ger, (-s), supporter, provider, fosterer, bread-winner; provisor (hist.).

versor'ging, maintenance, alimony; care, nurture; purveyance.

versor'gingsgestig, charitable home (institution).

versot', (~), besotted; keen on; *~ OP*, fond of, infatuated with; eager for; *~ RAAK op*, become enamoured of (infatuated with); **~heid**, fondness, infatuation; eagerness.

versover', in so far as, as far as; *~ (vir sover) dit moontlik is*, as far as it is possible.

versout', (~), make salt, salinize.

verspaans', (~), become (make) Spanish; **~ing**, becoming (making) Spanish.

verspan', (~), harness otherwise, change position (of draught-animals); brace; *~ de boog*, braced arch; **~ning**, wiring; bracing; change (of animals) in a team; **~ningsdraad**, bracing-wire; **~ningswinkel**, wiring-shed; **~stang**, brace rod; **~stuk**, brace, bracing.

verspeel', (~), gamble away; trifle away; lose; *die kans ~*, miss the opportunity.

versper', (~), block, choke, obstruct, barricade, encumber, foul, bar; *die weg ~*, bar the way; **~ring, (-e, -s)**, obstruction, barricade, entanglement, block(ing)-up, barrier, road-block, barrage (balloons); **~ringsdraad**, wire entanglement(s); **~ringspunt**, fouling-point.

verspied', (~), reconnoitre, spy, scout; **~er, (-s)**, spy, scout.

verspie'ding, espionage, spying, reconnaissance.

verspil', (~), squander, waste, dissipate; *sy geld en kragte ~*, waste one's money and energy; **~ler, (-s)**, waster, spiller; spendthrift; **~ing**, waste, squandering, dissipation; **~sug**, extravagance, wastefulness.

versplin'ter, (~), splinter, comminute, shatter, shiver; **~ing**, splintering; disintegration; comminution.

verspoel', (~), wash away; erode; **~ing, (-e, -s)**, wash-away; erosion.

verspoor', (~), rail.

verspot', (-te), ridiculous, silly, absurd, foolish, nonsensical, apish; **~(tig)heid**, folly, silliness.

verspreek', (~), speak incorrectly; say more than one intends to, commit oneself, make a slip of the tongue.

versprei', (w) (~), spread (rumour); scatter (seed); distribute (newspapers); propagate (belief); disseminate (doctrines); deploy, extend (troops); hawk (goods); stagger (holidays); radiate (light; heat); *deur die omroep ~*, broadcast (by radio); **~haar, (..bare)**, diffusible; **~(d), (-de)**, scattered (towns); sparse (population); straggling, dispersed; *~de BEVOLKING*, sparse population; staggered; *~de LAS*, distributed load; *~de LIG*, diffused light; *~de OPSTELLE*, stray (scattered) essays; *in ~de ORDE*, in extended order; *~de VERHARDING*, multiple sclerosis; *~de WINKELURE*, staggered shop-hours; **~dend, (-e)**, diffusive, spreading; **~der, (-s)**, spreader; diffuser; circulator; disseminator; propagator.

verspreid'heid, diffuseness.

versprei'ding, spreading, scattering, diffusiveness, dissipation; diffusion (of light); emission; occurrence (disease); circulation (newspapers); distribution (of plants); dissemination (of sedition); dispersion; propagation (of belief).

versprei'er, (-s) = **verspreider**.

verspre'king, (-e, -s), slip of the tongue, lapsus linguae.

ver'spring¹, (s) long jump; **(w) (-ge-)**, do the long jump; jump a good distance.

verspring'², (w) (~), leap (shift) out of position; sprain in jumping; **~end, (-e)**, staggered.

ver'springer, long jumper.

versprin'ging, staggering.

vers: ~reël, line of poetry; verse line; **~snede**, caesura; **~soort**, poetry type.

verstaal', (~), turn into steel; steel, harden; ~**kas**, case-hardening box.

verstaan', (~), understand, see, comprehend, gather, get (the hang of); *my is te* ~ *GEGEE*, I have been given to understand; *die KUNS* ~, know the art; know a trick well; *VERKEERD* ~, misunderstand; *WEL te* ~, it should be clearly understood.

verstaan'baar, (..**bare**), understandable, intelligible, comprehensible; distinct; *jou* ~ *maak*, make oneself understood; ~**heid**, intelligibility, comprehensibility.

verstaan'der, (-s), one who understands; *'n goeie* ~ *het net 'n halwe woord nodig*, a word to the wise is enough.

versta'ling, steeling.

verstand', sense, intellect, intelligence, discrimination, understanding, mind, reason; *hy is van sy* ~ *AF*, he is out of his mind; *iets aan die* ~ *BRING*, make something perfectly clear (understandable); *iem. na sy* ~ *laat GAAN*, leave someone to his own devices; *dit GAAN bo my* ~, it is beyond me; it beats me; *GEBRUIK jou* ~, use your common sense; *ek het my* ~ *uit GEPRAAT*, I talked until I was blue in the face; *GESONDE* ~, common sense; ~ *van 'n ding HÊ*, know a thing; understand something thoroughly; *hy is IN sy* ~, he is done for; ~ *kom met die JARE*, years know more than books; *JOU* ~! you're daft! met ~ *LEES*, read intelligently; *LOOP na jou* ~! go to the devil! go to blazes; *die* ~ *ONTWIKKEL*, develop the intellect; *hy het meer* ~ *in sy PINKIE as jy in jou hele lyf*, he has more brains in his little finger than you have in your head; *van jou* ~ *RAAK*, go out of one's mind; *my* ~ *STAAN stil*, it has me baffled (puzzled); *TRAAG van* ~, slow to understand; *sy* ~ *VERLOOR*, go off one's head; lose one's reason; *nie by sy VOLLE* ~ *nie*, not in his right mind; ~ *van WISKUNDE hê*, have a head for mathematics; ~**e**: *met dien* ~ *e*, on the understanding that.

verstan'delik, (-e), intellectual; mental, cerebral; noetic; ~ *AFWYKEND*, mentally deviate; ~ *VERTRAAG*, mentally retarded; ~**heid**, intellectuality, cerebralism, rationality.

verstand'eloos, (..**lose**), senseless, reasonless, stupid; ~**heid**, senselessness, stupidity; amentia.

verstand'houding, understanding; *'n BLIK van* ~, an understanding (knowing) look; *GEHEIME* ~, secret understanding; *GOEIE* ~, good feeling; *'n* ~ *hê met 'n NOOI*, be privately engaged to a girl; *ONDER die* ~ *dat*, on the understanding that; *'n goeie* ~ *SKEP*, create good feeling; *VRIENDELIKE* ~, friendly relationship.

verstan'dig, (-e), intelligent, sensible, discreet; politic, prudent(ial), rational, reasonable, wise, judicious; *dit is* ~ *om*, it is wise to; ~**heid**, intelligence, wisdom, good sense, judiciousness, prudence.

verstands': ~**kies**, wisdom-tooth; ~**leer**, noetics; ~**meting**, measurement of the intellect; ~**ontwikkeling**, enlightenment, intellectual development; ~**tand**, wisdom-tooth; ~**toets**, intelligence test, mental test; ~**verbystering**, mental derangement, insanity, mental alienation; ~**werk**, brainwork.

versta'ner, (-s), one who understands.

verstar', (w) (~), make (become) rigid or stiff, petrify; ~ *van skrik*, petrified with fear; ~**(d)'**, (b) (-**de**), rigid, inflexible; *'n* ~ *de sondaar*, a hardened sinner.

ver'ste, furthermost, furthest, farthest; hindmost.

verste'delik, (~), urbanize; ~**ing**, urbanization.

versteek'¹, (~), hide, conceal.

versteek'², change (shift) the pegs (pins).

versteen', (~), petrify, turn to stone, lapidify, fossilize; harden, set; ~**baar**, (..**bare**), petrifiable.

versteen(d)', (-**de**), petrified, fossilized, fossil; ossified; ~ *de HOUT*, petrified wood; *van SKRIK* ~, petrified with fear.

verstek'¹, (s) default; *by* ~ *veroordeel*, sentence (condemn) by default.

verstek'², (s) mitre (woodwork); ~**bak**, mitre-box; ~**balk**, jack-rafter; ~**blok**, mitre-block; ~**boog**, mitre arch.

verste'keling, (-e), stowaway.

verstek': ~**haak**, mitre square; mitre bevel; ~**hoek**, bevel mitre; ~**las**, mitre joint, diagonal joint; ~**saag**, mitre saw.

verstek'saak, default case.

verstek': ~**rat**, mitre wheel, mitre gear; ~**skaaf**, mitre plane; ~**steen**, mitre brick; ~**voeg**, mitre joint, diagonal joint.

verstek'vonnis, judgment by default.

verstek'werk, mitring.

verstel', (~), mend (clothes); alter; (re)adjust (engine); rearrange; change gears; ~**baar**, (..**bare**), adjustable; ~**bare** *LEER*, adjustable ladder; ~**bare** *MOERSLEUTEL*, shifting spanner; ~**baarheid**, adjustability, adaptability; ~**boor**, expansion bit.

versteld', dismayed, disconcerted, dumbfounded; ~ *staan oor die slegte nuus*, be staggered by the bad news; ~**heid**, dismay, perplexity.

verstel': ~**goed**, mending; ~**haak**, bevel protractor; ~**ler**, (-s), adjustor; ~**ling**, (-e, -s), adjustment; changing of gears; mending (clothes); ~**skroef**, (..**skroewe**), adjusting screw; ~**tang**, setter's tong; ~**werk**, mending.

verste'nend, (-e), petrifying, hardening, gorgonian.

verste'ning, (-e, -s), petrification, lapidification, fossilization, petrescence, ossification.

versterf', (s) death; *BY* ~, ab intestato, in case of intestacy; *ERFOPVOLGING by* ~, intestate succession; ~**reg**, law of succession; (w) = **versterwe**.

versterk', (w) (~), strengthen, invigorate (person); brace (mech.); fortify, reinforce (fortress); confirm, corroborate (statement); intensify, amplify (sound); heighten (delight); *iem. in sy KWAAD* ~, encourage someone in his wrong-doing; *dit* ~ *my in my OPVATTING*, this confirms me in my opinion; (b) (-**te**), strengthened; fortified; ~**te** *BETON*, reinforced concrete; *'n* ~**te** *STAD*, a fortified city; ~**baar**, (..**bare**), fortifiable; ~**band**, strengthening tape; ~**drank**, cordial; ~**end**, (-e), strengthening; bracing; intensive; corroborative; augmentative; invigorating, recuperative; analeptic; ~**ende middel**, restorative, bracer, tonic; ~**er**, (-s), amplifier, booster, intensifier, multiplier; tonic; ~**erbuis**, ~**erlamp**, amplifying valve.

verster'king, (-e, -s), support, reinforcement; recruitment; redoubt; fortification; corroboration; strengthening; consolidation; invigoration; amplification (sound).

verster'kings: ~**kuns**, art of fortification; ~**leër**, reinforcements; ~**middel**, tonic; invigorator; ~**troepe**, reinforcements; ~**werke**, fortifications.

versterk': ~**middel**, tonic, analeptic; ~**plaat**, stiffening (reinforcing) plate; ~**stuk**, bracing; gusset; ~**water**, spirits; *op* ~ *water sit*, place in spirits.

verster'we, (~), die out, mortify.

verster'wing, death; mortification, necrosis.

versteur', (~) = **verstoor**; ~**der**, (-s), perturber, disturber.

versteu'ring, (~) = **verstoring**.

verste'wig, (~), strengthen, stiffen, stag, make firm; consolidate.

verstik', (~), suffocate, choke, strangle, asphyxiate, smother; ~**kend**, (-e), suffocating, stifling, choking, asphyxiant; ~**king**, suffocation, asphyxia(tion); ~**kingsdood**, death by asphyxiation; ~**kingstoestel**, lethal chamber.

verstil', (~), become quiet (silent); be stilled; ~**ling**, stilling.

verstof', (w) (~), become dusty; (b) (-**te**), dusty, choked with dust.

verstof'lik, (~), materialize; ~**ing**, materialization.

verstok', (-**te**), obdurate, callous, confirmed (bachelor); unrepentant, hardened (sinner); ingrained (vice); ~ *te MISDADIGER*, an old lag; ~ *te OUJONGKÊREL*, confirmed bachelor; ~ *te SONDAAR*, hardened sinner.

versto'ke, concealed, hidden; ~ *INLATING*, stopped housing; ~ *VAN*, deprived of; devoid of, destitute of.

versto'king, burning up (fuel).

verstokt'heid, obduracy, hard-heartedness.

versto'le, secret, furtive.

verstom', (w) (~), become dumb, grow mute, dumb= found; strike dumb; amaze; (b) (-de), speechless, dumbfounded; astonished; ~ **staan**, be struck dumb; ~**ming**, speechlessness; amazement.

verstomp', (w) (~), blunt, stupefy, deaden, hebetate; (b) (-te), blunted, dull; blasé; ~**ing**, dullness, iner= tia; mental deficiency; blunting.

verstook', (~), burn, consume (coal).

verstoor', (w) (~), disturb (peace); upset (plans); vex, perturb, derange, break off (relations); interfere with, intrude upon (privacy); *die EWEWIG* ~, up= set the balance; *die openbare RUS* ~, disturb the peace; (b) (-de), vexed, annoyed, cross; ~**der**, (-s), disturber.

verstoord'heid, crossness, anger, annoyance; mad= ness.

verstoot', (~), disown (child); cast out; repudiate; re= ject, ostracize.

verstop', (w) (~), plug; engorge; obstruct, choke up, clog; hide; constipate; (b) (-te), clogged, blocked up; plugged; oppilate, costive, constipated; *'n* ~ *te riool*, a blocked sewer; ~**per**, (-s), obturator; ~**ping**, (-e, -s), stoppage; constipation, costiveness; obstruction; engorgement; clog(ging); oppilation.

verstopt'heid, constipation, costiveness.

versto'ring, (-e, -s), disturbance, interference, pertur= bation, derangement.

versto'teling, (-e), outcast, pariah.

verstout', (~), make bold, take courage (heart); have the impudence; embolden; *hom* ~ *om*, make bold to.

verstrak', (~), become tense, set (face).

verstram', (~), stiffen, become rigid; ~**ming**, stiffening.

verstrek', (~), furnish, supply, procure, provide with; *inligting* ~, furnish information.

verstre'ke, elapsed, expired; *'n week is reeds* ~, a week has elapsed already.

ver'strekkend, (-e), far-reaching.

verstrek'king, provision, supply.

verstren'gel, (~), entwine, intertwine, interlace; ~**ing**, intertwining, interlacing.

verstrik', (~), ensnare, entrap, entangle, entrammel, (en)mesh; ~**king**, ensnaring, trapping, enmesh= ment, entanglement.

verstrooi', (~), scatter, disperse; amuse, divert; dif= fuse; ~**(d)'**, (-de), scattered; absent-minded, distrait.

verstrooid'heid, wool-gathering, preoccupation, ab= sent-mindedness.

verstrooi': ~**end**, (-e), dispersive; ~**ing**, scattering, dispersal, dispersion; diversion, distraction, amusement; Diaspora (of Jews); diffusion; *Jode in die* ~ *ing*, the Diaspora.

verstryk', (~), elapse, expire; *twee maande het* ~, two months have elapsed; ~**ing**, expiry.

verstuif', (~), be blown away, fly away like dust; at= omize, spray, drift (sand).

verstuit', (~), dislocate, sprain (limb), ~**ing**, sprain(ing), luxation, dislocation.

verstui'we, (~) = **verstuif**; ~**r**, (-s), spray(er), atom= izer, pulverizer.

verstui'wing, dispersion; atomization; drifting.

verstui'wingstoestel, atomizer.

verstyf', **versty'we**, (w) (~), stiffen, grow stiff, tor= pify, grow numb; benumb; (b) (-de), stiffened.

verstyf'middel, stiffening agent.

versty'wend, (-e), cataleptic.

versty'wer, (-s), stiffener.

versty'wing, stiffening; benumbing; catalepsy.

versuf', (w) (~), grow dull, daze; begin to dote; (b) (-te), dull, dazed, doting.

versuft'heid, dotage; dullness; stupor.

versug', (~), sigh for; ~**ting**, (-e, -s), sigh, groan; ejaculatory prayer; *vrome* ~ *ting*, pious wish.

versui'ker, (w) (~), sugar; saccharify; become can= died, form sugar crystals; grain (jam, honey); ice (cake); gloss over; *'n bitter pil* ~, sugar a bitter pill; (b) (-de), candied; ~ *de SKIL*, candied peel; ~ *de VRUGTE*, candied fruit; ~**ing**, sugaring; sacchari= fication; icing (cake); crystallization (of fruit); graining (honey).

versuim', (s) omission, neglect; delay; negligence; de= fault; *deur 'n* ~, through an oversight; (w) (~), neglect, fail, default, omit; linger, tarry; delay; *'n* ~ *HERSTEL*, rectify an omission; *sy PLIG* ~, neglect one's duty; *'n VERGADERING* ~, fail to attend a meeting.

versuip', (w) (~), drown, be drowned; spend on drink; become waterlogged; (b) (-te), drowned; waterlogged (ground); ~**ing**, drowning; waterlog= ging.

versuk'kel, (~), exhaust in body or mind; tire out by bodily or mental strain; live in poverty; *sy het haar heeltemal* ~, she has worn herself out; ~ **(d)**, **(-de)**, weak and worn, in poor condition, decrepit.

versu'ring, acetification, acidulation.

ver'sus, versus, against.

versuur', (~), grow sour; embitter; acidify; *iem. se lewe* ~, be the bane of someone's life.

vers'voet, metrical foot.

verswaar', (~), aggravate (burden); make heavier (load); encumber (with debt); *'n vonnis* ~, make a sentence heavier.

verswa'er, (~), ally by marriage; ~**ing**, relationship by marriage.

verswak', (~), weaken (eyes); enervate, attenuate, devitalize, enfeeble, debilitate; run down (battery); ~ *te kragte*, weakened strength; ~**ker**, (-s), attenu= ator; ~**king**, attenuation, enervation, weakening, debilitation, enfeeblement.

verswa'rend, (-e), aggravating; ~ *e omstandighede*, aggravating circumstances.

verswa'ring, aggravation, weighting; strengthening.

verswe'ë, tacit, undisclosed; *cf.* **verswyg**.

verswéer', (~), fester, suppurate, ulcerate.

verswelg', (~), swallow, gorge, devour, engulf; ~**er**, (-s), swallower, devourer; ~**ing**, swallowing, devouring.

verswen'del, (~), squander, waste.

verswe'ring, (-e, -s), suppuration, festering; ulceration.

verswik', (~), sprain, dislocate (limb); twist; ~**king**, sprain, twisting, dislocation.

verswyg', (~), suppress, keep silent, conceal; *iets* ~, keep something mum; hold something back.

verswy'ging, suppression, concealment.

vertaal', (~), translate, render, construe; *uit DUITS in Afrikaans* ~, translate from German into Afri= kaans; *LETTERLIK* ~, translate literally; *WOORDELIK* ~, translate word for word; ~**baar**, (..bare), translatable; ~**buro**, translation bureau; ~**kuns**, art of translation; ~**kursus**, trans= lation course; ~**metode**, translation method; ~**oe= fening**, translation exercise; ~**reg**, right of transla= tion; ~**werk**, translation (work); ~**woede**, translation mania.

vertak', (w) (~), ramify, branch off, (bi)furcate, di= varicate; dichotomize; (b) (-te), branched, rami= fied, furcated; ~ *te weerlig*, forked lightning; ~**king**, (-e, -s), ramification, branch(ing), (bi)fur= cation, divarication, embranchment, filiation.

verta'ler, (-s), translator; *beëdigde* ~, sworn translator.

verta'ling, (-e, -s), translation; version, rendering; *vrye* ~, free translation.

vertan'ding, serration; toothing; tooth (gearing), cogging.

ver'te, (-s), distance; *IN DIE* ~, in the distance; *UIT die* ~, from a distance, from afar; *nie in die VERSTE* ~ *nie*, not in the least.

verte'der, (~), soften, dulcify, mollify, melt; ~ *deur haar trane*, mollified by her tears; ~**ing**, softening, mollification, melting; tenderness.

verteenwoor'dig, (~), represent; ~**end**, (-e), rep= resentative; ~**er**, (-s), representative; exponent; ~**ing**, representation, agency.

verteer', (~), digest (food); assimilate (knowledge); spend (money); consume, devour (by flames); fret; *deur JALOESIE* ~, eaten up with jealousy; *vandag* ~, *more ontbeer*, wilful waste makes woeful want; stuff today and starve tomorrow; (b) (-de), di= gested; ~**baar**, (..bare), digestible; consumable; ~**baarheid**, digestibility; ~**der**, (-s), digestor; con= sumer; ~**put**, septic tank; ~**toestel**, digestor.

verte'ken, (~), draw incorrectly (wrongly), distort.
vertel', (~), tell, relate, narrate; recount; *HULLE ~ dat; daar WORD ~ dat*, the story goes that; *dit LAAT ek my nie ~ nie*, you cannot tell me that; ~ kuns, narrative art; ~ ler, (-s), narrator, relator, story-teller; raconteur; ~ ling, (-e, -s), narration, narrative, tale, story; recital; ~ sel, (-s), story.
verte'ring, consumption; wasting away; digestion.
verte'ringsvog, digestive fluid.
vertien'voudig, (~), increase tenfold, decuple.
vertik', (~), refuse point-blank; *ek ~ dit om . . .*, I absolutely refuse to . . .
vertikaal', (s) perpendicular; (b) (..kale), vertical; plumb; *..kale LUGSTROOM*, vertical air current; *..kale SPORING*, camber.
vertim'mer, (~), alter, rebuild.
vertin', (~), tin, coat with tin; ~ ning, tinning; ~ sel, tinning.
vertoef', vertoe'we, (~), stay, linger, tarry, sojourn, abide.
vertolk', (~), interpret, explain (text); read; voice (feelings); render (music); *'n rol ~*, play the part of; ~ er, (-s), exponent (of doctrine); interpreter; performer; ~ ing, (-e, -s), interpretation; reading; rendering, rendition; version.
verto'ner, exhibitor; ~ ig, (-e), showy, ostentatious, flashy.
verto'ning, (-e, -s), show, ostentation, display, pageant, spectacle, performance; presentation; *'n MOOI ~*, a fine display; *'n TREURIGE ~*, a sorry spectacle; ~ s, shows; gauds.
vertoog', (..toë), treatise, essay; representation; discussion; remonstrance; *'n ~ INDIEN*, make representations, prefer a remonstrance; *vertoë RIG tot*, make representations to.
vertoon', (s) show, sight, display, array, ostentation, parade; flare; ~ *van GELEERDHEID*, a parading of learning; *met GROOT ~*, with a great show; *OP ~*, at sight; *UITERLIKE ~*, outward show; *net YDEL ~*, mere empty show; (w) (~), show, expose; enact, perform; play; flaunt, show off, flash, exhibit, display; produce (show); flare; ~ baar, (..bare), presentable; producible; ~ baarheid, presentability; producibility; ~ bord, poster; ~ dag, day of presentment (bills); day of showing (film); ~ duik, fancy dive; ~ huis, show house; ~ kamer, show room; ~ kas, display cabinet; ~ kuns, showmanship; ~ rugby, professional rugby; ~ stuk, show-piece; ~ sug, love of showing off; ~ venster, show window; ~ wedstryd, exhibition match.
vertoor', (~), change by conjuring.
vertoorn', (w) (~), incense, infuriate, anger, enrage; (~ d)', (b) (-de), irate.
verto'wer, (~) = vertoor.
vertraag', (w) (~), delay, slacken, decelerate, retard; *in jou ywer ~*, relax in one's zeal; (b) (-de), belated; ~ *de KABELGRAM*, deferred cablegram; ~ *de ONTSTEKING*, retarded ignition; ~ *de ONTWIKKELING*, arrested development; ~ *de ROLPRENT*, slow-motion picture.
vertra'ging, (-e, -s), retardation; lag (mech.); deceleration; delay; hang; drag.
vertra'gings: ~ aksie, delaying action; ~ geveg, delaying action; ~ rat, back gear; ~ taktiek, delaying (Fabian) tactics.
vertrap', (w) (~), trample upon, tread underfoot; (-te), downtrodden, trampled down.
vertrap'pel, (~), trample down, tread underfoot.
vertrap'ping, trampling upon.
vertre'ding, treading upon.
vertree', (~), tread upon; *in die stof ~*, trample underfoot.
vertrek¹, (s) (-ke), room, chamber, apartment.
vertrek'², (s) departure; *dag van ~*, day of departure; (w) (~), leave, depart, go (away), take one's departure, quit, shift, remove; distort, twist, pull (face); *geen spier ~ nie*, keep a straight face; display no emotion; ~ dag, day of departure; ~ datum, date of departure; ~ gesprek, exit interview; ~ hawe, port of departure; ~ king, (-e, -s), distortion, contortion; ~ rigting, direction of take-off; ~ sein, starting signal; ~ tyd, time of departure; ~ uur, hour of departure; ~ vlag, Blue Peter.
vertreu'sel, (ong.), (~), trifle away.
vertroe'bel, (~), stir up, make muddy; *die saak ~*, confuse the issue; ~ ing, confusion.
vertroe'tel, (w) (~), spoil, (over)indulge, (molly-)coddle, pet, pamper, cosset, fondle, mother; (b) (-de), bloated, pampered; *'n ~ de kind*, a pampered (indulged) child, a spoilt brat; ~ ing, spoiling, pampering, coddling, petting.
vertrok'ke, gone away, departed; distorted (face); *cf.* vertrek².
vertroos', (~), console, comfort, solace; ~ baar, (..bare), consolable; ~ tend, (-e), consolatory, comforting; ~ ter, (-s), comforter; ~ ting, (-e, -s), consolation, solace, comfort.
vertrou', (~), trust, confide in; rely upon, depend upon; ~ *op GOD*, trust in God; ~ *op 'n VRIEND*, rely on a friend; ~ baar, (..bare), reliable, to be depended upon; ~ baarheid, reliability, dependability; ~ baarheidsrit, reliability run; ~ d', (-e), well-acquainted, conversant; trustworthy, trusted, reliable; *jou ~ d MAAK met*, acquaint yourself with; ~ *d MET*, conversant with; *die ou ~ de OMGEWING*, the old familiar surroundings; ~ de, (-s), confidant; fiduciary.
vertroud'heid, trustworthiness; familiarity, knowledge.
vertrou'e, confidence, trust, assurance, credence, dependence, affiance, faith; *die volste ~ GENIET*, enjoy the fullest confidence; *op GOEIE ~*, in good faith; *IN ~*, confidentially, privately; ~ *INBOESEM*, inspire confidence; *MET ~*, confidently; *iem. in jou ~ NEEM*, take someone into one's confidence; ~ *STEL in*, place trust in, have faith in; *hulle ~ VESTIG op*, pin their faith on; ~ *WEK*, arouse confidence; *die ~ WEN (win) van*, gain the confidence of; ~ ling, (-e), confidant.
vertrou': ~ ensaak, matter of confidence, confidential matter; ~ enskwessie, question of confidence; ~ ensman, confidant; ~ ensmosie, confidence motion; ~ enswaar'dig, (-e), trustworthy, reliable.
vertrou'enswendel, confidence trick; ~ aar, confidence trickster.
vertrou'lik, (-e), confidential, private; confiding; fiduciary; ~ heid, confidentiality; intimacy, familiarity.
vertwy'fel, (~), despair; ~ *aan die toekoms*, despair of the future; ~ d, (-e), desperate; ~ ing, despair, desperation.
verui'terlik, (~), externalize; ~ ing, externalization.
veruitwen'dig, (~), superficialize.
vervaag', (w) (~), grow dim, fade away; (b) (-de), dim, faded; ~ *de herinneringe*, faded recollections.
vervaard', (-e), alarmed, fearful, afraid; ~ heid, alarm, fright, fearfulness.
vervaar'dig, (w) (~), make; compose; manufacture, fabricate, form; produce; construct; (b) (-de), manufactured; constructed; ~ er, (-s), maker, fabricator, manufacturer; ~ ing, making, manufacture; confection; fabrication; ~ ingsproses, proses of manufacture.
vervaar'lik, (-e), frightful, awful; huge; ~ heid, frightfulness, awfulness; hugeness.
verva'ging, dimming, fading (away), blurring.
verval', (s) decline, decay; escheat (property); maturity (of bill); dilapidation, deterioration, disrepair (of building); decrepitude (with age); decadence, degeneration (of morals); *in ~ RAAK*, fall into disrepair; *in 'n TOESTAND van ~*, in a state of decay (disrepair); (w) (~), decline; ebb; decay, fall into disrepair; fall (become) due, mature (bill); expire (lease); lapse (of right(s)); escheat (property); *in SONDE ~*, lapse into sin; *in die ander UITERSTE ~*, go to the opposite extreme; ~ baar, (..bare), lapsable; ~ dag, day of maturity, due date, date of expiry; ~ datum, due date.
verval'le, dilapidated, ramshackle (house); matured, overdue (bill); decayed; worn out, careworn (person); shrunken, haggard (face); forlorn; *van die troon ~*, deposed, dethroned.
verval'lendheid, dilapidation.

vervals', (w) (~), adulterate (food); falsify (documents); denature (alcohol); counterfeit (coins); fake (antiques); forge (signature); tamper with, doctor (accounts); load (dice); (b) (**-te**), adulterated; falsified; forged; ~ **baar**, (..**bare**), falsifiable.
verval'ser, (**-s**), falsifier; adulterator; forger, cooker (of accounts); counterfeiter; faker; huckster.
verval'sing, adulteration; falsification; faking; forgery, forging.
verval'singsmiddel, adulterant.
vervalst'heid, adulteration.
verval'tyd, due date; expiry; *op die* ~ , at maturity.
vervang', (~), replace, displace, substitute, supersede; deputize for; ~ **baar**, (..**bare**), commutable; replaceable; expendable; ~ **er**, (**-s**), substitute; replacement, refill; locum tenens; ~ **ing**, replacement; ~ **ingsmiddel**, substitute; ~ **ingswaarde**, replacement value; ~ **stuk**, replacement, spare part.
vervars', (~), freshen, make fresh.
vervas', certainly, surely.
vervat', (~), resume; take hold of otherwise, change the grip; ~ *in*, included in, implied in, contained in, couched in.
verveel', (~), bore, weary, irk; *ek het my GRUWELIK* ~ , I was bored to death; *JOU* ~ , be bored; ~ **d'**, (b) (**-e**), bored.
verveeld'heid, boredom, ennui.
verveelvou'dig, (~), multiply; ~ **ing**, multiplication.
verveer', (~), cast feathers, moult (birds); ~ **der**, (**-s**), moulter.
vervel', (~), slough, cast the skin, exuviate; desquamate; peel, blister (after sunburn).
verve'lend, (**-e**), boring, tedious, tiresome, dull, humdrum; *'n ~ e vent*, a regular bore; ~ **heid**, tediousness, boredom, ennui.
verve'lens, *tot ~ toe*, ad nauseam, to a sickening extent.
verve'l(er)ig, (**-e**), boring, wearisome, tedious, irksome, tiresome; ~ **heid**, tediousness, monotony, tedium, ennui.
verve'ling, ennui, tedium, boredom, tediousness.
vervel'ling, sloughing; desquamation; exuviation, ecdysis, peeling.
verve'ring, moulting.
ververs', (~), refresh; bait, ~ **ing**, (**-e**, **-s**), refection, refreshment.
verver'sings: ~ **departement**, catering department; ~ **diens**, catering service; ~ **hawe**, coaling-station; ~ **kamer**, ~ **lokaal**, refreshment room; ~ **kraampie**, refreshment stall; ~ **ontvangste**, catering receipts; ~ **plek**, refreshment room; ~ **tent**, canteen; ~ **uitgawes**, catering expenses; ~ **wa**, mobile canteen.
vervet', (~), turn into fat; ~ **ting**, becoming fat; fatty degeneration.
vervier'voudig, (w) (~), quadruplicate; (b) (**-e**), quadruple; ~ **ing**, quadruplication.
vervies', (~): *jou ~ OOR*, be annoyed at; *jou ~ VIR*, be vexed with
vervilt', (~), felt; ~ **ing**, felting.
vervlaams', (~), (make) Flemish; ~ **ing**, Flemishing.
vervlak', (~), fade away (colour); become shallow; superficial; ~ **king**, superficialization, becoming shallow (superficial).
vervlaks', (tw) confound it! hang (darn) it! drat it! deuced! downright; *ek sal dit ~ nie doen nie*, I'm hanged if I'll do it; ~ **te**, downright, damned, bally, blooming; *die ~ te dief*, the blooming (ruddy) thief.
vervlees', (~), carnificate.
vervleg', (w) (~), entangle; intertwine; (b) (**-te**), intertwined.
vervle'sing, carnification.
vervlie(g)', (~), pass rapidly (time); evaporate, volatilize; vanish (hope); ~ **ing**, vanishing; evaporation.
vervlo'ë, gone by; ~ *tye*, bygone times.
vervloei', (~), flow away; fade, run (colours); deliquesce; ~ **end**, (**-e**), diffluent; ~ **ing**, deliquescence; melting (of colours).
vervloek', (w) (~), curse, execrate, damn, anathematize, excommunicate, imprecate, blast; ban; (b) (**-te**), damned, cursed, accursed, confounded, blasted; ~ **er**, (**-s**), curser; ~ **ing**, (**-e**, **-s**), execration, curse, anathema, malediction, imprication, cursing; ban.
vervloeks', (tw), damn it! dash it! (bw) damned; ~ *dom*, damned stupid; ~ **te**, (b) damned, accursed.
vervloekt'heid, cursedness.
vervlug'tig, (~), volatilize, evaporate; etherealize; ~ **ing**, evaporation, volatilization.
vervoeg', (~), conjugate (verb); join; *hom ~ by*, apply to; join the company of; ~ **baar**, (..**bare**), capable of being conjugated, conjugable; ~ **ing**, (**-e**, **-s**), conjugation.
vervoer', (s) transport, traffic, carriage, cartage, conveyance, transmit, freight; porterage; railage; *per BOOT ~* , carriage by steamer; *KOSTE van ~* , transport charges; *MINISTERIE van V ~* , Ministry of Transport; *~ met PAKDIERE*, pack-animal transport; *~ van bederfbare PRODUKTE*, perishable traffic; *~ per SPOOR*, conveyance by rail; *VRY ~* , free transport; (w) (~), convey, transport, carry; *deur haat ~ word*, be transported with hatred; ~ **afdeling**, transportation department; ~ **baar**, (..**bare**), conveyable, transportable; portative, portable; ~ **band**, band-conveyor, conveyor belt; ~ **bedryf**, transport undertaking; ~ **bewys**, carrier's receipt; ~ **der**, (**-s**), conveyor, transporter, haulier.
vervoe'ring, enthusiasm, ecstasy, rapture; transport; *in ~ RAAK*, go into raptures; *in ~ WEES*, be enraptured.
vervoer': ~ **kontrak**, contract of carriage, ~ **koste**, carriage, cost of carriage, transport charges; ~ **maatskappy**, transport company; ~ **middel**, vehicle (means) of conveyance; ~ **moeilikhede**, transport difficulties; ~ **monopolie**, monopoly of transport; ~ **ondernemer**, carrier; ~ **onderneming**, transport undertaking; ~ **ontvangste**, traffic-receipts; ~ **prys**, cost of transport; ~ **skema**, transport scheme; ~ **staking**, transport strike; ~ **tarief**, rate of carriage; ~ **toelae**, transport allowance; ~ **verbod**, prohibition of transport; ~ **vraagstuk**, problem of transport; ~ **wa**, transport truck; pantechnicon; ~ **wese**, transport (matters).
vervolg', (s) (**-e**), continuation, sequel; future; *IN die ~* , in future, henceforth; *die ~ OP*, the continuation of; (w) (~), continue (narrative); follow; prosecute, proceed against (heretics); pursue, persecute; pester, plague; hound (the enemy); *wie ander ~ , STAAN self nie stil nie*, ill-doers are ill-deemers; *jou WEG ~* , continue (on) one's way; ~ **baar**, (..**bare**), liable to be prosecuted, indictable, suable, prosecutable; pursuable; ~ **baarheid**, suability; ~ **bundel**, sequel, continuation volume; ~ **de**, (**-s**), victim of persecution; ~ **deel**, sequel.
vervol'gens, further, then, thereupon, next, subsequently.
vervol'ger, (**-s**), pursuer; prosecutor; persecutor; *openbare ~* , public prosecutor; ~ **y**, persecution.
vervol'ging, (**-e**, **-s**), pursuit, chase; prosecution; persecution; *'n ~ INSTEL*, institute legal proceedings; *van ~ ONTSLAAN*, not subject to prosecution.
vervol'gings: ~ **gees**, spirit of prosecution (persecution); ~ **reg**, right of prosecution; ~ **waansin**, persecution mania, paranoia.
vervolg': ~ **klas**, continuation class; ~ **lys**, continuation list; ~ **nommer**, consecutive number; ~ **omsendbrief**, ~ **sirkulêre**, follow-up (circular); ~ **ster**, (**-s**), persecutrix; ~ **stuk**, continuation, sequel; ~ **sug**, spirit of persecution; ~ **sug'tig**, (**-e**), eager to persecute; ~ **vel**, continuation sheet; ~ **verhaal**, serial (story); ~ **werk**, serial work, sequel.
vervolle'dig, (~), complete, enlarge (upon), amplify; ~ **ing**, completion, amplification.
vervolmaak', (~), perfect.
vervolma'king, perfection.
vervorm', (w) (~), remodel, transform, recast; refashion; mould; distort; deform; (b) (**-de**), anamorphous (of crystals); ~ **baar**, (..**bare**), transformable, deformable; ~ **baarheid**, transformability; plasticity; ~ **ing**, (**-e**, **-s**), remodelling, recasting; deformation, distortion.

vervrag', (~), charter (out); ~**ter**, **(-s)**, charterer, freighter; ~**ting**, chartering, freighting.
vervreem', (w) (~), alienate (property); estrange, drift apart; *vriende van jou* ~, become estranged from your friends; (b) **(-de)**, alienated; estranged; ~**(d)'baar**, **(..bare)**, alienable; ~**(d)'baarheid**, alienability.
vervreem'ding, alienation, estrangement.
vervroeg', (~), fix at an earlier time, antedate (cheque); advance (date, spark); expedite, accelerate; ~*de ONTSTEKING*, advanced ignition; '*n VERGADERING* ~, put forward the time (date) of a meeting.
vervroe'ging, advancing (date); acceleration.
vervro'lik, (~), enliven, cheer up; ~**ing**, enlivenment.
vervrou'lik, (~), become effeminate, feminize; ~**ing**, feminization.
vervuil', (w) (~), grow foul; soil; become weedy, spread (as weeds), grow rank; *die tuin is heeltemal* ~, the garden has become choked with weeds; (b) **(-de)**, weedy, choked with weeds; dirty, filthy.
vervuild'heid, filth, filthiness; weediness
vervui'ling, foulness, dirtiness; weediness, spreading (of weeds).
vervul', (~), fulfil (promise); perform (duty); accomplish (desires); discharge (duties), execute (command); imbue; pervade; possess; redeem (pledge); fill, occupy (position); grant (wish); *HEELTEMAL* ~ *wees van iets*, be completely absorbed in something; *met SKRIK* ~, strike terror into; *iem. se WENS is* ~, someone has realized his ambition; ~**ling**, fulfilment, performance, discharge; realization; accomplishment; execution; *in* ~ *ling gaan*, be realized.
vervyf', (~), convert a try (rugby); ~**skop**, conversion of a try, goal; ~**voudig**, **(-de)**, quintuple; ~**voudiging**, quintuplication.
verwaai', (~), blow about (into disorder); (b) ~**(d)'**, **(-de)**, ruffled, dishevelled, blowzed, blowzy; blown about, wind-swept.
verwaand', **(-e)**, priggish, cocksure, cocky, conceited, pedantic, arrogant, overweening, stuck-up, flatulent (fig.), bumptious, hoity-toity; presuming; proud; presumptuous; pompous; ~**heid**, pedantry, arrogance, conceit(edness), presumption, presumptuousness, pomposity, priggishness.
verwaar'loos, (w) (~), neglect; (b) **(-de)**, neglected, unkempt; ~**baar**, **(..bare)**, negligible.
verwaar'losing, neglect, inobservance (of law), dilapidation; *met* ~ *van*, at the cost of, to the neglect of.
verwag', (w) (~), anticipate, await; expect (a baby); look forward to, apprehend; *soos te* ~*(te) was*, as was to be expected; (b) **(-te)**, anticipated (deficit); ~**tend**, **(-e)**, expectant, anticipatory; pregnant (woman).
verwag'ting, **(-e, -s)**, expectation, anticipation, prospect, promise, hope, expectance, expectancy; *teen ALLE* ~ *in*, contrary to expectation; *in BLYE* ~ *wees*, expecting; awaiting a happy event; *BO* ~, beyond expectation; *die* ~ *KOESTER*, cherish the hope; *alle* ~ *OORTREF*, exceed all expectations; *VOL* ~, in expectancy.
verwant', (s) **(-e)**, relative, relation; (b) **(-e)**, akin, allied; conjugate; related, connatural; associated, congeneric, congenerous, congenial; cognate, germane, kindred (languages); ~ *AAN*, related to; ~*e MAATSKAPPY*, associated company; *van MOEDERSKANT* ~, cognate; *van VADERSKANT* ~, agnate; ~*e VAKKE*, related subjects; ~*e WETENSKAPPE*, kindred sciences.
verwant'skap, relationship; affinity; alliance; consanguinity, kinship, agnation, cognation; ~ *AAN*, kinship with; ~ *MET*, affinity with.
verwant'skaps: ~**band**, family tie; ~**betrekking**, ~**verhouding**, relationship.
verwar', (w) (~), confuse, confound, complicate, muddle, perplex, ravel, bewilder, fog, distract, mix up, embarrass, entangle, embroil, disarrange; intertwine; *twee sake met mekaar* ~, confuse two matters with each other; (b) ~**(d)'**, **(-de)**, confused (ideas); disordered, embarrassed, confounded, complicated; disorderly; disarranged (hair); (en)tangled, fouled (fishing-line); perplexed, mazy; promiscuous; puzzled; '*n* ~ *de blik*, a bewildered look.
verward'heid, confusion, perplexity, maziness.
verwarm', (~), warm, heat; *jou by die vuurtjie* ~, warm oneself at a fire; ~**end**, **(-e)**, calefacient, calefactory; ~**er**, **(-s)**, heater; heating device, radiator; ~**ing**, heating, warming, calefaction; calorification.
verwar'mings: ~**buis**, heating tube; flue; ~**doeleindes**, heating purposes; ~**installasie**, heating installation; ~**oppervlak**, heating surface; ~**plaat**, warming-plate; hotplate.
verwar'mingstelsel, heating system.
verwar'mings: ~**toestel**, heating apparatus; radiator; ~**vermoë**, heating power; ~**waarde**, calorific value.
verwar'rend, **(-e)**, confusing, bewildering.
verwar'ring, **(-e, -s)**, confusion; embarrassment; disarray, disorder; revel(ling); disorganization; fluster, flutter, fuddle; jumble, pell-mell; entanglement, imbroglio; *in* ~ *bring*, throw into confusion.
verwa'te, arrogant, overbearing, overweening.
verwa'tenheid, arrogance, insolence, presumption.
verwa'ter, (w) (~), dilute, water down; weaken; ~**(d)'**, (b) **(-de)**, diluted, weakened; ~**ing**, watering down, weakening, dilution, adulteration.
ver'we, (ge-), paint; dye.
verwed', (~), wager, bet; lose in betting, gamble away.
verweef', (~), interweave, intertwine.
verweek', (~), soften; become soft.
verweek'lik, (~), enervate; make (become) effeminate; coddle; ~**ing**, enervation; mollification.
verweer'[1], (s) defence, resistance; (w) (~), defend, resist; *ek moet my* ~, I must defend myself.
verweer'[2], (w) (~), moulder away; erode, weather; (b) **(-de)**, weathered (rocks); weather-beaten (face).
verweer': ~**der**, **(-s)**, defender; defendant (in court); ~**deres**, **(-se)**, female defendant; ~**middel**, means of defence; ~**skrif**, written defence, apologia, plea.
verwees', **(-de)**, orphan(ed); ~**d'heid**, orphanhood.
verwek', (~), beget, father, procreate (children); sire (foal); generate (steam); stir up, raise, provoke (trouble).
verwe'king, softening.
verwek': ~**ker**, **(-s)**, procreator, begetter; author; causer, originator; ~**king**, begetting, procreation, progeniture, breeding (discontent), raising, stirring up.
verwelf', **(..welwe)**, vault.
verwelk', (w) (~), wither, fade; nutate (bot.); (b) **(-te)**, nutant, withered, wilted, faded; ~**baar**, **(..bare)**, witherable; ~**end**, **(-e)**, marcescent; ~**besie**, twigwilter.
verwelk'king, fading, withering.
verwelk'lik, **(-e)**, transitory, perishable.
verwel'kom, (~), welcome; extend (hand); ~**ing**, **(-e, -s)**, welcoming, welcome, reception.
verwelk'siekte, wilt(-disease).
verwen', (~), spoil, pamper, over-indulge, (molly-)coddle, pet, cosset; '*n* ~ *de kind*, a spoilt child; ~**ing**, spoiling, pampering, over-indulging; over-indulgence.
verwens', (~), curse, accurse, imprecate, execrate; beshrew; (b) **(-te)**, cursed; ~**end**, **(-e)**, imprecatory, execrative; ~**ing**, **(-e, -s)**, curse, oath; malediction, execration, imprecation.
ver'wer, **(-s)**, painter; dyer.
verwer'dig, (~), condescend, deign; *iem. met 'n ANTWOORD* ~, condescend to answer someone; *hy het hom* ~ *om met ons te GESELS*, he condescended to speak to us.
verwê'reldlik, (~), secularize; become worldly; ~**ing**, secularization.
verwe'rend[1], **(-e)**, erosive.
verwe'rend[2], **(-e)**, defending.
verwerf', (~), acquire, win (honour); obtain (degree); gain (knowledge); achieve, earn, get (honour); *see* **verworwe**.
verwe'ring[1], defence.

verwe'ring², weathering (rocks); erosion; disintegration, mouldering (crumbling) away, decomposition.

verwe'rings: ~ **laag**, patina; ~ **middel**, weathering agent.

verwerk', (~), take in; work into; elaborate; revise; metabolize (food); process; digest; assimilate; ~ **baar**, (..**bare**), adaptable; ~ **er**, processor, adaptor.

verwer'king, (-e, -s), digestion; working into; elaboration; recasting; adaptation (of novel); *die ~ v.d. leerstof*, the assimilation of what is taught.

verwerk'lik, (~), materialize, realize, actualize; ~ **ing**, realization, actualization.

verwerp', (~), reject (motion); decline (proposal); discard, cast off (out), disown, disapprove, disagree, disclaim, refuse; negative, defeat, vote down, disallow, overrule, throw out (motion); recuse (a judge); *'n voorstel ~*, reject a motion (proposal).

verwer'ping, rejection, repudiation, condemnation, reprobation, disclaimer.

verwerp'lik, (-e), rejectable, unacceptable, objectionable; ~ **heid**, rejectableness, unacceptableness, objectionableness.

ver'werswinkel, painter's shop.

verwer'we, (~) = **verwerf**.

verwer'wing, acquisition, purchase, gaining, acquirement, winning.

ver'wery, painting; dyeing; dye-works.

verwe'se, dismayed, disconcerted, dumbfounded, bewildered.

verwe'senheid, dismay, bewilderment.

verwe'senlik, (~), substantiate, realize, bring about, effect, bring into being, actualize, materialize, fulfil, effectuate; ~ **ing**, realization, actualization, materialization, fulfilment.

verwes'ters, (w) (~), westernize; (b) (-e), westernized; ~ **ing**, westernization.

verwe'we = **verweef**.

verwik'kel, (w) (~), embroil, enmesh, entangle, make intricate, complicate; *in moeilikhede ~*, involved in difficulties; ~ (**d**), (-**de**), involved, complicated; ~ **ing**, (-e, -s), intricacy, embroilment, complication, trouble; *die nuutste ~ inge*, the latest developments; ~ **ingsplan**, plot.

verwild', (-e), wild, dazed.

verwil'der, (~), grow wild; scare away, chase away; ~ (**d**), (-**de**), wild, savage-looking, ghostlike, dishevelled (hair); uncultivated, overgrown (garden); ~ **ing**, running wild; scaring away; degeneration.

verwis'sel, (~), exchange; alternate; commute; interchange; permute, change; *van KLERE ~*, change clothes; ~ **baar**, (..**bare**), interchangeable; permutable; commutable; convertible; ~ **baarheid**, interchangeability; commutability; ~ **ing**, (-e, -s), permutation, change, alternation; exchange; conversion; commutation; ~ **stuk**, spare part.

verwit'tig, (~), acquaint, inform, notify; ~ **ing**, warning, information, intelligence, notice.

verwoed', (-e), furious, mad, frantic, enraged, fierce; ~ **heid**, fury, madness, fierceness, rage.

verwoes', (w) (~), destroy; ruin (hopes); depredate, devastate, desolate, lay waste, ravage (country); (b) (-te), devastated, ruined, destroyed; ~ **baar**, (..**bare**), destructible; ~ **tend**, (-e), depredatory, destroying, destructive, disastrous, ravaging, devastating; ~ **ter**, (-s), destroyer; wrecker; devastator, ravager; depredator, annihilator; ~ **ting**, (-e, -s), destruction, desolation, devastation, havoc, ravage; blight; ~ **ting aanrig**, play (work) havoc.

verwond', (w) (~), wound, hurt; (b) (-e), wounded, hurt.

verwon'der, (~), astonish, amaze, surprise; *dit ~ MY nie*, I am not surprised; *jou ~ OOR*, be surprised at; ~ (**d**), (-**de**), astonished, surprised; ~ **ing**, astonishment, wonder, surprise; ~ **lik**, (-e), wonderful, astonishing; strange, amazing, odd, surprising; ~ **likheid**, wonderfulness; strangeness.

verwon'ding, (-e, -s), wound, hurt, wounding, trauma.

verwon'neling, (-e), vanquished person.

verwoord', (~), express, put into words; ~ **ing**, expression.

verword', (w) (~), decay, rot, decompose; degenerate; (b) (-e), changed for the worse, degenerate; ~ **ing**, decomposition; perversion, decadence, degeneration; ~ **ingsproses**, process of degeneration (decomposition).

verwor'pe, depraved, reprobate; rejected; ~ **ling**, (-e), outcast, castaway, waif, reprobate; ~ **ne**, (-s), outcast, pariah.

verwor'penheid, depravity.

verwor'we, acquired, gained, won; *DUUR ~*, hard-earned; ~ *EIENSKAPPE*, acquired characteristics; ~ *immuniteitsgebreksindroom (vigs)*, acquired immunity defect syndrome, Aids; *cf.* **verwerf**.

verwor'wenheid, (..**hede**), acquisition.

verwrik', (~), shift, move.

verwring', (~), distort, twist, wrench; ~ **ing**, distortion.

verwron'ge, distorted, twisted; ~ *styl*, involved style.

verwulf', (..**wulwe**), vault, cove.

verwurg', (~), strangle, throttle, bowstring; ~ **end**, (-e), choking; ~ **ing**, strangulation.

verwyd', (~), widen, enlarge, dilate.

verwy'der, (w) (~), remove (stains); eliminate (mistakes); discard (clothes); clear (weeds); enucleate (med.); absent, withdraw (oneself); alienate, estrange (friends); ~ **aar**, (-s), remover; ~ **baar**, (..**bare**), removable; (b) ~ (**d**), (-**de**), remote, distant; (bw) away; ~ **ing**, (-e, -s), removal; alienation, estrangement; elimination, clearing (rubbish).

verwy'ding, widening, dilation, dilatation; ~ **skroef**, dilatator.

verwyf', (w) (~), become effeminate; make effeminate, emasculate; (b) (-**de**), womanish, effeminate; much-married.

verwyfd'heid, effeminacy, philogyny; emasculation.

verwyl', (s) delay; *sonder ~*, without delay; (w) (~), stay, sojourn, linger, tarry.

verwys', (~), refer to (committee); relegate (matter to); *ter strafsitting ~*, commit for trial; ~ **nommer**, (-s), reference number.

verwy'sing, (-e, -s), reference; remand; relegation.

verwy'sings: ~ **kolom**, reference column; ~ **letter**, reference letter; ~ **metode**, method of reference; ~ **nommer**, reference number; ~ **teken**, reference (mark).

verwys'nommer, reference number.

verwyt', (s) (-e), reproach, blame, reproof, exprobation; *iem. 'n ~ van iets MAAK*, blame someone for something; *'n SAGTE ~*, a gentle reproach; (w) (~), reproach, objurgate, blame, upbraid; *MEKAAR ~*, exchange reproaches; *ek het my NIKS te ~ nie*, I bear no blame; ~ **end**, (-e), reproachful.

very'dol, ( ), frustrate, baffle, shatter, foil, balk, disappoint (hope); defeat (purpose); disconcert, discomfit, confound, blast, checkmate, cause to fail, counteract; ~ **end**, (-e), baffling; ~ **ing**, frustration, disappointment, defeat.

verys', (w) (~), freeze over; (b) (-**de**), frozen; ~ **ing**, freezing.

ve'sel, (-s), fibre, thread, filament, strand, fluff; ~ **ag'tig**, (-e), fibrous, filamentous; ~ **ag'tigheid**, fibrousness; ~ **bord**, fibre board; ~ **bos**, fibre bush; ~ **fabriek**, fibre factory; ~ **fyn**, subtle, elaborate; ~ **fynheid**, fibre fineness; ~ **gehalte**, fibre content; ~ **gewas**, fibre crop; ~ **glas**, fibre glass; ~ **ig**, (-e) = **veselagtig**; ~ **igheid** = **veselagtigheid**; ~ **isolasie**, fibre insulation; ~ **lengte**, staple, length of fibre; ~ **ontsteking**, fibrositis; ~ **perske**, mango; ~ **plank**, beaver board; ~ **plant**, fibrous plant; ~ **rig**, (-e), fibrous, stringy; ~ **ryk**, rich in fibre; ~ **skub**, scale, barb (of wool); ~ **staal**, stranded steel; ~ **stof**, fibrin; ~ **tjie**, (-s), filament, funicle; ~ **weefsel**, fibrous tissue; ~ **wortel**, root filament.

Vespasia'nus, Vespasian.

ves'per, (-s), evensong, vespers; ~ **boek**, vesperal; ~ **diens**, vespers; ~ **klok**, vesper bell; ~ **tyd**, vesper hour.

Vestaals', (-e), Vestal; ~ *e Maagd*, Vestal Virgin.

vestibu'le, (-s), entrance hall, lobby, vestibule.

ves'tig, (ge-), establish (business); settle, domicile, domiciliate; direct (attention); found; *die AAN= DAG op iets* ~, draw (direct) attention to some= thing; *hom ERENS* ~, settle somewhere; *sy HOOP* ~ *op*, pin one's hopes on; *die OË* ~ *op*, fix one's eyes on; ~**ing**, establishment, settling; installation; settlement.

ves'ting, (-e, -s), fortress, citadel, muniment, acro= polis, stronghold; ~**artillerie**, garrison artillery; ~**bou**, (building of a) fortification; ~**boukunde**, art of fortification; ~**boukundige**, fortress engineer; ~**geskut**, position guns; ~**muur**, fortress wall (mil.); embattled wall (archit.); ~**oorlog**, trench= warfare; ~**stad**, fortified town; ~**stelsel**, system of fortifications; ~**straf**, imprisonment in a fortress; ~**toring**, keep; ~**wal**, rampart; ~**werke**, fortifi= cations.

Vesuviaans', (-e), Vesuvian.

Vesu'vius, Vesuvius.

vet, (s) (-te), fat, lard; grease (for axle); suet (kidney); *die* ~ *v.d. AARDE*, the fat of the land; *iem. in sy eie* ~ *laat gaar BAK*, let someone stew in his own juice; *jou* ~ *sal BRAAI*, you'll be called to account; ~ *GEE*, step on it (motor-car); *HARDE* ~, suet; *hy IS vandag weer* ~, he is tipsy again; ~ *en maer JARE*, fat years and lean years; *so goed soos* ~ *op 'n warm KLIP*, of no avail at all; *van die* ~ *v.d. land LEWE*, draw a big salary, live on the fat of the land; *iem.* ~ *om die OË smeer*, throw dust into someone's eyes; *die* ~ *braai by my ORE uit*, my head is spinning; *SAGTE (uitgebraaide)* ~, drip= ping; *aan iem. is geen* ~ *te SMEER nie*, someone is past redemption; *op jou* ~ *TEER*, live on one's capital; *so WAAR soos* ~, as true as faith; (b) fat, corpulent, podge, pudsy, portly, obese (person); rich, fertile (land); bold, heavy (type); *in* ~ *LET= TERS (druk)*, in bold type; ~ *en MAER jare*, fat and lean years; *so* ~ *soos 'n VARK*, as fat as a pig; ~ *WEES*, be intoxicated; ~**afskeier**, grease sep= arator; ~**afval**, waste fat; ~**agtig, (-e)**, fattish, fat= ty; sebaceous (biol.); ~**arm**, low-fat (diet); ~**breuk**, steatocele, adipose hernia; ~**derm**, chit= terling(s); rectum; ~**dig, (-te)**, grease-proof; ~**druppel**, fat globule.

ve'te, (-s), quarrel, feud, bitter strife.

ve'ter, (s) (-s), lace, bootlace; (w) **(ge-)**, lace; give a hiding.

veteraan', (..rane), veteran, campaigner; ~**motor**, vintage car.

**ve'tergat, eyelet, hole (in uppers).

veterinêr', (-e), veterinary.

ve'ter: ~**punt**, tab; ~**ring(etjie)**, eyelet; ~**tang**, belt= punch; ~**werk**, lacing.

vet: ~**ganslewer**, foie gras; ~**gedruk**, printed in bold (heavy) type; ~**gehalte**, percentage of fat; ~**ge= swel**, fatty tumour; lipoma; ~**gewas**, wen; ~**heid**, fatness, obesity; plumpness; ~**horinkie**, ergot; ~**houdend, (-e)**, adipose; ~**kalk**, hot lime; ~**kers**, dip, tallow candle; ~**klier**, fat gland; ~**koek**, doughnut; suet dumpling; ~**kol**, grease spot; ~**kole**, bituminous coal; ~**laag**, layer of fat; ~**lam**, fat(ted) lamb, fatling; ~**lap**, grease rag; ~**lok**, fetlock; ~**lywigheid**, adiposity; ~**maag**, potbelly, tubby person; rennet bag; ~**maakbeeste**, store cattle; ~**maakdier**, fatling; ~**maakvark**, baconer; ~**maker**, feeder, fattening substance; ~**mes, (-ge-)**, fatten; ~**mesting**, fattening (up); ~**moer**, greaves.

ve'to, (s) (-'s), veto; (w) **(ge-)**, veto; ~**reg**, right of veto.

vet: ~**oplosmiddel**, grease solvent; ~**pan**, dripping-pan; ~**papier**, grease-proof paper; grease paper; ~**plant**, succulent; ~**plante**, *Crassulaceae*; ~**pot**, grease cup; dripping pot; ~**puisie**, blackhead, acne; ~**ryk, (-e)**, high-fat (diet); ~**sak**, fat (tubby) per= son, fatty, roly-poly, podge, humpty-dumpty; ~**salf**, cerate; ~**sel**, fat cell; ~**splitsing**, lipolysis; ~**spuit**, grease gun; ~**stertskaap**, fat-tailed sheep (Persian, Africander); ~**sug**, obesity, adiposity, lipomatosis; ~**sug'tig, (-e)**, obese; ~**suur**, sebacic acid, oil-acid; fatty acid; ~**sweet**, wool oil; ~**te en olies**, fats and oils.

vet'terig, (-e), greasy, fatty, fattish, tallowy; ~*e kos*, fatty food; ~**heid**, greasiness, fattiness.

vet'tig, (-e), fatty; fertile; ~**heid**, fatness; fertility, richness.

vet: ~**vanger**, grease-trap; ~**vark**, larder; ~**veeten= toonstelling**, fat-stock show; ~**verhouding**, harden= ing of fat; ~**vertering**, lipolytic digestion; ~**vlek**, grease stain; ~**voer, (-ge-)**, stall-feed: fatten; ~**vor= mend, (-e)**, fat-forming; ~**vry, (-e)**, grease-proof; ~*vrye gaarmaak*, fat-free cooking; ~**ware**, fats; ~**weefsel**, adipose (fat) tissue; ~**wol**, grease (in wool).

V: ~**-formasie**, V formation; ~**-geut**, arris-gutter; ~**-hals**, V neck.

vi'a, via, by way of; ~ *Pretoria*, via Pretoria.

viaduk', (-te), viaduct.

vibra'sie, (-s), vibration.

vibra'to, vibrato.

vibreer', (ge-), vibrate; ~**sif**, vibrating screen.

Victo'ria¹, Victoria; ~**kruis**, Victoria Cross; ~**water= val**, Victoria Falls.

victo'ria², (-s), victoria (coach).

Victoriaan', (..riane), Victorian; ~**s', (-e)**, Victo= rian.

vi'deo, (-'s), video; ~**band**, video tape; ~**bandop= nemer**, video tape recorder; ~**kasset**, video cas= sette; ~**kassetopnemer**, video cassette recorder; ~**opnemer**, video recorder.

vief, (viewe; viewer, -ste), lively, active, spruce; ~**heid**, spruceness, liveliness.

vier¹, (w) (ge-), celebrate, hold celebrations, com= memorate, observe, keep.

vier², (w) (ge-), veer out; ease, slacken (rope); off, lay out (anchor).

vier³, (telw) (-e, -s), four; quaternary; ~ *uur*, four hours; ~**armig, (-e)**, four-armed; ~**bal**, foursome; ~**benig, (-e)**, four-legged; ~**blaar**, quadrifolium; ~**bladig**, ~**blarig, (-e)**, tetrapetalous, quadriphyl= lous, quadrifoil.

vier'daags, (-e), of four days, four-day; ~*e koors*, quartan fever.

vier'dag, day of celebration, anniversary.

vier'de, (-s), fourth; *ten* ~, in the fourth place; ~**daags, (-e)**, every fourth day; ~*daags koors*, quartan fever.

vier'dekker, quadruplane.

vier'delig, (-e), quadripartite, tetramerous, quatern= ary, consisting of four parts.

vier'demagsvergelyking, biquadratic equation.

vier'demagswortel, fourth root.

vier'dens, fourthly, in the fourth place.

vier'derangs, (-e), fourth-rate.

vier'desimalig, (-e), four-figure (table).

vier'dimensionaal, (..nale), four-dimensional.

vier'draads, (-e), four-ply, four-thread.

vierdubbel(d), (-de), quadruple, fourfold.

vier'duims, (-e), four-inch; ~**pyp**, four-inch pipe.

vier'eenheid, quarternity.

vie'rendeel, (ge-), quarter; draw and quarter; ..**de= ling**, quartering.

vier'fasig, (-e), four-phase.

vier'gangratkas, four-speed gearbox.

vierhan'dig, (-e), quadrumanous, four-handed.

vier'hoek, quadrangle; tetragon; ~**ig, (-e)**, quad= rangular, quadrilateral, four-cornered.

vier'honderd, four hundred; ~**duisend**, four hundred thousand.

vierhoof'dig, (-e), four-headed.

vie'ring, (-e, -s), celebration; (Sabbath) observance.

vier'jaarliks, (-e), four-yearly, quadrennial.

vier'jarig, (-e), of four years, four years old, quadrennial.

vier'kaart, sequence of four cards.

vier'kamerhuis, four-roomed house.

vier'kant, (s) (-e), square; quadrangle; quadrate; quadratic; ~ *teen iets GEKANT wees*, be dead against something; ~ *teenoor mekaar STAAN*, be diametrically opposed to each other, be poles asun= der; (w) **(ge-)**, square; ~**beitel**, square-edged chisel; ~**geut**, flat gutter; ~**hout**, square timber.

vierkan'tig, (-e), square; four-square; quadrilateral; quadrangular; *jou* ~ *VERSET teen*, set one's face

against; be dead against something; ~ *e VYL*, square file; ~**heid**, squareness.
vier'kantmaat, square measure.
vier'kantsgetal, square number.
vier'kantsvergelyking, quadratic equation.
vier'kantswortel, square root; *die* ~ *trek*, extract the square root.
vier'klawer, four-leaf clover.
vierklep'pig, (-e), quadrivalvular.
Vier'kleur, flag of the late South African Republic.
vier'kleuredruk, four-colour printing.
vier'kleurig, (-e), four-coloured.
vier'kwartsmaat, quadruple time.
vier'laag, four-ply.
vierlafooi', vierlavink', *(kinderterm)*, fourth finger.
vierle'dig, (-e), consisting of four parts, quadripartite; ~ *e doel*, a fourfold object.
vierlettergre'pig, (-e), of four syllables, quadrisyl= labic, tetrasyllabic.
vier'ling, (-e), quadruplet.
vierlob'big, vier'lobbig, (-e), with four lobes, four-lobed.
vier'maandeliks, (-e), four-monthly.
vier'manskap, quadrumvirate; the Big Four.
vier'master, fourmaster.
vier'motorig, (-e), four-engined.
vier'pantbal, four-panel ball.
vier'perde: ~**kar**, cart drawn by four horses; ~**sweep**, whip used with a team of four; ~**wa**, light wagon for a team of four; bridal coach; *in die* ~ *wa ry*, in a coach and four; on the way to be married.
vier'ponder, (-s), four pounder.
vier'pondsbrood, quarter-loaf.
vierpo'tig, vier'potig, (-e), four-legged, tetrapod; ~ *e*, (-s), four-legged animal.
vierpun'tig, vier'puntig, (-e), four-pointed.
vierre'ëlig, vier'reëlig, (-e), of four lines; ~ *e gedig*, quatrain.
vier'sadig, viersa'dig, (-e), tetraspermous.
vier'sellig, viersel'lig, (-e), four-celled; quadrilocular.
vier'sitplek: ~**kar**, Cape cart; ~**motor**, four-seater (motor-car).
vier'skaar, tribunal; judgment-seat; *die* ~ *span*, sit in judgment.
vier'skelling, (hist.), ninepence.
vier'slag: ~**enjin**, four-stroke engine; ~**steek**, quad= ruple treble.
viersna'rig, (-e), having four strings.
vier'span, team of four, four-in-hand.
vier'spel, four-ball (match) (golf).
vier'spoor: *uit die* ~, from the start (beginning)
vier'sprong, four-way, cross-ways, crossroads; part= ing of the ways; *op die* ~ *van die lewe*, at the cross-roads of life.
vier'stemmig, vierstem'mig, (-e), arranged for four voices, four-part.
vier'stralig, vierstra'lig, (-e), tetrarch.
vier'stukbattery, four-gun battery.
vier'sydig, viersy'dig, (-e), quadrilateral, tetrahedral.
vier'takmotor, four-stroke motor.
vier'tal, (-le), four, tetrad, quaternity, quartet(te); quadruplet.
vier'talig, vierta'lig, (-e), in four languages, quadrilingual.
viertall'ig, (-e), quaternary.
vier'tandvurk, four-pronged fork.
vierter'mig, (-e), quadrinomial.
vier'tjie, (-s), (small) four; *'n* ~ *maak*, hole out in four.
vier'uur, four o'clock; ~ *hou*, have afternoon tea; ~ **tjie, (-s)**, afternoon lady *(Mirabilis jalapa)*, four-o'clock (flower); afternoon break.
vier'vinger, (-s), tetradactyle, four-fingered.
vier'vlak, tetrahedron.
vier'vlakkig, viervlak'kig, (-e), tetrahedral.
viervler'kig, viervleu'elig, (-e), four-winged.
vier'voet, on all four; ~ *KRUIP*, crawl on all fours; ~ *VASSTEEK*, stop in one's tracks.
vier'voeter, quadruped.
vier'voetig, viervoe'tig, (-e), quadruped, four-footed.
vier'vors, (-te), tetrarch.
vier'voud, (-e), quadruple; ~ **ig, (-e)**, fourfold, quad=
ruple, quadruplex; quadruplicate; ~**igheid**, quad= ruplicity.
vier'waardig, vierwaar'dig, (-e), tetravalent.
vier'weekliks, (-e), four-weekly.
vier'wiel: ~ **er, (-s)**, four-wheeler; ~ **ig, (-e)**, four-wheeled; ~**remme**, four-wheel brakes.
vies, (w) (ge-): *jou* ~, be disgusted; (b) nasty, offens= ive, filthy; vexed, disgusted; fed-up; foul (weather); ~ *maak*, annoy, vex.
vie'serig, (-e), somewhat disgusted, rather fed-up; dirty.
vies'heid, annoyance; dirtiness.
vie'sigheid, dirt, filthiness.
vies'lik, (-e), dirty, filthy, loathsome, disgusting; ~**heid**, loathsomeness, filthiness, dirt, nastiness.
Viët'nam, Vietnam; ..**namees'**, (..**mese)**, Viet= namese.
viets, (-e; -er, -ste), spruce, smart; ~**heid**, smartness, spruceness.
vie'werig, (-e), lively, gay, active.
vigeer', (ge-), be in force, obtain (laws).
vigilan'te, (-s), cab.
vigs (verworwe immuniteitsgebreksindroom), Aids, acquired immunity defect syndrome; ~ **virus**, Aids virus.
vikariaat', (..riate), vicarage, vicariate.
vika'ris, (-s), vicar; ~**-generaal, (-se-generaal)**, vicar-general; ~**skap**, vicarship.
vikto'rie, (-ë, -s), victory; *te gou* ~ *kraai*, rejoice too soon; ~**kraaiend, (-e)**, cock-a-hoop; ~**skote**, salvo of shots celebrating victory.
viktua'lieë, victuals, provisions.
vil, (ge-), flay, fleece, flench, flense, strip, skin; ~ **der**, (-s), skinner, fleecer.
vilet', (-te), gillyflower, stock *(Mathiolaincana)*.
vil'la, (-s), villa.
vil'mes, flayer's knife.
vilt, felt; ~**agtig, (-e)**, felty, felted; ~ **gare**, felted yarn; ~**hoed**, felt hat; ~ **ig, (-e)**, felted; villous (bot.); ~**igheid**, villosity (bot.); ~**skyfie**, felt disc; ~**was= ter**, felt washer.
vin, (-ne), fin, flapper (whale), flipper; *GEEN* ~ *ver= roer nie*, not lift a finger; *ROER jou* ~*ne*, get a move on! ~**ag'tig, (-e)**, finlike.
vind, (ge-), find, ascertain, come across, meet with, light upon, locate, hit upon; think, consider; *hy is nie DAARVOOR te* ~ *(e) nie*, he will not have any= thing to do with it; *HOE* ~ *jy dit?* how do you like it? *MOOI* ~, admire, like, find (it) attractive; *ek* ~ *dit VERKEERD*, I don't approve of it; *sal jy VIND*, you'll find what you're looking for; ~**baar**, (..**bare)**, findable; ~**baarheid**, findability.
vin'der, (-s), finder.
vin'dersreg: ~ *hê*, findings are keepings.
vindika'sie, vindication.
vin'ding, (-e, -s), invention; discovery; device; creative ability.
vin'dingryk, (-e), resourceful, shrewd, ingenious, cre= ative, inventive; ~**heid**, resourcefulness, ingenious= ness, ingenuity, inventiveness, creativeness.
vind'plek, find-spot, occurrence; source.
vin'ger, (-s), finger; digit; *die* ~*s AFLEK*, lick one's fingers; *dit kan jy op jou* ~ *s AFTEL*, it is as easy as pie; *sy* ~ *s BRAND*, burn one's fingers; *iem om sy* ~ *DRAAI*, twist someone round one's little finger; *tussen* ~ *en DUIM wegraak*, steal away quietly; slip away unnoticed; *deur die* ~ *s GLIP*, slip through the fingers; *die* ~ *van GOD*, the finger of God; *gee hom 'n* ~ *en hy vat die hele HAND*, give him an inch and he'll take an ell; *my* ~ *s JEUK om* ..., my fingers are itching to ...; *LANG* ~ *s hê*, have long fingers; be light-fingered; *LEKKER is net 'n* ~ *lank*, pleasure is short-lived; no joy so great but runneth to an end; *die MIDDELSTE* ~, the middle finger; *die* ~ *op die MOND lê*, hush some= one; *iem. met vyf* ~ *s MOSES gee*, give someone a smack; *met die* ~ *NAWYS*, point an accusing fin= ger at; *die* ~ *OPSTEEK*, hold up one's finger, *iets deur die* ~ *s SIEN*, overlook a mistake; turn a blind eye; *jy sal jou* ~ *s nie blou TEL aan die geld nie*, you won't have much money to play around with; *iem op die* ~ *s TIK*, rap someone over the knuckles; *jou*

~s VERBRAND, burn one's fingers; g'n ~ VER=
ROER nie, not lift a finger; die ~ op die WOND lê,
put one's finger on the spot; ~afdruk, fingerprint,
dactylogram; ~afdrukafdeling, fingerprint div=
ision; ~afdrukkundige, fingerprint expert; ~agtig,
(-e), dactyline; ~alfabet, manual alphabet, finger
alphabet; ~alleen, all alone, all by oneself; ~bak=
kie, finger-bowl; ~band, finger-dressing; ~been=
tjie, carpal, finger-bone; phalanx; ~breed, of a fin=
ger's breadth; ~breedte, finger's breadth; nie 'n
~breedte afwyk nie, not to deviate a hairbreadth;
~deurslag, leg-punch; ~dier, aye-aye (Chiromys
madagascariensis); ~dik, as thick as a finger;
~doek, small napkin; ~doekie, doily, finger-cloth;
~drukking, digital compression; ~gaatjie, finger-
hole; ~gewrig, finger joint; ~glas, finger-bowl;
~gras, finger-grass; ~hoed, thimble; ~hoedjie,
foxglove (flower); ~(hoed)kruid, digitalis;
~(hoed)pol, fingerpoll (Euphorbia caput medu=
sae); ~kappie, finger-stall; ~kommetjie, finger-
bowl; ~krul, pin curl; ~las, (-se), finger joint;
~ling, (-e), finger-tip; finger-stall; ~lit, finger-
joint; ~loos, (..lose), fingerless; ~maal, finger
lunch (supper); ~merk, finger-mark; ~nael, fin=
ger-nail; ~oefening, five-finger exercise; ~plaat,
push-plate (on door); ~ring, finger-ring; ~setting,
fingering (music); ~skerm, finger guard; ~spraak
= vingertaal; ~steen, belemnite; ~stok, glove-
stretcher; ~taal, finger-and-sign language, finger
alphabet; chirology, dactylology; ~top, finger-tip;
~trek, fingerhooks (game); ~vormig (-e), finger-
shaped, digitate(d); ~wysing, (-e, -s), hint, indi=
cation, warning.
vin'haai, dogfish.
vinjet', (-te), vignette, flourished illustration.
vink, (-e), finch, weaver-bird; ~eier, (-s), finch's egg.
vin'kel, fennel, dill; dis ~ en koljander, it is six of the
one and half a dozen of the other; it is as long as it is
broad; ~blom, love-in-a-mist; ~water, gripe-
water; ~wortel, vegetable (Carum capense).
vink'nes, (-te), finch's nest.
vin'kplaag, plague of finches.
vin'loos, (..lose), finless.
vin'nig, (-e), quick, fast, nippy, speedy; sharp (reply);
rapid; fast-moving; rattling (pace); presto; ready;
apace, at full speed, full-swing; light-heeled, nim=
ble; fleet of foot; biting (retort); short-tempered; 'n
~e afdraande, a sharp descent; ~heid, quickness,
sharpness; expedition; fastness.
vin'poot, flapper, flipper.
vint, (-e), boil.
vin: ~vis, fin-whale, fin-back (whale); ~vormig, (-e),
fin-shaped, pinniform.
vin'walvis, rorqual; blou ~, blue whale.
vio'la, (-s), viola.
violet', (s) (-te), violet; (b) mauve, violet; ~kleurig,
(-e), violet, mauve.
violier', (-e), stock (-gillyflower).
violis', (-te), violinist, fiddler; ~te, (-s), (lady) violin=
ist.
violonsel', (ong.) (-le), violoncello; ~lis', (-te), vi=
oloncellist; ~liste, (-s), (lady) violoncellist.
viool', (viole), violin, fiddle; EERSTE ~ wil speel,
want to rule the roost; 'n ou ~ kan ook nuwe LIED=
JIES speel, many a fine tune is played on an old
fiddle; an old fiddle can play a new tune; TWEEDE
~ speel, play second fiddle; be henpecked;
~boomhout, kingwood; ~haai, sand shark; ~har=
puis, ~hars, colophony; ~kam, bridge (violin);
~kas, body of violin; ~kis, violincase; ~konsert,
violin recital (concerto); ~krasser, gut-scraper;
~les, violin lesson; ~maker, violin-maker; ~mu=
siek, violin music; ~onderwyser(es), violin teacher;
~saer, gut-scraper; ~skroef, tuning-peg; ~sleu=
tel, violin (treble) clef; ~snaar, violin string;
~solo, violin solo; ~speelster, (-s), (lady) violinist;
~spel, violin-playing; ~speler, violin-player, fid=
dler; ~stuk, violin solo, piece for the violin.
viool'tjie, (-s), violet; GROEN ~, wild hyacinth; WIT
~, chinkerinchee.
viool'vis, sand shark, fiddle-fish.
vir, for, to; during; ~ ALTYD, for ever, for all time;

eens en ~ ALTYD, for ever and anon; ~ die hele
DAG, for the whole day; EEN ~ een, one at a time;
one by one; ~ EERS, to begin with; for the time
being; ~ GOED, permanently; ~ GOU, in a jiffy;
goed ~ HOOFPYN, good for a headache; ~ hom=
self HOU, keep to (for) himself; ~ LAAS, for the
last time; ~ LIEF neem, put up with; ek ~ MY, I,
for one; ~ OULAAS, for the (very) last time; SÊ
~ my, tell me; ~ SEKER, for sure; suiker ~ tien
SENT, ten cents' worth of sugar; ~ SOVER, in so
far; ~ VAS, certainly, surely; ~ sover ek WEET,
as far as I know.
Virgi'lius, Virgil.
Virgi'nië, Virginia; ~r, (-s), Virginian; ..nies, (-e),
Virginian; ..niese tabak, Virginian tobacco.
viriel', (-e), virile.
viriliteit', virility.
virologie', virology.
virtueel', (virtuele), virtual.
virtuoos', (..tuose), virtuoso, skilled musician; ..tuo=
siteit', virtuosity.
virulen'sie, virulence; ..lent', virulent.
vi'rus, (-se), virus; ~griep, virus flu; ~siekte, virus
disease.
vis, (s), (-se), fish; DIE V~se, Pisces; soos 'n ~
DRINK, drink like a fish; so FRIS (gesond) soos 'n
~, as fit as a fiddle; soos 'n ~ op droë GROND voel,
feel like a fish out of water; INGELEGDE ~, mari=
nated (tinned) fish; so LEWENDIG soos 'n ~, as
lively as a cricket; ~ moet SWEM, fish must swim
thrice; wine must be served with fish; nòg ~ nòg
VLEES, neither fish, nor flesh, nor good red her=
ring; (w) (ge-), fish; ~ na KOMPLIMENTE, fish
for compliments.
vi'sa, (-s), visa.
vis: ~aas, fish-bait; ~afval, fish-refuse, pomace;
~agtig, (-e), fish-like, ichthyoid; ~akkedis, ich=
thyosaurus; ~arend, fish eagle; ~balletjie, fish
ball; ~bank, fish-bank; fish-stall; ~bek, fish's
mouth; bird's-mouth (carpentry); ~bemesting, fish
manure; ~beskrywing, ichthyography; ~blaas,
fish-bladder; ~blik, fish tin; ~bord, fish plate;
~broeiery, fish hatchery; ~dam, fish-pond, her=
ring-pond; preserve (for fish); ~dieet, fish diet;
~dief, tern.
vi'se-admiraal, vice-admiral.
viseer', (ge-), visé (passport).
vis'eier, berry (in fish-roe); ~s, roe, spawn.
vi'se-kanselier, vice-chancellor.
vi'se-konsul, vice-consul.
vi'se-lugmaarskalk, air vice-marshall.
visenta'sie, search, inspection.
visenteer', (ge-), search, inspect; ~beampte, exam=
ining officer; ~brief, search-warrant; ~mes,
searcher (implement); ~offisier, examining officer;
~yster, searcher (implement).
visente'ring, search, inspection, examination.
vi'se-president, vice-president.
vi'se-prinsipaal, vice-principal.
vi'se-rektor, vice-rector; vice-principal (univ.).
vis'etend, (-e), fish-eating, piscivorous, ichthyopha=
gous.
vis'eter, fish-eater, ichthyophagist.
vi'se-voorsitter, vice-chairman.
vis: ~fabriek, fish factory; ~fossiel, ichthyolite;
~frikkadel, fishcake; ~fuik, fish-trap; ~gebied,
fishing grounds (waters); ~gereedskap, fishing-
tackle (-gear); ~gereg, dish of fish; fish-course;
~gerei, fishing-gear; ~gier, erne; ~graat, fish-
bone; ~graatpatroon, herring-bone pattern;
~graatrat, herring-bone gear; ~graatverband,
herring-bone bandage; herring-bone bond (mason=
ry); ~graatsteek, herring-bone stitch; ~grond,
fishing grounds; ~haak, gaff, fish-hook; ~hande=
laar, fishmonger, fish-dealer; ~hek, heck; ~hoek,
fish-hook, angle.
vi'sie, (-s), vision.
visier'¹, (-e, -s), vizier.
visier'², (-e, -s), gun-sight, backsight; visor, elevating-
sight; met HOË ~ skiet, brag, exaggerate, draw the
long bow; iem. met OOP ~ bestry, fight openly;
STEL jou ~ hoog, he who aims at the stars shoots

higher than he who aims at a tree; ~**hoogte,** elevation (of gun-sight); ~**keep,** hindsight; notch (of gun-sight); ~**klep,** leaf (of the backsight); ~**kyker,** sight-telescope; ~**lyn,** line of sight.

visioen', (-e), vision, dream, phantasm; ~**êr',** (-e), visionary.

visita'sie, visitation, search, examination; ~**kommissie,** visitation committee.

visita'tor, (-e, -s), visit(at)or, inspector.

visi'te, (-s), visit, call; *'n* ~ *maak,* pay a visit; ~**kaartjie,** visiting-card.

vis: ~**jag,** spear-fishing; ~**jagter,** spear-fisherman; ~**kar,** fish-cart; ~**kenner,** ichthyologist.

viskeus', (-e), viscous.

vis: ~**koekie,** fishcake; ~**kom,** fish bowl, fish globe; ~**kop,** fish-head; ~**koper,** fishmonger.

visko'se, viscose.

visko'simeter, (-s), viscosimeter.

viskositeit', viscosity.

vis: ~**kuit,** spawn, roe, milt; ~**kunde,** ichthyology; ~**kun'dig,** (-e), ichthyological; ~**kun'dige,** (-s), ichthyologist; ~**kweker,** fish-farmer; ~**kwekery,** pisciculture, hatchery; fish-breeding; ~**lepel,** fish-slice; ~**lug,** fishy smell; ~**lym,** fish-glue, isinglass; ~**lyn,** fishing-line; ~**maal,** fish-meal; meal of fish; ~**mandjie,** creel, fish-basket; ~**mark,** fish market, billingsgate; *dit gaan hier soos 'n* ~*mark,* it sounds like a fishmarket; ~**mayonnaise,** fish mayonnaise; ~**meel,** fish meal; ~**mes,** fish-knife, fish-slice; ~**moot,** fish fillet; ~**mot,** fishmoth, silver fish; ~**net,** fishing-net, flue; ~**olie,** fish-oil, cod-liver oil, sperm-oil, ichthyol; ~**pastei,** fish pie; ~**patee,** fish paste; ~**reg,** fishing-right; ~**reuk,** fishy smell; ~**ryk,** (-e), abounding in fish, fishy; ~**rykdom,** abundance of fish; ~**rys,** fish kedgeree.

vis'ser, (-s), fisherman.

vis'sers: ~**bevolking,** fishing population; ~**boot,** fishing-boat, dogger; pink; ~**dorp,** fishing village; ~**hawe,** fishing port.

vis'serskuit, fishing-boat.

vis'sers: ~**lewe,** fisherman's life; ~**lied,** fisherman's song; ~**vloot,** fishing fleet; ~**volk,** fishing community; nation of fishermen.

vissery', (-e), fishery; ~**bedryf,** fishing industry; ~**maatskappy,** fishing-company.

vis: ~**skep,** fish server; ~**skietery,** shooting fish; spear-fishing; ~**skob,** ~**skub,** scale (of a fish); ~**skyf(ie),** fish steak; ~**slaai,** fish salad; ~**smaak,** fishy taste; ~**smeer,** fishpaste; ~**so(e)p,** fish soup; ~**soort,** kind of fish; ~**souter,** fish-curer; ~**spaan,** fish-slice; ~**speer,** gig, fish-spear; ~**spies,** grains; ~**stalletjie,** fish-stall; ~**steen,** ichthyolite; ~**stel,** fish-set; ~**stert,** fishtail; ~**stok,** fishing-rod, angling-rod; ~**stokkatrol,** troll; ~**teelt,** fish-breeding, pisciculture; ~**teler,** fish-breeder; ~**terman,** (geselst) fisherman; ~**torpedo,** fish torpedo; ~**traan,** fish-oil; ~**tuig,** fishing-tackle (gear); ~**tyd,** fishing season.

visualiseer', (ge-), visualize.

visueel', (visuele), visual.

vis'uil, fishing owl.

vi'sum, (-s, visa), visa.

vis'valk, osprey, fish-hawk.

vis'vang, (-ge-), catch fish, angle; troll; doze, niddle-noddle, nod; *op droë GROND* ~, fish on dry ground; *SIT en* ~, sit and nod; ~**er,** (-s), fisherman; kingfisher (bird); *groot* ~*er,* sea-eagle; ~**er-spinnekop,** fishing spider; ~**ertjie,** (-s), fishing bird; ~**ery,** fishing, fishery; ~**kuns,** halieutics, the gentle art; ~**plek,** fishing-spot; ~**s,** fishing, haul, catch; ~**wedstryd,** fishing competition.

vis: ~**venter,** fish-hawker; ~**vergiftiging,** fish-poisoning; ~**verkoper,** fishmonger; ~**vinger,** fish finger; ~**vervoer,** fish-traffic; ~**vormig,** (-e), fish-shaped; ~**vrou,** fishwife; fishwoman; ~**vurk,** fish-fork; ~**vywer,** fish-pond; ~**water,** fishing place, piscary; fish-stock; ~**weer,** fish garth (weir), kiddle; ~**winkel,** fish-shop; ~**wyf,** fishwife, fishwoman; ~**wywetaal,** billingsgate.

vit, (ge-), find fault with, cavil, carp; *op iem. (iets)* ~, find fault with somebody (something).

vitaal', (vitale), vital.

vitalis', (-te), vitalist; ~**me,** vitalism; ~**ties,** (-e), vitalistic.

vitaliteit', vitality.

vitamien', (-e), **vitami'ne,** (-s), vitamin; ~**gebrek,** lack (deficiency) of vitamins, hypovitaminosis; ~**gehalte,** vitamin content; ~**ryk,** (-e), rich in vitamins; ~**tablet,** vitamin tablet.

vitellien', vitelli'ne, vitellin.

vitofilis', (-te), vitophilist, cigar-band collector.

vitrioel', vitriol; *BLOU* ~, sulphate of copper; *GROEN* ~, sulphate of iron; *WIT* ~, sulphate of zinc; ~**agtig,** (-e), vitriolic; ~**olie,** ~**suur,** oil of vitriol, sulphuric acid (concentrated).

vi'tro: *in* ~ *bevrugting,* in vitro fertilisation.

vit'sug, censoriousness, fault-finding, captiousness.

vitsug'tig, (-e), fault-finding, captious.

vit'ter, (-s), faultfinder, caviller, carper, hypercritic, hairsplitter; ~**ig,** (-e), carping, fault-finding, captious, cantankerous, cavilling, pettifogging; ~**igheid,** fault-finding, censoriousness, cavilling, criticism, hair-splitting; ~**y,** (-e) = **vitterigheid.**

vi'vat, long live! three cheers for!

vivipaar', (..pare), viviparous.

vivisek'sie, vivisection.

vi'vo: *in* ~ *-bevrugting,* in vivo fertilisation.

V'-kerf, V notch.

vla, custard.

vlaag, (vlae), sudden squall, gust (of wind), access, outburst (emotion); shower (of rain); fit (of rage); *BY vlae,* by fits and starts; ~ *van MISDAAD* crime wave; *'n* ~ *van WOEDE,* a fit of anger; ~**lyn,** squall-line.

Vlaams, (s) Flemish; (b) (-e), Flemish; ~*e verband,* Flemish bond (mech.); ~**gesind,** (-e), in favour of the Flemish movement, pro-Flemish.

Vlaan'dere, Flanders.

vla-appel, custard-apple.

vla'erig, (-e), gusty.

vlag, (s) (vlae), flag, colours, standard, ensign, vexillum; vane; *die* ~ *HYS,* hoist the flag; *die* ~ *dek die LADING,* the flag protects the cargo; free flag makes free bottom; *met die* ~ *SALUEER,* dip the flag; *die* ~ *STRYK,* strike one's colours; *die* ~ *SWAAI,* start flag-waving; *die* ~ *UITSTEEK,* hang out the colours; *onder valse* ~ *VAAR,* sail under false colours; *onder watter* ~ *VAAR hy?* whose banner does he follow? *die Engelse* ~ *VOER,* fly the English flag; *met* ~ *en WIMPEL,* with flying colours; *die WIT* ~ *opsteek,* hoist the white flag, surrender; (w) (ge-), hoist (hang out) flags; ~**berig,** semaphore message; ~**doek,** bunting; ~**gie,** pennon, pennant, pendant, small flag; ~**houer,** flagman; ~**hyser,** flag-hoister; ~**hysers,** colour party (mil.); ~**hysing,** flag-hoisting, hoisting of the flag; ~**jonker,** midshipman; ~**kaart,** flag chart; ~**kaptein,** flag-captain; ~**komitee,** flag-committee; ~**kwessie,** flag-problem; ~**luitenant,** flag lieutenant; ~**man,** linesman (tennis, football); ~**offisier,** superior (naval) officer; ~**paal,** flagpost; flagstaff; ~**pen,** pin; ~**salm,** grayling; ~**sein,** semaphore; ~**seiner,** flagman; ~**sersant,** colour-sergeant; ~**skip,** flagship; ~**stof,** bunting; ~**stok,** flagstaff; flagpost (in ground); ~**stryking,** retreat ceremony (mil.); ~**swaaier,** (-s), flag-waver; *'n regte* ~*swaaier,* a flag-wagger; a braggart; ~**swaaiery,** flag-waving, flag-wagging; ~**tou,** flag-line; ~**vertoon,** showing the country's flag; ~**voerder,** flag-waver; flagship; ~**vraagstuk,** flag-question (-problem); ~**wetsontwerp,** flag-bill.

vlak, (s) (-ke), plane, level, surface, flat (of the hand); sheet (of water); facet (of gem); *'n HELLENDE* ~, an inclined plane; *op HELLENDE* ~ *raak,* be going downhill; be on the downgrade; *op HOË* ~ *onderhandel,* conduct negotiations at a high level; *op HOOGSTE* ~, at the highest level; (w) (ge-), level, flatten; face; (b) shallow, flat, plane; ~ *PLOOI,* open fold (geol.); ~ *SLOT,* flush lock; ~ *VOEG,* flush (flat) joint; (bw) flatly; ~ *AGTER hom,* immediately behind him; ~ *BO,* directly above; ~ *BY,* close up, near; *in sy GESIG,* bang in his face; ~ *NAAS my,* immediately next to me; ~ *VOOR hom,* right in front of him; ~**afmetings,**

superficial dimensions; ~**bakvoertuig**, low-sided vehicle; ~**beitel**, carving-chisel; chipping-chisel; ~**blok**, surface plate; ~**bol**, (-le), plano-convex; ~**bok**, steenbok *(Raphicerus campestris)*; ~**bord**, platter; ~**braai**, shallow frying; ~**gom**, India rubber, eraser; ~**by-opname**, close-up (picture); ~**druk**, offset (in printing); ~**haas**, (Cape) hare; ~**hamer**, set-hammer; ~**heid**, flatness; shallowness; ~**hoek**, plane angle; ~**hol**, (-le), plano-concave; ~**kerig**, (-e), rather shallow; ~**klinknael**, flush rivet; ~**kop**, countersunk head; ~**maat**, superficial dimension; ~**maker**, surfacer; ~**meetkunde**, plane geometry; planimetry; ~**papier**, blotting-paper; ~**slypmasjien**, face-grinding machine.
vlak′te, (-s), plain, flats, champaign, stretch, surface; *op die* ~ *sit*, be destitute; ~**bewoner**, plainsman; ~**-inhoud**, area; ~**maat**, surface measure, square measure; ~**meter**, planimeter; ~**meting**, planimetry; ~**snelheid**, areal velocity; ~**vorming**, planation.
vlak: ~**toets**, boning; ~**vark**, warthog; ~**versiering**, flat ornament; ~**voël**, spike-heeled lark *(Chersomanes albofasciata)*; pipit; ~**vyl**, stub file.
vlam, (s) (-me), flame, blaze, flare; grain, figure (in wood); vein (in marble); *'n OU* ~ *van hom*, an old flame of his; *in* ~ *me STAAN*, be ablaze; ~ *VAT*, catch fire; become enthusiastic; (w) (ge-), flame, blaze, burn; ~**bek**, jet; ~**blom**, phlox; red-hot poker; ~**boog**, electric arc; ~**boom**, flamboyant (tree); ~**dig**, (-te), flame-proof; ~**glas**, blazed glass; ~**gooier**, flame-projector.
Vla′ming, (-e), Fleming.
vlam: ~**kas**, fire-box; combustion chamber; furnace; ~**kleur**, flame (colour); ~**kleurig**, (-e), flame-coloured; ~**kole**, long-flame coal; ~**medood**, death by fire; ~**mend**, (-e), flaming, blazing; ~**mesee**, sheet of flame; ~**metjie**, (-s), small flame; ~**oond**, reverberating (heating) furnace; ~**punt**, flashpoint; point of ignition; ~**pyp**, blast-pipe; flue; fire-tube; ~**pypketel**, tubular boiler; ~**siekte**, bacterial blight; ~**skilder**, (ge-), grain; ~**skildering**, graining; ~**steenkool** = **vlamkole**; ~**stof**, inflammables; ~**stofpakhuis**, combustible stores; ~-**van-die-vlakte**, pride of De Kaap *(Bauhinia galpinii)*; ~**vanger**, flametrap (aero.); ~**vas**, (-te), ~**veilig**, (-e), flame-proof; ~**werper**, (-s), flame-projector.
vla: ~**poeier**, custard powder; ~**roomys**, custard ice-cream.
vlas, flax; ~**afval**, flax waste, boon; ~**agtig**, (-e), flaxy, flaxen; ~**baard**, flaxy beard; milksop; ~**bewerker**, flax-dresser; ~**blom**, flax flower; ~**boerdery**, flax culture, flax-growing; ~**braak**, flax-breaker (machine); ~**breker**, flax-dresser; flax-brake; ~**dodder**, false flax *(Camelina sativa)*; ~**draad**, flax-thread; ~**fabriek**, flax-mill; ~**handel**, flax trade; ~**handelaar**, flax-dealer; ~**hare**, flaxen hair; ~**hekelaar**, hackler; ~**kam**, flax-comb; ~**kleur**, flax(en) colour; ~**kleurig**, (-e), flaxen; ~**koper**, flax-dealer; ~**kruid**, flax-weed; ~**repel**, ripple (-cloth); ~**rok**, distaff; ~**saad**, flax-seed, linseed; ~**sig**, (-e), flaxy.
vla: ~**skyf**, custard slice; ~**sous**, custard sauce.
vlas′spinner, flax-spinner; ~**y**, flax-mill.
vlas: ~**stingel**, flax-stalk; ~**vesel**, flax-fibre; ~**vink**, linnet.
vla: ~**tert**, custard-pie; ~**vulsel**, custard filling.
vle′ël, (-s), flail; cur, boor, churl; ~**agtig**, (-e), currish, boorish, churlish; ~**jare**, awkward age.
vlees, *(see* **vleis**), flesh, meat; pulp; *ons eie* ~ *en BLOED*, our own flesh and blood; *die* ~ *DOOD*, deny the flesh; *alle* ~ *is soos GRAS*, all flesh is as grass; *die* ~ *is SWAK*, the flesh is weak; ~**geworde**, incarnate; ~**kleur**, flesh-colour; ~**kleurig**, (-e), flesh-coloured; ~**lik**, (-e), carnal; animal; fleshy; ~*like LUSTE*, carnal desires; ~*like OMGANG*, carnal intercourse; ~**likheid**, carnalism, carnality, concupiscence; fleshliness; ~**vormend**, (-e), flesh-building; ~**wording**, incarnation; transubstantiation.
vleet, (**vlete**), herring-net; skate (fish); *by die* ~, galore, tons of.

vleg, (s) (-te), braid, plait; tress; plexus; (w) (ge-), plait (hair); wreathe (garland); weave (mat); twine (plants).
vleg: ~**mat**, braided rug; ~**sel**, (-s), string (of plaited hair); tress; queue (pigtail); (gastric) plexus; ~**spar**, lacing-dropper; ~**strooi**, plait-straw; ~**ter**, (-s), plaiter; weaver; ~**werk**, wickerwork; interlacing; plaiting; ~**werkboot**, coracle.
vlei^1, (s) (-e), valley, vale, glen, marsh, swamp, vlei.
vlei^2, (w) (ge-), flatter, coax, blandish, adulate, butter, fawn, cringe, wheedle, soft-soap, cajole.
vlei: ~**agtig**, (-e), swampy, marshy; ~**disa**, vlei disa.
vlei: ~**end**, (-e), flattering, bland, complimentary, adulatory, cringing, fawning; ~**er**, (-s), flatterer, flunkey, blandisher, cajoler, adulator, bootlicker, fawner, cringer.
vlei′erig^1, (-e), marshy.
vlei′erig^2, (-e), flattering, cringing, honeymouthed, insinuating.
vlei′erigheid^1, marshiness.
vlei′erigheid^2, flattery, cajolery.
vlei′ery, flattery, blandishment, cajolery, adulation, butter, fawning, flummery, cringing, apple-pie sauce.
vlei: ~**gousblom**, marsh marigold; ~**gras**, reed-grass; ~**grond**, marshy ground, bog; ~**kuiken**, fluff-tail; ~**loerie**, coucal, rainbird.
vlei′naam, pet name.
vlei: ~**rosie**, meadow sweet; ~**rot**, marsh rat.
vleis, flesh, meat; pulp (of fruit); *BEVRORE* ~, frozen meat; *moenie die* ~ *BRAAI voor jy die wild geskiet het nie*, don't count your chickens before they are hatched; first catch your hare, then cook him; *GOED in die* ~, in good condition; *die* ~ *het 'n KRAKIE*, the meat has gone off; *weet watter* ~ *jy in die KUIP het*, know whom one is dealing with; *in die* ~ *SNY*, cut to the quick; *WILDE* ~, proud flesh; ~**aftreksel**, meat stock; ~**afval**, butcher's offal; ~**agtig**, (-e), fleshy, meaty, beefy; ~**bal**, meatball; ~**balk**, meat-bar; ~**bees**, beefer; ~**beskuit**, meat-biscuit; ~**beuker**, tenderizer; ~**blok**, butcher's block, meat-block; ~**blokkies**, cubed meat; ~**bolletjie**, croquette; ~**bord**, meat-dish; ~**braaiaand**, ~**braaiery**, barbecue; ~**braaiplek**, (place for) barbecue; ~**bredie**, goulash; ~**brood**, meatloaf; ~**byltjie**, meat-chopper; ~**dag**, meat-day; ~**deksel**, meat-cover; ~**dieet**, meat-diet; ~**ekstrak**, extract of meat, stock, essence of beef, beef tea; bovril (registred trade name); ~**erig**, (-e), meaty; ~**etend**, (-e), carnivorous; ~*etende diere*, carnivora; ~**eter**, carnivore; ~**frikkadel**, meatball; ~**gereg**, meat course (dish); ~**haak**, cambrel, meat-hook; ~**hal**, meat market; ~**hammer**, meat-bat; ~**handel**, meat trade; ~**jellie**, aspic; meat-jelly; ~**kant**, grain (leather); flesh side (of skin); ~**kar**, meat-cart (-wag(g)on), butcher's cart; ~**kas**, meat-safe; ~**keurder**, inspector of meat; ~**kleur**, flesh-colour; ~**kleurig**, (-e), flesh-coloured; ~**klopper**, meat bat; steak hammer; ~**koekie**, meat patty; ~**kop**, blockhead, num(b)skull; ~**kos**, meat dish; ~**kuip**, meat tub; ~**lappies**, grenadine; ~**loos**, (..lose), meatless; ~**maaier**, maggot; ~**maal**, meat dinner; ~**mandjie**, meat-basket; ~**mark**, meat market; ~**masjien**, mincer, mincing-machine; ~**meel**, meat meal; ~**mes**, butcher's knife; carving-knife; ~**meul(e)**, mincing-machine; V~**merino**, German merino; ~**naald**, trussing needle; ~**nat**, beef tea; ~**nood**, dearth of meat; ~**pan**, saucepan; meat pan; ~**pastei**, meatpie, meat-pasty; ~**pen**, meat-skewer; ~**plank**, chopping-board; ~**pot**, flesh-pot; *verlang na die* ~*potte van Egipte*, hanker after the flesh-pots of Egypt; ~**rantsoen**, meat ration; ~**ras**, beef breed; mutton breed; pork breed; ~**rasram**, mutton-ram; ~**rekening**, butcher's bill; ~**rol**, galantine; meat roll; ~**rolletjie**, beef olive; ~**saag**, kitchen saw; ~**sagmaker**, meat-tenderizer; ~**sap**, meat juice; pot liquor; ~**skottel**, meat dish; ashet, platter; ~**smeer**, meat paste, meat spread; ~**sny**, carving; ~**snyer**, meat slicer; ~**so(e)p**, meat-juice, stock; consommé; ~**sous**, gravy; ~**stuk**, joint; cut of meat; ~**uier**, big udder giving little milk; ~**uitwas**, caruncle; ~**vark**,

vleitaal 603 **vlieg**

porker; ~ **verbruik,** consumption of meat; ~ **vergiftiging,** meat-poisoning; ~ **vratjie,** caruncle; ~ **vulsel,** forcemeat; ~ **vurk,** meat-fork; ~ **wond,** flesh-wound.
vlei'taal, flattery, adulation, blarney.
vlei: ~ **-uil,** marsh owl; ~ **valk,** marsh harrier.
vlek¹, (s) (-ke), hamlet.
vlek², (s) (-ke), blot, spot, splodge, blotch, smut (of soot); stain, blemish (on character); macula(tion), freckle; cataract; blur; feather (in gems); gout (wheat); (w) (ge-), soil, blot, stain, mottle, spot, smudge; *dit sal gou* ~ , it will soil easily.
vlek³, (w) (ge-), flay, gut (fish).
vlek: ~ **haai,** spear-eye shark; ~ **kerig,** (-e), spotty, patchy, blotchy; ~ **kie,** (-s), small stain, smudge; dab (of paint); ~ **koors,** spotted fever; scarlet fever; ~ **loos,** (..lose), spotless, immaculate, fleckless; blameless; ~ *lose ontvangenis,* immaculate conception; ~ **loosheid,** spotlessness, immaculateness; purity; ~ **siekte,** swine erysipelas; dotiness (in timber); ~ **tifus,** typhus-fever, spotted typhus; ~ **verdeling,** maculation; ~ **voor,** open furrow; ~ **vry,** (-e), stainless; ~ *vrye staal,* stainless steel; ~ **wol,** stained wool.
vlerk, (-e), wing, pinion, flipper; aisle (of church); aerofoil; *sy* ~ *e HANG,* he is crestfallen (down in the mouth); *iem. se* ~ *e KNIP,* clip someone's wings; *sy* ~ *by 'n NOOI sleep,* pay one's court to a girl; *hoër vlieg as sy* ~ *e LANK is,* try to fly too high; fly higher than one's wings can carry one; *afstand,* gap of wing; ~ **dak,** single pitch roof; ~ **ie,** (-s), winglet; ~ **loos,** (..lose), wingless, apterous; ~ **moer,** wing(ed) nut; ~ **skild,** wing-cover; ~ **sleep,** (-ge-), court, go courting, make love; ~ **spanning,** wing-span; ~ **spits,** wing-tip; ~ **styl,** wing-strut; ~ **tip,** wing-tip; ~ **trilling,** wing-flutter; ~ **tuig,** all-wing aircraft; ~ **voetig,** (-e), aliped; ~ **vormig,** (-e), wing-shaped; ~ **winkel,** aerofoil shop; ~ **wortel,** wing-root; ~ **wydte,** wing-span, spread.
vler'muis, bat, noctule, flitter-mouse; pipistrel(le); ~ **mis,** bat guano; ~ **mou,** bat-wing sleeve; ~ **valk,** bat-hawk.
vle'sig, (-e), fleshy, beefy; pulpy; ~ **heid,** fleshiness; pulpiness.
vlet, (-te), punt (boat).
vleu'el, (-s), wing, pinion; vane; aisle, side-aisle; horn, flank (army); limb (building); wing threequarter, winger (sport); grand piano; *iem. se* ~ *s KORT,* clip someone's wings; *iem. onder sy* ~ *s NEEM,* take someone under one's wing; *die* ~ *s UITSLAAN,* spread one's wings; ~ **adjudant,** wing-adjutant, aide-de-camp; ~ **bevelvoerder,** wing-commander (S.A.); ~ **deur,** folding door; ~ **driekwart,** wing threequarter (football); ~ **klavier,** concert piano; grand piano; *groot* ~ *klavier,* concert grand; ~ **klep,** butterfly valve; ~ **klitser,** wing-whip; ~ **kommandant,** ~ **kommandeur,** wing-commander, ~ **kraan,** butterfly cock, ~ **lam,** broken-winged; *iem.* ~ *lam maak,* clip someone's wings; ~ **loos,** (..lose), wingless, apterous; ~ **man,** file-leader, fugleman; ~ **moer,** thumb nut, winged nut, butterfly-nut, fly-nut; ~ **nerf,** nervure; ~ **neut,** winged fruit, samara; ~ **piano,** concert (grand) piano; ~ **punt,** pinion; ~ **rat,** impellor (aero.); ~ **rug,** fastback (motor); ~ **rugstoel,** wing-backed chair; ~ **skild,** wing-case; ~ **skroef,** butterfly-screw; ~ **slag,** wing-stroke, wing-beat; ~ **spanning,** wing-span; ~ **spel,** wing-play (rugby); ~ **vormig,** (-e), wing-shaped, aliform, alar; ~ **wydte,** wing-spread.
vleug, (vleue), vleu'gle, (-s), last flicker, flash, flare-up.
vlie, (ge-), fly, aviate; career; *aan brand* ~ , catch fire.
vlied, (ge-), flee, fly.
vlie'ë: ~ **bossie,** fly-bush *(Roridula dentata);* ~ **deksel,** meat-screen; ~ **dig,** (-te), fly-proof; ~ **gaas,** wire gauze; ~ **gif,** fly-poison; ~ **kas,** meat-safe.
vlie'ënd, (-e), flying; *die V* ~ *e HOLLANDER,* the Flying Dutchman; ~ *e HOND,* flying fox; ~ *e PATROLLIE,* flying squad(ron), mobile patrol; ~ *e PIERING,* flying saucer; ~ *e TERING,* galloping consumption; *met* ~ *e VAANDELS,* with flying colours; *in* ~ *e VAART,* in a great hurry; at breakneck speed; ~ *e VIS,* flying fish.
vlie'ënet, fly-net.
vlieënier', (-s), airman, pilot, aviator, aeronaut.
vlie'ë: ~ **papier,** flypaper; ~ **plaag,** fly-plague, nuisance; ~ **plak,** (-ke), fly-swatter; ~ **poeier,** insect-powder.
vlie'ër, (-s), kite; aviator, flyer, airman, pilot; *daardie* ~ *gaan nie op nie,* that trick won't work; that horse won't run; ~ **ballon,** kite balloon; ~ **kaart,** aeronautical map; ~ **sertifikaat,** pilot's certificate.
vlie'ërs: ~ **helm,** pilot's helmet; ~ **kenteken,** flying-badge, pilot's emblem.
vlie'ërskool, flying- (training-) school.
vlie'ërs: ~ **lisensie,** pilot's license; ~ **mus,** flying cap; ~ **pak,** flying-suit; ~ **toets,** pilot's test.
vlie'ëry, flying, aviation.
vlie'ë: ~ **skerm,** fly-screen; ~ **slaner,** fly-swatter; ~ **swam,** fly-agaric, fly-trap; ~ **vanger,** (-s), fly-catcher, fly-trap; sundew *(Drosera cistiflora);* fly-catcher (bird); ~ **vry,** (-e), fly-proof; ~ **waaier,** fly-flap.
vlieg¹, (s) (vlieë), fly; drake (fishing); *iem. 'n* ~ *AFVANG,* get the better of someone; steal a march on someone; *so seker as 'n HANDVOL vlieë,* most unlikely; *'n mens vang meer vlieë met HEUNING as met asyn,* fair and softly goes far; *soos 'n* ~ *lyk wat in KARRINGMELK geval het,* to be all in white; *twee vlieë in een KLAP slaan (vang),* kill two birds with one stone; *ek KOM nie hier om vlieë te vang nie,* I have not come here just to pass the time of day; *hy sal geen* ~ *KWAAD doen nie,* he will not hurt a fly; *dit lyk of daar 'n* ~ *oor sy NEUS geloop het,* something seems to have bitten him; *van 'n* ~ *(muggie) 'n OLIFANT maak,* make a mountain out of a molehill; *die* ~ *in die SALF,* the fly in the ointment; *daar SIT jy met jou hand vol vlieë,* you have had your trouble for nothing; *vlieë VANG,* sit with one's mouth agape.
vlieg², (w) (ge-), fly; aviate; *in BRAND* ~ , catch fire; *moenie HOOG* ~ *nie,* don't fly too high; *in die LUG* ~ , explode; *hoog* ~ *en LAAG val,* go up like a rocket and come down like a stick; *op iem. se WENKE* ~ , carry out orders quickly.
vlieg'afstand, flying distance.
vlieg'agtig, (-e), musciform.
vlieg: ~ **baan,** aerodrome; flight-path; ~ **basis,** flying base; ~ **bereik,** action radius, flying range; ~ **bewys,** pilot's certificate; ~ **boot,** flying boat; ~ **bootbasis,** flying-boat base; ~ **brandstof,** aviation spirit; ~ **dek,** flying deck, flight-deck; ~ **dekskip,** aircraft carrier; ~ **demonstrasie,** flying demonstration; ~ **diens,** flying- (air-) service.
vlieg'dig, (-te), fly-proof.
vlieg: ~ **dril,** air-drill; ~ **duur,** flying time; ~ **eenheid,** flying unit.
vlieg'eler, fly-blow.
vlie'gend = **vlieënd.**
vlie'gensnel, as quick as lightning.
vlieg: ~ **eskader,** air squadron; ~ **gevaar,** flying risk; ~ **gewig,** flyweight; ~ **hawe,** airport; ~ **helm,** flying helmet; ~ **hindernis,** airway obstruction; ~ **hoogte,** flight level.
vlie'gie, (-s), small fly, gnat.
vlieg: ~ **ingenieur,** aero-engineer; flight engineer; ~ **instrukteur,** flying instructor; ~ **kamp,** flying camp, aviation camp; ~ **kampskip,** aircraft carrier; ~ **klere,** flying kit; ~ **klub,** aero-club; ~ **koers,** flight path; ~ **korps,** flying corps; ~ **kuns,** aviation, airmanship; ~ **leer,** theory of flight; ~ **les,** flying lesson, ~ **masjien,** aeroplane; flying machine; ~ **oefening,** flying practice; air-drill; ~ **offisier,** flying officer; ~ **onderrig,** flight instruction; ~ **ongeluk,** air disaster, flying accident; ~ **opleiding,** flying training; ~ **pak,** flying suit; ~ **park,** aircraft park; ~ **personeel,** air-going crew; ~ **ramp,** air disaster; ~ **rekord,** flying record; ~ **rigting,** direction of flight; ~ **risiko,** flying risk.
vlieg'siekte, nagana.
vlieg: ~ **skool,** flying- (training-) school; ~ **skou(ing),** aerial display; ~ **snelheid,** flying speed; ~ **sport,** aviation; ~ **stasie,** air station; ~ **ster,** (-s), aviatrix,

airwoman; ~ **styl**, flying technique; ~ **tegniek**, aerotechnics; ~ **tegnies**, (-e), aerotechnical; ~ **terrein**, aerodrome, aviation ground, flying area; ~ **terreinwerker**, groundsman (aerodrome); ~ **toer**, air-tour; ~ **toestande**, flying conditions; ~ **toets**, flight test; ~ **tog**, flying expedition, air-trip, flight; ~ **toggie**, flip, joy-flight.

vlieg'tuig, (..tuie), aeroplane, aircraft; ~ **bemanning**, aircraft crew; ~ **berig**, air report; aeroplane control; pilotage; ~ **bestuurder**, air pilot; ~ **bou**, aeroplane construction; ~ **boukunde**, aeromechanics; ~ **brandstof**, aviation fuel (spirit); ~ **dekking**, aircover; ~ **draer**, aircraft carrier; ~ **fabriek**, aircraft factory; ~ **herstelafdeling**, aircraft-repair section; ~ **industrie**, aircraft industry; ~ **loods**, aeroplane shed, hangar; ~ **model**, aeroplane model; ~ **moederskip**, aircraft carrier; ~ **monteur**, air-mechanic; ~ **motor**, aero-engine; ~ **nywerheid**, aircraft industry; ~ **ongeluk**, aeroplane accident; ~ **ontwerp**, aircraft design; ~ **raam**, airframe; ~ **ramp**, air disaster; ~ **skroef**, aeroplane propeller; airscrew; ~ **skuur**, hangar; ~ **stasie**, aircraft station; ~ **sterkte**, aircraft establishment.

vlieg: ~ **tyd**, flying time; ~ **uitrusting**, flying kit; ~ **uur**, flying hour; ~ **vaardig**, (-e), air-ready; ~ **veer**, oar feather; ~ **veilig**, (-e), safe for flight, airworthy; ~ **veld**, aerodrome; ~ **velddiens**, ground-control; ~ **veldmerke**, ground marks; ~ **veldpersoneel**, aerodrome staff, ground-control; ~ **veldwag**, (areo)drome-guard; ~ **vertoning**, aerial (flying) display.

vlieg'vlies, wing-membrane.

vlieg'vry, (-e), fly-proof.

vlieg: ~ **wa**, flying box-car; ~ **wedstryd**, air-race (meeting); ~ **week**, aviation week; ~ **weer**, flying weather; ~ **werk**: *met kuns en* ~ *werk,* with clever devices; by hook or by crook; ~ **werktuigkundige**, air mechanic; ~ **wese**, aeronautics, aviation, flying; ~ **wiel**, flywheel, balance (watch); flyer (machine).

vlier: ~ **blom**, elder-flower; ~ **boom**, elder-tree.

vlie'ring, (-s), garret, attic, loft.

vlies, (-e), fleece (of sheep); membrane (in body); cuticle, pellicle; coat, (in)tegument; film (over eyes); *die GULDE V* ~ , the Golden Fleece; ~ **agtig**, (-e), membranous, filmy, fleecy, (in)tegumentary.

vlie's(er)ig, (-e), membranous, membranaceous; filmy.

vlie'sie, (-s), pellicle, thin (filmy) membrane; cuticle.

Vlies'ridder, Knight of the Golden Fleece.

vlies: ~ **stof**, fleece; ~ **vlerkig**, ~ **vleuelig**, (-e), hymenopterous; ~ **vlerkige**, ~ **vleuelige**, (-s), hymenopteron; ~ **wolk**, fleecy cloud.

vliet, (s) (-e), brook, rivulet, rill; (w) (ge-), flow, stream, pass, fleet; *trane* ~ *oor haar wange,* tears stream down her cheeks; ~ **end**, (-e), flowing, fleeting; *die* ~ *e jare,* the fleeting years.

vlin'der, (-s), butterfly; coquette; ~ **agtig**, (-e), like a butterfly; papilionaceous; fickle; ~ **blommig**, (-e), papilionaceous; ~ **dak**, butterfly roof; ~ **das**, butterfly, cravat; ~ **net**, butterfly-net; ~ **slag**, butterfly stroke (in swimming); ~ **vormig**, (-e), butterfly-shaped, papilionaceous.

Vlis'singen, Flushing.

vloed, (-e), stream, flood (of tears); inundation, torrent, gust; gush (liquid); menorrhagia (med.); ~ **deur**, flood-gate; ~ **gety**, flood-tide; ~ **golf**, tidal wave, bore; ~ **hawe**, tidal harbour; ~ **hoogte**, high-tide level; ~ **lyn**, high-water line; ~ **strand**, foreshore; ~ **streep**, foreshore; ~ **water**, tide-water, flood-water, storm-water.

vloei, (s) flow; yield (of fountain); (w) (ge-), flow, stream, course; run (ink); fleet (time); blot (ink).

vloei'baar, (..bare), fluid, liquid; fluent; ~ **maak**, liquefy; ~ **heid**, liquidity, fluidity; ~ **making**, ~ **wording**, liquefaction.

vloei'blok, blotter, blotting-pad.

vloei'end, (-e), flowing, fluent, smooth, easy, glib; ~ *e LETTERS,* the liquids (letters); ~ *Engels PRAAT,* be fluent in English; ~ *e VERSE,* flowing verses; ~ **heid**, fluency; liquidity, smoothness.

vloei: ~ **ing**, (-e, -s), flowing, streaming; fluency; menorrhagia (med.); ~ **lyn**, flow-line; ~ **middel**, flux;

~ **papier**, blotting-paper; ~ **punt**, pour-point; ~ **pyp**, flow pipe; ~ **seep**, liquid soap.

vloei'spaat, fluorspar; Derbyshire spar; ~ **glas**, murrhine glass; ~ **suur**, hydrofluoric acid.

vloei'staal, mild steel; ingot steel.

vloei'stof, liquid, fluid; dip (disinfectant); ~ **kompas**, fluid compass; ~ **koppeling**, fluid drive; ~ **ons**, fluid ounce; ~ **rem**, hydraulic brake.

vloei: ~ **stuk**, fillet (architecture); ~ **vernis**, liquid veneer; ~ **weerstand**, water-resistance; ~ **yster**, ingot iron.

vloek, (s), (-e), curse, oath, malediction, damn, swearword; rascal; *met twee* ~ *e en 'n DRAFSTAP,* in two shakes of a lamb's tail; *JOU* ~ *!* you rascal; *in 'n* ~ *en 'n SUG,* in a trice; (w) (ge-), swear, curse, use profane language; *die KLEURE* ~ *teen mekaar,* the colours clash; ~ *soos 'n MATROOS,* swear like a trooper; ~ **bek**, ~ **er**, (-s), swearer, curser; ~ **genoot**, accessory, fellow criminal; ~ **psalm**, imprecatory psalm; ~ **waar'dig**, (-e), accursed, damnable; ~ **waar'digheid**, accursedness, damnability; ~ **woord**, swearword, oath, curse; ~ **woorde**, abusive language, profane language, profanities.

vloer, (-e), floor; pavement (geol.), threshing-floor; ground; apron (sea); *'n mens kan daar van die* ~ *EET,* the place is scrupulously clean; one can dine from the floor; *die* ~ *v.d. HOF,* the well of the court; *dikwels oor die* ~ *KOM by,* haunt someone's doorstep; *cf.* **verdieping**; ~ **balk**, floor-joist; ~ **bedekking**, floor-covering; ~ **beits**, floorstain; ~ **dweil**, floor mop; ~ **grond**, seat-clay; ~ **hoogte**, floor-level; ~ **kleedjie**, carpet, floor-cloth; ~ **klip**, flooring-stone; seat-stone (geol.); ~ **knie**, housemaid's knee; ~ **kraan**, floor crane; ~ **kussing**, pouffe; ~ **lap**, floor-cloth, polishing-cloth; ~ **lat**, floor-slat; ~ **lys**, skirting-board, base-mould; ~ **mat**, floor-mat; *iem. as* ~ *mat gebruik,* use someone as a door-mat; ~ **matstof**, rugging, matting; ~ **oppervlakte**, floor-space (-area); ~ **plank**, floor(-ing-) board; ~ **poets**, ~ **politoer**, floor-polish; ~ **ruimte**, floor-space; ~ **seil**, floor-cloth; ~ **spyker**, brad (nail); cut-nail; casing-nail; floor-nail; ~ **steen**, paving-stone; ~ **tapyt**, carpet; ~ **teël**, floor-tile, paving-tile; flagstone; ~ **vernis**, liquid veneer; ~ **vrywer**, floor-polisher; ~ **waks**, floor-polish; ~ **was**, floor-wax; ~ **wol**, sweepings.

vlok, (s) (-ke), flock, floccule (of wool); flake; tuft; villus (bot.); (w) flake; ~ **agtig**, (-e), flocculent, floccose; ~ **gare**, ~ **garing**, flake yarn; ~ **kie**, (-s), flakelet, small flake; floccule (of wool); ~ **kig**, (-e), flocky, flocculent, floccose; flaky; ~ **kigheid**, flakiness; ~ **middel**, flocculent; ~ **seep**, soap-flakes; ~ **sy**, floss silk; ~ **sneeu**, fleecy snow; ~ **wol**, flock (-wool); ~ **wolk**, cirrus (cloud).

vlooi, (-e), flea; hopper; *'n* ~ *in die BROEK hê,* be on edge; be on pins and needles; *as die* ~ *e BYT, moet 'n mens krap,* needs must when the devil drives; *'n* ~ *het oor sy LEWER geloop,* something has bitten him; *julle sal* ~ *e in die MAAG kry,* coffee is not meant for children; *van 'n* ~ *'n OLIFANT maak,* make mountains out of molehills; ~ **agtig**, (-e), like a flea; ~ **byt**, flea-bite; ~ **fliek**, (sl.) cafe bio; ~ **kewertjie**, flea-beetle *(Chrysomelidae);* ~ **kruid**, flea-bane; ~ **poeier**, insect-powder; ~ **tjie**, (-s), small flea.

vloot, (vlote), fleet, navy; ~ **admiraal**, admiral of the fleet; ~ **basis**, naval base; ~ **beperking**, naval reduction; ~ **blou**, navy blue; ~ **bou**, naval construction; building up of a navy; ~ **eenheid**, naval unit; ~ **eskader**, naval squadron; ~ **geskut**, naval battery; ~ **jie**, (-s), flotilla; ~ **liga**, naval (navy) league; ~ **lugbasis**, naval aviation base; ~ **lugmag**, fleet air-arm; ~ **lugvaart**, naval aviation; ~ **maneuver**, fleet manoeuvre; ~ **oefening**, naval exercise; ~ **operasie**, naval operation; ~ **personeel**, naval staff; ~ **politiek**, naval policy; ~ **program**, naval programme; ~ **skou**, naval review; ~ **soldaat**, marine; ~ **staf**, naval staff; ~ **stafhoof**, chief of naval staff; ~ **sterkte**, naval strength; ~ **steunpunt**, naval base; ~ **stof**, navy cloth; ~ **voog**, commander of the fleet, admiral.

vlos, floss silk; ~**sig, (-e),** flossy, fluffy; ~**sy,** floss silk, embroidery floss, filoselle.

vlot, (s) (-te), raft, balsa, float; **(w) (ge-),** float; drift; succeed; move easily, go smoothly; become airborne; *hout wat na die see ge~ word,* timber which is floated to the sea; (b, bw) fluent, facile, easy; expeditious; glib; afloat (ship); *'n skip ~ KRY,* float a ship; *'n ~ PEN,* a facile pen; *~ PRAAT,* speak fluently; *~ VERLOOP,* proceed smoothly; ~**baar, (..bare),** floatable; ~**balke,** timber rafts; ~**brenging,** refloating; ~**brug,** raft, floating bridge; raft-bridge; ~**teling, (-e),** marine; ~**gaand, (-e), (of)** shallow draught; ~**heid,** fluency, smoothness; ~**hout,** driftwood.

vlot'tend (-e), drifting, floating; *~e BATE,* floating capital; *~e BEVOLKING,* floating population; *~e SKULD,* floating debt.

vlot'ter, (-s), float (in carburettor); floating gauge; raftsman; ~**hoogte,** float level; ~**kamer,** float-chamber; ~**klep,** float valve; ~**kraan,** ball cock; ~**naald,** float-needle; ~**pen,** float-tickler; ~**prikkelaar,** float-tickler; ~**val,** float drop.

vlug¹, (s) covey, bevy, flock (birds); *'n HOË ~ neem,* indulge in a flight of fancy; *'n ~ PATRYSE,* a covey of partridges; *in die ~ SKIET,* shoot on the wing.

vlug², (s) flight, escape, decampment; chase (of cannon); *op die ~ GAAN (slaan),* take to flight; *op die ~ JAAG,* put to flight; **(w) (ge-),** flee, take to flight, decamp, fly; *~ is goed, maar begin betyds,* go while the going is good; running away may be a good thing but you had better give yourself a good start; (b) quick, swift, nimble, adroit (fingers); apt (reply); smart (boy); deft (hands); agile (movement); prompt (service); expeditious (performance); *~ van begrip,* quick-witted; ~**baan,** flight path (bomb); ~**bal,** volleyball; ~**duur,** flying time; time of flight.

vlug'gat, bolt(ing)-hole.
vlug'geheue, flight recorder.
vlug'hawe, port of refuge.
vlug'heid, swiftness, quickness, fleetness, celerity; brightness; activity; handiness, agility; promptness; readiness.
vlug'heuwel, safety island (zone); refuge.
vlug: ~**hou,** volley (in tennis or cricket).
vlug'kapitaal, flight capital.
vlug: ~**kommandant,** flight-commander (-leader); ~**meter,** flight-analyser; ~**offisier,** flight-officer.
vlug'oord, place of refuge.
vlug'opnemer, flight recorder, black box.
vlug'rekenaar, ready reckoner; ~**sand,** quicksand(s); ~**sersant,** flight-sergeant; ~**skrif,** pamphlet; ~**snelheid,** flying speed; ~**sout,** smelling-salts, volatile salts.
vlug'teling, (-e), fugitive, refugee; absconder.
vlug'kamp, refugee camp.
vlug'tig, quick, (-e), volatile (salt); hasty (farewell); glancing (weapon); momentary, fleeting (glance); superficial, cursory (examination); transitory (illness); evanescent (impression); *'n ~e BESOEK,* a flying visit; *~e OLIES,* volatile (essential, ethereal) oils; ~**heid,** hastiness, cursoriness, transitoriness, fugacity.
vlug'tyd, flying time.
vly, (ge-), snuggle (up to, against), nestle, lay down, cuddle; *die kind ~ hom teen sy moeder,* the child nestles close to his mother.
vlym, (-e), lancet; fleam (for bleeding horses); ~**end, (-e),** poignant (grief); biting, keen, very sharp, acute; stinging, scathing (criticism); ~**skerp,** sharp as a razor; scathing.
vlyt, diligence, industry.
vly'tig, (-e), industrious, hard-working, diligent, studious; ~**heid,** industriousness, diligence.
vod, (-de, -dens), rag, tatter; *'n ~ jie papier,* a scrap of paper; ~**dehandel,** rag-trade; ~**dehandelaar,** ~**dekoper,** ragman, rag-hand, rag-merchant; ~**demark,** rag fair; ~**deraper,** rag-picker, rag-and-bone man; ~**dery,** tatters; ~**desmous,** rag-picker; ~**dewol,** softs, shoddy.

voed, (ge-), feed, nourish; suckle (child); entertain, cherish (hope); *'n kind self ~,* breast-feed a child; ~**baar, (..bare),** nourishable; ~**end, (-e),** nutritive, nourishing, alimentary; ~**er, (-s),** feeder, nourisher.

voe'ding, feeding, nourishment, alimentation, nurture, nutrition; nursing (child); ~**kun'dige,** nutritionist, dietitian.

voe'dings: ~**artikel,** article of food; ~**bestanddeel,** alimentary substance; ~**bodem,** nutrient medium; matrix; breeding-ground; fertile soil (fig.); ~**bottel,** feeding-bottle, feeder; ~**bron,** source of nutrition; ~**doeleindes,** feeding purposes; ~**gebrek,** innutrition; nutritional deficiency; ~**kanaal,** alimentary canal; feeder (mech.); ~**koste,** cost of the food; ~**krag,** nutritive power; goodness (cookery); ~**lawement,** nutrient enema; ~**leer,** theory of nutrition; dietetics; ~**middel,** aliment; article of food; ~**oogpunt:** *uit 'n ~,* from a nourishment (feeding) point of view; ~**orgaan,** organ of nutrition; ~**plant,** nutritious plant; ~**proses,** digestion.

voe'ding: ~**sorg,** nutritional care; ~**stof,** nutritious matter, nutrient, foodstuff; ~**stoornis,** alimentary disturbance, dystrophy.

voe'dings: ~**verhouding,** nutritive ratio; ~**waarde,** nutritive value; food value; ~**ware,** foodstuffs; ~**wetenskap,** science of nutrition.

voed'saam, (..same), nutritious, pabulary, wholesome, nourishing, nutritive, alimental; ~**heid,** nutritiousness, nutritiveness.

voed'sel, food, pabulum, nutriment, nutrition, nourishment, aliment, nurture; provender; *~ en DEKSEL,* food and clothing; *~ gee aan iem. se EERSUG,* feed someone's vanity; *GEESTELIKE ~,* mental pabulum, ~**afval,** refuse food; ~**bedryf,** food trade; ~**bereiding,** preparation of food; ~**bestanddeel,** food element, food constituent; ~**bry,** chyme; ~**gebrek,** food shortage; ~**hantering,** food handling; ~**higiëne,** food hygiene; ~**kaart,** food-chart; ~**kontaminasie,** food contamination; ~**kontroleur,** food controller; ~**opname,** ingestion; ~**opsigter,** food supervisor; ~**pakket,** food parcel; ~**preservering,** food preservation; ~**produksie,** food-production; ~**prosesseerder,** food-processor; ~**prosessering,** food-processing; ~**rantsoenering,** food-rationing; ~**reëling,** dietary; ~**skaarste,** food-shortage; ~**tegnologie,** food-technology; ~**tegnoloog,** food-technologist; ~**tekort,** shortage of food; ~**toelae,** messing allowance; ~**uitslag,** food rash; ~**verbruik,** food-consumption; ~**vergiftiging,** food-poisoning, ptomaine poisoning, ~**verwerker,** food-processor; ~**verwerking,** food-processing; ~**vet,** food-fat; ~**voorraad,** food-stock, food-supplies; ~**voorsiening,** food-supply; ~**vrieser,** (food-) freezer; ~**ware,** foodstuffs, foods; ~**weieraar,** hunger-striker; ~**weiering,** hunger-strike; ~**wetenskap,** nutrition science, food-science; ~**wetenskaplike,** nutrition scientist, food-scientist.

voed'ster, (s), (wet-)nurse, foster-mother; fosterer; host (plant, animal); ~**by,** mother bee; nurse bee; ~**kind,** foster-child; ~**ling, (-e),** foster-child; ~**moeder,** foster-mother; ~**plant,** host (-plant); ~**vader,** foster-father.

voe'ë, (ge-) = **voeg, (w).**

voeg, (s) (voeë), join(t); seam, commissure; *in DIER ~e, (voeë),* in that manner; *uit die voeë RUK,* put out of joint so as to; *~e (voeë) STRYK,* point; **(w) (ge-),** join, add, include; fit in; weld; seam; point (masonry), flush; suit, become; *dit ~ JOU nie,* it does not become you; *jou by jou VROU ~,* join your wife; *jou ~ na die WENS van,* comply with the wish of; ~**bry,** grout; ~**gat,** mortise; ~**ing, (-e, -s),** joining; joinder (law); ~**kant,** close-string (stairs); ~**lat,** lathe.

voeg'lik, (-e), becoming, suitable, seemly, proper; ~**heid,** becomingness, suitability, seemliness, propriety.

voeg: ~**lood,** flashing (in roof-joint); ~**groef,** raggle; ~**plaatjie,** expansion piece, joint plate; ~**ring,** joint ring; ~**saag,** joiner saw.

voeg'saam, (..same), decent, suitable, befitting,

proper, fitting, civil, pertinent; ~**heid**, decency, propriety, decorum, suitability.

voeg: ~**sel**, (-s), joint; ~**skraper**, raker; ~**spyker**, joining nail; ~**stryker**, jointer (building); ~**stryking**, pointing (masonry); ~**troffel**, jointer; ~**vlak**, joining area; ~**waster**, joint washer; ~**werk**, pointing; ~**woord**, conjunction; ~**yster**, jointer.

voel, (ge-), feel; touch; be aware of; realize; probe; ~ *AAN 'n kledingstof*, tell by the feel of a cloth; *g'n GROND meer ~ nie*, be out of one's depth; *hy het my LAAT ~*, he stated clearly; *TUIS ~*, feel at home; *VIR iem. ~*, be partial to someone; *VIR iets ~*, be in favour of something.

vo'ël, (-s), bird; *'n ~ tjie hoor FLUIT*, hear it rumoured; have it from a little bird; *ek het dié ~ tjie al vroeër hoor FLUIT*, I've heard that story before; *'n ~ sing soos hy GEBEK is*, each man lives according to his lights; dogs bark as they are bred; *een ~ in die HAND is beter as tien in die lug*, a bird in the hand is worth two in the bush; *is daar 'n ~ tjie onder jou HOED?* why don't you take off your hat? *'n ou ~ met KAF probeer vang*, try to catch an old bird with chaff; *'n mens vang die ou ~ s nie met KAF nie*, you cannot catch old birds with chaff; *soos 'n ~ op 'n TAK sit*, like a bird of passage; *vry soos 'n ~ tjie op 'n TAKKIE*, free as a bird on the wing; *hulle is ~ s van eenderse VERE*, they are birds of a feather; *soos 'n ~ VLIEG, kan jy hom skiet*, a bird on the wing is fair game; *so VRY soos 'n ~*, as free as a bird on the wing; ~**agtig**, (-e), bird-like.

voel'baar, (..**bare**), tangible, palpable, tactile; ~**heid**, tangibility, palpability, tactility.

voël: ~**bak**, bird-bath; ~**bek**, bill, beak (of a bird); ~**bekdier**, duck-bill; ~**beskerming**, protection of birds; ~**beskrywing**, ornithology; ~**boer**, bird fancier; ~**boerdery**, aviculture; ~**eier**, bird's egg.

voe'lend, (-e), feeling, sentient; ~*e wese*, sentient being.

vo'ëlent, bird-lime; mistletoe.

voe'ler, (-s), feeler; antenna; tentacle, groper, palp; ~*s uitgooi*, throw out feelers; ~**proef**, feeler-trial.

vo'ëlgesang, birds' song, bird-song.

voel'haar, tactile hair.

vo'ël: ~**handelaar**, bird-seller, bird-fancier; ~**hawe**, bird-sanctuary; ~**hok**, bird-cage, aviary.

voel'horing, feeler; tentacle, antenna, tenter, horn (of insect); palp; *die ~s uitsteek*, throw out a feeler.

voel'horingdraend, (-e), palpigerous.

vo'ëlhuis, aviary.

voe'ling, touch, contact; feeling, groping; ~ *HÊ met*, be in touch with; ~ *KRY met*, come into contact with; get into touch with; *in ~ MET*, in touch with; ~ *VERLOOR met*, lose touch with.

vo'ël: ~**jaer**, scarecrow, bird-scarer; ~**jag**, bird-shooting; fowling; bird-scaring (from wheat field); ~**kenner**, (-s), ornithologist; ~**kloutjie**, nerina (a flower); ~**kooi**, ~**kou**, bird-cage, aviary; ~**kunde**, ornithology; ~**kun'dig**, (-e), ornithological; ~**kun'dige**, (-s), ornithologist; ~**lewe**, bird-life; ~**liefhebber**, bird-fancier; ~**lym**, bird-lime; ~**mark**, bird-market; ~**melk**, star of Bethlehem (flower); ~**mis**, guano; bird-dung; ~**nes**, bird's nest; ~**opstopper**, taxidermist.

voel'orgaan, tactile organ.

vo'ëlpark, bird sanctuary.

voel'pen, probe.

vo'ëlperspektief, bird's-eye view.

voel'rat, contact wheel.

vo'ël: ~**rek**, catapult; ~**reservaat**, bird-sanctuary; ~**roep**, bird-call; ~**saad**, canary-seed, bird-seed; ~**sang**, singing of birds, warbling; ~**soort**, species of bird; ~**slang**, bird-snake.

voel'spriet, feeler; tentacle, antenna, tenter, palp.

vo'ëlteelt, aviculture.

vo'ëltjie, (-s), little bird, birdie; birdie (golf).

vo'ël: ~**val**, bird-trap; ~**vanger**, bird-catcher; ~**vangery**, bird-fowling; ~**verskrikker**, (-s), scarecrow; tatterdemalion, fright, bogy; ~**vlug**, bird's-eye view.

voel'-voel, (w) (ge-), grope; (bw) gropingly; ~ *loop*, grope one's way, find it by feeling.

vo'ël: ~**vormig**, (-e), aviform; ~**vry**, (-e), outlawed;

free as a bird; ~*vry verklaar*, outlaw a person; ~**vryverklaarde**, (-s), outlaw, bandit; ~**vryverklaring**, outlawry, proscription; ~**waarnemer**, bird-watcher; ~**waarneming**, bird-watching, ornithoscopy; ~**wêreld**, bird-world; avifauna; ~**wiggelaar**, (-s), augur, ornithomancer; ~**wiggelary**, augury, ornithomancy; ~**wip**, bird-trap.

voer¹, (s) fodder, forage, provender, (poultry) food; (w) (ge-), feed (animal); *vet ~*, fatten (animal).

voer², (w) (ge-), conduct; make, wage (war); lead; ply; bear (name); carry on; fly (flag); wield (pen); line; *BRIEFWISSELING ~*, conduct correspondence; *'n GESPREK ~*, carry on a conversation; *'n slegte LEWE ~*, lead a bad (sinful) life; *OORLOG ~*, wage war; *die PEN ~*, wield the pen.

voer: ~**bak**, manger; feeding-trough; feeding hopper; ~**der**, feeder; feed mechanism; ~**gang**, feed passage; ~**gat**, feed-hole; ~**gewasse**, fodder crops.

voe'ring, (-s), lining (clothes); gasket; doubling; ~**linne**, scrim; ~**pyp**, casing; ~**stof**, lining; ~**sy**, sarsenet; ~**vel**, basil.

voer: ~**klamp**, rick-yard; ~**koste**, feeding charges; ~**kraal**, feed lot, feeding pen; ~**krip**, cratch; ~**kuil**, silo.

voer'man¹, (-ne), feeder.

voer'man², driver (of delivery van), haulier, wa(g)-goner; *'n ou ~ hoor graag die klop v.d. sweep*, an old hunter likes to talk of game.

Voer'man³: *die ~*, Auriga, the Wag(g)oner.

voer'middel, vehicle, medium.

voer: ~**plaat**, feed plate; ~**pyp**, feed(ing-) pipe; ~**rak**, hay rack; ~**reserwe**, feed-reserve, fodder-bank; ~**sak**, nosebag.

voer'sies: *iem. ~ slaan*, beat someone to a pulp.

voer'sis, printed calico.

voer: ~**snyer**, forage-cutter; ~**soeker**, forager.

voer'straal, radius vector.

voert, go! be gone! off with you! clear out!

voer'taal, medium of instruction; ~**kwessie**, ~**vraagstuk**, language-medium question.

voer: ~**toring**, silo; ~**tregter**, feed-hopper; ~**trog**, feeding-trough.

voert'sek, get away! be off! footsack!

voer'tuiepark, vehicle park.

voer'tuig, (..**tuie**), vehicle, carriage.

voer: ~**verskaffer**, forager; ~**vark**, porker.

voet, (-e), foot; footing; foothold; basis; bottom; ~*e in die AARDE hê*, have snags; *op BESKEIE ~*, in a modest way; *nie 'n ~ buite die DEUR sit nie*, not to stir out of the house; *op DIESELFDE ~*, on the same footing; *aan die ~ van GAMALIËL*, sit at the foot of a master; *op GELYKE ~*, on an equal footing; *op ~ van GELYKHEID*, on equal terms; *op GESPANNE ~*, at daggers drawn; *op GOEIE ~ wees*, be on good terms; *iem. iets voor die ~ GOOI*, cast something in a person's teeth; *met een ~ in die GRAF*, with one foot in the grave; *op GROOT ~ lewe*, live in style; *JOU ~! my foot!* ~*e KRY*, disappear mysteriously; vanish into thin air; *iem. die ~ LIG*, cut someone out; *iem. met die ~ LIG*, kick someone out; *te ~ LOOP*, ride Shanks's mare; ~*jie vir ~jie LOOP*, move but a foot at a time; tread warily; *jou uit die ~e MAAK*, run away; *iem. die ~ op die NEK hou*, keep one's foot on someone's neck; *op ~ van OORLOG*, on a war footing; *OP die ~ van*, in accordance with; *PER ~*, by the foot; *onder die ~e RAAK*, be trampled underfoot; *iem. die ~ dwars SIT*, thwart someone; put a spoke in someone's wheel; *iem. die ~e SPOEL*, make someone walk the plank; *op jou ~e STAAN*, stand on one's own feet; *op STAANDE ~*, on the spot; immediately; *sy ~ in die STIEBEUEL hê*, have one's foot in the stirrup; have found one's footing; ~ *by STUK hou*, stick to one's guns; *met die ~e onder 'n ander man se TAFEL sit*, be beholden to another; *TE ~*, by foot; *iem. TEN ~e uit skilder*, paint a full-length portrait of someone; *oor sy eie ~e VAL*, fall over one's own feet; *iem. te ~ VAL*, throw oneself at the feet of; *VASTE ~ kry*, get a firm footing (foothold); *met die VERKEERDE ~ uit die bed klim*, get out of bed the wrong side; *geen ~ VERSIT nie*, not stir a foot;

voetbreed 607 *voldoendheid*

met die ~*e VERTRAP*, trample underfoot; *op die* ~ *VOLG*, follow close on the heels; *VOOR die* ~, as they come; without picking and choosing; *die beste* ~ *VOORSIT*, put one's best foot forward; *op VRYE* ~ *e stel*, set free; ~ *aan WAL sit*, set foot on shore; ~ *in die WIND slaan*, take to one's heels; ~*e WARM maak*, step it out; ~**afdruk**, footprint; ~**afstand**, footage; ~**angel**, mantrap; crow's-foot (*Euphorbia ferox*), caltrop; ~**bad**, foot-bath; ~**bal**, football; ~**balblaas**, football bladder; ~**balbroek**, football shorts; ~**balie**, foot (-washing) tub; ~**balklere**, football togs; ~**balklub** football club; ~**balkstuk**, dragon-tie; ~**balskoen**, football boot; ~**balspel**, football (game); ~**balspeler**, football player; ~**baltrui**, football jersey; ~**balunie**, football union; ~**balveld**, football field; ~**balwedstryd**, football match; ~**bank**, footstool; ~**bedekking**, footwear; ~**blok**, foot-block; ~**boeie**, leg-irons, fetters; ~**boog**, crossbow, arbalest.

voet'breed: *g'n* ~ *wyk nie*, not budge an inch.
voet'brug, foot-bridge.
voe'tenent, (-e), foot- (lower) end (bed).
voet: ~**feil**, foot-wiper; ~**fout**, foot fault (tennis).
voet'ganger, (-s), pedestrian; hopper, wingless locust; infantryman, foot soldier; ~**sprinkaan**, hopper, wingless locust; ~**s**, infantry; pedestrians; ~**verkeer**, pedestrian traffic.
voet: ~**gestamp**, stamping of feet; ~**gewrig, (-te)**, ankle; ~**hamer**, oliver; ~**heelkunde**, chiropody; ~**heelkun'dige, (-s)**, chiropodist; ~**hotnotjie, (-s)**, tarsal bone.
voe'tjie, (-s), little foot; *vir* ~ *loop*, walk at a snail's pace; cautiously.
voe'tjie-voe'tjie, slowly, cautiously; ~ *speel*, attract attention by the touching of feet.
voet: ~**jig**, gout in die foot, podagra; ~**kleedjie**, footrug; ~**klep**, foot valve; ~**klier**, pedal gland; ~**kneg**, foot-soldier; ~**kolonne**, marching column; ~**konstabel**, foot constable; ~**kroon**, coronet (horse); ~**kruik**, foot-warmer; ~**kussing**, hassock; ~**lig**, footlight; *AGTER die* ~ *lig*, behind the footlights; *voor die* ~ *lig BRING*, put on the stage; *voor die* ~ *ligte VERSKYN*, appear before the footlights; ~**luis**, foot-louse; ~**lyn**, base line; ~**lys**, baseboard, skirting-board; plinth; ~**maat**, foot-measure; ~**matjie**, foot-mat; ~**noot**, footnote; ~**omloop**, athlete's foot; ~**oog**: *ou* ~ *oog*, the bogy man; ~**oorgang**, crosswalk; pedestrian crossing; ~**pad**, foot-path; pathway; ~**patrollie**, foot patrol; ~**perd**, scooter; ~**plaat**, footplate, base-plate; ~**plank**, footboard; ~**poeier**, foot-powder; ~**polisie**, foot police; ~**pomp**, foot-pump; ~**pond**, foot-pound; ~**punt**, tip of the toes; nadir (astron.); ~**puntsdriehoek**, pedal triangle; ~**rand**, kerb; ~**reis**, walking-tour; hike; ~**reisies**, foot-race; ~**rem**, foot-brake, service brake; ~**rif**, basal reef; ~**ring**, anklet; ~**rug**, instep; ~**rus**, footrest; ~**seer**, footsore; ~**skerm**, foot guard; ~**skimmel**, athlete's foot; ~**skraper, (-s)**, mud scraper; ~**slaan, (-ge-)**, footslog, hoof (leg) it, tramp, walk, hike; ~**slaner, (-s)**, hiker; ~**snee** bottom edge (of book); ~**soeker, (-s)**, squib, petard, cracker; ~**sool**, sole of the foot; ~**spoor**, footprint; *iem. se voetspore volg (druk)*, follow in another's footsteps; ~**stap**, footstep; *in iem. se* ~ *stappe volg*, follow in another's footsteps; ~**stoof**, footwarmer; ~**stoots**, as it stands, off-hand, without picking and choosing, with all defects; ~ *stoots verkoop*, sell without any guarantee; ~**straatjie**, pavement; ~**stuk**, sill (mining); base, pedestal; block (backsight); foot; *op 'n* ~ *stuk plaas*, place on a pedestal; ~-**ton**, foot-ton; ~**val**, prostration; obeisance; *'n* ~ *val doen*, kneel before someone; ~**veeg**, doormat; *iem. soos 'n* ~ *veeg BEHANDEL*, treat someone as if he were a doormat; *iem. se* ~ *veeg WEES*, be someone's drudge (doormat); ~**veër, (-s)**, foot-wiper; ~**volk**, infantry, foot soldiers; ~**vormig, (-e)**, foot-shaped; pediform; ~**vry, (-e)**, leaving the feet free (e.g. gown); ~**warmer**, footwarmer; ~**wassing**, washing of the feet; maundy (R.C.); ~**werk**, footwork; ~**wortel**, tarsus; metatarsal; ~**wortelbeen**, tarsal bone; ~**wreef**, instep.

vog, (-te), liquid, fluid, moisture, juice, humor (biol.); ~**afskeiding**, gleet; ~**bepalend, (-e)**, hygrometric; ~**bepaling**, hygrometry; ~**brandwond**, scald; ~**dig, (-te)**, damp-proof; moisture-proof; ~**digt'heidsmeter**, hydrometer; ~**digting**, damp-proofing.
Voge'se: *die* ~, the Vosges.
vog: ~**gehalte**, moisture content, percentage of moisture; humidity; ~**houvermoë**, hygroscopicity; ~**krommend, (-e)**, hydrotropic; ~**kromming, (-s)**, hydrotropism; ~**laag**, damp course; ~**maat**, liquid measure; ~**meter**, hygrometer; areometer; ~**meting**, hygrometry; areometry; ~**ryk**, juicy; ~**spanning**, turgor.
vog'tig, (-e), damp, moist, humid; ~**heid**, dampness, moistness, humidity.
vog'tigheids: ~**bepaling**, hygrometry; ~**leer**, hygrology; ~**meter**, hygrometer.
vog: ~**trekkend, (-e)**, hygroscopic; ~**vry, (-e)**, damp-proof; ~**werend, (-e)**, damp-resisting (paint).
voile, voile; veil.
vokaal', (s) (..**kale**), vowel; (b) (..**kale**), vocal; *vokale musiek*, vocal music; ~**kaart**, vowel chart; ~**stelsel**, vowel system.
vokabulêr', (-e), vocabulary.
vokalisa'sie, vocalization.
vokaliseer', (ge-), vocalize.
vokalis'me, vocalism; vowel system.
vo'katief, (..**tiewe**), vocative.
vol¹, (w) (ge-), (-te), full, mill (cloth).
vol², (b, bw), (-le), full, filled, rich (tone), fully, completely; plenary; *iem. vir* ~ *AANSIEN*, consider someone a sensible person; ~ *le BELASTING*, full load; ~ *BESPREEK*, house full, booked out; ~ *BLOED*, covered with blood; *uit* ~ *le BORS*, at the top of one's voice; ~ *le DAGLIG*, broad daylight; *in* ~ *le ERNS*, in dead(ly) earnest; *'n* ~ *le FILIAAL*, wholly owned subsidiary; *sy GEMOED skiet* ~, he was deeply moved; *'n GLAS* ~ *skink*, fill a glass to the brim; ~ *le GROOTTE*, full size; ~ *le HOEKLAS*, full-fillet weld; ~ *le MAALTYD*, table d'hôte meal; full meal; *my* ~ *le NEEF*, my first cousin; *jou PLEK* ~ *staan*, pull one's weight; ~ *PUNTE kry*, get full marks; *die SAAL was goed* ~, the hall was well-filled; *'n* ~ *SEE*, a high sea; *in* ~ *le SITTING*, in plenary session; ~ *STAAN*, take up; *TEN* ~ *le*, in full, fully; *iets TEN* ~ *ste geniet*, enjoy something thoroughly; *in* ~ *le VAART*, at full speed; *in* ~ *le VLAM staan*, be ablaze; *TWEE* ~ *le dae*, two clear days; ~ *WEES vir iem.*, be fed-up with someone; ~ *le WYN*, full-bodied wine.
vol'aarde, fuller's earth.
Volapük', Volapuk.
vol'bal, full toss (cricket).
vol'bek, full-toothed, full-mouthed (sheep); *sy is al* ~, she is no chicken; ~**skaap**, full-mouthed sheep.
vol'bloed, (s) (-e), thoroughbred; (b) thoroughbred (animal); true blue, full-blooded, hundred per cent, out and out; *'n* ~ *liberalis*, an out and out liberalist; ~**dier**, thoroughbred animal.
volbloe'dig, (-e), full blooded, plethoric; ~**heid**, plethora; hypostasis.
vol'bloedperd, thoroughbred (horse).
volbrag', (-te), performed, finished; *na* ~ *te taak*, after having completed his task.
volbren'ging, accomplishment, fulfilment, implementing, implementation, execution (of duty).
volbring', (~), perform, fulfil, accomplish, complete, achieve; ~**er, (-s)**, performer.
voldaan', (s) (..**dane**), receipt; *'n* ~ *toon*, produce a receipt; (b) (..**dane**), satisfied, content; received (payment); paid; *'n voldane rekening*, a receipted account; ~**heid**, satisfaction, contentment.
vol'der, (-s), fuller.
vol'diensmotorhawe, full-service garage.
voldoen', (~), satisfy, gratify; do; pay, discharge (debt); comply with; answer; ~ *aan VEREISTES*, conform to requirements; *aan 'n VERSOEK* ~, comply with a request; ~**de**, satisfactory, adequate, enough, sufficient; *dis* ~ *de om te sê*, suffice it to say.
voldoend'heid, adequacy.

voldoe'ning, satisfaction, gratification; atonement; payment; quittance; *ter ~ AAN,* in compliance with; *~ GEE,* give satisfaction; *~ HÊ,* have the satisfaction; *ter ~ VAN,* in settlement of.

voldon'ge, accomplished; *'n ~ feit,* an accomplished fact.

voldra'e, mature.

voldra'enheid, ripeness, maturity.

volein'der, (-s), accomplisher, finisher; *V~ v.d. geloof,* Finisher of our faith.

volein'dig, (~), accomplish, finish, complete, end, perfect; ~**ing,** completion, finishing, accomplishment, end.

volg, (ge-), follow (person); shadow (criminal); pursue (studies); *KLASSE ~,* attend classes; *sy LAAT daarop ~,* she added; *SLOT ~,* to be concluded in next issue; *ek kan die SPREKER nie ~ nie,* I cannot understand (follow) the speaker.

volgaar'ne, (ong.), most willingly.

volg: ~ **afstand,** following distance; ~ **baanvorm,** continuous stationery; ~ **beurt,** follow-on (cricket).

vol'gehoue, sustained, unfailing.

vol'gelaai, (-de), fully loaded.

vol'geling, (-e), adherent, follower, supporter, attendant, hanger-on, henchman, minion, disciple; pursuivant (poetic).

vol'gend, (-e), following, next, sequent; *~ e week,* next week; ~ **erwys(e),** as follows, in the following way.

vol'gens, according to; under; *~ ARTIKEL 137,* under article 137; *~ die jongste BERIGTE,* according to the latest reports; *~ die MANIER van,* a la mode, after the style of; *~ die MODE,* in the fashion.

vol'ger, (-s), follower.

vol'gestort, (-e), fully paid-up.

volg'kaart, following-up card; *~e,* sequence of cards.

volg'nommer, serial (consecutive) number; progressive number.

volg'orde, sequence, consecutive order, gradation, consecution.

volgroeid', (-e), full-grown, mature; ~**heid,** maturity.

volg'saam, (..same), docile, tractable, obedient; ~**heid,** docility, tractableness, obedience.

volhard', (~), persevere, persist, continue (action); *wie ~ tot die einde toe,* he that shall endure unto the end; ~**end, (-e),** persevering, persistent, pertinacious; assiduous, perseverant.

volhar'der, (-s), perseverer, persister.

volhar'ding, perseverance, persistence; assiduity; insistence, patience, pertinacity.

volhar'dingsvermoë, perseverance, persistency, stamina, power of endurance.

vol'heid, ful(l)ness, abundance; body (of wine); plenitude; flush (of youth); *uit die ~ van sy HART praat,* speak out of the fullness of his heart; *die ~ van die TYE,* the fullness of time.

vol'hou, (-ge-), persevere, maintain, endure, face out; hold, keep up, stand, sustain; *ek hou vol dat . . .,* I maintain (insist) that . . .; ~**'dend, (-e),** perseverant; ~ **er, (-s),** perseverer.

volk, (-e, -ere), people, nation; *'n ~ is 'n kulturele EENHEID,* a nation is a cultural unity; *die UITVERKORE ~,* the chosen people, the elect.

vol'kebeskrywing, ethnography.

vol'kekunde, ethnology, ethnography.

volkekun'dig, (-e), ethnological; ethnographical; *~ e,* **(-s),** ethnologist; ethnographer.

Vol'ke(re)bond, League of Nations.

vol'kery, international law, public law.

volkereg'telik, (-e), under (concerning) international law.

vol'kery, comity of nations.

vol'kie, (-s), small nation.

volko'me, complete, perfect, absolute; entire, radical; outright; clear; quite; dead right; exquisite; fully; *ek het ~ gelyk,* I am quite right.

volko'menheid, perfection, completeness, entireness, fullness.

vol'koring, whole wheat; ~**brood,** whole-wheat bread.

volk'ryk, (-e), populous; ~**heid,** populousness.

volks, (-e), of the people, national.

volk'saak, national question, public affair.

volks'aard, national character.

volk'sang, national song; community singing.

volks: ~ **bank,** people's loan bank; ~ **begrip,** popular notion; ~ **belang,** public interest; common weal; ~ **beskrywing,** demography; ~ **bestaan,** national existence; ~ **bestuur,** popular government; ~ **beweging,** popular movement; ~ **bewussyn,** sense of nationhood, national consciousness; ~ **biblioteek,** free library; ~ **blad,** popular paper; ~ **boek,** popular book, chap-book; ~ **bou,** building of a nation; ~ **buurt,** people's quarter; ~ **bygeloof,** national superstition; ~ **dans,** popular (national, folk-) dance; ~ **danser,** folk-dancer; ~ **deel,** section of the community; ~ **diens,** services to the people; ~ **digter,** national (popular) poet; ~ **drag,** national dress; ~ **drank,** national drink; ~ **dwaling,** popular error; ~ **edisie,** popular edition; ~ **eenheid,** national unity; ~ **eie,** national identity; ~ **eienaardigheid,** national characteristic; ~ **epos,** national epic; ~ **etimologie,** popular (folk) etymology; ~ **fees,** national festival; ~ **front,** people's front, popular front; ~ **gebruik,** national custom; ~ **gees,** national spirit; mentality of the nation; ~ **gebruik,** national custom; ~ **geloof,** national religion; popular belief; ~ **geneeskunde,** folk medicine; ~ **genoot,** fellow citizen; ~ **geskiedenis,** national history; ~ **gesondheid,** public health; ~ **gewoonte,** folk-custom, popular (national) custom; ~ **groep,** national group; ~ **guns,** popularity, popular favour; ~ **haat,** popular hatred; ~ **heerskappy,** democracy; ~ **held,** national hero; ~ **himne,** national anthem; ~ **hof,** people's court; ~ **hoop,** mob; national desire; ~ **huishouding,** national economy; ~ **huisvesting,** housing of the people; ~ **humor,** popular wit.

volk'siekte, epidemic; national disease.

volk'siel, national spirit, soul of the people.

volks: ~ **inkomste,** national income; ~ **instelling,** national institution; ~ **justisie,** mob law; ~ **kanker,** national depravity; ~ **karakter,** national character; ~ **kerk,** national church; ~ **klasse,** lower classes; ~ **kommissaris,** ombudsman; ~ **konsert,** popular concert.

volk'skool, (national) public school.

volks: ~ **kultuur,** national culture; ~ **kunde,** folklore; ~ **kun'dig, (-e),** folkloristic; ~ **kun'dige, (-s),** folklorist; ~ **kuns,** popular art; ~ **leër,** irregular army; ~ **leier,** leader of the people; ~ **leuse,** popular cry; ~ **lewe,** life of the people; ~ **lied,** national anthem; national song; folk-song; ~ **mag,** power of the people; ~ **man,** popular leader; leader of the people; ~ **massa,** masses (of the people); ~ **meerderheid,** popular majority; ~ **menigte,** crowd, mob; ~ **mening,** popular opinion; ~ **menner,** demagogue; ~ **mite,** popular myth; ~ **mond:** *in die ~ mond,* in the language (idiom) of the people; in popular parlance; ~ **moord,** genocide; ~ **musiek,** folk-music; ~ **naam,** popular name; name of a people; ~ **nood,** national emergency; ~ **nywerheid,** national industry; ~ **onderwys,** public education; ~ **ontwikkeling,** national development; ~ **oorlewering,** popular tradition, folklore; ~ **oproer,** riot, insurrection; popular revolt; ~ **opruier,** agitator; ~ **opvoeding,** national education; ~ **opvoedkun'dig, (-e),** adult educational; ~ **party,** democratic party, people's party.

volk'spele, folk-dances; *~ r,* folk-dancer.

volks: ~ **planter,** colonist; settler; ~ **planting,** colony, settlement; colonizing, colonization; ~ **plantkunde,** ethnobotany.

Volks'raad, House of Assembly, Parliament; ~ **sitting,** Parliamentary session.

Volks'raadslid, Member of Parliament (S.A.).

volks: ~ **redenaar,** demagogue; ~ **regering,** democracy; ~ **republiek,** people's republic; democratic republic; ~ **rykdom,** national wealth; ~ **taal,** vernacular; popular language; national language.

volk'stam, tribe, race.

volks'teller, enumerator (of people).

volks'telling, census; *'n ~ hou,* take a census.

volk'stem, voice of the people; ~**ming**, plebiscite, referendum.
volks'tribuun, tribune of the people.
volks: ~ **trots**, national pride; ~**uitdrukking**, popular expression; ~**uitgawe**, popular edition; ~**vader**, patriarch, father of the people; ~**verdrukker**, oppressor of the people; ~**vergadering**, national assembly; ~**verhaal**, folk-tale; ~**verhuising**, migration of the nations; ~**vermaak**, public amusement; ~**versekering**, national insurance; ~**verteenwoordiger**, representative of the people; ~**verteenwoordiging**, representation of the people; parliament; ~**vlyt**, national industry; ~**voorligting**, popular enlightenment; ~**vooroordeel**, popular prejudice; ~**vriend**, friend of the people; ~**vyand**, enemy of the people; ~**weldoener**, public benefactor; ~**welsyn**, national welfare (well-being); ~**welsynsbeampte**, social-welfare officer; ~**welvaart**, public welfare; national prosperity; ~**wil**, will of the people; ~**woede**, national fury; ~**wysheid**, popular wisdom; ~**wysie**, popular tune; ~**wyn**, cheap wine.
volle'dig, (-e), complete, full (payment); plenary (session); exhaustive (enquiry); entire, complete (set of books); ~**heid**, completeness, entirety, entireness; ~**heidshalwe**, for the sake of completeness.
volleerd', (-e), proficient, accomplished, well-trained, a past master in, full-fledged; *'n* ~ *e skurk*, an out-and-out rogue.
vol'(le)maan, full moon.
vol'(le)maansgesig, pudding-face, full (round) face.
vol'ler, (-s), fuller.
vol'lers: ~**aarde**, fuller's earth; ~**kuip**, fulling-trough.
vol'lery, (-e), fulling mill.
vol'ling, fulling.
volmaak: (w) (~), perfect; (b) (-te), complete, perfect, finished; exquisite; ~ *TEENWOORDIGE tyd*, perfect tense; ~ *TOEKOMENDE tyd*, future perfect tense; ~ *VERLEDE tyd*, pluperfect tense; ~**baar**, (..**bare**), perfectible.
volmaakt'heid, perfection, completeness; perfectibility.
vol'maan = **vollemaan**; ~**gesig**, pudding face.
vol'mag, power (of attorney); warrant, authorization, procuration, authority, plenary powers, proxy (to vote); breve (from pope); brief (law); *BY* ~, by proxy; ~ *GEE*, authorize, empower; give power of attorney; ~**gewer**, warrantor; ~**hebber**, attorney; proxy; ~**'tig**, (ge-), give power of attorney; warrant; *ge* ~ *de minister*, minister plenipotentiary; ~**verlening**, authorization, empowering.
volma'king, perfection.
vol'masjien, fulling machine.
vol'matroos, able-bodied seaman, A.B.
vol'melk, whole milk; ~**kaas**, whole-milk cheese.
vol'meule, fulling mill.
volmon'dig, (-e), unhesitatingly, frank, candid; unqualified.
volontaris'me, voluntaryism.
volontêr', (ong.), (-s), voluntary (unsalaried) clerk; voluntaryist; volunteer.
vol'op, in abundance, plentiful, lavish, abundant, flush, galore; hearty; *die seelug* ~ *GENIET*, enjoy the sea air to the full; *die* ~ *SEISOEN*, the flush season; ~ *TYD*, plenty of time; *VANDAG* ~, *môre glad (skoon) op*, feast today and fast tomorrow; stuff today and starve tomorrow; ~**heid**, plenty, abundance.
vol'prese, surpassing; *nooit* ~ never given its due; never fully appreciated.
vol'prop, (-ge-), cram, stuff; cloy, (en)gorge, glut; *leerlinge* ~ *met feite*, stuff scholars with facts.
vol'ryp, fully matured; ~**heid**, full maturity.
volsa'lig, (-e), blessed.
vol'sin, complete sentence, full period.
vol'skaduwee, umbra.
Vol'sker, (-s), Volscian; ~**s**, Volsci; **Volskies**, (-e), Volscian.
volsla'e, entire, complete, full-fledged, utter (misery); absolute (nonsense); clean (sweep); *'n* ~ *FIASKO*, a complete fiasco; *'n* ~ *SUKSES*, a complete success.

volstaan', (~), suffice; *ek kan* ~ *deur te sê*, suffice it for me to say; for **vol staan** see **vol**.
vol'stof, milled fabric.
vol'stop, (-ge-), cram, crowd into, stuff; pack (a council).
vol'stort, (-ge-), pay in full; fill (by overflow); *volgestorte aandele*, fully paid-up shares; ~**ing**, payment in full.
volstrek', (b) (-te), absolute; ~ *te FOUT*, absolute fault; ~ *te MEERDERHEID*, absolute (clear) majority; (bw) absolutely, quite; ~ *geen staanplek*, strictly no parking.
volstrekt'heid, absoluteness.
volstruis', (-e), ostrich; *soos 'n* ~, *waar hy kom, is hy tuis*, he makes himself at home wherever he goes; ~**boer**, ostrich farmer; ~**boerdery**, ostrich-farming; ~**eier**, ostrich-egg.
volstrui'sie, (-s), small ostrich, ostrich chick; ~**s**, *Cotula sororia*.
volstruis': ~**kamp**, ostrich-camp; ~**kos**, ostrich feed; ~**kuiken**, ostrich chick; ~**leer**, ostrich leather; ~**maag**, ostrich stomach; *'n* ~ *maag hê*, have the stomach of an ostrich; ~**nek**, ostrich neck; *Euphorbia clandestina;* ~**nes**, ostrich nest; ~**politiek**, ostrich policies; ~**skop**, ostrich's kick; mule-kick, flying kick; ~**toon**, ostrich's toe; *Gibbaeum spp*.; ~**veer**, ostrich feather; ~**voël**, ostrich.
vol'suig, (-ge-), suck full; engorge; ~**ing**, engorgement.
volt, (-s), volt; ~**ies**, (-e), voltaic.
vol'tal, maximum; possible (point); ~**'lig**, (-e), complete, plenary; full; ~ *lige vergadering*, plenary (fully-attended) meeting; ~**ligheid**, completeness.
vol'tameter, (-s), voltameter.
volt'ampère, volt-ampere.
vol'te, crowd, crush; fullness.
vol'te face, volte-face.
volte'ken, (~), fully subscribe; *die lening is* ~, the loan is fully subscribed.
voltigeer'perd, vaulting-horse.
volt'meter, volt meter.
voltooi', (~), complete, finish, consummate, perfect; ~**d'**, (-e), accomplished; ~**d** *TEENWOORDIGE tyd*, perfect tense; ~**d** *TOEKOMENDE tyd*, future perfect tense; ~**d** *VERLEDE tyd*, pluperfect (tense); ~**er**, (-s), finisher; ~**ing**, completion, accomplishment, consummation.
vol'treffer, (-s), direct hit; hit.
voltrek', (~), execute (sentence); solemnize, perform (marriage ceremony); consummate; ~**ker**, executor; solemnizer; performer; ~**king**, execution; solemnization; consummation (of marriage).
voltrok'ke, solemnized; carried out; executed.
vol'tyds, (-e), full-time; *'n* ~ *e betrekking*, a full-time post.
volubiliteit', (ong.), volubility.
vol'uit, in full; at full length, unabridged; *'n woord* ~ *skrywe*, write a word in full.
volu'me, (-s), volume, bulk; ~**-eenheid**, unit of volume; ~**reëling**, volume control.
volume'tries, (-e), volumetric.
volu'meverhouding, volume ratio.
volumineus', (-e), capacious, voluminous, bulky.
Voluntaris'me = **Volontarisme**.
voluntêr' = **volontêr**.
voluptueus', (-e), voluptuous.
voluut', (**volute**), volute(d), volutoid.
volvaar'dig, (-e), quite willing, ready.
vol'vet, full-cream (cheese).
vol'vloertapyt, wall-to-wall carpet.
volvoer', (~), perform, fulfil, accomplish, perfect; ~**der**, (-s), accomplisher, performer; ~**ing**, performance, fulfilment, accomplishment.
volwaar'dig, (-e), able-bodied (worker); undepreciated (money); with full and equal status (university); full (member); full-fledged; ~**heid**, full status; maturity.
volwas'se, adult, grown-up, full-grown; ~**ne**, (-s), full-grown person, adult, grown-up; *DOOP van* ~ *nes*, adult baptism; *ONDERWYS vir* ~ *nes*, adult education; *STEMREG vir* ~ *nes*, manhood suffrage.

volwas′senheid, maturity, adulthood.
volwig′tig, (-e), of full weight.
voly′werig, (-e), zealous, assiduous.
vomeer′, (ge-) = vermeer.
vomitief′, (..tiewe), emetic; *grou* ~, tartar emetic.
von′deling, (-e), foundling; *'n kind te* ~ *lê,* abandon a child, lay a child on somebody's doorstep.
von′delingshuis, foundling home.
vonds, (-te), find, discovery, strike, treasure trove; *twee belangrike olie* ~ *te,* two important oil-strikes.
vonk, (s) (-e), spark, sparkle, *die* ~ *e sal SPAT,* the sparks will fly; *die* ~ *VERVROEG,* advance the spark; (w) **(ge-),** spark, sparkle; ~ **baan,** ~ **brug,** spark gap; ~ **brugstuk,** gap-unit; ~ **draad,** ignition wire.
von′kel, (ge-), sparkle, scintillate, emit sparks; glare; ~ **end, (-e),** coruscant, sparkling; glaring; ~ **ing,** scintillation, sparkling; ~ **nuut, (..nuwe),** brand-new; ~ **wyn,** sparkling wine.
von′keteller, scintillation counter.
vonk: ~ **gaping,** spark gap; ~ **ie, (-s),** spark, sparklet; ~ **indukteur,** spark inductor; ~ **ontlading,** spark discharge; ~ **ontsteking,** spark ignition; ~ **opening,** spark gap; ~ **prop,** sparking-plug; ~ **propdraad,** plug-wire; ~ **punt,** plug-point; ~ **reëlaar,** spark= (-regulator); ~ **reëling,** firing order; ignition tim= ing; ~ **skakelaar,** ignition switch; ~ **spoel,** spark coil; ~ **sprong,** flash-over; ~ **steller,** spark lever; ~ **stel= ling,** timing; ~ **stelsel,** ignition system; ~ **toets,** spark test; ~ **vanger,** spark arrester; ~ **verdeler,** (ignition) distributor; ~ **vervroeging,** ignition (spark) advance.
vonk′vry, (-e), non-sparking, sparkless; ~ *e vuurhout= jies,* safety matches.
von′nis, (s) (-se), sentence, judg(e)ment, decree, ad= judgment, adjudication; doom; *toe is sy* ~ *GE= VEL,* then his doom was sealed; *'n* ~ *HERSIEN,* review a judg(e)ment (sentence); *ONBEPAALDE* ~, indeterminate sentence; *'n* ~ *UITSPREEK,* pass sentence, pronounce judg(e)ment, give a ver= dict; *'n* ~ *VEL,* pass sentence on someone; *'n* ~ *VERNIETIG,* quash a conviction; (w) **(ge-),** sen= tence, condemn, pass judg(e)ment, decree; doom.
vont, (-e), (baptismal) font.
voog, (-de), guardian; trustee; custodian; curator; *NATUURLIKE* ~, natural guardian; *TESTA= MENTÊRE* ~, guardian by will; ~ **des′, (-se),** curatrix; ~ **dy′,** guardianship; ~ **dy′maatskappy,** trust company; ~ **dy′raad,** board of guardians; ~ **dy′skap,** guardianship, tutelage, ward.
voor¹, (s) (vore), furrow, gutter, ditch; chase; wrinkle; (w) **(ge-),** furrow; wrinkle; *'n ge=de gesig,* a wrinkled face.
voor², (s): *ALLES het sy* ~ *en teë,* everything has its good and bad points; *die* ~ *en die TEË,* the pros and cons; *VAN* ~ *af begin,* begin at the beginning; (bw) in front, in the lead, ahead; *EK is daar nie* ~ *nie,* I am not in favour of that; *LOS* ~ *wees,* have a good lead; *ONS is hulle* ~, we have anticipated them, we have a start on them; *jou OORLOSIE is* ~, your watch is fast; *een PUTJIE* ~, one hole up (golf); ~ *RY,* ride (drive) in front; *10 TREE* ~ *kry,* get 10 yards start; (vs) before, in front of; ~ *ANKER gaan,* anchor; ~ *die HUIS,* in front of the house; ~ *NUWEJAAR,* before New Year's Day; ~ *die PAALTJIES,* at the wicket; ~ *die VEN= STER,* at the window; (vgw) before; ~ *hy gepraat het, wis ek dit al,* before he spoke, I knew it.
voor′aan, foremost; in front, ahead.
voor′aand, early evening; eve, threshold; *aan die* ~ *van sy HUWELIK,* on the eve of his wedding; *in die* ~ *VERTREK,* leave in the early evening.
voor′aanmaak, (-gemaak), pre-mix.
voor′aansig, front view, front elevation.
voor′aanstaande, prominent, leading, notable; ~ *lid,* prominent member; ~ *persone,* distinguished persons.
voor′aanvoeging, prefixion.
voor′af, vooraf′, previously, beforehand; ~ *GIET,* precast; ~ *GEGOTE beton,* precast concrete; ~ *MENG,* pre-mix; *iem.* ~ *WAARSKU,* warn some= one beforehand.

voor′afbepaal, (~), decree beforehand, predetermine, pre-establish.
voor′afberaam, (w) (~ **beraam**), preconcert; (b) **(-de),** preconcerted.
voor′afbeskik, (~), preordain; ~ **te,** preordained.
voor′afbespreek, (~), pre-engage; book in advance, prebook.
voor′afbestaan, (~), pre-exist; ~ **de,** pre-existent.
voor′afbetaling, prepayment.
vooraf′gaan, (-gegaan), precede, go before; forerun, forego; *wat die geveg voorafgegaan het, weet ek nie,* I don't know what happened before the fight; ~ **de,** foregoing, preceding (sentence); preliminary (in= vestigation); precedent, anterior, prior, previous.
voor′afkapping, aphaeresis.
voor′afkies, (-gekies), pre-elect.
voor′afskadu, (-geskadu), foreshadow; adumbrate; ~ **wing,** adumbration, foreshadowing.
voor′afverbind, (~), pre-engage.
voor′afvereis, (-te), prerequisite.
voor′afveroordeel, (~), predoom; **..deling,** precon= demnation.
voor′afvervaardig, (-de), prefabricated; ~ **ing,** prefa= brication.
voor′afvoelend, (-e), presentient.
voor′afwetend, (-e), prescient.
voor′arbeid, preliminary work, spade work, prepara= tory work.
voor′arm, forearm; ~ **dryfhou,** forearm drive; ~ **hou,** forehand stroke.
voor′arres, preliminary imprisonment; *in* ~ *HOU,* remand; *in* ~ *WEES,* be awaiting trial.
voor′as, front axle, forward axle, fore-axle.
voorasnog′, as yet, at the present moment, for the present; ~ *is daar geen haas by nie,* at the present moment it is not urgent.
voor′baan, fore-width, front panel (of a dress), front width, skirt-front.
voor′baat, advance; *by* ~, in advance, in anticipation.
voor′band, front tyre.
voor′bank, front seat; ~ **er, (-s),** front-bencher (parliament).
voorba′rig, (-e), untimely, rash, premature; forward, saucy, presumptuous; *'n* ~ *e vent,* a forward fellow; ~ **heid,** rashness, prematurity; forwardness, sauci= ness, presumption.
voor′bedag, (-te), premeditated, afore-thought, in= tentional; *met* ~ *te rade,* with malice aforethought, of malice prepense, with premeditation; ~ ′**telik,** premeditatedly, on purpose, wilfully, knowingly.
voor′bedagtheid, premeditation.
voor′bede, intercession; *op* ~ *van,* on the intercession of.
voor′beding, (s) (-e), provisional condition, proviso; *onder* ~ *van,* on the proviso that; (w) (~), stipulate beforehand.
voor′bedui, (~), prefigure.
voor′beeld, (-e), example, illustration, instance; ex= emplar; model; copy; specimen; precedent; *as* ~ *AANHAAL,* quote as an example; *BY* ~, for example, for instance; *as* ~ *DIEN,* serve as an example; *'n* ~ *GEE,* set (give) an example; *SON= DER* ~, without precedent; *tot* ~ *STREK,* serve as example to.
voorbeel′deloos, (..lose), matchless, without pre= cedent, unparalleled.
voorbeel′dig, (-e), exemplary; ideal; model; ~ **heid,** exemplariness.
voor′been, front leg, foreleg.
voor′behoedend, (-e), preven(ta)tive; preservative; prophylactic (med.).
voor′behoeding, prevention; contraception.
voor′behoedmiddel, preven(ta)tive, prophylactic; precautionary measure, precaution; contraceptive.
voor′behoud, (-e), reservation, reserve, condition; *'n* ~ *MAAK,* make a reservation; *ONDER* ~ *dat,* subject to the reservation (proviso); on condition that; *SONDER* ~, unreservedly, without reserve.
voor′behoudsbepaling, proviso.
voor′behoudsklousule, escalator clause.
voor′bekap, (~), waste (away); ~ **ping,** wasting.

voorbelasting

voor'belasting, preload.
voor'berei, (~), prepare, coach (for examination); predispose, prime; *jou OP die ergste* ~, prepare oneself to hear the worst; *jou* ~ *VIR 'n taak*, prepare oneself for a task.
voor'bereidend, (-e), preparatory; propaedeutic; preparative, preliminary; ~*e MAATREËL*, preparative act; ~*e SKOOL*, preparatory school; ~*e WERK*, preliminary work, spade-work.
voor'bereider, (-s), preparator, preparer.
voor'bereidheid, preparedness.
voor'bereiding, (-e, -s), preparation; arrangement; predisposition.
voor'bereidingsdiens, service preparatory to Holy Communion.
voor'bereidingskool, preparatory school.
voor'bereidingskursus, preparatory course.
voor'bereidsel, (-s), preparation; preparative (act); ~**s**, disposition; ~*s tref vir*, make preparations for.
voor'berig, (-te), preface, foreword.
voor'besigtiging, preview, private view.
voor'beskik, (~), predestinate, (pre)destine, preordain, foreordain; ~**king**, predestination, foreordination; predetermination.
voor'beskiktheid, predisposition.
voor'beskouing, preview.
voor'bespreking, pre-engagement; prebooking.
voor'bestaan, pre-existence, previous existence.
voor'bestem, (~), (pre)destine, foreordain; ~(d), (-e), (pre)destined; ~**ming**, predestination.
voor'bid, (-ge-), lead in prayer; ~**der**, (-s), intercessor; leader in prayer; ~**ding**, intercession; praying.
voor'bind, (-ge-), tie on, put on.
voor'blaas, (-ge-), blow first (orchestra).
voor'blad, front page; vamp (of shoe); ~ **foto**, cover-photo; ~ **nuus**, front-page news.
voor'bly, (-ge-), remain in front (ahead), keep the lead; keep ahead of; outpace; maintain (supplies).
voor'bode, (-s), forerunner, precursor; omen, presage, portent, augury, foretoken, harbinger.
voor'bok[1], bell-wether; (ring)leader; *die* ~ *ke v.d. BEWEGING*, the leaders of the movement; *die* ~ *WEES*, be the cock of the walk.
voor'bok[2], waggon-seat.
voor'boom: ~ *steek*, post, ride standing up in the stirrups.
voor'bou, catch crop.
voor'brand, (s) (-e), fire-break, fire-path; counter-fire; ~ *MAAK*, make the first approach; ~ *MAAK teen gevare*, take precautions against dangers, (w) (-ge-), make a fire-break.
voor'bring, (-ge), bring forward; propose, broach (a subject); bring on the tapis, bring up (in court).
voor'buik, preabdomen.
voor'christelik, (-e), pre-Christian.
voor'dans, (-ge-), lead the dance; ~**er**, (-s), dance-leader.
voor'dat, before, ere.
voor'dateer, (-ge-), antedate; .. **tering**, antedating.
voor'deel[1], (voordele), foremost (front) part
voor'deel[2], (voordele), profit, gain, benefit, avail, good advantage; pull; ~ *AFWERP*, yield a profit; *'n* ~ *BEHAAL*, gain an advantage; ~ *BRING*, yield profit (advantage); *sy* ~ *DOEN met*, put to good use; profit by; ~ *GENIET van*, have the benefit of; *'n* ~ *HÊ oor*, have an advantage over; *MET* ~, at a profit; *'n ONVERWAGTE* ~, a windfall; ~ *OPLEWER (afwerp)*, yield profit; ~ *PLUK van*, have the benefit of; ~ *SLAAN uit*, turn to one's own advantage; *SONDER* ~, without profit; *daar STEEK geen* ~ *in nie*, there is no advantage to be gained from that; *tot* ~ *STREK van*, be to someone's advantage; ~ *TREK van*, benefit from, take advantage of; *die* ~ *van die TWYFEL*, the benefit of the doubt; *met* ~ *VERKOOP*, sell at a profit; *ten VOORDELE van*, for the benefit of; ~**trekker**, gainer, beneficiary.
voor'dek, foredeck, forward deck.
voorde'lig, (-e), profitable, advantageous; lucrative, gainful; ~*e saldo*, credit balance; ~**heid**, profitableness, advantageousness.

voorgewel

voor'denkbeeld, prenotion.
voorde'se, (vero.), previously, before; ~ *het hy anders gepraat*, formerly he told a different tale.
voor'deur, front door; ~**sleutel**, front-door key.
voor-die-hand'-liggend, (-e), evident, obvious; clear, patent; *'n* ~*e oplossing*, an obvious solution.
voor-die-voet, without exception, without selection.
voor'doen, (-ge), appear, represent oneself, want to pass for: arise, crop up; show (as an example); *sy kan haar GOED* ~, she is good in creating an impression; *hy het hom as 'n RYK man voorgedoen*, he pretended to be a rich man; *'n SOM op die bord* ~, work out a sum on the blackboard.
voor'dorp, suburb.
voor'dra, (-ge-), recite, declaim, give an item, perform; bring up, present (a case).
voor'draagster, (-s), female reciter, elocutionist; diseuse.
voor'draer, (-s), reciter, entertainer, performer, elocutionist; diseur.
voor'drag, (-te), lecture, address, speech; acting; declamation; delivery, recital, recitation (of poem); elocution; presentation (of a matter); *'n prediker met 'n goeie* ~, a preacher with a good delivery; ~**bundel**, reciter (book); ~**kuns**, art of reciting, elocution; ~**kunstenaar**, elocutionist; declaimer.
voor'dragsleer, elocution.
voor'drag: ~**versameling**, reciter; ~**wedstryd**, recitation (elocution) competition.
voor'eergister, three days ago.
voor'eksemplaar, advance copy
voor'ent, forefront, forepart, fore-end.
voor'esel, (-s), leader (in a team of mules or donkeys), front mule.
voor'fluit, (-ge-), whistle (to someone).
voor'gaan, (-ge-), precede, go before, lead, set an example, take precedence, have preference; ~ *in (die) GEBED*, lead in prayer; *'n GRYSAARD laat* ~, give an old man precedence; *die VOLK se belang moet* ~, the nation's interest must come first; ~**de**, preceding, previous, antecedent.
voor'gang, front passage.
voor'ganger, (-s), predecessor; minister; antecessor (in office); leader, foregoer.
voor'gangster, (-s), female antecessor.
voor'gebed, prayer before the sermon.
voor'gebergte, promontory, headland, bluff, naze, ness.
voor'geboortekliniek, prenatal clinic.
voor'geboortelik, (-e), prenatal.
voor'geborgte, limbo.
voor'gebou, front part of a building.
voor'gedraene, (-s), presentee.
voor'gee, (s), start, handicap; yield (traffic sign); *blinde* ~, sealed handicap; (w) (-ge-), pretend, assume, purport, affect, profess to be; give odds, give a start (sport); *siekte* ~, pretend illness, malinger, ..**geër**, (-s), handicapper; ~**ren**, handicap race; ~**slag**, handicap stroke; ~**spel**, handicap; ~**wedstryd**, handicap match.
voor'gegewe, pretended.
voor'gemeld, (-e), **voor'genoem(d)**, (-de), above-mentioned.
voor'genome, intended, projected, proposed; *'n* ~ *reis*, a planned journey.
voor'gereg, (-te), hors d'oeuvre.
voor'gesang, first hymn (of the service).
voor'geskiedenis, antecedents (of person); past history, prehistory.
voor'geskrewe, prescribed, set, formulary; preceptive.
voor'geslag, (-te), ancestors, forefathers.
voor'gestel, proposed; introduced; ~ *word*, be confirmed (in church); ~**de**, (-s), presentee; person proposed.
voor'gestoelte, front seat, prominent place; *in die* ~ *wees*, be in the limelight.
voor'gevallene: *die* ~, what has happened, the occurrence.
voor'gevoel, presentiment, premonition, suspicion, prescience, presage, foreboding, divination.
voor'gewel, front gable, facade, frontage, forefront, front wall, frontal.

voor'gewend, (-e), feigned, professed, sham, pretended, simulated, put-on, counterfeit, false, fictitious, make-believe, assumed, meretricious; ~**heid,** fictitiousness, sham.
voor'gif, (-te), odds, handicap.
voor'graads, (-e), undergraduate.
voor'grond, foreground; forefront; *iets op die* ~ *BRING,* bring something into prominence; *jou op die* ~ *DRING,* force (thrust) oneself to the fore; seek publicity; *op die* ~ *HOU,* keep in the forefront; *op die* ~ *SKUIF,* push into the front; *dit STAAN op die* ~, with me it comes first; *jou op die* ~ *STEL,* thrust oneself on the foreground; *op die* ~ *TREE (kom),* come to the fore.
voor'haak, (-ge-), hook on in front; assist financially; *iem.* ~, advance someone a loan; ~**sel,** aid, loan, advance.
voor'haker, (-s), helper; advancer; lender (of money); mechanical horse.
voor'hal, foyer, vestibule, lobby.
voor'hamer, sledge-hammer.
voor'hand, forehand; leading hand (cards); *ek sit aan die* ~, it is my lead; ~**dryfhou,** forehand drive.
voorhan'de, on hand; in stock; extant, available; at hand; forthcoming; *nie* ~ *nie,* sold out, not in stock.
voor'hang, (s) (-e), veil (of the temple); curtain; front drape (of dress); (w) **(-ge-),** hang in front; ~**sel, (-s),** curtain; veil (of the temple).
voor'hê, (-gehad), have a lead; wear (apron); intend, propose, drive at; *iets op 'n ANDER* ~, have certain advantages over another person; *BAIE* ~ *op,* have many advantages over; *wat het jy DAARMEE voor?* what do you intend to do with that? *dit GOED met iem.* ~, mean it well.
voor'heen, formerly, erstwhile; late; anciently; ~ *van die firma X,* formerly of X's (firm).
voor'hel, limbo; purgatory.
voor'heuwel, foothill.
voor'histories, (-e), prehistoric; ~*e werktuig,* prehistoric implement.
voor'hoede, (-s), van, vanguard, advance guard; forefront; forwards, pack (rugby); *in die* ~ *staan,* be in the van; ~**geveg,** advance-guard fighting.
voor'hoef, forehoof.
voor'hoek, advancing angle.
voor'hof, forecourt, outer court, atrium (Roman).
voor'hoof, (-de), forehead; front.
voor'hoofsbeen, coronal bone, frontal bone.
voor'hou, (-ge-), hold before; present; exhort; impress on; use as (an excuse); *iem. sy PLIG* ~, exhort someone to do his duty; ~ *as 'n VOORBEELD,* hold up as an example.
voor'huid, foreskin, prepuce.
voor'huis, living-room; lounge; front room; atrium (Roman).
voor'huweliks, (-e), antenuptial, premarital.
voor'in, in the front; in at the front.
Voor'-Indië, Nearer India, Hither India.
voor'ingang, front entrance.
voor'ingenome, prejudiced, partial (to), bia(s)sed; predisposed.
voor'ingenomenheid, prejudice, bias, prepossession, partiality.
voor'jaar, spring.
voor'jaars: ~**blom,** spring flower; ~**hout,** spring wood.
voor'jaarskoonmaak, spring-cleaning.
voor'jaars: ~**nagewening,** vernal equinox; ~**opruiming,** spring clearance (sale); ~**reën,** ~**reent,** spring rain; ~**weer,** spring weather; ~**wol,** spring wool.
voor'joggie, fore-caddy.
voor'juk, front yoke.
voor'kajuit, fore-cabin.
voor'kamer, front room; sitting-room; reception room, drawing-room, parlour; anteroom, antechamber; vestibule; atrium (of heart).
voor'kant, front (side), face, frontage, foreside, forefront; forehand (of horse).
voor'kap, (-ge-), rough-hew; ~**per,** rough-hewer.
voor'kasteel, forecastle.

voor'keer, (-ge-), bar, stand in the way, stop; turn back (cattle); dam up (water).
voor'kennis, foreknowledge, precognition, prescience, foresight.
voor'keur, preference; priority; first choice; predilection; yield (traffic sign); *BY* ~, preferably, by preference; *die* ~ *GEE aan,* give preference to; *die* ~ *GENIET,* have preference; ~**aandeel,** preference share; ~**behandeling,** preferential treatment; ~**effek, (-te),** preference share; ~**reg,** preferential right; preference, priority; ~**stem,** preferential vote; ~**tarief,** preferential tariff.
voor'kies, premolar.
voor'kieser, preselector.
voor'kind, child by a previous marriage; illegitimate child.
voor'kis, front box, box-seat (on ox-wagon); coachbox; boot (wagon).
voor'klamp, (-ge-), clamp in front (before).
voor'kleur, advancing colour.
voor'klep, pilot valve.
voor'koel, (-ge-), precool; ~**ing,** precooling; ~**kamer,** precooling store.
voor'kom¹, (-ge-), appear; occur to; exist; happen; come before; gain the lead; appear in court; appear as defendant; *A kom voor B,* A comes before B; *dit gaan nog BAIE* ~, this will happen again and again; *hy sal MÔRE* ~, he will be tried tomorrow; *dit WIL my* ~, it appears to me.
voorkom'², (~), anticipate; avert, preclude; forestall, prevent; ward off; obviate; *'n ONGELUK* ~, avert an accident; *iem. se WENSE* ~, forestall someone's wishes; ~**baar, (..bare),** preventable.
voor'kome, appearance, mien, air, bearing, port; face, countenance.
voor'komend¹, (-e), occurring; *by* ~*e geleenthede,* when opportunities occur.
voorko'mend², (-e), obliging, affable, complaisant; ready to please, debonair; ~**heid,** willingness to oblige, affability, considerateness, complaisance.
voorko'mer, (-s), preventer.
voorko'ming, prevention; anticipation; preclusion; ~ *is beter as GENESING,* prevention is better than cure; *TER* ~, in order to prevent.
voor'koms, occurrence, incidence; ~**syfer,** incidence.
voor'koms(te), appearance, look, bearing, air; *die nuwe* ~, the new look.
voor'koop, pre-emption; ~**reg,** pre-emptive right.
voor'kop, forehead; *dit staan op sy* ~ *geskryf,* it is written all over him.
voor'koppelaar, front clutch.
voor'kou, (-ge-), chew for another; explain in detail for someone's benefit; spoon-feed.
voor'krimpstof, preshrunk material.
voor'kry, (-ge-), rebuke, reprimand; cross-examine; receive odds; *iem.* ~, call someone to account; take someone to task.
voor'kwart, (-e), forequarter.
voor'laag, precoating.
voor'laaier, (-s), muzzle-loader (rifle).
voor'laasnag, the night before last.
voor'laaste, last but one, second-last; semifinal, penultimate (syllable).
voor'laasweek, the week before last.
voor'lading, preliminary charge.
voor'lamp, headlight, headlamp; front lamp.
voor'land, fate, destiny; *BANKROTSKAP was baie se* ~, many were destined to go bankrupt; *dis JOU* ~, that is in store for you; *VERDWAAL is jou* ~, you are sure to lose your way.
voor'lê¹, (-ge-), submit (plan); state (facts); propound, put (question); hand in (resignation); present, lay before; *'n dokument vir ondertekening* ~, submit a document for signature.
voor'lê², (-ge-), await, lie in ambush, waylay; *ons weet nie wat vir ons* ~ *nie,* we do not know what awaits us.
voor'leer¹, front upright (on wagon).
voor'leer², front leather (of shoe).
voor'lees, (-ge-), read to; read out.
voor'legging, submission, reference.
voor'lengte, front length.

voor'leser, (lay) reader, prelector.
voor'lesing, (-e, -s), reading, lecture.
voor'letters, initials.
voor'liefde, special liking, bent, bias, preference, predilection, propensity; *iets met* ~ *DOEN*, do something by preference; *'n groot* ~ *HÊ vir*, have a special preference for.
voor'lieg, (-ge-), teach (a child) to tell lies; lie to.
voor'lig¹, (s) headlight.
voor'lig², (w) (-ge-), enlighten; give information; light (with lantern or torch); beacon; ~ **ter**, guide, adviser.
voor'ligting, information; enlightenment; *ter* ~ *van*, for the information (guidance) of; ~ **sbeampte**, (agricultural) extension officer, information officer; (school) guidance officer; ~ **sdiens**, information service; (school) guidance service.
voor'lik, (-e), forward (for its age), precocious; ~ **heid**, forwardness, precocity.
voor'linie, front line.
voor'loop, (s) first flow (distillation of brandy); (w) (-ge-), lead, walk in front; gain; be fast (watch); ~ **hoek**, angle of advance.
voor'loper, (-s), precursor, harbinger, herald, leader, forerunner; foreplane; prototype; ~ **installasie**, pilot plant; ~ **proef**, pilot experiment; ~ **skaaf**, jack-plane.
voorlo'pig, (b) (-e), preliminary, provisional, interim, precursory; preparatory; tentative; provisory; ~ *e reëlings tref*, make temporary arrangements; (bw) for the present, for the time being, in the interim (meantime), provisionally, temporarily.
voor'lyf, front half of the body.
voor'maag, rumen, fore-stomach.
voor'maals, formerly.
voorma'lig, (-e), former, sometime, quondam, one-time, ex-.
voor'man, (-ne), leader, foreman; fugleman; leading man; protagonist; ~ **laaimeester**, foreman-checker.
voor'mars, foretop (ship); ~ **seil**, fore-topsail.
voor'mas, foremast.
voor'meet, (-ge-), measure in the presence of.
voormeld', (-e), before-mentioned, aforesaid, fore-quoted.
voor'melk, colostrum.
voor'meng, (-ge-), premix; ~ **sel**, premix(ture).
voor'middag, forenoon, morning; ~ **diens**, morning service; ~ **preek**, morning service (sermon); ~ **wag**, forenoon watch.
voor'moeder, ancestress.
voor'muur, front wall.
voor'naaf, front hub.
voor'naam, Christian name, given name, first name.
voor'naamwoord, pronoun; *AANWYSENDE* ~, demonstrative pronoun; *BESITLIKE* ~, possessive pronoun; *BETREKLIKE* ~, relative pronoun; *ONBEPAALDE* ~, indefinite pronoun; *PERSOONLIKE* ~, personal pronoun; *VRAENDE* ~, interrogative pronoun.
voornaamwoor'delik, (-e), pronominal.
voor'nag, first half of the night.
voor'neem, (-ge-), intend, resolve, make up one's mind; *ek het my voorgeneem*, I have resolved.
voor'neme, (-ns), intention; resolve, purpose, plan, design, counsel; *die* ~ *BESTAAN*, it is the intention to; *vol GOEIE* ~ *ns wees*, be full of good resolutions (intentions); *die* ~ *HÊ*, have in mind; *hy is* ~ *ns om*, it is his intention to; *die* ~ *te KENNE gee*, express one's intention; *die* ~ *OPVAT om*, make up one's mind to; *sy VASTE* ~ *om*, his firm intention to; *van* ~ *WEES*, ~ *ns WEES*, have it in mind to.
voor'nemend, (-e), prospective; potential; ~ *e kopers*, prospective buyers.
voor'noem(d), **voornoem(d)'**, (-de), abovementioned, aforesaid, (a)fore-mentioned, afore-cited, (a)fore-named, foregoing.
voor'onder, forecastle.
voor'ondersoek, preliminary inquiry, preparatory examination.
voor'onderstel, (~), presuppose; premise; ~ **ling**, (-e, -s), presupposition.

voor'ontsteking, advanced ignition, pre-ignition; ~ *gee*, advance the ignition.
voor'oor, bending (leaning) forward; head first; ~ *buk*, stoop, bend forward.
voor'oordeel, prejudice, bias, preconception, prepossession, preapprehension.
voor'oorledene, (-s), predeceased.
vooroor'leend, vooroor'liggend, (-e), procumbent.
voor'oorlogs, (-e), pre-war.
voor'oorly, (ong.), (~), predecease; ~ **de**, ~ **ding**, predecease; *by* ~ *ding*, in the event of previous death.
voor'op, in front, ahead.
voor'opgaan, (-ge-), lead the way; go in front.
voor'opgeset, (-te), preconceived (opinion).
voor'opleiding, preliminary training.
voor'opstaan, (-ge-), be in front; be of great importance.
voor'opstand, front elevation.
voor'opstel, (-ge-), premise, postulate, place first; *'n vooropgestelde idee*, a preconceived notion.
voor'os, front ox, leader; forward (rugby).
voor'ou(d)erlik, (-e), ancestral.
voor'ouers, ancestors, forefathers, ancestry.
voor'pant, front panel (gore, width of skirt).
voor'perd, front horse; leader; stalwart, mainstay; *die* ~ *jie wees*, be the ringleader.
voor'piek, forepeak.
voor'plasing, preplacement.
voor'plein, forecourt, front square.
voor'poort, front gate, outer gate; propylaeum (of temple).
voor'poot, front leg, foreleg, pud.
voor'portaal, porch, hall, lobby, portico, vestibule, foyer, entrance hall, galilee (of church).
voor'pos, outpost; outguard; *op die* ~ *te wees*, man the front line; ~ **diens**, outpost duty; ~ **geveg**, outpost skirmish; ~ **troepe**, outpost troops.
voor'praat, (-ge-), prompt; speak up for, side with; tell what to say; put words into someone's mouth; *hy praat die kinders altyd voor*, he always sides with the children.
voor'pratery, prompting; siding with.
voor'prent, supporting film.
voor'proef, foretaste, pregustation, prelibation; earnest (law).
voor'proewer, food-taster.
voor'program, supporting programme.
voor'punt, van, forefront, outskirts; foible (of sword); gully (cricket); *op die* ~ *van die beskawing*, in the vanguard of civilization.
voor'raad, (..rade), stock; provisions, supply; holding; hoard; fund; *GOEDERE in* ~, stock-in-trade; *GROOT voorrade hou*, carry large supplies; *voorrade OPGAAR*, stockpile; *die* ~ *OPNEEM*, take stock; *UIT* ~, out of stock; *van voorrade VOORSIEN*, stock provision, furnish with supplies, ~ **boek**, stock-book; ~ **bord**, tally-board; ~ **houer**, dispenser; ~ **kamer**, store-room; ~ **klerk**, provision clerk; ~ **lys**, stores-list; ~ **magasyn**, store-room; ~ **opgaring**, stock-piling; ~ **opname**, stock-taking; ~ **opnemer**, stock-taker; ~ **patroon**, stock pattern; ~ **rekening**, stock account; ~ **skip**, supply-ship; ~ **skuur**, storehouse; warehouse; ~ **tenk**, reservoir tank; ~ **vorming**, stock-piling.
voor'raam, front window.
voor'radewa, chuck-wagon.
voorra'dig, (-e), in stock, on hand, in store.
voor'rand, front edge.
voor'rang, precedence; anteriority; antecedence; priority, pre-eminence, primacy; *iem die* ~ *BETWIS*, contend with someone for the first place (the upper hand); vie with someone for superiority; *die* ~ *GEE aan*, give preference to; *sy* ~ *laat GELD*, enforce his priority; *die* ~ *GENIET (hê)*, enjoy (have) preference; *REG van* ~, right of way; ~ **lys**, order of precedence.
voor'rede, preface, proem, foreword; preamble, prologue.
voor'reg, (-te), privilege, prerogative, advantage; charter; franchise.
voor'reken, (-ge-), reckon out (calculate) for (someone), prove.

voor'rem, (-me), front brake.
voor'rib, fore-rib, wing rib.
voor'rit, right of way.
voor'ruim, forehold.
voor'ruimer, roughing-reamer.
voor'ruit, windscreen.
voor'ry, (s) front row (scrum); (w) (-ge-), ride in front; ~er, (-s), leader (of a group of horsemen); outrider; postillion; ~man, front-ranker; prop (rugby).
voor'saal, front hall, foyer.
voor'saat, (..sate), ancestor, forbear.
voor'sanger, (-s), leader in singing, cantor, precentor.
voor'sê[1], (-ge-), prompt, whisper to; *ek sal vir jou* ~, say it after me.
voorsê[2], (~), predict, prophesy, presage.
voor'sêer[1], (-s), prompter.
voorsê'er[2], (-s), predictor.
voorseg'ging, (-e, -s), prophecy, prediction.
voor'setsel, (-s), preposition.
voorsien'[1], (~), provide, supply, furnish, equip; feed; *in 'n GEBREK* ~, supply a deficiency; *in 'n BEHOEFTE* ~, meet a need, *in eie ONDERHOUD* ~, pay one's own way; *RUIM* ~, well-stocked (-equipped); ~ *VAN*, provide with.
voorsien'[2], (~), foreknow, forecaste, anticipate; *dit was te* ~, that was to be anticipated (expected); ~baar, (..bare), foreseeable, predictable.
Voorsie'nigheid, Providence.
voorsie'ning, provision; supply; purveyance; ~ *IN 'n behoefte*, filling a need; ~ *MAAK vir*, make provision for.
voorsie'ningsbron, source of supply.
voor'sin, protasis.
voor'sing, (-ge-), lead in singing, precent; sing (to someone); ~er, leader in singing, percentor, chanter; ~ersamp, precentorship.
voor'sit[1], (-ge-), preside, take the chair.
voor'sit[2], (-ge-), serve (food); put in front of, place before.
voor'sitster, (-s), chairwoman, lady president; *geagte* ~, Madam Chair, Chairlady.
voor'sitter, (-s), president, chairman; foreman (jury); prolocutor; *u moet die* ~ *AANSPREEK*, you must address the chair; *MENEER die* ~, Mr. Chairman.
voor'sittershamer, chairman's hammer, gavel.
voor'sitterskap, chairmanship; presidency; prolocutorship; *die* ~ *BEKLEE*, take the chair, preside; *ONDER die* ~ *van*, presided by.
voor'sittersrede, presidential speech (address).
voor'sitterstoel, (president's) chair.
voor'skaaf, jack-plane.
voor'skeen, front of shin; ~been, anterior tibia.
voor'skenkelbeen, fore-knuckle (of animal).
voor'skiet, (-ge-), advance, lend (money); ~er, (-s), money-lender.
voor'skip, forepart, stem (of ship), foreship.
voor'skools, (-e), pre-school.
voor'skoot, (..skote), apron, pinafore; gremial (of bishop); ~rok, pinafore dress; dungaree skirt.
voor'skot, (-te), advance, advancement, accommodation; imprest; *'n* ~ *GEE*, advance money; *OP* ~, in advance; ~bank, loan bank; loan office; ~biljet, advance-note; ~kas, loan fund; ~maatskapppy, loan company; ~stelsel, imprest system; ~wissel, accommodation bill.
voor'skou, (-e), preview.
voor'skrif, (-te), prescription (of doctor); instruction, order, directive, direction; formula; manual; recipe.
voor'skryf, **voor'skrywe**, (-ge-), prescribe (medicine); instruct, direct, lay down (the law); dictate (terms); write (as example); *BOEKE vir 'n eksamen* ~, prescribe books for an examination; *ek LAAT my nie deur jou* ~ *nie*, I won't allow you to dictate to me; vgl. **voorgeskrewe**.
voor'skrywend, (-e), prescriptive.
voor'skuif, **voor'skuiwe**, (-ge-), push in front of, use as a screen.
voor'skyn: *te* ~ *BRING*, produce, bring to light; *te* ~ *HAAL*, produce; *te* ~ *KOM*, appear; *te* ~ *ROEP*, create, cause (tension); call into existence (party); *te* ~ *TREE*, appear, come into the limelight.
voor'slaan, (-ge-), suggest; strike first.
voor'slag, whiplash; grace-note (music); suggestion, proposition; *hy KLAP die* ~ *te hard*, he drives too hard (fast); *iem. onder die* ~ *laat DEURLOOP*; *iem. onder die KRY*, make someone feel the lash; *soos 'n* ~ *WEES*, be as nimble as a squirrel; ~bediende, a first-class servant; ~riempie, whiplash; ~vel, prepared (cured) skin from which to cut whiplashes.
voor'slaner, striker (blacksmith), hammerman.
voor'slip, front opening.
voor'smaak, foretaste; han(d)sel, pregustation, prelibation.
voor'snee, fore-edge (of book).
voor'sny, (-ge-), carve (meat); intercept; cut in ahead; ~er, (-s), cutter (plane); carver; roughing-tool; ~mes, carving-knife; ~stel, carving-set; ~vurk, carving-fork.
voor'somer, early part of summer, spring.
voor'sorg, precaution, provision, foresight, providence, forethought; ~ *MAAK*, make provision; ~ *voorkom nasorg*, prevention is better than cure; ~fonds, provident fund.
voor'sorgmaatreël, precautionary (preventive) measure; precaution; ~*s tref*, take precautionary steps.
voor'span, (-ge-), put (horses) to (cart), inspan; ~lokomotief, banking-engine, pilot engine; ~motor, truck tractor; mechanical horse; ~ning, relay (of horses), fresh horses.
voor'spatbord, splash-board (cart).
voor'speel, (s): *jou* ~, your lead (bridge); (w) (-ge-), lead in playing; play for others to imitate.
voor'spel[1], (s) forward play (rugby).
voor'spel[2], (s) (-le), overture; prolusion; prologue; proem, introduction; curtain-raiser.
voorspel'[3], (w) (~), predict, prophesy, prognosticate, divine, adumbrate, foretell, presage, bode, forebode, foreshadow (good or ill); portend, foreshow, foretoken, forecast (doom).
voor'spel[4], (w) (-ge-), spel out to (for).
voorspel'baar, (..bare), predictable.
voor'speld, (-ge-), pin on; ~er, (-s), bib.
voor'speler, (-s), forward (rugby).
voorspel'lend, (-e), prognostic, predictive.
voorspel'ler, (-s), prophet, predictor, prognosticator, diviner.
voorspel'ling, (-e, -s), prophecy, prediction, prognostication, forecast, augury, auspice, bodement, adumbration, foreboding, divination; *die* ~ *is BEWAARHEID (het uitgekom)*, the prophecy came true; *'n* ~ *DOEN*, predict, forecast; *hom aan 'n* ~ *WAAG*, venture to prophesy.
voor'spieël, (-ge-), put in an attractive way; hold out (false hopes), delude (with false hopes); *jou IETS* ~, indulge in an illusion; *hy het hulle groot WINSTE voorgespieël*, he held out visions of great profits; ~ing, (-e, -s), raising false hopes, delusion.
voor'spin, (-ge-), slub (wool); rove (cotton); ~linne, slub linen; ~masjien, rover, roving-frame; ~ner, rover; ~reep, slubbing-end; ~sel, slub, rove.
voor'spoed, prosperity, success, bonanza, (good) fortune; *ALLE* ~, good luck! *IN* ~ - *en teenspoed*, for better or for worse; in prosperity or adversity; ~golf, boom.
voorspoe'dig, (-e), prosperous, felicitous, flourishing, fortunate, successful; ~heid, prosperity.
voor'spoedsbond, prosperity league.
voor'spooksel, (-s), bad omen; foreboding; ~*s maak*, don't ask for trouble.
voor'spraak, intercession, advocacy; mediator, advocate, interceder, paraclete; *OP* ~ *van*, at the intercession of; ~ *vir iem. WEES by*, hold brief for someone; put in a good word for someone.
voor'spring, (-ge-), forestall, steal a march on, anticipate.
voor'sproeier, pilot jet.
voor'sprong, advantage, pull (fig.), start; *sy* ~ *BEHOU*, retain one's lead; *die* ~ *HÊ op iem.*, have an advantage over someone; *die* ~ *INHAAL op iem.*,

voorspys   615   *voortsê*

catch up with someone, reduce someone's lead; *'n ~ KRY*, get a lead.
voor'spys, hors d'oeuvre.
voor'staan¹, (-ge-), advocate, champion, stand for (a scheme); preach, espouse (cause).
voor'staan², (-ge-), await, lie (stand) in ambush; *jou op iets LAAT ~*, pride oneself on; *dit staan my NOG voor*, I can still remember; *daar staan my iets VAN voor*, I have a vague recollection of it; *ek WIL my so iets ~*, I seem to remember something of that kind.
voor'stad, (..stede), suburb.
voor'stander, (-s), advocate, defender, supporter, partisan, adherent, advocator, champion; ~**klier**, prostate gland.
voor'ste, (-s), foremost, first, front (seat); forward, headmost.
voorste'delik, (-e), suburban.
voor'steek¹, (s) running stitch.
voor'steek², (w) (-ge-), put (stick) out in front; pin on (an emblem); *jou voet ~*, trip up; ~**els**, bradawl.
voor'steier, falsework.
voor'stel¹, (s) (-le), proposal, proposition; *'n ~ AANNEEM*, adopt a proposal; *'n ~ GOEDKEUR*, approve a resolution; *'n ~ INDIEN*, introduce a proposal; *'n ~ INTREK*, withdraw a proposal; *'n ~ MAAK*, propose, make a proposal; (w) (-ge-), propose, move; introduce, present (a person); express; propound; (im)personate; imagine, picture, represent; *'n AMENDEMENT ~*, move an amendment; *ek kan my DIT nie ~ nie*, I cannot imagine that; *ek wil my ~ dat hy GESE het*, I rather have an idea that he said, *voorgestel WORD*, be confirmed (in church).
voor'stel², (-le), limber (gun-carriage); fore-carriage (waggon).
voor'stel: ~**brief**, letter of credence; ~**ler**, (-s), proposer, mover; proponent; presenter; propounder; ~**ling**, (-e, -s), introduction; performance; confirmation; conception, idea, notion, fancy; (im)personation; presentation, presentment (at court); figuration; image; ~**lingsdiens**, confirmation service (in church); ~**lingsparade**, passing-out parade; ~**(lings)tabberd**, confirmation dress; ~**lingswyse**, manner (way) of representing (things).
voor'stem, (-ge-), vote in favour; ~**mer**, (-s), voter in favour.
voor'steng, fore-topmast.
voor'stewe, (-ns), prow, stem, head, bow(s) (of ship).
voor'stoep, front veranda(h).
voor'stoot, (s) first stroke; (w) (-ge-), push in front of; push forward (to place of honour); play first (billiards).
voor: ~**stotend**, (-e), protrusive; ~**stoting**, protrusion.
voor'straat, main street.
voor'strand, foreshore.
voor'studie, preliminary study.
voor'stuk, front piece; curtain raiser; vamp (of shoe).
voor'swaarte, bow heaviness (vessel); nose heaviness (aero.).
voor'sy, front side.
voor'syfer, (-ge-), reckon out (calculate) for (someone).
voort, forward, onwards, along, forth.
voor'taan, voortaan', in future, henceforth, from this day forth.
voor'tand, front tooth, foretooth, incisor.
voor'tang, front fork (of an ox-wagon).
voort'babbel, (-ge-), prattle on.
voort'bestaan, (s) existence, survival, (w) (~), survive, continue to exist.
voort'beweeg, (~), move forward; propel; *jou ~*, move on.
voort'beweging, moving forward, locomotion.
voort'bou, (-ge-), continue building; ~ *op*, build on; ~**ing**, building on; progradation (geol.).
voort'brengend = voortbringend.
voort'brenging, production; creation, generation.
voort'brengsel, (-s), product; birth; produce, production; creation.
voort'bring, (-ge-), produce, yield, bring forth, originate; grow (fruit); procreate, beget (children); evolve, (en)gender, create (plans); ~**end**, (-e), procreative, progenitive; productive; proliferous; ~**er**, (-s), producer, evolver; generator; (pro)creator; ~**ing**, production, creation; procreation.
voort'dring, (-ge-), press forward; bore (horseracing).
voort'dryf, voort'drywe, (-ge-), drive on, goad onward, spur on, urge on; float along; propel.
voort'drywend, (-e), propulsive; floating along.
voort'drywing, propulsion.
voortdu'rend, (-e), continuous, incessant, continual(ly), perennial, constant, permanent.
voort'during, continuance, duration, permanence, continuation; *by ~*, continuously.
voort'duur, (-ge-), continue, last.
voor'teken¹, (s) (-s), omen, augury, foretoken, portent, presage, bodement, boding; symptom (of disease).
voor'teken², (w) (-ge-), draw (for others to copy).
voor'tel, (-ge-), count to; count down; *kleingeld ~*, count down change.
voor'terrein, fore-field; front area.
voort'gaan, (-ge-), continue, proceed, pursue, go on, go along; ~**de**, progressional; proceeding.
voort'gang, progress, advance, progression.
voort'geset, (-te), continued; ~ *te onderwys*. post-elementary education; continuation classes.
voort'help, (-ge-), help on, push.
voort'hol, (-ge-), run on, rush along.
voort'huppel, (-ge-), hop (skip) along.
voort'jaag, (-ge-), hurry along.
voor'tjie, (-s), drill (for seeds), little furrow.
voort'kanker, (-ge-), fester away, spread like cancer.
voort'kom, (-ge-), get along, make progress; grow, arise, result, emanate, spring from; *daar sal bog tery uit ~*, trouble will result from that.
voort'kruie, (-ge-), trundle along.
voort'kruip, (-ge-), crawl along, creep forward.
voort'leef, (-ge-), live on; be remembered; *sy naam sal bly ~*, his name will be remembered.
voort'lei, (-ge-), lead on.
voort'maak, (-ge-), make haste, hurry up, hustle.
voort'marsjeer, (-ge-), march on.
voor'toneel, proscenium.
voor'tou, lead; *die ~ neem*, take the lead.
voort'plant, (-ge-), spread, propagate (belief); progenerate, reproduce (race); transmit (disease); *die GELUID word voortgeplant deur golwings*, the sound is transmitted by waves; *die enigste SEUN moet die geslag ~*, the only son must propagate the race, ~**end**, (-e), progenitive; procreative; ~**er**, propagator; procreator; ~**ing**, propagation; transmission (of sound); reproduction, procreation (of race); ~**ingsel**, reproductive cell; ~**ingsklier**, reproductive gland; ~**ingsnelheid**, velocity of reproduction; ~**ingsorgaan**, reproductive organ; ~**ingsvermoë**, reproductive power (capacity).
voort'ploeter, (-ge-), plod on.
voort'ratel, (-ge-), rattle on; rumble on.
voortref'lik, (-e), transcendent, exquisite; excellent, (pre-)eminent, admirable, first-rate; with distinction, exemplary; ~ *e diens*, meritorious service; ~**heid**, excellence, merit, (pre-)eminence; transcendency, exquisiteness, perfection.
voor'trein, first part of a train; earlier train.
voor'trek, (-ge-), treat with favour, single out as favourite; differentiate; accept; pull (draw) into the front position.
Voor'trek, beginning of the Great Trek (1833); ~**ker**, (-s), Voortrekker; pioneer; ~**kerbeweging**, Voortrekker movement; ~**kerdrag**, Voortrekker dress (fashion); ~**kermonument**, Voortrekker Monument; ~**ker(s)lied**, Voortrekker song.
voor'trekkery, favouritism, nepotism.
voor'troep, main guard.
voort'rol, (-ge-), roll on.
voort'ruk, (-ge-), march on; pull (jerk) along.
voorts, moreover, besides, further; ~ *moet ons onthou*, moreover we should remember; *cf.* **ensovoorts**.
voort'sê, (-ge-), make known; spread (news); pass on

(information); *sê dit voort!* tell your friends! pass it on!
voort'setter, (-s), continuator, prosecutor.
voort'setting, (-e, -s), continuation, extension, prosecution (of studies); pursuance, continuance.
voort'settings: ~ **klas**, continuation class; ~ **komitee**, continuation committee.
voort'settingskool, continuation school.
voort'sit, (-ge-), continue (studies); carry on; pursue, prosecute (enquiry); proceed (on journey).
voort'skop, (-ge-), kick forward (along).
voort'skry, (-ge-), walk on, proceed, advance; ~ **dend, (-e)**, proceeding, advancing; ~ **ding**, advance, progress.
voort'skuif, voort'skuiwe, (-ge-), slide along; push on.
voort'sleep, (-ge-), drag along; drag on, linger on (life); *hy het hom voortgesleep*, he dragged himself along.
voort'slenter, (-ge-), lounge along.
voort'sleur, (-ge-), drag along; sweep along; drag on (without completing).
voort'sluip, (-ge-), steal (slink) forward, sneak along.
voort'snel, (-ge-), rush (hurry) on.
voort'speel, (-ge-), play on.
voort'spoed, (-ge-), hurry along, speed on.
voort'spruit, (-ge-), arise from, spring from; accrue (issue) from; *hieruit het baie moeilikhede voortgespruit*, many troubles resulted from this.
voort'stamp, (-ge-), push forward (along); hurtle along.
voort'stap, (-ge-), walk on.
voort'stoom, (-ge-), steam on.
voort'stoot, (-ge-), push along (forward).
voort'storm, (-ge-), rush on, storm forward.
voort'strompel, (-ge-), stumble along.
voort'stroom, (-ge-), stream on.
voort'stu, (-ge-), propel, drive forward.
voort'stuif, voort'stuiwe, (-ge-), rush along (forward).
voort'stuwend, (-e), impulsive, propellent, propulsive.
voort'stuwing, propulsion.
voort'sukkel, (-ge-), drudge (plod) on, jog along.
voort'swoeg, (-ge-), toil along, plod on.
voort'teel, (-ge-), (continue to) multiply, breed, progenerate, propagate.
voort'telend, (-e), genital, progenitive, procreative, reproductive.
voort'teling, procreation, reproduction, prolificity.
voort'trippel, (-ge-), trip along (forward).
voor'tuin, front garden.
voort'vaar, (-ge-), sail along; continue.
voortva'rend, (-e), impulsive, impetuous, dashing, eager, rash, full of push, pushing; ~ **heid**, impetuosity, impulsiveness, energy, push, go, rashness.
voort'vloei, (-ge-), flow on; result, arise, emanate; *uit hierdie feit vloei voort*, from this fact follows; ~ **ing**, emanation, result; ~ **sel**, result, consequence.
voortvlug'tig, (-e), fugitive, fleeting; ~ **e, (-s)**, fugitive, prison-breaker.
voort'werk, (-ge-), continue working.
voort'woed, (-ge-), go on raging.
voort'woeker, (-ge-), eat into (like cancer into the flesh); spread, fester; ~ **ing**, rampancy.
voort'worstel, (-ge-), struggle on.
voor'tyd, the dim past, foretime, prehistoric times; ~ **elik, (-e)**, prehistoric; ~ **s, (-e)**, formerly.
voort'yl, (-ge-), hasten (rush) forward.
vooruit', in front of; in advance, beforehand; ahead; along; forward; progressive; ~ ! forward! go ahead! ~ *BETAALBAAR*, payable in advance; *'n* ~ *DORP*, a progressive (go-ahead) town; ~ *REKEN is dubbel reken*, don't count your chickens before they are hatched; *die TYD* ~ *wees*, be ahead of one's time; ~ *WEET*, know beforehand; *nie* ~ *of agteruit WEET nie*, be quite at a loss.
vooruit'bepaal, (~), determine beforehand, preordain.
vooruit'bespreek, (~), book in advance.
vooruit'bestel, (~), order in advance; ~ **ling, (-e, -s)**, advance order.

vooruit'betaal, (~), pay in advance, prepay; ~ *is dubbel betaal*, pay beforehand was never well served; ~ **baar, (..bare)**, payable in advance; prepayable; **..betaling**, advance payment, prepayment, fore-payment.
vooruit'beur, (-ge-), go ahead, make progress, slog on, forge ahead.
vooruit'boer, (-ge-), be a successful farmer; get on, make good progress.
vooruit'bring, (-ge-), advance, help on, bring improvement.
vooruit'dateer, (-ge-), postdate (cheque).
vooruit'dink, (-ge-), think ahead.
vooruit'dring, (-ge-), push forward (on).
vooruit'dryf, vooruit'drywe, (-ge-), drive forward, drive on in advance of.
vooruit'gaan, (-ge-), proceed, get on, prosper, get along, make progress, improve (patient); go on in advance of, lead the way; ~ **de**, progressive.
vooruit'gang, progress, prosperity, advance, headway; advancement, improvement.
vooruit'geskuif, (-de), advanced.
vooruit'hê, (-gehad), have an advantage over, have a pull on; have in advance; *hy het heelwat vooruit op sy MEDEDINGERS*, he has a great advantage over his rivals; *hy wil sy SALARIS* ~, he wants his salary in advance.
vooruit'help, (-ge-), help on.
vooruit'ja(ag), (-ge-), drive forward, drive on in advance of; race ahead of.
vooruit'kom, (-ge-), make headway, gain ground, get on, forge ahead.
vooruit'loop, (-ge-), anticipate (trouble); walk on in front of, go first; *moenie ons PLANNE* ~ *nie*, don't anticipate our plans; *die TYD* ~, be premature.
vooruit'lopend, (-e), anticipatory.
vooruit'reken, (-ge-), reckon (count) beforehand; ~ *is dubbel reken*, there's many a slip betwixt the cup and the lip; the best-laid schemes o' mice and men gang aft agley.
vooruit'ry, (-ge-), ride on in advance of.
vooruit'sê, (-ge-), foretell.
vooruit'sien, (-ge-), foresee; look far ahead; previse; ~ **de**, prescient.
vooruit'siendheid, foresight, prescience.
vooruit'sig, (-te), prospect; chance, outlook; expectance; prognosis (med.); expectancy; perspective; *GEEN* ~ *te nie*, no prospects; *IN* ~, in prospect; *MET die* ~ *op verbetering*, with the prospect of improvement; *'n beroep SONDER* ~ *te*, a blind-alley occupation; *in die* ~ *STEL*, envisage; hold out the prospect of; *die* ~ *op goeie WEER*, the prospect of good weather.
vooruit'skat, (-ge-), forecast; ~ **ting**, forecast, projection.
vooruit'skiet, (-ge-), shoot ahead (forward).
vooruit'skop, (-ge-), kick on in front, kick forward.
vooruit'skuif, vooruit'skuiwe, (-ge-), move (shove) forward, advance.
vooruit'snel, (-ge-), hasten on ahead, rush forward.
vooruit'spring, (-ge-), jump forward; project, jut out; ~ **end, (-e)**, projecting; prominent (lit.); salient.
vooruit'staan, (-ge-), protrude, project.
vooruit'steek, (-ge-), put forward, advance; stick out, protrude, project; **..stekend, (-e)**, protuberant, prognathous (jaws), protrusive.
vooruit'stoot, (-ge-), push forward; pole; punt; propel.
vooruit'streef, vooruit'strewe, (-ge-), forge ahead, push forward, strive onward.
vooruitstre'wend, (-e), progressive, go-ahead, aspiring, ambitious; pushful, thrustful; forward, advanced; ~ *e boere*, progressive farmers; ~ **heid**, progressiveness, ambitiousness.
vooruit'stuif, (-ge-), rush forward.
vooruit'stuur, (-ge-), send on ahead (in advance).
vooruit'trek, (-ge-), advance, trek on ahead.
vooruit'veroordeel, (~), prejudge.
vooruit'vlieg, (-ge-), fly on ahead; plunge forward.
vooruit'weet, (-ge-), know beforehand.
vooruit'werkend, (-e), prospectively.
voor'vaart: *in die* ~, at the outset.

voor'vader, ancestor, primogenitor, forefather, for(e)bear.
voorva'derlik, (-e), ancestral.
voor'val, (s) (-le), incident, event, occurrence, episode; circumstance; (w) **(-ge-),** take place, occur, happen; ~**le,** happenings; ~**leboek,** occurrence book; ~**letjie,** (little) incident.
voor'vegter, champion, advocate; protagonist.
voor'venster, front window.
voor'verhit, preheat; ~ *te oond,* preheated furnace (oven); ~**ting,** preheating.
voor'verhoog, apron (of stage), proscenium.
voor'vereiste, prerequisite.
voor'vering, front suspension.
voor'verkoeling, precooling.
voor'verlede, before last; ~**nag,** the night before last; ~**week,** the week before last.
voor'versterker, preamplifier (of sound).
voor'vertoning, preview.
voor'vertrek, front room, anteroom.
voor'verwarm, (~), warm up (engine); preheat; ~**ing,** warming up; preheating.
voor'vinger, index finger, forefinger, trigger-finger, pointer.
voor'vlak, face, front face.
voor'voeg, (-ge-), prefix; ~**ing,** prothesis, prefixing; ~**sel, (-s),** prefix, affix.
voorvoel', (~), have a presentiment; ~**end, (-e),** presentient.
voor'voer, (-ge-), prime; ~**der,** primer.
voor'voet, forefoot; front (part of) foot.
voor'vrou, forewoman, leading (prominent) woman.
voor'vurk, front fork (bicycle).
voor'wa, limber (gun-carriage).
voorwaar', indeed, truly, surely, in truth, forsooth; ~! ~! verily! verily!
voor'waarde, (-s), condition, precondition, proviso, stipulation; article; *op* ~ *DAT,* on condition that; ~*s van OOREENKOMS,* articles of agreement; ~*s OPLÊ,* impose terms; ~*s STEL,* make terms, stipulate.
voorwaar'delik, (-e), conditional, contingent; provisory; ~*e OORGAWE,* conditional surrender; ~*e WYSE,* conditional mood.
voor'waarts, (-e), forward; on, ahead; onward(s); ~ *mars!* quick (forward) march!
voor'wag, quarter-guard.
voor'warm, (-ge-), preheat; ~**er, (-s),** preheater; ~**ing,** preheating.
voor'was, propolis.
voor'wedstryd, curtain-raiser; preliminary contest, heat.
voor'weerstand, head-resistance.
voor'wend, (-ge-), pretend, profess, feign, (dis)simulate, affect, dissemble, sham, make believe; *siekte* ~, malinger, sham sickness.
voor'wendsel, (-s), pretext, pretence, pretension, sham, blind, make-believe, subterfuge; *onder* ~ *van,* on the pretext of.
voor'wêreld, prehistoric world; ~**lik, (-e),** prehistoric, primeval.
voor'werk, (s) preliminary work, spadework; face (of watch); facing, introduction (of book); (w) **(-ge-),** lead, work in front; ~**klip,** facing stone; ~**muur,** faced wall.
voor'werp, (-e), object, thing; *BELANGHEBBENDE* ~, indirect object; *LYDENDE* ~, direct object; ~ *van SPOT,* object of ridicule, laughing-stock; ~**glas,** objective slide; ~'**lik, (-e),** objective, pertaining to an object; ~**sin,** objective clause.
voor'werpsnaam, name of an object (thing).
voor'wete, prescience, foreknowledge; *sonder my* ~, without my prior knowledge.
voor'wetend, (-e), prescient; ~**heid,** prescience, foreknowledge.
voor'wetenskap, foreknowledge, prescience; ~'**lik,** prescientific, pretheoretic.
voor'wiel, front wheel; nose wheel; ~**aandrywing,** front-drive, forewheel-drive; ~**naaf,** front hub.
voor'wind, front squall; head wind.
voor'winter, early (part of) winter, autumn.
voor'woord, preface, foreword, proem, prologue.

voor'ylhefboom, combination lever.
voos, (vose; voser, -ste), spongy, pulpy (fruit); woolly; sickly, unsound, weakish; ~**heid,** sponginess; sickliness; rottenness; unsoundness.
vor'der, (-ge-), make progress; get along; demand, claim, exact; ~**baar, (..bare),** demandable; ~**end, (-e),** progressional.
vor'dering, (-e, -s), progression, headway, improvement (of patient); dun (money), exaction, claim, demand (debt); ~ *MAAK,* progress; *ONVERHAALBARE* ~, bad debt.
vo're: *na* ~ *BRING,* raise, put (bring) forward; *NA* ~, to the front.
vorendag': ~ *kom,* appear.
vo'rentoe, to the fore, forward; *nie* ~ *of AGTERTOE weet nie,* be in a quandary; not to know which way to turn; ~ *BOER,* make good progress; ~ *GOOI,* throw (pass) forward (rugby); *'n* ~ *NOOI,* a smart girl; *dit SMAAK* ~, it tastes good; ~ *kan ons nog erger dinge VERWAG,* in future we can expect worse things.
vo'rige, former, past, last, previous; prevenient; *die* ~ *DAG,* the previous day; *die* ~ *WEEK,* last week.
vorm, (s) (-e, -s), form (of word); mould (for cake); (con)figuration, conformation, cast (iron), shape, chase (metal); matrix (for type); formality; voice (grammar); *vaste* ~ *AANNEEM,* take definite shape; ~ *GEE aan,* give shape to; *in alle* ~ *e GIET,* try everything possible; *iets in 'n ander* ~ *GIET,* remould something; *IN die* ~ *van,* in the shape of; *na* ~ *en INHOUD,* in form and contents, *LYDENDE en bedrywende* ~, passive and active voice; *sonder enige* ~ *van PROSES,* summarily; without trial; *VIR die* ~, merely as a matter of form; (w) **(-ge-),** shape, form, fashion (character); frame (theory); mould (lit. and fig.); configure; constitute, create, model; *'n FONDS* ~, set up a fund; ~ *NA,* model on (after); ~**afdruk,** cast; ~**baar, (..bare),** plastic; mouldable; ~**baarheid,** plasticity; ~**bank,** moulder's bench; ~**beitel,** shaping tool; ~**blok,** former; ~**boë,** centres; centring; ~**boom,** topiary; ~**drag,** foundation garments; ~**end, (-e),** instructive, forming, formative; ~**er, (-s),** moulder, shaper, framer, modeller; ~**erstroffel,** slicker; ~**gebrek,** formal defect; ~**gereg,** mould; ~**getrou, (-e),** conformal; ~**gewing,** shaping; design; ~**gieter,** moulder; ~**hael,** moulded shot; ~**hout,** templet, template.
vor'ming, forming, shaping, elaboration, moulding; formation; education, cultivation (mind); constitution; ~**swyse,** morphosis.
vorm: ~**kas,** casting-box; ~**kleding,** foundation garments; ~**klei,** moulding-clay, modelling clay; ~**klip,** ashlar; ~**koekie,** cupcake; ~**krag,** formative (creative) power; ~**leer,** accidence (gram.); morphology.
vorm'lik, (-e), formal, conventional; ceremonious, ceremonial; prim; frigid; ~ *wees,* stand upon ceremony; ~**heid,** formality, ceremonialism, conventionality, ceremony; primness.
vorm'loos, (..lose), shapeless, amorphous; ~**heid,** shapelessness, amorphism.
vorm: ~**masjien,** moulding-machine; ~**opmaker, (-s),** compositor; ~**pie, (-s),** little form; ~**plank,** moulding-board; ~**poeding,** moulded pudding; ~**raam,** moulding-frame; ~**rekking,** stretching; ~**sand,** moulding sand; ~**sel,** confirmation, chrism (R.C.); ~**skool,** training-school; ~**smee, (ge-),** drop-forge; ~**smeedsel,** drop-forging; ~**snyer,** form-cutter, moulder; ~**steek,** scribe; ~**steen,** cast brick; ~**stryktroffel,** slicker; ~**troffel,** spoon tool; ~**vas, (-te),** form-retaining; shape-retaining; ~**verandering,** change of form, metamorphosis; strain; ~**verminking,** disruption; ~**werk,** moulding.
vors¹, (s) (-te), ruler, potentate, prince, pendragon (hist.); *die* ~ *v.d. duisternis,* the prince of darkness.
vors², (s) (-te), ridge (of roof); capping (of wall); frieze.
vors³, (s) (-te), frost.
vors⁴, (w) (ge-), investigate, inquire, search; *met*

vors / **vrede**

~*ende BLIK*, with a searching glance; *na GE=HEIME* ~, ferret out secrets.
vors: ~**balk**, ridge-pole; ~**bedekking**, ridging.
vors: ~**er, (-s)**, scientific investigator; ~**ing**, scientific investigation.
vors'pan, ridge-tile; barge-board.
vors: ~**tebloed**, royal blood; ~**tedom**, principality; princedom; ~**teguns**, royal favour; ~**tehuis**, dynasty.
vors'telik, (-e), princely, royal, majestic; princelike, queenly; ~*e beloning*, princely reward; ~**heid**, princely state; princeliness, royalty.
vors'temoord, regicide; ~**er**, regicide.
vors: ~**terang**, princehood; ~**teseun**, prince (of the blood), royal son; ~**tin', (-ne)**, queen, empress.
vort, gone away; ~! clear out! move on! ~**gaan, (-ge-)**, go away, be off; ~**maak, (-ge-)**, hurry.
vos, (s) (-se), fox; sorrel, chestnut (bay) horse; rascal; *as die* ~ *die PASSIE preek, boer, pas op jou ganse*, beware of your geese when the fox preaches; '*n SLUWE* ~, a shrewd rascal; (b) bay (horse); reddish; ~**aap**, lemur; ~**blond**, light blond; ~**bont**, fox fur; ~**hare**, red hair; ~**kop**, light blonde; redhead; ~**perd**, chestnut horse, bay horse; ~**sejag**, fox-hunting; ~**sie, (-s)**, small fox; jackal; ~**skimmel**, chestnut (strawberry) roan.
votief', (votiewe), votive; ~**steen**, votive stone (R.C.).
vo'tum, (-s), votum, prayer (at the beginning of divine service), opening prayer.
vou, (s) (-e), crease, fold; ply; ruck, pleat; doubling, plication; *iets in die beste* ~ *e lê*, present something in the best light; (w) **(ge-)**, fold; pleat; *met ge* ~ *de arms*, with folded arms; ~**arm**, folding arm; ~**baar**, (..**bare**), foldable; collapsible; pliable; ~**baarheid**, collapsibility, pliability; ~**bed**, stretcher, camp-bed; ~**been**, folder; paper-knife; ~**blad**, folder; ~**boot**, collapsible boat; ~**deur**, folding door, accordion door, extension door; ~**duimstok**, folding rule; ~**er, (-s)**, folder, pleater; ~**gleuf**, folder (of sewing machine); ~**hek**, extension gate; ~**kap**, calash, folding hood; ~**katel**, folding bedstead; ~**leer**, folding ladder; ~**lyn**, crease; ~**masjien**, folding machine; ~**perforasiepapier**, (samfold) tractor set paper; ~**poot**, folding leg; ~**poottafel**, gate-leg(ged) table; ~**skerm**, folding screen; ~**spieël**, folding mirror; ~**staak**, creasing-stake; ~**stoel**, camp-chair, folding chair; ~**sweis, (ge-)**, faggot-weld; ~**tafel**, folding table; ~**tjie, (-s)**, small fold, crease; ~**vlerk**, folding wing; ~**yster**, double iron.
vra, (ge-), ask, question, query, interrogate, inquire, request; charge (price); ask to marry, propose; *EK* ~ *my af*, I am beginning to wonder; *LAAT hom* ~, send someone to ask him; let him ask; *NA iem.* ~, inquire after a person; *ge~: 'n ONDERWYSER*, wanted, a teacher; *OUERS* ~, ask parents' consent to marriage; ~ *om RAAD*, ask advice; ~ *is VRY en weier daarby*, there is no harm in asking; *WAT* ~ *jy hiervoor?* what do you charge for this?
vraag, (vrae), question, query; request; demand (for commodity); interrogation; ~ *en AANBOD*, demand and supply; *op 'n* ~ *ANTWOORD*, answer a question; *'n* ~ *BEANTWOORD*, answer a question; *vrae v.d. DAG*, current affairs; *DIS die* ~, that is the question; *daar is* ~ *NA*, it is in demand; *vrae STEL*, put questions; ~**al**, inquisitive person, quidnunc; ~**baak**, (..**bake**), book of reference; guide, adivser, oracle; ~**brief**, questionnaire; ~**gesprek**, interview; ~**punt**, point in question.
vraags'gewys(e), by way of question.
vraag: ~**siek**, inquisitive; ~**sin**, interrogative sentence; ~**stuk**, problem, question; rider; puzzle; riddle; ~**sug**, inquisitiveness; ~**sug'tig, (-e)**, inquisitive; ~**teken**, question (interrogation) mark; query; *'n* ~ *teken word agter sulke beweringes geplaas*, a query is placed against such statements; ~**woord**, interrogative word.
vraat, (vrate), glutton, gormandizer, gourmand, cormorant (fig.); *vrate word GEMAAK en nie gebore nie*, gluttons are made, not born; *sê GROETNIS vir die vrate*, my greetings to the gluttons; ~**agtig, (-e)**, gluttonish; ~**agtheid**, gluttony; ~**sug**, gluttony;

~**sug'tig, (-e)**, gluttonous, greedy, edacious, voracious, ravenous; ~**sug'tigheid**, edacity, voracity.
vra'e: ~**boek**, catechism; ~**bus**, question box; ~**lys**, list of questions, interrogatory, questionnaire.
vra'end, (-e), inquiring, questioning, interrogative; ~**erwys(e)**, interrogatively, by questions.
vra'er, (-s), questioner, interrogator; inquirer; querist; demander; ~**ig, (-e)**, inquisitive; ~**igheid**, inquisitiveness.
vra'estel, examination paper; ~**ler**, questioner; heckler (at political meetings); quiz master.
vra'etyd, question time.
vrag, (-te), load (on waggon); freight(age) (by water); cargo (on boat); carriage, portage (by land); ~ *BETAAL(D)*, carriage paid; ~ *TE betaal*, carriage forward; ~**agent**, freight agent; ~**boot**, barge; cargo boat; freighter; ~**brief**, consignment note (rail); bill of lading (boat); ~**diens**, cargo service; carrier service; ~**eenheidsvorming**, unitization.
vra'genderwys(e) = vraenderwys(e).
vrag: ~**geld**, cartage, freight; ~**goed**, goods, cargo; ~**kontrak**, charter-party; ~**koste**, rate of freight; ~**loods**, freight shed; ~**lys**, manifest; way-bill (train); ~**meter**, load-gauge; ~**motor**, motor lorry, truck; ~**motorryer**, lorry driver; ~**polis**, policy on freight; ~**prys**, carriage; fare; freight(age); ~**rekening**, freight account; ~**ryer**, carrier, cartage contractor; ~**skip**, transport ship, freighter, cargo liner; ~**skipper**, bargee, bargeman; ~**soeker**, tramp (boat); ~**stukke**, freight; ~**tarief**, railway rates, freight rate; ~**trein**, goods train; ~**vaarder**, freighter; ~**vaart**, carrying trade; ~**verdeling**, load distribution; ~**versekering**, cargo insurance; ~**vervoer**, freight traffic, freightage; haulage, cartage; ~**vliegtuig**, cargo plane, air-freight carrier, freighter; ~**vry, (-e)**, carriage paid, post-free; prepaid; ~**wa**, truck, lorry; delivery-van; transport wagon.
vrank, acrid, sour, acid, tart; harsh; astringent; ~**erig, (-e)**, rather acid (sour); ~**heid**, astringency; acidity, harshness; ~**wortel**, green hellebore.
vrat, (-te), wart, pustule, verruca; scab (in timber); ~**agtig, (-e)**, warty, verrucose.
vra'terig, (-e), gluttonous, greedy.
vra'tjie, (-s) = vrat.
vre'de, peace, calm; quiet; ~ *BEWAAR*, keep peace; *DAAR het ek* ~ *mee*, that is no concern of mine; *'n GEWAPENDE* ~, an armed peace; *met* ~ *LAAT*, leave in peace; *in* ~ *LEEF*, live in peace; *om die LIEWE* ~, for the sake of peace; ~ *SLUIT*, make peace, bury the hatchet; ~ *STIG*, make peace; ~**bode**, messenger of peace; ~**bond**, peace-union; ~**breuk**, breach of the peace; ~**fees**, peace celebration; ~**gereg**, court of equity; ~**kus**, kiss of peace.
vredelie'wend, (-e), peaceable, peaceful, peace-loving; irenic(al); ~**heid**, peaceableness, peacefulness, pacifism.
vre'de: ~**maker**, peacemaker; ~**offer**, peace-offering; ~**regter**, justice of the peace.
vre'des: ~**aanbod**, peace offer; ~**afgevaardigde**, peace delegate; ~**afkondiging**, proclamation of peace; ~**apostel**, apostle of peace; ~**beampte**, peace officer; ~**behoeftes**, peace requirements; ~**beweging**, peace movement; ~**byeenkoms**, peace-meeting; ~**duif**, dove of peace; ~**effek**, peace-time footing (of army); ~**engel**, angel of peace; ~**konferensie**, peace conference; ~**kongres**, peace congress.
vre'desluiting, conclusion of peace; peace-making.
vre'des: ~**naam**: *in* ~ *naam*, for heaven's sake; ~**onderhandelaar**, peace negotiator; ~**onderhandelinge**, peace negotiations; ~**opleiding**, peace(-time) training; V ~ **paleis**, Palace of Peace; ~**party**, peace party; ~**plan**, peace plan; ~**poging**, peace-move; ~**politiek**, peace policy; ~**propaganda**, peace propaganda; ~**pyp**, pipe of peace, calumet; *die* ~**pyp aanbied**, offer (smoke) the pipe of peace; ~**tempel**, temple of peace.
vre'de: ~**sterkte**, peace establishment; peace-footing; ~**steurder**, disturber of the peace; ~**stigter**, peacemaker, pacifier; ~**stigting**, pacification.

vre'destoorder = vredesteurder.
vre'des: ~**traktaat**, peacy treaty; ~**tyd**, time of peace; ~**verbond**, league of peace; ~**verdrag**, peace treaty; ~**vlag**, flag of truce; ~**voet:** *op* ~ *voet BRING*, put on a peace-time basis; *op* ~ *voet VERKEER*, be on a piecetime footing; ~**voorstander**, pacifist; ~**voorstel**, proposal of peace; eirenicon; ~**voorwaardes**, peace terms, conditions of peace.
vr'edesversteurder, vre'desvoorstoorder, (-s), disturber of the peace.
vre'devlag, flag of truce.
Vre'devors, Jesus, the Messiah, Prince of Peace.
vre'dig, (-e), quiet, peaceful, halcyon; ~**heid**, peace(fulness).
vreed'saam, (..same), peaceful, calm; peaceable, placid; ~**heid**, peacefulness, calmness.
vreemd, (-e), strange (person); bizarre; queer, odd, peculiar (occurrence); peregrine, extraneous, foreign, alien (from another country); exotic (plants); *die* ~*e DAARVAN is*, the strange part of it is; *DIS* ~, that is queer; ~*e GODE*, strange gods; *IN die* ~*e*, abroad, in foreign lands; *'n* ~*e TAAL*, a foreign language; ~*e VOORWERP*, foreign (extraneous) body (med.); ~**bevrugting**, exogamy.
vreem'de, (-s), stranger; outsider; foreigner; *in die* ~, in foreign parts; ~**godediens**, allotheism; **V**~**legioen**, Foreign Legion.
vreem'delinge: ~**boek**, visitors' book; ~**buro**, tourist information bureau, ~**haat**, xenophobia; ~**hater**, xenophobe; **V**~**legioen**, Foreign Legion; ~**verkeer**, tourist traffic; **V**~**wet**, Aliens' Act
vreem delingskap, alienism, alienship, state of being an alien; *IN* ~, in exile; *die JARE van my* ~, the years of my pilgrimage; *die LAND van jou* ~, the land where thou art a stranger; *die LAND van hulle* ~, the land where they sojourn (Bibl.).
vreem'delinkie, (-s), little stranger.
vreemd'heid, strangeness, queerness, extraordinariness, peculiarity; foreignness.
vreemdsoor'tig, (-e), strange, quaint, singular, odd; heterogeneous, motley; ~**heid**, quaintness, oddity, singularity; heterogeneity.
vrees, (s) (vrese) awe; fright; dread; apprehensiveness; funk; fear; ~ *AANJA*, terrify; *die* ~ *van GOD*, the fear of God; *die* ~ *v.d. HERE is die beginsel v.d. wysheid*, the fear of the Lord is the beginning of wisdom; ~ *KOESTER vir*, be afraid of; *RIDDER sonder* ~ *of blaam*, knight without fear or reproach; *die* ~ *UITSPREEK*, express the (one's) fear; (w) (ge-), fear, dread, be afraid; apprehend; ~**aanja(g)end, (-e),** terrifying, intimidating, appalling, fearsome, alarming; ~**aanjaging**, intimidation.
vreesag'tig, (-e), timid, timorous, chicken-hearted; ~**heid**, timidity, fearfulness.
vrees'bevange, panic-stricken.
vrees'lik, (b) (-e), terrible, horrible, dreadful, awful, fearful, horrid, ghastly, frightful, appalling, direful), fearsome; (bw) confoundedly, horribly, fearfully, terribly, awfully; ~ *stadig*, terribly (dead) slow; ~**heid**, dreadfulness, terribleness, direness, direfulness, horridness.
vreeswek'kend, (-e), awe-inspiring, terrifying.
vreet, (ge-), eat (animals); gorge, gut(tle), guzzle, gormandize, gluttonize; corrode, fret (by acid); *vretende SEER*, rodent ulcer; *vretende UITSLAG*, lupus; ~**baar**, edible (e.g. grass); ~**kaart**, rummy (card game); ~**middel**, corrosive; ~**saam**, (..same), (skertsend), gluttonous; ~**sak**, glutton; ~**werking**, corrosive action.
vrek[1], (s) (-ke), miser, cheeseparer, curmudgeon, skinflint, churl.
vrek[2], (w) (ge-), die (of animals); (b) dead; *die DIER is* ~, the animal is dead; *GAAN* ~! go to the devil! (bw) extremely; *dit is* ~ *VER*, it is very far; *jou* ~ *WERK*, work oneself to death.
vrek'agtig = vrekkerig.
vrek'bang, extremely afraid; in a blue funk.
vrek: ~**kerig, ~kig, (-e),** miserly, avaricious, stingy, scrimpy, cheeseparing, close-fisted, niggardly, costive (fig.), penurious; ~**kerigheid**, ~**kigheid**, cheeseparing, closeness, miserliness, avarice,

stinginess; ~**maer**, as thin as a rake; ~**sel, (-s),** scoundrel; ~**suinig, (-e),** extremely miserly, skinflinty, iron-fisted.
vrek'te, mortality (animals).
vre'se, apprehension, dread, fear; *die* ~ *van die HERE*, the fear of God.
vre'ter, (-s), glutton; ~**ig, (-e),** gluttonous; ~**igheid**, gluttony; ~**y**, gorging.
vreug'(de), joy, gladness, happiness; *DRONK van* ~, intoxicated with joy; *met DUIWELSE* ~, gloatingly; *SING van* ~, sing for joy.
vreug'de: ~**bederwer**, spoil-sport, kill-joy; ~**bedryf**, rejoicing, festivity; ~**betoon**, rejoicings; ~**dronk**, drunk with joy; ~**fees**, festivity; ~**klokke**, joy-bells; ~**kreet**, shout of joy; ~**lied**, song of joy; ~**loos, (..lose),** joyless, cheerless; ~**sang**, song of joy; ~**skoot**, festive salute; feu de joie; ~**teken**, sign of joy; ~**traan**, tear of joy; ~**vol, (-le),** joyful, joyous; ~**vuur**, bonfire, bale-fire, feu de joie.
vriend, (-e), friend; *ALLEMANS* ~ *is niemands* ~, a friend to everybody is a friend to nobody; ~*e BLY met*, remain friends with; *DIK* ~ *e wees*, be inseparable friends; ~*e praat in my GESIG*, honde blaf *agter my rug*, friends speak to my face, dogs bark behind my back; *iem. aan sy* ~*e KEN*, know a person by the company he keeps; ~ *nog MAAG hê*, have neither kith nor kin; ~*e MAAK*, make (gain) friends; *'n* ~ *in NOOD*, a friend in need; *TOON my jou* ~ *e en ek sal jou sê wie jy is*, *sê my wie is jou* ~ *e en ek sal jou sê wie jy is*, a man is known by the company he keeps.
vrien'de: ~**diens**, good turn; ~**kring**, circle of friends.
vrien'delik, (b) (-e), friendly, affable, kind, suave, decent, amicable, good, polite, kindly-disposed; (bw) gently; ~*e groete*, kind regards; ~**heid**, kindness, friendliness, affability, amicability, politeness, affableness; ~*heid kos geen geld nie*, civility costs nothing.
vrien'deloos, (..lose), friendless, ~**heid**, friendlessness.
vriendin', (-ne), lady friend; ~**netjie, (-s),** girl friend.
vriend: ~**jie, (-s),** little friend; ~**lief**, my dear friend (fellow).
vriend'skap, friendship, amity; favour, good turn; *iem.* ~ *'n* ~ *BEWYS*, do someone a favour (a kind turn); *die EEN* ~ *is die ander werd*, one good turn deserves another; ~ *SLUIT met*, make friends with; *UIT* ~, for the sake of friendship.
vriendskap'lik, (-e), friendly, amicable, chummy, neighbourly; *'n* ~*e wedstryd*, a friendly match; -**heid**, friendliness, amicableness, amity.
vriend'skaps: ~**band**, tie of friendship; ~**betoon**, expression of friendship; ~**betrekking**, friendly relation; ~**betuiging**, expression of friendship; ~**bewys**, token (proof) of friendship; ~**diens**, kindness, kind turn, friendly office; ~**gevoel**, feeling of friendship; ~**verbond**, bond of friendship; ~**verdrag**, treaty of friendship; ~**verhouding**, friendly relation; ~**vertoon**, display of friendship.
vries, (ge-), freeze; ~**bars**, frost crack; ~**diepte**, frostline; ~**eier**, frozen egg; ~**end, (-e),** frozen; frosty; ~**glas**, arctic glass; ~**hoogte**, freezing level; ~**ing**, freezing, freeze; ~**kamer**, freezing-chamber; ~**kas, (-te),** deep-freeze(r); ~**kis**, chest food-freezer; ~**mengsel**, freezing-mixture; ~**middel**, freezing-agent; ~**punt**, freezing-point, *BO (onder)* ~*punt*, above (below) freezing-point; ~*punt van LUG*, freezing temperature of air; ~**puntverlaging**, depression of freezing-point; ~**stof**, freezing-agent; ~**vleis**, frozen meat; ~**weer**, frosty weather; ~**weermiddel**, antifreeze (mixture); ~**wering**, antifreeze.
vrind = vriend.
vroed, (-e), wise, discreet; *die* ~*e vaders*, the city fathers; ~**meester**, accoucheur; ~**vrou**, midwife, accoucheuse.
vroe'ë: ~**pampoen**, squash, vegetable marrow; ~**perske**, early peach.
vroe'ër, (-e), (b) former, late, previous; earlier, prior, pristine; *my* ~*e BAAS*, my former master (head, chief); *in* ~ *DAE*, in bygone days; (bw) formerly,

previously; earlier; pristine, prior; before; quondam, erstwhile, sooner; ~ *was die gewoonte ANDERS*, formely there was a different custom; ~ *of LATER*, sooner or later; ~**ig**, rather early.

vroeg, (vroeë), early, timely, betimes, matutinal; *'n vroeë DOOD*, an untimely death; ~ *GENOEG*, in good time; ~ *en LAAT*, early and late; sooner or later; *vroeë METTE*, matins; *OORMÔRE op sy (die)* ~*ste*, the day after tomorrow at the earliest; *jy sal* ~ *moet OPSTAAN*, you will have to work hard; you will have to be wide awake; *'n vroeë PAMPOEN*, an early pumpkin; *SMÔRENS* ~, early in the morning; ~**aand**, (in the) early evening; ~**-Christelik, (-e)**, early Christian; ~**diens**, early service; ~**erig, (-e)**, somewhat early; ~**geboorte**, premature birth; ~**gebore**, prematurely born; ~**kos**, breakfast; ~**mis**, early mass, matins; ~**oggend**, early in the morning; ~**opstaner**, early riser; ~**ryp, (-e)**, early (fruit); precocious, premature, forward, sophisticated; ~**rypheid**, precocity, prematurity.

vroeg'ste, earliest, primary; *cf.* **vroeg**.

vroeg'te, early morn(ing); *in die* ~, early in the morning.

vroegty'dig, (-e), early, in good time, in advance, betimes; ~**heid**, earliness.

vroeg'-vroeg, very early.

vroe'kos = **vroegkos**.

vroe'pampoen = **vroeëpampoen**.

vroe'perske = **vroeëperske**.

vroe'tel, (ge-), root, tootle (of swine); grovel; wallow, scratch up the soil, burrow; rummage; fidget; pry into (affairs); ~**end, (-e)**, fossorial.

vro'lik, (-e), merry, gay, cheerful, chirpy, jolly, blithe, festive, frolic(some), hilarious, jocund, jovial, joyful, mellow, cheery, genial, gleeful, bobbish, hearty, high (spirits); tipsy; *jou* ~ *maak oor iets*, poke fun at something.

vro'likheid, cheerfulness, gaiety, mirth, cheeriness, cheer, glee, geniality, gladness, merriness, merriment, jocundity, jollification, jollity, jolliness, conviviality, exhilaration, frolicsomeness, hilarity, hilariousness, joviality, joyfulness; pleasantry; gay party; *na* ~ *kom OLIKHEID*, grief treads upon the heels of pleasure; sadness and gladness succeed each other; *ONDER groot* ~, amidst great hilarity.

vro'me, (-s), pious person; saint; pietist; *die* ~ *uithang*, play the saint; look pious.

vroom, (vrome), pious, devout, saintly, religious, godly, holy; ~ *praatjies*, claptrap, hypocritical talk; ~**heid**, piousness, piety, saintliness, devotion, devoutness, godliness.

vrot, (w) (ge-), rot, putrefy, decay; (b) rotten, decayed, bad, putrid, putrescent; ~**heid**, rottenness, putridity, putridness, badness; ~**pootjie(s)**, black-leg, root-rot (potatoes), potato-rot; wart; eelworm; foot-rot (animals).

vrot'sig, (-e), inefficient, hopeless, worthless (fellow); rotten (idea); beastly; ~**heid**, rottenness, inefficiency, hopelessness.

vrot'terd, (-s), rotter, no-good.

vrot'tigheid, rottenness; incompetence.

vrot'vel, blackguard, mean fellow, rotter, good-for-nothing.

vrou, (-e, -ens), woman; wife, spouse, better half; queen (cards); *soos 'n ou* ~ *se DANS*, of short duration; *die* ~ *van die HUIS*, the mistress (lady) of the house; *versadig eers* ~ *en KIND en sorg dan vir jou goeie naam*, charity begins at home; *MAN en* ~, husband and wife; *NIEMAND mag twee* ~*ens hê nie*, no one is allowed two wives; *my OU* ~, my old dutch (woman); *soos 'n OU* ~, like an old woman; ~ **ag'tig, (-e)**, womanish, effeminate; ~ **ag'tigheid**, womanishness, effeminacy.

vrou'e: ~**aard**, woman's nature; ~**afdeling**, women's ward; ~**arbeid**, woman's work; female labour; ~**arts**, specialist in women's diseases, gynaecologist; ~**beeld**, image of a woman; ~**beul**, wife-beater; ~**bevryding**, women's liberation; ~**beweging**, women's movement, feminist movement; suffragette movement; ~ **blad**, women's magazine; ~ **bond**, women's league; ~ **bors**, woman's breast; ~**bossie**, mountain-tea *(Geranium incanum)*; ~**deug(de)**, womanly virtue(s); ~ **dissel**, milk-thistle; ~**dokter**, gynaecologist; lady doctor; ~**drag**, women's wear; ~ **dubbelspel**, women's doubles; ~**figuur**, female figure; ~ **gedaante**, female figure; ~**gek**, philanderer, dangler after women, ladies' man; ~**geselskap**, women's society; ~**gril**, woman's whim; ~ **grootte**, woman's size; *groot* ~ *grootte*, outsize; *ekstragroot* ~ *grootte*, extra outsize; ~**gelykstelling**, women's lib: ~**haar**, woman's hair; ~**haarvaring**, maidenhair fern; ~**haat**, misogyny; ~**hand**, woman's hand; woman's handwriting; ~**handel**, trade in women, white-slave traffic; ~**handelaar**, white-slaver; ~**hart**, woman's heart; ~**hater, (-s)**, woman-hater, misogynist; ~**hemp**, chemise; ~**hoed**, lady's hat; ~**hoedemaker**, (man-)milliner; ~**hospitaal**, hospital for women; ~**jagter**, philanderer, wolf; ~**kamp**, concentration camp; ~**kampioen**, women's champion; ~**kiesreg**, women's suffrage; ~ **klere**, women's wear; ~**klooster**, nunnery; ~ **koor**, choir of female voices, ladies' choir; ~**liefde**, woman's love; ~**lis**, female cunning, woman's guile; ~**logika**, female logic (reasoning); ~**mantel**, lady's coat.

Vrou'emonument, Women's Monument (to the memory of the women and children who died in die refugee camps, 1899-1902).

vrou'ensaal, side-saddle; pillion.

vrou'e: ~**naam**, feminine name; ~**party**, women's (political) party; ~**partytjie**, ladies' party, hen party; ~**portret**, female portrait; ~**raad**, women's council; woman's advice; ~*raad is goeie raad*, a woman's advice is no great thing but he who won't take it is a fool; ~**reg**, women's lib; ~**regering**, petticoat government, gynocracy; ~**regte**, women's rights; ~**rok**, skirt, (women's) dress; ~**rol**, woman's role (part); ~**roof**, abduction of women; ~**rower**, woman-snatcher.

vrou'esaal¹, (-s), side-saddle; pillion.

vrou'esaal², (..sale), women's ward.

vrou'e: ~ **siekte**, women's disease; ~ **skender**, violator (ravisher) of women; ~**skending**, rape, violation, ravishment (of a woman); ~**skoen**, lady's shoe; ~**skoentjie**, lady's slipper; ~**stem**, female voice; ~**stemreg**, women's suffrage; ~ **tehuis**, women's home; ~**verblyf**, women's quarters; zenana (India); gynaeceum (Rome); harem; ~**vereniging**, sorority, women's society; ~**verering**, woman-worship; ~**vryheidsbeweging**, women's lib (liberation); ~**werk**, women's work.

vrou'lief, wife dear, my dear wife.

vrou'lik, (-e), womanly (manners); female; feminine (gender); *die ewig* ~ *e*, the eternal woman; ~**heid**, womanliness, femininity, muliebrity.

vrou'mens, female, woman; vixen, hussy.

vrous'persoon, female, woman.

vrou'siek, uxorious, excessively fond of one's wife.

vrou'tjie, (-s), little wife, wifie dear, little woman.

vrou'volk, womenfolk.

vrug, (-te), fruit; result, effect; embryo, foetus; *goeie* ~ *te AFWERP*, bear good fruit; *aan die* ~ *ken 'n mens die BOOM*, a tree is known by its fruit; ~ *te DRA*, bear fruit; yield results; *MET* ~, successfully, fruitfully; *ONGEBORE* ~, foetus; *die* ~ *te PLUK*, pluck the fruit; *as 'n mens 'n* ~ *RYP wil druk, word dit vrot*, no success can be expected by forcing matters; *SONDER* ~, fruitlessly, without avail; *VERBODE* ~ *te smaak die soetste*, stolen fruits (kisses) are the sweetest; ~ *te VORM*, form fruit; *WRANGE* ~ *te*, dead sea fruit; ~**afdrywend, (-e)**, abortifacient, abortive; ~**afdrywing**, abortion.

vrug'baar, (..bare), fruitful (year); prolific (writer); rich, fertile, fructuous, productive (soil); ~ *maak*, fertilize, fecundate; enrich; ~**heid**, fruitfulness, fertility, fatness, productivity, fecundity; ~**making**, fertilizing, fertilization, fecundation.

vrug'bed, stroma (biol.)

vrug: ~**beginsel**, ovary; germ, germen; ~**bekledend, (-e)**, amniotic; ~**bekleedsel, (-s)**, capsule, amnion; ~**blaar**, carpel; ~**bodem**, receptacle (bot.); ~**bren-**

vruggebruik 621 *vryheids*

gend, (-e), fructiferous, fruit-bearing; ~**draend, (-e),** fruit-bearing, fruitful, fructiferous, fructuous, frugiferous; ~**etend, (-e),** carpophagous, frugivorous.
vrug'gebruik, usufruct; royalty; ~**er, (-s),** usufructuary.
vrug: ~ **gie, (-s),** small fruit; ~**holte,** locule, loculus; ~**hulsel,** husk; ~**kiem,** embryo, germ; ~**knop,** fruit bud; ~**pluis,** pappus; ~**reg,** royalty (mine); ~**ryk, (-e),** fructuous, fruitful; ~**set,** fruit set; ~**stuk,** fruit still-life.
vrug'te: ~**bak,** fruit dish; ~**blatjang,** fruit chutney; ~**boer,** fruit-farmer; ~**boerdery,** fruit-farming; ~**boom,** fruit-tree; fruiter; ~**boord,** fruit grove, orchard; ~**bord,** fruit plate; ~**botter,** fruit butter; ~**compote,** compote of fruit; ~**dieet,** fruit diet; ~**drank,** fruit cordial, sherbet; ~**droging,** fruit drying; ~**-ete,** fruit lunch; ~**-eter,** fruit-eater; fruitarian; ~**fees,** fruit feast; ~**fles,** preserving-jar; ~**handel,** fruit trade; ~**handelaar,** fruiterer; ~**-inmaak,** fruit-canning; ~**jellie,** fruit jelly; ~**kassie,** fruit box; ~**kelkie,** fruit cocktail; ~**kiem,** fruit-germ; ~**kissie,** fruit box; fruit tray; ~**koek,** fruit cake; ~**kunde,** carpology; pomology; ~**kun'dig, (-e),** pomological; ~**kun'dige, (-s),** pomologist; ~**kweker,** fruit-grower, fruit-farmer; fruiter; ~**kwekery,** fruit-growing, orcharding; pomiculture; fruit farm; ~**lekkers,** fruit sweets.
vrug'teloos, (b) (..lose), ineffectual, vain, futile; abortive; purposeless; (bw) without avail; ~**heid,** futility, ineffectualness.
vrug'te: ~**maaltyd,** fruit lunch; ~**mandjie,** fruit basket, ~**messie,** fruit knife; ~**moer,** marc; ~**moes,** fruit-pulp; ~**-oes,** fruit crop; ~**pakker,** fruit-packer; ~**pakkery,** fruit-packing; ~**pannekoekie,** fruit fritter; ~**pastei,** fruit pie; fruit cobbler; ~**pit,** pip; ~**pias,** fruit farm; ~**puree,** fruit purée; ~**reep,** fruit slab; ~**ruspe(r),** canker-worm; ~**sap,** fruit juice; ~**servet,** fruit napkin; ~**skuim,** fruit whip; ~**slaai,** fruit salad, angels' food; ~**smeer,** fruit leather; ~**solder,** fruit loft; ~**sous,** fruit sauce; ~**sout,** fruit salts; ~**stalletjie,** fruit stall; ~**stellasie,** drying-tray; ~**stoompoeding,** plum pudding; ~**stroop,** fruit syrup; ~**suiker,** fructose; ~**tameletjie,** fruit leather; ~**teelt,** fruit-growing; ~**tentoonstelling,** fruit show; ~**tert,** fruit tart; ~**vlek,** fruit stain; ~**vlieg,** fruit fly; ~**vlies,** chorion; ~**vulsel,** fruit filling; ~**vurk,** fruit fork; ~**winkel,** fruit shop; ~**ys,** fruit ice.
vrug: ~**val,** fruit fall; ~**vormig, (-e),** fructiform; ~**vorming,** setting, fructification; ~**wand,** pericarp, fruit-wall; ~**water,** amniotic fluid.
vry¹, (w) (ge-), woo, make love, keep company, court, spoon, flirt; *na 'n BETREKKING* ~, solicit one's appointment to a post; *LANK gevry, niks gekry,* after all the wooing there is nothing doing; *met 'n MEISIE* ~, make love to a girl; *na 'n NOOI* ~, court a girl; *na STEMME* ~, canvass (solicit) votes, try to catch votes.
vry², (bw) ([-e]), free, at liberty, disengaged; emancipated (slave); gratis, free (admission); off-duty, at leisure; heart-whole (girl); unoccupied, vacant (seat); complimentary (ticket); clear, unobstructed (view); ~ *aan BOORD,* free on board; *'n* ~ *e DAG,* a day off; ~ *van DIENS,* off duty; *uit* ~ *e GENADE,* as an act of grace; *iem. die* ~ *e HAND laat,* allow someone a free hand; *uit die* ~ *e HAND teken,* draw freehand; ~ *HEFBOOM,* idle lever; *'n LESUUR* ~ *hê,* have a free period; ~ *e LIEFDE,* free love; ~ *LOSIES hê,* have free board; be lodged at the state's expense; *hy het 'n* ~ *e SÊ,* he is at liberty to say what he likes; ~ *van siekte,* immune from disease; ~ *van sorg,* care-free; ~ *e STAD,* free city; ~ *TOEGANG,* admission free; ~ *e TYD,* leisure (spare) time; ~ *soos 'n VOËL,* free as air; *mag ek so* ~ *WEES,* may I take the liberty? (bw) rather; freely; fairly, tolerably; ~ *wat BETER,* much better; ~ *GOED,* fairly good; ~**af,** free off; ~ *af HÊ,* have a holiday; *'n DAG* ~ *af neem,* take a day off.
vrya'sie, (-s), courtship, love-making, flirtation.
vry'blywend, (-e), without obligation (engagement).

vry'boer, free farmer, peasant proprietor.
vry'brief¹, passport, permit; licence.
vry'brief², love-letter.
vry'buit, (ge-), practise piracy, freeboot; ~**er, (-s),** freebooter, pirate, buccaneer; ~**ery,** freebooting.
Vry'burger, (-s), Free Burgher.
vry'burger, freeman; free burgher.
Vry'dae, on Friday(s).
Vry'dag, (..dae), Friday; *Goeie* ~, Good Friday; ~**aand,** Friday evening; ~**middag,** Friday afternoon; ~**môre,** Friday morning; ~**oggend,** Friday morning; ~**s,** (b) (-e), Friday; (bw) on Friday.
vry'denker, (-s), free-thinker, latitudinarian, libertine; ~**y,** free-thinking, libertinism.
vry: ~**dom,** freedom, exemption; franchise; ~**draai, (-ge-),** idle (of motor-car).
vry'draend, (-e): ~ *e BALK,* cantilever; ~ *e BRUG,* cantilever bridge.
vry'e, (-s), freeman; *in die* ~, in the open air.
vry'(e)lik, freely; *gebruik* ~, use freely.
vry'er, (-s), lover, suitor, wooer, adorer, boy-friend, sweetheart; ~**ig, (-e),** amorous, inclined to make love; spoony, flirtatious, flirty; ~**igheid,** amorousness, flirtatiousness; ~**y, (-e),** wooing, courtship, love-making, flirtation; ~**ytjie, (-s),** amourette.
vry'(e)tydsbesteding, utilization (utilizing) of leisure.
vryf, (ge-) = vrywe.
vryf: ~**doek,** mop, polishing-cloth; ~**dokter,** masseur; ~**klop, (ge-),** cream, beat to cream; ~**kuur,** massage; ~**lap,** polishing-cloth (-rag); ~**las, (-se),** rubbed joint; ~**middel,** rub; embrocation; ~**paal,** rubbing-post; ~**plank,** float (plasterer); ~**steen,** float-stone; rub-stone; muller; ~**vastheid,** fastness against rubbing; ~**waks,** polishing wax; ~**was(sing),** friction-washing.
vry'gebore, free-born; ~**ne, (-s),** free-born person, freeman.
vry: ~**gee, (-ge-),** give a holiday; give leave; release (for publication); clear, free, ~**gees,** free-thinker; libertine.
vrygees'tig, (-e), liberal, free-thinking; ~**heid,** free-thinking, liberalism.
vry'gelaat, (..late), released, freed.
vry'gelatene, (-s), emancipist, freed man.
vry'geleide, escort; safe conduct; protection; *onder 'n* ~, under safeguard.
vry'gesel, (-le), bachelor.
vry'gestelde, (-s), exempted (released) person.
vry'gewes, (-te), dominion.
vryge'wig, (-e), generous, open-handed, liberal; ~**heid,** liberality, generosity, munificence, freeness; prodigality.
vry'gooi, (-e), free throw.
vry'handel, free trade; ~**aar,** free-trader; ~**stelsel,** system of free trade.
vry'handskets, freehand drawing.
vry'hawe, (-ns), open port.
vry'heer, baron; ~**lik, (-e),** baronial; ~**likheid,** harmony.
vry'heid, (..hede), liberty, freedom, independence; immunity; exemption; licence; *die* ~ *BEHOU om,* remain free to; ~ *van BEWEGING,* liberty of movement; *dit is hier* ~ *BLYHEID,* it is Liberty Hall here; *DIGTERLIKE* ~, poetic licence; ~ *LAAT,* allow some latitude, give scope; *die* ~ *NEEM om,* make bold to; take the liberty to; ~ *v.d. PERS,* freedom of the press, *in* ~ *STEL,* release, set free; *VEG vir die* ~, fight for independence; *hom vryhede VEROORLOOF,* take liberties with; *die* ~ *VOORBEHOU,* reserve the liberty to; ~**lie'wend, (-e),** fond of liberty, liberty-loving.
vry'heids: ~**apostel,** apostle of liberty; ~**beperking,** restriction of freedom; ~**berowing,** deprivation of liberty; ~**boom,** liberty pole, tree of liberty; ~**droom,** dream of freedom; ~**fakkel,** torch of freedom; ~**gees,** spirit of liberty; ~**gesind, (-e),** libertarian; ~**gesinde, (-s),** libertarian; ~**hoed,** cap of liberty.
vry'heidsin, spirit of liberty.
vry'heids: ~**liefde,** love of liberty (independence); ~**maagd,** goddess of liberty; ~**moord,** ~**moordenaar,** liberticide; ~**oorlog,** war of independence.

vry'heidsug, spirit of liberty.
vry'heids: ~ **vaan,** ~ **vlag,** flag of liberty; ~ **waansin,** eleutheromania.
vry: ~ **hoek,** angle of clearance; ~ **hoogte,** clearance, free height; ~ **hou, (-ge-),** keep free (open, vacant).
vry'kaartjie, complimentary ticket, free ticket; railway warrant, free pass; ~ **houer,** deadhead.
vry: ~ **kamer,** best (guest-) room, spare (bed)room; ~ **kom, (-ge-),** get off, go free, escape; become vacant; ~ **koop, (-ge-),** redeem, ransom, buy off; ~ **koping,** redemption; ~ **korps,** body of volunteers, volunteer corps; ~ **kwartier,** first quarter (her.); ~ **laat, (-ge-),** release, free, liberate, set at liberty (captive); emancipate, manumit (slave); absolve from blame; give (someone) a free hand; ~ **lating,** liberation, release (of captives); emancipation, manumission (of slaves); ~ **leen,** freehold; ~ **lekker, (-s),** motto kiss.
vry'loop, (-ge-), escape, get off scot-free; coast (motor); free-wheel (bicycle); idle (of engine); ~ **sproeier,** idling jet.
vry'loot, (-ge-), draw a lucky number; be exempted from military training.
vry'lustig, (-e), amorous, hot-stuff.
vry'maak, (-ge-), liberate, disencumber; (set) free, emancipate (slave); decontrol; *jou van 'n slegte gewoonte* ~ , free oneself of a bad habit.
vrymag'tig, (-e), almighty.
vry: ~ **maker, (-s),** liberator, emancipator, liberationist; absolver; ~ **making,** freeing, liberation, emancipation; affranchisement; disembarrassment.
Vrymes'selaar, Freemason.
Vrymes'selaars: ~ **losie,** Freemason's lodge; ~ **orde,** order of Freemasons.
Vrymesselary', Freemasonry.
vrymoe'dig, (-e), candid, frank, bold, outspoken; ~ **heid,** candour, confidence, frankness, candidness, freeness.
vry'party, petting party.
vry'pas, free pass.
vry'passing, clearance fit.
vry'peperment, (-e), motto kiss.
vry'perd, wooer's horse; showy horse.
vry: ~ **plaas,** sanctuary, refuge, asylum; ~ **pleit, (-ge-),** exonerate, exculpate, clear; obtain the discharge of an accused.
vry'plek¹, courting- (wooing-) place.
vry'plek², asylum, sanctuary, refuge; complimentary seat.
vrypos'tig, (-e), impudent, pert, forward, free, familiar, bold; ~ **heid,** forwardness, impudence, freeness, pertness.
vry: ~ **ruimte,** clearance; ~ **ry, (-ge-),** free-wheel; ~ **setting,** affranchisement; liberation.
vrysin'nig, (-e), liberal, broad, latitudinous, latitudinarian, liberal-minded; ~ **heid,** liberalism, latitudinarianism, liberality.
vry'skel(d), (-ge-), exempt; let off; *iem. sy skuld* ~ , cancel someone's debt.
vry'skut, freelance, independent journalist.
vry'slaapkamer = **vrykamer.**
vry'slag, free-style (swimming); ~ **suier,** piston-clearance.
vry'spraak, acquittal, discharge, absolution, exculpation.
vry'spreek, (-ge-), acquit, discharge, clear, exonerate, absolve, exculpate; ~ *van,* find not guilty of; **..spreker,** absolver.
vry'spring, (-ge-), escape, evade, get off free, dodge.
vry'staan, (-ge-), be free to; be permitted to; *dit staan jou vry om . . .,* you are free to . . .; ~ **de,** free-standing (exercises); detached (house); ~ *de KRAAN,* independent crane; ~ *de MUUR,* selfsupporting wall; ~ *de STOOF,* island range.
vry'staat, free state.
Vry'staat, (s) Free State; (tw) **Vrystaat'!,** well done! press on regardless! whacko!; ~ **s, (-e),** (of the) Free State.
vry'stad, (..stede), free city; city of refuge.
Vry'stater, (-s), Free Stater.
vry'stel, (-ge-), exempt, let off; free, release (news, film, slave); excuse; dispense; *vrygestel van belasting,* exempt from taxation; ~ **ling, (-e, -s),** exemption; freeing, freedom; dispensation; franchisement; ~ *ling vir die pers,* press release; ~ **lingsbewys,** certificate of exemption.
vry'ster, (-s), sweetheart; spinster.
vry'stoei, catch-as-catch-can.
vry'tog, courting expedition.
vry'tydsbesteding = **vry(e)tydsbesteding.**
vry: ~ **uit,** frankly, freely, without restraint; ~ **veg, (-ge-),** free, fight to liberate; ~ **verklaar, (~),** declare free, acquit, discharge; emancipate.
vry'verklaring, (-e, -s), release, acquittal, discharge; emancipation; ~ *van die slawe,* emancipation of the slaves.
vry'waar, (ge-), protect, guard; guarantee; indemnify (legal); *teen (vir) verlies* ~ , safeguard against loss; ~ **der, (-s),** guarantor.
vry'waring, protection, safeguard; guarantee; indemnification.
vry'warings: ~ **vorm,** indemnity form; ~ **wet,** indemnification (indemnity) law.
vry'we, (ge-), rub, massage; polish, burnish; *FYN* ~ , pulverize; *die HANDE* ~ , rub one's hands; *deur 'n SIF* ~ , pass through a strainer.
vry'wel, fairly well, pretty much, well-nigh, more or less; *dis* ~ *onmoontlik,* it is practically impossible.
vry'wer, (-s), masseur.
vry'wiel, free-wheel; ~ **stelsel,** free-wheel system.
vrywil'lig, (-e), voluntary; gratuitous; of one's own free will.
vrywil'liger, (-s), volunteer; ~ **er-offisier,** volunteer officer.
vrywil'ligers: ~ **korps,** volunteer corps; ~ **reserwe,** volunteer reserve.
vrywil'ligerstelsel, volunteer system.
vrywil'lig: ~ **heid,** voluntariness; free will; ~ **lik,** voluntarily, freely.
vry'wing, rubbing.
vry'wording, liberation.
vry'worp, (-e), free throw.
v''tjie, (-s), small v.
vuig, (-e; -er, -ste), low, sordid, mean, base, vile; ~ **heid,** meanness, vileness, baseness.
vuil, (s) dirt, filth, grime; (b) dirty (hands, clothes); smutty (talk); foul (weather); filthy, grimy; fly-blown (window); impure, indecent (jokes), obscene (language); *sy hande* ~ *MAAK (smeer),* dirty (soil) his hands; ~ *SPEL,* foul play; ~ *TAAL gebruik,* use obscene language; *die TUIN is* ~ , the garden is full of weeds; ~ *WATER,* slops; *'n ander se* ~ *WERK doen,* do someone else's dirty work; ~ *WOL,* dingy wool; ~ **bek,** user of obscene language; scabby mouth (animal disease); ~ **bekkig, (-e),** foul-mouthed.
vui'lerig, (-e), rather dirty, scruffy.
vuil'goed, filth, dirt, rubbish, dust; dirty person, bad egg (sl.); contemptible fellow, skunk; raffle; weeds; pus (wound); placenta (of animal); *jou lae* ~ *!,* you dirty swine!; ~ **blik,** rubbish bin, dustbin; ~ **hoop,** refuse-heap, dunghill, midden; ~ **kar,** dust-cart, rubbish cart; ~ **oond,** destructor, incinerator; ~ **sak,** soiled-linen bag; ~ **verwydering,** rubbish removal.
vuil: ~ **heid,** foulness, impurity, mess, dirt(iness), squalor, filth(iness); obscenity; ~ **igheid,** garbage, ordure, smut.
vui'lis, rubbish, filth, dirt; pus; **(-se),** mean fellow, skunk, bad egg (sl.); ~ **bak,** dustbin, dirt-box; ~ **eter,** coprophagist; ~ **hoop,** refuse-heap; ~ **kar,** dust-cart, rubbish (refuse-) cart.
vuil: ~ **maak, (-ge-),** go to stool, defecate; ~ **put,** cesspool, cesspit; ~ **pyp,** cesspipe, soil-pipe; ~ **riool,** sewer; ~ **siekte,** venereal disease, syphilis; ~ **skrywery,** pornography.
vuil'water, ditch-water; ~ **bak,** (slop-)sink; ~ **emmer,** slop-pail; ~ **pyp,** waste-pipe.
vuil'wit, dirty white; off-white.
vuis, (-te), fist; *'n mens kan nie* ~ *maak sonder HAND nie,* omelets are not made without the breaking of eggs; *iem. met die KAAL* ~ *bydam,* go for someone hammer and tongs; *in sy* ~ *LAG,* laugh up one's sleeve; ~ *MAAK,* clench the fist; challenge; *alles*

voor die ~ *NEEM,* take whatever comes to hand; *uit die* ~ *PRAAT,* make an impromptu speech; speak extempore (without notes); speak off the cuff; *uit die* ~ *SKIET,* fire without taking proper aim; *VOOR die* ~, impromptu; *'n* ~ *van YSTER,* a rod of iron; a mailed fist; ~**dik,** much, very thick; *dit sit* ~ *dik agter die ore,* he is not as green as he is cabbage-looking; ~**geveg,** boxing-match, mill; sparring bout; ~**handskoen,** boxing-glove; mitten; ~**hou,** punch; ~**ie,** (-s), little fist; ~**reg,** fist-law; ~**slaan,** (-ge-), fight with the fists; ~**slanery,** fisti= cuffs; ~**tedik** = **vuisdik;** ~**steenkool,** cobbles; ~**vegter,** (-s), boxer, pugilist; ~**vegtery,** boxing, prize-ring; pugilism, fisticuffs; ~**vol, (vuistevol),** handful; ~**voos,** punch-drunk; ~**yster,** knuckle= duster.
vul[1]**,** (s) (-le, -lens), foal; colt (male); filly (female); (w) **(ge-),** foal.
vul[2]**,** (w) **(ge-),** fill (glass); stuff (chicken); stop, fill (tooth); flush (cistern); ~**bak,** hopper; ~**blok,** packing block.
Vulca'nus, Vulcan.
vul: ~**diens,** refuelling service; ~**dop,** filter-cap.
Vulgaat' = **Vulgata.**
vulgariseer', (ge-), vulgarize.
vulgaris'me, (-s), vulgarism.
vulgariteit', vulgarity.
vul'gat, filler; filler hole; filling hole.
Vulga'ta, Vulgate.
vulgêr', (-e), vulgar; ~**heid,** vulgarity.
vulkaan', (-, kane), volcano; *uitgedoofde* ~, extinct volcano; ~**as,** volcanic ash; ~**modder,** moya; ~**pyp,** volcanic pipe.
vulka'nies, (-e), volcanic.
vulkaniet', vulcanite.
vulkaniseer', (ge-), vulcanize.
vulkanise'ring, vulcanization.
vulkanis'me, vulcanism.
vulkanologie', vulcanology.
Vulka'nus, Vulcan.
vul'klei, puddle.
vul'ler, (-s), filler.
vul'lertuit, filler spout.
vul'letjie, (-s), little foal; side-car; *moenie die* ~ *se RUG afry voordat jy die groot perd het nie,* don't discard old clothes before you have new ones; don't be off with the old love before you are on with the new; *toe jy nog 'n* ~ *WAS,* when you were still a mere chit.
vul'ling, (-e, -s), filling, stopping, impletion, stuffing, plugging; ~**halk,** filler joist.
vul'lingspomp, bilge-pump.
vul'lis = **vuilis.**
vul'pen, fountain-pen; ~**ink,** fountain-pen ink.
vul'plaat, packing plate; ~**jie,** shim.
vul'potlood, propelling pencil.
vul'pyp, filler hose (pipe).
vul'sel, (-s), stuffing (chicken); force (meat), dressing; stopping, filling (tooth); filler, padding, gasket, fill= ing material.
vul: ~**stasie, (-s),** filling-station, petrol station; ~**steek,** filling stitch; ~**steen,** jamb-stone; ~**stof,** bulk (food); filler; filling material; ~**stuk,** filler piece; liner; packer; slip; ~**tregter,** hopper funnel, chute, shoot; ~**vliegtuig,** refuelling-plane; ~**werk,** padding.
vun'sig, (-e), musty, fusty, mouldy; ~**heid,** mustiness, fustiness.
vu'rig, (-e), fiery (eyes); animated, eager, (hot-)spirit= ed, hot-blooded, keen (person); mettlesome (horse); perfervid, glowing, fervent, ardent (desire); ~**heid,** ardour, spiritedness, keenness, fieriness, fervency, fire.
vurk, (s) (-e), fork; prong; pitchfork; clevis; bifur= cation; *met 'n* ~ *SOP eet,* attempt the impossible; *hy weet hoe die* ~ *in die STEEL (hef) steek,* he knows the ins and outs of the matter; (w) **(ge-),** bifurcate; pitchfork; ~**been,** wishbone, merry= thought; ~**bliksem,** forked lightning; ~**ie, (-s),** small fork; ~**las, (-se),** forked joint; ~**pen,** clevis-pin; ~**senter,** fork-chuck.
vurks'gewyse, dichotomal.

vurk: ~**skakel,** fork-link; ~**sleutel,** fork-spanner, fork-wrench; ~**stang,** fork-rod; ~**tand,** tine, prong; ~**taplas, (-se),** bridle joint; ~**verbinding,** clevis-fitting.
vuur, (s) (vure), fire; flame; match; ardour, fervency, gusto, impressment, ardency; mettle (horse); gangrene (disease); *die* ~ *AANBLAAS,* fan the flames; *'n* ~ *AANLÊ,* build (make) a fire; *die* ~ *is in die GRAS,* the fat is in the fire; ~ *GEE,* blaze away; fire at; *die GROOT* ~, hell-fire; *onder* ~ *KOM,* go into action; *vir iem. deur die* ~ *LOOP,* go through fire and water for someone; *soos 'n LO= PENDE* ~ *tjie,* like wildfire; ~ *MAAK,* make (light) a fire; *ONDER* ~, under fire; *onder iem.* ~ *MAAK,* make someone hurry up; *wie die naaste aan die* ~ *SIT, word die warmste,* a friend at court makes the process short; *langs een* ~ *SIT,* be at one; *hulle SIT nie langs een* ~ *nie,* they cannot hit it off with one another; *tussen twee VURE SIT,* be= tween the devil and the deep blue sea; *iem. die* ~ *aan die SKENE lê,* make it hot for someone; ~ *SLAAN,* strike fire; extinguish a veld-fire; *met* ~ *SPEEL,* play with fire; play with edged tools (fig.); play with ardour (orchestra); play with spirit (foot= ball); *te* ~ *en te SWAARD,* by fire and sword; ~ *VAT,* catch fire; *iem. is* ~ *en VLAM,* someone is fired with enthusiasm (going into raptures); ~ *en VLAM spoeg,* breathe fire and brimstone; *VOL* ~ *wees oor,* be (wildly) enthusiastic about; *soos* ~ *en WATER wees,* be like fire and now; (w) **(ge-),** fire; shoot at someone; ~**aanbidder,** fire-wor= shipper; ~**aanbidding,** fire-worship, pyrolatry; ~**aansteker,** fire-lighter; ~**baken,** beacon light; ~**bal,** fireball; ~**bessie,** hawthorn berry; ~**blik,** brazier; ~**blom,** hibiscus; ~**blusmiddel,** fire-extin= guisher; ~**bok,** andiron, dog-iron; ~**bol,** meteor; ball of fire; ~**buis,** fire-tube; fire-tube; ~**deur,** fire-door; ~**digtheid,** fire-density; ~**dood,** death by fire (at the stake); ~**doop,** maiden engagement, baptism of fire; crucial test; *die* ~ *doop ontvang,* re= ceive one's baptism of fire; ~**doring,** fire-thorn; Christ's thorn; ~**erd** = **vuurherd;** ~**eter,** fire-eater; ~**gang,** flue; ~**gedroog, (-de),** fire-cured; ~**gees,** salamander; ~**geveg,** fire-fight; ~**gloed,** glow of (the) fire, glare, blaze; ~**gordel,** fire belt; ~**gordyn,** fire curtain; ~**haak,** poker; ~**hark,** fire-rake, forge-rake; pricker.
vuur(h)erd, hearth, grate, fireside, fireplace; ~**besem,** hearth-broom; ~**grafie,** fire-shovel; ~**rand,** fend= er; ~**stel,** fire-irons; ~**yster,** fire-dog.
vuur'houtjie, (-s), match; ~**dosie,** match box; ~**fa= briek,** match factory; ~**maker,** match-maker.
vuur: ~**kas,** ~**ketel,** ~**kis,** fire-box; ~**klei,** fire-clay; ~**kleur,** flame-colour; ~**kleurig, (-e),** fire-coloured; ~**klip,** fire-stone, flint-stone; ~**klipge= weer,** ~**klipslot,** flintlock; ~**koeël,** fireball; ~**ko= lom,** column (pillar) of fire; ~**konka,** fire-pot, dev= il; brazier; ~**koord,** slow-match; ~**kopkaffervink,** fire-crowned bishop-bird; ~**kruis,** fiery cross, fire-cross; ~**lak,** black japan; ~**leer,** pyrology; ~**lei= dingsvliegtuig,** gunnery-spotter; ~**lelie,** fire-lily *(Cyrtanthus sanguineus);* ~**linie,** firing-line; ~**lo= pery,** fire-walking; ~**lyn,** fire-line.
vuur'maak: *onder iem.* ~, egg someone on; urge someone to buck up; ~**goed,** fuel; ~**hout,** fire-wood; ~**plek,** fireplace, fire-box; comprehension, ability; *dis bokant my* ~*plek,* it is beyond me.
vuur: ~**maker,** firer, fire-lighter; ~**makerskuns,** pyrotechny; ~**massa,** mass of flames; ~**meter,** pyrometer; ~**mond,** gun-tube; gun cannon; ~**oond,** furnace; ~**opaal,** girasol, fire-opal; ~**pelo= ton,** firing party, firing squad; ~**plaat,** furnace-plate; ~**poel,** sea of fire, inferno; ~**pot,** devil; ~**proef,** crucial test, (fire-)ordeal; acid test; *die* ~ *proef deurstaan,* survive one's baptism of fire; ~**punt,** fire-point.
vuur'pyl, sky rocket, rocket projectile; red-hot poker (flower); ~**kanon,** sky-rocket cannon; ~**stok,** rocket-mould; ~**vliegtuig,** rocket-propelled air= craft; ~**werk,** rocketry.
vuur: ~**rat,** Catherine wheel; ~**reën,** rain of fire; ~**roer,** firelock; ~**rooi,** red as fire; ~**root word,**

blush, turn scarlet (person); ~**salamander**, spotted salamander; ~**see**, sea of fire; ~**skerm**, fire-guard, fire-screen; baffle plate; ~**skip**, fire-ship; ~**skop**, forge-slice; ~**slag**, flint, steel and tinder; ~**slaner**, factotum; ~**snelheid**, rate of fire; ~**spu'wend, (-e)**, belching fire, volcanic; ~*spuwende berg*, volcano, volcanic mountain; ~**staking**, ceasefire; ~**stappery**, fire-walking; ~**steen**, flint; emery wheel; ~**straal**, flash of fire; ~**stroom**, stream of fire; ~**swam**, amadou; ~**tang**, fire-tongs, forge-tongs; ~**tempo**, rate of fire; ~**tessie**, fire-pan, chafingdish; ~**toring**, lighthouse, light-beracon, pharos; ~**toringwagter**, lighthouse-keeper.

vuur'vas, (-te), fireproof, fire-resisting; refractory; ~*te KLEI*, fire clay; ~ *STEEN*, fire brick; ~*te STOF*, refractory; ~*te TEËL*, fire tile.

vuur: ~**vastheid**, refractoriness; fireproofness; ~**verlegging**, lift (gunnery); ~**vermoë**, fire-power; ~**vlam**, flame (of fire); ~**vlieg**, firefly; ~**vonk**, spark; ~**vreter**, fire-eater (fig.); firebrand, hothead; ~**wa**, locomotive; ~**wapen**, firearm; ~**warm**, very hot, red-hot, aflame; broiling; intoxicated; *hy was ~ warm*, he was all aflame; he was as drunk as a lord; ~**water**, firewater; spirituous liquors; ~**werk**, fireworks, pyrotechnics; ~**werker**, forgeman; ~**werkkuns**, pyrotechnics; ~**werkmaker**, pyrotechnist; ~**werkmakerskuns**, pyrotechny; ~**werkvertoning**, pyrotechnic display; ~**yster**, firebar; poker.

V'-vormig, (-e), V-shaped.

vy, (-e), fig; *laat vye*, late figs; donkeys.

vy'and, (-e), enemy, adversary, foe(man); *'n GE= SWORE ~*, a professed enemy, a sworn foe; *onder die ~ MAAI*, mow the enemy down; *die ~ van die MENS*, the enemy of mankind.

vyan'delik, (-e), hostile, enemy, inimical; ~*e DAAD*, act of hostility; ~*e OPTREDE*, enemy action; ~**heid**: *die vyandelikhede begin*, open hostilities.

vyan'dig, (-e), hostile, antagonistic, adverse, inimical; ~ *teenoor iets staan*, be hostile to something; ~**gesind**, hostile-minded, inimical; ~**heid**, enmity, hostility, animus, animosity.

vy'andseiendom, enemy property.

vy'andskap, hostility, animosity, malice, enmity.

vy'ands: ~**onderdaan**, enemy subject; ~**vreemdeling**, enemy alien.

vy'eblaar, vy'eblad, fig-leaf; excuse; *jou met vyeblare DEK*, try to cover up; *vyeblare SOEK*, look for excuses.

vy'eboom, fig-tree; *onder jou ~ woon*, live under your own fig-tree.

vy'ebossie, *Mesembryanthemum spp*.

vyf, (vywe, -s), five; ~ *MAAL*, five times; ~ *UUR*, five hours; ~**ar'mig, (-e)**, five-armed.

vyf'blad, cinqfoil; ~**ig, (-e)**, pentapetalous; quinquefoliate.

vyf'daags, (-e), five-day, of five days, lasting five days; quintan (fever); ~*e werkweek*, five-day week.

vyf'de, (-s), fifth; ~*e KOLONNE*, fifth column; ~ *PART*, a fifth; *TEN ~*, fifthly; ~**kolonner**, fifthcolumnist.

vyf: ~**delig, (-e)**, fivefold, quinary, quinquepartite; ~**dens**, in the fifth place, fifthly; ~**derangs, (-e)**,fifth-rate; ~**draads, (-e)**, five-ply; ~**dubbel(d), (-de)**, fivefold; ~**duifies**, columbine; ~**duims, (-e)**, five-inch; ~**duimspyp**, five-inch pipe.

vyf'duisend, five thousand; ~**ste**, five-thousandth (part).

vyf'eeuefees, quincentenary.

vyf'ganger, (-s), vyf'gangperd, five-gaiter.

vyf'hoek, pentagon.

vyf'hoekig, vyfhoe'kig, (-e), pentagonal, quinquangular, five-angled.

vyf'honderd, five hundred; ~**jarige, (-e)**, quincentenary; ~**ste**, five-hundredth (part).

vy'fie, (-s), small five.

vyf: ~ **jaarliks, (-e)**, five-yearly, quinquennial; ~**jaarplan**, five-year plan; ~**jarig, (-e)**, of five years, five years old, five-year, quinquennial; ~**kaart**, sequence of five cards; ~**kamp**, pentathlon.

vyf'kant, pentahedron.

vyf'kantig, vyfkan'tig, (-e), pentahedral, five-sided.

vyf'ledig, vyfle'dig, (-e), quinary, quinquepartite.

vyf'lettergrepig, (-e), five-syllabled, of five syllables, quinquesyllabic.

vyf: ~ **ling, (-e)**, quintuplets; ~**lobbig, (-e)**, five-lobed.

vyf'man, pentarch; ~**skap**, pentarchy.

vyf: ~**ponder, (-s)**, five-pounder; ~**randnoot**, fiver.

vyf'reëlig, vyfre'ëlig, (-e), of five lines.

vyfsa'dig, vyf'sadig, (-e), pentaspermous.

vyf'sellig, vyfsel'lig, (-e), quinquelocular.

vyf'snarig, vyfsna'rig, (-e), five-stringed.

vyf'stemmig, vyfstem'mig, (-e), for five voices.

vyf'sydig, vyfsy'dig, (-e), five-sided, pentagonal, quinquelateral.

vyf'tal, five; pentad; quintet(te).

vyf'tallig, vyftal'lig, (-e), quinary.

vyf'tien, (-e), fifteen; ~**de**, fifteenth; ~**de-eeus, (-e)**, fifteenth-century; ~**hoek**, quindecagon.

vyf'tienhoekig, vyftienhoe'kig, (-e), quinary.

vyf'tien: ~**jarig, (-e)**, of fifteen years; fifteen years old; ~**tal**, fifteen; *'n ~ tal*, about fifteen; ~**voud**, multiple of fifteen; ~**voudig, (-e)**, fifteenfold.

vyf'tig, fifty; ~**er**, person of fifty; *in die ~erjare*, in the fifties; ~**jarig, (-e)**, of fifty years, fifty years old, quinquagenarian; ~**ste**, fiftieth; ~**tal**, fifty, about fifty; ~**voud, (-e)**, multiple of fifty; ~**voudig, (-e)**, fifty-fold.

vyf: ~**tonig, (-e)**, pentadactyl; ~**uur**, five o'clock.

vyf'vingerig, vyfvin'gerig, (-e), five-fingered, pentadactyl(ic).

vyf'vlak, pentahedron.

vyf'vlakkig, vyfvlak'kig, (-e), pentahedral.

vyf'voetig, (-e), five-footed; ~*e reëls*, pentameters.

vyf'voud, quintuple.

vyf'voudig, vyfvou'dig, (-e), fivefold, quintuple.

vyf'yster, (no.) 5 iron (golf).

vy'gie, (-s), vygie *(Mesembryanthemum)*.

vyl, (s) (-e), file; (w) **(ge-)**, file; ~**angel**, file-tang; ~**blok**, filing-block; ~**borsel**, file-carding; ~**doring**, file-tang; ~**er, (-s)**, filer; ~**handvatsel**, fileholder; ~**saag**, slitting-saw; ~**sels**, fillings, scobs; ~**skag**, file-body; ~**slang**, file-snake.

vy'sel, (-s), mortar; screw-jack; ~**kop**, die; ~**stamper**, pestle; *hy het die ~ stampers en die kriewelkrappers*, he is on pins and needles.

vy'tjie, (-s), small fig.

vy'wer, (-s), pond, pool.

W

w, (-'s), w.

wa, (-ens), wag(g)on; carriage, van, truck; *DIE Wa*, Charles's Wain; *krakende ~ens loop die LANG= STE*, creaking doors hang the longest; *die ~ voor die OSSE span*, put the cart before the horse(s); *voor op die ~ WEES*, be forward; be bumptious.

waad, (ge-), wade, ford; ~**baar**, (..bare), fordable; ~**voël**, wading-bird, wader.

waag, (ge-), venture, dare, risk, have a fling, hazard, stake, chance; *DURF dit tog ~!* just you dare do it! *jy kan dit GERUS ~*, you can safely chance (risk) it; *'n GEWAAGDE grap*, an improper joke; *'n KANS ~*, take a chance; *sy TOEKOMS aan iets ~*, stake his future on something; *wie ~, die WEN*, fortune favours the bold; *wie nie ~ nie, WEN nie*, nothing venture, nothing gain; faint heart never won fair lady; *aan mekaar ge~ WEES*, be wellmatched; ~**duiwel**, daredevil; ~**geld**, risk money, risk-capital.

waag'hals, (-e), daredevil, desperado, risker, adven=

waagkapitaal / **waarde**

turer, venturesome person; ~'(er)ig, (-e), reckless, daredevilish, breakneck, venturesome, foolhardy; ~ery', ~'igheid, recklessness, foolhardiness, daredevilry.

waag'kapitaal, risk-capital.

waag'moed, audacity, daring, pluck, daredevilry; ~ig, (-e), plucky, daredevilish.

waag'skaal = weegskaal.

waag'spel, game of hazard (chance); venture; ~er, (-s), punter.

waag'stuk, rash act, hazardous undertaking, daring feat, adventure, tour de force, plunge, enterprise, gamble.

waai[1], (s) (-e), slap, smack; *iem. 'n ~ gee*, give someone a smack.

waai[2], (s) (-e), bend, hollow, crook (of the knee, arm).

waai[3], (w) (ge-), blow, fan; float; flutter, flap (with wings); run off, go quickly; *die vlae ~ HALFSTOK*, the flags are flying at half-mast; *KOM ons ~*, let us be off; *NIKS met iem. uit te ~ e hê nie*, have no truck with someone; have nothing to do with a person; *hy sal NOG ~*, he will be thrown (chucked) out; ~ *soos 'n vrot VEL*, go (be sent) flying; ~**boom**, umbrella-tree *(Cussonia spicata)*; ~**bos**, acacia.

waai'er, (-s), fan (of woman); blower; ~**agtig, (-e)**, fanlike; ~**as**, fan-spindle; ~**band**, fan-belt; ~**bandwiel**, fan-pulley; ~**blad**, fan-blade; ~**gewelf**, fan-vault; ~**kap**, fan-cowl; radiator cowl; ~**katrol**, fan-pulley; ~**koppelaar**, fan-clutch; ~**palm**, fan-palm, palmyra; ~**riem**, fan-belt; ~**riemskyf**, fan pulley; ~**rogewys(e)**, fanlike, fanwise; ~**skuim**, spindrift; ~**spil**, fan-spindle; ~**stertduif**, fan-tail(ed) pigeon; ~**stertmeerkat**, fan-tailed meercat, ground-squirrel; ~**stertmuis**, dormouse; ~**tjie, (-s)**, small fan; ~**ventilator**, ventilation-fan; ~**vormig, (-e)**, fan-shaped; flabellate, flabelliform (bot. & zool.); ~**wiek**, fan-blade.

waai: ~**golf**, blow-wave; ~**gras**, waving grass, tall grass; ~**sand**, drift-sand; ~**sandduin**, shifting dune.

waak, (s) (**wake**), watch; vigil; *die tweede ~*, the second watch; (w) (ge-), watch, be awake; sit up with (invalid); take care of; ~ *oor GELDSAKE*, watch over financial matters; *'n wakende OOG hou oor*, keep a watchful eye on; ~ *TEEN*, be on one's guard against; ~**eenheid**, intensive care unit; ~**hond**, watchdog; ~**lig**, police-light.

waak'saam, (..same), alert, vigilant, watchful, wakeful; lynx-eyed; ~**heid**, alertness, wakefulness, watchfulness, vigilance; ~**heidskomitee**, vigilance committee.

Waal, (Wale), Walloon; ~**s** (b) (-e), Walloon, French.

waan, (s) fancy, delusion; idolum (logic); hallucination, conceit, erroneous idea; *in die ~ BRING*, lead to think; *uit die ~ HELP*, undeceive; *in die ~ KOM dat*, be led to believe that; *onder die ~ VERKEER, be* under the delusion that; (w) (ge-), fancy, imagine, think, ~**beeld**, fantasy, delusion; ~**denkbeeld**, false notion (idea); ~**geloof**, superstition; ~**sin**, phrenitis, insanity, madness, lunacy, dementia, mania, craziness; distraction; fury, frenzy, delirium.

waansin'nig, (-e), insane, deranged, maniacal, frenzied, mad, demented; furious, distraught, distracted, frantic; ~**e, (-s)**, madman, lunatic, maniac; ~**heid**, lunacy, madness; deliriousness.

waan'voorstelling, hallucination, delusion.

waan'wys, (-e), conceited, pedantic, opinionated, presumptuous; ~**heid**, presumption, self-conceit; presumptuousness.

waar[1], (s) (**ware**) = ware, commodity, ware; *goeie ware prys hulself*, good wine needs no push.

waar[2], (w) (ge-), (ong.), wander, haunt; *spoke ~ hier*, this place is haunted.

waar[3], (b) (**ware**), true, real, genuine; *vir ~ AANNEEM*, accept as correct; *dit BLY altyd ~*, this always holds good; *dit is HALF ~*, it is only partly true; *dit is HEELTEMAL ~*, that is quite true; *jy sal dit moet MAAK*, you will have to prove that; *niks is MINDER ~ nie*, nothing is further from the truth; *jy het dit gesien, NIE ~ nie?* you have seen it, haven't you? *NIKS van ~ nie*, not a word of truth (in it); *'n ware WELDAAD*, a veritable boon; (bw) really; *regtig ~*, really, truly.

waar[4], (bw) where; ~ *gaan jy heen?* where are you going?

waar[5], (vgw) where; *die skool ~ ek gematrikuleer het*, the school where I matriculated.

waaraan'[1], of which, about which, of whom; *die gebeurtenis ~ ek dink*, the event I am thinking of, of which I am thinking.

waar'aan[2], by what? to (of) which? how? ~ *DINK jy?* what are you thinking about? ~ *KEN jy hom?* how do you know him?

waarag'ter[1], behind which (whom); *die muur ~ hy wegkruip*, the wall behind which he is hiding; ~ *is jy nou*, what are you after now?

waar'agter[2], behind what (which)? ~ *skuil hy?* what is he hiding behind?

waarag'tig, (b) (-e), real, true, veritable, genuine; *die ~e waarheid*, the gospel truth; (bw) really, truly, veritably, actually; *ek weet dit ~ nie*, I am blessed if I know it; ~**heid**, trueness, veracity, genuineness.

waar'bo[1], above which? over what? beyond which? ~ *vlieg ons nou?* over which place are we flying now?

waarbo'[2], above which; *die boom ~ die toring uitsteek*, the tree above which the tower projects.

waar'borg, (s) (-e), guarantee, warrant, security; avouchment; caution; safeguard; *'n ~ eis*, demand a guarantee; (w) (ge-), warrant, avouch, certify; guarantee; ensure, safeguard; *dit kan ek jou ~*, I'll warrant you; ~**fonds**, guarantee fund, guaranty-fund; caution money; ~**kapitaal**, guarantee capital; ~**lys**, guarantee list; ~**maatskappy**, trust company; ~**som**, security, caution money; ~**stempel**, hallmark.

waarby'[1], by which, whereby; *'n middel ~ ek baat gevind het*, a remedy which gave me relief.

waar'by[2], whereby? near which? ~ *is hy betrokke?* in what matter is he involved?

waard, (-e), host, landlord, innkeeper; *BUITE die ~ reken*, reckon without one's host; *soos die ~ is, vertrou hy sy GASTE*, one is inclined to judge others by oneself; ill-doers are ill-deemers.

waarda'sie, (-s), assessment, valuation; ~**lys**, valuation roll.

waar'de, (s) (-s), worth, worthiness, caliber, merit, price, value; ~ *heg AAN*, attach value to; *BELASBARE ~*, ratable value; *die ~ BEPAAL van*, determine the value of; *die ~ van GELD ken*, know the value of money; *GEMIDDELDE ~*, mean (average) value; *INTRINSIEKE HÊ*, de ~; *INTRINSIEKE ~*, intrinsic value; *NOMINALE ~*, face value; *van NUL en gener ~*, quite worthless; of no value at all; ~ *ONTVANG*, value received; *TEENSWOORDIGE ~*, present value; *TER ~ van*, to the value of; (b) worthy; ~ *HEER*, dear sir; *my ~ VRIEND*, my worthy friend; ~**bepaling**, assessment, appraisement, valuation, ratal; ~**berekening**, calculation of value; ~**daling**, depreciation; ~**eenheid**, unit of value.

waardeer', (ge-), value, estimate, appraise; esteem, price, rate; prize, cherish, appreciate; ~**baar**, (..**bare**), valuable; appreciable, ratable; ~**der, (-s)**, appraiser, valuator, estimator, taxing-master.

waar'deleer, theory of values.

waar'deloos, (..**lose**), worthless, feckless, dud (cheque), valueless; ~**heid**, worthlessness, nullity.

waar'de: ~**meter**, standard of value; ~**oordeel**, value-judgment; ~**papier**, security; negotiable instrument (law).

waarde'rend, (-e), appreciative, appreciatory.

waarde'ring, (-e, -s), valuation, appraisal, ratal, estimate, estimation, esteem, regard, appreciation; recognition; *MET ~*, with appreciation; *UIT ~ vir*, in appreciation of.

waar'derings: ~**graad**, degree of appreciation; ~**hof**, valuation court; ~**koste**, cost of valuation, valuation charges; ~**lys**, valuation roll; ~**vermoë**, appreciative power, faculty of appreciation.

waar'de: ~**skatting**, valuation; appreciation;

~ **skommeling,** fluctuation in values; ~ **styging,** rise, appreciation (in value).
waardeur'[1], by which (means), whereby, on account of which; *die venster ~ die dief gekom het,* the window by which the thief entered.
waar'deur[2], by what? whereby? through what (which)? ~ *het dit so gebeur?* what caused it to happen in this way?
waar'de: ~ **verandering,** change in (of) value; ~ **verhoging,** appreciation, revalorization (of coins); ~ **verhouding,** ratio of values; parity; ~ **vermeerdering,** increase in value; *toevallige* ~ *vermeerdering,* unearned increment; ~ **verminderend, (-e),** depreciatory; ~ **vermindering,** depreciation, devaluation, decrease in value; ~ **verskil,** difference in value; ~ **vol, (-le; -ler, -ste),** valuable, of great value, worthwhile.
waar'dig, (-e), worthy; grand, dignified; ~ *e gedrag,* dignified behaviour; ~ **heid,** dignity; worthiness; *BENEDE sy* ~ *heid,* infra dig(nitatem), beneath his dignity; *MET* ~ *heid,* with dignity; ~ **heidsbekleër, (-s),** dignitary, high offical; ~ **lik,** worthily, with dignity, dignified.
waardin', (-ne), landlady, hostess; stewardess.
waardy', value, worth.
waarheen', where, whither; ~ *hy ook mag GAAN,* wherever he may go; *die PLEK* ~ *hy gaan,* the place where he is going.
waar'heen, whither? where? in which direction? to what place? ~ *gaan hy?* where is he going?
waar'heid, (..hede), truth, veracity, verity; reality; truism; *die* ~ *in die AANGESIG slaan,* violate the truth; disguise facts; *BESYDE die* ~, far from the truth; *die* ~ *BEWIMPEL (verbloem),* disguise the truth; *die* ~ *wil nie GESÊ wees nie, die* ~ *GEWELD aandoen,* violate the truth; *die HEILIGE* ~, the gospel truth; *die* ~ *IS,* as a matter of fact; the truth is; *'n* ~ *soos 'n KOEI,* a fact as plain as a pikestaff; a truism; *die* ~ *te KORT doen,* not to tell the whole truth; *agter die* ~ *KOM,* get to the bottom of; *NA* ~, truthfully; *die NAAKTE* ~, the unvarnished truth; *die RONDE* ~, the blunt truth; *iem. goed die* ~ *SÊ,* tell someone some home truths; *om die* ~ *te SÊ,* as a matter of fact; the truth is; *om die* ~ *te SÊ, moet ek lieg,* I really don't know; I couldn't say; *die* ~ *SPAAR,* be sparing of the truth; *in STRYD met die* ~, in conflict with the truth; *iem. goed die* ~ *VERTEL,* give someone a bit of one's mind; *iem. kaalvuis die* ~ *VERTEL,* tell someone the truth bald-headed; ~ **lie'wend, (-e),** truth-loving, truthful, veracious; ~ **lie'wendheid;** truthfulness, veracity; ~ **serum,** truth serum; ~ **gaping,** credibility gap; ~ **sin,** sense of truth.
waar'heids: ~ **kloof,** credibility gap; ~ **leër,** truth-legion; ~ **liefde,** veracity, love of truth.
waar'in[1], wherein, in what (which)? ~ *GLO jy?* what do you believe in? ~ *GOOI jy dit?* in what do you pour this?
waarin'[2], in which; *die huis* ~ *ek woon,* the house in which I live.
waarkrag'tens, on the strength (by virtue) of which; *die wet* ~ *ek handel,* the law by virtue of which I act.
waarlangs', along which; *die PAD* ~ *hy loop,* the road along which he is walking; *die VUUR* ~ *hy sit,* the fire next to which he is sitting.
waar'langs, along which? past which? ~ *gaan jy?* which way are you taking?
waar'lik, indeed, verily, truly, actually, real(ly); marry! upon my conscience! *dis* ~ *waar REG,* it is indeed correct; *hy kry SO* ~ *'n kolhou,* he actually gets a hole in one.
waar'maak, (-ge-), prove, make good; *dit sal jy moet* ~, you'll have to prove that.
waar'maker, (-s), a person whose word is his bond; *God is 'n* ~ *van Sy woord,* the Lord speaketh truth.
waar'making, proving, substantiation.
waar'mee[1], with what (which)? ~ *speel jy?* what are you playing with?
waarmee'[2], with (on) which; *die skip* ~ *ek gereis het,* the boat on which I travelled.
waar'merk, (s) (-e), stamp, hallmark (gold); (w) **(ge-),** stamp, hallmark (silver); authenticate, check, certify; aver, attest (document); *'n gewaarmerkte getuigskrif,* a certified testimonial; ~ **ing,** stamping; authentication.
waarna'[1], after which, whereafter, whereupon; at which; *die ding* ~ *ek verlang,* the thing I am longing for.
waar'na[2], where to? at what? ~ *kyk jy,* what are you looking at?
waar'naas[1], beside what? next to what? ~ *het jy geloop?* next to what did you walk?
waarnaas'[2], beside which; *die kerk* ~ *sy motor gestaan het,* the church beside which his motor-car stood.
waarnatoe'[1], to(wards) which; *die plaas* ~ *ek wou gaan,* the farm to which I wanted to go.
waar'natoe[2], where to? whither? to which? ~ *loop julle nou?* where are you going now?
waar'neem, (-ge-), perceive, discern, notice, eye, observe; perform; avail oneself of, make use of; act in temporary capacity; *die BELANGE* ~ *van,* look after the interests of; *hy neem vir DOKTER A.* ~, he is acting as locum tenens for Dr. A.; *'n GELEENTHEID* ~, avail oneself of an opportunity; *die HUISHOUDING* ~, keep house; *die KANS* ~, seize the opportunity; *sy PLIGTE* ~, perform one's duties; ~ **'baar, (..bare),** cognizable, appreciable; perceivable, palpable, perceptible; *uiterlik* ~ *baar,* very noticeable; ~ **'baarheid,** perceptibility.
waarne'mend, (-e), acting, temporary; percipient; ~ *e direkteur,* acting director.
waar'nemer, (-s), observer; substitute, locum tenens (of doctor); deputy.
waar'neming, (-e, -s), observation, percept, percipience, (ap)perception; locum-tenency; *uit eie* ~, from personal observations.
waar'nemings: ~ **ballon,** observation balloon; ~ **fout,** error in observation; ~ **hoek,** angle of sight; ~ **lugskip,** blimp; ~ **pos,** observation post; ~ **vermoë,** perceptive faculty, power of observation, perceptivity, sentience.
waarne'wens, (ong.), beside which.
waar'om[1], why? wherefore? *die ewige* ~ *s,* the eternal whys and wherefores.
waarom'[2], round which; *die pakkie* ~ *die tou was,* the parcel round which the string was tied.
waar'omheen[1], round what (which)? ~ *het jy die draad gedraai?* round what did you wind the wire?
waaromheen'[2], round which; *die huis* ~ *hy verdwyn het,* the house round which he disappeared.
waaromtrent'[1], about which; whereabout; *die saak* ~ *ek ondersoek instel,* the case about which I am making investigations.
waar'omtrent[2], about what? about which? ~ *wil jy my spreek?* what do you want to see me about?
waar'onder[1], among which (whom)? under which? beneath what? ~ *het jy nou verval?* among whom have you fallen (landed) now?
waaron'der[2], among whom, beneath which; *die rots* ~ *hy geskuil het,* the rock under which he took shelter.
waar'oor[1], about what? why? over which? ~ *huil jy?* why are you crying?
waaroor'[2], over which, across which; *die sloot* ~ *ons gespring het,* the furrow over which we jumped.
waar'op[1], upon which (what)? ~ *sit jy?* on what are you sitting?
waarop'[2], on which, whereupon, after which; *die vraag* ~ *hy geen antwoord gehad het nie,* the question to which he had no answer.
waar'sê, (-ge-), tell fortunes, foretell.
waar'sêer, (-s), fortune-teller, diviner, soothsayer; ~ **y,** fortune-telling, geomancy, augury, divination, gyromancy.
waar'segging, (-s), fortune-telling, prophecy.
waar'segster, (-s), fortune-teller, soothsayer.
waar'sku, (ge-), warn, caution, alarm, admonish; *iem.* ~ *TEEN gevaar,* warn somebody of danger; ~ *TEEN 'n stap,* warn against a measure; *WEES ge* ~, take care; ~ **wend, (-e),** warning, (ad)monitory, expostulative, expostulatory, dehortative;

precautionary; ~'n ~ wende TEKEN, a warning sign; ~ wende VERSKYNSELS, premonitory symptoms; ~ wer, (-s), warner, monitor, expostulator; call-boy (theatre).
waar'skuwing, (-e, -s), warning, caution, admonishment, dehortation, admonition, reminder; met 'n ~ daarvan afkom, be dismissed with a caution.
waar'skuwings: ~ bel, call-bell; ~ bord, caution signboard.
waar'skuwingsein, warning signal.
waar'skuwings: ~ teken, danger signal; ~ toestel, warning device; ~ woord, word of caution.
waarskyn'lik, (-e), probable, likely; prospective; nie EERS ~ nie, not very likely; HEEL ~, most likely; ~ heid, (..hede), probability, likelihood, odds, chance; na alle ~ heid, most likely, in all probability; ~ heidskromme, probability curve; ~ heidsleer, ~ heidsrekening, ~ heidsteorie, theory of probabilities, probabilism.
waar'so? where?
waar'sonder,[1] without which (what)? ~ kan jy nie vorder nie? what is it without which you cannot make headway?
waarson'der[2], without which; 'n boek ~ ek nie kan klaarkom nie, a book without which I cannot manage.
waar'teen,[1] against which (what)? ~ het jy GESKUUR? against what did you rub? ~ VEG ons? what are we fighting against?
waarteen'[2], against which: 'n boek ~ niks gesê kan word nie, a book against which nothing can be said.
waarteenoor'[1], opposite (against) which; ~ gesê moet word dat . . ., against which it must be said that . . .
waar'teenoor[2], opposite (to) what? ~ lê die kerkhof? opposite to what does the churchyard lie?
waar'toe[1], whereto? to what end? for what? ~ dien dit? what is the use of this?
waartoe'[2], to which; die PUNT ~ ons gekom het, the point to which we have come; 'n peil ~ hy hom nooit VERLAAG het nie, a level to which he never stooped.
waar'tussen[1], between (among) which (whom)? ~ lê die plaas? between which (mountains) is the farm situated?
waartus'sen[2], between (among) which (whom); die pale ~ die bal deurgetrek het, the goal posts through which the ball went.
waar'uit[1], out of which (what)? ~ haal jy aan? out of which (what) book are you quoting?
waaruit'[2], from (out of) which; die saal ~ hy gekom het, the hall out of which he came.
waar'van[1], of which? from which? whereof? ~ praat jy? what are you talking about?
waarvan'[2], whose, of which; die motor ~ die band pap is, the car of which the tyre is flat.
waar vandaan'[1], from which; ~ ons nou verder sal gaan, from which point we shall now proceed.
waar'vandaan[2], whence? from where? wherefrom? ~ af? from where? whence?
waar'volgens, according to what?
waarvol'gens, according to which, whereby; 'n wet ~ bepaal word dat . . ., a law by which it is laid down that . . .
waar'voor, wherefore? why? for which (what)? ~ is jy bang? of what are you afraid?
waarvoor', in front of which, before which; die spieël ~ jy staan, the mirror in front of which you are standing.
waas, (atmospheric) haze, mist; flush, bloom (on fruit, varnish); 'n ~ van GEHEIMSINNIGHEID, a veil (shroud) of mystery; 'n ~ van TREURIGHEID gooi oor, cast a gloom over.
wa'-as, waggon-axle, axle-tree.
waatlemoen', water-melon.
wa: ~ band, hoop of a waggon-wheel; ~ boom, waggon-tree (Protea grandiflora); ~ buik, flooring of a waggon, waggon-bed; ~ burg, laager, barricade of waggons; ~ disselboom, waggon pole; ~ drif, waggon drift; ~ drywer, waggon-driver, waggoner.
wa'e, (ge-) = waag.
wa'enhuis, waggon-house, coach-house, cart-shed;

~ deur, coach-house door; ~ spinnekop, house-spider.
wa'entjie, (-s), little waggon.
wa'fel, (-s), waffle, wafer, goffer; iem. met 'n groot ~, someone with a big trap; ~ pan, waffle-iron; ~ stof, waffle cloth; ~ yster, waffle-iron.
waf'fer = watter.
waf'fers, (-e), grand, wonderful; die KONSERT was nie te ~ nie, the concert was not up to much; 'n ~ e SPORTMAN, some sportsman.
wag, (s) (-te), watchman, sentry, guard; watch (on ship); die ~ AFLOS, relieve guard, relieve the watch; die ~ BETREK, mount guard; ~ HOU, keep guard, keep a sharp look-out; sit 'n ~ voor my MOND, set a watch before my mouth; die ~ OORNEEM, take over guard (the watch); (op) ~ STAAN, be on guard; stand watch; ~ te UITSIT, post sentries; (w) (ge-), wait, pause; ~ 'n BIETJIE, wait a bit (a moment); iem. LAAT ~, keep someone waiting; jy kan LANK ~, you may whistle for it; OP (vir) 'n antwoord ~, wait for an answer; STAAN en ~, stand and wait, be waiting; iets TE ~ te wees, expect something; 'n groot VERRASSING ~ op hom, he is in for a big surprise; ~ jou VIR sakkerollers, beware of pickpockets; nie WEET wat jou te ~ te staan nie, not know what is in store for one; not know what one is in for; ~ diens, guard-duty, watch (at sea).
wag'gel, (ge-), totter, stagger, reel; waddle (of geese); toddle (young child); joggle; die lugskroef ~, the airscrew is out of true; ~ aar, (-s), dodderer; ~ aartjie, (-s), toddler.
wag'geld, part-pay, retaining fee.
wag'gel: ~ end, (-e), out of true; unsteady, wobbly; ~ ende tafels, rickety tables; ~ gang, wobble, staggering gait; ~ ing, waddle, wobbling, tottering; ~ meter, truth-gauge (airscrew); ~ wiel, wobbly wheel.
wag: ~ glas, hour glass; ~ hebbend; ~ hebbende offisier, officer of the watch; ~ hond, watchdog; ~ hou (wag ge-), be on guard; keep watch, keep cave, guard.
wa'ghries, waggon-grease.
wag'huis, guardhouse; ~ ie, sentry-box.
wag: ~ kamer, waiting-room; guardhouse, guardroom, antechamber, anteroom (mayor); ~ lys, waiting-list; ~ lyster, sentinel rock-thrush; ~ meester, troop sergeant.
wag-'n-bietjie, (s) (-s), acacia thorn (Acacia caffra); ~ boom, acacia thorn, wait-a-while (wag-'n-bietjie)-tree, ~ -bos, wait-a-while-bush; ~ doring, Zizyphus mucronata.
wag: ~ offisier, guard officer; ~ parade, guard-parade; ~ personeel, duty staff; ~ -plek, waiting-place, place of waiting; ~ pos, picket, guard-post; ~ rol, watch-bill, list of crew divided into watches; ~ rooster, duty list; ~ skip, tender; receiving-ship; guard-ship, ~ stanery, standing guard, picketing; ~ suster, sister in charge; ~ ter, (-s), watchman, keeper; herd; satellite (of planet); ~ teres, (-se), female watcher; ~ tertjie, herdboy; ~ tery, waiting, ~ toring, barbican, watch-tower; conning-tower (ship); ~ tyd, watch; waiting-time; ~ vuur, camp-fire, watch-fire; ~ woord, watchword, password, parole, catchword; cue (play-production); countersign.
wak, (-ke), air-hole (in ice).
wa'kap, waggon-hood.
wa'kend, (-e), wakeful, watchful, vigilant, waking; 'n ~ e oog hou op (oor), keep a watchful eye on.
wa'ker, (-s), watcher; keeper.
wa'kis, waggon-box.
wak'ker, awake; alive, vigilant, smart, brisk, spry, alert, on the job; ~ BLY, remain awake (alert); stay up; spoon; HELDER (nugter) ~, wide awake; 'n ~ KÊREL, a wide-awake fellow; ~ KRY, awaken; ~ LÊ, lie awake; jy sal moet ~ LOOP, you'll have to be wide awake; ~ MAAK, awaken, wake up; ~ ROEP, rouse (with a call); ~ SKRIK, start out of (from) sleep, wake up; ~ SKUD, shake up, rouse; ~ WORD, awake, wake

up; ~heid, alacrity, liveliness, alertness, briskness, vigilance.
waks, (s) (-e), polish; blacking; (w) (ge-), polish, black (shoes), shine; ~spreier, wax distributor.
wal, (-le), bank; embankment, mound; beach, shore; quay; rampart; *op see en AAN* ~, at sea and ashore; *aan* ~ *GAAN*, land, go ashore; ~ *GOOI, dam up*; ~ *GOOI teen,* offer resistance; try to stem the tide; *aan HOËR* ~ *kom*, be doing well; *aan* ~ *KOM*, go ashore; *aan LAER* ~ *geraak*, be thrown on one's beam ends; be doing badly; *aan LAER* ~ *wees*, be on one's beam ends; ~ *le onder die OË*, bags under the eyes; *PRYS aan* ~, landed cost; *v.d.* ~ *in die SLOOT help*, assist from the frying-pan into the fire; *van* ~ *STEEK*, set off; get off the mark; (set) sail; embark upon.
wa'laer, laager of waggons.
Walden'se, Waldenses, Vaulois.
wald'horing, French horn.
wa'leer, rail.
Wa'leland, Wallonia.
walg, (s) disgust, loathing; *'n* ~ *van kafpraatjies hê*, be nauseated by tittle-tattle; (w) (ge-), loathe; disgust, make sick, nauseate; *tot* ~ *ens toe*, ad nauseam; ~end, (-e), loathsome.
wal'ging, loathing, distaste, disgust, aversion, nausea; *'n* ~ *van iets hê*, have a loathing of something; ~wekkend, (-e), nauseating.
walg'lik, (-e), disgusting, loathsome, distasteful, nauseous, gross, foul, sickening, nauseating, beastly, fulsome, odious, offensive, nasty; ~heid, loathsomeness, nastiness, fulsomeness, mawkishness, nauseousness, odiousness.
wal'gooier, ditcher.
Walhal'la, Valhalla.
wal: ~kant, quayside; ~kaptein, marine superintendent.
Walku're, (-s), Valkyrie.
Wallagy'e, Wallachia; ~r, (-s), Wallachian.
Wallagys', (-e), Wallachian.
Wal'lies, (s) Welsh (language); (b) (-e), Welsh.
Wal'lis, Wales; ~er, (-s), Welshman.
Wallo'nië, Wallonia.
walm, (s) (-s), dense smoke, gush, reek, vapour; fume; (w) (ge-), emit smoke, give off vapour, smoke.
wal'rif, barrier reef.
wal'rus, (-se), walrus, morse.
wals[1], (s) (-e), waltz; (w) (ge-), waltz, dance.
wals[2], (s) (-e), roll; flatting-roller; (w) (ge-), roll; *gewalste staal*, rolled steel; ~breker, gyratory breaker.
wal'ser[1], (-s), roller.
wal'ser[2], (-s), waltzer.
wals'meul(e), rolling-mill, roll.
wals'musiek, waltz music.
wals'werk(e), rolling-mill.
wa'luns, linch pin.
wal'vis, whale; ~ag'tig, (-e), whale-like, cetaceous, cetacean; W~ag'tiges, Cetacea.
Walvisbaai', Walfish Bay
wal'vis: ~baard, whale-fin; ~been, whalebone; ~boot, whale-boat; ~bul, bull whale; ~fabriek, whalery; ~haai, whale shark; ~jag, whaling, whale-hunting; ~jagter, whaler, whale-hunter; ~kalf, whale-calf; ~kanon, whale-gun; ~koei, cow whale; ~ruiter, horse-marine; ~skip, whaler, whaling-ship; ~spek, blubber, speck, junk, fenks; ~stasie, whaling-station; ~traan, whale-oil; ~vaarder, (-s), whaler; ~vaart, whale-fishing; whalery; ~vanger, (-s), whale-catcher; ~vangs, whale-fishery, whaling; ~vleis, whale-meat.
wa'maker, waggon-builder, cartwright, coachbuilder, wheelwright; ~y, coachbuilder's shop, cartwright's shop.
wan[1], (s) (-ne), winnowing-fan; (w) (ge-), winnow.
wan[2], (bw): *dan en* ~, now and then, off and on.
wan: ~aangepaste, (-s), (social) misfit; ~aanpassing, maladjustment, maladaptation; ~balans, imbalance; ~bedryf, offence, outrage, malfeasance; ~begrip, misconception, erroneous idea, false notion; ~beheer, mismanagement, maladministration, malconduct (of business); ~beleid, mis-

direction, mismanagement; ~bestee, (~), misapply; ~besteding, misapplication; ~bestuur, mismanagement, misgovernment, misrule, maladministration; ~betaler, (-s), defaulter.
wan'betaling, non-payment, default; *by* ~, in default of payment.
wand, (-e), wall.
wan'daad, misdeed, outrage, malpractice, misdoing.
wand: ~arm, wall-bracket; ~been, parietal bone; ~breuk, side-wall fracture (tyre).
wan'del, (s) walk; hike; conduct, behaviour, mode of life; (w) (ge-), walk; hike; take a walk; promenade; *'n entjie gaan* ~, go for a short walk; ~aar, (-s), walker, pedestrian, hiker; ~dek, promenade deck; ~duin, barkhan.
wan'delend, (-e), walking, ambulatory, wandering; *'n* ~*e ENSIKLOPEDIE*, a walking encyclopedia; *'n* ~*e GERAAMTE*, a walking skeleton; *die W*~*e JOOD*, the Wandering Jew; *'n* ~*e KOERANT*, a newsmonger; ~*e NIER*, floating kidney; ~*e TAK*, stick-insect.
wan'delgang, lobby; ~politikus, lobbyist.
wan'del: ~hoof, pier; ~ing, (-e, -s), walk, stroll; hike; ramble; *'n* ~*ing DOEN*, go for a stroll; *IN die* ~*ing genoem*, commonly called; commonly referred to; ~inkie, (-s), stroll, short walk; ~kostuum, walking-dress; ~laan, walk; pedestrian avenue; ~paadjie, ~pad, footway, walk, promenade; hiking-road; ~pak, lounge suit; ~pier, promenade pier; ~plek, mall, esplanade; ~sport, hiking; ~stok, cane; walking-stick; ~tog, hiking-tour; ~weg, pathway, walk.
wan'derlus, wanderlust.
wand: ~gesteente, wall-rock; ~kaart, wall-map; ~luis, bug; ~skildering, fresco, mural painting; ~stan'dig, (-e), parietal; ~tapyt, tapestry; gobelin; ~teks, mural text; ~versiering, mural decoration.
wang, (-e), cheek; jamb, chap; ~ *aan* ~, cheek by jowl; ~been, cheek-bone; ~bekleding, jamb lining.
Wanganel'la, Wanganella (breed of Merino sheep).
wan: ~gebruik, wrong use, abuse; ~gedrag, misconduct, misbehaviour, misdemeanour, malpractice; demerit; *jou aan* ~*gedrag SKULDIG maak*, be guilty of misconduct; *WEENS* ~ *gedrag*, because of misconduct; ~gedrog, monster; ~geloof, misbelief; superstition; ~geluid, jarring note, dissonance, cacophony.
wan: ~gerig, (-te), misaligned (mech.); ~gespoor, (-de), misaligned (wheels).
wang: ~etjie, (-s), small cheek; ~holte, buccal cavity; ~klier, cheek-gland, buccal gland; ~klip, jamb stone (of fireplace); ~kuiltjie, (-s), dimple in the cheek; ~plooi, jowl; ~prop, plumper; ~sak, cheek-pouch; ~sakmuis, pouched mouse; ~spier, buccinator; ~suil, jamb shaft.
wan'guns, envy; ~'tig, (b) (-e), envious; (bw) grudgingly.
wang'wol, cheek wool.
wan'hoop, (s) despair, desperation; *met die moed v.d.* ~, with the courage of despair; (w) (ge-), despond, despair; ~ *aan iem. se herstel,* despair of someone's recovery.
wan'hoops: ~daad, act of desperation; ~kreet, cry of despair; ~maatreël, desperate measure.
wanho'pend, (-e), despairing.
wanho'pig, (-e), desperate, despairing, forlorn; ~e, (-s), desperado; ~heid, desperation, despair, forlornness.
wan'hou, (-e), mishit.
wan'kante, wan(e)y edges (of timber).
wankan'tig, (-e), wan(e)y.
wan'kel, (w) (ge-), totter, waver, stagger; reel, vacillate; *'n partylid wat begin te* ~, a member of a party who begins to waver; (b) (-e), uncertain, tottering, unstable, wavering, rickety, wobbly; *die* ~*e GE LUK*, fickle fortune; ~*e GESONDHEID*, delicate health; indifferent health; ~*e SKREDES*, faltering steps; ~baar, (. . bare), wavering, unstable, tottering; ~baarheid, instability, unsteadiness; ~end, (-e), frail; tottering, unstable; wavering; ~heid, shakiness, instability; ~ing, tottering; vacillation.
wankelmoe'dig, (-e), faint-hearted; fickle; irresolute,

wankelrig vacillating; ~ **e**, (-s), waverer; ~ **heid**, fickleness; irresolution; instability; faint-heartedness.

wan'kelrig, (-e), unsteady, shaky.

wan'klank, dissonance, discord(ance), disharmony, false (discordant) note, cacophony; *'n ~ laat hoor*, strike a discordant note.

wanklink'end, (-e), **wanlui'dend**, (-e), dissonant, inharmonious, disharmonious, discordant, absonant, cacophonous; ~ **heid**, disharmony, dissonance.

wan'maat, off-size.

wan: ~ **mandjie**, winnowing-basket; ~ **masjien**, winnowing-machine; ~ **meul(e)**, winnowing-mill.

wan'neer, when, at what time; if; *al van ~ af staan en wag*, have been waiting a long time; (vgw) when, by which time; *kom ~ dit vir jou geleë is*, come when it suits you.

wan'ner, (-s), winnower.

wan'opvatting, misconception, mistaken idea.

wan'orde, disorder, confusion; dishevelment, disarray, disarrangement; flutter; anarchy; bedevilment; disorganization; *in ~ BRING*, throw into confusion; *haar HARE was in ~*, her hair was dishevelled; *IN ~*, in disorder; *~ STIG*, create disorder; *in ~ TERUGTREK*, retreat in disorder.

wanor'delik, (-e), disorderly; messy; irregular; deranged; ~ **heid**, rowdyism, disorderliness; ~ **hede**, riots.

wan'oriëntasie, disorientation.

wan: ~ **praktyk**, malpractice, corrupt practice; ~ **regering**, bad government; ~ **rigting**, misalignment.

wanor die REËN *sommer uit ~ uit*, it is coming down in buckets; *UIT ~ uit*, straight away, then and there; without further ado.

wanska'pe, deformed, miscreated, misformed, malformed, misshapen, monstrous.

wanska'penheid, malformation, deformity, abnormity.

wan'skottel, winnowing-dish (-basin).

wan'smaak, bad taste; taint; *~ 'lik*, (-e), in bad taste.

wan'sporing, misalignment (of wheels).

wanstal'tig, (-e), deformed, misshapen, formless; ~ **heid**, deformity, abnormity, misshapenness.

want¹, (s) rigging.

want², (s) (-e), mitt.

want³, (vgw) because, for, as; *ek gaan nie ~ dit reën*, I am not going because it is raining.

wan'toepassing, misapplication.

wan'toestand, bad condition, irregularity; *~ e heers op die mark*, irregularities occur on the market.

wan'trou, (ge-), distrust, mistrust, suspect; ~ **e**, distrust, mistrust(fulness), suspicion; *met ~ e AANSIEN*, view with suspicion; *diep ~ e KOESTER jeens*, harbour dark suspicions against; *'n MOSIE van ~ e*, a motion of no-confidence; *~ e SAAI*, sow distrust; *met ~ e VERVUL*, fill with mistrust; *~ 'end*, (-e), suspicious, distrustful.

wantrou'ig, (-e), suspicious, mistrustful, distrustful; ~ **heid**, suspiciousness, distrustfulness.

wants, (-e), bed-bug, house-bug.

wan'verdeling, maldistribution.

wan'verhoor, mistrial.

wan'verhouding, disparity, disproportion, discrepancy; incongruity; malconformation.

wan'vloer, winnowing-floor.

wan'voeding, malnutrition.

wanvoeg'lik, (-e), unsuitable; indecent, unseemly; ~ **heid**, indecency.

wan'voorstelling, gloss, misrepresentation.

wa'pad, (..paaie), waggon-road, cart-road, carriage-road; *hy is IN die ~*, he has taken to the road; he has no fixed abode; *so oud soos die KAAPSE ~*, as old as the hills; *in die ~ VAL*, get going; set off.

wa'pen, (s) (-s), weapon, gun, arm(s); bearing (her.); badge (of school); *na die ~ s GRYP*, take up arms; *onder die ~ KOM*, be called to arms; *die ~ s NEERLÊ*, lay down one's arms; *ONDER die ~ s*, under arms, armed; *die ~ s OPNEEM*, take up arms; *onder die ~ s ROEP*, call to arms; *te ~ SNEL*, rush to arms; (w) (ge-), arm; reinforce; *ge ~ de BETON*, reinforced concrete; *'n mens moet jou ~ teen jou VYANDE*, one should arm oneself against one's enemies; ~ **balk**, bar (her.); ~ **bediening**, gun-crew; ~ **beeld**, heraldic figure; ~ **beskrywing**, blazon; ~ **boek**, armorial; ~ **bord**, (e)scutcheon; hatchment; ~ **broer**, comrade-in-arms; companion-in-arms; fellow-soldier; ~ **dans**, wardance; ~ **dos**, full armour; ~ **draer**, (-s), armour-bearer; ~ **fabriek**, munition-factory; ~ **fabrikant**, arms manufacturer; ~ **feit**, feat of arms; martial exploit (achievement); ~ **figuur**, bearing (her.); ~ **gedruis**, clash of arms; force of arms; ~ **gekletter**, clash of arms, clang of arms; ~ **geluk**, good fortune in the field, victory; ~ **geweld**, force of arms; armed force; ~ **handel**, trade in munitions; blazonry; ~ **handelaar**, arms-dealer; ~ **huis**, (arsenal); ~ **industrie**, arms-industry; ~ **ing**, (-s), arming, equipping, armament; reinforcing, reinforcement (of concrete); ~ **kamer**, armoury; ~ **kneg**, armour-bearer, armourer; ~ **koepel**, gun-turret; ~ **koning**, king of arms; ~ **krans**, gun-ring; ~ **kreet**, battle-cry; ~ **kunde**, heraldry; armory; ~ **kun'dig**, (-e), heraldic; ~ **kun'dige**, (-s), heraldist; arms expert; ~ **loop**, chamber; ~ **magasyn**, arsenal, magazine; ~ **maker**, armourer; ~ **makker**, comrade-in-arms; ~ **monteur**, armament-fitter; ~ **oefening**, military exercise; ~ **riem**, shoulder-belt; ~ **roem**, military glory; ~ **rok**, military coat; ~ **rusting**, armour; hauberk; panoply; armature; ~ **s**, armaments; ~ **saal**, armoury, arsenal; ~ **skild**, (coat of) arms, armorial bearings, blazon, (e)scutcheon; coat-armour; ~ **skou**, (-e), ~ **skouing**, (-s), military review; Wapens(c)haw; ~ **skouingsdag**, field-day; ~ **smid**, armourer; ~ **spreuk**, heraldic device (motto); ~ **stilstand**, armistice, cease-fire, truce; ~ **stok**, truncheon; ~ **teken**, crest; ~ **tuig**, arms, weapons; ~ **veld**, field of an escutcheon; ~ **vervaardiging**, armament industry.

wapi'ti, (-'s), wapiti *(Cervus canadensis)*.

wap'per, (ge-), fly out, float, flutter, flaunt (one's colours), wave.

war, confusion, muddle; *ALLES is in die ~*, everything is in a muddle; *in die ~ BRING*, confuse; disarrange (hair); put out (person); *EK is in die ~*, I am completely confused; *in die ~ RAAK*, become confused; become muddled; *in die ~ STUUR*, throw into confusion; upset; *in die ~ WEES*, be in a muddle; ~ **boel**, confusion, chaos, clutter, imbroglio, litter, muddle, tangle, maze, puddle (fig.), mix-up, mess.

wa're¹, *as 't ~*, as it were.

wa're², wares, goods, commodities, merchandise, lines (commerce); ~ **huis**, warehouse, department store; ~ **kennis**, knowledge of goods.

wa: ~ **reling**, waggon rail; ~ **rem**, waggon-brake.

warem'pel, truly, surely, really.

war'hoof, scatter-brain, mophead; ~ **'dig**, (-e), scatter-brained, addle-pated, muddle-headed.

warin'gin, (-s), banyan.

war'kop, (-pe), scatter-brain, mophead, muddler; ~ **'pig** = **warhoofdig**; ~ **'pigheid**, muddle-headedness.

war'kruid, dodder.

warm, (b, bw), warm, hot, heated; fervent; generous (colour); ~ *AANBEVEEL*, recommend warmly (strongly); *dit sal daar het ~ GAAN*, they are in for a hot time; *so ~ dat die KRAAIE gaap*, stiflingly hot; ~ *KRUIEWYN*, mulled wine; *dit vir iem. ~ MAAK*, make things hot for someone; ~ *OMSLAG*, (hot) fomentation; *'n ~ (e) ONTVANGS*, a hot reception; a cordial welcome; *iem. na die ~ PLEK stuur*, send someone to blazes; *hy kom nie ~ by die WATER nie*, he is very slow, he is lazy; *hy WORD gou ~*, his anger is easily roused; he is quick-tempered.

warm'as, (-se), ~ **sie**, (-s), midge.

warm'bad, (~ **baaie**), hot (thermal) spring; ~ **inrigting**, thermal bath.

warm; ~ **beitel**, hot chisel; ~ **bespuiting**, hot spraying; ~ **bloe'dig**, (-e), warm-blooded; ~ **bros**, hot-short (steel); ~ **doek**, a children's hiding-game, hide-and-seek; ~ **dompeling**, hot dipping; ~ **droging**, hot-air process; ~ **erig**, (-e), slightly warm; ~ **fles**, vacuum flask; hot-water bottle.

warm'hakskeentjies, cooked onion salad.
warm'loop, (-ge-), run hot; overheat.
warm'lug: ~ **buis,** hot air duct; ~ **gang,** hot-air passage; ~ **inlaat,** hot-air intake; ~ **leiding,** hot-air duct.
warm'pan, warming-pan.
warm'patat = **warmdoek.**
warm'pies, cosily, warmly; *daar* ~ *in sit,* be comfortably off.
warm'te, heat, warmth; hot weather; fervency, ardour; ~ *AFGEE,* emit heat; *EIE* ~ , caloricity; *GEBONDE* ~ , latent heat; ~ **behandeling,** thermotherapy, heat treatment; ~ **behoud,** conservation of heat; ~ **bron,** source of heat; ~ **buis,** caloriduct; ~ **deurlaatvermoë,** diathermancy; ~ **deurlatend, (-e),** diathermic; ~ **-eenheid,** calorie, thermal unit, heat unit; ~ **-elektrisiteit,** thermo-electricity; ~ **gejeuk,** prickly heat; ~ **geleidend, (-e),** heat-conductive; ~ **geleiding,** thermal conduction; convection; ~ **geleier,** heat-conductor, conductor of heat; ~ **gewend, (-e),** calorific; ~ **golf,** heat-wave; ~ **graad,** degree of temperature, heat; ~ **leer,** theory of heat; ~ **leiding,** heater duct; ~ **makend, (-e),** calorific; ~ **meter,** thermometer; pyrheliometer, calorimeter; ~ **meting,** thermometry; ~ **reëling,** heat-regulation; ~ **stof,** caloric; ~ **straal,** heat-ray; ~ **straling,** heat radiation; ~ **stroming,** convection; ~ **toevoer,** heat-supply; ~ **-uitsetting,** heat expansion; ~ **-uitstraling,** radiation of heat; ~ **verbruik,** heat consumption; ~ **vermoë,** calorific power; ~ **verspreiding,** distribution of heat; ~ **verwekkend, (-e),** thermogenetic; ~ **verwekking,** ~ **voortbrenging,** thermogenesis; ~ **waarde,** calorific value; ~ **wol,** thermal wool.
warm'water: ~ **aanleg,** hot-water installation; ~ **bad,** hot bath, bain-marie; ~ **baaie,** thermal baths; ~ **bord,** water-plate; ~ **fles,** hot-water bottle; ~ **kors,** hot-water crust; ~ **kraan,** hot-water tap; ~ **kruik,** hot-water bottle; ~ **sak,** hot-water bag; ~ **-tert(deeg),** hot-water pastry; ~ **toestel,** waterheater; ~ **verband,** fomentation; ~ **voorsiening,** hot-water supply.
war'net, maze, labyrinth.
war'rel, (ge-), whirl, swirl, reel; ~ **ing,** eddy, whirl, swirl; ~ **stroom,** slip-stream; ~ **wind,** whirlwind.
wars, loath; ~ *van,* averse to; ~ **heid,** averseness.
War'schau, War'skou, Warsaw.
war'taal, gibberish, jargon, abracadabra, balderdash.
wart'lemoen = **waterlemoen.**
was¹, (s) wax.
was², (s) rise (of river); growth; (w) **(ge-),** grow (person); rise (water); wax (moon).
was³, (s) laundry, wash(ing); *my HEMP is in die* ~ , my shirt is in the wash (at the laundry); *sy SOKKIES het in die* ~ *weggeraak,* his socks got lost in the wash; (w) **(ge-),** wash; clean, scour (wol); shuffle (cards); swab (wound); van (mining); *hy GAAN hom* ~ , he is going to have a wash.
was⁴, (w) *verl. tyd van wees; hy is weer wat hy* ~ , he is himself again.
was: ~ **afdruk,** impression in wax; ~ **agtig, (-e),** waxy (potato).
was: ~ **baar, (bare),** washable; ~ **baarheid,** washableness; ~ **bak,** wash-basin, lavabo, laver, sink; trough, dolly; ~ **balie,** wash-tub.
was'beeld, wax figure; ~ **espel,** waxworks show.
was'beer, raccoon *(Procyoninus),* wash(ing)-bear.
was'beker, ewer, toilet-jug.
was: ~ **bessie,** wax-berry *(Myrica cordifolia);* ~ **blom,** wax-flower; ~ **boetseerder,** wax-modeller; ~ **boetseerkuns,** wax-modelling; ~ **boom,** waxmyrtle.
was'dag, wash(ing)-day.
was'doek¹, wash-cloth.
was'doek², waxcloth, cerecloth.
was'dom, growth.
was'draad¹, waxed thread.
was'draad², clothes-line.
was'eg, (-te), fast-dyed, washable; ~ **theid,** colourfastness.
wa'sem, (s) **(-s),** vapour, steam; breath, reek, exhalation, halitus; (w) **(ge-),** steam, reek, give off vapour; ~ **vry, (-e),** non-fogging.
was-en-stryk'werk, laundry-work.
wa'serig, (-e), gauzy.
was'figuur, wax figure.
was: ~ **fles,** wash-bottle; ~ **geld,** laundry charges; ~ **geleentheid,** lavatory, washing-place; ~ **goed,** washing, laundry; ~ **goedknyper,** clothes-peg; ~ **goedlyn,** clothes-line; ~ **goedmandjie,** soiled-linen basket, clothes-basket; ~ **goedpennetjie,** clothespeg; ~ **goedstander,** clothes-horse, clothes-rack; ~ **hok,** laundry; ~ **huis,** wash-house, laundry.
wa'sig, (-e), hazy, foggy, filmy, dim, bleary, blurred; ~ **heid,** haziness, fogginess, mistiness.
was: ~ **inrigting,** laundry; ~ **kamer,** lavatory; ~ **kan,** ewer.
was: ~ **kers,** wax candle, taper; ~ **kleur,** waxen colour; ~ **kliertjie,** wax-pocket.
was: ~ **klip,** washing stone; ~ **kom,** wash-basin, lavabo, laver.
was'kryt, wax crayon.
was: ~ **kuip,** washing tub; ~ **kunde,** laundrywork (as subject).
was'laag, wax coating, waxy layer; bloom (on fruit); *met 'n* ~ *bedek,* glaucous (bot.).
was: ~ **lap,** wash-cloth; ~ **lyn,** clothes-line, ~ **lys,** laundry-list; ~ **mandjie,** soiled-linen basket; laundry-basket; ~ **masjien,** washing-machine.
wa'smeer, axle-grease.
was: ~ **merk,** laundry mark; ~ **middel,** washing agent, detergent.
was: ~ **model,** model in wax; ~ **modellering,** ceroplastics; ~ **mot,** bee moth *(Gallena mellonella);* ~ **museum,** wax museum; ~ **neus,** wax nose; a mere formality (pretext); *dis maar 'n* ~ *neus,* it is purely a facade (mask); ~ **palm,** wax-palm; ~ **papier,** wax-paper; ~ **pitjie,** night-light, wax-light, taper.
was'plank, wash-board.
was'pleister, wax-plaster, cerate.
was'poeier, washing-powder.
was'politoer, wax polish.
wa'spoor, (. .spore), wag(g)on-rut (-track).
was'pop, wax doll.
was'send, (-e), waxing, growing, crescent (moon); rising; *die* ~ *e maan,* the waxing moon.
was: ~ **ser, (-s),** washer, laundry-hand; ~ **sery, (-e),** washing, laundry; ~ **sing,** (act of) washing.
was: ~ **skildering,** ~ **skrif,** cerography.
was: ~ **soda,** washing soda, carbonate of soda; ~ **spaan,** dolly; ~ **stamper,** dolly; ~ **stel,** toilet-set; ~ **stok,** battledore.
was'tafel¹, wash-stand.
was'tafel², wax tablet.
was'ter, (-s), washer (ring).
was: ~ **trog,** washing-trough; ~ **vas, (-te),** fast to wash; ~ **vastheid,** washing resistance (fastness); ~ **vat,** trommel (mining); buddle.
was'vel, wax sheet, stencil.
was: ~ **verlies,** sinkage (wool); ~ **vertrek,** lavatory.
was: ~ **vlies,** cere; ~ **vorm,** wax mould.
was'vrou, (-e, -ens), washerwoman, laundress.
was'vuurhoutjie, fusee.
was'water, water for washing.
was'werk¹, laundry-work.
was'werk², waxwork.
wat, (vr. vnw) what? ~ *wil jy HÊ?* what do you want?; ~ *NOU?,* what shall we do now?; ~ *TRAAK dit my?,* what do I care?; ~ *WOU!,* no fear! (betr. vnw) who, that, which, what; *AL* ~ *ek besit,* all that I possess; *die HUIS* ~ *verkoop word,* the house which is for sale; *die MAN* ~ *hier was,* the man who was here; *die VROU* ~ *gepraat het,* the woman who spoke; (onbep. vnw.) whatever, something; *ALLES en nog* ~ , all sorts of things; *BLY kalm,* ~ *ook al gebeur,* keep calm, whatever may happen; *'n STUK of* ~ , a few; *dis nie* ~ *WONDERS nie,* it is nothing much; (tw) ~ *! het hy DIT gesê?,* what! did he actually say that?; *NEE* ~ , *ek glo dit nie,* no, I don't believe it.
wa'teer, axle-grease.
wa'tent, waggon-tent (-hood); ~ **dak,** tilt roof.

wa'ter, (s) water; dropsy; urine; ~ *AFSLAAN*, urinate; *BO* ~ *wees*, be in easy street; have nothing to worry about; *hy BRAND hom aan kou* ~, he is overcautious; *in DIEP* ~ *raak*, get into deep water (trouble); *soos* ~ *op 'n EEND se rug*, like water off a duck's back; *'n vabond v.d. EERSTE* ~, a rogue of the first water; *GODS* ~ *oor Gods akker laat loop*, let things slide; ~ *HÊ*, suffer from dropsy; *hy KOM nie warm by die* ~ *nie*, he never overworks himself; *KOUE* ~ *op iem. se planne gooi*, throw cold water on someone's plans; *te* ~ *LAAT*, launch; *wanneer die* ~ *tot aan die LIPPE kom*, when one is reduced to the last extremity; *aan* ~ *LY*, suffer from dropsy; ~ *in 'n MANDJIE dra*, carry water in a sieve; ~ *op sy MEUL*, grist to his mill; *koue* ~ *op iem. OMKEER*, give someone a cold douche; *koue* ~ *op iem. se PLANNE gooi*, pour cold water on someone's plans; ~ *loop altyd SEE toe*, money begets money; *die* ~ *v.d. SEE kan hom nie skoon was nie*, the sea can't cleanse him; *daar sal nog baie* ~ *in die SEE loop*, lots of water will flow under the bridge; ~ *in die SEE dra*, carry coals to Newcastle; *onder* ~ *SIT*, flood, inundate; *'n SKELM v.d. eerste* ~, a rogue of the first water; *onder* ~ *STAAN*, be under water; *op STERK* ~ *sit*, lay up in lavender; *STILLE* ~*s, diepe grond*, still waters run deep; *'n diamant v.d. SUIWERSTE* ~, a diamond of the first water; ~ *TRAP*, tread water; *in die* ~ *VAL*, fall through; *in troebel* ~ *VISVANG*, fish in troubled waters; *soos* ~ *en VUUR wees*, like fire and tow; be sworn enemies; *in WARM* ~ *wees*, be in hot water; *in WARM* ~ *kom*, get into hot water; *moenie vuil* ~ *WEGGOOI voor jy skone het nie*, cast not out the foul water before you bring in the clean; ~ *in jou WYN gooi*, be less demanding; climb down a peg or two; (w) (ge-), water; make water, urinate; *sy oë* ~, there are tears in his eyes; his eyes are watering; ~ **aanvoer,** water-supply; ~ **aanwyser,** dowser, water-diviner; ~ **aanwysing,** rhabdomancy; ~ **aar,** subterranean watercourse; vein of water; ~ **afskeiding,** emiction, urination; ~ **afvoer,** draining (of water); ~ **agtig, (-e),** watery, aqueous, insipid; ~ **agtigheid,** aqueousness, aquasity; insipidity; ~ **anker,** drogue; ~ **arm,** dry, arid, with little water; ~ **bak,** cistern; water-trough; ~ **balie,** water-tub, cowl; ~ **ballas,** water-ballast; ~ **behandeling,** water-treatment, water-cure, hydropathy; ~ **beits,** water stain; ~ **beker,** ewer; ~ **bel,** water-bubble; ~ **belasting,** water-rate; ~ **beskrywing,** hydrography; ~ **besem,** squeegee; ~ **bessie,** water-berry (*Syzygium cordatum*); ~ **bestand,** water-resisting (paint); ~ **bestuif, (-de),** aquatic, hydrophile; ~ **bewaring,** water conservation; ~ **bewoner,** aquatic animal; ~ **biesie,** spike-rush; ~ **blaas,** (water-)blister; water-bubble; urinary bladder; ~ **blasie, (-s),** hydatid; ~ **blommetjie,** water-lily (*Castalia odorata*); ~ **bobbejaan,** dog-otter; ~ **bok,** waterbuck (*Kobus ellipsiprymnus*); ~ **bokooi,** waterbuck cow; ~ **bokram,** waterbuck bull; ~ **boom,** whitewood-tree; milkwood (*Ilex mitis*); ~ **boor,** waterdrill; ~ **bord,** watering-board; ~ **bottel,** water-bottle; ~ **boukunde,** hydraulic engineering, hydraulics; ~ **boukun'dig, (-e),** hydraulic; ~ **boukun'dige, (-s),** hydraulic engineer; ~ **boukuns,** hydrotechnics; ~ **breuk,** hydrocele; ~ **bron,** spring; ~ **buffel,** water-buffalo; ~ **damp,** water vapour; ~ **dier,** aquatic animal; ~ **dig, (-te),** impermeable, waterproof (clothes); watertight (boots); ~ **digtheid,** watertightness; impermeability, imperviousness (to water); ~ **digting,** waterproofing; ~ **dokter,** hydropathist; ~ **dorp,** marina.

Wa'terdraer¹, Aquarius, the Waterman.
wa'terdraer², drone; water-carrier; aquifer; ~*s en houtkappers*, hewers of wood and drawers of water; ~ **by,** bumble-bee, drone.
water: ~ **drag,** draught (of ship); ~ **druk,** water-pressure; ~ **druppel,** drop of water; ~ **eier,** poached egg; ~ **emmer,** water-bucket, water-pail; ~ **erf,** water erf; ~ **ewewigsleer,** hydrostatics; ~ **fiskaal,** water-bailiff; ~ **fles,** carafe, water-bottle; ~ **fontein,** water fountain; ~ **gas,** water-gas; ~ **gat,** pool (in river); ~ **gebrek,** water-famine; water content; ~ **gees,** water-sprite, nix(ie), kelpie; ~ **gehalte,** water content; ~ **geleiding,** water-conducting; ~ **gemak,** water-closet, w.c.; ~ **geneesinrigting,** hydropathic establishment; ~ **geneeskunde,** hydropathy, hydrotherapy; ~ **geneeskun'dig, (-e),** hydropathic; ~ **gesig,** waterscape; ~ **geswel,** oedema.

Wa'tergeus, (hist.), Sea-Beggar (80 Years' War).
wa'ter: ~ **geut,** gutter; ~ **glas,** tumbler, drinking-glass; water-glass; ~ **god,** water-god; ~ **godin,** naiad; ~ **graf,** Davy Jones's locker; watery grave; ~ **gras,** water-grass, watercress, sedge; ~ **grip,** water-furrow, gutter; ~ **harding,** water-hardening; ~ **harpuis,** resin-bush; ~ **hart,** disease of apples; ~ **hoender,** moorhen; ~ **hof,** water-court; ~ **holte,** water-pocket; ~ **hondjie, (-s),** whirligig (beetle) (*Syrnus natans*); ~ **hoof, (-de),** hydrocephalus; ~ **hoofdig, (-e),** hydrocephalous; ~ **hoogte,** water-line, high-water mark; ~ **hoos,** water spout; ~ **houdend, (-e),** aqueous, hydrous; ~ **hout** = **waterboom;** ~ **houvermoë,** water-retaining capacity; ~ **ig, (-e),** watery, hydrous; washy (food); rheumy (eyes); ~ **igheid,** wateriness; rheum; washiness.
wa'ter: ~ **inhoud,** water capacity; ~ **inlaatpyp,** water (-inlet) pipe; ~ **kalk,** water-lime, hydraulic lime; ~ **kan,** jug, ewer; ~ **kannetjie,** canteen; ~ **kant,** waterside; waterfront; ~ **kar,** water-cart; ~ **kartel,** water-wave (hair); ~ **keerplank,** weather-board; ~ **kering,** barrage, dam, weir; groyne.
wa'terkers¹, (-e), home-made candle, dip.
wa'terkers², watercress.
wa'ter: ~ **kerwel,** cow-bane; ~ **ketel,** boiler; kettle; ~ **klawer,** buck-bean; ~ **klep,** water-valve; ~ **kleur,** colour of water; ~ **klip,** aquifer; ~ **klipblom,** water crassula; ~ **klok,** water-clock, clepsydra; ~ **koedoe,** sitatunga (*Tragelaphus spekei*); ~ **koeling,** water-cooling; ~ **kolom,** column of water; ~ **kom,** water-basin; ~ **kraan,** water-tap; water-cock; water-crane; ~ **kraf(fie),** (water-)decanter, water-bottle, carafe; ~ **krag,** water-power; ~ **kragmynbou,** hydraulic mining.
wa'ter: ~ **kriek,** mole-cricket; ~ **kruik,** pitcher, monkey; ~ **kuil,** pool (of water); water-hazard (golf); ~ **kuip,** water-tub; ~ **kultuur,** soilless culture, hydroponics; ~ **kunde,** hydrology; ~ **kun'dig, (-e),** hydrologic; ~ **kuur,** water-cure, hydropathy; ~ **kwekery,** tank-farming; ~ **kweking,** hydroponics; ~ **laag,** water-bed.
wa'terlander, (-s), tear; *toe kom die* ~ *s*, then the waterworks were turned on.
wa'ter: ~ **leer,** hydrology; ~ **lei, (-ge-),** irrigate; ~ **leibeurt,** regular irrigation rights; ~ **leiding, (s),** water-installation, water-main, aquaduct, conduit; water system; ~ **lelie,** water-lily, hyacinth; ~ **leliedam,** water-lily pond, hyacinth pond; ~ **lemoen,** water-melon; ~ **liewend, (-e),** hydrophile; aquatic (animal); ~ **linie,** waterline; ~ **long,** water lung (zool.); ~ **loop,** watercourse, flume; ~ **loopkunde,** hydrodynamics, hydraulics; ~ **loos, (..lose),** anhydrous, waterless; ~ **loot,** sucker, water-shoot; ~ **losing,** drainage; urinating, passing water; ~ **lyn,** water-line; ~ **lynpapier,** laid paper, water-lined paper; ~ **lys,** window-drip.

Wa'terman¹, Aquarius.
wa'terman², waterman.
wa'ter: ~ **mantel,** water-jacket; ~ **massa,** mass of water; ~ **matras,** water-bed; ~ **meid,** water-witch; ~ **meetkunde,** hydrometry; ~ **meetkun'dig, (-e),** hydrometric; ~ **merk,** watermark; ~ **meter,** water-meter; hydrometer; ~ **meul(e),** water-mill; ~ **mol,** water-mole; ~ **molekule,** water-molecule; ~ **mot,** caddisfly; ~ **nat,** dripping wet, soaked, wet all over; ~ **nawel,** pennywort; ~ **nimf,** water-nymph, naiad, undine; ~ **nood,** water-famine; scarcity of water; ~ **nooi(en)tjie,** mermaid; ~ **omhulsel,** hydrosphere; ~ **onttrekking,** dehydration; ~ **oog,** watery eye; ~ **opaal,** moonstone; ~ **oplossing,** aqueous solution; ~ **opname,** water survey; ~ **oppervlak,** surface of water; ~ **oppervlakte,** area of water; ~ **opsplitsing,** hydrolysis; ~ **opsuiend, (-e),** hydrophile; ~ **palm,** macaw palm.
wa'terpas, (s) (-se), (spirit) level, waterlevel, plumb-rule; (b) level, horizontal; ~ *MAAK*, level, true up;

iem. ~ *in die OË kyk*, look someone straight in the eye; ~**sing**, levelling; ~**instrument**, levelling-instrument.
wa'ter: ~**peil**, water-gauge; watermark; water-level; ~**peilglas**, water-gauge; ~**pers**, hydraulic press; ~**pes**, *Elodea canadensis;* ~**plaas**, watered farm; ~**plant**, aquatic (plant), hydrophyte, water-plant; ~**plas**, pool, puddle; ~**plek**, urinal; ~**ploeër**, skimmer (bird); ~**poel**, pool of water; ~**pokkies**, chicken-pox; varicella; ~**polo**, water polo; ~**pomp**, water-pump; ~**poort**, water-gate; ~**proef**, ordeal by water; ~**put**, draw-well; ~**putter**, drawer of water; ~**pyp**, water-pipe; culvert (underground); ~**raad**, water-board; ~**ram**, hydraulic ram; ~**rat**, water-wheel; ~**reg**, water-right; ~**regter**, water-judge; ~**rookpyp**, hookah, water-pipe; ~**rot**, water-rat; ~**ruimte**, water-space; ~**ryk, (-e)**, abounding in water; ~**saak**, water-case (-suit); ~**sak**, water-bag; ~**salamander**, newt; ~**sement**, hydraulic cement; ~**skaarste**, water-famine, scarcity of water; ~**skade**, damage caused by water; ~**skeiding**, watershed, divide; ~**ski**, water ski; ~**skiër**, water skier; ~**skilpad**, turtle, water-tortoise, terrapin; ~**skisport**, water-skiing; ~**sku, (-we)**, hydrophobic, afraid of water; ~**skuheid**, hydrophobia; ~**slag**, water-hammer; ~**slagplank**, weather-board; ~**slang**, hydra, water-snake; hose; ~**sloot**, water furrow; ~**sluis**, water gate; ~**snip**, snipe; judcock.
wa'tersnood, floods, inundation.
water: ~**soeker**, water-diviner, dowser; ~**sopnat**, dripping wet; ~**spieël**, sea-level, water-level; ~**sport**, aquatic sports, aquatics; ~**sproeiing**, water-blast; ~**spuit**, water-spout, gargoyle; ~**stand**, height of the water, water-level; ~**stewel**, knee-boot, wader, wellington; ~**stof**, hydrogen; ~**stofatoom**, atom of hydrogen; ~**stofbom**, hydrogen bomb, H-bomb; ~**stofperokside**, ..**sied**, hydrogen peroxide; ~**stok(kie)**, dowsing-rod, divining-rod; ~**straal**, jet (spurt) of water; water spout; ~**stroom**, current, stream; ~**sug**, anasarca, oedema, dropsy; ~**sug'tig, (-e)**, hydropic, oedematose, dropsical; ~**suil**, column of water; ~**tand, (ge-)**, (make the mouth) water; *dis om van te ~ tand*, that's enough to make my mouth water; ~**tenk**, water-tank; ~**toevoer**, water-supply; ~**tog**, boating excursion; ~**toring**, water-tower; ~**trap, (-ge-)**, tread water, swim upright; ~**trapper**, Peter's finfoot (bird); ~**trek, (-ge-)**, deliquesce; ~**tuit**, water spout; ~**uintjie**, nutgrass, water hawthorn; pondweed *(Aponogeton distachyus);* ~**uitlaat**, water escape; ~**uurwerk**, water-clock, clepsydra; ~**vaatjie**, water-cask; ~**val**, waterfall, cataract, chute, cascade; *die Victoria~val*, the Victoria Falls; ~**vat**, water-cask; ~**verband**, water-dressing; ~**verbruik**, consumption of water.
wa'terverf, water-colour; ~**laag**, wash; ~**skildery**, aquarelle, water-colour painting; ~**tekening**, water-colour drawing.
wa'ter: ~**verkeer**, water traffic; ~**verkwisting**, waste of water; ~**verontreiniging**, water pollution; ~**verplasing**, water displacement; ~**versagter**, water softener; ~**verversing**, refreshing of water; ~**verwarmer**, geyser (for heating water); ~**verwydering**, hydroextraction; ~**vlak**, water-surface; sheet of water; ~**vliegtuig**, water-plane, sea-plane; ~**vloed**, flood, deluge, inundation; ~**vlooi**, water-insect *(Daphnea);* ~**voël**, aquatic bird, water-fowl; ~**vog**, aqueous humour; ~**voor**, water-furrow; mill-race; flume; ~**voorraad**, supply of water; ~**voorsiening**, water-supply; ~**vrees**, hydrophobia; rabies (in dogs); ~**vry, (-e)**, free from water, anhydrous; ~**wa**, water-waggon; ~**waarde**, water equivalent; ~**weg**, water-way; ~**werke**, water-works; ~**werktuigkunde**, hyraulics, hydrodynamics; ~**wese**, water affairs; *Minister van W~wese*, Minister of Water Affairs; ~**wiel**, water-wheel; ~**wilg(erboom)**, osier; ~**wolk**, water cloud; ~**wyser, (-s)**, dowser, water-diviner.
wat'jie, (-s), wad of cotton wool.
wa'tros, waggon-train.
watt, (-s), watt.

wat'te, wadding, cotton wool; ~**agtig, (-e)**, like cotton wool; floccose.
watteer', (ge-), wad; quilt, pad; ~**sel**, wadding, padding.
wat'tel: ~**bas**, wattle-bark; ~**boom**, wattle(-tree).
wat'teprop, plug of wadding.
wat'ter, which, what; ~ *EEN?*, which (one)?; ~ *ONSIN!*, what nonsense!; ~ *ROK moet ek aantrek?*, which dress must I wear?; *hy WEET van ~ (waffer)*, he knows what's what.
wat'testof, wadding; wadded cloth.
watt: ~**meter**, wattmeter; ~**verbruik**, wattage.
watwon'ders, (-e), jolly good, startling; *nie 'n ~e boek nie*, not a wonderful book.
wa: ~**vrag**, waggon-load; ~**wiel**, waggon-wheel; ~**wielhoed**, cart-wheel hat; ~**wielore**, ears like cart-wheels.
wa'wyd, very wide; wide open; ~ *oop*, ~ *ope*, open as wide(ly) as possible.
wê, so there!
web, (-be), web.
wed, (ge-), wager, gage, bet, punt, stake money on; *ek ~ JOU*, I bet you; *op 'n PERD ~*, back a horse; *WAT ~ jy*, what's the bet?; ~**denskap, (-pe)**, wager, bet; *'n ~denskap aangaan*, lay a wager; ~**denskapbelasting**, betting-tax; ~**der, (-s)**, better (bettor), punter, bookie; ~**dery**, betting, wagering, punting.
we'derdiens, return service; *iem. 'n ~ bewys*, return a service.
we'derdoop, anabaptism; rebaptism.
We'derdoper, (-s), (Ana)baptist; dipper; ~**s, (-e)**, (Ana)baptist; ~**y**, Anabaptism.
we'dereis, counter-claim.
we'dergeboorte, regeneration, conversion, new birth, rebirth, palingenesis, regenesis.
we'dergebore, born again, reborn, regenerate; ~**ne, (-s)**, convert, one reborn.
we'dergif, return present.
we'derhelf, (-te(s)), better half, other half, half-section, helpmate, helpmeet, spouse.
wederke'rend, (-e), reflexive; recurrent, periodic; ~*e voornaamwoord*, reflexive pronoun.
wederke'rig, (-e), mutual, reciprocal; ~**heid**, reciprocity, reciprocalness, mutuality.
we'derkoms, return; second coming (of Christ), Advent.
we'derliefde, mutual love, love in return.
we'derom, again, anew; *(tot) ~*, so long! see you again!
we'(d)eropbou(ing), re-erection, rebuilding.
we'(d)eroprigting, re-establishment, restoration, reconstruction.
we'(d)eropsegging: *tot ~*, until further notice.
we'(d)eropstanding, resurrection.
we'derparty, opponent, antagonist, adversary.
wederreg'telik, (-e), illegal, unlawful, wrongful; extrajudicial; ~**heid**, illegality.
we(d)erstre'wig, (-e), refractory, obstinate; ~**heid**, refractoriness.
we'(d)ersyds, (-e), mutual, reciprocal; ~*e GOEDVINDE*, by mutual consent; ~*e KENNISGEWING*, notice given on either side; ~*e LIEFDE*, mutual affection.
wedervaar', (~), befall, meet with, betide, happen to; occur; *reg laat ~*, allow justice to prevail.
wederva're, (-ns), wederva'ring, (-e, -s), occurrence, incident; adventure, experience.
we'dervergeld, (~), retaliate; ~**ing**, retribution, recompense, retaliation.
we'derverskyning, reappearance, emersion.
we'(d)ervraag, counter-question.
wederwaar'digheid, (..hede), adversity, vicissitude, tribulation; adventure; *die ..hede v.d. lewe*, the vicissitudes (ups and downs) of life.
we'(d)erwoord, counter-word, reply.
wed'kantoor, betting-shop.
wed'loop, (..lope), (foot-)race; *ek het die ~ voleindig*, I have finished my course; ..**loper, (-s)**, runner, racer.
wed'ren, (-ne), race; ~ *met hindernisse*, obstacle-race;

~**klub**, turf club, racing club, jockey club; ~**program**, race-card, book (turf).

wed'stryd, (-e), match, fixture, game, event, competition, contest, bout, tournament; *'n ~ uitskryf*, arrange a competition; ~**bepalings**, match regulations; fixtures; ~**datum**, fixture; ~**reeks**, fixtures (of matches); ~**vliegtuig**, racing aeroplane.

wed'syfer, (betting) odds.

we'duskap = **weduweeskap**.

we'duvrou, (-e, -ens), widow.

we'duwee, (-s), widow, relict; dowager; *'n onbestorwe ~*, an unofficial widow; ~**fonds**, widow's fund; ~**geld**, (widow's) dower; ~**goed**, jointure; ~**moeder**, widowed mother; ~**pensioen**, widow's bounty (pension); ~**rou**, widow's weeds; ~**skap**, widowhood; ~**verbranding**, suttee, widow-burning.

wed: ~**vaart**, sailing competition; ~**vlug**, air-race.

wed'ywer, (s) competition, rivalry, contention, emulation; (w) **(ge-)**, compete, vie, contend, cope with; bandy, compare; emulate; ~ *met*, compete, vie with; ~**end, (-e)**, emulative, emulous.

wee¹, (s) (weë), woe, throe, grief, pain; labour (at birth).

wee², weë, (w) (ge-), = **weeg**.

wee³, (b) (weë), (w.g.), faint, queer, mawkish; *'n weë ruik*, a mawkish smell.

wee¹, (tw) woe! ~ *jou GEBEENTE as . . .*, heaven help if you . . .; ~ *jou, o LAND, as jou koning 'n kind is*, woe to thee, O land, when thy king is a child; ~ *MY!*, woe is me!

wee blaar, waybread, ribwort, lamb's-tongue *(Plantago)*.

wee'dom, woe, grief, sorrow, sadness.

weef, (ge-), weave; ~**behangsel**, tapestry; ~**binding**, weave structure; ~**fabriek**, power-mill; ~**getou**, weaving-loom; ~**kuns**, textile art; ~**leer**, leather cloth; ~**loon**, weaver's wages; ~**lyne**, ratlines; ~**masjien**, power loom; ~**nywerheid**, weaving industry, textile industry.

weef'sel, (-s), (con)texture, fabric, membrane, tissue, grain; ~**asemhaling**, internal respiration; ~**bloeding**, suffusion; ~**herstel**, regeneration; ~**leer**, histology; ~**ontsteking**, cellulitis; ~**oorplanting**, graft (med.); ~**opbou**, anabolism; ~**spanning**, tissue tension; ~**stowwe**, woven fabrics; ~**vorming**, histogeny.

weef; ~**skool**, weaving-school; ~**spoel**, shuttle; ~**ster, (-s),** female weaver; ~**stoel**, loom.

weef'stof, (..stowwe), woven fabric; textile; ..stowwe, textiles, dry goods; ~**handel**, mercery; ~**handelaar**, mercer.

weef'toestel, loom.

weeg, (ge-), weigh, balance; poise; *ge~ en te LIG bevind*, weighed and found wanting; *wat die SWAARSTE is, moet die swaarste ~*, the most important matter must come first; ~ *jou WOORDE*, weigh your words; ~**baar, (..bare)**, weighable, ponderable; ~**baarheid**, ponderability; ~**brug**, platform-balance, weigh-bridge; bascule; ~**haak**, weigh-beam; ~**huis**, weigh-house; ~**loon**, weighage; metage (coal), ~**masjien**, weighing-maching; ~**skaal**, balance, (pair of) scales; *DIE W~skaal*, Libra (astron.); *jou LEWE is in die ~skaal*, your life is at stake; *jou LEWE in die ~skaal stel*, put one's life in the balance; ~**stoel**, weighing-chair; ~**toestel**, weighing-machine.

wee'heid, faintness, queerness, qualmishness, mawkishness.

wee'ïg, (-e), queer (feeling), faint, qualmish; ~**heid**, queerness, faintness, qualmishness.

week¹, (s): *wasgoed in die ~ LAAT*, leave washing to soak; *in die ~ SIT*, put in to soak; let soak; (w) **(ge-),** steep in, soak, soften; liquor (malt) ret (hemp); (b) **(weke),** soft, flabby, tender.

week², (s) (weke), week; *(al) om die ANDER ~*, every second week; *BY die ~*, by the week; *vandag OOR 'n ~*, today week; *TWEE weke*, a fortnight; ~ *in ~ UIT*, week in week out; ~**aand**, evening of a weekday; ~**berig**, weekly report; ~**blad**, weekly (paper); ~**daags, (-e),** (of a) weekday; ~**dag**, weekday; ~**diens**, weekly service.

week'dier, mollusc (pulpy animal).

week'geld, weekly allowance, weekly pay.

weekhar'tig, (-e), tender-hearted, soft-hearted; effeminate; ~**heid**, tender-heartedness.

week: ~**heid**, softness, milkiness, weakness; tenderness; ~**hoewig, (-e),** tender-hoofed; ~**hui'dig, (-e),** soft-skinned.

week: ~**huur**, weekly rent; ~**kaartjie**, weekly ticket.

week'kuip, soaking-vat.

wee: ~**klaag, (ge-),** wail, lament, moan, groan; elegize; ~**klag, (-te),** wailing, lament(ation), moan(ing).

week: ~**liks, (-e),** weekly, once a week; ~**loon**, weekly wages.

week(s)'dag, weekday.

week: ~**soldeersel**, soft solder; ~**staal**, mild (soft) steel.

week'staat, weekly return.

week'tenk, soaking tank.

weel'de, luxury; profusion, abundance, copiousness; wealth, affluence, opulence; *iets nie uit ~ DOEN nie*, to be forced by circumstances; *in ~ GEBORE*, born with a silver spoon in his mouth; *'n ~ van KLEURE*, a riot of colours; *in ~ LEWE*, live in the lap of luxury; *hom die ~ VEROORLOOF*, be able to afford something; allow oneself the luxury; ~**artikel**, article of luxury; ~**artikels**, fancy goods; luxuries; ~**bedryf**, luxury trade; ~**belasting**, sumptuary duties; ~**bus**, luxury bus; ~**hotel**, luxury hotel; ~**lewe**, life of luxury; ~**rig, (-e),** exuberant, luxuriant; sumptuous, opulent; lush, luxurious; ~**righeid**, luxuriance, luxuriousness; exuberance; ~**wette**, sumptuary laws.

wee'luis, (bed-)bug, cimex.

wee'moed, grief, sadness, melancholy.

weemoe'dig, (-e), sad, melancholic; ~**heid**, sadness, melancholy.

ween, (ge-), weep, cry, shed tears.

Wee'nen, Weenen (Natal).

weë'net, road network.

Weens¹, (b) (-e), Viennese; ~*e worsies*, Vienna sausages.

weens², (vs) on account of, for, because of; ~ *GEBREK aan geld*, for want of money; ~ *SIEKTE*, on account of illness.

we'ër, (s) (-s), weigher.

weer¹, (s) weather; *deur die ~ GETREF*, struck by lighting; *by GUNSTIGER ~*, weather permitting; *MOOI ~ speel met 'n ander se geld*, play ducks and drakes with someone else's money; *die ~ maak VIER*, it is making up for rain.

weer², (s) defence; *DRUK in die ~ wees*, be astir, be very busy; *jou te ~ STEL*, offer resistance; defend oneself; *vroeg in die ~ WEES*, be up and doing; (w) **(ge-),** defend (oneself); exclude, avert, prevent (disaster); exert (oneself), strain every nerve; *jy MOET jou ~*, you must exert yourself; ~ *die RAMP van ons*, avert the disaster from us; *die SOLDATE het hulle dapper ge~*, the soldiers put up a brave fight.

weer³, (bw) again, afresh, anew, a second time; ~ *EENS*, again; *HEEN en ~*, to and fro; ~ *HIER?*, here again?; ~**aanhegting**, reannexation; ~**aanneming**, reassumption.

weer'baar, (..bare), able-bodied, fit; resistant; defensible; ~**heid**, defensibility; ability to defend oneself; resistance.

weerbars'tig, (-e), unruly, intractable, recalcitrant, refractory, forward; ~**heid**, unruliness, intractibility, refractoriness, recalcitrance, obstreperousness.

weer: ~**bebossing**, reafforestation; ~**bekering**, reconversion.

weer'berig, weather-report; ~**gewing**, reporting the weather.

weer: ~**bestand, (-e),** weatherproof; ~**buro, (-'s)**, weather bureau.

weer'dam, barrage, coffer-dam.

weer: diens, weather service; ~**dig, (-te),** weather-proof.

weer'ga, rival, match, fellow, peer, equal; *sonder ~*, matchless, unrivalled; without equal.

weer'galm, (s) echo, reverberation; (w) **weergalm',**

(~), echo, resound, reverberate, re-echo; peal (bells).
weer'galoos, (..**lose**), matchless, peerless, without example, unparalleled; ~**heid**, matchlessness.
weer'gawe, (-s), reproduction, rendering.
weer'gebore, born again, regenerated, reborn.
weer'gee, (-ge-), reproduce, render (music); express (feelings); interpret (conception); convey (impression); capture (spirit of a work); echo (someone's words).
weer'gety, ebb-tide.
weer'gevoel, weather-sense.
weer'gewer, (-s), sound-box; reproducer (radio).
weer'glans, reflection.
weer'glas, barometer, (weather-)glass.
weer'haak, barb(ed hook), grapple-hook; beard.
weer'haan, weathercock (fig. & lit.); turncoat.
weerhou', (~), keep back, refrain from, deter, detain, restrain; *jou van iets* ~, refrain from doing something; ~**ding**, restraint.
weer: ~**indiensneming**, reinstatement; ~**inskeping**, re-embarkation; ~**instorting**, relapse.
weer'invoer, re-importation; ~**ing**, restoration, re-introduction (gold standard).
weer'kaart, weather-chart.
weerkaats', (~), reflect, flash back (light); re-echo (sound); ~ *te weerlig*, sheet lightning; ~**baar**, (..**bare**), reflexible; ~**baarheid**, reflexibility; ~**end**, (-e), reflective, catoptric; ~**er**, reflector; ~**ing**, reflection; echo, re-echo(ing) (sound).
weerkaat'sings: ~**hoek**, angle of reflection; ~**vermoë**, reflectivity; ~**wet**, law of reflection.
weerkaats'strook, reflecting strip.
weer'keer, (-ge-), return, come back, recur.
weer'kenner, (-s), meteorologist.
weer'kennis, weather lore.
weer'klank, echo, resonance, reverberation; ~ *vind*, find a ready response.
weerklink', (~), resound, (re-)echo, reverberate; ring (with), peal (bells); ~ *van*, resound with.
weer'krag, military strength.
weer'kry, (-ge-), find again, recover.
weer'kunde, meteorology.
weerkun'dig, (-e), meteorological; ~*e AFDELING*, meteorological section; *BOERE is* ~*e mense*, farmers are weather-wise; ~*e DIENS*, meteorological service; ~*e KANTOOR*, meteorological office; *ons* ~*e MEDEWERKER*, our weather-correspondent; ~**e**, (-s), meteorologist; weather-prophet.
weerlê', (~), refute, dispose of (argument), disprove, contradict, rebut, controvert (statement), counter, impugn, confute (theories); ~**baar** = **weerlegbaar**; ~**er**, (-s), refuter.
weerleg'baar, (..**bare**), disprovable, confutable, impugnable, opposable, refutable; ~**heid**, refutability.
weerleg'ging, (-e, -s), refutation, disproval, rebuttal, disproof, impugnment, confutation, contradiction; ~ *van BEWYS*, rebuttal of evidence; *TER* ~ *van*, in refutation of.
weer'liefde, returned love.
weer'lig, (s) lightning; *deur die* ~ *getref*, struck by lightning; (w) (ge-), lighten, flash; ~**afleier**, lightning-conductor; ~**skynsel**, heat lightning; ~**straal**, flash of lightning.
weer'loos, (..**lose**), defenceless; ~**heid**, defencelessness.
weer'mag, armed force, army and navy, fighting services; defence force.
weer'magskleur, service colour.
weer'man[1], private (mil.).
weer'man[2], meteorologist, weatherman.
weer'middel, means of defence.
weer'om, again, back, return; *tot* ~, au revoir; ~**slag**, recoil, rebound; reaction; ~**spel**, return match; ~**stuit**, (s) recoil, reaction; (w) (ge-), rebound, recoil.
weer'ontmoeting, reunion; return match.
weer'opbou(ing) = **wederopbouing**.
weer: ~**oplegging**, reimposition; ~**oplewing**, revival, recovery.

weer'oprigting, = **we(d)eroprigting**.
weer'opsegging: *tot* ~, until further notice.
weer: ~**opstanding**, resurrection; ~**opsuiging**, reabsorption; ~**opvoering**, revival (of play).
weer'plank, fender.
weer'plig, compulsory military service; ~'**tig**, (-e), liable to military service; ~'**tigheid**, liability to military service.
weer: ~**pos**, weather station; ~**profeet**, weather-prophet.
weer'pyn, sympathetic pain.
weers'gesteldheid, state of the weather, weather conditions.
weer'sien, (s), meeting again, reunion; *tot* ~*s*, so long! till we meet again! au revoir! (w) (-ge-), meet again.
weer'sin, repugnance, antipathy, dislike, aversion; ~ *in iem. KRY*, take a dislike to someone; *MET* ~, with aversion, reluctantly, with a bad grace; ~ *TEEN iets*, aversion to something.
weers'invloed, influence of the weather (on rheumatism).
weersinwek'kend, (-e), loathsome, repugnant, revolting, fulsome, antipathetic.
weers'kante, both sides; *AAN* ~, on both sides; *VAN* ~, from both sides.
weerskan'tig, (-e), ambilateral, bilateral.
weer'slag, recoil; return stroke.
weer'skyn, reflection, lustre; ~**sel**, reflection; ~**stof**, changeant; ~**sy**, shot silk.
weers'omstandighede, weather conditions.
weerspan'nig, (-e), refractory, insubordinate, rebellious; ~**e**, (-s), rebel, recalcitrant; ~**heid**, refractoriness; recalcitrance, rebelliousness.
weerspie'ël, (~), mirror, reflect; ~**end**, (-e), reflective; ~**ing**, (-s), reflection.
weer'spraak, contradiction.
weerspreek', (~), contradict, gainsay, deny, belie; *'n bewering* ~, deny an allegation.
weerspre'ker, (-s), contradictor, denier.
weerspre'king, (-e, -s), contradiction, denial, disclaimer.
weerstaan', (~), withstand, resist, cohibit, oppose.
weer'stand, resistance; drag (aero.); opposition; recalcitrance; ~ *BIED*, resist, offer resistance; *MAGNETIESE* ~, reluctance; *SOORTLIKE* ~, resistivity; ~**skaal**, drag-balance.
weer'stands: ~**klos**, rheostat; ~**koppeling**, resistance coupling; ~**lyn**, line of resistance; ~**moment**, moment of resistance; ~**toets**, resistance test; ~**vermoë**, power of resistance, stamina, staying-power, resistability, endurance.
weer'standsweising, resistance welding.
weer'stasie, weather station.
weers'toestand, condition of weather.
weerstreef', **weerstre'we**, (~), resist, strive against, struggle against, go counter to, oppose.
weerstre'wig, (-e), recalcitrant; ~**heid**, recalcitrance.
weerstre'wing, opposition, resistance.
weers'verandering, (-e, -s), change of weather.
weers'verskynsel, phenomenon of the weather.
weer'sy, (-e), reverse, back side; *aan* ~*e*, on both sides.
weer'syds, (-e), mutual, reciprocal.
weer'tabel, (-le), weather-chart.
weer'toelating, readmission, readmittance.
weer'uitbreking, recrudescence.
weer'vas, (-te), weatherproof; all-weather; *'n* ~ *te tennisbaan*, an all-weather tennis court.
weer'vastheid, state of being weatherproof.
weer: ~**vergelding**, retaliation, requital; ~**verhuring**, reletting; subletting; ~**verhuur**, (~), relet; sublet; ~**verkiesbaar**, (..**bare**), re-eligible; offered for re-election; ~**verskyning**, reappearance.
weer: ~**voorspeller**, weather-forecaster; ~**voorspelling**, weather-forecast; ~**vooruitsigte**, weather prospects.
weer'vraag, counter-question.
weer'wag, meteorological station; ~**ter**, meteorological observer.
weer'wil: *in* ~ *van*, in spite of, despite, notwithstanding.

weerwolf, wer(e)wolf; lycanthrope; scarecrow, ogre, bogeyman, bugbear; spotted hyena; ~**waansin**, lycanthropy.
weer'woord, reply, answer.
weer'wraak, revenge, retaliation; ~ *NEEM op*, retaliate against; *UIT* ~ *vir*, in retaliation for.
weer: ~**wys, (-e)**, weather-wise; ~**wyser**, weather-glass.
wees¹, (s) (wese), orphan; (b) without parents; ~ *opgroei*, grow up as an orphan.
wees², (w) (is, was, ge-), be: *AS dit nie was dat ek daarvan gehoor het nie (was dit nie dat . . .)*, if it had not been that I had heard about the matter; but for the fact that . . .; *die DOKTER sal nou-nou hier* ~, the doctor will be here immediately; *EK is Jan*, my name is John; *hy is in die GEVEG gewond*, he was wounded in the battle; *GOD is*, God is (exists); *LAAT dit* ~ *soos dit wil*, be that as it may; ~ *'n MAN*, be a man! *hy is PROKUREUR*, he is a lawyer; *die vergadering was al VERBY toe ek daar kom*, the meeting had already been closed when I arrived there; *WAAR was jy?* where were you? *soos die WET nou is*, as the law now stands.
wees'boom, boom device used for steadying a wagon-load of sheaves.
Wees'heer, Master of the Supreme Court.
wees'fonds, orphan's fund.
wees: ~**huis**, orphanage; protectory (R.C.); ~**(huis)moeder**, matron of an orphanage; ~**(huis)vader**, warden of an orphanage; ~**inrigting**, orphanage; ~**jongetjie**, orphan boy; W~**kamer**, Orphan Chamber; ~**kind**, orphan; ~**kindertjies**, little orphans; linaria (flower); several wild flowers (e.g. *Tritonia spp.*); ~**meisie**, orphan girl; ~**seun**, orphan boy.
weë'-soet, mawkish.
weet, (ge-), know, be conscious of, have knowledge of, be aware of, be apprised; *BETER* ~, know better; *nie* ~ *wat jy aan iem. HET nie*, not to know what to make of someone; ~ *wat jy het en nie wat jy KRY nie*, be sure of the present, but not of the future; not to know what the future may hold; *LAAT* ~, send word; inform; *dit MOET jy* ~, you can be sure of that! *ek wil NIKS van hom* ~ *nie*, I don't want to have anything to do with him; *'n mens kan NOOIT* ~ *nie*, one never can tell; one never knows; *NUGTER* ~, goodness knows; *SONDER om dit self te* ~, unwittingly, unconsciously; *vir SOVER ek* ~, as far as I know; for all I know; *VAN iets* ~, know about something; *hy* ~ *nie VAN beter nie*, he does not know any better; *hy wil nie* ~ *dat hy VERKEERD is nie*, he won't admit that he is wrong; *hy* ~ *my te VERTEL*, he informs me; I have it from him; *vir my om te* ~, *vir jou om uit te VIND*, I know, but I am not going to tell you; that is for you to find out; ~ *jy WAT?* do you know what?; *see* **wete;** ~**al, (le)**, wiseacre, know-all, ~**baar, (..bare)**, knowable; ~**baarheid**, knowability; ~**gie'rig, (-e)**, inquisitive, curious; eager to learn; ~**gie'righeid**, eagerness to learn; curiosity, inquisitiveness; ~**lus**, desire for knowledge; curiosity; ~**niet, (-e)**, ignoramus, dunce.
weg, (s) (weë), way, road, path, route; *die* ~ *BAAN tot*, open the gate to; *die* ~ *BAAN vir*, pave the way for; *die* ~ *BEREI vir*, prepare the way for; *die BREË* ~, the primrose path; *goed met iem. oor die* ~ *KOM*, get on well with someone; *as niks in die* ~ *KOM nie*, if nothing unforeseen crops up; *die KONINKLIKE* ~, the royal road; *die KONINKLIKE* ~ *gaan*, be straightforward; *LANGS hierdie* ~, in this way; *dit LÊ nie op my* ~ *nie*, it is not my duty, *weë en MIDDELE*, ways and means; *alle weë gaan (lei, voer) na ROME*, all roads lead to Rome; *so oud soos die* ~ *na ROME*, as old as the hills; *moeilikhede uit die* ~ *RUIM*, smooth over difficulties; remove obstacles; *iets in die* ~ *SIT*, put something in someone's way; *daar STAAN vir my geen ander* ~ *oop nie*, I have no choice; *in iem. se* ~ *STAAN*, stand in someone's way; *aan die* ~ *TIMMER*, appear in public; *die* ~ *VERSPER*, bar the way; *die* ~ *van alle VLEES gaan*, go the way of all flesh; *die weë v.d. VOORSIENIGHEID*, the ways of Providence; *mooi op* ~ *WEES OM*, be in a fair way to; (bw) away, off, gone; mislaid, lost; apart; *EK moet* ~, I must go; *iets* ~ *HÊ van sy vader*, have something of his father in him; *die boom het* ~ *v.d. HUIS geval*, the tree fell clear of the house; *nou dat hy moet WERK, is hy baie* ~, now that he has work to do, he can be found nowhere; (tw) go, get away; off; ~ *IS jy!* clear off! off with you! ~ *MET hom!* away with him! *te VER* ~, too far away; ~**aanleg**, road-construction.
weg'ban, (-ge-), banish, drive away.
weg'baner, trail-blazer.
weg'belasting, road-tax.
weg'bêre, (-ge-), hide, put away, box, lock up, pocket; tuck in.
weg'bereider, (-s), herald; pioneer; forerunner.
weg'blaas, (-ge-), blow away.
weg'blaker, (-ge-), shoot away.
weg'bly, (s) non-appearance; non-attendance; **(w) (-ge-)**, stay away, absent (oneself) (from school); hold off, abstain (from drink); ~**er**, absentee; ~**ery**, absenteeism.
weg'boender, (-ge-), bundle (away), drive off, chase away, shoo away.
weg'borsel, (-ge-), brush off (away).
weg'brand, (-ge-), burn away.
weg'breek, (s) (..breke), (-ge-), off-break (cricket); **(w) (-ge-)**, break away; ~**bal**, off-break; ~**bouler**, off-spinner.
weg'bring, (-ge-), take away, escort (out, away).
weg'brokkel, (-ge-), crumble away.
weg'buig, (-ge-), deflect; ~**ing**, deflection.
weg'buk, (-ge-), duck.
weg'dink, (-ge-), eliminate in thought, shut one's mind to, think away.
weg'doen, (-ge-), do away (with), dispose of; *ons sal die motor moet* ~, we'll have to get rid of the motor-car; ~**'baar, (..bare)**, disposable; ~**ing**, disposal; removal; ~**plek**, disposal site.
weg'dra, (-ge-), carry away; *die prys* ~, carry off the prize.
weg'draai, (-ge-), turn away; branch off.
weg'drae = **wegdra**.
weg'draf, (-ge-), trot away, trot off.
weg'drentel, (-ge-), shuffle off.
weg'dring, (-ge-), push away (aside), hustle away.
weg'dros, (-ge-), abscond, desert.
weg'druip, (-ge-), drop away; slink off.
weg'druk, (-ge-), push away (aside).
weg'dryf, weg'drywe, (-ge-), drive away; float away, drift off.
weg'duik, (-ge-), duck; dive away, jink (aero.).
weg'fladder, (-ge-), flutter away.
weg'fluit, (-ge-), hiss away (off); whistle away (off).
weg'gaan, (-ge-), go (away), depart, get (go) off, leave, make one's exit.
weg'gee, (-ge-), give away (lit.); part with.
weg'gegooi, (dc), discarded, cast-off.
weg'gevoer, (-de), rapt; ~**de, (-s)**, evacuee.
weg'gly, (-ge-), slip (away), slide away.
weg'gooi, (-ge-), discard (lamb); fling aside; discard (card); chuck away, cast away (forth); waste (money) throw away; *JOUSELF* ~, lower oneself; *'n KANS* ~, let an opportunity slip; *sy VROU het hom weggegooi*, his wife left him; ~**goed**, rubbish, cast-offs, discards; ~**lam**, lost lamb; lamb refused by its mother; refuse (lamb); ~**ooi**, ewe that refuses to suckle her lamb; ~**sakkie**, disposal bag.
weg'graaf, weg'grawe, (-ge-), dig away.
weg'gryp, (-ge-), whisk away, snatch away.
weg'haak, (-ge-), hook away.
weg'haal, (-ge-), take away, fetch away; *ek sal die meubels laat* ~, I will have the furniture removed.
weg'haas, (-ge-), hurry away; *ek moet my nou* ~, I must now hurry away.
weg'hardloop, (-ge-), run away, flee.
weg'hark, (-ge-), rake away.
weg'help, (-ge-), assist in getting away; attend to; *iem.* ~ *met GELD*, assist someone with money; *KLANTE gou* ~, serve customers quickly.
weg'hol, (-ge-), run away, take to one's heels, bolt, stampede; *die wilde* ~ *kry*, panic.

weg'hou, (-ge-), keep away.
weg'inspekteur, road-inspector.
weg'ja(ag), (-ge-), drive (chase) away, drum out; extrude; dislodge, turn out; sack (servant); expel (child from school); dispel; race away.
weg'jaend, (-e), expulsive.
weg'kaap, (-ge-), pilfer, purloin, filch.
weg'kaart, road-map.
weg'kam, (-ge-), comb away.
weg'kant, off-side (cricket).
weg'kap, (-ge-), cut away, lop off, hew off.
weg'keer, (-ge-), drive away; ward off.
weg'knaag, (-ge-), gnaw away; erode.
weg'knip, (-ge-), lop, clip off, cut away (with scissors); flick away (with a finger).
weg'kom, (-ge-), get away; *maak dat jy ~!* be gone! be off with you!
weg'krap, (-ge-), scratch away.
weg'krimp, (-ge-), shrink away, dwindle away; *~ van pyn,* writhe with pain.
weg'kruip, (-ge-), hide oneself, lie low, be in hiding, take cover; crawl away; ~**er, (-s),** stowaway; ~**ertjie,** hide-and-seek, I spy, bo-peep; ~**plek,** hide-out, hiding-place.
weg'krummel, (-ge-), crumble away.
weg'kry, (-ge-), get (something) away (from).
weg'kwyn, (-ge-), fade away; pine (waste) away, dwindle; languish; atrophy; ~**ing,** pining away, languishing, atrophy (med.).
weg'kyk, (-ge-), look away; *iem. ~,* freeze a person out, stare someone out of countenance.
weg'laat, (-ge-), leave out, eliminate, miss out, omit; ~**'baar, (..bare),** omissible.
weg'lag, (-ge-), laugh away, make light of, pooh-pooh.
weg'lating, (-s), leaving out; omission; pretermission.
weg'latingsteken, apostrophe, caret.
weg'lê, (-ge-), put away; lay away from nest (hen); eat ravenously, tuck in; lay away (corpse); lay aside (money); *~ by 'n NOOI,* try to win a girl; *die seuns het weggelê aan die VRUGTE,* the boys made a feast of the fruit; *dit WAS nie vir hom weggelê nie,* it was not destined for him; ~**horings,** widespread horns.
weg'lei, (-ge-), lead away; ~**put,** inverted well.
weg'lê: ~**snor,** handle-bar moustache; ~**tone,** splayed toes.
weg'lok, (-ge-), entice away, decoy, lure away.
weg'loop, (w) (-ge-), walk away; desert, run away, make off, levant, take French leave, abscond, decamp; elope; *sy GAAN met hom ~,* she is going to elope with him; *ons span sal met al die PUNTE ~,* our team will win all the points; *~ VAN, ~ VIR,* run away from; ~**paar,** eloping couple.
weg'loper, (-s) deserter, absconder, fugitive, levanter; ~**y,** eloping; desertion; fleeing.
weg'maai, (-ge-), mow (down), decimate.
weg'maak, (-ge-), do away with, dispose of, remove; chloroform.
weg'meter, pedometer.
weg'moffel, (-ge-), shuffle away; pilfer; hide.
weg'neem, (-ge-), take away, remove; obviate; fetch away; allay (pain); *dit NEEM nie weg dat ...,* that does not alter the fact that ...; *STILLETJIES ~,* remove on the sly, steal.
weg'neming, excision; removal; taking away.
weg'oorgang, level crossing.
weg'paaltjie, off-stump (cricket).
weg'pak, (-ge-), pack away; garner; snatch away; tuck away (food).
weg'pik, (-ge-), peck away.
weg'pink, (-ge-), brush away (tears).
weg'pluk, (-ge-), snatch (pluck) away.
weg'praat, (-ge-), talk out of (plans); talk away from (person); explain away (fears).
weg'raak, (-ge-), get lost, disappear.
weg'ratel, (-ge-), rumble away.
weg'redeneer, (-ge-), explain (reason) away, gloss (over).
weg'roei, (-ge-), row away.
weg'roep, (-ge-), call away.
weg'roes, (-ge-), rust away.

weg'rol, (-ge-), roll away.
weg'roof, weg'rowe, (-ge-), pilfer, purloin, rob.
weg'ruim, (-ge-), clear away (snow); dispel (illusions); dispose of (objections); ~**ing,** obviation (difficulties); clearing, removing, removal; ~**trein,** pick-up train.
weg'ruk, (-ge-), tear away, snatch away, pluck away; *in die bloei van sy jare weggeruk,* cut off in the prime of his life.
weg'ry, (-ge-), ride off, drive away; cart away.
weg'saag, weg'sae, (-ge-), saw (cut) away.
weg'sak, (-ge-), sink away, cave in, subside; ~**king,** subsidence.
weg'seil, (-ge-), sail away.
weg'sending, dismissal.
weg'sien, (-ge-), see off (at station, boat).
weg'sink, (-ge-), sink away; ~**ing,** subsidence; submergence (mining).
weg'sit, (-ge-), put away; save.
weg'skaaf, weg'skawe, (-ge-), plane off (away); abrade.
weg'skeer, (-ge-), shave (shear) away (off); clear off.
weg'skenk, (-ge-), give away, make a present of.
weg'skeur, (-ge-), tear away.
weg'skiet, (-ge-), shoot away.
weg'skink, (-ge-), pour away.
weg'skop, (-ge-), kick away.
weg'skram, (-ge-), ricochet; *die PROJEKTIEL het weggeskram,* the projectile was deflected; *VAN iem. ~,* avoid someone; give someone a wide berth; *van 'n VRAAG ~,* evade a question; ~**skoot,** ricochet (shot).
weg'skuif, (-ge-), push (shove) away; move away.
weg'skuil, (-ge-), hide oneself.
weg'skuiwe, (-ge-) = **wegskuif.**
weg'slaan, (-ge-), strike (beat) away; swallow, gulp down (brandy, medicine); *dit laat 'n mens se ASEM ~,* it takes one's breath away; *'n BAL ~,* hit away a ball; *'n KALF v.d. uier af ~,* hit a calf away from the udder; *'n SOPIE ~,* toss off a drink; *'n groot skottel VLEIS ~,* devour a large plate of meat.
weg'sleep, (-ge-), drag away; enrapture, fascinate, carry away (fig.).
weg'slepend, (-e), fascinating, rapturous; *'n ~ e melodie,* a captivating melody.
weg'sleur, (-ge-), drag away; sweep away (floods).
weg'slinger, (-ge-), hurl away; stagger away (off).
weg'sluip, (-ge-), steal away, sneak off, do a bunk.
weg'sluit, (-ge-), lock away, enshrine; encase.
weg'sluk, (s) swallowing, deglutition; **(w) (-ge-),** gulp down.
weg'slyt, (-ge-), wear off (away).
weg'smelt, (-ge-), melt away, deliquesce; *in trane ~,* dissolve in tears; ~**ing,** melting away.
weg'smyt, (-ge-), fling (chuck) away; abandon, desert (wife); waste (money).
weg'snel, (-ge-), hurry off, hasten away.
weg'snoei, (-ge-), prune, lop off.
weg'sny, (-ge-), cut away; pare; recess; ~**ding, (-e, -s),** cutting away; recess (in building).
weg'soen, (-ge-), kiss away.
weg'spat, (-ge-), splash away; scatter (sheep).
weg'spoel, (-ge-), wash away.
weg'spring, (-ge-), jump away; take (be) off, go, start off; ricochet, bounce off; make a dash; *ongelyke ~,* false start; ~**plek,** starting-place; jumping-off place.
weg'staan, (-ge-), stand away; *~ van,* (fig.), dissociate oneself from.
weg'stap, (-ge-), walk away, stride away.
weg'steek, (s) retention; **(w) (-ge-),** hide, cache, conceal; camouflage; dig away (with spade); hold, retain (milk); *die koei steek haar melk weg,* the cow is retaining her milk.
weg'steekgoed, cache (of provisions).
weg'steel, (-ge-), steal away.
weg'steker, concealer.
weg'sterf, weg'sterwe, (-ge-), die away (down), fade (sound).
weg'stoom, (-ge-), steam off, steam out (train).
weg'stoot, (-ge-), push away, jockey (out of position).
weg'stop, (-ge-), conceal, hide, put away.

wegstorm — 637 — **weldadig**

weg'storm, (-ge-), storm (dash) away (off).
weg'stroom, (-ge-), flow (stream) away; leave (in great numbers).
weg'stryk, (-ge-), brush away (tears); iron out (creases); march away (off).
weg'stuif, (-ge-), blow away (dust); hurry away.
weg'stuur, (-ge-), despatch, send away, pack off; discharge, dismiss.
weg'swaai, (-ge-), swing away (off).
weg'sweef, weg'swewe, (-ge-), glide (soar) away.
weg'syfer, (-ge-), eliminate, set aside, ignore; reason away; seep away; *'n FEIT probeer* ~, try to reason away a fact; *JOUSELF* ~, obliterate (efface) oneself; ~ **ing,** seepage.
weg'teer, (-ge-), waste away, become emaciated.
weg'toor, weg'tower, (-ge-), conjure (spirit) away.
weg'trap, (-ge-), trample out (spoor); wear away (by walking); kick away.
weg'trek, (-ge-), pull away; draw away; drive off; flit; depart, go (away); leave, move (out of the neighbourhood); ~ **spier,** abductor muscle.
weg'trippel, (-ge-), scamper away, trip away.
weg'troon, (-ge-), lure (entice) away.
weg'vaag, (-ge-), blot out; sweep away; fan away.
weg'vaar, (-ge-), sail away.
weg'val, (-ge-), drop off, fall out (away); be omitted; fall to (at meal); die; *dié BEPALING het weggeval,* this clause has been omitted; *haar OUERS het vroeg weggeval,* she lost her parents early in life; *môre moet ons VROEG* ~, we must start early tomorrow.
weg'vang, (-ge-), catch (snatch) away.
weg'vat, (-ge-), take away.
weg'vee(g), (-ge-), wipe away, flick away (tears); sweep away (dust).
weg'vlie(g), (-ge-), fly away (bird); shy (horse).
weg'vloei, (-ge-), flow away; ~ **end,** (-e), diffluent.
weg'vlug, (-ge-), flee (from enemy); fly (away) (out of country).
weg'voer, (-ge-), lead away; carry off, cart away; abduct, kidnap; ~ **ing,** removal; abduction, kidnapping.
weg'vreet, (-ge-), eat away, canker; corrode (by acids); erode (by floods).
weg'vretend, (-e), erosive; corrosive.
weg'vreting, erosion, ablation; corrosion; fretting away.
weg'vryf, weg'vrywe, (-ge-), rub away, massage away.
weg'vyl, (-ge-), file away.
weg'waai, (-ge-), blow away; be blown away; wave away.
weg'werk, (-ge-), clear away, get rid of, shift away, manoeuvre away; freeze out; work off.
weg'werp, (-ge-), throw away, cast off.
wegwerp'lik, (-e), rejectable.
weg'wis, (-ge-), wipe away (out).
weg'wys¹, (w) (-ge-), refuse, reject (at confirmation).
weg'wys², (bw); ~ *wees,* know the ropes.
weg'wys: ~ **er,** (-s), guide post, signpost; cicerone, guide; handbook; ~ **ing,** rejection (at confirmation); exclusion; warning off.
wel¹, (s) whey; serum (med.).
wei², (s) (-e), pasturage, meadow; (w) (ge-), feed, graze; *KOEIE laat* ~, let cows graze; *jou oë laat* ~ *oor,* let one's eyes travel over.
wei'agtig, (-e), serous (med.); whey-like.
wei'de, (-s) = **wei²,** (s).
wei'dend, (-e), grazing.
wei'ding, (-s), grazing, pasture, pasturage.
weids, (-e; -er, -ste), grand, showy, stately; *'n* ~ *e uitsig,* an imposing view; ~ **heid,** stateliness, grandeur, splendour.
wei'er, (ge-), decline, refuse, disallow, deny; dishonour (cheque); misfire (gun); *'n AANBOD* ~, turn down an offer; *die GEWEER het ge* ~, the gun misfired; *die REM het ge* ~, the brake failed; *VRA is vry en* ~ *daarby,* there can be no harm in asking; ~ **aar,** (-s), refuser; recusant; ~ **agtig,** ~ **ag'tig,** (-e), unwilling to grant a request; ~ **end,** (-e), recusant; ~ **ing,** (-s), refusal, rebuff, disallowance, denial, negation, failure (motor); misfire (motor, gun); ~ **skoot,** misfire.

wei'fel, (-ge-), waver, doubt, demur, flinch, dilly-dally, shilly-shally, pendulate, fluctuate, vacillate, hesitate, boggle, falter; balance; ~ **aar,** (-s), vacillator, demurrer, waverer; ~ **agtig,** ~ **ag'tig,** (-e), hesitating, dubitative, vacillating; ~ **agtigheid,** ~ **ag'tigheid,** hesitation, vacillation, indecision; ~ **end,** (-e), wavering, wavery, dubious, fluctuant, faltering, double-minded, hesitative, hesitant, hesitating, undecided, vacillating; ~ **ing,** (-e, -s), wavering, hesitancy, irresolution, hesitation, dubitation, vacillation, dubiousness, demurring, doubt, fluctuation.
weifelmoe'dig, (-e), vacillating, irresolute, wavering; ~ **heid,** irresolution, vacillation.
wei: ~ **geld,** grazing-fee; pannage (pigs); ~ **gras,** grazing-grass.
wei'kaas, skimmed-milk cheese; green cheese.
wei: ~ **kamp,** paddock; ~ **kool,** rape (vegetable), kale; ~ **land,** pasture land, meadow-land.
wei'nig, (-e, **minder, minste**), little, few; modicum; ~ *of NIKS,* little or nothing; *met* ~ *TEVREDE wees,* be satisfied with very little; *VEEL te* ~, much too little; ~ *WAARHEID,* a modicum of truth; ~ **e,** (-s), few; the little bit; *die* ~ *e wat MYNE is,* the little bit that belongs to me; ~ *es is UITVERKORE,* few are chosen; ~ **heid,** fewness, small number (amount).
wei: ~ **plaas,** cattle-range; ~ **reg,** (-te) grazing right(s); ~ **veld,** pasture, meadow; pannage (pigs); feeding-ground, grass, grazing-ground.
wei'vlies, serous membrane.
wek, (ge-), wake, awake(n), challenge (admiration), call, rouse, raise, excite, stir (curiosity); create (suspicion).
we'kelange, continuing for weeks.
we'king, soaking, impregnation.
wek: ~ **gesang,** rousing song; ~ **ker,** (-s), alarm-clock; knocker-up; ~ **pen,** alarm adjuster; ~ **roep,** clarion call; ~ **stem,** rousing (stirring) voice, loud voice.
wel¹, (s) weal; *die* ~ *en wee,* the weal and woe; (b, bw) well, (all)right; *ek het* ~ *so GEDINK,* I thought as much; *wat* ~ *GEVAARLIK is,* what really is dangerous; *as ek dit* ~ *HET,* if I am not mistaken; if I remember correctly; *LET* ~, nota bene; ~, *ou MAAT,* well, old chap; *jy's nie MOEG nie? Ek* ~, you don't feel tired? I do; *ek MOET* ~, I ought to; ~ *te RUSTE!* good night! sleep well! ~ *RYK, maar nie gelukkig nie,* wealthy all right, but far from being happy; ~ *SEKER,* yes, to be sure; of course; *'n man* ~ *TER TALE,* a fluent speaker; *alles* ~ *TUIS?* all well at home? *dit mag jy* ~ *VRA!* you may well ask (that)! *dit kan* ~ *WEES,* that may be; (tw) well!
wel², (w) (ge-), weld.
wel³, (w) (ge-), simmer, well up, bubble (water).
wel⁴, (w) (ge-), scald (milk); draw (butter).
welaan', well then, very well.
wel'af, rich, well off, well to-do.
wel'baar, (..bare), weldable.
wel'bedag, (-te), well-considered (thought out).
wel'begrepe, well understood; *in die* ~ *belang van,* in the proper interest of.
welbehaag'lik, (-e), comfortable, pleased, complacent, at ease; ~ **heid,** complacency.
wel'behae, feeling of pleasure, complacence; *in mense 'n* ~, goodwill towards men.
wel'bekend, (-e), well-known, noted, familiar (fact).
wel'bemind, (-e), well-beloved.
wel'bereid, (-e), well-prepared.
wel'beskou(d), after all, all things considered.
wel'besnede, well-cut; ~ *gelaatstrekke,* clear-cut features.
wel'bespraak, (-te), eloquent; glib, fluent; honey-mouthed, honey-tongued; *'n* ~ *te redenaar,* a fluent speaker.
wel'bespraaktheid, eloquence; fluency, glibness.
wel'besteed, (..stede), well-spent; *welbestede geld,* well-spent money.
wel'bewus, (-te), deliberate (attempt); conscious.
wel'daad, kindness, kind action; boon, benefit, benefaction.
welda'dig, (-e), charitable, beneficent, benevolent;

bounteous; salutary, beneficial (influence); *dit doen* ~ *aan*, it has a pleasing effect, it does one good.
welda'digheid, benevolence, charity, beneficence, benignity, benefaction.
welda'digheids: ~ **basaar,** charity bazaar; ~ **genootskap,** benevolent society; ~ **instelling,** charitable institution; ~ **konsert,** charity concert; ~ **posseël,** charity-stamp; ~ **vereniging,** benevolent society.
welden'kend, (-e), right-minded; ~ **heid,** right-mindedness.
wel'deurdag, (-te), well-considered, well thought-out (plan).
wel'deurvoed, (-e), well-fed.
wel'doen, (-ge-), do good; philanthropize; ~ **er,** benefactor; ~ **ster, (-s),** benefactress.
wel'dra, presently, soon, shortly.
wele'del, (-e), honourable; *W* ~ *e Heer*, dear sir, esquire; ~ **ag'bare,** (right) honourable; ~ **gebo're,** honourable (form of address); ~ **gestren'ge,** right honourable; *W* ~ *gestrenge Heer*, Dear Sir.
wel'eens, ever, at any time, once.
weleer', (s) the past; (bw) formerly.
weleerwaar'de, (right) reverend.
welf, (ge-), vault, cove, arch; ~ **sel, (-s),** vault, coving.
wel'gaan, (-ge-), prosper, fare well, thrive; *dit gaan HOM wel*, he is prospering; *dit gaan JOU wel*, goodbye! good luck to you!
wel'gebore, well-born, high-born.
wel'gedaan, (..dane), well-fed; sleek, plump, portly; ~ **heid,** state of being well-fed; sleekness, portliness.
wel'geleë, beautifully situated.
welgeluksa'lig, (-e), blessed; ~ **heid,** blessedness.
wel'gemaak, (-te), well-made, well-built.
wel'gemanierd, (-e), well-mannered, polished, well-bred; ~ **heid,** good manners, good breeding.
wel'gemeen(d), (-de), well-meant; ~ *de raad*, well-meant advice.
wel'gemoed, (-e), cheerful, contented, in good cheer; ~ **heid,** cheerfulness.
wel'gemuts, (-te), in good humour.
wel'geordend, (-e), well-regulated (household); well-governed.
wel'gesind, (-e), well-disposed; ~ **heid,** goodwill, friendly feeling.
wel'geskape, well-formed, well-made.
wel'geslaag, (-de), successful.
wel'gesteld, (-e), opulent, easy, well-off, well-to-do, in easy circumstances; ~ **heid,** opulence, good financial position, competence; comfort.
wel'geval: *jou iets laat* ~ , put up with something, approve, accept without protest.
wel'gevalle, pleasure, liking; *na sy* ~ , to his liking, as one pleases.
welgeval'lig, (-e), pleasing, agreeable; ~ **heid,** agreeableness.
wel'gevoed, (-e), well-fed.
wel'gevorm(d), (-de), well-formed, shapely, clean-limbed; ~ **heid,** shapeliness.
wel'haas, well-nigh; soon, shortly.
we'lig, (-e), luxuriant, rank, exuberant, rampant; fertile; ~ **heid,** luxuriance, fertility, rankness.
wel'ingelig, (-te), well-informed; *uit 'n* ~ *te bron verneem*, hear from an inspired quarter.
wel'ingerig (-te), well-appointed, well-arranged.
weliswaar', indeed, actually, in truth, admittedly; *ek het dit* ~ *belowe, maar* . . ., I did indeed promise that, but . . .
welk, (ge-), wither, fade.
wel'ke, which, what; *cf.* **watter.**
wel'kom, (s) welcome; (b) **(-e),** welcome, desired; agreeable; acceptable; *iem.* ~ *HEET*, extend a welcome to someone; ~ *TUIS!* welcome home!
wel'koms: ~ **geskenk,** welcoming gift; ~ **groet,** welcome; ~ **lied,** song of welcome; ~ **rede,** speech (address) of welcome; ~ **woord,** word of welcome.
welle'wend, (-e), courteous, well-mannered, well-bred, urbane; ~ **heid,** courtesy, good breeding; ~ **heidshalwe,** for courtesy's sake; ~ **heidsvorme,** etiquette.
wel'lig, wellig', perhaps, may be; ~ *gebeur dit nog*, perhaps it will still happen.

wellui'dend, (-e), melodious, harmonious, musical, melodic, consonant, harmonic, euphonious; ~ **heid,** melodiousness, harmoniousness, harmony, chime, euphony; ~ **heidshalwe,** for the sake of harmony.
wel'lus, (-te), delight, bliss; sensual pleasure, lechery, lust, voluptuousness, concupiscence, carnal pleasures, prurience, venery, sensuality; *'n* ~ *vir die oë*, a feast for the eyes; ~ **siekte,** satyriasis; ~ '**teling,** sensualist, debauchee, lecher, satyr, sybarite, voluptuary.
wellus'tig, (-e), voluptuous, concupiscent, carnal, lewd, libidinous, lecherous, sensual, prurient, lustful, lascivious; ~ **heid,** voluptuousness, sensuality.
welme'nend, (-e), well-meaning; ~ **heid,** good intention, goodwill.
wel'naat, weld.
wel'omskrywe, well-defined.
wel'oond, simmering oven.
wel'oorwoë, weloorwo'ë, well-considered, deliberate, judicious.
wel'opgevoed, (-e), well-bred, polite, well-educated; ~ **heid,** good breeding.
welp, (-e), cub, whelp.
welrie'kend, (-e), sweet-scented, fragrant, ambrosial, perfumed, aromatic, odoriferous, redolent; ~ **heid,** fragrance, redolence.
Wels, (s) Welsh; (b) **(-e),** Welsh.
welsa'lig, (-e), blessed; ~ **heid,** blessedness, heavenly joy.
wel'sand, quicksand.
wel'slae, success; *'n taak met* ~ *voltooi*, complete a task successfully.
welspre'kend, (-e), eloquent; well-spoken; ~ **heid,** eloquence, oratory; elocution.
wel'staanshalwe, for the sake of decency.
wel'stand, welfare, health, well-being; *in* ~ *LEWE*, live in comfort; *na iem. se* ~ *VERNEEM*, enquire after someone's health.
wel'syn, well-being, good, welfare; health; *vir die algemene* ~ , for the common (public) weal; ~ **beampte,** welfare officer; ~ **organisasie,** welfare organization.
wel'syns: ~ **fonds,** welfare fund; ~ **gevoel,** euphoria.
wel'syn: ~ **staat,** welfare state; ~ **werk,** welfare work.
wel'tergewig, welterweight; ~ **bokskampioen,** welterweight boxing champion.
wel'tevrede, well-satisfied, well-pleased, quite content.
Welt'schmerz, sentimental pessimism about life in general, Weltschmerz.
wel'vaar, (-ge-), be in good health; be successful, thrive.
wel'vaart, welfare, prosperity; ~ **beampte,** welfare officer; ~ **werkster,** welfare worker (lady).
wel'vare, good health.
welva'rend, (-e), prosperous, flourishing, thriving; healthy; ~ **heid,** prosperity; good health.
wel'verdiend, (-e), well-deserved, merited, just (reward).
wel'versnede: *'n* ~ *pen*, a facile pen.
wel'versorg, (-de), well-tended, well-cared for; ~ **dheid,** immaculateness, good grooming.
welvoeg'lik, (-e), proper, becoming, decorous, decent.
welvoeg'likheid, decency, propriety, decorum.
welvoeg'likheidshalwe, for the sake of decency.
wel'voorsien, (-e), well-supplied, well-stocked.
wel'water, well water, spring water.
wel'we, (ge-), vault.
welwil'lend, (-e), kind, kindly disposed, benevolent, favourable, sympathetic (consideration); ~ **heid,** goodwill, kindness, benevolence, consideration; ~ **heidsbesoek,** courtesy (goodwill) visit; ~ **heidswaarde,** goodwill value.
wel'wing, (-s), vault, archway; camber (road).
we'mel, (ge-), swarm, abound in, teem with; *dit* ~ *van FOUTE*, it bristles with mistakes; *die PERSKE* ~ *v.d. wurms*, the peach is alive with worms; *die WATER* ~ *v.d. visse*, the water teems with fish; ~ **end, (-e),** alive; ~ **ing,** swarm, crowd.
wen¹, (s) **(-ne),** windlass.

wen², (s) (-ne), wen, goitre.

wen³, (w) (ge-), accustom, make used to, habituate, familiarize, inure to; *ek is daaraan gewend*, I am accustomed to it.

wen⁴, (w) (ge-), win, gain; (out)distance; reap, harvest; land (a prize); gain the victory; *500 sak KORING* ~, reap 500 bags of wheat; *R400 OP die verkoop* ~, gain R400 on the transaction; *'n SETEL v.d. opposisie* ~, gain a seat from the opposition; *TYD* ~, gain time; *VER* ~, win hands down; *'n WEDSTRYD* ~, win a match.

wen'akker, headland, ba(u)lk.

wen'as, windlass; winch.

wend, (ge-), turn, put about; *hoe jy dit ook* ~ *of KEER*, whichever way you turn; *jou tot iem. om RAAD* ~, turn to someone for advice.

wen'dag, field-day.

wen'dam, catch(ment)-dam.

wend'baar, (..bare), manoeuvrable; ~**heid**, manoeuvrability; docility.

Wen'dies, (s) Wendic, Wendish (language); (b) (-e), Wendish, Wendic.

wen'ding, (-e, -s), turn; bent; jink (aero.); *'n ANDER* ~ *gee*, turn into another channel; *'n GUNSTIGE* ~ *neem*, take a turn for the better.

wen'dingspunt, turning-point, crisis.

We'nen, Vienna (Austria).

We'ner, (-s), Viennese.

wen'gees, spirit of victory.

wen'hou, winning stroke.

we'uling, lamentation, weeping; ~ *en knersing van tande*, weeping and gnashing of teeth.

wenk, (-e), hint, sign, nod, tip, cue, point, pointer, intimation, inkling; *hy word op sy* ~ *e BEDIEN*, his every wish is gratified; *op die EERSTE* ~ *van*, at the first hint; *iem. 'n* ~ *GEE*, drop someone a hint; make a suggestion; *'n* ~ *ter HARTE neem*, take a hint; follow up a suggestion; *'n* ~ *KRY*, receive a hint; ~ **brou = winkbrou**; ~ **vlies**, haw (of animal); ~ **vraag**, leading question.

wen'lansering, winch-launching.

wen'ner, (-s), winner; gainer.

wen'paal, winning-post; straining-post; ~ **foto**, photo-finish.

wen'punt, game point.

wens, (s) (-e), wish, desire; *die* ~ *te KENNE gee*, express a desire; *die opregte* ~ *KOESTER om*, have an honest desire to; *NA* ~, as desired (wished); *die* ~ *is VADER v.d. gedagte*, the wish is father to the thought; *die* ~ *VERVUL van*, gratify the wish of; (w) (ge-), wish, desire, want; *veel te* ~ *e OORLAAT*, leave much to be desired; *VROME* ~, an idle wish; a vain hope; ~ *ende WYS(E)*, optative mood; ~ **denkery**, wishful thinking; ~ **droom**, pipe-dream.

wen'skoot, draw (bowls); winning shot (stroke).

wens'lik, (-e), desirable, expedient; *al wat* ~ *is*, everything of the best, ~ **heid**, desirability, desirableness; *die* ~ *heid uitspreek*, express the wish.

wen: ~ **span**, winning team; ~ **streep**, finish (ath.).

wen'tel, (ge-), roll over; revolve (round sun); rotate (on own axis); gyrate (in circles); welter, wallow (in mud); ~ **as**, reverse (tumbling-) shaft; ~ **baan**, orbit; ~ **bom**, orbital bomb; ~ **ing**, (-e, -s), rotation, revolution; ~ **krediet**, revolving credit; ~ **trap**, spiral (winding) staircase, circular staircase; ~ **vlug**, orbital flight.

wen'tol, winch barrel.

wen'tou, winding-rope.

werd, worth; *die MOEITE* ~, well worth the trouble; *NIE die moeite* ~ *nie*, not worthwhile.

wer'da, halt! who goes there? ~ **komitee**, vigilance committee.

wê'reld, (-e), world; cosmos, universe; part of country, region; *die ANDER* ~, the hereafter; *na die ANDER* ~, gone to kingdom come; *die* ~ *se BELOOP*, the way of the world; *die* ~ *is BOOS*, it is a cruel world, it is an uncharitable world; *in die (ter)* ~ *BRING*, give birth to; bring into the world; *hy het die* ~ *DAARAAN*, he has an intense dislike for something; *die* ~ *van iem. DINK*, think the world of someone; *die DERDE W* ~, the Third World; *die* ~ *DRAAI met hom*, he is reeling; *die* ~ *wil GEE*, be prepared to give anything in the world; *die GELEERDE* ~, the learned world; *hy was by toe die* ~ *GEMAAK is*, he thinks he knows everything; *die GROOT* ~, the fashionable world; the world at large; *uit die* ~ *HELP*, give the quietus to, kill; dispose of; *iem. na die ander* ~ *HELP*, send someone to kingdom come; *die* ~ *INSTUUR*, send out into the world; launch upon the sea of life; *iem. KEN sy* ~, someone knows his way around, is a man of the world; *KLAAR met die* ~ *wees*, be done for; *die* ~ *is baie KLEIN*, it is a small world; *ter* ~ *KOM*, come into the world; be born; *weet wat in die* ~ *te KOOP is*, know the ways of the world; *die* ~ *staan op sy KOP*, everything is topsy-turvy; *die* ~ *is vir A te KOUD*, there is nothing too good for A; *die* ~ *het toe LANGWERPIG geword*, things became difficult; *'n MAN v.d.* ~, a man of the world; *MY* ~! good heavens! my goodness! *vir NIKS ter* ~, not for all the world; *die OU (Nuwe)* ~, the Old (New) World; ~ *e aan mekaar PRAAT*, talk for hours on end; *die* ~ *is 'n PYPKANEEL*, all the world is a stage; *'n REIS om die* ~, a voyage round the world; *wat sal die* ~ *SÊ?* what will Mrs. Grundy (the world, people) say? *die* ~ *SIEN*, see the world; *die* ~ *SKEUR*, run for dear life; *die* ~ *het toe SMAL geword*, he did not know which way to turn; *die* ~ *is 'n SPEELTONEEL*, all the world is a stage; *die hele* ~ *is SYNE*, he has the world at his feet; the world shines for him alone; *jou* ~ *VERSTAAN*, know one's world; *WAAR ter (in die)* ~ *is ons?* where on earth are we? *van die ander* ~ *WEES*, be dead; *die hele* ~ *WEET dit*, the whole world knows about it; *die WYE* ~ *ingaan*, go out into the world; *die* ~ *WYS sy verkeerde kant*, the world seems upside down; (tw): *wêreld!* well I never! ~ **as**, axis of the world; ~ **beeld**, world picture; ~ **beheerser**, master of the world; ~ **beheersing**, world domination, ~ **bekend**, (-e), world-famed; ~ **beroemdheid**, world fame; ~ **beskouing**, philosophy, (view, conception) of life; ~ **beskrywer**, cosmographer; ~ **beskrywing**, cosmography; ~ **betekenis**, world importance; ~ **beweging**, world movement; ~ **bewoner**, earth-dweller; ~ **bol**, globe; ~ **bond**, world federation; ~ **brand**, world war; ~ **burger**, cosmopolitan, cosmopolite; ~ **burgerskap**, cosmopolit(an)ism; ~ **deel**, part of the world; continent; ~ **gebeurtenis**, world event, event of international importance, great event; ~ **gerig**, the last judgement; ~ **geskiedenis**, history of the world; ~ **goudprys**, world gold-price; ~ **handel**, international trade; ~ **heerskappy**, world dominion; ~ **hervormer**, world reformer; ~ **hof**, world (international) court; ~ **kaart**, map of the world; ~ **kampioen**, world champion; ~ **kampioenskap**, world championship; ~ **kennis**, knowledge of the world; ~ **klas**, world class; ~ **kunde**, cosmology; ~ **kundig**, (-e), universally known; ~ **kundig maak**, spread abroad; ~ **lik**, (-e), worldly (goods); temporal (power); secular (music); ~ **ling**, (-e), worldling; ~ **literatuur**, world literature; ~ **mag**, world power; ~ **mark**, world market; ~ **moondheid**, world (great) power; ~ **naam**, world-wide repute, world figure; ~ **omroep**, world service; ~ **onderneming**, world concern; ~ **ontvlugter**, escapist; ~ **ontvlugting**, escapism; ~ **oorheersing**, world domination; ~ **oorlog**, world war; ~ **orde**, world order, cosmogony; ~ **organisasie**, world organization; ~ **politiek**, world politics; ~ **prys**, world price; ~ **reis**, world tour; ~ **reisiger**, globetrotter, world traveller; ~ **rekord**, world record; ~ **rond**, world globe; ~ **ruim**, infinite space; universe; ~ **ryk**, world empire; ~ **s**, (-e), worldly, earthly, carnal; mundane, earthly-minded, secular.

wê'reldsbeloop, way of the world.

wê'reldsee, ocean.

wê'reldsgesind, (-e), worldly-minded; ~ **heid**, worldly-mindedness, secularity; concupiscence (N.T.).

wê'reldsgoed, worldly things; ~ *is EB en vloed*, our worldly goods do not endure; ~ *is soos 'n handvol VLIEË*, worldly goods are like a handful of dust.

wê'reldsheid, mundaneness, worldliness.

wê'reld: ~ **skaarste,** world-wide scarcity; ~ **skepper,** demiurge; ~ **skokkend, (-e),** world-shaking; ~ **smart,** Weltschmerz, sentimental pessimism about things in general; ~ **spil,** axis of the world; ~ **staat,** world power; great (universal) power; ~ **stad,** metropolis; ~ **statebond,** world federation; ~ **stelsel,** cosmic system; ~ **streek,** zone; ~ **taal,** universal language; ~ **tekort,** world shortage; ~ **tentoonstelling,** international exhibition; ~ **toneel,** stage of the world; ~ **verbeteraar,** would-be world reformer; ~ **verbruik,** world consumption; ~ **verkeer,** world traffic; ~ **vermaard, (-e),** world-famed; ~ **veroweraar,** conqueror of the world; ~ **versaking,** renunciation of the world; ~ **voleinding,** end of the world; ~ **voorraad,** world('s) supply; ~ **vraag,** world demand; ~ **vrede,** universal peace; ~ **vreemd, (-e),** strange to the ways of the world; ~ **wonder,** wonder of the world; ~ **wyd,** (.. **wye**), mondial, world-wide; ~ **wys, (-e),** philosophic; world(ly)-wise; sophisticated; ~ **wyse, (-s),** philosopher; ~ **wysheid,** wide experience of life; philosophy; sophistication.

werf¹, (s) (werwe), barnyard, farmyard; shipyard; yard; premises.

werf², (w) (ge-), enlist, enrol, recruit, raise (troops); *stemme* ~, canvass for votes; ~ **agent,** recruiting agent, canvasser; ~ **geld,** recruiting-money; ~ **kantoor,** recruiting office; ~ **krag,** drawing power; ~ **offisier,** recruiting officer.

we'ring, prevention (of disease); exclusion (of cold); fender (fire).

werk, (s) (-e), work, labour, employment, job; *'n* ~ *AANNEEM,* undertake a job, contract for a job; accept a post; ~ *soos BOSSIES,* a mountain of work; *te* ~ *GAAN,* set about doing something; *iem.* ~ *GEE,* find work for someone; ~ *onder HANDE hê,* have work in hand; *hy het meer* ~ *as HARE op die kop,* he is snowed under with work; *dis alles* ~ *wat die KLOK slaan,* work is the order of the day; ~ *KRY,* obtain employment; *baie* ~ *van iem. MAAK,* make a great fuss of someone; *daar* ~ *van MAAK,* set about (see to) it; *MOOI te* ~ *gaan,* proceed in a friendly fashion; *ONDANKBARE* ~, a thankless task; *ONDER die* ~, while at work; *iem.* ~ *OPDRA,* set someone a task; ~ *tot oor jou ORE hê,* be up to one's ears in work; *'n* ~ *PLATLOOP,* get a job done; ~ *SOEK,* seek employment; *SONDER* ~ *wees,* be out of work, be unemployed; *in die* ~ *STEEK,* put someone to work; *alles in die* ~ *STEL,* leave no stone unturned; ~ *maak STERK,* labour warms, sloth harms; ~ *op TYD maak welbereid,* a stitch in time saves nine; ~ *maak VAN iets,* see to something; *VERKEERD te* ~ *gaan,* set about something the wrong way; *iem. anders se VUIL* ~ *doen,* do someone else's dirty work; (w) **(ge-),** work, labour, function; operate (machine); be effective, act; ferment (jam); have diarrhoea; *wie nie* ~ *nie, sal nie EET nie,* idle hand has empty belly; no mill, no meal; *die BIER* ~, the beer is fermenting; *dit sal ten GOEDE* ~, it will be all to the good; *my MAAG* ~, I am suffering from diarrhoea; *die MEDISYNE* ~ *al,* the medicine is already taking effect; *my REM* ~ *nie,* my brake has failed; *die geraas* ~ *op 'n mens se SENUWEES,* the noise gets on one's nerves; *VOEDSEL na binne* ~, eat ravenously; ~ **afbakening,** job reservation; ~ **as,** operating shaft; ~ **baas,** foreman; ~ **bank,** carpenter's (work-) bench; ~ **besparend, (-e),** labour-saving; ~ **besparing,** economy of labour; ~ **broek,** working-trousers; overall, dungarees; ~ **by,** worker bee, honey-bee.

werkda'dig, (-e), active, effective, operative, efficient, practical, efficacious; ~ **heid,** activity, efficaciousness.

werk: ~ **dag,** working day; weekday; ~ **dele,** working parts; ~ **dier,** beast of burden; ~ **doos,** work-box; ~ **druk,** operating pressure; ~ **eloos, (**..**lose),** idle, inactive; ~ **eloosheid,** idleness, inactivity; ~ **end, (-e),** operating, operative, working, active (volcano); acting; *die* ~ *ende STAND,* the working classes; *'n* ~ *e VENNOOT,* an active partner; ~ **ent, (-e),** work(ing) end.

wer'ker, (-s), worker, workman, employee, operator; ~ **s,** labour.

wer'kers: ~ **bond,** trade union, workers' union; ~ **klas,** proletariat.

werk: ~ **esel,** drudge, grub, slave, plodder, glutton for work; ~ **front,** stope face (mining); ~ **geefster,** employer (lady); ~ **gees,** working mood, zeal; ~ **geleentheid,** opportunity for work; ~ **gemeenskap,** working party, study group; ~ **gereedskap,** tools; ~ **gesant,** shop-steward; ~ **geselskap,** Dorcas meeting, working party; ~ **gewer, (-s),** (task)master; employer; ~ **gewersbond,** employer's union; ~ **groep,** working group; ~ **heilig, (-e),** legal; ~ **heilige, (-s),** legalist; ~ **heiligheid,** legalism; ~ **hipotese,** working hypothesis; ~ **huis,** workhouse; ~ **ie, (-s),** little job; *los* ~ *ies,* odd jobs.

wer'king, (-e), action, working, functioning, operation; efficacy, efficiency; effect; *sonder* ~ *BLY,* be inefficient, have no effect; *BUITE* ~ *wees,* be out of action (operation); be idle; *die* ~ *e van die gemoed,* the workings of the mind; *IN* ~, in action; *in* ~ *STEL,* put into action; *buite* ~ *STEL,* suspend; put out of action; *in* ~ *TREE,* take effect; come into operation (force); *in VOLLE* ~, in full swing.

werk: ~ **kaart,** job-card; work ticket; ~ **kamer,** workroom; ~ **kamp,** labour (work-) camp; ~ **kant,** face side; ~ **kapitaal,** working capital; ~ **klere** = **werksklere;** ~ **kolonie,** labour colony; ~ **krag,** energy, capacity for work; ~ **kragte,** manpower; ~ **kring,** field of activity; department; occupation; province; ~ **lamp,** jack-lamp; ~ **las, (-te),** working load; ~ **lewe,** working life; ~ **liede,** workmen, hands.

werk'lik, (b) (-e), real, true, actual; practical; ~ *e DISKONTO,* true discount; ~ *e TREK,* effective pull; (bw) in fact, indeed; ~ *waar,* actually.

werk'likheid, reality; bustle, activity; *dit is 'n HELE* ~, it is quite a to-do; *IN* ~, in reality; in fact; *die* ~ *onder die OË sien,* look facts in the face.

werk'loon, wages, pay.

werk'loos, (..**lose),** unemployed, disemployed, out of work (employment); inoperative, dull, idle, inactive; ~ **heid,** inaction, inactivity; unemployment.

werk'loosheids: ~ **fonds,** unemployment fund; ~ **toelae,** dole; ~ **uitkering,** unemployment benefit; ~ **versekering,** unemployment insurance; ~ **vraagstuk,** unemployment problem.

werk'lose, (-s), unemployed (person).

werk'lui: *see* **werksman.**

werk: ~ **lus,** zest for work; ~ **maat,** fellow-worker, workmate.

werk'man, (-ne, ..**liede,** ..**lui, werksmense),** workman, labourer, artisan, hand, operative, employee.

werk: ~ **mandjie,** work-basket; ~ **manstand,** working class(es); ~ **meester,** overseer, work-master; ~ **meisie,** (work-)maid, housemaid; ~ **merk,** face-mark (woodwork); ~ **mier,** worker ant; ~ **monster,** working sample; ~ **nemer (-s),** employee; *los* ~ *nemer,* jobber, casual workman; ~ **nemersvereniging,** labour association; ~ **nemersverteenwoordiger,** employees' representative.

werkolis', (-te), workaholic.

werk: ~ **ontleding,** job-analysis; ~ **opsigter,** job-clerk; overseer; clerk of works; ~ **pak,** overalls; working-suit, everyday clothes; ~ **pas,** work-seeking pass; ~ **peloton,** fatigue party; ~ **perd,** working (dray-) horse; ~ **plaas,** workshop, work-room; ~ **plan,** working plan, scheme to work on; ~ **plek,** work-shop, work-room; factory; ~ **plig,** obligation to work; ~ **ploeg,** shift, relay of labourers; working party, gang; ~ **program,** working programme, scheme to work on; ~ **put,** (garage) pit; ~ **rand,** working edge; ~ **rat,** actuating gear; ~ **rooster,** work-schedule, timetable; ~ **ruimte,** working space; ~ **saal,** work-room.

werk'saam, (..**same),** active, industrious, laborious, diligent; effective; *NUTTIG* ~ *wees,* be usefully employed, do useful work; *op (in) 'n fabriek* ~ *WEES,* be employed in a factory; ~ **heid,** activity, business, work; agency; laboriousness; ~ *hede van die vergadering,* the business before the meeting.

werk'sakkie, housewife (sewing-)case, tidy.

werks: ~ **broek** = **werkbroek;** ~ **klere** = **werkklere.**

werk: ~**skool,** continuation school for workers; ~**sku, (-we),** work-shy; ~**skuheid,** work-shyness, work-dodging; ~**skuwe, (-s),** spiv, shirker.
werks'man, (-ne, ..liede, ..lui, ..mense) = **werkman.**
werk'soeker, work-seeker.
werk: ~**span,** gang (of labourers); ~**spanning,** operating stress.
werks'perd = **werkperd.**
werk'spil, actuating spindle.
werk: ~**staker, (-s),** striker; ~**staking, (-e, -s),** strike; ~**stang,** operating rod; ~**stel,** actuating gear; ~**ster, (-s),** worker (female); charwoman; ~**student,** working student; ~**stuk,** piece of work; problem.
werks'toestand, working condition.
werks'winkel = **werkwinkel.**
werk: ~**tafel,** work-table; ~**tekening,** working drawing; ~**tempo,** tempo of work; ~**terapie,** occupational therapy.
werk'tuig, tool, implement; cat's-paw, creature, puppet; organ; engine; ~**kunde,** mechanics; mechanical(-engineering) science; ~**kun'dig, (-e),** mechanical; ~**kun'dige, (-s),** mechanician, engine-builder, mechanic, mechanical engineer; ~**'lik, (-e),** mechanical, automatic(al); ~**'likheid,** mechanicalness; ~**masjien,** machine tool; ~**staal,** tool-steel; ~**tekene,** machine-drawing; ~**tekening,** machine drawing.
werk: ~**tyd,** hours of work, working hours; ~**uur,** working hour; ~**vakansie,** busman's holiday; ~**veer,** actuating spring; ~**verdeling,** division of work; ~**vermoë,** capacity (machine), working capacity; ~**verrigting,** performance; ~**verskaffing,** (providing of) employment, relief-works; ~**verskaffingsdiens,** employment service; ~**verskaffingskantoor,** employment office; ~**vlak,** work face, face side; ~**volk,** labourers, workmen; ~**voorskoot,** work-apron; ~**vrou,** charwoman; ~**week,** working week; ~**weerstand,** resistivity; ~**willig, (-e),** willing to work; ~**willige, (-s),** non-striker; ~**winkel,** workshop; ~**woord,** verb; ~**woor'delik, (-e),** verbal; ~**wyse,** method of work, procedure; plan of action; ~**ywer,** zest for work, industry, diligence.
werp, (s),(-e), throw; (w) **(ge-),** cast, throw, fling; project; litter; *'n AANTYGING van jou* ~, repudiate a charge; *ANKER* ~, cast blame on someone; *'n BLIK op iem.* ~, cast a glance at someone; *LIG op iets* ~, throw light on something; *die SKULD op iem.* ~, lay the blame on someone; ~**anker,** kedge; grapnel; stream-anchor; ~**draad,** woof; ~**er, (-s),** flinger, thrower; ~**garing,** woof; ~**geskut,** mangonel; ~**hout,** boomerang; ~**koord,** lasso; ~**lood,** sounding-lead; plumb-bob; ~**lyn,** painter; pilot line; ~**net,** cast(ing)-net; ~**pyltjie,** dart; ~**ring,** quoit; ~**sel,** litter; farrow (piglets); ~**skyf,** quoit; disc(us); ~**spies,** javelin; dart; ~**tros,** warp; ~**tuig,** projectile, missile; ~**verligting,** flood-lighting; *onder* ~ *verligting,* flood-lit.
wer'skaf, (ge-), do, make, be busy; *wat* ~ *jy?* what are you doing? ~**fery,** being busy, bustling, bustle, working, fuss.
werst, (-e), verst.
wer'waarts, whither.
wer'we, (ge-) = **werf².**
wer'wel, (s) (-s), window-fastener; (cupboard-)button, hasp, thumb-latch; swivel; vertebra (anat.); *die deur is op* ~, the door is on the latch; (w) **(ge-),** eddy, whirl, swirl; ~**been,** vertebra; ~**beweging,** vortex motion; ~**dier,** vertebrate animal; ~**ing,** vortex, swirl, whirl; ~**kamer,** whirl chamber; ~**kolom,** spinal column; ~**kop,** turbulence head; ~**storm,** cyclone, tornado; ~**stroom,** vagrant current (elec.); ~**vormig, (-e),** shaped like vertebrae; ~**wind,** whirlwind.
wer'wer, (-s), recruiter; canvasser; tout, barker.
wer'wing, (-s), recruiting; canvassing; enrolment; enlistment; touting.
wer'wings: ~**depot,** recruiting depot; ~**offisier,** recruiting officer.
wes, west; ~ *van,* west of.

Wes'-Afrika, West Africa.
Wes'-Afrikaan, (..kane), West African; ~**s, (-e),** West African.
Wes'-Australië, Western Australia.
Wes'-Australies, (-e), West Australian.
Wes'-Duits, West(ern) German.
Wes'-Duitsland, West(ern) Germany.
we'se, (-ns), being, creature; nature; existence; entity; essence; face, looks; *in* ~ *LAAT,* leave in existence; *geen LEWENDE* ~ *nie,* not a living soul; *die man se* ~ *LYK my bekend,* he looks familiar to me; *die instelling het in* ~ *VERANDER,* the character of the institution has changed entirely.
we'sefonds, orphans' fund.
wes'einde, west end.
we'sel, (-s), weasel, mink; ~**agtig, (-e),** musteline; ~**bont,** mink (fur); ~**bontjas,** mink coat.
we'senlik, (-e), elemental, essential, real, actual, fundamental, constitutive, substantial, material; *die* ~*e BEDOELING,* the actual aim; ~*e BESTANDDEEL,* constituent; ~**heid,** reality, essentiality; quiddity.
we'senloos, (..lose), senseless, blank, stupid, vacant, expressionless; *iem.* ~ *aanstaar,* stare vacantly at someone; ~**heid,** vacancy, vacuity, blankness, inanimation.
we'sensleer, ontology.
we'senstrek, facial expression, lineament, feature.
we'sensvol, (-le), full of expression, expressive, meaningful; ~**heid,** expressiveness, meaningfulness.
we'sentjie, (-s), small creature, diminutive being.
we'sentlik = **wesenlik.**
Wes'-Europa, Western Europe.
Wes'-Europeaan, (..peane), ..peër, (-s), Western European.
Wes'-Europees, (..pese), West European.
Wesfaals', (-e), Westphalian.
Wesfa'le, Westphalia; ~**r, (-s),** Westphalian.
Wes'-Friesland, Western Friesland.
Wes'gote, Visigoths.
Wes'-Goties, (-e), Visigothic.
wes'grens, western boundary (frontier).
wes'halwe, wherefore, on which account.
we'sie, (-s), little orphan.
Wes-In'dië, the West-Indies; ~**r, (-s),** West Indian.
Wes-In'dies, (-e), West-Indian.
Wes-In'diëvaarder, (-s), West Indiaman.
Wes'-Kaapland, the Western Cape.
wes'kus, west coast.
Wesleyaan', (..ane), Wesleyan; ~**s', (-e),** Wesleyan.
wes'moeson, west monsoon.
wes'noordwes, west-north west; ~**telik, (-e),** west-north-westerly.
wesp, (-e), wasp, hornet; ~**e-angel,** wasp's sting; ~**enes,** wasp's (hornet's) nest, vespiary.
Wes'-Pruis, West Prussian; ~**e,** West Prussia; ~**ies, (-e),** West Prussian.
Wes'-Romeins, West Roman; ~*e Ryk,* Roman Empire of the West.
wes'suidwes, west-south-west; ~**telik, (-e),** west-south-westerly.
Wes'te¹: *die* ~, the Occident; the Western Powers.
wes'te², west, occident.
wes'te³: *buite* ~, senseless.
wes'te: ~**hoek,** west corner; ~**kant,** west side; ~**lik, (-e),** westerly, western, Hesperian.
wes'terfront, western front.
wes'tergrens = **wesgrens.**
wes'tering, westing.
wes'ter: ~**kim,** western horizon; ~**lengte,** west(ern) longitude.
Wes'terling, (-e), Westerner.
Wes'ters, (-e), Western, Occidental.
wes'tewind, west wind.
Wes'-Transvaal, the Western Transvaal.
Wes'-Virginië, West Virginia.
Wes'-Vlaams, (-e), West Flemish.
Wes'-Vlaandere, Western Flanders.
wes'waarts, (-e), westward.
wet¹, (s) (-te), law; act; *'n* ~ *AANNEEM,* pass an act (a law); *by* ~ *BEPAAL,* stipulate (define) by law; *die* ~ *maak DOOD,* the letter killeth; ~ *van GE-*

MIDDELDES, law of averages; *'n ~ INDIEN*, introduce a bill; *KRAG van ~ kry*, become (aquire the force of) law; *die ~ van MEDE en PERSE*, the law of the Medes and Persians; *die MOSAÏESE ~*, the Mosaic law; *'n ~ OORTREE*, contravene a law; *'n ~ OPHEF*, repeal a law; *binne die PERKE van die ~*, within the limits of the law; *iem. die ~ STEL*, lay down the law; *die ~ TOEPAS*, apply the law; *die ~ UITVOER*, carry out the law; *geldig VOLGENS die ~*, valid at law; *VOOR die ~*, in the eyes of the law; *iem. die ~ VOORSKRYF*, lay down the law for someone; *~ WORD*, become law.

wet², (w) **(ge-)**, sharpen, whet; *die tande ~*, look forward eagerly (keenly).

wet'boek, law-book; statute-book; code of law; codex; *BURGERLIKE ~*, civil code; *in die ~ OPNEEM*, place on the statute-book; *~ van STRAFREG*, criminal code.

wet: ~ **breker**, law-breaker; ~ **breuk**, breach of the law.

we'te, knowing, knowledge; *teen BETER ~ hoop*, hope against hope; *teen jou BETER ~*, against one's better knowledge; *BUITE my ~*, without my knowledge; *BY my ~*, as far as I know; *iem. die ~ DOEN*, inform someone; *te ~ KOM*, come to know; *NA my ~*, as far as I know; *TE ~*, namely, to wit, viz.

we'tens, knowlingly.

we'tenskap, **(-pe)**, science, knowledge, learning; ~ **'lik**, (-e), scientific; ~ **'like**, (-s), scientist; ~ **'likheid**, scientific character.

we'tenskap: ~ **leer**, theory of science; ~ **mens**, man (woman) of science, scientist.

wetenswaar'dig, (-e), worth knowing, interesting; ~ **heid**, (..hede), something worth knowing.

wet'gehoorsaam, (..same), law-abiding.

wet'geleerd, (-e), versed in the law; knowing; *iem. is ~*, someone knows all the answers; ~ **e**, (-s), lawyer, jurist; ~ **heid**, jurisprudence, law.

wet'getrou, (-e), law-abiding; ~ **heid**, law-abidingness.

wet'gewend, (-e), legislative, law-making; constitutive; *~ e LIGGAAM*, legislature; *~ e MAG*, constitutive power, legislature.

wet: ~ **gewer**, (-s), legislator, law-giver; ~ **gewing**, (-s), legislation; legislature; ~ **houer**, alderman; ~ **kenner**, lawyer, jurist.

wet'lik, (-e), legal, jural; lawful (proof); statutory (provisions); ~ **heid**, legality, lawfulness.

wetma'tig, (-e), according to law.

wets: ~ **agent**, law-agent; ~ **artikel**, clause of a law; section of an act; ~ **bepaling**, stipulation of the law; ~ **gehoorsaam**, (..same), law-abiding; ~ **gehoorsamig**, (-e), law-abiding; ~ **gelykheid**, isonomy; ~ **genootskap**, law society; ~ **getroue**, law-abiding; ~ **hersiening**, revision of the law; ~ **interpretasie**, interpretation of the law.

wet'skender, violator of the law.

wet'skennis, law-breaking.

wets: ~ **kennis**, legal knowledge; ~ **konsep**, draft bill; ~ **kwessie**, question of law; ~ **misbruik**, abuse of the law; ~ **ontduiker**, evader of the law; ~ **ontwerp**, bill, draft act; measure; ~ **oortreder**, (-s), law-breaker; ~ **oortreding**, breach of law, delict, offence; ~ **opsteller**, legal draftsman; ~ **praktyk**, practice of the law; legal practice (office); ~ **punt**, *see* **regspunt**; ~ **reël**, rule of law; ~ **rol**, scroll of the law; ~ **taal**, legal language.

wet: ~ **staal**, butcher's steel, knife-sharpener; ~ **steen**, whetstone; ~ **stoeptassing**, law enforcement.

wet'teks, text of a law.

wet'teloos, (..lose), lawless, anarchic(al); ~ **heid**, lawlessness, anarchy, anarchism.

wet'tereg, statute law; ~ **telik**, (-e), statutory.

wet'term, legal term.

wet'ties, (-e), keeping the letter of the law; orthodox, rigid; ~ **heid**, legalism.

wet'tig, (w) **(ge-)**, justify, warrant; regularize, authorize, legalize, legitimatize (a child); *dit ~ nie so 'n stap nie*, that does not justify such a measure; (b) **(-e)**, legal, legitimate, genuine; *~ e BETAALMID-*

DEL, legal tender; *~ e EGGENOOT*, lawful spouse; *~ e ERFGENAAM*, heir-at-law; *~ e HOUER*, holder in due course; *~ e OPVOLGING*, testamentary succession; ~ **heid**, legitimacy, legality; ~ **ing**, legitimation, justification, legalization; ~ **lik**, lawfully, legally; ~ **verklaring**, legitimation.

wet: ~ **toepassing**, law enforcement; ~ **uitlegging**, interpretation of the law; ~ **uitvoering**, administration of the law; ~ **verandering**, change of the law; ~ **verbreker**, law-breaker; ~ **verbreking**, breach of the law; ~ **verdraaiing**, perversion of the law; ~ **vereniging**, law society; ~ **verklaring**, legitimation; ~ **verkragter**, (-s), law-breaker; ~ **verkragting**, violation of the law; ~ **voorstel**, legislative proposition bill; ~ **wysiging**, amendment of the law.

we'we, **(ge-)**, weave.

we'wenaar, (-s), widower; ~ **s**: *see* **knapsekerwels**.

we'wenaarsbeentjie, funny-bone.

we'wer, (-s), weaver.

we'wers: ~ **boom**, weaver's beam; loom tree; ~ **gilde**, weavers' guild; ~ **kam**, reed; ~ **knoop**, weaver's knot.

we'wer, ~ **tjie**, (-s), weaver-bird; chuck; ~ **voël**, bishop-bird; ~ **y**, (-e), weaving-mill, cotton factory.

whê! so there!

whis'ky, whisk(e)y; ~ **-en-soda**, whisk(e)y and soda.

whist, whist (cards).

wie, (vr vnw) who; *~ is DAAR?* who's there? *~ kon dit DINK?* who could imagine that? *met ~ PRAAT ek?* with whom am I speaking? (onbep. vnw): *~ dan ook*, whoever; (betr. vnw), whom, he who.

wie'bel, **(ge-)**, wobble, wiggle, rock.

wied, **(ge-)**, weed.

wieg, (s) **(wieë, -e)**, cradle, cot; launching-cradle (ship); *vir iets in die ~ GELÊ wees*, destined to; born to; *van die ~ tot in die GRAF*, from the cradle to the grave; *in die ~ SMOOR*, stifle in the cradle; nip in the bud; *VAN die ~ af*, from one's cradle-days; (w) **(ge-)**, rock, jiggle, dandle, lull to sleep; *aan die slaap ~*, rock to sleep.

wie'g(e)druk, incunabulum, cradle-book.

wie'gel, **(ge-)**, rock, wiggle.

wie'g(e)lied, lullaby, cradle-song, berceuse.

wieg'klip, rocking-stone.

wie'geling, (-s), rocking, (oscillating) movement, wobbling.

wieg'sif, baby (diggings).

wiek¹, (-e), wing (of bird); vane (of propeller); pinion; wick (of candle); *op eie ~ e DRYWE*, paddle one's own canoe; *die ~ e KORT*, clip the wings.

wiek², (-e), vetch; ~ **hooi**, vetch hay.

wiek: ~ **slag**, beat(ing) of wings; ~ **wiel**, vane wheel.

wiel, (-e), wheel; *iem. in die ~ e RY*, thwart a person, put a spoke in someone's wheel; *tussen die ~ e SIT*, be travelling; *die ~ e SPOOR nie*, the wheels are out of alignment; *'n VYFDE ~ aan die wa*, a fifth wheel to the coach; ~ **as**, wheel axle; ~ **band**, tyre, hoop of the wheel; ~ **basis**, wheel-base; ~ **bedding**, wheel seat; ~ **beslag**, wheel trim; ~ **besturing**, wheel-control; ~ **blok**, chock; ~ **breedte**, wheel-tread; ~ **diertjie**, wheel-animal (cule); rotifer; ~ **dop**, hub-cap; ~ **dryfas**, axle-shaft.

wie'letjie, (-s), small wheel; rowel (on spur); castor (on chair), trundle.

wie'lewaal, (..wale), oriole.

wiel'flens, wheel-flange.

wie'l(i)ewaai, **(ge-)**, wheel round and round in a circle; wheel, mill, spin (round).

wiel(i)ewa'lie, merry-go-round (children's wheeling game).

wie'ling, (-e, -s), eddy, whirlpool, wheeling.

wiel: ~ **katrol**, gin wheel, gin block; ~ **ketting**, tyre chain, wheel chain; ~ **klep**, wheel valve; ~ **leer**, ladder on wheels; ~ **maker**, (-s), wheelwright; ~ **moer**, wheel nut; ~ **naaf**, nave of wheel; ~ **rem**, wheel-brake.

wiel'ryer, (-s), cyclist.

wiel: ~ **sak**, sun-cover (on spare wheel); ~ **skrop**, carrying-scraper; ~ **sleutel**, wheel-spanner; ~ **speek**, spoke; ~ **spoor**, rut; ~ **sporing**, wheel alignment; ~ **stoomboot**, paddle-steamer; ~ **stut**, wheel strut;

wier 643 *wimpel*

~**tand**, mill cog; ~**trekker**, wheel puller; ~**vlug**, camber; ~**vormig, (-e)**, wheel-shaped.
wier, seaweed, alga.
wie'rook, (frank)incense; fume, olibanum; *iem.* ~ *toeswaai*, laud someone to the skies; ~**bak**, censer; ~**brander**, incense burner; ~**damp**, incense vapour; ~**draer**, thurifer; ~**geur**, smell of incence; ~**offer**, incense offering; ~**skaal**, censer, incense boat; ~**stokkie**, joss-stick; ~**swaaier, (-s)**, thurifer; ~**vat**, censer, thurible; ~**voortbrengend, (-e)**, thuriferous; ~**walm**, fumes of incense; ~**wolk**, cloud of incense.
wies(i)ewa'sie, (-s), trifle; whim, caprice; nonsense.
wig[1], **(wie, -ge)**, wedge, cleat, chock, quoin, key (archit.); scotch (before wheel); *'n* ~ *indryf tussen*, drive a wedge between.
wig[2], **(-te)**, baby, child.
wig'been, sphenoid bone.
wig'gel, (ge-), divine (water); foretell, predict, augur (from omens); ~**aar, (-s)**, diviner, soothsayer, astrologer, augur; ~**ary'**, augury, divination; ~**roede**, ~**stok**, divining-rod, dowsing-rod, dowser.
wig: ~**hak**, wedge heel; ~**hoek**, angle of wedge; ~**holte**, key-bed; ~**las, (-se)**, wedged joint; ~**skrif**, cuneiform writing; ~**steen**, quoin; ~**stuk**, saddleback; wedge piece; ~**vormig, (-e)**, wedge-shaped, cuneiform, cuneal, cuneate; ~**werk**, keying.
wig'wam, (-s), wigwam
wik, (ge-), reflect, weigh, poise; *die MENS* ~, *maar GOD beskik*, man proposes, but God disposes, *en WEEG*, weigh the pros and cons.
Wi'king, (-s), Viking.
wik'ke, vetch, chickling; *see* **wiek**[2].
wik'kel, (ge-), wrap, wind round; wobble, rock, waggle, move from side to side; engage, involve (in war); envelop; move (along); hurry up; *aan 'n SPYKER* ~, try to prize a nail loose; *in 'n TWIS ge*~ *raak*, become involved in a quarrel; ~**aar, (-s)**, winder; ~**ing**, involving; wrapping (parcels); winding (elec.); wobbling, rocking; ~**doedie**, go-go girl; ~**rig, (-e)**, wobbly; ~**wa**: *ounooi se* ~*wa*, the iron horse, train.
wiks, (s) (-e), slap, smack, blow; (w) **(ge-)**, beat, flog, slap, smack.
wil, (s) will, wish, desire, volition; *met die BESTE* ~ *van die wêreld*, with the best will in the world; *die* ~ *vir die DAAD neem*, take the will for the deed; *teen* ~ *en DANK*, in spite of oneself; *jou* ~ *staan agter die DEUR*, wishers and woulders make no good householders; shall and will are for the king; *sy* ~ *DEURDRYF*, assert one's will; *uit EIE (vrye)* ~, of one's own accord; *U* ~ *GESKIED*, Thy will be done; *'n klein* ~ *dra 'n groot GEWIG weg*, a little willingness can work wonders; *GOEIE* ~, goodwill; ~ *is KAN*, where there is a will there is a way; *'n mens se wil is 'n mens se LEWE*, to be free to do as one wishes is to live; *TER* ~ *le van*, for the sake of; *UITERSTE (laaste)* ~ *(en testament)*, someone's last will; *teen die* ~ *VAN*, against the wishes of; *uit VRYE* ~, of one's own free will; *iem ter* ~ *le WEES*, comply with someone's wishes; *waar 'n* ~ *is, is 'n WEG*, where there is a will there is a way; *met die beste* ~ *ter WÊRELD*, with the best will in the world; *sy* ~ *is WET*, his will is law; (w) **(wou, ge-)**, wish, want to desire, be willing, intend; *dit* ~ *by my nie IN nie*, I simply can't believe it; ~ *is KAN*, where there's a will there's a way; *die LOT het dit anders ge* ~, fate decreed otherwise; ~ *jy nou MEER!*, well, I never! *dit* ~ *SÊ*, that is to say; *dit* ~ *my VOORKOM*, it seems to me; *wat* ~ *daardie WOORD sê?* what does that word mean?
wild, (-e) game; venison; chase; quarry; *in die* ~*e weg*, at random, indiscriminately; (b) **(-e)**, wild (country); untamed, savage, feral, ferine, ferocious (animal); frantic (attempt); unruly (child); fierce (passion); boisterous (wind); coltish, hare-brained, hoydenish (girl); ~**agtig, (-e)**, inclined to be wild; gamelike; ~**bewaarder**, game warden; ~**dief**, poacher; ~**diewery**, poaching.
wil'de, (-s), savage; (b), wild; ~**als'**, wormwood *(Artemisia afra)*; ~**aman'del**, African almond; *Brabeium stellatifolium*; ~**appel**, crab-apple; ~**appelkoos**, wild apricot *(Donyalis tristis)*; ~**banana**, wild banana *(Strelitzia augusta)*; ~**bees**, wildebeest, gnu; ~**beesgras**, lemon-grass; ~**bras**, filly; wild (unruly) boy (girl); tomboy; ~**druif**, wild grape *(Rhoicissus spp.)*; ~**eend**, wild duck; mallard; broad-bill; ~**-er'tjie**, vetch *(Dolichos gibbosus)*; ~**-esel**, wild ass, onager; ~**gans**, wild-goose, booby; ~**hawer**, wild oats *(Avena fatua)*; cow-grass; ~**hoender**, guinea-fowl; water-fowl, coot, moorhen; ~**hond**, wild dog, (Cape) hunting-dog; ~**kalkoen**, bald ibis; ~**kapok**, wild cotton *(Asclepias fruticosa)*; ~**kastai'ing**, wild chestnut *(Brabeium stellatifolium)*; ~**kat**, wild cat; catamountain; ~**katjiepiering**, *Gardenia Thunbergia*; ~**katoen'**, wild cotton *(Gossypium herbaceum)*; ~**kerwel**, cow-parsley; ~**klawer**, cow-grass; ~**klawersaad**, burg; ~**knoffel**, wild garlic *(Tulbaghia alliacea)*; ~**kopi'va**, *Bulbine asphodeloides*; ~**makou'**, spurwing goose; ~**mal'va**, *Pelargonium culcullatum*.
wil'deman, savage, barbarian.
wilde: ~**moer'bei**, Cape mulberry; ~**perd**, zebra; zebra-fish; ~**perske**, porkwood, wild peach *(Kiggelaria africana)*; ~**pie'sang** = **wildebanana**; ~**pou**, bustard; ~**pruim'**, bullace, wild plum *(Ximenia caffra)*.
wil'dernis, (-se), wilderness, waste.
wil'de: ~**sa'go**, South African plantain; ~**salie**, *Salvia spp.*; ~**sering'**, wild seringa *(Burkea africana)*; ~**stokroos**, Deccan hemp; ~**suring**, oxalis; ~**tabak'**, wild tobacco plant *(Nicotiana glauca)*.
wil'devarkjag, pig-sticking; ~**ter**, pig-sticker (-hunter).
wil'de: ~**vrug**, bullace; ~**vy**, wild fig *(Ficus capensis)*; ~**weghol(stuipe)**, panic; ~**wingerd**, *Cliffortia odorata*; Virginia creeper; bryony; ~**wol'haarpraatjies**, irresponsible talk, trash, nonsense; ~**wrag'tig, (s)**, scarecrow; woman with untidy hair; hothead, firebrand.
wild: ~**heid**, ferocity; savageness, wildness; ~**leer**, antelope leather; ~**opsigter**, gamekeeper; ~**park**, ~**reservaat**, game reserve; ~**ryk, (-e)**, abounding in game ~**sang**, warbling; tomboy.
wilds: ~**biltong**, game biltong; ~**blad**, shoulder of venison; ~**bok**, wild buck, antelope; ~**boud**, leg of venison; ~**braad**, roast venison; ~**vleis**, game; venison; ~**vleispastei**, game pie.
wild: ~**skade**, damage caused by game; ~**skut**, hunter; ~**smaak**, gamy taste; ~**sop**, game soup; ~**stelery**, poaching; ~**stroper**, poacher; ~**tuin**, game reserve; ~**vanger**, game catcher; game capture officer; ~**vreemd, (-e)**, completely strange; ~**vuur**, wildfire (in tobacco); ~**wagter**, game warden.
wilg, (-e), wil'ger, (-s), willow.
wil'ge(r): ~**boom**, willow-(tree); ~**bossie**, osier-bed; ~**groen**, celadon; ~**katjie**, catkin; ~**lat**, osier; ~**tak**, willow-twig.
wil'lekeur, arbitrariness; discretion; despotism; *na* ~ *arbitrarily, at will*.
willekeu'rig, (-e), arbitrary; discretionary; gratuitous; voluntary (muscles); despotic; *neem 'n* ~*e AANTAL*, take any number; ~*e SPIER*, voluntary muscle; ~**heid**, arbitrariness.
wil'lens, on purpose; ~ *of ONWILLENS*, willy-nilly; ~ *WEES*, intend; ~ *en WETENS*, deliberately, with full knowledge and intent.
wil'lie, (-s), green (sombre) bulbul *(Andropodus importunus)*.
wil'lig, (-e), willing, docile; of easy virtue (woman); animated (of market); ~**heid**, willingness; firmness (market); ~**lik**, voluntarily.
wil'loos, (..lose), without a will of one's own, passive, irresolute; ~**heid**, irresolution, passivity.
wil'sand = **welsand**.
wils'beskikking, (last) will, testament; *sy uiterste* ~, his last will.
wils: ~**daad**, act of volition; ~**inspanning**, effort of will; ~**krag**, will-power; ~**uiting, (-e, -s)**, ~**verklaring**, declaration of intention; ~**vryheid**, free will.
wil'swak, (ke), weak willed; ~**te**, weakness of will.
wim'pel, (-s), pennant, pennon, pendant, banderol(e),

streamer (on flag); ~**vis**, angel-fish *(Heniochus acuminatus)*.
wim'per, (-s), eyelash; ~**kruller**, eyelash curler.
win, (ge-), win, gain; enlist (sympathy); recover (mining); harvest, reap; *jou BROOD* ~, earn one's living; *aan DUIDELIKHEID* ~, gain in clearness; *'n vriend se VERTROUE* ~, gain a friend's confidence; *see* **wen**; (w), ~**baar**, (..**bare**), recoverable.
wind[1], (s) (-e), wind, breeze; flatulence; fart; ~ *AF seil*, sail before the wind; *die* ~ *van AGTER hê*, have a following wind; *DEUR die* ~ *wees*, talk airy nonsense; be confused; *dit GAAN met iem*. ~ *op*, it's uphill work for someone; *dit GAAN voor die* ~, it is plain sailing; ~ *op GAAN*, be making heavy weather; *die* ~ *waai v.d. GARSLAND af*, there's an icy wind blowing; *iem. die* ~ *van voor GEE*, take someone to task; *so GOU soos die* ~, as quick as lightning; *waai die* ~ *uit daardie HOEK uit?* is that how the land lies? *die* ~ *waai uit die verkeerde HOEK*, the wind is in the wrong quarter; *'n* ~ *jie HOOR waai*, hear it rumoured; *die* ~ *van voor KRY*, be taken to task; *'n* ~ *LAAT*, pass a wind, fart; *'n mens kan van* ~ *alleen nie LEEF nie*, one can't live on air; *van* ~ *LEWE*, live on air; ~ *op LOOP*, walk against the wind; ~ *MAAK (sonder stof)*, brag; bluster; blow off hot air; *ONDERKANT die* ~ *hou*, keep on die lee side (of game); *'n* ~ *OPBREEK*, break a wind; *in die* ~ *PRAAT*, preach to the winds; waste one's breath; *dis alles PURE* ~, it's all empty talk; *die* ~ *kom die REËN*, sadness and gladness succeed each other; *met elke* ~ *SAAMWAAI*, be a weathercock (fig.); *iem die* ~ *uit die SEILE neem*, take the wind out of someone's sails; *raad in die* ~ *SLAAN*, throw advice to the winds; *die* ~ *SNY*, run like the wind; *vir iem*. ~ *SNY*, lend someone a helping hand; make smooth the way for someone; *hy is SOOS die* ~ *waai*, he is opportunistic (capricious); *SOOS die* ~, like the wind; ~ *sonder STOF*, empty boasting; *wie* ~ *saai, sal die STORMWIND maai*, he who sows the wind, shall reap the whirlwind; *'n mens kan VAN* ~ *alleen nie leef nie*, one can't live on air; *die* ~ *VERSKRAAL*, the wind is becoming icy; *VLAK teen die* ~, in the teeth of the wind; *die* ~ *van VOOR kry*, run into trouble; make heavy weather; *daar WAAI geen* ~ *nie of dit is iem. van nut*, it's an ill wind that blows nobody good; *soos die* ~ *WAAI*, as variable as the wind; *'n kind vir* ~ *en WEER grootmaak*, let a child run wild; *in* ~ *en WEER*, in all weathers.
wind[2], (w) (ge-), wind, swathe.
wind: ~**afdryfmiddel**, carminative; ~**afdry'wend**, (-e), carminative; ~**afsetting**, aeolian deposit.
win'dam = **wendam**.
wind'as, windlass, gin, wheel and axle, whim, crab.
wind: ~**barsie**, (-s), chap, crack (on the hands); surface crack; ~**beskrywing**, anemography; ~**bestuif**, (-de), wind-pollinated; ~**bestuiwing**, wind-pollination; ~**blom**, anemone; ~**boom**, capstan-bar; ~**breker**, windscreen; ~**bui**, gust of wind; ~**buks**, (-e), air-gun; boaster, gasbag, popinjay, windbag; ~**dig**, (-te), wind-proof; ~**drif**, wind-drift; ~**droging**, natural seasoning (wood); ~**droog**, (..**droë**), partially dry, almost dry; air-dried; ~**druk**, wind pressure.
win'de, convolvulus; ide (fish).
wind'ei, wind-toy (fish).
wind'eier, soft-shelled egg; wind-egg; farce, failure; *dit sal nie vir hom 'n* ~ *lê nie*, that will earn him a pretty penny.
win'derig, (-e), windy, breezy, gusty; puffy; flatulent; ~**heid**, windiness; flatulence; puffiness.
wind: ~**erosie**, aeolian erosion; wind erosion; ~**gat**, (-te), gasbag, windbag, boaster; ~(-**e**), air-hole; ~**geweer**, air-gun; ~**god**, wind-god, Aeolus; ~**handel**, stock-jobbing, bubble, gambling on the Stock Exchange; ~**harp**, Aeolian harp; ~**heining**, windbreak, windscreen; ~**hoek**, quarter from which the wind blows; windy corner; ~**hond**, greyhound, whippet; ~**hoos**, tornado, wind spout.
win'ding, (-e, -s), winding; coil (cable); convolution (shell); gyrus (cerebrum).

wind: ~**jie**, (-s), breeze, breath of air; *'n* ~ *jie HOOR waai*, hear a rumour that ...; *'n* ~ *jie LAAT*, break wind; ~**kaart**, wind-chart; ~**kant**, windy side, weather-side; ~**klep**, air-valve, vent; ~**koliek**, tympanites; ~**korrel**, vane-sight; ~**kous**, drogue, wind-sock; ~**krag**, wind-power; ~**kussing**, air-cushion, air-pillow; ~**lawaai**, boaster, gasbag, windbag; ~**leer**, anemology.
wind'maak, (-ge-), boast, brag, swank, show off.
wind'maker, (s) (-s), boaster, gasbag, windbag; coxcomb, dandy, showman; (b) smart, posh; ~**bos**, *Passerina filiformis*; ~**goed**, hot stuff; ~**ig**, (-e), boasting, bragging; dandy, nobby, flashy, swaggering, dressy, hot-stuff, ostentatious; ~**igheid**, ostentatiousness, gasconade; ~**y**, coxcombry, swank.
wind'meter, wind-gauge, anemometer.
wind'meting, anemometry.
wind'meul(e), windmill; *teen* ~ *e(n)s veg*, tilt against windmills; ~**pomp**, windmill; ~**vliegtuig**, autogyro, gyroplane, helicopter.
wind: ~**orrel**, wind organ; empty-headed person, gasbag, windbag; ~**pasteitjie**, vol-au-vent; ~**rigting**, direction of the wind; ~(**rigting**)**wyser**, anemoscope; ~**roer**, air-gun; ~**roos**, compass-card, rhumb-card; wind rose; anemone; ~**ruk**, gust of wind; ~**ry**, wind row; ~**sak**, gasbag; wind sock; bladder (football).
wind'sel, (-s), bandage, swathe, dressing.
wind: ~**skade**, damage caused by wind; ~**skeef**, (..**skewe**), skew, slightly crooked, lopsided, wry; ~**skerm**, windbreak; windscreen (of car); ~**skermveër**, windscreen wiper; ~**skoot**, fresh-air shot (golf); ~**skuif**, wind-gauge (of a rifle); ~**skut**, windscreen; ~**snelheid**, velocity of the wind; ~**spil**, windbreak; capstan; ~**sprong**, wind-shift; ~**sterkte**, force of the wind; ~**stil**, calm; windless; ~**stilte**, calm, lull; *streek van* ~ *stilte*, doldrums, calm-belt; ~**stilteken**, no-wind signal; ~**stoot**, gust of wind; ~**streek**, rhumb, point of the compass; ~**sug**, tympanites; ~**swa(w)el**, swift; ~**tonnel**, wind-tunnel; wind-channel; ~**uit**, winded; breathless; ~**vaan**, weather vane; ~**veer**, barge-board; ~**verwering**, eolation, wind corrosion; ~**vlaag**, squall, gust; ~**vry**, (-e), sheltered; ~**waarts**, (-e), windward; ~**wakker**, wide awake; ~**weerstand**, wind resistance; ~**wolk**, fleece cloud; ~**wyser**, weathercock, vane; anemograph.
win'gerd, (-e), vineyard; *hy het deur die* ~ *geloop*, he is three sheets in the wind; he has been bitten by the brewer's horse; ~**bemesting**, manuring of a vineyard; ~**besmetting**, vineyard infection; ~**boer**, grape-farmer; ~**bou**, viticulture; ~**dou**, vine-disease *(Plasmopora viticola)*; ~**fees**, vintage festival; ~**kwekery**, viticulturist, vine nursery; ~**loot**, vine-shoot; ~**luis**, phylloxera; ~**plantasie**, vineyard; ~**produk**, vine-product; ~**rank**, vine-shoot; ~**ry**, row of vines; ~**siekte**, vine-disease; ~**skêr**, pruning shears; ~**snoeier**, vine-dresser; ~**stok**, vine-cutting; vine; ~**trekker**, vineyard tractor.
win'gewes, (-te), annexed (conquered) territory; colony.
wink, (s) (-e), wink, nod; wave; (w) (ge-), wink, beckon; ~**brou**, (-e), eyebrow; ~**broupotlood**, ~**broustiffie**, eyebrow pencil.
win'kel, (s) (-s), shop, store, business, emporium; workshop; canteen (police); *gaan* ~ *s kyk*, go window-shopping; (w) (ge-), shop; ~**bank**, counter; ~**bediende**, shop-assistant, counter-jumper; ~**bedryf**, retail trade; ~**beskadig**, (-de), shop-soiled; ~**brand**, shop fire; ~**buurt**, shopping centre; ~**dief**, shop-lifter; ~**diefstal**, shop-lifting; ~**front**, shop front; ~**gang**, arcade; ~**haak**, set-square; try-square, carpenter's square; dog-leg (golf); three-cornered tear (in cloth); ~**huur**, shop-rent; ~**ier'**, (-s), shopkeeper, dealer; ~**inbraak**, shop-breaking; ~**inrigter**, shopfitter; ~**inrigting**, shopfitting; ~**inspekteur**, shop-inspector; ~**juffrou**, shop-girl, saleswoman; ~**ketting**, chain store; ~**klerk**, shop-assistant; ~**kykery**, window-shopping; ~**laai**, till; ~**mandjie**, shopping-basket; ~**meisie**, shop-girl; ~**merk**, shop serial number; ~**net**, string bag; ~**opstand**, shop fixtures; ~**personeel**,

shop staff; ~**prys,** retail price, selling price, sale price; ~**raam,** ~**ruit,** shop window; show-window; ~**skip,** coper; ~**skuld,** shop debts; ~**sluiting,** closing of shops; ~**straat,** chief business (shopping) street; ~**tande,** false teeth; ~**tas,** shopping-bag; ~**tjie, (-s),** small shop; kiosk; boutique; ~**toonbank,** shop-counter; ~**uitstalling,** display (exhibit) in shop-windows; ~**ure,** business hours; shop hours; ~**venster,** shop window; ~**versiering,** shop decoration; ~**voorraad,** stock-in-trade; ~**ware,** shop-goods; ~**week,** shopping week; ~**wyk,** shopping quarter (district).

wink'vlies, nictitating membrane, haw, third eyelid (of horse, dog); ~**ontsteking,** haws.

win'ner, (-s), winner; recoverer (mining).

win'ning, production; reclamation (land); saving (time); recovery (by-products); extraction (ore); winning, gaining (prize); working; advantage.

wins, (-te), profit, gain, winnings, proceeds, booty, benefit; conquest; *'n AANDEEL in die ~,* a share in the profits; *~ AFWERP,* yield a profit; *~ MAAK,* make a profit; *'n ~ NEEM,* take a profit; *~ OPLEWER,* yield a profit; *~ SLAAN uit,* profit from; gain by; *met ~ VERKOOP,* sell at a profit; ~**aandeel,** share in profits; ~**aanwending,** allocation of profits; ~**bedrag,** amount of profit; ~**bejag,** profiteering, pursuit of gain; *iets uit ~ bejag doen,* act from motives of gain; ~**belasting,** profits tax; taxation of profits; ~**berekening,** calculation of profits; ~**botrekking,** office of profit; ~**deling,** profit sharing; ~**drempel,** break-even point.

wins'-en-verlies'rekening, profit and loss account; *die ~ opmaak,* cast up the profit and loss account.

wins: ~**ge'wend, (-e),** lucrative, profitable, gainful, paying, remunerative; *~gewende dienste,* profitable services; ~**ge'wendheid,** profitability; ~**grens,** margin of profit; mark-up; ~**jagter,** profiteer; ~**kopie, (-s),** bargain, good buy; ~**maker,** profit-maker; ~**motief,** profit motive; ~**nemer,** profit-taker; ~**neming,** profit-taking (-snatching); ~**oogmerk,** profit motive; *sonder ~ oogmerk,* not for gain (profit); ~**pot,** jackpot; ~**raming,** estimation of profits; ~**ruimte,** margin of profit, profit margin; ~**saldo,** profit balance; ~**syfer,** (margin of) profit.

wins'sug, lust for gain, mercenariness; ~**'tig, (-e),** gainful, bent on gain.

wins: ~**uitkering,** distribution of profits; ~**vasstelling,** declaration of profits; ~**verdeling,** distribution of profits; ~**verdelingsrekening,** appropriation account.

win'ter, (-s), winter; *die ~ DEURBRING,* pass the winter; hibernate; *IN die ~,* in (during) winter; ~**aand,** winter evening; ~**agtig, (-e),** wintry, brumal, brumous; ~**appel,** winter apple; ~**aster,** chrysanthemum; ~**bene,** chilblained legs; ~**(blom)kool,** broccoli; ~**bui,** winter shower; ~**dag,** winter day; ~**drag,** winter wear; ~**druif,** chicken-grape; ~**gesig,** winterscape; ~**gewasse,** winter crops; ~**goed,** winter clothes; ~**groen,** evergreen; ~**hakskene,** chilblained heels; *swerende ~ hakskeen,* kibe; ~**hande,** chilblained hands; ~**hard,** winter-hardened; hardy; ~**hare,** winter coat; ~**jas,** winter overcoat, greatcoat; ~**klere,** winter clothes; ~**koninkie,** wren; ~**koring,** winter corn; ~**kou(e),** cold of winter; ~**kwartier,** winter quarters; ~**lam,** winter lamb; ~**landskap,** winter landscape; ~**lug,** winter sky; wintry air; ~**maand,** winter month; ~**mantel,** winter coat; ~**môre,** winter morning; ~**mot,** winter moth; ~**nag,** winter night; ~**olie,** winterized oil, winter oil; ~**opruiming,** winter sale; ~**ore,** chilblained (chilled) ears; ~**pak,** winter suit; ~**paleis,** winter palace; ~**pampoen,** winter pumpkin; ~**peer,** winter pear; ~**plaas,** farm with winter grazing; ~**provisie,** winter store; ~**reën,** winter rain; ~**reën(val)streek,** winter-rainfall area; ~**rok,** winter dress; ~**rus,** winter rest; hibernation; ~**s, (-e),** wintry; ~**saffraanpeer,** saffron pear; ~**seisoen,** winter season.

win'tershande — **winterhande**

win'ter: ~**slaap,** hibernation; ~**slaper,** hibernant; hibernating animal; ~**snoei,** winter pruning; ~**son,** winter sun; ~**sonstilstand,** winter solstice.

win'tersore = **winterore.**

win'ter: ~**sport,** winter sports; ~**storm,** winter gale.

win'tersvoete = **wintervoete.**

win'ter: ~**tabberd,** winter gown (dress); ~**tuin,** winter garden; ~**tyd,** winter time; ~**uitverkoop,** ~**uitverkoping,** winter sale; ~**vakansie,** winter holidays (vacation); ~**veld,** winter pasture; Lowveld; ~**veldtog,** winter campaign; ~**verblyf,** winter residence; ~**vermaak,** winter sports (amusement); ~**vlaag,** winter storm; ~**voer,** fodder (forage) for use during winter; ~**voete,** chilblained feet; ~**voorraad,** winter supply; ~**weer,** wintry weather.

wip, (s) (-pe), seesaw; snare, trap, gin; tilt, skip; *IN 'n ~,* in a jiffy, in half-a-tick; *op die ~ SIT,* be in danger of getting the order of the boot; *'n ~ vir iem. STEL,* set a trap for someone; **(w) (ge-),** hop, tip, wobble, seesaw; tilt; whisk; dandle (child on knee); *moenie jou ~ nie,* don't get cross (snobbish); ~**bak,** tipper; ~**brug,** drawbridge; tipping bridge; ~**emmer,** tipping bucket; ~**gatmier,** variety of black ant; ~**hout,** lever; ~**kar,** tip-cart; ~**klip,** rocking stone; ~**lat,** tilting (arris) fillet; ~**lig,** diplight (motor); ~**mat,** trampoline; ~**neus,** snub nose, tip-tilted nose; ~**per, (-s),** tippler, tipping-gear; ~**perig, (-e),** given to hopping (wobbling, tipping); uppish, snobbish, pert; ~**perigheid,** wobbliness; uppishness; ~**plank,** seesaw; ~**ploeg,** swing plough; ~**rooster,** pop up toaster; ~**rif,** jig; ~**skaal,** bascule; ~**smeltoond,** tilting-furnace; ~**stert, (s)** wagtail; robin; **(b)** cross-grained, easily offended spiteful; uppish; ~**stertmier** = **wipgatmier;** ~**stoel,** rocking-chair; ~**stuk,** chantlate (of eaves); sprocket; ~**styging,** jump start; ~**vragwa,** tip-lorry; ~**wa,** tip-waggon; ~**waentjie,** roller-coaster.

wir'war, whirl, jumble, tangle.

wis¹, (w) (ge-), wipe.

wis², (w) *verlede tyd* van **weet;** *ek ~ dit al,* I knew it long ago.

wis³, (b) (-se), certain, sure; *iem. van ~ se ondergang RED,* save someone from certain failure (disaster); *dis ~ en SEKER,* it is an absolute certainty; *VIR die ~ en (of) die on ~,* just (in case), to make quite sure, on the safe side.

wisent', (-e), aurochs, European bison.

Wisj'noe, Vishnu.

wis'kunde, mathematics; ~**les,** lesson in mathematics; ~**onderwyser,** mathematics master (teacher).

wiskun'dig, (-e), mathematical; ~**e, (-s),** mathematician.

wiskuns'tig, (-e), (ong.), mathematical.

wispeltu'rig, (-e), fickle, inconsistent, flighty, capricious, changeable, freakish, crotchety; desultory; ~**heid,** inconstancy, fickleness, capriciousness, freakishness, changeability, inconsistency.

wis'sel, (s) (-s), bill (of exchange), draft; points, switch (railway); *'n ~ AKSEPTEER,* honour a bill; *'n ~ BETAAL,* take up a bill; *'n ~ DISKONTEER,* discount (buy) a bill; *'n ~ HONOREER,* honour (meet) a bill; *~s en KRUISSTUKKE,* points and crossings; *'n ~ PROTESTEER,* protest a bill; *~ op SIG,* bill payable at sight; *'n ~ op iem. TREK,* draw on someone; *'n ~ VERDISKONTEER,* discount (sell) a bill; *die ~ VERSIT,* shift the points; **(w) (ge-),** exchange, change (money); interchange; fluctuate (market); cash (cheque); shift (gears); bandy (words); reciprocate; negotiate, encash; shed (teeth); *GEDAGTES ~,* exchange ideas; *TANDE ~,* shed teeth; *WOORDE ~,* bandy words; exchange a few words; ~**aar, (-s),** money-changer; oscillator; gear lever; ~**afdeling,** bill-department; ~**agent,** exchange broker; ~**arbitrasie,** arbitration of exchange; ~**baar, (..bare),** interchangeable; negotiable; commutative; ~**baarheid,** exchangeability; ~**bak,** interchangeable body; gearbox; ~**bank,** exchange bank; ~**bedrag,** amount of a bill; ~**bedryf,** exchange business; ~**beker,** floating trophy (cup), challenge cup; ~**betrekking,** correlation; ~**beweiding,** rotational grazing; ~**hoek,** bill-book; ~**bord,** switchboard; ~**bou,** rotation of crops, rotational cropping; convertible husbandry; ~**boustelsel**, rotational cropping; ~**brief**, bill of exchange; ~**dans**, Paul Jones (dance); ~**dele**, spare parts; ~**diskonto**, rate of discount; ~**end**, (-e), fluctuating, reciprocating; variable, changing, varying; ~**fonds**, cash float; ~**geld**, change; ~**gids**, cambist; ~**handel**, bill-broking, exchange business; ~**handelaar**, bill-broker; cambist; ~**hefboom**, gear (lever); gear-shift lever; switch lever; ~**hoek**, alternate angle; ~**houer**, holder of a bill.

wis'seling, (-e, -s), interchange, (ex)change, reciprocation; vicissitude; flux (prices); *by die ~ v.d. JAAR*, at the turn of the year; *die ~ v.d. JAARGETYE*, succession of the seasons; *die ~e v.d. NOODLOT*, the vicissitudes of fortune.

wis'sel: ~**jare**, change of life; ~**kantoor**, exchange office; ~**kind**, changeling; elf-child; ~**koers**, rate of exchange; course of exchange; ~**koste**, bill of charges; ~**krediet**, paper credit; ~**kruising**, traffic interchange; ~**lam**, hogget; ~**lamwol**, hoggets, hogget wool; ~**loon**, bill-brokerage, agio; ~**makelaar**, bill-broker; ~**maker**, discount (exchange) broker; ~**nemer**, payee; ~**notering**, rate of exchange; ~**ooi**, maiden ewe; ~**pari**, par of exchange; ~**provisie**, commission; ~**rat**, variable gear; ~**reg**, law of exchange; ~**rekening**, bill account; calculation of exchange; ~**ruiter**, kite-flier; ~**ruitery**, kiteflying; cross-accommodation; ~**rym**, alternate rhyme; ~**sake**, agiotage; ~**sang**, antiphony; ~**seël**, bill-stamp; ~**skaal**, sliding scale; ~**spelling**, alternative spelling; ~**spoor**, side-rails; shunt-line; ~**stang**, control rod; ~**stroom**, alternating current; ~**stroomdinamo**, alternator; ~**tand**, milk-tooth; ~**trofee**, floating trophy; ~**tyd**, staggering.

wisselval'lig, (-e), changeable, uncertain, erratic, precarious, variable, unsteady, inconstant, patchy (play); contingent; ~**heid**, (..**hede**), inconsistency, vicissitude, hazard, changeableness, precariousness; *die ~ hede van die lewe*, the vicissitudes of life.

wis'sel: ~**vervalser**, (-s), bill-forger; ~**vervalsing**, forging of bills; ~**vorm**, variant; ~**waarde**, exchange value; ~**wagdiens**, point-duty; ~**wagter**, pointsman, switchman, pointer; ~**weiding**, pasture rotation; ~**werking**, (-e, -s), interaction, reciprocal effect; reciprocation; ~**wiel**, spare wheel; exchange wheel; ~**wind**, alternating wind.

wis'ser, (-s), wiper, eraser; sponge; pull-through; ~**stok**, cleaning rod.

wis'skut, (ong.), sure shot.

wit, (s) white(ness); white (of egg); pith (of orange); *~ van die EIER*, white of the egg; *in ~ GEKLEED*, dressed in white; *gee dit vir my SWART op ~*, put it down in writing (in black and white); (w) (**ge-**), lime(wash), whitewash, distemper; (b) white; hoar(y), frosty; blank; grey (horse); *~ BIER*, pale ale; *~ BROODJIES bak*, eat humble pie; *~ MAAK*, whiten; *~ OLIFANT*, white elephant; *~ VERF*, Chinese white; *die ~ VLAG*, the white flag, flag of truce; *~ WORD*, go white, turn pale; ~**aarsiekte**, foot-rot (in plants); ~**aas**, white bait; ~**aasvoël**, griffin, griffon; ~**agtig**, (-e), whitish; ~**appeltjie**, *Patchystigma pymaea*; ~**baard**, greybeard; ~**baardsuikerbos**, giant woolly-bearded protea; ~**been**, milk-leg, white leg (med.); ~**bek**, biliary fever; ~**bestuif**, (-de), covered with (white) dust; ~**blits**, home-distilled brandy, "dop" brandy; ~**bloedig**, (-e), white-blooded, leucaemic; ~**bloedigheid**, leucaemia; ~**boek**, white paper; ~**bont**, piebald; miniver; ~**boom**, silver-tree; ~**borskraai**, parson crow; ~**bos(hout)**, *Maerua caffra*; ~**bossie**, favourite, pet; blue-eyed boy; ~**damp**, white damp; ~**den**, white (nothern) pine.

Wit'donderdag, Maundy Thursday.
wit'doringboom, white thorn (*Acacia karroo*).
wit'dragte, white heel (horse).
wit'eik, white oak.
wit'els, white elder (*Platylophus trifoliatus*).
wit'gansvoet, white goosefoot; lamb's quarters.
wit'gat, white rump; ~**boom**, shepherd's tree (*Capparis albitrunca*); ~**jie**, sandpiper; greenshank; ~**koffie**, coffee from the roots of the shepherd's tree; ~**spreeu**, pied starling; ~**wortel**, root of shepherd's tree (used as coffee substitute) (*Capparis albitrunca*).

wit: ~**geglans**, (-de), white-glazed; ~**gelak**, (-te), white-lacquered; ~**gepleister**, (-de), whitewashed; ~*gepleisterde grafte*, whited sepulchres; ~**gloeiend**, (-e), white-hot; ~**goud**, platinum; ~**greinhout**, white deal; ~**haak**, white-thorn acacia (*Acacia spirocarpoides*); ~**haar**, ~**harig**, (-e), white-haired; ~**heid**, whiteness; hoariness; ~**hitte**, white heat; ~**hond**, Cape smoke (brandy); ~**hout**, Cape holly (*Ilex mitis*): ~**jie** = **witte(tjie)**.

wit: ~**kalk**, whitewash, distemper; whiting; ~**klawer**, Dutch clover; ~**klei**, kaolin; ~**kool**, Savoy cabbage; ~**kook**, (-ge-), blanch; ~**kop**, white-haired (grey-haired) person, blonde; *rooi ~ kop*, male red stumpnose; ~**kraai**, white crow; ~**kruisarend**, black eagle; ~**kryt**, white chalk; ~**kwas**, whiting-brush, lime-brush; cow with white bush on tail; ~**kwasjakkals**, side-striped jackal; ~**lag**, (-ge-), laugh merrily; ~**lof**, French endive, chicory; ~**lood**, white lead, putty; ceruse; ~**loog**, diluted sulphuric acid; ~**looi**, taw; ~**looier**, tawer; ~**looiery**, tawery; ~**luis**, mealy-bug; ~**lyn**, white line (anat.); ~**maak**, (-ge-), blanch.

wit'man, (..**mense**), white man.

wit: ~**metaal**, Babbit-metal, bearing-metal, anti-friction metal; white metal; ~**mielie**, white mealie (maize); ~**mieliemeel**, white maize meal; ~**mielieproduk**, white maize product; ~**mier**, termite; ~**miernes**, termitary; ~**ogie**, white-eye; ~**lyf**, wild fuchsia (*halleria lucida*); ~**oog**, wall-eye; ~**ooievaar**, white stork; ~**papier**, white paper (official document); ~**peer**, white pear; ~**populier**, abele; ~**roes**, mildew (*Odium tuckeri*); ~**rugaasvoël**, white-backed vulture; ~**rys**, polished rice; ~**rysheide**, rice heath (*Erica tenuifolia*).

Wit'rus, White Russian; ~**land**, White Russia; ~**sies**, (-e), White Russian.

wit: ~**seerkeel**, diphtheria; ~**sel**, whiting, whitewash; ~**sig**, white-out; ~**skimmel**, light-grey horse; ~**skrif** = **witpapier**; ~**sous**, white sauce; ~**spar**, Canadian spruce; ~**stam** = **witgatboom**; ~**stertspreeu** = **witgatspreeu**; ~**stof**, white matter (med.); ~**streep**, whiting line.

wit'tande: *~ lag*, laugh with joy.
wit'teboom, silver-tree.
wit'tebroods: ~**dae**, ~**weke**, honeymoon; ~**kamerstel**, bridal suite; ~**paar**, honeymoon couple; ~**reis**, honeymoon trip.
wit'terig, (-e), whitish; albescent.
wit'te(tjie), (-s), jack (bowls); white one.
wit'valk, chanting goshawk; ~**ie**, black-shouldered kite.
wit'verf, lithopone.
wit'vis, dace, whitebait, whitefish, minnow.
wit'vleis, white meat.
wit'vloed, leucorrhoea, the whites.
wit'voet, white-footed (cat, horse, etc.); *~jie soek*, toady to someone, flatter, cringe, curry favour; ~**jiesoeker**, lickspittle, cringer, flatterer, toady; ~**jiesoekery**, toadyism.
wit: ~**vrot**, fungus plant-disease; ~**water**, white water (paper factory); ~**werk**, whitewash(ing); ~**wortel**, parsnip.
Wo'dan, Odin.
wod'ka, vodka.
woed, (ge-), rage, work havoc, rage fiercely (storm, epidemic, fight).
woe'de, rage, orgasm, fury, choler; *BUITE jouself van ~*, beside oneself with rage; *sy ~ KOEL op*, vent one's anger on; *MAGTELOSE ~*, impotent rage; *STIK van ~*, be boiling with rage; *~bui*, fit of anger, tantrum.
woe'dend, (-e), furious, violent, raging, like mad, frantic, enraged, infuriated; *~ AANKYK*, look daggers at; *~ MAAK*, enrage, infuriate; *~ WEES op*, be furious with; *~ WEES oor*, be furious (enraged) about; infuriated; *~ WORD*, become enraged, fly into a passion.
woef, bow-bow.

woe'fie, (-s), doggy.
woe'ker, (s) usury; *geld op* ~ *uitsit*, lend money on usury; (w) **(ge-)**, practise usury; parasitize; grow rank (plants), multiply rapidly; make the most of; ~ *met sy talent*, make the most of one's talent; ~ **aar**, (-s), extortioner, usurer; huckster; profiteer; ~ **agtig**, (-e), usurious, exorbitant; ~ **dier**, parasite; ~ **end**, (-e), epiphytal, epiphytic; ~ **geld**, money obtained by usury; ~ **handel**, usurious trade; ~ **huur**, rack-rent; ~ **huurbaas**, rack-renter; ~ **ing**, (-e, -s), parasitic growth; parasitism; ~ **plant**, epiphyte, aerophyte, parasitic plant; ~ **pot**, totalisator jackpot; ~ **prys**, usurious price; ~ **rente**, usurious interest; ~ **sug**, spirit of usury; ~ **sug'tig**, (-e), usurious; ~ **vlees**, proud flesh; ~ **wet**, usury act; ~ **wins**, usury, usurious gain, exorbitant profit; profiteering; ~ **winsmaker**, profiteer.
woel, (ge-), bustle, bestir oneself; wind round, twist; fasten; fidget, toss about (in bed); work hard; burrow, root; rummage; ~ *om BETYDS daar te wees*, bestir oneself to get somewhere in time; ~ *HOM*, make it hot for him; *'n tou om 'n PAAL* ~, wind a rope round a post; ~ **beuel**, lashing-handle; ~ **er**, (-s), hustler, bustler; ~ **(er)ig**, (b) (-e), restless, active; choppy (sea), turbulent, busy, riotous (meeting); bustling, fussy, fidgety (child); rackety; (bw) busily; ~ **(er)igheid**, turbulence, unrest, restlessness; ~ **gees**, agitator, factionist, stormy petrel; ~ **haak**, lashing-hook; ~ **ig** = **woelerig**; ~ **ing**, (-e, -s), agitation, disturbance, turbulence; lashing; ~ **ingo**, riots, disturbances, ~ **ketting**, lashing chain; ~ **muis**, vole; ~ **riem**, twist-string; ~ **siek**, (-e), turbulent, riotous, restless, fidgety; ~ **sug**, turbulence, restlessness, agitation; ~ **tou**, lashing rope; ~ **water**, (-s), restless person (child), flibbertigibbet, disturber, fidget, bustler, hustler (Amer.); ~ **yster**, pry-bar.
Woens'dag, Wednesday; ..**dae**, on Wednesdays; ~ **aand**, Wednesday evening; ~ **môre**, ~ **more**, Wednesday morning; ~ **(na)middag**, Wednesday afternoon; ~ **oggend**, Wednesday morning; ~ **s**, (b) (-e), Wednesday; (bw) on Wednesdays.
woeps, flop!
woerts, there! whiz!
woer-woer', (-e), whirr-whirr (a boy's toy), whirligig, bull-roarer.
woes, (-te), desolate, desert, waste (country); frantic, feral, ferine, ferocious, hectic, fell (struggle); unruly, rampageous (behaviour); rabid (hate); truculent (temper); furious (mirth); wild (tribe); savage, fierce (persecution); *'n* ~ *te RYER*, a reckless driver; ~ *TE kere gaan*, storm, raise the devil.
woest'aard, (-s), savage, barbarian, ruffian.
woes: ~ **teling**, (-e), brute, desperado, ruffian, berserker; ~ **teny'**, (-e), wilderness, desert, wild(s), desolate tract.
woest'heid, fury, ruffianism, ferociousness, truculence, savageness, fierceness, wildness, desolateness.
woestyn', (-e), desert, wilderness; *SKIP van die* ~, ship of the desert (camel); *'n STEM roepende in die* ~, a voice crying in the wilderness; *'n VERSKRIKLIKE* ~, a howling wilderness; ~ **ag'tig**, (-e), desert-like; ~ **bewoner**, desert-dweller (Bedouin); ~ **muis**, jerboa; ~ **plant**, desert plant, xerophyte; ~ **sand**, desert sand; ~ **wind**, desert wind, simoon.
wol, wool; *pilage*; pile; *in die* ~ *GEVERF*, dyed in the wool; *onder die* ~ *KRUIP*, go off to bed; ~ **afmaker**, fellmonger; ~ **afval**, noil wool waste; ~ **ag'tig**, (-e), woolly; ~ **baal**, wool-bale wool-pack; ~ **baardsulkerbos**, woolly-bearded protea; ~ **bak**, wool-bin; ~ **bederf**, fleece-rot; ~ **bedryf**, wool industry; ~ **bereider**, wool-dresser; ~ **bereiding**, wool-dressing; ~ **beurs**, wool exchange; ~ **boer**, wool-grower; wool-farmer; ~ **boerdery**, sheep-farming; ~ **borduurwerk**, crewel-work; ~ **damas**, moreen; ~ **deskundige**, wool expert; ~ **distrik**, wool district; ~ **draad**, wool yarn; ~ **draend**, (-e), wool-bearing, laniferous; ~ **drifsels**, swimmings.
Wolf¹, Lupus (astron.).
wolf², (**wolwe**), wolf; devil (weaving); *met die wolwe in die BOS huil*, trim one's sails to the wind; run with the hare and hunt with the hounds; *soos 'n* ~ *EET*, eat like a horse; *vir die wolwe GOOI*, throw to the wolves; *so HONGER soos 'n* ~, as hungry as a hunter; *'n* ~ *in SKAAPSKLERE*, wolf in sheep's clothing; *vir* ~ *SKAAPWAGTER maak*, set a fox to keep the geese; give the wolf the wether to keep.
wol: ~ **fabriek**, wool-factory, wool-mill; ~ **fabrikant**, wool-manufacturer; ~ **fabrikasie**, woollen-manufacture.
wolf: ~ **ag'tig**, (-e), wolfish, lupine; ~ **ent**, hipped end; ~ **entdak**, hipped roof; ~ **entgewel**, jerkin head; ~ **hoek**, hip (on roof); ~ **hok**, pitfall; **W** ~ **hond**, wolf-hound, Alsatian; ~ **huis**, wolf-trap; ~ **kuil**, wolf-trap; pitfall.
wol'fluweel, plush.
wolf'ram, tungsten, wolfram(ite); ~ **aat'**, (..**ate**), wolframate; ~ **iet'**, wolframite; ~ **staal**, tungsten steel; ~ **suur**, tungstic acid.
wolfs'boontjie, lupin.
wolfs'dak, hip and gable roof.
wolfs: ~ **klou**, lycopod(ium); ~ **kruid**, wolf's-bane; ~ **kuil** = **wolfkuil**; ~ **melk**, spurge; ~ **tand**, wolf's tooth; dog-tooth (brickwork); gullet-tooth (saw); ~ **vel**, wolfskin; ~ **wortel**, aconite, wolf's-bane, monk's-hood.
Wol'ga, Volga.
wol: ~ **goed**, woollen clothing, woollens, hosiery; ~ **gare**, ~ **garing**, wool yarn; ~ **gesig**, woolly face; ~ **gras**, cotton-grass *(Eriophorum);* ~ **haak**, bale-hook.
wol'haar, woolly hair; *die lyf* ~ *hou*, to be smitten; ~ **hond**, woolly dog.
wol'haarwoorde, wol'haarstories: *wilde* ~, irresponsible words, tales, nonsense, wild talk.
wol'hakie, bale-fastener.
wol'handel, wool-trade; ~ **aar**, (-s), wool-merchant.
wol: ~ **heffing**, wool levy, levy on wool; ~ **industrie**, wool-industry.
wolk, (-e), cloud; *DONKER* ~ *e*, storm clouds; *'n* ~ *van GETUIES*, a cloud of witnesses; *IN die* ~ *e wees*, be beside oneself with joy; be up in the clouds; *uit die* ~ *e VAL*, drop from the clouds; *iem. tot in die* ~ *e VERHEF*, praise someone to the skies.
wol'kaard, wool-card; ~ **er**, (-s), wool-carder; ~ **ery**, wool-carding.
wolk'agtig, (-e), cloudy, cloud-like.
wol'kam, wool-comb; ~ **mer**, (-s), wool-comber; ~ **sels**, wool noils.
wol: ~ **kant**, wool lace; ~ **katoen**, linsey-woolsey.
wolk: ~ **baan**, track of the clouds, cloud trail; ~ **bank**, bank of clouds; ~ **bou**, cloud formation; ~ **breuk**, cloud-burst, deluge; ~ **(e)bank**, bank of clouds; ~ **(e)dak**, cloud canopy; ~ **(e)dek**, cloud cover(ing).
wol'kekrabber, (-s), skyscraper.
wolki: ~ **erig**, (-e), cloudy, fleecy, foggy (photo); ~ **erigheid**, nebulousness.
wol'kestapel, cloud-rack.
wolk: ~ **gevaarte**, mass of clouds; ~ **ig**, (-e), cloudy; ~ **kolom**, pillar of clouds.
wol'kelaag, cloud layer.
wol'keleer, nephology.
wolk'meter, nephoscope.
wol: ~ **kombers**, woollen blanket; ~ **koper**, wool-merchant; ~ **koring**, *Triticum aestivum;* ~ **krep**, wool crêpe; ~ **kundige**, wool expert; ~ **kweker**, (-s), wool-grower; ~ **lengte**, staple.
wol'l(er)ig, (-e), woolly, nappy, fleecy, fleeced, flocose; lanate; ~ **heid**, woolliness, fleeciness.
wol'letjie, (-s), piece of fluff, small tuft of wool, flock.
wol: ~ **lig**, (-e), woolly, fleecy; ~ **luis**, mealy-bug; ~ **makelaar**, wool-merchant, wool-broker; ~ **mark**, wool-market; ~ **matras**, wool mattress; ~ **menger**, wool-mixer; ~ **moeselien**, mousseline de laine; ~ **muis**, chinchilla; ~ **nywerheid**, wool industry; woollen-industry; ~ **oes**, wool clip; ~ **olie**, wool oil; ~ **onderbaadjie**, cardigan; ~ **onderklere**, woollen underwear; ~ **opbrengs**, wool clip; ~ **pak**, wool suit; ~ **pakhuis**, wool warehouse, wool store; ~ **pers**, wool press; ~ **poeier**, devil's dust; ~ **produksie**, wool production; ~ **produserend**, (-e), wool-growing; ~ **prys**, wool price.

Wol'raad, Wool Board.
wol'reep, sliver of wool.
wol: ~ **sak,** woolsack; wool-bale; jumbo, fat (big) person; ~ **satyn,** satin de laine; ~ **serp,** comforter; ~ **skaap,** wool-bearing sheep, merino; ~ **skeersel,** wool clip; ~ **skuur,** wool-shed; ~ **sorteerder,** wool-sorter; ~ **spinner,** wool-spinner; ~ **spinnery,** (wool-)spinning factory; ~ **stapel,** wool staple; ~ **stertmuis,** bushy-tailed mouse (rat); ~ **stof,** (..**stowwe**), woollen material; *suiwer* ~ *stof,* all-wool material; ~ **sweet,** suint.
Wol'toon, nickname for an inhabitant of the Cape Province.
wol: ~ **trui,** wool pullover; ~ **veiling,** wool-auction (-sale); ~ **vel,** merino skin, wool-fell; ~ **verwer,** wool-dyer; ~ **verwery,** wool-dyeing (works), wool-dye works; ~ **vesel,** wool fibre; ~ **vet,** yolk (wool); lanolin, wool-fat.
wolvin', (-ne), she-wolf.
wol'vingergras, woolly finger-grass *(Digitaria eriantha* or *smutsii).*
wol'was, wool wax.
wol'was: ~ **masjien,** wool-scouring machine; ~ **ser,** wool-washer; ~ **sery,** wool-washing (works), wool-refinery; scouring mill.
wol'we: ~ **aard,** wolfish nature; ~ **byt,** bite of a wolf; ~ **dak,** hip-roof; ~ **doring,** wolf's-thorn *(Scolopia zeyheri);* ~ -**ent** = **wolfent;** ~ **gat,** (-e), wolf's lair; ~ **gif,** strychnine; ~ **hoek,** hip (of roof); ~ **hok,** ~ **huis,** wolf-trap; ~ **jag,** wolf-hunt(ing); ~ **kap,** hip truss; ~ **kos,** ink-plant *(Hyobanche sanguinea).*
wol'wewer, (-s), wool-weaver; ~ **y,** wool-weaving factory.
wond, (s) (-e), wound, injury, cut, stab; *ou* ~ *e OOP= KRAP,* reopen old wounds; *'n onbeduidende* ~ *OPLOOP,* receive a minor injury; *diep* ~ *e SLAAN,* hurt deeply; ~ *e TOEBRING aan,* inflict injuries to; (w) (**ge-**), wound, hurt, injure, disable; ~ **baar,** (..**bare**), vulnerable; pregnable; ~ **baar= heid,** vulnerability; ~ **balsem,** vulnerary balm.
won'der, (s) (-e, -s), wonder, marvel, miracle; prodigy; portent; phenomenon; *iem. as 'n* ~ *BESKOU,* look upon someone as a miracle; regard someone as a tin-god; ~ *BO* ~, miracle of miracles; amazingly enough; ~ *s DOEN,* work miracles; *GEEN* ~ *dat,* no wonder that; *'n* ~ *van GELEERDHEID,* a prodigy of learning; a genius; *die SEWE* ~ *s van die wêreld,* the seven wonders of the world; *hy VER= BEEL hom wat* ~, he is full of himself; *die motor is glad nie WAT* ~ *s nie,* the car is nothing much; ~ *s is nog nie uit die WÊRELD nie,* wonders never cease; (w) (**ge-**), wonder; *ek sit en* ~ *of dit waar is,* I am wondering whether it is true.
won'derbaar, (..**bare**), strange, wonderful, wonder= ous; ~ **lik,** (-e), wonderful, strange, providential; phenomenal, marvellous, miraculous; ~ **likheid,** miraculousness.
won'der: ~ **beeld,** miraculous image; ~ **blom,** marvel of Peru, afternoon lady; ~ **boom,** wonder-tree *(Fi= cus salifolia);* ~ **daad,** wonder; miracle; ~ **da'dig,** (-e), miraculous; ~ **dier,** prodigious beast, freak, monster; ~ **doener,** thaumaturge, wonder-worker; ~ **doenery,** thaumaturgy; ~ **dokter,** quack; witch-doctor, medicine man; ~ **essens,** wonder-essense; ~ **gawe,** miraculous gift; ~ **genesing,** miracle cure; ~ **jaar,** year of wonders; ~ **kind,** wonder-child, in= fant prodigy; ~ **krag,** thaumaturgy, miraculous power; ~ **kruid,** St. John's herb; ~ **kuur,** quack cure; ~ **lamp,** Aladdin's lamp; ~ **land,** wonderland, fairyland.
won'derlik, (-e), marvellous, miraculous, strange, odd, amazing, curious, wonderful, wondrous; ~ **heid,** fantasticalness, marvellousness, strange= ness, queerness, wonderfulness.
won'der: ~ **mag,** miraculous power; ~ **mens,** prodigy; phenomenon, human wonder; ~ **middel,** wonder= ful remedy; heal-all, arcanum, panacea; quack medicine; ~ **mooi,** exceedingly beautiful, exquisite; ~ **olie,** castor oil; ~ **peper,** allspice, pimento; ~ **plant,** castor-oil plant; ~ **skoon,** (..**skone**), ex= quisite, marvellously beautiful; ~ **spreuk,** paradox; magic formula; ~ **sprokie,** fairy tale; ~ **steen,** won=

derstone; ~ **teken,** miracle; miraculous sign; ~ **veel,** exceedingly much; ~ **verhaal,** miraculous story; ~ **verrigter,** wonder-worker, miracle-worker; ~ **vol,** (-le), marvellous, wonderful; ~ **water,** water with medicinal properties; ~ **wel,** wonderfully well; ~ **werk,** miracle; ~ **werke,** mighty works; ~ **wiel,** thaumatrope.
wond: ~ **heelkunde,** surgery; ~ **koors,** wound-fever, traumatic fever; ~ **kramp,** tetanus, lockjaw; ~ **kruis,** wound-wort, vulnerary, arnica; ~ **merk,** cicatrice, cicatrix; ~ **middel,** vulnerary, cure for wounds; ~ **naat,** suture; ~ **pleister,** vulnerary plas= ter; ~ **roos,** erysipelas, the rose, St. Anthony's fire; ~ **salf,** healing ointment; ~ **skêr,** probe-scissors; ~ **verband,** dressing; ~ **water,** vulnerary water; ~ **weefsel,** callus (bot.) ; ~ **yster,** probe.
wo'ning, (-s), dwelling, residence, abode, habitation, house; ~ **aanleg,** housing scheme; ~ **argitektuur,** domestic architecture; ~ **bou,** house-building, ~ **buro,** house-agent's office; ~ **gebrek,** housing shortage; ~ **gids,** (house-)directory; ~ **huur,** house-rent; ~ **nood,** house-famine; ~ **s,** quarters; ~ **skaarste,** scarcity of houses; ~ **subsidie,** housing subsidy; ~ **tekort,** housing shortage; ~ **toelae** house-allowance; ~ **toestande,** housing conditions; ~ **verskaffing,** provision of houses; ~ **vraagstuk,** housing problem; ~ **wet,** housing act; ~ **wetgewing,** housing legislation.
wo'ninkie, (-s), small dwelling-house, cottage.
woon, (ge-), live, dwell, domiciliate, reside, abide, do= micile, stay; ~ **ag'tig,** (-e), resident, domiciled; ~ **baar,** (..**bare**), inhabitable; ~ **blok,** block of flats; ~ **boot,** houseboat; ~ **buurt,** residential area; ~ **erf,** residential site; ~ **gebied,** residential area; ~ **gebou,** domestic building; ~ **geleentheid,** housing accommodation; ~ **huis,** dwelling(-house), home-stead, residence; ~ **kamer,** living-room, lounge; ~ **kaserne,** tenement house; ~ **plaas,** ~ **plek,** resi= dence, dwelling-place; habitation, domicile, lodg= ing, home, abode; habitat (of plants, animals); ~ **reg,** right of occupation; ~ **ruimte,** living-space; ~ **skuit,** houseboat; ~ **stel,** flat, maison(n)ette; ~ **stelgebou,** flat-building; ~ **vertrek,** living-room; ~ **volk,** resident labourers; ~ **wa,** caravan, living-wagon, house on wheels, gipsy wagon; ~ **wyk,** resi= dential quarter.
woord, (-e), word; term; tidings, message; promise; *wie is AAN die* ~ *?,* who has the floor?; *met ANDER* ~ *e,* in other words; *sy* ~ *BREEK,* break one's word; *iets onder* ~ *e BRING,* put something into words; *met* ~ *en DAAD,* by word and deed; *die* ~ *by die DAAD voeg,* suit the deed to the word; *van* ~ *e tot DADE kom,* come to blows; act; *'n* ~ *jie DOEN vir iem.,* put in a good word for someone; *in EEN* ~, in a word; in short; *op my* ~ *van EER,* on my word of honour; *iem. die* ~ *GEE,* request some= one to speak; *jou* ~ *GEE,* give one's word; *die GESPROKE* ~, the spoken word; *sy* ~ *GE= STAND doen,* keep one's word; *sy* ~ *GOED kan doen,* have the gift of the gab; *so GOED as sy* ~ *wees,* be as good as one's word; *GOEIE* ~ *e kos geen geld nie,* courtesy costs nothing; *'n GOEIE* ~ *vind 'n goeie plaas,* a kind word is never out of sea= son; *'n GROOT* ~, a swear-word; *HARDE* ~ *e,* hard words; ~ *HÊ,* have words; *die* ~ *HÊ,* have the floor; *die HOOGSTE* ~ *voer,* have the greatest say; do most of the talking; *die HOOGSTE* ~ *moet uit,* the trush will out; *die HOOGSTE* ~ *is uit,* the cat is out of the bag; *iem. aan sy* ~ *HOU,* keep someone to his word; ~ *HOU,* honour one's word, keep a promise; *iem. sy* ~ *e laat insluk,* make some= one swallow his words; *sy eie* ~ *e INSLUK,* eat one's words; *sy* ~ *is JA en amen,* his word is law; *sy* ~ *e KIES,* choose one's words; ~ *e KORTKOM,* be at a loss for words; *sy* ~ *e was nog nie KOUD nie,* his words were hardly cold; *hy kon geen* ~ *tussenin KRY nie,* he could not get in a word edgeways; ~ *e KRY,* have words, quarrel; *sy LAASTE* ~ *e,* his dying words; *altyd die LAASTE* ~ *wil hê,* want to have the last word always; *die LEWENDE* ~, the living word; *'n MAN van sy* ~, a man of his word; *geen* ~ *e MEER nie!,* not another word!; *die hoog=*

ste ~ *MOET uit*, the secret must be revealed; it must be acknowledged; *die ~ e uit iem. se MOND neem*, take the words out of someone's mouth; *iem. ~ e in die MOND lê*, put words into someone's mouth; *~ e uit die MOND kan die hart verwond*, words cut more than swords; *~ e en MUSIEK*, words and music, libretto and score; *die ~ NEEM*, take the floor; *OP my ~ !*, on my word of honour!; *jou ~ e OPEET*, be made to eat one's words; *die ~ is (lê) op die PUNT van my tong*, the word is on the tip of my tongue; *jy kan op sy ~ REKEN*, you can rely on what he says; *die ~ RIG tot*, address oneself to; *daaroor kan ek 'n ~ jie SAAMPRAAT*, I can also say something about that; *~ e maak nie SEER nie*, words can never hurt one; *na ~ e SOEK*, look for words; *~ e SOEK*, pick a quarrel; *geen SPAANSE ~ nie*, not a single word; *iem. te ~ STAAN*, give someone a hearing; *'n ~ STEMREG verleen*, give a word recognition; *geen STOMME ~ sê nie*, say not a single word; *~ e van dieselfde STREKKING*, words to the same effect; *geen ~ kan UITBRING nie*, be unable to utter a word; *iem. met sy eie ~ e VANG*, trip someone up with his own words; *sy ~ VERPAND*, give his word; *~ VIR ~*, word for word; *die ~ VOER*, be the speaker; *~ e wek maar VOORBEELDE trek*, example is better than precept; *die ~ VRA*, beg leave to say a few words; *die VRYE ~*, free speech; *WEEG jou ~ e*, you should weigh your words; *aan die ~ WEES*, have the floor; be speaking; *die laaste ~ WIL hê*, want to have the last word; *~ e WISSEL*, exchange a few words; bandy words; ~ **afleiding**, (word-)derivation; etymology; ~ **aksent**, word accent; ~ **armoede**, lack of vocabulary; ~ **beeld**, written word; ~ **bepaling**, definition; ~ **betekenis**, word-meaning; ~ **betekenisleer**, semantics, semasiology; ~ **blind**, word-blind; ~ **blindheid**, word-blindness, alexia; ~ **breker**, promise-breaker, defaulter; ~ **breuk**, breach of promise; ~ **buiging**, (word-)inflection, declension; ~ **doof**, word-deaf; ~ **doofheid**, word-deafness.

woor'de: ~ **boek**, dictionary, lexicon; *VERKLARENDE ~ boek*, explanatory dictionary; *WANDELENDE ~ boek*, a walking dictionary; ~ **boekskrywer**, compiler of a dictionary, lexicographer; ~ **keus**, choice of words; ~ **kramery**, word-spinning.

woord'element, word element.

woor'de: ~ **lik, (-e)**, literal, verbal, verbatim; ~ **lys**, list of words, vocabulary, glossary; ~ **praal**, flourish (pomp) of diction, bombast, ~ **ryk, (-e)**, verbose, wordy; ~ **rykdom**, wealth of words; stock of words, vocabulary; ~ **skat**, vocabulary; ~ **spel**, pun; quibble; ~ **stroom**, torrent of words; ~ **stryd**, (verbal) dispute, quibble, altercation; logomachy; debate; ~ **tal**, wordage; ~ **tolk**, dictionary (of foreign terms); ~ **twis**, (verbal) dispute, altercation; ~ **vloed**, flow (torrent) of words (language); verbosity; ~ **wisseling**, dispute, debate, altercation.

woord: ~ **familie**, family of words; ~ **gegoël**, word-juggling; ~ **groep**, group of words; phrase; ~ **herhaling**, repetition of words, tautology; ~ **jie, (-s)**, (little) word; *hieroor KAN ek 'n ~ jie saampraat*, I can speak from experience about this matter; *ek WIL ook 'n ~ jie saampraat*, I too would like to have a say in the matter; ~ **keuse**, choice of words; phraseology; ~ **kramer**, word-monger; ~ **kuns**, literary art (poetry, prose); literature; ~ **kunstenaar**, literary artist (poet, prose writer); ~ **misbruik**, catachresis, misuse of words; ~ **omsetting**, inversion, transposition; ~ **omskikking**, hyperbaton, ~ **omspanning**, hypallage; ~ **ontleding**, parsing; ~ **orde**, order of words; ~ **paar**, word-couple; ~ **raaisel**, word-puzzle, charade, logogryph; ~ **register**, word-index; ~ **ryk, (-e)**, verbose, voluble; ~ **rykdom**, ~ **rykheid**, volubility, wordiness, verbosity; ~ **sifter**, hair-splitter; verbalist; ~ **siftery**, quibbling, hair-splitting; ~ **skikking**, order of words; ~ **skildering**, word-painting; ~ **skildery**, word-picture; ~ **smeder, (-s)**, coiner of words, neologist; ~ **soort**, word-class, part of speech; ~ **spelling, (-s)**, play upon words, pun, quibble, quodlibet, equivoque, paronomasia; ~ **tarief**, word-tariff; ~ **uitlating**, ellipsis; ~ **verandering**, change of words; ~ **verbuiging**, declension; ~ **verdraaier, (-s)**, word-twister, equivocator, contortionist (of words); ~ **verdraaiing**, word-twisting, distortion (of words); ~ **verklaring**, explanation (definition) of words, glossology; ~ **vervoeging**, conjugation; ~ **voeging**, syntax; ~ **voerder, (-s)**, spokesman, mouthpiece; protagonist; prolocutor; ~ **vorm, (-e)**, form of a word, word form; ~ **vorming**, formation of words, word-building; ~ **vorser**, etymologist; ~ **vorsing**, etymology; scientific word-study.

Worces'tersous, Worcester sauce.

word, (ge-), become, get, take place, grow, turn; *BLEEK ~*, turn pale; *DRONK ~*, get drunk; *OUD ~*, grow old; *SIEK ~*, take ill; *WAT wil jy ~ ?*, what do you want to become?; ~ **end, (-e)**, becoming, nascent.

wor'ding, origin, beginning, origination, genesis, evolution.

wor'dings: ~ **geskiedenis**, genesis; ~ **jare**, formative years; ~ **leer**, ontogeny; genetics; ~ **tyd**, formative stage.

worp, (-e), cast (fishing-line); fling, chuck, hurl, litter (of young).

wors, (-e, -te), sausage; *'n ~ het twee ENTE*, there are two sides to every question; *so skaars soos ~ in 'n HONDEHOK*, extremely scarce (rare); *~ in 'n HONDESTAL soek*, look for a needle in a haystack, try to cut a silk purse out of a sow's ear; *van iem. ~ MAAK*, make mincemeat of someone; ~ **boom**, sausage-tree *(Kigelia pinnata);* ~ **broodjie**, hot-dog; ~ **derm**, sausage-skin (-casing); ~ **fabriek**, sausage-factory; **W-hond(jie)**, Dachshund; ~ **horinkie**, sausage-filler; ~ **masjien**, ~ **meul**, sausage-machine; ~ **rolletjie**, sausage roll; ~ **steek**, bullion stitch; ~ **stopper**, sausage-filler.

wors'tel, (ge-), wrestle, flounder (in water), struggle (against disease); battle against; combat (difficulties); contend (with waves); grapple; *met die dood ~*, wrestle with death; ~ **aar, (-s)**, wrestler; ~ **ing, (-e, -s)**, conflict, wrestling (with death), struggle, fight, scuffle (in fight); ~ **kamp**, wrestling-match; ~ **kuns**, wrestling; ~ **perk**, arena, pal(a)estra, ring; ~ **stryd**, struggle for life; wrestling-match; ~ **wedstryd**, wrestling-match.

wors: ~ **vark**, sausager; ~ **vel**, sausage-casing (-skin); ~ **vergiftiging**, botulism; ~ **vleis**, sausage-meat; ~ **vormig, (-e)**, sausage-shaped.

wort, wort (of malt).

wor'tel, (s) (-s), root; carrot; radical; *die ~ v.d. KWAAD*, the root of the evil; *tot die ~ van die SAAK gaan*, go to the root of the matter; *iets met ~ en TAK uitroei*, eradicate root and branch; ~ **TREK**, extract the root; (w) **(ge-)**, take root; *~ in*, be rooted in; ~ **aal**, eelworm (disease); ~ **agtig, (-e)**, root-like, carrot-like; ~ **blaar**, ~ **blad**, radical leaf; ~ **boom**, mangrove; ~ **draad**, fibril, root-hair; ~ **getal**, surd, exponent, rational; ~ **gewasse**, root crop, tuber plants; ~ **groente**, root vegetables; ~ **grootheid**, radical quantity; ~ **haar**, fibril; ~ **hout**, root-wood; ~ **ing**, radication; ~ **kiem**, radicle, caulicle; ~ **klank**, ~ **klinker**, radical vowel; ~ **knol**, root tuber; ~ **knoop**, root knot; ~ **krul**, curled carrot; ~ **lof**, (..**lowwe**), carrot leaves; ~ **loos**, (..**lose**), rootless; ~ **luis**, sucker; ~ **nek**, crown (of root), root-neck; ~ **punt**, tip of the root; ~ **siekte**, root-disease; ~ **skeut**, tiller, stolon; ~ **skiet, (-ge-)**, take root, strike root; radicate; ~ **skieting**, radication; ~ **skimmel**, root fungus; ~ **sop**, carrot soup; ~ **stand**, radication, ~ **stelsel**, root-system; ~ **stok**, rhizome, root stock; ~ **stomp**, stump (of a tooth); ~ **teken**, radical sign; ~ **tjie, (-s)**, rootlet; small carrot; ~ **trekking**, extraction of roots; evolution; ~ **verrotting**, root-rot; ~ **vesel**, root fibre; fibril; ~ **vorm**, shape of root; surd, radical quantity; ~ **vormig, (-e)**, root-shaped; ~ **vrot**, root-rot; ~ **woord**, radix, root-word; stem.

wou, *verlede tyd van wil*, would; *ek ~ hom so GRAAG ontmoet*, I was so keen on meeting him; *ek ~ mos*

SÊ, I thought as much; *sy* ~ *gaan SIT,* she wanted to sit down; *WAT* ~ *!*, not at all! no fear!
woud, (-e), forest, wood; ~**bewoner,** forest-dweller, woodsman; ~**duif,** wood-pigeon; ~**duiwel,** mandrill; ~**esel,** wild ass; ~**gebergte,** wooded mountains; ~**klimaat,** forest climate; ~**loper,** bushranger; ~**reus,** giant of the forest.
wou′terklou′ter, jungle-gym.
wraak, (s) revenge, vengeance, retaliation; *sy* ~ *KOEL op,* wreak one's vengeance on; ~ *NEEM,* take vengeance, avenge oneself; *om* ~ *ROEP,* cry for vengeance; ~ *SWEER,* vow vengeance; *UIT* ~, vindictively, in retaliation; **(w) (ge-),** censure, declare unworthy, reject, take exception to, challenge; recuse (a judge); *ge* ~ *te uitdrukkings,* expressions complained of; ~**baar, (..bare),** challengeable; censurable; ~**engel,** avenging angel; ~**gevoel,** feeling of revenge, vindictiveness; ~**gie′rig, (-e),** revengeful, vindictive; ~**gie′righeid,** revengefulness, thirst for revenge; ~**godin,** avenging goddess, fury, Nemesis; ~**lus,** lust for vengeance, vindictiveness; ~**lus′tig, (-e),** revengeful; ~**maatreël,** measure of revenge; ~**neming,** revenge, retaliation; ~**oefening,** revenge; ~**plan,** scheme of vengeance; ~**sug,** desire for revenge, vindictiveness; ~**sug′tig, (-e),** revengeful, vindictive.
wrag′gies, wrag′tie, indeed, surely, truly, actually; ~ *WAAR,* truly, really, actually; *hy is* ~ *WEG,* he has actually gone!
wrak, (s) (-ke), wreck, derelict; debris; *LIGGAAMLIKE* ~, physical wreck; *MAATSKAPLIKE* ~, social wreck (outcast); **(b) (-ke),** rickety (chair); infirm, shaky (health); ~**goed,** flotsam and jetsam, wreckage; ~**hout,** driftwood, wreckage.
wra′king, (-e, -s), challenging (of juryman); censuring (of conduct); recusation (of a judge); ~ *sonder opgawe van rede,* peremptory challenge.
wrak: ~**stuk,** piece of wreckage; ~**werf,** scrapyard.
wrang, (-e), acrid, astringent, acid, tart, harsh (taste), unpleasant; bitter; *die* ~ *e vrugte pluk,* reap the bitter fruits; ~**heid,** bitterness; acridity; tartness; acerbity, acidity, astringency.
wreed, (wrede), cruel, barbarous, brutish, inhuman, heartless, ferocious, fell (purpose), bloody-minded, truculent; raw (taste); *die wrede werklikhede v.d. lewe,* the grim realities of life; ~**aard, (-s),** cruel person, brute, barbarian, butcher.
wreedaar′dig, (-e), cruel, inhuman, brutal, barbarous, atrocious; ~**heid,** cruelty, atrocity.
wreed′heid, (..hede), cruelty, ferociousness, ferocity, brutality, brutishness, barbarity, barbarousness, truculence; *'n* ~ *BEGAAN,* perpetrate a cruelty; *'n* ~ *PLEEG,* commit a brutality.
wreef, (wrewe), (-s), instep; ~**band,** shoe-strap.
wreek, (ge-), revenge, avenge; *JOU* ~, take one's revenge; *jou* ~ *OP,* take vengeance on.
wre′ker, (-s), avenger, revenger.
wre′wel, resentment, rancour, irritation, animus, pique, spite; *'n* ~ *oor iets koester,* feel indignation about something; ~**daad,** evil deed; ~**(r)ig, (-e),** resentful, rancorous, spiteful, irritable, ill humoured, testy; *'n* ~ *ige haat,* a bitter hatred; ~**(r)igheid,** resentfulness, peevishness, rancour, ill humour.
wrie′mel, (ge-), swarm, abound in; wriggle; teem; ~**ende wurms,** wriggling worms.
wrik, (ge-), shake, move, jerk; *aan 'n klip* ~, try to prize a stone loose; ~**baar, (..bare),** unstable.
wring, (ge-), wring (one's hands); wrest, wrench (from someone); writhe, wriggle (from pain); *jou deur 'n opening* ~, wriggle through an opening; ~**buis,** torque tube; ~**draai, (-e),** torque-tighten; ~**er,** wringer; ~**hoek** = **wringingshoek; ~ing, (-e, -s),** wringing, wrenching; writhing, torsion, twist; ~**ingsbalans,** torsion balance; ~**ingshoek,** angle of torsion; ~**krag,** torque; ~**masjien,** clotheswringer; ~**moment,** moment of torsion; ~**sleutel,** torsion wrench; ~**spanning,** torsional stress; ~**streek,** torsion area; ~**vastheid,** torsional strength; ~**yster,** tap-wrench.
wrin′tie, wrin′tig, wrint′lik, really, surely, truly, actually; *hy het dit* ~ *INGESLUK,* he has actually swallowed it! ~ *WAAR,* actually, honestly and truthfully.
wroe′ging, (-s), remorse, contrition, self-reproach, compunction; prick (of conscience); ~ *van die gewete,* qualms; pricks of conscience.
wroet, (ge-), burrow, grub; investigate (mysteries); *in die verlede* ~, burrow in the past.
wrog, (ge-), create, work.
wrok, (s) (-ke), grudge, rancour, hatred, spite, animosity; pique; *'n GEVOEL van bittere* ~, a feeling of bitter rancour; *sy* ~ *KOEL,* wreak one's vengeance; *'n* ~ *KOESTER teen,* bear a grudge against; ~ *TOON jeens,* show resentment against; ~ *VOEL jeens,* feel resentment towards; **(w) (ge-),** fret, sulk, chafe; ~**kend,** ~**kig, (-e),** spiteful, resentful.
wrong, (-e), roll; wreath (flowers); knot, coil (hair), chignon.
wrong′el, curd(s).
wryf: ~**aandrywing,** friction drive; ~**blok,** friction block; ~**koppelaar,** friction clutch; ~**veer,** friction spring; ~**vlak,** friction surface; ~**vonk,** friction spark.
wry′wing, friction, rubbing; ~**loos, (..lose),** frictionless.
wry′wings: ~**brandwond,** brush-burn; ~**elektrisiteit,** frictional electricity; ~**hoek,** angle of friction (repose).
wry′wings: ~**plaat,** friction plate; ~**rots,** sheer rock; ~**vlak,** friction surface; ~**vry, (-e),** frictionless; ~**weerstand,** frictional resistance (drag); ~**wiel,** friction-wheel.
w′′tjie, (-s), small w.
wuf, (-te), frivolous, fickle, feather-brained.
wuft′heid, frivolity, fickleness.
wuif, wui′we, (ge-), wave, beckon; *wuiwende koringhalms,* waving cornstalks.
wulf, (wulwe), transom (naut.), ~**balk,** wingtransom.
wulfeniet′, wulfenite.
wulk, (-e), whelk.
wulp, (-e), curlew.
wulps, (-e; -er, -ste), wanton, sexy, rank, prurient, libidinous, lascivious, concupiscent, lewd; ~**heid,** wantonness, prurience, lasciviousness, lewdness, concupiscence.
wurg, (ge-), strangle, throttle, garrotte, choke (gun); be strangled; *iem.* ~ *om deur te KOM,* someone has to contend with many (financial) difficulties; ~**bedryf,** thuggery; ~**berowing,** garrotte; ~**end, (-e),** choky; ~**er, (-s),** strangler, choker, garrotter, thug; ~**geswel,** quinsy; ~**greep,** stranglehold; ~**ing,** strangling, throttling, choking; ~**ketting,** choke chain; ~**knoop,** knot to prevent throttling; ~**koord,** garrotte; ~**nek,** choke-throat (banana); ~**paal,** strangling-post; ~**patat,** choke sweet potato *(see* **teëhouer);** ~**peer,** choke-pear; ~**plek,** bottle-neck; ~**roof, (ge-),** mug, garrotte; ~**rower,** mugger; garrotter; ~**siekte,** croup; ~**strop,** tourniquet; ~**-wurg:** *dit gaan* ~ *-wurg,* it is a struggle at times; ~**yster,** garrotte.
wurm, (s) (-s), worm, maggot, grub; helminth; **(w) (ge-),** worm, twist, wriggle; ~**aandrywing,** wormdrive; ~**afdrywend, (-e),** anthelminthic; ~**afdrywer,** vermifuge; ~**agtig, (-e),** vermicular, helminthoid; lumbricoid; wormlike; ~**artseny,** vermifuge; ~**as,** worm shaft; ~**besmetting,** verminosis; worm-infestation; ~**boorsel,** frass; ~**drywend, (-e),** vermifugal; ~**frees,** hob (mech.); ~**gat,** worm-hole; ~**hopie,** worm-cast(ing); ~**koekie,** worm-tablet; ~**kruid,** tansy *(Matricaria multiflora);* ~**kunde,** helminthology; ~**laer,** worm bearing; ~**middel,** vermifuge, worm-killer, vermicide, anthelmintic; ~**parasiet,** helminth; ~**pie, (-s),** little worm; mite (fig.); ~**rat,** worm wheel, worm gear; ~**siekte,** vermination; helminthiasis; ~**skroef,** endless screw; ~**stekig,** ~**ste′kig, (-e),** worm-eaten; ~**stekigheid,** ~**ste′kigheid,** worminess; ~**vormig, (-e),** vermiform, helminthoid, lumbricoid, wormshaped; ~**vretend, (-e),** vermivorous; ~**vry, (-e),** worm-proof; ~**wiel,** worm wheel.

Wur'temberg, Wurtemburg; ~er, (-s), Wurtemburger; ~s, (-e), (of) Wurtemburg.
wurtziet', wurtzite.
wy, (ge-), devote, consecrate, bless, hallow, dedicate (building), ordain (minister); *gewyde GESKIEDENIS,* sacred history; *jou aan die STUDIE ~,* devote oneself to study.
Wyandot'tehoender, Wyandotte fowl.
wyd, (wye; wyer, -ste), wide, broad, spacious, roomy, ample, expansive, large; *'n wye GEWETE,* an elastic conscience; *~ OOP,* wide open; *~ en SYD,* far and wide; ~**beroemd,** (-e), far-famed, famous.
wy'der, (-s), dedicator.
wy'ders, (ong.), further, moreover, besides.
wyd'gesprei(d), (-de), straggling.
wyd'gestrek, (-te), far-flung, wide-spreading.
wyd'heid, wideness, roominess, broadness.
wy'ding, (-e, -s), consecration, sanctification, ordination; devotion.
wy'dings: ~**diens,** consecration service; ~**plegtigheid,** consecration ceremony; ~**tablet,** memorial tablet.
wydlo'pig, (-e), verbose, prolix, diffuse, digressive, excursive, expatiatory, long-winded, circuitous; ~**heid,** prolixity, verbosity, copiousness, long-windedness, detour (in speech), expatiation, diffuseness.
wyds'been, astraddle, astride, stride-legged; *~ RY,* ride astride a horse; *~ SIT,* sit astride; *~ STAAN oor,* straddle.
wyd'te, (-s), width, breadth; gauge (rails); calibre (gun).
wyd'uitgestrek, (-te), vast, expansive, widely extended.
wyd'uitspreidend, (-e), brachiate, widespread.
wyd'vermaard, (-e), famous, widely known, far-famed, famous.
wyd'versprei, (-e), widely diffused, widely known; far-flung.
wyd'vertak, (-te), widespread.
wy'etandsaag, rack saw.
wyf, (wywe), mean woman, vixen, shrew, termagant, beldam(e); ~**ag'tig,** (-e), shrewish; effeminate.
wy'fie, (-s), female (animal); doe (of deer); cow (of rhinoceros); hen (of birds); ~**dier,** female animal; ~-**eend,** duck; ~**jakkals,** female jackal, vixen; ~**kat,** she-cat; ~**konyn,** doe (rabbit); ~**leeu,** lioness; ~**papegaai,** poll parrot; ~**pou,** peahen.
wy'fieskemphaan, reeve.
wy'fieskilpad, female tortoise.
wy'fiesmansmens, effeminate person.
wy'fle: ~**swaan,** pen; ~**tarentaal,** guinea-hen; ~**varing,** lady-fern; ~**volstruis,** hen ostrich.
wyk¹, (-e), ward, quarter, area, district, beat (of policeman); *die ~ neem,* flee, take oneself off.
wyk², (w) (ge-), withdraw, retire, give ground, yield, give way; *na BUITE ~,* seek refuge outside; *geen DUIMBREED ~ nie,* not budge an inch; *vir NIEMAND ~ nie,* yield to no-one; *die SPANNING ~ reeds,* the tension is lessening already.
wyk: ~**besoek,** ward-visit; ~**besoeker,** ward visitor; ~**bestuur,** district board, ward committee; ~**kleur,** retiring (receding) colour; ~**meester,** warden; ~**plaas,** asylum, refuge.
wyks: ~**geneesheer,** district surgeon; ~**kraamverpleegster,** district midwife.
wyk: ~**suster,** district nurse; ~**verpleegster,** district nurse; ~**verpleging,** district nursing.
wy'kwas, aspergillum.
wyl¹, (s) moment, while; *onder die ~,* while, meanwhile.
wyl², (w) (ge-), sojourn, stay.
wyl³, (vgw) because, since, as.
wy'le¹, (s) moment, while; *by ~,* sometimes, at times; now and then.
wy'le², (b) late, deceased; *~ my vader,* my late father.
wyn, (-e), wine; *HELDER ~ skink,* be quite open about something; be frank; *die ~ het 'n KRAKIE,* the wine has turned sour; *goeie ~ het g'n KRANS nodig nie,* good wine needs no bush; *goeie ~ PRYS homself,* good wine needs no bush; *ROOI ~,* red wine; claret; *WIT ~,* white wine; hock; *~ in die man, WYSHEID in die kan,* when the wine is in, the wit is out; ~**ag'tig,** (-e), winelike, vinous; ~**aksyns,** duty on wine; ~**asyn,** wine-vinegar; ~**bak,** winepress; ~**beker,** winecup; ~**belasting,** wine-duty; ~**bereiding,** wine-making; ~**bessie,** wine-berry; ~**boer,** wine-farmer; ~**boerdery,** wine-farming, viticulture; ~**bottel,** wine-bottle; ~**bou,** vine-growing, viniculture; ~**bouer,** viniculturist; ~**distrik,** wine-district; ~**drinker,** wine-drinker, wine-bibber; ~**droesem,** wine-dregs, lees; ~**druif,** wine grape; ~**fees,** wine-festival; ~**gaard,** vineyard (fig.); ~**gees,** spirit of wine; alcohol; ethanol; ~**geesvernis,** spirit varnish; ~**glas,** wineglass.
wyn'handel, wine-trade; ~**aar,** wine-seller, wine-merchant, vintner.
wyn: ~**huis,** tavern, bar; ~**jaar,** wine-year, year of vintage; ~**kaart,** wine-list; ~**kan,** wine-jug, wine-tankard; ~**kelder,** wine-cellar, wine-vault; ~**kelkie,** wineglass; ~**kelner,** wine steward (waiter); ~**kenner,** judge (connoisseur) of wine; ~**kleur,** wine-colour; ~**kleurig,** (-e), wine-coloured, claret; ~**koek,** tipsy-cake; ~**koper,** wine-buyer; ~**kraffie,** wine decanter; ~**kruik,** wine-jar; ~**kuip,** wine-vat; ~**kunde,** oenology; ~**kun'dig,** (-e), oenological; ~**kun'dige,** oenologist; ~**land,** wine-country; ~**lied,** (-ere), drinking-song; ~**lug,** winy smell; ~**maat,** wine-measure; ~**makery,** wine-making; ~**meter,** vinometer; wine-gauger (person); ~**moer,** lees (of wine); wine-marc; ~**mos,** must; ~**oes,** vintage; ~**offer,** wine-offering, libation; ~**pers,** wine-press; ~**plaas,** wine-farm; ~**proef,** wine-tasting; ~**proewer,** wine-taster; ~**roeier,** gauger (person); ~**rooi,** wine red, maroon; ~**ruik,** vinous smell.
wyn'ruit, rue (*Ruta graviolens*); ~**haakdoring,** hook-thorn (*Acacia detinens*).
wyn: ~**sak,** wineskin, winebag; tippler, winebibber; ~**smaak,** taste of wine; ~**soort,** kind of wine; ~**sop,** caudle; ~**sous,** wine-sauce; ~**spiritus,** rectified spirit(s); ~**steen,** wine-stone, tartar; ~**steensuur,** tartaric acid.
wyn'stok, vine; ~**bladluis,** vine-fretter, phylloxera.
wyn: ~**streek,** wine-district; ~**suiper,** winebibber; ~**suipery,** winebibbing.
Wyn'tjie: *van ~ en Tryntjie hou,* be fond of wine and women.
wyn: ~**vaatjie,** wine-barrel, wine-cask; ~**vervalsing,** adulteration of wine; ~**vlek,** wine-stain; ~**vlieg,** wine-fly; wine bibber; tippler; ~**vlies,** beeswing; ~**vomitief',** impecacuanha wine.
wys¹, (s) (-e), manner, way; mood (gram.); type; *AANTONENDE ~,* indicative mood; *LANDS ~, lands eer,* when in Rome, do as the Romans do.
wys², (w) (ge-), show, demonstrate, indicate, point out, direct; *waar DAWID die wortels gegrawe het,* give someone a dressing-down; *iem. die DEUR ~,* show someone the door; *~ NA,* point at; *iem. OP iets ~,* call someone's attention to something; *ek SAL hom ~!* I'll show him!
wys³, (h) (-e; -er, -ste), prudent, sage, wise; *die oier wil ~er wees as die HEN,* want to teach one's grandmother to suck eggs; *iem. ~e RAAD gee,* give someone sound advice; *nie REG ~ wees nie,* be not quite all there; he hasn't all his wits about him; *na die VOORVAL ~ wees,* be wise after the event; *ek kan hier niks uit ~ WORD nie,* I cannot make head or tail out of this; I am none the wiser.
wys⁴, (b, bw) (-e; -er; -ste), obstinate; impertinent; vicious (animals); ~ *wees,* be impudent; be cheeky; be unruly; be vicious.
wys'begeerte, philosophy.
wy'se¹, (-s) = **wys¹;** *na my ~ van SIEN,* as I see things; *by ~ van SPREKE,* in a manner of speaking; *by ~ van UITSONDERING,* by way of exception.
wy'se², (-s), wise man, sage; *die W~s uit die Ooste,* the Wise Men of the East.
wy'ser, (-s), index, hand (of a clock); needle (compass), (weather)cock; indicator; *GROOT ~,* minute-hand; *KLEIN ~,* hour-hand; *MET die ~s,* clockwise; ~**meter,** dial gauge; ~**plaat,** dial, hour-plate, (clock-)face; reader-plate.
wys'geer, (wysgere), philosopher.

wysge'rig, (-e), philosophical.
wys'heid, wisdom; judiciousness; prudence; *die ~ is in die KAN*, it's the wine talking; *hy maak asof hy die ~ in PAG het*, he acts as though he has a lien on wisdom; he thinks that he knows everything.
wys'heidskies(tand), wisdom-tooth.
wy'sie, (-s), melody, air, tune, aria; *iem. van die ~ BRING*, put someone off his stroke; confuse someone; throw someone off his stride; *nie kan ~ HOU nie*, not be able to sing in tune; *van die ~ RAAK*, lose one's head; lose the thread of one's discourse; become flustered; *van sy ~ af WEES*, he is all at sea.
wy'sig, (ge-), modify, amend, alter, change, recast; *ge~de omstandighede*, altered circumstances; ~**baar**, (..**bare**), modifiable, amendable; ~**end**, (-e), alterative; qualificative; ~**er**, modifier.
wy'siging, (-e, -s), amendment, modification, qualification, alteration, change; *'n ~ AANBRING in*, amend to; *~ van 'n BEVEL*, variation of an order (law); *'n ~ ONDERGAAN*, undergo a change; ~**swet**, amending act; ~**swetsontwerp**, amending bill.
wys'kleur, advancing colour.
wys'lik, wisely.
wys'maak, (-ge-), make belief; bluff; impose on; *'n mens kan hom ALLES ~*, he is very easily imposed upon, he is easily bluffed; *probeer dit aan jou GROOTJIE ~*, tell that to the marines; *iem. IETS ~*, spin someone a yarn; *ek LAAT my dit nie ~ nie*, nobody can tell me that.
wys'maker, bluffer; ~**y**, make-believe.
wys'neus, wiseacre, know-all, pedant, prig, malapert.
wysneu'sig, (-e), pedantic, cocky, pert, conceited; ~**heid**, pedantry, conceit, pertness.
wys'pennetjie, indicator (scales).
wys'stok, fescue.
wys'ter = **wyser**.
wys'vinger, index finger, forefinger.
wyt, (ge-), impute, accuse, blame; attribute; *te ~e AAN*, due to; ascribable to; *IETS aan iem. ~*, blame someone for something; *jy het dit aan JOUSELF te ~e*, it is your own fault, you have only yourself to blame.
wy'ting, whiting (fish); merlin.
wy'water, lustral water, holy water; ~**bakkie**, holy-water basin (font), aspersorium; ~**kwas**, aspergillum; ~**vaatjie**, holy-water font, stoup, aspersorium.
wy'we: ~**beul**, (-s), wife-beater; ~**praatjie**, (-s), chit-chat, gossip; old wives' tale.

X

x, (-'e), x.
xantaat', (**xantate**), xantate.
xanteen', xanthene.
xanteïen', **xanteï'ne**, xanthein.
xanthidrol', xanthydrol.
Xanthip'pe, Xanthippe, shrewish wife.
xantien', **xanti'ne**, xanthine; ~**suur**, xanthic acid.
xantofiel', xanthophyll.
xantogeen', xanthogen.
X'-as, X-axis (math.).
X'-bene, knock-knees.
xe'nium, (**xenia**), xenium; present to (from) a guest.
xenoblas', (-te), xenoblast.
xenofobie', xenophobia.
xenogamie', xenogamy, cross-fertilization.
xenograaf', (..**grawe**), xenographer.
xenografie', xenography.
xenokrist', (-te), xenocryst.
xenoliet', xenolith.
xenomanie', xenomania, xenophobia.
xenomorf', (s) (-e), xenomorph; (b) (-e), xenomorphic.
xe'non, xenon.
xenotiem', xenotime.
xe'res, xeres, sherry.
xerofiel', (-e), xerophilous.
xe'rofiet, (-e), xerophyte; ..**fi'ties**, (-e), xerophytic.
xeroftalmie', xerophthalmia.
xerografie', xerography.
xero'se, xerosis.
X'-hakke, cow-hocks.
Xho'sa, (-s), Xhosa.
x'ie, (-s), small x.
xi'leem, xylem.
xilofoon', (..**fone**), xylophone.
xilograaf', (..**grawe**), xylographer.
xilografie', xylography; ..**fies**, (-e), xilographic(al).
xiloliet', xylolite.
xilologie', xylology.
xi'lometer, (-s), xylometer.
xiloon'suur, xylon acid.
xilo'se, xylose.
X'-straal: ~**behandeling**, X-ray treatment; ~**fotografie**, X-ray photography.
X'-strale, X-rays.
X'-sweislas, double V-weld.

Y

y, (-'s), y.
yak, (-ke), yak.
Yale'slot, Yale lock.
Yan'kee, (-s), Yankee.
yard, (-s), yard.
Y'-as, Y axis.
y'del, (**|-e|**; **-er**, **-ste**) idle (word), empty, useless, futile; vain (person), foppish, conceited, coquettish; *'n ~e nooi*, a vain girl.
y'delheid, (..**hede**), vanity, futility, emptiness; self-conceit, foppishness, ostentatiousness, trumpery; *ALLES is ~*, all is vanity; *~ DER ydelhede*, vanity of vanities.
y'dellik, vainly; *die HERE se naam ~ gebruik*, take the name of God in vain.
y'deltuit, (-e), fop; coquette, vain woman; ~(**er)ig**, (-e), vainglorious; coquettish; ~**ery**, vainglory, vanity; coquetry.
yf, (**ywe**), yew(-tree).
yk, (s) gauge, verification of weights and measures; (w) (ge-), test, adjust; hallmark, stamp (and verify), assize; calibrate; standardize; *'n geykte uitdrukking*, a standard (stereotyped) phrase; ~**brief**, bill of lading; ~**er**, (-s), inspector of weights and measures, assizer, gauger; ~**geld**, assizer's fee; ~**gewig**, standard weight; ~**ing**, assizement, calibration; ~**instrument**, calibrating instrument; ~**kantoor**, weights-and-measures office, gauging-office; ~**kromme**, calibration curve; ~**loon**, assizer's fee; ~**maat**, standard measure, gauge; ~**meester**, gauger, assizer; assayer; ~**merk**, stamp, seal; ~**wese**, assizing; ~**wet**, assize law.
yl¹, (s) haste, hurry; *in aller ~*, with all haste, at top speed; (w) (ge-), hasten, hurry.
yl², (w) (ge-), be delirious, rave.
yl³, (b) thin (hair); rarefied (air); fine; rare; tenuous

(air); *die mielies staan* ~ *op die land*, the mealies are scattered here and there on the land.
yl: ~ **bode**, express messenger; ~ **diens**, **(-te)**, express service.
yl: ~ **end**, **(-e)**, delirious; ~ **gif**, deliriant.
yl'goed, express goods.
yl'heid, rarefaction, rarity, thinness.
yl'hoof, rattle-brain.
ylhoof'dig, **(-e)**, delirious, light-headed; ~ **heid**, delirium, deliriousness.
y'ling, raving, delirium.
y'lings, in great haste, hurriedly.
yo'ga, yoga.
yo'gi, **(-'s)**, yoga.
young'bessie, youngberry.
yp'silon, **(-s)**, ypsilon (Greek letter y).
ys, (s) ice; *die* ~ *BREEK*, break the ice; *iem. gaan nie oor* ~ *van een NAG nie*, one should not skate on thin ice; *op gladde* ~ *STAAN*, be in danger; be on slippery ground; *VRY van* ~, clear of ice; *jou op gladde* ~ *WAAG*, skate on thin ice; (w) **(ge-)**, freeze, ice; shudder; ~ **afsetting**, accretion of ice; ~ **ag'tig**, **(-e)**, icy; ~ **baan**, skating-rink; ~ **bank**, icebank; ~ **bedekking**, ice-cap; ~ **been**, aitchbone; ~ **beer**, polar bear; ~ **berg**, iceberg; ~ **bestryder**, anticer, de-icer; ~ **beweging**, ice-movement; ~ **blink**, iceblink; ~ **blok**, ice-floe; ~ **blom**, frost-flower; ~ **breker**, ice-breaker (-boat); ice-pick; ~ **bultjie**, hummock; ~ **dek**, ice-cap; ~ **drank**, cobbler (iced drink); ~ **drif**, ice-drift; ~ **duiker**, loon (bird); ~ **eend**, noddy (bird)
y'sel, glazed frost.
y'ser, **(-e)**, (fig.), iron; hard; *die Y~e HERTOG*, the Iron Duke; *die Y~e KANSELIER*, the Iron Chancellor.
ys: ~ **fabriek**, ice-factory; ~ **gang**, ice-drift; floating ice; ~ **gevaar**, ice-peril; ~ **glas**, frosted glass; ~ **grot**, ice-cave; ~ **hokkie**, ice hockey.
y'sig, **(-e)**, ice (icy) cold; ~ **heid**, iciness.
ysingwek'kend, **(-e)**, horrifying, ghastly, appalling, horrific.
ys: ~ **kamer**, refrigerating chamber; ~ **kap**, ice-cap; ~ **kar**, ice-cream cart; ~ **kas**, refrigerator, ice-chest, freezer; ~ **keël**, ~ **kegel**, icicle; ~ **kelder**, icehouse; ~ **kis**, ice-chest; ~ **kors**, crust of ice.
ys'koud, (b) (..**koue**), icy cold, cold as ice, frigid, gelid, clay-cold (corpse); (bw) frostily, icily; *hy het daar* ~ *van GEWORD*, it struck a chill to his heart; *dit LAAT my* ~, it has no effect on me; it leaves me cold; *hy het 'n yskoue ONTVANGS by haar gehad*, she gave him an icy reception; *van iets* ~ *WORD*, go cold all over; ~ **heid**, iciness.
ys'laag, ice stratum.
Ys'land, Iceland; ~ **er**, **(-s)**, Icelander; ~ **s**, **(-e)**, Icelandic; ~ *se papawer*, Iceland poppy; ~ **spaat**, Iceland spar.
ys'lik, **(-e)**, tremendous, enormous; horrible, dire, ghastly; ~ **heid**, enormity; horror.
ys: ~ **loper**, iceman; ~ **masjien**, freezing-machine, freezer; ~ **massa**, icepack; ~ **modder**, slush, sludge ice; ~ **muur**, ice-barrier; ~ **naald**, ice-needle; ~ **omslag**, ice-compress; **Y** ~ **periode**, Ice Age, glacial period; ~ **ploeg**, ice-plough; ~ **rand**, icefoot; ~ **reën**, sleet; ~ **rot**, ice-rat; ~ **ryp**, glazed frost; ~ **sak**, ice-pack.
Ys'see, Polar Sea; *die Noordelike Y*~, the Arctic Ocean; *die Suidelike Y*~, the Antarctic Ocean.
ys: ~ **skade**, ice damage; ~ **skeur**, crevasse; ~ **skol**, ~ **skots**, floe of ice, ice-floe, flake of ice, ice-float; ~ **slee**, luge, ice-sledge; ~ **spaat**, sanidine, glassy felspar; ~ **spoor**, crampon; ~ **sport**, ice sports; ~ **steen**, cryolite; ~ **stokkie**, ice-sucker.
ys'ter, **(-s)**, iron; flat iron; branding-iron; horse-shoe; runner (of sledge); blade (of skate); *BEWERKTE* ~, manufactured iron; *GEDEË* ~, native iron; *GEGOTE* ~, cast iron; *GESMEDE* ~, wrought iron; *GEPLETTE* ~, rolled iron; ~ *met die HANDE wil breek*, attempt the impossible; one can't squeeze blood out of a stone; *RU* ~, pig-iron; *SES jaar in die* ~ *s*, six years' hard labour; *iem. in* ~ *s SLAAN*, put someone in irons; *SMEE die* ~ *terwyl dit heet is*, make hay while the sun shines; *hy is van* ~ *en STAAL*, he has muscles of steel; he is all thews and sinews; *te veel* ~ *s in die VUUR hê*, have too many irons in the fire; ~ **aar**, iron vein (lode); ~ **aarde**, ferruginous earth; ~ **afval**, scrap-iron; ~ **agtig**, **(-e)**, ferreous, ferric, iron-like, ferruginous; ~ **balk**, steel girder; ~ **band**, ferrule, iron (steel) hoop; ~ **bank**, iron seat; iron pan (soil); ~ **bedryf**, iron industry; ~ **bek**, bean-bug; ~ **beslag**, iron mounting; ~ **beton**, ferroconcrete; ~ **bint**, iron tie; ~ **byter**, old war-horse; ~ **draad**, iron wire; ~ **erts**, iron ore; ~ **fabriek**, ironworks, steelworks; ~ **fabrikant**, ironmaster; ~ **gaas**, iron gauze; ~ **ghwano**, basic slag, scoria; ~ **gieter**, iron-founder; ~ **gietery**, iron-foundry; ~ **glans**, specular iron ore; ~ **gordyn**, iron curtain; ~ **gras**, forget-me-not *(Anchusa riparia)*; ~ **grou**, iron-grey; ~ **haak**, gaff; ~ **hak**, iron heel; ~ **hand**, mailed fist; ~ **handel**, ironmongery, iron trade; ~ **handelaar**, ironmonger, hardware-man; ~ **hard**, hard as iron; ~ **hiel**, iron heel; ~ **hoed**, gossan; ~ **hok**, iron cage; ~ **hou'dend**, **(-e)**, ferruginous, ferreous, ferriferous, chalybeate; ~ **hout**, ironwood; ~ **industrie**, iron (steel) industry; ~ **katel**, iron bedstead; ~ **kies**, pyrite, iron pyrites; ~ **kleur**, iron-colour, iron-grey; ~ **kleurig**, **(-e)**, iron-grey; ~ **klip**, diabase; dolerite; ironstone.
ys'terklou: ~ *in die grond slaan*, (i) take to one's heels; (ii) dig in one's heels.
ysterkruid, verbena.
Ys'terkruis, Iron Cross.
ys'ter: ~ **lees**, (shoemaker's) last; ~ **legering**, ferrous alloy; ~ **long**, iron lung; ~ **marmer**, basalt; ~ **myn**, iron mine; ~ **okside**, ~ **oksied**, ferric oxide; ~ **paal**, iron standard (pole); ~ **perd**, bicycle; train; locomotive; ~ **pil**, Blaud's pill; ~ **plaat**, iron plate; ~ **ploeg**, iron plough; ~ **punt**, gad; ~ **pyp**, iron tubing; ~ **ring**, iron ring; ~ **roes**, iron mould; ~ **ryk**, **(-e)**, rich in iron; ~ **saag**, hack-saw; ~ **sintel**, iron cinder; ~ **skaaf**, iron plane; ~ **skêr**, iron shears; ~ **skimmel**, iron-grey horse; ~ **slak**, dross, slag; ~ **smedery**, forge; ~ **smeltery**, iron-foundry; ~ **smid**, iron smith; ~ **spaat**, siderite; ~ **spyker**, frostnail, calk; ~ **staaf**, iron bar; ~ **sterk**, strong as iron; ~ **stok**, iron (golf); ~ **sulfaat**, copperas; green vitriol; ~ **suur**, ferric acid; **Y** ~ **tydperk**, Iron Age; ~ **vark**, porcupine; *gaan* ~ *vark slaan*, go a-wooing; ~ **varkgat**, nest (hole) of a porcupine; ~ **varkpen**, porcupine-quill, ~ **verblinding**, iron compound, ~ **vernis**, Berlin black; ~ **vitrioel**, copperas, iron sulphate; ~ **vreter**, fire-eater, swashbuckler, bully, hector; ~ **vuis**, iron fist; ~ **ware**, hardware; ironmongery; ~ **werk**, ironwork; ~ **winkel**, ironmonger's shop, hardware shop.
Ys'tyd(perk), Ice Age, glacial period.
ys: ~ **veld**, ice-field, ice-sheet; ~ **vlakte**, expanse of ice; ~ **vleis**, frozen meat; ~ **voël**, halcyon kingfisher; ~ **voëlblou**, kingfisher blue; ~ **vorming**, glaciation; ice accretion; ice-formation; ~ **vos**, Arctic fox; ~ **vry**, **(-e)**, ice-free; ~ **wafel**, ice-wafer; ~ **water**, ice(d) water; ~ **werk**, ice-work; ~ **werking**, ice-action; ~ **wolk**, ice-cloud.
y'tjie, **(-s)**, small y.
ytter'bium, ytterbium.
yt'trium, yttrium.
y'wer, (s) diligence, zeal, ardour, ardency, eagerness, fire, fervency, gusto, intentness, mettle, earnestness, industry; *blinde* ~, fanaticism; (w) **(ge-)**, devote oneself to, be zealous, display zeal; *jou vir 'n saak (be)* ~, devote oneself body and soul to a cause; ~ **aar**, **(-s)**, zealot, devotee, enthusiast; ~ **end**, **(-e)**, fervid; ~ **ig**, **(-e)**, diligent, industrious, earnest, eager, assiduous, fervent, keen, zealous; ~ **igheid**, diligence, zealousness; ~ **sug**, envy, jealousy; ~ **sug'tig**, **(-e)**, jealous, envious; ~ **sug'tigheid**, envy, jealousy.

Z

z, (-'s) z; *van A tot Z*, from A to Z, from beginning to end.
Zambe'zi, Zambezi.
Zam'bië, Zambia; ~ **r**, (-s), Zambian.
Zam'bies, (-e), Zambian.
Zan'zibar, Zanzibar.
Zarathoes'tra, Zoroaster, Zarathustra.
ze'boe, zebu.
Ze'phyrus, Zephyr.
zeppelin', (-s), zeppelin.
ze'ro, (-'s), zero, naught.
Zeus, Zeus.
zig'goerat, (-s), ziggurat.
Zimbab'we, Zimbabwe.
zinkeniet', zinkenite.
zirko'nium, zirconium.
zits, (ge-), hit all of a sudden; sting (like a bee); whizz.
Zoe'loe, (-s), Zulu; ~ **beeste,** Zulu cattle; ~ **gewoonte,** Zulu custom; ~ **hoof,** Zulu chief; ~ **impie,** (-s), Zulu army; ~ **land,** Zululand; ~ **opperhoof,** Zulu chief; ~ **taal,** Zulu language.
zoem, (tw) buzz! whizz!
zoem, (s) buzz(ing), drone; (w) (ge-), buzz, whizz, drone, zoom; ~ **er,** (-s), buzzer; ~ **pie,** (-s), blue duiker; ~ **vlieg,** (ge-), zoom; ~ **vlug,** zoom.
Zoroas'ter, Zoroaster, Zarathustra.
Zoroastris'me, Zoroastrianism.
Zouaaf', (Zouawe), Zouave.
Z'-staaf, Z bar.
z'tjie, (-s), small z.
Zu'lu = **Zoeloe.**
Zwingliaan', (..liane), follower of Zwingli; ~ **s',** (-e), Zwinglian.
Zwinglianis'me, Zwinglianism.
zy'liet, zylite.
Z'-yster, Z iron.

1. AFKORTINGS

A

Afrikaans		Engels
A	ampère	ampere
Å.	angström	angström
a.	aan	to
a	aar	a
a., adj.	adjektief; adjektiwies	a.; adj.
AA	Automobiel-Assosiasie	AA
AA	Alkoholiste Anoniem	AA
AAK	Algemene Armesorgkommissie	—
aand.	aandeel	share
aanget.	aangeteken	regd.
aanh.	aanhangsel	app.
aank.	aankoms	arr.
aanm.	aanmerking	rem.
aansl.	aansluiting	junc.
aant.	aantonend	ind.
aant.	aantekening	note, n.
aanvr.	aanvraag	demand
aanw.	aanwysend	dem.
aard.	aardkundig(e)	geol.
Aardk.	Aardkunde (as vak)	Geol.
Aardr.	Aardrykskunde (as vak)	Geog.
antw. asb.	antwoord asseblief	RSVP
a.b.	aan boord	o.b.
A/B	afleweringsbrief	D/O
A.B.	Algemeen-Beskaaf	standard speech
ABC	alfabet	A.B.C.
ab init.	*ab initio* (van die begin af)	ab init.
abl.	ablatief; ablaut	abl.
ABM	Aktiewe Burgermag	ACF
abs.	absoluut	abs.
ACVV	Afrikaanse Christelike Vrouevereniging	ACVV
a.d.	*ante diem* (voor die dag); *a dato* (vanaf datum)	a.d.
A.D.	*Anno Domini* (in die jaar van ons Here)	A.D.
ad fin.	*ad finem* (tot die einde)	ad fin.
ad inf.	*ad infinitum* (tot die oneindige)	ad inf.
adj.	adjektief	adj.
adjk.	adjunk	adj.
adj.-off.	adjudant-offisier	W./O.
adjt.	adjudant	A.D.C., Adj.
ad lib.	*ad libitum* (na verkiesing)	ad lib.
admin.	administrasie; administrateur	Admin.
adml.	admiraal	Adm., A.F.
adv.	advokaat; adverbium; adverbiaal; advies, adviseur	adv.
ad val.	*ad valorem* (volgens waarde)	ad val.
advt.	advertensie	ad., advt.
advv.	advokate	advocates
aet.	*aetatis* (oud)	aet., aetat.
afb.	afbeelding	illus.
afd.	afdeling	div.
afdb.	afdelingsbestuur	divisional council
afk.	afkorting	abbr.
afl.	aflewering	dely.
afl.	afleiding	der.
Afr.	Afrikaans; Afrikaner	Afr.
afs.	afsender	sender
A.G.	adjudant-generaal	A.G.
agb.	agbare	Hon.
AGS	Apostoliese Geloofsending	AGS
a.i.	*ad interim* (vir die tussentyd; waarnemend)	ad. int.
Akad.	Akademie	Acad.
akk.	akkusatief	acc.
aks.	akseptasie; aksepteer	acc.
al.	*alias* (anders)	alias
al.	*alinea* (reël)	line
ald.	aldaar	ib., ibid.
Alg.	Algebra (as vak)	Alg.
alg.	algebraïes	alg.
alg.	algemeen	gen.
Am.	Amerika; Amerikaans	Amer.
A.M.D.G.	*ad majorem Dei gloriam* (tot meerdere eer van God)	A.M.D.G.
amp.	ampère	amp.
and.	*andante* (stadig)	and.
Angl.	Anglikaans; Anglisisme	Angl.
anon.	anoniem; anonimus	anon.

Afrikaans		Engels
anorg.	anorganies(e)	inorg.
ANS	Afrikaans-Nasionale Studentebond	—
antw.	antwoord	ans.
antw. bet.	antwoord betaal	R.P.
ANV	Algemeen Nederlands Verbond	—
apk.	asperdekrag	b.h.p.
a.p.k.	aangeduide perdekrag	i.h.p.
app.	appellant	app.
appl.	applous	appl.
Apr.	April	Apr.
Arab.	Arabies	Arab.
Arb.	Arbeid(er)	Lab.
arg.	argaïes; argaïsme	arch.
Argeol.	Argeologie (as vak)	Archaeol.
argeol.	argeologies	archaeol.
argit.	argitektuur; argitektonies	arch.
ARM	Assistent-Resident-Magistraat	ARM
art.	artikel	art.
As.	Angel-Saksies	A.S.
a.s.	aanstaande	prox.
ASB	Afrikaanse Studentebond	ASB
asb.	asseblief	please, s.v.p.
ASK	Algemene Sendingkommissie	—
ass.	assuransie	ass(ur).; ins.
asst.	assistent	asst.
asste.	assistente	asst.
Astr.	Astronomie (as vak)	Astr(on).
ATG	Afrikaanse Taalgenootskap	—
ATKV	Afrikaanse Taal- en Kultuurvereniging	—
atm.	atmosferies	atmos.
attr.	attributief	attrib.
ATV	Afrikaanse Taalvereniging	—
a.u.b.	as u blief (asseblief)	s.v.p.
Aug.	Augustus	Aug.
avdp.	avoirdupois	avdp.
a.w.	aangehaalde werk	op.cit.

B

B	bel	bel
B.A.	*Baccalaureus Artium*	B.A.
bal.	balans	bal.
bar.	barometer; barometries	bar.
B. Arch.	*Baccalaureus Architecturae*	B. Arch.
bat.	bataljon	bat.
batt.	battery	batt.
bb.	broeder(s)	Bros., brethren
b.b.a.	betaling by aflewering	COD
BBC	British Broadcasting Corporation	BBC
BBP	baie belangrike persoon	VIP
B.Ch.	*Baccalaureus Chirurgiae*	B.Ch.
B.Ch.D.	*Baccalaureus Chirurgiae Dentium*	B.Ch.D.
B.C.L.	*Baccalaureus Communis Legis*	B.C.L.
B.Com.	*Baccalaureus Commercii*	B.Com.
bd.	boulevard	Bd.
B.D.	*Baccalaureus Divinitatis*	B.D.
B.Econ.	*Baccalaureus Economiae*	B.Econ.
B.Ed.	*Baccalaureus Educationis*	B.Ed.
B.Ed.Ph.	*Baccalaureus Educationis Physicae*	B.Ed.Ph.
bedr.	bedrag	amt.
bekl.	beklaagde	acc.
Belg.	België; Belgies	Belg.
ben.	benaming	name
bep.	bepaling	def.
bes.	besending	cons.
bes.	besitlik	poss.
bes.	besonder(e)	spec.
besk.	beskuldigde	acc.
best.	bestelling	order
bes. vnw.	besitlike voornaamwoord	poss. pron.
bet.	betaal	pd.
bet.	betekenis	meaning
betr. vnw.	betreklike voornaamwoord	rel. pron.
BF&W	behoudens foute en weglatings	E.&O.E.
bg.	bogenoemde(e)	above-mentioned
BGSA	Bybelgenootskap van Suid-Afrika	BSSA
bibl.	biblioteek	lib.
Biol.	Biologie (as vak)	biol.
BHF	baie hoë frekwensie	VHF
B.Ing.	*Baccalaureus in Ingenieurswese*	B.Eng.
bk.	bank	bank
bk.	boek	bk.
b.k.	bokas	u.c.

Afrikaans		Engels
bl.	bladsy	p.
B.Litt.	*Baccalaureus Litterarum*	B.Litt.
bll.	bladsye	pp.
bls.	balansstaat	b.s.
B.M.	*Baccalaureus Medicinae*	B.M., M.B.
B.Mil.	*Baccalaureus Militaris*	B.Mil.
B.Mus.	*Baccalaureus Musicae*	B.Mus., Mus.B(ac).
b.nw.	byvoeglike naamwoord	a., adj.
B.O.	bevelvoerende offisier	C.O., O.C.
b.o.	blaai om	P.T.O.
boe.	boesel	bush.
boekh.	boekhandel	book-trade
Boekh.	Boekhou (as vak)	bkk.
Bot.	Botanie (as vak)	bot.
bot.	botanies	bot.
Bouk.	boukunde (as vak)	arch.
bouk.	boukunde	arch.
B.Phil.	*Baccalaureus Philosophia*	B.Phil.
Bpk.	Beperk	Ltd.
br.	broer; broeder	Bro.
Br.	Brits; Britse	Br.
B.R.	Britse ryk	B.E.
brig.	brigade; brigadier	Brig.
brig.-genl.	brigade-generaal	Brig.-Gen.
br. in X.	broeder in Christus	Br. in X
brs.	broeders	Bros., brethren
bs.	balansstaat	b.s.
B.S.A.	Birmingham Small Arms	B.S.A.
B.Sc.	*Baccalaureus Scientiae*	B.Sc.
B.Sc.Agric	*Baccalaureus Scientiae Agriculturae*	B.Sc.Agric
bst.	bostaande	above
btd.	betaald	pd.
bto.	bruto	gross
burg.	burgemeester	mayor
bv.	byvoorbeeld	e.g.
b.v.p.	been voor paaltjie (krieket)	l.b.w.
B.V.Sc.	*Baccalaureus Veterinariae Scientiae*	B.V.Sc.
bw.	bywoord	adv.
B.W.	Betaalbare Wissels	B/P
byl.	bylae	encl.
byv.	byvoeglik	adj.
byv.	byvoegsel	suppl.

C

C.	curie	C.
c.	sent	c
ca.	*circa* (ongeveer)	c.
cal.	kalorie	cal.
cap.	*caput* (hoofstuk)	cap., chap.
cet. par.	*ceteris paribus* (alles gelyk synde)	cet. par
c. ex.	*cum expenses (met koste)*	c. ex.
cf.	*confer* (vergelyk)	cf.
Ch.B.	*Chirurgiae Baccalaureus*	Ch. B.
Chem.	Chemie (as vak)	Chem.
Ch.M.	*Chirurgiae Magister*	Ch.M.
CHO	Christelike Hoër Onderwys	C.H.E.
Chr.	Christus	Christ
CJMV	Christelike Jongmannevereniging	YMCA
CJV	Christelike Jongliedevereniging	YMCA; YWCA
CMR	Christelike Maatskaplike raad	—
CNO	Christelik Nasionale Onderwys	—
cos	kosinus	cos
cosec	kosekans	cosec
cot	kotangens	cot
cresc.	*crescendo* (toenemend in sterkte)	cresc.
c.s.	*cum suis* (met die syne)	c.s.
CSV	Christelike Strewersvereniging	C.E.S.
CSV	Christen-Studentevereniging	C.S.A.
cum. div.	*cum dividendo* (met dividend)	cum div.
cwt.	sentenaar	cwt.
CI	Christelike Instituut	CI

D

d.	*denarius* (pennie)	d.
D/A	Dokumente teen Akseptasie	D/A
DALRO	Dramatiese, Artistieke en Letterkundige Regte-Organisasie	Dramatic, Artistic and Literary Rights Organization.
Dan.	*Daniël*	Dan.
dat.	datief	dat.
d.a.v.	daaraanvolgende	et seq., et sq,
D/b	debietbrief	D/N

Afrikaans		Engels
D/B	Dokumente teen Betaling	D/P
DBV	Dierebeskermingsvereniging	SPCA
D.C.	*da capo* (herhaal van die begin af)	D.C.
D.C.L.	*Doctor Communis Legis*	D.C.L.
d.d.	dae na datum	d.d.
d.d.	*de dato* (gedateer)	dated
D.D.	*Doctor Divinitatis*	D.D.
DDT	dichloordifenieltrichlooretaan	DDT
D.Econ.	*Doctor Economiae*	D.Econ.
D.Ed.	*Doctor Educationis*	D.Ed.
def.	definisie	def.
dekl.	deklinasie	decl.
del.	*deleatur* (op drukproewe: skrap); *dileneavit* (op tekeninge: het dit geteken)	del.
Dem.	Demokraat; Demokraties(e)	Dem.
dep.	depot	dep.
dept.	departement	dept.
des.	deser	cur., inst.
Des.	Desember	Dec.
Deut.	*Deuteronomium*	Deut.
D.G.	*Dei gratia* (deur Gods genade); *Deo gratias* (God sy dank); Direkteur-Generaal	D.G.
dgl.	dergelike	such
d.i.	dit is	i.e., q.e.
di.	*domini* (predikante)	Revs.
Di.	Dinsdag	Tues.
dial.	dialek(ties)	dial.
diensw.	dienswillig	obed.
Dierk.	Dierkunde	Zool.
dierk.	dierkundig(e)	zool.
dies.	dieselfde	id.
digk.	digkuns	poetry
dim.	*diminuendo* (afnemend in sterkte)	dim.
dim.	diminutief	dim.
dipl.	diploma	dipl.
Dir.	Direkteur	Dir.
disk.	*diskonto* (afslag)	disc.
dist.	distrik	dist.
div.	diverse	sundry
div.	dividend	div.
dl.	deel	vol., pt.
D.Litt.	*Doctor Litterarum*	D.Litt.
D.M.	*Doctor Medicinae*	D.M., M.D.
dm.	duim	in.
d.m.v.	deur middel van	by means of
D.Med. Vet.	*Doctor Medicinae Veterinariae*	D.Met. Vet.
D.Mus.	*Doctor Musicae*	D.Mus., Mus.D(oc.)
dnr.	dienaar	serv.
Do.	Donderdag	Thur(s).
do.	*ditto* (dieselfde)	do.
D.O.	Direkteur van Onderwys	D.E.
Dom. Sc.	*Domestica Scientia* (Huishoudkunde)	Dom.Sc.
dos.	dosyn	doz.
DPW	Department (van) Publieke Werke	PWD
D.Phil.	*Doctor Philosophiae*	D.Phil., Ph.D.
dr.	dokter; doktor	Dr.
dr.	debiteur	Dr.
dr.	druk	ed.
dr.	dragme	dr.
dra.	*doctoranda*	Dra.
Dr. Med.	*Doctor Medicinae*	D.M., M.D.
drr.	doktors; doktore	Drs.
drs.	*doctorandus*	Drs.
Dr. Theol.	*Doctor Theologiae*	D.Th(eol)., Th. D.
ds.	*Dominus* (predikant); dominee	Rev.
D/S	dae na sig	d/s.
D.Sc.	*Doctor Scientiae*	D.Sc.
dt.	*debet* (is verskuldig)	dr.
d.t.	*delirium tremens* (dronkaardsberoerte)	D.T.(s)
D.T.D.	Decoratie voor Trouwe Dienst	—
Dui.	Duitsland; Duits	Ger.
DV	*Deo Volente* (as God wil)	DV
DVD	Dekorasie vir Voortreflike Diens	DMS
D.V.Sc.	*Doctor Veterinariae Scientiae*	D.V.Sc.
dw.	dienswillig	obed.
dw.	deelwoord	part.
dw. dnr.	dienswillige dienaar	obdt. serv.
d.w.s.	dit wil sê	viz.
dwt.	pennyweight	dwt.

E

| e.a. | en ander(e) | et al. |

Afrikaans		Engels
e.d.	en dergelike	etc.
ed.	edisie; *edit* (het uitgegee)	ed.
Ed.	edele	Hon.
Ed. Agb.	Edelagbare	Hon.
Ed. Gestr.	Edelgestrenge	Rt. Hon.
e.d.m.	en dergelike (dies) meer	etc.
Edms.	Eiendoms	Pty.
e.e.	en elders	et al.
EEG	Europese Ekonomiese Gemeenskap	EEC
eerw.	eerwaarde	Rev.
Ef.	Efesiërs	Eph.
e.g.	eersgenoemde	the former
e.g.	*exempli gratia* (byvoorbeeld)	e.g.
EGM	Europese Gemeenskapsmark	ECM
eint.	eintlik(e)	actual.
e.k.	eerskomende	next, prox.
E.K.	eerste kwartier	F.Q.
Ekon.	Ekonomie	Econ.
eks.	eksemplaar	copy
Eks.	Eksellensie	Exc.
ekv.	enkelvoud	sing.
e.l.	elektriese lig	e.l.
elektr.	elektries; elektrisiteit	elec.
Em.	Eminensie	Em.
em.	*emeritus* (rustend)	emeritus
Eng.	Engels; Engeland	Eng.
enkl.	enklities	encl.
ens.	ensovoorts	etc.
Entom.	Entomologie	Entom.
e.o.	*ex officio* (ampshalwe)	e.o.
e.o.w.	eerste op water	f.o.w.
epk.	elektriese perdekrag	e.h.p.
er.	eienaarsrisiko	O.R.
eresekr.	eresekretaris	Hon. Sec.
Eseg.	Esegiël	Ezek.
esk.	eskader; eskadril; eskadron	sqn.
e.s.m.	en so meer	etc.
etc.	*et cetera* (ensovoorts)	etc.
Etim.	Etimologie	Etym.
Etnol.	Etnologie	Ethnol.
Eur.	Europees	Eur.
ev.	eersvolgende	next, prox., foll.
Ev.	Evangelie	Gospel
E.V.	*En ville* (alhier)	E.V.
e.v.	en volgende	et. seq.
EVKOM	Elektrisiteitsvoorsieningskommissie	ESCOM
Ex.	*Exodus*	Exod.

F

F	Fahrenheit; faraday; farad	F.
f	*forte* (hard; luid)	f
f(l).	floryn (gulden)	f.
FAK	Federasie van Afrikaanse Kultuurvereniginge	—
fakt.	faktuur	inv.
fam.	familie	fam.
Febr.	Februarie	Feb.
fec.	*fecit* (het dit gemaak)	fec.
F & WU	foute en weglatings uitgesonderd	E. & O.E.
ff	*fortissimo* (baie hard)	ff
Fid. Def.	*Fidei Defensor* (Defender of the Faith)	F.D.
fig.	figuur(lik)	fig.
Fil.	Filemon	Philem.
filat.	filatelie	philat.
Filip.	Filippense	Phil.
Filos.	Filosofie	Phil.
fl.	floryn	f.
FM	frekwensiemodulasie	FM
Fonet.	Fonetiek	Phonet.
Fonol.	Fonologie	Phonol.
fol.	folio	fol., fcp.
fot.	foto; fotografies	phot
fr.	frank	fr.
Fr.	Frans; Frankryk	Fr.
Fri.	Fries	Frisian
Frk.	Frankies	Frank.
fur.	furlong	fur.
fut.	*futurum* (toekomende tyd)	fut.

G

g, gell.	gallon, gelling	gal.
Gal.	*Galasiërs*	Gal.
Gall.	Gallies	Gall.

Afrikaans		Engels
gall.	gallon, gelling	gal.
GB	Groot-Brittanje	GB
geadr.	geadresseer	add.
geb.	gebore; geboul; gebou	b.
gebr.	gebroeders	Bros.
geb. wys	gebiedende wys	imp.
ged.	gedateer	d.d.
ged.	gedeelte	pt.
geïll.	geïllustreer	illus.
gell.	gelling, gallon	gal.
gel. str.	gelykstroom	D.C.
gem.	gemiddeld(e)	av.
gen.	genitief	gen.
Gen.	Genesis	Gen.
Geneesk.	Geneeskunde	Med.
genl.	generaal	Gen.
genl.-maj.	generaal-majoor	Maj.-Gen.
geod.	geodesie; geodeties	geod.
geogr.	geografies	geog.
Geogr.	Geografie	Geog.
Geol.	Geologie	Geol.
geol.	geologies	geol.
gep.	gepensioneer(d)	ret.
Geref. K.	Gereformeerde Kerk	R.C.
gereg.	geregistreer(d)	regd.
Germ.	Germaans; Germanisme	Ger.
Ges.	Gesang	hymn
geselst.	geselstaal	colloq.
Gesk.	Geskiedenis (as vak)	hist.
gesk.	geskiedkundig	historical
gest.	gestorwe	ob.
get.	geteken	sgd.
get.	getuie	W.
gev. (en geb)	gevang (en geboul)	c.(and b.)
gew.	gewig	wt.
gew.	gewestelik	dial.
gew.	gewoonlik	usu.
GG	Goewerneur-Generaal	GG
GGD	grootste gemene deler	GCF, GCM, HCF
ghn.	ghienie	g.
gimn.	gimnasium; gimnastiek	gym.
G.K.	Gekose Komitee	S.C.
G.K.	Goewermentskennisgewing	G.N.
glos.	glossarium	gloss.
goew.	goewerneur	Gov.
G(oew).-G(enl).	Goewerneur-generaal	G(ov)-G(en).
Got.	Goties	Goth.
gr.	graad	deg.
gr.	grein	gr.
Gr.	Grieks	Gr.
GRA	Genootskap van Regte Afrikaners	—
gram.	grammatika	gram.
GR (SA)	Geoktrooieerde Rekenmeester (Suid-Afrika)	CA (SA)
G.S.	Generale Staf	G.S.
gs.	gelykstroom	D.C.
G.T.	Greenwichtyd	G.T.
g.v.	goed vir	good for
G.W.	geldwissel	M.O.
G.W.	Griekwaland-Wes	G.W.

H

H	henry	H
H.	Heilige	St., S.
Hab.	*Habakuk*	Hab.
Hag.	*Haggai*	Hag.
Hand.	*Handelinge*	Acts
h.c.	*honoris causa* (eregraad)	h.c.
Hd.	Hoogduits	H.G.
hdbk.	handboek	hdbk.
H.d.L.	Heil die Leser	L.S.
Hebr.	Hebreeus	Heb.
Hebr.	*Hebreërs*	Heb.
H.Ed.	Hoogedele	Hon.
H.Eerw.	Hoogeerwaarde	Rt. Rev.
H.Eks.	Haar Eksellensie	H.E.
her	heraldiek; heraldies	her.
Herv.	Hervormd	Ref.
hfl.	hoofletter	cap.
hfst.	hoofstuk	cap., chap., ch.
H.G.S.	Hoof van die Generale Staf	C.G.S.
hh.	menere, die here	Messrs.
H.H.	Haar Hoogheid	H.H.

Afrikaans		Engels
HH.HH.	Hulle Hooghede	T.H.
HK	hoofkwartier	HQ
HKH	Haar Koninklike Hoogheid	HRH
h.l.	hoc loco (op die plek)	hoc loc.
hm	hektometer	hm
HM	Haar Majesteit	HM
HMK	Historiese Monumentekommissie	HMC
HMS	Hoër Meisieskool	GHS
HNP	Herstigte Nasionale Party	H.N.P.
H.O.	Hoër Onderwys	H.E.
HOD	Hoër Onderwysdiploma	HED
HOIK	Hollandse Oos-Indiese Kompanjie	DEIC, NEIC
Holl.	Hollands	Du.
Hoogl.	*Hooglied*	Cant.
hoogl.	hoogleraar	prof.
Hos.	*Hosea*	Hos.
hosp.	hospitaal	hosp.
H.P.K.	hoofposkantoor	G.P.O.
hr.	heer	Mr.
H.R.R.	Heilige Romeinse Ryk	H.R.E.
H.S.	Heilige Skrif	H.S.
hs.	handskrif	MS.
hss.	handskrifte	MSS.
hulpww.	hulpwerkwoord	aux.
h/v	hoek van	cor.
Hz, hz	hertz	Hz

I

IAO	Internasionale Arbeidsorganisasie	ILO
ib(id.)	*ibidem* (dieselfde)	ib(id).
i.c.	*in casu* (in hierdie geval)	i.c.
id.	*idem* (dieselfde)	id.
Ide.	Indo-Europees	I.E.
Idg.	Indo-Germaans	I.G.
i.e.	*id est* (dit is)	i.e.
iem.	iemand	someone
i.e.w.	in een woord	in short
i.f.	*ipse fecit* (hy het dit self gemaak)	i.f.
I.G.J.	Internasionale Geofisiese Jaar	I.G.Y.
I.K.	intelligensiekwosiënt	I.Q.
i.l.	*in loco* (ter plaatse)	in loc.
ill.	illustreer	illus.
I.M.	*in memoriam* (ter nagedagtenis)	I.M.
IMF	Internasionale Monetêre Fonds	IMF
imp.	imperatief	imp.
impf.	*inperfektum*	imperf.
impr.	*imprimatur* (laat dit gedruk word)	impr.
incog.	*incognito* (onbekend)	incog.
I.N.D.	*In Nomine Dei* (in Gods naam)	I.N.D.
Ind.	Indië; Indies(e)	Ind.
ind.	indikatief	indic.
ind.	indeks	ind.
Indon.	Indonesië	Indon.
inf.	infinitief; infanterie	inf.
infra dig.	*infra dignitatem* (benede sy waardigheid)	infra dig.
inkl.	inklusief	incl.
inl.	inleiding	intro.
in loc. cit.	*in loco citato* (ter aangehaalde plaats(e)	(in) loc. cit.
ins.	insonderheid	esp.
insl.	insluitend	incl.
insp.	inspekteur	Insp.
insp.	inspeksie	insp.
instr.	instrument; instruksie; instrukteur	instr.
intr.	intransitief	intr.
i.p.v.	in plaas van	instead of
I.R., IR.	*Imperator Rex* (Keiser-Koning)	R.I.
ir.	ingenieur	eng.
I.R.K.	Internasionale Rooikruis	I.R.C.
i.s.	in sake	re
Isr.	Israel(ities)	Israel(itic)
It.	Italiaans	It.
i.t.	*in transito* (gedurende vervoer)	in transit
i.v.	*in voce (verbo)* (by daardie woord)	i.v.
i.v.m.	in verband met	re

J

j.	jaar	yr.
J	joule	J
J	jodium	iodine
Jak.	Jakobus	Jam.; Jas.
Jan.	Januarie	Jan.
Jap.	Japan; Japannees	Jap.

Afrikaans		Engels
Jav.	Javaans	Jav.
J.C.	Jesus Christus	J.C.
Jer.	*Jeremia*	Jer.
Jes.	*Jesaja*	Is.
jg.	jaargang	vol.
jhr.	jonkheer	Bart.; Bt.
jl.	jongslede	ult.
Joh.	Johannes	John
Jos.	Josua	Josh.
jr.	junior	Jr.
jt.	jaart	yd.
Jud.	Judas	Judas
juf.	juffrou	Miss
Jul.	Julie	Jul.
Jun.	Junie	Jun.
jur.	juridies	jud.
Jurisp.	Jurisprudensie	Jurisp.
Just.	Justinianus	Just.

K

K	Kelvin	K
kal	kalorie	cal.
Kan.	Kanada; Kanadees	Can.
kap.	kapitaal	cap.
kap.	kapittel	chap., ch.
kapt.	kaptein	Capt.
kar.	karaat	ct.
kat.	katalogus	cat.
k.a.v.	koste, assuransie, vrag	c.i.f.
K.B.	kunsmatige bevrugting	A.I.
K.B.	kasboek	C.B.
K/B	kredietbrief	C/N, L/C
k.b.a.	kontant by aflewering	C.O.D.
kg	kilogram	kg
K.G.	Kommandant-Generaal	C.G.
K.G.V.	kleinste gemene veelvoud	L.C.M.
KJV.	Kerkjeugvereniging	—
K.I.	kunsmatige inseminasie	A.I.
Kie.	Kompanjie	Co.
kk	kerskrag	c.p., cd
kl	kiloliter	kl
Klaagl.	*Klaagliedere*	Lam.
klass.	klassiek(e)	class.
klemt.	klemtoon	acc.
km	kilometer	km
k.m.b.	kontant met bestelling	c.w.o.
kmdmt.	kommandement	Cmd.
kmdo.	kommando	cmdo.
kmdoor.	kommodoor	Cmdre.
kmdr.	kommandeur	Cmdr.
kmdt.	kommandant	Comdt.
KMG	kwartiermeester-generaal	Q.M.G.
Kol.	Kollossense	Col.
kol.	kolonel	Col.
koll.	kollektief; kollektiewe	coll.
koll.	kollege	Coll.
kom.	komitee	Com.
komm.	kommissie; kommissaris	Comm.
komp.	komparatief	comp.
Kon.	Konings	Kings
kon.	koninklik	royal
konj.	konjunksie; konjunktief	conj.
konkr.	konkreet	concr.
kons.	konsonant	cons.
Kons.	Konserwatief	Cons.
kons.-genl.	konsul-generaal	Cons.-Gen.
konst.	konstabel	const.
koöp.	koöperasie; koöperatief	Co-op.
kooph.	koophandel	comm.
Kor.	Korinthiërs	Cor.
korr.	korrespondensie; korrespondent	corr.
K.P.	Kaapprovinsie	C.P.
K.P.A.	Kaapse Provinsiale Administrasie	C.P.A.
kpl.	korporaal	Corp., Cpl.
K.P.L.U.	Kaaplandse Landbou-Unie	C.P.A.U.
kr.	krediteur; krediteer	Cr.
kr.	kroon	cr.
Kron.	Kronieke	Chron.
KRUIK	Kaaplandse Raad vir die Uitvoerende Kunste	CAPAB
Krygsk.	Krygskunde	Mil. Sc.
krygsk.	krygskundige	mil.
k.s.	kredietsaldo	C.B.

Afrikaans		Engels
k.s.b.	kombuis, spens, badkamer	k.p.b.
kt.	krediet	Cr.
kub.	kubiek	c., cu.
kurs.	kursief	ital.
K.v.K.	Kamer van Koophandel	C.C.
kw.	kwartaal	qr.
kwal.	kwaliteit	qual.
kwan.	kwantiteit	qty.
K.W.V.	Koöperatiewe Wynbouersvereniging	K.W.V.

L

L	Lengtegraad; Linnaeus	L
lab.	laboratorium	lab.
Landb.	Landboukunde	Agric.
landb.	landboukundig(e)	agric.
Lat.	Latyn	L.
L/B	ladingsbrief	B/L
lb	*libra(e)* (pond gewig)	lb(s).
L.B.S.	Lopende Betaalstelsel	P.A.Y.E.
LD	landdros	M.
L.D.	*Laus Deo* (Lof aan God)	L.D.
leerl.	leerling	L; sch.
letg.	lettergreep	syl.
Lett.	Lettere	Lit.
lett.	letterlik	lit.
Lettk.	Letterkunde	Lit.
lettk.	letterkundige	lit.
Lev.	Levitikus	Lev.
lg.	laasgenoemde	the latter
lh.	linkerhand	l.h.
Lib.	Liberaal	Lib
lis.	lisensie	lic.
Lis.	Lisensiaat	L.
Litt.D.	*Literarum Doctor*	Litt.D.
L.K.	laaste kwartier	L.Q.
lk.	lewenskoste	C.O.L.
lkt.	lewenskostetoelae	C.O.L.A.
ll.	laaslede	ult.
LL.B.	*Legum Baccalaureus*	LL.B.
LL.D.	*Legum Doctor*	LL.D.
LL.M.	*Legum Magister*	LL.M.
l.n.r.	links na regs	l. to r.
L.O.	Laer Onderwys	Prim. Ed.
L.O.	Liggaamlike Opvoeding	Phys. Ed.
l(oc). c(it).	*loco citato* (op die aangehaalde plek)	loc. cit.
log.	logaritme	log.
Log.	Logika	Logic
l.r.	lopende rekening	curt. a/c
L.S.	*Lectori Salutem* (heil die leser)	L.S.
l.s.	*loco sigilli* (in die plek van seël)	l.s.
L.s.d.	*librae, solidi, denarii* (ponde, sjielings, pennies)	L.s.d.
lt., luit.	luitenant	Lt.
lt.-genl.	luitenant-generaal	Lt.-Gen.
lt.-kmdr.	luitenant-kommandeur	Lt.-Com.
lt.-kol.	luitenant-kolonel	Lt.-Col.
lugv.	lugvaart; lugvaartkundige	avn.
luit.	luitenant	Lt.
Luk.	Lukas	Luke
Luth.	Luther(s)	Luth.
L.U.K.	Lid van die Uitvoerende Komitee	M.E.C.
L.V.	Lid van die Volksraad	M.P.
L.W.	Let Wel	N.B.
lw.	lidwoord	art.
L.W.R.	Lid van die Wetgewende Raad	M.L.A., M.L.C.
L.W.V.	Lid van die Wetgewende Vergadering	M.P.
L.X.X.	Septuagint	L.X.X.
lyd. (vorm)	lydende vorm	pass. (voice)

M

M.	Monsieur	M.
M	mark (Duitse munt)	m., Mk., D.M.
m.	manlik; myl	m.
m	meter	m
m., ml.	manlik	masc.
m., min.	minuut	min.
M.A.	*Magister Artium*	M.A.
Ma.	Maandag	M(on).
mA	milliampere	mA
mag.	magistraat	R.M.
maj.	majoor	Maj.
maks.	maksimum	max.
Mal.	Maleis	Malay

Afrikaans		Engels
Mal.	*Maleagi*	Mal.
Mal.-Port.	Maleis-Portugees	Malayo-Portuguese
Mark.	Markus	Mark
Mat.	Matesis	Maths.
matriek	matrikulasie	matric.
Matt.	Matteus	Matt.
m.a.w.	met ander woorde	in other words
M.B.	*Medicinae Baccalaureus*	M.B.
mbar	millibar	mbar
m.b.t.	met betrekking tot	with reference to
M.Com.	*Magister Commercii*	M.Com.
m/d	maande na datum	m/d
md(e).	maand(e)	mo(s).
M.D.	*Medicinae Doctor*	D.M., M.D.
M.Div.	*Magister Divinitatis*	M.Div.
Me.	Middeleeue	Middle Ages
M.Econ.	*Magister Economiae*	M.Econ.
M.Ed.	*Magister Educationis*	M.Ed.
med.	medies; medisyne	med.
Meetk.	Meetkunde	Geom.
me.	dame	Ms.
mej.	mejuffrou	Miss.
mejj.	mejuffroue	Misses
mem(o).	memorandum	memo.
Me.	Middelengels	M.E.
metaf.	metafoor, metafories	—
Meteor.	meteorologie (as vak)	met.
meton.	metonimie(s)	meton.
mev.	mevrou	Mrs.
mevv.	mevroue	Mmes.
mf	*mezzo forte* (matig luid)	mf
mg	milligram	mg.
mgr.	monseigneur	Mgr.
M.G.T.	Middelbare Greenwichtyd	G.M.T.
Mhd.	Middelhoogduits	M.H.G.
m.i.	myns insiens	in my view
mil.	militêr(e)	mil.
Mil. Akad.	Militêre Akademie	Mil. Acad.
min.	minuut; minimum	min.
min.	minister	Min.
Miner.	Mineralogie (as vak)	minerology
M.Ing.	Meester in Ingenieurswese	M. Eng.
misk.	miskien	perhaps
mit.	mitologies	myth.
m.i.v.	met ingang van	commencing
m.k.	met koste	c.ex.
m(l).	manlik	m(asc).
m.m.	*mutatis mutandis* (met die nodige veranderinge)	mutatis mutandis
mme.	madame	Mme.
M.Med.	*Magister Medicinae*	M.Med.
m.n.	met name	viz
Mnl.	Middelnederlands	M.D.
mnr.	meneer	Mr., Esq.
mnre.	menere	messrs., MM.
M.O.	Middelbare Onderwys	S.E.
mod.	modern	mod.
mol.	molekule	mol.
M.P.	Militêre Polisie	M.P.
mp	*mezzo piano* (matig sag)	mp
m.p.g.	myl per gelling	m.p.g.
m.p.u.	myl per uur	m.p.h.
mr.	meester (in die regte)	—
Mrt.	Maart	Mar.
m/s	maande na sig	m/s
ms.	manuskrip	MS.
MS.	motorskip	M.V.
M.Sc.	*Magister Scientiae*	M.Sc.
M.Sc.Agric.	*Magister Scientiae Agriculturae*	M.Sc.Agric.
M.Theo.	*Magister Theologiae*	M.Theo.
ms.	dame	Ms.
mss.	manuskripte	MSS
mun.	munisipaliteit	mun.
Mus.	Musiek	Mus.
Mus. B.	*Musicae Baccalaureus*	B.Mus., Mus. B(ac)
Mus. D.	*Musicae Doctor*	D.Mus., Mus. D(oc).
mv.	meervoud	pl.
m.v.	*messa voce* (met halwe stem)	m.v.
My., Mpy.	Maatskappy	Co.
Mx	Maxwell	Mx
Mynw.	Mynwese	Min.

N

Afrikaans		Engels
N.	noord	N.
N	normaal (by oplossings)	N
n.	*nomen* (selfstandige naamwoord)	n.
n.	namens	p.
n.	neutrum	n., neut.
N.A.	Noord-Amerika; Noord-Afrika	N.A.
n.a.	noukeurige afdruk	f.co.
Nah.	*Nahum*	Nah.
NAROBS	Nasionale Adviserende Raad vir Opvoeding buite Skoolverband	NACES
NARUK	Natalse Raad vir die Uitvoerende Kunste	NAPAC
nas.	nasionaal	nat.
Nat.	Natuurkunde	Phys.
nat.	natuurkundig	phys.
n.a.v.	na aanleiding van	ref. to
N.A.V.O.	Noord-Atlantiese Verdragsorganisasie	N.A.T.O.
N.B.	*Nota Bene* (let wel)	N.B.
N.Br.	noorderbreedte	N.Lat.
n.C.	na Christus	A.D.
N.C.V.V.	Natalse Christelike Vrouevereniging	—
n/d	na datum	a/d
N.D.	natuurdokter	N.D.
Ndl.	Nederlands	Neth.
N(ed).G(eref).	Nederduits Gereformeerde	D.R.
Ned.Herv.	Nederduits Hervormde	D.R.
neg.	negatief	neg.
Neh.	*Nehemia*	Neh.
N.Germ.	Noord-Germaans(e)	N.Germ.
nem. con.	*nemine contradicente* (sonder teëstem)	nem. con.
net.	netto	nett
neut.	neutrum	n(eut).
N.G.K.	Nederduitse Gereformeerde kerk	D.R.C.
Nhd.	Nieu-Hoogduits	N.H.G.
N.H. of G.K.	Nederduits Hervormde of Gereformeerde Kerk	D.R.C.
N.L.	noorderlengte	N.Long.
n.l.	*non licet* (dit mag nie)	non licet
nl.	naamlik	viz.
N.L.U.	Natalse Landbou-unie	N.A.U.
nm.	namiddag	p.m.
N.M.	Nasionale merk; nuwe maan	N.M.
N.N.	*nomen nescio* (onbekend)	N.N.
N.N.O.	noord-noordoos	NNE.
N.N.W.	noord-noordwes	NNW.
no.	nommer	No.
n.o.	naam onbekend	n.u.
NO.	noordoos	N.E.
N.O.	*nomine officii* (pligshalwe)	N.O.
N.O.D.	Natalse Onderwysdepartement	N.E.D.
N.O.I.K.	Nederlands-Oos-Indiese Kompanjie	D.E.I.C., N.E.I.C.
N.O.K.	Nywerheidsontwikkelingskorporasie van Suid-Afrika, Bpk.	I.D.C.
nol. pros.	*nolle prosequi* (opskorting van vervolging)	nol. pros.
nom.	nominatief	nom.
nom. kap.	nominale kapitaal	nom. cap.
N.O.U.	Natalse Onderwysersunie	—
Nov.	November	Nov.
n.p.	nuwe paragraaf	n.p.
N.P.	Nasionale Party	N.P.
nr.	nuwe reël	n.l.
nr.	nommer, numero	No.
n/s	na sig	a/s
NS.	naskrif	P.S.
N.S.	Nieu-Seeland	N.Z.
N.S.	Nuwe Styl	N.S.
nste	tot die naaste (enige) mag	nth
N.S.W.	Nieu-Suid-Wallis	N.S.W.
N.T.	Nuwe Testament	N.T.
N.T.O.	Nasionale Teaterorganisasie	N.T.O.
N.U.	Natalse Universiteit	N.U., U.N.
Num.	*Numeri*	Num.
N.U.S.A.S.	Nasionale Unie van Suid-Afrikaanse Studente	N.U.S.A.S.
N.V.	Nuwe Verbond	N.T.
N.V.R.	Nasionale Vroueraad	N.C.W.
nv.	naamval	c.
N.W.	noordwes	NW.
nw.	naamwoord	n.
N.Y.	New York	N.Y.
N.Z.A.S.M.	Nederlandsch Zuid-Afrikaansche Spoorwegmaatschappij	—
N.Z.A.V.	Nederlandsch Zuid-Afrikaansche Vereeniging	—

O

Afrikaans		Engels
O.	ooste; oostelik	E.
o.	onsydig	neut.
o.a.	onder andere	i.a.
OAE	Organisasie vir Afrika-Eenheid	OAU
ob.	*obiit* (oorlede)	ob.
o/b	oorgebring	B/F, b.f.
O.B.	Ossewa-Brandwag	O.B.
Obad.	*Obadja*	Obad.
obj.	objek; objektief	obj.
O.D.H.	Onwettige Diamanthandel	I.D.B
Oe.	Oud-Engels	O.E.
oef.	oefening	ex.
Oerg.	Oergermaans	—
Ofr.	Oud-Frans	OF.
off.	offisier	off.
Ohd.	Oud-Hoogduits	O.H.G.
O.I.	Oos-Indië	E.I.
o.i.	onses insiens	in our view
okt.	oktavo	8vo
Okt.	Oktober	Oct.
O.L.	Oos-Londen	E.L.
O.L.	oosterlengte	E.Long.
o.l.v.	onder leiding van	cond.; u.d.o.
o.m.	onder meer	i.a.
On.	Oud-Noors	ON.
onbep.	onbepaald	indef.
onderv.	ondervoorsitter	V.C.
onderw.	onderwerp	subj.
ong.	ongeveer	c.
ongew.	ongewoon	unusual
O.N.O.	oosnoordoos	ENE
onoorg. ww.	onoorganklike werkwoord	intr.
onpers.	onpersoonlik	impers.
ons.	onsydig	n(eut).
ontl.	ontleding	anal.
ontl.	ontlening	der.
ontv.	ontvang	recd.
onvolm.	onvolmaak	imperf.
onvolt.	onvoltooi(d).	imperf.
oordr.	oordrag	tr.
oordr.	oordragtelik	fig.
oorg.	oorganklik	trans.
oorl.	oorlede	late
oorspr.	oorspronklik	orig.
oortr.	oortreffende	sup.
op.	*opus* (werk)	op.
o.p.	op proef	u.p.
O.P.	Oostelike Provinsie	E.P.
op. cit.	*opere citato* (in die genoemde werk)	op. cit.
openb.	openbaar	pub.
Openb.	*Openbaring*	Apocalypse
opm.	opmerking	rem.
o.p.m.	omwentelinge per minuut	r.p.m.
opt.	optatief	opt.
o.r.	op rekening	o/a
ord.	ordonnansie	ord.
o/s	onder sorg	c/o
O.S.	Ou Styl	O.S.
ost.	onderstaande	foll.
Os.	Ou(d)-Saksies	O.S.
O.S.O.	oossuidoos	ESE
O.T.	Ou Testament	O.T.
oud.-genl.	ouditeur-generaal	Aud.-Gen.
Oudhk.	Oudheidkunde	Arch.
oudhk.	oudheidkundig	arch.
oudl.	ouderling	elder
O.V.	Ou Verbond	O.T.
O.V.S.	Oranje-Vrystaat	O.F.S.
O.V.S.B.	Oranje-Vrouesendingbond	—
O.V.S.L.U.	Oranje-Vrystaatse Landbou-Unie	O.F.S.A.U.
O.V.S.O.V.	Oranje-Vrystaatse Onderwysersvereniging	O.F.S.T.A.
O.V.V.	Oranje-Vrouevereniging	—
o.v.v.	onbekende vlieënde voorwerp	u.f.o.
O/W	ontvangbare wissel	B/R
O.W.	Openbare Werke	P.W.
o.w.	onder wie	among whom
oz.	ons	oz.

P

P.	pater	Fr.
P.	parkering	P.

Afrikaans		Engels
p	*piano* (sag)	p
p.	*pagina* (bladsy); *per* (vir; met)	p.
p.	paaltjie (krieket)	w.
p.a.	per adres	c/o
p.a.	*per annum* (per jaar)	p.a.
par.	paragraaf	par.
parl.	parlement	Parl.
Patol.	Patologie	Path.
p.d.	per dag	p.d.
pd	pond	£, L., sov.
pd.	pond (gewig)	lb.
P.E.	Port Elizabeth	P.E.
penm.	penningmeester	Treas.
perf.	perfectum	perf.
per pro.	*per procurationem* (by volmag)	per pro., p.p.
Pers.	Persies	Pers.
pers.	persoonlik	pers.
pers. vnw.	persoonlike voornaamwoord	pers. pron.
P.G.	prokureur-generaal	A.G.
Ph.D.	*Philosophiae Doctor*	D. Phil., Ph.D.
p.j.	per jaar	p.a.
p.jt.	per jaart	per yd.
P.K.	Provinsiale Kennisgewing	P.N.
pk.	perdekrag	h.p.
Pk.	Poskantoor	P.O.
pl.	*pluralis* (meervoud)	pl.
Plantk.	Plantkunde	Bot.
P.M.	posmeester	P.M.
p.m.	per maand; plus minus; per minuut	p.m.
P.M.D.	Padmotordiens	R.M.S.
P.M.G.	posmeester-generaal	P.M.G.
P.O.	posorder	P.O.
Port.	Portugal; Portugees	Port.
Potch.	Potchefstroom	Potch.
p.p.	*per procurationem* (by volmag)	per pro.
p.p.	per persoon	p.p.
pp.	paginas (bladsye)	pp.
pp	*pianissimo* (baie sag)	pp
P.O.	pakketpos; Progressiewe Party	P.P.
p.p.c.	*pour prende congé* (om afskeid te neem)	p.p.c.
ppp	*pianissimo* (baie sag)	ppp
p.p.p.d.	per persoon per dag	p.d. each
pqpf.	*plusquamperfectum* (volt. verl. tyd)	plup.
P.R.	Poste Restante	poste restante
P.R.	Provinsiale Raad	P.C.
Pr., Prot.	Protestant(s)	Prot.
P.R.C.	*post Roman conditam* (na die stigting van Rome)	P.R.C.
praes.	*praesens* (teenwoordige tyd)	pres. tense
praet.	*praeteritum* (verlede tyd)	pret.
Pred.	*Prediker*	Eccl(es).
pred.	predikant	Rev.
prep.	preposisie; preposisioneel	prep.
pres.	president	Pres.
pres.	presens	pres.
pred.	predikant; predikatief	pred.
pret.	preteritum (onv. verl. tyd)	pret.
prim.	*primarius* (eerste)	prim.
prin.	prinsipaal	prin.
priv.	privaat	private
pro.	professioneel	pro.
prof.	professor	prof.
proff.	professore	proff.
Prog.	Progressief	Prog.
prok.	prokureur	atty., N.P.
prok.-genl.	prokureur-generaal	A.G.
prom	promesse	P/N
prop.	proponent	—
Prot., Pr.	Protestant	Prot.
prot.	protokol	protocol
pro tem.	*pro tempore* (tydelik)	pro tem.
prov.	provinsie; provinsiaal	Prov.
prox.	*proximo* (aanstaande)	prox.
P.S.	*post scriptum* (naskrif)	P.S.
P.S.	Provinsiale Sekretaris	P.S.
ps.	privaat(pos)sak	P.B
Ps.	Psalm	Ps.
p.s.	present	p.c.
Psig.	Psigologie (as vak)	psych.
psig.	psigologies	psych.
p.st.	pond sterling	£ stg.
pt.	pint; punt	pt.

Afrikaans		Engels
PU v CHO	Potchefstroomse Universiteit vir Christelike Hoër Onderwys	P.U. for C.H.E.
pub.	publiek	pub.
P.W.	poswissel	P.O.
P.W.	Publieke Werke	P.W.
p.w.	per week	p.w.

Q

q.a.	*quod attestor* (waarvan ek getuie is)	q.a.
q.e.	*quod est* (wat beteken)	q.e.
q.e.d.	*quod erat demonstrandum* (wat bewys moes word)	Q.E.D.
q.e.f.	*quod erat faciendum* (wat gedoen moes word)	Q.E.F.
q.q.	*qualitate qua* (in die hoedanigheid van)	q.q.
q.s.	*quantum sufficit* (soveel as genoeg is)	q.s.
qt.	kwart	qt.
q.v.	*quod vide* (sien aldaar)	q.v.

R

r.	radius; reël; regs	r.
R	Rand; Réamur; röntgen	R
R.	Reuter	R.
rab.	rabat, diskonto	reb.
rall	*rallentando* (verlangsamend)	rall
R.O.K.	Raad op Atoomkrag	C.A.E.
RAU	Randse Afrikaanse Universiteit	RAU
Rd.	ryksdaler, riksdaler	Rd.
R.D.B.	Reddingsdaadbond	—
red.	redakteur; redaksie.	ed.
redupl.	reduplikasie; redupliserend	redup(l).
ref.	referensie; referent	ref.
refl.	refleksief	refl.
reg.	regering	govt.
Regsg.	Regsgeleerdheid	Jurisp.
regsg.	regsgeleerde	jurist
regt.	regiment	regt.
rek.	rekening	a/c, acc.
rek. van	rekening van	a/o
Rekenk.	Rekenkunde	Arith.
rekenk..	rekenkundige	arith.
rel.	relatief	rel.
Rep.	republiek; republikeins	Rep.
resp.	respektiewelik; respondent	resp.
R.G.N.	Raad vir Geesteswetenskaplike Navorsing	H.S.R.C.
rh.	regterhand	r.h.
Rigt.	*Rigters*	Judg.
R.I.P.	*requiescat in pace* (rus in vrede)	R.I.P
rit	*ritardando* (langsamer)	rit
riv.	rivier	R(iv).
R.I.V.	rus in vrede	R.I.P.
R.K.	Rooms-Katoliek	R.C.
R/K.	rekening-koerant	A/C.
rl.	radiaal	radial
R.M.	resident-magistraat	R.M.
RM	Reichsmark	RM
r.p.m.	rewolusies per minuut	rpm
rom.	Romeinse lettertipe	rom.
Rom.	*Romeine*	Rom.
RP	Regter-president	J.P.
rpk.	remperdekrag	b.h.p.
rr	*reservatis reservandis* (met die nodige voorbehoud)	r.r.
R.S.A.	Republiek van Suid-Afrika; Radio Suid-Afrika	R.S.A.
R.S.V.P.	*répondez s'il vous plaît* (antwoord asseblief)	R.S.V.P.
R/T	verwys na trekker	R/D
R.U.	Rhodes-universiteit; Rugbyunie	R.U.
Rus.	Russies	Russ.
Rusl.	Rusland	Russ.
RVK	rugbyvoetbalklub	R.F.C.

S

s.	saldo	bal.
s.	sjieling; sekonde	s.
S.	suid; suidelik	S.
Sa.	Saterdag	Sat.
S.A.	Suid-Afrika; Suid-Amerika	S.A.
S.A.	Senior Advokaat	S.C. (K.C., Q.C.)
s.a.	*sine anno* (sonder jaartal van publikasie)	s.a.
Sabena	*Société anonyme belge d'exploitation de la navigation aérienne*	Sabena
SABRA	Suid-Afrikaanse Buro vir Rasseaangeleenthede	SABRA
S.A.B.S., SABS	Suid-Afrikaanse Buro vir Standaarde	SABS
Sag.	*Sagaria*	Zach.
S.A.L.	Suid-Afrikaanse Lugdiens	S.A.A.

Afrikaans		Engels
S.A.L.M.	Suid-Afrikaanse Lugmag	S.A.A.F.
S.A.L.U.	Suid-Afrikaanse Landbou-unie	S.A.A.U.
Sam.	Samuel	Sam.
SAMPI	Suid-Afrikaanse Mielieprodusente-Instituut	SAMPI
SAMRO	Suid-Afrikaanse Musiekregteorganisasie	SAMRO
Sans.	Sanskrit	Skr.
S.A.O.U.	Suid-Afrikaanse Onderwysersunie	S.A.T.U.
S.A.P.	Suid-Afrikaanse Party; Suid-Afrikaanse Polisie	S.A.P.
SAPA	Suid-Afrikaanse Persassosiasie	SAPA
S.A.S.	Suid-Afrikaanse Skip	S.A.S.
S.A.R.B.	Suid-Afrikaanse Reserwebank	S.A.R.B.
S.A.S. & H.	Suid-Afrikaanse Spoorweë en Hawens	S.A.R. & H.
S.A.S.M.	Suid-Afrikaanse Staande Mag	S.A.P.F.
SASOL	Suid-Afrikaanse Steenkool-, Olie- en Gaskorporasie	SASOL
SASVIA	Suid-Afrikaanse Studentevereniging in Amsterdam	—
SATMAR	S.A. Torbanite Mining and Refining Company	SATMAR
S.A.U.K.	Suid-Afrikaanse Uitsaaikorporasie	S.A.B.C.
S.A.V.	Suid-Afrikaanse Vloot	S.A.N.
S.A.V.F.	Suid-Afrikaanse Vroue-Federasie	—
SAVO	Suid-Asiatiese Verdragsorganisasie	S.(E)A.T.O.
S.A.W.	Suid-Afrikaanse Weermag	S.A.D.F.
S.Br.	suiderbreedte	S.Lat.
sc.	*scillicet* (te wete)	sc.
S.C.	Senior Consultus	S.C.
s.d.	*sine die* (vir onbepaalde tyd)	s.d.
s.d.	sien daar	op.cit.
S.D.G.	*Soli Deo Gloria* (aan God alleen die eer)	S.D.G.
SDN	standaardnommer	S.W.G.
S.Ed.	Sy Edele	His Hon.
S.Ed.Agb.	Sy Edelagbare	His Hon.
seem.	seemyl	sea mile, naut. mi.
S.Eerw.	Sy Eerwaarde	His Rev.
Sef.	Sefanja	Zeph
sek.	sekonde; sekundus	sec.
sekr.	sekretaris	Sec.
sekre.	sekretaresse	Sec.
S.Eks.	Sy Eksellensie	H.E.
S.Em.	Sy Eminensie	H.Em.
sen.	senaat; senator	Sen.
Sept.	September	Sept.
seq.	*sequens, sequentes* (wat volg)	foll., seq(q).
sers.	sersant	Sgt.
sert.	sertifikaat	cert.
sfz	*sforzando* (steeds sterker) (mus.)	sf
sg.	sogenaamd	so called
s.g.	soortlike gewig	sp.gr.
S.H.	Sy Heiligheid; Sy Hoogheid	H.H.
S.H.Ed.	Sy Hoogedele	The Rt. Hon.
S.H.Eerw.	Sy Hoogeerwaarde	The Rt. Rev.
s.i.	syns insiens	in his view
S.I.H.	Sy Imperiale Hoogheid	H.I.H.
sill.	sillabe	syl.
sin	*sinus* (in algebra)	sin
sin.	sinoniem	syn.
sing.	*singularis* (enkelvoud)	sing.
sit.	sitasie	cit.
s.j.	sonder jaartal	s.a.
S.J.	*Societatis Jesu* (Jesuïeteorde)	S.J.
Skand.	Skandinawië; Skandinawies	Scand.
Skeik.	Skeikunde	Chem.
skeik.	skeikundige	chem.
S.K.H.	Sy Koninklike Hoogheid	H.R.H.
S.K.H	Sy Keiserlike Hoogheid	H.I.H.
S.K.M.	Sy Koninklike Majesteit	H.M.
skr.	skrywer	author
Skt.	Sanskrit	Skt.
S.L.	*suo loco* (op sy plek)	suo loco
S.L.	suiderlengte	S. Long.
Slaw.	Slawies	Slav.
S.M.	Sy Majesteit	H.M.
S.M.	Suiderkruismedalje	D.M.
S.M.	stasiemeester	S.M.
SM	Staande Mag	P.F.
sn.	seun	son
s.nw.	selfstandige naamwoord	n.
S.O.	suidoos	SE
So.	Sondag	Sab., S(un).
SOEKOR	Suidelike Olie-Eksplorasiekorporasie	SOEKOR
Soöl.	Soölogie	Zool.
Sos.	Sosiologie (as vak)	Soc.
sos.	sosiologies	soc.
S.O.S.	sien ommesyde	P.T.O.

Afrikaans		Engels
SOS	internasionale noodsein	SOS
S.P.	Staatspresident	S.P.
Sp.	Spanje; Spaans	Sp.
spes.	spesiaal	spec.
S.P.Q.R.	*Senatus Populusque Romanus* (die Senaat en Volk van Rome)	S.P.Q.R.
spr.	spreker	speaker
Spr.	*Spreuke*	Prov.
sprw.	spreekwoord(elik)	proverb
S.R.	Studenteraad	S.R.C.
sr.	senior	sen.
ss.	stoomskip	s.s.
ss.	samestelling	comp.
S.S.O.	suid-suidoos	SSE
S.S.W.	suid-suidwes	SSW
St.	Sint (Heilige)	St.
st.	standerd	Std.
st.	sterk	strong
sta.	stasie	station
Staatk.	Staatkunde	Pol. Sc.
staatk.	staatkundig(e)	pol.
Stelk.	Stelkunde	Alg.
stelk.	stelkundig	alg.
Sterrek.	Sterrekunde	Astr(on).
sterrek.	sterrekundig	astr(on).
stg.	sterling	stg.
St.-Gen.	State-Generaal	—
sth.	stemhebbend	voiced
stl.	stemloos	unvoiced
str.	straat	St.
S.T.R.	spesiale trekkingsregte	S.D.R
stud.	student; studie	stud.
subj.	subjek; subjunktief	subj.
SUKOVS	Streekraad vir die Uitvoerende Kunste O.V.S.	PACOFS
sup.	superlatief	sup(erl).
sup.	*supra* (bo)	sup.
supt.	superintendent	Supt.
s.v.	*sub voce* (onder die woord)	s.v.
s.v.p.	*s'il vous plaît* (asseblief)	s.v.p., please
S.V.R.	Spesiale Vrederegter	S.J.P.
S.W.	Suidwes	SW
sw.	swak	weak
s.w.	soortlike warmte	sp. ht.
S.W.A.	Suidwes-Afrika	S.W.A.
SWARUK	Suidwes-Afrikaanse Raad vir die Uitvoerende Kunste	SWAPAC

T

T.	absolute temperatuur	T
t.	ton; tarra; tempo; tyd	t.
Taalk.	Taalkunde	Ling.
tab.	*tabula* (lys)	table
taf.	tafel	table
tan	tangens	tan
Tandk.	Tandheelkunde	Dent.
tandk.	tandheelkundig(e)	dent.
t.a.p.	ter aangehaalde plaas (plaatse)	(in) loc. cit.
tar.	tarief	tar.
t.a.r.	teen alle risiko	a.a.r.
t.à.t.	*tout à toi* (geheel die uwe)	yours sincerely
t.à.t.	*tout à vous* (geheel die uwe)	yours sincerely
t.a.v.	ten aansien van	in respect of
t.b.c.	tuberkulose	T.B.
t.b.v.	ten behoewe van	for the sake of
t.b.v.	ter bevordering van	for the advancement of
t.b.v.	ter beskikking van	at the disposal of
t.d.e.	te dien einde	for that purpose
teenst.	teenstelling	contrast
teenw.	teenwoordig	pres.
tegn.	tegnies	tech.
tegnol.	tegnologies	technol.
tel.	telefoon	tel.
tel. ad.	telegramadres	tel. add.
telegr.	telegram; telegrafies	tel.
telw.	telwoord	num.
t.e.m.	tot en met	up to & incl.
temp.	temperatuur	temp.
Teol.	Teologie	Theol.
tes.	tesourier	Treas.
t.g.t.	te geleëner tyd	—
t.g.v.	ten gevolge van	in consequence of

Afrikaans		Engels
t.g.v.	ten gunste van	i.f.o.
t.g.v.	ter geleentheid van	on the occasion of
Th(eol) D(r).	*Theologiae Doctor*	D. Th(eol)., Th.D.
Thess.	*Thessalonicense*	Thess.
Tim.	*Timoteus*	Tim.
Tit.	*Titus*	Tit.
t.l.	ten laaste	lastly
T.L.U.	Transvaalse Landbou-Unie	T.A.U.
TNT	trinitrotoluol	TNT
t.o.	telegrafiese oordrag	T.T.
T.O.	Transvaalse Onderwysersvereniging	—
T.O.D.	Transvaalse Onderwysdepartement	T.E.D.
toej.	toejuiging	appl.
toek.	toekomend; toekoms	fut.
t.o.v.	ten opsigte van	with regard to
tr.	transponeer	trs.
Trig.	Trigonometrie	Trig(on).
Truk	Transvaalse Raad vir die Uitvoerende Kunste	PACT
t.s.	ter sake	ad rem
t.s.	ter see	at sea
t.s.t.	te syner tyd	in his own time
t.t.	*totus tuus* (geheel die uwe)	yours sincerely
Tuinb.	Tuinbou	Hort.
Tvl.	Transvaal	Tvl.
tw.	tussenwerpsel	interj.
t.w.	te wete	viz.
t.w.v.	ter waarde van	to the value of

U

u.	uur	h.
U dw.	U dienswillige	yours faithfully
U dw. dnr.	U dienswillige dienaar	your obedient servant
U Ed.	U Edele	Your Hon.
u.i.	*ut infra* (soos onder)	u.i.
uitbr.	uitbreiding	ext.
uitdr.	uitdrukking	expr.
U.K.	Universiteit van Kaapstad	U.C.T.
U.K.	Uitvoerende Komitee	E.C., Ex. Co.
ult.	*ultimo* (laaslede)	ult.
U.N.	Universiteit van Natal	N.U., U.N.
UNESCO	United Nations Educational, Scientific and Cultural Organisation	UNESCO
UNISA	Universiteit van Suid-Afrika	UNISA
univ.	universiteit	Univ.
U.O.V.S.	Universiteit van die Oranje-Vrystaat	U.O.F.S.
U.P.	Universiteit van Pretoria; Unie-Parlement	U.P.
U.P.E.	Universiteit van Port Elizabeth	U.P.E.
U.R.	Uitvoerende Raad	E.C., Ex. Co.
u.s.	*ut supra* (soos bo)	u.s.
U.S.	Universiteit van Stellenbosch	U.S.
U.S.S.R.	Unie van Sosialistiese Sowjetrepublieke	U.S.S.R.
U.V.	Universiteit van die Vrystaat	U.F.
U.V.M.	Unie-Verdedigingsmag	U.D.F.
U.W.	Universiteit van die Witwatersrand	U.W., Wits.

V

v	volt	V
v.	vers; *vide* (kyk, sien)	v.
v.	vroulik	f(em).
v.a.b.	vry aan boord	f.o.b.
val.	valuta	val.
V.A.R.	Verenigde Arabiese Republiek	V.A.R.
V/B	vragbrief	B/L (ships); C/N (on land)
vb.	voorbeeld	ex.
v.b.	van bo	from above
v.b.b.	volgens bygaande brief	acc. to accomp. letter
V.C.	Victoria Cross	VC
v.C.	voor Christus	B.C.
v.d.	van die	of the
V.D.M.	*Verbi Dei (Divini) Minister* (leraar van die Goddelike Woord) (predikant)	Rev.
v.d.S.	van die skrywer	from the author
veldm.	veldmaarskalk	F.M.
ver.	vereniging	ass., soc.
verb.	*verbum* (woord)	v.
verb.	verbinding	comp.
verb.	verbuiging	dec.
verg.	vergadering	meeting
verg. tr.	vergrotende trap	comp.

Afrikaans		Engels
verklw.	verkleinwoord	dim.
verl.	verlede	past
verl. dw.	verlede deelwoord	p.p.
verl.t.	verlede tyd	pret.
Verlosk.	Verloskunde	Obstet.
verlosk.	verloskundige	obstet.
versk.	verskillend	dif.
versk.	verskuldig	Dr.
vert.	vertaling; vertaler, vertaal(d)	transl.
vert.	vertrek	dep.
verv.	vervoeging	conj.
verw.	verweerder; verwysing	def.
vgl.	vergelyk	cf., cp.
vgw.	voegwoord	conj.
v/h	voorheen	late
v.h.	vryhandel	F.T.
v.h.t.h.	van huis tot huis	—
vk.	veldkornet; voetbalklub	F.C.
vk.	vierkant	sq.
V.K.	Verenigde Koninkryk	U.K.
V.K.	Vise-Kanselier	V.C.
Vl.	Vlaams	Flem.
vlg.	volgende	foll., seq(q).
vlgs.	volgens	according to
v.l.n.r.	van links na regs	(f.) l. to r.
v.l.s.	vry langs skip	f.a.s.
V.L.U.	Vrouelandbou-unie	W.A.U.
vm.	voormiddag	a.m.
V.M.	volmaan	F.M.
V.N.S.	Vereenvoudigde Nederlandse Spelling	—
vnw.	voornaamwoord	pron.
v.o.	van onder	from below
voegw.	voegwoord	conj.
V.O.I.C.	Vereenigde Oost-Indische Compagnie	U.E.I.C.
vok.	vokaal	vowel
vok.	vokatief	voc.
vol.	volume	vol.
volm.	volmaak	perf.
volt.	voltooi	completed
voors.	voorsitter	Chairman, Pres.
voors.	voorsetsel	prep.
voorw.	voorvoegsel	prefix
voorw.	voorwerp	obj.
v.o.s.	vry op skip	f.o.b.
v.o.s.	vry op spoor	f.o.r.
V.O.T.M.S.	Vereniging van Onderwysers in Transvaalse Middelbare Skole	T.H.S.T.A.
V.P.	Verenigde Party	U.P.
V.P.	vise-president	V.P.
V.R.	vrederegter	J.P.
V/R	verkoopsrekening	A/S
vr.	vroulik	f(em).
Vr.	Vrydag	F(ri).
v.r.n.l.	van regs na links	f.r.t.l.
vs.	vers	v.
vs.	*versus* (teen)	v.
V.S.A.	Verenigde State van Amerika	U.S.A.
V.S.A.N.P.	Verenigde Suid-Afrikaanse Nasionale Party	U.S.A.N.P.
V.S.B.	Vroue-sendingbond	—
V.S.R.	Verteenwoordigende Studenteraad	S.R.C.
V.S.V.	Verdedigingskietvereniging	D.R.A., D.R.C.
V/T	verwys na trekker	R/D
vt.	voet	ft.
Vulg.	Vulgata	Vulg.
vv.	(en) volgende	(et) sqq.
vv.	vragvry	carriage free
v.v.	*vice versa* (omgekeer)	v.v.
v.v.b.	vry van beskadiging	f.f.d.
V.V.	Verenigde Volke	U.N.
V.V.O.K.	Verenigde Volke se Oproep vir Kinders	U.A.C.

W

W.	wes	W
W.	wissel	bill
w.	week; woord	w.
W.A.T.	Woordeboek van die Afrikaanse Taal	—
W.B.	wisselboek	B.B.
wbl.	weekblad	weekly
wd.	woord	wd.
wdb.	woordeboek	dict., lex.
wed.	weduwee	widow
wederk.	wederkerend	reflex.

Afrikaans		Engels
WelEd.	Weledele	Hon.
WelEerw.	Weleerwaarde	Rt. Rev.
w. & k.	warm en koud	h. & c.
wetb.	wetboek	Stat.
wew.	wewenaar	widower
w.g.	was geteken	sgd.
W.G.O.	Wêreldgesondheidsorganisasie	W.H.O.
W.I.	Wes-Indië	W.I.
Wisk.	Wiskunde	Maths.
wisk.	wiskundig	math.
Wits.	Witwatersrandse Universiteit	U.W., Wits.
wk.	week	wk.
wk.	wisselkoers	rate of exchange
W.L.	westerlengte	W.Long.
wnd.	waarnemende	acting
W.Nfr.	Wes-Nederfrankies	W.L. Frankish
W.N.N.R.	Wetenskaplike en Nywerheidsnavorsingsraad	C.S.I.R.
W.N.T.	Woordenboek der Nederlandsche Taal	—
W.N.W.	wesnoordwes	WNW
wo.	waaronder	among which
Wo.	Woensdag	W(ed).
W.P.	Westelike Provinsie	W.P.
W.R.	Wetgewende Raad	Leg. Co.
W.S.	wisselstroom	A.C.
W.Tvl.	Wes-Transvaal	W.Tvl.
W.Vl.	Wes-Vlaams; Wes-Vlaandere	W.Fl.
ww.	werkwoord	v(b).
Wysb.	Wysbegeerte	Phil.

Y

| YSKOR | Suid-Afrikaanse Yster- en Staal- Industriële Korporasie | Iscor |

Z

| Z.A.R. | Zuid-Afrikaansche Republiek | S.A.R. |
| Z.A.R.P. | Zuid-Afrikaansche Republiek Politie | Z.A.R.P. |

2. SI- EN METRIESE EENHEDE

Afrikaans		Engels
A	ampère	A
C	1. Celsius	C
	2. coulomb	
°C	graad Celsius	°C
cc, cm³	kubieke sentimeter	cc, cm³
Kal.	kalorie	cal.
cg	sentigram	cg
cl	sentiliter	cl
cm	sentimeter	cm
kumec, m³/s	kubieke meter per sekonde	cumek, m³/s
db	decibel	db
Dg	dekagram	Dg
dg	desigram	dg
Dl	dekaliter	Dl
dl	desiliter	dl
Dm	dekameter	Dm
dm	desimeter	dm
g	gram	g, gm
gcm	gramsentimeter	gcm
gcs	gramsentimeter per sekonde	gcs
gm	gramme	gm
H	henry	H
h	uur	h
ha	hektaar	ha
Hg	hektogram	Hg(m)
Hl	hektoliter	Hl
Hm	hektometer	Hm
Hz	hertz	Hz
J	joule	J
K	kelvin	K
kg	kilogram	kg
kl	kiloliter	kl
km	kilometer	km
km/h	kilometer per uur	km/h
kV	kilovolt	kV
kVa	kilovolt ampère	kVa
kW	kilowatt	kW
kW.h	kilowatt-uur	kW.h
l	liter	l
m	meter	m
mbar	millibar	mbar
mg	milligram	mg
ml	milliliter	ml
mm	millimeter	mm
MVA	megavoltampère	MVA
N	newton	N
N.m	newtonmeter	N.m
Pa	pascal	Pa
S	siemens	S
V	volt	V
V.A	voltampère	V.A
W	watt	W
Wb	weber	Wb

3. SIMBOLE

&	ampersand	ampersand
@	teen	at
A1	eersteklas; die beste	first class; the best
B	swart (potlood)	black (pencil)

Afrikaans		Engels
t.g.v.	ten gunste van	i.f.o.
t.g.v.	ter geleentheid van	on the occasion of
Th(eol) D(r).	*Theologiae Doctor*	D. Th(eol)., Th.D.
Thess.	*Thessalonicense*	Thess.
Tim.	*Timoteus*	Tim.
Tit.	*Titus*	Tit.
t.l.	ten laaste	lastly
T.L.U.	Transvaalse Landbou-Unie	T.A.U.
TNT	trinitrotoluol	TNT
t.o.	telegrafiese oordrag	T.T.
T.O.	Transvaalse Onderwysersvereniging	—
T.O.D.	Transvaalse Onderwysdepartement	T.E.D.
toej.	toejuiging	appl.
toek.	toekomend; toekoms	fut.
t.o.v.	ten opsigte van	with regard to
tr.	transponeer	trs.
Trig.	Trigonometrie	Trig(on).
Truk	Transvaalse Raad vir die Uitvoerende Kunste	PACT
t.s.	ter sake	ad rem
t.s.	ter see	at sea
t.s.t.	te syner tyd	in his own time
t.t.	*totus tuus* (geheel die uwe)	yours sincerely
Tuinb.	Tuinbou	Hort.
Tvl.	Transvaal	Tvl.
tw.	tussenwerpsel	interj.
t.w.	te wete	viz.
t.w.v.	ter waarde van	to the value of

U

u.	uur	h.
U dw.	U dienswillige	yours faithfully
U dw. dnr.	U dienswillige dienaar	your obedient servant
U Ed.	U Edele	Your Hon.
u.i.	*ut infra* (soos onder)	u.i.
uitbr.	uitbreiding	ext.
uitdr.	uitdrukking	expr.
U.K.	Universiteit van Kaapstad	U.C.T.
U.K.	Uitvoerende Komitee	E.C., Ex. Co.
ult.	*ultimo* (laaslede)	ult.
U.N.	Universiteit van Natal	N.U., U.N.
UNESCO	United Nations Educational, Scientific and Cultural Organisation	UNESCO
UNISA	Universiteit van Suid-Afrika	UNISA
univ.	universiteit	Univ.
U.O.V.S.	Universiteit van die Oranje-Vrystaat	U.O.F.S.
U.P.	Universiteit van Pretoria; Unie-Parlement	U.P.
U.P.E.	Universiteit van Port Elizabeth	U.P.E.
U.R.	Uitvoerende Raad	E.C., Ex. Co.
u.s.	*ut supra* (soos bo)	u.s.
U.S.	Universiteit van Stellenbosch	U.S.
U.S.S.R.	Unie van Sosialistiese Sowjetrepublieke	U.S.S.R.
U.V.	Universiteit van die Vrystaat	U.F.
U.V.M.	Unie-Verdedigingsmag	U.D.F.
U.W.	Universiteit van die Witwatersrand	U.W., Wits.

V

v	volt	V
v.	vers; *vide* (kyk, sien)	v.
v.	vroulik	f(em).
v.a.b.	vry aan boord	f.o.b.
val.	valuta	val.
V.A.R.	Verenigde Arabiese Republiek	V.A.R.
V/B	vragbrief	B/L (ships); C/N (on land)
vb.	voorbeeld	ex.
v.b.	van bo	from above
v.b.b.	volgens bygaande brief	acc. to accomp. letter
V.C.	Victoria Cross	VC
v.C.	voor Christus	B.C.
v.d.	van die	of the
V.D.M.	*Verbi Dei (Divini) Minister* (leraar van die Goddelike Woord) (predikant)	Rev.
v.d.S.	van die skrywer	from the author
veldm.	veldmaarskalk	F.M.
ver.	vereniging	ass., soc.
verb.	*verbum* (woord)	v.
verb.	verbinding	comp.
verb.	verbuiging	dec.
verg.	vergadering	meeting
verg. tr.	vergrotende trap	comp.

Afrikaans		Engels
verklw.	verkleinwoord	dim.
verl.	verlede	past
verl. dw.	verlede deelwoord	p.p.
verl.t.	verlede tyd	pret.
Verlosk.	Verloskunde	Obstet.
verlosk.	verloskundige	obstet.
versk.	verskillend	dif.
versk.	verskuldig	Dr.
vert.	vertaling; vertaler, vertaal(d)	transl.
vert.	vertrek	dep.
verv.	vervoeging	conj.
verw.	verweerder; verwysing	def.
vgl.	vergelyk	cf., cp.
vgw.	voegwoord	conj.
v/h	voorheen	late
v.h.	vryhandel	F.T.
v.h.t.h.	van huis tot huis	—
vk.	veldkornet; voetbalklub	F.C.
vk.	vierkant	sq.
V.K.	Verenigde Koninkryk	U.K.
V.K.	Vise-Kanselier	V.C.
Vl.	Vlaams	Flem.
vlg.	volgende	foll., seq(q).
vlgs.	volgens	according to
v.l.n.r.	van links na regs	(f.) l. to r.
v.l.s.	vry langs skip	f.a.s.
V.L.U.	Vrouelandbou-unie	W.A.U.
vm.	voormiddag	a.m.
V.M.	volmaan	F.M.
V.N.S.	Vereenvoudigde Nederlandse Spelling	—
vnw.	voornaamwoord	pron.
v.o.	van onder	from below
voegw.	voegwoord	conj.
V.O.I.C.	Vereenigde Oost-Indische Compagnie	U.E.I.C.
vok.	vokaal	vowel
vok.	vokatief	voc.
vol.	volume	vol.
volm.	volmaak	perf.
volt.	voltooi	completed
voors.	voorsitter	Chairman, Pres.
voors.	voorsetsel	prep.
voorw.	voorvoegsel	prefix
voorw.	voorwerp	obj.
v.o.s.	vry op skip	f.o.b.
v.o.s.	vry op spoor	f.o.r.
V.O.T.M.S.	Vereniging van Onderwysers in Transvaalse Middelbare Skole	T.H.S.T.A.
V.P.	Verenigde Party	U.P.
V.P.	vise-president	V.P.
V.R.	vrederegter	J.P.
V/R	verkoopsrekening	A/S
vr.	vroulik	f(em).
Vr.	Vrydag	F(ri).
v.r.n.l.	van regs na links	f.r.t.l.
vs.	vers	v.
vs.	*versus* (teen)	v.
V.S.A.	Verenigde State van Amerika	U.S.A.
V.S.A.N.P.	Verenigde Suid-Afrikaanse Nasionale Party	U.S.A.N.P.
V.S.B.	Vroue-sendingbond	—
V.S.R.	Verteenwoordigende Studenteraad	S.R.C.
V.S.V.	Verdedigingskietvereniging	D.R.A., D.R.C.
V/T	verwys na trekker	R/D
vt.	voet	ft.
Vulg.	Vulgata	Vulg.
vv.	(en) volgende	(et) sqq.
vv.	vragvry	carriage free
v.v.	*vice versa* (omgekeer)	v.v.
v.v.b.	vry van beskadiging	f.f.d.
V.V.	Verenigde Volke	U.N.
V.V.O.K.	Verenigde Volke se Oproep vir Kinders	U.A.C.

W

W.	wes	W
W.	wissel	bill
w.	week; woord	w.
W.A.T.	Woordeboek van die Afrikaanse Taal	—
W.B.	wisselboek	B.B.
wbl.	weekblad	weekly
wd.	woord	wd.
wdb.	woordeboek	dict., lex.
wed.	weduwee	widow
wederk.	wederkerend	reflex.

Afrikaans		Engels
2B	dubbel swart (potlood)	double black (pencil)
3B	driedubbel swart (potlood)	treble black (pencil)
C	1. Romeinse 100 2. Celsius	1. Roman 100 2. Celsius, centigrade
D	Romeinse 500	Roman 500
$	dollar	dollar
=	is gelyk aan	equals
H	hard (potlood)	hard (pencil)
2H	dubbel hard (potlood)	double hard (pencil)
3H	driedubbel hard (potlood)	treble hard (pencil)
L	Romeinse 50	Roman 50
£	pond (geld)	pound (money)
M	Romeinse 1 000	Roman 1 000
V	Romeinse 5	Roman 5
×	vermenigvuldigingsteken	multiplication sign
X	Romeinse 10	Roman 10

MAJOR DICTIONARY

ENGLISH · AFRIKAANS

Thirteenth Edition
Revised by L. C. Eksteen

Earlier compilers
M. S. B. Kritzinger,
P. C. Schoonees, U. J. Cronjé

J. L. van Schaik

J. L. van Schaik (Pty) Ltd,
Libri Building, Church Street, Pretoria
All rights reserved

First edition 1926
Second edition 1928
Third edition 1937
Fourth edition 1946
Fifth edition 1951
Sixth edition 1954
Seventh edition, first impression 1956, second impression 1957
Eighth edition, first impression 1959, second impression 1960, third impression 1961
Ninth edition, first impression 1963, second impression 1966
Tenth edition, first impression 1968, second impression 1969, third impression 1970
Eleventh edition, first impression 1972, second impression 1977
Twelfth edition 1981
Thirteenth edition 1986

ISBN 0 627 01491 7

Typeset, printed and bound by
National Book Printers,
Goodwood, Cape

FOREWORD TO THE THIRTEENTH EDITION

This edition has been thoroughly revised and considerably expanded.
An attempt has been made to incorporate new words which have appeared in the press.
I express my appreciation to those readers who sent me comments and suggestions.
My thanks go to Mrs. A. Smith for her assistance in reading the galley proofs.

L.C.E.
Pretoria
July 1986

ABBREVIATIONS

a	= adjective		pl	= plural
adv	= adverb		prep	= preposition
conj	= conjunction		pron	= pronoun
interj	= interjection		sing	= singular
n	= noun		v	= verb

..   is used where the last syllable of a word has been changed:
    geklee, (..klede) = geklede;

~- denotes a hyphenated word, e.g.
    brake: ~-fluid = brake-fluid;

~   (separate) represents the key word, e.g.
    engine: ~ number = engine number;

~   (joined) means that the key word and the other word should be joined, e.g.
    club: ~man = clubman;

~   after certain Afrikaans verbs means that the verb does not take *ge-*, or *-ge-*, e.g.
    voorspel, (~), beskerm, (~) remain **voorspel** and **beskerm;**

=   is used at the end of a line to denote that the word must be written as one word, e.g.
    scout: ~=master = scoutmaster;

'   indicates that in pronouncing the word the accent falls on the syllable preceding the mark,
    e.g. **aback', ab'acus.**

A

a, (a's, as), a; A 1, eersteklas; puik; *FROM* ~ *to z*, van die begin tot die end; van alfa tot omega; *not KNOW A from B*, nie 'n (g'n) A voor (van) 'n B ken nie.

a, an, 'n, per; *see also* **an;** *he EARNS R5* ~ *week*, hy verdien R5 per week; *so MUCH* ~ *day*, soveel per dag; *it costs 10c* ~ *KILOGRAM*, dit kos 10c per kilogram; *TWICE* ~ *year*, twee maal per jaar.

Aa'chen, (Aix-la-Chapelle'), Aken.
aa' lava, aälawa.
aard'vark, erdvark.
aard'wolf, maanhaarjakkals, erdwolf.
aa'svoël, aasvoël.
a'ba, aba.
abaca', manillahennep.
aback', terug, agteruit; *taken* ~, verbluf, uit die veld geslaan, verras.
ab'acus, (..ci), telraam, abakus, rekenbord, dekstuk (argitektuur).
Abad'don, die hel; die duiwel.
abaft', agter, agteruit; op die agterskip.
abalo'ne, perlemoen.
aban'don, (n) oorgawe; losheid, losbandigheid; onverskilligheid, sorgelose vryheid; ongedwongenheid; (v) opgee; los ('n voertuig); verlaat; oorgee; wegsmyt; begeef, afsien van, laat vaar; ~ *all HOPE*, by die pakke gaan sit; ~ *ONESELF to*, hom oorgee aan; ~ *SHIP*, die skip verlaat; ~ed, verlate, oorgegee; losbandig; onopgeëis; ~ed *goods*, onopgeëiste goedere; ~ment, afstel, verlating, agterlating; oorgawe; opsegging; verslaafdheid; verlatenheid; losbandigheid; afstand (jur.), ~ee', sessionaris
abase', verlaag, verneder; ~ment, vernedering, verlaging.
abash', beskaam, uit die veld slaan, verbluf; ~ed, verleë, uit die veld geslaan, skaam; ~ment, verleentheid, beskaamdheid, verbluftheid.
abask', aan die sonbrand; luierend.
abat'able, onderhewig aan afslag.
abate', verminder (prys); verflou, uitwoed, minder word (siekte); matig; afslaan; lenig, bedaar; kragteloos word (wet); bekoel; *the wind has* ~ *d*, die wind het gaan lê; ~ment; vermindering, afslag; bedaring.
ab'atis, abatt'is, verkapping; taklaer.
abattoir', (-s), slaghuis, slagpale, slagplek, abattoir; ~ *dues*, ~ *fees*, slaggeld; ~ **system,** abattoirstelsel.
abax'ial, abaksiaal.
abb'a, vader; kloostervoog; ~cy, amp (ampsbekleding, gebied) van 'n ab, abskap.
abba'tial, abba'tical, abtelik.
ab'bé, geestelike, abbé.
abb'ess, (-es), abdis.
abb'ey, (-s), abdy, klooster(kerk).
abb'ot, ab, kloosterhoof; ~ **ship,** abskap.
abbrev'iate, verkort, afkort; verklein.
abbrevia'tion, verkorting, afkorting; verkleining.
abbrevia'tory, verkortend.
ABC, ABC, alfabet; allereerste beginsels; *not to KNOW one's* ~, die ABC nie ken nie; *the* ~ *OF*, die abc van; die allereerste beginsels van; *that's as SIMPLE as* ~, dis net ABC.
ab'dicant, afstand doende, aftredend.
ab'dicate, afstand doen van, neerlê, aftree.
abdica'tion, (troons)afstand, aftreding, neerlegging (van 'n amp); abdikasie (van 'n vors).
ab'dicator, (troon)verlater, aftreder, afstanddoener.
abdom'en, maag, (onder)buik; agterlyf (insek).
abdom'inal, buik=, maag=; ~ **belt,** buikband; ~ **cavity,** maagholte; ~ **hernia,** buikbreuk; ~ **ptosis,** buikversakking; ~ **region,** maagstreek; ~ **trocar,** buiktapnaald; ~ **wall,** buikwand.
abdom'inoscopy, abdominoskopie.
abdom'inous, swaarlywig, dikbuikig.
abdu'cent, afvoer=.
abduct', ontvoer, wegvoer, skaak, weggloop (met 'n vrou); ~ **ion,** ontvoering; vroueroof, skaking; ~ **or,** skaker, ontvoerder; afvoerder; (af)trekspier.
abeam', dwars (deur 'n skip); dwarsskeeps, in die dwarste.

abecedar'ian, (n) a-b-c-leerling; (a) alfabeties; elementêr; ongeletter(d).
abed', in die bed; in die vere; *lie* ~, nog in die vere lê.
abele', a'bele, witpopulier.
a'belmosk, a'belmusk, abelmos.
A'berdeen An'gus, Aberdeen Angus.
aberdevine', sysie.
Aberdon'ian, inwoner van Aberdeen; Aberdeener (S.A.).
abe'rrance, afdwaling, afwyking.
abe'rrant, afdwalend, afwykend.
aberra'tion, afwyking, afdwaling; misstap; brekingsafwyking.
abet', (-ted), aanhits, opstook; bystaan, help; *aid and* ~, aanhits en help; medepligtig wees; ~ **ment,** aanhitsing, aansporing; bystand, hulp; ~ **tor,** opstoker, aanhitser; handlanger, medepligtige.
abey'ance, opskorting; stilstand; *FALL into* ~, kragteloos (ongeldig) word; in onbruik raak; *IN* ~, opgeskort, hangende, onuitgemaak, onopgelos; *LEAVE in* ~, agterweë hou; opskort.
abhor', (-red), verfoei, verafsku.
abho'rrence, verfoeiing, (ver)afskuwing, afgryse, afsku, veragting; *hold someone (something) in* ~, 'n hekel aan iem. (iets) hê.
abho'rrent, verfoeilik, haatlik, afskuwelik; onverdraaglik.
abho'rrer, verafskuwer, verfoeier.
abid'ance, vashouding, aanhouding; volging; gehoorsaamheid (aan reëls, ens.).
abide', (abode), bly, woon, vertoef; uithou, verdra; afwag, jou neerlê by; ~ *BY*, jou neerlê by, bly by; *be unable to* ~ *EACH other,* mekaar nie kan veel nie; *be UNABLE to* ~ *someone (something),* hoog aan iem. (iets) hê; die land aan iem. (iets) hê.
abi'ding, duursaam, ewig, blywend.
ab'igail, kamermeisie, diensmeisie.
abil'ity, (..ties), bekwaamheid, vermoë, knapheid; (pl) geestesgawes, talente; *ACCORDING to* ~, na vermoë; *to the BEST of my* ~, na my beste vermoë; ~ *to LAUGH*, lagvermoë.
ab ini'tio, ab initio, van die begin.
abiogen'esis, selfontstaan, abiogenese.
abiogenet'ic, abiogeneties.
ab'ject, (n) ellendeling, verworpeling; (a) veragtelik, gemeen; kruipend, laag; ~ *OBEDIENCE,* willose gehoorsaamheid; ~ *POVERTY,* volslae armoede.
abject'ly, op 'n veragtelike (kruiperige) manier.
abjec'tion, ab'jectness, laagheid, veragtelikheid; kruiperigheid.
abjura'tion, afswering.
abjure', afsweer; herroep, verloën; ~r, afsweerder; verloënaar.
ablactate', speen; afspeen (vrugte).
ablacta'tion, spening, ablaktasie; (die) speen (wegneem van die bors).
abla'tion, afsetting, erosie, wegbreking, ablasie (geol.).
ab'lative, ablatief; ~ **case,** ablatief (naamval).
ab'laut, ablaut, vokaalwisseling.
ablaze', aan die brand, gloeiend; in ligtelaaie; skitterend; opgewonde; vuur en vlam (fig.).
a'ble, bekwaam, knap, bevoeg; sterk; *be* ~, kan, vermag, in staat wees; ~**-bodied,** frisgebou, kragtig, sterk, weerbaar; ~*-bodied seaman,* bevare (vol)matroos.
a'blet, alweertjie (vis).
abloom', in (volle) bloei.
ab'luent, (n) reinigingsmiddel; (a) reinigend.
ablu'tion, afwassing, afspoeling, reiniging; suiwering; ablusie; ~**-block,** waskamers; ~**-tub,** wasbalie.
ab'ly, knap, behendig.
ab'negate, ontsê, verloën, ontken; afsien van.
abnega'tion, ontkenning, (self)verloëning; selfversaking; ontsegging.
abnorm'al, onreëlmatig, teen die reël, abnormaal; gepikkewaan; gebreklik, misvorm; sieklik.
abnormal'ity, onreëlmatigheid; mismaaktheid, wanstaltigheid, gebreklikheid.

abnormally / absorber

abnorm'ally, buitengewoon, abnormaal.
abnorm'ity, wanstaltigheid; monstrositeit.
aboard', aan boord; *ALL ~?*, almal op? opklim!; *FALL ~*, teen 'n ander skip bots; *LAY ~*, langs die kant van 'n ander skip kom.
abode', verblyfplek, woning, woonplek, tuiste, verblyf; *of no fixed ~*, sonder vaste woonplek; in die wapad.
abol'ish, afskaf, ophef, vernietig, herroep; *~er*, afskaffer, vernietiger; *~ment*, afskaffing, opheffing.
aboli'tion, afskaffing, opheffing, abolisie; *~ism*, afskaffingstelsel; *~ist*, afskaffer.
A'-bomb, A-bom, atoombom, kernbom.
aboma'sum, melkpens, lebmaag.
abom'inable, afskuwelik, gruwelik, verfoeilik, walglik; *~ snowman*, afskuwelike sneeumens.
abom'inate, verfoei, verafsku, haat.
abomina'tion, gruwel, afskuwelikheid; verafskuwing.
abori'ginal, (n) (-s, ..gines), oerinwoner, inboorling; inlander; (a) oorspronklik, inheems.
Abori'gine, (-s), Aborigine.
abori'gine, oorspronklike inwoner, oerinwoner; inheemse plant (dier).
abort', ontydig beval, 'n miskraam kry; onontwikkeld bly (biol.); *~ed*, ontydig beval.
abortifa'cient, (n) aborsiemiddel; (a) afdrywend.
abor'tion, ontydige bevalling, misgeboorte, miskraam, aborsie, abortus, vrugafdrywing; monster, misgewas; agteruitgang; *~ist*, vrugafdrywer, aborteur.
abor'tive, ontydig gebore; mislukkend, vrugteloos; vrugafdrywend, abortief.
abou'lia, wilskragverlies.
abound', oorvloei van, oorvloedig wees, vol wees van, volop wees, wemel van.
about'¹, (v) ('n skip) laat omdraai, wend.
about'², (adv, prep) ongeveer, sowat, circa, omtrent; met betrekking tot; omstreeks, in om, rondom; *BE ~ something*, besig wees met iets; *BRING ~*, teweegbring, veroorsaak; *COME ~*, gebeur; *GO (set) ~ a thing*, iets aanpak; *HAVE money ~ one*, geld by jou hê; *much ado ~ NOTHING*, meer lawaai as wol; *be QUICK ~ it*, gou maak; *RIGHT ~!*, regs om!; *SET ~ a person*, iem. aanval; *STAND ~*, rondstaan; *be ~ TO*, van plan wees om; op die punt staan om; *~ TURN*, omkeer; *be UP and ~*, op die been wees; woel; besig wees; *WHAT ~ it?*, wat daarvan? wat dan nog?; *~-face*, ommekeer; *~-sledge*, voorhamer; *~-turn*, ommekeer; *make an ~-turn*, bolmakiesie slaan.
above', (adv. prep) bo, hoër, meer, bo-oor, omhoog, daar bo, bokant, meer as; bostaande, bogenoemde; *~ ALL*, bowenal, veral; *CAN'T get ~ C*, nie hoër as C kan sing nie; *FROM ~*, van bo (af); *GET ~ oneself*, verwaand wees; uit jou vel raak; *~ GROUND*, nog nie dood nie; *~ my HEAD*, bokant my vuurmaakplek; *be ~ ONESELF*, jouself nie meer ken nie; *honour ~ WEALTH*, eer bo rykdom; *~ board*, rondborstig; reguit, eerlik, onbewimpeld; *~-cited*, boaangehaalde, *~-deck*, bodek; eerlik; *~ ground*, bo die grond, in lewe; *~-mentioned*, bogenoemd, voor(ge)noem, voorgemeld; *~-named*, bostaande, bogemeld, bogenoem.
ab ov'o, ab a'vo, (vervelig herhaal) van die begin af.
abracadab'ra, abrakadabra, toorwoord; wartaal, onsin.
abrad'able, afslytbaar; afskuurbaar.
abra'dant, (n) skuurmiddel, skaafmiddel; (a) skrynend.
abrade', afskaaf, afskuur, afvrywe, skryn, wegskaaf.
A'braham: *in ~'s bosom*, in Abraham se skoot; geluksaligheid.
abranch'ial, sonder kuwe.
abra'sion, skaafplek; afskawing, afslyting; *~ mark*, skaafplek, skuurplek.
abra'sive, (n) skaafmiddel, skuurmiddel; (a) afskawend; slyp=
abreast', langs mekaar, in gelid, op 'n ry; *~ of AFFAIRS*, op hoogte van sake bly; *keep (be) ~ of the TIMES*, op die hoogte van jou tyd wees.
abridge', verkort, afkort, beperk; beknopter maak; inkort.

abridg(e)'ment, verkorting, beperking, bekorting; uittreksel; inkorting.
abroach', oopgetrek, oopgesit.
abroad', buite, buitekant; buitelands, in die vreemde; in omloop; *FROM ~*, uit die buiteland; *GET ~*, rugbaar word, in omloop kom; *GO ~*, oorsee gaan; *at HOME and ~*, binne- en buitelands; *the NEWS is all ~*, die nuus is orals bekend; *there is a RUMOUR ~*, 'n gerug is in omloop (doen die rondte); *SPREAD (rumour) ~*, rondstrooi.
ab'rogate, herroep, afskaf, ophef, intrek; *~d by disuse*, deur onbruik verval.
abroga'tion, herroeping, afskaffing, opheffing, intrekking, abrogasie.
abrupt', afgebroke; plotseling, onverwags; afgebete, kortaf; steil; *~ion*, afbreking van 'n deel van die massa, wegbreek; *~ly*, skielik, kortaf; dwarsweg; *~ness*, kortheid; skielikheid; afgebetenheid; driftigheid.
ab'cess, (-es), geswel, ettergeswel, etterbuil, sweer, abses.
abscind', afsny.
ab'sciss, (-es), **absci'ssa**, (-s), absis.
absci'ssion, afsnyding, afskeuring; *~-layer*, skeidingslaag.
abscond', wegloop, (weg)dros, vlug, die plaat poets; *~er*, wegloper, vlugteling, droster; *~ing*, drostery.
ab'seil, afklim(ming) (van 'n steil rotsrand).
ab'sence, afwesigheid; gebrek; *APOLOGY for ~*, verskoning vir afwesigheid; *be CONSPICUOUS by one's ~*, skitter deur afwesigheid; *IN the ~ of*, by gebrek aan; by afwesigheid van; *~ of MIND*, afgetrokkenheid, verstrooidheid; *~-record*, aantekeninge oor afwesigheid; *~-study*, studie oor afwesigheid (fabriek).
absent'¹, (v) verwyder; wegbly; afwesig wees, absenteer; *~ oneself*, jou absenteer, afwesig wees.
ab'sent², (a) afwesig, absent; verstrooid, afgetrokke; *long ~, soon forgotten*, uit die oog, uit die hart; *~ee'*, afwesige; *~ee landlord*, elderswonende grondbesitter; *~ee'ism*, absentisme, werkafwesigheid, gewoonte-afwesigheid; *~ly*, ingedagte.
absen'tia: *DEGREE in ~*, graad in absentia; *IN ~*, by verstek (jur.); in afwesigheid.
ab'sent: *~-minded*, afgetrokke, verstrooid; *~-mindedness*, afgetrokkenheid, verstrooidheid, gedagteloosheid.
ab'sinth, absint, als(em), alsbrandewyn; *~ine*, alsembitter.
absol'utary, vrymakend; vergewend.
ab'solute, volstrek, volslae, onbeperk; volkome; pure, skone, absoluut; heeltemal; *~ DISCRETION*, volstrekte goeddunke; *~ MAJORITY*, volstrekte meerderheid; *this is ~ NONSENSE*, dis pure onsin; *THE ~*, die absolute (volstrekte); *~ ceiling*, bereikte hoogtegrens; *~ density*, absolute digtheid; *~ly*, heeltemal, volkome, ten ene male, totaal, glad en al; (facetious) opsluit; *~ly nothing*, hoegenaamd niks; *~ monarchy*, absolute koningskap; *~ness*, onbeperktheid, volstrektheid, onbeperkte mag; willekeur; *~ term*, konstante term; *~ zero*, absolute nulpunt.
absolu'tion, vryspraak, vergifnis, kwytskelding, absolusie; *~ of the instance*, absolusie van die instansie.
ab'solutism, absolutisme, alleenheerskappy.
ab'solutist, absolutis.
absolve', vryspreek, kwytskeld, vrylaat, vergewe, loslaat; *~ from a promise*, van 'n belofte ontslaan; *~r*, vrymaker, vryspreker.
ab'sonant, wanklinkend, wanluidend; teenstrydig.
absorb', (op)suig, intrek; opneem, absorbeer; insluk; verslind; *~abil'ity*, verslindbaarheid, opsuigbaarheid, absorbeerbaarheid; *~able*, verslindbaar, opsuigbaar.
absorb'ed, versonke, verdiep in; opsuig, versink; *in a BOOK*, in 'n boek verdiep; *be ~ in THOUGHT*, in gedagte versink.
absorb'ent, absorbeermiddel, opsuigmiddel; *~ LINT*, verbandlinne; *~ PAPER*, vloeipapier; *~ cotton WOOL*, opsuigwatte.
absorb'er, demper; verslinder.

absor'bing, interessant, boeiend; ~-**well**, dreineerput.
absorp'tion, opsuiging, inslukking, absorpsie; demping (geluid); *power of* ~, absorpsievermoë; ~-**bands**, absorpsiebande; ~-**curve**, absorpsiekromme; ~ **meter**, absorpsiemeter.
absorp'tive, absorberend, opsuigend; ~**ness**, suigkrag, absorbeerkrag, absorpsievermoë.
absquat'ulate, laat spat, padgee.
abstain', hom onthou van; afskaf; wegbly; ~ **er**, onthouer; afskaffer; *total* ~ *er*, geheelonthouer.
abstem'ious, matig; onthoudend; ~ **ness**, matigheid.
absten'tion, onthouding; onttrekking; matigheid.
absten'tious, matig; onthoudend.
absterge', suiwer, reinig, abstergeer.
abster'gent, (n) reiniger, suiweraar; (a) reinigend, suiwerend.
abster'sion, reiniging, suiwering.
abster'sive, reinigend, suiwerend.
ab'stinence, afskaffing, onthouding; matigheid; *total* ~, geheelonthouding.
ab'stinency, onthouding.
ab'stinent, onthoudend; matig.
ab'stract[1], (n) uittreksel; aftreksel; samevatting; afgetrokkenheid; afgetrokke begrip; *in the* ~, in teorie; abstrak beskou.
abstract'[2], (v) aftrek, skei, uittrek; ontleen, hom toeëien; uittreksel maak; abstraheer; ~**ed**, afgesonder, verstrooid, diepsinnig; ~**edness**, afgetrokkenheid, diepsinnigheid; ~**er**, opsommer; ~**ion**, aftrekking; afgetrokkenheid, verstrooidheid; abstraksie; ontvreemding, onttrekking; ~**ly**, abstrak (gesproke).
ab'stract[3], (a) afgetrokke; diepsinnig; abstrak; ~ *number*, onbenoemde getal.
abstrict', afsnoer; ~ **ion**, afsnoering.
abstruse', verborge, diepsinnig, duister; ~ **ness**, duisterheid, diepsinnigheid, verborgenheid.
absurd', onbestaanbaar, ongerymd, belaglik, dwaas, onsinnig, verspot, absurd; ~**ity**, ongerymdheid, onsinnigheid, dwaasheid, belaglikheid, absurditeit; ~**ly**, dwaas.
abu'lia = **aboulia**.
abun'dance, oorvloed, volheid, veelheid, menigte, rykdom.
abun'dant, oorvloedig, baie, volop, ryk.
abuse', (n) misbruik, wangebruik, mishandeling; verguising, belediging, smaad; geskel, skeldtaal; ~ *of POWER*, ampsoortreding, misbruik van gesag; *TERM of* ~, skeldwoord; (v) misbruik, mishandel; bedrieg, mislei; skend; verguis, (uit)skel, beledig; ~ *someone's HOSPITALITY*, 'n lêplek êrens maak; ~ **d**, verguis.
abus'ive, misbruikend; beledigend; smalend, lasterend; verkeerd, onjuis; *BECOME* ~, begin skel, ~ *LANGUAGE*, beledigende taal, skeldtaal; ~ *NAME*, skimpnaam; ~ *TERM*, skimpwoord; ~**ness**, beledigende manier.
abut', (-ted), grens aan; raak aan; stoot.
abu'tilon, bebroeide-eiers (plant).
abut'ment, grens, begrensing; steunpunt, steunpilaar; landhoof, oewerondersteuning; ~ **hinge**, voetskarnier; ~ **piece**, voetplaat; ~ **ring**, stootring; ~ **tooth**, ankertand.
abut': ~ **tal**, begrensing, grensskeiding; ~ **ter**, eienaar van aangrensende eiendom; ~ **ting**, aangrensend.
abysm' = **abyss**.
abys'mal, grondeloos, onpeilbaar.
abyss', afgrond, bodemlose diepte; ingewande van die aarde; ~ **al**, diepsee-; bodemloos.
Abyssin'ia, Abessinië; ~ **n**, (n) Abessiniër, Abessyn; (a) Abessinies, Abessyns.
aca'cia, akasia.
a'cademe, (lit.), universiteit.
acade'mic, (n), akademikus; geleerde.
academ'ic(al), akademies; onprakties, teoreties; ~ **field**, akademiese gebied (terrein); ~ **sector**, akademiese sektor.
academ'icals, akademiese drag.
academi'cian, lid van 'n akademie.
academ'icism, akademisme.
academ'ics, teoretiese redeneringe; akademiese gewaad.

acad'emism, akademisme.
Aca'demy, Akademie; ~ **for Arts and Science**, Akademie vir Wetenskap en Kuns.
aca'demy, (..**mies**), akademie; genootskap; ~ **figure**, modeltekening.
Aca'dia, Akadië, Nieu-Skotland; ~ **n**, (n) bewoner van Nieu-Skotland; (a) Akadies.
ac'aleph(e), seekwal, seenetel.
acana'ceous, doringagtig, van dorings voorsien.
acan'thus, beerklou, akant(us) (plant); nabootsing v.d. plant as versiering (argitektuur).
a cappel'la, (It.), a cappella, sonder begeleiding.
acap'sular, sonder kapsule.
acar'diac, sonder 'n hart.
aca'ricide, mytdoder.
a'carid, myt, luis, akaride (fam. *Acaridae*).
acarp'ous, nie-vrugdraend.
acatalec'tic, volkome (versreël), akatalekties.
acatalep'sy, onbegryplikheid, akatalepsie.
acathar'sy, bloedonsuiwerheid, akatarsis.
acaud'al, stertloos.
acaul'ous, stamloos.
Accad'ian, (n) Akkadiër; Akkadies (taal), (a) Akkadies.
accede', toestem; toestaan, instem; (die troon) bestyg; toegee; aanvaar ('n amp); ~ *to*, inwillig, gehoor gee aan, voldoen aan.
accelera'ndo, (It., mus.), accelerando, met geleidelike tempoversnelling.
accel'erate, versnel, vet gee (motor); verhaas; bespoedig; vervroeg; akselereer; ~ **d**, versnel(de).
accelera'tion, versnelling; bespoediging, verhaasting; vervroeging (ontsteking), akselerasie; ~ **lane**, versnellingsbaan; ~ **power**, versnelvermoë.
accel'erative, versnellend.
accel'erator, versneller, gaspedaal; dryfspier (dierkunde); ~ **lever**, versnellerhefboom; ~ **y**, versnellend.
accelero'meter, versnellingsmeter.
ac'cent, (n) nadruk, klem, klemtoon; uitspraak; stembuiging; klemteken, aksent; (pl) toon, woorde.
accent', (v) nadruk lê op, beklemtoon, aksentueer; ~ **or**, soort spreeu (geslag *Prunella*); ~ **ual**, geaksentueer(d); ~ **uate**, nadruk lê op, verskerp, beklemtoon, betoon; op die voorgrond bring; ~ **ua'tion**, aksentuasie, verskerping, beklemtoning, betoning.
accept', aanneem, aanvaar, goedkeur; ontvang, aksepteer; voortrek; ~ *BATTLE*, die geveg aanvaar; ~ *a PROPOSAL*, 'n voorstel aanneem; ~ **abil'ity**, aanneemlikheid; ~ **able**, aanneemlik, aanvaarbaar; aangenaam, welkom; ~ *able in the best circles*, aanneemlik (welkom) in die beste (hoogste) kringe; ~ **ableness** = **acceptability**.
accep'tance, aanname, ontvangs, aanvaarding; aksepsasie; geaksepteerde wissel; ~ **house**, aksepbank; ~ **test**, aanneemtoets.
accepta'tion, aanneming; aangenome betekenis; akseptasie.
accep'ted, aangenome; gangbaar, geldend.
accep'ter, aannemer; ontvanger.
accep'tor, akseptant (van wissel).
ac'cess, (n) nadruk; toename, vermeerdering; aanval, vlaag; ~ *of AIR*, lugtoevoer; *EASE of* ~, maklik genaakbaar; *HAVE* ~ *to*, toegang hê tot; *an* ~ *of PASSION*, 'n vlaag van woede.
acces'sary, (n) (..**ries**), bykomstigheid; vereiste; onderdeel, byehoorsel; medepligtige; ~ *AFTER the fact*, begunstiger van 'n misdaad; ~ *BEFORE the fact*, aanstigter van 'n misdaad; ~ *to a CRIME*, medepligtige aan 'n misdaad; (pl) bybehore, toebehore; (a) medepligtig; bybehorend; *kyk* **accessory**.
accessibil'ity, toeganklikheid, genaakbaarheid; ontvanklikheid.
acces'sible, toeganklik, genaakbaar, bereikbaar; ontvanklik.
acces'sion, toetreding; aanwins; ampsaanvaarding; uitbreiding; troonsbestyging; ~ **al**, bykomend, bybehorend.
acces'sory, (n) (..**ries**), medepligtige, bykomstigheid, vereiste onderdeel; (pl) toebehore, bybehore, onderdele, toebehoorsels, bybenodighede; (a) byko-

mend, bykomstig; medepligtig, aandadig; *accessories LIST*, lys van bykomende benodigdhede; ~ *MUSCLE*, byspier; *kyk* **accessary.**
ac'cess road, toegangspad.
acciaccatu'ra, (It., mus.), acciaccatura.
ac'cidence, vormleer, buigingsleer; eerste beginsels.
ac'cident, toeval; ongeluk, misslag; bykomstigheid; gedaante (Eucharistic); *BY* ~, toevallig; *a CHAPTER of* ~ *s*, onvoorsiene gang van sake; ~ *s happen in the best-regulated families*, 'n ongeluk kan enigeen oorkom; ~ *s of the GROUND*, terreinoneffenhede; *be KILLED in an* ~, verongeluk; *MEET with an* ~, 'n ongeluk oorkom, 'n ongeluk kry; ~ *RATE*, ongeluksyfer.
acciden'tal, (n) bysaak, iets toevalligs; (a) toevallig; as bysaak; ondergeskik; bykomend; ~ *COLOURS*, aanvullingskleure, komplementêre kleure; ~ *DEATH*, dood deur 'n ongeluk; ~ **ly,** per ongeluk; toevallig.
ac'cident insur'ance, ongevalleversekering, versekering teen ongelukke.
ac'cident-prone, ongeluksvatbaar.
a'ccidie, luiheid, traagheid; apatie.
accip'itral, valkagtig; roofsugtig; skerpsiende.
acclaim', (n) toejuiging; goedkeuring; (v) toejuig; uitroep; begroet as.
acclama'tion, byval, toejuiging, applous; *by* ~, met luide toejuiging.
acclam'atory, byvals=, toejuigend; ~ *shouts*, vreugdekrete.
acclim'ate, *kyk* **acclimatize.**
acclimatiza'tion, gewoondwording aan klimaat, akklimatisering, aanpassing.
acclim'atize, aanpas by (aan) 'n klimaat, wen aan 'n klimaat, akklimatiseer.
accliv'ity, (..ties), helling, steilte, opdraand.
accliv'ous, steil, opdraand.
accolade', ridderslag, akkolade; krulhakie, akkolade, verbindingshakie.
accom'modate, aanpas, skik; onder dak bring, herberg, inneem; voorsien; versoen, akkommodeer.
accom'modating, toeskietlik, (in)skiklik, tegemoetkomend; aanneemlik; ruim (bv. gewete).
accommoda'tion, skikking, aanpassing, skiklikheid; losies, huisvesting, plaasruimte, akkommodasie; gerief; ~ *for the night*, nagverblyf; ~ **bill,** voorskotwissel, akkommodasiewissel; ~ **bridge,** hulpbrug; ~ **ladder,** touleer, valreeptrap, noodleer; ~ **road,** tydelike pad.
accom'modative, inskiklik, gerieflik, aanpassend.
accom'paniment, begeleiding; vergeselling; toebehore, bybehore.
accom'panist, begeleier.
accom'pany, (..nied), vergesel van, begelei deur; saamgaan, in verband staan met; *be ..panied by*, vergesel (begelei) word deur (van).
accom'panying, bygaande; ~ *CIRCUMSTANCES*, bykomende omstandighede; ~ *DOCUMENTS*, bylaes, bygaande stukke.
accom'plice, medepligtige, mededader; vloekgenoot; handlanger.
accom'plish, uitvoer, volbring, tot stand bring, vervul, volvoer; ~ **ed,** voltooid; welopgevoed, beskaaf; talentvol; volmaak; bedrewe; *an* ~ *ed FACT*, 'n voldonge feit, 'n uitgemaakte saak; *an* ~ *ed GENTLEMAN*, 'n beskaafde heer, 'n agtermekaar (talentvolle) kêrel; ~ **er,** volvoerder; ~ **ment,** voltooiing, totstandbrenging, bewerkstelliging, uitvoering; beskawing; vervulling; talent, begaafdheid, kundigheid.
accord', (n) ooreenstemming; ooreenkoms, verdrag; harmonie; *of its OWN* ~, vanself; *of one's OWN* ~, op eie houtjie, uit eie beweging; *WITH one* ~, eenparig; (v) ooreenstem, akkordeer; laat ooreenstem; vereffen; toestaan, vergun; ~ *a WELCOME*, welkom heet; ~ **ance,** ooreenstemming; *in* ~ *ance with*, in ooreenstemming met, ooreenkomstig; ~ **ant,** ooreenstemmend; harmoniërend.
accord'ing, ooreenkomstig, volgens; ~ *AS*, namate, na gelang, in soverre as; ~ *TO*, na, volgens, luidens, ooreenkomstig; gevolglik, bygevolg, dus, daarna, desgelyks.

accor'dion, akkordeon, handharmonika, trekklavier; ~ **door,** voudeur, konsertinadeur; ~ **pleat,** ~ **wall,** konsertinaplooi.
accost', (n) begroeting; (v) aanspreek; begroet; aanklamp, bydam.
accouch'ement, accouchement, bevalling, verlossing.
accoucheur', verloskundige, vroedmeester, accoucheur.
accoucheuse', vroedvrou, "ouvrou".
account', (n) rekening; berig, verhaal, verslag; rekenskap, verklaring, rede; belang, betekenis; uittreksel; *BRING to* ~, in rekening bring; rekenskap eis; *CALL to* ~, tot verantwoording roep; iem. voorkry; *be CALLED to* ~, aan die pen ry; les opsê; *be CALLED to one's* ~, finale verantwoording moet doen; *to CAST* ~ *s*, 'n rekening optel; *CHARGE to someone's* ~, op iem. se rekening bring (sit); *CHECK an* ~, 'n rekening kontroleer; 'n rekening nasien (toets); *GIVE a good* ~ *of oneself*, hom goed weer, hom nie onbetuig laat nie; *GONE to his* ~, hy is oorlede (dood); *KEEP* ~ *of*, rekening hou van; *go to one's LAST* ~, die ewigheid ingaan; die tyd met die ewigheid verwissel; *LAY to someone's* ~, aan iem. toeskryf; *LEAVE out of* ~, buite rekening (beskouing) laat; *MAKE out an* ~, 'n rekening uitskryf (opmaak, uitmaak); *of NO* ~, van geen belang nie; *on NO* ~, om die dood nie; *on* ~ *OF*, weens, vanweë, ter oorsake van, ter wille van; *ON* ~, op rekening; *OPEN an* ~, 'n rekening open; *OVERDRAW an* ~, 'n rekening oortrek; *on one's OWN* ~, vir eie rekening; op eie houtjie; *as PER* ~, volgens rekening; *RENDER an* ~, verslag doen; 'n rekening stuur; ~ *RENDERED*, gelewerde rekening; *RUN up an* ~, 'n rekening laat oploop; *SAY more than one can* ~ *for*, meer sê as wat jy krediet voor het; *SELL for* ~, vir rekening verkoop; ~ *of SETTLEMENT*, finale afrekening; *of SMALL* ~, van min belang; *SQUARE (settle) an* ~, 'n rekening vereffen (betaal); *TAKE* ~ *of*, rekening hou met; *not to TAKE into* ~, buite rekening laat; *TURN to good* ~, soveel voordeel moontlik daaruit haal; *on no* ~ *WHATEVER*, onder geen omstandighede nie; (v) reken, oordeel, ag, beskou as; rekenskap gee, ophelder, verklaar; verantwoord; skiet; afreken met; ~ *FOR*, verantwoord; verklaar.
accountabil'ity, verantwoordelikheid, toerekenbaarheid.
account'able, verantwoordelik, aanspreeklik, toerekenbaar, rekenpligtig; ~ **ness** = **accountability.**
accoun'tancy, rekeningkunde; rekenmeestersvak, boekhou.
accoun'tant, rekenmeester; boekhouer; rekenkontroleur; rekeningkundige.
account: ~ **book,** skuldboek, rekeningboek; ~ **day,** betaaldag.
accoun'ting, verrekening; rekeningkunde; ~ *DEPARTMENT*, rekeninge-afdeling; ~ *OFFICER*, rekenpligtige amptenaar; ~ *POLICY*, boekhoubeleid, rekeningkundige beleid; ~ *SERVICES*, rekenmeestersdienste; *there is no* ~ *for TASTES*, oor die smaak val nie te twis nie.
accou'ter, accou'tre, uitrus; uitdos; ~ **ment,** uitrusting, kleding; opskik; mondering; ~ **ments,** toebehore (mil.).
accred'it, glo, erken; krediet gee; magtig; ~ *with*, toeskryf aan, ~ **a'tion,** akkreditering; *letters of* ~ *ation*, geloofsbriewe; ~ **ed,** offisieel erken, toegelaat; algemeen aangeneem; geakkrediteer.
accres'cent, groeiend, aanwassend, toenemend.
accrete', saamgroei; opneem; aanslib.
accre'tion, aanwas, aangroei, samegroeiing, aangroeisel, vermeerdering.
accre'tive, aanwassend, aangroeiend.
accru'al, opgehoopte bedrag; aanwas; toevalling.
accrue', voortspruit; aangroei, toeneem; toekom; oploop; ~ *d interest*, opgeloopte (opgelope) rente; ~ **ment,** toename, aanwassing, oploping.
accul'turate, akkultureer.
accultura'tion, akkulturasie.
accum'bent, leunend.
accu'mulate, ophoop, opgaar, openhoop, byeen

bring; versamel; oploop (rente); vermenigvuldig; ~ **d**, opgeloop (rente); opeengehoop; ~ **d funds**, opgehoopte fondse.

accumula'tion, ophoping, opeenstapeling; vermeerdering; hoop, stapel; akkumulasie; *point of* ~, verdigtingspunt (mat.).

accum'ulative, toenemend, opgeloop, opstapelend, ophoopbaar, akkumulatief.

accum'ulator, versamelaar; oppotter, geldmaker; opgaarbattery, akkumulator (elek.).

acc'uracy, noukeurigheid, stiptheid, juistheid, striktheid, sekuurheid, presiesheid, trefsekerheid, akkuraatheid; ~ *of AIM*, rigjuistheid; ~ *of FIRE*, trefsekerheid.

acc'urate, noukeurig, nougeset, stip, presies, akkuraat, juis, strik, sekuur; net; ~ **ly**, noukeurig; *shoot* ~ *ly*, net skiet.

accur'sed, accurst', vervloek, gedoem tot ondergang; verfoeilik, ellendig.

accu'sable, laakbaar, aanklaagbaar.

accu'sal, accusa'tion, beskuldiging, aanklag, aantyging, telastelegging, betigting.

accusativ'al, akkusatief=.

accus'ative, akkusatief; ~ **case**, akkusatief (naamval).

accusator'ial, akkusatoriaal.

accus'atory, verwytend, beskuldigend.

accuse', beskuldig, aankla; verkla; wyt, aantyg; betig; ~ **d**, beskuldigde, aangeklaagde, beklaagde; ~ **r**, aanklaer, beskuldiger.

accus'tom, gewoond maak, wen, aanwen; ~ *oneself to SOMETHING*, jou aan iets wen; *(to)* ~ *TO*, gewoond maak aan; ~ **ed**, gewoon(d), gebruiklik; gewend; gesout.

ace, aas; oom kool (kaartspel), een; kleinigheid; baasvlieër, kampioenvlieër, baasjaer, ens.; kishou (tennis); uitblinker; kampioen; meester; *BATE an* ~, twyfel; 'n kans gee; ~ *of CLUBS*, klaweraas; *DEUCE* ~, twee en een (met dobbelsteentjies); ~ *of DIAMONDS*, ruite(n)aas; ~ *s EASY*, ase gelyk; ~ *of HEARTS*, harte(n)aas; ~ *of SPADES*, skoppe(n)aas, bloukoos; *WITHIN an* ~ *of*, op 'n haar (nerf) na, so hittete, nerfskeel.

ace'dia = **accidie**.

Acel'dama, Akeldama, bloedakker.

acen'tric, asentries, uitmiddelpuntig.

aceph'alous, koploos.

a'cer, es(doring).

acerb', bitter, wrang, suur.

a'cerbate, wrang (suur) maak.

acerb'ity, suurheid, bitterheid; bits(ig)heid, skerpheid; wrangheid.

ac'erose, naaldvormig.

aces'cent, suurderig.

aceta'bulum, (..la), (hist.), asynbeker; (dierk.), acetabulum, potjie.

acetal'dehyde, aldehide, aldehied.

a'cetate, asynsuursout, asetaat.

acet'ic, suur, soos asyn; ~ **acid**, asynsuur.

acetifica'tion, versuring, verandering in asyn.

acet'ify, (..fied), versuur; suur word, in asyn verander.

acet'imeter, asetimeter.

a'cetone, asetoon, asyngees.

a'cetous, asynsuurhoudend, asynagtig, suur.

a'cetyl, asetiel.

acet'ylene, asetileen.

acetylsalicyl'ic: ~ **acid**, asetielsalisielsuur.

achar'nement, (F.), acharnement, vuur, vurigheid, animo.

ache, (n) pyn, smart; *full of* ~ *s and pains*, vol skete; (v) pyn, seer wees, pyn ly; *my HEAD* ~ *s*, my kop is seer; *my HEART* ~ *s for him*, ek is hartseer oor hom; ek het medely(d)e met hom.

achene', dopvrug.

Acheu'lian, ..lean, Acheuls.

à cheval, (F.), skrylings; gelykkansig.

achiev'able, uitvoerbaar, doenlik; bereikbaar.

achieve', volbring, uitvoer; behaal, verrig, verwerf, bereik, presteer; ~ **ment**, verrigting, uitvoering; wapenfeit; daad; prestasie, sukses; *man of* ~ *ment*, man van betekenis, man van naam; ~ *ment rating*, prestasiemeting.

Achil'les: ~ **heel (tendon)**, Achilleshiel, hakskeensening; kwesbare plek.

achil'ous, liploos.

a'ching, (n) pyn, smart; (a) seer; *an* ~ *heart*, 'n seer hart.

achon'drite, achondriet.

achoo! aitsjie! atsjoe! (niesgeluid).

ach'roma, velkleurloosheid.

achromat'ic, kleurloos, achromaties.

achromati'city, kleurloosheid.

achrom'atism, kleurloosheid, achromatisme.

achromato'sis, kleurblindheid.

achro'matous, kleurloos.

a'chy, pynlik, seer, seerderig.

aci'cular, naaldvormig.

a'cid, (n) suur; (a) suur, bitter, vrank, wrang; skerp, bitsig; *the* ~ *test*, die vuurproef; ~ **-bath**, suur=, fikseerbad; ~ **-drop**, suurklontjie.

acidi'fic, suurvormend, suur; verbitterd; ~ **a'tion**, suurvorming.

acid'ify, (..fied), suur maak, versuur; tot 'n suur verander; suur word.

acidim'eter, suurmeter.

aci'dity, suurheid; suurgehalte; wrangheid; suur (van die maag); skerpheid, bitsigheid; asiditeit.

acido'sis, suurvergiftiging (by suikersiekte), asidose.

a'cid: ~ **-proof**, suurvas, suurbestand; ~ **-pump**, suurpomp; ~ **-resistant**, ~ **-resisting**, suurwerend; ~ **test**, suurtoets; vuurproef; ~ **-tolerant**: ~ **-tolerant crops**, gewasse teen suur bestand; ~ **-tube**, suurbuisie.

acid'ulate, suur maak; verbitter; ~ **d**, suur, suurderig.

acidula'tion, versuring.

acid'ulous, suurderig, suuragtig.

a'ciform, naaldvormig.

ack'-ack, lugafweergeskut.

a'ckee, akee, tropiese boomsoort *(Blighia sapida)*.

acknow'ledge, erken, beken; berig; bedank vir, beantwoord; ~ *DEFEAT*, die stryd gewonne gee; ~ *RECEIPT of a letter*, ontvangs van 'n brief erken; ~ *a SALUTE*, teruggalueer; ~ **d**, erkende.

acknow'ledg(e)ment, erkenning, eerbiediging, erkentenis, huldiging; bewys; berig van ontvangs; dank, bedanking; beantwoording; *with* ~ *s to*, met erkenning van; ~ **register**, ontvangsregister.

aclin'ic, magneties; ~ **line**, magnetiese linie (ewenaar).

ac'me, toppunt, summum, krisis, glanspunt; keerpunt.

ac'ne, puisie, huidvyn; puisiesiekte, aknee; ~ **-remover**, puisiemiddel.

acock', skuins, op een oor (van hoed gesê).

ac'olyte, altaardienaar, misdienaar; beginner, akoliet; aanhanger.

acon'dylose, acon'dylous, gewrigloos

ac'onite, wolfswortel, akoniet.

a'corn, akker, eikel; ~ **-coffee**, akkerkoffie; ~ **-cup**, akkerdoppie; ~ **-nut**, dopmoer; ~ **-shaped**, akkervormig; ~ **-shell**, akkerdop.

acotyled'on, plant sonder saadlobbe, akotiel; ~ **ous**, sonder saadlobbe.

acous'tic, gehoor=, akoesties; ~ *DUCT*, gehoorbuis; ~ *GUITAR*, akoestiese kitaar; ~ *GUITARIST*, akoestiese kitaarspeler; ~ *NERVE*, gehoorsenuwee; ~ *TELESCOPE*, luistertrompet; ~ *WAVE*, klankgolf, geluidsgolf; ~ **'ian**, akoestikus; ~ **on**, akoestikon (gehoorapparaat); ~ **s**, geluidsleer, gehoorleer, akoestiek; klank.

acquaint', bekend maak, berig, in kennis stel, meedeel; ~ *with*, onderrig, in kennis stel.

acquaint'ance, bekendheid; kennis; *have some* ~ *with*, 'n mate van kennis hê van; ~ **ship**, kennis, bekendheid.

acquaint'ed, bekend; *be* ~ *with*, ken, bekend wees met.

acquiesce', berus; toestem, skik, inwillig; ~ *in the DECISION*, berus by die beslissing.

acquiesc'ence, gelatenheid, berusting; instemming.

acquiesc'ent, toegewend, berustend; instemmend.

acquir'able, verkrygbaar.

acquire', verkry, erlang; verwerf; aanleer; oorneem, aankoop.

acquired', aangeleer; verworwe; ~ *CHARACTERISTIC(S)*, verworwe eienskap(pe); ~ *DEFORMITY*, opgedane misvorming; ~ *HERNIA*, verworwe breuk; ~ *REFLEX*, aangeleerde refleks; ~ *TASTE*, aangeleerde smaak; ~ *immunity defect syndrome (AIDS)*, verworwe immuniteitsgebreksindroom, vigs.
acquire'ment, verkryging; verwerwing; aanwins; bekwaamheid; kennis; ~s, talente, bevoegdhede.
acquisi'tion, verwerwing, aanskaffing; oorneming; aanwins.
acquis'itive, hebsugtig, begerig; ~ness, begeerte (vermoë) om te verwerf, hebsug.
acquit', (-ted), ontslaan, vryspreek, vryverklaar, kwytskeld; ~ *oneself of a CHARGE*, hom van 'n las (plig) kwyt; ~ *a DEBT*, 'n skuld betaal; ~ *oneself OF*, jou kwyt van; ~ *oneself WELL*, jou knap gedra; ~**tal**, vrysprak, vryverklaring, ontslag; verrigting; ~**tance**, kwytskelding; ontslag; kwitansie.
acra'nia, skedelloosheid, akranie.
acra'nial, skedelloos.
a'cre, akker, halwe morg; ~**age**, oppervlakte; grootte in akkers; ~**d**, welgesteld, ryk in grondbesit; ~**-foot**, akkervoet (water).
ac'rid, bitter; wrang, vrank; skerp, bytend, bits.
a'cridine, akridine, akridien, koolteerverbinding.
acrid'ity, bitterheid; vrankheid; wrangheid; skerpheid; bitsigheid.
acriflav'ine, akriflavien, akriflavine, antiseptiese poeier.
acrimo'nious, skerp, bits(ig); bitter.
ac'rimony, bitterheid; skerpheid, stekeligheid, bits(ig)heid.
ac'robat, kunstemaker, akrobaat; kunsvlieër.
acrobat'ic, akrobaties; ~ *DISPLAY*, kunsvlugvertoning; ~ *FLYING*, kunsvlieëry; ~**s**, akrobatiek; kunstemakery.
ac'rogen, akrogeen.
ac'rolith, akroliet.
acrome'galy, akromegalie, reusegroei.
acrom'ion, skouer(blad)punt, akromion.
acro'nyc(h)al, (a.), nagtelik(s).
a'cronym, (-s), akroniem, letterwoord.
acrop'etal, akropetaal.
acrophob'ia, hoogtevrees, akrofobie.
acrop'olis, (..**poles**), akropolis, burg, vesting.
across', oor; dwars; oorkruis; deur, anderkant; in die dwarste; *COME (run)* ~ *somebody*, iem. teëkom (raakloop); ~ *the BOARD*, regdeur, oor die hele linie; ~ *the FACE*, oor die gesig; ~ *the GRAIN*, dwarsdraads.
acros'tic, naamdig, naamvers, akrostigon, lettervers.
acrot'omous, akrotomies.
acry'lic: ~ **acid**, akrielsuur; ~ **fibre**, akrielvesel; ~ **paint**, akrielverf; ~ **resin**, akrielhars.
act, (n) daad, handeling; akte, wet; verhandeling; bedryf (toneelstuk); *A* ~ *s (of the APOSTLES)*, Handelinge (v.d. Apostels); *he was CAUGHT in the* ~, hy is op heter daad betrap; ~ *of FAVOUR*, gunsbewys; ~ *of GOD*, natuurramp, Gods will; oormag, force majeure; ~ *of GRACE*, genadebewys; ~ *of INDEMNITY*, skadeloosstellingswet, vrywaringswet; ~ *of PARLIAMENT*, parlementswet; *PUT on an* ~, 'n rol speel; komedie speel; ~ *of STATE*, daad van staatsbeskerming; owerheidsdaad; ~*s inter VIVOS*, handeling onder lewendes; (v) handel, doen, te werk gaan; gedra; opvoer, speel, toneelspeel; fungeer, optree; ~ *upon an AGREEMENT*, volgens 'n ooreenkoms handel; ~ *as INTERPRETER*, as vertaler optree; ~ *a PART*, 'n rol speel; ~ *up to one's PROMISE*, volgens jou belofte handel; ~ *of VIOLENCE*, geweldsdaad; ~**able**, opvoerbaar (toneelstuk).
Ac'ta Sin'odi, Acta Sinodi; bepalings (besluite) v.d. Sinode.
ac'ting, (n) voordrag, toneelspel; onopregtheid; valsheid; fungering; (a) diensdoende, handelend; waarnemend, agerend, plaasvervangend; fungerend, werkend; vals, onopreg; *in an* ~ *CAPACITY*, in 'n waarnemende hoedanigheid; ~ *PARTNER*, beherende (werkende) vennoot; ~ *PRINCIPAL*, waarnemende hoof(onderwyser).
acti'nea, (~**e**), aktinea, see-anemoon.
actin'ic, aktinies; ~ **line**, magnetiese ewenaar; ~ **rays**, aktiniese strale.
actin'iform, straalvormig.
ac'tinism, aktinisme.
actin'ium, aktinium.
actino'graphy, aktinografie.
actin'olite, stralingsgesteente, straalsteen, aktinoliet.
actinom'eter, straalsterktemeter.
actinom'etry, aktinometrie, straalsterktemeting.
actinomycete', (..**tae**, ~**s**), straalswam.
actinomyco'sis, straalswamsiekte.
ac'tion, handeling, (in)werking, verrigting; aanklag, hofsaak; geveg; meganiek; aksie; optrede, handelwyse, daad; *ADVANCE into* ~, na die geveg opruk; *BRING an* ~ *against someone*, iem. laat dagvaar, 'n hofsaak teen iem. instel; *COME into* ~, begin veg; in werking tree; ~ *for DAMAGES*, aksie om skadevergoeding; *INSTITUTE an* ~, 'n hofsaak instel (aangaan); *be KILLED in* ~, sneuwel, op die veld van eer sterf; *MAN of* ~, man v.d. daad; *put OUT of* ~, buite geveg stel; *PUT in* ~, laat werk, in werking stel; *READY for* ~, strydvaardig; ~*s SPEAK louder than words*, baie myle lê tussen doen en sê; *man* ~ *STATIONS*, ammunisie insamel; jou slaggereed maak; *TAKE* ~, stappe doen, optree; tot die daad oorgaan; *UNITY of* ~, eenheid van handeling; *suit the* ~ *to the WORD*, die daad by die woord voeg; ~**able**, strafbaar, vervolgbaar, aksionabel; ~ **painting**, aksieskilder(y); ~**-post**, alarmpos; ~**-radius**, vaarbereik, aksiestraal; ~**s**, handelinge; ~**-song**, aksielied, sangspeletjie; ~ **station**, gevegspos.
ac'tivate, aktief maak; radioaktief maak, aktiveer; ~**d carbon**, geaktiveerde koolstof; ~**d sludge**, verlugte rioolvuil.
activa'tion, aansetting; aktivering.
act'ivator, opwekker, aktiveermiddel.
ac'tive, werksaam, aktief, bedrywig, besig; vief, vieweirg, werkdadig, werkend, energiek, roerig, woelig; bedrywend (gram.); ~ **interest**, daadwerklike belang; ~ **list**, aktiewe lys; ~**ly**, daadwerklik, regtig; ~ **mine**, gelaaide myn; ~ **service**, oorlogsdiens; ~ **stroke**, arbeidslag; ~ **trading months**, aktiewe handelsmaande; ~ **voice**, bedrywende vorm; ~ **volcano**, werkende vuurspuwende berg (vulkaan).
ac'tivism, aktivisme.
ac'tivist, aktivis.
activis'tic, aktivisties.
activ'ity, (..**ties**), werksaamheid, werkdadigheid, roerigheid, doenigheid, bedrywigheid; vlugheid; *AERIAL* ~, lugbedrywigheid; *in FULL* ~, in volle gang; *SPHERE of* ~, werkkring.
ac'ton, (hist.), pantserbaadjie, maliekolder.
ac'tor, toneelspeler, akteur; dader; doener; bewerker.
ac'tress, (-**es**), toneelspeelster, aktrise; bewerkster.
ac'tual, werklik, wesenlik, eintlik, feitlik, effektief; aktueel; teenwoordig, oombliklik; ~ **horsepower**, werklike perdekrag.
actual'ity, realiteit, werklikheid, aktualiteit, wesenlike toestand, feitlikheid; ~ **shot**, aktualiteitskoot, aktualiteitstoneel (TV).
actualiza'tion, verwesenliking, verwerkliking.
ac'tualize, verwerklik, wesenlik, aktualiseer; realisties beskryf.
ac'tually, waarlik (waar), werklik waar, waaragtig, eintlik, regtig, inderdaad, wraggies waar, wrintie waar, sowaar
actua'rial, aktuarieel.
ac'tuary, (..**ries**), aktuaris, wiskundige raadgewer.
ac'tuate, in beweging bring, aan die gang sit; aanpor; beweeg; aansit, drywe, aktueer.
ac'tuated, gedrewe, gedryf.
ac'tuating shaft, dryfas.
actua'tion, aandrywing; werkende krag; bediening.
acu'ity, skerpheid, hewigheid, akuutheid; ~ *of vision*, gesigskerpte.
acul'eate, met 'n angel; stekelig; skerp; gepunt.
acum'en, skerpheid, skerpsinnigheid, vernuf; speursin; *business* ~, sakevernuf, besigheidsvernuf.

acum'inate, (v) spits toeloop; (a) spits toelopend.
a'cupuncture, akupunktuur, naaldbehandeling.
acush'la, (Iers), liefling, hartedief.
acute', skerp; vlymend; fyn; vlug, gevat, skerpsinnig, skrander; hewig; akuut; ~ *ANGLE*, skerp hoek; ~ *CROSSING,* skerphoekkruising; ~ *DISEASE*, kwaai (ernstige, akute) siekte; ~ **accent,** akuut= (aksent); ~**ness,** skerpte, skerpsinnigheid; hewig= heid.
a'cyl, (chem.), asiel, akiel.
ad, (colloq.), advertensie, reklame.
ad: ~ *EUNDEM,* tot dieselfde; ~ *HOC,* vir dié doel gereël; ~ *INFINITUM,* tot in die oneindige; ~ *INTERIM,* vir die tussentyd, intussen; ~ *LIB,* ~ *LIBITUM,* uit die vuis; ~ *NAUSEAM,* tot wal= gens toe; ~ *REM,* ter sake, ~ *VALOREM,* vol= gens waarde (van goedere); ~ *VERBUM,* woord vir woord.
adac'tyl, toonloos, sonder tone.
ad'age, spreekwoord, spreuk, gesegde.
adag'io, adagio, stadig (mus.).
Ad'am, Adam; menslike swakheid; ~ *'s ALE,* water; ~ *'s APPLE*, adamsappel, komhalertjie; ~ *blamed EVE, Eve in turn the snake,* Adam sê dis Eva en Eva sê dis die slang; ~ *'s FIG,* adamsvy(g); *not know from* ~, nie van Adam af ken nie; *LAY aside the old* ~, die ou Adam aflê; *the OLD* ~, die ou Adam; *RELATED through* ~, familie van Adam se kant.
ad'amant, hard soos diamant, adamant; onwrikbaar; *he is* ~, hy is onwrikbaar; ~ **clinker,** plaveiklinker.
adaman'tine, diamantagtig, hard soos diamant; on= breekbaar, klipsteenhard.
ad'amine, adamien.
Ad'amite, naakloper, Adamskind; Adamiet.
ad'amsite, adamsiet.
adapt', geskik maak; aanpas, aanwend, verander, wy= sig (klere); bewerk (boek), adapteer; *BECOME* ~ *ed,* geskik word; *freely* ~ *ed from the FRENCH,* vry nagevolg uit die Frans; ~ *TO,* aanpas by (aan).
adaptabil'ity, geskiktheid; aanwendbaarheid; aan= passingsvermoë; bruikbaarheid; bewerkbaarheid; verstelbaarheid.
adapt'able, geskik, verwerkbaar, aanwendbaar, buigsaam, aanpasbaar.
adapta'tion, aanpassing; bewerking; aanwending; in= burgering, adaptasie; ~ **goggles,** ~ **spectacles,** adaptasiebril.
adap'ter, bewerker; aansluiter.
adap'ting ring, pasring.
adap'tor, nippel (van bom); pasring (vonkprop); pas= stuk; aansluiter; aftakker (elek.); ~ **piece,** aan= sluitstuk
ad captan'dum (vul'gus), ad captandum (vulgus), vir die massa (menigte).
add, byvoeg, optel, vermeerder; bysit (geld); aanvoeg; ~ *together,* optel, saamtel.
ad'dax, (-es), addaks.
adden'dum, (..da), bylae, toevoegsel, aanvoegsel, ad= dendum; kophoogte (latte).
ad'der¹, opteller; optelmasjien.
ad'der², adder, pofadder; *flying* ~, naaldekoker; *horned* ~, horingadder, horingsman(slang); ~ *'s* **tongue,** slangtong; ~ *'s* **wort,** slangwortel.
ad'dice, snymes; dissel.
ad'dict, (s) verslaafde.
addict', (v) toewy; oorgee aan; verslaaf raak (aan); ~ *ed,* verslaaf, oorgegee; toegewy; ~ *ed to drink,* aan drank verslaaf; ~**ion,** toegeneentheid, neiging (tot); verslaafdheid (aan).
ad'ding-machine, optelmasjien.
Ad'dison's disease', Addisonsiekte.
addi'tion, byvoeging, aanvulling, toegif; vermeerde= ring; optelling; byvoegsel; *in* ~ *to,* daarby, boon= op; ~ **al,** bygevoeg, bykomend(e), ekstra, addisio= neel; ~ **al expenditure,** bykomende (ekstra) uit= gawe; *pay an* ~ *al sum,* bybetaal; ~**s,** aanbou(sel), aanbouing; aanvulling; ~ **sum,** optelsom.
ad'ditive, byvoer; bymiddel.
ad'dle, (v) bederf, verwar; (a) leeg, misluk; bedorwe, deurgelê; ~**-brained,** warhoofdig; ~**d,** bedorwe, deurgelê; leeg; verward; ~ *d egg,* vrot eier; ~**-head=**

ed, ~**-pated,** dom, onnosel; warhoofdig; met 'n pampoenkop.
ad'dorsed, rug-teen-rug.
address', (n) **(-es),** adres; toespraak; spreekwyse; op= trede, gedrag; bekwaamheid; (v) wend (tot), rig, aanspreek, adresseer; toespreek; ~ *the BALL,* kor= relvat (gholfbal); *DELIVER an* ~, 'n redevoering hou; *PAY one's* ~ *es to,* komplimente maak; die hof maak; by iem. aanlê; vlerk sleep by; *PAY one's* ~ *es somewhere,* by iem. aanlê; ~ *oneself TO,* praat met; skryf aan; ~**-book,** adresboek.
addressee', geadresseerde.
addres'sograph, adresseermasjien, adressograaf.
adduce', aanvoer, aanhaal, bybring.
adduce'able, adduc'ible, aanvoerbaar.
adduct', saamtrek, byeentrek; ~**ion,** saamtrekking; ~ **or,** bytrekspier, aantrekspier; saamtrekker.
a'denine, adenine, adenien.
ad'enoid, (-s), (n) adenoïde, neusmangel; (a) klier= limf=; kliervormig.
adenol'ogy, klierkunde, adenologie.
adenom'a, kliergewas, adenoom.
ade'nosine, adenosine, adenosien, spierstof.
adept', (n) ingewyde, deskundige, doring; (a) ervare, ingewy, geoefen.
ad'equacy, geskiktheid, doelmatigheid; voldoend= heid, toereikendheid.
ad'equate, eweredig, gelyk; geskik, doelmatig, toe= reikend, doeltreffend; afdoende, voldoende; ade= kwaat; ~ **ly,** voldoende; op die regte manier.
aderm'in, adermien, adermine.
adhere', vasklewe, aankleef; aanhang, bly by, trou bly (party).
adher'ence, vasklewing; verkleefheid; vashoudend= heid; aanhang.
adher'ent, (-s), (n) aanhanger, volgeling, voorstan= der, aanklewer, geesverwant (politiek); getroue; kleefstof; ~**s,** aanhang(ers); (a) vasklewend; ver= bonde
adhe'sion, aanklewing, vasklewing; gehegtheid; ad= hesie; hegting (med.); vergroeiing; toetreding; instemming.
adhe'sive, (n) kleefmiddel; (a) vasklewend; klewerig; taai; ~ **bandage,** kleefverband; ~**ness,** klewerig= heid; aanhanklikheid; ~ **paper,** hegpapier, kleef= papier; ~ **patch,** plaklap (naaldw.); ~ **plaster,** heg= pleister, kleefpleister; ~ **power,** kleefkrag, kleefver= moë; ~ **strength,** kleefvastheid, kleefvermoë; ~ **substance,** kleefstof; ~ **tape,** kleefband.
adhib'it, aanheg; toedien.
adhibi'tion, aanwending, toediening; aanhegting.
ad ho'minem, ad hominem, persoonlik, op die per= soon af.
adiabat'ic, adiabaties.
adian'tum, adiantum, nooienshaarvaring, nôiens= haarvaring.
ad'iate, adieer.
adiather'mancy, ondeurdringbaarheid (vir warmte).
adia'tion, adiasie.
adieu', (-s, -x), vaarwel, adieu; *bid* ~, vaarwel sê.
ad infi'nitum, ad infinitum, oneindig; tot vervelens toe.
ad in'terim, ad interim, intussen, voorlopig, tydelik.
ad'ipocere, lykvet.
ad'ipose, (n) diervet; (a) vet, vethoudend; ~ *GLAND,* vetklier; ~ *HERNIA,* vetbreuk; ~ *LAYER,* vetlaag; ~ *TISSUE,* vetweefsel.
adipos'ity, vetheid, gesetheid, lywigheid.
ad'it, toegang; horisontale mynskag, (ingangs)ton= nel; *air* ~, lugtonnel,
adja'cency, nabyheid.
adja'cent, aangrensend, naby, naasgeleë; ~ *ANGLE,* aanliggende hoek; newehoek; ~ *SIDE,* aangren= sende sy.
adjecti'val, byvoeglik, adjektiwies.
ad'jective, (n) byvoeglike naamwoord, adjektief, epi= teton; (a) byvoeglik, adjektief=; ondergeskik.
adjoin', byvoeg; grens aan; ~**ing,** aangrensend, langsaan, daarnaas.
adjourn', uitstel, opskort, verdaag; verander van ver= gaderplek; uiteengaan, uitmekaargaan; ~ *a meet= ing till later,* 'n vergadering tot later verdaag;

adjudge 688 *adsorption*

~ment, uitstel, verdaging, skorting; verandering van vergaderplek.
adjudge', toeken; oordeel; veroordeel, beslis; ~ment, vonnis; oordeel; toekenning.
adju'dicate, uitspraak gee, oordeel, beoordeel, bereg, beslis; toeken, toewys; ~ *upon*, uitspraak doen oor.
adjudica'tion, uitspraak, beslissing, beoordeling; toekenning; vonnis, beregting.
adju'dicator, skeidsregter, beoordelaar.
ad'junct, (n) aanhangsel, byvoegsel; hegstuk; hoedanigheid; adjunk; (a) bygevoeg, toegevoeg; adjunk-; aangeheg; hulp-; ~-minister, adjunk-minister.
adjura'tion, beswering, eedoplegging; eed; dringende bede.
adjure', beveel, besweer; smeek.
adjust', in orde bring; reël; vereffen; vasmaak; stel, instel, verstel, regstel, in ooreenstemming bring met; 'n boekhoufout verbeter; monteer; yk; ~ *an ACCOUNT*, 'n rekening aansuiwer; ~ *the GRIP*, vervat.
adjustabil'ity, verstelbaarheid.
adjust'able, verstelbaar; afstelbaar; ~ clamp, stelbare klamp; ~ ladder, verstelbare leer; ~ seats, skuifsitplekke; ~ spanner, moerhamer, moersleutel, skroefsleutel; ~ table, afslaantafel; ~wrench, skroefhamer, stelbare sleutel.
adjus'ter, reëlaar; versteller.
adjust'ing, aanpassing; ~ arm, stelarm; ~ gear, stelrat; ~-machinery, montering; ~ nut, stelmoer; ~ plane, stelskaaf; ~ ring, stelring; ~ rod, stelstang; ~ screw, stelskroef.
adjust'ment, verstelling; reëling; aanpassing; skikking; montering; afrekening; vereffening; *COARSE* ~, grofinstelling; *FINE* ~, fyninstelling; ~ *OF account*, aansuiwering, storno; ~ account, verskillerekening; ~ voucher, eisstrook.
ad'jutage, mond(stuk), sproeistuk (van fontein).
ad'jutancy, adjudantskap; hulp.
ad'jutant, adjudant; stafoffisier; hulp; Indiese ooievaar; ~-general, adjudant-generaal; ~-officer, adjudant-offisier.
ad'juvant, (n) steun, hulp(middel); (a) helpend, hulps, behulpsaam; bevorderlik.
ad lib', ad lib, ad libitum, praat sonder voorbereiding.
ad li'bitum = ad lib.
ad li'tem, ad litem, vir die doel (van 'n hofsaak) aangestel.
ad'man, (..men), advertensieskrywer, reklameman.
admeas'ure, toewys, toedeel; ~ment, toewysing; vergelyking; afmeting.
admin'icle, iets wat help; stawende getuienis.
admin'ister, bestuur, beheer, handhaaf; bedien, toedien; afneem; administreer; beredder (boedel); ~ *JUSTICE*, regspreek; ~ *an OATH*, 'n eed afneem; ~ *the SACRAMENTS*, die sakramente bedien; ~ *TO*, toedien.
admin'istrate, administreer.
administra'tion, beheer, bewindvoering, administrasie; bediening, toediening; toepassing; ~ *of justice*, regspraak; ~ fee, administrasiegeld.
admin'istrative, bewindvoerend, administratief, besturend; ~ courts, administratiewe howe; ~ law, administratiewe reg.
admin'istrator, bestuurder, bewindvoerder; administrateur; boedelberedderaar; ~ship, administrateurskap.
admin'istratrix, (..trices), bestuurderes, administratrise.
ad'mirable, bewonderenswaardig, uitstekend, voortreflik.
ad'miral, admiraal; ~ *of the FLEET*, vlootadmiraal; *REAR* ~, skoutadmiraal, skout-by-nag; ~ship, admiraalskap; ~ty, admiraliteit; seeraad; admiraalskap; admiraliteitsgebou; *court of* ~*ty*, admiraliteitshof.
admira'tion, bewondering, verering.
admire', bewonder, vereer; ~r, bewonderaar, aanbidder, vereerder.
admissibil'ity, aanneemlikheid, toelaatbaarheid.
admis'sible, aanneemlik, toelaatbaar; geldig, geoorloof; ~ stress, toelaatbare spanning.

admi'ssion, toelating, aanneming; entree, toegang; admissie; toegangsprys; erkentenis, erkenning; *FREE* ~, vry(e) toegang; ~ *of GUILT*, skuldbekentenis; skulderkenning (jur.); *RIGHT of* ~, toegangsreg; ~ fee, toegangsgeld; ~ hopper, voerder; ~ money, toetredingsgeld, entreegeld, toegangsgeld; ~ pipe, inlaatpyp, instromingsbuis; ~ requirements, toelatingsvereistes; ~ register, toelatingsregister; ~ ticket, toegangskaartjie.
admit', (-ted), toestaan; toelaat, toegang verleen; aanneem; erken, beken, toegee; ~ *to the BAR*, tot die balie (as advokaat) toelaat; ~ *a FACT*, 'n feit erken; ~ *to a HOSPITAL*, in 'n hospitaal opgeneem word; in 'n hospitaal opneem; ~ table, toelaatbaar; ~tance, toegang; toelating; *no* ~*tance*, geen toegang nie, toegang verbode; ~ted, erken; ~tedly, soos erken word, weliswaar.
admix', vermeng, meng; ~ture, mengsel, bymenging, bymengsel, toevoegsel.
admon'ish, vermaan, teregwys, waarsku, aanmaan; ~er, vermaner; ~ment, vermaning, waarskuwing; raad; skrobbering.
admoni'tion, vermaning, waarskuwing, teregwysing, skrobbering.
admon'itory, waarskuwend, teregwysend, vermanend, skrobberend.
ad nause'am, ad nauseam, tot vervelens (satwordens, naarwordens) toe.
adnom'inal, attributief.
ad'noun, byvoeglike naamwoord; selfstandig gebruikte adjektief.
ado', ophef, gedoente, petalje, bohaai, rompslomp, drukte, omhaal; *without FURTHER* ~, sonder om gras oor iets te laat groei; op die daad; op die plek; *without MUCH* ~, sonder baie omhaal; sonder verdere omslag; sonder meer; *much* ~ *about NOTHING*, meer lawaai as wol, veel geskreeu en weinig wol.
adobe', rousteen; klei(steen), modder(steen).
adoles'cence, jongelingskap, ryper jeug, puberteitsjare, adolessensie.
adoles'cent, (n) jongeling, jongmeisie, jeugdige (persoon); (a) jeugdig, opgeskote, opgroeiend; ~ river, halfwasriver.
Ado'nis, Adonis, mooi jonkman; adoons (naam vir 'n aap of bobbejaan).
ad'onize, versier, opsmuk, opskik; laat bewonder, adoniseer.
adopt', aanneem; aanwend; goedkeur, aanvaar; inneem (standpunt); oorneem; ontleen (woorde); adopteer; ~able, aanneembaar; ~ed, aangenome; goedgekeur; ~*ed child*, aangenome kind; ~ion, aanneming; opname, adopsie, ingebruikneming; oorname; *the country of my* ~ *ion*, my tweede vaderland; ~ive, (a), aangeneem, aangenome; ~ive father, pleegvader.
ador'able, aanbiddelik.
adora'tion, aanbidding, verering, bewondering, adorasie.
adore', aanbid, vereer, vurig liefhê, verafgod; ~d, aangebedene; ~r, aanbidder, vereerder, bewonderaar, vryer.
adorn', (ver)sier, verfraai, (op)tooi, behang; ~ment, versiering, sieraad, opskik.
ad perso'nam, ad personam, persoonlik, aan die persoon.
ad rem', ad rem, ter sake, tersaaklik.
adren'al, bynier; ~in, adrenalien, adrenaline; ~in gland, adronalienklier, buislose klier.
adrenocorticotro'phic, adrenokortikotropies; ~ hormone, adrenokortikotrope hormoon, ACTH.
Adriat'ic, Adriaties; ~Sea, Adriatiese See.
adrift', drywend, los; *CUT* ~, die tou deurhak; *be TURNED* ~, aan sy lot oorgelaat word.
adroit', handig, behendig, vlug, knap; *be* ~, nie links wees nie; ~ness, handigheid, kunsvaardigheid; takt.
adry', droog; dorstig.
adsciti'tious, aangenome, ontleen, bygevoeg; aanvullend.
adsorb', adsorbeer.
adsorp'tion, adsorpsie.

adsum', adsum, ek is teenwoordig (aanwesig).
ad'ulate, vlei, bewierook; flikflooi, pamperlang, lek.
adula'tion, vleiery, flikflooiery, inkruipery, lekkery.
ad'ulator, inkruiper, vleier.
adula'tory, vleiend, kruiperig.
adul'lamite, adullamiet, afwykeling (polities).
ad'ult, adult', (n) grootmens, volwassene; (a) volwasse, uitgegroei; ~ *BAPTISM*, grootdoop, volwassenedoop; ~ *EDUCATION*, onderwys vir volwassenes; ~ *educational SERVICE*, volksopvoedkundige diens.
adul'terant, vervalsingsmiddel.
adul'terate, (v) bederf, knoei met; vervals; dokter (vloeistof); verdun; (a) vervals; verdun; geskandvlek; oneg; ~*d FOOD*, vervalste eetware; ~*d MILK*, verwaterde melk.
adultera'tion, vervalsing, verwatering.
adul'terator, vervalser; knoeier.
adul'terer, egbreker, owerspeler, hoereerder; afvallige.
adul'teress, (-es), owerspeelster, egbreekster, hoer.
adul'terine, oneg; vals; onwettig; ~ *child*, buite-egtelike kind.
adul'terous, owerspelig.
adul'tery, owerspel, egbreuk, ontug, hoerery; *commit* ~, owerspel bedryf, egbreek.
a'dulthood, volwassenheid, meerderjarigheid.
adum'bral, skaduryk.
ad'umbrate, oorskadu; afskadu, afskets; beskadu; aankondig, aandui, voorspel.
adumbra'tion (voor)afskaduwing; skets; voorloper (van gebeurtenis of toestand), voorspelling
adust'¹, verdroog, geskroei; bruin gebrand; somber.
adust'², verstof, bestof.
ad valo'rem, ad valorem, na die waarde; ~ **customs duty**, ad valorem-doeanereg.
advance', (n) voordeel, vooruitgang, vordering; oprukking, opmars, voortgang; voorskot; bevordering, verhoging, promosie; aantog; styging; *ANY* ~ *(on)?* niemand meer nie? ~ *BOOKING*, vooralbespreking; *an* ~ *COPY*, 'n vervroegde eksemplaar, 'n eksemplaar wat voor die verskyning gelewer is; *IN* ~, vooruit; *MAKE* ~*s*, toenadering soek, die eerste stappe doen; ~ *OF money*, voorskot; (v) aanruk, opruk, vooruitskry, vooruittrek, vooruitskuiwe, nader; verhaas; bevorder; verhoog; ('n mening) opper; vervroeg (vonk); voorskiet (geld); vorder; styg; ~ *ARGUMENTS*, beweer, argumente aanvoer; ~ *someone a LOAN*, iem. (voor)haak; ~ *MONEY*, geld voorskiet, ~ *PRICES*, pryse opskuif; ~ *the SPARK*, die ontsteking vervroeg; ~ *in YEARS*, ouer word.
advanced', gevorderd, vooruitstrewend, modern, geavanseer; ver; vooruitgeskufde; ~ *AGE*, gevorderde leeftyd; ~ *DEPOT*, voordepot; ~ *landing-GROUND*, frontvliegterrein; ~ *flying-SCHOOL*, hoër vliegskool; ~ *STUDIES*, gevorderde studie; ~ *VIEWS*, moderne opvattings; ~ *in YEARS*, op leeftyd.
advance'-guard, voorhoede; ~ **fighting**, voorhoedegeveg.
advance'ment, bevordering, promosie; voortgang, vooruitgang; voorskot; opskuiwing (med.).
advance': ~**-note**, voorskotbiljet; ~**-warning**, voorwaarskuwing.
advan'tage, (n) voordeel, gewin, voorreg; voorsprong, nut, wins; ~ *ALL*, gelykop (tennis); *to the BEST* ~, so voordelig moontlik; *ENJOY the* ~ *of*, die voordeel geniet van; *to GREAT* ~, baie voordelig; ~ *IN (server)*, afslaner voor (tennis); *MECHANICAL* ~, hefvoordeel; *to the* ~ *of*, tot voordeel van; *to OUR* ~, in (tot) ons voordeel; *have an* ~ *OVER someone*, op iem. iets voorhê; *SEEK one's own* ~, voordeel vir jouself soek; *SHOW to best* ~, op sy voordeligste voorkom; *TAKE* ~ *of*, voordeel trek uit; gebruik (misbruik) maak van; *TAKE* ~ *of another*, jou keteltjie by 'n ander se vuur sit; misbruik van iem. maak; *be TO someone's* ~, iem. tot voordeel strek; *TURN a thing to* ~, iets tot voordeel aanwend; jou voordeel doen met; voordeel slaan uit; *WITH* ~, met voordeel; voordelig, met vrug; (v) baat, bevoordeel, bevorder.
advanta'geous, voordelig, gunstig, nuttig, bevorderlik; ~**ly**, met vrug, voordelig; ~**ness**, voordeligheid.
advan'tage: ~ **server**, voordeelafslaner; ~ **striker**, voordeelontvanger (tennis).
advec'tion, adveksie, horisontale lugtoevoer.
advect'ive, advektief, horisontaal invloeiend.
Ad'vent, Advent(styd), die vier weke voor Kersfees.
ad'vent, koms, wederkoms, advent.
Ad'ventist, Adventis.
adventi'tious, toevallig, bykomstig, bykomend, adventief; ~ *BUD*, byknop; ~ *ROOT*, bywortel.
adven'ture, (n) voorval; avontuur; wederwaardigheid; waagstuk, kans, toeval; (v) waag; gevaar loop; onderneem; ~ **park**, avontuurpark; ~ **playground**, avontuurspeelplek, avontuurpark; ~**r**, waaghals, avonturier, fortuinsoeker, geluksoeker; ~ **some**, waaghalsig.
adven'turess, (-es), avonturierster, fortuinsoekster.
adven'turism, avonturisme; ..**rist**, avonturier.
adven'turous, gewaag, avontuurlik, roekeloos; ondernemend.
ad'verb, bywoord, adverbium.
adverb'ial, bywoordelik, adverbiaal.
ad ver'bium, ad verbium, verbatim, woordelik(s).
ad'versary, (..**ries**), teenstander, vyand, opponent, wederparty.
advers'ative, teenstellend.
ad'verse, teenstrydig; teenspoedig; vyandig; ongunstig; teengesteld; ~ *FATE (fortune)*, teenspoed; ~ *WIND*, teenwind.
adver'sity, teenspoed, ongeluk; wederwaardigheid.
advert'¹, verwys na, refereer na; ~ *to*, verwys na, terugkom op.
ad'vert², (-s), advertensie.
adver'tence, adver'tency, aandag, opmerksaamheid.
ad'vertise, bekend stel, adverteer, aankondig, reklame maak; *te koop loop met*.
advert'isement, aankondiging, advertensieberig; reklame, reklameberig.
ad'vertiser, adverteerder, aankondiger; advertensieblad.
ad'vertising, reklame, bekendstelling; ~ **agency**, advertensieburo; ~ **art**, adverteerkuns; ~ **matter**, advertensies, reklame; ~ **sign**, reklamebord.
advice', raad; meedeling, berig, aanrading, advies; *ACCORDING to last* ~, volgens die jongste berigte; *ASK* ~, raad vra; ~ *of DELIVERY*, aflewerringsadvies; *GIVE* ~, raad gee; *IF you'll take my* ~, as jy na my wil luister, as jy my raad wil volg; *LETTER of* ~, adviesbrief; *ON the* ~ *of*, op raad van; *RENDER* ~, raad gee; van raad dien; *SOUND* ~ *is a rare commodity*, goeie raad is duur; *TAKE* ~, raad aanneem, luister na; ~ **form**, adviesvorm; ~ **note**, adviesbrief; ~ **service**, adviesdiens; ~ **telegram**, adviestelegram.
advisabil'ity, raadsaamheid.
advis'able, raadsaam, gerade; dienstig; *deem* ~, dit gerade ag.
advise', raai, aanraai, raad gee; meedeel, berig, laat weet; ~**d**, berade, deurdag, oorwoë; *ILL* ~*d*, ondeurdag, onberade; *WELL* ~*d*, verstandig; ~**dly**, na ryp oorleg; met opset; ~**r**, raadsman, raadgewer, vraagbaak.
advi'sory, raadgewend, adviserend; ~ **council**, adviesraad.
ad'vocacy, voorspraak, verdediging; bepleiting; advokaatskap.
ad'vocate, (n) advokaat; raadsman; pleitbesorger, verdediger, voorspraak, bepleiter; voorstander; (v) bepleit, verdedig; voorstaan, aanraai, aanbeveel; ~ **ship**, advokaatskap.
ad'vocator, voorstander, pleitbesorger; ~**y**, pleitend, verdedigend.
advokaat', (D.), advokaat (drank), eierbrandewyn.
advow'son, kollasiereg.
ad'ytum, (..**ta**), heilige der heilige.
adze, (n) dissel; (v) met 'n dissel bewerk.
ae'dile, aedile, Romeinse magistraat.
Aege'an Sea, Egeïese See.

ae'gis, skild, skut; beskerming, hoede; *under the* ~ *of,* onder beskerming van.
ae'grotat, siektebewys; egrotateksamen, siekte-eksamen.
Aeol'ian, Eolies, ~ **harp,** Eoliese harp.
aeol'ian, eolies, wind-, waai-; ~ **erosion,** winderosie; ~ **soil,** waaisand.
aeolo'tropy, eolotropie, anisotropie, eienskapverandering.
ae'on, eeu; ewigheid.
aepyor'nis, epiornis, uitgestorwe vlerklose voël (grondvoël).
aer'adio, lugvaartradio.
aer'ate, belug, deurlug, van lug of koolsuur voorsien; ~**d,** deurlug; ~*d BREAD,* koolsuurbrood; ~*d WATER,* spuitwater, mineraalwater.
aera'tion, belugting, aërasie, deurlugting (grond).
aer'ial, (n) antenne, opvangdraad, lugdraad; (a) verhewe, eteries, denkbeeldig; lug-; ~ *BARRAGE,* lugversperring; ~ *BATTLE,* luggeveg; ~ *DERBY,* lugreisies, vliegwedstryd; ~ *DISPLAY,* vliegvertoning; ~ *FRAME,* antenneraam; ~ *MAST,* lugdraadmas; ~ *NAVIGATION,* lugvaart; ~ *PHOTOGRAPH,* lugfoto; ~ *RAILWAY,* lugspoor; ~ *RECONNAISSANCE,* lugverkenning; ~ *SURVEY,* lugopmeting; ~ *TERMINAL,* antenne-aansluiting; ~ *TOWER,* antennetoring, antennemas, antennepaal; ~ *TRAFFIC,* lugverkeer; ~ *TRANSPORT,* lugvervoer; ~ *WARFARE,* lugstryd.
a'erie, nes van 'n roofvoël; broeisel.
a'eriform, aërivormig, lugvormig, newelagtig; yl; gasvormig.
aer'obat, aërobaat, kunsvlieër, fratsvlieër.
aerobat'ic, aërobaties, kunsvlieg-; ~ **display,** kunsvliegvertoning; ~**s,** aërobatiek, kunsvlieëry; ~ **school,** kunsvliegskool.
a'erobe, aëroob.
aerob'ic, aëroob, aërobies; ~ **exercise,** aërobiese oefening; ~ **shoe,** aërobiese skoen.
aerobiol'ogy, lugbiologie, aërobiologie.
aer'oclub, vliegklub.
aer'odrome, vliegveld, lughawe; ~ **beacon,** vliegveldbaken; ~ **guard,** vliegveldwag; lughawewag; ~ **illumination,** lughaweverligting; vliegveldverligting; ~ **official,** vliegveldbeampte; ~ **staff,** vliegveldpersoneel, lughawepersoneel.
aerodynam'ic(al), aërodinamies.
aerodynam'icist, aërodinamikus.
aerodynam'ics, aërodinamika, lugdinamika.
ae'rodyne, aërodien, lugvaartuig (swaarder as lug).
aer'o-engine, vliegtuigmotor.
aer'ofoil, draagvlak; vlerk.
aer'ogram, draadlose telegram.
aer'ograph, aërograaf; tekenspuit.
aerog'rapher, lugbeskrywer.
aerog'raphy, lugbeskrywing.
aer'olite, aer'olith, meteoorsteen.
aerol'ogy, (hoog)lugkunde, aërologie.
aer'ometer, lugmeter, aërometer.
aerom'etry, lugmeting, aërometrie.
aer'omotor, lugmotor.
aer'onaut, lugskipper; vlieënier; aëronout.
aeronaut'ical, lugvaartkundig; ~ **engineer,** vlieginge-nieur; ~ **landmark,** lugvaartkoersbaken; ~ **map,** lugvaartkaart.
aeronaut'ics, lugvaartkunde; lugskeepvaart, vliegwese.
aer'ophone, radiotelefoon.
aer'ophyte, aërofiet, lugplant, woekerplant, epifiet.
aer'oplane, vliegmasjien, vliegtuig; ~ **accident,** vlieg(tuig)ongeluk; ~ **carrier,** vliegdekskip, vliegkampskip, moederskip; ~ **shed,** vliegtuigloods; ~ **ticket,** lugkaartjie, vliegtuigkaartjie.
aer'oscopy, aëroskopie, lugwaarneming, lugondersoek.
aer'oshow, lugvaartskou.
aer'osol, aërosol, gassol.
ae'rospace, lugruim(te).
aer'osphere, aërosfeer.
aer'ostat, aërostaat, lugvaartuig (ligter as lug).
aerostat'ics, ewewigsleer van gasse, aërostatika.

aerotech'nical, aërotegnies.
aerotech'nics, vliegtegniek.
aeru'ginous, groen, groenerig, roeskleurig.
ae'ry, (aeries) = **aerie.**
Aescula'pius, Aesculapius, Eskulaap.
Ae'sop, Esopus.
aesthes'ia, gevoeligheid.
aes'thete, estetikus, esteet; skoonheidsdweper.
aesthet'ic(al), esteties, skoonheids-; ~ **design,** estetiese ontwerp.
aestheti'cian, estetikus.
aesthet'icism, estetisisme.
aesthet'ics, skoonheidsleer, estetika, estetiek.
aes'tival, aestiv'al, somers, somer-.
aes'tivate, die somer (slapend) deurbring, oorsomer.
aestiva'tion, somerslaap; blomligging.
aet'atis, aetat'is, op die ouderdom (van).
aetiol'ogy, oorsaakleer, etiologie.
Aeto'lia, Etolië; ~**n,** (n) Etoliër; (a) Etolies.
afar', ver, in die verte; *FROM* ~, van ver af, uit die verte; ~ *OFF,* ver weg.
affabil'ity, voorkomendheid, vriendelikheid, minsaamheid, inskiklikheid.
aff'able, voorkomend, vriendelik, minsaam, toeskietlik, inskiklik; ~**ness,** vriendelikheid, minsaamheid.
affair', saak, besigheid, gedoente, aangeleentheid, ding, petalje, spul(letjie), affère; verhouding; ~ *s of a COUNTRY,* landsake; *DOMESTIC* ~*s,* binnelandse sake; *EVERYDAY* ~, alledaagse saak; *FOREIGN* ~*s,* buitelandse sake; *at the HEAD of* ~*s,* aan die hoof van sake; ~ *of HONOUR,* eresaak; *MAN of* ~*s,* sakeman; *that is MY* ~, dis my saak; *as* ~*s STAND,* soos sake staan.
affaire', liefdesverhouding; ~*de coeur,* (F.), liefdesverhouding.
affect'¹, (n) gevoelsinhoud, affek.
affect'², (v) (in)werk op, tref, raak, aantas; (be)roer; veins, voorgee, voorwend; aandoen; beïnvloed, affekteer; ~ *a CERTAIN style,* 'n sekere styl voorstaan (gebruik); *it DOES not* ~ *you,* dit raak jou nie; ~ *the RICH man,* die ryk man speel.
affecta'tion, aanstellery, aanstellings, gemaaktheid, fiemies, gekunsteldheid, affektasie.
affect': ~ **ed,** geroer, aangedaan, bewoë; geveins; gesind; gemanierd, onnatuurlik, gemaak, aanstellerig, geaffekteer; *PARTS* ~*ed,* aangetaste dele; ~*ed WITH,* aangetas deur; ~**edness,** gemaaktheid, aanstellerigheid; ~**ing,** rakend; roerend, aangrypend; ~**ion,** toegeneentheid, liefde(rykheid); aandoening, affeksie; siekte.
affec'tionate, toegeneeë, liefhebbend; hartlik, lief(deryk); beminlik; aandoenlik; ~**ly,** liefhebbend; ~**ness,** liefde, teerheid, beminlikheid, hartlikheid.
affec'tive, emosioneel, affektief, gemoeds-.
A'ffenpinscher, Affenpinscher (soort skoothondjie).
aff'erent, afferent, na binne voerend, toevoerend, sentripetaal; ~ **nerve,** afferente senuwee.
affi'ance, (n) verlowing, troubelofte; vertroue; (v) verloof; plegtig belowe.
affi'anced, (n) verloofde; (a) verloof.
affi'ant, (-s), affidavit(uit)maker.
affidav'it, beëdigde verklaring, affidavit.
affil'iate, (n) geaffilieerde (lid); sustermaatskappy; geaffilieerde maatskappy; (v) aanneem (lid), opneem; verbind; affilieer (by, met); as tak opneem (vereniging); 'n kind toewys aan die vader; 'n persoon aanwys as vader; ~**d,** aangeslote, geaffilieer.
affilia'tion, aanneming; erkenning; aansluiting, affiliasie; ~ *WITH,* affiliasie by (met); aansluiting by; ~ **order,** affiliasiebevel.
affined', verwant, verbind.
affin'ity, (aan)verwantskap; affiniteit; swaerskap, huweliksverwantskap; stamverwantskap; verband; ooreenkoms; aantrekking; ~ *by marriage,* swaerskap.
affirm', bevestig; beweer, verklaar; bekragtig; ~ **ant,** beweerder; bekragtiger.
affirma'tion, bevestiging; verklaring; versekering, bekragtiging.
affirm'ative, bevestigend; *answer in the* ~, bevestigend antwoord.
affix, (n) **(-es),** toevoegsel, aanhegsel; affiks, formans

(woordvorming); aanhangsel; agtervoegsel; voorvoegsel.
affix', (v) aanheg, opplak, aanbring (seëls); byvoeg; verbind; ~ **ture**, toevoeging, aanhegsel.
affla'tion, aanblasing, inspirasie.
affla'tus, ingewing, inblasing, inspirasie.
afflict', bedroef, smart; kwel; teister, besoek; ~ **ed**, geslae; aangetas; besoek; ~ **ed with**, gepla deur; lydende aan.
afflic'tion, droefheid, droefnis, geslaenheid, smart, leed; ramp, besoeking, plaag, straf, beproewing; *bread of* ~, brood van smarte.
aff'luence, oorvloed, rykdom, weelde; toevloed.
aff'luent[1], (n) tak (van 'n rivier); spruit, sytak.
aff'luent[2], (a) oorvloedig; ryk; toevloeiend.
aff'lux, toevloed; stroom; vermeerdering.
affor'ce, versterk, byvoeg (van deskundiges).
afford', verskaf, gee; oplewer; bekostig; *he CAN* ~ *to*, hy kan dit bybring (bekostig); hy kan hom die weelde veroorloof; ~ *an OPPORTUNITY*, 'n geleentheid gee om; *can you* ~ *the TIME?* het jy die tyd daarvoor?
affo'rest, bebos.
afforesta'tion, bosaanplanting, bebossing.
affran'chise, vry maak, bevry; ~ **ment**, vrymaking, vrysetting.
affray', (-s), vegparty, oploop, standjie, relletjie, bakleiery.
affreight', 'n skip huur; ~ **ment**, skeepshuur; skeepsbevragting.
a'fricate, (-s), affrikaat.
affront', (n) affront, belediging; *FEEL it an* ~, dit as 'n belediging beskou; *OFFER an* ~, 'n belediging aandoen; *iem. in sy gesig vat;* (v) affronteer, beledig; aandurf, trotseer; te woord staan.
affu'sion, begieting, besprinkeling.
Af'ghan, (n) Afgaan; (a) Afgaans; ~ **hound**, Afgaanse hond; ~ **istan**, Afganistan.
aficiona'do, (-s), aficionado, stiergevegliefhebber; liefhebber, ondersteuner.
afield', in die veld; te velde; *far* ~, ver van die huis af, ver weg, ver.
afire', aan die brand, in ligtelaaie; gloeiend.
aflame', aan die brand, in vlam, in ligtelaaie; gloeiend.
afloat', drywend; aan die gang, in omloop; onvas; in die vaart, in die see; onseker.
à fond, (F.), à fond, deeglik, deur en deur, indringend.
afoot', te voet; op die been; op tou; aan die gang; *there is something* ~, daar is iets gaande; daar broei iets.
afore', (adv, prep) voor, vantevore; eerder, liewers; ~ **cited**, voornoemd; ~ **going**, voorgaande, ~ **mentioned**, voornoemd, meergenoemde; ~ **named**, voornoemd; ~ **said**, bogemelde, voornoemd; ~ **thought**, voorbedag; *malice* ~ *thought*, bose opset.
a fortiori, meer oortuigend.
afraid', bang, lugtig, bangerig, bevrees; *I'm* ~ *I'm LATE*, ek vrees ek is laat; ~ *LEST*, bang dat; *MORTALLY* ~ *of*, so bang soos die duiwel vir 'n slypsteen; so bang soos 'n haas vir 'n hond; so bang soos 'n bok vir 'n skoot hael; bang soos die dood vir; ~ *OF*, bang vir; ~ *of one's own SHADOW*, vir koue pampoen skrik; vir 'n pampoenspook skrik; *I'm* ~ *THAT*, ek glo (dink, vermoed) dat; ~ *TO*, bang om.
afresh', opnuut, van voor af; weer; *start life* ~, 'n nuwe begin maak; weer van voor af begin.
Af'rica, Afrika.
Af'rican, (n) Afrikaan; (a) Afrikaans; *EAST* ~, Oos-Afrikaan; *NORTH* ~, Noord-Afrikaan; *SOUTH* ~, Suid-Afrikaner; *SOUTH-WEST* ~, Suidwes-Afrikaner, Suidwester; *WEST* ~, Wes-Afrikaan.
Africa'na, Africana.
Af'rican: ~ **a'lmond**, wildeamandel; ~ **elephant**, Afrikaanse olifant; ~ **gray**, jako *(Poittacus erithacus)*; ~ **ize**, Afrikaniseer, aan Afrikane oormaak; ~ **languages**, Afrikatale; tale van Afrika; ~ **spoonbill**, lepelaar; ~ **studies**, Afrikanistiek; ~ **violet**, saintpaulia; ~ **wattle**, huilbos *(Peltophorum africanum)*.
Af'ricanism, Afrikanisme.

Afrikaans', Afrikaans; ~ **ification**, verafrikaansing; ~ **ified**, verafrikaans, ~ **ify**, (..**fied**), verafrikaans; ~ **medium school**, Afrikaansmedium-skool.
Afrikan'er, (-s), Afrikaner; Afrikanerbees.
afrikan'er, afrikaner (blom); *BROWN* ~, bruin afrikaner, aandpypie; *PINK* ~, Sandveldlelie; *RED* ~, rooipypie; *WHITE* ~, bergpypie; *YELLOW* ~, (vlei)aandblom, trompetter.
Afrikan'erdom, Afrikanerdom.
Afrikan'erize, verafrikaans.
Afrika'ner, (n) Afrikaner; (a) Afrikaans.
Af'ro-hairstyle, Afrohaarstyl.
Af'ro-Asian, Afro-Asiaties.
aft, agter, agterskeeps.
af'ter, agter; naderhand; na, daarna, later; nadat; ~ *ALL*, tog, op die ou end, ten slotte, darem, welbeskou, per slot van rekening; *BE* ~, van plan wees, beoog; *in* ~ *DAYS*, later; ~ *a FASHION*, op 'n manier; *HANKER* ~, hunker na; *a man* ~ *my own HEART*, 'n man na my hart; *INQUIRE* ~, vra na; *in* ~ *LIFE*, op later leeftyd; in die hiernamaals; *LOOK* ~, kyk na, sorg vir; *ONE* ~ *the other*, na mekaar; *PIECE* ~ *piece*, stuk vir stuk; *be* ~ *the SAME thing*, na dieselfde stokkie mik; ~ *WHICH*, waarna; ~ **hours**, na-uurs; na werk; *work* ~ *hours*, na werktyd (werkure) werk; oortyd werk; ~ **birth**, nageboorte; ~ **-care**, nasorg, nabehandeling; ~ **-crop**, tweede oes, nadrag, naoes; ~ **damp**, stikgas, nadamp; ~ **-deck**, agterdek; ~ **-dinner**, na die ete; ~ **-dinner** *CALL*, besoek na ete; ~ **-dinner** *SPEECH*, tafelrede, redevoering na die ete; ~ **-effect**, nawerking, gevolg, nadraai, uitwerking; ~ **-glow**, nagloed (na die son onder is), naskynsel; ~ **-grass**, nagras, nawei; ~ **-growth**, nagewas; ~ **-guide**, agtertang; ~ **-hold**, agter(skeeps)ruim; ~ **-image**, nabeeld; ~ **life**, later leeftyd; lewe hiernamaals; ~ **math**, nasleep, naweë, gevolg; nagroei; ~ **math grazing**, nagras; ~ **most**, agterste.
af'ternoon, namiddag, agtermiddag; *GOOD* ~, goeiemiddag; *In the* ~ *of LIFE*, op middeljarige leeftyd; *THIS* ~, vanmiddag; *the WHOLE blessed* ~, die hele goddelike middag; ~ **nap**, middagdutjie; ~ **paper**, middagblad; ~ **performance**, middagvoorstelling; ~ **rest**, middagrus; ~ **service**, middagbeurt; ~ **sleep**, middagslapie; ~ **sun**, middagson; ~ **tea**, namiddagtee; ~ **train**, middagtrein; ~ **watch**, (na)middagwag.
af'ter: ~ **pains**, naweë; ~ **piece**, nastuk, naspel; ~ **play**, naspel; ~ **-pour**, nagiet; ~ **sales service**, naverkoopdiens; ~ **service**, onderhoudsdiens; ~ **-shave**, ~ **shave lotion**, naskeermiddel; ~ **-shock**, naskok; ~ **-tack**, naklewerigheid; ~ **taste**, bysmaak, nasmaak; ~ **thought**, nader oorweging; uitvlug; bygedagte, nagedagte; ~ **treatment**, nabehandeling; ~ **vintage**, nadruiwe; ~ **wards**, naderhand, daarna, later; ~ **word**, nawoord, besluit, epiloog; ~ **-years**, later jare.
ag'a, aga (titel); kommandeur (Turke); *A* ~ *Khan*, Aga Khan.
again', weer (eens), opnuut, nog eens, andermaal, nog, verder; aan die ander kant; vir die tweede maal; ~ *AND* ~, herhaalde male, dikwels; *HALF as much* ~, anderhalf maal soveel; *as MUCH* ~, nog 'n keer soveel; *NOW and* ~, af en toe; *TIME and* ~, herhaalde male; weer en weer; *WHAT do you call him* ~? wat noem jy hom nou ook weer?
against', teen, teë, strydig met; jeens; *AS* ~, in teenstelling met; *FIGHT* ~, veg teen; ~ *the GRAIN*, teen die draad in; met teësin; ~ *the HOUSE*, teen die huis; ~ *ODDS*, teen 'n oormag; *OVER* ~, jeens; teenoor; ~ *a RAINY day*, vir tye van nood; vir die oudag; *RUN* ~, raakloop; *STAND out* ~, uitstaan teen; ~ *the SUN*, teen die son in; *talk* ~ *TIME*, so vinnig moontlik praat; ~ *the WIND*, teen die wind, wind op.
agalac'tia, melkgebrek.
agalma'tolite, agalmatoliet, Chinese speksteen.
ag'ama, koggelmander.
ag'ami, ~ **agami**, trompettervoël.
agam'ic = **agamous**.
agamogen'esis, ongeslagtelike voortplanting.
ag'amous, geslagloos, ongeslagtelik.

agapan'thus, (-es), keiserskroon (blom), agapant, (konings)kandelaar, bloulelie, bruidslelie.
ag'ape¹, (n) liefde; liefdesmaal.
agape'² (adv) met oop mond, dronkgeslaan.
a'gar-a'gar, agar-agar.
ag'aric, boomswam; paddastoel; sampioen.
agas'tric, sonder maag of voedingskanaal.
ag'ate, agaat.
agav'e, garingboom, agave; sisal.
agaze', starend, kykend, aan die kyk.
ag'ba, agba (hout).
age, (n) ouderdom, leeftyd; eeu; ~s *AGO*, in die jaar nul; *BE your* ~, moenie kinderagtig (laf) wees nie; *(BE)COME of* ~, meerderjarig word; ~ *of DIS= CRETION*, jare van onderskeidingsvermoë (na 14); *FOR* ~s, eeue lank; *the GOLDEN* ~, die goue (gulde) eeu; ~ *before HONOUR (HONESTY)*, eers grootmense, dan langore; *LOOK one's* ~, so oud lyk soos 'n mens werklik is; *the MIDDLE A*~s, die Middeleeue; *OLD* ~, die ouderdom; *in his OLD* ~, op sy oudag; *OVER* ~, bokant die jare; *TAKE (be) an* ~, *TAKE (be)* ~s, nie warm by die water kom nie; iets by die Kaap gaan haal; *UNDER* ~, minderjarig; *WHAT is your* ~, hoe oud is jy? (v) verouder, oud word.
aged, oud, bejaard, bedaag, afgeleef; *the* ~, die oues van dae; ~**ness,** verouderdheid.
age'-group, leeftydsgroep.
age'ing = aging.
age'less, van alle tye, nooit verouderend; ~**ness,** tydeloosheid.
age: ~**-limit,** ouderdomsgrens; leeftydsgrens; ~**-long,** eeuelang.
a'gency, (..cies), werking, werksaamheid; verteen= woordiging, agentskap; bemiddeling, tussenkoms; *by the* ~ *of*, deur toedoen (tussenkoms) van.
agen'da, agenda, werksaamhede; sakelys.
a'gent, agent; tussenpersoon; spioen; rentmeester; be= werker; middel; agens (chem.); *sole* ~, alleenagent, enigste agent. ~ **general,** agent-generaal; ~ **pro= vocateur'** (F.), agent provocateur, lokvink.
age'-old, eeuelang, eeue-oud; ~ *question*, oeroue vraagstuk.
agglom'erate, (n) opeenhoping, agglomeraat; (v) op= eenhoop; (a) opeengehoop.
agglomera'tion, opeenhoping, versameling, saam= klontering.
agglut'inate, (v) aanmekaarlym; verbind; aggluti= neer, saamklonter; (a) saamklewend; ..*ting lan= guage,* agglutinerende taal.
agglutina'tion, agglutinasie.
agglut'inative, saamklewend.
aggradi'tion, aanwas; opvulling (van kanaal).
agg'randize, vergroot; verhoog; verheerlik; verfraai; ~**ment,** vergroting; verheerliking; verryking; ver= fraaiing.
agg'ravate, verswaar, vererger; verbitter; terg.
agg'ravating, ergerlik, onuitstaanbaar; verswarend; ~ *circumstances*, beswarende omstandighede; ~**ly,** tergend, ergerlik.
aggrava'tion, verergering, verswaring; terging; oor= drywing.
agg'regate, (n) totaal, geheel, aggregaat; versame= ling; betongruis; *in the* ~, as geheel; (v) versamel, saamvoeg; beloop; (a) gesamentlik; totaal (punte) ~ *FRUIT*, saamgestelde vrug; ~ *HORSE= POWER*, totale perdekrag; ~**s,** grondkrum= mels.
aggrega'tion, versameling; opneming, samevoeging.
aggress'ion, aanval, aanranding, aggressie.
aggress'ive, (n) aanval; *assume the* ~, tot die aanval oorgaan; (a) aanvallend, strydlustig, rusiemakerig, parmantig, aggressief, diknek.
aggress'or, aanvaller, aanrander, aangryper, aggres= sor.
aggrieve', grief; benadeel, veronreg; krenk; ~**d,** be= droef; gekrenk; benadeel.
ag'gro, (sl.) moeilikheidmakery, onrusstokery.
aghast', ontsteld, ontset.
a'gile, gou, rats, handig, lenig, vlug, rapat.
agil'ity, ratsheid, handigheid, vlugheid.
agin', (colloq.), teen, anti.

ag'ing, (n) veroudering; verwering; verharding; (a) verouderend; ouerig.
a'gio, koersverskil, opgeld, agio.
a'giotage, spekulasie; wisselsake; beursspekulasie, agiotage.
agist', (laat) wei.
a'gitate, beweeg; skud; beroer; agiteer; verontrus, kwaad stook; ~**d,** bewoë; opgewonde.
agita'tion, beweging; opskudding, opgewondenheid, beroering, agitasie, verontrusting, woeling, kwaad= stokery; woelsug.
agita'to, (It., mus.), agitato, opgewonde.
a'gitator, oproermaker, aanstoker, opstoker; agita= tor, volksopruier, woelgees, ophitser, roerder; roertoestel, roerstok.
ag'let, klossie, fraiing; metaalornament.
aglow', gloeiend, verhit; blosend.
ag'nail, geskeurde naelvleis; naelsweer.
ag'nate, (n) bloedverwant, agnaat; (a) verwant (van vaderskant).
agna'tic, verwant van vaderskant.
agna'tion, verwantskap.
agni'tion, agnisie.
agnom'en, (..mina), bynaam; erenaam.
agnos'tic, (n) agnostikus, godloënaar, vrydenker; (a) agnosties; ~**ism,** agnostiek, agnostisisme, vryden= kery.
Ag'nus Dei, (L.) Lam van God, eerste deel van die RK mis.
ago', gelede, terug; *3 days* ~, vooreergister.
agog', in beweging; verlangend; opgewonde; ~ *with*, aan die brand wees; vol vuur wees.
ago'ing, aan die gang; in omloop.
agon'ic, agonies.
ag'onize, folter, kwel; met die dood worstel; jag maak op effek; *agonizing pain,* onuithoubare pyn.
agonis'tic, atleties, sport=; strydlustig, polemies; stre= wend na effek.
ag'onizing, sielpynigend.
ag'ony, (agonies), angs, doodstryd, doodsangs; kwel= ling; sielsmart; ~ *of DEATH*, doodsangs; sielto= ging; ~ **column,** koerantkolom vir verdwene per= sone, ens.
agoraphob'ia, pleinvrees, ruimtevrees, agorafobie.
agou'tie, agoeti, goudhaas; S.-Amer. knaagdier (ge= slag *Dasyprocta*).
agram'matism, agrammatisme.
a'grapha, nie-kanonieke gesegdes van Jesus.
agra'phia, agrafie.
agra'rian, (n) agrariër, landbouer; (a) agraries, lande= lik, landbou=.
agree', instem, toestem; ooreenstem, saamstem, ak= kordeer, stryk, eensgesind wees; dit eens word, har= monieer; *they* ~ *ABOUT everything*, hulle boer onder een sambreel; ~, *for the LAW is costly*, as iem. jou wil prosedeer vir jou koei, gee die kalf ook daarby; *I could not* ~ *MORE*, ek is dit roerend eens; ~ *ON*, saamstem oor, ooreenstem; ~ *to a PROPOSAL*, met 'n voorstel meegaan; 'n voorstel aanneem; *not* ~ *WITH*, nie akkordeer nie met, nie saamstem nie met; ~**able,** aangenaam (wel)geval= lig; welkom; aardig; behaaglik, lief; ooreenkom= stig; *render* ~*able*, veraangenaam; ~**ableness,** (wel)gevalligheid; genoeglikheid; ~**d,** top! ak= koord! afgespreek! aangeneem!
agree'ment, ooreenkoms; verdrag; vergelyk; af= spraak, akkoord; *be in* ~, saamstem, akkoord gaan.
agres'tic, landelik; takhaaragtig, onbeskof, ru, boers.
a'gribusiness, landbouondernemings.
agric'olite, agrikoliet.
agricul'tural, landboukundig, landbou=; ~ **chem= istry,** landbouskeikunde; ~ **college,** landboukol= lege; ~ **credit,** landboukrediet; ~ **district,** land= boustreek; ~ **drain,** sugvoor, sugriool; ~ **educa= tion,** landbouonderwys; ~ **holding,** landbouhoewe, kleinhoewe; ~ **implement,** landbouwerktuig; ~ **in= struction,** landbouonderwys; ~ **journal,** landbou= joernaal; ~ **lime,** landboukalk; ~ **science,** land= bouwetenskap; ~ **show,** landboutentoonstelling; ~ **training school,** landbouvakskool.

agriculture   693   air

ag'riculture, landbou(bedryf); landboukunde, akkerbou.
agricul'turist, (graan)boer, landbouer; landboukundige.
ag'rimony, lewerkruid.
ag'rimotor, landboumotor.
ag'ro-ecological, agroëkologies.
ag'ro-economics, landbou-ekonomie.
ag'ronomic(al), akkerboukundig, agronomies.
agron'omist, agronoom.
agron'omy, agronomie, veldkunde; landboukunde, landhuishoudkunde.
agrostol'ogist, graskenner, grasdeskundige.
agrostol'ogy, grasbouleer.
aground', teen die grond, gestrand; in verleentheid; *run* ~, strand.
ag'ue, koors, kouekoors, rilling; ~-**cake,** miltvergroting.
Agul'has, Agulhas.
agu'ti = agouti
ah! ag! a! o!
aha'! ha! aha! nou toe nou! nou ja!
ahead'! vooruit, vorentoe; voorop; vooraan; *BREAKERS* ~, branders voor; *DANGER* ~, gevaar voor; *GO* ~, aangaan; vooruitgaan; ~ *of SOMEBODY,* voor iem.; *full STEAM* ~, met volle krag vooruit; *STRAIGHT* ~, reguit vorentoe.
aheap', op 'n hoop, inmekaar.
ahem'! hm!
ahim'sa, nie-geweld, geweldloosheid.
ahisto'rical, ahistories, nie-histories, ongeskiedkundig.
a-hun'ting, aan die jag.
ahoy'! haai! hêi! ahooi!
ai, aai, luidier.
aid, (n) hulp, bystand; subsidie; hulpmiddel; helper; ~ *s to BEAUTY,* skoonheidshulpmiddels; *FIRST* ~, eerstehulp (by ongelukke); *IN* ~ *of,* ten bate van, vir; ~ *to MEMORY,* geheue(hulp)middel, eselsbrug; ~*ed SCHOOL,* ondersteunde skool; *with the* ~ *of TOOLS,* met behulp van gereedskap; (v) help, steun, bystand verleen, bydra; ~ *and abet,* help, steun; handlanger wees.
aide, helper, hulp, adjudant.
aide-de-camp', (aides-de-camp), adjudant, aide-de-camp, vleueladjudant.
aide-memoire', aide-memoire, memorandum.
AIDS (aquired immunity defect syndrome), vigs, verworwe immuniteitsgebreksindroom; ~ **infection,** vigsbesmetting ~ **victim,** vigs-slagoffer
aid'er, helper, handlanger; *one's* ~*s and abettors,* jou gesante en trawante.
aig'rette, egret(reier); kuifreier; kuif, pluim.
ai'guille, (-s), rotspunt; rotsboor; ~-**tte,** aglet.
ai'kido, aikido, Japanse selfverdediging.
ail, makeer, skort, skeel; sukkel, siek wees; *what* ~*s you?* wat makeer jou?
ail'eron, rolroer; ~-**control,** rolstuur; ~-**drag,** rolroerweerstand.
ail: ~**ing,** sieklik, sukkelend, ~**ment,** siekte, kwaal, ongesteldheid.
ailu'rophil(e), ailurofiel, katteliefhebber.
ailu'rophobia, ailurofobie, kattevrees.
aim, (n) doelwit, doel, oogmerk, plan; *MAKE it one's* ~, jou ten doel stel; *POINT of* ~, aanlêpunt; ~*s of the SOCIETY,* oogmerke v.d. genootskap; *TAKE* ~ *at,* korrelvat op; (v) doel; rig, aanlê, korrel; beoog, mik; ~ *AT,* korrelvat op, mik op; aanstuur op; dit op iem. (iets) munt; ~ *to PLEASE,* probeer om voldoening te gee; ~**ing,** korreling; ~**less,** doelloos.
air, (n) lug, windjie; lied, aria, wysie, melodie; houding, gedrag; voorkome, voorkomste; *BE in the* ~, in die lug hang; *this shop is* ~-*CONDITIONED,* hierdie winkel is lugversorg; *live on FRESH* ~, van die oostewind moet leef; *don't GIVE yourself* ~*s!* jy moenie jou wip nie! *GIVE oneself* ~*s,* jou verbeel, jou aanstel; jou airs gee; *be full of* ~*s and GRACES,* vol komplimente wees; *have a HAUGHTY* ~, sy neus in die wind steek; *be IN the* ~, in die lug hang (sit); *LEAVE something up in the* ~, iets in die midde laat; *one can't LIVE on* ~, 'n mens kan van wind alleen nie leef nie; *be ON the* ~, uitgesaai word; *PUT on* ~*s,* vol krupsies wees; *TAKE the* ~, 'n luggie skep; *TAKE* ~, rugbaar word (raak); *TREAD on* ~, in die wolke wees; *be UP in the* ~, in die wolke wees; (v) lug, droogmaak (klere); uitdamp; uit(er), lug gee aan; *TO* ~ (one's learning, etc.), lug (jou geleerdheid, ens.); ~ *one's VIEWS,* jou mening lug; (a) lugwind=; ~-**action,** luggeveg; lugbeweging; ~ **adit,** lugtonnel; ~ **alarm,** lugalarm; koestoeter; ~-**ambulance,** lugambulans; ~-**apprentice,** lugvakleerling; ~-**armament,** lugbewapening; ~ **arms,** lugwapens; ~ **artillery,** lugartillerie, boordgeskut; ~-**bag,** lugsak; ~-**balloon,** lugballon; ~-**barrage,** vliegtuigversperring, lugversperring; ~-**base,** lugbasis; lugsteunpunt; lughawe, vliegveld; ~-**battle,** luggeveg; ~-**beacon,** lugvaartbaken, vliegtuigbaken; ~-**bed,** lugmatras; ~-**bells** = ~-**bubbles;** ~-**bladder,** lugblaas; ~-**board,** lugvaartraad; ~-**bomb,** lugbom, vliegtuigbom; ~-**bomber,** bomwerper; ~ **borne,** deur die lug vervoer; in die lug; *become* ~*borne,* vlot, opstyg; ~-**bottle,** lugbottel, lugfles; ~ **brake,** lugrem; ~-**brick,** lugrooster; ventilasierooster; ~-**bridge,** lugbrug; ~-**brigade,** lugbrigade; ~ **brush,** verfspuit; ~-**bubbles,** lugblasies; ~ **buffer,** lugbuffer; ~-**bump,** lugstamp; ~ **burst,** lugbars(ting); ~ **cargo,** lugvrag; ~ **cell,** lugsel, lugsakkie; ~-**carrier,** lugkarweier; ~-**cataract,** lugafstroming, lugstoring; ~ **chief marshal,** eerste lugmaarskalk; ~-**circulation,** lugsirkulasie; ~-**cleaner,** lugsuiweraar; ~-**cock,** lugkraan; **commodore,** lugkommodoor; ~ **column,** (druk)lugkolom; **company,** lugvaartmaatskappy; ~ **compressor,** lugpomp; ~ **condenser,** lugkondensator; lug(ver)koeler; ~-**conditioned,** lugversorg(de); ~-**conditioner,** lugversorger, lugversorgingsapparaat; ~-**conditioning,** lugversorging; lugreëling; klimaatreëling, ~-**conscious,** lugbewus, lugvaartgesind; ~ **container,** lughouer; ~ **controls,** stuurmiddele; ~-**conveyance,** lugvervoer; lugvervoermiddel; ~-**cooled,** deur die verkoel, lugverkoel(de), ~-**cooling,** verkoeling; ~-**cover,** vliegtuigdekking.
air'craft, lugvaartuig, vliegtuig; ~ **accident,** vlieg(tuig)ongeluk; ~-**carrier,** vliegdekskip, vliegtuigdraer, moederskip, vliegkampskip; ~ **casualties,** vliegtuigverliese; ~ **construction,** vliegtuigbou; ~ **controls,** stuurmiddele, roere (lugv.); ~ **crew,** vlieg(tuig)bemanning; vlugbemanning, lugbemanning, vlieg(tuig)personeel; ~ **design,** vliegtuigontwerp; ~ **designer,** vliegtuigontwerper; ~ **disaster,** lugramp, ~ **engine,** vliegtuigmotor; ~ **engineering,** vliegtuigboukunde, lugvaarttegniek; **establishment,** vliegtuigsterkte; ~ **factory,** vliegtuigfabriek; ~ **industry,** lugvaartnywerheid; ~ **inspection,** lugvaartinspeksie.
air'craftsman, lugwerktuigkundige.
air'craft: ~ **manufacturer,** lugvaartfabrikant; ~ **pilot,** vlieënier; ~ **station,** vliegtuigstasie.
air: ~ **crash,** vliegtuigongeluk; ~ **crew,** lugpersoneel, vlugpersoneel, vliegtuigbemanning (-personeel); ~-**cured,** luggedroog(de), lugdroë; ~-**current,** lugstroom; ~-**cushion,** lugkussing; ~-**damping,** lugdamping; ~ **defence,** lugverdediging; ~ **density,** lugdigtheid; ~ **disaster,** lugramp; vliegtuigramp; ~ **display,** vliegvertoning; ~ **door,** lugdeur; ~ **drag,** lugweerstand; ~ **drainage,** lugafvoer; ~-**dried,** luggedroog, lugdroë; ~-**drift,** lugtrek.
air' drill[1], vliegdril.
air' drill[2], (lug)drukboor; lugklopboor.
air: ~ **dry,** winddroog; ~ **drying,** lugdroging; ~ **duct,** lugleiding; lugbuis; ~ **duel,** lugtweegeveg; ~ **embolism,** lugembolie; ~-**escape,** ~-**exhaust,** luguitlaat; ~ **experience,** vliegondervinding; ~ **field,** vliegveld; ~-**fight,** luggeveg; ~ **fighter,** jagvliegtuig, vegvliegtuig, jagter, vegter; ~ **filter,** lugfilter, lugsuiweraar; ~ **fleet,** lugvloot; ~ **flow,** lugstroming; ~ **flue,** lugkanaal; ~-**foil,** draagvlak; ~ **force,** lugmag, lugstrydkrag(te), lugwapen; ~-**force chaplain,** lugmagkapelaan; ~ **frame,** vliegraam; ~ **freight,** lugvrag, lugvraggeld; ~ **freight building,** lugvraggebou; ~ **freight carrier,** vragvliegtuig; ~ **fuel,** vliegtuigbrandstof; ~-**gauge,** lugdrukmeter

~ glow, luggloed; ~-going crew, boordpersoneel; ~graph, lugposfotobrief; ~ gun, windbuks, lug=spuit; ~ gunner, boordskutter; ~-hole, luggat; kel=dergat, wak (in ys); ~ hostess, lugwaardin, reis=waardin; ~ily, lugtig, lughartig, vrolik; ~ iness, lugtigheid, lughartigheid, vrolikheid; ~ ing, lug; beweging in die buitelug; *take an* ~*ing,* 'n luggie skep; ~-**inlet cock**, luginlaatkraan; ~-**jacket**, lug=swemgordel; ~ **lane**, lugweg, luggang; ~-**law**, lug=reg; ~-**layer**, luglaag; luginlêer; ~ **less**, bedompig; lugleeg; ~ **level**, lugvlak; lugverspeiding (myn); (lugbel) waterpas; ~-**lift**, lugbrug; lugvervoer; ~-**light**, lugvaartlig; ~ **line**, vliegroete; lugdiens, lug=vaartlyn; luglyn; reguit lyn; ~ **liner**, passasiersvlieg=tuig, lugskip; ~-**lock**, gasprop; lugverstopping, dampsluiting, dampverspering; lugprop; ~ **mail**, lugpos; ~ **main**, hoofligleiding; ~**man**, (..**men**), vlieër, vlieënier, lugvaarder; ~ **manship**, vliegken=nis, vliegvaardigheid, vliegvermoë; ~ **map**, lug=kaart; ~ **marshall**, lugmaarskalk; ~ **mattress**, lug=matras; ~ **mechanic**, vliegtuigmonteur, lugwerk=tuigkundige; vliegtuigmeganikus, lugmeganikus; ~-**meeting**, vliegwedstryd; ~ **meter**, lugmeter, lug=vloeimeter; ~ **mileage**, lugmylafstand; ~-**minded**, lugbewus, lugvaartgesind; ~ **navigation**, lugvaart; ~ **navigator**, (lug)navigator; ~ **nozzle**, druklug=tuit, lugmondstuk; ~ **observer**, lugwaarnemer; ~ **operations**, lugbedrywighede; ~-**pact**, lugvaart=ooreenkoms; ~-**pageant**, vliegvertoning, vlieg=skou; ~ **photo**, lugfoto; ~-**pillow**, windkussing; ~ **pilot**, vlieër, vliegtuigbestuurder; lugvaarder; ~ **pipe**, lugpyp; ~ **plane**, vliegtuig; vliegmasjien; ~-**plant**, epifiet, lugplant; kanniedood; ~ **pocket**, lug=gat, lugholte, lugknik, lugblaas; ~ **pollution**, lugbe=soedeling; ~ **port**, lughawe, vliegveld; ~ **pressure**, lugdruk; ~ **proof**, lugdig; ~ **pump**, lugpomp; ~-**purifying**, lugsuiwerend; ~-**race**, vliegwedstryd, wedvlug; ~-**raid**, lugaanval; ~ **rally**, (**rallies**), lug=vertoning, vliegbyeenkoms.
air: ~-**ready**, vliegvaardig; ~ **reconnaissance**, lugver=kenning; ~-**regulation**, lugreëling; ~-**regulator**, lugreëlaar; ~-**release valve**, lug(uitlaat)klep; ~ re=port, vliegtuigberig; ~-**resistance**, lugweerstand; ~ **review**, vliegvertoning; ~-**root**, lugwortel; ~ **route**, luglyn; lugroete; ~ **rules**, lugverkeersreëls; ~ **sac**, lugsakkie; ~ **school**, vliegskool; ~ **screw**, lug=skroef; *lifting* ~*screw,* hefskroef; ~-**sense**, lugsin; ~ **service**, lugdiens; ~-**shaft**, luggang; ~ **ship**, lug=skip; ~ **sick**, lugsiek; ~-**slot**, luggleuf; ~ **space**, lugruimte; ~ **speed**, lugsnelheid; ~ **squadron**, (lug)eskader; ~ **station**, lugstasie; ~ **stewardess**, lugwaardin; ~ **strip**, (nood)vliegveld; ~ **supply**, lugtoevoer; ~ **supremacy** oppermag in die lug, lug=oormag; ~ **survey**, lugkartering; ~ **taxi**, lugtaxi; ~ **terminal**, lugeindpunt; ~ **thermometer**, lugter=mometer; ~-**threads**, herfsdrade; ~-**ticket**, lugreis=kaartjie; ~ **tight**, lugdig, hermeties, potdig; ~ **traf=fic**, lugverkeer; ~-**training**, vliegopleiding; ~ **transport**, lugvervoer; ~ **trap**, lugval; stankaf=sluiter; ~ **travel**, lugreise; ~ **traveller**, lugreisiger; ~ **truck**, vragvliegtuig; ~ **tube**, lugbuis; ~**tuck**, pofopnaaisel; ~ **umbrella**, lugbeskerming; ~-**valve**, lugklep, lugklappie; ~ **vent**, luggat, lug-uit=laat; ontlugter; ~ **war**, lugoorlog; ~ **warden**, lug=vaartwagter; ~ **wave**, luggolf; ~ **way**, lugroete; ~ **ways office**, lugdienskantoor; ~ **weapon**, boord=wapen; ~ **woman**, vrouevlieënier, vliegster; ~ **wor=thy**, lugwaardig; vliegveilig.
ai'ry, lugtig, vrolik; hoog in die lug; yl; ontasbaar; beuselagtig.
aisle, vlerk, vleuel (van 'n gebou); paadjie (tussen stoele of banke); beuk (argit.); moot, gang (bosb.).
ait, (rivier)eilandjie.
aitch, die letter h; *drop one's* ~ *es,* die *h* nie uitspreek nie; ~ **bone**, stuitjiestuk (beesvleis), stertstuk.
ajar', half oop, op 'n skrefie (kier).
akee = **ackee**
ak'erite, akeriet.
akim'bo: *with arms* ~, met die hande in die sy.
akin', (stam)verwant, vermaagskap.
ak'tian, akties.
al'abaster, (n) albaster, albas; (a) albaster=.

à la carté, a la carte (volgens spyskaart) ~ ~ ~ **menu**, a la carte-spyskaart.
alack' helaas! ~-**a-day**! helaas! ag!
alac'rity, lewendigheid, wakkerheid; gretigheid, bereidwilligheid.
Alad'din, Aladdin; ~ **'s lamp**, Aladdin se lamp.
ala'lia, spraakverlies.
à la mode', modieus, na die mode.
al'ar, vleuel=, vlerk=; vleuelvormig, vlerkvorming.
alarm', (n) alarm, alarmsein; angs, skrik; verontrus=ting; wekker; *CAUSE* ~, angs wek; *a FALSE* ~, 'n vals alarm; *GIVE the* ~, alarm maak; *SOUND the* ~, alarm blaas; *TAKE* ~, lont ruik; (v) bang maak, verontrus, alarmeer, verskrik; waarsku; die alarm gee; ~-**bell**, stormklok, alarmklok; ~-**clock**, wekker; ~ **ed**, vervaard; ~ **ing**, verontrustend, on=rusbarend, angswekkend, skrikbarend, sorgwek=kend, bedenklik (toestand), sorgbarend, alarme=rend; ~ **ingly**, onrusbarend, verontrustend; ~ **ist**, (n) alarmis, opruier; (a) skrikaanjaend, sorgwek=kend; ~-**post**, alarmplek; ~-**signal**, alarmteken, alarmsein.
ala'rum, *see* **alarm**, (n).
al'ary, vleuel=, vlerk=.
alas'! helaas! ~ *and alack!* o droefheid (treurigheid) op note!
alas'trim, amaas, kafferpokke.
al'ate(d), gevleuel(d).
alb, albe, koorhemp.
al'bacore, albakoor (vis), geelstert, halfkoord.
Alban'ia, Albanië; ~ **n**, (n) Albaniër; (a) Albanies.
Al'bany, Albany (Eng.); Albanie (K.P.).
alba'ta, albata, witmetaal, Duitse silwer.
al'batross, (-**es**), stormvoël, albatros; *wandering* ~, grootalbatros.
albe'it, (lit.), alhoewel, hoewel.
al'bert, kort oorlosieketting.
albes'cent, witwordend, witterig.
al'bian, albies.
Albigen'ses, Albigense.
al'binism, albinisme.
albi'no, (-s), albino.
Al'bion, Albion, Engeland.
al'bite, albiet, witveldspaat.
al'bite law, albietreg.
al'bitite, albitiet.
al'bolite, alboliet.
albugin'eous, eiwitagtig.
albu'go, wit (grou) staar.
al'bum, album; gedenkboek; bundel.
al'bumen, **al'bumin**, kiemwit, eiwit, albumien, albu=mine.
album'inates, albuminate.
album'inoid, eiwitstof, eiwit.
album'inous, eiwitagtig, eiwithoudend.
albuminur'ia, urine-eiwit, albuminuria.
al'burn, **alburn'um**, jonghout, lotehout.
alchem'ic(al), alchemisties.
al'chemist, Middeleeuse chemikus, goudmaker, al=chemis.
al'chemy, alchemie.
al'cohol, alkohol, wyngees; sterk drank.
alcohol'ic, (n) (-s), alkoholis, dranksugtig; (a) alko=holies; ~ **beverage**, alkohol(drank), sterkdrank; ~ **content**, alkoholgehalte; ~ **drink**, sterkdrank; ~ **poisoning**, alkoholvergiftiging.
al'coholism, alkoholisme.
al'coholize, suip, dronk wees, alkoholiseer.
alcoholom'eter, alkoholmeter.
Al'coran, (Al)koran.
al'cotester, alkoholtoetser.
al'cove, alkoof; somerhuisie, prieel.
al'dehyde, aldehied, aldehide.
al'der, elsboom, els; *red* ~, rooi-els; ~ **bush**, elsbos.
al'derman, (..**men**), raadsheer; ~ **ship**, raadsheer=skap.
al'derwood, elshout.
Al'dis: ~ **lamp**, aldislamp; ~ **lens**, aldislens; ~ **sight**, aldisvisier.
al'dose, aldose.
al'drin, aldrin.
ale, Engelse bier; *Adam's* ~, pompwater.

aleato'ric, a'leatory, (ewe)kansig; ~ **contract,** kansooreenkoms.
al'egar, suurbier; bierasyn.
ale'house, bierhuis.
alem'bic, distilleerkolf, alembiek.
alert', (n) alarmsein; *on the* ~, op sy hoede, wakker; (v) wakker maak, aansê, waarsku; (a) waaksaam, wakker, op die hoede; vlug; ~ **ness,** waaksaamheid, wakkerheid.
aleur'on = **aleurone.**
aleur'onate, aleuronaat.
aleur'one, aleuroon.
Aleu'tians, Aleoete.
alexan'drine, (n) aleksandryn; (a) aleksandryns.
alexan'drite, aleksandriet.
alex'ia, leesblindheid; aleksie.
alex'in, aleksine, aleksien.
alfal'fa, lusern, alfalfa.
al'fenide, alfenide, alfenied.
alfres'co, alfresko, in die buitelug, buiteluge.
al'ga, (-e), seewier, seegras.
al'gebra, algebra, stelkunde.
algebra'ical, algebraïes, stelkundig.
Alger'ia, Algerië, Algiers; ~**n,** (n) Algeryn; (a) Algeryns.
al'gicide, algdoder.
al'gid, koud.
algid'ity, koudheid, koue.
Algiers', Algiers, Algerië.
al'ginate, alginaat.
algi'nic acid, algiensuur, alginesuur.
Al'gol, Algol, algebraïese rekenaartaal.
algolag'nia, algolagnie, pyngenot.
al'gorism, al'gorithm, Arabiese syferstelsel; algorisme, algoritme.
al'ias, (n) **(-es),** aangenome naam, alias; (adv) anders genoem, alias.
al'ibi, alibi; (sl.) ekskuus.
al'idade, alidade.
al'ien, (n) vreemdeling, uitlander; (a) vreemd, uitlands; ~ **abil'ity,** vervreembaarheid; ~ **able,** vervreembaar; ~ **ate,** vervreem; afkonkel, verwyder.
aliena'tion, vervreemding, ontvreemding, verwydering, afkonkeling; *mental* ~, verstandsverbystering.
alienee', nuwe eienaar, persoon op wie eiendom oorgedra word.
al'ienism, psigiatrie.
al'ienist, psigiater, student van sielsiektes.
al'ienship, vreemdelingskap.
al'iform, vleuelvormig, vlerkvormig.
alight', (v) neerkom, land, gaan sit; afspring, uitklim; afstap (van trein), afstyg, uitstyg, neerstryk, grondvat; (a) aangesteek, aan die brand: *KEEP* ~, brandend hou; aan die brand hou; *SET* ~, aan die brand steek.
align', rig, op een lyn bring; in gelid staan; (wiele) spoor; ~ **er,** spoortoestel; ~ **ment,** rooilyn; rigtingslyn; opstelling; sporing; *the wheels are out of* ~ *ment,* die wiele spoor nie; ~ **ment gauge,** sporingsmeter.
alike', gelyk; eenders.
al'iment, kos, voedsel; leeftog; ondersteuning.
alimen'tal, voedsaam, voedings.
alimen'tary, alimentêr, voedend, voedings; ~ **canal,** spysverteringskanaal.
alimenta'tion, voeding; onderhoud; alimentasie.
al'imony, onderhoud; versorging; *sue for* ~, onderhoud eis.
aline' = **align.**
al'iped, vlerkvoetig (soos vlermuis).
aliphat'ic, alifaties, vets.
al'iquant, alikwant.
al'iquot, opgaande, ewematig, alikwot, eweredig.
alive', in lewe, lewendig; wakker; bewus, gevoelig; wemelend; *ANY MAN* ~, enigiemand; *the BEST man* ~, die beste man van die wêreld; *be* ~ *and KICKING,* springlewendig wees; *the LINE (MICROPHONE) is* ~, die lyn (mikrofoon) is lewendig, is aan; *LOOK* ~! roer jou riete! *MAN* ~! ou kêrel! ~ *TO,* bewus van; ~ *WITH* wemelend van.
aliz'arin, alisarine.

alkales'cent, brakwordend.
al'kali, (-(e)s), loogsout, alkali.
alkalim'eter, alkalimeter.
al'kaline, alkalies.
alkalin'ity, loogsoutinhoud, alkaliniteit, brakheid.
al'kalize, alkaliseer.
al'kaloid, alkaloïd.
all, (a) al die, alle, algar; die hele, gans(e), heel; ~ *DAY,* heeldag, die hele dag; *for* ~ *his CAPABILITIES,* nieteenstaande al sy bekwaamhede; *on* ~ *FOURS,* op hande en voete, handeviervoet; ~ *KINDS,* alle soorte; ~ *PEOPLE,* al die mense; *he of* ~ *PEOPLE,* juis hy; *it takes* ~ *SORTS to make a world,* die wêreld bestaan uit allerhande soorte; *be* ~ *THINGS to* ~ *men,* wees soos die wind waai; ~ *the WORLD,* die hele wêreld; (pron) alles; algar, almal; ~ *BUT one,* almal op een na; *AFTER* ~, op die (ou) end, darem, tog; *AT* ~, in die minste, maar enigsins; ~ *'s well that ENDS well,* end goed, alles goed; ~ *and EVERY,* almal sonder onderskeid; *for* ~ *I CARE,* wat my betref; ~ *CLEAR!* alles veilig! *once FOR* ~, finaal; *HANG it* ~! vervlaks! *IN* ~, ~ *IN* ~, alles tesaam; *for* ~ *I KNOW,* sover ek weet; bes moontlik; *NOT at* ~, glad nie, geensins; ~ *OF it,* alles; *ONE and* ~, almal; *it is* ~ *ONE,* dit is om die ewe; ~ *in ONE,* in een stuk; *ONE'S* ~, jou goed en bloed; ~ *in RED,* heeltemal in rooi; ~ *the SAME,* darem, tog, nietemin; ~ *on SIDE,* speelkant (rugby); ~ *and SUNDRY,* die hele klomp; algar; ~ *THERE,* nie mal nie, by jou positiewe; ~ *TOLD,* almal (alles) ingesluit (inbegrepe); ~ *square (even),* gelykop; *it is* ~ *UP with him,* dis klaar met kees; dit is klaarpraat met hom; ~ *of US,* ons almal; ~ *shall be WELL, and Jack shall have (his) Jill,* alles sal regkom (sê Jan Brand); (adv) totaal, heeltemal; ~ *ALONG,* al die tyd; ~ *the BETTER,* des te beter; ~ *BUT,* ampertjies, amper; almal behalwe; ~ *HAIL!* wees gegroet! ~ *at ONCE,* plotseling, meteens; *go* ~ *OUT,* uithaal, uit alle mag probeer; ~ *OVER,* oral(s); ~ *too SOON,* ver te gou; ~ *of a SUDDEN,* skielik, meteens; *not to be* ~ *THERE,* nie al jou varkies in die hok hê nie.
Al'lah, Alla.
allant'oid, worsvormig; allantoïed.
allan'toin, allantoïen, allantoïne.
all'-automatic, vol-outomaties.
allay', verlig, verminder, matig, wegneem, laat bedaar, versag, stil; ~ **ing,** stilling.
all comers, almal; *ready for* ~ ~, klaar vir enigeen.
all'-destroying, alverdelgend, alvernielend.
all'-devouring, alverslindend.
allega'tion, bewering; betoog.
allege', aanvoer, beweer; ~ **d,** beweerde; ~ *d crime,* beweerde misdaad; ~ **dly,** volgens bewering.
alle'giance, getrouheid; aanhanklikheid, onderdanigheid; *swear* ~, trou sweer.
allego'ric(al), sinnebeeldig, allegories; ~ *play,* sinnespel.
all'egorist, allegorieskrywer.
all'egorize, allegories voorstel.
all'egory, (..ries), sinnebeeld, allegorie.
allegret'to, (It. mus.), allegretto, redelik vinnig.
alle'gro, (It. mus.), allegro, vinnig.
al'lel(e), alle'lomorph, alleel, allelomorf.
allelu'ia, lofsang, halleluja.
al'lemande, allemande, Duitse dans.
all'-embracing, alomvattend.
all'ergen, allergeen, allergiestof, allergieveroorsaker.
aller'gic, allergies.
all'ergy, allergie; ~ **reaction,** allergiereaksie.
alleviate, verlig, versag, lenig, stil.
allevia'tion, versagting, verligting, leniging, stilling.
allev'iative, versagtend, verligtend.
allev'iator, verligter, versagter, leniger.
allev'iatory = **alleviative.**
alley, (-s), laan, laning; steeg, wandelbaan, dreef, allee, gang; kegelbaan; *BLIND* ~, omdraaistraatjie, doodloopstraatjie, keerweer; *blind-* ~ *OCCUPATION,* doodloopbaantjie.
All'-Father, Alvader.

All Hall'ows, Allerheilige.
All-Hi'ghest, Allerhoogste.
alli'ance, verbond, bondgenootskap, alliansie; verbintenis; verwantskap; huwelik.
al'lied, verbonde, geallieerd; verwant, aanverwant.
alliga'tion, alligasie; mengsel; vasbinding.
all'igator, kaaiman, alligator; ~ **clip,** katnael; ~**ing,** krokodilvelbarsies (verf); ~ **pear,** avokadopeer; ~ **wrench,** haaibek, pypsleutel.
all'-important, allerbelangriks.
all'-in, alles insluitende; *he is* ~, sy pê (gô) is uit; ~ **wrestling,** rofstoei.
allit'erate, allitereer.
allitera'tion, alliterasie, stafrym.
allit'erative, allitererend.
al'lium, allium.
all'-knowing, alwetend; *he thinks he is* ~, hy verbeel hom hy het die wysheid in pag.
all'-metal construc'tion, metaalbou.
all'-night, nag-; ~ *fun event,* nagvermaaklikheidsgebeurtenis; ~ **marathon,** nagmarathon.
all'ocate, aanwys; toebedeel, toewys; plek aanwys; ~**d,** toegewys; ~**d land,** toegewese grond.
alloca'tion, bedeling, vasstelling; plaasaanwysing; toewysing; aanwysing.
allo'chrous, van verskillende kleure.
allocu'tion, formele aanspreekvorm; toespraak (van die pous tot die kardinale); redevoering.
allod'ial, vry van leenreg, allodiaal.
allog'amous, kruisbestuiwend, allogaam.
allog'amy, kruisbestuiwing, allogamie.
all'omorph, allomorf; ~ **'ic,** allomorfies; ~**ism,** allomorfisme.
allonge', verlengstuk
all'opath, allopaat; ~ **'ic,** allopaties.
allop'athist, allopaat.
allop'athy, allopatie.
al'lophone, allofoon, klankvariant; ..**pho'nic,** allofonies.
allophyl'ian, uitheems; vreemdsoortig.
allot', (-ted), aanwys, toe(be)deel, toemeet, toeken; *one's* ~ *ted portion,* jou beskeie deel.
all'otheism, vreemdegodediens.
allothig'enous, allotigeen.
allot'ment, toekenning, toewysing; aandeel; erf, perseel.
all'otrope, allotroop.
allotrop'ic, allotropies, meervormig.
allotrop'ism, allotropie, meervormigheid.
allot'ropy, meervormigheid, allotropie.
allottee', toebedeelde, begunstigde.
allow', (toe)laat, vergun, veroorloof; bewillig; erken; gee; ~ *FOR,* in aanmerking neem; rekening hou met; ~ *OF,* toelaat, gedoog; ~ *ME,* vergun my; *THIS is not* ~ *ed,* dit word nie toegelaat nie; dit mag nie; ~**able,** geoorloof, toelaatbaar.
allow'ance, verlof, permissie; afslag; vergunning, toelating; toegewendheid; toelae; speelruimte; korreksie (by skiet); *MAKE* ~ *for,* in aanmerking neem; *WEEKLY* ~, weekgeld.
all'oy, (n) (-s), vermenging, mengsel; allooi, legering; gehalte, kwaliteit; alliasie; ~ *of COINS,* muntgehalte.
alloy', (v) meng; verslegt; temper; matig; legeer.
all'oy metal, legeermetaal.
all'-powerful, almagtig, oppermagtig.
all'-purpose, alsydig; meerdoelig.
all' right, pluis, goed, reg, in orde, in die haak, ôraait (geselst.).
all'-round, deur en deur; rondom; algeheel; veelsydig, alsydig; ~ **break,** alsydige seriestoot (biljart); ~ **er,** alsydige sportman; *be a good* ~ *er,* van alle markte tuis wees; ~ **player,** alsydige speler.
All' Saints' Day, Allerheilige(dag).
all'-seeing, alsiende.
all'spice, piment, wonderpeper, jamaikapeper, naelbol.
all'-star, net sterre; ~ **cast,** sterbesetting (rolprent, toneelstuk).
all'-steel body, staalbak.
all'-sufficiency, algenoegsaamheid.
all'-sufficient, algenoegsaam.

all'-time: ~ *high (low),* die hoogste (laagste) vir alle tye.
allude': ~ *to,* sinspeel op, doel op, verwys na.
allure', (n) aanloklikheid, aantreklikheid, sjarme; (v) lok, aanlok, verlok, uitlok, verlei; ~**ment,** aanloksel, verloklikheid, verleidelikheid; lokmiddel; bekoring, verlokking; ~**r,** verlokker.
allur'ing, verleidelik, aanloklik.
allu'sion, sinspeling, toespeling, skimp.
allu'sive, sinspelend, ryk aan toespelinge.
allu'sory, *kyk* **allusive.**
alluv'ial, (uit)gespoel, alluviaal, aangespoel; ~ **diamond,** spoeldiamant, alluviale diamant; ~ **diggings,** spoeldelwery, alluviale delwery; ~ **gold,** spoelgoud, alluviale goud; ~ **soil,** spoelgrond; alluvion.
alluv'ion, aanspoeling, aanspoelsel, (land)aanwas, aanslibbing, grondaanwas, vloed; opdrifsels, alluvie; alluvion.
alluv'ium, (-s, ..via), spoelgrond, aanslibsel, alluvium.
all'-wave, alle golflengtes.
all'weather, teen weer bestand, weervas; ~ **court,** weervaste tennisbaan.
All'-Wise, (die) Alwyse.
all'y¹, (allies), (groot) albaster, ellie.
ally'², (n) (allies), bondgenoot; *the Allies,* die Geallieerdes; (v) (allied), verbind, verenig; *allied by MARRIAGE,* verswaer, aangetroud; *allied WITH,* gepaard met, saam met.
Alma Mat'er, alma mater.
al'manac, almanak, kalender.
al'mandine, rooi granaat, almandien.
almi'ghtiness, almag, almoëndheid.
Almi'ghty: *the* ~, die Almagtige, die Allerhoogste.
almi'ghty, almagtig, almoënd, vrymagtig; kolossaal, tamaai; *an* ~ *pain,* 'n verskriklike pyn.
alm'ond, amandel; ~ **cream,** amandelroompie; ~ **custard,** amandelvla; ~ **emulsion,** amandelmelk; ~ **essence,** amandelolie; ~ **paste,** marsepein, amandelvulsel; ~ **rock,** banket, amandelklont; ~**-shaped,** amandelvormig; ~**-stone,** amandelpit.
al'moner, aalmoesenier, aalmoesgewer.
al'monry, aalmoeseniershuis, aalmoeshuis.
al'most, amper, byna, haas, bykans; ~ *but not quite,* amper maar nog nie stamper nie.
alms, aalmoes, liefdegawe; ~**-box,** aalmoeskassie; offerbussie; armbussie; ~ **house,** ouetehuis; armegestig.
almucan'ter, almacan'tar, almukantar, almakantar, hoogtesirkel.
al'noite, alnoïet.
al'oe, aalwyn, aalwee; ~ **bag,** aalwynsak.
aloet'ic, aalwyn-, aalweeagtig.
aloft', hoog, bo, omhoog; na bo.
alo'gical, alogies, onlogies.
alo'ha, aloha.
al'oin, aloïen, aalwynbitter.
alone', alleen, eensaam; net; enkel; *ALL* ~, stokalleen; stoksielalleen; moedersielalleen; *BE* ~, houtpop sit; *let* ~ *the EXPENSE,* om nie van die onkoste te praat nie; *LEAVE* ~, alleen laat, afbly; *QUITE* ~, moedersielalleen.
along', langs; deur; vooruit; voort; met; aan; *ALL* ~, aldeur, die hele tyd; *GET* ~, vooruitkom, aangaan; ~ *WHICH,* waarlangs; ~ *WITH,* saam met; ~**ship,** langsskeeps; ~**side,** naas, langsaan.
aloof', ver, op 'n afstand; opsy, apart, gereserveerd, afsydig; afgemete; *stand* ~, hom buite (op 'n afstand) hou; ~**ness,** gereserveerdheid, afsydigheid, teruggetrokkenheid.
alope'cia, kaalheid, kaalsiekte.
aloud', hardop, luid; *think* ~, hardop dink.
alp, bergtop; *the Alps,* die Alpe.
alpac'a, skaapkameel, alpakka; alpakkawol, lamawol; ~ **suit,** alpakkapak, witpak.
alparga'ta, (~ s), alpargata, espadril.
al'pen: alpe-; ~**glow,** alpegloed; ~**horn,** alpehoring; ~**stock,** alpestok.
al'pha, alfa; begin; *A* ~ *and OMEGA,* die alfa en die omega, die begin en die end.
al'phabet, abc, alfabet.

alphabet'ical, alfabeties; ~ly, in alfabetiese volg=
orde.
alphabetiza'tion, alfabetisering.
al'phabetize, alfabetiseer.
al'pha: ~me'ric, ~ nume'rical, alfameries, alfanume=
ries; ~ **particles**, alfadeeltjies; ~ **ray**, alfastraal.
Al'pine, Alpe=, Alpinies, Alpyns; ~ *flora*, Alpeflora.
al'pinist, alpinis, bergklimmer.
Alps, (die) Alpe.
alread'y, al, reeds, alreeds.
Alsace', (die) Elsas; ~**-Lorraine**, Elsas-Lotharinge.
Alsa'tia = **Alsace**.
Alsa'tian, (n) Elsasser; Wolfhond; (a) Elsassies.
al'sike (clover), basterklawer, alsike(klawer).
al'so, ook; eweneens, insgelyks; ~**-ran**, swak mede=
dinger, agterruiter.
alt = **alto**.
al'tar, altaar; *AT the* ~, voor die preekstoel; *HIGH*
~, hoogaltaar; ~ *of INCENSE*, reukaltaar;
LEAD to the ~, na die altaar voer, trou; ~**-boy**,
altaarknaap; ~**-bread**, altaarbrood, ouel; ~**-card**,
kanonbord; ~**-cloth**, altaarkleed; ~**-piece**, altaar=
skildery; ~**-rail**, kommuniebank; ~**-slab**, ~**-
stone**, altaarsteen.
alta'zimuth, altasimut, sterhoogtemeter.
al'ter, verander; wysig; verbou (huis); vermaak, ver=
stel (klere); vertimmer; *that cannot* ~ *the CASE*,
dit sal daar niks aan toe- of aandoen nie; ~ *one's
MIND*, van gedagte (mening) verander; ~**abil'ity**,
veranderlikheid; veranderbaarheid; ~**able**, veran=
derlik; veranderbaar.
altera'tion, verandering, wysiging; verbouing (huis);
~ *IN*, wysiging in; ~ *TO*, wysiging tot; ~ **hand**,
verstelwerker.
al'terative, (n) alteratief; (a) wysigend, veranderend.
al'tercate, twis, rusie maak, kibbel, woorde wissel.
alterca'tion, twis, rusie, woordewisseling, woorde=
stryd, krakeel.
alter eg'o, alter ego, jou ander ek, tweede ek.
altern'ate, (n) plaasvervanger, (a) afwisselend, alter=
natief; *on* ~ *days*, al om die ander dag.
al'ternate, (v) afwissel, omwissel, verwissel.
altern'ate: ~ **angle**, wisselhoek; ~ **husbandry**, wis=
selbou; ~**ly**, om die beurt, beurtelings, afwisse=
lend.
al'ternating, afwisselend; ~ **current**, wisselstroom;
~ **winds**, wisselwinde.
alterna'tion, afwisseling, alternering.
altern'ative, (n) keus, keuse, een van twee, alternatief;
uitweg; ~ *CHARGE*, alternatiewe aanklag; *we
HAD no* ~ *but* . . ., daar het vir ons niks anders
oorgebly nie as . . .; *IN the* ~, anders, so nie; *the
ONLY* ~, die enigste uitweg; (a) afwisselend; an=
der, alternatief; ~**ly**, so nie, anders; of.
al'ternator, alternator, wisselstroomdinamo.
alt'horn, althoring.
although', alhoewel, hoewel, ofskoon.
alt'igraph, altigraaf.
altim'eter, hoogtemeter, altimeter.
altim'etry, hoogtemeting, altimetrie.
al'tiscope, altiskoop.
altis'onant, hoogdrawend.
al'titude, hoogte; diepte; ~ **angle**, dieptehoek; ~
control, hoogtereëlaar; ~ **flight**, hoogtevlug; ~ **re=
cord**, hoogterekord; ~ **throttle**, hoogteversneller.
altitud'inal, hoogte=.
altitudinar'ian, hoogswewer.
al'to, alt tweede stem; ~ **clef**, altsleutel.
altocu'mulus, altocumulus, hoë cumulus(wolk).
altogeth'er, (n): *in the* ~, volkome naak; (adv) almal;
heeltemal, tesame, volkome, totaal, algeheel, alte=
gaar, altegader; (-s), alto-relievo; glad, skoon.
alto-relie'vo, (-s), alto-relievo, hoogreliëf, hoogrelief.
altostra'tus, altostratus.
al'to-viola, altviool.
altri'cial, (a), altrisieel, ouergevoed (voëls).
altrop'athy, meegevoel, medclyc, simpatic.
al'truism, altruïsme, naasteliefde, onselfsugtigheid.
al'truist, altruïs.
altruis'tic, altruïsties, onselfsugtig; ~ **ally**, altruïsties,
onselfsugtig.
alu'la, kleinvlerkie.

al'um, aluin; ~ **earth**, aluinaarde.
alum'ina, aluinaarde, aluminiumoksied.
aluminif'erous, aluinhoudend.
alum'inize, aluminiseer.
alumin'ium, aluminium; ~ **foil**, bladaluminium; ~
paint, aluminiumverf; ~ **paper**, aluminiumpapier;
~ **ware**, aluminiumware; ~ **wire**, aluminiumdraad.
alumin'othermy, aluminotermie.
alum'inous, aluinagtig.
alum'nus, (. . ni), alumnus, oud-leerling, oud-student;
~ **society**, alumnivereniging, oud-studentevereni=
ging.
al'umstone, aluinsteen, aluniet.
al'unite, aluniet, aluinsteen.
aluta'ceous, leerkleurig; leeragtig.
aluta'tion, looiery.
alve'olar, tandkas=, alveolêr; ~ **sound**, alveolêre
klank.
alve'olus, (. . li), alveolus, tandkas; tandholte; klier=
sakkie; longblasie.
al'veus, kom; trog.
al'ways, altyd, altoos, gedurig, deurentyd, te alle tye,
steeds, aljimmers; ~ **late**, altyd laat.
a'lyssum, alyssum.
am, *kyk* **be**.
amaas', pokke; amaas, alastrim.
amadavat', Indiese sangvoël.
am'adou, tontel.
amain', uit alle mag; haastig.
amala'ita, amalaita; ~ **gang**, amalaitabende.
amal'gam, amalgaam, metaalmengsel.
amal'gamate, (v) meng, verbind, amalgameer, saam=
smelt; (a) mengsel=, gemeng; ~ **language**, mengel=
taal.
amalgama'tion, samesmelting, amalgamasie, men=
ging.
amal'gam-filling, amalgaamvulsel.
amal'gamist, amalgamis.
amanuen'sis, (. . enses), (af)skrywer, sekretaris,
amanuensis.
am'arant(h), amarant; purper; ~ **ine**, amarantagtig,
onverwelkbaar.
amaryll'is, amarillis, amaril, narsinglelie.
am'asette, paletmes; tempermes.
amass', ophoop, versamel, vergaar, bymekaarmaak;
~ **riches**, skatte versamel.
am'ateur, liefhebber, amateur, dilettant; beginner; ~
concert, liefhebberykonsert.
amateur'ish, amateurs=, soos 'n amateur, dilettanties;
beginners=; amateuragtig; ~ **ness**, geliefhebber, di=
lettanterigheid.
a'mateurism, amateurisme; liefhebbery.
am'ateur: ~ **match**, amateurwedstryd; ~ **theatre**,
amateurteater; ~ **theatricals**, amateurtoneel.
am'ative, verliefderig; ~ **ness**, verliefderigheid.
am'atol, amatol, springstof.
am'atory, verlief, liefdes=; eroties.
amauro'sis, amaurose, gesigsverlies.
amaze', verbaas, dronkslaan, verwonder, verstom;
~ **d**, ontsteld, dronkgeslaan, verbaas; ~ **ment**, ver=
basing, verstomming.
ama'zing, verbasend, wonderlik.
Am'azon, Amasone(rivier); **a** ~, amasone, heldin;
mannetjiesvrou.
amazon'ian, amasoneagtig; strydbaar.
amaz'onite, amasonesteen, amasoniet.
amba'ges, kronkelpaaie; wydlopigheid.
ambass'ador, ambassadeur, gesant; ~**-extraor'di=
nary**, buitengewone gesant; . . **do'rial**, gesants=; ~**-
plenipotentiary**, gevolmagtigde gesant; ~**'s resi=
dence**, ambassadeurswoning.
ambass'adress, (-es), ambassadrise.
am'batch, ambatsj(boom).
am'ber, (n) amber, barnsteen; amberkleur; (a) amber=
kleurig; geel (lig); ~**-coloured**, amberkleurig;
~ **gris**, ambergrys, grys amber; ~ **ite**, amberiet; ~
pipe, barnsteenpyp; ~ **stem**, ambersteel (pyp).
ambidex'ter, **ambidex't(e)rous**, vaardig met albei
hande, dubbelhandig, ambidekster; dubbelhartig.
ambidexte'rity, ambideksteriteit, dubbelhandigheid;
dubbelhartigheid.
ambidex'trous = **ambidexter**; ~**ness**, ambidekstrie.

am'bient, omringend; ~ *temperature,* omringende temperatuur.
ambigu'ity, (..ties), dubbelsinnigheid.
ambig'uous, dubbelsinnig; twyfelagtig, duister, onduidelik.
am'bit, omvang, grense, bestek, omtrek; werkkring; uitgebreidheid; omgewing.
ambi'tion, eersug; ambisie; heerssug, eergierigheid, eersoekerigheid; doel.
ambi'tious, heerssugtig, eersugtig, eergierig, eersoekerig; ambisieus; vooruitstrewend; groots, pretensieus; ~**ness,** eersoekerigheid, ambisie, eersugtigheid, vooruitstrewendheid.
ambi'valence, ambi'valency, tweewaardigheid, ambivalensie; dubbelsinnigheid.
ambiv'alent, tweeslagtig, tweewaardig; dubbelsinnig.
ambiver'sion, ambiversie.
am'bivert, (~**s),** ambivert.
am'ble, (n) gang, telgang, pasgang; (v) 'n gang loop, 'n pasgang loop, op 'n gangetjie voortgaan, aftrippel; ~**r,** gangloper, pasganger, telganger.
am'bling, voortgang, voortstap, aanstap.
amblyo'pia, ambliopie, gesigsverswakking.
am'bo, (~**s),** ambo, preekstoel.
amboyna, amboina (hout).
ambro'sia, godespys, ambrosyn, ambrosia; ~**l,** ambrosies, heerlik, goddelik; welriekend.
ambs-ace', dubbele aas; teenspoed.
am'bulance, ambulans, veldhospitaal; ~**-aircraft,** ambulansvliegtuig; ~ **box,** noodhulpkas; ~**-man,** baardraer, hospitaalsoldaat; ~**-plane,** ambulansvliegtuig; ~ **room,** ambulanskamer.
am'bulant, trekkend, rondreisend, ambulant; niebedlêend.
am'bulate, rondtrek; rondloop.
am'bulator, afstandsmeter; meetwiel; ~**y,** (n) loopgang; (a) rondgaande, verplaasbaar, trekkend, wandelend, ambulant.
ambuscade', (n) hinderlaag; (v) in hinderlaag lê.
am'bush, (n) (-es), hinderlaag; strik; *LAY an* ~, 'n val stel; *LIE in* ~, in hinderlaag lê, voorlê, jou verdek opstel; (v) in hinderlaag lê; 'n val stel.
ame'ba = amoeba.
ameer', emir.
amel'iorate, verbeter, versag.
ameliora'tion, verbetering, veredeling, versagting.
amel'iorative, versagting; noodlenigend, noodlenigings=, verbeterend; ~ **meaning,** amelioratiewe (versagtende) betekenis.
amen', amen; *say* ~ *to everything,* op alles ja en amen sê.
amenabil'ity, geseglikheid, vatbaarheid.
amen'able, verantwoordelik; geseglik, vatbaar; ~ *to,* verantwoording skuldig aan; vatbaar vir; ~ **ness = amenability.**
amend', verbeter, amendeer; wysig; ~*ing act,* wysigingswet; ~ **able,** verbeterbaar.
amende honora'ble, (F.), amende honorable, openbare erkenning van skuld en apologie.
amend'ment, verbetering; wysiging, amendement; gewysigde voorstel; ~ *to (an act),* wysiging van ('n wet).
amends', vergoeding, vergelding; *make* ~, dit goedmaak (vergoed).
amen'ities, beleefdhede; geriewe, fasiliteite, genietings, genoëens; ~ *of life,* lewensgenietinge.
amen'ity, aantreklikheid, innemendheid; gerief, fasiliteit.
amenorrhoe'a, amenorrhe'a, amenorree, menstruasie-afwesigheid.
ament'[1]**,** ament(um), swaksinnige, imbesiel.
ament'[2]**,** amentum, blomkatjie.
amen'tia, amentia, verstandelooseid, imbesiliteit, swaksinnigheid.
amen'tum = ament[2]**.**
amerce', beboet, (be)straf; ..ciable, beboetbaar, strafbaar; ~**ment,** beboeting; boete.
Ame'rica, Amerika; ~**n,** (n) Amerikaner; (a) Amerikaans; ~*n BLIGHT,* bloedluis; ~*n SADDLE HORSE,* Amerikaanse saalperd.
Americana, Americana.
Amer'icanism, Amerikaanse taaleie, Amerikanisme.

Amer'icanization, Amerikanisering.
Ame'ricanize, veramerikaans, amerikaniseer.
Amerind', Amerin'dian, (n) Indiaan, Rooihuid; Eskimo; (a) Indiaans.
ameri'cium, amerikium.
ames-ace' = ambs-ace.
ames'ite, amesiet.
am'ethyst, ametis; purper; ~**-coloured,** ametiskleurig.
amet'ria, ametrie.
Amhar'ic, Amharies.
amiabil'ity, minsaamheid, beminlikheid, vriendelikheid, aanvalligheid.
am'iable, (be)minlik, lief, lieftallig, vriendelik, aanminlik, aanminnig, aanvallig; *an* ~ *mien,* 'n aanvallige (vriendelike) voorkoms; ~**ness,** (be)minlikheid.
amian't(h)us, amiantus, mineraalasbes.
amicabil'ity, vriendelikheid, vriendskaplikheid.
am'icable, vriendelik, minlik, amikaal; ~**ness,** vriendskaplikheid, vriendelikheid, aangenaamheid.
am'ice[1]**,** amictus, skouerdoek (R.K.).
ami'ce[2]**,** (L.), vriend, amice.
amicus cu'riae, (L., law), amicus curiae, vriend van die hof.
amid' = amidst.
a'mide, amied, amide.
a'midone, amidoon, metadoon.
amid'ships, in die middelskip, midskeeps.
amid(st)', te midde van, onder, tussen.
a'mine, amien, amine.
amin'o-acid, aminosuur.
amir = ameer.
A'mish, Amish (religieuse sekte).
amiss', verkeerd, uit die haak; onvanpas; kwalik; *not COME* ~, van pas wees; *NOT* ~, van pas; *there is SOMETHING* ~, daar is 'n steek aan los; daar haper iets aan; *TAKE* ~, kwalik neem; iets ten kwade dui; *WHAT is* ~?, wat makeer?
am'ity, vriendskap, vriendskaplikheid.
am'meter, ammeter, ampèremeter, stroommeter.
am'mo, (colloq.), ammunisie, skietgoed.
ammon'ia, ammoniak; ~**c,** ammoniak=; ..i'acal, ammoniakagtig; ~**-poisoning,** ammoniakvergiftiging; ~ **water,** ammoniakwater.
am'monite, ammoniet, slangsteen; ammonshoring.
ammo'nium, ammonium.
ammuni'tion, ammunisie, skietgoed, skietvoorraad, patrone; ~ **boot,** soldateskoen, soldatestewel; ~ **bread,** klinkers, soldatebrood; ~ **factory,** (am)munisiefabriek, wapenfabriek, patroonfabriek; ~ **leg,** vals been; ~ **magazine,** (am)munisiemagasyn.
amnes'ia, geheuverlies, amnesie.
am'nesty, vergifnis, begenadiging, amnestie; *grant an* ~, amnestie verleen.
am'nion, (..nia), vrugbekleedsel; binne(n)ste eiervlies; lamsvlies.
amniot'ic, vrugbekledend; ~ *fluid,* vrugwater.
amoeb'a, (-e, -s), amebe.
amoebi'asis, amebiase.
amoeb'ic, amebies; ~ *dysentery,* amebedisenterie, amebiese disenterie.
amoeb'oid, (n) ameboïed; (a) amebeagtig; amebevormig, amebies.
amok' = amuck.
amo'ng(st), onder, tussen, by; *they had seven CENTS* ~ *them,* hulle het alles tesaam sewe sent gehad; *FROM* ~ *them,* uit hulle; *one* ~ *MANY,* een van baie; ~ *OTHERS,* onder andere; ~ *OURSELVES,* onder ons; ~ *THESE,* hieronder.
amontilla'do, (Sp.), amontillado, (droë) sjerrie.
amo'ral, nie-sedelik, amoraal; amoreel; ~**ism,** amoralisme; ~**'ity,** amoraliteit.
am'orist, meisiegek, vrouejagter.
amoro'so, (Sp.), amoroso, soet sjerrie.
am'orous, verlief, liefdes=, minne=, amoreus; vryerig; ~**ness,** verliefdheid, verlieferigheid.
amor'phism, vormloosheid, amorfisme.
amor'phous, vormloos, amorf; ~**ness,** vormlooosheid, amorfie.
amortiza'tion, skulddelging, amortisasie; ~ **fund,** delgingsfonds.

amort'ize, afbetaal, amortiseer, delg, aflos.
am'osite, amosiet, grys asbes.
amount', (n) bedrag, som; hoeveelheid; opbrings; *CONSIDERABLE* ~, taamlike hoeveelheid; *any* ~ *of MONEY*, volop geld, geld soos bossies; *TO the* ~ *of*, tot die bedrag van; (v) bedra, beloop, uitwerk op; beteken; *it* ~ *s to the SAME thing*, dit kom op dieselfde neer; dit staan daarmee gelyk; *that is WHAT it* ~ *s to*, dit is waarop dit te staan kom; daarop kom dit neer.
amour', amour, minnary, liefdesavontuur.
amourette', liefdesavontuurtjie, minnarytjie, amourette.
amour prop're, (F.), amour propre, selfdunk; ydelheid.
amp, (-s) ampère.
ampelog'raphy, ampelografie.
ampelop'sis, ampelopsis, klimplant.
am'perage, stroomsterkte, ampèretal.
am'pere, ampère.
am'peremeter, ampero'meter, (elektriese) stroommeter, ampèremeter, ammeter.
am'persand, ampersand, &-teken.
amphet'amine, amfetamine, amfetamien, ~ **sulphate,** amfetamiensulfaat, benzedrine.
amphib'ia, tweeslagtige diere, amfibieë; ~ **n,** (n) amfibie, tweeslagtige dier; amfibievliegtuig; (a) tweeslagtig, amfibies.
amphibiolo'gical, amfibiologies.
amphibiol'ogy, amfibiologie.
amphib'ious, tweeslagtig, amfibies, halfslagtig; ~ **ness,** halfslagtigheid.
am'phibole, amfibool.
amphib'olite, amfiboliet.
amphibol'ogy, dubbelsinnigheid, amfibologie.
amphib'olous, amfibolies.
amphibrach', amfibrag; ~ **ic,** amfibraggies.
amphic'tyon, amfiktion.
amphi'gamous, (bot.) amfigaam, sonder geslagsorgane.
am'phipod, amfipode, tweevoetsoortige.
am'phitheatre, amfiteater; strydperk.
amphitheat'rical, amfiteatersgewyse.
am'phora, (-e) amfora, vaas met twee handvatsels, pul.
am'ple, breed(voerig), wyd; ruim; oorvloedig, oorgenoeg; uitvoerig; ~ **ness,** ruimheid; oorvloedigheid; breedvoerigheid.
amplifica'tion, uitbreiding; vergroting, aanvulling, versterking; verduideliking, uitweiding; ampliasie (jur.); amplifikasie.
am'plifier, uitbreider, vergroter; versterker.
am'plify, (..fied), uitbrei; toelig; versterk; vergroot, amplifiseer; ~ *ing valve*, versterkerlamp.
am'plitude, uitgestrektheid, omvang; uitwyking, oorvloedigheid; slingerwydte, trilwydte; prag, heerlikheid; ~ **modulation,** amplitudemodulasie.
am'ply, ruimskoots, volop, ruim.
am'poule, ampul.
amp'meter, stroommeter, ampèremeter.
ampull'a, (-e) pul, kannetjie met twee ore; sakkie; ampul.
am'putate, afsit, afsny, amputeer.
amputa'tion, afsitting, afsetting, afsnyding, amputasie.
Am'sterdam, (n) Amsterdam; (a) Amsterdams.
amuck', amok; *run* ~, amok maak, soos 'n rasende te kere gaan; hand-uit ruk.
am'ulet, amulet, towerkragtige voorwerp (om rampspoede af te weer); geluksteentjie, toorhoutjie.
amuse', vermaak, verstrooi, amuseer; besig hou; ~ *oneself*, jou besig hou, jou vermei (in), die tyd verdryf; ~ **ment,** vermaak, tydverdryf, vermaaklikheid, amusement, verstrooiing; ~ **ment park,** pretpark.
amus'ing, amus'ive, vermaaklik, onderhoudend, snaaks, amusant.
amyg'dale, amandel.
amygdal'ic, amandel-.
amyg'daline, amandelagtig.
amygdali'tis, mangelontsteking.
amyg'daloid, (n) amandelsteen; (a) amandelvormig; ~ **al,** amandelsteenvormig.

amyg'dule, amandel (geol.).
am'yl, amiel.
amyla'ceous, setmeelagtig.
am'ylase, amilase.
am'yloid, setmeel, amiloïed, amiloïde.
amylop'sin, amilopsien, amilopsine.
am'ylose, amilose.
amyl'um, setmeel, stysel.
an, 'n; *kyk ook* **a.**
an'a, (-s), versameling van gesegdes en anekdotes; segswyses, skinderpraatjies oor iemand.
anabap'tism, wederdoop, anabaptisme.
Anabap'tist, Wederdoper, Anabaptis.
Anabaptist'ic(al), Wederdopers-, Anabaptisties.
a'nabas, anabas, varswatervis.
ana'basis, anabasis, landtog, landopmars.
anabat'ic, anabaties, stygend; ~ **wind,** stygwind.
anabio'sis, anabiose, lewensterugkeer.
anabol'ic, opbouend, anabolies.
anab'olism, anabolisme, weefselopbou.
anacathar'tic, vomeermiddel.
anach'orite, anachoreet.
anachron'ic, anachronisties; uit die tyd.
anach'ronism, anachronisme, tydteenstrydigheid.
anachronis'tic, anachronisties.
anaclas'tics, straalbrekingsleer.
anaclin'ic, anaklien.
anacoluth'on, anakoloet.
anacon'da, luislang, anakonda.
anacreon'tic, (n) anakreontiese gedig; (a) anakreonties.
anacro'tic, anakroties; ~ **pulse,** hefpols.
anad'romous, trekkend (vis).
anaem'ia, bloedarmoede, bleeksug, anemie; *pernicious* ~, kwaadaardige bloedarmoede.
anaem'ic, bloedarm, bleeksugtig, anemies.
ana'erobe, anaërobiont, anaëroob.
anaerob'ian, anaëroob.
anaeroh'ic, anaërobies.
anaerobio'sis, anaërobiose.
anaesthes'ia, gevoelloosheid, ongevoeligheid; anestesie, verdowing, narkose; *GENERAL* ~, algehele verdowing; *LOCAL* ~, plaaslike verdowing.
anaesthet'ic, (n) verdowingsmiddel; *under an* ~, onder narkose; (a) ongevoelig; anesteties, verdowend.
anaes'thetist, anestetikus, narkotiseur.
anaes'thetize, gevoelloos maak, verdoof, anesteseer, onder narkose bring, doodspuit.
an'aglyph, anaglief, stereoskopiese prent.
anagno'risis, anagnorise, ontknoping, dénouement.
anago'ge, allegoriese vertolking, anagoge.
anago'gy, mistieke uitleg.
an'agram, anagram, letterkeer, letteromsetting.
anagrammat'ic, anagrammaties.
an'al, anaal.
analec'ta, an'alects, bloemlesing, analekte.
analep'tic, (n) versterkmiddel; (a) versterkend, analepties.
analges'ia, ongevoeligheid (vir pyn), analgesie.
analges'ic, pynstillend; ~ *balm*, pynstillende balsem, verdowingsbalsem.
a'nalog = analogue.
analog'ic(al), analogies, ooreenkomstig, gelykvormig.
anal'ogize, gebruik maak van analogie, analogiseer.
anal'ogous, ooreenkomstig, gelykvormig, analoog; gelyknamig.
an'alogue, ooreenkomstige vorm, analoog; ~ **computer,** analoogrekenaar.
anal'ogy, gelykvormigheid, analogie, ooreenstemming; *on the* ~ *of*, na analogie van.
analphabete', analfabeet, ongeletterde.
analphabet'ic, nie-alfabeties.
an'alysable, ontleedbaar, ontbindbaar; oplosbaar.
an'alyse, ontleed; oplos; analiseer; krities ondersoek; ~ **r,** ontleder.
ana'lysis, (analyses), ontleding, ontbinding, analise; oorsig; *in the final* ~, by die laaste ontleding; in laaste instansie.
an'alyst, ontleder; skeikundige; analis, analitikus.
analyt'ic, ontleedkundig, analities, ontledend; ~ **ally (ly),** op ontleedkundige wyse; ~ **s,** ontleedkunde.

anamnes'is, herinnering; siektegeskiedenis, anamnese.
anamorph'ism, anamorfose.
anamorph'osis, anamorfose.
anamorph'ous, verkeerd; vervorm.
anan'as, pynappel, ananas.
anan'drous, sonder meeldrade, anandries.
Anani'as, Ananias; *be an* ~, 'n Ananias wees; almanakke druk; lekker lieg.
anan'thous, sonder blomme.
an'apaest, anapes.
anapaes'tic, anapesties.
anaph'ora, anafoor, anafora.
anapho'ric, anafories, anafoor; ~ **word,** anafoor, anaforiese woord.
anaphylac'tic, anafilakties.
anaphylax'is, anafilaksie.
anaphrodis'ia, geslagtelike onmag; geslagsonderdrukking.
anaphylac'tic, anafilakties.
anaphylax'is, anafilakse.
anaplasmos'is, galsiekte, anaplasmose.
anaplas'ty, plastiese chirurgie.
anapleros'is, opvulsel, anaplerose.
anaplerot'ic, anapleroties.
anapodic'tic, anapodikties.
anapty'xis, anaptiksie, vokaalinvoeging.
an'arch, oproerleier, anargis.
anarch'ic(al), regeringloos; anargisties, wetteloos, ordeloos.
an'archism, wetteloosheid, anargie.
an'archist, anargis, oproermaker.
anarchis'tic, anargisties.
an'archy, regeringloosheid; anargie, wetteloosheid, wanorde.
anar'throus, gewrigloos, geleedloos, ongeleed.
anasar'ca, watersug.
anastat'ic, anastaties, in reliëf.
anastig'mat, (n) anastigmaat.
anastigmat'ic, (a) anastigmaties.
anastomose', (w), vertak, inmond.
anastomos'is, anastomose, inmonding.
anas'trophe, anastrofe.
anatase', anataas.
anatex'is, anateksis.
anath'ema, banvloek, banbliksem, ban, vervloeking, anatema; ~ **tize,** vervloek, in die ban doen.
Anato'lia, Anatolië; ~ **n,** (n) Anatoliër; (a) Anatolies.
anatom'ical, ontleedkundig, anatomies.
anat'omist, ontleedkundige, anatoom.
anat'omize, ontleed, anatomiseer; **..tomy,** ontleedkunde, ontleding; geraamte; bou, anatomie; liggaam; maer kraai.
an'cestor, voorvader, stamvader, voorsaat; (pl) stamouers.
ances'tral, voorvaderlik, erf=.
an'cestress, (-es), voormoeder, voorouer (vroulik).
an'cestry, voorouers, afkoms, afstamming, geboorte.
anc'hor, (n) anker (skip); steun, toeverlaat, behoud; *AT* ~, voor anker; *COME to* ~, *DROP (cast)* ~, die anker laat val; *LIE at* ~, voor anker lê; *WEIGH* ~, die anker lig; (v) (vas)anker, veranker, vasmaak; ~ **age,** aanlêplek, ankerplek, klouplek; ankergeld; ankering; ~ **age-bracket,** ankersteun; ~ **age-cell,** ankersel; ~ **-bolt,** ankerbout; ~ **-buoy,** ankerboei; ~ **-cable,** ankerkabel; ~ **ed,** geanker.
anc'horess, (-es), kluisenares.
anc'horet, kluisenaar.
anc'hor: ~ **-fluke,** ankerblad; ~ **-ice,** grondys.
anc'horite = **anchoret.**
anc'hor: ~ **-ground,** ankerplek; ~ **-knot,** vissersteek, visserslag, seeslag; ~ **-lamp,** anker-lamp; ~ **-link,** ankerkabel; ~ **-mast,** meermas; ~ **-pin,** ankerpen; ~ **-plate,** ankerplaat; ~ **-ring,** ankerring; ~ **-rope,** ankertou; ~ **-watch,** ankerwag; ~ **-wire,** ankerdraad.
anchove'ta, ansjoveta.
an'chovy, anchov'y, ansjovis; ~ **paste,** ansjovissmeer; ~ **sandwich,** ansjovis(toe)broodjie; ~ **-toast,** ansjovisroosterbrood.
anchu'sa, anchusa.
ancien' regime', (F.), ancien regime, Ou Orde.

an'cient, oud; outyds, alou(d)e, ouderwets; bejaard; *the A* ~ *s,* die Ou Volke; ~ **history,** ou geskiedenis; ou storie (verhaal); outyds; ~ **ly,** van ouds, voorheen, eertyds; ~ **ry,** oudheid; ouderwetsheid; ~ **times,** ou tye, outyd, vervloë tye.
ancill'ary, ondergeskik, diensbaar; by=, hulp=.
an'con, ankon, kraagsteen.
and, en; *there are BOOKS* ~ *books,* daar is baie soorte boeke; *walk MILES* ~ *miles,* myle ver loop; *for MONTHS* ~ *months,* maande lank; *walk TWO* ~ *two,* twee-twee loop.
Andalu'sia, Andalusië, ~ **n,** (n) Andalusiër; (a) Andalusies.
andan'te, (It., mus.), andante, nie te vinnig nie.
An'derson shelter, skuilkeldertjie.
An'des: *the* ~, die Andes(gebergte).
an'diron, vuurbok, esyster, haardyster.
andou'ille sausage, andoelie.
an'drogyne, hermafrodiet, trassie.
androg'ynism, tweeslagtigheid, androginie (bot.).
androg'ynous, tweeslagtig, trassie=, androgien.
androg'yny, androginie, tweeslagtigheid.
an'ecdotage, anekdoties; praatsug (van ou mense).
anecdot'al, anekdoties.
an'ecdote, kort verhaal, anekdote.
anem'ogram, anemogram, windkaart.
anem'ograph, windwyser, anemograaf; ~ **y,** windbeskrywing, anemografie.
anemol'ogy, anemologie.
anemom'eter, windmeter.
anemom'etry, anemometrie.
anem'one, anemoon, windblom.
anemoph'ilous, anemofiel, windbestuif(de).
anemophob'ia, anemofobie.
anem'oscope, anemoskoop; wind(rigting)wyser.
anem'ovane, windvaan.
anent', aangaande, betreffende, nopens.
an'eroid, aneroïed, doosbarometer, aneroïedbarometer.
an'ethol, anetol.
aneur'in, aneurien, aneurine, vitamine B_1.
an'eurism, slagaargeswel, slagaarbult, aneurisme.
anew', opnuut, weer, nog eens, van nuuts af.
anfractuos'ity, bogtigheid, kronkeling; verdraaidheid, anfraktuositeit.
anfrac'tuous, kronkelend; ingewikkeld, vol bogte.
ang'ary, angarie.
an'gel, engel, hemelbode, hemeling, engeltjie; *AVENGING* ~, wraakengel; ~ *of DEATH,* doodsengel, verderfengel; ~ *of DESTRUCTION,* verderfengel; *ENTERTAIN an* ~ *unawares,* sonder om te weet 'n belangrike persoon help; *talk of an* ~ *and you hear the FLUTTER of wings,* praat van die duiwel, dan trap jy op sy stert; *there is an* ~ *PASSING over,* daar gaan weer 'n Jood hemel toe; daar gaan 'n predikant verby; ~ **cake,** silwersuikerbrood; ~ **-fish,** engelhaai.
angel'ic, engelagtig, engele=.
angel'ica, engelwortel.
angelol'atry, engeldiens, angelolatrie, engelaanbidding.
angelol'ogy, angelologie, engeleleer.
angeloph'any, engelofanie.
an'gel's food, vrugteslaai.
angel: ~ **-shark,** engelhaai; ~ **-shot,** kettingkoeël.
an'gelus, angelus, bedeklok.
an'gel worship, engeleverering.
ang'er, (n) kwaadheid, toorn, gramskap, verbolgenheid, gebelgdheid, drif, vergramdheid; (v) vertoorn, vererg, kwaad maak.
angin'a, keelsweer; angina, beklemming; ~ *pectoris,* angina pectoris, hartkramp.
angiog'raphy, aardbeskrywing, angiografie.
angiol'ogy, angiologie.
angiop'athy, angiopatie.
an'giosperm, bedeksadige, angiosperm; ~ **ous,** bedeksadig, angiosperm.
Ang'le, Angel.
an'gle, (n) hoek; haak; vishoek; gesigspunt, oogpunt; *ACUTE* ~, skerp hoek; *ADJACENT* ~, aangrensende hoek; *ALTERNATE* ~, wisselhoek; ~ *of APPROACH,* binnesweefhoek, aanvlieghoek, na-

deringshoek; ~ *of ASCENT (climb)*, styghoek; ~ *of BACKING*, steunhoek; ~ *of CIRCUMFER=ENCE*, omtrekshoek; ~ *of CLEARANCE*, vry=hoek; ~ *of CONTACT*, aanrakingshoek (geom.); omspanningshoek (mynw.); ~ *of CURVATURE*, buigingshoek; ~ *of DEFLECTION*, afwykings=hoek; *I look at the matter from a DIFFERENT* ~, ek beskou die saak uit 'n ander oogpunt; *DI=HEDRAL* ~, tweevlakshoek; ~ *of INCIDENCE*, invalshoek; ~ *of INTERSECTION*, kruisings=hoek; (in)sny(dings)hoek; ~ *of MOVEMENT*, be=wegingshoek; *OBTUSE* ~, stomphoek; ~ *of RE=FLECTION*, uitvalshoek; ~ *of REFRACTION*, brekingshoek; ~ *of a SHOT*, hoek van 'n stoot (biljart); ~ *of SLOPE*, hellingshoek; (v) vis(vang), hengel; ~ *for a COMPLIMENT*, na 'n kompli=ment vis, komplimente uitlok; ~ *FOR*, hengel na.

an'gle: ~**-bar**, hoekstaaf, hoekstut; ~**-bead**, hoeklys; ~**-brace**, hoekstut; hoek(boor)omslag; hoekanker (houtw.); ~**-bracket**, hoekstut, hoeksteun; ~**-cleat**, hoekklamp; ~**-dividers**, hoekdeler; ~**-dozer**, skuinsstoter; ~**-gauge**, hoekmeter; ~**-hinge**, win=kelhaakskarnier; ~**-iron**, hoekyster; ~**-joint**, hoeklas; ~**-parking**, skuins parkering; ~**-piece**, hoekstuk; ~**-pipe**, hoekpyp; ~**-plane**, hoekstaaf; ~**-plate**, hoekplaat; ~**-post**, hoekpaal, hoekstyl.

an'gler, hengelaar, visvanger, visser, visserman, vis=terman; seeduiwel.

an'gle: ~**-rafter**, heupbalk; hoekkap(balk); ~ **sec=tion**, hoekprofiel, hoekdeursnee; ~**-smith**, hoekys=tersmid; ~ **standard**, hockpaal, ~**-stay**, hoek=anker; ~**-strut**, hoekstut; ~**-tie**, hoekanker.

An'gles: the ~, die Angele.
Ang'lican, (n) Anglikaan; (a) Anglikaans.
Ang'licism, Anglisisme, Engelsheid.
Angliciza'tion, verengelsing.
Ang'licize, verengels, angliseer.
ang'ling, hengelary, visvangs, hengel(sport); ~**-club**, hengelklub, hengelvereniging; ~ **competition**, hen=gelwedstryd, hengelkompetisie; ~**-fish**, hengelvis; ~**-rod**, visstok, hengelstok.

Ang'lo-, Engels, Anglo-; ~**-American**, Engels-Ame=rikaans, Anglo-Amerikaans; ~**-Boer War**, Tweede Vryheidsoorlog, Engelse Oorlog, Anglo-Boereoor=log, Boereoorlog.
Angloman'ia, Anglomanie, pro-Engelse gevoel; ~ **c**, Engelsgesinde.
Ang'lophil, Engelsgesind, Anglofiel.
Ang'lophobe, Engelsehater.
Anglophob'ia, Anglofobie, anti-Engelse gevoel, Engelschaat.
Anglo-Sax'on, (n) Angel-Sakser; (a) Angel-Saksies.
Ango'la, (n) Angola; (a) Angolees, Angools; ~ **pea**, Angola-ertjie, bambaragrondboontjie.
angor'a, angora, angorabok; ~ **cat**, angorakat; ~ **goat**, angorabok, sybok; ~ **rabbit**, angorakonyn; ~ **wool**, bokhaar, angorahaar.
angostur'a, angostura, bitter(s); ~ **bark**, angostura=bas, bitterbas; ~ **bitters**, (angostura)bitter(s).
ang'rily, kwaad, toornig.
ang'riness, kwaadheid, boosheid, toornigheid.
ang'ry, kwaad, boos, gramstorig, grimmig, driftig, toornig, vergram(d), verbolge; ~ *ABOUT*, boos om (oor); ~ *WITH*, die hamer in wees vir, kwaad vir.
Angst, (Germ.), angs, vrees.
ang'uine, slangagtig.
ang'uish, angs, foltering, smart, sielskwelling, (siele)= pyn, benoudheid.
ang'ular, hoekig, puntig; maer, hoekerig; ~ *AC=CELERATION*, hoekversnelling; ~ *DISTANCE*, boogafstand, hoekafstand; ~ *ERROR*, hoekfout; ~ *FEATURES*, skerp gelaatstrekke; ~ *FORCE*, draaikrag; ~ *LEAF-SPOT*, hoekvlek; ~ *MO=MENTUM*, hoekmoment; ~ *MOTION*, hoekbe=weging; ~ *ROTATION*, hoekwenteling; ~ *VEL=OCITY*, hoeksnelheid; ~ *WHEEL*, koniese rat.
angular'ity, hoekigheid, kantigheid.
angu'late, hoekig, gehoek; ~ *tortoise*, duinskilpad; bontskilpad.
anhed'ral, anhedries.
anhyd'ride, anhidried.
anhyd'rite, anhidriet.
anhyd'rous, watervry; waterloos, anhidries; ~ *COMPOUND*, watervrye verbinding; ~ *LIME*, ongebluste kalk.
anico'nic, anikonies.
anigh', (poet.), naby, digby.
an'il, aniel, indigo.
an'ile, kinds; ouvrouagtig; suf.
an'iline, anilien, aniline.
anil'ity, sufheid; kindsheid.
animadver'sion, opmerking; berisping, afkeuring, kritiek.
animadvert', kritiseer; opmerkings maak; bestraf, be=rispe, afkeur.
an'imal, (n) dier, bees; *the* ~ *kingdom*, die diereryk; (a) dierlik; vleeslik; sinlik; ~ **appetites**, vleeslike luste; ~ **charcoal**, beenkool.
animal'cule, mikroskopiese diertjie, animalkule, pro=tosoön.
an'imal: ~ **disease**, dieresiekte; ~**-drawn vehicle**, trekdiervoertuig, bespanne voertuig; ~ **fable**, dierefabel; ~ **husbandry**, veeteelt, ~**ism**, dierlik=heid, animalisme; sinlikheid.
animal'ity, dierlikheid, animaliteit; dierewêreld.
an'imalize, verdierlik, animaliseer.
an'imal: ~ **killer**, dieredoder; ~ **kingdom**, diereryk; ~ **life**, dierelewe; ~**-lover**, dierevriend; ~ **magne=tism**, hipnotisme, mesmerisme; ~ **nutrition**, diere=voeding; ~ **power**, trekdierkrag; ~ **saga**, diere=sage; ~ **science**, veekunde; ~ **spirits**, uitgelaten=heid; ~**-tamer**, dieretemmer; ~ **welfare**, dieresorg; ~ **worship**, dier(e)aanbidding.
ani'mate, (v) besiel, aanmoedig, bemoedig; aanwak=ker, opwek, beweeg; (a) lewendig; besield; ~ **d**, le=wendig, opgewek; besield, vurig; willig, lewendig (mark); ~ **d cartoon**, tekenprent; ~ **d film**, teken=film, tekenrolprent.
an'imating, lewewekkend.
anima'tion, besieling, aansporing, aanmoediging; le=wendigheid, animo; animasie (film).
an'imism, animisme.
an'imist, (n) animis, (a) animisties; ~ **'ic**, animisties.
animos'ity, verbittering, wrok; vyandigheid, vyand=skap, animositeit.
an'imus, gees, gesindheid, stemming; vyandigheid, wrewel.
an'ion, anioon; ~ **ic**, anionies.
an'ise, anys.
an'iseed, anyssaad; ~ **brandy**, anysbrandewyn; ~ **oil**, anysolie.
anisette', anyssopie, anyslikeur.
an'isol, anisol.
anisomet'ric, anisometries.
anisotrop'ic, anisotropies.
aniso'tropy, anisotropie, eolotropie.
An'kara, Ankara.
ank'er, anker (maat).
an'kle, enkel; onderbeen; ~**-boot**, stewel; ~**-deep**, tot aan die enkels; ~**-guard**, enkelskut, enkelskerm; ~**-joint**, enkelgewrig; ~**-length**, tot op (oor) die en=kels; ~ **t**, voetring, kort kamas; enkelverband.
ankylo'sis, ankilose, gewrigsverstywing.
ankylostomia'sis, ankilostomiase, haakwurmsiekte.
an'lace, steekmes.
ann'a, anna (sestiende deel van 'n roepee).
an'nalin, annalien, annaline; ~ **dye**, annalienkleur=stof, annalienkleursel.
ann'alist, kroniekskrywer.
ann'als, jaarboek, annale, kronieke, geskiedrol.
An'nam, An'am, Annam; ~ **ese'**, (n) Annamees, An=namiet; (a) Annamees, Annamities.
ann'ates, annate.
anna'to, kaaskleursel, annato.
anneal', uitgloei, temper; afkoel (glas na verhitting); ~**ing-box**, uitgloeikas; ~**ing-colour**, uitgloeikleur; ~**ing furnace**, koeloond; ~**-room**, boutery.
an'nelid(e), ringwurm, annelide, annelied.
annex', byvoeg, aanheg; annekseer, inlyf; ~ **a'tion**, aanhegting, inlywing, anneksasie; ~ **e**, bygebou, anneks; bylae.
annex'ure, bylae, aanhangsel.
anni'hilate, vernietig, verwoes, uitroei.

annihila'tion, vernietiging, uitroeiing, verdelging.
anni'hilator, verdelger, uitroeier, vernietiger.
annivers'ary, (n) (..ries), verjaar(s)dag; jaarfees; gedenkdag; (a) jaarliks; ~ **feast,** jaarfees; ~ **wind,** periodieke wind.
Anno Dom'ini, in die jaar van ons Heer.
ann'otate, aanteken, van aantekeninge voorsien, annoteer; verklarings skryf.
annota'tion, aantekening, opmerking; annotasie.
ann'otator, maker van aantekeninge; verklaarder.
announce', aankondig, aanmeld, aansê, afroep, bekend maak, verklaar, verkondskap; aandien; ~ **ment,** aankondiging, bekendmaking, aanseg-ging, melding; verklaring; aandiening (persoon); ~**r,** aankondiger, omroeper (radio); boodskapper.
annoy', lastig val, erg(er), hinder, pla, versondig, ontstig, tormenteer; neuk (plat); ~ **ance,** las, ergernis, gehaspel, geneuk (plat); ontstigting, hindernis, gegriefdheid; viesheid, mishae, neukery (plat); ~ **ed,** gegrief; *BE* ~ *ed,* kwaad (vies, gegrief) wees; *you're not EVEN* ~*ed!,* jy sing toe nie!; ~ **ing,** lastig, ergerlik, vervelig, hinderlik; tergagtig, tergerig.
ann'ual, (n) jaarboek, jaarblad; eenjarige plant; (a) jaarliks; eenjarig, jaar-; ~ **audit,** jaarlikse oudit; ~ **congress,** jaarlikse kongres; jaarkongres; ~ **crops,** jaargewasse; ~ **cycle,** jaarkring; ~ **fair,** jaarbeurs; ~ **financial statements,** finansiële jaarstate; ~ **fluctuation,** jaarlikse skommeling; ~ **general meeting,** algemene jaarvergadering; ~**ize,** op 'n jaarbasis bereken; ~**ly,** jaarliks; ~ **market,** jaarmark; ~ **meeting,** jaarvergadering; ~ **premium,** jaarpremie; ~ **rebate,** jaarkorting; jaarlikse korting; ~ **report,** jaarverslag; ~ **ring,** jaarring; ~ **salary,** jaarlikse salaris; ~ **subscription,** jaargeld; ~ **ticket,** jaarkaartjie.
annu'itant, gepensioeneerde, lyfrentenier, jaargeldtrekker.
annu'ity, (..ties), jaargeld, lyfrente, annuïteit; *deferred* ~, uitgestelde jaargeld; ~ **insurance,** annuïteitsversekering; ~ **tables,** annuïteittafels.
annul', (-led), vernietig; te niet doen; afskaf, ophef, herroep (wet).
ann'ular, ringvormig, ring-; ~ **eclipse,** ringverduistering; ~ **kiln,** ringoond; ~ **vessel,** ringvat; ~ **wheel,** binnetandrat.
annu'late(d), gering; ringvormig.
annula'tion, ringvorming.
ann'ulet, ringetjie.
annul'ment, nietigverklaring, vernietiging, opheffing, tenietdoening.
ann'uloid, ringvormig.
annu'lose, van ringe gevorm.
an'nulus, annulus, ring.
annun'ciate, aankondig, aanmeld.
annuncia'tion, aankondiging, verkondiging; boodskap; *A*~ *Day,* Mariaboodskap.
annun'ciator, boodskapper, verkondiger.
annus luc'tus, annus luctus, treurjaar.
annus mira'bilis, annus mirabilis, wonderjaar.
ano'a, anoa, wilde os.
an'ode, anode; positiewe pool (elektries); ~ *BATTERY,* anodespanningsbattery ~*-grid CAPACITY,* anoderoosterkapasiteit; ~ *CURRENT,* anodestroom; ~ *PART (piece, portion),* anodestuk; ~ *RAY,* anodestraal; ~ *RAY TUBE,* anodestraalbuis; ~-*voltage SUPPLY,* anodespanningsbron.
an'odyne, (n) pynstillende middel; (a) pynstillend.
anoe'sis, anoëse, sensasiebewussyn.
anoint', oliesel toedien; salf; ~ **ed,** (n) gesalfde; (a) gesalf; ~ **ing,** salwing; ~ **ing oil,** salfolie; ~ **ment,** salwing.
anomalis'tic, anomalisties, afwykend; ~ **month,** anomalistise maand; ~ **year,** anomalistiese jaar.
anom'alous, onreëlmatig, afwykend, abnormaal.
anom'aly, (..lies), onreëlmatigheid, afwyking, abnormaliteit, anomalie.
ano'mie, anomy, anomie, sosiale normversaking; ..'ic, anomies.
anon', binnekort, eerlank, netnou; *EVER and* ~, van tyd tot tyd; nou en dan; *TWO* ~*s and a by and by make half an hour,* van uitstel kom afstel.
an'onym, naamlose persoon, anonimus; skuilnaam.

anonym'ity, anonimiteit, naamloosheid.
anon'ymous, naamloos, anoniem; ~ *letter,* ongetekende (naamlose, anonieme) brief.
anoph'eles, anofeles, malariamuskiet.
a'norak, anorak, windbaadjie, parka.
anorec'tic, anorekties.
anore'xia, anoreksie, aptytverlies; ~ **nervosa,** anorexia nervosa, chroniese anoreksie.
anor'thosite, anortosiet.
anos'mia, reukverlies, anosmie.
anoth'er, 'n ander; nog een; *A.N. OTHER,* N.O.G. Een; *one AFTER* ~, een na die ander, agtereenvolgend; ~ *CUP of coffee,* nog 'n koppie koffie; *ONE* ~, mekaar; ~ *PLACE,* 'n ander plek, elders; *TAKEN one with* ~, deur die bank geneem; *one WITH* ~, gemiddeld.
anour'ous, stertloos (padda).
ano'vulant, anovulant, ovulasiebehoedmiddel.
anox(a)em'ia, suurstoftekort, anoksemie.
anox'ia, anoksie, versmoring.
an'schluss, anschluss, vereniging, inlywing.
an'serine, gansagtig; onnosel, dom; laf.
an'swer, (n) antwoord; oplossing; beskeid; verhoring (gebed); *IN* ~ *to,* in antwoord op; *KNOW all the* ~*s,* alle antwoorde ken, alle probleme kan oplos; ervaring hê; *have NO* ~ *for,* nie 'n antwoord op iets kan vind nie; nie weet hoe om iets te keer nie; *in* ~ *to PRAYER,* as gebedsverhoring; in antwoord op die gebed; *always have an* ~ *READY,* altyd 'n antwoord klaar hê; *not to have an* ~ *READY,* om 'n antwoord verleë wees; *SERVE someone with an* ~, iem. van 'n antwoord dien; (v) antwoord, beantwoord; hom verantwoord; instaan vir; boet vir; voldoen, voordeel afwerp; ooreenkom (met 'n beskrywing); ~ *BACK,* teëpraat; ~ *the BELL,* die deur oopmaak; iem. inlaat; ~ *to a CHARGE,* hom op 'n aanklag verantwoord; ~ *FOR,* verantwoord; ~ *a LETTER,* terugskrywe; 'n brief beantwoord; *have MUCH to* ~ *for,* heelwat op jou gewete hê, baie op jou boekie hê; baie op jou kerfstok hê; baie te verantwoord hê; ~ *no PURPOSE,* aan geen doel beantwoord nie; *I shall have to* ~ *for THAT,* dit kry ek nog op my dak; ~ **able,** verantwoordelik, aanspreeklik; geskik; beantwoordbaar; *be* ~ *able for something,* aanspreeklik wees vir iets; pa vir iets staan; ~ **er,** antwoorder; verhoorder (van gebed); ~ **ering,** beantwoording; ~ **ering service** antwoorddiens; boodskapdiens.
ant, mier; *go to the* ~, *thou sluggard,* gaan na die mier, jou luiaard; *have* ~*s in his pants,* miere hê.
antac'id, teensuur(middel); suurbinder.
antag'onism, vyandskap, stryd, teenstand, bestryding.
antag'onist, teenstander, teenparty, wederparty, bestryder, antagonis; teenspier.
antagonis'tic, vyandig; in stryd met, teenstrydig, strydig; ~ **ally,** vyandig, teenstrydig, strydig.
antag'onize, bestry, teëwerk; tot vyand maak, opstandig maak; in die harnas jaag.
antaphrodis'iac, antafrodities.
antarc'tic, suidelik; Suidpool-; *A*~ **a,** Antarktika; *A*~ **Circle,** Suidpoolsirkel; *A*~ **expedition,** Suidpoolekspedisie, Suidpooltog; *A*~ **explorer,** Suidpoolreisiger; *A*~ **navigator,** Suidpoolvaarder; *A*~ **ocean,** Suidelike Yssee; *A*~ **Pole,** Suidpool; *A*~ **regions,** Suidpoolstreke.
ant: ~**-bear,** erdvark, miervreter; ~**-destroyer,** miergif.
ante, (n) inset; (v) insit, (ver)wed.
ant: ~**-eating,** miervretend; ~**-eater,** miervreter; erdvark; ~**-eating chat,** swartpiek.
antebel'lum, vooroorlogs.
antecede', voorafgaan.
anteced'ence, voorrang.
anteced'ent, (n) antesedent; (pl) voorgeskiedenis; *his* ~*s,* sy verlede; (a) voorafgaande; ~ *river,* gehandhaafde rivier.
antecess'or, voorganger (in amp).
an'techamber, voorkamer; wagkamer.
antecha'pel, voorkapel.
antedate', vroeër dagteken, antedateer, vooruitdateer; vervroeg, verhaas.

antediluvian 703 *antimonarchic(al)*

antediluv'ian, voor die sondvloed, so oud soos die ark, antediluviaal, antediluviaans; *it is (looks)* ~, dit lyk of dit uit die ark gekom het; dit kom uit Noag se ark.
ant'-eggs, miereiers.
an'telope, wildsbok, antiloop.
antemerid'ian, voormiddag=.
antemun'dane, voorwêreldlik.
antenat'al, (van) voor die geboorte, voorgeboorte=; ~ *clinic,* kliniek vir aanstaande moeders.
antenn'a, (-e), antenne, lugdraad, vangdraad; voelhoring, voeler, spriet (van insek).
an'te mortem, ante mortem, voordoods; ~ *examination,* voordoodse ondersoek.
anten'nule, voelhorinkie; voelsprietjie.
antenup'tial, van voor die huwelik, huweliks=, antenupsiaal; ~ *contract,* huweliksvoorwaardekontrak.
antepen'dium, voorhangsel.
antepenult', antepenul'timate, derdelaaste, op twee na die laaste.
antepost', voor die wedren; ~ *bet,* voorweddenskap.
antepran'dial, van voor die ete.
anter'ior, voorafgaande, vroeër, voor.
anterio'rity, voorrang.
an'teroom, voorkamer; spreekkamer; wagkamer.
antes'ia bug, stinkvlieg.
ant'heap, miershoop.
anthel'ion, anthelium.
anthelmin'tic, (n) wurmmiddel; (a) wurmafdrywend.
an'them, koorsang; lofsang; *national* ~, volkslied.
anthe'mion, antemion, blommotief.
an'ther, meeldraad; helmknop; ~ *cell,* helmhok(kie); ~ *dust,* stuifmeel; ~ *mould,* helmknopskimmel.
ant'hill, miershoop, miernes.
anthol'ogy, (..gies), bloemlesing, (uitgesoekte) versameling.
an'thophyll, blaargeel.
an'thophyte, blomplant, antofiet.
anthozo'an, antosoön; koraal.
an'thracene, antraseen.
an'thracite, antrasiet, smeulkool, glanskool.
an'thracnose, anthracno'sis, swartroes (op druiwe), antraknose.
anthraco'sis, koolmyntering, antrakose.
an'thrax, bloedpuisie; negeoog; miltvuur, miltsiekte (by beeste), antraks.
anthropocen'tric, antroposentries.
anthropocen'trism, antroposentrisme.
anthropog'eny, ontwikkelingsleer v.d. mens, antropogenie.
anthrop'oglot, antropoglot.
anthropog'raphy, antropografie, rasverspreidingsleer.
an'thropoid, (n) antropoïed, antropoïede, mensaap; (a) menslik, mens=, antropoïed; ~ *ape,* mensaap.
anthropol'atry, antropolatrie.
anthrop'olite, fossielmens, antropoliet.
anthropolo'gic, antropologies, menskundig.
anthropol'ogist, antropoloog.
anthropol'ogy, menskunde, antropologie.
anthropomet'ric, antropometries.
anthropom'etry, antropometrie.
anthropomor'phic, menslik, antropomorfies.
anthropomor'phism, antropomorfisme.
anthropomor'phize, antropomorfiseer, vermenslik.
anthropomor'phous, antropomorfies.
anthropon'ymy, antroponomie, persoonsnaamkunde.
anthropop'athy, antropopatie.
anthropoph'agite, anthropoph'agus, antropofaag; menseter, mensvreter, kannibaal.
anthropo'phagy, antropofagie, kannibalisme, mensvretery.
anthropopho'bia, antropofobie, mensevrees.
anthroposo'phic(al), antroposofies.
anthroposo'phy, antroposofie.
anthropot'omy, antropotomie.
an'ti, anti, teen, strydig met.
anti-air'craft, lugafweer; ~ *artillery,* lugafweergeskut; ~ *ballistic missile,* antiballistiese missiel; ~ *battery,* lugafweerbattery; ~ *defence,* lugafweer; lugverdediging; ~ *gun,* lugafweergeskut; lugafweerkanon; ~ *protection,* lugbeskerming; ~ *searchlight,* lugafweersoeklig.
anti-apart'heid, anti-apartheid; ~ *measure,* anti-apartheidsmaatreël.
antibil'ious, galverdrywend.
antibio'sis, antibiose.
antibiot'ic, (n) (-s), antibiotikum; (a) antibioties; siektewerend.
an'tibody, teenstof, teenliggaam, antistof.
antibur'glar-wire, diefwering, diefdraad.
an'tic, (n) *kyk* **antics;** (a) snaaks, koddig, potsierlik.
antica'thode, antikatode.
antic'er, ysbestryder; ~ *pump,* sweetpomp.
an'tichlor, antichloor.
antichres'is, pandgenoot.
An'tichrist, Antichris.
antichris'tian, anti-Christelik.
anti'cipate, voorkom; voorspring, vooruitloop, verwag; voorsien; verhaas; ~ *payment,* voor die vervaldag betaal; betaling verwag.
anticipa'tion, voorgevoel, verwagting; voorsmaak; *BEYOND* ~, bo verwagting; *IN* ~, by voorbaat, vooruit; *in* ~ *OF,* in afwagting van; *POWER of* ~, voorgevoel; *THANKING you in* ~, by voorbaat dank.
anticipa'tory, vooruitlopend, verwagtend.
anticler'ical, (n, a), antiklerikaal; ~ *ism,* antiklerikalisme.
anticlimac'tic, antiklimakties.
an'ticlimax, antiklimaks.
anticlin'al, antiklinaal.
an'ticline, plooirug, antiklien, antikline.
anticlock'wise, links om, hot om, teen die wysers in, antikloksgewys(e).
anticoag'ulant, (n) stollingsteenmiddel, bloedstelpende middel; (a) stollingwerend.
anticonstitu'tional, strydig met die konstitusie, antikonstitusioneel.
An'ti-Convict-movement, Antibandietebeweging.
anticonvul'sant, stuipweerder, stuipwerende middel.
anti-corros'ive, (n) roeswerende middel, roesteenmiddel; (a) roeswerend.
anticreep', kruipwerend.
an'tics, grappe, klugte, kaskenades, kaperjolle, manewales.
anticy'clone, antisikloon, hoogdrukgebied, hoog.
anticyclon'ic, antisiklonaal.
anti-dazz'le, nie-verblindend.
antidemocrat'ic, antidemokraties.
antidepres'sant, (n), gemoedsverligter; opkikkeraar; (a) verligtend, opheffend; opkikkerend.
an'tidotal, gifwerend, as teengif.
an'tidote, teengif, antidoot.
anti-eme'tic, braakteenmiddel.
antifeb'rile, (n) koorsmiddel; (a) koorsverdrywend.
antifeb'rine, antifebrien.
an'tifreeze, vriesweerder, vrieswerende middel, antivries.
antifreez'ing, frieswerend.
antifric'tion, wrywingsvry; ~ *ball,* loopkoeël; ~ *metal,* witmetaal; laermetaal.
antifroth'ing, skuimwerend; ~ *agent,* skuimteenmiddel.
an'tigen, antigeen.
antigen'ic, antigeen, antigenies.
antiglare', skitterskerm.
an'ti-hero, antiheld, teenheld; papbroek, lafaard.
antihis'tamine, antihistamien, antihistamine.
anti-insur'gency, anti-insurgensie, teeninsurgensie; ~ *troops,* teeninsurgensietroepe.
an'tiknock, klopvry; klopwerend; ~ *AGENT,* klopweermiddel; ~ *FUEL,* klopvrye brandstof.
antilegom'ena, antilegomena.
antigen', antigeen.
antilitt'er-meeting, antirommelvergadering.
antilog'arithm, antilogaritme.
antil'ogy, teenstrydigheid, antilogie.
antimacass'ar, stoelkleedjie, antimakassar.
antimat'ter, antimaterie, teenmaterie.
antimonarc'hic(al), antimonargisties.

antimon'archism, antimonargisme.
antimon'archist, antimonargis.
antimon'ial, antimoonhoudend.
antim'onite, antimoonglans; antimoniet.
an'timonsoon, antimoeson.
an'timony, antimonium, antimoon, spiesglans.
antin'omy, teenstelling, teenstrydigheid, antinomie.
an'ti-novel, antiroman.
An'tioch, Antiochië.
antipap'al, strydig met die Roomse leer.
an'tiparticle, antipartikel, antideeltjie, teendeeltjie.
antipas'to, voorgereg, hors d'oevre.
antipathet'ic, antipaties, afstotend, weersinwekkend.
antip'athy, (..thies), natuurlike afkeer (van), teensin (in), weersin, antipatie.
anti-personnel', antipersoneel=; antimenslik; ~ **bomb**, mensdodende bom, personeelbom; ~ **mine**, mensdodende myn, personeelmyn.
antiper'spirant, (n) sweetweerder, sweetwerende middel; (a) sweetwerend.
antiphlo'gistic, koorsverdrywend.
antiphlo'gistine, antiflogistine.
an'tiphon, keervers, antifoon.
anti'phonal, antifonies.
antipho'nery, antifoonboek.
antiph'ony, (..nies), beurtsang, teensang, wisselsang, antifoon.
antip'odal, teenvoeter=; teengesteld, antipodies; ~ **triangle**, teëdriehoek.
antip'ode, teenvoeter; antipode.
an'tipole, teengestelde pool.
an'tipope, teenpous.
antipro'ton, antiproton.
antipyret'ic, (n) koorsweerder, koorswerende middel; (a) koorswerend, antipireties.
antipy'rine, antipirien, antipirine.
antiquar'ian, (n) oudheidkenner, antikwaar; antiekhandelaar; (a) oudheidkundig, antikwaries.
an'tiquary, (..ries), oudheidkundige, antikwaar; oudhedewinkel, antikwariaat.
an'tiquate, laat verouder, in onbruik bring; ~ **d**, verroes; verouderd, ouderwets, uit die ou doos; antikwaries.
antique', (n) antieke kunswerk; (a) ouderwets, antiek; ~ **dealer**, oudhedehandelaar, oudhedewinkel, antikwaar; ~ **gold** *(colour)*, geelgoud; ~ **ness**, oudheid, aloudheid; ~ **shop**, antiekwinkel, antikwariaat; oudhedewinkel.
antiq'uity, (..ties), die Oudheid, antikwiteit; ouderdom; (pl.) sedes en gewoontes van die Oudheid; oudhede; *in* ~, in die vroegste tyd.
antirat'tle, rammelwerend.
antiratt'ler, rammeldemper.
antireli'gious, antigodsdienstig, antireligieus.
antirepub'lican, antirepublikeins.
antirevolu'tionary, antirewolusionêr.
antirevolu'tionist, antirewolusionêr.
antiri'ot vehicle, onlustebeheervoertuig.
an'tiroll, rolwerend, kantelwerend.
an'tiroll bars, kanteldempers.
anti-roy'alist, antirojalis.
antirrhin'um, leeubekkie.
an'tirust, roeswerend.
antisabbatar'ian, antisabbatariër.
antiscorbut'ic, (n) middel teen skeurbuik; (a) skeurbuikwerend.
antiscrip'tural, onbybels, onskriftuurlik.
anti-Sem'ite, (n) anti-Semiet; (a) anti-Semities.
anti-Semit'ic, anti-Semities, anti-Joods.
anti-Sem'itism, anti-Semitisme.
antisep'sis, kiemwerende behandeling, antisepsis.
antisep'tic, (n) ontsmettingsmiddel, kiemdoder; (a) bederfwerend, kiemwerend, antisepties, ontsmettend; ~ **cream**, ontsmettingsroom; ~ **dressing**, ontsmettingsverband; ~ **lint**, ontsmettingslinne; ~ **plaster**, ontsmettingspleister.
a'ntiserum, antiserum, immuunserum.
an'tishine lotion, matmiddel.
an'tishrink, krimpwerend; ~ **agent**, krimpweerder, krimpmiddel; ~ **treatment**, krimpwering, krimpbehandeling.

antiso'cial, onmaatskaplik, antisosiaal; ~ **ist**, antisosialis; ~ **is'tic**, antisosialisties.
anti-South A'frica, anti-Suid-Afrika; ~ **n**, anti-Suid-Afrikaans.
antispasmo'dic, (n) krampweerder, krampmiddel, krampstiller; (a) krampwerend, krampstillend.
antispas'tic, krampstiller, krampmiddel.
an'tisqueak, piepweerder.
antista'tic, statiese elektrisiteitsweerder.
anti'strophe, antistrofe.
antisub'marine vessel, duikbootjagter.
antitank', vir gebruik teen gepantserde voertuie; ~ **ditch**, pantsersloot; ~ **mine**, pantserafweermyn; ~ **rifle**, pantsergeweer.
antite'tanus, tetanuswerend.
anti'theism, antiteïsme, anti-Godsbeskouing.
antith'esis, (..theses), teenstelling, antitese.
antithet'ic, teenstellend, antiteties; ~ **s**, antitetika.
antitick' chemical, bosluisweermiddel.
antitox'in, teengif.
an'titrade, antipassaat(wind).
antitrust', antitrust.
antitwist', vormvas.
an'titype, teenbeeld, antitipe.
antivenene', teengif (teen slangbyt), antivenien, antivenine.
an'tivibration, trillingwerend.
antivi'ral, viruswerend.
antivivisec'tionism, antiviviseksionisme.
antiwaste' organization, organisasie ter bestryding van verkwisting.
ant'ler, horing, tak; (pl.) horings, gewei (van 'n takbok).
ant'lion, mierleeu, joerie.
antonomas'ia, naamsverwisseling, antonomasia.
an'tonym, antoniem, teengestelde.
ant' poison, miergif.
ant' queen, mierkoningin.
an'trum, (..tra), antrum, beenholte.
an'trycide, antriside, antrisied.
anu'ria, anurie.
an'us, anus, fondament, aars, gat (plat).
an'vil, aambeeld; *be on the* ~, aandag geniet; ~ **chisel**, skrootbeitel; ~ **dross**, hamerslag.
anxi'ety, (..ties), angs, beangstheid, bekommerdheid, benoudheid, angsvalligheid, sorg, ongerustheid, bekommernis; begeerte; *cause* ~, sorg baar; ~ **complex**, ~ **neurosis**, angsneurose.
an'xious, begerig, verlangend, gretig; bang, beangs, ongerus, bevrees, angsvallig, besorg, kommervol; angstig; ~ *to HEAR the result*, nuuskierig om die uitslag te verneem; ~ *to HELP*, begerig om te help; ~ **ly**, angsvol; angstig.
an'y, elke, enige; iedereen; iemand; *is he* ~ *BETTER?* is hy iets beter? *in* ~ *CASE*, in alle geval; in elk geval; ~ *CHILD knows that*, elke kind weet dit; ~ *DISTANCE*, so ver as jy wil; ~ *LENGTH of time*, so lank as jy wil; ~ *PERSON*, elkeen, iedereen; *at* ~ *RATE*, in alle geval; in elk geval; *at* ~ *TIME*, te eniger tyd; ~ *of US*, enigeen van ons; *in* ~ *previous YEAR*, in enige vorige jaar.
an'ybody, enigeen, iemand, iedereen; *HAS* ~ *left?* het iemand vertrek? *NOT* ~, niemand . . . nie.
an'y: ~ **how**, (adv) in elk geval; hoe dan ook; sommerso, op 'n manier; (conj) hoe dit ook mag wees; in elk geval; *you will have to do it* ~ *how*, jy sal dit in alle geval moet doen; ~ **one**, elkeen; enigeen; iedereen; ~ **place**, enige plek.
an'ything, enigiets, alles; ~ *BUT*, allesbehalwe; *CRY like* ~, skreeu of jy betaal word; ~ *GOES*, alles is aanneemlik.
an'y: ~ **way**, hoe dan ook, in alle geval; ~ **where**, orals, êrens, op enige plek; *not* ~ *where*, nêrens . . . nie; ~ **wise**, hoe dan ook, op een of ander manier.
An'zac, Australiese of Nieu-Seelandse soldaat (in die Wêreldoorlog).
a'orist, onbepaald verlede tyd, aoristus.
aor'ta, groot slagaar, aorta; ~ **aneurism**, aorta-aneurisme.
aort'ic, aorties.
a'oudad, N. Afr. wilde skaap, aoedad.
apace', vinnig, hard; hand oor hand, by elke tree.

apa'che, straatskurk, apache; ~ dance, apachedans.
ap'anage = appanage.
apan'thropy, apantropie.
apart', afsonderlik, uitmekaar, apart; alleen; weg, opsy; ~ FROM, afgesien van; JESTING ~, gekheid op 'n stokkie; KEEP ~, uiteenhou; SET ~, afsonder; TAKE ~, uitmekaar maak; opsy neem; ~ heid, (rasse-)apartheid.
apart'ment, vertrek, kamer; FURNISHED ~, gemeubileerde kamer; ~ s to LET, kamers te huur; ~ building, deelhuisgebou; woonstelgebou; woonstelblok; ~ house, deelhuis.
apart'ness, apartheid; afsonderlikheid.
apathet'ic, gevoelloos, ongevoelig, apaties; onverskillig.
ap'athy, ongevoeligheid, apatie; flegma, traagheid, lusteloosheid; gevoelloosheid, onverskilligheid.
ap'atite, apatiet.
ape, (n) aap; na-aper, koggelaar; an ~ 's an ~, a varlet's a varlet, though they be clad in gold and scarlet, al dra 'n aap 'n goue ring, hy is en bly 'n lelike ding; (v) na-aap, uitkoggel.
apeak', vertikaal, loodreg, steil.
ape'man, aapmens.
Ap'ennines, (die) Apennyne.
apep'sy, slegte spysvertering, apepsie.
aperçu', (F), aperçu, samevatting, oorsig, opsomming.
ape'rient, (n) lakseermiddel, suiweringsmiddel, purgasie, afvoermiddel; (a) openend, purgerend.
aperiod'ic, aperiodies.
aperiodic'ity, aperiodisiteit.
ape'ritif, lusmakertjie, aperitief, aptytwekker, sopie, eetluswekker; ~ wine, aperitiefwyn.
ap'erture, opening; gaatjie, gleuf, spleet; ~-sight, gaatjievisier.
ap'ery, na-apery; apestreek.
apet'alous, sonder blomblare, kroon(blaar)loos.
ap'ex, (-es, apices), punt, top, toppunt, apeks; ~ beat, hartstoot, puntstoot; ~ stone, sluitsteen.
ap'felstrudel, (Ger.), apfelstrudel, appeltert.
aphae'resis, aferesis, voorafkapping.
aphas'ia, spraakverlies, afasie.
aphas'ic, afaties.
aphel'ion, aphelium, afelium.
aph'id, aph'is, (aphides), plantluis, bladluis; woolly ~, bloedluis.
aphon'ia, aph'ony, spraakloosheid, afonie; stemverlies.
aph'orism, spreuk, leenspreuk, gnoom, gedenkspreuk, aforisme.
aphoris'tic, aforisties, gnomies.
a'phrodine, afrodine, afrodien, johimbine, johimbien.
aphrodis'iac, seksstimuleermiddel; ~ al, geslagsprikkelend.
Aphrodite', Afrodite.
aphrolith'ic, afrolities; ~ lava, skuimsteen.
aph'tha, spru, afta.
aphyll'ous, blaarloos.
aphyll'y, blaarloosheid, afillie.
apiar'ian, bye-.
ap'iarist, byeboer; byekundige.
ap'iary, (..ries), byehok, byekamp; ~ house, byehuis, byestal.
a'pical, apikaal, top=; ~ beat, hartstoot, puntstoot.
apic'ulate, kortpuntig.
ap'iculture, byeteelt
apicul'turist, byeboer, byeteler.
apiece', per stuk, vir een, elk(een).
ap'ish, aapagtig; na-aperig; verspot; ~ ness, aapagtigheid; gemaaktheid.
aplas'tic, aplasties.
aplen'ty, volop, te kus en te keur.
aplomb', selfbewustheid, selfversekerdheid, parmantigheid; loodregte stand.
apoc'alypse, openbaring, apokalips.
apocalyp'tical, openbaring, apokalips.
apocalyp'tical, openbarend, apokalipties.
apoc'ope, apokopee, agterafkapping.
apoc'rypha, apokriewe boeke; ~ l, twyfelagtig, apokrief; verdag.

a'pod(e), pootlose dier.
apodeic'tic, apodic'tic, stellig, onweerlegbaar, apodikties.
ap'ogee, klimaks, hoogtepunt, apogeum.
apoli'tical, apolities.
Apol'lo, Apollo.
apologet'ic, verontskuldigend; verdedigend, apologeties; ~ s, apologetiek.
apolo'gia, verweerskrif.
apol'ogist, verdediger, apologeet.
apol'ogize, hom verontskuldig; verskoning maak; om verskoning vra; apologie aanteken.
ap'ologue, fabel.
apol'ogy, (..gies), verontskuldiging, apologie; ~ for ABSENCE, verskoning vir afwesigheid; an ~ for a NOSE, net die skyn van 'n neus, 'n sogenaamde neus; OFFER apologies, verontskuldiginge aanbied.
apomeco'meter, (-s), afstandsmeter.
ap'omorphine, apomorfien.
ap'ophthegm, sinspreuk, gedenkspreuk, kernspreuk.
apo'physis, (..ses), apofise.
apoplec'tic, apoplekties, onderhewig aan beroerte, beroerte ; an ~ fit, 'n aanval van beroerte.
ap'oplexy, beroerte, apopleksie.
a-port', aan bakboord.
aposiopes'is, (..peses), afbreking, aposiopesis.
apos'tasy, afvalligheid, geloofsversaking, afval, versaking, verloëning, apostasie.
apos'tate, (n) afvallige, verloënaar, versaker, renegaat, afgevallene, apostaat; (a) afvallig.
apos'tatize, afval, afvallig word, versaak.
apos'til, kantteckening, apostil.
apos'tle, apostel, godsgesant, verkondiger; ~ ship, apostelskap; ~ spoon, apostellepel.
apos'tolate, apostolaat; apostelskap.
apostol'ic, apostolies; A ~ Mission, Apostoliese Sending.
apos'trophe, afkappingsteken, weglatingsteken, apostroof; aanspreking; toespraak.
apostroph'ic, apostrofies.
apos'trophize, aanspreek, wend tot; afkap.
apoth'ecary, (..ries), apteker; female ~, aptekeres; ~ 's Latin, potjieslatyn, aptekerslatyn; ~ 's weight, aptekersgewig.
ap'othegm = apophthegm.
apotheos'is, (..theoses), verheerliking; vergoding, apoteose; vergeesteliking.
apo'theosize, verheerlik, verafgo(o)d.
appal', (-led), verskrik, ontstel; ~ ling, vreeslik, verskriklik, ontsettend, ysingwekkend.
app'anage, apanage, toelae aan prinse; besit, afhanklike gebied; voorreg; eienskap.
apparat'chik, (R.), apparatsjik.
apparat'us, (-es), toestel, gereedskap, samestel, apparaat; orgaan.
appa'rel, (n) kleding, drag, gewaad, uitrusting; (v) (-led), aantrek, uitrus, klee, tooi.
appa'rent, blykbaar, duidelik, kenlik, uiterlik, waarneembaar, skynbaar, vermoedelik; HEIR ~, regmatige troonopvolger; ~ LENGTH, skynlengte; ~ ly, klaarblyklik, oenskynlik, vermoedelik, blykbaar.
appari'tion, verskyning; spook, spokery, skim, gesig, gedaante; ~ al, spookagtig.
appar'itor, deurwaarder, bode.
appeal', (n) beroep; bede; appèl, hoër beroep; aantrekkingskrag, trekkrag; AESTHETIC ~, skoonheidswerking; CASE for ~, appèlsaak; COURT of A ~, hof van appèl; ENTER an ~, appèl aanteken, in hoër beroep gaan; (v) aantrek, aanlok; beroep, appelleer, in beroep gaan; 'n beroep doen (op); ~ AGAINST, appelleer; protes aanteken teen; ~ to the COUNTRY, 'n verkiesing uitskryf; 'n beroep op die kiesers doen; it DOES not ~ to me, dit staan my nie aan nie; PICTURES ~ to the eye, skilderye spreek tot die oog; ~ TO, 'n beroep doen op; it does not ~ TO him, hy voel daar nie baie voor nie; ~ able, vatbaar vir appèl; ~ court, appèlhof; ~ fund, insamelingsfonds; ~ ing, smekend; aantreklik, aanloklik.
appear', verskyn, optree, (op)daag; voorkom, skyn,

lyk, uitsien; ~ *for a CLIENT,* vir 'n kliënt verskyn; ~ *in COURT,* voorkom; *it WOULD* ~, dit lyk.
appear'ance, verskyning, verskynsel; optrede; aansien, aanskyn, skyn, voorkoms; aanslag (plante); *to ALL* ~*s,* soos dit lyk, blykbaar; ~*s ARE against him,* die skyn is teen hom; ~*s are DECEPTIVE,* skyn bedrieg; *at FIRST* ~, by die eerste oogopslag; *GO by* ~*s,* na die skyn oordeel; *JUDGE by* ~*s,* iem. op sy baadjie takseer; *KEEP up* ~*s,* die skyn bewaar; *PUT in (make) an* ~, sy verskyning maak, opdaag.
appear'er, komparant.
appease', bevredig, versadig, stil (honger), les (dors); stil maak; bedaar, kalmeer; paai; vermurf; tevrede stel; laat bedaar; ~ *one's conscience,* jou gewete sus; ~**ment**, bedaring, vermurwing; bevrediging, versadiging; *policy of* ~*ment,* paaibeleid.
appell'ant, (n) appellant; (a) smekend; appelerend.
appell'ate, appèl=; ~ **court**, ~ **division**, appèlhof.
appella'tion, benaming, naam.
appell'ative, (n) naam, benaming; soortnaam; (a) naams=, naamgewend; gemeen= (gram.).
append', aanhang, byvoeg, toevoeg; ~ **age**, aanhangsel, aanvoegsel, byvoegsel; ~ **ant**, (n) aanhangsel; gevolg; (a) begeleidend, bygevoeg.
appendec'tomy, blindedermoperasie, appendektomie.
appendicit'is, blindedermontsteking, appendisitis.
appendic'ular, appendikulêr, appendiks=; ~ *skeleton,* aanhangskelet.
appen'dix, (-es, ..dices), aanhangsel, bylae; blindederm, appendiks.
apperceive', appersipieer.
appercep'tion, appersepsie, waarneming.
appertain', behoort, toebehoort; betrekking hê op.
app'etence, app'etency, vurige begeerte, verlange; aantrekking.
app'etent, begerig (na); belus (op).
app'etite, eetlus, ete, begeerte, aptyt, lus.
ap'petitive, begerend; belus(tig); verlangend.
appe'tizer, aptytwekkertjie, opwekkertjie, skrikmakertjie, bittertjie, sopie, aperitief, luswekkertjie, snaps.
app'etizing, aptytlik, smaaklik, eetluswekkend; aantreklik.
App'ian, Appies; ~ **Way**, Appiese Weg.
ap'planate, afgeplat.
applaud', toejuig; prys, loof; ~ **ing**, applous; applouserend, toejuigend.
applause', byval, toejuiging, applous, handgeklap.
applaus'ive, byvals=, toejuigend, applouderend.
ap'ple, appel; *one BAD* ~ *destroys the whole basket,* een brandsiek skaap steek die hele trop aan; ~ *of DISCORD,* twisappel; ~ *of the EYE,* oogappel; *a ROTTEN* ~ *injuries its neighbours,* een vrot appel steek die ander aan; *STOLEN* ~*s (kisses) are sweetest,* verbode vrugte smaak die soetste; ~-**aphis**, appelbloedluis; ~ **blackspot**, appelskurfte, appelskurfsiekte; ~-**blossom**, appelbloeisel; ~ **brandy**, appelbrandewyn; ~-**cart**, appelkar; *upset a person's* ~-*cart,* iem. se planne in die war stuur; ~ **cider**, appelwyn; ~-**core**, kern van 'n appel, klokhuis; ~-**corer**, appelboorder; ~ **dumpling**, appelbolletjie; ~ **fritters**, appelkoekies, appelpoffers; ~-**green**, appelgroen; ~ **jack**, appelwyn; ~-**john**, gerimpelde winterappel; ~-**juice**, appelsap; ~ **meringue**, appelskuimpie, appelmeringue; ~-**orchard**, appelboord; ~-**pie**, appeltert; ~-*pie BED,* bed waarvan die lakens vir 'n poets so gevou is dat 'n mens nie kan inkom nie; *in* ~-*pie ORDER,* piekfyn; agtermekaar; so reg soos 'n roer; ~-*pie SAUCE* (n) vleiery; (interj) bog! kaf! ~ **pulp**, appelmoes; ~ **ring**, appelskyfie, appelring; ~ **sauce**, appelmoes; kaf, nonsens; ~-**scale**, appelskurfte; ~ **tree**, appelboom; ~-**whip**, appelskuim.
appli'able, *kyk* **applicable**.
appli'ance, aanwending, toepassing; toestel; instrument; apparaat; ~ **spares**, toesteltoebehore; apparaattoebehore.
applicabil'ity, toepaslikheid, aanwendbaarheid.
app'licable, toepaslik, bruikbaar, aanwendbaar; ~ *to,* van toepassing op; *whichever is* ~, na gelang van die geval; *delete whichever is not* ~, skrap waar nodig.
app'licant, aansoeker, sollisitant, applikant.
applica'tion, aanwending, toepassing; toediening; gebruik; vlyt, toewyding; inskrywing (aandele); aansoek, sollisitasie; versoek, aanvraag; *make* ~ *for,* aansoek doen om; ~ **of funds**, fondsbesteding; ~-**form**, aansoekvorm.
ap'plicator, (-s), toediener, aanbringer; (spons=) kwassie.
applied', toegepas; ~ *mathematics,* toegepaste wiskunde.
appli'er, (-s), aansoeker; toediener; aanbringer.
applique', (n) applikee(werk); appliek; (v) applikeer, applikeewerk doen; ~ **ornament**, oplegversiersel.
apply', (**applied**), aansmeer (salf); aanwend, aanlê (verband); oplê (versiersel); toepas (reëls); aanvra; hom rig tot; aansoek doen, skiet, sollisiteer (om betrekking); beywer, toelê op; ~ *BRAKES,* rem; *it DOES not* ~ *to,* dis nie van toepassing nie op; *it DOES not* ~ *to all cases,* dit geld nie vir alle gevalle nie; ~ *FOR,* aanvra, aansoek doen om; ~ *ONESELF to,* hom toelê op; ~ *a SUM of money,* 'n som geld gebruik (aanwend); ~ *TO,* aansoek (navraag) doen by.
appoint', bepaal, vasstel; benoem, aanstel; voorskrywe; ~ **ed**, bepaal, vasgestel; aangestel; uitgerus, ingerig; *an* ~*ed TASK,* 'n opgelegde taak; *at the* ~*ed TIME (and place),* op die bestemde tyd (en plek); *WELL* ~*ed,* uitstekend toegerus; ~ **ee'**, benoemde (persoon), aangestelde (persoon); benoeming; ~ **er**, aansteller, benoemer.
appoint'ment, bepaling; afspraak; benoeming; uitrusting; beskikking; *BREAK an* ~, 'n afspraak nie hou nie; *BY* ~, volgens afspraak; *the* ~*s of the HOUSE,* die uitrusting van die huis; *KEEP an* ~, 'n afspraak hou; *by* ~ *to his MAJESTY,* hoflewerransier; *MAKE an* ~, 'n afspraak maak; ~-**book**, afspraakboek(ie); ~-**club**, afspraakklub; ~-**service**, afspraakdiens.
apport', apport.
appor'tion, verdeel, bestem, toe(be)deel, afpas, afmeet; ~ **ment**, verdeling, toedeling; ~ **ment suit**, toedelingsgeding.
apposed', teen mekaar; naas mekaar.
app'osite, geskik, passend, toepaslik, saaklik; ~ **ness**, saaklikheid.
apposi'tion, bystelling, apposisie; aanhegting, byvoeging.
apposi'tional, bystellend, apposisioneel.
apprais'able, takseerbaar.
apprais'al, waardering, skatting, taksasie.
appraise', skat, takseer, waardeer; ~ **ment**, skatting, waardebepaling, taksasie; ~ **r**, skatter, waardeerder, taksateur; *sworn* ~ *r,* beëdigde taksateur.
appre'ciable, waardeerbaar, skatbaar; merkbaar; aansienlik, beduidend.
appre'ciably, merkbaar, waarneembaar, aanmerklik, heelwat.
appre'ciate, hoogskat; waardeer, op prys stel; waarneem; verstaan; in waarde toeneem, styg (prys).
apprecia'tion, skatting, waardering; beskouing; goeie mening; waardevermeerdering, waardestyging.
appre'ciative, appre'ciatively, appre'ciatory, waarderend.
apprehend', vat, aanvat; begryp, snap; verwag; vrees; gevange neem, arresteer; beskou.
apprehen'sible, bevatlik, begryplik.
apprehen'sion, gevangeneming, aanhouding, inhegtenisneming; bevatting, begrip; vrees, bedugtheid, bevreesdheid; *quick of* ~, vlug van begrip.
apprehen'sive, bevatlik; bevrees, bang, bedug; begrips=; ~ *FACULTIES,* begripsvermoë(ns); ~ *OF,* bang vir; ~ **ness**, bevatlikheid; vrees, besorgdheid.
appren'tice, (n) leerjonge, klerk; ingeboekte persoon; nuweling; vakleerling; leermeisie; (v) in die leer sit (doen), 'n ambag laat leer.
appren'ticeship, leertyd, leerjare, vakleerlingskap; *ARTICLES of* ~, leerkontrak; *SERVE an* ~, 'n leertyd deurmaak; *by iem.* in die leer wees; ~ **board**, vakleerlingraad; ~ **system**, leerlingstelsel.

appres'sed, teenaan geleë; teenaan gegloei.
apprise', laat weet, berig, in kennis stel; *be ~ d,* bewus wees van, weet.
ap'pro: *on ~,* op sig; *kyk* **approbation.**
approach', (n) nadering; toegang; toenadering; benadering; aantog; naderingswerk; benaderingswyse; binneswewing (vliegtuig); oprit; (v) naderkom; benader; lyk na; binneseil (boot); binnesweef; aanvlieg; aankom, aanspeel (gholf); *~ to LIFE,* lewensbeskouing; *~ to a MATTER,* benadering van 'n saak; *~* **altitude,** *~* **height,** naderingshoogte; *~* **light,** naderingslig, landingslig; aanlooplig; binneseillig; *~* **line,** binnesweeflyn; *~* **path,** naderingspad; naderingsbaan; binnesweefbaan; *~* **shot,** kaphou(tjie), naderhou (gholf); *~* **side,** naderingskant; *~* **signal,** naderingsein; nader(kom)sein.
approba'tion, goedkeuring; goedvinding, byval; *on ~,* op sig (approbasie).
approb'ative, goedkeurend.
app'robatory, goedkeurend.
approp'riable, toe-eienbaar; aanwendbaar.
approp'riate, (v) toe-eien, beslag lê op, inpalm; afsonder, bestem; *~ a GIRL,* 'n nooi stompoor merk; *~ MONEY for,* geld bestem (toewys) vir; (a) bestem; passend, geskik, aangewese, doelmatig; gevolglik, juis, toepaslik, eie; *the ~ AMOUNT,* die regte (nodige) bedrag; *the ~ COMMITTEE,* die betrokke komitee; *~* **ly,** toepaslik, passend; *~* **ness,** juistheid.
appropria'tion, toe-eiening, inpalming; aanwending; bestemming, bewilliging, aanwysing; *~* **account,** toewysingsrekening; *~* **act,** begrotingswet; *~* **committee,** geldsakekomitee; begrotingskomitee.
appro'priative, toe-eienend; beslagleend.
approp'riator, beslagleer.
approv'able, loflik, goedkeurenswaardig.
approv'al, goedkeuring, byval, beaming; *MEET with ~,* groot byval vind; *ON ~,* op sig.
approve', goedkeur; bevestig; bewys, billik; bekragtig, beaam; *~ of,* goedvind, goedkeur; *~* **d,** probaat; goedgekeur; beproef; erken, gangbaar; *~ d LOAN,* goedgekeurde lening; *in the ~ d STYLE,* op die gangbare wyse; *~* **r,** bevestiger; bekragtiger; goedkeurder.
approx'imate, (v) nader, naderby bring; naby kom; benader; (a) benaderend, geraam, geskat; *~* **ly,** naastenby, by benadering, ongeveer, plus-minus, so in dié geweste.
approxima'tion, benadering; nabyheid; begroting; (pl) benaderde waardes.
approx'imative, benaderend, ongeveer.
appur'tenance, aanhangsel, aanhang; toebehore, aanhorigheid; (pl) toebehore.
appur'tenant, bybehorend; verbonde.
ap'ricot, appelkoos; *~* **(colour),** appelkoos(kleur); *~* **jam,** appelkooskonfyt; *~* **kernel,** appelkoospit; *~* **leather,** appelkoossmeer; *~* **sickness,** appelkoossiekte; *~* **-tree,** appelkoosboom.
Ap'ril, April, Aprilmaand; *~* **-fool,** Aprilgek; velskoenblaar *(Haemanthus); ~* **fool's day,** 1e April, gekkedag. *~* **joke,** Aprilgrap.
a prio'ri, a priori, vooraf; **aprioris'tic,** aprioristies.
ap'ron, voorskoot, skort; borsplooi (van 'n skaap); sluis; skaafblok; voetlood (bouk.); vet maagvel van 'n gans; deklaag; dekkleed (vir bene); dekstuk (foto); aansitblad (vliegveld); *~* **ed,** met 'n voorskoot; *~* **-file,** rygpenomslag; *~* **leather,** leervoorskoot; leerskort; *~* **lining,** trapskort, drupskort; *~* **man,** ambagsman; *~* **-piece,** dekstuk; *~* **plate,** skortplaat; *~* **rail,** dekreling; *~* **stage,** voorverhoog; *~* **-string,** voorskootband; *tied to the ~ -string of someone,* onder die plak van iem. wees; aan iem. se leiband loop; aan iem. se rokbande vas wees.
apropos', apropos, toepaslik; terloops; *~ of,* aangaande.
apse, (-s), halfrond (agter die koor); apsis (argit.)
apsi'dal, apsis-, apsidaal.
ap'sis, (apsides), apsis (sterrek.), apsides, keerpunt; absis (wisk.).
apt, geskik, gepas; geneig; vlug, gevat; onderhewig aan; bekwaam; *~ to forget,* geneig om te vergeet; *~ to take offence,* liggeraak.

ap'teral, ap'terous, ongevleuel.
ap'titude, geskiktheid; geneigheid; bekwaamheid, aanleg; *~* **test,** aanlegtoets.
apt'ly, gepas.
apt'ness, toepaslikheid, juistheid.
apyret'ic, sonder koors.
apyr'ous, brandvry; vuurvas.
a'qua: *~ FORTIS,* salpetersuur; *~ REGIA,* koningswater; *~ VITAE,* brandewyn.
a'quacade, watersport(byeenkoms), waterfees.
a'qualung, duiklong.
aquamarine', (n) akwamaryn, blougroen beril; (a) blougroen, seegroen.
a'quaplane, (n) branderplank; (v) op 'n branderplank ry; *~* **r,** branderplankryer.
aqua re'gia, koningswater, aqua regia.
aquarelle', akwarel, waterverfskildery.
aquarellist', waterverfskilder, akwarellis.
aquar'ium, (..ria, -s), akwarium.
Aquar'ius, Aquarius, die Waterdraer (sterrek.).
aquat'ic, (n) waterdier; waterplant; (a) water-; *~* **animal,** waterdier, *~* **bird,** watervoël; *~* **s,** watersport.
a'quatint, akwatint.
a'queduct, waterleiding, akwaduk.
a'queous, waterig, water-, wateragtig; *~ HUMOUR,* glasagtige water (van die oog); *~* **ness,** waterigheid; *~ SOLUTION,* waterige oplossing; *~ VAPOUR,* wasem; waterdamp.
a'quifer, waterdraer.
a'quifuge, keerbank.
aquile'gia, akelei.
a'quiline, gebuig, krom, arends-; *~ nose,* arendsneus, bylneus, krom neus, haakneus.
Aquitan'ia, Akwitanië; *~* **n,** (n) Akwitaniër; (a) Akwitaans.
aquos'ity, waterigheid.
A'ra¹, Ara, die Altaar (sterrek.).
a'ra², ara, soort papegaai.
A'rab, Arabier; Arabiese perd.
arabes'que, (n) arabesk; (a) arabesk.
Arab'ia, Arabië; *~* **n,** Arabies; *the ~ n Nights,* Duisend-en-een-nag (verhale).
A'rabic, Arabies (taal); *~ numerals,* Arabiese syfers.
arabil'ity, beboubaarheid, ploegbaarheid, saaibaarheid; plantbaarheid.
A'rabist, Arabis, kenner v.d. Arabiese taal.
a'rable, ploegbaar, beboubaar, bewerkbaar; *~ land,* saaigrond, ploegland, landbougrond, saailand, bewerkbare grond.
a'rachis-oil, grondboontjie-olie.
arach'nid, (n) spinagtige; (a) spinagtig.
arach'noid, (n) spinnerakvlies; (a) spinnerakagtig; *~* **membrane,** spinnerakvlies; *~* **itis,** spinnerakvliesontsteking, aragnoïditis.
arag'onite, aragoniet.
Arama'ic, Aramees.
ar'balest, kruisboog, voetboog; *~* **er,** kruisboogskutter.
ar'biter, skeidsregter, skeidsman, arbiter.
ar'bitrage, arbitrasie, skeidsregterlike uitspraak.
ar'bitral, skeidsregterlik.
arbit'rament, skeidsregterlike uitspraak, arbitrasie.
ar'bitrariness, willekeur(igheid).
ar'bitrary, willekeurig, eiemagtig, arbitrêr.
ar'bitrate, besleg, deur arbitrasie beslis, uitspraak gee, arbitreer.
arbitra'tion, skeidsregterlike uitspraak, arbitrasie; *~ of EXCHANGE,* wisselkoersberekening; *SUBMIT to ~,* aan skeidsregterlike beslissing onderwerp; *~* **award,** skeidsregterlike uitspraak.
ar'bitrator, skeidsregter, skeidsman, arbiter.
ar'bitress, (-es), skeidsvrou.
ar'blast = arbalest.
ar'bor, spil, as; boom.
arbora'ceous, boomagtig; bebos.
Ar'bor Day, Boomplantdag.
arbor'eal, boomagtig, boom-.
arbor'eous, boomryk, bebos; boomagtig.
arbores'cent, boomagtig; boomvormig.
arboret'um, (..reta,) botaniese boomtuin, arboretum.
arboricul'tural, boomkweek-, boomkundig.

ar'boriculture, boomkwekery, boomteelt.
arboricul'turist, boomkweker.
ar'borist, boomkweker.
ar'bour, prieel, somerhuisie.
arbut'us, aarbeiboom.
arc, boog; vonk (elek.); ~ *of ACTION,* ingrypingsboog; ~ *of a CIRCLE,* sirkelboog; *DIURNAL* ~, dagboog; ~ *of VIBRATION,* trillingswydte, trillingsboog.
arcade', deurloop, boog, booggang, winkelgang, arkade, suilegang.
Arca'dian, (n) Arkadiër; (a) Arkadies, landelik.
Ar'cady, Arkadië.
arcane', geheimsinnig.
arcan'um, (..na), geheim; geheimmiddel; wondermiddel.
arc gap', boogbrug; booggaping.
arch¹, (n) (-es), boog, verwulf, (ge)welf; plooirug; *COSTAL* ~, ribbeboog; *FALLEN* ~, gesakte boog (van voet); *TRIUMPHAL* ~, praalboog; (v) welf, buig.
arch-², (a) aarts=, opperste.
archaeolo'gic(al), oudheidkundig, argeologies.
archaeol'ogist, oudheidkundige, argeoloog.
archaeol'ogy, oudheidkunde, argeologie.
archa'ic, oud, verouder(d), argaïsties.
arch'aism, verouderde woord of uitdrukking, argaïsme.
arch: ~ **angel,** aartsengel; engelwortel; bosnetel; soort duif; ~**-bar,** boogstaaf; ~ **bishop,** aartsbiskop; ~ **bishopric,** aartsbisdom; ~ **buttress,** (-es), steunboog; ~ **conservative,** aartskonserwatief; ~ **deacon,** aartsdeken; ~ **diocese,** aartsbiskopsetel; ~ **ducal,** aartshertoëlik; ~ **duchess,** (-es), aartshertogin; ~ **duchy,** aartshertogdom; ~ **duke,** aartshertog; ~ **dukedom,** aartshertogdom.
archebio'sis, argebiosis.
arched, gewelf, geboë, boog=; ~ *CULVERT,* boogduiker; ~ *NECK,* kromnek, sekelnek, swanehals.
archegon'iate, archegoniumdraend.
archegon'ium, (..nia), archegonium.
arch'-enemy, (..emies), aartsvyand; bloedvyand.
arch'er, boogskutter; *the A* ~, Sagittarius, die Boogskutter (sterrek.).; ~**y,** boogskiet(ery).
arc'hetype, oertipe, grondvorm, standaard.
arch'-fiend, Satan, aartsvyand.
arch'-foe, aartsvyand.
arch'-heretic, aartsketter.
arch'hypocrite, aartshuigelaar.
archidiac'onal, aartsdekendom.
archiepis'copal, aartsbiskoplik.
Archimed'es, Archimedes; *the principle of* ~, die wet van Archimedes.
archipel'ago, (-s), eilandsee, argipel, eilandgroep.
arc'hitect, argitek, boumeester; ~'**s profession,** argiteksberoep.
architecton'ic, boukundig, argitektonies; ~**s,** boukunde.
architec'tural, boukundig; ~ *assistant,* argiteksassistent.
arc'hitecture, boukunde, argitektuur, boustyl.
arc'hitrave, argitraaf, hoofbalk; deurlys.
arc'hives, argief, versameling oorkondes, argiefgebou; *keeper of the* ~, hoofargivaris; ryksargivaris.
arc'hivist, argivaris.
arch'-knave, aartsskelm, aartsskurk, aartsmisdadiger.
arch'-liar, aartsleuenaar.
arch'ly, skelmpies, ondeund; oulik.
arch'ness, ondeundheid, skelmheid, skalksheid.
ar'chon, argont; ~ **ship,** argontskap.
arch'priest, aartspriester.
arch: ~**-rail,** boogreling; ~**-rib,** boogrib, gewelrib; ~**-rival,** aartssteenstander; ~**-sight,** boogvisier; ~**-stone,** sluitsteen; ~**-support,** steunsool; ~**-typal,** argetipies; **archtype,** argetipe; ~ **way,** (-s), (suile)boog, welwing, gewelfde gang; ~ **wise,** boogsgewys(e), boog=.
arc'ing, boogvorming; boogvonking.
arc: ~ **lamp,** booglamp; ~ **light,** booglig.
ar'cose, arkoos.
arcta'tion, nouheid, saamgedrongenheid.

arc'tic, noordelik; Noordpool=; **A** ~ **Circle,** Noordpoolsirkel; **A** ~ **expedition,** (Noord)pooltog; **A** ~ **explorer,** poolreisiger; ~ **fox,** poolvos, ysvos; ~ **glass,** vriesglas; **A** ~ **navigator,** Noordpoolvaarder; **A** ~ **Ocean,** Noordelike Yssee; **A** ~ **pole,** Noordpool; **A** ~ **regions,** Noordpoolstreke.
arc transmitt'er, booglampsender.
arc'uate(d), boogvormig.
arc: ~ **welder,** (lig)boogsweiser; ~ **welding,** boogsweis(ing).
ard'ency, gloed; ywer, vuur.
Ardennes', Ardenne.
ard'ent, gloeiend, brandend; geesryk; vurig, ywerig, hartstogtelik; blakend; ~ *spirits,* sterk drank; ywer.
ard'our, hitte, vuur, gloed, warmte; vurigheid, ywer.
ard'uous, steil; moeisaam; moeilik, opdraand, swaar, hard; energiek.
are¹, (n) are (metrieke stelsel).
are², (v) *kyk* **be.**
ar'ea, (-s), oppervlakte; gebied, streek, wyk; oop ruimte; vlakte-inhoud; draagvlak (lugv.); ~ *of OPERATIONS,* operasiegebied; *PROHIBITED* ~, verbode gebied; ~ **bell,** kombuisbel, kelderbel; ~ **commander,** streekkommandant; ~ **wall,** voggangmuur; ~**-way,** luggang.
ar'eca (nut), areka(neut).
aren'a, (-s), strydperk, kampplek, arena; *ENTER the* ~, die strydperk binnetree.
arena'ceous, arenose', sanderig, sand=.
are'na: ~ **stage,** arenaverhoog; ~ **theater,** arenateater.
areola, areool, ring.
are'olar, are'olate(d), areolêr.
areom'eter, vogmeter, areometer.
areom'etry, vogmeting, areometrie.
Areop'agus, Areopagus, regbank.
arête', arête, mesrug.
ar'gent, (n) silwer; (a) wit, silwerwit; silwer.
argen'tan, argentankant.
argen'tic, silweragtig, silwerhoudend.
argentif'erous, silwerhoudend.
Ar'gentine¹, (n) Argentinië; (a) Argentyns.
ar'gentine², (n) nagemaakte silwer; namaaksilwer, argentaan; klein vissoort; (a) silwerkleurig, silwer=.
ar'gentite, argentiet, silwerglans.
argen'tous = **argentic.**
ar'gil, (sagte) klei, potklei.
ar'gillite, argilliet.
ar'ginine, arginine, arginien.
Ar'give, (n) Argeër, Griek; (a) Grieks.
ar'gle-bargle, stryery, kibbelry.
ar'gol, ruwe wynsteen.
ar'gon, argon.
Ar'gonaut¹, Argonout.
ar'gonaut², nautilus.
ar'gosy, (..sies), geldskip, skatskip; skat.
ar'got, diewetaal, boewetaal, argot.
ar'guable, betwisbaar, nog te bewys.
ar'gue, redeneer, redetwis, betoog, beweer; redekawel; argumenteer; bespreek, diskusseer; *it* ~ *s him to be a rogue,* dit dui daarop dat hy 'n uiterste vabond is; ~**r,** disputant, redeneerder.
ar'guing, geredeneer, geredekawel.
ar'gument, redenering, bewysgrond; diskussie, disputt; debat; onderwerp; argument; beredenering (jur.); hoofinhoud; *ADVANCE* ~ *s,* redes aantoon; *BEYOND* ~, buite twyfel; ~ **s!** kry jou sê goed reg!
argumenta'tion, redenering, bewysvoering, betoog, geredekawel, argumentasie.
argumen'tative, beredeneer(d) betogend; twisgraag, polemies, betoog=; ~ **ness,** stryerigheid, redeneerlustigheid.
Ar'gus, Argus, ~**-eyed,** met Argusoë.
argute', skel; skrander, skerpsinnig; skerp.
ar'gy-bargy = **argle-bargle.**
arhyth'mia, aritmie; ..mic, aritmies.
ar'ia, (-s), aria, lied, wysie.
Ar'ian, (n) Ariaan; (a) Ariaans.
ar'id, dor, droog, kaal; onvrugbaar.
arid'ity, a'ridness, droogte, dorheid.

ar'iel, gasel, ariëlbok.
aright', juis, tereg.
arise', (**arose, arisen**), ontstaan, intree, voortkom, voortspruit; opstaan; voordoen (moeilikheid); op= gaan (son); ~ *again (from the dead)*, herrys.
aris'ing; ~*from the minutes*, punte uit die notule.
aris'ta, (-e), baard, aar, borsel; ~ **te**, geborsel, geaar.
aristoc'racy, aristokrasie, adelstand; aansienlikes, hoëlui.
a'ristocrat, aristokraat; edelman.
aristocrat'ic, aristokraties; adellik.
Aristotel'ian, (n) Aristoteliaan; (a) Aristoteliaans.
Aristot'le, Aristoteles.
arith'metic, (n) rekenkunde, rekene; getalleleer; sy= ferkuns; *mental* ~, hoofrekene; (a) rekenkundig, reken=; ~ *mean*, rekenkundige gemiddelde.
arithmet'ical, rekenkundig, reken=; ~. *progression*, rekenkundige reeks.
arithmeti'cian, rekenkundige, rekenaar.
arithmom'eter, rekenmasjien.
ark, ark; *it CAME out of the Ark*, dit kom uit Noag se ark; *A* ~ *of the COVENANT*, Verbondsark.
arm¹, (n) arm (liggaam); mou (kledingstuk); tak (rivier); inham, golf (see); been (hoek); *ENFOLD another in one's* ~ *s*, iem. in die arms sluit; *FLING oneself into another's* ~ *s*, jou in iem. se arms werp; *with FOLDED* ~ *s*, met gevoue arms; ~ *IN* ~, ingehaak, gearm(d); *INFANT in* ~ *s*, suig(e)ling, kind op die skoot; *have a LONG* ~, lang arms hê; *the long* ~ *of the LAW*, die lang arm(s) van die gereg; *keep at* ~ *s LENGTH*, op 'n afstand hou; *with OPEN* ~ *s*, met oop arms; *within* ~ *'s REACH*, binne bereik; *the SECULAR* ~, die wê= reldlike mag.
arm², (n) wapen; wapensoort; (pl) wapens; *BEAR* ~ *s*, wapens dra; *COAT of* ~ *s*, familiewapen, wa= penskild; *HEAVY* ~ *s*, swaargeskut, artillerie; *LAY down* ~ *s*, die wapens neerlê; *SMALL* ~ *s*, kleingewere; *TAKE up* ~ *s*, die wapens opneem, opstaan; *UNDER* ~ *s*, onder die wapens wees; *be UP in* ~ *s*, opstandig wees; (v) wapen, van wapens voorsien.
arma'da, (-s), armada, vloot.
armadill'o, (-s), pantserdier, Amerikaanse ietermagô, armadil, skubdier.
Armagedd'on, Armageddon.
arm'ament, bewapening, krygstoerusting; krygsmag; swaargeskut; ~ **-fitter**, wapenmonteur; ~ **s man= ufacture**, wapenvervaardiging.
arm'ature, bewapening, pantser, wapenrusting; (magneet)anker (dinamo); poolstuk (magneet); ~ **- bar**, ankerstaaf; ~ **-coil**, ankerspoel; ~ **-head**, ankereindplaat; ~ **-shaft**, ankeras; ~ **-winding**, an= kerwikkeling; ~ **-wire**, ankerdraad.
arm'-bandage, armverband.
arm'-bone, armbeen.
arm'chair, (n) leunstoel, armstoel; (a) teoreties, on= prakties; ~ *COMMUNIST*, studeerkamerkom= munis; *an* ~ *POLITICIAN*, 'n politieke tingieter; 'n studeerkamerpolitikus.
armed, gewapen; gepantser; ~ *BOMB*, plofgerede bom; ~ *merchant CRUISER*, gewapende koop= vaartkruiser; ~ *FORCE*, gewapende mag; wapen= geweld; ~ *INTERVENTION*, gewapende tussen= koms; ~ *NEUTRALITY*, gewapende neutraliteit.
Armen'ia, Armenië; ~ **n**, (n) Armeniër; Armeens (taal); (a) Armeens; ~ *n stone*, lapis lazuli, lasuur= steen.
arm: ~ **-file**, armvyl; ~ **ful**, armvol; ~ **hole**, armsgat, mousgat.
armill'ary, ring=; ~ **sphere**, armillaarsfeer.
ar'mistice, wapenstilstand; *A* ~ *Day*, Wapenstil= standsdag.
arm'less¹, sonder wapens.
arm'less², sonder arms.
arm'let, armpie; armband; armring.
armoire', (spog)klerekas.
armor'ial, (n) wapenboek; (a) wapen=; ~ **bearings**, geslagswapen, wapenskild.
ar'morist, heraldikus.
arm'ory, (..ries), wapenkunde, heraldiek.
arm'our, (n) wapenrusting; pantser; duikerspak; *suit*

of ~, wapenrusting; (v) harnas, pantser; ~ **-bearer**, wapendraer; ~ **-clad**, gepantser.
arm'oured, gepantser; ~ *CABLE*, pantserkabel; ~ *CAR*, pantserwa; ~ *DECK*, pantserdek; ~ *DIV= ISION*, pantserdivisie; ~ *GLASS*, pantserglas; ~ *SCALE*, harde dopluis; ~ *TRAIN*, gepantserde trein; ~ *TROOPS*, pantsertroepe.
arm'our: ~ **er**, wapensmid; wapenkneg; geweer= maker; ~ **ing**, pantsering, wapening; ~ **plate**, pant= serplaat; ~ **y**, (..**ries**), wapenkamer, arsenaal.
arm: ~ **pit**, armholte, kieliebak, oksel; ~ **-rest**, arm= leuning.
arms, wapens; wapenskild; ~ **embargo**, wapenver= bod; ~ **factory**, wapenfabriek; ~ **manufacturer**, wapenvervaardiger; ~ **requirement**, wapenbehoef= te.
arm'sling, geweerband; armdraagdoek, draagband, hangverband; *have one's arm in an* ~, jou arm in 'n doek dra.
arm'-splint, armspalk.
arms'-rack, geweerrak.
arm'ure, pantserstof, armure.
ar'my, (..**mies**), leër(skare), heer; krygsmag, weer= mag; *JOIN the* ~, aansluit, in militêre diens tree; ~ **ant**, swerfmier; ~ **beef**, blikkiesvleis; ~ **biscuit**, klinker; ~ **bulletin**, leërberig; ~ **chaplain**, veldpre= diker; kapelaan; ~ **cloth**, leërstof; ~ **command**, leërbevel; ~ **commander**, leërhoof; ~ **contractor**, leërleveransier; ~ **corps**, leërafdeling, leërkorps; ~ **division**, leëraf deling; ~ **doctor**, militêre dokter; ~ **education**, militêre voorligting, leëropleiding; ~ **estimates**, oorlogsbegroting; ~ **language**, militêre taal, soldatetaal, ~ **list**, offisierslys; ~ **officer**, leer= offisier; ~ **order**, leërorder; ~ **-worm**, kommando= wurm; *lesser* ~ *-worm*, kleinkommandowurm.
ar'nica, valkruid, wondkruid, arnika.
aro'ma, (**-s**), aroma, geur.
aromat'ic, geurig, welriekend, aromaties.
arose, *kyk* **arise**.
around', (adv) rond; in die rondte, in die buurt; *a ru= mour is going* ~, 'n gerug doen die rondte; (prep) om, rondom; ~ *a HUNDRED*, om en by 'n hon= derd; ~ *our WAY*, by ons langs.
arous'al, opwekking; aansporing.
arouse', opwek; wakker maak; aanpor, aanspoor.
ar'quebus, (-es), haakbus, stutgeweer; *kyk* **harquebus**.
a'rrack, arak, rysbrandewyn.
arraign', aankla, beskuldig, daag; bestry, in twyfel trek; ~ **ment**, beskuldiging, aanklag; aanmerking.
arrange', skik, reël, inrig; voorberei; opstel; indeel; rangskik; orden; ooreenkom; afspreek, afpraat; be= dissel; regsien; arrangeer; ~ **d**, getroffe (maatreëls); ~ **ment**, rangskikking (van blomme); indeling, reë= ling; voorbereiding, inrigting; arrangement (mus.); ooreenkoms, skikking, vergelyk; bedisseling; ~ **ments**, planne, reëlings.
a'rrant, verstok, onvervals; deurtrap, berug, aarts=; ~ *KNAVE*, deurtrapte skurk; ~ *NONSENSE*, klinkklare onsin; ~ *ROGUE*, spitsboef; ~ *THIEF*, aartsdief.
A'rras, Atrecht.
a'rras, muurtapyt, behang.
array', (n) slagorde; troepe; dos, tooi, kledy; vertoon, prag; *in battle* ~, in slagorde; (v) skik; opstel, aan= voer (besware); tooi, versier, uitdos, opskik.
arrear', agterstand.
arrear'age, skuld(e); reserwe; agterstand.
arrears', agterstallige gelde; *IN* ~, agter; *be in* ~ *WITH*, agterstallig wees met sy betaling.
arrect', gespits (ore); wakker, op sy hoede.
arrest', (n) inhegtenisneming, gevangeneming, aan= houding, arrestasie; *under* ~, onder arres; (v) aan= hou, in hegtenis neem, vang, arresteer; teenhou, stuit, belemmer; die hande lê op; beslag lê op; boei, trek (aandag); ~ *the ATTENTION of*, die aandag trek van; ~ *ed DEVELOPMENT*, vertraagde ont= wikkeling; ~ *a'tion*, inhegtenisneming; stuiting; ~ **er**, aanhouer, vanger, vangtoestel; ~ **er-wire**, vangdraad; ~ **ing**, ophoudend; pakkend, boeiend.
a'rrha, handgif (reg)
a'rris, skerp kant; snykant (op hout); nok; ~ **gutter**, V-geut; ~ **-rafter**, driehoekspar.

arri'val, aankoms, landing; pasgeborene; aangekomene; *NEW* ~, nuwe aankomeling; *POINT of* ~, aankomspunt (ballistiek); ~ **hall**, aankomssaal.

arrive', aankom, aansit, (aan)land; grondvat, arriveer; bereik; aanbreek; gebeur; tref; naam maak; ~ *at a DECISION*, tot 'n besluit kom; *when the TIME* ~ *s*, wanneer die tyd aanbreek; ~ *somewhere UNEXPECTEDLY*, onverwags aankom, êrens aangesit kom.

a'rrogance, a'rrogancy, inbeelding, opgeblasenheid, aanmatiging, oormoed, verwaandheid, verwatenheid, hovaardy, hovaardigheid.

a'rrogant, aanmatigend, verwaand, hovaardig, verwate, oormoedig.

a'rrogate, jou aanmatig, toe-eien; ~ *to oneself*, wederregtelik vir jou opeis.

a'rrow, pyl; skig; *like an* ~ *from a BOW*, soos 'n pyl uit 'n boog; *have an* ~ *left in one's QUIVER*, nog 'n pyl in jou koker hê; ~**-disc**, rigtingskyf; ~ **head**, pylpunt; pylkruid; ~ **root**, pylwortel, araroet; pylwortelmeel; ~ **shaft**, pylstok; ~**-shaped**, pylvormig; ~**-shot**, pylskoot; ~ **worm**, pylwurm; ~**y**, pylsnel; pyl=.

arse, agterste, gat, aars (plat).

ars'enal, wapenhuis, (geweer)magasyn, arsenaal.

ars'enic, arsenik, rottekruid, arsenikum, arseen.

arsen'ic(al), arseen=, arseenhoudend; ~ *acid*, arseensuur.

arsen'ious, arseen=, arseenhoudend.

ars'enite, arseniet; ~ *of soda*, soda-arseniet, natriumarseniet.

ars'is, (arses), arsis; toonheffing.

ars'on, (moedswillige) brandstigting; *commit* ~, 'n brand stig; ~**ist**, brandstigter.

art¹, (n) kuns; lis, bedrog; slag, streek, kunsvaardigheid; gekunsteldheid; (pl) lettere; kunste; *BLACK* ~, toordery; ~ *s and CRAFTS*, kunsvlyt; ~ *s DEGREE*, graad in die lettere; *FINE* ~ *s*, skone kunste; *LIBERAL* ~ *s*, vrye kunste; ~ *NEEDLEWORK*, kunsnaaldwerk.

art², (v): *Thou* ~, U is.

art: ~ **dealer**, kunshandelaar; ~ **director**, dekorateur (film); ~ **education**, kunsonderrig.

art'efact, kunswerk, kunsproduk, artefak; werktuig.

artemis'ia, alsemkruid.

arter'ial, slagaar=; ~ **blood**, slagaarbloed; ~ **dilatation**, slagaarverwyding; ~ **haemorrhage**; slagaarbloeding; ~**ize**, aarbloed in slagaarbloed omsit; ~ **road**, grootpad, hoofverkeersweg; kolonnepad.

arterioscleros'is, aarverkalking, arteriosklerose.

arteriostenos'is, slagaarvernouing.

arteriot'omy, arteriotomie.

art'ery, (..ries), slagaar, arterie; hoofverkeersweg; *COELIAC* ~, buikslagaar; *MAIN* ~, hoofslagaar; *PULMONARY* ~, longslagaar; *TEMPORAL* ~, slaapslagaar.

arte'sian, artesies; ~ *well*, artesiese put (boorgat).

art'-exhibition, skilderytentoonstelling, kunstentoonstelling.

art'ful, kunstig; listig, slinks, slu, poliets, loos, deurtrap; ~**ness**, kunstigheid; deurtraptheid, slinksheid, sluheid, loosheid, listigheid.

art: ~ **gallery**, kunsgalery; kunsmuseum; ~ **historian**, kunshistorikus; ~**-historical**, kunshistories; ~ **history**, kunsgeskiedenis.

arthrit'ic, gewrigsontsteking=, artrities.

arthrit'is, gewrigsontsteking, artritis.

arthro'dia, glygewrig; ~**l**, glydend; ~*l joint*, glygewrig.

arthrop'oda, ar'thropods, geleedpotiges, artropode, geleedpotige diere.

arthro'sis, gewrigsaandoening, artrose.

art'ichoke, artisjok; *Jerusalem* ~, aardpeer, Jerusalemartisjok.

art'icle, (n) lidwoord (gram.); stuk, artikel; voorwaarde, ooreenkoms; klousule; ~ *s of APPRENTICESHIP*, leerkontrak, leerskap; ~ *s of ASSOCIATION*, statute van oprigting; *DEFINITE* ~, bepaalde lidwoord; ~ *of DRESS*, kledingstuk; ~ *s of FAITH*, geloofsartikels; ~ *of FURNITURE*, meubelstuk; *the GENUINE* ~, die ware Jakob; *INDEFINITE* ~, onbepaalde lidwoord;

LEADING ~, hoofartikel; ~ *of QUALITY*, kwaliteitsartikel; *SERIES of* ~ *s*, artikelreeks; *SERVE one's* ~ *s*, sy leerskap doen, sy leertyd uitdien (by 'n prokureur); (v) verdeel, indeel (in klousules); inskrywe (as vakleerling); ~ *d clerk*, leerklerk, ingeskrewe klerk.

artic'ular, gewrigs=, lit=.

artic'ulate, (v) duidelik uitspreek; verbind; bepaal; van litte voorsien; (a) duidelik verbonde; duidelik uitgespreek; geartikuleer; geleed, gelit.

articula'tion, duidelike uitspraak, artikulasie; geleding, aanhegting; verstaanbare klank.

art'ifact = **artefact**.

art'ifice, (jakkals)streek, lis; kunsgreep; ~**r**, kunstenaar; uitvinder; handwerksman, vakman.

artifi'cial, kunsmatig; oneg, vals, nagemaak, gekunsteld, kuns=; ~ **diamond**, kunsdiamant; ~ **fibre**, kunshars, kunsvesel; ~ **flower**, kunsblom; ~ **insemination**, kunsmatige bevrugting; ~ **leather**, kunsleer; ~ **leg**, kunsbeen; ~ **light**, kunslig; ~ **line**, hulplyn; ~ **pearls**, onegte pêrels; ~ **resin**, kunshars; ~ **respiration**, kunsmatige asemhaling; ~ **seasoning**, kunsmatige droging; ~ **silk**, kunssy; ~ **teeth**, kunsgebit, kunstande, winkeltande, valstande; ~ **wave**, nagebootste golf (swembad); ~ **wool**, kunswol.

artificial'ity, onnatuurlikheid, gekunsteldheid.

artifi'cialize, onnatuurlik maak.

artifi'cially, kunsmatig; ~ **sweetened**, kunsmatig versoet.

artifi'cialness = **artificiality**.

artill'erist, artilleris, kanonnier.

artill'ery, geskut, artillerie; *HEAVY* ~, grofgeskut; *LIGHT* ~, ligte geskut; ~**-bird**, geel kaffervink *(Ploceus capensis)*; ~ **duel**, grofgeskuttweegeveg; ~ **formation**, spikkelformasie; ~**-park**, kanonpark; ~**-piece**, vuurmond; ~**-range**, artillerieskietbaan; ~ **reservist**, artillerieserwis; ~**-train**, artillerietrein; ~**-wheel**, speelwiel (motor); kanonwiel.

artisan', (hand)werksman, ambagsman.

art'ist, kunstenaar, arties, artis; *COMMERCIAL* ~, handelskunstenaar; ~ *'s MATERIALS*, kunsgerei; ~ *'s MODEL*, beeldhouersmodel; skildersmodel; ~ *'s PROOF*, kunstenaarsproef.

artiste', (beroeps)kunstenaar.

artis'tic, kunsvol, kunstig, artistiek, fraai.

art'istry, kunssin; kunsvaardigheid.

art'less, kunsteloos; eenvoudig, naïef, ongekunsteld; onskuldig; ~**ness**, natuurlikheid, naïwiteit.

art: ~ **needlework**, kunsnaaldwerk; ~ **paper**, kunspapier; ~ **print**, kunsafdruk.

arts: ~ **block**, kunsgebou; letteregebou; ~ **building**, letteregebou, geesteswetenskappegebou; ~ **course**, letterekursus, geesteswetenskaplike kursus.

art'y, gemaak-kunstig, skyn-artistiek, artistiekerig.

ar'um lily, (..lies), varkblom, aronskelk, kalla.

Ar'yan, (n) Ariër; Ariese taal, Indo-Europese tale; (a) Aries.

aryte'noid, bekervormige kraakbeen, gieterkraakbeen.

as, as, soos, gelyk as, net soos, nes; terwyl; (de)wyl, deurdat, aangesien, vermits; namate; wat; ~ *we ADVANCE*, namate ons vorder; ~ *FAR* ~, tot, tot aan; so ver as; ~ *FOR*, wat betref; ~ *good* ~ *done*, feitlik (nagenoeg) afgehandel; ~ *IF*, asof, kastig, kamma; ~ *it IS*, soos sake nou staan; ~ *IT were*, so te sê, as't ware, kwansuis; ~ *I LEFT*, toe ek weggaan; ~ *we LIE!*, gelyk! (gholf); ~ *you LIKE*, soos jy wil; *I thought* ~ *MUCH*, net wat ek gedink het; ~ *ONE man*, soos een man; ~ *PER*, volgens; ~ *REGARDS*, wat betref; ~ *SOON* ~, so gou as; *SUCH* ~, sodanig as, soos; *such THINGS* ~, dinge soos; ~ *THOUGH*, asof; kastig, kamma; ~ *TO*, wat betref; ~ *USUAL*, soos gewoonlik; ~ *WELL* ~, so goed as; sowel as; saam met; ~ *you WERE!*, herstel!; ~ *it WERE*, so te sê; as't ware; ~ *and WHEN*, na gelang van; wanneer; ~ *YET*, nog, tot nog toe.

asafoet'ida, duiwelsdrek.

asbes'tine, asbes=, soos asbes, onbrandbaar.

asbes'tos, gareklip, asbes, doeksteen, steenvlas; **blue** ~, blou asbes, krosidoliet; **white** ~, wit asbes; ~

ascarid 711 *assail*

cement, asbessement, eterniet; ~ **cord,** asbestou; ~ **is,** asbestose, asbessiekte; ~ **paint,** asbesverf; ~ **powder,** poeierasbes; ~ **roof,** asbesdak; ~ **pulp,** asbespap; ~ **sheet,** asbesplaat; ~ **wire,** asbesdraad.
ascar'id, spoelwurm.
ascend', klim, oploop, opstyg, omhoog styg, rys, opvaar; ~ **able,** beklimbaar; ~ **ancy,** ~ **ency,** oorwig, gesag, meerderheid; ~ **ant,** ~ **ent,** (n) oorwig, meerderheid; invloed; horoskoop; voorvader; *IN the* ~ *ant,* aan die opgaan; aan die wenkant; *his STAR is in the* ~ *ant,* die geluk loop hom agterna; (a) opgaand, opdraand; oorheersend; ~ **er,** bosteelletter; ~ **ing,** stygend, opklimmend.
ascen'sion, bestyging; troonsbestyging; hemelvaart, opvaring.
Ascen'sion Day, Hemelvaartsdag.
ascen'sive, stygend; intensief.
ascent', steilte, opdraand; bestyging; beklimming; opgang; *ANGLE of* ~, styghoek, klimhoek; *RATE of* ~, stygsnelheid.
ascertain', verseker, vasstel, bepaal; navraag doen, vergewis, vind, uitvind; ~ **able,** bepaalbaar, naspeurbaar, vasstelbaar; ~ **ed,** uitgemaak, bepaald; ~ **ment,** bepaling, vasstelling, bevestiging.
ascet'ic, (n) kluisenaar, askeet; (a) asketies; ~ **ism,** strenge onthouding, askese; boetedoening.
asci'dian, bekerdier.
ascit'es, buikwatersug.
ascorb'ic acid, askorbinesuur, vitamien C.
ascrib'able, toe te skrywe aan, toeskryfbaar.
ascribe', toeskrywe, toeken, dank, toereken; *they* ~ *his fitness to intensive training,* hulle skryf sy fiksheid toe aan harde (gekonsentreerde) oefening.
ascrip'tion, toeskrywing.
as'cus, sporeblaas.
as'dic, sonar, duikbootopspoorder; ~ **beam,** sonarstraal, duikbootjagstraal.
asem'ia, asemie.
asep'sis, kiemvryheid, asepsis, asepsie.
asep'tic, (n) ontsmettingsmiddel; (a) ontsmettend, kiemvry, asepties.
asex'ual, geslagloos, aseksueel, ongeslagtelik.
ash[1], (n) (-es), as; *BRING back the A* ~ *es,* 'n krieketneerlaag uitwis; *IN* ~ *es,* afgebrand, in die as gelê; *PEACE be to his* ~ *es,* sy as rus in vrede; *REDUCE to* ~ *es,* in die as lê; *RISE from the* ~ *es,* uit die as verrys; *THE A* ~ *es,* die Asse, trofee van krieketkampioenskap tussen Australië en Engeland; (v) veras, verbrand.
ash[2], es(seboom); essehout.
ashamed', beskamend, skaam, skamerig, druipstert; *BE* ~, skaam wees; ~ *FOR,* skaam vir; ~ *OF,* skaam oor.
ash: ~ **-bin,** vuilgoedblik; ~ **blonde,** asblondine; ~ **-box,** asbak; ~ **-bucket,** ~ **can,** asemmer, vuilisbak; ~ **-colour,** askleur; ~ **-ejector,** asuitwerper.
ash'en[1], askleurig, as=, asvaal, vaal; doodsbleek.
ash'en[2], van essehout, es(se)=.
ash'lar, reggekapte klip, hardsteen, arduin; dukjuk; ~ **brick,** reggekapte steen.
ash'laring, rugstutwerk.
ashore', aan land, aan wal; gestrand; *run* ~, op die strand loop, strand.
ash: ~ **-pit,** asput; ~ **-receptacle,** asbakkie; ~ **-tray,** asbakkie; es.
Ash' Wednesday, Asdag.
ash'y, asagtig; asvaal, doodsbleek; asblond.
A'sia, Asië; ~ **Minor,** Klein-Asië; ~ **n,** (n) Asiër; Asiaat; (a) Asiaties.
Asiat'ic, (n) Asiaat; (a) Asiaties; ~ **flu,** Asiatiese (Oosterse) griep.
aside', (n) tersyde, syspraak, apartjie; (adv) tersyde, eenkant, opsy, aan die kant; *LAY* ~, wegbêre, spaar; *SET* ~ *a verdict,* 'n uitspraak vernietig; *SPEAK* ~, privaat met iem. praat; *STAND* ~, opsy staan.
as'inine, eselagtig, esels=; koppig, dom.
asinin'ity, eselagtigheid.
ask, (af)vra; versoek; eis; uitnooi; ~ *ABOUT,* vra na; ~ *for a DAY off,* 'n dag vry vra; ~ *a FAVOUR,* a guns vra; ~ *FOR,* vra om; *be HAD for the* ~ *ing,* uit die ashoop geskop kan word; ~ *for IT,* daarna

soek; *that is* ~ *ing too MUCH of me,* dit is anderkant my uitspanplek; dis bokant my vuurmaakplek; *be* ~ *ed OUT,* uitgenooi word; 'n skiet kry (studentetaal); ~ *a QUESTION,* 'n vraag vra (stel); ~ *to tea,* vir tee (uit)nooi; ~ *the TIME,* vra hoe laat dit is; ~ *for TROUBLE,* moeilikheid soek; daarna soek; sonde soek; *you are asking for TROUBLE,* jy soek moeilikheid; die ongeluk sal jou haal; *not have to be* ~ *ed TWICE,* jou nie laat nooi nie.
askance', askant', skuins, skeef; *look* ~ *at,* iem. agterdogtig (skeef) aankyk.
askar'i, (-s), askari.
askew', skeef, skuins.
aslant', skuins, dwars.
asleep', aan die slaap, in slaap; *fall* ~, aan die slaap raak.
aslope', skuins, hellend, afdraand.
aso'cial, asosiaal; antisosiaal; ~ *behaviour,* asosiale gedrag.
asp[1], esp, trilpopulier.
asp[2], aspis, slang, adder.
aspa'ragus, aspersie; *wild* ~, katbos, katnaels, katdoring; ~ **bed,** aspersiebed(ding); ~ **fern,** siervaring; ~ **gall,** bobbejaanappel.
as'pect, aanblik, vorm; ligging; gedaante, voorkoms; uitsig; kant; oogpunt, gesigspunt; aspek; *another* ~ *of the MATTER,* 'n ander kant v.d. saak; *in its TRUE* ~, in sy ware lig; ~ **'ual,** aspekties.
as'pen, (n) trilpopulier, abeel, esp; (a) espe=, populier=, abeel=; trillend; *shake like an* ~, hewig bewe(e)frees(d) wees; ~ **leaf,** espblaar.
aspergill'um, wywaterkwas.
aspergil'lus, kwasskimmel.
aspe'rity, ruheid, skerpheid; hardheid; strengheid; ~ *of tone,* skamperheid.
asperse', besprinkel; belaster, beswadder, beskinder.
asper'sion, bekladding, betigting, belastering; *cast* ~ *on,* beswadder.
aspersor'ium, wywatervaatjie.
as'phalt, (n) (pad)teer, asfalt, bergpik; (v) teer, asfalteer, asfalt lê; ~ *ed wire,* asfaltdraad; ~ **court,** asfaltbaan; ~ **ite',** asfaltiet; ~ **pavement,** asfaltsypaadjie; ~ **road,** teerpad.
as'phodel, daglelie, immortel.
asphyx'ia, verstikking, skyndood, asfiksie; versmoring; ~ **nt,** (n) stikgas; (a) versmorend; ~ **te,** verstik, versmoor; ~ **'tion,** verstikking; versmoring.
asphyx'y, verstikking, skyndood; asfiksie; versmoring.
as'pic, drilvleis, vleisjellie, aspiek.
aspidis'tra, aspidistra.
as'pirant, aspirant; kandidaat; mededinger.
as'pirate, (n) geaspireerde klank; h-klank; (v) met asemstoot uitspreek, aspireer; deursuig (gas); (a) aangeblaas; stemhebbend.
as'pirating, aspirasie=, aspirerend; suigend; ~ **action,** suigwerking.
aspira'tion, aanblasing, aftapping (gas); verlange, strewe, aspirasie.
as'pirator, suigbuis, lugsuier, aspirator; suigwaaier.
aspire', strewe, hunker, verlang, aspireer, ding, begeer; hom verhef; ~ *after (to),* streef na.
as'pirin, aspirien, asperine (geregistreerde handelsnaam); asetielsalisielsuur.
aspir'ing, eersugtig, vooruitstrewend; ~ **pump,** suigpomp.
asquint', skeel, oormekaar (oë).
ass, (-es), esel, donkie, langoor; domkop; *BE an* ~, 'n skaap (bobbejaan) wees; *A* ~ *s' BRIDGE,* esel(s)brug; *an* ~ *is but an* ~ *though laden with GOLD,* al dra 'n aap 'n goue ring, hy is en bly 'n lelike ding; ~ *'s HEAD,* eselskop; *every* ~ *likes to HEAR himself bray,* elkeen hoor homself graag praat; *MAKE an* ~ *of oneself,* jou belaglik maak; 'n gek van jouself maak; *make an* ~ *of SOMEONE,* iem. belaglik maak; die gek met iem. skeer; *you* ~ *!,* jou esel!
ass'agai, assegaai; *kyk* **assegai.**
assai', (It., mus.), assai, baie; *adagio* ~, adagio assai, baie stadig.
assail', aanval, aanrand; bestorm, bespring, bestook,

assassin   *assumption*

aangryp; ~**able,** aantasbaar; ~**ant,** aanrander, aanvaller, aangryper, bespringer; stormjaer.
assass'in, sluipmoordenaar; ~**ate,** vermoor, (sluip)moord pleeg.
assassina'tion, (sluip)moord.
assass'inator, (sluip)moordenaar.
assault', (n) aanval; aanranding, bedreiging; stormaanval, stormloop; *CARRY by* ~, stormenderhand verower; *COMMON* ~, gewone aanranding; *INDECENT* ~, onsedelike aanranding; ~ *with INTENT,* voorbedagte aanval; (v) aanval; aanrand, te lyf gaan; (be)storm, stormloop; ~**er,** aanrander, aanvaller; ~ **party,** stormafdeling.
assay', (n) toets, proef, keuring, essai; (v) toets, ondersoek, essaieer; onderneem; beproef, probeer; ~ **balance,** justeerskaal; ~**er,** ykmeester, toetser, keurder, essaieur; ~ **furnace,** proefoond; ~ **gold,** proefgoud; ~ **inch,** essaiduim; ~**ing,** keuring; toetsing (mineraal); ~ **master,** muntmeester; ~ **office,** ykkantoor; ~ **value,** essaiwaarde; ~**-weight,** toetsgewig.
ass'-driver, eseldrywer, donkiedrywer.
ass'egai, asgaai, assegaai; ~ **wood,** assegaaihout.
assem'blage, versameling, byeenkoms, vergadering, menigte; montasie.
assem'ble, versamel, vergader, byeenkom, saamkom; monteer, inmekaarsit; byeenroep, bymekaarmaak; saamstel; ~**r,** versamelaar; monteur.
assem'bling, montering; montasie; monteerwerk; ~**-plant,** monteerfabriek; ~**-work,** monteerwerk.
assem'bly, (..**blies),** byeenkoms, vergadering; party; inmekaarsetting, montering montasie (masjien); inrigting; meganiek; onderdeelgroep; *HOUSE of A* ~, Volksraad; *LEGISLATIVE A* ~, Wetgewende Vergadering; *POINT of* ~, versamelpunt; *RIOTOUS* ~, oproerige samekoms; ~ **belt,** monteerband, lopende band; ~ **hall,** vergadersaal; ~ **hangar,** montasieloods; ~ **line,** monteerbaan; ~ **plant,** monteerwerkplaas; monteerfabriek; ~ **room,** vergadersaal; konsertsaal, balsaal.
assent', (n) toestemming, instemming, inwilliging; bewilliging, goedkeuring, beaming; *Royal* ~, koninklike goedkeuring; (v) toestem, instem, bewillig, toestaan, inwillig; ~ *to,* toestem in (tot); instem met.
assenta'tion, slaafse goedkeuring, beaming.
assen'tient, instemmend, toestemmend.
assert', laat geld; aanspraak maak op; staande hou, handhaaf; beweer, bevestig; ~ *ONESELF,* jou laat geld; ~ *one's RIGHTS,* sy regte laat geld; ~**able,** verdedigbaar, beweerbaar; ~**ion,** handhawing; bewering; verklaring; ~**ive,** stellig, uitdruklik; selfbewus; aanmatigend.
ass'es' bridge, eselsbrug, pons asinorum.
assess', belasting oplê, aanslaan, belas, belasting vasstel; skat, raam; takseer, waarde bepaal (iets abstraks); ~ *DAMAGES,* skade vasstel; ~**able,** belasbaar; skatbaar; ~**ed,** aangeslaan; ~**ing office,** aanslagkantoor.
assess'ment, skatting, raming; waardebepaling, waardasie; belasting, aanslag; ~ *of damages,* skadebepaling; ~ **form,** aanslagvorm; ~ **rate,** eiendomsbelasting; skadebepaling.
assess'or, belastingheffer, skatter; assessor; ~ **member,** assessorlid; ~**ship,** assessorskap.
ass'et, besit, baat, bate; aanwins; (pl) boedel, nalatenskap; bates, activa; *BECOME an* ~, 'n aanwins wees; ~*s* and *LIABILITIES,* bates en laste.
assev'erate, plegtig verseker, betuig, verklaar, besweer.
assevera'tion, versekering, betuiging, swering.
assib'ilate, assibileer, as sisklank uitspreek, sis.
assibila'tion, assibilasie, uitspraak met 'n sisklank.
assidu'ity, volharding, naarstigheid, aanhoudende ywer; (..**ties),** voortdurende beleefdhede, attensies.
assid'uous, naarstig, volhardend, dienswillig, (vol)ywerig, aanhoudend; ~ *rain,* landsreën.
assign', (n) regverkryer, sessionaris; (v) aanwys; bepaal; aanstel; toebedeel, toewys, oormaak, opdrag gee; oordra; toeskryf; ~ *one's ESTATE,* sy boedel oordra; ~ *PROPERTY,* eiendom oordra; ~ *a REASON,* a rede opgee; ~ *a TASK,* 'n taak opdra (aan iemand); ~**able,** bepaalbaar, aanwysbaar, toeskryfbaar.
ass'ignat, assinjaat, papiergeld.
assigna'tion, toewysing; oordrag; afspraak; dagvaarding; aanwysing; toeskrywing.
assignee', gevolmagtigde, prokurasiehouer; kurator, boedelberedderaar; sessionaris; regverkrygende.
assign'ment, toewysing; oordrag; toeskrywing; opgawe; aanwysing; taak; boedelafstand.
assign'or, oordraer; boedelafstaner.
assim'ilable, opneembaar, assimileerbaar.
assim'ilate, gelykmaak; eie maak, opneem, verwerk; assimileer; verteer; gelyk word.
assimila'tion, gelykmaking; opname, assimilasie; vereenselwiging.
assim'ilative, assim'ilatory, gelykmakend; assimilerend.
assist', help, aanhelp, handjie bysit, byspring, bystaan, steun; meedoen, bevorder; ~**ance,** hulp, bystand, onderskraging; ondersteuning, handreiking; *with (without)* ~**ance,** met (sonder) ondersteuning; *without my* ~**ance,** sonder my toedoen; ~ **ant,** (n) helper, handlanger; hulponderwyser; assistent; (a) behulpsaam, helpend, hulp=; ~ **antdirector,** assistent-direkteur; assistent-regisseur; ~ *ant to the director (editor, rector),* assistent van die direkteur (redakteur, rektor); *female* ~, vroueassistent, assistente; ~**ed,** gerugsteun.
assize', (n) bepaling, gewigsbepaling; yking (van mate en gewigte); *the GREAT (last)* ~, die laaste oordeel; *THE* ~*s,* sitting v.d. rondgaande hof; (v) skat, raam; vasstel; yk (skaal); ~ **dues,** ykgeld; ~ **law,** ykwet; ~**ment,** yking; ~ **office,** ykkantoor; ~**r,** ykmeester, yker.
associabil'ity, verenigbaarheid.
asso'ciable, verenigbaar.
asso'ciate, (n) maat, (mede)genoot, metgesel; bondgenoot; medelid; assosiaat, newelid; vennoot; medepligtige; (v) *(with),* omgaan met; verenig, verbind; opneem; assosieer, vereenselwig; 'n vereniging aangaan; (a) verenig, verbonde; verwant, geassosieerde, mede=; ~ **member,** geassosieerde lid, assosiaat(lid); sociuss; ~ **professor,** adjunk-professor, mede professor; ~**ship,** assosiaatskap; ~ **society,** assosiaatvereniging.
associa'tion, verbinding; vereniging, genootskap; assosiasie; band; bond; omgang, kameraadskap; ~ *of CONSUMERS,* verbruikersvereniging; ~ *of IDEAS,* ideë-assosiasie; *MEMORANDUM (ARTICLES: DEED) of* ~, akte van oprigting; *in* ~ *WITH,* in oorleg met; ~ **football,** sokker.
assoil', vryspreek; vergewe; boet.
ass'onance, gelykluidendheid; klinkerrym, assonansie.
ass'onant, gelykluidend, assonerend.
assort', uitsoek, sorteer; groepeer, saamvoeg; verkeer met; pas by; ~ *with,* omgaan met; ~**ed,** allerhande, 'n verskeidenheid van; ~**ed sweets (chocolates),** lekkergoedverskeidenheid, sjokoladeverskeidenheid; lekkergoedmengsel, sjokolademengsel; ~**ment,** mengsel, sortering, verskeidenheid; *a large* ~**ment,** 'n groot verskeidenheid; ~ **ment tray,** vakkies(skink)bord.
assuage', versag, vermurf, lenig; laat bedaar; laat afneem; sus, kalmeer; ~ *HUNGER,* honger still; ~ *PAIN,* pyn stil (lenig); ~ *THIRST,* dors les; ~**ment,** versagting, leniging; vermurwing; ~**r,** leniger.
assua'sive, versagtend.
assum'able, aanneembaar, aanvaarbaar.
assum'ably, vermoedelik, blykbaar.
assume', aanneem, opneem; veins; veronderstel; voorgee; aanmatig; aanslaan; aanvaar; ~ *AUTHORITY,* gesag aanvaar; ~ *DUTY,* diens aanvaar; ~ *MANAGEMENT,* die leisels in hande neem; ~ *another NAME,* 'n ander naam aanneem; ~**d,** aangenome; toegeëien; ~*d name,* vals naam; skuilnaam.
assum'ing, aanmatigend, pretensieus; ~ *that,* aangeneem dat, gestel dat.
assump'tion, aanneming, aanvaarding; veronderstel=

ling; aanmatiging; toe-eiening; ~ *of DUTY (WORK)*, diensaanvaarding; *FEAST of the A*~, Hemelvaart van Maria (R.K.); ~ *of OFFICE*, ampsaanvaarding; *ON the* ~ *that*, uitgaande v.d. veronderstelling dat.
assump'tive, aangenome, veronderstel(d); aanmatigend.
assur'able, versekerbaar.
assur'ance, versekering; sekerheid; stoutmoedigheid; (lewens)versekering, assuransie; versekerdheid; vertroue, selfvertroue; gerusstelling; onbeskaamdheid, astrantheid; *GIVE* ~, die versekering gee; *MAKE* ~ *doubly sure*, jou heeltemal verseker (vergewis) dat.
assure', verseker, verassureer; beveilig; betuig; (jou) vergewis; ~ **d,** (n) versekerde; (a) verseker; selfbewus; stellig, seker.
assur'edly, vir seker, gewis, stellig, sekerlik.
assur'er, versekeraar; verassureerder.
assur'gent, opstygend; aanvallend.
Assyr'ia, Assirië; ~**n,** (n) Assiriër; Assiries (language); (a) Assiries.
Assyriol'ogist, Assirioloog.
Assyriol'ogy, Assiriologie.
asta'ble, onstabiel.
astar'board, na stuurboord.
astas'ia, astasie, staanonvermoë.
astat'ic, onvas; onbestendig; astaties; ~ **galvanometer,** astatiese galvanometer; ~**ism,** onvastheid, astatisisme; ~ **needle,** astatiese naald.
a'statine, kunsmatige radioaktiewe element, astaat *(At)*.
as'ter, aster, sterblom, krisant; · **dahlia,** veerdahlia.
aster'ial, sterrekundig; sterre=.
as'terisk, sterretjie, asterisk.
as'terism, drie-ster; gesternte.
astern', agteruit; agter; op die agterskip, agterskeeps.
as'teroid, (n) asteroïed, asteroïde, klein planeet; stervuurwerk; (a) ster=, stervormig; ~ **'al,** asteroïdaal, planetoïdaal.
asthen'ia, swakheid, astenie.
asthen'ical, astenies, swak.
asth'ma, asma, benoudebors; aamborstigheid; ~ **patient,** asmalyer; ~ **t'ic,** (n) asmalyer; (a) aamborstig, asmaties, asma=; ~ **treatment,** asmabehandeling.
As'ti, Asti, wit Italiaanse bruiswyn.
astigmat'ic(ally), astigmaties.
astig'matism, astigmatisme.
astil'be, astilbe.
astir', in beweging, op die been; in rep en roer, opgewonde.
astom'atous, mondloos.
aston'ish, verbaas, verwonder, dronkslaan; ~**ed,** verbaas, verwonder, verstom; *be* ~*ed at*, verbaas wees oor; ~**ing,** verbasend, verwonderlik, verwonder(d); ~**ment,** verbasing, bevreemding, ontsetting, verwondering.
astound', verbaas, dronkslaan; ~**ed,** verbaas, dronkgeslaan; ~**ing,** verbasend, ontstellend, asembenemend, asemberowend; *an* ~*ing performance*, 'n asemberowende uitvoering.
astrad'dle, wydsbeen, skrylings.
as'tragal, lyswerk; stylband.
astrag'alus, (..li), dolos, kootbeen, astragalus.
astrakhan', astrakan, karakoelwol.
as'tral, ster=, astraal; ~ **body,** astraalliggaam; ~ **globe,** hemelbol; ~ **lamp,** astraallamp; sterlamp; ~ **spirits,** astraalgeeste.
astray', verdwaal, afdwaal; *GO* ~, verdwaal, van die spoor raak; onklaar trap; die verkeerde pad opgaan; *LEAD* ~, verlei; verkeerd lei; op 'n dwaalspoor bring.
astrict', saamtrek; stelp; verstop.
astric'tion, saamtrekking; stelping; verstopping.
astric'tive, saamtrekkend; stelpend.
astride', wydsbeen, skrylings.
astringe', saamtrek, adstringeer; verstop, konstipeer.
astrin'gency, sametrekking; saamtrekkende hoedanigheid; strengheid; vrankheid.
astrin'gent, (n) saamtrekmiddel; stopmiddel, bloedstelper, bloedstelpende middel; (a) saamtrekkend, adstringerend; (bloed)stelpend; streng; vrank.
as'tro: ~ **botany,** astrobotanie; ~ **dome,** sterrekoepel, astrokoepel; ~ **'geny,** astrogenie; ~ **'graphy,** astrografie; ~ **hatch,** sterrekoepel, astrokoepel; ~ **labe,** sterrehoekmeter, astrolabium; ~ **latry,** astrolatrie; ~ **'loger,** astroloog, sterrewiggelaar; ~ **log'ical,** astrologies; ~ **'logy,** astrologie, sterrewiggelary; ~ **'meter,** astrometer, sterligmeter; ~ **'metry,** astrometrie.
as'tronaut, ruimtevaarder, ruimteman; ..**naut'ical,** ruim(te)vlug=, astronouties; ..**naut'ics,** ruimtevaart(kunde).
astron'omer, sterrekundige, astronoom.
astronom'ic, astronomies, sterrekundig; ontsaglik (getal).
astron'omy, sterrekunde, astronomie.
astrophotog'raphy, sterrefotografie, astrofotografie.
astrophys'ical, astrofisies.
astrophys'icist, astrofisikus.
astrophys'ics, astrofisika.
astute', slim, skerpsinnig; geslepe, skelm, slu; ~**ness,** slimheid, skerpsinnigheid; geslepenheid, sluheid.
asun'der, uitmekaar, vaneen, vanmekaar; afsonderlik; in stukke; uiteen; *BURST* ~; uiteenbars; *TEAR* ~, uitmekaarskeur.
As'wan, Aswan.
aswarm', aan die swerm.
asyl'um, (-s), skuilplek; asiel; toevlugsoord; toevlug; gestig; vryplaas, vryplek; *LUNATIC* ~, kranksinnigegestig; *MENTAL* ~, sielsiekegestig; *seek POLITICAL* ~, om politieke asiel aansoek doen.
asymmet'ric(al), ongelykmatig, asimmetries.
asymm'etry, oneweredigheid, asimmetrie.
as'ymptote, asimptoot.
asynde'tic, asindeties.
asyn'deton, asindetiese verbinding, asindeton.
at, tot; te, op, in; aan, by; teen; met; na; oor; *AIM* ~, mik na; *not* ~ *ALL*, glad nie, heeltemal nie; *ARRIVE* ~, aankom by (in); *BE* · ~ *it*, besig wees met; ~ *BEST*, op sy beste; ~ *BILLIARDS*, by biljart; ~ *BREAK of day*, met dagbreek; *BUSY* ~, besig met; ~ *a DISTANCE*, op 'n afstand; ~ *FIRST*, eers; *GET* ~ *someone*, iem. in die hande kry; ~ *their HANDS*, deur hulle; ~ *HOME*, tuis; ~ *LAST*, eindelik; ~ *the LATEST*, op die (ten) laatste; op sy laaste, uiterlik; *LAUGH* ~, lag vir (oor); ~ *LEAST*, ten minste, minstens; ~ *a LOSS*, teen 'n verlies; verleë, in die middel van die wêreld; ~ *someone's MERCY*, aan iem. se genade oorgelewer; ~ *MOST*, uiters; ~ *ONCE*, dadelik; ~ *ONE*, om eenuur; eensgesind, eens; ~ *PRESENT*, teenswoordig; nou; op die oomblik, tans; ~ *PRETORIA*, in (op) Pretoria; ~ *a PROFIT*, met (teen) 'n wins; ~ *ten RAND*, teen tien rand; ~ *my REQUEST*, op my versoek; *be* ~ *SEA*, heeltemal deurmekaar wees; ~ *SWORD'S point*, op die punt van die degen; ~ *THAT*, daarby, daarmee, nogtans; ~ *the VERY first*, heel in (aan) die begin; ~ *WORK*, aan die werk; ~ *WORST*, op sy slegste, op sy ergste.
atabrin(e) = atebrin(e).
ata'camite, atakamiet.
atarac'tic, kalmeermiddel.
atarax'ia, a'taraxy, ataraksie.
at'avism, atavisme, terugaarding, terugslag.
atavis'tic, atavisties.
ataxia = ataxy.
atax'ic, ataksies, onreëlmatig.
atax'y, ataksie, onreëlmatigheid, koördinasiesteuring; *locomotor* ~, motoriese ataksie, bewegingsteurnis.
a'tebrin(e), atabrine, atebrine, atabrien, atebrien.
atelier' ateljee.
a tem'po, (It., mus.), a tempo.
atha'nasy, atanasie, onsterflikheid.
ath'eism, godversaking, godloëning, ateïsme, vrydenkery.
ath'eist, godversaker, godloënaar, ateïs, vrydenker.
atheis'tic(al), ateïsties, godloënend.

athematic 714 *attention*

athema'tic, atematies, temaloos; sonder tematiese vokaal.
athenae'um, (-s), wetenskaplike of letterkundige vereniging; leessaal; atheneum.
Athen'ian, (n) Athener; Atheense (vrou); (a) Atheens.
Ath'ens, Athene.
athero'ma, ateroom, vetkliergewas, vetkliergeswel.
athirst', dorstig; gretig, verlangend.
ath'lete, atleet, sportman; ~ 's foot, voetskimmel; tinea; ~ 's heart, vergrote hart.
athlet'ic, atleties, sport=; frisgeboud, sterk, gespierd; ~ism, atletisisme; ~s, sport; atletiek; ~s track, atletiekbaan.
at-home', ontvangs, resepsie; ontvangdag.
athwart', dwarsoor; (oor)dwars; ~ -ships, dwarsskeeps.
atilt', skuins.
a-tin'gle, tintelend.
a-tip'-toe, op die punte v.d. tone.
atlant', atlant.
Atlan'tic, (n) Atlantiese Oseaan; (a) Atlanties; ~ *CHARTER*, Atlantiese Handves; ~ *OCEAN*, Atlantiese Oseaan.
atlan'tasaurus, atlantasourus.
at'las¹, (-es), atlas; draerwerwel, eerste halswerwel.
at'las², sysatyn.
atmol'ogy, verdampingsleer, atmologie.
atmol'ysis, gasontleding, atmolise.
atmom'eter, verdampingsmeter, atmometer.
at'mosphere, atmosfeer, dampkring, lug; *create an* ~, 'n stemming skep.
atmospher'ic, atmosferies, lug=, dampkrings=; ~ **density**, lugdigtheid; ~ **electricity**, lugelektrisiteit; ~ **haze**, dynserigheid, waas; ~ **pressure**, lugdruk; ~ **radiation**, atmosferiese straling; ~s, leer v.d. atmosfeer; lugverstoring, atmosferiese steurings, lugsteuring.
atoll', atol, lagunerif, ringeiland.
at'om, atoom, stofdeeltjie; stoffie, krieseltjie, sier, ietsie, greintjie; ~ **bomb**, atoombom.
atom'ic, atomies, atoom=; ~ **age**, atoomeeu; ~ **bomb**, atoombom; ~ **energy**, atoomenergie; ~ **era**, atoomtydperk; ~ **fission**, atoomsplitsing; ~ **nucleus**, atoomkern; ~ **pile**, atoomsuil; ~ **power**, atoomkrag; ~ **test**, atoomtoets; ~ **theory**, atoomteorie; ~ **war**, atoomoorlog; ~ **waste**, kernafval; ~ **weight**, atoomgewig. NB. *Kyk ook* **nuclear**.
at'om: ~ **ic'ity**, atomistiek; ~ **ism**, atomeleer, atomisme; ~ **is'tic**, atomisties; ~ **is'tics**, kernleer; ~ **iza'tion**, verstuiwing; ~ **ize**, atomiseer, tot atome teruglei; verdeel; verklein; ~ **izer**, neusspuit; verstuiwingstoestel; verstuiwer; ~ **plant**, atoominstallasie; kerninstallasie; ~ **-powered**, atoomaangedrewe; ~ **reactor**, atoomreaktor, kernreaktor.
at'omy¹, (atomies), geraamte, skelet.
at'omy², (obs.), atoompie, klein wesentjie.
aton'able, versoenbaar, wat goedgemaak kan word.
ato'nal, atonaal; ~ *music*, atonale musiek; ~ **'ity**, atonaliteit.
atone', boete doen, goedmaak, boet; versoen; ~ **ment**, boete(doening); vergoeding; versoening; voldoening; *Day of A* ~ *ment*, Versoendag.
aton'ic, (n) onbeklemtoonde (onbeklemtoonde) woord; (a) toonloos, atonies; slap.
aton'ing, versoenend; ~ **sacrifice**, soenoffer.
at'ony, toonloosheid, atonie; swakheid (van lid); atonie.
atop', bo-op.
atrabil'iar, atrabil'ious, swartgallig, bitter; ~ **ness**, swartgalligheid.
atramen'tal, inkswart, swart.
atrip', opgehys, uit die grond gelig (van anker).
at'rium, (..ria, -s), atrium, voorhuis; voorhof; hartboesem (fisiologie).
atro'cious, gruwelik, afgryslik, verskriklik, wreedaardig, snood; buitengewoon sleg, vrot; ~ **ness**, gruwelikheid, snoodheid.
atro'city, (..ties), gruweldaad, afgryslikheid, gruwelstuk, snoodheid, wreedaardigheid; flater.
at'rophy, (n) uittering, wegkwyning, atrofie; (v) uitteer, wegkwyn.
at'ropine, atropien, atropine.

at'ropism, belladonnavergiftiging.
a'trous, pikswart.
att'aboy! ryperd! ou haan! ou doring!
attach', vasmaak, aanheg; boei; aanhang; in beslag neem (eiendom); verbind; gevange neem; aanlas; ~ *BLAME to*, skuld gee aan; *DEEPLY* ~ *ed to his parents*, innig verknog aan sy ouers; *GREATLY* ~ *ed to one another*, baie geheg aan mekaar; *no blame* ~ *es to HIM*, hy dra geen skuld nie; ~ *IMPORTANCE to*, waarde heg aan; ~ **able**, aanhegbaar, waarop beslag gelê kan word.
atta'ché, (gesantskaps)attaché; ~ **case**, aktetas, handsak, dokumentetas.
attach'ed, verkleef, verknog, geheg.
attach'ment, band, verbinding; aanhegtoestel; hegstuk; geneentheid, gehegtheid, aanhanklikheid, verkleefdheid, verknogtheid; beslag(legging); inhegtenisneming; ~ *of DEBT*, skuldbeslaglegging; ~ *of GOODS*, beslaglegging op goedere; inbeslagneming van goedere; ~ **pin**, bevestigingspen; ~ **s**, toebehore, bybehore; ~ **screw**, hegskroef.
attack', (n) stormloop; aanval; aantasting; *LAUNCH an* ~, 'n aanval loods (rig op, tot); *ON the* ~, aanvallend; op die aanval wees; *POINT of* ~, aanvalspunt, aanvalsplek; *a SLIGHT* ~, 'n ligte aanval; *SOUND the* ~, die aanval blaas, begin aanval; *UNDER* ~, aangeval (word); (v) aanval, binneval; aanrand, aantas, aangryp, te lyf gaan, bevlieg; aanpak; ~ **able**, aantasbaar; ~ **er**, aanvaller, aangryper; ~ **ing force**, aanvalsmag.
attain', bereik, verkry; *he will not* ~ *his GOAL*, sy mes is stomp; ~ *TO*, kom tot; ~ **abil'ity**, bereikbaarheid; ~ **able**, bereikbaar, verkrygbaar; ~ **ableness = attainability**; ~ **der**, verlies van burgerreg weens hoogverraad, ontburgering; eerverlies; *bill of* ~ *der*, wetsontwerp ter veroordeling weens hoogverraad; ~ **ment**, bereik, verkryging; ~ **ments**, talente, kundighede, bekwaamhede.
attaint', besmet, besoedel; aankla weens hoogverraad; aansteek.
att'al = **attle**.
att'ar, roosolie, attar(olie).
attem'per, temper, matig, versag; aanpas by.
attempt', (n) poging, aanslag, probeerslag; onderneming; *CRIMINAL* ~, misdadige aanslag, poging tot misdaad; *MAKE an* ~, 'n poging aanwend; *MAKE an* ~ *on someone's life*, iem. na die lewe staan; 'n moordaanslag op iem. waag (uitvoer); *MURDEROUS* ~, moordaanslag, moordpoging; (v) probeer, trag, beproef; onderneem; 'n aanslag doen op; ~ *the IMPOSSIBLE*, sop met 'n vurk eet; ~ **ed**, beproef; ~ *ed MURDER*, moordaanslag, poging tot moord.
attend', ag gee, let op, oppas; bywoon; vergesel; oplet, aandag skenk aan; (be)dien; oor 'n sieke gaan, behandel (pasiënt); ~ *ed BY*, vergesel deur; gepaard met; ~ *CLASSES*, klasse bywoon; ~ *to DUTY*, plig(te) nakom; ~ *SCHOOL*, skoolgaan; ~ *TO*, let op; oppas; aandag skenk aan; ~ *as WITNESS*, as getuie verskyn.
atten'dance, bediening; behandeling; bywoning; *BE in* ~, bedien, oppas; diens hê; aanwesig wees; *COMPULSORY* ~, verpligte bywoning; *DANCE* ~ *on*, orals naloop, attensies opdring; *HOURS of* ~, diensure, kantoorure, dienstyd, kantoortyd; ~ *at MEETING*, bywoning van vergadering; ~ **fee**, presensiegeld; ~ **list**, presensielys; bywoningsregister; ~ **-officer**, skoolbesoekbeampte, ~ **register**, presensielys; bywoningsregister.
atten'dant, (n) geleier; bediende, oppasser; lid van gevolg, volgeling; (a) aanwesig; vergesellend; diensdoende; ~ *circumstances*, (bykomende) omstandighede; ~ *officer*, geleide-offisier.
atten'tion, (n) aandag, oplettendheid; sorg; (pl) beleefdhede, attensies; *ATTRACT* ~, aandag trek; *CALL for* ~, aandag vra; *DIRECT (call)* ~ *to*, die aandag vestig op; ~ *to DUTY*, pligsbetragting, pligsvervulling; *pay NO* ~ *to*, geen ag slaan nie op; geen aandag wy nie aan; *pay ONE'S* ~ *s to*, die hof maak; *PAY* ~, aandag gee; *with RAPT* ~, met gespanne aandag; *STAND to* ~, op aandag staan; (interj) ~!, aandag! gee ag!

atten'tive, oplettend, aandagtig; beleef(d); ~ **ly,** aandagtig, gespits; ~ **ness,** oplettendheid; opmerksaamheid; beleefdheid.
atten'uate, (v) verdun; verswak; maer word; uitteer, vermaer; versag; (a) dun, maer; swak; verswak; verdun.
attenua'tion, verdunning, verswakking; vermaering, uittering; demping (elek.).
atten'uator, verswakker, demper.
attest', (n) getuienis, verklaring, attes; (v) betuig, waarmerk, bevestig; tot getuie roep; beëdig; die eed aflê, attesteer; ~ *to,* getuig van; ~ **ant,** attesteerder; getuie.
attesta'tion, verklaring, getuienis; beëdiging; getuigskrif, bewys; attes(tasie), eedafneming.
attes'ted, gestaaf (deur getuienis).
attes'tor, verklaarder, getuie; beëdiger.
Att'ic¹, Atties; ~ *wit (salt),* Attiese geestigheid (sout).
att'ic², solderkamer, dakkamer, vliering; ~ *window,* soldervenster, dakvenster.
att'icism, attisisme.
att'ic window, soldervenster, dakvenster.
attire', (n) drag, kleding; opskik; (v) (aan)klee; versier, dos, optooi.
att'itude, gestalte, stand, houding; gesindheid; kyk (op sake); ~ *of MIND,* sienswyse, standpunt; gemoedstoestand; *STRIKE an* ~, poseer, 'n houding aanneem; hom aanstel; *TAKE up an* ~, 'n houding aanneem; 'n standpunt inneem; ~ *TOWARDS life,* lewenshouding.
attitudinar'ian, aansteller, poseerder, poseur.
attitud'inize, poseer, 'n aanstellerige houding aanneem; ~ **r,** poseur.
att'le, afvalerts.
attorn', oordra (wet); ~ **ment,** oordrag.
attorn'ey, (-s), prokureur; saakwaarnemer; *letter (power) of* ~, prokurasie, volmag; ~ **-general,** (~ **s-general),** staatsprokureur, prokureur-generaal; ~ **ship,** prokureurskap; prokurasieskap.
attorn'ment, oordrag(serkenning) (wet).
attract', aantrek; aanlok; boei; ~ **ed,** getrokke; ~ **ing,** aantreklik; aantrekkend.
attrac'tion, aantreklikheid, aantrekkingskrag; *CAPILLARY* ~, kapillêre aantrekking; *FORCE of* ~, aantrekkingskrag; ~ *of GRAVITY,* swaartekrag; *a GREAT* ~, iets baie verleideliks; 'n groot aantreklikheid; *MAGNETIC* ~, magnetiese aantrekking; *MOLECULAR* ~, molekulêre aantrekking.
attrac'tive, aantreklik, aanloklik; boeiend, bekoorlik; aantrekkend; aanhalig, ~ **ness,** aantreklikheid, aanloklikheid, aanhaligheid; bekoorlikheid.
attrib'utable, toeskryfbaar; te wyte (aan) (ongunstig); te danke (aan) (gunstig).
att'ribute¹, (n) hoedanigheid, kenmerk; eienskap; attribuut; byvoeglike (attributiewe) bepaling.
attrib'ute², (v) toeskryf aan; toedig; wyt.
attribu'tion, toeskrywing, toerekening.
attrib'utive, (n) attribuut; (a) attributief, ~ *adjective,* attributiewe byvoeglike naamwoord (adjektief).
attrit'ed, afgeslyt, glad gevryf
attri'tion, wrywing, afslyting; afskuring, skawing; berou; *war of* ~, uitputtingsoorlog.
attune', stem; in ooreenstemming bring; welluidend maak.
At'wood's machine, valmasjien.
atyp'ical, onreëlmatig, atipies.
aubade', oggendgedig, môrehulde, aubade, musikale môregroet.
auberge', (F.), herberg.
aub'ergine, eiervrug, brinjal.
aubrie'tia, aubrietia.
aub'urn, goudbruin, rooibruin, kastaiingbruin; ~ *hair,* rooibruin hare.
au courant', (F.), au courant, goed ingelig, op hoogte van sake.
auc'tion, openbare verkoping, vendusie, veiling; *AMERICAN* ~, Amerikaanse veiling; *DUTCH* ~, verkoping by afslag; *SELL by* ~, opveil; ~ **bridge,** brug, opjaagbrug, opveilbrug; ~ **dues,** venduregte.

auctioneer', (n) (vendu)afslaer; (v) opveil, vendusie hou; ~ **ing,** afslaery, vendusiewese; ~ **ing concern,** vendu(sie)saak, afslaersonderneming; ~ **'s stockyard,** vendusiekraal.
auc'tion: ~ **list,** vendulys, vendurol; ~ **mart,** vendusiesaal, verkooplokaal; ~ **room,** verkooplokaal; ~ **sale,** vendusie.
auda'cious, vermetel, stoutmoedig; astrant, onbeskaam; ~ **ness,** vermetelheid, driestheid, (oor)moed; waagmoed; onbeskaamdheid, astrantheid, brutaliteit.
auda'city = **audaciousness.**
audibil'ity, hoorbaarheid.
aud'ible, hoorbaar, verneembaar.
aud'ience, gehoor; publiek, toehoorders; oudiënsie; *GIVE* ~, gehoor verleen, oudiënsie gee, te woord staan; *RECEIVE in* ~, in oudiënsie ontvang.
aud'ile, (n) ouditiewe tipe; (a) ouditief.
au'dio, klankreproduksie.
aud'iofre'quency, gehoorfrekwensie.
aud'iogram, oudiogram.
aud'iograph, geluidmeter, oudiograaf.
audio'logist, oudioloog, gehoorkundige.
audio'logy, gehoorleer, oudiologie.
audiom'eter, gehoormeter, oudiometer.
audiomet'ric, oudiometries.
audiom'etrist, oudiometris.
audiom'etry, gehoormeting, oudiometrie.
aud'io-tac'tual, oudiotaktiel.
audio-vis'ual, oudiovisueel; ~ **education,** oudiovisuele onderrig.
aud'it, (n) oudit, verifikasie, ouditering, rekeningkontrole; (v) nasien, oudit, ouditeer, rekeninge nasien; verifieer; ~ **ing,** ouditkunde; nasien, ouditering.
audi'tion, gehoor; proefvoordrag, oudisie.
aud'itive, gehoors-, ouditief.
aud'itor, hoorder; ouditeur; ~ **'s report,** ouditverslag; ~ **-general,** (~ **s-general),** ouditeur-generaal.
auditor'ium, (..ria, -s), gehoorsaal, ouditorium; kloostersspreekkamer.
aud'itory, (n) (..ries), gehoorsaal, ouditorium; skip (kerk); toehoorders; (a) v.d. gehoor; gehoors-; ouditories; ~ **canal,** gehoorbuis; ~ **nerve,** gehoorsenuwee.
aud'it: ~ **query,** (..ries), ouditeursondersoek; ouditeurs(na)vraag; ~ **return,** ouditeeropgawe.
au fait': (F.), *be* ~, op hoogte van sake wees.
Auge'an, Augias-; ~ **stable,** Augiasstal; *cleanse the* ~ *stable,* die Augiasstal reinig.
aug'er, awegaar, swikboor, skroefboor, grootboor; ~ **-beetle,** boorkewer; ~ **bit,** spiraalboor, awegaarboor; ~ **file,** boorvyl, awegaarvyl.
aught, iet(s); *for* ~ *I know,* sover ek weet.
au gite, ougiet.
aug'ment¹, (n) (klinker)voorvoegsel (in ouer Ariese tale); ougment.
augment'², (v) vermeerder, uitbrei, toeneem, vergroot; ~ **ed choir,** versterkte koor; ~ **ed interval,** vergrote interval.
augmenta'tion, vermeerdering, vergroting, verhoging; toeneming; toevoegsel; aangroei.
augmen'tative, (n) ougmentatief; (a) vermeerderend, versterkend, aanvullend.
Augra'bies: ~ *Falls,* die Augrabieswaterval.
Augs'burg, Augsburg; *the* ~ *Confession,* die Augsburgse Geloofsbelydenis.
aug'ur, (n) waarsêer, voëlwiggelaar; (v) voorspel, wiggel, waarsê; *it* ~ *s well,* dit beloof veel (baie).
aug'ury, (auguries), waarsêery, voorspelling, voëlwiggelary; voorteken, voorbode; belofte.
Aug'ust¹, (n) Augustus(maand).
august'², (a) verhewe, majestueus, groots, deurlugtig.
Augus'tan, Augustyns; *the* ~ *AGE,* die eeu van Augustus; *the* ~ *CONFESSION,* die Augustynse Geloofsbelydenis.
Augus'tine, (n) Augustinus; Augustyner(monnik); (a) Augustyns.
august'ness, verhewenheid, grootsheid, deurlugtigheid.
auk, alk, papegaaiduiker.

auld, (Sc.), oud; *for* ~ *lang syne,* uit ou vriendskap, ter wille van die ou dae.
aul'ic, hof=.
aum, aam.
au naturel', (F.), au naturel, ongekook.
aunt, tant(e); *my SAINTED* ~*!,* liewe tyd!, magistraat!, hygend!, allamaggies!; *an A* ~ *SALLY,* die teiken of mikpunt van almal; ~ *SUSIE,* tant Sannie.
aun'tie, tannie.
au pair', (F.), au pair.
aur'a, aura; uitwaseming, uitstraling; gewaarwording.
aur'al¹, lug=; uitstralings=.
aur'al², oor=; gehoor=; ~ **nerve,** gehoorsenuwee.
aur'eate, goudagtig, goudgeel.
aure'ola, aur'eole,stralekrans, ligkrans, gloriekroon, heilige krans, oureool.
aureomy'cin, oureomisien, oureomisine.
au revoir', (F.), au revoir, tot siens, tot weersiens.
au'ric, goud=, goue.
au'ricle, oorskulp; hartvoorkamer; ourikel.
auric'ular, oor=; ~ **confession,** oorbieg; ~ **tradition,** mondelinge oorlewering (tradisie); ~ **tube,** praathoring.
auric'ulate, oorvormig; met ore, geoord.
aurif'erous, goudhoudend, gouddraend.
aur'iform, oorvormig.
Auri'ga, die Wadrywer (ster).
au'rin(e), ourien, ourine.
aur'iscope, oorspieël.
aur'ist, oordokter, oorspesialis.
aur'ochs, oeros, wisent.
auror'a, daeraad, dagbreek; rooidag; ~ **australis,** suiderlig; ~ **borealis,** noorderlig; ~**l,** noorderlig=.
ausculta'tion, ouskultasie, stetoskopiese ondersoek, beluistering.
ausculta'tory, ouskultaties.
au sérieux', (F.), ernstig, au serieux.
aus'picate, inwy; voorspel.
aus'pice, voorteken, voorspelling; (pl) bystand, beskerming, ouspisieë; *under the* ~ *s of,* onder beskerming van.
auspi'cious, gunstig, gelukkig, veelbelowend; ~**ness,** gunstigheid, veelbelowendheid.
Auss'ie, Australiër.
aus'tenite, austeniet.
austere', straf, (ge)streng; grimmig, nors; vrank; stemmig, eenvoudig, armoedig; ~ *life,* eenvoudige lewe; ~**ness,** ..**te'rity,** strengheid, hardheid, strafheid; ~ eenvoud(igheid); ..*terity measure,* besparingsmaatreël.
auste'rity building, spaarbou(wyse).
Au'stin friar, Augustyner(broeder).
aus'tral, suidelik, oustraal.
Australa'sia, Australasië.
Austral'ia, Australië, ~**n,** (n) Australiër, (a) Australies.
Australopi'thecus, Austrialopithecus.
Aus'tralorp, Australorp(hoender).
Aus'tria, Oostenryk; ~**n,** (n) Oostenryker; (a) Oostenryks.
autar'chic(al), outargies.
aut'archy, selfbestuur, outargie.
autar'kic(al), selfgenoegsaam, selfversorgend.
aut'arky, selfgenoegsaamheid, outarkie.
authen'tic, eg, opreg, outentiek, geloofwaardig, betroubaar; ~ **ate,** bekragtig, waarmerk; eg verklaar; die outeur vasstel, ~**a'tion,** bekragtiging, stawing; waarmerking.
authenti'city, egtheid, geloofwaardigheid, betroubaarheid.
auth'or, bewerker; skepper; verwekker; skrywer, outeur; dader; ~ *'s CORRECTION,* skrywerskorreksie, outeurskorreksie; ~ *'s FEES,* outeursaandeel, honorarium; ~ *'s RIGHTS,* outeursreg, vrugreg; ~**ess,** (-es), skryfster.
authoriza'tion, magtiging, outorisasie; volmag.
auth'orize, magtig; wettig, outoriseer; ~**d,** geoutoriseer(d); ~*d capital,* toegestane (statutêre) kapitaal.
autho'ritative, gesaghebbend, outoritêr; gebiedend;

~ **ly,** gebiedenderwys(e); gesaghebbend; *learn* ~ *ly,* uit gesaghebbende bron verneem.
autho'rity, (..**ties),** gesag, heerskappy, seggenskap, mag, invloed; vergunning; owerheidspersoon; outoriteit; mandaat, volmag, magtiging; segsman; bewysplek; (pl) owerheid, gesaghebbendes; *BY the* ~ *of,* met magtiging van; *on GOOD* ~ *,* op goeie gesag; van gesaghebbende bron; *on one's OWN* ~ *,* op eie gesag; *he is a RENOWNED* ~ *on nuclear physics,* hy is 'n beroemde deskundige op die gebied v.d. kernfisika; *by VIRTUE of the* ~ *conferred by,* ingevolge magtiging van; *by the WRITTEN* ~ *of,* op skriftelike magtiging van.
auth'orship, outeurskap, skrywerskap.
autis'm, outisme.
autis'tic, outisties; ~ *child,* outistiese kind; ~ *school,* skool vir outistiese kinders.
au'to, (-s), outo(mobiel), motor(kar).
auto-ana'lysis, selfontleding, selfanalise.
au'tobahn, (Ger.), autobahn, deurpad, snelweg.
aut'obike, outofiets.
autobiog'rapher, outobiograaf.
autobiograph'ic(al), outobiografies.
autobiog'raphy, (..**phies),** outobiografie, eielewensbeskrywing.
aut'obus, (-es), (outo)bus.
au'tocade, motoroptog.
aut'ocar, outo(mobiel), motor(kar).
autoceph'alous, onafhanklik.
autoch'thon, (-es, -s), outochtoon, inboorling; ~**ous,** inheems, outochtoon.
au'toclave, outoklaaf, stoomsterilisator, stoomsteriliseerder; stoomketel.
au'tocode, outokode.
autoc'racy, (..**cies),** alleenheerskappy, outokrasie.
aut'ocrat, alleenheerser, outokraat.
autocrat'ic(al), eiemagtig, outokraties.
au'tocross, veldmotor; ~ *race,* veldmotorwedren.
aut'ocycle, kragfiets, outofiets, motorfiets.
aut'o-da-fé', (autos-da-fé), auto-da-fé, ketterverbranding.
aut'odidact, outodidak; ~**ic,** outodidakties.
autodynam'ic, selfwerkend, outodinamies.
auto-e'rotism, outo-erotisme.
auto'gamy, outogamie, selfbevrugting.
autog'enous, spontaan voortbrengend.
autog'eny, spontane voortbrenging.
aut'ograph, (n) eie handskrif, handtekening, outograaf; litografiese afdruk; (v) eiehandig opstel; teken; litografies afdruk; ~ **'ic,** eiehandig.
autog'raphy, eiehandige skrif; oorspronklike handskrif; outografie, litografiese afdruk.
autogy'ro, (-s), (wind)meulvliegtuig, outogiro.
aut'oharp, harp.
aut'ohoist, hefbrug (motorhawe).
auto-igni'tion, selfontbranding.
auto-immu'ne, outo-immuun, selfimmuun.
auto-immuniza'tion, selfimmunisasie, outo-immunisasie, selfsouting.
auto-infec'tion, selfbesmetting.
auto-intoxica'tion, selfvergiftiging.
aut'olith, outoliet.
auto'lysis, outolise.
autoly'tic, outolities.
aut'omat, outomaat; muntoutomaat.
automat'ic, (n) outomatiese pistool; sarsiewapen; (a) selfbewegend; werktuiglik, vanself, outomaties; ~ **advance,** outomatiese vervroeging.
automat'ically, vanself, outomaties
automat'ic: ~ **clutch,** outomatiese koppelaar; ~ **device,** outomaat; ~ **feeder,** selfvoerder; ~ **gearbox,** outomatiese ratkas; ~ **level control,** outomatiese vlakkontrole; ~ **lift,** outomatiese hyser; ~ **pilot,** stuuroutomaat; ~ **release,** selfuitskakeling; ~ **system,** outomatiese stelsel; ~ **telephone,** outomatiese telefoon; ~ **traffic signal,** outomatiese verkeersein; ~ **transmission,** outomatiese ratwisseling; ~ **valve,** outomatiese klep; ~ **writing,** outomatiese skrif.
automati'city, outomatisiteit.
automa'tion, outomatisasie.
autom'atism, onwillekeurigheid (van beweging), onbewuste masjinale handeling, werktuiglikheid.

autom'atize, outomatiseer.
autom'aton, (-s, ..ta), selfbewegende werktuig, outomaat.
autom'etry, selfmeting; selfwaardering.
aut'omobile, automobile', outo(mobiel), motor(kar).
automo'bilism, automobilism', motorsport, outomobilisme.
automobilist', motorryer, outoryer, bestuurder.
automor'phic, eievormig, idiomorf, outomorf.
automo'tive supplies, motorvoorrade.
automo'tive work, motorwerk.
autonom'ic, auton'omous, selfbesturend, selfregerend, eiewetlik, outonoom.
auton'omy, selfbestuur, selfregering, selfstandigheid, outonomie.
aut'onym, eie naam, ware naam.
aut'opilot, outomatiese loods.
autop'sy, (..sies), lyskouing, lykopening, outopsie; kritiese ontleding.
autora'diograph, outoradiograaf, outoradiofoto.
autoregula'tion, selfreëling.
au'toroute, (F.), deurpad, snelweg, autoroute.
autostra'da, (It.), deurpad, snelweg, autostrada.
autosugges'tion, outosuggestie.
autote'lic, outoteles.
autother'apy, outoterapie.
autotoxica'tion, selfvergiftiging.
autoto'xin, outotoksien, outotoksine.
autotro'phic, outotrofies, outotroof.
aut'otype, faksimilee, troue weergawe, outotipe.
aut'umn, herfs, najaar; *in* ~, in die herfs.
autum'nal, najaars-, herfs-, herfsagtig; ~ **equinox**, herfsnagewening.
aut'umn: ~ **gale**, najaarstorm; ~ **sale**, najaarspruiming; ~ **time**, herfs(tyd).
auxil'iary, (n) helper; bondgenoot; hulpstuk; ..**ries**, hulptroepe; hulpmasjiene; **(a)** hulp-; ~ **army**, hulpleër; ~ **battery**, hulpbattery; ~ **chain**, noodketting; ~ **cruiser**, hulpkruiser; ~ **engine**, hulpmotor; ~ **fuel tank**, hulpbrandstoftenk; ~ **grid**, hulprooster; ~ **jet**, hulpstraler; ~ **language**, hulptaal; ~ **lever**, hulpliefboom; ~ **light**, hulplig; ~ **motor**, hulpmotor, bymotor; ~ **science**, hulpwetenskap; ~ **service**, hulpdiens; ~ **shaft**, hulpskag; hulpas; ~ **tank**, hulptenk; ~ **train**, hulptrein; ~ **troops**, hulptroepe; ~ **valve**, hulpklep; ~ **verb**, hulpwerkwoord; ~ **wire**, hulpdraad, bydraad.
aux'in, groeistof.
avail', (n) baat, nut, voordeel; *to LITTLE* ~, met min sukses, tevergeefs; *it is of NO* ~, dit baat nie; *WITHOUT* ~, tevergeefs, verniet; **(v)** help, baat, benut; ~ *oneself of an opportunity*, van 'n geleentheid gebruik maak, 'n geleentheid te baat neem; ~**abil'ity**, geldigheid; beskikbaarheid; *period of* ~**ability**, geldigheidsduur.
avail'able, nuttig, dienstig, geldig; disponibel; verkrygbaar, beskikbaar, voorhande; *MAKE* ~ beskikbaar stel; ~ *POWER*, beskikbare krag.
av'alanche, sneeuval, sneeustorting, sneeuverskuiwing, lawine.
avant-courier', voorloper, voorryer.
avant-gar'de, avant-garde, vernuwers, voorlopers.
av'arice, gierigheid, hebsug, skraapsug, vrekkigheid, goudduiwel, grypsug, inhaligheid; ~ *is the root of all evil*, gierigheid is die wortel van alle kwaad.
avari'cious, gierig, hebsugtig, skraapsugtig, vrekkig, inhalig.
avast'! stop! genoeg!
a'vatar, avatar, inkarnasie.
avaunt', (obs.), skoert, trap, maak dat jy wegkom.
avenge', wreek, wraak neem; *be* ~*d*, gewreek wees; ~**r**, wreker.
a'vens, naelkruid.
aven'turine, goudglassteen, aventurien.
av'enue, toegang; laning, laan; kanaal; ~ *of employment*, werk(geleentheid); ~ *of fire*, skietmoot.
aver', (-red), betuig, verseker; beweer; waarmaak.
av'erage, (n) gemiddeld; middelmaat; deursnee; awery; (pl) gemiddeldes; *GROSS* ~, algemene awery; *ON an* ~, gemiddeld, deur die bank; **(v)** die gemiddelde bereken; 'n gemiddelde behaal, gemiddeld kos, gemiddeld opbring, uitwerk op 'n gemiddelde; **(a)** middelslag-, gemiddeld; deursnee-; middelmatig; ~ *EXPOSURE*, gemiddelde beligting; *the* ~ *FRENCHMAN*, die gewone Fransman; ~ *SPEED*, gemiddelde snelheid (spoed); ~ *STUDENT*, gemiddelde student; ~ *VALUE*, gemiddelde waarde; ~**r**, awerytaksateur.
aver'ment, bevestiging, versekering; bewys; bewering.
averruncat'or, snoeimes, snoeiskêr, boomskêr.
averse', afkerig, onwillig; ~**ness**, afkerigheid, onwilligheid.
aver'sion, afkeer, teensin; afsku, walging, renons, weersin; afskrik; afkerigheid; haat; *HAVE an* ~ *to*, 'n broertjie dood hê aan; 'n afsku hê van; *my PET* ~, my doodsteek, die doring in my vlees.
avert', afwend, afkeer, voorkom; weer; afweer, afhou; ~**ible**, afwendbaar.
av'ertin, avertien (verdowingsmiddel).
av'ian, voël-.
av'iary, (aviaries), (groot) voëlhok, voëlkooi.
av'iate, vlieg, 'n vliegtuig bestuur.
avia'tion, lugvaart; vliegkuns, vliegwese, lugvaartkunde; ~ **beacon**, lug(vaart)baken; ~ **catastrophe**, vliegramp; ~ **company**, lugvaartmaatskappy; ~ **fuel**, vliegtuigbrandstof; ~ **insurance**, lugvaartversekering; ~ **lubricant**, vliegtuigsmeer; ~ **map**, lugtrajekkaart; ~ **medicine**, lugvaartgeneeskunde; ~ **school**, vliegskool; lugvaartskool; ~ **spirit**, vliegtuigbrandstof.
av'iator, vlieër, vlieënier; lugreisiger.
av'iatrix, (..trices), vlieenierster, vliegster.
av'iculture, voëlteelt, voëlboerdery.
av'id, begerig, gretig.
avid'ity, begerigheid, begeerte, gretigheid; gierigheid, hebsug.
a'vidly, gretig.
av'ifauna, voëlwêreld.
av'iform, voëlvormig.
avio'nics, lugvaartelektronika, avionika.
avi'so, adviesboot.
avitamino'sis, vitamiengebrek, vitamientekort, avitaminose.
avoca'do, (-s), avokado(peer), murgpeer.
avoca'tion, werk, beroep; afleiding; roeping.
av'ocet, bontelsie.
avoid', vermy, ontvlug, ontwyk; ongeldig maak, onwettig verklaar; *I COULD not* ~ *saying*, ek kon nie nalaat om te sê nie; *GO out of one's way to* ~ *something*, uit jou pad gaan om iets te vermy; ~**able**, vermybaar; afweerbaar; ~**ance**, vermyding; teenwerping (jur.).
avoid'ing, vermydend; uitwykend; ~ *ACTION*, uitwykbeweging; ~ *LINE*, uitwykspoor.
avoirdupois', gewone Engelse gewig, avoirdupois.
av'oset = **avocet**.
avouch', verseker, verklaar; waarborg, instaan vir; toegee, erken, beken; ~**ment**, erkenning; waarborg; versekering.
avow', bely, erken; *an* ~*ed enemy*, 'n verklaarde (openlike) vyand; ~**able**, erkenbaar; ~**al**, erkenning, bekentenis; ~**edly**, openlik, onbewimpeld, uitgesproke.
avul'sion, afskeuring, aanspoeling; ~**-forceps**, afskeurtang.
avun'cular, ooms-, van 'n oom.
await', verwag, afwag, afkyk ('n kans); voorlê, wag; te wagte staan; *a disappointment* ~*s him*, 'n teleurstelling wag vir hom.
awake', (v) (awoke, awakened), ontwaak, wakker word; wek, wakker maak; tot die besef kom; lewendig word; **(a)** wakker; opgewek; lewendig; *BE* ~ *to*, op sy hoede wees vir; besef; *you'll HAVE to be wide* ~, jy sal moet wakker loop; jy sal fyn moet loop; jy sal vroeg moet opstaan; jy sal op jou hoede moet wees; *be WIDE* ~, helder wakker wees; rapat wees.
awa'ken, wakker word, ontwaak; wakker maak; ~**ing**, ontwaking; *rude* ~*ing*, (wrede) ontnugtering.
award', (n) uitspraak, beslissing; beloning; toekenning; bekroning, prys; *MAKE an* ~, 'n uitspraak lewer; 'n toekenning doen; **(v)** toeken, uitreik, toe-

wys; beslis; uitspraak doen; ~ *COSTS*, koste toe=
ken; 'n prys toeken; ~ *a PRICE*, bekroon, 'n prys
toeken.
aware', bewus; bedag; wakker, belangstellend; *BE ~
of*, weet, bewus wees van: *BEFORE he was ~ of it*,
eer hy dit besef het; toe hy hom kom kry; *be made
PAINFULLY ~ of something*, iets aan die lyf voel;
~**ness**, bewustheid, besef.
awash', bespoel deur water; gelyk met die water.
away', weg; voort, van huis; verwyderd; uit (tennis);
DO ~ with, van kant maak, vernietig; *EXPLAIN
~*, goedpraat; *FAR and ~*, verreweg; *FIRE ~*,
trek maar los; *GIVE ~*, weggee; verraai; *OUT and
~*, ver weg; *RIGHT ~*, dadelik; *WASTE ~*,
wegkwyn, wegteer; ~ *WITH it*, weg daarmee; ~
with YOU! weg is jy, skoert! maak dat jy wegkom!
awe, (n) ontsag, eerbied; gedugtheid, vrees; *INSPIRE
~*, vrees aanjaag; *KEEP in ~*, in bedwang hou;
STAND in ~ of, bang wees vir; ontsag koester vir;
(v) ontsag inboesem; bang maak; ~**-inspiring**,
vreeswekkend; ~**less**, sonder ontsag, oneerbiedig;
onverskrokke; ~**some**, ontsagwekkend; verskrik=
lik; ~**struck**, vervaard, bang, verskrik.
aweigh', (los)hangend; *anchors ~!* ankers los!
aw'ful, ontsagwekkend, vervaarlik, eerbiedwekkend,
vreeslik, skrikwekkend; buitengewoon; *what an ~
BUSINESS*, wat 'n naarheid; *an ~ SCRAWL*, 'n
lelike skrif; ~**ly**, verskriklik, vreeslik, geweldig, da=
nig; bedroef; *get ~ly little*, bedroef min kry;
~**ness**, verskriklikheid; ontsaglikheid.
awhile', 'n tydjie, 'n tyd lank.
awk'ward, onhandig, onbeholpe, slungelagtig, lomp;
hinderlik, lastig; naar; ongemaklik; *the ~ AGE*,
die lummeljare, die vleëljare; *be placed in ~ CIR=
CUMSTANCES*, in verleentheid kom; *an ~ CUS=
TOMER*, 'n ongemaklike (moeilike) ou (vent,
kêrel, man); *at an ~ MOMENT*, op 'n ongeleë
oomblik; ~**-looking**, ongemaklik; ~**ness**, lomp=
heid, onbeholpenheid, linksheid, onhandigheid;
ongemanierdheid; ~ **squad**, baar klomp; rou span,
baar span.
awl, els; priem; ~**-haft**, elshef; ~**-shaped**, elsvormig,
skerp, puntig.
awn, angel, baard (aan 'n aar); *full of ~s*, angelrig;
~**ed**, baard=, gebaard.
awn'ing, seil, skerm; sonskerm, sonkap; agterdek.
a-woo'ing: *go ~*, gaan vry; die hof gaan maak.
awry', skeef, krom; verkeerd; *GO ~*, verkeerd loop;
with her HAT all ~, met haar hoed skeef.
ax, axe, (n) byl; kapding, kapper; *APPLY the ~*, die
byl inlê, die byl aan die stam sit; *have an ~ to grind*,
eiebelang soek; bybedoelings hê; *send the ~ after
the HELVE*, goeie geld agter slegte geld gooi; (v)
besnoei, besuinig; uitkap; ~**-hammer**, hamerbyl;
~**-handle**, bylsteel; ~**-head**, bylkop; ~**-man**, byl=
vegter; houtkapper; ~**-shaped**, bylvormig; ~**-stroke**,
bylhou.
ax'ial, as=, aksiaal; in die rigting v.d. as; ~ **angle**,

ashoek; ~ **centre**, magpunt (mat.); ~ **distance**,
asafstand; ~ **line**, aslyn, middellyn; ~ **plane**,
as(se)vlak; ~ **skeleton**, asskelet.
ax'iform, asvormig.
ax'il, (-s), oksel, boonste hoek tussen blaar en tak;
~**lary**, oksel=, aksillêr (plantk., anat.); ~*lary
artery*, okselslagaar.
axcil'la, (-e) = **axil**.
ax'inite, aksiniet.
axio'logy, aksiologie, waardeteorie.
ax'ion, grondwaarheid, aksioma, aksioom, (grond)=
stelling.
axiomat'ic, onweerspreeklik, onomstootlik, aksio-
maties.
ax'is, (axes), as, aslyn, spil; ~ *of DILATION*, uitset=
tingsas; ~ *of the EARTH*, aardas; ~ *of FOLD*,
plooias; ~ *of INCIDENCE*, invalsas; *MAJOR ~*,
hoofas; lang (groot) as; lengteas; *MINOR ~*, klein
(kort) as; breedteas; ~ *of OSCILLATION*, slin=
geras; *PAIR of axes*, assekruis; assepaar; *PIV=
OTAL ~*, draaiingsas; *PRINCIPAL ~*, hoofas;
~ *of ROTATION*, daaiingsas; *VISUAL ~*, gesigs=
as; ~ *of the WORLD*, wêreldas; wêreldspil; ~-
plane, asvlak; **A ~ Powers**, Spilmoonhede.
a'xle, wa-as, as; ~ **arm**, asarm; ~ **bearing**, aslaer; ~
bench, aspot; ~ **box, (-es)**, naafbus; ~ **cap**, naaf=
dop; ~ **casing**, ~ **housing**, ashulsel; ~**journal**, as=
tap; ~ **lathe**, asdraaibank; ~ **lining**, asvoering; ~
load, aslading, aslas, asbelasting; ~ **pin**, luns, luns=
pen; ~ **seat(ing)**, asbedding, asbodem; ~ **shaft**,
wieldryfas (mot.); binne-as; ~ **tree**, spil, as.
axunge', binnevet; varkvet; gansvet.
ay, (-es), ja; *the ayes HAVE it*, die meerderheid is
daarvoor; *SAY ~ to everything*, op alles ja en amen
sê; met almal saamblaf.
ay'ah, aia.
ayatol'lah, (-s), ajatolla.
aye¹, altyd, ewig; *for ~*, vir ewig.
aye² = **ay**.
aye'-aye, vingerdier.
Ayr'shire, Ayrshire (bees).
azal'ea, asalea; *A ~ City*, Pietermaritzburg.
aze'otrope, aseotroop; ..**tropic**, aseotropies.
az'imuth, topboog, asimut; ~**-instrument**, peil=
skyf.
azo'ic, sonder spoor van lewe.
Azores', (die) Asoriese Eilande, die Asore.
az'ote, stikstof.
Az'tec, (n) Asteek; (a) Asteeks.
az'ure, (n) hemelsblou, asuur; (v) hemelsblou verf; (a)
hemelsblou, lasuur, asuur; wolkloos; ~ **d**, hemels=
blou.
az'urine, grysblou.
az'urite, kopersuur, asuursteen, asuriet.
az'ygote, asigoot.
az'ym(e), Paasbrood, ongesuurde brood.
az'ymous, ongegis, ongesuur (brood).
azz'le-tooth, maaltand.

B

b, (bs, b's, bees), b; *not know a B from a BATTLE=
DORE*, g'n A van 'n B ken nie; *not know a B from a
BULL'S foot*, nie 'n A voor 'n B ken nie; g'n A van
'n B ken nie.
baa, (n) bê, geblêr; (v) (**-ed**), blêr.
Ba'al, (-im), Baäl; *bow the knees unto ~*, die knie voor
Baäl buig.
baa'lamb, lammetjie (kindertaal).
baas, baas, boss; ~ **skap**, baasskap.
baba'la, babala, kaffermanna.
ba'ba rum, babarum.
Bab'bitt, Babbitt, materialis, filistyn; **b ~ -metal**, bab=
bittmetaal, witmetaal.
babb'le, (n) kindergestamel; gebabbel, geklets, gesna=
ter; verklappery; gemurmel, gekabbel; (v) babbel,
klets; stamel, brabbel; verklap; kabbel; murmel

(water); ~**r**, prater, praatkous, babbelaar; verklik=
ker; katlagter (voël).
bab'bling, gemurmel; gebabbel.
babe, kindjie, baba(tjie); uilskuiken.
Bab'el, Babilon, Babel; *a perfect ~*, 'n toring van
Babel.
bab'el, verwarring, lawaai; spraakverwarring.
babia'na, bobbejaan(tjie), bobbejaantjie.
babirou'sas, babiru'sa, wildevark (Oos-Indië), babi=
roesa.
baboon', bobbejaan; ~ **spider**, bobbejaanspinnekop.
babouche', haklose pantoffel, baboesj.
ba'bu, ere-aanspreekvorm (Hindoe), baboe.
babush'ka, kopserp, baboesjka.
bab'y, (babies), kind, wig, baba, babatjie; wiegsif (del=
werye); ~ *in ARMS*, suigling; onervare mens; *have*

outgrown one's ~ CLOTHES, die kinderskoene ontgroei het; EMPTY the ~ with the bath, die kind met die badwater uitgooi; be LEFT holding the ~, met iets opgeskeep sit; met die gebakte pere bly sit; someone will have to NURSE the ~, iem. sal die babatjie moet vashou; ~ **bashing,** kindermishandeling, babamishandeling, babamokering; ~ **basket,** babamandjie, kapwieg; ~ **beef,** jongbeesvleis; ~ **bottle,** pypkan, bababottel; ~ **car,** klein motor; minimotor; ~ **carriage,** kinderwaentjie, stootwaentjie; ~ **chair,** babastoel; kinderwaentjie ~ **clothes,** babaklere; ~**-farmer,** kinderverkoper; ~**-farming,** kinderverkopery; ~ **fat,** babavet; ~ **food,** babavoedsel; babakos; ~ **grand,** klein vleuelpiano; ~**hood,** kleintyd, suigelingsjare, kindertyd; ~**ish,** kinderagtig; kleinserig; ~ **linen,** luiers; ~ **powder,** babapoeier.

Bab′ylon, Babilon, Babel.
Babylon′ian, (n) Babiloniër; (a) Babilonies.
ba′by sit, kroostroos, baba(s) oppas.
bab′y sitter, babawagter, kroostrooster, fopouer.
bab′y: ~ **spoon,** kinderlepel; ~ **talk,** kindertaal.
baccalaur′eate, baccalaureusgraad.
bac′carat, baccarat, kaartspel.
bacc′ate, bessies=.
Bacc′hanal, (n) suipparty, Bacchusfees; Bacchuspriester; dronklap; (a) Bacchus=; bacchanties.
Bacchanal′ia, Bacchusfees; swelgparty, Bacchanalieë; ~ **n,** (n) suiplap; wellusteling; (a) bacchanalies, swelgend; ~ **n song,** Bacchuslied.
Bacc′hant, volger van Bacchus, bacchant.
Bacc′hus, Bacchus, wyngod.
baccif′erous, bessiedraend.
bacc′iform, bessievormig.
bacciv′orous, bessie-etend.
bacc′y, (colloq.) twak, tabak.
bach′elor, jonkman, jonggesel, vrygesel; oujongkêrel; ~ **of ARTS (Science),** Baccalareus Artium (Scientiae); ~'**s BUTTONS,** patentknope; botterblom(me); KNIGHT ~, vrye ridder; ~'**s WIVES** and **old maids' children are the best trained,** die beste stuurlui staan aan wal; die beste touleier sit op die (wa se) voorbok; ~ **flat,** enkelwoonstel, eenpersoonswoonstel, eenvertrekwoonstel; ~ **girl,** vrygesellin; ~ **quarters,** enkelkwartier; eenmanswoonplek; ~**hood,** ~**ship,** jonkmanskap; oujongkêrelskap; baccalaureusgraad.
bacill′ary, basil=; stafies=, basillêr; ~ **white diarrhoea,** basillêre wit diarree.
bacillem′ia, basillemie.
bacill′icide, basillevernietiger, basilledoder.
bacill′iform, stafiesvormig, basilvormig.
bacill′iscopy, basilliskopie.
bacillos′is, basillose.
bacillur′ia, basillurie.
bacill′us, (..cilli), basil, staafdiertjie.
back, (n) rug, rugkant, agterkant; (rug)leuning (van stoel); agtergrond; agterspeler (rugby); heelagter (sokker); my ~ is ACHING, die hondjies byt (by bukwerk), AT the ~ of, agter; BEHIND one's ~, agterom, agteraf; agter iem. se rug; BREAK someone's ~, iem. te swaar belaai; BREAK one's ~, hard spook; jouself verrinneweer; FALL on one's ~, agteroor val; lie FLAT on one's ~, bene in die lug lê; plat op jou rug lê; GIVE ~, gee terug; terruggee; HAVE one's ~ up, op jou perdjie wees; jou stert wip; put one's ~ INTO something, jou kragte inspan; 'n kragtige poging aanwend; KNOW something like the ~ of one's hand, iets deur en deur ken; iets op jou duimpie ken; MAKE a ~, buk; be at the ~ OF something, agter iets sit; break the ~ OF something, iets baasraak; iem. onder die knie kry; oor die hond se stert wees; be ON one's ~, op die rug; bedlêend wees; die bed moet hou; ON the ~ of, boonop; PUT (get, set) a person's ~ up, iem. vererg (kwaad maak); PUT one's ~ into something, jou kragte inspan; 'n kragtige poging aanwend; ~ to ~, rug aan rug; TURN one's ~, rug toekeer; have one's ~ UP, op jou perdjie wees; with one's ~ to the WALL, met die rug teen die muur; in die knyp, in die noute; (v) ondersteun, rugsteun; agteruit laat gaan (vaar); agteruit ry (met motor), tru=

wed op; van 'n rug voorsien; ~ **DOWN,** terugkrabbel; toegee; kop uittrek; ~ **HOME,** terug by die huis; tuis; ~ a **HORSE,** op 'n perd wed; ~ **OUT,** kop uittrek; ~ **UP,** steun; ~ **WATER,** stryk, agteruit roei; (a) agterste; agterstallige; ~ **PAYMENT,** agterskot; PUT ~, sit terug, terugsit; take a ~ **SEAT,** tweede viool speel; would give one's ~ **TEETH,** wat sou wou gee; (adv.) terug, agteruit, gelede; ~ and FORTH, heen en weer; GET ~, terugkry; terugkom; staan terug!; GO (come) ~, gaan (kom) terug; some TIME ~, 'n tydjie gelede.
back: ~ **ache,** rugpyn; ~**-axle,** agteras; ~ **bench,** agterbank; ~**-bencher,** agterbanker; ~ **bite,** belaster, (be)skinder; ~ **biter,** lasteraar, agterklapper, hakskeenbyter, addertong; ~ **biting,** agterklap, skindery; ~ **board,** rugleuning; rugplank; ~ **bone,** ruggraat; beginselvastheid; a man without ~ BONE, 'n papbroek; iem. sonder pit; ~**-breaking,** uitputtend; ~ **chat,** teenpratery; astrantheid; ~ **cloth,** agterdoek; ~**-comb,** pluiskam; ~**-coupling,** terugkoppeling; ~ **court,** agterbaan; ~ **current,** teenstroom; ~ **date,** vroeër dateer, vervroeg; ~**-dip:** ~**-dip** neckline, lae agterhalslyn; ~ **door,** (n) agterdeur; get in by the ~-door, by 'n agterdeur insluip; (a) agterbaks; ~ **drop,** agterdoek; agtergrond; ~ **er,** aanhanger; ondersteuner, wedder (op 'n perd); ~ **fire,** (n) terugplof; terugslag (van motor); (v) terugslaan; terugplof; ~ **flow,** terugvloei(ing); ~**-fork,** agtervurk; ~ **gable,** agtergewel; ~**-gammon,** bakspel, t(r)ikt(r)ak, bordspel; ~ **ground,** agtergrond; keep in the ~ ground, op die agtergrond bly, terughou.
back′hand, dwarshand, handrug; botom (rolbal); ~ **drive,** handrughou; ~ **ed,** handrug=; ~ **ed compliment,** 'n beledigende aanmerking; ~ **grip,** handrugvat; ~ **stroke,** (hand)rughou; ~ **volley,** handrugvlughou.
back: ~ **hander,** (hand)rugspeler; handrughou; ~ **ing,** steun, ondersteuning; weddenskap; terugslaan (van wind); rugmateriaal (boek); versterking; ~ **ing strip,** keerstrook; ~ **joint,** agtervoeg; ~ **lash,** teenreaksie; speelruimte; dooiegang; ~ **less,** rugloos; ~ **line,** agterhoede, agterlyn, agterspelers (rugby); ~ **log,** agterstand (werk); make up the ~ log, die agterstand inhaal; die agterstallige skuld vereffen; ~ **most,** agterste; laaste; ~ **number,** ou tydskrifnommer; outydse persoon of metode; ~ **nut,** sluitmoer; ~ **pack,** (n) rugsak; (v) voetslaan; ~ **packer,** voetslaner; ~ **packing,** voetslaan; ~ **packing trail,** voetslaanpad, voetslaanroete; ~ **pay,** agterskot, agterstallige betaling; ~**-pedal,** terugtrap, terugkrabbel; terugneem; ~**-pedalling brake,** terugtraprem; ~ **pressure,** teendruk; ~ **projection,** truprojeksie; ~ **projector,** truprojektor; ~ **rent,** agterstallige huur; ~ **rest,** rugleuning; ~ **room,** agterkamer; ~**-room boy,** geheime navorser; uitvinder, stille werker; ~**s,** rugwol; ~**-saw,** rugsaag; ~ **scratch,** flikflooi, inkruip; ~ **scratcher,** rugkrapper; flikflooier, inkruiper; ~ **scratching,** rugkrap(pery) flikflooiery, (in)kruiping; vleiery.
back′seat, agterste bank; TAKE a ~ seat, op die agtergrond raak; ~ **driver,** bekbestuurder, bekdrywer.
back: ~ **set,** teenstroom; ~ **side,** agtersy, rug, agterkant; boud(e), agterste, sitvlak; ~ **sight,** agterste visier; terugles ing; ~ **slide,** afvallig word; terugval, weer tot sonde verval; ~ **slider,** afvallige, oorloper; ~ **spin,** terugkrul; terugtol, terugdraai; ~ **stage,** agter die skerms; agterverhoog; ~ **stair(s),** agterste trap; geheim, oneerlik; ~ **stand,** agterstaander (motorfiets); ~ **stay(s),** pardoen (skip); ~**-stroke,** terugslag; rugslag (swem); handrug (tennis); ~ **swing,** terugswaai; ~ **talk,** terugpraat, teenpraat, parmantigheid; ~ **tooth,** kiestand; ~**-track,** agteruit ry; terugtrek; ~ **tug,** agterband; ~**-up,** terugrugry; terugstoot; ondersteuning, steun; agtergrond; ~ **veld,** agterveld, agterwêreld; platteland; ~ **velder,** velskoendraer; plattelander; takhaar; ~ **view,** agteraansig; ~ **wall,** agterwand; ~ **ward,** agterlik, afteraf, lui, dom; bedees; agteroor; agteruit; ~ ward people, agteraf mense; ~ **warda′tion,** effektehuur, deport(handel); laat (af)lewering, ver=

traagde lewering; terugslag; ~ **wardness,** agterlikheid; traagheid; ~ **wards,** agteruit, terug; agteroor; ~ *wards and forwards,* heen en weer; ~ **wash,** (n) terugtrek(king), terugspoeling, boeggolf, stuwater, teensee; (v) terugspoel; ~ **water,** terugstromende water; staande water; dooierige toestand; water deur skepratte uitgegooi; kielwater; opdamwater; ~ **way,** sypaadjie; agterpaadjie; kortpad.

back'woods, onbewoonde boswêreld; agterveld, die gramadoelas; *COME from the* ~, van die gramadoelas (agterveld) kom; *IN the* ~, in die gramadoelas (agterveld); ~ **man,** agtervelder; takhaar; konserwatiewe persoon.

back'yard, agterplaas; ~ **yard mechanic,** tuiswerktuigkundige, werfwerktuigkundige.

bac'on, spek, varkspek; spekvleis, *bring HOME the* ~, die paal haal; die draai regkry; *SAVE one's* ~, daar heelhuids van afkom; *STREAKY* ~, streepspekvleis; ~ **beetle,** spektor; ~ **er,** spekvark; ~ **rind,** swoer(d); ~ **roll,** spekrolletjie; ~ **y,** spekagtig.

Baco'nian, (-s), Baconvolgeling.

bacter'ial, bakteries; ~ **blight,** vlamsiekte (druiwe); ~ **disease,** bakteriesiekte; ~ **wilt,** bakteriese verwelksiekte, moko.

bactericid'al, bakteriedodend, kiemdodend, ontsmettend.

bacte'ricide, bakteriedoder, kiemdoder.

bacteriol'ogist, bakterioloog, bakteriekundige.

bacteriol'ogy, bakteriologie, bakteriekunde.

bacteriol'ysis, bakteriolise.

bacteriolyt'ic, bakteriolities.

bacte'riophage, bakteriofaag, bakterievreter.

bacteriosta'sis, bakteriostase.

bacter'ium, (..ria), bakterie, kiem, staafdiertjie.

Bac'tria, Baktrië; ~ **n,** Baktries; ~ **n camel,** Baktriese kameel.

bac'ule, meetroede.

bac'uline, betreffend die tugroede; ~ **argument,** magsargument.

bad, (n) slegte; bose; *GO to the* ~, die verkeerde weg gaan; *take the* ~ *with the GOOD,* die slegte met die goeie neem; *R20 to the* ~, 'n verlies (tekort) van R20; *he that SPARES the* ~ *injures the good,* sagte dokters maak stinkende wonde; (a) **(worse, worst),** sleg, erg, snood; stout; nadelig; siek, naar; bederf, vrot; ongunstig; nagemaak; vals; ~ *AIR,* slegte lug; *a* ~ *BUSINESS,* 'n slegte saak; 'n ongelukkige gebeurtenis; *CAUSE* ~ *blood,* haat veroorsaak; ~ *COIN,* vals munt; *a* ~ *COLD,* 'n swaar verkoue; ~ *DEBTS,* dooieskuld, slegte skulde, oninbare vordering; *a* ~ *EGG,* 'n niksnuts; *a* ~ *EXCUSE is better than none,* 'n flou verskoning is beter as glad nie een nie; ~ *FAITH,* kwade trou; *in* ~ *FAITH,* te kwader trou; ~ *FOR,* skadelik (nadelig) vir; ~ *FORM,* gebrek aan goeie maniere; *GO* ~, bederf, sleg word; *with* ~ *GRACE,* teësinnig; *that will be JUST too* ~, dit sal darem te erg wees; ~ *in LAW,* regtens ongegrond; ~ *LOAN,* slegte lening; ~ *LUCK,* teenspoed; ~ *MANNERS,* ongemanierdheid; *a* ~ *MIXER,* 'n alleenloper, 'n eenspaaier; ~ *SHOT,* slegte skoot (hou); verkeerd geraai; ~ *TASTE,* wansmaak, slegte smaak; ~ *WEATHER,* onweer, slegte weer; ~ *WORKMEN always blame their tools,* 'n slegte ambagsman gee altyd sy gereedskap die skuld; *from* ~ *to WORSE,* van kwaad tot erger; *a* ~ *WOUND,* 'n lelike wond; ~ **dish,** slegterig.

bad blood, haat, haatgevoel; slegte verhouding.

bad'deleyite, baddeleyiet.

bad'die, (colloq.), slegte persoon, skurk.

bade, *see* **bid.**

badge, kenteken, kleurteken, ordeteken, insinje, wapen; skild; kokarde.

badg'er, (n) ratel; kunsvlieg; kwas; (v) koejeneer, kwel, pla, sar; ~ *someone,* iem. treiter (pla, sar, moveer); ~ **dog,** dashond; ~ **-legged,** krombeen= met ongelyke bene; ~ **-plane,** lysterskaaf, kantskaaf.

bad'inage, skerts, spotterny, gekskeerdery.

bad'lands, erosiegebied, dongaveld.

bad'ly, erg, danig; deerlik, skroomlik, sleg; *be* ~ *HURT,* lelik seerkry; *NOT be* ~ *off,* dit nie te sleg (kwaad) hê nie; *WANT* ~, vurig verlang na; baie nodig hê; ~ *WOUNDED,* swaar gewond.

bad'man, boef, skurk.

bad'minton, pluimbal, badminton.

bad'ness, slegtheid, slegtigheid; gevaarlikheid; verdorwenheid, vrotheid.

Bae'deker, Baedeker(gids).

baf'fle, (n) skot; (v) verydel; beskaam; oorbluf; dronkslaan, uitoorlê, verbluf; ~ **brick,** keersteen; ~ **drum,** demptrommel; ~ **ment,** verbystering; verbasing; verdwasing; ~ **plate,** ~ **r,** brandplaat, vuurskerm; leiplaat (lugv.); skotplaat (motor); ~ **spring,** terugslaanveer; ~ **window,** windskerm.

baf'fling, raaiselagtig, verydelend; oorstelpend, verbluffend; ~ **winds,** teenwinde.

baf'fy, (obs.) knots.

bag, (n) sak, tas; geldsak; possak, jagsak; borrievel; hoeveelheid geskiete wild; uier; ~ *and BAGGAGE,* met sak en pak; *be a* ~ *of BONES,* net vel en been wees; *give someone the* ~ *to HOLD,* iem. met die gebakte pere laat sit; *IN the* ~, feitlik afgehandel; uitgemaakte saak; suksesvol (poging, uitslag); ~ *s of MONEY,* sakke vol geld, hope geld; *the WHOLE* ~ *of tricks,* alles; die hele santepiek (santekraam); die hele spul; (v) **(-ged),** skiet; vang; in die sak stop; inpalm, inpik; knieë maak (broek); bol staan (seile); in sakke pak; toepak.

bagasse', uitgeperste suikerriet, ampas, bagasse.

bagatelle', kleinigheid; bakatel (spel).

ba'gel, bagel, broodrol.

bagg'age, bagasie, reisgoed; flerrie, ligtekooi; leërtrein; ~ **car,** goederewa; ~ **master,** bagasiemeester; ~ **office,** bagasiekantoor; ~ **room,** bagasiekamer; ~ **tag,** ~ **ticket,** bagasiekaartjie.

bagg'er, baber (vis).

bag: ~ **ging,** sakgoed, saklinne; ~ **gy,** sakkerig; slordig; bokknieërig (broek); *the trousers are* ~ *gy at the knees,* die broek maak bokknieë; ~ **gy trousers,** pap broek; slobberbroek; ~ **house,** sakfilterkamer; ~ **man,** handelsreisiger.

bagn'io, bordeel; tronk; bagnio; badhuis (Ooste).

bag'pipe, doedelsak.

bags, wye broek, sambalbroek; *Oxford* ~, wye broek.

bag'-snatcher, tasdief, grypdief.

baguette', (F.), Franse brood, baguette; reghoekige juweel.

bag'worm, sakwurm; rietwurm; kokerwurm.

bah! ba! ag! sies!

baig'noire, (F.), baignoire, teaterlosie.

bail¹, (n) borg, borgtog; *ALLOW* ~, borgtog toestaan; *ESTREAT one's* ~, sy borgtog verbeur; *be* ~ *FOR,* borg wees vir; *RELEASED on* ~, onder borgtog vrygelaat; (v) borgstaan; onder borg vrystel; ~ **out,** borgstaan vir.

bail², (n) staketsel, skutting.

bail³, (n) dwarspaaltjie; balkie (krieket); *knock off the* ~ *s,* die paaltjies laat spat.

bail⁴, (n) hingsel (van pot); hoepel.

bail⁵, (v) hoos (water); uitskep, uitgooi (met emmers); ~ **out,** uitspring (met 'n valskerm uit 'n vliegtuig).

bail, -ee', borgtoghouer.

bail bond, borglening.

bail'er¹, hoser.

bail'er², uitskepper; skepper; skepding.

bail'ey, buitevestingmuur, binneplein; kasteelmuur; *Old B* ~, strafhof in Londen.

Bai'ley bridge, baileybrug.

bai'lie, Skotse magistraat.

bail'iff, balju, geregsdienaar; agent, rentmeester.

bail'iwick, baljuskap.

bail'ment, vrystelling van gevangenes onder borgtog; aflewering van goedere onder borgstelling; bewaargewing; borgstelling.

bail'or, persoon wat goedere onder voorwaardes aflewer.

bails'man, (..men), borg.

bain-marie', (F.) potverwarmer, bain-marie.

bairn, kind, wig, kleintjie.

bait, (n) lokaas, aas; aanloksel; verversing; (v) aanlê; ververs, afsaal, voer gee; lok; aas aansit; aanhits; terg; aanval; ~ **-boy,** aasjong; ~ **er,** terger; kogge=

laar; ~-**hook**, aasstok; ~**ing**, tergery, koggeling; ~-**money**, lokgeld.
baize, baai (wolstof); poortlaken, biljartstof, groenlaken.
bake, bak; blaker; hard word; hard maak, uitdroog; ~-**apple**, bakappel, stoofappel; ~**d beans**, sousboontjies, sousbone; ~**d enamel**, brandemalje, moffelemalje; ~**d potato**, gebakte aartappel; ~**house**, bakkery, bakhuis.
bak'elite, bakeliet; ~ **ashtray**, bakelietasbak.
bak'er, bakker; ~**'s CART**, bakkerskar; *a* ~**'s DOZEN**, dertien; ~**'s LOAF**, bakkersbrood; ~**'s MAN**, bakkerskneg; ~**'s SHOP**, bakkerswinkel; ~**'s TROUGH**, bakkerstrog, bakkis; ~**'s VAN**, broodwa.
bak'ery, (..ries), bakkery; ~ **van**, broodlorrie.
Bakewell tart, Bakewelltert.
ba'king, bakwerk; baksel; ~-**dish**, bakskottel; ~-**mould**, bakvorm; ~-**oven**, uitdroogoond; bakoond; ~-**pan**, bakpan; ~-**powder**, bakpoeier; ~ **soda**, koeksoda.
bak'kie, (Afr.), (-s), bakkie, pick-up, light lorry.
bak'sheesh, fooi; aalmoes; omkoopgeld.
Bal'aam, Bileam (valse profeet, bondgenoot); kommerberig; koerantartikel oor iets buitenissigs (as bladvulling); ~**'s ass**, Bileamsesel.
balaclav'a, balaklawamus, bivakmus.
balalaik'a, balalaika, driehoekkitaar.
bal'ance, (n) saldo, balans (in bank); egaligheid, ewewig(tigheid); vliegwiel (oorlosie); teenwig; oorskot; (weeg)skaal; skommelwiel; *the* ~ *AMOUNTS to*, die saldo beloop; ~ *DUE*, bedrag uitstaande; ~ *in HAND*, batige saldo; *HANG in the* ~, in die weegskaal hang; *HOLD the* ~, die ewewig bewaar; die mag in hande hê; *set one's LIFE in the* ~, jou lewe in die weegskaal stel; *LOSE one's* ~, jou ewewig verloor; *ON* ~, by 'n vergelyking; ~ *of POWER*, magsewewig; *STRIKE a* ~, die balans opmaak; ~ *of TRADE*, handelsbalans; *TURN the* ~, die deurslag gee; (v) weeg; opweeg teen; vereffen; balanseer, sluit (begroting); die ewewig bewaar; skommel; weifel; die balans opmaak; afsluit (boeke); ~ **bob**, skietlood; ~ **bridge**, wipbrug; ~**d**, ewewigtig, gebalanseer(d); ~**d picture**, gebalanseerde (ewewigtige) voorstelling; ~**r**, koorddanser; balanseerder; stabilisator; ~ **sheet**, balansstaat; ~ **spring**, balansveer; ~ **weight**, balanseergewig; ~ **wheel**, skakelrat; onrus (in horlosie).
bal'ancing, balansering; ~-**pole**, balanseerstok.
ba'las, balas, roosrobyn.
bala'ta, balata(boom).
bal'cony, (..nies), balkon, loggia; galery; - **door**, balkondeur; ~ **guard**, balkonstut; ~ **rail**, balkonreling; ~ **seat**, balkonsitplek; ~ **window**, balkonvenster.
bald, kaal, kaalkop; onopgesmuk (styl); naak, bloot (feite); *as ~ as a COOT*, 'n groot soutplek hê; ~ *FACTS*, naakte feite; ~ *STYLE*, onopgesmukte styl.
bal'dachin, **bal'daquin**, troonhemel, baldakyn.
bal'derdash, geklets, onsin; vuil taal; *it IS* ~, dis alles kaf; *dis pure kaf*, *TALK* ~, twak(praatjies) verkoop.
bald: ~ **eagle**, kaalkoparend; ~**head**, kaalkop, pankop; ~-**head'ed**, bles, kaalkop; blindelings; *BE* ~*headed*, 'n groot soutplek hê; *GO* ~*headed for somebody*, iem. kaalkop die waarheid vertel; ~ **horse**, blesperd; ~ **ibis**, rooikopibis, wildekalkoen; ~**ing**, bles(wordend); ~**ly**, onopgesmuk, reguit; ~**ness**, kaalhoofdigheid; ~**pate**, kaalkop, pankop, bleskop.
bal'dric, gordel, skouerband, skouerriem.
bale¹, (n) baal; (v) in bale pak.
bale², (n) ellende, verderf.
bale³, (v) uitskep; ~ *out*, uitspring (uit vliegtuig).
baleen', balein; ~ **whale**, baleinwalvis.
bale'-fastener, wolhakie.
bale'fire, (lit.), vreugdevuur; brandstapel; sinjaalvuur.
bale'ful, nadelig, verderflik; droewig; noodlottig, heilloos, onheilspellend; ~**ness**, treurigheid, verderflikheid, heilloosheid.

bale'-hook, wolhaak.
bal'er¹, baalpers, baalmasjien.
bal'er², skeplepel; skepper.
balibun'tal, strooihoed.
bal'ing: ~-**paper**, pakpapier; ~-**press**, baalpers; ~-**wire**, baaldraad.
balk, (n) teleurstelling; balk; rand (tussen twee vore); doodvak (biljartspel); braakland; wenakker; bollyn (visnet); (v) teleurstel; vermy, verbygaan, oorslaan; hom onttrek aan; vassteek, wegspring (perd); nie wil weet nie; dwarsboom, verydel.
Bal'kan, Balkan=; *the* ~ *states*, die Balkanstate; ~**s**: *the* ~**s**, die Balkan.
balk'ing dog, sperklou.
balk'-ring, sperring.
bal'ky, skrikkerig; steeks.
ball¹, (n) bal, dansparty; *masked* ~, maskerbal, gemaskerde bal; *OPEN the* ~, die bal (dans) open; die saak aan die gang sit.
ball², (n) koeël (geweer); bal, bol; kluit; oogappel; muis (van duim); *ADDRESS the* ~, korrelvat (gholf); ~ *of the FOOT*, kussinkie (muis) v.d. voet; *HAVE the* ~ *at one's feet*, die spel in hande hê; op die punt staan om te slaag; *KEEP the* ~ *rolling*, die spel (die saak) aan die gang hou; *NO* ~, foutbal (krieket); *be ON the* ~, wakker, byderhand (gereed) wees; *PUT the* ~ *in the other court*, die verantwoordelikheid op jou teenstander skuif; *SET (START) the* ~ *rolling*, aan die gang sit, die baan open, die bal aan die rol sit, iets op tou sit, die eerste stoot gee, 'n klip aan die rol sit; ~ *and SOCKET*, bolskarnier; *the* ~ *is WITH you*, dis jou beurt; (v) tot 'n bal vorm; bal.
ball'ad, ballade; liedjie; ~-**eer**, liedjiesmaker; liedjiesanger; ~ **metre**, balladmetrum; ~ **poet**, balladedigter; ~-**singer**, liedjiesdigter; liedjiesanger.
balla'de, ballade.
ball' and claw: ~ **feet**, bal-en-kloupote.
ball' and socket: ~ **joint**, bolgewrig, koeëlgewrig.
ball'ast, (n) ballas; ballasskip; (v) ballas inlaai; ~-**stone**, klipballas; ~ **train**, ballastrein.
ball: ~ **bearing**, koeëlas, koeëllaer; ~-**bearing race**, koeëlbaan; ~-**boy**, baljoggie; ~ **catch**, koeëlknip; ~ **cock**, balvlotterklep; ~-**control**, balbeheer.
ballerin'a, balletdanseres, balletmeisie; *prima* ~, prima ballerina, hoofballetdanseres.
balleri'no, ballerino, balletdanser.
ball'et, ballet, toneeldans; ~-**dancer**, danseuse; balletdanser(es); ~-**dancing**, balletdans; ~-**girl**, balletdanseres; ~-**master**, balletmeester; ~-**mistress**, balletonderwyseres, ~-**music**, balletmusiek; ~-**omane**, balletliefhebber.
ball' float, bolvlotter (klep).
ball' frame, telraam; rekenraam, abakus.
ball' game, balspel; bofbal; *that's another* ~, dis 'n ander speletjie daai!, dis totaal 'n ander saak.
ball' hammer, bolhamer.
ballis'tic, ballisties; ~ **fruits**, skietvrugte; ~**s**, ballistiek.
ball' joint, koeëlgewrig.
ball' journal, koeëltap.
ball light'ning, bolblits, bolbliksem.
ball'onet, gassakkie; sakkie.
balloon', (n) ballon, lugballon; (v) ballonneer; opblaas; ~ **anchor**, ballonanker; ~ **apron**, ballongordyn; ~ **barrage**, ballonversperring; ~ **gas**, ballongas; ~**ist**, lugreisiger, ballonvaarder, ballonreisiger; ~ **tyre**, kussingband, ballonband.
ball'ot, (n) stembriefie; stemming; loting; stemmeaantal; *vote by* ~, met geslote briefies stem; (v) met geslote briefies stem; loot; ~-**box**, stembus; ~-**paper**, stembriefie.
ball: ~-**peen hammer**, rondekophamer; ~ **pivot**, koeëltap; ~ **player**, balspeler, bofbalspeler; ~ **point pen**, bol(punt)pen, rolpuntpen, koeëlpuntpen, balpunt(pen); ~-**proof**, koeëlvry; ~ **race**, koeëlring; koeëlbaan.
ball'room, danssaal, balsaal; ~ **dancing**, geselskapsdans.
ball: ~ **stud**, koeëltapbout; ~ **structure**, bolstruktuur; ~ **track**, koeëlbaan; ~ **valve**, koeëlklep, balklep.

ball'y, vervlakste, verdekselse, verduiwelde, bleddie.
ballyhoo', bohaai, advertensielawaai, reklamepraatjies, reklamelawaai, geraas, haaihoei, hoe(i)haai.
ball'yrag, (-ged, -ged), terg, vertoorn; beskimp; karnuffel.
balm, (n) balsem; balsemboom; balsemgeur; *POUR* ~ *onto the wounds,* balsem in die wonde giet; *that is* ~ *to his WOUNDS,* dit is 'n pleister (salfie) op sy wond; (v) balsem; ~ **cricket,** sikade, sonbesie; ~**ily,** sag, strelend; ~**iness,** balsemagtigheid, sagtheid; soelte, soelheid; gekheid, mallerigheid; ~**y,** soel; balsemagtig, gesond; geurig; kalmerend; getik.
balmo'ral, balmoral(pet).
balneol'ogy, balneologie, badgeneeskunde.
balneother'apy, waterbehandeling, balneoterapie.
balo'ney, nonsens, kaf.
balopay', betalingsbalans.
bal'sa, balsa(hout); ~ **wood,** balsahout.
bal'sam, balsem; balseminie (plant); smeergoed; ~ *of fire,* dennebalsem; ~ **fir,** balsemden; ~ **poplar,** balsempopulier.
bal'sa raft, balsavlot.
balsam'ic, (n) balsem; (a) balsemagtig; balsemiek.
Bal'tic, Balties; ~ **Sea,** Oossee; ~ **timber,** greinhout.
bal'uster, baluster, styl (van trapleuning), pilaar; relingpaal; (pl) trapleuning.
balustrade', leuning, borswering, balustrade, reling, tralie.
Bambar'a ground'nut, Angola-ertjie, bambaragrondboontjie.
bambi'no, (It.), bambino, kleintjie, kindjie.
bamboo', (n) **(-s),** bamboes; (a) bamboes=; ~ **curtain,** bamboesgordyn (van Rooi Sjina); ~**-fish,** mooinooientjie, stinkvis (*Box salpa);* ~ **mat,** bamboesmat; ~ **needle,** bamboesnaald.
bamboo'zle, bedrieg, fop, beetneem; ~**ment,** bedriegery.
ban¹, (n) vervloeking, ban; (v) **(-ned),** ban, in die ban doen; vervloek; verbied; ~ *someone with bell, book and candle,* iem. uit die sinagoge werp.
ban², (n) goewerneur, ban.
ban'al, banaal, afgesaag, alledaags, platvloers.
banal'ity, (..ities), alledaagsheid, banaliteit.
bana'na, banana, piesang; *wild* ~, wilde piesang, geel piesang; **B**~ **Boys** (joc.), Natallers; ~ **farmer,** piesangboer; ~ **leaf, (..leaves),** piesangblaar; ~ **peel,** piesangskil; ~ **plantation,** bananaplantasie; ~ **republic,** bananarepubliek, piesangrepubliek; ~ **skin,** piesangskil; ~ **split,** piesangroomys, roomyspiesang; ~ **trade,** piesanghandel, bananahandel.
band, (n) bende, groep; musiekkorps; orkes, benning; bef (van predikant); lynband, band, bindsel; dryfriem (masjien); windsel; *when the* ~ *BEGINS to play,* as die moeilikhede begin; as die poppe begin dans; *with the* ~ *PLAYING,* met volle musiek; ~ *of ROBBERS,* rowersbende; (v) 'n band omsit; verenig, verbind; ~*ed structure,* streepstruktuur; gelaagde struktuur.
ban'dage, (n) bindsel, verband; sluitband swagtel; (om)windsel; (v) verbind; blinddoek.
ban'daging, verbinding.
bandann'a, bandana.
band: ~ **box, (-es),** hoededoos; lintdoos; ~ **brake,** bandrem; ~ **conveyor,** vervoerband; ~ **course,** bandlaag.
bandeau', (-x), haarband; binneband (van hoed).
ban'ded: ~ *animal, stone,* bantom, bandom.
banderil'la, (Sp.), banderilla.
banderil'lo, (Sp.), stiervegter, bulvegter.
ban'derol(e), wimpel, vaantjie.
ban'dicoot, buideldas; Indiese rot.
ban'ding, gestreeptheid.
ban'dit, voëlvryverklaarde; struikrower; ~**ry,** struikrowery.
band'leader, orkesleier.
band'master, kapelmeester, orkesdirigent.
ban'dog, kettinghond.
bandoleer', bandolier', bandelier.
band'-saw, lintsaag, bandsaag.
bands'man, orkesspeler, musikant.

band: ~ **stand,** orkespodium; orkesverhoog; musiekkoepel; ~ **stitch,** randsteek; ~ **string,** hegdraad.
band'wa(g)gon, musiekwa, reklamewa; *be on the* ~, met die stroom saamgaan; die wenkant kies; aan die optog deelneem; ~ **effect,** optogeffek.
ban'dy¹, (n) **(bandies),** karretjie (in Indië).
ban'dy², (n) **(bandies),** hokkie (spel); hokkiestok; (v) **(..died),** oor en weer slaan; wissel, wedywer; ~ *ABOUT,* heen en weer kaats (slinger); ~ *WORDS,* oor en weer praat, stry.
ban'dy³, (a) met hoepelbene, hoepelbeen=; ~**-legged,** hoepelbeen=; ~ **legs,** snyersbene; O-bene, hoepelbene.
bane, vergif; verderf; pes, ondergang; ~ **berry,** bitterbessie, gifbessie; ~**ful,** verderflik, skadelik; giftig; ~ **fulness,** verderflikheid; giftigheid; ~**wort,** nastergal, nagskade, belladonna.
bang¹, (n) slag, knal, bons; (v) toeslaan, toegooi; klap; afransel, klop; (interj) paf! poef! pardoems! boems! *go* ~, ontplof; bankrot speel.
bang², (n) gordyntjiehare (oor voorkop gesny); (v) gordyntjiekop sny.
bang'ing, gebons, geknal, gesmyt.
Bangladesh', Bangladesh.
ban'gle, armband; voetring.
bang'tail, stompstert.
ban'ian, Hindoekoopman, Hindoemakelaar; kabaai; ~**-fig,** ~ **tree,** heilige vyeboom, waringin.
ban'ish, verban, uitsit, verdryf; ~**ment,** verbanning, uitsetting; ballingskap.
ban'ister, paaltjie, pilaartjie, trapleuning; (pl) trapleuning; ~ **brush,** handborsel, meubelborsel, stofborsel.
ban'jo, -(es), banjo; ~**ist,** banjospeler.
bank¹, (n) wal, oewer (rivier), bank, dyk, moel (van dam); dwarshelling, slagsy (vliegtuig); spoorwal; (v) opdam, wal maak; opstapel; ~ *up,* indam; bank; operd (aartappels).
bank², (n) bank; speelbank; pot; *BREAK the* ~, 'n bank bankrot laat raak; skoonskip maak; *as SAFE as the B~ of England,* so veilig soos die bank; *CENTRAL* ~, sentrale bank, reservebank; (v) geld in die bank sit; 'n bank hou; tot geld maak; banksake doen; ~ *on,* staatmaak op.
bank³, (n) span (silinders); groep (hysers).
bank⁴, (n) skuinste; (v) laat oorhel, kantel (vliegtuig).
bank: ~ **able,** bankwaardig; ~ **agent,** bankagent; ~ **analyst,** bankontleder.
bank' angle, dwarshellinghoek.
bank: ~ **balance,** bankbalans, banksaldo; ~ **bill,** bankwissel, bankbiljet; ~ **book,** kassiersboek; bankboekie; ~ **building,** bankgebou; ~ **card,** bankkaart, kredietkaart; ~ **commission,** bank(iers)kommissie; ~ **cormorant,** bankduiker; ~ **credit,** bankkrediet; ~ **deposit,** bankdeposito; ~ **discount,** bankdiskonto; ~ **draft,** (geld)wissel; ~**er,** bankier, geldhandelaar, finansier; bankhouer; vissersboot; ~**er's hours,** bankure.
banket', banket.
bank' holiday, openbare vakansiedag.
bank'ing¹, bankwese, bankiersake, bankbedryf; geldhandel.
bank'ing², opdamming.
bank'ing³, skuinsvlug.
bank'ing account, bankrekening.
bank'ing-engine, hulplokomotief.
banking hours, bankure.
bank: ~**ing industry,** bankwese; ~**ing practice,** bankbedryf; ~ **interest,** bankrente; ~ **loan,** banklening; ~ **manager,** bankbestuurder; ~ **note,** banknoot; ~ **official,** bankbeampte=; ~ **overdraft,** bankoortrekking; ~ **rate,** bankdiskonto, bankkoers; leningskoers; ~**-robbery,** bankberowing, bankroof.
bank'rupt, (n) bankrotspeler, bankroetier; (v) bankrot maak; (a) bankrot, insolvent; *become* ~, uitboer; insolvent (bankrot) raak.
bank'ruptcy, (..cies), bankrotskap, insolventskap, faillissement; *file a petition of* ~, boedel oorgee; ~ **rate,** bankrotskapsyfer.
bank'sia, banksia.
banks'man, opsigter; seingewer; skagwagter.

bank' staff, bankpersoneel.
bank' statement, bankstaat.
ban'ned, verban, verbode; ~ **book**, verbode boek; ~ **person**, verbanne persoon.
ban'ner, banier, vaan, vaandel, vlag; *what* ~ *does he FOLLOW?* onder watter vlag vaar hy? *JOIN the* ~, by die gevolg aansluit; die saak dien; ~ *stretched across a STREET*, spandoek; ~ **cloud**, wimpelwolk; ~ **et**, baanderheer; ~ **headline**, reuse= opskrif, reusekopstuk; ~ **streamer**, spandoek.
ban'ning, verbod; uitsluiting.
ban'nister = **banister**.
bann'ock, garsbrood; roosterkoek.
banns, huweliksgebooie; *FORBID the* ~, die gebooie stuit; *have the* ~ *PUBLISHED*, die gebooie laat gaan.
ban'quet, (n) banket, fees, gasmaal, feesmaaltyd; (v) feestelik onthaal; feesvier; eet en drink; ~ **er**, fees= vierder, feesgenoot, banketteerder; ~ **te**, (opge= stopte) bankie.
ban'shee, doodsbode.
bant, verslank.
ban'tam, kapokhoendertjie, bantam(hoender); band= om, bantom (diamant); ~ **weight**, kapokgewig, bantamgewig.
ban'ter, (n) skerts, plaery, persiflage, gekskeerdery; (v) skerts, korswel, gekskeer; vir die gek hou; ~ **er**, gekskeerder, plaer; skertser.
ban'ting, vermaeringskuur.
bant'ling, babatjie, suigeling; snuiter.
Ban'tu, Bantoe; Afrikaan.
Ban'tuist, Bantoeïs.
Ban'tu language, Bantoetaal, Afrikataal, Swart= taal.
Ban'tustan, (derog.), Bantoestan.
ban'yan = **banian**.
banzai', (Jap.), banzai, oorlogskreet.
ba'obab, kremetartboom, baobab.
bap'tism, doop; doopseel; ~ *of BLOOD*, martelaar= skap; ~ *of FIRE*, vuurdoop; *receive one's* ~ *of FIRE*, jou vuurdoop deurmaak.
baptis'mal, doop=; ~ **ceremony**, doopplegtigheid; ~ **certificate**, doopseel; ~ **font**, doopvont, doopbek= ken, doopbak; ~ **name**, doopnaam; ~ **vow**, doop= gelofte; ~ **water**, doopwater.
bap'tist, (n) doper; **B**~, Baptis; Wederdoper; Doops= gesinde; *B*~ *CHURCH*, Baptistekerk; *John the B*~, Johannes die Doper; (a) Doopsgesind; Bap= tiste=.
bap'tist(e)ry, (..tries), doopkapel; doopvont; baptis= terium.
bap'tize, doop; onderdompel.
bar, (n) draaiboom, sper(boom), slagboom, sluit= boom (oorgang); hinderpaal; bout; staaf, tralie; stang; (dwars)balk (her.); dwarsstreep; steen; reg= bank, balie (reg.); kantien, drinkplek, kroeg, hoe= kie, gelagkamer; gebitrand (stang); arm (visier); steunsel (perdehoef); steeg (rysaal); sandbank; maat(streep) (mus.); buffet; (pl) balkies (voetbal= skoene), *APPEAR at the* ~, voor die gereg ver= skyn; *AT the* ~, voor die vierskaar; *BEHIND* ~ *s*, agter die tralies; *in die hok*; vry losies; agter slot en sleutel; *be CALLED to the* ~, as advokaat toege= laat word; *CROSS the* ~, die tydelike met die ewi= ge verwissel; *GOLD* ~ *s*, staafgoud; *at the* ~ *of HISTORY*, voor die vierskaar v.d. geskiedenis; *HORIZONTAL* ~, rekstok; *READ for the* ~, in die regte studeer; ~ *SINISTER*, skuinsbalk, *a* ~ *of SOAP*, 'n steen seep; (v) **(-red)**, uitsluit, belet; teenhou, belemmer; voorkeer, stuit; verhinder, voorkom; barrikadeer; (prep) behalwe, buite; ~ *one*, op een na.
barb[1], (n) Barbaryse perd.
barb[2], (n) weerhaak; prikkelbaard (vis); angel (in ha= werkorrel); doring, haak, prikkel; (v) weerhake aansit; ~ *ed-wire CLOTH*, duiwelsterk; ~ *ed-wire ENTANGLEMENT*, doringdraadversperring; ~ *ed WIRE*, doringdraad; prikkeldraad, ~ *ed WIRE FENCE*, doringdraad.
barbar'ian, (n) barbaar; woestaard; wreedaard; (a) barbaars, onbeskaaf.
barbar'ic, barbaars, onbeskaaf.

barb'arism, onbeskaafdheid, woestheid, barbaars= heid, wreedheid; barbarisme.
barbar'ity, wreedheid, barbaarsheid.
barb'arous, wreedaardig, barbaars; ~ **ness**, barbaars= heid.
Barb'ary, (n) Barbarye; (a) Barbarys; ~ **ape**, Bar= baryse aap, Turkse aap, magot.
barb'ate, gebaard.
barb'ecue, (n) groot rooster; dier wat heel gebraai is; braaistel; braaihoek; vleisbraai(ery), vleisbraai= aand; droogvloer; (v) heel braai, oor die kole braai; vleis braai; ~ **nook**, braaivleishoekie, vleisbraai= hoekie.
barb'el, baber, moggel.
bar'bell, staafgewig.
barb'er, barbier, haarsnyer, haarkapper; ~ *'s CHAIR*, skeerstoel; ~ *'s ITCH*, baarduitslag; ~ *'s POLE*, barbierpaal; ~ *'s SHOP*, skeerwinkel, haarkapperswinkel.
barb'er(r)y, (..ies), suurbessie, suurdoring; berberis (boom).
Bar'berton: ~ *daisy*, Barbertonse madeliefie.
barb'et, houtkapper.
barbette', barbet, geskutbank, geskuttoring.
bar'bican, wagtoring.
bar'bit, stang.
barb'ital, barbital.
barbit'urate, barbituraat.
barbitu'ric acid, barbituursuur.
barbo'la, barbola; ~ **work**, barbolawerk.
barb'ule, baardjie, stekel.
barc'arol(l)e, gondellied, barcarolle.
bar: ~ **clamp**, staafklamp; ~ **code**, strepieskode; ~ **coding**, strepieskodering; ~ **copper**, staafkoper; ~ **council**, balieraad; ~ **coupling**, stangkoppeling.
bard[1], digter, skald, sanger.
bard[2], borswapen (perd).
bare, (v) ontbloot, kaal maak; aan die lig bring; (a) bloot, kaal, naak; oop en bloot; leeg; haarloos; ~ *CONDUCTOR*, kaal geleier; *with one's* ~ *HANDS*, sonder gereedskap; *the* ~ *IDEA*, die ge= dagte alleen; *the* ~ *NECESSARIES of life*, die al= lernodigste; *the* ~ *TRUTH*, die naakte waarheid; ~ **back**, bloots; kaalrug; ~ **-faced**, met onbedekte gesig; onbeskaam; skaamteloos; *faced lie*, 'n skaamtelose leuen; ~ **-foot(ed)**, kaalvoet; ~ **-head= ed**, kaalkop, blootshoofs; ~ **-legged**, met kaal bene; ~ **ly**, ternouernood, skaars; alleen maar; openlik; ~ **ness**, naaktheid, kaalheid, blootsheid.
barège, (F.), barège, sygaas.
barette'-file, kantvyl; platvyl.
bar-fag'gotting, leerlasstoek.
bar'fly, kroegvlieg, kantienvlieg, kroegloper, kan= tienloper, drinker.
bar'gain, (n) goeie slag, (wins)kopie; keurkoop; oor= eenkoms; *a BAD* ~, 'n slegte koop; die slegste daarvan afkom; *he made the BEST of a bad* ~, hy het hom so goed moontlik na omstandighede ge= skik; *DUTCH (wet)* ~, 'n kopie wat met drank beklink word; *a bad* ~ *is dear at a FARTHING*, goedkoop is duurkoop; *GET (receive, obtain) into the* ~, toekry; *a GOOD* ~, 'n winskoop, winsko= pie; 'n slag; *drive a HARD* ~, iem. die vel oor die ore trek; *INTO the* ~, op die koop toe; *it IS a* ~, dis afgepraat; dis 'n kopie; top! *STRIKE a* ~, 'n slag slaan; *he STRUCK a* ~, hy het 'n goeie slag geslaan; *WHAT a* ~*!* wat 'n slag! (v) onderhandel; kwansel, afding, sjaggel, sjagger, knibbel, ooreen= kom, 'n koop sluit; ~ *AWAY*, verkwansel; *I did not* ~ *FOR that*, ek het my nie daarvoor klaargemaak nie; *get MORE than one* ~ *ed for*, jou druiwe teë= kom; jou heiland leer ken; ~ **basement**, winskoop= afdeling; ~ **er**, verkoper; knibbelaar, sjaggelaar, sjaggeraar, kwanselaar; ~ **-hunter**, kopiesoeker, kopiejagter.
bar'gaining, bedinging, kwanselary, smousery; *COL= LECTIVE* ~, gesamentlike bedinging; *HARD* ~, knibbelary; ~ *POWER*, beding(ings)vermoë, be= dingingsmag.
bar'gain price, spotprys, winskoopprys.
barge, (n) trekskuit, aak; landingsvaartuig; vragboot; sloep; (v) bots; ~ *in*, indring, indringerig wees; in=

druk (in verkeer); ~ -**board,** pan op die vors; wind=veer; ~ -**course,** gewellaag.
bargee', (-s), **barge'man,** (..**gemen**), skipper, skuit=voerder, vragskipper; ~ 's *MATE,* skipperskneg; *SWEAR like a* ~, soos 'n viswyf (matroos) vloek.
barge'-pole, skippersboom; *I wouldn't touch him with a* ~, ek sal hom nie met 'n tang aanraak nie.
bar: ~ **gold,** staafgoud; ~ **iron,** staafyster.
baril'la, (Sp.), barilla.
bar'ite, swaarspaat, bariet.
ba'ritone, bariton; ~ **singer,** baritonsanger.
bar'ium, barium; ~ **meal,** bariummaal; ~ **nitrate,** bariumnitraat.
bark[1]**,** (n) bas (boom); skil; (v) bas afmaak; 'n kors vorm; (jou) skawe; nerf-af word.
bark[2]**,** (n) driemasseilskip, bark.
bark[3]**,** (n) geblaf (hond); *his* ~ *is worse than his bite,* blaffende honde byt nie; (v) blaf, aanblaf; hoes; ~ *AT,* blaf vir; ~ *against the MOON,* vir die maan blaf; ~ *up another TREE,* oor 'n ander boeg gooi; ~ *up the WRONG tree,* aan die verkeerde adres wees.
bark: ~ **beetle,** baskewer; ~ **bound,** deur bas verwurg (boom); ~ **bush,** bergbas; ~ **cloth,** basmateriaal.
bar'keep, bar'keeper, hotelhouer, kantienman, kroeghouer, kroegman.
bar'keeping, kroegbedryf.
bar'kentine, barkie, klein bark.
bark'er, blaffer; klantelokker, werwer; pistool; kanon; *great* ~ *s are no biters,* blaffende honde byt nie.
bark'ing, geblaf; ~ *DOGS seldom bite,* blaffende honde byt nie; ~ *against the MOON,* 'n geblaf vir die maan.
bark'-pit, looikuip.
barl'ey, gars; gort; ~ **beer,** garsbier; ~ **bread,** gars=brood; ~ **corn,** garskorrel; ¼ duim; korrel (geweer); *John B* ~ *corn,* sterk drank; ~ **cream soup,** gort=melksop; ~ **flour,** garsmeel; ~ **porridge,** garspap; ~ **soup,** gortsop; ~ **sugar,** draaisuiker, borssuiker; ~ **water,** gortwater; ~ **wheat,** barlewiet, kaalgars.
bar'-line, maatstreep.
bar: ~ **lounge,** ~ **parlour,** (drank)sitkamer, drink=kamer, buffetlokaal.
barm, biergis, bierskuim, bolaaggis.
bar: ~ **magnet,** staafmagneet; ~ **maid,** kroegmeisie, skinkjuffrou, buffetjuffrou; ~ **man,** (..**men**), kan=tienman, kroeghouer, kroegman, kroegbaas, buf=fetman.
barmit'zvah, barmitswa.
barm'y, skuimerig; moerderig; simpel, mal, getik, gek.
barn, skuur, loods; *have been born in a* ~, in die kerk gebore.
barn'acle, brandgans; suigmossel; eendskulp, eende=mossel (skip); (pl) neusknyper (van perde); knyp=bril.
barn: ~ **board,** muurplank; ~ **dance,** volkspeledans; boeredans; ~ **door,** skuurdeur; groot skyf; ~ -**door fowl,** mak hoender; ~ **floor,** dorsvloer; ~ **owl,** nonnetjiesuil; ~ **storm,** rondtrek; op 'n toneelreis gaan; 'n politieke reis onderneem; ~ **storming,** in die toneel (die politiek) reis; lawaai en skree; ~ **yard,** agterplaas, werf.
ba'rogram, barogram.
ba'rograph, barograaf.
barol'ogy, gewigsleer, barologie.
barom'eter, weerglas, barometer.
baromet'ric(al), barometer=, barometries.
barom'etry, barometrie.
ba'ron, baron, vryheer; ~ *of beef,* rugstuk (van 'n bees); ~ **age,** baronskap; adel; adelboek; ~ **ess,** (-es), barones; ~ **et,** baronet; ~ **etcy,** (..**cies**), baro=netskap.
baron'ial, baron=, baroniaal.
ba'rony, (baronies), vryheerlikheid; baronie.
Baro'que, Barok.
baroque', (n) barokstyl; (a) barok; ~ **music,** barok=musiek.
ba'roscope, swaartemeter, baroskoop.
barouche', vierwielige rytuig, barouche.
bar'que(ntine), driemasseilskip, bark; barkie.

bar'racan, barrakan.
barr'ack, (n) barak; hut; (pl) kaserne, (v) in barak lê; uitjou; ~ **ing,** uitjouery; ~ **room,** kasernekamer; ~ **square,** kaserneplein; ~ **yard,** kasernewerf.
barracou'ta, snoek *(Thyrsitis atun).*
barracud'a, katonkel, barrakuda.
barr'age, barrage, afsluitdam, sluisdam, weerdam; studam, waterkering, afdamming; damwal; sper=vuur (oorlog); ~ -**lane,** spervuurmoot.
ba'rrator, twissoeker; lastige prosedeerder.
ba'rratry, baratterie; lastige prosedeerdery; moeds=willige beskadiging van 'n skip deur die beman=ning; *commit* ~, baratteer.
barre, barre (ballet).
barred, belet, uitgesluit; gestreep; *no holds* ~, alles (word) toegelaat.
ba'rrel, (n) vaatjie; geweerloop; trommel (oorlosie); buis, pyp; stam (van boom); romp (van perd); ke=telwand; skietligkoker; keel (vergasser); *neither* ~ *the BETTER herring,* dis vinkel en koljander; *EMPTY* ~ *s make the most noise,* hoe kleiner brak, hoe groter geraas; *have someone OVER the* ~, iem. laat deurloop; iem. ooptrek; (v) (-led), inkuip; in vate gooi; ~ **arch,** tongewelf; ~ **bolt,** skuifie, skuif=grendel; ~ **chest,** breë bors(kas); ~ **organ,** straat=orrel, draaiorrel; ~ -**roll,** spiraalrol; ~ **roof,** tonnel=dak; ~ **saw,** dingsaag; ~ **vault,** tonnelgewelf.
ba'rren, dor; onvrugbaar, gus, steriel; kaal; skraal; ~ **cow,** kween; ~ **ness,** onvrugbaarheid, steriliteit; kaalheid, dorheid.
ba'rret, baret, plat mus; biretta.
barricade', (n) verskansing, versperring, barrikade; (v) versper, verskans, barrikadeer.
ba'rrier, (n) sperboom; slagboom, sluitboom, sluit=paal; grenspaal; skeidsmuur; hinderpaal; verskan=sing; versperring; (pl) grense; (v) afsluit; ~ -**cream,** keerroom, beskermende room (vir hande); ~ -**fort,** sperfort; ~ **line,** sperstreep, versperringstreep; ~ **reef,** koraalbank, koraalrif, walrif.
barr'ing, behalwe, uitgenome, uitgesonderd, behou=dens.
bar'rio, Spaanse kwartier, barrio.
bar'rister, pleiter, juris, advokaat; ~ -**at-law,** (..**ters-at-law**), advokaat.
bar' room gelagkamer, kantien, kroeg.
ba'rrow[1]**,** kruiwa; stootkar; draagbaar.
ba'rrow[2]**,** grafheuwel, hunebed.
ba'rrow[3]**,** burg (vark).
ba'rrow-way, kabeltrem (myne).
Bar'sac, Barsac, soet witwyn.
bar' shoe, balkyster, brugyster.
bar'sight, stangvisier.
bar' silver, staafsilwer.
bar' soap, seepsteen, steenseep.
bar'tack, balkhegting, balkhegsel.
bar takings, kroeginkomste.
bar'tender, kroegman, kroegbaas; kroegbediende.
bart'er, (n) ruil(handel); *article OF* ~, ruilartikel; *TREATY of* ~, ruilverdrag; (v) (in)ruil; verruil; kwansel, verhandel; ~ *AWAY,* verkwansel; ver=ruil; ~ **agreement,** ruilooreenkoms; ~ **er,** kwanse=laar, ruiler; ~ **ing,** gekwansel; inruiling, gesmous.
bar'tin, staaftin, bloktin.
bar'-waiter, drankkelner, kroegbediende; kelner.
bar'wood, rooiverfhout.
ba'ryon, barion.
ba'rysphere, barisfeer.
baryt'a, barietaarde, bariumoksied.
baryt'es, bariet, swaarspaat.
ba'rytone, bariton.
bas'al, fundamenteel; grond=; basaal; voet=; ~ **cover,** grondbedekking; ~ **leaf,** wortelblaar; ~ **reef,** voet=rif, basaalrif.
basalt', ystermarmer, basalt; ~ **ic,** basaltagtig, ba=salt=; ~ **ine,** basaltien.
bas bleu', (F.) bloukous.
bas'cule, weegbrug, ophaalbrug; ~ **bridge,** wipskaal, brugbalans, baskule.
base[1]**,** (n) grondslag, basis; voetstuk; staanspoor, uit=gangspunt; bodem; patroonrand; eindvlak; bof (bofbal); steunpunt; uitgangslyn (dril); ~ *of a CYLINDER,* silinderbasis; *RETURN to* ~, na die

basis terugkeer; ~ *of SKULL*, onderskedel; (v) baseer, grond, grondves; stasioneer; ~ *d at Pretoria*, gestasioneer in Pretoria.
base², (a) sleg, laag; snood, vuig, onedel; minderwaardig; vals (geld); laagstaande; diensbaar; waardeloos.
base: ~ **aerodrome**, vliegpark; ~ **ball**, bofbal (spel); ~ **ball field**, bofbalveld; ~ **ball player**, bofbalspeler; ~ **board**, voetlys, spatlys.
base'born, van lae afkoms; oneg.
base' coat, onderlaag, eerste laag.
base'-coin, vals munt.
base: ~ **course**, voetlaag; ~ **hospital**, sentrale hospitaal; basishospitaal; ~ **less**, ongegrond; ~ **line**, agterlyn; grondlyn.
base'ly, laag, gemeen.
base: ~ **map**, basiskaart; ~ **ment**, fondament; benedevertrek, kelder(verdieping); ~ **ment parking**, kelderparkering; ~ **ment room**, kelderkamer; ~ **ment shop**, kelderwinkel; ~ **metals**, onedele metale.
base: ~ **-minded**, laaghartig; ~ **money**, vals munt.
base'mould, vloerlys.
base'ness, laag(hartig)heid, gemeenheid, vuigheid; onegtheid; minderwaardigheid
Basen'ji, Basenji.
base: ~ **plate**, voetplaat; ~ **port**, uitgangshawe, tuishawe; ~ **station**, tuisstasie, basisstasie; ~ **value**, basiswaarde.
bash, (n) slag, hou; (v) slaan, bons, moker, indeuk.
bash'ful, skaam, verleë, bedees, beskimmeld, skamerig, sku(erig); *be* ~, beskimmeld (skamerig) wees; - ness, skamerigheid, verleentheid, skugterheid, inkennigheid.
bash'ing, slaan; mokering; **child** ~, kindermishandeling, kindermokering.
ba'sic, grond-, basies, grondliggend, fundamenteel; *the* ~ *cause*, die grondliggende oorsaak; ~ **difference**, basiese verskil, grondverskil; ~ **error**, basiese fout, grondfout; ~ **industry**, hoofnywerheid, hoofbedryf, hoofindustrie; ~ **ally**, basies, fundamenteel; ~ **dye**, grondkleur, hoofkleur; ~ **English**, Basic English; ~ **freight**, grondvrag; ~ **idea**, grondidee, basiese idee.
basi'city, basisiteit.
basic: ~ **industry**, hoofnywerheid, hoofbedryf, hoofindustrie; ~ **lead acetate**, loodasyn, basiese loodasetaat; ~ **material**, grondstof; ~ **number**, grondgetal; ~ **pattern**, grondpatroon, basiese patroon; ~ **pay**, grondsalaris; ~ **principle**, basiese beginsel, grondbeginsel; ~ **rate**, grondtarief; ~ **right**, grondreg; ~ **slag**, slakmeel; ysterghwano; ~ **steel**, basiese staal; ~ **tax**, insetbelasting; ~ **time**, basistyd; ~ **training**, beginopleiding; ~ **truth**, grondwaarheid; ~ **year**, basisjaar.
basi'dium, basidium.
ba'sil¹, tiemie; balsemkruid; **sweet** ~, soetkruid
bas'il², voeringvel; skaapvel.
ba'silar, basilêr.
basil'ica, basiliek.
bas'ilisk, basilisk, draak; kuifakkedis.
bas'in, kom, skottel, wasbak; hawekom; vallei; bekken; stroomgebied (van 'n rivier); ~ **ed**, kômvormig.
bas'(i)net, staalhelm.
basi'petal, basipetaal.
bas'is, (bases), grondslag; grondlyn; voetstuk (monument); fondament; voet; basis; *on a DAILY* ~, by die dag; ~ *of OPERATIONS*, operasiebasis; *on a* ~ *of RECIPROCITY*, op die grondslag van wederkerigheid.
bask, koester, stowe, bak (in die son)
bas'ket, (n) mandjie, korf; skansmandjie; *the pick of the* ~, die eerste uitsoekkans; die allerbeste; (v) in 'n mandjie sit; ~ **ball**, korfbal; basketbal; ~ **chair**, rottangstoel; ~ **factory**, (..tories), mandjiesmakery; ~ **ful**, mandjievol; ~ **hilt**, handvatsel, oor (van mandjie); - **maker**, mandjiemaker, mandjievlegter; ~ **-stitch**, maassteek; ~ **trade**, mandjiehandel; ~ **try**, mandjiewerk; ~ **weave**, mandjieweef; ~ **work**, vlegwerk, mandjiewerk.
bas'king, bak, braai (in die son); sonbraai.
Basque¹, (n) Baskies (taal); Baskiër; (a) Baskies.

basque², (n) lyfie; onderent van lyfie.
bas-relief', basreliëf, vlakreliëf, basrelief, vlakrelief.
bass¹, (-s), basstem, bas; basviool.
bass², seebaars (vis).
bass³, binnebas (v.d. Amerikaanse lindeboom).
bass' broom, stalbesem, basbesem.
bass' drum, groot (Turkse) trom.
bass'et, ~ **-hound**, Basset, Franse dashond.
bas'set-horn, tenoorklarinet, bassethoring.
bass' fibre, basvesel.
bassinet', kinderwaentjie; kapwieg(ie); drawiegie.
ba'ssist, basvioolspeler, basviolis.
bass'-note, basnoot.
bas'so, (It.) bas; ~ **ostinato**, basso ostinato; ~ **profundo**, basso profundo; ~ **-relievo**, basso relievo, basreliëf.
bassoon', fagot; ~ **ist**, fagottis, fagotspeler.
bas(s)'-relief, basreliëf, basrelief.
bass' viol(in), basviool, kontrabas.
bass'wood, Amerikaanse lindehout(boom).
bast, binnebas, floëem; baston.
bas'tard, (n) baster, hibried; (a) hibridies, baster-; buite-egtelik.
bastardiza'tion, bastardering, bastering.
bas'tardize, oneg verklaar; verbaster, hibridiseer.
bas'tard: ~ **mackerel**, marsbanker; ~ **reef**, jammerriffie; ~ **size**, bastergrootte; ~ **thread**, basterskroefdraad.
bas'tardy, basterskap, onegtheid; buite-egtelikheid; hibriditeit.
haste¹, (aan)ryg; - *together*, aaneenryg.
baste², slaan, moker, uitlooi.
baste³, vet drup op, bedruip.
Bast'er, Baster (van Rehoboth).
bastille', bastille; vesting; tronk, gevangenis.
bastinad'o, (n) (-es), bastonnade, slae (op voetsole); (v) met stokslae straf.
bas'ting-ladle, skuimspaan.
bas'tion, bolwerk, bastion.
bas'ton, torus (bouk.)
Basu'to pony, (..nies), Basoetoponie.
bat¹, (n) vlermuis; *have* ~ *s in the BELFRY*, van lotjie getik wees; 'n krakie hê; 'n klap v.d. windmeul weg hê; in die bol gepik wees; *as BLIND as a* ~, so blind soos 'n mol; *like a* ~ *out of HELL*, baie vinnig, helvinnig.
bat², (n) knuppel; kolf(stok); krieketstok; kolwer, slaner; *CARRY one's* ~, na 'n beurt nie uit wees nie; *do something OFF one's own* ~, iets op eie houtjie doen; (v) **(-ted)**, slaan (bal); kolf.
bat³, (n) vleishamer.
bat⁴, (n) passteen, stuk baksteen.
bat⁵, (v) **(-ted)**, knip(oog); *without* ~ *ting an eyelid*, sonder om 'n spier te vertrek.
batat'a, patatta, patat.
Batav'ia, Batavia; ~ **n** (n) Batavier, Bataaf, Bataviaan; (a) Bataafs; Batavies.
batch, (s) **(-es)**, klomp; baksel; broeisel; besending; gasmengsel; *ALL of the same* ~, almal van die selfde soort; *BOILING* ~, kooksel; *BREWING* ~, brousel; (v) groepeer.
bat'chy = **batty**.
bate¹, (n) loog; (v) loog (velle); in die loog sit.
bate², (n) woede; (v) verlaag, verneder; afkort, verminder; opgee (hoop); inhou (asem); afstaan; *with* ~ *d breath*, in spanning, angsvol, met ingehoue asem, met gespanne aandag.
bat'-eared: ~ **jackal**, bakoor(jakkals).
ba'teau, (F), platboomrivierboot.
ba'teleur (eagle), berghaan, stompstertarend
bat'-fowling, voëlvangery (snags).
Bath: ~ **bun**, suikerbolletjie; ~ **chair**, rolstoel; ~ **metal**, pinsbek, Bathmetaal.
bath, (n) bad; badkamer, badhuis; badplek, badinrigting; *Roman* ~, Romeinse badhuis, *Turkish* ~, Turkse (bad) (huis); (v) bad; ~ **brick**, skuursteen; ~ **-cleanser**, badskoonmaker.
bathe, (n) bad; baai(ery); (v) bad; baai (in die see); besproei, natmaak; laaf; afspoel; bet (wond).
bath'er, baaier, badgas.
bathet'ic, bateties, banaal.
bath: ~ **gown**, badjapon; ~ **house**, badhuis.

bath'ing, swem(mery), baai(ery); ~ **beauty,** ~ **belle,** strandskoonheid, strandpop(pie); ~**-booth,** bad=huisie; baaihokkie; ~**-box, (-es),** badhuisie; ~**-cabin,** baaihokkie; ~**-cap,** baaimus; ~**-costume,** badklere, baaiklere, swemklere, swemkostuum, swempak; ~**-cubicle,** badhokkie; ~**-cure,** bad=kuur; ~**-dress,** baaipak, baaikostuum; ~**-estab**=**lishment,** badhuis, badinrigting; ~**-machine,** bad=waentjie, badkoets; ~**-place,** baai, strand(oord), swemplek; ~**-resort,** badplek, badplaas; ~**-season,** badseisoen; ~**-stone,** puimsteen; ~**-suit,** swemkos=tuum, swemklere, badklere; ~**-ticket,** badkaartjie; ~**-trunks,** swembroek; ~**-tub,** badbalie; ~**-wear,** badklere.
bath'-mat, badkamermat(jie).
bath'olith, batoliet.
bathom'eter, dieptemeter.
bat'-horse, pakperd.
bath'os, batos; antiklimaks; banaliteit.
bath: ~ **room,** badkamer; ~ **s,** warmbad, spa; ~ **salts,** badsout; ~**-soap,** badseep; ~**-sponge,** badspons; ~**-towel,** badhanddoek; ~ **tub,** badkuip, bad.
bath'yal, diepsee=.
bath'yscaphe, duiktoestel.
bath'ysphere, batisfeer.
bat'ik, batik(werk); ~ **artist,** batikkunstenaar.
bat'ing, behalwe, uitgesonderd.
bat'is, bontrokkie.
batiste', batis.
bat'man, (..men), agterryer, lyfbediende (van offi=sier).
bat'-money, bagasietoelae.
bat'-mule, pakmuil.
bat'on, dirigeerstok; baton, knuppel; (maarskalk)=staf; *UNDER the* ~ *of,* gedirigeer deur; ~ **charge,** knuppelstormloop, batonstormloop.
batra'chian, (n) padda; (a), padda=.
bats'man, (..men), slaner, kolwer (krieket); ~**'s crease,** kolfperk, kolfkampie; ~ **ship,** kolfvernuf.
battal'ion, bataljon; *God is for the big* ~ *s,* mag is reg; ~ **commander,** bataljonkommandant, bataljon=aanvoerder.
batt'els, losiesgeld.
batt'en¹, (n) (heg)lat; naald; dun plank, strooklat; (v) van naalde voorsien; met latte vasslaan; vassit; (be)lat; ~ *down the hatches,* die luike vasskroef; ~*ed wall,* latmuur, lattemuur.
batt'en², (v) vet word; vet mes; swelg.
batt'en-door, klampdeur.
batt'ening, belatting; ~ *on the country,* die land uit=suig, vet word uit die land.
batt'en-light, bolig, solderlig.
batt'er¹, (n) beslagdeeg; dun deeg.
batt'er², (n) kolwer (bofbal); (v) beuk; bestook, be=skiet, bombardeer; vernief; duik; slaan, moker; mishandel.
batt'er³, (n) skuinste, oorhelling, hang; (v) oorhel, hang.
batt'ered, gehawend, gebreek, geduik; vernief; ge=slaan, mishandel.
batt'ering, gebeuk, gebons; beskieting; **child** ~, kin=derslaan, kindermishandeling; ~ **charge,** volle la=ding; ~**-gun,** beleëringsgeskut; ~**-ram,** stormram, rammei, muurbreker; ~**-train,** beleëringstrein.
batt'ery, (..ries), battery; aanranding, handtastelik=heid; stel kopergereedskap; *CHARGE a* ~, 'n bat=tery laai; ~ *of TESTS,* toetsbattery; ~ **cable,** bat=terykabel; ~ **cell,** batterysel; ~ **charger,** battery=laaier; ~ **director,** hoekmeter; ~ **ignition,** battery=ontsteking; ~ **mud,** batteryafsaksel; ~ **pieces,** bat=terygeskut; ~ **plates,** batteryplate; ~ **shop,** batte=rywinkel; ~ **switch, (-es),** batteryskakelaar; ~**-terminal,** poolklem, batteryaansluiter; ~ **tester,** batterytoetser; ~ **voltage,** batteryspanning.
batt'ing, kolfwerk, slaan (krieket); ~ **average,** kolf=gemiddelde; ~**-crease,** kolflyn, kolfkampie.
bat'tle, (n) (veld)slag, geveg, stryd; *it is A* ~, dit gaan maar wurg-wurg; *DRAWN* ~, onbesliste slag; *FALL in* ~, sneuwel, in die slag bly; *FIGHT one's own* ~*s,* op eie kragte steun; jou eie boontjies kan uitdop; *GIVE* ~, slag lewer; *that's HALF the* ~, daarna is die saak al half gewonne; *JOIN* ~, die stryd begin (aanknoop); *LINE of* ~, slaglinie; *PITCHED* ~, gereëlde veldslag; ~ *ROYAL,* alge=mene geveg; ~ *of WITS,* vernufstryd; *the* ~ *has been WON,* die slag is gelewer; (v) veg, slag lewer; ~ *with,* veg teen; ~ **array,** slagorde; ~**-axe,** stryd=byl, hellebaard; ~**-cruiser,** slagkruiser; linie=kruiser; ~**-cry,** (..**cries),** oorlogskreet, strydkreet.
bat'tledore, raket (pluimbal); wasstok, wasklopper.
bat'tle: ~ **dress,** gevegstenue, vegklere; ~ **ensign,** ge=vegsvlag; ~ **exercise,** gevegsoefening; ~ **fatigue,** vegmoegheid, vegafgematheid; ~ **field,** slagveld; ~**-front,** gevegsfront; ~ **ground,** gevegsgebied, strydgebied, strydtoneel; ~ **honours,** gevegsonder=skeiding.
bat'tlement, kanteel, borswering; trans, omgang.
bat'tle: ~**-piece,** oorlogskildery; ~**-plane,** vegvlieg=tuig, vegter; ~**-ready,** strydvaardig; ~**-regiment,** linieregiment; ~ **royal,** titaniese geveg (stryd); ~=**ship,** slagskip, slagbodem; ~**ships,** oorlogskepe (spel); ~**-troops,** linietroepe; ~**-zone,** gevegstrook.
battue', dryfjag, klopjag, bloedbad.
batt'y, getik, simpel.
bau'ble, kleinigheid, snuistery, tierlantyntjie; narre=septer, sotskolf.
baulk = **balk:** *be* ~ *ed by nothing,* jou deur niks laat stuit nie.
baux'ite, bauxiet, aluminiumerts.
Bavar'ia, Beiere; ~**n,** (n) Beier; (a) Beiers.
baw'bee, (Sc.) stuiwer.
bawd, koppelaar(ster), sielverkoper; ~**iness,** ontug=tigheid; ~**ry,** smerigheid, vuil praatjies; ontug; ~**y,** (n) ontugtige taal; (a) ontugtig, liederlik, onkuis; ~*y talk,* vuil praatjies; ~**y-house,** bordeel, hoer=huis.
bawl, joel; skreeu (mens); bulk (beeste); brul (van pyn); ~ *FORTH,* uitblêr; ~ *one's HEAD off,* 'n keel opsit; ~ *(even) LOUDER,* (nog) 'n groter keel opsit; (nog) harder skree; ~**er,** skreeuer; skreeu=bek; ~**ing,** (n) gegalm; skreëry; (a) joelend; skreeuend.
bawn, ringmuur; kraal.
bay¹, (n) baai, inham.
bay², (n) plek, sone.
bay³, (n) vosperd; (a) vos, bruinrooi; ~ *BROWN,* donkerbruin; *DARK* ~, donkerbruin; ~ *HORSE,* vosperd; *LIGHT* ~, ligbruin; *MEALY* ~, vaal=bruin.
bay⁴, (n) lourier(boom); lourierkrans.
bay⁵, (n) opening in muur, nis, uitbousel (aan huis), erker.
bay⁶, (n) (skiet)vak.
bay⁷, (n) blaf (van hond); *BRING to* ~, in die nou bring, vaskeer; *KEEP at* ~, op 'n afstand hou; van sy lyf afhou; *STAND at* ~, jou te weer stel; klaar staan; (v) blaf, aanblaf; ~ *at the moon,* vir die maan blaf.
bay'-bar, skoorwal.
bay'berry, (..berries), lourierbesie.
bay' line, hokspoor.
bay'onet, (n) bajonet; *with fixed* ~, met gevelde ba=jonet; (v) met 'n bajonet steek, deursteek; ~**-attack,** bajonetaanval; ~**-cap,** bajonetdop; ~ **catch, (-es),** bajonetsluiting; ~ **fight,** bajonetgeveg; ~ **needle,** bajonetnaald; ~ **nipple,** bajonetnippel; ~ **scabbard,** bajonetskede; ~ **thrust,** bajonetsteek.
bay' rum lourierwater, brumium.
bay' salt, growwe sout, baaisout.
bay'-tree, lourierboom; *flourish like the green* ~, tot groot bloei kom.
bay' window, boograam, uitbouvenster, komvenster, erker, boogvenster.
bazaar', basaar, bazaar; alleswinkel.
bazook'a, antitenkvuurpyl, pantservuis, basoeka.
bdell'ium, bdellium, balsemgom.
be, (was, has been), wees; bestaan; *his BRIDE-to-* ~, sy aanstaande bruid; *LET him* ~, laat hom staan; *don't* ~ *LONG,* moenie lank wegbly nie; ~ *that as it MAY,* hoe dit ook al sy; *how MUCH will it* ~*?* hoeveel sal dit kos? ~ *OFF with you!* trap! skoert! voertsek! *the POWERS that* ~, die owerheid; *SO* ~ *it,* dit sy so; *THE to-* ~, die toekoms.
beach, (n) (-es), kus, strand; wal; (v) op die strand laat

beacon — bearing

loop (trek); ~ **attraction**, strandattraksie; strand=
vermaaklikheid; ~ **ball**, strandbal; ~ **buggy**,
duinebesie; ~**-cabin**, strandhokkie, strandhut; ~**-
chair**, strandstoel; ~ **comber**, stranddief, rond=
loper, struikrower, sandrot, strandloper, strandjut;
~ **combing**, strandroof; ~ **cottage**, strandhuis; ~**-
dress**, (-es), strandrok; ~**-flea**, strandvlooi; ~**-
frock**, strandrok; ~ **front**, seekant; ~ **gown**, strand=
jas; ~**-grass**, duinegras; ~**-head**, strandhoof; ~
hyena, strandjut; ~**-master**, strandkommandant;
~**-la-mar**, beach-la-mar; ~ **mine**, strandmyn; **B** ~
ranger, Strandloper; ~**-rest**, strandleuning; ~
road, strandweg; ~**-sandals**, strandsandale; ~**-
wrap**, strandmantel, strandjas.

beac'on, (n) baken; vuurtoring; seinvuur; (v) afba=
ken; voorlig; verlig; bebaken; ~ **landing**, baken=
landing; ~ **light**, ligbaken; ~ **point**, bakenpunt; ~
station, bakenstasie, bakentoring; ~**-tower**, baken=
toring.

bead, (n) kraal; pêrel; belletjie, blasie; druppel
(sweet); korrel (geweer); knoppie; hiel, flens, span=
rand (van motorband); stootlat (houtwerk); (pl)
rosekrans; *DRAW a* ~ *upon*, aanlê op; ~*s of PER=
SPIRATION*, sweetdruppels, (v) inryg; laat perel;
druppels vorm; ~ *over*, omkraal (buis); ~ **form**,
kraalvormig; ~**-heel**, flenshiel.

bead'ing, kraallys; omkraling; lyswerk; ~ **embroi=
dery**, kraalborduurwerk; ~**-plane**, lysskaaf; ~ **rail**,
lysreling.

bea'dle, pedel, stadsbode, (geregs)bode; koster;
~ **dom**, omslagtigheid; bemoeisug.

bead: -moulding, kraallys; ~**-plane**, kraalskaaf; ~**-
seat**, spanrandvoet; ~ **sight**, visier.

beads'man, (..men), gehuurde bidder; provenier.

bead'work, kraalwerk, kralewerk.

bead'y, kraalagtig, kraal=; pêrelend; ~ *eyes*, kraal=
ogies.

bea'gle, speurhond; jaghondjie, brakkie; spioen.

beak¹, magistraat; skoolmeester.

beak², bek, snater, snawel (voël); tuit (ketel); neus;
krom neus; voorskip; ~ **ed**, gesnawel, gebek; krom.

beak'er, beker, drinkbeker.

beak'-iron, speekhaak.

beak-moulding, papegaailys.

beak-shaped, snawelvormig.

beak'whale, snoetdolfyn.

be'-all, einddoel; alles; wese; *the* ~ *and end-all*, die
begin en die einde; die hoofdoel.

beam, (n) balk (gebou); disselboom (wa); juk (skaal);
ewenaar (stringe); boom; wewersboom; ploegbalk;
dryfstand; dekbalk (skip); stam van takbokgewei,
grootste breedte van skip; straal (van son); *not
CONSIDER the* ~ *that is in one's own eye*, die balk
in jou eie oog nie raaksien nie; ~ *of LIGHT*, lig=
bundel; *first REMOVE the* ~ *from one's own eye*,
verwyder eers die balk uit jou eie oog; vee eers voor
jou eie deur; (v) straal, breed glinslag; ~ *FORTH*,
uitstraal; ~ *ON them*, vir hulle toelag; ~ *WITH*,
straal van; ~ **compasses**, stokpasser.

beam'-ends, kant, sy; *be on one's* ~, lelik in die knyp
sit, aan laer wal wees; platsak.

beam: -er, lyfbal; ~ **indicator**, skerpligklikker;
~ **ing**, stralend; ~**less**, sonder strale, dof; sonder
balke; ~ **radio**, rigstraalradio; ~ **service**, rigstraal=
diens; ~ **station**, rigstraalstasie; ~ **system**, (rig)=
straalstelsel; ~ **track**, rigstraal; ~ **tube**, straalbuis;
~ **width**, straalbreedte (radio); ~ **wind**, sywind,
kantwind; ~ **wireless**, rigstraaldraadloos; ~ **wood**,
balkhout; ~**y**, breed; stralend.

bean, (n) boontjie; (pl) boontjies; pitte (geld); *every* ~
has its BLACK, elkeen het sy foute, elke gek het sy
gebrek; *not work for DRY* ~*s*, nie om dowe neute
iets doen nie; *he knows how many* ~*s make FIVE*,
he is ouer as twaalf; hy weet waar Dawid die wortels
gegrawe het; *FRENCH* ~, snyboontjie; *FULL of*
~*s*, opgeruimd, uitgelate; op sy stukke; *be GIVEN*
~*s*, ingekluim word; dadels gegee word; blouboon=
tjies kry; *GREEN* ~, groenboontjie; *I HAVEN'T a*
~, ek het nie 'n bloue duit nie; *LARGE ever-bear=
ing* ~, heerboontjie; *OLD* ~, ou kêrel; *SPILL the*
~*s*, met die hele mandjie patats voor 'n dag kom;
~**-bug**, ysterbek; ~ **cake**, sojakoek; ~**-feast**, fees,

fuif; ~**-fed**, met boontjies gevoer; in sy noppies,
opgewek; ~**-field**, boontjieland; ~ **goose**, akker=
gans; ~**-oil**, soja-olie; ~ **plot**, boontjieakker; ~
pod, boontjiepeul; ~ **pole**, boontjiestok, boontjie=
stut; skraalhans, skarminkel; ~ **s**, korrelsteenkool;
~ **salad**, boontjieslaai; ~ **stalk**, boontjierank,
boontjiestoel; ~ **stew**, boontjiebredie.

bean'o, fees, fuif, feesviering.

bear¹, (n) beer; lomperd, brommerige kêrel; *CATCH
the* ~ *before you sell its skin*, moenie die vel ver=
koop voor die beer geskiet is nie; *the GREATER
and the Lesser B* ~, die Groot en Klein Beer; *he is
like a* ~ *with a sore HEAD*, 'n vlieg het oor sy neus
geloop; *as angry as a* ~ *with a sore HEAD*, van
boosaardigheid kan moor; *THE B* ~, die Beer,
Rusland.

bear², (n) daalspekulant; (v) spekuleer op daling.

bear³, (v) **(bore, borne)**, dra, tors, gedra, voer; verdra,
deurstaan, duld, uitstaan, veel; besit; gee (rente);
stut; druk; aanhou; **(bore, born)**, baar, voortbring;
~ *ARMS*, wapens voer; ~ *AWAY*, wegtrek; weg=
dra; *BRING to* ~, toelê, toepas; aanwend, laat
geld; ~ *one's BURDENS*, jou laste dra; *I CAN=
NOT* ~ *him*, ek kan hom nie verdra nie; ~ *CHIL=
DREN*, kinders voortbring (baar); ~ *COMPANY*,
geselskap hou; ~ *a DATE*, gedateer wees; ~
DOWN, onderdruk, oorwin, verdruk; ~ *somebody
a GRUDGE*, iem. 'n wrok toedra; ~ *a HAND*,
help; *it is HARD to* ~, dit hang swaar aan 'n mens;
dis 'n swaar las; ~ *to the LEFT*, links draai, ~ *a
LIKENESS to*, lyk na; ~ *in MIND*, (goed) onthou;
~ *ON*, betrekking hê op; ~ *OUT*, staaf, bevestig;
~ *PART of the blame*, 'n deel van die skuld dra; *be
unable to* ~ *SOMEONE*, iem. nie kan veel nie;
hoog aan iem. hê; ~ *UP against*, die hoof bied aan,
uithou teen; ~ *WITH*, verdra, duld; ~ *WIT=
NESS*, getuie wees.

bear'able, (ver)draaglik, duldbaar, redelik, skaflik.

bear: -account, baisse; daalspekulantrekening; ~
animalcule, mosbeertjie, beerdiertjie; ~**-baiting**,
beerterging, beertergery.

beard¹, (n) baard; weerhaak; ~ **ed**, baard=, gebaard,
bebaard; van weerhake voorsien; ~ *ed VULTURE*,
lammergier; ~ *ed WHEAT*, baardkoring, emmer=
koring.

beard², (v) trotseer; belediq; ~ *the lion in his den*, iem.
op sy eie werf aandurf; iem. openlik trotseer, uit=
tart.

bear'die, (colloq.), baardman.

beard'less, baardloos; kaal; gladgeskeer.

bear'er, draer, aandraer, bringer; pilaar; lykdraer,
bode; toonder (tjek); draagbaar; vrugtedraer
(boom); *BY* ~, per bringer; *a GOOD* ~, 'n boom
wat goed dra; *TO* ~, aan toonder; ~**-beam**; draag=
balk; ~ **bill**, toonderwissel; ~ **certificate**, toonder=
sertifikaat; ~ **cheque**, toonder tjek; ~ **option**, toon=
deropsie; ~ **party**, draers, draergroep; ~**-rail**,
draagreling; ~ **share**, toonderaandeel; ~**-spring**,
draagveer.

bear'garden, beretuin; lawaaimakery, onstuimige
vergadering, deurmekaarspul, harwar.

bear'-hug, groot (sterk) omhelsing.

bea'ring, (n) gedrag, houding, voorkome, voorkoms;
strekking, verband; draagplek; ligging; peiling;
rigting, drag, wapen; wapenfiguur (heraldiek);
druk; neiging, aanleg; draagwydte; laer (masjien);
ARMORIAL ~*s*, wapenbeeld; *BEYOND* ~, on=
(ver)draaglik; *it HAS a* ~ *on the matter (case)*, dit
staan in verband met die saak; *LOSE one's* ~*s*, uit
die koers raak; die kluts kwyt wees; die spoor bys=
ter wees; *have a* ~ *ON*, betrekking hê op; *his* ~ *was
REGAL*, sy voorkoms was koninklik; *TAKE one's*
~*s*, vasstel waar jy is; poolshoogte neem (fig.);
TREE in full ~, boom in volle drag; (a) draend; ~**-
arch**, peilboog; ~**-area**, draagvlak; laeropper=
vlakte; ~**-block**, draagblok; ~**-bush**, laerbus; ~**-
cap**, laerdop; ~ **capacity**, dravermoë; ~**-collar**,
laerkraag; ~**-compass**, (-es), peilkompas; ~**-cone**,
binnekeëlring; ~**-cup**, buitekeëlring; ~**-housing**,
laerhulsel; ~**-insert**, laervoering; ~**-ledge**,
dra(ag)lys; ~**-liner**, laervoering; ~**-metal**, laerme=
taal, witmetaal; ~**-plate**, dra(ag)plaat; ~**-race**,

laerbaan; laerring; ~-rein, springteuels; ~ ring, laerring; ~s, koeëllaer; rigting; ligging, posisie, oriëntasie; peiling: ~-shaft, langwa; ~-sleeve, laerhuls; ~ spigot, laertap, ~ spring, draveer; ~-strength, dravermoë; ~ stress, dra(ag)spanning; ~ surface, dra(ag)vlak; laervlak, laeroppervlakte; ~ wall, dra(ag)muur, stutmuur.

bear: ~ish, ongemanierd, lomp; iesegrimmig; ~-leader, beerleier; ~like, beeragtig; ~ market, beermark; Bearnais'e (sauce), Bearnaisesous, ryk witsous; ~'s-breech, akant; ~'s-foot, (soort) belladonna; ~'s-grease, beervet; ~ skin, beervel; beermus, kolbak.

beast, bees; dier; onbeskofte mens; ~ of BURDEN, lasdier; ~ of PREY, roofdier; ~liness, beesagtigheid; smeerboel; ~ly, beesagtig, dierlik, walglik; ~ly DRUNK, smoordronk; a ~ly NUISANCE, ellende, naarheid, narigheid; ~ly SCOUNDREL, ellendige skurk.

beat, (n) klap; roffel (trom); tik; slag, maatslag (musiek); polsslag; ritme; ronde, rondgang, wyk, patrollie; jagveld; off ~, uit die maat; (v) (beat, -en), klop, slaan, pak gee, strop, striem, wiks, vel; (af)klop (tapyt); bons, beuk, klots (golwe); teen die wind seil; roer (trom); laat klink; kneus; uitklop, uitstof (in spele), wen; klits (eiers); deursoek (vir wild); ~ the AIR, in die lug skerm; ~ BLACK and blue, bont en blou slaan; ~ one's BRAINS, jou kop krap, jou inspan; ~ about the BUSH, afwykend wees, rondval; ~ a CARPET, 'n tapyt klop; one ~s the bush and another CATCHES the bird, die perd wat die are (hawer) verdien, kry die strooi; the sun ~s DOWN, die son staan stil; die son skroei die aarde; ~ back the ENEMY, die vyand terugslaan; that ~s EVERYTHING, dis nog die ergste; dis nog die mooiste van alles; that HAS him ~, dis bo sy vuurmaakplek; ~ someone HOLLOW, iem. ver oortref; iem. ver uitstof; ~ IT! voertsek! gee pad! skoert! that ~s ME, dit slaan my dronk; ~ OFF, verdryf, afslaan; ~ OUT, uitklop (metaal); ~ OUT the flames, 'n vuur doodslaan; 'n vuur blus; ~ the PISTOL, te gou wegspring (atletiek); ~ down the PRICE, op die prys afding (afknibbel); ~ a RETREAT, die aftog blaas, vlug; ~ the ROBOT, die robot voorspring; ~ the RUFFLE, roffel; ~ the STREETS, deur die strate slenter; what ~s even THAT . . .! nou nog mooier! follow the ~en TRACK, die gebaande weg volg; ~ UP, aanrand, aanval; slaan; ~ against the WIND, laveer.

bea'ten, verslaan, gewen; afgesaag; geslaan; platgetrap; ~ GOLD, bladgoud; ~ METAL, dryfwerk; gedrewe metaal; the ~ PATH (TRACK), die platgetrapte paadjie, die gebaande weg.

beat'er, klopper; opjaer, drywer (van wild); kloppik; slaner; stamper; klitser (vir eiers).

beat genera'tion, beatgenerasie, beatgeslag, beatniks.

beatif'ic, saligmakend, geluksalig.
beatifica'tion, saligmaking, saligverklaring, saligspreking, heiligverklaring.
beat'ify, (..fied), salig maak, salig verklaar.
beat'ing, slanery, kloppery; loesing, pak slae; getrommel (trom); geklots (golwe); take a ~, 'n nederlaag ly; pak kry.
beat'itude, saligheid, geluksaligheid, gelukstaat; saligspreking; ~s, saligsprekinge.
beat'nik, beatnik.
beau, (-x), pronker; saletjonker, modegek; kêrel, minnaar; ~ IDEAL, ideaal; ideale skoonheid; MY ~, my kêrel.
Beauf'ort scale, Beaufortskaal, windskaal.
beau ge'ste, (F.), beau geste, groothartigheidsgebaar.
beau ideal', (F.) beau ideal, hoogste ideaal.
Beau'jolais, Beaujolais, rooi Boergondiese wyn.
beau mon'de, (F.) beau monde, deftige kringe.
Beaune, Beaune, rooi Boergondiese wyn.
beaut, pragtige (mooi) ding.
beaut'eous, skoon, mooi, beeldskoon.
beauti'cian, skoonheidsdeskundige, kosmetikus.
beautifica'tion, vermooiing.
beaut'ifier, verfraaier; skoonheidsmiddel.

beaut'iful, mooi, fraai(tjies), sierlik, pragtig, beeld(er)ig, skoon; ~ness, mooiheid, skoonheid, fraaiheid.
beaut'ify, (..fied), versier, opsier, mooi maak, verfraai.
beaut'y, skoonheid, fraaiheid, bevalligheid, mooiheid; prageksemplaar; (..ties), mooi meisie; iets moois; ~ is but a BLOSSOM, skoonheid vergaan; ~ without BOUNTY avails nought, skoonheid vergaan, maar deug bly staan; that's the ~ OF it, dis die mooiste daarvan; ~ knows no PAIN, mooi maak seer; ~ is but SKIN DEEP, skoonheid vergaan, maar deug bly staan; uiterlike skoon is slegs vertoon; ~ aid, skoonheidsmiddel; ~ competition, skoonheidswedstryd; ~ culture, skoonheidskunde; ~ parlour, skoonheidsalon; ~ sleep, eerste slaap, voornagslaap; ~-specialist, skoonheidspesialis(te), skoonheidskundige; ~ spot, (skoonheids)moesie; mooi plekkie; ~ treatment, skoonheidsbehandeling, kosmetiese behandeling. ~-wash, (-es), skoonheidswater.
beaux arts, (F.), skone kunste, beeldende kunste.
beav'er¹, helmklap.
beav'er², bewer; bewerhaarhoed; kastoorhoed; eager ~, vlytige vent, fluks buks.
beav'er: ~-board, geperste houtvesel, veselplank, kunsplank.
beav'er: ~ fur, bewerbont; ~ hat, bewerhaarhoed; ~ lamb, bewerwol.
bebop', bop (musiek), bop(dans).
becalm, stil, bedaar; bevredig; be ~ed, deur windstilte oorval word.
became', kyk become.
because', omdat, want, deurdat, (de)wyl, daar; ~ of, weens, om, vanweë.
bêche-de-mer', seekomkommer; beach-la-mar.
beck¹, (n) wink, knik; I am not at your ~ and CALL, het jy my gister gehuur, dan het jy my vandag gehad; be at someone's ~ and CALL, tot iem. se diens wees; iem. se Klaas wees; altyd vir iem. klaar moet staan; (v) wink, knik.
beck², (n) stroompie.
beck'on, wink, knik, sein, wuif; ~ to, toewink.
becloud', bewolk, verdonker, verduister; ~ the issue, 'n saak vertroebel.
become', (..came, ..come), word; betaam, voeg, pas, goed staan.
becom'ing, betaamlik, oorbaar, paslik, behoorlik, voeglik, welvoeglik, passend; netjies; ~ly, netjies; van pas; innemend; ~ness, gepastheid, betaamlikheid, voeglikheid.
be'cquerel, becquerel, eenheid van radioaktiwiteit.
bed, (n) bed, kooi, katel, mat, ledekant; lêplek; bedding (rivier); huwelik; perk, bedding (in tuin); onderlaag; laag; blok, skoen (aambeeld); rolmat (van kruiptrekker); mat (van draagbaar); voetstuk (visier); ~ and BOARD, kos en inwoning; ~ and BREAKFAST, bed en ontbyt; be BROUGHT to ~, beval van ('n kind); DIE in one's ~, 'n natuurlike dood sterf; GET out of ~ on the wrong side, met die verkeerde voet uit die bed stap; GO to ~, inkruip, gaan lê; KEEP (to) one's ~, in die bed bly; die bed hou; get out of ~ with the LEFT leg foremost, met die verkeerde voet uit die bed klim; as you make your ~, so you must LIE on it; one must LIE in the ~ one has made, wat jy saai, sal jy maai; MAKE the ~, die bed opmaak; early to ~ and early to RISE, makes a man healthy, wealthy and wise, die môrestond het goud in die mond; no ~ of ROSES, geen bed van rose nie; ~ of STATE, praalbed; TAKE to one's ~, gaan lê; (v) (-ded), na bed gaan; na bed bring; 'n bed vorm; vassit, lê; inlaat; uitplant; inbed; ~ DOWN, gaan slaap; 'n kooi maak; ~ IN, vassit; pasmaak; ~ OUT, uitplant.
bedab'ble, bespat, besprinkel.
bedash', bespat.
bedaub', besmeer, beklad.
bedaz'zle, verblind; verruk, betower.
bed: ~-bug, weeluis; ~ cabinet, bedkassie; ~ chamber, slaapkamer; ~ clothes, beddegoed, kooigoed; ~ cover, (bed)deken; ~-cradle, bedwieg; ~ dable,

bedding 729 **beggar**

seksueel aantreklik; ~**der,** beddingplant; ~**-die,** matrys.
bedd'ing, beddegoed, kooigoed (ook vir diere); ~**-attendant,** beddegoedbediende; ~ **plane,** laevlak; ~ **surface,** oppervlak; ~ **ticket,** beddegoedkaart= jie, bedkaartjie.
bedeck', opskik, tooi, optakel.
bedel(l)', pedel.
bedev'il, mishandel; oorduiwel, uitvloek, beheks, toor; in die war bring; ~**ment,** beduiweling; wan= orde; heksery.
bedew', bedou, bevogtig.
bed: ~ **fast,** bedleênd; ~ **fellow,** bedgenoot, slaap= maat; ~**-frame,** slaapbankraam; ~ **gown,** nagrok; ~**-hangings,** bedgordyne; ~ **head,** koppenent.
bedim', (-med), verduister, verdonker, verdof.
bediz'en, opsier, uitdos, optakel.
bed: ~ **jacket,** bedjakkie; ~ **joint,** strykvoeg.
bed'lam, kranksinnigegestig, malhuis; oproer; lawaai; ~ *broke loose,* daar was 'n helse kabaal; ~**ite,** kranksinnige.
bed: ~ **lamp,** bedlamp, leeslamp; ~ **linen,** bedlinne; ~ **maker,** beddeopmaker; bedvervaardiger; ~ **making,** beddeopmaak; ~ **mould,** patroon, vorm; ~ **moulding,** dra(ag)lys; ~ **night,** oornag= ting.
Bed'ouin, (sing and pl), Bedoeïen, woestynbewoner, swerwer.
bed: ~ **pan,** steekpan, bedpan; ~**post,** katelstyl.
bedrab'bled, bemodderd, besmeer.
bedrag'gle, bevuil, betakel, besmeer.
bed: - **rest,** bedstut, rugsteun; ~ **ridden,** bedlêerig; bedlêend; ~**rock,** (n) rotsbedding; grondlaag, vaste gesteente; grondslag; (a) allerlaagste; *get down to* ~ *rock,* ter sake kom; tot die wese van 'n saak deurding.
bed'room, slaapkamer; ~ **farce,** stout klug; ~ **slip= per,** pantoffel, muil(tjie); ~ **suite,** (slaap)kamerstel.
bed: ~**-screen,** bedskerm; ~**-settee,** slaaprusbank; ~ **side,** bed, sponde; ~**side manner,** siekekamer= maniere; ~ **sitter,** ~**-sitting-room,** sitslaapkamer; ~**sore,** bedseer, deurlêseer; *become* ~ *sore,* jou deurlê; ~ **spread,** bedsprei, deken; ~ **spring,** bed= veer; ~**stead,** katel, ledekant, slaapstee; ~**stone,** fondamentklip, draagsteen; ~ **tick,** bedtyk; ~ **time,** slaaptyd, slapenstyd; ~**-wetting,** bedwate= ring, bednatmaak, enurese.
bee, by; byeenkoms, vergadering; *have a* ~ *in one's bonnet,* oor een ding sanik, gedurig oor een ding maal; ~**-bread,** broodkoek, byebrood ~**-eater,** byevanger.
beech, (-es), beukeboom; boeken(hout)hoom, berg= swoel (S.A.); ~**en,** beuke=; ~**-mast,** beukeneutjies; ~ **nut,** beukeneut; ~ **wood,** beukehout, boekenhout (S.A.) *(Faurea saligna).*
bee culture, byeteelt.
beef, beesvleis; spierkrag, sterkte.
bee'-farming, byeboerdery.
beef: ~ **biltong,** beesbiltong; ~**burger,** biefburger, lamburger; ~**cake,** manlike krag(tigheid); man= likheid; ~ **cattle,** vleisbeeste, slagbeeste; ~ **cattle breed,** vleisbeesras.
Beef'eater¹, lyfwag (Engeland).
beef'-eater², buffelsvoël; buffelsvriend.
beef: ~ **er,** vleisbees, slagbees; ~ **essence,** vleisek= strak; ~ **olive,** blindevink, gevulde beesvleisrolle= tjie; ~ **roll,** (bees)vleisrol; ~**steak,** biefstuk; ~ **stew,** gestoofde beesvleis, beesvleisbredie; ~**-suet,** beesniervet; ~ **tea,** boeljon, bieftee; ~**-witted,** suf; ~**-wittedness,** sufheid; ~**-wood,** kasuarishout; ~ **y,** soos beesvleis; frisgebou; vleisagtig; bot, suf.
bee: ~ **fly,** by(e)vlieg; ~ **glue,** bye(werk), propolis; ~ **hanger,** by(e)hanger; ~ **hive,** byenes, byekorf; ~ **house,** byekorfhuis; ~**-keeper,** byeboer, imker; ~ **-keeping,** byeboerdery.
bee'-line, reguit lyn, luglyn; *make a* ~ *for,* reguit af= gaan (afpyl) op.
Beel'zebub, Beëlsebul.
bee: ~**-master,** byehouer; ~ **moth,** wasmot, bymot, motby.
been, *kyk* **be.**
beep, (n) biep(geluid); (v), biep; ~ **er,** bieper.

bee-pir'ate, byevanger.
beep tone, bieptoon.
beer, bier; *life is not all* ~ *and SKITTLES,* dis nie altyd kermis nie; die lewe is nie alles rosegeur en maneskyn nie; *SMALL* ~, ligte bier; beuselagtig= hede; *STRONG* ~, sterk bier; *he THINKS no small* ~ *of himself,* hy dink baie van homself; ~**-barrel,** biervat; bierbuik; ~ **bottle,** bierbottel; ~ **can,** bier= blik; ~**-cask,** biervat; ~**-drinker,** bierdrinker; bier= suiper; ~**-engine,** bierpomp; ~ **garden,** biertuin; ~**-glass, (-es),** bierglas; ~**hall,** bierhuis, biersaal; ~ **house,** bierkroeg; ~**-jug,** bierkan; ~ **party,** bier= party(tjie), bierdrinkery; ~**-pot,** bierpot; ~**-shop,** kantien, drinkhuis; ~ **trade,** bierhandel; ~ **y,** bier= agtig.
bee: ~ **smo'ker,** rookpomp; ~**'s nest,** by(e)nes; ~**-sting,** (by)esteek; angel, by(e)angel; ~**-sting (bush),** by(e)angel, naaibos, naaldbos; ~**stings,** bies= (melk), kolostrum; ~**s wax,** (n) by(e) was; (v), po= leer, smeer; ~ **swine,** ou wyn, wynvlies.
beet, beet; ~ **greens,** beetlowwe.
beet'le¹, (n) kewer, tor; *BLACK* ~, swart kewer.
beet'le², (n) rammei (werktuig); stamper, heiblok; klereklopper; (v) stamp.
beet'le³, (n) bysiende persoon.
beet'le⁴, (v) oorhang; vooruitsteek.
beet'le: ~**-brain,** domkop; ~**-browed,** met 'n frons, nors, suur; met ruie winkbroue; ~**-crusher,** groot voet (skoen); doodkis.
beet'le-eyed, bysiende.
beet'le-poison, kewergif.
beet'ling, oorhangend.
beet'root, beet(wortel); ~**-sugar,** beetsuiker.
beeves, beeste, grootvee; *kyk* **beef.**
bee'zer, (sl.), neus; mens, persoon.
befall', (..fell, -en), gebeur, geskied; oorkom, wedevaar.
befit', **(-ted),** pas, deug, betaam; ~ **ting,** passend, be= taamlik
beflag', **(-ged),** bevlag, vlae hang.
befoam', met skuim oordek.
befog', **(-ged),** benewel, verduister, in mis hul.
befool', vir die gek hou, mislei, bedrieg, kul, bedot.
before', (adv.) voor, vooruit; vroeër, vantevore; voor= heen; ~ *and BEHIND,* voor en agter; *GO* ~, voor= afgaan; *LONG* ~, lank tevore.
before', (prep) voor; in teenwoordigheid van; ~ *ANOTHER year,* voor die verloop van 'n jaar; ~ *ANYTHING else,* heel eerste, voor wat ook al; *CARRY all* ~ *one,* slaag; *go* ~ *the HEADMAS= TER,* voor die prinsipaal verskyn; ~ *LONG* hin= nekort, een van die dae; ~ *NOON,* voor die mid= dag; ~ *TIME,* voorheen, vanmelewe, eertyds, vroeër.
before', (conj) voordat, voor, alvorens.
before'hand, vantevore, vooraf, vooruit; *PAY* ~ *was never well served,* vooruitbetaal is dubbel betaal; *be* ~ *WITH,* voor wees met; voorspring met
before'mentioned, voormeld, meergemeld, meerge= noemd.
befoul', besoedel, bevuil; ~ **ed,** vuil.
befriend', begunstig, help, ondersteun, guns bewys.
befringe', met fraiings versier.
befud'dle, benewel (fig.); ~ **d:** *be* ~ *d,* deur die wind wees; ~ **ment,** beneweling (fig).
beg, **(-ged),** versoek; mooipraat, bontlê, (af)smeek, bid; bedel; *I* ~ *to DIFFER,* ek is dit nie daarmee eens nie; ~ *to DO,* die vryheid neem om; ~ *FOR,* vra (bedel) om; *GO* ~ *ging,* ongebruik verbygaan; gaan bedel; *I* ~ *to INFORM you,* ek het die eer om mee te deel; ~ *someone OFF,* iem. los soebat (pleit); *I* ~ *your PARDON,* ekskuus; ek vra u om verskoning; ~ *the QUESTION,* as bewys aanneem wat nog bewys moet word; iets as uitgemaak aan= vaar.
begad'! sowaar! wraggies!
began', *kyk* **begin.**
beget', (..got, ..gotten), verwek, genereer, teel, voortbring; ~ **ter,** verwekker, vader.
begg'ar, (n) bedelaar, skooier; stumper; (pl) bedel= dom; skooiery; ~ *s cannot be CHOOSERS,* as daar nie 'n keuse is nie, moet 'n mens maar tevrede wees

met wat jy kan kry; as jy verleë is, kan jy nie kies=keurig wees nie; *set a ~ on HORSEBACK and he'll ride at a gallop* (or *to the gallows* or *to the devil*), as niet kom tot iet, ken iet homselwe niet; as 'n nego=siekas 'n stoel word; as dikmelk kaas geword het; **LITTLE** ~, klein vabond; (v) verarm; doodarm maak; *it ~ s description*, dit gaan alle beskrywing te bowe; dis onbeskryflik; ~**liness**, armoede, armoedigheid; ~**ly**, bedelagtig; armoedig; armsa=lig, berooid; ~ **tick**, knapsekêrel, wewenaar; ~-**woman**, (..**men**), bedelvrou; ~**y**, bedel(a)ry; ar=moede; *reduced to ~ y*, tot die bedelstaf gebring.

begg'ing, (n) smekery, bedel(a)ry; (a) smekend, bedelagtig; ~ **friar**, bedelmonnik; ~-**hand**, oupa-pyp-in-die-bek *(Herschelia spatulata);* ~ **letter**, bedelbrief.

begin', (**began, begun**), begin, 'n aanvang neem met; aan die gang sit; aangaan; aanhef (lied); aanvoor; ~ *AGAIN*, hervat; ~ *AT*, begin by; ~ *UPON*, êrens (mee) begin; *to ~ WITH*, in die eerste plek, om mee te begin; ~**ner**, beginner, beginneling, groentjie, nuweling; aankomeling; stigter; leerling.

beginn'ing, begin, wording, aanvoorsel, aanvang; aanhef; aangang; aanvaarding; *it is BUT a ~*, dit is maar net die begin; *without ~ or END*, sonder kop of stert; *every ~ has an END*, waar 'n begin is, is 'n end; *FROM the ~*, van meet af, uit die staanspoor; *a GOOD ~ makes a good ending*, goed begin, is halfpad gewin; goed begonne, is half gewonne; *a good ~ is HALF the battle*, 'n goeie begin sit voor=deel in; *one must START at the ~*, 'n mens moet voor (by die begin) begin.

begird', omgord; omring, omsluit.
begone'! voort! trap! voert! maak dat jy wegkom!
begon'ia, begonia.
begor'ra! wragtie! by my siel! gedorie(waar)!
begot'ten, gebore, verwek, voortgebring; *only ~ Son*, eniggebore Seun; *kyk* **beget**.
begrime', bemors, bevuil, betakel.
begrudge', beny, misgun.
beguile', bedrieg, mislei, verskalk, bedot; bekoor; ~ *one INTO*, iem. verlei tot; ~ *the TIME*, die tyd verdryf; ~**r**, misleier, verskalker; ~**ment**, verlei=ding, bekoring.
beg'uine[1], begyntjie.
beguine[2], beguine (dans).
beg'um, (Indiese) vorstin.
begun', *kyk* **begin**; *well ~, half done*, goed begonne, is half gewonne; goeie begin is halfpad gewin; 'n goeie begin sit voordeel in.
behalf': *on ~ of the COUNTRY*, van landsweë; *on HIS ~*, vir hom, om sy ontwil.
behave', (jou) gedra; ~ *oneself*, jou gedra; ~**d**, or=dentlik, fatsoenlik.
behav'iour, bedrag, houding; wandel, doentjie, optre=de; *be on one's best ~*, die beste beentjie voorsit; ~**ism**, gedragsleer, gedragsuiting, behaviorisme.
behead', onthoof, kop afkap.
behe'ld, *kyk* **behold**.
behem'oth, behemot.
behest', bevel, voorskrif, opdrag.
behind', (n) agterste, agterwêreld, sitvlak; (adv) agter; van agter, agteraan; agterna; agterom; *BE ~ what is happening*, agter die skerms sit (werk); *FALL ~*, agterbly; *FROM ~*, van agter; ~ *with PAY=MENT*, agterstallig wees; *STAY ~*, agterbly; (prep) agter; agterkant; ~ *one's BACK*, agter iem. se rug; agterbaks; *there IS something ~ it*, daar sit (steek, skuil) iets agter; ~ *the SCENES*, agter die skerms; *think that there is SOMETHING ~ it all*, êrens iets daaragter soek; *be ~ TIME*, te laat in=kom; agterlik wees; ~ *the TIMES*; agterlik; oumo=dies, verouderd; ~**hand**, agterlik; agter(stallig).
behold', (v) (**beheld**), aanskou, sien, beskou; (interj) siedaar!
behol'den, verplig, verskuldig; *be ~ to someone*, iem. na die oë kyk; iem. dank verskuldig wees.
behoof', voordeel, nut; *for (on) ~ of, for the ~ of*, ten behoewe van, ten bate van.
beho(o)ve', betaam; pas; *it ~ s you*, dit pas jou, jy behoort.
beige, beige.

beigel = **bagel**.
be'ing, (n) aansyn, bestaan; wese; kreatuur, skepsel; *BRING into ~*, in die lewe roep; *COME into ~*, ontstaan; (v) (particle of **to be**), synde; *that ~ SO*, aangesien dit so is; *for the TIME ~*, vir die oom=blik, tydelik.
Beirut, Beiroet.
bei'sa, beisa(gemsbok).
beja'b(b)ers, liewe magtig!
bejew'el, (**-ed**), met juwele behang.
belab'our, bewerk; afransel, toetakel; afjak.
belat'ed, te laat opgehou, deur die nag oorval; ver=traag, laat.
belaud', hemelhoog prys, ophemel.
belay', vasmaak, vasknoop, vasdraai; ~ *there!* hou op! skei uit! ~**ing pin**, belegpen.
bel can'to, (It.), bel canto, vol ryk sang.
belch, (n) wind, oprisping; (v) wind opbreek; braak; losbars; uitbars (vlamme); ~**er**, windopbreker; nekdoek.
bel'dam(e), wyf, feeks; helleveeg.
beleag'uer, beleër, insluit; ~**er**, beleëraar.
bel'emnite, belemniet, dondersteen.
bel esprit', (F.), spitsvondige persoon, bel esprit.
bel'fry, (..**fries**), kloktoring; klokkamer.
bel'ga, belga (vyf Belgiese frank).
Bel'gian, (n) Belg; (a) Belgies; ~ **hare**, Belgiese haas.
Bel'gium, België.
Bel'grade, Belgrado.
Bel'ial, Belial, die Duiwel.
belie', loënstraf, weerspreek; belieg; (hoop) teleurstel.
belief', geloof, mening, oortuiging; geloofsbelydenis; *to the BEST of my ~*, na my beste wete; *BEYOND ~, PAST all ~*, ongelooflik.
believ'able, geloofbaar, gelooflik.
believe', glo; vertrou; veronderstel, van mening wees; *CAN you ~ it!* bid (begryp) jou aan! *I DON'T ~ in*, ek is geen ondersteuner van, ek is daarteen dat; *not ~ one's EYES*, jou oë nie glo nie; ~ *d KILLED*, vermoedelik dood; *MAKE ~*, maak asof; wys=maak; *I QUITE ~ it*, dit wil ek hê; *I'll ~ you but THOUSANDS wouldn't*, al honderd-en-tien.
believ'er, gelowige; ~ *in*, voorstander van.
believ'ing, gelowig; gelowigheid.
belike', waarskynlik, miskien.
belit'tle, verklein; afkam, verkleineer; gering ag.
bell, (n) klok; sein; bel, blomkelk; lugbel; (pl) *ook* gla=se (skeepsterm); *ANSWER the ~*, oopmaak (deur); *CARRY away (bear) the ~*, eerste wees; *as CLEAR as a ~*, klokhelder; *RING the ~*, lui die klok; *as SOUND as a ~*, perdfris, fris en gesond; (v) skel; van klokke voorsien; belletjie aanbind; ~ *the cat*, die kat die bel aanbind; die voortou neem in gevaar.
belladonn'a, belladonna; nagskade, nastergal.
bell'-bottom trousers, tregterbroek, matroosbroek, klokbroek.
bell: ~ **boy**, hoteljoggie, page; ~ **buoy**, klokboei, bel=boei; ~ **cage**, klokstoel; ~ **cord**, klokkoord; ~ **crank**, kniehefboom.
belle, mooi vrou; mooiste meisie; belle; *the ~ of the ball*, die mooiste meisie op die dansparty.
bell'-end, klokent.
belle épo'que, (F.), belle époque, tydperk voor die Eerste Wêreldoorlog.
belles-lett'res, belletrie, skone lettere.
bellet'rist, beoefenaar (kenner) van belletrie, belle=tris.
belletris'tic, belletristies.
bell: ~-**flower**, klokblom; ~-**founder**, klokgieter; ~-**foundry**, (..**ries**), klokgietery; ~-**glass**, (**-es**), stolp; stulp; ~-**hammer**, klokhamer; ~-**heath**, lantern=heide; ~-**heather**, dopheide; ~-**hop**, hoteljoggie, page; ~-**housing**, klokhulsel.
bell'icose, oorlogsugtig, strydlustig; bakleisoekerig; ~**ness**, oorlogsugtigheid, strydlustigheid.
bell'ied, dikbuikig; geswolle.
bell'ies, penswol.
belli'gerence, **belli'gerency**, staat van oorlog; oorlog=voering.
belli'gerent, (n) strydende party, oorlogvoerende; (a) oorlogvoerend.

bell: ~-jar, klokglas; ~-knob, drukknoppie; ~ man, klokluier; ~-master, beiaardier, klokkespeler; ~-metal, klokmetaal.
bellom'bra, belhambra, bellombra *(Phytolacca dioica).*
bell'ow, (n) gebulk; gebrul; gebulder; (v) bulk; brul; bulder; dreun; ~ ing, gebulk, geloei.
bell'ows, blaasbalk; *pair of ~*, blaasbalk; ~-blower, blaasbalktrekker; orreltrapper; ~-blowpipe, soldeerbrander; ~ tongue, uitsteektong.
bell: ~ pepper, soetrissie; ~-pull, kloktou, skelkoord, klokkoord; ~-puller, klokluier; ~-punch, kaartjieknipper; ~-push, (-es), drukknoppie, klokknoppie; ~-ringer, klokluier; ~-rope, kloktou; ~-shaped, klokvormig; ~-signal, kloksein; ~-tent, ronde tent; ~ tower, kloktoring, kampaniel; ~ wether, voorbok, belhamel.
bell'y, (n) (bellies), buik, maag, pens; eetlus; holte; klankkas (viool); *live for one's ~*, 'n afgod van sy maag maak; (v) (bellied), swel; uitstaan; ~-ache, maagpyn; ~-acher, klaagpot, kermkous; ~-band, buikgord; sluitband; ~ board, branderplank; ~ button, naeltjie; ~ dance, buikdans; ~ dancer, buikdanseres; ~ful, bekoms; buik (maag-) vol, *to have had a ~ful,* buikvol (maagvol) wees vir iets; ~-god, likkebaard, likkebroer; smulpaap; ~ landing, buiklanding; ~ laugh, diep lag, buiklag, maaglag; ~-pinched, uitgehonger; ~ scope, onderspieël; maagspieël; ~-timber, mondvoorraad, maagvoorraad; ~ wool, *kyk* bellies; ~-worship, buikdiens, maagvergoding, ooreting.
belong', behoort; toebehoort; tuis behoort; ~ ing, behorend; betreffend; · ings, besittings, goed, eiendom; toebehorens, toebehoorsels.
bel'onite, beloniet.
beloved', (n) beminde, geliefde; (a) bemind.
below', (adv) onder, benede; omlaag; onderkant; onderaan; *FROM ~,* van onder af; *HERE ~,* hier benede; (prep) onder, benede, onderkant; ~ *STANDARD,* benede peil.
bel pae'se, (It.), bel paese, wit roomkaas.
belt, (n) gordel, gord, riem, lyfband, seintuur (om lyf); strook, streek (land); dryfriem; dwarsband; (patroon)band; (sabel)koppel; ~ *of FIRE,* vuurgordel; *HIT below the ~,* te laag slaan, op gemene manier baklei; *TIGHTEN the ~,* die gort (gordel) stywer trek; *have something UNDER one's ~,* iets agter die ribbes hê; iets in jou besit hê; iets op jou kerfstok hê; (v) omgord; omring; afransel, streep; ~ *ed CRUISER,* gordelkruiser; ~ *SOMEONE,* iem. afransel; iem. met die platriem gee; iem met die strop gee; iem. 'n drag slae gee; ~-armour, gordelpantser; ~-conveyor, vervoerband; lopende band; ~-drive, bandaandrywing; ~-drive turntable, bandaangedrewe plateselger; ~ ed, gegord, met 'n gordel gestreep, bantom-; ~ *ed cattle,* bandombeeste; ~-fastener, bandverbinder; riemverbinder; ~-feed, bandaanvoer(ing); ~-fork, riemvurk; ~ ing, dryfriem, dryfband; styfband; *give someone a ~ ing,* iem. met die platriem gee; iem. 'n drag slae gee; ~ joint, riemverbinding; ~-pulley, bandskyf, riemskyf, bandkatrol; ~-punch, (-es), vetertang, gattang; ~-race, lasriem; ~-rivet, bandnael; ~-saw, bandsaag, lintsaag.
Bel'tel, Beltel; ~ system, Beltelstelsel.
Belt's' body, liggaampies van Belt, mierbroodjies.
belt'-shifter, bandskuif.
belu'ga, beloega, wit dolfyn.
bel'vedere, belvedere, uitkyktoring; brandendebos (plant).
bem'a, altaarruimte, verhoog (in kerk).
bemed'alled, vol medaljes, medaljebehang.
bemire', beslyk, bemodder.
bemist', benewel, toemis.
bemoan', beween, beklaag, betreur.
bemuse', benewel, verwar, verbyster.
bench, (n) (-es), bank; sitbank; setel; skaafbank; regbank; regter(s); ~ *of JUDGES,* regbank; *RAISE to the ~,* tot regter benoem; biskop maak; ~ *of STILLS,* stookbattery; (v) op 'n bank neersit; van banke voorsien; ten toon stel (hond); ~ clamp, klou; bankklamp; ~ mark, hoogtemerk; beginpunt; ~-plane, bankskaaf; ~-saw, voegsaag; ~-vice, bankskroef; ~-worker, bankwerker; ~ working, bankafbouing (mynw.).
bend¹, (n) knoop (see); balk (heraldiek).
bend², (n) kromming, bog (rivier); waai (van bene); draai (in pad); *round the ~,* om die draai; getik; klarpraat; (v) (bent, bended), buig, verbuig; oorhang; span (boog); knoop; rig; buk; geneig wees; draai; *either ~ or BREAK,* buig of bars; ~ *ENERGIES,* kragte inspan; ~ *the KNEE to,* die knie buig vir; onderdanig wees aan; *bent on MISCHIEF,* geneig tot kattekwaad, uit op kattekwaad; ~ able, buigbaar; ~ er, buiger; ~ ing, buiging; kromtrekking; ~ ing machine, buigmasjien; ~ ing stress, buigspanning; ~-leather, soolleer; ~ moment, buigmoment; ~-spanner, draaisleutel.
beneath', (adv) onder, benede; onderaan; ondertoe; (prep) benede, onder(kant); ~ *CONTEMPT,* nie werd om te verag nie; nie werd dat die son op hom skyn nie; benede kritiek; ~ *his DIGNITY,* benede sy waardigheid.
ben'edick, pasgetroude (man); vrygestel wat trou.
Benedic'tine, Benediktyner; benediktien (likeur).
benedic'tion, seening, benediksie; gebed, seënwens.
benedic'tory, seënend, seën-.
benefac'tion, weldaad, skenking, beweldadiging; weldadigheid.
ben'efactor, weldoener.
ben'efactress, (-es) weldoenster.
ben'efice, beneficium, predikantsplek; leen(goed).
benef'icence, weldadigheid; weldaad, liefdadigheid.
benef'icent, weldadig; heilsaam, voordelig.
benefi'cial, voordelig, heilsaam, seënryk.
benefi'ciary, (n) (..ries), begunstigde, bevoordeelde, genotstrekker; bedeelde; geldtrekker; ontvanger van weldade; iem. in besit van 'n kerklike bediening; (a) leenroerig, benefisiêr.
benefi'ciate, benefisieer; veredel; reduseer.
beneficia'tion, benefisiëring.
ben'efit, (n) voordeel, nut, wins; weldaad; uitkering; voorreg, beneficie; benefiet (teater); *the ~ of the DOUBT,* die voordeel van die twyfel; aanneem dat iem. gelyk kan hê; *REAP the ~ of,* voordeel trek uit; *WITHOUT ~ of clergy,* sonder kerklike sanksie, ongekerk; (v) bevoordeel; voordeel trek, profiteer, baat; bevorder; ~ *from,* voordeel trek uit; ~ concert, fonds(insamelings)konsert; ~ fund, bystandsfonds; ~ match, fondswedstryd, ondersteuningswedstryd; ~ night, fondsaand; ~ society, (..ties), hulpvereniging, bystandsvereniging.
Ben'elux, Benelux(lande).
benev'olence, welwillendheid, liefdadigheid, weldadigheid.
benev'olent, welwillend, weldadig; goedgunstig; ~ depotism, verligte despotisme; ~ fund, ondersteuningsfonds, uitkeringsfonds; ~ society, liefdadigheidsgenootskap, hulpvereniging.
Bengal', Bengale; ~ ee, ~ ese', ~ i, (n) Bengalees; (a) Dengaals.
Bengal': ~ lights, Bengaalse vuur; b~ ine, bengalien, bengaline; ~ tiger, Bengaalse tier.
benight'ed, deur die nag oorval; in duisternis gehul; verblind; onbeskaaf.
benign', goed, minsaam, vriendelik; goedgunstig; sagaardig; goedaardig; heilsaam; ~ *tumor,* goedaardige gewas; ~ ancy, goedaardigheid; goedhartigheid; heilsaamheid; ~ ant, goedgunstig, goedaardig, liefderyk, vriendelik, weldadig; ~ ity, goedgunstigheid, vriendelikheid, sagtheid, weldadigheid, heilsaamheid.
be'nison, seën(ing).
Ben'jamin, Benjamin.
ben'jaminite, benjaminiet.
ben'net, naelkruid.
ben'ni, sesam(plant).
bent¹, (n) rietgras; ruigte.
bent², (n) draai, buiging, wending; aanleg, neiging, voorliefde; strekking; *FOLLOW one's ~,* doen soos jy geneë voel; *he has a ~ for MATHEMATICS,* hy het aanleg vir wiskunde; *to the TOP of his ~,* na hartelus, tot die uiterste; (a) inmekaar; gebuig, geboë, krom, gebukkend; daarop uit om; *BE*

COME ~ on, tuk word op; with ~ HEAD, met geboë hoof; ~ on MISCHIEF, geneig tot katte= kwaad; ~ callipers, krompasser; ~ gouge, krom= guts; ~ lever, kromhefboom, tuimelaar.
ben'thal, bentaal.
benthos', bentos, bodemplante en -diere.
ben'tonite, bentoniet.
bent pipe, krom(steel)pyp; geboë pyp.
bent' saw, geboë saag.
bent' spanner, draaisleutel.
bentwood, buighout; ~ **chair,** buighoutstoel, kom= buisstoel.
bent' wrench, (-es), kromneksleutel.
benumb', verkluim, verstywe; verdoof; ~ **ing,** versty= wing.
Benzedrine', Benzedrine.
ben'zene, benseen.
benzidine', bensidien, bensidine.
ben'zine, bensien, bensine.
ben'zoate, bensoaat, bensoësuursout.
benzo'ic acid, bensoësuur.
ben'zoin, bensoïen, bensoïne; ~ **gum,** bensoïnehars, bensoïenhars.
ben'zol(e), bensool, benseen.
ben'zyl, bensiel.
bequeath', bemaak, vermaak, nalaat, legeer, legateer; ~ *by will,* by testament bemaak; ~ **er,** bemaker, nalater; ~ **ment,** bemaking, nalatenskap.
bequest', bemaking, erfporsie, erflating, vermaking, legaat.
berate', uitskel, slegsê, raas, skrobbeer.
berb'erin(e), berberien, berberine.
berceuse', berceuse, wiegelied.
bereave', (-d, bereft), berowe; ontneem; ~ **d,** beroof; diep bedroef, swaar beproef; *the* ~ *d children,* die bedroefde kinders; ~ **ment,** berowing; verlies; sterf= geval, ontvalling.
bereft, beroof; ~ *of one's senses,* van jou sinne beroof.
be'ret, baret, mus.
berg, berg; ysberg.
ber'gamasque, bergamask, wilde dans.
berg'amot¹, bergamotpeer.
berg'amot², bergamotolie; bergamot (sitroen).
ber'gie, (Afr.), bergie (gew.).
berg'schrund, gletsergaping.
ber'gylt, Noorse skelvis.
berg'wind, bergwind, landwind.
beribe'ri, berrie-berrie, beri-beri.
berke'lium, berkelium.
Berlin', Berlyn; ~ **black,** ystervernis; ~ **blue,** berlyns= blou; pruisiesblou; ~ **gloves,** gehekelde handskoe= ne; ~ **wool,** fyn breiwol.
berlin(e)', perdewa, perdekar.
berm, berm; sypaadjie.
Bermud'as, Bermuda-eilande.
be'rry, (n) (berries), bessie; viseier; pit (van vrug); (v) **(berried),** bessies kry; bessies insamel; ~ **wax,** bessiewas.
berserk', berserk, wild, woes, rasend, waansinnig; ~ **er,** beserker, woesteling; waansinnige; *go* ~, soos 'n besetene te kere gaan; mal word.
berth¹, amp, betrekking.
berth², (n) slaapplek, lêplek; kooi (skip); laaiplek, an= kerplek; ruimte tussen seilende skepe; *give a wide* ~ *to,* uit die pad bly van, vermy; lig loop vir iem.; uit iem. se vaarwater bly; (v) aanlê, vasmaak (skip); 'n slaapplek aanwys; aan 'n baantjie help; ~ **ing,** vas= mering; ~ **master,** ankermeester.
be'ryl, beril, seewatersteen; ~ **-green,** berilgroen;. ~ **li'ferous,** berilhoudend.
beryl'lium, berillium.
beseech', (besought), versoek, smeek, afsmeek, bid; ~ **ing, (n)** smekery; (a) smekend.
beseem', betaam, voeg, pas; ~ **ing,** passend, betaam= lik, voegsaam.
beset', (beset), in besit neem; beset, insluit, omring; ~ *ting sin,* boesemsonde.
beset'ment, boesemsonde; insluiting, ingeslotenheid.
beshrew', vervloek, verwens.
besiclom'eter, besikilometer.
beside', langs, naas, neffens; digby; by; behalwe, bui=

ten; *be* ~ *oneself with ANGER,* buite jouself wees van woede; uit jou vel kan spring van woede; uit jou klere kan klim van kwaadheid; *BE* ~ *oneself,* uitbundig wees, uit sy vel bars (van . . .); *that is* ~ *the MARK (question),* dit kom nie ter sprake nie.
besides', bowendien, behalwe, buiten, buitendien, te= wens, daarbenewens, daarby, boonop, voorts, daarenbowe.
besiege', beleër, insluit, omsingel; ~ **r,** beleëraar.
beslav'er, bekwyl; lek, flikflooi.
beslobb'er, bekwyl; geesdriftig soen.
beslubb'er, bemors; beslobber.
besmear', besmeer, bevuil, betakel.
besmirch', beklad, beswadder, besoedel, bemodder; ~ *the good name of others,* met roet (modder) gooi; die goeie naam van ander beswadder.
bes'om, (n) besem; (v) (uit)vee.
besot', (-ted), verdwaas, verblind, versot maak; ~ **ted,** verdwaas, versot; benewel.
bespang'le, versier; besaai; ~ *d with stars,* met sterre besaai.
bespatt'er, bespat, beklad, bevuil.
bespeak', (bespoke, bespoke(n)), bespreek; bestel; in beslag neem; versoek om; getuig van.
bespoke', op die maat gemaak; ~ **boots,** maatskoene; ~ **department,** maatafdeling; ~ **tailor(ing),** maat= kleremaker(y).
bespok'en, bespreek.
besprin'kle, besprinkel, besaai.
Bes'semer: ~ **converter,** bessemerpeer; ~ **process,** bessemerproses; ~ **steel,** bessemerstaal.
best, (n) bes, beste; *to the* ~ *of my ABILITY,* na my beste vermoë, so goed as ek kan; *AT* ~, op sy beste, hoogstens; *BE at one's* ~, op sy beste wees; *to the* ~ *of my BELIEF,* na my beste wete, sover ek weet; *DO one's* ~, sy bes (uiterste) doen; *he DOES it for the* ~, hy meen dit goed; *the* ~ *is the ENEMY of the good,* 'n te hoë standaard belemmer die vooruit= gang; *FOR the* ~, ten goede; *GET the* ~ *of it,* die oorhand kry; *HAVE the* ~ *of it,* die beste daaraan toe wees; *to the* ~ *of his KNOWLEDGE,* sover hy weet; *MAKE the* ~ *of it,* jou daarin skik; dit vir lief neem; jou daarmee versoen; jou daarby neerlê; *the NEXT* ~, op een na die beste; *he is ONE of the* ~, hy is 'n pure man; ~ *POSSIBLE,* beste, hoogste; *he can SING with the* ~ *of them,* hy sing net so goed soos enigeen; *in his SUNDAY* ~, in sy kisklere; (v) uitoorlê; (a) beste; *put one's* ~ *FOOT foremost,* die beste beentjie voor sit; *his* ~ *GIRL,* sy nooi; (adv) liefs, die beste.
bestead', baat, help.
bested', geplaas; *ill (hard)* ~, in die knyp, in die moeilikheid.
bes'tial, dierlik, beesagtig; sinlik.
bestial'ity, bestialiteit, beesagtigheid, verdierliking.
bes'tialize, verdierlik.
bestir', (-red), gou maak, roer; ~ *ONESELF,* jou roer; *you WILL have to* ~ *yourself,* jy sal vroeg moet opstaan.
best'man, (. . men), strooijonker, bruidsjonker.
bestow', skenk (in huwelik); besteë (aandag); verleen; bedeel; bêre; ~ **al,** gif, skenking; verlening (ge= nade); opberging (goedere); besteding.
bestrew', (-ed, -n). bestrooi, rondstrooi.
bestride', (bestrode, bestridden), wydsbeen sit; bery; bestyg, opklim.
best'seller, treffer, trefferverkoper, trefferboek, suk= sesboek, blitsverkoper; trefferskrywer, treffer= outeur.
bestud', met spykers beslaan; besaai (fig.).
bet, (n) weddenskap; *MAKE a* ~, 'n weddenskap aangaan, wed; *WHAT'S the* ~? wat wed jy? (v) **(bet),** wed, verwed; ~ *your BOOTS,* doodseker wees; ~ *one's bottom DOLLAR,* alles waag; ~ *YOU!* dit kan jy glo!
be'ta, beta; ~ **particle,** betadeeltjie; ~ **ray,** beta= straal; ~ **tron,** betatron.
betake', (betook, -n), begewe, die toevlug neem tot, wend tot; ~ *oneself to,* jou toevlug neem tot; gaan na.
bet'el, betel(neut); ~ **-nut,** betelneut, pienang.

bête noire, (F.), bête noire, gehate persoon, gehate ding, nagmerrie.
Beth'el, Bet-el, heilige plek.
beth'el, matrosekerk.
bethink', (bethought), bedink, oorweeg; ~ *oneself OF*, jou iets herinner, aan iets dink; ~ *ONESELF*, jou bedink.
betide', oorkom, gebeur, wedervaar; *WHATE'ER* ~, wat ook al gebeur; *WOE* ~ *him!* wee hom! wee sy gebeente!
betimes', vroegtydig, betyds, vroeg.
betok'en, aandui, voorspel, beteken.
bet'on, beton.
bet'ony, betonie (plant).
betook', *kyk* **betake**.
betray', verraai, in die steek laat; mislei, bedrieg; verlei (meisie); skend (geheim); dui op, aandui (gevoelens); ~ *someone's CONFIDENCE*, iem. se vertroue skok (misbruik); ~ *one's DUTY*, sy plig versaak; ~ *no SIGN of something*, iets nie laat merk nie; ~ **al**, verraad, troubreuk, judasstreek; ~ **er**, verraaier; verleier.
betroth', verloof raak; belowe om te trou; ~ **al**, verlowing; ~ **ed**, verloofde.
bett'er[1], (n) wedder.
bett'er[2], (n) meerdere; oorhand; *CHANGE for the* ~, verandering ten goede; *GET the* ~ *of*, iem. die loef afsteek; uitoorlê, die oorhand kry oor; *ONE'S* ~ *s*, jou meerderes; *for* ~, *for WORSE*, in lief en leed; in voor- en teëspoed; (v) verbeter; oortref; ~ *oneself*, jou posisie verbeter; (a) *(comp. of good)* beter; *on - ACQUAINTANCE*, by nader kennismaking, *the* ~ *the DAY, the* ~ *the deed*, hoe gouer die geleentheid, hoe beter die daad; hoe eerder, hoe beter; *that is EVEN* ~, nou nog mooier; *he is the* ~ *FOR it*, hy trek daar voordeel uit; hy vind daar baat by; *GET* ~, beter word; ~ *HALF*, wederhelf; *MUCH the* ~, des te beter; ~ *PART*, leeueaandeel, grootste gedeelte; *one's* ~ *SELF*, jou beter natuur; *TAKE each other for* ~ *or worse*, hulle velletjies bymekaargooi; ~ *WEAR out than rust out*, jou liewer doodwerk as verroes, liewer uitslyt as verroes; *be* ~ *than one's WORD*, meer doen as wat beloof is; (adv) beter; liewer; *GO one* ~ *than someone else*, iem. (oor)troef; *you HAD* ~ *go*, jy moet liewer gaan; *KNOW* ~, beter weet; ~ *LATE than never*, liewer laat as nooit; ~ *OFF*, ryker, daar beter aan toe wees; *be* ~ *OFF*, in beter omstandighede wees, meer gegoed wees; ~ *some of the PUDDING than none of the pie*, liewer net 'n korsie as glad geen brood nie; *THINK* ~ *of*, van gedagte verander.
bett'erment, verbetering; verhoogde waarde.
bett'ing, weddery; ~ **-book**, wed(denskap)boek; ~ **-shop**, wedkantoor; ~ **tax**, wedbelasting.
bett'or = **better**[1].
between', tussen, tussenin; onder; ~ *the DEVIL and the deep blue sea*, tussen twee vure; *FEW and far* ~, dun gesaai; seldsaam; ~ *OURSELVES*, so onder ons meisies; dit bly tussen ons meisies; onder ons gesê; ~ *WHILES*, by tussenpose, tussendeur; ~ *YOU and me and the gate-post*, onder ons mans; ~ **-decks**, tussendeks; ~ **-maid**, hulpbediende, hulp.
betwixt', tussen; ~ *and between*, middelmatig; so-so, so half en half; tussen die boom en die bas; so tussen die by en die koek.
bev'el, (n) skuinskant, skuinste; swaaihaak; hoekmeter; faas; (v) (-led), skerphoekig maak; afplat; afpunt; afskuins; skuins maak; afsteek; (a) hoekig; skuins; ~ *led CHISEL*, steekbeitel; ~ *ed GLASS*, spieël met geslypte rand; ~ **angle**, afskuinshoek; ~ **drive**, keëlrataandrywing; ~ **edge**, skuins kant (rand); ~ **gauge**, swaaihaak; swei; ~ **-gear**, koniese rat; ~ **ling**, afskuinsing; ~ **-mitre**, ~ **-protractor**, verstekhaak; ~ **-square**, swaaihaak; swei; ~ **-tool**, afkantgereedskap; ~ **-wheel**, keëlrat.
bev'erage, drank; ~ **wine**, tafelwyn.
bev'y, (bevies), swerm, trop (bokke); aantal, troep (meisies); vlug (patryse); ~ *of beauties*, klomp mooi meisies.
bewail', betreur, beween, beklaag.
beware', oppas, op sy hoede wees, in ag neem; ~ *of the DOG*, pas op vir die hond; *I WILL* ~, ek sal oppas; ek sal versigtig wees.
bewigged', gepruik, met 'n pruik op.
bewil'der, verwar, verbyster, desoriënteer, deurmekaar maak; ~ **ed**, verwar(d); oorstuur; deurmekaar; verwese; ~ **ing**, verwarrend, ontstellend; ~ **ment**, (sins)verbystering, verwildering; verwarring.
bewitch', betower, bekoor; toor, doepa, beheks, begoël; ~ **ing**, (n) begoëling; (a) betowerend; ~ **ment**, betowering, bekoring; begoëling.
bey, Turkse goewerneur, bei.
beyond', (n) oorkant; *the BACK of* ~, die verste uithoek, (aan) die ander kant van die wêreld, die gramadoelas; *COME from the back of* ~, v.d. gramadoelas (agterveld) kom; *THE* ~, die hiernamaals; (adv) verder; *go* ~, verder gaan; (prep) oorkant, anderkant; bo; oor; buite; verby; *it is* ~ *my COMPREHENSION*, dis bokant my vuurmaakplek; *it is* ~ *ENDURANCE*, dit is ondraaglik; ~ *HELP*, reddeloos; ~ *HOPE*, hopeloos; buite hoop; *that is* ~ *ME*, my verstand staan stil; dit gaan my verstand te bowe; dis anderkant my uitspanplek, dit gaan my begrip te bowe; dis bokant my vuurmaakplek; ~ *MEASURE*, uitermate; ~ *REACH*, buite bereik; ~ *REDEMPTION*, hopeloos verlore.
bezant', sierskyf; ou goue munt(stuk).
bez'el, skuins kant (van beitel); kassie (vir edelsteen); gleufie (vir oorlosieglas), groefie; faset.
bezique', bezique (kaartspel).
be'zoar, maagbal; beeswart; besoar; ~ **antelope**, besoarbok, ~ **stone**, besoarsteen.
bhang, Indiese hennep, dagga.
bi'angular, tweehoekig.
biann'ual, halfjaarliks, twee maal per jaar.
biarti'culate, tweedelig.
bi'as, (n) oorhelling; neiging; eensydige verswaring (van rolbal); skuinste; onewewigtigheid; vooringenomenheid; voorliefde, vooroordeel, partydigheid; drang, invloed; *cut on the* ~, skuins knip; (v) bevooroordeel; beïnvloed, vooringenome (partydig) maak; laat voordeel kry; *be* ~ (*s*)*ed*, bevooroordeel(d) wees; ~ **band**, ~ **binding**, skuinsomboorsel, skuinsstrook, skuinsband; ~ **sed**, bevooroordeel(d), partydig; ~ **strip**, skuins (oorhoekse) strook.
bi'athlon, tweekamp.
biax'ial, tweeassig.
bib[1], (n) vissoort.
bib[2], (n) borslappie; beffie; moffelplaat; *in one's best* ~ *and tucker*, fyn uitgevat (uitgepiets).
bib[3], (v) (-bed), drink, suip; slurp; ~ **ber**, dronklap, suiplap; ~ **cock**, ~ **tap**, tapkraan.
Bi'ble, Bybel, Gods Woord; ~ **oath**, eed op die Bybel; ~ **reading**, Skriflesing; ~ **scholar**, Bybelgeleerde, Bybelkenner; ~ **Society**, Bybelgenootskap; ~ **study**, Bybelstudie; ~ **translation**, Bybelvertaling.
Bib'lical, Bybels, Bybel-; ~ **language**, Bybeltaal; ~ **scholar**, Bybelkenner.
Bib'licism, Biblisisme.
Bib'licist, Biblisis.
bibliog'rapher, boekbeskrywer; bibliograaf.
bibliograph'ic(al), bibliografies.
bibliog'raphy, (..phies), bibliografie, literatuurlys; leeslys.
bibliol'ater, boekaanbidder.
bibliol'atrous, boekaanbiddend.
bibliol'atry, boekaanbidding, bibliolatrie.
biblioman'cy, bibliomansie.
biblioman'ia, boekwoede, boekmanie, bibliomanie; boekversamelingsmanie.
biblioman'iac, bibliomaan, boekgek.
bib'liophil(e), boekversamelaar, boekliefhebber, bibliofiel.
biblioph'ilism, bibliofilie, boekeliefhebbery, bibliofilisme.
bib'liopole, boekantikwariaat.
bib'ulous, sponsagtig; opslurpend; dranksugtig.
bicam'eral, tweekamer-, bikameraal.
bicar'bonate, bikarbonaat, dubbelkoolsuursout; ~ *of soda*, koeksoda, natriumbikarbonaat.
bicaud'ate, tweestert-.

bice, bergblou.
bicen'tenary, (n) (..ries), tweede eeufees, tweehonderdjarige fees (gedenkdag); (a) tweehonderdjarig.
bicentenn'ial, tweehonderdjarig, twee-eeue-.
biceph'alous, tweehoofdig.
biceph'aly, dubbelkoppigheid, tweehoofdigheid, bisefalie.
bi'ceps, (-es), tweehoofdige armspier, biseps.
bichrom'ate, bichromaat.
bick'er, (n) rusie; gekletter; geflikker; (v) kibbel, twis, skermutsel; flikker; ~**ing,** gekibbel, gekrakeel, stryery, gestry, gekyf.
bicol'oured, tweekleurig.
bicon'cave, dubbelkonkaaf, dubbelhol, bikonkaaf.
bicon'vex, dubbelkonveks, dubbelbol, bikonveks; ~'**ity,** dubbelbolheid.
bicor'nous, tweehoringrig, tweehoring-.
bicus'pid, tweepuntig.
bi'cycle, (n) fiets, rywiel, ysterperd; (v) fiets ry; ~ **bell,** fietsklokkie; ~ **handle(s),** fietshandvatsel(s); ~ **lamp,** fietslamp; ~ **pedal,** fietstrap; ~ **pump,** fietspomp; ~ **rack,** fietsrak; ~**shed,** fietsafdak; ~ **tour,** fietstog; ~ **tyre,** fietsband.
bi'cyclist, fietsryer.
bid, (n) bod; *make a* ~, 'n bod maak; 'n poging aanwend; (v) **(bid,** or **bad(e), bid** or **-den),** aanbied; beveel, gebied; versoek, nooi, uitnooi; sê, heet (welkom); bied; ~ *AGAINST,* bie teen; *he* ~*s fair to BECOME a man of note,* hy beloof om 'n man van betekenis te word; *DO as you are* ~, doen soos jy beveel word; ~ *FAREWELL,* vaarwel sê; ~**dable,** geseglik, gehoorsaam; biedbaar (kaarte); ~**den,** uitgenooi, ontbied, geroep; ~**der,** bieër; ~**ding,** uitnodiging; bevel, gebod; bieëry, bod; versoek; *without* ~ *ding,* uit eie beweging.
bide, afwag, verdra, verduur; hom hou aan; ~ *one's time,* jou tyd afwag.
bi'dent, biden'tal, tweetand-.
bi'det, bidet, sitbad.
Bie'dermeier, (n), Biedermeier (styl); (a): konvensioneel, (klein)burgerlik.
bienn'ial, (n) tweejarige plant; (a) tweejarig; ~**ly,** elke twee jaar.
bien'nium, tweejaartydperk, tweejaarperiode, biennium.
bier, (draag)baar, lykbaar; dwarsstyl.
biff, (n) opstopper, klap; (v) klap, opstopper gee.
bif'fin, Norfolkappel, kookappel.
bif'id, gevurk, gesplits.
biflo'rous, tweeblommig.
bifoc'al, bifokaal, dubbelbrandpuntig; ~**s,** ~ **spectacles,** bifokale bril, dubbeldoorbrilglase.
bifol'iate, tweeblarig.
bi'furcate, in twee takke, verdeel, vurk, vertak, splits; ~**d,** gevurk, gaffelvormig, gesplete.
bifurca'tion, vertakking, splitsing, bifurkasie; vurk, gaffel; tweesprong, padmik; ~ **pole,** aftakpaal.
big, groot; swaar; dik; *B*~ *BEN,* Big Ben; *B*~ *BER= THA,* die Dik Bertha; *get (grow) too* ~ *for one's BOOTS,* te groot vir sy skoene word, hoogmoedig word; ~ *BROTHER,* outokratiese heerser, diktator; ~ *BUSINESS,* handel op groot skaal; groot sakelewe; oorheersing deur die groot sakeondernemings; ~ *with CHILD,* swanger; ~ *END,* dryfstangkop; suierstangkop; grootkop (werktuigk.); ~ *GAME,* grootwild; ~ *GUNS,* (die) groot base; *a* ~ *MAN,* 'n groot man; *the* ~ *STICK,* magsvertoon; ~ *with YOUNG,* dragtig.
big'amist, bigamis, tweewywer.
big'amous, bigamies, tweewywig.
big'amy, tweewywery, bigamie.
big: ~ **band,** grootorkes; ~ **bang,** groot ontploffing; ~**-bellied,** dikbuikig, grootmaag-; ~**-boned,** grof gebou; ~ **brother,** ouboet; ~ **bug,** grootpiet, grootmeneer; groot persoon, vooraanstaande persoon; ~ **deal!,** dit imponeer my nie!; ~ **end,** grootkop; ~ **end bearing,** grootkoplaer; ~**-framed,** groot (grof) gebou; ~ **game,** grootwild; ~**-game hunter,** grootwildjagter; ~ **gun,** groot kanon; grootkanon, grootmeneer; ~ **head,** dikkopsiekte; geswolle hoof; ~**-headed,** verwaand; ~**-hearted,** vrygewig, gul, groothartig; ~ **house,** groot huis.

bight, (see)bog, baai; lus, oog (van tou).
big: ~ **money,** grootgeld; groot geldbase; ~ **mouth,** grootprater, grootbek; ~**-mouthed,** grootpraterig, grootbek; ~ **name,** beroemdheid; ~ **ness,** grootheid, omvangrykheid; ~ **noise,** grootpiet, belangrike ou.
bignon'ia, trompetblom.
big'ot, yweraar; dweper; geesdrywer; skynheilige; ~**ed,** skynheilig; dweperig, dweepsiek, bekrompe; ~**ry,** bygelowigheid, skynheiligheid; dwepery, bigotterie.
big: ~ **pot,** hoë koejawel, hoë piet; ~ **shot,** groot kokkedoor, hoë ou, belangrike ou, grootpiet, hoë piet; ~ **sister,** ousus; ~ **stick,** straf(toediening); ~ **talk,** groot pratery, spog(gery); ~ **time,** eerste rang (bv. in sport, in die teater, in die musiek); ~ **toe,** groottoon; ~ **top,** sirkustent; ~ **way,** hoë (groot) mate; ~ **wheel,** kermiswiel; ~**wig,** groot kokkedoor, groot meneer; hoë piet, hoë (belangrike) ou.
bijou', (-x), juweeltjie; ~**terie,** juweliersware.
bij'ugate, bij'ugous, dubbeljukkig, tweejukkig; tweeparig.
bike, fiets, rywiel; ~ **track,** fiets(ren)baan.
biki'ni, bikini; ~ **swim-suit,** bikini(baaikostuum), bietjie-nie.
bilab'ial, tweelippig, bilabiaal.
bilat'eral, tweekantig, tweesydig, bilateraal; ~ **contact,** bilaterale kontak.
bil'berry, (..rries), bloubosbessie.
bil'bo, (-s), swaard, sabel.
bil'boes, (hist.), boeie.
bile, gal; knorrigheid, gehumeurdheid; *stir up the* ~, in die harnas jaag, kwaad maak; ~**-duct,** galbuisie; ~ **salts,** galsout; ~**-stone,** galsteen.
bilge¹, (n) buik (van vat, skip); kaf, onsin.
bilge², (v) 'n lek kry; opswel.
bilge: ~**-keel,** kimkiel; ~**-pump,** lenspomp, ruimpomp; ~**-water,** ruimwater, rioolwater, skottelgoedwater, vuil water.
bilhar'zia, bilharziaparasiet, rooiwaterparasiet.
bilharzios'is, rooiwater, bilharziose.
bil'iary, gal-; ~ **calculus,** galsteen; ~ **fever,** galkoors, witbek.
bilin'ear, bilineêr.
biling'ual, tweetalig; dubbeltalig; ~**ism,** tweetaligheid; ~ **gentleman,** tweetalige man; ~ **lady,** tweetalige vrou (dame); ~ **person,** tweetalige persoon.
bil'ious, galagtig, gallerig, mislik, naar; knorrig, oplopend; *feel* ~, mislik voel; ~**ness,** mislikheid; galagtigheid, naarheid, gallerigheid.
bilirub'in, galrooi, bilirubien, bilirubine.
biliverd'in, galgroen, biliverdien, biliverdine.
bilk, bedrieg, fop; betaling ontduik; ~**er,** glyjakkals; ~**ing,** bedrieëry, kullery.
bill¹, (n) bek, snawel (voël); (v) met die bek streel; ~ *and coo,* trekkebek (voëls); minnekoos, by gesonde mense waak.
bill², (n) rekening, faktuur; wissel; bewys; aanplakbiljet; wetsvoorstel, wetsontwerp; ~ *of COSTS,* onkostelys, rekening; ~ *of CREDIT,* skatkisbiljet; kredietbrief; ~ *of DISCOUNT,* diskontowissel; ~ *of DIVORCE,* skeibrief; ~ *of EXCHANGE,* wissel(brief); ~ *of FARE,* spyskaart; ~ *of FARES,* vragtarief; ~ *of HEALTH,* gesondheidspas; ~ *of LADING,* (skeeps)vragbrief, ladingsbrief; ~ *of PARCELS,* faktuur; *PASS a* ~, 'n wetsontwerp aanneem; ~ *PAYABLE,* betaalwissel; ~ *of QUANTITIES,* bestek, hoeveelheidslys; ~ *RECEIVABLE,* ontvangswissel, baatwissel, inbare wissel; ~ *of SALES,* koopbrief.
bill³, (n) kapmes; ankerklou; strydbyl.
bill⁴, (v) aankondig; aanplak; in rekening bring; 'n rekening stuur.
bi'llabong, (Austr.), billabong, riviersytak.
bill: ~ **board,** reklamebord, skutting, advertensiebord; ~**-book,** wisselboek; ~**-broker,** wisselhandelaar; ~ **charges,** wisselkoste; ~**-clerk,** wisselklerk.
bill'et¹, (n) biljet, briefie; baantjie, betrekking; kwartier, leëring; inkwartieringsbevel; *every BULLET has its* ~, as jy vir 'n koeël gebore is, sal jy nie in troebel water verdrink nie; ~*s for PALS,* baantjies vir boeties; (v) inkwartier, plaas (in betrekking).

bill'et², (n) houtblok, stuhout.
billet-doux', minnebriefie.
bill'eting, inkwartiering; leëring.
bill'fold, sakportefeulje, beursie.
bill'hook, snoeimes, kapmes.
bill'iard: ~**-ball,** biljartbal; ~**-cue,** keu, biljartstok; ~**ist,** ~**-player,** biljartspeler; ~ **marker,** biljarttel= linghouer; ~**-rest,** biljartbok; ~**-room,** biljartka= mer; ~**s,** biljart(spel); ~**-table,** biljarttafel.
bill'ing¹: ~ *and cooing,* gevry, vryery, liefkosery.
bill'ing², aankondiging, reklame.
bill'ingsgate, billingsgate, vismark; gemene taal, skeldwoorde, viswywetaal, matroostaal, straattaal.
bill'ion, biljoen; miljard (Amerika).
bi'llon, goud- of silwerlegering.
bill'ow, (n) golf, baar, brander; (v) golf, dein; ~**y,** golwend.
bill: ~**-paper,** waardepapier; ~ **poster,** ~ **sticker,** (aan)plakker, biljetplakker, plakkaatplakker; ~-**walker,** wisselklerk.
bill'y, (billies), (Australiese) keteltjie; kookblik; ~**can,** kookblik, kosblik; keteltjie.
bill'ycock, hardebolkeil; mosdoppie.
bill'y-goat, bokram.
bilob'ate, bilo'bed, tweelobbig.
bil'tong, biltong; ~ **meat,** biltongvleis.
bim'anal, bim'ane, bim'anous, tweehandig.
bim'bo, (sl.), persoon; vrou.
bimetall'ic, bimetaal; ~ **strip,** tweemetaalstrook (ter= mostaat).
bimet'alism, bimetallisme.
bimonth'ly, (n) tweemaandelikse tydskrif; (a, adv) tweemaandeliks; veertiendaags.
bin, meelkis; blik, bak.
bin'ary, (n) dubbelster; (a) dubbel, tweeledig, tweetal= lig, binêr; ~ **alloy,** binêre legering, tweemetaallege= ring; ~ **compounds,** binêre verbindings, twee-ele= mentverbindings; ~ **digit,** binêre syfer; ~ **fission,** binêre deling, tweedeling; ~ **measure,** tweeslags= maat; ~ **star,** dubbelster; ~ **system,** binêre stelsel; ~ **theory,** binêre teorie.
bin'ate, paarsgewys(e).
binaur'al, twee-oor=.
bind, (n) boog (musiek); (v) **(bound),** bind, vasmaak; verbind (wond); bekragtig; inbaker (babatjie); om= gord; verplig; inbind (boek); *I'll* BE *bound,* ek wed, ek sweer; *be bound to DO it,* gedwing wees om dit te doen; *in DUTY bound,* na eer en gewete verplig; ~ *OFF,* afkant; ~ *OVER,* onder geregte= like verbintenis stel; ~ *UP,* verbind, vasbind, opbind.
bin'der, (boek)binder; bindmasjien; verband, bindsel, bindmiddel; nawelband; bindbalk; bindsteen; om= slag; ~ **course,** bindlaag (pad); ~ **twine,** bindtou.
bin'dery, (..ries), boekbindery.
bin'ding, (n) binding, hindsel; omlegsel, omboorsel; stootkant (rok); band (van 'n broek); (a) bindend, geldig (gereg), verpligtend; ~**-agent,** bindmiddel; ~**-beam,** moerbalk; ~**-joist,** bindbalk; - **screw,** klemskroef; ~**-stay,** spanstaaf; ~**-wire,** bind= draad.
bind'weed, klimplant, klimop, akkerwinde, convol= vulus.
bine, (hop)rank; stam.
binge, fuif; *on the* ~, aan die fuif.
binn'acle, kompashuisie; naghuisie.
bin'ocle, toneelkyker; verkyker; binokel.
binoc'ular, (n) verkyker; toneelkyker, binokel; (a) twee-ogig, biokulêr.
binom'ial, (n) binoom, tweeterm, tweeledige groot= heid; (a) tweeledig; binomiaal; ~ **theorem,** bino= miaalformule.
bint, (sl.), meisie, vrou.
bio: ~ **chemical,** biochemies; ~ **chemist,** biochemikus; ~ **chemistry,** biochemie; ~ **coenosis,** biosenose, plantgemeenskap; ~ **degradability,** verval, ver= gaanbaarheid; ~ **degradable,** vergaanbaar; ~ **degra= dation,** vergaanbaarheid, verval; ~ **dynamics,** bio= dinamika; ~**-electricity,** bioëlektrisiteit; ~**-engineering,** bio-ingenieurswese; ~ **feedback,** bioterugvoer; ~ **genesis,** biogenese; ~ **genetic,** bio= geneties; ~ **genic,** biogenies, biogeen; ~ **geography,** biogeografie, bioaardrykskunde; ~ **graph,** kinema= tograaf; ~ **grapher,** biograaf, lewensbeskrywer; ~ **graphic(al),** biografies, lewensbeskrywend; ~ **graphy,** biografie, lewensbeskrywing; lewensge= skiedenis; ~ **lite,** bioliet; ~ **logical,** biologies; ~ **logical clock,** biologiese klok; ~ **logical control,** biologiese bestryding (beheer); ~ **logical warfare,** biologiese oorlogvoering; ~ **logist,** bioloog; ~ **logy,** biologie; ~ **luminescence,** bioluminessensie; ~ **magnetism,** biomagnetisme; ~ **mass,** biomassa; ~ **mathematics,** biowiskunde; ~ **metric(al),** biome= tries; ~ **metrician,** biometrikus; ~ **metrics,** ~ **metry,** biometrie, biometrika; ~ **morph,** bio= morf; ~ **nic,** bionies; ~ **nics,** bionika; ~ **nomic,** bio= nomies, ekologies; ~ **nomics,** bionomie, ekologie; ~ **nomy,** bionomie; ~ **physical,** biofisies; ~ **physics,** biofisika; ~ **plasm,** bioplasma; ~ **plast,** bioplas(t); ~ **psy,** biopsie, weefselondersoek, weefselverwyde= ring; ~ **rhythm,** bioritme; ~ **scope,** bioskoop, fliek, filmvertoning, kinema; ~ **sphere,** biosfeer; ~ **stat= istics,** biostatistiek; ~ **synthesis,** biosintese; ~ **ta,** biota, plante en diere van 'n streek (gebied); ~ **tic,** bioties, lewens=; ~ **tics, biotika,** biotiek, lewensleer; ~ **tin,** biotien, biotine; ~ **tite,** biotiet; ~ **tope,** bio= toop; ~ **type,** biotipe.
bip'arous, tweelinggewend.
bipart'isan policy, tweepartybeleid.
bipart'ite, tweedelig; ~ **treaty,** tweesydige verdrag.
bip'ed, tweevoetige dier; ~ **'al,** tweevoetig.
bipinn'ate, dubbelgeveer.
bi'plane, tweedekker, dubbeldekker.
bi'pod, stander.
bipol'ar, bipolêr, tweepolig, dubbelpolig.
bipyr'amid, bipiramide; ~ **al,** bipiramidaal, bipira= midies.
biquadrate, vierdemag.
biquadrat'ic, vierdemags=, bikwadraat.
birch, (-es), (n) berk(eboom); lat; (v) slaan, tugtig, klop; ~**-rod,** lat; ~**-tree,** berk(eboom).
bird, voël; nooi; *an old* ~ *is not caught with CHAFF,* 'n ou voël laat hom nie met kaf vang nie; *the EARLY* ~ *catches the worm,* die môrestond het goud in die mond; ~*s of a FEATHER,* voëls van eenderse vere; ~*s of a FEATHER flock together,* soort soek soort; *FINE feathers make fine* ~*s,* die klere maak die man; *the* ~ *is FLOWN,* die skelm is skoonveld; die dader is dood; *be GIVEN the* ~, uitgejou, uitgelag, uitgefluit word; *a* ~ *in the HAND is worth two in the bush,* een voël in die hand is beter as tien in die lug; ~ *of JOVE,* adelaar, arend; ~ *of JUNO,* pou; *a LITTLE* ~ *has told me,* ek het 'n voëltjie hoor fluit; ~ *of MINERVA,* uil; *an OLD* ~, 'n wakker persoon; ~ *of PARADISE,* paradysvoël; ~ *of PASSAGE,* trekvoël; ~ *of PREY,* roofvoël; *PROTECTION of* ~*s,* voël= beskerming; *a RUM* ~, 'n eienaardige vent; *SPE= CIES of* ~, voëlsoort; *kill two* ~*s with one STONE,* twee vlieë met een klap slaan; ~**-bath,** voëlbak; ~**-cage,** voëlkooi, voëlkou, voëlhok; ~**-caging,** noodstuk (spoorweg); ~**-catcher,** voël= vanger; ~**-fancier,** voëlliefhebber; voëlboer; voël= handelaar; ~ **guano,** voëlmis.
bird'ie, voëltjie (gholf); klein voëltjie.
bird: ~**-fancier,** voëlliefhebber; voëlboer; ~**-life,** voëlewe; ~**-hospital,** voëlhospitaal; ~ **like,** voëlag= tig; ~**-lime,** voëllym, voëlent; ~**-sanctuary,** voël= park, voëlhawe; ~*'s-brandy, Lantana salviaefolio Jacq.;* ~**-scarer,** voëljaer; ~ **seed,** kanariesaad; voëlsaad.
bird's: ~ egg, voëleier; ~ **eye, veronica, growwe ta=** bak; ~**-eye view,** voëlvlug, voëlperspektief.
bird: ~**-shot,** donshael; ~ **snake,** stokslang, voëlslang (in bome).
bird's: ~ **nest,** voëlnes(sie); ~**-nesting,** die uithaal van voëlneste.
bird'-song, bird's song, voëlgesang.
bird'-trap, voëlwip.
bird'-watch, voëlwag; ~ **er,** voëlwaarnemer; ~ **ing,** voëlbespieding, voëlwaarneming.
bird'-weed, akkerwinde.
birefrin'gence, dubbelbreking.
birefrin'gent, dubbelbrekend.

bi'reme, tweedekker, bireem.
birett'a, baret.
birth, geboorte; oorsaak, ontstaan, voortbrengsel; stand, afkoms; *BY* ~, van geboorte; van huis uit; *GIVE* ~ *to,* die lewe skenk aan, baar; *a MAN of* ~, 'n man van goeie afkoms; *NEW* ~, wedergeboorte; *STILL* ~, dooie geboorte; *STRANGLE at* ~, in die geboorte smoor (fig.); ~ **certificate,** geboortesertifikaat, geboortebewys; ~**-control,** geboortebeperking, gesinsbeperking.
birth'day, geboortedag, verjaar(s)dag; *celebrate one's* ~, verjaar; ~ **book,** verjaar(s)dagalbum; ~ **cake,** verjaar(s)dagkoek; ~ **dinner,** verjaar(s)dagmaal; ~ **honours,** onderskeiding met die koning(in) se verjaar(s)dag; ~ **party,** (..ties), verjaar(s)dagparty; ~ **present,** verjaar(s)daggeskenk, verjaar(s)dagpresent; ~ **suit,** adamspak; *wearing one's* ~ *suit,* in adamsklere, in adamspak, kaal.
birth: ~**-mark,** moedervlek; ~**-pain,** geboortepyn; ~**-pangs,** barensweë; ~**-place,** geboorteplek; ~**-rate,** geboortesyfer; ~**-register,** geboorteregister; ~**-registration,** geboorteregistrasie; ~ **right,** eersgeboortereg; erfenis; *DEPRIVE someone of his* ~ *right,* iem. sy eersgeboortereg ontneem; *SELL one's* ~ *right for a mess of pottage,* sy eersgeboortereg vir 'n pot lensiesop verkoop; ~**-roll,** geboorteregister; ~**-sin,** erfsonde.
bis, twee maal.
Bis'cay, Biskaje.
bis'cuit, droë koekie; beskuitkleur; ongeglasuurde erdewerk; ~**-barrel,** beskuithouer; ~**-box, (-es),** beskuittrommel; ~ **colour,** beskuitkleur; ~**-throw,** hanetreetjie; ~**-tin,** beskuitblik, koekblik, trommel(tjie).
bisect', in twee deel, halveer, middeldeur sny; splits; ~ **ion,** deling in twee, halvering; ~ **or,** deellyn, halveerlyn, bisektor; ~ **rix,** bisektriks (myn).
bisex'ual, tweeslagtig, hermafrodities, biseksueel.
bish'op, biskop; raadsheer, loper (skaak); biskopwyn; ~**-bird,** wewervoël, flap, vink; ~ **ric,** bisdom.
bisk, kragsop, roomsop; neuteroomys.
bis'ley, (-s), skietoefening; skietwedstryd, prysskiet.
bismil'lah, (Ar.), bismillah.
bis'muth, bismut; ~ **ite,** bismutiet; ~ **ochre,** bismutoker; ~ **oxide,** bismutas.
bis'on, bison, Amerikaanse buffel.
bisque¹, (n) ongeglasuurde erdewerk, beskuitporselein.
bisque², (n) skelvissop; *kyk* **bisk.**
bisque³, (sports), bisk, bisque.
bissex'tile, (n) skrikkeljaar; (a) skrikkeljaar=.
bista'ble, bistabiel.
bis'toury, (..ries), opereermes, bistouri.
bis'tre, roetbruin, bister.
bi'stro, kroegie, restourantjie; straatkafee, sypadkafee.
bi'sulc, tweehoewige dier; ~ **ate,** tweehoewig.
bisul'phate, bisulfaat.
bisul'phite, bisulfiet.
bit¹, (n) stang; trens; (v) **(-ted),** 'n toom aansit; beteuel; skaafbeitel; sleutelbaard; gebit; booryster (masj.); skroefdraad; knyper (van 'n tang); kalibreerboor (geweer); snede (beitel); *TAKE the* ~ *between the teeth,* die stang vasbyt; hom nie meer laat regeer nie.
bit², (n) bietjie; stukkie, happie; entjie (tou); sier, snars, brokkie; ~ *BY* ~, stappie vir stappie, stadig, bietjie-bietjie, stuksgewys(e); *DO one's* ~, sy deeltjie doen; *EVERY* ~ *as good,* net so goed; *a* ~ *of a FOOL,* nogal dwaas (onverstandig); *I shall give him a* ~ *of my MIND,* ek sal hom wys waar Kaïn Abel vermoor het, ek sal hom goed die waarheid vertel; *a* ~ *of NEWS,* 'n nuusbrokkie; *NOT a* ~, glad nie, heeltemal nie; ~*s and PIECES,* stukkies en brokkies; *a WEE* ~, 'n mondjievol, 'n klein bietjie.
bit: ~ **auger,** awegaar(boor); ~ **brace,** (boor)omslag.
bitch, (-es), teef, wyfie; feeks, slet; ~**y,** honds.
bite, (n) byt; beet, hap; stukkie ete; skerpte; invreting; greep; *that's a LARGE* ~ *out of the cherry,* dis 'n hele sluk op die bottel; *a* ~ *of SOMETHING,* iets om te eet; (v) **(bit, bitten),** byt, hap; wond, kwes,

invreet; brand, steek; bedrieg; ~ *AT,* hap na; *don't* ~ *off more than you can CHEW,* moenie verder spring as wat jou stok lank is nie; ~ *the DUST,* in die stof byt; grond eet (vreet); baken steek; die grond ploeg; sandruiter word; ~ *the HAND that fed one,* iem. met stank vir dank beloon; ~ *IN(TO),* inbyt; ~ *one's LIPS,* op jou lip byt; ~ *someone's NOSE off,* iem. se kop afbyt; ~ *OFF,* afbyt; *PUT the* ~ *on,* afpers; geld leen (van iem.); *mind, it will* ~ *YOU!,* as dit 'n slang was, het dit jou al lankal gebyt.
bit'er, byter; bedriër; *the* ~ *bit,* die bedrieër bedroë.
bit'ing, bytend, bits, snerpend, skerp; invretend; *a* ~ *wind,* 'n snerpende wind.
bitt'en, gebyt; verlief, been-af; gefop; aangesteek; *once* ~, *twice SHY,* 'n esel stamp (stoot) hom nie twee maal aan dieselfde steen nie; *SOMETHING seems to have* ~ *him,* dit lyk of daar 'n vlieg oor sy neus geloop het; *WHAT has* ~ *you?,* waarom is jy op jou perdjie? wat het jou gebyt?
bitt'er, (n) bitterbier; bitter; *the* ~ *with the sweet,* die soet met die suur, in lief en leed; (a) bitter; skerp; griewend; warm (trane); skamper, verbitterd; *to the* ~ *end,* tot die bitter einde; tot die uiterste; ~ **apple,** bitterappel, kolokwint; ~ **bush,** bitterbossie; kaalsiektebossie *(Chrysocoma);* ~**-earth,** magnesia; ~ **ish,** bitteragtig; ~**ly,** bitter, griewend.
bitt'ern, roerdomp; moederloog.
bitt'erness, bitterheid, wrangheid; skamperheid, verbittering.
bitt'ers, maagbitter, bittertjie.
bitt'er-sweet, (n) nagskade; (a) bitter-soet.
bitt'er water, bitterwater (geol.).
bitt'erwort, bitterwortel.
bitts, kabelpale (op skip).
bit'ty, stuk-stuk.
bit'umen, berghars, aarpik, asfalt, bitumen, aardhars, Jodelym.
bitum'inize, asfalteer, bitumineer.
bitum'inous, asfalt=, harsagtig, harpuisagtig, bitumineus.
bi'valve, (n) skulpdier; oester; (a) tweekleppig, tweeskalig.
biv'ouac, (n) kamp, bivak; (v) **(-ked),** bivakkeer, kampeer.
bi'weekly, tweeweekliks, veertiendaags; twee maal weekliks, halfweekliks.
biz, (sl.), besigheid, sake.
bizarre', grillig, oordrewe, fantasties, ongewoon, vreemd, bisar; ~ **rie,** bisarheid.
blab, (n) verklikker, verklapper; kletser; (v) **(-bed),** uitflap, verklap, verklik; ~ **ber,** babbelaar, verklapper.
Black, (n) Swarte, Swartmens, Swartman; (pl) Swartes, Swartmense.
black¹, (n) swart; swartsel; swart vlek; brandkoring; roet; swart klere, rouklere; (v) swart smeer; waks (skoen), swart maak; ~ *out,* onleesbaar maak; verdonker; uitvee; (a) swart, donker, somber; duister; ~ *AMBER,* git; *the* ~ *ART,* toordery, die swart(e) kuns; *beat* ~ *and BLUE,* bont en blou slaan; pimpel en pers slaan; *the* ~ *CAP,* die swart mus; *suit of* ~ *CLOTH,* swartlakense pak; *B~ CONSCIOUSNESS,* Swart Bewustheid; *B~ DEATH,* pes; ~ *DESPAIR,* diepe bedroefdheid; ~*-and-white DRAWING,* pentekening; *a* ~ *EYE,* 'n blouoog; ~ *in the FACE,* blou in die gesig; ~ *JAPAN,* swart muurlak; *give someone a* ~ *LOOK,* iem. skeef aankyk; ~ *MARK,* ordemerk; ~ *SHEEP,* swart skaap; skande; ~ *as SOOT, as* ~ *as the ace of SPADES,* so swart soos die nag; ~ *STINKWOOD,* swart stinkhout; ~ *and TAN,* swart en bruingeel; *in* ~ *and WHITE,* swart op wit; ~ **agama,** swart koggelmander; ~ **albatross,** swart albatros, stinkpot; ~ **amoor,** Neger, Swarte; *try to wash a* ~ *white,* monnikewerk doen; dit vat van die Danaïde vul; ~ **and white,** swart en wit; ~ **ant,** swartmier; ~ **art,** swart kuns, toorkuns; ~ **ash,** swart as; ~ **avised,** met 'n donker gelaatskleur; ~**-backed jackal,** rooijakkals; ~**-backed seagull,** swartrugmeeu; ~ **ball,** (n), teenstem, uitsluiting, veto; ~ **ball** (v), uitstem, uitsluit, afstem, veto; ~

bark, swartbas(boom); ~ **bass,** swartbaars; ~ **bear,** swartbeer, baribal; *Asiatic* ~, Asiatiese swartbeer, kragbeer; ~**-bearded protea,** swartbaardprotea; ~**-beetle,** kakkerlak; ~ **berry,** braambessie, braambos; ~ **bird,** swartvoël, lyster; slaaf; *European* ~ *bird,* merel; ~ **birding,** slawedrywing, slawejag; ~ **board,** swartboard, skryfbord, skoolbord; ~ **board duster,** borduitveër, bordwisser; ~ **body,** swartliggaam; ~ **bolt,** swartbout; ~ **book,** swart boek(ie); strafregister; *in a person's ~ book(s),* in onguns wees by 'n persoon; ~ **border,** swart rand, rou rand; ~ **box,** vlugopnemer, vluggeheue; vlugopname; ~ **boy,** Australiese boomsoort; ~ **bread,** rogbrood, swartbrood; pumpernickel; ~**-browed albatross,** malmok(albatros); ~**-brown,** swartbruin, ~ **buck,** swartbok; ~ **bulb thermometre,** stralingstermometer; ~ **cap,** swart mus, swart pet; swartkopbosvoël, swartkoppie, kuifkop(voël); ~**-cap pudding,** korintepoeding; ~ **coat worker,** klerk, kantoorwerker; ~ **cobra,** swartkobra, swartslang; ~ **cock,** Europese korhaan; ~ **coffee,** swart koffie; ~ **copper,** swartkoper; ~ **crow,** swartkraai; ~ **currant,** swart(aal)bessie; ~ **damp,** koolsuurgas; ~ **diamond,** swartdiamant; ~ **disease,** gasedeem; ~ **dog,** terneergedruktheid; ~ **draught,** purgeermiddel; swart sennamengsel; ~ **eagle,** witkruisarend; ~ **earth,** swartgrond, turf, tjernosem; ~**-edged,** swartgerand; (v) swart maak; swartsmeer; poleer; ~ *someone's name,* iem. swartsmeer, slegmaak; ~ **eye,** blou oog (a.g.v. 'n stamp, besering), swart oog; *give a person a* ~, iem blouoog slaan; ~**-eyed,** swartoog=, met swart oë; ~**-eyed bean,** swartbekboontjie; ~**-eyed pea,** swartoogertjie; ~**-eyed Susan,** black-eyed Susan (soort ertjie); thunbergia; rudbeckia; ~ **face,** swart gesig, swartgesig(skaap); swart grimering; ~ **fellow,** Australiese aborigine; ~ **fever,** swartkoors; ~ **fibre,** kleurvesel (wol); ~ **fin needlefish,** swartvinnaaldvis; ~ **fin shark,** swartvinhaai; ~ **fish,** swart vis; salmvissie; ~ **flag,** swart vlag; seerowersvlag; ~ **fly,** trips, swartvlieg; ~**-footed cat,** swartpoot(wilde)kat; ~**-fronted bulbul,** swartkopgeelgat; ~ **frost,** swartryp, skroeiryp; ~ **gam,** ~ **grouse,** Europese korhaan; ~ **guard,** (n) deugniet, skurk, smeerlap, skobbejak, derduiwel; (v) uitskel, swartsmeer; ~ **guardism,** gemeenheid, skurkagtigheid; ~ **guardly,** laag, gemeen; ~**-haried,** met swart hare; swarthaar=; ~ **hawk,** kuifkopvalk; ~ **head,** swartkopvoël; swartkoppie, puisie, aknee; mee-eter; ~ **head canary,** swartkop(kanarie), swartkoppie; ~**-headed gull,** swartkopmeeu; ~**-headed heron,** swartkopreier; ~**-headed sheep,** swartkopskaap; ~ **headed Persian sheep,** swartkop-Persie; ~**-hearted,** kwaadgesind, wreed; verdorwe; ~ **hole,** donker plek (kamer, ens.); swartgat, swartkuil (sterrek.); ~ **ice,** dun ys; ~**ing,** swartsel, swart politoer; ~ **ingratitude,** growwe ondankbaarheid, ~ **iron,** swartyster; ~**-ish,** swarterig, swartagtig; ~ **ivory,** swart slawe; ~ **jack,** wynsak; leerknuppel; seerowersvlag; kaartspel; ~ **jacks,** knapsekêrels, wewenaars; ~ **japan,** muurlak; ~ **kite,** swartwou; ~ **lead,** (n) grafiet, (v) poleer (met grafiet); ~ **leg,** (n) onderkruiper; swendelaar; sponssiekte (beeste); vrotpootjie (aartappels); (v) onderkruip; swendel; ~**-legging,** onderkruiping; swendelary; ~**-legine,** sponssiekteentstof; ~ **leopard,** swartluiperd, panter; ~ **letter,** Gotiese letter; swart (gedrukte) letter; ~**-letter day,** belangrike dag; ongeluksdag; ~ **light,** swartbestraling, ultraviolet bestraling, infrarooi bestraling; ~ **list,** (n) swartlys; (v) op die swartlys plaas; verdink; ~ **magic,** swart kuns, nigromansie, toorkuns; ~ **mail,** (n) afpersing; (v) afpers; ~ **er,** afperser; ~ **man,** Swartman; ~ **mark,** swart merk, kruisie (van diskrediet, by iem. se naam); ~ **market,** swartmark, swarthandel, sluikhandel, smokkelhandel; ~ **marketeer,** sluikhandelaar, smokkelhandelaar, smokkelaar; ~ **marketing,** sluithandelary, smokkelhandelary, smokkeling; ~ **mongoose,** swart muishond; ~ **mould,** swartskimmel; ~ **mustard,** swart mosterd; ~ **ness,** swartheid; donkerte, nag, duisternis; ~ **nightshade,** galbessie; nastergal.

Black²: ~ **Africa,** Swart Afrika, Afrika suid van die Sahara; ~ **chief(tain),** Swart stamhoof (opperhoof); ~ **Circuit,** (die) Swart Ommegang; ~ **consciousness,** Swartbewustheid, swartbewussyn; ~ **Death,** (die) Swart Dood; ~ **foot (Indian),** Blackfoot(indiaan); ~ **forest,** Swartwoud; ~ **friar,** Dominikaner(monnik), Dominikaan; ~ **Hand,** (die) Swart Hand; ~ **Hills,** Black Hills; ~ **labour,** Swart arbeid; ~ **labour organization,** Swart arbeidsorganisasie; ~ **man,** Swartman; ~ **Maria,** (polisie) vangwa, rookgranaat; ~ **Monk,** Dominikaner(monnik), Dominikaan; ~ **people,** Swartmense, Swartes; ~ **Pete,** Swart Piet (kaartspel); ~ **Poll,** Swartpoenskop; ~ **Pope,** Swart Pous, hoof van die Jesuïete; ~ **Power,** Swartmag; ~ **Rod,** Swart Roede; draer van die Swart Roede; ampswag; ~**s,** Swartes, Swartmense; ~ **Sash,** Black Sash; ~ **Sea,** Swart See; ~ **shirt,** Swarthemp; ~ **states,** Swartstate; ~ **township,** Swart woonbuurt; ~ **trade union,** Swart vakbond; ~ **Watch,** Black Watch; ~ **woman,** Swartvrou; ~ **wood,** Blackwood (brugspel).

black'-out, verdonkering, verduistering; (brein)floute, floute-aanval; ~ *MATERIAL,* verdonkeringstof; *NEWS* ~, nuusverbod; ~ *REGULATIONS,* verduisteringsvoorskrifte; *SUFFER a* ~, 'n floute ondergaan (kry); **black out,** (v) verdonker; uitwis.

black: ~ **pepper,** swartpeper; ~ **powder,** swart kruit; ~ **pudding,** bloedwors; ~ **quarter,** sponssiekte; ~ **rat,** swartrot (soort rot); swart rot; ~ **rhinoceros,** swartrenoster; ~ **rot,** swartvrot; ~ **rust,** stamroes (graan); swartroes (druiwe); ~ **salsify,** skorsenier(wortel); ~ **sand,** swartsand; ~ **sheep,** swart skaap; ~**-shoulder kite,** blouvalk; ~ **smith,** smid, grofsmid; ~ **smith's coal,** smeekool; ~ **snake,** swartslang; ~ **spot,** swart muf; swartvlek(siekte); ~ **squall,** storm(wind); ~ **stork,** swart sprinkaanvoël; ~ **swan,** swart swaan; ~ **tail,** kolster *(Diplodus capensis);* ~ **tea,** swart tee; ~ **tea bush,** swarttee(bos); ~ **thorn,** sleedoring; ~**-throated canary,** bergkanarie; ~ **tie,** aandpak; ~**-tipped wool,** teertipwol; ~ **tit,** swartmees; ~ **top,** teerpad; ~ **tracker,** soeker; ~ **treason,** snode verraad; ~ **type,** vet (letter); ~ **udder,** blou-uier; ~ **varnish,** teervernis; ~ **vulture,** swartaasvoël; ~**-water (fever),** swartwater(koors); ~ **wattle,** basboom, wattelboom *(Acacia mollissima);* ~ **widow (spider),** knopiespinnekop; ~ **wildebeest,** swartwildebees; ~**-winged bishop (bird),** vuurkopprooivink; ~**-winged stilt,** rooipoot-elsie; ~ **wood,** swarthout; ~ **wool,** swart wol.

bladd'er, blaas; binnesak, binnebal (van 'n voetbal), windsak; ~**-disease,** blaaskwaal, ~**-nosed seal,** klapmusrob; ~**-worm,** blaaswurm.

blade, skeerlemmetjie, lem (van 'n mes); messie; halm (gras); blaadjie; grasspriet; blaar; blad van skroef; graaf, ens.; degen; *GAY* ~, vrolike vent, *MAIN* ~, hoofblad; ~**-bone,** skouerblad; ~ **d,** met 'n lem; lemvormig; ~**-file,** sleutelvyl; ~**-holder,** saagbladhouer; ~ **terracer,** skraperlem.

blah(-blah), kaf, bla-bla.
blain, blaar, blaas; sweer.
blam'able, berispelik, laakbaar.
blame, (n) blaam, skuld; berisping; *BEAR the* ~, die skuld dra; *one SHIFTS the* ~ *onto the other,* die een skuil agter die ander; die een gee die ander die skuld; (v) blameer; afkeur; beskuldig, laak, wyt; berispe; ~**ful,** laakbaar; afkeurend; ~ **less,** onberispelik; skuldeloos, onskuldig; ~**worthy,** laakbaar, berispelik, afkeurenswaardig; ~**worthiness,** laakbaarheid, berispelikheid.

blam'ing, laking.
blanch, bleik, wit maak, ontkleur; skil; witkook, blansjeer; pel (neute); ~ **over,** verbloem, vergelik.
blancmange', blancmange, blamaans.
blan'co, poeiersteen, blanko.
bland, sag, vriendelik, minsaam; vleiend; ironies; neutraal (med.); ~ **diet,** neutrale diet.
blan'dish, vlei, pamper, skouerblad; ~ **er,** vleier; ~ **ment,** vleiery, streling; verleidelikheid.
bland'ness, minsaamheid; beleefdheid.
blank, (n) oop plek; leemte; teleurstelling; ru-stuk; nul; muntplaatjie; *DRAW a* ~, 'n nul trek; *FIRE*

~s *at*, met loskruit skiet; *his MIND was a* ~, sy geheue was skoon weg; hy kon nie dink nie; (v) toemaak; vloek; ~ *off*, afdig; (a) blank, bleek; onbeskrewe, oningevul (vorm); blanko (tjek); dof (aar); leeg; rymloos (vers); yl; onbetekenend, onbelangrik; sonder uitdrukking; wesenloos, verbluf, sprakeloos, verbyster(d); *look* ~, verbouereerd (verbluf) lyk; ~ **cartridge,** loskruitpatroon; ~ **cheque,** blanko tjek; ~ **ear,** dowwe aar.

blank'et, (n) kombers; deken; *CRAWL under the* ~ *s*, in die vere kruip; onder die wol kruip; *a WET* ~, 'n droogstoppel; 'n spelbederwer; *born on the WRONG side of the* ~, oneg, buite-egtelik; (v) bedek, toemaak; stil hou; die loef afsteek (skip); beesvel gooi; (a) omvattend, algemeen, allesinsluitend; ~ *action*, oorkoepelende optrede, omvattende optrede; ~ **cloth,** kombersstof; ~ **ing,** kombersgoed, kombersstof, dekenstof; ~ **stitch,** kombersteek; ~-**vote,** kombersstem.

blank: ~ **flange,** blinde flens; ~ **key,** ru-sleutel.
blank'ly, wesenloos, beteuterd; botweg; *refuse* ~, botweg weier.
blank'ness, wesenloosheid.
blank: ~ **round,** loskruitskoot; ~ **space,** leë ruimte; ~ **verse,** rymlose poësie; ~ **wall,** blinde muur.
blare, (n) gebrul; lawaai, gesketter; ~ *of trumpets*, trompetgeskal; (v) bulk, brul (dier); skal, sketter.
blarn'ey, (n) mooipraatjies, vleitaal, flikflooiery; (v) vlei, flikflooi.
blasé', blasé, sat, verstomp, geblaseer(d).
blaspheme', laster; (ver)vloek; spot (met godsdiens); ~**r,** lasteraar, vloeker.
blas'phemous, godslasterlik, hemeltergend.
blas'phemy (..mies), godslastering, heiligskennis, lastertaal; *gross* ~, ergerlike godslastering.
blast, (n) wind, rukwind; geskal; lugtrilling, windstroom; plaag, verderf; lading; ontploffing; skoot; brand (koring); *let someone have it FULL* ~, iem. die volle lading gee; *GIVE someone a* ~, iem. skrobbeer; ~ *of TRUMPETS,* basuingeskal; (v) verseng, verdor; laat ontplof, (met) dinamiet skiet; uitbars, vernietig, verydel; vervloek; ~ *someone's CREDIT,* iem. se krediet wegneem; ~ *a TUNNEL through the mountain,* 'n tonnel deur die berg met dinamiet skiet; ~**ed,** vervloek, vervlaks; *the* ~*ed fellow!,* so 'n blikskater!; ~ **effect,** lugslag(werking); ~**er,** dinamietskieter; ~-**furnace,** smeltoond, hoogoond; ~ **hole,** boorgat (vir plofstof), skietgat.
blast'ing, wegskiet, dinamietskietery, springwerk; ~-**agent,** springmiddel, springstof, plofstof, skietmiddel; ~-**cap,** slagdoppie; ~-**cartridge,** springpatroon; ~-**certificate,** skietsertifikaat; ~-**charge,** skietlading; ~-**compound,** mynplofstof; ~ **effect,** lugslag; ~-**furnace,** smeltoond, hoogoond; ~-**gelatine,** skietgelatien, ontploffingsgelatien; ~-**material,** ontploffingsmiddel; ~ **operations,** skietwerk; ~ **powder,** mynkruit, skietkruit.
blastocar'pous, blastokarp(ies).
blast'ocyst, kiemblaas, blastosis.
blas'toderm, kiemskyf, blastoderm; ~-'**ic,** blastodermies.
blast off, (v) lanseer, opstyg; (n) lansering, opstyging.
blastogen'esis, blastogenese.
blast: ~-**pipe,** vlampyp; ~ **pressure,** winddruk; ~ **ula,** blastule, selbal; ~-**valve,** lugklep.
blat'ancy, skreeuerigheid.
blat'ant, skreeuend; skreiend, lawaaierig, luidrugtig; volslae; ~ *FOOL,* afgedankste gek; ~ *NONSENSE,* klinkklare onsin.
blath'er = **blether.**
bla'therskate = **bletherskate.**
blaze¹, (n) vlam, gloed (van kleure); volle lig; uitbarsting; prag; ~ *of COLOUR,* kleureprag; *GO to* ~ *s,* loop na die hoenders (duiwel); *IN a* ~, in ligtelaaie; *LIKE* ~ *s*, soos blits (die bliksem); ~ *of PASSION,* hartstogtelike vlaag; *WHAT the* ~*s!,* wat die drommel!; (v) vlam, oplaai, brand, skitter, uitbars; ~ *up,* opvlam, in woede uitbars.
blaze², (n) bles (dier); (v) bles, 'n wit streep maak; blek(boom); ~ *a TRAIL,* die weg baan; ~ *a TREE,* 'n boom merk (blek).

blaze³, (v) skiet, losbrand; ~ *away,* losbrand, lostrek.
blaze⁴, (v) rondvertel, uitbasuin; ~ *ABROAD,* rondbasuin; ~ *FORTH,* uitbasuin.
blaz'er, kleurbaadjie, klubbaadjie, skoolbaadjie; yslike leuen.
blaz'ing, gloeiend, brandend, vlammend.
blaz'on, (n) blasoen, wapenskild; praal, lofverkondiging; wapenbeskrywing; (v) 'n wapenskild skilder; afmaal; opsier; uitbasuin, openbaar maak; versier, beskilder; ~ *something forth*, iets uitbasuin; hoog opgee van iets; ~**er,** heraldikus; ~**ry,** heraldiek, wapenkunde; praal, prag.
bleach,' (n) bleikmiddel; (v) bleik, uitbleik, op die bleik lê, blansjeer; ~-**field,** bleikery, bleikveld.
bleach'ing, bleikend; ~-**agent,** bleikmiddel; ~ **ground,** bleikveld; ~-**liquid,** bleikwater; ~-**paste,** bleikpap; ~-**powder,** bleikpoeier.
bleak¹, (n) alwertjie, bliek (vis).
bleak², (a) koud, skraal, oop, onbeskut; aaklig, naar; troosteloos; guur; *a* ~ *OUTLOOK,* 'n treurige vooruitsig; ~ *WEATHER,* (on)gure weer, slegte weer; *a* ~ *WIND,* 'n skraal windjie; ~**ness,** guurheid; onherbergsaamheid.
blear, (v) dof maak, verduister; laat traan; verblind; (a) tranend; dof; duister; wasig; ~-**eyed,** leepoog-, met leepogies, leepogig, druipogig; ~**y,** dof; tranerig.
bleat, (n) geblêr; getjank; (v) blêr; tjank; ~**ing,** geblêr.
bleb, blasie, blaar; spikkel.
bleed, (**bled**), bloedlaat; aarlaat; bloei, bloed stort; lug laat; traan, huil (wingerdstok); uitgooi (sakkie); te duur laat betaal, te veel vra; ~ *to DEATH,* doodbloei; ~ *someone DRY,* iem. se bloed tap; iem. uitsuig; ~**er,** bloeier; luglater; ~ **hole,** luglaatgat; ~**ing,** (n) bloedlating; bloei (verf); luglating; (a) bloeiend; ~**ing-heart,** muurblom *(Cheirinia cheiri);* gebrokehartjies *(Dicentra spectabilis);* dolksteekduif.
bleep, (-**ed**), biep, bliep; ~**er,** blieper, bieper, roeper, roepradio.
blem'ish, (n) vlek, smet, klad; gebrek; (v) misvorm, skend; vlek.
blench, wyk, terugdeins, die oë sluit vir; ontwyk, vermy.
blend, (n) mengsel; vermenging; (v) meng, vermeng; saamvloei; versmelt, ineensmelt, in mekaar oorgaan (kleure).
blende, blende (erts).
blend: ~**er,** menger, bereider; ~**ing,** menging, vermenging; ineenvloeiing, samesmelting.
blenn'y, (**blennies**), slymvis.
blephari'tis, blefaritis, ooglidontsteking.
bles'bok, .. **buck,** blesbok.
bless, (**-ed** or **blest**), seën, loof, wy; gelukkig maak; *don't* ~ *the DAY before it is over,* moenie die dag voor die aand prys nie; ~ *ME! liewe tyd; not a PENNY to* ~ *oneself with,* geen bloue duit besit nie.
bless'ed, goddelik, geseën(d), gelukkig, geluksalig, gebenedy; vervloekte, vervlakste; saliger; *the whole* ~ *DAY,* die hele goddelike dag; *a* ~ *FOOL,* 'n verbrande gek; *of* ~ *MEMORY,* van saliger (na)gedagtenis; *it is MORE* ~ *to give than to receive,* dis saliger om te gee as om te ontvang; *THE* ~ , die gesaligdes; ~ *THISTLE,* geseënde distel *(Carbenia benedictus);* ~**ness,** saligheid; geluksaligheid; *single* ~ *ness,* ongehude staat.
bless'ing, seën(bede), seënwens; seëning; tafelgebed; *ASK a* ~, bid, 'n seën vra; *a* ~ *in DISGUISE,* 'n bedekte seën; *GIVE one's* ~ *to something,* jou seën aan iets gee.
blest = **blessed.**
bleth'er, geklets, kafpraatjies.
bletherskate, kletser, kafprater, windsak.
blew, *kyk* **blow,** (v).
blight, (n) heuningdou, meeldou, roes; skimmel (by ertappels, tamaties); brand (by koring); plantluis; plaag, pes, verwoesting; (v) bederwe; vernietig; laat verdor, verwoes; ~**er,** rakker, snuiter; skobbejak, asgat, blikslaer, bog.
Blight'y, (sl.), vaderland; **b**~, vleiswond.
blim'ey, (vulgar) vervlaks!

blimp, waarnemingslugskip, ballonskip.

blind, (n) blinding, rolgordyn, hortjie; skerm; blind=doek; oogklap; voorwendsel, oëverblindery; *in the LAND of the ~ the one-eyed man is king*, in die land van die blindes is eenoog koning; *if the ~ LEADS the ~ both shall fall into the ditch*, as 'n blinde 'n ander blinde lei, sal altwee in die sloot val; *VENETIAN ~*, hortjiesblinding; (v) verblind, blind maak; bedrieg; (a) blind, verblind; donker; verborge; sonder blom (vrug); *as ~ as a BAT*, so blind soos 'n mol; *~ DRUNK*, stomdronk; *turn a ~ EYE to*, maak of jy dit nie sien nie; iets oogluikend toelaat; iets deur die vingers sien; *~ man's HOLIDAY*, die skemering; *there are NONE so ~ as those who will not see*, niemand is so blind as dié wat nie wil sien nie; *one's ~ SIDE*, jou onbeskermde kant; **~age,** blindering; **~ alley,** blinde steeg, omdraaipad, doodlooppaadjie; **~-alley occupation (work, job),** doodloopbaantjie; **~ angle,** blinde hoek; **~ approach,** blinde nadering; **~ bombing,** blindbombwerping; **~ coal,** blinkkool, antrasiet; **~ corner,** blinde hoek; **~ date,** molafspraak; **~ door,** blinde deur; **~ed,** verblind; blind gemaak; **~er,** oogklap; sinjaalskyf; blinde klip; blinde golf; **~-fly, (~-flies),** blindevlieg; **~-flying,** blindvlieg; **~ fold,** (v) blinddoek, die oë toebind; (a) geblinddoek; blindelings, roekeloos; **~ god,** blinde god, Eros, Kupido; **~ gut,** endelderm, sakderm; **~ hinge,** luikskarnier; **~ hookey,** blindekaart(spel); **~ing,** verblindend; **~-landing,** blindlanding; **~ letter,** onbestelbare brief; **~ lode,** verborge ertsspleet; **~ly,** blindweg, blindelings, roekeloos; **~ man's buff,** blindemannetjie, blindemol; **~ness,** blindheid; **~ nut,** blinde moer; **~ printing,** blinddruk; **~ purchase,** ongesiene koop; **~ quarter,** opgedroogde uierkwart; **~ rise,** blinde bult (opdraand); **~ rock,** blinde (verborge) klip; **~-school,** blinde-instituut; **~ shaft,** doodloopskag; **~ shell,** onontplofte bom; **~ side,** swak kant, skeelkant; steelkant (rugby); **~ siding,** uitwykspoor; **~ snake,** blindeslang; **~ spot,** blindvlek, geelvlek; **~ staggers,** malkopsiekte; **~-stamping, ~-tooling,** blinde afwerking; **~ trial,** blinde toets; **~ window,** blinde venster; **~-worm,** blindewurm.

blink, (n) flikkering, flits, skynsel, glans; oogwenk, lonk; (v) knipoog; gluur; skemer; flits; ontwyk (oorweging); *~ one's eyes*, die oë knip.

blink'er, kniplig, kyker; (pl) oogklappe; *wear ~s*, 'n pampoenbril dra; oogklappe aanhê.

blip, radarbeeld.

bliss, saligheid, geluk, heil; **~ful,** salig, gelukkig; *seem fully unaware (ignorant)*, v.d. duiwel geen kwaad weet nie; jou doodluiters hou; v.d. hele moord niks weet nie; **~fulness,** saligheid, geluksaligheid.

blis'ter, (n) blaar, bobbel, blaas; trekpleister; bleek kol (koelkamervleis), blasieskoper (min.); (v) blaar trek, bobbel; skilfer (rots); blase vorm (op tertdeeg); trekpleiser opsit; afblaar (verf); afdop (sement), verveel; tyd verkwis; **~-beetle,** spaansvlieg; **~ copper,** ru-koper; **~ed,** beblaar(d); **~ gas,** blaargas; **~ing,** (n) blaasvorming (verf); (a) blaartrekkend; **~ plaster,** trekpleister; **~ steel,** sementstaal.

blithe, bly, vrolik, blymoedig, opgeruimd, **~ness,** blyheid, opgeruimdheid.

blith'ering, onsinnig spraaksaam; veragtelik; *~ idiot*, volslae idioot, uilskuiken, stomme dwaas.

blithe'some, lustig, opgeruimd.

blitz, blitsaanval; **~ krieg,** blitsoorlog.

blizz'ard, sneeustorm, sneeujag.

bloat, (n) trommelsug, buikswelling, opblaas(siekte); (v) opswel; laat opswel; opblaas; sout en rook (haring); **~ed,** opgeblaas; gerook (vis); **~er,** gerookte haring, bokkem; **~ing,** geilsiekte.

blob, druppel; klont; blaas; nul (krieket); **~ by,** klonterig.

bloc, (politieke) blok (van partye).

block, (n) blok; vleisblok; hoedvorm; hysblok; katrol; drukplaat; blok huise; massa; opblokking, hindernis; versperring; belemmering; aantekeningboek; bot persoon; belemmering; aantekeningboek; blokgat; *~ and CHAIN tackle*, kettingtakel; *a CHIP of the old ~*, 'n aardjie na sy vaartjie; *~ of FLATS*, blok woonstelle, woonstelgebou; *~ of LORRIES*, lorrietrein; *cut ~s with a RAZOR*, water in 'n mandjie dra; *STERLING ~*, sterlinggroep; *~ and TACKLE*, katrolstel, takel(stel); *~ of TICKETS*, 'n blok kaarte (v) afsluit, versper, afsper (pad); toespyker; blokkeer; belemmer; dwarsboom; vorm (hoed); obstruksie voer; blok (krieket); *~ IN*, ru skets; *~ OUT*, ru skets, ontwerp; *~ UP*, insluit, versper.

blockade', (n) insluiting, blokkade; *RAISE a ~*, 'n blokkade ophef; *RUN a ~*, deur 'n blokkade breek; (v) insluit, blokkeer; **~r,** blokkeerder; **~-runner,** blokkadebreker; **~ ship,** blokkadeskip.

block: ~ age, versperring, verstopping; **~ board,** rugplank; blokkiesbord; **~-brake,** blokrem; **~ brush,** teerkwas, koolborsel; **~-buster,** brisantbom, blokbom; asembenemende gebeurtenis; **~ calendar,** skeurkalender; **~ chain,** blokketting; **~ check,** blokruit; **~-chisel,** blokbeitel; **~-ed,** geblokkeerd; *~ed rand,* blokrand; **~ er-ring,** sperring; **~-flooring,** blokkiesvloer; **~ grant,** bloktoekenning.

block'head, domkop, stommerik, esel, domoor, aartsappelkop, swaap, uilskuiken; pampoenkop; **~ ed,** dom, onnosel.

block: ~ hole, kolfstaanplek (krieket); **~ house,** blokhuis; **~ing,** blokkering, blokkasie, versperring, afsluiting; bloklaswerk; **~ish,** ongevoelig, bot; **~ joint,** bloklas; **~-lava,** aä-lawa; **~ letter,** blokletter; **~-maker,** blokmaker, lichémaker; **~ man,** blokman; **~ mountain,** blokberg; **~ piece,** hoekklamp; **~-plane,** blokskaaf; **~ printing,** blokdruk, **~ puzzle,** raaiselblok; blokraaisel; **~-shears,** stokskêr; **~ ship,** blokskip; **~-sight,** platvisier, lêvisier; **~ signal,** bloksein; **~-signalman,** blokwagter; **~ silver,** bloksilwer; **~ system,** afsluitingstelsel, blokstelsel (spoorweë); **~-telephone,** bloktelefoon; **~-time,** afsluittyd; **~-up,** versperring; **~ vote,** blok, groepstem; **~-window,** blokvenster; **~ writing,** blokskrif.

bloke, kêrel, vent, jafel.

blond, blond, lig.

blonde, blondine, witkop; soort kant.

blood, (n) bloed; verwantskap, familie; sap; humeur; temperament; fat, snuiter; *make BAD ~*, slegte gevoelens veroorsaak; *BLUE ~*, hoë afkoms; *make one's ~ BOIL*, 'n mens se bloed laat kook; *his ~ BOILED*, hy kon slange vang; hy het hom bloedig vererg; *one's ~ BOILS*, jou bloed kook; *CLOT= TED ~*, dooi(e) bloed; *in COLD ~*, opsetlik, koelbloedig; *make someone's ~ turn COLD*, iem. se bloed in sy are laat stol; *draw FIRST ~*, die eerste voordeel behaal; die eerste hou inkry; *FRESH ~*, nuwe bloed; *FULL ~*, volbloed; *HIS ~ be on us, and our children*, laat sy bloed op ons en ons kinders kom; *LET ~*, bloedlaat; *~ ROYAL*, koninklike afkoms; *by (of) ROYAL ~*, van adellike (koninklike) bloed wees; *it RUNS in the ~*, dis in die familie; dis erflik; *SHED ~*, bloed vergiet; *try to squeeze ~ out of a STONE*, yster met jou hande probeer breek; *get ~ out of a STONE*, uit 'n klip bloed tap; *SUCK someone's ~*, iem. bloedlaat; *SWEAT ~*, bloed sweet; *TASTE ~*, bloed ruik; *THIRST for ~*, na bloed dors; *make someone's ~ TURN cold*, iem. se bloed in sy are laat stol; *his ~ was UP*, sy bloed het gekook; die hoenders in wees; *~ is thicker than WATER*, bloed kruip waar dit nie kan loop nie; *YOUNG ~*, snuiter; nuwe lewe (bloed); (v) bloedlaat; met bloed besoedel; bloed laat proe; **~ and iron (policy),** militêre mag= (sbeleid); **~ and thunder,** melodramaties, sensasioneel; **~ and thunder film (book),** skop-skiet-en-donderprent (-boek); **~-apple,** bloedappel; **~ bank,** bloedbank; **~ baptism,** bloeddoop (martelaars); **~ bath,** bloedbad; *plunge into a ~ bath,* in 'n bloedbad dompel; **~-bay,** rooi-bruin; **~ blister,** bloedblaar, bloedblaas; **~-brother,** bloedbroer; **~ cast,** bloedsilinder; **~-cattle,** stamboek; **~ cell,** bloedsel; **~ circulation,** bloedsomloop; **~ cleansing,** bloedsuiwerend; **~-clot,** bloedklont; **~-corpuscle,** bloedliggaampie; **~ count,** bloedsyfer; **~-curdling,** bloedstollend; **~ disk (disc),** bloedskyfie; **~-donor,**

bloody 740 blue

bloedskenker; ~**ed,** volbloed; opreg; ~ **feud,** bloedwraak; bloedvete; ~ **film,** bloedsmeer; ~**-flower,** bloedblom; ~**-group,** bloedgroep; ~**-guilt,** bloedskuld; ~**-guilty,** skuldig aan moord; ~**-heat,** bloedwarmte; ~**-horse,** volbloedperd; ~**hound,** speurhond; bloedhond; ~**ily,** bloedig; ~**iness,** bloederigheid; ~ **less,** sonder bloed, bloedloos; ~**-letting,** bloedlating; aarlating; ~**-lust,** bloeddorstigheid; moordgierigheid; ~**-money,** bloedgeld; soengeld; ~ **orange,** bloedlemoen; ~**-plasm,** bloedplasma; ~ **platelet,** bloedplaatjie; ~**plum,** bloedpruim; ~**-poisoning,** bloedvergifti= ging; ~ **polony,** bloedwors; ~**-pressure,** bloed= druk; ~**-pudding,** bloedwors; ~**-red,** bloedrooi; ~ **relation,** eie familie, bloedverwant; ~**-rings,** bloed= ringe; ~ **royal,** koninklike bloed; ~ **sausage,** bloedwors; ~**-serum,** bloedwei, bloedserum; ~**-shed,** bloedstorting; moord; ~**shot,** bloed-belope: rooi; ~**-smeer,** bloedsmeer(sel); ~**-spavin,** bloed= spat, aarspat; ~ **sports,** jag(sport); ~**-stain,** bloed= kol; bloedvlek; ~**-stained,** met bloed bevlek; ~**stock,** volbloedvee; ~**stone,** bloedsteen; ~**-stream** bloedstroom; ~**-sucker,** bloedsuier; uit= suier; ~ **sugar,** bloedsuiker; ~**-test,** bloedtoets; ~**-test kit,** bloedtoetsapparaat; ~**thirstiness,** bloeddorstigheid; ~**thirsty,** bloeddorstig; ~**-trail,** bloedspoor; ~ **transfusion,** bloedoortapping, bloedtransfusie; ~**-transfusion service,** bloedoor= tappingsdiens; ~ **type,** bloedgroep; ~**-vessel,** bloedvat, aar; ~**-warm,** bloedheet; ~ **wood,** bloed= hout; ~ **worm,** bloedwurm; ~**wort,** drakebloed.
blood'y, (v) bloederig maak; (a) bloedig; bloederig; rooi; wreedaardig; vervloekste; ~ **diarrhoea,** bloedpersie; ~ **dysentry,** bloedpens; ~ **flux,** persie, bloedpersie; ~ **gang fight,** bloedige bendegeveg; **B** ~ **Mary,** wodka en tamatiesap; ~**-minded,** bloeddorstig, moorddadig, wreed; ~ **sweat,** bloed= sweet.
bloom¹, (n) bloeisel, blom; fleur, krag, bloei; blos; uit= slag (op mure); aanslag (op glas); waslaag, dons, waas (op vrugte); frisheid; *the* ~ *IS off,* die fleur is daarvan af; *TAKE the* ~ *off,* die fleur verwyder; (v) bloei, uitbot; voorspoedig wees; blom.
bloom², (n) wolf (yster); glasmassa.
bloom'er¹, blommer, bloeier.
bloom'er², blaps, bok, fout, stommiteit.
bloom'ers, kniebroek, rokbroek, toebroek.
bloom'ing, bloeiend; blosend; vervlaks(te).
Bloomsbury Group, Bloomsburygroep.
bloom'y, bloeiend.
bloss'om, (n) bloeisel, blom; bloesem; bloei; (v) bloei, blom; ~ *out into,* ontwikkel tot; ~**ing,** bloeiend; ~**-time,** bottyd.
blot, (n) klad, vlek; skandvlek, smet; (v) **(-ted),** be= klad; vlek; uitvee; uitwis; onsigbaar maak, verduis= ter; vloei; droogmaak (ink); onteer; ~ *one's COPYBOOK,* jouself oneer aandoen; afbreuk doen aan jou goeie naam; ~ *OUT,* uitwis, uitvee; uitdelg.
blotch, (-es), vlek; puisie; klad; vloeipapier; ~**y,** klad= derig; vlekkerig.
blott'ed, geklad.
blott'er, vloeiblok, kladblok.
blott'ing-pad, vloeiblok.
blott'ing-paper, vloeipapier, kladpapier, vlakpapier.
blouse, bloes(e); hempbaadjie.
blow¹, (n) windstorm; geblaas (walvis); eierlêery (in= sekte); vliegeiers.
blow², (n) slag, klap; hou, wiks, raps; ramp; skok; (pl) dodelikhede; *COME to* ~*s,* handgemeen raak; tot handtastelikhede oorgaan; slaags raak; mekaar in die hare vlieg; *DEAL a* ~ *to,* 'n slag toedien aan; *a* ~ *of a HAMMER,* 'n hamerslag; *a HEAVY* ~, 'n swaar slag; *that IS a* ~, dis 'n skade in die boedel; dis 'n geweldige slag; *STRIKE a* ~ *for,* vir iem. (iets) veg; *deliver TELLING* ~*s,* spykers met kop= pe slaan; *WITHOUT a* ~, sonder slag of stoot; (v) waai (wind); blaas (met mond); hyg; snuit (neus); spuit (walvis); te kere gaan; bloei, oopgaan (blom); uitblaas; toeter, sketter (trompet); aanblaas, op= blaas (vuur); eiers lê (vlieë); smelt (sekering); ~ *AWAY,* wegblaas; wegskiet; *I'll BE* ~*ed if I will,* ek

verseg om dit te doen; ~ *out one's BRAINS,* self= moord pleeg; jouself deur die harsings skiet; ~ *DOWN,* omwaai; ~ *the EXPENSE,* vergeet maar die onkoste; ~ *great GUNS,* 'n hewige stormwind woed; ~ *HOT and cold,* uit twee monde praat; ~ *IN,* aangewaai kom; ~ *a KISS,* 'n kushandjie gee; ~ *one's NOSE,* jou neus snuit; ~ *OUT,* bars; uit= waai; uitbrand (gloeilampie); ~ *OVER,* verbytrek, oorwaai; vergeet raak; omwaai; ~ *off STEAM,* stoom afblaas; ~ *one's TOP,* (colloq.), teen iem. uitvaar; losbrand; ~ *one's own TRUMPET,* sy eie lof verkondig; ~ *UP,* in die lug laat vlieg; oppomp; uitsak.
blow³, (n) bloeisel; (v) blom, bloei, oopgaan.
blow: ~**-all,** (sl.), toetentaal niks, boggerol; ~**ball,** perdeblomsaad; ~**-by,** lek (suier); ~**-cock,** af= blaaskraan; ~**-dry,** blaasdroog, droogblaas; ~**er,** blaser, blaasbalk; luggat; waaier; ~ **fish,** blaasop= pie; ~**fly,** (..**flies),** brommer; ~**-hard,** spogger, grootprater; ~**hole,** blaasgat; trekgat; gasholte; ~**ing,** (n) geblaas, gestorm; (a) blasend; ~**lamp,** blaaslamp.
blown, uitgeput, uitasem; opgeswel; bederf; ~ *FUSE,* (deur)gesmelte sekering; *a* ~ *HORSE,* 'n flou perd; ~ *OIL,* geoksideerde olie.
blow'-out, bandbars (motor); ontploffing; fuif; ~ *charge,* blaasskoot.
blow: ~ **over,** oorgaan, verby waai; ~**pipe,** blaas= pyp(ie); sweispyp; ~**pipe flame,** steekvlam; ~**torch,** blaaspyp; ~**-up,** (n), ontploffing; ~ **up,** (v), opblaas, die lug in blaas; ~ **wave,** waaigolf; blaas= krul, waaikrul.
blow'y, winderig.
blowzed, blowz'y, rooi, verhit; bloesend; verwaai, deurmekaar.
blub, tjank, grens.
blubb'er, (n) walvisspek; getjank; (v) grens, snotter, huil; huil-huil praat; ~**ed,** dik gehuil, geswel; ~**ing,** getjank.
bludg'eon, (n) knuppel, knopkierie; (v) met 'n kierie slaan.
blue, (n) blou; asuur; blousel; kenteken, insinje (van sportman); lug; *like a BOLT from the* ~, soos 'n bliksemstraal uit die helder lug; *a FIT of the* ~*s,* 'n neerslagtige bui; *drop OUT of the* ~, uit die lug val; (v) in die blousel steek; verkwis; (a) blou; bleu (van vlag); neerslagtig; geleerd; *talk until one is* ~ *in the FACE,* jou verstand af praat; praat tot jy blou word; *be in a* ~ *FUNK,* doodbang wees; *LOOK* ~, terneergedruk lyk; *things LOOKED* ~, sake het maar oes gelyk; ~ *MONDAY,* blou Maandag; *in a* ~ *MOOD,* neerslagtig; *once in a* ~ *MOON,* baie selde; *yell* ~ *MURDER,* moord en brand skree; *the deep* ~ *SEA,* die blou dam; *TRUE* ~, volbloed; getrou; ~ **antelope,** bloubok; ~ **asbestos,** blou= asbes, krosidoliet; ~ **baby,** blou baba; ~**backs,** Transvaalse papiergeld (1865); hakskeenpleister; ~ **bag,** blouselsakkie; ~ **bear,** bloubeer; **B** ~**beard,** Bloubaard; ~ **bell,** rietpypie; grasklokkie; pypie; ~**-bird,** blou(sang)voël; ~ **blindness,** bloublind= heid; ~ **blood,** blou bloed, hoë afkoms; ~**-book,** bloubock; ~ **bottle,** koringblom; brommer; kaster= olie; **blouhlasie;** ~ **buck,** bloubok; ~ **butterfish,** Kaapse nôientjie, bloubottervis; ~ **cheese,** blou kaas, Roquefort; ~ **chip,** sekuriteitsaandeel, prima aandeel; ~**-collar worker,** dagloner; ~ **crane,** blou= kraan; ~ **devils,** neerslagtigheid; ~ **duiker,** blou= bokkie, blouduiker; ~ **dun,** blouvaal; ~ **ebony,** amaranthout; ~**-eyed,** met blou oë, blouoog=; ~**-eyed boy,** witbroodjie, troetelkind; gunsteling; ~ **film,** bloufilm; ~**-fin tuna,** blouvintuna; ~ **fish,** pampelmoes; ~**-flame burner,** bloubrander; ~ **funk,** groot vrees; ~ **gill,** varswatervis; ~ **grass,** blougras; ~**-green,** blougroen; ~ **ground,** blou= grond, kimberliet; ~**-gum,** bloekom, eukaliptus= (boom); ~**ing,** aanblouing; ~**jacket,** matroos; pik= broek; ~ **joke,** blougrap, gewaagde grap, skurwe grap; ~ **lead,** loodglans; ~ **light,** blou seinlig; ~ **mould,** blouskimmel (sitrus); ~ **mud,** bloumodder; ~**ness,** blouheid; ~**-nose,** farisecër; jandooi; heilige boontjie; ~ **ointment,** kwiksalf; ~**-pencil,** die blou potlood gebruik; iets drasties verbeter; **B** ~ **Peter,**

bluff vertrekvlag (op skepe); ~ **pill,** kwikpil; blouboon= tjie; ~ **pointer (shark),** wit doodshaai; blouvinhaai; ~ **print,** bloudruk, ligdruk; fotodruk; ~ **ribbon,** Orde van die Kousband; afskafferknoop; kam= pioenprys, blou lint; ~ **roan,** blouskimmel; ~ **shark,** blouhaai; B ~ **Shirt,** Blouhemp; ~ **spar,** blouspaat; ~**-speckeld,** blouskilder; ~ **stocking,** bloukous, geleerde vrou; ~**-stone,** blouvitrioel; blouklip; ~ **streak,** vetgesmeerde blits; ~ **t,** koring= blom; ~ **tick,** blouboslius; ~ **tongue,** bloutong; B ~ **Train,** Blou Trein; ~ **vitriol,** blouvitrioel; ~ **water,** blouwater, see; ~ **waxbill,** blousysie; ~ **whale,** blouwalvis; ~**-whale unit,** blouwalviseen= heid; ~**-white (diamond),** blouwit diamant; ~ **wil= debeest,** blouwildebees; ~ **wool,** blouwol; ~ **y,** blouerig; blouagtig.

bluff¹, (n) grootpratery, opskeppery, oorbluffing; *call his* ~, sy uitdaging aanvaar; iem. ontmasker; (v) grootpraat, opsny; afsnou; oorduiwel, oorbluf, bangmaak; wysmaak, uitoorlê.

bluff², (n) voorgebergte, steil kaap; steil oewer; klif (geogr.).

bluff³, (a) grof; steil; stomp, bot; gulhartig, openhar= tig, hartlik.

bluff: ~ **er,** bangmaker; sketterbek; ~ **ness,** hartlik= heid; steilheid.

blu'ish, blouagtig, blouerig.

blun'der, (n) flater, bok, stommiteit, (growwe) vergis= sing; misgreep, fout; (v) flaters maak, 'n bok skiet; struikel; ~ *AWAY,* verknoei; ~ *UPON,* by toeval afkom op; ~ **buss, (-es),** haakbus, donderbus; san= na; ~ **er,** domkop, knoeier, sukkelaar, lomperd; ~ **ing,** (n) vergissing, brouspul; (a) onbesonne, on= nadenkend.

blunge, (v) klei meng (potteb.).

blunt, (n) stomp naald; pitte, duite; (v) afstomp, ver= stomp, stomp maak, afrond; ongevoelig maak; (a) stomp, bot; nors, stoets, kortaf; plomp; reguit, on= omwonde; ~ *ing of feelings,* gevoelsafstomping; ~ **ly,** platweg, botaf, botweg, kortaf, reguit; ~ **ness,** stompheid; botheid, norsheid; eerlikheid; ~ **side,** rugkant (van mes).

blur, (n) vlek, smet; wasige voorkoms; (v) **(-red),** be= klad, vlek, besmet; verdof, onduidelik maak, ver= duister.

blurb, flapteks, omslagaanbeveling, omslagadverten= sie; aanprysing.

blurred, gevlek, geklad; onduidelik, wasig, dof.

blurt, uitflap, uitblaker, verklap.

blush, (n) **(-es),** blos; gloed; *at the FIRST* ~, op die eerste gesig; *PUT someone to the* ~, iem. lelik laat skaam kry; iem, lelik skaam maak; *WITHOUT a* ~, sonder blik of bloos; (v) bloos, rooi word; ~ *to the roots of one's hair,* tot agter die ore bloos; ~ **ing,** blosend; gesond; ~ *ing bride,* trots van Fransch= hoek, bergbruidjie *(Serruria florida);* ~**-pink,** lig= rooi.

blus'ter, (n) getier, geraas; lawaai; geswets; (v) storm, wind maak (sonder stof), lawaai maak, snoef, raas, tier; ~ *out,* uitbulder; ~ **er,** lawaaimaker, basjan, grootbek, swetser, baasspeler; windorrel; windba= lie; vlagswaaier, snoeshaan; ~ **ing,** (n) gebulder; (a) snoewend, baasspelerig, bulderend; ~ **ous,** snoe= wend.

BMX bike, BMX-fiets.

bo! boe! *not say* ~ *to a goose,* nie boe of ba sê nie; nie pê sê nie; nie pruim (kan) sê nie.

bo'a, boa; ~ **constrictor,** boakonstriktor, luislang, piton.

boar, beer; wildevark; *castrated* ~, burg.

board, (n) plank; dis, tafel; kosgeld, losies, ete, kos; boord, bestuur, raad, kommissie; aanplakbord; bordpapier, karton; *it was not all ABOVE* ~, daar het suurlemoensap deurgeloop; ~ *of CENSORS,* sensuurraad; *FREE on* ~, vry aan boord (gelewer); *GO by the* ~, oorboord val; uitgegooi word; oor= tref word, geslaan word (rekords); ~ *of GUARD= IANS,* voogdyraad; *ON the* ~s, op die toneel; *SWEEP the* ~, alles opstryk (wen); *B* ~ *of TRADE,* Handelsraad; (v) met planke bespyker, beplank; loseer, inwoon; kos gee; aanklamp; aan boord gaan, enter (skip); instap (trein); *BE* ~*ed,*

liggaamlik afgekeur word; na 'n geneeskundige raad verwys word; ~ *OUT,* buitenshuis eet; ~ *a SHIP,* aan boord gaan; 'n skip aanklamp (binne= dring); ~ **book,** kartonboek; ~ **er,** kosganger; lo= seerder; ~ **fence,** plankheining, skutting; ~ **game,** bordspel.

board'ing, losies; skutting, beskot; ~**-house,** losies= huis; koshuis; ~**-joist,** kinderbalk; ~**-party,** enter= afdeling, -troep; ~**-pass,** instapkaart (vliegtuig); ~**-point,** opklimplek; ~**-school,** kosskool.

board: ~ **meeting,** bestuursvergadering; raadsverga= dering; direksievergadering; ~ **money,** kosgeld; lo= sies(geld); ~ **room,** bestuurskamer, raadsaal, raad= kamer; direksiekamer; ~**-saw,** kloofsaag; ~ **wages,** kosgeld; ~ **walk,** plank(voet)pad.

boar: ~**-hunt,** swynejag; ~ **ish,** onbeskof; swynagtig, dierlik; ~**'s' head,** swynskop, varkkop.

boast, (n) spoggery, grootpratery; trots, roem; *an IDLE* ~, 'n ongegronde bewering, pure bekpraat= jies; *MAKE a* ~ *of,* hom beroem op; hom verho= vaardig op; *great* ~, *small ROAST,* hoe minder harsings in sy kop, hoe hoër pluiskeil sit hy op; hoe kaler, hoe rojaler; hoe kaler jonker, hoe groter pronker; hoe kaler heer(tjie), hoe groter meneer= (tjie); hoe kaler jakkals, hoe groter stert; (v) spog, windmaak, grootpraat, bluf, boog, praal, snoef; trots wees op, roem; ~ **ed,** veelgeprese; ~ **er,** groot= prater, bekprater, windbuks, opsnyer, blaffer, bluf= fer, snoewer, windmaker, windlawaai; klipbeitel; ~ **ful,** spoggerig, windmakerig; ~ **fulness,** spogge= righeid; ~ **ing,** (n) gebral, gesnoef, pralery, spogte= ry; (a) varkgooierig, windmakerig.

boat, (n) boot, skuit, skip; souspotjie, souskom; *BURN one's* ~s, jou skepe agter jou verbrand; *you've MISSED the* ~, jy is laat; jy vis agter die net; *have an OAR in another's* ~, sy neus in 'n an= der man se sake steek; *ROCK the* ~, die rus ver= stoor (versteur); onaangenaamheid veroorsaak; *be in die SAME* ~, in dieselfde omstandighede ver= keer; *we are all in the SAME* ~, ons sit in die skuit en moet meevaar; (v) roei, in 'n skuit vaar; ~ **age,** vrag; boottransport; bootvervoer; ~**-bill,** ~**-billed heron,** Suid-Amerikaanser reier; ~**-bridge,** skip= brug; ~ **builder,** bootbouer; ~ **building,** bootbou= (ery); ~**-deck,** bootsdek; ~ **drill,** bootoefening; ~ **el,** botel, boothotel; ~ **er,** strooihoed; roeier, vaarder; ~**-hook,** boothaak; ~**-house,** skuithuis; boothuis, huisboot; ~ **ing,** vaar (met 'n boot); roei; ~ **man,** skipper; roeier; bootverhuurder; ~ **race,** roeiwedstryd; ~**-shaped,** bootvormig; ~**-song,** bootlied, ~ **swain,** (spreek uit *bo'sn*), bootsman; ~ **swain's mate,** onderbootsman; ~**-train,** boottrein.

bob¹, (n) opstopper; ruk.

bob², (n) sjieling.

bob³, (n) slingergewig; lood (van dieplood).

bob⁴, (n) pruik; bossie; bolla (hare); stompstert; kort haarbos, kortgesnyde hare; (v) kort afsny (hare).

bob⁵, (n) buiging; (v) **(-bed),** heen en weer slinger; op een neer gaan, dobber; ruk aan, pluk.

bob⁶, (n) melodie, refrein (by klokke).

bobbed hair, polkahare.

bobb'ery, oproer, rusie, geraas.

bobb'in, spoel, klossie, tolletjie, garingdraer; ~ **bolt,** tolbout; ~ **carrier,** skietspoel; toldraer; ~ **cheek,** tolwang; ~ **cylinder,** spoelsilinder; ~ **lace,** klos= kant.

bob'bish, opgeruimd, vrolik.

bobb'y, (bobbies), konstabel, polisiedienaar; ~ **pin,** haarspeld; ~**-socks,** ~**-sox,** enkelsokkies; ~**- soxer,** tienderjarige, tiener; bakvissie.

bo'bolink, rysvoëltjie.

bobo'tie, bobotie.

bob'sled, bob'sleigh, bobslee.

bob'tail, stompstert; ~ **ed,** met kort hare; stompstert=.

bob'-wig, kort pruik.

boca'ge, bocage, bostoneel (keramiek).

Boche, (F., neerh.), Duitser; die Duitsers.

bock, bock(bier).

bode, voorspel, vooruit voel; ~ **ful,** onheilspellend.

bodeg'a, bodega, wynwinkel.

bode'ment, voorspelling, voorteken.

bodge = **botch.**

bodice 742 bolting

bod'ice, lyfie.
bod'iless, sonder liggaam, onliggaamlik.
bod'ily, liggaamlik, lyflik, in lewende lywe; kompleet, heeltemal, met kop en pootjies; ~ *presence,* aanwesigheid in lewende lywe.
bod'ing, voorteken, voorgevoel.
bod'kin, haarspeld; els; dolk; rygnaald; *LIE* ~, lepelê; *RIDE (sit)* ~, gepak sit soos sardientjies.
bod'y, (n) **(bodies),** liggaam, lyf, bas; persoon; lyk; romp (skip); lyfie; kern; hoofinhoud, hoofdeel (van dokument, brief); versameling; massa; stof, materie; skag (van boute); huis (van klep); volheid (van wyn); krag; bak, bostel (van motor); meerderheid; bende, trop, vereniging; stertstuk (van vuurwapen); hart (van skroef); lywigheid, dekvermoë (van verf); ~ *CORPORATE,* regspersoon(likheid); ~ *of FOOT,* voetvolk; *FOREIGN* ~, vreemde liggaam (voorwerp, stof, materiaal); *HEAVENLY* ~, hemelliggaam; *a* ~ *of HORSES,* 'n afdeling ruitery; *IN a* ~, in 'n klomp; *the* ~ *POLITIC,* die staat; *keep* ~ *and SOUL together,* siel en liggaam aanmekaar hou; ~ *of TROOPS,* troepemag; *WINE of good* ~, volle (lywige) wyn; (v) **(bodied),** beliggaam; ~ **blow,** harde hou; ~**-bolt,** bakbout; ~ **build,** liggaamsbou; ~**er,** spierbouer; koetsbouer; ~ **building,** liggaamsopbou; ~ **cavity,** liggaamsholte; ~**-cloth,** dekkleed, perdedeken; lyflinne; ~**-colour,** dekkleur; dekverf; ~ **corporate,** regsliggaam; regsinstelling; regspersoonlikheid; ~**-design,** bakontwerp; ~ **exercise,** liggaamsoefening; ~ **fluids,** liggaamsvloeistowwe; ~**-guard,** lyfwag; ~**-hair,** lyfhaar, lyfhare; ~**-heat,** liggaamshitte; ~ **language,** liggaamstaal, houdingstaal; ~ **line bowling,** lyfboulwerk; ~ **linen,** onderlinne; ~ **louse,** lyfluis; ~ **maker,** bakmaker; ~ **odour,** liggaamsreuk, lyfreuk; ~ **politic,** staatsliggaam, staatsbestel; ~ **pressings,** bakstukke, bakdrukstukke; ~ **receipt,** lyfkwitansie; ~ **region,** liggaamstreek; ~**-servant,** persoonlike bediende; lyfkneg; ~ **shirt,** lyfhemp, kleefhemp; ~**-snatcher,** lykdief; ~ **stocking,** lyfkous; ~ **suspension,** bakvering; bakmontering; ~ **sweep,** bakronding; ~ **wall,** liggaamswand; ~**-work,** bak(werk); ~ **wrinkle,** lyfplooi(tjie).
Boeo'tia, Beosië, ~**n,** (n) Beosiër; (a) Beoties; onnosel, dom.
Boer, Boer.
boer: ~ **biscuit,** boer(e)beskuit; ~ **goat,** boerbok; ~**-meal,** growwe meel, boermeel; ~ **millet,** boermanna; B ~ **orchestra,** Boereorkes; B ~ **saddle,** nierknyper; ~ **sausage,** boerewors; ~ **tobacco,** boeretwak, boeretabak.
Boer War, Engelse Oorlog, Tweede Vryheidsoorlog, Driejarige Oorlog, Boereoorlog.
bof'fin, wetenskaplike, navorser, uitvinder.
bog, (n) moeras, vlei; (v) **(-ged),** in die modder dompel; vasval.
bog'ey, **(-s),** syfer, baansyfer (gholf).
bog'eyman, paaiboelie; Antjie Somers; weerwolf.
bogg'iness, moerassigheid, drassigheid.
bog'gle, (n) draai; (v) skrik; mopper; draai; weifel, vassteek, aarsel; veins; *my mind* ~*s at the thought,* ek deins terug by die gedagte; ~**r,** lafaard.
bogg'y, moerassig, vleiagtig, deurslagtig, flodderig.
bog'ie, skamelwa; onderstel, draaistel, bogie; ~**-carriage,** bogiewa; ~**-cart,** skamelkar; ~**-centre,** draaibord; ~**-engine,** bogiemasjien; ~**-truck,** draaisteltrok, bogietrok, skamelwa; ~**-wag(g)on,** draaisteltrok.
bog'iron, moerasyster.
bo'gle, kabouter, gogga, boeman, paaiboelie, skrikbeeld, spook, gees, voëlverskrikker.
bog'-ore, moeraserts.
bog'us, vals, oneg; sogenaamde; *a* ~ *COMPANY,* 'n swendelmaatskappy; *a* ~ *WEDDING,* skynhuwelik; ~ **bomb,** vals bom.
bo'gy, (bogies), gogga, spook, gees, skrikbeeld, paaiboelie, voëlverskrikker; *the* ~ *man,* gô, kinderverskrikker.
boh! = **bo!**
bohea', swart tee.
Bohem'ia, Boheme; artiestewêreld; ~**n,** (n) Bohemer;

losbolkunstenaar, bohémien; (a) Boheems; bohémien, losbandig; **b** ~ **nism,** artiestebestaan.
boil¹, (n) pitsweer; bloedvin(t); steenpuis(ie).
boil², (n) kook; *OFF the* ~, v.d. kook af; *ON the* ~, aan die kook; (v) kook; ~ *AWAY,* verdamp, verkook; *his BLOOD* ~*s,* hy is baie kwaad; ~ *CLEAN,* uitkook; ~ *DOWN,* afkook; slink; verkort; *it* ~*s DOWN to this,* dit kom hierop neer; ~ *OVER,* oorkook; woedend word; ~*ed SHIRT,* stywe hemp.
boil'er, ketel, stoomketel; koker, warmwatertenk; kookgroente; *double* ~, dubbele kookpot; ~ **bearer,** ketelstoel; ~**-capacity,** ketelvermoë; ~ **deposit,** ketelsteen, ketelaanpaksel; ~**-flue,** rookkanaal; ~ **furnace,** vuurkas; ~ **maker,** ketelmaker; ~**-man,** stoker; ~ **plate,** ketelplaat; ~**-pressure,** keteldruk; ~**-pump,** ketelpomp; ~**-room,** ketelkamer; ketelruim; ~ **scale,** ketelaanslag; ~ **shop,** ketelmakery, ketelwerkswinkel; ~**-suit,** ketel(werks)pak; ~**-tube,** hittepyp, ketelpyp.
boil'ing, (n) kokery, kook; kooksel; (pl) kooklekkers; (a) kokend; warm; ~ *HOT,* baie warm, so warm dat die kraaie gaap; *KEEP the pot* ~, die skoorsteen aan die rook hou; ~ **bag,** uitkooksakkie; ~**-flask,** kookfles; **kookkolf;** ~**-hot,** kookwarm, vuurwarm; ~ **point,** kookpunt; ~**-water reactor,** kookwaterreaktor; ~**-water starch,** kookwaterstysel, gaar stysel.
bois'terous, onstuimig, wild, stormagtig; luidrugtig, rumoerig; uitgelate, dartel, uitbundig; ~ *talker,* skreër, skreeuer; ~**ness,** onstuimigheid, rumoer.
Bok'keveld, Bokkeveld; *COLD* ~, Kouebokkeveld; *WARM* ~, Warmbokkeveld.
bokmakie'rie, bokmakierie.
bok'o, (sl.) neus.
Boks, Bokke, Springbokke (sport).
bo'las, bolas, vangriem, gooiriem.
bold, stout(moedig), dapper; vry, vrymoedig, onbeskroomd, vrypostig, astrant, vermetel, onbeskaam; opvallend; sterk, duidelik (skrif); *be as* ~ *as BRASS,* astrant en onbeskaamd wees; *MAKE* ~, die vryheid neem, hom verstout; *SPEAK* ~*ly,* reguit praat; ~**-faced,** onbeskaamd, domastrant; ~**-(faced) type,** vet letter(s); ~**ly,** reguit, vrypostig, vrymoedig; ~**ness,** moed, stoutmoedigheid, stoutheid; vermetelheid, onbeskaamdheid; ~ **wool,** oorsterk wol; lywige wol.
bole, (boom)stam; suil; nis.
bole'ro, bolero (kledingstuk; dans).
bo'lide, vuurbal, meteoor.
Boliv'ia, Bolivië; ~**n,** (n) Boliviaan; (a) Boliviaans.
boll, saadbolletjie.
boll'ard, meerpaal, bolder.
boll'-weevil, boll'-worm, bolwurm, bolkewer.
bo'lo, bolo, bladstuk.
bolo'meter, bolometer, hittestralingsmeter.
bolon'ey, kaf, onsin, bog.
Bol'shevik, (n) Bolsjewiek; (a) Bolsjewisties.
Bol'shevism, Bolsjewisme.
Bol'shevist, (n) Bolsjewis; (a) Bolsjewisties.
bol'ster, (n) kussing; peul; stut; skamel (draaistel), kompres; (v) ondersteun; rugsteun; met 'n kussing slaan; ophou; ~ *up one's courage,* iem. 'n riem onder die hart steek; ~**-bar,** kussingslaanpaal; ~**-case,** kussingsloop, peulsloop; ~ **ing,** ondersteuning; ~**-truck,** skameltrok.
bolt, (n) pyl; grendel, bout, (deur)skuif, knip, afsluiter; skig, bliksemstraal; lang koeël; sprong; vlug; *that* ~ *never came from your BAG,* dit het nooit uit jou koker gekom nie; *a* ~ *from the BLUE,* 'n donderslag uit die helder hemel; *he has SHOT his* ~, sy kruit is weggeskiet; (v) met boute grendel; die knip opsit; spring (perd); weghol, op loop sit; insluk (kos); haastig wegsluk; vasklink; sif, ondersoek; ~ *down (together),* vasbout; (adv): ~ *upright,* penregop; ~ **body,** boutskag; ~ **chisel,** ritsbeitel; ~ **cutter,** boutsnyer; ~**ed,** gegrendel; toe.
bol'ter¹, (n) sif, meelsif.
bol'ter², (n) skrikkerige perd; weglopper, droster.
bolt: ~**-head,** boutkop; ~**-hole,** sluipgat; boutgat.
bolt'ing: ~**-cloth,** buillinne; ~**-mill,** builmeule.

bolt: ~ **lock,** grendelslot; ~ **nut,** moer; ~ **-on,** vasgebout.
bolt'shank, boutskag.
bolt'-sprit, boegspriet.
bol'us, (-es), groot pil; bitter pil; kosbal, bolus; *red* ~, rooibolus.
bom'a, kraalheining; distrikskantoor; polisiepos.
bomb, (n) bom; *high-explosive* ~, brisantbom; (v) bombardeer, bomme gooi; granate gooi; ~ **-aimer,** bomrigter.
bombard', bombardeer, bestook; ~ **er,** bombardeerder; ~ **ier',** bombardier; ~ **ier-beetle,** bombardeerkewer, poepgogga (sl.); ~ **ment,** beskieting, bombardement.
bom'bardon, bombardone', bombardon, bronsmusiekinstrument (met lae toon), brombas; basuin (orrel).
bom'basine, bombasyn.
bom'bast, hoogdrawende taal, bombas.
bombas'tic, bombasties, hoogdrawend, geswolle.
bomb'-attack, bomaanval.
Bombay', Bombaai; ~ *duck,* kerrievis.
bomb: ~ **-bay,** bomafskorting; ~ **carrier,** bomrak; ~ **casing,** bomdop; ~ **crater,** bomtregter, homgat, bomkrater; ~ **damage,** bomskade; ~ **dropper,** bomlosser; ~ **dropping,** bomwerping.
bomb'er, bomwerper, bomvliegtuig; granaatgooier; **B** ~ **Command,** bevelsgebied vir bomwerping; ~ **force,** bomwerpmag; ~ **pilot,** bomvlieënier; ~ **squadron,** bom-eskader.
bomb: ~ **explosion,** bomontploffing; ~ **-happy,** met bomskok; ~ **hit,** bomtreffer; *direct* ~ *hit,* voltrefter; ~ **hoist,** bomhyser.
bomb'ing, bomwerping; bombardering; ~ **aircraft,** bomwerper; ~ **attack,** bomaanval; ~ **plane,** bomwerper; ~ **raid,** bomaanval; ~ **sequence,** bomreeks.
bomb: ~ **-load,** bomlading, bomvrag; ~ **-outrage,** bomaanslag; ~ **proof,** bomvry; ~ **raid,** bomaanval; ~ **-release,** bomlostoestel; ~ **shell,** bom, bomdop; *drop a* ~ *shell,* 'n bom los; 'n knuppel in die hoenderhok gooi; ~ **shelter,** bomvaste kelder; ~ **-shock,** bomskok; ~ **-sight,** bomvisier; ~ **-splinter,** bomskerf; ~ **squad,** bomeenheid; ~ **station,** bompos; ~ **-thrower,** bomgooier; ~ **-throwing,** bomgooiery.
bona fide, te goeder trou, solied, bona fide; ~ **farmer,** bona fide-boer; ~ **student,** bona fide-student; ~ **s,** opregtheid, eerlikheid.
bonan'za, voorspoed, geluk; goudmyn; ryk myn.
bon-bon', bonbon; ~ **s,** lekkergoed, bonbons.
bond, (n) band; verbond, ooreenkoms; verband (in steenwerk); verbintenis, kontrak, pakhuis, entrepot; verpligting; samevoeging, verband, hipoteek (op huis); borgakte; skuldbewys, obligasie; *GOODS in* ~, goedere in entrepot; *IN* ~ *s,* in boeie gevang; *TAKE out of* ~, uit die pakhuis los; *an honest man's WORD is as good as his* ~, 'n man se woord, 'n man se eer; *his WORD is his* ~, jy kan op sy woord reken; sy woord is ja en amen; (v) verbind; onder verband plaas, verband, beswaar, verband neem op; in entrepot opslaan; inmessel; ~ **age,** gebondenheid; slawerny, diensbaarheid, knegskap; gevangenskap; ~ **course,** verbandlaag; ~ **ed,** verpand, onder verband; in 'n pakhuis; versterk, gebind, verbind; ~ **ed brake lining,** geplakte remvoering; *CONTINUOUS COVERING* ~, deurlopende dekverband; ~ *ed DEBT,* obligasieskuld; ~ *ed GOODS,* goedere in entrepot; ~ *ed WAREHOUSE,* entrepot; ~ **er,** bindsteen; opslaner (in pakhuis); ~ **-holder,** verbandhouer; verbandnemer; ~ **maid,** slavin; ~ **man,** slaaf, lyfeiene; ~ **paper,** bond(papier), hoëgehaltepapier; ~ **s,** skuldbriewe, obligasies; ~ **service,** slawediens; ~ **sman,** = **bondman;** ~ **stone,** bindsteen; ~ **-store,** doeanepakhuis; ~ **(s)'woman,** vroulike lyfeiene; ~ **-timber,** bindbalk, verbandhout.
bone, (n) been; graat (vis); balein (walvis); bot; (pl) beendere, gebeente; dobbelstene; *devour something* ~ *s and ALL,* iets met huid en haar verslind; *what is BRED in the* ~ *will come out in the flesh,* 'n jakkals verloor wel sy hare maar nie sy streke nie; *a* ~ *of CONTENTION,* 'n twisappel; *DRY as a* ~, kurk-

droog; *FEEL in one's* ~ *s,* doodseker wees; iets aan jou broek (se naat) voel; *a HORSE with plenty of* ~, 'n goed ontwikkelde perd; *MAKE no* ~ *s about,* nie weifel nie; geen swarigheid maak nie; *he will NEVER make old* ~ *s,* hy sal nie oud word nie; ~ *of OUR* ~ *and flesh of our flesh,* been van ons been, vlees van ons vlees; *PICK a* ~, 'n appeltjie skil; *RADIAL* ~, speekbeen; *SKIN and* ~, vel en been; *THROW the* ~ *s,* dolosse gooi; *TO the* ~, tot op die been; in murg en been, deur en deur; *WORK oneself to the* ~, jou oorhoeks werk; jou boeglam werk; (v) bene (grate) uithaal, ontbeen; skaai; (a) been=, van been; ~ **ash,** beenas; ~ **bank,** beenbank; ~ **-black,** beenswart; ~ **callus,** beeneelt, beengroeisel; ~ **cancer,** beenkanker; ~ **-charcoal,** beenswart; ~ **china,** been(der)porselein; ~ **coal,** leikool, swaarkool; ~ **-dry,** horingdroog; kurkdroog; ~ **-dust,** beenmeel; ~ **-glass,** beenglas; ~ **head,** domkop; ~ **lazy,** aartslui, vrek lui; ~ **less,** sonder bene; pap; sonder ruggraat; ~ **manure,** beenmis, kunsmis; ~ **marrow,** beenmurg; ~ **meal,** beenmeel; ~ **-milling,** beenmalery; ~ **plate,** beenplaat; ~ **r,** ontbener; stommiteit; lawwe fout; dom fout; ~ **setter,** beenspalker; ~ **-shaker,** rammelkas, lewerskudder (fiets); ~ **spavin,** splint in die been, beengewas (by perde), spat; ~ **splint,** spalk; ~ **-thrower,** dolosgooier; ~ **-throwing,** dolosgooiery; ~ **-tired,** ~ **-weary,** doodmoeg, stokflou, tam.
bon'fire, vreugdevuur, segevuur.
bon'go, trom.
bon'homie, gulhartigheid, gemoedelikheid.
bon'ing, ontbening; ontgrating; vlaktoets.
bon'ism, bonisme.
bonit'o, katonkel *(Sarda sarda).*
bon'kers, (sl.), gek, mal, getik, die kluts kwyt.
bon mot, (F.), bon mot, kwinkslag.
bonn'et, (n) vrouehoed, mus, kappie; enjinkap, motordeksel; kap (lamp); lokvoël, handlanger; *have a bee in one's* ~, eksentries wees oor iets, (v) hoed oor die oë trek; mus opsit; ~ **lacing,** enjinkapomlysting, kapwyfstrook; ~ **-monkey,** hoedaap *(Macacus radiatus).*
bonn'y, lief, aanvallig, vrolik, dartel.
bonsai', bonsai, dwergboom.
bonsel'la, pasella, geskenk.
Bons'mara, Bonsmara (beesras).
bont'bok, bont(e)bok.
bont'legged tick, bont(poot)bosluis.
bon ton, (F.), bon ton, die regte aanslag; goeie opvoeding.
bon'us, (-es), bonus, premie, ekstra; ~ **bond,** bonusobligasie; ~ **offer,** bonusaanbod.
bon vivant', (F.), bon vivant, lekkerbek, gourmand.
bon viveur', vrolike ou; lewensgenieter.
bon'y, ben(er)ig, beenagtig; vol grate; langbeen=; maer; ~ *tissue,* beenweefsel.
boo, (v) naflult; (uit)jou, uitkoggel; bulk; (interj) boe!
boob, swaap, esel.
hoobs, (colloq.), vroueborste.
boob'y, (boobies), lummel, domoor, swaap, slungel; (soort) wildegans; ~ **hatch, (-es),** skuifluik, ~ **ish,** dwaas, gek, onnosel; ~ **prize,** poedelprys, spotprys; ~ **trap,** verneukmyn, fopmyn, lokval, deurval.
boo'dle, boel, klomp; omkoopgeld; (sl.), geld, malie.
boogie-woo'gie, boogie-woogie.
boohoo', grens, tjank
boo'ing, gejou (by vergadering).
book, (n) boek; geskrif, werk; wedrenprogram; Bybel; *be in someone's BAD* ~ *s,* by iem. in 'n slegte blaadjie staan; *BRING to* ~, tot verantwoording roep; *be BROUGHT to* ~, aan die pen ry; *COPY from the* ~, laat afskryf; *GET into someone's bad* ~ *s,* in onguns raak; *GO beyond one's* ~, sy boekie te buite gaan; *be in someone's GOOD* ~ *s,* in 'n goeie blaadjie by iem. staan; by iem goed aangeskryf staan; in iem. se goeie boeke wees; *the GOOD B* ~, die Groot Boek; *KISS the* ~, op die Bybel sweer; *take a LEAF out of someone's* ~, iem. se voorbeeld volg; ~ *of LIFE,* lewensboek, *ON the* ~ *s,* ingeskryf; *READ someone like an open* ~, iem. soos 'n boek lees; ~ *of REFERENCE,* naslaanwerk; *a SEALED*

~, 'n geslote boek; *SPEAK (talk) like a* ~, praat of dit gedruk is, soos 'n boek praat; *SUIT one's* ~, jou pas; (v) boek, noteer; inskryf, opskryf; bespreek; *BE* ~ *ed for,* nie kan loskom nie; bespreek hê na; ~ *a CABIN,* 'n kajuit bespreek; ~ *IN,* inskryf, inteken; ~ *OFF,* afboek; ~ *OUT,* ten volle bespreek; ~**binder,** boekbinder; ~ **binding,** boekbindery; ~**case,** boekrak; boekkas; ~ **club,** boekklub; ~**-cover,** boekband; stofomslag, boekomslag; ~**-debt,** boekskuld; ~**-edge,** snee; ~**-end,** boekstut; ~**-fancier,** boekliefhebber; ~ **fold,** bladvou; ~**-hawker,** kolporteur; ~ **ie,** beroepswedder; ~**ing,** inboek, registrasie; plekbespreking; ~**ingclerk,** besprekingsklerk, besprekingsbeampte, kaartjiesklerk; ~**ing-fee,** besprekingsgeld; ~**inghours,** besprekingstyd, loket-ure; ~ **ing-hall,** besprekingsaal; ~**ing-office,** kaartjieskantoor, loket, besprekingskantoor; ~**ish,** geleerd; boekagtig; ~*ish language,* boek(e)taal; ~**-jacket,** boekomslag; stofomslag; ~**-keeper,** boekhouer; ~**-keeping,** boekhou; boekhouding; ~**-keeping teacher,** boekhouonderwyser; ~ **language,** boektaal; ~**-learned,** belese; ~**-learning,** boekgeleerdheid; ~**let,** boekie; brosjure; pamflet; ~**-lined,** met baie boeke teen die mure; ~**-louse,** stofluis; ~ **lover,** boekevriend; ~**-lung,** boeklong; ~ **maker,** boekmaker; beroepswedder; ~ **maker's tax,** belasting op beroepswedders; ~ **making,** boekemakery; beroepsweddery; ~ **man,** letterkundige; leser; ~ **mark(er),** leeswyser, bladwyser; ~**-muslin,** neteldoek; ~**plate,** boekmerk, ex-libris; ~**-post,** drukwerk; *send by* ~*-post,* as drukwerk stuur; ~**-rack,** boekerak; ~**-rest,** boekstander(tjie); boekstut; ~ **salesman,** kolporteur; ~ **seller,** boekhandelaar; ~ **selling,** boekhandel; ~ **shelf,** boekrak; ~**-shop,** boekwinkel; ~ **stall,** boekstalletjie; boekwinkeltjie; ~ **stand,** boekkas; ~**-stock,** boekvoorraad; ~**-store,** boekwinkel; ~**sy,** (sl.), boekerig, pretensieus geleerd; ~ **token,** boekbewys; ~ **trade,** boekhandel; ~**-value,** boekwaarde; ~ **work,** boekwerk; studie; ~ **worm,** boekwurm.

Boo'lean al'gebra, Boole-algebra, Booleaanse algebra.

boom[1], (n) sluitboom, slagboom; valhek, valboom (spoor); haweboom; weesboom; (v) (voort)boom.

boom[2], (n) gebulder, gedonder, gedreun; ophemeling, aanprysing; oplewing, groot aanvraag, handelshoogty, plotselinge prysstyging, hoogkonjunktuur; (v) bulder, dreun, dawer, donder; floreer, bloei; opgaan, omhoog gaan; reklame maak vir, ophemel, aanprys; sukses hê.

boo'mer, reklamemaker; kangaroemannetjie; bergbewer.

boom'erang, (n) boemerang, werphout; (v) terugspring.

boom'ing, (n) gedonder; golfgedruis; gebom (klokke); dreun(ing); (a) bulderend; bloeiend.

boom: ~ **let,** klein oplewing, dwergoplewing; ~ **price,** opgejaagde prys; ~ **sail,** gaffelseil; ~ **slang,** boomslang; ~ **town,** paddastoeldorp (=stad), bloeidorp (=stad); ~ **vessel,** sperboomvaartuig.

boom' swinger, boomswaaier, boomkontroleur, hengelman (TV).

boon, (n) geskenk; guns(bewys); genade, seën, weldaad; uitkomste; vlasafval; *this is a* ~ *to us,* dis 'n onverwagte uitkoms vir ons; (a) vrolik, vriendelik; mild, weldadig; ~ *companion,* boesemvriend; vrolike kêrel, 'n vrolike Frans.

boor, lummel, lomperd, vleël, onbeskofte vent, gaip, buffel, gawie, ghwar; ~**ish,** lomp, onbeskof, ongemanierd, buffelagtig, vleëlagtig, torrerig.

boost, (n) reklame, ophemeling; aanjadruk; (v) aanjaag, druk; reklame maak, ophemel, aanprys; versterk, verstewig; ~ **er,** aanjaer; opvyselaar; reklamemaker; ~ **er fuel,** aanja(ag)brandstof; ~ **er pump,** aanja(ag)pomp; ~ **er rocket,** aanja(ag)vuurpyl; ~ **ing battery,** versterkingsbattery, aanja(ag)battery.

boot[1], (n) stewel, laars; sitplek (op koets); bagasiebak, agterbak (motor); voorkis, bok; ~ *s and ALL,* met kop en pootjies; met kop en stert; (met) pens en pootjies; *BE in someone's* ~ *s,* in iem. se skoene staan; *too BIG for one's* ~ *s,* te groot vir sy skoene; *DIE in one's* ~ *s,* nie in jou bed sterf nie; *the* ~ *is on the other FOOT (leg),* dit is net andersom; *GET the* ~, *GET the order of the* ~, uitgeskop word; in die pad gesteek word; die trekpas ontvang (kry); *his HEART is in his* ~ *s,* sy hart het in sy skoene gesak; ~ *and SADDLE!* opsaal! opklim! *over SHOES, over* ~ *s,* as 'n mens A sê, moet jy ook B sê; (v) skop.

boot[2], (n) baat, voordeel; *to* ~, op die koop toe, bowendien; (v) baat.

boot: ~ **black,** skoenpoetser; ~**-blacking** (swart) skoenpolitoer; ~**-brush,** skoenborsel; ~ **ed,** geskoei, met skoene aan, gelaars; ~ *ed and spurred,* gelaars (gestewel) en gespoor; ~ **ee',** vroueskoen; kinderskoentjie.

booth, hut, tent; stalletjie; kiosk; badhuis.

boot: ~ **jack,** stewelkneg, skoenkneg; ~ **lace,** skoenveter, skoenriem; ~**-last,** skoenlees; ~**-leather,** skoenleer; ~ **leg,** smokkel; ~ **legger,** (drank)smokkelaar; ~ **legging,** (drank)smokkelary.

bootless[1], sonder skoene, ongeskoei, kaalvoet.

bootless[2], vrugteloos, vergeefs.

boot: ~ **licker,** vleier, kruiper; ~ **maker,** skoenmaker; ~ **making,** skoenmakery; ~**-polish,** (skoen)waks, skoensmeersel; ~**-protector,** skoenyster, soolbeslag; ~ **s,** skoenpoetser, skoenskoonmaker; stewelkneg; ~ **splint,** spalkstewel; ~ **stage,** stoelstadium; ~**-store,** skoenwinkel; ~ **strap,** skoenlus; skoenveter; ~**-stretcher,** skoenrekyster; ~**-trade,** skoenhandel; ~**-tree,** skoenstut.

boot'y, (booties), buit, roof.

booze, (n) fuif, drinkparty; lawaaiwater, drinkgoed; *on the* ~, aan die swier, aan die fuif; (v) fuif, bedrink, (be)suip, bras, drink, boemel; ~ **r,** suiplap, suiper; swierbol.

booz'ing, suipery.

booz'y, dronkerig, hoenderkop; drinklustig.

bop, bop (dans).

bo-peep', wegkruipertjie.

bop'per, bopper, bopdanser.

bo'ra, bora, droë Adriatiese wind.

bora'cic, boraks=, boor=; ~ **acid,** boorsuur; ~ **lint,** boorpluksel; ~ **lotion,** boorwater; ~ **ointment,** boorsalf; ~ **powder,** boorpoeier.

bor'acite, borasiet.

bo'rage, komkommerkruid, bernagie.

bo'ran(e), booretaan.

bo'rate, boorsout, boraat.

bo'rax, boraks; ~ **bead,** borakspêrel.

bor'azon, boorasoon.

borboryg'mus, maaggerammel, winde in die buik.

Bordeaux', Bordeaux; Bordeauxwyn; ~ **mixture,** bordeauxmengsel.

bordel'(lo), bordeel.

bord'er, (n) rand; randakker; blomrand; kant, grens; stootkant; soom; (v) omsoom; grens aan; begrens; van 'n rand voorsien; ~ *(up)on,* grens aan; ~ **area,** grensgebied; randgebied; ~ **ed,** gerand; ~ **er,** grensbewoner; ~**-flourish,** randversiering; ~ **gate,** grenshek; ~ **guard,** grenswag; ~ **industry,** grensnywerheid; ~ **land,** grensland; ~ **line,** grenslyn; ~ **line case,** grensgeval; ~ **state,** randstaat; grensstaat; ~ **stitch,** randsteek.

bore[1], (n) boorgat; boring; kaliber; boorwydte (geweer); (v) boor, uitboor, deurboor.

bore[2], (n) vloedgolf.

bore[3], (n) vervelende mens of saak; seurkous, lolpot, las; (v) verveel, neul.

bore[4], (v) voortdring; die kop vooruitsteek (perd); van die baan dring (perdewedloop).

bor'eal, noordelik, noorder=, boreaal, borealies.

Bor'eas, noordewind.

bore' bit, boorstaal; boorpunt.

bore'cole, boerkool, krulkool.

bore: ~ **d,** geblaseer; verveel; geboor; ~ **dom,** verveling, verveeldheid.

borehole, boorgat; ~ **cartridge,** boorpatroon; ~ **charge,** boorlading; ~ **core,** boorkern.

bor'er, boor; boorder; houtwurm, boorwurm; boorkewer.

bo'ric, boor=; ~ **acid,** boorsuur.

bor'ing[1], (n) boordery; boor; (pl) boorsel; (a) boor=.

bor'ing², (a) vervelig, vervelend, vervelerig.
bor'ing: ~ apparatus, boortoestel; ~ bar, boorspil; ~ bit, boorstuk.
bor'ingly, uitentreure, treurig.
bor'ing, ~ machine, boormasjien; ~ mill, uitboormasjien; ~ rod, boorstaaf; ~ tower, boortoring.
born, gebore; ~ AGAIN, wedergebore; BE ~, gebore word, die lewenslig aanskou; ~ and BRED, gebore en getoë; *in all my* ~ *DAYS*, my hele lewe; *be* ~ *under an EVIL star*, vir die ongeluk gebore wees; *a* ~ *FOOL*, 'n dwaas gebore; ~ *OF*, afkomstig van; *a* ~ *ORATOR*, 'n gebore redenaar; *a PERSON* ~ *under an evil star*, 'n ongelukskind; ~ *with a SILVER spoon in the mouth*, van ryk familie; ~ *TO*, gebore vir; *not* ~ *YESTERDAY*, nie gister se kind nie; nie onder 'n kalkoen (volstruis, skilpad) uitgebroei nie; nie van gister nie; ouer as tien.
borne, gedra; *kyk* bear³.
born'eol, borneol.
born'ite, borniet.
bo'ron, boron, borium, boor.
bo'rough, stad, dorp; kiesafdeling; munisipaliteit; ~ council, stadsraad.
bo'rrow, leen van; ontleen aan; toelaat (vir helling in gholf); ~ *ed LIGHT*, steelig; ~*ed PLUMES*, geleende vere; ~er, lener; *neither a* ~ *er nor a lender be*, borge baar sorge.
bor'rowing, leen, lenery; ontlening; ~ *POWERS*, leenbevoegdheid; *he who goes a-* ~, *goes A-SORROWING*, borge baar sorge; ~-pit, steelgat.
bo'rrow word, leenwoord.
borsch(t), bortsch, bortsj, beetsop.
Bor'stal: ~ *school*, tugskool.
hort, diamantgruis, boort.
borz'oi, Russiese wolfhond, Borzoi.
bos'cage, boskasie.
bosh, onsin, bog, kaf; koelbak.
bosk, bos'ket, ruigte, kreupelbos.
bo'sky, bosagtig, bosryk.
bo's'n, bo'sun = boatswain.
Bos'nia, Bosnië; ~ n, (n) Bosniër; (a) Bosnies.
bo'som, boesem, bors; hart, watervlak; *in the* ~ *of the CHURCH*, in die skoot v.d. kerk; *the* ~ *of mother EARTH*, die skoot v.d. aarde; *be* ~ *FRIENDS*, dik maats wees; boesemvriende wees; ~ **friend**, boesemvriend; ~y, met groot borste.
bos'quet = bosk.
boss¹, (n) (-es), baas, meester; leier; (v) bestuur, die hoof wees; baasspeel; ~ *the show*, baasspeel, die leiding neem.
boss², (n) knop, bult; (oog)verdikking; (v) met knoppe versier.
boss³, (n) (-es), naaf.
boss'age, kragsteen.
bos'sa no'va, (Port.), bossa nova (dans; mus.).
boss'-bolt, naafbout.
boss'-boy, hoofwerker, voorwerker.
bossing'-stick, bosseleerstok.
bos'sy¹, baasspelerig.
bos'sy², bulterig, knopperig.
Bos'ton: ~bread, bostonbrood; ~crab, Bostongreep; ~terriër, Bostonterriër.
bo'son, boson.
bo'sun = boatswain.
bot, papie; *the* ~*s*, papies (in perde).
botan'ic(al), plantkundig, botanies; ~ **case**, botaniseertrommel(-houer); ~ **garden**, botaniese tuin, plantetuin; ~ **name**, botaniese naam, plantnaam.
bot'anist, plantkundige, botanis.
bot'anize, botaniseer, plante versamel en bestudeer.
bot'any, plantkunde, botanie.
Bo'tany wool, Botanywol, fyn merinowol.
botar'go, visgereg.
botch, (n) (-es), geswel; knoeiwerk; (v) (op)lap; knoei, brou, (ver)konkel; ~ *the job*, die hele ding verfoes; ~er, knoeier, afskeper; ~ing, afskepery, knoeiwerk, gebrou.
botel' = boatel.
bot'-fly, (. . flies), perdevlieg, papievlieg.
both, beide, altwee, albei; ~ *AND*, èn . . . èn, sowel as; *you cannot HAVE it* ~ *ways*, jy moet een van die twee kies; ~ *of US*, ons altwee.

both'er, (n) las, kwelling, geneul, gesanik, getob; beslommering; (v) neul, lastig val, lol, versondig, foeter, seur, neuk (sl.), moeite maak; hom bekreun oor; ~ *IT!* vervlaks! *not be* ~*ed WITH someone or something*, nie veel omslag met iem. of iets maak nie; ~ation, gesanik, kwelling, geduiwel, gedonder, gehaspel, gefoeter, gelol, geneuk (sl.), foetery, gesukkel; ~some, lastig, vervelend, dwingerig, seurderig.
botryoid(al), druiwetrosvormig.
bot'ryolite, druiwesteen.
botry'tis, botritis.
Botswan'a, Botswana.
bott = bot.
bot'tle¹, (n) knop, botsel.
bot'tle², (n) bondel (strooi).
bot'tle³, (n) bottel, fles; pypkan; *be ADDICTED to the* ~, aan drank verslaaf wees; *have been AT the* ~, van Noag se sap gedrink het; *BRING up on the* ~, met die fles grootmaak; *OVER a* ~, oor 'n glasie; *PLY the* ~, in die bottel kyk; die bottel aanspreek; te veel v.d. bottel hou; lief wees vir die bottel; die karba lig; in die kalbas (kan) kyk; *have TAKEN to the* ~, aan drank verslaaf wees; (v) in bottels tap, bottel; insluit (skepe); inlê (vrugte); ~ up, opkrop; vaskeer; ~-baby, hansbabatjie, bottelbaba; ~-blower, bottelblaser; ~-brush, bottelborsel; baakhout *(Gregia sutherlandii)*; ~ cap, botteldop(pie); ~d, gebottel; ~d beer, bottelbier; ~d gas, vloeibare gas; ~-fed baby, bottelbaba; ~-fed calve (lamb), hanskalf (-lam); ~-green, donkergroen, bottelgroen; ~ heath, dopheide, bottelheide; ~-holder, sekondant, helper, handlanger; ~-imp, Cartesiaanse duikertjie; ~-jaw, dikkeel (siekte); ~ label, botteletiket; ~-neck, knelpunt; knyppunt, nou uitgang, knypgangetjie, wurgplek; ~-nose, knopneus, brandewynneus, dikneus; ~-nose(d) dolphin, stompneusdolfyn; bottelneusdolfyn; ~-party, drinkparty, ~r, bottelaar; bottelleerder; ~-rearing, hans grootmaak (diere); ~-screw, kurktrekker; spanmoer; (motor); ~-store, drankwinkel; bottelstoor; ~-thrower, bottelgooier; ~-throwing, bottelgooi(ery); ~-tissue, bottelsy; ~-washer, handlanger; bottelspoeler; ~ wrapper, bottelomslag.
bott'ling, inlêery, inmakery; intappery, vullery; ~ company, bottelmaatskappy, botteleringsmaatskappy, bottelary; ~ machine, flesvulmasjien; bottelvulmasjien; ~ works, botteleerfabriek, bottelary; koeldrankfabriek.
bott'om, (n) boom, bodem; agterste; fondament, grond(slag); kiel (skip); onderkant; vallei; diepte; onderste, onderent; sitting (stoel); *AT* ~, in die grond; in wese; *the* ~ *of the BAG*, boomskraap; die troefkaart; *BE at the* ~ *of*, die oorsaak wees van; *agter iets sit; GET to the* ~ *of*, tot die kern van 'n saak deurdring; iets uitvis; *GOOD at* ~, goed van inbors (hart); *FROM the* ~ *of my HEART*, uit die grond van my hart; *KNOCK the* ~ *out of something*, iets in duie laat val; iets die boom inslaan; *SEND to the* ~, tot sink bring; *STAND on its own* ~, op eie bene (pote) staan; *TOUCH* ~, grond raak; (v) grondves; deurgrond; 'n boom insit; (a) onderste, laaste; *bet your* ~ *dollar*, alles waag; ~ **board**, buikplank; ~ **cover**, oliebak, oliedekstuk (motor); ~ **dollar**, laaste stukkie geld, laaste sent; ~ **drawer**, onderste laai; bêrelaai; droomlaaitjie; ~-dump truck, losservragmotor; ~ **edge**, voetsnee (boek); onderste kant; ~ **flue**, onderste rookkanaal; ~ing, onderbou, grondbaan; ~ing drill, boomboor; ~ layer, (n) onderste laag; ~less, bodemloos; (a) grondeloos; ~most, heel onderste; ~ plate, onderplaat; ~-ramming machine, bodemstampmasjien; ~ rib, onderrib (suier).
bott'omry, bodemery, lening (met die skip as waarborg).
bott'om view, onderaansig.
bot'ulism, botulisme, voedselvergiftiging; gallamsiekte (by vee), lamsiekte.
bou'bou (shrike), waterfiskaal.
bouclé, (F), bouclé, boeklee.
bou'doir, (F.), boudoir, sitkamer, damesvertrek.

bou'ffant, (F.), uitgepof, opgepof, bouffant.
bougainvillae'a, ..**vill'ea,** bougainvillea, papierblom.
bough, tak.
bought, *kyk* **buy.**
boug'ie, prop, staaf; kersfilter; waskers; kateter.
bouillabai'sse, (F.), bouillabaisse, visbredie, vissop.
bouil'lon, boeljon, (vleis)sop.
boul'der, rotsblok, groot klip; rolblok, rolsteen; ~ **clay,** keileem; ~ **conglomerate,** rolsteenkonglomeraat, rolblokkonglomeraat.
boule, (F.), boule, Franse rolbal.
boul'evard, boulevard, boomstraat, boomweg.
boul'ter, lang vislyn, stellyn; sif.
bounce, (n) terugslag, hou; opslag, sprong; bluf, opsnyery, gespog; (v) huppel, terugspring, spring, opspring; aanbons; grootpraat, windmaak; stuit; *the CHEQUE* ~ *d,* die tjek is geweier; ~ *into a ROOM,* 'n kamer instorm; ~ **r,** springer; opslagskoot; opslagbal (krieket); onbeskaamde leuen; knewel; windmaker; windbuks; uitsmyter.
boun'cing, elasties, veerkragtig; stewig; groot, kolossaal; windmakerig; *a* ~ *baby,* 'n groot, gesonde baba.
bound¹, (n) grens, grenslyn; *BREAK* ~ *s,* die grense oorskry; *EXCEED the* ~ *s,* die perke oorskry; *GO beyond the* ~ *s of reason,* die redelike grense oorskry; *KEEP within* ~ *s,* jou beperk; die maat hou; *dit binne perke hou; OUT of* ~ *s,* op verbode grond; oor die grens(lyn); buite perke; *SET* ~ *s to,* perk en paal stel aan; (v) begrens, beperk, afpaal, die grens vorm.
bound², (n) sprong, opslag; *on the FIRST* ~ , by die eerste opslag; (v) spring; 'n opslag maak; huppel.
bound³, (a) klaar (om te vertrek), gereed; bestem; verbonde, skuldig, verplig; *I'll BE* ~ , ek sweer; ~ *for the CITY,* met die stad as bestemming; *HOMEWARD* ~ , op pad huis toe; ~ *to SUCCEED,* seker van sukses.
bound⁴, gebonde, ingebind; *a* ~ *COPY,* 'n ingebinde eksemplaar; ~ *POCKET,* omgeboorde sak.
boun'dary, (..ries), grens, (land)skeiding; grenshou (sport); ~ **condition,** randtoestand; ~ **dispute,** grensgeskil; ~ **farm,** grensplaas; ~ **fence,** grensskeiding; grensdraad, lyndraad; ~ **gate,** grenshek, lynhek; ~ **hit,** grenshou; ~ **layer,** grenslaag; ~ **light,** grenslig; ~ **limit,** landpaal; ~ **line,** grenslyn, grensskeiding; kantlyn; ~ **mark,** grensteken; ~ **post,** grenspaal; ~ **settlement,** grensreëling; ~ **wall,** grensmuur.
boun'den, verskuldig, verplig; *your* ~ *duty,* jou dure plig.
boun'der, niksnuts, swernoot, rakker, ondeug.
bound'less, grensloos, onbeperk.
boun'teous, mild, weldadig, vriendelik; oorvloedig.
boun'tiful, mild, milddadig; oorvloedig, rojaal; ~**ness,** mildheid, milddadigheid, oorvloed.
boun'ty, (..ties), milddadigheid, goedheid; (uitvoer)premie; gif, geskenk.
bouquet', ruiker, bos blomme; boeket, geur (van wyn).
bour'bon, Amerikaanse whisky.
bour'don, brombas (mus.); baspyp.
bour'geois, (n) bourgeois, iem. uit die burgerstand; drukletter; (a) burgerlik; ~**ie',** middelklas, burgerstand, bourgeoisie.
bourn, stroompie.
bourn(e), grens; doel, eindpaal; ~ *from which no traveller returns,* die graf.
bourré'e, bourrée (dans).
bourse, (F.), effektebeurs; geldmark.
boustrophe'don, boestrofedon.
bout, keer, beurt; rondjie; partytjie; rondte; roes; stryd; wedstryd; aanval (siekte).
boutique', boetiek; modewinkel; ~ **print,** boetiekmateriaal.
boutonnière', (F.), knoopsgatruiker.
bouzou'ki, (Gr.), boesoeki, Griekse mandolien (kitaar).
bov'ine, (n) bees; (a) bees=; beesagtig; dom, vadsig; ~ **parabotulism,** gallamsiekte, lamsiekte; ~ **tuberculosis,** beestuberkulose, beestering.
bow¹, (n) boog (skiet); strykstok (viool); strikdas; *keep the* ~ *BENT too long,* die snare te styf span; *DRAW the long* ~ , met spek skiet; met 'n hoë visier skiet; nie alleen met spek skiet nie, maar met die hele vark gooi; *a* ~ *long bent GROWS weak,* die boog kan nie altyd gespan bly nie; *MAKE a* ~ , 'n strik maak; (v) stryk (met 'n strykstok).
bow², (n) stewe, boeg (van skip).
bow³, (n) buiging; groet; beuel, hingsel; drilboor; *make one's* ~ , vir die eerste keer optree; (v) buig, buk, groet; jou onderwerp; laat buig; *have a* ~ *ing ACQUAINTANCE,* mekaar op 'n afstand ken; ~ *one's ASSENT,* met 'n buiging toestem; ~ *DOWN,* buk, neerbuig; gebuk gaan onder; ~ *one's HEAD,* die hoof buig; jou berus.
bow'-anchor, boeganker.
bow: ~ **compass(es),** orillonpasser, boogpasser, veerpasser; ~ **dividers,** nulverdeelpasser.
bowd'lerize, suiwer, ekspurgeer (boek).
bow' drill, boogdril.
bow'el: ~ **action,** ontlasting, opelyf; ~**-complaint,** ingewandskwaal; ~**-movement** = **bowel-action.**
bow'els, ingewande; hart; medelye; ~ *of COMPASSION,* medelye; *EVACUATION of* ~ , ontlasting, opelyf; *LOOSENESS of the* ~ , loslywigheid.
bow'er¹, boeganker (skip).
bow'er², boer (kaartspel).
bow'er³, verblyf, oord; somerhuisie, (lus)prieel; damesvertrek.
bow'er anchor, boeganker.
bow'ery, skaduryk.
bow'fin, Amerikaanse varswatervis.
bow' frame, spansaagraam.
bow: ~**-fronted,** met 'n komvenster, uitgebou; ~**-head (whale),** baardwalvis; baleinwalvis; Groenlandse walvis; ~**-heaviness,** boegswaarte; ~**-heavy,** boegswaar.
bow'ie knife, jagmes, herneutermes.
bow'ing, strykwerk (viool); ~ **mark,** strykteken (mus.).
bowl¹, (n) skaal, bak, kom; beker; pypkop; blad (van roeispaan); spoelkom.
bowl², (n) rolbal; bal; (v) bal gooi; boul (krieket); rol; ~ *OUT,* uitboul; ~ *OVER,* hulpeloos maak; omgooi; onder stof loop; onderstebo loop.
bow'-legged, hoepelbeen=, met hoepelbene, O-benig; nie 'n vark kan vang nie.
bow-legs, hoepelbene, O-bene.
bowl'er, bouler (krieket); rolbalspeler, keëlaar; hardebolkeil, dophoed; ~**'s crease,** boulstreep; ~ **hat,** hardebolkeil(tjie); dophoedjie; ~**-hat** *someone,* iem. oor die hoof sien; iem. uitskuif.
bow'line, boeglyn, booglyn; ~ **knot,** boogknoop.
bowl'ing, boul(werk) (krieket); rolwerk; ~**-alley,** keëlbaan; ~ **analysis,** boulontleding; ~ **average,** boulgemiddelde; ~**-club,** rolbalklub; ~**-crease,** boulstreep; ~**-green,** ~**-rink,** rolbalbaan.
bowls, rolbal; *those who play at* ~ *must look for rubs,* wie kaats, moet die bal terug verwag.
bowl'-shaped, komvormig.
bow'man¹, (..men), boogskutter.
bow'man², boegroeier.
bow'-net, fuik.
bow' saw, boogsaag, spansaag, beuelsaag.
bow'ser, petrolpomp; petroltenkwa.
bow: ~**-shackle,** D-harp; ~ **shot,** boogskot; pylsko(o)t; ~ **sprit,** boegspriet; ~ **stick,** dakboog; ~**-string,** (n) boogpees, boogsnaar; (v) verwurg; ~**-tie,** strikdas, stropdas; ~**-window,** boogvenster, komvenster, uitbouvenster, erker; ~**'-wow',** woefwoef, waf-waf; hond; ~ **yer,** boogmaker, boogverkoper; boogskutter.
box¹, (n) **(-es),** doos, kas, kis, koffer; bussie; afskorting (koffiehuis); kamertjie, vertrekkie; kompashuisie; sinjaalhuisie; naafbus (wiel); voorkis (wa); spaarpot, offerbus; loge (teater); bossing (deur); bank (hof); (pos)bus, briewebus; vak; bok (voertuig); ~ *and NEEDLE,* kompas; *he is in the WRONG* ~ , hy verkeer in 'n ongemaklike posisie; (v) in 'n kas sit; opmekaar druk (pak); afskort, wegbêre; ~ *the compass,* die 32 windrigtings v.d. kompas opnoem; omspring, draai.
box², (n) klap, opstopper; *a* ~ *on the ear,* 'n oorveeg

(oorkonkel, oorwaks); (v) met die vuis veg, boks; klap, 'n opstopper gee; ~ *someone's ears*, iem. 'n oorveeg gee.
box³, (n) buksboom.
box: ~**-barrage**, afkampspervuur; ~**-bed**, opklap=bed, alkoofbed; ~ **calf**, kalfsleer;. ~ **camera**, doos=kamera, bokskamera, handkamera; ~**-car**, goe=derewa; ~**-chisel**, koubeitel; ~**-clamp**, spanklos; ~**-cloth**, rybroekstof; ~**-coat**, swaar oorjas; ~**-coupling**, mofverbinding; ~ **ed**, verpak; ingepak; afgeskort; ingekas.
box′er, vuisvegter, bokser; (in)pakker; Boxer(hond); *B* ~ *rebellion*, Bokseropstand (in Sjina).
box: ~**-file**, doosleêr; pamfletkassie; ~**-fish**, oskop, seevarkie *(Lactoria spp.)*; koffervis; ~ **hide**, bees=leer, ~**-hole**, laaigat; ~**-in**, inkoker (balke).
box′ing, vuisslaan, boks; houtbekleding; ~ **coach**, boksafrigter; **B** ~**-day**, Tweede Kersdag, Gesins=dag; ~**-gloves**, bokshandskoene; ~ **injury**, boksbe=sering; ~**-match**, bokswedstryd; ~ **promotor**, bokspromotor, vegventer, vegknoper; boksbe=stuurder; ~**-ring**, bokskryt.
box: ~**-iron**, hol strykyster; ~ **jacket**, regaf baadjie; ~**-kite**, kasvlieër; ~**-mattress**, binnevecrmatras, ~ **measure**, meetdoos; ~**-office**, kaartjieskantoor, loket; besprekingskantoor; ~**-office hit (success)**, suksesstuk, kasstuk, lokettreffer; ~ **ottoman**, ge=stoffeerde kis; ~**-piece**, kantstrook; ~**-pleat**, plat=plooi, stolpplooi; ~**-rib**, kasrib (lugv.); ~ **room**, pakkamer; ~ **seat**, voorkis (wa); ~**-shaped**, kas=vormig; doosvormig; vierkantig; reghoekig; ~**-spanner**, sokssleutel, pypsleutel, kokersleutel, dop=sleutel; ~**-spring**, kisveer; ~ **spur**, polvyspoor; ~**-type frame**, kokerraam; ~ **wagon**, goederewa.
box′-wood, bukshout.
boy, jongetjie(skind), seun, knaap; klonkie; *OLD* ~, ou kêrel; ~*s WILL be* ~ *s*, 'n seun bly maar 'n seun.
boyar′, bojaar.
boy′cott, (n, v) boikot, afsluit; ~ **er**, boikotter; ~ **ing**, boikot.
boy: ~ **friend**, kêrel; vryer, vriend; ~ **hood**, seunsjare; ~ **ish**, seunsagtig; ~ *ish MANNERS*, seunsmanie=re; ~ *ish TRICK*, jongenstreek; ~ **ishness**, seunsag=tigheid; ~**-like**, seunsagtig; ~ **s' book**, seunsboek, seunstorie; ~ **s' choir**, seunskoor; **B** ~ **Scout**, Boy Scout, Padvinder; ~ **s' double**, seunsdubbelspel.
boys′: ~ **high school**, hoër seunskool; ~ **hostel**, seunskoshuis; ~ **school**, seunskool; ~ **singles**, seunsenkelspel.
boy′sen berry, boysenbessie.
bra, buustelyfie; *kyk* **brassière**,
braal, braaivleis; vleisbraai; braai; ~ **facilities**, braai=geriewe; ~ **vleis**, braaivleis.
Brabant′, Brabant.
bracc′ate, veerpoot=.
brace, (n) band, bras (op skuit); haak; koppel, paar (voëls); anker; boor, omslag; boog, spanning; beuel, koppeling; stut; klamp; trommelspanner; booghaak; versterking; akkolade (drukw.); ~ *and BIT*, omslag en boor; *SPLICE the main* ~, 'n dop steek; ekstra rumrantsoen (aan skeepsbemanning) toelaat; (v) vasbind; span; verspan; versterk, staal; verbind; ~ *oneself up*, hom verman, hom sterk maak; ~**-bit**, boorystêr; ~**-chuck**, omslagklembus; ~**-crank**, booromslag.
brace′let, armband; handboei (misdadigers).
brac′er, armplaat, lusmakertjie, oprissertjie, ver=sterkmiddel.
brac′es, kruisbande; tandbande (om kinders se tande reg te laat groei); krulhakies, akkolades.
bra′chial, arm=, tot die arm behorende.
bra′chiate, wyduitspreidend, bragiaat.
brach′iopod, (n) armvoetige, armpotige; (a) armpo=tig, armvoetig.
brachiosau′rus, bragiosourus.
brachycephal′ic, kortkoppig, bragisefaal, bragisefa=lies.
brachyceph′al(ous), breedhoofdig, kortkoppig.
brachyl′ogy, beknoptheid, beknopte uitdrukking, bragilogie.
brachyp′terous, kortvlerkig.

brac′ing, (n) verspanstuk, verspanning; (a) verster=kend, opfrissend; ~ **wire**, spandraad.
brack, brak, souterig, soutagtig.
brack′en, adelaarsvaring.
brack′et, (n) skragie, hakie, arm; rakkie; klamp; stoel (vere); proefskoot; *IN* ~ *s*, tussen hakies; *higher INCOME* ~, hoër inkomstegroep; *ROUND* ~, ronde hakie; *SQUARE* ~, vierkantige hakie; (v) tussen hakies sit; in een asem noem, op een lyn stel; koppel, saamvoeg; ~ **ing**, samevoeging, samekop=peling; steunwerk, stutwerk; ~ **joint**, hoeklas; ~ **plate**, steunplaat, stutplaat; ~ **turn**, skaatsdraai; ~ **wheel**, kettingskyf.
brack′ish, brak, souterig; ~ *spot*, brak (kol).
bract, dekblaar, dekblad, skutblaartjie, skutblad; braktee; ~ **eate**, met skutblaartjies; ~ **eole**, steel=blaartjie; ~ **if′erous**, skutblaardraend; ~ **scale**, dekskub.
brad, vloerspyker; kleinkopspyker; ~ **awl′**, skoenma=kersels; priem, voorsteekels; houtels; bros; ~ **punch**, spykerpons.
bradycar′dia, bradikardie, hartvertraging.
brae, (Sc.), steilte, hang.
brag, (n) gespog, windmakery, bluf; *GREAT* ~, grootpratery; *B* ~ *is a good dog, but HOLD FAST is a better*, grootpraat is niemand se maat nie; (v) (**-ged**), spog, opsny, snoef, pog, sy lyf grootman hou, boog, windmaak, grootpraat; ~ *of something*, hoog opgee oor iets.
braggado′cio, grootpratery, bluffery, windmakery, blaaskakery.
brag: ~ **gard**, ~ **ger**, bluffer, blaaskaak, grootprater, windmaker, spogter, praler, blaser, opsnyer, groot=bek, bekprater; ~ **ging**, (n) gebluf, grootpratery, poggery, gesnoef, gebral, windmakery, gespog; (a) pronkend, spoggerig.
bragg′ite, braggiet.
Brah′man, **Brah′min**, Brahmaan; ~ **cattle**, Brah=maanbeeste.
braid, (n) vlegsel, haarvleg; koord, galon, omboorsel; sierband, stootband, passement; haarband, veter=band; (v) vleg; aaneenvleg; omboor, galonneer; ~ **ed**, gevleg; met koord om, omgeboor; omgevleg; ~ *ed CABLE*, omvlegte kabel; ~ *ed RUG*, vlegmat; ~ *ed WIRE*, omvlegte draad; ~ **er**, omboorder; ga=lonvoetjie (van naaimasjien); ~ **ing**, vlegwerk; ga=lon; ~ **work**, galonwerk, koordwerk.
braille, braille(skrif), blindeskrif.
brain, (n) brein, harsings, bol; verstand, oordeel; *BLOW out one's* ~ *s*, jou deur die kop skiet; *CUD=GEL one's* ~ *s*, jou harsings afmartel; *he HAS* ~ *s*, hy het 'n goeie kop, hy het verstand; *HAVE it on the* ~, gek wees oor iets; oor iets maal; *PICK (suck) a person's* ~, iem. uithoor; iem. se idees steel; *SOFTENING of the* ~, harsingverweking; *TURN someone's* ~, iem. hoogmoedig en verspot maak; (v) die kop inslaan; ~ **box**, ~ **case**, ~ **cav=ity**, breinholte, harsingholte, breinkas. harsingkas, harsingpan; ~ **child**, geesteskind; ~ **drain**, talent=verlies; ~**-fag**, oorspanning, harsingvermoeienis; ~**-fever**, harsingkoors; - incss, intelligensie; ver=stand, breinvermoë, harsingvermoë; ~ **less**, ver=standeloos; harsingloos; ~ **matter**, breinmassa, harsingmassa; ~**-pan**, harsingpan; harspan; ~ **power**, geesteskrag; denkvermoë; ~**-racking**, hoof=brekend; ~ **s**, harsings; verstand; ~**-sick**, kranksin=nig; ~**-softening**, harsingverweking; ~**-specialist**, breinspesialis; ~ **stem**, harsingstam; breinstam; ~**-storm**, harsingstoornis; ~**-teaser**, lastige probleem; ~ *s trust*, breintrust, voorligtingspan; gedagtewis=seling; ~**-wash**, die verstand suiwer; ~**-washing**, breinspoeling, weerstandsafbreking; ~ **wave**, breintriling; ingewing, blink gedagte; ~ **work**, ver=standswerk, breinwerk; ~**-worm**, bolwurm (ska=pe); ~ **y**, slim, skrander.
braise, (n) smoor; (v) smoor, braaistoof, ~ **d meat**, gesmoorde vleis; ~ **d fish**, smoorvis.
brake¹, (n) briek, rem; remskoen; *apply the* ~ *s*, briek aandraai (rem), (v) rem, briek.
brake², (n) vlasbraak; vlasbreker, eg; (v) (vlas) braak.
brake³, (n) ruigte, boskasie, bossies; varings.
brake⁴, (n) brik (voertuig).

brake: ~ **action,** remwerking, briekwerking; ~ **adjuster,** remsteller, brieksteller; ~ **band,** briekband, remband; ~ **block,** briekblok, remblok; ~ **cam,** brieknok, remnok; ~ **chain,** briekketting, remketting; ~ **check,** brieketoets, remtoets; ~ **cheek,** briekwang, remwang; ~ **control,** briekbeheer, rembeheer; ~**-control valve,** briekbeheerklep, rembeheerklep; ~ **cylinder,** brieksilinder, remsilinder; ~ **device,** briektoestel, remtoestel; ~ **drum,** briektrom(mel), remtrom(mel); ~ **failure,** briekweiering, remweiering; ~ **fluid,** briekvloeistof, remvloeistof; ~ **force,** briekkrag, remkrag; ~ **gear,** briektoestel, remtoestel; briekwerk, remwerk; ~ **horsepower,** remperdekrag, briekperdekrag; ~ **lag,** naloop; ~ **less,** sonder brieke (remme); ~ **lever,** briek, rem; briekhefboom, remhefboom; briekhandvatsel, remhandvatsel; ~ **light,** brieklig(gie), remlig(gie); ~ **lining,** briekvoering, remvoering; ~ **load,** remlas, brieklas; ~ **man,** briekwerker, remwerker, remmer, brieker; ~ **mechanism,** briektoestel, remtoestel; ~ **pad,** briekkussing, remkussing; ~ **pedal,** briek(pedaal), rem(pedaal); ~ **power,** briekkrag, remkrag, ~**pressure,** briekdruk, remdruk; ~ **pulley,** briekskyf, remskyf; ~ **rod,** briekstang, remstang; ~**s,** briek(e), remme; ~ **shaft,** briekas, remas, ~ **shoe,** briekskoen, remskoen; ~**s man,** brieker, remmer, briekdraaier, remdraaier; ~ **spider,** briekstel, remstel; ~ **spindle,** briekspil, rempsil, ~ **squeal,** briekgeskreeu, remgeskreeu, briekgeluid, remgeluid; ~ **system,** briekstelsel, remstelsel; ~ **test,** brieketoets, remtoets; ~ **torque,** briekwringing, remwringing; ~ **tube,** briekpyp, rempyp; ~ **valve,** briekklep, remklep; ~ **van,** kondukteurswa, goederewa.
bra'king, briek, gebriek, remming; briekwerking remwerking; ~ **effort** briekkrag, remkrag; ~ **force,** ~ **power,** briekkrag, remkrag; ~ **propeller,** briekskroef, remskroef; ~ **surface,** briekvlak, remvlak.
brak'thorn, brakdoring.
brak'y, ru, doringrig, woes.
bram'ble, braam(bos).
bran, semels; ~ **bread,** semelbrood.
bran'card, draagbaar.
branch, (n) (-es), tak; vertakking, arm, sytak; filiaal, bykantoor, takkantoor; stand, been; vak, afdeling; (v) takke gee; vertak, in takke verdeel; ~ *AWAY,* vertak; ~ *OFF,* wegdraai; vertak, afdraai; ~ **bank,** takbank; ~ **business,** bykantoor, filiaal; ~ **circuit,** takkring, takbaan.
branch'ia, kieu; ~**l,** kieu-; ~**l arch,** kieuboog; ~**l cleft,** kieuspleet.
branch: ~**ing,** vertakkend; ~**less,** sonder takke; ~ **line,** sylyn, taklyn; ~ **manager,** takbestuurder; ~ **meeting,** takvergadering; ~ **office,** takkantoor; ~ **railway,** takspoorweg; ~ **road,** uitdraaipad; ~ **wire,** aansluitdraad; ~**y,** met baie takke.
branch'iopod, kieupotige.
brand[1], (n) merk, brandmerk; stigma, skandvlek; brandende hout; toorts (digterlik); kwaliteit; soort, fabrikaat, handelsmerk; (v) brand(merk); kenmerk; uitbrand; onteer; inbrand; merk; ~ *some one,* iem. brandmerk.
brand[2], (n) swaard.
brand,[3] (n) brand(siekte); roes.
brand'(ing) iron, brandyster; drievoet.
bran'dish, swaai, slinger.
brand'-new, (spik)splinternuut, vonkelnuut, blinknuut, gloednuut.
brand switching, produkwisseling, produkruil.
bran'dy, (...dies), brandewyn, hardehout, lawaaiwater; *home-distilled* ~, witblits, mampoer; ~**-ball,** likeurlekker; ~**-snap,** gemmer-ouel.
bran: ~ **food,** semelkos; ~ **gruel,** semelkos, semelwater; ~ **mash,** semelvoer, semelpap; ~**ny,** semelagtig; ~ **poultice,** semelpap; ~ **tea,** semelwater.
brash, (n) gruis, brokkelrots; rommel (met snoeityd); (a) parmantig, domastrant; ~**ness,** parmantigheid, domastrantheid, vermetelheid.
brass, geelkoper; hardestel; koperinstrumente; messing; skaamteloosheid; pitte; geld; brons; offisier; *BIG* ~, leërowerheid; *as BOLD as* ~, oormoedig;

not one ~ *FARTHING,* geen blou(e) duit nie; *get down to* ~ *TACKS,* tot die kern van 'n saak gaan; spykers met koppe slaan; **B**~ **Age,** Bronstyd- (perk); ~**ie,** (obs.), tweehout (gholf); ~ **age,** muntkoste; ~**ard',** armband; armplaat; ~ **band,** blaasorkes; ~**erie,** bierhuis; bierkroeg; ~**-foil,** klatergoud; ~ **founder,** kopergieter; ~ **foundry,** kopergietery; ~ **furniture,** geelkoperbeslag; ~ **hat,** offisier; ~**ie,** houtstok (gholf).
bras'sica, brassica.
brass'ière, buustelyfie, brassière.
brass: ~ **ingot,** geelkoperstaaf; ~**-knuckles,** boksyster; ~ **pipe fittings,** geelkoperpyptoebehore; ~ **plate,** naambord; ~**-rod,** geelkoperstaaf; ~ **rule,** geelkoperlynstafie (drukk.); ~**-sheet,** geelkoperplaat; ~ **strip,** geelkoperreep; ~ **tape,** messingband; ~**ware,** geelkoperware; ~ **wedding,** koperbruilof; ~ **wire,** koperdraad; ~**-works,** kopergietery; ~**y** (a) koperagtig, koper-; onbeskaamd, astrant.
brat, rakker, snuiter, skreeubek, snotneus; *a spoilt* ~, 'n bedorwe brokkie.
bratt'ice, afskorting, skerm.
braun'ite, brauniet, mangaanerts.
brava'do, (-es, -s), grootpratery, bluf, snoewery, bravado.
brave, (n) dappere, held; Indiaanse vegter (krygsman); (v) uitdaag, braveer; tart; trotseer; ~ *it out,* die hoof bied, uithou; (a) dapper, stoer, moedig; flink, kranig, onverskrokke.
brave'ly, moedig, dapper.
brav'eries, opsmuk.
brav'ery, dapperheid, moed, stoerheid, onverskrokkenheid; pronkery, opskik, praal.
braviss'imo! baie mooi!; bravissimo!
bra'vo, (n) (-es, -s), sluipmoordenaar, gehuurde moordenaar; (interj) pragtig! skote P(r)etoors! mooi! mooi skoot! bravo!
bravur'a, bravour(sang)stuk.
brawl, (n) rusie, twis, relletjie; lawaai; (v) twis, rusie maak; lawaai maak; bruis, kletter; ~ **er,** rusiemaker; bakleier; breker; ~**ing,** skreeuend, twistend.
brawn, spier; spierkrag; sult, hoofkaas; ~**iness,** spierkrag; gespierdheid.
brawn'y, gespier(d), sterk.
brax'y, miltvuur (in skape); dooie skaap.
bray, (n) gebalk (van esel); gesketter (van trompette); (v) skreeu soos 'n esel, balk; sketter; fyn stamp (in vysel); ~**ing,** geskal.
braze, verbrons, staal; sweissoldeer, (hard)soldeer.
braz'en, (v) brutaal maak; ~ *it out,* brutaal volhou; jou astrant gedra; (a) koper-; brons-; hard, metaalagtig; astrant, onbeskaamd; *the* ~ *ALTAR,* die koperaltaar; *BE* ~, 'n bord voor die kop hê; *the* ~ *SERPENT,* die koperslang; ~**-faced,** onbeskaamd; ~**ness,** koperagtigheid; onbeskaamdheid.
bra'zier[1], (n) kopersmid.
bra'zier[2], (n) konfoor; vuurblik, kolepan, konka.
Brazil', Brasilië; ~**ian,** (n) Brasiliaan; (a) Brasiliaans.
brazilin', brasilien (kleurstof); ~ **acid,** brasiliensuur.
Brazil': ~**-nut,** kokeleko, paraneut, Brasiliaanse neut; ~**-wood** Brasiliaanse hout.
braz'ing, hardsoldering; sweissoldering; ~ **alloy,** sweissoldeersel; sweislegering, sweisallooi; ~ **lamp,** (hard)soldeerlamp; ~ **metal,** sweissoldeersel; ~ **solder,** sweissoldeersel; ~ **soldeertang;** ~ **wire,** hardsoldering; sweissoldeerdraad.
breach, (n) (-es), breuk; bres; skeur; gat; deurbraak (van dyk); verbreking (van troubelofte); rusie; oortreding; ~ *of CONTRACT,* kontrakbreuk; ~ *of DUTY,* pligsversuim; ~ *of FAITH,* troubreuk; ~ *of PEACE,* vredebreuk, burgerrug, rusverstoring; ~ *of PROMISE,* verbreking van troubelofte; *STAND in the* ~, in die bres tree; *STEP into the* ~ *for someone,* in die bres tree vir iem.; ~ *of TRUST,* misbruik van vertroue; (v) 'n gat deur maak, deurbreek; opspring uit die water (walvis).
bread, (n) brood; (v) paneer, met krummels (voor)berei; *eat the* ~ *of ADVERSITY,* brood der smarte eet; *eat the* ~ *of AFFLICTION,* die brood der verdrukking eet; *man cannot live by* ~ *ALONE,* 'n mens kan van brood alleen nie leef nie; *BREAK* ~,

bread-and-butter

eet; Nagmaal gebruik; *BROWN* ~, growwebrood, bruinbrood; ~ *and BUTTER*, brood en botter; bestaan, broodwinning; ~ *and BUTTER affairs*, sake wat jou bestaan raak; *know on which side one's* ~ *is BUTTERED*, sy eie voordeel ken; *his* ~ *is BUTTERED on both sides*, sy mes sny aan albei kante; *eat the* ~ *of CHARITY*, genadebrood eet; *COARSE* ~, growwebrood; *EARN one's* ~, sy brood verdien; *EAT the* ~ *of idleness*, ledig wees; *LEAVENED* ~, gerysde (gesuurde) brood; ~ *of LIFE*, lewensbrood; *a* ~ *-and-butter MISS*, skooldogter; *QUARREL with one's* ~ *and butter*, in jou eie lig staan, jouself benadeel; ~ *and SCRAPE*, dun gesmeerde brood; *ask for* ~ *and be given a STONE*, klippe vir brood kry; *TAKE the* ~ *out of someone's mouth*, die brood uit iem. se mond neem; *better half a loaf THAN no* ~, 'n halwe eier is beter as 'n leë dop; *cast your* ~ *upon the WATERS*, werp jou brood op die waters; *WHITE* ~, witbrood.
bread-and-butter, brood-en-botter, nuttig, alledaags; prakties; ~ **education,** beroepsonderig, beroepsonderwys, praktiese onderrig (onderwys); brood-en-botteronderrig, brood-en-botteronderwys; ~ **miss,** skoolmeisie, bakvissie; ~ **politics,** brood-en botterpolitiek, praktiese politiek; ~ **pudding,** broodpoeding; ~ **study,** brood(-en-botter)studie, praktiese studie.
bread: ~ **-and-cheese,** brood-en-botter, botter-enbrood (soort malva); ~ **and milk,** brood-en-melk(pap), broodpap; ~ **bag,** broodsak; ~ **baker** (brood)bakker; ~ **-baking,** broodbak(kery); ~ **-basket,** broodmandjie, maag, pens; *hit someone in the* ~ *-basket*, iem. op (in) sy maag slaan, iem. in sy ete-en-drinke slaan; ~ **bin,** broodtrommel, broodblik; ~ **board,** broodbord, broodplank; ~ **cart,** broodkar, broodwa; ~ **cloth,** brooddoek; ~ **corn,** broodkoring; ~ **crumb,** (brood)krummel; ~ **-crumb machine,** krummelmeul; ~ **crumbs,** (brood)krummels; paneermeel; ~ **crust,** (brood)korsie; ~ **cube,** broodblokkie; ~ **cutter,** broodsnyer; ~ **-cutting machine,** broodsnymasjien; ~ **delivery truck,** brood(afleverings)wa; ~ **dish,** broodbak, broodbord; ~ **flour,** broodmeelblom; ~ **-fruit,** broodvrug; broodboom; ~ **-fruit tree,** broodboom, sikadee; ~ **grain,** broodgraan, broodkoring; ~ **ing,** (brood)krummels; ~ **knife,** broodmes; ~ **less,** sonder brood, broodloos; ~ **less diet,** dieet sonder brood, broodlose dieet; ~ **lessness,** broodloosheid; ~ **line,** broodlyn, behoeftepeil, bestaansminimum; *live under the* ~ *line*, onder die broodlyn (bestaansminimum) lewe; ~ **-making,** broodbak(kery); ~ **pan,** broodpan; ~ **plate,** broodbord; broodplaat; ~ **poultice,** broodpap; ~ **queue,** broodtou; ~ **roll,** broodrol(letjie); ~ **sauce,** broodsous; ~ **slicer,** broodsnyer, broodsnymasjien; ~ **soup,** broodsop; ~ **stick,** broodstok(kie); stokbrood; ~ **stuffs,** broodmeel, broodkoring, broodgraan; bakgoed.
breadth, breedte; wydte, uitgestrektheid, wydheid; ruimte; strook, baan; visie, breë blik, ruime siening (opvatting); *to (within) a hair's* ~, op 'n haar, uiters noukeurig (presies); ~ **ways,** ~ **wise,** breedweg; *in die breedte*
bread: ~ **tin,** broodblik; ~ **tray,** broodbord; ~ **truck,** broodwa; ~ **winner,** broodwenner, broodwinner, broodgediener.
break¹, (n) brik (rytuig).
break², (n) steuring, leemte, serie (spel); verbreking, skeur, breuk; pouse, rus, onderbreking; oorgang (mus.); afskeiding; afbrekingsteken; breekslag (rugby); breekbal (kriek.); *at* ~ *of DAY*, met dagbreek; *all ROUND* ~, afsydige seriestoot (biljart); ~ *in SERVICE*, diensonderbreking; *WITHOUT a* ~ *or pause*, een stryk deur; aan een stuk; sonder onderbreking; (v) **(broke, broken),** breek, verbreek, verstoor, versteur; fnuik (planne); deurslaan (stem); vernietig; geleidelik meedeel (nuus); leer (perd), afrig; aanbreek (dag); uitput (kragte); uitbars; bot; hom voordoen aan; kleinmaak (geld); laat bankrot raak (bank); daal (mark); ophou (met reën); ~ *ADRIFT*, losbreek; ~ *AWAY*, losbreek; hande-uit ruk; afsplits; ~ *a BANK*, 'n bank laat spring; ~ *the BACK of*, oor die hond se stert wees;

~ *BOUNDS*, wegloop; ~ *BREAD with someone*, met iem. saameet; ~ *CAMP*, kamp (laer) opbreek; ~ *COVER*, uit sy skuilplek kom; ~ *of DAY*, dagbreek; ~ *DOWN*, inmekaarsak, beswyk; in trane uitbars; bly steek; teëspoed kry; onklaar raak; ontleed; ~ *EVEN*, sonder verlies uitkom; ~ *a FLAG*, 'n vlag ontplooi; ~ *a lance FOR*, 'n lansie breek vir; ~ *FORTH*, losbars; ~ *GROUND*, met iets begin, aanvoor; ~ *oneself of a HABIT*, 'n gewoonte afleer; ~ *into a HOUSE*, inbreek; ~ *the ICE*, die ys breek; ~ *IN*, touwys maak, mak maak, tem; afrig; inloop, inry (motor); ~ *a JOURNEY*, 'n reis onderbreek; ~ *a LAW*, 'n wet oortree; ~ *LOOSE (free)*, uitbreek, hand-uit ruk; ~ *NEWS*, tyding meedeel; ~ *OFF*, uitmaak, afbreek; ~ *OFF an engagement*, 'n verloofskap uitmaak; ~ *an OFFICER*, 'n offisier ontslaan; ~ *OPEN*, oopbreek; ~ *OUT*, losbreek, uitbreek; uitbars; ~ *a PROMISE*, 'n belofte breek; ~ *a RAND*, 'n rand kleinmaak; ~ *the RANKS*, uit die gelid tree; ~ *a RECORD*, 'n rekord slaan (verbeter); ~ *REIN*, stilhou; ~ *a horse to the REIN*, 'n perd touwys maak; ~ *the SABBATH*, die Sabbat ontheilig; *SCHOOL* ~ *s up*, die skool sluit; ~ *SOMEONE*, iem. se nek breek; iem. ten onder bring; ~ *SURFACE*, opkom, bo kom; ~ *UP*, sloop; *it* ~ *s in UPON me*, ek word daarvan bewus; *his VOICE begins to* ~, sy stem begin wissel (deurslaan); ~ *on the WHEEL*, radbraak, ledebraak; ~ *a (butter)fly on the WHEEL*, 'n muggie met 'n hamer doodslaan; mossies met kanonne skiet; ~ *a lance WITH someone*, teen iem. redeneer; ~ *WITH someone*, vriendskap met iem. beëindig, aan iem. vaarwel sê; ~ *one's WORD*, die gegewe woord breek; ~ **-able,** breekbaar; ~ **-action revolver,** nekbrekerrewolwer; ~ **age,** breek; brekasie; breekskade; wat gebreek het; ~ **away,** (v), wegbreek; afbreek; afskei; afsplinter, rus, ontspan; (n), wegbreek, wegbreking; afbreking; afskeiding; afsplintering, ontspanning, rus; ~ **-away movement,** wegbreekbeweging (rugby); ~ **-away state,** afgeskeide staat; ~ **-bone fever,** beenbreekkoors.
break'down, instorting; defek; teenspoed, oponthoud; ongeluk; bedryfsteuring; ontleding; indeling; uiteensetting; ~ **crane,** noodkraan; ~ **gang,** noodspan, hulpspan, noodhelpers; ~ **lorry,** teëspoedwa, takelwa, hulpwa; herstelmotor; ~ **party,** noodspan; ~ **service,** teenspoeddiens, (in)sleepdiens; ~ **team,** noodspan; ~ **tractor,** uitsleeptrekker; ~ **train,** hulptrein; ~ **truck,** ~ **van,** herstelwa, sleepwa, noodwa.
break: ~ **er,** breker, afbreker; verbreker; golf, brander; temmer; ~ **ers,** branders, branding; ~ **er strip,** skokstrook.
break-even, (v), gelykbreek; ~ **point,** gelykbreekpunt; winsdrempel.
break'fast, (n) ontbyt, môre-ete, agtuur; *AT* ~, aan (by) die ontbyt; *it is ONLY a* ~, dis 'n klein sakie; dis 'n nietigheid; ~ *ONly* ontbyt; die oggendete nuttig; ~ **cereal,** ontbytgraan; ~ **nook,** eethoekie; ~ **roll,** broodrolletjie; ~ **room,** ontbytkamer; ~ **run,** ontbytrit (motorfietse).
break'ing, breek, breking, brekery; ~ **burden,** breeklas; ~ **-in,** temming; ~ **-load,** breekbelasting; ~ **-point,** breekgrens; *NEAR (the)* ~ *-point*, tot bregkens toe; *REACH the* ~ *-point*, die breekpunt bereik; ~ **-stress,** breekspanning; ~ **-through,** deurbraak; ~ **-up value,** sloopwaarde; ~ **-weight,** breekbelasting.
break'neck, gevaarlik, halsbrekend; waaghalsig; *at* ~ *speed*, in dolle vaart; ~ **pace, speed,** woeste (dolle) vaart.
break: ~ **-out,** ontsnapping, uitbraak; ~ **-through,** deurbraak; *make a* ~ *-through*, 'n deurbraak maak.
break'-up, ontbinding, splitsing (van party); uitmekaargaan; sluiting (van skole).
break'water, hawehoof, seehoof, golfbreker, seewering, stroombreker.
bream¹, (n) brasem, blinkvis.
bream², (v) skoon brand (skip)
breast, (n) bors; boesem, skoot; gemoed; gewete; *MAKE a clean* ~ *of it*, alles opbieg; alles bely (er-

ken); ~ *the TAPE*, die lint breek; (v) die hoof bied aan, trotseer; klief (water); ~ **bone**, borsbeen; ~ **cancer**, borskanker; ~**-collar**, borsboog; ~**-fed baby**, borsbaba; ~**-feed**, aan die bors voed; ~*-feed a child*, 'n kind self voed; ~**-high**, borshoogte; ~**-piece**, borsplaat; ~**-pin**, dasspeld; ~**-plate**, borsplaat, borsharnas; ~**-plough**, omslagploeg; ~ **pocket**, borssak; ~**-pump**, ~**-reliever**, borspomp; ~**-shield**, borsskild; ~**-stoping**, horisontale afbou(ing); ~**-stroke**, borsslag, borshaal; ~**-wall**, borswering; skans; ~**-wheel**, skeprat; ~**-work**, borswering, skans.

breath, asem, luggie, windjie; asemhaling, ademtog, asemstoot; klank; wasem; *ALL in one* ~, in een asem; *AT a* ~, in een asem; *a* ~ *of FRESH air*, vars lug; *GASP for* ~, na asem snak; *GET one's* ~, op asem kom; *HOLD one's* ~, die asem ophou; *KEEP your* ~ *to cool your porridge*, stil bly, swyg; ~ *of LIFE*, 'n noodsaaklikheid; *MENTION in one* ~, in een asem noem; *OUT of* ~, uit-asem; *PAUSE for* ~, asem skep; *RECOVER one's* ~, weer op asem kom; *TAKE (draw)* ~, asemhaal; *it TOOK his* ~ *away*, dit het hom verstom laat staan; *UNDER (below) one's* ~, fluisterend, binnensmonds; *WASTE one's* ~, jou asem mors; in die wind praat; verniet vra; *you're WASTING your* ~, jy vra verniet; ~ **alyser**, ~ **analyser**, asemtoetser, asemontleder, asemverklapper; ~**-consonant**, stemlose konsonant; ~ **control**, asembeheer.

breathe, asem, asemhaal; slaak, lug gee; laat blaas (perde); blaas; uitasem; uit, fluister; ~ *AGAIN*, weer kan asemhaal; ~ *FIRE*, vuur en vlam spoeg; ~ *FREELY*, vry (kan) asemhaal; ~ *one's LAST*, die laaste asem uitblaas; die gees gee; *don't* ~ *a WORD of it*, moenie 'n woord daarvan rep nie.

breath'er, luggat; ruspouse, blaaskans; ~ **pipe**, asempyp, lugpyp; ~ **plug**, gaatjieprop; ~ **ring**, gaatjiering.

breath'ing, asemhaling, asemtog, aspirasie; ~ **apparatus**, asemhalingstoestel; ~**-control**, asem(halings)beheer; ~**-exercise**, asemhalingsoefening; ~**-hole**, luggat; ~**-mark**, asemteken (musiek); ~**-pore**, asemporie; ~**-space**, blaastyd, blaaskans; versagting; rustyd; (oop) ruimte; *allow* ~*-space*, laat blaas; 'n blaaskans gee; ~**-time**, rustyd; ~**-tube**, asemslurp (gasmasker).

breath'less, asemloos, ingespanne; uitasem; leweloos; ~ **ness**, leweloosheid; aamborstigheid.

breath'-taking, asembenemend, asemrowend.

breath'y, ruiserig; asemrig.

brec'cia, breksie, breccia; ~ **te**, breksieer.

bred, *kyk* **breed**, (v).

breech, (n) (-es), agterste; agterlaaier; slot (geweer); broek, boud (van dier); agterstuk (kanon); *wear the* ~*es*, die broek dra, baasspeel; (v) pak gee, ooptrek; broek aantrek; ~**-action**, sluittoestel; ~ **block**, slot, sluitstuk, agterstuk; ~ **bolt**, grendel; ~ **buoy**, broekboei; ~ **ed**: *before he was* ~ *ed*, toe hy nog 'n snuiter was; toe hy nog kortbroek gedra het; ~ **es**, broek; broekwol; ~ **ing**, pak slae; rybroekmateriaal; kanontou; broek (van 'n tuig); ~**-laces**, rybroekveters; ~ **less**, sonder broek; broekloos; ~**-loader**, afbreekgeweer, agterlaaier; ~**-loading**, agterlaaier=; ~ **mechanism**, sluittoestel; sluitmeganisme; ~ **presentation**, stuitligging (geboorte); ~ **wool**, broekwol.

breed, (n) geslag, ras, soort; (v) **(bred)**, (aan)teel, voortteel; (uit)broei; baar; veroorsaak; voortbring; oplei, opvoed; ~ *bad BLOOD*, kwaad bloed set; rusie veroorsaak; ~ *IN*, inteel, in dieselfde bloed teel; *WHAT is bred in the bone*, wat ingebore is, oorerflike trekke; ~ **er**, teler, veeboer; kweker; ~ **er reactor**, kweekreaktor; ~ **er material**, kweekstof; ~ **ers**, aanteelvee, aanteelgoed.

breed'ing, verwekking; veroorsaking; teelt; opvoeding, beskawing; beesboerdery, veetelery; *GOOD* ~, goeie maniere, welgemanierdheid; *a MAN of good* ~, 'n welopgevoede persoon; *for* ~ *PURPOSES*, vir aanteel; ~**-animal**, teeldier; ~**-bird**, broeivoël; ~**-cattle**, aanteelvee; ~**-ewe**, teelooi; ~**-ground**, broeiplek; ~**-pen**, aanteelhok; broeitoom (hoenders); ~**-place**, broeiplek; ~**-pond**, (aan)teel=

dam; ~**-season**, paartyd; ~**-stock**, aanteelvee, aanteelgoed; ~**-time**, teeltyd.

breeze[1], (n) bries, luggie, windjie; standjie, rusie; (v) sag waai.

breeze[2], (n) steekvlieg, perdevlieg.

breeze[3], (n) kooks, smidskool; sintel, gruis; ~**-block**, ~**-brick**, assteen, sintelsteen; ~**-coal**, smidskole; ~**-concrete**, sintelbeton.

breez'y, lugtig, winderig; lewendig.

Bren: ~**-carrier**, Brenvegrusper; ~ **gun**, Brenmasjiengeweer; ~**-gunner**, Brenskutter.

brent'(-goose), (..geese), brandgans, boomgans, rotgans.

brer, (Am. E.) broer.

breth'ren, broeders; ampsbroers.

breve, volmag, mandaat; dubbelnoot; kortteken; brevis.

brev'et, (n) brevet, rang; (v) rang verleen.

brev'iary, (..**ries**), brevarium, brevier, getydeboek.

brevican'date, kortstert=.

brevier', brevier (lettertipe).

brev'iped, kortpotig.

brevipenn'ate, kortvlerkig.

brev'ity, kortheid, beknoptheid; ~ *is the soul of wit*, kort maar kragtig; vernuf word deur kortheid gekenmerk; kortheid is die kern van vernuf.

brew, (n) treksel; brousel; mengsel; (v) laat trek; brou; gis; broei; opstook; *as you* ~, *so you will BAKE*, soos jy saai, sal jy maai; ~ *MISCHIEF*, kwaad stig; ~ **age**, brousel, treksel; ~ **er**, brouer; ~ **er's grains**, brouersgraan; ~ **ery**, (..**ries**), brouery; ~**-house**, brouery; ~ **ing**, brou; gebrou; *something is* ~ *ing*, daar is iets aan die broei, daar broei iets; ~ **ing-vat**, broukuip.

bri'ar = **brier**.

bribabil'ity, omkoopbaarheid.

brib'able, omkoopbaar.

bribe, (n) omkoopgeld, omkoopprys; (v) omkoop; ~ **e'**, omgekoopte (persoon); ~ **r**, omkoper; ~ **ry**, omkopery.

bric'-a-brac, snuisterye, rariteite, bric-a-brac.

brick, (n) baksteen; staatmaker, doring, ryperd; blok; *A* ~, 'n regte ou doring; 'n agtermekaar kêrel; *you ARE a* ~ *!* jy is 'n doring! *DROP a* ~, sy mond verbrand (verbypraat); *a REGULAR (an absolute)* ~, 'n regte ou doring; *one cannot make* ~ *s without STRAW*, 'n mens kan nie sonder 'n hand vuis maak nie; *TRY to make* ~ *s without straw*, met nat hout wil vuur maak; (v) (toe)messel; ~ *up*, toemessel; (a) baksteen=, van baksteen; ~ **bat**, stuk baksteen; kritiek; onvriendelike opmerking (aanmerking); ~**-coloured**, baksteen(kleurig); ~**-dust**, steengruis; ~**-field**, steenbakkery, steenmakery; ~**-floor**, steenvloer; ~**-hammer**, bikhamer; ~**-house**, (bak)steenhuis; ~**-kiln**, steenoond; ~ **layer**, messelaar; ~ **layer's hammer**, steenhamer; ~**-laying**, messel(werk); ~**-lining**, steenvoering; ~**-maker**, steenmaker, steenbakker; ~**-making**, steenbakkery; ~**-mould**, steenvorm; ~**-moulder**, steenvormer; ~**-nogging**, steenvoering, steeninvoeging; steenlaag; ~**-red**, (bak)steenrooi; ~ **road**, klinkerpad; ~ **trowel**, messeltroffel; ~ **veneer**, oplegbou; ~ **wreath**, bruidsblom (krans).

brid'al, (n) troufees; bruilof; (a) bruids=, trou=; ~**-cake**, bruidskoek; ~ **chamber**, bruidskamer; ~ **couple**, bruidspaar; ~ **heath**, heide (uit Albertinia); ~ **suite**, wittebroodskamerstel; ~ **veil**, bruidsluier; ~ **wreath**, bruidsblom (krans).

bride[1], band (van kappie); netwerk (van kant).

bride[2], bruid; ~ *to BE*, aanstaande bruid; *BLUSHING* ~, trots van Franschhoek, bergbruidjie *(Serruria florida)*; *the* ~ *is GOTTEN*, die bruid is in die skuit, nou is die mooi praatjies uit; ~**-bed**, bruidsbed; ~**-cake**, bruidskoek; ~ **groom**, bruidegom.

brides'maid, strooimeisie, bruidsmeisie; *be always the* ~, *never the bride*, nooit die paal eerste haal nie.

brides'man, (..**men**), strooijonker, bruidsjonker.

bride'well, verbeteringsgestig.

bridge[1], (n) brug; oorloop (trein); vioolkam; brug (van neus); *never cross a* ~ *until you come to it*, moenie die bobbejaan agter die bult gaan haal nie, moenie moeilikhede vooruitloop nie; (v) oorbrug; 'n brug slaan (lê) oor; ~ *over*, oorbrug.

bridge², brug (kaartspel); *AUCTION* ~, opjaagbrug, opveilbrug, gewone brug; *CONTRACT* ~, kontrakbrug.

bridge: ~-**builder**, brugbouer; ~-**building**, brugbou, brugkonstruksie; ~ **deck**, brugdek.

bridge'drive, brugparty, brugwedstryd.

bridge: ~ **engineering**, brugboukunde; ~ **head**, brughoof, vastrapplek; ~ **keeper**, ~ **man**, brugwagter; ~ **piece**, spanstuk; ~ **pipe**, brugpyp; ~ **plate**, brugplaat; ~ **player**, brugspeler; ~ **train**, ponttrein; ~ **work**, brugwerk; brugkonstruksie.

bridg'ing, brugbou, brugmateriaal; koppelbalk; ~-**beam**, koppelbalk; ~-**joist**, stutbalk; ~-**party**, brug(slaan)span; ~-**site**, brugopslagplek.

bri'dle, (n) toom, teuel; beteueling; breidel; beuel (myn); *put the* ~ *on someone*, 'n stang in die bek sit; iem. met 'n stang ry; (v) 'n toom aansit, optoom; beteuel; intoom, inhou; ~-**bit**, toomstang; ~-**hand**, linkerhand; ~-**joint**, toomboeg, dubbelpenvoeg, breidelvoeg; ~-**lock**, toomsluiting; ~-**path**, rypad; voetpad; ~-**rein**, teuel; ~-**shy**, kopsku.

bridoon', trens.

brief¹, (n) opdrag; volmag; uiteensetting, dossier; instruksie; pouslike nabetragting; (pl) o.a. knapbroekie; *I HOLD no* ~ *for*, ek verdedig nie; ek het nie opdrag nie; *OBTAIN a* ~, 'n saak kry, 'n opdrag kry; (v) in hoofpunte saamvat; 'n saak aan 'n advokaat gee, opdrag gee, instrueer.

brief², (a) kort; beknop, bondig; *to BE* ~, om kort te gaan; *IN* ~, kortom; ~ *and to the POINT*, kort en bondig.

brief: ~-**bag**, ~-**case**, aktetas; boeksak; dokumentetas; advokaattas; ~ **ing**, opdrag, instruksie; ~ **less**, sonder opdrag; sonder praktyk; ~ *less barrister*, advokaat wat nie sake kry nie.

brief: ~ **ly**, kortom, kortliks; ~ **ness**, kortheid, beknoptheid, bondigheid.

bri'er, wilderoos, doringstruik, ~-**pipe**, heidewortelpyp; ~ **y**, doringrig.

brig, brik, seilskip.

brigade', brigade.

brigadier', brigadier; brigadier-kommandant; **b** ~-**general**, (~ **s-general**), brigadegeneraal.

brig'and, rower; struikrower; ~ **age**, struikrowery.

brig'antine, skoenerbrik, brigantyn.

bright, helder, skitterend, glansend; lig; skoon; opgewek, geestig, lewendig, vernuftig, verstandig; ~ *LOOKS*, opgeruimde voorkoms; *the* ~ *SIDE*, die ligkant; die blink kant; ~ **bolt**, blinkbout.

bright'en, verlig, verhelder, helder maak; opklaar; opvrolik; ~ *up*, optleur, opvrolik; opklaar; blink maak.

bright'-eyed, helderogig, blinkoog=.

bright'ness, helderheid, glans; opgeruimdheid; vlugheid, lewendigheid; verstandigheid, knapheid.

Bright's disease, siekte van Bright.

brill, griet, platvis.

brill'iance, bril'liancy, glans, luister, skittering, helderheid, blinkheid, genialiteit, briljantheid, skranderheid.

brill'iant, (n) juweel; geslypte diamant, briljant; diamantletter; (a) glinsterend, glansryk, skitterend; skrander, geniaal, briljant; *a* ~ *CONVERSATIONALIST*, 'n skitterende geselser; ~ *DUST*, blinkstof, skitterstof, briljantstof; ~ **ine**, haarolie, haarpommade, brilliantine.

brim, (n) rand, boord, kant; (v) (-med), vol maak, vol skink; oorloop; ~ *with*, oorloop van; ~ **ful**, propvol, boordevol, oorlopens toe vol; ~ **less**, sonder rand; ~ **mer**, vol glas (koppie); ~ **ming**, propvol; ~ *ming over with mischief*, vol kattekwaad.

brim'stone, swa(w)el, sulfer; **fire and** ~! vuur (donder) en bliksem!

brin'dle(d), geelbruin, gestreep, gespikkel(d), briekwa=; ~ **gnu**, blouwildebees.

brine, (n) pekel(water), soutwater; die see; trane; (v) insout, pekel; ~ **deposit**, pekelafsetting, soutafsetting.

bring, (**brought**), bring, saambring; veroorsaak; aanvoer; opbring; aanbring; ~ *ABOUT*, teweegbring; tot stand bring; *to be brought ABOUT*, sy beslag kry; ~ *an ACTION (charge) against*, 'n saak maak teen; ~ *BACK*, terugbring; herinner; ~ *to BEAR*, laat geld; ~ *to BOOK*, afreken met; ~ *a CLAIM against*, 'n eis instel teen; ~ *to COURT*, voor die gereg bring; ~ *up to DATE*, bywerk; ~ *DOWN*, afbring; neerskiet, omkap; verminder; ~ *someone DOWN heavily*, iem. plant (rugby); iem. plattrek; ~ *FORTH*, voortbring, baar; ~ *FORWARD*, oordra, transporteer (boekhou); indien; aanvoer; voortbring; ~ *in (a verdict of) GUILTY*, skuldig verklaar; ~ *up by HAND*, met die bottel grootmaak; hans grootmaak; ~ *HOME*, iem. iets inskerp; iets op die hart druk; oortuig van; ~ *down the HOUSE*, algemene byval vind; ~ *to LIGHT*, aan die lig bring; ~ *LOW*, laat agteruitgaan; ~ *to MIND*, in herinnering roep; ~ *OFF*, red; 'n sukses maak van; ~ *ON*, veroorsaak; opbring; laat anker; te voorskyn bring; ~ *it ON oneself*, jou iets op die hals haal; ~ *OUT*, uitbring; aan die dag bring; publiseer; uitdruk, duidelik vertoon; ~ *OVER*, oorbring, vervoer; oorhaal; bekeer; ~ *to PASS*, teweegbring; tot stand bring; ~ *into PLAY*, aan die gang sit; ~ *up the REAR*, agteraan kom, die agterhoede vorm; ~ *ROUND*, (iem. weer) bybring; meebring; ~ *THROUGH*, deurhaal; ~ *UNDER*, baasraak; ~ *UP*, grootmaak; opvoed; voorbring (saak), voor die hof bring; onder die aandag bring; op die lappe kom; ~ *something UPON oneself*, daarna soek; self die oorsaak wees van iets; ~ *in a VERDICT*, uitspraak gee (doen); ~ *into the WORLD*, in die wêreld bring; ~ **and buy sale**, bring-en-koopveiling; ~ **and buy tea**, bring-en-koop-tee(party); ~ **er**, bringer.

bring'ing-up, opvoeding.

brin'iness, siltigheid, soutigheid.

brin'jal, brinjal, eiervrug.

brink, rand, (water)kant; *on the* ~ *of*, op die rand van.

brink'manship, risikoneming, risikobeleid.

brink' of death, op die randjie.

brin'y, (n): *the* ~, die see; (a) pekelagtig, sout(erig), silt.

briquet, briquette', briket.

brisk, (v) verlewendig, aanwakker; versnel; (a) lewendig, monter, wakker, opgewek, flink, gou; ~ *up*, aanwakker, aanvuur.

brisk'et, bors, borsstuk, borsvleis; onderbors (perd).

brisk'ly, flink.

brisk'ness, lewendigheid, wakkerheid, opgewektheid.

bri'stle, (n) varkhaar, borsel, (pl) borselhare; *set up one's* ~ *s*, kwaad word; (v) van borsels voorsien, kwaad (verontwaardig) word; styf maak; regop staan; ~ *UP*, opvlieg; ~ *WITH*, wemel van, vol wees van; ~**d**, borselrig, stekelrig, hard; ~ **grass**, steekgras; - **worm**, borselwurm.

brist'ling, vererg, kwaad.

Brit'ain, Brittanje; *Great* ~, Groot-Brittanje.

Britann'ia, Britannia; ~ *metal*, britanniametaal.

Britann'ic, Brittannies.

britch, broek; ~ **wool**, broekwol (vgl. **breech(es)**).

Brit'icism = **Britishism**.

Brit'ish, Brits; ~ **er**, Brit.

Brit'ishism, Britse uitdrukking; Britse eienaardigheid.

British raj, Britse raj, Britse regering (bestuur) (Indië).

Brit'on, Brit.

Britt'any, Bretagne.

brit'tle, (a), bros, breekbaar; broos; brokkelrig; (n), broslekker; ~ **ness**, brosheid, breekbaarheid, broosheid.

broach, (n) spit; rubeitel; els, (tand)priem, (stoot)ruimer; boor; toringspits; (v) ter sprake bring, opper; aansteek, oopmaak (vat); aanboor, deurstoot; oopslaan; na die wind draai; ~ *a subject*, iets ter sprake bring; iets te berde bring.

broad, (n) breedte; vroumens (Am.); *the* ~ *of the BACK*, die naat van die rug; (a) breed, wyd, ruim, groot, uitgebrei; helder, grof, plat; onomwonde, onverbloemd; vry, ongewonge; algemeen; vrysinnig, verdraagsaam, liberaal; ru, smerig; *a* ~ *AC*=

CENT, 'n breë uitspraak; ~ *DAYLIGHT*, helder oordag; ~ *DIALECT*, egte dialek; ~ *GAUGE*, breë spoor; *a* ~ *HINT*, 'n duidelike wenk; *in* ~ *OUTLINE(S)*, in breë trekke; *as* ~ *as it is LONG*, om die ewe, so lank as wat dit breed is; ~ *SCOPE*, breë veld; *a* ~ *SMILE*, 'n stralende glimlag; *a* ~ *STARE*, 'n onbeskaamde aanblik; *a* ~ *STORY*, 'n growwe verhaal; ~ **acres**, wye velde; ~ **arrow**, hoenderspoor; ~ **axe**, strydbyl; houtkappersbyl; ~**-beaked**, met 'n breë bek, breëbek=; ~ **bean**, boer= boon; ~**-bill**, lepelaar; wilde-eend; swaardvis; ~**-breasted**, breed van bors, breëbors=; ~**-brimmed**, breërand=, met breë rand.

broad'cast, (n) uitsending; (v) **(-ed,** ~**)**, rondstrooi; uitsaai; saai; (a, adv) wyd en syd versprei; ~ **application**, saaitoediening; ~ **band**, uitsaaiband; ~ **er**, omroeper, uitsaaier; ~**ing corporation**, uitsaaikor= porasie; ~**ing service**, radiodiens, uitsaaidiens, om= roep; ~**ing station**, uitsaaistasie, radiostasie; ~ **speech**, radiorede; ~ **talk**, radiopraatjie.

broad: ~**cloth**, swartlaken; ~**en**, breed maak, ver= breed; verruim (die gees); rek; ~**ened**, verbreed; ~**ening**, verbreding, verruiming; ~**loom**, (n) breedgetou; (a) breedgeweef; ~**ly**, breed, onbe= krompe, breedgesind; duidelik; globaal; ~ **minded**, ruimhartig, onbekrompe; ~**mindedness**, ruimheid van opvatting, ruimhartigheid, liberaliteit, onbe= krompenheid; ~**ness**, breedte, wydte; grofheid; platheid (spraak); ~**side**, lang kant; volle laag; ~**sword**, slagswaard; ~ **tail**, breëstertpels; ~**-tail sheep**, vetstertskaap; ~**wise**, in die breedte.

brocade', brokaat, goudlaken; ~**d**, brokaat=; gebor= duur; geblom.

broc'(c)oli, spruitkool, spruitjies, winter(blom)kool.

brochure', brosjure, pamflet.

brock, ratel; stinkerd.

brock'et, tweejarige hert, spieshert, spiesbok.

brog, els.

brogue[1], gewestelike spraak; Ierse aksent.

brogue[2], lae skoen; (soort) velskoen; brogue.

broil[1], (n) braaivleis; (v) braai, rooster; bak (in die son).

broil[2], (n) rusie, rumoer, getwis; (v) twis, rusie maak.

broil'er[1], braaihoender, roosterkuiken, jong slag= hoender.

broil'er[2], rusverstoorder.

broil'ing, vuurwarm; ~ *hot*, skroeiend warm.

broke[1], (n) penswol, stukkies.

broke[2], (v) *kyk* **break**; as makelaar optree; (a) ge= breek; bankrot, platsak.

bro'ken, gebreek, stukkend, geknak, morsaf; touwys (perd); moedeloos, verslae; ongesteld; gebroke, on= gelyk (veld); ~ *white LINE*, onderbroke wit streep; *be* ~ *OFF*, uitraak; *he is a* ~ *REED*, jy kan nie op hom staatmaak nie; ~ *SLEEP*, versteurde slaap; *SPEAK* ~ *English*, gebroke Engels praat; ~ *AFRIKAANS*, gebroke (geradbraakte) Afrikaans; ~ **brick**, steenslag; ~ **colours**, saamgestelde kleure; ~ **country**, rantjiesveld; bankeveld; ~**-down**, inge= stort; gebroke, terneergeslae, ellendig; ~ **fleece**, ge= breekte vag (wol); ~ **ground**, gebroke terrein; on= gelyke grond; ~**-hearted**, met 'n gebroke hart, ver= pletter(d); baie treurig, hartseer; ~ **home**, gebroke (ontwrigte) huis(gesin); ~ **line**, gebroke lyn; los ar= tikels; ~ **lot**, los klompie; ~ **ly**, onsamehangend, met rukke en stote; ~ **man**, moedelose man; ~ **meat**, oorskietvleis; ~ **money**, kleingeld; ~ **num= ber**, breuk(getal); ~ **promise**, gebroke belofte; ~ **range**, onvolledige reeks; ~ **reed**, gebroke (ge= knakte) riet; ~ **soil**, weggevrete grond; ~ **tea**, fyn tee; ~ **time**, verlore tyd; ~ **water**, onstuimige wa= ter; ~ **weather**, onsekere weer; ~**-winded**, kort= asem, flou; dampig; ~**-winded horse**, floukop; ~**-windedness**, dampigheid; ~ **wing**, gebreekte vlerk.

bro'ker, makelaar, agent; ~ **age**, makelaarsloon; agentskoste; provisie; ~ **age firm**, makelaarsfirma; ~ **'s note**, koopbriefie.

brokes, brokkies (wol).

brok'ing, makelary.

broll'y, (brollies), sambreel.

brom'al, bromaal.

brom'ate, bromaat.

brom'ic, broom=.

brom'ide, bromied, bromide.

brom'inate, bromeer.

brom'ine, broom.

bronc'hial, lugpyp=; brongiaal; ~ **tube**, lugpyp.

bronch'iole, longpypie, brongiool.

bronchit'ic, brongities.

bronchit'is, lugpypontsteking, brongitis.

bronch'ium, (..**chia**), longpyp, lugpyp.

bronch'opneumonia, lugpypontsteking, brongitis.

bronch'oscope, longpypspieël, brongoskoop.

bronch'us, longpyp.

bron'co, (-s), halfwilde perd; perd, bronco; ~**-buster**, perdetemmer.

bronto'meter, brontometer, onweermeter.

brontosaur'us, brontosourus.

bronze, (n) brons; bronsfiguur; bronskleur; (v) ver= brons, 'n brons kleur gee; verbrand; bruin brand, sonbrand; (a) brons=; bronskleurig; **B** ~ **Age**, Bronstydperk; ~ **bearing**, bronslaer; ~ **bushing**, bronsbussing; ~**-coloured**, bronskleurig; ~ **cuc= koo**, diederik; ~ **medal**, bronsmedalje; ~ **welding**, bronssweis.

bronz'ing, sonbrand, bruinbrand; verbronsing; bronspoeier; ~ **ite**, bronsiet.

bronz'ite, bronsiet.

bronz'itite, bronsitiet.

brooch, (-es), borsspeld.

brood, (n) broeisel; gebroedsel; gespuis; jongby; (v) broei; uitbroei; bedreig; sin, peins, oordink, be= peins; ~ **body**, broeiliggaam(pie), broeiknop; ~ **cell**, broeisel; ~ **chamber**, broeikas; ~ **er**, kuns= moeder; broeikas; ~**-hen**, broeihen; ~ **iness**, broeisheid; ~ **ing**, broei; ~**-mare**, aanteelmerrie; ~ **stock**, teelvee; ~**-time**, broeityd; ~ **y**, broeis.

brook[1], (n) spruit, lopie, beek.

brook[2], (v) verdra, uitstaan, veel, doog, duld; ~ *no interference*, geen bemoeiing duld nie.

brook'ite, brookiet.

brook'let, stroompie, spruitjie.

broom, (n) besem; veër; brem (plant); *new* ~ *s sweep clean*, nuwe besems vee skoon; (v) vee, besem; ~**-corn**, heidekoring, besemkoring. ~ **cupboard**, be= semkas; ~ **grass**, besemgras.

broom'stick, besemstok; *JUMP (marry) over the* ~ , agter die bos trou; oor die puthaak trou; *PLY the* ~ , onder die besemstok steek.

broth, kragsop.

broth'el, hoerhuis, bordeel, huis van ontug.

broth'er, (-s, brethren), broer, boet; vriend; ~ *of the BRUSH*, medeskilder; ~ *GERMAN* volle broer; *HALF* ~ , halfbroer; ~ *of the QUILL*, medeskry= wer; *SMITH Bro(ther)s*, gebr(oeders) Smith; ~ *UTERINE*, broer van moederskant; ~**hood**, bro(ed)erskap; ~**-in-arms**, wapenbroer; ~**-in-law**, **(-s-in-law)**, swaer; ~**liness**, broederlikheid; ~ **ly**, broederlik.

brough'am, (geslote) koets.

brought, *kyk* **bring**: *be* ~ *about*, beslag kry.

brow, wysbrou, winkbrou; voorkop; kruin, rand (berg); lip (van myn); *knit one's* ~ *s*, frons; ~ **beat**, **(browbeat, browbeaten)**, kwaai aankyk; oorbluf, oordonder, intimideer, uit die veld slaan; ~**-box**, lipkas.

brown, (n) bruin (kleur); (v) bruin maak; bruin word; bruin braai; bruineer; (a) bruin; donker; somber; ~ *ed OFF*, kwaad; buikvol; ~ *ed POTATOES*, bruingebraaide aartappels; *in a* ~ *STUDY*, diep in gedagte; ~ **beans**, bruin boontjies; ~ **bear**, bruin= beer; ~ **booby**, bruinmalgas; ~ **bread**, growwe= brood, bruinbrood; ~ **coal**, bruinkole, ligniet; ~**-eyed**, bruinoog=; ~ **fleck**, bruinvel(siekte); ~ **hyena**, strandjut; ~ **ibis**, hadida.

brown'ie, gees, kabouter, aardmannetjie; padvind= ster; (klein) kamera.

Brow'nian movement, Brownbeweging, beweging van Brown, Browniaanse beweging.

brown: ~ **ing**, bruineersel; bruinsel; bruining (vleis); bruinwording; ~**ish**, bruinerig, bruinagtig; ~ **loaf**, bruinbrood; ~ **locust**, bruinsprinkaan; ~ **mite**, bruinmiet; ~**ness**, bruinheid; ~ **paper**, pakpapier,

bruinpapier; ~ **rust**, roes (by koring); **B** ~ **Shirt,**
Bruinhemp; ~ **stone**, bruinsteen; ~ **sugar**, bruin=
suiker, goewermentsuiker; ~**ware**, bruin erde=
werk; ~ **wool**, lieswol.
browse, (n) eerste uitspruitsels, jong lote; takvoer; (v)
(op blare) wei, afvreet, afknabbel; grasduin.
brow'sel, kaiings.
brow'ser, blaarvreter.
brr, brr, soe, sjoe.
brucello'sis, brusellose, maltakoors.
bru'cin(e), brusien, brusine.
bru'cite, bruciet.
Bruges, Brugge; ~ **lace,** Brugse kant.
Bru'in, Bruin (die beer).
bruise, (n) kneus(plek), stamp(plek); (v) kneus, stamp; seermaak (gevoelens); ~**d**, gekneus, ge=
kraak, gestamp; ~**r**, vegter, bokser.
brui'sing, kneusing; ~ **action,** kneusing.
bruit, (n) gerug; geruis, gedruis (med.); *much* ~ *little FRUIT,* groot lawaai, weinig wol, meer lawaai as wol; (v): ~ *about*, iets aan die groot klok hang.
brum'al, winteragtig; mistig.
brume, mis, newel.
brum'ous = **brumal**
brunch, (sl.) noenontbyt; vroeë middagmaal.
brunette', brunet, swartkop, swartoog.
Bruns'wick, Brunswyk.
brunt, skok, heftigheid; hewige aanval; hoogtepunt, krisis; skerpte; *bear the* ~ *of the ATTACK,* die spit afbyt in die aanval; *he will have to BEAR the* ~, alles sal op hom neerkom.
brush, (n) (**-es**), borsel; penseel, kwas; jakkalsstert; kreupelhout; skermutseling; (v) borsel; verf, aan=
raak, stryk langs, skuur langs; vee; skaaf (vel); ~ *ASIDE,* opsy stoot, verbygaan; ~ *AWAY,* wegvee, wegpink (traan); wegborsel; negeer; ~ *BACK,* ag=
tertoe (agteroor) borsel; ~ *OUT,* uitborsel; ~ *OVER,* stryk langs; oorverf; ~ *PAST,* verbyskuur; ~ *UP,* opfris, opknap; ~ *UP knowledge,* kennis opknap; ~ **fabric,** pluisstof; ~ **fire,** veldbrand; ~**-fire war,** veldoorlog, plaaslike oorlog; ~**ing,** bor=
sel, borselwerk; ~**ing-boot,** aanklapkous, aanklap=
kussinkie (perd); ~**less,** sonder kwas; ~ *less cream,* skeersmeer; ~**-off,** (v), afjak, afsnou; ~ **pencil,** penseel; ~ **plate,** borselplaat; ~ **resistance,** borsel=
weerstand; ~ **rocker,** borseltuimelaar; ~**-set,** bor=
selstel; ~ **spring,** borselveer; ~ **stroke,** kwashaal; penseelstreep; ~**ware,** borselware; ~**-wire,** borsel=
draad, ~**wood,** ruigte, fynruigte, kreupelhout; ~**work,** skilderwerk; penseeltegniek, kwastegniek; ~**y,** stekelrig; ruig.
brusque, kortaf, ru, bruusk; ~**ness,** kortafheid, bruuskheid.
Bruss'els, Brussel; ~ *LACE,* Brusselse kant; ~ *SPROUTS,* spruitkool, Brusselse spruitjies.
brut'al, dierlik, honds, onmenslik, beesagtig, wreed=
aardig, onbeskof; brutaal; *the* ~ *FACTS,* die naak=
te feite; *a* ~ *MURDER,* 'n wreedaardige moord.
brutal'ity, onmenslikheid, dierlikheid, wreedheid.
brutaliza'tion verdierliking, ontaarding.
brut'alize, verdierlik; verlaag.
brute, (n) redelose dier; onbeskofte mens; woesteling, wreedaard, onmens, derduiwel, onverlaat, ondier; (a) redeloos; dierlik, ru, onbeskof, sinlik, bruut; dom; *the* ~ *CREATION,* die onbesielde skepping; *use* ~ *FORCE,* brute geweld gebruik.
brut'ish, dierlik, wreed, bruut, ru; dom; ~**ness,** dier=
likheid, wreedheid, domheid.
bryol'ogist, brioloog, moskenner.
bryol'ogy, briologie, moskunde.
bry'ony, wildewingerd, brionie.
bub, (colloq.), pram.
bub'ble, (n) waterblaas; blasie; lugbel; seepbel; skyn; iets verganklik; hersenskim; windhandel; bobbel; *prick the* ~, die seepbel prik; (v) borrel, blaas, prut=
tel, (op)wel, bobbel, bruis, opborrel; ~ *over with LAUGHTER,* uitbars van die lag; ~ *OVER,* oor=
loop, oorborrel; ~ *UP,* uitborrel; ~ *and squeak,* opgewarmde groentegereg; oorskietkoolgereg; ~ **car,** doppie(motor); ~**-company,** swendelmaat=
skappy; ~ **gum,** blaasgom, bobbelgom, klapkou=
gom.

bub'bling, (n) borreling (verf); (a) borrelend, kokend.
bub'bly, (n) sjampanje; (a) borrelend; ~**-jock,** kal=
koenmannetjie.
bub'o, (**-es**), kliergeswel.
bubon'ic, buile=; ~ *plague,* builepes, rottepes.
buc'cal, wang=; ~ *cavity,* wangholte.
buccaneer', (n) seerower, boekanier, vrybuiter; (v) 'n seerowersbestaan voer; ~**ing,** vrybuitery, seerowe=
ry.
bucc'inator, wangspier.
Buch'arest, Boekarest.
buch'u, boegoe; ~**-brandy,** boegoebrandewyn.
buck¹, (n) bokram; mannetjie; fat, modegek; *old* ~! ou doring! (v) spring; bokspring; steeks wees, kop tussen die bene steek (perd); ~ *one OFF,* iem. af=
gooi; *it* ~*s YOU up,* dit gee jou moed; dit fleur jou op; ~ *UP,* gou maak.
buck², (n) loogwater (looiery); (v) in loog was.
buck³, (n) bak, buik, fuik.
buck⁴, (n) saagbok.
buck⁵, (n) dollar (Am.); *pass the* ~, verantwoordelik=
heid ontduik (afskuif).
buck'-ashes, loogas.
buck'bean, boksboon; waterklawer.
buck'board, ligte karretjie.
buck: ~**ed,** opgemonter, uitgelate; in sy noppies; ~**er,** springer.
buck'et¹, (n) emmer; bak; pompsuier; koker (vir sweep); *kick the* ~, bokveld toe gaan; (v) skep (by roei).
buck'et², (v) ja, vinnig ry.
buck'et: ~**-chain,** emmerketting; ~ **conveyor,** bak=
vervoerder; ~ **elevator,** bakkieshyser; ~**ful,** em=
mervol; ~**-hook,** puthaak; ~**-measure,** emmer=
maat; ~**-pump,** bakkiespomp; ~ **seat,** komsitplek= (motor); komstoel; ~**-shop,** knoeikantoor vir aan=
delespekulasie; dobbelkantoor, onwettige wed=
plek; ~ **system,** emmerstelsel; ~ **tilting,** vaatjie=
steek; ~ **valve,** bakklep; ~**-wheel,** skeprat.
buck'ing, bokspring.
buck'ing-tub, loogbak, loogkuip.
buck'ish, fatterig, hanerig, windmakerig.
buck'jump, bokspring.
buc'kle, (n) gespe; beuel; verbuiging (wiele); (v) vas=
gespe; omgord; baktrek, kromtrek, omkrul; buig; ~ *TO,* aangord; 'n werk aanpak; ~ *UP,* opkrul; inmekaarsak; vasgord.
bu'ckled, gebuig; gegespe; ~ **shoe,** gespeskoen; ~ **wheel,** gebuigde (krom) wiel.
buck'ler, skild, beukelaar, rondas.
buck'ling, buiging, (ver)kromming; ~ **load,** kniklas, knikbelasting; ~ **strength,** kniksterkte; ~ **stress,** knikspanning.
buck' rabbit, mannetjieskonyn.
buck'ram, (n) stywe linne, styflinne, boordjiegaas, hoedestyfgaas; stywigheid; (a) styf.
buck' reef, dooierif.
buck'sail, bokseil.
buck'-saw, boksaag.
buck: ~**shot,** bokhael, lopers; ~**-skin,** bokvel, bokskyn; ~ **skins,** rybroek; ~**-stick,** grootprater; ~**-tooth,** uitsteektand; *have* ~*-teeth,* haaitande hê.
buck'-waggon, bokwa.
buck'wheat, bokwiet, bokweit.
bucol'ic, (n) herdersang, herdersdig; (a) herderlik, landelik, bukolies; ~**s,** herdersgedigte.
bud, (n) knop, bot, uitloopsel; ent; *be IN* ~, in die knop staan; *NIP in the* ~, in die kiem smoor; (v) (**-ded**), bot, uitloop; ontluik; ent.
Buddh'a, Boeddha.
Buddh'ism, Boeddhisme.
Buddh'ist, (n) Boeddhis; (a) Boeddhisties.
budd'ing, (n) ent, okulering; (a) in die dop; ontlui=
kend; aankomende; ~ **feeling,** ontluikende gevoel; ~**-knife,** okuleermes; ~ **politician,** politikus in die dop.
bud'dle, (n) wasvat, wastoestel; (v) erts was.
budd'y¹, (n) (**buddies**), vriend, maat.
budd'y², (a) vol bloeisels.
budge, verroer, beweeg; *not* ~ *an inch,* g'n voetbreed wyk nie; geen duimbreed padgee nie; *refuse to* ~, viervoet vassteek, nie kopgee nie.

budgerigar   754   *bullion*

budgerigar', parkiet, budjie, grasparkiet.
budg'et, (n) leersak; pak; begroting; (v) begroot, voorsiening maak; ~ *for,* daarvoor beraam (begroot); ~ **ary**, begrotings~; ~ **committee**, begrotingskomitee; ~**ing**, begroting; ~*ing method,* begrotingsmetode; ~ **sale**, spaaruitverkoping; ~ **shop**, spaarwinkel, afslagwinkel; afbetalingswinkel; ~ **speech**, begrotingsrede.
budg'ie = budgerigar.
bud: ~ **rot**, knopvrot (siekte); ~ **union**, okuleerlas; ~ **wood**, enthout, okuleerhout.
buff, (n) buffelleer; buffelsvel; (lig)geel beesleer; afskuurder; paradyskleed; fynskuurskyf; *in the ~,* naak, in Adam se pak (klere); (v) afskuur (buiteband); fynskuur; poleer, polys; (a) liggeel, dofgeel.
buff'alo, (-es), buffel; ~**-bean**, hokkiespeul; ~**-fly**, ~**-gnat**, buffelvlieg; ~**-grass**, buffel(s)gras; ~**-hunt**, buffeljag; ~**-nut**, olieneut; ~**-thorn**, blinkblaar-wag-'n-bietjie; ~ **weaver**, buffelwewer.
buff'er[1], sukkelaar; *old ~,* ou sufferd, ou sukkelaar.
buff'er[2], stampkussing, stootkussing, stootblok, buffer.
buf'fer: ~ **beam**, stootbalk; ~ **block**, stootblok; ~ **cell**, tussensel; ~**ing**, bufferwerking; ~ **pad**, stootkussing; ~ **plate**, stootplaat; ~ **state**, bufferstaat; ~ **strip**, bufferstrook.
buff'et[1], (n) klap, slag, hou; (v) slaan, beuk; worstel.
buff'et[2], (n) buffet, toonbank; ~ **supper**, buffetete.
buff'ing, afskuring, polering, polysting; ~ **machine**, poleermasjien, polysmasjien.
buff' leather, poetsleer.
buffoon', (n) grapmaker, fratsemaker, harlekyn, nar; (v) die gek skeer; jou bespotlik maak; ~**ery**, grapmakery, gekskeerdery, apespel, harlekynstreke.
bug, (n) gogga, insek; kewer; (wee)luis; luistervink, afluisteraar, meeluisteraar; *big ~,* hoë meneer, grootmeneer, belangrike ou; (v), afluister, meeluister, inluister.
bug'aboo, bug'bear, paaiboelie, gogga, gô, weerwolf, skrikbeeld.
bugg'er, bokker, vent, bees, swernoot; sodomiet; ~**y**, sodomie.
bug'ging, afluistering, meeluistering; ~**-device**, klikapparaat, klikker; afluistertoestel, luisterapparaat.
bugg'y[1], (n) **(buggies)**, bokkie (rytuig); besie, insek, gogga.
bugg'y[2], (a) vol weeluise.
bug'-hunter, goggasoeker, insektekundige.
bu'gle[1], slingerplant.
bu'gle[2], glaskraal.
bu'gle[3], (n) beuel, trompet; (v) op 'n horing blaas; ~ **band**, beuelkorps; ~ **bead**, buiskraal; ~**-call**, beuelgeblaas; ~**-horn**, beuel; ~**r**, trompetter, beuelblaser; ~ **sound**, beuelgeskal; oproep (tot aksie); ~**-string**, beuelkoord; ~**-weed**, senegroen.
bug'loss, ostong (plant).
bug'-tree, luisboom.
buhl, buhl-inlêwerk, boule.
buhr'stone, braamsteen.
build, (n) bou, liggaamsbou, vorm, gestalte; boustyl; (v) **(built)**, bou; stig, aanlê; slaan (brug); oprig; maak; ~ *IN,* inmessel, toebou; ~ *ON,* aanbou; verhoogde pad; ~ *UP,* opbou; ~ *UPON,* hom verlaat op; ~ **er**, bouer, kontrakteur, bouaannemer; ~**er's knot**, kniehalterslag; ~**er's staging**, bousteierwerk.
buil'ding, gebou; bouwerk, bouery; konstruksie; ~ **alteration**, verbouing; ombouing; ~ **bee**, bouby; ~ **block**, boublok; bousteen; ~ **board**, boubord; ~ **bylaw**, bouverordening; ~ **clerk**, bouklerk; ~ **committee**, boukomitee; boukommissie; ~ **company**, boumaatskappy; ~ **contractor**, bouaannemer; ~ **concern**, bouersfirma, bouonderneming; ~ **control**, boubeheer; ~ **density**, terreindekking, bebouingsdigtheid; ~ **engineer**, bouingenieur; ~ **industry**, boubedryf, bounywerheid; ~ **inspector**, bouinspekteur; ~ **land**, bougrond; ~ **leasehold**, boureg; woonreg; ~ **lime**, messelkalk; boukalk; ~ **line**, bougrens; ~ **material**, boumateriaal; ~ **plan**, bouplan; ~ **plot**, bouperseel; ~ **programme**, bouprogram; ~ **project**, bouplan; ~ **regulation**, bouregulasie, bouverordening; ~ **sand**, bousand; ~ **site**,

bouterrein; ~ **society**, bouvereniging, bougenootskap; ~ **stone**, bouklip; ~ **surveyor**, bourekenaar; bouopmeter; ~ **timber**, bouhout; ~ **trade**, boubedryf, bouvak; ~ **worker**, bouwerker, bouvakarbeider.
build'-up, ophemeling.
built'-in, ingebou; ~ *cupboard,* ingeboude kas.
built'-up, bebou (gebied); opgebou; verhoog (pad); ~ **area**, beboude gebied; ~ **road**, verhoogde pad.
Bulaway'o, Bulawayo.
bulb, bol, bolletjie; blombol; knol; gloeilamp; peer (van 'n termometer); horingbal (perdepoot); *electric ~,* gloeilamp.
bulba'ceous, bolvormig.
bulb'ar, bulbêr.
bulb: ~**-end**, dik ent (paal); ~ **if'erous**, boldraend; ~ **iform**, bolvormig; ~ **let**, bolletjie; ~ **ose**, bolagtig, bol-; ~ **nose**, knopneus; ~ **ous**, bolagtig, bol-; ~ *ous plant,* bolgewas; ~ **rot**, bolvrot; ~ **scale**, bolskub; ~ **tube**, glaskolf, bolbuis.
bul'bul, geelgat, tiptol, pietkluitjiekorrel.
Bulgar'ia, Bulgarye; ~**n**, (n) Bulgaar; (a) Bulgaars.
bulge, (n) buik (van 'n vat); ruim (van 'n skip); bult, knop; uitsetting; boepens; *get the ~ on,* die oorhand kry oor; (v) swel, uitsit; uitpeul; bult, puil, laat uitstaan; uitbol; ~ **eye**, uitpeuloë (skaapsiekte).
bul'gy, uitpuilend, uitstaande, bol.
bulim'ia, bul'imy, geeuhonger, sieklike vraatsug.
bulk, (n) omvang, volume, grootte; grootmaat; (skeeps)lading; vrag; klomp; massavoorraad; massa, gevaarte; meerderheid; vulstof (voedsel); *BUY in ~,* by die groot maat koop; *IN ~,* los; in grootmaat; (v) lyk, vertoon; ~ *LARGE,* groot lyk; ~ *UP,* ophoop, opstapel; ~ **cargo**, massavrag; stortvrag; ~ **density**, massadigtheid; ~ **grain**, los graan; stortgraan; ~**head**, (be)skot, afskorting; ~*head type,* skottipe; ~**iness**, dikte; grootte; ~ **storage**, massaopberging; ~ **stores**, stortgoedere; ~**-test**, massatoets, grootmaattoets; ~**y**, groot, swaarlywig, dik; omvangryk, groot; ~**y wool**, digvselwol.
bull[1], (n) bul; mannetjie; *a ~ in a CHINA SHOP,* 'n aap in 'n porseleinkas (glaskas); 'n bul in 'n glashuis; 'n kalf in die wingerd; *HIT the ~ 's-eye,* in die kol skiet; pastersteek skiet; *take the ~ by the HORNS,* die bul by die horings pak; *SCORE a ~ (~ 's eye),* die doel tref.
Bull[2], (n) Stier (sterrek.).
bull[3], (n) pouslike bul.
bull[4], (n) stygspekulant; ~ *s and bears,* styg- en daalspekulante; (v) op styging spekuleer.
bull[5], (n) kolskoot, kol.
bull[6], (n): *an Irish ~,* 'n bewering met 'n grappige teenstrydigheid.
bull'ace, wildevrug; wildepruim.
bull: ~**ary**, bullarium; ~**-baiting**, bultergery; ~**-calf**, bulkalf; uilskuiken; ~ **dog**, Bulhond, boelhond; dapper persoon; ~ **doze**, (v) stootskraap, plat stoot, gelyk stoot (skraap); oorrompel; intimideer, afknou; ~ **dozer**, stootskraper, olifantstoter, olifantskrop, olifantskraper; oorrompelaar, platveêr; afknouer, intimideerder; dwangmiddel; ~ **elephant**, olifantbul.
bull'et, koeël, bloubonntjie; hak (perd); *every ~ has its BILLET,* elke koeël het sy bestemming; *all his ~ s are SPENT,* al sy kruit is verskiet (weggeskiet); al sy pyle is weggeskiet; *STOP (be given) a ~,* 'n koeël kry; ~**-case**, koeëlhuls; ~**-head**, ronde kop; dikkop; ~**-headed**, rondkoppig, rondekop-.
bull'etin, daaglikse rapport, bulletin; pamflet.
bull'et: ~**-jacket**, koeëlmantel; ~ **mould**, koeëlvorm; **proof**, koeëlvry, koeëlvas; ~ **wound**, koeëlwond.
bull: ~**fight**, stiergeveg, bulgeveg; ~**fighter**, stiervegter, bulvegter, matador; ~**fighting**, stiervegtery, bulvegtery; stiergeveg, bulgeveg; ~**finch**, (-es), geelvink, goudvink; ~ **frog**, brulpadda, donderpadda; ~**-headed**, koppig; ~ **hippopotamus**, seekoeibul; ~**-holder**, neusknyper; ~ **horn**, luidspreker.
bull'ion[1], goudfraaing, silwerfraaing.
bull'ion[2], spesievoorraad, edelmetaal, staafgoud,

staafsilwer, ongemunte goud of silwer; muntme=
taal; *trade in* ~, spesiehandel; ~ **stitch,** roossteek.
bullish, bulagtig; stygend.
bull: ~ **ock,** os; ~ **ock cart,** oskar; ~ **market,** bul=
mark, stygmark; ~ **mastiff,** kettingbul(hond),
bulbyter; ~**neck,** bulnek, dik nek; ~**nose,** ronde
neus, stompneus; ronding; ~*nosed brick,* stomp=
neussteen; ~*nosed plane,* stompneusskaaf; ~ **pup,**
bulhondjie; ~ **ray,** bulrog; ~ **ring,** stierarena, stryd=
perk; neusring; boegring; ~**-roarer,** woer-woer; ~
session, groepsbespreking.
bull's eye, kol; teiken; kolskoot; lensvormige glas;
dekglas (skip); handlantern; deklamp; tieroog (lek=
ker); oog (storm); ~ **lamp,** springhaaslamp; brand=
glaslamp; ~ **target,** kolskyf.
bull: ~ **shit,** (vulg.), stront, kak, onsin, nonsies, non=
sens; ~ **terrier,** Bulterriër, boelterriër; ~ **thistle,**
akkerdistel; ~ **trout,** salmforel.
bull'y¹, (n) **(bullies),** rusiemaker, baasspeler, voorveg=
ter, bullebak, afknouer; donderjaer; (v) **(bullied),**
rusie soek, karnuffel, bluf, treiter, baasspeel, af=
knou; donderjaag.
bull'y², (n) skerm, kap, instok (hokkie); (v) **(bullied),**
skerm, kap, instok (hokkie).
bull'y³, (a) eersteklas, piekfyn.
bul'ly: ~**beef,** boeliebief, blikkiesvleis; ~ **boy,** ge=
huurde sterkman; ~**ing,** (n), afknouery, baasspe=
lery; mishandeling; (a) geniepsig, afknouerig; ~
rag = **bully rag;** ~ **seedeater,** dikbekkanarie, dik=
beksysie; ~ **tree,** bolata.
bul'rush, **(-es),** biesie, matjiesgoed, papkuil, palmiet.
bul'wark, bolwerk, skans, verskansing; hawehoof.
bum, (n) agterste, agterwêreld, sitvlak; rondloper,
klaploper (Amer.); (v) **(-med),** klaploop; leeglê; be=
del; (a) prul=; niksbeduidend.
bum'ble, bode, pedel; parmantige amptenaartjie; ~**-
bee,** hommel(by); ~**dom,** amptenary, burokrasie;
gewigtigdoenery; ~**-foot,** horrelvoet; boetson
(hoendersiekte); ~**-puppy,** knoeispel; ~ **r,** knoeier.
bum'boat, provisieboot.
bumf, (sl.), snipperjag; toiletpapier; paperasse.
bummer, luiaard, leegleër; bedelaar.
bump, (n) slag, stamp; knop; geswel, knobbel; stoot,
bons; *come down to earth with a* ~, skielik die har=
de feite (naakte waarheid) in die aangesig moet
staar; (v) stamp, bots; opspring; ~ *INTO someone,*
teen iem. vasloop; iem. raakloop; ~ *one's HEAD,*
jou kop stamp; ~**-ball,** opslagbal.
bum'per, (n) vol glas, vol beker; buffer, stamper; sto=
ter (van motor); stampveer; (a) oorvloedig, pronk=;
~ **crop,** rekordoes; ~ **crowd,** rekordskare; ~ **sale,**
groot uitverkoping, reuse-uitverkoping; ~ **sticker,**
stamperplakker, bufferplakker; ~ **to bumper,** teen
mekaar, stamper-teen-stamper, buffer-teen-buffer.
bumph, (sl.), gemors, twak.
bump'iness, stamperigheid, hobbelrigheid.
bump'ing, klopwerk (paneelwerk); stampery, ge=
stamp.
bump'kin, lomperd; japie, knop; pampoen(kop);
country ~, plaasjapie.
bump'tious, verwaand, aanmatigend, domastrant,
aanstellerig; *to be* ~, domastrant wees; ~**ness,** ver=
waandheid, domastrantheid; aanstellerigheid.
bum'py, hobbelrig, stamperig.
bun, bolletjie; konyntjie; kondee, haarwrong, bolla
(hare); *that takes the* ~, dit span die kroon; *hot
cross* ~, Paasbolletjie.
Bun'a, Boena.
bunch, (n) **(-es),** bos(sie); bondel; tros (druiwe); rits;
a ~ *of CROOKS,* 'n klomp skelms; *a* ~ *of
GRAPES,* 'n druiwetros; *the WHOLE* ~, die hele
spul; die hele kasarm; die hele santepetiek; (v) bos=
sies maak; openhoop, (saam)bondel; tros (drui=
we); ~**ing,** ophoping; ~**y,** verfrommel, geplooi;
~**y-top (disease),** trostopsiekte (tamaties).
bun'combe = **bunkum.**
bund, kaai, esplanade.
Bun'destag, Bundestag, Duitse parlement.
bun'dle, (n) bondel, gerf, bos, pak, hoop; *a* ~ *of
nerves,* 'n senuweeorrel; (v) inpak; saambind; op 'n
hoop smyt; wegboender; ~ *in,* inboender; ~ *out,*
uitboender.

bund'ling, bondeling; baling; ~**-wire,** baaldraad.
bun'du, gramadoelas, boendoe.
bung, (n) spon (van 'n vat), prop, swik, bom (vat),
tap; (v) toesteek, toemaak; toeprop.
bung'alow, landhuis, (buite)huisie, huthuis, bunga=
low; *seaside* ~, strandhuis, strandbungalow.
bung'-hole, spon(ning)gat, swikgat, sponsgat, bom=
gat.
bun'gle, (n) broddelwerk, knoeiwerk, brouwerk;
lompheid; misoes; (v) brou, (ver)knoei, konkel, op=
dons, verfoes, afjakker; (a) verfoes; ~ **r,** knoeier,
verknoeier, stumper(d), sukkelaar, haspelaar, am=
braal; ~*rs work in the dark,* donkerwerk is konkel=
werk.
bungl'ing, (n) geknoei, knoeiwerk, knoeiery, brou=
werk (a) knoeiend; brou=, knoei=.
bun'ion, toonknobbel, eeltknobbel, knobbeltoon,
knokkel(eelt).
bunk¹, (n) slaapbank, kooi, slaapplek.
bunk², (n) kaf, onsin.
bunk³, (n): *do a* ~, wegsluip; (v) stokkies draai, klas
versuim; dros.
bunk'-bed, kajuitbed, slaapbank.
bunk'er, (n) kolehok (in skip); hinderns; kuil (gholf);
bunker (mil.); (v) kole laai, bunker; ~ **coal,** skeeps=
kool, bunkerkool; ~ **ed,** gekuil; ~ **ing,** bunkering.
bunk'light, kooilig.
bunk'um, onsin, geklets, bogpraatjies; kullery.
bunn'y, (bunnies), konyntjie, hasie; ~ **wool,** donswol.
bun'sen burner, bunsenlamp, bunsenbrander.
bunt¹, buik.
bunt², koringroes, stinkbrand.
bun'-tin, kolwyntjiepan.
bun'ting¹, dundoek, vlagdoek; vlae, vlagversiering,
vlagwappering.
bun'ting², streepkoppie (voël).
buoy, (n) baken (in see), boei; dryftou; (v) drywe; on=
dersteun; ~ *UP,* steun, opbeur, staande hou;
~ **ancy,** dryfbaarheid; veerkrag(tigheid); dryfver=
moë, dryfkrag, stygingsvermoë; hefkrag; lewendig=
heid (mark); ~**ant,** drywend; veerkragtig; opge=
ruimd, lewendig.
bup'restid, pragkewer.
bur, klitsgras; steeksaad; wildeklawersaad; kwas;
baard (van metaal).
bur'ble, borrel; brabbel.
burb'ot, barbot.
bur' clover, klitsklawerplant *(Medicago denticulata).*
burd'en, (n) las, vrag, pak, drag; serwituut (op land);
verantwoordelikheid; beswaar; deklaag (myn); la=
ding, tonne-inhoud; refrein; hooftema (lied),
BEAR one's ~*s,* jou laste dra; *REAST of* ~, las=
dier; *BURDEN of* ~, skuld(e)las; ~ *of PROOF,*
bewyslas; ~ *of SIN,* sondelas; *none knows the
WEIGHT of another's* ~, ander mense se boeke is
duister om te lees; (v) belaai, belas, bevrag; ~**-
bearer,** lasdraer; ~**some,** lastig, beswarend, druk=
kend.
burd'ock, klitsgras; klitskruid.
bu'reau, bureau', (-x), kantoor; buro; skryftafel; *B* ~
of Standards, Buro vir Standaarde.
bureau'cracy, burokrasie, amptenaredom; ampte=
naarsgees; amptenary.
bureau'crat, burokraat, amptenaar; voorstander v.d.
burokrasie; ~**ic,** burokraties; ~**ize,** burokratiseer.
burette', maatglas, buret.
burg, burg, kasteel; stad; dorpie.
burgee', jagvlag.
bur'geon, (n) knop; (v) bot, ontluik.
bur'gess, (-es), burger, kieser.
burgh, dorp, stad.
burg'her, burger; ~**-right,** burgerreg; ~**-watch,** bur=
gerwag.
burg'lar, inbreker; ~**-alarm,** inbraakalarm; ~**'ious,**
soos 'n inbreker; ~**-proof,** diefvry, inbraakvry,
diefdig; ~**-proofing,** diefwering; ~**-proof wire,**
diefdraad; ~**y,** huisbraak; inbraak; ~**y** *IN=
SURANCE,* versekering teen huisbraak; ~**y**
POLICY, inbraakpolis; ~ *RATE,* inbraaksyfer.
bur'gle, inbreek.
burg'omaster, burgemeester.
bur'grave, burggraaf.

Burg'undy, Boergondië.
burg'undy, boergonje(wyn), boergondiese wyn.
bu'rial, begrafnis; ∼-**fund,** begrafnisfonds; ∼ **ground,** begraafplaas, kerkhof; ∼ **hill,** ∼ **mound,** grafheuwel; ∼-**service,** lykdiens, begrafnisdiens; ∼ **site,** graf; ∼ **vault,** grafkelder.
bu'ried, begrawe, onder die sooie; blind (van 'n klip).
bur'in, graveernaald, radeernaald, buryn.
burke, versmoor, smoor; doodswyg; ∼ *the issue,* die saak smoor; iets doodswyg.
burl, (n) (k)nop, knoop; (v) nop (tekstiel); ontklits (wol).
burl'ap, goiing, sakgoed.
burlesque', (n) bespotting, burlesk, parodie; klug; (v) parodieer, bespotlik voorstel; (a) bespottend, kod=dig, grapp(er)ig, burlesk.
bur'ler, nopster.
burl'iness, lompheid; grootheid, omvang; dikte.
bur'ling, ontklitsing; nopwerk.
burl'y, dik, swaarlywig; stewig.
Burm'a, Birma.
Burm'an, Burmese', (n) Birmaan; Birmaans (taal); (a) Birmaans.
burn¹, (n) brandplek, brandwond; (v) (**-t** or **-ed),** (ver)brand, seng; blaker (in son); byt (op tong); gloei, blaak; sterk verlang; aanbrand; verbrou (rolbal); ∼ *AWAY,* verbrand, uitbrand; ∼ *one's BOATS,* sy skepe agter hom verbrand, die terugtog onmoontlik maak; ∼ *the CANDLE at both ends,* jou krag ooreis; vroeg en laat studeer; ∼ *DAYLIGHT,* kunsmatige lig bedags gebruik; ∼ *DOWN,* afbrand; *his EARS* ∼, sy ore tuit; ∼ *one's FINGERS,* die vingers verbrand; ∼ *IN,* inbrand; ∼ *LOW,* flou brand; ∼ *the MIDNIGHT oil,* snags laat werk; *MONEY* ∼ *s holes in his pockets,* geld brand in sy sakke; ∼ *OUT,* doodgaan, uitbrand; ∼ *UP,* verbrand.
burn², (n) stroompie.
burn: ∼-**dressing,** brandwondverband; ∼**er,** brander; pit, lamp.
burn'et, pimpernel.
burn'ing, (n) verbranding; (a) brandend, verlangend; *a* ∼ *question,* 'n brandende vraagstuk; ∼ **bush,** vlamklimop; essekruid; kardinaalsmus; ∼-**glass,** brandglas; ∼-**mirror,** brandspieël; ∼ **pain,** brandpyn; ∼-**point,** brandpunt, vlampunt; ∼ **question,** brandende vraag(stuk); ∼ **scent,** sterk reuk; ∼ **shame,** skreiende skande; ∼ **skin,** branderige vel.
burn'ish, glansend maak, bruineer, polys, poleer, skuur, vryf; glans; ∼**er,** blinkmaker, bruineerder; politoerder; bruineerstaal; bruineernaald; ∼**ing,** glans, bruineersel; skuring, (die) blinkmaak; ∼*ing tool,* bruineerstaal.
burnous(e)', boernoes, Arabiese wit jas.
burnt, verbrand; gebrand; *a* ∼ *child dreads the fire,* ondervinding is die beste leermeester; ∼ **brick,** baksteen; ∼-**ear,** brandkoring; ∼ **flavour,** brandsmaak; ∼ **lime,** gebrande kalk, ongebluste kalk; ∼ **offering (sacrifice),** brandoffer; ∼-**out,** uitgebrand; ∼ **sienna,** gebrande siënna; ∼ **sugar,** karamel.
burp, (n) oprisping, windopbreek, wind; (v), wind opbreek, oprisp; ∼ **gun,** outomatiese geweer (pistool); ∼**less,** windvry.
burr¹, (n) kring om die maan, newelring; bry (spraak); baard (metaal); ongelykheid; skaafplek; saaldroes; braam (beitel); (v) bry (uitspraak van r); onduidelik praat; afbaard.
burr², (n): *stick like a* ∼ *to someone,* soos 'n klits aan iem. klou (vassit); *kyk ook* **bur.**
bur'ro, donkie.
bur'row, (n) (konyne)hol, gat, lêplek; (v) omvroetel, dowwel, woel, vroetel; grawe; in 'n gat woon; 'n loopgraaf maak; ∼ *up,* uitwoel; ∼**ing,** gewroet; ∼**ing animal,** graafdier; ∼**ing insect,** boorder, boorinsek.
burr'y, bebaard, klits=; ∼ *wool,* klitswol.
burs'a, slymbeurs; ∼**l,** slymbeurs=; ∼*l cyst,* slymbeurssak.
burs'ar, penningmeester, tesourier; beurshouer; ∼**y,** (..**ries),** (studie)beurs, stipendium.
bursit'is, slymbeursontsteking.

burst, (n) skeur, bars; uitbarsting, losbarsting; inspanning; fuif; vlaag; springpunt (granaat); sarsie; *ON the* ∼ *(bust),* aan die swier (fuif); (v) **(burst),** bars, skeur; oopbreek; verbreek; oopbars; onderbreek; laat bars; ontluik; afspring; spring (granaat); ∼ *ASUNDER,* uimekaarbars, uiteenbars; ∼ *upon enemy's COUNTRY,* vyandelike gebied oorstroom; *be* ∼*ing with INDIGNATION,* van verontwaardiging kook; ∼ *one's sides with LAUGHTER,* skaterlag; ∼ *OPEN,* oopbars; ∼ *OUT,* losbreek, losbars, uitbars; ∼ *into the ROOM,* die kamer binnestorm; ∼ *into TEARS,* in trane uitbars; ∼ *UPON,* skielik te voorskyn kom; oorval, oorrompel; ∼**er,** springlading; ∼**ing bomb,** springende bom, brisantbom.
burth'en = burden.
bur'weed, boetebossie, pinotiebossie *(Xanthium spinosum).*
bu'ry, (buried), begrawe, bylê; bedek; graaf; verloor (familielede); ∼ *the hatchet,* die strydbyl begrawe; vrede sluit; die swaard in die skede steek.
bu'rying, begrawe; ∼-**ground,** ∼-**place,** begraafplaas, kerkhof.
bus, (-es), (n) bus; *miss the* ∼, die bus nie haal nie; na die maal kom; 'n misoes maak; die kans laat verbyglip; die kans verkyk; *take a* ∼, die bus haal, met die bus ry; (v) **(-sed),** bus ry.
bus'bar, geleistang.
bus'by, (busbies), husaremus, kolbak.
bus: ∼ **conductor,** buskondukteur; ∼ **driver,** busbestuurder, busdrywer.
bush¹, (n) **(-es),** bos(sie), struik; haarbos; bosveld; *BEAT about the* ∼, uitvlugte soek, kleitrap; om iets heen praat; *one beats the* ∼ *and another CATCHES the birds,* die perd wat die hawer (voer) verdien, kry dikwels die strooi; (v) met struike beplant; ruig groei.
bush², (n) bossing (deur); naafbus; (v) bus, bus insit.
bush: ∼ **baby, (..bies),** nagapie, bosapie; ∼ **buck,** bosbok; ∼ **cart,** boskar; ∼ **clearance,** ontbossing; ∼ **country,** bosveld, boswêreld; ∼ **cow,** tapir; Wes-Afrikaanse buffel; ∼ **craft,** veldkennis, veldkuns.
bushed, gebus; bebos; verbaas, verbyster; poot-uit, pê.
bush'el, skepel, boesel, koringmaat; *BY the* ∼, by die vleet; *HIDE your talents under a* ∼, jou lig onder 'n maatemmer verberg; ∼-**basket,** skepelmandjie.
bush: ∼ **fight,** bosgeveg, guerillageveg; ∼-**fighting,** bosoorlog, guerillaoorlog(voering); ∼-**fire,** bosbrand; ∼-**hammer,** beeldhouershamer; klipkappershamer; ∼ **hat,** veldhoed; ∼-**hog,** bosvark; ∼**iness,** bosagtigheid, ruigheid; ∼ **jacket,** bosbaadjie.
bushling, naafbus; bossing (deur); asblokvoering.
bush: ∼ **knife,** kapmes; ∼-**locust,** bossprinkaan; ∼ **man,** (Australiese) bosvelder; veldkenner.
Bush'man (..men), San, Boesman; ∼ **arrow,** Boesmanpyl; ∼ **grass,** boesmangras; ∼ **hare,** vleihaas; ∼ **land,** Boesmanland; ∼ **painting,** Boesmanskildery; Boesmantekening; ∼ **rice,** hottentotsrys, boesmanrys; ∼ **woman,** Boesmanvrou.
bush: ∼-**partridge,** bospatrys; ∼-**pumpkin,** bospampoen; ∼-**ranger,** boswagter; struikrower, bandiet; boslanser; ∼-**rope,** bobbejaantou; ∼ **shirt,** boshemp; bosbaadjie; ∼-**shrike,** boslaksman; ∼ **sickness,** gebreksiekte (diere); ∼-**tea,** blomtee, bossiestee; ∼ **telegraph,** bostelegraaf; ∼-**tick,** bosluis; *B*∼**veld,** Bosveld; ∼-**wacker,** boslanser; ∼ **willow,** vaarlandswilg, rooibos; raasblaar *(Combretum zeyheri);* ∼**y,** bosagtig, ruig; ∼**y tail,** borselstert.
bus'ily, bedrywig, besig, woel(er)ig.
bu'siness, besigheid; handel; beroep; saak, bedryf, werk; (sake)onderneming, winkel; besigheidslewe, sakelewe, besigheidswêreld, sakewêreld; bedryfslewe, bedryfswêreld; handeling, optrede, aktiwiteite (teater); affêre, gedoente; manewales; werskaffery; werskaamheid; ∼ *ACUMEN,* sakebedrewenheid; *no ADMITTANCE except on* ∼, toegang slegs vir sake, slegs vir bevoegdes; *AWAY on* ∼, weg vir sake; uitstedig; *it's a BAD* ∼, dis 'n slegte affêre (gedoente, aangeleentheid); *at the CLOSE of* ∼, by

kantoor=, winkelsluiting; by beurssluiting; ~ *of the DAY*, sakelys, agenda; punt(e) op die agenda; *there being no FURTHER* ~, geen verdere sake word (is) geopper nie (notule); *GET down to* ~, 'n saak (werk) met mening aanpak, jou (ernstige) aandag aan 'n saak wy; ter sake kom, jou by die aange= leentheid bepaal; *do GOOD* ~, goeie (winsgewen= de) sake (besigheid) doen; ~ *in HAND*, lopende sake; *HAS no* ~ *to*, geen reg hê om; *HAVE no* ~ *with*, niks te doen hê met; *be IN* ~, sake doen, 'n saak bedryf; 'n sakeman (winkelier) wees; in werking (aan die gang) wees; ~ *IS* ~, besigheid is besigheid, sake kry voorrang; *MAKE it your* ~, gee aandag aan, sorg vir; dra sorg dat iets gebeur; *MAN of* ~, sakeman, besigheidsman; *MEAN* ~, in erns (ernstig) wees; sake wil doen; dit ernstig be= doel; *MIND your own* ~, bemoei jou met jou eie sake; dit het niks met jou te doen nie, dit traak jou nie; hou jou neus uit my sake uit; *NEW* ~, nuwe besigheid; *you have NO* ~ *to (here)*, jy het geen reg om (hier nie); jy het niks hier te doen (te soek) nie; *like NOBODY'S* ~, buitengewoon, uitsonderlik; *it is NONE of your (my)* ~, dit het niks met jou (met my) te doen nie; *OPEN a* ~, 'n saak (winkel, besig= heid) begin; *make a* ~ *PAY*, 'n saak (besigheid) lonend (betalend) maak; ~ *before PLEASURE*, werk voor plesier, plig gaan voor alles; *PROCEED to* ~, met die werk (sakelys) begin; *PUT out of* ~, 'n nekslag gee; 'n konkurrent (mededinger) uitska= kel; *a QUEER* ~, 'n snaakse besigheid (affêre, ge= beurtenis); *do a ROARING* ~, flink besigheid (sake) doen; 'n florerende bedryf hê, *SEND some= one about (on) his* ~, iem. op sy plek sit (na die hoenders laat gaan); iem. wegja, in die pad steek; *SET up in* ~, begin met sake ('n bedryf, winkel, besigheid); *SICK of the (whole)* ~, moeg (sat vir die (hele) affêre; *a good STROKE of* ~, 'n goeie slag; 'n winskopie; ~ *as USUAL*, sake (besigheid) soos gewoonlik; *WHAT a* ~, wat 'n affêre (ge= mors)!; *sick (and tired) of the WHOLE* ~, siek (en sat vir die hele affêre (die hele spul); ~ **acumen,** sakevernuf, besigheidsvernuf; ~ **address,** sake=, besigheidsadres; ~ **administration,** bedryfsleiding; besigheids=, sakebestuur; bedryfsleer; ~ **area,** sake=, besigheidsbuurt; ~ **arithmetic,** handelsre= kene; ~ **capital,** bedryfskapitaal; ~ **circles,** sake= kringe; ~ **college,** handelskool; ~ **community,** sa= kegemeenskap; ~ **concern,** besigheids=, sakeonder= neming; ~ **course,** bedryfs=, sake=, besigheidskur= sus; kursus in bedryfsleer; ~ **cycle,** besigheidsiklus, besigheidskringloop, sakesiklus, sakekringloop; ~ **economics,** bedryfsekonomie; ~ **executive,** sake= bestuurder, sakeleier; bedryfsleier; besigheidsbe= stuurder; ~ **experience,** sakekennis; besigheidsver= nuf, sakevernuf; besigheids=, sake-ervaring; ~ **girl,** kantoormeisie; ~ **hours,** kantoorure; winkelure; werksure; ~ **interests,** sake=, besigheidsbelange; ~ **leader,** sakeleier; ~ **letter,** sakebrief, besigheids= brief; ~ **like,** metodies, presies; saaklik, saakkun= dig; prakties; ~ **machine,** kantoormasjien; ~ **man,** sakeman, besigheidsman; handelaar; winkelier; ondernemer, entrepreneur; ~ **management,** sake=, besigheidsbestuur; bedryfsleiding; ~ **manager,** be= dryfsleier; sakebestuurder, besigheidsbestuurder; ~ **meeting,** huishoudelike vergadering; ~ **name,** saak=, firmanaam, besigheidsnaam; ~ **place,** besig= heidsplek, sakeplek; ~ **premises,** sake=, besigheids= perseel; ~ **relations,** sake=, handels=, besigheidsbe= trekkinge; ~ **reply card,** besigheidsantwoordkaart; ~ **reply service,** besigheidsantwoorddiens; ~ **science,** handelswetenskap, handelsleer; ~ **sign,** uithangbord; naambord; besigheidsnaam, firma= naam; ~ **studies,** bedryfsleer; ~ **suit,** dagpak, kan= toorpak; ~ **transaction,** sake=, besigheidstransak= sie; ~ **undertaking,** besigheid, saak; sake=, besig= heidsonderneming; ~ **woman,** besigheids=, sake= vrou; ~ **world,** sake=, besigheids=, handelswêreld.
busk¹, (n) balein.
busk², (v) op straat sing, voordra.
busk'er, straatkomediant, straatsanger.
bus'kin, toneelstewel, broos, koturn; tragedie.
bus'man, (..men), busbestuurder; ~ **'s holiday,** werk=

vakansie, vakansie waarin iem. sy gewone werk verrig.
bus: ~ **route,** busroete; ~ **shed,** busloods; ~ **stop,** bushalte.
bust¹, (n) borsbeeld; buuste, bors.
bust², (n) (sl.) fuif; *on the* ~, aan die fuif.
bust³, (v) (sl.) bars; *go* ~, op die fles gaan.
bust'ard, korhaan, (duin)pou; *EUROPEAN* ~, trap= gans; *GIANT* ~, gompou.
bust'-bodice, buustehouer, buustelyfie.
bu'stle¹, bussel, heupbolla, tournure.
bu'stle², (n) gewoel, lewe, rumoer; drukte, bedrywig= heid, gedoe, gejaag; gedruis, gewerskaf; (v) lewe maak, bedrywig wees, stommel, woel; opdruk, aan= ja; ~ *ABOUT*, heen en weer woel, draf; ~ *and FIDGET*, maai en pagaai; ~**r,** woelwater.
bu'stling, (n) werskaffery; (a) woel(er)ig, bedrywig.
bus'y, (v) (**busied**), jou besig hou, jou bemoei; (a) be= sig, onledig; woelig, bedrywig, in die weer, doende, doenig; beset; *he is as* ~ *as a BEE*, hy is hard besig; *GET* ~, aan die gang raak (kom); ~ *HOUR of the day*, spitsuur van die dag; *the busiest men have the most LEISURE*, hoe besiger, hoe meer tyd; hoe besiger die mens, hoe meer vrye tyd maak hy; *be VERY* ~, druk besig wees; ~ *WORK SCHEDULE*, besige (besette) werksprogram; ~ **body,** (..**dies),** bemoeial, albedil, bedilal; kwaadstoker; ~ **ness,** be= sig wees; besetheid; woeligheid, lewendigheid, drukte.
but, (n) maar; ~ *me no* ~ *s*, moenie besware maak nie; ek wil geen maar ("mare") hoor nie, geen mare nie.
but, (adv, prep) maar, dog, immers, egter; slegs, net; behalwe; *ALL* ~, almal behalwe; byna; *ANY= THING* ~, alles behalwe; *there is no DOUBT* ~, daar is geen twyfel nie of; ~ *FOR*, was dit nie; *who* ~ *HE*, wie anders as hy; *who* ~ *KNOWS*, wie is daar wat nie weet nie; *he says* ~ *LITTLE*, hy sê maar min; *NOT only* ..., ~ *also*, nie alleen ... nie, maar ook; *the last PAGE* ~ *one*, op een na die laaste bladsy; ~ *YET*, maar tog.
but'ane, butaan.
butch'er, (n) slagter; janfiskaal, laksman; wreedaard; (v) slag; 'n slagting aanrig, doodmaak, vermoor; ~**-bird,** laksman, janfiskaal; ~**ly,** wreed, onmens= lik, moorddadig; ~**'s axe,** slagtersmes; ~**'s bill,** on= gevallelys; slagtersrekening, vleisrekening; ~**'s block,** kapblok; ~**'s business,** slagtersaak; ~**'s man,** slagterskneg; ~**'s meat,** slaghuisvleis; ~**'s shop,** slagterswinkel; ~**y** (..**ries),** slaghuis, slagte= ry; slagting, moord(ery).
but'ler, bottelier; skinker; hoofbediende.
butt¹, (n) dik gedeelte; skyf, kol; mikpunt, stomp kant (biljart); koeëlvanger; tergery; voorwerp van spot.
butt², (n) stukvat, vat, pyp.
butt³, (n) muis (van hand); kolf; stomp (van boom); (sigaret)stompie.
butt⁴, (n) platvis.
butt⁵, (v) stoot, stamp, ~ *IN*, jou inlaat met; jou neus steek in; iem. in die rede val; ~ *UP against*, bots teen.
butte, spitskop, pramkop; los kop.
butt'-end, kolf, agterkant; stuikent; stam-ent, dikent (paal).
butt'er¹, stoter, stamper.
butt'er², (n) botter; vleiery; *those who have plenty of* ~ *can LAY it on thick*, van dik hout saag 'n mens dik planke; *he looks as if* ~ *would not melt in his MOUTH*, hy lyk of hy nie 'n vlooi kan kwaad doen nie; (v) botter smeer; heuning om die mond smeer, vlei; ~ *one's BREAD on both sides*, op groot voet lewe; *soft words* ~ *no PARSNIPS*, praatjies vul geen gaatjies nie; ~ *up PEOPLE*, met die stroop= kwas rondloop; ~**-bean,** botterboontjie; ~ **biscuit,** botterkoekie; ~**-boat,** souskommetjie; ~**-bream,** pampelmoes (vis); ~ **cup,** botterblom; ~ **dish,** bot= terpotjie; ~ **fat,** bottervet; ~**-fingered,** lomp, on= handig; ~**-fingers,** bottervingers; ~**-firkin,** botter= vaatjie.
butt'erfly, (..**flies),** skoe(n)lapper, vlinder; wispeltu= rige persoon; *have butterflies in the STOMACH*, dit op jou senuwees hê; *break a* ~ *on the WHEEL*,

'n vlieg met 'n voorhamer slaan; ~ **collar**, weg=staanboordjie; ~ **flower**, skoenlapperblom; ~-**kiss**, vlugtige soentjie; soen op die oë; ~-**net**, vlindernet; ~-**nut**, vleuelmoer; ~-**spaniel**, Eekhoringhondjie; ~-**shaped**, vlindervormig; ~ **stroke**, vlinderslag; ~ **tie**, vlinderstrikkie; ~-**valve**, vleuelklep, smoorklep; ~ **weed**, woestyntulp.
butt'erine, kunsbotter, margarien.
butt'er: ~-**knife**, bottermes; ~-**milk**, karringmelk; ~-**mould**, bottervorm; ~ **muslin**, melkdoek; ~-**paper**, botterpapier; ~-**pat**, botterspaantjie; ~-**pear**, botterpeer; ~-**scotch**, borsplaat (lekkers), botterkaramel; ~-**trade**, botterhandel; ~ **tree**, botterboom; ~-**tub**, bottervaatjie; ~ **wort**, vetkruid, smeerblaar; ~ **y**, (n) (..**ries**), spens; (a) botteragtig; ~ **y-hatch**, kosdeurtjie.
bu'tteris, hoefmes.
butt'-hinge, deurskarnier.
butt'-joint, stuikvoeg, stuiklas, stootvoeg.
butt'ock, boud, agterdeel; broek (perd); ~**s**, sitvlak, agterste, boude.
butt'on, (n) knoop; knop; knoppel; werwel; doppie; (pl) livreikneg; *not have ALL his* ~*s*, nie al sy varkies in die hok hê nie; *not CARE a* ~, g'n flenter omgee nie; *TOUCH the* ~, net 'n knoppie druk; *not WORTH a* ~, geen blou duit werd wees nie, geen sent werd nie; (v) toeknoop; vasknoop; knope aansit; ~ **boot**, oprygskoen; ~ **box**, knoopdosie; ~ **bush**, knoopbos; ~-**fastening**, knoopsluiting; ~ **head**, rondekop (skroewe); ~ **hole**, (n) knoopsgat; ruiker; (v) knoopsgate maak; (iem.) aanklamp, bydam; ~ *hole scissors*, knoopsgatskêr; ~*hole stitch*, knoopsgatsteek; ~*hole twist*, knoopgatsy; ~-**hook**, knoophakie; ~ **mushroom**, dwergsampioen; ~-**punching**, knoopponsing; ~ **quail**, boskwartel; ~**s**, livreikneg; ~ **shoe**, knoopskoen; ~ **spider**, knopiespinnekop; ~-**switch**, knopskakelaar; ~**wood**, koeëlblomplataan.
butt'ress, (n) (-es), stutmuur, steunmuur; stut, steun= (pilaar); beer; steunwal, skoormuur; (v) stut, steun; ~ *up*, skraag; ~ **root**, stutwortel; ~-**thread**, trapesiumdraad.
butt'-seam, stuiknaat.
butt'-weld, stuiklas; ~**ing**, stompsweis, stuiksweis.
butt'y, maat.
bu'tyl, butiel.
bu'tyne, butyn.
buty'ric, botteragtig; botter=; ~ **acid**, bottersuur.
but'yrin, butirien, butirine, botterstof.
butyrom'eter, bottervetmeter.
bux'om, mollig, vet; vrolik, lewendig.
buy, **(bought)**, koop, inkoop; omkoop; aankoop; aanskaf; ~ *on CREDIT*, op krediet koop; ~ *DEARLY*, duur betaal vir; ~ *IN*, terugkoop; opkoop; *NOT* ~*ing that*, nie daarvoor te vinde nie; ~ *OFF*, loskoop, afkoop; ~ *OUT*, uitkoop; ~ *OVER*, omkoop; ~ *UP*, opkoop; ~**able**, koopbaar; ~-**aid**, koophulp; ~**er**, koper; aankoper; ~**er**, prospective ~*er*, moontlike koper; ~**ers' market**, kopersmark; ~**ers' resistance**, kopersweerstand; ~**ing**, koop; ~*ing ASSOCIATION*, koopvereniging; *CONSUMER'S* ~*ing association*, verbruikerskoopvereniging; ~**ing power**, koopkrag.
buzz, (n) gegons; gerug, gefluister; geroesemoes; drukte; *the* ~ *of applause*, die geruis van applous; (v) gons, suis(el), zoem, brom; fluister; praatjies versprei; smyt; afdwing; ~ *ABOUT someone*, om iem. draai; ~ *about someone's EARS*, aan iem. se ore lol; ~ *OFF!* trap! ~ *in and OUT again*, 'n kooltjie vuur kom haal.

buzz'ard, muisvalk.
buzz: ~ **bike**, bromfiets; kragfiets; ~ **bomb**, vlieënde bom, gonsbom.
buzz'er, oorblaser, fluisteraar; gonser, zoemer; stoomfluit; kletskous.
buzz group, gonsgroep.
buzz'ing, (n) gegons, gefluister, gesuis; suis(el)ing; (a) gonsend, fluisterend; suiserig.
buzz: ~ **saw**, sirkelsaag, rondesaag; ~ **word**, modewoord; slagwoord; wagwoord.
bwana, (Swah.), baas; meneer.
by, (adv, prep) deur; tot; met; na; by; op; volgens; langs, naby; verby; per; ~ *AND* ~, later, netnou, strakkies, dalkies; ~ *BIRTH*, van geboorte; ~ *CHANCE*, by toeval; ~ *CHEQUE*, per tjek; ~ *DAY*, bedags; *DAY* ~ *DAY*, dag vir dag; ~ *DEFAULT*, by verstek; ~ *DEGREES*, trapsgewyse; *DIVIDE* ~, deel deur; *do one's DUTY* ~, sy plig doen teenoor; ~ *FAR*, verreweg; ~ *HEART*, uit die kop, van buite; ~ *HUNDREDS*, by die honderde; ~ *LAND and sea*, op land en see; ~ *and LARGE*, oor die algemeen; alles in aanmerking geneem; *LAY* ~, bêrekoop; wegsit, opsy sit; ~ *your LEAVE*, met u verlof; *LITTLE* ~ *little*, bietjie vir bietjie; ~ *no MEANS*, volstrek nie; glad nie; *MULTIPLY* ~, vermenigvuldig met; ~ *MYSELF*, ek alleen; ~ *the NAME of*, genoem, genaamd, onder die naam van; *NEAR* ~, naby; ~ *the NEAREST road*, met die kortste pad; ~ *NIGHT*, snags; ~ *NOW*, teen hierdie tyd; nou; ~ *ONESELF*, alleen; sonder hulp; ~ *RAIL*, per spoor, per trein; ~ *RIGHT of birth*, kragtens (sy) geboorte; *SWEAR* ~, sweer by; *TAKEN* ~ *itself*, op sigself beskou; ~ *THE* ~, terloops; tussen hakies, van die os op die esel; ~ *my WATCH*, volgens my oorlosie; ~ *the WAY*, terloops; tussen hakies; van die os op die esel; ~ *WAY of*, by wyse van; ~ *next WEEK*, teen aanstaande week; *WRITTEN* ~, geskryf deur.
by'alite, basaltglas.
by'-blow, dwarshou; onegte kind, buitebeentjie.
bye¹, (n) iets ondergeskiks; loslopie (krieket); loslootjie; orige speler (in wedstryd); *draw a* ~, orige lootjie trek, vryloot.
by(e)², (a) onder=, ondergeskik, sub=; geheim; sydelings.
bye'-bye¹, deedoe.
bye-bye'², tot siens.
by: (=e)-**law**, verordening (munisipaliteit), reglement, regulasie; dorpswet; ~-**election**, tussenverkiesing; ~-**end**, byoogmerk.
by: ~**gone**, (n, pl) gedane sake; *let* ~*gones be* ~ *gones*, moenie ou koeie uit die sloot haal nie; gras oor iets laat groei; vergewe en vergeet; (a) verby, vergange; uitgesterf; ~-**lane**, sygangetjie; ~**line**, getekende bydrae (in koerant); ~-**name**, bynaam; ~-**pass**, (n) omweg, ontwyking; omloopleiding; verbypas; (v) verbygaan; verbyry; oor die hoof sien; ~ **pass road**, verbypad; ~ **pass-valve**, omloopklep; ~ **path**, dowwe paadjie, sypad; ~ **play**, stille spel (toneel); syspel; ~-**product**, neweproduk, afvalproduk, byproduk.
byre, koeistal.
by: ~**road**, ompad, bypad, dowwe paadjie; ~**stander**, omstander, toeskouer; ~**street**, agterstraatjie; systraatjie; ~**way**, kort paadjie; sypad; minder bekende terrein; ~**word**, spreekwoord; skimpwoord; spotnaam, aanfluiting; ~-**work**, bywerk, bysaak.
Byza'ntine, (n) Bisantyn; (a) Bisantyns.
Byza'ntium, Bisantium.

C

c, (**cs**, **c's**, **cees**), c.
Caaba, Kaäba.
cab¹, (n) huurmotor, keb; kap (van lokomotief); kajuit (van bestuurder); (v) **(-bed)**, 'n rytuig huur, met 'n huurrytuig gaan.
cab², (n) afskryfpapiertjie; (v) afskrywe.

cabal', **(n) kabaal, intrige, kuipery; kliek; politieke samespanning; (v) **(-led), saamsweer, konkel, intrigeer; ~ **ler,** kuiper, intrigant.
cab'aret, kabaret.
caba'ya, kabaai.
cabb'age, kool, kopkool; ~**-head,** koolkop; ~**-lettuce,** k(r)opslaai; ~ **palm,** koolpalm; ~ **patch,** groentetuintjie; ~**-plant,** koolplant; ~**-rose,** maagderoos; koolroos; ~ **stalk,** koolstronk; ~ **tree,** kiepersol *(Cussonia thyrsiflora);* ~ **wood,** kiepersol- (hout).
cab(b)'ala, kabbala; geheime leer.
cab(b)'alist, kabbalis.
cab(b)alis'tic, kabbalisties, geheim, verborge.
caba'na, skuiling, hut, hokkie; strandhuis, cabana.
cabb'y, (cabbies), huurkoetsier.
cab'-driver, huurkoetsier.
ca'ber, (Sc.) kaber.
cab'in, (n) kajuit, hut; (v) insluit, vasknel; ~ **aeroplane,** kajuitvliegtuig; toevliegtuig; ~ **boy,** kajuitseun, kajuitbediende; ~ **class,** kajuitklas; ~ **cruiser,** kajuitmotor; motorwoonskuit.
cab'inet, kabinet, ministerie; kas; skryn; kamertjie; kantoor; raadskamer; ~ **council,** kabinet; ministerraad; ~ **crisis,** kabinetskrisis; ~ **decision,** kabinetsbesluit; ~ **edition,** kabinetuitgawe; ~**-maker,** meubelmaker; ~**-making,** meubelmakery; ~ **minister,** minister van die staat; ~ **photograph,** ~ **portrait,** kabinetsportret; ~**-size,** kabinetgrootte, kabinetformaat; ~ **varnish,** meubellak; ~ **work,** kabinetwerk.
cab'in, ~**-hole,** patryspoort; ~**-hook,** deurhaak; sluithaak; ~ **luggage,** hutbagasie; ~ **scooter,** kajuitfiets; ~ **trunk,** kajuitkoffer, skeepskoffer, hutkoffer; ~ **window,** patryspoort.
ca'ble, (n) kabel; kabel berig; kabeltou; ankertou; kabellengte; *flexible* ~, buigsame kabel; (v) kabel; vasmaak; ~ **armour,** kabelpantser; ~ **balloon,** kabelbalon; ~ **brake,** kabelrem; ~ **car,** kabelkar(retjie); ~**-clip,** kabelklem; ~**-coil,** kabelrol; ~ **compound,** kabelpasta; ~ **core,** kabelkern; ~ **deck,** kettingdek; ~**-duct,** kabelkanaal; ~**-foul,** kinkel in die kabel; ~ **gland,** kabelinleistuk; ~**-gram,** kabelgram; ~ **joint,** kabellas; ~ **jointer,** kabellasser; ~ **layer,** kabellêer; ~**-laying,** kabellegging; ~**-letter,** briefkabel; ~ **railway,** kabelspoor, sweefspoor; ~**-route,** kabelroete; ~**-run,** kabelloop; ~ **saw,** kabelsaag; ~ **service,** kabeldiens; ~ **sleeve,** kabelmof; ~ **stitch,** kabelsteek; ~**-strand,** kabelstring; ~ **suspender,** kabelhanger; ~ **suspension wire,** kabelhangdraad; ~**-thimble,** kabelklem; ~ **way,** sweefspoor, kabelspoor; ~ **winch,** kabelwindas, ~**-wire,** staalkabel.
ca'bbing, kabelaanleg; kabelversending.
cab'man, (..men), huurkoetsier.
cabob', sosatie, kabab, kebab.
cabochon', cabochon; *en* ~, en cabochon.
cabood'le, spul, boel, sitsewinkel, kaboedel, santepetiek, sous, pakaas; *the whole* ~, die hele spul; die hele boel; die hele sous.
caboose', skeepskombuis; kaboes.
cab'otage, kushandel.
cabotin', tweederangse akteur, cabotin.
cab' rank, huurmotorstaanplek.
cab'riole, boogpoot, kabriool.
cabriolet', kabriolet (rytuig).
cab' stand, huurmotorstaanplek.
caca'o, kakao; kakaoboom; kakaoboontjie.
cach'alot, potvis, masvis.
cache, (n) geheime wegsteekplek; wegsteekgoed; (v) wegsteek, verberg.
cachec'tic, swak, ongesond, uitgeput.
cach'et, stempel, cachet, kasjet; pildoppie, kapsule.
cachex'ia, cachex'y, cachexia, ongesonde toestand (van liggaam).
cach'innate, hard lag, skater, uitskater.
cachinna'tion, geskater, skaterlag.
ca'cholong, (Mong.) soort opaal, kasjolong.
cach'ou, (geur)pilletjie, cachou.
cack, (n, v) kak.
cac'kle, (n) gekekkel, gesnater; gebabbel; (v) kekkel; babbel; ~ *OFTEN but never lay an egg,* grootpraat, maar niks uitvoer (uitrig) nie; ~ **r,** kekkelbek, babbelaar.
cack'ling, gekekkel.
cacodem'on, bose gees; kwaadwillige persoon.
caco'epy, slegte uitspraak.
cacog'raphy, kakografie, slegte spelling; gekrap, slegte handskrif.
cacol'ogy, kakologie, slegte uitspraak.
cacoph'onous, onwelluidend, wanluidend, wanklinkend.
cacoph'ony, wangeluid, wanklank, onwelluidendheid, kakofonie.
cac'toblastis, turksvymot.
cac'tus, (-es, cacti), kaktus; *JOINTED* ~, litjieskaktus; *SPINELESS* ~, kaalbladturksvy; ~ **dahlia,** veerdahlia.
cad, gemene vent, gemenerd, ploert, lunsriem, smeerlap.
cadas'ter, kadaster.
cadas'tral, kadastraal; ~ *MAP,* kadasterkaart.
cadas'tre = **cadaster.**
cadav'er, kadawer; lyk; ~**ous,** lykagtig; lykkleurig; lyk-.
cadd'ic, (n) joggie; (v) stokke dra; joggie; ~ **car(t),** joggiekar, wieljoggie; ~**-master,** joggiebaas.
cadd'is[1]**,** kokerwurm.
cadd'is[2]**,** kaddis (wolstof).
cadd'is-fly, watermot.
cadd'ish, gemeen, laag, ploerterig, skurkagtig.
cadd'is-worm, sprokkelwurm.
cadd'y, (caddies), teebus.
cade, hanslam, hansdier.
cad'ence, kadans, toonval, ritme; stembuiging; aksent.
caden'za, cadenza, kadensa.
cadet', jonger seun; kadet; ~ **camp,** kadetkamp. ~ **corps,** kadet- korps; ~ **officer,** kadetoffisier; ~ **ship,** kadetskap; leerlingskap.
cadge, bedel; rondsmous; ~ **r,** bondeldraer, smous, marskramer, bedelaar, klaploper skuimer.
cad'ging, klaplopery, gebedel.
cad'i, kadi, regter.
cad'mium, kadmium; ~**-plate,** verkadmium; ~**-yellow,** kadmiumgeel; ~ **red,** kadmiumrooi.
ca'dre, kader, raamwerk.
cadu'ceus, (..cei), Merkuriusstaf, Hermesstaf, boodskapperstaf, slangstaf.
cadu'city, verganklikheid; afgeleefdheid, kaduksheid; verval van kragte.
cadu'cous, verganklik, verbygaande; afvallend.
caec'um, (..ca), blindederm; blindesak.
Caes'ar, Caesar; keiser, outokraat; *render unto* ~ *the things which are* ~ *'s,* betaal aan die keiser wat die keiser toekom; ~ **weed,** caesaronkruid (*Urena lobata).*
Caesa'rean, Caesa'rian, Caesariaans; ~ **birth,** ~ **operation,** keisersnee.
Caes'arism, Caesarisme, outokrasie, alleenheerskappy, diktatorskap.
caes'ious, blougroen, grysgroen.
caesur'a, (-e, -s), sesuur, verssnede; snee; ~ **l,** verssnede-, sesuur-.
cafe', kafee, koffiehuis; ~ **au lait,** koffie met melk, melkkoffie, wit koffie, cafe au lait ~ **bio(scope),** vloofliek, kafeebioskoop; ~ **chantant,** cafe-chantant; ~ **owner,** ~ **proprietor,** kafeebaas; ~ **restaurant,** kaffeerestourant (-restaurant).
cafeter'ia, kafeteria.
caff'eine, kafeïne, kafeïen.
Caffrar'ia, Kaffrarië.
Caff're, Kafir.
caf'tan, kaftan.
cage, (n) voëlkou, kooi, kou, voëlhok; gevangenis; filmhouer (fotografie); hyshok; hok; (v) opsluit (in 'n hok); ~ **bird,** kouvoël(tjie); ~**-type,** kooitipe; ~**-work,** traliewerk.
cag(e)y, (sl.), slinks; slim; versigtig.
cahoots': *be in* ~, kop in een mus wees.
Cain, Kain; *bear the MARK of* ~, die Kainsteken dra; *RAISE* ~, lawaai opskop; 'n herrie opskop.
caïque, kaïk.
Cairene', Kaïreens.

cairn, klipstapel, baken; ~ '**gorm,** cairngorm, rooktopaas; ~ **terrier,** Cairnterriër.
Cair'o, Kaïro.
caiss'on, ammunisiewa; caisson; fondamentkas; dryfhek; ~ **disease,** duikersiekte.
cait'iff, (n) skelm, skurk; lafaard, ellendeling; (a) laag, skurkagtig.
cajole', vlei; ompraat, troggel, omkonkel; aanhaal, stroop (heuning) om die mond smeer; flikflooi; ~ **r,** vleier, flikflooier; ~ **ry,** vleiery, geflikflooi, mooipraatjies, aanhaligheid.
caj'uput (oil), kajapoet(olie).
cake, (n) koek, gebak; *his* ~ *is DOUGH,* sy kruit is nat; *you cannot EAT your* ~ *and have it,* jy moet een van twee kies; *it's a PIECE of* ~, dis tog te maklik; ~ *of SOAP,* koekie seep; *TAKE the* ~, die prys behaal; die toppunt wees; die kroon span; almal se moses wees; sy (haar) gelyke nêrens vind nie; (v) koek, tot 'n koek vorm; klont; ~ **batter,** koekbeslag; ~ **-cooler,** afkoelrak; ~ **d,** gekoek; ~ **-dish,** koekbord; ~ **flour,** koekmeel, banketmeel ~ **-fork,** koekvurkie; ~ **-lifter,** koekspaan, koekskep, koekskoppie; ~ **mix,** koekmengsel; ~ **mould,** koekvorm; ~ **pan,** koekpan; ~ **-rack,** afkoelrooster; ~ **tin,** koekblik; ~ **walk,** Negerdans.
cal'abash, (-es), kalbas; ~ **milk,** kalbasmelk.
cal'aber, eekhoringbont; ~ **bean,** kalabarboon.
calaboose', tronk.
calamen'co, kalmink (wolstof).
calaman'der, harde Oosterse meubelhout, koromandelhout.
cal'amine, kalamyn, galmei; ~ **lotion,** kalamynmelk.
cal'amint, kattekruie; kalamint; ~ **balm,** kattekruiesalf.
calam'itous, rampspoedig, ongelukkig.
calam'ity, (. . ties), rampspoed, ramp, onheil, ellende; *that was a* ~, dit was 'n skade in die boedel.
cal'amus, (. . mi), kalmoes; rietpen, skryfstif.
calash', (-es), kales (rytuig); (vou)kap, hoepelkap.
calcan'eum, hakbeen.
calcar'eious, calcar'ious, kalkagtig, kalkhoudend, kalk=.
calceolar'ia, pantoffelboom, pantoffelplant.
cal'ceolate, pantoffelvormig.
calcif'erous, kalkhoudend.
calcifica'tion, verkalking.
calciflo'ral, kelkbloemig.
cal'cify, (. . fied), verkalk, uitdroog; verbrand.
cal'cimine, kalsimien.
calcina'tion, verkalking, verbranding.
cal'cine, verkalk; (ver)brand (bene) verfyn; ~ **r,** gloeioond, kalkbrander, kalsineeroond.
cal'cite, kalsiet.
cal'cium, kalsium.
calculabil'ity, berekenbaarheid.
cal'culable, berekenbaar, oorsienbaar.
cal'culate, bereken, reken, beraam; uitwerk; glo, dink (Amer.).
cal'culated, berekend, voorbedag, koelbloedig; geskik; *with* ~ *CRUELTY,* met voorbedagte wreedheid; ~ *FOR,* bereken op; ~ *HORSEPOWER,* berekende perdekrag; ~ *RISK,* berekende risiko; ~ *TO,* bereken om.
cal'culating, berekend, reken=; ~ **-machine,** rekenmasjien.
calcula'tion, berekening, beraming; ~ *on the DECI= MALS,* staffel; ~ *of PROFITS* winsberekening.
cal'culator, rekenaar; rekenmeester; rekenmasjien, rekentafel; sakrekenaar, drarekenaar.
cal'culous, steenagtig, graweelagtig (med.).
cal'culus, (. . li). (graweel)steen; rekenwyse, rekenmetode; rekening; kalkulus; *BILIARY* ~, galsteen; *DIFFERENTIAL* ~, differensiaalrekening; *INTEGRAL* ~, integraalrekening.
calde'ra, kaldera, krater.
cal'dron, *kyk* **cauldron.**
Caledon'ia, Skotland; ~ **n,** (n) Skot; (a) Skots; ~ *n market,* rommelverkoping.
calefa'cient, verwarmend.
calefac'tion, verhitting, verwarming.
calefac'tor, klein kookoond; ~ **y,** verhittend, verwarmend.

cal'embour, calembour, (dubbelsinnige) woordspeling.
cal'endar, (n) kalender, almanak; rol (van heiliges); (v) opteken; rangskik; ~ **er,** optekenaar; ~ **month,** kalendermaand; ~ **year,** kalenderjaar.
cal'ender, (n) lakenpers, kalander; (v) oor warm rolle trek, pers, mangel; ~ *ed paper,* glanspapier; ~ **ing,** glansdruk.
cal'endry, kalandery; kalandermeul.
cal'ends, eerste dag van die maand (by die Romeine), calendae; *on the Greek* ~, nooit, in die jaar nul.
calen'dula, (-e), gousblom.
cal'enture, tropiese ylkoors.
calf¹, (calves), kuit (been).
calf², (calves), kalf (dier); kalfsleer; snuiter; *kill the FATTED* ~, die gemeste kalf slag; *worship the GOLDEN* ~, die goue kalf aanbid; *IN (with)* ~, dragtig, grootuier, gedek; *SLIP her* ~, 'n dooie kalf kry; ~ **-bound,** kalfsleer=, in kalfsleer gebind; ~ **-bush,** kalwerbossie *(Pelargonium aidoides);* ~ **knees,** hol knieë (perd); krom knie; ~ **-love,** kalwerliefde; ~ **meal,** kalfsmeel; ~ **'s foot,** kalfspoot; kalfsvoet (plant); ~ **skin,** kalfsleer; ~ **'s liver,** kalfslewer; ~ **'s teeth,** melktande.
cal'iber, *Amer. spelling of* **calibre.**
cal'ibrate, kalibreer, yk; ~ **d,** gekalibreer.
calibra'tion, yking, kalibrering, graadverdeling.
cal'ibre, deursnee, wydte (geweerloop); gewigsposisie; gehalte, soort, waarde, kaliber; *a man of different* ~, 'n man van ander stoffasie.
cal'icle, kelkie (van blom).
cal'ico, (-es), katoen, kaliko; ~ **-printer,** katoendrukker; ~ **-printing,** katoendrukkery.
cal'if = **caliph;** ~ **ate** = **caliphate.**
Californ'ia, Kalifornië; ~ **n,** (n) Kaliforniër; (a) Kalifornies; ~ *n poppy,* botterkelk.
cal'ipash, skilpadvleis (donkergroen vleis onder boonste dop van skilpad).
cal'ipee, skilpadvleis (liggeel vleis aan onderste dop van skilpad).
cal'iph, kalief; ~ **ate,** kalifaat.
cal'ix, (calices), blomkelk.
calk¹, (n) hoefysterpen, klou, ysspyker; (v) skerp penne aansit; *kyk ook* **caulk.**
calk², (v) kalkeer, natrek.
call, (n) roep, geroep; lokstem, lokfluitjie; kuier; besoek, visite; bod (kaarte); oproep, uitnodiging; sinjaal; beroep (predikant); eis, vraag; aanleiding; roepstem; opsegging, aflossing; *AT* ~, op aanvraag; *at one's BECK and* ~, tot iem. se diens; *a DUTY* ~, 'n verpligte besoek; *ON* ~, dadelik opvraagbaar (opvorderbaar); have *NO* ~ *to,* geen aanleiding hê nie; *PAY a* ~, 'n besoek aflê; *WITH= IN* ~, byderhand; sommer naby; (v) roep; noem, heet (naam); beroep (predikant); aankom, besoek, kuier, besoek aflê; troef maak, bie (kaarte); afkondig; byeenroep, belê (vergadering); opsê (verband); uitlees (naam); opbel, oplui (telefoon); aangaan, aanroep; ~ *to ACCOUNT,* tot verantwoording roep; ~ *AFTER,* naroep; noem na; ~ *to ARMS,* tot (onder) die wapens roep; ~ *AT,* aanloop (kuier) by; ~ *ATTENTION to,* die aandag vestig op; ~ *AWAY,* wegroep; ~ *BACK,* terugroep; herroep; voor die gees roep; ~ *to the BAR,* tot die balie toelaat, as advokaat toelaat; ~ *into BEING,* in die lewe roep; ~ *over the COALS,* oor die kole haal; berispe; *COME as if* ~ *ed,* kom of jy geroep is; ~ *it a DAY,* ophou; uitskei; ~ *DOWN,* berispe; uitdaag; ~ *FOR,* roep om; vereis; kom haal; ~ *FORTH,* te voorskyn roep; uitbring; veroorsaak; ~ *a HALT,* halt roep; laat stilstaan; ~ *to HEAVEN,* tot die hemel roep, ten hemel skrei; ~ *IN,* oproep, opsê (geld); inroep, ontbied; ~ *for IN= FORMATION,* inligting vra; ~ *a MEETING,* 'n vergadering belê; ~ *to MIND,* jou herinner, byval; onthou; ~ *a person NAMES,* iem. uitskel; ~ *OFF,* wegroep; aflei; af(ge)las; ~ *ON,* aanspreek; 'n besoek aflê by; 'n beroep doen op; ~ *OUT,* oproep; kommandeer; uitroep; uitdaag; ~ *OVER,* aflees; ~ *into PLAY,* geleentheid bied vir; ~ *in QUES= TION,* in twyfel trek; ~ *the ROLL,* appèl hou; ~ *ROUND,* aanloop; ~ *UP,* oproep; opbel; voor die

gees roep; ~ *UPON*, 'n beroep doen op; ~ *UPON someone to do something*, iem. versoek om iets te doen; ~ *for VOLUNTEERS*, oproep om vrywilligers; ~ *to WITNESS*, as getuie oproep; ~**-bell**, (op)roepklok(kie); ~**-bird**, lokvoël; ~**-box**, telefoonhokkie; ~**-boy**, aanseër; waarskuwer; teater=, hoteljoggie; ~ **ed**, genoem; getitel; gesegde; geroep; beroep (predikant); ~ **er**, besoeker, kuiergas; roeper; ~**-girl**, foondoedie, telefoonliefie; foonsnol; kontakmeisie.
call'a lily, varkoor, varkblom.
callig'rapher, callig'raphist, skoonskrywer.
call'igraphy, skoonskryfkuns, skoonskrif, kalligrafie.
call'ing, geroep; roeping; bedryf, beroep; ~**-off**, af(ge)lasting; ~**-signal**, oproepsein (teleg.); oproepsinjaal (telef.).
cal(l)'iper, tang; diktemeter; skuifpasser; stangpasser; ~ **compasses**, passer, krompasser; diktemeter; ~**-gauge**, speermaat, stangpasser; ~**-rule**, kaliberstok; ~ **s**, meetpasser; ~**-square**, skuifpasser.
callisthen'ic, kallistenies, gimnastiek=; ~ **s**, kamergimnastiek, kallistenie.
call: ~**-lamp**, oproeplamp (telef.); ~**-loan**, (te eniger tyd) opvraagbare lening; ~ **man**, (..**men**), oproeper; ~**-money**, opvraagbare geld; daggeld; ~**-office**, telefoonhokkie, oproepkantoor.
callos'ity, (..**ties**), eeltagtigheid, kallositeit, harderigheid, eelt; dikhuidigheid.
call'ous, verhard, vereelt, eeltagtig, geëelt; ongevoelig, dikvellig, verstok; ~ **ness**, hardheid, ongevoeligheid.
call'-over, rollesing, appèl.
call'ow, kaal, sonder vere, onervare, baar, groen; *be* ~, nog nat agter die ore wees.
call: ~**-sign**, roepnaam; roepletters; ~**-tune**, kenwysie; ~**-up**, oproep(ing).
call'us: (..**li, -es**), eelt, vereelting, kallus; wondweefsel.
calm, (n) kalmte, vrede, stilte; windstilte; gevegstilte; (v) kalmeer, tot bedaring bring, bedaar; stilmaak; ~ *down*, bedaar; (a) kalm, effe, gerus; besadig, rustig, bedaard, stil; *quite* ~, perdgerus, houtgerus; ~ **ative**, (n) kalmerende middel; (a) kalmerend; ~**-belt**, windstilte(streek); ~ **ly**, goedsmoeds, doodluiters; bedaard, kalmpies; ~ **ness**, kalmte, stilte, stilheid.
cal'omel, kalomel, merkurochloried.
calor'ic, (n) warmtestof; (a) warmte=, kalories; ~**-engine**, lugenjin, enjin wat deur warm lug gedryf word; ~'**ity**, eie warmte; ~**-unit**, warmte-eenheid.
calor'iduct, warmtebuis.
cal'orie, warmte-eenheid, kaloric.
calor'ifere, verwarmingstoestel.
calorif'ic, verwarmend, warmtegewend; ~ **a'tion**, verwarming, verhitting; ~ **rays**, warmtestrale.
calorim'eter, kaloriemeter, warmtemeter.
calorim'etry, kaloriemeting, kaloriemetrie, warmtemeting.
calotte', kalotjie.
calque, leenvertaling, calque.
cal'trop, val, voetangel, hoefangel; draadduwweltjie; sterdistel.
cal'umet, vredespyp, kalumet.
calum'niate, belaster, beskinder, beswadder.
calumnia'tion, belastering, beskindering.
calum'niator, lasteraar.
calum'niatory, lasterlik, lasterend.
calum'nious, lasterlik, lasterend, lastersiek.
cal'umny, laster, skindertaal, agterklap; eerrowing, eerroof.
calva'dos, appelbrandewyn, calvados.
Cal'vary, Golgota, Kruisberg, Kalvarieberg; Kruisgang.
calve, kalf, kalwe; ~ *IN*, inkalf, inkalwe; ~ *OUT*, uitkalf, uitkalwe; *kyk* **calf**.
calves'-foot jelly, kalfspootjellie.
Cal'vin, Calvyn; ~ **ism**, Calvinisme; ~ **ist**, Calvinis; ~ **is'tic**, Calvinisties, gereformeerd.
calvi'ties, kaalhoofdigheid.
calx, (**calces**), kalsiumoksied, kalsiumokside; hakskeenbeen.

cal'yciform, kelkvormig.
calyc'inal, kelkvormig, komvormig (bot.).
cal'ycoid, kelkvormig, bekervormig (bot.).
calyp'so, kalipso; ~ **dance**, kalipsodans; ~ **song**, kalipsolied.
cal'ypter, dek(sel)skub, kalipter.
cal'yx, (**-es, calyces**), blomkelk.
cam, kam (van 'n kamrat); nok, tand, spilhaak; duim (mynwese); ~ **angle**, nokhoek.
camaraderie', kameraadskap, kameradie.
camaron', varswaterkrewel, kamaron.
cam'ber, (n) kromming, welwing, kruipronding (pad); bakspoor (wiele); ronding; ashelling, askanteling; wielvlug; vertikale sporing; kromhout; houthawe; (v) (af)rond, rondte gee, welf; ~ *ed ROAD*, geronde pad; ~ *ed ROOF*, geronde dak; ~ **alignment**, wielvlugstelling; ~ **angle**, wielvlughoek.
cam'bial, ruit, kambiaal.
cam'bist, wisselhandelaar; wisselgids.
cam'bium, kambium, teellaag.
Cambo'dia, Kambodja; ~ **n**, (n) Kambodjaan; (a) Kambodjaans.
cam' box, (**-es**), nokkas.
Cam'bray Kamcryk.
cam'brel, vleishaak.
Cam'bria, Kambrië, Wallis; ~ **n**, (n) Walliser; (a) Kambries, Wallies.
cam'bric, (n) kamerdoek, batis; (a) kamerdoeks, batis=; ~ **paper**, satynpapier.
Cam'bridge: ~ **blue**, ligblou; ~ **sausage**, knakwors.
cam' bush, nokasbus.
Camdeboo, Kamdeboo; ~ **Mountains**, Kamdebooberge; - (**white**) **stinkwood**, Kamdeboostinkhout.
cam: ~ **disc**, nokskyf; ~ **drum**, noktrommel.
came, (n) vensterlood; (v) *kyk* **come**.
cam'el, kameel, die skip van die woestyn; ~**-back**, loopvlakrubber; boggelrug; ~ **eer'**, kameeldrywer; ~**-hair brush**, kameelhaarkwas; kameelhaarborsel.
camell'ia, japonika, kamelia.
cam'elopard, kameelpeerd, giraf, langnekkameel.
cam'el: ~ **ry**, kameelkorps, kameelruitery; ~'**s hair**, kameelhaar; ~**-thorn**, kameeldoring(boom) *(Acacia giraffae)*.
camembert', camembert(kaas).
cam'eo, (**-s**), kamee, edelsteen met reliëfsnywerk.
cam'era, kamera, fototoestel; *in* ~, agter geslote deure, in kamera; ~ **case**, kamerates; ~**-man**, kameraman, rolprentfotograaf; persfotograaf.
camerlin'go, Poussekretaris, camerlingo.
Cameroon', Kameroen.
ca'miknickers, hempbroek, lyfbroek(ie).
cam'ion, vragwa, vragmotor.
cam'isole, onderlyfie, kamisool.
cam'let, kamelot, kameelhaarstof.
cam: ~ **lever**, nokhefboom; ~ **lobe**, nokneus.
cam'omile, kamille; ~ **daisy**, (cgte) kamille.
cam'ouflage, (n) vermomming, maskering, kamoeflage, kamoeflering; skutkleur; rooskerm; (v) vermom, wegsteek, onherkenbaar maak, kamoefleer; ~ *d battery*, vermomde battery; ~ **artist**, momskilder; ~ **net**, momnet; ~ **painting**, skutkleuring; ~ **screen**, momskerm.
camp, (n) laer, leërplaas, kamp; *AT* ~, in die kamp; *BREAK* ~, kamp opbreek; *IN* ~, in die kamp; *PITCH* ~, kamp opslaan; *QUIT* ~, die kamp verlaat; (v) kampeer, laer trek; ~ *OFF*, afkamp; ~ *OUT*, kampeer.
campaign', (n) veldtog, kampanje; *plan of* ~, veldtogsplan; (v) veldtog voer; op kommando wees; propaganda maak; ~ **er**, soldaat; veteraan, kryger, stryder.
campanil'e, kloktoring, kampaniel.
campanol'ogist, klokspeler, kampanoloog.
campanol'ogy, klokspeelkuns, klokkunde, kampanologie.
campan'ula, klokkiesblom; ~ **te**, klokvormig.
camp: ~**-bed**, veldbed, voubed; ~**-chair**, veldstoel, voustoel.
Cam'peachy (wood), blouhout.
camp: ~ **ed**, gelaer; ~ **er**, kampeerder; ~**-fever**, laerkoors, tifus; ~**-fire**, laervuur; kampvuur; ~**-follower**, laernaloper,

cam'phor, kanfer; ~**ated,** gekanfer; kanfer=; ~**ated oil,** kanferolie; ~**-ball,** kanferbal; ~**-tree,** kanfer=boom; ~**-wood,** kanferhout.
camp'-hospital, kamphospitaal.
camp'ing, kampeerdery; ~ *HOLIDAY,* kampeer=vakansie; ~ *KITCHEN,* kookskerm; ~ *SITE,* kampeerterrein.
camp: ~**-meeting,** kampdiens; ~**-shedding,** ~**-sheeting,** ~**-shot,** deklaag, beskoeiing; ~**-stool,** voustoel; ~**-stretcher,** leërbed, voubed, veldbed.
camp'tonite, kamptoniet.
cam'pus, kampus, universiteitsterrein.
cam: ~ **ring,** duimring; ~ **shaft,** nokas, drukasspil, duimspil; ~**-shaft bush,** nokasbus; ~ **spindle,** nok=spil; ~ **wheel,** kamrat.
can¹, (n) kan, blik; (v) inlê, inmaak (in bottels), verduursaam.
can², (v) **(could),** kan; in staat wees; mag; *you ~ not but know it,* jy moet dit weet.
Can'aan, Kanaän; ~**ite,** Kanaäniet; ~**it'ic,** Kanaänities.
Can'ada, Kanada; ~ **thistle,** Kanadese distel *(Cuicus arvensis).*
Canad'ian, (n, a) Kanadees; ~ **spruce,** witspar, Kanadese spar.
canaill'e, gepeupel, Jan Rap en sy maat.
canal', (n) kanaal, grag, vaart, vaarwater; buis; groef; (v) **(-led),** kanaliseer; ~ **boat,** kanaalboot.
canalic'ulate(d), gegroef.
canalisa'tion, kanalisasie, deurgrawing.
can'alize, kanaliseer.
canal: ~ **lock,** kanaalsluis; ~ **shipping,** kanaalvaart.
can'apé, ansjovishappie; kanapee.
can'ard, vals gerug, foppery, riemtelegram; eendvliegtuig.
Canar'ies: *The ~,* die Kanariese Eilande; ..**ry creeper,** Oos-Indiese kers, kappertjie.
canar'y, (..ries), kanarie; Kanariese wyn; *Cape ~,* Kaapse kanarie; ~ **bird,** kanarie(voël), tronkvoël; ~**-coloured,** kanariekleurig; ~ **creeper;** kappertjie, Oos-Indiese kers; ~ **grass,** kanariegras; ~ **pudding,** kanariepoeding; ~**-seed,** kanariesaad, voëlsaad; ~ **tree,** kanarieboom; ~ **wood,** tulpehout.
canas'ta, kanasta (kaartspel).
canas'ter, tabakmandjie; growwe tabak.
can'can, cancan', cancan(dans).
can'cel, (n) vervanging van 'n bladsy; (v) **(-led),** kanselleer, afsê; verklein (breuke); herroep, intrek (verlof); afstempel (dokument); uitkrap, deurhaal (woorde); vernietig; rojeer; afskryf; afstel; ~ *an APPOINTMENT,* 'n afspraak afsê, 'n benoeming terugtrek; ~ *a BOND,* 'n verband rojeer; ~ *a CONTRACT,* 'n kontrak opsê; ~ *a DEBT,* 'n skuld delg; *the FRACTIONS must be ~ led out,* die breuke moet verklein word; ~ *LEAVE,* verlof intrek; ~ *OUT,* mekaar ophef; ~ **la'tion,** kansellasie, kansellering, herroeping, intrekking; vernietiging; afsegging, afskrywing, deurhaling, rojering; ~**ling-machine,** rojeermasjien.
can'cer, kanker, krap; ~ *of the HOOF,* straalkanker, hoefkanker; ~ *of the LUNG,* longkanker; *TROPIC of ~,* Kreefskeerkring; ~**ate,** verkanker; ~**a'tion,** verkankering; ~**-bush,** kankerbos *(Sutherlandia frutescens);* ~ **growth,** kankergeswel; ~**ous,** kankeragtig.
can'crene, krapagtig; krapvormig.
can'crinite, cancriniet.
can'croid, (n) soort kanker; soort kreef; skaaldier; (a) kankeragtig; kreefagtig.
cande'la, kandela.
candela'bra, kandelaber, kandelaar; ~ **flower,** kandelaarblom.
candela'brum, (..bra), kandelaber, kandelaar, kroonlugter; kandelaarsblom, koningskandelaar.
candes'cence, gloed, gloeiing.
candes'cent, gloeiend.
can'did, eerlik, opreg, openhartig, vrymoedig, rondborstig, reguit, trouhartig; volmondig.
can'didacy, kandidatuur, kandidaatskap.
can'didate, kandidaat; sollisitant, aansoeker; ~ *for confirmation,* katkisant; ~**-minister,** proponent.
can'didature, kandidatuur, kandidaatskap.

candid: ~ **camera,** steelfotografie, geheime fotografie; afloerkamera; ~ **friend,** eerlike (kritiese) vriend.
can'didness, openhartigheid, opregtheid, eerlikheid, vrymoedigheid.
can'died, versuiker; soet; vleiend; ~ **peel,** sukade, suikerskil.
can'dle, kers; *BURN the ~ at both ends,* jou ooreis; verkwistend te werk gaan met jou kragte; *hold a ~ to the DEVIL,* iem. in sy kwaad sterk; *not fit to HOLD a ~ to someone,* nie in iem. se skaduwee kan staan nie; nie kers vir iem. kan vashou nie; nie werd om iem. se skoenriem los te maak nie; *his ~ has been SNUFFED,* iem. se lewensdraad is geknip; *hold a ~ to the SUN,* water na die see dra; ~ **berry,** bankoelneut; ~**berry-tree,** kersbessieboom; ~ **bracket,** kershouer; ~**-bush,** kersbos; ~**-ends,** kersstompies; kleinighede; ~ **factory,** kersfabriek; ~ **flame,** kersboom; ~ **grease,** kersvet; ~**light,** kerslig.
Can'dlemas, Marialigmis, Vrouedag (2 Februarie).
can'dle, ~ **mould,** kersvorm; ~ **nut,** bankoelneut, ~ **plant,** kersplant; ~**-power,** kerskrag, kersligsterkte; ~**-snuff,** snuitsel; ~**-snuffer,** kerssnuiter; ~ **stick,** blaker, kandelaar; ~ **stick lily,** kandelaarlelie; ~ **tree,** kersboom; ~**-wax,** kerswas; ~**-wick,** kerspit; ~ **wood,** kershout, aapsekos.
candling test, kerstoets, ligtoets.
can'dour, opregtheid, trouhartigheid; onbevangenheid, openhartigheid, rondborstigheid.
can'dy, (n) kandy, sukade; suikerklontjies; (v) (..**died),** versuiker; laat versuiker; ~**-floss,** spookasem, suikerdons; ~**-hook,** lekkergoedhaak; ~ **sugar,** kandysuiker, teesuiker; ~**tuft,** skeefblommetjie, grafblommetjie, heuningblom.
cane, (n) riet, rottang, lat; suikerriet; wandelstok, kierie; bamboes; *ply the ~,* die lat inlê, streepsuiker gee; (v) slaan, pak gee, uitklop; mat (stoel); ~**-bottom,** rietmat; ~ **chair,** rottangstoel; rietstoel; ~ **cutter,** rietmes; ~**-drill,** stokdril; ~ **furniture,** rietmeubels; ~**-juice,** rietsap; ~ **knife,** rietmes; ~ **mill,** suiker(riet)meul; ~**-rat,** rietrot; ~**-seat,** rottangmat; ~ **spirit,** rietblits, rietspiritus, rietsnaps; ~**-sugar,** rietsuiker, sukrose; ~**-thrash,** uitgeperste suikerriet, ampas; ~**-work,** rottangwerk.
cang(ue), nekplank, nekhout.
can'icide, hondemoord(enaar).
canic'ular, Hondster=; ~ **days,** hondsdae.
can'ine, (n) hond; hoektand, oogtand; (a) hondagtig; ~ **incisor,** hoeksnytand; ~ **teeth,** oogtande, hoektande.
can'ing, loesing, pak slae; *give someone a ~,* iem. streepsuiker gee.
can'ister, trommel, blik; *gas ~,* gasbottel, gashouer; ~**-shot,** kartets, skroot(vuur).
cank'er, (n) kanker; pes; mondseer; hoefseer; knaende wurm; blaarvlek (tamaties); (v) wegvreet, verkanker; verpes; ~**ed,** verkanker; ingevreet, bederf; boos(aardig); giftig; verbitter; ~**ous,** kankeragtig, verbitterd; venynig; ~ **spider,** kannibaalspinnekop.
cann'a, kanna, (Indiese) blomriet.
cann'abis, kannabis, hennep; dagga.
canned, ingelê, ingemaak; ~ **fruit,** ingelegde vrugte, gebottelde vrugte; ~**-fruit, bottle,** vrugtefles; ~ **goods,** blikkieskos; verduursaamde ware; ~ **vegetables,** ingelegde groente.
can'nel (coal), kerssteenkool.
cann'er, inmaker; ~**y,** (..**ries),** inmaakfabriek.
cann'ibal, menseter, kannibaal; ~**ism,** kannibalisme; ~**is'tic,** kannibalisties; ~**ize,** beroof; kannibaliseer; roofmontasie toepas; ~ **spider,** kannibaalspinnekop.
cann'ikin, kannetjie.
cann'ily, uitgeslape; versigtig.
cann'ing, inmaak, inlê (vrugte), verduursaming; ~ **bottle,** vrugtefles.
cann'on, (n) kanon, geskut, artillerie; skrootstuk; karamboel, raakstoot (biljart); (v) raakstoot (biljartspel), karamboleer; teen mekaar stamp; ~ **ade',** (n) kanonnade, beskieting; (v) beskiet, kanonneer; ~**-ball,** kanonkoeël; ~**-bone,** kanonbeen; ~ **eer',**

kanonnier; ~**-fire,** kanonvuur; ~**-fodder,** kanonvoer, kanonvleis; ~**-shot,** kanonskoot.
cann'ot, kan nie; *there is no such word as* ~, kannie is dood.
can'nula, kan(n)ule, holnaald; tapbuis, dreineerbuis.
cann'y, versigtig; slim, oulik; spaarsaam; bedaard, kalm; *ca'* ~, stadig oor die klippers.
canoe', (n) kano, bootjie; *paddle one's own* ~, jou eie potjie krap; op eie bene staan; (v) in 'n kano vaar; ~**ing,** kanovaart; ~**ist,** kanovaarder; ~ **trip,** kanorit.
cañ'on, cañon; *kyk* **canyon.**
can'on, kanon; kerkwet, reël; domheer; kanon (letter); die kanonieke boeke (v.d. Bybel).
canon'ical, kanoniek, kerklik; kerkregtelik; ~**s,** kerklike gewaad.
canoni'city, kanonisiteit, egtheid.
cano'nics, kanonieke.
can'on: ~**ist,** kerkregsgeleerde; ~**iza'tion,** heiligverklaring; ~**ize,** heilig verklaar, kanoniseer; ~ **law,** kerklike reg; ~**ry,** domheerskap.
canoo'dle, (sl.) kafoefel, vry.
can'-opener, bliksnyer, blikoopmaker.
can'opy, (..**pies),** (troon)hemel; blaredak; hemeldak; oordekking; baldakyn; kap, tent; ~ **bed,** hemelbed, kapbed; ~ **pick-up,** tentvangwa.
canor'ous, sangerig; welluidend, melodieus.
Canos'sa: *go to* ~, na Canossa gaan.
can't = cannot.
cant¹, (n) stamp, stoot.
cant², (n) jargon; vaktaal; wartaal, gebrabbel, (geheime) boewetaal, geheimtaal; huigeltaal, gofemel, femelary, geveinsdheid; (v) teem; brabbel; huigelagtig praat, femel.
cant³, (n) helling, skuins kant; (v) kantel, omkantel; laat oorhel; skuins maak; omgooi, skuins lê.
cant⁴, (v) swaai, 'n draai maak.
Can'tab, Cantabri'gian, gegradueerde (student) van Cambridge.
canta'bile, (It., mus.), cantabile, vloeiend
can'taloup(e), spanspek.
cantank'erous, rusiemakerig, prikkelbaar, dwarskoppig, nors, suur, vitterig, befoeterd.
canta'ta, kantate.
can'tatrice, kantatrise, beroepsangeres.
cant'-board, kantblok (spoorbaan).
canteen', personeelwinkel; veldfles, waterkannetjie; veldkombuis; winkel; ~ *of CUTLERY,* stel (kassie) tafelgereedskap; *MOBILE* ~, verversingswa; mobiele soldatewinkel.
canter¹, (n) huigelaar.
can'ter² (n) kort galop, handgalop; *PRELIMINARY* ~, oefening, proefrit; *WIN at a* ~, fluit-fluit wen, draf-draf wen; (v) op 'n kort galoppie (handgaloppie) ry; ~ *home,* maklik wen, fluit-fluit wen.
can'terbury¹, musiekkassie.
Can'terbury², Kantelberg; *Archbishop of* ~, Aartsbiskop van Kantelberg, ~ **bells, klokkies,** koppies-en-pierings, mariëtteklokkie.
cant' file, kantvyl.
cantha'rides, (med.) spaansvlieg, kantaried, kantaride.
cantha'ris, groenvlieg, spaansvlieg.
cant'-hook, rolhaak, kantelhaak.
can'thus, ooghoek.
can'ticle, lofsang.
Can'ticles, Hooglied.
cantile'na, cantilena, deurlopende melodie.
can'tilever, vrydraer, vrydraende balk, stut, modiljon, balkkraan; ~ **beam,** vrydraerbalk; ~ **bridge,** vrydraerbrug.
can'tillate, kantelleer, musikaal resiteer.
cantin'a, kroeg, kantien; wynwinkel.
can'tle, (n) stuk; saalboog, agterboom; uitvalgrond; (v) omrol.
can'to, (-s), sang, kanto; gedeelte van 'n gedig.
canton', (n) kanton, provinsie, afdeling; skildhoek (heraldick); (v) in kantons (wyke) verdeel; in 'n skildhoek plaas; inkwartier; ~**ment,** troepekwartier, kamp, barakke, kantonnement.
can'tor, voorsanger, kantor.
cant: ~ **phrase,** modewoord; slimpraatjie; hol geseg-

de; ~**-rail,** hoër spoorstaaf, kantreling; ~ **term,** vakterm, beroepsterm.
Canuck', (Frans-)Kanadees.
can'vas, (-es), seil(doek); skilderdoek; skildery; *under* ~, in tente; ~**-back,** Amerikaanse see-eend; ~ **bag,** seilsak; ~ **bed,** seilmat; ~ **bucket,** seilemmer; ~ **chair,** dekstoel, seilstoel; ~ **cloth,** seildoek, seilstof; ~ **embroidery,** gaasborduurwerk; ~ **leggings,** seilkamaste; ~ **pocket,** seilsak.
can'vass, (n) ondersoek; huisbesoek, werwing, stemwerwery; (v) ondersoek, uitpluis, bespreek; kolporteer; bewerk; stemme werf; klante werf; pols; ~**er,** stemwerwer, werwer; lappiesmous, bestellingswerwer.
can'vas shoes, seilskoene, tekkies, tennisskoene;
can'vassing, (stem)werwery, bearbeiding (van kiesafdeling).
can'y, rietagtig; rottangagtig.
can'yon, bergkloof, diep kloof, canyon.
canzonet'(ta), kort ligte liedjie, kansonet.
caout'chouc, gomlastiek, kaoetsjoek.
cap, (n) mus, hoed, pet, baret; doppie; pakpapier; beskermer, dekking, deklaag, deklaag, kap; kapsule; ~ *and BELLS,* narrekap; *If the* ~ *FITS, wear it,* as die skoen pas, trek hom aan; ~ *and GOWN,* toga en baret; ~ *in HAND,* nederig; met die hoed in die hand; *SET one's* ~ *at someone,* iem. probeer aanlok; *put on one's THINKING* ~, jou gedagtes laat gaan; *TURKISH* ~, bandietjiespampoen; (v) **(-ped),** 'n mus opsit; beslaan; oortref; 'n graad toeken; bekroon, bedek, kroon; oordek; ~ *an ANECDOTE,* 'n anekdote troef; ~ *SOMETHING,* die kroon op iets sit, dek (doppie).
capabil'ity, (..**ties),** bekwaamheid, vermoë, aanleg, bevoegdheid.
cap'able, bekwaam; geskik, vatbaar; kapabel; ~ *of contracting,* handelsbevoeg.
capa'cious, ruim, (veel)omvattend; ~**ness,** omvang, ruimheid.
capa'citance, kapasitansie.
capa'citate, bekwaam, in staat stel.
capac'itor, kondensator, kapasitor.
capa'city, (..**ties),** bekwaamheid, vatbaarheid, vermoë, bevoegdheid; hoedanigheid; inhoud, volume; bakmaat (dam); laaivermoë; dravermoë (wa); draagvermoë; *CONTRACTUAL* ~, handelingsbevoegdheid; *FILLED to* ~, propvol; *at FULL* ~, op volle sterkte (krag); *IN the* ~ *of,* in die hoedanigheid van; *MEASURE of* ~, inhoudsmaat; ~ **crowd,** tjokvol saal (stadion); maksimumopkoms; ~ **house,** stampvol saal; ~ **test,** vermoëtoets; ~ **yield,** hoogs moontlike (optimum) opbrengs.
cap-à-pie', van kop tot toon.
capa'rison, (n) uitrusting, mondering; (v) uitdos, uitrus, optuig.
cape, kaap, landpunt; (skouer)mantel, kraag; muurvors.
Cape, (n) Kaap; (a) Kaaps; ~ *of Good Hope,* Kaap die Goeie Hoop; ~ **almond,** wildeamandel; ~ **ash,** es(se)hout; ~ **bamboo,** wildebamboes; ~ **barn-owl,** nôiensuil; ~ **beech,** boekenhout(hoom); ~ **boxwood,** buig-my-nie, bukshout; ~ **bulbul,** geelgat, witoogtiptol; ~ **bunting,** streepkoppie; ~ **cart,** kapkar, Kaapse kar; ~ **cherry,** koeboebessie; ~ **chestnut,** wildekastaiing; ~**-chisel,** ritsbeitel; ~ **cobra,** koperkapel, geelslang; ~ **cod,** Kaapse kabeljou; ~ **Colony,** Kaapkolonie; ~ **cormorant,** trekduiker; ~ **cowslip,** naeltjie; groenviooltjie; ~ **cranberry,** wynbessie, suurbessie; ~ **cress,** sterkgras, sterkkos; ~ **cycad,** kafferbroodboom; ~ **dabchick,** Kaapse duikertjie; ~ **daisy,** wit botterblom; ~ **date,** bokdrolletjie; ~ **doctor,** Kaapse dokter, suidoos(ter); ~ **Flats,** die Kaapse Vlakte; ~ **forget-me-not,** ystergras; ~ **fox,** silwerjakkals; ~ **fritillary,** aasuintjie; ~ **gannet,** malgas, molgans; ~ **gooseberry,** appelliefie; ~ **grasshird,** grasvoël; ~ **hare,** vlakhaas; ~ **hedgehog,** krimpvarkie; ~ **jasmine,** jasmyn; ~ **lark,** kalkoentjie; ~ **lady,** jakopewer; Kaapse nooientjie; ~ **laurel** stinkhout; ~ **lobster,** kreef; ~ **plane,** rooihout; ~ **polecat,** stinkmuishond, streepmuishond; ~ **Province,** Kaapprovinsie, Kaapland.

ca'per¹, (n) kappertjie (plant).
ca'per², (n) sprong, kapriol, bokkesprong; *cut a* ~, 'n flikker gooi; (v) (rond)spring, bokspring, kapriolle maak.
capercai'llie, capercail'zie, auerhaan, auerhoender.
cap'er sauce, kappersous.
Cape: ~ saffron, geelblom(metjies); ~ salmon, geelbek, kabeljou (diepseevis).
Cape: ~ sheep, Afrikanerskaap; ~ shoveller, Kaapse slopeend; ~ siskin, pietjiekanarie; ~ skin, Kaapse skaappleer (skaapvel); ~ smoke, withond (brandewyn); ~ sparrow, mossie; ~ starling, glansspreeu; ~ spitz, Kaapse spitskool; ~ sugar-bird, Kaapse suikerbosvoël; ~ sumach, jakkalspruim; ~ tea, bossie(s)tee; ~ teak, kiaat(hout); ~ ton, Kaapse ton; ~ ton'ian, (n) Kapenaar; (a) Kaapstads; Kaaps; ~ Town, Kaapstad; ~ vulture, kransaasvoël; ~ turtle-dove, tortelduif; ~ weaver, Kaapse wewer, geelvink; ~-weed, gousblom; ~ widowbird, geelkruisvink; ~ wi(d)geon, teeleentjie; ~ wild cat, groukat; ~ wild dog, wildehond.
cap'-gun, knalpistool.
cap'ias, bevelskrif tot inhegtenisneming.
capillarectas'ia, haarvatverwyding.
capillar'ity, kapillariteit, haarbuiswerking.
capill'ary, haarvormig; haarfyn; kapillêr; ~ action, kapillariteit; ~ attraction, kapillêre aantrekking; ~ tube, haarbuisie; ~ vessel, haarvat.
capill'iform haarvormig.
cap' iron, keerbeitel, dekbeitel.
cap'ita: *per* ~, per kop, per hoof.
cap'ital, (n) hoofstad; hoofsom, kapitaal; hoofletter; kapiteel, suilhoof (bouk.); *FIXED* ~, vaste kapitaal; *FLOATING (circulating)* ~, vlottende kapitaal; *MAKE* ~ *out of something*, munt slaan uit iets; *PAID-UP* ~, volgestorte kapitaal; (a) hoof-, agtermekaar, eersteklas, uitstekend; belangrik; *that's a* ~ *idea*, dis 'n uitstekende idee; ~ account, kapitaalrekening; ~ appreciation, kapitaalaanwas; ~ charge, beskuldiging van moord, moordaanklag; ~ city, hoofstad; ~ crime, halsmisdaad; ~ commitment(s), kapitaalverpligting(e); ~ consumption, kapitaalverbruik; ~ creation, kapitaalskepping, kapitaalvorming; ~ crime, halsmisdaad; ~ debt, kapitaalskuld; ~ error, fatale fout; ~ expenditure, kapitaaluitgawe; ~ formation, kapitaalvorming; ~ fund, hoofsom, kapitaal; ~ gain, kapitaalwins; ~ gains tax, kapitaalwinsbelasting; ~ goods, kapitaalgoedere; ~ grant, hoofdelike toelae; ~ income, inkomste uit kapitaal; ~-intensive, kapitaalintensief; ~ investment, kapitaalbelegging; ~ism, kapitalisme; ~ist, (n) kapitalis; goudmagnaat; geldman, geldbaas; (a) kapitalisties; ~ iza'tion, kapitalisasie; ~ ize, kapitaliseer; in geld omsit; met 'n hoofletter skryf; ~ letter, hoofletter; ~ levy, kapitaalheffing; ~ market, kapitaalmark; ~ needs, kapitaalbenodigdhede; ~ outlay, kapitaalbesteding; ~ punishment, doodstraf, halsstraf; ~ receipts, kapitaalontvangste; ~ sentence, doodstraf; ~ ship, slagskip; ~ sin, doodsonde; ~ stock, aandelekapitaal.
cap'itate(d), kop-.
capita'tion, hoofbelasting; ~ grant, hoofdelike toelae.
Cap'itol, Kapitool; Kongresgebou (Amer.).
capit'ular, kapittel-.
capit'ulate, oorgee, kapituleer.
capitula'tion, kapitulasie, oorgawe; opsomming (van hoofde); voorwaarde, verdrag.
ca'po, capo.
ca'poc, *kyk* kapok.
cap'on, kapoen, gesnyde hoenderhaan; ~ize, sny, kastreer.
capote', kapotjas, kapmantel.
capouch', monnikskap; mantelkap.
capped, gekop; gemus; ~ fuse, doppielont; ~ wheatear, skaapwagter(tjie).
cap(ping) piece, dekstuk.
capp'ing, wasdeksel; indraaiprop; dekplaat, vors (van 'n muur); dwarshout; graadverlening; ~ brick, deksteen; sluitsteen; ~ iron, dekbeitel.

cappucci'no, (It.), cappuccino, expresso, koffie met melk.
cap'ric, bokagtig, bok-; ~ acid, kapriensuur.
cappric'cio, (It., mus.) capriccio, lewendig.
capriccio'so, (It., mus.) capriccioso, vry en impulsief.
caprice', luim, bevlieging, gril, fiemies, nuk, gier; wies(i)ewasie, frats; (pl) hipokonders.
capri'cious, buierig, vol giere, wispelturig, eiesinnig, grillig, nukkerig, humeurig, fiemiesrig; ~ness, eiesinnigheid, wispelturigheid, buierigheid, fiemies, humeurigheid.
Cap'ricorn, die Steenbok; *Tropic of* ~, Steenbokskeerkring.
cap'rine, bokagtig, bok-.
cap'riole, (n) bokkesprong, kaperjol, kapriol; (v) bokspring, kapriole (kaperjolle) maak.
cap' screw, dopskroef.
capse'lla, dopvrug.
cap'sicum, rissie(s), Spaanse peper.
cap'size, omval, omslaan, omkantel, oorval.
cap' sleeve, kapmou.
cap'stan, kaapstander; gangspil; ~-bar, windboom; ~-head, spilkop; ~-socket, spilbed.
cap'stone, dekklip, sluitsteen.
cap'-stud, doptapbout.
cap'sular, doosvormig; in 'n vliesie, kappie-; ~ fruit, kokervrug, doosvrug.
cap'sulate, inkapsel.
capsula'tion, inkapseling.
cap'sule, saadhuisie, kapsel, saaddoos, doosvrug, vrugbekleedsel; kappie, dop(pie); omhulsel; skaaltjie; kapsule; smeltkroes.
capsuli'tis, kapselontsteking.
cap'tain, (n) kaptein; aanvoerder; leier; ~ *of industry*, groot nyweraar; (v) aanvoer, lei; ~cy, (..cies), kapteinskap; kapteinsrang; ~ship, kapteinsrang; kapteinskap.
capta'tion, kaptasie, inpalming; apploussoekery, flikflooiery; slinkse inpalming.
cap'tion, opskrif, titel; onderskrif, byskrif (rolprent); gevangeneming, arrestasie.
cap'tious, bedrieglik, misleidend; spitsvondig; aanmerkerig, bedilsiek, vitterig; ~ness, vitsug; bedrieglikheid.
cap'tivate, bekoor, betower, inneem, boei, inpalm; ~d, geboei(d).
captiva'tion, bekoring, betowering.
cap'tive, (n) gevangene; (a) gevanklik; gevang, geboei; ~ balloon, kabelballon.
captiv'ity, gevangenskap.
cap'tor, vanger, gevangenemer; buitmaker.
cap'tress, (-es), vangster.
cap'ture, (n) vangs, roof; inname, gevangeneming, vermeestering, verowering; prys; buit, beslagname; ~ team, wildvangspan; (v) vang (mense); beslag lê op, buitmaak (wapens); roof; inneem, jou meester maak van, vermeester, verower (stad); ~ *the imagination*, die verbeelding aangryp; ~d river, geroofde rivier.
Cap'uchin, Kapusyner.
cap'uchin, (-s), kapmantel; mantelkap, kap; ~ capers, kapper(tjie)s; ~ monkey, kapusyneraap, rolaap, mantelaap; ~ pigeon, mantelduif.
car, rytuig, kar; trem; spoorwa; motor(kar).
car'abid, loopkewer, grondkewer.
car(a)bineer', karabinier.
ca'racal, rooikat, karakal *(Felis caracal)*.
car accident, motorongeluk, karongeluk.
ca'racol(e), (n) swaai; halwe swenking; bokkesprong; draaitrap; (v) swaai; bokspring.
Ca'racul, Karakoel.
carafe', kraf, kraffie, karaf, waterfles.
car'ambole, karambool, raakstoot (biljart).
ca'ramel, karamel, gebrande suiker; ~ize, karamelliseer.
ca'rapace, rugdop, rugskild; bodop (skilpad), karapaks.
ca'rat, karaat.
ca'ravan, caravan', karavaan; woonwa, toerwa; ~ner, woonwatoeris, karavaantoeris; ~ning, woonwatoerisme, karavaantoerisme; ~ park, woonwapark, karavaanpark.

caravan'serai, (-s), caravan'sary, (..ries), karavaan= herberg, karavanserai.
caravan site, woonwaterrein, karavaanterrein.
ca'ravel, karveel (ligte skip).
ca'raway, karwy; komyn; ~ **seed,** karwysaad, koek= saad.
car'bamid(e), karbamied, karbamide, ureum.
carb'ide, karbied.
carb'ine, kort geweer, buks, karabyn.
car'bineer, karbinier.
carbohyd'rate, koolhidraat.
carbol'ic, karbol; ~ *ACID,* karbolsuur; ~ *OIL,* kar= bololie; ~ *SOAP,* karbolseep.
carbolin'eum, carbolineum (geregistreerde handels= naam).
car'bolize, karboliseer.
carb'on, koolstof; ilmeniet; ~ **a'ceous,** koolstofhou= dend; koolsofagtig; ~ **ade,** karbonado.
carb'onate, (n) karbonaat; ~ *of soda,* wassoda; (v) verkool.
carb'on: ~ **a'tion,** verkoling; ~ **atite,** karbonatiet; ~ **bisulphide,** koolstofdisulfide, koolstofdisulfied; ~ **- black,** koolswart, roetswart; ~ **book,** deurslag= boek; ~ **compound,** koolstofverbinding; ~ **con= tent,** kool(stof)gehalte; ~ **copy,** deurslag, bloutjie; ~ **dating,** koolstofdatering; - **deposit,** roetaan= korsting, koolaanslag; ~ **diamond,** karbonado; ~ **dioxide,** koolsuurgas, kooldioksied; ~ **electrode,** koolelektrode; ~ **filament,** kooldraad (gloeilamp); ~ **formation,** koolstofvorming; ~ **-free,** kool= stofvry; ~ **gland,** kooldrukstuk; ~ **ian,** karbonies.
carbon'ic, koolstofhoudend; koolsuur=; ~ **acid,** koolsuur.
carb'on: ~ **if'erous,** koolstofhoudend; ~ *iferous age,* steenkooltydperk; ~ **ify,** karboniseer; ~ **iza'tion,** aankoling, verkoling; ~ **ize,** karboniseer, aankool, verkool; ~ **izing,** karbonisering, verkoling, aanko= ling; ~ **-knock,** koolklop; ~ **monoxide,** koolmon= oksied, kooldamp; ~ **paper,** deurslagpapier, kool= drukpapier, bloutjie; ~ **point,** koolspits; ~ **print= (ing),** kooldruk; ~ **steel,** kool(stof)staal; ~ **stick,** koolspits; ~ **tetrachloride,** kool(stof)tetrachloride; ~ **tip,** koolspits.
carborun'dum, karborundum.
carb'oy, mandjiefles, karfles; karba; suurfles.
carb'uncle, karbonkel; negeoog, steenpuisie.
carburet', (-ted), met koolstof vermeng, karbureer, vergas; ~ **ting,** vergassing, karburering.
carburett'er, carburett'or, karburateur, vergasser; ~ **action,** vergasserwerking; ~ **choke,** vergasser= smoorder; ~ **float,** vlot, dobber; ~ **needle,** vergas= sernaald; ~ **plug,** vergasserprop.
carburiza'tion, dopverharding (in)koling (van staal).
car'burize, dopverhard; karbureer
car'cajou, veelvraat (dier).
carc'ase, (-s), carc'ass, (-es), geraamte, karkas, kada= wer; romp; geslagte dier; wrak; lyf, liggaam; raam= werk (van model); *where the* ~ *is, there the vultures will gather, waar die aas is, vergader die arende;* ~ **ply,** karkaslaag (buiteband).
carcin'ogen, karsinogeen, kankerverwekker; ~ **'ic,** karsinogeen, kankerverwekkend.
carcinom'a, (-ta), karsinoom, kankergeswel.
car coat, motorjas; heupjas.
card¹, (n) kaart; program; visitekaartjie; spyskaart; *have the* ~ *s in one's HAND,* die hef in die hand hê; *HOUSE of* ~ *s,* kaarthuis; *LAY one's* ~ *s on the table,* (met) oop kaarte speel; helder wyn skink; *it is ON the* ~ *s,* dit sal waarskynlik gebeur, daar be= staan 'n moontlikheid; *PLAY one's* ~ *s well,* met oorleg te werk gaan; met politiek werk; *a QUEER* ~ , 'n snaakse vent; *he's a REAL* ~ , hy is 'n ou grapmaker; *SHOW one's* ~ *s,* in jou kaarte laat kyk; jou planne openbaar; *a* ~ *up one's SLEEVE,* 'n slag om die arm; 'n plan agter die hand; *SPEAK by the* ~ , jou woord goed doen; *a SURE* ~ , iets waarop 'n mens kan reken; *put one's* ~ *s on the TABLE,* jou plan(ne) openbaar; (met) oop kaarte speel; *THROW up one's* ~ *s,* tou opgooi, opgee; (v) op 'n kaart aanteken.
card², (n) wolkam, kaardwol; (v) uitkam, kaard.
card'amom, kardamom; *wild* ~ , pramdoring.

card'an: ~ **joint,** kruiskoppeling, kardankoppeling; ~ **shaft,** kardanas, dryfas.
card: ~ **board,** bordpapier, karton; ~ **box,** kaartdo= sie; ~ **-carrying,** ingeskrewe; ~ *-carrying member,* ingeskrewe lid; ~ **case,** kaartboekie; ~ **catalogue,** kaartkatalogus.
card'er, (wol)kaarder, wolkammer; (wol)kaardster.
car'dia, hort; maagmond, maagingang.
card'iac, (n) hartlyer; hartversterking; (a) hart=, hart= versterkend, kardiaal; ~ **abnormality,** hartafwy= king; ~ **arrest,** hartstilstand; hartversaking; ~ **failure,** hartverlamming; ~ **lesion,** hartletsel; ~ **murmur,** hartgeruis; ~ **muscle,** hartspier; ~ **sac,** hartsak; ~ **valve,** hartklep.
cardial'gia, kardialgie, maagkramp; sooibrand.
card'igan, gebreide onderbaadjie, wolonderbaadjie, middelbaadjie, knooptrui.
card'inal, (n) kardinaal; damesmantel; (a) kardinaal, vernaamste; hoof=; dieprooi; ~ *NUMBER,* hoof= getal; ~ *POINT,* hoofpunt; hoofwindstreek; ~ *VIRTUES,* hoofdeugde; ~ **ate,** ~ **ship,** kardinaal= skap; ~ **'s hat,** kardinaalshoed.
card' index, (n), kaartregister; (v) 'n kaartregister aanlê (maak); ~ **system,** kaartstelsel, kaartsisteem.
card'ing, kaardery, kaarding; (pl) kaardsels; ~ **ma= chine,** kaardmasjien; ~ **wool,** kaardwol.
card'iogram, kardiogram.
card'iograph, kardiograaf; **..dio'graphy,** kardiogra= fie.
card'ioid, (n) kardioïed, kardioïede; (a) hartvormig.
cardiolog'ical, hart=, kardiologies.
cardiol'ogist, hartspesialis, kardioloog.
cardio'logy, kardiologie.
cardiom'etry, hartmeting, kardiometrie.
cardit'is, ontsteking van die hart.
cardoon', kardoen.
card: ~ **party,** kaartaand; ~ **reader,** kaartlêer, =legster.
car-driver, motorbestuurder, karbestuurder.
card: ~ **room,** kaartkamer; ~ **-sharp(er),** valsspeler; ~ **-table,** speeltafeltjie; ~ **tray,** kaartbak; ~ **-trick,** kaartkunsie; ~ **-vote,** blokstem; ~ **-wire,** fyn staal= draad; ~ **-wool,** kaardwol; ~ **wreck,** kraaines (rekenaar).
care, (n) sorg, oplettendheid, sorgvuldigheid; inagne= ming, hoede, toesig; versorging; bekommernis, be= sorgdheid, ongerustheid; (pl) beslommernis(se); *with the GREATEST* ~ , met die grootste versigtig= heid, met die meeste sorg; *HAVE a* ~ , oppas; *HAVE the* ~ *of,* belas wees met; ~ *KILLED the cat,* kommer maak 'n mens gedaan; ~ *OF,* per adres; *TAKE* ~ , oppas; sorg vir; *UNDER his* ~ , onder sy sorg, in sy hoede; (v) omgee, hom bekom= mer; sorg vir, sorg dra; versorg; hou van; graag wil hê; ~ *ABOUT,* omgee; *for AUGHT (ALL) I* ~ , wat my betref; *I COULD not* ~ *less,* ek gee geen flenter om nie; *he DOES not* ~ , hy gee nie om nie; *I DON'T* ~ , dit traak my nie; ~ *FOR,* oppas; omgee vir, hou van; *not* ~ *in the LEAST,* geen flenter om= gee nie; - *for NOTHING,* nêrens voor omgee nie; *I don't* ~ *a RAP,* dit kan my nie skeel nie; ek het daar maling aan; ek gee geen flenter om nie; *I don't* ~ *a STRAW,* ek gee geen flenter om nie; *WOULD you* ~ *to?* het jy lus om te?
careen', (n) kentering, oorhelling; kanteling, kieling; (v) oorhel, kenter (skip); kielhaal, kantel; op een kant seil; ~ **age,** kieling; ~ **ing,** kanteling, kente= ring, (oor)helling; kieling.
career', (n) loopbaan, voortgang; vaart; *CARVE out a* ~ *for oneself,* jou weg baan, vooruitgaan in die wêreld; *in FULL* ~ , in volle vaart; *in MID* ~ , in volle vaart; (v) jakker, hol, rondhardloop; vlieg; snel; ~ *ABOUT,* rondjakker; rondvlieg; ~ *ALONG,* voortsnel; ~ **diplomat,** beroepsdiplo= maat; ~ **girl,** beroepsvrou; sakevrou; ~ **guidance,** beroepsleiding, beroepsvoorligting; ~ **-guide,** loop= baangids; ~ **ist,** baantjiesjaer, baantjiesoeker, eer= gierige; ~ **-minded,** ambisieus; ~ **officer,** beroeps= offisier; ~ **woman,** beroepsvrou.
care'free, onbesorg, sorgvry; *a* ~ *person,* 'n sieltjie sonder sorg; ~ **spirit,** sorgvrye gees, sorgvryheid.
care'ful, sorgvuldig, versigtig; bedag, sorgsaam, op=

passend; *be ~ of*, ontsien; ~ **ness**, sorgvuldigheid, versigtigheid.
care'less, sorgeloos, nalatig, agteloos, agtelosig; slordig; roekeloos; onbedagsaam; ~ **ness**, sorgeloosheid, onverskilligheid, agtelosigheid; slegtigheid.
caress', (n) (-es), liefkosing, omhelsing, streling; (v) liefkoos, aai, streel; aanhaal; ~ **ing**, gestreel.
ca'ret, invoegteken, inlasteken, uitlatingsteken, weglatingsteken, karet; skilpaddop.
care'taker, opsigter, oppasser, saalwagter, bewaarder; ~ **cabinet**, ~ **government**, tussentydse regering.
care'worn, uitgeput, afgesloof, afgetob, vervalle.
car'fare, tremgeld; busgeld.
carg'o, (-es), (skeeps)lading, vrag(goed); ~ **boat**, vragboot; ~ **capacity**, laairuim; ~ **-carrying**, vragdraend; ~ **-carrying capacity**, vragvermoë; laaivermoë; ~ **clerk**, laaiklerk; ~ **hatchway**, laaihoof; ~ **hold**, laairuim; ~ **plane**, transportvliegtuig, vragvliegtuig; ~ **ship**, vragskip, vragboot; ~ **space**, laairuimte; ~ **steamer**, vragstoomskip, vragstoomboot.
car hire, motorhuur; motorhuursaak.
Caribbe'an, Karibies.
Caribbees', Karibiese Eilande.
cariboo', **caribou'**, rendier, kariboe.
caricature', (n) karikatuur, spotprent; (v) 'n spotprent maak van, karikaturiseer.
caricatur'ist, spotprenttekenaar, karikaturis.
ca'ries, beenbrand, beenvreter, beenettering, kariës; *dental* ~, tandbederf, tandkariës.
carill'on, **ca'rillon**, klokkespel, kariljon, beiaard; ~ **eur'**, klokkespeler, beiaardier, klokkenis.
cari'na, kiel (biol.); kielbeen.
ca'rinate, kielvormig.
car'ious, aangevreet, verrot, karieus.
cark'ing, drukkend; ~ **care**, knaende sorg.
car' licence, motorlisensie.
carl'ine, driedissel; daksteunrib, dakboog.
car load, motorvrag, karvrag.
Carlovin'gian, (n) Karolinger; (a) Karolingies.
car'man, voerman; karweier; besteller.
Carm'elite, Karmeliet.
carm'inative, (n) maagwindmiddel; (a) windafdrywend.
carm'ine, karmosyn, karmyn.
carmin'ic acid, karmynsuur.
carn'age, slagting, bloedbad.
carn'al, vleeslik, sinlik, wellustig; stoflik, wêrelds, dierlik; ~ *CONNECTION*, vleeslike omgang; ~ *KNOWLEDGE*, geslagtelike ervaring; ~ *PLEASURE*, wellus.
carn'alism, **carnal'ity**, sinlikheid, vleeslikheid.
carn'alize, versinlik.
car'nallite, karnalliet.
carn'ally, vleeslik; *know* ~, geslagsomgang hê.
carna'tion, (n) angelier; (a) vleiskleur, ligrooi.
carnel'ian, karneool, kornalyn.
carn'ey, *kyk* **carny**.
carnif'icate, vervlees.
carnifica'tion, vervlesing.
car'nify, (..fied), vervlees, vlees word.
carn'ival, karnaval; feesviering; uitspanning.
Carniv'ora, Karnivore, Carnivora, vleisetende diere.
carn'ivore, vleiseter, karnivoor.
carniv'orous, vleisetend.
car'notite, karnotiet.
carn'y, (carnied), flikflooi, paai, pamperlang.
ca'rob, ~ **-tree**, karob(boom), Johannesbrood(boom) *(Ceratonia siliqua)*.
caroche', stasiewa.
ca'rol, (n) lofsang, lied; voëlsang; *C ~ s by CANDLELIGHT*, Kersliedere by kerslig; (v) (-led), vrolik sing, vreugdeliedere sing; kwinkeleer.
Carolin'gian = **Carlovingian**.
ca'roller, sanger.
ca'rom, karamboleer.
car'otene, karoteen.
carot'id, nekslagaar; ~ **artery**, nekslagaar; ~ **gland**, karotisklier.
carous'al, suipparty, fuif, drinkgelag, slemmpaal; ~ **-song**, slampamperliedjie.

carouse', (n) brasparty, drinkgelag; (v) fuif, slemp, slampamper, gloria hou, drink, suip, boemel, swel.
car(r)ousel', mallemeule.
carou'ser, drinker, fuiwer; suiplap, suiper.
carp¹, (n) karp.
carp², (v) vit, lol, brom.
carp'al, (n) handwortelbeen, polsbeen, hotnotjie, vingerbeentjie; (a) hand-, gewrigs; pols-; ~ **bones**, handhotnotjies, polsbeentjies, handwortelbene; ~ **joint**, polsgewrig.
car'-park, motorpark; parkeerterrein.
Carpath'ian, Karpaties; ~ **Mountains**, (die) Karpate.
carp'el, vrugblaar.
carp'enter, (n) timmerman; (v) timmer; ~ **ant**, houtkappermier; ~ **bee**, houtkapperby; ~ **ing**, timmerwerk; ~ **'s bench**, skaafbank; ~ **'s brace**, omslag; ~ **'s gauge**, kruishout; ~ **'s measure**, duimstok; ~ **'s shop**, timmermanswinkel; ~ **'s square**, winkelhaak; ~ **'s tools**, timmermansgereedskap; ~ **'s work**, timmerwerk.
carp'entry, houtwerk; timmerwerk; timmermansambag.
carp'er, vitter, loller.
carp'et, (n) tapyt, mat, vloerkleed(jie); deklaag, bladlaag (pad); *BRING on the* ~, ter bespreking bring; *PUT someone on the* ~, iem tot verantwoording roep; *the RED* ~ *was laid out for him*, die wêreld was vir hom te koud; (v) met tapyte belê; skrobbeer; ~ **-bag**, reissak, tapytsak; ~ **-bagger**, politieke indringer; ~ **-beater**, matteklopper; ~ **binding**, ~ **braid**, tapytomboorsel; ~ **broom**, tapytbesem, matbesem; ~ **brush**, tapytborsel, matborsel; ~ **-dance**, danspartyjie; ~ **drive**, grondhou; ~ **ing**, tapytgoed; tapytstof, matstof; tapytwerk; ~ **-knight**, sitkamerheld, saletjonker, salonheld; ~ **-rod**, tapytstang, matstang; traproede; ~ **runner**, tapytloper; ~ **slipper**, tapytskoen; ~ **strip**, tapytlat; ~ **-stud**, tapytskroef; ~ **-weaver**, tapytmaker; ~ **-weaving**, tapytwewery; ~ **wool**, tapytwol.
carp'ing, gevit.
carpol'ogy, vrugtekunde, karpologie.
carpoph'agous, vrugetend.
car'port, motorafdak, motoroordak, motorskuiling, karskuiling.
carp'us, (..pi), handwortel.
car: ~ **-racing**, motor(wed)renne; ~ **-rally**, tydren.
ca'rriable, dra(ag)baar.
ca'rriage, wa, rytuig, voertuig; vervoer; vrag; frankeerkoste, vervoerkoste, vraggeld; houding; gedrag; uitvoering; aanneming (voorstel); rolstel (van tikmasjien); onderstel; affuit (van kanon); ~ *by AIR*, lugvervoer; ~ *of BODY*, houding van liggaam; ~ *FORWARD*, verskuldig, te betaal; verskuldigde vraggeld; ~ *and FOUR*, 'n rytuig met vier perde, vierspan; ~ *FREE*, vragprys betaal(d), vragvry; ~ *PAID*, vrag betaal; ~ **-builder**, rytuigmaker; ~ **-drive**, oprylaan; ~ **ful**, karvrag; ~ **-horse**, karperd, trekperd; ~ **road**, rypad; ~ **way**, wapad; rypad, rybaan; ~ **works**, voertuigfabriek.
ca'rrier, transportryer, bevragter, karweier; (aan)draer; motorwa; draagblok; kiemdraer (siekte), siekteoorbringer; drasak (patrone); tassie; rak (vir bomme); vervoerder; posduif; afvoerbuis; karretjie; dakrak (motor); bagasierak (rywiel); vliegdekskip, moederskip; vegrusper (mil.); ~ **bicycle**, transportfiets; ~ **-bracket**, draagstuk; ~ **-cone**, moerkeël; ~ **current**, dragolf; ~ **frequency**, dra(ag)frekwensie; ~ **-pigeon**, posduif; ~ **-plate**, dra(ag)plaat; ~ **rocket**, abbavuurpyl; ~ **-service**, vragdiens, karweidiens; ~ **tricycle**, besteldriewiel; ~ **wave**, dragolf.
ca'rrion, aas, kreng; ~ **-beetle**, aaskewer; ~ **crow**, swartkraai; ~ **-eating**, aasvretend; ~ **flower**, aasblom; ~ **-lily**, aaslelie.
car'rom = **carom**.
carrona'de, karronade.
ca'rron oil, carronolie.
ca'rrot, (geel)wortel; ~ **leaves**, wortelblare, -lowwe; ~ **s**, wortels; rooikop, rooi hare; ~ **-tree**, wortelboom; ~ **y**, geelagtig; rooihaar-.
ca'rry, (n) dra(ag)wydte; trekvermoë; drastand

(mil.); haal (gholf); (v) **(carried)**, dra, vervoer; bring; gedra; neem; leen (rekenkunde); oordra, oorhou; inpalm; bevat, inhou; verdien (rente); ~ *ASHORE,* aanspoel; aan wal dra; ~ *a WAY*, meevoer, wegdra, wegvoer, skaak; ~ *BACK*, terugvoer, terugbring; ~ *everything BEFORE one,* alles oorwin, meesleep; ~ *on a BUSINESS,* sake doen; ~ *CONVICTION,* oortuig; ~ *the DAY,* seëvier; ~ *into EFFECT,* ten uitvoer bring; ~ *into EXECUTION,* uitvoer; *FETCH and* ~ *for someone,* iem. se handlanger wees; ~ *a FORTRESS,* 'n vesting inneem; ~ *FORWARD,* oorbring; ~ *one's HEARERS with one,* jou toehoorders meevoer; ~ *INTEREST,* rente opbring (dra); *loans* ~ *INTEREST,* lenings verdien rente; ~ *a MOTION,* 'n voorstel aanneem; ~ *OFF,* die paal haal; jou goed van 'n taak kwyt; wen; wegvoer; ~ *ON,* voortsit; voortgaan; te kere gaan; ~ *ON in the same old way,* die ou slentergang gaan; die ou sleur volg; ~ *ONESELF well,* 'n mooi houding hê; ~ *OUT,* uitvoer; ~ *OVER,* oordra; ~ *PAST,* verbydra; ~ *one's POINT,* sy sin kry; ~ *RIGHT on to the end,* end-uit volhou; ~ *STOCKS,* voorrade aanhou; ~ *THROUGH,* deursit; voltooi; ~ *UNANIMOUSLY,* met algemene stemme (sonder teenstemme) aanneem; ~ *it off WELL,* jou dapper gedra; ~**-bag,** drasak, dratas, drakoffer; ~**-cot,** drawieg(ie), kapwieg(ie).
ca'rrying, vervoer; dra(ag)-; verdraend (stem); ~**-agency,** karweionderneming; oorbringmiddel; ~**-capacity,** draagkrag (stem); drakrag (veld); laaivermoë; ~**(s)-on,** wangedrag; streke; gedoente; ~**-out,** (taak)verrigting; uitvoer; ~**-pole,** dra(ag)-stok; ~ **scraper,** wielskrop; ~**-spring,** draveer; ~**-trade,** vragvaart; vragvervoer.
ca'rry-shaft, dra-as, draagas.
car'-sick, motorsiek; karsiek; ~**ness,** motorsiekte, karsiekte.
cart, (n) kar, rytuig; *put the* ~ *before the horse,* agterstevoor te werk gaan; die wa voor die osse inspan; die perde agter die wa span; (v) met 'n kar vervoer, ry; ~ *away,* wegvoer, wegry.
cart'age, vraggeld, ryloon; besteldiens, vervoer; ~ **area,** bestelgebied; ~ **contractor,** besteldiensaannemer; ~ **rate,** besteltarief; ~ **service,** besteldiens; ~ **station,** afleweringstasie; ~ **trailer,** karweisleepwa.
cart: ~ **box,** karkis; ~ **cushion,** karkussing; ~ **driver,** kardrywer.
carte: *GIVE someone* ~ *blanche,* iem. vry spel gee, iem. carte blanche gee; *a LA* ~, keusespyskaart.
cart'el, uitdaging; verdrag; kartel, ring; ooreenkoms.
carteliza'tion, kartellering, kartelvorming.
cart'elize, kartelleer.
cart'er, voerman, karweier.
Carte'sian, (n) aanhanger van Descartes, Cartesiaan; (a) Cartesiaans; ~ **devil,** ~ **diver,** Cartesiaanse duikertjie; ~**ism,** Cartesianisme.
Carth'age, Carthago, Kartago.
Carthagin'ian, (n) Carthager, Kartager; (a) Carthaags, Kartaags.
cart: ~ **horse,** karperd; ~**-house,** waenhuis.
Carthu'sian, Kartuiser.
cart'ilage, kraakbeen.
cartila'ginous, kraakbenig, kraakbeenagtig; ~ *tissue,* kraakbeenweefsel.
cart'-load, karvrag; hoop, baie.
cartog'rapher, kaartmaker, kartograaf.
cartograph'ical, kartografies.
cartog'raphy, kartografie, kaarttekenkuns.
cart'omancy, kaartwaarsêery.
cart'on, bordpapierdosie, doos, karton(houer); kartonpapier; hartjie van die kol.
cartoon', spotprent; grapprent; tekenprent; karikatuur; *animated* ~, verlewendigde spotprent; ~**ist,** spotprenttekenaar, karikatuurtekenaar.
cartouch(e)', krulwerk, randversiering, cartouche.
cart'-pole, disselboom.
cart'ridge, patroon; *blank* ~, loskruitpatroon; ~**-bag,** patroonsak; ~**-belt,** bandelier; patroonband; ~**-box,** patroondoos; patroonkis; ~**-cap,** patroondoppie; ~**-case,** patroonsak; patroondop; ~ **clip,** (in) laaiplaatjie; ~ **drum,** patroontrommel; ~**-ejec**-**tor,** dopuitwerper; dopuittrekker; ~**-extractor,** patroontrekker; ~ **paper,** kardoespapier; ~**-pouch,** patroontas.
cart: ~ **road,** wapad; ~ **rut,** karspoor; ~ **shed,** waenhuis; ~ **track,** karspoor; karpaadjie, middelmannetjie.
cart'ulary, (..ries), register, oorkondeboek, katalogus.
cart: ~**-wheel,** karwiel; bolmakiesie; groot muntstuk; *TURN* ~*-wheels,* bolmakiesie slaan; ~**-wheel penny,** dikoulap; ~**-whip,** peits; ~**-wright,** wamaker, karmaker.
ca'runcle, kam (haan); bel (kalkoen); vleisuitwas, vleisvratjie.
car'-valet, motorversorger, karversorger.
carve, kap; uitsny, beeldhou, graveer; voorsny (vleis); ~ *out a CAREER for oneself,* jou weg in die wêreld baan; ~*d WOOD,* gesnede hout; ~*d WORK,* sneewerk.
carv'el, karveel (ligte skip).
carv'en, gebeeldhou, gesnede.
car'vene, karween.
carv'er, voorsnyer; houtsnyer; beeldsnyer; grootmes; leuningstoel; (pl) grootmes en vurk.
carv'ing, snywerk; vleis sny, voorsny; ~**-chisel,** vlakbeitel, houtbeitel; ~**-fork,** voorsnyvurk, grootvurk; ~**-gouge,** houtsnyguts; ~**-knife,** grootmes, voorsnymes, transeermes, vleismes; ~ **set,** voorsnystel, transeerstel.
car wheel, motorwiel, karwiel.
caryat'id, steunbeeld, vrouefiguur (as steunpilaar), kariatide.
caryop'sis, graanvrug.
Casano'va, Casanova.
cas'bah, kasba.
cascade', (n) waterval, kaskade, stroom; menigte; (v) neergolf; neerklater.
cascar'a (sagra'da), kaskara.
case¹, (n) kis, kas, tas, doos, trommel; etui; letterkas; oortreksel, feodraal, koker; huisie, dop; stolp; handkoffer; boeksak; sloop; *LOWER* ~, onderste kas, onderkas, klein letters; *UPPER* ~, boonste kas, hoofletters; (v) beklee, oortrek; aanklam (tabak).
case², (n) geval; omstandigheid; aanklag; hofsaak; naamval (gram.), casus; pasiënt, sieke, gewonde; *in ANY* ~, in alle geval; *AS the* ~ *may be,* soos die geval mag wees; ~ *of CONSCIENCE,* gewetensaak; *in EVERY* ~, in elke geval; *put up a GOOD* ~, goeie (afdoende) redes aanvoer; *the* ~ *in HAND,* die onderhawige geval; *he HAS no* ~, sy klag is ongegrond, *IN* ~, ingeval; *LEADING* ~, sleutelvonnis; *MAKE out one's* ~, sy saak bewys; *that MEETS the* ~, dit voldoen aan die eise; *in NO* ~, onder geen omstandighede nie; *in* ~ *OF,* in geval van; *a* ~ *in POINT,* 'n geval wat as voorbeeld dien; *PUT the* ~, die saak stel; *in THAT* ~, in daardie geval.
casea'tion, verkasing.
case: ~**-book,** gevalleboek; verslagboek; pasiënteboek; ~ **bottle,** veldfles; mandjiefles; ~ **clock,** staanklok; ~**-ending,** naamvalsuitgang; ~**-harden,** dopverhard; verhard maak; ~**-hardened,** (dop)verhard; verstok; ~ **history,** gevallestudie, praktykgeval; siekteverslag.
cas'ein, kaasstof, kaseïen, kaseïne.
case'-knife, (..knives), skedemes.
case'-law, uitspraakreg, presedentereg.
case'-lock, kasslot.
case'mate, kasemat.
case'ment, raam, draaivenster; swaairaam; ~ **cloth,** gordyngoed; ~**-moulding,** hollys; ~ **window,** knipraam, swaaivenster.
cas'eous, kaasagtig, kaas-.
case'-rack, letterkas.
case-record, siekteverslag; gevalleverslag.
casern(e)', kasern.
case'-room, lettersettery.
case-sheet, bedkaart.
case'-shot, kartets, skroot; kartetslading.
case'work, gevallestudie.
case'-worm, kokerwurm.

cash, (n) kontant(geld), spesie; kas, kasgeld; ~ *and CARRY*, koop-en-loop, haal-en-betaal, kontanten afhaalstelsel; *CONVERT something into ready* ~, iets tot geld maak; ~ *on DELIVERY*, kontant by aflewering; ~ *DOWN*, kontant; botter by die vis; *FOR* ~, teen kontant; ~ *in HAND*, kontantgeld (voorhande); *HARD* ~, klinkende munt, kontant; *LOOSE* ~, kleingeld; *pay* ~ *on the NAIL*, met klinkende munt betaal; ~ *with ORDER*, kontant by bestelling; *be OUT of* ~, sonder blik wees; platsak wees; sleg by kas; *READY* ~, kontant voorhande; *SHORT of* ~, sonder geld; kort by kas; *SPOT* ~, klinkende munt; kontant betaling; (v) inwissel, kleinmaak; inkasseer; trek; honoreer, realiseer, uitbetaal; *in* ~ *or KIND*, in geld of goed; ~ *in ON*, munt uit iets slaan; voordeel trek uit; ~ **able**, uitwisselbaar; ~ **account**, kasrekening; kontantrekening; ~ **aperture**, loket; ~ **balance**, kontantsaldo; ~**-book**, kasboek; ~**-box**, (**-es**), geldkissie; ~ **clearances**, kontantvereffenings; ~ **crop**, kontantgewas; ~ **desk**, kas(toon)bank; ~ **disbursement**, kontantuitbetaling; ~ **discount**, kontantkorting; ~**-drawer**, geldlaai.
cash'ew, kasjoe; ~**-nut**, kasjoeneut.
cash: ~ **float**, kontant; wisselfonds; ~ **flow**, kontantvloei, kontantbeweging.
cashier'¹, (n) kassier, inner, teller.
cashier'², (v) afsit, afdank, ontslaan; kasseer (mil.).
cash'ing, uitwisseling.
cash' issues, kontantuitreikings.
cash' keeper, kassier.
cash'mere, kasjmier, kassemier; ~ **shawl**, kasjmiersjaal.
cash: ~ **office**, kassierskantoor; ~ **payment**, kontantbetaling; ~ **price**, kontantprys; ~ **register**, kasregister; ~ **resources**, kasmiddele, kontantmiddele; ~ **sale**, kontantverkoop; ~ **till**, geldlaai.
cas'ing, koker; aanklam (tabak); oortreksel, dekkleed; skerm (toneel); omhulsel; worsderm; skuifie (naaldw.); buitewand; voering; verpakking, bekledingsbuis, huls, kas; bekisting; ~**-nail**, vloerspyker; ~**-spring**, hulselveer.
casi'no, (**-s**), kasino, speelbank, dobbelsaal.
cask, vat, vaatjie, kuip.
cas'ket, dosie, kassie, kissie; (doods)kis; urn.
Cas'lon, Caslon (lettertipe).
Cas'pian, Kaspies.
casque, helm; valhelm; ooryster.
Cassan'dra, Kassandra, doemprofeet.
cassa'ta, cassata, roomys.
cassa'tion, vernietiging, kassasie.
cassa'va: ~ **root**, boordwortel, kassawe, maniok.
cass'erole, kastrol, (vuurvaste) oondskottel, erdekastrol, bakskottel; oondstoofgereg.
cassette', kasset; kassetband, bandkasset; filmkasset; videokasset; ~ **music**, kassetmusiek; ~ **player**, kassetspeler; ~ **video**, (kasset)video(band).
ca'ssia, kassia, (wilde)kaneel; seneblare; senepeule; ~ **oil**, kassia-olie, Chinese kaneelolie.
cassi'terite, tinsteen, kassiteriet.
cass'ock, priesterkleed, toga, soutane, soetane.
cas'soulet, (F.), cassoulet, ragout, vleis-en-boontjiebredie.
cass'owary, (..**ries**), kasuaris.
cast, (n) gooi, worp; lot; afgietsel, bou, vorm; staaltjie; wurmhopie; paar (valke); berekening; rolverdeling, besetting (toneelstuk); gietvorm; afgietsel, vormafdruk; aanleg, karakter; trek, sweem, soort; *a* ~ *in the EYE*, effens skeel kyk; *the* ~ *of his FEATURES*, sy gelaatstrekke; (v) (**cast**), gooi, werp; strooi; veroordeel, verwerp; uitwerp; neergooi; oorwin; afwerp; verloor (vel); laat val (vrugte); verskiet, verbleik (kleure); afdank, afkeur (soldaat); optel (syfers); bedink; rangskik (feite); die rolle verdeel; vorm; wend (see); opwerp; uitbring (stem); giet (metaal); kromtrek (hout); ~ *ABOUT*, rondval; ~ *ACCOUNTS*, rekenings opmaak; ~ *ADRIFT*, aan sy lot oorlaat; ~ *ANCHOR*, die anker laat val; ankergooi; ~ *ASHORE*, uitwerp; op die strand uitgooi; ~ *ASIDE*, verwerp, opsy gooi, wegsmyt; ~ *AWAY*, weggooi; verkwis; ~ *BACK*, teruggooi; ~ *the BLAME on*, die skuld laai op; ~ *DOUBT*, in twyfel trek; ~ *DOWN*, neergooi, omgooi; ontmoedig; terneergeslae, moedeloos, neergedruk; ~ *one's EYES over something*, jou oë laat gaan (wei) oor iets; ~ *FEATHERS*, verveer; ~ *FIGURES*, syfers optel; ~ *FORTH*, uitwerp, versprei; ~ *LOOSE*, losmaak; ~ *in one's LOT with*, jou skaar aan die kant van; aansluit by; jou lot inwerp met; ~ *LOTS*, loot; ~ *METAL*, giet; ~ *OFF*, verwerp, uitwerp; afheg (breiwerk); ~ *ON*, oorgee aan; steke opsit; ~ *OUT*, uitwerp, verstoot; ~ *the SKIN*, vervel; ~ *a SPELL on*, betower; ~ *in one's TEETH*, iem. iets voor die kop gooi; ~ *UP*, optel; bereken, opmeet (drukkery); opgooi; ~ *a VOTE*, stem, 'n stem uitbring; (a) gegote.
castanet', kastanjet, dansklepper, klaphoutjie.
cast'away, (n) verwerpeling; skipbreukeling; (a) gestrand; onbruikbaar.
cast: ~ **brass**, gietmessing; ~ **brick**, vormsteen.
caste, kaste, stand; *lose* ~, afsak, jou aansien verloor (kwytraak); jou stand verloor.
cas'tellan, burgheer, burgvoog, slotvoog.
cas'tellated, kasteelagtig, met torinkies; gekartel; ~ **nut**, kartelmoer, kroonmoer.
cas'ter, (n) rekenaar; gooier; pootrollertjie (onder meubels); peperbus, strooier; ashelling, askanteling; nasporing; (v) naspoor; ~ **angle**, naspoorhoek.
cast' fleece, uitskotvag.
cas'tigate, straf, kasty, tugtig; die teks verbeter, emendeer, kuis, suiwer.
castiga'tion, kastyding, tugtiging; teksverbetering, suiwering.
cas'tigator, kasty(d)er, tugtiger; teksverbeteraar.
Castile', Kastilië; ~ *soap*, Spaanse seep.
Castil'ian, (n) Kastiliaan; Kastiliaans (taal); (a) Kastiliaans.
cast'ing, gooi; lyngooi (hengel); gietsel, gietstuk; gietwerk; storting (beton); *continuous* ~, stringgiet; ~**-box**, vormkas; ~**-frame**, gietkas; ~**-metal**, gietsels; ~**-net**, werpnet; ~**-rod**, katrolstok (hengel); ~**-vote**, beslissende stem; ~**-yard**, gietery, gietwerf.
cast'-iron, (n) gietyster, gegote yster, potyster; (a) klipsteenhard; onbreekbaar; onveranderlik; onomstootlik, onaantasbaar.
ca'stle, (n) kasteel; burg; slot; toring (skaak); ~ *in the AIR*, lugkasteel, toekomsmusiek; *build* ~ *s in the AIR (in Spain);* (v) rokeer (skaak); ~**-builder**, fantas; dromer; ~ **gate**, kasteelpoort; ~**-keeper**, slotbewaarder; ~**-nut**, kroonmoer.
castling, rokering (skaak).
cast'-off, (n) verwerpeling; (pl) afgedankte klere; (a) onbruikbaar; weggegooi.
cas'tor¹, bewer; kastoorhoed.
cas'tor², strooier, bussie.
cas'tor³, pootrollertjie, rolwieletjie.
Cas'tor⁴, Castor (ster).
casto'reum, bewergeil, castoreum.
cas'tor-oil, kasterolie; ~ **bush**, (**-es**), kasteroliebom; ~ **plant**, wonderbom.
cas'tor sugar, strooisuiker.
castramenta'tion, kampvorming.
cas'trate, (n) ontmande, gesnyde, eunug; (v) sny, ontman, kastreer, regmaak, onder die mes kry; ~**d cock**, kapoen; ~**d goat**, bokkapater; ~**d horse**, reun(perd); ~**d person**, eunug, gesnedene; ~**d sheep**, hamel.
castra'tion, sny, ontmanning, kastrasie, emaskulasie.
castra'to, (It., mus.), castrato.
castrat'or, snyer, kastreerder.
cast shadow, slagskadu(wee).
cast' steel, gietstaal, gegote staal.
ca'sual, (n) toevallige bewoner; arme; (a) toevallig, terloops; onseker; los, ongereeld; onverskillig; kasueel (ong.); slenter=, dra= (klere); ~ **clothes**, slenterdrag; ~ **expenditure**, toevallige (onvoorsiene) uitgawes; ~**ism**, terloopsheid; ~ **labour**, los arbeid; los werk(ies); ~ **labourer**, los werker; ~ **leave**, los verlof; ~**ly**, toevalligerwys, terloops; ~**ness**, toevalligheid; onverskilligheid; ongeërgdheid; ~ **shoe**, slenterskoen.

ca'sualty, (..ties), toeval, ongeluk; verlies, sterfgeval; gewonde, buitegeveggestelde; afwesige (soldaat); ongeval, beseerde, dooie, slagoffer; ~ **insurance**, ongevalleversekering; ..**ties**, dooies en gewondes; *list of* ..*ties*, ongevallelys; ~ **list**, verlieslys; sneuwellys; sterftelys; krukkerlys (sport); ~ **ward**, ongevalleafdeling, ongevallesaal.
ca'sual visitor, toevallige besoeker.
ca'sual water, spoelwater (gholf).
casuari'na (tree), kasuaris(boom).
ca'suist, sofis, haarklower, kasuïs, drogredenaar.
casuis'tic, spitsvondig, kasuïsties.
ca'suistry, spitsvondigheid, haarklowery, kasuïstiek, drogredenering.
casus be'lli, casus belli, oorlogsrede.
cat¹, (n) kat; kats (straf); ankerkraan; kennetjie; *he let the* ~ *out of the BAG*, hy het die aap uit die mou laat kom; *BELL the* ~, die kat die bel aanbind; *the BIG* ~*s*, die leeus, tiers en luiperds; *like a* ~ *on hot BRICKS*, op hete kole; *CARE killed the* ~, dit help nie om te huil nie; *in the DARK all* ~*s are grey*, in die donker (snags) is alle katte grou; *live like* ~ *and DOG*, in onmin lewe; soos kat en hond leef; *it is raining* ~ *s and DOGS*, dit reën aanmekaar; *wait to see which way the* ~ *JUMPS*, die kat uit die boom kyk; *fight like KILKENNY* ~*s*, mekaar doodbaklei; *there are more ways of KILLING a* ~ *than drowning it in butter*, daar is meer as een manier om jou doel te bereik; *a* ~ *may look at a KING*, kyk is vry; *an old* ~ *LAPS as much as a young kitten*, 'n ou bok het ook nog lus vir 'n groen blaartjie; *a* ~ -*and-dog LIFE*, 'n rusieagtige lewe; lewe soos kat en hond; *when the* ~ *is away the MICE will play*, wanneer die kat weg is, is die muis baas; *set a* ~ *among the PIGEONS*, 'n knuppel in die hoenderhok gooi; *PLAY* ~ *and mouse with someone*, iem. aan 'n lyntjie hou; *there is not ROOM enough to swing a* ~, 'n mens kan jou daar nie draai nie; daar is g'n plek vir 'n muis nie; *TURN* ~ *in the pan*, van kleur verander; *he thinks he is the* ~ *'s WHISKERS*, hy dink hy is die koning se hond se oom (neef)
cat², (v) vermeer, opgooi, jongosse inspan.
cat³, (v) die anker optrek.
catabol'ic, katabolies.
catab'olism, katabolisme.
catachres'is, foutiewe woordgebruik, katachrese.
catacla'sis, kataklase, rotsbreuk.
cat'aclasm, splitsing, skeuring.
cat'aclysm, omwenteling, opskudding, beroering; sondvloed, oorstroming; ~'**ic**, rampspoedig, ontsettend.
cat'acomb, katakombe, onderaardse grafkelder.
catacous'tics, geluidhreking.
cata'dromous, katadroom, seebrociend.
cat'afalque, katafalk; lykwa.
Ca'talan, (n) Katalaan, Kataláans; (a) Kataláans, Katalonies.
catalec'tic, katalekties, onvolledig.
cat'alepsy, katalepsie; verstywing.
catalep'tic, katalepties, verstywend.
cat'alogue, (n) katalogus, pryskoerant, pryslys; naamlys; (v) katalogiseer, 'n lys maak; ~ **r**, lysmaker, katalogiseerder.
cat(t)alo, bees-buffelkruising.
catalo'guing, katalogisering.
catal'pa, catalpa(boom).
cat'alyse, kataliseer.
catal'ysis, katalise, katalisering.
cat'alyst, katalisator, kataliseermiddel.
catalyt'ic, katalities.
catamaran'¹, houtvlot, vlotboot, tweerompskuit, tweeromper, katamaran.
catamaran'², feeks; hellevoeg.
catamen'ia, maandstonde.
ca'tamite, sodomietersknaap, skandknaap.
catamount'(ain), wildekat; luiperd.
cat-and-mouse' (game), kat-en-muis(speletjie).
cataphore'sis, kataforese.
ca'taphyll, katafil, (onderste) oorgangsblaar.
cat'aplasm, kataplasma, omslag, kompres, pap, pleister.
ca'taplexy, katapleksie, tydelike verlamming.

cat'apult, (n) rek(ker), slingervel, katapult; (v) met 'n rek skiet; lanseer, afskiet.
cat'aract¹, waterval, stortvloed.
cat'aract², katarak, oogpêrel, ster, oogvlek; (grou)staar (perd).
catarrh', katar, verkouentheid, slymvliesontsteking; ~ **al**, katarraal; *malignant* ~ *al fever*, snotsiekte; ~ **cough**, slymhoes.
catas'trophe, ramp, groot ongeluk; ontknoping (drama); katastrofe, onheil.
catastroph'ic, rampspoedig, katastrofies.
cataw'ba, catawba, glippertjies (druifsoort).
catato'nia, ..**to'ny**, katatonie.
cat: ~ **bear**, katbeer, klein panda; ~ **bird**, spotlyster; ~ **boat**, eenmaster; ~ **brier**, katdoring.
cat' burglar, klouterdief; sluipdief; klimdief.
cat'call, (n) kattegetjank; gesis; (pl) uitjouery, gefluit (v) tjank; uitfluit, uitjou.
catch, (n) vangs, buit; aanwins, voordeel; greep; beurtsang; gewilde persoon of ding; haak, knip, klink (deur); strikvraag; brokstuk (van lied); vanghou (krieket); *a GOOD* ~, 'n goeie party (huwelik); 'n mooi vangs; *no GREAT* ~, nie van danige betekenis nie; *MISS a* ~, 'n vangkans verbrou; *with a* ~ *in the VOICE*, met 'n stem wat stok; (v) **(caught)**, vang (bal); gryp, vat, beetpak; snap (betekenis); haal (trein); betrap (dief); opvang; raakslaan; besmetlik wees (siekte); trek, raak; inhaal; *be caught in the* ~, op heter daad betrap; ~ *AT*, gryp na; ~ *ATTENTION*, aandag trek; ~ *him a BLOW*, hom 'n klap gee; ~ *a COLD*, koue vat; ~ *the EYE*, aandag trek; in die oog spring; ~ *FIRE*, vuur vat, aan die brand raak; ~ *FISH*, visvang; vis; ~ *a GLIMPSE of*, skrams raaksien; vlugtig sien; ~ *HOLD of*, vasgryp; *you'll* ~ *IT!* jy sal dit kry! jou gal sal waai! ~ *someone in a LIE*, iem. op 'n leuen betrap; ~ *someone's MEANING*, iem. verstaan (begryp); ~ *someone NAPPING*, iem. aan slaap kry; iem. onverwags betrap; ~ *ON*, inslaan, populêr word; ~ *up with a PERSON*, iem. inhaal; ~ *SIGHT of*, te sien kry; ~ *the SPEAKER'S eye*, die woord kry; ~ *a TARTAR*, sy moses teëkom; ~ *a TRAIN*, 'n trein haal; ~ *UP*, inhaal; ~ -**as-catch-can**, vrystoei; ~ **basin**, vangbak; ~ **bolt**, vangknip; ~ -**contact**, knipkontak; ~ **crops**, vangoes, tussenoes, tussengewas; voorbou; ~ **dam**, wendam, opvangdam; ~ -**drain**, afvoerkanaal, oorloop; ~ **er**, vanger, opvanger; ~ **fly**, vlieëbos; ~ **hook**, vanghaak; ~ **ing**, aansteeklik; besmetlik; aantreklik; pakkend; ~ **line**, oogvanger; trefferopskrif; merkreël, kenreël; ~ **ment**, opvanggebied; ~ -**ment-area**, ~ -**ment-basin**, neerslaggebied, stroomgebied, opvanggebied; ~ -**ment-dam**, bewaardam; ~ **penny**, goedkoop, advertensieagtig; bedrieglik; ~ -**phrase**, slagwoord; ~ -**plate**, meeneemskyf; ~ -**points**, vangwissel; ~ -**question**, strikvraag; ~ -**rod**, knipstang (motor); ~ **stitch**, oorkruisrygsteek; visgraatsteek; ~ -**title**, verkorte titel; trefferopskrif; ~ -**water drain**, afkeersloot; ~ **word**, wagwoord, trefwoord; leuse, partyleuse; bladwagter (drukw.).
catch'y, aantreklik, pakkend; bedrieglik; aansteeklik; -*question*, strikvraag.
cat'echesis, kategese.
catechet'ic, kategeties; ~ **s**, kategetiek.
cat'echism, kategismus; vraeboek; ~ -**book**, katkisasieboek.
cat'echist, katkiseermeester; ondervraer, kategis; kategeet.
cat'echize, katkiseer; kruisvra, ondervra.
cat'echol, katesjol.
cat'echu, katesjoe.
catechum'en, katkisant.
categor'ical, kategories, uitdruklik, stellig, beslis, op die man af, padlangs, direk.
cat'egory, (..ries), kategorie, klas, soort.
cate'na, reeks; kettingreeks, katena.
cate'nary, (..ries), kettinglyn.
cat'enate, aaneenskakel.
cat'enate(d), aaneengeskakel.
catena'tion, aaneenskakeling, kettingskakeling.
cat'er, spysenier, spyseneer; proviandeer; voorsien;

~ *FOR,* voorsiening maak vir; ~ *for the public TASTE,* die openbare smaak bevredig.

ca'tercorner(ed), diagonaal.

cat'erer, spysenier, proviandeerder, leweransier.

cat'ering, spyseniering, spysenering; verversingsvoorsiening, proviandering, ete; ~ **department,** verversingsdepartement, spyseniersafdeling; ~ **manager,** spysmeester, proviandmeester; ~ **service,** spyseniersdiens, verversingsdiens; ~ **staff,** verversingspersoneel; ~ **store,** verversingsmagasyn; ~ **trade,** verversingsbedryf.

cat'erpillar, ruspe, miswurm; rusper (voertuig); vegwa; ~**-drive,** rusperaandrywing; ~ **tank,** ruspertenk; ~ **tractor,** rusperbandtrekker, kruiptrekker; ~ **tread,** kruipband, rusperband; ~ **wheel,** rusper(band)wiel.

cat'erwauling, katmusiek, kattegetjank, gemiaau.

cat'fish, platkop, (see)baber; seekat, katvis.

cat'gut, katderm; (derm)snaar; strykinstrumente.

cathar'sis, suiwering, reiniging, katarsis, purgering.

cathart'ic(al), (n) purgeermiddel; (a) suiwerend, purgerend, katarties.

cat'head, katrolbalk.

cathed'ra, kateder, biskopstoel; ~**l,** (n) domkerk, katedraal; (a) katedraal; gesaghebbend; ~**l church,** katedraalkerk; ~**l tower,** domtoring.

Cath'erine wheel, roosvenster; vuurrat; bolmakiesie.

cath'eter, kateter; ~**ize,** kateteriseer.

cathetom'eter, katetometer.

cathe'tus, loodlyn; loodregte stand; reghoeksy.

cathe'xis, kateksie, konsentrasie.

cath'ode, negatiewe pool, katode; ~ **ray,** katodestraal; ~**-ray tube,** katodestraalbuis.

catho'dic, katodies, katode-.

Cath'olic, (n) Katoliek.

cath'olic, (a) algemeen, onbevooroordeeld, omvattend; katoliek.

cathol'icism, katolisisme.

catholi'city, algemeenheid; veelomvattendheid; katolisiteit.

Catholi'city, Roomsheid, Katolisiteit.

cathol'icize, katoliseer, verrooms.

cathol'icon, panasee.

cat'house, stormkat (mil.); hoerhuis, bordeel.

ca'tion, katioon; ~**ic,** kationies.

cat'kin, katjie (wilgerboom); saadjie.

cat: ~ **ladder,** dakleer; ~**-lap,** kasaterwater, flou drinkgoed; ~**like,** sag, onhoorbaar; katagtig; ~**ling** katjie; fyn snaar; opereermes; ~ **lover,** katteliefhebber, kattevriend; ~**-mint,** kattekruid; ~**-nap,** dutjie; ~**nip,** kattekruid, -kruie; ~**-o'-nine-tails,** kats.

catop'tric, spieël--, weerkaatsend, katoptries.

cat's: ~**-cradle,** uitvalspeletjie; ~**-eye,** katoog (steen); blinkogies (pad), padogie, blinker; ~ **meat,** kattevleis, afvalvleis; ~ **paw,** katpoot; windjie, luggie; dupe, werktuig; *be made a* ~, vir iem. kastaings uit die vuur moet haal; as handlanger gebruik word; ~ **purr,** (katte)gespin; ~**-tail,** katstert; kaffertjie (blom); ~ **whiskers,** kattebaard; *he thinks he is the* ~ *whiskers (pyjamas),* hy reken (dink) hy is net te wonderlik.

cat'sup = **ketchup.**

cat'-tail, duikertjie.

cat'-thorn, katdoring; kaffer-wag-'n-bietjie *(Acacia caffra).*

ca'ttery, kattebewaarplek.

cattiness, katterigheid.

catt'ish, katterig; ~**ness,** katterigheid.

catt'le, vee, grootvee, beeste; domkoppe, stommerike; ~**-breeder,** beesboer, veeteler; ~**-breeding,** veeteelt, beesboerdery; ~**-cake,** veekoek; ~**-crossing,** veeoorgang; ~**-dealer,** veehandelaar, veekoper; ~**-disease,** veesiekte; ~ **egret,** bosluisvoël, veereier, witreier; ~ **farm,** beesplaas; ~ **farmer,** beesboer; ~**-farming,** beesboerdery; ~**-grid,** motorhek; ~ **guard,** veekeerder (lokomotief); ~ **herd,** veewagter; ~ **jaundice,** geelsiekte; ~**-kraal,** veekraal; ~**-leader,** neusring; ~ **lick,** beeslek; ~**-lifting,** veediefstal; ~ **man,** beesboer; ~**-market,** vee-mark; ~**-pen,** veekraal; ~**-plague,** veesiekte, runderpes; ~ **population,** beesstapel; ~**-raiding,** beesdiefstal, veediefstal; ~**-ranching,** veldbeesboerdery; ~**-range,** veeplaas, weiplaas; ~**-rustler,** veedief; ~**-shed,** veestal; ~**-show,** beestentoonstelling, veetentoonstelling; ~**-station,** veepos; ~**-trade,** veehandel; ~ **trailer,** veeslaapwa; ~**-truck,** veetrok, beestrok.

catt'y¹, (n) kattie (gewig).

catt'y², (n) **(catties),** rek, kettie; *kyk* **catapult.**

catt'y³, (a) katterig.

cat: ~**walk,** kruipgangetjie; looplys; ~**whisker,** deteksieveertjie.

Cauca'sian, (n) Kaukasiër; (a) Kaukasies.

Cauc'asus, Kaukasus.

cauc'us, (n) **(-es),** koukus, partyvergadering; (v) 'n koukus hou.

caud'al, stertagtig, stert-; ~ **fin,** stertvin.

caud'ate, gestert.

caudil'lo, (Sp.), caudillo, leier.

cau'dle, kandeel, wynsop.

caught, *kyk* **catch,** (v); *be* ~ *in the act,* op heter daad betrap word.

cauk, cawk, swaarspaat, bariet.

caul, netjie, haarnet; agterstuk (van kappie); helm; teenplaat; dermnet; netvet; *born with a* ~, met die helm gebore.

caul'dron, kookketel, kookpot.

caules'cent, stam-, gesteel.

caul'icle, wortelkiem.

caul'iflower, blomkool; ~ **ear,** frommeloor, sportoor, skrumoor, perskeoor.

caul'iform, stingelvormig.

cau'linar, stingelstandig.

caul'ine, stam-.

cau'lis, stam, stingel.

caulk, kalfater, toestop (barste in skip), toemaak; ~**ing,** kalfatering; ~**ing compound,** kalfaatsel; ~**ing hammer,** stophamer; ~**ing iron,** kalfaatyster.

caus'al, oorsaaklik, redegewend, kousaal; ~ *nexus,* oorsaaklike verband.

causal'ity, oorsaaklike verband, kousaliteit; oorsaaklikheidsleer; *doctrine of* ~, oorsaaklikheidsleer.

causa'tion, veroorsaking; ~**ism,** oorsaaklikheidsleer.

caus'ative, oorsaaklik, kousatief; veroorsakend.

cause, (n) oorsaak, bron, beweegrede, grond, rede, aanleiding; saak; veroorsaker; *make COMMON* ~ *with,* gemene saak maak met; ~ *and EFFECT,* oorsaak en gevolg; *in a GOOD* ~, vir 'n goeie doel; *PLEAD a* ~, 'n saak bepleit; *PRIME* ~, aanleidende oorsaak; *SHOW* ~, bewys lewer; *WITH-OUT* ~, sonder oorsaak, sonder grond; *WORK for a* ~, vir 'n saak ywer; (v) veroorsaak, bewerkstellig, aanlei (tot); laat bewerk, teweegbring, laat maak dat; gee (moeilikheid); ~ *to FAIL,* verydel; ~ *a HUBBUB,* rumoer, 'n lawaai opskop; ~ **célèbre,** cause célèbre, opspraakwekkende (hof)saak; ~**less,** sonder rede, ongegrond; ~**-list,** sakerol; ~**r,** verwekker.

causerie', causerie, praatjie.

cause'way, caus'ey, straatweg; laagwaterbrug, spoelbrug; verhoogde pad.

caus'ing, veroorsaking.

caus'tic, (n) brandmiddel; helsteen; (a) bytend, stekelig, skerp; sarkasties; ~ **holder,** helsteen.

causti'city, bytende eienskap; sarkasme.

caus'tic: ~ **lime,** ongebluste kalk; ~ **potash,** bytpotas; bytkali, etsnatron; ~ **retort,** snydende antwoord; ~ **soda,** seepsoda, bytsoda; ~**-soda solution,** natronloog, sodaloog.

cau'ter, brandyster; ~**iza'tion,** uitbranding, toeskroeiing; verharding; ~**ize,** toeskroei, (dig)skroei, doodbrand; uitbrand; verhard; ~**izing iron,** skroei-yster; ~**y,** (..ries), brand; brandyster; toeskroeiing.

cau'tio, sekerheidstelling (jur.).

cau'tion, (n) versigtigheid, omsigtigheid; waarborg, pand, sekerheid; waarskuwing; skrobbering; borggeld; voëlverskrikker, snaakse persoon; *he is a* ~, hy is 'n snaakse entjie mens; (v) waarsku; skrobbeer, vermaan; ~ *and discharge,* met 'n berisping ontslaan; ~**ary,** waarskuwend; ~ **money,** skadevergoedingsfonds, waarborgfonds; waarborgsom.

cau'tious, versigtig, behoedsaam, omsigtig, beleidvol; ~ness, versigtigheid, omsigtigheid, behoedsaamheid.

cavalcade', perdekommando, ruiterstoet, kavalkade.

cavalier', (n) ruiter, kavalier, ridder; kêrel; (a) ruiterlik, ongedwonge; kortaf; hooghartig, laatdunkend, trots, uit die hoogte; ~ *treatment,* hooghartige (kortaf) behandeling.

cav'alry, (..ries), ruitery, kavallerie; ~ **attack,** ruiteraanval, kavallerieaanval; ~ **captain,** ritmeester; ~ **charge,** ruiteraanval; ~ **man,** kavalleris; ~ **school,** ruiteryskool, kavallerieskool; ~ **sword,** sleepsabel; ~ **twill,** ruiterykeper.

cavati'na, (It.), cavatina.

cave, (n) grot; gat, spelonk, aardholte; afgeskeidenes, skeurders(party); *open* ~, holkrans; (v) uithol, uitkalwe; indeuk; afskei; ~ *in,* instort, insak, toeval, afkalwe; inkalwe(r).

cav'e! pas op! *keep* ~, kywie, wag hou, spioen speel.

cav'eat, (regterlike) waarskuwing; protes; ~ *EMPTOR,* die verantwoordelikheid rus by die koper; *ENTER a* ~, protes aanteken.

cave: ~ **disease,** grotsiekte, histoplasmose; ~**-dweller,** grotbewoner, troglodiet; ~ **dwelling,** grot= (woning); ~**-in,** inkalwing; insakking; instorting; ~ **man,** (..men), grotbewoner; haasspeler.

cav'endish, tamaryn(tabak), koektabak.

cave painting, grotskildery, grottetekening.

cav'ern, hol, grot, spelonk; ~**ous,** hol, spelonkagtig; ~ **water,** grotwater.

caves(s)on, neusband.

cavett'o moul'ding, hollys.

caviar(e)', cav'iar(e), kaviaar, sout viseiers; viskuit; ~ *to the general,* pêrels vir die swyne.

cav'icorn, holhoring (dier).

cav'il, (n) haarklowery, spitsvondigheid; vittery; (v) (-led), vit; haarklowe, spykers op laagwater soek; ~**ler,** drogredenaar, haarklower; vitter, foutsoeker, lettersifter, albedil; ~**ling,** haarklowery; vittery, gehekel; *there can be no* ~*ling at that,* daaroor kan daar geen haarklowery wees nie; daaroor kan daar nie gevit word nie.

cav'ity, (cavities), holte; ~ **brick,** hol steen; ~ **wall,** hol muur.

cavort', bokspring, steier (perd).

ca'vy, marmot(jie).

caw, (n) gekras; (v) skreeu (soos 'n kraai), krys, kras.

cay, bank, eiland(jie), (koraal)rif.

cayenne' (pepper), rooipeper, helpeper, rissies, cayennepeper, paprika.

cay'man, kaaiman.

ceano'thus, ceanotus.

cease, ophou, laat staan, staak; tot 'n end kom, eindig; ~ *FIRE,* vuurstaking, skietstaking; *die vuur staak; the FIRING* ~ *d,* die skietery het tot 'n end gekom; *WITHOUT ceasing,* sonder ophou; ~**-fire order,** bevel tot vuurstaking; ~**less,** onophoudelik.

ceb'us, rolaap.

ce'city, blindheid.

ced'ar, seder; ~**-wood,** sederhout.

cede, afstaan, opgee, afstand doen van, sedeer, oordra, toestaan (regte); toegee (argument); ~**nt,** sedent (jur.).

cedill'a, cedille.

ced'rine, sederagtig, seder=.

ceil, plafon insit.

cei'ling, solder(ing), plafon; dakprys; styghoogte, hoogtegrens; *ABSOLUTE* ~, absolute hoogtegrens; *PRACTICAL* ~, praktiese hoogtegrens; *REDUCED* ~, verminderde hoogtegrens (lugv.); ~**-beam,** plafonbalk; solderbalk; ~**-board,** plafonplank; ~**-calco,** duiwelsterk; ~**-cornice,** plafonlys; ~**-fan,** plafonwaaier; ~**-fixer,** plafonneerder; ~**-joist,** solderrib; ~**-lamp,** solderlamp, plafonlamp; ~**-light,** kaplig, plafonvenster; ~**-mop,** raagbol; ~**-price,** maksimumprys, topprys; plafonprys; ~**-trap,** solderluik, plafonluik.

cein'ture, gordel, seintuur.

cel'adon, seladon, wilgergroen; ~**ite,** seladoniet, groenaarde.

Cel'ebes, Cele'bes, Celebes.

cel'ebrant, selebrant, priester by die misdiens.

cel'ebrate, feesvier, vier, herdenk; besing, verheerlik; ~**d,** beroemd, vermaard.

celebra'tion, viering, herdenking; verheerliking; (pl) feestelikheid.

celeb'rity, (..ties), beroemdheid, roem, vermaardheid; beroemde persoon, beroemdheid, kalkligvanger, selebriteit; ~ **concert,** beroemdheidskonsert.

cele'riac, koolseldery, knolseldery.

cele'rity, spoed, snelheid, vlugheid; vinnigheid.

cel'ery, seldery; ~ **cabbage,** selderykool; ~ **salt,** selderysout.

celes'ta, (mus.), celesta.

celeste', hemelsblou.

celes'tial, (n) hemelbewoner, hemeling; (a) hemels, bowemaans, boaards, hemel=; *the C* ~ *City,* Rome; ~ **bodies,** hemelliggame; ~ **chart,** sterrekaart; *C* ~ **Empire,** China, Sjina; ~ **equator,** hemelsewenaar; ~ **globe,** hemelbol; ~ **hemisphere,** hemelhalfrond; ~ **host,** hemelheer, hemelskare; ~ **mechanics,** fisiese sterrekunde; ~ **navigation,** ruim(te)navigasie; ~ **pole,** hemelpoort; ~ **sphere,** hemelbol.

celesti'na, (mus.), celestina.

cel'ibacy, ongetroude staat, selibaat, agamie; *state of* ~, ongehude staat.

celibata'rian, selibatêr.

cel'ibate, (n) oujongkêrel, vrygesel; oujongnooi; (a) selibatêr, ongetroud.

cell, sel; kamertjie; hokkie; vakkie; element; graf (digterlik); *CONDEMNED* ~, dodesel, sel van terdoodveroordeeldes; *DRY* ~, droë sel.

cell'ar, (n) kelder; (v) in 'n kelder bewaar; ~ **age,** kelderruimte; ~**er,** keldermeester; ~ **et',** likeurkeldertjie; ~**-flap,** kelderluik; ~ **man,** keldermeester, keldernan; ~**-vault,** keldergewelf.

cell: ~**-box,** selkas; ~**-clip,** selklem; ~ **division,** seldeling; ~ **fusion,** selversmelting.

cell'ist, tjellis, tjelliospeler.

cell' lid, seldeksel.

cell'o, (-s), tjello, violonsel.

cell'ophane, sellofaan (geregistreerde handelsnaam), glaspapier.

cell: ~ **lumen,** selholte; ~ **plate,** batteryplaat; ~ **theory,** selteorie.

cell'ular, selvormig, sel=; ~ **tissue,** selweefsel.

cell'ulate, sel=; selvormig.

cell'ule, selletjie.

cellulif'erous, sel=, selvormig.

celluli'tis, weefselontsteking, sellulitis.

cell'uloid, (n) selluloïed, selluloïde; (a) selagtig.

cell'ulose, (n) sellulose, selstof; (a) selvormig; ~ **nitrate,** nitrosellulose; ~ **paint,** spuitverf.

cell: ~ **voltage,** selspanning; ~ **wall,** selwand; selmuur.

celo'sia, hanekam (blom).

celt[1], (voorhistoriese) beitelvormige gereedskap.

Celt[2], Kelt; ~**ic,** (n) Kelties (taal); (a) Kelties; ~**ol'ogist,** Keltoloog.

cem'balo, (mus.), cembalo, harpsikord.

cement', (n) sement; band; lym; lak; (v) verbind; sementeer, met sement messel, saamvoeg, saamhang, vaslym, toelak, aanlym; ~*ed together,* innig verbind; ~ **a'tion,** sementering, sementasie; verbinding; ~ **ation process,** bindingsproses; ~ **block,** sementblok; ~**-buyer,** sementkoper; ~ **copper,** sementkoper; ~ **floor,** sementvloer; ~**-gun,** sementspuit; ~**-gunning,** sementspuitwerk; ~ **ing,** binding; ~**ing furnace,** sementeeroond; ~**ing material,** bindmiddel; ~ **iron,** sementyster; ~ **i'tious,** sementagtig; ~ **lining,** sementbekleding; ~ **slab,** sementplatstuk; ~ **stucco,** sementgips; ~ **wash,** sementwas, sementstryksel.

cem'etery, (..ries), kerkhof, godsakker, dodeakker, begraafpark, begraafplaas.

ce'nacle, eetsaal, senakel.

cen'obite, kloosterling, monnik.

cen'otaph, praalgraf, senotaaf; gedenksteen.

cense, bewierook; ~**r,** wierookskaal, wierookvat, reukvat; bewieroker.

cen'sor, (n) sensor; tugmeester, sedemeester; (v) senseer, onder sensuur bring, keur; ~ **able,** sensureerbaar, ~ **ed,** deur die sensor nagesien.

censor'ial, sensoragtig; streng.

cen'soring, sensuurwerk.
censor'ious, vitterig, berispend, bedilsiek; streng; ~ness, vitsug.
cen'sorship, sensorskap; sensuur; ~ *of books*, boekesensuur, publikasiesensuur.
cen'surable, berispelik, laakbaar, sensurabel, wraakbaar.
cen'sure, (n) sensuur, berisping, afkeuring, blaam, bestraffing; *motion of* ~, mosie van afkeuring; (v) onder sensuur sit, sensureer; bestraf, berispe; laak, afkeur, bedil, wraak.
cen'suring, wraking, laking.
cen'sus, (-es), (volks)telling, sensus; ~**-paper**, sensusvorm; ~ **return**, sensusopgawe; ~**-taker**, sensusopnemer.
cent, sent; duit; honderd; *PER* ~, per honderd, persent; per (by die) sent; *not worth a RED* ~, geen bloue duit werd nie.
cen'tal, sentenaar.
cen'taur, perdmens, sentour, kentour.
centa'vo, centavo.
centenar'ian, (n) honderdjarige; (a) honderdjarig.
centen'ary, (n) (..ries), eeufees; (a) honderjarig, honderd-, eeufees-.
centenn'ial, (n) eeufees; (a) honderdjarig.
cen'ter = **centre**.
centes'imal, honderdste, sentesimaal.
cen'tigrade, Celsius; honderdgradig; *4 degrees* ~, 4 grade Celsius; ~ **thermometer**, Celsiustermometer.
cen'tigram(me), sentigram.
cen'tilitre, sentiliter.
cen'time, centime (Franse munt).
cen'timetre, sentimeter.
centi'mo, centimo.
cen'tipede, oorkruiper *(Chilopoda)*.
cent'o, (-s), sento, kompilasiewerk.
cen'trage, gewigsverdeling.
cen'tral, sentraal, middelste, midde-, middel-; vernaamste, hoof-; **C**~ **Africa**, Midde(l)-Afrika; ~ **bank**, sentrale bank; reserwebank; ~ **business district**, sakesentrum; ~ **canal**, rugmurgkanaal; ~ **exchange**, hoofsentrale; ~ **figure**, hooffiguur, hoofkarakter, sentrale figuur, sentrale karakter; ~ **heating**, sentrale verwarming; ~ **housing-board**, sentrale woningraad; ~ **idea**, hoofgedagte, sentrale gedagte, kerngedagte; ~ **island**, middelstrook; ~**iza'tion**, sentralisasie; ~**ize**, sentraliseer, sentreer, in een punt verenig; ~**izer**, sentreerder; ~ **lubrication**, sentraalsmering; ~ **nervous system**, sentrale senuweestelsel; ~ **projection**, perspektiefvoorstelling; ~ **shadow**, slagskaduwee.
cen'tre, (n) middelpunt, sentrum, senter, middel; hoof; as, spil; hoofkantoor; hartlyn; kern, middelste trefpunt; hart; (pl) vormboë; ~ *of ATTRACTION*, aantrekkingspunt; middelpunt van belangstelling; ~ *of EQUILIBRIUM*, ewewigspunt; ~ *of FORCE*, kragsentrum; ~ *of GRAVITY*, swaartepunt; ~ *of MOTION*, bewegingsdraaipunt; ~ *of PRESSURE*, drukkingspunt, drukmiddelpunt; (v) sentreer, op een punt saamtrek, in 'n middelpunt verenig; *his interests* ~ *round sport*, sy belange is toegespits op sport; ~ **aisle**, middelpaadjie; ~ **bearing**, middellaer (motor); ~**-bit**, senterboor; ~ **board**, middelswaard (boot); ~ **bolt**, toringbout (veer); ~**-boyancy**, drukkingspunt; ~ **court**, middelbaan; ~ **distance**, middelafstand; ~ **drill**, senterboor; ~ **fire**, senterslag (patroon); ~ **forward**, (middel-) voorspeler; middelvoor; ~ **furrow**, holvoor; ~**-gauge**, middelpuntsoeker, sentermaat; ~ **gear**, middelrat; ~ **half**, middelskakel; ~**-jumper**, middelspeler; ~ **left**, middellinks; ~ **line**, as, middellyn; hartlyn; middelstreep (pad); ~ **party**, sentrumparty; ~**-piece**, taffelloper; middelstuk; ~**-pin**, spil; skamelpen; ~ **point**, middelpunt; ~ **pop**, kornaelmerk; ~**-punch**, senterpons, kornael; ~ **row**, middelry; ~ **section**, middelmoot; ~ **spread**, dubbelblad; ~ **spring**, middelveer; ~**-square**, sentreerhaak; ~**-studding**, middeltrappe; ~ **threequarter**, senter.
cen'tric, sentraal, middelpuntig.
centrif'ugal, middelpuntvliedend; ~ **force**, middelpuntvliedende krag, sentrifugale krag; ~ **pump**, middelpuntvliedende pomp, sentrifugale pomp.
cen'trifuge, (n) sentrifuge, swaaimasjien; wenteldroër; toldroër; (v) sentrifugeer.
centrif'ugence, vlug, uitswaai (van middelpunt).
cen'tring, vormboë, sentrering; ~**-screw**, sentreerskroef.
centrip'etal, middelpuntsoekend; ~ **force**, middelpuntsoekende krag, sentripetale krag.
cen'trist, (a), gematig; sentristies; (n), sentris; gematigde.
cen'tum language, centumtaal, kentumtaal.
cen'tumvir, centumvir; ~**ate**, centumviraat.
cen'tuple, (v) verhonderdvoudig; (a) honderdvoudig.
centur'ion, hoofman (oor honderd).
cen'tury, (..ries), eeu, honderd jaar; honderdtal (krieket); *at the turn of the* ~, by die eeuwisseling (eeuwending); ~ **plant**, garingboom.
cephalal'gia, hoofpyn.
cephal'ic, hoof-; ~ **vein**, hoofslagaar.
cephalit'is, breinontsteking; harsing(vlies)ontsteking.
ceph'alopod, (n), koppotige dier, kefalopode, sefalopode; (a) koppotig.
cera'ceous, wasagtig.
cera'go, byebrood.
ceram'ic, keramies, pottebakkers-; ~**s**, pottebakkerskuns; keramiek, erdeware; pottebakkery.
ce'ramist, pottebakker, keramis.
ce'rasin, serasine.
ceras'tes, horingsman.
ce'rate, vetsalf, waspleister.
ce'ratin, horingweefsel.
ce'ratite, horingsteen.
ceratit'is, horingvliesontsteking.
ce'ratoma, horingsuil.
Cerb'erus, helhond, Kerberos.
cerca'ria, serkarie.
cer'cus, anale aanhangsel.
cere, (n) wasvlies, (v) met was bedek; in 'n (was)doodskleed wikkel.
ce'real, (n) graan; graansoort; ontbytgraan, ontbytkos, graankos; (a) graan-; *breakfast* ~, ontbytgraan; ~ **culture**, graanbou, graanverbouing; ~ **food**, graankos; ~ **mix(ture)**, graanmengsel, ontbyt(graan)mengsel; ~**s**, graan, grane; ontbytgraan, ontbytkos, graankos.
cerebell'um, kleinharsings, serebellum.
ce'rebral, harsings-, serebraal; verstandelik; ~ **cortex**, harsingskors; ~ **concussion**, harsingskudding; ~ **h(a)emorrhage**, breinbloeding; ~ **hemisphere**, breinhelfte; ~**ism**, verstandelikheid; ~ **membrane**, harsingvlies; ~ **palsy**, serebrale gestremdheid, breinverlamming.
cerebra'tion, breinwerking, breinaktiwiteit.
cerebrit'is, breinontsteking, harsing(vlies)ontsteking.
ce'rebro-spinal, rugmurg-, serebrospinaal; ~ **fluid**, harsing-rugmurgvog; ~ **meningitis**, rugmurgmeningitis, harsingvliesontsteking, harsing-en-rugmurgvliesontsteking.
ce'rebrum, grootharsings, serebrum.
cere'cloth, cere'ment, wasdoek; grafdoek; doodshemp.
ceremon'ial, (n) pligpleging, seremonie, seremonieel; seremoniebook; (a) seremonieel, plegstatig, vormlik; ~**ism**, vormlikheid.
ceremon'ious, vormlik, deftig, plegtig, (pleg)statig; ~**ness**, hoofsheid, plegstatigheid.
ce'remony, (..nies), seremonie, pligpleging, plegtigheid; vormlikheid; *MASTER of ceremonies*, seremoniemeester; *NOT stand upon* ~, jou tuis maak; die vormlikheid laat vaar; *STAND upon* ~, vormlik wees, die afstand bewaar; *WITHOUT* ~, sonder komplimente, sonder pligpleginge; kaalkop.
ce'resin, witwas, hardewas.
cerise', (n) kersiekleur, cerise; (a) kersiekleurig, kersierooi.
cer'met, keramieklegering, hittebestande legering, kermet.
cerog'raphy, wasskrif, wasskildering, serografie.
ceroplas'tics, wasmodellering, wasboetseerkuns, seroplastiek.

cert, (sl.), sekerheid; *a dead* ~, doodseker, heeltemal seker (geselst.).
cert'ain, seker, gewis, wis, stellig, vas; vasstaande; *FOR* ~, stellig, sekerlik; *SAY for* ~, as 'n feit meedeel; *of THAT you can be* ~, dis nou nie almaskie nie; daarvan kan jy seker wees; ~**ly**, sekerlik, beslis, juistement, vervas, ongetwyfeld; ja, seker, bepaald; ~**ty**, sekerheid, stelligheid; *absolute* ~ *ty*, volkome sekerheid.
cert'es, (arch.), ongetwyfeld, seker.
cert'ifiable, sertifiseerbaar.
certi'ficate, (n) getuigskrif, sertifikaat, diploma; bewys, akte, verklaring, attes; ~ *of COMPETENCE*, bevoegdheidsertifikaat; ~ *of DOMICILE*, domisiliebewys; ~ *of FITNESS*, geskiktheidsertifikaat; ~ *of MERIT*, verdienstelikheidsertifikaat; ~ *of ORIGIN*, sertifikaat van herkoms; ~ *of REGISTRY*, seebrief; ~ *of SERVICE*, dienssertifikaat; (v) 'n sertifikaat verleen, diplomeer; ~**d**, gekwalifiseer(d).
certifica'tion, versekering, attestasie, verklaring, sertifikasie.
cert'ified, gediplomeerd (rekenmeester); gewaarmerk; ~ **accountant**, geoktrooieerde rekenmeester; ~ **cheque**, ge(waar)merkte tjek; ~ **copy**, gesertifiseerde (gewaarmerkte) afskrif; ~ **lunatic**, kranksinnigverklaarde.
cert'ify, (..fied), verseker, betuig; verklaar, sertifiseer; waarmerk (afskrif); aangee (by hof); (kranksinnig) verklaar; attesteer, waarborg; *certified CORRECT*, as dit gewaarmerk, as korrek gesertifiseer; ~*ing OFFICER*, waarmerkingsbeampte.
cert'itude, sekerheid; versekerdheid.
cerul'ean, hemelsblou, diephlou.
cerum'en, oorwas.
cer'use, witlood, loodwit.
cer'usite, witlooderts, serussiet.
cer'velat, gerookte varkwors, cervelat.
cervic'al, nek-, hals-; ~ **region**, halsstreek, nekstreek; ~ **vertebra**, nekwerwel, halswerwel.
cerv'ine, hert-, hertagtig.
cerv'ix, nek, hals.
ces'ium, sesium.
cess, skatting, syns; belasting; *bad* ~ *to you*, mag die duiwel jou haal.
cess'ation, ophouding, staking, stilstand, einde.
cess'er, einde.
ce'ssion, afstanddoening, (boedel)afstand, sessie; ~**ary**, (..ries), sessionaris, regverkryer, regverkrygende.
cess'pipe, vuilpyp.
cess'pit, cess'pool, (sink)put, beerput, (stink)poel, geutput; ~ **closet**, putkleinhuisie.
ces'toid, lintwurm.
ces'tus, venusgordel; boksring, boksyster.
Ceta'cea, Walvisagtiges.
ceta'cean, (n) walvisagtige, setasee; (a) walvisagtig.
ceta'ceous, walvisagtig.
ce'tane, setaan; ~ **number**, setaangetal.
Ceylon', Ceylon; ~ **ese'**, (n, a) Ceylonees; ~ **pumpkin**, selonspampoen; ~ **rose**, oleander, selonsroos; ~ **tea**, Ceylontee.
cha, (sl.), tee.
Cha'blis, Chablis, wit boergondiese wyn.
cha'-cha (-cha'), (n) cha-cha, baldans; (v) cha-cha (dans).
chac'ma (baboon), (Kaapse) bobbejaan.
chaconne', chaconne.
chad, elf (vis).
chae'ta, borselhaar.
chae'topod (worm), borselwurm.
chafe, (n) wrywing; skaafplek, skawing; ergernis, wrok; (v) (deur)skaaf, (deur)skuur, (deur)vrywe; kwaad maak, wrok, erger; kloek; woed; aankap (perde); ~ *against the restrictions*, vererg wees oor die beperkings.
chaf'er, kewer.
chaf'er-strip, skaafstrook.
chaff, (n) kaf; skerts; plaery; iets waardeloos; bog, twak; (geselst.), vry na, aanlê by; *CAUGHT with* ~, met die kaf gevang; *like* ~ *before the WIND*, soos kaf voor die wind; (v) gekskeer, terg, pla; ~

bale, kafbaal; ~ **barn**, kafhok; ~**-cutter**, ~**-cutting machine**, kafsnyer, kerfmasjien.
chaff'er, (n) plaer; gekskeerder, grapmaker; vryer; (v) knibbel, afding; skarrel; verkwansel; ~**er**, knibbelaar, smouser.
chaf'finch, boekvink *(Fingilla coelebs)*.
chaff'y, kafagtig; prullerig.
chaf'ing, plaery; skawing; deurskaaf; ~**-beam**, skuuryster; ~**-dish**, konfoor; (vuur)tes(sie); ~**-plate**, skuurplaat.
Cha'gas ('s) disease, Chagas se siekte, slaapsiekte.
chagrin', cha'grin, (n) verdriet, hartseer, kwelling, ergernis; boosheid, kwaadheid; (v) hartseer maak, erger.
chain, (n) ketting; ry, reeks; (pl) boeie, kettings; gevangenskap; *a* ~ *of EVENTS*, gebeure; 'n reeks voorvalle; *a* ~ *'s weakest LINK is the measure of its strength*, 'n ketting is net so sterk soos sy swakste skakel; ~ *of OFFICE*, ampsketting; (v) bind, boei, aan die ketting lê; ~**age**, kettingmaat, kettingmeting; ~**-armour**, malie(kolder); ~ **attack**, kringaanval, beurtaanval; ~ **axle**, kettingas; ~ **bolt**, kettinggrendel; ~ **bond**, kettingverband; ~ **bridge**, kettingbrug; ~ **cable**, ankerketting; ~ **case**, kettingkas; ~ **coupling**, kettingkoppeling; ~ **dog**, kettingklou; ~ **drive**, kettingaandrywing; ~ **edge**, kettingrand; ~ **eye**, kettingoog; ~ **forge**, kettingsmedery; ~**-gang**, kettingboewe; ~**-grate**, kettingrooster; ~**-guard**, kettingskerm; ~**ing**, vasketting; ketening; kettingmeting; ~**-jack**, kettingdomkrag; ~ **less**, sonder ketting; ~ **let**, kettinkie; ~**-letter**, kettingbrief; ~**-lightning**, sigsagblits, kettingblits, vurkblits; ~**-link**, kettingskakel; ~**-mail**, maliekolder; ~ **man**, landmetershulp, kettingdraer; ~**-organization**, ketting(skakel)organisasie; ~**-pulley**, kettingkatrol; ~ **pump**, kettingpomp; ~ **reaction**, kettingreaksie; ~ **rhyme**, kettingrym; ~**-saw**, kettingsaag; ~ **shackle**, kettingharp; ~**-shot**, kettingkoeëls; ~**-sling**, kettingstrop; ~**-smoker**, kettingroker; strawwe roker, aanhoudende roker; ~**-stitch**, (cs), kettingsteek; ~ **store**, kettingwinkel; ~ **vice**, kettingskroef; ~**-wheel**, kettingrat; ~**-wrench**, kettingsleutel, aapstert.
chair, (n) stoel, gestoelte; setel; voorsitter(stoel); leerstoel, professoraat; plat (spoor); kapgebint; stoelbed (vir tappe); *ADDRESS the* ~, die voorsitter aanspreek; *APPEAL to the* ~, hom op die voorsitter beroep; *JOINT* ~, lasstoel; *MADAM* ~, geagte voorsitter; *TAKE a* ~, gaan sit; *take THE* ~, voorsit, die voorsitterstoel inneem, presideer; (v) in 'n stoel sit; in triomf ronddra; ~**-back**, stoelleuning; ~**-bottom**, stoelmat; ~**-bottomer**, stoelmatter; ~**-caning**, (stoel)vlegwerk; ~**-cover**, (stoel)oortreksel; stoelbekleedsel; ~**-cushion**, stoelkussing; ~ **leg**, stoelpoot; ~**-lift**, hysstoel; ~**man**, (..men), voorsitter; president; ~ **man's address**, voorsittersrede; ~**manship**, voorsitterskap; ~ **rail**, stoellys; ~**-saw**, stootsaag; ~**woman**, voorsitster.
chaise, plesierrytuig, karretjie; ~ **longue**, sofa.
chala'za, eiervoet, vaatmerk; haelsnoer, chalaza.
chala'zion, karkatjie.
chal'canite, blouvitrioel.
chalced'ony, chalcedoon, chalsedoon, kalsedoon, melksteen.
chal'cocite, chalkosiet.
chalcog'raphy, kopergraveerkuns, plaatsnykuns.
chal'copyrite, chalkopiriet, koperpiriet, koperkies.
Chalde'an, Chaldee', (n) Chaldeër; Chaldeeus (taal); (a) Chaldeeus.
chald'ron, 36 boesel, hoed (steenkoolmaat).
chal'et, chalet; berghut.
chal'ice, kelk, altaarkelk, (verbond)beker, Nagmaalsbeker; miskelkie; ~**d**, kelkvormig.
chalico'sis, silikose, pneumokoniose, kiesel(stof)long.
chalk, (n) kryt; *as like as* ~ *and CHEESE*, soos dag en nag verskil; hemelsbreed verskil; heeltemal verskillend; *FRENCH* ~, talkaarde, kleremakerskryt; *by a LONG* ~, ver(re)weg; *NOT by a long* ~, op verre na nie; (v) met kryt teken; aanteken; ~ *up on the CALENDAR*, 'n kruisie aan die balk maak; ~ *OUT*, in ruwe trekke ontwerp; ~ *UP*, opskryf;

challenge 774 *chanty*

~ **bed,** krytlaag; ~**-block,** blok kryt; krytblok; ~ **cliff,** krytrots; ~ **deposit,** krytafsetting; ~**iness,** krytagtigheid; ~**ing,** verpoeiering (verf); ~**like,** kalkagtig; ~ **line,** krytstreep; ~**-pit,** krytgroef; ~**-stone,** krytklip; jigknobbel; ~ **white,** krytwit; ~**y,** krytagtig; vol jigknobbels.
chall'enge, (n) uitdaging, uittarting; eksepsie, protes, wraking, betwisting (jur.); aansporing; *not take a* ~ *lying down,* jou nie onbetuig laat nie; (v) uitdaag, vuis maak, (uit)tart, betwis; aanhou, aanroep; ter verantwoording roep; wraak; eis; roep om; wek (bewondering); ~**able,** betwisbaar; aanvegbaar; ~ **cup,** uitdaagbeker, wisselbeker; ~**r,** uitdager; ~ **round,** uitdaaggronde.
chall'enging, wraking; uitdaging, uittarting.
chal'lis, sagte kleremateriaal.
chalon', sjalon, bedsprei, deken.
chalyb'eate, ysterhoudend; staalhoudend; ~ **drops,** staaldruppels; ~ **pill,** staalpil; ~ **spring,** staalbron; ~ **water,** staalwater.
cham: *great* ~, groot kokkedoor; outokraat.
cham'ber, (n) kamer, vertrek; kantoorlokaal; sittingsaal; wapenloop; (kamer)pot; (pl) kamers; kantoor; ~ *of COMBUSTION,* verbrandingskamer; *C*~ *of COMMERCE,* Kamer van Koophandel; Sakekamer; ~ *of HORRORS,* gruwelkamer, gruwelmuseum; *JUDGE in* ~*s,* regter op kamerhof; *C*~ *of MINES,* Kamer van Mynwese; (v) opsluit; sitting hou; ~ **acid,** loodkamersuur; ~ **concert,** kamerkonsert; ~ **counsel,** kamer(regs)praktisyn; ~ **court,** kamerhof; ~**ing,** lis, bedrog; ~**ed vein,** kameraar; ~**lain,** kamerheer, kamerdienaar; ~**maid,** kamermeisie, kamenier; ~ **music,** kamermusiek; ~ **orchestra,** kamerorkes; ~**-pot,** kamerpot, pispot (plat), (blou)koos; ~**-stool,** stilletjie, stelletjie.
Chambertin', Chambertin, droë rooi Boergondiese wyn.
cham'bray, chambray, kambrai.
chamel'eon, trapsuutjies, trapsoetjies, verkleurmannetjie; manteldraaier; oorloper, tweegatjakkals.
cham'fer, (n) groef; riggel; skuins kant; afkanting; (v) afskuins, afkant; 'n groef (riggel) skaaf; ~**-bit,** afkantboor; ~**-clamp,** klemhaak; ~**ed,** afgekant, gegroef; ~ **plane,** afkantskaaf, randskaaf.
cham'my, seemsleer, seemslap.
cham'ois, gems(bok) *(Rupicapra rupicapra);* seemslap; seemsleer; ~ **leather,** seemsleer.
cham'omile, *kyk* **camomile.**
champ¹, (n) gekou; (v) kou, knaag, byt.
champ², (n) (sl.), kampioen, bobaas.
champagne', sjampanje, bruiswyn, vonkelwyn.
cham'paign, vlakte, veld.
cham'pers, (sl.), sjampanje.
champi'gnon, sampioen.
cham'pion, (n) kampioen, oorwinnaar; uithaler; voorstander; voorvegter, baas; (v) verdedig; voorstaan, bepleit, veg vir; (a) eerste, beste; baas~; ~**ship,** kampioenskap; baasskap; bepleiting, voorspraak; ~**ship meeting,** kampioenskapsbyeenkoms; ~**ship tournament,** kampioenskapswedstryd, kampioenskapstoernooi.
champlevé, champlevé, enemmelwerk.
chance, (n) kans; toeval, geluk; moontlikheid, gebeurlikheid, waarskynlikheid; vooruitsig; *the* ~*s are AGAINST it,* die kanse is daarteen; *let a* ~ *go BEGGING,* 'n kans verkyk; 'n geleentheid laat verbygaan; *BY* ~, toevalligerwyse; *the* ~ *has been LOST,* die kans is verkyk; dis neusie verby; *take NO* ~*s,* niks waag nie; *ON the* ~ *that,* met die oog op die moontlikheid dat; *what are his* ~*s of PROMOTION?* hoe staan sy kanse op verhoging? *STAND a good* ~, 'n goeie kans hê; *his* ~*s are SLENDER,* sy kanse is maar skraal; *let a* ~ *SLIP (through one's fingers),* nie van 'n geleentheid gebruik maak nie; *TAKE a* ~, 'n kans vat (waag); *TAKE one's* ~, jou kans neem; *TAKE* ~*s,* jou aan risiko blootstel, waag; (v) gebeur, geskied, toevallig plaasvind; waag, riskeer; ~ *one's ARM,* dit waag; *AS it* ~*d,* soos dit voorgeval het; ~ *ON,* teëkom; ~ *UPON,* toevallig kry (afkom op); (a) toevallig; ~**ful,** gewaag, gevaarlik.

chan'cel, kansel; koor (deel van 'n kerk); ~**lery,** (..ries), kanselary; gesantskap.
chance'less, kansloos, sonder 'n kans; foutloos; onberispelik.
chan'cellor, kanselier; *C*~ *of the Exchequer,* Minister van Finansies (Engeland); ~**ship,** kanselierskap.
chan'cel screen, kanselskerm, koorhek.
chanc'er, dobbelaar, opportunis, waaghals; kansvatter; onbevoegde, beunhaas.
chan'cery, kanselary; *COURT of* ~, Kanselaryhof; *IN* ~, voor die hof; met die kop onder die arms van die teenstander (boks).
chan'cre, sjanker, veneriese seer.
chan'croid, sagte sjanker.
chan'cy, onseker, gewaag.
chandelier' kandelaar, kroonlugter; ~**-lily,** kandelaarblom, koningskandelaar.
chand'ler, kersmaker; kruidenier; ~**y,** kersmakery.
'Change¹, (die) Beurs.
change², (n) verandering; ruil; oorgang; oorstapping; wysiging; veromkleding; variasie; kleingeld; uitkeergeld; skoon klere; *all* ~*s are not for the BETTER,* alle veranderings is nie veranderings ten goede nie; ~ *of CLOTHES,* 'n verskoning; ~ *in CONDITION,* toestandsverandering; ~ *of LIFE,* oorgangsjare; klimakterium; *get NO* ~ *out of him,* verniet probeer om hom die loef af te steek; *a* ~ *is as good as a HOLIDAY,* verandering van spys laat eet; *RING the* ~*s,* die klok lui; die moontlike metodes uitput; (v) verander; ruil, omruil, verruil; (ver)= wissel; afwissel; verklee; oorstap; wysig; kleinmaak (geld); oorskakel (motor); verstel; afstap (van onderwerp); draai (mening); ~ *one's COAT,* jou baadjie omruil; verhaar; ~ *COLOUR,* bloos; bleek word; verkleur; verbleik; ~ *one's CONDITION,* in die huwelik tree; ~ *DOWN,* afskakel; in laer versnelling bring; ~ *FRONT,* van mening verander; ~ *GEARS,* oorskakel, ratte wissel; ~ *HANDS,* in ander hande oorgaan; verkoop word; ~ *one's MIND,* van gedagte (plan) verander; ~ *HORSES,* omspan; ~ *a NAME to,* 'n naam verander na; ~ *TRAINS (carriages),* oorstap, oorklim; ~ *one's TUNE,* 'n ander liedjie sing; ~**ability,** veranderlikheid; ~**able,** veranderlik, ongestadig, wisselvallig, onegaal (die weer); veranderbaar; wispelturig; ~**ableness,** veranderlikheid, wisselvalligheid; wispelturigheid; ~**ant,** (F.), weerskynstof, changeant; ~**ful,** veranderlik, onbestendig; ~**less,** onveranderlik; ~**ling,** wisselkind; ~**man,** onderbaas.
change'over, verandering, oorskakeling, vervanging; ~ **cock,** wisselkraan; ~ **switch,** omskakelaar.
change: ~**s,** veranderings; maandstonde; ~**-voucher,** kleingeldbewys; ~**-wheel,** wisselrat (motor).
chang'ing, verandering; oorskakeling (ratte); ~**-light,** draailig (by vuurtoring); ~**-room,** kleedkamer.
chann'el, (n) kanaal, sloot, loop; bedding; straat (see); vaarwater, geul; groef; grip; geut; ~ *of COMMUNICATION,* kommunikasiekanaal; verbindingskanaal; (v) **(-led),** uitgrawe; rimpel; met vore deurploeg; ~ **bar,** U-yster; ~**er,** skietbeitel; groefmasjien; ~ **iron,** U-yster; ~**ize,** kanaliseer; ~**-light,** kanaallig; ~**ling,** sponning (motor); ~**-plate,** riffelplaat; ~ **rail,** groepspoor; ~ **steel,** U-staal; geutstaal; ~ **width,** kanaalwydte; rifspanwydte.
chan'son, chanson.
chant, (n) gesang, lied; kerkgesang; sangerige spraak; dreun, gegalm; (v) sing, besing; sing-praat; (op)= dreun; ~ *the praises of,* gedurig die lof sing van.
chan'tage, chantage, afpersing.
chan'ter, koorsinger; voorsinger; fluit.
chanteuse', chanteuse, kabaretsangeres.
chan'ticleer, haan, kantekleer.
Chantil'ly, Chantillykant.
chan'ting, singspraak; gesang, gesing; ~ **goshawk,** singvalk.
chant'late, wipstuk (van dakrand).
cha'ntress, (-es), sangster, sangeres.
chan'try, (..ries), koorkapel.
chan'ty, (chanties), matroosliedjie.

cha'os, chaos, baaierd; warboel, deurmekaarspul, dolliewarie, deurmekaarheid.
chaot'ic, verward, chaoties.
chap¹, (n) bars, windbars(ie) (hande); skeur, kraak (droë grond); (v) **(-ped)**, bars; skeur; ~ *ed hands*, gebarste hande, skurwe hande.
chap², (n) kêrel, ou(tjie); *a LITTLE* ~, 'n buksie; 'n kêreltjie; *OLD* ~, ou kêrel, ou man.
chap³, (n) onderkaak (van vark); wang; (pl) kake (van diere).
chaparral', (digte), struikgewas, kreupelbos, kreupelhout; dwergeikebos.
chap'-book, volksboek.
chape, haak; beslag (swaard); skedegespe.
chapeau-bras, (F.), chapeau-bras, driekanthoed.
chap'el, kapel; kerkie; drukkery; byeenkoms; ~ *of ease*, hulpkerkie.
chapelle ardente, (F.), staatsiekapel.
chap'eron, (n) beskermster, begeleidster, chaperone, reismoeder, duenna; begeleider, chaperon, reisvader; (v) begelei, beskerm, chaperonneer; ~ **age**, begeleiding.
chap'-fallen, verleë; ontmoedig, uit die veld geslaan; bek-af; *he is* ~, sy ore hang; hy is bek-af.
chap'iter, kapiteel(kroon).
chap'lain, kapelaan, veldprediker; ~cy, kapelaanskap.
chap'let, krans; rosekrans; haarband, snoer; eierlys (bouk.).
chap'man, (..men), bondeldraer, smous; handelaar.
chap'pal, (Indiese) leersandaal.
chapped, gebars, vol barsies.
chap'pie, chap'py, snoeshaan; kêreltjie, mannetjie.
chap'ter, hoofstuk, kapittel; domkapittel; vergadering; *a* ~ *of ACCIDENTS*, opeenhoping van ongesiene gebeurtenisse (ongelukke); *DEAN and* ~, domkapittel; *to END of* ~, tot die end; vir ewig; *quote* ~ *and VERSE*, man en perd noem; met vers en kapittel bewys; ~**-house**, kapittelhuis; ~**ization**, hoofstukverdeling; ~**ize**, in hoofstukke verdeel; ~**-room**, kapittelsaal.
char¹, (n) dagwerk, loswerk; skoonmaakster, werkvrou; (v) los werkies doen; skoonmaak, huiswerk doen.
char², (n) rooi forel.
char³, (n) sintel; (v) **(-red)**, verkool; brand, skroei.
cha'rabanc, (groot) motorbus, toerbus, janplesier.
cha'racter, karakter, tipe, aard; kenmerk, stempel; getuigskrif; reputasie; karakterisering; *ACT out of* ~, strydig met sy karakter handel; uit jou rol val; *a DANGEROUS* ~, 'n gevaarlike klant; *IN* ~, in die rol; ~**is'tic**, (n) kenmerk, kenteken; eienaardigheid; eienskap, karaktertrek, eienheid; (a) karakteristiek, kenmerkend, tekenend; ~*istic of*, kenmerkend vir (van); ~**or**, karakterakteur (-aktrise), karakterspeler; ~ **assassin**, karakterskender; ~ **assassination**, karakterskending; ~**-building**, karaktervorming; ~**iza'tion**, karakteruitbeelding, karaktertekening; ~**ize**, karakteriseer, tipeer, kenmerk; skilder, beskryf; ~**less**, karakterloos; alledaags; sonder getuigskrif; ~**ology**, karakterkunde, karakterologie; ~ **part**, ~ **role**, karakterrol; ~**sketch**, karakterskets; karakteristiek; ~ **training**, karaktervorming, karakterbou(ing).
charade', charade; raaisel; absurde voorstelling.
char'coal, houtskool; ~**-biscuit**, houtskoolbeskuit; ~**-burner**, koolbrander; ~**-cooler**, houtskoolkoelkas; ~**-iron**, houtskoolyster.
chard, artisjokkelof; *Swiss* ~, spinasiebeet, blaarbeet.
charge, (n) opdrag, bevel; bewaring; beskuldiging; aanval, bestorming; aantyging, aanklag; las, vrag; opdrag, taak, plig; pleegkind; leerling; koste, uitgaaf; prys; lading (geweer, battery); heraldiese figuur; beswaring; sorg, toesig, vermaning; (pl) beskuldigings; *lay a* ~ *AGAINST*, iem aangee; 'n (aan)klag inbring teen iem.; *BAYONET at the* ~, gevelde bajonet; *BE in* ~, toesig hou; in beheer wees; *BILL of* ~ *s*, onkosterekening; ~ *upon a FUND*, las teen 'n fonds; *GIVE in* ~, laat arresteer; toevertrou; *IN* ~ *of*, onder toesig van; *LAY to someone's* ~, iem. ten laste lê; ~ *for MAKING*,

maakloon; *NO* ~, gratis, verniet; *NOTE of* ~ *s*, onkostenota; *RETURN to the* ~, die aanval hernuwe; (v) opdra, beveel; storm, aanval; belas; hef; beskuldig; vra, vorder; aantyg; debiteer, in rekening bring; laai (battery), vul; 'n wapenfiguur aanbring op; toespreek (jurie); aanklá, beskuldig, bereken; ~ *AT*, losstorm op; ~ *d PERSON*, aangeklaagde; ~ *with THEFT*, van diefstal aankla; *WHAT do you* ~ *for this?* wat vra u hiervoor? ~ *a person WITH*, iem. beskuldig van; iem. iets nagee; iem. aankla weens; ~**abil'ity**, verantwoordelikheid; belasbaarheid; ~**able**, te wyte aan, te laste van; verantwoordelik; belasbaar; vorderbaar; ~ **account**, ope rekening.
charg'é d'affaires', (**chargés d'affaires**), chargé d'affaires, saakgelastigde.
charge: ~**hand**, ~**man**, werk(s)opsiener, voorman; ploegbaas, spanbaas; ~ **nurse**, eerste verpleegster, toesighoudende verpleegster; ~**-office**, aanklagkantoor, klagtekantoor, polisiekantoor.
char'ger¹, perd, strydros; laaier; laaiplaatjie.
char'ger², vleisskottel.
charge: ~ **rate**, laaisterkte; ~**-sheet**, klagstaat, aanklagakte.
char'ging: ~ **crane**, laaikraan; ~ **current**, laaistroom; ~ **platform**, laaivlak, laaiplatform; ~ **rate**, laaitempo; ~ **voltage**, laaispanning.
char'ily, versigtig; teësinnig.
char'iness, versigtigheid, behoedsaamheid; suinigheid.
cha'riot, koets; triomfwa; strydwa; ~**eer'**, (strydwa)drywer, koetsier, menner; ~ **race**, strydwawedren, karwedren.
charis'ma, charisma.
charismat'ic, oorredend, charismaties.
cha'ritable, liefdadig, weldadig, offervaardig, vrygewig; mensliewend; barmhartig; ~ *institution*, liefdadigheidsinrigting, liefdadige instelling; ~**ness**, liefdadigheid; mensliewendheid; barmhartigheid.
cha'ritably, mededeelsaam, vrygewig, mildelik.
cha'rity, liefdadigheid, weldadigheid; naasteliefde, barmhartigheid, mensliefde; sagtheid; aalmoes; *ACT of* ~, liefdadigheid; ~ *begins at HOME*, die hemp is nader as die rok; begin eers by Jerusalem; *LIVE on* ~, van genadebrood leef; van assebliéf en dankie lewe; *OUT of* ~, uit barmhartigheid; *WORK of* ~, liefdadigheidswerk; liefdeswerk; ~**child**, armskoolkind; ~ **concert**, liefdadigheidskonsert; ~ **performance** liefdadigheidsvoorstelling; ~ **school**, armskool; ~**-stamp**, weldadigheidseël, welsynseël.
charivar', chariva'ri, ketelmusiek; lawaai.
char'lady, skoonmaakster, werkvrou.
charl'atan, kwaksalwer, charlatan; ~**ism**, ~**ry**, kwaksalwery, boerebedrog, charlatanerie.
Charl'emagne, Karel die Grote.
Charles's Wain', die Ploeg, Groot Beer.
Char'leston, charleston (dans).
char'lie, japie, skaap, haas, dommerd.
charl'ock, geelmosterd (plant); *joined* ~, ramenas.
char'lotte, charlotte(poeding); ~ **russe**, charlotte russe, vla(spons)koek.
charm, (n) betowering, bekoring, sjarme, begoëling, doepa; aanminlikheid, aantreklikheid, aanvalligheid; gelukbringer, amulet, talisman; toormiddel, toorspreuk; sieraad, snuistery; (pl) aantreklikhede; (v) betower, besweer; inneem, bekoor; verruk; toor; aanlok; ~**ed**, verruk, opgetoë; *REAR a* ~ *ed life*, onkwesbaar wees; *I SHALL be* ~ *ed*, dit sal vir my 'n genoeë doen; ~**er**, heks, towenaar; bekoorster, aanlokster; ~**euse'**, charmeuse, sjarmeuse (materiaal); ~**ing**, betowerend, bekoorlik, innemend, aanloklik, aanminlik, bevallig, aanminnig, aanvallig (persoonlikheid); verruklik (musiek); ~**less**, onbehaaglik; ~**-school**, verfyningskool, afrondingskool.
charn'el-house, beenderehuis, knekelhuis, dodehuis.
Charol(l)ais' (cattle), Charol(l)ais(bees(te)).
char'poy, (Indiese) katel, bed.
charred, verbrand, verkool; ~ **stubble**, swartbaard.
charr'ing, verkoling.

chart, (n) (see)kaart; tabel (inligting); (v) in kaart bring; tabelleer; ~ *a COURSE,* 'n koers vasstel (vaslê); ~ *SOMETHING,* iets in kaart bring; ~-**book,** seekaartboek.
chart'er, (n) oktrooi, grondwet; voorreg, privilege; vrybrief, handves, magtigingsbrief, oorkonde; (v) 'n oktrooi toestaan, oktrooieer; huur; verhuur; bevoorreg.
chart'ered: ~ **accountant,** geoktrooieerde reken= meester; ~ **company,** geoktrooieerde maatskappy.
chart'er: ~**er,** bevragter; ~ **flight,** huurvlug; C~ **house,** Kartuiserklooser; ~**ing,** bevragting; ~ **member,** stigterslid; stigtingslid; ~ **party,** bevrag= tingsooreenkoms, cherteparty; ~ **service,** huur= diens.
chart: ~**house,** ~**room,** kaartkamer.
chartreuse', chartreuse (likeur).
char'woman, (..**men**), werkvrou, werkster, skoon= maakster; los bediende.
char'y, versigtig, behoedsaam; ongeneë; spaarsaam, suinig, karig.
Charyb'dis, Charibdis.
chase¹, (n) jag; vervolging; vervolgde skip; wild; jag= veld; *give* ~, jag maak op; agtervolg; (v) jag; agter= volg, (na)jaag; uitdryf; ~ *AWAY,* verjaag, weg= jaag; ~ *OUT of,* uitwoel, verdryf.
chase², (n) vorm, raam (in drukkery); (v) nasny (skroefdraad); siseleer; graveer; inlê; groef; insit; ~ *METALS,* gedrewe werk maak; ~*d WORK,* dryf= werk.
chase³, (n) groef (geweer); voor (pyp); vlug (kanon); ~-**girdle,** kanonring; ~-**mortise joint,** dryftap= voeg.
chas'er, verjaer; drywer; graveur; spoeldrankie; ~-**plane,** jagvliegtuig; ~-**squadron,** jageskader.
chas'ing¹, agtervolging.
chas'ing², gravering; dryfwerk; ~-**chisel,** dryfbeitel; ~-**hammer,** dryfhamer; ~-**punch,** graveerpons; ~-**tool,** skroefstaal.
chasm, afgrond; (berg)kloof; diepte, gaping.
chasse, (F.), chasse, likeur.
chasseur', (F.), chasseur, jagter.
chass'is, (sing. and pl.), onderstel; geraamte, raam= werk, chassis; bakwerk; monteerplaat (radio).
chaste, kuis, rein, eerbaar, vlekloos; ~**ness,** kuisheid, reinheid.
cha'sten, kasty, straf; reinig, suiwer, temper, matig.
chastis'able, strafbaar.
chastise', kasty, tugtig; *we* ~ *those whom we love,* dié wat 'n mens liefhet, kasty jy; ~**ment,** kastyding, tugtiging, straf; ~**r,** strawwer, kastyder.
chas'tity, kuisheid, reinheid; keurigheid (styl); eer= baarheid; suiwerheid; ~ **belt,** kuisheidsgordel.
chas'uble, altaargewaad, kasuifel.
chat¹, (n) praatjie; gebabbel; *have a* ~, 'n praatjie maak; (v) **(-ted),** gesels, babbel, keuwel.
chat², (n) spekvreter, bergwagter; *FAMILIAR* ~, dagbrekertjie; *MOCKING* ~, dassievoël.
chât'eau, (-x), buiteverblyf, kasteel, lusslot.
chat'elaine, sleutelketting; burgvrou; gasvrou; ~-**bag,** beueltassie.
chatoy'ant, katoogagtig, katogig.
chatt'el, losgoed, los besitting; (pl) hawe, huisraad, besittings, losgoed; *ALL his* ~*s,* sy hawe en goed; *GOODS and* ~*s,* roerende goedere; ~ **mortgage,** losgoedverband; ~**s,** los goed(ere), roerende goed(ere).
chatt'er, (n) geklets, gebabbel; trilling (van gereed= skap); (v) babbel, klets; snater; klappertand (van koue); klapper (koppelaar), ratel; ~ *away time,* tyd verbabbel; ~**box,** (-**es**), babbelkous, snaterbek, flapuit, babbelaar, babbelbek, kekkelbek, veel= prater; Kaatjie Kekkelbek, Antjie Tatterat; klets= kous; ~**er,** kletsmajoor; veelprater; *kyk* **chatter= box;** ~**ing,** gesnater; gebabbel, gekeuwel; gesnap, geklapper.
chat: ~**tiness,** geselserigheid; spraaksaamheid; ~**ting,** geselsery; kletsery; pratery.
chatt'y, praterig, spraaksaam, geselserig.
chaud-froid', (F.), chaud-froid, koue vleis in jellie (sous).
chauff'er, vuurbak, konfoor.

chauffeur', motorbestuurder, chauffeur.
chauffeuse', chauffeuse, motorbestuurderes.
chaulmoo'gra, ..**mug'ra,** kalmoegra(boom); ~ **oil,** kalmoegraolie.
chauv'inism, chauvinisme, jingoïsme.
chauv'inist, (n) chauvinis, jingo; *male* ~, manlike chauvinis; (a) chauvinisties; ~ **'ic,** (a) chauvinisties, jingoïsties.
chaw', (n) pruimpie; (v) kou, pruim; ~ *up,* 'n groot pak gee; ~-**bacon,** gomtor; pruimpie.
chayote', soesoe.
cheap, goedkoop, spotkoop; nietig, veragtelik; *DIRT* ~, spotgoedkoop; *FEEL* ~, sleg voel; *HOLD* ~, geringskat; *MAKE oneself* ~, jou status verlaag; *ON the* ~, goedkoop; *SELL something* ~, iets vir 'n appel en 'n ei verkoop; iets spotgoedkoop ver= koop; ~**en,** afding; goedkoop word (maak); af= slaan; kleineer; ~**jack,** smous, marskramer; ~**ness,** goedkoopheid, goedkoopte; ~**skate,** vrek, suinigaard.
cheat, (n) opligter, fopper, afsetter, verneuker (sl.), bedrieër; (v) bedrieg, oplig, toesit, toetrap, intrek, betrek, fop, kierang, verneuk (sl.), flous, kul, mis= lei, pier; ~ *someone into the BELIEF,* iem. in die waan bring; ~ *the TIME,* die tyd verdryf; ~ *OUT of,* beroof van; ~**ed,** gepier; ~**ing,** bedrog, kullery opligtery, foppery, flousery, kulwerk, afsettery, verneukery.
check¹, (n) skaak; verifikasie, kontrole; stuiting, be= lemmering, teenwerking; teenspoed, nederlaag; on= derbreking, rem; beperking; kontroleur; keerder, stuiter; ontvangbewys; verwyt, berisping; waar= merk; *HAND in one's* ~, sterf; *KEEP in* ~, in toom hou; (v) nagaan, nareken, kontroleer (opga= wes); nasien, natel, deursien, deurloop (rekeninge); waarmerk; inhou, bedwing, beteuel, intoom (perd, woede); ophou (jaghonde); teëgaan; berispe; be= lemmer, stuit; skaak; ~ *BOOKS,* boeke nagaan; ~ *into a HOTEL,* by 'n hotel inteken; *IT* ~*s,* dit klop; ~ *UP,* optel; vergelyk, kontroleer, toets.
check², (n) windbarsie (in verf); (v) windbarsies vorm (verf).
check³, (n) ruit; blokkiesgoed, geruite goed.
check⁴, (v) tot stand kom.
check: ~**able,** kontroleerbaar; ~-**action,** remming; ~-**analysis,** kontroleanalise; ~-**ball,** keerkoeël; ~-**bearing,** kontrolepeiling; ~-**bolt,** stelbout; ~-**book,** kontroleboek; ~-**chain,** noodketting; ~-**col= lar,** wurgketting.
checked, geruit; ~ *square,* haaks gekeep.
check'er, beteuelaar; kontroleur, opsigter, nasiener, nateller; laaimeester; *kyk* **chequer.**
check'ered, geruit; ~ *materiaal,* skotsbont.
check'ers, dambord; albasterdambord.
check'er-work, inlêwerk.
check: ~-**in,** (n), aankoms, aanmelding; ~ **in,** (v), aanmeld; ~-**in counter,** aanmeldtoonbank, ver= trektoonbank; ~-**key,** loper; ~**list,** kontrolelys; ~ **mate;** (n) (skaak)mat; (v) skaakmat sit; verydel, uitoorlê; *be* ~*mated,* skaakmat wees; ~-**nut,** sluit= moer; ~-**out bag,** winkelsak; ~-**pattern,** ruitpa= troon; ~-**plate,** keerplaat, sluitplaat; ~-**point,** kontrolepunt, bestek; snypunt; ~-**rail,** keerstaaf; ~-**rein,** binneleisel; ~-**sample,** kontrolemonster; ~-**screw,** sluitskroef; ~-**strap,** keerstrop; keer= band; ~-**till,** kasregister; ~-**up,** roetine-ondersoek, kontrole; toets, inspeksie; ~-**valve,** afsluitklep, keerklep; ~-**word,** kontrolewoord.
chedd'ar, cheddar(kaas).
chedd'ite, cheddiet.
chee'-chee, pietjiekanarie.
cheek, (n) wang; brutaliteit, astrantheid, parmantig= heid; onbeskaamdheid; *HAVE the* ~ *to,* die verme= telheid hê om; ~ *by JOWL,* wang aan wang, sy aan sy; (v) parmantig wees teenoor; ~-**bone,** wang, juk= been; ~-**gland,** wangklier.
cheek'iness, parmantigheid, astrantheid.
cheek: ~-**muscle,** kouspier; ~-**pouch,** kies, wangsak; ~-**tooth,** kiestand; ~-**wool,** wangwol.
cheek'y, brutaal, parmantig, diknek, (dom)astrant; onbeskaamd; ~ *person,* parmant.
cheep, (n) getjilp, gepiep; (v) tjilp, piep.

cheer, (n) onthaal, spys; vrolikheid, blydskap; *the FEWER the better* ~, elke minder eter maak dit beter; *be of GOOD* ~, opgeruimd wees; moed hou; *MAKE* ~, vrolik wees; feesvier; *THREE* ~ *s*, drie hoera's; (v) onthaal; opbeur, troos, opvrolik, moed inpraat; toejuig, hoera roep, jubel, joel; ~ *ON*, aanmoedig; ~ *UP*, moed skep; opfleur, opvrolik, vervrolik; ~**ful**, vrolik, opgeruimd, blygeestig, (op= ge)monter, blymoedig, welgemoed; ~**fully**, goeds= moeds; ~**fulness**, opgeruimdheid, blygeestigheid; blymoedigheid, opgewektheid; ~**ily**, vrolik; lustig; ~**iness**, opgewektheid, vrolikheid; ~**ing**, (n) op= wekkende woorde; toejuiging, applous, gejoel, ge= jubel; (a) aanmoedigend, opwekkend; ~**io!** alles ten beste; tot siens! ~**-leader**, rasieleier, sangleier, dirigent; ~ **less**, neerslagtig, moedeloos, trooste= loos, vreugdeloos; somber; ~ **s**, gejubel, gejuig; (in= terj.), gesondheid!; ~**y**, vrolik, opgewek, lustig, op= geruimd.
chee'sa-stick, laaistok, fakkelstok, tjiesa(stok).
cheese[1], kaas; *GREEN* ~, jong kaas; *RIPE* ~, beleë kaas; ~ *and WINE party*, kaas-en-wynparty.
cheese[2], (v): ~ *it!* hou op!
cheese: ~ **agitator**, kaasroerder; ~ **and wine**, kaas en wyn; ~ **and wine party**, kaas-en-wynparty(tjie); ~ **biscuit**, kaasbeskuitjie; ~ **board**, kaasbord; ~**bur= ger**, kaas(ham)burger; ~ **cake**, stremselkoek, kaas= koek; prikkelfoto; prikkelpop; ~**-cloth**, gaasdoek, kaasdoek; ~**-cover**, kaasstolp; ~**-curing**, kaasry= ping; ~**-cutter**, kaasmes, kaassnyer; strooihoed; ~ **dish**, kaasgereg; ~**factory**, kaasfabriek; ~**finger**, kaasstokkie, kaasvinger; ~**-fly**, kaasvlieg; ~**head**, dikkop (boute); ~**-maggot**, kaasmaaier, kaas= wurm; ~**-maker**, kaasmaker; ~**-making**, kaasma= kery, kaasbereiding; ~**-milk**, kaasmelk; ~**-mite**, kaasmyt; ~ **monger**, kaaskoper; ~**-mould**, kaas= vorm; ~ **nip**, kaashappie, southappie; ~**-parer**, vrek, gierigaard; ~**-paring**, (n) suinigheid, vrekkig= heid; (pl) kaaskorsies; rommel; (a) suinig, vrekkig; ~**-press**, kaaspers; ~**-skipper**, kaasmaaier; ~**-slicer**, kaasskaaf; ~ **spread**, kaassmeer; smeerkaas; ~**-straw**, kaasstokkie; ~ **twist**, kaaskrul; ~**-vat**, kaasvat; ~**-weed**, kiesieblaar.
chee'siness, kaasagtigheid; (sl.), goorheid, baklei= erigheid; minderwaardigheid.
chee'sy, kaasagtig; agtermekaar; goor, bakleierig; minderwaardig.
cheet'ah, jagluiperd, cheetah.
chef, hoofkok, sjef.
chef-d'oeu'vre, (chefs-d'oeuvre), meesterstuk.
cheili'tis, cheilitis, lipontsteking.
cheiloschi'sis, cheiloskise, haaslip, haasspleet.
chek'a, tsjeka (Rus.).
che'la, knyper (skaaldiere); ~**te**, chelaat; ~**'tion**, chelasie.
cheli'sera, knyper, kloukaak.
chem'ical, (n) skeikundige stof; (a) skeikundig, che= mies; ~ **agent**, reagens; ~ **compound**, skeikundige (chemiese) verbinding; ~ **food**, chemiese voedsel; ~**ly**, skeikundig, chemies; ~ **reaction**, skeikundige (chemiese) reaksie; ~ **s**, chemikalieë.
chemise', vroue(onder)hemp, chemise.
chemisette', onderlyfie, chemiset.
chem'ist, apteker; skeikundige, chemikus.
chem'istry, skeikunde, chemie.
chem'ist's shop, apteek.
chemi'type, chem'itypy, chemitipie.
chemother'apy, chemoterapie.
chemo'tropism, chemotropie.
chomurg'io(al), chemurgies.
chem'urgy, chemurgie.
che'nevixite, cheneviksiet.
chenille', fluweelkoord, chenille.
cheong'sam, spleetrok.
cheque, tjek, wissel; *BLANK* ~, blanko tjek; *CROSSED* ~, gekruiste tjek; *STOP a* ~, 'n tjek keer; ~**-book**, tjekboek; ~**-book farmer**, tjekboek= boer; ~ **counter**, los tjek; ~**-guarantee**, tjekwaar= borg.
cheq'uer, (n) ruit (patroon); skakering; *Chinese C* ~ *s*, Chinese dambordspel; (v) ruit; skakeer; ~**-board**, dambord; ~**ed**, geruit; geskakeer; *a* ~ *ed*

CAREER, 'n bewoë lewe; ~*ed PLATE*, geruite plaat; ~**s**, dambord(spel).
cheque'-stub, tjekteenblad, tjekstrokie.
che'rish, koester, liefkoos; liefhê, bemin; versorg; waardeer; ~**ed**, bemind; kosbaar; ~**er**, minnaar; begeerder.
cheroot', seroet
che'rry, (n) **(cherries)**, kersie; kersieboom; *make two BITES at a* ~, nie ondernemend wees nie, te ver= sigtig te werk gaan; *cherries are BITTER to the sur= feited bird*, as die muis dik (vol) is, is die meel bitter; (a) kersiekleurig; ~**-bay**, lourier; ~**-bob**, tweeling= kersie; ~ **brandy**, kersiebrandewyn; ~**-laurel**, lou= rierkersie; ~ **orchard**, kersieboord; ~**-pie**, helio= troop; sonsoekertjie (plant); kersietert; ~**-red**, ~**-ripe**, kersierooi; ~**-stone**, kersiepit; ~**-tree**, ker= sieboom; ~**-wood**, kersiehout.
cher'sonese, skiereiland.
chert, onsuiwere kwarts, horingsteen, chert.
che'rub, **(-im, -s)**, gerub(yn), engel.
cheru'bic, engelagtig.
cherv'il, kerwel.
chervo'nets, tsjerwonets (munt).
chess[1], pontbrugplank.
chess[2], skaak(spel); *a* ~ *EVENING (party)*, skaak= party; *PLAY* ~, skaak speel; ~ **board**, skaakbord; ~ **champion**, skaakkampioen ~ **column**, skaakru= briek; ~ **competition**, skaakwedstryd, skaakkom= petisie.
chess'el, kaasvorm, kaasvat.
chess: ~ **man**, skaakstuk; ~ **master**, skaakmeester; ~ **move**, (skaak)set, skuif; ~ **piece**, skaakstuk; ~ **player**, skaakspeler; ~ **set**, skaakstel; ~ **tourna= ment**, skaaktoernooi, skaakwedstryd.
chest, bors(kas); borsholte (perd); kis, koffer; kas; *GET off one's* ~, van die hart kry; ~ *of DRAWERS*, laaikas, klerekas, spieëlkas; *PUSH out one's* ~, jou bors uitstoot; die hoed uit die oë stoot; ~**-bone**, borsbeen; ~**-cavity**, borsholte; ~ **complaint**, borskwaal; ~**ed**, gebors, van die bors.
ches'terfield, rusbank; jas.
chest: ~**-expander**, borsontwikkelaar; ~ **measure= ment**, borsmaat.
chest'nut, (n) kastaiing; vos (perd); ou grap; horing= vrat, swilvrat (perd); *PULL the* ~ *s out of the fire*, die kastaiings uit die vuur haal (krap); *his* ~ *s are in the FIRE*, hy is in die knyp, sy akkers brand; (a) vos=, kastaiingbruin; *DARK* ~, sweetvos; *LIGHT* ~, ligvos; ~ **colour**, kastaiingbruin; ~ **roan**, vos= skimmel; ~**-tree**, kastaiingboom; ~**-wood**, kastai= inghout.
chest: ~**-on-chest**, (hoë) laaikas; ~**-protector**, bors= beskermer; ~**-trouble**, borskwaal, borsaandoe= ning; ~**y**, verwaand.
cheval'-glass, (-es), draaispieël.
chevalier', ridder; ruiter; fortuinsoeker; ~ *of in= dustry*, swendelaar.
chev'erel, jong bok; seemsleer.
chev'ron, rangstreep, moustreep; chevron, sjevron; keper (heraldiek); ~ **stitch**, chevronsteek, sjevron= steek.
chev'y, (n) Jag; (v) **(chevied)**, nasit, jaag.
chew, (n) koutjie; pruim; (v) kou; pruim; ~ *the CUD*, herkou; oorpeins; ~ *OVER*, oorpeins, oordink; ~ *the RAG*, klets; land en sand aanmekaar praat; ou koeie uit die sloot haal; ~ *TOBACCO*, van sy kies 'n looikuip maak; pruim; ~**er**, kouer; pruimer; ~**ing-gum**, kougom; ~**ing-tabacco**, pruimtwak.
chi, chi (Griekse letter).
chiaroscur'o, chiaroscuro, lig-en-skaduwee, lig-en-donker.
chias'ma, chias'mus, chiasma (biol.); kruising; chias= ma, chiasmus (gram).
chias'tic, oorkruis=.
chias'tolite, holspaat, chiastoliet.
chibouk', (Turkse) langsteelpyp.
chic, chic, modieus, sjiek, elegant.
chicane', haarklowery, uitvlug, foppery; regsver= draaiing, chicane; hand sonder troewe; (v) uitvlug= te soek; twis soek; fop, kul; ~**ry**, slim streke, haar= klowery; regsverdraaiing.
chi'chi, opgesmuk; verwyf; aanstellerig.

chick, (-s), kuiken; kind; aster, meisie; *started* ~ *s,* halfwaskuikens, opgeskote kuikens; ~ **abid'dy,** liefling, hartlam; ~ **adee,** swartkopmees.

chick'en, kuiken; hoendervleis; snuiter, kind; *go to BED with the* ~ *s,* saam met die hoenders gaan slaap; *Mother CARY's* ~, stormvoël; *COUNT one's* ~ *s before they are hatched,* die vel verkoop voordat die beer geskiet is; *a MERE* ~, sommer 'n kuiken, 'n piepjong ventjie; *he is NO* ~, hy is nie meer so jonk nie; hy is nie vandag se kind nie; *look like a PLUCKED* ~, soos 'n natgereënde hoender lyk; lyk soos 'n haan waarvan die stertvere uitgepluk is; *his* ~ *s have come home to ROOST,* boontjie kom om sy loontjie; kiering (kierang, kurang) het gebraai; *as TENDER as a* ~, baie sag, mollig; ~ **-breasted,** spitsborstig, met 'n misvormde bors; ~ **broth,** hoendersop; ~ **cholera,** hoendercholera; ~ **-coop,** hoenderhok; kuikenhok; ~ **corn,** kuikenkos (plant); ~ **curry,** kerriehoender; ~ **feed,** hoenderkos; kuikenkos; kleinigheidjie (geld); ~ **grain,** kuikensaad; ~ **grape,** winterdruif; ~ **grass,** kuikenkos *(Sorghum drummondii);* ~ **-hearted,** lafhartig; kleinhartig; papbroekig, bang, vreesagtig; ~ **maize,** kiepiemielies; ~ **mash,** hoenderkos; kuikenkos; ~ **mite,** hoendermyt; ~ **pie,** hoenderpastei; ~ **piri-piri,** piri-pirihoender; ~ **-pox** waterpokkies (mens); hoenderpokkies (pluimvee); ~ **soup,** hoendersop; ~ **wire,** hoender(hok)draad.

chick'ling[1], kuikentjie.
chick'ling[2], wieke *(Vicia sativa).*
chick'-pea, dwerg-ertjie *(Cicer arietinum).*
chick'-weed, sterremuur, muurkruid.
chic'ory, sigorei, witloof, Brusselse lof.
chide, berispe, knor; afjak, uitskel.
chief, (n) hoof, baas; opperhoof; owerste, kaptein, leier; skildhoof (herald.); *IN* ~, vernaamlik; (a) vernaamste, hoogste, eerste, hoof=, opperste; ~ **accountant,** hoofrekenmeester; ~ **agent,** hoofagent; ~ **character,** hoofkarakter; ~ **clerk,** hoofklerk; ~ **constable,** hoofkonstabel; ~ **contents,** hoofinhoud; ~ **dish,** hoofgereg; ~ **dom,** kapteinsgebied; hoofskap; leierskap; ~ **engineer,** hoofingenieur; ~ **executive,** hoofamptenaar; *C* ~ *Justice,* hoofregter; ~ **leader,** hoofleier; ~ **ly,** veral, hoofsaaklik, grotendeels, vernaamlik; ~ **mate,** eerste stuurman; ~ **matron,** hoofmatrone; ~ **medical officer,** hoof mediese beampte; ~ **merit,** hoofverdienste; ~ **officer,** eerste offisier (op skip); ~ **priest,** owerpriester; ~ **rabbi,** opperrabyn; ~ **secretary,** hoofsekretaris; ~ **steward,** hoofkelner; hooftafelbediende.

chief'tain, hoof, aanvoerder; ~ **cy,** bevelhebberskap, opperhoofskap; ~ **ess,** vroulike opperhoof; ~ **ry,** ~ **ship,** opperhoofskap, kapteinskap.

chief: ~ **witness,** hoofgetuie; ~ **work,** hoofwerk, magnum opus.
chiff'on, dun gaas, chiffon; ~ **ier,** sierlaaikas.
chigger, sandvlooi.
chig'non, bolla, kondee, haarmassa (op die agterhoof).
chihua'hua, chihuahua.
chil'blain(s), winterhande, winterore, wintervoete.
child, (-ren), kind, wig; *BE with* ~, swanger wees; *the BURNT* ~ *dreads the fire,* ondervinding is die beste leermeester; *the* ~ *is FATHER to the man,* so vader, so kind; *the FIRST* ~, die eerste hoepel om die vaatjie; *FROM a* ~, van kindsbeen af; ~ *of GOD,* kind van God; ~ *of the IMAGINATION,* kind (vrug) v.d. verbeelding; ~ *of NATURE,* natuurkind; *that is* ~ *'s PLAY,* dis kinderspeletjies; *it is no* ~ *'s PLAY,* dis nie kinderspeletjies nie; *a* ~ *of his TIME(S),* 'n kind van sy tyd; ~ **-bearing,** swangerskap; baring; ~ **bed,** kraambed; kinderbed; ~ **birth,** bevalling; *C* ~ **ermas,** Allerkinderdag; ~ **hood,** kinderjare; *SECOND* ~ *hood,* kindsheid; *SINCE* ~ *hood,* van kindsbeen af; ~ **ish,** kinderagtig; ~ **ishness,** kinderagtigheid; ~ **less,** kinderloos; ~ **like,** kinderlik; ~ **prodigy,** wonderkind.

chil'dren, kinders; ~, *when little, make parents FOOLS,* gaan jy met kinders uit, kom jy met kinders tuis; klein kinders, klein sorge, groot kinders groot sorge; *he that has* ~ *can call NOTHING his own,* kinders is 'n seën v.d. Here, maar hulle hou die mot uit die klere; ~ *should be SEEN and not heard,* kinders moet gesien, maar nie gehoor word nie; ~ *and fools SPEAK the truth,* uit die mond v.d. kinders sal 'n mens die waarheid verneem; ~ *WILL be* ~, kinders bly maar net kinders; *C* ~ **'s act,** Kinderwet; ~ **'s choir,** kinderkoor; ~ **'s court,** kinderhof; ~ **'s service,** kinderdiens.

child: ~ **'s play,** kinderspel; ~ **'s portion,** kindsdeel (jur.); ~ **-welfare,** kindersorg; ~ **-wife,** meisie-vroutjie.

Chil'e, Chili.
Chil'ean, (n) Chileen; (a) Chileens.
chil'i, *kyk* **chilli.**
chil'iad, duisend; duisend jaar, millennium.
chil'iasm, chiliasme.
chil'iast, chilias, verwagter van die millennium; ~ **'ic,** chiliasties.
chili'tis = **cheilitis.**
chill, (n) koue; verkoue(ntheid); kilheid, koudheid; onvriendelikheid; gietvorm; *CAST a* ~ *over,* demp; *CATCH a* ~, koue vat; *HAVE a* ~, verkoue wees; *TAKE the* ~ *off,* die ergste koue wegneem; (v) verkluim, verstyf; koud maak, verkoel; ontmoedig, neerdruk; afkoel; die oppervlak hard maak; (a) yskoud, verkluim, koel, koud; ongevoelig.

chilled, koud; afgekoel; koudgesmeed; ~ *EGG,* koeleier; ~ *MEAT,* koel(kamer)vleis; ~ *STEEL,* verkoelde staal.

chill'i, rissie, paprika.
chill'iness, koelheid; huiwerigheid.
chill'ing, (n) verkoeling; (a) verkoelend; kil, ontmoedigend.
chill'y[1], (a) verkluimerig, kouerig, koud, koulik, naterig; koel; *a* ~ *reception,* 'n onvriendelike ontvangs.
chill'y[2], (n) *kyk* **chilli.**
Chiltern Hun'dreds: *apply for the* ~, bedank as parlementslid (in Engeland).
chim(a)er'a, skrikbeeld, chimera, paaiboelie, droombeeld, hersenskim, drogbeeld.
chime[1], (n) rand (van 'n vat), kim.
chime[2], (n) klokkespel; klokke; melodie, deuntjie, harmonie; ooreenstemming; welluidendheid; (v) speel (klokke), lui, beier, laat klink, klokke bespeel; rym; napraat; harmonieer; ~ *in with EVERY= THING,* met alles saamstem, altyd saamblaf; ~ *IN,* in die rede val; ~ *in WITH,* instem met; ~ **r,** klok(ke)speler.

chime'rical, denkbeeldig, hersenskimmig, ingebeeld.
chimes, speeluurwerk; klokkespel.
chim'ing, lui, gelui; klokkespel; ~ **alarm (clock),** deuntjiewekker; ~ **watch,** slaghorlosie.
chim'ney, (-s), skoorsteen; lampglas; opening; *smoke like a* ~, van jou mond 'n skoorsteen maak; soos 'n skoorsteen rook; ~ **-arch,** vuurherdboog; ~ **-back,** agterherd; ~ **-base,** skoorsteenvoet; ~ **-bonnet,** skoorsteenkraag; ~ **-corner,** hoekie v.d. haard; ~ **-cowl,** skoorsteenkap; ~ **-flue,** skoorsteenpyp; ~ **-grate,** herdrooster; ~ **-hook,** herdhaak; ~ **-jack,** skoorsteenkap; ~ **-mantle,** skoorsteenmantel; ~ **-petticoat,** skoorsteensluk (lokom.); ~ **-piece,** skoorsteenmantel, kaggel; ~ **-pot,** skoorsteenpyp; ~ **-pot hat,** keil, pluishoed; ~ **-shaft,** kaggelpyp, skoorsteenpyp; ~ **-stack,** fabriekskoorsteen; ~ **-stalk,** fabriekskoorsteen; ~ **-sweep(er),** skoorsteenveër; ~ **-trap,** skoorsteenklep, roetvanger.

chimp, chimpanzee', sjimpansee, mensaap.
chin, ken, kin; *DOUBLE* ~, onderken; *KEEP one's* ~ *up,* goeie moed hou; jou taai hou; *UP to the* ~, tot oor die ore.
Chin'a, Sjina, China.
chin'a, porselein, breekgoed.
Chin'a aster, someraster.
chin'a: ~ **cabinet,** glaskas; ~ **chest,** porseleinkas; ~ **clay,** porseleinklei; ~ **closet,** uitstalkas, ~ **egg,** porseleineier.
Chin'a-ink, (Oos-)Indiese ink.
Chin'aman[1], (..men, Chinese), Sjinees, Chinees.
chin'aman[2], krulbal (krieket).
Chin'a rose, Chinese roos.
chin'a shop, porseleinwinkel.

Chin'a tea, Chinese tee.
chin'aware, porseleingoed, porseleinware.
chin'beard, kenbaard(jie).
chinchill'a, chinchilla (konyn), wolmuis.
chin-chin'! tot siens! gesondheid!
chin'-deep, tot oor die ore.
chine, (n) rugstring; ruggraat; kim (vliegboot); kambene (koei); (v) die ruggraat breek; ~ **biltong,** garingbiltong.
Chinese', Sjinees, Chinees; ~ **aster,** someraster; ~ **cabbage,** Chinese kool, selderykool; ~ **checkers,** Chinese albasterbord (dambord); ~ **fish,** sneesvis; ~ **lantern,** papierlantern; lampion; stuipebossie; ~ **rose,** eikerosie; ~ **white,** wit verf.
Chink[1]**,** Snees (neerh.).
chink[2]**,** (n) spleet, naat, skeur, kraak; (v) splits.
chink[3]**,** (n) kontantgeld, duite; (v) klink, rammel; laat klink.
chinkerinchee', tjienkerientjee, Septemberblom, witviooltjie.
chink'y, vol krake,
chin: ~ **less,** kenloos; karakterloos; ~ **music,** grootpratery, bluf; ~ **stay,** ~ **strap,** kenriem; kenband; stormband.
chintz, sis; **glazed** ~, glanssis.
chip, (n) spaander, splinter, skerf (van breekgoed); stuk, snipper; skaar (in beitel); tikhou, polshou, kaphou (gholf); skyfie, vlokkie (elektronika); (pl) snippertjies, stukkies; *a ~ of the old BLOCK,* 'n aardjie na sy vaartjie; 'n riempie v.d. ou vel gesny; uit die ou soort hout; *CASH one's ~s,* lepel in die dak steek; *DRY as a ~,* onsmaaklik, onaantreklik; *FISH and ~s,* vis en aartappelskyfies; *he has HAD his ~s,* sy doppie het geklap; *have a ~ on the SHOULDER,* 'n kruidjie-roer-my-nie wees; liggeraak wees; met 'n voortdurende grief; (v) **(-ped),** kap, bik (klip); afsny; afsplinter, afskilfer; afskerf, afbrokkel; tik, kaphou speel (gholf); ~ *AWAY,* wegskram; ~ *ped CUP,* koppie met happe; ~ *ped BEEF,* snippervleis; blikkiesbiltong; ~ *FLUSH,* gelyk afbeitel; ~ *IN, die rede val;* altyd 'n eiertjie byle, 'n stuiwer in die armbeurs gooi; ~ *OFF,* afbreek.
chip: ~ **-axe,** kapbyl(tjie); ~ **board,** spaanderbord; ~ **-carving,** kerfsny; kerfwerk; ~ **guard,** splinterskerm; gruisskerm; ~ **hat,** strooihoed; ~ **munk,** eekhorinkie; ~ **ped,** afgeskerf; afgesplinter; geskaar, gehap, met happe.
chipp'er, (n) kapper; kapmes; (a), opgewek, vrolik.
chipp'iness, katterigheid.
chipp'ing, snipper, spaander; barsvorming; kaphouspel, naderspel (gholf); ~ **chisel,** bikbeitel; ~ **hammer,** bikhamer; ~ **s,** spaanders; gruis.
chipp'y, splinterig; droog; katterig.
chips, geld, malie; (aartappel)skyfies, slap skyfies, klipgruis; spaanders.
chip: ~ **shield,** splinterskerm; ~ **shot,** kapskoot, naderhou, tikhou (gholf); ~ **stone,** bougruis, betonklip.
chirog'nomy, lees van die karakter uit die hand, chirognomie.
chir'ograph, chirograaf, formeel geskrewe en getekende stuk.
chirog'raphy, chirografie, handskrif.
chirol'ogist, chiroloog.
chirol'ogy, vingertaal, gebaretaal, chirologie.
chir'omancer, handwaarsêer, chiromant.
chi'romancy, chiromansie, handwaarsêery.
chirop'odist, voetversorger, voetheelkundige, chiropodis, liddoringsnyer.
chirop'ody, voetversorging, chiropodie.
chiroprac'tic, (n) chiropraktyk; (a) chiropraktics.
chiroprac'tor, chiropraktisyn.
chirp, (n) gepiep; (v) tjilp, piep, kwetter; ~ **ing,** getjirp, gekriek; getjilp, gepiep; ~ **y,** vrolik, opgewek; *be ~y,* hups wees.
chirr, (n) tjir; (v) tjir.
chi'rrup, tjilp, fluit, kweel; ~ **ing,** getjilp, gekwetter.
chis'el, (n) beitel; *COLD ~,* koubeitel; (v) **(-led),** uitbeitel; beeldhou; fop, verneuk; ~ **-blade,** beitellem; ~ **-handle,** beitelhef; ~ **led,** uitgebeitel; ~ *ed features,* fynbesnede gelaatstrekke; ~ **ler,** bedrieër,

fopper; verneuker (plat); ~ **ling,** gebeitel; beitelwerk; ~ **-shaped,** beitelvormig; ~ **tooth,** (.. **teeth),** snytand.
chit[1]**,** briefie; getuigskrif; skuldbewys, teenblad.
chit[2]**,** kind, kleinding, buksie; ~ *of a GIRL,* bakvissie; *a MERE ~,* 'n snuiter, sommer 'n boggie (kuiken).
chit'-chat, gebabbel, gepraat, gesels(ery).
chi'tin, chitien, chitine; ~ **ous,** chitienagtig.
chi'ton, chitoon.
chit' system, bewysstelsel.
chitt'erlings, eetbare binnegoed; varkdermpies.
chiv'alric, ruiterlik; ridderlik.
chiv'alrous, ridderlik; ruiterlik; hoflik; ~ **ly,** hoflik; ridderlik.
chiv'alry, ridderskap; ridderlikheid; ruiterlikheid; hoflikheid; *AGE of ~,* riddertyd(perk); *SPIRIT of ~,* riddergees; *TALE of ~,* ridderverhaal.
chive, grasui; ~ **garlic,** uiegras.
chiv'y, jaag, agternasit.
chloas'ma, lewervlek.
chlor'al, chloraal.
chlor'ate, chloraat, chloorsuursout.
chlor'ic, chloor-; ~ **acid,** chloorsuur.
chlor'ide, chloried, chloride; ~ *of LIME,* chloorkalk, bleikpoeier; ~ *of MANGANESE,* mangaanchloried, mangaanchloride.
chlor'inate, chloreer; ~ **d lime,** chloorkalk, bleikpoeier.
chlorina'tion, chlorering, chloorbehandeling.
chlor'ine, chloor.
chlor'ite, chloriet.
chlor(o)aceto'phenone, traangas, traanrook.
chlor'odyne, chlorodien.
chlor'oform, (n) chloroform; (v) onder chloroform sit, bewusteloos maak, narkotiseer; ~ **mask,** chloroformkap, chloroformmasker.
chloroge'nic, chlorogeen.
chlorom'eter, chloormeter.
chloromyc'etin, chloormisetine, chloormisetien.
chlor'ophyll, bladgroen, chlorofil; ~ **'ose,** ~ **'ous,** bladgroenagtig, bladgroenhoudend.
chlor'oplast, bladgroenkorrel, chloroplast.
chlo'roprene, chloorpreen.
chloros'is, bleeksug, bloedarmoede, chlorose.
chlorot'ic, bleeksugtig.
chlo'rous acid, chlorigsuur.
choa'na, choaan; keel-neusopening; tregter.
chock, wig; wielblok; klamp; klik (van roer); keerblok (lugv.); stopblok; ~ **-a-block,** ~ **-full,** stampvol, tjokvol, stikvol, propvol; ~ **valve,** afsluiter, afsluitklep.
choc'olate, sjokolade; ~ **cake,** sjokoladekoek, ~ **cream,** sjokoladelekkergoed; ~ **pudding,** sjokoladepoeding; ~ **slab,** sjokoladereep.
choice, (n) keus(e); keur; verkiesing; beste, fynste; *AT ~,* na keuse; *FOR ~,* by voorkeur; *the GIRL of one's ~,* jou uitverkorene; *I HAVE no ~ but,* ek kan niks anders doen nie as; *HOBSON'S ~,* geen keuse hê nie; *MAKE one's ~,* jou keuse doen; *TAKE your ~,* kies; ~ *of WORDS,* woordkeuse; (a) keurig, mooi, uitgelese; fyn; *a ~ morsel,* 'n lekker stukkie; ~ **butter,** keurbotter; ~ **grade,** keurgraad; ~ **ness,** keurigheid; ~ **st,** keurigste, fynste; ~ **wool,** fyn wol, keurwol.
choir, koor, rei; koorruimte; ~ **boy,** koorknaap; ~ **leader,** voorsinger; ~ **loft,** koorgalery; oksaal; ~ **master,** koordirigent; ~ **music,** koormusiek; ~ **singer,** koorsanger; ~ **stall,** koorbank.
choke, (n) smoorklep, smoorder, demper; vernouing (geweer); (v) stik, wurg, versmoor, verstik (mens); smoor (motor); onderdruk; belemmer, versper (kanaal); volprop; vernou; wurg (geweer); ~ *with ANGER,* stik van woede; ~ *OFF,* afsnou, deur die mosterd trek; die mond snoer; ~ *UP,* verstop; ~ *d with WEEDS,* toegegroei van vuilgoed; ~ **chain,** wurgketting; ~ **coil,** smoorspoel; ~ **control,** smoorklepsteller; ~ **damp,** stikgas, myngas; ~ **pear,** wurgpeer; ~ **piston,** smoorsuier; ~ **(sweet) potato,** wurgpatat; ~ **r,** wurger; hoë boordjie; stropdas; doodskoot (as antwoord); smoorder, halsdoek; ~ **screw,** smoorskroef; ~ **throat,** wurg

nek (piesang); ~ **tube**, smoorpyp, smoorbuis; ~ **valve**, smoorklep.
chok'ing, verstikkend, verwurgend; ~**-coil**, smoorspoel.
chok'ka, tjokka.
chok'y¹, (n) **(chokies)**, tjoekie, tronk.
chok'y², (a) verstikkend, wurgend.
chol'agogue, gal(af)drywer.
cholecysti'tis, galblaasontsteking.
chol'er, woede, driftigheid, prikkelbaarheid, opvlieëndheid; galagtigheid (fig.).
chol'era, cholera; ~ **epidemic**, cholera-epidemie; ~ **germ**, cholerakiem; ~ **patient**, choleralyer.
choleret'ic, (n) gal(af)drywer; (a) galafdrywend.
chol'eric, driftig, choleries, opvlieënd; galagtig (fig.).
chol'erine, buikloop, cholerine, cholesterien.
choles'terin, cholesterien, cholesterine, galvet.
chol'esterol, cholesterol.
chol'iamb, hinkvers.
cho'lin(e), cholien, choline.
chomp, kou, hard kou.
chon'drin, kraakbeenstof, chondrine, chondrien.
chon'drite, chondriet.
chon'drule, chondrule.
choose, (chose, chosen), kies, 'n keuse doen, verkies; *there is not MUCH to* ~ *between them*, hulle is vinkel en koljander, die een is so goed (sleg) soos die ander; *PICK and* ~, noukeurig uitsoek; ~**r**, uitkieser; ~**y**, uitsoekerig, kieskeurig.
chop¹, (n) hou, kap, slag; homp, dik sny; (v) kap, hou, kloof; maal (vleis); ~ *AT*, kap na; ~ *AWAY*, wegkap; ~ *DOWN*, afkap; ~ *THROUGH*, deurkap; ~ *UP*, stukkend kap.
chop², (n) skaapribbetjie, ribstuk, karmenaadjie, tjop.
chop³, (n) golfslag.
chop⁴, (n) tjap, stempel; (v) tjap, stempel.
chop⁵, (n) kake (van diere); wang, lip; *lick one's* ~ *s*, jou lippe aflek; jou tande slyp.
chop⁶, (v) ruil; ~ *BACK*, skielik terugswenk; ~ *and CHANGE*, weifel, telkens verander, rondspring.
chop-chop', tjoptjop, vinnig, gou-gou.
chop'-house, goedkoop eetplek.
chop'per, kapper; handbyl; vleisbyl.
chop'ping, kap; ~**-block**, kapblok; ~**-board**, hakbord, kapplank; ~**-knife**, kerfmes, hakmes, kapmes.
chop'py, vol skeure; woelig, veranderend; rukkerig (see); ~ *sea*, joppelsee.
chop'-service, kapafslaan (tennis).
chop'stick, eetstokkie.
chop'-suey, Sjinese vleisgereg.
chor'al, koraal, koor=; ~**e'**, koraal; ~**ist**, koorsanger; ~ **society**, sanggeselskap, sangvereniging; ~ **speech**, koorspraak.
chor-chor', tjortjor.
chord¹, snaar, lyn, tou, string, koorde (mat.); *touch the RIGHT* ~, die regte snaar aanraak (roer); *striking the SAME old* ~, dis elke dag dieselfde ou deuntjie; *SPINAL* ~, rugstring; *STRIKE a* ~, 'n snaar aanroer; *VOCAL* ~, stemband.
chord², akkoord (mus); *common* ~, akkoord v.d. grondtoon; ~**al**, akkoord=.
chore, (n) (los) werkie; (v) los werkies doen; huiswerk doen.
chore'a, senuweetrekkings, St. Vitusdans, chorea.
chor'ee, trogee.
cho'reograph, choreog'rapher, dansontwerper, choreograaf.
choreog'raphy, choreografie, dansbeskrywing.
chore'us, trogee.
cho'riamb, choriam'bus, choriambus (metriese voet).
chor'ic, koor=; ~ **dance**, reidans, koordans.
chor'ion, vrugvlies, vlokvlies.
choripe'talous, choripetaal, loskroonblarig, loskroonbladig.
cho'rister, koorlid, koorsanger.
chorog'raph(er), landskapbeskrywer, chorograaf.
chorog'raphy, landskapbeskrywing, chorografie.
chor'oid, (n) vaatvlies; (a) vaatvlies=.
cholog'ic, chorologies.
chorol'ogy, chorologie.

chor'tle, skaterlag; ginnegaap.
chor'us, (n) **(-es)**, koor, rei; refrein; (v) in koor sing (praat); ~ **conductor**, koordirigent; ~ **girl**, koriste, koormeisie; musiekblyspelfigurant; koordanseres; ~ **master**, koordirigent, koorleier.
chos'en, gekies, uitverkore; *the* ~ *people*, die uitverkore volk.
chou, roset; soesie.
chough, Alpekraai *(Pyrrhocorax alpinus)*, steenkraai.
chou' paste, soesiebeslag.
chouse, bedrieg, kul.
chow¹, Chinese keeshond.
chow², (sl.) kos, eetgoed, kougoed; ete.
chow'-chow, mengelmoes, allegaartjie, tjou-tjou, bredie.
chow'der, visbredie; vissop; seekossop.
chrestom'athy, (..**thies**), bloemlesing, chrestomatie.
chrism, salfolie, heilige olie, vormsel, chrisma.
chris'om, doopkleed; ~**-child**, doopkind.
Christ, Christus; ~**-child**, Christuskind.
chri'sten, doop, naam gee; *when you* ~ *the bairn, you should know what to call it*, eers kindjie sien, dan vader staan; **C**~**dom**, Christendom, Christenheid; ~**ing**, doop; ~*ing ROBE*, dooprok.
Christian, (n) Christen; Christin; (a) Christelik; ~ **church**, Christelike kerk; ~ **doctrine**, Christelike leer; ~ *Endeavour Society*, Christelike Strewersvereniging (hist.); ~ **era**, Christendom; Christenheid; ~**iza'tion**, kerstening; ~**ize**, tot die Christendom bekeer, kersten; ~ **name**, voornaam, doopnaam, ~ **Science**, Christian Science; ~ **Science Church**, Christian Science-kerk; ~ **year**, kerklike jaar.
Christ'mas, (-es), Kersfees, Krismis (geselst.), Kersmis (ong.); ~ **anthem**, Kerslied, Kersgesang; ~ **beetle**, somerbesie; ~ **bells**, Kersgelui, Kersklokke; ~ **berry**, bitterbos(sie), aambeibos (sie); dronkbessie; ~**-box**, Kerspresent, Kersgeskenk; Kersfooi(tjie); ~ **cake**, Kerskoek, Krismiskoek; ~ **cantata**, Kerskantate; ~ **card**, Kerskaart; ~ **carol**, Kerslied; ~ **celebration(s)**, Kersfees(vie=ring); Kersviering; ~ **cheer**, Kersvreugde; Kerspret; ~ **club**, Kersfeesklub; ~ **cracker**, Kersklapper; ~ **crib**, Kerskrip; ~ **day**, Kers(fees)dag; ~ **dinner**, Kersmaal, Kersete; ~ **disease**, Christmassiekte; ~ **edition**, Kersuitgawe; ~ **Eve**, Kersaand, Oukersaand; dag voor Kersfees; ~ **evening**, Kersaand; ~ **fern**, dolkvaring; ~ **flower**, krismisroos, hortensia, hortensie; poinsettia; winterakoniet; ~ **function**, Kersfunksie, Kersbyeenkoms; ~ **fund**, Kersfonds; ~ **gift**, Kersgeskenk, Kerspresent; ~ **greeting(s)**, Kerswens(e), Kersgroete; ~ **hamper**, Kersmandjie; ~ **holdiday(s)**, Kersvakansie; ~ **message**, Kersboodskap; ~ **morning**, Kersoggend, Kersmôre (-more); ~ **moth**, pouoogmot; ~ **night**, Kersnag, Kersaand; ~ **number**, Kersnommer; ~ **party**, Kersparty(tjie); ~ **present**, Kerspresent, Kersgeskenk; ~ **pudding**, Kerspoeding; ~ **rose**, kersroos, kersfeesroos; krismisroos, krismisblom, hortensia, hortensie, hydrangea; ~ **season**, Kerstyd; ~ **stamp**, Kersseël; ~ **stocking**, Kerskous; ~**-tide**, Kerstyd; ~ **time**, Kerstyd, Kersseisoen; ~ **tree**, Kersboom, krismisboom; *she looks like a* ~ *tree*, sy lyk soos 'n (regte) krismisboom; *Kalahari* ~ *tree*, sekelbos; ~ **week**, Kersweek; ~ **wish(es)**, Kerswens(e).
Christolog'ic, Christologies.
Christol'ogy, Christologie.
Chris'ty min'strels, Negersangers.
chrom'a, chroma, kleurgehalte.
chrom'ate, chroomsuursout.
chromat'ic, chromaties, kleur=, ~**s**, kleurleer, chromatiek; ~ **scale**, kleurskaal; chromatiese toonleer.
chromatog'raphy, chromatografie, kleuredruk.
chromatol'ogy, chromatologie, kleurleer.
chromatom'eter, chromatometer, kleurmeter.
chromat'ophore, kleurdraer, kleursel.
chrom'atrope, kleurwisselaar; kleurfotografie.
chrome, chroom; ~ **acid**, chroomsuur; ~ **alum**, chroomaluin; ~ **leather**, chroomleer; ~ **ochre**,

chromaatgeel; ~ **steel**, chroomstaal; ~ **yellow**, chroomgeel.
chromif'erous, chroomdraend.
chrom'ite, chromiet, chroomystersteen.
chrom'ium, chroom; ~-**plate**, verchroom; ~-**plated**, verchroom, met chroom oorgeblaas.
chromoli'thograph, kleursteendruk, chromolitografie.
chromolithog'rapher, chromolitograaf.
chromolithograph'ic, chromolitografies.
chromolithog'raphy, kleurlitografie, kleursteendruk.
chromophotog'raphy, chromofotografie.
chrom'osome, chromosoom, kernlis.
chrom'osphere, chromosfeer.
chrom'otherapy, chromoterapie.
chrom'ule, chromule.
chron'ic, chronies, langdurig, slepend; ~ **fever**, slepende koors; ~ **invalid**, chroniese invalide.
chron'icle, (n) jaarboek; kroniek; (v) te boek stel, boekstaaf, opteken; ~ *small beer*, oor koeitjies en kalfies gesels (praat); ~**r**, kroniekskrywer.
Chron'icles, Kronieke.
chron'ogram, chronogram, jaardig.
chronogrammat'ic, chronogrammaties.
chron'ograph, chronograaf, (akkurate) tydmeter.
chronog'rapher, tydbeskrywer, chronograaf.
chronog'raphy, tydbeskrywing, chronografie.
chronolog'ical, chronologies, in tydsorde.
chronol'ogist, tydrekenaar, chronoloog.
chronol'ogy, tydrekening, chronologie, jaartelling.
chronom'eter, tydmeter, chronometer; skeepsoorlosie.
chronomet'ric, chronometries, tydmeetkundig.
chronom'etry, tydmeetkunde, chronometrie.
chronophotog'raphy, chronofotografie.
chron'oscope, chronoskoop, snelheidsmeter.
chrys'alid, (-(e)s), **chry'salis**, (-es), papie.
chrysan'themum, krisant, aprilblom, winteraster.
chrys'idid, goudwesp.
chrysobe'ryl, chrisoberil.
chrys'olite, chrisoliet, wit ashes, peridoot.
chrys'ophyll, chrisofil.
chrys'oprase, chrisopraas.
chrys'ote, chrisoot.
chrys'otile, chrisotiel.
chrys'otype, chrisotipe.
chtho'nic, chtonies.
chthon'isotherm, chtonisoterm.
chub, kopvoorn (riviervis), vetsak.
chubb, slot.
chubb'iness, molligheid, poeseligheid.
chubb'y, rond, vet, mollig, poeselig; ~-**cheeked**, dikwangig.
chuck¹, (n) klop; gooi, tik, worp; (v) gooi; opgee, laat staan; ~ *AWAY*, weggooi; ~ *under the CHIN*, iem. onder die ken aai; ~ *IT!* hou op! ~ *OUT*, uitgooi; ~ *up the SPONGE*, die poging laat vaar, tou opgooi; ~ *UP*, in wanhoop opgee.
chuck², (n) skat, liefste.
chuck³, (n) wewervoël (*Hyphantornis olivaceous*).
chuck⁴, (n) kloukop (draaibank), skroef, klembus (van omslag); ketelklep; (v) op 'n draaibank plaas; inbus.
chuck⁵, (n) bladstuk, dikrib (bees).
chuck⁶, (v) klap (met tong); aanspoor (perd); klo(e)k.
chuck⁷, kos, ete.
chu'cker, gooier; malie(spel).
chucker-out', uitsmyter.
chuck'ing, gooiery, gooiaksie.
chuck'-key, klouplaatsleutel.
chuck'lathe, kopdraaibank.
chuc'kle, (n) onderdrukte lag; geklok; (v) (saggies) lag; klok; ~ *with delight*, jou verkneukel; ~**head**, swaap, domkop.
chuck: ~ **face**, kloukopvlak; ~ **rib**, dikrib, armmansrib; ~-**ring**, klouplaatring; ~ **klouring**; ~-**spindle**, klouplaatspil; ~ **steak**, dikribskyf.
chuck'-wa(g)gon, voorradewa, koswa.
chuff, brompot; lomperd.
chug, poef-poef; puf; ronk; tjoef-tjoef.
chuk'ka, **chuk'ker**, kring; wiel, tjakker (polo).
chum, (n) maat, boesemvriend; *great ~s*, groot maats, dik vriende; (v) (-**med**), maats maak; saamwoon; kamermaats wees; ~ *up with*, maats maak met; ~**mery**, saamwonery; ~**miness**, (hegte) vriendskap; ~**my**, vriendskaplik, intiem.
chump, stomp, houtblok; kruisstuk (skaap); *OFF his* ~, van lotjie getik; *SILLY* ~, onnosele ding, domkop; ~ **chop**, kruiskarmenaadjie, rugskyf.
chunk, (n) stuk, bonk (ys), homp, byt, klomp; (v) in groot stukke sny; ~ **jam**, stukkonfyt; ~ **wool**, dikwol; ~**y**, bonkig, geset.
church, (n) (-**es**), kerk, Godshuis; ~ *of ENGLAND*, Anglikaanse Kerk; *ENTER the* ~, predikant word; *the* ~ *MILITANT*, die strydende kerk; *the NEARER the* ~, *the farther from God*, hoe nader by Rome, hoe slegter Christen; *C* ~ *of the PROVINCE*, Anglikaanse Kerk (in R.S.A.); *the* ~ *TRIUMPHANT*, die seëvierende kerk; (v) kerk toe bring (om dank te betuig vir herstel na bevalling); ~ **administrator**, saakgelastigde; ~ **attendance**, kerkbywoning, kerkgang; ~ **bell**, kerkklok; ~-**box**, (-**es**), kerkbussie; ~ **clock**, kerkoorlosie; ~ **council**, kerkraad; *appear before the* ~ *council*, voor die swart span kom; voor die kerkraad verskyn; ~**ed**: *married but not* ~ *ed*, getroud maar nie gekerk nie; ~-**goer**, kerkganger; ~-**going**, kerkgang; ~ **government**, kerkbestuur, kerkregering; ~ **history**, kerkgeskiedenis; ~**ify**, verkerklik; ~**iness**, kerksheid; ~**ism**, kerkisme; ~ **law**, kerkreg; ~**man**, (..**men**), kerkman; ~-**martin**, kerkswael(tjie); ~ **member**, gemeentelid; ~-**mouse**, kerkmuis; *as poor as a* ~*mouse*, so arm soos 'n kerkmuis; ~ **office**, kerkkantoor; ~ **organ**, kerkorrel; ~ **owl**, toringuil; ~ **parade**, kerkparade; ~ **register**, doopregister; ~ **service**, kerkdiens; ~ *service conducted by an elder*, leesdiens; ~ **spire**, kerktoringspits; ~ **square**, kerkplein; ~ **steeple**, kerktoringspits; ~-**text**, Gotiese letter; ~ **tower**, kerktoring; ~ **vestry**, konsistorie(kamer); ~ **warden**, kerkopsiener; langsteelerdepyp, langsteelkleipyp; ~**wards**, na die kerk, kerkwaarts; ~**woman**, kerkvrou, vroulike lidmaat; ~**y**, kerks; ~**yard**, kerkhof; ~**yard cough**, kerkhofhoes.
churl, lummel, vent, gawie, misbaksel, gomtor; 'n regte ou ta (tor), gaip, vleël; vrek; ~**ish**, lomp, honds, vleëlagtig, buffelagtig; inhalig, suinig; ~**ishness**, buffelagtigheid, lompheid, inhaligheid.
churn, (n) karring; (v) karring, afkarring; omwoel; bruis; ~-**dasher**, karringstok; ~**ing**, gekarring, karringsel.
chut! sjt!
chute, waterval, stroomversnelling; glybaan, glygeut; stortkoker, valpyp, (stort)geut.
chut'ney, blatjang.
chutz'pah, goetspa, vermetelheid.
chyle, chyl, limfvog, voedingsap, melksap.
chyme, maagbry, kospap, chymus, chym.
cibor'ium, hostiekis(sie) (R.K.), siboric.
cicad'a, **cica'la**, sonbesie, somerbesie, langasem (kriek), sikade, boomsingertjie.
cic'atrice, **cicat'rix**, (..**ices**), litteken, wondmerk.
cicatriza'tion, littekenvorming, toegroeiing.
cic'atrize, toegroei ('n wond), gesond word; merk, 'n litteken vorm.
cicerone', (..**roni**), gids, wegwyser, cicerone.
Ciceron'ian, Ciceroniaans.
ci'der, appelwyn, sider, appeldrank; ~ **vinegar**, appelasyn.
cig, (sl.), sigaret.
cigar', sigaar, seroet; ~ **ash**, sigaaras; ~ **band collector**, vitolfilis; ~ **box**, (-**es**), sigaarkissie, sigaardoos; ~ **case**, sigaarkoker; ~-**cutter**, sigaarknipper; ~-**end**, sigaarstompie; ~-**end rot**, sigaarendvrot.
cigarette', sigaret; ~ **ash**, sigaretas; ~ **butt**, sigaretstompie; ~ **case**, sigaretkoker, sigaretdosie; ~-**holder**, sigaretpypie, sigarethouer; ~-**lighter**, sigaretaansteker; ~ **paper**, sigaretpapier; ~ **tobacco**, sigarettabak.
cigar: ~ **factory**, sigaarfabriek; ~-**holder**, sigaarpypie; ~ **il'lo**, (-**es**), sigaar(tjie); ~-**shaped**, sigaarvormig; ~ **shop**, sigaarwinkel; ~ **smoke**, sigaarrook; ~ **trade**, sigaarhandel.
cil'ia, ooghare, wimpers; trilhare (insek); ~**ry**, (n)

ooglid; (a) ooghaar=, wimper=; sweephaar=, tril=
haar=; ~ **ted,** gewimper(d); met trilhare.
cil'ice, haarboetehemp, haarkleed, boetekleed.
Cili'cia, Cilicië; ~ **n,** (n) Ciliciër; (a) Cilicies.
ci'lium, ooghaar; trilhaar.
Cim'brian, (n) Kimber; Kimbries (taal); (a) Kim=
bries.
ci'mex, wants; weeluis, wandluis.
cinch, (n) buikgort; (sl.), sekerheid; (v) gord.
cinchon'a, kinaboom, kinabas.
cin'chonism, kinavergiftiging.
cinc'ture, (n) band, gord; lyfband, seintuur; krans; (v)
omgord, omgordel; omgewe; ringeleer; ~ **d,** met 'n
gordel (krans).
cin'der, sintel; kool, as; ~ **brick,** sintelsteen; ~ **chute,**
sintelvlapyp; ~ **concrete,** sintelbeton.
Cinderell'a, Aspoestertjie; ~ **dance,** voornagbal.
cin'der: ~ **frame,** vonkvanger; ~ **notch,** slakgat; ~
path, aspad; ~ **-sifter,** sintelsif; ~ **track,** sintelbaan,
asbaan.
ci'ne, rolprent, film; ~ **ast(e),** rolprentmaker; ~ **-
camera,** rolprentkamera, filmkamera; ~ **-film,** rol=
prentfilm; rolprent, film.
cin'ema, kinema, bioskoop; ~ **operator,** bioskoop=
masjinis; ~ **scope,** kinemaskoop; ~ **show,** bio=
skoopvoorstelling; ~ **tic,** kinematies, filmmatig;
~ **t'ograph,** (n) kinema, bioskoop; (v) verfilm; ~
tog'rapher, filmoperateur; ~ **tog'raphy,** filmkuns,
kinematografie, rolprentkuns.
cin'e-projector, rolprentprojektor, filmprojektor.
cinerar'ia, asblom.
cin'erary, as=; ~ **urn,** lykbus.
cinera'tion, aswording, verassing.
ciner'eous, asgrou, askleurig.
Cingalese', (n) Singalees; (a) Singalees, Ceylons.
cinn'abar, (n) vermiljoen, bergrooi; sinnaber; (a) ver=
miljoenkleurig; ~ **ite,** sinnaber.
cinn'amon, kaneel; *ground* ~, fyn kaneel; ~ **bear,**
baribal, ~ **dove,** kaneelduif; ~ **essence,** kaneel=
essens; ~ **stick,** pypkaneel.
cinq(ue), (die) vyf(kaartspel).
cinq(ue)'foil, vyfvingerkruid, vyfblad.
ciph'er, (n) syfer; nul; syferskrif; sleutel; naamsyfer;
monogram; naklank (orrel) geheimskrif; figurant;
a mere ~, 'n nul; (v) syfer; (be)reken; in syfers uit=
druk; naklink (orrel); ~ *out,* bereken, uitwerk; uit=
syfer; ~ **ing,** syfering, uitsyfering; ~ **key,** syfersleu=
tel; ~ **officer,** syferskrifoffisier; ~ **operator,** syfer=
skrifoffisier; syferskrifseiner.
circ'a, circa, ongeveer, omstreeks.
Circa'ssian, (n) Cirkassiër; (a) Cirkassies.
cir'cle, (n) sirkel, kring; baan; omtrek; kroon, dia=
deem; galery, balkon (teater); verkeerseiland;
stand, geselskap, kliek; *ARGUE in a* ~, in 'n kring=
(etjie) redeneer; ~ *of CONFUSION,* instelfout; *IN
a* ~, in 'n kringetjie; ~ *of LATITUDE,* breedtesir=
kel; ~ *of LONGITUDE,* lengtesirkel; *RUN* ~ *s
round someone,* iem. ver oortref; iem. disnis loop;
iem. kafloop; *SQUARE the* ~, die onmoontlike
probeer; *UPPER* ~, hoë kring; hoëlui; *VICIOUS*
~, bose kringloop; (v) omsingel; omvaar; in 'n
kring beweeg; 'n kring vorm; swenk; rondgaan; ~
the room, rondgaan in die kamer; ~ **plane,** sirkel=
vlak; ~ **t,** kringetjie, sirkeltjie, ringetjie; band, ring.
circ'ling, ronddraaiend; ~ **disease,** listerellose.
cir'clip, klemring; klemveer; borgring.
circ'uit, omloop, omtrek, grens; ompad, rondreis;
stroombaan, stroomkring (elek.); kring; terrein;
rondgang, sirkelgang, omgang, kringloop; *BE on*
~, met die rondgaande hof reis; *the BLACK C* ~,
die Swart(e) Om(me)gang; *CLOSED* ~, geslote
baan; *MAKE a* ~, rondgaan; *SHORT* ~, kortslui=
ting; ~ **-breaker,** stroombreker; ~ **-closer,** stroom=
sluiter; ~ **court,** rondgaande hof.
circu'itous, omlopend, wydlopig; onregstreeks, in=
direk; breedsprakig; *a* ~ *ARGUMENT,* 'n inge=
wikkelde argument; *a* ~ *ROAD,* 'n ompad, groot
draai.
circ'uit rules, kringvlugreëls.
circ'ular, (n) omsendbrief, sirkulêre; (a) sirkelvormig,
rond; rondgaande; sirkel=; ~ **motion,** sirkelbewe=
ging; ~ **hem,** sirkelsoom; ~ **ity,** rondheid, sirkel=
vormigheid; ~ **ize,** (laat) sirkuleer; sirkulêres rond=
stuur, 'n omsendbrief rig aan; ~ **letter,** ~ **minute,**
omsendbrief; ~ **note,** rondskrywe; ~ **pitch,** tand=
steek (ratte); ~ **plane,** hobbelaar, rondeskaaf; ~
protractor, graadboog; ~ **saw,** boogsaag; draai=
saag, sirkelsaag; ~ **seam,** ringnaat; ~ **staircase,**
wenteltrap; ~ **tour,** rondreis; ~ **wall,** ringmuur.
circ'ulate, in omloop bring (wees); sirkuleer, rond=
gaan; rondstrooi, uitstrooi.
circ'ulating, bewegend; rondgaande; uitleen=, lees=;
~ *DECIMAL,* repeterende breuk; ~ *LIBRARY,*
leesbiblioteek, uitleenbiblioteek.
circula'tion, omloop, verspreiding, sirkulasie; oplaag
(koerant); ruilmiddel (munt); ~ *of the BLOOD,*
bloedsomloop; *COME into* ~, in omloop kom;
loskom (geld); *WITHDRAW from* ~, buite om=
loop stel; ~ **branch,** sorteerafdeling.
circ'ulative, omloop=, sirkulasie=; sirkulerend.
circ'ulator, verspreier, rondstrooier; ~ **y,** omlopend,
sirkulerend.
circumam'bience, wydlopigheid.
circumam'bient, omgewend, kringend; wydlopig.
circumam'bulate, rondloop; rondom draai, om iets
heen praat (draai).
circumben'dibus, omslagtigheid, om-die-bos-draai=
ery.
circumcen'tral, sirkumsentries.
circ'umcise, besny; ~ **d,** besny, gereinig; ~ **r,** besnyer.
circumci'sion, besnyding, besnydenis; *feast of* ~,
besnydenisfees.
circum'ference, omtrek.
circumferen'tial, omtrek=; ~ **stress,** omtrekspan=
ning.
cir'cumflex, (-es), sametrekkingsteken, kappie.
circum'fluence, omstroming.
circum'fluent, omvloeiend, omstromend.
circumfuse', rondgiet, omgiet, oorgiet.
circumgyr'ate, ronddraai, wentel.
circumgyra'tion, omwenteling, ronddraaiing.
circumja'cent, omliggend.
circumlitt'oral, strand=, langs die strand.
circumlocu'tion, omskrywing; breedsprakigheid, om=
slagtigheid, om-die-bos-draaiery.
circumloc'utory, omslagtig, omskrywend; ontwy=
kend.
circumnav'igable, omvaarbaar.
circumnav'igate, omvaar, rondom vaar, omseil.
circumnaviga'tion, omvaring, omseiling.
circumnav'igator, omvaarder.
circumpol'ar, rondom die pool, sirkumpolêr.
circ'umscribe, omskryf; omgeef, omgrens; bepaal;
beperk; ~ **r,** omskrywer; omgrenser.
circumscrip'tion, omskrywing; afbakening; beper=
king; omtrek; gebied; omskrif; randskrif (op
munt).
circumscrip'tive, omskrywend, beperkend.
circ'umspect, omsigtig, bedagsaam, behoedsaam;
~ **'ion,** omsigtigheid, behoedsaamheid, bedag=
saamheid; ~ **'ive,** omsigtig, behoedsaam.
circ'umstance, omstandigheid; breedvoerigheid, om=
haal; voorval, gebeurtenis; ~ *s ALTER cases,* al die
omstandighede moet in ag geneem word; *be in
EASY (reduced)* ~ *s,* welgesteld (armoedig) wees;
the FORCE of ~ *(s),* die mag van omstandighede;
with MUCH ~, met baie omhaal; *under NO* ~ *s,*
hoegenaamd nie; *POMP and* ~, prag en praal;
plegstatigheid; *UNDER the* ~ *s,* onder die omstan=
dighede; *WITHOUT* ~, sonder pligpleging; ~ **d,**
gesitueer, in 'n toestand verkerend, gesteld, ge=
plaas.
circumstan'tial, bykomstig; omstandig, uitvoerig; ~
evidence, aanwysende getuienis, omstandigheids=
getuienis; ~ **'ity,** breedvoerigheid, uitgesponnen=
heid, omstandigheid.
circumstan'tiate, uitvoerig beskryf; deur omstandig=
hede staaf, bewys.
circumvall'ate, omwal, omskans.
circumvalla'tion, omwalling, omskansing.
circumvent', omtrek; uitoorlê, verskalk, mislei, be=
drieg; ~ **ion,** misleiding, bedrog, verskalking.
circumvolu'tion, omwenteling; omloop; kronkeling.
circumvolve', omwentel, omdraai.

circ'us, (-es), sirkus; arena; plein; ~ **proprietor,** sirkusbaas; ~ **rider,** kunsryer; ~ **tent,** sirkustent.
cirque, (natuurlike) amfiteater (digt.); kaar, keteldal.
cirrho'sis, sirrose, verskrompeling (v.d. lewer).
cirro-cum'ulus, cirro-cumulus, skaapwolk, veerwolk.
cirro-stra'tus, cirro-stratus, sluierwolk.
ci'rrus, (cirri), rank (plant); baard (dier); cirrus, veerwolk, vlokwolk, skaapwolk.
cis, duskant; **~-al'pine,** duskant die Alpe, Cisalpyns.
cis'elure, gravering, siselering.
Cis'kei: *the* ~, die Ciskei; ~'**an,** Ciskeis; Ciskeier.
ciss'ing, kruip (verf).
ciss'y, (cissies), lafaard, papbroek.
cist, sarkofaag, doodkis (argeol.).
Cister'cian, Cisterciënser.
cis'tern, tenk, vergaarbak, waterbak; spoelbak; dam; kuip; ~ **barometer,** bakbarometer.
cistico'la, tinktinkie; klopkloppie.
cit'able, daagbaar; aanhaalbaar.
cit'adel, burg, vesting, slot, sitadel.
cit'al, dagvaarding, daging.
cita'tion, dagvaarding, sitasie (reg); aanhaling, sitaat.
citat'ory, dagvarend; ~ **letter,** skriftelike dagvaarding.
cite, dagvaar; siteer, aanhaal; aanvoer.
citha'ra, (Griekse) kitaar.
cith'er(n), siter; luit.
ci'tify, verstedelik.
cit'izen, burger; stadsbewoner; (pl) burgery; *JOHN* ~; *the ORDINARY* ~, Jan Burger; ~ *of the WORLD,* wêreldburger; ~ **army,** volkskleër; **~-band radio,** burgerbandradio; **~-ess,** burgeres, ~ **force,** burgermag; **~-ry,** burgery; **~ship,** burgerskap; ~ **soldier,** burger(soldaat).
cit'rate, (n) sitraat, sitroensuursout; (v) sitreer.
cit'reous, sitroengeel.
cit'ric, sitroen=; ~ **acid,** sitroensuur.
citricul'ture, sitrusbou.
cit'rine, (n) geelkwarts, sitrien; (a) sitroengeel.
cit'ron, sitroen, siter, lemoenkleur, liggeel.
citronell'a oil, sitronellaolie.
cit'ron: ~ **peel,** suurlemoenskil; ~ **tree,** sitroenboom, siterboom; **~wood,** geelhout, sitroenhout.
cit'rus, sitrus; ~ **bug,** sitruswitluis *(Planococcus citri);* ~ **cancer,** sitruskanker; ~ **export,** sitrusuitvoer; ~ **fruit,** sitrusvrugte; ~ **nematode,** sitrusmatode; ~ **thrips,** sitrusblaaspootjie.
citt'ern, *kyk* **cither(n).**
cit'y, (cities), stad; *C~ EDITOR,* stadsredakteur; *the ETERNAL C~,* die Ewige Stad, Rome; *the C~ of GOD, the HEAVENLY C~,* die Paradys; *the HOLY C~,* die Heilige Stad; ~ *of REFUGE,* vrystad; *THE C~,* die (sakedeel van 'n) stad; **~-bred,** stads=; **~-bred child,** stadskind; **~-bred person,** stadsmens, stadsbewoner; ~ **centre,** stadsentrum, stadskern, middestad; ~ **clerk,** stadsklerk; ~ **council,** stadsraad, munisipaliteit; ~ **councillor,** stadsraadslid; **~-dweller,** stadsbewoner; ~ **engineer,** stadsingenieur; ~ **fathers,** stadsvaders; ~ **gate,** stadspoort; ~ **hall,** stadhuis, stadsaal; ~ **residence,** stadshuis, stadswoning; **~-slicker,** windmakerige nikadooner; **state,** stadstaat, Platostaat; ~ **treasurer,** stadstesourier.
ci'vet, sivet; ~ **bean,** sewejaarsboontjie, goewerneursboontjie; ~ **(cat),** sivetkat.
civ'ic, burgerlik, burger=; stads=; stedelik; ~ **aviation,** burgervliegwese; ~ **centre,** burgersentrum; ~ **duty,** burgerplig; *C~* **Foundation,** Burgerstigting; ~ **guard,** burgerwag; ~ **lunch,** burgemeestersnoenmaal; ~ **loyalty,** burgertrou; ~ **pride,** burgertrots; ~ **reception,** burgemeestersonthaal; ~ **right,** burgerreg; **~s,** burgerkunde; burgerleer; ~ **spirit,** burgersin; ~ **theatre,** stadskouburg; ~ **virtue,** burgerdeug.
civ'il, burgerlik, burger=; siviel; beleef; *it pays to be* ~, met die hoed in die hand kom 'n mens deur die hele (ganse) land; ~ **action,** siviele geding (saak); ~ **administration,** burgerlike bestuur; ~ **authorities,** burgerlike owerheid; ~ **air-board,** burgerlugvaartraad; ~ **aviation,** burgerlugvaart; ~ **code,** burgerlike wetboek; ~ **commissioner,** siviele kommissaris; ~ **court,** siviele hof, burgerlike hof, burgerhof; ~ **debtor,** siviele gyselaar; ~ **defence,** burgerlike beskerming (verdediging); ~ **disturbance(s),** burgerlike oproer, burgerlike onrus; ~ **engineer,** siviele ingenieur; ~ **government,** burgerregering.
civil'ian, (n) burger; (pl) burgers; *armed ~s,* burgermag; (a) burgerlik, burger=; ~ **clothes,** burgerklere.
civ'il imprisonment, siviele gyseling.
civil'ity, wellewendheid, beleefdheid; (pl) beleefdheidsbetuigings; ~ *costs nothing and it goes a long way,* met die hoed in die hand kom 'n mens deur die (hele) land.
civiliza'tion, beskawing.
ci'vilize, beskawe, verfyn, siviliseer; ~ *away,* kwytraak (barbaarsheid).
civ'il: ~ **law,** burgerlike reg; ~ **list,** Britse kroontoelae.
civ'illy, as burger; beleef(d); voegsaam.
civ'il: ~ **marriage,** burgerlike huwelik; ~ **power,** burgerlike gesag; ~ **procedure,** burgerlike regsvordering; ~ **process,** siviele prosesakte; ~ **protection,** burgerlike beskerming; ~ **rights,** burgerlike regte; ~ **servant,** staatsamptenaar; *C~* **Service,** staatsdiens; *C~* **Service Commission,** (hist.), Staatsdienskommissie; ~ **strife,** burgertwis; ~ **war,** burgeroorlog; ~ **year,** kalenderjaar.
civv'ies, burgerklere, burgerdrag; *RETURN to* ~, die soldaterok uittrek; *return to civvy STREET,* tot die burgerlike (gewone) lewe terugkeer, na burgerstraat terugkeer; **civvy street,** burgerstraat.
claf'fer, (n), dikmelk; (v) klont.
clack, (n) geratel; ratel; klep; geklap, gebabbel; (v) klepper; babbel; kekkel; **~ing,** geklak; **~-valve,** skarnierklep, valklep.
clad, gekleed; *kyk* **clothe.**
cla'dode, kladode, blaaragtige stingel.
claim, (n) eis, (skuld)vordering, aanspraak; reg; bewering; ~ *in CONVENTION,* hoofeis; ~ *for DAMAGES,* eis om skadevergoeding; skade-eis; *LAY* ~ *to,* aanspraak maak op; (v) eis, opeis, lig (attestaat), vorder, opvorder, aanspraak maak op; ~ *BACK,* opeis, terugeis; ~ *THAT,* beweer dat; ~ *the VICTORY,* aanspraak maak op die oorwinning; **~able,** opeisbaar; **~ant,** reklamant, aanspraakmaker, eiser; pretendent; **~-holder,** kleimhouer; **~ing,** opvordering; **~-jumper,** kleimsteler; **~s section,** eisafdeling.
clairaud'ience, helderhorendheid.
clairaud'ient, (n) helderhorende; (a) helderhorend.
clairvoy'ance, clairvoyance, heldersiendheid.
clairvoy'ant, claivoyant, heldersiende; **~e,** waarsegster, heldersiende vrou.
clam¹, gapermossel, gaapskulp; *shut up like a* ~, tjoepstil wees.
clam², diepseelood.
clam³, *kyk* **clamp.**
clam'ant, raserig, luidrugtig, aanhoudend; dringend.
clam'ber, klouter, met hande en voete klim; **~er,** klouteraar; **~ing,** geklouter.
clamm'iness, klammigheid, natterigheid, klewerigheid.
clamm'y, nat, klam, klewerig; ~ **wool,** kleefwol.
clam'orous, raserig, lawaaierig, luidrugtig, uitbundig; **~ness,** raserigheid, lawaaierigheid, luidrugtigheid.
clam'our, (n) geskreeu, misbaar, getier, geherrie, lawaai, geroep; (v) skreeu, roep; ~ *for,* roep om; **~er,** skreeuer, lawaaimaker; **~ing,** (n) skreeuery; (a) skreeuend.
clamp, (n) klamp; klem, skroef; klemring, klembeuel; *adjustable* ~, plaatklem; (v) klamp; (vas)klem; las; oppak (stene); ~ *down on,* beteuel, aan bande lê, **~-bolt,** klembout, klampbout; ~ **connection,** klamplasstuk, klampverbinding, klemverbinding; gespeverband; **~-down,** vasklamping; verbod; on= derdrukking; **~-down on news,** nuusverbod; **~-hook,** klemhaak; **~ing,** vasklamping; vasklemming; **~ing nut,** klemmoer; **~ing screw,** klampskroef, klemskroef; **~-nut,** klemmoer.
clan, clan, (familie)stam, sibbe, stamgroep; geslag, bende, kliek.
clandes'tine, heimlik, stil, verhole, ongeoorloof; ag

terbaks, slinks; klandestien; ~ *marriage*, geheime huwelik.
clang, (n) geratel; gekletter; geskal, gelui; ~ *of ARMS*, wapengekletter; ~ *of TRUMPETS*, trompetgeskal; (v) skal, kletter, klink, lui; laat klink; ~**er**, kletteraar; flater; ~**ing**, geklank, geskal; ~**orous**, kletterend; ~**our**, gekletter, geklank, galm, geskal.
clank, (n) gerammel, gerinkel; (v) rammel, ratel, raas.
clan: ~**nish**, aaneengeslote, stamvas; kliekerig; ~**nishness**, aaneengeslotenheid; kliekerigheid; ~**ship**, bond; stamgenootskap; partyverdeling; gehegtheid (aan 'n leier).
clans′man, clanlid, stamgenoot.
clap¹, (n) druiper, gonorree.
clap², (n) klap, slag; donderslag; knal; handegeklap; (v) **(-ped)**, klap; hande klap, toejuig; toeslaan (deur); klapwiek; klop; ~ *on the BACK*, op die skouer klop; ~ *EYES on*, sien; ~ *one's HANDS*, die hande klap; ~ *ON*, toeklap; opsit; ~ *into PRISON*, in die tronk smyt; ~ *on all SAILS*, alle seile bysit; ~ *SPURS to*, die spore gee; ~**-board**, waterslagplank; klapper, klapbord (film); ~**-net**, slagnet; ~**per**, klepel, bengel (klok); klapper, ratelaar.
clapp′erclaw, krap en byt; vit, uitskel; toetakel.
clap′perboard, klapper, klapbord (film).
clapp′er lark, klappertjie, klapperlewerkie.
clap′ping, handegeklap, applous.
clap′trap, effekbejag; knaleffek; slimpraatjies, vroompraatjies, boerebedrog; *it is MERE* ~, dis alles pure kaf; *TALK* ~, slimpraatjies verkoop.
clap′-valve, valklep.
claque, gehuurde toejuigers, claque.
cla′ret, (n) klaret, bordeauxwyn, rooi wyn; *tap someone's* ~, iem. bloedneus slaan (sl.); (a) wynkleurig; ~**-coloured**, wynkleurig.
clarifica′tion, suiwering, opheldering, verheldering, opklaring; afsakking; brei (van wyn).
cla′rified butter, geklaarde botter.
cla′rifier, suiweringsmiddel; melkreiniger; breimiddel (vir wyn).
cla′rify, (..fied), suiwer, opklaar, reinig, verhelder, ophelder; besink, afsak, helder word.
cla′rinet, klarinet; ~ **′ist**, klarinetspeler, klarinettis.
cla′rion, klaroen, (skel)trompet; ~ **call**, klaroengeskal, wekroep.
clarionet′ = **clarinet**.
cla′rity, duidelikheid, helderheid, ondubbelsinnigheid.
clash, (n) **(-es)**, bons, stamp; skok; gekletter; stoot; gerammel; botsing; ~ *of opinions*, meningsverskil; (v) stamp, bons, bots; in botsing kom; saamval (vergaderings); aandruis; stry; in stryd wees met; kletter; *COLOURS* ~, kleure bots; kleure vloek teen mekaar; ~ *WITH*, in botsing kom met; indruis teen; ~**ing**, (n) gekletter; (a) kletterend; botsend.
clasp, (n) haak, gespe, knyper, knip, klamp; omhelsing; handdruk; oorslag, sluithaak; *a medal and two* ~*s*, medalje met twee tonge op die lint; (v) vashaak, toegespe, toeknoop, sluit; omhels, omarm, omklem; ~ *HANDS*, mekaar se hande druk; ~ *ONE's hands*, die hande vou; ~**er**, rank; boikpoot; ~**ers**, buikpote (by insekte); ~**-knife**, (..knives), knipmes; ~**-lock**, knipslot.
class, (n) **(-es)**, klas, orde; stand; lesuur; kursus; rang; *she HAS* ~, sy is 'n deftige nooi; *IN* ~, in die klas; *the LOWER* ~*es*, die laagste stande; *not be in the SAME* ~ *as another*, nie in iem. se skaduwee kan staan nie; nie by 'n ander se stof kom nie; *TAKE a* ~, 'n klas onderrig; *UPPER* ~*es*, hoër stande; (v) indeel, rangskik, klassifiseer, klasseer, klas (wol); ~ **book**, klasboek, skoolboek; ~**-conscious**, klas(se)bewus; ~**-consciousness**, klas(se)bewussyn; klas(se)trots; ~**-distinction**, standverskil; ~ **domination**, klasseoorheersing; ~**er**, klasseerder; ~**-feeling**, standsgees, klassegevoel; ~**-fellow**, klasmaat; ~ **hours**, skoolure.
class′ic, (n) klassieke werk (skrywer); meesterwerk; (a) klassiek; ~**al**, klassiek; ~ *al music*, klassieke musiek, musiek v.d. meesters; ~**ism**, klassisisme;

studie van die klassieke tale; ~**ist**, kenner van die klassieke, klassikus; ~**s**, klassieke.
class′ifiable, verdeelbaar in klasse, indeelbaar.
classifica′tion, klassifikasie, indeling.
class′ifier, klassifiseerder.
class′ify, (..fied), in klasse verdeel, klassifiseer, rangskik, indeel, orden; klas (wol).
class′is, **(classes)**, kerkring, klassis; groep.
class: ~**less**, klas(se)loos, sonder klasse; ~**-list**, klaslys; ~ **master**, klasonderwyser; ~**-mate**, klasgenoot, klasmaat; ~ **name**, ~ **noun**, soortnaam; ~ **prejudice**, klassevooroordeel, standsvooroordeel; ~**-room**, klaskamer; ~ **struggle**, klassestryd; ~ **teacher**, klasonderwyser; ~ **teaching**, klasonderwys; ~ **war**, klassestryd; ~**y**, van goeie stand, deftig; puik, netjies.
clas′tic, klasties.
clatt′er, (n) lawaai, gerammel, geratel; getrappel; ~ *of arms*, wapengekletter; (v) klater, rammel; trappel; ~ *by*, verbyratel; ~**ing**, gekletter, geklepper, geklikklak.
claudica′tion, kreupelheid.
clause, sinsdeel; klousule; bysin (gram.); artikel; paragraaf.
claus′tral, kloosteragtig; klooster=; bekrompe; afgesonder; ~ *life*, kloosterlewe.
claustrophob′ia, kloustrofobie, opsluitingsvrees, noutevrees, engtevrees.
cla′vate, knotsvormig.
clav′ecin, klavesimbel.
clav′ecinist, klavesinis.
clav′iature, toetsbord, klaviatuur, klawerbord.
clav′ichord, klavichord.
clav′icle, sleutelbeen.
cla′vier, klawerbord, toetsbord, klaviatuur.
clav′iform, knotsvormig, sleutelvormig.
cla′vis, sleutel.
claw, (n) klou, poot; knyper, vangarm; *CLIP (cut) the* ~*s of*, ontwapen; *by his* ~*s you may know the LION*, as die klou uitsteek, is die leeu daaragter; (v) gryp, klou; ~**-and-ball leg**, klou-en-balpoot; ~**-bar**, klouyster, kloukoevoet; ~ **bolt**, kloubout; ~ **chisel**, tandbeitel; ~ **clutch**, kloukoppelaar; ~**ed**, met kloue, geklou; verskeur, toegetakel; ~**-end**, klouent; ~**-hammer**, klouhamer; ~ **hatchet**, kloubyl; ~**less**, sonder kloue; ~ **plate**, tandplaat; ~**-sickness**, klouseer, klousiekte; ~**-spanner**, haaksleutel; ~**-tongs**, kloutang; ~**-wrench**, haaksleutel; dekhamer.
clay, (n) klei; erd; stoflike oorskot; *FEET of* ~, kleivoete; *be* ~ *in someone's HANDS*, deeg in iem. se hande wees; *WET one's* ~, 'n dop steek, die keel smeer; (a) van klei, klei=; ~ **bed**, kleilaag; kleibedding; ~ **brick**, kleisteen; ~**-cold**, yskoud (lyk); ~**ey**, kleiagtig; ~ **fever**, mok; ~**-hole**, kleigat; ~**ish**, kleiagtig; ~**-modelling**, kleiwerk; ~ **more**, (Skotse) slagswaard; ~ **pigeon**, kleiduif, piering; ~**-pigeon shooting**, kleiduifskiet, pieringskiet; ~ **pipe**, kleipyp, erdepyp; ~ **pit**, kleigat; ~ **ware**, aardewerk, erdewerk.
clean, (n) skoonmaak; opruiming; (v) reinig, skoonmaak, opruim, poets, afpoets, was; ~ *DOWN*, afwas, afstof; ~ *OUT*, uitstof; kaal (sonder geld) laat; ~ *someone OUT*, iem. kaal maak; iem. kaal uittrek; ~ *UP*, opruim; (a) skoon, helder, suiwer, sindelik; welgevorm (liggaam); totaal, volslae; *be given a* ~ *BILL of health*, 'n gesondheidspas kry; *make a* ~ *BREAST*, eerlik beken; *show a* ~ *pair of HEELS*, op loop sit; ~ *PROOF*, revisie; skoon proof; ~ *RATE*, vaste tarief; *make a* ~ *SWEEP*, totale opruiming hou; ~ *TIMBER*, hout sonder kwaste; *as* ~ *as a WHISTLE*, silwerskoon; (adv) skoon, glad, heeltemal; ~ *BOWLED*, skoon geboul; *GET* ~ *away*, skoonveld raak; ~ *GONE*, skoon op (weg); ~ **copy**, skoon afskrif (kopie); ~**-cut**, skerp omlyn; fynbesnede; ~**er**, skoonmaker; reiniger, poetser; ~**-fingered**, eerlik; ~**-handed**, onskuldig.
clean′ing, skoonmaak; ~ *CLOTH*, poetslap; ~ *FRENZY*, skoonmaakwoede; ~ **agent**, skoonmaakmiddel, reiniger.
clean: ~**-limbed**, mooigebou; ~**-lined**, vaartbelyn,

cleanse 785 climacteric

stroombelyn; ~ **liness,** reinheid, sindelikheid; ~ *liness is next to godliness,* reinheid kom naby goddelikheid; 'n rein liggaam is die naaste aan 'n rein hart; ~ **-looking,** met 'n oop (skoon) gesig; ~ **ly,** netjies, sindelik; skoontjies; ~ **ness,** skoonheid, sindelikheid; suiwerheid; onskuld.
cleanse, suiwer, reinig, skoonmaak, afwas (sonde); ~ **r,** skoonmaker; reinigingsmiddel, suiwerende middel, suiweraar.
clean'-shaven, kaalgeskeer, gladgeskeer.
clean'sing, reiniging; ~ **cream,** reinigingsroom.
clean' up, (v), skoonmaak; (n) opruiming.
clear, (v) reinig; (af)klaar (skepe); ophelder; vryspreek (van blaam); verwyder, wegruim (vuilgoed); opruim, ontruim (kamer); (af)los; klaarmaak; ooptrek (weer); afneem, afdek (tafel); helder maak; verduidelik; oorspring (hekkies); verreken, aansuiwer, afbetaal (rekeninge); uitklaar, inklaar (goed); wegraak, trap; uitverkoop; ~ *ACCOUNTS,* die rekening vereffen; ~ *the AIR,* onplesierigheid uit die weg ruim; die lug suiwer; ~ *AWAY,* verwyder; ~ *the COURSE!* van die baan af! *two DAYS* ~, twee volle dae; ~ *the DECKS for action,* in slaggereedheid bring, slaggereed maak, klaarmaak om te veg; ~ *a GATE,* oor 'n hek spring; ~ *the GROUND,* opstyg; net bokant die grond vlieg; ~ *LAND,* land skoonmaak; ~ *OFF,* trap, loop, skoert; ~ *OUT,* opruim; kaal maak; trap! loop! voert! vort! ~ *the ROAD,* gee pad; ~ *the TABLE,* die tafel afdek; ~ *one's THROAT,* keel skoonmaak, kug, ~ *UP,* los (skepe); opklaar, ooptrek (weer); uitlê; netjies maak; oplos (vraagstuk); ~ *out of the WAY,* uit die weg ruim; (a) helder, duidelik, suiwer; skoon, leeg, oop, skerp; onskuldig, rein; onbeswaard; volkome; vry; glad, vol; *as* ~ *as a BELL,* helderklinkend; *the COAST is* ~, alles veilig; ~ *CONSCIENCE,* rein gewete; *as* ~ *as CRYSTAL,* skitterend; *as* ~ *as DAYLIGHT,* so helder as glas, so klaar as die dag; ~ *MAJORITY,* 'n besliste meerderheid; ~ *PROFIT,* skoon wins; ~ *SOUP,* helder sop; (adv) skoon; totaal, opsy, los; duidelik; *GET* ~, losraak; *KEEP* ~ *of,* bly buite bereik van; *MAKE* ~, verduidelik; *STAND* ~, wegstaan; *STEER* ~ *of,* vermy, verbystuur.
clear'ance, opruiming, uitverkoop; (uit)klaring (doeane); oorgangshoogte; speelruimte, speling (suier); keerwerk (sokker); klaring (wissels); ruimte (myn); vry ruimte, grondhoogte, vry hoogte (voertuig); opheldering; tussenruimte; opruiming (dorpsaanleg); ~ **angle,** vryloophoek; ~ **card,** klaringskaart; ~ **certificate,** uitklaringsbrief, inklaringsbewys (doeane); ontslagbewys, kwytbrief; belasting(s)bewys; lisensiebewys; skoonbewys, terugbesorgingsbewys; lisensiebewys; ~ **fee,** klaringskoste; ~ **fit,** vrypassing; ~ **height,** vryhoogte (van brug); ~ **hole,** vrypasgat; ~ **indicator,** ruimtemerk; ~ **lamp,** breedtelamp; ~ **note,** rolbrief; ~ **price,** uitverkopingsprys; ~ **sale,** uitverkoping, uitverkoop; ~ **volume,** skadelike ruimte.
clear; ~ **-cut,** duidelik omskrewe, skerp omlyn; ~ **glass,** helder glas; ~ **-headed,** slim, knap, helder (van verstand).
clear'ing, oop plek; verwydering, wegruiming; skoonmaak; verrekening; ~ **agent,** klaringsmiddel; klaringsagent; ~ **-agreement,** verrekeningsooreenkoms; ~ **-bank,** verrekeningsbank; ~ **-chisel,** stokbeitel; ~ **-fee,** klaringskoste; verreken(ings)geld; ~ **-hospital,** afvoerhospitaal; ~ **-house,** verrekenkantoor; ~ **-plough,** hakploeg; ~ **-rod,** haakstok; ~ **-signal,** sluitsein (teleg.); afbelsein (telef.).
clear: ~ **ly,** duidelik, klaarblyklik; ~ **ness,** helderheid, duidelikheid, suiwerheid; aanskoulikheid; oopheid; ~ **sighted,** helder van blik, heldersiende; ~ **signal,** afbelsein; ~ **-starch,** styf; ~ **-stuff,** gawe hout.
cleat, (n) klamp; wig; greep; (v) vasklamp; ~ **-insulator,** klemisolator; ~ **nail,** (vas)klampspyker.
cleav'able, kloofbaar.
cleav'age, skeiding; klowing (van diamante); splyting, kliewing (hout), *lines of* ~, skeidingslyne, klooflyne; ~ **plane,** splytvlak, kliefvlak, kloofvlak.

cleave¹, (v) (**clove** or **cleft, cloven** or **cleft**), klowe, splits, deursny, (deur)klief (hout), kloof.
cleave², (v) klou, vaskleef; ~ *together,* aan mekaar klou; getrou bly.
cleav'er, kloofmes, kloofbyl, hakmes.
cleek, (obs.) klik (gholf); klouhaak; ~ **shot,** klikhou.
clef, (sang)sleutel (musiek); *BASS* ~, bas- of F-sleutel; *TREBLE* ~, G- of sol- of vioolsleutel.
cleft, (n) kloof, skeur, reet, bars; (a) gekloof; gesplete; *in a* ~ stick, in die knyp; nie vooruit of agteruit weet nie; ~ **-grafting,** spleetenting; ~ **leaf,** gesplete blaar; ~ **lip,** gesplete lip, haaslip; ~ **palate,** gesplete verhemelte; ~ **stick,** knypstok; *in a* ~ *stick,* in die knyp; *kyk* **cleave.**
cleg, perdevlieg.
cleistogam'ic, kleistogaam, met geslote bestuiwing (blomme).
clema'tis, lemoenklimop, diewekruid, hegbosdruif, clematis.
clem'ency, goedertierenheid, lankmoedigheid, genade; sagtheid (weer).
clem'ent, toegewend, genadig, lankmoedig, medelydend; sag (weer).
clench, (n) (-es), kram, haak; klinknael, omklinkspyker; omgeklinkte stuk; beseëling; (v) aaneenklink; (om)klink; vasklem, vasgryp; omklem, vasklou; op mekaar klem (tande); beklink, beseël (saak); bal (vuis); ~ **er,** *kyk* **clincher;** ~ **-joint,** klinknaat.
clep'sydra, waterklok.
cler'estory, bobeuk; sondak.
cler'gy, geestelikheid, predikante; ~ **man,** (..**men**), predikant, geestelike; *RETIRED* ~ *man,* emeritus; ~ **men's pension,** emeritaat; ~ **woman,** predikantsvrou; predikantsdogter; non.
cle'ric, geestelike.
cle'rical, geestelik; klerikaal; klerk-, klerklik; ~ *ERROR,* skryffout; ~ *STAFF,* klerklike personeel; ~ *WORK,* klerkwerk; skryfwerk; ~ **ism,** klerikalisme.
cle'rihew, onsinrympie, clerihew.
cle'risy, geestelikheid.
clerk, klerk; winkelbediende; geleerde; koster; sekretaris; griffier; opsigter (van werke); *ARTICLED* ~, ingeskrewe prokureursklerk, leerlingprokureur, kandidaat-prokureur; *CHIEF* ~, eerste klerk, hoofklerk; ~ *of the COURSE,* baanmeester; ~ *of the COURT,* hofgriffier; ~ *of (the) WEATHER,* weervoorspeller; ~ *of (the) WORKS,* opsigter, bouopsigter; ~ **dom,** klerkedom; ~ **ly,** klerklik; geleerd; ~ **ship,** klerkskap.
clev'er, slim; handig, oorlams; knap, oulik; gevat, gewiks, skrander; knaphekwaam; *he too* ~ *by half,* so slim soos die houtjie v.d. galg, slim verby wees; ~ **ish,** slimmerig; ~ **ly,** knap, oulik, slim; ~ **ness,** snuggerheid, oorlamsheid, slimheid, knapheid; handigheid.
clev'is, trekstang, haak, vurk, beuel (disselboom); ~ **pin,** vurkpen (motor).
clew, (n) leidraad; bol (wol); bewys; (v) oprol; *kyk* **clue.**
cliché', metaalafdruk, drukplaat, blok; cliché, afgesaagde uitdrukking.
click, (n) getik; klink; aanslag; klapklank, suigklank, klik (gram.); opmaker, meesterkneg (drukw.); pal (masj.); aantrapper, snyer (skoenmaker); (v) tik; klink; klik, klap (met tong); aantrap, aankap (met agterhoefyster); geluk hê; bevriend raak; ~ **heels,** hakke aanslaan; ~ **beetle,** kniptor, springkewer; ~ **-clack,** (ge)klikklak; ~ **er,** opmaker (drukw.); klikpal (masj.); uitsnyer (skoenm.); ~ **ety clack,** klikklak, rikketik; ~ **ing,** getik; ~ **-lock,** slot met pal, klikslot; ~ **-wheel,** plarat.
cli'ent, kliënt; klant; ~ **age,** klante, kliënteel; kliëntskap; ~ **ed,** goedbeklant; ~ **ele',** gevolg; klante, praktyk, kliënteel; ~ **ship,** kliëntskap; ~ **-state,** vasal(staat).
cliff, krans; ~ **dweller,** grotbewoner; ~ **hanger,** avontuurstuk, spanningstuk; baie gelyke wedstryd.
cliffs'man, bergklimmer.
cliff'-swallow, windswael, familieswael.
climac'teric, (n) hoogtepunt, krisis; oorgangsleeftyd; klimakterium; *a grand* ~, 63-jarige leeftyd; (a) klimakteries; kritiek.

climac'tic, op die hoogtepunt, klimakties.
clim'ate, klimaat, weersgesteldheid, lugstreek.
climat'ic, klimaats=, klimaties; ~ *CONDITION*, klimaatstoestand; ~ *ZONE*, klimaatgordel.
climatograph'ical, klimaatsbeskrywend, klimatografies.
climatog'raphy, klimaatsbeskrywing, klimatografie.
climatol'ogist, klimaatkenner, klimatoloog.
climatol'ogy, klimaatkunde, klimatologie.
clim'ax, toppunt, hoogtepunt, klimaks.
climb, (n) klim, klimvermoë, stygvermoë (vliegtuig); stygvlug; *rate of* ~, klimsnelheid; (v) klim, klouter, beklim, opklim; ~ *down*, 'n toontjie laer sing; afklim; ~ **able**, (be)klimbaar; ~ **er**, klimmer; klimplant; klimvoël; *social* ~*er*, opdringer, klimvoël; ~-**indicator**, stygingsmeter.
cli'mbing, klimmend, klouterend; ~ **ability**, klimvermoë; ~ **angle**, styghoek, klimhoek; ~ **fish**, kloutervis; ~-**iron(s)**, klimyster(s); ~ **lane**, klimbaan; ~ **perch**, klimbaars; ~ **plant**, klimop, slingerplant, klimplant; ~ **position**, stygstand, klimstand; ~ **rope**, klimtou; ~ **rose**, rankroos; ~ **speed**, stygsnelheid; klimsnelheid; ~ **turn**, stygdraai, klimdraai.
clime, klimaat; gewes, streek.
clinch, (n) greep, handvat(sel); ombuiging, beklinking; (v), vasgryp, vasvat; vasval; ~ **bolt**, klinkbout.
clin'cher, kram, haak; klinknael, omklinkspyker; beklinking, beseëling; dronkslaner, magswoord, doodhou, dooddoener (argument); ~ **tyre**, flensband; ~-**work**, klinkwerk.
clin'ching, (die) vasslaan, klink; beseëling; ~-**nail**, klinknael, omklinkspyker.
cline, klien.
cling, (clung), vashou, vasklewe, vasklem; span (klere); ~ *together*, aanmekaarklou; ~**ing**, lief, aanhanklik; vryerig, vatterig; nousluitend; ~ *ing garments*, nousluitende klere; ~ **stone**, taaipit(perske); ~ **y**, klewerig.
clin'ic, (n) kliniek; (a) klinies.
clin'ical, klinies; ~ **thermometer**, koorstermometer, koorspen(netjie).
clink, (n) geklink, gerinkel, geklingel; tronk; (v) klink; rymel; aanstoot; ~ *glasses*, glase klink.
clink'er[1], klinker, harde baksteen; sinter; slak, metaalskuim.
clink'er[2], hamerslag; resounding blow; thumping lie.
clink'er[3], prageksemplaar.
clink'er: ~-**built**, vasgeklink dat die ente oormekaar val, oornaats (gebou, bote); ~ **concrete**, sinterbeton; ~ **fork**, klinkervurk (loko.); ~**ing**, sintering; ~ **shovel**, klinkergraaf (loko.).
clink'ing, verbrands, besonderlik; eersteklas.
clink'stone, fonoliet.
clin'ograph, klinograaf.
clinom'eter, hellingmeter, klinometer.
clin'tonite, klintoniet, clintoniet.
cliome'trics, kliometrika.
clip[1], (n) knipsel, skeersel (wol); (v) **(-ped)**, (be)snoei (muntstuk); knip (kaartjie); snoei (bome); skeer (skape); kortwiek (vleuels); weglaat (woorde); ~ *someone's wings*, iem. kortwiek; ~ **ped**, gekortwiek, geskeer; geknip; ~ *ped coin*, besnoeide muntstuk.
clip[2], (n) klem, klou, tang, knyper; (v) omgeef, omklem, onarm; vasklou.
clip[3], (n) hou, klap; *give someone a* ~ *on the ear*, iem. 'n oorveeg gee.
clip: ~ **board**, knyperbord, klembord, klampbord; ~ **bolt**, klembout; ~ **card**, knipkaart(jie); ~-**clop**, geklepper; geklop; ~ **hooks**, muishake; ~ **joint**, (sl.), vermaaklikheidsplek met buitensporige pryse; ~-**on**, geknip, met 'n knip(pie) vas.
clipp'er, knipper; skêr; skeermasjien; klipper (boot); prageksemplaar.
clipp'ing, (n) uitknipsel; skeersel; afknipsel, afnysel; die geknipte; (a) uitstekend.
clip: ~ **plate**, klemplaat; ~ **tongs**, kloutang.
clique, kliek, aanhang; ~ **y**, kliekerig.
cli'quish, kliekerig, uitsoekerig; ~ **ness**, kliekerigheid, uitsoekerigheid.
clit'oris, (..rides), kittelaar, klitoris.

cloa'ca, (-e), riool, sinkput; opening, aarsopening, kloaak.
cloak, (n) mantel; dekmantel; laag (sneeu); *cover something with the* ~ *of CHARITY*, iets met die mantel van liefde bedek; *UNDER the* ~ *of*, onder die dekmantel van; (v) mantel omhang; bedek; bemantel; ~-**and-dagger**, spioenasie=, spioen=; ~**ing**, mantelstof; bemanteling; ~ **room**, bagasiekmaer, bewaarkamer; kleedkamer; ~-**room ticket**, bewaarkamerkaartjie.
clobb'er[1], (n) (sl.) sportklere; werksklere; ~ *tique*, rommelwinkel.
clobb'er[2], (v) (sl.) moker; plat slaan; 'n afgedankste pak gee; neerstort (vliegtuig).
cloche (hat), klokhoed(jie).
clock[1], (n) pyltjie (op kous).
clock[2], (n) klok(uurwerk), horlosie, oorlosie; *PUT back the* ~, tot die verlede terugkeer; *ROUND the* ~, ure aaneen; *it is SIX o'* ~, dit is sesuur; (v) tyd aanteken; ~ *IN*, aankoms (outomaties) aanteken, inklok; ~ *OFF (out)*, vertrek (outomaties) aanteken, uitklok; ~-**card**, loonkaart; ~-**face**, wyserplaat; ~-**hand**, wyser; ~**ing-hen**, broei(s)hen, klokhen; ~-**like:** *someone of* ~-*like punctuality*, 'n man van die klok; ~-**ray**, uurstraal; ~ **wise**, saam met die wysers, haar om, regs om; ~ **wise rotation**, regsomdraaiing, kloksgewyse rotasie; ~ **work**, uurwerk; ratwerk; *like* ~ *work*, baie gereeld, so gereeld soos 'n klok; ~ **work toy**, opwenspeelgoed, -speelding.
clod, (n) kluit, klont; stof; ondernek (beesvleis); 'n siel van potklei, domkop, 'n dooie kluit; (v) **(-ded)**, met kluite gooi; ~ **dish**, gevoelloos; dom; ~ **dishness**, gevoelloosheid; domheid; ~ **dy**, kluiterig, klonterig; ~-**hopper**, gomtor, ghwar; lomperd, kleitrapper; ~-**hopping**, lomp, onbeholpe; ~-**pate**, ~ **poll**, klipkop, lummel, stommerik.
clog, (n) blok (aan been); hindernis; klomp; kaparrang; (v) **(-ged)**, hinder, belemmer; 'n blok aan die been bind; verstop (raak); ~-**dance**, klompedans; ~ **gy**, hinderlik; kluiterig; taai, klewerig.
clogue, (F.), clogue.
cloisonné', cloisonne, enemmelwerk.
clois'ter, (n) klooster(gang); suilegang; (v) in 'n klooster sit; opsluit, afsonder; omgewe deur 'n suilegang; ~ *ed life*, kluisenaarslewe.
clois'tral, kloosteragtig, klooster=.
clone, (n, v), kloon.
clo'nal, klonaal.
clo'ning, kloning; kloonvorming.
clo'nus, klonus, herhalingskramp.
cloop, klok (van hen); floep (van prop).
clop'-clop, klipklap, klopklop, rikketik.
close, (n) end, slot; speelterrein; omheining; handgemeen; *at the* ~ *of DAY*, teen die aand; *at the* ~ *of the SEASON*, aan die end van die seisoen; (v) sluit, toemaak, toesluit (deur); afsper (pad); digmaak; toegroei, dig groei (woud); eindig, afboek, afsluit (rekening); toegaan; ooreenkom; aaneensluit; handgemeen (slaags) raak (geveg); afdig (kan); ~ *a BARGAIN*, die koop sluit; ~ *one's DAYS*, sy dae afsluit; sterwe; ~ *IN*, insluit; ~ *UP*, sluit, toemaak; (a, adv) gesluit, toe, dig (deur); beslote (korporasie); agterhoudend, geslote; benoud, duf, swoel, bedompig (lug); naby; geheim, afgesonder; gierig, vashoudend; bondig; skerp; innig, intiem; diep (geheim); noukeurig; byna gelyk (wedstryd); trompop; *upon* ~ *r ACQUAINTANCE*, by nader kennis; ~ *ANALYSIS*, fyn ontleding; ~ *ATTACK*, stormaanval, 'n tromp-op aanval; ~ *BILLETS*, huisbivakke; *a* ~ *CALL*, so ampertjies (dodelik); by die stert af; *a* ~ *CONTEST*, 'n stryd tussen byna gelyke partye; *a* ~ *FRIEND*, 'n intieme vriend; *have* ~ *at HAND*, byderhand hê; *KEEP* ~, geheim hou; naby bly; *LIE (keep)* ~, wegkruip; naby lê (bly); *in* ~ *ORDER*, in geslote geledere; *he is as* ~ *as an OYSTER*, hy is so dig soos 'n pot; ~ *PRISONERS*, streng bewaakte prisoniers; *at* ~ *QUARTERS*, van naby, tromp-op; ~ *QUESTIONING*, skerp ondervraging; ~ *RANGE*, kort afstand; klein skootafstand, stormafstand; ~ *RESEMBLANCE*, groot ooreenkoms; ~ *SEASON*,

geslote seisoen; *it was a* ~ *SHAVE*, dit het naelskraap gegaan, dit het min geskeel; dit was so hittete; *TOO* ~, by, naby; ~ *TOGETHER*, bankvas; ~ *WEATHER*, drukkende weer; ~ **adviser**, vertrouensman, vertroude raadgewer; ~ **analysis**, presiese ontleding, presisieanalsie; ~ **argument**, presiese argument, stap-vir-stapredenering; ~ **arrest**, geslote arres; ~ **attention**, noukeurige (nouletende) aandag; ~**-barred**, toegesluit; ~ **call**, noue ontkoming; ~ **column**, geslote kolonne (formasie); ~ **combat**, handgeveg; handgemeen; kontakgeveg; ~ **contest**, taai geveg (mededinging, wedstryd); ~ **corporation**, geslote (private) maatskappy; ~**-cropped**, kortgeknip.
closed, toe, geslote; ~ *CIRCUIT*, russtroombaan, geslote kringloop, geslote baan; ~ *CIRCUIT television*, geslotebaantelevisie, toekringtelevisie; kabeltelevisie; ~ *JOINT*, geslote las; ~ *SHOP*, geslote geledere; ~*-shop SYSTEM*, stelsel van geslote geledere.
close: ~ **fertilisation**, selfbestuiwing; ~**-fisted**, suinig, vrekkerig, vrekkig, gierig; ~ **finish**, gladde (fyn) afwerking; kop-aan-kopuitslag; ~ **fit**, presiese passing; *it was a* ~ *fit*, dit het net gepas; dit het net deurgegaan (geslaag); ~**-fitting**, nousluitend; ~ **formation**, geslote geledere; ~**-grained**, fyn van draad; digkorrel(r)ig; ~**-knit**, aaneengeslote; dig; ~**-ly**, digby, strykelings; noukeurig; innig; ~**-mouthed**, dig, swygsaam; ~**ness**, digtheid; terugggetrokkenheid; swoelheid, bedompigheid (weer); dufheid (kamer); nabyheid; noukeurigheid; vrekkigheid; ~ **observer**, noukeurige (presiese) waarnemer; ~ **order**, geslote orde; ~ **pass**, kort aangee; ~ **prisoner**, (streng) bewaakte gevangene.
clos'er, (n) sluitsteen; (a) nader; ~ *investigation*, nader ondersoek.
close: ~**-stool**, stilletjie, stelletjie.
clos'et, (n) kabinet, studeerkamer; priewie, kleinhuisie; (v) verberg, opsluit; *be -ed with*, 'n geheime onderhoud hê met; ~ **play**, leesdrama; ~ **student**, kamergeleerde.
close'-up, (n) nabyheid; digbyopname; vlakbyopname; (a) vlak by.
clos'ing, (n) sluiting, afsluiting, einde; (a) sluitings=; ~ **address**, slotwoord; ~ **argument**, slotpleidooi; ~ **date**, sluitingsdatum; ~ **hour**, sluitingsuur; ~ **number**, slotnommer; ~ **prices**, slotkoers; ~ **remarks**, slotopmerkings; ~ **scene**, slottoneel; ~ **sentence**, slotsin; ~**-time**, toemaaktyd; ~ **words**, slotwoorde.
clo'sure, sluiting; slot; debatsluiting; klousure, sluitingsreg (op 'n debat); genesing (wond); **-rail**, sluitspoorstaaf.
clot, (n) klont; klodder; bloedklont; dommerik, houtkop; ~ *of blood*, bloedprop, bloedklont; (v) **(-ted)**, stol, klont (bloed, melk); vasplak; vaskoek (hare).
cloth, **(-s)**, kledingstof; tafellaken, laken; kleed, doek, lap; ampskleed, gewaad; ~ *of GOLD*, goudlaken; *LAY the* ~, die tafel dek; *THE* ~, die geestelikheid; predikante; ~**-binding**, linneband; ~ **boards**, linneomslag; ~ **bolt**, stoflengte; ~ **cap**, lappet, lapkeps; ~ **duster**, stoflap; ~**-dyer**, lakenverwer.
clothe, klee(d), dos, beklee; inklee; bedek; ~ *ideas in words*, idees in woorde inklee (uitdruk); ~*d with powers*, met bevoegdhede beklee; bevoegdheid besit (om).
clothes, klere; kleding; *the* ~ *make the MAN*, die vere maak die voël; *still in SWADDLING* ~, nog 'n baba; ~**-bag**, kleresak; wasgoedsak; ~ **basket**, wasgoedmandjie; ~ **brush**, klereborsel; ~**-drainer**, droograk; ~**-hanger**, klerehanger, skouertjie; ~**-horse**, droograam, droograk; ~ **line**, wasgoedlyn, droogtou; ~ **man**, klerekoper; ~**-moth**, kleremot; ~ **peg**, wasgoedpennetjie, wasgoedknyper; ~ **press**, klerekas; ~**-rack**, droograk; klerestander; ~ **stick**, droogstok; **wire**, wasgoeddraad; ~**-wringer**, wringmasjien, wringer.
cloth' factory, lakenfabriek.
cloth'ier, lakenfabrikant; klerehandelaar.
cloth'ing, kleding, klere, klerasie; aankleding, inkleding, isolering (stoommasjien); ~ **industry**, klerebedryf; ~ **manufacture**, klerasievervaardiging; ~

wool, klerewol, kaardwol, stofwol; ~ **worker**, klerewerker.
cloth: ~ **length**, stuklengte, stoflengte; ~ **manufacturer**, lakenfabrikant; ~ **merchant**, handelaar in kledingstowwe; ~**-weaver**, lakenwewer; ~**-yard shaft**, lang pyl.
clott'ed, geklont, geronne (bloed); ~ **cream**, room wat van opgekookte melk geskep is; Devonshireroom.
clott'y, klonterig.
cloud, (n) wolk; *DROP from the* ~*s*, uit die lug val; ontnugter word; *arrive in a* ~ *of DUST*, êrens oopen-toe aankom; *every* ~ *has a silver LINING*, elke moeilikheid het sy ligkant; daar is altyd 'n geluk by 'n ongeluk; geen kwaad sonder baat; agter die wolke skyn die son; *be IN the* ~*s*, in die lug swewe; *be UNDER a* ~, onder verdenking wees; in onguns wees; (v) bewolk, benewel; donker maak; ~ **bank**, wolkbank; ~ **burst**, wolkbreuk; ~ **canopy**, wolk(e)dak; ~**-capped**, met wolke bedek; ~ **ceiling**, wolkhoogte; ~ **chamber**, newelkamer, wolkkamer; ~ **cover**, wolkbedekking; bewolking; ~**-cuckooland**, droomwêreld; ~**ed**, bewolk, betrokke; somber, bedruk; *his BROW* ~*ed over* hy het stuurs (neerslagtig) geword; *a* ~*ed SKY*, 'n betrokke lug; ~ **formation**, wolkformasie; wolkvorming; ~**-gas**, blaasgas; ~ **height**, wolkhoogte; ~**iness**, bewolktheid; dynserigheid; ~ **layer**, wolk(e)laag; ~**less**, onbewolk, wolkloos; ~**-rack**, wolkestapel; ~ **scape**, skildery van wolke; ~ **veil**, wolk(e)sluier; ~ **warbler**, klopkloppie; ~**y**, dynserig, bewolk; troebel; donker, onduidelik, duister.
clough, kloof.
clout, (n) hou, slag; vadoek; lap; (v) lap; slaan; ~**-nail**, platkopspyker.
clove[1], skyfie, huisie.
clove[2], naeltjie; ~**-brandy**, naeltjie(s)brandewyn.
clove' hitch, maswerkknoop; ~**ing**, maswerk.
clov'en, gesplete, gekloof, verdeel; *show the* ~ *hoof*, sy duiwelse (ware) geaardheid openbaar; ~ **footed**, met gesplete hoewe; *kyk* **cleave**.
clove'-oil, naeltjie(s)olie.
clov'er, klawer; *BE in* ~, lekker lewe; die vet v.d. aarde geniet; *GO from* ~ *to rye-grass*, hertrou; ~**-leaf**, klawerblaar; ~**-leaf interchange**, ~**-leaf intersection**, ~**-leaf junction**, klawer(blaar)wisselaar, klaweraansluiting; klawerring.
clove'-tree, naeltjieboom.
clown, grapmaker, hanswors, nar, uilspieël, harlekyn; maltrap, mal bobbejaan; ~**ery**, hansworstery, narrestreke; ~**ish**, dwaas, naragtig; lomp, onhandig; ~**ishness**, hansworstery.
cloy, volprop, oorlaai; oorversadig; (laat) walg; *be* ~*ed with*, uitgeëet (oorversadig) wees; ~**ing**, stroperig, walglik; soetlik.
club, (n) knuppel, knopkierie; vereniging, klub; (gholf)stok; klawer (kaartspel); haarknoop; (v) **(-bed)**, slaan, knuppel; met 'n geweerkolf slaan; ~ *together*, saamspan, saamwerk; ~**bable**, gesellig, gemoedelik; verkiesbaar as lid van 'n klub; ~**bed**, met 'n knop; knuppelvormig; ~**building**, klubgebou; ~**-easy**, gemakstoel, klubstoel; ~**-fellow**, klubgesel, klubmaat; ~**-foot**, horrelvoet (mens); horrelpoot (dier); ~**-hammer**, (moker)hamer; ~**-head**, stokpunt, stokvoet (gholf); ~ **house**, klubgebou; ~**-law**, vuisreg; ~**-length**, stoklengte; ~ **man**, klublid; ~**-moss**, kolfmos; wolfsklou; ~**-room**, klubkamer; ~**-root**, goudknol (plantsiekte); knopwortel; ~**-shaped**, knotsvormig, knuppelvormig.
cluck, kloek, klok (van 'n hen); ~**ing**, (n) geklok; (a) klokkend, broeis; ~**ing hen**, broeis hen, klokhen.
clue, (lei)draad (ondersoek), aanwysing, spoor; *FIND no* ~, nie op die spoor kom nie, geen leidraad vind nie; *HAVE no* ~, geen idee hê nie; ~**less**, dom, onnosel; oningelig; toe.
clump, (n) blok; klomp; bome; groep; ekstra (dubbele) sool; (v) bymekaar plant; van dik sole voorsien; swaar loop; ~**ing**, verklomping; klontvorming; ~**-sole**, ekstra sool, dubbele sool.
clum'sily, lomp, onhandig.
clum'siness, onhandigheid, lompheid, stokkerigheid, onbeholpenheid.

clum'sy, onhandig, lomp, slungelagtig, houterig, stokkerig.
clung, *kyk* **cling**.
clus'ter, (n) tros, bos; trop, hoop, menigte, swerm; groepie (hekelterm); bondel (plantk.); (v) in trosse groei; in trosse bind; swerm; ~ **bomb**, trosbom; ~-**bug**, stinkvlieg; groen stinkbesie; ~-**ed**, in groepe; gebondel, saamgetros; opmekaar; ~ **fig**, trosvy; ~ **gear**, veelrat; ~ **houses**, meenthuise, korfhuise; ~ **housing**, meentbehuising, korfbehuising; ~ **pine**, seeden; ~ **raisins**, trosrosyntjies; ~-**shaped**, trosvormig.
clutch[1], (n) (-es), broeisel; (v) uitbroei.
clutch[2], (n) (-es), koppeling, koppelaar (motor); friksieskyf; greep; klou; *want to have EVERYTHING in one's ~ es,* alles wil insluk (inpalm), inhalig wees; *FALL into the ~ es of,* in die hande kom (val) van; (v) gryp, beetpak; vashou; ruk; omvat; ~ *one's heart,* jou hart vashou; ~ **bag**, handsak(kie), armsak(kie), handtassie; ~-**brake**, koppelaarrem; ~-**coupling**, kloukoppeling; ~-**flange**, koppelaarflens; ~ **gear**, koppelrat; ~-**lever**, koppelaarhefboom; ~-**lining**, koppelaarvoering; ~-**pedal**, koppelpedaal; ~-**pencil**, drukpotlood; ~-**plate**, koppelaarplaat; ~-**rod**, koppelaarstang; ~-**shaft**, koppelaaras; ~-**sleeve**, koppelaarhuls; ~-**spring**, koppelaarveer.
clutt'er, (n) geraas; warboel; (v) geraas maak, stommel, rammel; rommel; ~ *up,* verstop; volprop; vol rommel prop; ~-**ed**, opeengehoop; deurmekaar; rommel(r)ig; ~-**ing**, openhoping; deurmekaarheid; rommel(r)igheid.
clyp'eate, skildvormig.
clype'us, kopskild.
clys'ma, klisma, lawement.
clys'ter, (n) klisma, lawement; (v) klisteer, 'n lawement (klisma) toedien; ~ **pipe**, klisteerspuit.
co'accused, medebeskuldigde.
coacervate', opstapel, ophoop.
coacerva'tion, opstapeling, samehoping, ophoping.
coach, (n) (-es), rytuig, koets; passasierswa; drilbaas, drilmeester, driller; privaatonderwyser; oefenmeester, afrigter, breier (sport), dresseerder; *one can drive a ~ and six through,* Kaapse draaie maak deur; (v) vervoer (met rytuig); oefen, dresseer, dril, afrig, brei; voorberei, klaarmaak vir eksamen; ~ *for an examination,* vir 'n eksamen oplei (voorberei); ~-**box**, (-es), bok, voorkis; ~-**builder**, wamaker; rytuigmaker; ~-**builder's shop**, rytuigfabriek; ~-**dog**, Dalmasiër; ~-**horse**, koetsperd, karperd; ~-**house**, waenhuis; ~-**ing**, afrigting; dressering; brei; ~-**maker**, wamaker; ~-**man**, koetsier; ~-**screw**, spoorskroef; ~ **stand**, staanplek vir rytuie; ~-**work**, bakwerk; ~-**works**, rytuigfabriek.
coact', dwing; saamwerk; ~-**ion**, dwang, geweld; samewerking; ~-**ive**, samewerkend.
coad'jutor, medewerker, medehelper, assistent.
coad'jutress, (-es), **coad'jutrix**, (..trices), helpster.
coadmini'istrator, mede-beredderaar.
coag'ency, medewerking, hulp.
coag'ent, medewerker, helper.
coag'ulant, stolmiddel, koaguleermiddel, stremstof.
coag'ulate, stol, strem, verdik, stulp.
coagula'tion, stolling, stremming, verdikking.
coag'ulator, stolmiddel, stremsel.
coag'ulum, stolsel.
coak, taptand.
coal, (n) (steen)kool, kole; *BLOW the ~ s,* vuur aanwakker, ophits; *CARRY ~ s to Newcastle,* water na die see dra; uile na Athene bring; *heap ~ s of FIRE on,* vurige kole hoop op; *HAUL over the ~ s,* iem. berispe; iem. voor stok kry; (v) kole inneem, kole laai, bunker; ~ **basin**, steenkoolbekken; ~-**bearing**, steenkoolhoudend; ~-**bed**, steenkoollaag, koolbedding; ~-**black**, koolswart; ~-**box**, (-es), kolebak; ~-**bunker**, kolehok, steenkoolruim; ~-**burning**, met steenkool gestook; ~-**cellar**, kolehok; ~-**chute**, kolestortgeut; ~-**cleaning**, steenkoolsuiwering; ~-**consumption**, koleverbruik; ~-**cutter**, steenkoolsaag; ~-**dross**, steenkoolgruis; ~-**dust**, steenkoolas, steenkoolgruis; ~-**er**, steenkoolskip; steenkooltrein.

coalesce', verenig, saamvloei, saamsmelt.
coales'cence, vereniging, samevloeiing, samesmelting.
coales'cent, saamsmeltend, saamvloeiend.
coal: ~-**face**, oop steenkoollaag; ~ **field**, steenkoolveld; ~-**forming age**, steenkooltydperk; ~-**gas**, koolgas; ~-**hammer**, (steen)koolhamer; ~-**heaver**, ~-**ie**, koledraer; ~-**hold**, koleruim; ~-**hole**, kolegat; ~ **ing**, kole inneem; ~ **ing-stage**, steenkoolsteier; ~ **ing-station**, verversingshawe, kolestasie.
coali'tion, verbond, vereniging, koalisie, samesmelting, bondgenootskap.
coal: ~-**layer**, steenkoollaag; ~-**less**, sonder steenkool, koolloos; ~-**master**, eienaar van 'n koolmyn; ~-**measure**, steenkoolmaat; steenkoollaag; ~-**meter**, kolemeter; ~-**mine**, steenkoolmyn; ~-**miner**, steenkoolmynwerker; ~-**mining**, steenkoolmynbou; steenkoolbedryf; ~ **oil**, keroseen; ~-**owner**, eienaar van 'n koolmyn; ~-**pit**, koolmyn; ~-**production**, koolproduksie, kole-opbrengs; ~-**ring**, steenkoolring; **C**~-**Sack**, Koolsak (in Melkweg); ~-**screen**, koolsif; ~-**scuttle**, kolebak; ~-**seam**, steenkoollaag; ~-**shed**, steenkoolloods; steenkoolhok, kolehok; ~-**shovel**, koleskop; ~-**slack**, steenkoolas; ~-**smoke**, steenkooldamp; ~ **stove**, steenkoolstoof; ~-**supply**, steenkoolvoorraad; ~ **tar**, koolteer; ~-**tender**, steenkoolwa; ~-**tongs**, steenkooltang; ~-**trade**, steenkoolhandel; ~-**truck**, kolewa; ~-**vein**, steenkoolaar; ~-**whipper**, koollaaier; ~-**y**, steenkoolagtig; ~-**yard**, steenkoolwerf.
coam'ing, luiklys; spoelboord; luikhoof.
coarse, ru; grof (draad); lomp (gedrag); plat, onbehoorlik (taal); ~ *FILE,* skropvyl; ~ *SALT,* growwe sout, kombuissout; ~ *WOOL,* growwe wol; ~ **bread**, growwe brood, semelbrood; ~ **fodder**, ruvoer; ~-**grained**, grof van draad; ~ **ness**, ruheid; grofheid; lompheid, platheid; ~ **ning**, vergrowwing; ~ **quick**, litjieskweek; ~ **wool**, ruwol, growwe wol.
coast, (n) lus, strand; *the ~ is CLEAR,* die gevaar is verby; die kans is mooi; alles is veilig; *the ~ is NOT clear,* daar is kapers langs die kus; (v) langs die kus vaar; vrywiel ry, vry loop (motor); ~ **al**, kus=; ~ *al BELT,* kusstreek; ~ *al FORTIFICATION,* kusversterking; ~ **battery**, kusbattery; ~ **belt**, kusstrook; kusstreek; ~ **defence**, kusverdediging; ~ **er**, kusvaarder; voetrus; skinkbord; kusbewoner; ~ **er brake**, terugtraprem; ~ **fort**, seevesting; ~ **grass**, hoenderspoor; ~ **guard(sman)**, (..smen), kuswag; ~ **ing**, vryloop; ~ **ing trade**, kusvaart; ~ **line**, kuslyn; ~ **partridge**, namakwapatrys; ~ **rat**, sandmol; ~ **road**, kuspad; ~ **trade**, kushandel; ~ **ward**, na die kus; ~ **ways**, ~ **wise**, langs die kus, kuslangs.
coat, (n) baadjie; jas; skil (vrug); vleis (spier); laag (verf); manel; damesmantel; vel, vag, (dek)hare, harekleed, pels (dier); ~ *of ARMS,* wapenskild; *CUT your ~ according to your cloth,* sit die tering na die nering; *DUST someone's ~,* iem. 'n pak gee; *FINAL ~,* deklaag; ~ *of MAIL,* pantser; ~ *of PAINT,* laag verf, verflaag; ~ *and SKIRT,* baadjiepak, mantelpak; *TRAIL one's ~,* twis soek; *if you TRAIL your ~ you must expect someone to tread on it,* wie kaats, moet die bal verwag; *TURN one's ~,* met alle winde meewaai; van kleur verander; *WEAR the king's ~,* soldaat wees; (v) beklee, bedek; oortrek; verf, bestryk; ~ **armour**, wapenskild; ~ **collar**, baadjiekraag; jaskraag; ~ **dress**, jasrok; ~-**ed**, beslae; met baadjie aan; beklee, omhul; aangeslaan (tong); ~-**ee**, kort baadjie; jakkie, damesbaadjie; ~-**hanger**, baadjiestok; klerehanger, skouertjie.
coa'ti, **coatimun'di**, neusbeer.
coat'ing, stof, materiaal; (beskermings)laag (verf); aanpaksel (tong); oortreksel; aansetsel; ~ *BATTER,* dekbeslag; *FIRST ~,* grondlaag.
coat: ~-**less**, sonder baadjie, in hempsmoue; ~ **pocket**, baadjiesak; ~ **shirt**, toeknoophemp; ~-**tail**, manelpant.
coau'thor, medeouteur, medeskrywer.
coax, vlei, pamperlang, mooipraat, paai; bontlê (om guns); troggel, flikflooi, soebat; ~ *ALONG,* mee=

troon; ~ *one INTO*, deur vleiery verkry; ~ **er**, flikflooier; mooiprater.
coax′ial, eenassig, koaksiaal; ~ **cable**, konsentriese (koaksiale) kabel.
coax′ing, flikflooiery.
cob[1], mieliekop; kopstronk; ponie; mannetjieswaan; *corn on the* ~, groenmielies.
cob[2], strooiklei.
cob[3], (v) slaan, dors; gooi.
cob′alt, kobalt; ~ **bloom**, kobaltblom; ~ **blue**, kobaltblou; ~ **bomb**, kobaltbom; ~ **glance**, kobaltglans, kobaltiet; ~ **glass**, blouglas; ~ **green**, kobaltgroen; ~**ian**, kobalt-, kobaltics; ~**ine**, kobaltien, kobaltine; ~**ite**, kobaltiet; ~**yellow**, kobaltgeel.
cobb′ing, ertsafkapping.
cob′ble[1], (n) kei, klip, straatsteen; stuk steenkool; (pl) stukkieskool; (v) met klippe uitlê.
cob′ble[2], (v) lap, saamflans.
cob′ble-coal, stukkieskool, haardkool.
cobb′ler, skoenmaker, skoenlapper; knoeier; ysdrank; ~, *stick to your last*, skoenmaker, hou jou by jou lees.
cob′blestone, grint, straatklip, straatsteen.
cob′ brick, strooisteen.
cobb′y, stompieagtig, kort en dik.
cobellig′erant, medeoorlogvoerende.
cob′ nut, haselneut.
cob′-pipe, stronkpyp.
cob′ra, koperkapel, geelslang, kobra; *BLACK (ringed)* ~, rinkhals(slang), bakkopslang; *BROWN* ~, bruinkapel; *CAPE* ~, geelslang; *spectacled* ~, brilkobra.
cob′web, (n) spinnerak; *BLOW away the* ~ *s*, 'n luggie skep; *have a mind FULL of* ~ *s*, die kop vol muisneste hê; (a) ragfyn; yl; ~**bing**, ragvorming; ~**by**, vol spinnerakke; ragfyn; ~**like**, spinnerakagtig.
cob′worm, kopwurm.
coc′a, koka (plant).
cocaine′, kokaïen, kokaïne.
coccidios′is, koksidiose.
coc′coid, kokkusvormig.
coc′cus, (cocci), kokkus, koeëlbakterie; splytvrug.
coccyg′eal, stuitbeen-; ~ *region*, stuitstreek, stuitjie.
coc′cyx, (coccyges), stuitbeentjie, stertbeen.
coch′ineal, cochenille.
coch′lea, skulp (van oor); diggerolde peul.
coch′lear, skroefvormig; skulpvormig.
cock[1], (n) haan (van geweer); hoenderhaan; mannetjie; doring, haantjie; wyser; kraan; *a* ~ *is always BOLD on its own dunghill*, elke haan is op sy ashoop baas; *as the old* ~ *CROWS, the young one learns*, soos die oude songe, so piepe de jonge; *every* ~ *crows best on his own DUNGHILL*, elke haan is koning op sy eie mishoop; *elke hond is baas op sy eie plaas* (werf); *that* ~ *won't FIGHT*, daardie plan sal nie stryk nie; daardie vlieër sal nie opgaan nie; *live like FIGHTING* ~ *s*, 'n koninklike lewe lei; *at HALF-*~, met die haan in die rus; *at FULL-*~, oorgehaal, ~ *of the WALK*, haantjie die voorste; *he wants to be* ~ *of the WALK*, sy haan moet altyd koning kraai; (v) oorhaal, span (geweer); opslaan (hoed), skuins sit; optrek (neus); spits (ore); windmaak, grootmeneer speel; ~ *the EARS*, die ore spits; ~ *an EYE at*, 'n blik op iem. slaan; ~ *a GUN*, 'n geweer oorhaal; ~ *one's HAT*, die hoed opslaan; ~ *a SNOOK*, die neus optrek.
cock[2], (n) graanhoop, opper, drooghopie (hooi); (v) graan in hopies sit, oppers maak
cock[3], (v) opwaartse swaai; knipoog.
cockade′, kokarde.
cock-a-doodle-doo′, koekelekoe.
cock-a-hoop′, uitgelate, viktoriekraaiend; hanerig, astrant; *be* ~ *about something*, opgewonde wees oor iets.
Cockaigne′ = **Cockayne**.
cock-a-leek′ie (soup), hoender-en-preisop.
cockalor′um, krielhaantjie, parmantige ventjie; *high* ~, bok-bok-staan-styf.
cock′-and-bull: *a* ~ *story*, 'n wolhaarstorie.

cockateel′, cockatiel′, kokketiel *(Nymphicus hollandicus)*.
cockatoo′, kaketoe (kaketoea), (soort) papegaai.
cock′atrice, basilisk.
Cockayne′, Kokanje, Luilekkerland.
cock: ~ **bird**, haan; mannetjie(s)voël; ~ **bead**, deklys; ~**boat**, sloep; ~**-brained**, onbesonne, roekeloos; ~ **chafer**, meikewer; ~**-crow(ing)**, hanekraai, hanegekraai; dagbreek.
cocked, opgeslaan (hoed); oorgehaal (geweer); ~ *HAT*, hoed met 'n opgeslaande rand; driekantige hoed; *KNOCK into a* ~ *hat*, papslaan, onherkenbaar verniel; volkome oorwin.
Cock′er[1], (n) Patryshond; ~ *spaniel*, Basterpatryshond, Sniphond.
cock′er[2], (v) vertroebel, bederf, verwen.
cock′erel, haantjie, jong haan.
cock′-eyed, skeel; krom; dwaas.
cock′fight, hanegeveg; ~**ing**, hanevegtery.
cock′horse, houtperd, hobbelperd.
cock′iness, parmantigheid, eiewysheid.
coc′kle[1], (n) kammossel; *warm the* ~ *s of one's heart*, bly maak, verheug.
coc′kle[2], (n) koringblom, brand (in koring).
coc′kle[3], (v) krul; rimpel.
coc′kle: ~**-boat**, klein bootjie; ~**-shell**, mosselskulp.
cock′loft, solder.
Cock′ney, (-s), Londenaar, Cockney; Londense dialek.
cock′ ostrich, volstruismannetjie.
cock′pit, hanemat, veglek; boegkajuit; stuurhut, stuurkuip, stuurkajuit (vliegtuig); siekeboeg (op skip); stutbak; ~ **canopy**, kajuitkoepel.
cock′roach, (-es), kakkerlak; meikewer.
cocks′comb, hanekam (plant); windmaker; dwaas, sot.
cock′s′comb, hanekam.
cocks′foot[1], kropaargras.
cock′s′foot[2], haanpoot.
cock: ~**-shy**, mikpunt, kol; gooi; ~ **sparrow**, 'n haantjie, kapokhaantjie; ~ **spur**, hanespoor; ~ **sure**, positief, selfvertrouend, verwaand.
cock′swain, *kyk* **coxswain**.
cock′sy = **cocky**.
cock′tail, halfbloedreisiesperd; kewer; parvenu; skommeldrank, mengelsopie, skemerkelkie; ~ **bar**, drankbuffet, kelkiekroeg; huiskroegie, dranktoonbank; ~ **cabinet**, drankkabinet; ~**-frock**, skemerrok; ~ **hat**, skemerhoed(jie); ~**-lounge**, kelkiekamer; ~**-mixer**, skinker, kroegman; ~ **party**, skemer(kelk)partytjie; ~ **stick**, hapstokkie, snoepstokkie, peuselstokkie.
cock′-up, hoofletter, grootletter.
cock′y, verwaand, eiewys, hanerig; *be* ~, jou lyf grootman hou.
coc′o(a), kakao; kokospalm; klapper; ~ **bean**, kakaosaad; ~ **matting**, klapperhaar.
coc′o(a)-nut, klapper, kokosneut; ~ **cake**, klapperkoek; ~ **filling**, klappervlisel; ~ **ice**, klapperys; ~ **milk**, kokosmelk, klappermelk; ~ **oil**, kokosolie, klapperolie; ~ **palm**, kokospalm; ~ **pudding**, klapperpoeding.
cocoon′, kokon, papie.
co′copan, koekepan.
cocotte′, ligtekooi, cocotte.
coc′tile, deur vuur gehard.
cod[1], (n) kabeljou; *dried* ~, gedroogde vis.
cod[2], (n) sakkie; teelsak; balsak; sakvet (bees).
cod[3], (n) foppery; (v) beetneem, vir die gek hou.
cod′a, coda, koda.
co′damine, kodamien, kodamine.
cod′dle[1], (ver)troetel, verwen, verweeklik, oppiep.
cod′dle[2], wel; ~**d egg**, gewelde eier.
cod′dling, troeteling, verwenning; *spoil by* ~, verpiep.
code, (n) wetboek, kode, reglement, gedragslyn; ~ *of ETHICS*, gedragskode; ~ *of HONOUR*, erekode; *THE* ~, skoolregulasies; (v) kodeer; ~ **book**, kodeboek.
co′defendant, medeverweerder.
cod′eine, kodeïen, kodeïne.
code: ~ **language**, kodetaal; geheimtaal; ~**r**, kodeer-

der; ~ **strip**, seinlap; ~ **telegram**, kodetelegram; ~**-writing**, syferskrif; geheimskrif, kodeskrif.
cod'ex, (codices), wetboek; handskrif, kodeks.
cod: ~**-fat**, boudvet; ~**fish**, kabeljou.
cod'ger, vent, kêrel, snaar.
cod'icil, kodisil, aanhangsel; ~**l'ary**, kodisilêr.
codico'logy, kodikologie, manuskripstudie, manuskripleer.
codifica'tion, kodifikasie.
cod'ify, (..**fied**), kodifiseer.
codille', kodille (kaartspel).
cod'ing, kodering.
co'director, mededirekteur.
cod'ling¹, kabeljoutjie.
cod'lin(g)², stoofappel; ~**-moth**, appelmot, kodlingmot.
cod'-liver oil, lewertraan, visolie.
co'don, kodon.
co'donee, medebegiftigde.
co'donor, medeskenker.
co'driver, medebestuurder
cods(wallop), (sl.), kaf, nonsens, nonsies.
co'ed, meisieleerling, meisiestudent (in 'n koëdukasieinrigting).
co'editor, mederedakteur.
coeduca'tion, koëdukasie; ~**al**, gemeng; ~**al school**, gemengde skool.
coeffi'cient, koëffisiënt; ~ *of ELASTICITY*, rekgetal; ~ *of EXPANSION*, uitsettingskoëffisiënt.
coel'acanth, selakant, doringholtevis.
coel'enterate, holtedier.
coelen'teron, liggaamsholte.
coel'iac, buikholte=; ~ **artery**, ingewandslagaar.
coel'om, seloom, rompholte.
coe'lostat, selostaat.
coenti'tled, medegeregtig.
coen'zyme, koënsiem.
coe'qual, gelyk, gelykwaardig.
coequal'ity, gelykheid.
coerce', dwing, forseer; ~**r**, (be)dwinger.
coer'cion, dwang, bedwang.
coer'cive, beteuelend; dwingend, dwang=.
coessen'tial, een in wese.
coeter'nal, mede-ewig, wat ewig naas 'n ander bestaan het.
coev'al, (n) tydgenoot; (a) net so oud; tydgenootlik.
coexec'utor, mede-eksekuteur.
coexec'utrix, (..**trices)**, mede-eksekutrise.
coexist', gelyktydig bestaan; ~ **ence**, medebestaan; gelyktydige bestaan; naasbestaan; *peaceful* ~*ence*, vreedsame naasbestaan; ~**ent**, gelyktydig bestaande.
coexten'sive, van gelyke omvang; van gelyke duur.
coff'ee, koffie, boeretroos, Afrikanertroos; ~ **bag**, koffiesak(kie); ~ **bar**, koffiekroeg; ~ **bean**, koffieboontjie; koffiepit; ~ **berry**, koffiebessie, koffieboontjie; ~ **bibber**, koffiepens; ~ **cake**, koffiekoek; ~ **colour**, koffiekleur; ~**-coloured**, koffiebruin; ~ **cup**, koffiekoppie; ~ **essence, extract**, koffie-ekstrak; ~**-grinder**, koffiemeul(tjie); ~**-grounds**, koffiemoer; ~ **house**, koffiehuis; ~ **mill**, koffiemeul; ~ **mould**, koffievorm; ~ **percolator**, sypelkan; ~ **plant**, koffieplant; ~ **plantation**, koffieplantasie; ~**-planter**, koffieplanter; ~ **pot**, koffiekan, koffieketel; ~ **room**, koffiekamer; ~ **rust**, koffieroes; ~ **shop**, koffiehuis; ~ **stall**, koffiekraampie; ~**-strainer**, koffiesakkie, =siffie, =filtreerder; ~ **table**, koffietafeltjie; ~**-table book**, koffietafelboek, grootformaatboek, duur boek; ~ **tin**, koffieblik; ~ **tree**, koffieboom.
coff'er, kis, kas, koffer; skatkis; geldkas; sluiskamer; ~*s of the state*, staatskas.
coff'er-dam, kisdam, vangdam, keerwal, afsluitdam, weerdam, kofferdam.
coff'er-panel, kofferpaneel.
coff'in, (n) doodskis; (v) kis; ~**-bone**, hoefbeen; ~**ing**, bekisting; ~**-joint**, hoefgewrig; ~ **nail**, sigaret; ~**-plate**, kisplaatjie; ~**-ship**, onveilige skip.
co'ffle, slawetou.
co'founder, medestigter.
co'ffret, koffertjie, tassie, kissie.

cog¹, (n) tand (van 'n wiel); kamrat; (v) **(-ged)**, van tande voorsien; ~*ged wheel*, tandrat.
cog², (n) bedrog; leuen; (v) vals speel; dobbelstene vervals; *play with* ~*ged dice*, met dobbelstene vals speel.
co'gency, bewyskrag, oortuigingskrag.
co'gent, kragtig, oortuigend, klemmend.
cogg'ing, tanding.
co'gitable, denkbaar, voorstelbaar.
co'gitate, oordink, bepeins, oorweeg.
cogita'tion, oorpeinsing, oorweging.
cog'itative, peinsend, nadenkend.
co'gito, cogito (filos.).
cogn'ac, konjak, fransbrandewyn.
cog'nate, (stam)verwant, aanverwant.
cogna'tion, verwantskap.
cogni'tion, kennis, besef; kenvermoë; bewustheid; kognisie.
cog'nizable, kenbaar, waarneembaar; beregbaar.
cog'nizance, kennis; kennisneming; waaneming; erkenning; kenteken; kenmerk; jurisdiksie; *HAVE* ~ *of*, kennis dra van, bekend wees met; *TAKE* ~ *of*, kennis neem van.
cog'nizant, bekend (met), bewus (van).
cognize', ken, kennis hê van, waarneem.
cognom'en, (..**mina, -s)**, bynaam; van.
cognoscen'ti, kenners, connoisseurs, ingeligtes, cognoscenti.
cognos'cible, kenbaar.
co'guardian, medevoog.
cog'wheel, kamrat, tandrat, vangrat.
cohab'it, (buitenegtelik) saamwoon; saamhuis (as man en vrou); ~ **ant**, medebewoner; ~**a'tion**, samewoning; vleeslike omgang.
coheir', mede-erfgenaam; ~**ess, (-es)**, mede-erfgename.
cohere', saamhang, saamklewe.
coher'ence, coher'ency, samehang, verband.
coher'ent, samehangend.
coher'er, fritter (teleg.).
cohe'sion, samehang, verband, kohesie.
cohes'ive, samehangend; ~ *power*, kohesie.
cohib'it, intoom, teëhou, weerstaan.
co'hort, krygsbende, kohort.
coif, hooftooisel; kappie; mus.
coiffeur', kapper, haarsnyer, barbier, coiffeur.
coiffeuse', haarkapster, coiffeuse.
coiffure', kapsel, coiffure.
coign, hoek; wig; buitehoek; ~ *of vantage*, geskikte punt, geskikte uitkykplek.
coil¹, (n) kronkeling, winding, klos, draai, spiraal; rank (plant); rol (draad); metaaldraad; lok (hare); induksiespoel; (v) inmekaarkronkel, oprol, opdraai; krul.
coil², (n) verwarring; *this mortal* ~, hierdie aardse wirwar.
coiled hair, kondee, bolla.
coil'ing drum, draadtrommel.
coil-shanked cultivator, krulstertskoffel, varkstert= (skoffel).
coil' spring, krulveer, kronkelveer.
coin, (n) muntstuk, spesie, geld; *COUNTERFEIT* ~, vals munt; *CURRENT* ~, gangbare munt; *FORGING of* ~*s*, muntvervalsing; *MELT down* ~, muntspesie versmelt; *PAY someone in his own* ~, iem. in sy eie (gelyke) munt betaal; (v) (aan)munt, tot munt slaan; smee, versin; baie geld verdien; ~ *MONEY*, hope geld verdien; ~ *a WORD*, 'n nuwe woord skep.
coin'age, gemunte geld; geldmunting; muntwese, muntstelsel; nuwe woord; versinsel, uitvindsel; *RIGHT of* ~, muntreg; *STANDARD of* ~, muntvoet; ~ **act**, muntwet; ~ **collar**, muntring; ~ **die**, muntmatrys; ~ **stamp**, muntstempel.
coincide', ooreenkom; ooreenstem; saamtref, saamval.
coin'cidence, ooreenstemming, sameloop; toeval.
coin'cident, ooreenstemmend; saamvallend.
coinciden'tal, toevallig; ooreenstemmend; ~**ly**, toevallig.
coin: ~ **circulation**, muntomloop; ~**-clipper**, muntsnoeier; ~ **collection**, muntversameling; ~ **ed**, ge=

munt, gesluan; verdig; gemaak, geskep (woord); ~ **er**, (geld)munter; valsmunter; uitvinder; skepper (woord).
coin'ing, aanmunting, (die) munt; uitvinding; skepping (woorde); *FALSE* ~, muntvervalsing; *be* ~ *MONEY*, geld soos water verdien; ~ *press*, muntpers.
coin: ~ **mould**, muntvorm; ~ **plate**, muntplaatjie; ~-**shaped**, muntvormig; ~-**slot screw**, gleuf(kop)skroef.
coinstantan'eous, gelyktydig.
coir, klapperhaar; ~ **mattress**, klapperhaarmatras.
coi'tion, coit'us, geslagsgemeenskap, byslaap, paring, koïtus.
coke, (n) kooks; (v) verkooks; ~-**breeze**, kooksgruis; ~ **coal**, kookskool; ~ **fire**, kooksvuur; ~ **furnace**, kooksoond; ~ **oven**, kooksoond; ~ **pocket**, kookssak; ~ **waste**, afvalkooks.
cok'ing, verkooksing; ~ **coal**, kookssteenkool; ~-**plant**, kooksaanleg.
col, (berg)nek; hoogpas.
co'la, kolaboom.
col'andor, sif, gaatjiesbak; haelvorm
cola: ~ **nut**, kolaneut; ~ **seed**, kolasaad, kolaneut.
cold, (n) kou(e), koudheid; verkoue(ntheid); *BITING* ~, snerpende koue; *CATCH* ~, koue vat; *HAVE a* ~, verkoue wees; *leave someone out IN the* ~, iem. verontagsaam; iem. laat fluit; *be LEFT out in the* ~, opsy gestoot word; *OUT in the* ~, verwaarloos; verontagsaam; (a, adv) koud, guur; koel; onvriendelik, onhartlik (ontvangs); onverskillig; *in* ~ *BLOOD*, koelbloedig; met voorbedagte rade; onverskillig; ~ *as CHARITY*, so koud soos ys; ~ *COMFORT*, 'n skamele troos; *have* ~ *FEET*, bang wees; papbroek(er)ig wees; *GET a person* ~, iem. in sy mag kry; *GO* ~ *all over*, yskoud word; *LEAVE one (stone-)* ~, jou koue klere nie raak nie, jou koud laat; *give the* ~ *SHOULDER*, met die nek aankyk, die rug toekeer; *a* ~ *SNAP*, onverwagte koue (weer); *put something in* ~ *STORAGE*, iets op die lange baan skuif; *TURN* ~ *with fear*, jou yskoud skrik; *a* ~ *WAR*, 'n koue oorlog; gewapende vrede; *the WORDS were barely (hardly)* ~, die woorde was nog nie koud nie; ~-**blooded**, koelbloedig; koudbloedig (diere); onverskillig, ongevoelig; ~-**bloodedness**, koelbloedigheid; ~ **Bokkeveld**, Koue Bokkeveld; ~ **cathode**, koue katode; ~-**chisel**, koubeitel; ~ **colour**, koue kleur; ~ **comfort**, skraal troos; ~ **compress**, kouekompress; ~ **control**, kouereëlaar; ~ **cream**, koelpommade; koelroom; ~ **cuts**, koue vleis; ~-**drawn**, koudgetrokke; ~ **drink**, koekdrank; ~ **feet**, bang(ig)heid, lafhartigheid; ~ **fish**, koue vis, emosielose mens; ~ **front**, kouefront; ~-**hearted**, koud, onverskillig, ongevoelig; ~-**ish**, koelerig, kouerig; ~ **lime**, maerkalk; ~-**ly**, koud, koel; ~ **meats**, koue vleis(soorte); ~-**ness**, kou(e), koudheid; koelheid; onvriendelikheid; onverskilligheid; ~ **patch**, koue lap (binneband); ~ **perspiration**, angssweet, koue sweet; ~ **pressure**, koue druk; ~ **proof**, verkouevry; ~-**saw**, kousaag; ~-**set**, koue sethamer; ~ **short**, koudbros; ~ **shoulder**, (n) afsydigheid, koue behandeling; ~-**shoulder**, (v) verontagsaam, ignoreer; ~ **snap**, ~ **spell**, koue vlaag, vlaag koue; ~ **spring**, koue fontein; ~ **steel**, swaard, bajonet.
cold' storage, koelbewaring; ~ *PLANT*, koelinrigting; ~ *SPACE*, koelruimte; ~ *WAREHOUSE*, koelruimte.
cold: ~ **store**, koelkamers; ~ **sweat**, angssweet, koue sweet; ~-**valve**, koelklamp; ~ **war**, koue oorlog; ~ **water**, koue water; ~-**water cure**, kouewaterkuur, -behandeling; ~ **waving**, koue golwing.
cole, kool; raap; seekool.
Cole'brooke (pig), Kolbroek(vark).
co'legatee, mede-erfgenaam.
coleop'terous, skildvleuelig.
cole: ~ **rape**, koolraap; ~-**seed**, raapsaad; koolsaad.
co'leus, coleus, Josefskleed.
coli'bri, kolibrie.
col'ic, (n) koliek; buikkramp; (a) ydikerm-, kolon-; ~ **ky**, koliekagtig.
Colise'um, Coliseum.

colit'is, dikdermontsteking, kolitis.
collab'orate, saamwerk, meewerk.
collabora'tion, samewerking, medewerking.
collab'orator, medewerker; meeloper, kollaborateur (met vyand).
collage', plakskildery, collage; ruborduurwerk.
col'lagen, kollageen, lymstof.
collapse', (n) instorting, ineensinking; mislukking, insakking, debakel; (v) instort, ineenstort, inmekaarval; omdop, neerstort, neersyg; insak, inval; misluk.
collap'sible, (op)voubaar, saamvoubaar; ~ **gate**, konsertinahek, vouhek; ~ **boat**, vouboot; ~ **gate**, vouhek, konsertinahek; ~ **target**, klapskyf.
coll'ar, (n) boordjie; kraag (hemp); halsband; skouer (masj.); wortelnek (bot.); ring (munt); tapring; halsstuk; *BLUE-* ~ *worker*, arbeider; *wear a very HIGH* ~, oor 'n wit muur kyk; *SLIP the* ~, losraak (hond); ontspan; *WHITE-* ~ *worker*, salaristrekker; (v) vang; neertrek, plant (rugby); by die nek vat; (vleis) oprol; ~-**band**, kraagband; ~-**beam**, stutbalk, hanebalk, dwarsbalk, bindbalk; ~-**bearing**, kraagblok; kraaglaer; ~-**bolt**, borsbout; ~-**bone**, sleutelbeen; ~ **ed**, gekraag; gevang; opgerol; met 'n boordjie.
collaret(te)', kragie.
coll'ar: ~-**key**, spiltap; dwarsbout; ~-**level**, aanvoorhoogte (geol.); ~-**plate**, kraagplaat; ~-**rot**, kraagvrot; ~-**stud**, boordjieknoop; ~-**tie**, binthout; ~-**tongue**, gerolde tong; ~-**work**, swaar werk.
collate', vergelyk, kollasioneer; byeenbring; insorteer
collat'eral, (n) bloedverwant (in sylinie); (a) sydelings, sy aan sy; indirek; ewewydig, parallel; verwant in die sylinie; kollateraal; by-, bykomstig; sy-; ~ **branch**, sytak; ~ **facts**, meegaande feite; ~**ly**, sydelings; ~ **security**, onderpand, bykomende sekuriteit; aanvullende sekerheid.
colla'tion, vergelyking, kollasie; ligte maaltyd, tussenmaaltyd.
collat'or, naleser, vergelyker; kollator; skenker.
coll'eague, kollega, konfrater, ampsgenoot, medeamptenaar, ampsbroer; ~ **ship**, ampgenootskap.
coll'ect¹, (n) formuliergebed.
collect'², (v) bymekaarmaak; vergader; in, ingaar, insamel, versamel; kollekteer; afhaal (briewe); ~ *ONESELF*, bedaard nadink; jouself beheers, jou regruk; ~ *TAXES*, belasting in; *he can't* ~ *his THOUGHTS*, hy is deur die wind; ~ **able**, inbaar; ~ **call**, kollekteeroproep.
collecta'nea, collectanea, versamelwerk.
collec'ted, versamel; bedaard; *when I had* ~ *my wits*, toe ek my kom kry; ~**ly**, bedaard; ~**ness**, bedaardheid; selfbeheersing; ~ **works**, versamelde werke.
collec'ting, (n) versameling; inkassering; (a) versamelend; ~ **agency**, invorderingsagentskap; ~ **bank**, invorderingsbank; ~ **box**, kollektebus; versamelingskassie (bot.); ~ **depot**, versameldepot; inwinningsdepot; ~ **fee**, invorderingsgeld, kollekteergeld; ~ **point**, versamelpunt, versamelplek, versameldepot; ~ **station**, versamelstasie (radio); ~ **van**, afhaalwa; ~ **wire**, opvangdraad.
collection, versameling, kollekte; insameling; inning; busligting; afhaling; inkassering; ~ **bag**, kollektesakkie; ~ **box**, kollektebus, geldbussie; ~ **charge**, afhaalkoste; ~ **fee**, invorderingsgeld; ~ **plate**, kollektebord.
collec'tive, versamelend, tesame; versamel-; gesamentlik, gemeenskap; kollektief; verenig; ~ **bargaining**, gesamentlike onderhandeling (bedinging); ~ **farm**, gemeenskapsplaas; kibboets; ~ **fruit**, samegestelde vrug; ~**ly**, gesamentlik; ~**ness**, kollektiwiteit; ~ **noun**, versamelwoord; ~ **ownership**, gesamentlike besit; ~ **protection**, gesamentlike beskerming; ~ **work**, versamelwerk.
collec'tivism, kollektivisme.
collec'tivist, (n) kollektivis; (a) kollektivisties.
collectiv'ity, gemeenskaplikheid; gemeenskap.
collec'tor, versamelaar, ontvanger; kollektant; gaarder, inner (belastings); heffer; sleepkontak; kollektor (elek.); ~-**ring**, sleepring (lugv.); ~**'s mania**, versamelwoede.

colleen', nooi, meisie.
coll'ege, kollege; raad, genootskap; ~ **cap**, studentepet; ~ **days**, studentedae; ~ **life**, studentelewe.
colle'gial, kollegiaal, kollege-.
colle'gian, kollegestudent, kollegelid; ~-**like**, studentikoos.
colle'giate, kollegiaal, kollege-; korporasie-; ~ **humour**, studentikose grappigheid, studente= humor.
coll'et, halsband, splitkraag; vatsel, ring.
collide', bots, teen mekaar stamp, in botsing kom, aanvaar (skepe); ~ **head-on**, kop teen kop bots.
Coll'ie, Skaaphond, Kollie.
coll'ier, steenkoolwerker; matroos op 'n koleskip; koleskip; ~-**jetty**, steenkoolhawehoof.
coll'iery, (..ries), steenkoolmyn.
coll'igate, saambind, verbind.
coll'igative, saambindend.
coll'imate, rig, peil; parallel maak, kollimeer.
collima'tion, kollimasielyn, peillyn; rigting.
coll'imator, kollimator.
collin'ear, saamlynig, op een reguit lyn.
colling'ual, van dieselfde taal.
coll'iquate, smelt.
coll'iquation, versmelting, vervloeiing.
colli'sion, botsing, aanvaring, aanseiling.
coll'ocate, plaas, rangskik.
colloca'tion, rangskikking, plasing.
coll'ocutor, medespreker.
collod'ion, kollodium.
coll'ogue, saamspan.
colloid', lymstof, kolloïed; ~ **al**, lymagtig, kolloïdaal; ~ **chemistry**, kolloïedchemie.
coll'op, snytjie, lappie vleis; plooi (huid).
collo'quial, alledaags, gemeensaam; spreektaal-; ~ **speech** *(language)*; omgangstaal, geselstaal; ~ **ism**, spreektaaluitdrukking, geselstaaluitdrukking; ~ **ly**, in die omgangstaal (spreektaal).
coll'oquist, saamprater.
collo'quium, colloquium, kollokwium, seminaar; (akademiese) konferensie.
coll'oquy, samespraak; gesprek, colloquium.
coll'otype, gelatineplaat; ligdruk, kollotipe.
collude', saamspan, onderhands saamwerk, saamknoei, ooreenkom, heul.
collu'sion, geheime verstandhouding, kollusie; heuling, samespanning.
collu'sive, heimlik, onderhands; samespannend, kollusief; ~ **dealings**, samespanning, onderhandse handelinge.
collu'vial, kolluviaal.
collu'vium, kolluvium.
coll'y, (collies) ~ **collie**.
colly'rium, (..ria), oogsalf; setpil; oogwater.
coll'ywobbles, maaggeluide; bangheid.
co'lobus, colobus(aap), stompaap.
col'ocynth, kolokwint, bitterappel, gifappel.
Cologne,' Keulen; *eau-de-*~, oliekolonie, Keulse (reuk)water.
col'on¹, dubbelpunt.
col'on², grootderm, dikderm, kolon.
colonel, kolonel; ~**cy, (**..cies**)**, ~**ship**, kolonelskap, kolonelsrang.
colon'ial, (n) kolonis, kolonialer; (a) koloniaal; ~**ism**, kolonialisme; ~**ist**, kolonialis.
colo'nic, kolon-, derm-; ~ **irrigation**, dermspoeling.
col'onist, kolonis, volksplanter, nedersetter.
coloniza'tion, kolonisasie.
col'onize, koloniseer; ~**r**, koloniseerder, volksplanter.
colonnade', suilery, suilegang, kolonnade.
col'ony, (..nies), kolonie, wingewes; volksplanting, nedersetting; kweekgroep; trop; groep (voëls); ~ **weaver**, versamelvoël.
col'ophon, slottitel, eindtitel, kolofon; *from title-page to* ~, van begin tot end.
coloph'ony, spieëlhars, vioolhars, harpuis.
coloquin'tida, *kyk* **colocynth**.
Colora'do beetle, Koloradokewer, aartappelkewer.
colora'tion, kleuring, kleursel.
coloratur'a, koloratuur(sopraan).
col'orature, koloratuur, sangkleur.

colorif'ic, kleurgewend, kleur-; kleurvol.
colorim'eter, kleurmeter, kolorimeter.
coloss'al, kolossaal, reusagtig.
Colosse'um, Colosseum.
Coloss'ians, Kolossense.
coloss'us, (-es, ..ssi), gevaarte, reus, kolos.
colos'tomy, kolostomie.
colos'trum, bies(melk); eerste moedersmelk, voormelk.
colo'tomy, kolotomie.
col'our, (n) kleur, tint, gelaatskleur; voorkome; voorwendsel, dekmantel; skyn; verf; karakter, aard; *CHANGE* ~, van kleur verander; bloos; bleek word; *COMPLEMENTARY* ~, komplementêre kleur, aanvullingskleur; *DESERT one's* ~s, die vaandel verlaat; *FAST* ~s, vaste kleure; *with FLYING* ~s, met vlieënde vaandels; *keep the* ~s *FLYING*, die banier hoog hou; *JOIN the* ~s, diens neem; *LEND* ~ *to*, 'n skyn van waarheid gee aan; *LOCAL* ~, plaaslike kleur; *NAIL one's* ~s *to the mast*, pal staan, voet by stuk hou; *be OFF* ~, van stryk af wees; kroeserig (sleg) voel; *PAINT in false* ~s, in die verkeerde lig stel; *PRIMARY* ~s, grondkleure; *REGIMENTAL* ~s, regimentsvlag; *SAIL under false* ~s, onder 'n valse vlag vaar; *SECONDARY* ~, sekondêre kleur; *SEE the* ~ *of one's money*, betaal word; *SERVE with the* ~s, as soldaat dien; *SHOW one's* ~s, kleur beken; *TROOPING the* ~s, vaandelparade hou; *TRUE* ~s, in sy ware gedaante; *UNDER* ~ *of*, onder die naam van, onder voorwendsel van; (v) kleur, verf; inkleur; verbloem, bewimpel; bloos; deurrook (pyp); ~**able**, aanneemlik; skynbaar, gefingeer, voorgewend; ~**a'tion**, *kyk* **coloration**; ~ **atlas**, kleurkaart; ~ **bar**, kleurslagboom; ~-**blind**, kleurblind; ~-**blindness**, kleurblindheid, daltonisme; ~ **box**, verfdoos; ~ **card**, kleur(e)monster; ~ **chart**, kleurkaart; ~ **coat**, kleurlaag; ~ **code**, kleurkode; ~-**consciousness**, kleurbewustheid; ~ **consultant**, kleurkonsultant; kleuradviseur; ~ **disc**, kleurskyf; ~ **dispersion**, kleurskifting, kleurspreiding; ~**ed**, (gekleur(d), geverf, getint; aangedik, opgesier; *C*~*ed people*, Kleurlinge; Bruinmense; ~ **effect**, kleureffek; ~-**fast**, kleurvas, kleureg; ~ **fastness**, kleurvastheid, -egtheid; ~ **film**, kleurfilm; ~**ful**, kleurryk, kleurvol; ~**ing**, kleur, kleursel; vals skyn; ~*ing matter*, kleurstof; ~**fulness**, kleurigheid; kleurvolheid, kleurrykheid; ~ **harmony**, kleurharmonie; ~ **index**, kleurindeks; kleursyfer; ~ **intensity**, kleurdiepte; ~**ist**, koloris; ~**istic**, koloristies; ~**less**, vaal, kleurloos; neutraal; achromaties; ~ **line**, kleurslagboom, kleur(skeids)lyn; ~ **man**, verfhandelaar; ~ **matcher**, kleurpasser; verfmenger; ~ **party**, vaandelwag, vlaghysers; ~ **photograph**, kleurfoto; ~ **photography**, kleurfotografie; ~ **print**, kleurafdruk; kleurprent; ~-**printing**, kleurdruk; ~ **range**, kleur(e)reeks, kleuromvang; ~s, vlag; *call to* ~s, opkommandeer; ~ **scheme**, kleurskema; ~ **screen**, kleurfilter; ~ **sense**, kleurgevoel; ~-**sensitive**, kleur(e)gevoelig; ~ **sergeant**, vlagsersant; ~-**slide**, kleurskyfie; ~ **spectrum**, kleurspektrum; ~ **supplement**, kleurbylae; ~-**value**, kleurwaarde; ~ **wash**, kleurkalk.
Col'oured: ~ **people**, Kleurlinge, Bruinmense; ~s, Kleurlinge, Bruinmense.
co'louring, kleuring, kleur, kleursel; koloriet; skakering, tint; vals(e) skyn.
col'portage, kolportasie.
colporteur', kolporteur, boeksmous, boekverkoper.
col poscope, skedespieël, kolposkoop.
Colt¹, rewolwer, Colt.
colt², jong hings; nuweling; stuk tou, slaantou; ~ **foal**, hingsvul; ~**ish**, wild, jonk.
colts'foot, hoefblad.
colt's' tooth, (..teeth), melktand; lekkerbek; *he hasn't cast his* ~ *yet*, 'n ou bok lus ook nog 'n groen blaartjie.
col'ubrine, slangagtig.
columba'rium, kolumbarium, urnkelder.
col'umbine, (n) akelei, vyfduifies, duifie(blom), koningklokkie; (a) duifagtig.
colum'bium, columbium.

munt, geslaan; verdig; gemaak, geskep (woord); ~ **er,** (geld)munter; valsmunter; uitvinder; skepper (woord).

coin'ing, aanmunting, (die) munt; uitvinding; skepping (woorde); *FALSE* ~, muntvervalsing; *be* ~ *MONEY,* geld soos water verdien; ~ *press,* muntpers.

coin: ~ **mould,** muntvorm; ~ **plate,** muntplaatjie; ~**-shaped,** muntvormig; ~**-slot screw,** gleuf(kop)skroef.

coinstantan'eous, gelyktydig.

coir, klapperhaar; ~ **mattress,** klapperhaarmatras.

coi'tion, coit'us, geslagsgemeenskap, byslaap, paring, koïtus.

coke, (n) kooks; (v) verkooks; ~**-breeze,** kooksgruis; ~ **coal,** kookskool; ~ **fire,** kooksvuur; ~ **furnace,** kooksoond; ~ **oven,** kooksoond; ~ **pocket,** kookssak; ~ **waste,** afvalkooks.

cok'ing, verkooksing; ~ **coal,** koolsteenkool; ~**-plant,** kooksaanleg.

col, (berg)nek; hoogpas.

co'la, kolaboom.

col'ander, sif, gaatjiesbak; haelvorm.

cola: ~ **nut,** kolaneut; ~ **seed,** kolasaad, kolaneut.

cold, (n) kou(e), koudheid; verkoue(ntheid); *BITING* ~, snerpende koue; *CATCH* ~, koue vat; *HAVE a* ~, verkoue wees; *leave someone out IN the* ~, iem. verontagsaam; iem. laat fluit; *be LEFT out in the* ~, opsy gestoot word; *OUT in the* ~, verwaarloos; verontagsaam; (a, adv) koud, guur; koel; onvriendelik, onhartlik (ontvangs); onverskillig; *in* ~ *BLOOD,* koelbloedig; met voorbedagte rade; onverskillig, ~ *as CHARITY,* so koud soos ys; ~ *COMFORT,* 'n skamele troos; *have* ~ *FEET,* bang wees; papbroek(er)ig wees; *GET a person* ~, iem. in sy mag kry; *GO* ~ *all over,* yskoud word; *LEAVE one (stone-)* ~, jou koue klere nie raak nie, jou koud laat; *give the* ~ *SHOULDER,* met die nek aankyk, die rug toekeer; *a* ~ *SNAP,* onverwagte koue (weer); *put something in* ~ *STORAGE,* iets op die lange baan skuif; *TURN* ~ *with fear,* jou yskoud skrik; *a* ~ *WAR,* 'n koue oorlog; gewapende vrede; *the WORDS were barely (hardly)* ~, die woorde was nog nie koud nie; ~**-blooded,** koelbloedig; koudbloedig (diere); onverskillig, ongevoelig; ~**-bloodedness,** koelbloedigheid; ~ **Bokkeveld,** Koue Bokkeveld; ~ **cathode,** koue katode; ~**-chisel,** koubeitel; ~ **colour,** koue kleur; ~ **comfort,** skraal troos; ~ **compress,** kouekompress; ~ **control,** kouereëlaar; ~ **cream,** koelpommade; koelroom; ~ **cuts,** koue vleis; ~**-drawn,** koudgetrokke; ~ **drink,** koekdrank; ~ **feet,** bang(ig)heid, lafhartigheid; ~ **fish,** koue vis, emosielose mens; ~ **front,** kouefront; ~**-hearted,** koud, onverskillig, ongevoelig; ~**-ish,** koelerig, kouerig; ~ **lime,** maerkalk; ~**-ly,** koud, koel; ~ **meats,** koue vleis(soorte); ~**-ness,** kou(e), koudheid; koelheid; onvriendelikheid; onverskilligheid; ~ **patch,** koue lap (binneband); ~ **perspiration,** angssweet, koue sweet; ~ **pressure,** koue druk; ~ **proof,** verkouevry; ~**-saw,** kousaag; ~**-set,** koue oothamer; ~ **short,** koudbros; ~ **shoulder,** (n) afsydigheid, koue behandeling; ~**-shoulder,** (v) verontagsaam, ignoreer; ~ **snap,** ~ **spell,** koue vlaag, vlaag koue; ~ **spring,** koue fontein; ~ **steel,** swaard, bajonet.

cold' storage, koelbewaring; ~ *PLANT,* koelinrigting; ~ *SPACE,* koelruimte; ~ *WAREHOUSE,* koelruimte.

cold: ~ **store,** koelkamers; ~ **sweat,** angssweet, koue sweet; ~**-valve,** koelklamp; ~ **war,** koue oorlog; ~ **water,** koue water, ~**-water cure,** kouewaterkuur, -behandeling; ~ **waving,** koue golwing.

cole, kool; raap; seekool.

Cole'brooke (pig), Kolbroek(vark).

co'legatee, mede-erfgenaam.

coleop'terous, skildvleuelig.

cole: ~ **rape,** koolraap; ~**-seed,** raapsaad; koolsaad.

co'leus, coleus, Josefskleed.

coli'bri, kolibrie.

col'ic, (n) koliek; buikkramp; (a) dikderm-, kolon-; ~ **ky,** koliekagtig.

Colise'um, Coliseum.

colit'is, dikdermontsteking, kolitis.

collab'orate, saamwerk, meewerk.

collabora'tion, samewerking, medewerking.

collab'orator, medewerker; meeloper, kollaborateur (met vyand).

collage', plakskildery, collage; ruborduurwerk.

col'lagen, kollageen, lymstof.

collapse', (n) instorting, ineensinking; mislukking, insakking, debakel; (v) instort, ineenstort, inmekaarval; omdop, neerstort, neersyg; insak, inval; misluk.

collap'sible, (op)voubaar, saamvoubaar; ~ **gate,** konsertinahek, vouhek; ~ **boat,** vouboot; ~ **gate,** vouhek, konsertinahek; ~ **target,** klapskyf.

coll'ar, (n) boordjie; kraag (hemp); halsband; skouer (masj.); wortelnek (bot.); ring (munt); tapring; halsstuk; *BLUE-* ~ *worker,* arbeider; *wear a very HIGH* ~, oor 'n wit muur kyk; *SLIP the* ~, losraak (hond); ontspan; *WHITE-* ~ *worker,* salaristrekker; (v) vang; neertrek, plant (rugby); by die nek vat; (vleis) oprol; ~**-band,** kraagband; ~**-beam,** stutbalk, hanebalk, dwarsbalk, bindbalk; ~**-bearing,** kraagblok; kraaglaer; ~**-bolt,** bolsbout; ~**-bone,** sleutelbeen; ~ **ed,** gekraag; gevang; opgerol; met 'n boordjie.

collaret(te)', kragie.

coll'ar: ~**-key,** spiltap; dwarsbout; ~**-level,** aanvoorhoogte (geol.); ~**-plate,** kraagplaat; ~**-rot,** kraagvrot; ~**-stud,** boordjieknoop; ~**-tie,** binthout; ~ **tongue,** gerolde tong; ~**-work,** swaar werk.

collate', vergelyk; kollasioneer; byeenbring; insorteer.

collat'eral, (n) bloedverwant (in sylinie); (a) sydelings, sy aan sy; indirek; ewewydig, parallel; verwant in die sylinie; kollateraal; by-, bykomstig; sy-; ~ **branch,** sytak; ~ **facts,** meegaande feite; ~**ly,** sydelings; ~ **security,** onderpand, bykomende sekuriteit; aanvullende sekerheid.

colla'tion, vergelyking, kollasie; ligte maaltyd, tussenmaaltyd.

collat'or, naleser, vergelyker; kollator; skenker.

coll'eague, kollega, konfrater, ampsgenoot, medeamptenaar, ampsbroer; ~ **ship,** ampgenootskap.

coll'ect¹, (n) formuliergebed.

collect'², (v) bymekaarmaak; vergader; in, ingaar, insamel, versamel; kollekteer; afhaal (briewe); ~ *ONESELF,* bedaard nadink; jouself beheers, jou regruk; ~ *TAXES,* belasting in; *he can't* ~ *his THOUGHTS,* hy is deur die wind; ~ **able,** inbaar; ~ **call,** kollekteeroproep.

collecta'nea, collectanea, versamelwerk.

collec'ted, versamel; bedaard; *when I had* ~ *my wits,* toe ek my kom kry; ~**ly,** bedaard; ~**ness,** bedaardheid; selfbeheersing; ~ **works,** versamelde werke.

collec'ting, (n) versameling; inkassering; (a) versamelend; ~ **agency,** invorderingsagentskap; ~ **bank,** invorderingsbank; ~ **box,** kollektebus; versamelingskassie (bot.); ~ **depot,** versameldepot; inwinningsdepot; ~ **fee,** invorderingsgeld, kollekteergeld; ~ **point,** versamelpunt, versamelplek, versameldepot; ~ **station,** versamelstasie (radio); ~ **van,** afhaalwa; ~ **wire,** opvangdraad.

collection, versameling, kollekte; insameling; inning; busligting; afhaling; inkassering; ~ **bag,** kollektesakkie; ~ **box,** kollektebus, geldbussie; ~ **charge,** afhaalkoste; ~ **fee,** invorderingsgeld; ~ **plate,** kollektebord.

collec'tive, versamelend, tesame; versamel-; gesamentlik, gemeenskap, kollektief; verenig; ~ **bargaining,** gesamentlike onderhandeling (bedinging); ~ **farm,** gemeenskapsplaas; kibboets; ~ **fruit,** samegestelde vrug; ~**ly,** gesamentlik; ~**ness,** kollektiwiteit; ~ **noun,** versamelwoord; ~ **ownership,** gesamentlike besit; ~ **protection,** gesamentlike beskerming; ~ **work,** versamelwerk.

collec'tivism, kollektivisme.

collec'tivist, (n) kollektivis; (a) kollektivisties.

collectiv'ity, gemeenskaplikheid; gemeenskap.

collec'tor, versamelaar, ontvanger; kollektant; gaarder, inner (belastings); heffer; sleepkontak; kollektor (elek.); ~**-ring,** sleepring (lugv.); ~**'s mania,** versamelwoede.

colleen', nooi, meisie.
coll'ege, kollege; raad, genootskap; ~ **cap,** studentepet; ~ **days,** studentedae; ~ **life,** studentelewe.
colle'gial, kollegiaal, kollege=.
colle'gian, kollegestudent, kollegelid; ~**-like,** studentikoos.
colle'giate, kollegiaal, kollege=; korporasie=; ~ **humour,** studentikose grappigheid, studentehumor.
coll'et, halsband, splitkraag; vatsel, ring.
collide', bots, teen mekaar stamp, in botsing kom, aanvaar (skepe); ~ **head-on,** kop teen kop bots.
Coll'ie, Skaaphond, Kollie.
coll'ier, steenkoolwerker; matroos op 'n koleskip; koleskip; ~**-jetty,** steenkoolhawehoof.
coll'iery, (..ries), steenkoolmyn.
coll'igate, saambind, verbind.
coll'igative, saambindend.
coll'imate, rig, peil; parallel maak, kollimeer.
collima'tion, kollimasielyn, peillyn; rigting.
coll'imator, kollimator.
collin'ear, saamlynig, op een reguit lyn.
colling'ual, van dieselfde taal.
coll'iquate, smelt.
col'liquation, versmelting, vervloeiing.
colli'sion, botsing, aanvaring, aanseiling.
coll'ocate, plaas, rangskik.
colloca'tion, rangskikking, plasing.
coll'ocutor, medespreker.
collod'ion, kollodium.
coll'ogue, saamspan.
colloid', lymstof, kolloïed; ~ **al,** lymagtig, kolloïdaal; ~ **chemistry,** kolloïedchemie.
coll'op, snytjie, lappie vleis; plooi (huid).
collo'quial, alledaags, gemeensaam; spreektaal=; ~ **speech (language);** omgangstaal, geselstaal; ~ **ism,** spreektaaluitdrukking, geselstaaluitdrukking; ~ **ly,** in die omgangstaal (spreektaal).
coll'oquist, saamprater.
collo'quium, colloquium, kollokwium, seminaar; (akademiese) konferensie.
coll'oquy, samespraak; gesprek, colloquium.
coll'otype, gelatineplaat; ligdruk, kollotipe.
collude', saamspan, onderhands saamwerk, saamknoei, ooreenkom, heul.
collu'sion, geheime verstandhouding, kollusie; heuling, samespanning.
collu'sive, heimlik, onderhands; samespannend, kollusief; ~ **dealings,** samespanning, onderhandse handelinge.
collu'vial, kolluviaal.
collu'vium, kolluvium.
coll'y, (collies) = collie.
colly'rium, (..ria), oogsalf; setpil; oogwater.
coll'ywobbles, maaggeluide; bangheid.
co'lobus, colobus(aap), stompaap.
col'ocynth, kolokwint, bitterappel, gifappel.
Cologne,' Keulen; *eau-de-*~, oliekolonie, Keulse (reuk)water.
col'on[1]**,** dubbelpunt.
col'on[2]**,** grootderm, dikderm, kolon.
colonel, kolonel; ~ **cy,** (..cies), ~ **ship,** kolonelskap, kolonelsrang.
colon'ial, (n) kolonis, kolonialer; (a) koloniaal; ~ **ism,** kolonialisme; ~ **ist,** kolonialis.
colo'nic, kolon=, derm=; ~ **irrigation,** dermspoeling.
col'onist, kolonis, volksplanter, nedersetter.
coloniza'tion, kolonisasie.
col'onize, koloniseer; ~ **r,** koloniseerder, volksplanter.
colonnade', suilery, suilegang, kolonnade.
col'ony, (..nies), kolonie, wingewes; volksplanting, nedersetting; kweekgroep; trop; groep (voëls); ~ **weaver,** versamelvoël.
col'ophon, slottitel, eindtitel, kolofon; *from title-page to* ~, van begin tot end.
coloph'ony, spieëlhars, vioolhars, harpuis.
coloquin'tida, *kyk* **colocynth.**
Colora'do beetle, Koloradokewer, aartappelkewer.
colora'tion, kleuring, kleursel.
coloratur'a, koloratuur(sopraan).
col'orature, koloratuur, sangkleur.

colorif'ic, kleurgewend, kleur=; kleurvol.
colorim'eter, kleurmeter, kolorimeter.
coloss'al, kolossaal, reusagtig.
Colosse'um, Colosseum.
Coloss'ians, Kolossense.
coloss'us, (-es, ..ssi), gevaarte, reus, kolos.
colos'tomy, kolostomie.
colos'trum, bies(melk); eerste moedersmelk, voormelk.
colo'tomy, kolotomie.
col'our, (n) kleur, tint, gelaatskleur; voorkome; voorwendsel, dekmantel; skyn; verf; karakter, aard; *CHANGE* ~, van kleur verander; bloos; bleek word; *COMPLEMENTARY* ~, komplementêre kleur, aanvullingskleur; *DESERT one's* ~*s,* die vaandel verlaat; *FAST* ~*s,* vaste kleure; *with FLYING* ~*s,* met vlieënde vaandels; *keep the* ~*s FLYING,* die banier hoog hou; *JOIN the* ~*s,* diens neem; *LEND* ~ *to,* 'n skyn van waarheid gee aan; *LOCAL* ~, plaaslike kleur; *NAIL one's* ~*s to the mast,* pal staan, voet by stuk hou; *be OFF* ~, van stryk af wees; kroeserig (sleg) voel; *PAINT in false* ~*s,* in die verkeerde lig stel; *PRIMARY* ~*s,* grondkleure; *REGIMENTAL* ~*s,* regimentsvlag; *SAIL under false* ~*s,* onder 'n valse vlag vaar; *SECONDARY* ~, sekondêre kleur; *SEE the* ~ *of one's money,* betaal word; *SERVE with the* ~*s,* as soldaat dien; *SHOW one's* ~*s,* kleur beken; *TROOPING the* ~*s,* vaandelparade hou; *TRUE* ~*s,* in sy ware gedaante; *UNDER* ~ *of,* onder die naam van, onder voorwendsel van; (v) kleur, verf; inkleur; verbloem, bewimpel; bloos; deurrook (pyp); ~ **able,** aanneemlik; skynbaar, gefingeer; voorgewend; ~ **a'tion,** *kyk* **coloration;** ~ **atlas,** kleurkaart; ~ **bar,** kleurslagboom; ~**-blind,** kleurblind; ~**-blindness,** kleurblindheid, daltonisme; ~ **box,** verfdoos; ~ **card,** kleur(e)monster; ~ **chart,** kleurkaart; ~ **coat,** kleurlaag; ~ **code,** kleurkode; ~**-consciousness,** kleurbewustheid; ~ **consultant,** kleurkonsultant; kleuradviseur; ~ **disc,** kleurskyf; ~ **dispersion,** kleurskifting, kleurspreiding; ~ **ed,** (gekleur(d), geverf, getint; aangedik, opgesier; *C*~*ed people,* Kleurlinge; Bruinmense; ~ **effect,** kleureffek; ~**-fast,** kleurvas, kleureg; ~ **fastness,** kleurvastheid, -egtheid; ~ **film,** kleurfilm; ~ **ful,** kleurryk, kleurvol; ~ **ing,** kleur, kleursel; vals skyn; ~ *ing matter,* kleurstof; ~ **fulness,** kleurigheid; kleurvolheid, kleurrykheid; ~ **harmony,** kleurharmonie; ~ **index,** kleurindeks; kleursyfer; ~ **intensity,** kleurdiepte; ~ **ist,** koloris; ~ **istic,** koloristies; ~ **less,** vaal, kleurloos; neutraal; achromaties; ~ **line,** kleurslagboom, kleur(skeids)lyn; ~ **man,** verfhandelaar; ~ **matcher,** kleurpasser; verfmenger; ~ **party,** vaandelwag, vlaghysers; ~ **photograph,** kleurfoto; ~ **photography,** kleurfotografie; ~ **print,** kleurafdruk; kleurprent; ~**-printing,** kleurdruk; ~ **range,** kleur(e)reeks, kleuromvang; ~**s,** vlag; *call to* ~*s,* opkommandeer; ~ **scheme,** kleurskema; ~ **screen,** kleurfilter; ~ **sense,** kleurgevoel; ~**-sensitive,** kleur(e)gevoelig; ~ **sergeant,** vlagsersant; ~**-slide,** kleurskyfie; ~ **spectrum,** kleurspektrum; ~ **supplement,** kleurbylae; ~**-value,** kleurwaarde; ~ **wash,** kleurkalk.
Col'oured: ~ **people,** Kleurlinge, Bruinmense; ~**s,** Kleurlinge, Bruinmense.
co'louring, kleuring, kleur, kleursel; koloriet; skakering, tint; vals(e) skyn.
col'portage, kolportasie.
colporteur', kolporteur, boeksmous, boekverkoper.
col'poscope, skedespieël, kolposkoop.
Colt[1]**,** rewolwer, Colt.
colt[2]**,** jong hings; nuweling; stuk tou, slaantou; ~ **foal,** hingsvul; ~ **ish,** wild, jonk.
colts'foot, hoefblad.
colt's' tooth, (..teeth), melktand; lekkerbek; *he hasn't cast his* ~ *yet,* 'n ou bok lus ook nog 'n groen blaartjie.
col'ubrine, slangagtig.
columba'rium, kolumbarium, urnkelder.
col'umbine, (n) akelei, vyfduifies, duifie(blom), koningklokkie; (a) duifagtig.
colum'bium, columbium.

colum'bite, columbiet.
columel'la, suiltjie.
col'umn, kolom; kolonne; pilaar, suil; ry; rubriek (nuusblad); *FIFTH* ~, vyfde kolonne; ~ *of SMOKE,* rooksuil; *SPINAL* ~, ruggraat.
colum'nar, kolomvormig; suilvormig, pilaar=; ~ **structure,** suilbou.
co'lumn: ~-**base,** suilvoet; ~-**bolt,** pilaarbout; ~-**heading,** kolomhoof; ~ **ist,** rubriekskrywer.
colure', snypunt, kolure.
col'y, (colies), muisvoël.
col'za, koolsaad; raapsaad; ~-**oil,** koolsaadolie; raapolie.
com'a¹, bewusteloosheid, koma, swym, slaapsug, vaste slaap.
com'a², saadpluimpie.
com'a³, newelkring (komeet).
co'manager, medebestuurder.
com'atose, slaapsugtig, bewusteloos.
comb, (n) kam, haarkam; heuningkoek, raat; skroef= staal; *CUT someone's* ~, iem. 'n toontjie laer laat sing; *SEARCH with a fine* ~, fynkam; deursnuffel; van hoek tot kant deursoek; (v) kam; hekel (vlas); opkam; kaard (wol); ~ *someone's HAIR,* iem. af= ransel; ~ *OUT,* uitkam; afskei; uitsoek.
com'bat, (n) stryd, geveg; *single* ~, tweegeveg; (v) veg, (be)stry, bekamp, worstel.
com'batant, (n) stryder, bakleier, vegter, vegsman; (a) strydbaar, strydend; ~ **duties,** vegdiens; ~ **offi= cer,** vegoffisier, frontoffisier.
com'bat-general, veggeneraal.
com'bating, bestryding.
com'bative, vegterig, veg=, strydbaar; strydend, -ness, veglus, strydlus(tigheid).
comb'er, kammer; kammasjien, kaarder; krulgolf.
comb' honey, koekheuning.
combin'able, verenigbaar.
combina'tion, verbinding, vereniging, kombinasie; komplot, samespanning; samespel (rugby); motor= fiets met syspan(wa); (pl) hempbroek; ~ **calipers,** kombinasiepasser; ~ **(harvester),** stroper; ~ **lever,** voorylhefboom; ~ **lock,** kodeslot, letterslot; ~ **plane,** kombinasieskaaf; ~ **pliers,** steltang; ~ **pump,** kombinasiepomp; ~ **square,** allegaar; ~ **yarn,** saamgestelde garing.
combine'¹, (n) stroper (graan), snydorsmasjien.
combine'², (n) vereniging, trust, kartel, sindikaat; (v) verbind, verenig; sameslut; kombineer; in onder= linge verband bring.
combined', gekombineerd, verenig, verbonde; ~ *CY= LINDER,* saamgestelde silinder; ~ *OPER= ATIONS,* gesamentlike ondernemings.
comb: ~**ing mill,** kammery; ~-**ing-process,** kam= proses; ~**ings,** kamhare, kamwol; ~**ings wool,** kamwol; ~-**out,** uitkamming.
com'bo, combo, kombinasie (jazzmusiek).
combret'um, hardekool.
comb: ~-**roof,** geweldak; ~-**shaped,** kamvormig.
combustibil'ity, brandbaarheid, ontvlambaarheid, kortgebondenheid.
combus'tible, (n) brandstof; (a) brandbaar, ver= brandbaar; ontvlambaar; kortgevat; ~ **stores,** ont= vlambare goedere; vlamstofpakhuis.
combus'tion, verbranding, brand; *SLOW* ~, smeul= branding; *SPONTANEOUS* ~, selfontbranding; ~ **chamber,** verbrandingsruim(te); ~ **stove,** smeul= stoof.
come, (came, come), kom; aankom; nader, aanbreek; daartoe geraak; oorkom; ~ *ABOUT,* gebeur; ~ *ACROSS,* teëkom; ~ *of AGE,* mondig word; ~ *ALONG,* saamgaan; maak gou; *AS they* ~, soos hulle by die hek uitkom; voor die voet; ~ *AT,* in die hande kry; ~ *AWAY,* wegkom; ~ *BACK,* terug= kom; ~ *into BEING,* tot stand kom; - *to BLOWS,* handgemeen raak, vuisslaan; ~ *BY,* ver= bykom; in die hande kry; ~ *BY something,* aan iets kom; iets in besit kry; *when does the COMPETI= TION* ~ *off?,* wanneer vind die wedstryd plaas?; ~ *down with a handsome CONTRIBUTION,* 'n groot bydrae lewer; ~ *DOWN,* afkom; ~ *DOWN on someone,* iem. uittrap; op iem. se dak afklim; ~ *to an END,* ophou; *FIRST* ~, *first served,* eerste kom, eerste maal; ~ *FORTH,* te voorskyn kom; ~ *FORWARD,* vorentoe kom; hom aanmeld; ~ *to GRIEF,* verongeluk; in die moeilikheid beland; ~ *to HAND,* bereik; toekom; ~ *in HANDY,* te pas kom; ~ *to HARM,* beseer word; ~ *HELL and high water,* al bars die bottel en al buig die fles; ~ *HOME to someone,* iem. intiem raak; ~ *IN for,* 'n deel kry, kry; ~ *INTO,* erf; ~ *to KNOW,* te wete kom; ~ *to be KNOWN,* bekend word; *LIGHTLY* ~, *lightly go,* so gewonne, so geronne; erfgeld is swerfgeld; ~ *what MAY,* kom wat wil; wat ook al mag gebeur; ~ *into MONEY,* geld erf; ~ *to NO= THING,* misluk; ~ *under one's NOTICE,* onder iem. se aandag kom; ~ *to NAUGHT,* op niks uit= loop; ~ *OFF,* slaag, suksesvol wees; ~ *OFF badly,* daar sleg van afkom; ~ *OFF it!,* sak Sarel!; ~ *ON,* aankom; komaan!; ~ *OUT,* uitkom; ~ *OUT with,* voor die dag kom met; ~ *OVER,* oorkom; ~ *into one's OWN,* sy erfdeel kry; kry wat jou toekom; in sy reg kom; ~ *of rich PARENTS,* van ryk ouers afstam; ~ *to PASS,* gebeur; ~ *down a PEG or two,* 'n toontjie laer sing; ~ *into POWER,* aan die be= wind kom; ~ *ROUND,* aankom, besoek; bykom (na floute); *be coming ROUND to,* al hoe meer ge= neig wees; ~ *out in SPORTS,* 'n uitslag kry; ~ *out (on STRIKE),* staak, die werk neerlê; ~ *it too STRONG,* die pap te dik aanmaak; ~ *to THINK of it,* daaraan begin dink; ~ *THROUGH,* deur= kom; ~ *TO,* bykom (na floute); *if it* ~ *s TO that,* as dit so ver kom; ~ *TRUE,* uitkom; waar word; ~ *UP,* opkom; ~ *UPON something,* iets raakloop; iets op die lyf loop; ~ *in USEFUL,* te pas kom; ~ *WEAL,* ~ *woe,* laat kom wat wil; ~ *WELL out of something,* daar goed van afkom; *WHERE do I* ~ *in?,* waar bly ek nou? watter voordeel trek ek daar uit?; *WIND, weather,* al bars die bottel en al buig die fles; ~ *into the WORLD,* in die wêreld kom; gebore word; *if the WORST* ~ *s to the worst,* as die ergste gebeur; *not for YEARS to* ~, nie vir jare nie; ~ **across,** kry, ontdek, vind; ~-**along clamp,** trekklamp (elek.); ~-**and-go',** die kom-en-gaan; ~-**at'-able,** toeganklik, bereikbaar; ~-**back; stage a** ~-*back,* weer op die voorgrond tree, terug= keer.
comed'ian, komediant, grapmaker; blyspelskrywer.
comedienne', blyspelaktrise; toneelspeelster; komedi= ante, comedienne.
com'edist, blyspelskrywer, komedieskrywer.
co'medo, swartkoppie; mee-eter.
come'-down, val, vernedering; *have a* ~, verneder word, 'n vernedering ondergaan.
com'edy, (..dies), komedie, blyspel; ~ *of manners,* sedeblyspel.
come-hi'ther, aanloklik, verloklik; ~ **look,** uit= nodigende blik.
come'liness, bevalligheid, aantreklikheid.
come'ly, bevallig, aantreklik; gepas; **come-on',** lok= middel, aas.
com'er, aankomer, aankomeling; *ALL* ~ *s,* almal wat kom; *the FIRST* ~, die eerste aankomeling; ~ *s and GOERS,* dié wat kom en gaan.
come'-sit-by-me, affronteerspeletjie.
comes'tibles, eetware.
com'et, komeet, roeister, dwaalster, stertster; ~ **ary,** komeet=, komeetagtig; ~-**year,** komeetjaar.
come-up'pance, verdiende loon, terugbetaling.
com'fit(s), versuikerde vrugte, konfiture.
com'fort, (n) troos, aanmoediging, vertroosting; on= besorgdheid, welgesteldheid; steun, opbeuring; ge= rief, gemak; *BE a* ~ *to someone,* iem. tot troos wees; ~ *in the HOUR of sorrow,* 'n soet druppel in iem. se beker; *LIVE in* ~, in gemak lewe; welge= steld wees; ~ *in the hour of SORROW,* 'n soet druppel in iem. se beker; *TAKE* ~, hom troos; moed skep; *WORD of* ~, trooswoord; (v) troos, vertroos, opvrolik, opbeur.
com'fortable, gemaklik, gerieflik; aangenaam; ge= noeglik, (wel)behaaglik; gerus; *the CHAIRS are* ~, die stoele sit lekker; *FEEL* ~, behaaglik voel; ~**ness,** gemaklikheid.
com'fortably: *be* ~ *OFF,* daar goed in sit; welgesteld wees; daar warmpies in sit; ~ *WARM,* lekker warm.

com'fort: ~ **ed,** getroos; ~ **er,** trooster, vertrooster; fopspeen, foppertjie; serp; ~ **ing,** gemoedelik; troostend, troosryk; ~ **less,** troosteloos; ongerieflik; ~ **lessness,** troosteloosheid; ongerieflikheid; ~ **station,** openbare toilet.
com'frey, (Russiese) smeerwortel.
com'fy, knus, behaaglik.
com'ic, (n) grapmaker, komiek; (a) grapperig, komiek, snaaks, komies; ~ *OPERA,* komiese opera; ~ **al,** snaaks, koddig, komieklik, potsierlik, komies; ~ *al incident,* koddige voorval; ~ **al'ity,** (..ties), snaaksheid, grapperigheid; ~ **ally,** grappenderwys(e); ~ **ness,** potsierlikheid, snaaksigheid, snaaksheid, komieklikheid; ~ **opera,** komiese opera, blyspelopera; ~ **s,** ~ **-strip,** tekenstorie, prentverhaal, strokiesverhaal.
com'ing, (n) koms, aankoms; ~ *of AGE,* mondigwording; ~ *into FORCE,* vankragwording; *one's* ~ *s and GOINGS,* iem. se doen en late; iem. se handel en wandel; *not KNOW whether one is – or going,* nie weet waar jy aan of af is nie; (a) komend, toekomstig; aanstaande, ~! ek kom; ~ *EVENTS cast their shadows before,* naderende gebeurtenisse kondig hulleself aan; *a* ~ *MAN,* 'n man v.d. toekoms.
co'minister, medeleraar.
Com'intern, Komintern.
com'ity, (..ties), beleefdheid, hoflikheid.
comm'a, komma; *inverted* ~ *s,* aanhalingstekens; ~ **bacillus,** cholerakiem, kommabasil.
comm'anche bridle, leiriem.
command', (n) bevel, gebod; opdrag; mag, meesterskap, beheersing; aanvoering; beskikking; kommandement, bevelsgebied; *AT your* ~, tot u diens; *BE in* ~, die bevel voer; *BY* ~ *of,* op bevel van; ~ *of LANGUAGE,* taalbeheersing, meesterskap oor 'n taal; *have* ~ *of ONESELF,* selfbeheersing besit; *UNDER* ~ *of,* onder bevel van; (v) beveel, gebied, gelas; kommandeer; beheers; afvorder (eerbied); aanvoer, die bevel voer oor; beskik oor; bestryk; uitsien op; ~ *your man, and do it yourself,* kommandeer jou eie honde en blaf self; ~ **able,** gebiedbaar, geseglik; beheerbaar; aanvoerbaar.
commandant', kommandant, bevelvoerder; ~ **-general,** kommandant-generaal; ~ **ship,** kommandantskap.
commandeer', (op)kommandeer.
comman'der, bevelhebber, aanvoerder, bewindvoerder, gesaghebber, gesagvoerder (op see); kommandeur (rang); kommandant; ~ *of the fleet,* vlootvoog; **C** ~ **-in-Chief, (Commanders-in-Chief),** opperbevelhebber, hoofaanvoerder; ~ **ship,** bevelhebberskap.
comman'ding, gebiedend; magtig; bevelend, beheersend; indrukwekkend; bevelvoerend; ~ *FEATURE,* beheersende terreinvorm; ~ *OFFICER,* bevelvoeder; ~ *POSITION,* beheersende stelling.
command'ment, gebod, bevel; *ELEVENTH* ~, elfde gebod; *the TEN C* ~ *s,* die verbondswet, die Tien Gebooie.
command' night, toneelvoorstelling op hoë bevel, galakonsert.
comman'do, (-s), kommando; skoktroepe.
command' performance = **command night.**
commedia dell'ar'te, (It.), commedia dell'arte.
comme il faut', (F.), comme il faut, soos dit moet wees.
commem'orable, gedenkwaardig.
commem'orate, herdenk, vier; gedenk.
commemora'tion, herdenking, (gedagtenis)viering; *in* ~ *of,* ter nagedagtenis aan.
commem'orative, herinnerings-, herdenkings-.
commence', begin, aanvang; *commencing NUMBER,* aanvangsyfer; aanvangsnommer; *commencing SALARY,* aanvangsalaris; ~ **ing (on),** met ingang van; ~ **ment,** begin, aanvang, aangang; inwerkingtreding (van wet).
commend', aanbeveel, prys, aanprys, opdra; *it has much to* ~ *it,* daar is baie hiervoor te sê; ~ **able,** loflik, aanbevelenswaardig, aanbeveelbaar, prysenswaardig; ~ **a'tion,** lof, loftuiting, aanbeveling; *letter of* ~ *ation,* aanbevelingsbrief; ~ **atory,** aanbevelend, lowend.

commen'sal, tafelgenoot, kosganger; kommensaal; ~ **ism,** tafelgenootskap; kommensalisme.
commensurabil'ity, vergelykbaarheid; meetbaarheid.
commen'surable, meetbaar, verdeelbaar, eweredig.
commen'surate, eweredig; gelykmatig; ~ *to (with),* eweredig aan.
commensura'tion, eweredigheid.
comm'ent, (n) aanmerking, kritiek, kommentaar; uitlegging; (v) verklaar; aanmerk, opmerkings maak, kritiseer, kommentaar lewer; ~ **ary, (..ries),** uitlegging, kommentaar; ~ **ate,** kommentaar lewer (op); uitsaai; ~ **ator,** uitlêer, verklaarder; kommentator; aantekenaar; uitsaaier; omroeper.
comm'erce, handel, verkeer; omgang; gemeenskap; *Chamber of C* ~, Kamer van Koophandel.
commer'cial, handels-, handeldrywend, kommersieel, bedryfs-; ~ **advance,** handelsvoorskot; ~ **advice,** handelsberig; ~ **(aero)plane,** handelsvliegtuig; ~ **affair,** handelsaangeleentheid; ~ **agency,** handelsagentskap; ~ **agreement,** handelsooreenkoms; ~ **alliance,** handelsverbond; ~ **arithmetic,** handelsrekene; ~ **art,** handelskuns; reklamekuns; reklamewerk; ~ **artist,** handelskunstenaar, reklamekunstenaar; ~ **aviation,** handelslugvaart; ~ **bank,** handelsbank; ~ **banking,** handelsbankwese; ~ **bounty,** handelspremie; ~ **broadcasting,** handelsradio; ~ **career,** sakeloopbaan, handelsloopbaan; ~ **circles,** handelskringe; ~ **claims,** handelsvorderinge; ~ **class,** handelstand, sakestand; ~ **college,** handelskool; ~ **connections,** handelsbetrekkinge, sakebetrekkinge; ~ **convention,** handelsooreenkoms; ~ **credit house,** handelskrediethuis; ~ **credit instruments,** handelskredietstukke; ~ **crisis,** handelskrisis; ~ **custom,** handelsgebruik; ~ **directory,** handelsadresboek; ~ **economy,** handelsekonomie, markekonomie; ~ **education,** handelsonderwys; ~ **empire,** handelsryk; ~ **enterprise,** handelsonderneming, ~ **ese,** handelstaal(gebruik), handelsjargon; ~ **establishment,** handelsaak; handelsbedryf; ~ **exchange,** handelsbeurs; ~ **geography,** handelsaardrykskunde; ~ **intercourse,** handelsverkeer; ~ **interest,** handelsbelang(e); ~ **ism,** handelsgees, kommersialisme; merkantilisme; ~ **iza'tion,** kommersialisering; ~ **ize,** tot handelsvoorwerp maak; kommersialiseer; ~ **knowledge,** handelskennis; ~ **law,** handelsreg; ~ **news,** handelsberig; ~ **pilot,** handelsvlieër; ~ **photographer,** handelsfotograaf; ~ **policy,** handelspolitiek; ~ **radio,** handelsradio; ~ **school,** handelskool; ~ **spirit,** handelsgees; ~ **system,** handelstelsel; ~ **teacher,** handelsonderwyser; ~ **training,** handelsopleiding; ~ **traveller,** handelsreisiger; ~ **treaty,** handelsverdrag; ~ **undertaking,** handelsonderneming, handelsaak; ~ **union,** tolverbond; ~ **vehicle,** handelsvoertuig.
commère', commère, seremoniemeesteres.
Com'mie, (sl.), Kommunis, Rooie.
commi'nate, dreig, bedreig (met banvloek).
commina'tion, dreiging, bedreiging.
comm'inatory, dreigend, bedreigend.
commin'gle, meng, vermeng.
comm'inute, verbreek, vergruis; (eiendom) verdeel in klein stukkies, versplinter; ~ *d fracture,* vergruisingsbreuk.
comminu'tion, vergruising; versplintering.
commis'erable, bejammerenswaardig, deerniswaardig.
commis'erate, beklaag, medelye hê, bejammer.
commisera'tion, medelye, roubeklag, bejammering.
com'missar, kommissar; ~ **iat,** kommissariaat, kosdiens, intendans (leër); voedselvoorraad.
com'missary, (..ries), gemagtigde, kommissaris; koskommandant.
commi'ssion, (n) kommissie; lasgewing, brevet; opdrag; aanstelling; offisierspos; kommissieloon, aanbringpremie, aanbringgeld; die begaan (van 'n misdaad), pleging; *GO beyond one's* ~, buite sy boekie gaan; *GOODS on* ~, goed in kommissie; *HOLD a* ~, 'n offisiersrang beklee; *hold a* ~ *of INQUIRY into,* 'n kommissie van ondersoek instel na; *OUT of* ~, buite diens; *PUT in* ~, in bedryf

commissioner   795   *commutation*

(diens) stel; *SHIP in* ~, skip in aktiewe diens; (v) opdra, bevel oor 'n skip gee; in diens stel; aanstel; volmag gee; ~ **agent**, kommissieagent; ~ **aire'**, toesighouer, portier; bode; kruier; opsigter; deurwagter; ~ **ed**, opgedra; ~ *ed OFFICER*, (kommissie)offisier; ~ *ed RANK*, offisiersrang.

commi'ssioner, kommissaris, kommissielid; opsiener (eksamens); saakgelastigde (N.G. Kerk); *HIGH C* ~, Hoë Kommissaris; *C* ~ *of INLAND Revenue*, Kommissaris van Binnelandse Inkomste; ~ *of OATHS*, kommissaris van ede.

comm'issure, voeg, naat, verenigingslyn.

commit', (**-ted**), bedrywe, uitvoer; begaan, pleeg (moord); toevertrou, toebetrou, betrek; toewys, kommitteer (kind na inrigting); blootstel; ~ *to the CARE of*, aan die sorg toevertrou van; (volgens kinderwet) kommitteer aan die sorg van; ~ *to MEMORY*, uit die hoof leer, van buite leer; ~ *MURDER*, moord pleeg; ~ *ONESELF*, jou verbind; jou vergalopeer; jou blootgee; jou verpraat, jou verspreek; jou kompromitteer; ~ *PERJURY*, meineed pleeg; ~ *to PRISON*, tot gevangenisstraf veroordeel; in die tronk sit; ~ *for TRIAL*, ter strafsitting verwys; ~ *to WRITING*, op skrif stel; swart op wit sit; ~ **ment**, (die) toevertrou; gevangesetting, veroordeling; verbintenis; verpligting; pleging; ~ **ment fee**, bindgeld; ~ **table**, begaanbaar, pleegbaar.

commit'tal, afspraak; toewysing; aanbeveling; inhegtenisneming; verpligting; belofte; ~ **warrant**, lasbrief tot gevangesetting.

commit'ted, verbind, verbonde; ~ *to a cause*, verbonde tot 'n saak.

committ'ee, komitee; bestuur; *SELECT* ~, gekose komitee (van parlement); *SERVE (sit) on a* ~, in 'n komitee dien, lid wees van 'n komitee; ~ **man**, bestuurslid, komiteelid; ~ **meeting**, komiteevergadering; ~ **member**, komiteelid; ~ **room**, bestuurskamer; ~ **woman**, (vroulike) komiteelid, bestuurslid.

commix', (ver)meng.

commix'ture, mengsel.

commoda'tion, bruikleen.

commode', laaitafel; klein buffet; stelletjie, stilletjie; ~ **handle**, opklimhandvatsel, styghulp.

commod'ious, gerieflik, ruim; ~ **ness**, gerieflikheid, ruimte, ruimheid.

commod'ity, (..**ties**), handelsartikel; (pl) ware, goedere; ~ **price**, goedereprys, wareprys.

comm'odore, kommodoor; president; aanvoerder.

comm'on, (n) (die) gewone; meent, dorpsgrond; *ABOVE the* ~, meer as gewoon; bo die gemiddelde; *HOUSE of C* ~ *s*, die (Engelse) Laerhuis; ~ *or GARDEN*, doodgewoon; alledaags; *IN* ~, gesamentlik; *have MUCH in* ~, baie gemeen hê, *have NOTHING in* ~, niks met mekaar gemeen hê nie; *OUT of the* ~, ongewoon; buitengewoon; *on SHORT* ~ *s*, van min kos voorsien; met verminderde rantsoen; *in* ~ *WITH*, net soos; op dieselfde wyse as; (a) gemeenskaplik; ordinêr, gemeen, alledaags, gewoon; openbaar, publiek, verbreid; gemeenslagtig; sleg, plat, goedkoop; *make* ~ *CAUSE with*, gemene saak maak met; *by* ~ *CONSENT*, eenparig; *of* ~ *GENDER*, gemeenslagtig; ~ *INTERESTS*, gemeenskaplike belange; *be* ~ *KNOWLEDGE*, algemeen bekend wees; ~ *LANGUAGE*, gemeenskaplike taal; ~ *TO*, eie aan; gemeen hê met; ~ *WEAL*, algemene welsyn; ~ **age**, dorpsveld, dorpsgrond, (dorps)meent; weireg; burgery; ~ **alty**, (die) volk; ~ **assault**, gewone aanranding; ~ **boundary**, gemeenskaplike grens; ~ **brick**, pleistersteen; ~ **bud**, gemengde knop; ~ **carrier**, karweier, vragryer; ~ **cause**, gemene saak; ~ **chickweed**, gewone voëlkruid *(Stellaria media)*; ~ **chord**, gewone drieklank; ~ **decency**, gewone ordentlikheid; ~ **denominator**, gemeenskaplike (gemene) noemer; ~ **divisor**, gemene deler; ~ **divisor**, gemene deler; ~ **er**, burger; lid van (Engelse) Laerhuis; ~ **estate**, gemeenskaplike boedel; ~ **factor**, gemene deler; ~ **fraction**, gewone breuk; ~ **gender**, gemene geslag; ~ **ground**, gemeenskaplike terrein; *to be on* ~ *ground*, dit met mekaar eens

wees; ~ **honesty**, gewone eerlikheid; ~ **knowledge**, algemene kennis; ~ **law**, gemene reg; ~ **-law husband**, houman; ~ **-law wife**, houvrou; ~ **ly**, deurgaans, gewoonlik, in die reël; gewoon; ~ **multiple**, gemene veelvoud; ~ **name**, gewone naam; volksnaam; ~ **ness**, gemeenheid; algemeenheid, alledaagsheid; ~ **noun**, selfstandige naamwoord; soortnaam; ~ **place**, (n) gemeenplaas; treffende gesegde; (a) alledaags, banaal; verslyt; *C* ~ **Prayer**, gebedeboek; ~ **rafter**, dakspar; ~ **-room**, personeelkamer, geselskamer; ~ **s**, die (gewone) volk; kos, ete; ~ **salt**, tafelsout; ~ **sense**, gesonde verstand; ~ **stock**, gewone aandele; ~ **tangent**, gemeenskaplike raaklyn; ~ **use**, gewone gebruik; ~ **variety**, gewone soort.

comm'onwealth, gemenebes, statebond; republiek; ryk; *the C* ~ *(of Nations)*, die Gemenebes (van Nasies), Statebond.

commo'tion, beweging; (be)roering, drukte, opspraak, opskudding, opstand; *in* ~, in rep en roer.

commove', moveer, ophits; beweeg, beroer.

comm'unal, gemeente-, dorps-; gemeenskaps-; ~ **council**, gemeenskapsraad; ~ **customs**, volksgewoontes; stamgewoontes; gemeenskaplike gebruike; ~ **development**, gemeenskapsontwikkeling; ~ **ism**, kommunalisme; ~ **ize**, onder gemeenskaplike beheer bring; ~ **ly**, gesamentlik; ~ **sense**, saamhorigheidsgevoel; gemeenskapsgevoel; ~ **spirit**, groepsgees.

com'munard, kommunelid.

comm'une[1], (n) gemeente; gemeenskap; kommune.

commune', **comm'une**[2], (v) raadpleeg, bepraat; geestelike gemeenskap hê; Nagmaal gebruik.

communicabil'ity, medeedeelbaarheid.

commun'icable, mededeelbaar; aansteeklik; oordraagbaar; spraaksaam.

commun'icant, Nagmaalganger; mededeler, beriggewer, segsman.

commun'icate, meedeel; gemeenskap hou; Nagmaal vier; verkeer; in verbinding stel, in verbinding staan; inmekaarloop (kamers).

commu'nicating door, tussendeur, verbingingsdeur.

communica'tion, mededeling, omgang, gemeenskap; kommunikasie; verbinding; aansluiting; verkeersweë; *LINE of* ~, verbindingslinie; *evil* ~ *s corrupt good MANNERS*, meng jou met semels dan vreet die varke jou; kwade samesprekinge bederf goeie sedes; *MEANS of* ~, verbindingsmiddel; kommunikasiemiddel; ~ **cord**, noodrem, noodkoord; ~ **flight**, verbindingsvlug; ~ **line**, verbindingslyn; ~ **passage**, verbindingsgang; ~ **s**, berigte; verbindingslyne; ~ **satellite**, kommunikasiesatelliet; ~ **squadron**, verbindingseskader; ~ **system**, verbindingsnet; verkeersnet, verkeerstelsel.

commun'icative, mededeelsaam, spraaksaam.

commun'icator, segsman, mededeler, sleutel, kommunikator (elek.).

commun'ion, Nagmaal, Avondmaal; gemeenskap; verbinding, omgang, verkeer; aandeel; *Holy C* ~, Nagmaal; ~ **-cup**, Nagmaalsbeker; ~ **-service**, Nagmaalsdiens; aksiediens; ~ **-table**, Nagmaalstafel; ~ **-wine**, Nagmaal(s)wyn.

communiqué', offisiële berig, amptelike mededeling, communiqué.

Comm'unism, Kommunisme; *c* ~, kommunisme.

Comm'unist, Kommunis (partylid); *c* ~, kommunis.

Communis'tic, Kommunisties; *c* ~, kommunisties.

Com'munist Party, Kommunistiese Party.

communita'rian, kommunitariër.

commun'ity, (..**ties**), gemeenskap, maatskappy; gemeente; ~ *of INTERESTS*, gemeenskaplikheid van belange; *the JEWISH* ~, die Joodse gemeenskap; *the MERCANTILE* ~, die handelsgemeenskap; *OUT of* ~ *of property*, buite gemeenskap van goedere; *with (in)* ~ *of PROPERTY*, in gemeenskap van goedere; *THE* ~, die publiek; ~ **centre**, gemeenskapsentrum; ~ **chest**, gemeenskapskas; ~ **life**, gemeenskapslewe; ~ **singing**, volksang, gemeenskaplike sang; massasang.

commutabil'ity, verwisselbaarheid.

commut'able, verwisselbaar, vervangbaar.

commuta'tion, verwisselbaarheid; verruiling; veran=

commutative 796 *complaisant*

dering; omsetting, omskakeling; versagting; kom*mutasie; ~ of PENSION*, omsetting van pensioen; *~ of PUNISHMENT*, strafverandering, strafversagting; **~ ticket**, seisoenkaartjie.
commut'ative, wisselbaar, ruil=.
comm'utator, omskakelaar, stroomwisselaar, stroomwender, kommutator; **~ base**, kommutatorvoetstuk; **~ segment**, kollektorstrook.
commute', verander, verwissel, verruil; versag; om=set, afkoop, kapitaliseer (pensioen); pendel; **~ r**, seisoenkaartjiehouer (trein); pendelaar, dagreisiger.
commu'ting, heen-en-weerreis, pendeling; **~ service**, pendeldiens.
comose', harig; met 'n koma (sterrek.).
com'pact[1], (n) verdrag, ooreenkoms, verbond; poei=erdosie.
compact'[2], (v) nou verbind, saamdring, aaneensluit; verkort; opmaak; toeslaan; verdig (grond); (a) vas, dig; beknop, gedronge; bondig; stewig; kompak; **~ ion**, verdigting (grond); **~ ness**, digtheid, vast=heid, saamgedrongenheid; beknoptheid.
compan'ion, (n) maat, (met)gesel, kameraad; gesel(lin); pendant; ridder; geselskapsdame; kampanjetrap; kapluik; (v) vergesel; omgang hê met; (a) by=behorende; *~ volume*, bybehorende deel; **~ able**, gesellig; **~ ableness**, geselligheid; kameraadskaplikheid; **~ ate marriage**, proefhuwelik; **~ flange**, begeleidingsflens; **~ hatch**, luikdeur; **~ -in-arms**, wapenbroer; **~ -ladder**, kampanjeleer; kajuittrap; **~ less**, alleen, onvergesel; sonder kameraad; **~ picture**, teenhanger; **~ piece**, teenstuk; maatstuk; **~ set**, vuurysterstel; **~ ship**, geselskap; kameraadskap; **~ -way**, kajuittrap.
com'pany, (n) (..nies), geselskap; aanspraak; gaste; bemanning, vendel (soldate); maatskappy, kompan(j)ie; mense; omgang; gilde; toneelgeselskap; *BAD ~*, slegte maats; *BEAR ~*, geselskap hou; *~ in DISTRESS makes sorrow less*, gedeelde smart is halwe smart (gedeelde vreugde is dubbele vreugde); *in GOOD ~*, in goeie geselskap; *HAVE ~*, gaste hê; *IN ~*, in geselskap; *one is JUDGED by the ~ one keeps*, waar jy mee verkeer, word jy mee geëer; *KEEP ~ with*, omgaan met; gesels met; vry na; vergesel; *a man is KNOWN by the ~ he keeps*, sê my wie is jou vriende en ek sal jou sê wie jy is; *'n mens word aan sy vriende geken*; *~ MANNERS*, gemanierdheid; *PART ~*, vanmekaar gaan; *PRESENT ~ excluded*, alle aanwesiges uitgesluit; *SUBSIDIARY ~*, dogtermaatskappy; *TWO is ~, three is none*, twee is 'n paar, drie onpaar; (v) (..nied), omgaan met.
com'parable, vergelykbaar; *not ~ to*, nie te vergelyk nie met.
compa'rative, (n) vergrotende trap; (a) vergelykend; vergelykbaar; betreklik; **~ degree**, vergrotende trap; **~ ly**, betreklik, vergelykenderwys(e); **~ standards**, vergelykbare standaarde.
compare', (n) vergelyking; *beyond ~*, onvergelyklik, sonder weerga; (v) vergelyk; gelyk wees; trappe van vergelyking gee; wedywer; gelyk word; *~ FAVOURABLY with*, goed vergelyk met; *~ NOTES*, mekaar hulle bevindings meedeel; **~ d**, vergeleke; *~ d with*, teenoor.
compa'rison, vergelyking; *there is no ~ BETWEEN them*, hulle kan nie vergelyk word nie; *BEYOND ~*, nie te vergelyk nie; *BY ~*, vergelykenderwys(e); *DEGREES of ~*, trappe van vergelyking; *DRAW a ~*, 'n vergelyking tref (maak); *IN ~ with*, vergeleke met; *MAKE a ~*, 'n vergelyking maak; *~ s are ODIOUS*, vergelykings is haatlik.
compart'ment, afdeling; vak; koepee, kompartement (trein); **~ 'alize**, kompartementaliseer, rubriseer, afhok; **~ aliza'tion**, kompartementalisering, rubrisering, afhokking.
com'pass, (n) ruimte, bestek; grens, gebied; omweg; omtrek, omvang; (-es), kompas; *FETCH (go) a ~*, iets by die Kaap gaan haal; *POINTS of the ~*, hemelstreke; *in SMALL ~*, in klein bestek; (v) om=vat; verkry; beraam; bedink; omsluit, bevat; reg=kry, tot stand bring; rondom gaan; begryp; bereik; **~ able**, bereikbaar; **~ -base**, kompasskyf; **~ -bear=ing**, kompaspeiling; **~ -bowl**, kompasdoos; **~ -box**, (-es), kompashuisie; **~ -brick**, boogsteen; **~ -card**, kompasroos, windroos; kompaskaart; **~ correction**, kompasvasstelling, -korreksie; **~ -course**, kompaskoers; **~ deflection**, kompasuitwyking; **~ deviation**, kompasafwyking; **~ -error**, kompasfout.
com'passes: *DIVIDING ~*, verdeelpasser; *PAIR of ~*, passer; *beam ~*, standpasser; *bow ~*, veerpasser; *cal(l)iper ~*, meetpasser; *spherical ~*, holpasser; *spring ~*, veerpasser.
com'passface, kompasroos, windroos, kompasplaat.
compa'ssion, medelye, erbarming, meewarigheid, me(d)edoënheid, barmhartigheid; *have ~ on us*, wees ons barmhartig; **~ ate**, (v) medelye hê met, bejammer; (a) deelnemend, meewarig, me(d)e=doënd, medelydend; *~ ate leave*, menslikheidsver=lof, troosverlof.
com'pass: **~ -needle**, kompasnaald; **~ -pin**, kompas=pen; **~ -plane**, vellingskaaf, hobbelskaaf; **~ -point**, kompasstreek, windstreek; passerpunt; **~ -reading**, kompasstand; **~ -rose**, kompasroos, windroos; **~ -saw**, steeksaag, spitssaag, figuursaag, sirkelsaag; **~ window**, halfmaanerker; kompasglas.
compatibil'ity, bestaanbaarheid; verenigbaarheid.
compat'ible, bestaanbaar; verenigbaar; kruisbaar (bot.).
compat'riot, landgenoot.
compeer', gelyke, maat, ewknie, konfrater, portuur.
compel', (-led), verplig, noodsaak, forseer, (af)dwing; **~ lable**, verplig; afdwingbaar; **~ ling**, gebiedend, dwingend; meeslepend, onomstootlik.
compen'dious, beknop, kort, saaklik; **~ ness**, beknoptheid, saaklikheid.
compen'dium, (..dia, -s), uittreksel, kort begrip, samevatting, kompendium.
com'pensate, skadeloos stel, vergoed, goedmaak, kompenseer; opweeg (teen).
com'pensating, vergoedend; **~ -beam**, ewenaar; **~ current**, kompensasiestroom; **~ error**, balanseer=fout, teenfout; **~ -gear**, ewenaar (motor); **~ -jet**, kompensasiesproeier; **~ -magnet**, kompensasie=magneet; **~ -pendulum**, kompensasieslinger; **~ -valve**, kompenseerklep; **~ -wave**, rusgolf.
compensa'tion, vergoeding, kompensasie, skadeloos=stelling; **~ al**, skadeloosstellend, kompenserend; **~ pendulum**, kompensasieslinger.
compen'sative, vergoedend; neutraliserend.
com'pensator, vergoeder, skadeloossteller; ewenaar (werktuigkunde).
com'père, (n) opsteller; aankondiger, compère, sere=moniemeester; (v) opstel; aankondig.
compete', meestry, wedywer, (mee)ding.
com'petence, com'petency, bevoegdheid, geskikt=heid; genoegsaamheid; regsbevoegdheid, kompe=tensie (reg); welgesteldheid, gegoedheid.
com'petent, bevoeg, bekwaam, geskik, gepas, toerei=kend.
competi'tion, mededinging, wedywer; kompetisie, wedstryd; prysvraag.
compet'itive, mededingend; konkurrerend; vergely=kend (eksamen); *~ price*, me(d)edingende prys; konkurrerende prys; **~ spirit**, wedywering.
compet'itor, mededinger, deelnemer.
compila'tion, versameling, kompilasie, samestelling; *~ work*, kompilasiewerk.
compile', saamstel, bymekaarmaak, versamel; opstel; kompileer; bymekaarslaan, aanteken (krieket); **~ r**, versamelaar, kompilator; bewerker, samestel=ler; slaner (krieket).
compla'cence, compla'cency, selftevredenheid, wel=behae, selfvoldoening, welbehaaglikheid.
compla'cent, selftevrede, (self)voldaan, welbehaaglik.
complain', kla; beklaag; *I can't ~*, ek kan nie kla nie; ek het niks te kla nie; **~ ant**, klaer, eiser, aanklaer; **~ er**, klaer; **~ ing**, (n) gekla(ag); (a) klaerig, klaend; **~ t'**, (be)klag; kwaal, ongesteldheid; beskuldiging; beswaarskrif; *~ ts book*, klagteboek.
complais'ance, voorkomendheid; inskiklikheid, tegemoetkomendheid; hoflikheid, beleefdheid; onbe=kommerdheid.
complaisant', inskiklik; voorkomend; beleef, hoflik; onbekommerd.

complement 797 *compromise*

com'plement, (n) aanvulling, aanvulsel, byvoegsel, komplement; voleindiging; vol getal, sterkte, bemanning; ~ *of OFFICERS*, offisiersterkte.
com'plement, (v) aanvul, byvoeg, voltallig maak.
complemen'tal, aanvullend.
complemen'tary, aanvullend, aanvullings-, komplementêr; ~ **angle,** aanvullingshoek; ~ **colour(s),** komplementêre kleur(e), aanvullingskleur(e).
complete', (v) voltooi, klaar maak; voltallig maak, aanvul; afdoen, afrond, voleindig, afwerk; (a) volkome; totaal, volslae; volledig; voltallig; volmaak; (ge)heel, kompleet; ~ *CIRCUIT*, voltooide baan; ~ *LOAD*, volle belasting (elektr.); vol vrag; ~ *OVERHAUL*, algehele opknapping; ~ *ROUND*, volledige ammunisie; ~ *STRANGER*, wildvreemde; ~ *UNIFORM*, volle uniform; ~**ly,** volkome, volslae, totaal, heeltemal, glattendal, ten volle, ten ene male; ~**ness,** volledigheid, voltalligheid; volmaaktheid.
comple'tion, voltooiing, afwerking; aanvulling.
complet'ive, aanvullend.
com'plex, (n) (-es), samestel, geheel; kompleks; (a) saamgestel(d), ingewikkeld; gekompliseer(d); ~ *fraction*, saamgestelde breuk; ~ *sentence*, saamgestelde sin.
comple'xion, gelaatskleur, huidkleur; aansien, voorkome; aard; *that puts another* ~ *on the matter*, dit gee die saak 'n ander aansien; ~**less,** kleurloos.
complex'ity, (..ties), ingewikkeldheid, samegesteldheid, gekompliseerdheid.
compli'able, buigsaam, inskiklik.
compli'ance, inskiklikheid, toegewing, inwilliging; nakoming; inagneming; ooreenstemming; *in* ~ *with*, ooreenkomstig, ingevolge.
compli'ant, inskiklik, toegewend, toegeeflik.
com'plicacy, (..cies), ingewikkeldheid.
com'plicate, (v) verwikkel; verwar; ingewikkeld maak; (a) ingewikkeld, gekompliseer(d); verward; ~**d,** ingewikkeld; verward; gekompliseerd; ~*d fracture*, saamgestelde breuk.
complica'tion, verwikkeling, ingewikkeldheid; verwarring, komplikasie.
compli'city, medepligtigheid.
compli'er, onderdanige persoon, jabroer.
com'pliment, (n) pligpleging, kompliment; pluimpie, beleefdheid; (pl) groetnis; beleefdheidsbetuiging; *with the AUTHOR'S* ~*s*, met die komplimente van die skrywer; *MY* ~*s to*, groete aan; *be PAID a* ~, 'n pluimpie kry; *PAY one's* ~*s*, pligplegings waarneem; sy opwagting maak; *RETURN the* ~, 'n guns met 'n guns vergeld; *the* ~*s of the SEASON*, geseënde Kersfees en voorspoedige Nuwe Jaar, Kers- en Nuwejaarsgroete; *SHOWER* ~*s on someone*, iem. bewierook; *pay SOMEONE a* ~, iem. 'n pluimpie gee.
com'pliment, (v) gelukwens, komplimenteer; 'n kompliment maak; *be* ~*ed*, 'n pluimpie kry
complimen'tary, gelukwensend; groetend; wellewend, vleiend; vry (kaartjie, boek); ~ **copy,** komplimentêre eksemplaar; presenteksemplaar; ~ **ticket,** komplimentêre kaartjie, vrykaartjie.
complimen'ter, komplimenteerder, komplimentmaker.
com'pline, kompletorium (R.K.), kerklike aandgebed.
comply', (..lied), nakom, inwillig, toestem; ~ *with*, voldoen aan, toestem in; ~**ing,** inskiklik.
compon'ent, (n) bestanddeel, onderdeel; (a) samestellend; ~ **part,** bestanddeel.
comport', gedra; ~ *with*, ooreenstem met; ~**ment,** gedrag, houding, optrede.
compose', (saam)stel; opstel, skryf; toonset, komponeer, set (drukwerk); kalmeer; bylê (geskil); tot rus bring; ~ *oneself*, bedaar.
compo'sed, kalm, bedaard, besadig, geset (drukkery); *be* ~ *of*, bestaan uit; ~**ly,** kalm, rustig; ~**ness,** kalmte.
compo'ser, toonsetter, komponis, toondigter; samesteller; opsteller; lettersetter.
compo'sing, samestelling; vervaardiging; ~ **frame,** setraam; ~-**machine,** setmasjien; ~-**rule,** setlyn; ~-**stick,** sethaak, letterhaak.

Compo'sitae, Compositae.
com'posite, (n) mengsel, samestelling; (a) saamgestel(d), gemeng; deelbaar; ~ **carriage,** gemengde spoorwa; ~ **column,** gemengde kolonne; ~ **construction,** mengbou; ~ **flower,** saamgestelde blom; ~ **number,** deelbare getal; ~ **photograph,** saamgestelde foto.
composi'tion, samestelling; geskrif, opstel; toonsetting, rangskikking, komposisie (musiek); aard, formasie, konstruksie; geaardheid; akkoord (reg); sas (plofstof); vergelyk, ooreenkoms, skikking; afkoping; set(tery), setwerk; ~ **al,** komposisioneel, kompositories; ~ **exercise,** styloefening, opstel; ~ **fuse,** dryfsas.
compos'itive, samestellend.
compos'itor, (letter)setter, vormopmaker.
com'pos men'tis, compos mentis, by sy volle verstand; *non* ~, mal, van sy verstand af, non compos mentis.
com'post, (n) mengsel; kompos; (v) kompos maak.
compo'sure, kalmte, bedaardheid, besadigdheid.
compota'tion, saamdrinkery, fuif.
com'pote, ingelegde (gestoofde) vrugte, compote.
com'pound¹, (n) mynkamp, kampong.
com'pound², (n) samestelling, mengsel; verbinding; (v) saamstel, inmekaarsit; verenig; belê, vereffen; 'n skikking maak; saamvoeg, vermeng; 'n vergelyk tref; ~ *a CRIME*, 'n misdaad afkoop; ~ *a DEBT*, 'n skuld verminder kry; ~ *with the DEVIL*, 'n ooreenkoms met die duiwel aangaan; ~ *for SINS*, sondes afkoop; (a) saamgestel(d); ~ **addition,** optelling met ongelyke breuke; ~ **beam,** saamgestelde balk; ~ **cal(l)ipers,** kombinasiepasser; - **dynamo,** gemengde dinamo; ~**ed,** saamgestel; ~**ed oil,** saamgestelde olie; ~**er,** menger; bemiddelaar; vereffenaar; ~ **eye,** saamgestelde oog, fasetoog; ~ **fraction,** samegestelde breuk; ~ **fracture,** saamgestelde breuk; ~ **interest,** saamgestelde rente; ~ **pendulum,** saamgestelde slinger; ~ **roof,** wolweentdak; ~ **sentence,** saamgestelde sin; ~ **word,** samestelling.
comprehend', verstaan, snap, begryp; omvat, insluit, bevat; ~**er,** verstaner, begryper.
comprehensibil'ity, verstaanbaarheid, bevatlikheid.
comprehen'sible, verstaanbaar, begryplik, bevatlik.
comprehen'sion, bevatting, begrip; omvang, omvatting; bevatlikheid; *above my* ~, bo(kant) my vuurmaakplek; ~ **test,** begripstoets.
comprehen'sive, (veel)omvattend, omvangryk, allesomvattend, uitgebreid; verstands-; ~**ness,** veelomvattendheid, uitgebreidheid; vlugheid van begrip.
com'press, (n) kompres; (nat) doek, omslag.
compress', (v) saamdruk, saampers, verdig, saamknyp, saamvat; ~**ed,** ineengedronge, verdig; ~*ed AIR*, saamgeperste lug, druklug; ~*ed GAS*, drukgas; ~*ed YEAST*, geperste suurdeeg; ~**ibil'ity,** samedrukbaarheid, samevatbaarheid; ~**ible,** saamdrukbaar; ~**ing rod,** spanstaaf, drukstaaf.
compre'ssion, samedrukking, kompressie; persing; verdigting, druk; beknoptheid; ~ *of the earth*, afplatting v.d. aarde; ~ **beam,** drukbalk; ~ **chamber,** kompressiekamer; ~ **leg,** veerstyl (lugv.); ~ **member,** drukstaaf; ~ **pump,** perspomp; ~ **reinforcement,** druk(be)wapening; ~ **rib,** drukrib; ~ **rod,** drukstang; ~ **strain,** drukbelasting; ~ **strength,** drukvastheid; drukstertke; ~ **stress,** drukspanning; ~ **stroke,** drukslag; ~ **strut,** veerstyl; ~ **valve,** drukklep; ~ **wood,** pershout.
compress': ~**ive,** saamdrukkend, saampersend; ~**ive strength,** drukvastheid; druksterkte; ~**ive stress,** drukspanning.
compress'or, saamdrukkende spier; samedrukker; kompressor; *air* ~, lugperspomp; ~-**drill,** lugdrukboor.
compris'al, insluiting.
comprise', bevat, omvat, insluit; beslaan; bestaan uit.
compris'ing, bevattende; bestaande uit.
com'promise, (n) ooreenkoms, vergelyk, dading (juridies), skikking, kompromis, kompromie; tussending; (v) skik, bylê; ooreenkom; 'n kompromie (kompromie) aangaan, tegemoetkom; kompromit-

comptometer

teer, in opspraak bring, blootstel; tot 'n vergelyk kom; ~ **r**, skikker.
comptom'eter, rekenmasjien.
comptroll'er, *kyk* **controller**.
compul'sion, dwang, nooddwang, dwingery, geweld; *upon (under)* ~, (nood)gedwonge.
compul'sive, dwingend, gedwonge; ~ *DRINKER*, gewoontedrinker; ~ *EATER*, eetslaaf; ~ *INSANITY*, dwangwaansin; ~ *NEUROSIS*, dwangneurose.
compul'sory, gedwonge, onvrywillig, verpligtend; dwang=; verplig; ~ **attendance**, leerdwang, verpligte skoolbesoek; ~ **education**, skoolplig, leerplig, verpligte onderwys; ~ **labour**, gedwonge arbeid; ~ **service**, diensplig; ~ **stop**, verpligte stilhou; verpligte stilhouplek; ~ **subject**, druipvak; ~ **voting**, stemdwang.
compunc'tion, wroeging, gewetensknaging, spyt, berou.
compunc'tious, berouvol, berouhebbend.
com'purgator, eedhelper.
computabil'ity, berekenbaarheid.
comput'able, berekenbaar, skatbaar.
computa'tion, berekening, skatting, raming.
computa'tor, *kyk* **computer**.
compute', bereken, uitreken, besyfer; begroot, skat.
compu'ter, rekenaar; rekenoutomaat; syferrekenaar; ~ **science**, rekenaarwetenskap; ~ **service**, rekenaardiens; ~ **term**, rekenaarterm.
compu'terize, rekenariseer.
compu'ting, (be)rekening; ~ **list**, rekenaarlys; ~ **machine**, rekenmasjien; ~ **scale**, berekeningskaal.
com'rade, maat, mieta, genant, makker, kameraad; spitsbroer; ~**-in-arms**, wapenbroer; ~**ship**, kameraadskap, kameraderie, maatskap.
com'sat, komsat, kommunikasiesatelliet.
con¹, (n): *pros and* ~*s*, die voor- en nadele.
con², (v) **(-ned)**, bestudeer; uit die kop leer.
con³, (v) **(-ned)**, bestuur (skip).
con⁴, (v) bedrieg, kul, verneuk.
con⁵, (prep) met; teen.
con amo're, (It., mus.), con amore, toegewy, met toewyding.
cona'tion, strewe.
con'ative, wils=, konatief.
con bri'o, (It., mus.), con brio, met geesdrif, geesdriftig.
concat'enate, aaneenskakel, skakel, aanmekaarskakel.
concatena'tion, aaneenskakeling, skakeling.
conc'ave, (n) holte; gewelf; (a) konkaaf, hol(rond); ~ **joint**, holvoeg; ~ **saw**, holsaag.
concav'ity, (..ties), holte, holheid.
concav'o-con'cave, bikonkaaf, dubbelhol, dubbelkonkaaf.
concav'o-con'vex, holrond-bolrond, konkaaf-konveks, holbol.
conceal', wegsteek, wegstop; bewimpel; versteek, verberg; verheel, geheim hou; verswyg; ~*ed lighting*, skuilverligting; ~**able**, verbergbaar; ~**ed**, verborge; ~*ed drive(way)*, verborge (verskuilde) oprit (inrit); ~**ed road**, verborge pad; ~**er**, wegsteker, verbloemer, verheler; ~**ment**, verheling, verberging, agterhouding; verheim(e)liking, geheimhouding; skuilplek; *place of* ~*ment*, wegkruipplek.
concede', toestem, toegee, inwillig, toestaan; ~ *the point (victory)*, dit gewonne gee.
conceit', waan, verwaandheid, aanstellerigheid, ydelheid, wysneusigheid, inbeelding, verbeelding; bogtery, gier; *out of* ~, ontevrede.
conceit'ed, verwaand, eiewys, ydel, wysneusig, laatdunkend, nuffig, waanwys, trots; *BE* ~, aanstellerig wees; ~ *GIRL*, verwaande meisie, nuffie; ~**ness**, verwaandheid, waanwysheid, aanstellings, eiewaan, eiewysheid.
conceiv'able, denkbaar, versinbaar, begryplik.
conceivabil'ity, denkbaarheid.
conceiv'ably, moontlik, denklik.
conceive', begryp, denkbeeld vorm; bedink; uitdink; opvat; swanger raak (word); ~ *OF*,'n begrip vorm van; ~ *ed in SIN*, in sonde ontvang(e).
conce'lebrate, (die mis) saamlees, konselebreer (R.K.).

conciliator

con'centrate, (n) konsentraat; pitkos, kragvoer; (v) konsentreer, versterk, saamtrek, bymekaartrek (troepe); ~ *on*, jou toelê op; ~**d**, gekonsentreerd; kragtig, ingespanne; versadig.
con'centrates, kragvoer, pitkos.
concentra'tion, vereniging, sametrek(king), konsentrasie; ~ *of troops*, troepesametrekking; ~ **camp**, konsentrasiekamp; vrouekamp (hist.).
con'centrator, konsentreerder, konsentrator.
concen'tre, konsentreer, verenig.
concen'tric, konsentries, eenmiddelpuntig; gelykmiddelpuntig; ~ **cable**, ringkabel; ~**'ity**, konsentrisiteit.
con'cept, ontwerp; konsep, begrip, denkbeeld, idee; konsepsie; ~**'acle**, vrugholte.
concep'tion, voorstelling, begrip, benul, opvatting, gedagte; bevatting; ontvangenis, bevrugting.
concep'tive, begrips=; bevattings=; konsepsioneel; ontvanklik.
concep'tual, konsepsioneel, begrips=, voorstellings=; ~**ism**, konseptualisme.
concern', (n) onderneming; belang; deelneming; sorg, besorgdheid; betrekking; saak (handel); geld; aangeleentheid; aandeel; *with DEEP* ~, met groot besorgdheid; *FLOURISHING* ~, bloeiende saak; *GOING* ~, saak in bedryf, gevestigde saak; *HAVE a* ~ *in*, geïnteresseer(d) wees in; belang hê by; *I HAVE no* ~ *with it*, ek het daar niks mee te maak nie; *it is no* ~ *of MINE*, daar het ek vrede mee; ek soek nie wat ek nie verloor het nie; *of NO* ~, van min (geen) belang; *it is his OWN* ~, dis sy eie saak; *the WHOLE* ~, die hele saak; *it is no* ~ *of YOURS*, dit gaan jou nie aan nie; dit traak jou nie; (v) betref; aangaan; aanbelang, aanbetref; raak; verontrus; *it DOES not* ~ *me*, dit raak my nie; dit het geen betrekking op my nie; ~ *ONESELF*, jou bekommer; jou bemoei; *to WHOM it may* ~, wie dit mag aangaan.
concerned', betrokke; belangstellend; gemoeid, besorg; *ALL (everyone)* ~, alle belanghebbendes; wie dit ook al raak; *be* ~ *AT*, jammer (besorg) wees oor; *BE* ~ *in*, betrokke wees in (by); ~ *for his SAFETY*, besorg oor sy veiligheid; ~**ly**, bekommerd, met kommer.
concern': ~**ing**, rakende, aangaande, nopens, betreffende; belangende; ~**ment**, saak; aangeleentheid; belang, gewig; aandeel; betrekking; besorgdheid.
con'cert, (n) ooreenstemming; samewerking; konsert; *work in* ~, goed saamwerk.
concert', (v) ooreenkom; beraadslaag; skik; oorlê; ~**ed**, beraam; geskik; gesamentlik; ~*ed action*, gesamentlike optrede, vooraf beraamde stap(pe).
con'cert-goer, konsertganger, konsertbesoeker.
con'cert grand, groot vleuelklavier, konsertvleuel, konsertpiano.
con'cert hall, konsertsaal, konsertgebou.
concerti'na, konsertina, trekorrel; ~ **crash**, konsertinabotsing.
concertin'o, (It. mus.), concertino.
con'cert master, konsertmeester.
concert'o, concerto, konsert; ~ **grosso**, (It., mus.), concerto grosso.
con'cert: ~ **pitch**, orkestoon(hoogte); gereedheid; slagvaardigheid; ~ **tour**, konsertreis.
conce'ssion, toegewing, inwilliging, konsessie, vergunning; *make a* ~, 'n toegewing doen; tot iets inwillig; ~**ary**, konsessie-; ~ **(n)aire'**, konsessionaris, begunstigde; ~**-ticket**, konsessiekaartjie.
concess'ive, toegewend, konsessief.
conch, skulpdier; seeskulp; trompetskulp; ~**a**, oorskulp; ~**if'erous**, skulpdraend; ~**iform**, skulpvormig; ~**oid'**, skulpkromme, kongoïde; ~**oi'dal**, skulpvormig, kongoïdaal; ~**ol'ogy**, skulpkunde.
con'chie, con'chy, (conchies), (sl.), diensweieraar.
con'cierge, deurwagter, opsigter; concierge.
concil'iate, versoen; bevredig; win vir, paai, oorhaal; uit die weg ruim.
concilia'tion, versoening, konsiliasie, bevrediging; ~ **board**, versoeningsraad.
concil'iative, versoenend, bemiddelend.
concil'iator, bemiddelaar, versoener; ~**y**, versoenend, bemiddelend.

concinnity 799 conduct

concinn'ity, sierlikheid, verfyning, swier (van styl).
concise', kort, bondig, beknop, kernagtig; saaklik; ~**ness**, kortheid, bondigheid, beknoptheid.
conci'sion, afsnyding, besnoeiing; besnydenis; verminking; beknoptheid, bondigheid.
conc'lave, geheime vergadering; kardinaalsvergadering; konklaaf; *in (secret)* ~, in geheime sitting.
conclude', besluit, beslis; aflei, opmaak; 'n gevolgtrekking maak; afsluit, eindig, beëindig; sluit (toespraak); ~**d**, geëindig; afgelei; gesluit; geslote (verdrag); beslis; *to be* ~*d*, slot volg.
conclud'ing, laaste; ~ *verse*, slotvers.
conclu'sion, besluit, slotsom; sluiting; gevolgtrekking, konklusie; afloop, einde, end, slot; *COME to the* ~, tot die slotsom kom; *DRAW the* ~, die gevolgtrekking maak; *a FOREGONE* ~, 'n uitgemaakte saak; *IN* ~, ten besluite, ter afsluiting van; ten slotte; *JUMP to* ~*s*, sonder meer aanvaar; *TRY* ~*s with*, jou kragte meet met.
conclu'sive, oortuigend, beslissend, afdoende; ~ *ARGUMENT*, magspreuk; ~ *PROOF*, afdoende bewys; ~**ness**, afdoendheid, bewyskrag.
concoct', beraam, smee; brou, saamkook; saamflans; uitbroei, versin, opmaak, bekonkel, bekook; berei; ~**ion**, fabrikasie, versinsel, verdigsel; brousel; gebrou.
concom'itance, concom'itancy, gelyktydige bestaan, koëksistensie, konkomitansie.
concom'itant, (n) metgesel; meegaande verskynsel; (a) vergesellend, bykomend, wat gepaard gaan met, konkomitant, samegaande; ~ *circumstances*, saamgaande (bykomende) omstandighede.
con'cord, eendrag; ooreenstemming, harmonie; kongruensie; *rules of* ~, kongruensiereëls; ~'**ance**, ooreenkoms; ooreenstemming; gelyktonigheid; konkordansie (boek); ~**ant**, ooreenstemmend, saamstemmend, gelyktonig, gelykluidend, harmonies; konkordant; ~'**at**, konkordaat, verdrag, ooreenkoms; ~**ial**, eensgesind, harmonies.
con'course, samestroming, toeloop; menigte; binneplein, hal, konjunksie (astr.).
concres'cense, samegroeiing.
concres'cent, samegroeiend.
con'crete, (n) beton; *BOUND* ~, omwikkelde beton; *IN the* ~, in werklikheid; *PRESTRESSED* ~, spanbeton; *REINFORCED* ~, gewapende beton; (a) konkreet; vas, tasbaar; kompak.
concrete', (v) tot een massa vorm, stol; met beton bewerk, vassit; betonneer.
conc'rete: ~ **bed**, betonbed; ~ **jungle**, betonoerwoud, stadsoerwoud; ~ **mixer**, betonmenger; ~ **music**, konkrete musiek; ~ **nail**, muurspyker; ~ **noun**, konkrete selfstandige naamwoord; ~ **number**, benoemde (konkrete) getal; · **paint**, sementverf; ~ **poetry**, konkrete poësie; ~ **road**, betonpad; ~ **stone**, betonklip.
concre'tion, vasworming, verharding; saamgroeiing, stolling; vaste massa; aansetsel, aanpaksel.
concub'inage, konkubinaat; onwettige saamwoning, buite-egtelike saamlewing; bywywery.
conc'ubine, bywyf, hysit, byvrou, houvrou.
concup'iscence, seksuele lus, wellus, wulpsheid, ontug; wêreldgesindheid (N.T.); vleeslikheid; seksualiteit.
concup'iscent, wellustig, ontugtig, wulps, seksbelustig.
concur', (-red), saamval; meewerk; ooreenkom, instem, akkoord gaan met; ~ *in a JUDG(E)MENT*, 'n uitspraak onderskryf; ~ *with a PERSON*, met iem. saamstem; ~ *WITH*, nasê; ~**rence**, instemming, ooreenkoms, medewerking; ~*rence of lines*, sameloping van lyne; ~**rency**, vereniging, samewerking; ~**rent**, (n) meewerkende oorsaak; (a) parallel lopend; konkurrent; gelyktydig.
concuss', skok, skud; intimideer.
concu'ssion, skok, botsing, skudding; ~ *of the brain*, harsingskudding.
concu'ssion: ~ **break**, ~ **fracture**, slagbreuk (buiteband).
condemn', veroordeel; afkeur; berispe; (ver)doem, skuldig verklaar; ~ *to death*, tot die dood veroordeel; ~**able**, laakbaar, afkeurenswaardig, doemwaardig; skuldig; ~**a'tion**, veroordeling; verwerping, afkeuring; vonnis; ~**atory**, veroordelend; afkeurend; ~**ed**, (n) veroordeelde; (a) skuldig; veroordeel; afgekeur; ~*ed CELL*, dodesel; ~*ed PERSON*, veroordeelde; ~**er**, veroordelaar.
condensabil'ity, verdigbaarheid; kondenseerbaarheid.
condens'able, verdikbaar, verdigbaar; kondenseerbaar.
condens'ate, kondensaat.
condensa'tion, kondensasie; verdigting; samepersing; bekorting; verdikking; ~ **point**, verdigtingspunt.
condense', kondenseer, verdig, verdik; saampers; saamvat; verkort; ~**d**, ineengedronge; gekondenseer; saamgevat; verkort; ~*d book*, verkorte boek; ~*d milk*, blikkiesmelk, gekondenseerde melk, kondensmelk.
conden'ser, verdikker; kondensator (elek.); koeler; verdigter, kondensor (stoom); ~ **lens**, kondensorlens, versamellens; ~ **microphone**, kapasitormikrofoon; ~ **motor**, kondensatormotor; ~**y**, blikkiesmelkfabriek.
conden'sing, samevatting; verkorting; verdikking; kondensasie, kondensering; ~ **agent**, kondenseermiddel; · **coil**, koelpyp; ~ **surface**, kondenseervlak.
condescend', jou verwerdig, afdaal tot, neerbuig; jou inlaat met (jou minderes); ~**ing**, neerbuigend; minsaam.
condescen'sion, afdaling, verwerdiging; neerbuiging; minsaamheid; neerbuigendheid.
condign', verdiend; afdoende, genoegsame; ~ *punishment*, verdiende straf; afdoende straf.
con'diment, kruiery, spesery, smaakmiddel.
condi'tion, (n) voorwaarde, stipulasie; stand; gesteldheid, toestand, kondisie; beding(ing); *CHANGE one's* ~, in die huwelik tree; ~ *of EQUILIBRIUM*, ewewigstoestand; *under EXISTING* ~*s*, onder bestaande omstandighede; *in GOOD* ~, blink verhaar (by diere); in goeie toestand; ~*s of LIVING*, lewenstoestande; *ON* ~ *that*, op voorwaarde dat; *in POOR* ~, verpot; ~*s of SERVICE*, diensvoorwaardes; (v) bepaal; voorwaardes maak; gewoond maak; kondisioneer; in kondisie bring; aanklam (tabak); *BECOME* ~*ed to*, gewoond raak aan; ~ *ONESELF to*, jou gewoond maak aan; ~ **al**, (n) voorwaardelike wys(e); (a) voorwaardelik, kondisioneel; ~*al selling*, koppelverkoop; ~**ed**, aangeleer, gewoond gemaak aan; gekondisioneer(d); gesteld, beding; ~*ed REFLEX*, aangeleerde (gekondisioneerde) refleks; ~**ing**, kondisionering, voorbereiding; vogbepaling (wol); ~**ing cellar**, aanklamkelder.
condol'atory, kondolerend, mee(ge)voelend, simpatiek, vol roubeklag, kondoleansie-; ~ **letter**, brief van deelneming.
condole', simpatie betuig, saamtreur, betreur, beklaag, kondoleer.
condol'ence, roubeklag, simpatiebetuiging; *motion of* ~, mosie van roubeklag.
condol'ent, meetreurend.
condol'er, kondoleerder.
con'dom, kondoom, voorbehoedmiddel.
condomi'nium, kondominium; meenthuisblok; deelgebou, deeleiendom.
condo'nable, verskoonbaar, vergeeflik.
condona'tion, vergifnis, kwytskelding, verskoning, kondonasie.
condone', vergewe, kwytskeld; deur die vingers sien, kondoneer; ~**ment** = **condonation**.
con'dor, kondor, Suid-Amerikaanse aasvoël.
condottie're, (It.) condottiere, huurleier (hist.).
conduce', lei, strek (tot); bydra tot.
condu'cible, bevorderlik, nuttig, diensig.
condu'cive, bevorderlik, diensig; ~**ness**, diensigheid, bevorderlikheid.
con'duct, (n) gedrag; optrede, handeling, handelwyse; wandel; leiding; houding; geleide; beheer; *GOOD (bad)* ~, goeie (slegte) gedrag; *SAFE* ~, vry geleide.
conduct', (v) lei, aanvoer (aanval); hou (winkel); drywe (sake); behartig, bestuur; gedra; afneem (eksa-

men); aflei, gelei (elektr.); voer (proses); dirigeer; ~ an *ATTACK,* 'n aanval lei; ~ an *EXAMINATION,* 'n eksamen afneem; ~ an *INQUIRY,* 'n ondersoek instel; ~ an *ORCHESTRA,* 'n orkes dirigeer; ~ *oneself WELL,* jou goed gedra; ~ **ance,** geleibaarheid, konduktansie.
con'duct book, gedragboek.
conduct': ~ **ed,** gelei, begelei; ~ **ibil'ity,** geleibaarheid; ~ **ible,** geleibaar.
conduc'ting tissue, geleidingsweefsel.
conduc'ting wire, geleiding, geleidraad.
conduc'tion, geleiding, konduksie.
conduc'tive, geleidend.
conductiv'ity, geleidingsvermoë, geleibaarheid.
con'duct money, getuiegeld.
conduc'tor[1], weerligafleier, bliksemafleier; kondukteur; bestuurder; leier, gids; orkesmeester; (orkes)dirigent; kapelmeester.
conduc'tor[2], oorbringer, geleier; geleidraad (elektr.); *bad* ~ *of heat,* swak (slegte) warmtegeleier.
conduc'tor: ~ **'s baton,** dirigeerstok; ~ **ship,** leiding; dirigering; dirigentskap.
conduc'tress, (-es), bestuurderes, direktrise; geleister; leidsvrou; orkesleidster; konduktrise.
con'duit, (lei)pyp, geleiding, waterleiding, buis.
condup'licate, in die lengte gevou (plantk.).
con'dyle, gewrigsknobbel.
Con'dy's crys'tals, natriumpermanganaat.
cone, horing, horinkie (vir roomys); kegel, keël; dennebol; konus; tregter; ~ *of light,* ligkeël; ~ **-bearer,** keëldraer; ~ **bearing,** (n) keëllaer; (a) keëldraend; ~ **-bearing tree,** keëldraende boom; ~ **drawing,** keëlafdunning; ~ **joint,** keëlverbinding; ~ **pulley,** koniese skyf; ~ **-section,** keëldeursnee; ~ **-shaped,** keëlvormig; ~ **wheel,** koniese rat.
con'ey = cony.
confab', confab'ulate, keuwel, praat, babbel, gesels; konsistorie hou, met mekaar oorlê.
confabula'tion, praatjie, gebabbel, geselsery; oorleg.
confab'ulatory, pratend, babbelend.
confec'tion[1], (n) vervaardiging; die meng, aanmaak; klaargemaakte klerasie; (v) berei, maak.
confec'tion[2], (n) banket, suikergoed; lekkergoed.
confec'tionary[1], (n) lekkergoed.
confec'tionary[2], (a) klaargemaak, klaargekoop.
confec'tioner, koekbakker, suikerbakker, banketbakker; lekkergoedmaker, ~ **y,** suikerbakkery; soetgebak, banket, suikergoed; lekkers, lekkergoed; ~ **y shop,** lekkergoedwinkel.
confed'eracy, (..cies), verbond; konfederasie; bondgenootskap; komplot.
confed'erate, (n) bondgenoot, eedgenoot, medepligtige; (v) 'n verbond aangaan; (a) verbonde.
confedera'tion, konfederasie; (ver)bond; bondgenootskap; ~ *of labour,* vakverbond.
confer'[1]**, (-red),** beraadslaag, ruggespraak hou; ~ *together,* beraadslaag.
confer'[2], verleen, toeken (graad); opdra; ~ *a degree,* 'n graad toeken.
conferee', persoon met wie geraadpleeg word, geraadpleegde; konferensieganger.
con'ference, onderhoud, gesprek; beraadslaging; samespreking, konferensie, byeenkoms; *the* ~ *table,* die groen tafel; konferensietafel; ~ **hall,** vergadersaal, konferensiesaal; ~ **room,** vergaderkamer, konferensiekamer.
confer'er[1], beraadslaer.
confer'er[2], verlener, toekenner.
confer'ment, toekenning, verlening.
confess', bely, beken, erken; bieg; die bieg afneem; getuig; ~ *sins,* bieg, sonde bely; ~ **ant,** biegteling, biegkind; ~ **ed,** erken, onteenseglik; erkende; ~ **edly,** onteenseglik; soos algemeen bekend; volgens eie getuienis.
confe'ssion, bekentenis; belydenis, bieg; erkenning; ~ *of FAITH,* geloofsbelydenis; ~ *of GUILT,* skuldbekentenis; *OPEN* ~ *is good for the soul,* liewer bieg as lieg; ~ **al,** (n) biegstoel; (a) belydenis-, konfessioneel; ~ **ary,** belydend; bieg-; ~ **novel,** biegroman.
confess'or, belyer; biegvader.
confetti'i, confetti.

confidant', vertroueling, vertroude; vertrouensman, boesemvriend.
confidante', vertroude, boesemvriendin.
confide', vertrou; toevertrou; meedeel.
con'fidence, vertroue, geloof, sekerheid, fidusie; gerustheid; selfvertroue; vrymoedigheid; oormoedigheid; vertroulike mededeling; *MATTER of* ~, vertrouensaak; *TOLD in* ~, in vertroue gesê; *VOTE of* ~, mosie van vertroue; *VOTE of no* ~, mosie van wantroue; ~ **man,** bedrieër, verneuker; ~ **motion,** mosie van vertroue (parlement); ~ **trick,** vertrouenswendel, opligtery, verneukery; ~ **trickster,** (vertrouen)swendelaar, bedrieër, verneuker.
con'fident, (n) vertroueling, vertroude; (a) vertrouend; seker, oortuig; astrant; hoopvol; vrymoedig.
confiden'tial, vertroulik, konfidensieel; geheim; ~ **clerk,** vertroude amptenaar (klerk); geheimskrywer.
confidential'ity, vertroulikheid.
confiden'tially, vertroulik, in vertroue.
confid'ing, vertroulik, vol vertroue.
configura'tion, uiterlike; gedaante, vorm; gesteldheid, formansie, konfigurasie, gestalte; planetestand.
config'ure, skik, gedaante gee; vorm.
con'fine[1], (n) grens, gebied; uiterste.
confine'[2], (v) begrens, beperk; opsluit, gevangesit; ~ *oneself to,* jou bepaal tot (by).
confined', beperk, eng, nou; gevang; *BE* ~, beval, 'n bevalling hê; *be* ~ *to the HOUSE,* nie kan uitgaan nie; huisarres hê; *be* ~ *to one's ROOM,* die kamer moet hou; ~ *SPACE,* beperkte ruimte.
confine'ment, opsluiting, gevangenskap; beperking; bevalling; ~ *to CAMP,* kamparres; ~ *to one's HOME,* huisarres; *PLACE in* ~, laat opsluit; ~ **fees,** bevallingskoste.
confirm', bevestig, bekragtig, goedkeur; versterk; bewaarheid; aanneem, as lidmaat voorstel; ~ *on oath,* besweer; met 'n eed bevestig; ~ **and,** katkisant, aanneemling.
confirma'tion, bevestiging, stawing; bekragtiging, goedkeuring; aanneming; vormsel (R.K.); ~ **candidate,** aanneemling, kategeet, katkisant; ~ **class(es),** kategese, katkisasie; ~ **dress,** voorstel(lings)rok, voorstellingstabberd; ~ **lesson,** kategeseles, katkisasie(les); ~ **service,** voorstellingsdiens.
confirm'ative, confirm'atory, bevestigend.
confirmed', beslis; verstokte; *a.* ~ *BACHELOR,* 'n verstokte oujongkêrel; *BE* ~, belydenis doen (aflê); *a* ~ *DRUNKARD,* 'n verstokte dronkaard, 'n suiplap; ~ *INVALID,* chroniese invalide.
confirmee', katkisant, aanneemling, kategeet.
confis'cable, verbeurbaar, konfiskeerbaar.
con'fiscate, verbeurd verklaar, konfiskeer, beslag lê op, in beslag neem.
confisca'tion, verbeurdverklaring, konfiskasie.
con'fiscator, verbeurdverklaarder, konfiskeerder.
confis'catory, verbeurdverklarend.
conflagra'tion, groot brand; ontbranding; oorlogsbrand.
conflate', saamsmelt.
confla'tion, samesmelting (van twee variante).
con'flict, (n) botsing, stryd, worsteling, geskil, teenstrydheid, konflik; *COME into* ~, (met mekaar) bots; *INWARD* ~, innerlike tweestryd (konflik); ~ *of LAWS,* strydigheid van regsbeginsels; *in* ~ *WITH,* in teenstryd met, strydig met.
conflict', (v) bots, worstel; in stryd wees met, indruis teen, in botsing kom; ~ **ing,** teenstrydig; ~ **ion,** teenstrydigheid, botsing.
con'fluence, sameloop, samevloeiing.
con'fluent, (n) bystroom; systroom; (a) saamvloeiend.
con'flux, samevloeiing.
conform', (v) ooreenkomstig maak; instem met; skik, hom voeg na, aanpas (by), konformeer; (a) gelykluidend (beskrywings).
conformabil'ity, gelykvormigheid; inskiklikheid; gedweeheid.
conform'able, inskiklik, plooibaar; gedwee; ooreenkomstig; gelykvormig, ooreenstemmend; konform;

ooreenkomend met; passend; ~ *to*, in ooreenstemming met; ~**ness**, *kyk* **conformability.**
conforma'tion, vorm, bou, aard; ooreenstemming, aanpassing; konformasie.
confor'mism, konformisme; meelopery.
conform'ist, konformis; lidmaat van die Engelse Staatskerk.
conform'ity, gelykvormigheid, ooreenkoms; inskiklikheid, plooibaarheid; *in* ~ *with*, ooreenkomstig.
confound', verwar; verydel, vernietig; verleë maak, beskaam maak; ~ *it!*, vervlaks! verbrands!
confound'ed, verward; oorbluf, vervloek, verduiweld, drommels, afgedankste, vervlakste; ~**ly**, skandelik, vreeslik, ellendig; verdeksels, vervlaks.
confratern'ity, broederskap; bende.
con'frère, kollega, medelid, konfrater.
confront', konfronteer, teenoor mekaar stel; te staan kom, te kampe hê met; vergelyk; ~ *a person with facts*, iem. teenoor feite stel; ~**a'tion**, teenoorstelling, konfrontasie.
Confu'cian, (n) Confuciaan; (a) Confuciaans; ~**ism**, Confucianisme.
Confu'cius, Confucius.
confuse', verwar; onthuts, dronkslaan, deurmekaar maak, verbyster; verleë maak; ontstel; ~ *the issue*, die saak vertroebel; ~**d**, verward; verleë, verboueerd, deurmekaar, onthuts, dronkgeslaan; bedremmeld, beteuterd; *BECOME* ~ *d*, onthuts (verleë) word; onklaar trap; ~ *d FLOUR-BEETLE*, malkopmeelkewer.
confus'edness, verwardheid, verwarring.
confus'ing, verwarrend; (sin)storend.
confu'sion, verwarring; verbouereerdheid, verleentheid, beskaming; warboel, wanorde, dolliewarie, dikkedensie, deurmekaarheid; rommel; ondergang, verderf; ~ *of MIND*, sinsverbystering; ~ *of TONGUES*, spraakverwarring; ~ *WORSE confounded*, chaotiese verwarring, 'n deurmekaarspul.
confut'able, weerlêbaar, weerlegbaar.
confuta'tion, weerlegging.
confute', weerlê, oortuig van dwaling.
con'ga, conga, Latyns-Amerikaanse dans; ~ **drum**, congatrom.
con'gé, ontslag; verlof, congé.
congeal', strem, stulp, stol, laat stol; bevries; hard word; dik word; ~**able**, bevriesbaar; ~**ed**, gestol; ~**ing**, stolling; ~**ing point**, stolpunt; vriespunt; ~**ment**, stremming; bevriesing; stolling; verharding.
con'gee, ryswater, water waarin rys gekook is; *kyk ook* **congé**.
congela'tion, stolling; bevriesing; bevrore toestand; verharde massa.
con'gener, (n) soortgenoot; (a) verwant, gelyksoortig.
congene'ric, gelykslagtig.
congen'erous, gelyksoortig; verwant; van dieselfde soort; saamwerkend (spiere).
congen'ial, gelyksoortig, verwant; geesverwant, simpatiek; passend, aangenaam; ~ *spirit*, geesverwant.
congenial'ity, gelyksoortigheid, gelykheid; geesverwantskap; geskiktheid.
congen'ital, aangebore, van nature, oorgeërf; ~ **defect**, aangebore (kongenitale) afwyking; ~ **idiot**, gebore idioot; ~**ly**, van geboorte af, kongenitaal.
cong'er, seepaling; ~ **eel**, seepaling.
conge'ries, (sing and pl), hoop, massa, versameling.
congest', ophoop, strem; saamdring; ophoping van bloed veroorsaak; ~**ed**, saamgedring, saamgedronge; oorbevolk; oorlaai; oorvol; met opgehoopte bloed; ~ *ed district*, oorbevolkte distrik; ~**ion**, ophoping; oorlading; kongestie; stremming; bloedstuwing; ~ *ion of traffic*, verkeersopeenhoping.
con'globate, conglobe', (v) bolvormig word; bolvormig maak; (a) bolrond, bolvormig.
conglom'erate, (n) sameklontering, konglomeraat; openhoping; (v) saamwikkel, versamel, saamklonter; openhoop; (a) saamgepak.
conglomera'tion, samepakking, ophoping, konglomerasie, massa; sameflansing.
conglu'tinate, saamlym, aaneenplak; toegroei (wond).

conglutina'tion, sameklewing, aaneenhegting.
conglut'inative, sameklewend.
Cong'o, Kongo; ~**lese'**, (n, a) Kongolees; ~ **pea**, duif-ert=jie; duiweboon *(Cajanus indicus)*.
congrat'ulate, gelukwens, felisiteer.
congratula'tion, gelukwensing, felisitasie.
congrat'ulator, gelukwenser, felisiteerder; ~**y**, gelukwensend, gelukwensings=; ~ *y letter*, felisitasie= brief, brief van gelukwensing.
cong'regate, vergader, bymekaarkom, versamel.
congrega'tion, vergadering; gemeente; versameling; kongregasie; ~**al**, gemeentelik; **C**~**alism**, Kongregasionalisme; **C**~**alist**, Kongregasionalis.
cong'ress, (-es), kongres; vergadering.
Cong'ress, Amerikaanse wetgewende liggaam, die Kongres; ~**'ional**, Kongres=; ~**man**, Kongreslid, lid v.d. Amerikaanse Kongres.
cong'ruence, cong'ruency, ooreenstemming, kongruensie, ooreenkoms; bestaanbaarheid.
cong'ruent, ooreenstemmend, saamvallend, passend, kongruent, gelyk en gelykvormig; bestaanbaar.
congru'ity, gepastheid, kongruensie.
cong'ruous, ooreenkomstig; gepas, behoorlik.
con'ic(al), kegelvormig, keëlvormig, konies; ~ *ant's nest*, tuitmiershoop; ~ **cap**, puntmus; ~ **section**, keëlsnee; ~ **sleeve**, ~ **sock**, ~ **streamer**, windkeël, windkegel; ~ **wheel**, koniese rat, keëlwiel.
co'nics, leer van die keëlsnee.
coni'dium, somerspoor, konidium, konidie.
coni'dio: ~ **phore**, lugspoordraer, konidiofoor; ~ **spore**, lugspoor, konidiospoor.
con'ifer, keëldraende gewas; naaldboom, konifeer; ~ **forest**, naaldwoud, naaldbos; ~ **tree**, naaldboom, konifeer; **C** ~ **ae**, keëldraende plante.
conif'erous, boldraend, keëldraend; ~ **tree**, naaldboom, konifeer.
con'iform, keëlvormig.
con'iine, con'ine, koneïen, koneïne.
conio'sis, koniose, stofsiekte.
conjec'turable, vermoedbaar, raaibaar.
conjec'tural, vermoedelik, na gissing.
conjec'ture, (n) vermoede, veronderstelling, gissing, raaiery; (v) vermoed, veronderstel, gis, raai.
con'jee, ryswater.
conjoin', saamvoeg; verbind, verenig; ~**ed**, verbonde; ~**t'**, verenig, verbonde; gesamentlik; toegevoeg; aangeslote; ~**t'ly**, gesamentlik, tesaam; gemeenskaplik.
con'jugal, egtelik, huweliks=; ~ **bliss**, huweliksgeluk; ~ **duty**, huweliksplig; ~ **fidelity**, huwelikstrou; ~**'ity**, egtelike staat; ~ **love**, huweliksliefde; ~ **rights**, huweliksregte.
con'jugate, (v) vervoeg; saamvlooi; gemeenskap hê; (a) verbonde; gepaard; korresponderend; verwant; ~ **angles**, aanvullende hoeke; ~**d**, vervoeg.
con'jugating, vervoegend; verbindend; ~ **tube**, konjugasiebuis.
conjuga'tion, vervoeging (gram.); verbinding; versmelting, samevloeiing; ~**al**, vervoegings=; ~ **canal**, konjugasiebuis.
conjunct', (n) byvoegsel; metgesel; (a) verenig; saamgevoeg; toegevoeg; ~**ion**, verbinding, versmelting, vereniging; sameloop; toestand; voegwoord; *in* ~ *ion with*, in verbinding met, tesame met; ~**ional**, voegwoordelik.
conjunctiv'a, bindvlies.
conjunc'tive, (n) aanvoegende (konjunktiewe) wys(e); bindwoord; (a) verbindend; byvoegend; aanvoegend; konjunktief.
conjunctivit'is, konjunktivitis, bindvliesontsteking.
conjunc'ture, sameloop (van omstandighede), krisis, tydsgewrig, konjunktuur.
conjura'tion, beswering; towerformule; goëlery.
con'jure, beswer; smeek; oproep; toor; goël; ~ *AWAY*, wegtoor; *a NAME to* ~ *with*, 'n naam wat wonders kan verrig; *conjuring TRICK*, goëltoer; ~ *UP*, oproep.
con'jurer, con'juror, geestebesweerder, goëlaar, towernaar.
con'juring, goëltoere; goëlery, toordery; ~ **trick**, goëltoer(tjie).
conk[1], (n) knopneus.

conk², (v) defek raak; ~ *out*, defek raak; bewusteloos word; uitgeput raak.
conk: ~ **er**, kastaiing; hou op die neus; ~ **y**, (n) (..**kies**), knopneus; (a) knopneus=.
con'man, (vertrouen)swendelaar, bedrieër.
conn'ate, aangebore, gelyktydig ontstaan; verwant.
conna'tural, aangebore; gelyksoortig, verwant.
connect', verbind, aaneenheg, aaneenvoeg, in verband bring; aansluit, koppel; in verbinding tree; skakel; ~ *ACROSS*, oorkruis verbind; ~ *UP*, aaneenskakel; ~ **ed**, verenig, verbonde; samehangend; aaneengeskakel; *WELL* ~ *ed*, van goeie familie; *be* ~ *ed WITH*, verwant aan; betrokke by.
connect'ing, verbindings=, verbindend; ~ **arm**, koppelarm; ~ **bolt**, koppelbout; ~ **door**, tussendeur; ~ **hose**, koppelslang; ~ **line**, verbindingslyn; ~ **link**, koppelskakel; ~ **main**, hooftoevoerdraad (-pyp); ~ **passage**, verbindingsgang; ~ **piece**, verbindingstuk; ~ **road**, verbindingspad; ~ **rod**, dryfstang, suierstang, trekstang; ~ **shaft**, koppelas; ~ **terminal**, verbindingsklem; ~ **tube**, verbindingspyp; ~ **wire**, verbindingsdraad; ~ **word**, verbindingswoord.
connec'tion, betrekking; naasbestaande, familie(betrekking); (vleeslike) gemeenskap; geleiding (elektr.); aansluiting (spoorweg); groep; klandisie; konneksie; (pl) bekendes, konneksies; verbinding, lasplek; samehang, verband; *CATCH a* ~, aansluiting kry; *in CLOSE* ~ *with*, in (noue) verband met; *IN this* ~, in verband hiermee; in hierdie verband; *POINT of* ~, aansluitpunt; ~**s**, bloedverwante, familie; konneksies, verhoudings, relasies; ~ **spring**, aansluitveer.
connec'tive, (n) verbindingswoord; helmbindsel (bot.); (a) verbindend, bind=; ~ **tissue**, bindweefsel.
connec'tor, verbinder; ~ **box**, koppelingskas; ~ **link**, koppelskakel; ~ **rod**, koppelstang; ~ **strip**, verbindstrook (battery).
conne'xion = **connection**.
con'ning: ~ **bridge**, kommandobrug; ~ **orders**, leibevele; ~ **tower**, kommandotoring, uitkyktoring.
connip'tion, (sl.), aanval van raserny, histerie; ~ **fit**, histeriese aanval.
conniv'ance, oogluikende toelating, oogluiking.
conni'vant, saamneigend.
connive', oogluikend toelaat; ~ *(at)*, oogluikend toelaat.
connoisseur', (kuns)kenner, fynproewer, connoisseur; ~ **of art**, kunskenner; ~ **of food**, koskenner, fynproewer; ~ **of wine**, wynkenner.
connota'tion, bybetekenis, konnotasie; inhoudsbepaling; gevoelswaarde (woord).
connote', insluit; (tegelyk) beteken, bybetekenis hê, konnoteer.
connub'ial, egtelik, huweliks=.
connubial'ity, egtelike staat; handeling(e) van gehudes.
con'oid, (n) konoïed, konoïde; geknotte keël; (a) keëlvormig, konies.
co'noscope, konoskoop.
con'quer, oorwin, verower, baasraak, bemagtig, verslaan, onderwerp; seëvier; *stoop to* ~, jou verlaag om jou doel te bereik; ~ **able**, oorwinlik; ~ **ed**, verslaan, oorwin; ~ *ed territory*, wingewes; ~ **or**, oorwinnaar, veroweraar.
con'quest, oorwinning, verowering, onderwerping, vermeestering; wins; *make a* ~ *(of)*, iem. se liefde (vriendskap) win.
conquis'tador, conquistador, veroweraar.
consang'uine, consanguin'eous, bloedverwant.
consanguin'ity, bloedverwantskap.
con'science, gewete, konsensie; *in ALL* ~, waarlik, seker, op my woord; *a GOOD* ~ *is a soft pillow*, wie 'n skoon gewete het, slaap rustig; 'n skoon gewete laat rustig slaap; *GUILTY* ~, skuldige gewete; *HAVE the* ~ *to*, so astrant wees om; die brutaliteit hê om; *have ON one's* ~, op sy gewete hê; *QUESTION of* ~, gewetensvraag; *a QUIET* ~ *sleeps in thunder*, wie 'n skoon gewete het, slaap soos 'n klip; 'n skoon gewete laat soos 'n klip slaap; *for* ~*'s SAKE*, gewetenshalwe; *SALVE one's* ~, jou gewete sus; ~ **clause**, gewetensklousule; ~**-keeper**,

biegvader; ~**less**, gewetenloos; ~ **money**, gewetensgeld; ~**-smitten**, ~**-stricken**, gewetensbeswaard.
conscien'tious, nougeset, konsensieus, pligsgetrou; angsvallig; ~**ness**, nougesetheid, pligsgetrouheid; ~ **objection**, gewetensbeswaar; ~ **objector**, diensweieraar (oorlog), gewetensbeswaarde.
con'scious, bewus; ~ *of GUILT*, skuldbewus; ~ *OF*, bewus van.
con'sciousness, bewustheid, bewussyn; ~ *of GUILT*, skuldbesef; *LOSE* ~, die bewussyn verloor; *REGAIN* ~, die bewussyn herwin; bykom.
conscribe', opkommandeer; beperk.
con'script, (n) ingeskrewene, dienspligtige; (a) ingeskrewe, opgekommandeer, dienspligtig.
conscript', (v) opkommandeer.
con'script fathers, vroede vadere.
conscrip'tion, konskripsie, opkommandering; inskrywing; diensplig.
con'secrate, (v) (in)wy, inseën, heilig; toewy; (a) geheilig, gewyd; ~**d**, gewyd, ingeseën; toegewy; ~*d wafer*, hostie, oblaat.
consecra'tion, wyding, inseëning; ingebruikneming (van kerk).
con'secratory, inseënend, wydend; toewydend.
consecu'tion, opeenvolging; opvolging, reeks; volgorde, samehang.
consec'utive, opeenvolgend, gereeld, volgend; gevolgaanduidend; ~**ly**, agtereenvolgens, na mekaar; onafgebroke, aaneen, aanmekaar; ~**ness**, onafgebrokenheid; ~ **number**, (ver)volgnommer.
consenes'cense, ouderdomsverval.
consen'sual, eenstemmig, konsensueel.
consen'sus, eenstemmigheid; ooreenstemming, algemene mening, konsensus; ~ *of opinion*, algemene opinie, eenstemmigheid.
consent', (n) toestemming, inwilliging, bewilliging, goedkeuring, jawoord, konsent; berusting; *AGE of* ~, ouderdom van toestemming (vir meisies); *by COMMON* ~, eenparig, eenstemmig; *GIVE* ~, toestem, konsent gee; *with ONE* ~, met algemene stemme, eenstemmig; *SILENCE gives* ~, wie swyg, stem toe; (v) toestem, inwillig, bewillig, goedkeur; toegee; ooreenstem, instem; ~ *to a request*, 'n versoek inwillig.
consentane'ity, eenparigheid, ooreenstemming; gepastheid.
consentan'eous, ooreenstemmend (met), passend (by); gepaardgaande met; eenparig; ~**ness**, ooreenstemming, gepastheid.
consen'tient, saamstemmend, instemmend, ooreenstemmend.
consent'ingly, toestemmend, inwilligend.
con'sequence, gevolg, uitvloeisel, uitwerking; belang, gewig; gevolgtrekking; gewigtigheid; konsekwensie; *IN* ~, bygevolg, dientengevolge; *IN* ~ *of*, as gevolg van; *it is of LITTLE* ~, dit beteken nie baie nie; *of NO* ~, onbelangrik, onbeduidend; van geen belang nie; *OF* ~, gewigtig; *PERSONS of* ~, vername persone; persone van gewig (gesag); *this will have SERIOUS* ~*s*, dit sal ernstige gevolge hê; dié muisie sal 'n stert hê; *TAKE the* ~*s*, die gevolge aanvaar; ly wat daarop volg.
con'sequent, (n) gevolg; sluitterm (wis.); (a) konsekwent, logies; gevolglik; (adv) gevolglik, as gevolg.
consequen'tial, volgend, daarmee gepaardgaande; gewigtig; verwaand; ~ *damage*, voortvloeiende skade.
con'sequently, gevolglik, bygevolg.
conserv'ancy, toesig, beskerming; raad van toesig; bewaargebied (bosbou).
conserva'tion, behoud, bewaring, instandhouding, konservasie; ~ *of ENERGY*, behoud van arbeidsvermoë; ~ *of HEAT*, warmtebehoud; ~ *of MATTER*, stofbehoud; ~**-farming**, bewaringsboerdery.
conserv'atism, konserwatisme, behoudendheid; behoudsug.
conserv'ative, (n) preserveermiddel; behoudsman, konserwatief; vastrapper; (a) konserwatief, behoudend; Dopperagtig; ~ **estimate**, versigtige (matige) raming; ~**ly**, op behoudende wyse; ~*ly furnished*, stemmig gemeubileer; ~**ness**, konserwatisme, behoudendheid.

conservatoire', musiekskool, konservatorium.
con'servator, bewaarder; opsigter, opsiener; ~ *of forests,* bosbewaarder.
conservator'ium, musiekskool, konservatorium.
conserv'atory, (..ries), bewaarplaas; konservatorium; broeikas, blomhuisie.
conserve', (n) ingelegde vrugte (groente); stukkonfyt, heelkonfyt; konserf; (v) bewaar; inlê; in stand hou, konserveer; ~ *the soil,* die grond bewaar.
consid'er, in ag neem; dink, skat, oorweeg, bedink (saak, besluit); beskou, in aanmerking neem; erken; ontsien; meen; *ALL things* ~*ed,* alles wel beskou, alles in aanmerking geneem; ~ *my GREY hairs,* ontsien my grys hare; *only* ~ *ONESELF,* net aan jouself dink, net jouself in ag neem; ~*ed OPINION,* weloorwoë mening; ~**able,** aanmerklik, aansienlik; flink; geruim; diskreet; aardig (som geld); ~**ably,** heelwat, aansienlik, aanmerklik.
consid'erans, doelstelling (van wet), aanhef, considerans.
consid'erate, sorgvuldig; sorgsaam, omsigtig, bedagsaam, hoflik, voorkomend, besonne; kies; ~**ness,** sorgsaamheid; oplettendheid; kiesheid; voorkomendheid; diskresie, bedagsaamheid, hoflikheid.
considera'tion, oorweging, oordenking, beraad, gedagte; aanmerking, bedenking; vergoeding, beloning, koopsom, teenprestasie; konsiderasie; bedagsaamheid; welwillendheid; agting, aansien; *after DUE* ~, na rype beraad; *FOR a* ~, om 'n beloning; *GIVE* ~ *to,* oordink, oorweeg; *IN* ~ *of,* weens; ter wille van; as teenprestasie; nademaal; *after MATURE* ~, na rype beraad; *OUT of* ~ *for,* met die oog op; ter wille van; *TAKE into* ~, in aanmerking neem; *UNDER* ~, in oorweging.
consid'ering, (aan)gesien, in aanmerking nemende; ~ *that,* gelet op die feit dat.
consign', toevertrou, in bewaring gee; onderwerp; opdra; oordra, oorlewer; toestuur, oorstuur, versend, afsend; ~ *to OBLIVION,* aan die vergetelheid prysgee; ~ *to WRITING,* op skrif bring; ~**able,** versendbaar.
consigna'tion, oordrag; toesending.
consign: ~**ed,** in bewaring gegee; ~*ed to,* geadresseer aan; ~**ee',** ontvanger, geadresseerde; agent.
consign'ment, (be)sending, afsending, versending, lading; oordrag, oorlewering; ~ **note,** laaibrief, vragbrief.
consignor', (ver)sender, afsender.
consist', bestaan, bestaanbaar wees met, saamgaan; ~ *IN,* bestaan in; ~ *OF,* bestaan uit.
consis'tence, consis'tency, digtheid; lywigheid; stewigheid; vastheid; gebondenheid; ooreenstemming; volharding, beginselvastheid; konsistensie; nie strydigheid (wisk.).
consis'tent, duursaam, bestendig, vas, stewig; steekhoudend, konsekwent; ~ *with,* verenigbaar met; ~**ly,** steekhoudend, konsekwent.
consistor'ial, konsistoriaal, kerkraads=.
consis'tory, (..ries), konsistorie; kerkraad, kerklike raad; kardinaalsvergadering.
consol'able, troosbaar.
consola'tion, troos, gerusstelling; opbeuring, vertroosting; ~ **prize,** troosprys; ~ **race,** verloordersꞏwedloop.
consol'atory, troostend, vertroostend, troos=.
con'sole¹, (n) steunstuk; konsole.
console'², (v) troos, vertroos, opbeur, bemoedig.
con'sole bracket, draagsteun; steunstuk.
consoled', getroos.
con'sole mirror, konsolespieël.
consol'er, trooster, vertrooster.
con'sole table, muurtafel.
consol'idate, stewig word, hard word; bevestig; saamgroei; konsolideer; verenig; ~ *a position,* 'n stelling verseker; ~**d,** gekonsolideer, bevestig, verseker.
consolida'tion, verdigting, konsolidasie; vaswording (van grond); vereniging, bevestiging, versterking.
consol'ing, troostend, opbeurend.
con'sols, consols (effekte v.d. Britse gekonsolideerde staatskuld).
consommé', helder sop, consommé.

con'sonance, ooreenstemming, harmonie, gelykluidendheid, konsonansie.
con'sonant, (n) medeklinker, konsonant; (a) ooreenkomstig, gelykluidend; saamstemmend; welluidend.
con'sort¹, (n) maat; gemaal, gemalin, gade; geleiskip, konvooivaarder; **prince** ~, prins-gemaal.
consort'², omgaan met; verkeer; vergesel; saamlewe; ooreenstem, klaarkom (met).
consor'tium, konsortium; geselskap.
conspecif'ic, gelyksoortig.
conspec'tus, (-es), oorsig, algemene blik; opsomming.
conspicu'ity, sigbaarheid; ooglopendheid.
conspic'uous, opsigtig; merkwaardig, beroemd; ooglopend, opvallend; in die oog lopend; *be* ~ *by one's ABSENCE,* skitter deur jou afwesigheid; *BE* ~, opval; ~ *GALLANTRY,* uitnemende dapperheid; *MAKE oneself* ~, die aandag trek; jou op die voorgrond dring; ~**ness,** sigbaarheid, duidelikheid; opvallendheid; opsigtigheid, ooglopendheid.
conspi'racy, (..cies), sameswering, komplot, samerotting.
conspi'rator, samesweerder, eedgenoot; (pl) saamgesworenes; samesweerders.
conspire', saamsweer, saamspan, saamrot, beraam; ~**r,** samesweerder.
conspure', hoon.
con'stable, konstabel, polisiedienaar, polisieman; slotvoog; *OUTRUN the* ~, in skuld raak; *SPECIAL* ~, spesiale konstabel.
constab'ulary, polisie(mag).
con'stancy, standvastigheid, volharding; trou; bestendigheid; ooreenstemming (fis.).
con'stant, (n) konstante; onveranderlike (grootheid); (a) standvastig; gestadig; voortdurend, gedurig, bestendig; onveranderlik; getrou; aanhoudend; ~ *CHATTER,* aanhoudende gebabbel.
con'stantan, koper-nikkellegering.
Constan'tia, Constantia; ~ **wine,** Constantiawyn.
Con'stantinople, Konstantinopel.
con'stantly, voortdurend, onafgebroke, gedurig, steeds; dikwels.
con'stant: ~ **speed,** konstante spoed; ~ **wind,** bestendige (egalige) wind.
constata'tion, konstatering, vasstelling.
con'stellate, 'n sterrebeeld vorm, konstelleer.
constella'tion, gesternte, sterrebeeld, konstellasie.
con'sternate, ontstel, onthuts; ~**d,** ontsteld, verslae, onthuts.
consterna'tion, ontsteltenis, verbouereerdheid, verslaenheid, konsternasie.
con'stipate, hardlywig maak, verstop, konstipeer; ~**d,** hardlywig.
constipa'tion, hardlywigheid, verstopping, konstipasie.
constit'uency, (..cies), kiesafdeling; kieserskorps.
constit'uent, (n) kieser; wesenlike bestanddeel; lasgewer; (a) samestellend; konstituerend; kies=; ~ **part,** bestanddeel.
con'stitute, uitmaak; saamstel, stig, vorm, konstitueer, aanstel, benoem; ~*d AUTHORITIES,* die gestelde magte; ~ *oneself a JUDGE,* jou as regter opwerp.
constitu'tion, gestel, liggaamsgesteldheid; vorming; reëling, bepaling, inrigting, samestelling; grondwet, staatsreëling, konstitusie; grondreëls (van 'n vereniging); *written* ~, geskrewe konstitusie (grondwet).
constitu'tional, (n) gesondheidswandeling; (a) grondwetlik, konstitusioneel; gestels=; essensieel; aangebore; ~ *law,* staatsreg.
constitu'tionalism, konstitusionalisme.
constitu'tionalist, konstitusionalis, aanhanger v.d. grondwet.
constitu'tionalize, grondwettig maak; 'n gesondheidswandeling doen.
con'stitutive, samestellend; konstituerend; wesenlik; bepalend; wetgewend; ~ *PARTS,* bestanddele; ~ *POWER,* wetgewende mag.
con'stitutor, samesteller, aansteller, konstitueerder.
constrain', dwing, noodsaak, afdwing; opsluit; druk (uitoefen op); ~**able,** bedwingbaar; ~**ed,** onnatuurlik; gedwonge; verleë.

constraint', dwang; opsluiting; gedwongenheid, bevangenheid; beperking, inperking; *put under ~*, die vryheid inperk; onder dwang plaas.
constrict', saamtrek, saamdruk; toedruk; beknel, insnoer, toesnoer; *~ed*, beklem, nou; *~ion*, sametrekking; beklemming, engheid; vernouing; strik=tuur; *~or*, sametrekker; kringspier, sluitspier, trekspier; luislang; *~or muscle* = **constrictor**.
constringe', saamtrek, vernou; toetrek.
constrin'gency, sametrekking, vernouing.
constrin'gent, sametrekkend, vernouend, knellend.
construct', bou, oprig, inrig, timmer, vorm, aanlê, inmekaarsit; saamstel, konstrueer; teken (mat.).
construc'tion, uitleg, verklaring; sinsbou (gram.); samestelling; bouwerk; aanleg; bou, aanbou (bv. spoorweg); inrigting; konstruksie, maaksel; *in COURSE of ~*, in aanbou; *PUT a false ~ on*, 'n verkeerde uitleg gee aan; *UNDER ~*, in aanbou.
construc'tional, aanleg=; bou=, konstruksie=; *~ steel*, konstruksiestaal, boustaal; *~ work*, bouwerk.
construc'tion: *~ company*, konstruksiemaatskappy, boumaatskappy; *~ engineer*, konstruksie-ingenieur, bou-ingenieur; *~ train*, konstruksietrein, boutrein.
construc'tive, samestellend; bou=; boukundig; afleibaar; opbouend; *~ criticism*, opbouende kritiek; *~ desertion*, veronderstelde (afgeleide) verlating (jur.); *~ness*, samestellingsvermoë.
construc'tor, samesteller, bouer, boumeester; oprigter.
con'strue, verklaar, uitlê; vertaal, opvat; verbind.
consubstan'tial, een in wese, eenstoflik.
consubstan'tiate, tot een stof saamvoeg.
consubstantia'tion, konsubstansiasie.
con'suetude, gewoonte, gebruik; gewoontereg; omgang.
consuetud'inary, (n) (. . ries), handboek oor gewoontes; (a) gewoonte; gebruiklik, geyk deur gewoonte; *~ law*, gewoontereg.
con'sul, konsul; *~ar*, konsulêr; *~ate*, konsulaat; **C~-General, (Consuls-General)**, konsul-generaal; *~ ship*, konsulskap.
consult', raadpleeg; beraadslaag; oorleg pleeg, konsulteer, ruggespraak hou; in aanmerking neem; *~ a DOCTOR*, 'n dokter raadpleeg; *~ TOGETHER*, onderling raadpleeg; *~ant*, raadpleger, konsultant; raadgewer, raadsman, adviseur; raadplegende geneesheer.
consulta'tion, raadpleging; inspraak; ruggespraak; konsult, konsultasie; *HAVE a ~*, beraadslaag; *in ~ WITH*, in oorleg met; na raadpleging met; *~ fee*, konsultgeld.
consul'tative, consul'tatory, konsulterend, raadplegend; raadgewend, adviserend.
consultee', raadgewer; gekonsulteerde.
consul'ter, raadpleger, konsultant.
consul'ting, (n) raadpleging; raadgewing; (a) raadgewend; raadplegend; *~ engineer*, raadgewende ingenieur; *~ hours*, spreekure; spreektye; *~ physician*, raadplegende geneesheer; *~ room*, spreekkamer.
consum'able, verteerbaar; *~ stores*, verbruiksgoedere.
consume', verteer, verbruik, uitleef, verorber, opgebruik; verkwis; verbrand; verslind; uitput; deurbring; uitteer; *BECOME ~d*, opraak; *~d with CURIOSITY*, brand van nuuskierigheid; *~d with RAGE*, verwoed; *~dly*, uitbundig, oordadig.
consu'mer, verbruiker, konsument; gebruiker; *~ goods*, verbruik(er)sgoedere; *~ price*, verbruikersprys; *~ research*, verbruik(er)snavorsing; *~ resistance*, verbruikersweerstand; verkoopsweerstand; *~ society*, verbruikersvereniging; *~ spending*, verbruik(er)sbesteding; *~'s terminal*, verbruikerspunt.
consum'ing, verterend; *~-device*, verbruiktoestel (elek.); *~ power*, koopkrag.
con'summate¹, (v) volmaak, voltooi, voltrek; *~ a marriage*, 'n huwelik volvoer deur omgang.
consumm'ate², (a) deurtrap, geraffineer (skelm); volkome, voltooid, volslae; *~ scoundrel*, deurtrapte skurk.
consumma'tion, voltooiing, vervolmaking, voltrekking, vervulling; oplossing, doel; einde; hoogste punt, toppunt; gewenste einddoel; *~ of a marriage*, volvoering v.d. huwelik deur omgang.
consump'tion, verbruik, verorbering, vertering; tering; uittering; *ARTICLE of ~*, verbruiksartikel; *~ of CURRENT*, stroomverbruik; *FALL in ~*, verbruiksdaling; *GALLOPING ~*, galoptering; *HUMAN ~*, menslike verbruik; *PULMONARY ~*, longtering; *RISE in ~*, verbruiksstyging; *~-figure*, verbruiksyfer; *~ record*, verbruikrekord; *~ test*, verbruiktoets.
consump'tive, (n) teringlyer; (a) teringagtig, tuberkuleus; verslindend, verterend; *~ness*, teringagtigheid.
con'tact, (n) aanraking, voeling, kontak; tussenpersoon; *BREAK ~*, kontak verbreek; *COME into ~ with*, in aanraking kom met; ontmoet; *MAKE ~*, aansluit; kontak maak; ontmoet; *POINT of ~*, raakpunt; *in ~ WITH*, in aanraking met; (v) aanraak, voel, vat aan; nader, in aanraking bring (kom) met; skakel, in verbinding tree; *~-breaker*, stroomverbreker; stroomsluiter; *~ lens*, *(-es)*, kontaklens; *~ level*, raakvlak; *~-maker*, kontakmaker; *~ man*, tussenpersoon; skakelman; *~ mine*, trapmyn; skokmyn; *~ plug*, kontakprop; *~ point*, kontakpunt; raakpunt; *~ prints*, kontakafdruk; *~ reef*, kontakrif; *~ situation*, kontaksituasie; *~ sport*, kontaksport; *~ spring*, kontakveer; kontakbron; *~ surface*, raakvlak; *~ wheel*, voelrat; *~ wire*, stroomdraad, boleiding, kontakdraad.
contadi'no, (It.), contadino, Italiaanse boer.
conta'gion, (kontak)besmetting; besmetlike invloed; aansteeklike siekte; aansteking; smetstof.
conta'gious, besmetlik, aansteeklik; *~ ABORTION*, besmetlike misgeboorte; *C~ Diseases ACT*, Wet op Besmetlike Siektes; *~ness*, besmetlikheid, aansteeklikheid.
contain', bevat, insluit, behels; inhou, beheers, bedwing, in toom hou; *~ your ANGER*, nie kwaad word nie; beheers jou kwaadheid; *~ed ANGLE*, ingeslote hoek; *~ ONESELF*, jou inhou.
contain'er, houer, blik, potjie, doos, koker, huls, fles; *~iza'tion*, houerverpakking, houervrag; behouering; *~ ship*, houerskip; *~ trailer*, pakwa; *~ vessel*, houerskip.
contain'ment, insluiting; indamming.
contam'inant, besmetter, besmettingsfaktor.
contam'inate, besoedel, bevlek, besmet, bederf, verpes, verontreinig; vergas.
contamina'tion, besoedeling, bevlekking, besmetting, kontaminasie; vergassing.
contan'go, (-s), contango, verlengingspremie.
con'té, conté(kryt); *~ crayon*, contékryt.
conte, (F.), conte, (kort)verhaal.
contemn', verag, minag, geringskat; *~er*, versmader, veragter.
con'template, beskou; bepeins, oorpeins, oorweeg; verwag; aanskou; dink oor, van plan wees; *~ a journey*, 'n reis oorweeg; *~d*, voorgenome, oorwoë.
contempla'tion, beskouing, aanskouing; bespieëling; kontemplasie, oordenking, oorweging, oorpeinsing.
con'templative, oordenkend, bespieëlend; beskouend.
con'templator, beskouer, dinker; mymeraar.
contemporane'ity, gelyktydigheid; eietydsheid, kontemporêrheid.
contemporan'eous, gelyktydig; kontemporêr, van dieselfde tyd; *~ness*, gelyktydigheid.
contem'porary, (n) (. . ries), tydgenoot; (a) gelyktydig; eietyds, kontemporêr, van dieselfde tydvak (leeftyd); hedendaags; *~ author*, hedendaagse (kontemporêre) skrywer; skrywer van dieselfde tydvak; *~ music*, eietydse (kontemporêre) musiek.
contem'porize, laat saamval, gelyktydig maak; tot tydgenoot maak.
contempt', veragting, minagting, versmading; *BENEATH ~*, benede kritiek; *~ of COURT*, minagting v.d. hof; *HOLD in ~*, verag, minag; *~ibil'ity*, veragtelikheid; *~ible*, veragtelik; *~iblenes*, veragtelikheid.

contemptuous

contemp'tuous, veragtend, honend, smalend; veragtelik; parmantig; ~**ness**, veragtelikheid; veragting.
contend', stry; worstel; wedywer; betwis, bestry; aanvoer, betoog, beweer; ~**er**, stryer, vegter; ~**ing**, strydend; ~*ing parties,* gedingvoerende partye (jur.); strydende partye.
con'tent¹, kapasiteit, volume; gehalte; (pl) inhoud; omvang; *CUBICAL* ~, kubieke inhoud; *the* ~*s OF,* die inhoud van; *TABLE of* ~*s,* inhoudsopgawe.
content'², (n) voldaanheid, tevredenheid; *to one's HEART'S* ~, na hartelus; ~ *LODGES more often in cottages than in palaces,* hoe groter huis, hoe groter kruis; (v) bevredig, tevrede stel; ~ *oneself,* jou tevrede stel; (a) tevrede, vergenoeg, voldaan.
content'ed, tevrede, vergenoeg, welgemoed; ~**ness**, tevredenheid, vergenoegdheid.
conten'tion, stryd, twis; bewering; wedywer; standpunt; *this is my* ~, dis wat ek beweer; dis my standpunt.
conten'tious, twissiek, moeilik; betwisbaar, aanvegbaar, kontensieus, netelig; *a* ~ *matter,* 'n aanvegbare saak; ~**ness**, aanvegbaarheid, omstredenheid; stryerigheid.
content'ment, tevredenheid, voldaanheid.
conterm'lnal, conterm'inous, tesamekomend; met dieselfde grense, aangrensend.
contes'sa, (It.), contessa, Italiaanse gravin.
con'test, (n) wedstryd; debat; twis, stryd.
contest', (v) betwis, beanveg, beveg; redetwis; wedywer; ~ *a seat,* 'n setel betwis; ~**able**, betwisbaar; ~**ant**, teenstander; deelnemer (wedstryd); ~**a'tion**, betwisting; stryd, woordestryd; wedywer.
contest'ed, bestrede; ~ *election,* bestrede verkiesing; ~ **seat**, betwiste (bestrede) setel.
con'text, konteks, samehang, (gedagte)verband; sameweefsel; *IN* ~, in samehang; in (sy) verband; in konteks; *PUT into proper* ~, in die regte verband bring; *TAKE something out of its* ~, iets uit sy verband ruk; buite konteks beoordeel.
contex'tual, kontekstueel.
contex'ture, samehang; verband; bou, samestelling; weefsel.
contigu'ity, samehang, aanraking; nabyheid, aangrensing.
contig'uous, aangrensend, naby, aanliggend, rakend, naburig, naasgeleë; ~ *angles,* aanliggende hoeke.
con'tinence, matigheid, selfbeheersing, onthouding; kuisheid.
con'tinent¹, (n) vasteland, kontinent, wêrelddeel.
con'tinent², (a) matig, onthoudend; kuis.
continen'tal, (n) bewoner van 'n vasteland, vastelander; (a) kontinentaal, vastelands-; ~ *CLIMATE,* vastelandsklimaat; ~ *SHELF,* vastelandsplat; ~ *SYSTEM,* kontinentale stelsel; ~**ist**, vastelandsbewoner, kontinentbewoner.
contin'gency, toevalligheid; toevallige gebeurtenis, geval; moontlikheid, gebeurlikheid; eventualiteit; onvoorsiene uitgawe; ~ **fee**, gebeurlikheidsgeld; ~ **fund**, gebeurlikheidsfonds, fonds vir onvoorsiene uitgawes; ~ **plan**, gebeurlikheidsplan; ~ **reserve (fund)**, gebeurlikheidsreserwe(fonds).
contin'gent, (n) afdeling, kontingent; bypassing; (a) gebeurlik, onseker, wisselvallig; afhanklik van; toevallig; voorwaardelik; ~ **claim**, moontlike (voorwaardelike) eis; ~ **debt**, beladingskuld; ~ **liability**, voorwaardelike aanspreeklikheid, voortvloeiende verpligting; ~ **lien**, beladingskuld; ~ **payment**, voorwaardelike betaling; ~ **probability**, gebeurlikheidskans; ~ **services**, bykomstige dienste.
contin'ual, gedurig, voortdurend, gestadig, aanhoudend, onophoudelik; ~**ly**, voortdurend, aanhoudend, onophoudelik, ewigdeur, deurentyd, gedurig, heeltyd, altyddeur, almaardeur, steeds.
contin'uance, voortduring, duur; voortsetting, aanhoudendheid, aanhouding.
contin'uant, kontinuant, duurklank.
continua'tion, voortsetting; vervolg; voortduring, verlenging; ~ **class**, voortsettingsklas; ~ **committee**, voortsettingskomitee; ~ **education**, voortsettingsonderwys; ~ **list**, vervolglys; ~ **page**, vervolgblad-

contradict

sy; ~ **school**, voortsettingskool; ~ **sheet**, vervolgblad, vervolgvel; ~ **volume**, vervolgbundel.
contin'uator, voortsetter.
contin'ue, voortsit; aanhou, laat voortduur, aangaan, verleng; volhard; vervolg (storie); aanbly; ~**d**, onafgebroke, voortdurend, aanhoudend, gedurig; vervolg-; *to BE* ~*d*, word vervolg; ~*ing COVERING security,* deurlopende dekpand; ~*d FRACTION,* kettingbreuk.
continu'ity, samehang, bestendigheid, onafgebrokenheid, kontinuïteit.
contin'uous, deurlopend, onafgebroke, voortdurend, aanmekaar, aanhoudend, volgehoue, kontinu; ~ *CROPPING,* roofbou; ~ *white LINE,* ononderbroke wit streep; ~ *WAVE,* gelykgolf; ~**ly**, pal, voortdurend, aaneen, heeltyd, eenstreep, eenstryk.
contin'uum, kontinuum.
contort', verdraai, verwring; ~**ion**, verdraaiing; vertrekking; kronkeling; ~**ionist**, (woord)verdraaier; slangmens; kunstemaker.
con'tour, (n) omtrek; hoogtelyn; kontoer; (v) met hoogtelyne merk; pad langs die kontoer van 'n heuwel maak; ~ **feather**, kontoerveer; ~**ing**, aanlê van kontoerwalle; kontoerploeëry; ~ **line**, hoogtelyn, omtreklyn; grenslyn; ~ **map**, hoogtelynkaart, kontoerkaart; ~ **plan**, kontoerplan; ~ **ploughing**, kontoerploeg; ~ **survey**, kontoeropmeting.
con'tra, teen, teenoorgestel(d), kontra; *per* ~, per contra, op die teenoorgestelde kant; ~ **account**, teenrekening.
con'traband, (n) smokkelhandel, sluikhandel, kontrabande; smokkelware; ~ *of war,* oorlogskontrabande; (a) smokkel-; verbode; ~ **goods**, smokkelgoedere; ~**ist**, smokkelhandelaar, smokkelaar; ~ **trade**, smokkelhandel.
con'trabass, (-es), kontrabas, basviool; ~**oon**, kontrafagot.
contracep'tion, geboortebeperking, voorbehoeding, voorkoming van swangerskap.
contracep'tive, (n) middel teen swangerskap, voorbehoedmiddel; (a) voorbehoedend.
con'tract, (n) verdrag, ooreenkoms, verbintenis, kontrak, aanbesteding; ~ *of AFFREIGHTMENT,* bevragtingsooreenkoms; *BY* ~, by aanbesteding; *ENTER into a* ~, 'n kontrak aangaan (sluit); *GIVE out on* ~, aanbestee; ~ *of LEASE,* pagakte.
contract', (v) ooreenkom; aanbestee; inkrimp, bymekaartrek, saamtrek; kry, opdoen (siekte); vat, aanwen (gewoonte); ~ *the BROWS,* frons; ~ *DEBT,* skuld maak, in skuld raak; ~ *a DISEASE,* 'n siekte opdoen (kry); ~ *FOR,* aanneem; ~ *a MARRIAGE,* 'n huwelik aangaan; ~ *OUT,* jou onttrek aan.
con'tract bridge, kontrakbrug (kaartspel).
contrac'ted, saamgetrokke; eng; bekrompe, beknop, verkort; ~ **hoof**, klemhoef; ~**ness**, bekrompenheid, beknoptheid.
contractibil'ity, sametrekbaarheid, krimpbaarheid.
contract'ible, saamtrekbaar; krimpbaar.
contrac'tile, saamtrekkend; sametrekbaar, krimpbaar.
contractil'ity, sametrekbaarheid.
contrac'tion, sametrekking; verkorting; vernouing; krimp, (in)krimping; oploop (siekte); ~ *of bad habits,* vorming van slegte gewoontes; ~ **crack**, krimpskeur; ~ **joint**, krimpvoeg.
contrac'tor, kontraktant; kontrakteur, aanbesteder, aannemer; saamtrekker; saamtrekspier; ~ *to,* leweransier aan; *building* ~, boukontrakteur, bouaannemer.
con'tract price, aanbestedingsom, aannemingsbedrag, kontrakprys (-geld).
contrac'tual, kontrak-, kontraktueel; ~ *capacity,* handelingsbevoegdheid.
con'tract work, kontrakwerk, aannemingswerk.
contradict', weerspreek, teenspreek, weerlê, ontken, in die kontramine wees; teëpraat; ~**ion**, teenspraak; teenstrydigheid; weerspraak, weerlegging; ~*ion in terms,* teenstrydigheid in die woorde; selfweerspreking; ~**or**, weerspreker, teenspreker, teenprater, weerlêer; ~**ory**, (n) teenstrydigheid,

contradistinction teenspreking; ontkenning; (a) teenstrydig, teensprekend; ontkennend.
contradistinc'tion, teenstelling; *in* ~ *to,* in teenstelling met.
contradisting'uish, onderskei.
con'trail, dampspoor, kondensasiespoor.
contra-in'dicate, teenaandui; *..-indica'tion,* kontraindikasie, teenaanduiding.
contral'to, (-s), contralto, alt; tweede stem.
contrapolarisa'tion, teenpolarisasie.
contraposi'tion, teenoorstelling; kontras, opposisie; kontraposisie.
contrapo'sitive, kontrapositief, gekontrasteer(d).
contrap'tion, uitvindsel, toestel, gedoente, affêring; kontrepsie (geselst.); ~s, gereedskappe, toestelle; kontrepsies (geselst).
contrapun'tal, kontrapuntaal.
contrar'iant, gekant; teenstrydig, teengestel(d).
contrari'ety, teenstrydigheid; weerspreking; ongunstigheid; teenspraak.
con'trarily, teen, daarenteen, op teenoorgestelde wyse.
contrar'iness, weerspannigheid; teenstrydigheid; koppigheid, dwarsheid, dwarstrekkerigheid, dwarstrekkery; dwarsdrywery.
contrar'ious, weerbarstig; teenstrydig; ongunstig.
contra'riwise, inteendeel; daarteenoor; omgekeerd; pervers, dwarstrekkerig.
con'trary, (n) teendeel; teenoorgestelde; *ON the* ~, inteendeel, daarenteen; *PROOF of the* ~, teenbewys; (a) teenoorgestel(d), strydig; teen; eiesinnig, koppig, dwars, strydend, dwarstrekkerig, stroomop; *BE* ~, altyd hot om wil kom, in die kontramine wees, altyd stroom-op wil wees; ~ *ORDER,* teenbevel; ~ *TO,* in stryd met; teen, in teenstelling met; ~ *WIND,* teenwind.
con'trast, (n) teenstelling, kontras.
contrast', (v) teenstel; afsteek by; stel teenoor; verskil; kontrasteer; ~*ing COLOURS,* teengestelde kleure; *as* ~*ed WITH,* in teenstelling met; ~**ing,** kontrasterend, teenstellend; ~**ive,** kontrasterend, teenstellend, kontrastief; ~**y,** kontrasryk, vol teëstellings.
contra-sugges'tible, kontrasuggestief.
con'trate wheel, kroonrat, kroonwiel.
contravalla'tion, teenverskansing.
contravene', in teenspraak wees; inbreuk maak op, oortree; teëwerk; betwis; ~**r,** oortreder.
contraven'tion, teenstand; oortreding; *in* ~ *of,* in stryd met.
con'tretemps, ongelukkige voorval; haakplek; contretemps.
contrib'utary, bydraend, skatpligtig.
contrib'ute, bydra; bevorder; meewerk; ~ *to,* bydra tot; bevorder; ~**d,** bygedra.
contribu'tion, bydrae, kontribusie; skatting; medewerking; *LAY under* ~, laat betaal; skatpligtig maak; *MAKE a* ~ *to,* 'n bydrae lewer tot.
contrib'utive, medewerkend; bydraend.
contrib'utor, medewerker, insender; donateur, bydraer.
contrib'utory, (n) (..ries), deelhebber; (a) bydraend, medewerkend; bykomstig; ~ *CAUSE,* medeoorsaak; aanleidende oorsaak; ~ *NEGLIGENCE,* meewerkende nalatigheid.
con'trite, berouvol, berouhebbend, boetvaardig; ~**ness,** berou, boetvaardigheid.
contri'tion, berou, wroeging.
contriv'ance, uitvinding; uitvindsel, bedenksel; plan, lis, middel; toestel; kunsgreep.
contrive', planne maak, smee(d), bedink, uitdink; uitvind; versin; bewerk, regkry; bestuur; beraam; ~**r,** uitvinder, planmaker; intrigant.
control', (n) bestuur, kontrole; beteueling; mag; beheer; besturing, toesig; bestryding; beperking; (self)beheersing; beheerskakel; *BE in* ~ *of,* die beheer voer oor; *have the FIRE under* ~, die vuur onder beheer hê; *GET out of* ~, hand-uit ruk; *HAVE no* ~ *over yourself,* jou nie kan beheers nie; *KEEP under* ~, in bedwang hou; onder beheer hou; *OUT of* ~, buite beheer, hand-uit, nie te regeer nie; (v) (-led), in bedwang hou; kontroleer, nagaan; bedwing, regeer, beheers, beteuel; ~ *traffic,* verkeer reël; ~ **arm,** kontrolearm; ~ **board,** beheerraad; kontrolebord; ~ **button,** kontroleknoppie; ~ **cabin,** stuurkajuit; ~ **cable,** stuurkabel; ~ **catch,** kontroleknip; ~ **column,** stuurkolom; ~-**drag,** stuurweerstand; ~ **experiment,** kontrole-eksperiment, kontroleproef; ~ **flag,** verkeersvlag; ~ **gear,** reëlinrigting; ~ **group,** kontrolegroep; ~**lable,** bedwingbaar, beheerbaar, bestuurbaar; narekenbaar; ~**ler,** kontroleur; opsigter; ~**lership,** kontroleurskap; ~ **lever,** stuurhefboom, wisselaar, wisselhefboom.
control'ling, rig=, beheer=, beherend, kontrole=; ~ **company,** beheermaatskappy; ~ **force,** rigkrag; ~ **interest,** beherende aandeel; meerderheidsbelang(e); ~ **magnet,** rigmagneet; ~ **station,** kontrolestasie.
control': ~**ment,** kontrole, beheer, bedwang; ~ **officer,** verkeersbeampte; ~-**plunger,** reëlingsdompelaar; ~ **point,** beheerpunt; ~ **post,** beheerpos; ~ **rod,** wisselstang; ~ **room,** beheerkamer; verkeerskamer; ~**s,** stuurtoestel; beheermiddels; ~ **seat,** stuurstoel; ~ **shaft,** kontrole-as; stelstang; ~ **station,** beheerstasie; ~ **stick,** stuurstok, stuurknuppel; ~ **tender,** kontrolewa; ~-**tower,** verkeerstoring, beheertoring; ~ **valve,** skakelklep, stuurklep; ~ **wire,** stuurdraad.
controver'sial, strydveroorsakend, polemies, twissiek; betwisbaar, stryd=; ~ *QUESTION,* twisvraag; ~ *WRITINGS,* twisgeskryf; ~**ist,** polemikus, twisredenaar; strydvoerder.
con'troversy, (..sies), kontrovers(e), twispunt, strydvraag, dispuut, geskil; twisgeskryf; strydpunt, getwis, polemiek; *CARRY on a* ~, polemiseer; *RELIGIOUS* ~, geloofstryd.
con'trovert, betwis, bestry; weerlê, ontken.
controvert'ible, betwisbaar; weerlegbaar.
contuma'cious, weerspannig, koppig, weerbarstig.
con'tumacy, weerbarstigheid, styfkoppigheid.
contume'lia, contumelia (jur.).
contumel'ious, onbeskaamd; spottend, smadend, honend, smadelik, skimpagtig.
con'tumely, (..lies), onbeskaamdheid; hoon, gesmaal, smaad; skande; skimp; smadelikheid.
contuse', kneus; ~*d wound,* kneuswond.
contu'sion, kneusing, kneuswond.
conun'drum, strikvraag, raaisel, konundrum.
conurba'tion, aaneenskakeling van dorpsgemeenskappe; stedegroep.
co'nure, (Amerikaanse) papegaai.
convalesce', herstel, beter word, aan die beter hand wees, sterker word (sieke).
convales'cence, herstel, genesing, beterskap.
convales'cent, (n) herstellende sieke; *home for* ~*s,* herstel(lings)oord; (a) genesend, herstellend; ~ **diet,** hersteldieet; ~ **home,** herstel(lings)oord.
convalida'tion, bekragtiging.
convec'tion, konveksie, warmtestroming; ~ **current,** konveksiestroom, geleidingstroom (elek.).
conven'able, saamroepbaar, belegbaar (vergadering).
con'venance, betaamlikheid, gepastheid.
convene', saamroep, byeenroep, bymekaarroep, oproep, belê; ~**r,** saamroeper, oproeper, belêer, konvener.
conven'ience, geskiktheid; gemak, gerieflikheid; stoflike voordeel; kleinhuisie; *at your EARLIEST* ~, sodra dit u pas; *FOR* ~, vir die gemak; *MAKE a* ~ *of somebody,* misbruik van iem. se goedheid maak; *MARRIAGE of* ~, huwelik uit stoflike oorweegings; *PUBLIC* ~, openbare gemakhuis; ~ **circuit,** geriefbaan.
conven'ient, gemaklik; geskik, geleë; by die hand; gerieflik; *FIND it* ~, dit gerieflik vind; *MAKE it* ~ *to,* dit so skik; ~**ly,** gerieflik; gerieflikheidshalwe.
conve'ning, oproepend; *notice* ~ *a meeting,* kennisgewing van 'n vergadering.
con'vent, klooster; ~ **cloth,** kloosterstof.
conven'ticle, geheime vergaderplek; geheime samekoms.
conven'tion, byeenkoms, kongres; ooreenkoms, verdrag, traktaat; vergadering, konvensie; gebruik; gewoonte; *claim in* ~, hoofeis; ~**al,** gebruiklik, konvensioneel; vormlik; ~*al tyre,* gewone buite=

band; ~**alism**, konvensionalisme; ~**alist**, konvensionalis; ~**al'ity**, gebruiklikheid; vormlikheid; ~**alize**, konvensioneel voorstel.
convent: ~**like**, kloosteragtig; ~**school**, kloosterskool.
conven'tual, (n) kloosterling; (a) kloosterlik, klooster=.
converge', in een punt saamloop; mekaar nader (lyne); konvergeer.
conver'gence, conver'gency, sameloping, konvergensie.
conver'gent, conver'ging, samelopend, konvergerend.
conver'ging fire, middelpuntvuur.
conver'sable, spraaksaam; onderhoudend, gesellig.
con'versance, con'versancy, deurkneedheid.
con'versant, bekend met, bedrewe, tuis (in), ervare, vertroud (met), op die hoogte (van).
conversa'tion, gesprek; gesels, mondgesprek, geselskap, konversasie; ~**al**, konversasie=; gemeensaam, gesellig, spraaksaam; gespreksmatig; ~**alist**, prater, konverseerder, causeur, geselser; ~**exercise**, ~**lesson**, spreekoefening, spreekles; ~**lozenge**, leeslekker; ~**piece**, groepportret, groepskildery; geselsonderwerp; gespreksonderwerp.
conversazlon'e, (..ni, -s), conversazione, byeenkoms v.d. intelligentsia, gesellige byeenkoms.
converse'[1] (n) gesprek; (v) gesels, omgaan met, verkeer, gedagtes wissel, konverseer.
con'verse[2], (n) teenstelling; die omgekeerde; (a) teenoorgesteld, omgekeerd; ~**ly**, omgekeer(d).
conver'sion, omkering; ombouing (motor); verandering; omsitting (elek.); herleiding; omrekening; omskakeling; bekering (tot Christen); verduistering, toe-eiening (reg); · *of a try* (rugby), vervytskop; ~ **loan**, omsettingslening; ~ **set**, omboustel; ~ **table**, omrekeningstafel, herleidingstafel.
con'vert, (n) bekeerde, bekeerling.
convert', (v) ('n drie) vervyf (rugby); omskakel, omsit (hout); aanwend; omkeer; verander, ombou, omwissel, herskep; bekeer (sondaar); wissel (geld); atwerk (weefstowwe); herlei (breuke); omreken, verduister, onwettig toe-eien (geld); ~*ed into CENTS*, tot sente omgereken; ~*ed STEEL*, sementstaal; ~**er**, omvormer, omsitter, konvertor; ~**er pump**, omsitpomp; ~**er valve**, mengbuis.
convertibil'ity, veranderbaarheid; inwisselbaarheid, omsetbaarheid; ~ *of sterling*, omsetbaarheid van sterling.
convert'ible, veranderbaar, verwisselbaar, omskakelbaar, omsetbaar, ruilbaar; omkeerbaar; ~ *BED*, opklapbed; ~ *CAR*, afslaankapmotor; ~ *COUPE*, afslaankapkoepee; ~ *CURRENCY*, inwisselbare valuta; ~ *HUSBANDRY*, wisselbou; ~ *TERMS*, verwisselbare terme; ~ *VEHICLE*, veranderbare voertuig.
con'vex, bolrond, bolvormig, konveks; ~ *slope*, hellingbult.
convex'ity, bolheid, bolvormigheid, bolrondheid, gewelfdheid, konveksiteit.
convex'o con'cave, bolrond-holrond, konveks-konkaaf.
convex'o-con'vex, dubbelkonveks, dubbelbol.
convey', vervoer, deurvat, oordra, oorbring; meedeel; gee; transporteer; beteken; ~ *across*, oorsit; ~**able**, vervoerbaar, oordraagbaar.
convey'ance, vervoer; rytuig, vervoermiddel; oordrag; grondbrief, transport; afvoer; mededeling, oorbrenging, geleiding; *DEED of* ~, akte van oordrag; *LETTER of* ~, bewys van oordrag.
convey'ancer, transportuitmaker, transportbesorger, aktebesorger.
convey'ancing, transportuitmakery, aktemakery, transportwerk.
convey'er, oorbringer, transporteur, vervoerder.
convey'or belt, vervoerband, transportband, lopende band.
con'vict[1], (n) bandiet, dwangarbeider, prisonier, gevangene.
convict'[2], (v) vonnis, veroordeel; oortuig (van skuld); skuldig vind; ~ *of*, skuldig bevind aan; ~**ed**, veroordeel; ~*ed criminal*, veroordeelde misdadiger.

convict'ion, skuldigverklaring; vonnis; skuldigbevinding; oortuiging (van sonde); veroordeling; *CARRY* ~, oortuig; *have the COURAGE of one's* ~, die moed van jou oortuiging hê; *IN the* ~, oortuig; *LIVE up to one's* ~*s*, volgens jou oortuiging leef.
convic'tive, oortuigend; voldoende, afdoende.
convict: ~ **labour**, bandietarbeid, gevangenearbeid; ~ **prison**, (straf)gevangenis; ~ **settlement**, strafkolonie; strafkamp.
convince', oortuig.
convin'cible, oortuigbaar.
convin'cing, oortuigend; ~**ness**, oortuigingskrag.
conviv'ial, (n) feestelikheid, feestelike byeenkoms; (a) feestelik, gesellig; ~**'ity**, feestelikheid; vrolikheid.
convoca'tion, sameroeping, oproeping; uitskrywing; ring (kerk); byeenkoms; konvokasie (universiteit).
convoke', saamroep, oproep, belê (vergadering).
con'volute, ineenrol, oprol.
con'volute(d), ineengerol, opgerol, gedraai, kronkelend.
convolu'tion, (harsing)winding; kronkeling.
convolve', saamrol, oprol.
convol'vulus, (**-es**), trompettertjie, driekleurige winde, akkerwinde, trompetterblom, convolvulus.
con'voy, (n) konvooi; geleide; geleiskip, konvooivaarder.
convoy', (v) (be)gelei, konvooieer.
convul'sant, stuipgif.
convulse', krampagtig saamtrek; skok; stuiptrek; *be* ~*d with laughter*, skud v.d. lag, jou 'n ongeluk lag, jou slap lag.
convul'sion, stuip, stuiptrekking; aardbewing, ~**ary**, krampagtig; okokkend, ~**s**, stupe; *HAVE (go off into)* ~*s*, die stuipe kry; *IN* ~*s*, stuiptrekkend.
convul'sive, stuipagtig, stuiptrekkerig; krampagtig; ~ *twitch*, senutrekking.
con'y, (**conies**), das; (Europese) konyn; ~**-catcher**, bedrieër, afsetter, skelm; dassievanger; ~ **fur**, konynbont, konynpels.
coo, koer, kir; *bill and* ~, mekaar liefkoos.
co'-obligee', medeskuldeiser.
coo'ee, coo'ey, haai! jy daar!
coo'ing, gekoer.
cook, (n) kok; kookster; *too many* ~*s spoil the broth*, te veel koks bederf die bry; (v) kook; klaarmaak; gaarmaak; vervals, dokter, knoei; ~ *ACCOUNTS*, rekeninge vervals; ~ *the BOOKS*, die boeke verknoei; *not to* ~ *one's CABBAGES twice*, jou ertappels nie twee keer skil nie; ~ *one's GOOSE*, jou kanse bederf; ~*ed STARCH*, gaar stysel; ~ *UP*, versin; die gewenste resultaat lewer; ~*ed VEGETABLES*, gaar groente; ~**book**, kookboek; ~**boy**, koksmaat.
cooke'ite, cookeïet.
cook'er, kooktoestel; veldkombuis; kookding; stoofvrug; vervalser; *waterless* ~, stoomkastrol, drukkoker, stoompot.
cook'ery, kookkuns, kokery; ~ **book**, reseptebook, kookboek; ~ **demonstration**, kookdemonstrasie; ~ **school**, kookskool.
cook'house, kookhuis.
cook'ie, koekie.
cook'ing, (die) kook, gekook; gaarmaak; ~ **apparatus**, kooktoestel ~ **apple**, kookappel; ~ **fat**, kookvet; ~ **odour**, kosreuk; ~ **oil**, kookolie; ~ **range**, stoof; ~ **utensils**, kookgereedskap.
cook: ~**-room**, kombuis; ~**'s apron**, koksvoorskoot, kombuisvoorskoot; ~**'s cap**, kokskmus; ~**-shop**, eetplek; ~**'s mate**, koksmaat; ~**'s store**, spens; ~ **stove**, kookstoof; ~**y**, koekie; kok.
cool, (n) koelte; (v) afkoel; bedaar; verkoel; ~ *DOWN*, afkoel; ~ *one's HEELS*, wag; ~ *a HORSE*, 'n perd koudlei; (a) fris, koel kouerig; lugtig (klere); kalm, bedaard; onverskillig; onbeskaamd; astrant; *be* ~ *and COLLECTED*, doodkalm (doodbedaard) wees; *be as* ~ *as a CUCUMBER*, doodbedaard wees; *a* ~ *HUNDRED*, 'n kleinigheidjie van R100, net mooi R100; *KEEP* ~, bedaard (kalm) bly; *a* ~ *RECEPTION*, 'n onvriendelike ontvangs; ~**ant**, koelmiddel; ~ **bag**, koelsak; ~ **colours**, koel kleure; ~ **customer**, koel

klant, astrante vent; ~ **drink,** koeldrank; ~**er,** koeldrank; koelbalie; watersak; koeler; tronksel; ~ **hand,** ou kalant, koelkop; ~**-headed,** koel; doodbedaard; ~**-headedness,** koelheid, kalmte, bedaardheid.
cool'ie, (derog.), koelie, arbeider.
cool'ing, (ver)koeling; ~**-agent,** koelmiddel; ~**-chamber,** koelkamer; ~**-coil,** koelslang; ~**-fin,** koelvin; ~**-gill,** koelkieu (lugv.); ~**-jacket,** koelmantel; ~**-medium,** afkoelmiddel; ~**-off,** afkoeling; ~**-off period,** afkoeltydperk; ~**-oven,** koeloond; ~**-plant,** koelinrigting; ~**-system,** afkoelstelsel; ~**-tower,** koeltoring; ~**-tray,** afkoelrak, -rooster; ~**-unit,** koeleenheid; ~**-vane,** koelvin; ~**-vat,** koelvat; ~**-water,** koelwater.
cool: ~ **iron,** lou strykyster; ~**ish,** (taamlik) koel; ~**ly,** ongeërg, doodluiters, koeltjies, kalmpies; ~**ness,** kalmte, onverskilligheid; lugtigheid; koelheid; onhartlikheid, stroefheid.
cool'y = **coolie.**
coom, koolroet; waghries.
coomb(e), bergkloof, vallei.
coon, slimmerd, jakkals; wasbeer; Neger (neerh.); *he is a gone* ~, dis klaar met kees; ~ **band,** klopse; ~**s,** klopse; ~**skin,** beervel; ~ **song,** klopseliedjie; Negerliedjie.
coop, (n) fuik; hoenderhok; (v) opsluit, inhok; *be* ~*ed up,* tussen vier mure ingehok wees.
coop'er, (n) kuiper, vatmaker; mengeldrank; (v) kuip; opknap; ~**age,** kuiperswerk; kuiperswinkel; kuipersloon.
co-op'erate, saamwerk, meewerk, meearbei, koöpereer.
co-operation, samewerking, medewerking; saamwerk; koöperasie; *in* ~ *with,* in oorleg met; in samewerking met.
co-op'erative, koöperatief, samewerkend; ~**ness,** samewerking, behulpsaamheid; tegemoetkomendheid; ~ **society,** koöperatiewe vereniging, saamwerk; ~ **store,** koöperasiewinkel.
co-op'erator, medewerker, saamwerker.
co-opt', koöpteer, tot medelid kies; assumeer; ~**a'tion,** koöptasie, koöptering.
co-ord'inate, (n) koördinaat; (v) in ooreenstemming bring; gelykstel; neweskikkend orden; koördineer; (a) van dieselfde orde (mag); newegeskik; koördinaat.
co-ord'inating, neweskikkend; ~ **conjunction,** neweskikkende voegwoord; ~ **officer,** koördinasieoffisier.
co'-ordina'tion, neweskikking; gelykstelling; koördinasie.
co-ord'inator, koördineerder.
coot, bleshoender (S.A.); meerkoet (Europees) *as bald as a* ~, kaalkop.
coo'tie, lyfluis.
cop, (sl.), (n) konstabel, polisiedienaar; (v) **(-ped),** vang, gryp, in die hande kry; *you'll* ~ *it,* jou gal sal waai.
copai'ba, copai'va, kopiva; ~ **bal(se)m,** balsem kopiva.
cop'al, kopal, harpuis.
copartic'ipant, medegeregtigde.
copart'ner, deelhebber; medebelanghebbende, vennoot; ~**ship,** deelgenootskap, vennootskap.
cope[1], (n) bedekking (myne); kap; mantel (van gebou); dak, gewelf; deklaag; priestermantel; (v) bedek (van dak), oorwelf.
cope[2], (v) wedywer, meeding; regkry, baasraak; *be able to* ~ *with,* opgewasse wees teen; jou kan meet met; mans genoeg wees vir.
cop'eck, kopek.
cope level, deklaaghoogte.
Co'penhagen, Kopenhagen.
cop'er, perdekoper, perdesmous.
Copern'ican, Copernicaans; ~ *theory,* Copernicus se teorie.
Copern'icus, Copernicus.
cope'-stone, kopsteen, dekklip, sluitsteen; kroon op die werk.
co'pier, kopiïs, afskrywer; na-aper.
co'-pilot, medevlieënier, medeloods.

cop'ing, kap (gebou); deksteen, dekking, dekplaat, deklaag; ~ **brick,** deksteen; ~ **chisel,** kloofbeitel; ~ **punch,** kloofpons; ~ **saw,** figuursaag, patroonsaag, kurwesaag; ~ **slab,** dekklip, dekstuk; ~ **stone** = **cope-stone;** ~ **tile,** dekteël.
cop'ious, oorvloedig; ruim; uitvoerig; ~**ly,** ruimskoots; ~**ness,** oorvloedigheid; breedvoerigheid, uitvoerigheid; wydlopigheid; weelde, oordaad.
copi'ta, sjerrieglas.
cop'la, (Sp.), kopla, koeplet.
copla'nar, saamvlakkig.
copo'lymer, kopolimeer.
copp'er[1], (n) koper; kopergeld; rooikoper; ketel; *hot* ~*s,* nadors, haarpyn, babalas; (v) met koper beslaan; verkoper; (a) koper-.
copp'er[2], (sl.), (n) konstabel, polisieman.
copp'eras, ystersulfaat, ystervitriool, groenvitriool.
copp'er: ~ **bar,** staafkoper; koperstaaf; ~**-bearing,** koperhoudend; ~ **beech,** bruinbeuk; C ~ **Belt,** Kopergordel, Koperstreek; ~ **bit,** soldeerbout; ~ **bottom,** bodem met koper beslaan; ~ **captain,** kammakaptein; ~**-clad,** met koper beklee(d); ~**-coated,** met koper beslaan; ~**-coloured,** koperkleurig; ~ **compound,** koperverbinding; ~**-engraver,** kopersnyer; ~ **foil,** bladkoper; ~**-foundry,** kopergietery; ~ **glance,** chalkosiet, koperglans; ~**head,** mokassinslang; ~**-leaf,** koperblaar(boom); ~ **ore,** kopererts; ~ **piping,** koperpyp.
copp'erplate (n) koperplaat, kopergravure; plaatdruk; netjiese skrif; (v) verkoper; ~ *PRINTER,* plaatdrukker; ~ *WRITING,* netjiese skrif.
copp'er: ~ **plated,** verkoper; ~ **plating,** verkopering; ~ **sheet,** koperplaat; ~ **smith,** koperslaer; ~ **sulphate,** kopersulfaat, blouvitriool; ~ **tube,** koperpyp; ~**ware,** koperware; ~ **wire,** koperdraad; ~**y,** koperagtig.
copp'ice, ruigte, fynruigte, kreupelhout; stamlote; ~ **forest,** stomplootbos.
cop'ra, kopra, gedroogde klapper; ~**-bee'tle,** hamkewer, koprakewer (*Necrobia rufipes*).
coprin'cipal, medeprinsipaal; mededader; ~ **debtor,** medehoofskuldenaar.
co'prolith, koproliet, dreksteen.
coprol'ogy, koprologie, behandeling van vuil sake (letterkunde, kuns).
coproph'agist, misvreter; vuilgoedvreter, vuilisvreter (torre).
coproph'agy, lus vir vuilis.
corpse, kreupelbos; ~ **wood,** boskasie.
Cop'tic, Kopties.
cop'ula, koppelwoord; kopula, koppelwerkwoord; band, verbinding; ~ **furnace,** koepeloond.
cop'ulate, verbind, koppel; paar.
copula'tion, verbinding; paring; byslaap.
cop'ulative, (n) koppelwoord, verbindingswoord; (a) verbindend, koppel-, aaneenskakelend; parend; ~ **verb,** koppelwerkwoord.
cop'ulatory, parend.
cop'y, (n) **(copies),** kopie, afskrif, afdruk, eksemplaar; uitskrywing; manuskrip; namaaksel; (koerant)stof; afgietsel; afskrif; *CERTIFIED* ~, gewaarmerkte afskrif; *CLEAR* ~, netskrif, netkopie; *ROUGH* ~, klad; (v) **(copied),** afskrywe, kopieer; naboots, namaak; naskilder; oorskrywe; afkyk.
cop'y-book, (skoon)skryfboek; *BLOT one's* ~, jou goeie naam besoedel; ~ *MAXIMS,* afgesaagde spreuke; skoolse wyshede; ~ *WRITING,* skoonskrif, fraaiskrif.
cop'y-cat, na-aper; afskrywer.
cop'yhold, erfpag; ~**er,** erfpagter; kopiehouer.
cop'ying, kopieer; ~ **fee,** kopieergeld; ~ **ink,** kopieerink; ~ **machine,** afrolmasjien; ~ **paper,** kopieerpapier; ~ **pencil,** inkpotlood; ~ **press,** kopieermasjien; kopieerpers.
cop'y: ~**ist,** kopiïs, oorskrywer, afskrywer; ~ **paper,** kopieerpapier; skryfpapier; ~**right,** (n) outeursreg, eiendomsreg, kopiereg; *DRAMATIC* ~*right,* reg van opvoering; ~*right LIBRARY,* bewaarbiblioteek; (v) outeursreg voorbehou; (a) met verbode nadruk; ~**-typist,** kopieertikster; ~**-work,** kopieerwerk; ~**-writer,** teksskrywer.

coq au vin', (F.), coq au vin, hoender in wyn gaargemaak.
coquet', (v) **(-ted)**, koketteer; (a) koket, behaagsiek.
co'quetry, koketterie, behaagsug, ydeltuitery.
coquette', koket(te), behaagsieke vrou, ydeltuit.
coquett'ish, koket, behaagsiek, ydel; ~ **ness** = **coquetry**.
coqui'na, padkalksteen.
coq'ui partridge, swempie(patrys).
coquito, Chileense palmboom, coquito.
cor, (interj.), (sl.) hemel! herder!
co'racle, vlegwerkboot, mandjieboot.
cor'acoid, (n) kraaibekbeen; (a) kraaibekvormig.
co'ral, koraal; kreeftekuit; *red* ~, bloedkoraal; ~ **bells**, koraalbos; ~ **creeper**, koraalklimop; bokhorinkies, kannetjies; ~**-diver**, koraalvisser; ~ **insect**, koraaldiertjie; ~ **island**, koraaleiland; ~ **lif'erous**, koraalhoudend; ~ **lily**, koraallelie; ~ **line**, (n) koraalmos; koraaldier; (a) koralyn, koraal-; ~ **lite**, koraliet, koraalverstening; ~ **loid**, koraalagtig; ~ **polyp**, koraalpoliep; ~ **reef**, koraalrif; ~ **root**, koraalwortel; ~ **sea**, koraalsee; ~ **stitch**, Duitse knoopsteek; ~ **tree**, kafferboom, koraalboom.
cor anglais', (F.), Engelse horing, althobo.
cor'beil, skanskorf.
corb'el, karbeel, draagsteen, balkdraer, korbeel, kraagsteen; ~**led house**, korbeelhuis; ~ **ling**, korbeelwerk.
corb'ie, raaf, kraai; ~**-gable**, trapgewel; ~**-steps**, geweltrap(pie).
cord¹, (n) band, tou, lyn, koord, snoer; rib; *FLEXIBLE* ~, snoer (elek.); ~ *ed SILK*, geribde sy, *SPINAL* ~, rugstring; *UMBILICAL* ~, naelstring; *VOCAL* ~, stemband; ~ *of WOOD*, vaamhout; (v) bind; van 'n koord voorsien.
cord², (n) ferweel.
cord'age, touwerk, takeltoue.
cord'ate, hartvormig.
cor'ded, gekoord; gerib; met tou(e); ~ **fabric**, koordstof.
cord'ial, (n) hartversterking; versterkdrank; likeur; (vrugte)stroop; (a) hartlik, gul, hartsterkend; van harte, gulhartig.
cordial'ity, hartlikheid, gulhartigheid.
cor'dierite, cordieriet, dichroïet.
cord'iform, hartvormig.
cordille'ra, cordillera, bergreeks.
cord'ing foot, koorddrukvoet.
cord'ite, kordiet.
cord'on, (n) kordon; muurkrans; snoer; ordeband, lint; (v) afset, 'n kordon trek (slaan) om; ~ **bleu**, eersterangse kok; ~ **sanitaire**, beskermende kordon; ~ **net**, kordonnet.
cord'ovan, fyn bokleer, Corduaanse (Spaanse) leer.
cord'uroy, koordferweel, riffelferweel; duiwelsterk; (pl) ferweelbroek; ~ **road**, knuppelpad; ~**s**, ~ **trousers**, ferweelbroek.
core, (n) kern, hart, binneste, pit, klokhuis (van 'n appel); sweer; binnevorm (gietwerk); kabelstring; *HEALTHY to the* ~, kerngesond; *ROTTEN to the* ~, vrot tot in die binneste; deur en deur verrot; *TO the* ~, in murg en been; deur en deur; (v) die binneste uithaal; die kern of klokhuis uithaal; boor; ontkern; ~*d SECTION*, gevulde dop; ~ **bar**, kernspil; ~**-flush**, kernverbruining.
core'gent, mederegent.
corelig'ionist, geloofsgenoot.
core: ~ **machine**, kernmasjien; ~**-making**, kernmakery (staalfabriek).
cor'er, vrugteboor; pitboor; kernboorder.
core' sample, kernmonster, boorkern.
coreli'gionist, medegelowige, geloofsgenoot.
coreop'sis, coreopsis.
corespon'dent, ko-respondent, medeaangeklaagde, medebeskuldigde, medeverweerder.
coresponsibil'ity, medeaanspreeklikheid.
corespon'sible, medeaanspreeklik.
core' syllabus, kernsillabus.
corf, (corves), mandjie, korf.
Cor'fu, Corfu.
Cor'gi, Corgi, Walliese herdershond.
coria'ceous, leeragtig.

corian'der, koljander; ~ **seed**, koljander(saad).
Corin'thian, (n) Korinthiër; (a) Korinthies.
co'rium, leerhuid, middelhuid.
cork, (n) kurk; prop; dobber; (v) toekurk; 'n kol gee; (a) kurk=; ~ **age**, kurkgeld; ~**-cutter**, kurkmes; ~ **ed**, gekurk; kurkagtig; gekol; ~ **er**, dooddoener; kolossale leuen; doodhou; bul (fig.); puik voorbeeld; ~ **iness**, kurkagtigheid; ~ **ing**, (a) uitstekend; groot; ~ **ing-pin**, paknaald; ~ **jacket**, reddingsbaadjie; ~ **joint**, kurkpakking; ~ **lino**, kurklino; ~ **packing**, kurkpakking; ~ **rubber**, skuurkurk; ~ **screw**, (n) kurktrekker; (v) slinger; uitwurm; kul; (a) draai=, spiraalvormig; ~**-screw stairs**, wenteltrap; ~ **sock**, kurkbinnesool; ~ **surface**, kurkvlak; ~ **tipped**, met kurkmondstuk; ~**-tree**, kurkboom; ~ **washer**, kurkwaster; ~ **wood**, pimpernel; balsahout; ~ **y**, kurkagtig, droog; ligsinnig, lewendig; na kurk smakend; ~*y scab*, bruinskurfsiekte (by ertappels).
corm, bol (swaardlelie), stingelknol.
corm'ophyte, stingelplant.
corm'orant, kormorant; aalskolwer, seeraaf; duiker; vraat; 'n regte aasvoël.
corn¹, (n) saadkorrel; graan, mielies; koring; ~ *in EGYPT*, baie kos; *INDIAN* ~, mielies; *MEASURE other people's* ~ *with one's own bushel*, ander na jouself oordeel.
corn², (n) liddoring; steengal (med.); *tread on someone's* ~*s*, op iem. se tone trap.
corn³, (v) insout; ~*ed beef*, soutbeesvleis; blikkiesvleis; boeliebief.
corn: ~ **beetle**, koringkewer; ~**-belt**, koringstreek; ~ **brandy**, koringbrandewyn; ~ **bread**, mielie(meel)brood; ~**-chandler**, koringhandelaar; ~**-cob**, mieliekop; ~**-cob pipe**, mieliestronkpyp; ~**-cracker**, mieliebreker; ~ **crake**, kwartelkoning.
corn'-cure, liddoringmiddel.
corn'ea, horingvlies.
corned, gekorrel, gesout; ~ **beef**, blikkiesvleis; soutvleis, boeliebief.
cornel'ian, kornalyn, karneool.
corn'eous, horingagtig.
corn'er¹, (n) opkopersgroep, spekulantekliek; opkoopspekulasie; (v) opkoop.
corn'er², (n) hoek, draai; *DRIVE someone into a* ~, iem. in 'n hoek jaag; iem. vastrek; *DRIVEN into a* ~, in die noute gebring, vasgekeer; *DO something in the* ~, iets om die hoekie doen; *around EVERY* ~, om elke hoek en draai; *from the* ~ *of his EYE*, so onderlangs, skrams, met een oog; *OUT of the* ~ *of one's MOUTH*, uit die kant v.d. mond; *JUST around the* ~, met om die draai; net agter die bult; *have the* ~*s KNOCKED off*, afgerond word; ~ *of the MOUTH*, mondhoek; *just ROUND the* ~, net om die draai; net agter die bult; om die hoek (draai); *be in a TIGHT* ~, in die knel sit; in die knyp sit (wees); in die noute wees; *TURN the* ~, die ergste verby wees; *have TURNED the* ~, deur die ergste heen wees; oor die bult wees; oor die hond se stert wees; *have a WARM* ~ *in one's heart for someone*, 'n warm plekkie vir iem. in sy hart hê; (v) in 'n hoek sit; in die nou dryf; vaspraat; in 'n hoek saamkom; ~ *someone*, iem. in 'n hoekie jaag; ~ **beacon**, hoekbaken; ~**-boy**, hoekstaner, straatloper; ~ **bracket**, hoeksteun; ~ **chair**, hoekstoel; ~ **chisel**, swaelsterbeitel; ~ **cupboard**, hoekkas; ~ **ed**, hoekig; vasgekeer, in 'n hoekie gedryf; *BE* ~*ed*, in 'n hoekie wees; *HAVE someone* ~*ed*, iem. vas hê; iem. in 'n hoek gedryf hê; ~ **flag**, hoekvlag; ~ **halflap**, hoekinlating op halwe hout; ~ **house**, hoekhuis; ~ **ing**, opkoopspekulasie; ~**-joint**, hoeklas; ~**-judge**, hoekbeampte; ~**-kick**, hoekskop; ~ **penalty**, strafhoekskop; ~ **pillar**, hoekpilaar; ~ **plate**, hoekplaat; ~ **post**, hoekpaal, hoekstander; ~ **radius**, hoekronding; ~**-short**, kort hoek; ~ **stone**, hoeksteen; ~**-tooth**, hoektand; ~ **wise**, oorhoeks.
corn'et, kornet; kardoes; blaashoring; horinkie (vir roomys); ~ **ist**, ~**-player**, kornetblaser; kornettis.
corn: ~**-exchange**, graanbeurs; ~**-factor**, graanhandelaar; ~ **field**, koringland; ~ **flakes**, graan-

vlokke; ~ **flour,** mieliemeelblom; ~**-flower,** ko=
ringblom; mielieblom; ~**-fly,** koringmot.
corn'ice, kroonlys, lyswerk, gewellys; ~ **plane,** kraal=
skaaf, kroonlysskaaf.
cor'niche (load), kus(uitsig)pad.
cornifica'tion, verhoorning.
corn'ified, verhoring(de).
Corn'ish, (n) Cornies (taal); (a) Cornies; ~ *pasty,*
Corniese pasteitjie.
corn: ~**-law,** koringwet, graanwet; ~**-loft,** graansol=
der; ~ **meal,** mieliemeel; ~**-pad,** liddoringkussin=
kie; ~**-plane,** liddoringskaaf; ~**-plaster,** liddoring=
pleister; ~ **poppy,** klaproos; ~ **ration,** pitvoer
(diere); ~**-razor,** liddoringmes; ~**-remover,** liddo=
ringverwyderingsmiddel; ~**-sheaf,** koringgerf; ~**-
stack,** koringmied; ~ **stalk,** graanstingel; ~**-trade,**
koringhandel.
corn'u, (-a), horing, horingvormige uitwas.
cornucop'ia, horing van oorvloed; roomhoring.
cornut'ed, gehoring; horingagtig.
corn'-weevil, kalander.
cor'ny¹, graanagtig.
cor'ny², liddoringagtig.
cor'ny³, vol clichés, afgesaag; kinderagtig; verspot,
laf.
coroll'a, blomkroon, blomhart.
coroll'ary, (n) (..ries), aanhangsel; afleiding, resul=
taat, gevolgtrekking; aanvulling; (a) bykomstig,
bykomend.
co'rollate(d), gekroond(d); kroondraend.
coroman'del wood, koromandelhout.
coron'a, (-e), kroonlys (boukuns); kroon (bot.); koro=
na (sterrek.); ligkroon.
co'ronach, lyksang.
coro'nagraph, koronagraaf.
co'ronal, (n) krans, kroon, korona; (a) kroon=, koro=
naal.
co'ronary, kroon=, koronêr; ~ **artery,** kroonslagaar;
~ **thrombosis,** kroonslagaartrombose, koronêre
trombose; ~ **vein,** kroonaar.
corona'tion, kroning, ~**-ceremony,** kroningsplegtig=
heid.
co'roner, lykskouer; ~**'s inquest,** lykskouing.
co'ronet, voetkroon (perd); kroon(tjie); krans; *white*
~, withoefkroon; bykroon (plantk.).
coro'zo, corozo, (S. Amer.) palmboom; ~**nut,**
corozoneut.
corp'oral, (n) korporaal.
corp'oral², (n) misdoek, hostiedoek.
corp'oral³, (a) liggaamlik; lyf=, liggaams=; persoonlik;
~ *punishment,* lyfstraf, liggaamstraf.
corporal'ity, liggaamlikheid, stoflikheid; liggaam;
(pl) liggaamlike behoeftes.
corp'oras, misdoek.
corp'orate, geïnkorporeer, verenig, verbonde; *BODY*
~, verenigde liggaam, regspersoonlikheid; regslig=
gaam; *in a* ~ *CAPACITY,* as regspersoon; ~
MEMBER, stemgeregtigde lid; maatskappy.
corpora'tion, stadsbestuur; liggaam; ghoempie,
pokkel, vaatjie, korporasie; *C* ~ *for Economic De=
velopment,* Ekonomiese Ontwikkelingskorpora=
sie.
corp'orative, korporatief.
corp'orator, korporasielid.
corpor'eal, liggaamlik; stoflik; tasbaar; ~**'ity,** lig=
gaamlikheid; stoflikheid.
corpore'ity, stoflikheid; liggaamlikheid.
corp'osant, St. Elm(u)svuur.
corps, (sing. and pl) korps, afdeling; *DIPLOMATIC*
~, diplomatieke korps; ~ *of ENGINEERS,* die
geniekorps; ~ *of MARINES,* mariniersorps; ~
of OFFICERS, offisierskorps; ~ *de ballet,* ballet=
(dans)groep.
corpse, lyk; kadawer; ~**-candle,** kerkhoflig.
corp'ulence, corp'ulency, swaarlywigheid, gesetheid,
korpulensie.
corp'ulent, swaarlywig, vet, buikig, geset, dik(lywig),
korpulent; ~ *woman,* gesette dame; soustanne.
corp'us, (corpora), liggaam; korpus; versameling.
corp'uscle, liggaampie; atoom, stofdeeltjies.
corpus'cular, atoom=, atomies, uit atome bestaande;
korpuskulêr.

cor'pus delic'ti, corpus delicti; misdaadbewys.
corral', (n), kraal; laer, kamp; (v) **(-led),** laer trek; in
die kraal jaag.
corra'sion, korrasie, uitholling (deur water); afslyting
(deur wind); afskuring (deur water).
correct', (v) verbeter, dokter; bestraf, straf, tugtig;
herstel; regsit; nasien, korrigeer; (a) presies, suiwer,
juis, netjies, noukeurig, korrek; ~**ed,** gekorrigeer=
de; *I stand* ~*ed,* ek erken my fout; ~**ing fluid,** fla=
terwater, korreksievloeistof.
correct'ion, verbetering, korreksie; berisping, tugti=
ging; *HOUSE of* ~, verbeterhuis; *MAKE* ~ *s,* ver=
beteringe aanbring; *ROD of* ~, tugroede; *UNDER*
~, onder voorbehoud (korreksie).
correct': ~**ional,** verbeterings=; ~**itude,** korrektheid
(van gedrag); ~**ive,** (n) verbetermiddel; korrektief;
(a) verbeterend, korrektief; ~**ly,** tereg, presies, juis,
korrek; ~**ness,** juistheid, korrektheid; noukeurig=
heid; ~**or,** verbeteraar, korrigeerder; proefleser;
berisper.
co'rrelate, (n) korrelaat; wederkerige betrekking; (v)
wederkerig in betrekking staan (bring); korreleer,
saamknoop.
correla'tion, korrelasie, samegaan, wisselbetrekking;
~ **curve,** korrelasiekromme.
correl'ative, (n) korrelaat; (a) korrelatief, wedersyds
betreklik.
correspond', ooreenstem, ooreenkom, klop (met);
briewe wissel; korrespondeer.
correspon'dence, briefwisseling, korrespondensie;
ooreenstemming, ooreenkoms; aansluiting; *BE in*
~ *with,* briewe wissel met; *ENTER into* ~ *with,* in
korrespondensie tree met; ~ **course,** korrespon=
densiekursus; ~ **school,** korrespondensieskool.
correspon'dent, (n) korrespondent, beriggewer; (a)
ooreenkomstig, korresponderend.
correspond'ing, ooreenstemmend; geëweredig; oor=
eenkomstig; ~ **angles,** ooreenkomstige hoeke; ~
member, korresponderende lid; ~ **sides,** ooreen=
komstige sye.
corri'da, corrida, stiergeveg, bulgeveg.
co'rridor, (breë) gang; korridor; ~ **disease,** korridor=
siekte; ~ **rug,** gangmat; ~ **train,** deurlooptrein,
gangtrein.
corrigen'dum, (..da), verbetering.
co'rrigible, verbeterlik, verbeterbaar; mak.
corrob'orant, versterkend, bevestigend.
corrob'orate, bevestig, stawe, versterk, bekragtig, be=
aam; ~ *under oath,* onder eed bevestig.
corrobora'tion, bevestiging, stawing, versterking, be=
kragtiging, beaming.
corrob'orative, corrob'oratory, versterkend, bevesti=
gend, stawend.
corrode', invreet, deurvreet, uitbyt, aanvreet, inbyt,
korrodeer, inkanker (metaal), (weg)vreet; verroes,
roes, deurroes.
corrod'ible, corros'ible, invreetbaar.
corro'sion, aanvreting, invreting, wegvreting; ver=
roesting, korrosie; ~**-resistant,** korrosievas, korro=
siebestand.
corros'ive, (n) bytmiddel, vreetmiddel, etsmiddel; (a)
bytend, invretend; ~ **acid,** bytsuur, etssuur; ~ **ac=
tion,** bytwering; ~**ness,** invreting; ~ **poison,** bytgif;
~ **power,** bytvermoë, invreetvermoë; ~ **sublimate,**
kwiksublimaat.
co'rrugate, riffel, golf; sinkplaat ry; rimpel; frons.
co'rrugated: ~ **cardboard,** riffelkarton; ~ **forehead,**
gefronste voorhoof; ~ **iron,** riffelsink, (gegolfde)
sinkplaat, golfyster; ~ **paper,** riffelpapier; ~ **road,**
sinkplaatpad, geriffelde pad, riffelpad; ~ **roof,**
sinkdak; ~ **section,** geriffelde deel; ~ **sheet,** sink=
plaat; ~ **sides,** gekartelde rande; ~ **spring,** riffel=
veer; ~ **washer,** riffelwaster.
corruga'tion, rimpeling, golwing, golfvorming, riffel,
golf; (pl) riffels, sinkplaat.
corrupt', (v) bederwe; verlei; verbaster; omkoop; ver=
ontreinig; (a) bedorwe, omkoopbaar; verknoei,
oneg, korrup; ~**er,** verleier, bederwer, omkoper;
~**ibil'ity,** venaliteit, veilheid, omkoopbaarheid; be=
derflikheid; ~**ible,** veil, omkoopbaar, verganklik;
bederflik; ~**ion,** bederf; verdorwenheid; omko=
ping; verbastering; verknoeiing; slegtheid; korrup=

corsage 811 *cotton*

sie; ~ **ive,** bederwend; verleidend; ~ **ness,** bedorwenheid; verdorwenheid.
cors'age, lyfie, keurslyf; ruikertjie; corsage.
cors'air, seeskuimer, seerower; roofskip, kaperskip.
cors'(e)let, borsharnas, korselet.
cors'et, korset, borsrok, keurslyf; ~ **eer',** borsrokmaker; ~ **ry,** vormdrag; korsetwerk; korsetware.
cortège, stoet, gevolg, cortège.
cort'ex, (cortices), kors, bas; skors.
cort'ical, basagtig, bas=; skors=; ~ *tissue,* skorsweefsel.
cort'icate, skorsagtig; met bas.
cort'isone, kortisoon.
corun'dum, korund(um).
corus'cant, flikkerend, vonkelend, glinsterend.
co'ruscate, flikker, glinster, blink, vonkel.
corusca'tion, glinstering, flikkering, vonkeling.
corvée', herediens(te), corvée.
corvette', korvet.
corv'ine, raafagtig, kraaiagtig.
coryban'tic, woes, uitgelate.
co'rymb, tuil, stingeltros.
corymb'iate, tuilvormig.
corymbose', tuildraend.
coryphae'us, (.aei), korifee, koorleier.
co'ryphee, (F.), hoofdanser(es) (ballet).
coryz'a, neusverkoue, katar.
cos¹, bindslaai.
cos², kosinus.
cosec'(ant), kosek(ans), cosec.
co'set, koset (wisk.).
cosh, (n) knuppel; jeugmisdadiger; (v) platslaan, neerslaan; ~ **-boy,** jeugmisdadiger.
co'sher, troetel, pamperlang.
cosig'natory, (..ries), medeondertekenaar.
cosig'nature, medeondertekening.
co'sily, knus(sies), behaaglik.
co'sine, kosinus.
co'siness, knusheid, behaaglikheid.
cos' lettuce, bindslaai.
cosmet'ic, (n) kosmetiek, skoonheidsmiddel; (a) skoonheids=; ~ *BAG,* kosmetieksakkie; ~ *ROOM,* grimeerkamer; ~ *SURGERY,* plastiese snykunde.
cosmetic'ian, skoonheidsdeskundige, kosmetikus.
cosme'tics, kosmetiek; skoonheidsmiddels.
cos'mic, kosmies, wêreld=; ~ **dust,** kosmiese stof, ruimtestof; ~ **radiation,** kosmiese straling; ~ **rays,** kosmiese strale.
cosmog'ony, wêreldskepping; skeppingsteorie, kosmogonie.
cosmog'rapher, wêreldbeskrywer, kosmograaf.
cosmograph'ic, kosmografies.
cosmog'raphy, kosmografie, wêreldbeskrywing.
cosmol'ogist, kosmoloog.
cosmol'ogy, wêreldkunde, kosmologie.
cos'monaut, ruimtevaarder, ruimteman, ruimtereisiger, kosmonout.
cosmo'polis, kosmopolis, kosmopolitaanse stad.
cosmopol'itan, (n) wêreldburger, kosmopoliet; (a) kosmopolities; ~ **ism,** kosmopolitisme, wêreldburgerskap.
cosmop'olite, wêreldburger, kosmopoliet.
cosmopolit'ical, kosmopolities.
cosmora'mia, kosmorama, kykspel.
cosmoram'ic, kykspelagtig, kosmoramies.
cos'mos, wêreld, kosmos, heelal; wêreldstelsel; kosmos(blom), nooientjie-in-die-gras.
Coss'ack, Kosak; ~ **choir,** Kosakkekoor.
cos'set, (n) hanslam; liefling; (v) liefkoos, verwen, vertroetel; ~ **ing,** vertroeteling.
cost, (n) prys; koste; uitgawe; skade, verlies; boete; (pl) koste; *at ALL ~ s,* tot elke prys, teen alle koste, laat dit kos wat dit wil; *at ANY ~,* teen enige prys; *AT ~,* teen kosprys; *AT the ~ of,* ten koste van; ~ *of CARRIAGE,* vervoerkoste; *COUNT the ~,* die koste (kanse) bereken; ~ *of LIVING,* lewenskoste, lewensduurte, lewensonderhoud; ~ *of PRODUCTION,* produksiekoste; ~ *of REGISTRATION,* registrasiekoste; ~ *of (legal) SUIT,* regskoste; *TO my ~,* tot my skade; ~ *of UPKEEP,* onderhoudskoste; (v) kos; te staan kom op; prys vasstel; ~ *someone a good DEAL,* iem. duur te staan kom; ~

DEARLY, duur te staan kom; duur kos; ~ **accountancy,** kosteberekening; ~ **accountant,** kosteberekenaar; ~ **accounting,** kosteberekening.
cos'tal, rib(be), kostaal; ~ **-nerved,** ribnerwig; ribarig, gerib.
co'star, medester (film).
cos'tard, groot appel.
cos'tate, gerib; generf (bot.).
cost clerk, kosteklerk.
costean', 'n mynskag maak.
cost'ed, berekende.
cost-effective, lonend, betalend.
cos'termonger, straatsmous, (straat)venter.
cost'ing, kosteberekening; ~ **clerk,** kosteklerk.
cos'ting account, prysbepalingsrekening; ~ **ant,** kosterekenmeester; kosteberekenaar.
cos'tive¹, hardlywig, verstop.
cos'tive², vrekkig, suinig.
cos'tiveness¹, hardlywigheid.
cos'tiveness², suinigheid, vrekk(er)igheid.
cost: ~ **-ledger,** kostegrootboek; ~ **less,** kosteloos; ~ **ly,** kosbaar; kostelik, duur; ~ **-of-living,** lewenskoste, lewensduurte; ~ **of living allowance,** duurtetoeslag; lewenskostetoelae; ~ **price,** inkoopprys, kosprys; ~ **s,** koste, onkoste; hofkoste.
cost'ume, (n) kleredrag, kostuum; pak; rok; (v) kostumeer, aanklee; ~ **jewellery,** kleedjuwele, kostuumjuwele; ~ **piece,** ~ **play,** kostuumstuk.
costum'er, costum'ier, modiste, kostumier.
cosure'ty, medeborg.
co'sy, co'zy, (n) **(cosies),** teemus; hoekbankie; (a) gesellig, behaaglik, knus.
co'syl group, kosielgroep.
cot¹, (n) kinderkateltjie, wieg; hangmat.
cot², (n) hut; kraal; skuiling; (v) in die hok jaag.
cot³, (n) veldbed.
cotan'gent, kotangens.
cot'-bar, ronderoei.
cot' death, wiegdood, wiegsterfte.
cote, hok, kraal, skuur.
coten'ant, medehuurder.
cot'erie, kliek, koterie.
coterm'inous = **conterminous.**
cothurn'(us), (..ni), koturn(e), hoë toneelstewel.
coti'dal, gety=; ~ **line,** getylyn.
cot'ill(i)on, kotiljons.
cotoneas'ter, dwergmispel, cotoneaster.
cot' plum, appelkoospruim.
cotrustee', medevoog.
cott, steekhaarkombers; brosvag.
cott'age, klein buitehuisie, woninkie; hut; kothuis; villa; huis; ~ **cheese,** dikmelkkaas; maaskaas; ~ **home,** villa, huisie; ~ **hospital,** klein hospitaal, huishospitaal; ~ **industry,** huisvlyt, tuisnywerheid; ~ **loaf,** koringbrood, boerebrood; ~ **piano,** pianino; ~ **pie,** boerepastei, ertappelpastei, herderspastei; ~ **pudding,** koekpoeding; ~ **r,** hutbewoner; ~ **roof,** hanskapdak; ~ **weave,** volksweefbinding.
cott'ar, bywoner.
cott'ed, gekoek (wol).
cott'er, sleutel, wig, spy, dwarsspy; ~ **bolt,** spybout; ~ **pin,** spypenneljie, dwarsspy; ~ **stud,** spytapbout; ~ **washer,** spywaster; ~ **-way,** spygleuf.
cott'ier, bywoner.
cott'on, (n) katoen; garing; katoenstof; pluis; (v) wollig word; met watte opvul; vriende word, maats word; harmonieer; ~ *on to something,* iets snap; iets verstaan; ~ *TO someone,* dadelik van iem. hou; sin in iem. kry; 'n plan goedvind; (a) katoen=; ~ **bale,** katoenbaal; ~ **cake,** katoensaadkoek; ~ **crop,** katoenoes; ~ **culture,** katoenbou; ~ **factory,** katoenfabriek; ~ **flannel,** katoenflanel, flanelet; ~ **gin,** katoenpluismeul; ~ **grass,** wolgras, katoengras; ~ **-grower,** katoenplanter; ~ **-growing,** katoenverbouing, katoenboerdery; ~ **merchant,** katoenhandelaar; ~ **mill,** katoenfabriek; ~ **plant,** katoenplant; ~ **plantation,** katoenplantasie; ~ **press,** katoenpers; ~ **print,** bedrukte katoen; ~ **seed,** katoensaad; ~ **-seed oil,** katoenolie; ~ **spinner,** katoenwewer; ~ **thread,** katoendraad; rugaring; garingdraad, garedraad; ~ **trade,** katoenhandel; ~ **velvet,** katoenfluweel; ~ **waste,** poets=

cotty

katoen, afvalkatoen; ~**wood,** Amerikaanse populier, cottonwood; ~ **wool,** boomwol, watte; ~y, katoenagtig; ~ **yarn,** katoendraad.
cot'ty, gekoek (wol).
co'tutor, medevoog.
cot'yle, gewrigsholte.
cotyled'on, saadlob, kiemblaar, kiemlob, kotiel; ~**ous,** saadlobbig, kiemblarig.
cot'yloid, komvormig.
cou'cal, vleiloerie.
couch, (n) (-es), rusbank, sofa; sponde; leërstede, (rus)bed; (v) lê; vel (lans); neerdruk, laat lê; uitdruk, inklee (in woorde); met gouddraad bestik; ~ *a person's eye (for a cataract),* 'n pêrel van iem. se oog verwyder.
couch'ant, lêend, neerhurkend; couchant (her.).
couched, gevel (lans).
couch'-grass, kweekgras.
couch'ing: ~ *a cataract,* staarligting; ~ **stitch,** kruipsteek.
coug'ar, poema, cougar, bergleeu.
cough, (n) hoes, kug; (v) hoes, kug, blaf; ~ *OUT,* uithoes; ~ *it UP,* voor die dag haal; alles opbieg; ~ **drop,** hoesklontjie; ~**ing,** hoes, (ge)kug, geblaf; ~**ing fit,** hoesbui; ~ **lozenge,** hoesklontjie; ~ **mixture,** borsdrankie, borsdruppels; hoesmiddel; ~**relieving,** hoesstillend; ~ **remedy,** hoesmiddel; ~ **syrup,** hoesstroop; ~ **tablet,** hoespil, hoestablet.
could, *kyk* **can.**
coulée', lawavloei; ravyn.
coulisse', toneelskerm, coulisse.
coulomb', coulomb, elektrisiteitseenheid; ~ **meter,** coulombmeter.
coulo'metry, coulombmeting.
coul'ter, kouter; *rolling* ~, kouterwiel.
cou'marin, coumarine.
coun'cil, konsilie, raad; raadsvergadering; *IN* ~, in rade; *MEMBER of* ~, raadslid; *PRIVY* ~, Geheime Raad; ~ *of WAR,* krygsraad; ~**-board,** bestuur; ~ **chamber,** raadsaal; ~ **lor,** raadslid; skepen; ~**lorship,** raadslidskap; ~**man,** raadslid; ~ **meeting,** raadsvergadering; ~ **room,** raadskamer.
co'undersigned, medeondergetekende.
coun'sel, (n) raadgewer; advokaat; plan; voorneme; beraadslaging, raad; ~ *for the DEFENCE,* advokaat vir die verdediging; *HOLD* ~ *with,* raad inwin van; *KEEP one's own* ~, jou gedagtes vir jouself hou; iets vir jouself hou; stilbly; *take* ~ *with one's PILLOW,* oor iets slaap; *TAKE* ~, raadpleeg; oorleg pleeg; ~ **lee,** raadontvanger; ~ **ler,** raadgewer; berader (sielkunde); ~**ling,** raadgewing, voorligting; ~*'s* **opinion,** regsadvies, regsgeleerdeadvies; *take* ~*'s opinion,* regsadvies inwin.
count¹, (n) graaf (edelman).
count², (n) rekening; telling, aantal, getal, som; (punt van) aanklag; *on ALL* ~*s,* in alle opsigte; *go DOWN for the* ~, uitgetel wees (bokser); *KEEP* ~ *of,* rekening hou met; *LOSE* ~, die tel kwytraak; *take NO* ~ *of,* oor die hoof sien; buite rekening laat; *TAKE the* ~, uitgetel wees (bokser); (v) tel; reken, ag; meetel; afpas; beskou; ~ *the DAYS,* die dae tel; ~ *FOR,* tel; bereken; beteken; ~*ing FROM today,* van vandag af; ~ *for NOTHING,* nie tel nie; ~ *ON,* reken op; ~ *OUT,* uittel; *be* ~*ed OUT,* uitgetel word; ~ *SHEEP,* skape tel; ~ *in TWOS,* in twee tel; twee-twee tel; ~ *UP,* optel; ~ *UPON someone,* op iem. staatmaak; ~ **able,** telbaar; ~**able noun,** telbare naamwoord.
coun'tenance, (n) gesig, voorkome, aangesig, gelaat; gelaatsuitdrukking; selfbeheersing; *CHANGE* ~, verbleek; *his* ~ *FELL,* hy het verslae gelyk; *KEEP one's* ~, kalm bly; jou lag inhou; jou goed hou; *PUT out of* ~, verleë maak; van sy stukke bring; (v) toelaat, steun, aanmoedig, begunstig; *refuse to* ~, weier om te steun.
coun'ter¹, (n) toonbank; teller; rekenaar; winkelbank; *sell over the* ~, in klein maat verkoop.
coun'ter², (n) parade (skermkuns); teenstoot, teenset; teenmaatreël; (v) teenwerk; afweer, afslaan; pareer (skermkuns); teenspreek; 'n teenset doen; weerlê; antwoord; (a) teen=; (adv) teen in; *run* ~ *to,* indruis teen, teenwerk.

coun'ter³, (n) bors (perd); hakstuk (skoen); agterleer.
counteract', teenwerk; verydel, neutraliseer; ~**ion,** teenstand, teenwerking, opheffing.
coun'ter: ~**-ag'ent,** teenwerkende krag; ~**-arch,** (-es), kontraboog; ~**-argument,** teenargument; ~**-attack',** (n) teenaanval; (v) 'n teenaanval doen; ~**-attrac'tion,** kontra-aantreklikheid; ~**bal'ance,** (n) teenwig; eweewig; (v) opweeg teen; goedmaak; ophef; ~**-barr'age,** teenspervuur; ~**-bid,** teëbod; ~**blast,** antwoord, repliek; teenverklaring; ~**bluff,** (n) terugstoot; (v) terugstoot; ~**-bore,** teenboor; ~**-bracing,** teenverspanning; ~**charge,** teenbeskuldiging; teenklag; ~ **check,** stuiting, teenbelemmering; rem; kontrole, kontrabiljet; ~**-claim,** teeneis; ~**-clock'wise,** teen die wysers in, agteruit; links om; ~ **culture,** teenkultuur; ~**-current,** teenstroom; ~**-demand,** teeneis; ~**-demonstration,** teenbetoging; ~ **display,** toonbankvertoonkaart; ~**-drill,** teenboor; ~**-entry,** teenpos, storno; *make* ~ *entry,* storneer; ~**-es'pionage,** teenspioenasie; ~**-ev'idence,** teenbewys.
coun'terfeit, (n) namaak, afdruk; afbeeldsel; bedrog, huigelary; (v) namaak, bedrieg, huigel; (a) voorgewend, vals, nagemaak; ~**er,** namaker; vervalser (munt); bedrieër.
coun'ter: ~**-fire,** voorbrand; ~ **foil,** teenblad, teenstrokie, bewysstuk, kontrabewys; teëbewys; ~**-force,** teenkrag; ~**-fort,** steunmuur, klipbeer; ~**-grip,** teengreep; ~**-guard,** bolwerk; ~**-hem,** sluitsoom; ~**-insurgence,** teeninsurgensie; ~**-i'rritant,** teenprikkel(middel); ~**-jum'per,** winkelbediende, elleridder; ~**mand',** teenbevel; afsegging; (v) herroep; afskryf; afsê, intrek; af(ge)las, afbestel; ~**march,** (n) (-es), teenmars; (v) 'n teenmars maak; ~**-mark,** teenmerk, kontramerk; ~**measure,** teenmaatreël; ~ **mine,** (n) teenmyn; teenlis; (v) teenmyn; teenwerk, ondergrawe; ~**-motion,** teenvoorstel; teenbeweging.
coun'termove, teenset; ~**ment,** teenbeweging.
coun'ter, ~**-nut,** teenmoer; ~**-objection,** teenbeswaar; ~**-offensive,** teenoffensief; ~**-offer,** teenaanbod; ~**-ord'er,** teëbevel, afbestelling; ~ **pane,** deken, bedsprei; ~**part,** teenstuk; teenstem (mus.); teenparty (reg); teenhanger, eweebeeld, teëbeeld; ~**plea,** repliek; ~**-plot,** (n) teenlis; (v) (-ted), teenwerk, 'n eweewig bring; ~**-poison,** teengif; ~**-pre's-sure,** teendruk; ~**-promise,** teenbelofte; teëbelofte; ~**-proof,** teenbewys; ~**-proposal,** teenvoorstel; ~**-ques'tion,** wedervraag; ~**-reformation,** kontrarefor mas ie; ~**-report,** teenberig; ~**-resolution,** teenvoorstel; ~**-revolution,** teenomwenteling, teenrewolusie; ~**-scarp,** teenwal; ~**-seal,** weer van 'n seël voorsien, herseël; ~**shaft,** tussenas.
coun'tersign, (n) wagwoord; herkenningsteken; medeondertekening; *execute in* ~, in duplo uitmaak; (v) medeonderteken; goedkeur.
coun'ter-signal, kontrasein, kontrateken.
coun'ter: ~**-signature,** medeondertekening; ~**-signer,** medeondertekenaar.
coun'tersink, (n) spitsboor, versinkboor, versinkyster; (v) (..**sank** or ..**sunk**), ruim; inlaat, versink; ~**-bit,** versinkboor; ~**ing,** versinking.
coun'ter-slope, teenhelling, teenhang.
coun'ter-statement, teenverklaring.
coun'ter-stock, toonbankvoorraad.
coun'terstroke, teenstoot, teenset.
coun'ter-suit, teenproses.
coun'tersunk: ~**-head,** versinkkop; ~**-rivet,** versinkklinknael; ~**-screw,** versinkskroef.
coun'ter-tenor, hoë tenoor, kontratenoor.
coun'tervail, opweeg teen; ~*ing duties,* kontraregte.
coun'ter: ~**-value,** teenwaarde; ~**-vote,** teenstem; ~**-wall,** teenmuur; ~**-weight,** teenwig; ~**-work,** (n) teenwerking; (v) teenwerk, dwarsboom.
coun'tess, (-es), gravin.
coun'ting, tellery, telling; ~**-house,** ~**-room,** (bankiers)kantoor; ~**-out rhyme,** uittelrympie.
count'less, ontelbaar, talloos.
count'-out, uittelling (boks).
coun'trified, boers, landelik, plattelands.
coun'try, (n) (..**tries**), land, streek, kontrei, gewes; vaderland; platteland; buitedistrik; *GO (appeal) to*

the ~, 'n beroep doen op die volk; *IN the* ~, op die platteland; *the OLD* ~, moederland; *UNDERDEVELOPED* ~, onderontwikkelde land; *UP* ~, in die binneland; (a) plattelands, boere-; ~**-andwestern,** countrymusiek, cowboymusiek; ~**-bumpkin,** plaasjapie, boslanser, sandtrapper, boerkwagga; ~ **cheque,** buitetjek; ~ **church,** buitekerk; ~ **club,** buiteklub; ~ **cousin,** plaasjapie, buitemens, takhaar; ~ **dance,** boeredans, kontradans; ~ **district,** buitedistrik; ~**-dweller,** plaasboer, plattelander, landbewoner, buiteman; ~ **estate,** landgoed; ~**-folk,** plaasmense; buitemense, plattelanders; ~ **friend,** buitevriend; ~ **girl,** boermeisie; ~ **house,** buiteverblyf, landhuis; ~ **life,** buitelewe, plaaslewe, boerelewe; ~ **man,** landgenoot; boer; landbewoner; ~ **member,** buitelid; ~ **party,** boereparty(tjie); ~ **people,** plaasmense, boeremense, buitemense; ~ **residence,** buiteverblyf, plattelandse woning; ~ **road,** veldpad, plaaspad; ~ **rock,** newensgesteente, omliggende gesteente; ~ **scholar,** buiteleerling; ~ **school,** buiteskool, plaasskool; ~ **schoolmaster,** plaasonderwyser; ~**'s climate,** landsklimaat; ~**-seat,** plaas, landgoed; ~ **side,** platteland; ~ **sports,** boeresport; ~ **squire,** landjonker; ~**'s service,** landsdiens; ~ **store,** buitewinkel, plaaswinkel; ~ **town,** ~ **village,** dorp; ~**-wide,** landswyd; ~ **woman,** landgenote; boer(e)vrou; ~ **youth,** landjeug, plattelandse jeug.
count'ship, graafskap; graaflikheid.
coun'ty, (counties), graafskap; provinsie, distrik.
coup, gelukkige slag; onverwagte set; coup; ~ *D'ÉTAT,* staatsgreep; ~ *de GRÂCE,* genadeslag; ~ *de MAIN,* oorval.
coupé', koepee.
cou'ple, (n) paar, span, tweetal; egpaar; koppel (masj.); hanskap (in dak); *a* ~ *of DAYS,* 'n paar dae; *MARRIED* ~, egpaar; (v) saamvoeg; verbind; paar; skakel, (aaneen)koppel; ~ *TOGETHER,* vaskoppel; ~ *WITH,* paar aan; ~ **d,** gekoppel; ~ *d with,* gepaard met; ~ **r,** koppelketting, koppelaar; koppeling (mus.).
coup'let, koeplet, tweereëlige vers.
coup'ling, verbinding; koppeling; aaneenkoppeling; *FLEXIBLE* ~, gewrigskoppeling; *VERNIER* ~, vernierkoppeling; ~**-bar,** koggelstok; koppelstang; ~**-belt,** koppelriem; ~**-bolt,** koppelbout; ~**-box,** mof; ~**-disc,** koppelskyf; ~**-hook,** koppelhaak; ~**-hose,** koppelslang; ~**-nut,** koppelmoer; ~**-pin,** koppelpen, kettingbout; ~**-rod,** koppelstang; ~**-shaft,** koppelas; ~**-socket,** koppelsok; ~**-strap,** koppelriem.
coup'on, koepon; kaartjie; ~**-book,** koeponboek(ie).
cou'rage, moed, dapperheid, koerasie; *the* ~ *of one's CONVICTIONS,* die moed van sy oortuiging; *his* ~ *FAILED him,* sy moed het in sy skoene gesink; *take one's* ~ *in both HANDS,* die stoute skoene aantrek; al sy moed bymekaarskraap; *INSPIRE with* ~, moed inboesem (inpraat); *LOSE* ~, moed verloor; *PLUCK up* ~, moed vat, moed skep; *TAKE* ~, moed skep.
cou'rag'eous, moedig, dapper, manhaftig, heldhaftig; ~**ness,** moedigheid.
courgette', murgpampoentjie, vingerskorsie, courgette.
cou'rier, koerier, renbode; posryer.
Cour'land, Koerland.
course, (n) loop; vaart; gereg (ete); renbaan; kuur (gesondheid); opeenvolging, aantal, ry; laag; kursus; leergang; verloop, beloop; roete, koers; reeks, serie; handelswyse, gedragslyn; ~ *of ACTION,* gedragslyn, handelswyse; ~ *in AGRICULTURE,* landboukursus; *ALTER one's* ~, die roer omgooi; 'n nuwe rigting inslaan; *CLEAR the* ~! v.d. baan af! *in* ~ *of CONSTRUCTION,* in aanbou; *a DANGEROUS* ~, 'n gevaarlike rigting; *in DUE* ~, op sy tyd; ~ *of EVENTS,* (ver)loop van sake; ~ *of EXCHANGE,* wisselkoers; *FOLLOW a* ~, 'n kursus volg; *IN* ~, in gereelde orde; *a* ~ *of LESSONS,* 'n reeks lesse; ~ *of LIFE,* lewensloop; *a MATTER of* ~, natuurlik; *during the* ~ *of the MEETING,* staande (tydens) die vergadering; *OF* ~, natuurlik; *the illness must RUN its* ~, die siekte moet sy loop neem; *in*

the ~ *of his SPEECH,* in die loop van sy toespraak; *steer a STEADY* ~, koers hou; *steer a STRAIGHT* ~, reg deur see gaan; ~ *of STUDY,* kursus; *I will let it TAKE its* ~, ek sal dit sy gang laat gaan; *let THINGS take their* ~, Gods water oor Gods akker laat loop; *in* ~ *of TIME,* in die loop v.d. tyd; mettertyd; *during the* ~ *of the YEAR,* in die loop v.d. jaar; (v) vloei, loop (water); laat loop; ja(a)g, najaag; ~ **bet,** baanweddenskap; ~**ed stonework,** gelaagde klipwerk; ~ **fee,** kursusgeld; ~**-indicator,** koers(aan)wyser; ~**-light,** koerslig.
cours'er, reisiesperd, renperd; drawwer(tjie) (voël).
courses, bane; kursusse; maandstonde; *horses for* ~, die gepaste man vir die gepaste werk.
cours'ing, jaag.
court[1]**,** (n) speelveld, baan; binneplaas, voorplein (gebou); hofhouding; (geregs)hof, magistraatshof, landdroshof, hofsaal; hofhouding; *C* ~ *of Appeal,* Appèlhof; *C* ~ *of CHANCERY,* Kanselaryhof; *CIRCUIT* ~, Rondgaande Hof; *GO to* ~, 'n hof saak maak; *HOLD* ~, hof hou; ~*of HONOUR,* ereraad; ~ *of INJUSTICE,* skynhof; ~ *of JUSTICE,* gereghof, regbank; *OUT of* ~, buite geding, buite die gereghof; *SETTLE out of* ~, (in der minne) skik, buite die regbank om reël; *TAKE a matter to* ~, 'n hofsaak maak; hof toe gaan.
court[2]**,** (n): *pay* ~, 'n dame die hof maak; (v) die hof maak, soetlandsit (aanlê, draai) by 'n nooi, vry na, vlerksleep, opsit; soek (toejuiging); lok, weglok, verlok; ~ *DANGER,* gevaar trotseer; ~ *DISASTER,* ramspoed (moeilikheid) soek; *GO* ~*ing,* 'n dame die hof maak.
court: ~ **attendant,** hofbediende; ~ **ball,** hofbal; ~ **capital,** hofstad; ~ **card,** prentkaart; ~ **case,** hofsaak, regsgeding; ~ **chancellor,** hofkanselier; ~ **chaplain,** hofprediker, hofkapelaan; ~ **circular,** hofberig; ~ **clique,** hofkliek.
court' craft, baankennis, baanvernuf.
court: ~**-dance,** hofdans; ~ **day,** hofdag; ~ **dress,** groot tenue, galakleding; hofklere, ~ **eous,** hoflik, galant, hups, beleef, beskaaf, wellewend; ~ **eously,** hoflik, beleef; ~ **eousness,** beleefdheid, hoflikheid, wellewendheid; ~ **er,** vryer.
courtesan', ligtekooi, bysit, courtisane.
court'esy, (..sies), wellewendheid, hoflikheid, galanterie, hupsheid, tegemoetkomendheid, pligpleging, beleefdheid; buiging; *BY* ~ *of,* deur die guns van; goedgunstig afgestaan deur; ~ **bus,** kliëntebus, diensbus; ~ **call,** hoflikheidsbesoek; ~ **car,** gastemotor, gastekar; ~ **card,** voorkeurkaart; ~ **ticket,** hoflikheidskaartjie; ~ **title,** beleefdheidstitel; ~ **visit,** beleefdheidsbesoek.
court: ~ **etiquette,** hofetiket; ~ **fool,** hofnar; ~ **hairdresser,** hofkapper; ~**-house,** landdroskantoor; geregshof; ~ **ier,** howeling; ~ **ing,** die hof maak; vlyery; hofmakery; ~ **lady,** hofdame; ~ **life,** hoflewe; ~ **liness,** hoflikheid; ~ **ly,** hoflik, elegant; ~ **martial, (n)** krygsraad; (v) voor die krygsraad bring; ~ **messenger,** geregsbode; ~ **mourning,** hofrou; ~ **official,** hofbeampte; ~ **order,** hofbevel; ~ **orderly,** hofordonnans; ~ **physician,** hofarts, ~ **plaster,** trekpleister; hegpleister; ~ **retinue,** hofstoet; ~ **roll,** sakerol, ~**-room,** hofsaal, regsaal.
court'ship, vryery, hofmakery.
court: ~ **shoe,** hofskoen; ~ **tennis,** kaatstennis, kaatsspel; ~ **term,** hoftermyn; ~ **yard,** binneplaas, binnehof.
cous'cous, koeskoes, bredie.
cou'sin, neef, niggie, oomskind; *we are DISTANT* ~*s twice removed,* ons is familie van Adam se kant; *FIRST* ~, *GERMAN,* volle neef (niggie); *SECOND* ~, kleinneef, kleinniggie; ~ **hoodship,** neef- of niggieskap.
couth, beskaaf(d), goedgemanier(d).
coutur'e, modeontwerp, modemakery, couture.
couva'de, couvade.
couvert', dekplek; ~ **charge,** plekgeld.
cova'lent, kovalent.
cove[1]**,** (n) inham, baai, (ge)welf; beskutte hoekie; (v) verwelf, welf.
cove[2]**,** (n) drommel, vent.

co'ven, heksevergadering.
co'venant, (n) verdrag, verbond; handves; gelofte; ARK of the C~, Verbondsark; DAY of the C~, Geloftedag; GOD of the C~, Verbondsgod; ~ of GRACE, genadeverbond; LAW of the C~, Verbondswet; (v) verbond maak; ooreenkom, 'n verdrag aangaan; ~-breaker, verbondbreker; ~ed, in 'n verbond getree; ~ee', verbondene; ~er, verbondene; ~ theology, verbondsteologie.
Cov'entry: send to ~, 'n uitgebyte bobbejaan maak, iem. uit die sinagoge werp, iem. uit die maatskappy ban.
co'ver, (n) sitplek (aan tafel); boekband, omslag, koevert; buiteblad (van boek); buiteband (van motor); oortreksel; voorwendsel; beskerming; dekkleed (van diere); skerm, skuilplek, skuiling, skuilhoek; stolp, stulp; deksel, dop, deksblad, (be)dekking; FIRST-DAY ~, eerstedagkoevert; ~s were LAID for four, die tafel was vir vier (mense) gedek; under ~ of NIGHT, onder die sluier v.d. nag; READ from ~ to ~, v.d. begin tot die end lees; SEEK ~, skuiling soek; TAKE ~, skuil, wegkruip; UNDER ~, in die geheim; UNDER ~ of, onder dekking van; onder die skyn van; in die geheim; onder dekmantel van; (v) oortrek (kussing); beskut, beslaan, omvat; begeef; rapporteer (vir koerante); deurloop, aflê (afstand); bedek, oordek; dek (van diere); bestry (koste); beskerm teen; afdoen (werk); toegooi; omgeef; beskiet; bestryk (met kanonne); ~ with a FIREARM, 'n vuurwapen (op iem.) gerig hou; ~ IN, toemaak; ~ UP, bedek, toemaak, geheim hou.
co'ver: ~ age, dekking (assuransie); afsetgebied (handel); reklamegebied (advertensie); strekvermoë (verf); ~ age of news, nuusdekking; ~ band, dekband, dekstrook; ~ beading, deklys; ~ charge, bedieningsgeld; plekgeld; ~ crop, dekgewas; ~ design, bandontwerp; ~ drive, dekpunthou (krieket).
co'vered, oordek, met 'n dak; verbloem; gedek (dier); ~ trench, gedekte loopgraaf; ~ wa(g)gon, tentwa; ~ way, oordekte pad.
co'ver: ~ girl, fotomodel, buitebladmeisie, buitebladpop; ~ glass, dekglas.
co'vering, (n) bedekking, omhulsel, oortreksel; dekking; (a) (be)dekkend; ~ action, dekkingsgeveg; ~ authority, dekkende magtiging; ~ board, dekplank; ~ fee, dekgeld (vir bul, hings); ~ fire, dekkingsvuur; ~ iron, dekbeitel; ~ letter, bygaande (meegaande, begeleidende) brief; ~ list, inhoudslys; ~ note, sluitnota, begeleidende brief; ~ power, dekvermoë; ~ strip, dekstrook.
co'ver: ~let, deken, sprei; oortreksel; ~-pho'to, voorbladfoto; ~-plate, dekplaat; ~ point, dekpunt; ~ strip, dekstrook.
co'vert, (n) skuilplek, lêplek, ruigte, kreupelhout; (a) verborge, skelm, geheim; ~ coat, somerjas; ~ly, bedek, onderlangs; ~s, dekvere.
co'verture, bedekking, beskutting; dekking; staat van getroude vrou.
co'vet, begeer, verlang, hunker (na), najaag; ~ all, lose all, wie die onderste uit die kan wil hê, kry die deksel op sy neus.
co'vetous, begerig, skraapsugtig, gewinsugtig, geldgierig, inhalig; begeerlik; ~ly, begeerlik; hunkerend, verlangend; eye something ~ly, iets begerig (hunkerend) aanstaar; ~ness, begerigheid; inhaligheid, gewinsug, geldsug, (geld)gierigheid, skraapsug, hebsug.
co'vey, (-s), swerm, trop, klompie, vlug (patryse).
co'ving, sywande; welfsel.
cow¹, (n) koei; wyfie; till the ~s come HOME, tot die perde horings kry; tot in die oneindige; STERILE ~, kween.
cow², (v) bang maak, vrees inboesem, intimideer.
cow'ard, (n) lafaard, touopgooier, bangbroek; (a) lafhartig; ~ice, lafhartigheid; ~ly, lafhartig, blo.
cow: ~ bane, waterkerwel; ~ bell, beesklok; ~ berry, rooibosbessie; ~ boy, cowboy, beeswagter; ~ boy song, cowboyliedjie; ~ cabbage, beeskool; ~-calf, verskalf; ~-catcher, baanveër, baanruimer, baanskuimer; ~-dung, koeimis, beesmis; ~-elephant, olifantkoei.

cow'er, ineenkrimp; beef; koes, hurk.
cow: ~-fish, oskop, seekoei (vis); ~-grass, wildeklawer; ~-heel, beeskloutjie; sult; ~ herd, beeswagter; ~hide, beesvel; sambok, karwats; ~-hocks, aankaphakke; ~ hippopotamus, seekoeikoei; ~-house, koeistal.
cowl¹, waterbalie.
cowl², skoorsteenkap; tussenkap (motor); torpedofront (motor); monnikskap; py; it is not every ~ that hides a FRIAR, dit is nie almal koks wat lang messe dra nie; the ~ does nog make the MONK, hulle is nie almal heilig wat baie kerk toe gaan nie; ~ed, met 'n kap, gekap.
cow: ~lick, kroontjie, kuif; ~pea, kafferboontjie; ~pox, koeipokkies; ~-puncher, beeswagter; cowboy.
cowr'ie, cowr'y, (..ries), muntskulp, kauri.
cow: ~ shed, koeistal; ~ shot, veegskoot (krieket); ~'s-lick, kroontjie, kuif; ~ slip, sleutelblom; ~ tail, beesstert, koeistert; broekwol.
cox, cox'swain, (n) stuurman; bootsman; (v) bestuur.
cox'a, (-e), heupgewrig; ~l, heup=.
cox'comb, ingebeelde gek, sot, dwaas; windmaker, pronker; snuiter; ~ry, pronkery, windmakery.
coxit'is, heupgewrigsontsteking.
cox'swain = cox.
cox'y, kyk cocky.
coy, skaam(agtig), verleë, sedig, bedees, jonkvroulik, skugter; afgesonder (plek); ~ness, skaamheid, sedigheid, skaamagtigheid, bedeesdheid, preutsheid, skugterheid.
coyot'e, (Amerikaanse) prêriewolf, coyote.
coy'pu, bewerrot, nutria.
coz = cousin.
coze, gesels, babbel.
co'zen, bedrieg, beetneem, bedot; ~ age, bedrog, kullery.
crab¹, (n) krap; kreef; dwarsloper (meganika), kruisloper; windas; the C~, die Kreef (sterrek.).
crab², (n) suurpruim, suurknol; nors mens, iesegrim; wilde appel; ~-apple, houtappel, wildeappel; ~ bed, stuurs, nors, prikkelbaar; onduidelik (skrif); ruig; ingewikkel(d), gedwonge (styl); ~ bedness, stuursheid, norsheid; ~-tree, houtappelboom.
crab³, (v) (-bed), krap, baklei; uitmekaartrek; bekritiseer; bederf.
crab: ~ grass, jongosgras; ~like, krapagtig; ~-louse, platluis; ~-spider, krapspinnekop.
crack, (n) pronkery; praatjie; uithaler, (bo)baas; inbreker; kraak, knak, bars, skeur; windbars(ie) (op hande); klap; at the ~ of DAWN, teen dagbreek; a ~ on the HEAD, 'n hou oor die kop; (v) kraak; skeur, bars; gesels; grootpraat; benadeel; afbreek; afspring; klap (sweep); breek (stem); BE ~ed, 'n krakie hê; ~ a BOTTLE, 'n bottel aanspreek; ~ JOKES, grappe verkoop; ~ someone (something) UP, hemelhoog prys; tot die hemel verhef; ~ UP, onklaar raak; in duie stort; instort; his VOICE is ~ing, sy stem breek; ~ a WHIP, klap met 'n sweep; (a) uitstekende, beste, uithaler=, baas=, kranig, windmaker, knap; a ~ PLAYER, 'n pronkspeler, baasspeler; a ~ SHOT, 'n baasskut.
crack: ~-brained, kranksinnig, getik, in die bol gepik; naatlos; dwaas; roekeloos; ~-down, streng maatreëls; vinnige ingryping; ~ down (on), streng maatreëls tref; vinnig ingryp; ~ed, gekraak; getik, gek; ~ed wheat, gebreekte koring; ~er, kraker, neutkraker; pronker; kraakkoekie; ongeluk; voetsoeker, sisser, klapper; leuen; (pl) velbroek; ~erjack, bobaas, uithaler; ~ing, kraking; barsvorming; ~-jaw, tongknoper.
crac'kle, (n) gekraak, geknetter; (v) knetter, rinkel, kraak, ritsel.
crack'ling, geknetter; gekraak; spek, sooltjie; kaiings.
crack'nel, krakeling (gebak); swoerd, spek.
crack: ~ pot, (n), dweper, malkop, maljan, gek, getikte vent; (a), mal, dwaas, van lotjie getik; ~ regiment, keurkorps; ~ shot, baasskut; ~ sman, inbreker; ~-up, uiteenbarsting, instorting; debakel, affêre; ~-willow, broswilg(er); ~y, gekraak, gebars; gek, getik, mal.

cra'dle, (n) spalk; skaafrusblok; horing (van dom=krag); slee (op skeepswerf); stapel; sif; radeernaald; wieg; bakermat, geboortegrond; *FROM the* ~, *van jongs af; from the* ~ *to the GRAVE,* van die wieg tot die graf; *the* ~ *of a NATION,* die baker=mat van 'n volk; *he is* ~*-SNATCHING,* hy wil gaan popspeel; (v) wieg, in die wieg lê; ~**-book,** wieg(e)druk; ~ **scaffold,** hangsteier; ~**-snatcher,** kuikendief; ~ **song,** wiegelied.

crad'ling, kruiswerk, raamwerk (plafon); betimme=ring.

craft, lis, arglistigheid, sluheid; werk, gilde; hand=werk; ambag; vaartuig; vliegtuig; kunsvaardigheid; *the gentle* ~, visvangkuns; ~**-brother,** vakmaat; ~**-guild,** handwerkgilde; ~**ily,** geslepe, listig; ~**iness,** geslepenheid, arglistigheid, lis(tigheid); deurtraptheid.

crafts'man, vakman, ambagsman; handwerker; handkunstenaar; ~ **ship,** bedrewenheid; handwerk; handkuns.

craft'-work, kunshandwerk; kunsvlyt; ~ **er,** kuns=handwerker.

craf'ty, behendig; deurtrap, slu, geslepe, arglistig.

crag, klip, rots, krans; ~**ged,** klipperig; ru; steil; ~ **gedness,** ~ **giness,** rotsagtigheid; ruheid; ~**gy,** klipperig; ru.

crags'man, (..men), rotsklimmer, alpinis.

crake, kwartelkoning; riethaan.

cram¹, (n) leuen.

cram², (n) gedrang; inpompery, blokkery; (v) (**-med**), volprop, opprop, instop, opvul; gulsig eet; inpomp, blok, dril (vir eksamen); ~ *it down his throat,* iem. iets opdring; in iem. se keel afdruk.

cram'bo, rymspeletjie.

cram: ~**-full, -med,** stikvol; stampvol; ~ **mer,** blok=ker; inpomper; ~ **ming,** inpomping, oppropping; blok, studie; ~ **ming, system,** impompstelsel.

cramp¹, (n) kramp; (v) kramp veroorsaak.

cramp², (n) beperking, belemmering; (v) beperk, be=lemmer, druk; vaskram; beklem; (a) eng, beperk; ~ **ed,** nou, beperk, saamgedruk; inmekaar gedruk, onduidelik (skrif); *be* ~ *ed for room,* min ruimte hê.

cramp: ~**-fish,** drilvis; ~**-iron,** kram, klemhaak; muuranker.

cram'po(o)n, sneeuspoor; balkanker; kram, anker; hegwortel; klingster, crampon.

cramp'y, krampagtig.

cran, (Sk.), haringmaat.

cran'age, kraangeld.

cran'berry, (..rries), bosbessie; ~ **sauce,** bosbessie=sous.

crane, (n) kraan; hysmasjien; hewel, sifon; kraanvoël; *BLUE* ~, bloukraan; *CROWNED (wattled)* ~, mahem; lelkraan; *MOBILE* ~, loopkraan; (v) he=wel; oplig; uitrek (nek); ~**-bill,** ooievaarsbek; kraanbek (instr.); malva; ~ **driver,** kraanmasjinis; kraandrywer; ~ **flower,** kraanblom; ~ **fly,** pui=siebyter; aardvlieg, langpoot; ~ **gantry,** kraan=baan; ~ **girder,** kraanbalk; ~**-jib,** kraanarm; ~ **rail,** kraanbaanspoor; ~**'s bill,** kraanbek(tang); ooievaarsbek, malva, geranium.

cran'ial, skedel=; ~ **fracture,** skedelbreuk; ~ **index,** skedelindeks; ~ **nerve,** harsingsenuwee; ~ **suture,** skedelnaat.

cra'niate, skedeldier.

craniog'raphy, skedelbeskrywing, kraniografie.

craniol'ogist, skedelkundige, kranioloog.

craniol'ogy, skedelleer, kraniologie, skedelkunde.

craniom'eter, skedelmeter, kraniometer.

craniom'etry, kraniometrie.

cranio'scopy, skedelbeskouing, kranioskopie.

cran'ium, (..nia, -s), skedel, kopbeen, kranium.

crank¹, (n) slinger, arm, handvatsel, kruk; krukas; draai; (v) draai; ~ *up,* aanslinger.

crank², (n) sonderling, gek; gril, luim; inval; *he is an absolute* ~ *about physical fitness,* hy is dol oor lig=gaamlike fiksheid.

crank³, (a) skuins, skeef; los; lendelam.

crank: ~ **axle,** krukas; ~ **brace,** swingelboor; ~ **case,** krukkas; ~**-case stay,** krukkassteun; ~ **ed,** gekruk; ~ *ed chimney,* gekrukte rookgang; ~**(ing) handle,** slinger (motor); ~ **le,** kronkel, wring, draai;

~ **lever,** krukarm; ~ **pin,** krukpen; ~ **pulley,** kruk=riemskyf; ~ **rod,** krukstang; ~ **shaft,** krukas; ~ **support,** slingersteun.

crank'y¹, skielik, swak, knorrig; eksentriek, vol fie=mies; lendelam; bogtig.

crann'ied, vol skeure.

crann'y, (crannies), skeur, spleet, bars.

crap¹, (n) (vulg.), ontlasting; stront, kak; (v), jou ont=las; kak.

crap², dobbelsteenspel; *shoot* ~ *(s),* die dobbelsteen=spel speel.

crape, (n) krip, lanfer, (rou)floers, rouband; (v) met krip opmaak; befloers; ~ **cloth,** floerskleed; ~ **myrtle,** skubliesroos.

crap'pie, sonvis.

craps = **crap².**

crap'ulence, onmatigheid; mislikheid; oorlading.

crap'ulent, crap'ulous, onmatig; mislik.

cra'quelure, krakelering, kraaknetwerk.

crash¹, (n) gekraak, gerinkel; geraas; verplettering (masjien); groot bankrotskap; neerstorting; ramp; botsing; (v) kraak; 'n geraas maak; dawer; val; ban=krot raak; verbrysel, verpletter; ~ *into,* vasry teen, bots teen, neerstort (vliegtuig).

crash², (n) growwe linne; handdoekgoed.

crash: ~ **bar,** skermreling; ~ **barrier,** botsreling; ~ **boat,** pletterboot; ~ **course,** blitskursus; ~ **dive,** snelduik; ~ **helmet,** valhoed, valhelm; pletterpet; ~ **landing,** pletterlanding, buiklanding; ~ **pad,** botskussing; ~ **programme,** blitsprogram (bv. sko=le); ~**-proof,** breekvry; ~ **van,** pletterwa.

cra'sis, krasis, vokaalsamctrekking.

crass, grof, dik, sterk; kras; ~ **'itude,** ~ **'ness,** dikte, lompheid; grofheid; krasheid.

crass'ula, ko(e)snaatjie, klipblom, crassula.

Crassula'ceae, Crassulaceae.

cratch, voerkrip.

crate, hok, hoenderhok; krat; mandjie; houtraam, latwerk.

crat'er, krater; (bom)tregter; ~ **wall,** kraterwand.

cravat', nekdoek, halsdoek, krawat.

crave, smeek; hunker; verlang; ~ *for a thing,* na iets hunker.

crav'en, (n) lafaard; (a) lafhartig; ~ **ly,** lafhartig.

crav'er, smeker; soeker; hunkeraar.

crav'ing, vurige wens, lus (vir); sterk verlange, drang (na); hunkering.

craw, krop.

craw'fish = **crayfish.**

crawl¹, (n) (vis)kraal.

crawl², (n) gekruip; sukkelgang, stadige gang; kruip=slag (swem); gekriewel; (v) kruip; kruie; sluip; aan=sukkel; kruipswem, krioel; wemel; skarrel; kriewe=lig voel; ~ *ALONG,* stadig loop (ry); soos 'n slak aansukkel; ~ *BEFORE someone,* jou voor iem. verneder; voor iem. kruip; ~ *WITH,* wemel van; ~ **er,** kruiper; kruipende dier; morspak, kruippak (vir kind); ~ **er tractor,** kruiptrekker; ~ **loader,** kruiperlaaigraaf.

crawl'ing, gekrioel, gekriewel; ~ *with vermin,* van weeluise (ongedierte) wemel.

crawl: ~**-stroke,** kruisslag; kruiphou; ~**-trench,** kruiploopgraaf.

crawl'y, kriewelrig; kruipend.

cray'ferine, kreefmeel.

cray'fish, varswaterkreef, rivierkreef; (see)krap; ~ **cocktail,** kreefkelkie.

cray'on, (n) tekenkryt, vetkryt, crayon; pastelteke=ning; koolspits (lamp); (v) skets; ~**-drawing,** kryt=tekening; ~**-holder,** tekenpen; ~**-paper,** pastel=papier.

craze, (n) gier, manie, passie, hartstog, modegril; kranksinnigheid; *be the* ~, hoog in die mode wees; (v) breek, bars, kraak; barsies veroorsaak; verbry=sel; krenk; gek maak; ~ **d,** gek, getik.

craz'iness, waansin, kransinnigheid; bouvalligheid; dolheid.

craz'ing, diep windbarsies; barsvorming; ~ **mill,** stampmeul.

craz'y, wrak; lendelam; gek, mal, (be)dol, kranksin=nig; *be* ~, van lotjie getik wees; ~ **art,** malkuns; ~ **flying,** dolvlieëry; ~ **pattern,** hobbelpatroon; ~

pavement, breekklippaadjie; ~ **paving,** lapbestrating, plaveipaadjie.

creak, (n) gekraak, geknars; (v) kraak, knars, kras; ~**-ing,** gekraak, geknars; ~**y,** krakend, piepend; ~*y voice,* kraakstem.

cream, (n) room; blom, die beste, uitsoek=; crème; *the* ~ *of the ARMY,* die blom v.d. leër; *the* ~ *of the JOKE,* die beste v.d. grap; *SKIM the* ~, die room afskep; *the* ~ *of SOCIETY,* die hoë lui; ~ *of TARTAR,* kremetart; (v) afroom; room byvoeg; sag klop (botter); (a) liggeel; ~ **cake,** roomkoek; roomsoesie; ~ **caramel,** roomkaramel; ~ **cheese,** roomkaas; ~**-coloured,** roomkleurig; ~ **cracker,** botterkoekie; krakeling; ~**ed:** ~*ed potatoes,* geroomde aartappels; ~**er,** roomafskeier; ~**ery,** (..ries), melkkamer; botterfabriek; suiwelfabriek; melkery; ~**ery butter,** fabrieksbotter; ~ **filling,** roomvulsel; ~ **gauge,** roommeter; ~ **horn,** roomhorinkie; kraakhorinkie; ~**iness,** romerigheid, roomagtigheid; ~**-laid,** roomkleurig gerib (papier); ~**-like,** romerig, roomagtig; ~ **of tartar,** krematart; ~ **puff,** roomsoesie; ~ **separator,** roomafskeier; ~ **shade,** roomkleur; ~ **sherry,** crèmesjerrie; ~ **soda,** sodacrème; ~ **tart,** roomtert; ~**-wove,** roomkleurig geweef; ~**y,** soos room, romerig; roomkleurig.

crease, (n) vou, plooi, kreukel; streep (kriekel); (v) (ver)kreukel, vou, frommel, plooi; ~**d,** kreukelig, gerimpel; ~**less,** kreukelvry; ~**-proof,** kreukeltraag, kreukelvry; ~**-resistant,** kreukeltraag.

creas'ing, verkreukeling; ~**-hammer,** plooihamer; hakhamer; ~**-iron,** plooiyster; ~**-stake,** voustaak.

creas'y, gekreukel, kreukelig, vol plooie.

create', skep; vorm; maak, voortbring, formeer, instel, te voorskyn roep, kreëer; berokken (kwaad); benoem tot; wek, opwek; ~ *a certain IMPRESSION,* 'n sekere indruk wek; ~ *a PEER,* iem. tot die adelstand verhef; ~ *STRIFE,* stryd wek.

crea'tion, skepping, heelal; instelling; benoeming; kunswerk, gewrog, skeppingswerk, kreasie; ~**ism,** skeppingsleer.

creat'ive, kreatief, skeppend, skeppings=, vindingryk; ~ **ability,** skeppingsvermoë, kreatiewe vermoë; ~ **deed,** skeppingsdaad; ~ **energy,** skeppingskrag; ~ **impulse,** skeppingsdrang; ~**ness,** vindingrykheid, skeppingsvermoë, kreatiwiteit; ~ **power,** skeppingsvermoë; ~ **urge,** skeppingsdrang.

cre'atin(e), kreatine, kreatien.

creati'vity, skeppingsvermoë, kreatiwiteit.

creat'or, skepper, voortbringer, formeerder; ontwerper; *the C*~, die Skepper.

crea'ture, skepsel; kreatuur; wese; dier; werktuig; handlanger; ~ **comforts,** stoflike (menslike) behoeftes (geriewe), genietinge.

crèche, kinderhuis, kinderbewaarhuis, kinderhawe, crèche, bewaarplek, bewaarskool; kleuterskool.

cred'ence, geloof, vertroue; Nagmaalstafeltjie; *GIVE* ~ *to,* geloof heg aan; *LETTER of* ~, voorstelbrief; geloofsbrief; *not to PLACE much* ~ *in,* nie veel vertroue heg aan nie.

creden'tials, geloofsbriewe; getuigskrifte.

credibil'ity, geloofwaardigheid; aanneemlikheid, geloofbaarheid; ~ **gap,** ongeloofwaardigheid, glogaping, geloofkloof.

cred'ible, geloofwaardig, geloofbaar, gelooflik, aanneemlik; ~**ness,** geloofwaardigheid.

cred'it, (n) kredit (ong.), bate, krediet; geloof, invloed, vertroue, eer, naam, aansien; (pl.) krediteringe; kredietposte; *BE a* ~ *to,* 'n eer wees vir; tot eer strek; *BUY on* ~, op rekening koop; *DEAL on* ~, goed laat opskryf; op krediet handel dryf (sake doen); *DO* ~ *to,* tot eer strek; *GET* ~ *for,* erkenning (krediet) ontvang vir; in staat beskou word tot; *GIVE him* ~ *for,* hom die eer gee; hom iets as 'n verdienste toereken; hom in staat ag om; *LETTER of* ~, kredietbrief; *ON* ~, op krediet; *REVOLVING* ~, wentelkrediet; (v) glo, vertrou; krediteer; aanreken; *I did NOT* ~ *him with that,* dit het ek nie by hom gesoek nie; ~ *TO,* toeskryf aan; ~ *him WITH,* hom krediteer met; ~**able,** verdienstelik, betroubaar, eervol, geloofwaardig, agbaar; ~ **accommodation,** kredietakkommodasie; kredietverle=

ning; ~ **advice,** kredietbewys; ~ **analysis,** kredietanalise, kredietontleding; ~ **association,** kredietvereniging, koopvereniging; ~ **balance,** batige saldo, tegoed; ~ **bank,** kredietbank; ~ **basis,** kredietbasis; ~ **bondsman,** pandeling; ~ **book,** kredietboek; ~ **business,** krediettransaksies; ~ **card,** kredietkaart; ~ **ceiling,** kredietperk, kredietplafon; ~ **check,** kredietwaardigheidskontrole; ~ **contraction,** kredietinkrimping; ~**-creating,** kredietskepping; ~ **creep,** kredietoename; ~ **directive,** kredietvoorskrif; ~ **entry,** kredietboeking; ~ **facilities,** kredietvoorsiening; ~ **item,** kredietpos; ~ **letter,** kredietbrief; ~ **limit,** kredietbeperking, kredietgrens; ~ **manager,** kredietbestuurder; ~ **note,** kredietnota; ~**or,** krediteur, skuldeiser; ~ **side,** batesy, kredietsy; ~ **squeeze,** kredietbeperking; ~ **stock,** kredietvoorraad; ~ **voucher,** kredietbewys; ~**worthy,** kredietwaardig.

cred'o, (-s), credo, geloof, geloofsbelydenis.

credul'ity, liggelowigheid, goedgelowigheid; eenvoudigheid.

cred'ulous, liggelowig, goedgelowig; eenvoudig; ~**ness,** liggelowigheid.

creed, geloofsbelydenis, geloof.

creek, inham, draai, bog; spruit; kiel; ~**y,** kronkelend, vol bogte.

creel, vismandjie.

creep, (n) krieweling; kruipgat; *give someone the* ~ *s,* iem. laat gril; iem. hoendervleis laat kry; (v) (**crept**), kruip, sluip; seil; opkruip; aansukkel; kriewel; *FIRST* ~ *and then go,* eers kruip, dan loop; *make one's FLESH* ~, iem. hoendervel laat kry; ~ *into one's SHELL,* in sy dop kruip; ~**er,** klimop; slingerplant; rolmat (motor); skuiwer (tennis); dreg; ~ **age,** kruiping; kruipverlenging; ~**-hole,** wegkruipplek; voorwendsel; ~**ing,** langsaam; kruipend; ~*ing BARRAGE,* golwende spervuur; ~*ing THISTLE,* kruipdistel; ~ **resistance,** kruipweerstand; ~**-resistant,** kruipvas; ~**-washer,** kruipwasser; ~**y,** grillerig, grieselig; ~*y crawly,* gogga.

creese, kris, Javaanse dolk.

cremate', verbrand, veras.

crema'tion, lykverbranding, verassing, kremasie, dodeverbranding.

crema'tor, verbrander; lykoond.

cremator'ium, (-s, ..ia), crem'atory, (..ries), krematorium.

crème, crème, room; ~ *de menthe,* pepermentlikeur, jangroentjie.

Cremon'a (violin), Cremona(viool).

crena'te(d), getand, gekartel; geskulp.

crena'tion, karteling, gekarteldheid; krimping (anat.).

cren'el, skietgat, kanteelkeep.

cren'el(l)ate, van skietgate voorsien; ~**d,** gekanteel.

crenella'tion, kanteel, kanteling; getandheid.

cren'ulate(d), fyn gekartel.

Cre'ole, (n) Kreool; (a) Kreools; ~ **language,** Kreoolse taal.

creoliza'tion, kreolisering.

cre'olize, kreoliseer.

cre'olism, kreolisme.

cre'osol, kreosol.

cre'osote, kreosoot.

crep'ance, aankapplek (perd).

crêpe, lanfer, crêpe, krep, (rou)floers, rouband; gekrinkelde materiaal; ~ **bandage,** crêpeverband; ~ **de Chine,** crêpe de chine, Sjinese krep; ~ **paper,** kreukelpapier; ~ **rubber,** spekgomlastiek; ~ **sole,** speksool; ~ **wool,** krepwol.

crep'itate, knetter, kners, kraak.

crepita'tion, knettering, kraakgeluid.

crep'itus, knersing.

crep'on, soort lanfer, krepon.

crept, *kyk* **creep.**

crepus'cular, skemer=; skemerend, skemeragtig; half ontwikkel.

crescen'do, crescendo.

cres'cent, (n) halfmaan, sekelmaan; Turkse halfmaan; Mohammedaanse godsdiens; halfmaanvormige blok huise; singel (straat); (a) toenemend, *cresol* 817 *croak*

groeiend, wassend; halfmaan=; ~-*shaped earmark*, halfmaantjie (oormerk).
cre'sol, kresol.
cress, bronkors, waterkers, bronslaai.
cress'et, ligbaken, vuurbaken.
crest, (n) kuif, kam; maanhaar; kruin, kop (van brander); skuim; helmkam; helmteken (herald.); wapen; (v) kam (kuif) opsit; die top bereik; koppe vorm; ~**ed,** gekuif, met 'n kam; ~**ed guinea-fowl,** kuifkoptarentaal; ~**ed partridge,** Bosveldpatrys; ~**fallen,** ontmoedig, bedruk, terneergeslae, bek-af, druipstert, kop onderstebo; *he is* ~*fallen,* dit lyk of die hoenders sy kos afgeneem het; ~ **line,** kruinlyn.
creta'ceous, krytagtig, kryt=.
Cret'an, (n) Kretenser; (a) Kretensies.
Crete, Kreta.
cret'in, idioot, kretin, kropmens; ~**ism,** skildkliergebrek, kretinisme.
cret'onne, meubelsis, kreton.
crevasse', gletserkloof, ysskeur.
crev'ice, skeur, bars, spleet.
crew[1], (n) gespuis, bende; trop; (skeeps)bemanning, skeepsvolk; bediening (geskut); ~-**cropped head,** ~-**cut (hair),** borselkop.
crew[2], (v) *kyk* **crow,** (v).
crew'el, borduurwol; ~ **needle,** borduurnaald; ~ **stitch,** steelsteek; ~-**work,** borduurwerk; ~ **yarn,** kamborduurwol.
crew'man, spanlid, spanwerker; matroos.
crib, (n) stal; hutjie, huisie; rivierdam; balkstapel; raam; krip; kinderbedjie; plagiaat, letterdiewery, afkykwerk; (v) (**-bed),** bedreig; afkyk, afskryf; opsluit, inperk.
cribb'age, (soort) kaartspel, cribbage.
cribb'ing, afkykery, afskrywery; bedrog.
crib'-biter, kripbyter.
crib'ble, (n) growwe sif; growwe meel; (v) sif.
crib' rail, vloerreling.
crib'riform, sifagtig, sifvormig.
crick, (n) spierkramp; styfheid; stywe nek; spit (in rug); ~ *in the neck,* 'n stywe nek; (v) verrek.
crick'et[1], kriek; langasemsprinkaan; *as lively as a* ~, springlewendig.
crick'et[2], krieket; *not* ~, geen eerlike spel nie; ~ **bag,** krieketsak; kolfsak; ~ **bat,** krieketkolf; ~**er,** krieketspeler; ~ **field,** veldwerkers; krieketveld; ~ **ground,** krieketveld; ~ **ing,** krieket speel, krieket; ~ **match,** krieketwedstryd; ~ **pitch,** kolfblad; ~-**player,** krieketspeler; ~ **team,** krieketspan.
cri'coid, ringvormig; ~ **cartilage,** ringkraakbeen.
cri de coeur', (F.), cri de coeur, hartekreet.
cri'er, omroeper, afroeper; skreeuer.
crik'ey! allawêreld! magtig!
crime, misdaad, euweldaad; gruweldaad; *CAPITAL* ~, halsmisdaad; *INCIDENCE of* ~, misdadigheid; *WAVE of* ~, vlaag van misdade; ~ **rate,** misdaadsyfer; ~ **sheet,** strafregister; ~ **wave,** misdaadgolf.
Crime'a, (die) Krim; ~*n War,* Krimoorlog.
crim'inal, (n) misdadiger, boef; *habitual* ~, gewoontemisdadiger; (a) misdadig, strafregtelik, krimineel; ~ *NEGLIGENCE,* strafbare nalatigheid; ~ *INVESTIGATION,* speurwerk; ~ *case,* strafsaak; ~ **code,** strafwetboek; ~ **connection,** owerspel; ~ **investigation department,** speurafdeling, speurdiens; ~**ist,** kriminalis; ~'**ity,** misdadigheid, kriminaliteit; ~ **judge,** halsregter; ~ **jurisdiction,** strafregtelike jurisdiksie (bevoegdheid); ~ **justice,** strafregspleging; strafregter; ~ **law,** strafreg; ~ **lawyer,** straf(reg)advokaat; ~**ly,** op misdadige wyse, misdadig, krimineel; ~ **offence,** misdryf, misdaad; ~ **procedure,** strafproses; ~ **proceedings,** strafgeding; strafsaak; ~ **record,** strafregister; oortredingsrekord; ~ **session(s),** strafsitting; ~ **tribunal,** strafgereg.
crim'inate, beskuldig, aantyg, berispe; skuldig maak.
crimina'tion, aanklag, beskuldiging, berisping; skuldigmaking.
crim'inative, beskuldigend.
criminolog'ic(al), misdadig, kriminologies.
criminol'ogist, bestudeerder van misdadigers; kriminoloog.

criminol'ogy, misdaadleer, kriminologie.
crimp[1], (n) sielverkoper; ronselaar, soldate= of matrosewerwer; (v) ronsel, aanwerf (soldate, matrose).
crimp[2], (n) kartel(ing) (papier, wol); (v) rimpel; krul; plooi, friseer, riffel (papier).
crimp: ~-**formation,** kartelformasie; ~**ing-iron,** krulyster, friseertang, plooitang.
crimp'iness, karteling.
crim'son, (n) karmosyn; (v) rooi word; bloos; (a) hoogrooi, karmosyn; ~-**breasted shrike,** rooiborslaksman, -fiskaal.
cringe, (n) kruipery; (v) vlei, witvoetjie soek; ineenkrimp; kruip, lek; ~ *before someone,* voor iem. kruip; ~**r,** witvoetjiesoeker, vleier, kalfakter, lekker, kruiper.
cring'ing, kruipend; kruiperig.
crin'gle, ring (oog) (in 'n tou).
crin'ite, haaragtig, behaard, harig.
crin'kle, (n) kronkel; plooi; golf; (v) inmekaarfrommel, kreukel; golf; ruis; kronkel; rimpel; ~**d paper,** rimpelpapier, kreukelpapier; ~ **skin,** kraakskil (sitrus).
crin'oid, lelievormig.
crinolette', krinolet.
crin'oline, hoepelrok; krinolien, torpedonet; ~ **band,** krinolienband; ~ **petticoat,** krinolienonderrok.
crin'ose, harig, haaragtig, harerig.
criol'lo, kakao.
cripes, (interj.), genugtig, magtig, vervlaks.
crip'ple, (n) kreupele, gebreklike, manke; (v) kruppel maak; verlam, lamslaan, fnuik, belemmer; (a) kruppel, mank; ~ **care,** kreupelsorg; ~**d,** onmagtig, verminh, geknak, afbeen=; mank, kreupel; ~**ness,** kreupelheid, mankheid.
cripp'ling, verlamming; *a* ~ *blow,*'n mokerhou, 'n verpletterende slag.
cris, kris.
cris'is, (crises), keerpunt, toppunt, wendingspunt, krisis, hoogtepunt; ~ **politics,** krisispolitiek.
crisp, (n) bros happie; bros lekker; (v) krul; bros maak; (a) kroes, krullerig; krakerig; fris; brokkel(r)ig, bros; kraakvars; skerp, pittig (styl); tintelend, lewendig; beslis (van manier); veerkragtig; *potato* ~, aartappelskyfie, bros skyfie.
cris'pate, gekrul, gekroes, gegolf.
crispa'tion, krul; golwing, rimpeling; hoendervel (fig.).
crisp' bread, brosbrood.
crisped, gekroes, gekrul (hare).
crisp'ing-iron, krulyster, friseertang.
crisp'ness, brosheid, kroesheid; frisheid; beslistheid; beknoptheid.
crisp'y, gekrul, gekroes; bros; fris; lewendig.
criss'-cross, (n) kruising (van lyne ens.); (v) kruis; (a) kriskras; deurmekaar, gekruis, kruis en dwars; ~ **patch,** kriskraslap.
cris'ta, kuif; rif.
cris'tate, gekuif.
cristo'balite, cristoballet.
criter'ion, (..**teria),** kenmerk, standaard, maatstaf, toets, kriterium.
cri'tic, beoordelaar, kritikus; resensent.
cri'tical, krities, beoordelend; vitterig, kritiek, bedenklik, sorgbarend, haglik; netelig; ~ *ANGLE,* grenshoek; *in a* ~ *CONDITION,* in 'n bedenklike toestand; ~ *LIMIT,* breekgrens; *a* ~ *OPERATION,* 'n gevaarlike operasie; *a* ~ *REVIEW,* a kritiese beskouing; ~ *SPEED,* kritieke snelheid; ~ *STATE,* neteligheid; kritiese toestand; ~ *TEMPERATURE,* kritiese hittegraad; ~'**ity,** kritikaliteit.
cri'tic: ~**as'ter,** vitterige kritikus, kritikaster; ~**ism,** kritiek, beoordeling, resensie; afkeuring, vittery; aanmerking; ~**ize,** kritiseer, resenseer, beoordeel; bedil.
critique', kritiek, beoordeling; **critiquing,** kritiklewering, kritisering.
croak, (n) gekras, gekwaak; (v) kwaak (padda); kras (voël); ongeluk voorspel; doodgaan; ~**er,** knorpot, ongeluksprofeet; ~**ing,** gekras, gekwaak; ~**y,** kwakend.

Croa'tia, Kroasië.
Croa'tian, (n) Kroaat; (a) Kroaties.
croc, krokodil.
cro'ceate, saffraankleurig.
cro'chet, (n) hekelwerk, haakwerk; *DOUBLE* ~, kortbeen; *SINGLE* ~, glipsteek; (v) hekel, haak; ~ **book,** hekelboek; ~ **cotton,** hekelgaring; ~ **ed,** gehaak; ~ **hook,** hekelpennetjie; ~ **needle,** hekelnaald; ~ **stitch,** (-es), hekelsteek, haaksteek; ~-**work,** hekelwerk, haakwerk.
cro'cidolite, krosidoliet, blou asbes.
crock¹, (n) erdepot.
crock², (n) krukker; kruik; ou nooi; ou perd, knol; sukkelaar; rammelkas (motor); (v) seermaak; breek; ~ **ed,** gebreek, kapot; gekruk.
crock'ery, breekgoed, erdewerk, erdegoed, porseleinware; eetgereedskap, eetgerei.
croc'ket, loofversiering (argit.).
croc'odile, krokodil; tou (van meisies); ~ **cloth,** krokodilstof; ~-**jaw,** kraaibek; ~ **leather,** krokodilleer; ~ **tears,** voorgewende smart, bobbejaanhartseer, krokodiltrane.
crocodil'ian, krokodilagtig.
croc'odiling, krokodilvelbarsies (verf).
croc'oite, loodchromaat.
croc'us, (-es), krokus.
Croes'us, Croesus, rykaard.
croft, tuintjie, saailandjie; ~ **er,** pagter, kleinboer.
croi'ssant, croissant, broodrol.
crom'bec, stompstertjie *(Sylvietta rufescens).*
crom'lech, hunebed, cromlech.
crone, ou-ooi; ou vrou; heks.
cron'y, (cronies), boesemvriend, kameraad, kornuit; *be cronies,* boesemvriende wees; dik maats wees.
crook, (n) skelm, dief; herderstaf; biskopstaf; haak; kromte; bog, kromming; (v) buig; fop, bedrieg; ~-**back,** boggelrug.
crook'ed, krom, gebuig, geboë; verdraai; oorhoeks; mismaak; slinks, oneerlik; skeef; geboggel; *go through a wood and pick up a* ~ *stick,* beter soek en slegter kry; langs die laning afloop en die kromste lat sny; ~ **ness,** kromheid; skeefte, skeefheid; skurkery, oneerlikheid; ~ **shy,** skewe ingooi (rugby).
crook: ~-**neck squash,** kromnekpampoen; ≈kalbas; ~ **stick,** haakstok, haakkierie.
croon, (n) neurietoon, geneurie; (v) neurie(sing); ~ **er,** neuriesanger, sniksanger, kermsanger.
crop, (n) krop (van voël); stok (van sweep); gelooide vel; kortgeknipte hare; oes, drag; (krop)gewas; gesaaide; opbrings; pluksel (volstruisvere); *there was a large* ~ *of failures,* daar was 'n slagting onder die kandidate; (v) (-ped), kort sny, afsny (hare); top; oes; afvreet (gras); opbring, dra (gesaaides); ~ *OUT,* uitkom, opkom; ~ *UP,* onverwags; ~-**ear,** afoor; ~ **stompoor**≈; ~ **estimates,** oesskatting; ~ **farming,** saaiboerdery; ~-**full,** maagvol, keelvol; ~ **grass,** vingergras, kruisgras; mannagras; ~-**headed,** stompkop≈; borselkop≈; ~ **management,** gewasbestuur; ~ **page,** bebouing; beplanting; ~ **ped,** gekort, afgesny, stomp.
cropp'er, kropduif; knipper; mislukking; draer (boom); *COME a* ~, sandruiter word; baken steek; deur die mat val, die pot mis sit; daar baie sleg van afkom; *a HEAVY (light)* ~, 'n goeie (slegte) skieter of draer (graan, bome).
cropp'ing, afsny; oes; ~ **waste,** skeerafval.
cropp'y, (croppies), stompkop, kaalkop.
croq'uet, kroket, kroukie, croquet; ~ **ball,** croquetball, kroketbal, kroukiebal.
croquette', kroket, bolletjie (vleis, ens.).
cro'sier, biskopstaf, kromstaf, herderstaf.
cross, (n) (-es), kruis; moeite; kruising, kruisras (diere); baster; foppery; *no* ~, *no CROWN,* geen kroon sonder kruis nie; ~ *of MERIT,* erekruis; *ON the* ~, skuins; *PECTORAL* ~, borskruis; (v) 'n kruis trek; deursny; dwarstrek; 'n kruis slaan; oorbring; verbykom; dwarsboom; kruis (plante; tjek); mekaar kruis; oorsteek, dwarsoor loop; deurkruis, deurtrek; streep; met 'n kruis merk; oorloop, oorgaan; teenwerk; ~ *her HAND (palm) with silver,* die waarsegster geld gee; ~ *my HEART and hope to die,* mag ek dood neerval (as dit nie so is nie); ~ *the LINE,* oor die ekwator gaan; ~ *one's MIND,* te binne skiet; ~ *ONESELF,* 'n kruis slaan; ~ *OUT,* uitkrap, deurhaal, skrap, deurstreep; ~ *the PATH of,* iem. ontmoet; iem. dwarsboom; ~ *SOMEONE,* iem. die voet dwars sit; ~ *SWORDS,* met mekaar veg; (a) suur, nors, kwaad, spytig, boos; kwaai, teenstrydig; *as* ~ *as two sticks,* briesend; ~ **accommodation,** wisselruitery; ~ **action,** teeneis; ~ **aisle,** dwarsbeuk (kerk); ~ **appeal;** teenappèl; ~-**arm,** dwarshout; ~ **balance,** (n) kruisbalans; (v) kruisbalanseer; ~-**bar,** draaghout, nekhoutjie; swingel; dwarshoutjie, dwarspyltjie; dwarsstuk; dwarspaal; ~-**barred,** getralie; ~-**barred snake,** bandomslang; ~ **bat,** dwars kolf (krieket); ~ **beam,** dwarsbalk, kruisbalk, dekbalk; ~-**bearer,** dwarsdraer; kruisdraer; ~ **bedding,** diagonale gelaagdheid (geol.); ~ **bench,** dwarsbank; ~-**bencher,** dwarsbanker; ~ **bill,** kruisbek (voël); teeneis (reg); ~-**bolt,** dwarsbout; ~-**bond,** kruisverband; ~-**bones,** gekruiste bene (simbool v.d. dood); ~ **bow,** kruisboog, handboog; ~ **brace,** kruiverspanstuk; ~-**bred,** van gekruiste ras; ~-**breed,** (n) kruisras; (v) (-bred), kruis; ~-**bun,** Paasbolletjie; ~-**cast,** kruisoptelling; ~-**channel steamer,** kanaalstoomboot; ~-**check,** dubbele kontrole; ~ **connection,** dwarsverbinding; ~-**country,** landre(i)sies; veldwedloop; landloop; ~-*country race,* landloop; ~-**court shot,** dwarshou (tennis); ~-**current,** dwarsstroom.
cross'-cut, (n) dwarssny; dwarsgang; dwarshaakhou (tennis); (a) dwarsgesny; dwarssny≈; dwars≈; ~ **chisel,** ritsbeitel; ~ **file,** kruiskapvyl; ~ **saw,** mootsaag, treksaag, dwars(sny)saag.
cross: ~ **dip,** dwarsduik (in pad); ~ **ditch,** dwarssloot; ~ **drain,** dwarsduik (in pad); ~ **ed,** gekruis; *a* ~ *ed cheque,* 'n gekruiste tjek; ~ **entry,** teenpos, kontraboeking; ~-**examination,** kruisverhoor; ~-**examine,** kruisvra, onder kruisverhoor neem; voorkry; ~-**eyed,** skeel; ~-**feathered hen,** verkeerde veerhoender; ~-**feed,** dwarsvoeding; ~ **fertilization,** kruisbestuiwing; ~-**fertilize,** kruisbestuif, kruisbevrug; ~-**fibre,** dwarsdraad; ~-**fire,** kruisvuur; ~-**firing,** wisselruitery (bankwese); ~ **fish,** seester; ~ **flower,** kruisblom; ~ **flute,** dwarsfluit; ~-**garnet,** T-skarnier; ~-**girder,** dwarsbalk; ~-**grain,** hopshout; ~-**grained,** dwars(trekkerig); teen die draad, dwarsdraads; onhandelbaar, stuurs; *a* ~-*grained fellow,* 'n dwarstrekker; 'n jantjie kontrarie; ~ **hair,** kruisdraadjie; ~-**haulage,** kruisvervoer (spoorw.); ~ **head,** kruiskop; ~ **heading,** dwarshofie; ~-**head pin,** kruiskoppen; ~-**index,** (n) kruisregister; (v) kruisverwysings maak; ~ **ing,** kruising (vee; trein); oorloop, oortog (see); oorweg, oorgang (spoorweg); kruispad, oorgaanplek; oorsetting; kruisstuk (spoorbaan); ~ **ing-loop,** kruisuitwykspoor; ~**ing-sweeper,** straatveër; ~-**joint,** dwarsnaat; ~-**key,** dwarspen; ~-**kick,** dwarsskop; ~-**legged,** met die bene oormekaar; kruisbeen; ~ **let,** kruisie; ~-**level,** dwarshellingmeter; dwarswaterpas; ~-**light,** dwarslig; nuwe lig (op onderwerp); ~-**line,** dwarsstreep; ~-**member,** dwarsbalk (motoronderstel); ~ **ness,** verstoordheid, kwaadheid; knorrigheid; norsheid; ~-**pass,** dwarshou (hokkie); ~ **passage,** dwarsgang; ~-**patch,** dwarskop, korrelkop, iesegrim, kruidjie-roer-my-nie; ~-**peen hammer,** dwarskophamer; ~ **petition,** teenpetisie; ~-**piece,** dwarsstuk; ~-**ply tyre,** kruislaagband; ~ **pollination,** kruisbestuiwing; ~ **purposes,** misverstand; *be at* ~ *purposes,* mekaar misverstaan; in mekaar se vaarwater wees; in die kontramine wees; ~-**question,** (n) kruisvraag; (v) kruisvra; ~-**questioned,** onder kruisverhoor; ~-**rail,** dwarsreling; ~-**reef,** dwarsrif; ~ **reference,** kruisverwysing, verwysing oor en weer; ~ **road,** dwarspad, oorweg; (pl) kruispaaie; *at the* ~ *roads,* op die tweesprong; op die keerpunt; ~ **rut,** knikspoor; ~ **saddle,** mansaal; ~ **seam,** dwarsnaat; ~-**section,** (dwars)deursnee; ~-**shaft,** dwarsas; ~-**shaped,** kruisvormig; ~ **shot,** dwarsskoot, kruisskoot; ~-**staff,** graadboog; ~-**stay,** dwarsanker; ~ **spindle,** T-spil; ~-**stitch,** (-es), kruissteek; ~ **street,** dwarsstraat; ~ **talk,** (n) geselsprogram;

gesprekstoring; (v) kruisklets; ~-tempered, brommerig; ~-tie, dwarslêer; dwarssteun; bindbalk; dwarsmars (skeepsterm); ~ tube, dwarspyp; ~ vault, dwarsgewelf; ~ voting, deurmekaar stemmery; ~-walk, voetoorgang; ~-way, dwarspad, kruisweg; ~ weave, kruisbinding; ~-wind, teenwind; ~ wires, kruisdrade; ~ wise, oorkruis; in die dwarste; kruislings; ~ word (puzzle), blokkiesraaisel, rebus.
crotch, (-es), mik; kruis (van liggaam).
crot'chet, hakie; kwartnoot; gril; ~eer', sonderling, dweper.
crotch'ety, wispelturig; vol grille, buiering; *be* ~, rebels wees, buierig wees, vol grille wees.
crotch'wood, blomhout.
cro'ton, kroton; ~ **aldehyde,** krotonaldehied.
crouch, laag buk; kruip; gebukkend staan; hurk.
croup¹, kruis (van 'n perd); rug (saal).
croup², kroep, wurgsiekte.
croup'ier, croupier; ondervoorsitter (eetmaal).
croute, croute.
croû'ton, braaibroodbrokkie, crouton.
crow, (n) kraai; gekraai; *the* ~ *thinks her BIRD the fairest,* elkeen meen dat sy uil 'n valk is; *EAT* ~, iets doen wat uiters onplesierig is; *as the* ~ *FLIES,* reguit; *HOODED* ~, bontkraai; *PIED* ~, bontkraai; *have a* ~ *to PLUCK with someone,* met iem. fout vind; 'n appeltjie te skil hê; *WHITE* ~, wit kraai, sonderlinge verskynsel; (v) **(-ed** or **crew, -ed),** kraai; pronk, spog; *nothing to* ~ *ABOUT,* niks om oor te roem nie; ~ *OVER someone,* oor iem. viktorie kraai; ~**bar,** koevoet; ligterhout; breekyster; ~**berry,** kraaibessie; kraaiheide; ~-**hill,** koeëltang.
crowd, (n) menigte, wemeling, klomp, duisternis, swetterjoel; gewoel, gedrang; gepeupel; *IN* ~ *s,* in klompe; *he might PASS in a* ~, hy's niks besonders nie; *a POOR* ~, 'n swak opkoms; 'n treurige klomp (spul); (v) volprop; (saam)dring, saampak, drom, toepak, ophoop; ~ *IN on,* verdring; ~ *INTO,* volstop; indruk, indring; ~ *OUT,* uitdruk; ~ *ROUND,* toedam; ~ *SAIL,* alle seile bysit; ~ *TO= GETHER,* saamskool, saamrot; ~ *THROUGH,* deurdruk; ~ *WITH,* volprop met; ~ **behaviour,** skaregedrag, massagedrag; ~**ed,** vol, opgehoop; oorbevolk; oorlaai; saamgedronge; ~**ing,** gekrioel.
crow'foot, kraaipoot; ranonkel; hanepoot (skeepsterm); voetangel; ~ **grass,** hoenderspoor, Natalkweek.
crow's: ~ **foot,** lagrimpel, oogplooitjie; kreukeltjie; kraaines; ~ **nest,** kraaines; maskorf.
crow: ~-**step gable,** trapgewel.
crown, (n) kroon (ook Engelse geldstuk); kruin; (hoe= de)bol; top, kop; boorkroon; (v) (be)kroon; voltooi; die kroon sit op; koning maak (dambord); *to* ~ *ALL,* om die kroon op die werk te sit; tot oormaat van ellende; *that* ~*s EVERYTHING,* dit kroon alles; ~ *a TOOTH,* 'n kroon op 'n tand sit; ~ **burst,** sterbreuk; ~ **circle,** kroonbrood; ~ **colony,** kroonkolonie; ~**ed crane,** mahem(kraanvoël); ~ **gall,** kroongal; ~ **glass,** kroonglas; ~**ing,** (n) kroning, (a) hoogste, grootste; ~*ing madness,* toppunt van dwaasheid; die opperste dwaasheid; ~ **jewels,** kroonjuwele; ~ **knot,** kruisknoop; ~ **land,** staatsgrond, kroongrond; ~ **moulding,** kroonlys; ~ **nut,** kruinmoer; ~ **octavo,** kroonoctavo; ~ **paper,** kroonpapier; ~ **piece,** kroon; kopriem; ~ **pinion,** kroonrondsel; ~ **plate,** kruinplaat; ~ **prince(ss),** kroonprins(es); ~ **prosecutor,** staatsaanklaer; ~ **roast,** kroonbraaistuk; ~ **rot,** kroonverrotting; ~ **rust,** kroonroes; ~ **saw,** kroonsaag, kommetjiesaag; ~ **stay,** ankerbaar; ankerplaat ~ **stone,** kroonsteen; ~ **wheel,** kroonrat; ~ **witness,** staatsgetuie.
crozier = **crosier.**
cru, cru (wyn); *grand* ~, grand cru.
cru'cial, kruisvormig; kritiek, beslissend; *kruis=; ~ test,* vuurproef.
crucian, geelvis.
cru'ciate, kruisvormig.
cru'cible, smeltkroes; vuurproef; *pass through the* ~, deur die smeltkroes gaan; ~ **tongs,** kroestang.

crucif'erous, kruisdraend; kruisblommig.
cru'cifix, (-es), kruisbeeld; kruis.
crucifi'xion, kruisiging, kruisdood.
cru'ciform, kruisvormig.
cru'cify, (..fied), kruisig, kruis.
cru'cite, kruissteen, holspaat.
cruck, kapstyl (dak).
crude, (a) rou; ru, grof, onafgewerk; primitief; kru; onryp; onbeholpe; onbekook; onverfyn; onverteer; onsuiwer; (n) ru-olie.
crude'ness, crud'ity, ruheid, kruheid; rouheid; onbekooktheid; onsuiwerheid.
crude: ~ **oil,** ru-olie; ~ **ore,** ru-erts.
cru'el, wreed, wreedaardig, hardvogtig; *BE* ~, 'n swaar hand hê; *BEING* ~ *to be kind,* iets onaangenaams (pynliks) doen vir die daaruitspruitende voordeel; sagte heelmeesters maak stinkende wonde; ~-**hearted,** wreedaardig, hard; ~ **ty,** wreedheid, wreedaardigheid, onmenslikheid.
cru'et, flessie, kruikie; standertjie; ~-**set,** ~-**stand,** sout-en-peperstel, -standertjie.
cruise, (n) (kruis)vaart, tog; rondvaart; kruisvlug; (v) kruis; rondvaar; ~ **r,** kruiser; ~**rweight,** ligswaargewig; ~ **ship,** toerskip.
cruis'ing, kruis=; ~ **level,** kruishoogte; ~ **power,** kruisvermoë; ~ **range,** kruisbereik (lugv.); ~ **speed,** kruissnelheid, kruispoed.
crull'er, wildebeeskaiing, kruller.
crumb, (n) krummel; brokkie; (v) krummel, paneer; ~ **brush,** tafelborsel; ~ **cake,** krummelkoek; ~ **cloth,** morskleedjie; ~ **crust,** krummelkors; ~**ed chop,** krummelkarmenaadjie.
crum'ble, krummel; brokkel; ~ *AWAY,* uitmekaarval; afbrokkel; ~ *into DUST,* tot niet gaan; ~ **crust,** krummelkors.
crum'bly, krummel(r)ig, bros, brokkel(r)ig.
crumbs, (interj.), maggies, genugtig.
crumb' tray, tafelskoppie.
crumb'y, crumm'y, krummelrig; sag, mollig; vuil; miserabel.
crump, (n) moerhou; swaar granaat; (v) moker.
crum'pet, plaatkoekie, flappertjie; klapperdop.
crum'ple, (ver)kreukel, verfrommel, frommel.
crunch, (n) gekraak, geknabbel, geknars; (v) vermorsel, knars; hard kou, knabbel; ~**ie,** knapkoekie; knappertjie (lekkergoed); ~**y,** korrel(r)ig; krakerig.
crupp'er, stertriem; kruis (perd).
crur'al, been=, dybeen=; ~ **hernia,** dybreuk.
crusade', (n) kruistog; (v) op 'n kruistog gaan; te velde trek; ~ **r,** kruisvaarder; stryder.
cruse, kruik.
crush, (n) gedrang; botsing, skok, verplettering; volte; minnekoors; *have a* ~ *on someone,* verlief wees op iem.; (v) verfrommel, verbrysel, vermaal, vernietig, verpletter, fynmaak; stamp; saampers; platlê, platdruk; indruk (eier); breek (mielies); vermorsel; verkreukel; onderdruk; ~ *to DEATH,* dooddruk; ~ *INTO,* binnedring; ~ *OUT,* uitpers; ~ *a REBEL= LION,* 'n opstand onderdruk; ~ *UP,* verfrommel, ~ *a cup of WINE,* 'n kelkie wyn wegslaan; ~**able,** breekbaar; ~-**barrier,** skareversperring; drukversperring.
crushed, gekneus, vergruis; onderdruk; ~ *FRAC= TURE,* splinterbreuk; ~ *MAIZE,* gebreekte mielies; gruis; ~ *WHEAT,* stampkoring.
crush: ~**er,** breker; stamper; breekmasjien; klipmeul; ~**er station,** ertsbrekery; ~ **fracture,** knypbreuk (buiteband); ~ **hat,** klaphoed, deukhoed.
crush'ing, verpletterend, vernietigend; ~ *DEFEAT,* verpletterende nederlaag; ~ *REPLY,* vernietigende antwoord; ~ **plant,** ertsbrekery; klipbreek=, ~ **station,** ertsbrekery; ~ **strength,** drukvastheid; ~ **test,** druktoets; vergruisingstoets.
crust, (n) kors, korsie; aanpaksel; roof; aanbrandsel; aansetsel (wyn); *live on* ~*s and crumbs,* van brood en water lewe; (v) oorkors, 'n kors vorm; met 'n korsie toemaak; aanbrand.
Crusta'cea, Skaaldiere, Krustaseë.
crusta'cean, (n) skaaldier; (a) skaaldier=.
crusta'ceous, geskaal, geskub; ~ *animal,* skaaldier.
crust: ~ **a'tion,** oorkors(t)ing; aanpaksel; aanbrand=

sel; ~**ed**, omkors; aangesit (wyn); ingewortel (gewoonte); verroes, verouderd, eerbiedwaardig; ~**ifica'tion**, verkorsting; ~'**ify**, verkors; ~**iness**, kwasterigheid, kors(ter)igheid, norsheid; stuursheid; ~**y**, kors(t)ig; nors, stuurs, bits, rebels.
crutch, (n) (**-es**), kruk, stut; kruis (van liggaam); mik (van skaap); *a pair of* ~*es*, krukke; (v) mikskeer; ~**ing**, mikskeer (skape); ~ **wool**, mikwol.
crux, kruis; knoop, (groot) moeilikheid; *the* ~ *of the matter*, die kern van die saak; die spil waarom alles draai.
cry, (n) (**cries**), skreeu, gil, geroep; gehuil; kreet; gebrul; straatroep; roepstem, bede; ~ *of ALARM*, noodkreet; *a FAR* ~, 'n lang ent; 'n groot verskil; *be in FULL* ~, in volle vaart agter iem. of iets aan wees; *MUCH* ~ *and little wool*, groot lawaai, weinig wol, meer lawaai as wol; ~ *of VICTORY*, segekreet; (v) (**cried**), smeek; roep; skreeu; huil, skrei, grens, ween; aanprys; omroep, te koop aanbied; ~ *ABOUT*, huil oor; ~ *out AGAINST*, protesteer teen; ~ *DOWN*, vergruis, verkleineer; ~ *with one EYE and laugh with the other*, deurmekaar huil en lag; ~ *one's EYES out*, bitter huil, trane met tuite huil; ~ *stinking FISH*, sy eie nes bevuil; ~ *HALVES*, sy deel eis; ~ *to (high) HEAVEN*, ten hemel skrei; ~ *for JOY*, van vreugde huil; ~ *with one eye and LAUGH with the other*, deurmekaar huil en lag; ~ *for the MOON*, die onmoontlike verlang; ~ *OFF*, terugtrek, kop uittrek; ~ *OUT*, uitroep; ~ *QUARTER*, om genade vra; ~ *QUITS*, 'n end maak aan 'n bakleiery; ~ *SHAME upon*, skande roep oor; ~ *oneself to SLEEP*, jou aan die slaap huil; *it is no use* ~*ing over SPILT milk*, gedane sake het geen keer nie; wat verby is, is verby; ~ *UP*, ophemel; ~ *your WARES*, jou goedere te koop aanbied (aanprys); ~ *WOLF*, 'n vals alarm gee; ~**-baby**, tjankbalie, grensbalie, brulbek, skreeubek.
cry'ing, (n) geskreeu; geskrei, grensery, gehuil; *start* ~, 'n keel opsit; (a) skreeuend, hemeltergend; dringend (behoefte); huilend; ~ *INJUSTICE*, skreiende onreg; *a* ~ *NEED*, 'n dringende behoefte; *a* ~ *SHAME*, 'n skreiende skande.
cryo: ~**biology**, kriobiologie; ~**gen**, kriogeen; ~**genic**, kriogeen, kriogenies; ~**genics**, ~**geny**, kriogenie; ~**lite**, krioliet; ~**nics**, krionika; ~**pump**, vakuumpomp; ~**stat**, kriostaat; ~**surgery**, kriochirurgie; ~**therapy**, hipotermie, krioterapie.
crypt, grafkelder, kripta; klierholte; ~**ic(al)**, geheim, duister, verborge; kripties; ~**o-Communist**, kriptokommunis; ~**ogam**, kriptogaam, spoorplant; ~**ogam'ic**, bedekbloeiend; ~**ogram**, ~**ograph**, stuk in geheimskrif; kriptogram; ~**og'rapher**, geheimskrywer, kriptograaf; ~**ograph'ic**, geheimskrifkundig; kriptografies; ~**og'raphy**, geheimskrif, kriptografie; ~**ol'ogy**, geheime taal.
cryp'ton, kripton.
cryp'torchid, klophings; klopram.
crys'tal, kristal; ~ **ball**, kristalbal; ~**-clear**, kristalhelder; ~ **form**, kristalvorm; ~**-gazer**, kristalkyker; ~**-gazing**, kristalkykery; ~ **glass**, kristalglas; ~ **grape**, kristaldruif; ~**line**, kristal-, kristalhelder; kristalvormig; ~ **line lens**, kristallens; ~ **liza'tion**, kristallisasie.
crys'tallize, kristalliseer; sandsuiker word; ~*d FRUIT*, versuikerde vrugte, suikervrugte; ~*d SUGAR*, sandsuiker.
crys'tal: ~**log'raphy**, kristalbeskrywing, kristallografie; ~**loid**, kristalvormig; ~**lo'metry**, kristallometrie; ~ **receiver**, kristalontvanger; ~ **set**, kristalstel; ~ **structure**, kristalstruktuur.
csar'das, czar'das, csardas, czardas, Hongaarse dans.
cten'oid, kamvormig.
C'-transmission, C-uitsending.
C'-transmitter, C-sender.
cub, (n) welp; kleintjie (van roofdier); ongepoetste vent; klein Padvinder; (v) (**-bed**), kleintjies kry, jong.
Cub'a, Kuba; ~**n**, (n) Kubaan; (a) Kubaans.
cub'age, cub'ature, inhoudsmeting, kubieke inhoud.
cub'anite, kubaniet.
cubb'y-hole, (bêre)hokkie, oondjie, paneelkassie; gesellige hoekie.

cube, (n) blokkie; dobbelsteen; kubus; derdemag; (v) tot die derde mag verhef; die inhoud bereken; ~ **gunpowder**, dobbelsteenkruit; ~ **root**, derdemagswortel; ~ **sugar**, klontjiesuiker, blokkiesuiker.
cu'beb(s), sterkpeper.
cub'ic, kubiek, van die derde mag; ruimte-, inhouds-; ~ *CONTENT*, kubieke inhoud; ~ *EQUATION*, derdemagsvergelyking; ~ *FOOT*, kubieke voet; ~ *INCH*, kubieke duim; ~ *MEASURE*, kubieke maat, ruimtemaat; ~**al**, kubies, kubusvormig.
cub'icle, kamertjie, hokkie, afskortinkie.
cub'iform, kubusvormig.
cub'ism, kubisme.
cub'ist, (n) kubis; (a) kubisties.
cub'it, elmbooglengte, voorarmlengte.
cub'oid, (n) kuboïed; (a) kubusvormig.
cub' **reporter**, leerlingverslaggewer.
cuck'old, (n) horingdraer, bedroë eggenoot; (v) horings opsit, bedrieg.
cu'ckoo, koekoek, diederik; idioot; *red-chested* ~, piet-my-vrou *(Notococcyx solitarius)*; ~ **clock**, koekoekklok; ~ **falcon**, koekoekvalk; ~ **finch**, koekoekvink; ~ **flower**, koekoeksblom; ~**-fly**, goudwesp; ~**-pint**, aronskelk, varkoor; ~**-shrike**, katakoeroe; ~**-spit**, slangspoeg; ~ **wasp**, goudwesp.
cu'cullate, kapvormig.
cuc'umber, komkommer; *as cool as a* ~, doodbedaard; ~ **tree**, komkommerboom.
cucurb'it, kalbas; distilleerkolf.
cud, herkoutjie; *chew the* ~, herkou; bepeins.
cud'dle, (n) omhelsing; (v) omhels; (ver)troetel; bevoel, betas; vas teen mekaar sit (lê), lepellê; ~ **some**, mollig.
cudd'ly, mollig.
cudd'y[1], (**cuddies**), eetkajuit; muurkas.
cudd'y[2], (**cuddies**), esel; hefboom.
cud'gel, (n) knopkierie; knots; *TAKE up (the)* ~*s*, die stryd aanbind; *take UP (the)* ~*s for someone*, dit vir iem. opneem, in die bres tree vir iem., party trek vir iem., iem. se saak bepleit; (v) (**-led**), knuppel, afransel; ~ *one's BRAINS*, die hoof breek, die kop krap, die harsings afmartel.
cue[1], (haar)stert, end; keu, stootstuk, biljartstok, snoekerstok.
cue[2], wenk, aanwysing, wagwoord (toneel); gedragslyn; *give someone his* ~, iem. iets in die mond gee.
cue: ~**-ball**, speelbal; ~ **chalk**, biljartkryt; ~**ist**, biljartspeler, snoekerspeler.
cuff[1], (n) vuisslag, opstopper.
cuff[2], (n) mou-opslag (baadjie); mansjet; los handboordjie, mouboordjie; (pl) handboeie; *OFF the* ~, uit die vuis; *ON the* ~, op skuld; ~**-leg panties**, kraagbroekie; ~ **link**, mansjetknoop.
cuirass', (**-es**), kuras, pantser, borsharnas; ~**ier'**, kurassier.
cuish = **cuisse**.
cuisine', kookkuns, cuisine; kookwyse; *excellent* ~, goeie ete, goeie tafel.
cuisse, dyharnas.
cul'-de-sac, doodloopstraat, blinde straatjie, keerweer; doodlooppunt (motor); blinde sak.
cul'inary, kombuis-, kook-; ~ *ART*, kookkuns; ~ *PLANTS*, eetplante, eetbare plante.
cull, (n) uitgooidier, swak dier; uitskot-, uitvangdier; (v) uitgooi, uitvang, uitsoek; pluk; uitdun.
cull'ender = **colander**.
cull'et, glasafval.
cull'ing, uitgooing; uitdunning.
cull'y, (n) (**cullies**), kêrel; vent; domkop; (v) (**cullied**), kul, bedrieg.
culm[1], steenkoolstof.
culm[2], grashalm; stingel.
cul'minant, hoogste; kulminerend.
cul'minate, toppunt bereik, kulmineer.
cul'minating point, hoogtepunt, toppunt, kulminasie.
culmina'tion, toppunt, kulminasie(punt), hoogtepunt.
culotte', broekrok, culotte.
culpabil'ity, strafbaarheid, strafskuldigheid, skuld, toerekenbaarheid.

culp'able, strafbaar (dader); strafwaardig, strafskul=
dig (daad); ~ *HOMICIDE,* strafbare manslag; ~
NEGLIGENCE, stafbare versuim (nalatigheid).
cul'prit, skuldige, beskuldigde, oortreder.
cult, kultus; mode; erediens; verering; ~ **figure,** kul=
tusfiguur; modefiguur; ~ **ic,** kulties.
cul'tivable, beboubaar, ploegbaar, bewerkbaar
(grond); verboubaar (gewas).
cul'tivar, kultivar.
cul'tivate, bewerk, bearbei, verbou; bebou; kweek;
teel, kultiveer; ontwikkel (stem); beoefen, beskaaf,
veredel; aankweek; aanplant (gewasse); ~
FRIENDSHIP, vriendskap aankweek.
cul'tivated, bebou, bewerk; beskaaf; ~ *LAND,* lan=
dery; ~ *PEOPLE,* beskaafde mense.
cultiva'tion, bebouing; teelt; verbouing; aankweking;
teling; beoefening; ontwikkeling, beskawing; aan=
planting (gewasse); bewerking, bearbeiding.
cul'tivator, boer; beoefenaar; verbouer; kweker;
landbouer; beskawer; skoffelploeg, skoffelwerk=
tuig; skoffeleg; grondbreker.
cul'trate, cul'triform, mesvormig.
cul'tural, kultuur=, kultureel, beskawings=, beska=
wend; ~ **value,** kulturele waarde.
cul'ture, (n) kweking, verbouing; aanbou; kultuur;
beskawing; ontwikkeling; *PHYSICAL* ~, lig=
gaamlike opvoeding; (v) bebou; aankweek; beska=
we; ontwikkel; ~ **area,** kultuurgebied; ~ **d,** bebou;
beskaaf, ontwikkeld; ~ *d pearl,* gekweekte pêrel; ~
flask, kweekfles; ~ **language,** kultuurtaal; ~ **me=
dium,** kweekbodem; ~ **plate,** kweekplaat; ~ **vul=
ture,** kultuurdier, kultuurhiëna.
cul'ver, houtduif.
cul'verin, veldslang (kanon).
cul'vert, riool; duiker, duiksluis, duiksloot; waterpyp;
deurlaat, deurloop.
cum, cum, met.
cum'bent, agteroorleunend.
cum'ber, (n) las, hindernis; (v) kwel, bemoeilik, be=
lemmer; ~ **some,** lastig, moeilik, hinderlik, beswa=
rend, swaar, lomp, log, onhandelbaar; omslagtig;
~ **someness,** omslagtigheid; lompheid.
cum'brance, las, hindernis.
cum'brous = **cumbersome.**
cu'mec, kumek.
cum grano salis, (L.) met 'n knypie sout, cum grano
salis.
cum'merbund, kamarband, lyfband.
cum(m)'in, komyn.
cum'quat, koemkwat.
cum'ulate, (v) ophoop, opstapel; toeneem; (a) opeen=
gehoop, opgestapel.
cumula'tion, ophoping, opstapeling, toename.
cum'ulative, ophopend, toenemend; kumulatief; ~
distribution function (stat.), kumulatiewe distribu=
siefunksie; ~ *preferent shares,* kumulatiewe voor=
keuraandele.
cum'ulo-nimbus, cumulonimbus, donderwolk.
cum'ulus, (..li), stapel, hoop; stapelwolk, cumulus.
cun'eal, cun'eate, wigvormig.
cun'eiform, wigvormig, ~ *CHARACTERS,* pylskrif;
~ *WRITING,* spykerskrif.
cunn'ing, (n) lis, sluheid, arglistigheid, jakkalostreke,
looshcid; rattinement; bedrewenheid, behendig=
heid; uitgeslapenheid; (a) (arg)listig, geslepe, uitge=
slape, loos, poliets, slinks, slu, slim, skelm; bedre=
we, behendig; *as ~ as a fox,* so slim soos 'n jakkals.
cup, (n) koppie; beker (sport); kelk (blom); dop (ak=
ker); kommetjie; lydenskelk; uitholling; *a BITTER*
~, 'n bittere kelk; *the ~ that CHEERS but not
inebriates,* tee; *DASH the ~ from someone's lips,*
iem. se hand in die as slaan; *one's ~ is FULL,* iem.
se beker is vol; *IN one's ~ s,* in die takke, aange=
klam; *OVER their ~ s,* onder 'n glasie; *a PART=
ING ~,* 'n glasie tot afskeid; *his ~ RUNS over,* sy
beker loop oor; (v) **(-ped),** grond skep (gholf); aar=
laat, bloedlaat (pasiënt); baktrek (hout); ~ *ped
END,* hol (versonke) ent; ~ *ped HANDS,* bakhan=
de, gekelkte hande; ~ **-and-ball joint,** koeëlgewrig;
~ **barometer,** bakbarometer; ~ **-bearer,** skinker.
cup'board, kas, muurkas, rakkas, koskas; ~ **button,**
werwel; ~ **love,** baatsugtige liefde; ~ **shelf,** kasrak.

cup'-cake, kolwyntjie, vormkoekie.
cup'el, kupel, smeltkroes; ~ **late,** kupelleer; ~ **-fur=
nace,** dryfhaard, kupelleeroond.
cup'ferron, kupferron.
cup: ~ **ful,** koppievol; ~ **grease,** dopsmeer; ~ **-
headed,** rondekop (boute); ~ **holder,** bekerwenner,
trofeehouer.
Cup'id, Cupido; liefdesgod.
cup'id, cupido'tjie.
cupid'ity, hebsug, lus, begerigheid; begeerlikheid.
cup'-match, bekerwedstryd.
cup'ola, koepel; vlamoond.
cupp'ing, aarlating, bloedlating.
cuprammo'nium, kuprammonium.
cup'r(e)ous, koperagtig, koper=.
cup'ric, koperhoudend, koper=; ~ **acid,** koper=
suur.
cuprif'erous, koperhoudend.
cuprine', koperagtig, koperkleurig.
cu'prite, kupriet, rooikopererts.
cu'pro-nickel, kopernikkel.
cu'prous, koper=.
cup: ~ **-shake,** ringskeur; ~ **-shaped,** dopvormig, ge=
kelk (hande).
cup'ule, koppie, doppie (bot.); suiertjie (soöl.).
cur, brak; skobbejak, vleël, lafaard.
cur'able, geneesbaar, geneeslik, heelbaar; ~ **ness,**
heelbaarheid.
cur'açao, cur'açoa, curaçao (likeur).
cur'acy, (..ies), predikantskap.
curar'e, kurare (gif).
cur'ate, hulpprediker; hulppriester (R.K.), onderpas=
toor; sieketrooster.
cur'ative, (n) geneesmiddel; (a) genesend; genees=
kragtig, heelkragtig; ~ *method,* geneeswyse.
curat'or, voog, opsigter; beheerder, kurator; ~
BONIS, curator bonis; ~ *DATIVE,* kurator da=
tief; ~ *ad LITEM,* curator ad litem; ~ **'ium,** kura=
torium; ~ **ship,** voogdyskap.
cur'atrix, (..trices), kuratrise.
curb, (n) kenketting (toom); beteueling, rem; be=
dwang; haasbak (perd); *ride a horse on the ~,* 'n
perd op die stang ry; (v) (be)teuel, in toom hou,
intoom, rem, bedwing; ~ **chain,** kenketting; ~ **ing,**
beteueling; ~ **roof,** gesplete dak; ~ **strap,** ken=
band; ~ **weight,** sleepgewig.
curc'uma, borrie, kurkuma.
curd, (n) stremsel, dikmelk, wrongel; ~ *s and whey,*
wrongel en wei; (v) strem, stol; dik word (melk).
cur'dle, skif, klonter, dik word, stulp, strem (melk);
stol (bloed); ~ *the BLOOD,* die bloed laat stol; ~ *d
MILK,* dikmelk, gestremde melk.
cur'dling, skifting.
cure[1], (n) snaakse persoon, eksentrieke mens.
cure[2], (n) geneesmiddel, kuur; genesing; geneeswyse;
raat; sorg; (die) droogmaak; *be beyond ~,* onge=
neeslik wees; (v) genees, heel, gesond maak; ryp
maak (kaas); sweet (tabak); sout, rook (vis); brei
(vel); verduursaam; insout, berei (spek); droog=
maak (tabak); indroë (lemoene); verouder; ~
CONCRETE, beton laat verhard; *what cannot be
~ d must be ENDURED,* 'n mens moet jou in die
onvermydelike skik; ~ *SKINS,* velle brei; ~
SOMEONE of something, iem. iets afleer; ~ **-all,**
panasee, wondermiddel; ~ **less,** ongeneesbaar, on=
geneeslik; ~ **r,** geneser, arts; insouter.
curette', (n) skraper, kuret (med.); (v) skraap.
curf'ew, aandklok, nagklok; aandklokreël; ~ **bell,**
aandklok.
cur'ia, curia (R.K.); ~ **l,** kuriaal.
cur'ie, curie.
cu'rine, kurien, kurine.
cur'ing, (die) genees; insout; inpekeling; brei; rypwor=
ding; bewerking, bereiding.
cur'io, (-s), kuriositeit, snuistery, antikwiteit, rariteit,
curio; ~ **'sa,** kuriositeite, curiosa.
curios'ity, (..ties), nuuskierigheid; sonderlingheid,
seldsaamheid; merkwaardigheid, curiosum, be=
sienswaardigheid, rariteit; weetgierigheid; ~ *killed
the cat,* van nuuskierigheid is die tronk vol, nuus=
kierige agies hoort in die wolwehok, dit is husse
met lang ore; ~ **shop,** rariteitswinkel.

cur'ious, nuuskierig, weetgierig, leergierig; benieud; sonderling, seldsaam; snaaks; merkwaardig, wonderlik; ~**ness**, merkwaardigheid; weetgierigheid.
cu'rite, curiet.
curl, (n) krul, haarlok; kronkeling, kinkel; golwing; (v) krul, friseer; oprol; kronkel; ~ **ed**, gekrul, gekroes (hare); ~**er**, haarkruller, krulyster, krulpen.
cur'lew, wulp (voël); ~ **sandpiper**, krombekstrandloper.
curl'ing, (n) krulling; Skotse ysspel, ysbal; (a) krullend, golwend; ~ **iron**, krulyster; ~ **paper**, papillot, krulpapier; ~ **pin**, krulpen, krulspeld; ~ **tongs**, krultang, friseertang.
cur'ly, krullerig; krul=; gelok; gekrul, gekroes; ~ **hair**, krullerige hare; ~ **head**, krulkop; ~**-headed**, krulkop=; ~ **pate**, krulkop.
curmudg'eon, vrek, gierigaard; suurpruim.
cur'rach, **cur'ragh**, mandjieboot.
cu'rrant, korint, korent; aalbesie; *BLACK* ~, swartbessie; *DRIED* ~*s*, korente; ~ **bread**, korentebrood; ~ **bun**, korentebolletjie; ~ **cake**, korentekoek; ~ **jelly**, korentejellie; ~ **juice**, aalbessiesap; ~ **pudding**, korentepoeding; ~ **wine**, aalbessiewyn.
cu'rrency, (..cies), loop; omloop; looptyd (wissel); duur (note); duurte (kontrak); koers (geld); geldigheidsduur (lisensie); gangbaarheid, valuta, betaalmiddel; geld, muntwese; ~ *of BILL*, termyn (looptyd) van wissel (lening); *HARD* ~, sterk (skaars) betaalmiddel; *SOFT* ~, swak betaalmiddel; ~ **control**, valutabeheer; ~ **country**, muntland; ~ **note**, muntbiljet; ~ **realignment**, valutaaanpassing.
cu'rrent, (n) loop, stroom; stroming; *ALTERNATING* ~, wisselstroom; *DIRECT* ~, gelykstroom; *ELECTRIC* ~, elektriese stroom; *RATED* ~, ontwerpstroom; *SWIM (go) with the* ~, saam met die stroom gaan; (a) lopend; geldend, geldig, gangbaar, in omloop; algemeen, verbreid; ~ *AFFAIRS*, lopende sake; sake v.d. dag; *sell BELOW* ~ *prices*, onder die mark verkoop; ~ **account**, ope rekening, lopende rekening; ~ **assets**, bedryfsbates; lik(w)iede bates; ~**-breaker**, stroomonderbreker; ~ **consumption**, stroomverbruik; ~ **expenses**, lopende uitgawe(s); ~ **flow**, stroomvloei; ~ **issue**, jongste uitgawe (seëls, tydskrif); ~ **liabilities**, bedryfslaste; ~ **ly**, teenswoordig, tans; ~ **price**, geldende (heersende) prys; ~ **rating**, ontwerpstroom; stroomdravermoë; ~ **season**, huidige seisoen; ~ **supply**, stroombron; stroomtoevoer; ~ **value**, markwaarde.
cu'rricle, ligte rytuig.
curric'ulum, (..la), kurrikulum, leergang, leerplan; ~ **vitae**, curriculum vitae, lewensbesonderhede; biografiese skets.
Cur'rie: ~ **Cup**, Curriebeker; ~ **Cup competition**, Curriebekerkompetsie; ~ **Cup match**, Curriebekerwedstryd.
cu'rried, met kerrie; ~ *CHICKEN*, kerriehoender; ~ *EGGS*, kerrie-eiers; ~ *FISH*, kerrievis.
cu'rrier, leerlooier, leerbereider, velbreier.
cu'rrish, gemeen, lafhartig; vleëlagtig; ~**ness**, hondsheid.
cu'rry¹, (n) kerrie; (v) **(curried)**, kerrie, met kerrie berei.
curry², (v) **(curried)**, roskam (perd); brei (leer); afransel, looi; ~ *favour with someone*, iem. se guns probeer win, witvoetjie soek by iem., mooibroodjies bak.
cu'rry-comb, (n, v), roskam.
curse, (n) vloek, verwensing, lastering; ramp; *not worth a* ~, geen stuiwer (sent) werd nie; (v) (uit) vloek, verwens; swets, laster; ~ *by bell and candle*, uit die kerk ban, onder sensuur sit; ~**d**, vervloek; bedonderde, vervloekste; verwenste; ~*d with*, gestraf met.
curs'edness, vloek, ellendige staat, vervloektheid.
curs'er, vervloeker; sweerder; vloeker, vloekbek.
curs'ing, swetsery, geknoop, gevloek; verwensing, vervloeking.
curs'ive, lopend; kursief; ~ **letter**, skryfletter; kursief(letter).
curs'or, loper.

cursor'es, loopvoëls.
cursor'ial, loop=, lopend; ~ **bird**, loopvoël.
curs'oriness, vlugtigheid, haastigheid; oppervlakkigheid.
curs'ory, vlugtig; oppervlakkig, haastig; terloops.
curt, kortaf, bits.
curtail', besnoei, verkort, bekrimp, verminder, afsny; inperk, inkort; ~ **ed**, besnoei, verkort; ~ **ment**, besnoeiing, verkorting, bekorting, inkorting, bekrimping, inperking.
curt'ain, (n) gordyn; klappie (motor); voorhang(sel); doek, skerm; *BEHIND the* ~*s*, agter die skerms; *BRING down the* ~, die gordyn laat sak; *DRAW the* ~*s*, die gordyne toetrek; *DRAW a* ~ *over*, die gordyn oor iets laat val; *DROP the* ~, die gordyn laat val (sak); *LIFT the* ~, die sluier oplig; *it was* ~*s WITH him*, dit was klaarpraat met hom; (v) met gordyne behang, omhul; ~**-call**, buiging (voor gehoor); ~ **cord**, gordynkoord; ~ **fastener**, klapknippie; ~ **fire**, spervuur, skermvuur; ~**ing**, gordynstof; ~ **lecture**, bedsermoen; ~**less**, sonder gordyne; ~ **pin**, gordynhakie; ~**-raiser**, voorspel; voorstuk; voorwedstryd; ~ **ring**, gordynring; ~ **rod**, gordynstok; gordynstaaf; ~ **tape**, gordynband; ~**-wall**, bekledingsmuur; skermmuur.
curt'ilage, erf, binneplaas, werf.
curt'ly, kortaf, bitsig.
curt'ness, kortheid, bitsheid, stugheid.
curt'sey, **curt'sy**, (n) (..sies), (knie)buiging, knieknik (van dames); *drop a* ~, 'n buiging maak; voor iem. 'n voetval doen; (v) 'n kniebuiging (knieknik) maak.
curva'ceous, gerond, vol rondings; mollig.
curv'ate, reëlmatig gebuig.
curva'tion, boog, kromming.
curv'ature, buiging; booglyn; kromming, kromte; kurwatuur.
curve, (n) boog; kromme (grafiek), kromming, krom lyn; buiging; draai (in pad); bog; (v) buig, krom, draai, 'n bog maak.
curved, gebuig, gerond, (ge)krom; ~ *BRACKET*, ronde hakie; ~ *BRICK*, ronde steen; ~ *RIB*, boogrib; ~ *SAW*, kromsaag; ~ *TRACK*, kromspoor; ~ *WASHER*, saalwaster.
curve' resistance, boogweerstand.
curv'et, **curvet'**, (n) bokkesprong, boksprong, boogsprong; (v) (-(t)ed), bokspring.
curv'icaudate, krulstert=.
curv'identate, met krultande (krom tande).
curv'iform, boogvormig.
curvilin'ear, kromlynig.
cus'cus¹, mottekruid, akkerwanie.
cus'cus², vlieënde vos, koeskoes.
cus'cus³, kuskusgras.
cuscut'a, dodder.
cu'sec, kusek (kubieke voet per sekonde).
cush, band (biljart, snoeker).
cush'at, houtduif, ringduif.
cu'shion, (n) kussing (biljart)band, stootband; buffer; straal (van hoef); haarkussinkie; (v) van kussings voorsien; met 'n kussing steun; demp, smoor; bal by die band bring (biljart); ~ **cover**, kussingoortreksel; ~ **ed**, van kussings voorsien; ~ **point**, demppunt; ~ **spring**, kussingveer; ~ **tyre**, kussingband.
cush'y, maklik, lekker, lig; ~ *job*, ligte werkie; maklike baantjie.
cusp, horing (v.d. maan); uitstekende punt; knobbel (op die kroon van 'n tand); keerpunt; ~**idal**, gepunt, spits.
cus'pidor, kwispedoor, spoegbakkie.
cuss, (n) kêrel, vent; (v) (sl.) vloek; ~**ed**, befoeterd, nukkerig, vervloek; ~**edness**, dwarstrekkery; dwarskoppigheid, befoeterdheid; *pure* ~*edness*, skone befoeterdheid; ~**-word**, vloekwoord.
cus'tard, vla; ~ **apple**, vla-appel; kaneelappel; suikerappel; ~ **cup**, vlaglasie; ~ **pie**, vlatert; ~ **powder**, vlapoeier; ~ **sauce**, vlasous.
custod'ian, voog, bewaarder, konservator, opsigter; kurator (museum); ~ **ant**, wagtermier; ~**ship**, kuratorskap; bewaring.
cus'tody, bewaring, voogdy, gevangenskap; hegtenis;

GET ~ *of a child,* toesig oor 'n kind kry; *IN* ~, in hegtenis, onder arres; *PLACE in* ~, in bewaring gee; *SAFE* ~, veilige bewaring; *TAKE into* ~, gevange neem.
cus'tom, klandisie; tol, inkomende regte; (pl) invoerregte, tol, doeane; gewoonte, sede, gebruik; aanwensel; *AS is the* ~, ouder gewoonte; *the* ~ *s of the TRADE,* handelsgebruike; ~ **arily,** gewoonlik, gebruiklik; ~ **ary,** (n) gebruiksboek (R.K.); (a) gewoon, gebruiklik; ~ **dues,** doeaneregte.
cus'tomer, klant, koper, afnemer; *a COOL* ~, 'n onverskrokke vent; *a queer* ~, 'n snaakse vent; *a TOUGH* ~, 'n harde koejawel; 'n lastige klant.
cus'tom, ~ **-free,** belastingvry; ~ **-house,** doeanekantoor; ~ **-house officer,** tolbeampte, doeaneamptenaar; ~ **-made,** volgens maat (bestelling) gemaak.
cus'toms: ~ **agreement,** doeane-ooreenkoms; ~ **area,** tolgebied; doeanegebied; ~ **clearance,** doeaneklaring; ~ **declaration,** doeaneverklaring; ~ **dues,** doeaneregte; ~ **duty,** doeaneregte; ~ **form,** doeanevorm; ~ **office,** doeanekantoor; ~ **officer,** doeaneamptenaar, doeanebeampte; ~ **tariff,** doeanetarief; ~ **union,** tolverbond, tolunie.
cut, (n) sny; keep; snit, snede (van mes), inbraak (myne); fatsoen; kap; kaphou; hakhou (krieket); moot (vis; stuk (vleis); hou, raps (sweep); besnoeiing, prysverlaging; *a* ~ *ABOVE,* 'n entjie beter; *the* ~ *of JIB,* sy bakkies; *SHORT* ~, kortpad, kortpaadjie; ~ *and THRUST,* handgemeen; tweegeveg; *a* ~ *of TOBACCO,* 'n string tabak; (v) (cut), sny, afsny, stukkend sny, opsny; kap, wegsny; kerf (twak); raps (met sweep); knip (hare); oopsny; besnoei (salaris); graveer; graaf (kanaal), seermaak; aankap (perd); negeer, verbygaan sonder groet, nie aankyk nie; verminder, verlaag (pryse); afskaf; afneem (kaarte); deursteek (dyk); slyp (glas); opbreek (spoorweg); uitgraaf, deurgraaf; *the ARGUMENT* ~ *s both ways,* die argument geld vir albei kante; ~ *ASUNDER,* in twee sny; ~ *BACK,* terugsny; *it* ~ *s BOTH ways,* die mes sny albei kante toe; dit geld vir albei kante; ~ *CAPERS,* flikkers gooi; ~ *a CONNECTION,* 'n kennismaking afbreek; ~ *a CORNER,* kort om 'n hoek stuur; ~ *DOWN,* besnoei; bespaar; neersabel; afmaai; neervel; vel, afkap; *everything is* ~ *and DRIED,* alles is in kanne en kruike; alles is kant en klaar; ~ *a sorry FIGURE,* 'n treurige figuur slaan; ~ *it FINE,* amper laat wees; die minimum toelaat; ~ *one's FINGER,* jou vinger sny; ~ *for the FIRST time,* aansny; ~ *the GROUND from under someone's feet,* iem. se voete onder hom uitslaan; die gras voor iem. se voete wegmaak; ~ *to the HEART,* diep grief; ~ *no ICE,* geen indruk maak nie; geen hond haar-af maak nie; geen ingang vind nie; ~ *IN,* in die rede val; indraai; (onverwags) tussen ander motors instuur; *be able to* ~ *with a KNIFE,* met 'n stok kan voel; ~ *the Gordian KNOT,* die (Gordiaanse) knoop deurhak; ~ *LOOSE,* vreeslik huishou; woes te kere gaan; ~ *a LOSS,* 'n verlies so klein moontlik maak; ~ *OFF with a shilling,* onterf; ~ *OUT,* uitknip; ignoreer; afdruk (koekie); die voet lig; iem. se hand in die as slaan; *be* ~ *OUT for,* uitgeknip wees vir; ~ *it OUT!* skei uit! ag, man! hou op! ~ *for PARTNERS,* trek vir maats, loot (kaartspel); ~ *a PERSON,* iem. nie wil raaksien nie (negeer); ~ *to PIECES,* in die pan hak (milit.); stukkend sny; ~ *up ROUGH,* uitvaar, briesend word; ~ *and RUN,* laat spat; die rieme neerlê (bêre); ~ *large SHIVES of another's loaf,* van 'n ander man se vel breë rieme sny; ~ *SHORT,* in die rede val; bekort; ~ *SOMEONE out,* iem. koudsit; iem. se hand in die as slaan; ~ *SQUARE,* haaks sny; *to* ~ *a long STORY short,* om kort te gaan; ~ *TEETH,* tande kry; ~ *UP,* stukkend sny; *be* ~ *UP,* erg ontsteld wees; omgekrap wees; ~ *out the WHOLE business,* die hele affère laat vaar; ~ **-and-thrust weapon,** kap-en-steekwapen.
cutan'eous, vel=, huid=; ~ *disease,* huidsiekte, velsiekte.
cut'-away, swa(w)elstertbaadjie; ~ **view,** oopwerkaansig.

cut: ~ **-back,** besnoeiing, terugsnyding; ~ **diamond,** geslypte diamant.
cute, skerpsinnig, skerp, fyn, glad, uitgeslape; oulik, geslepe; *very* ~, so slim soos die houtjie v.d. galg; ~ **ness,** oulikheid, geslepenheid, slim(mig)heid; glad(dig)heid, fynheid.
cut: ~ **-flower,** snyblom; ~ **glass,** geslypte glas; ~ **holes,** inbraakgate.
cut'icle, nerf (bot.); opperhuid; horinghuid; vlies; naelvelletjie, naelriem; *with* ~ *abraded,* nerf-af; ~ **-scissors,** naelvelskêr.
cutic'ular, kutikulêr.
cut'ie, poppie.
cut'ine, kurkstof, kutine, kutien.
cutiniza'tion, kurkstofvorming, verkurking.
cut'inize, verkurk.
cut'-in speed, inskakelspoed.
cut'is, onderhuid.
cut'lass, (-es), kort sabel, hartsvanger.
cut'ler, mesmaker; ~ **y,** mesmakery, meshandel; mesware, messegoed.
cut'let, kotelet; ~ **frill,** kotelettooisel.
cut: ~ **-nail,** vloerspyker; ~ **-out,** sekering, stroom(ver)breker; knalopening; uitskakelaar; uitsnysel; ~ **-out speed,** uitskakelspoed; ~ **purse,** sakkeroller; dief; ~ **-shot,** krulhou.
cut'ter, snyer; snymasjien; kapper; kotter; deegsnyer, koekafdrukker; uitsteekvorm; ~ *and polisher,* snyer en slyper; ~ **bar,** boorspil; ~ **block,** boorkop.
cut'throat, (n) ouderwetse skeermes; moordenaar, keelsnyer; boef; (a) genadeloos, meedoënloos; ~ **competition,** genadelose mededinging.
cutt'ing, (n) uitgrawing, deurgrawing (spoorweg); sny; uitknipsel (koerant); afsnysel; stiggie (plant); ~ *and polishing,* sny en slyp (diamante); (a) snydend; skerp, snedig, bitsig; ~ **angle,** snyhoek (in gereedskap); ~ **block,** kapblok; ~ **chisel,** snybeitel; ~ **circle,** snysirkel; ~ **edge,** snykant; ~ **face,** snyvlak; ~ **gauge,** snykruishout; ~ **machine,** afsnymasjien; ~ **plane,** snyvlak; ~ **pliers,** draadtang; ~ **s,** afsnysels; ~ **tongs,** snytang; ~ **tools,** snygereedskap.
cut'tle(fish), inkvis, seekat, sepia, tjokka.
cut: ~ **water,** golfbreker, boeg van skip; ~ **work,** uitknipwerk; ~ **worm,** miswurm, snywurm.
cyan'ic, siaan=; ~ **acid,** siaansuur.
cyan'ogen, siaan; sianied proses.
cy'anide, sianied.
cyano'sis, blousiekte, sianose.
cyberne'tic, kuberneties.
cybernet'ics, kubernetika.
cy'cad, sikade, broodboom.
cy'clamate, siklamaat.
cyc'lamen, alpevioolt jie, siklaam.
cy'cle, (n) kringloop; periode (elek.); (tyd)kring; een, siklus, reeks; fiets, rywiel; ~ *of action,* arbeidsperiode; (v) 'n kringloop volbring; fiets ry; ~ **lane,** fietslaan; ~ **path,** fietspad; ~ **racing,** fietsre(i)sies; ~ **track,** fietsbaan; ~ **tyre,** fietsband.
cyc'lic(al), siklies, kring=.
cyc'ling, ry (met 'n fiets), fietsry; ~ **race,** fietswedren.
cyc'list, fietser, wielryer, fietsryer.
cy'clograph, siklograaf.
cyc'loid, (n) sikloïed, sikloïde, ratlyn; (a) sikloïdaal.
cy'clometer, siklometer.
cyc'lone, werwelstorm, sikloon; depressiegebied, laag(drukgebied).
cyclon'ic, siklonies, siklonaal.
cyclop(a)ed'ia, afkorting vir **encyclopa(e)d'ia.**
Cyclope'an, Cyclop'ian, Siklopies.
Cyc'lop(s), (. . ops, . . opses, . . opes), Sikloop, Eenoog.
cyclora'ma, siklorama.
cy'clostyle, (n) afrolmasjien; (v) afrol, kopieer.
cyc'lotron, siklotron, kernreaktor, kernsplitser.
cyg'net, swaankuiken, jong swaan.
cyl'inder, silinder; ~ **barrel,** silinderromp; ~ **bloc(k),** silinderblok; ~ **boiler,** silindriese ketel; ~ **boot,** silinderkous (motor); ~ **bore,** silinderboring, silinderdeursnee; ~ **capacity,** silinderinhoud; ~ **cover,** silinderdeksel; ~ **head,** silinderkop; ~ **jacket,** silin-

dermantel; ~ **lining,** silindervoering; ~ **press,** silinderpers; ~**-shaped,** silindervormig; ~ **skirt,** silinderrok; ~ **sleeve,** silindervoering; ~ **wall(s),** silinderwand(e); ~ **watch,** silinderhorlosie.
cylin'drical, silindervormig, silindries.
cylin'driform, silindervormig.
cyl'indroid, (n) silindroïed; (a) silindervormig.
cym'a, (-e), cyma, ojief; ~ **recta,** regte ojief, klokojief; geutlys; ~ **reversa,** omgekeerde ojief, hielojief.
cym'bal, simbaal; ~**ist,** simbalis.
cym'biform, bootvormig.
cyme, byskerm (bot.).
cym'ose, byskerm=.
Cym'ric, Wallies, Kimries.
cyn'ic, (n) sinikus, vitter, menshater; (a) sinies; ~**al,** ongevoelig, sarkasties, skerp; hondagtig; sinies; ~**ism,** sinisme; hondagtigheid; ~ **spasm,** lagkramp.
cynophob'ia, hondevrees.
cyn'osure, poolster, lei-ster; aantrekking; *the* ~ *of all eyes,* die aantrekkingspunt van alle oë; die middelpunt van bewondering.
cyph'er, syfer; nul.
cyp'raea, porseleinslak.
cyp'ress, (-es), sipres.

Cyp'rian, (n) Cipriaan, Sipriaan; (a) Cipries, Sipries.
Cyp'riot, (n) Ciprioot, Siprioot; (a) Cipries, Sipries.
Cyrena'ic, (n) Cireneër; (a) Cireneïes.
Cyrena'ica, Cirenaïka, Sirenaïka.
Cyre'ne, Cirene.
Cyp'rus, Ciprus, Siprus.
Cyrill'ic, Cirillies.
cyst, ettersak, sist, sak, blaas; saksweer; ~**ic,** blaas=; sisties; ~ *ic duct,* (gal)blaasbuis; ~**iform,** blaasvormig.
cysticerc'us, blaaswurm.
cystit'is, blaasontsteking, sistitis.
cyst'oscope, sistoskoop.
cystot'omy, blaasoperasie.
cytogen'esis, selontwikkeling, selvorming.
cytogenet'ics, sitogenetika.
cytol'ogy, selleer, sitologie.
cyto'lysis, selvervloeiing, sitolise.
cyt'oplasm, selplasma, sitoplasma.
cytotox'in, selgif, sitotoksien, =ine.
czar, tsaar.
czarin'a, tsarina.
Czech(oslov'ak), (n) Tsjeg; (a) Tsjeggies.
Czechoslovak'ia, Tsjeggo-Slowakye; ~**n (n)** Tsjeggo-Slowaak; (a) Tsjeggo-Slowaaks.

D

d, (ds, d's, dees), d; *d*~ *!* verdomp!
da, paps, pappie.
dab¹, (n) tikkie, kloppie; stekie; vlekkie; klodder; slier, slons; (v) **(-bed),** tik, sag aanraak; smeer; bet, dep (wond).
dab², (n) platvis, skar.
dab³, (n) stuk vleis.
dab⁴, (n) uithaler, doring; (a) bedrewe; uithaler=; ~ *hand,* uithaler(speler).
dab⁵, (n) doppie (kompasnaald).
dab'ber, depper.
dab'bing, sprinkeling; skimmelverfwerk; geprikte klipwerk.
dab'ble, sprinkel; plas, bemors; natmaak; 'n bietjie doen aan, liefhebber; ~**r,** morser; knoeier; diletant; stumperd, beunhaas; liefhebber.
dab'bling, geliefhebber,
dab'chick, duiker(tjie); seilbootjie.
da ca'po, (It., mus.), da capo, herhaal van die begin af.
dace, witvis.
da'cha, villa, daga.
dachs'hund, worshond(jie); Dashond.
dacoit', struikrower; ~**y,** benderoof; struikrowery.
dacryo'ma, druipoog.
dac'tyl, daktiel; ~**ic,** daktilies.
dactyl'ogram, vingerafdruk, daktilogram.
dactylog'raphy, daktilografie.
dactylol'ogy, vingerspraak, daktilologie.
dad, pa, vadertjie, paps.
Dad'a, Dada; ~**ism,** Dadaïsme.
dadd'y, (daddies), pa, vadertjie; ~**-long'-legs,** langbeenspinnekop, hooiwa, langpoot.
dad'o, (-s), beskot, lambrisering; dado; sokkel (suil); ~ **board,** dadoplank; dadobord; ~ **cutter,** groefsnyer, keepsnyer; ~ **moulding,** dadolys; ~ **plane,** groefskaaf.
daed'al, geheimsinnig, ingewikkeld, kunstig, vernuftig.
daemon = **demon.**
daff'odil, affodil, môresterretjie, plaaslelie.
daf'fy, mal, gek.
daft, dwaas, bekonkel, mal; *you're* ~ *!* jy is mal! jy is skoon besimpeld (bekonkeld)!; ~**ness,** dwaasheid, malheid.
dagg'a, dagga *(Cannobis sativa);* ~ **pipe,** daggapyp; ~ **smoker,** daggaroker.
dagg'er, dolk, ponjaard; kruisie; *be at* ~ *s DRAWN,* bitter vyande wees, op gespanne voet met mekaar

wees, mekaar in die hare sit; met mekaar oorhoop wees; soos vuur en water wees; *LOOK* ~ *s at someone,* iem. woedend aankyk; iem. stukkend kyk; ~**-shaped,** dolkvormig; ~ **stab,** dolksteek.
da'gha, dagha, messelklei.
dag'o, (-s), Amerikaanse Spanjaard (Italianer, Portugees), dago.
dags, misklosse.
dague'rreotype, daguerreotipe.
dahl'ia, dahlia; *blue* ~, onmoontlike saak.
Dail Ei'reann, Ierse Laerhuis, Ierse Landdag.
dail'y, (n) (dailies), dagblad; (a, adv) daagliks, dag=; per dag; aldag, aldae; daags; ~ *BALANCE,* dagsaldo; ~ *BREAD,* daaglikse brood; ~ *DOZEN,* liggaamsoefeninge; *D*~ *ORDERS,* dagbevel; ~*-PAID worker,* dagloner; ~ *PAPER,* dagblad; ~ *PAY,* dagloon; ~ *PRESS,* dagbladpers; ~ *REPORT,* dagverslag; ~ *TASK,* dagwerk, dagtaak; ~ *WAGE(S),* dagloon; ~ *WOMAN,* skoonmaakster.
dain'tily, kraaksindelik; fyntjies; kieskeurig; keurig.
dain'tiness, sierlikheid, fynheid, netheid; kieskeurigheid; keurigheid.
dain'ty, (n) (..ties), lekkerny, delikatesse, snoepery, versnapering; (a) kieskeurig; kraaksindelik; fyn, sierlik; presies; netjies; delikaat; *FOND of* ~ *dishes,* lekkerbekkig; *a* ~ *MORSEL,* die neusie v.d. salm.
dair'y, (dairies) melkkamer; melkery; ~ **beef breed,** melkvleisras; ~ **breed,** melkras; ~ **cattle,** melkbeeste; ~ **cow,** melkkoei, ~ **factory,** suiwelfabriek; ~ **farm,** melkboerdery, melkery; ~ **farmer,** melkboer, suiwelboer; ~**-farmers' union,** suiwelbond; ~**-farming,** melkboerdery, suiwelboerdery; ~ **herd,** melkkudde; ~ **industry,** suiwelnywerheid, suiwelbedryf; ~**ing,** melkboerdery, suiwelboerdery; ~ **maid,** melkmeisie; ~ **man,** melkboer; melkverkoper; ~ **meal,** suiwelmeel; ~ **nut,** kragvoerkoekie; ~ **produce,** suiwelprodukte; ~ **product,** suiwelproduk ~ **ranching,** veldmelkboerdery; ~ **woman,** melkboerin; melkverkoopster.
dais, dais, podium, verhewe sitplek, verhoog; troonhemel.
dais'y, (daisies), grasblom, (geel) margriet, gousblom, botterblom; madeliefie; pragstuk; ~**-cutter,** kruipbal; sleepvoet; skeerhou; ~ **lawn,** klawerkweek, margrietgras.
dale, dal, laagte, kom, vlei.
dales'man, dalbewoner.

dall'iance, gedartel, gebeusel; getalm, liefkosing; uitstel.
dall'y, (dallied), stoei, dartel, speel; draai, talm; ~ *away*, verbeusel; ~**ing**, getalm; gedartel.
Dalma'tian, (n) Dalmasiër; Dalmasiese hond; (a) Dalmasies.
dalmat'ic, dalmatika (kledingstuk), dalmatiek.
dal'tonism, kleurblindheid, daltonisme.
dam[1], (n) dam; damwal; (v) opdam, stuit; ~ *up*, opdam, stuit, keer.
dam[2], (n) maai, moeder, moer (diere); *the devil and his* ~, die duiwel en sy moer.
dam'age, (n) skade, nadeel; awery (versekering); beskadiging, afbreuk; (pl) onkoste, skadevergoeding; ~ *CAUSED by hail*, haelskade; *to the* ~ *OF*, ten nadele van; *PAY* ~, skadevergoeding betaal; *RECOVER* ~*s*, skadevergoeding kry; *SUSTAIN* ~, skade ly; (v) beskadig, skaad, benadeel, in diskrediet bring; ~**able**, breekbaar, beskadigbaar; ~**d**, geskonde, beskadig.
dam'aging, beswarend, beledigend; skadelik; ~ *evidence*, beswarende getuienis.
Da'mara, Damara; ~ **cattle**, Damarabeeste.
Damascene', (n) Damassener; (a) Damasseens.
damascene', (v) damasseer.
dam'ask, (n) damas; damaskusrooi; damassenerstaal; (v) damasseer, versier; (a) gedamasseer; rooi; ~ **een'** = **damascene**; ~ **linen**, damaslinne; ~ **plum**, damaspruim; ~ **rose**, damasroos; ~ **silk**, damassy, sydamas; ~ **steel**, damassenerstaal; ~ **weaver**, damaswewer.
dame, dame; huisvrou; vrou; damestitel; matrone; *D~ FORTUNE*, voorspoed, geluk; *D~ NATURE*, Moeder Natuur.
damm'ar, dammar (harpuis).
damn, (n) vloek; *I don't CARE a* ~, dit traak my niks; *not WORTH a* ~, geen flenter werd nie; ~! verduiwels! verduiweld; (d) veroordeel; benadeel; vloek; verdoem; ~ *with faint praise*, deur skamele lof verdoem; iem. op 'n mooi manier slegsê; ~**abil'ity**, doemwaardigheid; ~**able**, verdoemlik, doemwaardig, vloekwaardig, verdoemenswaardig; sleg; vervloekste; ~**ableness**, verdoemlikheid; slegtheid; ~**a'tion**, verdoeming, verdoemenis; veroordeling, afkeuring; (interj) vervloeks! verdomp! ~**atory**, verdoemend, veroordelend; ~**ed**, (n) (die) verdoemdes; (a) verdoem; veroordeel; vervloek; bliksems, donders; vermaledyd, verdomd; *life is just one* ~ *ed thing after another*, hoe meer dae hoe meer dinge.
dam'nify, (..fied), beskadig, bederf, benadeel.
damn'ing, (n) verdoeming; (a) verdoemend, veroordelend, beswarend; vernietigend (getuienis).
Dam'ocles: *the sword of* ~, die swaard van Damokles.
da'mosel, da'mozel, (arch.), meisie, dame.
damp, (n) myngas; moedeloosheid, neerslagtigheid; vogtigheid, klamheid; (v) ontmoedig, bekoel; vogtig maak, natmaak; smoor, doof, demp (geluid); (a) vogtig, klam; neerslagtig; ~ **course**, voglaag.
damp'en, klam maak, klam word; ~ *one's ardour*, 'n demper op iem. sit (plaas); iem. se geesdrif demp; ~**er**, demper.
dam'per, demper, sleutel, skuif (in kaggelpyp); sordino, klankverdower (mus.); ontmoediging, bekoeling; domper; klammerder (vir seël); teleurstelling (fig); *put the* ~ *on someone (something)*, 'n demper op iem. (iets) sit; ~ **spring**, dempveer; ~ **valve**, dempklep.
damp: ~**ing**, damping; ~**ish**, klammerig, vogtig; ~**ness**, vogtigheid, klamheid; ~**-proof**, vogvry, vogdig; ~*-proof course*, vogdigte laag, voglaag; ~**-resisting**, vogwerend; ~**squib**, fiasko, mislukking, misoes; sisser.
dam'sel, meisie; maagd, jonkvrou.
dam'son, damaspruim.
Dan, Dan; *from* ~ *to Beersheba*, van Dan tot Berseba.
dance, (n) dans, bal, dansparty; ~ *of DEATH*, dodedans; *LEAD someone a* ~, vir iem. die wêreld moeilik maak; *LEAD the* ~, voor dans; (v) dans, skoffel; ~ *ABOUT*, ronddans, rondspring; ~ *ATTENDANCE on a person*, iem. op sy wenke bedien;

iem. agternaloop; *make someone* ~ *on NOTHING*, iem. ophang, iem. se keel laat weet hoe swaar sy agterlyf is; ~ *to someone's TUNE (pipes)*, na iem. se pype dans; ~ **band**, dansorkes; ~ **floor**, dansvloer; ~ **hall**, danssaal; ~**-leader**, voordanser; ~ **music**, dansmusiek; ~**r**, danser; danseres, ~ **step**, danspas(sie); ~ **tune**, danswysie.
danc'ing, dans, gedans, dansery; geskoffel; ~ **academy**, dansinrigting; ~ **card**, dansboekie; ~ **couple**, danspaar; ~ **girl**, danseres; ~ **instructor**, dansonderwyser(es); ~ **lesson**, dansles; ~ **master**, dansmeester; ~ **mistress**, dansmeesteres; ~ **partner**, dansmaat; ~ **room**, danssaal; ~ **school**, dansskool; ~ **shoe**, dansskoen; ~ **song**, danslied.
dan'delion, molslaai, perdeblom.
dan'der, slegte humeur; *get one's* ~ *up*, iem. se bloed laat kook.
dandi'acal, dan'dified, fatterig, opgetooi, opgesmuk.
dan'dify, (..fied), opskik, optakel.
dan'dle, wieg, wip; liefkoos, vertroetel.
dan'druff, skilfers; *full of* ~, skilferig; ~ **lotion**, skilfer(was)middel; ~**y**, skilferagtig.
dan'dy[1], (n) **(dandies)**, hangmat.
dan'dy[2], (n) **(dandies)**, modegek, laventelhaan, swierbol, heertjie, fat, windmaker; (a) windmakerig, spoggerig; keurig; ~ **brush**, perdeborsel; denne-bros; ~ **cart**, veerkarretjie; ~**ish**, fatterig, pronkerig; ~**ism**, fatterigheid; swierigheid; pronkerigheid; ~ **roll(er)**, gaaswals.
Dane, Deen; Noorman; Deense hond; *Great* ~, Deense hond; **d~wort**, wilde vlier.
dan'ger, gevaar; *on the* ~ *list*, in lewensgevaar; ~ **area**, gevaargebied; ~ **man**, waarskuwer, rooivlagdraer.
dan'gerous, gevaarlik, gewaag; ~ *FORK*, gevaarlike vurk; ~ *to LIFE*, lewensgevaarlik.
dan'ger: ~ **point**, gevaarpunt; ~ **sign(al)**, gevaarteken, gevaarsein; ~ **zone**, gevaarsone, gevaarstrook.
dan'gle, bengel; los hang; naloop; voorspieël; ~**r**, meisiegek, naloper; ~ **tag**, hangkaatser.
dan'gling, geslinger.
Dan'ish, Deens.
dank, vogtig, nat; ~**ish**, vogtig, natterig; ~**ness**, vogtigheid, natheid.
danse maca'bre, (F.) danse macabre, dodedans.
danseur', (F.), balletdanser.
danseu'se, (F.), balletdanseres.
Dan'ube, Donau, Donou.
dap, (n) keep, inkeping; (v) **(-ped)**, (laat) opspring ('n bal); laat dobber; inkeep.
daph'ne, soort lourier.
dap'-joint, keeplas.
dapp'er, fiks, lewendig; keurig, agtermekaar, netjies, vief.
dap'ple, (v) spikkel, bont maak; vlek; (a) bont, gespikkel(d), gevlek; ~ **bay**, appelbruinperd, ~**d**, gespikkel(d), geappel (perd); ~ **grey**, appelblou; appelblouskimmel.
dar'by, (darbies), stryktroffel, (pl) boeie.
Darb'y and Joan, 'n nog verliefde ou egpaar.
Dard'anelles, Dardanelle.
dare, (n) uitdaging; (v) (aan)durf, waag; uitdaag, tart, trotseer; *I* ~ *SAY*, ek veronderstel; *let "I* ~ *not" WAIT upon "I would"*, jou aan kou water brand.
dare'devil, (n) waaghals, durfal; (a) doldries, roekeloos; ~**ish**, waaghalsig; ~**ry**, waghalsery, doldapperheid.
dar'ing, (n) astrantheid, vermetelheid, onverskrokkenheid, waagmoed, stoutheid, durf(krag); (a) onverskrokke, (stout)moedig, vermetel, koen, astrant; ~ *ACT*, vermetele daad; ~ *ASSURANCE*, stoutmoedigheid.
dark, (n) donker, duisterheid, duisternis; *AT* ~, teen die aand; *BE in the* ~, in die duister wees; van niks af weet nie; *in the* ~ *all CATS are grey*, in die donker is alle katte grou; *GROPE in the* ~, in die donker rondtas, in die donker soek; *IN the* ~, in die donker; *KEEP one in the* ~, iem. in die duister hou; *a LEAP in the* ~, 'n sprong in die onbekende; (a) donker, duister; somber; sleg; onheilspellend; onwetend; onverlig; onbekend (perd); *the D~*

AGES, die Middeleeue; *the D~ CONTINENT*, die Donker Vasteland; *the ~est hour is that before the DAWN*, dit is droogte net voor die reën; hoe steiler die opdraand, hoe nader die end; *a ~ HORSE*, 'n onbekende mededinger; *KEEP ~* , verberg, geheim hou; *as ~ as PITCH*, so donker soos die nag; pik-donker; *the ~ SIDE of things*, die donker kant v.d. lewe; ~ **blue**, donkerblou; ~ **brown**, donkerbruin; ~**-coloured**, donkerkleurig.
dark'en, donker word; verdonker, benewel, donker maak, verduister; *don't ~ my door*, bly van my huis weg; moenie jou pote oor my drumpel sit nie; ~**ing**, verduistering, verdonkering.
dark: ~**-eyed**, donkeroog~; ~ **glasses**, donker bril; ~ **green**, donkergroen; ~ **grey**, donkergrys; ~**-haired**, donkerharig; ~ **horse**, buiteperd; onsekerheid; ~**ish**, donkeragtig, donkerig, skemerig; ~ **lantern**, diewelantern; ~**le**, donker word; verborge lê; ~**ling**, in die donker; ~**ly**, donker, in die geheim; onheilspellend; in duistere taal; ~**ness**, duisternis, donkering, donkerte, duisterheid, donkerheid; *PRINCE of D~ness*, Satan; *the POWERS of ~ness*, bose geeste; ~ **picture**, donker prentjie; ~ **purple**, donkerpers; ~ **red**, donkerrooi; ~ **room**, donkerkamer (fot.); ~ **side**, donker sy, skadusy (fig.); ~**-skinned**, donkervellig, soel; **D~y**, (..**kies**), Neger; ~ **suit**, donkerpak; ~ **weather**, dreigende onweer.
dar'ling, (n) liefling, hartlam, liefste, skat; soetlief; (a) liefste, geliefde, liewe.
darn¹, (n) stop; stopplek; (v) stop, maas; heelmaak.
darn², (v): ~ *it!* vervlaks! ~**ed**, verduiweld, deksels; *it's a ~ed nuisance*, dis 'n vervlakste hindernis.
darn'el, drabok.
darn'er, stopper.
darn'ing, stopwerk; ~ **ball**, maasbal; ~ **cotton**, stopwol; ~ **needle**, stopnaald; ~ **stitch**, stopsteek; ~ **wool**, stopwol.
dart, (n) pyl, (werp)spies; veerpyltjie, werppyltjie; skig, gooipyl(tjie), speelpyl(tjie); sprong, skielike beweging; (v) skiet; gooi; wegspring, pyl, pylsnel beweeg; ~ **board**, pylskyf.
dart'er¹, gooier.
dart'er², slanghalsvoël.
dar'tle, skiet, vonkel.
dart' pistol, dwelmpistool.
darts, pyltjiesgooi, werppyltjies.
Darwin'ian, (n) Darwinis; (a) Darwinisties.
Dar'winism, Darwinisme.
Dar'winist, Darwinis; ~**'ic**, Darwinisties.
dash, (n) (-es), slag; storm, botsing; sweem; stoot; skik; golfslag, geklots (golwe); veeg, streep; skeut (drank); haal; snelle beweging; vuur, flinkheid, durf, fut; swier, bevalligheid; vertoon; aandagstreep; afbrekingsteken; *a ~ of BRANDY*, 'n rapsie brandewyn; *CUT a ~* , 'n flikker maak; jou lyf windmaker hou; *MAKE a ~ for*, na iets snel; vlieg na; *a ~ OF*, 'n ietsie van; 'n rapsie van; ~ *of the PEN*, penstreep; (v) wegstoot; slaan, gooi, smyt, bons; kletter; platslaan; uit die veld slaan, verleë maak; hol, snel; klots (golwe); bespat; meng (wyn met water); verpletter, vernietig; teleurstel; ~ *AGAINST*, stamp teen; ~ *AT*, aanvlieg op; ~ *the CUP from someone's lips*, iem. hokslaan; iem. 'n genot ontneem; ~ *one's HOPES*, sy hoop verydel; ~ *INTO*, bots teen; ~ *IT!* vervlaks! ~ *OFF*, haastig teken (skryf); weghol; ~ *ON*, voortstorm; ~ *OUT*, uithardloop; uitstreep; ~ *to RUIN*, in die verderf stoot; ~ *away TEARS*, trane afvee; ~ *UPON one*, losstorm op iem.; ~ *WITH*, vermeng; 'n skeutjie bygooi van; ~ **board**, spatbord; instrumentebord, paneelbord; ~ **brace**, paneelverspanstuk; ~**ed**, vervlaks, verbrands; ~**er**, roerstok; karringstok; ~**ing**, (n) geklots (a) haastig, voortvarend; kranig; vurig; swierig, modieus; ~ **lamp**, spatbordlamp; paneellamp; ~ **plate**, stootplaat; ~ **pot**, slagdemper; ~ **switch**, paneelskakelaar; ~ **tank**, gravitasietenk; ~ **unit**, paneeleenheid; ~**y**, swierig.
das'sie, dassie; ~ **rat**, klipmuis.
das'tard, (n) lafaard; (a) lafhartig, bang; ~**liness**, lafhartigheid, bangheid; ~**ly**, lafhartig, laag, gemeen.

dat'a, gegewens, data; ~ **bank**, databank.
dat'able, dateerbaar.
data: ~ **processing**, dataverwerking; ~ **retrieval**, data-ontsluiting.
date¹, (n) dadel (vrug).
date², (n) datum, dagtekening; afspraak; jaartal; tydperk; *BEAR the ~* , gedateer wees; *BRING up to ~* , (boeke) bywerk; *BLIND ~* , onbeplande afspraak, lukraak afspraak, toe-oë-afspraak, molafspraak; ~ *of EXPIRY*, vervaldatum; *FIX the ~* , jaar en dag bepaal; ~ *of ISSUE*, datum van uitgifte; *KEEP up to ~* , byhou; ~ *of MATURITY*, vervaldag; *OUT of ~* , verouder; ouderwets, uit die mode; *UP to ~* , nuwerwets, modern; by (tot op) datum; op hoogte van die tyd; (v) dateer, dagteken; reken; die datum vasstel; afspraak maak (met nooi); ~ *from*, dagteken van; reken van; met ingang van; ~**d**, gedateer, verouderd; *be ~d*, genooi word (deur 'n man), geskied word (stud.); ~**less**, ongedateer, sonder datum; ~ **line**, datumgrens; datering; **international ~ line**, internasionale datumgrens; ~ **loaf**, dadelbrood; ~ **mark**, jaarmerk, datummerk; datumstempel; ~ **oil**, dadelolie; ~ **palm**, dadelpalm; ~ **plum**, dadelpruim; ~ **press**, stempelmasjien, datummasjien; ~**r**, stempelmasjien; ~ **stamp**, datumstempel; ~**-stone**, dadelpit; ~ **wine**, dadelwyn.
dat'ive, (n) datief; (a) geregtelik aangestel; *executor ~* , eksekuteur datief.
dat'um, (data), gegewe; datum; meetpunt (in gebou); (pl) gegewens, data; ~ **level**, stelhoogte; uitgangspeil, -vlak; ~ **line**, uitgangslyn, nullyn, stellyn; ~ **point**, aanvangspunt, basispunt.
datur'a, stinkblaar, stinkolie.
daub, (n) klei; smeer, veeg, knoeiwerk; smeerlaag (verf); gooipleister; (v) besmeer, bepleister, beplak; klad; pleister aangooi; verf aansmeer; ~**er**, kladskilder; ~**ing**, smeerdery; kladskildering; gooipleistering; ~**y**, kladderig.
daught'er, dogter; *he that would the ~ win, must with the mother first begin*, as jy die dogter wil kry, moet jy eers na die moeder vry; ~**hood**, dogterskap; ~**-in-law**, **(daughters-in-law)**, skoondogter; ~**ly**, dogterlik.
daunt, verskrik, ontmoedig, afskrik; *he is not EASILY ~ed*, hy laat hom nie met 'n blaas vol ertjies op loop jaag nie; *NOTHING ~ed*, onvervaard; ~**less**, onverskrokke, onbevrees, moedig; ~**lessness**, onverskrokkenheid, moedigheid.
dauph'in, kroonprins (Frankryk), dauphin; ~**ess**, kroonprinses, dauphine.
dav'enport¹, groot rusbank; bed-sofa.
dav'enport², skryftafeltjie.
Da'vid, Dawid; ~ *and Jonathan*, soos Dawid en Jonathan.
dav'it, dowe jut; kraanbalk; dawit, davit; hysmasjien.
Davy Jo'nes's locker, die diepte van die see; watergraf; *go to ~* , na die kelder gaan, na die haaie gaan.
Dav'y lamp, Davylamp, veiligheidslamp.
daw, kraai, kerkkraai.
daw'dle, tyd vermors, talm, draai, draal, lanterfanter, sloer, leuter, treusel, (ver)beusel, lol; ~ *away*, verbeusel, vermors; ~**r**, leuterkous, treuselaar, beuselaar, draaikous, drentelaar, draaier.
daw'dling, gesloer, getreusel, getalm; beuselwerk.
dawn, (n) dagbreek, rooidag, daeraad, sonsopgang, sonop, daglumier; *at the CRACK of ~* , douvoordag; *after the DARKNESS comes the ~* , die dag kom uit die nag; *before the LIGHT of ~* , douvoordag; (v) lig word, aanlig, aanbreek (dag), daag; *it ~ed upon me*, daar het vir my 'n lig opgegaan; dit het my bygeval; ~**ing**, daeraad, dagbreek, daglumier.
day, dag; daglig; ontvangdag; *A ~ , per dag*; ~ *AFTER ~* , dag na dag; *the ~ AFTER tomorrow*, oormôre; *AFTER two ~s*, na twee dae; *this ~ and AGE*, vandag, hierdie dag; *two ~s AGO*, naaseergister; *ALL ~ (long)*, die hele dag, heeldag; *the ~ BEFORE yesterday*, eergister; *have known BETTER ~s*, beter dae geken het; *BROAD ~* , helder oordag; ~ *BY ~* , dag vir dag; *CALL it a ~* , dit daarby laat, uitskei; *CALL it a ~!* dis genoeg! hou

daylight 827 *dead*

nou op! skei nou uit! *CARRY the* ~, die pyp rook; seëvier; *in* ~*s to COME*, in die toekoms; ~ *of CREATION*, skeppingsdag; *at DAWN of* ~, teen dagbreek; *the better the* ~ *the better the DEED*, vir 'n dringende saak is enige dag die regte dag; *their* ~ *is DONE*, hulle kers is uit; *DON'T bless the* ~ *before it is over*, moenie die dag voor die aand prys nie; *DURING the* ~, oordag, in die dag; *EVERY* ~, elke dag; ~-*to*-~ *EXPENSES*, lopende uitgawes; *the* ~ *after the FAIR*, na alles verby is; *FALL on evil* ~*s*, swaar dae deurmaak; in armoede verval; *one FINE* ~, op 'n goeie dag; *FOR* ~*s*, dae lank; *this* ~ *FORTNIGHT*, vandag oor veertien dae; *FROM* ~ *to* ~, van dag tot dag; *what one* ~ *GIVES, another takes away (from us)*, as dit op een reën, drup dit op 'n ander; ~*s of GRACE*, uitsteldae, respytdae; *he has HAD his* ~, sy tyd is verby; *IN my* ~, in my tyd; *IN the* ~, oordag, bedags; ~ *IN* ~ *out*, dag in dag uit; *IN the* ~*s of*, in die tyd van; *the* ~ *of JUDGEMENT*, die jongste dag; *KEEP one's* ~, presies op tyd wees; *the LAST* ~, die laaste der dae; *it will be a LONG* ~ *before*, daar sal nog baie water in die see loop voor; *the LORD'S* ~, die dag van die Here; Sondag; *LOSE the* ~, die stryd verloor, die onderspit delf; *MEN of the* ~, vername mense v.d. dag; *NAME the* ~, die (trou)= dag bepaal (vasstel); *differ like* ~ *and NIGHT*, soos dag en nag verskil; *his* ~*s are NUMBERED*, hy het nie meer lank om te lewe nie; hy sal binnekort sy betrekking verloor; *in the* ~*s OF*, in die tyd van; *the* ~*s of OLD*, vanmelewe; *ONE* ~, eendag; *ONE of these* ~*s*, een v.d. mooi dae; *every OTHER* ~, al om die ander dag; *the OTHER* ~, nou die dag, onlangs; *the* ~ *is OURS*, die oorwinning is ons s'n; *his* ~*s are OVER*, sy dag is verby; sy kerk is uit; *PER* ~, per dag, by die dag; *at the PRESENT* ~, teenswoordig; *his* ~ *of RECKONING will come*, sy dag sal kom; *SOME* ~, eendag; *SUFFICIENT unto the* ~ *is the evil thereof*, elke dag het genoeg aan sy eie kwaad; *THIS* ~, vandag, hede; *to THIS* ~, tot vandag; *within a* ~ *or TWO*, môre-oormôre; *WIN the* ~, die oorwinning behaal; *that is all in the* ~'s *WORK*, dit vorm deel v.d. spel; dis maar die normale gang van sake; dis daarby ingesluit; *a* ~'s *WORK of*, 'n vrag (boel); *in the* ~*s of YORE*, vanmelewe, in die dae van olim; ~ **bed**, dagbed, rusbed; ~-**blind**, dagblind; ~-**blindness**, dagblindheid; ~-**boarder**, kosleerling; kosganger; ~-**bomber**, dagbomwerper (lugv.); ~-**book**, dagregister, dagboek; joernaal; ~ **break**, dagbreek, sonop, daglumier; rooidag; ~ **dream**, lugkasteel, dromery; ~-**dreamer**, dagdromer; ~ **dreaming**, dagdromery; ~ **dress**, draroK; - **flight**, dagvlug; ~ **labourer**, dagloner.
daylight, daglig; *as CLEAR as* ~, so klaar soos die dag; ~ *ROBBERY*, skaamtelose roof; ~ *SAVING*, daglighesparing; ~ *TRAIN*, dagtrein.
day: ~ **lily**, daglelie; ~-**long**, die hele dag; daglang(e); ~ **nurse**, dagverpleegster; ~ **nursery**, bewaarskool, crèche, bewaarplek; ~ **old**, dagoud, eendaags; ~-**old chick**, dagoudkuiken, eendagskuiken; ~ **scholar**, buiteleerling, dagskolier, dagleerling; ~ **school**, dagskool; ~ **shift**, dagploeg, dagskof; ~**spring**, daeraad; ~ **star**, môrester; ~ **suit**, dagpak, drapak; ~ **ticket**, dagkaartjie; ~-**time**, dag, oordag; ~-**work**, dagwerk.
daze'on, (n) (sins)verbystering, versuftheid, bedwelming; (v) verblind; versuf, in verwarring bring, verbyster; ~**d**, suf; verwese; ~ **d'ly**, verbyster, katswink.
daz'zle, verblind, verbyster; ~ **painting**, verblindskildering, -skildery.
daz'zling, verblindend; stralend; glansend; skitterend; ~ *smile*, stralende glimlag.
D'-day, aanvalsdag, D-dag, beslissingsdag.
deac'on, diaken; armeversorger; ~ **ate**, diakenskap; diakonaat; ~**ess**, (-**es**), diakones; ~**ship**, diakenskap; ~'s **pew**, diakensbank; ~'s **ward**, diakenswyk.
deac'tionate, skadeloos stel (maak), deaktiveer.
dead, (n) (die) dood; dooie, oorledene; gesneuwelde; *let the* ~ *BURY their* ~, laat die dooies hulle dooies begrawe; *FROM the* ~, uit die dood; *the* ~

of WINTER, die hartjie v.d. winter; (a) dood; doods, (af)gestorwe, leweloos; onvrugbaar; uitgebrand (vulkaan); dof, mat, blind; eentonig; diep, volkome; dom, styf (vingers); buite werking; swaar (gewig); volslae; seker; *more* ~ *than ALIVE*, op sterwe na dood; lewendig dood; ~ *and ALIVE*, dood vervelig; lewendig dood; ~ *ASLEEP*, vas aan die slaap; *there was a* ~ *CALM*, dit was doodstil; *a* ~ *CERTAINTY*, absolute sekerheid; ~ *as the DODO*, morsdood; *as* ~ *as a DOORNAIL*, so dood soos 'n klip (mossie); *in* ~ *EARNEST*, in alle erns; *a* ~ *END*, 'n dooie punt; 'n doodloopnunt; *be* ~ *and GONE*, ter siele wees; bokveld toe wees; *a* ~ *LANGUAGE*, 'n dooie taal; *a* ~ *LETTER*, 'n dooie letter (v.d. wet); onbestelbare brief; *a* ~ *LOSS*, 'n totale verlies; volslae (pure) verlies; *he is a* ~ *MAN*, hy is 'n kind des doods; *wait for a* ~ *MAN's shoes*, ongeduldig op iem. se dood wag; wag op wat daar te erwe is; ~ *MARINES*, leë botels; ~ *as MUTTON*, so dood soos 'n klip (mossie); ~ *from the NECK up*, onnosel; *at* ~ *of NIGHT*, in die holte (middel) v.d. nag; *QUITE* ~, morsdood; *the* ~ *SEASON*, die stil seisoen; *kom= kommertyd; he is a* ~ *SHOT*, hy is 'n uithaleiskut; *he is the* ~ *SPIT of his father*, hy is sy pa se ewebeeld; *STONE* ~ *hath no fellow*, dooie honde byt nie; dooies praat nie; *a* ~ *STOP*, 'n dooiepunt; doodstil; ~ *men tell no TALES*, 'n dooie praat nie; dooie honde byt nie; *I WOUNDN'T be seen* ~, ek sou liewer sterwe; (adv) erg, totaal, in erge graad; *be* ~ *AGAINST something*, vierkant teen iets gekant wees; ~ *SURE*, so seker as wat; ~ *on the TARGET*, op die kol vasgesuig; ~-**alive**, lewendigdood; ~ **angle**, blinde hoek; ~-**arm disease**, streepvleksiekte; ~ **axle**, dooie as; ~ **bat**, slap kolf (krieket); ~-**beat**, doodmoeg, boeglam, dood-af, poot-uit; bek-af; *BE* ~-*beat*, poot-uit wees; doodmoeg wees; *he is* ~-*beat*, sy gô is uit; hy is boeglam; ~ **beer**, verslane bier; ~ **body**, lyk, dooie liggaam; ~ **bolt**, slotgrendel, ~ **calm**, doodstil, doodkalm; ~ **capital**, dooie kapitaal; ~ **centre**, dooiepunt; presiese middelpunt; ~ **certainty**, volstrekte sekerheid; ~-**clothes**, doodsklere; ~ **coil**, dooie kronkel; dooie spoel; ~ **colour**, eerste verflaag (skildery); ~ **colouring**, doodverf; ~ **dog**, bobbejaankos, jakkalskos, kannip; ~ **door**, blinde deur; ~ **drunk**, stomdronk, smoordronk; ~ **duck**: *he is a* ~ *duck*, hy is op sterwe na dood; hy is 'n lewende lyk.
dead'en, verswak, kragteloos maak; demp (geluid), verminder; ongevoelig maak; dof maak, verdoof; afstomp, verstomp.
dead: ~ **end**, doodloopspoor; ~-*end job*, doodloopbaantjie; ~-*end kid*, agterbuurtskind; ~-*end street*, doodloopstraat; ~ **eye**, baasskut; ~-**face**, blinde gewel; ~ **fingers**, verkluimde vingers; ~ **finish**, matafwerking; ~ **flat**, heeltemal plat; spieëlglad; ~ **freight**, foutvrag, ballasvrag; dooie vrag; ~ **furrow**, uitstrykvoor; ~ **gold**, dowwe goud; ~ **ground**, dooie grond (mynb.); ~ **head**, vrykaarthouer; ~ **heat**, gelykop, kop aan kop; ~-**house**, dodehuis; ~ **knot**, dooie kwas; ~ **language**, dooie taal; ~ **latch**, nagslot; ~ **letter**, dooie letter; onbestelbare brief; ~ **level**, waterpas, heeltemal gelyk; ~ **light**, daklig; dwaallig; stormklap; ~ **line**, spertyd, perktyd, krytstreep; grenslyn; ter-perse-gaantyd, saktyd; ~ **liness**, dodelikheid; ~ **load**, dooiegewig, dooielas; eiegewig; ~ **lock**, absolute stilstand; dooie punt; enkelslot; *reach a* ~ *lock*, 'n dooiepunt bereik; ~ **loss**, dooie verlies; ~ **ly**, dodelik; ~ *ly sin*, doodsonde; ~ **man's bones**, doodsbeendere; ~ **man's eye**, ronde daklig; juffer; ~ **march**, treurmars, dodemars; ~ **ness**, doodsheid; dofheid; flouheid; onbeweeglikheid (van water); ~-**office**, lykdiens; ~ **pan**, nikseggende blik; uitdrukkinglose gesig; ~ **point**, dooie punt; ~ **reckoning**, gisbestek; presiese berekening; ~ **rest**, dooierus; ~ **stock**, dooie kapitaal; ~ **stop**, volslae stilstand; ~ **sure**, doodseker; ~-**tired**, flou, pootuit; ~ **wall**, blinde muur; ~ **water**, stilstaande water; ~ **weight**, swaargewig, dooiegewig; ~ **white**, matwit; ~ **window**, blinde venster; ~ **wood**, dooie hout; ~ **wool**, dooie wol.

dea'erate, ontlug.
deaera'tion, ontlugting.
deaf, doof; gehoorgestrem(d); ~ *as an ADDER,* soos 'n dowe adder; horende doof; *ARE you* ~? het jy pluisies in jou ore? ~ *and DUMB,* doofstom; ~ *in one EAR,* doof in een oor; *that didn't fall on* ~ *EARS,* dit het jy aan geen dowe gesê nie; *turn a* ~ *EAR to,* nie wil luister nie; geen gevolg gee nie aan; *a* ~ *NUT,* 'n dowe neut; ~ *as a POST,* so doof soos 'n kwartel; stokdoof; *STONE* ~, so doof soos 'n kwartel; stokdoof, potdoof; ~ *TO,* doof vir; *none are so* ~ *as THOSE who will not hear,* daar is niemand dower as dié wat nie wil hoor nie; ~**-aid,** gehoortoestel; ~**-and-dumb alphabet,** vingeralfabet; ~**-and-dumb language,** vingertaal; ~**en,** verdoof, doof maak; ~**ening,** oorverdowend; ~**mute,** (n) doofstomme; (a) doofstom; ~**mutism,** doofstomheid; ~**ness,** doofheid, hardhorendheid; ~ **nut,** dowwe neut; ~ **person,** dowe mens, dowe, ~ **school,** skool vir dowes, skool vir gehoorgestremdes.

deal¹, (n) greinhout, deel; plank; (a) greinhout-.
deal², (n) kopie, slag; afslaan (tennis); beurt, (uit)gee (kaarte); *NEW D*~, Nuwe Bedeling (V.S.A.); *a RAW* ~, slegte behandeling; *a SQUARE* ~, 'n eerlike transaksie; (v) deel, ronddeel; sake doen, handel, verhandel, handel drywe; afslaan (tennis); toebedeel; ~ *a person a BLOW,* iem. 'n slag toedien; ~ *IN,* handel drywe in; *REFUSE to* ~ *with,* weier om te doen te hê met; ~ *WITH,* handel met, koop by; behandel; omgaan met; aandag gee aan.
deal³, (n) klomp, aantal, hoeveelheid; *a great* ~, 'n groot hoeveelheid, baie.
deal'er, uitgeër (kaarte); handelaar, winkelier, koopman; ~ *in BONES,* benehandelaar.
deal'ing, handelwyse; verkeer; omgang; *DOUBLE* ~, valsheid; *PLAIN* ~, eerlikheid, reguit manier; (pl) transaksie; *have* ~*s with,* te maak hê met; omgang hê met; sake doen met.
dean, deken (Engelse kerk); dekaan (universiteit); ~ *and chapter,* domkapittel; ~**ery,** dekanaat, amp (huis) van 'n deken; dekanie; ~**ship,** dekenskap (kerk); dekaanskap (universiteit).
dear, (n) hartjie, skat, liefling; (a) lief, dierbaar, gelief, bemind; duur (pryse), kosbaar; ~ *ME!* goeie genugtig! allawêreld! ~ *OH* ~! liewe hemel! o hening! ~ *as SIN,* geweldig duur; ~ *SIR,* Meneer; Geagte Heer (Meneer); Waarde Heer; ~**est,** liefste; *nearest and* ~*est,* dierbares; naasbestaandes; ~**ie,** liefste, skat; ~**ly,** innig, teer; baie; duur; ~*ly beloved,* dierbaarste, innig gelief; teerbeminde; ~**ness,** duurte; dierbaarheid.
dearth, duurte; skaarste, gebrek.
death, dood, sielsverhuising, uiteinde, end, versterwing; sterfte; oorlye; sterfgeval; *AFTER* ~ *the doctor,* mosterd na die maal; *APPARENT* ~, skyndood; *be in AT the* ~, die end meemaak; *BE the* ~ *of,* die dood veroorsaak van; *BORED to* ~, doodverveel(d); ~ *keeps no CALENDAR,* die dood kom soos 'n dief in die nag, die dood kom te eniger tyd; *nothing is CERTAIN but* ~, niks is so seker as die dood nie; *CONDEMN to* ~, ter dood veroordeel; ~ *will have no DENIAL,* die dood is nie te keer nie; *at* ~'*s DOOR,* op sterwe na dood; op die randjie v.d. graf; *be at* ~'*s DOOR,* in doodsgevaar verkeer; op sterwe na dood wees; *put the FEAR of* ~ *into somebody,* iem. die dood voor oë hou; *FIELD of* ~, slagveld; *FLIRT (gamble) with* ~, sy dood soek; die dood trotseer; *FRIGHTEN to* ~, laat doodskrik; *like GRIM* ~, op lewe en dood; *that will be the* ~ *of HIM,* dit sal sy dood kos; dit sal hom in sy graf bring; *the JAWS of* ~, die kake v.d. dood; ~ *is the great LEVELLER,* die graf maak almal gelyk; *MEET* ~, die dood tegemoetgaan; *be PLAYING with* ~, roekeloos wees; *PUT to* ~, ter dood bring; *there is no REMEDY against* ~, teen die dood groei geen kruid nie; *SURE as* ~, doodseker; so waar as mens leef; *die a THOUSAND* ~*s,* 'n duisend dode sterf; *TO the* ~, tot die dood; *sign one's own* ~ *WARRANT,* jou eie doodvonnis vel, jou eie dood op die hals haal; ~ **agony,** doodsangs; ~**bed,** sterfbed; ~**bed repentance,** sterfbedberou;
~**-bell,** doodsklok; ~**-blow,** nekslag, doodhou, doodsteek; doodslag, genadeslag; *GIVE someone a* ~*-blow,* iem. 'n genadeslag (nekslag) toedien; *RECEIVE a* ~*-blow,* 'n genadeslag ontvang; ~ **cell,** dodesel; ~ **certificate,** sterfsertifikaat, doodsertifikaat; ~ **claim,** sterfeis; ~ **colour,** doodskleur; ~ **cup,** slangkos; duiwelsbrood; ~ **damp,** doodsweet; ~ **dance,** dodedans; ~**-dealing,** dodelik; ~ **duties,** sterfregte; ~**-knell,** doodsklok; ~**less,** onsterflik; ~**like,** doodstil, doods; ~**liness,** doodsheid; ~**ly,** dodelik; ~ **mask,** dodemasker; ~ **notice,** doodstyding, doodsberig; ~ **penalty,** doodstraf; ~ **rate,** sterfte(syfer); ~ **rattle,** doodsroggel; geroggel; ~**-ray,** doodstraal; ~ **register,** sterfregister; ~ **roll,** dodelys; ~ **room,** sterfkamer; ~ **sentence,** doodstraf; ~'**s-head,** doodskop, doodshoof; ~'**s head moth,** doodshoofvlinder; ~ **song,** swanesang; ~ **stroke,** doodslag, genadeslag; ~ **struggle,** ~ **throes,** doodstryd; doodsworsteling; sieltoging; ~ **toll,** dodetal; ~ **trap,** lewensgevaarlike plek; ~ **warrant,** doodvonnis; ~**-watch,** houtkewer, kloptor; dodewaak; ~**-watch beetle,** kloptor, doodslopertjie.

deb, debutante.
débâ'cle, losbreking (van ys); val, ineenstorting, mislukking, debakel.
debag', (-ged), iem. se broek uittrek.
debar', (-red), verhinder, uitsluit.
debark', ontskeep, land, los; ~**a'tion,** ontskeping, landing, lossing.
debase', verneder, verlaag; vervals; ~**ment,** vernedering; verlaging; vervalsing.
debat'able, betwisbaar, onuitgemaak, aanvegbaar, omstrede, kwestieus.
debate', (n) debat, twisgesprek, bespreking, redetwis, woordestryd; *beyond* ~, onbetwisbaar, onteenseglik; (v) debatteer, beraadslaag, verhandel; bestry; betwis; ~**r,** disputant, debatteerder, disputeerder.
deba'ting, debattering; ~ **chamber,** raadsaal; parlement; ~ **point,** debatspunt; ~ **society,** debatsvereniging.
debauch', (n) losbandigheid, uitspatting, brassery; (v) verlei, verliederlik, losbandig maak, verlaag; ~**ed,** losbandig; uitspattend; liederlik; ~**ee',** losbandige mens, brasser, smeerlap; ligmis, wellusteling; ~**er,** deurbringer, smeerlap, dronklap; ~**ery,** losbandigheid, liederlikheid, uitspatting, brassery; brasparty.
deben'ture, obligasie, skuldbrief; *issue of* ~*s,* obligasie-uitgifte; ~ **holder,** obligasiehouer, skuldbriefhouer; ~ **loan,** obligasielening; ~ **stock,** obligasies.
de'bile, swak, kragteloos.
debil'itate, verswak.
debilita'tion, verswakking.
debil'ity, (..ties), swakheid, kragteloosheid, astenie, atonie, liggaamswakheid.
deb'it, (n) debiet, debietkant, debet (ong.); (v) debiteer; belas; ~ *him with,* hom debiteer met; ~ **amount,** debietbedrag; skuldbedrag; ~ **balance,** nadelige saldo; ~ **book,** debietboek; ~ **entry,** skuldpos, debietpos; ~ **note,** debietnota; ~ **side,** debietsy; ~ **voucher,** debietbewys.
debonair', lewenslustig, opgewek, joviaal; sjarmant; windmakerig.
debone', ontbeen; ~*d meat,* ontbeende vleis.
debouch', uitmond, uitkom, uitwater, uitloop; ~**ment,** uitwatering, uitmonding.
debrief', ondervra (na 'n sending).
deb'ris, puin, wrak, wrakstukke, brokstukke, afbreeksel; steengruis; oorskot; opdrifsel.
debt, skuld; *BAD* ~, onverhaalbare vordering; *BE in* ~, verpligting hê teenoor, skuld aan; *be up to one's EARS in* ~, hard v.d. skuld wees, diep in die skuld wees; *FUNDED* ~, gefundeerde (gekonsolideerde) skuld; ~ *of HONOUR,* ereskuld; *he IS in my* ~, hy is iets aan my verplig; *NATIONAL* ~, staatskuld; *OUT of* ~, sonder skuld; *PAY the* ~ *of nature,* die tol van die natuur betaal; *RUN into* ~, skuld maak; ~ **collector,** skuldinvorderaar; ~ **obligation,** skuldverbintenis; ~**or,** skuldenaar, debiteur; ~*or's LEDGER,* debiteurs(groot)boek; ~ *SIDE,*

debunk — declension

debietsy; ~ **redemption,** skulddelging; ~ **settlement,** skuldreëling.
debunk', aan die kaak stel, van sy voetstuk haal, aftakel, ontmasker, ontluister; ~ **ing,** ontmaskering, ontgoding, ontluistering, aftakeling.
debur', (-red), ontklits; afbaard; ~ **ring,** ontklitsing.
debus', (-sed), uitklim (uit 'n voertuig); 'n voertuig aflaai.
début', debuut, eerste optrede; *make one's* ~, sy debuut maak; ~ **ant,** debutant; ~ **ante,** debutante.
dec'adal, dekadies.
dec'ade, tiental (jare), dekade, desennium.
dec'adence, dec'adency, verval, verwording, agteruitgang, dekadensie.
dec'adent, afnemend, in verval, dekadent.
dec'adic, dekadies.
deca'ffeinate, dekafeïneer.
dec'agon, tienhoek, dekagoon; ~ **al,** dekagonaal.
dec'agram(me), dekagram.
decahed'ral, tienvlakkig, dekahedraal.
decahed'ron, tienvlak, dekahedron.
decalcifica'tion, ontkalking.
decal'cify, (..fied), ontkalk.
dec'alitre, dekaliter.
dec'alogue, die Tien Gebooie, Dekaloog.
dec'ametre, dekameter.
decamp', kamp opbreek; wegloop, trap, vlug, op loop sit; ~ **ment,** vlug; opbreking, aftog.
decant', afgooi (vloeistof); oorskink, afskink, dekanteer; afklaar; ~ **a'tion,** afgieting; afklaring; ~ **er,** (wyn)kraffie; (water)kraffie.
decap'itate, onthoof, dekapiteer; ~ **d,** afkop (hoender).
decapita'tion, onthoofding, dekapitasie.
dec'apod, (n) tienpotig(e) dier: (a) tienpotig.
decarboniza'tion, ontkoling.
decarb'onize, ontkool, dekarboniseer.
decasyllab'ic, tienlettergrepig, tiensillabies.
decasyll'able, tienlettergrepige reël.
dec'athlon, dekatlon, tienkamp.
decay', (n) verval, afgetakeldheid, agteruitgang; afslyting; afneming, afname, aftakeling, verrotting, bederf; *fall into* ~, in verval raak; (v) verval, vergaan; verword; verswak; bederf, verrot, vrot; ~ **ed,** v(er)rot, sleg, kaduks, vervalle, bouvallig.
Decc'an hemp, wilde stokroos.
decease', (n) oorlye, dood; (v) sterwe, doodgaan; ~ **d,** (n) afgestorwene, oorledene; (a) oorlede, dood, wyle, (af)gestorwe; ~ *d estate,* uitgestorwe boedel.
deceit', bedrog, lis, misleiding, verskalking, bedrieglikheid; ~ **ful,** bedrieglik, misleidend, vals, valshartig; ~ **fully,** bedrieglik, vals; ~ **fulness,** valshartigheid, valsheid
deceiv'able, bedriegbaar, bedrieglik, misleibaar.
deceive', bedrieg, mislei, fop, onderdeurspring, toetrap, toetrek, flous, pier; teleurstel; verlei; ~ *someone,* iem. in die nek kyk; ~ **r,** bedrieër, verleier.
decel'erate, vertraag, stadiger gaan, spoed verminder.
decelera'tion, vertraging, spoedvermindering; ~ **lane,** spoedverminderingsbaan.
Decem'ber, Desember; *the month of* ~, Desembermaand.
decem'vir, (-i, -s), lid van 'n tienmanskap, decemvir; ~ **ate,** tienmanskap, decemviraat.
de'cency, (..cies), fatsoenlikheid, ordelikheid, betaamlikheid, oorbaarheid, welvoeglikheid, eerbaarheid.
decenn'ary, (n) (..aries), tienjarige tydperk; dekade; (a) tienjarig.
decenn'iad, (-s), desennium, tydperk van 10 jaar.
decenn'ial, tienjarig, tienjaarliks.
decenn'ium, (..cennia) = **decenniad.**
de'cent, fatsoenlik, ordentlik, betaamlik, welvoeglik, behoorlik; vriendelik.
decentraliza'tion, desentralisasie.
decen'tralize, desentraliseer.
deceptibil'ity, bedrieglikheid.
decep'tion, bedrog, bedrieëry, misleiding, verskalking.
decep'tive, misleidend, bedrieglik; ~ **ness,** bedrieglikheid.
dechlor'inate, ontchloor.

dechlorina'tion, ontchloring.
dechristianiza'tion, ontkerstening.
dechris'tianize, ontkersten.
de'ciare, desiaar.
dec'ibel, desibel.
decid'able, beslisbaar, beslegbaar.
decide', beslis, besleg, bepaal, vasstel; besluit, 'n besluit neem; oordeel; ~ *AGAINST,* besluit teen; uitspraak doen teen; ~ *FOR,* besluit ten gunste van; ~ *ON,* besluit om; ~ *the ISSUE,* die deurslag aan iets gee; ~ **d(ly),** beslis, nadruklik, bepaald, sekerlik, positief, stellig; *a* ~ *d DIFFERENCE,* 'n merkbare verskil; *a* ~ *d IMPROVEMENT,* 'n besliste verbetering; *a* ~ *dly modern STYLE,* 'n ontwyfelbaar moderne styl; ~ **r,** beslissingswedstryd; beslisser.
deci'duous, sporelossend; bladwisselend, afvallend; verganklik; ~ *fruit,* sagte vrugte.
de'cigram(me), desigram.
de'cilitre, desiliter.
de'cimal, (n) tiendelige breuk, desimaal; (a) desimaal, tientallig, tiendelig; ~ **coinage,** desimale muntstelsel; ~ **fraction,** desimaalbreuk, desimale breuk; ~ **point,** desimale punt, desimaalpunt; ~ **system,** tiendelige stelsel, desimaalstelsel, desimale stelsel.
decimaliza'tion, omrekening in desimale, desimalisasie.
de'cimalize, desimaliseer, tiendelig maak.
de'cimate, een uit tien doodmaak, desimeer; wegmaai, uitdun.
decima'tion, uitdunning, desimering
de'cimetre, desimeter.
deciph'er, (n) ontsyfering, (v) ontsyfer; ontraaisel; ~ **able,** leesbaar, oplosbaar; ~ **er,** ontsyferaar; ~ **ing,** ~ **ment,** ontsyfering.
deci'sion, beslissing, besluit; beslistheid; uitslag; uitspraak (regter); ~ **taker,** besluitnemer; ~ **taking,** besluitneming.
decis'ive, beslissend, afdoende, beslis, deurslaggewend, deurtastend, definitief; ~ **battle,** beslissende veldslag; ~ **ness,** beslistheid, afdoendheid.
deciv'ilize, barbaars maak.
deck, (n) dek; pak (kaarte); *CLEAR the* ~ *s,* klaarmaak om te veg; *a DOUBLE* ~, twee pakke kaarte; (v) oortrek; bedek; versier, (uit)dos, tooi; van 'n dek voorsien; ~ **-beam,** dekbalk, skeepsbalk; ~ **boy,** dekjonge; ~ **-cargo,** bolas, deklading; ~ **-chair,** dekstoel, seilstoel; ~ **-crane,** dekkraan; ~ **-hand,** dekmatroos; dekmanskap; ~ **-house,** roef; ~ **-landing,** deklanding.
dec'kle, kartel; ~ **-edge,** onafgesny; met kartelrand (seël).
deck: ~ **-light,** dakvenster (passasierswa); ~ **-load,** deklas; ~ **-plate,** dekplaat; ~ **-quoits,** skyfgooi; ~ **-roof,** lanterndak; ~ **-seam,** deknaat; ~ **-swab,** dweil; ~ **-tennis,** ringtennis
declaim', opsê, voordra; deklameer; uitvaar; ~ **er,** deklameerder, voordragkunstenaar.
declama'tion, redevoering; deklamasie; voordrag; vurige rede.
declam'atory, retories, hoogdrawend, geswolle.
declar'able, verklaarbaar, bewysbaar.
declar'ant, verklaarder, deklarant.
declara'tion, verklaring; deklarasie (jur.); afkondiging, aandiening; bekendmaking; aangifte; beurtsluiting (kr.); ~ *of LOVE,* liefdesverklaring; ~ *of WAR,* oorlogsverklaring.
declar'ative, bevestigend, verklarend.
declar'atory, verklarend, ophelderend.
declare', verklaar, betuig; aankondig; aangee (doeane); bekend maak; bie, roep (kaartspel); deklareer (jur.), die beurt sluit (kr.); ~ *FOR,* hom verklaar vir, party kies; ~ *OFF,* afsê, afskryf; ~ *ONESELF bankrupt,* jou bankrot verklaar; ~ *a STATE of emergency,* 'n noodtoestand afkondig; ~ *d VALUE,* aangegewe waarde; ~ *WAR,* oorlog verklaar; ~ **dly,** rondborstig, openlik, onbewimpeld; ~ **r,** verklaarder, aankondiger; troefmaker.
declass', verlaag.
de'classify, verwyder (van geheime lys).
declen'sion, verval; afwyking; afneming; verbuiging (gram.).

declin'able, verbuigbaar.
declina'tion, afhelling; deklinasie, afwyking (astr.); afwysing; vermindering; verbuiging; *angle of* ~, hoek van afwyking; ~ **needle,** deklinasienaald.
dec'linator, afwykingsmeter.
declin'atory, weierend, afwysend.
decline', (n) verval, agteruitgang, ondergang; afdraand; afname; daling (prys); aftakel; (v) verval, afwyk; afhang; afdraand loop, afhel; buig, hang; afslaan, afwys (versoek); verwerp (voorstel); minder word, daal; weier, bedank vir; verbuig (gram.); afloop, agteruitgaan, verminder; ~ *to DO,* weier om te doen; ~ *with THANKS,* met dank afwys (iron.).
declin'ing, afnemend; ~ *years,* hoë leeftyd.
decliv'itous = **declivous.**
decliv'ity, (..ties), helling, glooiing, steilheid, steil afdraand; afgang; *a gradual* ~, 'n skotige afdraand.
decliv'ous, afhellend, oorhangend.
declutch', uitskakel, ontkoppel.
decoct', afkook, brou; ~ **ion,** afkooksel, uittreksel, brousel, aftreksel, uitkooksel.
decode', ontsyfer, dekodeer.
decoke', ontkool.
decoll'ate, onthoof.
decolla'tion, onthoofding.
décolletage', lae halslyn (rok), décolletage.
décolleté', met lae halslyn, décolleté.
decoloniza'tion, dekolonisasie.
decolo(u)ra'tion, ontkleuring, verkleuring.
decol'o(u)rize, ontkleur.
decommis'sion, buite diens stel; ontslaan.
decompos'able, ontbindbaar; oplosbaar.
decompose', ontleed; oplos; vergaan, ontbind; verrot; ~ **d,** vergane; verrot, ontbind; ~ **d body,** ontbinde lyk.
decomposi'tion, oplossing; ontleding; ontbinding, bederf; verwording; verwering; dubbele samestelling.
de'compound, (n) dubbele samestelling; (v) dubbel saamstel; (a) saamgestel(d).
decompress', ontlas (enjin); die druk verlig.
decompress'ion, drukverligting, dekompressie; ~ **disease,** dekompressiesiekte, borrelsiekte.
deconges'tant, dekongestiemiddel, ontstumiddel.
decon'secrate, ontheilig, ontwy; sekulariseer.
deconsecra'tion, ontheiliging; sekularisering.
decontam'inate, reinig, ontsmet; ontgas.
decontamina'tion, reiniging, ontsmetting; ontgassing.
decontrol', vrymaak, aan beheer onttrek.
déc'or, dekor.
dec'orate, opsier, (ver)sier, dekoreer, tooi; ~ **d,** opgeskik, versier, getooi.
decora'tion, opsiering, versiering; (ver)siersel; sieraad, smuk; ereteken, ordeteken; *interior* ~, binneargitektuur, binne(ns)huise versiering.
dec'orative, dekoratief, versierend, sier=; ~ **art,** sierkuns; ~ **artist,** sierkunstenaar; ~ **candle,** sierkers; ~ **stitch,** siersteek; ~ **wood,** fineerhout.
dec'orator, versierder, dekorateur, huisskilder, plakker; *interior* ~, binneversierder; binneargitek.
de'cor: ~ **builder,** dekorbouer; ~ **designer,** dekorontwerper.
dec'orous, decor'ous, welvoeglik, fatsoenlik.
decort'icate, uitdop; ontbas, bas aftrek; afskil, pel; ontvesel (stokroos).
decortica'tion, uitdopping; afskilling; ontveseling (stokroos); pellery.
decor'um, welvoeglikheid, voegsaamheid, betaamlikheid, fatsoenlikheid, dekorum.
dé'coupagé, papierknipsel(versiering), decoupage.
decou'ple, ontkoppel.
decou'pling, ontkoppeling.
decoy', (n) lokaas, lokmiddel, aanloksel; eendekooi; (v) aanlok, verlok; weglok, mislei; ~-**bird,** lokvoël; ~-**duck,** lokeend.
dec'rease, (n) vermindering, afname; *a* ~ *in value,* waardevermindering.
decrease', (v) verminder, minder maak; slink, afneem.

decrea'sing, verminderend; afnemend; ~ *moon,* afnemende maan.
decree', (n) besluit, bepaling, verordening, gebod, insetting; uitvaardiging, edik, dekreet, vonnis; ~ *of BANISHMENT,* uitsettingsdekreet, verbanningsvonnis; ~ *NISI,* voorwaardelike egskeidingsvonnis, bevel nisi; (v) verorden, bepaal, vasstel, uitvaardig, dekreteer.
dec'rement, afname, verlies, vermindering, dekrement.
decrep'it, afgeleef, oud, vervalle, lendelam, uitgeleef, versukkeld, kaduks; gebreklik; ~ **ate,** laat uitknetter, dekrepiteer; ~ **ness,** ~ **ude,** afgeleefdheid, verval; gebreklikheid.
decres'cent, afnemend.
decret'al, (n) pouslike bevel, dekreet, dekretaal; (a) dekreet=.
decri'al, afkamming, afkeuring; minagting.
decri'minalize, ontkriminaliseer.
decrusta'tion, ontkorsting.
decry', (**decried**), uitskreeu, kleineer, blameer, laak, beskinder; in minagting bring; verketter; uitkryt, afkeur, bekritiseer; ~ **ing,** verkettering.
decu'bitus (**ulcer**), bedseer, lêseer.
decum'bence, decum'bency, ligging, lêende toestand.
decum'bent, kruipend; liggend; slepend.
dec'uple, (n) tienvoud; (v) vertienvoudig; (a) tienvoudig, tiendubbel(d).
decurr'ent, decurs'ive, aflopend.
decuss'ate, (v) oorkruis, deursny, kruis; (a) oorkruis, kruiselings.
decussa'tion, deursnyding, kruising.
deden'dum, voethoogte (ratte).
dedes'ignate, intrek, herroep (benoeming).
ded'icate, toewy, opdra; inseën; (in)wy.
dedica'tion, (toe)wyding, opdrag; inseëning, inwyding; ~ **ceremony,** toewydingsplegtigheid.
ded'icator, toewyder, opdraer, inwyder.
ded'icatory, (toe)wydend, opdraend, inwydings=; ~ **sermon,** inwydingsrede.
dedolomatiza'tion, dedolomatisasie, dedolomatisering.
deduce', aflei; 'n gevolgtrekking maak; opmaak; nagaan; herlei; ~ *from,* aflei uit; ~ **ment,** afleiding.
deduc'ible, afleibaar.
deduct', aftrek, verminder; *after* ~ *ing EXPENSES,* na aftrek van (die) onkoste; *to be* ~ *ed from the PRINCIPAL,* ter vermindering van die hoofsom.
deduc'tion, aftrekking, vermindering; gevolgtrekking, afleiding; korting; herleiding; ~ **formula,** herleidingsformule.
deduc'tive, deduktief; ~ **method,** deduktiewe metode.
dee, letter d; D-vormige ring.
deed, daad, handeling, doening; akte, dokument; ~ *of ASSIGNMENT,* akte van boedelafstand; *DRAW up a* ~, verly; ~ *of GIFT,* skenkingsakte; ~ *of HYPOTHECATION,* verbandakte; ~ *of LEASE,* huurakte, pagbrief; *NOTARIAL* ~, notariële akte; ~ *of SALE,* koopbrief; ~ *of SETTLEMENT,* beskikkingsakte; ~ *of TRANSFER,* transportakte; ~-**poll,** eensydige akte; ~ **s box,** aktetrommel; ~ **s office,** aktekantoor; registrasiekantoor; ~ **s registry,** registrasiekantoor; ~-**stamp,** akteseël.
deem, oordeel, dink, ag, reken, skat; ~ *it one's duty,* dit as sy plig beskou.
deep, (n) diepte; see; *the* ~, die see; (a) diep; diepsinnig; swaar; donker; verdiep; grondig, diepgaande; glad, geslepe; *GO off the* ~ *end,* woedend word; ~ *INSIGHT,* grondige kennis; ~ *MOURNING,* diep rou; *a* ~ *SIGH,* 'n swaar sug; in ~ *WATERS,* in die moeilikheid; op gevaarlike grond; (adv) diep; ~ *in DEBT,* swaar in die skuld; *DRINK* ~, swaar drink; *still waters RUN* ~, stille waters diepe grond; *TEN* ~, tien diep; ~ *in THOUGHT,* in gedagtes verdiep; *THREE* ~, drie agter mekaar; ~ **blue,** donkerblou; ~-**coloured,** donker; ~-**drawing,** diepgaan (skip); ~ **en,** dieper maak, verdiep; vererger, vermeerder; ~ **fine leg,** diep skerpby (kr.); ~-**freeze(r),** vrieskas, hardvries; hardvriesbak; ~-**frozen,** hardbevries, hardbevrore; ~-**frying,** diep(vet)=

braai; ~-laid, listig, fynbedag; ~ learning, grondige geleerdheid; ~ level, diep vlak; ~ly, diep; innig; ~ most, diepste; ~ mourning, diep rou, swaar rou; ~ platteland, agterland, diep (ver) platteland; ~ regret, innige (groot) spyt; ~-roasted, deurgebak; ~-rooted, ingewortel(d), diepgewortel; ~ sea, diepsee; ~-seated, ingewortel, diepliggend; vas; ~ shine, diepglans; ~ space, buitenste ruim(te); ~ thought, diep gedagte; ~-toned, diep van toon; ~-water channel, vaargeul; ~ yellow, donkergeel.

deer, takbok, hert; red ~, takbok; ~-forest, takbokbos; ~-hound, jaghond, herthond; ~-lick, brak(p)lek, lekplek (vir wild); ~-park, takbokkamp; ~ skin, takbokvel; ~-stalker, jagter; ~-stalking, jag op takbokke.

deface', skend, ontsier, vermink; uitwis, deurtrek; rojeer (seël); ~d, geskend, ontsier; vermink; ~d document, geskonde dokument; ~ment, ontsiering; verminking; uitwissing; skending; ~r, skender; ontsierder; uitwisser.

de fac'to, (L.), feitelik (bestaande), de facto.

def'aecate = defecate.

defaeca'tion = defecation.

def'alcate, verduister, verdonkermaan (geld).

defama'tion, eerrowing, laster, belastering, eerskennis, eerroof.

defam'atory, eerrowend, lasterlik, skendig; ~ LANGUAGE, lastertaal; ~ LETTER, skendbrief; ~ PAPER, skendblad.

defame', laster, kwaadspreek, beskinder, swartsmeer; onteer; ~r, eerrower, eerdief, lasteraar, faamrower, faamskender.

default', (n) versuim, gebrek; verstek; nalatigheid; wanbetaling; afwesigheid; ~ of APPEARANCE, nie-verskyning; BY ~, by verstek; IN ~ of, by gebreke van; by ontstentenis van; MAKE ~, nie verskyn nie; ~ of PAYMENT, wanbetaling; (v) versuim, in gebreke bly; by verstek veroordeel; nie verskyn nie, afwesig wees; faal, nie betaal nie; ~ case, versteksaak; ~er, woordbreker; oortreder, nalatige, wanbetaler; nie-verskyner, afwesige; gestrafte; ~ judg(e)ment, veroordeling by verstek; verstekvonnis.

defeas'ance, herroeping, nietigverklaring, opheffing.

defeas'ible, vernietigbaar, herroepbaar.

defeat', (n) neerlaag; verydeling, vernietiging; INFLICT ~ on someone, iem. 'n nederlaag toedien (laat ly); SUFFER ~, die neerlaag ly; (v) verslaan; verydel, te niet doen; verwerp (voorstel); ~ the LAW, die wet ontduik; ~ one's OBJECT, jou doel verbystreef; ~ism, défaitisme, pessimisme, touopgooigees, lamsakgees; ~ist, (n) lamsak, touopgooier, pessimis, défaitis, papbroek; (a) défaitisties, moedeloos.

defea'ture, onkenbaar maak, misvorm.

def'ecate, suiwer; ontlas, vuilmaak, defesseer.

defeca'tion, suiwering; ontlasting, stoelgang, detekasie.

defect', (n) gebrek, defek, mankement; euwel, tekort, onvolkomenheid, fout, HAVE a ~, aan 'n euwel mank gaan; ~ of the MIND, sielsgebrek; (v) afval, afvallig word; ~ion, afvalligheid, afval, ontrou; weglopery.

defec'tive, gebrekkig, onvolkome; defek(tief); ~ness, onvolledigheid; geskondenheid; gebrekkigheid; ~s, gebrekkiges.

defect'or, afvallige, renegaat, oorloper, deserteur.

defence', verdediging, afweer; verweer, verweermiddel; beskerming; bolwerk, verdedigingswerk; COUNSEL for the ~, advokaat vir die verdediging; ~ of the COUNTRY, landsverdediging; IN ~ of, ter verdediging van; LINE of ~, verdedigingslinie; STUBBORN ~, handhawing; ~ bond, verdedigingsobligasie; ~ force, weermag, verdedigingsmag; ~ less, weerloos, onbeskerm, verlate; ~ lessness, weerloosheid; ~ mechanism, verweer(meganisme), verdediging; ~s, skanse, verskansings, verdedigingswerke.

defend', verdedig, beskerm, (ver)weer; behoed, bewaar; ~ant, verweerder, beskuldigde, aangeklaagde, gedaagde, beklaagde; APPEAR for the ~ant, vir die verweerder verskyn; FEMALE ~ant, ver=

weerderes; ~er, verdediger, beskermer, voorstander; D~er of the Faith, Verdediger v.d. Geloof.

defe'nestrate, (iem.) by 'n venster uitgooi.

defe'nestration, defenestrasie.

defense' = defence.

defensibil'ity, weerbaarheid, verdedigbaarheid.

defen'sible, verdedigbaar, weerbaar, houbaar.

defen'sive, (n) defensief; be on the ~, 'n verdedigende houding aanneem; (a) verdedigend, defensief, beskermend; ~ war, verdedigingsoorlog.

defer', (-red), uitstel; verskuiwe; jou neerlê by, jou onderwerp aan; ~red PAY, agtergehoue salaris; ~red PAYMENT, agterskot, uitgestelde betaling; ~red SHARES, slapende aandele.

def'erence, eerbiediging, ontsag, agting; onderwerping; IN ~ to, uit agting vir; WITH due ~ to, met alle respek vir.

def'erent, (n) geleier; (a) leidend, afvoerend.

deferen'tial, eerbiedig, onderdanig, respekvol.

defer'ment, uitstel.

defi'ance, uitdaging, trotsering, tarting; oortreding; BID ~ to, tart, trotseer; in ~ OF, trots, ten spyte van, ondanks, ongeag; SET at ~, tart, trotseer.

defi'ant, uitdagend, tartend, trotserend.

defib'rinize, defibriniseer.

defi'ciency, (..cies), gebrek, tekort; leemte; onvolkomenheid; defek; make up a ~, 'n tekort aanvul; ~ disease, gebreksiekte.

defi'cient, gebrekkig; ontoereikend, onvoldoende; mentally ~, swaksinnig.

def'icit, tekort, nadelige saldo; ~ budgeting, begroting vir 'n tekort; ~ spending, leningsbesteding, leningsuitgawe.

defi'er, uitda(g)er, tarter, trotseerder.

defilad'e, defilade.

defile'¹, (n) (berg)engte, poort, nou nekkie; defileermars; (v) defileer.

defile'², (v) besmet, skend (eer), bevlek, vuil maak, verontreinig, besoedel, onteer; ~d, geskonde.

defile'ment¹, defilement (mil.).

defile'ment², verontreiniging, besmetting, bevlekking, besoedeling.

defil'er, skender, onteerder.

defin'able, bepaalbaar, omskryfbaar, definieerbaar.

define', bepaal, omskryf, begrens, afbaken, omlyn, verklaar, beskryf, belyn, definieer; afpaal; ~d, geset (ure); ~r, omskrywer, verklaarder, beskrywer.

defin'ing, omlyning, bepaling.

def'inite, bepaald, stellig, definitief; begrens, skerp omlyn, presies, noukeurig; uitdruklik; ~ article, bepaalde lidwoord; ~ly, uitdruklik; beslis, definitief, bepaald, positief; ~ ness, bepaaldheid.

defini'tion, (woord)bepaling, (woord)omskrywing, definisie; skerpte (van beeld); duidelikheid.

defin'itive, bepalend, beslissend, uitgemaak, definitief; ~ issue, vaste uitgawe (seël).

de'flagrate, vinnig uitbrand, opvlam.

deflagra'tion, verbranding, opvlamming.

de'flagrator, deflagrator.

deflate', pap maak (bal), afblaas, lug uitlaat; deflasie veroorsaak; ~d, pap (binneband).

defla'tion, uitlating van lug; geldskaarste, deflasie; ~ of currency, deflasie; ~ary, deflasionisties.

deflect', afwyk, buig, wegbuig, deflekteer; uitslaan (vere); afskram; ~ion, afwyking, buiging, defleksie; uitslag (vere); angle of ~ion, afwykingshoek; ~or, deflektor, straalbreker.

deflex', afbuig, uitbuig.

defle'xion = deflection.

deflex'ure, sywaartse buiging.

deflora'tion, ontering, skending, ontmaagding, deflorasie, verkragting, ontwyding.

deflow'er, onteer, verkrag, defloreer; ontwy; van blomme beroof.

de'fluent, afstromend.

deflu'xion, afvloeiing.

defo'cus, ontfokus.

defol'iate, ontblaar.

defolia'tion, ontblaring.

defol'iator, blaarvreter, blaaswurm.

defor'est, ontbos; ~a'tion, ontbossing.

deform', mismaak, lelik maak, ontsier, vervorm,

skend; ~ **able,** vervormbaar; ~ **a'tion,** mismaking, deformasie, verminking; vervorming; ~ **ed,** mismaak, gebreklik, lelik, wanstaltig, wanskape; ~ **er,** mismaker; ~ **ity,** (..**ties**), mismaaktheid, wanstaltigheid, wanskapenheid, gebrek; misbaksel.
defraud', bedrieg, kul, beroof van, ontroof; verneuk (plat); ~ **a'tion,** bedrog; ~ **er,** bedrieër, kuller.
defray', betaal, bekostig, (die koste) bestry (dek); vergoed (onkoste); ~ **al,** bestryding, betaling; bekostiging; ~ **er,** bekostiger; ~ **ment,** bekostiging, bestryding.
defrock', *kyk* **unfrock.**
defrost', ontys; ontvries (voedsel); ~ **er,** ontvriestoestel, ontyser; ~ **er switch,** ontdooiskakelaar; ~ **ing,** ontdooiing; ontvriesing.
deft, handig, behendig, slim, knap, vaardig, vlug; ~ **ness,** behendigheid, vaardigheid.
defunct', (n) (die) oorledene; (a) oorlede, dood; verouder(d); afgehandel (saak).
defy', (**defied**), uitdaag, (uit)tart, trotseer; ~ *descrip tion,* onbeskryflik wees.
degas', (**-sed**), ontgas.
degauss's, degausseer, ontmagnetiseer.
degen'eracy, ontaarding, verwording.
degen'erate, (n) ontaarde, gedegenereerde; (v) ontaard, versleg, verbaster, verword, agteruitgaan, degenereer; (a) ontaard, versleg, gedegenereer.
degenera'tion, ontaarding, verval, verwording, verbastering, verslegting, degenerasie, agteruitgang; *fatty* ~ *of the heart,* hartvervetting.
degen'erative, degeneratief.
degerm', kiemvry maak; ~ **inate,** ontkern.
deglut'inate, ontlym, losweek.
degluti'tion, sluk, wegsluk, inswelging, inslukking.
degrada'tion, verlaging, skande, vernedering, degradasie, verslegting, afsetting.
degrade', verneder, verlaag, versleg, afgradeer, degradeer, afsit; ~ **d,** verneder, verlaag, afgesit.
degrad'ing, verlagend, vernederend.
degrease', ontvet; ghries verwyder.
degree', graad, rang, trap, stand; *BY* ~ *s,* trapsgewyse, geleidelik; *to a CERTAIN* ~, in sekere mate; ~ *s of COMPARISON,* trappe van vergelyking; ~ *of HEAT,* warmtegraad; *to the HIGHEST* ~, in die hoogste mate; *HONORARY* ~, eregraad; ~ *of LATITUDE,* breedtegraad; ~ *of LONGITUDE,* lengtegraad; ~ *of TEMPERATURE,* hittegraad; warmtegraad; *THIRD* ~, polisie-inkwisisie; *TO a* ~, in groot mate; *he TOOK his* ~, hy het 'n graad behaal; hy het gepromoveer; ~ **day,** gradedag; ~ **minute,** boogminuut; ~ **scale,** gradeskaal; ~ **second,** boogsekonde; ~ **sheet,** gradevel; ~ **square,** gradevierkant; ~ **subject,** eksamenvak.
degre'ssion, vermindering; dalende skaal.
degres'sive, afnemend, degressief.
degum', (**-med**), ontgom.
dehisce', oopbars, oopspring.
dehis'cence, oopbarsting.
dehis'cent, oopbarstend; ~ *fruit,* splitvrug.
dehorn', onthoring; ~ **er,** onthoorner; ~ **ing,** onthoorning.
dehort', afraai; waarsku; ~ **a'tion,** ontrading, waarskuwing, afraaiing; ~ **ative,** waarskuwend.
dehumaniza'tion, verdierliking, dehumanisering.
dehum'anize, ontmens, verdierlik, dehumaniseer.
dehumidifica'tion, ontvogting.
dehumid'ify, ontvog.
dehusk', uitdop; ~ *maize,* mielies afmaak.
dehy'drant, wateronttrekkingsmiddel.
dehyd'rate, ontwater, dehidrateer; dehidreer; ~ *d lime,* ongebluste kalk.
dehydra'tion, ontwatering, dehidrasie.
dehyp'notize, wek (uit hipnotiese toestand).
de-ice', ontys; ~ **r,** ysbestryder; ontyser.
de'icide, godsmoord; godsmoordenaar.
deic'tic, aanwysend, deikties.
deifica'tion, vergoddeliking, vergoding.
de'ifier, vergoder, afgodsdienaar.
de'iform, goddelik van gedaante.
de'ify, (**deified**), vergoddelik, verheerlik, vergood, aanbid.
deign, verwerdig, toelaat.

deipno'sophist, deipnosoof, tafelgeselser.
de'ism, deïsme; natuurlike godsdiens.
de'ist, deïs.
deis'tic, deïsties.
de'ity, (..**ties**), godheid.
déjà vu, (F.), déjà vu, herkenningservaring, herkenningskok; oorbekendheid.
dei'xis, deiksis, aanwysing.
deject', neerslagtig maak, ontmoedig.
dejec'ta, uitwerpsels.
deject': ~ **ed,** neerslagtig, swaarmoedig, triestig, droef, droefgeestig, gedruk, bedruk, bek-af; *he is* ~ *ed,* sy ore hang; ~ **edness,** ~ **ion,** neerslagtigheid, moedeloosheid, verslaenheid, swaarmoedigheid.
de ju're, (L.), de jure, regtens, volgens die reg.
dek'ko, dekko, kykie, dophouding.
delab'ialize, ontrond.
delacta'tion, spening; droog word (van ooi, koei, ens.).
delaine', wolmoeselien, delaine.
delate', aankla, verklik; bekend maak.
dela'tion, aanklag.
delat'or, beskuldiger; verklikker.
delay', (n) uitstel, oponthoud, verlet, versuim, vertraging; *without* ~, onmiddellik, onverwyld; (v) uitstel; vertraag; teenhou, verskuif; versuim; weifel; talm; ~ *ed ACTION,* vertraagde werking; *all is not LOST that is* ~ *ed,* uitstel is nie afstel nie; ~ **er,** uitsteller; ~ **fuse,** talmlont; ~ **ing,** (die) uitstel, vertraging; ~ **ing action,** vertragingsgeveg (mil.).
del'e, (n) uitlaatteken; (v) haal deur.
delec'table, lekker, verruklik, heerlik, genotvol.
delecta'tion, genot, genoeë.
delec'tus, bloemlesing.
del'egacy, (..**cies**), kommissie, delegasie, afvaardiging; afgevaardigdes.
del'egate, (n) afgevaardigde, gevolmagtigde, delegaat, deputaat, gedeputeerde; (v) afvaardig, volmag gee; oordra, delegeer; ~ *d authority,* oorgedrae (gedelegeerde) regsbevoegdheid.
delega'tion, afvaardiging, deputasie; volmag, opdrag, delegasie; ~ *of DEBT,* oorsetting van skuld; ~ *of POWERS,* oordrag van bevoegdhede.
delete', skrap, uitkrap, uitwis, deurstreep, deurhaal, doodtrek, doodkrap, deurstryk; rojeer; ~ *whichever is not APPLICABLE,* skrap waar nodig.
delete'rious, verderflik, verwoestend, nadelig, skadelik.
dele'tion, uitwissing, skrapping, deurhaling.
Delft, Delftse erdewerk.
delib'erate, (v) oorweeg, beraadslaag, delibereer; ~ *with,* ruggespraak hou met; oorleg pleeg met; (a) bedagsaam, weloorwoë; bedaard, besadig, opsetlik; tydsaam; ~ **ly,** bedagsaam; met voorbedagte rade, opsetlik, willens en wetens; tydsaam; ~ **ness,** bedagsaamheid; vasberadenheid; opsetlikheid; kalmte.
delibera'tion, oorweging, oorleg; bedagsaamheid; bedaardheid; gewik en geweeg, deliberasie, beraad (slaging); *COME under* ~, ter sprake kom; *after MUCH* ~, na baie gewik en geweeg; *TAKE into* ~, in oorweging neem.
delib'erative, beraadslagend, oorleggend.
del'icacy, kiesheid; keurigheid; fyngevoeligheid; fynheid, tingerigheid, teerheid; swakheid; (..**cies**), versnapering, lekkerny, delikatesse.
del'icate, lekker, fyn; tinger; kies delikaat; netelig; net, sierlik; teer, gevoelig; *a* ~ *matter,* 'n netelige saak.
delicatess'en, fynkos, delikatesse; ~ **shop,** delikatesewinkel, fynkoswinkel.
deli'cious, heerlik, lekker, aangenaam, verruklik, smaaklik; ~ **ly,** heerlik, aangenaam, verruklik; ~ **monster,** geraamteplant, mielievrug, gaatjieblaarplant *(Monstera deliciosa);* ~ **ness,** heerlikheid, verruklikheid, lekkerheid.
delict', wetsoortreding, vergryp, misdaad, delik.
deliga'tion, verbinding, afbinding.
delight', (n) genoeë, genot, verrukking; *take a* ~ *in,* behae skep in; jou verlekker in; (v) verheug, behaag, verruk, vermaak, verbly.
delight'ed, verruk, bly, verheug, opgetoë; *I shall be* ~

to, dit sal vir my aangenaam wees om; ~ WITH, opgetoë met; baie in jou skik wees; hoogs ingenome wees.
delight'ful, genotvol, genotryk, heerlik, verruklik; ~ness, heerlikheid; genotvolheid.
delight'some, genotvol.
delim'it, delimiteer, afbaken, afpaal.
delimita'tion, afbakening, delimitasie; grensreëling; ~ commission, afbakeningskommissie.
delin'eate, afbeeld, uitbeeld, verbeeld, ontwerp, skets, uitteken, skilder, afteken.
delinea'tion, skets, tekening, afbeelding, aftekening, deliniasie, uitbeelding; afskildering (fig.).
delin'eator, tekenaar, sketser, afbeelder, skilder.
delin'quency, pligsversuim; oortreding, misdaad, vergryp; *juvenile* ~, jeugmisdaad, jeugmisdadigheid.
delin'quent, (n) skuldige, oortreder; stokkiesdraaier, delinkwent; *juvenile* ~, jeugmisdadiger; (a) skuldig.
deliquesce', smelt; vervloei, wegsmelt.
deliques'cence, vervloeiing, smelting.
deliques'cent, smeltend.
deli'riant, ylgif.
deli'rious, ylhoofdig; deliries, deurmekaar, ylend; opgetoë; dol, rasend; *be* ~, yl; ~ness ylhoofdigheid; waansinnigheid.
deli'rium, ylhoofdigheid, waansin, delirium; ~ *tremens,* dronkmanswaansin, delirium tremens, blouduiwel, horries.
delitesc'ent, sluimerend, latent.
deliv'er, verlos, bevry; oorlewer, oorhandig; lewer; voordra, bestel (briewe), besorg, ter hand stel; uitreik; verlos (vrou); ~ *BATTLE,* slag lewer; *BE* ~*ed of,* ter wêreld bring; verlos word van; die lewe skenk aan; ~ *the GOODS,* presteer, resultate kry; bestelde goedere aflewer; ~ *JUDGEMENT,* uitspraak gee; ~ *a SPEECH,* 'n toespraak hou; ~ *in TRUST,* toevertrou; ~ *UP,* uitlewer, oorgee; ~*able,* (af)lewerbaar, bestelbaar; ~**ance,** bevryding, uitredding, verlossing; oorlewering; uitspraak (jurie); ~**er,** bevryder, verlosser; besorger; besteller.
deliv'ery, (..ries), aflewering; afgifte; verlossing, bevalling; voordrag (toespraak); boulmanier (krieket); afslaan (tennis); bevryding; vrymaking; oordrag, oorgawe; uitdeling, besorging; oorlewering; *CASH on* ~, kontant by aflewering; *for FUTURE* ~, op lewering; *TAKE* ~ *of,* in ontvangs neem; ~ **bicycle,** bestelfiets, afleweringsfiets; ~ **boy,** besteljonge, afleweringsjonge; ~ **charge,** afleweringsgeld; ~**man,** besteller, afleweraar; ~ **note,** bestelbrief, afleweringsbrief; ~ **order,** volgbrief; bestelbrief; ~ **pipe,** afvoerpyp; toevoerpyp; ~ **room,** kraamkamer; ~ **van,** bestelwa, bestelbakkie; afleweringswa, afleweringsbakkie; ~ **vehicle,** bestelvoertuig, afleweringsvoertuig.
dell, dal, vallei.
delouse', ontluis.
delous'ing-tent, ontluisingstent.
Del'phian, Del'phic, Delfies; duister, raaiselagtig; ~ *oracle,* orakel van Delfi.
del'phinine, delfinien, delfinine.
delphin'ium, delfinium, pronkridderspoor.
del'ta, delta; ~ **aircraft,** deltavliegtuig; ~**fica'tion,** deltavorming; ~ **lake,** deltameer; ~ **metal,** deltametaal; ~ **wing,** deltavlerk.
del'toid, (n) deltaspier; (a) deltavormig; deltaïes; ~ **muscle,** deltaspier.
delud'able, maklik misleibaar.
delude', mislei, bedrieg, begoël, voorspieël, beetneem; ~ *oneself into the belief that,* jou wysmaak dat; jou laat verlei om te glo dat; ~**r,** misleier, bedrieër.
del'uge, (n) sondvloed, stortbui, wolkbreuk, oorstroming; *it dates back to before the* ~, dis nog van voor die sondvloed, dis horingoud; (v) oorstroom; oorstelp.
delu'sion, (sins)bedrog; begoëling, oogverblinding, voorspieëling, misleiding, dwaling, waan; ~ *of GREATNESS,* grootheidswaansin; *be SUFFER= ING from* ~ *s,* aan dwalings onderhewig wees; *be UNDER the* ~ *of,* 'n oordrewe denkbeeld hê van; ~**al** = **delusive.**
delus'ive, misleidend; bedrieglik; ~**ness,** bedrieglikheid.

delus'tre, ontglans.
delve, grawe, spit, dolwe, delf; ~**r,** grawer, spitter, delwer.
demagnetiza'tion, ontmagnetisasie, onmagnetisering.
demag'netize, ontmagnetiseer, demagnetiseer; ~**r,** ontmagnetiseerder.
demagog'ic, demagogies.
dem'agogue, opruier; agitator, demagoog.
dem'agogy, demagogie, volksmennery.
demand', (n) vraag; gewildheid; eis; versoek, aanskrywing, (skuld)vordering; behoefte; *be MUCH in* ~, baie gesog wees, opgeld doen, in trek wees; *ON* ~, op aanvraag; *PAYABLE on* ~, betaalbaar aan toonder (op sig); *by PUBLIC* ~, op aandrang v.d. publiek; ~ *and SUPPLY,* vraag en aanbod; (v) eis, afverg, opvorder; (af)vorder, opvra (geld); verlang; terugvra; aftrek; ~ *AGAIN,* terugvorder; ~ *BACK,* terugeis; ~**able,** vorderbaar, opeisbaar; billik; ~ **ant,** eiser, klaer; ~ **draft,** aanvraagwissel; sigwissel; ~**er,** eiser, vraer; ~**ing,** veeleisend; eisend; ~ **note,** aanmaning; aanvraagpromesse; ~ **notice,** aanmaning.
deman'toid, groen granaat, demantoïed.
de'marcate, afbaken; skei.
demarca'tion, afbakening, afperking; grenslyn, demarkasie; *line of* ~, grenslyn.
dé'marche, (F.) démarche, beleidsvernuwing, beleidswysiging.
demater'ialize, vergeestelik.
demean'[1], verlaag.
demean'[2], gedra; ~**our,** gedrag, houding, handelswyse.
dement', kranksinnig (gek) maak, ~**ed,** kranksinnig, waansinnig, uitsinnig, gek.
démen'ti, (amptelike) ontkenning, démenti.
demen'tia, kranksinnigheid, waansin, demensie; ~ *praecox,* dementia praecox, skisofrenie.
demer'it, gebrek, wangedrag, fout; slegte beloning; ~ **or'ious,** onverdienstelik.
demer'sal fish, bodemvis.
demersed', onder water.
demesne', gebied, landgoed, besit, eiendom, domein; *royal* ~, kroongrond.
dem'i: ~ **god,** heros, halfgod; ~**john,** karba; mandjiefles.
demilitariza'tion, demilitarisasie.
demil'itarize, demilitariseer.
dem'i: ~-mondaine', vrou van die demi-monde; ~**-monde,** demi-monde, klas vroue van verdagte sedes; ~**-rep,** vrou van verdagte sedes.
demis'able, bemaakbaar.
demise'[1], oorlyding, heengaan, dood.
demise'[2], (n) oordrag, bemaking, vermaking; (v) oordra, bemaak.
dem'isemiquaver, 1/32e noot.
demi'ssion, afstand; ontslag, afsetting, afdanking; demissie; verlaging.
demist', ontwasem; ~**er,** ontwasemer, missmelter.
demit', (-ted), ontslaan; sy ontslag neem, (sy amp) neerlê, aftree.
de'mitasse, (F.), koffiekoppie; koppie koffie.
dem'iurge, wêreldskepper; ondergod; demiurg.
dem'o, (-s), betoger.
demob', demobiliseer.
demobiliza'tion, demobilisasie, ontbinding (van 'n leër).
demob'ilize, demobiliseer, ontbind.
democ'racy, (..cies), volksregering, demokrasie.
dem'ocrat, demokraat.
democrat'ic, demokraties, volks=.
democratiza'tion, demokratisering.
democ'ratize, demokratiseer, demokrasies inrig.
demo'grapher, demograaf.
demograph'ic, volks=.
demog'raphy, volksbeskrywing, demografie.
demol'ish, afbreek, verniel, sloop, vernietig; ~**er,** vernieler, sloper, afbreker.
demoli'tion, vernieling, verwoesting, sloping, afbraak, slegting, afbreking; ~ **charge,** vernielingslading; ~ **work,** sloopwerk.
dem'on, bose gees, duiwel, demon; *he is a* ~ *for work,* hy werk soos 'n esel.

demonetiza'tion, ontmunting, demonetisasie, demonetisering.
demo'netize, ontmunt, demonetiseer.
demon'iac, (n) besetene; (a) demonies, duiwels.
demoni'acal, duiwels, besete.
demon'ic, demonies; besete; geïnspireerd.
dem'onism, demonisme.
dem'onize, verduiwel, demoniseer.
demonol'atry, duiwelverering.
demonol'ogy, duiwelleer, geesteleer, demonologie.
demonoman'ia, demonomanie.
demon'omist, duiweldienaar.
demonstrabil'ity, bewysbaarheid; onloënbaarheid.
demons'trable, bewysbaar, verklaarbaar; onloënbaar; aantoonbaar.
demon'strant, betoger, betoër.
dem'onstrate, bewys, aantoon, uitlê, betoog; demonstreer, wys.
demonstra'tion, bewys; betoging; demonstrasie, vertoning; verklaring; ~ **leader,** betogingsleier; ~ **plot,** demonstrasieveld, demonstrasieperseel.
demon'strative, bewysend; demonstratief; klaarblyklik; aanwysend; betogend; *a ~ person,* persoon wat met sy gevoelens te koop loop; aanstellerige persoon; ~ **pronoun,** aanwysende voornaamwoord, demonstratief.
dem'onstrator, demonstrateur, demonstreerder, bewysvoerder; betoër, betoger; assistent, demmie.
demoraliza'tion, sedebederf, demoralisasie, bederf, verwildering.
demor'alize, bederf, bederwe; demoraliseer; ontmoedig.
demor'alizing, demoraliserend, sedebederwend; ontmoedigend.
Demos'thenes, Demosthenes, goeie spreker.
demote', terugsit, in rang verlaag, demoveer, degradeer.
demot'ic, populêr, vulgêr; demoties, volks.
demo'tion, demosie, terugsetting, verlaging (in rang)
demount', afhaal (buiteband); ~ **able,** afneembaar.
demul'cent, (a), versagtend, lenigend; (n) stilmiddel, versagtende middel.
demul'sion, versagting.
demur', (n) aarseling, weifeling, bedenking, beswaar; (v) (-red), aarsel, weifel; beswaar maak, eksepsies maak (opwerp).
demure', stemmig, sedig; preuts; ~ **ness,** stemmigheid, sedigheid; preutsheid.
demu'rrable, aanvegbaar, betwisbaar.
demu'rrage, lêgeld, oorlêgeld; staangeld; *days of ~,* lêdae.
demu'rrer[1], weifelaar; beswaarmaker.
demu'rrer[2], teenwerping; eksepsie (reg.)
demu'rring, weifeling.
dem'y, (demies), klein mediaan, demi (papier).
demytho'logize, ontmitologiseer.
den, werkkamer; privaat vertrek; gat, lêplek, hol; ~ *of ROBBERS,* rowershol; ~ *of THIEVES,* diewenes, rowershol; ~ *of VICE,* huis van ontug.
denar'ius, (..rii), denarius; pennie.
den'ary, tientallig.
denationaliza'tion, denasionalisering.
dena'tionalize, denasionaliseer.
dena'turalize, denaturaliseer.
dena'ture, vervals, verbrou; dokter, denatureer.
denaz'ify, (..fied), denazifiseer.
den'driform, boomagtig; boomvormig.
den'drite[1], dendriet; naaldstruktuur (chem.).
den'drite[2], senuseltak, dendriet.
dendrit'ic, boomvormig, dendrities.
den'droid, boomvormig, dendroïed.
den'drolite, fossielboom, dendroliet.
dendrol'ogist, boomkenner, dendroloog.
dendrol'ogy, boombeskrywing, boomkunde, dendrologie.
dendrom'eter, boommeter, dendrometer.
denega'tion, ontkenning.
dene-hole, krytgrot.
deng'ue (fever), dengue(koors), uitslagkoors, sonkoors, knokkelkoors.
deni'able, betwisbaar, loënbaar.
deni'al, ontkenning, weerspreking, verloëning, dementi; weiering; *meet with a flat ~,* die aanklag onomwonde ontken.
denier'[1], gewigseenheid van (kuns)sy, draaddikte, denier.
deni'er[2], ontkenner, verloënaar.
den'igrate, swartsmeer, beskinder, beklad.
denigra'tion, swartsmeerdery.
de'nim, denim; ~ **s,** denimbroek; jannas, jeans; ~ **suit,** denimpak.
denit'rate, denit'rify, denitrifiseer.
den'izen, (n) inwoner; (genaturaliseerde) burger; bewoner; inheemse woord (plant, ens.); (v) naturaliseer, inburger, opneem, vestig; ~ **ship,** burgerskap.
Den'mark, Denemarke.
denom'inate, 'n naam gee, noem, benoem, benaam, betitel, aandui.
denomina'tion, gesindheid; sekte, denominasie; benaming, benoeming; klas; soort; *REDUCE to the same ~,* gelyknamig maak; *money of SMALL ~s,* kleingeld.
denomina'tional, sektaries, sekte=; ~ **education,** kerklike (sektariese) onderwys; ~ **school,** kerkskool; sekteskool.
denom'inative, (n) denominatiewe werkwoord, denominatief; (a) benoemend, aanduidend; denominatief.
denom'inator, aanduier; noemer (breuk), deler; *reduce to the same ~,* gelyknamig maak.
denota'tion, aanduiding, aanwysing; teken; kognitiewe betekenis; denotasie; betekenis; omvangsbepaling.
denot'ative, aanduidend.
denote', aandui, aanwys, beteken; denoteer; aangee, te kenne gee.
dénoue'ment, ontknoping, afloop, denouement.
denounce', aankondig, aansê; bedreig; betig; uitvaar (teen); opsê (verdrag); veroordeel, afkeur; aankla, beskuldig, aanbring, aangee (wet); uitmaak, aan die kaak stel; ~ *as,* aan die kaak stel as; ~ **ment,** bedreiging; aanklag; aangifte; veroordeling, afkeuring; ~ **r,** beskuldiger, veroordelaar, aanklaer, aanbringer.
de nov'o, van voor af, opnuut, de novo.
dense, stom, stompsinnig, dom; dig, dik; suf; ~ **fog,** digte (dik) mis; ~ **ness,** digtheid; domheid, stomheid.
densim'eter, densimeter, digtheidsmeter.
densito'meter, densitometer, digtheidsmeter (fot.).
den'sity, (..ties), digtheid, densiteit, vastheid; stomheid, domheid; *BULK ~,* gemiddelde digtheid; *bruto digtheid; UNIFORM ~,* egalige digtheid.
dent, (n) deuk, moet, duik; kerf; (v) duik, indeuk; kerf, uittand.
den'tal, (n) tandletter, dentaal; (a) dentaal, tand=; ~ **drill,** tandboor; ~ **forceps,** tandtang; ~ **formula,** tandformule; ~ **hygiene,** tandhigiëne; ~ **letter,** tandletter; ~ **mechanic,** tandtegnikus; ~ **moulding,** tandlys ~ **nerve,** tandsenuwee; ~ **plate,** verhemelteplaat; ~ **powder,** tandpoeier; ~ **science,** tandheelkunde; ~ **surgeon,** tandarts, tandedokter, tandheelkundige.
den'tate, getand; tandvormig.
dent'ed, gebult.
den'ticle, tandjie, puntjie.
dentic'ular, dentic'ulate, getand.
den'tiform, tandvormig.
den'tifrice, tandepoeier; tandepasta.
den'til, tandjie; ~ **moulding,** tandlys.
den'tine, tandbeen.
den'tist, tandedokter, tandarts; ~ **profession,** tandartsberoep.
den'tistry, tandheelkunde.
denti'tion, tandekry; tandstelsel.
dent maize (mealies), duikpitmielies, deukmielies.
den'ture, (kuns)gebit, kunstande, valstande; (tand)plaat.
denu'clearize, kernwapens verwyder.
denuda'tion, ontbloting, afstroping, kaalmaking, blootlegging, denudasie.
denude', kaal maak, ontbloot, beroof, denudeer.
denun'ciate, aankla, veroordeel; opsê (kontrak).
denuncia'tion, bedreiging; aangifte, aanklag, beskul=

diging; ontbloting; veroordeling; opsegging (kontrak).
denun'ciator, beskuldiger, aanbringer, aangewer, aanklaer, veroordelaar.
denun'ciatory, beskuldigend; veroordelend; bedreigend; aanklaend; afkeurend; gispend.
deny', **(denied),** ontken, teenspreek, weerspreek; (ver)loën, misgun; ontsê, weier; ~ *ACCESS,* toegang weier; ~ *the CHARGE,* die beskuldiging ontken; ~ *oneself the LUXURY,* jou die weelde ontsê; daarsonder klaarkom; ~**ingly,** ontkennend.
de'odand, godsgif (jur.).
de'odar, Himalajaseder, deodar.
deod'orant, (n) reukverdrywer, deodorant; ontsmettingsmiddel; (a) reukverdrywend; ontsmettend.
deodoriza'tion, reukverwydering.
deod'orize, ontsmet; reukloos maak; ~**r,** reukverdrywer; ontsmettingsmiddel.
deontol'ogy, sedeleer, deontologie, etiek.
De'o volen'te, as God wil, Deo volente.
deox'idize, van suurstof ontneem, deoksideer.
deo'xygenate, suurstof verwyder, deoksigineer.
depart', vertrek, heengaan, verlaat; wegtrek, afreis; afvaar; afwyk van; ~ *FROM,* afwyk van; vertrek van; ~ *this LIFE,* sterf, doodgaan; ~**ed,** (n) (die) oorledene; (a) oorlede; vertrokke; vergane; ~**ing,** vertrek, weggaan.
depart'ment, werkkring; departement, afdeling; gebied; *D~ of EDUCATION,* Departement van Onderwys; *D~ of MINES,* Departement van Mynwese.
departmen'tal, departementeel, departements-, afdelings-; ~ **chief,** ~ **head,** departementshoof; ~ **instruction,** departementsvoorskrif, afdelingsvoorskrif; ~**ism,** omslagtigheid.
depart'ment store, afdelingswinkel.
depar'ture, vertrek, trek, afreis; opstyging (van vliegtuig); afwyking; afvaart (van skip); afsterwing, heengaan, oorlye; *DATE of ~,* vertrekdatum; *a NEW ~,* iets nuuts; *POINT of ~,* uitgangspunt; beginpunt; uitvaarspunt (van koeël); *PORT of ~,* vertrekhawe; *TAKE your ~,* vertrek; *TIME of ~,* vertrektyd; ~ **desk,** vertrektoonbank.
depas'ture, kaal wei, afwei; laat wei.
depaup'erate, verarm, arm maak.
depaup'erize, ophef (uit armoede), op die been bring.
depend', afhang van; vertrou, staatmaak op, reken op; *he CAN be ~ed upon,* hy is vertroubaar, jy kan op hom staatmaak; *THAT ~s,* dit hang daarvan af; ~ *UPON,* afhanklik wees van; reken op; ~ **abil'ity,** vertroubaarheid; ~ **able,** betroubaar, vertroubaar; ~ **ant,** afhanklike, ondergeskikte, aanhorige.
depen'dence, afhanklikheid; samehang; aanhangsel; onderhorigheid; vertroue; aanhorigheid.
depen'dency, (..cies) bygebou; aanhang; kolonie, afhanklike staat; *kyk ook* **dependence.**
depen'dent, (n) = **dependant;** (a) afhanklik; afhangend; onderhorig.
depen'ding, afhanklik.
depersonaliza'tion, ontpersoonliking.
deper'sonalize, ontpersoonlik.
depict', (af)skilder, skets, afteken, afbeeld, uitbeeld.
depic'ter, skilder, uitbeelder.
depic'tion, skildering, afbeelding, uitbeelding.
depic'tor = **depicter.**
depic'ture = **depict.**
dep'ilate, onthaar, afhaar; ~**d,** haar-af.
depila'tion, ontharing, kaalheid.
de'pilator, ontharingsmiddel.
depil'atory, (n) (..ries), onthaarmiddel; (a) ontharend.
deplane', uit 'n vliegtuig stap, ('n vliegtuig) uitlaai.
deplen'ish, leeg maak; ontruim.
deplete', leeg maak, uitput, ledig; ontlas; uitdun.
deple'tion, vermindering; bloedlating; uitputting, lediging.
deplor'able, beklaenswaardig, betreurenswaardig, bedroewend, bejammerenswaardig, erbarmlik; ~**ness,** betreurenswaardigheid, erbarmlikheid, jammerlikheid.
deplore', betreur, beklaag, bejammer.

deploy', ontplooi, ontrol, versprei; ~**ment,** ontplooiing, verspreiding.
deplume', vere uittrek.
deplu'ming itch, hoenderbrandsiekte.
depolariza'tion, depolarisasie.
depol'arize, depolariseer; ontwrig; ~**r,** depolarisator.
depon'ent, (n) getuie, deponent; deponens (gram.); (a): ~ *verb,* deponens.
depop'ulate, ontvolk.
depopula'tion, ontvolking.
deport', oor die grense sit, deporteer; gedra; ~ *oneself,* jou gedra; ~ **able,** deporteerbaar; ~ **a'tion,** verbanning, uitsetting, deportasie; ~**ee',** gedeporteerde, verbannene.
deport'ment, houding, gedrag, maniere; houdingleer (vak).
depos'able, afsitbaar; as getuie dienende.
depos'al, afsetting.
depose', (onder eed) getuig, verklaar; afsit, ontslaan (uit 'n amp).
depos'it: (n) besinksel, neerslag, afsetsel, aanslibsel, afsaksel; aanpaksel; ertslaag, afsetting (geol.); storting; belegging, pand; deposito; *IN ~,* in deposito; *MAKE a ~,* iets deponeer; 'n deposito stort; *WITHDRAW a ~,* 'n deposito trek; (v) neerlê; neerslaan (elek.); laat besink; in bewaring gee; stort, inlê, deponeer (geld); ~ **account,** depositorekening; ~ **ary,** (..ries), bewaarder; ~ **ary library,** bewaarbiblioteek; ~ **bank,** depositobank; ~ **book,** kassiersboek; inlêboek; spaarboek(ie); ~**ed,** gedeponeer; ~**ee',** depositaris.
deposi'tion, verklaring (onder eed), getuienis; afsetting, onttroning; ontsetting; kruisafname; belegging, plasing, deposisie; afsetsel, neerslag, aanspoeling.
depos'it: ~ **money,** gedeponeerde geld; ~**or,** storter, deposant, deponeerder, belêer; ~**ory** (..ries), bewaarplaas, depot; depositaris, bewaarnemer, bewaarder, ~ **receipt,** ~ **slip,** inlêstrokie, depositobewys, stortingsvorm.
dep'ot, bêreplek, opslagplek, stapelplaas, magasyn, skuur; depot; kwartiere; ~ **fat,** vetreserwe; ~ **ship,** moederskip.
deprava'tion, bederf; verdorwenheid; ontaarding.
deprave', bederwe, versleg; demoraliseer; ~**d,** karakterloos, sleg, bedorwe, verdorwe; verworpe, ontaard, gesonke; ~**ment,** bederf, verdorwenheid.
deprav'ity, ondeug, slegtheid, bedorwenheid, verdorwenheid; verworpenheid; sedeloosheid, onsedelikheid; bederf.
dep'recate, smeek; afwend (deur smeking); berou; afkeur; afbid.
depreca'tion, afbidding; afwending; berou; protes; afkeuring.
dep'recative, smekend, afbiddend, afkeurend; ~ *letter,* smeekbrief.
dep'recator, afbidder, smeker; ~**y** = **deprecative.**
depre'ciate, laer skat; in waarde verminder; depresieer; kleiner, onderskat, minag.
deprecia'tion, depresiasie, waardevermindering; daling; afkamming, minagting, geringskatting; afskrywing.
depre'ciatory, geringskattend, minagtend, neerhalend, kleinerend; waardeverminderend.
dep'redate, plunder, buit maak, verwoes.
depreda'tion, plundering, roof.
dep'redator, plunderaar, verwoester.
dep'redatory, plunderend, verwoestend.
depress', neerdruk; laat daal; verlaag; neerslagtig maak, ontmoedig, deprimeer; verneder; ~ **ant,** kalmerende middel; ~**ed,** neerslagtig, bedruk; gedruk, ingedruk; ~**edness,** gedruktheid; ~**ing,** drukkend; ontmoedigend; ~**ion,** neerdrukking; neerslagtigheid, bedruktheid, laagdrukgebied; (terrein)insinking, grondversakking; diepte, laagte, duik, holte; gedruktheid, daling (barometer); slapte (in sake), depressie; ~**ion angle,** drukhoek, diephoek; ~**or,** onderdrukker, neerdrukker, omlaagdrukker.
depriva'tion, berowing, verlies; afsetting.
deprive', ontneem; ontroof; beroof; afsit ~ *d OF,* verstoke van, sonder; ~ *ONESELF of,* jou ontsê.

de'proclaim, deproklameer.
deproclama'tion, deproklamasie.
de profun'dis, de profundis, uit die diepte (van smart).
depth, donkerheid; diepte; diepsinnigheid; (pl) afgronde; diepsinnigheid; ~ *of FOCUS*, brandpuntafstand; *GET out of one's* ~, in diep water raak; iets bo sy vuurmaakplek vind; *in the* ~ *of WINTER*, in die hartjie v.d. winter; ~**-bomb**, ~**-charge**, diepgelading, dieptebom; ~**-gauge**, dieptemaat; ~ **psychology**, dieptesielkunde, dieptepsigologie.
dep'urate, suiwer, louter.
depura'tion, loutering, suiwering.
depur'ative, (n) suiweringsmiddel; (a) louterend, suiwerend.
de'purator, suiweraar.
deputa'tion, afvaardiging, deputasie.
depute', afvaardig, deputeer; oordra; magtig.
dep'utize, as plaasvervanger optree, vervang.
dep'uty, (..ties), afgevaardigde, gesant, gevolmagtigde; adjunk, waarnemer, gelastigde, deputaat, plaasbekleër, plaasvervanger; gedeputeerde; ~ **chairman**, ondervoorsitter; tweede voorsitter; ~ **commissioner**, adjunk-kommissaris; ~ **governor**, ondergoewerneur; ~ **leader**, onderleier; ~ **mayor**, onderburgemeester; ~ **minister**, adjunk-minister; ~ **premier**, adjunk-premier; ~ **sheriff**, onderskout, onderbalju; ~ **speaker**, adjunk-speaker.
derac'inate, ontwortel, uitroei; verdelg.
deracina'tion, ontworteling, uitroeiing; verdelging.
derail', (n) skilpad, ontspoorder; (v) ontspoor; laat ontspoor; ~**ment**, ontsporing.
derange', verwar; versteur, ontwrig, deurmekaar maak; mal maak; krenk; ~**d**, wanordelik; malend; gekrenk; waansinnig, mal; ~**ment**, steuring, storing, verwarring; kranksinnigheid, sinsverwarring.
derate', van belasting onthef.
Der'by¹, Derby(wedren)
der'by² (..bies), dophoed, hardebolkeil; ~ **boot**, kapstewel.
Der'byshire: ~ **neck**, kropgeswel; ~ **spar**, vloeispaat.
dereg'ister, registrasie intrek, skrap, deregistreer.
deregistra'tion, skrapping, deregistrasie.
de'relict, (n) wrak, verlate skip; (a) verlate, opgegee; ~ **land**, verlate grond.
derelic'tion, versaking; pligsversuim; verlating; ~ *of duty*, pligsversuim.
derestric'tion, opheffing.
deride', uitlag, (be)spot; belaglik maak, uitkoggel; ~**r**, bespotter, spotvoël.
deri'sion, bespotting, (ge)hoon, spot; *be HELD in* ~, bespot word; *IN* ~, spottenderwys(e).
deris'ive, deris'ory, spottend, honend.
deriv'able, afleibaar.
deriva'tion, afleiding; herleiding; afkoms, herkoms, derivasie.
deriv'ative, (n) afleiding; afgeleide woord; derivaat (chem.); derivatief (gram.); (a) afgelei, derivatief; ~ **wire**, aftakkingsdraad.
derive', aflei (van, uit); ontleen (aan); afstam (van); spruit, voortkom uit; ~ *from*, aflei van.
derm, huid, onderhuid; ~**al**, huid-, vel-, dermaal; ~**atit'is**, huidontsteking, dermatitis; ~**atol'ogist**, huidarts, dermatoloog; ~**atol'ogy**, huidsiekteleer, dermatologie; ~**atos'is**, dermatose, huidsiekte.
dernier cri, (F), dernier cri, die jongste mode.
der'ogate, afbreuk doen, benadeel, derogeer; verminder; ontaard; te kort doen; inkort; agteruitgaan; jou verlaag.
deroga'tion, afbreuk, nadeel; verkorting; agteruitgang; verlaging.
derog'atory, nadelig; verkortend; veragtelik; vernederend, geringskattend, kleinerend.
der'rick, kraan; boortoring; katrolboom, laai(boom)bok; ~ **crane**, galgkraan.
derrière, (F), derrière, boude, agterstewe.
derring-do', dapperheid, waaghalsigheid.
der'ringer, sakpistool, derringer.
der'vish, derwisj, bedelmonnik (Moslem).
desal'inate, desalt', uitvars, ontsout.
desalina'tion, desalta'tion, uitvarsing, ontsouting.
des'cant, (n) rede(voering); lied (digterlik); verhandeling; diskant.

descant', (v) breedvoerig praat, uitwei.
descend', afstam; afklim; neerdaal; afkom; afsink, neerstryk; land (vliegtuig); afstyg; neerkom; afdaal; ~*ing GRADE*, afdraande; ~*ing series of NUMBERS*, getalle van die algemena na die besondere; ~ *ON*, op iem. toesak, iem. toeval, oorgaan op; afdaal; ~ *TO*, hom verlaag tot; afgaan (afstap) tot; ~ *UPON*, oorval; ~ **ant**, afstammeling, nakomeling; ~ **ed**: *be* ~*ed from*, afkomstig wees van, afstam van; ~**ent**, afstammend; ondertoe gaande; ~**er**, ondersteelletter (drukk.); ~**ible**, oorerfbaar.
descen'sion, neerdaling, neerkom(s); afkoms.
descent', neerdaling, afstyging; afneming (van kruis); afgang; inval; landing, (af)daling; afdraand; oorval; oorgang (van regte); geslag; vererwing; afkoms, herkoms; nakomelingskap; ~ **theory**, afstammingsleer.
describ'able, beskryfbaar.
describe', beskrywe; omskrywe; afbeeld; aandui; ~**r**, beskrywer.
descri'er, bespieder, ontdekker, bespeurder.
descrip'tion, beskrywing; soort, slag, aard, klas; *it BEGGARS* ~, geen pen kan dit beskryf nie; *no FOOD of any* ~, hoegenaamd geen voedsel nie; *PERSONAL* ~, sinjalement; persoonlike beskrywing.
descrip'tive, beskrywend, deskriptief; ~ **botany**, beskrywende plantkunde (botanie); ~ **linguistics**, beskrywende taalkunde.
descry', **(descried)**, bespied, ontdek, gewaar, bespeur, ontwaar.
des'ecrate, (ver)ontheilig, ontwy.
desecra'tion, skending, (ver)ontheiliging, heiligskennis, ontwyding.
des'ecrator, verontheiliger, ontwyer.
dese'gregate, desegregeer, integreer.
desegrega'tion, desegregasie, integrasie.
desensitiza'tion, desensitisasie, ongevoeligmaking.
desen'sitize, ongevoelig maak.
de'sert¹, (n) woestyn, woesteny; (a) woes, verlate, onbewoon: dor.
de'sert², (n) verdienste; (pl) verdiende loon; *GET one's* ~*s*, sy verdiende loon kry; *one's JUST* ~*s*, jou verdiende loon; *according to ONE'S* ~*s*, na verdienste; ~ *and REWARD seldom go together*, die perd wat die korrels verdien, kry dikwels die strooi.
desert'³, (v) verlaat, (weg)dros, wegloop, deserteer, oorloop.
de'sert country, dorsland.
desert': ~ **ed**, verlate, uitgestorwe, uitgesterf; ~ **er**, droster, wegloper, deserteur.
de'sert is'land, woestyneiland.
deser'tion, verlatenheid; afvalligheid, versaking; oorloop, desersie; verlating, drostery; ~ *of SERVICE*, diensverlating; *WILFUL* ~, kwaadwillige verlating.
desert: ~ **people**, woestynbewoners; ~ **plant**, woestynplant; ~ **rat**, woestynrot; ~ **spray**, swartstorm; ~ **tract**, woestyngebied; woesteny.
deserv'e, toekom (eer); verdien, werd wees.
deserv'edly, na verdienste; tereg.
deserv'ing, verdienstelik; *be* ~, verdienstelik wees.
déshabille' = **dishabille.**
des'iccant, (n) opdroënde middel; (a) opdroënd.
des'iccate, (uit)droog, opdroog.
desicca'tion, uitdroging, opdroging, desikkasie.
des'iccative, opdroënd, uitdroënd.
des'iccator, uitdroër, droogtoestel, desikkator.
desid'erate, (ernstig) begeer, nodig hê, verlang, mis.
desid'erative, desideratief.
desiderat'um, (..ta), gevoelde behoefte, gewenste iets, vereiste, desideratum.
design'¹, (n) ontwerp, plan, patroon, tekening; (v) ontwerp, skets.
design'², (n) voorneme; toeleg, oogmerk, opset; *BY* ~, met opset, opsetlik; *HAVE* ~*s upon*, 'n oog hê op, iets in die skild voer (teen); (v) beoog; bestem, aanwys.
des'ignate, (v) aanwys, aandui; bestem; noem; ~ *by name*, by name aandui; (a) aangewese, pasbenoemde.

designa'tion, aanwysing, aanduiding; bestemming, doel; benoeming; betiteling, naam.
design'edly, opsetlik, voorbedagtelik.
design'er[1], (patroon)ontwerper.
design'er[2], intrigant, konkelaar.
design'ing[1], (n) tekenkuns, patroontekening; ontwerp; (a) ontwerpend.
design'ing[2], arglistig, slu.
desilica'tion, desilikasie.
desil'verize, ontsilwer.
desip'ience, dwaasheid; speelsheid, kinderagtigheid.
desirabil'ity, wenslikheid; gewenstheid.
desir'able, wenslik, verkieslik, begeerlik; ~**ness,** wenslikheid.
desire', (n) begeerte, verlange, verlangste, lus, wens, wil; (v) begeer, verlang, wil, wens; versoek; *LEAVE much to be* ~*d,* veel te wense oorlaat; ~ *him to WAIT,* hom versoek om te wag; ~**d,** gewens, gewild, welkom; ~**r,** verlanger, versoeker.
desir'ous, begerig, verlangend; ~ *OF,* verlangend na; *be* ~ *TO,* verlang om.
desist', laat staan, ophou, aflaat (van), uitskei (met).
desk, lessenaar, skryftafel; spreekgestoelte; skoolbank; ~ **calender,** tafel-almanak; ~ **dictionary,** handwoordeboek, tafelwoordeboek; ~ **encyclopedia,** tafelensiklopedie; ~ **pad,** vloeiblok, blok vloeipapier; notablok; ~ **telephone,** tafeltelefoon; ~ **work,** kantoorwerk; skryfwerk.
des'man, watermol (*Desmana moschata*).
desmo'logy, verbandleer, desmologie.
des'olate, (v) verwoes, eensaam maak; ontvolk; (a) verlate, eensaam, ontvolk; woes, (haai)kaal; desolaat; doods, troosteloos; *nothing grows on these hills,* niks groei teen hierdie verlate (haaikale) berge nie; ~**ness,** eensaamheid; troosteloosheid, doodsheid, eensaamte.
desola'tion, verwoesting; verlatenheid; ontvolking; troosteloosheid.
des'olator, verwoester.
despair', (n) wanhoop, radeloosheid; troosteloosheid, vertwyfeling; *be driven to* ~, tot wanhoop gebring word; (v) wanhopig maak; wanhoop, versaak; in vertwyfeling raak, moed opgee; ~ *of,* wanhoop aan, vertwyfel.
despair'ing, wanhopend; wanhopig, desperaat.
despatch' = **dispatch.**
desperad'o (-es), waaghals; wanhopige woesteling, desperado.
des'perate, wanhopig, desperaat; roekeloos; radeloos; *be* ~, wanhopig (desperaat) wees; ~**ly,** hopeloos; in hoë mate, buitengewoon.
despera'tion, wanhoop, wanhopigheid, radeloosheid, vertwyfeling; woestheid; *act of* ~, wanhoopsdaad.
despi'cable, veragtelik, laag, gemeen, verfoeilik; ~**ness,** laagheid, gemeenheid.
despis'able = **despicable.**
despise', verag, versmaad, verfoei; ~**r,** veragter, versmader, verfoeier.
despite', (n) kwaadwilligheid; hoon, minagting; gekrenktheid; (prep) in weerwil van, nieteenstaande; ondanks; *in* ~ *of,* in weerwil van, ten spyte van; ~**ful,** boosaardig, nydig.
despoil', plunder, beroof, berowe; ~**er,** plunderaar, (be)rower.
despolia'tion, roof, plundering.
despond', wanhoop, moed verloor, tou opgooi; ~**ence,** ~**ency,** moedeloosheid, wanhopigheid, kleinmoedigheid, verslaenheid, swaarhoofdigheid, neerslagtigheid; ~**ent,** moedeloos, mismoedig, swaarhoofdig, neerslagtig, kleinmoedig; ~**ing,** terneergedruk.
des'pot, despoot, dwingeland.
despot'ic, despoties, willekeurig, heerssugtig.
des'potism, despotisme, dwingelandy.
des'pumate, afskuim.
despuma'tion, afskuiming.
des'quamate, afskilfer; vervel.
desquama'tion, afskilfering; vervelling.
dessert', dessert, toespys, nagereg; ~**-apple,** tafelappel; ~**-fork,** dessertvurk; ~**-knife,** (..knives), dessertmes; ~**-plate,** dessertbord; ~**-service,** dessertservies; ~**-spoon,** dessertlepel; ~**-wine,** dessertwyn.
destarch', ontstysel.
destina'tion, bestemming, destinasie; lot.
des'tine, bestem, voorbestem, bepaal, bedoel; toewy; ~**d,** voorbestem(d), voorbeskik.
des'tiny, (..nies), lot, noodlot, bestemming, voorland; *man of* ~, man met 'n roeping.
des'titute, ontbloot; doodarm, behoeftig, nooddruftig, (brand)arm; beroof; verlate; verstoke (van); ~ *OF,* sonder, ontbloot van: ~ *of POPULATION,* ontvolk; *THE* ~, die misdeeldes, die hulpbehoewendes.
destitu'tion, gebrek, armoede, behoeftigheid, ontbering, nood(druf).
destroy', verniel, verdelg, vernietig, verderf, verwoes: doodmaak, afmaak; afbreek; ~ *oneself,* jou ruïneer; jou van kant maak, selfmoord pleeg; ~**able,** vernielbaar; ~**er,** vernieler, verdelger; torpedojaer; ~**ing,** verwoestend, vernietigend; *the* ~*ing angel,* die verderfengel.
destructibil'ity, vernielbaarheid, verdelgbaarheid.
destruc'tible, vernielbaar, verwoesbaar, vernietigbaar.
destruc'tion, vernieling, vernielery, verwoesting, verdelging; verderf; *be heading for* ~, op die afdraand wees (met die rem los); ~**ist,** vernielal, verwoester.
destruc'tive, vernielend, vernielsiek, vernielsugtig, afbrekend, destruktief, verderflik; dodelik, boosaardig; ~ *criticism,* afbrekende kritiek; ~**ness,** skadelikheid; vernielsug.
destruc'tor, vernieler, verwoester, vuilgoedoond, verbrandingsoond, verbrander.
desuc'kering, ontsuiering.
desuda'tion, uitsweting.
des'uetude, ongewoonte, onbruik; *fall into* ~, in onbruik raak.
desul'pherize, ontswa(w)el.
des'ultoriness, ongestadigheid, onbestendigheid.
des'ultory, onsamehangend, wispelturig, oppervlakkig, sonder metode; van die os op die esel, rond en bont, rondspringerig; ongestadig.
detach', losmaak, afhaak, afsonder, detasjeer, skei; afdeel (mil.); ~**able,** skeibaar; afneembaar, los; ~*able BOOKLET,* losmaakboekie; ~*able RIM,* afneembare velling; ~*able WHEEL,* afneembare wiel; ~**ed,** afgeskeie, alleenstaande; objektief, onbevooroordeel; onbevange, los; ~*ed dwellings,* losstaande huise; ~**ment,** losmaking; afdeling (mil.); afgetrokkenheid; skeiding; objektiwiteit; isolement, afsondering, losheid; ~*ment of retina,* netvliesloslating.
det'ail, (n) besonderheid; uiteensetting; diensorder (mil.); klein puntjie; omstandigheid; detail; *GO into* ~*s,* in besonderhede afdaal; *in GREAT* ~, van hawer tot gort; *IN* ~, breedvoerig; haarfyn; omstandig; in besonderhede; *KNOW something in great* ~, tot in die fynste besonderhede ken; *that is MERE* ~, dis van min(der) belang.
de'tail, (v) omstandig vertel, uitvoerig meedeel; opsom; aanwys, afsonder, bestem.
det'ailed, uitvoerig, omstandig; gedetailleerd; ~ *account,* uitvoerig verhaal; gespesifiseerde rekening.
detain', terughou, weerhou, vashou; gevange hou; ophou; op skool hou; ~ *in custody,* in hegtenis hou; ~**ee,** aangehoudene; ~**er,** vashouer; onwettige besit; geregtelike beslag; bevel tot gevangehouding; ~**ment,** terughouding; gevangehouding.
detect', uitvind, bespeur, betrap, agterkom, ontdek, opspoor; verklik (maj.); ~**able,** te betrap, bespeurbaar; bemerkbaar; ~**ion,** ontdekking, betrapping, opsporing; verklikking, bespeuring; vasstelling.
detec'tive, (n) speurder; *AMATEUR* ~, amateurspeurder; *PRIVATE* ~, privaatspeurder; (a) detektief, speurend; ~ *department,* speurafdeling; ~ *force,* speurdiens; ~ **novel,** ~ **story,** speurverhaal.
detec'tograph, verklikker.
detec'tor, ontdekker; openbaarder; opspoorder; verklikker, detektor (elek.).
detent', drukker, ligter, klink, knip; stuiter.

détente', ontspanningspolitiek, ontladingspolitiek, afkoelingspolitiek, détente.
deten'tion, terughouding; aanhouding, gevangehouding, hegtenis, opsluiting; oponthoud; skoolsit; agterhouding (deur polisie), detensie; *in* ~ , in bewaring; ~ **barracks**, militêre tronk, detensiekaserne; ~ **cell**, aanhoudingsel; ~ **centre**, bewaarplek; aanhoudingsplek; ~ **room**, gevangekamer, arrestantelokaal; ~ **work**, strafwerk.
deter', (-red), afskrik, terughou, weerhou.
deterge', suiwer, skoonmaak, reinig; ~**nce**, ~**ncy**, reiniging.
deter'gent, (n) suiweringsmiddel, reiniger; (a) suiwerend.
deter'iorate, slegter word, bederwe; ontaard; agteruitgaan; afbrokkel, vererger, versleg; ~**d**, ontaard; sleg.
deteriora'tion, verslegting, agteruitgang, verval; ontaarding; bederf.
deter'ment, afskrik(king).
determinabil'ity, bepaalbaarheid.
determ'inable, bepaalbaar.
determ'inant, (n) determinant; (a) beslissend, bepalend.
determ'inate, bepaald; beslissend; vasgestel; beperk.
determina'tion, bepaling; beslissing; vasstelling; rigting, koers; beëindiging; neiging; vasberadenheid; determinasie.
determ'inative, (n) kenmerk, determinatief; (a) bepalend; beslissend.
determ'ine, bepaal, besluit, determineer, uitmaak; beslis, vaslê, eindig; vasstel; rigting gee, beweeg; ~ *on*, besluit tot; ~ **d**, vas, onwankelbaar, gedetermineerd, vasberade, vasbeslote, stellig; *be* ~ *d*, vasbeslote wees.
determ'inism, determinisme.
determinis'tic, deterministies.
dete'rrence, afskrikking.
dete'rrent, (n), afskrikmiddel; *act as a* ~, as afskrikmiddel dien; (a) afskrikkend; afskrikwekkend.
dete'rring, afskrikkend, ontmoedigend.
deter'sion, suiwering, reiniging.
deters'ive, suiwerend(e middel).
detest', verfoei, verafsku, haat; ~ **able**, verfoeilik, afskuwelik, haatlik; ~ **a'tion**, verfoeiing, afsku; *hold in* ~ *ation*, verfoei, verafsku, 'n broertjie daaraan dood hê; ~**ed**, gehaat; ~**er**, hater.
dethrone', onttroon, afsit; van die troon verval; ~**ment**, onttroning, afsetting; ~**r**, afsitter, onttroner.
det'onate, ontplof, knal; laat ontplof, detoneer.
detona'tion, ontploffing, knal, detonasie.
det'onator, ontploffer, knalpatroon; dinamietpatroon; slaghoedjie, knaldoppie; slagdoppie; springbus; donderbuisie (granaat); pistool (torpedo).
detor'sion, verdraaiing.
de'tour, omweg, ompad, uitwykpad; kronkelpad; wydlopigheid; uitweiding; *make a* ~, 'n ompad gaan.
detract', te kort doen, ontneem; afbreuk doen; (ver)kleineer, belaster, beskinder; ~ *nothing from some= one's merits*, niks aan iem. se verdienste afdoen nie; ~**ing**, lasterlik, kleinerend; ~**ion**, benadeling; belastering, verkleinering; ~**ive**, kleinerend; lasterend; ~**or**, afbreker; lasteraar; ~**ress**, (-es), skinderbek, Antjie Taterat.
detrain', afstap, uitstap (v.d.trein); uitlaai.
detribaliza'tion, ontstamming.
detrib'alize, ontstam; ~**d**, ontstam.
det'riment, nadeel, skade.
detrimen'tal, (n) ongewenste vryer; (a) nadelig, skadelik.
detrit'al, puin=, gruis=, detritaal.
detri'tion, afslyting.
detri'tus, rotsgruis, afslytsel, puin, afval, detritus.
detrun'cate, verkort, afsny, snoei.
deuce¹, gelykop (tennis); twee.
deuce², drommel; duiwel; ~ *KNOWS*, joos weet; *a* ~ *of a MESS*, 'n vreeslike warboel; *at a* ~ *of a PACE*, vreeslik vinnig; *there will be the* ~ *to PAY*, die poppe sal dans; daar sal 'n lelike nadraai wees; *PLAY the* ~ *with*, roekeloos te werk gaan met; deurbring;

the ~ *TAKE you*, mag die duiwel jou haal (ry)! *WHAT the* ~? wat de drommel; ~**d**, drommels, duiwels; *in a* ~ *d hurry*, baie haastig.
deus ex machina, (L.), deus ex machina, toevallige tussenkoms (tussentrede).
deuterag'onist, deuteragonis, tweede speler.
deu'terate, deutereer, deuteriuminvoeging.
deut'eric, deuteries.
deute'rium, swaarwaterstof, deuterium.
deuterog'amy, tweede huwelik.
deuteron'omist, medewerker, samesteller.
Deuteron'omy, Deuteronomium.
deval'uate, in waarde verminder, devalueer.
devalua'tion, waardevermindering, devaluasie.
Devana'gari, Devanagari, Sanskritalfabet.
dev'astate, verwoes, verniel.
devasta'tion, verwoesting, vernieling.
dev'astator, vernieler, verwoester.
devel'op, ontwikkel, uitgroei, ontvou, ontplooi, ontgin; begin ontwikkel; *POWER to* ~, ontwikkelingsvermoë; ~ *a TUMO(U)R*, 'n gewas ontwikkel; ~**er**, ontwikkelaar; ontginner, ontsluiter; ontginnende myn.
deve'loping, ontwikkelend; ~ **country**, ontwikkelende land; ~ **tray**, ontwikkelingsbak.
devel'opment, ontwikkeling; ontplooiing; ontsluitingswerk (myn); *AWAIT* ~ *s*, verdere verwikkelinge afwag; *COURSE of* ~, ontwikkelingsgang; *HISTORY of* ~, ontwikkelingsgeskiedenis; *POSSIBILITY of* ~, ontwikkelingsmoontlikheid; ~ **'al**, ontwikkelings; ~ **bank**, ontwikkelingsbank; ~ **company**, ontwikkelingsmaatskappy; ~ **plan**, ontwikkelingsplan, bebouingsplan.
deverb'ative, deverbatief.
deverm'inize, ontluis.
dev'iate, (v) afwyk, uitwyk, afdwaal; afbuig (pad); (a) afwykend; ~ *children*, afwykende kinders.
devia'tion, afwyking, deviasie; verlegging (pad); koersafwyking (lugv.); afdrywing; afleiding (water); sypad, syspoor; *angle of* ~, deviasiehoek; ~ **chart**, deklinasiekaart; ~**ism**, afwyking; ~**ist**, afwykeling; ~ **line**, vermyspoor, uitwykspoor.
dev'iator, afwyker.
device', sinspreuk, (leen)spreuk, motto, leuse; oogmerk; byskrif, devies; toestel, ontwerp; *LEFT to one's own* ~ *s*, aan jouself oorgelaat; *RESORT to devious* ~ *s*, van twyfelagtige middele gebruik maak; krom spronge maak, krom paaie bewandel.
dev'il, (n) duiwel, satan; swernoot, josie, drommel, broesa, bloukoos, duiwelstoejaer; vuurpot; loopjong; assistent; wolf(spinnery); kruiekos; *A* ~ *of a* . . ., 'n vervlakste . . .; 'n duiwelse . . .; *the* ~ *'s AD= VOCATE*, duiwelsadvokaat, vitter, afkammer; *CAST out the* ~ *by Beelzebub*, die duiwel met Beëlsebub uitdryf; *BETWEEN the* ~ *and the deep (blue) sea*, tussen twee vure; tussen hamer en aambeeld; *the* ~ *'s BONES*, dobbelsteentjies; ~ *'s BOOKS*, speelkaarte; *the* ~ *and his DAM*, die duiwel en sy moer; *better the* ~ *that you know than the* ~ *you DON'T know*, liewer 'n bekende as 'n onbekende ergernis; *not give the* ~ *his DUE*, die duiwel nie gee wat hom toekom nie; *FEAR someone like the very* ~, vir iem. so bang wees soos die duiwel vir 'n slypsteen; *GIVE the* ~ *his due*, gee die duiwel wat hom toekom; *GO to the* ~, te gronde gaan; *GO to the* ~, loop na jou moer; ~ *take the HINDMOST*, laat elkeen vir homself sorg; *as the* ~ *loves HOLY water*, so lief soos die duiwel vir 'n slypsteen; *the* ~ *finds work for IDLE hands to do*, ledigheid is die duiwel se oorkussing; *the* ~ *INCARNATE*, die baarlike duiwel; *the* ~ *only KNOWS*, dit weet joos alleen; *LIKE the very* ~, soos 'n besetene; *the* ~ *is NEVER given his due*, die duiwel word altyd swarter gesmeer as wat hy is; *the* ~ *looks after his OWN*, die duiwel sit sy voete reg; *there will be the* ~ *to PAY*, daar lê die groot moeilikheid voor; *PLAY the* ~ *with*, roekeloos omspring met; ruïneer; *POOR* ~, arme drommel; *be like one POSSESSED by the* ~, jou gedra of die duiwel in jou gevaar het; *the PRIN= TER'S* ~, die drukkersduiwel; *RAISE the* ~, 'n lawaai opskop; *RUN as if the* ~ *were at one's heels*, loop of die duiwel agter jou is; *between the* ~ *and*

the deep blue SEA, tussen twee vure; tussen Farao en die Rooi See; tussen hamer en aambeeld; *the ~ among the TAILORS*, 'n helse lawaai; *the ~ TAKE you*, mag die josie jou haal; *TALK of the ~ (and he will appear)*, praat v.d. duiwel (dan trap jy op sy stert); *beat the ~ 's TATTOO*, met die vingers (voete) trommel; *a ~ of a TEMPER*, 'n briesende humeur; *~ 's THORN*, dubbeltjie; *go TO the ~*, te gronde gaan; *the ~ is beating his WIFE*, jakkals trou met wolf se vrou; (v) **(-led)**, duiwels maak; peper, sterk krui; werk afskuif; **~-dodger**, duiweljagter, hemeldragonder; **~-fish**, seeduiwel; duiwelvis; **~-in-a-bush**, duiwel-in-die-bos; **~ish**, duiwels, duiwelagtig; **~ishness**, duiwelagtigheid; **~ led**, gekrui(de); **~ led kidneys**, gepeperde niertjies; **~-may-care'**, roekeloos; onverskillig, astrant; geen duiwel en sy moer ontsien nie; **~ment**, duiwelary; guitigheid; uitgelatenheid, grap; spokery; **~-ray**, duiwelvis, duiwelrog; **~ry**, duiwelary, duiwelskunste; slegtheid; tergagtigheid; roekeloosheid.
dev'il's: ~ **advocate**, duiwelsadvokaat; ~ **bedpost**, klawervier; ~ **bit**, blouknoop; ~ **bones**, dobbelstene; ~ **claw**, duiwelsklou; ~ **dirt**, ~ **dung**, duiwelsdrek; ~ **dozen**, dertien; ~ **dust**, wolpoeier; ~ **egg**, stinkswam, ~ **grass**, renosterkweek, kwaggakweek; ~ **grip**, duiwelsklou; ~ **gut**, meetketting; ~ **guts**, duiwelsnaaigaring; ~ **snuff-boxes**, duiwelsnuif; ~ **wool**, kunswol; ~ **work**, duiwelswerk.
devil: try = devilry; ~ **worship**, satansaanbidding, duiwelsaanbidding.
dev'ious, afwykend; afgeleë; dwaal=; verdwaal; slinger=; kronkel=, kronkelend; ~ *way*, 'n omweg; ~ **ly**, langs 'n omweg.
devise'¹, (n) erflating, bemaking; (v) bemaak.
devise'², (v) uitdink, versin, smee(d), beraam, bedink.
devis'er, uitvinder, planmaker, uitdinker.
devisee', erfgenaam, legetaris.
devis'or, erflater, bemaker.
devit'alize, verswak; demonteer, onskadelik maak.
devitrifica'tion, ontglasing, devitrifikasie.
devit'rify, ontglaas, devitrifiseer.
devoc'alize, stemloos maak.
devoid', leeg, ontbloot; ontdaan; ~ *of FEAR*, sonder vrees; ~ *of SHAME*, skaamteloos; ~ *of UNDER-STANDING*, sonder verstand.
dev'oir, plig; **~s**: *pay one's ~ to*, jou opwagting maak by.
dev'olute, oordra.
devolu'tion, tebeurtvalling; oordrag, devolusie; oorgang; **~ist**, afstigter.
devolve', neerkom; oordra; toeval, te beurt val; afskuif op; ~ *upon*, neerkom op; oorgaan op.
Devon'ian, (n) Devoon; (a) Devonies.
devote', toewy, wy, bestee, opoffer; oorlewer; ~ *oneself to*, jou toelê op.
devot'ed, toegewy, toegeneë; geheg; verkleef, verknog; verslaaf; gedoem; ~ *FRIEND*, getroue vriend; ~ *THINGS*, bangoed; **~ness**, toegeneentheid, gehegtheid.
devotee', toegewyde, aanhanger, aartsliefhebber, dweper; yweraar; slaaf.
devo'tion, gehegtheid, toegeneentheid; (toe)wyding, devosie, eerbiediging; godsdienstigheid; vroomheid, godsvrug; godsdiensoefening; (pl) godsdiensoefening, gebede; ~ **al**, godsdienstig, stigtelik; vroom; godvrugtig; eerbiedig; opreg; **~alist**, godsdienstige, voorbidder.
devour', verslind, opvreet, verorber, verteer; kafdraf, kafloop (koek); ~ *ed by curiosity*, brand van nuuskierigheid; **~er**, verslinder, vernieler; deurbringer; **~ing**, (n) verorbering; (a) begerig, gulsig; verslindend; ~ *ing passion*, verterende hartstog.
devout', godsdienstig, vroom; **~ness**, godsvrug, vroomheid; eerbied.
dew'ar flask, dewarfles, vakuumfles.
dewa'ter, ontwater; **~ing**, ontwatering.
dewax', ontwas; **~ing**, wasverwydering.
dew, (n) dou; (v) nat dou; **~berry**, braam; **~-claw**, valskloutjie; **~ drop**, doudruppel; **~iness**, douerigheid; klamheid; **~ lap**, hangwang (hond); keelvel (bees); **~less**, sonder dou.
dewool', ontwol, bloot; **~ing**, velbloting.

deworm', ontwurm; **~ing**, ontwurming.
dew: ~ **point**, doupunt; **~-worm**, erdwurm; **~y**, nat gedou, bedou, douerig; klam.
dex'ter, regter=, regs.
dexte'rity, handigheid, vaardigheid, gouigheid, handvaardigheid, behendigheid; regsheid, regshandigheid.
dex't(e)rous, behendig, rats, vaardig, handig; regs.
dex'trin, dekstrien, dekstrine, styselgom.
dex'trose, druiwesuiker, dekstrose.
dey, dei (hist.)
d(h)ow, Arabiese skip, dau.
diabase', diabaas.
diabet'es, suikersiekte, diabetes.
diabet'ic (n) suikersiektelyer; (a) diabeties, suikersiekte=.
diabetom'eter, diabetometer.
dia'blerie, toordery; roekeloosheid; duiwelkunde, duiwelary, duiwelswerk.
diabol'ic(al), duiwelagtig, diabolies, duiwels.
diab'olism, duiwelswerk, toordery; duiwelaanbidding.
diab'olist, duiwelvereerder.
dia'bolo, diabolo, tolspel.
diachro'nic, diachronies; ~ **linguistics**, diachroniese taalkunde (linguistiek); **~s**, diachronie.
dia'conal, diakonaal, diaken=.
dia'conate, diakonaat.
diacrit'ical, onderskeidend, onderskeidings=, diakrities; ~ **mark (sign)**, diakritiese teken.
diac'tinal, diaktinaal.
diactin'ic, diaktinies.
di'adem, kroon, diadeem; **~-spider**, tuinspinnekop; **~ed**, gekroon, versier.
di(a)er'esis, (..eses), deelteken, skeiteken, afskeidingsteken; trema; diërese.
diagen'esis, diagenese.
diagenet'ic, diageneties.
diagnose', 'n diagnose maak, diagnoseer, vasstel (siekte).
diagnos'is, (..noses), diagnose, siektebepaling.
diagnos'tic, (n) kenteken, simptoom; (a) kenmerkend, diagnosties.
diagnosti'cian, diagnostikus.
diagnos'tics, diagnostiek.
diag'onal, (n) hoek(punt)lyn, diagonaal; (a) diagonaal, oorhoeks; ~ **arch**, kruisboog; ~ **course**, klamplaag; ~ **grain**, oorhoekshout; ~ **joint**, versteklas; ~ **rib**, kruisrib; ~ **scale**, transversaalskaal; ~ **stay**, steekskoor, oorhoekse anker; ~ **stitch**, skuinssteek; ~ **tie**, oorhoekse anker.
di'agram, figuur, skets, tekening, diagram; ~ **and title deeds**, kaart en transport.
diagrammat'ic, skematies, diagrammaties, grafies, met sketse.
diagramm'atize, skematies voorstel.
di'agraph, diagraaf, tekenaap.
di'al, (n) sonwyser; wyserplaat; skakelskyf (telef.); bakkies; (v) (**-led**), meet; aanwys; skakel (telefoon).
di'alect, dialek, tongval, streekspraak; *regional ~*, streekstaal; **~al**, dialekties; ~ **atlas**, dialekatlas; ~ **dictionary**, dialekwoordeboek.
dialec'tic, (n) dialektiek; (a) dialekties, dialek=.
dialec'tical, dialekties; ~ **materialism**, dialektiese materialisme.
dialecti'cian, logikus, dialektikus.
dialec'tics, logika, dialektiek.
dialectol'ogist, dialektoloog.
dialectol'ogy, dialekleer, dialekstudie, dialektologie.
dialect word, dialekwoord, streekwoord.
dial face, wyserplaat.
di'allage, diallaag.
dialo'gic, dialogies.
dial'ogist, skrywer van samesprake.
di'alogue, dialoog, samespraak, tweegesprek; colloquium.
di'al: ~ **plate**, wyserplaat; **~-telephone**, outomatiese telefoon; **~-tone**, skakeltoon.
dial'ysis, (..lyses), dialise.
dialyt'ic, halfdeurdringbaar, dialities.
diamagnet'ic, diamagneties.
diamag'netism, diamagnetisme.

diamanté, diamanté, blinkerstof.
diam'eter, middellyn, deursnee, diameter.
diam'etral, diametral.
diamet'ric(al), lynreg, diametraal; ~ *ly opposed,* in lynregte teenstelling; vierkant teenoor mekaar staan.
di'amond, diamant; ruite(ns); glassnyer; diamantletter; *BLACK* ~, swart diamant; steenkool; ~ *CUT* ~, baas bo baas, meester bo meester; *ROUGH* ~, ongeslypte diamant; ~ *s are TRUMPS,* ruite(ns) is troef; ~**-cleaver,** diamantklower; ~**-cutter,** diamantslyper; diamantwerker; ~**-cutting,** diamantslyping; ~ **digger,** diamantdelwer; ~ **drill,** diamantboor; ~**-driller,** diamantboorder; ~ **dust,** diamantpoeier; diamantgruis; ~ **field,** diamantveld; ~ **frame,** ruitraam; ~ **grit,** diamantgrint; ~**if'erous,** diamanthoudend; ~ **interchange,** diamantwisselaar; ~ **jubilee,** sestigjarige jubileum; ~ **letter,** diamant(letter); ~ **merchant,** diamanthandelaar; ~ **mine,** diamantmyn; ~ **ore,** diamantgrond; ~ **pipe,** diamantpyp; ~ **point,** graveernaald; ~**-polishing,** diamantslypery; ~ **powder,** diamantpoeier; ~ **setter,** diamantsetter; ~**-shaped,** ruitvormig; ~ **stitch,** ruitsteek; ~**-trade,** diamanthandel; ~ **type,** diamantsetsel; ~ **wedding,** diamantbruilof; ~**-worker,** diamantwerker, diamantslyper.
dian'drous, tweehelmig, diandries.
diapas'on, oktaaf, harmonie; toonomvang, diapason; toonhoogte.
di'apause, diapouse, vertraagde ontwikkeling.
di'aper, (n) damas, servetgoed, geblomde (geruite) linne; banddoek; pellegoed; luier; (v) skakeer, figure omweef; ~ **pattern,** blompatroon; ~ **pavement,** geblomde bestrating; mosaïekvloer; ~**-work,** geblomde werk.
diaphane'ity, ligdeurlatingsvermoë, deurskynendheid.
diaph'anous, deurskynend, diafaan.
diapho'nics, diafonie.
diaphore'sis, sweting, diaforese.
diaphoret'ic, (n) sweetmiddel; (a) sweetdrywend.
di'aphragm, middelrif, diafragma, mantelvlies; lensopening; ~ **hernia,** diafragmabreuk.
dia'physis, diafise, beenpyp.
diapos'itive, diapositief, skyfie.
di'archy, tweehoofdige regering, diargie.
dia'rial, dagboek-.
di'arize, opteken, opskryf, diariseer.
di'arist, dagboekskrywer.
di'arize, 'n dagboek hou, aanteken in 'n dagboek.
diarrhoe'a, diarree, persie, buikloop, maagwerking, appelkoossiekte.
di'ary, (diaries), dagboek.
di'ascope, diaskoop.
dias'pora, verstrooiing, diaspora.
di'astase, diastase.
diastat'ic, (diasties), diastasies.
dias'tole, uitsetting, diastool.
diastol'ic, diastolies; ~ **murmur,** diastool(ge)ruis.
diatherm'al, diatermies.
diatherm'ic, diatermies.
di'athermy, diatermie.
diath'esis, (..**theses),** vatbaarheid vir siekte, diatese.
di'atom, diatoom; diatomee, kristalwier.
diatoma'ceous, diatomeëhoudend; ~ **earth,** diatomeëaarde, diatomiet.
diatom'ic, diatomies.
diat'omite, diatomiet.
diaton'ic, diatonies.
di'atribe, skimprede, spotrede, smaadrede, hekelskrif, diatribe.
Di'az, Dias.
dib, dolos.
dibas'ic, tweebasies, dibasies.
dibb'er, plantyster, graafstok.
dib'ble, (n) plantstok; (v) gate maak; plant.
di'branch, tweekiewige; ~'**iate,** tweekiewig.
di'bromide, dibromied, dibromide.
dibs, klipspel (met skaaphotnotjies of skaapdolosse); pitte (geld).
dice, (n) dobbelstene; blokkies; *the* ~ *are LOADED,* met die lot is gepeuter; dis vals dobbelstene; *the* ~ *were LOADED against him,* alles was teen hom; (v) dobbel; in dobbelsteentjies (blokkies) sny; ~**-box,** dobbelbeker, dobbeldosie; ~**d,** in blokkies gesny; ~*d carrots,* wortels in blokkies gesny; ~**-player,** dobbelaar; ~**-play(ing),** dobbelspel; ~ **r,** dobbelaar; ~**y,** onseker, moeilik; gevaarlik.
dicho'rial twins, onpaar tweeling.
dichotom'ic, vurksgewyse.
dichot'omize, splits, vertak.
dichot'omous, tweedelig; gegaffel, gevurk (plant).
dichot'omy, gaffelsplitsing, digotomie.
dichro'ic, dichroma'tic, tweekleurig, dichromaties.
di'cing, dobbel(a)ry.
dick[1], speurder.
dick[2], woord; *take one's* ~, sweer, bevestig (Amer.).
dick'ens, drommel, duiwel; *what the* ~ *are you doing?,* wat op aarde doen jy?
dick'er[1], (n) tiental.
dick'er[2], (v) ruil, knibbel.
dick'ey[1], **(-s), dick'y, (dickies),** leervoorskoot; borsie (japon).
dick'ey[2], **(-s), dick'y, (dickies),** bok (rytuig); agterbak, kattebak (motor); esel, donkie; ~**-bird,** tinktinkie; ~**-seat,** kattebak, agterbak.
dic'ky, moeg, klaar, gedaan.
dicotyled'on, tweesaadlobbige plant, dikotiel; ~ **ous,** tweesaadlobbig, dikotiel.
dicro'tic pulse, tweeslagpols.
dic'taphone, diktafoon, dikteermasjien.
dic'tate[1], (n) voorskrif, gebod, bevel; *the* ~ *s of CONSCIENCE,* die stem van die gewete; ~ *s of the HEART,* ingewing v.d. hart, inspraak.
dictate'[2], dikteer; gebied, voorskryf; ingee.
dicta'tion, diktaat, diktee; voorskrif, bevel.
dictat'or, dikteerder; gebieder, diktator, alleenheerser.
dictator'ial, gebiedend, diktatoriaal.
dictat'orship, diktatorskap, diktatuur, alleenheerskappy.
dictat'ress, (-es), vroulike diktator.
dic'tion, voordrag, styl, diksie, segswyse; uitdrukking.
dic'tionary, (..ries), woordeboek; ~ *of idioms,* idiotikon, idioomwoordeboek; ~ **maker,** leksikograaf, woordeboekmaker.
dic'tograph, diktograaf.
dic'tum, (-s, dicta), voorskrif; gesegde; uitspraak.
did, kyk **do;** ~ *you ever?* het jy dit nou ooit? nou nog mooier!
didac'tic, (n) didaktikus; (a) didakties, lerend, strekkings-, tendens-; ~ **poem,** leerdig; ~ **s,** onderwyskunde, didaktiek.
did'apper, duiker (voël).
did'dle, bedrieg, kul, fop, flous; *be* ~ *d,* gepier (uitoorlê, gefop) wees.
did'o, (-es), kaperjol, flikker, bokkesprong.
die[1], (n) **(dice),** dobbelsteen, teerling; **(-s),** muntstempel; matrys; snymoer, snyblok, skroefsny-yster (bouk.); vorm; *the* ~ *is CAST,* die teerling is geu werp; die besluit is onherroeplik geneem; die kalf is verdrink; die koeël is deur die kerk; *as STRAIGHT as a* ~, pylreguit, so reguit soos 'n roer.
die[2], (v) **(-d),** doodgaan, sneuwel (op slagveld); inslaap, die tol aan die natuur betaal, sterf, wegval, verhuis; vrek (diere); ~ *AWAY,* wegkwyn; doodgaan; wegsterf; ~ *BACK,* terugsterf, kwyn; ~ *in one's BED,* in jou bed sterf; van ouderdom of siekte sterf; ~ *DOWN,* verloop; verdoof; ~ *FOR,* sterf vir; brand van verlange; ~ *GAME,* al vegtende ondergaan (sterf); ~ *HARD,* swaar sterf; ~ *in HARNESS,* in die tuig sterf; ~ *by INCHES,* geleidelik sterf; wegkwyn; ~ *of LAUGHTER,* jou doodlag; ~ *OF,* sterf aan; ~ *OFF,* uitsterf; *we* ~ *but ONCE,* ons is net een dood skuldig; ~ *OUT,* versterwe, uitsterwe; *never SAY* ~, moet nooit moed verloor (opgee) nie; *want to* ~ *for SHAME,* jou oë uit jou kop skaam; ~ *in one's SHOES,* deur geweld omkom; 'n geweldaddige dood sterf; ~ *by the SWORD,* deur die swaard omkom.
die: ~ **block,** stempelblok; ~ **cutter,** stempelsnyer; ~ **design,** stempelontwerp.

die'-hard, onversoenlike; bittereinder, vastrapper, kanniedood.
diel'drin, dieldrin.
dielec'tric(al), diëlektries, isolerend; ~ **constant**, diëlektriese konstante.
die: ~ **-nut**, draadsnymoer; ~ **-plate**, snyplaat.
dies'el, diesel; ~ **engine**, dieselmotor; ~ **fuel**, dieselbrandstof; ~ **ine**, ~ **oil**, dieselolie.
die: ~ **-sinker**, stempelsnyer, stempelmaker; ~ **-stamp**, stempelblok; muntstempel.
di'et¹, (n) ryksdag, landdag.
di'et², (n) leefreël; dieet; (v) voed; op dieet stel, eetwyse voorskryf; kos gee; dieet volg; ~ **ary**, (n) (..**ries**), dieetboek; rantsoen; voedselreëling, dieetreëling; (a) dieet=, kos=; dieetmatig.
dietet'ic, diëteties, voedings=; ~ **s**, voedingsleer, diëtetiek; dieetkunde, dieetreëls.
diet: ~ **education**, dieetonderrig; ~ **food**, dieetkos, verslankingsdieet.
dieti'cian, dieti'tian, dieetkundige, diëtetis.
diff'er, verskil, uiteenloop, dit nie eens wees nie; *AGREE to* ~, ooreenkom om te verskil; *I BEG to* ~, ek is dit nie daarmee eens nie; moenie glo nie; ~ *FROM*, verskil van.
diff'erence, verskil, afwyking, uiteenlopendheid; onderskeid; strydigheid; onenigheid, geskil; differensie; *there is a year's* ~ *in AGES*, hulle skeel 'n jaar; ~ *of OPINION*, meningsverskil; *POINT of* ~, geskilpunt; *SPLIT the* ~, die verskil deel; ~ **column**, differensiekolom; ~ **equation**, differensievergelyking.
diff'erent, verskillend, onderskeie, afwykend, anders; *in a* ~ *DIRECTION*, in 'n ander rigting; ~ *FROM*, verskillend van; *of a* ~ *KIND*, andersoortig; *speaking a* ~ *LANGUAGE*, andertalig.
differen'tia, onderskeidingsmerk(e), kenteken(s), kenmerk(e).
differen'tial, (n) ewenaar, differensiaal; (a) differensiaal; differensieel; ewenaar=; *block of* ~ *pulley*, differensiaaltakel; ~ **bearing**, ewenaarlaer; ~ **calculus**, differensiaalrekening, -rekene; ~ **casing**, ewenaarhulsel, ~ **development**, eiesoortige ontwikkeling; ~ **duties**, differensiële regte; ~ **equation**, differensiaalvergelyking; ~ **heating**, wisselverhitting; ~ **housing**, ewenaaromhulsel; ~ **movements**, differensiële bewegings; ~ **pinion**, ewenaarkleinrat; ~ **rate**, differensiële tarief; ~ **ratio**, ewenaarverhouding; ~ **wage**, differensiële loon (nywerheid); ~ **weathering**, differensiële verwering.
differen'tiate, onderskeid maak, onderskei, verskil maak, gaan verskil, differensieer; voortrek, begunstig.
differentia'tion, onderskeiding, splitsing; voortrekkery, begunstiging; differensiasie, differensiëring.
diff'erently, anders, verskillend.
diff'ering, verskillend.
diff'icult, moeilik, moeisaam, lastig, swaar, opdraand; *BE* ~, moeilik wees; *BECOME* ~, moeilik word; *MAKE things* ~, die wêreld moeilik maak; ~ **y**, (..**ties**), moeilikheid, moeite, strawasie, swarigheid; engte, haakplek; swaar; *with the GREATEST* ~ *y*, met die grootste moeite; tussen hange en wurge; *MAKE* ~ *ies*, besware opper; *PRESENT many* ~ *ies*, heelwat voete in die aarde hê; baie probleme vertoon.
diff'idence, verleentheid, nederigheid, beskroomdheid, gebrek aan selfvertroue.
diff'ident, verleë, skaam, skroomvallig, beskroomd, nederig.
diff'luence, wegvloeiing, vervloeiing.
diff'luent, wegvloeiend, vervloeiend.
diffract', buig, in onderskeie kleure opbreek; ~ **ion**, diffraksie, straalbreking, (straal)buiging.
diffuse', (v) versprei, verstrooi, uitstraal, diffundeer (natuurk.); (a) omslagtig, langdradig, diffuus, breedsprakig, wydlopig; versprei, uitgesprei; onreëlmatig; ~ *d light*, gedempte lig, strooilig; ~ **ness**, verspreidheid; langdradigheid, wydlopigheid; ~ **r**, verspreider; uitstroombuis.
diffusibil'ity, verstrooibaarheid, verspreibaarheid, diffusievermoë.
diffus'ible, verstrooibaar, verspreibaar.

diffu'sion, uitstorting, verstrooiing, verspreiding, uitstraling, diffusie.
diffus'ive, verspreidend, uitstrooiend; uitgebrei; omslagtig; ~ **nes**, verspreiding, verspreidheid.
dig, (n) stoot, stamp; spitwerk; *HAVE a* ~ *at someone*, iem. 'n steek gee; *a* ~ *in the RIBS*, 'n stamp in die ribbekas; (v) (**dug**), delf, grawe, spit; snuffel; ~ *DOWN*, ondermyn; ~ *up the HATCHET*, die stryd hervat; ~ *IN*, ingrawe; ~ *ONESELF in*, jou vestig; ~ *OUT*, uitgrawe; uithol; ~ *THROUGH*, deurgrawe; ~ *in one's TOES*, vasskop, ysterklou in die grond slaan; ~ *UP the past*, ou koeie uit die sloot grawe.
dig'amy, tweede huwelik.
di'gest¹, (n) oorsig, opsomming, uittreksel (van boeke of nuus); keurblad; digesta; versameling wetboeke.
digest'², (v) sluk, duld; opsom; oordink, verwerk, rangskik; verteer; verkrop, verdra; laat verteer; *be able to eat and* ~ *anything*, 'n maag soos 'n volstruis hê; ~ **ed**, verteer; *easily* ~ *ed*, lig verteerbaar; ~ **er**, verteerder, verteertoestel; ontbindingstoestel; ~ **ibil'ity**, verteerbaarheid; ~ **ible**, verteerbaar; ~ **ion**, spysvertering, vertering, digestie.
diges'tive, goed vir die spysvertering; spysverterings=; ~ **canal**, spysverteringskanaal; ~ **juices**, spysverteringsappe; ~ **organs**, spysverteringsorgane; ~ **tract**, spysverteringskanaal.
digg'er, delwer; grawer; graaftoestel.
digg'ing, graafwerk, spittery; graafplek; ~ **s**, kamers, woonplek, losiesplek; delwery.
di'git, vinger; toon; vingerbreedte; syfer.
di'gital, (n) vinger, toets, noot; (a) vinger=, tot die vingers behorende; toon=
di'gitalin, digitalin.
digital'is, vingerhoedkruid, digitalis.
di'gitate(d), vingervormig, gevinger; handvormig.
di'gitigrade, (n) toonloper; (a) op die tone lopend.
dig'nified, waardig, deftig, statig; verhewe.
dig'nify, (..**fied**), met eer beklee, verhef, vereer; sier, deftig maak.
dig'nitary, (..**taries**), (hoog)waardigheidsbekleër, dignitaris.
dig'nity, amp; waardigheid, fierheid, deftigheid; adel; *BENEATH his* ~, benede sy waardigheid; *the* ~ *of LABOUR*, die adel v.d. arbeid; *STAND on his* ~, op sy eer gesteld wees; toon dat hy sy eiewaarde besef.
dig'raph, dubbelletter, digraaf.
digress', afdwaal, afwyk, uitwei; ~ **ion**, afwyking, uitweiding; ~ **ive**, uitweidend, wydlopig.
digs, (sl.), losiesplek, blyplek, tuiste.
dig'ynous, tweeslagtig (plantk.).
dihed'ral, tweevlaks=; ~ **angle**, tweevlakshoek, standhoek.
dike, (n) damwal; dyk; sloot; lawamuur; gang (geol.); (v) indyk; afdam; walle gooi; ~ **burst**, dykbreuk.
di'king, (be)dyking; ~ **system**, dykstelsel.
dik'kop, dikkop, kommandovoël.
dilac'erate, verskeur, van mekaar skeur.
dilacera'tion, verskeuring.
dilap'idate, (laat) verval; bouvallig word; verwaarloos; ~ **d**, vervalle, bouvallig, gehawend.
dilapida'tion, verval, verwaarlosing; bouvalligheid, inmekaarstorting, agteruitgang, vervallenheid.
dilatabil'ity, rekbaarheid, uitsettingsvermoë.
dilat'able, uitsetbaar, rekbaar.
dilata'tion, uitsetting, uitrekking; uitweiding; dilatasie.
dilatat'or, rekspier, dilatator; verwydingskroef, verwyder.
dilate', uitsit (uit)swel; uitrek, vergroot, verwyd; ~ *d EYES*, oopgespalkte oë; ~ *UPON*, uitwei oor.
dila'tion, uitsetting, uitrekking, verwyding, dilatasie.
dilat'or *kyk* **dilatator**.
dil'atoriness, traagheid, talmrigheid, getalm, draaierigheid.
dil'atory, stadig, draaierig, uitstellerig, vadsig, traag, talmrig, talmend.
dilemm'a, dilemma, verleentheid, verknorsing; *be on the horns of a* ~, tussen twee vure; in 'n lastige parket wees.
dilettan'te, dilettant, liefhebber.

dilettan'tism, dilettantisme, liefhebbery.
dil'igence¹, reiswa, veerwa, diligence.
dil'igence², ywer, fluksheid, arbeidsaamheid, vlyt, ywerigheid, noestheid, naarstigheid.
dil'igent, ywerig, fluks, naarstig, vlytig, werksaam, arbeidsaam.
dill, vinkel; dille (*Anethum graveolens*); ~ **cucumber,** dillekomkommer; ~ **pickle,** dillesuurtjie; ~-**water,** vinkelwater.
dil'li, dil'ly (bag), (rug)sak.
dil'ly, (sl.) (n), bul, ramkat, doring, (a), laf, geklik.
dill'y-dally, (*kyk ook* **dally**), draai, talm, weifel, besluiteloos wees; ~**ing,** gedraai, uitstellery.
dil'uent, (n) verdunningsmiddel, verdunner (verf); (a) verdunnend, verflouend.
dilute', verdun, verslap, verwater; aanmeng, aanleng.
dilut'ent, verdunner.
dilu'tion, verdunning, verwatering.
dilu'vial, diluviaal, spoel=, vloed=.
dilu'vium, diluvium, spoelgrond.
dim, (v) (**-med**) donker maak, domp, demp (ligte); benewel; verdof, dof maak; ~ *lights,* ligte neerslaan (domp, demp); (a) donker, dof, skemerig; gedemp, flou; flets (oë); wasig; suf; *GROW* ~, vervaag; *TAKE a* ~ *view of,* nie veel dink nie van.
dime, tien sent (Amer.); ~ **novel,** sensasieroman, snertroman.
dimen'sion, afmeting, grootte, omvang, dimensie; *the FOURTH* ~, die vierde afmeting (dimensie); *of GREAT* ~*s,* met groot afmetings; *LINEAR* ~, lengtemaat; *SUPERFICIAL* ~, vlakmaat; *the THREE* ~*s,* die drie afmetings (dimensies); ~**al,** dimensionaal; ~**ed,** maat=.
dim'erous, tweedelig.
dim'eter, tweevoetige vers, dimeter.
dimid'iate, in twee dele verdeel, halveer.
dimin'ish, verminder, verklein; slink, inkrimp; ~ *BY,* verminder met; ~ *RIGHTS,* regte inkort; ~**ed,** verklein, verneder.
diminu'tion, vermindering, verlaging, verkleining; ~ *of rights,* inkorting van regte.
dimin'utive, (n) verkleinwoord; (a) klein, gering, diminutief; verkleinings=; miniatuur=; verminderend; ~**ness,** kleinheid, geringheid.
dim'ity, diemit.
dimmed, gedemp, verdof, gedomp; ~ **light,** gedempte (gedompte) lig.
dim: ~**mer,** verdoffer, domper; ~**ming,** verdoffing, domping (ligte); ~**mish,** dowwerig; ~**ness,** dofheid; skemer; donkerheid, duisterheid; dowwigheid; flouheid.
dimorph'ic, dimorf, tweevormig.
dimorph'ism, dimorfisme, dimorfie, tweevormigheid.
dimorph'ous = **dimorphic.**
dim'ple, (n) (wang)kuiltjie; (v) kuiltjies vorm; ~**d,** met kuiltjies.
dim'ply, vol kuiltjies.
dim'-switch, (-es), skemerskakelaar, dofskakelaar; dompskakelaar.
dim'-witted, dom, onnosel, stompsinnig.
din, (n) geraas, geroesemoes, gedreun, lawaai; (v) (**-ned**), raas, lawaai maak, baljaar, te kere gaan; ~ *something into a person's ears,* aanhoudend dieselfde ding vir iem. sê.
di'nar, dinar.
dine, eet, dineer; op 'n ete onthaal; *he* ~*ed with DUKE Humphrey,* die hond was in die pot; ~ *off MUTTON,* skaapvleis vir ete geniet; ~ *with the crosslegged KNIGHTS,* droëbek sit; ~ *OUT,* uiteet; ~ **r,** eter, dineerder; eetwa; eetsalon; ~ **r out,** uiteter, restourantbesoeker.
dinette', eethoekie; ontbythoekie.
ding, slaan, afransel; gooi; ~**bat,** gooiding, dinges, watsenaam. ~-**dong,** bimbam (soos 'n klok maak), klink-klank; ~-**dong match,** saai wedstryd, gelykopwedstryd.
ding'ey, (-s), dingh'y, (dinghies), rubberbootjie, skuitjie, jol(boot), dinghie.
din'giness, duisterheid; vuiligheid, morsigheid; somberheid.
din'gle, vallei, kloof, dal, bosklofie.
ding'o, (-es), Australiese wildehond, dingo.

din'gus, (sl.) dinges, watsenaam.
din'gy, morsig, vuil; somber, rokerig, donker.
din'ing, eet; ~-**car,** eetsalon, eetwa; ~-**hall,** eetsaal; ~-**room,** eetkamer; eetvoorhuis; ~ -*room suite,* eetkamerstel; ~-**saloon,** eetsalon; ~-**table,** eettafel.
din'kum, (colloq.), eg, puik, regtig.
dink'y (colloq.), mooi, netjies, aantreklik, viets.
din'ner, (n) middagmaal, (middag)ete; dinee, eetmaal; feesmaal, hoofmaal; ~ *is served,* die kos is op tafel; (v) dineer, die middagete gebruik; ~-**bell,** etensklok; ~-**dance,** dinee-dansparty; ~-**fork,** tafelvurk; ~-**hour,** etenstyd, eetuur, twaalfuur; ~-**jacket,** dineebaadjie, aandbaadjie, stompstertbaadjie; ~-**pail,** kosemmer; ~-**party,** dinee; dineegeselskap; ~-**service,** ~-**set,** eetservies, dineeservies; ~-**table,** eettafel; ~-**time,** etenstyd, twaalfuur; ~-**wa(g)gon,** dientafel, dienwaentjie, eetwa=(entjie), rolwaentjie; ~ **ware,** eetservies; eetgerei.
din'osaur, dinosourus; ~ **ian,** dinosouries.
dint, (n) krag, mag; *by* ~ *of,* deur krag van, deur middel van; (v) = **dent,** (v).
deo'cesan, (n) biskop; (a) biskops=, bisdoms=, bisdomlik, diosesaan.
di'ocese, bisdom, biskoplike gebied, dioses.
di'ode, diode.
dioe'cian, tweehuisig.
di'ol, diool.
diop'tase, dioptaas.
diop'ter, diopter, kykspleet, visier (sterrek.).
diop'tric(al), dioptries, straalbrekend; ~ **glass,** verkyker.
diop'trics, straalbrekingsleer, dioptriek.
diora'ma, diorama, kykspel.
dioram'ic, dioramies.
di'orite, diabaas, groensteen, dioriet.
diox'ide, dioksied, diokside.
dip, (n) dip (vee); dipstof, dipmiddel; vetkers; inklinasie (kompasnaald); duik, laagte; indomping, indompeling, bad; ~ *on the HORIZON,* kimdiepte, kimduiking; *LUCKY* ~, donkervat; verrassingspak(kie); *MAGNETIC* ~, duiking v.d. kompas; ~ *of the NEEDLE,* duiking v.d. kompas; *TAKE a* ~, gaan swem, induik; ~ *of an OAR,* slag van 'n roeispaan; (v) (**-ped**), dip (van vee); doop; laat hel, inklineer; laat sak (vlag, seil); duik; indoop, indompel; skep; insteek; oppervlakkig kennis maak; domp; ~ *into a BOOK,* 'n boek deurblaai; ~ *the FLAG,* met die vlag salueer; ~ *into the FUTURE,* 'n blik in die toekoms slaan; ~ *one's pen in GALL,* jou pen in gal doop; ~ *INTO,* induik; ~ *LIGHTS,* ligte domp, ligte neerslaan; ~ *into one's POCKET,* jou geld met 'n milde hand spandeer; ~ **candle,** vetkers; ~ **circle,** ~ **compass,** inklinasiekompas.
dipet'alous, tweekroonblarig, dipetaal.
diphe'nic acid, difeensuur.
diphther'ia, witseerkeel, difterie.
diphther'ic, difteries.
diphtherit'is = **diphtheria.**
diph'thong, tweeklank, diftong; ~**al,** diftongies; ~**ize,** diftongeer.
diple'gia, dubbelsydige verlamming.
dip'-light, domplig (motor).
di'ploid, (n) diploïde; (a) tweekernig, diploïed.
diplom'a, diploma, sertifikaat; bul; getuigskrif.
diplom'acy, diplomasie; behendigheid, sluheid.
diplom'aed, gediplomeer(d).
dip'lomat, diplomaat, staatsman.
dip'lomated, gesertifiseer, gediplomeer(d).
diplomat'ic, diplomaties; poliets, oulik; diplomatiek; ~ **corps,** diplomatieke korps; ~ **service,** diplomatieke diens.
diplom'atist, diplomaat, staatsman.
diplom'atize, diplomaties optree.
diplo'pia, diplopie, dubbelsiendheid.
dip: ~-**needle,** inklinasienaald; ~-**net,** skepnet.
di'pody, dipodie.
dipp'er, duiker (voël), dipper (vee); skepper, skepding; potlepel; dempskakelaar; wederdoper; ~ **switch,** dompskakelaar.
dipp'ing, (die) dip, dippery; doop; ~-**needle,** inklinasienaald; ~-**pen,** dipkraal, diphok; ~-**tank,** dipbak, dip, dipgat.

dip plane, hellingsvlak.
dipp'y, (sl.) mal.
diprismat'ic, disprismaties.
dip: ~**-rod,** handstok (hengel); ~ **slope,** duikhelling, laagvlakglooiing.
dipsoman'ia, dranksug, dipsomanie; ~ **c,** (n) drank= sugtige, dipsomaan; (a) dranksugtig, dipsomanies.
dip'-stick, maatstok (olie); meetstok.
Dip'tera, Diptera, Tweevlerkiges; **d**~**l,** tweevlerkig.
dip'terous, tweevlerkig, dipteraal.
dip'tych, diptiek, tweeluik.
dire, vreeslik, aaklig; yslik; ~ **necessity,** absolute noodsaak; ~ **need,** uiterste behoefte.
direct', (v) rig; vestig (aandag); afstuur; bestuur; lei; adresseer; beveel, voorskryf; die pad beduie, wys; aanstuur; ~ *attention to,* die aandag vestig op; (a) regstreeks, reguit; onmiddellik; openhartig, opreg, ondubbelsinnig; uitdruklik; direk; *in* ~ *PROPOR= TION to,* in regstreekse (direkte) verhouding met; *a* ~ *ROUTE,* 'n reguit pad; ~ **current,** gelykstroom; ~ **drive,** regstreekse aandrywing; ~**ed,** gerig; ~ **hit,** voltreffer; ~**ing,** beherend; besturend; aandui= dend; ~**ing-post,** padwyser; naambord.
direc'tion, rigting; leiding, bevel, voorskrif; aanwy= sing; diensaanwysing; bepaling (in testament); be= stuur (van handelsaak); *BY* ~ *of,* op las van; ~ *of FLIGHT,* vliegrigting; *SPIRITUAL* ~, geestelike leiding; ~ **aerial,** gerigte lugdraad (antenne).
direc'tional, leidend; rigtinggewend, besturend; rig= tings=, gerig(te); ~ *GYROSCOPE,* koerstol; ~ *LAMP,* koerslamp; ~ *TRANSMISSION,* gerigte uitsending.
dlrec'tlon: ~**-disc,** koersskyf; ~**-finder,** rigtingsoe= ker; peiler; ~**-finding,** rigtingbepaling; ~*-finding BEARING,* rigtingspeiling; ~*-finding SERVICE,* rigdiens; ~**-indicator,** rigtingwyser; ~**-light,** rig= tingpyltjie, rigtingliggie; ~**-line,** rigtingslyn; ~**- post,** padwyser, predikant; ~**-signal,** rigtingwyser.
direc'tive, (n) amptelike instruksie, opdrag; (a) bestu= rend, reëlend, leidend, rigtend; ~ **techniques,** voor= skriftelike tegnieke.
direc'tly, (adv) direk; aanstons, flus(sies); onmiddel= lik, dadelik; sodra; reguit; regstreeks; *LEAVE* ~, onmiddellik vertrek (weggaan); *they live* ~ *OPPO= SITE,* hulle woon regoor mekaar; (conj) so gou as, sodra.
direc'tness, eerlikheid, ondubbelsinnigheid, rondbor= stigheid; direktheid.
direc'tor, bestuurder, bewindvoerder, direkteur, leier, produksieleier; regisseur (drama); *board of* ~*s,* direksie; ~**ate,** direkteurskap; direksie, direk= toraat; ~'**s fees,** direkteursgelde; ~'**s report,** di= rekteursverslag.
direc'torship, direkteurskap; direksie, direktoraat.
direc'tory, (n) (..ries), adresboek; voorskrifboek (R.K.); gids; (a) besturend; aanwysend; advise= rend.
direc'tress, (-es), direktrise.
direc'trix¹, (..trices), direktrise.
direc'trix², (..trices), riglyn (meetk.)
direct': ~ **route,** regstreekse roete; ~ **speech,** direkte rede.
dire'ful, vreeslik, verskriklik, aaklig; ~**ness,** vreeslik= heid, aakligheid.
dirge, klaagsang, treursang, treurlied, lyksang.
dir'igible, (n) bestuurbare lugballon; lugskip; (a) be= stuurbaar.
dirk, (n) dolk, hartsvanger; (v) doodsteek.
dirndl, dirndl; ~ **dress,** dirndlrok; ~ **skirt,** dirndl= skirt, dirndlhalfrok.
dirt, vuilgoed, smerigheid, viesigheid, gemeenheid; vuilis; slyk, modder; grond; vuilheid; gemeenheid; *EAT* ~, in 'n belediging berus; *FLING* ~, met modder gooi; beklad; *FLING enough* ~, *and some will stick,* as baie modder gegooi word, sal daarvan bly sit; *THROW* ~ *at,* met modder gooi na; *YEL= LOW* ~, goud; ~**-bag,** vullissak; ~**-bin,** vullisblik, -houer; ~**-box,** vullisbak, vuilisbak, asbak; ~**- cheap,** spotgoedkoop; ~**-heap,** vuilishoop; ashoop; ~**iness,** vuilheid, morsigheid; vervuiling; ~ **road,** grondpad; ~**-track,** asbaan, sintelbaan; grondpad.
dirt'y, (v) **(dirtied),** bevuil, (be)mors, besmeer; besoe=

del; (a) vieslik, morsig, smerig, vuil; gemeen, laag, skunnig, goor, liederlik; ~ *LOOK,* dreigende blik; ~ *PERSON,* vuilgoed, luns(riem), vuil mens; ~ *PLAY,* vuil spel; *WASH one's* ~ *linen in public,* private sake onwenslike publisiteit gee; ~ *WORDS,* vuil taal; *do the* ~ *WORK,* die vuil werk doen.
dis'a, bakkiesblom, disa; *BLUE* ~, blou disa; *MAUVE* ~, blou moederkappie; *RED* ~, bak= kiesblom, rooi disa *(Disa uniflora).*
disabil'ity, (..ties), onbekwaamheid, ongeskiktheid; diskwalifikasie; onvermoë; gebrek, nadeel; ~ **al= lowance,** ~ **grant,** ongeskiktheidstoelae.
disa'ble, onbekwaam maak; onbruikbaar maak, on= geskik maak; buite geveg stel; diskwalifiseer; uit= sluit; vermink, wond; onttakel (skip); vernael (kanon).
disa'bled, ongeskik, gebreklik; gekwes, gewond; *a* ~ *SHIP,* 'n ontredderde skip; ~ *SOLDIER,* buitege= veggestelde soldaat.
disa'blement, ongeskiktheid; diskwalifikasie, on= bevoegdheid; onbekwaammaking; **permanent** ~, permanente ongeskiktheid; ~ **act,** invaliditeits= wet.
disabuse', ontnugter, uit die droom help, reghelp.
disaccomm'odate, in ongeleentheid bring; ongeleent= heid veroorsaak.
disaccord', verskil, rusie maak, dit oneens wees.
disaccord'ance, onenigheid.
disaccus'tom, afwen, ontwen.
disacknowl'edge, nie erken nie, verloën.
disadvan'tage, nadeel; skade; verlies; *LABOUR un= der a* ~, met moeilike omstandighede te kampe hê; *SELL to* ~, teen 'n verlies verkoop; *TAKE (catch) one at a* ~, iem. oorrompel.
disadvanta'geous, nadelig, onvoordelig, ongunstig, skadelik; ~ **ness,** skadelikheid.
disadven'ture, teenspoed, ongeluk.
disadven'turous, ongelukkig.
disaffect', afkerig maak, vervreem.
disaffect'ed, (n) (die) ontevredenes; (a) ontevrede, af= kerig, misnoeg; ontrou; ~**ness,** afkerigheid, onte= vredenheid.
disaffec'tion, afkeer, weersin, ontevredenheid; on= trou; ongunstige gesindheid.
disaffirm', ontken, teenspreek; vernietig, verwerp, loën (jur.); ~**a'tion,** ontkenning; loëning.
disaffo'rest, ontbos; status van bos ontsê; ~**a'tion,** ontbossing.
disa'gio, disagio.
disagree', nie ooreenstem nie, verskil, dit oneens wees; verwerp; *CABBAGE* ~ *s with me,* kool ak= kordeer nie met my nie; *I* ~ *with you,* ek verskil van jou; ek stem nie met jou saam nie.
disagree'able, onaangenaam, onplesierig; onvriende= lik; ~ *PERSON,* dwarskop; *a* ~ *TASK,* 'n onaan= gename taak; ~ **ness,** onaangenaamheid, onplesie= righeid.
disagree: ~**ing,** onenig; ~**ment,** verskil, onenigheid, misverstand.
disallow', nie toelaat nie, afwys, verwerp, weier; ver= bied, afkeur; ~ *an act,* 'n wet verwerp; ~**ance,** weiering, verbod.
disambi'guate, dubbelsinnigheid verwyder, ondub= belsinnig maak.
disambigua'tion, ondubbelsinnigmaking.
disame'nity, nadeel; onaangename kenmerk.
disan'imate, ontsiel; ontmoedig.
disanima'tion, ontsieling; ontmoediging.
disannul', (-led), vernietig, kanselleer, ophef; ~**ment,** vernietiging, opheffing, afskaffing.
disappear', verdwyn, tenietgaan, wegraak; ~**ance,** verdwyning.
disappoint', teleurstel; verydel; ~**ed,** teleurgestel(d); ~**ing,** teleurstellend; *be* ~**ing,** teenval; ~**ment,** te= leurstelling; verydeling.
disapproba'tion, afkeuring, misprysing.
disapprov'al, afkeuring.
disapprove', afkeur, verwerp, nie saamstem nie; ~ *of,* afkeur, misprys.
disarm', ontwapen; onttakel (skip); onskadelik maak; paai; ~**ament,** ontwapening.

disarrange', deurmekaar maak, in wanorde bring, verwar; ~ **ment**, verwarring, wanorde.
disarray', (n) wanorde, verwarring; (v) uittrek, ontklee (poëties); in die war bring.
disartic'ulate, uitmekaar neem, uitmekaar val; disartikuleer, desartikuleer.
disassem'ble, uitmekaarhaal.
disassim'ilate, afbou (biol.).
disassimila'tion, afbouing (biol.), disassimilasie.
disasso'ciate = **dissociate**.
disas'ter, ramp, ongeluk, onheil; *court* ~, roekeloos wees, gevaar trotseer; moeilikheid soek; ~ **drought area**, rampdroogtegebied; ~ **fund**, rampfonds.
disas'trous, noodlottig, treurig, rampspoedig.
disattach', losmaak, ontbind; ~ **ment**, losmaking, ontbinding.
disavow', (ver)loën, versaak, ontken; afkeur; ~ **al**, verloëning, versaking, ontkenning.
disband', ontbind; afdank; uitmekaargaan; ~ **ment**, afdanking; ontbinding.
disbar', (-red), as regsbeoefenaar skrap, van die prokureursrol afneem; ~ **ment**, skrapping (van rol).
dis'belief, ongeloof, twyfel.
disbelieve', twyfel, nie glo nie; ~ **r**, ongelowige.
disbranch', takke verwyder.
disbud', (-ded), knoppe verwyder.
disburd'en, ontlas; aflaai; lug; ~ *OF*, ontlas van; ~ *ONE's mind*, jou hart lug.
disburse', voorskiet; betaal, uitbetaal, uitgee; ~ **ment**, voorskot; uitbetaling.
disc, skyf, werpskyf, diskus; blaadjie (kruit); kiesskyf (telef.); ploegskottel; *slipped* ~, skyfletsel; *kyk* **disk**.
discal'ced, kaalvoet, sonder skoene.
discard', (n) afval, skrot; weggooigoed; weglêkaart; *in the* ~, op die ashoop; (v) verwyder; aflê, weggooi, afdank, verwerp; afskud; ~ **ed**, afgedank; weggegooi (kaarte).
discarn'ate, liggaamloos, onstoflik.
disc: ~ **clutch**, skyfkoppelaar; ~ **-crusher**, skyfbreker; ~ **drill**, skyfboor.
discern', onderskei, opmerk, uitmaak, waarneem; ~ **ible**, sigbaar, kenbaar; ~ **ing**, skrander, oordeelkundig, skerpsiende, skerpsinnig; ~ **ment**, oordeel, insig, skranderheid, deursig.
discerp', skei; ~ **tibil'ity**, skeibaarheid; ~ **tible**, skeibaar; ~ **tion**, skeiding; skeistuk.
discharge', (n) ontslag; vryspraak, vryverklaring, invryheidstelling, loslating (van gevangene); kwytskelding, betaling, delging, ontheffing van skuld); die afskiet; ontlading (elek.); lossing (lading); afvoer (deur kliere); losbranding (met geweer); etter; uitmonding (rivier); rehabilitasie (na bankrotskap); delging (van skuld); vervulling, uitoefening, betragting (plig); *COST of* ~, losgeld; *HONOURABLE* ~, eervolle ontslag; (v) ontslaan, loslaat, vry verklaar, vryspreek; afvuur, afskiet, afgaan, losbrand (geweer); ontplof; afvoer (kliere); onthef, afdank, afmonster, wegstuur (soldate); voldoen, betaal, delg (skuld); los, aflaai, ontskeep (vrag); vervul (plig); etter, loop, dra (wond); uitmond (rivier); ontlaai (elek.); ~ *a BANKRUPT*, 'n bankrot persoon rehabiliteer; ~ *a DEBT*, 'n skuld vereffen; ~ *one's DUTIES*, jou pligte vervul; ~ *a GUN*, 'n geweer afvuur (afvuur); ~ *a PRISONER*, 'n gevangene ontslaan; ~ **current**, ontladingstroom; ~ **jet**, uitlaatstraler; ~ **pipe**, uitlaatpyp, afvoerpyp; ~ **r**, ontskeper, losser (van vrag); afskieter (van geweer); ontslaggeër (van gevangenes); betaler (van skuld); vonkbrug; ontlaaitang; ~ **valve**, afvoerklep, uitlaatklep.
discharg'ing: ~ **berth**, losplek; ~ **sluice**, afwateringsluis.
disc' harrow, skotteleg, roleg.
dis'ciform, skyfvormig.
disci'ple, leerling, volgeling, dissipel, dissipelin; ~ **ship**, dissipelskap.
disciplinar'ian, handhawer v.d. tug, tugmeester, ordehouer.
dis'ciplinary, dissiplinêr, tughandhawend, tug-; ~ **action**, tugmaatreël(s); ~ **case**, tugsaak; ~ **ordinance**, tugordonnansie; ~ **regulations**, tugregulasies.

dis'cipline, (n) tug, dissipline; oefening; kastyding; (v) tugtig; kasty; dril; dissiplineer.
disc'-jockey, platespeler, platedraaier, plaatprater.
disclaim', ontken, weerspreek, loën, verwerp; afstand doen van; ~ **er**, verwerping; teenspraak, ontkenning.
disclose', ontdek; onthul, openbaar (maak), uitpak, blootlê, verraai, uitbring.
disclo'sure, onthulling, openbaarmaking, blootlegging.
dis'co, (-s), disko(teek).
disco'bolus, (..**boli**), skyfgooier, diskobolos, diskuswerper.
dis'co dancer, diskodanser.
dis'coid, discoi'dal, skyfvormig.
discol'our, laat verkleur, laat verbleik; vlek; ~ **ed**, verkleur; ~ **ment** = **discolo(u)ration**.
discolo(u)ra'tion, verkleuring, verbleiking; (die) vlek.
discombo'bulate, (joc.), omkrap, steur.
discom'fit, verslaan, uit die veld slaan; verydel; ~ **ed**, onthuts, uit die veld geslaan; ~ **ure**, neerlaag, teenspoed; beskaming, verslaenheid.
discom'fort, (n) ongemak, ongerief; onbehaaglikheid; las, onaangenaamheid; (v) ongemaklik maak, ongerief veroorsaak, hinder.
discommend', afraai, afkeur, misprys.
discommode', lastig val, oorlas aandoen.
dis'co music, diskomusiek.
discompose', verontrus, ontstel, in die war bring, onthuts, erger.
discompos'ing, verontrustend, ontstellend.
discompo'sure, ontsteltenis, verwarring, verontrusting, ontstemming.
disconcert', verydel; ontstel, onthuts, verleë maak, verbouereerd maak, versteur, in die war stuur; ~ **ed**, verleë, ontsteld, verbouereerd, uit die veld geslaan, verslae; verwese; ~ **ion**, ~ **ment**, verydeling; verleentheid, verbouereerdheid, verwarring.
disconnect', skei; loskoppel, afsluit, uitskakel, losskakel; ~ **ed**, los; onsamehangend; ~ **ion**, ..**nexion**, skeiding, losskakeling; afbreking.
discon'solate, troosteloos, bedroef, mistroostig, ontroosbaar; ongetroos, verslae; ~ **ness**, ..**la'tion**, troosteloosheid, hartseer, ontroosbaarheid.
discontent', (n) ontevredenheid, misnoeë; (v) ontevrede maak; (a) ontevrede, misnoeg; ~ **ed**, misnoeg, ontevrede; ~ **ment**, ontevredenheid.
discontig'uous, nie aanmekaar sluitend nie.
discontin'uance, staking, storing, (die) ophou, afbreking; intrekking.
discontin'ue, ophou, laat staan, staak, afbreek, opsê.
discontinu'ity, staking, afbreking; onsamehangendheid; diskontinuïteit; onderbreking.
discontin'uous, gestaak; onsamehangend, onderbroke; afgebroke, diskontinu.
dis'cord, (n) wanklank, dissonant, disharmonie; onenigheid, tweespalt, tweedrag; *APPLE of* ~, twisappel; *FOMENT* ~, die vuur van tweedrag aanblaas; *SOW* ~, die vuur van tweedrag aanblaas; (v) 'n wanklank wees, nie harmonieer nie, dissoneer; verskil; bots, dit oneens wees; ~ **ance**, wanklank; dissonansie; onenigheid, strydigheid.
discor'dant, valsklinkend, wanluidend, dissonant, diskordant, disharmonies; onenig; ~ *NOTE*, dissonant; *STRIKE a* ~ *note*, 'n wanklank veroorsaak.
dis'co singer, diskosanger.
discothèq'ue, (-s), disko(teek).
dis'count, (n) korting, afslag, diskonto, rabat; *BE at a* ~, in diskrediet wees, van min belang geag word; ~ *for CASH*, afslag vir kontant; *GIVE* ~, korting toestaan.
dis'count, discount', (v) aftrek, afslaan; inwissel, (ver)diskonteer; ~ **able**, af te trek; diskonteerbaar, inwisselbaar; met voorbehoud ('n korreltjie sout) aanneem; buite rekening laat; vooruitloop op; afbreuk doen aan; verminder.
dis'count broker, wisselmakelaar.
discoun'tenance, koel afwys, ontmoedig, teenwerk, van sy stuk bring.
dis'count house, afslagwinkel; verdiskonteerbank, diskontobank.

dis'counting bank, diskontobank.
dis'count: ~ **price,** diskontoprys, afslagprys; ~ **rate,** diskontovoet, diskontokoers; ~ **store,** afslagwinkel.
discou'rage, ontmoedig, bang maak, afskrik, afraai; ~ **ment,** ontmoediging, teenwerking, afraaiing.
discou'raging, ontmoedigend.
dis'course, (n) gesprek, diskoers; onderhoud; redevoering, verhandeling; ~ *analysis,* gespreksontleding.
discourse', (v) bespreek, bepraat; gesels; die woord voer; uit.
discourt'eous, ongemanierd, lomp, onbeleef, ru; onvriendelik.
discourt'esy, onbeleefdheid, ongemanierdheid, onwellewendheid.
disco'ver, ontdek, aan die dag bring, onthul, openbaar maak; agterkom, uitvind; ~ *CHECK,* ontmasker (skaak); ~ *a DOCUMENT,* 'n stuk ter insae gee (jur.); ~ **able,** sigbaar; ontdekbaar; ~ **er,** ontdekker.
disco'vert, ongetroud; weduwee-.
disco'very, ontdekking, vonds; openbaring; ontknoping; ooplegging (van dokumente).
disc' plough, skottelploeg, skyfploeg.
discred'it, (n) oneer, skande, diskrediet; (v) tot skande strek, in minagting bring; in twyfel trek; ~ **able,** skandelik, onterend.
discreet', beskeie; oordeelkundig, taktvol, verstandig, omsigtig, vroed, beleidvol, diskreet, ingetoë, versigtig; ~ **ness,** beskeidenheid, versigtigheid, behoedsaamheid, sedigheid.
discrep'ancy (.. **cies**), verskil, teenstrydigheid; wanverhouding, diskrepansie.
discrep'ant, dis'crepant, verskillend, teenstrydig, uiteenlopend, diskrepant.
dis'crete, apart, onderskeie, afsonderlik; abstrak.
discre'tion, beskeidenheid; oorleg, oordeel; ingetoënheid, diskresie; skeiding; onderskeidingsvermoë; willekeur; verstand; wysheid, beleid; *AT the ~ of,* oorgelewer aan die willekeur van; *an OUNCE of ~ is worth a pound of learning,* gesonde oordeel is meer werd as geleerdheid; *on one's OWN ~,* na goedvinde; *SURRENDER at ~,* oorgee op genade of ongenade; *USE one's own ~,* na eie goeddunke handel; ~ *is the better part of VALOUR,* liewer bang Jan as dooie Jan; versigtigheid is die moeder van die wysheid; *it is WITHIN your ~,* u moet self oordeel; *YEARS of ~,* jare van onderskeidingsvermoë; *at YOUR ~,* dit is soos u wil; ~ **ary,** onbepaald, willekeurig, na eie goeddunke, diskresionêr; ~ *ary power,* mag om na goeddunke te handel.
discrim'inate, onderskei, diskrimineer; ~ *AGAINST,* agterstel, onderskei maak ten koste van; ~ *BETWEEN,* onderskei tussen.
discrim'inating, skerpsinnig, oordeelkundig; onderskeidend.
discrimina'tion, onderskeiding; skerpsinnigheid; onderskeid, diskriminasie, verstand, oordeel; *power of ~,* onderskeidingsvermoë.
discrim'inative, discri'minatory, onderskeidend.
discrown', afsit, die kroon ontneem.
disc: ~ *saw,* sirkelsaag; ~ **-shaped,** skyfvormig; ~ *spring,* skottelveer.
discul'pate, verontskuldig, regverdig.
discur'sion, bespreking; betoog; uitweiding.
discurs'ive, afdwalend, omslagtig; betoënd; beredeneerd, logies; ~ *faculty,* rede, oordeel(vermoë); ~ **ness,** omslagtigheid.
dis'cus, (-es, disci), werpskyf, diskus; ~ **-thrower,** diskusgooier, diskuswerper, skyfwerper.
discuss', beraadslaag, bepraat, bespreek, diskusseer, gesels, uitpluis; verhandel, gedagtes wissel; ~ **ed,** bespreek (onderwerp); *much ~ ed,* veelbesproke (persoon).
discuss'ion, bespreking, gedagtewisseling, samespreking; beredenering, uitpluising, diskussie; *come up for ~,* ter sprake kom.
disc' wheel, skyfwiel, skottelwiel.
disdain', (n) veragting, versmading, smadelikheid; *hold in ~,* verag; (v) verag, (ver)smaad, geringag;

disease', siekte, kwaal; *DESPERATE ~ s must have desperate remedies,* ernstige toestande eis drastiese maatreëls; *MENTAL ~,* geesteskrankheid; *OCCUPATIONAL ~,* bedryfsiekte; *VENEREAL ~,* geslagsiekte; ~ **-carrier,** kiemdraer; ~ **d,** ongesteld; sieklik, bekwaald.
disembark', ontskeep, land, aan wal sit; ~ *a'tion,* ontskeping, landing.
disemba'rrass, uit verleentheid uithelp; bevry, losmaak; ~ **ment,** bevryding, vrymaking; uithelping.
disembod'ied, onliggaamlik, onstoflik; afgedank.
disembod'iment, (ver)ontliggaming.
disembod'y, (.. **died**), ontbind, afdank; die siel v.d. liggaam bevry; losmaak; ontliggaam.
disembogue', uitmond, uitstroom, uitwater; uitstort, uitspuug, uitspoeg; ~ **ment,** uitmonding, uitwatering.
disembos'om, jou ontboesem; openbaar maak.
disembow'el, ontwei, die ingewande uithaal.
disembroil', ontwar; verlos.
disemployed', werkloos.
disenchant', ontgoël, ontnugter; ~ **ment,** ontgoëling, ontnugtering.
disencum'ber, vrymaak, bevry, verlos, ontlas.
disencum'brance, ontlasting, ontheffing, bevryding.
disendow', (kerklike) goedere ontneem.
disenfran'chisement, kyk **disfranchisement.**
disengage', skei, ontslaan, vrymaak, losmaak; uitskakel (ratte) ~ **d,** bevry, ontslaan; los, vry, onbeset; ~ **ment,** bevryding; afmaking; vryheid; onbesetheid; (die) uitmaak, afbreking (verlowing).
disenrol', ontkieser.
disentang'le, ontwar, losmaak; bevry; ~ **ment,** ontwarring; bevryding.
disenthral(l)', (.. **lled**), bevry; ontgoël; ~ **ment,** verlossing, bevryding.
disenti'tle, van 'n titel beroof; die reg ontneem.
disentomb', uit die graf haal, opgrawe; opdiep.
disep'alous, tweekelkbladig, disepaal.
disequilib'rium, onstandvastigheid, ongebalanseerdheid.
disestab'lish, ontbind, afskaf (fonds); afsit, afstig, van die staat skei (kerk); ~ **ment,** ontbinding; skeiding; afstigting.
disesteem', (n) minagting, geringskatting; (v) minag, geringskat.
diseur', voordraer, deklamator, diseur.
diseuse', voordraagster, diseuse.
disfav'our, (n) ongenade, onguns; nadeel; *FALL into ~,* in ongenade val; uitgebak raak; uitbak; *REGARD with ~,* nie graag gun nie, jaloers wees, afkeur; *TO his ~,* tot sy nadeel; (v) nie begunstig nie; nie aanmoedig nie.
disfea'ture, ontsier, skend, bederf.
disfigura'tion, mismaking, skending, verminking.
disfig'ure, mismaak, ontsier, vermink, skend; ~ **d,** geskonde; ~ **ment,** mismaaktheid, ontsiering, verminking.
disfo'rest, ontbos; ~ *a'tion,* ontbossing.
disfran'chise, ontkieser, die stemreg ontneem, van burgerreg beroof; ~ **ment,** berowing van die stemreg (burgerreg); stemregontneming; stemloosheid.
disfrock', afsit (as predikant); kyk ook **unfrock.**
disgorge', teruggee; opbring; uitbraak; uitstort.
disgrace', (n) skande, skandvlek; ongenade; *be IN ~,* in onguns wees; *GET into ~,* in die skande kom; *be a ~ TO somebody,* iem. tot skande strek; (v) in ongenade bring; te skande maak, in die skande steek, oneer aandoen; in ongenade verval; ~ **d,** geskandvlek; ~ **ful,** skandelik; ~ **fulness,** skandelikheid, skande.
disgrun'tled, ontevrede, brommerig; onvergenoeg(d), buierig.
disgrun'tlement, ontevredenheid, onvergenoegdheid.
disguise', (n) vermomming, omsluiering, dekmantel, masker, voorwendsel; *a BLESSING in ~,* 'n bedekte seën; *IN ~,* vermom; *THROW off the ~,* die masker afwerp; *WITHOUT ~,* sonder om daar doekies om te draai; (v) vermom; verklee(d); masker, verbloem, mislei, bewimpel, ontveins; verdraai

disgust 846 *disown*

(handskrif); ~**d,** vermom; verklee(d); gesimuleer; ~**ment,** verkleding; vermomming; ~**r,** vermommer; huigelaar.

disgust', (n) afkeer, walging, teensin; (v) walg, stuit, stuitlik wees.

disgust'ed, vies; *BE* ~, vies wees; *RATHER* ~, vieserig; *be* ~ *WITH (at),* walg van.

disgust': ~**ful,** ~**ing,** walglik, stuitlik, vieslik; *it is too* ~*ing for words,* dit gee 'n mens 'n pyn op jou naarheid.

dish, (n) (-es), skottel; gereg; *a standing* ~, 'n vaste skottel; (v) opdis, opskep, uitskep; uitoorlê; komvormig maak, uithol; bederwe; ~ *OUT,* bedien; uitdeel; ~ *one's PLANS,* jou planne bederf; ~ *UP,* opskep, opdis, voorsit.

dishabil'itate, onbevoeg maak.
dishabille', oggendjapon; huiskleding; *in* ~, onaangetrek.
dishabit'uate, ontwen, afleer.
dishallucina'tion, ontnugtering, ontgoëling.
disharmon'ious, wanluidend; vals.
disharmo'nize, wanluidend maak, vals laat klink, disharmonieer.
disharm'ony, wanluidendheid, wanklank, disharmonie, oneensgesindheid.
dish: ~ **cloth,** vadoek, afvryflap, bordedoek; ~**cover,** deksel.
disheart'en, ontmoedig, afskrik; ~**ment,** ontmoediging.
dished, komvormig; uitoorlê (in politiek); gepier.
dishe'rison, onterwing.
dishev'el, (-led), verfoes, verfomfaai, verpluk; deurmekaarmaak (hare); ~**led,** los, verfoes, verfomfaai, verpluk, verwaaid, deurmekaar, onordelik, slordig, verwilderd; ~**ment,** wanorde, onordelikheid.
dish' mop, afwasstokkie, stokdweil.
dishon'est, oneerlik, bedrieglik; ~**y,** oneerlikheid, bedrog.
dishon'our, (n) oneer, skande, skandvlek; (v) onteer, te skande maak; weier, nie honoreer nie, dishonoreer (wissel); ~ **able,** skandelik, oneervol, eerloos, onterend, oneerlik; ~ *able discharge,* oneervolle ontslag.
dishorn', onthoring, die horings verwyder.
dishorse', afgooi, afsmyt (deur 'n perd), uit die saal lig.
dishouse', op straat sit, uit die huis sit.
dish: ~ **washer,** bordewasser, skottelgoedwasser; ~**water,** skottelgoedwater; kasaterwater.
disillu'sion, (n) ontnugtering, ontgoëling; (v) ontnugter, die illusie beneem, ontgoël; ~**ment,** ontnugtering, ontgoëling, desillusie.
disinclina'tion, ongeneentheid (van), teensin (in), afkeer (van).
disincline', afkerig maak, teensin wek; ~**d,** ongeneig, afkerig, teensinnig, ongeneë.
disincorp'orate, ontbind; van voorregte beroof.
disincorpora'tion, ontbinding; opheffing van voorregte.
disinfect', ontsmet; ~**ant,** ontsmettingsmiddel; ~**ion,** ontsmetting; ~**or,** ontsmetter; ontsmettingstoestel.
disinfest', ontluis.
disinfla'tion, disinflasie.
disingen'uous, onopreg, vals, oneerlik; ~**ness,** onopregtheid, valsheid.
disinhab'ited, onbewoon.
disinher'it, onterf; ~**ance,** onterwing.
disin'tegrate, tot ontbinding oorgaan; uitmekaarval, verbrokkel, verval, disintegreer; oplos.
disintegra'tion, ontbinding, verwording, verwering, verbrokkeling, disintegrasie; ontwrigting; ~**bomb,** spatbom, splinterbom.
disinter', (-red), opgrawe.
disin'terest, (n) belangeloosheid; onverskilligheid; nadeel; (v) van belang ontbloot.
disin'terested, belangeloos, onpartydig, onbaatsugtig; ~**ness,** belangeloosheid, onbaatsugtigheid, onpartydigheid.
disinter'ment, opgrawing.
disinvolve', ontwar.

disjecta membra, (L.), disjecta membra, fragmente, stukkies.
disjoin', skei, losmaak.
disjoint', verrek, ontwrig; verbrokkel, opbreek; ~ **ed,** los, onsamehangend; ontwrig; ~**edness,** onsamehangendheid; ontwrigting.
disjunct', los, afgesonder, geskei; ~**ion,** splitsing, skeiding, ontwrigting, disjunksie; ~**ive,** skeidend, splitsend, ontwrigtend, disjunk, disjunktief; ~**or,** uitskakelaar.
disk = disc; ~ **harrow,** skotteleg; ~ **jockey,** platedraaier, platespeler, plateprater; ~ **plough,** skottelploeg; ~ **wheel,** skottelwiel.
dislike', (n) afkeer, teensin, weersin, hekel, afkerigheid; *take a* ~ *to,* 'n afkeer kry van; teensin kry in; 'n hekel hê aan; (v) nie van hou nie; 'n afkeer hê van; 'n hekel hê aan; ~ *a person,* 'n weersin in iem. hê.
dis'locate, ontwrig, verrek, verstuit, verswik; uit sy verband ruk; ~**d,** verswik, uit lit (uit), ontwrig; uit sy verband geruk.
disloca'tion, ontwrigting, verswikking, verrekking, dislokasie; verplasing.
dislodge', laat trek, verjaag, wegjaag, verdryf; loswikkel.
dislodg(e)'ment, verdrywing, wegjaging; loswikkeling.
disloy'al, ontrou, troueloos, dislojaal; ~**ty,** ontrou, troueloosheid, dislojaliteit, ongetrouheid.
dis'mal, somber, treurig, droewig, troosteloos, naar, aaklig, naargeestig; *the* ~ *SCIENCE,* staathuishoudkunde; *THE* ~*s,* neerslagtigheid; ~**ness,** neerslagtigheid.
disman'tle, afbreek, sloop; uitmekaarneem, aftakel (gebou); uitmekaarhaal, ontredder, onttakel (skip); ontmantel (fort); demonteer; ~**ment, dis= man'tling,** afbreking, sloping; onttakeling (skip).
dismask', ontmasker.
dismast', ontmas.
dismay', (n) skrik, verslaenheid, onstelttenis, ontmoediging, versteldheid; *be in* ~, verslae wees; in angs verkeer; (v) bang maak, verslae maak; ontmoedig; onthuts; ~**ed,** verwese; verslae, ontsteld.
dismem'ber, verbrokkel, uitmekaarruk; vermink; in stukke sny (lyk); ~**ment,** verbrokkeling, verdeling, verminking.
dismiss', ontslaan, afdank, afsit, laat gaan, uitskop; ontbind (vergadering); ophef (sitting); laat vaar ('n idee); afwys (jur.); wegstuur; verstoot; uit die hoof sit; uitvang (krieket), uitkry; verdaag (mil.); ~ **al,** ontslag, afdanking, afsetting; ontbinding; afwysing (jur.); wegsending; val; afhandeling; demissie (predikant); ~**ion,** ontslag, afdanking.
dismount', afklim, afstyg; uit die saal lig; demonteer; neerdaal; afhaal (buiteband); ontbind (wagte); ~ **ed,** onberede, te voet; opgevou (affuit).
disobed'ience, ongehoorsaamheid.
disobed'ient, ongehoorsaam, ongeseglik.
disobey', ongehoorsaam wees; veronagsaam; *be* ~ *ed,* nie gehoorsaam word nie.
disoblige', onbeleef wees; 'n ondiens doen (aan iem.); weier om iem. tegemoet te kom.
disoblig'ing, ongedienstig, ontoeskietlik, ondiensvaardig, onbehulpsaam; onbeleef, onvriendelik; ~**ness,** ongedienstigheid; onbeleefdheid.
disord'er, (n) wanorde, verwarring; ongereeldheid; opstootjie, oproer; ongesteldheid; gekrenktheid (verstand); *mental* ~, geestelike gekrenktheid; (v) in wanorde bring, in die war maak; krenk; ~**ed,** ongereeld; verwar(d); van stryk; gekrenk; ~**liness,** wanordelikheid, onordelikheid; ongereeldheid; rusverstoring; ~**ly,** wanordelik, ordeloos, onordelik; ongereeld; verward; uitgelate, rumoerig; ~ *ly GOINGS-ON,* uitspattings; ~ *ly HOUSE,* hoerhuis, bordeel.
disorganiza'tion, verwarring, disorganisasie, wanorde, ontreddering.
disor'ganize, ontbind; in wanorde bring, ontredder, in die war stuur, disorganiseer.
diso'rientate, disoriënteer, iem. die kluts laat kwytraak.
disown', verloën, ontken, verstoot, verwerp.

dispa'rage, verkleineer; beskinder; afbreuk doen aan; onderskat, geringskat; bekritiseer, neerhaal; afkam, uitkryt, verketter; ~**ment**, verkleinering; afkammery, afkamming; minagting; verkettering, verlaging; oneer; ~**r**, beskinderaar.

dispa'raging, kleinerend, minagtend.

dis'parate, ongelyk(soortig), disparaat; ~**ness**, ongelyksoortigheid.

dis'parates, ongelyksoortige sake.

dispa'rity, ongelykheid, verskil, dispariteit, strydigheid, wanverhouding.

dispart'¹, (n) (visier van 'n kanon).

dispart'², (v) skei; verdeel; splits; kloof.

dispa'ssionate, bedaard, kalm, onpartydig, besadig; ~**ness**, besadigdheid, onpartydigheid.

dispatch', (n) bespoediging, haas, spoed; doodmaak; **(-es)**, dépêche, berig, rapport; afsending; uitsending; versending; afdoening, verrigting; *with ALL* ~, met bekwame spoed; *HAPPY* ~, harakiri; (v) wegstuur, afsend, uitsend; afdoen; afstuur; haastig verrig; bespoedig; uitvaardig; afhandel; wegsluk; doodmaak; ~**-case**, aktetas; ~**ed**, gestuur; afgehandel; doodgemaak; ~**er**, afsender; ~**-rider**, rapportryer; ~**-runner**, bode, ordonnans; ~**-service**, rapportdiens.

dispel', **(-led)**, wegjaag, verban, verdryf; wegruim; ~**ler**, verbanner, verdrywer.

dispen'sable, ontbeerlik, misbaar; verslapbaar (wet, eed).

dispen'sary, (..ries), apteek.

dispensa'tion, uitdeling; ontheffing, dispensasie, vrystelling; bedeling, bestel, bestier, (Gods)beskikking; beheer; stelsel; *CHRISTIAN* ~, Christelike (nuwe) bedeling; *GRANT* ~ *from*, vrystelling verleen van.

dispense', uitdeel, toedien; klaarmaak; dispenseer, opmaak, toeberei (medisyne); onthef, vrystel; dispensasie verleen; daarsonder klaarkom; *dispensing CHEMIST*, apteker, resep-apteker; ~ *WITH*, daarsonder klaarkom; ~**r**, voorraadhouer; uitdeler; apteker.

disper'mous, tweesadig.

disper'sal, verstrooiing; verspreiding; ~ **officer**, ontslagamptenaar.

disperse', verstrooi; versprei; uitmekaargaan, uiteengaan, uiteenstuif; rondstrooi, verbrei; verdryf, uitmekaardryf, uiteendryf, uiteenjaag, verjaag; *be* ~*d*, uitmekaargegaan; uitmekaargespat; ~**dly**, verstrooi(d).

disper'sion, verstrooiing, verstuiwing, spreiding; dispersie; ~ *of LIGHT*, kleurskifting; *THE D* ~, Diaspora, verstrooiing v.d. Jode onder die heidene.

disper'sive, verstrooiend, verspreidend.

dispi'rit, moedeloos maak, ontmoedig, deprimeer.

dispi'rited, neerslagtig, swak, moedeloos; ~**ness**, moedeloosheid, neerslagtigheid.

dispit'eous, meedoënloos.

displace', verplaas (van water); vervang; verlê; afsit (betrekking); ~*d person*, ontwortelde (ontheemde) persoon; ~**ment**, verplasing; verlegging; vervanging; waterverplasing (skip); ~**ment current**, verplasingstroom.

display', (n) tentoonspreiding, vertoning, etalage; pragvertoon; uitstalling; groot drukwerk; *aerial ACROBATIC* ~, kunsvliegvertoning; *AERIAL* ~, vliegvertoning; *MAKE a* ~ *of*, ten toon sprei; (v) ten toon sprei, ten toon stel, vertoon, uitstal; pronk; etaleer; openbaar; aan die dag lê; ~ **cabinet**, vertoonkas, toonkas; ~ **compositor**, smoutsetter; ~ **counter**, uitstaltoonbank; ~ **window**, toonvenster; uitstalvenster.

displease', mishaag, vererg; ~**d**, ontevrede, kwaad, vererg.

displeas'ing, onaangenaam.

displea'sure, mishae, misnoeë, ontevredenheid, ongenoeë; *CAUSE* ~ *to someone*, iem. mishaag; *INCUR* ~, in ongenade val.

displume', ontveer.

disport', (n) ontspanning, spel, tydverdryf; (v) speel, jou vermaak, jou verlustig, jou vermei; dartel; ~**ment**, tydverdryf, ontspanning.

disposabil'ity, verhandelbaarheid, verkoopbaarheid.

dispos'able, beskikbaar; verhandelbaar, afsetbaar, verkoopbaar; weggooibaar.

dispos'al, beskikking; skikking, reëling; wegdoening, opruiming, verkoop; toewysing, toekenning; *BE at somebody's* ~, tot iem. se beskikking wees; *the DIVINE* ~, Godsbestier; *HAVE the* ~ *of*, beskik oor; ~ **bag**, weggooisakkie; ~ **depot**, ontslagdepot.

dispose', beskik, toebeskik, disponeer; reël, inrig, orden; jou gereed maak; in 'n stemming bring, stem (tot vreugde); (troepe) opstel; verkoop; weerlê (argument); kwytraak; wegmaak, van die hand sit, vervreem, wegruim; *MAN proposes, God* ~*s*, die mens wik, maar God beskik; ~ *OF*, afdoen, afreken met; verkoop, vervreem; ~ *by WILL*, by testament bemaak.

disposed', geneë, geneig, gesind, gestem.

dispos'er, beskikker.

disposi'tion, neiging, aanleg, natuur, inbors, aard, gesindheid; skikking; disposisie, geneentheid, gemoedsaard, (gemoeds)gesteldheid; reëling; inrigting; beskikking; opstelling (troepe); (pl) voorbereidsels, reëlings.

dispossess', uit die besit verdrywe, onteien, berowe; ~ **ion**, berowing, onteiening, ontvreemding.

dispraise', (n) misprysing; blaam; (v) misprys, laak, verwyt.

disprais'ing, afkeurend.

disproof', weerlegging, teenbewys.

dispropor'tion, oneweredigheid, wanverhouding; ~**al**, oneweredig, ongelyk; ~**ate**, oneweredig, nie passend nie, nie in verhouding nie met; ~**ateness**, ongelykmatigheid.

dispropor'tioned, oneweredig, ongelyk; sleg gebou.

disprov'able, weerlegbaar.

disprov'al, weerlegging.

disprove', weerlê.

dis'putable, betwisbaar.

dis'putant, betwister, redetwister, disputant, disputeerder.

disputa'tion, redetwis, twisgeding, twisrede, disputasie.

disputa'tious, disput'ative, twissiek, redeneersiek.

dispute', (n) twis, struweling, disputasie, dispuut; geskil; bespreking, redenasie, woordewisseling; *BEYOND all* ~, onbetwisbaar; *the MATTER in* ~, die geskilpunt; *SETTLE a* ~, 'n geskil besleg (bylê); *WITHOUT* ~, sonder twyfel, buite kyf; (v) twis, betwis, redeneer oor; hom verset teen; afstry, ontstry; redetwis, disputeer.

disput'ed, betwis; ~ **case**, twissaak; ~ **point**, geskilpunt.

disqualifica'tion, ongeskiktheid, diskwalifikasie; uitsluiting, ongeskikverklaring.

disqual'ify, **(..fied)**, ongeskik maak; uitsluit, diskwalifiseer, ongeskik (onbevoeg) verklaar.

disqui'et, (n) onrus, ongerustheid, verontrusting; (v) verontrus, ontrus, ongerus maak; (a) ongerus, verontrus; ~**ing**, onrusbarend, verontrustend; ~**ness**, ~**ude**, verontrusting; besorgdheid, onrus.

disquisi'tion, uiteensetting, ondersoek, verhandeling.

disrate', verlaag in rang, degradeer (vloot).

disregard', (n) veronagsaming, geringskatting, minagting; (v) veronagsaam, minag; in die wind slaan, buite rekening laat, geringskat; ~**ful**, minagtend, agteloos.

disrel'ish, (n) afkeer (van), teensin (in); (v) nie van hou nie, teensin hê in.

disremem'ber, nie onthou nie.

disrepair', vervalle staat, verval.

disrep'utable, berug, skandelik, in slegte reuk; ~**ness**, berugtheid.

disrepute', slegte naam, oneer, skande, berugtheid; *fall into* ~, in 'n slegte reuk kom, 'n slegte naam kry.

disrespect', (n) oneerbiedigheid, minagting; (v) minag; ~**ful**, oneerbiedig, onbeleef, eerbiedloos; ~**fulness**, oneerbiedigheid, onbeleefdheid.

disrobe', jou ontklee, jou ontdoen (van klere).

disroot', ontwortel.

disrupt', uiteenspat; laat bars, verbrokkel, stukkend skeur; ~ **ion**, bars, splitsing, skeiding; skeuring,

dissatisfaction 848 **distract**

verbrokkeling, ontwrigting, afskeiding; verbryseling, vormverminking; ~ **ive**, skeurend, skeurings=.
dissatisfac'tion, ontevredenheid, onvoldaanheid.
dissatisfac'torily, op onbevredigende wyse.
dissatisfac'tory, onbevredigend.
dissat'isfy (..**fied**), ontevrede maak, mishaag, teleurstel.
disseat', ontsetel.
dissect', ontleed; in stukke sny, deursny, dissekteer.
dissect'ing, (n) ontleding; (a) ontleed=; ~ **knife**, ontleedmes; ~ **room**, ontleedkamer; ~ **table**, snytafel.
dissec'tion, ontleding; disseksie.
dissect'or, ontleder.
disseise', **disseize'**, wederregtelik uit die besit stoot, onteien.
disseis'in, **disseiz'in**, wederregtelike inbesitneming.
disseis'or, **disseiz'or**, iem. wat wederregtelik in besit neem.
dissem'ble, voorwend, veins, huigel; verheel; ~ **r**, huigelaar, veinser, geveinsde.
dissem'bling, geveins, huigelagtig, gehuigel.
dissem'inate, verbrei, versprei, uitstrooi, uitsaai; ~ **d sclerosis**, veelvuldige sklerose.
dissemina'tion, verbreiding, verspreiding, uitstrooiing, deurspikkeling.
dissem'inator, verspreider, uitstrooier.
dissen'sion, verdeeldheid, tweedrag, oneensgesindheid, onenigheid.
dissent', (n) verskil van mening; afskeiding; (v) van opinie verskil; doleer, afskei (godsdiens); ~ **er**, afgeskeidene, andersgesinde (godsdiens).
dissen'tient, (n) andersdenkende, afgeskeidene; (a) afwykend (hofuitspraak); andersdenkend (godsdiens); *with one* ~ *vote*, met een teëstem.
dissent'ing, afgeskeie; andersdenkend; afwykend; ~ *judg(e)ment*, afwykende uitspraak.
dissep'iment, tussenafskorting, tussenskot.
dissert', **diss'ertate**, 'n verhandeling hou, uitwei.
disserta'tion, verhandeling, dissertasie, proefskrif.
disserve', 'n ondiens bewys.
disserv'ice, ondiens.
dissev'er, (af)skei; ~ **ment**, (vaneen)skeiding.
diss'idence, onenigheid, twis.
diss'ident, (n) afgeskeidene, andersdenkende; (a) afwykend, verskillend.
dissim'ilar, ongelyk(vormig), nie eenders nie, verskillend; ~ *to*, verskillend van.
dissimilar'ity, verskil, ongelykheid, andersheid.
dissim'ilate, ongelyk maak (klanke).
dissimil'itude = **dissimilarity**.
dissim'ulate, ontveins, huigel, verberg, voorwend.
dissimula'tion, veinsery, huigelary, geveinsdheid, dissimulasie.
dissim'ulator, veinser, huigelaar.
diss'ipate, verkwis, verspil, verboemel, verbras; buitensporig wees; versprei, verjaag, verstrooi; laat wegvlieg; verniel; ~ **d**, buitensporig, losbandig; verstrooi(d); uitspattend.
dissipa'tion, verkwisting, vermorsing, verspilling; verspreiding, verstrooiing; losbandigheid, uitspatting.
disso'ciable, ongesellig.
disso'ciate, ontbind, skei, losmaak, dissosieer, distansieer, vanmekaar maak, nie mee verenig nie; ~ *oneself from*, jou losmaak van, jou distansieer van.
dissocia'tion, ontbinding, skeiding, dissosiasie.
dissolubil'ity, oplosbaarheid, ontbindbaarheid, verbreekbaarheid.
dissol'uble, oplosbaar, ontbindbaar, smeltbaar.
diss'olute, los; losbandig, bandeloos, uitspattend; liederlik; ~ **ness**, buitensporigheid, uitspatting, losbandigheid; liederlikheid.
dissolu'tion, smelting, oplossing; ontbinding; dood; ~ *of marriage*, ontbinding van 'n huwelik, egskeiding.
dissolv'able, oplosbaar, ontbindbaar, smeltbaar.
dissolve', oplos, (ver)smelt; ontbind; ~ *PARLIAMENT*, die Parlement ontbind; ~ *in TEARS*, in trane versmelt.
dissol'vent, (n) oplossende middel; (a) ontbindend, oplossend.

diss'onance, wangeluid, wanluidendheid, wanklank; dissonansie; onenigheid.
diss'onant, wanluidend, vals; strydig.
dissuade', afraai, ontraai, omkonkel, uit die kop praat.
dissua'sion, afraaiing, ontrading.
dissuas'ive, afraaiend, ontradend.
dissyll'able, *kyk* **disyllable**.
dissymmet'rical, onsimmetries.
dis'taff, spinrok, vlasrok; vrouewerk; die vrou, *the* ~ *side*, moederskant.
dis'tal, na die uiteinde toe, weg v.d. middelpunt, distaal.
dis'tance, (n) afstand, ent, distansie; verheid, verte; verskiet; tussenruimte; terughoudendheid; *AT a* ~, op 'n afstand; ~ *lends ENCHANTMENT to the view*, op 'n afstand lyk dit aanlokliker; die verste berge is altyd die blouste; *IN the* ~, in die verte; *KEEP one's* ~, jou op 'n behoorlike afstand hou; *WITHIN striking* ~, binne trefafstand; (v) verwyder; distansieer; wen, uitstof; ~ **lighting**, afstandverligting; ~ **perception**, afstandsin.
dis'tant, ver weg, afgeleë; terughoudend; verwaand, koel; ~ *ages*, vervloë tye; ~ **ly**, ver(af), verwyderd; ~ *ly related*, ver langs familie.
distaste', teensin, walging; ~ **ful**, onsmaaklik, sleg, walglik.
distem'per[1], (n) siekte, kwaal, ongesteldheid; politieke beroering; distemper, hondesiekte; slegte humeur; (v) siek maak; krenk; *a* ~ *ed fancy*, 'n verwarde verbeelding.
distem'per[2], (n) grondverf, distemper, witkalk, kalkverf, muurkalk; kleursel; (v) kalk, verf, wit (met distemper); ~ **brush**, muurkwas, witkwas.
distem'pered, siek; van stryk.
distend', (laat) swel, uitsit, rek, sper (oë).
distensibil'ity, rekbaarheid.
disten'sible, rekbaar.
disten'sion, uitrekking, spanning, opswelling, uitsetting.
dis'tich, (-es), tweereëlige vers, distigon.
dis'tichous, tweeryig, tweesydig (plantk.)
distil', (-led), distilleer; neerdrup; stook; oorhaal; suiwer; ~ **late**, distillaat; ~ **la'tion**, distillasie; stoking; ~ **lation flask**, distilleerfles; ~ **latory**, distilleer=; ~ **latory furnace**, distilleeroond; ~ **led**, gedistilleer.
distil'ler, distilleerder, distilateur, stoker; distilleerketel; distilleertoestel.
distill'ery, (..**ries**), stokery, distilleerdery.
distill'ing-flask, distilleerfles.
distinct', onderskeie; eie, afsonderlik, apart; helder, duidelik, verstaanbaar; bepaald; *as* ~ *FROM*, in teenstelling met; *a* ~ *LOSS*, beslis 'n verlies.
distinc'tion, onderskeiding; rang, aansien, vernaamheid, aansienlikheid, distinksie, eerbetoon; onderskeid; *a* ~ *without a DIFFERENCE*, 'n onbeduidende verskil; *a MAN of* ~, 'n man van aansien; *OF* ~, vernaam, gedistingeerd; *WITHOUT* ~, sonder onderskeid.
distinc'tive, apart, eiesoortig; onderskeidend, kenmerkend; vernaam; distinktief; ~ **mark**, onderskeidingsmerk; ~ **ness**, vernaamheid; kenmerkendheid; ~ **number**, onderskeidingsnommer.
distinc'tness, duidelikheid.
distingue', gedistingeerd.
disting'uish, uiteenhou, uit mekaar hou; onderskei, kenmerk; naam maak; ~ *oneself*, jou onderskei, 'n naam maak; ~ **able**, maklik te onderskei, kenbaar.
disting'uished, aansienlik, vernaam, beroemd; uitnemend, voortreflik; onderskei; ~ *BY*, onderskei deur, kenbaar aan; *a* ~ *COMPANY*, 'n uitgelese geselskap; *as* ~ *FROM*, in teenstelling met.
distort', verbuig, verdraai; verwring; baktrek, krom trek; ~ **ed**, skeef, verwronge, verdraai(d); ~ **ing**, verwringing; ~ **mirror**, verwringingspieël, drogspieël; ~ **ion**, verdraaiing; distorsie, verwrongenheid, verwringing; verdraaidheid; vervorming; vertrekking.
distor'tionist, slangmens, karikatuurtekenaar, spotprenttekenaar.
distract', verwar, steur; verbyster, gek maak; aftrek, aflei, weglok; ~ **ed**, kransinnig; deurmekaar;

waansinnig; afgetrokke; *his attention was* ~ *ed,* sy aandag is afgetrek.
distrac'tion, verbystering; waansin, kranksinnigheid; afleiding, verstrooiing; *drive to* ~, waansinnig maak.
distrain', in beslag neem, beslag lê op; ~ **ee',** geëksekuteerde; ~ **er,** ~ **or,** beslagleer.
distraint', inbeslagneming, beslag, beslaglegging, eksekusie.
distrait', verstrooi(d), afgetrokke, onagsaam.
distraught', verbysterd, radeloos, waansinnig, geweldig ontstel.
distress'[1], (n) beslag (jur.); *levy a* ~, beslag lê op.
distress'[2], (n) ellende, nood; verknorsing; gevaar; *BE in dire* ~, lelik in die knyp sit; lelik in die nood wees; *there is DIRE* ~, die nood is hoog; *a SHIP in* ~, 'n skip in nood; *SIGNAL of* ~, noodsein; (v) in verleentheid bring, in nood bring; kwel, sorg baar; ~ **communication,** noodberig; ~**ed,** behoeftig, benepe, noodlydend; ~**ful,** ellendig, ongelukkig, angsvol, kommervol; ~ **gun,** noodskoot; ~**ing(ly),** smartlik, beangstigend; ~ **sign(al),** noodsein.
distrib'utable, uitdeelbaar, verdeelbaar, verspreibaar; uitkeerbaar.
distrib'utary, verspreidingstroom.
distrib'ute, uitdeel, verdeel, versprei, uitgee, uitreik, verbrei, distribueer; *distributing DEPOT,* uitdeeldepot; *distributing MAIN,* hoofverdeelpyp.
distribu'tion, uitdeling, verdeling, verspreiding, verbreiding, distribusie; ~ *of LOAD,* lasverdeling; ~ *of POPULATION,* bevolkingsdigtheid; ~ *of PRIZES,* prysuitdeling; ~ **box,** splitsmof, aftakkas, verdeelkas; ~ **valve,** verdeelklep.
distrib'utive, verdelend, verspreidend, indelend, distributief.
distrib'utor, uitdeler, ronddeler, distribueerder; verdeler (tegn.); verdeelskyf, (stroom)verdeler (elek.); ~ **brush,** verdelerborsel; ~ **cam,** verdelernok; ~ **cap,** verdelerdop; ~ **clip,** verdelerklem; ~ **head,** verdelerkop; ~ **jet,** verdelersproeier; ~ **terminal,** verdeleraansluiter; ~ **tube,** verdeelbuis.
dis'trict, distrik; wyk, gebied, (land)streek; ~ **commandant,** distrikskommandant; ~ **midwife,** wykskraamverpleegster; ~ **nurse,** wyksverpleegster; ~ **nursing,** wyksverpleging; ~ **surgeon,** distriksgeneesheer, distriksdokter.
distrust', (n) wantroue, argwaan, agterdog; (v) mistrou, wantrou, verdink; ~**ful,** wantrouig, agterdogtig, argwanend, mistrouig; ~**fulness,** mistrouigheid, wantroue.
disturb', versteur, verontrus, hinder, steur, stoor, beroer, pla; verskuif, verlê; ~ **ance,** verskuiwing; versteuring, verwarring, rusverstoring, beroering, busregerug, opstootjie, onrus, opskudding; ~**ed,** verstoor, verontrus; ~**er,** versteurder, verstoorder; ~ *er of the peace,* rusverstoorder; woelwater; ~**ing,** hinderlik, steurend, verontrustend.
disun'ion, onenigheid, tweedrag.
disunite', skei, verdeel; onenig word; onenig maak; ~**d,** onenig, verdeeld, oneensgesind.
disun'ity, verdeeldheid.
disuse', (n) onbruik; afwenning, ongewoonte, ontwenning; (v) afwen; nie meer gebruik nie.
disyllab'ic, tweelettergrepig, disillabies.
disyll'able, tweelettergrepige woorde, disillabe.
ditch[1], (n) (-es), sloot; greppel, grip, voor; skans, grag; *die in the LAST* ~, hom tot die uiterste verdedig; *THE D* ~, die Engelse Kanaal, die Noordsee; *help someone OUT of a* ~, iem. uit die modder help; (v) slote grawe; 'n grondwal opwerp; dreineer; ~ **board,** slootplank; ~**er,** slootgrawer, walgooier; ~**landing,** ploustranding; ~ **water,** vuilwater; slootwater; *dull as* ~ *water,* stomvervelend.
ditch[2], (v) dreineer; vernietig; in die steek laat; ~ *someone's PLAN,* iem. se plan vernietig; ~ *SOMEONE,* iem. in die steek laat.
dith'er, (n) gebibber, bewing; *be all in a* ~, bibber en beef, die ritteltits hê; (v) beef, bibber.
dith'yramb, ditirambe, lofsang.
dithyram'bic, (n) Bacchuslied; (a) ditirambies, besield.
di'tone, tweetoon, ditoon.

dit'tany, essekruid.
ditt'o, dieselfde, idem, dit(t)o; *SAY* ~ *to,* beaam; *SUIT of dittoes,* pak klere heeltemal uit een soort stof.
ditt'y, (ditties), liedjie, deuntjie, slampamperliedjie; *vulgar* ~, straatdeuntjie.
ditt'y: ~ **bag,** matrosesak; gereedskapsak; naaldwerksak(kie); ~ **box,** trommel, visserskis, vissersak, naaidosie, naaldwerkdosie.
diure'sis, diurese.
diuret'ic, (n) urineafskeidende middel, urinedrywer; (a) urinedrywend, diureties.
diur'nal, (n) dagvlinder; daggetyeboek; (a) daaglikse, dag=; ~ *CIRCLE,* dagsirkel; ~ *FLOWER,* dagblom, dagbloeier; ~ *MOTION,* daaglikse gang.
di'va, (dive), prima donna, diva.
div'agate, afdwaal, uitwei, divageer.
divaga'tion, afdwaling, divagasie.
dival'ence, tweewaardigheid, divalensie.
dival'ent, tweewaardig, divalent.
divan', sofa, rusbank, divan; (Oosterse) raadsvergadering; raadsaal; rookkamer, sigaarwinkel.
diva'riant, divariant.
diva'ricate, (v) splits, vertak; (a) vertak, gesplits.
divarica'tion, splitsing, vertakking.
dive, (n) duik; duikvlug; skuilplek vir skobbejakke; *make a* ~ *for,* gryp na; (v) duik, dompel, onderduik; insteek; jou verdiep in; ~ *INTO,* naspoor; ~ *into one's POCKET,* die hand in die sak steek; ~**bomber,** duikbomwerper; ~**-bombing,** duikbombardement, duikbombardering; ~ **pass,** duikaangee; ~**r,** duiker, ondersese navorser; duikelaar.
diverge', afwyk, splits; divergeer; uiteenloop; ~ **nce,** ~ **ncy,** afwyking, splitsing; uiteenlopendheid, uiteenloping; ~ **nt,** uiteenlopend, divergerend.
div'ers, verskeie, diverse, etlike.
diverse', onderskeie, uiteenlopend, verskillend.
diversifica'tion, verandering, wysiging, verskeidenheid; afwisseling, diversifikasie.
divers'ified, verskillend; afgewissel(d); ~ *farming,* gemengde boerdery.
divers'ify, (..tied), afwisselend maak; verander; wysig; afwissel; verskeidenheid besorg, diversifiseer.
diver'sion, afwending; ontspanning, vermaak, vermaaklikheid; uitwykpad, verlegging; uitwyking, afleiding; ~**ary,** afleidend; ~*ary attack,* afleidingsaanval, skynaanval; ~ **railway,** vermyspoor.
divers'ity, variëteit, diversiteit, afwisseling, verskeidenheid; verskil, uiteenlopendheid, ongelykheid; ~ *of opinion,* meningsverskil.
divert', aflei, afwend; onttrek; aftrek (aandag); uitkeer, wegkeer; verlê ('n pad); ontspan, vermaak; ~**er valve,** omleikep.
diverticuli'tis, divertikulitis.
diverti'culum, uitstulping, divertikulum.
diver'ting, vermaaklik, grappig; afleidend, omleidend.
Div'es, (die) ryk man.
divest', beroof, ontbloot, ontklee; ontdoen van; ~ *oneself,* jou uittrek; afle; ~**iture,** ~ **ment,** ontbloting, ontkleding; berowing.
dive'-tackle, duik, laagvat, duikvat.
divide', (n) verdeling; skeiding; grens; waterskeiding; *the Great D* ~, die dood; (v) deel, verdeel; skif, skei; klief; afskei, afbaken; ~ *BY,* deel deur; ~ *INTO,* deel in.
divid'ed, gedeel, afgeskeie; onenig; ~ *AMONG themselves,* onderling verdeel; ~ *HIGHWAY,* verdeelde (hoof)pad; ~ *four-lane HIGHWAY,* verdeelde vierbaanpad; ~ *SKIRT,* broekrok.
div'idend, deeltal (wisk.); uitdeling, uitkering; dividend; *CUM* ~, met dividend; *CUMULATIVE* ~, kumulatiewe dividend; *DECLARE a* ~, 'n dividend verklaar; *EX* ~, sonder dividend; *PAY a* ~, 'n dividend uitbetaal (uitkeer); ~ **list,** dividendelys; ~ **payment,** dividendbetaling; ~ **tax,** duikaanbelasting; ~ **warrant,** dividendkoepon; dividendbewys, dividendmandaat.
divid'er, deler (wisk.); uitdeler; skeier (battery); (pl) verdeelpasser; steekpasser.
divid'ing, (n) deling; skifting, skeiding (a) skeidend; ~ **compasses,** verdeelpasser; ~ **line,** skeidingslyn;

~ **pinion,** verdeelrondsel; ~ **rib,** verdeelrib; ~ **wall,** skeidingsmuur, skeidsmuur.
divid'ual, gedeel; afsonderlik.
divina'tion, voorspelling, waarsêery, divinasie; gissing; voorgevoel.
divine', (n) geestelike, godgeleerde; (v) voorspel, divineer; gis, raai, vermoed; wiggel, water wys; 'n voorgevoel hê; (a) aanbiddelik, goddelik; ~ *RIGHT of kings,* goddelike reg van konings; ~ *SERVICE,* godsdiensoefening; ~ *WORSHIP,* openbare godsdiens; ~ **ness,** goddelikheid.
divin'er, voorspeller, waarsêer; watersoeker, waterwyser, wiggelaar.
div'ing, duiksport, duikery, duikwerk; ~ **apparatus,** duiktoestel; ~ **beetle,** duikkewer; ~ **bell,** duik(er)klok; ~ **board,** duikplank; ~ **chair,** duikstoel; ~-**dress,** duik(er)pak; ~ **gear,** duiktoerusting; ~ **goggles,** duikbril; ~ **helmet,** duikhelm; ~ **mask,** duikmasker; ~ **suit,** duikpak; ~ **test,** duiktoets; ~ **turn,** duikdraai.
divin'ing rod, wiggelstok, waterstokkie.
divin'ity, godheid; goddelikheid, goddelike wese; aanbiddelikheid; godgeleerdheid, teologie.
divisibil'ity, deelbaarheid.
divis'ible, deelbaar.
divi'sion, verdeling; verdeeldheid; onenigheid; (hoofdelike) stemming; afbakening; skeiding; afdeling; smaldeel, divisie (mil.); ~ *of LABOUR,* arbeidsverdeling; *LONG ~,* lang deling; *MOBILE ~,* ligte divisie; *POINT of ~,* deelpunt.
divi'sional, divisie=, deel=; afdelings=; ~ **council,** afdelingsraad.
divi'sion: ~ **bell(s),** stemklokkie(s) (parlement); ~ **plate,** verdeelskyf; ~ **sign,** deelteken; ~ **sum,** deelsom; ~ **wall,** skeidingsmuur, skeidsmuur.
divis'or, deler.
divorce', (n), egskeiding, huweliksontbinding; ~ *from BED and board,* skeiding tussen tafel en bed; *BILL of ~,* skeibrief; *SUE for ~,* 'n egskeiding aanvra; (v) skei, 'n huwelik ontbind; *be ~ d FROM,* geskei wees van; *~d from REALITY,* ver v.d. werklikheid; ~ **case,** egskeidingsaak; ~ **court,** skeihof; ~**e',** geskeie persoon; ~ **ment,** egskeiding; *bill of ~ment,* skeibrief; ~ **suit,** egskeidingsproses.
div'ot, kluit, sooi; *replace the ~ (turf),* sit die sooi= (tjie) terug.
divulga'tion = **divulgence.**
divulge', rugbaar maak, wêreldkundig maak, versprei, onthul, openbaar, verklap; verraai; ~ **ment,** ~ **nce,** onthulling, openbaarmaking, verklapping; ~ **r,** verklapper; verraaier (van geheime).
dix'ie, dix'y, (dixies), kommandokastrol, veldketel.
Dixieland, Suidelike State, Dixieland (V.S.A.); *d ~* **(jazz),** dixieland(jazz).
diz'en: ~ *out (up),* optooi, opskik, opsmuk.
dizz'iness, duiseligheid.
dizz'y, (v) **(dizzied),** duiselig maak; verbyster; (a) duiselig, dronk, draaierig; duiselingwekkend; *become ~,* duiselig word, dronk word.
do¹, (n) gedoente; fuif(partytjie); foppery, skelmstuk.
do², (v) **(did, done),** doen, maak, verrig, aanrig, werskaf; voldoende wees, baat; handeldrywer; voldoen, beantwoord; ~ *AWAY with,* wegmaak; afskaf; ~ *AWAY with oneself,* die hand aan jou eie lewe slaan; ~ *BADLY,* daar sleg van afkom; sleg vaar; ~ *BATTLE,* slag lewer; *BE done for,* geruineer (gedaan) wees; ~ *in BRONZE,* in brons uitvoer; ~ *as you would be done BY,* behandel ander soos jy graag behandel wil word; *I CAN ~ with a drink,* ek het dors; ek sal graag iets drink; ~ *COME,* kom tog; kom tog asseblief; ~ *to DEATH,* tot vervelens toe doen; doodmaak; ~ *or DIE,* buig of bars; ~ *someone DOWN,* iem. te kort doen; iem. uitoorlê; ~ *FOR,* deug vir; genoeg wees vir; ~ *in FURNITURE,* in huisraad handel drywe; ~ *GOOD,* goed doen; die goeie doen; ~ *one's HAIR,* die hare opmaak; ~ *HARM,* kwaad doen; *HAVE to ~ with,* te make hê met; betrokke wees in; *HAVE done with,* klaar wees met; *HAVE nothing to ~ with someone,* met iemand niks te doen (uit te waai, uit te staan) wil hê nie; ~ *HONOUR,* eer bewys; *I ~ HOPE,* ek hoop regtig; *HOW ~ you*

~? hoe gaan dit? bly om u te ontmoet; *have done with IT!* hou nou op! skei nou uit! *I ~ not KNOW,* ek weet nie; ~ *your LEVEL best,* jou inspan, jou uiterste bes doen; ~ *MEAT,* vleis gaar maak; ~ *MISCHIEF,* kattekwaad aanrig; ~ *unto OTHERS as you would have them ~ unto you,* behandel ander soos jy graag behandel wil wees; ~ *OUT of,* uitoorlê, kul; ~ *OVER,* weer doen, oordoen; *PLEASE ~,* toe tog! ~ *as you PLEASE,* maak soos jy wil; maak soos jy lekker kry; ~ *the POLITE,* die beleefde man uithang; ~ *oneself PROUD,* jou te goed doen aan; ~ *you SEE?* verstaan jy? ~ *SHOPPING,* winkels toe gaan, inkopies doen; ~ *the SIGHTS of a place,* die besienswaardighede van 'n plek besigtig; ~ *for SOMEONE,* iem. se nek breek; iem. ruïneer; *can ~ with a new SUIT,* 'n nuwe pak nodig hê; ~ *TIME,* sy tyd uitsit (in die tronk); ~ *UP,* inpak; versien (huis); agtermekaar maak; vasmaak (knope); ~ *away WITH oneself,* die hand aan jou eie lewe slaan; ~ *WITHOUT,* daarsonder klaarkom; *that WON'T ~,* dit sal nie gaan (betaal) nie; dis nie voldoende nie.
do³, (n) = **doh.**
do'able, doenbaar; maakbaar; moontlik.
dobb'in, werkperd, trekperd.
Do'bermann (pin'scher), Dobermann(-pinscher).
dob'o-lily, brandlelie.
doc, (colloq.), dok, dokter; kwak
Docete', Dosetis, Doketis.
Doce'tism, Dosetisme, Doketisme.
doch' an do'ris, afskeidsglasie.
do'cile, leersaam, handelbaar, mak, geseglik, gewillig, volgsaam, gehoorsaam.
docil'ity, leersaamheid, handelbaarheid, volgsaamheid, geseglikheid.
dock¹, (n) beskuldigdebank; getuiebank.
dock², (n) stompstert (perd); stertholte; stertwortel; stertpit; stertriemlis (tuig); (v) stert afsny, afsny, koepeer; inkort.
dock³, (n) steenboksuring; wilde suring; klits.
dock⁴, (n) dok, skeepsdok; (v) in die dok bring, dok (skip); aanlê, vasmeer; ~ **age,** hawegeld; ~ **charges,** ~ **dues,** dokgeld, lêgeld, hawegeld.
dock'er¹, bootwerker, dokwerker, stuwadoor.
dock'er², knipper, besnoeier.
dock'et, (n) briefie, etiket; rol, uitspraakregister (reg); dossier; kort inhoud, uittreksel; (v) kort inhoud maak; merk en nommer; op die rol plaas; inskryf (in register).
dock: ~ **hand,** ~ **labourer,** dokwerker; ~-**lift,** hefbrug; ~-**master,** dokmeester.
dock-tailed, met 'n stomp stert, stompstert=.
dock: ~ **train,** doktrein; ~ **yard,** skeepswerf, marinewerf.
doc'tor, (n) dokter, geneesheer; doktor (regte, lettere, ens.); gepromoveerde; kunsvlieg; *who shall decide if ~ s disagree?* wie kan tot 'n besluit kom, as die geleerdes dit nie eens is nie? (v) dokter, regmaak; tot doktor bevorder; knoei met, vervals; ~ **al,** doktoraal, doktor(s)=; ~ **ate,** doktoraat, doktorsgraad; ~ **hood,** ~ **ship,** dokterskap; doktorskap.
doc'tor's: ~ **advice,** doktersraad, doktersadvies; ~ **bill,** doktersrekening; ~ **degree,** doktorsgraad; ~ **visit,** doktersbesoek.
doc'tress, (-es), doktores.
doctrinaire', (n) doktrinêr, teoretikus; (a) doktrinêr, leerstellig.
doc'trinal, leerstellig, geloofs=, dogmaties.
doctrinar'ian = **doctrinaire.**
doc'trine, leer, leerstelling, dogma; *the ~ of average(s),* die leer van awery.
doc'ument, (n) dokument, akte, geskrif (bewys)stuk; (v) dokumenteer, van bewysstukke voorsien.
documen'tary, (n) dokumentêre boek (stuk); (a) deur dokumente gestaaf, dokumentêr; ~ **film,** feitefilm.
documenta'tion, dokumentasie, dokumentering.
dodd'er¹, (n) dodder, warkruid, duiwelsnaaigaring *(Cuscuta sp.).*
dodd'er², (v) bewe; waggel; strompel.
dodd'ered, afgeknot, sonder top.
dodd'erer, sufferd.

dodec'agon, twaalfhoek, dodekagoon; ~**al,** twaalfhoekig.
dodecahed'ral, dodekaëdries, twaalfvlakkig.
dodecahed'ron, twaalfvlak, dodekaëder.
dodge, (n) ontwyking, lis, (slenter)draai; slenter(slag), streek, kunsie, foefie, handigheid; *be on the* ~, vir die gereg vlug; (v) ontwyk, fop, uitdraai; uitvlugte soek; verbyglip; uit die weg gaan; uitoorlê; vryspring, ontglip; *try to* ~ *the issue,* die saak probeer ontwyk, jakkalsdraaie maak; ~**r,** draaier; bedrieër, skelm, voortvlugtige.
dod'o, (-es, -s), dodo; *as dead as the* ~, morsdood; dood en begrawe.
doe, (bok)ooi (wild); hinde, ree; wyfie.
do'er, dader, verrigter, man van die daad; *talkers are no great* ~ *s,* praatjies vul g'n gaatjies nie.
doe' rabbit, wyfiekonyn.
doe'skin, hertevel.
doff, uittrek; afhaal (hoed); wegsit; laat vaar.
dog, (n) hond; reun; mannetjie; haak, klemhaak, klou, kram; vuurherdyster; haan (van 'n geweer); klink, pal (by masjiene); vent, skurk; ~ *s BARK as they are bred,* elke voël sing soos hy gebek is; *go about like a* ~ *in search of a BONE,* doelloos rondsoek (ronddwaal); *it is raining CATS and* ~ *s,* dit reën ou meide met knopkieries; *not a* ~ *'s CHANCE,* nie die minste kans nie; *every* ~ *has his DAY,* elke hond kry sy beurt; *a live* ~ *is better than a DEAD lion,* liewer bang (blo) Jan as dooie Jan; *DIE like a* ~, 'n ellendige (skandelike) dood sterf; *a DULL* ~, 'n saai Piet; ~ *will not EAT* ~, kwaai honde byt mekaar nie, diewe besteel mekaar nie; *GO to the* ~ *s,* te gronde gaan; *take the HAIR of the* ~ *that bit you,* van dieselfde drank drink as wat jou dronk gemaak het; *help a LAME* ~ *over a stile,* iem. help; *LEAD someone a* ~ *'s life,* iem. se lewe suur maak (verbitter), iem. 'n hondelewe laat lei; *he who LIES down with* ~ *s will rise with fleas,* as jy jou met semels meng, dan vreet die varke jou op; wie met pik omgaan, word daarmee besmeer; *there's LIFE in the old* ~ *yet,* hy is nog lank nie dood nie; *every* ~ *is a LION at home,* elke hond is baas op sy eie werf; *a LIVE* ~ *is better than a dead lion,* liewer bang (blo) Jan as dooie Jan; *LOVE me love my* ~, wie A sê moet ook B sê; *LUCKY* ~, geluksvoël; *MALE* ~, reun; *be a* ~ *in the MANGER,* iem. wat 'n ander niks gun nie, 'n ander nie die bene gun wat jy self nie kan kou nie; *give a* ~ *a bad NAME and hang him,* een die persoon wat in 'n slegte reuk staan; *you cannot teach an OLD* ~ *new tricks,* 'n ou mens leer nie maklik iets nuuts aan nie; *an OLD (sly)* ~, 'n ou kalant; *as SICK as a* ~, so siek soos 'n hond; *let SLEEPING* ~ *s lie,* moenie slapende honde wakker maak nie; *while the* ~ *s are SNARLING at each other the wolf devours the sheep,* terwyl die herders twis, vang die wolf die skape; *THE* ~ *s,* hondewedrenne; *while two* ~ *s are fighting, the THIRD takes the spoil,* twee honde baklei om 'n been, die derde loop daarmee heen; *THROW to the* ~ *s,* wegsmyt; *TREAT someone like a* ~, iem. soos 'n hond behandel; *TWO* ~ *s strive for a bone, and a third runs away with it,* twee honde baklei om een been, die derde loop daarmee heen; *the* ~ *returns to his VOMIT,* 'n hond keer na sy uitbraaksel terug; (v) (-ged), naspeur, navolg, agtervolg; ~ *someone's footsteps (heels),* soos 'n hondjie agter iem. aandraf; iem. soos 'n skaduwee volg.
dog: ~ **anchor,** haakanker; ~ **berry,** lysterbessie; ~ **biscuit,** hondebeskuit(jie), hondekoekie; ~ **bite,** hondebyt; ~-**box,** hokkiestrein; hondehok; ~ **briar,** hondsroos; ~ **cart,** hondekar; ~-**catcher,** hondevanger; ~-**cheap,** spotgoedkoop; ~ **collar,** hondehalsband; predikantsboordjie; ~ **clutch,** kloukoppelaar; ~-**days,** hondsdae; ~-**eared,** beduimeld; ~-**fancier,** hondekenner, hondeboer; ~ **fight,** hondegeveg; verbitterde geveg; luggeveg; ~ **fish,** sandhaai, vinhaai; ~ **flea,** hondevlooi; ~ **fox,** mannetjiesjakkals.
dogares'sa, dogaressa.
do'gate, dogeamp.
doge, doge.
dogg'ed, koppig, hardnekkig; vashoudend; taai; *it's*

~ *does it,* aanhou wen; ~**ness,** vashoudendheid, vasberadenheid, taaiheid.
dogg'er, dogger, vissersboot.
dogg'erel, rymelary.
dog: ~ **giness,** hondeliefde; ~ **gish,** honds, hondagtig, onbeskof; ~ **go:** *lie* ~ *go,* jou skuilhou; jou doodstil hou.
do-goo'der, (-s), goeddoener.
dog: ~ **grass,** kweek; ~-**grate,** vuurbok; ~ **gy,** honde=; gek na honde; ~ **kennel,** hondehok; ~ **latin,** potjieslatyn, brabbellatyn; ~-**lead,** hondeleiriem, hondetou; ~-**leg,** elmboogswaai (gholf); ~ **like,** honds, hondagtig.
dog'ma, (-s, -ta), leerstuk, dogma.
dogmat'ic, leerstellig, dogmaties; aanmatigend; ~**s,** dogmatiek.
dog'ma: ~ **tism,** dogmatisme, leerstelligheid; ~ **tist,** dogmatikus; ~ **tize,** dogmatiseer, stellig beweer.
dog: ~ **nut,** kloumoer; ~-**otter,** waterbobbejaan; ~-**plum,** esse(n)hout; ~ **rose,** wilde roos; ~ **('s)-ear,** (n) vou, eselsoor; (v) omvou; ~ **sleep,** ligte, onrustige slaap; ~**'s-meat,** stukkiesvleis, afvalvleis; ~ **spike,** spoorspyker; haakspyker; **D**~ **Star,** Hondster; ~-**tick,** hondebosluis; ~-**tired,** doodmoeg, pootuit; ~-**tooth,** oogtand, slagtand; ~-**trainer,** hondeafrigter; ~-**trot,** hondedraffie; sukkeldraffie; ~-**watch,** hondewag; *second* ~-*watch,* platvoetwag; ~-**whip,** hondesweep; ~ **wood,** kornoelie.
do(h), do, ut (ong.) (mus.).
doil'y, (doilies), vingerdoekie; melklappie, bekerlappie, doilie.
do'ing, doen, daad, werk, bedryf, doenigheid; *NOTHING* ~ *!* puur verniet! *it is your OWN* ~, dis jou eie skuld; *it TAKES some* ~, dit wil gedaan wees; dis geen kleinigheid(jie) nie; ~**s,** besigheid, bedryf; gedrag; doen en late; doenigheid.
doit, duit; *not care a* ~, geen duit (flenter) omgee nie.
do'jo, judomat; judosaal.
dolce far nien'te, niksdoenery, plesierige tydverwyl.
dolce vi'ta, (It.), dolce vita, die soete lewe, plesierjagtery, plesiersoekery.
dol'drums, ekwatoriale stiltegordel, (streke van) windstilte; neerslagtigheid; *be in the* ~, neerslagtig wees.
dole¹, (n) aalmoes; deel; uitdeling; porsie; lot; werkloosheidstoelae; *be on the* ~, werkloosheidstoelae trek; (v) uitdeel.
dole², (n) gejammer, droefheid, verdriet; ~**ful,** treurig, jammerlik, droewig; ~**fulness,** treurigheid, droewigheid.
dol'erite, doleriet, ysterklip.
doles'man, (..men), steuntrekker.
doles'woman, (..women), steuntrekster.
dol'ichocephal'ic, langskedelig, langkop=.
doli'na, dolin'e, sinkgat, dolina.
doll, pop; 'n mooi pop (nooi); *play with* ~ *s,* popspeel (v); ~ *up,* uitdos.
doll'ar, (Amerikaanse) dollar; *the almighty* ~, die almagtige dollar; ~ **area,** dollargebied; ~ **diplomacy,** handigheid, kunsvaardigheid, takt, sluheid.
doll'ish, popperig; ~**ness,** popperigheid
doll: ~-**like,** popperig; ~**'s house,** pophuis; ~-**show,** poppetentoonstelling.
doll' signal, kortsinjaal.
doll'y, (dollies), poppie; wasstamper; wasbak; sethamer; ~ **shop,** lommerd; skeepswinkel; ~ **wheel,** steunwiel.
dol'ma, dolma, druiweblaargereg.
dol'man, Turkse mantel, dolman.
dol'men, hunebed, dolmen.
dol'omite, dolomiet, olifantsklip, jonasklip.
dol'orous, smartlik, pynlik.
do'los, dolos; gety(beton)steen.
dol'our, smart, leed (digterlik).
dol'phin, dolfyn, bruinvis; aanlegpaal, meerboei.
dolt, domkop, sukkelaar; stommerik; ~**ish,** dom, dwaas, onnosel; ~**ishness,** domheid, onnoselheid.
domain', gebied, domein; grondbesit.
dome, koepel, dom; helm, dom (loko.); ~-**lamp,** daklamp; kaplamp (motor); ~-**light,** kaplig (motor); ~-**shaped,** koepelvormig.
domes'tic, (n) huishulp; dienskneg, diensbode; (pl)

personeel; (a) huislik, huishoudelik; huis=; mak; in= heems, binnelands; ~ *AFFAIRS*, huislike (binne= landse) aangeleenthede; ~ *ANIMAL*, huisdier; ~ *ECONOMY*, huishoudkunde; binnelandse ekono= mie; ~ *INFLATION*, binnelandse inflasie; ~ *SCIENCE*, huisvlyt, huishoudkunde; ~ *SER= VANT*, huishulp; ~ *TRADE*, binnelandse handel; ~ *WAR*, burgeroorlog.
domes'ticate, huislik maak; tem, mak maak; inbur= ger; tot huisdier maak; ~**d**, getem, makgemaak; ~**d** animal, huisdier, makgemaakte dier.
domestica'tion, (die) makmaak, temming; huisdier= wording.
domesti'city, huislikheid; huislike lewe.
domes'tics, huisvlyt; huishulpe.
dom'icile, (n) verblyf, woonplek; domisilie; (v) woon; jou vestig, domisilieer; ~**d**, woonagtig, gehuisves, gevestig.
domicil'iary, huis=; ~ *visit (search)*, huissoeking.
domicil'iate, jou vestig; woon.
dom'inance, oorheersing, dominansie.
dom'inant, (n) dominant, botoon; (a) heersend, oor= heersend; hoof=; dominant (mus.); ~ *figure*, hoof= figuur.
dom'inate, heers, oorheers; bestryk (kanon); uitsteek bo; domineer.
dom'inating, oorheersend, dominerend.
domina'tion, oorheersing; heerskappy.
dom'inator, oorheerser, baasspeler, beheerser.
domineer', baasspeel, oorheers, domineer; ~**ing**, baasspelerig, baserig, dominerend.
domin'ical, van die Here; ~ *letter*, Sondagsletter (R.K.); ~ *prayer*, die Onse Vader.
Domin'ican, (n) Dominikaner; Dominikaan; (a) Do= minikaans.
dom'inie, onderwyser, meester (Amer.).
domin'ion, heerskappy, gesag; gebied, vrygewes, do= minium; besitreg.
dom'ino, (-es) domino; dominosteen; los mantel; ~ **pieces,** dominostene; ~ **theory,** dominoteorie.
don¹, (n) don (Spaanse titel); doring; hoof, don, do= sent (Eng. kollege).
don², (v) (-ned), aantrek; opsit.
donate', skenk; begiftig.
donat'ing, begiftiging; skenking.
dona'tion, geskenk, gif, skenking, gawe, donasie; *DEED of* ~, skenkingsakte; *MAKE a* ~, 'n sken= king doen.
don'ative, (n) skenking; (a) geskenk.
don'atory, (..ries), begiftigde, ontvanger.
dona'tress, (-es), geefster, skenkster.
done, gedaan, gekook, gaar; klaar; ~! top! ~ *BROWN*, bruin gebraai; *be* ~ *BROWN*, gefop (geflous, gekul, bedrieg) wees; *he is* ~ *FOR*, hy is poot-uit; dis klaar met hom; sy kerk is uit; dit is doppie in die emmer met hom; *HAVE* ~ *with it*, los dit; doen dit nie meer nie; *be* ~ *IN*, gedaan wees; uitgeput wees; *it's OVER and* ~ *with*, wat gebeur het, het gebeur; ~ *to a TURN*, goed gaar; ~ *UP*, doodmoeg; opgemaak; *WHAT is* ~ *cannot be un*~, gedane sake het geen keer nie.
donee', begiftigde, ontvanger.
don'ga, sloot, donga.
don'ite, doniet.
don'jon, slottoring, donjon.
Don Ju'an, losbol, Don Juan.
donk'ey, (-s), donkie, groutjie; domkop, swaap; *as DENSE as a* ~, so onnosel soos 'n esel; *one can only expect a KICK from a* ~, van 'n esel kan jy altyd 'n skop verwag; *talk the hind LEG off a* ~, praat soos 'n langasemsprinkaan; *not for* ~*'s YEARS*, nie in lang jare nie; ~**-boiler**, donkie(ke= tel); ~**-crane**, donkiekraan; ~**-driver**, eseldrywer; ~**-engine**, hulpmotor; hulpstoommasjien; ~**-pump**, donkiepomp; ~**-wa(g)gon**, donkiewa, esel= wa; ~ **work**, harde werk.
donn'a, donna.
donn'ish, professoraal.
don'or, gewer, geër, donateur, skenker, begiftiger; donatrise; ~ **member**, donateurlid.
do'-nothing, leegloper, luiaard.
don't = do not; moenie; verbod.

doo'dle, krabbel; uilskuiken; ~**r**, krabbelaar.
dool'ie, doo'ly (..lies), Indiese draagbaar; dra(ag)= stoel.
doom, (n) vonnis, oordeel; noodlot, lot; verdoemenis, verderf(e)nis, ondergang; (v) vonnis, veroordeel, verdoem; *day of* ~, dag van gerig, oordeelsdag; ~**ed**, gedoem, verdoem; ~**sayer**, onheilsprofeet, doemprofeet.
dooms'day, oordeelsdag; *PUT off till* ~, op die lange baan skuif; *wait UNTIL* ~, jou ou peetjie afwag; *you can WAIT until* ~, jy kan lank wag.
door, deur, ingang; *ALL* ~*s are open to him*, alle deu= re staan vir hom oop; *CLOSE the* ~ *upon*, die deur toemaak vir; afsluit; *behind CLOSED* ~*s*, agter ge= slote deure; *CREAKING* ~*s hang longest*, kraken= de waens loop die langste; *at DEATH'S* ~, aan die rand van die graf; *a FEW* ~*s away*, 'n paar huise verder; *FORCE an open* ~, 'n oop deur intrap; *KEEP open* ~*s*, jou deure vir almal laat oopstaan; *LAY at one's* ~, iem. die skuld gee; iem. iets ten laste lê; iem. iets voor die voete gooi; *NEXT* ~, langsaan, naasaan; *OPEN the* ~ *to*, dit moontlik maak vir; *OUT of* ~*s*, buitekant; *SHOW someone the* ~, iem. die deur wys; *SLAM a* ~ *in someone's face*, die deur voor iem. se neus toemaak (toesmyt); *THROW open the* ~ *to someone*, iets vir iem. moontlik maak; *WITHIN* ~*s*, binnenshuis; ~**bell**, deurklokkie; ~**-bolt**, deurgrendel; ~**button**, (deur)werwel; ~**-case**, deurkosyn; ~**-catch**, deur= knip; ~ **check**, deurkeerder; deursluiter; ~**-chimes**, deuntjieklok; ~**-fastening**, deurgrendel; ~**-frame**, deurraam; deurkosyn; ~ **furniture**, deur= beslag; ~**-guide**, deurbaan; ~**-handle**, deurknop, deurhandvatsel; ~**-head**, bodrumpel; ~**-hood**, deurkap; ~**-jamb**, deurstyl; ~**-keeper**, portier, deurwagter; ~**-knob**, deurknop; ~**-latch**, deur= knip, slot; deurklink; ~**-light**, deurlig; ~**-lock**, deurslot; ~**mat**, deurmat; *be someone's* ~ *mat*, deur iem. vertrap (verdruk) word; ~**-money**, in= treegeld, toegang; ~**-moulding**, deurlys; ~**nail**, deurbout; *dead as a* ~ *nail*, so dood soos 'n mossie; ~**-number**, deurnommer; ~**-panel**, deurpaneel; ~**-pawl**, deurklink; ~**-plate**, naamplaat, naambordjie.
door'post, kosyn, deurstyl; *BETWEEN you and me and the* ~, tussen ons meisies; *as DEAF as a* ~, so doof soos 'n kwartel.
door: ~**-ramp**, deurhelling (trok); drumpel, drempel; ~**-runner**, deurbaan; ~**-sill**, drumpel; ~ **step**, drumpel; trappie; ~**-stop**, deuraanslag; deurstui= ter; ~ **way**, ingang; poort; deuropening.
dop'-brandy, witblits, dopbrandewyn.
dope, (n) verdowingsmiddel; ghries; vernis; geheime inligting; (v) bedwelm, bedwelemende drank ingee; verlok; vervals, dokter, doepa; lak; met spanlak be= stryk; ~ **addict**, dwelmsugtige; ~ **fiend**, doepage= bruiker; dwelmsugtige; dwelmverslaafde; daggaro= ker; ~**d:** ~*d wine*, doepawyn; ~ **peddler**, pedlar, dwelmsmous; ~**-peddling**, dwelmhandel; ~ **ey**, be= newel(d), dronk(erig), bedwelm(d); ~**r**, lakspuit; lakskilder; doepaman; dwelmtoediener; ~**y**, bene= wel(d); dronk(erig), bedwelm(d).
dop'pelgänger, dubbelganger, doppelgänger.
Dopp'er, Dopper.
Doppler effect, ~ **shift**, Dopplereffek.
dor, kewer, tor.
dora'do, (-s), swaardvis, dorado, goudmakriel.
Dorc'as, vrouewerkgeselskap, Dorkas.
doree', goudvis, sonvis.
Dor'ian, (n) Doriese dialek; Doriër; (a) Dories.
Do'ric, Dories.
dorm, slaapsaal.
dorm'ancy, rus; slaap; rustyd.
dorm'ant, slapend, rustend, stil; ~ *PARTNER*, stille vennoot; ~ *PERIOD*, rustydperk; ~ *TOWN*, slaapdorp; ~ *TREATMENT*, winterbehandeling; ~ *WOOD*, rushout.
Dor'mer (sheep), Dormer.
dorm'er window, dakvenster.
dor'mie = dormy.
dormi'tion, slaap; ontslaping, dood.
dorm'itory, (..ries), slaapsaal, slaapvertrek, groot slaapkamer.

dorm'ouse, (..mice), waaierstertmuis.
dorm'y, doedoe (gholf).
dor'othy bag, handsak.
dorp, dorp.
Dorp'er (sheep), Dorper.
dors'al, (n) rugwerwel; (a) rug=, dorsaal; ~ **artery**, wreefslagaar; ~ **fin**, rugvin.
Dors'ian, Dorper, Dorsie.
dor'siventral, dorsiventraal, tweekantig.
dort'er, dort'our, slaapsaal.
dor'y¹, (dories), kano, platboomskuit.
dor'y², (dories), goudvis, sonvis.
dos'age, dosis, dosering.
dose, (n) dosis; *give someone a ~ of his own medicine*, iem. met gelyke munt betaal; (v) (ver)meng; toedien, ingee, dokter, doseer.
doss'-house, slaaphuis.
doss'ier, dossier; dokumente; strafregister (van veroordeelde).
dot, (n) punt, stippel, dotjie, vlek, stip(pie); kindjie; *~s and DASHES*, punte en strepe; *OFF one's ~*, malkop, mallerig, halfgaar; *ON the ~*, op die kop, presies betyds; *from the YEAR ~*, in die jaar nul; uit die jaar toet; (v) **(-ted)**, puntjies (kolletjies) opsit; stippel; besaai; slaan; ~ *one's I's*, puntjies op die i's sit; *~ted LINE*, stippellyn; ~ *OUT*, uitstippel; *~ted WHEEL*, stippelwiel; *~ted WITH*, besaai met.
dot'age, kindsheid, suffery, versuftheid, sufferigheid; versotheid.
dot'-and-go-one, mankpoot, hinkepink.
dot'ard, kindse grysaard; sufferd, dooierd.
dota'tion, begiftiging, skenking.
dote, kinds word; suf wees; ~ *on*, dol (versot) wees op, dweep.
dot'ing, versot; kinds; simpel, versuf, suf(ferig).
dot'ish, kinds; suf; versot.
dot'tel = **dottle**.
dott'(e)rel, domkiewiet, strandloper.
dot'tiness, getiktheid, onnoselheid.
dot'tle, tabakprop; pypmoer.
dott'y, gestippel; versprei; suf; onnosel, gepik, getik, simpel.
dou'ble, (n) duplo, duplikaat; dubbelganger; die dubbele; skerp draai; koppel (wedrenne); dubbelspel; (pl) dubbelspel; *AT the ~*, in looppas; hardloop; *MIXED ~s*, gemengde dubbelspel; ~ *quick PACE*, stormpas; (v) verdubbel; dubbel vou; ombuig; doebleer (kaartspel); skielik omvlieg, draai; omseil; die pas versnel, hardloop (soldate); (die vuis) bal; terugspring (bilj.); ~ *BACK*, terughardloop (op jou spore); ~ *the CAPE*, die Kaap omvaar; ~ *UP*, bymekaar slaap; inmekaarkrimp (van pyn); (a, adv) dubbel, verdubbeld; tweeledig, tweemaal; dubbelhartig, vals; *lead a ~ LIFE*, dubbelslagtig lewe; *RIDE ~*, twee op een perd ry; *SEE ~*, dubbel sien; *in ~ TIME*, in stormpas, vinnig; **~-action**, wisselwerking; dubbelslag; natrek (geweer); **~-action pump**, perssuigpomp; tweeslagpomp; **~-angle cutter**, dubbelhoekfrees; ~ **axe**, alkantbyl; **~-banded sandgrouse**, dubbelbandsandpatrys.
dou'ble barrel, tweeloop, dubbelloop; *~led GUN*, tweeloopgeweer; *~led NAME*, dubbele naam (van).
double: **~-bass**, kontrabas, basviool; ~ **bed**, dubbelbed, tweepersoonsbed; **~-bit axe**, alkantbyl; **~-bitted**, met twee snykante; ~ **boiler**, dubbelstoompot; ~ **bond**, dubbelbinding; dubbelverband; **~-breasted**, oorknoop=; ~ **cable stitch**, sigsagkabelsteek; ~ **cal(l)ipers**, vierbeenpasser; ~ **check**, dubbele kontrole; ~ **chin**, onderken; ~ **column**, dubbele kolom (drukk.); dubbele kolonne (mil.); ~ **crochet**, kort beentjie; **~-cross**, verraai, laat omkoop; bedrieg; verneuk; **~-dealer**, huigelaar; bedrieër; **~-dealing**, huigelary, dubbelhartigheid; draaiery; kullery; **~-decker**, dubbeldekker; **~-deck road**, dubbeldekkerpad, dubbelverdiepingpad; ~ **digit**, tweesyfer(getal); **~-distilled**, dubbel oorgehaal; ~ **door**, dubbeldeur; **~-dyed**, deurtrap; *a ~-dyed villain*, 'n deurtrapte skelm; ~ **eagle**, tweekoparend; Amerikaanse munstuk; **~-edged**, tweesnydend; *a ~-edged sword*, 'n tweesnydende swaard; **~-ended spanner**, dubbelbeksleutel; **~-engined**, tweemotorig; **~-entendre**, dubbelsinnigheid; dubbelsinnige grap; ~ **entry**, dubbele boekhouding; **~-faced**, dubbelvlakkig; huigelagtig, geveins; *BE ~-faced*, met twee monde praat; **~-faced PERSON**, iem. met 'n Janusgesig; 'n tweegatjakkals; iem. wat met twee monde praat; ~ **flat**, dubbelmol; ~ **fault**, dubbelfout (tennis); **~-furrow plough**, tweevoorploeg; ~ **gear**, dubbelrat; ~ **harness**, (die) getroude lewe; **~-hearted**, vals, bedrieglik, dubbelhartig; ~ **ignition**, dubbelontsteking; **~-jointed**, slaplittig; ~ **line**, dubbelspoor; **~-line road**, tweebaanpad; **~-lock**, nagslot; ~ **meaning**, dubbelsinnigheid; ~ **medium**, dubbelmedium; **~-minded**, weifelend, dubbelhartig; besluiteloos; ~ **parking**, dubbele parkering; **~-plane**, blokskaaf; ~ **play**, tweekuns (bofbal); **~-printing**, dubbelafdruk; **~-quick**: *in ~-quick time*, met versnelde pas; in die looppas (mil.); **~r**, doebleerder; twynmasjien; **~-refined**, twee maal gesuiwer; **~-refracting**, (n) dubbelbreking; (a) dubbelbrekend; ~ **rhyme**, vroulike rym; ~ **road**, dubbelpad; deurpad, snelweg; vierbaanpad; ~ **roof**, basterkap; ~ **room**, tweepersoonskamer; ~ **seat**, dubbelbank; ~ **screw**, ringskroef; **~-sharp**, dubbelkruis; **~-shared plough**, dubbelvoorploeg; ~ **sleeve**, dubbelhuls; ~ **standard**, dubbele standaard; ~ **storey**, dubbelverdieping.
doub'let, tweelingwoord; paar; dubbelvorm; doeblet; onderkleed; wambuis (hist.).
dou'ble: **~-talking**, huigelagtig; oneg; **~-tenon joint**, dubbeltapvoeg; ~ **ticket**, dubbele kaartjie; ~ **time**, looppas, **~-tongued**, dubbeltongig, met twee monde; ~ **tote**, koppeltoto; ~ **track**, dubbelspoor; ~ **treble**, dubbelslagsteek; dubbellangbeentjie, dubbelslagbeentjie; **~-treble stitch**, dubbelslagsteek; ~ **window**, dubbelvenster; **~-woven**, dubbelgeweef; ~ **yolk**, dubbeldoor.
dou'bling, voering; vou, soom; lis, uitvlug, kunsgreep; verdubbeling.
doubloon', doebloen (Spaanse muntstuk).
dou'bly, dubbel(d).
doubt, (n) twyfel, twyfeling, bedenking, argwaan; twyfelary, dubio, onsekerheid, aarseling; *BEYOND a ~*, ongetwyfeld, sweerlik, sonder twyfel; *CAST ~ on*, in twyfel trek; *HAVE doubts about*, bedenkings hê oor; *HAVE no ~*, seker voel; *MAKE no ~ about it*, wees seker daarvan; *there is NO ~*, dit ly geen twyfel nie; *WITHOUT ~*, ongetwyfeld, sweerlik, sonder twyfel; (v) twyfel, betwyfel; argwaan koester; nie vertrou nie; ~ **er**, twyfelaar.
doubt'ful, twyfelagtig, onseker; onuitgemaak; dubieus; *be ~ of*, in twyfel staan oor; **~ly**, twyfelagtig; **~ness**, twyfelagtigheid, onsekerheid.
doubt'less, ongetwyfeld, stellig.
dou'ceur, fooi, omkoopgeld.
douche, spuit; stortbad; douche, uitspoeling.
dough, deeg; geld; pitte (Amer.); **~-baked**, kleierig; ~ **boy**, kluitjie, maagbom; soldaat (Amer.); ~ **gun**, rubberlymspuit; ~ **mixer**, deegmenger, kniemasjien; ~ **nut**, oliebol, oliering.
dought'ily, manhaftig, moedig.
dought'iness, kloekheid, onverskrokkenheid, dapperheid, manhaftigheid.
dought'y, dapper, onverskrokke, manhaftig; ~ **fighter**, dapper vegter.
dough'y, deegagtig, papperig; neergeslaan (koek).
doum (palm), doempalm.
dour, streng, nors; hardnekkig; **~ness**, strengheid, norsheid; hardnekkigheid.
dour'ine, doerine *(Polyneuritis infectiosa)*, slapsiekte.
douroucou'li, grootoognagaap, douroucouli.
douse, doodmaak (lig); duik; begiet, natgooi; neerplof; neerlaat, laat sak (seile).
dove, duif; **~-colour(ed)**, grys, **~-cot(e)**, duiwehok; *CAUSE a flutter in the ~-cot(e)*, 'n knuppel in die hoenderhok gooi; *FLUTTER the ~-cot(e)s*, bedeesde mense verontrus; 'n beroering in die hoenderhok veroorsaak; **~-grey**, duifgrys, duifvaal, vaalgrys; ~ **like**, sagaardig; ~ **prion**, walvisvoël.
dove'tail, (n) swa(w)elstert; (v) las (met swa(w)el-

stert); inmekaargryp, inmekaarvoeg; ~-file, swa=(w)elstertvyl; ~-housing, swa(w)elstertinlating; ~-joint, swa(w)elstertvoeg; ~-plane, swa(w)elstert=skaaf; ~-saw, swa(w)elstertsaag; ~-tenon, swa=(w)elstert-tap.
dow'ager, adellike weduwee, douairiere.
dowd'y, (n) (dowdies), slodderkous, slons, sloerie, sleggeklede vrou; (a) slordig, smakeloos, uit die mode, vaal, verslons.
dow'el, (n) klinkbout; houtnael, (tap)pen; (v) klink, pen; tap; ~ling, tapwerk, tapverbinding; ~ pin, tappen; ~ screw, tapskroef.
dow'er, (n) nalatenskap, weduweegeld; bruidskat; gawe; (v) bruidskat gee; begiftig; ~ house, wedu=weehuis; ~less, sonder bruidskat; onbedeeld.
down¹, (n) dons (voëls); donshaartjies.
down², (n) duin; grasbult.
down³, (n) teenslag; HAVE a ~ on someone, 'n wrok koester teen iem.; UPS and ~s, wederwaardig=hede; (v) onder kry; neerlê; laat val; plant (rug=by); neergooi; ~ tools, staak; (a) afdraand; afgaan=de; mismoedig, neerslagtig; ~ GRADE, afdraand; ~ on one's LUCK, teenspoed ly; he is ~ in the MOUTH, sy lip hang; sy ore hang; sy kop hang; ~ and OUT, totaal platsak; verloop, aan laer wal; (adv, prep), af, neer, na onder toe; langs af; BE ~ for, aan die beurt wees vir; op die agenda staan; BEAR ~, lywaarts seil; a BOOK goes ~, 'n boek vind byval; BREAD is ~, brood is goedkoper; CALM ~, afkoel, kalmeer; COME ~, afkom; die prys verminder; ~ COUNTRY, in die onderveld; FALL ~, platval; ~ to the GROUND, heeltemal, uitstekend; HAND ~, nalaat; bring someone ~ HEAVILY, iem. plant (rugby); iem. plattrek; KNOCK ~, platslaan; omry; toeslaan (bod); LIE ~, gaan lê; ~ with MEASLES, met masels in die bed; PAY (money) ~, kontant betaal; PULL ~, aftrek; PUT ~, neersit; onderdruk (opstand); RUN ~, inhaal; omry; afhardloop; slegmaak; SET ~, neerskrywe; neerplaas; SHOUT ~, doodskreeu; die swye oplê; SIT ~, gaan sit; THROW ~, neergooi; ~ to our TIME, tot op ons tyd; ~ TOWN, die mid=destad; UP and ~, op en af; ~ WIND, saam met die wind; ~-and-out, platsak, penniloos; verarm; ~-at-heel, slordig, toiingrig, slonserig.
down'cast, neerslagtig, mismoedig; look ~, verlep lyk; bek-af lyk; ~ AIR, intreklig; neerslagtige hou=ding; ~ shaft, aftrekskag.
down: ~comer, sakpyp; ~ current, valwind; ~-draught, valstroom; trek na onder; ~er, terneer=drukking; ~fall, instorting, val; ondergang; reën=bui; bring about someone's ~fall, iem. se val be=werk; ~-grade, neertrek, verlaag.
down'hearted, neerslagtig, terneergeslae, bek-af, be=druk; BE ~, hangoor wees; terneergedruk wees; someone IS ~, iem. se lip hang.
down'hill, afdraand, berg af; be going ~, op die af=draand wees; die kreeftegang gaan.
down: ~-pipe, aflooppyp, reënwaterpyp, reënwater=geut; ~pour, stortreën, stortbui.
down'right, reguit, reëlreg, pure, verregaand(e), ge=woonweg; a ~ LIE, 'n onbeskaamde leuen; ~ NONSENSE, pure onsin; ~ PRETTY, werklik pragtig; in een woord pragtig.
down: ~slide, afglyding, afglying; ~stairs, (n) be=nedehuis, benedeverdieping; (a) onder, benede, on=dertoe, die trappe af; ~-stream, stroom af; ~-stroke, ~ throw, afhou; afskuiwing(stratum); ~-to-earth, nugter, realisties; ~-town, middestad; ~-train, afgaande trein; ~-trodden, vertrap, verdruk; ~ ward(s), (na) ondertoe; neerwaarts; afwaarts; ~-wash, valstroom (lugv.); ~-wind, wind af, onder die wind.
Down's syndrome, Downsindroom, mongolisme.
down'y¹, donsagtig, dons(er)ig, sag.
down'y², slim, oulik.
down'y³, heuwelagtig.
dowr'y, (dowries), bruidskat, huweliksgoed, huwe=liksgif; talent.
dowse¹ = douse.
dowse², (met wiggelstok) water (minerale) wys; ~r, waterwyser, watersoeker.

dows'ing-rod, wiggelroede, waterstok.
doxol'ogy, (..gies), lofsang, doksologie.
dox'y¹, (doxies), liefie, minnares.
dox'y², godsdienstige opinie (skerts.).
do'yen, doyen, deken, oudste lid (gesant).
doyl'ey = doiley.
doze, (n) sluimering, dommeling, dutjie; (v) sluimer, soes, dut; visvang, dommel; ~ off, indut.
do'zen, dosyn; twaalf; CHILDREN by the ~, kinders soos orrelpype; talk NINETEEN to the ~, onafge=broke babbel.
doz'iness, dromerigheid, vaakheid, dommeling.
doz'ing, dommeling.
doz'y, slaperig, lomerig, vaak, dommelig.
drab¹, (n) sloerie, slet, ligtekooi; (v) hoer(eer).
drab², (n) vaalheid; eentonigheid; (a) vaal, vaalbruin, ligbruin; saai, eentonig; kleurloos.
drab'ble, bemors, bespat, plas.
drab'ness, eentonigheid.
drabs, vaal vere.
drachm, dragme (gewig).
drach'ma, drachma (munt).
Dracon'ian, Dracon'ic, drakonies, oordrewe streng (wette).
drac'onite, drakoniet.
draff, oorskiet; draf; grondsop, moer; afval; there is much that is ~, daar is baie kaf onder die koring.
draft, (n) skets, plan; ontwerp, klad, konsep; wissel; afdeling (soldate), ligting; diepgang (van skip); (v) teken, opstel, ontwerp, formuleer, afsonder, uit=soek; onttrek; troepe afdeel, uitstuur; ~ act, ont=werpwet, konsepwet, wetskonsep; ~ee, dienspligtige; ~er, opsteller; ~ing, formulering; ~ing-pen, uitkeerhok; ~ law, konsepwet; ~ resolution, be=skrywingspunt; ~ sheep, uitkeerskape, -skaap.
drafts'man, (..men), ontwerper, opsteller; tekenaar (vgl. draughtsman).
drag, (n) haak; rytuig; eg; ruikspoor (vir honde); sleepnet, dreg; belemmering; remskoen; sleepsel; rem; sleepweerstand (lugv.); blok aan die been (fig.); be a ~ on someone, 'n las wees vir iem.; (v) (-ged), sleep, dreg; piekel, sleur; omkruip (tyd); kam (klipwerk); rem; agterbly; eg; ~ AWAY, weg=sleur; ~ one's FEET, jou voete sleep; soos 'n trap=suutjies wees; tydsaam wees; ~ IN head and shoul=ders, iets by die hare insleep; ~ ON, voortsleep; sloer; ~ OUT, uittrek; the SHIP ~s her anchor, die skip sleep sy anker; ~ UP a child, 'n kind vir wind en weer grootmaak; ~-anchor, sleepanker; ~-ba=lance, weerstandskaal; ~ car, stampkar, stampmo=tor; ~-chain, remketting; sleepketting; ~ fault, sleepfout; ~ fold, skeurplooi (geol.); ~ged, ge=sleep; gepiekel; ~ged up, agter die bossies opgegroei.
drag'gle, agteraan sukkel; bemodder, deur die mod=der sleep, bevuil; ~-tail, slodderkous, slordige vroumens, slons; ~-tailed, slonsagtig.
drag: ~ hook, gryphaak, trekhaak; dreghaak; ~-line, sleeptou; treklyn; ~-link, trekstang; stuur=stang (motor); ~-net, sleepnet, treknet; dregnet; treil.
drag'oman, (..men, -s), tolk, dragoman.
drag'on, draak; dasadder; sow ~'s teeth, tweedrag (draketande) saai; ~-fly, naaldekoker; ~ish, ~-like, draakagtig.
dragonnade', onderdrukking, vervolging, dragon=nade.
drag'on, ~'s blood, drakebloed; ~'s teeth, tenkver=sperring; ~-tie, voetbalkstuk; hoeksparbint; hoek=anker; ~-tree, drakebloedboom.
dragoon', (n) dragonder, soldaat; (v) aan soldate oor=gee; vervolg; met geweld dwing.
drag: ~-rope, trektou, sleeptou; ~-shoe, remskoen; ~ster, stampmotor(jaer); ~ster bike, stamp=motorfiets.
drain, (n) sloot, riool, afleidingskanaal, sugsloot, af=leivoor, grip; afwatering, afwateringsput, geutpyp, dakpyp, afvoerpyp, aftappyp (motor); dwarsgeut (pad); uitputting; DOWN the ~, na sy grootjie (peetjie); na die maan; a GREAT ~ on, 'n groot las op; be a ~ on one's PURSE (pocket), iem. se beur=sie uitput; 'n roes in iem. se sak wees; (v) droog=

maak, drooglê; afvoer, afwater, aftap; leegdrink, uitdrink; rioleer; uitloop; aflei; dreineer; uitput, sloop (kragte); ~ *AWAY*, afvoer; lek; ~ *to the DREGS*, tot die bodem toe drink.

drain'age, droogmaking; dreinering, afvloeiing, (water)afvoer; afwatering; riolering, rioolstelsel; ~ **area,** ~ **basin,** opvanggebied (van rivier); ~ **switch,** afleiskakelaar; ~ **system,** afwateringstelsel; ~ **tube,** dreineerbuis.

drain, ~**-cock,** aftapkraan; ~**-ditch,** afvoergrippie, ~**er,** droograk, droograam; vergiet (Ndl.).

drain'ing, drooglegging; ~**-board,** (af)drupblad; ~**-pen,** afdroogkraal; ~**-race,** afloopgang (vir beeste).

drain: ~**-pan,** aftapbak; ~**-pipe,** geutpyp; aftappyp; rioolpyp, afvoerpyp; ~**-plug,** aftaprop; ~**-trap,** sinkput; rioolsperder; ~**-valve,** aftapklep.

drake¹, mannetjieseend.

drake², dagvlieg.

dram, dragme; 'n bietjie; slukkie, sopie.

dra'ma, toneelstuk, drama; toneelkuns.

drama'tic, dramaties, toneel-; ~**ally,** op dramatiese wyse; ~ **art,** toneelkuns; ~ **censor,** toneelsensor; ~ **change,** dramatiese (opvallende) verandering; ~ **criticism,** toneelkritiek; ~ **performance,** dramaopvoering, toneelopvoering; ~**s,** dramatiek; toneelspelery; ~ **school,** dramaskool, toneelskool; ~ **society,** toneelvereniging.

dra'ma: ~ **tist,** toneelskrywer, dramaturg; ~**tiza'tion,** toneelbewerking, dramatisering; ~**tize,** dramatiseer, vir die toneel bewerk; ~**turge,** dramaturg, dramaskrywer, toneelskrywer; ~**turgy,** dramaturgie.

dram'shop, kroeg.

drank, *kyk* **drink.**

drape, (n) *kyk* **drapery;** (v) met draperie beklee, drapeer; oortrek, versier, omhang.

drap'er, klerasiehandelaar, handelaar in sagte goed (draperie); draperder; ~**'s shop,** klerewinkel.

drap'ery, sagte stowwe, draperie; klerasiehandel; klerasie, kledingstowwe; aankleding, draperings; behangsel.

drap'ing, drapering.

dras'tic, kragtig, drasties, deurtastend; ~**ally,** ingrypend, drasties.

drat, vervlaks.

draught, (n) trek, tog; trekking; stroom, lugstroom; spanvermoë; drankie, teug, skeut, dronk, sluk; vangs (visse); spanning; vaardiepte, diepgang (skip); *BEER on* ~, bier uit die vat; *FEEL the* ~, 'n trek voel; onder skadelike toestande ly; in die knyp sit; (v) afstuur; ontwerp; ~ **animal,** trekdier; ~ **beer,** vatbier; ~ **board,** dambord; ~ **cable,** trektou; ~ **horse,** trekperd, ~**iness,** trekkerigheid; ~**-ox,** jukos, trekos; ~ **proof,** trekvry; ~ **s,** damspel, dambord; trekke; ~**-screen,** togskerm, trekskerm, windskerm.

draughts'man, sketstekenaar, ontwerper; dam(bord)skyf; ~**ship,** (ontwerp)tekenkuns.

draught: ~ **strip,** trekstrook; ~ **wheel,** spanwiel (sinjale); ~ **window,** trekvenster; ~**y,** togtig, trekkerig.

drav'ite, draviet.

draw, (n) trek; skuifie (rook); aantrekking, trekpleister; vangs, gelykospel; lot, lootjie; plekloting (perde); trekking (lote); eis; *quick one the* ~, vinnig met 'n pistool; (v) **(drew, -n),** trek, sleep, span; aantrek, skep, put, tap; tap; trek (wissel; skoorsteen); vertrek (gesig); uittrek; ophaal (brug); intrek; ooptrek; toetrek (gordyn); gelykop speel (sport); trek, opvra (geld); teken, skets; opstel (dokument); ~ *ALONG,* aansleep; ~ *BACK,* terugtrek; ~ *a BEAD on,* die korrel vassuig op; ~ *a BLANK,* niks kry nie; ~ *BLOOD,* 'n bloeiende wond veroorsaak; ~ *a BOW,* 'n boog span; ~ *BREATH,* asemhaal; inasem; asem optrek; ~ *a BRIDLE,* 'n perd inhou; ~ *a BYE,* 'n loslootjie trek; ~ *a CHEQUE,* 'n tjek trek; ~ *to a CLOSE,* na die end toe loop; ~ *the CLOTH,* die tafel afdek; ~ *COMPARISONS,* vergelykings maak; ~ *a CONCLUSION,* tot 'n gevolgtrekking kom; ~ *a CURTAIN,* 'n gordyn trek; ~ *a DIVIDEND,* 'n dividend trek; ~ *to an END,* na die end toe loop; ~ *FEET of water,* 'n diepgang hê; ~ *FORTH,* uitlok; ~ *on one's IMAGINA*

TION, uit jou verbeelding put; ~ *IN,* intrek, oorhaal; aanhaal (laers); ~ *INSPIRATION,* besieling put; ~ *LEVEL,* kop-aan-kop (gelyk) kom; ~ *the LINE,* 'n grens stel; nie verder gaan nie; *know where to* ~ *the LINE,* weet hoe ver om te gaan; ~ *the LONG bow,* spek skiet; ~ *LOTS,* lootjies trek; ~ *it MILD,* moenie oordryf nie; sak, Sarel! ~ *NEAR,* naderkom; ~ *OFF,* aflei; wegtrek; ~ *someone OUT,* iem. aan die praat kry; ~ *and QUARTER,* vierendeel; ~ *REIN (bridle),* inhou, beteuel; ~ *a SIGH,* sug; *the TEA* ~ *s,* die tee trek; ~ *TIGHTER,* vaster trek; ~ *TOGETHER,* saamtrek; ~ *TRUMPS,* troewe vra; ~ *UP,* ontwerp, opstel; optrek (gesig); ~ *the WOOL over someone's eyes,* iem. bedrieg; ~ *a PRIZE,* 'n prys trek; ~**-back,** hinderpaal, hindernis, nadeel, beswaar; ~**-bar,** (t)rekstang; koppelstang; ~**-bridge,** ophaalbrug; ~ **card,** trekpleister, attraksie;

drawee', akseptant, nemer, betrokkene.

draw'er, tekenaar; laai(tjie); trekker; (pl) onderbroek; *CHEST of* ~ *s,* spieëlkas, laaikas; *PAIR of* ~ *s,* onderbroek; *out of the TOP* ~, uit die boonste rakke; v.d. beste; ~ *of WATER,* waterputter.

draw: ~**-file,** trekvyl; ~**-frame,** spanraam; rekbank; ~**-gear,** trekgoed.

draw'ing, tekening, tekenwerk, tekenkuns; trekking; ~ *LOTS,* loting; ~ *and QUARTERING,* vierendeling; ~ **board,** tekenbord; ~ **card,** attraksie; ~ **chalk,** tekenkryt; ~ **compasses,** tekenpasser; ~ **instruments,** tekengereedskap; ~ **knife,** trekmes, hoefmes; ~**-master,** tekenmeester; ~ **materials,** tekenbenodigdhede; ~ **office,** tekenkantoor; ~ **paper,** tekenpapier; ~**-pen,** tekenpen, trekpen; ~**-pin,** duimspykertjie, duimdrukker, drukspykertjie; ~**-power,** trekkrag; ~ **requisites,** tekengerei; ~**-room,** sitkamer, tekenkamer; ~**-school,** tekenskool; ~**-table,** tekentafel.

draw'-knife, trekmes, stokmes, snymes, hoefmes.

drawl, (n) geteem, temerige spraak, spreektoon; (v) teem, temerig praat; ~**er,** temer; ~**ing,** (n) geteem, temery; (a) prekerig.

drawn, onbeslis, onbesleg (spel); gelykop; getrek; vertrokke (van pyn); ~ *BATTLE,* onbesliste slag; ~ *CURTAINS,* toe gordyne; *a* ~ *GAME,* gelykop spel; gelykspel; remise; ~ *(-thread) WORK,* draadtrekwerk (in middel); siersoomsteek (op soom); rafelwerk.

draw: ~**-net,** sleepnet; ~**-sheet,** spanlaken; treklaken; ~**-shutter,** skuifluik; ~**-vice,** spanskroef; ~**-well,** put.

dray, brouerswa; slepersswa; karweikar; ~**-horse,** trekperd.

dread, (n) skrik, vrees, bedugtheid, ontsetting; (v) bang wees, dug, skroom, vrees; (a) verskriklik, vreeslik; ~**ed,** gevrees, gedug.

dread'ful, (ver)skriklik, ontsettend, afgryslik; ~**ness,** vreeslikheid, (ver)skriklikheid, afgryslikheid.

dread'nought, slagskip, duiwelsterk (kledingstof); stormjas.

dream, (n) droom; hersenskim; iets wat wonderskoon is; ~ *s go by contraries,* drome kom altyd andersom uit; (v) **(dreamt,** or **-ed),** droom; ~ *AWAY,* verdroom; *never* ~ *of DOING such a thing,* nooit droom om so iets te doen nie; *he LITTLE* ~ *t that,* min het hy geweet dat; *who could have* ~ *t of SUCH a thing?* wie het dit nou ooit kon droom? ~**-book,** droomboek; ~**er,** dromer; ~**iness,** dromerigheid; ~**-land,** land van drome, droomland; ~ **less,** droomloos; ~**-life,** droomlewe; ~**-like,** droomagtig, soos 'n droom; ~**-reader,** droomuitlêer; ~**-world,** droomwêreld. ~**y,** dromerig, vaak, soeserig.

drear, *kyk* **dreary.**

drear'iness, treurigheid, aakligheid, somberheid, doodsheid, naargeestigheid, troosteloosheid.

drear'y, treurig, aaklig, somber, troosteloos, doods, naar, vervelig, triestig; *a* ~ *business,* 'n oes affêre.

dredge¹, (n) sleepnet, dreg; moddermeul, baggermasjien; (v) uitbagger, dreg, dieper maak; met 'n baggernet vang.

dredge², (n) strooier; (v) bestrooi, besprinkel.

dredg'er¹, baggermasjien, moddermeul.

dredg'er², meelstrooier, strooibus.

dredg'ing¹, strooiing.
dredg'ing², baggerwerk.
dredg'ing: ~**-box**, meelstrooier, strooibus; ~ **company**, baggermaatskappy; ~ **machine**, baggermasjien; moddermeul; ~ **net**, baggernet; ~ **operations**, baggerwerk; ~ **work**, baggerwerk.
dreg, dregs, sediment, droesem; (pl) moer, afsaksel, grom; uitvaagsel; (be)sinksel, droesem, gromsop; die orige bietjie; *the* ~ *of the NATION*, die skuim van 'n volk; *TO the* ~, tot op die boom.
dregg'y, troebel, vuil, modderig.
drench, (n) drank; bad; stortbui; (v) deurweek; papnat maak; drenk, laat drink; (diere) medisyne ingee; *be* ~ *ed to the skin*, geen droë draad aan jou lyf hê nie; ~ **er**, stortbui; drinktoestel; ~ **er pipe**, stortpyp.
dress, (n) (-es), kleed, rok, jurk, japon, tabberd; kleding, klere, tenue, (klere)drag; *full* ~, in galaklere; in groot tenue; (v) aantrek, aanklee; dresseer (dier); klaarmaak, aanmaak; mis gee (plante); opmaak (hare); skoonmaak (vis); verbind (wond); snoei, skaaf (hout); uitdos, optooi; afwerk; bik, kap (klip); roskam (perd); leer, afrig (dier); berei, brei, bewerk (leer); smeer (kabels); etaleer (venster); ~ *a CARCASS*, 'n karkas skoonmaak; ~ *DOWN*, pak gee, afstof; roskam, skrobbeer; ~ *a PIG*, 'n vark krap; ~ *SALAD*, slaai maak; ~ *up SMARTLY*, jou uitpiets, opdirk; ~ *UP*, aantrek; vermom; ~ **age**, afrigting, dressuur, dressering; dressage; ~ **allowance**, kleregeld; ~ **circle**, balkon, eerste galery (in teater); ~ **coat**, manel; swaelstertbaadjie; ~ **collar**, aandboordjie; ~ **designer**, modemaker; ~**designing**, modemakery; ~ **ed**, uitgedos, geklee; afgerig, skoon, verbind; potklaar (hoender); ~ *ed CHICKEN*, skoongemaakte (potklaar) hoender; ~ *ed STONE*, gekapte (bewerkte) klip; ~ *ed WEIGHT*, skoongewig; slaggewig.
dress'er¹, uitstaller, kleder; (wond)verbinder.
dress'er², kombuiskas.
dress: ~ **form**, paspop; ~**-goods**, tabberdgoed; ~**-guard**, jasbeskermer; kettingplaat (fiets); ~**-hanger**, klerehanger; ~**iness**, gekleedheid.
dress'ing, styflinne; toebereiding; bewerking; smeersel; (die) aantrek (van klere); verbandgoed, verband; wonddekking; sous; skrobbering; loesing; *give someone a* ~ *DOWN*, iem. roskam (uittrap); *be GIVEN a* ~ *down*, geskrobbeer word,'n taai tameletjie kry; ~**-box**, verbandkis; ~**-case**, toiletdoos; ~**-glass**, kapspieël; ~**-gown**, huiskleed; kamerjas, kamerjapon; ~**-room**, kleedkamer; ~**-table**, spieëltafel.
dress: ~ **maker**, naaister, kleremaakster, modiste, modemaakster; kleremaker; ~ **making**, kleremakery; ~ **material**, tabberdgoed; ~ **parade**, modetentoonstelling; ~ **rehearsal**, kleedrepetisie; ~ **ring**, sierring; ~**-shield**, sweetlappie; rokbeskermer; ~**maker's dummy**, paspop; ~**maker's pin**, kopspeld; ~ **shirt**, borshemp; ~ **suit**, swaelstertpak; aandpak; ~ **sword**, pronkswaard; ~ **uniform**, galauniform.
dress'y, keurig gekleed; smaakvol, agtermekaar, swierig; windmakerig.
drew, *kyk* **draw**, (v).
drey, nes van eekhorinkie.
drib, druppel; *in* ~ *s and drabs*, drupsgewyse.
drib'ble, (n) kwyl; gedruppel; (v) drup; kwyl; dribbel (voetbal).
drib(b)'let, druppeltjie; kleinigheid; *by* ~ *s*, drupsgewyse.
dried, gedroog; ~ **fruit**, droëvrugte, gedroogde vrugte; ~ **peach**, droëperske; ~ **sausage**, droëwors; ~ **up**, verdroog.
dri'er, droër, droogmasjien; droogmiddel.
drift, (n) neiging, aandrif; aanspoelsel, opdrifsel; strekking, doel; drif (deur 'n spruit); stroming; dryfyster (werktuigkunde); hoop, massa; (die) dryf; *CATCH the* ~, die bedoeling snap; ~ *of a CURRENT*, snelheid van 'n stroom; ~ *of the DISCUSSION*, bedoeling v.d. bespreking; (v) drywe, opdrywe, wegdryf; aanspoel, ophoop, op 'n hoop dryf; ~ *ABOUT*, ronddrywe; ~ *APART*, vanmekaar gaan; uitmekaardryf; vervreem; *LET things*

~, Gods water oor Gods akker laat loop; ~ **age**, aandryfsel; ~ **er**, dryfnetboot; swerwer; ~ **hammer**, deurdryfhamer; ~**-ice**, dryfys; ~ **ing**, verstuiwing; galerybou; (weg)drywing; (rond)dobbering; ~ **ing snow**, jagsneeu; ~ **net**, dryfnet; ~**-sand**, dryfsand, waaisand, swerfsand; ~ **way**, galery; ~ **wood**, dryfhout, wrakhout.
drill¹, (n) (dril)boor; militêre oefening; *tubular* ~, holboor; (v) boor; dril, oefen; afrig, dresseer; ~ *out*, uitboor.
drill², (n) grippie, ry, voortjie; saaitoestel.
drill³, (n) dril, duiwelsterk (soort stof).
drill: ~**-bit**, boorpunt; boorbeitel, booryster; ~**-blade**, boorlem; ~**-borer**, drilboor; ~**-bow**, drilboog; ~**-brace**, booromslag; ~**-chuck**, boorklembus; ~**-clamp**, boorbeuel; ~**-core**, boormonster, boorpit; ~**-cuttings**, boorgat; ~ **ed**, geoefen; geboor; ~**-er**, afrigter, drilmeester; boorman; boorder; ~**-hall**, drilsaal; ~ **hole**, boorgat; ~ **ing**, dril(lery); boor(werk); ~ **(ing) ground**, oefenveld, ~ **ing-machine**, boormasjien; ~ **ing-post**, boorbeuel; ~ **ings**, boorgruis; ~ **ing-tools**, boorgereedskap; ~**-pipe**, boorbuis.
drill'-plough, saaiploeg.
drill: ~**-press**, staanboor; ~**-rod**, boorstang; ~**-sergeant**, drilsersant, drilmeester; ~**-sharpener**, boorslyper; ~**-socket**, klembus; boorvoering; boorbeuel, boorkop; ~**-spindle**, boorspil; ~ **squad**, drifafdeling.
dril'y, droogweg, droog, drogies, droogkomiek, droogkomies.
drink, (n) dronk; drank, sopie, aitsatjie; (pl) drinkgoed; *IN* ~, dronk; *MEAT and* ~, spys en drank; *REFRESHING* ~, verfrissende drank; *STAND a* ~, op 'n glasie trakteer; *STRONG* ~, sterk drank; *be the WORSE for* ~, dronk wees; (v) **(drank, drunk)**, drink, suip, swa(w)el; *one must* ~ *as one BREWS*, soos jy saai, sal jy maai; ~ *oneself to DEATH*, jou dooddrink; ~ *DEEP*, 'n lang teug neem; baie drink; ~ *too DEEP*, die lepel te vol skep; ~ *like a FISH*, drink soos 'n vis; kwaai stook; baie deur die kraag jaag; ~ *away a FORTUNE*, 'n plaas deur jou keel jaag; ~ *the HEALTH of*, op iem. se gesondheid drink; ~ *IN*, indrink, jou verlustig in; *have had too MUCH to* ~, te veel kromhoutsap gedrink het; ~ *someone under the TABLE*, iem. onder die tafel drink; ~ *TO*, drink op; ~ *the WATERS*, 'n badkuur ondergaan; ~ **able**, drinkbaar; ~ **ables**, drinkgoed, drank; ~**-demon**, drankduiwel; ~ **er**, drinker, suiper, dronkaard.
drink'ing, drinkery, suipery, dronkenskap; *given to* ~, aan die drank verslaaf; ~**-bout**, drinkgelag; suipparty; ~**-cup**, drinkbeker; ~**-glass**, drinkglas; dronkbeker; ~**-party**, dronkparty, dronknes; ~**-place**, suiping, suipplek (diere); kroeg; ~**-song**, drinklied; ~**-straw**, suigstrooitjie; ~**-trough**, drinkbak; ~**-water**, drinkwater.
drink: ~**-mixer**, drankmenger; ~**-money**, drinkgeld; ~**-offering**, drankoffer; plengoffer.
drip, (n) druppyp; druplys, dakrand (huis); drupvent, jafel; gedrup; (v) **(-ped)**, drup; lek; druip, laat drup; ~ **can**, lekkan; ~ **cock**, drupkraan, lekkraan; ~ **coffee**, sypelkoffie, drupkoffie; ~ **coffeepot**, filtreerkan; ~ **disa**, blou moederkappie; ~**-drop**, gedwep, dweppery; bietjies; ~**-dry shirt**, droogdruphemp; ~ **irrigation**, drupbesproeiing; ~**-loop**, drupring; ~**-mould**, druplys; ~**-pan**, lekbak.
dripp'ing, (n) lek; gedrup; uitgebraaide vet, braaivet; *constant* ~ *WEARS away the stone*, 'n gedurige gedrup maak 'n gat in 'n klip; ~ *WET*, papnat, waternat; ~ **pan**, braaipan; lekbak; opvangpan; ~ **s**, afdrupsel; (a) nat, papnat; druipend.
drip: ~**-proof**, drupdig; ~ **rail**, druppreling; ~**-sheet**, natlaken; ~ **stone**, druplys, afdak; druipsteen; ~**-tray**, drupbak, drupplaat, lekbak; ~**-valve**, drupklep, lekklep.
drive, (n) rytoertjie, ritjie; stoot, slag; harde hou, dryfhou, dryfskoot (gholf); stootkrag, dryfkrag (fig.); aandrywing; neiging; swer; poging, kollekteerkampanje; pad, rylaan; rifgang, myngang; *TAKE a* ~, gaan ry; *a* ~*-YOURSELF car*, huurmotor; (v)

(drove, driven), dryf, drywe; inslaan (spyker); dwing; bestuur (motor); dryf (osse); ry, leisels hou; grawe, tonnel, boor; vervolg, jaag; uitjaag (wild); ~ *AT*, van plan wees; beoog, in die skild voer; ~ *AWAY*, verdryf; wegry; ~ *BACK*, terugdryf; ~ *a BARGAIN*, 'n koop sluit; ~ *into a CORNER*, vaskeer; ~ *to DESPAIR*, tot wanhoop bring; ~ *someone to DISTRACTION*, iem. gek maak; ~ *the fact HOME to him*, die feit sterk onder sy aandag bring; ~ *HOME an argument*, 'n argument laat inslaan; ~ *HORSES*, leisels hou; ~ *IN*, inja; inry; ~ *MAD*, gek maak; ~ *a NAIL in*, 'n spyker inslaan; ~ *ON*, voortdrywe, aanjaag; aanry; ~ *the PEN*, skrywe, die pen voer; ~ *a TRADE*, handel dryf; ~ *a TUNNEL*, 'n tonnel graaf; ~ *a WEDGE between*, inkeil; vervreem van mekaar; *WHAT are you driving at?*, wat bedoel jy?; ~ **end,** dryfent; ~ **gear,** dryfwerk.
drive'-in theatre, inrybioskoop, inryteater, motorfliek, veldfliek.
driv'el, (n) gewawel, geklets; kwyl; (v) **(-led),** kwyl, klets; ~**ler,** dwaas; kwyler; ~**ling,** gekwyl.
driv'en, gedrewe; ~ **gear,** gedrewe rat; ~ **sprocket,** kettingrat.
driv'er, drywer (wa); leisehouer, meenemer (draaibank); masjinis (trein); bestuurder (motor); dryfwiel; dryfstok (gholf); dryfyster; hoepelhamer; aandrywer, aanjaer (van vee); koetsier, voerman (perde); ~'s **cab(in),** stuurkajuit, stuurkap; ~'s **compartment,** masjinishokkie; ~'s **licence,** rybewys, bestuurderslisensie; ~'s **seat,** stuurstoel.
drive: ~ **shaft,** dryfas, ~ **spring,** aandrywingsveer; ~ **way,** ryweg, oprit, rylaan, inrit; ~**-yourself car,** huurmotor.
driv'ing, (die) ry, gery; drywery; besturing, stuurkuns; *be* ~ *pigs*, balke saag, snork; ~**-axle,** dryfas; ~**band,** dryfriem, dryfband; ~**-belt,** dryfband, dryfriem; ~**-box,** bok; ~**-cam,** dryfnok; ~**-chain,** dryfketting; ~ **disc,** dryfskyf; ~ **dog,** dryfklou; ~ **force,** dryfkrag; ~ **gear,** drywerk; ~ **hammer,** aantikhamer; ~ **instructor,** ry-instrukteur; ~**-iron,** dryfyster; ~**-lesson,** ryles; ~ **licence,** bestuurslisensie, dryflisensie; ~ **pin,** dryfpen; ~**-pinion,** dryfrondsel; ~ **power,** dryfkrag; ~**-pulley,** dryfkatrol; ~ **rain,** stortbui; ~**-reins,** leisels; ~**-rod,** dryfstang; ~**-rope,** dryftou; ~ **school,** ryskool; bestuurskool; ~**-shaft,** dryfas; ~ **skill,** ryvaardigheid; stuurbehendigheid; ~ **spring,** dryfveer; ~ **time,** rytyd; ~ **wheel,** stuurwiel (motor); dryfwiel (van lokomotief); dryfrat; ~**-whip,** peits, karwats.
driz'zle, (n) motreën, stuifreën, misreën; (v) stuiwe, motreën.
drizz'ling rain, motreën.
driz'zly, mistig, motreënerig.
drogue, windkousie, lugsleepteiken; wateranker, dryfanker.
droit, reg.
droll, (n) grapmaker, spotvoël; (v) skerts, gekskeer; (a) koddig, droogkomiek, droogkomies, potsierlik, snaaks; ~**ery,** grappigheid, gekskeerdery, snaaksheid, koddigheid; ~**ness,** snaaksheid.
drome, (abbr. of **aerodrome**), vliegveld, lughawe.
drom'edary, (..ries), dromedaris.
drone, (n) waterdraerby, hommel(by); luiaard; vervelige spreker; gebrom, gegons, gedreun, eentonige geluid; (v) gons, zoem, brom; snor (dinamo); dreun; ronk; leeglê; (v) lui wees; ~**-fly,** brommer; hommelvlieg.
dron'go(-shrike), byvanger (voël).
dron'ing, gegons, gedreun; jaagsiekte.
drool, kwyl; klets; ~**er,** kletser.
droop, (n) kwyning; pap houding; insinking; (v) afhang, neerhang; kwyn; sink; ~ *ing EARS*, hangore (hond); ~ *ing SPIRITS*, neerslagtigheid; *LOOK* ~ *y*, verlep lyk.
drop, (n) druppel; sopie, snapsie; oorbel; agteruitgang, afname, prysdaling; loonsvermindering; skepskop; klontjie; drop, hondebloed (lekkergoed); val, verval; valluik; valluik (galg); *to the last* ~ *of BLOOD*, tot sy laaste druppel bloed; *every* ~ *COUNTS*, alle bietjies help; *have taken a* ~ *of the CREATURE*, met die leeu deurmekaar gewees het;

the last ~ *makes the CUP run over*, die laaste druppel laat die emmer oorloop; *at the* ~ *of a HAT*, in 'n oogwink; *HAVE had a* ~ *too many*, te diep in die bottel gekyk het; 'n goeie raps weghê; te veel geskep het; *he has had a* ~ *too MUCH*, sy tee was te sterk; hy het tiermelk gedrink; *a* ~ *in the OCEAN*, nie noemenswaardig nie; 'n druppel in die emmer; 'n druppel water in die see; *the* ~ *hollows the STONE not by force but by often falling*, 'n gedurige gedrup maak 'n gat in die klip; *have had a* ~ *or TWO*, in die glas gekyk hê; (v) **(-ped),** drup; ophou (wind), neerval; laat val; ~ *ANCHOR*, anker gooi; ~ *ASTERN*, agterraak; ~ *AWAY*, afval; ~ *BEHIND*, agter raak; ~ *a BRICK*, jou mond verbypraat; ~ *DEAD*, dood neerval; ~ *DOWN*, neerval; ~ *a GOAL*, 'n skepskop oorstuur; ~ *a NOTE (line)*, 'n brief(ie) skryf; ~ *one's H's*, die h's nie uitspreek nie; ~ *into a HABIT*, in 'n gewoonte verval; ~ *a HINT*, 'n wenk gee; ~ *IT!*, hou op!; ~ *OFF*, dut; aan die slaap raak; ~ *OUT*, uitval, uitsak; afskop (rugby); ~ *a PERPENDICULAR*, 'n loodlyn neerlaat; ~ *a REMARK*, jou 'n opmerking laat ontval; ~ *from the SKIES*, êrens uitslaan; ~ *a SUBJECT*, van 'n onderwerp afstap; ~ *one's VOICE*, die stem laat sak, sagter praat; ~**-arch,** sakboog; ~**-arm,** stuurarm; ~**-bottle,** drupfles; drupbottel; ~**-colour,** lakverf; ~**-compasses,** sakbeenpasser; ~ **curtain,** valgordyn, slotgordyn; ~ **door,** valdeur; ~ **ear,** hangoor; ~ **end,** klap-op; ~**-end truck,** agterklaplorrie; ~**-foot,** hangvoet; spitsvoet; ~**-forge,** vormsmee; ~**-forged steel,** ~**-forging,** vormsmeedsel; ~ **handle,** laaihingsel; ~**-kick,** skepskop; ~ **hammer,** valhamer (grofsmid); ~**-ledge,** druplys; ~ **let,** druppeltjie; hangdraad, hangpaaltjie, bindhoutjie, spar, spanpaal; ~**-letter,** hangletter; ~**-light,** valvenster; ~ **per,** hangertjie, spar, stutpaaltjie; druppelaar; ~ **ping batter,** drupbeslag; ~ **ping bottle,** druppelflessie; ~ **ping funnel,** tregter; ~ **pings,** mis, uitwerpsels; ~**-pit,** herstelput; ~ **scene,** slottoneel, valskerm (toneel); ~**-scone,** plaatkoekie; ~**-shot,** valhoutjie (tennis); ~ **shutter,** valsluiter.
drop'sical, watersugtig.
drop: ~ **side,** klapsy; ~**-stopper,** druppelprop.
drop'sy, (water)sug, water (siekte), edeem.
drop: ~ **table,** klaptafel; ~ **test,** valtoets; ~ **window,** valvenster; ~ **wire,** invoerdraad (elek.).
dros'dy, drosdy.
drosom'eter, doumeter, drosometer.
dross, skuim, aardse slyk; slak, metaalskuim, droes, afval, afvalkole; onsuiwerheid; vuilgoed; *there is much that is* ~, daar is baie kaf onder die koring; ~**y,** skuimerig; vuil; sleg.
drought, droogte; ~ **area,** droogtegebied; ~**-resistant,** droogtebestand; ~**-stricken,** droogtegeteister; ~**y,** droog, dorstig.
drove¹, (n) trop, kudde; messelaarsbeitel.
drove², (v) kyk **drive,** (v).
drov'er, veeaanjaer; beeskoper, veesmous.
drown, verdrink; versuip (dier); smoor; oorstem; oorstroom (lande); ~ *OUT*, uitdryf (met 'n vloed); *like a* ~ *ed RAT*, so nat soos 'n kat; *they WERE* ~ *ed*, hulle het verdrink; ~**ing,** verdrinking; *a* ~ *ing PERSON*, 'n drenkeling; *a* ~ *ing man will catch at a STRAW*, 'n drenkeling gryp na 'n strooihalm.
drowse, (n) sluimering; (v) vaak wees, soes, drommel, sluimer.
drow'sily, vakerig, slaperig, lomerig.
drow'siness, slaperigheid, soeserigheid, doeseling, lomerigheid.
drow'sy, vaak, lomerig, soeserig, slaapdronk, dommelig; doeselig, slaperig; ~**-head,** slaapkous, jandooi.
drub, (-bed), slaan, pak gee, uitlooi; ~ **bing,** slae, loesing; *give someone a* ~ *bing*, iem. 'n afgedankste loesing gee; iem. opdons; iem. bloots ry; iem. opkeil.
drudge, (n) slaaf, ploeteraar, swoeër, werkesel; (v) swoeg, voortsukkel, (om)swoeë, ploeter, (uit)sloof, hard werk; ~**ry,** swaar werk, geslaaf, gesloof, sloofwerk, sleur, swoeëry, eselswerk.
drudg'ing, geploeter; geswoeg; swaarkry.

drug, (n) geneeskruid, artsenymiddel, medisyne; droëry; doepa; dwelmmiddel, bedwelmingsmiddel, verdowingsmiddel; *a* ~ *on the market,* 'n onverkoopbare artikel; (v) **(-ged),** medisyne toedien; bedwelm, verdoof; vervals; 'n bedwelmende middel toedien; oorversadig; ~ **addict,** dwelmslaaf; ~ **fiend,** dwelmslaaf; verslaafde; ~ **gist,** apteker; ~ **gist's shop,** apteek; ~ **habit,** verslaafdheid aan verdowingsmiddele; narkomanie; ~ **pedlar, peddler,** ~ **pusher,** dwelmsmous; ~ **ring,** dwelmnet; ~ **store,** apterswinkel, drogistery, apteek; apteek en kafee (in Amerika); ~**-taker,** verslaafde, morfinis; ~ **trade,** ~ **traffic,** dwelmhandel.

drugs, dwelmmiddels, dwelms.

Drui'd, Druïde.

Druid'ical, Druïdies.

drum, (n) tamboer, trom, drom, ghomma (Kaaps-Maleis); oorvlies, (oor)trommel, trommelvlies; blik, bus; konka (petrol); kan; tol (kabels); riemskyf; *BEAT the big* ~, die groot trom roer; *with* ~*s beating and COLOURS flying,* met vlieënde vaandels en slaande trom; (v) **(-med),** trommel, tamboer slaan; ~ *INTO,* inhamer; ~ *OUT,* wegjaag; ~ *UP,* bymekaar trommel; ~**-armature,** trommelanker; ~**-axle,** trommelas; ~**-beat,** trommelslag; ~ **brake,** trommelrem; ~ **fire,** trommelvuur; ~**-fish,** trommelvis; ~**head,** trommelvel, trommelvlies; hoenderboud(jie); ~**head court martial,** standregtelike krygsraad; ~ **major,** tamboermajoor; ~**-majorette,** tamboernooi, tamboerpoppie, trompoppie; ~**mer,** tromslaner; trommelaar; tamboerslaner; ~**ming,** gedreun; getrommel; ~**-roll,** roffel; ~**-saw,** silindersaag, kroonsaag; ~**-skin,** trommelvlies (anat.).

drum'stick, trommelstok; hoenderboud(jie).

drunk, (n) suipparty; dronklap, beskonkene; (v) *kyk* **drink,** (v); (a) dronk, besope, gekoring, hoenderkop, beskonke; *DEAD* ~, smoordronk; *as* ~ *as a LORD (fiddler, fish, mouse, wheelbarrow),* smoordronk; ~**ard,** dronkaard, dopsteker, dronklap, elmboogligter.

drunk'en, dronk, besope, beskonke; ~ **brawl,** dronkemansrusie, dronkemanstandjie; ~ **fit,** roes; ~**ness,** dronkenskap; gesuip.

drupe, pitvrug, steenvrug, steenkern.

dry, (v) **(dried),** droog, droë; droog word; droogmaak; opdroog; uitdroog; verdroog; ~ *UP,* opdroog; stilbly; (a, adv) droog, dor; dors; droog (wyn); ongeërg; vervelig; *BECOME* ~, uitdroog, droog word; *not* ~ *behind the EARS,* nog nat agter die ore; *a* ~ *HUMOR,* 'n droë humor(sin); *on* ~ *LAND,* op droë grond; *RUN* ~, opdroog; vasbrand; *he is a* ~ *old STICK,* hy is 'n regte ou remskoen.

dry'ad, bosnimf, boomnimf.

dry: ~ **arch,** funderingsboog; ~ **area,** voggang.

dry'asdust, (n) droogstoppel; (a) horingdroog.

dry: ~ **bread,** droë brood; ~**-bulb thermometer,** droëboltermometer; ~ **cell,** droë sel; ~**-clean,** uitstoom, droogskoonmaak, chemies reinig; ~**-cleaner,** droogskoonmaker; ~**-cleaning,** uitstoming (klere); droogskoonmakery, droogskoonmaak; ~ **compass,** droëkompas; ~ **cough,** droë hoes; ~**-cure,** insout; ~**-dock,** droogdok; ~ **ewe,** droë (gus=)ooi; ~**-eyed,** met onbetraande oë; ~**-fry(ing),** droogbraai; ~ **goods,** weefstowwe; ~**-goods canteen,** pelisiewinkel, militêre winkel; ~ **humour,** droë humor; ~ **ice,** droë-ys.

dry'ing, (die) droog, droging; ~**-agent,** droogmiddel; ~**-bed,** droogbed; ~**-board,** droogplank; ~**-frame,** droograam; ~**-horse,** droogstok, droograk; ~**-kiln,** droogoond; ~**-loft,** droogsolder; ~**-machine,** droogmasjien; ~**-oven,** uitdroogoond; ~**-rack,** droogstok, droograk; ~**-room,** droogkamer; ~**-tower,** droogtoestel; ~**-up,** verdroging.

dry: ~ **land,** droëland; ~**-land farming,** droëlandboerdery; ~ **measure,** droëmaat; ~**ness,** droogheid, droogte, dorheid; vervelighed.

dry'-nurse, (n) baker; (v) hans grootmaak; met die fles grootmaak.

dry: ~ **paint,** verfpoeier; ~**-point,** fyn etsnaald; ~ **potash,** bytende potas; ~**-rot,** molm; droëvrot;

houtswam; ~ **salter,** handelaar in blikkiesware (ingesoute ware); ~**-shod,** droog, droogvoets; ~ **steam,** droë stoom; ~ **stick,** droogstoppel; ~**-throated,** droëlewer; ~ **wall,** stapelmuur; ~ **weight,** drooggewig; ~ **well,** wegsyferput; ~ **wine,** droë wyn.

du'al, (n) dualis; (a) tweeledig, dubbel; duaal; ~ **control,** dubbelbesturing, dubbelkontrole; ~**-control aeroplane,** dubbelstuurvliegtuig; ~ **flight,** dubbelstuurvlug; ~ **ignition,** dubbelontsteking; ~**ism,** dualisme; ~**is'tic,** dualisties; ~**'ity,** dualiteit, dubbelheid; ~ **medium,** dubbelmedium.

du'al purpose, dubbeldoel=; ~ **breed,** dubbeldoelras; ~**-vehicle,** tweedoelvoertuig.

du'al road, dubbele pad.

dub¹, (-bed), tot ridder slaan; verhef tot; noem, doop.

dub², **(-bed),** smeer.

dub³, **(-bed),** inklank; oorklank; ~ *a film,* 'n nuwe klankbaan byvoeg, oorklank.

dubb'ing¹, ridderslag.

dubb'ing², afsny van kam en belle (haan).

dubb'ing³, inklanking; oorklanking.

dubb'ing, smeersel, leersmeer, leervet.

dubi'ety, twyfelagtigheid, twyfel.

dub'ious, twyfelagtig, dubieus, onseker; weifelend; *a* ~ *COMPLIMENT,* 'n twyfelagtige kompliment; *a* ~ *LIGHT,* 'n dowwe lig; *a* ~ *UNDERTAKING,* 'n twyfelagtige onderneming; *VIEW it in a* ~ *light,* dit as twyfelagtig beskou; ~**ness,** weifeling.

dubita'tion, twyfel, weifeling.

dub'itative, aarselend, twyfelend, weifelagtig.

duc'al, hertoëlik, hertogs=.

duc'at, dukaat.

duc'atoon, dukaton.

Duce, Duce, hoof, diktator (Italië).

duch'ess, (-es)!, hertogin; *grand* ~, groothertogin.

duch'y, (duchies), hertogdom; *grand* ~, groothertogdom.

duck¹, (n) seildoek, tentlinne; (pl) seildoekse broek.

duck², (n) eend, eendvoël; liefling; nul (krieket); *a fine DAY for* ~*s,* eendeweer; ~ *and DRAKE,* koei en kalf (gooi met plat klip oor water); *look like a DROWNED* ~, lyk soos 'n haan waarvan die stertvere uitgetrek is; *like a DYING* ~ *in a thunderstorm,* soos 'n natgereënde (verkluimde) hoender; *a LAME* ~, 'n verminkte persoon; iem. wat sy verpligtings (op aandelemark) nie kan nakom nie; *make* ~*s and drakes with someone else's MONEY,* mooi weer speel met 'n ander se geld; *PLAY* ~*s and drakes with,* mooiweer speel met; (geld) in die water gooi, verkwis; *take to it like a* ~ *to WATER,* iets ongewoons doodnatuurlik doen; *like WATER off a* ~*'s back,* soos water van 'n eend se rug; (v) onderdompel, doop; wegbuk, koe(t)s, (weg)duik; ~**bill,** voëlbekdier; ~**er,** eendeboer; duiker; ~**ing,** (die) duik, onderdompeling; ~**-legged,** kortbeen=; ~**ling,** eendjie; ~**-pond,** eendedam; ~**tail (boy),** eendstert.

duck' trousers, seildoekbroek; witbroek.

duck: ~ **weed,** eendekroos; ~**y-~y!,** pielie-pielie.

duc'o, (n) spreiverf, spuitverf, sproeiverf; (v) duko (geregistreerde handelsnaam).

duct, pyp, geleibuis, kanaal; leiding; geut; gang; *biliary* ~, galbuis; ~**less,** buisloos; ~ *less gland,* buislose klier.

duc'tile, smeebaar, rekbaar; buigbaar, handelbaar, duktiel, buigsaam; inskiklik.

ductil'ity, smeebaarheid, rekbaarheid, duktiliteit, handelbaarheid.

dud, (n) dowe neut; esel, domoor, dommerik, domkop; (pl) toiings, flenters (klere); (a) dof (neut); sleg, waardeloos; ~ *joint,* slegte las.

dude, windmaker, fat.

dudg'eon, verontwaardiging, ergernis, toorn; *be in high* ~, die duiwel in wees.

due¹, (n) reg, eis; verskuldigde, verdiende; (pl) tol, belasting; kerkverpligtings; ledegeld; *never given its FULL* ~, nooit gegee word wat hom toekom nie; *GIVE everyone his* ~, elkeen gee wat hom toekom; *it is HIS* ~, dit kom hom toe.

due², (a, adv) skuldig, verskuldig; behoorlik, gepas, betaamlik; betaalbaar; *BE* ~ *to him,* hom toekom; aan hom te danke wees; *BECOME* ~, verval; ~

CONSIDERATION, na rype beraad; na grondige oorweging; in ~ COURSE, mettertyd, op sy tyd; the MAIL is ~, die pos moet nou aankom; his ~ REWARD, sy verdiende loon, sy regmatige beloning; in ~ TIME, op die regte tyd; ~ TO, te danke aan (gunstig); te wyte aan (ongunstig); ~ WEST, pal (reg) wes.
due: ~-**bill**, promesse; ~ **date**, vervaldatum.
du'el, (n) tweegeveg, duel; (v) (-**led**) duelleer; ~**ling**, duellering; ~**list**, duellis, duelleerder.
duenn'a, goewernante; chaperon, duenna.
duet', duet, tweesang; paar; woordestryd; ~**ist**, duetsanger(es).
duff¹, (n) doekpoeding, jan-in-die-sak.
duff², (n) koolstof, steenkoolgruis.
duff³, (v) ploeg (gholf); poets; vervals; oorbrand (vee).
duff'-coal, steenkoolgruis, koolstof.
duff'el, duffel (growwe wolstof); ~ **bag**, duffelsak.
duff'er, uilskuiken, stommerd; sufferd; makou (gholf); smous; verneuker, bedrieër, valsmunter; vals munt.
duf'fle = **duffel**.
dug¹, (n) tepel, speen, tiet, tet; uier.
dug², (v) *kyk* **dig**.
dug'-out, uitgrawing, hol; boomkano; (bomvry) skuilplek, spreeunes; oud-stryder (wat weer op die aktiewe lys geplaas is).
duik'er, duiker; *Natal (red)* ~, rooi duiker.
duke, hertog; *royal* ~, koninklike hertog; ~**dom**, hertogdom.
dul'cet, soet, strelend.
dul'cify, (..**fied**), soet maak; verteder; versag.
dul'cimer, hakbord, dulsimer.
dul'cis, dulsies.
dull, (v) bot (stomp) maak, afstomp (gees), verstomp; verdoof; verflou; ~ *the EDGE of*, stomp maak; (a) bot, dom, stompsinnig, onbevatlik; dof, loom, suf; somber, donker, doods; geesdodend, droog, vervelend, eentonig; ongevoelig; gevrek (plat); traag, slaperig; lusteloos; betrokke (lug); dood (kleur); moedeloos, neerslagtig; slap (mark); *BE* ~, jou verveel; dom wees; *as* ~ *as DITCHWATER*, stomvervelend; ~ *of HEARING*, hardhorend; *the* ~ *SEASON*, die slap tyd, komkommertyd; ~**ard**, domkop, stommeling, sufferd; ~-**brained**, dom, swaar van begrip, onnosel; ~-**eyed**, dof van blik; ~ **finish**, mat afwerking; ~**ness**, dofheid, dowwigheid; stompheid, verstomping; domheid, stompsinnigheid; onlustigheid; somberheid, bedruktheid; loomheid, slapheid; ~-**sighted**, swak van gesig; ~-**witted**, swaar van begrip, hardleers.
dul'y, behoorlik, noukeurig, tereg, op tyd, betyds.
du'ma, doema.
dumb, stom, spraakloos, geluidloos, stemloos, stilswygend; ~ *ANIMALS*, stomme diere; *the DEAF and* ~, die doofstommes; *a* ~ *DOG*, 'n domkop; vervelende mens; *STRIKE* ~, dronkslaan, verbaas; *be STRUCK* ~, dronkgeslaan wees; heeltemal oorbluf wees; verstom wees; ~-**bells**, handgewigte; ~-**found**, verstom, beteuter, oorbluf, verbluf, ~-**founded**, verstel(d), verstom, verwese; *BE* ~ *founded*, heeltemal oorbluf wees; dronkgeslaan wees; *LOOK* ~ *founded*, lyk of jy v.d. ape gekul is; ~ **insolence**, domastrantheid; ~-**iron**, veerhand; ~-**ness**, stomheid; ~ **show**, stilvertoning, gebarespel; ~ **waiter**, dientafel.
dum'dum (bullet), dumdumkoeël, loodneus(koeël).
dumm'y, (n) (**dummies**), stom mens; figurant; formaatboek, drukmodel, blokboek (in boekery); fopspeen, foppertjie, trooster(tjie); neusplankie (kalf); blindehand, blindeman (kaartspel); pop (mil.); *SELL a* ~, liemaak, pypkan (ougly), *SIT like a* ~, soos 'n houtpop sit; (a) oneg; nagemaak; vals, skyn-; ~ **bomb**, valsbom; ~ **cartridge**, valspatroon; ~ **load**, skynbelasting; ~ **shaft**, monteeras; ~ **tank**, nagemaakte vegwa (tenk).
dump¹, (n) kort, dik ding of persoon; stompie.
dump², (n) (myn)hoop; opslagplek, depot; slag; bons; (v) neerval, neergooi, (af)gooi, aflaai, neersmyt; pers (wol); stort; dump (op mark); ~ **body**, stortbak; ~-**cart**, stortkar; ~-**door**, stortdeur; ~ **er**, storter.

dump'ing, ophoping; uitgooiing; dumping (handel); *no* ~, gooi van afval verbied, storting verbode; ~-**ground**, mishoop, ashoop, stortplek, stortterrein; ~-**place**, stapelplaas.
dump'ling, kluitjie; ~ **soup**, kluitjiesop; ~ *cooked in fat*, stormjaer.
dump lorr'y, stortvragmotor.
dumps, bedruktheid, somberheid; *be in the DOLEFUL* ~, op moedverloor se vlakte wees; *be DOWN in the* ~, op moedverloor se vlakte wees; moedeloos wees; bek-af wees; op die ashoop sit.
dump: ~ **valve**, stortklep; ~ **wa(g)gon**, stortwa.
dum'py, propperig, kort en dik; ~ **level**, nivelleerder.
dun¹, (n) skuldeiser, aanmaner; vordering; (v) (-**ned**), betaling eis, aanmaan, opdruk.
dun², (a) donkerbruin, vaalbruin, vaalgrys, muisvaal, muisgrou; *BLUE* ~, vaalblou; ~ *DIVER*, duikergans; *YELLOW* ~, geel (perd).
dunce, domkop, stommerik, botterkop, botterik, domoor, donkie, druiloor, swaap.
dun'derhead, domkop; ~**ed**, oerdom, stom, stompsinnig.
dune, duin; ~ **lake**, duinmeer; ~ **mole**, duinemol; ~ **rat**, duinmol; ~ **rose**, duinroos.
dung, (n) mis; (v) bemes, mis gee.
dung'aree, growwe Indiese kaliko; ~**s**, oorpak, oorbroek.
dung: ~-**beetle**, miskruier; ~-**cart**, miskar.
dun'geon, (n) tronk, kerker, onderaardse sel; (v) opsluit, kerker.
dung: ~ **floor**, misvloer; ~ **fork**, misvurk; ~**heap**, ~**hill**, mishoop; ~ **lock**, mieskos; ~ **worm**, miswurm.
dun'ite, platina-erts, duniet.
dunk, week (brood in melk), indoop.
Dunkirk', (n) Duinkerken; (v) duinkerk.
dunn'age, pakhout, stugoed, stumateriaal.
dunn'er, aanmaner.
du'o, duet (stuk); duo, tweesang.
duode'cimal, twaalftallig, duodesimaal.
duode'cimo, duodesimo (drukkery).
duoden'al, duodenaal, duodenum-; ~ **ulcer**, duodenumsweer.
duoden'um, twaalfvingerderm, duodenum.
du'ologue, tweespraak.
dup'ability, liggelowigheid.
dup'able, liggelowig, maklik om te fop.
dupe, (n) slagoffer, dupe; *become the* ~ *of*, die slagoffer (dupe) van iets word; (v) bedrieg, mislei, dupeer, flous.
dup'lex, tweevoudig, dubbel; dupleks; ~ **chain**, dubbelketting; ~ **flat**, verdiepingwoonstel, dubbelverdiepingwoonstel, tweevlakwoonstel, dupleks (woonstel); ~ **gauge**, dubbelmeter; ~ **lamp**, lamp met dubbelpit; ~ **telegraphy**, tweerigtingtelegrafie.
dup'licate, (n) duplikaat, afskrif; *in* ~, in tweevoud, in duplo; (v) verdubbel; in duplo opmaak, dupliseer, 'n duplikaat maak; (a) dubbel, duplikaat; ~ **folios**, kopieblaaie.
duplica'tion, verdubbeling, duplikasie.
dup'licator, duplikator, afdrukmasjien, afrolmasjien, kopieermasjien; ~ **ink**, afrolink.
dupli'city, dubbelhartigheid, valsheid.
dur'a: ~ **mater**, harde harsingvlies, rugmurgvlies, dura mater.
durabil'ity, duursaamheid, deugdelikheid.
dur'able, duursaam, durabel; deugdelik; sterk; bestendig; ~**ness**, duursaamheid.
duram'en, kernhout.
dur'ance, gevangenskap, hegtenis; *in* ~ *vile*, in gevangenskap.
dura'tion, duur(te); duurtyd, voortduring; *for the* ~, vir die duur van; ~ **flight**, duurvlug.
durb'ar, hof van Indiese vors.
dur'ess(e), duress(e)', dwang; gevangenskap; *under* ~, onder dwang.
dur'ian, doerian (vrug).
dur'ing, gedurende; onder, ten tyde van, tydens, in.
dur'ite, duriet.
du'rra, graansorghum *(Andropogon sorghum)*.
du'rum wheat seed, durumkoringsaad.
dusk, (n) duisterheid; skemerdonker, skemeraand,

skemering; *at* ~, teen skemer(aand); (v) verdonker; (a) skemer, duister, halfdonker; ~**iness,** skemeragtigheid; ~**y,** skemer, halfdonker, skemeragtig; donker (kleur).

dust, (n) stof; stuifmeel; vuilgoed; stoflike oorskot; beroering; verwarring; *turn to* ~ *and ASHES,* tot stof en as vergaan; *BITE the* ~, in die stof byt; sandruiter word; *CLOUDS of* ~, stofwolke; *make the* ~ *FLY,* 'n stofwolk opskop; *HONOURED* ~, stoflike oorskot; *HUMBLED to the* ~, tot in die stof verneder; *KICK up* ~, stof opskop; lawaai maak; *LICK the* ~, in die stof kruip; *never mind, it is only a LITTLE* ~, die perdjie het maar net gespring; *MAKE someone bite the* ~, iem. in die stof laat byt; *RAISE* ~, stof maak, drukte maak; *not be SEEN for* ~, loop dat die stof so staan; *SHAKE the* ~ *off one's feet,* die stof van die skoene skud; *THROW* ~ *in a person's eyes,* sand (snuif) in iem. se oë strooi; *TRAMPLE in the* ~, met voete vertree; (v) afstof; afborsel; opvee; bestuif; bestrooi; uitlooi; ~ *someone's JACKET,* iem. op sy baadjie gee; iem. uitlooi; ~ *someone's TROUSERS, give someone's TROUSERS (jacket) a dusting,* iem. op sy baadjie gee; iem. se baadjie vir hom uitborsel; ~**-basket,** vuilgoedmandjie; ~**-bin,** vuilgoedblik; ~**-board,** stofskerm; ~**-bowl,** stofkom; ~**-brand,** brand (koring); ~**-brush,** stofborsel; ~**-cap,** afdigbus, stofdop; ~**-cart,** vuilgoedkar; ~**-cloak,** stofjas, stofmantel; ~**-cloud,** stofwolk; ~ **coat,** stofjas; ~**-coloured,** stofkleurig; ~ **content,** stofgehalte; ~**-cover,** (stof)omslag; stofdeksel; ~ **devil,** warrelwind, warrelwind; ~**-dry,** stofdroog (verf); ~ **er,** stofdoek, stoflap; stofbesem, stoffer; stowwer; ~**-excluder,** stofkeerder; ~**-free,** stofvry; ~**-gun,** stuifkop; ~**iness,** stowwerigheid; ~**ing,** loesing; stormweer; ~**ing-brush,** afstofkwas; ~**ing-powder,** stuifpoeier; lyfpoeier; ~ **jacket,** stofomslag; ~**less,** stofloos; ~**man,** asryer, Klaas Vakie; *the* ~*man has arrived,* Klaas Vakie is hier; ~ **pan,** stofpan; ~**-preventing,** stofwerend; ~**-proof,** stofvry; ~**-proofing,** stofdigting; ~**-sheet,** stoflaken; ~**-shield,** stofskerm; ~**-shot,** donshael; ~**-storm,** stofstorm; ~**-trap,** stofnes; ~**-trouble,** stofplaag; ~**-up,** rusie, bakleiery; lawaai; ~ **wrapper,** stofomslag; ~**y,** stowwerig; stofkleurig; stormagtig; winderig; *verveiend; not so* ~*y,* nie te sleg nie.

Dutch, (n) Nederlands, Hollands; *CAPE* ~, Kaaps-Hollands; *DOUBLE* ~, koeterwaals; *GO* ~, botjie by botjie lê; *HIGH* ~, *HOLLAND* ~, Hooghollands; *LOW* ~, Platduits; (a) Hollands, Nederlands; *STUDENT of* ~ *literature,* Neerlandikus; *talk to someone like a* ~ *UNCLE,* iem. 'n vaderlike skrobbering gee; ~ **auction,** afslagveiling; verkoping by afslag; ~ **barn,** oop skuur; ~ **brick,** klinkersteen; ~ **cheese,** Hollandse kaas; suurmelkkaas; weikaas; ~ **church(es),** Hollandse (Hollands-Afrikaanse) Kerk(e); ~ **clock,** koekoekklok; ~ **clover,** witklawer; ~ **comfort,** slegte troos; ~ **concert,** groot lawaai; ~ **courage,** jenewermoed; ~ **doll,** Hollandse pop, houtpop; ~ **drops,** haarlemmerolie; ~ **East Indies,** Nederlands-Oos-Indië; ~**ifica'tion,** verhollandsing; ~**ify,** (..**fied)** verhollands, verdiets; ~ **interior,** Hollandse interieur (skildery); ~**ism,** Hollandisme, Nederlandisme.

Dutch'man, (..**men),** Hollander, Nederlander; Afrikaner; *the FLYING* ~, die Vlieënde Hollander; *I'm a* ~ *if.* . ., my naam is bles as . . .; ~ **'s pipe,** Oom-Paul-se-pyp.

Dutch: ~ **metal,** klatergoud; ~ **studies,** Neerlandistiek; ~ **treat,** betaling vir jouself; ~ **uncle,** vermaner; ~ **woman,** Nederlandse vrou.

dut'eous = **dutiful.**

dut'iable, belasbaar, tolpligtig; aan invoerreg onderhewig.

duti'ful, gehoorsaam, dienswillig, onderdanig; pligmatig; ~**ly,** pligshalwe; ~**ness,** gehoorsaamheid, onderdanigheid; pligmatigheid.

dut'y, (duties), plig; diens, taak, werk; agting; gehoorsaamheid, onderwerping; reg; *ASSUME* ~, in diens tree; diens aanvaar; *BE on* ~, diens hê; op wag wees; *in* ~ *BOUND,* verplig, genoodsaak; *DEVOTION to* ~, pligsgetrouheid; *DO* ~ *for,* diens doen vir; *DO one's* ~, sy plig doen; *NEGLECT of* ~, pligsversuim; *be OFF* ~, vry wees, geen diens hê nie; *the OFFICER on* ~, die diensdoende beampte; *ON* ~, in diens, in die werk; op sy pos; *PERFORMANCE of* ~, pligsvervulling; ~ *before PLEASURE,* die werk gaan voor alles; *his duties PREVENT him,* sy werk verhinder hom; *SENSE of* ~, pligsgevoel; ~ **book,** diensboek; ~**-bound,** verplig; gebonde; pligshalwe; ~ **bus,** diensbus; ~ **call,** hoflikheidsbesoek; ~ **clerk,** diensklerk; ~**-free,** belastingvry; doeanevry; tolvry; ~ **list,** dienslys; ~ **load,** dienslas; ~ **officer,** diensoffisier; ~**-paid,** diensvry; ~ **room,** dienskamer; ~ **roster,** diensrooster; ~ **staff,** wagpersoneel; ~ **stamp,** belastingseël.

duum'vir, (-i, -s), duümvir, duumvir, tweeman; ~**ate,** tweemanskap, duümviraat, duumviraat.

dux, eerste; leier, dux.

dwarf, (n) dwerg, buks(ie), pigmee; (v) verdwerg; in die groei belemmer; klein laat lyk; in die skaduwee stel; (a) klein, miniatuur=, dwerg=; ~ **bean,** stamboontjie; ~ **beech,** dwergbeuk; ~ **bittern,** dwergreier; ~ **goose,** dwerggans; ~ **grass,** haasgras; ~**-ish,** dwergagtig; ~**ishness,** dwergagtigheid; ~ **mouse,** dwergmuis; ~ **oak,** dwergeik; ~ **pea,** kekerertjie; ~ **plant,** dwergplant; ~ **rose,** dwergroos, struikroos; ~ **tree,** dwergboom; kreupelboom; bonsai; ~ **willow,** dwergwilg(er).

dwell, woon, bly; ~ *(up)on,* stilstaan by; uitwei oor; ~**er,** bewoner.

dwell'ing, woning, woonhuis; ~**-house,** woonhuis; ~**-place,** woonplek; ~**-unit,** wooneenheid.

dwin'dle, inkrimp, kleiner word, verminder; wegkwyn, verdwyn; verklein; agteruitgaan; ~ *AWAY,* wegkrimp; ~ *DOWN to,* slink tot op.

dy'ad, (die getal) twee; atoom, element; paar; diade; ~**'ic,** tweewaardig, uit twee bestaande, diadies.

dye, (n) verf, kleurstof, kleursel; kleur, beits, tint; *of the deepest* ~, van die gemeenste soort (fig.); (v) verf, kleur; ~**-bath,** verfbad; ~**d,** geverf, gekleur, getint; ~ **d-in-the-wool,** in die wol geverf, was-eg; deurtrapte, verstokte; deurwinter(d); ~**ing,** verwery, kleuring; ~**ing process,** kleurproses; ~**-pistol,** kleurpistool; ~**r,** kleurder, verwer; ~**-stuff,** verfstof; ~**-works,** verwery.

dy'ing, (n) sterwe, dood; (a) doods=, sterf=, sieltogend, sterwend; *be* ~, op sterwe lê; ~ **bed,** sterfbed; ~ **day,** sterfdag; ~ **hour,** sterwensuur; ~ **moments,** laaste oomblikke; ~ **oath,** plegtige eed; sterfbedwoord.

dyke, *kyk* **dike.**

dynam'ic, dinamies; bewegings=, bewegend; kragtig; ~**s,** kragteleer; dinamika; bewegingsleer.

dyn'amism, dinamisme.

dy'namist, dinamis.

dyn'amitard, bomgooier; dinamietman.

dyn'amite, (n) dinamiet, springstof; (v) met dinamiet verniel, opblaas, laat spring; ~ **attack,** dinamietaanval; dinamietaanslag; ~ **cap,** dinamietdoppie; ~ **cartridge,** dinamietpatroon; ~ **charge,** dinamietlading; ~ **factory,** dinamietfabriek; ~ **fuse,** dinamietlont; ~ **outrage,** dinamietaanslag; ~**r,** bomgooier; dinamietman.

dyn'amo, (-s), dinamo, opwekker; ~ **drive,** dinamoaandrywing.

dynamom'eter, kragmeter, dinamometer.

dynamom'etric(al), dinamometries.

dynamo'metry, kragmeting (fis.).

dyn'amo: ~ **pulley,** dinamoskyf; ~ **spindle,** dinamospil; ~ **strap,** dinamoband.

dyn'ast, heerser.

dynas'tic, dinasties, stam=, dinastiek.

dyn'asty, (..**ties),** dinastie, vorstehuis, regerende stamhuis.

dyne', dine.

dysente'ric, buikloop=, disenteries.

dys'entery, disenterie, buikloop, bloedpersie; ~ **herb,** naaldbossie.

dysfunc'tion, disfunksie.

dysgra'phia, skryfstoring, disgrafie.

dysle'xia, disleksie, woordblindheid.

dysmenorrhoe'a, pynlike menstruasie, dismenorree.

dyspep'sia, dyspep'sy, slegte spysvertering, dispep=
sie.
dyspep'tic, (n) lyer aan slegte spysvertering; (a) met
slegte spysvertering, dispepties; neerslagtig.
dyspla'sia, displasie, weefselwanvorming.

dyspnoe'a, kortasemigheid, dispnee.
dystroph'ic, distrofies.
dystroph'y, kwyning, distrofie.
dysur'ia, pynlike watering, disurie.
dzig'getai, dziggetai, wilde esel.

E

e, (es, e's), e; *little* ~, e'tjie.
each, (a) elke, iedere; (pron) elk, elkeen, ieder(een);
stuk; *one CENT* ~, een sent stuk; ~ *and EVERY*,
elk en ieder; ~ *OTHER*, mekaar; ~ *of US*, elkeen
van ons.
eag'er, gretig, graag; happ(er)ig, begerig; ywerig, vu=
rig; skerp, voortvarend, onstuimig; ~ *FOR*, bege=
rig na, belus op, verlangend na, tuk op; ~ *TO*, be=
gerig om; ~ **ly,** gretig, vurig; verlangend; ~ **ness,**
verlange; graagheid, graagte; happ(er)igheid, gre=
tigheid; ywer; versotheid.
ea'gle, arend (ook gholf); adelaar; *BLACK* ~, dassie=
vanger; *BOOTED* ~, dwergarend; *CROWNED*
~, kroonarend; *DOUBLE* ~, twintigdollarstuk
(Amer.); *GOLDEN* (~-*bearded*) ~, lammervan=
ger; *MARTIAL* ~, breëkoparend; ~-**eyed,** skerp
van gesig, met arendsoë; met oë van agter en van
voor; ~ **owl,** ooruil; ~ **ray,** duiwelvis, duiwelrog;
~-**sighted,** met arendsoë, skerpsiende; ~**'s nest,**
arendsnes; ~**t,** arendjie, jong arend; ~-**winged,**
met arendsvlerke; ~ **wood,** aalwynhout.
ea'gre, vloedgolf.
ear¹, (n) aar; kop (mielie); saad; (v) in die aar kom,
saad skiet.
ear², (n) oor; gehoor; handvatsel (beker); *be ALL* ~ *s*,
belangstellend luister, een en al oor wees; *BIG* ~,
wawieloor; *a BOX on the* ~, 'n oorkonkel, 'n oor=
waks; *BRING something down about one's* ~ *s*, jou
iets op die hals haal; *were your* ~ *s BURNING last
night?* het jou ore gisteraand getuit? *CHILLED* ~,
winteroor; *COME to one's* ~ *s*, iets ter ore kom;
turn a DEAF ~, nie wil luister nie; *be up to one's* ~ *s
in DEBT*, skuld soos sand (bossies) hê; tot oor die
ore in die skuld wees; soveel skuld hê soos hare op
jou kop; *DELIGHT the* ~, die oor streel; *it did not
FALL on deaf* ~ *s*, dis aan geen dowe gesê nie; *send
away with a FLEA in his* ~, iem. kort en klaar die
waarheid vertel; *GAIN the* ~ *of*, gehoor vind by;
GIVE ~ *to*, die oor leen aan; *I would GIVE my* ~,
ek sou wat wou gee; *it GOES in at one* ~ *and out at
the other*, by die een oor in, by die ander oor uit;
have an ~ *close to the GROUND*, sake fyn dophou
(beluister); *listen with HALF an* ~, met 'n halwe
oor luister; *he that HATH* ~ *s to listen, let him hear*,
wie ore het om te hoor, laat hom hoor; *HAVE a
person's* ~, iem. se belangstelling geniet; *over
HEAD and* ~ *s*, tot oor die ore; *INCLINE one's* ~,
die oor neig, luister; *have ITCHING* ~ *s*, graag na
skinderpraatjies luister; *LEND one's* ~ *s*, die oor
leen; *have LONG* ~ *s*, lang ore hê; *have an* ~ *for
MUSIC*, musikaal wees; *have NO* ~ *s*, geen ore aan
jou kop hê nie; geen oor vir iets hê nie; *PLAY by* ~,
op gehoor speel; *PRICK up one's* ~ *s*, die ore spits;
SET by the ~ *s*, aanhits; *SMALL* ~, muisoor;
TICKLE the ~ *s*, die ore streel; *you should WASH
out your* ~ *s*, het jy dan nie ore nie? *a WORD in
your* ~, 'n woordjie privaat; *be up to one's* ~ *s in
WORK*, werk tot oor jou ore hê; werk soos bossies
hê; toegegooi wees met werk; ~-**ache,** oorpyn; ~
bone, gehoorbeentjie, oorbeentjie; ~ **canker,** oor=
verswering (diere); ~-**cap,** oorskerm; ~-**cleaner,**
oorreiniger; ~-**drop,** oorkrabbetjie, (oor)hanger,
oorbel; ~-**drops,** oordruppels; ~-**drum,** trommel=
vlies, oortrommel.
eared¹, met are, geaar.
eared², met ore.
ear: ~-**flap,** oorklappie; ~-**guard,** oorskut, oor=
skerm; ~-**hole,** oorgat.
earl, graaf.

ear'-lap, oorlel.
earl'dom, graafskap.
ear'less¹, sonder are (koring), aarloos.
ear'less², sonder ore.
earl'iest, vroegste; *at your* ~, so gou moontlik.
earl'iness, vroegtydigheid; vroegheid.
ear'-lobe, oorskulp, oorbel.
earl'y, vroeg, tydig; spoedig; vroegryp, vroegtydig; *an
HOUR* ~, 'n uur te vroeg; *KEEP* ~ *hours*, vroeg
opstaan en vroeg na bed gaan; *(both)* ~ *and
LATE*, vroeg en laat; *as* ~ *as OCTOBER*, al in
Oktober; *the* ~ *PART*, die begin; ~ *PEACHES*,
vroeë perskes; *E* ~ *ROSE*, ellierose (spel); *in* ~ *TI=
MES*, in die vroegste tye; ~-**bearing,** vroeg(dra=
end) (plant, boom); ~ **bird,** vroegopstaner; ~-
flowering, vroeg(bloeiend); ~**ish,** vroeërig; ~
mass, vroegmis; ~-**warning system,** vroegwaarsku=
stelsel, vinnige alarmstelsel.
ear'mark, (n) (oor)merk, (v) merk, afsonder, bestem
(fondse); ~ *funds for*, fondse bestem (uittrek, af=
sonder) vir; ~**ed,** gemerk; gebêre, opsy gesit, be=
stem.
ear-muff, oorskut.
earn, verdien; verwerf; ~ *one's DAILY bread*, aan die
kos kom, 'n bestaan maak; *PAY as you* ~, algaan=
de betaal; *PAY as you* ~ *system*, lopende (belas=
ting)betaalstelsel; ~-**er,** verdiener.
earn'est¹, (n) voorproef, belofte; pand, paaiement,
handgeld.
earn'est², (n) erns; (a) ernstig, ywerig, gretig, begerig;
be in ~, dit ernstig bedoel; ~**ly,** ywerig; ernstig;
toegewy(d); in erns, opreg.
earn'est-money, handgeld; handgif, begingeld.
earn'estness, erns, ernstigheid; innigheid; ywer.
earn'ing: *he and his wife are both* ~ *money*, sy mes sny
aan albei kante; ~ **power(s),** verdienvermoë.
earn'ings, verdienste, loon; inkomste.
ear: ~-**phone,** koptelefoon; kopstuk; (ge)hoorbuis;
~-**piece,** oorstuk (telef.); brilraam, veer; gehoor=
buis; ~-**piercing,** oorverdowend; ~-**plug,** oorplui=
sie; ~ **protector,** oorbeskermer; oorklap; ~ **ring,**
oorring, (oor)krabbetjie.
ear'-rot, kopvrot.
ear: ~ **shell,** klipkous; ~-**shot,** hoorafstand, gehoor,
be within ~ *shot*, nie ver weg wees nie, binne hoor=
afstand wees; ~ **space,** oorspasie; ~-**splitting,** oor=
verdowend; ~-**syringe,** oorspuit; ~-**tag,** oorplaat=
jie.
earth, (n) aarde, grond; aardryk; aardbol, wêreld;
hol, gat; grondsluiting; *come BACK to* ~, tot jou=
self kom; ontnugter word; *how on* ~ *COULD you?*
hoe kon jy tog? *what on* ~ *!* wat in die wêreld! op die
aarde! *RUN to* ~, in 'n gat jaag; na 'n lang soektog
ontdek; *feel as if the* ~ *could SWALLOW one*, voel
of jy in die aarde kan sink; *WHO on* ~ *?* wie op
aarde? wie die duiwel? (v) begrawe; aard (elek.);
operd; in 'n gat kruip; in sy gat jag; na die grond
aflei (elek.); ~ *up*, ophoop; operd; ~-**bank,** grond=
wal; ~-**board,** strykbord; ~-**born,** aards; sterflik;
~-**bound,** aardvas; ~-**bred,** aards; laag; ~-**cable,**
aardkabel; ~ **circuit,** aardkring; ~-**connection,**
aardgeleiding; ~ **contact,** aardverbinding; ~-**cur=
rent,** aardstroom; ~-**dam,** gronddam; ~**ed,** ge=
aard; ~-**electrode,** aardelektrode.
earth'en, grond=, aarde=, erde=; ~ **floor,** grondvloer;
~ **pipe,** erdepyp; ~ **ware,** (n) breekgoed, erdewerk;
(a) erde=.
earth: ~-**fall,** aardstorting, grondverskuiwing; ~ **fis=
sure,** aardspleet, grondspleet; ~-**flax,** asbes, gare=

klip, steenvlas; ~ **flea,** sandvlooi, erdvlooi; ~ **floor,** grondvloer; kleivloer.

earth'iness, aardsgesindheid, aardsheid.

earth'ing, aarding, aardgeleiding; ~ **chain,** afleiketting; ~ **connection,** aardverbinding; ~ **lead,** aardleiding.

earth: ~**liness,** aardsgesindheid; ~**ling,** aardbewoner.

earth'ly, aards, stoflik; *there is no* ~ *CHANCE,* daar is nie die minste kans nie; *for no* ~ *REASON,* sonder die minste aanleiding daartoe; *of no* ~ *USE,* hoegenaamd van geen nut nie; ~**-minded,** wêrelds, aardsgesind.

earth: ~**-mound,** grondhoop; ~**-moving,** grondverskuiwing; ~**-nut,** grondboontjie; ~ **pig,** erdvark; ~ **plate,** aardingsplaat; ~**quake,** aardbewing; ~ **return circuit,** aardterugleiding; ~ **road,** grondpad; ~**-satelite,** kunsmaan; ~**'s axis,** aardas; ~ **sciences,** aardwetenskappe; ~**'s crust,** aardkors; ~**-scoop,** damskrop; ~ **shadow,** aardskadu(wee); ~**-shaking,** aardskuddend, ontsaglik, geweldig; ~**-shine,** aardlig; ~**-shock,** aardskok, ~ **slide,** grondverskuiwing; ~**-snake,** erdslang; ~ **terminal,** aardaansluiter; ~**'s surface,** aardbodem, aardoppervlak; aardklem; ~**-tremor,** aardskok; ~**ward,** aardewaarts; ~**-wire,** aardleiding, aarddraad; ~ **work,** aardwerk, skans, bolwerk; ~**worm,** erdwurm; kruiperige persoon; ~ **y,** grondagtig, gronderig; aards, wêrelds.

ear: ~**-training,** gehooroefening; ~**-trumpet,** gehoorpyp; gehoorbuis (telef.); ~**-wax,** oorwas.

ear'wig¹, (n) oorwurm *(Euplexoptera en Dermaptera).*

ear'wig², (v) **(-ged),** bewerk, influister.

ear: ~**-witness,** oorgetuie; ~**-wool,** oorwatte.

ease, (n) gemak; rus; verligting; ongedwongenheid; gegoedheid; *AT* ~, maklik, vry; op jou gemak; *at HIS* ~, op sy sloffies; *ILL at* ~, nie op sy gemak nie; *do SOMETHING with the greatest of* ~, iets speel-speel doen; *STAND at* ~! (op die) plek rus! *WITH* ~, maklik; op jou gemak; (v) gerustel; versag, verlig; vergemaklik; laat skiet, skiet gee; lenig; verlos; losser maak; skotig insit (inwerk) (kleremakery)); ~ *AWAY a rope,* 'n tou geleidelik laat skiet (uitvier); ~ *on'es HUNGER,* sy honger stil; ~ *someone's MIND,* iem. gerusstel; ~ **ful,** kalm, rustig; gemaksugtig, traag.

eas'el, (bord)esel; skilderesel; ~**-peg,** eselpen; ~**-piece,** paneeltjie.

ease'ment, bygebou; serwituut.

eas'er, hulpgat.

eas'ily, maklik, fluit-fluit, speel-speel.

eas'iness, gemaklikheid, gemak; ~ *of mind,* gerustheid van gemoed.

eas'ing, gerusstellend; ~**-gear,** ligtoestel.

east, oos; ooswaarts; ooste; *the E* ~, die Ooste; *the FAR E* ~, die Verre Ooste; *the MIDDLE E* ~, die Midde(l)-Ooste; *the NEAR E* ~, die Nabye Ooste; (a) oos-; ooste-; oostelik; (adv) oos; ~ **coast,** ooskus; ~**-coast fever,** ooskuskoors.

Eas'ter, Pase, Paasfees; Paasvakansie; ~ **Day,** Paasdag; ~ **egg,** Paaseier; ~ **holidays,** Paasvakansie; ~ **lily,** Maartlelie, belladonnalelie.

Eas'terling, Oosterling.

Eas'ter loaf, Paasbrood.

eas'terly, oostelik; ooswaarts.

Eas'ter Monday, Paasmaandag.

eas'tern, oostelik, ooste-, oos-; ~**er,** Oosterling; ~**most,** oostelikste.

Eas'ter: ~ **offerings,** Paasoffergawe; ~ **sermon,** Paaspreek; ~ **show,** Paastentoonstelling; ~ **stamp,** Paaseël; ~ **Sunday,** Paassondag; ~ **tide,** ~ **time,** Paastyd; ~ **week,** Paasweek.

East Germ'any, Oos-Duitsland.

East In'dia, Oos-Indië; ~ **man,** Oos-Indiëvaarder; ~ **n,** Oos-Indiër; Oos-Indies.

East In'dies, Oos-Indië.

eas'ting, oostelike rigting, afstand na die ooste.

east'ward(s), ooswaarts.

eas'y, maklik, lig; inskiklik; gerus; rustig; ongedwonge; welgesteld; bedaard; flou (mark); ~ *of ACCESS,* genaakbaar; ~ *of BELIEF,* liggelowig; *in* ~ *CIRCUMSTANCES,* welgesteld; ~ *COME,* ~ *go,* so gewonne, so geronne; ~ *on the EYE,* mooi; iets vir die oog; *it is as* ~ *as FALLING off a log,* dis so maklik as koek eet; dis kinderspeletjies; dit is geen kuns nie; *MAKE* ~, gerusstel; ~ *MANNERS,* ongedwonge maniere; ~ *MARKET,* willige mark; ~ *MONEY,* maklik verdiende geld; ~ *PAYMENTS,* paaiemente, maklike afbetalings; *as* ~ *as PIE,* so maklik soos botter en brood; geen kuns nie; *TAKE it* ~, kalm opneem; ~ *THERE!* stadig oor die klippe! *of* ~ *VIRTUE,* van los sedes; ~ **chair,** gemakstoel, leunstoel, russtoel, luistoel.

eas'y-going, gemaksugtig; sorgeloos; *an* ~ *fellow,* 'n vent wat dinge maklik opneem.

eat, (ate, eaten), eet, opeet, nuttig; wei; invreet ('n suur); ~ *AWAY a fortune,* alles deur die keelgat jaag (laat gaan); ~ *one's DINNERS,* in die regte studeer; ~ *one's FILL,* jou versadig eet; ~ *out of one's HAND,* geseglik wees; *I'd* ~ *my HAT if that were true,* as dit waar is, eet ek my hoed op; ~ *one's HEART out,* bitter ly; jou verknies; vergaan van verdriet; ~ *a person out of HOUSE and home,* iem. die ore van die kop af eet; ~ *HUMBLE pie,* 'n nootjie laer sing; ~ *INTO,* invreet; *make someone* ~ *the LEEK,* iem. sy woorde laat insluk; ~ *what you LIKE and face the consequences,* eet wat jy lus en ly wat daarop volg; *as LONG as there is something to* ~, so lank as die lepel in die pappot staan; *MAKE someone eat his words,* iem. sy woorde laat insluk; ~*en up with PRIDE,* deur hoogmoed verteer; ~ *(drink) SOMETHING,* die inwendige mens versterk; ~ *UP,* opeet; opvreet; ~ *one's WORDS,* jou woorde terugtrek; ~ **able,** eetbaar; ~ **ableness,** eetbaarheid; ~ **ables,** eetware; ~ **er,** eter; *a GOOD* ~*er,* 'n goeie eter; *a POOR* ~*er,* 'n slegte (swak) eter.

eat'ing, (die) eet; etery; kos; *what is* ~ *you?* wat het oor jou lewer geloop? ~ **apple,** eetappel; ~ **competition,** eetwedstryd, moesoek eet; ~ **grapes,** tafeldruiwe; ~ **house,** eetplek, restourant.

eats, eetgoed.

eau-de-Cologne', laventel, eau-de-cologne, oliekolonie.

eua-de-vie', brandewyn.

eaves, dakrand, (dak)drup, dakgeut; ~**-drip,** dakdrup.

eaves'drop, (n) dakdrup; (v) **(-ped),** afluister; ~ **per,** afsluiteraar, luistervink; ~ **ping,** afluistery; ~**-gutter,** dakgeut; ~**-lath,** wiplat; ~**-moulding,** dakrandlys; ~**-purlin,** dakrandlat.

ebb, (n) eb, laag(ge)ty; ~ *and FLOW,* eb en vloed; *at a LOW* ~, op 'n lae peil; (v) afloop, afneem, eb; verval; ~ *away,* afneem, wegvloei; ~**-tide,** weergety, ebgety, laagwater.

E'-boat, torpedoboot, E-boot.

eb'onite, eboniet.

eb'onize, swartbeits.

eb'ony, (n) ebbehout; (a) ebbehout=; swart, donkerkleurig.

ebri'ety, dronkenskap, beskonkenheid.

e'brious, dronk, beskonke.

ebull'ience, opbruising; lewendigheid.

ebull'ient, kokend, opbruisend, opborrelend; opgewek.

ebull'ioscope, ebullioskoop.

ebulli'tion, (op)koking, opbruising, opwelling, opborreling; uitbarsting.

eb'urine, eb'urite, kunsivoor, eburiet.

ebur'neous, ivoorkleurig.

eca'rinate, kielloos (dierk.).

éscarté', éscarté, kaartspel.

ecbol'ic, (n) afdrywingsmiddel; (a) afdrywend.

eccen'tric, (n) eksentriek, sonderling (persoon); (a) snaaks; oordrewe, buitensig; eksentriek, sonderling; uitmiddelpuntig, eksentries; ~ **bolt,** eksentriekbout; ~ **gab,** eksentriekstang; ~ **gear,** eksentriektoestel; ~ **groove,** eksentriese groef.

eccentri'city, uitmiddelpuntigheid; afwyking; eksentrisiteit, buitensigheid; sonderlingheid.

eccen'tric: ~ **ring,** eksentriekring; ~ **rod,** eksentriekstang; ~ **shaft,** eksentriekstang; eksentriek-as.

Ecclesias'tes, Prediker.

ecclesiastic 863 *education*

ecclesias'tic, (n) geestelike; (a) geestelik, kerklik, ek=
klesiasties; ~ **al,** geestelik, kerklik; ~ *al law,* kerk=
reg; ~ **ism,** kerkisme.
ecclesiol'ogy, kerkboukuns.
ecdy'siast, ontkleedanseres.
ec'dysis, (ecdyses), vervelling.
e'chelon, echelon.
echid'na, mierystervark.
echid'nine, slanggif.
ech'inate(d), gestekel, stekelhuidig; stekel=, prikkelig.
echin'oderm, stekelhuidige.
ech'inoid, seekastaiing.
echin'us, see-eier; seekastaiings; see-egel; eierlys´ (argit.)
ech'o, (n) (-es), weerklank, weergalm, nagalm, eggo, weerkaatsing; nabootsing; *cheer to the* ~, uitbun= dig toejuig; (v) weergalm, weerklink, herhaal, na= boots, napraat; ~ *what EVERYBODY else says,* met elke hond saamblaf; ~ *someone's OPINIONS,* iem. napraat; ~ **ism,** klanknabootsing.
echola'lia, eggolalie.
e'cho-virus, echovirus.
éc'lair, roomtertjie, éclair.
eclat', glans, luister; skitterende sukses, éclat.
eclec'tic, (n) eklektikus; uitkieswedstryd (gholf); (a) uitkiesend, eklekties; ~ **ism,** eklektisisme.
eclipse', (n) verduistering, eklips; *he IS in* ~, dis klaar met hom; sy son het ondergegaan; ~ *of the MOON,* maansverduistering; *PARTIAL* ~, ge= deeltelike verduistering; *TOTAL* ~, algehele ver= duistering; (v) verduister, verdonker; oorskadu; eklipseer.
eclip'tic, (n) ekliptika, sonweg; (a) eklipties.
ec'logue, herdersdig, ekloge.
ecolog'ical, ekologies.
ecol'ogist, ekoloog.
ecol'ogy, ekologie.
econometric: ~ **al,** ekonometries, ~ **s,** ekonometrika, ekonometrie.
econom'ic, staathuishoudkundig, ekonomies; spaar= saam; huishoudelik; **E** ~ **Advisory Council,** Ekono= miese Adviesraad; ~ **al,** huishoudelik; suinig, spaarsaam, ekonomies; ~ **ally,** suinigies; op spaar= same wyse; ~ **burner,** suinigheidsbrander; ~ **enter= prise,** lonende onderneming; ~ **factors,** ekonomie= se faktore; ~ **life** (of machine), bruikduur, lewensduur; ~ **s,** (staat)huishoudkunde, ekono= mie; spaarsaamheid; besuiniging.
econ'omist, staathuishoudkundige, ekonoom; spaar= same persoon.
economiza'tion, versobering, besuiniging.
econ'omize, spaar, besuinig, spaarsaam wees, ekono= miseer, snoei, suinig met iets werk, uitspaar, uitsui= nig; ~ **r,** besuiniger; (brandstof)bespaarder.
econ'omy, ekonomie, staathuishoudkunde; huis= houdkunde, huishouding; suinigheid, spaarsaam= heid; (..**mies**), besparing, besuiniging, uitsparing; inrigting; *DOMESTIC* ~, huishoudkunde; *POLI= TICAL* ~, ekonomie, staatshuishoudkunde, staats= leer; *for the SAKE of* ~, suinigheidshalwe; ~ **measure,** suinigheidsmaatreël; ~ **run,** besparings= rit; ~ **valve,** bespaarklep.
e'cosphere, ekosfeer.
e'cosystem, ekosisteem, ekostelsel.
ecru', e'cru, kleur van ongebleikte linne.
ec'stasy, (..**sies**), verrukking, (geestes)vervoering, opgetoënheid, geesdrif, ekstase, sielsverrukking, sielsvervoering.
ecstat'ic, verruk, geesdriftig, verruklik, ekstaties, opgetoë.
ec'toderm, ektoderm; ~ **'al,** ektodermies, ektoderma= ties.
ec'toplasm, ektoplasma.
ec'type, afdruk (munt).
E'cuador, Ecuador.
Ecuador'ian, (n) Ecuadoriaan; (a) Ecuadoriaans.
ecumene', ekumene.
ecumen'ic(al), ekumenies.
e'cumenism, ekumenisme.
ec'zema, ekseem, huiduitslag; douwurm; roos.
eda'cious, gulsig, vraatsig.
eda'city, vraatsugtigheid, gulsigheid.

Ed'am, Edam; ~ **cheese,** Edammerkaas.
Edd'a, Edda.
edd'y, (n) (**eddies**), draaikolk, maling; warreling, wie= ling; (dwarrel)wind; (v) (**eddied**), ronddraai, dwar= rel, maal; ~ **current,** werwelstroom; ~ **ing,** dwarre= ling, ronddraaiing.
ed'elweiss, edelweiss (Alpeblom).
ede'ma, edeem, watergeswel, watersug.
Ed'en, Eden, paradys.
Ed'enburg, Edenburg (O.V.S.).
eden'tate, eden'tulous, tandeloos.
edge, (n) skerpte, skerp kant (gereedskap); snit (mes); snee (byl); kant, boord, rand; *give an* ~ *to the AP= PETITE,* die eetlus opwek; *BE on* ~, opgewonde (geprikkel) wees; *the* ~ *of BEYOND,* die ander= kant v.d. wêreld; *GIVE an* ~, skerp maak; *HAVE an* ~ *on someone,* 'n voorsprong op iem. hê; iem. vooruit wees; *the KNIFE has no* ~, die mes is stomp; *ON* ~, op sy kant; *SET an* ~ *on,* slyp, skerp maak; *it SETS one's teeth on* ~, dit gaan deur murg en been; dit laat 'n mens gril; *STRAIGHT* ~, rei(hout); *the thin* ~ *of the WEDGE,* die skerp kant v.d. wig; *TAKE the* ~ *off something.* (let. en fig.) stomp maak, afstomp; (v) skerp maak, slyp; ongemerk voorwaarts dring; om= geef, insluit; omklink, afkant, afbrand; omsoom (materiaal); ~ *AWAY,* wegskuif; ~ *IN,* indruk; ~ *IN a word,* 'n woord tussenin kry; ~ *ON,* aanhits; ~ **bone,** stertstuk.
edged, skerp, puntig, getand; omgesoom; ~ *TOOL,* skerp gereedskap; *play with* ~ *TOOLS,* met vuur speel.
edge: ~ **finish,** randafwerking; ~ **grain,** langshout; ~ **plane,** randskaaf; ~ **plate,** randplaat; ~ **r,** sny= werktuig; randsnyer; ~ **-stress,** randspanning; ~ **tool,** snywerktuig; kantsnyer; ~ **way,** smalkant; ~ **ways,** ~ **wise,** op sy kant, skuins; *not get a word in* ~ *ways,* geen kans kry om iets te sê nie; ~ **weapon,** snywapen.
edg'ing, soom; rand; omlegsel, omboorsel, randver= siersel, randversiering, randafwerking; velrand (seëls); ~ **-shears,** grasknipper; ~ **-tool,** randsnyer.
edg'y, skerp, kantig; krities, byterig; senu(wee)= agtig.
edibil'ity, eetbaarheid.
ed'ible, eetbaar; ~ **s,** eetware, eetgoed.
ed'ict, gebod, edik, bevelskrif, dekreet, plakkaat; *col= lection of* ~ **s,** plakkaatboek.
edic'tal, ediktaal, geregtelik; ~ **citation,** geregtelike dagvaarding.
edifica'tion, stigting, opbouing, lering, stigtelikheid.
ed'ifice, gebou.
ed'ifier, stigter, opbouer; onderrigter, geesverheffer.
ed'ify, (..**fied**), geestelik verbeter, onderrig, stig, op= bou; ~ **ing,** opbouend, stigtend, stigtelik; geesver= heffend.
Ed'inburgh, Edinburg (Skotland); ~ **rock,** klipsor= bet, sorbetlekker.
ed'it, redigeer, persklaar maak; bewerk; ~ *ed by,* on= der redaksie van, geredigeer deur.
ed'iting, redaksiewerk, redigering.
edi'tion, uitgawe, edisie, druk, oplaag; ~ **de luxe,** luukse-uitgawe.
ed'itor, redakteur; bewerker; *financial* ~, finansiële medewerker (redakteur).
editor'ial, (n) hoofartikel, inleidingsartikel; (a) re= daksioneel; van die redaksie; ~ **staff,** redaksie.
ed'itor-in-chief, hoofredakteur.
ed'itorship, redakteurskap; leiding; *under the* ~ *of,* onder redaksie van.
ed'itress, (-es), redaktrise.
educabil'ity, onderwysbaarheid, opleibaarheid.
ed'ucable, opvoedbaar, leersaam, ontvanklik.
ed'ucand, opvoedeling.
ed'ucate, opvoed; onderwys, leer, opkweek, oplei; grootmaak; ~ **d,** opgevoed, (skrif)geleerd, ontwik= keld, geleerd.
educa'tion, opvoeding, opleiding, ontwikkeling, on= derwys, edukasie; skoolwese; opvoedkunde; *CLASSICAL* ~, klassieke opleiding; *COMPUL= SORY* ~, leerdwang; *your* ~ *has been sadly NEG= LECTED,* jy moet jou skoolgeld gaan terugvra;

educational

SYSTEM of ~, onderwysstelsel; **VISUAL** ~, aanskouingsonderrig; ~ **act**, onderwyswet.
educa'tional, opvoedkundig; onderwys~; ~ **ADVANCEMENT FUND**, studieaanspoorfonds; ~ **APPLIANCES**, leermiddele; ~ **INSITUTION**, opvoedingsinrigting; ~ **MATTERS**, onderwyssake; ~ **PAPER**, onderwysblad; ~ **TOUR**, studiereis; skoolreis; ~**ist**, opvoedkundige; ~ **ly**, in opvoedkundige opsig, op opvoedkundige gebied.
educa'tion department, departement van onderwys, onderwysdepartement.
educa'tionist, opvoeder, opvoedkundige, pedagoog.
ed'ucative, onderwys~; opvoedend, leersaam.
ed'ucator, opvoeder, onderwyser, opvoedkundige.
educe', uittrek; te voorskyn bring; aflei; afskei.
edu'cible, afleibaar; af te skei; af te trek.
educ'tion, afvoering; afleiding; uitlating; afvoer (vloeistof); ~ **pipe**, afvoerpyp, uitlaatbuis; ~ **valve**, afvoerklep, uitlaatklep.
edul'corate, reinig, suiwer; ontsuur; ontsout.
edulcora'tion, suiwering; ontsuring; ontsouting.
eel, paling, aal; *as slippery as an* ~, so glad soos 'n paling, so glad soos seep; ~**-like**, palingagtig; ~-**monger**, palingverkoper; ~**-pie**, palingpastei; ~-**pot**, palingfuik; ~**-shaped**, palingvormig; aalvormig; ~**-worm**, aalwurm, aaltjie, nematode; knopwortel, vrotpootjie; ~**-worm disease**, knopwortel; ~**y**, aalagtig, palingagtig; glad.
e'en *abbr. of* **even; evening**.
e'er, *abbr. of* **ever.**
eer'ie, eer'y, bygelowig, bang; benouend, grieselig, grillerig; huiweringwekkend, onheilspellend; grillig.
eer'iness, onheilspellendheid; bangheid, grieseligheid.
effa'ce, uitwis, uitvee; verdelg; oorskadu, in die skaduwee stel; ~ *oneself*, jou terugtrek, jou op die agtergrond hou; ~ **able**, uitwisbaar; ~**ment**, uitwissing; terugtrekking.
effect', (n) uitwerking, uitslag, gevolg; effek; algemene indruk; (pl) bate, besittinge, goed, klere, effekte; *BE of no* ~, geen uitwerking hê nie; *CALCULATED for* ~, op effek bereken; *CARRY into* ~, ten uitvoer bring; *CAUSE and* ~, oorsaak en gevolg; *FOR* ~, om indruk te maak; *GIVE* ~ *to*, uitvoering gee aan; *IN* ~, feitlik, inderdaad; in werklikheid; *to NO* ~, tevergeefs; *it has a PRETTY* ~, dit vertoon mooi; *a RESOLUTION to the* ~ *that*, 'n besluit wat daarop neerkom dat; *TAKE* ~, uitwerking hê; in werking tree; *WITH* ~ *from*, met ingang van; *WITHOUT* ~, geen uitwerking hê nie; (v) uitwerk, bewerk, teweegbring, bewerkstellig, doen, verwesenlik; (af)sluit (assuransie); ~ *an ARRANGEMENT*, 'n skikking tref; ~ *a CHANGE*, 'n verandering aanbring; ~ *IMPROVEMENTS*, verbeterings aanbring; ~ *a POLICY*, 'n polis aangaan.
effec'tive, (n) effektief; diensdoende (strydbare) manskappe; (a) kragdadig; doeltreffend, dienstig, werksaam, effektief, werkdadig; treffend; afdoende; ~ *FORCE*, effektiewe krag; ~ *HORSEPOWER*, effektiewe perdekrag; ~ *PRESSURE*, effektiewe druk; ~ *PULL*, effektiewe trekkrag, werklike trekkrag; ~ *RANGE*, effektiewe reikwydte, uitwerkingsafstand; ~**ness**, doeltreffendheid, doelmatigheid; dienstigheid.
effec'tual, doeltreffend; kragtig, kragdadig; afdoende; ~**ly**, met sukses, op doeltreffende wyse.
effec'tuate, uitvoer, volbring, bewerkstellig, verwesenlik, teweegbring.
effectua'tion, uitvoering, bewerkstelliging, verwesenliking.
effem'inacy, verwyfdheid, verweekliking.
effem'inate, (v) verwyf maak; week maak; (a) verwyf, ouvrouagtig; weekhartig; *become* ~, verweeklik; vervroulik.
effen'di, effendi.
eff'erent, efferent, afvoerend, wegvoerend, uitvoerend.
effervesce', opkook, gis, opbruis, opborrel; ~**nce**, opkoking, gisting, opbruising, gebruis; ~**nt**, (n) bruispoeier; (a) opbruisend, opborrelend; ~ *nt powder*, bruispoeier.

egg

effete', afgeleef, uitgeput; kragteloos; nie meer vrugbaar nie; ~**ness**, afgeleefdheid; futloosheid.
effica'cious, werksaam, werkdadig; kragtig, doelmatig, probaat, doeltreffend; ~**ness**, kragdadigheid; doeltreffendheid, werkdadigheid.
eff'icacy, krag, kragdadigheid; werksaamheid, werking; doeltreffendheid, doelmatigheid.
effi'ciency, werking; doeltreffendheid, doelmatigheid; bedrewenheid, bekwaamheid; kragdadigheid; deeglikheid; prestasievermoë; fiksheid; rendement (werktuigkunde); nuttigheidsgraad (meganies); geoefendheid, strydbaarheid (mil.); *mechanical* ~, nuttigheidsgraad; ~ **bonus**, diensbonus, prestasiebonus; ~ **curve**, nuttigheidskromme; ~ **expert**, doeltreffendheidsekspert, doeltreffendheidskundige; bedryfsingenieur; rasionaliseerder; ~ **plan**, doeltreffendheidsplan; ~ **system**, doeltreffendheidstelsel.
effi'cient, werkdadig; bekwaam, doelmatig, doeltreffend, geskik, vir sy taak bereken, bruikbaar, effisiënt; saakkundig.
eff'igy, (..gies), afbeeldsel, beeld, beeltenis, pop, effigie; *burn in* ~, in beeld verbrand.
ef'filate, uitdun, effileer (hare).
effloresce', kristalliseer; uitslaan (muur); skimmel; uitbot, ontluik, bloei, uitkom, effloresseer; ~**nce**, bloei, bloeityd; bloeisel, effloressensie; kristallisering, kristallisasie; uitslag, skimmel; ~**nt**, (n) skimmel; (a) bloeiend; kristalliserend; skimmel; ontluikend.
eff'luence, uitvloeiing, uitvloeisel.
eff'luent, (n) afval (fabriek); syrivier, tak; afstroming; uitvloeisel, uitloop; afvalwater, uitvloeiwater; effluent; rioolwater; (a) uitvloeiend.
effluv'ient, uitvloeiend.
effluv'ium, (..via), uitstroming, uitvloeiing; uitwaseming, fluïdum, effluvium.
eff'lux, efflu'xion, verloop (van tyd); uitvloeiing, uitstroming, uitvloeisel.
eff'ort, poging, inspanning, probeerslag; *MAKE an* ~, 'n poging aanwend; *by one's OWN* ~ *s*, deur eie inspanning; ~ **less**, sonder inspanning, passief; ongedwonge, natuurlik, maklik, met gemak.
effron'tery, (..ries), onbeskaamdheid, brutaliteit, astrantheid, parmantigheid.
effulge', skitter, glinster; ~**nce**, glans, skittering; ~**nt**, glansryk; skitterend, stralend.
effuse', uitgooi, uitgiet, uitstort; versprei, uitstraal.
effu'sion, uitstorting; ontboeseming; effusie.
effu'sive, uitstortend, oorlopend; rojaal, danig, kwistig, effusief; oordrewe hartlik; ~**ness**, danigheid.
E' flat, E-mol, es.
eft, sal(a)mander, molg.
egad'! op die aarde! by my kool!
egalita'rian, (n), gelykmaker, egalitariër, egalis; (a), gelykmakend, egalitaries, egalitêr; ~**ism**, egalitarisme.
egg, (n) eier; *BAD* ~, vrot eier; niksnuts, persoon met skadelike invloed, skobbejak; *put all one's* ~ *s in one BASKET*, alles in een onderneming waag; alles op een kaart sit; *FRIED* ~, gebakte eier; *as FULL as an* ~ *is of meat*, propvol; *better an* ~ *today than a HEN tomorrow*, een voël in die hand is beter as tien in die lug; *NEWLAID* ~ *(s)*, pasgelegde eier(s); *POACHED* ~, kalfsoog; *what has that to do with the PRICE of* ~ *s?* hoe raak dit die saak? *SCRAMBLED* ~ *(s)*, roereier(s); struifeier(s); *as SURE as* ~ *s are* ~ *s*, so waar as vet; *TREAD on* ~ *s*, op eiers loop; (v) met eiers gooi; met eiers bedek; eiers versamel; ~ *on*, aanhits, aanspoor, aanpor; ~ **and spoon race**, eier-in-die-lepel(wedren); ~**-basket**, eiermandjie; ~**-beater**, eierklitser; ~**-boiler**, eierkokertjie; ~**-bound**: *be* ~**-bound**, lê nood hê; ~**-box**, eierkissie; ~**-cake**, eierkoek; ~**-cell**, eiersel; ~**-circle**, eierkring; ~**-cosy**, eiermussie; ~**-cup**, eierkelkie; ~**-custard**, eiervla; ~**-dance**, eierdans; ~**-dealer**, eierkoper; ~**-dish**, eiergereg; ~**-eater**, eiervreter; ~**-flake**, eiervlokkie; ~**-flip**, geklitste eier, eierdrankie, eierbrandewyn; ~**-fruit**, eiervrug, brinjal; ~**-glass**, sandlopertjie; ~**-grenade**, eierhandgranaat; ~**-in-the-hat**, eier-in-die-hoed; ~**-lifter**, eierspaan; ~**-money**, eiergeld; ~**-moulding**,

eierlys; ~-**nest**, eiernes; ~-**nog**, eiermelkdrank; ~-**noodles**, eiersnysels; ~-**plant**, eierplant, brinjal; ~-**plum**, eierpruim; ~-**pouch**, eiersak; ~-**powder**, eierpoeier; ~-**pulp**, eierpulp; ~-**rack**, eierrakkie; ~-**sac**, eiersak(kie); ~-**sauce**, eiersous; ~-**shaped**, eiervormig; eierrond; ~-**shell**, eierdop; ~-**shell china**, kraakporselein; ~-**slice**, eierspaan; ~-**spoon**, eierlepel; ~-**stand**, eierstander, eierstelletjie; ~-**timer**, sandloper; ~-**tray**, eierrak, eierlaai; ~-**tube**, lêbuis; ~-**whip**, eierklopper; ~-**whisk**, eierklopper, eierklitser; ~-**white**, ei(er)wit; ~-**yolk**, dooier, eiergeel.
eglan'dulous, klierloos.
eg'lantine, eglantier, wilde kanferfoelie.
eg'o, ek, ego; ekheid, eie ek.
egocen'tric, egosentries, selfgerig; .. **tri'city**, egosentrisiteit.
eg'oism, selfsug, eieliefde, egoïsme; eksug, ekkerigheid.
eg'oist, selfsugtige mens, egoïs.
egotis'tic(al), selfsugtig, baatsugtig, egoïsties; ekkerig.
eg'otism, ekkerigheid, eiedunk; selfgenoegsaamheid, egotisme, eielof.
eg'otist, ekkerige mens.
eg'rappoir, ontstingelaar, égrappoir.
egre'gious, skokkend; kolossaal (ook ironies); reusagtig, uitblinkend.
eg'ress, uitgang.
egre'ssion, uitgang, uittog.
eg'ret, egret, wit reier *(Ardeidae)*; saadpluim.
E'gypt, Egipte; *as dark as ~'s night*, die Egiptiese duisternis.
Egyp'tian, (n) Egiptenaar; (a) Egipties; ~ **goose**, kolgans.
Egyptol'ogist, Egiptoloog.
Egyptol'ogy, Egiptologie.
eh? wat? nè? hè?
eid'er, eider(gans); eider(dons); ~**down**, eiderdons; veerkombers, donskombers; ~ **duck**, eidereend, donseend; ~ **goose**, eidergans, donsgans.
eid'ograph, eidograaf, .. **g'raphy**, eidografie.
eidol'on, (-s, .. la), drogbeeld, skim, spookbeeld; gogga; geïdealiseerde figuur.
eight, ag(t); *have had one over the ~*, die kruie was te sterk; 'n goeie raps weghê; hoog veertien wees; lekkerlyf wees; ~-**cylinder car**, agtsilindermotor.
eighteen', agt(t)ien; ~ **th**, agt(t)iende.
eight'fold, agtvoudig.
eighth, ag(t)ste; ~ **ly**, ten ag(t)ste; ~ **man**, agtsteman (rugby).
eight hour day, agtuurwerkdag.
eight'ieth, tagtigste.
eight'-seater, agtsitplekmotor.
eight'y, tagtig; *in the eighties*, in die jare tagtig, in die tagtigerjare.
ein'korn, koringsoort, einkorn.
einstei'nium, einsteinium.
eiren'icon, ire'nicon, vredevoorstel.
eisteddfod, (-s, -au), kunswedstryd, eisteddfod.
ei'ther, (pron) albei; een van twee (beide); ~ *of US*, enigeen van ons twee; ~ *of YOU must go*. een van julle twee moet gaan; (a) albei; een van twee; *in ~ CASE*, in albei gevalle; (adv) of; ook; *I don't know ~*, ek weet ook nie; *NOT that ~*, dit ook nie; (conj) of; ook; ~ *come or go*, kom of trap.
ejac'ulate, uitspuit, skiet; uitroep; uitstoot; uitskiet.
ejacula'tion, uitwerping; uitstorting, ejakulasie; uitroep, skreeu; uitskieting.
ejac'ulatory, uitstortend, uitwerpings-; ~ *prayer*, skietgebedjie.
eject', uitgooi, uitknikker, uitsmyt, uitwerp, uitsit, uitdrywe; skiet; ~ **a**, uitwerpsels; ~ **ion**, uitgooiing; uitwerping, uitdrywing; afsetting; (uit)skiet; ~ **ion seat**, uitskietstoel; ~ **ive**, uitwerpend; ~ **ment**, uitwerping, uitsetting; verdrywing; ~ **ment order**, uitsettingsbevel; ~ **or**, uitstoter, uitwerper, ejekteur; uitgooier, uitsmyter; uitskieter; ~ **or seat**, uitskietstoel.
eke, vermeerder, vergroot; aanvul; rek; ~ *out an EXISTENCE*, met moeite 'n bestaan maak; ~ *OUT*, aanvul; bymekaarkrap.

ekis'tics, ekistiek, nedersettingsleer.
ek'ka, ekka, eenperdrytuig.
elab'orate, (v) noukeurig uitwerk; deeglik bearbei; deurwerk, uitwerk, verwerk; (a) deurwrog; uitvoerig, noukeurig; ~ **ness**, uitvoerigheid; afwerking.
elabora'tion,verwerking, bearbeiding, noukeurige uitwerking (afwerking); vorming.
élan', fierheid, vurige ywer, besieldheid, fut, vuur, élan.
elapse', verloop, verbygaan, verstryk; ~ **d**, verstreke, verby.
elasmosau'rus, elasmosourus.
elas'tic, (n) rekker; gomlastiek, elastiek, rek; (a) veerkragtig, elasties, rekbaar; ~ **anklets**, gomlastiekvoetringe; ~ **bandage**, rekverband; ~ **conscience**, rekbare gewete; ~ **force**, spankrag.
elasti'city, veerkragtigheid, rekbaarheid, elastisiteit; spankrag, veerkrag.
elastic: ~ **limits**, rekgrens, elastisiteitsgrens; ~ **plaster**, rekpleister; kleefpleister; ~ **stocking**, rekkous; ~ **tissue**, rekweefsel.
elate', (v) verhef; opwek; opgeblase maak; aanmoedig; (a) hoogmoedig, trots, opgeblase; opgetoë, verblyd.
ela'terine, elaterien, -ine.
elat'erite, elateriet.
ela'tion, opgeblasenheid; verheffing, aanstellery; lewenslus; opgetoënheid; trots.
Elber'ta peach, Elberta(perske).
el'bow, (n) kromming, bog (van rivier); kniestuk; elmboog; elmboogstuk; *out AT ~ s*, met die elmboë deur die moue; in behoeftige omstandighede; armoedig gekleed; *LIFT the ~*, in die bottel kyk; te veel v.d. bottel hou; die bottel aanspreek; *more POWER to your ~*, sterkte; *at YOUR ~*, binne bereik, byderhand; (v) stoot, dring, druk, stamp (met die elmboog); ~ *someone OUT*, iem. uitstoot, verdring; ~ *one's WAY in*, jou indring; ~-**bend**, elmboogswaai; ~-**chair**, armstoel; ~-**fitting**, elmboog; ~-**grease**, moeilike handearbeid; spierkrag; poetswerk, ~-**joint**, elmbooggewrig; ~-**linings**, vensterbeskot; ~-**pipe**, elmboogpyp; ~-**rest**, armleuning; ~-**room**, speling, ruimte, bewegingsvryheid, speelruimte; ~ **spring**, hangveer.
eld, die ou tyd; ouderdom.
el'der¹, (n) ouer persoon; ouderling; (a) ouer; *the ~ of the two*, die oudste v.d. twee.
el'der², (n) vlier(boom); ~-**berry**, vlierbessie; ~-**flower**, vlierblom.
el'dership, ouderlingskap.
el'derly, ouerig; bejaard, bedaag.
el'der-tree, vlierboom.
el'dest, oudste.
El Dorad'o, Eldorado; eldorado, goudland.
elect', (n) uitverkorene; (v) kies, uitkies; uitverkies; verkies, ~ *as chairman*, tot voorsitter kies, (a) uitgekies; verkore; gekose; *bride ~*, aanstaande bruid; ~ **ed**, verkose.
elec'tion, keuse; kiesing; verkiesing, eleksie; *general ~*, algemene verkiesing; ~ **agent**, verkiesingsagent; ~ **bureau**, verkiesingsburo; ~ **contest**, verkiesingstryd; ~ **cry**, verkiesingsleuse, verkiesingskreet; ~ **day**, stemdag.
electioneer', stemme werf; deelneem aan 'n verkiesing; ~ **ing**, stemwerwery; verkiesingswerk; ~ **ing address**, verkiesingsrede; ~ **ing agent**, verkiesingsagent.
elec'tion: ~ **expenses**, verkiesingskoste; ~ **fever**, verkiesingskoors; ~ **fight**, verkiesingstryd; ~ **law**, kieswet; ~ **malpractices**, verkiesingsmaneuver; ~ **meeting**, eleksievergadering, verkiesingsbyeenkoms; ~ **programme**, verkiesingsprogram; ~ **promise**, eleksiebelofte; ~ **propaganda**, verkiesingspropaganda; ~ **result**, verkiesingsuitslag; ~ **shock**, verkiesingskok; ~ **speech**, (-es), bokwatoespraak, verkiesingstoespraak; ~ **time**, eleksietyd.
elec'tive, kies-; verkiesings-; verkose; verkiesend; keur-.
elec'tor, kieser; keurvors.
elec'toral, kies-; kiesers-; keurvorstelik; ~ **college**, kieskollege; ~ **district**, kiesdistrik, kiesafdeling; ~

electorate 866 *eliminate*

law, verkiesingswet; kieswet; ~ **officer,** kiesbeampte; ~ **system,** kiesstelsel.
elec'torate, kiesers, kieserskorps; keurvorstedom.
elec'tress, (-es), kieseres; keurvorstin, keurprinses.
elec'tric, elektries.
elec'trical, elektries, elektrisiteits=; ~ *ENGINEER,* elektriese ingenieur; ~ *ENGINEERING,* elektriese ingenieurswese; ~ *UNIT,* elektriese eenheid.
elec'tric: ~ **arc,** vlamboog, ligboog; ~ **battery,** elektriese battery; ~ **blue,** staalblou; ~ **bulb,** gloeilamp; ~ **cable,** elektriese kabel; ~ **chair,** elektriese stoel; ~ **charge,** elektriese lading; ~ **circuit,** elektriese (stroom)kring; ~ **comb,** elektriese kam; ~ **control,** elektriese beheer; ~ **current,** elektriese stroom; ~ **eel,** sidderaal, beefaal, trilpaling.
electri'cian, elektrisiën.
electri'city, elektrisiteit; *FRICTIONAL* ~, wryswingselektrisiteit; *GALVANIC* ~, galvaniese elektrisiteit; *MAGNETIC* ~, magnetiese elektrisiteit; *NEGATIVE* ~, negatiewe elektrisiteit; *POSITIVE* ~, positiewe elektrisiteit; *STATIC* ~, statiese elektrisiteit; *THERMAL* ~, termoëlektrisiteit.
elec'tric: ~ **jar,** Leidse fles; ~ **light,** elektriese lig; ~ **meter,** elektrisiteitsmeter; ~ **motor,** elektromotor; ~ **plant,** elektriese installasie; ~ **ray,** drilvis; ~ **razor,** elektriese skeermes; ~ **shock,** elektriese skok; ~ **sign,** reklamelig; ~ **skate,** drilvis, sidderrog; ~ **socket,** steeksok; ~ **standard,** elektriese paal; ligpaal; ~ **storm,** elektriese storm, kwaai donderstorm; ~ **torch,** flitslig, toorts; ~ **van,** elektriese wa; ~ **welding,** elektriese sweising; ~ **wire,** elektriese draad.
electrifi'able, elektrifiseerbaar.
electrifica'tion, elektrifikasie, elektrifisering; elektrisering.
elec'trify, (..fied), elektriseer, elektrifiseer; ontstel, skok; ~**ing-machine,** elektriseermasjien.
electrobiol'ogy, elektrobiologie.
electrocard'iogram, elektrokardiogram.
electrocard'iograph, elektrokardiograaf.
electrocardiog'raphy, elektrokardiografie.
electrochem'istry, elektrochemie.
elec'trocute, elektries teregstel; doodskok.
electrocu'tion, elektrokusie.
elec'trode, elektrode; ~ **holder,** elektrodetang.
electrodynam'ics, elektrodinamika.
electro-ence'phalograph, elektroënkefalogram, -ënsefologram.
electro'graphy, elektrografie.
electrokinet'ics, elektrokinetika.
electrolier', elektriese kroonlugter.
electrol'ogy, elektrisiteitsleer.
electrol'ysis, galvaniese ontleding, elektrolise.
elec'trolyte, elektroliet, batterysuur.
elec'trolyze, elektroliseer.
electromag'net, elektromagneet; ~**'ic,** elektromagneties; ~**ism,** elektromagnetisme.
elektrom'eter, elektrometer.
elec'tromotive, elektromotories.
electromot'or, (n) elektromotor; **(a)** elektromotories.
elec'tron, elektron.
electron'ic, elektronies; ~ **computer,** elektroniese rekenaar; ~ **data processing,** elektroniese dataverwerking (EDV); ~ **microscope,** elektronmikroskoop; ~ **systems analyst,** elektroniese stelselontleder.
electron'ics, elektronika; elektroneleer, elektronestudie.
elec'tron volt, elektronvolt.
electrop'athy, elektroterapie.
elec'trophore, electroph'orus, elektrofoor.
elec'troplate, (n) pleetwerk, galvanies versilwerde ware; (v) (galvanies) versilwer; verpleet, elektroplateer; ~**r,** elektroversilweraar, verpleter, elektroplateerder.
elec'troplating, elektroplatering, verpleting.
elec'troscope, elektroskoop.
electrostat'ics, elektrostatika.
electrotech'nical, elektrotegnies.
electrotech'nics, elektrotegniek.
electrotechno'logy, elektrotegnologie.
electrother'apist, elektroterapis.

electrotherapeut'ics, elektroterapie.
electrother'apy, elektroterapie.
electrotherm'al, elektrotermies.
elec'trotropism, elektrotropie.
elec'trotype, elektrotipie; ~ **plate,** galvano.
elec'trotypy, elektrotipie; galvanoplastiek.
elec'trum, elektrum, silwerhoudende gouderts.
elec'tuary, lekmedisyne, lekstroop.
eleemos'ynary, liefdadigheids=, gratis; van aalmoese lewende.
el'egance, ..**gancy,** sierlikheid, bevalligheid, statigheid, swier(igheid), elegansie; keurigheid, fraaiheid, vernaamheid.
el'egant, sierlik, bevallig, smaakvol, statig, elegant, verfyn, keurig, swierig, fraai, grasieus.
elegi'ac, (n) elegiese digmaat; **(a)** elegies; ~ **poet,** treurdigter; ~**s,** elegiese poësie.
el'egist, treursangdigter.
el'egize, 'n treursang skrywe; weeklaag.
el'egy, (..gies), elegie, treursang, treurlied, roudig, (dode)klaaglied.
el'ement, element; grondbestanddeel, grondstof; (pl) elemente; beginsels; *be IN one's* ~, in jou element wees, gelukkig wees, jou tuis voel; *be OUT of one's* ~, jou ontuis voel, ongelukkig wees.
elemen'tal, (n) elementaal; **(a)** aanvanklik, oorspronklik; wesenlik, onvermeng, elementaal, fundamenteel.
elemen'tary, elementêr, eenvoudig; aanvanklik, allereerste; grond=, aanvangs=; ~ **school,** laerskool.
e'lemi, elemi, reukhars.
ele'nchus, elenchus.
elenc'tic, elenkties.
el'ephant, olifant; *a WHITE* ~, 'n lastige en kosbare besitting (gebou); ~ **bull,** olifantbul; ~ **cow,** olifantkoei; ~ **disease,** globidiose (beeste); ~ **ear,** olifantsoor; ~ **fish,** doodskop, ~ **gun,** olifantgeweer; ~ **hunt,** olifantjag; ~ **hunter,** olifantjagter.
elephanti'asis, olifantsiekte, elefantiase.
elephan'tine, olifantagtig; ontsaglik, tamaai; lomp.
elephant: ~ **seal,** see-olifant; ~**'s ear,** bobbejaanoor; olifantsoor; skeefblaarvaring; ~**'s fern,** skeefblaarvaring, begonavaring; ~**'s foot,** olifantpoot, skilpad (plant); spekboom; ~ **shrew,** klaasneus; ~ **skin (disease),** olifantvel(siekte), besnoitose; ~**'s trunk** olifantslurp; halfmens, noordappel; ~ **tusk,** olifanttand; ~ **wood,** loodhout.
eleuth'eromania, vryheidswaansin.
el'evate, ophef, optel, verhef, verhoog; veredel.
el'evated, verhewe; aangeklam; ~ *with,* besiel met; ~ **railway,** lugspoor(weg).
el'evating, besielend, verheffend; ~ **bar,** hoogtestang; ~ **plane,** hefvlak; ~ **screw,** hoogtestelskroef; ~ **sight,** visier.
eleva'tion, opheffing, verheffing, verhoging; verhewenheid; hoogte (graad); hoogheid; elevasie; opstand; hoek, visierhoogte (van kanon); aansig; vertikale projeksie; ~ **angle,** hoogtehoek, elevasiehoek.
el'evator, verheffer; ligter; hyser, elevator, (hys)kraan, hysbak, hystoestel, hysmasjien; hefspier; hoogteroer (vliegtuig); graansuier; ~ **cable,** hystou; ~ **casing,** hyserhulsel; ~ **chute,** graansuierstortgeut; ~ **door,** hyserdeur; ~ **pipe,** hyserpyp; ~ **pump,** hyspomp; ~ **worm,** hyserwurm.
elev'en, elf; elftal; (kriekettspan; ~**fold,** elfvoudig.
elev'enses, voormiddagtee, elfuur(tee).
elev'enth, elfde; *at the* ~ *hour,* ter elfder ure; op die tippie.
elf, (elves), elf, kaboutermannetjie, dwerg; ~**-child,** wisselkind; ~ **in, (n)** elf, dwerg, kleuter; **(a)** elfagtig, feëriek, dwergagtig; ~**ish,** elfagtig, ondeund, plaerig; ~**-lock,** heksevlegsel.
eli'cit, te voorskyn bring, aan die lig bring, uitlok.
elide', uitlaat; elideer.
eligibil'ity, (ver)kiesbaarheid, geskiktheid, aanneemlikheid, paslikheid.
el'igible, verkiesbaar, verkieslik, wenslik; paslik, geskik; *an* ~ *BACHELOR,* 'n goeie party; ~ *for MEMBERSHIP,* tot lid verkiesbaar; ~ *for RE-ELECTION,* herkiesbaar.
elim'inate, uitlaat, weglaat, verwyder, elimineer, uit=

elimination 867 **embrangle**

skakel, uithaal; oor die hoof sien; verdryf (mat.), wegsyfer.
elimina'tion, uitlating, weglating, uitskakeling; verdringing, verwydering, eliminasie; verdrywing (mat.).
eli'sion, elisie, uitlating, weglating.
élite', keur, blom, elite; ~ **corps,** keurkorps.
elix'ir, afkooksel; hartversterking, elikser.
elk, elk, Europese eland.
ell¹, el.
ell², elmboog (van pyp); vleuel (van gebou).
ellipse', ellips.
ellip'sis, (..ipses), woorduitlating, ellips.
ellip'sograph, ellipsograaf.
ellip'soid, ellipsoïed, ellipsoïde.
ellip'soid, ellipsoid'al, ellipsoïdaal.
ellip'tical, ellipties, ovaal; ~ **hull,** elliptiese romp; ~ **spring,** elliptiese veer; ~ **wing,** elliptiese vlerk.
elm, olm, iep.
El'mo: *St.* ~ *'s fire,* St. Elmsvuur.
elocu'tion, voordragleer, spreekonderwys, elokusie; welsprekendheid, voordrag; ~**ary,** voordrags-; ~ **contest,** voordragwedstryd; ~**ist,** spraakonderwyser; kunsredenaar; voordraer; deklamator; ~ **teacher,** elokusieonderwyser(es).
el'ongate, (v) uitrek; verleng; langer maak; (a) langwerpig, spits; ~**d,** verleng; ~*d shell,* myngranaat.
elonga'tion, verlenging; elongasie (sterrek.); afstand; ~ **stage,** pypstadium.
elope', wegloop met 'n minnaar; dros; (haar laat) skaak; ~**ment,** wegloop; skaking, ontvoering; ~**r,** skaker, ontvoerder.
el'oquence, welsprekendheid.
el'oquent, welsprekend, (wel)bespraak; veelseggend.
else, anders; *ANYONE* ~, iem. anders? nog iem.? enigeen anders? *ANYTHING* ~, iets anders; nog iets; *EVERYBODY* ~, al die ander; *NOTHING* ~, niks anders nie; *SOMEWHERE* ~, êrens anders; *WHERE* ~? waar anders? *WHO* ~? wie anders? ~ **where,** êrens anders, anderpad (kyk), elders.
elu'cidate, ophelder, toelig, verklaar, uitlê, verhelder, verduidelik, opklaar.
elucida'tion, opheldering, toeligting, verduideliking, verheldering, uitleg.
elu'cidative, ophelderend, verklarend.
elu'cidator, toeligter, uitlêer, verklaarder; ~**y,** ophelderend, toeligtend.
elude', ontwyk, ontduik; ontgaan; ontsnap; vermy.
elu'sion, ontwyking, ontduiking.
elus'ive, ontduikend, ontwykend; onbegrypbaar; misleidend, bedrieglik; ~**ness,** ontwyking, ontduiking; slimstreke.
elus'ory, elu; ontwykend, bedrieglik, misleidend.
elu'tion, uitwassing, elusie.
elutria'tion, uitwassing (mynb.)
el'ver, jong paling.
el'vish, elfagtig; ondeund.
Elys'ian, Elisies, verruklik, geluksalig.
Elys'ium, Elisium, Elisiese velde, hemel.
el'ytron, (clytra), rugskild; elitron, skede (van vrou); dekvlerk.
em, em.
ema'ciate, (v) uitmergel, maer maak; (a) uitgemergel, uitgeteer, vermaer; *become* ~*d,* wegteer, uitteer.
emacia'tion, vermaering, uitmergeling, uittering.
emalange'ni, emalangeni (Swazi-geldeenheid).
em'anate, uitgaan van, afkomstig wees van; uitvloei, voortvloei, voortkom; uitstraal, emaneer; uitwasem.
emana'tion, uitvloeiing, voortvloeiing; emanasie; uitstraling; uitwaseming.
eman'cipate, vrymaak, vrystel, vry verklaar, bevry, mondig maak, emansipeer; ~**d,** vry; modern.
emancipa'tion, vrymaking, vrylating, vryverklaring, emansipasie; handligting; meerderjarigheidsverklaring.
eman'cipator, vrymaker, bevryder, emansipator, emansipeerder.
eman'cipist, vrygelatene, ontslaande gevangene.
emar'ginate, uitgerand.
emas'culate, (v) ontman, sny, regmaak; emaskuleer;

ontsenu, verswak, verwyf maak; (a) gesny, reggemaak; verwyf.
emascula'tion, ontmanning, sny, emaskulasie; verwyfdheid.
embalm', balsem; ~**er,** balsemer; ~**ing,** balseming; ~**ment,** balseming.
embank', indyk, opdam; ~**ment,** opdamming, indyking; dyk, skoorwal, wal, damwal.
embarg'o, (n) (-es), verbod, beslag, embargo, inbeslaglegging (skepe); (v) beslag lê op.
embark', skeepgaan, aan boord gaan, inskeep; jou begeef in; aanvaar; aanpak; ~ *on a project,* 'n saak aanpak, jou in 'n saak begeef.
embarka'tion, inskeping; aanpakking; ~ **duties,** inskepingsdiens; ~ **establishment,** inskepingsinrigting; ~ **leave,** inskepingsverlof, skeepgaanverlof; ~ **officer,** inskepingsoffisier; ~ **order,** inskepingsbevel; ~ **port,** inskepingshawe; ~ **return,** inskepingstaat.
embar'rass, verleë maak; hinder, belemmer; verwar, bemoeilik; in verleentheid bring; ~**ed,** verleë, verbouereerd, verbysterd, verward, soos 'n natgereënde hoender; met iets in sy maag sit; op sy neus staan en kyk; in die skuld; ~**ing,** moeilik, pynlik; belemmerend; *vague and ~ing,* vaag en verwarrend; ~**ment,** verleentheid, belemmering, verbystering, verwarring; hindernis; skuld.
em'bassy, (..ssies), gesantskap; afvaardiging; gesantskapsgebou; ambassade.
embat'tle, in slagorde opstel; versterk; van kantele voorsien; ~*d wall,* vestingmuur.
embay', in 'n baai opsluit; insluit; **ment,** baaivorming, insluiting.
embed', (-ded), insluit, laat sak in; vassit.
embell'ish, mooi maak, versier, opsier, verfraai; ~**er,** verfraaier; ~**ment,** verfraaiing, vermooiing, opsiering, versiering; sieraad.
em'ber, stukkie gloeiende kool; (pl) warm as, sintels, gloeiende kole; ~ **days,** vasdae.
embez'zle, bedrieglik toe-eien, verduister, verdonkermaan, steel, ontvreem; ~**ment,** bedrieglike toe-eiening, verduistering, ontvreemding; ~**r,** bedrieër, verduisteraar.
embitt'er, verbitter, versuur, vergal; ~**ment,** verbittering, vergalling, gebetenheid.
emblaz'on, (opsigtig) versier; blasoeneer; verheerlik; ophemel, uitbasuin; ~**ry,** blasoenering; prag, praal.
em'blem, (n) sinnebeeld, simbool, embleem; (v) versinnebeeld; ~**at'ic(al),** sinnebeeldig, emblematies.
em'blematize, versinnebeeld, sinnebeeldig voorstel, as simbool dien, emblematiseer.
em'blements, grondopbrengs, wins uit gesaaides.
embod'iment, beliggaming.
embod'y, (..died), beliggaam, verpersoonlik; inlyf, omvat, insluit.
embog', (-ged), in 'n moeras stort (raak).
embogue', uitmond.
em'bolden, verstout; aanmoedig.
em'bolism, embolie, bloedvatverstopping; propvorming.
em'bolus, klont, embolus.
embonpoint', gesetheid.
embos'om, omhels; omsluit.
emboss', in reliëf maak, siseleer, bosseleer; ~**ed,** gedrewe, verhewe, reliëf-; ~*ed printing,* reliëfdruk, verhewe druk; ~**ing,** hoogdruk; ~**ing board,** dryfplank; reliëfbord; ~**ment,** reliëfwerk; verhewenheid.
embouchure', mond (van rivier); mondstuk (van fluit).
embow'el = **disembowel.**
embow'er, met bome insluit (omgeef).
embrace', (n) omarming, omhelsing; (v) omarm, omhels; omklem, aangryp; aansluit; insluit, omvat; aanvaar; ~ *an OFFER,* 'n aanbod aanvaar; *the REPORT* ~*s,* die rapport sluit in; ~ *SOMEONE,* iem. omhels, om die hals val; ~**able,** omhelsbaar; aangrypbaar; ~**ment,** omhelsing; aangryping; ~**r,** omhelser.
embranch'ment, vertakking.
embrang'le, verwar, verwikkel.

embra'sure, skietgat; indieping; afskuinsing.
embrit'tle, bros maak; ~**ment**, broswording.
em'brocate, invryf, invrywe, insmeer.
embroca'tion, smeergoed, vryfmiddel, embrokasie.
embroid'er, borduur, bestik; opsier, versien; voort= borduur, uitwei; ~**ed**, geborduur; ~*ed lace*, bor= duurkant; ~**er**, borduurder; ~**ess, (-es)**, borduur= ster.
embroid'ery, borduurwerk, borduursel; borduur= kuns; uitweiding; opsiering; ~ **canvas**, borduur= gaas; ~ **cotton**, borduurgaring; ~ **floss**, vlossy; ~ **frame**, borduurraam; ~ **scissors**, borduurskêr; ~ **stitch**, borduursteek; ~ **thread**, borduurgaring, -gare.
embroil', verwar, verwikkel; in stryd (onenigheid) bring; ~**ment**, verwikkeling; onenigheid, rusie.
embrown', bruin maak.
em'bryo, (-s), kiem, embrio; saadkiem; vrugkiem; *in* ~, in wording, in die dop.
embryogen'ic, embriogeen.
embryog'eny, embriogenie.
embryolog'ic, embriologies.
embryol'ogist, embrioloog.
embryol'ogy, embriologie, ontwikkelingsleer.
em'bryo nation, embriovolk, volk-in-wording.
embryon'ic, embrionies, embrionêr, embrionaal; in wording.
em'bryo sac, kiemsak.
embryot'omy, embriotomie.
embui'a, imbuia.
embus', (-sed), op 'n bus klim (sit); ~**sing**, instap (bus, trein).
emcee', (sl.), seremoniemeester, compère.
emend', emendeer, verbeter; ~**a'tion**, verbetering, emendasie.
em'endator, verbeteraar, emendator.
ęm'endatory, verbeterend, emenderend.
em'erald, (n) smarag; (a) smaraggroen, smarag=; *E*~ *Isle*, Ierland; ~ **copper**, dioptaas; ~ **cuckoo**, mooi= meisie(koekoek); ~ **green**, smaraggroen.
emerge', opkom, opduik, te voorskyn kom; verrys, oprys; ontstaan; jou voordoen; blyk.
emer'gence, opduiking, verskyning; uitwas (bot.); *angle of* ~, uittredingshoek.
emer'gency, (..cies), oprysing; onverwagte gebeurte= nis; dringende geval, noodgeval; *in CASE of* ~, in geval van nood; *PROCLAIM a state of* ~, 'n noodtoestand afkondig; ~ **act**, noodwet; ~ **aero= drome**, noodvliegveld; ~ **airport**, noodlughawe; ~ **brake**, noodrem; ~ **committee**, dagbestuur; ~ **coupling**, noodkoppeling; ~ **debate**, spoeddebat; ~ **door**, nooddeur; ~ **dwelling**, noodwoning; ~ **embankment**, noodwal; ~ **exit**, nooduitgang; ~ **expenses**, onvoorsiene uitgawe(s); ~ **fund**, nood= hulpfonds; ~ **halt**, noodhalte; noodhalthouding; ~ **ladder**, noodleer; ~ **landing**, noodlanding; ~ **lighting**, noodverligting; ~ **man**, noodhulp; ~ **measure(s)**, noodmaatreël(s); ~ **meeting**, spoedver= gadering; ~ **money**, noodgeld; ~ **nursing**, nood= verpleging; ~ **operation**, noodoperasie; ~ **power**, noodbevoegdheid; ~ **rations**, noodrantsoen; ~ **re= gulation(s)**, noodregulasie(s); ~ **run**, noodvaart; ~ **session**, spoedsitting; ~ **shaft**, noodskag; ~ **squad**, noodploeg; ~ **stair(s)**, brandtrap, noodtrap; ~ **station**, noodhulppos; ~ **stock**, noodvoorraad; ~ **switch**, noodskakelaar; ~ **tank**, noodtenk; ~ **transport**, noodvoertuig.
emer'gent, oprysend; dringend; voortkomend, verry= send.
eme'ritus, rustend, emeritus; ~ **professor**, emeritus= (professor), professor emeritus.
em'erods, aambeie.
emer'sion, tevoorskynkoming; (weer)verskyning, emersie, sigbaarwording.
em'ery, skuursteen, amaril; ~ **bag**, amaril(poeier)= sakkie; ~**-board**, amarilbord; skuurpapier; skuur= bord; ~**-cloth**, skuurlap, amarildoek; skuurlinne; ~ **dust**, amarilpoeier; ~**-paper**, skuurpapier; ~ **paste**, amarilpasta; ~ **stick**, amarilvyl; polyshout; ~**-wheel**, slypskyf, vuursteen, amarilskyf.
emet'ic, (n) braakmiddel, vomitief, emetikum; (a) braak=, opbringend.

émeute', (f.), emeute, oproer, volksopstand.
emic'tion, waterafskeiding; urine.
em'igrant, (n) landverhuiser, emigrant, trekker; (a) trekkend, uitwykend, verhuisend, emigrerend.
em'igrate, trek, uitwyk, verhuis, emigreer.
emigra'tion, landverhuising, trek, uitwyking, emigra= sie.
em'igratory, trekkend, emigrerend.
é'migré, emigré, uitgewekene.
em'inence, verhewenheid; hoogte; uitstekendheid, voortreflikheid; eminensie, hoogwaardigheid, be= roemdheid; onderskeiding; ~ **grise**, eminence gri= se, vertrouensman, vertroulike agent.
em'inent, hoog, verhewe; uitstekend, voortreflik; eminent, hoogwaardig; ~**ly**, uiters, besonder, hoogs, by uitstek.
emir', emir.
em'issary, (..ries), afgesant; handlanger; agent, spioen.
emi'ssion, uitsending, uitstorting; uitgifte; uitlating (gas); uitstraling (elek.); verspreiding, emissie; af= skeiding; ~ *of LIGHT*, liguitstraling; *SEMINAL* ~, saadlosing.
emiss'ive, uitstralend; uitsendend.
emit', (**-ted**), uitstuur, uitgee, uitvaardig, afgee; uit; uitstraal.
em'mer, koringsoort, emmer.
em'met, mier.
emoll'iate, versag; ontspan; ondoeltreffend maak; verwyf maak.
emoll'ient, (n) versagter, versagtende middel; (a) ver= sagtend; verwekend; ~ *lotion*, versagtingsmiddel.
emol'ument, verdienste, besoldiging, salaris, loon, emolument(e); byverdienste; ~**s**, byverdienste, emolumente.
emo'tion, aandoening, emosie, gevoel, ontroering; ~**al**, gevoelig; aandoenlik; gevoels=, emosioneel; liggeroer; ~**alism**, oorgevoeligheid; gevoelsuitstor= ting, emosionalisme; ~**al'ity**, gevoeligheid, emosi= onaliteit; ~**alize**, tot 'n gevoelsaak maak, emosio= naliseer.
emot'ive, gevoels=, emosioneel; emotief; ~ **meaning**, emotiewe betekenis, gevoelswaarde, gevoelsbete= kenis.
empale', palissadeer.
empan'el, (-led), op 'n naamrol plaas; ~ *a jury*, 'n jurie saamstel.
em'pathy, invoeling, empatie.
em'peror, keiser; ~ **moth**, pouoogmot; ~**ship**, keiser= skap.
em'phasis, (..phases), nadruk, klemtoon, klem.
em'phasize, met nadruk uitspreek, met klem verse= ker, beklemtoon; aandik.
empha'tic, nadruklik, uitdruklik, met klem, emfaties; ~ **accent**, emfatiese klem; ~ **al(ly)**, nadruklik; ~ *not*, volstrek nie; ~ **form**, nadruksvorm.
emphyse'ma, luggeswel, emfiseem.
emphyteus'is, erfpagreg.
emphyteut'a, erfpagter.
em'pire, ryk, keiserryk; heerskappy; *E*~, Empire (styl); *E*~ *Marketing BOARD*, Ryksbemarkings= raad; ~ *BUILDER*, ryksbouer; *E*~ *EXHIBI= TION*, Rykstentoonstelling, Rykskou; *Holy ROMAN E*~, Heilige Romeinse Ryk.
empir'ic, empirikus.
empi'ric(al), empiries, proefondervindelik, op onder= vinding gegrond; ~ **remedy**, huismiddel.
empi'ricism, empirisisme, empirie, ervaringsleer; kwaksalwery.
empi'ricist, empirikus, empiris; kwaksalwer.
empi'rics, ervaringsleer.
emplace', verskans, opstel; ~**ment**, terrein; stelling; geskutstand; plasing.
emplane', inlaai; instap, aan boord gaan (vlieg= tuig).
employ', (n) diens; besigheid; *IN the* ~ *of*, in diens van; *OUT of* ~, sonder werk, werkloos; (v) besig; gebruik; werk gee, emplojeer; besig hou; in diens hê; in diens neem; aanwend; ~ *ONESELF*, jou be= sig hou; ~ *your TIME*, jou tyd bestee; ~**able**, bruikbaar, diensbaar; aanwendbaar.
employ'ed, werksaam; *BE* ~, werksaam wees; ~

employ   869   *encyclop(a)edist*

ON, besig met; *SELF* ~, selfgeëmplojeer; *THE* ~, werkers, persone in diens.
employ': ~ **ee**, beampte, werksman, werker, bediende, werknemer; ~ **er**, werkgewer, baas.
employ'ment, werk, besigheid; diens; gebruik, aanwending; beroep, amp; werkverskaffing, werkvoorsiening; diensgeleentheid; werkverband, diensverband, werkbesetting; inwerkneming, indiensneming; *BE in* ~, werk hê; ~ *of CAPITAL*, aanwending (gebruik) van kapitaal; *OUT of* ~, sonder werk, werkloos; ~ **agency**, werkverskaffingsagentskap, arbeidsburo; ~ **bureau**, arbeidsburo; ~ **contract**, dienskontrak; ~ **exchange**, werkverskaffingsburo; arbeidsuitruiling; ~ **injury**, besering by werk; ~ **office**, werkverskaffingskantoor; ~ **opportunity**, werk(s)geleentheid; ~ **service**, werkverskaffingsdiens.
empois'on, verbitter; vergiftig.
empor'ium, (..ria, -s), mark, handelsplek, emporium, stapelplaas, entrepot; magasyn; grootwinkel.
empow'er, magtig, volmag gee, opdra; in staat stel; ~ *ed to*, gemagtig om.
em'press, (-es), keiserin.
emprise', (ridderlike) avontuur.
emp'ties, leë houers.
emp'tiness, leegheid, leegte; ydelheid; holheid.
emp'ty, (v) (..tied), leegmaak, lig (uit briewebus); ontlas; uithaal; uitmond (rivier); leegloop, leeg word; (a) leeg, boomskraap; ydel; sinledig, betekenisloos; leeghoofdig; ~ *COW*, nie-dragtige koei; ~ *THREAT*, holle dreigement; ~ *VESSELS make the most noise*, leë vate klink die holste; die hen wat die hardste (mooste) kekkel, lê nie die meeste eiers nie; ~ *WEIGHT*, leeggewig; ~ *WORDS*, hol woorde; ~ **-handed**, met leë hande; ~ **-headed**, dom, onnosel, leeghoofdig; ylhoofdig; onwetend; ~ **ing**, lediging; ~ **returns**, (teruggestuurde) leë houers.
empur'ple, purper (pers) verf.
empyre'al, hoogverhewe; hemels.
empyre'an, (n) hoogste hemel; (a) hoogverhewe.
em'u, emoe.
e'mulate, nastrewe, wedywer met, ewenaar.
emula'tion, nastrewing, wedywer, ewenaring.
em'ulative, wedywerend.
em'ulator, mededinger; nastrewer.
em'ulous, naywerig; mededingend, wedywerend.
emul'gent, (n) emulgator, emulgeermiddel; (a) emulgerend.
emul'sify, (..fied), emulsifiseer, emulgeer, emulseer.
emul'sion, emulsie.
emul'sive, versagtend, emulsie=.
emunc'tory, (n) (..ries), afskeidingsorgaan; afvoerkanaal; (a) afvoerend; snuit=, snultings=; atvoerend, afvoer=.
en¹, en.
en², (Fr.), in; ~ *BLOC*, in een klomp; ~ *ROUTE*, op pad, onderweg; ~ *VILLE*, (Eur.), *E.V.* (op koeverte), alhier, hier ter stede.
ena'ble, in staat stel, bekwaam maak, help, *enabling act*, magtigingswet.
enact', afspeel, vertoon; vasstel, verorden, uitvaardig, verordineer; bekragtig; opvoer, speel (rol); ~ *ing clauses*, nadere bepalings; ~ **ment**, verordening, bevel, uitvaardiging; ~ **or**, uitvaardiger; uitvoerder.
enam'el, (n) glasuur (tande); emalje, brandverf, enemmel, erd; smeltglas; brandskilderwerk; (v) (-led), emaljeer, verglaas, vererd; brandskilder; ~ **dish**, emaljeskottel; ~ **led**, verglaas, vererd; ~ *led work*, brandskilderwerk; enemmelwerk, emaljewerk; ~ **ler**, brandskilder, verglaser; emaljeerder; ~ **ling**, enemelwerk, emaljewerk; ~ **paint**, emaljeverf; enemmelverf; glansverf, glasuurverf; ~ **work**, brandskilderwerk; enemmelwerk, emaljewerk.
enam'our, verlief maak, bekoor; ~ *ed of*, verlief op; verruk oor, bekoor deur.
enathe'ma, enatema.
enantiomorph'ic, enantiomorf.
en'argite, energiet.
enarthros'is, koeëlgewrig.
e'nate, uitgloei.
ena'tion, uitgloeiing, uitgloeisel.

encage', opsluit, in 'n hok sit.
encamp', leër, laer trek, kampeer; ~ **ment**, kamp, leërplaas; staanplek.
encap'sulate, inkapsel; insluit; opsom.
encapsula'tion, inkapseling; insluiting; opsomming, oorsig.
encase', oortrek; wegsluit; insluit, inwikkel.
encash', wissel, inkasseer; in kontant ontvang.
encaus'tic, (n) enkoustiek; (a) ingebrand, enkousties.
enceinte', (n) omwalling, ringmuur; (a) swanger.
encephal'ic, harsing=, brein=.
encephalit'is, harsingontsteking, ensefalitis, enkefalitis.
enceph'alogram, ensefalogram, enkefalogram.
enceph'alograph, ensefalograaf, enkefalograaf.
encephalomalac'ia, harsingverweking.
encephalomeningi'tis, harsing-en-harsingvliesontsteking.
encephalomyeli'tis, harsing-en-rugmurgontsteking.
encephalomeningi'tis, harsing-en-rugmurgontsteking.
enceph'alon, brein, harsings.
enchain', boei, in kettings slaan.
enchant', betower, verruk, bekoor; ~ **ed**, betowerd; verruk; ~ *ed ring*, towerring; ~ **er**, towenaar; bekoorder; ~ **ing**, verruklik, betowerend, bekoorlik; ~ **ment**, bekoring, bekoorlikheid, betowering; ~ **ress**, (-es), towenares; bekoorster.
encir'cle, omsingel, omring, omgewe; ~ **ment**, omtrekking.
encir'cling, omsluiting
enclasp', omvat, omsluit, omhels.
enclave', ingeslote grondgebied, enklave.
enclis'is, enklise.
enclit'ic, (n) enklitiese woord, enklise, aanhangsel; (a) enklities.
enclose', insluit; indam (water); omhein, inkamp, afperk; ~ **d**, bygaande, ingeslote; ingekamp; ~ *d letter*, bygaande (newensgaande) brief.
enclo'sing, insluitend, insluiting=; ~ *LETTER*, ingeslote brief; ~ *WALL*, ringmuur.
enclo'sure, omheining, staketsel; afgekampte plek; speelveld; afperking; klousuur (R.K.); hok, kamp; bylae, bygaande stuk, bybrief.
encloud', in wolke hul.
enco'de, (en)kodeer.
encod'ing, (en)kodering.
encom'iast, lofredenaar.
encomias'tic, prysend.
encom'ium, lofrede, lofspraak.
encom'pass, omring, omvat; ~ **ment**, insluiting, omvatting.
encore', (n) herhaling; herhaalnommer; (geroep om 'n) toegif; (v) toejuig, terugroep, om 'n herhaling vra; (interj) encore! bis!
encoun'ter, (n) geveg, skermutseling; ontmoeting; (v) slaags raak, aanval; ontmoet, teenkom; ~ *friends*, vriende raakloop, vriende op die lyf loop.
encou'rage, aanmoedig, aanspoor, aanvuur, aanwakker, bemoedig, moed inpraat; ~ **ment**, aanmoediging, aansporing; ~ **r**, aanmoediger
encou'raging, aanmoedigend, opwekkend, bemoedigend, aansporend.
encroach', inbreuk maak, oortree, die grense oorskry; indring, insluip; ~ *on*, steel (pad); oortree op; ~ **ment**, inbreukmaking, oortreding; indringing.
encrust', omkors; aanpak; ~ **a'tion**, omkorsting; korsvorming; ~ **ment**, korsaanpaksel, bekorsting.
encum'ber, belemmer, verswaar, bemoeilik; versper; belas, met 'n verband beswaar.
encum'brance, belemmering, beswaring, hindernis, oorlas, skuldelas, hipoteek, verband; ~ **r**, hipoteekhouer.
encyc'lic(al), (n) (pouslike) omsendbrief, rondskrywe, ensikliek; (a) rondgaande.
encyclop(a)ed'ia, ensiklopedie.
encyclop(a)ed'ic(al), ensiklopedies, veelsydig; ~ *knowledge*, veelsydige (ensiklopediese, omvattende) kennis.
encyclop(a)ed'ist, ensiklopedis, ensiklopediemaker, -skrywer.

encyst, inkapsel; omkors; insluit (in 'n sist); ~**a'tion**, ~**ment**, inkapseling; omkorsting.

end, (n) end, ent, uiteinde; slot; afloop; doel, eindpunt, oogmerk; entjie (tou); puntjie (sigaar); punt (seil); *he will never hear the* ~ *of the AFFAIR*, hy sal nooit die end v.d. saak hoor nie; *at AN* ~, afgeloop, voleindig; *AT the* ~, aan die end; *come to a BAD* ~, aan 'n ongelukkige einde kom; *BE someone's* ~, iem. se dood wees; *BEGIN at the wrong* ~, agterstevoor begin; *BIG* ~, suierstangkop; *to the BITTER* ~, tot die bitter einde toe; *COME to an* ~, end kry; tot 'n end kom, eindig; opraak; *a DEAD* ~, 'n dooie spoor; *DEFEAT its own* ~ *s*, sy eie doel verydel; *go off the DEEP* ~, kwaad word; *the* ~*s of the EARTH*, die uithoeke v.d. aarde; *there is an* ~ *to EVERYTHING*, aan alles kom 'n end; *he is no* ~ *of a FELLOW*, hy is 'n gawe kêrel; *FROM* ~ *to* ~, van begin tot end; *find it HARD to make* ~ *s meet*, dit nie breed hê nie; *there is no* ~ *to HIM*, hy is sonder end; *come out at the little* ~ *of the HORN*, aan die kortste end trek (wees); *ten HOURS on* ~, tien uur oor 'n boeg (aanmekaar); *IN the* ~, per slot van rekening; op die lang duur; *and that is the* ~ *of IT*, en daarmee basta; *KEEP one's* ~ *up*, jou goed weer; jou nie onbetuig laat nie; *be at a LOOSE* ~, nie besig wees nie; met jou siel onder jou arm loop; *MAKE an* ~ *of it*, daar 'n stokkie voor steek; *the* ~ *justifies the MEANS*, die doel heilig die middele; *make (both)* ~*s MEET*, die tering na die nering sit; rondkom; *he is NEARING his* ~, hy gaan end se kant toe; *NO* ~ *of*, verskriklik baie; besonder groot; *ON* ~, regop; orent; *PUT an* ~ *to it*, daar 'n end aan maak; *be at the* ~ *of one's TETHER*, ten einde raad wees; raadop wees; *to THAT* ~, met dié doel; *THERE'S no* ~ *to it*, daar kom nie 'n end aan nie; ~ *TO* ~, met die punte teen mekaar; *to WHAT* ~? waarvoor? *have the WRONG* ~ *of the stick*, iets aan die verkeerde end beethê; (v) eindig, beëindig, ophou met; aan 'n end kom; ~ *in a POINT*, in 'n punt uitloop, spits toeloop; *near the* ~ *of the TETHER*, sy rieme styfgeloop hê; gedaan wees; ten einde raad wees; ~ *UP by marrying the girl*, uitloop op 'n trouery; *all's WELL that* ~*s well*, end goed, alles goed.

enda'mage, beskadig.
endan'ger, in gevaar bring, blootstel (aan gevaar).
end: ~ **clip**, spanlem; ~ **door**, enddeur.
endear', lief maak, bemind maak; ~ **ing**, innemend, beminlik; ~ *ing ways*, innemende maniere.
endear'ment, dierbaarmaking; liefkosing, streling; gehegtheid; *term of* ~, lieflingsnaam(pie), troetelwoord.
endeav'our, (n) poging, beywering, strewe; (v) poog, probeer, trag, streef, jou beywer.
end'-elevation, syaansig, syopstand.
endem'ic, (n) endemie, inheemse siekte; (a) inheems, eielands, endemies.
end: ~ **frame**, endraam; ~ **gable**, sygewel; ~ **grain**, endhout.
end'ing, slot; afloop, end; einde; uitgang (gram.); *HAPPY* ~, gelukkige einde; goeie afloop; *QUARTER* ~ *Sept.* 30, kwartaal eindigende 30 Sept.
en'dive, andyvie; *curly* ~, krulandyvie.
end'-joint, stuiklas.
end'less, eindeloos, sonder end (einde), baie, oneindig; ~ *BELT*, dryfband; ~ *SAW*, bandsaag, lintsaag; ~ *SCREW*, wurmskroef; ~**ness**, eindeloosheid.
end: ~-**long**, oorlangs, in die lengte; ~ **moraine**, endmoreen; ~**most**, agterste, laaste; ~ **movement**, endspeling.
en'docrine, buisloos (klier).
endocard'iac, hartvlies=.
endocardit'is, hartvliesontsteking, endokarditis.
endocard'ium, binneste hartvlies, endokardium.
endocarp', endokarp.
endoderm'is, kernskede, vaatbondelskede, setmeelskede, endodermis (plantk.).
endoderm'al, **endoder'mic**, endodermies.
endog'amy, stamhuwelik, endogamie; inteelt.
endogenet'ic, endogeneties.
endogen'ic, endogeen.

endog'enous, inwendig, endogeen.
en'domorph, endomorf.
endomorph'ic, endomorf.
endomorph'ism, endomorfisme, endomorfie, endomorfose.
endopa'rasite, inwendige parasiet.
endorse', oordra; rugteken, endosseer; goedkeur, onderskryf, bevestig; ~ *a cheque*, 'n tjek rugteken (endosseer); ~**e'**, (n) endossant; (a) geëndosseerde; ~**ment**, endossement, onderskrywing, rugtekening; goedkeuring; ~**r**, endossant, rugtekenaar.
endors'ing, endossering.
endosmos'is, endosmose.
en'dosperm, kiemwit, endosperm.
endow', skenk, begiftig; toerus; ~ *ed with reason*, met rede begaaf; ~**er**, skenker.
endow'ment, begiftiging, skenking; gawe, talent; vermaking, bemaking; ~ **fund**, skenkingsfonds; ~ **policy**, (..**cies**), uitkeerpolis; skenkingspolis.
end: ~ **plate**, endplaat; ~ **play**, entspeling; ~-**terminal**, eindstandig (plantk.); ~-**tipping lorry**, wipbakvragmotor.
endue', aantrek, beklee; voorsien van.
endur'able, uitstaanbaar, draaglik.
endur'ance, lydsaamheid; ontbering; voortduring; verduring, uithouvermoë, weerstandsvermoë, duurvermoë; ~ **flight**, duurvlug; ~ **limit**, uithougrens; ~ **record**, duurrekord; uithourekord; ~ **test**, duurtoets, uithoutoets.
endure', volhou, aanhou, bly bestaan; uithou, deurstaan, verduur, uitstaan, veel, duld, sluk, verdra; *be unable to* ~ *someone*, iem. nie kan verdra nie; 'n hekel aan iem. hê.
endur'ing, duursaam, blywend; ~**ness**, duursaamheid.
end'ways, **end'wise**, met die punt (ent) vorentoe; oorlangs; punt aan punt.
en'ema, (-s, -ta), lawement, dermuitspoeling, enema, klisma; ~ **syringe**, lawementspuit.
en'emy, (n) (..**mies**), vyand; duiwel; teenstander; (a) vyandelik; vyands=; ~ **action**, vyandelike optrede; ~ **property**, vyandseiendom; ~ **subject**, vyandsonderdaan.
energet'ic, bedrywig, kragtig; daadliewend; nadruklik, ferm; flink; deurtastend, energiek; ~**s**, energetiek.
en'ergize, besiel, energie gee, aanwakker; kragtig handel; ~**r**, energiewekker.
energum'en, dweper; besetene.
en'ergy, (..**gies**), krag, werkkrag, daadkrag; nadruk; energie; werklus; arbeidsvermoë; kragsuiting; arbeidspotensiaal; *CHEMICAL* ~, chemiese energie; *CONSERVATION of* ~, behoud van energie; *KINETIC* ~, kinetiese energie; *MOLECULAR* ~, molukulêre energie; *POTENTIAL* ~, potensiële energie; *RADIANT* ~, stralingsenergie; ~ **food**, kragvoedsel, energievoedsel, energiekos.
en'ervate, (v) ontsenu, verswak, verweeklik, verslap; (a) swak, slap, kragteloos.
en'ervating, senuweeverslappend.
enerva'tion, ontsenuwing, verswakking, verslapping, verweekliking.
enface', op die voorkant stempel (beskryf).
en'fant terrible', (**enfants terribles**), enfant terrible, flapuit, losbek.
enfee'ble, verswak, verslap; ~**ment**, verswakking, swakheid.
enfeoff', oordra, oorgee; beleen; ~**ment**, leenbrief; belening.
enfett'er, boei, kluister, bind.
enfilade', (n) syvuur, dwarsvuur, enfilade; (v) enfileer, beskiet, onder dwarsvuur neem.
enfold', inwikkel, invou, omsluit; rimpel, plooi.
enforce', afdwing, dwing, aandring; toepas, deurdryf, bekragtig; opdwing; ~ *the LAW*, die wet uitvoer (handhaaf); ~ *PAYMENT*, na die hof gaan vir betaling; betaling afdwing; ~ *SILENCE*, stilte oplê; ~**able**, afdwingbaar; ~**ment**, bekragtiging; toepassing, uitvoering, afdwinging, dwang, geweld; handhawing; ~**r**, bekragtiger; aandringer.
enframe', raam.
enfran'chise, burgerreg skenk, stemreg gee; vry

maak, bevry; ~ d, stemgeregtig; ~ ment, verlening van burgerreg, stemgeregtigheid; vrymaking, be= vryding; ~ r, bevryder.

engage', verbind, verpand; aanwerf, in diens gaan by; jou verloof; besig hou (aandag); aanval, aanpak, veg; beslag lê op; beset (stoel); bespreek (plek); huur; daarvoor instaan; inmekaargryp, inskakel (tegnies); ~ *GEARS*, inskakel; ~ *IN*, jou inlaat met; jou meng in; ~ *TO*, jou verbind om; ~d, be= sig; verloof; slaags (geveg); beset (telefoon); *BE* ~ *d to*, sy woord gegee het; verloof wees aan (met); be= sig wees; beset wees (telefoon); *BE* ~ *d in*, betrokke wees in; besig wees met.

engage'ment, verbintenis, verpligting; verlowing; slag, geveg; spreekbeurt; afspraak; inskakeling, in= koppeling (rat); bedrywigheid; *BREAK an* ~ , 'n verlowing uitmaak (verbreek); *BREAK off an* ~ , 'n geveg staak; *TERMINATE an* ~ , 'n dienskontrak beëindig; *WITHOUT an* ~ , vry, sonder verbinte= nis; ~ **festivity**, verlowingsfees; ~ **ring**, verloof= ring.

engag'ing, innemend, aantreklik; skakelend; verbin= dend; ~ spring, inskakelveer.

engar'land, omkrans.

engen'der, teel, voortbring, kweek; veroorsaak.

en'gine, werktuig, enjin, masjien; lokomotief; toestel; motor; *AUXILIARY* ~ , hulpmotor; ~ of DE= STRUCTION vernielingswerktuig; *HIGH-SPEED* ~ , snelmotor; *LONG-STROKE* ~ , lang= slagmotor; ~ *of WAR*, oorlogswerktuig; ~ **bed**, enjinbedding; ~ **block**, enjinblok; ~ **bonnet**, mo= torkap; ~ **breakdown**, teenspoed; masjiendefek; motordefek; ~ **builder**, werktuigkundige; ~ **cam= shaft**, enjinnokas; ~-**car**, motorgondel (lugskip); ~ **cooling**, enjin- (verl)koeling; ~ **construction**, masjienbou; ~ **cradle**, enjinwieg; ~ **driver**, masji= nis; enjindrywer.

engineer', (n) ingenieur (met graad); werktuigkundi= ge, masjinis (op skip); genie-offisier; *CHIEF* ~ , hoofingenieur; eerste masjinis (op skip); hooftegni= kus (in lugmag); *CIVIL* ~ , siviele ingenieur; *ELECTRICAL* ~ , elektrotegniese ingenieur; *ME= CHANICAL* ~ , werktuigkundige (meganiese) in= genieur; *NAUTICAL* ~ , skeepsboukundige inge= nieur; (v) die werk van 'n ingenieur verrig; bou, uitvoer; bewerk, op tou sit, beraam.

engineer'ing, ingenieurswese; werktuigkunde; ~ corps, geniekorps; ~ draughtsman, masjienteke= naar; ~ drawing, masjientekening; ~ industry, masjienbou(bedryf); ~ school, ingenieurskool; ge= nieskool (mil.); ~ shop, konstruksiewinkel, kon= struksiewerkplaas; ~ works, masjienfabriek.

en'gine: ~ failure, masjienweiering; ~ fitter, motor= monteur; ~-house, loko(motief)loods; masjienka= mer; brandweerstasie; ~-men, lokomotiefperso= neel; ~ number, enjinnommer; ~ oil, enjinolie; ~ power, masjienkrag; motorkrag; ~ room, masjien= kamer; ~ ry, masjinerie, ratwerk; ~ shed, masjien= loods; ~ sump, oliebak; ~ trouble, enjinmoeilik= heid; ~ union, metaalwerkersvakbond; ~ unit, enjineenheid; ~ worker, metaalwerker; ~ works, masjienfabriek; metaalfabriek; ~ wright, masjien= bouer; lokomotiefbouer.

engir'd(le), omgord.

Eng'land, Engeland.

Eng'lish, (n) Engels; *BASIC* ~ , Basiese Engels; *BROKEN* ~ , krom (geradbraakte) Engels; *the KING'S* ~ , Standaardengels; *MIDDLE* ~ , Mid= del-En=gels; *NEW* ~ , Nieu-Engels; *OLD* ~ , Oud-Engels; *SPEAK* ~ , Engels praat; ~ *as she is SPOKE*, geradbraakte Engels; (a) Engels; *the* ~ *Channel*, die Engelse Kanaal; ~ **horn**, cor anglais, althobo; ~ **man**, (..**men**), Engelsman, Rooinek (spotnaam); ~ **master**, Engelsonderwyser; ~ **me= dium**, Engelsmedium=; ~-**medium school**, Engels= mediumskool; ~-**speaking**, Engelssprekend, Engelstalig; ~ **woman**, Engelse vrou.

engorge', opsluit; verstop; volsuig; volprop; *be* ~ *d*, volgeprop wees; volgesuig; *fully* ~ *d tick*, volge= suigde bosluis; ~ **ment**, verslinding; verstopping, kongestie; volsuiging.

engraft', ent; inprent; byvoeg; inlyf; ~ **ment**, inenting.

engrail', inkerf; kartel.

engrain', diep indruk; in die wol verf; ~ ed, deurtrap, verstok.

engrave', graveer, insny, inkap (woorde in rots), grif; ~ r, graveur, graveerder, stempelmaker.

engrav'ing, (die) graveer; gravure, kunsplaat, gra= vering.

engross', in groot maat opkoop; met groot letters skryf; monopoliseer; toe-eien; in beslag neem; boei; besig hou; grosseer; ~ *ed in*, verdiep in; ~ **er**, opko= per; ~ **ing**, inbeslagnemend, monopoliserend; boei= end; ~ **ment**, inbeslagneming; opkoping.

engulf', opslurp, inswelg, insluk.

enhance', verhoog, vergroot, verhef, versterk; duur= der maak; ~ **ment**, verhoging, vermeerdering.

enharmon'ic, enharmonies.

enig'ma, (-s), raaisel, enigma; ~ **t'ic**, duister, raaisel= agtig, enigmaties; ~ **tize**, raaisels opgee; raaiselag= tig praat.

enisle', tot 'n eiland maak; op 'n eiland sit; isoleer, afsonder.

enjamb'ment, enjambement, oorvloeiing, deurloop (versreël).

enjoin', oplê, inskerp, op die hart druk; beveel, ver= bied (reg); ~ **er**, inskerper; ~ **ment**, inskerping; ver= bod.

enjoy', geniet, hou van, jou verheug, vermaak; smaak; gebruik (vleis); hê, ondervind; *I* ~ *ed MY= SELF very much*, ek het dit baie geniet; ~ *ONE= SELF*, plesier hê; van iets geniet; ~ *SOME= THING*, plesier in iets vind, iets geniet; ~ **able**, aangenaam, genotvol, genotryk; vermaaklik; ~ **ableness**, aangenaamheid, genotrykheid; ~ **ment**, genot, genieting, vermaak, vermaaklik=

enkin'dle, aansteek, aan die brand steek; opwek, aanstook.

enlace', inmekaarstrengel, omvat.

enlarge', vergroot, vermeerder, verruim; uitbrei, gro= ter maak; uitwei; ~ *on a STORY*, 'n stertjie aanlas; ~ *UPON*, uitwei oor; ~ **d**, vergroot; ~ **ment**, ver= groting, verruiming; uitbreiding; uitweiding; ~ **r**, vergroter.

enlight'en, verlig, voorlig, inlig; ophelder; ~ **ed**, ver= lig; ~ **ment**, voorligting; inligting; verligting; ver= standsontwikkeling.

enlink', inmekaarskakel, nou verbind.

enlist', aansluit, in diens neem, werf; registreer; in= roep (hulp); inskrywe, (aan)werf; ~ **ment**, inskry= wing; werwing, aanwerwing; indiensneming, aan= monstering.

enliv'en, opvrolik, verlewendig, vervrolik.

en masse', in een klomp, in 'n hoop, almal (alles) tesa= me, en masse.

enmesh', verstrik, inwikkel, verwikkel.

en'mity, (..ties), vyandskap, vyandigheid.

enn'ead, negetal.

en'neagon, negehoek.

enno'ble, veredel; adel; tot die adelstand verhef; ~ **ment**, veredeling; verheffing tot die adelstand.

ennui', verveling, vervelendheid, ennui.

eno'logy = oenology.

enorm'ity, (..ties), ontsaglikheid, yslikheid, enormi= teit; afskuwelikheid, verskriklikheid; gruwel.

enorm'ous, ontsaglik, enorm, tamaai, yslik, geweldig, kolossaal; ~ **ness**, ontsaglikheid.

enough', genoeg, voldoende, toereikend; ~ *to make a CAT laugh*, 'n groot rede gee om te lag; ~ *(noise) to wake the DEAD*, 'n geweldige rumoer; ~ *is as good as a FEAST*, genoeg is oorvloed; *when you have had* ~ , *FOOD is no longer appetizing*, as die muis dik is, smaak die meel bitter; *you KNOW well* ~ , jy weet baie goed; *ODDLY* ~ , vreemd genoeg; *we had* ~ *and to SPARE*, ons het oorgenoeg gehad; ons het meer as te veel gehad; *and SURE* ~ *there he was!* en wraggies (warempel) daar was hy! *THAT is* ~ *! basta! she sings WELL* ~ , sy sing taamlik goed.

enounce', uitdruk, uitspreek, verklaar; ~ **ment**, uit= drukking, uitspraak.

enow' = enough.

en pass'ant, in die verbygaan, terloops; en passant.

enquê'te, enquête, ondersoek.

enquire' = inquire.

enrage', kwaad word; vertoorn, woedend maak; ~ **d,** woedend, verwoed, smoorkwaad.
enrap'ture, verruk, in verrukking bring; wegsleep; ~ **d,** ekstaties, opgetoë.
enre'giment, tot 'n regiment verenig; dril.
enrich', tooi, verfraai; verryk, vrugbaar maak; verhoog (kleure); vermeerder, verhoog; ~ **ed,** verryk; verhoog; ~ *ed bread,* verrykte brood; ~ **er,** verryker (mengsel); ~ **ment,** verryking; versiering, sieraad, ornament.
enrobe', klee, uitdos.
enrol', (-led), inskrywe, aanwerf, aanmonster, in diens neem; aansluit; registreer, op die lys sit; ~ **ler,** aanwerwer, inskrywer; ~ **ment,** inskrywing, (aan)werwing, registrasie, aanmonstering; ~ **ment form,** inskryfvorm.
en route', op pad, op die deurreis, en route.
ens, (entia), wese, entiteit.
ensang'uined, bloedig, bebloed.
ensconce', verskans, verskuil; beskut; ~ *oneself,* jou nestel; 'n aangename posisie inneem.
ensem'ble, geheel; algemene indruk; ensemble; samespel (musiek, spele); ~ **-playing,** samespel, ensemblespel; ~ **-singing,** samesang.
enshrine', in 'n skryn plaas; wegsluit; heilig bewaar.
enshroud', omhul, omklee, inwikkel.
en'siform, swaardvormig.
en'sign, onderskeidingsteken; vaandrig, vaandeldraer; vaan, vaandel, vlag, standaard; waarnemende onderluitenant; ~ **-bearer,** vaandeldraer.
ensi'lage, (n) inkuiling; kuilvoer; (v) inkuil.
ensile', inkuil.
enslave', tot slaaf maak, verslaaf; ~ *d to,* verslaaf aan; ~ **ment,** slawerny, verslawing; ~ **r,** verslawer; bekoorster, hartedief, verleidster.
ensnare', verstrik, verskalk, verlei, verlok; ~ **ment,** verstrikking.
ensoul', besiel.
ensphere', omring, omsluit; bolvormig maak.
en'statite, enstatiet.
ensue', volg, voortkom, voortvloei; intree.
ensu'ing, daaropvolgende, navolgende; ~ *EVENTS,* later gebeurtenisse; ~ *YEARS,* volgende jare.
ensure', verseker, waarborg; beveilig.
enswathe', omhul, toewikkel.
entab'lature, dekstuk, entablement.
enta'blement, entablement, stutstuk, stutplatform.
entail', (n) onvervreemdbare erfgoed, fideicommissum; (v) onvervreemdbaar maak; onder fideikommis bemaak; meebring, veroorsaak, ten gevolge hê; ~ **ment,** oordrag as fideicommissum, vassetting; gevolg, uitvloeisel.
entang'le, verwar, in die war bring; verstrik; verwikkel; ~ **d,** verwar(d); *get* ~ *d,* jou vaswoel; ~ **ment,** verwarring; verwikkeling; verstrikking, versperring.
en'tasis, entasis.
ente'lechy, entelegie; vervollediging.
entente', eensgesindheid, ooreenkoms, verstandhouding, entente; ~ **cordiale,** entente cordiale (vriendskaplike verstandhouding tussen twee regerings).
en'ter, ingaan, intree, binnegaan, binnetree, binnekom, binneloop, betree; deurdring; aangaan, aanknoop; byhou; inskrywe, aanteken, registreer, boek; ~ *into an AGREEMENT,* 'n ooreenkoms aangaan; ~ *an APPEARANCE,* sy verskyning aanteken; ~ *the ARMY,* soldaat word; ~ *up the CASHBOOK,* die kasboek byhou; ~ *into a CONTRACT,* 'n kontrak (ooreenkoms) aangaan; ~ *into a CONVERSATION,* 'n gesprek aanknoop; ~ *the CHURCH,* predikant word; ~ *on one's DUTIES,* in funksie tree; sy werk aanvaar, sy werksaamhede begin; *HAVE something* ~ *ed,* iets op die boek sit; ~ *into NEGOTIATIONS,* onderhandelinge aanknoop; ~ *a PROTEST,* 'n protes indien; ~ *for a RACE,* jou laat inskryf vir 'n wedloop; ~ *into SERVICE,* in diens tree; ~ *it TO,* op rekening skryf van; ~ *into a TREATY,* 'n verdrag aangaan; ~ *UPON,* begin, aanvaar.
ente'ric, derm=, ingewands=; ~ **fever,** ingewandskoors.
en'tering, ingaan, ingang; *breaking and* ~ , inbraak.

enterit'is, dermontsteking, enteritis.
en'terocele, liesbreuk, dermbreuk.
en'teron, spyskanaal.
enteros'tomy, enterostomie, dermopening.
en'terotomy, derminsnyding, enterotomie.
enterotox(a)e'mia, dermvergiftiging (mense); bloednier (by diere).
en'terprise, onderneming; waagstuk; ondernemingsgees.
en'terprising, ondernemend.
entertain', onderhou; ontvang, onthaal, trakteer, vermaak, voed; koester, omdra ('n denkbeeld); in oorweging neem; amuseer, aangenaam besig hou; ~ *CORRESPONDENCE,* briefwisseling onderhou; ~ *a FEELING,* 'n gevoel koester; ~ *an OFFER,* 'n aanbod in oorweging neem; ~ **er,** gasheer; onthaler; voordraer; vermaaklikheidskunstenaar; ~ **ing,** onderhoudend, vermaaklik; ~ **ingness,** vermaaklikheid, onderhoudendheid.
entertain'ment, onthaal; vermaaklikheid, amusement; ~ **allowance,** onthaaltoelae; ~ **tax,** vermaaklikheidsbelasting; ~ **unit,** vermaaklikheidseenheid.
en'thalpy, entalpie, hitte-inhoud.
enthral(l)', (..**led),** tot slaaf maak; betower, boei, bind; ~ **ment,** verslawing; betowering.
enthrone', op die troon plaas; ~ **ment,** troonsverheffing, troonsbestyging.
enthroniza'tion = **enthronement.**
enthuse', (n) ekstase raak, dweep (met).
enthu'siasm, geesdrif, entoesiasme, ywer, vervoering.
enthu'siast, geesdriftige, yweraar, warme vereerder, liefhebber, dweper, entoesias.
enthusias'tic, geesdriftig, entoesiasties.
entice', verlok, verlei, aanlok, aflok; uitlok; in versoeking bring; ~ *away,* omkoop, oorhaal; wegtoor; weglok, aftroggel; ~ **ment,** verleiding, versoeking, aanlokking; aanloklikheid; lokmiddel; verlokking; ~ **r,** verlokker, verleier; aanlokker.
entic'ing, verloklik, verleidelik; begeerlik.
entire', (n) ongesnyde dier; hings; (a) heeltemal, volledig, volslae, gans, totaal, volkome; heel, onbeskadig; ongesny; ongedeel; gaafrandig (plantk.); ~ **ly,** heeltemal, volkome, ten ene male; ~ **ness,** volkomenheid, volledigheid; ongeskondenheid; ~ **ty,** geheel; *in its* ~ *ty,* in geheel.
enti'tle, betitel, noem; reg gee op; geregtig wees; ~ **d,** getitel, genaamd; geregtig op, gewettig; *be* ~ *d to,* reg hê op; ~ **ment,** reg op (besoldiging).
en'tity, (..**ties),** wese, entiteit, eenheid, geheel.
entomb', begrawe, bysit; toeval (in myn); ~ **ment,** begrawing; begrafnis, teraardebestelling.
entom'ic(al), insektekundig, insekte=.
entomog'rapher, entomograaf.
entomog'raphy, entomografie.
entomolo'gic(al), entomologies, insektekundig.
entomol'ogist, entomoloog, insektekenner, insektekundige; goggadokter (skerts.).
entomol'ogize, insekte versamel (bestudeer).
entomol'ogy, insektekunde, entomologie.
entomoph'agous, insekte-etend, entomofaag.
en'tophyte, entofiet.
entourage', gevolg; hofstoet, entourage; omgewing.
entozo'on, (..**zoa),** entosoön, lintwurm, rondewurm.
en'tr'acte, tussenbedryf, tussenspel, entr'acte.
en'trails, ingewande, binnegoed, harslag.
entrain', instap (in trein); inlaai, oplaai; ~ **ing point,** laaiplek (trein); instapplek.
entramm'el, verstrik, hinder, belemmer.
en'trance¹, (n) ingang, portaal; binnekoms; inkoms; intrede; aanvaarding (amp); aanvang (werk); toegang, toelating; inskryfgeld; *GIVE* ~ *to,* inlaat, laat binnekom; *MAKE one's* ~ , binnekom.
entrance'², (v) verruk, vervoer, in geesvervoering bring.
en'trance: ~ **door,** ingangsdeur; ~ **examination,** toelatingseksamen; admissie-eksamen; ~ **fee,** toetreegeld, toelatingsgeld, inskrywingsgeld; ~ **hall,** vestibule, voorportaal.
entran'cement, verrukking, vervoering.
en'trance: ~ **money** = **entrance fee;** ~ **ramp,** inrit; ~ **requirement,** toelatingsvereiste.

entrancing 873 epistaxis

entran'cing, verruklik.
en'trant, binnetredende; ingeskrewene; deelnemer, inskrywer.
entrap', **(-ped)** vang, betrap, verstrik.
entreat', smeek, soebat, bid, besweer, dringend versoek; ~**ing,** soebattery; ~**ingly,** smekend; ~**y,** (..**ties**), (smeek)bede, smeking, versoek; aandrang.
en'trecôte, entrecot, ribfilet, lendeskyf.
en'trée, toegang; voorgereg, entrée; ~**-dish,** entréeskottel.
en'tremets, tussengereg, entremets.
entrench', verskans, jou ingraaf; inbreuk maak op; ~*ed clauses,* verskanste klousules; ~**ment,** verskansing; inbreuk; loopgraaf, ingrawing.
entre nous', onder ons, entre nous.
en'trepôt, pakhuis; handelsentrum, entrepot.
entrepreneur', entrepreneur, ondernemer.
en'tresol, tussenverdieping.
en'tropy, entropie.
entrust', toevertrou; opdra; ~ *something to,* iets aan iem. toevertrou.
en'try, (..**ries**), ingang, toegang, intrede, intog, binnetreding, binnekoms; inskrywing, registrasie; pos; boeking; inbesitneming, aanvaarding (reg); *BILL of* ~, inklaringslys; *DOUBLE* ~, dubbele boekhouding; *MAKE un* ~, Inkom; 'n intrede doen; inskryf, 'n inskrywing maak; *NO* ~, geen toegang; spesiale aantekening (jur.); ~ **fee,** inskrywingsgeld; toegangsgeld; ~ **form,** inskryfvorm; ~ **money,** toegangsgeld; ~ **ticket,** toegangskaartjie.
entwine', omwind, omstrengel; deurvleg.
entwist', inmekaarvleg (-strengel).
enuc'leate, ontwar, ophelder, blootlê; verwyder, uithaal; ontkern.
enum'erate, opsom, opnoem; tel.
enumera'tion, opsomming; optelling, opnoeming.
enum'erative, opsommend.
enum'erator, opsommer, opteller; sensusopnemer.
enun'ciate, uit; verklaar, uitspreek; formuleer; verkondig; uitdruk.
enuncia'tion, uiting, verklaring; uitspraak; stelling.
enun'ciator, verkondiger.
enure', *kyk* **inure.**
enures'is, bednatmaak, bedwatering, enurese.
envel'op, (om)wikkel, omsluit, inwikkel, omklee, omhul; omsingel; ~**ing movement,** omsingelingsbeweging.
en'velope, omslag, omhulsel; koevert, envelop.
envel'opment, omsluiting, omhulling; omhulsel.
enven'om, vergiftig; vergal, verbitter.
en'viable, benydenswaardig, benybaar.
en'vier, benyer.
en'vious, afgunstig, ywersugtig, nydig, jaloers, *be* ~, jaloers wees, jannie se baadjie aanhê, jantjie wees; ~**ness,** afguns, jaloesie.
envir'on, omgeef, omring, omsingel, insluit; ~**ment,** omgewing; entourage.
environmen'tal, omgewings=; ~ **education,** omgewingsonderrig; ~**ist,** omgewingsdeskundige; ~ **pollution,** (omgewings)besoedeling; omgewingskending; ~ **study,** -studies, omgewingsleer.
envi'rons, omgewing; omstreke; buurgebied, aangrensende gebied.
envis'age, envi'sion, beskou; in die oë kyk; voor die gees roep; beoog, voor oë stel.
en'voy[1], gesant, afgesant; ~ *extraordinary,* buitengewone gesant.
en'voy[2], slotwoord; slotvers.
en'vy, (n) afguns, jaloesie, jaloersheid, ywersugtigheid, nyd, naywer; *BE the* ~ *of,* beny word deur; *EYE with* ~, met lede oë aanskou; *FROM (out of)* ~, uit afguns; (v) **(envied),** afgunstig wees, beny; misgun; *better envied than pitied,* liewer beny as beklaag.
enwind', (..wound), omwind.
enwomb', in die skoot sluit, verberg.
enwrap', **(-ped),** inwikkel, omhul; toedraai.
enwreathe', omkrans; deurvleg.
enzoot'ic, (n) plaaslike siekte (onder vee); (a) plaaslik, ensoöties.
en'zyme, ensiem.
E'ocene, Eoseen(tydperk).

eola'tion, windverwering.
e'olith, eoliet.
Eolith'ic, (n) Eolitikum, Vroeë Steentyd(perk); (a) Eolities.
e'ozoon, eosoön.
ep'act, epakta.
ep'arch, **(-es),** Griekse goewerneur; biskop.
ep'aulet(te), epoulet; rangstrepie; *win his* ~*s,* offisier word.
épée', degen (vir tweegeveg); skermdegen.
epen'thesis, epentese, inlassing, invoeging.
epenthet'ic, epenteties, ingelas, ingevoeg.
epergne', tafelmiddelstuk, epergne.
e'phedrine, efedrien, efedrine.
ephem'era, **(-s),** eendagsvlieë, insekte van een dag; efemera; ~**l,** eendaags, kortstondig, efemeer; ~*l records,* kortstondige (waardelose) dokumente.
ephem'eris, (..**merides**), sterrekundige tafel (almanak).
Ephe'sians, Efesiërs.
eph'od, efod.
ep'ic, (n) epos, heldedig; epiek; (a) epies, verhalend; ~ *ARTIST,* epikus; ~ *POEM,* heldedig; ~ *POETRY,* epiek; ~**al,** epies.
e'picallyx, bykelk.
ep'icene, gemeenslagtig.
epicen'tre, epicen'trum, episentrum.
epiclas'tic, epiklasties.
epicris'is, epikrisis.
ep'icure, epikuris, lekkerbek, smulpaap.
epicure'an, (n) genieter; (a) epikuries, lekkerbekkig, epikuristies, genotsoekend; ~**ism,** leer van Epicurus.
ep'icurism, epikurisme, genotsug, leer van Epicurus.
ep'icycle, bysirkel.
epicyc'lic, episiklies.
epidem'ic, (n) heersende siekte, epidemie; (a) besmetlik, epidemies.
epidemiolog'ical, epidemiologies.
epidemio'logist, epidemioloog.
epidemiol'ogy, leer van epidemiese siektes, epidemiologie.
epiderm'al, opperhuid=, epidermies.
epiderm'ic, epidermies.
epiderm'is, opperhuid, epidermis.
epidi'ascope, epidiaskoop.
epid'osite, epidosiet.
ep'idote, epidoot.
epid'otize, epidotiseer.
ep'ig(a)eal, landbewonend.
epigas'trium, bobuik.
ep'igene, epigeen.
epigen'esis, epigenese.
epigenet'ic, epigeneties.
epiglott'is, keelkleppie, strotklep, sluk, epiglottis.
ep'igone, epigoon; na-aper, nabootser.
ep'igram, puntdig, sneldig, epigram; ~**mat'ic,** epigrammaties; ~**m'atist,** puntdigter; ~**matize,** epigramme maak.
ep'igraph, opskrif; motto; ~**ist,** mottoskrywer.
ep'ilepsy, vallende siekte; epilepsie; *fit of* ~, toeval.
epilep'tic, (n) epileptikus, lyer aan vallende siekte; (a) epilepties; ~ *fit,* toeval.
epil'ogist, skrywer (voordraer) van epiloog.
ep'ilogue, narede, slottoespraak, epiloog; naberig.
Epiph'any, Driekoningefees, Driekoninge.
epi'physis, epifise.
epiphyt'al, woekerend, epifities.
ep'iphyte, epifiet, woekerplant; ..*t'ic* = **epiphytal.**
epis'copacy, biskoplike kerkbestuur; episkopaat.
epis'copal, biskoplik, episkopaal; ~ *town,* myterstad.
episcopa'lian, (n) lid van 'n episkopaalse kerk; (a) episkopaal(s), biskoplik.
epis'copate, bisdom; biskopsamp; biskopswyding; gesamentlike biskoppe; episkopaat.
ep'iscope, episkoop.
episep'alous, kelkstandig, episepaal.
ep'isode, tussenverhaal; voorval, episode.
episod'ic(al), episodies, bykomstig.
epispas'tic, (n) blaar; (a) blaartrekkend.
ep'isperm, saadhuid.
epistax'is, neusbloeding.

epistemolog'ical, kenteoreties.
epistemol'ogy, kennisleer, epistemologie.
epis'tle, brief, sendbrief, epistel.
epis'tolary, brief=; skriftelik; ~ *style*, briefstyl.
ep'istyle, argitraaf.
ep'itaph, grafskrif.
epithalam'ic, bruilofs=.
epithalam'ium, (..mia, -s), bruilofsdig (=lied), huweliksdig.
epithel'ium, epiteel, boonste huidlaag, bedekkingsweefsel, dekweefsel.
ep'ithet, byvoegsel, bynaam, toenaam, epiteton.
epit'ome, uittreksel, kort samevatting, kort begrip.
epit'omist, verkorter.
epit'omize, verkort, saamvat.
epivaginit'is, epivaginitis.
epizoot'ic, episoöties.
ep'och, tydperk, epog; tydstip; ~ **al**, besonder gewigtig; ~-**making**, buitengewoon gewigtig, epogmakend.
ep'ode, slotsang, epode.
ep'onym, naamgeër, stigter.
epon'ymous, naamgewend.
ep'opee, heldedig, epopee, epos.
ep'os, heldedig, epos.
Ep'som salt(s), Engelse sout.
equabil'ity, gelykheid, gelykvormigheid, eweredigheid.
eq'uable, gelykmatig, eweredig; *an ~ temperament*, 'n gelykmatige geaardheid.
eq'ual, (n) (syns)gelyke, ewekenie, weerga; portuur; *he has no ~*, sy maters is (klein) dood; sy moses is dood; (v) gelykmaak; gelyk wees aan; ewenaar, dieselfde wees, gelyk wees; *NEVER ~ someone*, nooit naby iem. kom nie, nooit iem. se gal ruik nie; *NOTHING ~s it*, niks haal daarby nie; sy moses is dood; (a) dieselfde, gelykvormig; egalig, eweredig; gelyk; *BE ~ to*, gelyk wees aan; in staat wees tot; ~ *to the HONOUR*, die eer waardig wees; ~ *LANGUAGE rights*, taalgelykheid; ~ *to the OCCASION*, teen die moeilikhede opgewasse; ~ *RIGHTS*, gelyke regte; ~ *SIGN*, gelykteken; *not ~ to the TASK*, nie bereken vir die taak nie; te lig in die broek vir die taak; *all THINGS being ~*, in gelyke omstandighede; *the VOTING was ~*, die stemme het gestaak.
equaliza'tion, gelykmaking, vereffening; ~ **fund**, vereffeningsfonds.
e'qualize, gelykmaak, effen; gelykstel; die telling gelykmaak (sport); ewenaar; ~**r**, ewenaarder, effenaar, gelykmaker.
equal'ity, (..ties), gelykheid, gelykvormigheid.
e'qually, gelyk(lik), eenders, net so, ewe(seer), in gelyke mate, sonder onderskeid; regverdig.
equanim'ity, gelykmatigheid, gelatenheid, gelykmoedigheid, sielsrus.
equate', tot 'n gemiddelde bring; gelykmaak; gelykstel; ~ **d**, gelykstaande.
equa'tion, vergelyking, ekwasie (wisk.); gelykmaking; ewewig.
equat'or, ewenaar, ekwator, linie, sonlyn, ewenagslyn; *magnetic ~*, magnetiese ekwator, akliniese lyn.
equator'ial, ekwatoriaal, ewenaars=; ~ **altitude**, ekwatoriaalshoogte; ~ **current**, ekwatoriaalstroom.
e'querry, (equerries), stalmeester; koningsruiter (Britse vorstehuis).
equest'rian, (n) perderuiter, ruiter; (a) ruiter=; ~ *sport*, ruiterkuns; ~ *statue*, ruiterstandbeeld.
equestrienne', damesruiter.
equiang'ular, gelykhoekig.
equidis'tant, ewe ver, op gelyke afstand; ewe wyd.
equigran'ular, gelykkorrelig.
equilat'eral, gelyksydig; ~ **triangle**, gelyksydige driehoek.
equilib'rate, in ewewig bring (hou), balanseer; opweeg teen.
equilibra'tion, ewewig.
equilib'rious, ewewigtig.
equilib'rist, koorddanser; akrobaat.

equilib'rium, ewewig(stoestand), balans; ~ *position*, ewewigstand.
equimul'tiple, dieselfde veelvoud.
e'quine, perde=.
equinoc'tial, (n) ewenagslyn; hemelekwator; (a) nagewenings=, ekwinoksiaal; ~ **gales**, ewenagstorms; ~ **line**, ewenagslyn; ~ **point**, nageweningspunt.
e'quinox, dag-en-nag-ewening.
equip', (-ped), uitrus, inrig, toerus, voorsien, beman (skip); bewapen.
e'quipage, uitrusting; benodigdhede; rytuig met perde en bediendes, ekwipasie.
equip'ment, inrigting, uitrusting, toerusting, instalasie, benodigdhede; bewapening; bepakking (mil.); ~ **expenses**, inrigtingskoste.
e'quipoise, (n) ewewig; teëwig; (v) in ewewig hou; opweeg teen; in onsekerheid laat.
equipoll'ence, gelykwaardigheid.
equipoll'ent, ekwivalent; (a) gelykwaardig.
equipon'derance, gelykwigtigheid.
equipon'derant, (n) teenwig; (a) gelykwigtig, ewe swaar, gelyk.
equipon'derate, balanseer; opweeg teen.
equipoten'tial, ekwipotensiaal.
equipped', uitgerus, toegerus.
e'quitable, billik, redelik, regverdig.
equita'tion, rykuns, ruiterskap.
e'quity, (..ties), billikheid, onpartydigheid; billikheidsreg; (pl) aandele, ekwiteite, effekte; *COURT of ~*, vredesgerig; *IN ~*, billikerwyse(e); ~ *of REDEMPTION*, inlossingsreg; ~ **capital**, ondernemingskapitaal.
equiv'alence, gelykwaardigheid, ekwivalensie.
equiv'alent, (n) ekwivalent; (a) eweredig, ekwivalent; ~ *to*, ewe veel werd as, gelyk aan.
equiv'ocal, dubbelsinnig, onseker, verdag, twyfelagtig; ~ *generation*, spontane ontwikkeling; ~ **ness**, dubbelsinnigheid, verdagtheid, onsekerheid.
equiv'ocate, dubbelsinnig maak; dubbelsinnig praat, uitvlugte soek.
equivoca'tion, dubbelsinnigheid, uitvlug.
equiv'ocator, woordverdraaier, dubbelsinnige mens.
e'quivoke, e'quivoque, woordspeling; dubbelsinnigheid.
er'a, tydperk; jaartelling; era; *the Christian ~*, die Christelike jaartelling.
erad'iate, uitstraal; skitter.
eradia'tion, uitstraling; glinstering.
erad'icable, uitroeibaar.
erad'icate, ontwortel, uitroei, verdelg.
eradica'tion, verdelging, uitroeiing, vernietiging.
eras'able, uitwisbaar.
erase', uitkrap, deurhaal, doodvee, skrap, uitwis, uitvlak, uitvee; ~ **r**, uitveër, wisser; radeerder.
era'sing knife, radeermes.
era'sion, era'sure, uitkrapping, uitwissing, uitveging, deurhaling.
ere, (prep) voor; (conj) eerder, voor, voordat; ~ **long**, binnekort, eerlank.
erect', (v) oprig; stig; bou, optrek; opstel, vestig; (a) regop, penregop, penorent; ~ **ile**, oprigbaar; ~ **ion**, bouwerk, gebou; oprigting, stigting; opbouing; optrekking; montering (masjien); opswelling, verstywing, ereksie; ~ **ness**, opregtheid; loodregtheid; regop houding; ~ **or**, oprigter; trekspier; monteur (masjien).
e'remite, kluisenaar.
eremit'ic, kluisenaars=.
e'rethism, sieklike oorprikkeling.
ere'while, voorheen, vroeër, eertyds.
erf, (erven), erf; *dry ~*, droë erf.
erg'o, dus, ergo, bygevolg.
erg'(on), erg, arbeidseenheid.
ergonom'ics, ergonomie.
erg'ot, roes, brand (in graan); ergot; moederkoring; swelvrat; spoor; vethorinkie; ~ **ism**, ergotvergiftiging; ergotisme.
e'rica, heide, erika.
E'rin, Ierland.
e'rinose, knoppiesblaar.
eriom'eter, eriometer.
eris'tic, (n) redeneerkuns; (a) polemies, strydlustig.

erm'ine, hermelyn; hermelynbont.
erne, seearend.
erode', wegvreet, verweer, wegknaag; uitkalf; wegspoel; uitmaal; erodeer.
Er'os, Eros.
ero'sion, invreting, wegspoeling, wegvreting, erosie; verwering; verspoeling; uitkalwing; uitmaling, slyting; *dental ~,* tand(ver)slyting.
eros'ive, wegvretend, invretend, verwerend, wegspoelend.
erot'ic, (n) minnedig; (a) eroties; ~**ism,** erotisme, erotiek.
erotoman'ia, minnewaansin, erotomanie; ~**c,** erotomaan.
err, 'n fout maak, fouteer, faal, feil; (af)dwaal; jou vergis; sonde begaan; *to ~ is human, to forgive divine,* 'n mens is maar 'n mens; dis menslik om te dwaal; 'n perd met vier bene struikel, wat nog 'n mens met net een tong; die beste perd struikel ook.
e'rrand, boodskap; opdrag; *a FOOL's ~,* 'n dwase onderneming; *be SENT on an ~,* op 'n boodskap gestuur word; ~**-boy,** loopjonge, boodskapper.
e'rrant, swerwend, rondtrekkend, dolend, dwalend; ~**ry,** omswerwing, ronddoling; ~ **star,** dwaalster.
errat'ic, dwalend, swerwend, ongereeld, ongedurig, ongelyk, wisselvallig; ~ **block,** swerfsteen; swerfblok.
errat'um, (..ta), (druk)fout, vergissing, erratum.
err'ing, feilbaar, sondig, afdwalend.
erron'eous, verkeerd, afwykend, onjuis, foutief; ~ *notion (idea),* dwaalbegrip; ~**ly,** foutief, foutiewelik, per abuis; ~**ness,** onjuistheid, verkeerdheid.
e'rror, fout, misgissing, feil, dwaling, vergissing, abuis; oortreding; *BE in ~,* verkeerd wees; *CLERICAL ~,* skryffout; *~ in COUNTING,* telfout; *FALL into ~,* 'n fout begaan, onklaar trap; *~ in FACTS,* feitedwaling; *IN ~,* per abuis; *~ of JUDG(E)MENT,* oordeelsfout; misgissing, mistasting, misskatting; *the LAST ~ is worse than the first,* die laaste dwaling is erger as die eerste; *~s and OMISSIONS excepted (E. & O. E.),* behoudens foute en weglatings (F. & W.); ~ **signal,** foutsein, vergissingsein; ~ **variance,** foutvariansie (stat.).
ersatz', substituut, plaasvervanger.
Erse, (n) dialek van Skotse Hooglande; (a) Ers, Iers, Gaelies.
erst, vroeër, voorheen; ~**'while,** vroeër.
erubes'cent, rooi wordend, blosend.
eructa'tion, oprisping, opbraaksel; sooibrand; uitbarsting (vulkaan).
e'rudite, geleerd; grondig; belese.
erudi'tion, geleerdheid, erudisie; belesenheid.
erupt', uitbars (vulkaan); deurkom (tande); uitbreek (sweer); ~**ion,** uitbarsting, uitbreking, erupsie; uitslag; deurbraak (tande); brand; ~**ive,** uitbarstend; uitslaande; eruptief; vulkanies; opvlieënd; *~ ive rock,* stollingsgesteente.
erysip'elas, belroos, Antoniusvuur, wondroos, erisipelas.
ery'throcyte, rooibloedsel (=liggaampie).
escadrille', eskadrielje, lugeskader.
escalade', (n) aanval met stormleer, beklimming, eskalade; (v) bestorm, beklim.
es'calate, met 'n vervoerband beweeg; eskaleer; uitbrei.
es'calating clause, aanpasklousule, eskaleerklousule, voorbehoudsklousule.
escala'tion, uitbreiding; eskalasie; verhoging (pryse).
es'calator, roltrap; hystrap.
escall'op, *kyk* **scallop.**
escap'able, ontvlugbaar.
escapade', eskapade, moedswillige streek, malkopdaad; *indulge in boyish ~s,* kattekwaad aanrig (doen).
escape', (n) ontsnapping, ontvlugting, ontkoming; lek (gas); wilde uitloper; opslag; reddingstoestel (brand); nooduitgang, nooddeur; *MAKE one's ~,* vlug, ontsnap; *have a NARROW ~,* ternouernood ontkom; *there is NO ~,* daar is geen uitweg nie; (v) ontsnap, ontvlug, ontkom; ontval (woorde); vryspring (berisping); aan iets ontkom; ontgaan; lek (gas); *his NAME ~s me,* sy naam het my ontgaan;

~ *NOTICE,* nie raakgesien word nie; ~ *UNHURT,* daar ongedeerd van afkom; ~ **clause,** uitkomsklousule, voorwaardelike klousule; ~ **cock,** afblaaskraan, suiskraan; ~ **door,** nooddeur; ~**e',** ontsnapte, ontsnapper, ontvlugter; ~ **hatch,** noodluik; ~ **hole,** uitlaatgat; ~ **ladder,** brandleer, noodleer; ~ **ment,** veiligheidsklep, gang (oorlosie); ontvlugting; uitweg; ~ **shaft,** ontvlugtingskag; noodskag; ~ **valve,** veiligheidsklep, uitlaatklep.
escap'ism, lewensontvlugting.
escap'ist, ontvlugter, ontsnapper; ~ **entertainment,** ontvlugtingsvermaak.
escapol'ogist, boeiekoning, ontsnapkunstenaar.
escar'got, (eetbare) slak.
es'carole, volhartandyvie.
escarp', (n) binnewal; eskarp; skuinste, hang, glooiing; platorand, kransreeks; (v) steil afgrawe, eskarpeer.
escarp'ment, valskerpte, kransrand, platorand, eskarp.
es'char, brandkors, brandrofie.
eschatolog'ic(al), eskatologies.
eschatol'ogist, eskatoloog.
eschatol'ogy, eskatologie, leerstuk omtrent die laaste dinge.
escheat', (n) vervalle eiendom, verval; (v) verval; verbeurd verklaar, in beslag neem, beslag lê op, konfiskeer.
eschew', vermy, sku, ontwyk; ~**er,** vermyer, ontwyker.
eschscholtz'ia, eschscholtzia, goudpapawer *(Papa veraceae).*
es'cort, (n) geleide, vrygeleide; *under ~,* onder (vry)geleide.
escort', (v) (be)gelei, wegbring, vergesel, geleide doen, eskorteer.
es'cort vessel, geleiskip, konvooiskip.
escribe', aanskrywe; *~d circle,* aangeskrewe sirkel.
es'critoire, skryftafeltjie, lessenaar.
escud'o, (-s), escudo (Portugese muntstuk).
es'culent, eetbaar.
Escur'ial, Eskuriaal.
escutch'eon, melkspieël (koei); beslag, sleutelgatplaat; skild, familiewapen; naambord; *a blot on his ~,* 'n klad op sy naam (eer); ~ **pin,** skildspyker.
e'skar, es'ker, esker, smeltwaterrug.
Es'kimo, (-es), Eskimo; ~ **pie,** eskimoroomys.
eso'phagus, slukderm.
esote'ric, net vir ingewydes, geheimsinnig; geheim; esoteries.
espace', spasieer; ~**ment,** spasiëring.
espagnole', Spaans; ~ **sauce,** Spaanse sous.
espal'ier, latwerk; leiboom.
espart'o, esparto, Spaanse gras, alfagras, draadgras.
espe'cial, besonder; ~**ly,** veral, vernaamlik, in die besonder, bepaald, spesiaal.
Esperan'to, Esperanto.
espi'al, bespieding.
espi'er, bespieder, spioen.
es'pionage, spioenasie, bespieding, verspieding.
esplanade', plein, wandelplek, esplanade.
espous'al, bruilof, huwelik; verlowing; ondersteuning, omhelsing (van 'n saak); verlowing; ~ **s,** troubeloftes.
espouse', trou, in die huwelik gee, uithuwelik; omhels, aanneem, voorstaan; ~ *someone's cause,* die handskoen vir iem. opneem.
espres'so, espresso(koffie); espressokoffiemaker; koffiekafee, espressokafee.
esprit', gees, lewendigheid; ~ **de corps,** samehorigheids(gevoel), korpsgees, spangees, esprit de corps.
espy', (espied), bespied, opmerk.
Es'quimau, (-x) = Eskimo.
esquire', skildknaap; heer; weledele heer, meneer; *J. Smith Esq.,* Weledele heer J. Smith.
ess, es (letter s); s-vormige voorwerp.
ess'ay, (n) proef; poging; vertoog, verhandeling; opstel, essay.
essay', (v) beproef, toets, keur, essaieer (minerale); probeer; ~**er,** keurder, ondersoeker, essaieur; ~**ist,** essayis; opstelskrywer.
ess'ence, reukwerk, reukgoed; geur, geursel; wese,

gees; grondbestanddeel; krag, ekstrak, essens(ie), aftreksel, beste deel, kern; ~ *of LIFE*, lewensessens; *be the ~ of POLITENESS*, die beleefdheid self wees; 'n toonbeeld van beleefdheid wees; *TIME is of the ~*, alles hang v.d. tyd af.

essen'tial, (n) (die) wesenlike, kern, hoofsaak; essensiële; (pl) noodsaaklikhede; *the ~ s*, die hoofsake; (a) wesenlik, essensieel, hoofsaaklik, noodsaaklik, onontbeerlik, belangrik; ~ *CHARACTER*, belangrikste (vernaamste) eienskap; ~ *ELEMENTS*, noodsaaklike elemente; *an ~ ERROR*, 'n wesenlike dwaling; ~ *OIL*, vlugtige olie; ~ *RESISTANCE*, werklike weerstand; ~ *SERVICES*, noodsaaklike dienste.

essential'ity, wesenlikheid, (die) essensiële, noodsaaklikheid.

essen'tially, in hoofsaak, hoofsaaklik, wesenlik.

es'senwood, esse(n)hout.

ess'onite, kaneelsteen, essoniet.

estab'lish, instel (pad), oprig, vestig, stig, tot stand bring; ~ *a FACT*, 'n feit vasstel; ~ *ONESELF*, jou vestig; ~ *a SUIT*, 'n kleur losspeel (kaarte); in die lewe roep; bewys, staaf; vasstel.

estab'lished, vas, vasgestel, bewese; gevestig, gestig, opgerig; ~ *CHURCH*, staatskerk; *an ~ FACT*, 'n voldonge feit; ~ *LAWS*, bestaande wette; ~ *STAFF*, vaste personeel; ~ *TRUTH*, uitgemaakte waarheid.

estab'lishment, grondvesting, nedersetting; ontstaan, stigting; totstandkoming; oprigting; invoering; instelling; getalsterkte; gestig; handelshuis, saak; personeel; vestiging, bevestiging; huishouding; bedryf, onderneming; liggaam; stigting, aanleg; vasstelling, bestendiging; diensstaat; *CHURCH E~*, staatskerk; *THE E~*, die (Britse) gesagsorde; die gevestigde orde; die gevestigdes (toonaangewendes); ~ *a'rian*, gevestigde (persoon).

estafette', renbode, hardloper (in oorlog); estafet.

estate', besitting; landgoed; huis en erf; (erf)goed; eiendom; boedel; staat, rang; toestand; *DECEASED ~*, bestorwe boedel; *FOURTH ~*, die pers; *the HOLY ~*, die huwelikstaat; *come to MAN'S ~*, die manlike jare bereik; mondig word; *PERSONAL ~*, roerende goed; *REAL ~*, grondbesit, vaste eiendom, onroerende goedere; *SURRENDER one's ~*, boedel oorgee; *the THIRD ~*, die derde stand; ~ **agent**, eiendomsagent; ~ **car**, stasiewa; landgoedmotor; ~ **duty**, boedelbelasting; ~ **fee**, boedelgeld(e); ~ **holder**, boedelhouer; ~'**s branch**, eiendomsafdeling; ~ **wine**, landgoedwyn.

esteem', (n) agting, waardering, skatting, aansien, hoogagting; *be held in HIGH ~*, hoog in aansien wees; hoog geag word; *HOLD in ~*, hoogag; (v) ag, hoogag, op prys stel, waardeer; skat; ~ed, geag, gesien.

es'ter, ester.

esterifica'tion, verestering, estervorming.

es'terify, (..fied), verester.

Est(h)on'ia, Estland; ~n, (n) Estlander; (a) Estnies, Est(lands).

es'timable, agtenswaardig.

es'timate, (n) raming, prysopgawe; skatting, waardering; begroting; (v) beraam, benader, bereken; skat, waardeer, op prys stel; 'n begroting opstel; ~*d LOAD*, beraamde belasting (elek.); *THE ~ s*, die begroting; ~*d TIME of arrival*, berekende (vermoedelike) tyd van aankoms.

estima'tion, begroting, berekening, skatting; waardering; hoogagting, estimasie; mening.

es'timator, skatter, waardeerder; berekenaar.

es'tival = **aestival**.

estop', (-ped), belemmer, belet (reg); ~ **page**, ~ **pel**, belemmering, estoppel (jur.).

esto'vers, estovers, gemeenskaplike eiendom(sreg).

estrade', trappie, verhoog, estrade.

estrange', vervreem, afsterf; ontvreem, verwyder; ~ **ment**, afsterwing, vervreemding, verwydering.

estreat', (n) afskrif, kopie; (v) kopieer, 'n afskrif maak; verbeurd verklaar (borgtog); ~ **ment**, verbeuring; verbeurdverklaring.

es'tuarine, estuaries.

es'tuary, (..ries), riviermond, tregtermonding; seearm, estuarium.

esur'ient, hongerig, begerig, gulsig.

état': **coup d'** ~, staatsgreep.

et cet'era, (etc.), ensovoort(s) (ens.); ~ **s**, ekstratjies; ekstra onkoste; ander dinge.

etch, (-es), ets; ~ *out*, uitets, uitbyt; ~ **er**, etser.

etch'ing, ets(kuns); etswerk; ~-**iron**, etsyster; ~-**needle**, etsnaald; ~-**water**, etswater.

Etern'al, (die) Ewige; *the ~ City*, die Ewige Stad, Rome.

etern'al, ewig; ~ *LIFE*, die ewige lewe; ~ *PUNISHMENT*, ewige straf; *enter one's ~ REST*, jou ewige rus ingaan; *the ~ TRIANGLE*, die ewige driehoek; ~**ize**, verewig; ~**ly**, ewig, ewigdurend.

etern'ity, ewigheid; ~ **ring**, middelring.

etern'ize, verewig.

eth'anol, wyngees, etielalkohol, etanol.

eth'er, eter; lugruim.

ether'eal, hemels, eteries; eteragtig, vlugtig; ~**ize**, vergeestelik; vervlugtig.

eth'erize, met eter verdoof, eter gee.

eth'ic(al), sedekundig, eties, sedelik; *ethical dative*, etiese datief.

eth'ics, sedeleer, sedekunde, etiek, etika.

Ethiop'ia, Etiopië, Abessinië.

Ethio'pian, (n) Etiopiër; (a) Etiopies.

eth'moid, sifagtig; ~ **bone**, sifbeen.

eth'narchy, etnargie, provinsieregering.

eth'nic, etnies, etnologies, volkekundig; heidens; ~ **character**, etniesheid; ~**alism**, heidendom.

ethnobot'any, volksplantkunde, etnobotanie.

ethnocen'tric, etnosentries.

ethnog'rapher, volkekundige, etnograaf.

ethnograph'ic(al), volkekundig, etnografies.

ethnog'raphy, volkekundig, etnografies.

ethnolog'ic(al), volkekundig, etnologies; etnies.

ethnol'ogist, volkekundige, etnoloog.

ethnol'ogy, volkekunde, etnologie.

ethnomusico'logy, etnomusikologie.

ethol'ogy, karakterkunde, etologie, sedekunde, gedragskunde.

eth'os, karakter, gebruik; sedes, etos.

eth'yl, etiel; ~ **alcohol**, etielalkohol, etanol; ~ **chloride**, chlooretiel.

et'iolate, kleur verloor (bot.), verbleik, etioleer.

etiola'tion, verble(i)king, eteolering.

etiol'ogy, etiologie, oorsaakleer.

etiquette', wellewendheidsvorme, etiket, fatsoen.

et'na, pompstofie, spiritusstofie.

Et'on, Eton; ~ **crop**, seunskop.

ê'triere, touleer, ètrier.

Etrur'ia, Etrurië; ~**n**, (n) Etruriër; (a) Etruries.

Etrus'can, (n) Etruskiër, Etruriër; (a) Etruries, Etruskies.

étude', etude, musiekstudie, musiekstuk.

étui', koker, doos, etui.

etymolog'ic(al), etimologies.

etymol'ogist, etimoloog.

etymol'ogize, etimologiseer.

etymol'ogy, etimologie, woordafleiding, woordvorming, woordverklaring, woordvorsing.

et'ymon, (-s, **etyma**), etimon, grondwoord, stamwoord.

eubiot'ics, eubiotiek.

eucalyp'tus, eukaliptus, gomboom, bloekom(boom); ~ **oil**, bloekomolie, eukaliptusolie.

Eu'charist, Nagmaal; eucharistie; danksegging.

Euchari'stic, Nagmaals=; eucharisties.

euchlor'ine, chloordioksiedmengsel.

eu'chre, (n) Amerikaanse kaartspel; (v) wen.

Eu'clid, Euklides; meetkunde.

eud(a)em'onism, geluksaligheidsleer, eudaimonisme.

eudiom'eter, eudiometer, luggehaltemeter; gasmeetbuis.

eugen'ic, eugeneties, volksteelt=; ~ **s**, rasverbeteringsleer, eugenese, eugenetiek.

eu'genist, eugenetikus.

euhed'ral, idiomorf.

euhe'merism, euhemerisme, miteverklaring.

eul'ogist, lofredenaar, aanpryser.

eul'ogize, loof, prys, roem, aanprys, ophemel.

eul'ogy, (..gies), lofspraak, lof, ophemeling, aanprysing.
eun'uch, gesnyde, gekastreerde, ontmande, eunug.
eupep'tic, met 'n goeie spysvertering, eupepties.
euph'emism, eufemisme, verbloeming, versagting; versagtende uitdrukking.
euphemis'tic, eufemisties, versagtend (taal); bedek.
eu'phemize, eufemisties (versagtend) uitdruk.
euphon'ic, euphon'ious, welluidend, soetklinkend, eufonies.
eupho'nium, eufonium, tenoortuba.
euph'onize, welluidend maak.
euph'ony, welluidendheid, eufonie.
euphor'bia, melkbos; noordsdoring; naboom, euforbia; vingerpol.
euphor'ia, behaaglikheid, welsynsgevoel, euforie.
eupho'riant, euforiant, opkikker.
eupho'ric, eufories, behaaglik.
eupho'ry = **euphoria**.
euph'rasy, oëtroos, eufrasie.
Euphrat'es, Eufraat.
euph'uism, blo(e)mrykheid, eufuïsme.
Eurafr'ican, (n) Eurafrikaan; (a) Eurafrikaans, halfbloed=.
Euras'ian, (n) Eurasiër; (a) Eurasies, halfbloed=.
eurek'a!, eureka! ek het dit!
eur(h)yth'mic, euritmies; euritmiek.
euryth'mics, euritmiek, bewegingsleer.
Eur'omart, Euromark.
Eu'rope, Europa.
Europe'an, (n) Europeaan, Europeër (inwoner van Europa); witman, blanke; (a) Europees.
euro'pium, europium.
eu'sol, eusol (Edinburgh University solution of lime).
Eustachian tube, buis van Eustachius, keel-oorbuis.
eu'stasy, eustasie, seevlakverandering.
eutec'tic, eutekties.
euthanas'ia, genadedood; middel vir genadedood; eutanasie.
eutro'phic, eutrofies, voedingsryk (meer, dam).
eu'trophy, eutrofie.
evac'uant, (n) purgeermiddel; (a) suiwerend, purgerend.
evac'uate, leegmaak, ontlas; (ont)ruim, evakueer.
evacua'tion, ontlasting, stoelgang; lediging; ontruiming, evakuasie.
evacuee', ontruimeling, weggevoerde.
evade', vermy (vraag); versuim (werk); ontloop, ontwyk, ontduik (gereg); uitvlugte soek.
eva'ginate, omdop, uitstulp.
evagina'tion, uitstulping, omdopping.
eval'uate, in syfers uitdruk, besyfer; die waarde bepaal van, bereken, beoordeel.
evalua'tion, skatting, berekening, waardebepaling, raming, evaluasie.
evanesce', verdwyn; verdamp; in rook opgaan; wegsterwe.
evanes'cence, verdwyning; kortstondigheid, verganklikheid.
evanes'cent, verdwynend; onmerkbaar; kortstondig, verganklik, vlugtig.
evan'gel, evangelie, goeie boodskap.
evangel'ic(al), evangelies; Luthers.
evangel'icalism, leer van die Evangeliese kerk.
evan'gel: ~**ism**, evangelieleer; evangeliegesindheid; ~**ist**, evangelieprediker, evangelis; ~**is'tic**, evangelisties; ~**iza'tion**, evangelisasie, verbreiding van die evangelie; ~**ize**, evangeliseer, die evangelie verkondig.
evan'ish, verdwyn; ~**ment**, verdwyning.
evap'orable, verdampbaar.
evap'orate, uitwasem; verdamp, vervlugtig, vervlieg; verkook; bokveld toe gaan; ~ *DOWN*, indamp; ~*d MILK*, ingedampte melk.
evap'orating, verdampend; ~ **dish**, verdamp(ings)bak; ~ **pan**, verdamppan.
evapora'tion, uitwaseming; verdamping; indamping; damp; *HEAT of* ~, verdampingswarmte; *SURFACE of* ~, verdampingsoppervlak; ~ **gauge**, verdampingsmeter; ~ **point**, verdampingspunt.
evap'orative, verdampings=.
evaporativ'ity, verdampingsvermoë.

evap'orator, verdampingstoestel, verdamper.
evapori'meter, evaporom'eter, verdampingsmeter.
eva'sion, ontwyking, ontduiking, jakkalsdraaie, vermyding, ontvlugting, uitvlug.
evas'ive, ontwykend, ontduikend, rondspringerig, vol uitvlugte; ~ *talk*, slimpraatjies; ~**ness**, ontwykendheid, vaagheid.
Eve, Eva; *daughters of* ~, Evasgeslag.
eve,' aand; vooraand; *on the* ~ *of*, aan die vooraand van.
evec'tion, afwyking (maan).
e'ven[1], (n) aand.
e'ven[2], (v) gelykmaak, effen, vereffen; ~ *OUT*, uitstryk; gelykmaak; (a) effe, glad; egalig, egaal, gelykmatig, reëlmatig; kalm; onpartydig; *they ARE* ~, hulle staan gelyk; *of* ~ *DATE*, van dieselfde datum; *GET* ~ *with someone*, jou wreek op iem.; iem. met gelyke munt betaal; met iem. afreken; *on an* ~ *KEEL*, met gelyke kiel, gelyklastig; ~ *MONEY*, gelyke kanse; gelykop weddenskap; ~ *NUMBER*, gelyk getal; *ODD and* ~, gelyk en ongelyk.
e'ven[3], (adv) eers, ook, eweneens, selfs; ~ *AS*, ewe(n)as, soos; ~ *IF*, selfs al, al was (dit dat); ~ *MORE*, selfs nog meer; *NOT* ~, nie eers (eens) nie; ~ *NOW*, op die oomblik; selfs nou; nou net; ~ *SO*, nietemin, ewenwel; almaskie; ~ *THOUGH*, selfs al.
e'ven: ~**-aged**, gelykjarig, ewe oud; ~**-handed**, onpartydig.
eve'ning[1], gelykmaking.
eve'ning[2], aand; awend (digt.); *GOOD* ~, naand, goeienaand; *LAST* ~, gisteraand; *OF an* ~, saans, in die aand; een aand; *ON the* ~ *of*, die aand van; *THIS* ~, vanaand; ~ **bag**, aandsak(kie), aandtassie; ~ **class**, aandklas; ~ **dress**, aandtoilet, aandkostuum; aandjapon, aandtabberd, aandrok, dansrok; aanddrag, swaelstert, aandpak (van mans); aandtenue (mil.); ~ **glow**, aandgloed, aandrooi; ~ **lesson**, aandles; ~ **meal**, aandete; ~ **paper**, aandkoerant, aandblad; ~ **prayer**, aandgebed; ~ **primrose**, nagkers; ~ **shift**, aandskof; ~ **shirt**, aandhemp, borshemp; ~ **star**, aandster; ~ **wedding**, aandhuwelik; ~ **worship**, aandgodsdiens.
e'ven: ~**ly**, gelykweg; gelykop; effe, egalig; ~**minded**, gelykmoedig; ~**ness**, gladheid, gelykheid, gelykmatigheid, egaligheid; bedaardheid; ~**-numbered**, eenders genommer.
e'vensong, aandlied, aandgesang, vesper; aanddiens.
event', uitslag, afloop; evenement; ontknoping; wedstryd, sportnommer; gebeurtenis, voorval, geval; *at ALL* ~*s*, in alle geval; *in ANY* ~, in alle geval; *CHAIN of* ~*s*, reeks gebeure; *the COURSE of* ~*s*, die loop van gebeurtenisse; *in EITHER* ~, in alle geval; *GREAT* ~, wêreldgebeurtenis; *awaiting a HAPPY* ~, in die blye verwagting wees; *IN the* ~ *of*, in geval van; *QUITE an* ~, 'n hele gebeurtenis; *coming* ~*s cast their SHADOWS before*, naderende gebeurtenisse kondig hulle self aan; *in THAT* ~, as dit gebeur; as dit sou gebeur dat; *be WISE after the* ~, na die voorval wys wees; ~**ful**, merkwaardig, avontuurlik, veelbewoë, belangrik.
e'ven-threaded, effedraads.
e'ventide, avondstond, awendstond.
event'less, stil, kalm, rustig.
even'tual, toevallig, moontlik, gebeurlik; gevolglik, slot=; eventueel; eindelik.
eventual'ity, (..ties), gebeurlikheid, eventualiteit.
even'tually, per slot van rekening, ten slotte, uiteindelik.
even'tuate, afloop, uitloop op, eindig; ~ *from*, voortvloei uit.
ev'er, ooit, altoos, altyd, ewig; ~ *AFTER*, van dié tyd af; ~ *and ANON*, telkens, nou en dan, by tye; *the BEST* ~, die allerbeste; *for* ~ *and a DAY*, vir altyd; *DID you* ~?, het jy ooit?; *FOR* ~, ewig, vir altyd; *FOR* ~ *and* ~, tot in alle ewigheid, vir altyd; *as GOOD as* ~, so goed soos altyd (ooit); *HARDLY* ~, byna nooit; *as MUCH as* ~, so veel as ooit; *thank you* ~ *so MUCH*, baie, baie dankie; *NOTHING* ~ *happens*, daar gebeur nooit iets nie; *SELDOM or* ~, selde of nooit; ~ *SINCE*, van dié

tyd af; van toe af; *as SOON as* ~ *you can*, so gou as jy maar kan; *as WELL as* ~, so goed as ooit; *WHY* ~ *not?*, waarom ter wêreld nie?; *YOURS* ~, altyd joue: ~**-bearing** = **everlasting**; ~ **green,** (n) meerjarige plant; (a) groenblywend, altydgroen, immergroen, blaarhoudend; ~**-increasing,** steeds groeiend (toenemend); ~ **last'ing,** (n) ewigheid; sewejaartjie; strooiblom, immortelle; kanniedood; (a) ewig(durend); ~ **more,** vir altyd, ewig, altyd weer; ~**sharp,** altyd skerp.
ever'sion, omdopping, omkering.
evert', omdop, binnestebuite keer, omkeer.
ev'ery, elke, ieder; alle; ~ *BIT*, heeltemal, alles, volkome, deur en deur; ~ *other DAY*, (al) om die ander dag; ~ *man JACK*, almal; ~ *bit as MUCH*, ruim soveel; ~ *NOW and then*, so af en toe, telkens; *on* ~ *SIDE*, aan al(le) kante; ~ *TIME*, telkens; elke slag (keer); *in* ~ *WAY*, in alle opsigte; ~ **body,** almal, elkeen, 'n iegelik, iedereen; ~**day,** aldae, daagliks; gewoon; ~**one,** algar, almal, elkeen, iedereen, 'n iegelik.
ev'erything, alles; ~ *COMES to him who waits*, wie geduldig wag, kry alles; ~ *possible*, al die moontlike, alles wat moontlik is (was).
ev'ery: ~ **way,** in alle opsigte; ~**where,** oral(s), alom, allerweë.
evict', geregtelik uitsit; geregtelik ontneem; uitwin (jur.); ~**ion,** uitsetting; ontsetting.
ev'idence, (n) bewys; getuienis; bewyslewering; (getuie)verklaring; bewysstuk; blyk; klaarblyklikheid; *BE in* ~, die aandag trek; op die voorgrond wees; in die oog val; *BEAR* ~, getuienis aflê; *CIRCUMSTANTIAL* ~, omstandigheidsgetuienis, aanwysende getuienis; *FURNISH* ~ *of*, die bewys lewer vir; *GIVE* ~, getuienis aflê; blyk gee; *RECORD of* ~, getuienis(verslag); *there is not the SLIGHTEST* ~, daar is hoegenaamd geen bewys nie; (v) getuienis aflê, bewys, staaf, getuig.
ev'ident, duidelik, klaarblyklik.
eviden'tial, bewysend, tot bewys dienend.
e'vidently, klaarblyklik, begryplikerwyse, blykbaar, glo.
ev'il, (n) kwaad, bose; euwel, slegtheid, bedorwenheid, sonde; ramp, ongeluk; ~ *to him who* ~ *DOES (thinks)*, wie kwaad doet, kwaad ontmoet; *the KING'S* ~, kliersiekte; *choose the LESSER* ~, van twee kwade die minste kies; *do* ~ *and look for the LIKE*, die kwaad loon sy meester; *NECESSARY* ~, noodsaaklike kwaad; (a) verkeerd, lelik, boos, kwaad, sondig, snood, erg, sleg; *put off the* ~ *DAY*, die kwade dag uitstel; *the* ~ *EYE*, die bose oog; *FALL on* ~ *days*, teenspoed kry; *have no* ~ *INTENT*, geen kwaad bedoel nie; dit nie sleg meen nie; *the* ~ *ONE*, die duiwel; *of* ~ *REPUTE*, berug; *don't RETURN* ~ *for* ~, moenie kwaad met kwaad vergeld nie; *SEE no* ~ *in someone*, geen kwaad in iem. sien nie; *SPEAK* ~ *of*, sleg praat van; iem. beskinder; *an* ~ *TONGUE*, 'n lastertong; ~**-doer,** boosdoener, kwaaddoener; ~*-doers are* ~*-thinkers*, as jy iem. jaag, staan jy self nie stil nie; ~ **genius,** bose gees; ~**ly,** ten kwade, sleg; ~*ly disposed*, kwaadgesind; ~**-minded,** kwaaddenkend; sleggesind, boosaardig; vol liederlike gedagtes; ~**ness,** verdorwenheid, slegtheid, goddeloosheid; ~**-smelling,** slegruikend, stinkend; ~**-speaking,** kwaadsprekery, agterklap, skindery; ~**-worker,** boosdoener, kwaadstoker.
evince', bewys, betoon, aantoon; aan die dag lê, openbaar.
ev'irate, ontman, kastreer; verswak (fig.).
evis'cerate, die ingewande uithaal, ontwei.
ev'ocate, oproep, besweer.
evoca'tion, oproeping, evokasie, beswering.
evoc'ative, oproepend, evokatief, beswerend.
evoke', evoseer, oproep, beswer; uittart, uitlok; voor 'n hoërhof bring.
evolu'tion, worteltrekking; maneuver, swenking; ontvouing, ontrolling; ontwikkeling, evolusie; ontplooiing; *theory of* ~, evolusieteorie; ~**al,** ~**ary,** evolusie-, ontwikkelings-; ~**ism,** evolusieleer, evolusionisme; ~**ist,** evolusionis; ~**is'tic,** evolusionisties.

ev'olutive, evolusie-, evolutief.
evolve', aflei, trek; vorm; voortbring; ontvou, ontplooi; ontwikkel; ~**ment,** ontplooiing; ~**r,** ontvouer; voortbringer.
evul'sion, uitrukking, uittrekking.
ewe, ooi; ~ *with HORNS*, horingmansooi; ~ *with YOUNG*, lammerooi.
ewe' lamb, ooilam; hooggewaardeerde besitting; *one's* ~, jou enigste ooilam.
ewe'-necked, (perd) met 'n skaapnek, holnek.
ew'er, waskan, lampetkan, lampetbeker, wasbeker, waterbeker, gorletbeker.
ex^1, (prep) uit; sonder; ~ *GRATIA*, by wyse van guns; ~ *OFFICIO*, ex officio, ampshalwe; ~ *PARTE*, uitgaande van net die een kant.
ex-^{2}, (pref.) gewese, oud-, voormalige, eks-.
exa'cerbate, vererg, verskerp; verbitter, prikkel.
exacerba'tion, verergering; verbittering.
exact'^{1}, (v) afpers; vorder, eis; verg, afverg, afdwing; ~ *VENGEANCE from*, wraak uitoefen op.
exact'^{2}, (a) noukeurig, sekuur, juis, stip, presies, eksak; gelykluidend (afskrif); ~ *COPY*, getroue afskrif; ~ *SCIENCES*, die eksakte wetenskappe.
exact'er = **exactor.**
exact'ing, streng, veeleisend; ~ *CIRCUMSTANCES*, moeilike omstandighede; *TOO* ~, te veeleisend.
exact'ion, vordering, eis; afpersing, afdwinging.
exact': ~**itude,** noukeurigheid, juistheid, stiptheid; ~**ly,** (adv) noukeurig, presies, op 'n haar; (interj) presies, juistement; *not* ~ *ly*, nie juis nie; ~**ness,** juistheid, presiesheid, eksaktheid.
exact'or, eiser; afperser.
exa'ggerate, oordrywe, vergroot, breed uitmeet; aanlas (storie); *DON'T* ~*!*, sak, Sarel!; ~ *SOMETHING*, iets oordryf, van 'n vlooi 'n olifant maak; ~**d,** oordrewe, hiperbolies.
exa'ggerating, oordrywend.
exaggera'tion, oordrywing, vergroting, oordrewenheid.
exa'ggerative, oordrywend.
exalt', verhef, verhoog, prys, ophemel; verdiep (kleure); ~ **a'tion,** verdieping; verheffing, opheming; verrukking; geestesvervoering; eksaltasie.
exalt'ed, verhewe, hoog, verhoog, groots; ~ *IDEAS*, verhewe begrippe; ~ *RANK*, hoë rang; ~**ness,** verhewenheid, grootsheid.
exalt'ing, hartverheffend.
exam' = **examination.**
exam'inant, ondervraer, ondersoeker.
examina'tion, eksamen; ondersoek; verhoor, ondervraging; *BE under* ~, verhoor word; *on CLOSER* ~, by nader ondersoek; *FAIL in an* ~, in 'n eksamen sak; ~ *INTO*, ondersoek na; *PASS an* ~, in 'n eksamen slaag, 'n eksamen met goeie gevolg aflê; *SIT for an* ~, eksamen doen (skrywe); ~ *of WITNESSES*, getuieverhoor; *WRITE an* ~, eksamen skrywe; ~ **book,** eksamenskrif, eksamenboek; ~ **centre,** eksamensentrum; ~ **committee,** eksamenkommissie; ~ **fee,** eksamengeld; ~ **fever,** eksamenkoors; ~ **fright,** eksamenvrees; ~ **mark,** eksamensyfer; ~ **number,** eksamennommer; ~ **paper,** eksamenvraestel; ~ **position,** eksamenposisie; ~ **question,** eksamenvraag; ~ **results,** eksamenuitslae; ~ **returns,** eksamenopgawes; ~ **system,** eksamenstelsel; ~ **test,** eksamentoets; ~ **time table,** eksamenrooster.
exam'ine, ondersoek, deurkam, deursoek, in oënskou neem; eksamineer; bekyk; deurloop (rekeninge); toets; ondervra, uitvra, verhoor, 'n ondersoek instel.
examinee', geëksamineerde, eksaminandus, kandidaat.
exam'iner, ondersoeker; eksaminator; ondervraer; kontroleur.
exam'ining, ondersoekend, eksaminerend; ~ **board,** eksamenkommissie; ~ **body,** eksaminerende liggaam; ~ **officer,** visenteerbeampte (hawe).
exam'ple, (n) voorbeeld, model; monster, proef, eksemplaar; *FOR* ~, byvoorbeeld; *MAKE an* ~ *of*, as voorbeeld laat dien; ~ *is better than PRECEPT*, woorde (leringe) wek, maar voorbeelde trek; *SET*

exanimate 879 *exculpate*

an ~, 'n voorbeeld stel; *TAKE* ~ *by*, 'n voorbeeld neem aan; *by WAY of* ~, as voorbeeld; *WITHOUT* ~, weergaloos, sonder voorbeeld; (v) as voorbeeld aanhaal.
exan'imate, (v) doodmaak; ontmoedig; (a) dood, sielloos, ontsiel, leweloos.
ex an'imo, met geesdrif, hartlik, graag.
exanthe'ma, uitslag, eksanteem.
exas'perate, kwaad maak, terg, verbitter, vererg; ~ *someone*, iem. se siel uittrek.
exas'perating, tergend, ergerlik.
exaspera'tion, gramskap, ergernis, terging, verbittering.
excarn'ate, ontvlees.
ex cathed'ra, op 'n toon van gesag, uit die hoogte; ex cathedra.
ex'cavate, uithol, uitdelf, uitgrawe, opgrawe.
excava'tion, uitgrawing, opgrawing, uitholling; holte, gat.
ex'cavator, opgrawer; slootgrawer, masjiengraaf, grondvreter.
exceed', oortref; oorskry; te bowe gaan; te buite gaan; ~ *his POWERS*, buite sy bevoegdheid handel; ~ *the SPEED limit*, die snelheidsperk oorskry; ~**ing(ly)**, buitengewoon, bomate, bomatig, verskriklik, uitbundig, uitermate, uiters, buitemate.
excel', (-led), oortref; uitmunt, uitblink.
ex'cellence, voortreflikheid, uitmuntendheid, deug.
ex'cellency, eksellensie; *His E* ~, Sy Eksellensie.
ex'cellent, uitstekend, voortreflik, eersteklas, puur, puik, eksellent, uitmuntend, gaaf; *most* ~, uitstekend, opperbes.
excel'sior, altyd hoër, excelsior.
excen'tric, eensydig (bot.); ʌʌ *eccentric*.
except' ¹, (v) uitsonder, uitsluit; 'n eksepsie opwerp; *present company* ~ *ed*, almal hier teenwoordig uitgesluit.
except' ², (prep) uitgesonderd, uitgenome, behalwe; *ALL* ~ *him*, almal buiten hom, almal behalwe hy; ~ *FOR*, behoudens, behalwe, met die uitsondering van; (conj) tensy.
except'ing, uitgesonderd, behalwe, uitgenome.
excep'tion, uitsondering; eksepsie; teenwerping; *the* ~ *PROVES the rule*, die uitsondering bevestig die reël; *RAISE* ~*s to*, besware opwerp teen; *an* ~ *to the RULE*, 'n uitsondering op die reël; *SUSTAIN an* ~, 'n eksepsie handhaaf; *TAKE* ~ *to*, aanstoot neem aan; protes aanteken teen; *WITH the* ~ *of*, uitgesonderd; *WITHOUT* ~, sonder uitsondering; voor die voet; ~ **able**, aanstootlik, laakbaar; betwisbaar; ~ **al**, besonder, buitengewoon, spesiaal (geval), eksepsioneel, uitsonderlik; ~ **ally**, buitengewoon; weergaloos; by wyse van uitsondering.
ex'cerpt, (n) uittreksel, verkorting, aanhaling, ekserp.
excerpt', (v) uitsoek, ekserpeer, 'n uittreksel maak; ~ **ion**, uittreksel; bloemlesing; ~ **or**, ekserptemaker, ekserpeerder.
excess', te veel, oorskot, saldo; oorskryding (reg); oordaad, oormaat; buitensporigheid, onmatigheid; *CARRY to* ~, oordryf; *IN* ~, oordadig; *IN* ~ *of*, meer as; ~ **air**, oortollige lug; ~ **amount**, byslag; ~ **baggage**, ekstra bagasie, oorbagasie; ~ **charge**, byslag; ekstra betaling; ~ **depot**, skutloods; ~ **fare**, ekstra betaling, toeslag, bybetaling; ~ **freight**, oorvrag, oorgewig.
excess'ive, oormatig, oordrewe, mateloos, uitbundig, buitensporig, oordadig; ~ **charge**, buitensporige prys; oorlading (battery); ~ **ly**, uiters, besonder, uitermate; ~ **ness**, oordrewenheid, mateloosheid; ~ **speed**, buitensporige snelheid (spoed); ~ **wear**, buitensporige slytasie.
excess': ~ **load**, oorvrag; ~ **luggage**, oorbagasie, oorgewig (bagasie), oorvrag; ~ **payment**, oorbetaling; ~ **pressure**, oordruk; ~ **profit**, oorwins.
exchange', (n) ruil(ing); verwisseling, omruiling; wisseling; intlewering; telefoonsentrale; beurs; wisselkoers; valuta; *BILL of* ~, geldwissel; *FOREIGN* ~, buitelandse betaalmiddel (valuta); *IN* ~, in ruil; *MEDIUM of* ~, ruilmiddel; (v) (ver)wissel; (ver)ruil; omruil; uitwissel; ~ *BLOWS*, mekaar slaan; handgemeen raak; ~ *WHEELS*, wiele om-

ruil; ~ *WORDS*, woorde wissel; ~ **abi'lity**, (ver)ruilbaarheid, wisselbaarheid; ~ **able**, ruilbaar, inwisselbaar; ~ **barrier**, valutaversperring; ~ **broker**, wisselmakelaar; ~ **control**, valutabeheer; ~ **copy**, ruilnommer; ~ **girl**, telefoonjuffrou, telefoniste; ~ **list**, ruilingslys; koerslys; ~ **rate**, wisselkoers; beursnotering; ~**s**, spelverwisseling; ~ **value**, ruilwaarde.
exche'quer, skatkis, landskas, tesourie; *CHANCELLOR of the E*~, Minister van Finansies (Engeland); *THE* ~, die skatkis; Jan Taks (skerts.); ~ **account**, skatkisrekening; ~ **bill**, skatkisbiljet.
exci'piable, eksipieerbaar (jur.).
excip'ient, eksipiënt (jur.); mengmiddel (med.).
excis'able, belasbaar, synsbaar, (ver)aksynsbaar.
ex'cise¹, (n) aksyns; (v) aksyns laat betaal, belas; afset, oorvra.
excise'², (v) uitsny, afsny, skrap.
ex'cise: ~ **dues**, aksynsregte; ~ **duties**, aksyns; ~ **office**, aksynskantoor; ~ **officer**, ontvanger van aksyns, aksynsbeampte.
exci'sion, uitsnyding; wegneming; skrapping.
excitabil'ity, prikkelbaarheid, opgewondenheid.
excit'able, prikkelbaar, liggeraak.
ex'citant, (n) prikkel, opwekkende middel; (a) prikkelend.
excita'tion, aansporing; opwekking; opwinding, opgewondenheid; eksitasie (med.).
excit'ative, excit'atory, opwekkend, prikkelend; veroorsakend; opwindend.
excite', aanspoor; opwind, in spanning bring; prikkel; (op)wek, opruf; gevoelig maak (plaat), gaande maak; eksiteer (med.); ~ *adoration*, bekoor; bekoring (op)wek; ~ **d**, opgewonde, ~ **ment**, opwinding, opgewondenheid; agitasie; opwekking, aansporing; prikkeling; gemoedsaandoening, spanning; ~ **r**, opwekker.
excit'ing, opwindend, spannend; ~ **dynamo**, opwekdinamo, velddinamo.
exclaim', uitroep, uitskreeu; ~ *against*, uitvaar teen; ~ **er**, uitroeper, uitskreeuer.
exclama'tion, uitroep, kreet, skreeu; *note of* ~, uitroepteken.
exclam'atory, uitroepend, skreeuend, luid.
exclude', uitsluit, uitsonder; weer.
exclud'ing, met uitsondering van, uitgesonder(d).
exclu'sion, uitsluiting; wering; eksklusie.
exclus'ive, uitsluitend; kieskeurig; deftig; eksklusief; *MUTUALLY* ~, onverenigbaar; ~ *OF*, met uitsluiting van, ongerekend; ~ *RIGHT*, alleenreg; ~ **ly**, uitsluitend, uitsluitlik; ~ **ness**, uitsluitendheid, eksklusiwiteit, afsonderlikheid.
exclus'ivism, eensydigheid, eksklusiwisme.
Ex'co, Uitvoerende Komitee, UK.
exco'gitate, uitdink, versin; bepeins, oordink.
excogita'tion, bepeinsing; uitvinding, bedenksel.
excommun'icate, uit die kerk of gemeenskap ban, ekskommuniseer, ekskommunikeer.
excommunica'tion, (kerklike) ban, sensuur, ekskommunikasie, verbanning.
excommun'icative, ban-.
excommun'icator, banopleër; ~ **y** = *excommunicative*.
exco'riate, afskil; vel-af maak; afskraap, afskaaf.
excoria'tion, ontvelling; afskawing; afskilling.
ex'crement, uitwerpsel, ontlasting, ekskrement; uitvaagsel.
excremen'tal, excrementi'tious, uitwerpsel-, drek-; ~ *diseases*, ontlastingsiektes.
excres'cence, uitwas, uitgroeisel.
excres'cent, uitwassend; oortollig.
excret'a, uitwerpsels; uitskeidingstowwe.
excrete', afskei, uitwerp, uitskei.
excre'tion, afskeiding, uitwerping, uitskeiding, ekskresie.
excret'ive, excret'ory, afskeidings-, afskeidend.
excru'ciate, martel, folter, pynig.
excru'ciating, folterend, ondraaglik; afgryslik; *an* ~ *ly hot day*, 'n uitermate warm dag.
excrucia'tion, foltering, marteling, pyniging.
ex'culpate, verontskuldig, skoonpraat; vryspreek, van blaam onthef.

exculpa'tion, verontskuldiging; vryspraak.
excul'patory, verontskuldigend.
excu'rrent, uitstromend, afvoerend.
excur'sion, afdwaling, afwyking; uitstappie, ekskursie, (plesier)tog, toer; ~ **fare,** ekskursiereisgeld; ~**ist,** plesierreisiger; ~ **ticket,** ekskursiekaartjie; ~ **train,** plesiertrein, ekskursietrein.
excur'sive, afdwalend, wydlopig, breedsprakig, uitweidend.
excus'able, vergeeflik, verskoonbaar.
excus'atory, verontskuldigend.
excuse', (n) verontskuldiging; verskoning; uitvlug, ekskuus, vyeblad, smoesie; *by way of* ~, ter (as) verskoning; (v) verontskuldig, vergoelik, verskoon; vrystel; (ver)ekskuseer; *BEG to be* ~ *d,* vra om verskoon te word; ~ *FROM,* vrylaat van; ~ *ME!,* ekskuus!; pardon.
excuss', uitwin (jur.); ~**ion,** uitwinning (jur.).
ex'eat, exeat, verlof om uit te gaan.
ex'ecrable, afskuwelik, verfoeilik, ellendig.
ex'ecrate, verfoei, vervloek, verafsku, verwens.
execra'tion, verfoeiing, verafskuwing, vervloeking, verwensing.
ex'ecrative, ex'ecratory, verwensend, vloek=.
ex'ecutable, uitvoerbaar; vatbaar vir eksekusie; uitwinbaar (eiendom).
exec'utant, uitvoerder, eksekutant; speler (musiek).
ex'ecute, verrig, vervul; passeer, verly (akte); fusilleer; teregstel, ter dood bring; uitvoer, speel, ten gehore bring (musiek); voltrek, ten uitvoer bring (vonnis); ~ *orders,* bestellings uitvoer; ~**d,** voltrokke (vonnis); tereggestel; gedood.
execu'tion, uitvoering; beslaglegging; eksekusie; spel, voordrag; teregstelling, onthoofding; slagting; verrigting, vervulling; verlyding (van akte); volbrenging; voltrekking (van doodstraf); *CARRY into* ~, ten uitvoer bring; *PLACE of* ~, strafplaas; ~ *of PUNISHMENT,* strafpleging, strafvoltrekking; *PUT into* ~, ten uitvoer bring; uitvoering gee aan; *SALE in* ~, eksekutoriale verkoping; ~**er,** skerpregter, beul, laksman.
exec'utive, (n) uitvoerende amptenaar, uitvoerende beampte, bestuurshoof, bestuursleier, bedryfsleier; uitvoerende mag; dagbestuur; uitvoerende raad; (a) uitvoerend, eksekutief; *E*~ *COMMITTEE,* Uitvoerende Komitee; ~ *suite,* bestuurstel; bestuursuite; ~ *WRITING desk,* bestuurslessenaar.
exec'utor, uitvoerder, voltrekker; eksekuteur, (boedel)beredderaar, boedelbesorger; ~ *DATIVE,* eksekuteur datief; *LITERARY* ~, letterkundige eksekuteur; ~ *TESTAMENTARY,* eksekuteur testamentêr.
executor'ial, eksekuteurs=, eksekutoriaal.
exec'utorship, eksekuteurskap.
exec'utrix, (..trices), eksekutrise.
exeges'is, (teks)uitlegging, skrifverklaring, eksegese; Bybelverklaring, (Bybel)uitleg(ging).
ex'egete, eksegeet, skrifverklaarder, teksuitlêer, (Bybel)uitlêer.
exeget'ic(al), eksegeties, uitlêend, verklarend.
exeget'ics, uitlegkunde, eksegese.
exeget'ist, *kyk* **exegete.**
ex-el'der, oud-ouderling.
exem'plar, voorbeeld; model, eksemplaar; toonbeeld; ~**iness,** voorbeeldigheid.
exem'plary, voorbeeldig, voortreflik, navolgenswaardig; waarskuwend; ~ *CONDUCT,* voorbeeldige gedrag; ~ *DAMAGES,* bestraffende skadevergoeding; ~ *PUNISHMENT,* afskrikkende straf.
exemplifica'tion, verklaring, opheldering; afskrif, kopie.
exem'plify, (..fied), voorbeelde gee, met voorbeelde verduidelik; 'n gewaarmerkte afskrif maak; sertifiseer.
exempt', (n) vrygestelde, verskoonde; (v) vrystel, verskoon, ontslaan, onthef; (a) vrygestel, bevry; ~ *from service,* diensvry verklaar; ~**ion,** vrystelling, verskoning; ~**ion certificate,** vrystelllingsbewys.
exen'terate, ontwei, die ingewande verwyder.
exequat'ur, erkenning (van konsul); erkenningsbesluit, eksekwatur.

ex'equies, begrafnisplegtighede, uitvaart.
ex'ercisable, uitvoerbaar, uitoefenbaar.
ex'ercise, (n) uitoefening; opgawe, tema; godsdiensoefening; oefening; liggaamsbeweging; eksersisie; *RELIGIOUS* ~, godsdiensoefening; *TAKE* ~, oefen, oefeninge doen; (v) beoefen, gebruik, uitoefen, aanwend; oefen; ekserseer, dril; liggaamsoefening doen; ~ *an OPTION,* 'n opsie uitoefen; ~ *PATIENCE,* geduld beoefen; ~ *a RIGHT,* 'n reg uitoefen; ~ **book,** skrif, skryfboek, oefenskrif.
exercita'tion, beoefening; verhandeling.
exert', aanwend, inspan, laat geld, uitoefen; ~ *oneself,* uithaal wat jy kan, jou benaarstig, jou bes doen, jou inspan; ~**ion,** inspanning, poging, uitoefening, beywering.
ex'eunt (omnes), (pl) hulle gaan (almal) af (v.d. toneel).
exfol'iate, afskilfer, afblaar.
exfolia'tion, afskilfering.
exfol'iative, afskilferend.
exhala'tion, uit(w)aseming, uitdamping; wasem, damp, ekshalasie.
exhale', uit(w)asem, uitdamp; lug gee, laat verdamp.
exhaust', (n) afvoer; uitlaatpyp; knalpot, knaldemper (motor); (v) uitput, afmat; uitpomp; uitlaat; leegmaak; ~ *oneself,* jou uitput, jou afsloof; ~ **box,** knaldemper; ~ **brake,** uitlaatrem; ~ **cam,** uitlaatnok; ~ **cock,** afblaaskraan; ~**ed,** poot-uit, tam, boeglam, gedaan, kapot, uitgeput; uitgewerk; verbruik; uitverkoop; *mentally (physically)* ~ *ed,* uitgeput; versukkel(d); ~ **flame,** uitlaatvlam; ~ **gas,** uitlaatgas; ~**ible,** uitputlik; ~**ion,** uitputting, afmatting, afgemoatheid; ~**ive,** uitputtend; volledig, uitvoerig, allesomvattend; ~**less,** onuitputlik; ~ **manifold,** uitlaatverdeelklep; ~ **nozzle,** blaaspypknop; ~ **pipe,** afvoerpyp; uitlaatpyp; ~ **silencer,** knaldemper; ~ **steam,** afgewerkte stoom, uitlaatstoom; ~ **stroke,** uitlaatslag; ~ **valve,** afvoerklep, uitlaatklep; ~ **vent,** uitlaatgat.
exher'idate, onterf.
exhib'it, (n) uitstalling; bewysstuk; insending; toonstuk; (v) blootlê; indien; vertoon, ten toon stel, eksposeer, uitstal; aan die dag lê.
exhibi'tion, oorlegging; indiening; studiebeurs; openbare les; vertoning, tentoonstelling, ekshibisie, eksposisie; ~ *of ILL TEMPER,* galbrakery, galbraking; *MAKE an* ~ *of oneself,* jou belaglik maak; ~ **battle,** spieëlgeveg; ~**er,** beurshouer; ~ **flight,** demonstrasievlug; ~**ism,** ekshibisionisme; ~**ist,** ekshibisionis; ~**is'tic,** ekshibisionisties; ~ **match,** vertoonwedstryd.
exhib'itive, vertonend, tentoonstellend.
exhib'itor, vertoner, tentoonsteller; insender; eksponent; ~**y,** *kyk* **exhibitive.**
exhil'arant, opwekkend, vermaaklik.
exhil'arate, vrolik maak, opvrolik, opwek, verfris.
exhil'arating, opwekkend, verfrissend.
exhilara'tion, vrolikmaking; opgewektheid, vrolikheid, lewenslustigheid.
exhil'arative = **exhilarant.**
exhort', aanmaan, vermaan, aanspoor; aandring op; voorhou; ~**a'tion,** vermaning, aanmaning, aansporing; toespraak; ~**ative,** ~**atory,** vermanend, aansporend; ~**er,** vermaner.
exhuma'tion, opgrawing, uitgrawing.
exhume', opgrawe, uitgraaf; opdiep.
ex'igence = **exigency.**
ex'igency, (..cies), behoefte, dringende noodsaaklikheid, vereiste; eis; nood; drang; *IN an* ~, in geval van nood; *MATTER of* ~, dringende aangeleentheid; *exigencies of the SERVICE,* vereistes v.d. diens.
ex'igent, dringend; veeleisend.
ex'igible, invorderbaar, opeisbaar.
exigu'ity, kleinheid, geringheid.
exig'uous, klein, gering, onbeduidend; ~**ness** = **exiguity.**
ex'ile, (n) verbanning, ballingskap; banneling; *go into* ~, uitwyk; (v) verban, uitban.
exi'lity, dunheid; fynheid; verfyning.
exist', bestaan, lewe, wees, voorkom.

exis'tence, bestaan, eksistensie; aansyn, wese; voort= bestaan; *the best in* ~, die beste wat bestaan.
exis'tent, bestaande, aanwesig, voorhande.
existen'tialism, eksistensialisme.
existen'tialist, (n) eksistensialis; (a) eksistensialisties.
exis'ting, bestaande, aanwesig.
ex'it, (n) uitgang; heengang; *make one's* ~, weggaan, uitgaan; (v) uitgaan, afgaan, v.d. toneel verdwyn; ~ **interview**, vertrekgesprek; ~ **ramp**, uitrit, afrit; ~ **ticket**, uitgangskaartjie.
ex-lib'ris, ex libris; boekmerk, biblioteeketiket.
Ex'odus, Exodus (Bybelboek).
ex'odus, eksodus, uittog.
ex-officer, oud-offisier.
ex offi'cio, ampshalwe, ex officio.
exogam'ic, exo'gamous, eksogaam.
exog'amy, eksogamie, huwelik buite die stam.
ex'ogen, eksogeen.
exogenet'ic, exogen'ic, eksogenies.
exog'enous, van buitekant aangroeiend, eksogeen.
exon'erate, onthef, ontslaan, vryspreek; ontlas; sui= wer; vrypleit.
exonera'tion, suiwering; ontlasting; ontheffing.
exophthal'mia, ooguitpuiling.
exor'able, vermurfbaar (deur gebed).
exorb'itance, exorb'itancy, buitensporigheid.
exorb'itant, buitensporig, erg, hoog, verregaande.
ex'orcise, uitdrywe, uitwerp, besweer, bespreek, uit= ban.
ex'orcism, (duiwel)beswering, uitdrywing, duiwel= banning.
ex'orcist, duiwelbanner, geestebesweerder.
exord'ial, inleidend.
exord'ium, (-s, . .dia), inleiding, aanhef, eksordium.
exoskel'eton, huidskelet.
exosmo'sis, eksosmose.
ex'ospore, eksospoor.
exote'ric, uiterlik, openbaar, eksoteries, populêr, be= gryplik vir oningewydes.
exot'ic, (n) uitheemse plant, woord, ens.; (a), uit= heems, uitlands, vreemd; eksoties; ~**ism**, eksoti= sisme.
expand', uitsprei, uitbrei; uitdy, uitsit, swel; ontwik= kel; ontdooi, vriendelik word; ~ *out of all recogni= tion*, onherkenbaar ontwikkel (uitbrei); ~**ed metal**, plaatgaas; ~**er**, uitdyer; pyproller.
expand'ing: ~ **suitcase**, verstelbare reistas; ~ **uni= verse**, uitdyende heelal; ~ **washer**, digring; ~ **wedge**, uitdywig.
expanse', uitgestrektheid, ruimte; *the* ~, die uitspan= sel.
expansibil'ity, uitsetbaarheid, uitsettingsvermoë, rekbaarheid.
expan'sible, expan'sile, uitsetbaar, rekbaar.
expan'sion, swelling; uitdying, uitsetting; uitsprei= ding; uitbreiding, ekspansie, uitstrekking, uitge= strektheid; *power of* ~, uitsettingsvermoë; ~ **bit**, verstelboor; ~ **chamber**, ekspansiekamer; ~ **gap**, uitsettingsruimte; ~ **joint**, uitsitvoeg, ekspansie= koppeling; ~ **link**, skêr (loko.); ~ **piece**, voeg= plaatjie; ~ **pipe**, ekspansiepyp; ~ **plug**, uitdyprop; ~ **reamer**, uitdyruimer; ~ **sleeve**, uitsettingshuls; ~ **steam**, ekspansiestoom; ~ **valve**, uitsitklep, eks= pansieklep.
expan'sive, uitsettend, rekbaar; uitsettings=; wyd uit= gestrek, uitgebrei, wyd, ruim, omvattend, breed, ekspansief; vertroulik, medeelsaam; ~ *force*, spankrag; ~**ness**, uitsetbaarheid; uitgesetheid; uit= gebreidheid; medeelsaamheid.
expansiv'ity, uitsetbaarheid, uitsettingsvermoë.
ex part'e, ex parte, van een kant, eensydig.
expa'tiate, uitwei, breedvoerig wees; rondwandel; ~ *on*, uitwei oor.
expatia'tion, uitweiding, wydlopigheid.
expa'tiatory, uitweidend, wydlopig.
expat'riate, (n) banneling; uitgewekene; (v) uitwyk, verhuis; verban, ekspatrieer.
expatria'tion, verbanning; uitsetting, ekspatriasie; uitwyking.
expect', verwag; veronderstel, vermoed; ~ *him when you SEE him*, verwag hom wanneer jy hom sien; ~ *VISITORS*, mense verwag (kry); ~**able**, te wagte;

~**ance**, ~**ancy**, verwagting, hoop; vooruitsig; ~**ant**, (n) vermoedelike opvolger; verwagtende; kandidaat; (a) afwagtend; hopend, verwagtend; aanstaande, swanger (moeder); vermoedelik (op= volger).
expecta'tion, verwagting, vooruitsig, afwagting; *CONTRARY to* ~ *s*, teen die verwagting in; *IN* ~ *of*, in afwagting van; ~ *of LIFE*, vermoedelike le= wensduur, lewenskans.
expec'ting, swanger; verwagtend.
expec'torant, hoesmiddel; spoegmiddel.
expec'torate, spu(ug), spoeg.
expectora'tion, spuug, spoeg, spuwing; ~ *prohibited*, moenie spoeg nie.
exped'ience¹, exped'iency, gepastheid, geskiktheid; doelmatigheid; berekening; geradenheid.
exped'ience², **exped'iency**, eiebelang, opportunisme.
exped'ient, (n) hulpmiddel(tjie), uitweg, redmiddel, toevlug; (a) geskik, dienstig, raadsaam, wenslik; *it is* ~ *that he should go*, dit is raadsaam dat hy gaan.
ex'pedite, verhaas, bespoedig, bevorder, aanhelp; af= stuur, afdoen.
expedi'tion, vinnigheid, vaardigheid, spoed; aansen= ding; (veld)tog, ekspedisie; ~**ary**, ekspedisie=; ~ *ary force*, ekspedisieleër.
expedi'tious, gou, skielik, haastig, vlug, glad, snel, vlot.
expel', (-led), verdrywe, uitsit, verban, wegjaag, uit= werp, uitbesem, uitboender, uitskop, uitstoot; ~ *from school*, uit die skool sit (verban); ~**lable**, uit= dryfbaar, uitwerpbaar; ~**lee'**, uitgeworpene; ~**ler**, uitdrywer, verbanner, uitwerper.
expend', verbruik; uitgee, bestee, deurbring; ~*ed re= serves*, ingesette reserwe, ~**able**, misbaar, verhan= delbaar, opofferbaar, ontbeerlik.
expen'diture, uitgawe, onkoste; besteding; verbruik; ~ *of ENERGY*, energieverbruik; *GOVERN= MENT* ~, owerheidsbesteding; ~ *ON*, uitgawe aan (vir); besteding aan.
expense', koste, uitgawe, prys; *AT someone's* ~, op iem. se onkoste; *AT the* ~ *of*, ten koste van; teen die koste van; *GO to considerable* ~, baie koste aangaan; *INCIDENTAL* ~*s*, onvoorsiene uitga= wes; *LAUGH at someone's* ~, iem. uitlag; *MEET an* ~, (on)koste bestry; *PUT someone to* ~, iem. onkoste veroorsaak; *SAVE on* ~*s*, onkoste be= spaar; ~ **account**, uitgawerekening.
expen'sive, duur, duurkoop, kosbaar; ~**ness**, kos= baarheid, duurte, duurheid.
exper'ience, (n) ondervinding, wedervaring, ervaren= heid; gewaarwording, belewenis, (lewens)ervaring; (pl) ondervindings; *BY* ~, by ondervinding, uit ervaring; ~ *makes FOOLS wise*, deur skade en skande word 'n mens wys; *FROM* ~, uit ervaring; ~ *is the MISTRESS of fools*, ondervinding is die beste leermeester; *PAY heavily for one's* ~, duur leergeld betaal; ~ *is the mother (father) of WIS= DOM (knowledge)*, ondervinding is die beste leer= meester; (v) ondervind, ervaar, deurmaak, deur= gaan, deurleef, beleef; ~**d**, ervare, bedrewe, geroetineerd; *an* ~*d man*, 'n man van ondervin= ding.
experien'tial, ervarings=; ~ **philosophy**, ervaringsfi= losofie.
expe'riment, (n) proef(neming), probeerslag, eksperi= ment; *make an* ~, 'n proefneming doen; (v) be= proef, probeer, eksperimenteer, proewe neem (doen).
experimen'tal, proefondervindelik, eksperimenteel, tentatief; ~ **aircraft**, proefvliegtuig; ~ **farm**, proef= plaas; ~ **flight**, proefvlug; ~**ist**, proefnemer, waar= nemer; ~**ize**, proefnemings doen, eksperimenteer; ~ **plant**, proefaanleg; ~ **stage**, proefstadium; ~ **station**, proefstasie.
experimenta'tion, proefneming.
experimen'ter, proefnemer, eksperimenteerder.
ex'pert, (n) deskundige, ekspert, vakman; (a) bedre= we, geoefen, ervare, deskundig, vakkundig, eks= pert; ~ *advice*, ekspertadvies, deskundige advies; ~**ise**, vernuf, kundigheid; ~**ly**, knaphandig, vak= kundig; ~**ness**, bedrewenheid, deskundigheid, vakkundigheid.

expiable   882   exquisite

ex'piable, waarvoor geboet kan word.
ex'piate, boet; weer goedmaak; boete doen vir.
expia'tion, boetedoening; goedmaking, versoening, soen=.
ex'piator, boeteling; ~ **y,** boetend, versoenend, soen=; ~ *y death,* versoeningsdood; ~ *y sacrifice,* versoeningsoffer, soenoffer.
expira'tion, uitaseming; ademtog; afloop; vervaltyd, verstryking.
expir'atory, uitasemings=.
expire', uitasem, uitadem; verval, afloop (tydperk); verstryk, eindig (wapenstilstand); sterwe, doodgaan; ~ *d period,* verstreke tydperk.
expir'ing, sterwend, aflopend.
expir'y, verval, afloop; vervaltyd; verstryking; *at ~ of period,* aan die einde (by afloop) v.d. tydperk.
explain', uitlê, verklaar, duidelik maak, ophelder, belig, uiteensit; ~ *AWAY,* goedpraat, wegredeneer; ~ *ONESELF,* jou nader verklaar; ~ **able,** verklaarbaar; ~ **er,** verklaarder, uitlêer.
explana'tion, uitleg(ging), verklaring, verduideliking; glos; *in ~ of,* ter verduideliking van.
explan'atory, verklarend.
exple'tive, (n) vloek, kragterm; stoplap; stopwoord; (a) aanvullend, afrondend, stop=.
expli'cable, verklaarbaar.
ex'plicate, verklaar, ontvou.
explica'tion, ontwikkeling, ontvouing, verklaring, verduideliking.
ex'plicative, ex'plicatory, verklarend, ophelderend.
expli'cit, duidelik, uitdruklik, stellig, glashelder, beslis, openhartig; ~ **ly,** duidelik, uitdruklik; ~ **ness,** duidelikheid, stelligheid, uitdruklikheid.
explode', laat ontplof; ontplof, uiteenvlieg, uitmekaarbars, uitmekaarspat, bars; laat spring; ~ *a THEORY,* 'n teorie omverwerp; *an ~ d THEORY,* 'n uitgediende teorie; ~ **r,** ontsteker, plofstofwerker.
ex'ploit¹, (n) daad, heldedaad, prestasie, kordaatstuk; wapenfeit.
exploit'², (v) uitbuit, eksploiteer; ontgin, bewerk, in bedryf stel.
exploita'tion, uitbuiting; bewerking, ontginning, eksploitasie.
exploit'er, uitbuiter; ontginner.
explor'able, ondersoekbaar.
explora'tion, ondersoek(ing), navorsing, eksplorasie; ontdekking; *journey of ~,* ontdekkingsreis.
explor'ative, explor'atory, ondersoekend, ondersoekings=; ontdekkend.
explore', verken, bespied; ondersoek, navors, naspoor, eksploreer, deursoek; sondeer (wond); ~ **r,** ondersoeker, navorser; ontdekkingsreisiger.
explo'sion, ontploffing, uitbarsting, losbarsting; slag, knal, eksplosie; ~ **chamber,** ontstekingskamer.
explos'ive, (n) plofstof, ontploffingsmiddel, springstof, springmiddel; ploffer, klapper, eksplosief (fonetiek); *high ~,* kragtige springstof; (a) ontplofend, eksplosief; losbarstend; ontplofbaar; ontploffings=, knal=; opvlieënd; ~ **area,** springstofgebied; ~ **chamber,** ladingskamer; ~ **charge,** springlading; ~ **cotton,** skietkatoen; ~ **drinks,** gasdranke; ~ **distance,** slagwydte; ~ **force,** ontploffingskrag; ~ **gas,** knalgas, plofgas; ~ **mixture,** plofmengsel; ~ **ness,** ontplofbaarheid; ~ **oil,** nitrogliserien, nitrogliserine; ~ **shell,** springgranaat; ~ **signal,** knalsein.
expon'ent, wortelgetal; eksponent, verklaarder, vertolker; verteenwoordiger; magsaanwyser.
exponen'tial, eksponensiaal; ~ **equation,** eksponensiaalvergelyking.
ex'port, (n) uitvoer; uitgevoerde artikels; eksport.
export', (v) uitvoer, eksporteer; verskeep; ~ **able,** uitvoerbaar; ~ **a'tion,** uitvoer, eksportasie.
ex'port: ~ **duty,** uitvoerreg; ~ **entry,** uitklaringsbrief; ~ **er,** uitvoerder, eksporteur; ~ **ing,** uitvoer=; ~ **ing country,** uitvoerland; ~ **rate,** uitvoertarief; ~ **tax,** uitvoerbelasting; ~ **trade,** uivoerhandel, eksporthandel.
exposé', (n) onthulling; exposé; blootstelling, aandiekaakstelling.
expose', (v) oopmaak, blootstel; uitstal, ten toon stel;

vertoon; ooplaat; aan die kaak stel, openbaar, verklap; ontwikkel, belig (plaat); ooplê (kaarte); aan sy lot oorlaat (kind); uiteensit; ontbloot; ~ *a CHILD,* 'n kind te vondeling lê; ~ *oneself to DANGER,* jou aan gevaar blootstel; ~ *onself to DEATH,* jou lewe waag; ~ *ONESELF,* jou ontbloot; ~ *for SALE,* te koop uitstal; ~ *his TREACHERY,* sy verraad (valsheid) openbaar; ~ **d,** onbeskut; blootgestel; ontbloot; ~ **r,** tentoonsteller; verklaarder.
exposi'tion, blootstelling; ooplegging; uitstalling, tentoonstelling; uiteensetting; verklaring; eksposisie (drama).
expos'itive, verklarend, beskrywend, uitleggend.
expos'itor, verklaarder, tolk, uitlêer; ~ **y** = **expositive.**
ex post fac'to, ex post facto, terugwerkend.
expos'tulate, opkom teen, jou bekla oor, protesteer; vermaan, kapittel.
expostula'tion, betoog, beklag, beswaar; vermaning, waarskuwing.
expos'tulative, vermanend, waarskuwend.
expos'tulator, vermaner, waarskuwer; ~ **y,** vermanend, waarskuwend.
expo'sure, blootstelling; tentoonstelling, uitstalling; ontmaskering, onthulling, aandiekaakstelling; dagsoom (geol.); versaking (van kind); ontbloting (van liggaam); beligting (foto); *death by ~,* dood deur blootstelling; ~ **meter,** beligtingsmeter; ~ **table,** beligtingstabel; ~ **time,** beligtingstyd.
expound', uitlê, verklaar, uiteensit, verkondig, blootlê; ~ **er,** uitlêer, verklaarder.
ex-pres'ident, oud-president.
express', (n) snelbode; sneltrein, eksprestrein; (v) uitdruk, uitpers; aandui, weergee, voorstel; verklank (musiek); uit, bewoord; betuig; ~ *doubt,* twyfel uitspreek; (a) uitdruklik, duidelik; bepaald; opsetlik; uitgeknip; spesiaal; ekspres; ~ **company,** bestelhuis; ~ **factor,** blootstellingsfaktor; ~ **freight,** snelvrag; ~ **goods,** snelgoedere; ~ **ly,** uitdruklik; met opset, ekspres, aspris; spesiaal.
expre'ssion, uiting, betuiging, ekspressie; spreekwyse, gesegde; uitdrukking; *BEYOND ~,* onbeskryflik; *a FIXED ~,* 'n staande uitdrukking; ~ **al,** uitdrukkings=; ~ **ism,** ekspressionisme; ~ **is'tic,** ekspressionisties; ~ **less,** toonloos; wesenloos, sonder uitdrukking, uitdrukkingloos; niksseggend; onbewoë.
express'ive, uitdruklik; beeldend, betekenisvol, veelbetekenend, ekspressief, veelseggend, wesensvol; ~ *LANGUAGE,* beeldende taal; ~ *OF,* uitdrukkend; ~ *POWERS,* seggingskrag; ~ **ness,** uitdruklikheid, seggingskrag; wesensvolheid.
express': ~ **letter,** spoedstuk, spoedbrief; ~ **-letter service,** snelbriewediens; ~ **ly,** uitdruklik; met opset; ekspres; ~ **messenger,** ylbode, renbode; ~ **post,** spoedpos; ~ **service,** sneldiens; ~ **train,** sneltrein; ~ **van,** snelwa; ~ **way,** snelpad, snelweg, deurpad.
exprobra'tion, verwyt, verwytende taal.
exprop'riate, onteien, uit sy besittings sit, eksproprieer.
expropria'tion, onteiening, ekspropriasie; *law of ~,* onteieningsreg; ~ **act,** onteieningswet.
exprop'riator, onteienaar.
expul'sion, verdrywing; uitdrywing; uitsetting; verbanning, ekspulsie.
expul'sive, verdrywend; verbannend, wegja(g)end, ekspulsief.
expunc'tion, skrapping, uitwissing, weglating.
expunge', uitwis, uitvee, skrap, uitkrap.
ex'purgate, skoonmaak, suiwer; kuis; skrap; ekspurgeer.
expurga'tion, suiwering; skrapping, ekspurgasie.
ex'purgator, suiweraar.
expurgator'ial, expurg'atory, suiwerend; ~ **index,** lys van verbode boeke, indeks (R.K.).
ex'quisite, (n) windmaker, modepop; fat; (a) uitgesoek, keurig, voortreflik, uitgelese; (oor)heerlik, lekker; fyn, wondermooi, wonderskoon; volkome, volmaak; groot, buitengewoon; hewig (pyn); ~ *PLEASURE,* besondere genot; ~ *TASTE,* fyn

exsanguniate 883 *extraterrestrial*

smaak; ~ **ness**, keurigheid, voortreflikheid; fyn=heid; hewigheid.
exsang'uniate, bloed aftap, bloedlaat.
exsang'uine, exsang'uinous, bloedarm, bloedloos.
ex-schol'ar, oud-leerling; oud-student.
exscind', uitsny, skrap.
exsert'ed, uitgestoot.
ex-serv'iceman, (..**men**), oud-stryder, oud-gediende.
ex'siccant, droogmiddel, opdroënde middel.
ex'siccate, opdroog, laat uitdroog; verdroog.
exsicca'tion, uitdroging, opdroging.
ex-sol'dier, oud-soldaat.
ex'tant, extant', nog bestaande, voorhande.
extemporan'eous, extem'porary, onvoorbereid, uit die vuis.
extem'pore, onvoorbereid, uit die vuis; *speak* ~, uit die vuis praat.
extemporiza'tion, improvisasie, ekstemporisasie.
extem'porize, uit die vuis praat, improviseer, ekstem=poriseer.
extend', (uit)rek; uitbrei, uitsit (grens); verleng (tyd, spoorweg); versprei (troepe); duur (tyd); beslag lê op (reg); opdraand kry; bied, verleen, toesteek (hand); ~ *the BOUNDARIES*, die grense uitbrei (uitsit); ~ *MERCY*, jou ontferm; ~ *ONESELF (at sport)*, jou beste gee; alles uithaal; ~ *a WELCOME*, verwelkom.
extend'ed, uitgestrek; uitgebrei; verleng; *in* ~ *order*, uitmekaar, versprei (soldate), in verspreide orde.
exten'der, aanvuller (verf).
extensibil'ity, rekbaarheid.
exten'sible, exten'sile, verlengbaar; (uit)rekbaar, uit=setbaar.
exten'sion, uitstrekking, omvang; uitbreiding, ver=breiding; verlenging; vergroting, rekking; uitgestrektheid; bepaling (spraak); *GRANT* ~, uit=stel verleen; ~ *TO*, uitbreiding aan; ~ **bandage**, rekverband; ~ **classes**, uitbreidingsklasse; ~ **course**, uitbreidingskursus; ~ **door**, verlengdeur, vou=deur; ~ **flash**, afstandsflits; ~ **gate**, vouhek; ~ **ladder**, skuifleer; ~ **lecture**, skuitlesing; ~ **officer**, uitbreidingsbeampte; ~ **piece**, verlengstuk; ~ **rule(r)**, skuifliniaal; ~ **table**, aanlastafel; ~ **tele=scope**, skuifteleskoop; ~ **trestle**, skuifbok, skuif=tafel.
exten'sive, uitgestrek, uitgebreid, omvangryk, veel=omvattend, ekstensief; ~ *FARMING*, ekstensiewe boerdery; *for* ~ *USE*, vir gebruik in ruim kringe; ~ *WARFARE*, uitgebreide oorlogvoering; ~**ly**, uitgebreid, op groot skaal; ~**ness**, uitgestrektheid, uitgebreidheid, omvangrykheid.
extenso'meter, ekstensometer, vervormingsmeter.
exten'sor, (s) trekspier; ~ **tendon**, streksening, strek=pees (perd).
extent', beslaglegging, skatting (reg); uitgestrektheid, omvang; mate; *to a CERTAIN* ~, in sekere mate; *to the FULL* ~, in sy hele omvang; *to a GREAT* ~, in 'n groot mate; *IN* ~, groot; *to a LARGE* ~, grotendeels; in 'n groot mate; *to a LARGER* ~, in meerdere mate; *to a LESSER* ~, in mindere mate; *to SOME* ~, in sekere mate; *TO* ~ *of*, tot die bedrag (omvang, grootte) van; *to WHAT* ~? in hoever(re)? in watter mate?
exten'uate, verminder, verklein, verswak; verdun; versag, vergoelik.
exten'uating, versagtend, vergoelikend; ~ *circum=stances*, versagtende omstandighede.
extenua'tion, versagting, vergoeliking, verontskuldi=ging; *in* ~ *of*, tot verontskuldiging van, ter versag=ting van.
exten'uatory, versagtend, vergoelikend.
exter'ior, (n) uiterlik; buitekant, eksterieur; (a) uit=wendig; buitenste; uiterlik; buite=; ~ *ANGLE*, buitehoek; ~ *LINES*, buitelinies; ~ *WALL*, buite=muur; ~**'ity**, uiterlike; uiterlikheid; ~**ize**, uitlig, uitbring, eksterioriseer, 'n uiterlike vorm gee, belig=gaam; ~ **mirror**, buitespieël.
exterm'inable, uitroeibaar, verdelgbaar.
exterm'inate, uitroei, verdelg.
extermina'tion, uitroeiing, uitdelging, verdelging; *war of* ~, vernietigingsoorlog.

exterm'inator, uitroeimiddel; uitroeier, verdelger; ~**y**, verdelgend, verdelgings=.
extern', uitwendig, ekstern, buite=; nie-inwonende student.
extern'al, (n) (die) uiterlike; (pl) uiterlikhede; uitwen=digheid; bykomstige dinge; (a) uitwendig; buite=kants(e); uiterlik; ekstern; buitelands; *for* ~ *USE*, vir uitwendige gebruik; *the* ~ *WORLD*, die wêreld om ons; die eksterne wêreld; ~ **affairs**, buitelandse sake; ~ **brake**, buiterem; ~ **dimensions**, buiteafme=tings; ~ **ear**, uitwendige oor; ~ **gauge**, buitekali=ber; ~ **'ity**, uitwendigheid; uiterlikheid; ~**ize**, 'n uiterlike vorm gee, veruiterlik.
exterritor'ial, eksterritoriaal; ~ **'ity**, eksterritoriali=teit.
extinct', dood; uitgeblus; uitgewerk (vulkaan); uitge=sterf; afgeskaf; *BECOME* ~, uitsterf; ~ *VOLCA=NO*, uitgedoofde vulkaan; ~ **ion**, blussing; uitster=wing; verdelging; verjaring (van skuldbewys); on=dergang, verdwyning (van volke); vernietiging, demping; delging (van skuld).
exting'uish, doodblaas, uitblaas, (uit)doof, (uit)blus, doodgooi (vuur); in die skaduwee stel; vernietig; delg (skuld); uitroei; ~**able**, blusbaar; ~**er**, uit=blusser, domper, blusmasjien, doofpot.
ex'tirpate, uitroei, verdelg; uitsny (gewas).
extirpa'tion, uitroeiing, verwoesting, verdelging, uit=delging; verwydering, uitsnyding.
ex'terpator, uitroeier, verdelger.
extol', (-led), prys, verhef, aanprys, opvysel, roem, loof, ophemel; ~**ler**, lofredenaar, verheerliker; ~**ment**, verheerliking, aanprysing.
extort', afpers, afdwing, afdreig, nitwring; uitsuie; ~ *from*, ontwring van; ~**ion**, ontwringing (van be=kentenis); afpersing; afsettery; uitsuiging; ~**ionary**, afpersend, afdreigend; ~**ionate**, buitensporig; af=persings=; ~*ionate price*, buitensporige prys; ~**ioner**, afperser; bloedsuier, uitsuier, woekeraar; ~**ive**, afpersend.
ex'tra, (n) ekstratjie, iets ekstra, toegif; figurant (to=neel); *no* ~*s*, geen verdere koste nie; alles inbe=grepe; (a) buitengewoon; bykomend, ekstra; be=sonder; aanvullend, addisioneel; ~**-strongs**, peper=mente, brandlekkers.
ex'tract, (n) uittreksel, ekserp; aanhaling, ekstrak; af=treksel; afkooksel (vleis, ens.).
extract', (v) uittrek (tand); uithaal, ekstraheer; 'n ek=strak maak; 'n uittreksel maak; ~**able**, uittrek=baar.
extract'ion, uittrekking; afkoms, afstamming; ek=strahering, ekstraksie; *of DUTCH* ~, van Hol=landse afkoms; ~ *of ORE*, ertswinning; ~ *of ROOT*, worteltrekking (mat.).
extract': ~**ive**, uittrekbaar, trek=, ekstraktief; ~**or**, tang; trekker; patroontrekker; perser (sap); uittrek=selmaker.
extradit'able, uitlewerbaar.
ex'tradite, uitlewer; uitlewering verkry van.
extradi'tion, uitlewering, ekstradisie, ~ **act**, uitlewe=ringswet; ~ **treaty**, uitleweringstraktaat.
extrajudi'cial, buite(n)geregtelik; wederregtelik; ~ **confession**, verklaring buite die hof afgelê; onwetti=ge verklaring.
extramar'ital, buite-egtelik.
extramun'dane, bo(we)aards, nie uit hierdie wêreld (afkomstig) nie.
extramur'al, buitemuurs; ~ **student**, buitemuurse student.
extran'eous, vreemd, uitheems, van buite.
extranu'clear, buitekernig.
extraord'inarily, buitengewoon, snaaks, seldsaam.
extraord'inariness, ongewoonheid, vreemdheid, son=derlingheid.
extraord'inary, buitengewoon, ongewoon, snaaks; verregaande; merkwaardig.
extraparoch'ial, buite die gemeente.
extrap'olate, ekstrapoleer.
extrapola'tion, ekstrapolering.
extrasen'sory, buitesintuiglik; ~ *perception*, buite=sintuiglike waarneming.
extrastat'utory, buitewetlik.
extraterres'trial, buiteaards.

extraterritor'ial, ekstraterritoriaal; ~'ity, ekstraterritorialiteit.

extrav'agance, uitspatting, buitensporigheid, oordrewenheid; verkwisting, verspilling, spandabelheid, spilsug, oordadigheid, oordaad; ongerymdheid; (pl) ongerymdhede.

extrav'agant, oormoedig; buitensporig, oordrewe; ongerymd; onmatig, verkwistend, oordadig, spandabel(rig), spilsiek; *live ~ly,* in oordaad lewe.

extravagan'za, fantastiese stuk (taal, gedrag); buitensporigheid, extravaganza.

extrav'asate, uitdwing (vloeistof); uitvloei, uitsyfer.

extravasa'tion, uitsyfering, ekstravasasie.

extreme', (n) uiterste; uiteinde, uiterste punt; *CARRY to an ~,* op die spits dryf; *be DRIVEN to ~s,* in uiterstes verval; *IN the ~,* uiters; *~s MEET,* die uiterstes ontmoet mekaar; *from one ~ to the OTHER,* v.d. een uiterste na die ander; (a) uiters, uitermate, bomatig; laaste; groot, heftig; oordrewe; *~ old AGE,* baie hoë ouderdom; *an ~ CASE,* 'n uiterste geval; *in ~ DANGER,* in buitengewone (baie groot) gevaar; *~ PENALTY,* doodstraf; *~ UNCTION,* laaste (heilige) oliesel; *~ly,* uiters, besonder; hoogs, uitermate, buitemate, erg; goddeloos.

extrem'ist, ekstremis; *~'ic,* ekstremisties.

extrem'ity, (..ties), uiterste, uiteinde, end, tip; hoogste graad; uiterste nood; ellende; (pl) uiterste maatreëls; arms en bene, ekstremiteite; *be in an ~,* in die uiterste nood wees.

ex'tricable, ontwarbaar; helpbaar.

ex'tricate, uittrek, uithelp, uitred; loswikkel, ontwar, bevry, losmaak.

extrica'tion, uitredding; ontwarring, loswikkeling.

extrin'sic, uiterlik, uitwendig, buitekant; bykomend, toevallig.

extrorse', na buite gerig (takbokgewei).

ex'trovert, (n) ekstrovert; (a) ekstrovert, na buite lewend.

extrude', uitdrywe, uitstoot; wegjaag; *~d moulding,* deurgedrukte lys.

extru'sion, verdrywing, uitstoting, ekstrusie.

extru'sive, ekstrusie-; *~ rock,* vulkaniese gesteente, ekstrusiegesteente.

exub'erance, oordrywing, uitgelatenheid; oorvloed, oortolligheid; weelderigheid.

exub'erant, oorvloedig, welig, weelderig, oordrewe; geesdriftig, uitbundig, danig; uitgelate.

exub'erate, oorvloedig wees, oorvloei.

ex'udate, uitsweetstof, eksudaat.

exuda'tion, uitsweting, uitwaseming.

exud'ative, uitswetings-.

exude', uitsweet; afskei; uitwasem; vog afgee.

exult', juig, jubel; *~ IN,* verheug wees oor; *~ OVER,* triomfeer oor, kraai oor, juig oor; *~ancy,* opgetoënheid; *~ant,* opgetoë, uitgelate, juigend, jubelend; *~a'tion,* opgetoënheid, uitgelatenheid, gejuig, verheuging, gejubel.

exuv'iae, kors, roof, afgeworpe vel; oorblyfsels.

exuv'iate, afwerp, vervel.

exuvia'tion, vervelling.

ey'as, jong valk.

eye, (n) oog; ring (van tou); oog (van naald); maas (van net); *ALL ~s,* een en al oog; *BEFORE the very ~s of,* vlak voor die oë van; *his ~s are BIGGER than his belly,* sy oë is groter as sy maag; *~s like BILLIARD balls,* jakopeweroë; *BLACK ~,* blouoog; *BLIND in one ~,* blind in een oog; *CAST an ~ over something,* iets in oënskou neem; *CATCH the ~,* in die oog val, in die oog lopend wees; *not CLOSE an ~ (in sleep),* geen oog toemaak nie; *be all ~s and EARS,* oog en oor vir iets hê; *have ~s and EARS for only one thing,* net vir een ding oog en oor hê; *FAR from ~, far from heart,* uit die oog, uit die hart; *have an ~ FOR something,* 'n oog vir iets hê; *GET one's ~,* mooi kan sien; *give someone the GLAD ~,* vir iem. ogies maak; *see with HALF an ~,* met een oogopslag sien; *HAVE an ~ for,* 'n oog hê vir; *have ~s at the back of one's HEAD,* van voor en agter oë hê; *KEEP an ~ (up)on,* dophou; 'n oog hou oor; *in the ~s of the LAW,* voor die wet; *MAKE ~s at,* ogies maak vir; *MIND your ~,* pas op; *all MY ~,* alles pure bog; alles pure kaf; *the NAKED ~,* die blote oog; *the ~ of the NEEDLE,* die oog van 'n naald; *~s and NO ~s,* siende blind; *have an ~ ON someone,* iem. in die oog hê, 'n oog op iem. hê; *shut ONE'S ~s to something,* die oë sluit vir iets; *OPEN someone's ~s,* iem. se oë laat oopgaan; *you are not keeping your ~s OPEN,* jy kyk al weer teen jou ooglede vas; *keep one's ~s OPEN,* jou oë oophou; *one's ~s are being OPENED,* jou oë gaan oop; *you must keep your ~s PEELED,* jy moet jou oë oopmaak; jy moet wakker loop; *be in the PUBLIC ~,* algemene aandag trek; *PUNCH someone in the ~s,* iem. op die oë slaan; *keep one's ~s RIVETED on,* stip kyk na; *SEE ~ to ~ with,* van dieselfde mening wees as; dit volkome eens wees met; *what the ~ does not SEE, the heart craves not,* wat die oog nie sien nie, deer die hart nie; *they do not SEE ~ to ~,* hulle sit nie langs een vuur nie; *I never SET ~s on him again,* ek het hom nooit weer onder die oë gekry nie; *SHUT one's ~s to something,* die oë sluit vir iets; *be able to do something with one's ~s SHUT,* iets toe-oog kan doen; *keep one's ~s SKINNED,* jou oë oophou; *be able to do SOMETHING with one's ~s shut,* iets toe-oog kan doen; *his ~s are bigger than his STOMACH,* sy oë is groter as sy maag; sy oë is te groot vir sy maag; *THEY do not see ~ to ~,* hulle sit nie langs een vuur nie; *with an ~ TO,* met die oog op; *an ~ for an ~ and a TOOTH for a tooth,* oog om oog en tand om tand; *TURN a blind ~,* een oog toemaak; *UNDER the ~s of,* onder die oog van; *UP to one's ~s,* tot oor die ore; *not to USE one's ~s,* teen jou oogvelle vaskyk; *WALK with your ~s shut,* teen jou oogbanke vaskyk; *keep a WATCHFUL ~ on,* 'n wakende oog hou op; dophou; *keep one's WEATHER ~ open,* 'n ogie in die seil hou; *WHAT the ~ sees not, the heart does not crave,* wat die oog nie sien nie, deer die hart nie; *WHITE of the ~,* oogwit; *WITH an ~ to,* met die oog op; (v) waarneem, sien, nakyk, aanskou, begluur, bekyk, dophou, beskou, gadeslaan; *~ something COVETOUSLY,* iets begerig begluur; *~ with ENVY,* met lede oë aansien (aanskou); *~ball,* oogappel, oogbol; *~ bank,* oogbank; *~ bath,* oogbad; *~ black,* maskara; oogswart; *~ bolt,* oogbout; *~-bright,* oëtroos, *~ brow,* winkbrou; wenkbrou; *PENCILLED ~brow,* bestrykte winkbrou; *RAISE the ~brows,* verbaas of geskok opkyk; *~brow PENCIL,* winkbroustiffie; *~ care,* oogsorg; *~-catching,* opvallend; *~ cup,* oogbakkie; *~-drops,* oogdruppels; *~ end,* oogend; *~ flap,* oogklap; *~ glass,* oogglas; *~ guard,* oogskerm; *~ hole,* oogkas; kykgat; *~ joint,* oogkoppeling; *~ lash,* ooghaar, wimper; *hang on by one's ~lashes,* net-net kan uithou; *~ less,* blind; sonder oë; *~ let,* ogie; vetergaatjie; *~ let embroidery,* gaatjiesborduurwerk; *~ let material,* gaatjiesgoed; *~-level,* ooghoogte; *~ lid,* ooglid; *without batting an ~ lid,* sonder blik of bloos; sonder om 'n gesig te trek; *~ lotion,* oogwasmiddel; oogwater; oogsalf; *~-opener,* (n) openbaring; *~ operation,* oogoperasie; *~ piece,* lens; oogglas; verkyker; *~ pit,* oogholte; *~ rhyme,* oogrym; *~ salve,* oogsalf; *~ servant,* oëdienaar; *~ service,* oëdiens; *~ shade,* oogklap; *~ shadow,* oogkleursel; *~ shield,* oogskerm, oogklap; *~ shot,* oogafstand, gesigsafstand; *~ sight,* gesig(svermoë); *~ slit,* kykgleuf; *~ socket,* oogholte, oogkas; *~ sore,* iets ontsierends, 'n doring in die oog; *~ specialist,* oogarts, okulis; *~ strain,* gesigsoorspanning; *~ string,* oogsenu(wee); *~ sufferer,* ooglyer; *~ tooth,* oogtand; slagtand; *have CUT one's ~ teeth,* iets v.d. wêreld geleer het, volleerd wees; *DRAW someone's ~ teeth,* iem. se stertvere uittrek; iem. kaal daarvan laat afkom; *~ wash,* oogwater; smoesie, skyn, kaf, vroom praatjies; *~ water,* oogwater; trane; *~ witness,* ooggetuie, aanskouer.

ey'ot, eilandjie.

eyre, (hist.), rondgaande hof.

eyr'ie, eyr'y, (eyries), nes van 'n roofvoël, arendsnes.

Ezek'iel, Esegiël.

F

f, (fs, f's), f.
fa, fa.
fa(a)fee', *kyk* **fa(h)fee.**
Fabian', (n) Fabianus; (a): ~ *tactics*, vertragingstaktiek.
fa'ble, (n) fabel, sprokie; versinsel, verdigsel; verhaal; *BOOK of* ~ *s*, fabelboek; *old WIVES'* ~ *s*, ouwyfse verhale; (v) verdig, fantaseer; ~ **d,** vermaard; legendaries; ~ **r,** verdigter; fabelskrywer; ~ **writer,** fabelskrywer.
fab'ric, (ge)bou, struktuur; maaksel, fabrikaat; stof, kleedstof, materiaal; goed, weefsel, doek; ~ **ate,** maak, vervaardig, fabriseer; bedink, versin, verdig; ~ **a'tion,** vervaardiging; samestelling; fabrikasie; versinsel, verdigsel; ~ **ator,** versinner, uitvinder; maker, vervaardiger; ~ **glove,** stofhandskoen, geweefde handskoen; ~ **shop,** bekleërswerkplek; ~ **worker,** bekleër.
fab'ulist, fabeldigter, fabelskrywer; versinner.
fabulos'ity, fabelagtigheid.
fab'ulous, fabelagtig; ongelooflik, oordrewe; fabuleus, verdig; ~ **ness,** fabelagtigheid.
façade', gewel, voorgewel, fasade, voorkant.
face, (n) gesig, gelaat, aangesig; eet-en-drink, snoet; werkfront (myn); wyserplaat (oorlosie); kant; slaanvlak (hamer); aanskyn, wese, voorkome, aansien; aanblik; gedaante, vorm; (af)dekking; voorkant; oppervlak; gewel (van gebou); parmantigheid; onbeskaamheid; *BEFORE one's* ~ , vlak voor die oë, *FLY in the* ~ , trotseer; ~ *DOWN,* onderstebo; met die vóórkant onder; *her* ~ *is her FORTUNE,* sy het net 'n mooi gesiggie; sy is baie mooi; *FULL* ~ , en face; *put a GOOD* ~ *on something,* 'n saak v.d. gunstige kant laat sien; *his* ~ *HARDENED,* sy gesig het 'n vasberade uitdrukking aangeneem; *HAVE the* ~ , die vermetelheid hê om; so astrant wees; *IN the* ~ *of,* ten spyte van; teenoor; *pull (wear) a LONG* ~ , ernstig (verslae) lyk; *LOOK someone squarely in the* ~ , iem. in die oë kyk; *LOSE* ~ , in aansien daal; *put a NEW* ~ *on,* 'n ander kleur gee aan; *ON the* ~ *of it,* op die eerste gesig; oënskynlik; *PULL a* ~ , 'n gesig trek; *PULL* ~ *s at someone,* vir iem. skewebek trek; *PUT a good* ~ *on the affair,* 'n saak van die gunstigste kant laat sien; die onvermydelike met moed aanneem; *SAVE one's* ~ , die skyn red; *SEE someone* ~ *to* ~ , iem. onder vier oë sien; *SET one's* ~ *against,* hom versit teen; *SHOW one's* ~ , sy gesig laat sien; *not to SHOW one's* ~ *again,* nie weer jou gesig laat sien nie; nie weer jou stof wys nie; *SHUT a door in a person's* ~ , 'n deur voor iem. se neus toeslaan; *a SOUR* ~ , 'n suur gesig; ~ *TO* ~ , van aangesig tot aangesig; onder vier oë; en face; *TO one's* ~ , in iem. se gesig; *have TWO* ~ *s,* uit twee monde praat; *take something at* ~ *VALUE,* iets woordelik glo; iets sonder meer aanvaar; onder die oë kom, aankyk; dek, beklee (met teëls); lê na; uitsien op, kyk na; staan teenoor; omdraai, vermetel brat, trotseer, die hoof bied (gevaar); afsit (met lint); omsoom, omboor (met materiaal); ~ *a CARD,* 'n kaart omkeer; *have to* ~ *the FACTS,* die feite onder oë sien; ~ *the MUSIC,* die gevolge dra; ~ *OUT,* uithou, volhou; ~ *UP to something,* front maak teen; iets onder die oë sien; ~ **-about:** *turn* ~ *-about,* regsomkeer maak; ~ **ache,** (aan)gesigspyn; ~ **angle,** gyhoek; ~ **brick,** siersteen; ~ **card,** prentkaart; ~ **cloth,** gesigsvadoek; waslappie; ~ **cream,** gesigsroom; ~ **dimension,** vlakafmeting, vlakdimensie; ~ **-grinding machine,** vlakslypmasjien; ~ **-guard,** masker; ~ **hammer,** vlakhamer; ~ **joint,** voorvlakvoeg; ~ **-lifting,** gesigsverjonging gesigskuur, ontrimpeling; ~ **-mark,** werkmerk (houtw.); ~ **-mask,** gesigsmasker; ~ **massage,** gesigsmassering; ~ **-moulder,** profielmaker; ~ **pack,** gesigskerm; ~ **plate,** spanplaat; stempelplaat (van telefoon); ~ **powder,** gesigspoeier; ~ **r,** klap, hou; teleurstelling; ~ **side,** werkvlak; ~ **stone,** breuksteen; voorwerkklip.

fa'cet, ruitjie; faset; vlak, slypvlak; ~ **ed,** met ruitjies geslyp; gefasetteer.
face'tiae, grappe, geestighede, aardighede.
face'tious, grappig, geestig; snaaks; ~ **ly,** grappenderwys(e); ~ **ness,** vrolikheid, grappigheid; snaaksheid.
face'-towel, gesighanddoek.
face' value, nominale waarde, sigwaarde (posseël); *accept at* ~ , woordelik glo; sonder meer aanvaar.
face: ~ **wall,** voormuur; ~ **work,** skoonwerk (by messel).
fa'cia, naambord, gewelplaat, fassieplaat.
fa'cial, (n) gesigsmassering; (a) aangesigs-, gelaats-; ~ **angle,** gelaatshoek, gesigshoek; ~ **artery,** gesigslagaar; ~ **expression,** gelaatsuitdrukking; ~ **hair,** gesigshare; ~ **muscle,** gelaatspier; ~ **paralysis,** gelaatsverlamming.
facile, maklik, gou, vlot; ongedwonge; minsaam, vriendelik, inskiklik; meegaande, gedwee.
fa'cile prin'ceps, maklik die eerste.
facil'itate, maklik maak, vergemaklik, verlig.
facilita'tion, vergemakliking, bevordering, verligting.
facil'ity, (..ties), gemak(likheid); vaardigheid; toegewendheid, inskiklikheid, geneigdheid; voordeel, geleentheid; (pl) hulpmiddels, fasiliteite.
fa'cing, (n) voorkant, front, sigkant, voorwerk (bouk.); sluitrand, laag, omslag, boordlint, omboorsel, bies, belegsel (uniform); oplegsel; bekleding; uitmonstering; *trim with* ~ *s,* uitmonster; (adv) teenoor, uitsiende op, regoor, reg voor; ~ **brick,** siersteen; ~ **hammer,** vlakhamer; **page,** blad teenoor; ~ **points,** puntwissels, inrywissels.
facsim'ile, faksimilee, reproduksie.
fact, feit; daad; werklikheid; ~ *s ARE* ~ *s,* dit is nou eenmaal so; *you cannot ESCAPE the* ~ , dit is nou eenmaal so; *FACE* ~ *s,* realisties wees; die moeilikhede onder die oë sien; *IN* ~ , inderdaad ja; om die waarheid te sê; *KNOW for a* ~ , met sekerheid weet; *the* ~ *s of LIFE,* besonderhede oor voortplanting; *as a MATTER of* ~ , in werklikheid; om die waarheid te sê; *the* ~ *of the MATTER is,* die waarheid is; *in POINT of* ~ , in werklikheid; ~ **-finding,** (n) feiteondersoek; (a) feitebepalend; ~ **-finding commission,** feitekommissie.
fac'tion, party, partyskap, faksie; verdeeldheid, onenigheid; ~ **fight,** partystryd; stamgeveg; ~ **ist,** onrusstoker; woelgees.
fac'tious, onrusstokend, oproerig, partysugtig, klieerig; ~ **ness,** partysugtigheid; oproerigheid.
facti'tious, kunsmatig, nagemaak.
fac'titive, faktitief.
fac'tor, faktor; deler (mat.); ~ **age,** kommissieloon; ~ **ing,** faktorering; ~ **iza'tion,** ontbinding in faktore, faktorisasie; ~ **ize,** in faktore ontbind, faktoriseer; ~ **ship,** agentskap.
fac'tory, (..ries), fabriek(sgebou), werkplek; ~ **act,** fabriekswet; ~ **girl,** fabrieksmeisie; ~ **goods,** fabrieksware; ~ **hand,** fabrieksware; ~ **-made,** fabrieks-; ~ **masjinaal vervaardig;** ~ **owner,** fabrieksbaas; ~ **-reject,** fabrieksuitskot; ~ **-reject store,** uitskotwinkel; ~ **work,** fabrieksarbeid, fabriekswerk.
factot'um, faktotum, regterhand, handlanger, jan-knaphand, huishulp, kantoorhulp.
fac'tual, feitlik, feite-; fakties, saaklik.
fac'ultative, fakultatief, volgens keuse, opsioneel.
fac'ulty, (..ties), fakulteit (van 'n universiteit); vermoë; bekwaamheid, talent, aanleg; gawe; *MENTAL faculties,* verstandelike vermoëns; *VITAL* ~ , lewenskrag.
fad, stokperdjie, gril, manie, gier, buitensigheid; *be full of* ~ *s and fancies,* vol streke wees; vol draadwerk wees; ~ **ding,** aansmering (vernis); ~ **dish,** vol grille, vol fiemies; dweperig; ~ **dist,** stokperdjieryer; maniak; dweper, oordrywer; (v) beusel; ~ **dy,** vol fiemies.
fade, (n) welk, verlep; verbleik, verbleek, verflens, verskiet (kleure); uitbleik, verkleur; doof (radio); verflou, wegsterwe (geluid); ~ *AWAY,* wegkwyn, vervaag, sterwe, heengaan; wegraak (radio); ~

fading 886 *fall*

AWAY to nothing, in die niet versink; ~ *DOWN*, afdoof; ~ *IN*, indoof, geleidelik verskyn (film); ~ *INTO*, saggies oorgaan in; ~ *OUT*, uitdoof; ~ *UP*, opdoof; ~ **d**, verbleik; verwelk; verflens, vaal, flets; ~ **dness**, fletsheid; ~ **less**, onverwelkbaar; on= verganklik; kleurhoudend, onverkleurbaar, kleur= vas, eg.

fa'ding, wegsterwing, verdowwing, geluidsverswak= king; dowing, sluiering (radio); verdwyning; ver= skieting (kleure).

fa'do, fado, Portugese volksliedjie.

faec'al, ontlastings=, fekaal.

fae'ces, uitwerpsels, fekalieë, faeces; besinksel, moer.

fa'erie, fa'ery, (n) feëland; (a) feeagtig, feëriek, denkbeeldig.

fag, (n) swaar werk, geswoeg; groentjie; slaaf, werk= esel; sigaret; (v) (**-ged**), swoeg, jakker, afsloof, af= beul, afmat; vuil werkies doen; ~ **-end**, rafelkant (van 'n stuk sis); oorskot; aanhangsel; stert, slot; ~ **ged**, vermoeid, uitgeput, afgesloof, afgemat; *be* ~ *ged out*, uitgeput wees.

fag(g)'ot, (n) bondel, drag; (v) in bosse bind, in dragte maak; ~ **ing**, leersteek, geknoopte graatsteek (naaldw.); ~ **-weld**, vousweis.

fa(h)'fee, fa(h)fee.

Fahr'enheit, Fahrenheit; ~ **thermometer**, Fahren= heittermometer.

fa'ience, porseleinware, erdeware, faïence.

fail, (n) fout, feil; *without* ~, seker; (v) te kort kom; begeef; faal; wegsterf; verswak; mis; nalatig wees; nalaat; bankrot raak; weier (geweer); onderbreek; onklaar raak; beswyk; misluk; in gebreke bly; te= leurstel, in die steek laat; verongeluk, misluk; sak, nie slaag nie, druip, dop (eksamen); ~ *to ANS= WER*, die antwoord skuldig bly; *one CANNOT* ~ *to*, 'n mens kan nie anders nie as; *the CROPS* ~ *ed*, die oes het misluk; *his HEART* ~ *ed him*, sy moed het hom begeef; *IF it* ~ *s*, as dit nie geluk nie; *he* ~ *ed to KEEP his word*, hy het nie sy woord gehou nie; *don't* ~ *to let me KNOW*, moenie nalaat om my te laat weet nie; *the MOTOR* ~ *ed*, die motor het gaan staan; *WORDS* ~ *me*, ek kom woorde kort.

fail'ing, (n) fout, swak, gemis; tekortkoming; (a) ont= brekend; agteruitgaande; mislukkend; ~ *to AP= PEAR*, in gebreke bly om te verskyn; *NEVER* ~, onfeilbaar, onuitputlik; *a* ~ *SUBJECT*, 'n druip= vak; (prep) by gebrek aan; ~ *WHICH*, anders, in gebreke waarvan, so nie; ~ *WHOM*, by wie se ontstentenis.

faille, falie.

fail'ure, onderbreking; breuk (buiteband); gebrek, te= kortkoming; druipeling, doppeling (eksamen); ver= suim; weiering (motor); mislukking, slegte uitslag, fiasko; bankrotskap, staking van betaling; fout; nalatigheid; windeier, gemors; *END in* ~, op 'n mislukking uitloop; *it WAS a hopeless* ~, dit was 'n misoes; dit was 'n hopelose mislukking.

fain, graag; gewillig; *he WOULD* ~, hy sou graag.

fain'eant, niksdoener, loodswaaier.

faint, (n) floute; (v) flou val, (be)swym; tou opgooi; ~ *dead away*, flou val; (a) swak; onduidelik; flou; on= magtig, benoud; dof; gering; *GROW* ~, dof word; flou word; moedeloos word; *not have the* ~ *est IDEA*, nie die flouste benul hê nie; ~ **-hearted**, laf= hartig; versaag, skroomhartig, flouhartig; wankel= moedig; ~ **-heartedness**, lafhartigheid; flouhartig= heid, versaagdheid, wankelmoedigheid; ~ **ing**, floute, beswyming; ~ **ing fit**, floute; ~ **ly**, floutjies, swakkies; ~ **ness**, swakte, kragteloosheid; flouheid; moedeloosheid; weeheid; onmag; onduidelikheid; dofheid; ~ **-ruled**, met waterlyne.

faints, (onsuiwer) voorloop, naloop (stokery).

fair[1], (n) jaarmark, kermis; *commercial* ~, jaarbeurs.

fair[2] (a), mooi, fraai, skoon; blank, blond, lig; goed; billik; regmatig; eerlik; vlekloos; helder (lug); op= reg; *BE in a* ~ *way to*, mooi op pad wees om; ~ *COPY*, foutlose eksemplaar; ~ *FIELD and no fa= vour*, almal is gelyk; ~ *of FOUL weather*, mooi of slegte weer; ~ *GAME*, geoorloofde wild; 'n geoor= loofde mikpunt; *all's* ~ *in LOVE and war*, in liefde= sake en in oorlog is enige middel geregverdig; *the* ~

SEX, die skone geslag; *a* ~ *SHARE*, 'n billike aan= deel; ~ *and SOFT goes far in a day*, met die hoed in die hand kom 'n mens deur die hele (ganse) land; ~ *and SQUARE*, reguit, rondweg; ~ *WEAR and tear*, billike slytasie; (adv) mooi; beleef; eerlik; taamlik, net, skaflik; *it BIDS* ~ *to*, dit beloof om; dit wek die beste verwagtings om; *it is ONLY* ~, dis niks meer as billik nie; *PLAY* ~, eerlik te werk gaan; ~ **-dealing**, opregtheid; eerlikheid; ~ **-haired**, lig, blond.

fair'-ground, kermisterrein.

fair'ing[1], bekleding (kabels); stroomlynkap (silinder).

fair'ing[2], kermisgeskenk.

fair'lead, geleiding; touleier (skeepvaart).

fairly, goed, behoorlik, taamlik; heeltemal, glad; *he was* ~ *BESIDE himself*, hy was heeltemal buite homself (van woede); ~ *EMPTY*, leërig; *this is* ~ *GOOD*, dit is taamlik goed.

fair: ~ **-minded**, opreg; billik; ~ **ness**, mooiheid; blondheid; regverdigheid, billikheid, skaflikheid; eerlikheid; ~ **play**, (n) eerlike (skoon) spel; (a) reg= verdig, reg, eerlik, ferplie (plat); ~ **-sized**, ordentlik; ~ **-spoken**, hoflik, beleef, vriendelik.

fair' stitcher, soolnaaier.

fair'way, vaarwater, vaargeul; skoonveld (gholf).

fair' weather, mooi weer; ~ *friend*, 'n vriend in voor= spoed, mooiweersvriend.

fair'y, (..ries), (n) fee, elf; towergodin; *the fairies are baking*, die jakkalse trou; (a) feeagtig, feëriek; to= wer=; ~ **bell**, grasklokkie; ~ **dance**, elwedans; ~ **godmother**, towertante; ~ **lamp**, sierlampie; **F** ~ **land**, towerland, feëryk, sprokiesland; ~ **-like**, feëriek, feeagtig, soos 'n fee; ~ **queen**, feëkoningin; ~ **ring**, heksekring; ~ **-tale**, sprokie; praatjie vir die vaak.

fait: ~ *ACCOMPLI*, voldonge feit; *QUITE au* ~, goed op hoogte van.

faith, (n) geloof; vertroue; erewoord, belofte; *ARTI= CLE of* ~, geloofsartikel; *BAD* ~, kwade trou; *BREACH of* ~, troubreuk; *BREAK* ~ *with*, jou woord nie gestand doen nie; *BY my* ~, op my woord van eer; *CONFESSION of* ~, geloofsbely= denis; *in GOOD* ~, te goeder trou; *KEEP* ~, jou belofte nakom; woord hou; *having LITTLE* ~, swakgelowig; ~ *will move MOUNTAINS*, geloof kan berge versit; *PIN one's* ~ *on*, jou vertroue stel in; jou verlaat op; *PUT one's* ~ *in*, vertroue stel in; *UPON my* ~, op my woord van eer; *break* ~ *WITH*, jou woord nie gestand hou nie; (interj) reg= tig! sowaar! ~ **-cure**, geloofsgenesing.

faith'ful, gelowig; getrou; ~ **ly**, getrou; *PROMISE* ~ *ly*, hand en mond belowe; *YOURS* ~ *ly*, die uwe; ~ **ness**, getrouheid.

faith: ~ **-healer**, geloofsgeneser; ~ **-healing**, geloofs= genesing; ~ **less**, troueloos, onbetroubaar; ongelo= wig; ~ **lessness**, ontrou, trouelooosheid; ongelowig= heid; onbetroubaarheid.

fake[1], (n) ontduiking, bedrog, slenterslag, lis; na= maaksel; (v) oplap; vervals; namaak, opsmuk; ~ **d**, nagemaak; ~ **ment**, swendel; namaak.

fake[2], (n) slag, kinkel (in kabel); (v) opdraai, oprol, opskiet (kabel).

fak'ing, swendel, namaak.

fakir', fakir, bedelmonnik.

Falang'ism, Falangisme.

Falang'ist, Falangis.

fal'bala, versiersel, garneersel, falbala.

fal'cate, sekelvormig.

fal'ces, vangtoestel (spinnekop).

fal'chion, kromswaard.

fal'ciform, sekelvormig.

fal'con, valk; ~ **er**, valkjagter, valkenier; ~ **ry**, valk= jag.

fal'deral, tierlantyntjie, snuistery.

fald'stool, bidstoel, faldistorium.

fall, (n) sondeval (v.d. mens); helling, afdraande; dood; reënval; lammeroes; herfs; najaar; uitgang (van jaar); daling, neerdaling; prysdaling, agteruit= gang, verval; val, verval; (pl) waterval; ~ *in CON= SUMPTION*, verbruiksdaling; *HAVE a* ~, val, in die grond ploeg; *the* ~ *of MAN*, die sondeval; *be RIDING for a* ~, roekeloos handel; ~ *of ROCK*, *fallacious* 887 *family*

rotsstorting; *SPECULATE for a* ~, op 'n daling spekuleer; *TRY a* ~ *with someone,* iem. probeer onder kry; (v) **(fell, -en),** instort; afval; verval; val; uitval; ingeneem (verower) word (vesting); afhel, afhang; sak, agteruitgaan; bedaar (wind); daal (pryse); sneuwel; ~ *AMONG,* verval onder; ~ *among thieves,* onder diewe verseil raak; ~ *ASLEEP,* in slaap val; aan die slaap raak; ~ *ASTERN,* agterraak; ~ *AWAY,* wegval; afvallig word; ~ *BACK,* terugval, terugtree; ~ *BACK on someone,* jou op iem. verlaat; jou toevlug tot iem. neem; ~ *BACK on something,* gebruik maak van; jou met iets anders behelp; ~ *BACKWARDS,* agteroorval; ~ *in BATTLE,* sneuwel; ~ *BEHIND,* agter raak; terugval; ~ *to BITS,* uitmekaarval; ~ *into CONVERSATION,* in gesprek raak; ~ *to the CROWN,* aan die kroon (staat) verval; ~ *into DISUSE,* in onbruik raak; ~ *DOWN,* val, (af)duiwel, afval; ~ *DUE,* verval; ~ *into ERROR,* verkeerd gaan; ~ *on EVIL days,* slegte tye deurmaak; ~ *on one's FEET,* op jou voete te lande kom; ~ *FLAT,* 'n misoes wees; op niks uitloop nie; *it has* ~ *en FLAT,* dit het nie ingeslaan nie; dit het misluk; die koek het in die as geval; ~ *FOR,* verlief raak op; ingenome wees met; geflous word; val daarvoor; instem (met argument); *a FORTRESS* ~ *s,* 'n vesting word ingeneem; ~ *FOUL of,* in botsing kom met; ~ *to the GROUND,* in duie stort; ~ *ILL,* siek word; ~ *IN,* inval, laat aantree; instort; verval; ~ *IN with,* teen die lyf loop; stoot op; hom voeg na; saamgaan met; instem met; akkoord gaan met; ~ *INTO,* uitloop in; ~ *into LINE with,* akkoord gaan met; jou aansluit by iets; ~ *to one's LOT,* iem. ten deel val; ~ *in LOVE,* verlief raak; ~ *into OBLIVION,* in vergetelheid raak; ~ *OFF,* afval, slink, agteruitgaan; ~ *ON,* aanval; aantref; ~ *OUT with someone,* met iem. oorhoeks raak; dit aan die stok kry met iem.; met iem. rusie kry; ~ *OVER,* omval; ~ *OVER one another,* oormekaar val om; ~ *to PIECES,* uitmekaar val; *the PLANS fell to the ground,* die planne het misluk; ~ *as if POLE-AXED,* soos 'n bees (os) neerslaan; ~ *(a) PREY to,* 'n slagoffer word van; ~ *into a RAGE,* woedend word; *he that* ~ *s today may RISE tomorrow,* jy moet eers val voordat jy kan opstaan; ~ *SHORT,* kortkom; ~ *SHORT of,* te kort skiet; nie beantwoord aan nie; agterstaan by; *have SOMETHING to* ~ *back upon,* 'n agterdeurtjie oophou; nog 'n toevlug (neseier) hê; ~ *to TALKING,* begin praat; ~ *amongst THIEVES,* onder diewe beland; ~ *THROUGH,* in duie stort; deur die mat val; ~ *TO!* aanpak! val weg! ~ *UNDER,* behoort tot; val onder; ~ *VICTIM to,* 'n slagoffer word van; ~ *WITHIN,* binne (onder) val.
falla'cious, bedrieglik, misleidend; verkeerd, vals; ~**ness,** bedrieglikheid; verkeerdheid.
fall'acy, (..cies) bedrog; drogrede, drogargument; misleiding, vergissing, dwaalbegrip; valse redenering.
fal-lal', tierlantyntjie, prul.
fall'en, (n) gevallene; (a) gevalle; ~ **angel,** gevalle engel; ~ **arches,** platvoete; ~ **woman,** gevalle meisie.
fall guy, slagoffer, prooi; swaap, haas.
fallibil'ity, feilbaarheid.
fall'ible, feilbaar.
fall'ing, (n) val; (a) vallende; ~ **door,** valdeur; ~ **glass,** dalende barometer (weerglas); ~ **hair,** uitvallende hare; ~ **leaf,** vallende biaar; blaarvlug (lugv.); ~**-off,** agteruitgang, vermindering; ~ **sickness,** vallende siekte; ~ **star,** vallende ster, skietster; ~ **stone,** meteoorsteen; ~ **tide,** afgaande (vallende) gety.
fall'-off, vermindering; agteruitgang; teruggang.
Fallop'ian tube, eierleier.
fall'-out, uitval, rusie; afval (stowwe); *radioactive* ~, radioaktiewe neerslag (afval).
fall'ow¹, (n) braakland; (v) braak; (a) braak; *lie* ~, braak lê; onbewerk lê.
fall'ow², (a) vaalbruin; ~ **deer,** damhert; ~**ing,** braking, dries; ~ **time,** braaktyd.
fall: ~ **plate,** klapplaat; ~ **trap,** valluik; ~ **wind,** daalwind; herfswind (Am.).

false, vals, skynheilig; onwaar, ongegrond; valshartig, trouteloos; bedrieglik; geveins; geniepsig; geaffekteerd(d), voorgewend; ontrou; nagemaak (munte), oneg; *sail under* ~ *COLOURS,* onder valse vlag vaar; *PLAY one* ~, iem. kul (bedrieg); ~ *NOTION,* dwaalbegrip; ~ *POSITION,* 'n skewe verhouding; *under* ~ *PRETENCES,* onder valse voorwendsels; ~ *PRIDE,* valse hoogmoed; ~ *START,* ongelyke wegspring (atletiek); *take a* ~ *STEP,* 'n misstap begaan; ~ **alarm,** vals alarm; blinde alarm; ~ **axis,** skynas; ~ **bark,** skynbas; ~ **bedding,** diagonale gelaagdheid (geol.); ~ **bottom,** dubbele boom; ~ **card,** kulkaart; ~ **coin,** vals munt; ~ **conception,** skynswangerskap; bedrogswangerskap; ~ **dawn,** skyndaeraad; ~ **doctrine,** dwaalleer; ~ **door,** blinde deur; ~ **face,** mombakkies; vals gesig; ~ **foot,** skynvoet; ~ **friendship,** vals(e) vriendskap, skynvriendskap; ~ **fruit,** skynvrug; ~ **hair,** vals hare; ~**-hearted,** vals; bedrieglik; ~ **heath,** valsheide; ~ **hem,** stootkant; ~ **hood,** valsheid; leuen; ~ **idea,** dwaalbegrip; waandenkbeeld; ~**ly,** vals; *swear* ~ *ly,* vals sweer; ~**ness,** valsheid, onopregtheid; ~ **move,** misstap, verkeerde stap; ~ **notion,** dwaalbegrip, waandenkbeeld; vals(e) idee (gedagte); ~ **peace,** skynvrede; ~ **position,** skewe posisie; vals(e) (swak) standpunt; ~ **pretences,** valse voorwendsels; ~ **prophet,** vals(e) profeet; ~ **rib,** vals rib; ~ **shame,** valse skaamte; ~ **start,** verkeerde begin; foutwegspring; ~**-swearing,** meineed; ~ **teeth,** valstande; ~ **work,** stutwerk; voorwerk.
falsett'o, kopstem, falset.
fals'ie, fopborsie, foppertjie.
falsifi'able, vervalsbaar.
falsifica'tion, vervalsing.
fal'sifier, vervalser.
fal'sify, (..fied), vervals, namaak; loënstraf; beskaam (verwagtings); ~ *hopes,* verwagtinge teleurstel; ~**ing,** sofistikasie (van metale); vervalsing.
fal'sitas, falsiteit, falsitas (reg).
fal'sity, (..ties), valsheid, leuenagtigheid.
fal'ter, stamel, hakkel, stotter; strulkel; aarsel, weifel; ~**ing,** stamelend; weifelend; strompelend; ~**ing prayer,** stamelgebed.
fame, roem, faam, glorie, groot naam; befaamdheid, vermaardheid; gerug; *HOUSE of ill* ~, bordeel; *ILL* ~, berugtheid; ~**d,** beroemd, vermaard; ~*d for,* vermaard weens.
famil'ial, familiaal.
famil'iar, (n) boesemvriend; (a) goed bekend, welbekend; vertroulik, familiaar; huislik, alledaags; mak; ongedwonge; eie, danig, vrypostig, gemeensaam, familiêr; *BE* ~ *with,* bekend wees met; vertroulik omgaan met; vertroud wees met; vrypostig wees met; ~ *LANGUAGE,* omgangstaal; ~ *SPIRIT,* gediensfige gees; *be TOO* ~ *with,* te vrypostig (gemeensaam) wees met; ~ **chat,** spekvreter (soort voëltjie).
familiar'ity, ongedwongenheid; bekendheid; vertroudheid; voorbarigheid; vertroulikheid, eieheid, gemeensaamheid, familiariteit; ~ *breeds contempt,* alte goed is buurman se gek; te goed bekend maak onbemind.
famil'iarize, bekend maak (met); wen (aan); oriënteer; gemeensaam maak.
fam'ily, (..lies), familie, gesin, vrou en kinders; geslag, stam, afkoms; orde, groep; *HAVE you a* ~? het u kinders? *IN a* ~ *way,* gemeensaam; *it RUNS in the* ~, dis 'n familietrek; dis in die familie; dis 'n kenmerk v.d. familie; *be TREATED like one of the* ~, soos 'n kind in die huis wees; *be in the* ~ *WAY,* in geseënde omstandighede wees; ~ **affairs,** huislike aangeleenthede; familieaangeleenthede; ~ **allowance,** gesinstoelae; ~ **altar,** huisaltaar; ~ **arms,** familiewapen; ~ **Bible,** Huisbybel; Familiebybel; ~ **budget,** gesinsbegroting; ~ **butcher,** (algemene) slagter; ~ **celebration,** gesinsfees; ~ **circle,** familiekring; ~ **coat of arms,** familiewapen; ~ **complaint,** familiekwaal; F ~ **Day,** Gesinsdag; ~ **doctor,** huisdokter; ~ **feeling,** familiegevoel, gesinsgevoel; familiehegtheid, gesinshegtheid; ~ **feud,** familietwis; ~ **friend,** huisvriend; ~ **grave,** familiegraf; ~ **like-**

ness, familietrek; ~ **man,** huisvader; huislike man; ~ **name,** van, familienaam, geslagsnaam, stamnaam; ~ **planning,** gesinsbeperking; ~ **tie,** gesinsband; ~ **tree,** stamboom; ~ **worship,** huisgodsdiens, boekevat.

fam'ine, hongersnood; gebrek, nood; ~ **fever,** vlektifus.

fam'ish, verhonger, doodhonger; uithonger; ~ **ed,** uitgehonger, doodhonger; *BE* ~ *ed,* baie honger hê; *be* ~ *ed FOR,* smag na.

fam'ous, uitstekend; beroemd, vermaard, befaamd; ~ **ly,** skitterend, pragtig.

fam'ulus, (..lie), famulus, towenaarhandlanger, towernaarhulp; gedienstige.

fan¹, (n) skermplank (steier); lugskroef, lugwaaier; skroefblad; waaier; wan; (v) (-ned), koel waai; uitwaai; wan; aanwakker; aanstook, aanblaas; ~ *the flames,* die vlamme aanwakker.

fan², (n) bewonderaar, dweper (sl.).

Fanagalo', Fanakalo', Fanakalo, Fanagalo.

fanat'ic, (n) dweper, (gees)drywer, fanatikus; (a) dweepsiek, dweepagtig, fanatiek; ~ **ism,** drywery, dwepery, dweepsug, fanatisme; *religious* ~ *ism,* godsdienswaansin; ~ **ize,** dweep, dweepsiek handel.

fan: ~ **belt,** waaierband; ~ **blade,** waaierblad.

fan'cied, geliefkoos, gelief, lieflings=; ingebeeld, gewaand, vermeend; *be* ~ , gewild wees; in trek wees.

fan'cier, liefhebber; kweker, teler.

fan'ciful, fantasties, grotesk; vol giere, grillig, ingebeeld, hersenskimmig; denkbeeldig; ~ **ness,** denkbeeldigheid.

fan: ~ **clutch,** waaierkoppelaar; ~ **cowl,** waaierkap.

fan'cy, (n) (..cies), verbeelding, fantasie; inbeelding, denkbeeld, voorstelling; bedenksel, versinsel; inval, waan; sin; lus, neiging, smaak; sinnigheid, nuk, fiemies, gril, gier; liefhebbery; verbeeldingskrag; *CATCH the* ~ *of,* in die smaak val van; *HAVE a* ~ *for,* sinnigheid in iets hê; groot trek in iets hê; *STRIKE one's* ~ , in jou smaak val; *SUIT one's* ~ , iem. geval; *TAKE a* ~ *to,* hou van; aangetrokke voel tot; (v) (..cied), verbeel, waan, inbeeld; meen, glo; kweek; baie hou van; *BE fancied,* gewild wees; in trek wees; ~ *ONESELF,* jou verbeel; hoogmoedig wees; meen dat jy 'n paspoort hemel toe het; jou verbeel dat jy die goewerneur se hond se oom is; *RATHER* ~ , meen, glo, 'n spesmaas hê; (a) mode=, fantasie=; oordrewe; oulik, fraai, spoggerig; (interj) dink, bid jou aan; verbeel jou; ~ **articles,** modeartikels, snuisterye, fantasiegoed; ~ **bread,** lukesebrood; ~ **breed,** sierteelt; ~ **cloth,** sierstof; ~ **dog,** sierhond; ~ **dress,** fantasiekostuum; ~ **-dress ball,** gekostumeerde bal; ~ **fair,** liefdadigheidsbasaar; ~ **fold,** siervou; ~ **-free,** nie verlief nie; ~ **girl,** nooi(e)ntjie, minnares; ~ **goods,** modeartikels, snuisterye, galanterieë, galanterieware, fantasiegoed; ~ **letter,** sierletter; ~ **man,** minnaar; ~ **name,** boeknaam; modenaam; ~ **paper,** luuksepapier; ~ **pigeon,** sierduif; ~ **price,** buitensporige prys; ~ **skating,** kunsskaats; ~ **shop,** galanteriewinkel; ~ **shot,** spoghou; ~ **weave,** sierbinding; ~ **work,** borduurwerk, fraai handwerk; ~ **yoke,** sierskouerstuk.

fan dance, waaierdans; ~ **r,** waaierdanseres.

fandang'le, malligheid, tierlantyntjie.

fandang'o, (-es), fandango (Spaanse dans).

fane, tempel, kerkgebou (digterlik).

fan'fare, fanfare, trompetgeskal.

fanfaronade', grootspraak, pronkery; fanfare.

fang¹, klou; slagtand; giftand; tandwortel.

fang², (v) laai; oppomp.

fang: ~ **ed,** met slagtande getand; ~ **bolt,** hakkelbout; ~ **less,** sonder giftande; sonder slagtande.

fan: ~ **hub,** waaiernaaf; ~ **light,** tuimelraam, bolig; ~ **-like,** waaieragtig; waaiersgewys(e); ~ **mail,** bewonderaarspos, lofpos; ~ **-nerved,** waaiernerwig; ~ **ny,** agterstewe, boude; ~ **ning,** gewaai; aanwakkering; ~ **-palm,** waaierpalm; ~ **-pulley,** waaierriemskyf; ~ **-scoop,** waaierskoep; ~ **-shaft,** waaieras; lugskag; ~ **-shaped,** waaiervormig; ~ **shroud,** waaiermantel; ~ **spindle,** waaieras, waaierspil (motor); ~ **ta'bulous,** (sl.), fantabuleus, ongelooflik

goed; ~ **tail,** waaierstert; ~ **tail pigeon,** pronkduif, poustertduif.

fan'tan, fantan, Chinese dobbelspel.

fanta'sia, fantasia (musiek).

fan'tast, dromer, fantas.

fantas'tic, ingebeeld, grillig, fantasties, denkbeeldig; ~ **al'ity,** grilligheid; ~ **alness,** ingebeeldheid; wonderlikheid; grilligheid, denkbeeldigheid; ~ **ate,** fantasties maak.

fan'tasy, (..sies), inbeelding; verbeeldingskrag; hersenskim; fantasie, gril, inval.

fan: ~ **tracery,** waaierloofwerk; ~ **vault,** waaiergewelf; ~ **window,** waaiervenster; ~ **wise,** waaiergewys(e).

far, (n): *BY* ~ , verreweg; *FROM* ~ , uit die verte; *NOT by* ~ , op verre na nie; (a, adv) ver, afgeleë; baie, veel; *AS* ~ *as,* sover as; vir sover; ~ *AWAY,* ver weg; ~ *and AWAY,* verreweg; ~ *BE it from me,* dit sy ver(re) van my; *you will have to go* ~ *to BEAT him,* nie maklik sy weerga kry nie; *a* ~ *CRY,* 'n groot afstand (verskil); ~ *FROM it,* ver daarvandaan; dis glad nie so nie; *GO* ~ *to,* baie bydra tot; dit ver bring; ~ *GONE,* ver gevorder; mooi dronk; ernstig siek; hoog swanger; ~ *from GOOD,* lank (glad) nie goed nie; *so* ~ *so GOOD,* tot sover gaan dit goed; ~ *from GOOD,* lank (glad) nie goed nie; *HOW* ~ *?* in hoeverre? hoever? *IN so* ~ *as,* vir sover; ~ *INTO the night,* diep in die nag; ~ *MORE,* baie meer; ~ *OFF,* ver weg; ~ *ON in years,* op gevorderde leeftyd; ~ *OUT,* ver weg; ver gevorder; ver verkeerd; *the* ~ *SIDE,* die ander kant; *SO* ~ , tot dusver; *THUS* ~ *and no further,* so ver en nie verder nie; ~ *and WIDE,* wyd en syd; heinde en ver.

fa'rad, farad; ~ **ad'ic,** faradies; ~ **ism,** induksie-elektrisiteit.

far'-away, dromerig; afgeleë; ~ *look,* afwesige (dromerige, starende) blik.

far' between, af en toe; selde; baie min.

farce¹, (n) klug, klugspel; sotterny; windeier.

farce², (n) vulsel; (v) opstop, vul.

farceur', (F.), grapmaker; klugskrywer.

farce writer, klugskrywer.

far'cical, klugtig; belaglik, bespotlik; denkbeeldig; ~ **ity,** ~ **ness,** belaglikheid, klugtigheid.

far'cy, (huid)droes.

far'cing, vulsel.

fard'el, pak, drag, bondel.

fare, vraggeld, reisgeld, passasiersgeld; passasier; vrag; kos; *bill of* ~ , spyskaart; (v) gaan, vaar, gebeur, oorkom, eet; ~ *BADLY,* daar sleg van afkom; ~ *FORTH,* begin; op reis gaan; ~ *WELL,* dit goed tref.

farewell', (n) vaarwel, afskeid; *bid* ~ , vaarwel sê; (a) afskeids=; (interj) vaarwel; ~ **dinner,** afskeidsmaal, afskeidsete; ~ **party,** afskeidsparty; ~ **speech,** afskeidsrede.

far: ~ **-famed,** wydvermaard; ~ **-fetched,** vergesog; ~ **-flung,** uitgestrek, wydversprei.

farin'a, (set)meel; stysel; stuifmeel.

farina'ceous, melerig, meelagtig, meel=, meelhoudend, farineus; poeieragtig; ~ **food,** meelkos.

fa'rinose, melerig, farineus.

farm, (n) plaas, boerdery, boereplaas; kindertehuis; (v) boer; bebou; verpag, verhuur; uitbestee; ~ *out,* verpag; uitbestee; ~ **able,** beboubaar; ~ **animal,** plaasdier; ~ **buildings,** opstal, plaasgeboue; ~ **butter,** plaasbotter; ~ **colony,** boerderykolonie.

farm'er, boer; landman, landbouer; pagter; ~ *'s BANK,* landbank; ~ *'s CLASS,* boerestand; ~ *'s town HOUSE,* tuishuis; ~ *'s town ROOM,* tuiskamer.

farm: ~ **foreman,** plaasvoorman; ~ **gaol,** plaastronk; ~ **hand,** boerkneg, plaashulp, plaaswerker; ~ **-hold,** pagbrief; ~ **horse,** boerperd, plaasperd; ~ **house,** boerewoning, plaashuis, opstal.

farm'ing, boerdery, landbou; *the* ~ *COMMUNITY,* die (plaas)boere; ~ *INTERESTS,* boerderybelange.

farm: ~ **labour,** plaasarbeid; plaaswerk; plaaswerkers; ~ **labourer,** plaaswerker; ~ **lad,** plaaseun; boerkêrel; boerseun; ~ **-lands,** landerye; ~ **life,**

faro

plaaslewe; boerelewe; ~ **manure,** kraalmis, stalmis; ~ **prison,** plaastronk, plaasgevangenis; ~ **life,** plaaslewe; ~ **produce,** landbouprodukte; ~ **product,** plaasproduk; ~ **remedy,** boerereaat; ~ **road,** buitepad, plaaspad; ~ **school,** plaasskool; ~ **stall,** plaaskiosk, plaasstalletjie; ~ **stead,** opstal, boerewoning; ~ **wife,** plaasvrou; boerevrou; ~ **woman,** boerevrou; ~ **wool,** werfwol; ~ **yard,** werf.
far'o, faro(spel) (kaarte).
Far'oe Islands, Faröer-eilande.
far'-off, afgeleë, ver.
farouche', stug, bot; skamerig.
farra'ginous, gemeng, deurmekaar.
farra'go, mengelmoes, brousel, allegaartjie.
far'-reaching, verreikend verstrekkend, ingrypend.
fa'rrier, hoefsmid; ~ **'s hammer,** beslaanhamer, hoefhamer; ~ **y,** smidswinkel; hoefsmedery; perdedoktery.
fa'rrow, (n) drag, werpsel, nes kleintjies (varke) (v) jong, kleintjies kry.
far: ~ **-seeing,** vooruitsiende; ~ **-sighted,** versiende; ~ **-sightedness,** versiendheid; ~ **-sought,** vergesog; gedwonge; ~ **-spent,** byna verby.
fart, (vulg.), (n) poep, wind; (v) poep, 'n wind laat.
farth'er, (a) verder, meer afgeleë; ~ **most,** verste; (adv) verder, buitendien.
farth'est, verste, mees afgeleë.
farth'ing, oortjie; *be without a BRASS* ~, geen duit besit nie; heeltemal platsak wees; *he does not CARE a brass* ~, hy gee niks (geen flenter) om nie; *not WORTH a brass* ~, nie 'n pyp dagga werd nie, geen sent werd nie.
farth'ingale, hoepelrok, fardegalyn.
far'tlek, langafstandatletiekoefening.
fas'ces, staafbundel, bylbondel, houtbundel.
fa'scia, band; (plat)lys, fassie (bouk.); gordel; streep.
fa'sciated, saamgegroei; gestreep.
fascia'tion, samegroeiing; swagteling; streping.
fas'cicle, bundeltjie, bondeltjie, tros, bossie; bondel (plantk.); aflewering (van 'n boekwerk).
fascic'ular, bondelvormig; bundelsgewys(e).
fas'cinate, betower, fassineer, bekoor, wegsleep, meesleep, boei; biologeer.
fas'cinating, boeiend, bekoorlik, aantreklik, betowerend, wegslepend, meeslepend, fassinerend.
fascina'tion, betowering, bekoring.
fas'cinator, bekoorder, towenaar.
fascine', latbos; ~ **dwelling,** paalwoning.
Fas'cism, Fascisme.
Fas'cist, (n) Fascis; (a) Fascisties.
fash, (n) omslag, moeite; (v) kwel, pla, moeite aandoen.
fas'hion, (n) drag, vorm; fatsoen, manier, trant, wyse; mode; *AFTER a* ~, tot op seker(e) hoogte; op 'n manier; *BE in* ~, in die mode wees; in swang wees; *BECOME the* ~, in swang kom; *DO something after a* ~, iets op 'n manier doen; *after the FRENCH* ~, na die Franse mode; *IN such* ~, op dié manier; *OUT of* ~, uit die mode; *PEOPLE of* ~, mense van stand; *SET the* ~, die toon aangee; *as good be out of the WORLD as out of* ~, liewer dood as uit die mode; (v) vorm; fatsoeneer, bewerk; inrig, maak; reël; ~ **able,** na die mode; deftig, grootsteeds, modieus, modies, chic; ~ **ableness,** deftigheid; modieusheid; ~ **able complaint,** mode-siekte; ~ **able word,** modewoord; ~ **board,** glansbordpapier; ~ **ed,** gefatsoeneer, gevorm; ~ **house,** modewinkel; ~ **mad,** modemal; ~ **magazine,** modetydskrif; ~ **-monger,** modegek; ~ **parade,** modeparade, modeskou; ~ **plate,** modeplaat; modegek; ~ **-sheet,** modeplaat; ~ **shop,** modewinkel; ~ **show,** modeskou.
fast¹, (n) vas; *break one's* ~, ophou vas; (v) vas.
fast², (a) vinnig, snel, hard, gou, skielik; vas, standvastig, stewig, sterk; eg; kleurvas; losbandig; *the CLOCK is* ~, die klok is (loop) voor; *a* ~ *COLOUR,* 'n vaste kleur; ~ *FRIENDS,* dik vriende; ~ *HEADSTOCK,* vaste kop; *a* ~ *HORSE,* 'n vinnige perd; *a* ~ *LIVER,* 'n deurbringer; ~ *TRAIN,* sneltrein; *a* ~ *WOMAN,* 'n losbandige vrou; (adv) vas; ferm; vinnig, stewig; dig; styf; los; vry; ~ *ASLEEP,* vas aan die slaap; ~ *and FURIOUS,* le-

father

wendig, kragtig; ~ *BIND,* ~ *find,* toesluit wat jy nie wil verloor nie; ~ *IDLE,* snel luier; *as* ~ *as your LEGS can carry you,* so vinnig as jy kan; *MAKE* ~, vasmaak; *PLAY* ~ *and loose,* onbetroubaar wees; *TAKE* ~ *hold of,* vasvat; ~ **back,** vloeirug (motor); ~ **bowler,** snelbouler; ~ **breeder (reactor),** snel-kweekreaktor; ~ **colour,** vaste kleur; ~ **court,** hardebaan.
fast'-day, vasdag.
fast'-dyed, waseg, kleurvas.
fa'sten, aanknoop; vasmaak, vasbind; aanbind, sjor, aanhaak; aanknoop; sluit, verbind; toebind, (be)vestig; inprent; vas gaan sit; ~ *DOWN,* vasmaak; ~ *one's EYES (up)on,* die oë vestig op; ~ *a QUARREL upon,* rusie soek met; ~ *TOGETHER,* saambind; ~ *UPON,* toedig, toeskryf aan; neerkom op; aangryp; 'n houvas kry; ~ **er,** vasbinder, vasmaker; knip, skuif, grendel; drukknopie; ~ **ing,** verbinding; sluiter, sluiting, bevestiging; haak, kram, knip; aaneenhegting; ~ **ing lever,** grendelhefboom.
fast'er¹, (n) vaster, persoon wat vas.
fast'er², (a) vinniger.
fast: ~ **friends,** dik (goeie) vriende; ~ **friendship,** hegte (troue, goeie) vriendskap.
fastid'ious, kieskeurig, uitsoekerig, lekkerbekkig; nousiende, punteneurig; ~ **ness,** kieskeurigheid, punteneurigheid, nousiendheid; lekkerbekkigheid.
fast'ing, vas.
fast-mov'ing, vinnig, snel.
fast'ness, vastheid; vlugheid; losheid (van sede); sterkte, vesting.
fat, (n) vet; smout; *the* ~ *is in the FIRE,* die poppe is aan die dans; *LIVE on the* ~ *of the land,* die vettigheid v.d. aarde geniet; *live on ONE'S* ~, op jou binnevet teer; (v) **(-ted),** vet maak, mes; *the* ~ *ted calf,* die gemeste (vetgemaakte) kalf; (a, adv) dik, vet; traag; ryk, vrugbaar; *CUT it* ~, 'n vertoning maak; *a* ~ *LOT,* baie min; *VERY* ~, hard v.d. vet; ~ *YEARS and lean years,* vet en maer jare; ~ **acid,** vetsuur.
fat'al, noodlottig, dodelik; ongelukkig; noodwendig; onvermydelik; rampspoedig; veeg; fataal; ~ *ACCIDENT,* dodelike ongeluk; ~ *CASES,* dodelike gevalle; ~ *CASUALTY,* dooie, gesneuwelde; *the* ~ *SHEARS,* die dodelike skêr, *the F* ~ *SISTERS,* die Skikgodinne; ~ *STROKE,* genadeslag; *the* ~ *THREAD,* die lewensdraad; *that is* ~ *TO their plans,* dit sal hulle planne in duie laat stort; ~ *WOUND,* dodelike wond; ~ **ism,** fatalisme; ~ **ist,** fatalis; ~ **is'tic,** fatalisties.
fatal'ity, (..ties), noodlottigheid; fataliteit; noodlot; onvermydelikheid; rampspoed; dodelike ongeluk; (pl) dooies; ~ **-rate,** sterftesyfer.
fata morga'na, lugspieëling, opgeefsel, fata morgana, mirage.
fat'-brained, dom, onnosel.
fat cat, rykaard, vet ryke, gladde ryke.
fate, noodlot, lot, bestemming; voorland, ondergang, dood; *there is no ARMOUR against* ~, die noodlot kan nie ontvlug (afgeweer) word nie; *DIVINE* ~, Godsbestuur; *I LEAVE someone to his* ~, iem. aan sy lot oorlaat; *his* ~ *is SEALED,* sy lot is beslis; dis klaar met kees; *TEMPT* ~, roekeloos wees; *THE Fates,* die Skikgodinne; ~ **d,** voorbeskik; noodlottig; tot ondergang gedoem; *he was not* ~ *d to,* dit was nie vir hom weggelê nie; dit was hom nie besko-re nie; ~ **ful,** noodlottig; fataal; gewigtig, beslissend; onvermydelik; ~ **fulness,** noodlottigheid.
fat: ~ **-free,** vetvry; ~ **-free diet,** vetvrye dieet; ~ **-free food,** vetvrye kos; ~ **gland,** vetklier; ~ **-guts,** dik-sak; ~ **-head,** dommerik, domkop, pampoenkop, uilskuiken; ~ **-headed,** dom, stomonnosel; ~ **-headedness,** domheid, onnoselheid.
fa'ther, (n) vader; pater (priester); *be GATHERED to one's* ~ *s,* tot jou vaders vergader wees; *the* ~ *of LIES,* die Satan; *LIKE* ~ *like son,* 'n aardjie na sy vaartjie; die appel val nie ver v.d. boom nie; ~ *of the PEOPLE,* landsvader; (v) verwek; as kind aanneem; verantwoordelik wees vir; vaderlik sorg vir; die vaderskap toeskryf; ~ **confessor,** biegvader; ~ **figure,** vaderfiguur; ~ **hood,** vaderskap; ~ **-in-law,**

fathom 890 **feather**

(fathers-in-law), skoonvader; ~**land**, vaderland; ~**less**, vaderloos; ~**like**, *kyk* **fatherly**; ~**liness**, vaderlikheid; ~**ly**, vaderagtig, vaderlik; ~**ship**, *kyk* **fatherhood**.

fath'om, (n) vaam, vadem; (v) omvat, deurskou, deurgrond, peil, deursien, begryp; afpeil, die dieplood uitgooi; ~ *someone or something*, iem. of iets deurgrond; ~**able**, begryplik; peilbaar; ~**age**, vaammaat; vaamloon; ~**ing lead**, dieptemeter; ~**less**, bodemloos, onpeilbaar; ondeurgrondelik; ~**line**, dieplood.

fatigue', (n) moegheid, vermoeienis, afgematheid, afmatting, vermoeidheid; korvee (mil.); (v) moeg maak, vermoei, afmat; aftob; lastig val; ~ **cap**, korveepet; ~ **company**, strafkompanie, korveekompanie; ~**d**, vermoeid, boeglam; ~ **dress**, werkpak; korveedrag; ~ **drill**, strafdril; ~ **duty**, korvee; ~ **limit**, vermoeidheidsgrens; ~ **party**, werkpeloton, korvee; ~ **resistance**, vermoeidheidsweerstand; ~ **test**, uitputtingstoets; vermoeidheidstoets.

fati'guing, afmattend, vermoeiend.

fat: ~**less**, vetvry; ~**-like**, vetagtig; ~ **lime**, vetkalk; ~**ling**, vetgemaakte dier; ~ **mouse**, vetmuis; ~**ness**, vetheid; vrugbaarheid; ~ **part**, groot rol (toneel); ~**-soluble**, oplosbaar in vet; ~ **stock**, slagvee; ~**-tailed**, vetstert=; ~ **ted**, vetgemaak; gemes; ~ **ten**, mes, vet maak, opvoer; vet word; vrugbaar maak, bemes; *what does not kill*, ~ *tens*, wat nie doodmaak nie, maak vet; ~**tish**, vetterig, dikkerig; ~ **tissue**, vetweefsel.

fat'ty, (n) (..**ties**), diksak, vaatjie, vetsak, potjierol; (a) vetterig; smerig; ~ *ACID*, vetsuur; ~ *DEGENERATION*, vetsug, vervetting; ~ *TISSUE*, vetweefsel.

fatu'ity, gekheid, dwaasheid, onbenulligheid.

fat'uous, onnosel, dom, dwaas, onbenullig; mal; ~**ness**, onbenulligheid.

fat'-witted, onnosel, stom.

fauc'al, strot=, keel=.

fau'ces, keelholte (anat.); keel (bot.); gang (bouk.).

fau'cet, tapkraan; ~ **pipe**, sokpyp.

faugh, ga! gang! sies!

fault, (n) lekplek, steuring (telegram); onderbreking (elek.); afskuiwing (myn); afbreking (mynrif); fout, gebrek, mankement, tekortkoming, skuld, defek, feil; misstap; *BE at* ~, ongelyk hê; die spoor kwyt wees; *DOUBLE* ~, dubbelfout; *FIND* ~, vit; kla; foutvind; *FIND* ~, vit; kla; foutvind; *through NO* ~ *of his*, nie deur sy skuld nie; buite sy toedoen; *TO a* ~, tot oordrywens toe; *WITH all* ~*s*, met alle gebreke; (v) 'n fout maak, te kort skiet; laak; fouteer; bestraf; breek, verskuif (geol.); (a) aanmerkerig, vitterig, vitsugtig, bedilsiek, twissiek; ~ **finder**, bedilaar, bediller, vitter; ~ **finding**, vitsug, foutvindery; ~ **iness**, gebrekkigheid; verkeerdheid; skuldigheid; ~**ing**, foute maak; ~**less**, onberispelik; feilloos, fouteloos; ~**lessness**, feilloosheid; ~ **pit**, breukkuil; ~ **plane**, breukvlak; verskuiwingsvlak (geol.); ~**s**, breuke (in rots); ~**y**, gebrekkig; verkeerd, foutief.

faun, bosgod, faun.

faun'a, (-e, -s), fauna, dierewêreld.

fauteuil', (teater)stalle, fauteuil.

faux' pas, fout, misstap, mistrap, faux pas.

fa'veolate, heuningkoekagtig.

fav'our, (n) guns, bevoorregting, grasie, begunstiging, genade; kleur; verlof; voorkome; vriendelikheid; vriendskap; partydigheid; gedagtenis, aandenking; gewildheid; *BE in* ~ *of*, ten gunste wees van; *BE in* ~ *with*, in die guns staan by; *BY your* ~, met u verlof; *BY* ~ *of*, deur vriendelike tussenkoms van; *COUNT in one's* ~, ten goede kom; tot voordeel strek; as verdienste toereken; *CURRY* ~, witvoetjie soek; *DO one a* ~, iem. 'n diens bewys; *FIND* ~ *with*, genade vind; *GRANT a* ~, 'n guns bewys; *IN* ~ *of*, ten gunste van; *LOOK with* ~ *on*, goedkeur, begunstig; *OUT of* ~ *with*, in onguns by; *WIN general* ~, gewild word; die goedkeuring wegdra; *YOUR* ~, u brief; gunsbewys; (v) bevoordeel; gunstig gesind wees; hou van; steun, aanmoedig; aanslag; gunstig wees vir; voortrek, begunstig; bevoorreg; lyk op; *you* ~ *your FATHER*, jy lyk na jou pa; ~ *SOMEONE*, vir iem. partytrek; iem. begunstig; ~ *WITH*, begunstig met, gee, verleen; ~**able**, gunstig, welwillend; bevorderlik; ~**ably**, gunstig; ~**ed**, begunstig, bevoorreg; gewild; begaaf, bedeel; *most* ~ *ed NATION*, mees begunstigde land; ~**ing**, bevoorregting.

fav'ourite, (n) gunsteling; lieflíng, geliefde; kansperd; (a) lieflings=; geliefkoosde, gelief(de), voorkeur=; ~ *AUTHOR*, lieflingskrywer; *HOT* ~, grootste gunsteling; ~ *SON*, geliefde seun, gunstelingseun; ~ *STUDY*, lieflingstudie; ~ *SUBJECT*, lieflingsvak; ~ *TOPIC*, geliefkoosde onderwerp; stokperdjie; ~ *WORK*, lieflingswerk.

fav'ouritism, begunstiging, gunsbetoon, voortrekkery, favoritisme.

fawn¹, (n) jong takbok; reebokkalf; jong damhert; (v) lam; (a) vaal(bruin).

fawn², (v) pamperlang, vlei, witvoetjie soek, lek, kruip.

fawn: ~**-colour(ed)**, geelbruin, vaalbruin (gekleur); ~**er**, kruiper, vleier; ~**ing**, (n) vleiery, aankwispeling, flikflooiery, lekkery, inkruiperigheid, kruipery; (a) (in)kruiperig, vleiend.

fay, fee (digterlik).

fay'alite, fayaliet.

faze, van stryk bring.

fe'alty, (leenpligtige) trou; *swear* ~ *to*, eed van trou sweer aan.

fear, (n) vrees, angs, bangheid; *BE in* ~ *of*, bang wees vir; iets vrees; vrees koester vir; *put the* ~ *of DEATH into someone*, iem. die dood voor oë hou; *without* ~ *or FAVOUR*, onpartydig; *FOR* ~ *of*, uit vrees vir; *INSPIRE* ~, vrees inboesem; *he KNOWS no* ~, hy het geen bang haar op sy kop nie; ~ *LEST*, bang wees dat; *the* ~ *of the LORD is the beginning of wisdom*, die vrees v.d. Here is die beginsel v.d. wysheid; *be in MORTAL* ~ *of someone*, doodbang vir iem. wees; so bang vir iem. wees soos 'n bok vir 'n skoot hael; *NO* ~! daar is geen gevaar nie; moenie glo nie! *STAND in* ~ *of*, bang wees vir; (v) bang wees, dug, skroom, vrees; *NEVER* ~, wees maar nie bang nie; *I* ~ *you are WRONG*, ek dink (reken, vermoed) jy is verkeerd; ~**ful**, vreeslik, skrikbarend; bang, dugtig, vervaard, vreesagtig, beangs; ~**fully**, vreeslik; ~**fulness**, vreesagtigheid, bangheid, vervaardheid; vreeslikheid; ~**less**, onbevrees, onverskrokke; ~**lessness**, onverskrokkenheid; ~**nought**, duiwelsterk; ~**some**, angswekkend, vreeslik; ~**someness**, vreeslikheid; ~**-stricken**, beangs, angsbevange.

feasibil'ity, uitvoerbaarheid, moontlikheid, lewensvatbaarheid; ~ **study**, gangbaarheidstudie, uitvoerbaarheidstudie, lonendheidsondersoek.

feas'ible, uitvoerbaar, prakties, doenlik, lewensvatbaar.

feast, (n) fees, feesmaal, gasmaal; feesviering; fuif, smulparty; *a* ~ *of the eyes*, 'n lus vir die oë; (v) smul, feesvier; onthaal; geniet, jou verlustig; fuif; ~ *one's EYES on*, die oë laat wei oor; ~ *today and fast TOMORROW*, die een dag fiks en die ander dag niks; vandag volop, môre skoon op; ~ **er**, feesvierder; gas; gasheer; ~**ing**, onthaal, smulparty, gefuif, gesmul.

feat, daad; kordaatstuk, heldedaad; kunsgreep, toer; behendigheid; ~ *of arms*, wapenfeit.

feath'er, (n) veer; pluim; dos; leispy; vin (van buiteband); vlek (in edelgesteente); *BIRDS of a* ~, voëls van eenderse vere; *BUNCH of* ~*s*, veerbos; *a* ~ *in one's CAP*, 'n pluimpie vir hom; 'n veer op iem. se hoed; *CROP someone's* ~*s*, iem. verneder; iem. se stertvere uittrek; *be in FINE* ~, in 'n goeie bui wees; in 'n feestelike stemming wees; *FINE* ~*s make fine birds*, die klere maak die man; *birds of a* ~ *FLOCK together*, soort soek soort; *in HIGH* ~, in 'n goeie bui, in feestelike stemming; *you could have KNOCKED me down with a* ~, jy kon my omgeblaas het; ek was skoon verbaas; *as LIGHT as a* ~, so lig soos 'n veer; *show the WHITE* ~, lafhartig wees; papbroekig wees; (v) veer; vol vere maak, beveer, met vere versier; ~ *one's NEST*, jou skapies op die droë bring; *as you* ~ *your NEST, you* *must lie in it,* wat jy saai, sal jy maai; ~ **bed,** veree= bed, bulsak; ~**-brained,** ylhoofdig; wuf, lossinnig; dom, onnosel; ~ **cloth,** veerstof; ~ **cushion,** vere= kussing; ~**-dealer,** veerhandelaar; ~ **duster,** vere= stoffer; ~**ed,** geveer; gou, vinnig.

feath'er edge, (n) skuinskant; (v) wegrand; ~ **file,** insnyvyl; ~ **d:** ~ **d horseshoe,** aanknyp(hoef)yster.

feathered: ~ **freight,** pluimvrag; ~ **oars,** plat spane; ~ **pitch,** ~ **position,** vaarstand.

feath'er: ~**ing,** vere; veerbekleedsel; bevering; vin= vorming (buiteband); ~ **joint,** veerlas, veervoeg; ~**less,** kaal; ~**-light,** veerlig; ~**-like,** veervormig, veeragtig; ~ **lure,** lokveer; loklig; ~ **market,** vere= mark; ~ **mattress,** verematras; bulsak; ~ **pillow,** verekussing; ~ **stitch,** sigsagsteek, heen-en-weer= steek, veersteek; ~ **trade,** veerhandel; ~**way,** ge= leigleuf, geleigroef; ~**weight,** veergewig; ~**y,** veer= agtig; geveer; ~ *y wool,* veerwol.

fea'ture, (n) gelaatstrek, wesenstrek, trek; gelaat; ter= rein, gesteldheid, terreinbakens; kenmerk, eien= skap, eienaardigheid; hooftrek, glanspunt; artikel; (pl) gesig, gelaatstrekke; *physical* ~*s,* terreinge= steldheid; (v) uitbeeld, teken; gekenmerk word; 'n beeld gee van; vertoon; in die hoofrol optree; die rol speel van; ~ **article,** glansartikel; ~ **film,** hoof= film, hoofprent; speelprent; ~**less,** sonder afwisse= ling, eentonig, saai; ~ **programme,** glansprogram; hoorbeeld; ~**s editor,** artikelredakteur; ~ **writer,** artikelskrywer.

fea'turing: ~ *a great star,* met 'n groot ster in die hoofrol.

febrifa'cient, koors(op)wekmiddel.
febrif'ugal, koorsverdrywend.
feb'rifuge, koorsverdrywende middel, koorsdrank.
feb'rile, koorsig, koors=, febriel.
Feb'ruary, Februarie, Skrikkelmaand.
fecal, feces = **faecal, faeces.**
feck'less, swak, onbekwaam, waardeloos, kragte= loos, flou; ~**ness,** swakheid, flouheid.
fec'ulence, troebelheid, modderigheid.
fec'ulent, troebel, moederig, modderig.
fec'und, vrugbaar; ~**ate,** vrugbaar maak; bevrug; ~**a'tion,** vrugbaarmaking.
fecun'dity, vrugbaarheid.
fed, gevoed; ~ *UP,* vies, sat; *be* ~ *up WITH,* sat wees vir; buikvol wees van.
fedayeen', fedayeen, Arabiese guerillas.
fed'eral, federaal, bonds=; ~ **council,** federale raad; ~ **government,** federale regering; ~**ism,** federalis= me; ~**ist,** federalis; ~ **republic,** bondsrepubliek; ~ **state,** federale staat.
fe'derate, (v) verenig, tot 'n statebond maak, fede= reer; (a) verenig, gefedereer, verbonde.
federa'tion, verbond, statebond, bondgenootskap, federasie; ~ *of trade unions,* vakverbond.
fed'erative, bonds=, verbonde, federatief.
fedo'ra, vilthoed, deukhoed, fedora.
fee, (n) loon, geld, honorarium, vergoeding; intree= geld, skoolgeld, eksamengeld, kollegegeld, leen= (goed); *LEGAL* ~ *s,* regskoste; *PAY* ~ *to,* betaal, vergoed, *without* ~ *or REWARD,* sonder enige vergoeding; *WHAT will your* ~ *be,* wat sal dit kos? (v) vergoed, betaal.
fee'ble, swak, kragteloos, flou(tjies), verboep, pap, kleinmoedig; *a* ~ *affair,* 'n oes affêre; ~**-minded,** swaksinnig, swakhoofdig, misdeeld van verstand; ~**-mindedness,** swaksinnigheid; ~**ness,** swakheid, slegtigheid, swakte.
fee'bly, swakkies.
feed, (n) voer; kos; voeding; toevoer; *off one's* ~ , jou eetlus kwyt wees; (v) **(fed),** voer; voed; onderhou; laat wei; vreet; voorsien; afwei; ~ *off the LAND,* op die veld wei; *the MOTHER* ~ *s the baby herself,* die moeder soog die kind; ~ *ON,* leef van; ~ *his VANITY,* by jou flikflooi; sy eiewaan versterk; ~**back,** terugkoppeling, terugvoer(ing); ~ **bag,** voersak; ~ **band,** patronenband; ~ **belt,** voerband; ~ **box,** voerbak.
feed'er, pypkan, suigfles, kinderbottel; eter; voedingskanaal; gasheer (biol.) borslap; voerder; vetmaker; syrivier; voedingsleiding (elek.); sylyn (spoorweg); aanbringer; ~ **arm,** voedingsarm; ~

line, toevoerlyn; ~ **plane,** toevoervliegtuig; ~ **road,** toevoerpad; ~ **service,** toevoerdiens.
feed: ~ **grain,** voergraan; ~ **ground,** weiveld; ~ **hole,** voergat; ~ **hopper,** laaitregter.
feed'ing, (n) voeding; (a) voer=; voedings=; ~ **bottle,** pypkan, suigbottel; ~ **cake,** veekoek; ~ **charge,** voerkoste; ~ **cup,** tuitkoppie; ~ **device,** aanbrin= ger; ~ **ground,** weiveld; ~ **hopper,** voerbak; ~ **line,** toevoerlyn; ~ **pen,** voerhok; ~ **stuff(s),** veevoer; ~ **tongs,** aanvoertang; ~ **trough,** eetbak; voerbak, voertrog.
feed: ~ **mechanism,** voerder; ~ **passage,** voergang; ~ **phosphate,** voerfosfaat; ~ **pipe,** aanvoerpyp; ~ **pump,** perspomp; toevoerpomp; ~ **screw,** aanset= skroef; ~ **system,** toevoerstelsel; ~ **tank,** toevoer= tenk; ~ **valve,** toevoerklep; ~ **water,** toevoerwater.
fee-faw-fum', paaiboelie; spook.
feel, (n) gevoel; *FIRM to the* ~, stewig (hard) voel; (v) **(felt),** aanvoel; ondersoek, nagaan; voel; betas, bevoel; meen, dink, vermoed, ondervind; waar= neem; ervaar; ~ *in one's BONES,* aan 'n mens se broek voel; ~ *like DOING,* lus voel om te doen; ~ *FOR,* voel vir, medelye hê met; ~ *one's GROUND,* voel-voel te werk gaan; ~ *the PULSE of,* die pols voel van; ~ *STRONGLY,* sterk oortuig wees; ~ *UP to,* in staat voel tot; ~ *one's WAY,* die terrein verken; voel-voel voortgaan; op die tas afgaan; *not* ~ *WELL,* nie lekker voel nie; ~**er,** voelhoring, voelspriet; voeler; proefballon, verkenner; *throw out a* ~*er,* die gevoel toets; 'n proefballon oplaat.
feel'ing, (n) gevoel; gesindheid; beskouing, opvatting; gedagte; gewaarwording; aandoening, gees, stem= ming, opinie; (pl) gevoelens, gemoed; *GOOD* ~ , goeie gesindheid; *HURT someone's* ~ *s,* iem. so gu= voel kwes; iem. seermaak; aanstoot gee; ~ *RAN high,* die gemoedere het hoog geloop; (a) gevoelvol; gevoelig; ~**ly,** gevoelvol, met gevoel; ~ **tone,** ge= voelswaarde.
fee' simple, onbeperkte eiendom.
feet, *see* **foot.**
feign, veins, voorgee, voorwend, huigel; verdig, fin= geer, versin; ~ *IGNORANCE,* jou dom (onnosel) hou, onkunde voorhou; ~ *ILLNESS,* maak of jy siek is, jou siek hou; ~**ed,** versin, gefingeer(d); ge= waand, voorgewend, geveins, kastig; ~*ed ATTACK,* skynaanval; ~*ed VIRTUE,* skyndeug; ~**edly,** kastig, kwansuis; ~**er,** valsaard.
feint, (n) voorwendsel; skynbeweging; (v) 'n skynaan= val doen; liemaak, skrikmaak, flous.
feint, (a) dof; *ruled* ~ , met waterlyne.
feint attack, skynaanval.
fel(d)'spar, veldspaat.
fel'icide, kattemoord.
felicif'ic, gelukkigmakend.
feli'citate, gelukwens, felisiteer.
felicita'tion, gelukwensing, felisitasie.
feli'citous, gelukkig, voorspoedig; toepaslik.
feli'city, (..**ties),** geluk; geluksaligheid, seën, voor= spoed; raakheid, goeie inval.
fel'id, lid van die kattegeslag *(Felidae).*
fel'ine, kat=, katagtig, soos 'n kat.
fell¹, (n) vel; vag, haarvel; ~ *of hair,* boskasie, bosgasie.
fell², (n) heuwel, kop.
fell³, (v) laat val, (neer)vel, plat kap (boom); plat slaan; plat maai.
fell⁴, (a) wreed, woes, fel; hewig.
fell'ah, (-in, -s), Egiptiese boer, fella(h).
fell: ~**er,** houtkapper; maat; kêrel; ~**ing,** kap(pery); afkap; ~**ing axe,** grootbyl, houtkappersbyl.
fell'-monger, wolafmaker, velbloter, velkoper, vel= handelaar.
fell'oe, velling.
fell'ow, maat, (soort)genoot, outjie, kameraad; mede= mens, kêrel; weerga, gelyke; heerskap; vent; lid, lid= maat; vennoot; genoot, medelid (van 'n instituut of vereniging); *a* ~ *can't do this ALONE,* 'n mens kan dit darem nie alleen doen nie; *stone DEAD hath no* ~ , 'n dooie man praat nie; *a GOOD* ~ , 'n gawe kêrel; *a JOLLY* ~ , 'n gawe kêrel; *OLD* ~ , ou kê= rel; *a SORRY* ~ , 'n arme drommel; ook 'n mens! *THAT* ~ , dié vent; ~ **artist,** medekunstenaar; ~

being, medeskepsel, medemens; ~ **believer,** medegelowige, geloofsgenoot; ~ **Christian,** mede-Christen; ~ **citizen,** medeburger, stadsgenoot, volksgenoot; ~**-countryman,** landgenoot; ~ **creature,** medemens; medeskepsel; ~ **culprit,** medeskuldige; ~ **elector,** medekieser; ~**-feeling,** meegevoel; ~ **fighter,** medestryder; ~ **heir,** mede-erfgenaam; ~ **labourer,** medearbeider, medewerker; ~ **man,** (ewe)naaste, medemens; ~ **member,** medelid; ~**-men,** ewemens; ~**-passenger,** reisgenoot; ~**-prisoner,** medegevangene; ~**-scholar,** medeleerling; ~ **ship,** deelgenootskap, gemeenskap; kameraadskap; geselskap; broerskap; bond; beurs, toelae; lidmaatskap; genootskap; *good* ~*ship,* kameraadskap; ~**-soldier,** wapenbroer, krygsmakker, strydgenoot; ~ **student,** medestudent; studentemaat; skoolmaat; ~ **sufferer,** lotgenoot, deelgenoot in lyding; ~**-townsman,** stadgenoot; dorpsgenoot; ~ **traveller,** reisgenoot, toggenoot, medereisiger; ~ **warrior,** medekrygsman; ~ **witness,** medegetuie; ~**-worker,** medewerker; medearbeider.

fell'y, (fellies) = **felloe.**

felo de se', selfmoord; **felo(ne)s de se,** selfmoordenaar.

fel'on¹, (n) fyt.

fel'on², (n) kwaaddoener; misdadiger; skurk; (a) misdadig, wreed.

felon'ious, misdadig, boosaardig; troueloos, snood; ~**ness,** misdadigheid; snoodheid.

fel'ony, (..nies), misdaad, felonie, snoodheid; *compound a* ~, 'n misdaad afkoop.

fel'site, felsiet.

felt¹, (n) vilt; (v) vilt, vervilt, tot vilt maak, met vilt voer.

felt², (v) *kyk* **feel.**

felt'ed, vervilt; viltagtig, vilt=; ~ **yarn,** viltgaring.

felt: ~ **hat,** vilthoed; ~**-like,** viltagtig; ~ **packing,** viltpakking; ~ **paper,** boupapier; ~ **pen,** viltpen; ~ **washer,** viltwaster; ~ **work,** viltwerk; ~ **worker,** viltwerker; ~**y,** viltagtig.

felucc'a, feloek (vaartuig).

fem'ale, (n) vrou(mens), vroupersoon; wyfie; *old COLOURED* ~, motjie; ~ *LEG of compasses,* stilstaande been van passer; (a) vroulik; vrou=; wyfie=; ~ **attendant,** begeleidster; oppasster; ~ **bend,** moerdraadbuigstuk; ~ **caretaker,** oppasster, huisbewaarster; ~ **child,** meisie, dogter; ~ **connection,** moerskroefverbinding; ~ **cook,** kookster; ~ **coupling,** oorpaskoppeling; ~ **die,** hol stempel; ~ **disciple,** dissipelin; ~ **dog,** teef; ~ **figure,** vrouegestalte, vrouegedaante; ~ **friend,** vriendin; ~ **part,** oorpasstuk (masj.); vrouerol; ~ **pills,** vrouepille; ~ **screw,** moer; ~ **servant,** diensmaagd; ~ **sextant,** kosteres; ~ **slave,** slavin; ~ **suffrage,** vrouestemreg; ~ **tank,** ligte vegwa (tenk); ~ **thread,** moerdraad.

feme co'vert, getroude vrou.

feme sole', ongetroude vrou; (finansieel) onafhanklike vrou.

feminal'ity, vroulikheid; vroulike geaardheid; snuistery.

femine'ity, vroulikheid; verwyfdheid.

fem'inine, vroulik; verwyf; ~ *ENDING,* vroulike uitgang; ~ *GENDER,* vroulike geslag; ~ *NAME,* vrouenaam, meisienaam; ~ *RHYME,* slepende rym, vroulike rym.

feminin'ity, vroulikheid; die vrouens.

fem'inism, feminisme, vrouebeweging.

fem'inist, feminis, voorstander van vrouereqte; ~**'ic,** feminities.

femin'ity = **femininity.**

feminiza'tion, vervroulikinq.

fem'inize, vervroulik; verwyf maak.

femme fatale, femme fatale, gevaarlik aantreklike vrou.

fem'oral, dy=; ~ **artery,** dyslagaar; ~ **hernia,** dybreuk.

fem'ur, (femora, -s), dybeen, skenkel(been), femur.

fen, moeras, vlei.

fence, (n) heining; draad; muur; heler; skermkuns; debat, woordestryd; bolwerk, omrastering, beskutting, skuilplek; *COME down on the right side of the* ~, by die wenkant aansluit; *one who SITS on the* ~, 'n draadsitter; *SIT on the* ~, die kat uit die boom kyk; (v) draad span, omhein; omgeef; met 'n perd oor 'n heining spring; probeer ontwyk, slim draaie maak; skerm; verdedig, debatteer; gesteelde goed verkoop; ~ *AGAINST,* skerm teen; ~ *IN (round, about, off),* afdraad, gorrel ('n pad), inkamp, toespan; omgewe; *a* ~*d ROAD,* 'n omheinde (gegorrelde) pad; (a) beskut; omhein; ~ **anchor,** draadanker; ~ **erector,** draadspanner; heiningmaker; ~ **less,** oop; onbeskut; hulpeloos; ~ **month,** geslote jagtyd; ~ **pin,** leipen (houtw.); ~ **season,** geslote jagtyd; ~**-sitter,** draadsitter; ~**-strainer,** draadtrekker; ~ **time,** geslote jagtyd; ~ **wire,** omheiningsdraad, heiningdraad.

fen'-fire, dwaallig.

fen'cing, omheining; skermkuns; debatteerkuns; ~ **club,** skermvereniging; ~ **cully,** heler; ~ **foil,** floret; ~ **glove,** skermhandskoen; ~ **law,** omheiningswet; ~ **lesson,** skermles; ~ **mask,** skermmasker; ~ **master,** skermmeester; ~ **material,** omheiningsmateriaal; ~ **pad,** plastron, borsleer; ~ **pole,** heiningpaal; ~ **post,** trekpaal; hoekpaal; ~ **rail,** vensterreling; ~ **sabre,** skermdegen; skermsabel; ~ **school,** skermskool; ~ **standard,** draadpaal; ~ **wire,** omheiningsdraad.

fend, afweer, weer, wegkeer, verdedig; ~ *FOR,* sorg vir; *LET someone* ~ *for himself,* iem. laat sien hoe hy die mas opkom; ~ *OFF,* afweer, afhou; ~ *for ONESELF,* self die mas opkom; jou eie potjie krap; jou eie mas ophaal; ~**er,** beskutting, weerplank, wering; stamptou; skutbalk, skutpaal; haardrand, haardskerm, haardyster; modderskerm, spatskerm, skutbord; ~**er beam,** stampbalk; ~**er board,** skutplank; ~**er wall,** herdskutmuur.

fene'stra, venstertjie, vensteropening.

fenes'tral, doekvenster; papiervenster; (a) venster=, met openinge.

fenes'trate(d), met vensters, gevenster; geperforeer; venster=.

fenestra'tion, vensterverdeling; fenestrasie.

fen'-fire, dwaallig.

fenks, walviskaiings; walvisspek.

fenn'el, vinkel; ~ **oil,** vinkelolie.

fenn'y, moeras=, moerassig.

fen'pole, springpaal.

fent, lap, reslap; spleet (kledingstuk); halsopening.

fen'ugreek, fenegriek, Griekse hooi.

feoff, (leen)goed; ~**ee',** leenman, besitter van leen; ~**ment,** oordrag van leengoed; ~**or,** leenheer.

fera'cious, vrugbaar.

fer'al, woes, dierlik, wild, wreed.

fe'retory, (..ries), graf, kapel; relikwieëkas.

fer'ial, weekdag=.

fer'ine, wild, woes; beesagtig.

ferm'ent, (n) gisting, ferment; suurdeeg, gis(stof), gismiddel; opstandigheid; *BE in a* ~, opgewonde wees; in beroering wees; *be THROWN into a* ~ *by something,* in jou siel versondig wees deur iets; (v) ophits; broei, sweet (tabak); gis, fermenteer; laat gis; ~ **able,** gisbaar; opsweepbaar; ~ **a'tion,** gisting, fermentasie; ~ **'ative,** gistend, gistings=, fermentatief; ~ **ing,** gistend, fermenterend.

fern, varing; ~**ery,** (..ries), varinghuis; ~ **moss,** varingmos; ~**y,** begroei met varings; varingagtig.

fero'cious, wild, wreed, woes, verskeurend; ~**ness,** wildheid, wreedheid, woestheid.

fero'city, wildheid, woestheid.

fe'rrate, ferraat.

fe'rreous, ysterhoudend; yster=; ysteragtig.

fe'rret¹, (n) floretband.

fe'rret², (n) fret *(Putorius furo);* snuffelaar; speurder; (v) verjaag; opspoor; vervolg; deursnuffel; ~ *out,* opspoor, uitvors, uitvroetel, uitpluis, nasnuffel, uitsnuffel; ~**er,** snuffelaar, snuffelgraag; ~**ing,** fretjag; gesnuffel.

fe'rriage, oorsetting; pontgeld, veergeld.

fe'rric, ysteragtig; yster=; ~ **acid,** ystersuur.

fe'rricrete, ouklip.

ferrif'erous, ysterhoudend.

ferrimagnet'ism, ystermagnetisme, ferrimagnetisme.

Fer'ris wheel, kermiswiel.

fer'rite, ferriet.

fe'rrochrome, ferrochroom.
ferroconc'rete, gewapende beton; ~ **glass,** glasbeton.
ferromagnet'ic, ferromagneties.
ferromang'anese, ferromangaan, mangaanyster.
fe'rrotype, foto op ysterplaat, ferrotipie.
fe'rrous, yster=; ysterhoudend.
ferrugina'tion, verystering.
ferru'ginous, ysterhoudend; ysteragtig; roesrooi, roeskleurig, ferrugineus.
fe'rrule, beslag, ysterband, noodring, beslagring; afstandspyp.
fe'rry, (n) **(ferries),** pont, veer; pontreg; (v) **(ferried),** oorsit; pontdiens doen; oorvaar; ~ **boat,** pont= boot, veerskuit; ~ **bridge,** veerpont, treinpont; ~ **man,** veerman, pontman, pontwagter; ~ **pilot,** veervlieër; ~ **service,** veerdiens.
fert'ile, vrugbaar, ryk aan; vettig, welig, geil; ~ *soil,* vrugbare grond; dankbare aarde.
fertil'ity, vrugbaarheid, weligheid, geilheid.
fertiliza'tion, bevrugting; bemesting; vrugbaar= making.
fert'ilize, vrugbaar maak; bevrug, fertiliseer; bemes; ~ **r,** misstof, kunsmis; bevrugter.
feru'la, reusevinkel.
fe'rule, plak, stok, kweperlat, platriem.
ferv'ency, vuur, gloed, ywer, vurigheid; innigheid.
ferv'ent, vurig, warm; ywerig; innig; ~ *desire,* sielsverlange.
ferv'id, brandend, hartstogtelik; ywerend; innig; ~ **'ity,** ~ **ness,** drif, ywer.
ferv'our, warmte, hitte; vurige ywer, gloed; innerlik= heid, innigheid.
fes'cue, wysstok; swenkgras.
fess(e), balk, faas (her.).
fes'tal, feestelik, fees=.
fes'ter, (n) verswering, sweer; kanker (fig.); (v) sweer, (ver)etter; invreet; voortwoeker; laat sweer; ver= sweer; kanker; ~ **ing,** etterend.
fes'tival, (n) fees, feesdag, feesviering; (a) feestelik, fees=.
fes'tive, feestelik, vrolik, fees=; ~ **board,** feesmaal, ~ **march,** feesmars; ~ **season,** feestyd, feesdae.
festiv'ity, (..ties), feestelikheid, vreugdebedryf, fees= vreugde.
festoon', (n) festoen, slinger, loofwerk; (v) met loof= werk versier, festoeneer.
fes'tschrift, festschrift, huldigingsbundel, feesuit= gawe.
fet'al, vrug=, fetaal.
fetch¹, (n) dubbelganger.
fetch², (n) kunsgreep, behendigheid; rek, inspanning; (v) gaan haal, bring; te voorskyn bring; behaal; op= bring; slaak, asemhaal; bereik; ~ *AWAY,* weg= neem; ~ *a BREATH,* asemhaal; ~ *and CARRY,* haal en dra, bediende wees; ~ *DOWN,* neerskiet; afhaal; ~ *IN,* inpalm; ~ *OUT,* laat uitkom; ~ *a PRICE of,* 'n prys behaal; ~ *a SIGH,* sug, 'n sug slaak; *THAT* ~ *ed him,* dit het sy hart gesteel; ~ *UP,* bly staan; vomeer; ~ **er,** haler; ~ **ing,** boeiend; aantreklik, innemend; ~ *ing ways,* innemende maniere.
fête, (n) fees, kermis, fête; (v) onthaal, fêteer, huldig; ~ **d,** gevier.
fet'id, stinkend, galsterig.
fet'ish, fetisj, aangebede voorwerp, afgod; ~ **er,** toor= dokter, fetisjis; ~ **ism,** fetisjisme; ~ **ist,** fetisjis; ~ **is'= tic,** fetisjistes.
fet'lock, vetlok, muishare (van perd).
fet'or, stank.
fett'er, (n) ketting, boei; voetboei; band; belemme= ring; kluister; (pl) bande, gevangenskap; (v) boei, vasbind; belemmer; kluister; ~ **less,** ongeboei(d), vry.
fet'tle, (n) kondisie; *in fine (good)* ~, op sy stukke; (v) regmaak; versier.
fet'us = foetus.
feud¹, leen, leengoed.
feud², vete, twis, rusie; *be at* ~ *with,* in vyandskap lewe met.
feud'al, leen=, leenroerig, feodaal; ~ **duty,** leenplig; ~ **estate,** leengoed; ~ **ism,** leenstelsel, feodalisme; ~ **'ity,** leenplig; leenreg; leenroerigheid; ~ **ize,** leen= pligtig maak, feodaliseer; ~ **law,** leenreg; ~ **lord,** leenheer; ~ **prince,** leenvors; ~ **service,** leendiens; ~ **system,** feodale stelsel, leenstelsel; ~ **tenant,** leenman; ~ **tenure,** leen.
feud'atory, (n) (..ries), leenman; leen; (a) leen=, leenroerig.
feu de joie', vreugdeskote; vreugdevure (milit.).
feui'lleton, feuilleton.
fev'er, (n) koors; onrus, opgewondenheid; *ENTERIC* ~, ingewandskoors, maagkoors; *REMITTENT* ~, op-en-afgaande koors; (v) koorsig maak (word); ~ **attack,** koorsaanval; ~ **blister,** koors= blaar; ~ **bush,** koorsbos; ~ **chart,** temperatuur= kaart, -lys; ~ **few,** moederkruid; ~ **germs,** koors= kieme; ~ **heat,** koorshitte; gejaagdheid; ~ **hospital,** koorshospitaal; ~ **ish,** ~ **ous,** koorsig (lett.); koorsagtig (fig.); ~ **ishness,** koorsigheid; ~ **powder,** koorspoeier; ~ **spot,** koorsvlek; ~ **the= rapy,** koorsbehandeling, koorsterapie; ~ **trap,** koorsnes, koorshol; ~ **tree,** koorsboom; ~ **wort,** driesteen.
few, weinig; party, 'n paar, min; *A* ~, 'n paar, 'n handjievol; *the* ~ *er the BETTER,* hoe minder hoe beter, *every* ~ *DAYS,* kort-kort; ~ *and FAR be= tween,* dun gesaai, seldsaam; *a GOOD* ~, baie, heelparty; *NO* ~ *er than,* nie minder nie as; *NOT a* ~, nie min nie; *SOME* ~, 'n klompie, 'n paar; *in a* ~ *WORDS,* kortom; *a man of* ~ *WORDS,* 'n man wat min praat; ~ **ness,** geringe aantal; klein hoe= veelheid; seldsaamheid.
fey, sterwende; tot die dood gedoem, veeg, sieal; deur= mekaar, uitbundig.
fez, fes, kofia.
fia'cre, vierwielrytuig, fiacre.
fian'cé, verloofde, galant, aanstaande (manlik); ~ **e,** verloofde, aanstaande (vroulik); *former* ~, gewe= sene.
fianchet'to, fianchetto(set) (skaak).
fias'co, (-s), mislukking, fiasko; *prove a* ~, op 'n mis= lukking uitloop.
fi'at, (n) bevel, fiat, magtiging; (interj) dit sy so.
fib¹, (n) slag, hou; (v) slaan, 'n hou gee.
fib², (n) leuen, kluitjie; *tell* ~ *s,* jok; kluitjies vertel; spekskiet; (v) **(-bed),** jok, spekskiet; ~ **ber,** jokker, spekskieter, duimsuier; ~ **bing,** spekskietery.
fi'bre, vesel; veselstof; wortelveseltjie; geaardheid, ka= rakter; *ARTIFFICIAL (synthetic)* ~, kunsvesel; *LENGTH of* ~, vesellengte; ~ **board,** veselbord; ~ **content,** veselgehalte; ~ **crops,** veselgewasse; ~ **fineness,** veselfynheid; ~ **gear,** veselrat; ~ **glass,** veselglas; ~ **insulation,** veselisolasie; ~ **less,** sonder drade.
fib'ril, veseltjie, wortelvesel, wortelhaar, fibril.
fibrilla'tion, vesel(r)igheid.
fi'brillate(d), veselagtig.
fi'brillose, veselbedek.
fi'brillous, veselagtig.
fib'rin, veselstof, fibrien, fibrine.
fib'roin, fibroïen, fibroïne.
fibrom'a, fibroom.
fibro'sis, fibrose.
fibrosit'is, fibrositis, veselontsteking.
fib'rous, veselagtig, draderig; ~ *ROOT,* haarwortel; ~ *TISSUE,* veselweefsel; ~ **ness,** draderigheid, ve= selagtigheid.
fib'ster, *kyk* **fibber.**
fib'ula, (-e, -s), kuitbeen, fibula.
ficelle', toukleurig.
fi'chu, kragie; skouermanteltjie, fichu.
fic'kle, wispelturig, veranderlik, buierig, ongedurig, ongaar, onbestendig, wuf, vlinderagtig, bontsin= nig; ~ **ness,** wispelturigheid, veranderlikheid, wuft= heid.
fic'tile, erde=; vormbaar; pottebakkers=; ~ **art,** pottebakkerskuns.
fic'tion, verdigting, versinsel, onwaarheid; fabel; ro= manliteratuur, romankuns, vertelkuns, verhaal= kuns, fiksie; ~ **al,** fiksie=, roman=; fiktief, denkbeel= dig; ~ **ist,** romanskrywer; ~ **writer,** fiksieskrywer; romanskrywer.
ficti'tious, verdig, denkbeeldig, versonne, gefin= geer(d), fiktief, uit die lug gegryp; oneg, gemaak,

vals; voorgewend; aangenome; ~ **ness**, denkbeeldigheid; onegtheid; voorgewendheid.

fic'tive, vormend, skeppend; verdig, versonne, gefingeerd; geveins.

fid, splitshoring; draaier, slothout; prop; pruimpie; stompie.

fid'dle, (n) viool, vedel, fiedel; slingerlat (skeepsterm); *a FACE as long as a* ~, met 'n lang gesig; *play FIRST* ~, eerste viool speel; *as FIT as a* ~, so reg soos 'n roer; so fris soos 'n vis; *HANG up one's* ~, jou onttrek aan sake; *an OLD* ~ *can play a new tune*, 'n ou viool kan ook nuwe liedjies speel; *play SECOND* ~, tweede viool speel; *play SECOND* ~ *to nobody*, by niemand agterstaan nie; (v) fiedel, viool speel; beusel, speel; peuter; vermors (tyd); ~ *ABOUT*, rondpeuter; jou tyd verkwansel; ~ *AWAY*, lostrek; verbeusel; ~ *while ROME is burning*, speel terwyl Rome brand; ~ *WITH*, peuter aan; ~**-back**, viool(rug)stoel; ~**-bow**, strykstok; ~**-case**, vioolkas; ~**-de-dee'**, onsin, malligheid, twak, kaf; ~ **drill**, drilboor; ~**-faddle**, (n) beuselary, kleinigheid; (v) klets, onsin praat, peuter; seur; (a) prullerig, niksbeduidend; kleingeestig; ~**-fish**, vioolvis; ~**-head**, stewenbeeld, skegbeeld; ~**r**, vioolspeler, vedelaar; krappie; ~**-stick**, strykstok; ~**sticks!** bog! onsin! ~ **string**, vioolsnaar; ~**-wood**, vioolhout.

fidd'ling, (n) vioolspelery; gepeuter; futsel(a)ry; (a) beuselagtig, prullerig, veragtelik, onbenullig.

fidei-commiss'um, fideicommissum, fideikommissaris.

fidel'ity, getrouheid, trou; eerlikheid; ~ *GUARANTEE insurance*, waarborgversekering; *HIGH* ~, werklikheidsweergawe, klankpresisie, klankgetrouheid (radio, grammofoon); ~ **bond**, waarborgakte, borgstelling.

fidg'et, (n) rustelose persoon, woelwater; onrustigheid, gejaagdheid; *have the* ~ *s*, miere hê, rusteloos wees; onrustig wees; tob; (v) woel, wriemel; tob; onrustig rondskuiwe; senuweeagtig op en af loop; ~ *over something*, bekommerd wees oor een of ander ding; ~**iness**, rusteloosheid; ~ **y**, rusteloos, ongedurig, onrustig, vol miere; *be* ~ *y*, miere hê.

fid'ibus, fidibus, papierrolletjie (om kerse, ens., op te steek), aansteker.

fidu'cial, vertrouend; stellig, seker; ~ **line**, basisvergelykingslyn; ~ **point**, basisvergelykingspunt.

fidu'ciary, (n) (..ries), vertroude; trustee; (a) vertrouend; toevertroud; fidusiêr, vertrouens-.

fidus achates, fidus achates, getroue vriend, toegewyde volgeling.

fie! foei! sies tog! skaam jou!

fief, leengoed; leen.

fie'-fie, onbehoorlik, skandelik.

field, kamp; land(ery), akker; speelveld; gebied; veld, vlakte; deelnemers; spelers; slagveld; veldslag; wapenveld; ~ *of BATTLE*, slagveld; *FAIR* ~ *and no favour*, dieselfde voorwaardes vir almal; ~ *of FIRE*, skootsveld; *die on the* ~ *of GLORY*, op die veld van eer sterf; *a GOOD* ~, baie deelnemers; *HOLD the* ~, die veld behou; *IN the* ~, te velde; in die veld; *KEEP the* ~, die veld behou; in die veld bly (mil.); *LEAD the* ~, op die voorpunt wees; die voorste in die jagstoet wees; ~ *of LITERATURE*, letterkundige gebied; *MAGNETIC* ~, magnetiese gebied; *remain in POSSESSION of the* ~, die slagveld behou; *PRODUCT of the* ~*s*, veldgewas; *TAKE the* ~, op die veld stap; optrek, te velde trek; ~ *of VISION*, gesigsveld; *cover a WIDE* ~, 'n groot gebied dek; *WIN the* ~, die slag wen; (v) veldwerk doen; vat, vang (rugby); ~**-allowance**, veldtoelae; ~**-ambulance**, veldambulans; ~ **army**, veldleër; leër te velde; ~ **artillery**, veldartillerie; ~ **badge**, veldteken; veldwapen; ~**-base**, veldbasis; ~ **battery**, veldbattery; ~**-bean**, stamboontjie; ~**-bed**, veldbed; ~**-book**, veldboek; ~ **boot**, veldstewel; ~ **censor**, veldsensor; sensor te velde; ~**-chaplain**, veldprediker; ~ **circuit**, veldbaan, veldkring; ~**-cornet**, veldkornet; ~**-cornetcy**, veldkornetskap; ~**-craft**, veldkuns; veldkennis, ~ **crop**, veldgewas, oesgewas; ~**-day**, wapenskouingsdag; maneuverdag; geluksdag, wendag; *he had a* ~ *day*, dit was sy geluksdag; ~**-dispensary**, veldapteek; ~ **distortion**, veldverwringing; ~ **dressing**, veldverband; ~**-duty**, veldwerksaamheid; gevegsdiens; ~ **equipment**, velduitrusting; ~ **event**, veldnommer; ~**er**, veldwerker (kr.); ~ **force**, veldmag; ~**-forge**, veldsmedery; ~**-glass(-es)**, verkyker; ~**-grey**, veldgrou; ~ **gun**, veldgeskut, veldstuk, veldkanon; ~ **hospital**, veldambulans; ~ **husbandry**, akkerbou; ~**ing**, veldwerk; versinkte skuinskant; ~ **inspection**, veldinspeksie (mil.); ~ **kit**, velduitrusting; ~ **labourer**, landarbeider; ~ **lens**, veldlens; ~**-magnet**, veldmagneet; ~**-markings**, terreinbakens; *F* ~ **Marshal**, veldmaarskalk; *F* ~ **Marhal's baton**, veldmaarskalkstaf; ~**-mouse**, streepmuis, veldmuis; ~ **officer**, hoofoffisier; ~ **operations**, krygsverrigtinge; ~ **piece**, veldstuk; ~ **preacher**, veldprediker; ~ **rank**, hoofoffisiersrang; ~ **representative**, veldverteenwoordiger, buiteverteenwoordiger; ~ **service**, velddiens; ~**-service uniform**, veldtenue.

fields'man, (..men), veldwerker.

field: ~ **sports**, veldsport; ~**-squadron**, veldeskader; ~ **staff**, veldpersoneel, buitepersoneel; ~**-stores**, frontbehoeftes; ~ **strength**, veldsterkte; ~ **telegraph**, veldtelegraaf; ~ **theory**, veldteorie; ~ **tile**, sponsteël; ~ **training**, veldopleiding; gevegsopleiding; ~ **winding**, veldwikkeling; ~**-work**, veldversterkings, veldskans; veldwerk; buitewerk; ~**-worker**, veldwerker; buitewerker.

fiend, bose gees, nikker, duiwel, demon, besetene; ~**ish**, hels, demonies, duiwels, besete, duiwelagtig; ~**ishness**, duiwelagtigheid.

fierce, wild, geweldig, woes, wreed, skerp, verbete; fel, verwoed; vurig, heftig; ~**ly**, woes, wreed; fel; ~**ness**, wildheid, geweldigheid, woestheid; verbetenheid, verwoedheid, wreedaardigheid; ~ **oven**, vuurwarm oond.

fieri fa'cias, dwangbevel, bevelskrif.

fi'eriness, drif, opvlieëndheid; vurigheid.

fi'ery, vurig, vuur-, warm; ontvlambaar; gloeiend, brandend; driftig, opvlieënd; ~ **death**, vlammedood; ~ **mine**, gasmyn; ontvlambare myn; ~ **temper**, opvlieëndheid; vurige humeur.

fiës'ta, feestelikheid; vakansie.

fife, (n) dwarsfluit, pyp; (v) fluit, pyp, speel; ~**r**, speler, fluitblaser.

fif'teen, vyftien; rugbyspan; ~**er**, inkunabel, wieg(e)druk; versreël van 15 lettergrepe; ~**th**, vyftiende.

fifth, (n) vyfde; kwint; (a) vyfde; ~ *wheel to a COACH*, vyfde wiel aan 'n wa; ~ *PART*, vyfde deel; *SMITE under the* ~ *rib*, doodslaan; ~ **column**, vyfde kolonne; ~**-column activities**, ondermyning, werksaamhede van 'n vyfde kolonne; ~**columnist**, vyfdekolonner; ~**ly**, ten vyfde, in die vyfde plek; ~ **rate**, vyfderangs; ~ **wheel**, skamel (motor); noodwiel.

fif'tieth, vyftigste.

fif'ty, vyftig; *the fifties*, die jare vyftig, die vyftigerjare.

fif'ty-fif'ty, half-om-half; *on a* ~ *BASIS*, op 'n gelyke basis; gelykop; *the CHANCES are* ~, die kanse is gelyk.

fif'tyfold, vyftigvoudig.

fig[1], (n) vy; vyeboom; *I don't CARE a* ~, dit traak my niks nie; ~ *s do not GROW on thistles*, van dorings pluk 'n mens tog nie vye nie.

fig[2], (n) mondering, kleding, uitrusting; *in FULL* ~, in volle mondering; *in GOOD* ~, op sy stukke; in goeie kondisie; *in GREAT* ~, op sy stukke; (v) (-ged), uitdos; opvrolik.

fight, (n) geveg, twis, rusie; bakleislag; stryd, veglus; boksgeveg, bokswedstryd; *a* ~ *to a FINISH*, 'n geveg end-uit; *GIVE* ~, teenstand bied; *he has PLENTY of* ~ *in him yet*, hy is nog pure man; *a RUNNING* ~, 'n lopende geveg; *SHOW* ~, 'n uitdagende houding aanneem; jou man staan; (v) **(fought)**, veg, twis; rusie maak; baklei, vuisslaan; beveg; stry; ~ *an ACTION*, 'n geveg voer; 'n regsaak verdedig; ~ *a BATTLE*, 'n slag lewer; ~ *a DUEL*, duelleer; ~ *an ELECTION*, 'n verkiesingstryd voer; ~ *OFF*, afweer, terugdryf, afslaan; ~ *it OUT*, dit uitbaklei; ~ *a SEAT*, 'n setel beveg; ~ *SHY of someone*, uit iem. sy pad bly; lig loop vir iem.; ~ *SHY of work*, jou lyf bêre; ~ *a WAR*, 'n oorlog voer; ~ *one's WAY*, 'n pad oopslaan; sy weg baan; ~ *with WINDMILLS*, teen windmeulens veg.

fight'er, bakleier, vegter; vegvliegtuig; ~ **bomber**, vegterbomwerper; ~ **cover**, vegterbeskerming; ~ **escort**, veggeleide; ~ **flight**, gevegsvlug; ~ **pilot**, vegvlieër; ~ **squadron**, vegeskader.

fight'ing, (n) geveg, stryd, spokery, vegtery; (a) veg=, vegtend; *a* ~ *chance*, 'n moontlike kans; ~ **cock**, veghaan, kemphaan; ~ **fit**, slaggereed; **forces**, strydmag; ~ **front**, gevegsfront; ~ **line**, gevegs= linie; ~ **spirit**, veglus, strydlus; ~ **strength**, oorlog= sterkte; ~ **unit**, vegeenheid.

fig: ~ **jam**, vyekonfyt; ~ **leaf**, vyeblaar; ~ **leather**, smeervye, vyetameletjie.

fig'ment, verdigsel, (ver)sinsel, bedenksel; ~ *of the imagination*, hersenskim.

fig'-tree, vyeboom.

figu'ra, figura.

fig'urant(e), balletdanser(es); figurant(e).

figura'tion, gedaantevorming; gedaante, vorm; voor= stelling, afbeelding; versiering, figurasie.

fig'urative, figuurlik, figuratief, oneienlik, oordragte= lik, sinnebeeldig; beeldryk; blomryk; beeldend, te= kenend; ~ *LANGUAGE*, figuurlike taal; ~ *NUM= BERS*, figuurlike getalle.

fig'ure, (n) gedaante; persoon; beeld; afbeelding; ge= stalte, vorm, figuur; postuur; bedrag; syfer; gram= matiese figuur; blom, vlam (van hout); *CUT a* ~, 'n figuur slaan; *DOUBLE* ~ *s*, getalle van twee sy= fers; *GOOD for the* ~, goed vir die slanke lyn; *GOOD at* ~ *s*, knap (slim) met syfers; hy kan goed reken; *KEEP one's* ~, nie vet word nie; *at a LOW* ~, teen 'n lae prys; *REACH four* ~ *s*, die duisende bereik; *cut a SORRY* ~, 'n droewige figuur slaan; ~ *of SPEECH*, beeldspraak; grammatiese figuur; ~ *-8 BANDAGE*, agtverband; ~ *-of-eight TEST*, syferagttoets; (v) vorm; figureer, afbeeld; figure maak, met figure versier; die rol speel van; optree; pryk; ~ *as*, optree as; die rol vervul van; ~ **d**, ge= blom, gewerk; ~ *d satin*, geblomde satyn; ~ **head**, beeld; skynhoof, nominale leier, strooipop; stewe= beeld, skegbeeld; ~ **less**, sonder gestalte; ~ **-skater**, sierskaatser; ~ **-skating**, sierskaats; ~ **stone**, Chi= nese speksteen; ~ **-work**, rekenwerk.

fig'urine, beeldjie.

fig'wort, hemelkruid, speenkruid.

Fi'ji Isl'ands, Fidji-eilande.

fike, jeuk(te), juk(te); gedoente.

fil'ament, veseltjie, draadjie (wortel), filament, helm= draad; gloeidraad; ry; streep; ~ **battery**, gloei= draadbattery; ~ **current**, gloeistroom; ~ **lamp**, gloeilamp.

filamen'tary, draadvormig; draad=, draderig.

fil'amented, van 'n draad voorsien, gedraad.

filamen'tose, **filamen'tous**, draderig, veselagtig.

fila'ria, nematode, filaria.

filari'asis, filariase.

fil'ate, draadvormig.

fil'ature, syspinnery, filatuur.

fil'bert, haselneut; haselneutboom; ~ **-tree**, haselaar, haselneutboom.

filch, steel, roof, kaap, gap(s), wegkaap.

file¹, (n) vyl; *BITE a* ~, onbegonne werk doen; *BEL= LIED* ~, buikvyl; *DEAD-CUT* ~, gladdevyl, dub= belsoetvyl; *FLAT* ~, platvyl; *SAFE-EDGE* ~, blindekantvyl, gladdekantvyl; (v) vyl; polys; ~ *away*, glad vyl.

file², (n) lêer, lias; papierhaak; papierknip; briefhou= er; dossier; lêer; omslag (om papiere in te bêre), inryer; lys; gelid; ry; *INDIAN* ~, agter mekaar; *KEEP on* ~, inryg; bewaar; *SINGLE* ~, agter me= kaar; op 'n streep; *STAND in* ~, toustaan; (v) lias= seer, inryg; in 'n lêer sit, bêre, opberg; twee-twee marsjeer, in geledere opruk; oorlê, deponeer (reg); ~ *OFF*, afmarsjeer; ~ *PAST*, twee-twee defileer; ~ *one's PETITION in bankruptcy*, die boeke oorgee.

file: ~ **-body**, vylskag; ~ **cover**, lêeromslag; ~ **-dust**, vylsels; ~ **-holder**, vylhandvatsel.

fil'emot, bruingeel, herfskleur.

file'-spike, liaspen.

fil'et, filet, (bees)haas; filet (haarnet); ~ **lace**, filet= kant.

file'-tang, vylangel, vyldoring.

fil'ial, kinderlik, filiaal; ~ *CELL*, dogtersel; ~ *LOVE*, ouerliefde; kinderliefde; ~ *PIETY*, ouer= verering.

filia'tion, afstamming, verwantskap; affiliasie; ver= takking, spruit.

fil'ibeg, (Skotse) rokkie.

fil'ibuster, (n) vrybuiter, rower; obstruksievoerder; vertragingstaktiek; (v) stroop, roof, vrybuitery uit= oefen; obstruksie voer; doodpraat; vertraag.

fil'iform, draadvormig.

fil'igree, filigraan, (goud= of silwer)draadwerk.

fil'ing¹, vylwerk; (pl) vylsels.

fil'ing², (n) liassering; (a) lias=; ~ **cabinet**, liasseerka= binet; opbergkas, bêrekas, lêerkas; ~ **clerk**, lias= seerklerk.

Filipi'no, Filippyn.

fill, (n) versadiging; bekoms; opvulling, opvulwerk; *DRINK one's* ~, jou vol eet; *EAT one's* ~, jou bekoms eet; *have EATEN one's* ~, oorgenoeg ge= had het; kan hou tot die mense v.d. land kom; *LOOK one's* ~, jou sat kyk; *a* ~ *of TOBACCO*, 'n stok tabak; (v) vol maak, vul; stop, plombeer (tand); versadig; digstop, opvul, laat vol loop; ver= vul; beklee, inneem (plek, pos); ~ *the BILL*, die enigste (vernaamste) nommer wees; aan alle eise voldoen; aan die doel voldoen; ~ *with DELIGHT*, verheug; ~ *IN*, invul; opstop; toemaak, toegooi; ~ *OUT*, uitdy, gevul word; opvul, aanvul; vetter (swaarder) word; ~ *a POST*, 'n betrekking beklee; ~ *UP*, aanvul; vol gooi, byskink; invul (form); demp.

fil'ler, stopwoord; bladvulling (in koerant); tregter; vulsel; (aan)vuller; ~ **cap**, vuldop; ~ **coat**, grond= laag (verf); ~ **coffee**, moerkoffie; ~ **hole**, vulgat; ~ **piece**, vulstuk; ~ **pipe**, vulpyp; ~ **spout**, vuller= tuit.

fill'et, (n) (haar)band, filet, kopband; (dek) lys, steun= lat (bouk.); moot, stuk; strook; dystuk, (bees)haas, vloeistuk (vliegtuig); ~ *of BEEF*, beeshaas, filet; ~ *of FISH*, vismoot(jie); ~ *of VEAL*, kalfskyf; (v) omlys, in mootjies sny; ontbeen; ~ **end**, haaskant; ~ **steak**, beeshaas, (bees)filet; ~ **weld**, hoeksweis= las.

fill'ing, aanvulling; plombeersel, vulsel; stopsel (tand); springlading (bom); ~ **cap**, vuldop; ~ **ma= terial**, vulsel, vulstof; ~ **orifice**, vulopening; ~ **sta= tion**, petrolstasie, vulstasie.

fill'ip, (n) knip, hou; prikkel, aansporing; opflikke= ring; (v) wegknip; opwek; optris; aanspoor; skiet (met duim).

fil'lis, losgedraaide tou.

fill'ister, verstelbare sponningskaaf.

fill'y, (**fillies**), (merrie)vul; rabbedoe, lewendige nooi.

film, (n) vlies; velletjie (op vloeistof), laag; (mis)= sluier; draad; rolprent, film; (v) vir die bioskoop bewerk, (ver)film, 'n rolprentopname maak, ~ **ac= tor**, rolprentakteur, filmakteur, filmspeler, rol= prentspeler; ~ **actress**, rolprentaktrise, filmaktrise, filmspeelster, rolprentspeelster; ~ **camera**, filmka= mera, rolprentkamera; ~ **cartoon**, tekenprent; ~ **cartridge**, filmrol, filmspoel; ~ **censor**, filmkeur= der, rolprentkeurder, filmsensor, rolprentsensor; ~ **clip**, filmklem, filmknip; rolprentuittreksel, film= uittreksel; ~ **er**, filmmaker, rolprentmaker, kineas; ~ **fan**, filmliefhebber; bioskoopmaniak; ~ **-goer**, bioskoopbesoeker; ~ **ic**, filmies; ~ **iness**, wasig= heid; ~ **ing**, opname, verfilming; ~ **ist**, kineas; ~ **let**, rolfilmpie, filmpie; ~ **library**, filmoteek; ~ **o'graphy**, filmografie, filmlys; ~ **pack**, filmpak; ~ **producer**, produksieleier; rolprentmaker, film= maker; ~ **projector**, filmprojektor; ~ **release**, film= uitreiking; ~ **set**, filmstel, rolprentstel; ~ **star**, rolprentster; ~ **strip**, strokiesfilm; filmstrook; ~ **strip library**, strokiesfilmbiblioteek; ~ **test**, film= toets, rolprenttoets; ~ **version**, rolprentweergawe, filmweergawe, rolprentbewerking; ~ **y**, vliesagtig; wasig.

fil'oplume, haarveer.

fil'oselle, vlossy, filosel.
fil'ter, (n) filter, filtreerder, filtreermasjien; suiweraar, sif; melkdoek; (v) filtreer; deurgiet, deurgooi; suiwer; deursyg, deursypel; ~ *through,* uitlek, deursyfer; ~ **bed,** filtreerbedding; ~ **body,** filterromp; ~ **bowl,** filterbak; ~ **cartridge,** filterpit; ~ **cloth,** sygdoek; ~ **coffee-pot,** sypelkan, filtreerkan, filtreerder; ~ **hair,** filterhaar.
fil'tering, filtrering, deursyfering; ~ **apparatus,** filtreertoestel; ~ **cloth,** melkdoek.
fil'ter: ~ **paper,** filtreerpapier; ~ **percolator,** sypelkan, sypelaar; ~ **plate,** filtreerplaat; ~ **pump,** filtreerpomp; ~ **sump,** filterslikbak; ~ **tip,** filtermondstuk; ~ **tray,** filterpan.
filth, vuilgoed, vuilis; vuiligheid, smerigheid; vervuildheid; vuilheid, liederlikheid; ~**iness,** vuilheid, smerigheid, viesigheid; vervuildheid.
filth'y, vuil, morsig, smerig, goor, vies(lik); ~ *LUCRE,* vuil gewin, aardse slyk (geld); ~ *PIGSTY,* swyneboel, varkhok.
fil'trate, (n) filtraat; (v) filtreer, suiwer.
filtra'tion, filtrering, deursyging, filtrasie, deursypeling, deursyfering.
fi'lum, draad.
fim'briate, uitgerafel, met fraiings.
fimbria'tion, fraiings.
fin, kielvlak (vliegtuig); vin.
fin'able, beboetbaar, strafbaar.
fina'gle, (v) knoei, kul; (n) knoeiery, kullery; ~**r,** knoeier, kuller.
fin'al, (n) finale; eindeksamen; laaste nuus (uitgawe); eindwedstryd; eindronde; (a) finaal; doel-; afdoende; laaste, eind-; beslissend; slot-; *that is* ~, dis finaal, dis die laaste woord; ~ **balance,** eindbalans; finale balansering (wiele); ~ **cause,** eindoorsaak; ~ **certificate,** einddiploma; ~ **chapter,** slothoofstuk; ~ **chord,** slotakkoord; ~ **clause,** doelbysin; slotklousule; ~ **consonant,** slotkonsonant, eindmedeklinker; ~ **decision,** eindbeslissing, eindbesluit; ~ **demand,** finale (laaste) aanmaning; ~ **destination,** eindbestemming; ~ **dividend,** slotdividend.
fina'le, finale, slot.
fin'al: ~ **examination,** eindeksamen; ~ **heat,** finale uitdunwedloop; ~**ist,** finalis; eindwedstrydspeler; ~**'ity,** einddoel; doelmatigheid; uitsluitsel, afdoendheid; eindresultaat; finaliteit; ~**ize,** afhandel; afrond, finaliseer; ~**ly,** ten slotte, laastelik, eindelik, op die ou end; afdoende; ~ **match,** eindwedstryd; ~ **note,** endnoot; ~ **payment,** laaste paaiement; agterskot; ~ **position,** eindstand; ~ **product,** eindproduk; ~ **purpose,** eindoel, eindoogmerk; ~ **race,** eindwedloop; ~ **result,** einduitslag; ~ **rhyme,** slotrym, eindrym; ~ **round,** eindronde; ~ **score,** eindtelling; ~ **sum,** eindbedrag; ~ **value,** eindwaarde; ~ **velocity,** eindsnelheid; ~ **victory,** eindoorwinning; ~ **whistle,** eindfluitjie.
finance', (n) inkomste; finansies, geldmiddele; fonds; geldwese, finansiewese; *Minister of F*~, Minister van Finansies; Jan Taks; (v) finansieer, finansier, geldelik steun; geldelik beheer; kapitaal verskaf; ~**r,** finansier.
finan'cial, geldelik, finansieel; *F*~ *Relations ACT,* Finansiële Verhoudingswet; ~ *CENTRE,* finansiële hart (sentrum); ~ *COMPANY,* leningsmaatskappy, beleggingsmaatskappy; ~ *DIFFICULTIES,* geldnood, geldgebrek; ~ *STATEMENT,* finansiële staat, geldstaat; ~ *YEAR,* boekjaar, bedryfsjaar.
finan'cier, (n) finansier, geldskieter, geldman; (v) geldelike operasies lei; kul, beetneem.
finan'cing, finansiëring, finansiering.
fin'-back, vinwalvis.
finch, (-es), vink.
find, (n) vonds, ontdekking; vangs; *make a* ~, 'n vonds doen; (v) **(found),** vind, kry; aantref; ontdek; verklaar; bevind; vel (vonnis); raakloop; agterkom; verskaf, voorsien van; ~ *AGAIN,* terugkry, weer kry; ~ *AGAINST,* uitspraak gee teen; *ALL found,* alles vry; alles ingesluit (inbegrepe); ~ *a true BILL,* regsingang verleen; ~ *EXPRESSION,* uitdrukking vind; ~ *FAULT with,* afkeur, vit, kapsie

maak op; ~ *FAVOUR,* genade vind; byval vind; ~ *one's FEET,* regkom; ~ *GUILTY,* skuldig vind; *he could not – it in his HEART,* hy kon dit nie oor sy hart kry nie; ~ *it IMPOSSIBLE,* dit onmoontlik vind; ~ *NECESSARY,* nodig vind; ~ *ONESELF,* jou bevind; in jou eie koste voorsien; ~ *OUT,* ontdek, uitvind, ontsyfer; agterkom, opspoor, naspoor, vasstel, nagaan; *you will be found OUT,* hulle sal uitvind wie jy is; ~ *a PERSON out,* iem. betrap; *take heed that you* ~ *not what you do not SEEK,* pas op om nie te kry wat jy nie soek nie; moenie soek wat jy nie verloor het nie; *you must TAKE us as you* ~ *us,* jy moet ons neem soos ons is; ~ *one's WAY,* sy weg vind; ~**able,** vindbaar; ~**er,** vinder; uitvinder; soekglas (kamera); afleespyltjie (op instrument); ~**ing,** vonds; uitspraak, bevinding; ~**ings,** optelgoed; ~ *ings keepings,* optelgoed is hougoed.
fin de siècle, (F.), fin de siècle, betreffende die eeuwending; dekadent.
fine¹, (n) geldboete, geldstraf; *in* ~, kortom, ten slotte, om op te som; (v) beboet; *I was* ~ *d R5,* ek is met R5 beboet.
fine², (n) (pl) fyngoed; fyn gruis; (v) verfyn; suiwer word; (a) fyn (meel, sand); suiwer, helder (vloeistof); mooi, fraai, keurig; deftig, vernaam; bedrewe, kranig, hups, flink; yl (lug); dun, skerp, spits; *that's ALL very* ~, dis alles goed en wel; ~ *ARTS,* skone kunste; *one* ~ *DAY,* op 'n goeie dag; *one of these* ~ *DAYS,* een van die dae; *a* ~ *DISTINCTION,* 'n baie klein onderskeid; *you're a* ~ *FELLOW,* jy's 'n mooi een; ~ *GOLD,* fyn goud; *you are a* ~ *ONE!,* jy is 'n mooi een; *a* ~ *PEN,* 'n skerp (dun) pen; *SAY* ~ *things about a person,* mooi dinge van iem. sê; ~ *WEATHER,* lieflike weer; ~**-draw,** (..drew, ..drawn), onsigbaar stop (aanmekaarnaai); ~**-drawn,** onsigbaar gestop; spitsvondig; subtiel; ~**-grained,** fynkorrelig; ~ **leg,** skerpby (krieket); ~**ly,** fyn; ~**ness,** skerpte; geslepenheid; mooiheid; gehalte; hupsheid.
fin'ery¹, (..ries), opskik, (op)smuk, sieraad, tooi, sierigheid; *dressed in all one's* ~, fyn uitgevat (uitgepiets) wees.
fin'ery², (..ries), affineeroond.
fine: ~ **slip,** skerpglip; ~**-spoken,** glad van tong; ~**-spun,** spitsvondig, subtiel; fyn; ~ **wool,** fynwol.
finesse', (n) finesse; geslepenheid; snyslag; (v) met lis te werk gaan; sny; uitoorlê (kaartspel).
fing'er, (n) vinger; *point an ACCUSING* ~ *at,* met die vinger wys na; *a* ~*'s BREADTH,* vingerbreed; *BURN one's* ~*s,* jou vingers verbrand; *be able to COUNT something on the* ~ *s of one hand,* dit op jou tien vingers kan aftel; *CROSS one's* ~*s, keep one's* ~*s CROSSED,* duim vashou; *FOURTH* ~, ringvinger; *he has GREEN* ~*s,* hy het 'n groeihand; *my* ~*s ITCH to,* my hande jeuk om; *LACE one's* ~*s,* die vingers inmekaarsluit; *LAY one's* ~ *on,* die vinger lê op; *LICK one's* ~*s,* die vingers aflek; *not LIFT a* ~, geen vinger verroer nie, nie eers 'n strooi breek nie, geen poot (wil) roer nie; *have LIGHT* ~*s,* lang vingers hê; *LITTLE* ~, pinkie; *LOOK through one's* ~*s,* deur die vingers sien; *she NEVER has to lift a* ~, sy steek haar hande nooit in koue water nie; *have a* ~ *in the PIE,* in die saak betrokke wees; *let SLIP through one's* ~*s,* deur die vingers laat glip; *SNAP one's* ~*s at someone,* iem. uittart (trotseer); *lay one's* ~ *on the SORE spot,* die vinger op die wond lê; *without STIRRING a* ~, sonder om 'n vinger te verroer; *as THICK as a* ~, vingerdik; *his* ~*s are all THUMBS,* hy is baie onhandig; *they are* ~*s and THUMBS,* hulle is kop in een mus; hulle boer onder een sambreel; *have at one's* ~ *TIPS,* op sy duim ken; *TURN round one's little* ~, om die vinger draai; *TWIST round one's (little)* ~, om jou (pinkie) vinger draai; (v) bevinger; bevoel, betas; beduimel; bespeel; van vingersetting voorsien; ~ *ed by,* met vingersetting van; ~ **alphabet,** vingertaal, doofstommetaal; ~ **board,** toetse, manuaal; toetsbord; ~ **bone,** vingerbeentjie; ~**-bowl,** vingerglas, vingerkom; ~**-breadth,** vingerbreedte; ~**-cloth,** vingerdoekie; ~**-dinner,** staanbuffet; ~**-dressing,** vingerband; ~ **ed,** vinger=

Fingo

vormig; gevinger; ~-**end,** vingertop; ~-**fish,** seester; ~-**glass** = **finger-bowl;** ~-**grass,** vingergras; ~ **guard,** vingerskerm; ~ **hole,** vingergaatjie; ~ **hooks,** vingertrek (spel); ~ **ing,** bevoeling, betasting; vingersetting (mus.); breiwol; blindset; vingertegniek; ~-**joint,** vingergewrig; vingerlit; ~ **language,** vingertaal, doofstommetaal; ~ **less,** vingerloos; ~ **ling,** vingerling; ~-**lunch,** vingermaal; ~-**mark,** vingermerk; ~-**nail,** vingernael; *to the* ~ *nails,* op en top; ~ **nut,** vleuelmoer; ~ **plate,** deurplaat; ~ **poll,** vinger(hoed)pol; ~-**post,** wegwyser, predikant; ~ **print,** vingerafdruk; ~-**shaped,** vingervormig; ~-**shield,** ~-**stall,** vingerkappie, vingerling; ~-**supper,** vingerete, buffetete; ~ **tip,** vingertop; *have something at one's* ~ *tips,* iets op die punte van jou vingers ken; iets op jou duimpie ken.
Fing'o, Fingo.
fin'ial, puntversiering, spitsversiering.
fin'ical, puntene(u)rig, peuterig, oornetjies, gekunsteld, kieskeurig, vol fiemies; ~ **ness,** peuterigheid.
fin'icking, fin'ikin = **finical.**
fin'icky: *be* ~, vol fiemies wees; puntene(u)rig wees.
fi'ning, klaarmiddel.
fin'is, end, slot.
fin'ish, (n) voltooiing, afwerking; afheid; kondisie (van diere); afronding, glans; end, einde, slot, beslissing; *BE in at the* ~, die end meemaak; *FIGHT to a* ~, uitveg, tot aan die end veg; (v) klaarmaak, eindig, voltooi, voleindig, afwerk, die laaste hand lê aan; ophou; beëindig, besluit; opdrink; opeet (kos); afmaak, doodmaak (dier); uitlees uitskei; ~ *off,* afwerk.
fin'ished, stokflou, gedaan; klaar, gereed; afgewerk, afgerond, volmaak; *I am* ~, ek is klaar; ek is gedaan.
fin'isher, voltooier, voleinder; afwerker, afronder; genadeslag.
fin'ishing, (n) afwerking; (a) finale, laaste; *give the* ~ *touches,* die laaste hand aan iets lê; ~ **agent,** afwerkmiddel; ~ **chisel,** afkantingsbeitel; ~ **coat,** deklaag, bolaag (verf); afwerklaag (pleister); ~ **industry,** veredelingsbedryf; ~ **line,** eindstreep; ~ **process,** veredelingsproses; ~ **school,** afrondingskool; ~ **stroke,** genadeslag; ~ **time,** uitskeityd; ~ **tools,** afwerkgereedskap; ~ **touches,** afwerking; finale afwerking (versorging); ~ **varnish,** glansvernis.
fin'ite, beperk, eindig, begrens; ~ **ness,** eindigheid, beperktheid.
fink, ploert, onaangename vent.
Fin'land, Finland, ~ **er,** Fin(lander).
fin'less, sonder vinne, vinloos.
fin'like, vinagtig, vinvormig.
Fin(n), Fin(lander).
fin'nan (haddock, haddie), gerookte skelvis.
finned, gevin, met vinne.
fin'ner, vinwalvis.
fin'nesko, finnesko, takbokskoen.
Finn'ic, Fins.
Finn'ish, (n, a) Fins.
finn'y, met vinne; *the* ~ *tribe,* die visse.
fin' whale, vinwalvis.
fi'no (Sp.), fino, droë sjerrie.
fiord, fjord, fjord.
fiouritu'ra, (mus., It.), fioritura.
fip'ple, fluitstop; ~ **flute,** stopfluit.
fir, den(neboom); ~-**apple,** ~-**cone,** dennebol.
fire, (n) vuur, vlam, brand; skietery; koors, gloed; vurigheid, drif, ywer, hartstog; *I AM on* ~ *to go,* ek brand om te gaan; die grond brand onder my voete; *BE all on* ~, aan die brand wees; *breathe* ~ *and BRIMSTONE,* vuur en vlam spoeg; *CATCH* ~, vuur vat; *CEASE* ~, die skietery staak; *HANG* ~, kets; *LINE of* ~, skootslyn; *MISS* ~, kets, weier (geweer); *OPEN* ~, begin skiet, losbrand; *PLAY with* ~, met vuur speel; *UNDER* ~, onder vuur; *PLAY with* ~ *until one burns one's fingers,* om die kers vlieg tot jy daarin val; *like RUNNING* ~, soos 'n lopende vuur; *SET on* ~, aan die brand steek; *STAND* ~, onder vuur kom; *STRIKE* ~, vuur slaan; ~ *and SWORD,* moord en brand; vuur in swaard; *TAKE* ~, brand, vlam vat; *be like* ~ *and*

fire

TOW, soos kruit en vuur wees; *between TWO* ~ *s,* van twee kante beskiet word; tussen hang en wurg; *go through* ~ *and WATER,* alle gevare trotseer; (v) aansteek, ontsteek, aan die brand steek; laat ontvlam, ontbrand; kwaad word; laat gloei; stook, aanvuur, aanwakker; losbrand, vuur, skiet; uitskop, afdank (werknemer); tak (erdewerk); droog (tee); vat (enjin); ~ *AT,* skiet op (na); ~ *AWAY!,* trek maar los!; *it* ~*s his BLOOD,* hy is vuur en vlam; ~ *a BROADSIDE,* 'n salvo afvuur; die volle laag gee; *it* ~*s his IMAGINATION,* hy is vuur en vlam; ~ *a MINE,* 'n myn laat spring; ~ *OFF,* afskiet; ~ *SOMEONE,* iem. in die pad steek; ~-**alarm,** brandklok, brandfluit; brandalarm; ~-**appliance,** brandblustoestel, brandblusser; ~-**arm,** vuurwapen; ~-**axe,** brandbyl; ~-**ball,** brandkoeël; granaat; meteoor; vuurbal; ligkoeël; ~-**bar,** roostersyster; roosterstaaf; ~-**beater,** brandslaner; vuurslaner; ~-**bell,** brandklok, brandalarm; ~-**belt,** brandgordel; vuurgordel; brandstrook; ~-**bomb,** brandbom; ~-**box,** vuurketel, vlamkas, vuurmaakplek; ~-**brand,** brandende stuk hout; onrusstoker, vuurvreter, stokebrand; ~-**break,** voorbrand, brandpad, brand(weer)strook; ~-**brick,** stoofsteen; vuurvaste steen; ~-**brigade,** brandweer; ~-**brush,** kaggelbesempie; ~-**bucket,** brandemmer; ~-**bug,** brandstigter; ~-**call,** brandalarm; ~ **chief,** brandweerhoof, brandmeester; ~-**clay,** vuurvaste klei; ~-**cock,** brandkraan; ~-**control,** vuurleiding; vuurbestryding; ~-**crack,** hittekraak; brandskerm; ~ **cross,** vuurkruis; ~-**crowned bishop,** vuurkonprooivink; ~-**cured,** gerook; vuurdroog; vuurgedroog; ~-**curing,** (be)roking; vuurdroging; ~-**curtain,** vuurgordyn (mil.); brandskerm; voorbrand; ~ **d:** *be* ~ **d,** die trekpas kry; in die pad gesteek word; ~ **damp,** myngas; ~ **density,** vuurdigtheid; ~-**detection appliance,** brandopsporingsapparaat; ~-**detection system,** brandopsporingstelsel; ~-**dog,** (vuur)herdyster; ~ **door,** branddeur; ~-**drake,** vlieënde draak; draak; dwaallig; ~-**drill,** brandoefening; ~-**eater,** vuureter; vuurvreter; ~-**engine,** brandspuit; brandweerwa; ~-**equipment,** brandweeruitrusting, blustoerusting, ~-**escape,** reddingstoestel; brandleer; brandtrap, noodtrap; ~-**exit,** nooddeur; ~-**extinguisher,** brandblusser; ~-**fighter,** vuurslaner, brandslaner; brandweerman; ~-**fighting,** brandbestryding; ~-**flue,** vlampyp; ~ **fly,** vuurvlieg; ~ **grate,** herdrooster; ~-**guard,** vuurskerm; ~ **hazard,** brandgevaar; ~-**hole,** stookgat (loko.); ~-**hose,** brandslang; ~-**hydrant,** brandkraan; ~ **installation,** stookaanleg; ~ **insurance,** brandassuransie, brandversekering; ~-**irons,** herdgereedstel; ~-**ladder,** brandleer; ~-**lane,** skietlaan; ~ **light,** vuurgloed, vuurkynsel, ~-**lighter,** vuurmaker; ~-**lock,** ou sanna, snaphaan; geweerslot; ~ **main,** hoofbrandweerpyp; ~ **man,** stoker; brandweerman; ~ *man's AXE,* brandbyl; ~ *man's RAKE,* stokershark; ~ **master,** brandweerhoof; ~-**office,** brandversekeringskantoor; ~-**opal,** vuuropaal; ~-**ordeal,** vuurproef; ~-**pan,** konfoor; ~ **partition,** brandafskorting; ~-**passage,** brandgang; ~-**path,** brandpad; voorbrand; ~ **place,** es, erd, stookplek, vuurmaakplek, kaggel, vuurherd; ~ *place and hearth,* kaggel en vuurherd; ~-**plug,** brandkraan; ~ **point,** vlampunt; ~-**policy,** brandpolis; ~-**pot,** vuurkonka; ~ **power,** vuurvermoë; ~ **prevention,** brandvoorkoming; ~-**proof,** brandvry, brandvas, vuurvas, teen vuur bestand; ~-**proof ceiling,** brandsolder; ~-**proof curtain,** brandskerm; ~-**proofing,** vuurvas maak; ~-**proofness,** vuurvastheid; ~ **protection,** brandbeveiliging; ~-**pump,** brandpomp; brandspuit; ~ **r,** vuurmaker; skutter; ~-**raising,** brandstigting; ~-**resistant,** ~-**resisting,** brandwerend; ~-**retarding,** brandvertragend; ~-**risk,** brandgevaar; ~-**screen,** vuurskerm; ~-**service,** brandwese; ~-**ship,** brander; ~-**shovel,** vuurherdgrafie, koleskop; ~ **side,** vuurherd, haard; ~-**signal,** brandsinjaal; ~ **station,** brandweerstasie; ~-**stone,** vuurklip; vuurvaste steen; ~-**system,** brandnet; ~-**tender,** brandweerwa; ~-**tongs,** smidstang; ~-**trap,** brandval; ~-**tube,** vlampyp; ~-**walker,** vuurloper, vuurstapper; ~-**walking,** vuurlopery, vuurstappery; ~ **wall,** brandmuur; ~-**watch,** brandwag; ~-**watcher,** brandbewaker; ~-**watching,** brandbewaking; ~-**water,** tiermelk, brandewyn; ~**wood,** brandhout, vuurmaakhout; ~**works,** vuurwerk; ~-**worship,** vuuraanbidding; ~-**worshipper,** vuuraanbidder; ~-**zone,** vuurstrook.

fir'ing, aanbrandsteking, ontsteek, ontsteking; vuur; afskieting, skietery, losbranding; vuurmaakgoed, brandhout; ontslag, afdanking; ~ **battery,** ontstekingsbattery (elek.); gevegsbattery; ~ **gear,** ontstekingsinrigting; ~-**interval,** skietpouse; ~ **iron,** vuuryster; ~-**line,** skootslyn, vuurlyn, vuurlinie; ~ **order,** ontsteekorde, vonkreëling; ~-**party,** vuurpeleton; ~-**point,** skietplek; ~-**pin,** slagpen; ~-**squad,** vuurpeloton; ~-**stroke,** ontstekingslag, kragslag.

firk'in, vaatjie.

firm[1]**,** (n) firma; handelsnaam; *long* ~, swendelfirma.

firm[2]**,** (v) bevestig; vasstamp, verstewig; hard maak; hard word; (a, adv) standvastig; stewig, sterk, heg, ferm; vasberade; onveranderlik; vas (mark); trou, koersvas; *have a* ~ *GRIP on,* 'n sterk houvas hê op; *with a* ~ *HAND,* met vaste hand; *a* ~ *HANDSHAKE,* 'n stewige handdruk; *HOLD* ~ *to,* pal staan, vastrap, onwrikbaar staan; ~ *MARKET prices,* bestendige pryse (mark); *a* ~ *OFFER,* 'n vaste aanbod; ~ *as a ROCK,* rotsvas; *STAND* ~, pal staan, vastrap, onwrikbaar staan.

firm'ament, uitspansel, firmament, hemelswerk.

firmamen'tal, van die uitspansel, hemel=, firmamentaal.

fir'man, ferman; pas(poort), vergunning, bevel.

firm'er-chisel, steekbeitel.

firm; ~ **joint,** stywe voeg; ~**ly,** flink; vas, stewig.

firm'ness, standvastigheid; willigheid (mark); vastheid, fermheid, hegtheid, stewigheid; vasberadenheid.

fir: ~ **needle,** dennenaald; ~ **nut,** dennepit; ~**ry,** dennerig, denagtig.

first, (n) (die) eerste, begin; eerste kwaliteit; ~ *of EXCHANGE,* primawissel; ~ *and FOREMOST,* allereers, voor alles; *FROM the* ~, van die begin af; ~ *and LAST,* voor alles; alles en alles; alles bymekaar geneem; *from* ~ *to LAST,* van begin tot end; ~ *or LAST,* eerste of laaste; *PROMISING* ~*s,* veelbelowende eerstelinge; (a) eerste; eerstegraads, kwaliteits=, puik, eersterangs, uitstekend, uitmuntend, prima; vernaamste; voorste; *draw* ~ *BLOOD,* die eerste voordeel behaal; die eerste hou inkry; *the* ~ *COAT,* die grondlaag; *a* ~ *COUSIN,* 'n bloedneef, 'n eie neef; ~ *DAY,* Sondag; *at* ~ *HAND,* uit die eerste hand; ~ *NAME,* voornaam; ~ *NIGHT,* première; ~ *OFFICER,* eerste offisier; *in the* ~ *PLACE,* in die eerste plek, eerstens, ten eerste; primo; *at* ~ *SIGHT,* op die eerste gesig; ~ *THINGS* ~, wat die swaarste is, moet die swaarste weeg; (adv) eers, eerste; eerder, liewer; ~ *of ALL,* in die eerste plek; *AT* ~, eers, in die begin; ~ *COME,* ~ *served,* eerste kom, eerste maal; *he who comes* ~ *to the HILL may sit where he will,* eerste kom, eerste maal; ~ *or LAST,* vroeër of later.

first-aid, noodhulp, eerstehulp; ~ **bandage,** noodverband; ~ **box,** noodhulpkissie; ~ **hold all,** noodhulpsakkie; ~ **outfit,** noodhulpuitrusting; noodhulpstel; ~**er,** noodhulpman.

first: ~-**born,** eersgeborene; ~ **class,** eerste klas; ~-**class coach,** eersteklaswa; ~-**comer,** die eerste, die beste; ~ **cost,** inkoopprys; aanvangskoste; ~-**day cover,** eerstedagkoevert; ~ **edition,** eerste uitgawe (edisie); ~ **floor,** eerste verdieping; ~ **fruits,** eerstelinge; ~-**grade,** eerstegraads; ~-**hand,** eerstehands, uit die eerste hand, direk; ~ **lieutenant,** (eerste) luitenant; ~**ling,** eersteling; ~**ly,** eerstens, ten eerste, in die eerste plek, primo; ~ **mate,** eerste stuurman; ~-**mentioned,** eersgenoemde; ~ **name,** voornaam; ~-**nighter,** premièreganger; ~-**offender,** eersteoortreder; ~ **officer,** eerste offisier; ~ **principles,** grondbeginsels; ~ **quarter,** eerste kwartier; ~-**rate,** eersteklas, prima, eersterangs; ~-**rate chap,** uitstekende kêrel; ramkat, bulperd, doring; ~-**rater,** bobaas; uitstaande presteer=

der, topppresteerder; ~ **refusal,** voorkoopreg; ~ **secretary,** eerste sekretaris; ~ **violin,** eerste viool; F ~ **Volksraad,** Eerste Volksraad; ~ **volume,** debuutbundel; ~ **watch,** eerste wag; ~ **year,** eerstejaars=; ~-**year student,** eerstejaar(student).

firth, seearm; riviermond.

fir'-tree, denneboom.

fisc, skatkis, fiskus.

fis'cal, (n) skatmeester, fiskaal; (a) fiskaal, belastings=, ~ **policy,** fiskale beleid; ~ **shrike,** janfiskaal, laksman; ~ **year,** belastingsjaar.

fish[1]**,** (n) las, klamp; spalklas; (v) las, klamp. spalk.

fish[2]**,** (n) (~, -es), vis; ~ *and CHIPS,* vis en aartappelskyfies; *DRINK like a* ~, soos 'n vis drink; *FEED the* ~*es,* verdrink; seesiek wees; *neither* ~ *nor FLESH (nor good red herring),* vis nòg vlees; *FLYING* ~*es,* vlieënde visse; *make* ~ *of one and FOWL of the other,* met twee mate meet; *have other* ~ *to FRY,* dinge van meer belang te doen hê; *there's as GOOD* ~ *in the sea as ever came out of it,* die see is vol visse, nooiens is nie geplant nie maar gesaai; *MAKE* ~ *of one and flesh of the other,* met twee mate meet; *all's* ~ *that comes to his NET,* alles is van sy gading; *a QUEER* ~, 'n snaakse vent; *better SMALL* ~ *than empty dish,* krummels is ook brood; liewer 'n halwe eier as 'n leë dop; *cry STINKING* ~, jouself slegmaak (verkleineer); *must SWIM thrice (first in the sauce, a second time in the wine, and a third time in the stomach),* vis moet swem; *like a* ~ *out of WATER,* soos 'n vis op droë grond; (v) visvang, hengel; uitvis; hengel na (komplimente); ~ *for a COMPLIMENT,* 'n kompliment soek; ~ *FOR something,* iets probeer uitvis; ~ *on dry GROUND,* op droë grond visvang; ~ *for INFORMATION,* na inligting vis; 'n hoek in die water gooi; die boer die kuns afvra; ~ *OUT,* opvis; uitvind; ~ *in TROUBLED waters,* in troebel water visvang.

fish: ~-**back,** pypwig; ~-**bait,** aas; ~ **ball,** visfrikkadel; ~-**basket,** vismandjie; ~-**bladder,** visblaas, swemblaas.

fish'-bolt, lasbout.

fish: ~-**bone,** (vis)graat; ~ **bowl,** viskom; ~-**breeding,** visteelt; ~-**cake,** viskoekie; ~-**carver,** vismes; ~ **club,** viskierie, -knuppel; ~-**course,** visgereg; ~ **croquette,** viskroket; ~-**culture,** visteelt; ~-**curer,** vissouter; ~-**cutlet,** visskyf, vismoot; ~-**dealer,** vishandelaar; ~ **dish,** visgereg; ~ **eagle,** visarend; ~-**eater,** viseter; ~**er,** ~**erman,** (..men), visser, hengelaar, visterman; ~ **folk,** vissers; ~**ery,** (..ries), vissery; ~-**eye (lens),** visooglens; ~ **farm,** vistelery, visboerdery; ~-**farmer,** visteler; ~ **fillet,** vismootjie; ~ **finger,** visvinger; ~ **fork,** visvurk; ~-**garth,** visdam; ~-**globe,** viskom; ~-**glue,** vislym; ~ **hatchery,** visbroeiery; ~ **hawk,** visvalk; ~-**hawker,** visventer; ~-**hook,** (vis)hoek; angel; ~-**horn,** vishoring; ~**iness,** verdagtheid, twyfelagtigheid; visagtigheid.

fish'ing, (n) visvangs; vissery; visplek; hengelary (na geheime); (a) vissers=, vis=; ~-**boat,** vissersboot; vissersskuit; hengelboot; ~-**company,** visserymaatskappy; ~ **competition,** vis(vang)wedstryd; ~ **expedition,** hengelekspedisie; vistog; ~-**fleet,** vissersvloot; ~-**fly,** kunsvlieg; ~-**gear,** visgereedskap, vistuig; ~-**ground(s),** visgrond, visgebied; ~-**hook,** (vis)hoek; ~-**industry,** vissersbedryf; ~-**line,** vislyn; ~-**net,** visnet; ~-**right,** visreg; ~-**rod,** visstok; ~-**tackle,** visgereedskap, vistuig, hengelgerei, visgerei; **vessel,** vissersvaartuig.

fish: ~ **kedgeree,** visrys; ~-**kettle,** viskastrol; ~-**knife,** vismes; ~-**like,** visagtig; ~-**line,** vislyn; ~-**market,** vismark; ~-**mayonnaise,** vismayonnaise; ~-**meal,** vismeel; ~ **monger,** viskoper; ~-**moth,** vismot; silwervissie; ~ **oil,** visolie, traan; ~-**paste,** vispatee, vissmeer; ~ **patty,** viskoekie; ~-**pie,** vispastei.

fish-plate[1]**,** klamp, bindplaat, lasplaat.

fish-plate[2]**,** visbord.

fish: ~ **pond,** visdam, visvywer; ~-**roe,** viskuit; ~-**salad,** visslaai; ~ **scale,** visskub; ~-**shop,** viswinkel; ~-**slice,** vismes, vislepel, visspaan; ~ **soup,** vissop; ~ **steak,** visskyf; ~-**stick,** visstokkie; ~ **stock,** vis=

aftreksel; ~-**tail**, visstert; ~-**tailed**, swaelstert; ~-**trap**, fuik; ~-**turner**, panspaan; ~-**weir**, visdam; ~ **wife**, visvrou, viswyf.

fish'y, visagtig; visryk; twyfelagtig, verdag; *there is something* ~ *ABOUT it*, daar is 'n geurtjie aan; ~ *SMELL*, vislug; *THINK that there is something* ~, iets verdag beskou; iets agter soek.

fisk = **fisc**.

fis'sate, gesplyt, gesplits.

fissibil'ity, kloofbaarheid, digsplytbaarheid.

fiss'ible, kloofbaar, digsplytbaar.

fiss'ile, splytbaar, kloofbaar.

fissil'ity = **fissibility**.

fi'ssion, splyting (fis.); deling (biol.); splitsing; ~ **bomb**, splytbom, kernbom, atoombom; ~ **fungus**, splytswam.

fissi'parous, splitsvermeerderend.

fiss'iped, met gekloofde tone (hoewe), spleethoewig.

fi'ssure, (n) speek, skeur, reet; kloof, bars, naat; (v) kloof, splyt, splits; ~ **lode**, ertsgang.

fist, (n) vuis; poot, handskrif; *GIVE us your* ~, gee ons die blad; *wave one's* ~ *under someone's NOSE*, vir iem. vuis maak; jou vuis onder iem. se neus druk; (v) met die vuis slaan; aanpak; hanteer; ~ **ed**, met vuiste; ~ **fight**, boksgeveg, vuisgeveg; ~-**fighting**, boks; vuisvegtery; ~**fuls**, hande vol; ~ **ic**, boks=; ~ **ic art**, bokskuns; ~**icuffs**, vuisslanery, boksery, vuisvegtery; ~ **law**, vuisreg.

fis'tula, (e, -s), buis (van insek); afleibuis; buis (by walvis); diep pypvormige sweer, fistel, ~ **r**, fistel=, pypvormig, buisvormig.

fis'tulous, fistelagtig; buisvormig.

fit¹, (n) toeval, floute; aanval, vlaag; bui, nuk, gril; (pl) stuipe; *a* ~ *of the BLUES*, 'n neerslagtige bui; *a DRUNKEN* ~, 'n roes; *GIVE someone a* ~, iem. die skrik op die lyf jaag; *GO into* ~ *s*, stuipe kry; dit op sy senuwees kry; *HAVE (throw) a fit*, stuipe kry; dit op die senuwees kry; *by* ~ *s and STARTS*, met horte en stote; met rukke en plukke; *a TREMBLING* ~, 'n bewerasie.

fit², (n) passing, (die) sit; snit; *it was a BAD* ~, dit het sleg gepas; *a CLOSE* ~, dit pas; *a GOOD* ~, dit sit goed; dit pas; (v) **(-ted)**, pas, byeenvoeg; laat pas; aanpas; aansit; monteer; inbou (enjin); ~ *CLOSELY*, nou sluit; ~ *IN with*, pas by, strook met; ~ *in NICELY*, presies pas; ~ *to a T*, net mooi nommer pas wees; ~ *TOGETHER*, inmekaarsit; byeenvoeg; inmekaargryp (tandwiele); aanpas; ~ *ON*, aanpas; ~ *OUT*, uitrus; ~ *UP*, agtermekaar maak, monteer, opstel, inrig; ~ *WELL*, goed pas; (a, adv) passend, geskik, dienstig, gevoeglik, behoorlik, gepas; fiks, flink en gesond; bruikbaar; weerbaar, afgerig, strydgereed; *BE* ~ *for*, deug vir; ~ *red BOLT*, pasbout; *DEEM* ~, goedvind, goedkeur; *as* ~ *as a FIDDLE*, so reg soos 'n roer, ~ *for a KING*, soos vir 'n koning; ~ *for OCCUPATION*, bewoonbaar, geskik vir bewoning; *THINK* ~, dit nodig oordeel; dit raadsaam ag.

fitch, fitch'ew, muishond.

fit'ful, ongestadig, ongereeld, veranderlik, buierig; ~ **ly**, ongereeld, by vlae; ~ **ness**, onbestendigheid.

fit'ly, behoorlik, passend.

fit'ment, meubelstuk; toerusting.

fit'ness, geskiktheid; betaamlikheid; gepastheid; fiksheid.

fit'-out, uitrusting.

fit'ter, passer; uitruster, toeruster; bankwerker; masjiensteller, monteur, aanlêer; ~ *and turner*, monteurdraaier; ~ **'s hammer**, bankhamer.

fitt'ing, (n) installasie; inrigting; beslag; passing, (die) aanpas; passtuk, montuur; (pl) toebehore(ns), bybehore, onderdele, toebehoorsels; meubels, uitrusting; ~ *s and fixtures*, los en vaste toebehore, binneinrigting; (a) passend; geskik, betaamlik, behoorlik, paslik, gepas; ~-**out**, uitrusting; ~-**room**, aanpaskamer; ~-**shop**, monteerwinkel; bankwerkery.

five, vyf; ~ *o'clock*, vyfuur; ~-**day week**, vyfdagweek, werkweek van vyf dae; vyfdaagse werkweek; ~-**eighths**, vyfagtstes; losskakel; ~-**finger exercise**, vyfvingeroefening; ~-**finger grass**, vyfvingerkruid; ~ **fold**, vyfdelig; vyfdubbeld, vyfvoudig; ~-**gaited**, vyfgang (perd); ~ **r**, vyfrandnoot; ~ **s**, kamerten=

nis; vywe, vyfs; ~-**sided**, vyfsydig; ~-**year plan**, vyfjaarplan.

fix, (n) verleentheid, knyp, verklitsing, moeilikheid, penarie, dikkedensie; bestek; oriënteringspunt (lugvaart); *BE in a* ~, sy as vasgebrand hê; in die knyp sit; in die moeilikheid wees; in die bone wees; *help one OUT of a* ~, iem. uit die nood help; (v) vasmaak, vasheg; toeskryf; deurboor; fikseer, verhelder, vaslê (foto); besluit, beslis, vasstel, bepaal, vestig; regmaak, agtermekaar maak, verrig; vas word; afreken met; ~ *(up)on a DAY*, 'n dag vasstel (kies); ~ *the EYES on*, die oë vestig op; ~ *one up for the NIGHT*, iem. vir die nag losies (verblyf, onderdak) gee; ~ *ON*, kies; ~ *ONESELF*, jou vestig; ~ *upon a RESOLUTION*, 'n besluit neem; ~ *UP*, regmaak; op tou sit; reël; ~ **ation**, vasstelling, vaslegging, bevestiging; fiksasie, fiksering; aanhegting; stolling, verdikking (van bloed); ~ **ative**, (n) vasmaker; bindmiddel, fikseermiddel, fiksatief; (a) klewend; fikserend; vasmaak=, vasmakend; ~ *ative hair cream*, haarlym; ~ **ature**, haargom.

fixed, seker; stewig; vasgesteld; onafgewend, star; gevestig, vas, strak, onbeweeglik; vasstaande; standvastig; gebonde (chem.); aard= en naelvas (jur.); ~ **address**, vaste adres; vaste verblyf; ~ **balloon**, kabelballon; ~ **bath**, ingemesselde bad; ~ **bayonet**: *with* ~ *bayonets*, met gevelde bajonette; ~ **beam**, ingeklemde balk; ~ **body**, vaste liggaam; ~ **capital**, vaste kapitaal; ~ **charge**, vaste koste; ~ **deposit**, vaste deposito; ~ **engine**, standmotor; ~ **establishment**, vaste personeelsterkte; ~ **focus**, vaste brandpunt; ~ **idea**, vaste idee, idée fixe; ~ **improvement**, vaste verbetering (eiendom); ~ **ly**, vas, strak; ~ **ness**, vastheid, starheid; ~ **oil**, nie-vlugtige olie; ~ **point**, vaste punt, uitgangspunt; ~ **property**, vaste eiendom; vasgoed; ~ **star**, vaste ster; ~-**time call**, afspraakoproep.

fix'er, bereddeelaar; fikseerder, fikseermiddel; vasmaker; reelaar, reëler.

fix'ing, vasmaak; fikseer, vaslegging, verheldering, fiksering; bepaling; ~ *of position*, plekbepaling, oriëntering; ~ **bath**, fikseerbad; ~ **fillet**, heglat; ~ **s**, uitrusting, toebehore, toestelle; meubels; bykomstighede; ~-**salts**, fikseersout; ~ **wire**, binddraad.

fix'ity, vastheid; duursaamheid; onveranderlikheid.

fix'ture, vasstaande ding; vastigheid; wat spykervas is, iets wat vasgeslaan is (toonbank, planke, ens.); vasgestelde datum; datumlys; afspraak; wedstryd; vasstelling; standplaas; (pl) wedstrydreeks; wedstrydbepalings; vaste uitrusting, installasie.

fiz'gig, geklike flerrie, prikkelpop.

fizz, (n) sjampanje; geborrel, gesis; (v) sis, bruis, borrel.

fiz'zle, (n) gesis; fiasko, mislukking; sisser; (v) sis, bruis; ~ *out*, op niks uitloop, doodloop.

fizz'y, bruisend, bruis=; skuimend; ~ *drinks*, bruisdrank

fjord, fjord.

flabb'ergast, beteuter(d), verbluf, dronkslaan; ~ *someone*, iem. dronkslaan (verbluf); ~ **ed**, verbouereerd; oorbluf; *be* ~ *ed*, heeltemal oorbluf wees.

flabb'iness, slap(perig)heid, papperigheid.

flabb'y, slap(perig), week, sag, pap.

flabell'ate, flabell'iform, waaiervormig.

flac'cid, slap, pap; ontspanne; ~ **'ity**, slapheid, slapte, papperigheid.

flag¹, (n) vlag, vaan; *DIP the* ~, met die vlag salueer; ~ *of DISTRESS*, noodvlag; *HOIST one's* ~, jou vlag hys; *LOWER the* ~, die vlag stryk; *the* ~ *PROTECTS the cargo*, die vlag dek die lading; *RED* ~, oproervlag; rooivlag; Russiese vlag; *SHOW the* ~, die vlag vertoon; *STRIKE the* ~, die vlag stryk; ~ *of TRUCE*, vredesvlag, wit vlag; ~ *of VICTORY*, oorwinningsvlag; *WHITE* ~, wit vlag; (v) vlag, sein.

flag², (n) flap (blom).

flag³, (n) plaveiklip, vloerteël; (v) bevloer; met klippe uitlê, plavei.

flag⁴, (n) slagveer, slagpen; (v) **(-ged)**, slap hang; verslap; sink; laat hang; verflou.

flag'boat, vlagboot; vlagskip.

flag'-captain, vlagkaptein.
flag'-day, kollektedag.
fla'ggellant, (n) geselbroeder, flagellant; (a) geselend, kastydend.
fla'gellate, (n) sweepdiertjie; (v) slaan, gesel.
flagella'tion, geseling.
flaggelli'form, sweepvormig.
flagell'um, flagellum, sweephaar.
flageolet', hoë viooltone; flageolet.
flag'-feather, slagveer, slagpen.
flagg'ing^1, (n) plaveisel; plaveiklippe.
flagg'ing^2, (n) verslapping; (a) verflouend, kwynend, verslappend.
flag'-hoisting, vlaghysing.
flagi'tious, misdadig, boosaardig, skandelik; ~ **ness,** misdadigheid, skandelikheid.
flag: ~-**lieuten'ant,** vlagluitenant; ~ **man,** vlaghouer; seinman, vlagseiner; baanwagter; ~-**officer,** vlag= offisier, vlagvoerder.
flag'on, tafelfles, skinkkan, flapkan.
flag'pole, ~ **post,** vlagpaal.
flag'rancy, in-die-oog-lopendheid, ooglopendheid, opvallendheid, onbeskaamdheid, berugtheid; (die) flagrante, flagrantheid.
flag'rant, in-die-oog-lopend, ooglopend, opvallend; verregaande, skaamteloos, berug; gloeiend; flag= rant.
flag: ~ **ship,** vlagskip, admiraalskip; ~-**signaller,** vlagseiner; ~ **staff,** vlagstok.
flag'stone, vloerteël, plaveisteen.
flag: ~-**wagger,** vlagswaaier; ~-**wagging,** vlag= swaaiery; ophitsery; ~-**waver,** onrusstoker, agita= tor; vlagswaaier; jingo.
flail, dorsstok, (dors)vleël; mynslaner, mynslaanket= ting; (v) dors; afransel; mynslaan; ~-**tank,** sweep= tenk.
flair, flair, aanleg; goeie neus, fyn ruik (instink); *have a ~ for,* aanleg hê vir; 'n goeie neus hê vir.
flak, lugdoelvuur, lugafweer; ~ **gun,** lugafweerka= non.
flake^1, (n) droograk, platformpie.
flake^2, gestreepte angelier.
flake^3, (n) vlok; vonk; skilfer; flentertjie; snysel, stuk= kie; laag, blad; ~ *of ICE,* ysskots; ~ *of SNOW,* sneeuvlok; (v) in vlokke val; afskilfer; streep; in dun blaaie afbreek; skoonmaak; pluis; ~*d FISH,* vlokkies vis, gevlokte vis; ~ *OFF,* afskilfer; ~-**white,** loodwit.
flak'iness, vlokkigheid, skilferigheid.
flak'ing, afskilfering.
flak'ship, lugdoelvuurboot.
flak'y, vlokkig; skilferig; ~ **pastry,** skilferkors (=deeg).
flam, versinsel, leuen, voorwendsel, smoesie.
flam'be, vlam=; ~ **pudding,** vlampoeding.
flam'beau, (-s, -x), fakkel, toorts, flambou.
flamboy'ancy, kleurigheid, kleurrykheid; praalsug= tigheid.
flamboy'ant, (n) vlamboom, flambojant *(Poinciana regia);* (a) vlammend, gevlam; opsigtig, kleurig, blomryk; praalsugtig, windmakerig; ~ **structure,** vlamstruktuur.
flame, (n) vlam; lig, gloed, vuur, hitte; beminde; *ALL a~,* in ligtelaaie, in volle vlam; *BE all on ~,* vuur en vlam wees; *BURST into ~s,* aan die brand slaan; *FAN the ~s,* die gloed aanwakker; die vuur aanblaas; *HOVER round the ~ until one singes one's wings,* om die kers vlieg tot jy daarin val; *IN ~s,* in ligtelaaie; *an OLD ~,* 'n ou vlam (nooi); (v) brand, vlam; laat vlam; blaak, gloei; oplaai; ~ *up,* hewig bloos; opstuif; ~ **bush,** vuurbos(sie); ~-**cleaning,** afbranding; ~-**colour,** vlamkleur; ~ **less,** sonder vlam; ~ **creeper,** vlamklimop; ~-**cut,** sny= brand; ~-**cutter,** snybrander; ~ **ed,** gevlam; ~ **flo= wer,** vuurblom; vlamblom, vuurpyl; ~ **lily,** vuurle= lie; ~-**projector,** vlamwerper, vlamgooier; ~-**proof,** vlamvas, vlamveilig; ~-**resistant,** brand= traag; ~ **thorn tree,** rank-wag-'n-bietjie; ~-**trap,** vlamvanger.
flam'ing, (n) opvlamming; (a) vlammend, brandend.
Flam'ingant, Flamingant.
flaming'o, (-es), flamink.

flammabil'ity, ontvlambaarheid, brandbaarheid.
flamm'able, ontvlambaar, brandbaar.
fla'my, vlammend, vurig.
flan^1, (n) oop tert; randkoek, flan.
flan^2, (v) (-ned), uitskuins; ~ **pan,** ~ **tin,** randpan.
Flan'ders, (n) Vlaandere; (a) Vlaams; ~ **poppy,** papa= wer; kunspapawer (op 11 Nov. verkoop tot steun van oud-stryders).
flange, (n) rand, flens; (v) omflens; ~-**angle,** rand= hoekyster; ~-**coupling,** flenskoppeling; ~ **d,** ge= flens, gerand; ~ **d coupling,** flenskoppeling; ~**d hole,** kraaggat; ~-**nut,** flensmoer; ~-**pipe,** flens= pyp; ~-**union,** flensverbinding; ~-**wrench,** flens= sleutel.
flang'ing, omflensing; ~ **machine,** flensmasjien.
flank, (n) sy, flank; grypkant (tand); vleuel; lies; (pl) lieswol; *THICK ~,* diklies; *THIN ~,* dunlies; (v) in die flank aanval; flankeer; die flank dek; ~ **at= tack,** flankaanval; ~ **defence,** flankdekking; ~ **er,** vleuelman; flankversterker; flankversterking; flank(voorspeler); ~ **fire,** flankvuur; ~ **guard,** flankhoede; ~ **man,** flankman; ~ **movement,** flank= beweging; ~ **steak,** liesskyf; ~ **wool,** lieswol.
flann'el, (n) flennie; flanel; (pl) lang broek; flennieon= derklere; (a) flanel=; flennie=; ~ **bandage,** flennie= verband; ~ **board,** flenniebord; ~ **cake,** rooster= koek; ~ **dance,** informele dans(party); ~**ette',** (n) flanelet; flennie; (a) flanelet=; flennie=; ~ **ly,** flennie= agtig; ~ **trousers,** flanelbroek.
flap, (n) klap, slag, flap; lel(letjie); deksel, valdeur, luik; inslag (van boek); afhangende rand; *BACK ~,* agterste inslag; *FRONT ~,* voorste inslag; *GET in a ~,* opgewonde raak; ~ *of a HAT,* rand van 'n hoed; (v) (-**ped**), slaan, waai, klap; flap(per), flad= der; ~ *the wings,* die vlerke klap; klapwiek; ~ **chart,** blaaikaart; ~ **doo'dle,** geklets, onsin, twak; ~-**door,** valluik; ~-**eared,** met hangore; ~-**hinge,** klapskarnier; ~ **jack,** poeierdosie; plaatkoekie; flappertjie; ~-**jacket,** sykant.
flapp'er, klap; vlieëplak, vlieëslaner; vin; stert; jong eend of patrys; ratelaar, klepper; bakvis(sie); nooi= (e)ntjie; opfrisser (vir geheue); ~ **bracket,** agter= saal (motorfiets); ~-**vote,** meisiestemreg, vroue= stemreg.
flapp'ing, geflap, geklap.
flap: ~ **pocket,** klapsak; ~ **seat,** klapstoel; ~ **table,** klaptafel; ~ **tile,** sluitteël, sluitpan; ~ **trousers,** klapbroek; ~ **valve,** skarnierklep, klapklep; ~ **win= dow,** klapvenster, tuimelvenster.
flare, (n) flikkerlig; nagsinjaal; fakkel; vlam; klokval; klokplooi (rok); pronkery, vertoon; oorhang (van boeg); (v) flikker, vlam, skitter; ronddraai; uitbol, bol staan; opstuif, opvlieg, woedend word; uitbars; ~ *up,* opflikker; ~-**bomb,** fakkelbom, ligbom; ~-**carrier,** fakkelhouer; ~**d skirt,** klokrok; ~ **light,** ligbol; fakkel, flikkerlig; observasielig; ~ **path,** fak= kelbaan; ~ **pistol,** fakkelpistool, ligpistool; ~ **sig= nal,** fakkelsein; ~-**up,** opflikkering, opvlamming; fuif; uitbarsting.
flar'ing, skitterend, flikkerend; ~ *COLOURS,* op= sigtige kleure; ~ *TOOL,* oopsperder.
flar'y, pronkerig, opsigtig; vulgêr.
flash^1, (n) vleug, golf.
flash^2, (n) (-**es**), blits, flits; flikkering, glans, skig, lig= straal; vleug, vlaag, golf; mondingsvlamme (ge= weer); skittering, vertoon; kleursel; flitsberig; kleurlappie (op helm); ketsskoot; stroom; ~ *of HOPE,* flikkering van hoop; *IN a ~,* in 'n kits, in 'n oogwink; ~ *of LIGHT,* bliksemstraal; *ORANGE ~,* rooi lus; *a ~ in the PAN,* 'n opflikkering; ~ *of WIT,* kwinkslag, 'n geestige inval; (v) flikker, skit= ter, flits; laat flikker; blitssnel vertoon; oordeel; op= vlam; ontvlam; sein; uitsprei; ~ *ACROSS,* te binne skiet; inval; opflits; pronk; stroom; voeë dek; ~ *BACK,* weerkaats; *his EYES ~ed FIRE,* sy oë het vonke geskiet; ~ *a MESSAGE,* 'n boodskap sein; *it ~ed UPON me,* dit het my te binne geskiet; (a) vals, diewe=; pronkerig, windmakerig nagemaak; ~ **language,** diewetaal.
flash: ~ **back,** terugflits; ~ **bulb,** blitsbol; ~ **butt wel= ding,** vlamboogstompsweis; ~ **card,** flitskaart; ~-**cartridge,** magnesiumpatroon; ~ **dry,** winddroog;

flask / fleecy

~ **er,** flitslamp; flitsseiner; knipoog (sein); ~ **fire,** flitsvuur; opslaanbrand, opslaanvuur; ~ **flood,** blitsvloed, skielike vloed; ~ **gun,** flitsapparaat; ~ **indicator,** rigtingflitser; ~ **iness,** opsigtigheid; spoggerigheid; ~ **ing,** voegloed; voegskort; skittering, geflikker, opflikkering; ~ **ing point,** vlampunt; ~ **lamp,** flitslamp; ~ **language,** boewetaal, bendetaal; ~ **light,** blitslig, flikkerlig, skitterlig; bliksemlig; magnesiumlig; flitslig; ligwerper; ~ **light portraiture,** blitsligopname; ~ **message,** flitsberig; ~ **money,** vals geld; ~ **-over,** vonksprong; ~ **photograph,** flitsfoto; ~ **photography,** flitsfotografie; ~ **point,** ontbrandingspunt; vlampunt; ontstekingstemperatuur; ontvlammingspunt, flitspunt (olie); ~ **-system,** oombliklike verhittingsmetode; ~ **y,** opsigtig, pronkerig, windmakerig.
flask, fles, bottel; kruithoring.
flask'et, kleremandjie; flessie.
flat, (n) plaat, gelykte, vlakte; plathoed; domkop; woonstel; platboomvaartuig; plat mandjie; handkar; skerm; tussenskerm (toneel); platdak (huis); plat kant; plat (van sabel); dowwe (mat) verf; mol (musiek); (pl) vlakte; plat kante; woonstelle; (v) **(ted),** plat maak; plet; (a) dof (verf); uitgewerk, verslaan, verskaal (bier); laf, flou; pap (wiel); onbewimpeld, onverbloem(d); vervelend, eentonig; lusteloos; plat, gelykvloers, effe; vals, mineur (mus.); *a* ~ *AFFAIR,* 'n vervelende affère; *a* ~ *DENIAL,* volstrekte ontkenning; *with the* ~ *HAND,* met die oop hand; *a* ~ *LIE,* 'n direkte leuen; *as* ~ *as a PANCAKE,* so plat soos 'n pannekoek; *at a* ~ *RATE,* teen 'n uniforme tarief; *give a* ~ *REFUSAL,* botweg weier; *a* ~ *WAGE,* 'n uniforme loon; ~ *WHITE paint,* mat (glanslose) wit verf; (adv) plat; vals; *the BATTERY went* ~, die battery het klaargeraak; *it FELL* ~, dit het in duie geval (misluk); *GO* ~, die geur verloor; *that IS* ~, dit is stellig; en daarmee uit, basta!; *LIE* ~, platlê; ~ *OUT,* dat dit so kraak; *RUN* ~ *out,* loop dat jy oop (plat) lê; ~ **angle,** gestrekte hoek; ~ **arch,** plat boog; ~ **attitude,** vlak stand (vliegtuig); ~ **-bed press,** platpers; ~ **-bit drill,** platboor; ~ **boat,** platboot; platskuit; ~ **bottom,** platboomskuit; ~ **-bottomed,** platboom-; ~ **building,** woonstelgebou; ~ **candlestick,** blaker; ~ **carving,** vlak reliëf; ~ **ceiling,** vlak plafon; ~ **-chested,** met 'n plat bors; ~ **chisel,** platbeitel; ~ **coat,** grondlaag; stryksellaag (bouk.); ~ **-coated,** met gladde hare; ~ **collar,** plat kraag; ~ **cost,** direkte koste; ~ **crown,** platkroon (boom); ~ **-cutting pliers,** plattang; ~ **-deck body,** plat bak; ~ **event,** baannommer; ~ **file,** platvyl; handvyl; ~ **-fish,** platvis; ~ **foot,** platvoet; polisieman (neerh.); ~ **-footed,** platvoet-, met plat voete; ~ **glass,** platglas; ~ **gutter,** vierkantgeut; ~ **hoof,** plat hoef; ~ **-hunting,** woonstelsoek; ~ **-iron,** strykyster, parsyster; platyster; ongegolfde sinkplaat; ~ **joint,** platvoeg; ~ **knot,** platknoop; ~ **ly,** plat; botweg, beslis, pront-uit, bot-af; ~ **ness,** platheid; gelykheid; lafheid, smaakloosheid; ~ **nose,** platneus; ~ **-out,** oop-en-toe, op volle spoed; ~ **part,** platte (van voete); ~ **pliers,** plat tang; ~ **race,** naelwedloop, baanwedloop; ~ **rate,** minimumtarief; ~ **rib,** platrib (van bees); ~ **roof,** plat dak; ~ **seam,** plat naat; ~ **season,** komkommertyd; ~ **spin,** plat tolvlug; *go into a* ~ *spin,* die kluts kwytraak; ~ **stake,** vlakstaak; ~ **surface,** gelyk oppervlak; mat vlak (verf).
flatt'ening, (die) platmaak; ~ **-press,** pletpers.
flatt'er¹, (n) plethamer.
flatt'er², (v) bewierook; vlei, iem. heuning om die mond smeer, flikflooi, pluimstryk, streel, pamperlang; flatteer (foto); ~ *only to DECEIVE,* liemaak; ~ *you* ~ *YOURSELF!,* jy lyk 'n mooi bobbejaan!; ~ **-er,** vleier, flikflooier, pluimstryker, oëdienaar, witvoetjiesoeker; ~ **ing,** (n) flikflooiery, gevlei, oëdiens; (a) vleiend, strelend, flatterend; ~ **y,** vleiery, gevlei, die gebruik v.d. heuningkwas.
flat'tie, flat'ty, plathakskoen.
flat: ~ **ting,** (die) platmaak; pletwerk; ~ **ting hammer,** plethamer; ~ **ing-mill,** plettery; pletmeul; ~ **tint,** effe kleur; ~ **t'ish,** platterig, gelykerig; ~ **-top desk,** skryftafel; ~ **trajectory,** vlak koeëlbaan; ~ **trowel,**

spatel; ~ **truck,** plat vragwa; plat goederewa; ~ **tyre,** pap band.
flat'ulence, flat'ulency, wind(erigheid); sooibrand; opgeblasenheid, verwaandheid.
flat'ulent, winderig, gasserig, opgeblaas; opgeblase, verwaand.
flat'us, (-es), (maag)wind.
flat: ~ **varnish,** mat vernis; ~ **wise,** plat; ~ **worm,** platwurm.
flaunt, (n) vertoon, gewapper; (v) wapper; praal, pronk; aanstel; te koop loop; ~ *one's FEATHERS,* bokspring; vertoon, spog, pronk; ~ *SOMETHING,* met iets pronk; te pronk loop met iets; ~ **ing(ly),** opsigtig, pronkend, pralend; opdringerig.
flaut'ist, fluitblaser, fluitspeler.
flaves'cent, geelagtig, gelerig; geelwordend.
flav'ine, flavine.
flavopro'tein, flavoproteïen, -proteïne.
flav'orous, geurig.
flav'our, (n) smaak, geur(tjie), aroma; (v) smaaklik maak; geurig maak; 'n geur gee, krui; ~ **ed,** smaaklik; gegeur; *highly* ~ *ed,* sterk gekruie; ~ **ing,** geuring; smakie, geursel; ~ *ing essence,* geursel; smaakmiddel; ~ **less,** geurloos, smaakloos; ~ **some,** geurig, smaaklik.
flavovir'ens, geelgroen.
flaw¹, (n) tekortkoming, fout, gebrek, vlek, gles (in diamant); dwarsskeurskuiwing (geol.); spleet, bars, skeur, kraak; *without* ~ *or blemish,* sonder smet of vlek (blaam); (v) bederf, skend; bars, skeur, splits; laat bars.
flaw², (n) windvlaag, reënvlaag.
flaw'less, vlekloos, onberispelik, gaaf.
flax, vlas; ~ *false* ~, vlasdodder; ~ **-breaker,** vlasbraak; ~ **-comb,** vlaskam; ~ **culture,** vlasbou, vlasverbouing; ~ **dresser,** vlasbewerker, vlasbreker; ~ **en,** van vlas; vlaskleurig; ~ *en hair,* ligblonde hare, vlashare; ~ **-growing,** vlasbou, ~ **-mill,** vlasfabriek; ~ **-raising,** vlasbou; ~ **-seed,** vlassaad; ~ **-thread,** vlasdraad; ~ **waste,** vlasafval; ~ **y,** vlassig.
flay, afslag, afstroop; vlek; vil; martel; uitkleed, afkam; ~ **er,** afslagter; afperser; afskiller; afkammer; ~ **er's knife,** slagmes, vilmes; ~ **-flint,** vrek, uitsuier; ~ **ing-knife,** slagmes.
F-layer, F-laag.
flea, vlooi; *COME away with a* ~ *in one's ear,* daar sleg van afkom; *HAVE a* ~ *in one's ear,* 'n skrobbering ontvang het; met iets in jou maag sit; *SEND someone away with a* ~ *in his ear,* teruggeslaan word; iem. met 'n berisping wegstuur; ~ **-bag,** (sl.), slaapsak, goor blypiek; ~ **bane,** vlooikruid; ~ **-beetle,** sandvlooi; erdvlooi *(Collembola);* ~ **vlooikewertjie;** springkewertjie *(Chrysomelidae);* ~ **-bite,** vlooibyt; kleinigheid; ~ **-bitten,** vol vlooibyte; gespikkeld; ~ **-bitten horse,** forelskimmel (perd); ~ **fair,** vlooimark.
fleam, vlym; tandhoek (saag).
flea: ~ **market,** vlooimark; ~ **wort,** vlooikruid.
fleck, (n) vlek; sproet; veeg; stippie; (v) spikkel, vlek; ~ **ed,** bont, gespikkeld; ~ **er,** stippel, bont maak; ~ **less,** vlekloos, smetloos.
flec'tion, *kyk* **flexion.**
fled, *kyk* **flee.**
fledge, veer, van vere voorsien; begin vlieg; *fully* ~ *d,* uitgegroei; volwasse, volgroei; ~ **ling,** jong voëltjie; snuiter, kuiken.
flee, (fled), vlug, sabander, duinkerk, ontvlug, wegvlug; vermy; padgee; sku, ontwyk; ~ *the country,* uit die land vlug.
fleece, (n) vlies, vag; skeersel; haardos; bossiekop; *golden* ~, gulde (goue) vlies; (v) skeer; bedek; **pluk;** die vel oor die ore trek, kaalmaak, uitbuit; ~ *a person,* iem. die vel oor die ore trek; iem. uitmelk; iem. kaal uitskud; ~ **able,** skeerbaar; plukbaar; ~ **clouds,** vlies-, veerwolke; ~ **d,** wollig; geskeer; uitgetrek, uitgebuit; ~ *d fabric* pluisstof; ~ **density,** vogdigtheid; ~ **line,** vagklas; ~ **rot,** wolbederf; wolvrot; ~ **wool,** skeerwol; vagwol.
flee'cing, skeer; pluising; uitmergeling.
flee'cy, wollerig, wollig; vliesagtig; wolkerig, vlokkig; ~ *CLOUDS,* ligte wolke; vlieswolke; ~ *SKY,* lug

vol skaapwolkies (vlieswolkies); ~ *SNOW*, vloksneeu; ~ *WOOL*, donswol.
fleer, (n) spottery, spotlag; gryns(lag); (v) spot, spottend lag, hoon, gryns.
fleet¹, (n) vloot; vlug; seearm; groot aantal, span; boel; ~ *of taxis*, 'n vloot huurmotors (taxi's).
fleet², (n) inham; stroompie, vliet.
fleet³, (v) vervlieg, vloei, vliet, verdwyn, heensnel, verbygaan; ~ *away*, verdwyn, wegsweef.
fleet⁴, (a) vinnig, snel, rats, haastig, lustig; verganklik; ~ *of foot*, vinnig.
fleet⁵, (a, adv) vlak; *plough* ~, vlak ploeg.
fleet' air-arm, vlootlugmag.
fleet: ~**-footed**, vinnig, snelvoetig; ~**ing**, verganklik, verbygaande; vlugtig; ~**ness**, snelheid, vlugheid, ratsheid.
Flem'ing, Vlaming.
Flem'ish, Vlaams; *the* ~, die Vlaminge; ~ **bond**, Vlaamse verband (bouk.); ~ **knot**, agtknoop.
flench, **flense**, (rob) afslag; vil (walvis); opsny; *kyk ook* **flinch**.
flesh, (n) vleis, vlees; liggaam; sinlikheid; *have the* ~ *off someone's BACK*, iem. ooptrek; iem. afransel; iem. met die sambok deurloop; *BE still in the* ~, nog in die lewe wees; *more than* ~ *and blood can BEAR*, meer as wat 'n mens kan verdra; *one's own* ~ *and BLOOD*, jou eie vlees en bloed; *make one's* ~ *CREEP*, jou hare regop laat staan; jou hoendervel laat kry; *DENY the* ~, die vlees dood; *GATHER* ~, vleis kry; *the ILLS that* ~ *is heir to*, menslike kwale; aardse sorge; *be IN* ~, goed in die vleis wees; *IN the* ~, in die liggaam; in lewende lywe; *LOSE* ~, afval, maer word; *ONE* ~, een vlees; *PROUD* ~, wilde vlees, woekervleis; *PUT on* ~, vet word; *SINS of the* ~, sondes v.d. vlees; *go the WAY of all* ~, die weg van alle vlees gaan; *the* ~ *is WEAK*, die vlees is swak; (v) vleislus (van hond) opwek, lus maak, laat bloed drink; 'n vleiswond toedien; inwy; ~**-brush**, lyfborsel; ~**-colour**, vleiskleur; ~**-coloured**, vleeskleurig, vleeskleur=; ~**-eaters**, vleiseters, carnivore; ~**-fly**, brommer; ~**-iness**, vleisigheid; ~**ing-iron**, ~**ing-knife**, skaafmes (looier), stootmes; ~**ings**, vleiskleurpakkie; ~**liness**, vleeslikheid; ~**ly**, vleeslik; sinlik; ~ **mark**, litteken; ~**pot**, vleispot; *hanker after the* ~*pots of Egypt*, na die vleispotte van Egipte verlang; ~ **side**, vleiskant (van vel); ~ **tights**, kaalpak; vleiskleurige kousbroek; ~ **wound**, vleiswond; ~**y**, dik, mollig, vleisagtig; gevleis; liggaamlik; goed in die vleis.
flet'cher, pylmaker.
fleur de coin', (F.), fleur de coin, pasmunt.
fleur-de-lis', **(-lys)**, fleur-de-lis.
fleu'ret, blomornament, flueret.
flew, *kyk* **fly**, (v).
flews, hanglippe (bloedhond).
flex, (n) (elektriese) koord of draad; (v) buig; ~ **break**, buigbreuk (buiteband); ~ **cord**, draaikoord, buigkoord.
flexibil'ity, buigsaamheid, lenigheid, slapheid, soepelheid; rigvaardigheid (wapen).
flex'ible, buigsaam, soepel, smedig, slap, lenig; rigvaardig; buigbaar; handelbaar; inskiklik; ~ **constitution**, buigsame konstitusie; ~ **cord**, elektriese draad; ~ **coupling**, gewrigskoppeling; ~ **drive**, buigsame aandrywing; ~ **pipe**, buigsame pyp; ~ **rule**, buigsame liniaal; ~ **shaft**, buigsame as; ~ **support**, buigsame onderlaag; ~ **thread**, liglei=draad.
flex'ile, beweeglik, buigsaam, handelbaar; ..**il'ity**, beweeglikheid, buigsaamheid, handelbaarheid.
fle'xion, (uit)buiging, kromming; verbuiging, fleksie; ~**al**, buigings=; ~**less**, onverbuigbaar.
fle'xitime, **flex'-time** skik(werks)tyd, fleksietyd.
flex'or, buigspier.
flex'uose, **flex'uous**, bogtig, kronkelend.
flex'ural, buig=, buigings=; ~ **fold**, buigingsplooi.
fle'xure, buiging, kromte; deurbuiging, fleksuur, bog, kromming; ~ **test**, buigtoets.
flibb'ertigibb'et, kekkelbek; woelwater.
flic, Franse polisieman, flic.
flick, (n) knip; klap; raps; veeg; fliek; ruk; tik, raps, piets; (v) klap; ~ *AWAY*, wegveeg; wegknip; ~ *ON*, aanskakel.
flick'er, (n) geblits, geflikker; geklap; getril; straal (van hoop); *the* ~*s*, die fliek; (v) flikker; tril; flapper, klap (vlerke); ~**ing**, trilling, flikkering, geflikker.
flick' knife, springmes.
flick'-roll, kitsrol.
fli'er, *kyk* **flyer**.
flight¹, vlug; ~ *of CAPITAL*, kapitaalvlug; *PUT to* ~, op loop jaag; ~ *of STAIRS*, trap (in 'n gebou); ~ *of STEPS*, trapleer; *TAKE* ~, op loop sit.
flight², vlug (groep vliegtuie); vliegafstand; vliegtog; trop; swerm (voëls); kaf; ~ *of BIRDS*, 'n trop (vlug, swerm) voëls; *a* ~ *of FANCY*, vlug v.d. verbeelding; *in the FIRST* ~, onder die belangrikste (bekwaamste); *IN* ~, in die vlug; *INVERTED* ~, rugvlug; (v) (in die vlug) skiet; ~**-analyser**, vlugmeter; ~ **bag**, vliegtuigsak; ~ **capital**, vlugkapitaal; ~ **commander**, vlugkommandant; ~ **controls**, stuurmiddels; ~ **crew**, vliegpersoneel; ~ **data recorder**, vlugdataregistreerder; ~**-deck**, vliegdek; ~ **engineer**, boordingenieur, boordtegnikus; ~**-feather**, slagpen, slagveer.
flight'iness, lossinnigheid, wuftheid, wispelturigheid.
flight: ~ **leader**, vlugkommandant; ~ **level**, vlieghoogte; ~ **lieutenant**, luitenantvlieër; vlugluitenant; ~ **mechanic**, boordwerktuigkundige; ~ **muscle**, vliegspier; ~ **officer**, offisiervlieënier; ~**-path**, vliegkoers; vlugbaan (van bom); ~ **recorder**, vlugopnemer, vluggeheue; ~ **strip**, aanloopbaan, stygbaan; ~ **time**, vliegtyd; ~ **trial**, proefvlug.
flight'y¹, vlug.
flight'y², vlugtig; lossinnig, wispelturig, grillig; fantasties; swaksinnig.
flim'flam, onsin, malpraatjies; foppery.
flim'siness, swakheid, niksbeduidendheid; dunheid; flenteragtigheid.
flim'sy, (n) deurslagpapier; deurslagkopie; banknoot; (a) dun, ragfyn, deursigtig; slap, niksbeduidend; oppervlakkig; flenterig; flou (ekskuus).
flinch, aarsel, terugdeins, versaag, weifel; *without* ~*ing*, onwrikbaar; sonder om 'n spier te trek.
flin'ders, flenters, toiings, splinters.
fling, (n) ongedwongenheid, vryheid; worp, gooi; Skotse dans; *HAVE a* ~ *at*, probeer; waag; vir die gek hou; *have ONE's* ~, op die boemel gaan; uitraas; jou uitlewe, die lewe geniet; jou aan losbandigheid oorgee; (v) **(flung)**, gooi, slinger, werp, smyt; slaan; afgooi; uitslaan (arms); ~ *ABOUT*, rondgooi; ~ *sound ADVICE to the winds*, goeie raad in die wind slaan; ~ *ASIDE*, opsy gooi, weggooi; ~ *AT*, gooi na; toesmyt, toewerp; ~ *AWAY*, wegsmyt; ~ *DOWN*, neersmyt, omgooi; ~ *to the GROUND*, teen die grond gooi; ~ *up one's HEELS*, agteropskop; ~ *OPEN*, oopgooi; ~ *OUT*, uitsmyt; ~ *into someone's TEETH*, iem. iets voor die kop gooi; ~**er**, werper, gooier.
flint, vuurklip, flint, vuursteen; blinkmieliepit; *set one's FACE like a* ~, vasberade wees; *SKIN a* ~, skraapsugtig wees, vrekkig wees; ~ *and STEEL*, vuurslag; *wring WATER from a* ~, bloed uit 'n klip tap; ~ **corn**, blinkpitmielie, rondemielie; ~**-glass**, flintglas; loodglas; ~ **gun**, pangeweer; ~**-hearted**, ongevoelig, hardvogtig; ~**-like**, vasberade; ~**lock**, vuurklipgeweer; vuurklipslot; ~ **lock gun**, sanna, pangeweer; ~**-lock musket**, pangeweer; ~ **maize**, ~ **mealie**, blinkpitmielie, rondepitmielie; ~ **paper**, vuurklippapier; ~ **steel**, vuurstaal; ~**-stone**, vuurklip; ~ **wort**, akoniet, wolwekruid; ~**y**, klipagtig, hard; hardvogtig.
flip¹, (n) ruk, raps, swaai; slag; skoot; plesiervluggie, vliegtoggie; (v) **(-ped)**, knip, klap, slaan, raps, tik.
flip², (n) flip (soort drank); eierbrandewyn.
flip'-flap, bolmaklesie, buiteling; klapper; geklikklak.
flip'-flop, terugspringskakelaar.
flipp'ancy, onbesonnenheid, ligsinnigheid, onverskilligheid; ligte spot; losheid.
flipp'ant, ligsinnig, oneerbiedig, lughartig, onbesonne, loslippig.

flipp'er, swempoot; vin; vlerk; spanrandkernhulsel (buiteband).
flipp'erty-flopp'erty, los, slingerend, swaai-swaai.
flirt, (n) flerrie, jongensgek, vryerige meisie, behaagsieke vrou, flirt; meisiegek; flirtery, vryery; ruk, swaai; (v) skerts; flankeer (met nooiens), koketteer, flirt; gekskeer; wegruk, swaai, fladder; ~ **a'tion,** behaagsug, koketterie, ligsinnigheid; geflirt, flirtasie, vryery, vryasie; ~ **a'tious,** vryerig, flirterig; ~ **ing,** geflirt, vryery, flirtery, flankeerdery; geskarrel; ~ **ish,** ~ **y,** vryerig, flirterig.
flit, (n) gefladder; verhuising; (v) **(-ted),** vlieg, fladder, swewe; verhuis; wegtrek; verbygaan (tyd).
flitch, (n) syspek, spekvleissy; moot, skyf; balk; ~ *of bacon,* syspek; (v) in skywe (mote) sny; ~ **beam,** botterhambalk.
flitt'er, fladder; ~ **-mouse,** (..**mice),** vlermuis.
flivv'er, tjorrie, blikmotor; blikvliegtuig.
flix, bont; bewerhaar.
float, (n) (die) drywe; dryfsel; sweef, swewing; vlot; dobber; vlotter (vergasser); drywer (seevliegtuig); skepbord, strykbord, vryfplank, strykplank (bouk.); sierwa; groefvyl; vlot; los kontant, (v) drywe; vlot; swewe; ronddryf; dobber; waai (vlag), wapper; laat drywe; vlot maak (skip); in omloop bring, uitstrooi (praatjie); stig, floteer, oprig (maatskappy); op tou sit; uitskrywe (lening); lanseer (vuurpyl); gelyk maak; stryk (pleister); marsjeer; vlot; ~ *a COMPANY,* 'n maatskappy oprig; ~ *a LOAN,* 'n lening uitskryf; ~ *on the SURFACE,* bo drywe; vlotbaar; ~ **abil'ity,** dryfvermoë; ~ **able,** dryfbaar; ~ **age,** seedrif; utgespoelde goed, wrakgoed; opdrifsels; dryfvermoë; deel bokant die diepgangsmerk; ~ **-and-wick,** dobber en pit; ~ **a'tion,** oprigting; uitgifte (van lening); ~ **board,** strykplank; skepbord; ~ **chamber,** vlotterkamer; dobbervaatjie; ~ **drop,** vlotterval; ~ **er,** drywer; drywende myn; swembal; strykplank (bouk.); staatsaandeel; ~**gauge,** vlotter.
float'ing, (n) die drywe; spoeling, afstryking; (a) drywend, vlottend; ~ **anchor,** dryfanker; ~ **assets,** vlottende bate(s); ~ **axle,** vry as; ~ **battery,** drywende battery; ~ **beacon,** dryfbaken; ~ **bridge,** skipbrug, dryfbrug; ~ **bush,** los bos; ~ **chamber,** vlotterkamer; ~ **crane,** dryfkraan; ~ **cup,** wisseltrofee; ~ **debt,** vlottende skuld; ~ **dock,** dryfdok; ~ **foundation,** vlot fondament; ~ **gauge,** vlotter; ~ **kidney,** wandelende nier, swerfnier; ~ **light,** ligboei; ~ **mine,** dryfmyn; ~ **population,** vlottende bevolking; ~ **power,** dryfvermoë, dryfkrag; ~ **rib,** vals rib; ~ **rig,** booreiland, boortoring; ~ **trophy,** wisseltrofee; ~ **vote,** vlottende stem(me).
float: ~ **level,** vlotterhoogte; ~ **-needle,** vlotternaald; ~ **-plane,** vliegboot; ~ **spindle,** vlotterspil; ~ **-tickler,** vlotterpen, vlotterprikkelaar; ~ **valve,** vlotterklep.
floc, vlokmassa, vlokke.
flocc'iform, pluisievormig; pluisierig.
floccinaucinihilipilifica'tion, (jok.), waardeloosverklaring.
flocc'ose, wollerig, vlokkig.
flocc'ulant, vlokmiddel.
flocc'ulate, (v) uitvlok; (a) vlokkig.
flocc'ule, vlok.
flocc'ulence, flocc'ulency, vlokkigheid.
flocc'ulent, vlokkig.
flo'cculus, vlokkie.
flocc'us, (flocci), donsvlokkie; bossie (hare); kwas (stert).
flock¹, (n) vlok, bossie; (pl) vlokwol.
flock², (n) trop, kudde; vlug (patryse); swerm; ~ *of sheep,* trop (kudde) skape; (v) bymekaarkom, saamkom; ~ *AFTER,* agternaloop; ~ *TO,* toestroom; ~ *TOGETHER,* saamstroom; ~**-master,** skaapboer; ~ **mattress,** donsmatras; wolmatras; ~ **paper,** donsmuurpapier; ~ **wool,** vlokwol.
flock'y¹, vlokkig.
flock'y², kuddeagtig.
floe, stuk dryfys, ysskots, skol; ~ **ice,** dryfys.
flog, (-ged), klop, wiks, vel, striem, uitwiks, (af)ransel, pak gee, slaan; ~ *a dead horse,* tevergeefse werk verrig; ~ **ging,** pak slae, afranseling, tugtiging, loesing, geseling, ranseling.

flong, matryspapier.
flood, (n) sondvloed; vloed, oorstroming; stortvloed; (v) oorstroom; laat oorloop; onder water sit; uitstort; stroom; ~ *the market,* die mark oorlaai; ~ **-anchor,** vloedanker; ~ **-beam,** dwarsdraer; ~ **control,** vloedbeheer; ~ **-ditch,** noodsloot; ~ **gate,** duiker, duiksluis; sluisdeur; *open the* ~ *gates,* die sluise ooptrek; ~ **ing,** (bloed)vloeiing; oorstroming; ~ **irrigation,** vloedbesproeiing; ~ **-level,** vloedpeil; vloedhoogte; ~ **-light,** spreiing; ~ **-lighting,** spreibeligting; ~ **-lit,** onder spreilig(te); ~ **-mark,** waterpeil; vloedlyn; ~ **plain,** vloedvlakte; ~ **-tide,** hoogwater, vloed; ~ **water,** vloedwater; spoelwater.
floor, (n) vloer; verdieping; buik (van wa); *FIRST* ~, eerste vloer, eerste vlak, eerste verdieping; *GET the* ~, aan die woord kom; *HAVE the* ~, die woord hê; aan die woord wees; *HOLD the* ~, op jou praatstoel sit; *TAKE the* ~, die baan open; die woord voer; *WIPE the* ~ *with someone,* iem. kafloop; (v) uitvloer, bevloer; vloer insit; neergooi, teen die grond gooi, onderkry; platslaan; ontstel, dronkslaan; uitoorlê (in eksamen); ~ *someone,* iem. dronkslaan; iem. troef, iem. koudsit; iem. kafloop; ~**-bearer,** moerbalk; ~**-board,** vloerplank; ~**-brush,** vloerborsel; ~ **casing,** vloerbekisting; ~**-cloth,** vloerkleed, linoleum; vloerlap; ~**-covering,** vloerbedekking; ~ **crane,** vloerkraan; ~ **duty,** saaldiens (in hospitaal); ~ **er,** uitklophou; teenvaller; dronkslaanvraag(stuk); ~**-guide,** deurbaan.
floor'ing, bevloering, vloer; vloerplanke; ~**-board,** vloerplank; ~**-brad,** vloerspyker.
floor: ~**-joist,** vloerbalk; ~**-lamp,** staanlamp; ~ **level,** vloerhoogte; ~**-mat,** vloermat; ~**-mop,** vloerdweil; ~ **nail,** vloerspyker; ~**-polish,** vloerwaks, vloerpolitoer; ~ **polisher,** vloervrywer, vloerpolitoerder, vloerpoleerder; ~ **price,** laagste prys; steunprys; ~ **rug,** (vloer)mat; ~ **sander,** vloerskuurder; ~ **show,** vloervertoning; vloeruitstalling; kabaret; ~**-slat,** vloerlat; ~**-space,** vloeroppervlakte, vloerruimte; ~ **stain,** vloerbeits; ~**-stop,** deuraanslag, deurstop; ~**-swab,** dweil; ~ **tile,** vloerteël; ~**-walker,** toesighouer, vloerbestuurder, vloeropsigter.
floo'zy, floo'zie, floo'sie, flerrie, ligtekooi.
flop, (n) klap; plof; misoes, mislukking, fiasko; *it was a* ~, dit was 'n misoes; (v) **(-ped),** fladder; klapwiek; swaai, slinger; neerplof; sak, druip; ~ *down,* neerplof; (interj) pardoems! flap! ~**py,** los, bakkerig, slap; ~*py DISC,* slapskyf, disket (reken.); ~*py HAT,* flaphoed; ~*py HOUSE,* slaaphuis.
flor'a, (-e, -s), plantegroei, flora.
flor'al, blom=, geblom; plante=; ~ **axis,** blomas; ~ **decoration,** blomversiering; ~ **envelope,** blomhulsel; ~ **fête,** blommefees; ~ **leaf,** blomblaar; ~ **material,** geblomde stof; ~ **offering,** blommehulde; ~ **tribute,** blommehulde; ~ **zone,** plantegordel.
Flor'ence, Florence (uitspraak Floraans).
Flor'entine¹, (n) Florentyn; (a) Florentyns.
flor'entine², systof, florentine.
flores'cence, bloei, bloeityd.
flores'cent, bloeiend.
flor'et, blommetjie; floret; ~ **silk,** floretsy, flossy.
flor'iate, met 'n blompatroon versier, blom=; ~**d,** geblom, blom=.
floribun'da, floribunda.
floribund'ant, blomryk.
flor'iculture, blomkwekery, blommeteelt.
floricul'turist, blomkweker; bloemis.
flo'rid, blomryk; swierig; opsigtig; kleurig, blosend.
Flo'rida, Florida; ~ **grape,** Floridadruif; ~ **grass,** Floridagras, Transvaalse kweekgras; ~ **moss,** oumansbaard, Spaanse mos.
florid'ity, flor'idness, blomrykheid, swierigheid.
florif'erous, blomdraend, blom=.
florile'gium, (..gia), bloemlesing.
flo'rin, floryn; gulden (Ned.).
flo'rist, blomkweker; bloemis.
florist'ic, floristies; ~**s,** floristiek.
flor'istry, bloemistery.
flor'uit, floruit (tyd waarin iem. geleef het).
flos'cular, met saamgestelde blomme.

flos'cule, blommetjie.
floss, dons, donsvere (volstruis); vlossy; ~ **flower,** ageratum; ~ **silk,** vlossy; ~**y,** vlossig; donserig.
flota'tion, oprigting, stigting, flottasie (van maatskappy); uitgifte, plasing (lening); optousetting; flottasie (van erts); ~ **costs,** ~ **expense(s),** oprigtingskoste; ~ **gear,** vlotuitrusting, dryfuitrusting; ~ **method,** flottasiemetode; ~ **process,** bedryfsproses, flotteringsproses.
flotill'a, flottielje, eskader; vlootjie.
flot'sam, seedrif, aanspoelsel, uitspoelsel, drifsel; afdrysel; dryfhout, wrakhout; strandgoed, opdrifsel; ~ *and jetsam,* rommel, afval, opdrifsel, wrakgoed; skuim (fig.).
flounce[1]**,** (n) breë val, sierstrook (op rok); (v) stroke aansit; 'n val maak.
flounce[2]**,** (v) flap; ruk, swaai; woel, spartel; struikel, strompel.
floun'der[1]**,** (n) bot(vis), platvis.
floun'der[2]**,** (n) gestrompel; gesukkel; (v) worstel, kleitrap, sukkel, spartel; knoei.
flour, meelblom, fynmeel; ~ *of wheat,* koringblom; ~**-bag,** meelsak; ~ **beetle,** meelkewer, kalander; ~**-bin,** meelblik; ~ **bomb,** meelbom; ~ **cake,** meelkoek; ~**-dredger,** meelstrooier; ~ **dust,** meelstof, stofmeel.
flou'rish[1]**,** (n) krul, haal; versiering; woordepraal; swierige beweging; sierletter; stylblom; fanfare, gesketter, geskal; prelude; bloei; glans, prag; voorspoed; (pl) fieterjasies; *BEGIN something with a* ~, iets met wapperende vaandels aanpak; *DO something with a* ~, iets spoggerig doen; iets windmakerig aanpak; ~ *of TRUMPETS,* trompetgeskal; (v) krulle maak; jou blomryk uitdruk; met sierletters skryf; blomryke taal gebruik; swaai; praal, pronk; trompet blaas.
flou'rish[2]**,** (n) prelude; (v) preludeer.
flou'rish[3]**,** (n) (-es), bloei, glans, prag; voorspoed; (v) (op)bloei, gedy, voorspoed hê; floreer; ~**ing,** bloeiend, florerend, welvarend, voorspoedig.
flour: ~**-mill,** koringmeule; ~ **porridge,** meelpap, hotom; ~ **scoop,** meelskoppie; ~ **sieve,** meelsif; ~ **trade,** meelhandel; ~ **wheat,** broodkoring; ~**y,** melerig; met meel bedek; *become* ~*y,* blus (ertappels).
flout, (n) hoon, spot, beskimping; (v) hoon, bespot, aanfluit, beskimp, beledig.
flow, (n) vloed, stroom; uitstroming; toevloed; loop, gang, eb; ~ *of CURRENT,* stroomloop; ~ *of LANGUAGE,* woordevloed; ~ *of SPIRITS,* opgewektheid; *TIDAL* ~, getystroming; (v) vloei, stroom; opkom (gety); oorvloei; laat oorloop; ~ *FROM,* voortvloei uit; ~ *IN,* toestroom; ~ *OFF,* afloop, wegloop; ~ *OVER,* oorloop; ~ **chart,** stroomkaart; vloeikaart; ~ **control,** vloeireëling; ~ **diagram,** stroomdiagram; vloeidiagram.
flow'er, (n) blom; bloeisel; bloei; keur, uitsoek; stylblom; *IN* ~, in bloei; ~ *of LIFE,* fleur (bloei) v.d. lewe; ~ *of a NATION,* die blom (keur) v.d. nasie; ~ *of SPEECH,* stylblom; ~*s of SULPHUR,* blomswa(w)el; *in the* ~ *of his YOUTH,* in die bloei van sy jeug; (v) blom; bloei; tooi; ~ **age,** bloei; ~ **arrangement,** blommerangskikking; ~**-bed,** blomakkertjie, blombeddinkie; ~ **bud,** blomknop; ~**-bulb,** blombol; ~**-child,** blomtjom; blommekind; ~**ed,** met blomme bedek; geblom; ~**er,** bloeier; ~**et,** blommetjie; ~ **garden,** blomtuin; ~**-girl,** strooimeisie; blommeisie; blomverkoopster; ~**-grower,** blommeboer; ~**-head,** blomhofie; ~**iness,** blomrykheid (lett.); bloemrykheid (fig.).
flow'ering, (n) (die) bloei; (a) bloeiend; ~ **almond,** Chinese pruim; ~ **peach,** blomperske, sierperske; ~ **plum,** blompruim, sierpruim; ~ **quince,** blomkweper, sierkweper; ~ **time,** bloeityd, blomtyd.
flower: ~**less,** sonder blom; ~ **pot,** blompot; ~**-show,** blommetentoonstelling; ~ **stalk,** blomstingel; ~**-stall,** blomstalletjie; ~**-stand,** blomtafel; ~**-time,** blomtyd, bloeityd; ~**-work,** blomwerk; ~**y,** blomryk; geblom; bloemryk (fig.).
flow'ing, vloeiend, stromend; golwend; lopend; ~ *GARMENTS,* sleepgewaad; ~ *LOCKS,* lang golwende hare; *land* ~ *with MILK and honey,* land wat vloei van melk en heuning; ~ *STYLE,* vloeiende styl; ~ *WATER,* lopende water.
flow: ~**-line,** vloeilyn; ~**-meter,** verbruiksmeter, stroommeter.
flown, *kyk* **fly,** (v).
flow: ~**-off,** afvoer, afloop; ~**-over,** oorloop; ~ **pipe,** vloeipyp; ~**-rate,** stroomsnelheid; ~**-sheet,** verloopkaart; vloeikaart.
flu, *kyk* **influenza.**
flub, verknoei, bebrou.
flub'dub, bombasme; swak taalgebruik.
fluc'tuant, weifelend; dobberend, swewend.
fluc'tuate, weifel; swewe, dobber; wissel, fluktueer, skommel; ~ *BETWEEN,* hang tussen; *fluctuating PRICES,* skommelende pryse.
fluctua'tion, weifeling; veranderlikheid, afwisseling; skommeling, wisseling, dobbering, fluktuasie; *liable to* ~ *s,* veranderlik, onderhewig aan verandering; *economic* ~, ekonomiese skommeling, wandelaksie van ekonomiese bewegings (konjunktuur).
flue[1]**,** (n) flou (visnet).
flue[2]**,** (n) dons, pluisie; (v) pluis.
flue[3]**,** (n) skoorsteenpyp, vlampyp; afkoelingspyp; orrelpyp; vuurgang; verwarmingsbuis.
flu(e)[4]**,** influensa, griep.
flue[5]**,** (v) wyer maak, afskuins.
flue: ~**-barn,** droog(oond)skuur; ~**-brush,** skoorsteenbesem; ~**-chamber,** uitlaatkamer; ~**-cure,** berook; ~**-curing,** oonddroging, beroking; ~**-dust,** skoorsteenstof; ~**-gas,** rookgas; ~**-hole,** skoorsteengat; ~**-passage,** vuurgang; ~**-pipe,** orrelpyp, lippyp; ~**-tube,** vlampyp.
flu'ency, vloeiendheid, vloeiing; welbespraaktheid, vaardigheid, vlotheid.
flu'ent, vloeiend, vloeibaar; ongestadig, vlottend; los, golwend; welbespraak, vlot; ~ **speech,** vlot taalgebruik.
fluff[1]**,** (n) halfgekende rol (toneel); (v) verknoei (gholf); 'n rol verknoei (toneel); oor jou woorde val.
fluff[2]**,** (n) dons, donshaartjies, pluisie, vesel; *a little bit of* ~, donsigheidjie; 'n oulike, popperige nooientjie; (v) pluis; sag maak; ~**iness,** donserigheid; ~**-louse,** donsluis; ~**-tail,** vleikuiken; ~**y,** donsagtig, donserig, vlossig; dons=; ~ *y paper,* donspapier.
flu'id, (n) vloeistof, vog, fluïdum; (a) vloeibaar; loperig; ~**-compass,** vloeistofkompas; ~**-drive,** hidrouliese aandrywing, vloeistofkoppeling; ~**ics,** vloeitegniek, fluïdika.
fluid'ify, vloeibaar maak.
fluid'ity, vloeibaarheid, fluïditeit.
fluid: ~ **mechanics,** vloeistofmeganika; ~ **ounce,** vloeistofons; ~ **pressure,** vloeistofdruk; ~ **resistance,** vloeistofweerstand; ~ **state,** fluïdum.
flu'idize, fluïdiseer.
fluke[1]**,** (n) ankertand, ankerklou, ankerblad; speerpunt; stert (walvis); (v) met die stert slaan.
fluke[2]**,** (n) bot (vis); slak (in lewer); slakwurm.
fluke[3]**,** (n) geluk, gelukslag, gelukskoot, bof; *by a* ~, per toeval, per geluk; (v) geluk hê, bof; 'n slag slaan.
fluk'y, gelukkig, geluk=.
flume, watervoor, waterloop.
flumm'ery[1]**,** bokwietpap.
flumm'ery[2]**,** vleiery, onsin, komplimentjies.
flumm'ox, van streek (stryk) bring, dronkslaan.
flump, plof, smyt.
flung, *kyk* **fling,** (v).
flunk, (n) mislukking; (v) sak, misluk (in eksamen).
flunk'ey, (-s), vleier, kruiper; ploert; livreikneg, lakei; agterryer; ~**ism,** agterryery; lekkery, pluimstrykery, kruipery.
fluoresce', fluoresseer.
fluores'cence, fluoressensie.
fluores'cent, fluoresserend; ~ **lamp,** fluoorlamp; ~ **light,** buislig; ~ **lighting,** fluoorverligting.
flu'oride, fluoried.
fluorina'tion, fluorinasie.
flu'orine, fluoor.
flu'orite, fluoriet.
fluoro'sis, fluorose, fluoorvergiftiging.

fluorspar / **focal**

flu'orspar, vloeispaat.
flu'rried, deurmekaar; verbouereerd; halsoorkop, gejaag, senuweeagtig, opgewonde.
flu'rry, (n) (**flurries**), bui, wind; doodstryd (van walvis); agitasie, gejaagdheid, verbouereerdheid; ~ *of BLOWS*, reën van houe; *a* ~ *of RAIN*, 'n reënvlaag; (v) (**flurried**), senuweeagtig wees; in die war bring; agiteer, deurmekaar maak; jou haas.
flush[1], (n) (**-es**), toevloed; deurspoeling; stroom; uitloop; kleur, blos; waas; (v) deurspoel, deurstroom, (uit)spoel; (v) laat kleur, bloos; (a) blosend.
flush[2], (n) stel, suite (kaarte), vyf kaarte van een kleur; *ROYAL* ~ , vyf opeenvolgende kaarte van een kleur tot die aas; *STRAIGHT* ~ , vyf opeenvolgende kaarte van een kleur.
flush[3], (n) opwelling, bloei; volheid; *in the first* ~ *of victory*, in die eerste opwinding v.d. oorwinning; (v) aanvuur, laat wortelskiet; na die hoof styg; opwind, dronk maak; gelyk maak; ~ *ed with JOY*, uitgelate (dronk) van vreugde; *he LOOKS* ~ *ed*, hy het 'n hoë kleur; ~ *ed with WINE*, deur wyn verhit; (a) effe, gelyk, gelykvlakkig, versonke (klinknael); kragvol; volop (geld).
flush[4], (n) vlug, trop (voëls); (v) wegvlieg; opjaag (voëls).
flush-deck, gladde dek.
Flush'ing[1], Vlissingen.
flushing[2], deurspoeling, uitspoeling; blosing.
flush' joint, inlaatvoeg, vlak voeg.
flush' production, beginproduksie.
flush riv'et, vlakklinknael.
flush' sanitation, spoelriolering.
flus'ter, (n) oorhaasting, verwarring, gejaagdheid; (v) oorhaas, in verwarring bring; benewel (deur drank); opgewonde maak; ~ **ed**, opgewonde, deurmekaar gemaak, deur die wind, gejaag.
flute, (n) groef; pypplooi; fluit; dwarsfluit; (v) uitgroef, uithol; siergroewe maak; pypplooie maak.
flut'ed, groef=, gegroef; gerib; ~ **column**, gegroefde suil; ~ **funnel**, gleuftregter; ~ **glass**, geribde glas; ~ **roller**, groefrol.
flute'-player, fluitspeler, fluitblaser.
flut'ing, groefwerk; ~ **plane**, groefskaaf.
flut'ist, fluitspeler.
flutter, (n) gefladder; verwarring; gejaagdheid, haas, onrus; wanorde; spekulasie; sensasie; gepopel, trilling (van hart); *have a* ~ , waag; spekuleer; (v) fladder, fletter; opjaag; in die war bring; wapper, waai (vlag), waai; heen en weer draf; tril, klop; flikker; beef, opgewonde wees; dwarrel; jaag (hart); agiteer; ~ *ABOUT*, rondfladder; ~ *AFTER*, natladder; ~ *the EYELIDS*, met die oë knipper; ~ **ing**, gewapper.
flut'y, fluitagtig, sag (van toon).
fluv'ial, **fluv'iatile**, rivier=, fluviaal.
fluviol'ogy, stroomkunde.
fluviom'eter, fluviometer, stroommeter.
flux, (n) stroming, vloeiing; smeltmiddel; samevloeiing; vloeimiddel; bloedstorting; stroom, vloed; kragstroom; wisseling, voortdurende verandering; *state of* ~ , toestand van veranderlikheid; (v) vloeibaar maak, smelt; saamvloei; stroom, vloei; ontsluit (chem.); ~ **ible**, smeltbaar, veranderlik; ~ **ion**, vloeiing, samesmelting; verandering; ~ **ional**, ongestadig, veranderlik, differensiaal.
fly[1], (n) gulp; onrus (van klok); huurrytuig; vlug, vliegtog; vliegafstand; tentklap; wydte van vlag; voorste (los) deel van vlag.
fly[2], (n) (**flies**), vlieg; kunsvlieg; *be the* ~ *on the COACH-WHEEL*, 'n orige jukskei wees; *he wouldn't HURT a* ~ , hy sal geen vlieg kwaad doen nie; *a* ~ *in the OINTMENT*, 'n vlieg in die salf; *there are no flies ON him*, hy is uitgeslape; *PLAGUE of flies*, vlieëplaag; *break a* ~ *on the WHEEL*, 'n kanon gebruik om 'n mossie te skiet.
fly[3], (v) (**flew, flown**), vlieg; vlug, ontvlug; ontwyk, vermy; vlag, laat waai (vlag); stuiwe; laat uitvlieg; fladder; wuif; ~ *ABOUT*, rondvlieg; ~ *an AEROPLANE*, 'n vliegtuig bestuur; ~ *APART*, uitmekaar vlieg; ~ *AT one*, iem. invlieg; op iem. lostrek; iem. onder die klippe steek; iem. onder die lat kry; ~ *AWAY*, wegvlieg; ~ *BACK*, agteruitspring; te=
rugvlieg; ~ *the COUNTRY*, uit die land vlug; ~ *the British FLAG*, die Britse vlag voer; ~ *the GARTER*, hasie-oor spring; ~ *off (at) the HANDLE*, opvlieg, opgewonde raak; ~ *HIGH*, hoog vlieg; ~ *a KITE*, 'n vlieër laat opgaan; *make MONEY* ~ , geld laat rol; ~ *OFF*, wegvlieg; ~ *OUT*, wegvlieg; ~ *into a PASSION*, woedend word; *make SPARKS* ~ , hare laat waai, vonke laat spat.
fly[4], (a) slim, oulik, oorlams, gevat.
fly: ~ **agaric**, ~ **amanita**, vlieëswam; ~ **-away**, ligsinnig; denkbeeldig; ~ **-away collar**, wegstaanboordjie; ~ **bane**, vlieëbos; ~ **-blow**, vliegeier; maaier; ~ **blown**, bederf, vol maaiers; vuil.
fly'boat, snelboot; vliegboot (hist.).
fly'-catcher, vlieëvanger; bontrokkie (voël).
fly: ~ **er**, vlieër; vlugteling; wegloper; reisiesperd; vliegwiel (masjien); ~ **-half**, losskakel; ~ **-hip**, kruisnok.
fly'ing, (n) vlieg, vlieëry; vliegkuns; vliegwese; *crazy* ~ , dolvlieëry; (a) vlieënd; ~ **accident**, vliegongeluk; ~ **badge**, vlieënierskenteken; ~ **base**, vliegbasis, lugbasis; ~ **bedstead**, vlieënde bed; ~ **boat**, vliegboot; ~ **bomb**, vlieënde bom; ~ **box car**, transportvlieëtuig; ~ **bridge**, noodbrug; pontonbrug; ~ **buttress**, steunboog, boogstut; ~ **camp**, vliegkamp; ~ **cap**, vliegpet; ~ **club**, vliegklub; ~ **colours**, vlieënde vaandels; *with* ~ *colours*, met vlieënde vaandels; triomfantlik; ~ **column**, vlieënde kolonne; ~ **conditions**, vliegtoestande; ~ **corps**, vliegkorps; ~ **deck**, vliegdek; ~ **display**, vliegvertoning; ~ **doctor**, vlieënde dokter; F~ **Dutchman**, Vlieënde Hollander; ~ **expedition**, vliegtog; ~ **experience**, vliegondervinding; ~ **fish**, vlieënde vis; ~ **fox**, vlieënde hond, kalong (vlermuis); ~ **gang**, snelspan; ~ **ground**, vliegveld, -terrein; ~ **helmet**, vlieghelm; ~ **hour**, vlieguur; ~ **instruction**, vlieg(kuns)onderrig; ~ **instructor**, vlieginstrukteur; ~ **jib**, jager; ~ **jump**, aanloopsprong; ~ **kit**, vliegklere; ~ **lesson**, vliegles; ~ **machine**, vliegmasjien; ~ **man**, vlieër, vlieënier; ~ **officer**, vliegoffisier; ~ **operations**, lugondernemings; lugbedryf; ~ **practice**, vliegoefening; ~ **range**, vliegbereik; ~ **risk**, vliegrisiko; ~ **saucer**, vlieënde piering; ~ **scaffold**, vliegsteier; ~ **school**, vliegskool; ~ **sense**, lugsin; ~ **service**, vliegdiens; ~ **sheet**, vlugskrif; traktaatjie; ~ **shuttle**, skietspoel; ~ **speed**, vliegsnelheid; ~ **squad**, blitspatrollie; ~ **squad car**, blitsmotor; ~ **squirrel**, vlieënde eekhoring; ~ **start**, aanloopwegspring; groot voorsprong; ~ **station**, vliegbasis, lugbasis; ~ **stress**, vliegspanningsdruk; ~ **stunt**, kunsvlug; ~ **suit**, vlieërpak; ~ **tackle**, duik; ~ **time**, vliegtyd, vlugtyd; ~ **tour**, vliegtoer; ~ **training**, vliegkunsopleiding; ~ **trick**, kunsvlug; ~ **trot**, harde draf; ~ **visit**, kort (vlugtige) besoek; ~ **weather**, vliegweer.
fly: ~ **-kick**, lugskop; ~ **-leaf**, skutblad; ~ **man**, huurkoetsier; toneelkneg.
fly' net, vlieënet.
fly: ~ **-nut**, vleuelmoer; ~ **-over (bridge)**, oorbrug, sneloorgang.
fly'paper, vlieëpapier.
fly'-past, defileervlug, défilé (van vliegtuie).
fly: ~ **poison**, vlieëgif; ~ **-proof**, vliegdig, vliegvry.
fly'sheet, traktaatjie.
fly'-swatter, vlieëslaner.
fly'-title, voortitel, korttitel.
fly'-trap, vlieëvanger.
fly'-wheel, vliegwiel.
fly'weight, vlieggewig.
f-number, f-getal.
foal, (n) vul; *in* ~ , dragtig; (v) vul.
foam, (n) skuim; (v) skuim, bruis, ~ *at the mouth*, skuimbek; ~ **beetle**, spoegbesie; ~ **(fire-)extinguisher**, skuimbrandblusser; ~ **iness**, skuimagtigheid; ~ **ing**, skuimend; ~ **ing tendency**, skuimneiging; ~ **less**, skuimloos; ~ **plastic**, skuimplastiek; ~ **rubber**, sponsrubber, skuimrubber; ~ **y**, vol skuim, skuimend, skuimagtig.
fob[1], (n) sakkie, oorlosiesakkie; (v) in die sak steek.
fob[2], (n) kullery, slenter; (v) (**-bed**), kul, mislei, fop; aansmeer, afsmeer; ~ *off upon*, afsmeer aan.
foc'al, brandpunt=, fokaal; ~ **depth**, fokusdiepte,

brandpuntafstand, fokusafstand; ~ **iza'tion**, instelling; ~ **ize**, in 'n brandpunt verenig, fokaliseer; ~ **length**, brandpuntafstand; ~ **plane**, beeldvlak; brandvlak (lens); ~ **point**, fokus, brandpunt.

fo'c's'le = **forecastle**.

foc'us, (n) **(foci, -es)**, brandpunt, fokus; haard (van siekte); ~ *the LIGHTS*, die ligte instel; *OUT of* ~, uit fokus, onskerp; swak ingestel; (v) saamtrek, saambring, instel, konsentreer; justeer, fokusseer; ~ **ing screen**, instelmatglas; ~ **ing slide**, rigskuifie (geweer).

fodd'er, (n) voer; (v) voer; ~ **crop**, voergewas; ~ **grass**, voergras, hooi(gras); ~ **plant**, voerplant; ~ **tree**, voerboom.

foe, vyand; teenstander; ~ **man**, vyand.

foet'al, fetaal.

foet'us, ongebore vrug, fetus.

fog¹, (n) nagras.

fog², (n) mis, newel; vlek (op foto); *in a* ~, buite raad wees; beneweld; (v) **(-ged)**, benewel; 'n missinjaal blaas; versluier, verbyster, verwar, vlek (van foto); mistig (wasig) maak; ~ **-bank**, misbank; ~ **-belt**, misgordel; ~ **-bound**, deur swaar mis opgehou; ~ **bow**, newelring.

fog'ey, (-s), remskoen (fig.); *old* ~, remskoen; ~ **ism**, remskoenagtigheid, ouderwetsheid.

fog: ~ **-flying**, misweervlieëry; ~ **ged**, gevlek, met vlekke (ou boek); beneweld; ~ **giness**, mistigheid, wasigheid; ~ **ging**, wasemvorming; aanslag (op ruit); ~ **gy**, mistig, newelig; benewel; gesluier, dof, vaag (foto); onduidelik; ~ **-horn**, mishoring; ~ **lamp**, mislamp; ~ **light**, mislig; ~ **-signal**, missinjaal; ~ **veil**, missluier.

fog'y, (fogies) = **fogey**.

foi'ble, swakheid, swak kant; voorpunt (swaard).

foie gras', ganslewer.

foil¹, (n) skermdegen, floret.

foil², (n) bladmetaal; kwikverf (agter spieël), foelie, foeliesel; bladgoud; (v) verfoelie; uitbring.

foil³, (n) spoor (van wild); verydeling; neerlaag, mislukking; (v) verydel, laat skipbreuk ly; v.d. spoor bring; oorwin, oortref, uitoorlê; teleurstel; in verleentheid bring; *be* ~ *ed*, die onderspit gedelf; van die spoor gebring.

foi'son, (arch.), oorvloed.

foist, iets onregmatig inskuif; aansmeer; ~ *IN*, onderskuif, binnesmokkel; ~ *oneself ONTO someone*, jou aan iem. opdring; ~ *SOMETHING on(to) someone*, aan iem. iets afsmeer.

fold¹, (n) vou; plooi; bog; kronkeling; (v) vou; plooi; opklap; ~ *ABOUT*, omsluit; toevou; ~ *in one's ARMS*, in die arms sluit; ~ *one's ARMS*, die arms vou; ~ *BACK*, omvou; ~ *to one's BREAST*, teen die bors druk; ~ *DOWN*, omplooi; afklap; ~ *one's HANDS*, die hande vou; niks doen nie; ~ *IN*, invou; insluit; ~ *in PAPER*, in papier toedraai; ~ *TOGETHER*, saamvou; ~ *UP*, toevou; opvou; bankrot raak; inmekaarsak.

fold², (n) skaapkraal, hok; die kerk, die gelowiges, kudde; skoot (v.d. kerk); *BACK in the* ~, terug onder die ou sambreel; *LEAVE the (political)* ~, uit die span spring; (v) op(sluit; in die kraal jaag.

fold: ~ **able**, voubaar; ~ **er**, vouer, voubeen; (gevoude) sirkulêre; soommasjien.

fold'ing, (n) vou, plooi(ing); kronkeling; (a) vouend, voubaar, vou=; ~ **arm**, vouarm; ~ **bed(stead)**, voubed, voukatel; ~ **boat**, vouskuit; ~ **camera**, klapkamera; ~ **chair**, voustoel; ~ **crops**, afweigewasse; ~ **door**, voudeur, oopslaande deur, dubbeldeur, konsertinadeur, portfisiedeur; ~ **hood**, voubare kap, voukap; ~ **ladder**, trapleer; ~ **leg**, voupoot; ~ **machine**, voumasjien; ~ **mirror**, vouspieël; ~ **rule**, vouduimstok; ~ **seat**, klapbank, klapstoel; ~ **screen**, vouskerm; ~ **sight**, klapvisier; ~ **table**, voutafel, klaptafel; ~ **wing**, vouvlerk.

fold' mountain, plooiingsberg.

folia'ceous, blaaragtig, bladvormig, blad=; ~ **moss**, blaarmos.

fol'iage, lommer, loof, blare, gebladerte, lower; ~ **leaf**, loofblaar; ~ **plant**, loofplant, blaarplant; ~ **tree**, lowerboom, loofboom.

fol'iar, blaar=, blad=; ~ **feed**, blaarvoedsel.

fol'iate, (v) baie dun slaan, plet; foliëer (blaaie van boek); dek, blare kry; versier met loofwerk; foelie (spieël); (a) geblaar, blaaragtig; blaarvormig.

folia'tion, botting, blaarvorming, uitloping (bot.); foliëring (drukwerk); pletwerk.

fol'ic acid, folinesuur, foliensuur.

fol'io, (n) **(-s)**, bladsy; folio; foliant; (a) folio=; ~ **book**, folioboek; ~ **edition**, folio-uitgawe; ~ **le**, blaartjie; ~ **page**, foliobladsy.

fol'iose, digblarig.

fol'io volume, foliant.

folk, (die) mense; volk; volksang; folk; *GENTLE* ~, die hoë mense; *LITTLE* ~ *s*, die kleintjies; *the OLD* ~ *s*, die ou mense; *OTHER* ~ *s*, ander; ~ *SAY*, hulle sê; ~ **art**, volkskuns; ~ **character**, volksaard; ~ **custom**, volksgewoonte; ~ **-dance**, volkspele; volksdans; ~ **dancer**, volkspeler; volksdanser; ~ **etymology**, volksetimologie; ~ **-lore**, volksoorleweringe, volkskunde, folklore; ~ **lorist**, volkskundige; **folkloris**; ~ **loristic**, folkloristies; ~ **medicine**, volksmedisyne; volksgeneeskunde; ~ **migration**, volksverhuising; ~ **music**, volksmusiek; folkmusiek; ~ **opera**, volksopera; ~ **song**, volksliedjie; folklied(jie); ~ **sy**, vriendelik, gesellig; ~ **tale**, volksvertelling, volksverhaal; sprokie.

foll'icle, saadhuisie, kokervrug; klier; blasie; follikel (anat.).

follic'ular, follikulêr.

foll'ow, volg; navolg; gehoorsaam; begryp (vraag); dien; aanhang, agteraan loop, naloop; uitoefen (beroep); gepaard gaan met; ~ *AFTER*, nastreef, najaag; *AS* ~ *s*, soos volg; ~ *someone CLOSELY*, op iem. se hakskene trap; *DO you* ~ ? verstaan jy? *it DOESN'T* ~, dit sê nie; dis nie te sê nie; ~ *the DRUM*, soldaat wees; *trade* ~ *s the FLAG*, handel volg die vlag; ~ *in his FOOTSTEPS*, in sy spoor volg; ~ *one's NOSE*, 'n willekeurige weg volg; ~ *ON*, volhard, volhou; 'n volgbeurt kry (kr.); ~ *the PLOUGH*, boer wees; ~ *the SEA*, matroos wees; ~ *SUIT*, dieselfde doen; kleur beken; ~ *THROUGH*, deurswaai (gholf); ~ *UP*, op iem. se hakke bly; voortsit; ondersteun; ~ *in the WAKE of*, onmiddellik volg op; navolg.

foll'ower, navolger; getroue volgeling; proseliet; vryer; drukstuk; (pl) aanhang; ~ **aircraft**, volgvliegtuig; ~ **plate**, drukplaat; ~ **ring**, drukring.

foll'owing, (n) gevolg; trein; aanhang; (a) volgende, eersvolgende, eerskomende, onderstaande; ~ **distance**, volgafstand; ~ **wind**, wind van agter.

foll'ow: ~ **-on**, opvolgbeurt (kr.); ~ **-up**, vervolgsirkulêre, opvolgbrief; voortsettingswerk, nabehandeling.

foll'y (follies), dwaasheid, dolheid, malstreek, stommiteit, sotheid, gekkewerk, gekkigheid.

foment', aankweek, koester; aanmoedig; aanwakker, aanhits; fomenteer, baai, met warm omslae behandel; ~ **a'tion**, koestering, aanmoediging; aanhitsing, aanstoking; warm omslag, warmwaterverband, fomentasie; ~ **er**, aanstoker.

fond, verlief; gek, sot, dwaas; oordrewe teer; innig, liefhebbend; ~ *CHILDREN*, liefhebbende kinders; ~ *DESIRE*, hartewens; *be* ~ *OF*, (baie) hou van; ~ *of READING*, graag lees.

fon'dant, borsplaat, fondant (soort lekker).

fon'dle, liefkoos, streel, vertroetel, aanhaal.

fond'ling, liefling, hartjie.

fond'ly, liefkosend; liefderyk; vurig, innig; dwaaslik.

fond'ness, versotheid; verliefdheid; geneentheid; gehegtheid; teerheid; liefde.

font, doopbakkie, doopbekken, doopvont; wywaterbakkie; oliebakkie; ~ **al**, eerste, oorspronklik; doop=.

fontanel(le)', fontanel.

food, kos, voedsel, eetware, ete, spyse; voer; ~ *and CLOTHING*, voedsel en deksel; ~ *and DRINK*, eet- en drinkgoed; *be* ~ *for the FISHES*, verdrink; kos vir die haaie; ~ *for the JOURNEY*, padkos; *one man's* ~ *is another man's POISON*, die een se dood is die ander se brood; *it PROVIDES* ~ *for thought*, dit stem tot nadenke; dit gee stof tot nadenke; ~ *for THOUGHT*, stof tot nadenke; *TIN= NED* ~, blikkieskos; *be* ~ *for WORMS*, dood *fool*   *foot*

wees; ~ **ball**, kosbal; ~ **card**, voedselkaart; ~ **chopper**, kosmeule; ~ **consumption**, voedselverbruik; ~ **fad**, kosgier; ~ **fish**, eetvis; ~ **fruit**, voedselvrug; ~ **hygiene**, voedselhigiëne; ~ **poisoning**, voedselvergiftiging; ~ **stuffs**, voedingstowwe; koswaare, eetware, eetgoed; ~-**supplies**, mondbehoeftes, proviand; voedselvoorrade; ~ **value**, voedingswaarde; ~-**warmer**, konfoor.

fool¹, (n) vrugteslaai; skuimnagereg.

fool², (n) dwaas, gek, sot; hofnar; gekskap (fig.); swaap; *I'd BE a ~ to do it*, ek sal dit nooit as te nimmer doen nie; ek sal gek wees om dit te doen; *a ~'s BOLT is soon shot*, 'n dwaas is gou uitgeredeneer; *go on a ~'s ERRAND*, vir die gek loop; *send one on a ~'s ERRAND*, iem. vir die gek laat loop; *not allow oneself to be MADE a ~ of*, nie met jou laat spot nie; *MAKE a ~ of oneself*, jou belaglik maak; jou mal aanstel; *PLAY the ~*, die gek skeer; *a ~ and his MONEY are soon parted*, 'n gek se geld brand 'n gat in sy sak; *no ~ like an OLD ~*, 'n ou gek is die ergste (dwaaste); oud mal gaan boweal; *be a ~ for one's PAINS*, verniet moeite doen; *every man is a ~ or a PHYSICIAN at forty*, 'n verstandige man het aan 'n dokter geen behoefte nie; *PLAY the ~ with someone*, die gek met iem. skeer; 'n lopie met iem. neem; *a ~ can ask more QUESTIONS in an hour than a wise man can answer in seven years*, een gek kan meer vrae stel as wat honderd wyses kan beantwoord; ~*s RUSH in where angels fear to tread*, 'n dwaas storm in waar 'n wyse huiwer; *TAKE someone for a ~*, meen dat iem. 'n bobbejaan is; *as the ~ THINKS, the bell clinks*, elke dwaas glo wat hy graag wil weet; (v) korswel, grappe verkoop, die gek skeer, gekskeer; vir die gek hou; bedrieg, kul, fop; ~ *ABOUT*, rondpeuter; ~ *AWAY*, vermors; ~**ery**, gekskeerdery; dwaasheid; ~**hardiness**, roekeloosheid, vermetelheid, waaghals(er)igheid; ~**hardy**, roekeloos, onbesonne, vermetel, waaghalsig; ~**ing**, gekskeerdery; foppery; ~**ish**, dwaas, mal, verspot, uitsinnig, simpel; belaglik; sot, stuitig, gek(lik); ~**ishly**, dwaas; ~**ishness**, dwaasheid, uitsinnigheid, dolheid; stuitigheid; ~**oc'racy**, regering deur dwase, gekkedom; ~**proof**, onvernielbaar, onbreekbaar; onfeilbaar; bestand teen slegte behandeling; bedryfseker; peutervry, flousvry.

fools'cap¹, foliopapier.

fool's cap², sotskap, narrekap.

fool's': ~ **mate**, gekkemat, narremat (skaak); ~ **paradise**, luilekkerland; gekkeparadys; *live in a ~ paradise*, in 'n droomwêreld leef.

foot¹, (n) versvoet.

foot², (n) (**feet**), voet; poot (van dier); voetstuk; onderent, voetenent; voet(maat); lettervoet; voetvolk, infanterie; *AT one's feet*, aan jou voete; *AT the ~*, onderaan; *put someone BACK on his feet*, iem. weer op die been help; *BE on one's feet*, op die been wees; 'n bestaan maak, *put one's REST ~ forward*, die beste beentjie voorsit; *have a ~ in both CAMPS*, op twee stoele sit; *CATCH someone on the wrong foot*, iem. onvoorbereid betrap; iem. onverwags in die verleentheid bring; *feet of CLAY*, kleivoete; *have COLD feet*, bang word; in die knyp sit; *FALL on one's feet*, op jou voete te lande kom; in die botter val; *FIND one's feet*, op die been kom; koers kry; *op dreef (stryk) kom*; *a mare with FOAL at ~*, 'n merrie met 'n vul; *GET someone on(to) his feet again*, iem. weer op die been help; *have one ~ in the GRAVE*, met die een voet in die graf staan; *have both one's feet firmly on the GROUND*, met albei voete vas op die grond staan; *HAVE something on ~*, iets aan die gang hê; *HELP someone find his feet*, *HELP someone to his feet*, iem. op die been help; *put one's ~ INTO it*, jou mond verbrand; jou mond verbypraat; 'n flater begaan; jou lelik vergaloppeer; skop (voetbal); *KEEP on one's feet*, op die been bly; *KNOCK someone's feet out from under him (someone off his feet)*, iem. se bene onder hom uitslaan; *KNOW as much as my ~*, soveel daarvan weet as 'n kat van saffraan; niks daarvan weet nie; *know (have) the LENGTH of someone's ~*, bewus wees van iem. se beperkings; weet wat iem. se swak

(kant) is; *sit at the feet of a MASTER*, aan die voete van Gamaliël sit; *unable to MOVE a ~*, geen voet kan versit (verroer) nie; *MY ~! onsin! kaf! pure bog!* *have set one's ~ on someone's NECK*, iem. die voet op die nek hou; *run someone OFF his feet*, iem. plat (disnis) loop (werk, speel); *ON ~*, te voet, met snaar en st(r)amboel; op die been; *be ON one's feet all the time*, die hele dag op die been wees; *PUT one's ~ down*, nie toelaat nie; sê tot hiertoe en nie verder nie; *RISE to one's feet*, opstaan; *SET on ~*, oprig; op tou sit; *set ~ on SHORE*, voet aan wal sit; *find no rest for the SOLE of one's ~*, geen rus vir die holte van 'n mens se voet vind nie; *STAND on one's own feet*, op jou eie bene staan; op eie wieke drywe; *SWIFT of ~*, vinnig; rats, vlug ter been; *thrust one's feet under another man's TABLE*, jou voete onder anderman se tafel sit; *THROW oneself at the feet of*, iem. te voet val; *TREAD under ~*, met die voete vertrap; *TRIP over one's own feet*, oor jou eie voete val; *UNDER ~*, in die pad; onder 'n mens se voete; *be UNSTEADY on one's feet*, hoog en laag trap; nie vas op jou bene wees nie; (v) betree, trap; met die pote gryp (valk); 'n voet aanbrei; loop, dans; skop (voetbal); ~ *the BILL*, opdok, betaal; *be the one who ~s the BILL*, die kind v.d rekening wees; ~ *IT*, te voet loop; afloop; dans, skoffel; ~ *UP to*, bedra, oploop tot; ~-**age**, voetmaat; lengte; voetafstand; filmlengte; ~ **and mouth disease**, bek-en-klouseer.

foot'ball, voetbal; *be the ~ of*, die speelbal wees van; ~ **bladder**, voetbalblaas; ~ **boot**, voetbalskoen; ~ **club**, voetbalklub; ~**er**, voetbalspeler; voetballer; ~ **field**, voetbalveld; ~ **jersey**, voetbaltrui; ~ **match**, voetbalwedstryd; ~ **player**, voetbalspeler; ~ **pool**, voetbalpot (geld); ~ **season**, voetbalseisoen; ~ **shorts**, voetbalbroek; ~ **togs**, voetbalklere; ~ **union**, voetbalunie.

foot: ~-**bath**, voetbad; voetbalie; ~-**block**, voetblok; ~-**blower**, trapblaasbalk; ~ **board**, staanplank, treeplank, voetplank; ~**boy**, livreikneg; ~-**brake**, voetrem; ~-**breadth**, voetbreedte; ~-**bridge**, voetbrug; ~-**control**, voetstuur; ~**ed**, met voete; *BARE-*~**ed**, kaalvoet; *FOUR-*~**ed**, viervoetig; ~**er**, stapper; sokker(voetbal); ~ **fall**, loopgeluid; stapgeluid; ~-**fault**, voetfout; trapfout (tennis); ~-**gear**, skoeisel; *F*~ **Guards**, lyfwag te voet; ~-**hill(s)**, uitloper(s); voetrantjie(s), voorheuwel(s); ~ **hold**, vastrapplek, houvas; basis, steunpunt; *gain a ~hold*, vaste voet kry.

foot'ing, vastrapplek; voetstuk; *on an EQUAL ~*, op voet van gelykheid; op gelyke voet; *FIND a firm ~*, vaste voet kry; *GET a ~*, 'n staanplek kry; *be on a GOOD ~ with someone*, op goeie voet wees met iem.; *(UP)ON the same ~*, op dieselfde voet; *on a WAR ~*, op voet van oorlog.

foot: ~-**irons**, klemysters; ~-**joint**, hoefgewrig; ~-**lathe**, trapdraaibank.

foo'tle, (n) kaf, onsin; (v) gekskeer; knoei.

foot: ~**less**, sonder voete; ~-**lever**, voetpedaal, voethefboom; ~ **light(s)**, voetlig(te); *appear before the ~ lights*, voor die voetligte verskyn.

foo'tling, beuselagtig.

foot: ~ **man**, huiskneg, lakei; infanteris, ~ **mark**, voetspoor; ~-**mat**, voetmatjie; ~-**muff**, voetsak; ~ **note**, voetnoot, verwysing, aantekening; ~ **pace**, stapsnelheid; ~ **pad**, struikrower; ~-**page**, page, hofknapie; ~-**passenger**, voetganger; ~-**path**, voetpad; sypad; wandelpaadjie; ~-**plate**, treeplank; staanbord; ~-**police**, voetpolisie; ~-**pound**, voetpond; ~-**powder**, voetpoeier; ~ **print**, spoor; ~-**pump**, voetpomp; ~-**race**, wedloop, hardlopery; ~-**rest**, voetrus; voetbankie; ~-**rot**, vrotpootjie (vee); stamvrot (by plante); ~-**rule**, duimstok; ~ **s**, besinksel, moer, afval; ~-**scraper**, voetskraper; ~-**screw**, stelskroef; ~-**slog**, voetslaan, stap; ~-**slogger**, stapper; ~-**soldier**, voetsoldaat; voetkneg; infanteris; ~ **sore**, deurgeloop, met seer voete; ~ **stalk**, bladsteel; ~ **step**, voetstap; *follow in another's ~ steps*, in iem. se voetspore volg; ~-**stone**, fondamentsteen; voetsteen (van graf); grafsteen; ~ **stool**, voetbankie; stofie, skabel, tabouret; ~-**stove**, (voet)stofie; ~ **sure**, vas op die

voete; ~**-tub**, voetbalie; ~**-valve**, bodemklep, suigklep; ~**-warmer**, voetstoof; voetkruik; ~**way**, looppad; voetpad, sypaadjie, wandelpaadjie; ~**wear**, voetbedekking, skoene, skoeisel; ~**wear factory**, skoenfabriek; ~**-wiper**, voetskraper; ~**-work**, voetwerk; ~**-worn**, deurgeloop, seervoer.

foo'zle, (n) knoeihou (gholf); (v) (ver)knoei, lomp slaan, opdons; ~**r**, knoeier.

fop¹, dwaasheid.

fop², modegek, ydeltuit; ~**pery**, pronkery, opskik.

fopp'ish, ydel, pronkerig, fatterig; ~**ness**, ydelheid, fatterigheid.

for, (prep) vir; weens, om; in plaas van; teen; namens; ten behoewe van; gedurende; ~ *ALL that*, in weerwil van dit alles; *AS* ~, wat betref; *things look BAD* ~ *you*, sake lyk vir jou lelik; *if it hadn't BEEN* ~ *him*, as hy nie gehelp het nie; as dit nie aan hom gelê het nie; *there is nothing* ~ *it BUT*, daar is geen ander plan nie as; *CARE* ~, omgee vir; ~ *all I CARE*, vir my part; ~ *COMPANY*, as geselskap; *leave* ~ *DEAD*, vir dood laat lê; ~ *EXAMPLE*, byvoorbeeld; *know* ~ *a FACT*, beslis weet; ~ *FEAR of*, uit vrees vir; *FIGHT* ~ *dear life*, veg so al wat jy kan; *GO* ~ *him*, pak hom; klim (in) hom in; *GO* ~ *a walk*, 'n end gaan loop; *all* ~ *her GOOD*, alles om haar beswil; ~ *GOODNESS' sake*, in hemelsnaam; *oh* ~ *a HORSE!* as ek maar 'n perd gehad het! ~ *HOURS*, ure lank; ~ *JOY*, van vreugde; ~ *all I KNOW*, bes moontlik, sover ek weet; *they have LEFT* ~, hulle het vertrek na; ~ *LIFE*, lewenslank; *I cannot do it* ~ *the LIFE of me*, ek kan dit nie doen nie, al slaan jy my dood; ~ *LONG*, lank; *LONG* ~, verlang na; *it is not* ~ *ME*, dit lê nie op my weg nie; ~ *as MUCH as*, vir sover; vir net soveel; *it is NOT for me to*, dit lê nie op my weg nie om; ~ *NOTHING*, verniet, tevergeefs; *ONCE* ~ *all*, eens vir altyd; *I* ~ *ONE*, wat my betref; ek vir my; ~ *ONE thing*, om maar een ding te noem; ~ *my PART*, wat my betref; ~ *the PRESENT*, vir eers, voorlopig, vir die teenswoordige; *READY* ~, klaar vir; ~ *this REASON*, om hierdie rede; ~ *the REST*, wat die res betref; ~ *SALE*, te koop; ~ *my SAKE*, om my ontwil; *it is not* ~ *me to SAY*, dit pas my nie om te sê nie; ~ *all you SAY*, ondanks alles wat jy sê; *time* ~ *SCHOOL*, tyd om skool toe te gaan; ~ *SHAME!* skande! skaam jou! *TAKE* ~ *granted*, as vanselfsprekend aanneem; ~ *a TIME*, 'n tyd lank; ~ *WANT of*, uit gebrek aan; *WHAT* ~, waarom? *WORD* ~ *word*, woord vir woord; *too beautiful* ~ *WORDS*, onbeskryflik mooi; ~ *all the WORLD*, presies; *not* ~ *the WORLD*, vir niks ter wêreld nie; ~ *YEARS*, jare lank; (conj.) want, omdat, omrede, aangesien; *he will succeed* ~ *he has talent*, hy sal slaag, want hy is talentvol.

fo'rage, (n) voer, kos; strooptog; (v) kos soek, snuffel; voer verskaf; stroop, roof, plunder; ~**-cap**, kwartierpet; ~**-cutter**, voersnyer; ~**-harvester**, voeroessnyer; ~**-machine**, voermasjien; ~**r**, voersoeker; voerverskaffer.

fo'raging-party, patrollie.

foram'en, (foramina), opening, gaatjie, foramen.

forasmuch' as, aangesien, nademaal.

fo'ray, (n) strooptog, inval; (v) roof, plunder.

forbear', **forb'ear¹**, (n) voorvader, voorstaat.

forbear'², (v) (..bore, ..borne), laat staan; nalaat; vermy; verdra; (jou) onthou (van); (jou) inhou; geduld hê; ~**ance**, nalating; onthouding; versaking; verdraagsaamheid; geduld; ~**ing**, verdraagsaam; geduldig; toegewend.

forbid', (..bad(e), -den), verbied, belet; verhinder; *HEAVEN* ~, mag God dit verhoed; ~ *HIM to go*, belet hom om te gaan; *SPACE* ~ *s*, die ruimte laat dit nie toe nie.

forbid'den, ongeoorloof, verbode; ~ *AREA*, verbode terrein; ~ *FRUIT*, verbode vrugte; ~ *fruit is SWEET*, verbode vrugte smaak die soetste; *he was* ~ *WINE*, wyn is hom belet.

forbid'ding, afskrikkend, afskuwekkend, verhinderend; bars, onaangenaam.

force, (n) krag; mag; geweld; dwang, noodsaak; oortuigingskrag; (pl) troepe, weermag; ~ *of ARMS*,

wapengeweld; *BE in* ~ *(laws)*, van krag wees, geldig wees; *BY* ~, met geweld; *BY* ~ *of*, deur middel van; *the* ~ *of CIRCUMSTANCES*, die druk van omstandighede; *COME into* ~, in werking tree; *COMING into* ~, vankragwording; *in FULL* ~, in volle krag; in groot getalle; ~ *of GRAVITY*, swaartekrag; *in GREAT* ~, kragtig, sterk; *by* ~ *of HABIT*, uit gewoonte; ~ *of IMPACT*, trefkrag; *IN* ~, van krag; in groot getalle; ~ *of LAW*, krag van wet, regsgeldigheid; *by MAIN* ~, met krag en mag; *by sheer* ~ *of NUMBERS*, eenvoudig deur oormag; *PUT into* ~, in werking stel; *what you SAY has* ~, daar sit iets in wat jy sê; *be a SPENT* ~, uitgebak wees; klaar wees; (v) dwing, dring, forseer, verplig; oorweldig, oormeester; oopbreek, laat spring, oopsluit (brandkas); onteer, verkrag; in 'n broeikas kweek; geweld aandoen; afdwing; ~ *BACK*, terugdrywe; ~ *FROM*, afdwing, afpers; ~ *the GAME*, gang in die spel bring; ~ *a GAP*, 'n bres slaan; ~ *someone's HAND*, iem. dwing; ~ *ON*, opdring; ~ *it ON someone*, dit opdring aan iem.; ~ *OPEN*, oopbreek; ~ *OUT of someone*, uit iem. pomp; ~ *the PACE*, hard aanjaag; ~ *a PASSAGE*, met geweld 'n deurtog baan; ~ *up PRICES*, pryse opdryf; ~ *a SMILE*, jou dwing om te glimlag; ~ *oneself UPON*, jou opdring aan; ~ *one's VOICE*, jou stem ooreis; ~ *one's WAY*, deurdruk, jou weg baan.

forced, gemaak, onnatuurlik, gesog, gekunsteld; gedwonge; ~ *FEEDING*, dwangvoeding; ~ *LABOUR*, dwangarbeid, gedwonge arbeid; ~ *LANDING*, noodlanding; ~ *LOAN*, gedwonge lening; ~ *MARCH*, noodmars; gedwonge tog; ~ *MOVE*, gedwonge set (skaak); ~ *SMILE*, gedwonge glimlag; ~ *STRAWBERRIES*, aarbeie uit 'n broeikas.

force: ~**-feed lubrication**, druksmering; ~**ful**, geweldig; kragtig; ~**ful language**, mannetaal; ~**fulness**, kragdadigheid; ~**less**, krag(te)loos; ~**meat**, vleisvulsel.

for'ceps, tang, tandetrekker; verlostang; pinset; *dental* ~, kiestang.

force'-pump, drukpomp.

for'cible, kragtig, heftig, geweldig; indrukwekkend; gewelddadig; ~ *language*, mannetaal.

for'cibly, met geweld; op indrukwekkende manier.

for'cing, forsering; ~ **frame**, broeiraam; ~ **house**, broeikas; ~ **tube**, spuitbuisie.

ford, (n) drif, deurgaanplek; (v) deurry, deurgaan, deurwaad; ~**able**, deurwaadbaar; passabel, oorgaanbaar; ~**age**, pontgeld.

fordone', uitgeput, klaar.

fore, (n) voorgedeelte, voorpunt, voorgrond; *COME to the* ~, op die voorgrond kom; *TO the* ~, reg; byderhand; op die voorgrond; (a) voor=; voorste; (adv., prep) voor; ~ *and aft*, voor en agter; langskeeps; (interj.) voor! oppas! pas op! (gholf).

fore'arm,¹ (n) voorarm.

forearm'², (v) vooruit wapen.

fore'-arm drive, voorarmhou.

fore'-axle, vooras.

fore'bear = **forbear¹**.

forebode', voorspel; 'n voorgevoel hê; ~**ment**, voorgevoel.

forebod'ing, voorspelling; voorspooksel; voorgevoel.

fore'-cabin, voorkajuit.

fore'-caddy, voorjoggie.

fore'-carriage, voorstel (van wa).

fore'cast, (n) plan, ontwerp; vooruitskatting; projeksie; voorspelling, beraming.

forecast', (v) (~), vooruitskat, projekteer, voorspel; raam; ontwerp; voorsien; ~**er**, voorspeller, vooruitskatter.

fore'casting, vooruitskatting; voorspelling; *long-range* ~, langtermynvooruitskatting; prognostika, prognostiek; futorologie.

fore'castle, voorkasteel; bak, vooronder.

foreclose', teenhou, afsny; onmoontlik maak; uitsluit; vooraf beslis; ~ *a mortgage*, 'n verband oproep.

foreclo'sure, preklusie, uitsluiting; verhindering; oproeping (van verband).

fore'court, voorhof, voorplein; voorbaan.

fore'date, vroeër dateer.
fore'deck, voordek.
foredoom', voorbeskik; voorspel; doem.
fore: ~-**end**, voorend; ~**father**, voorvader; (pl) voorgeslag, voorsate; ~-**field**, voorterrein; ~**finger**, voorvinger, wysvinger; ~**foot**, (..feet), voorpoot.
fore'front, voorgewel; voorkant, voorent; voorste gelid; voorhoede; *be in the* ~, op die voorpunt wees; in die voorhoede wees.
fore'gift, huurpremie.
forego', (**forewent**, **foregone**), voorgaan; ~**er**, voorganger; ~**ing**, voorafgaande, bostaande, voornoemde.
foregone', verby; afgedaan; ~ *conclusion*, 'n by voorbaat uitgemaakte saak; 'n deurgestoke kaart; bevooroordeelde gevolgtrekking.
fore'ground, voorgrond.
fore'hand, (n) voorhand; voorkant (van perd); (a) voorarm-; ~ **drive**, ~ **stroke**, voorarmhou; ~ **play**, voorarmspel.
fore'head, voorhoof, voorkop.
fore'hock, voorpootvleis (vark).
fore'hold, voorruim.
fo'reign, uitheems, buitelands; vreemd; *a* ~ *ACCENT*, 'n vreemde (uitheemse) uitspraak; *it is* ~ *to his NATURE*, dit is teen sy natuur; *in* ~ *PARTS*, in die vreemde; ~ **body**, vreemde stof; ~ **country**, buiteland; ~ **editor**, redakteur buiteland; ~**er**, uitlander, buitelander, anderlander, vreemdeling, andersoeman; ~ **exchange**, vreemde valuta; F~ **Legion**, Vreemdelingelegioen; ~ **matter**, vreemde stof; ~**ness**, vreemdheid, uitheemsheid; F~ **Office**, (Britse) kantoor vir buitelandse sake; F~ **Secretary**, minister van buitelandse sake; ~ **service**, buitelandse diens; ~ **vehicle**, buitelandse voertuig.
forejudge', voorbarig (vooruit) oordeel.
foreknow', (..knew, -n), voorsien; vooraf weet.
foreknow'ledge, voorkennis; voorwetenskap.
fo'rel, boekbindersperkament.
fore'land, landtong, kaap; voorland.
fore'leg, voorpoot; voorbeen.
fore'lock¹, (n) kuif; *take time by the* ~, die kans waarneem; as dit pap reën, moet jy skep; gebruik maak van die gunstige oomblik.
fore'lock², (n) wig, sluitspy; (v) 'n wig inslaan.
fore'man, (..men), voorsitter (van jurie); voorman, opsigter; (span)baas, ploegbaas; fabriekopsigter, mandoor; ~ *of works*, bouvoorman; ~-**checker**, voormanlaaimeester.
fore'mast, voormas, fokmas.
fore'mentioned, voornoem(d).
fore'milk, eerste melk.
fore'most, eerste, voorste, vernaamste; vooraanstaande; *first and* ~, in die allereerste plek.
fore'name, voornaam; ~**d**, voornoem(d).
fore'noon, voormiddag.
foren'sic, regs-, geregtelik, juridies, forensies; ~ **medicine**, geregtelike geneeskunde.
foreordain', voorbeskik, voorbestem.
foreordina'tion, voorbeskikking.
fore: ~-**payment**, vooruitbetaling; ~**peak**, voorender, piek (van skip); ~ **plane**, voorloper; ~ **quarter**, voorkwart.
fore'quoted, voormeld.
fore-reach', inhaal; wen op; verbygaan.
forerun', (..ran, ..run), voorafgaan, voorspel; ~**ner**, voorloper, voorbode, wegbereider.
foresaid', voormeld.
fore'sail, fok, fokseil, voorseil.
foresee', (..saw, -n), voorsien, vooruitsien; ~**able**, voorsienbaar, voorspelbaar; *in the able future*, binne afsienbare tyd.
foreshad'ow, dui, voorspel, voorafskadu; aankondig; ~**ing**, voorafskaduwing.
fore'ship, voorskip.
fore'shore, voorstrand, vloedstreep, strandgebied, (see)strand.
foreshort'en, verkort; in perspektief sien.
foreshow', (-ed, -n), voorspel, in die vooruitsig stel.
fore'side, voorkant.
fore'sight¹, vooruitsiendheid, voorkennis; oorleg, voorsorg.

fore'sight², korrel (van geweer).
fore'skin, voorhuid.
fo'rest, (n) bos, woud; *a* ~ *of masts*, 'n woud maste; (v) bebos; ~**al**, bos-; boswese-.
forestall', voorkom; voor wees; opkoop; voorspring; ~**er**, voorspringer; opkoper.
fore'stay, fokstag; ~ **sail**, stormfok.
fo'rest: ~-**blend** (**brick**), boombassteen; ~ **conservancy**, bosbewaring; ~ **conservator**, bosbewaarder; ~ **craft**, bosboukunde; ~-**dweller**, bosbewoner; ~**er**, bosbewoner; boswagter, bosopsigter, bosbouer, houtvester; ~ **fire**, bosbrand; ~-**fly**, perdevlieg; ~ **management**, bosbestuur; ~ **officer**, bos(bou)beampte; ~ **reserve**, bosreservaat; ~**ry**, houtvestery; boswese, bosbou; boswêreld; *DEPARTMENT of F~ry*, Departement van Bosbou; *SECRETARY for F~ry*, Sekretaris van Bosbou; ~-**tree**, bosboom.
fore'taste, (n) voorsmaak, voorproef.
foretaste', (v) vooraf proe; 'n voorsmaak kry van, by voorbaat geniet.
foretell', (..**told**), voorspel, vooruitsê, wiggel, profeteer, waarsê.
fore'thought, voorbedagtheid; voorsorg, oorleg.
fore'time, voortyd, oertyd.
fore'token, (n) voorteken; voorbode.
fore'tooth, (..**teeth**), voortand, snytand.
fore'top, voormars (skip); ~ **mast**, voorsteng; ~ **sail**, voormarsseil.
fore'type, voorloper, prototipe.
forev'er, ewig, vir altoos.
forewarn', vooruit waarsku; -*ed is forearmed*, voorkoming is beter as genesing.
fore'wheel, voorwiel; ~ **drive**, voorwielaandrywing.
fore'width, voorbaan (van rok).
fore'woman, voorsitster (van 'n vrouejurie), voorvrou; opsigster.
fore'word, voorwoord, inleiding, voorberig.
forf'eit, (n) verbeuring; boete; rougeld; pand, polfyntjie; (pl) pandspel; *DECLARE something* ~, iets verbeurd verklaar; *PLAY at* ~*s*, pand speel; (v) verbeur, boet, verloor; ~ *one's RIGHTS*, jou regte verbeur; ~ *one's WORD*, sy woord verbreek; ~**able**, verbeurbaar; verpandbaar; ~**clause**, verbeuringsbeding; ~ **money**, roukoop; ~**ure**, verbeuring, verbeurdverklaring; verlies; ~**ures**, verbeurdverklaarde geld.
forfend', verhoed.
forgath'er, vergader, bymekaarkom, versamel.
forgave', *kyk* **forgive**.
forge¹, (n) smidswinkel, (yster)smedery; smid; smidsoond; smeltoond; (v) smee; namaak, vervals (naamtekening); valsheid in geskrifte pleeg.
forge², (v) met moeite vooruitkom; 'n weg baan; ~ *AHEAD*, vooruitkom, vooruitbeur; ~ *one's WAY*, jou weg baan; jou indring.
forge: ~**abil'ity**, smee(d)baarheid; ~**able**, namaakbaar, vervalsbaar; smeebaar; ~-**bellows**, smidsblaasbalk; ~ **coal**, smidskole
forge: ~-**furnace**, smee-oond, ~-**hammer**, smidshamer; ~-**man**, (..men), smeder; vuurwerker; ~-**poker**, vuuryster; ~-**r**, namaker; (skrif)vervalser; valsmunter; ~-**rake**, vuurhark.
forg'ed, gesmee; vervals, nagemaak; ~ **cheque**, vervalste tjek; ~ **iron**, smeeyster; ~ **steel**, smeestaal.
forg'ery, (..**ries**), namaking; (skrif)vervalsing; vals handtekening; ~ *and uttering*, vervalsing en uitgifte.
forge'-slice, vuurskop.
forget', (..**got**, ..**gotten**), vergeet; in gebreke bly; afleer; ~ *ABOUT it*, vergeet dit maar; jy kan maar gaan slaap; ~ *ONESELF*, jou selfbeheersing verloor; onmanierlik wees; ~**ful**, vergeetagtig; ~**fulness**, vergeetagtigheid; nalatigheid; versuim; ~-**me-not**, vergeet-my-nietjie.
forge'-tongs, smeetang.
fogett'able, vergeetlik.
forge'-weld, smeelas.
forg'ing, smeding; naamvervalsing.
forgiv'able, vergeeflik.
forgive', (..**gave**, -**n**), vergeef, vergewe; kwytskeld (skuld); verskoon; begenadig; ~ *and forget*, vergewe en vergeet; ~**ness**, vergifnis; kwytskelding.

forgiv'ing, vergewensgesind; ~**ness,** vergewensgesindheid.
forgo', (**forwent, forgone,**) jou onthou van; laat vaar; afstand doen van; opgee, ontsê.
forgott'en, vergeet, vergete.
fo'rint, forint (munt).
fork, (n) vurk; gaffel; vertakking (van rivier); kruis (van broek); (v) gaffel; skei, splits, vertak; met 'n vurk werk; *have to* ~ *out,* moet opdok; jou hand in jou eie sak moet steek; jou sak moet skud.
forked, verdeel, getak, gesplits; gevurk; gaffelvormig; ~ **end,** gevurkte end; ~ **joint,** vurklas; ~ **lightning,** sigsagblits, streepbliksem; ~ **stick,** mikstok; ~ **yoke,** nekhoutjie.
fork: ~**-link,** vurkskakel; ~**-rod,** vurkstang; ~**-shaped,** vurkvormig; ~**-spanner,** vurksleutel; ~**-tailed drongo,** mikstertbyevanger; ~**-wrench,** vurksleutel.
forlorn', hopeloos, wanhopig; verlore, verlate; rampsalig; vervalle, ellendig; *ALL* ~, verlate; soos 'n uil op 'n kluit; ~ *HOPE,* wanhopige geval; laaste redmiddel; ~ **ness,** verlatenheid; wanhopigheid.
form, (n) fatsoen; skyn; gedaante; vorm, klas, standerd; (skool)bank; lêplek (van haas); drukvorm; formule, formulier; metode; stelsel; formaliteit, pligpleging; *BAD* ~, onbeskof, onmanierlik; nie passend nie; *GOOD* ~, manierlik, soos dit hoort; *be in GOOD* ~, op jou stukke wees; *in GREAT* ~, goed op stryk; *be IN* ~, op stryk wees; op jou stukke wees; *IN the* ~ *of,* in die gedaante (vorm) van; *a MATTER of* ~, 'n blote formaliteit; *OUT of* ~, van stryk af (sport); uit fatsoen; *STRIKE* ~, op slag kom; op dreef kom; op stryk kom; *play at the TOP of one's* ~, op jou beste speel; 'n barshou speel; *TRUE to* ~, vormgetrou; (v) vorm, formeer, maak, skep; vervaardig; afrig; opstel; fatsoeneer; kweek; set; stig; ~ *a COCOON round,* inspin; ~ *an ESTIMATE,* 'n begroting maak; ~ *a HABIT,* 'n gewoonte aanleer; ~ *PART of,* deel uitmaak van.
form'al, uitdruklik, stip, presies; formeel, amptelik, seremonieel; vormlik, stelselmatig; deftig, afgemete, styf; *a* ~ *CALL,* 'n besoek pligshalwe afgelê; *in a* ~ *TONE,* op afgemete toon.
formal'dehyde, formaldehied, formaldehide.
form'alin, formalien.
form'al: ~**ism,** gehegtheid aan vorme, vormdiens; formalisme; ~**ist,** slaaf van vorme; formalis.
formalis'tic, vormlik; formalisties.
formal'ity, (..ties), plegtigheid, afgemetenheid; formaliteit, vorm(likheid); beleefdheidsvorm.
form'alize, formeel maak; wettig; vorm gee aan.
form'ally, formeel, formalier (ong.).
form'ant, formant (fon.); formans.
form'at, formaat (van boek).
forma'tion, vorming, formasie oprigting; opstelling (by dril); afleidingsvorm; *GEOLOGICAL* ~, geologiese formasie; ~ *of GROUND,* terreingesteldheid; *POINT of* ~, opstellingspunt (by dril); ~**-commander,** formasiekommandant; ~ **flight,** formasievlug; ~**-flying,** formasievlieg.
form'ative, (n) formans; formasie (gram.); vormelement; (a) vormend, beeldend, formatief; formansties.
form'-drag, vormweerstand.
formed, gevorm; geset.
form'er, (n) vormer, vormblok, maker; drukvorm; vermoorbeitel; gietvorm; (a) vroeër; vorige, gewese, voormalige, eertydse; (pron) eerste, eertydse; eersgenoemde; *the* ~, die eerste, die eersgenoemde; ~ **ly,** voorheen, voormaals, voortyds, eertyds, vanmelewe, vroeër, eers.
form'-fitting, gefatsoeneer.
form'ic, miere=; ~ **acid,** mieresuur.
formica'tion, jeuking, krieweling.
formidabil'ity, gedugtheid.
form'idable, gedug, vreeslik, formidabel; ~**ness,** gedugtheid.
form'ing, (n) vorming, formering; (a) vormend; ~ **tongs,** vormtang; ~**-tool,** vormwerktuig.
form'less, vormloos; wanstaltig.
form'-master, klasonderwyser.
Formo'sa, Formosa; ~ **n,** (n) Formosaan; (a) Formosaans.

form'ula, (**-s, -e**), voorskrif, resep; formule, formulier; ~**ry,** (..**ries**), (n) formulier; formulierboek; (a) vormlik, voorgeskrewe.
form'ulate, omskrywe, bewoord, formuleer; in 'n formule saamvat.
formula'tion, formulering.
form'ulism, formulisme, gehegtheid aan formules.
form'ulist, formulis, aanhanger van formules.
form'ulize, *kyk* **formulate.**
forn'icate, ontug pleeg, hoereer.
fornica'tion, hoerery, owerspel, ontug.
forn'icator, owerspeler, hoereerder, ontugtige.
forn'icatress, (**-es**), hoer, ontugtige vrou.
fo'rrel = **forel.**
forsake', (..**sook, -n**), versaak, verlaat; in die steek laat; ~**n,** versaak, verlate.
forsak'ing, versaking, verlating.
forsooth', voorwaar, gewis, sowaar (ironies); kastig, konsuis.
forspent', uitgeput, doodmoeg.
forswear', (..**swore,** ..**sworn**), afsweer, verloën; ~ *oneself,* meineed pleeg.
forsworn', meinedig.
fort, vesting, skans, fort, sterkte.
for'te¹, (n) krag, sterkte; sterk kant; fort; agterhelfte (van swaard).
fort'e², (adv) luid, kragtig (mus.).
forth, voorwaarts, verder, vervolgens, voortaan, voort; *BRING* ~, voortbring; *CAST* ~, weggooi; *COME* ~, te voorskyn kom; *FROM this day* ~, van nou af; verder, voortaan; *HOLD* ~, betoog; *SAIL* ~, wegseil; *SET* ~, uiteengesit; in die lig gee; *and SO* ~, ensovoorts; ~**com'ing,** voorhande, aanstaande; *be* ~ *coming,* beskikbaar (voorhande) wees; op die punt wees om te verskyn; ~**-right,** reguit; ~**-rightness,** rondborstigheid; ~**with,** dadelik, onverwyld, op staande voet, meteens, terstond.
fort'ieth, veertigste.
fort'ifiable, versterkbaar.
fortifica'tion, versterking; verskansing, fortifikasie, vesting; versterkingskuns; ~ **s,** vestingwerke.
fort'ify¹, (..**fied**), versterk, sterk; bevestig; beskans, fortifiseer, met vestingwerke versterk; aanmoedig; *fortified AREA,* versterkte gebied; *fortified TOWN,* vestingstad.
fort'ify², aanmoedig.
fortiss'imo, fortissimo, baie hard (luid).
fort'itude, sielskrag, moed, sterkte, standvastigheid.
fort'night, veertien dae; *this DAY* ~, vandag oor veertien dae; *EVERY* ~, elke veertien dae; *a* ~ *HENCE,* oor veertien dae; ~ **ly,** veertiendaags, tweeweekliks, halfmaandeliks, al om die ander week.
fort'ress, (**-es**), vesting, fort.
fortu'itism, geloof in die toeval.
fortu'itist, gelower in die toeval.
fortu'itous, toevallig; ~**ness,** toevalligheid.
fortu'ity, toeval, onopsetlikheid.
fort'unate, gelukkig, voorspoedig, geseën; gunstig; ~ **ly,** gelukkig(erwys).
fort'une, geluk; lot; kans, bestemming; fortuin, voorspoed; rykdom; vermoë; *COME into one's* ~, jou erfdeel kry; ~ *DOGS his footsteps,* die geluk loop hom agterna; ~ *FAVOURS the bold,* wie nie waag nie wen nie; ~ *FAVOURS fools,* die gekke kry die kaarte; *GOOD* ~, voorspoed, geluk; *by GOOD* ~, gelukkigerwys(e); *MAKE a* ~, 'n fortuin maak; *MARRY a* ~, ryk trou; ~ *to one is MOTHER, to another stepmother,* as dit op een reën, drup dit op 'n ander; *a PERSON of* ~, 'n gegoede persoon; *a PIECE of good* ~, 'n geluk(slag); *SEEK one's* ~, sy geluk soek; ~ *SMILES on him,* die geluk loop hom agterna; *SOLDIER of* ~, 'n geluksoeker; *SPEND a* ~ *on,* 'n fortuin (massa geld) spandeer aan; *TELL one's* ~, sy toekoms voorspel, waarsê; *TELL someone his* ~, iem. goed die waarheid vertel; *TRY one's* ~, sy geluk beproef; ~ *of WAR,* oorlogskans; ~**-hunter,** ~**-seeker,** geluksoeker; ~**'s child,** gelukskind; ~**-teller,** gelukvoorspeller, waarsêer; ~**-telling,** waarsêery, voorspellery.
for'ty, veertig; *ROARING forties,* stormagtige seestreke (tussen 40° en 50° S. Br.); *SHE is in her for-*

forum 911 *fox*

ties, sy is in die veertig; *THE forties*, die jare veertig, die veertigerjare; ~ *WINKS*, haseslaap, 'n dutjie.
for'um, (-s), forum, tribune; regbank (fig.); markplein.
for'ward, (n) voorspeler, stoeier (rugby); *a* ~ *movement*, beweging v.d. voorhoede; (v) bevorder, verhaas, bespoedig (groei); afstuur, deurstuur, aanstuur, versend; (a) voorwaarts; vooruitstrewend, modern; verder, gevorder, vroeg; oulik, vroeg ryp, voorlik (kind); snipperig, parmantig; voorbarig, vrypostig, astrant (persoon); ~ *journey*, heenreis; (adv) vooruit, vorentoe, voort, voorwaarts; vooraan; op die voorskip; *BRING* ~, transporteer; oordra (rekening); *BROUGHT* ~, per transport; oorgedra, oorgebring; *CARRIAGE* ~, vraggeld verskuldig; *COME* ~, vorentoe kom; *DATE* ~, later dateer; *from this DAY* ~, van nou af; *LOOK* ~ *to*, vooruit kyk na; verlang na; *PUT* ~, vorentoe bring; aan die hand doen; ~ **axle**, vooras; ~ **behaviour**, vrypostige gedrag; ~**er**, bevorderaar; bespoediger; afsender, versender; ~ **exchange**, termynvaluta.
for'warding, afsending; versending; bevordering, bespoediging; ~ **agency**, versendingsaak; ~ **agent**, ekspediteur, aanstuurder, aanstuuragent, versender; ~ **charges**, versendingskoste; ~ **clerk**, versendingsklerk; ~ **list**, versendlys; ~ **office**, bestelkantoor; ~ **site**, laaiterrein; afsendingsterrein.
for'wardness, voorbarigheid, vrypostigheid, voorlikheid; bereidvaardigheid.
for'ward: ~ **pass**, vorentoe aangee (rugby); ~ **play**, voorspel.
for'wards, (n) voorspelers, voorhoede; (adv) vooruit, verder.
forwear'ied, afgemat, uitgeput.
fosse, grag, sloot.
foss'ick, minerale soek, prospekteer; (rond)snuffel; ~**er**, soeker, snuffelaar; prospekteerder; peuteraar.
foss'il, (n) verstening, fossiel; (a) fossiel, versteen; verouderd; ~**i'ferous**, fossielhoudend; ~**ist**, fossielkenner; ~**iza'tion**, verstening, fossilisasie; ~**ize**, laat versteen, fossileer.
fossor'ial, vroetelend, graaf=, fossoriaal.
fos'ter, grootmaak, oppas, aankweek, voed; koester, bevorder; ~ *discontent*, kwaad saai, opstook; ~ **age**, opkweking, grootmaak; opvoeding; bevordering; ~**-brother**, pleegbroer; ~**-child**, pleegkind, voedsterkind, voedsterling, aangenome kind; ~**-daughter**, pleegdogter, ~**er**, voedster, versorger; pleegouer; bevorderaar; ~**-father**, pleegvader; voedstervader; ~ **ling**, voedsterling, pleegkind, protégé; ~**-mother**, pleegmoeder, voedster, voedstermoeder; soogvrou; kunsmoeder; ~**-parents**, pleegouers; ~**-sister**, pleegsuster, ~**-son**, pleegseun, aangenome seun.
fougasse', slingermyn.
fought, gestrede; *kyk ook* **fight**, (v).
foul, (n) vuil spel; (opsetlike) fout; *through* ~ *and fair*, deur voor- en teenspoed; (v) vuil maak, bemors; onklaar maak; besmeer; in die war bring, verwar; belemmer, versper; omloop, platloop (hekkies); in botsing kom; ~ *one's own nest*, jou eie nes bevuil; (a) onrein, walglik, smerig, stink, vuil; lelik, sleg, gemeen, verfoeilik; bedorwe, oneerlik; modderig, troebel (water); ru, hard; onklaar; verward; ~ *COPY*, klad; ~ *DEED*, gemene daad; ~ *LANGUAGE*, vuil taal; ~ *LINEN*, vuil linne; ~ *MEANS*, ongeoorloofde middele; *no SUSPICION of* ~ *play*, geen misdaad word vermoed nie; ~ *WEATHER*, slegte weer; *a* ~ *WIND*, 'n teenwind; (adv) vuil; *FALL* ~ *of*, bots met; rusie maak met; *FALL* ~ *of someone*, in iem. se vaarwater kom; ~ **air**, bedorwe lug; ~ **berth**, slegte aanlêplek; ~ **bottom**, vuil skeepsbodem; ~**-dealing**, bedrog; ~ **drain**, vuil riool; ~ **fiend**, die bose vyand, die duiwel; ~ **ing**, besoedeling; aanpaksel; vuil; ~**-point**, versperringspunt; ~**ly**, op gemene (skandelike) manier; ~**-minded**, kwaaddenkend; van slegte inbors; ~**-mouthed**, vuilbekkig; ~**ness**, vuilheid, gemeenheid, skandelikheid; snoodheid; ~ **play**, oneerlike spel, vuil spel; skurkagtigheid; ~ **soil**, bevuilde grond; ~**-spoken**, met 'n vuil mond, vuilbekkig; ~**-tongued**, vuilbekkig.
foul'ard, foulard.
foum'art, muishond.
found¹, (v) stig, oprig, vestig, fundeer, fondeer, grondves; *well* ~ *ed*, gegrond; *kyk ook* **find**, (v).
found², (v) giet, smelt.
found³, (p.p. of **find**), gevind, gevonde; *all* ~, alles inbegrepe; met kos en inwoning.
founda'tion, grondslag, fondament; onderbou, fundering; grondlegging, fondering, grondvesting; fonds, stigting; (pl) grondveste; *on a FIRM* ~, op 'n vaste grondslag; *WITHOUT any* ~, heeltemal ongegrond; ~ **cream**, onderlaagroom; ~ **garment(s)**, korset; postuurdrag; vormdrag; onderklere (by vrouens); ~ **member**, stigterslid; ~**-muslin**, ~**-net**, styfgaas; ~ **pattern**, grondpatroon; ~ **seed**, kernmoere; ~ **stock**, stamvee; ~**-stone**, hoeksteen.
foun'ded, gegrond; opgerig, gestig.
foun'der¹, (n) oprigter, insteller, grondvester, stigter.
foun'der², (n) bevangenheid (by perde); hoefseer; (v) kruppel word.
foun'der³, (n) (metaal)gieter, smelter.
foun'der⁴, (v) sink, vergaan; inmekaarsak; vasval.
foun'der: *F* ~ *'s DAY*, Stigtersdag; ~ *'s SHARES*, oprigtersaandele.
foun'dering, bevangenheid (by perde).
foun'ding, oprigting, stigting.
found'ling, vondeling.
foun'dry, (foundries), gietery.
fount¹, bron, fontein, oorsprong.
fount², stel drukletters, tipe.
foun'tain, fontein, bron; oorsprong, oliebak; ~**-head**, bron(aar), oorsprong; ~**-pen**, vulpen.
four, vier; *on ALL* ~ *s*, op hande en voete, handeviervoet; *BE on all* ~ *s with*, klop (strook) met; *the BIG* ~, die viermanskap; *CARRIAGE and* ~, rytuig met vier perde; ~ *HOURS*, vier uur; ~ *TIMES*, vier maal (keer); *to the* ~ *WINDS*, wyd en syd; ~**-ball**, vierspel (gholf); ~**-bladed**, vierblad-, met vier lemme; ~**-celled**, viersellig; ~**-colour printing**, vierkleurdruk; ~**-cornered**, vierhoekig; ~**-corners**, kruisbessie; ~**-dimensional**, vierafmetings=, vierdimensie; ~**-door**, met vier deure; ~**-engined**, viermotorig; ~**-figure table**, vierdesimalige tafel; ~**-flusher**, grootprater, grootlawaai; bedrieër; ~ **fold**, viervoudig, vierdubbeld; ~**-footed**, viervoetig; ~ **furrow plough**, vierskaarploeg; ~**-gun**, met vier kanonne; ~**-handed**, vierhandig (aap); vierpersoon= (spel); ~**-inch**, vierduims=; ~**-in-hand**, vierspan; ~**-leaf clover**, vierklawer; ~**-legged**, vierpotig; ~**-lobed**, vierlobbig; ~**-master**, viermaster; ~**-monthly**, viermaandeliks; ~ *o' clock*, vieruur; vieruurtjie (blom); ~**-part**, vierstemmig; ~**-phase**, vierfasig; ~**-ply**, vierdraads; met vier lae; ~**-pointed**, vierpuntig, ~**-poster**, dubhelbed met vier style, hemelbed; ~**-pounder**, vierponder; ~ **score**, tagtig; ~**-seater**, viersitplekmotor; viersitplek=; ~**-seater plane**, viersitplekvliegtuig; ~ **some**, vierbal, vierspel; beurtspel; ~**-speed**, viergang=; ~**-square**, vierkantig; vas, flink, rotsvas; ~**-stroke**, viertak, vierslag; ~**-stroke motor**, viertakmotor, vierslagenjin
four'teen, veertien; ~ **th**, veertiende.
fourth, vierde; *every* ~ *DAY*, vierdedaags; elke vierde dag; al om die vierde dag; *the* ~ *ESTATE*, die pers; ~ *FLOOR*, vierde verdieping; ~ *ROOT*, vierdemagswortel; ~**-ly**, in die vierde plek, vierdens, ten vierde; ~**-rate**, vierderangs.
four'-thread, vierdraads.
four: ~**-way**, viersprong; ~**-wheel brakes**, vierwielremme, ~**-wheeled**, vierwielig, met vier wiele; ~**-wheeler**, vierwieler; ~**-yearly**, vierjaarliks.
fowl, (n) hoender; gevoëlte, wilde voël; hoendervleis; (pl) pluimvee; (v) voëls skiet; ~ **cholera**, hoendercholera; ~**er**, voëljagter, voëlvanger; ~**-food**, hoendervoer; ~ **giblets**, hoenderafval; ~**-house**, hoenderhok, hoenderhuis; ~ **ing**, voëljag; ~ **ing piece**, haelgeweer; ~ **manure**, hoendermis; ~**-perch**, hoenderstok; ~ **pox**, hoenderpokkies; ~**-run**, hoenderhok, hoenderhok; ~ **tick**, tampan; ~ **typhoid**, hoendertifus.
fox, (n) (-es), jakkals, vos; *set the* ~ *to keep the*

GEESE, van wolf skaapwagter maak; bobbejaan oppasser v.d. vyeboom maak; *an OLD* ~, 'n ou rot; *be a SLY* ~, 'n sluwe (geslepe) jakkals wees; *a* ~ *is not TAKEN twice in the same snare,* 'n esel stoot hom nie twee maal aan dieselfde klip nie; *a WILY* ~, 'n sluwe jakkals; (v) skelm handel; kul, flous, bedrieg; dronk maak; laat suur word; vlekkerig word, vlek (van boeke); ~**-bat**, vlieënde hond; ~**-brush**, jakkalsstert; ~ **ed**, vlekkerig, gevlek (boeke); ~ **ed tenon**, splytwigtap; ~ **fur**, vosbont; ~**-glove**, vingerhoedjie (plant), digitalis; ~ **hole**, skuilgat; ~ **hound**, jakkalshond; ~**-hunt**, jakkalsjag; ~**iness**, sluheid, jakkalsagtigheid; jakkalsstreke; ~ **tail**, jakkalsstert; ~**-tail saw**, foksswans; ~**-terrier**, terriërhond, Foksterriër; ~ **trot**, (n) jakkalsdraf, jakkalstrap; (v) die jakkalstrap dans; ~**-wedge**, tapsplytwig; ~ **y**, slu, deurtrap, jakkalsagtig; rooibruin, roeskleurig; suur; ~ *y oats*, vermufte hawer.
fo'yer, voorportaal, foyer.
frac'as, (sing and pl) opskudding, lawaai, rusie, relletjie.
frac'tion, brokstuk, onderdeel; gebroke getal, breuk (wisk.); breking; verbreking; ~ **al**, ~ **ary**, gebreek, gebroke; fraksioneel, gedeeltelik; breuk=; ~ *al PART*, onderdeeltjie; ~ *al STERILIZATION*, onderbroke sterilisasie; ~ **ate**, fraksioneer; ~ **a'tion**, fraksionering, (af)skeiding; ~ **ize**, verdeel.
frac'tious, lastig; kwaad, twissiek; weerspannig; ~ **ness**, twisterigheid; weerspannigheid.
frac'tural, breuk=.
frac'ture, (n) breuk, beenbreuk; fraktuur; ~ *of the skull*, skedelbreuk; (v) breek; bars, skeur, splyt; ~ **cleavage**, breuksplyting.
frac'turing, breukvorming; breking.
fr(a)en'um, (..na), frenum, band; ~ *of the tongue*, tongriem.
fra'gile, swak, teer; tingerig; bros, broos; breekbaar, fragiel.
fragil'ity, breekbaarheid; bro(o)sheid, swakheid; teerheid, tingerigheid.
frag'ment, (n) brok(stuk); fragment; (v) in stukkies breek, versplinter, fragmenteer; ~ **ariness**, onvolledigheid; ~ **ary**, fragmentaries, onvolledig; *what we know is* ~ *ary*, ons ken net ten dele; al ons kennis is stukwerk; ~ **a'tion**, splintering, skerfbreking, verbryseling, fragmentering, fragmentasie.
frag'rance, geurigheid, geur, welriekendheid.
frag'rant, geurig, welriekend.
frail¹, (n) biesiemandjie.
frail², (a) bro(o)s; rank, tingerig, swak, teer, pieperig; verganklik; ontrou; onkuis; ~ **ness**, ~ **ty**, bro(o)sheid; teerheid, swakheid; onstandvastigheid; verganklikheid; ontrouheid; onkuisheid.
fraise¹, uitboorsaag; ruimer, frees.
fraise², halskraag, geplooide kraag, stormpale; palissade.
fram'able, uitdinkbaar; raambaar.
framb(o)es'ia, framboesia, frambosesiekte (in Tropeë).
frame, (n) omtrek; skets; gestel, vorm, liggaamsbou; stelsel, inrigting; raam(werk), lys; montuur (bril); kosyn (bouk.); toestel, timmerasie; geraamte; bok (boekdr.); broeiraam (plante); gietvorm; ~ *of GOVERNMENT*, regeringsvorm; ~ *of MIND*, gemoedsgesteldheid; (v) omlys, in 'n lys sit, raam; saamstel; saamvoeg; vorm, ontwerp; opstel; bedink, beraam, versin; maak, inrig; verneuk, onderdeur spring; ~**-assembly**, raamwerk; ~ **construction**, skeletbou, raambou.
framed, omlys, geraam; ~ **bridge**, vakwerkbrug; ~ **building**, skeletbou.
frame: ~ **r**, bouer, maker; opsteller, ontwerper; vormer; lysmaker; ~**-saw**, spansaag, raamsaag; ~**-shears**, spanskêr; ~**-sight**, raamvisier; ~**-stretcher**, raamspanstuk; ~**-trunnion**, raamdra(ag)tap; ~**-up**, lis, sameswering; deurgestoke kaart; ~ **work**, lyswerk, geraamte, omlysting; opset; raamwerk; vakwerk.
fram'ing, raamwerk; omlysting; raamstelsel; vals beskuldiging; formulering; ~ **chisel**, tapbeitel; ~ **timber**, timmerasie; ~ **saw-horse**, saagbok.
franc, frank.

France, Frankryk.
fran'chise, stemreg, kiesreg; vrydom; voorreg; ~ **ment**, vrystelling.
Francis'can, (n) Franciskaner; (a) Franciskaans.
fran'cium, frankium.
Franc'o-Germ'an, Frans-Duits.
franc'olin, berghoender; (bos)fisant.
Francon'ia, Frankeland; ~ **n**, (n) Frank; Frankies (taal); (a) Frankies.
Franc'ophil(e), (n) Fransgesinde; Frankofiel; (a) Fransgesind, Frankofiel.
Franc'ophobe, (n) anti-Fransgesinde; (a) anti-Fransgesind.
franc tireur', franc tireur, guerrilla(stryder), vryskutter.
frangibil'ity, breekbaarheid, broosheid.
fran'gible, breekbaar.
fran'gipane, frangipan'i, frangipani; jasmyn(geur); amandelgebak; marsepein.
Frank¹, Frank.
frank², (n) offisiële stempel (handtekening op brief); (v) frankeer (brief); iem. 'n paspoort gee; kosteloos deurstuur; vrystel.
frank³, (a) vrymoedig, gulhartig, frank, rondborstig, openhartig, volmondig, reguit; vrygewig; bepaald.
franked, franko; gefrankeer(d).
frank'furter, frankfurter, frankfurtworsie.
frank'incense, wierook.
frank'ing machine, (brief)stempelmasjien (poskantoor).
Frank'ish, (n) Frankies (taal); (a) Frankies.
frank'ly, glyweg, vryuit, openhartig, ronduit, eerlik, reguit.
frank'ness, vrymoedigheid, openhartigheid, eerlikheid, rondborstigheid.
fran'tic, woedend, waansinnig, woes, rasend, dol, verwoed, wild; ~ *attempt*, verwoede (wanhopige) poging.
frap, (-ped), vasbind, vastrek, vaswoel.
frass, uitwerpsels (van larwes); boorsel (van insekte).
frat'e, (frati), monnik.
fratern'al, broederlik; ~ **ly**, broederlik.
fratern'ity, (..ties), broe(de)rskap, fraterniteit; vereniging, gilde.
fraterniza'tion, verbroedering.
frat'ernize, verbroeder; fraterniseer, soos broe(de)rs omgaan.
frat'ricidal, broedermoord=; broedermoordenaars=.
frat'ricide, broedermoord; broedermoordenaar.
fraud, bedrieër, verneuker; bedrog, bedrieëry, swendel(a)ry, verneukery; lis, valsheid; *pious* ~, bedrog om beswil; ~ **ulence**, ~ **ulency**, bedrieglikheid; bedrog; ~ **ulent**, oneerlik, slinks, bedrieglik; ~ **ulently**, op bedrieglike wyse.
fraught, belaai, ryk; vol, beswanger; ~ *with ANXIETY*, sorgwekkend; ~ *with DANGER*, vol gevaar.
Fraun'hofer lines, fraunhoferlyne.
fraus, fraus, bedrog.
fray¹, (n) twis, rusie, geveg; *eager for* ~, strydlustig.
fray², (n) skaafplek; rafel (materiaal); (v) verslyt, uittorring, (uit)rafel (stof); skaaf; *his nerves are badly* ~ *ed*, hy het dit op sy senuwees; ~ **ing**, rafeling.
fraz'zle, doodvermoeidheid; *WORK oneself to a* ~, jou boeglam werk; *WORN to a* ~, afgemat, afgetob, doodmoeg.
freak, nuk, inval, gier, gril; kuur; grilligheid, streek, (natuur)frats; sonderling; wonderdier; (wan)gedrog; ~ *of nature*, natuurgril, natuurfrats, speling v.d. natuur; ~ *OUT*, uit die juk spring; mal raak; alles net so los; jou eie pad gaan; dwelmiddels gebruik; ~ **ed**, gevlek, gestreep; ~ **ish**, grillig, nukkerig, wispelturig; ~ **ishness**, sonderlingheid; wispelturigheid; fiemies, grilligheid; ~ **weather**, fratsweer.
frec'kle, (n) sproet, vlek; (v) sproeterig maak (word); vlek, stippel; ~**-cream**, sproetroom; ~ **d**, met sproete; sproeterig; gespikkel; ~ **d face**, sproetgesig; ~**-faced**, (gesig) vol sproete.
free, (v) vry laat; vry veg; bevry, verlos, vrymaak; vrystel, ontslaan (gevangene); (a) vry, onbelemmerd; vrypostig; verniet, kosteloos, gratis; los, onge=

freedom

dwonge, vrywillig, gewillig; oorvloedig; vrymoe=
dig; *BE* ~ *to do it*, vry wees om dit te doen; ~ *on
BOARD*, vry aan boord; ~ *from CARE*, onbesorg;
~ *of CHARGE*, kosteloos, verniet, gratis; ~ *to
CONFESS*, gewillig om te bieg; ~ *and EASY*, on=
gegeneerd, ongedwonge, familiêr; ~ **ENTRAN=
CE**, vry(e) toegang; ~ *ENTRY*, vry(e) inskrywing;
a ~ *FIGHT*, algemene vegparty; *it is* ~ *FOR you
(to do so)*, dit staan jou vry (om so te maak); ~
FROM, vry van; *GIVE a* ~ *hand*, iem. die hande
vry laat; ~ *GRACE*, vrye genade; *have a* ~
HAND, carte blanche hê; ~ *LUGGAGE*, vry baga=
sie; *MAKE* ~ *with*, vryhede neem met; ~ *to do as
he PLEASES*, hy kan maak soos hy wil; die halter
is van die kop; ~ *on RAIL*, vry op spoor; ~ *from
RUST*, sonder roes; ontroes; *have* ~ *SCOPE*, die
hande vry hê; ~ *TRANSLATION*, vrye vertaling;
~ *from VIBRATION*, trillingvry; *as* ~ *as a bird on
the WING*, so vry soos 'n voëltjie op 'n takkie;
~ **board**, vryboord; ~ **booter**, vrybuiter; ~ **booting**,
vrybuitery; ~ -**born**, vrygebore; F ~ **Burgher**, Vry=
burger; ~ **city**, vry rykstad, vrystad; vrye stad; ~
dispensary, staatsapteek.

free'dom, vryheid; vrydom; gemak; vrystelling; (bur=
ger)reg, privilegie; vrypostigheid; ~ *of a CITY*,
ereburgerskap; *the FOUR* ~*s*, die vier vryhede
(spraak, godsdiens, vrees, gebrek); ~ *of the
PRESS*, persvryheid; *RESTRICTION of* ~ , vry=
heidsbeperking; ~ *of the SEAS*, die vrye see; ~ *of
SPEECH*, vryheid van spraak, die vrye woord;
TAKE ~*s with*, jou vryhede veroorloof met;
TORCH of ~ , vryheidsfakkel; ~ *of WORSHIP*,
godsdiensvryheid; ~ **fighter**, vryheidsvegter; ~ -
loving, vryheidsliewend.

free: ~ **fall**, vrye val; ~ **fight**, algemene bakleiery; ~ -
footed, onbelemmerd, vry; ~ -**for-all**, algemene ba=
kleiery; handgemeen; handgevegte; ~ **gift**, (gratis)
geskenk; ~ -**hand**, uit die vrye hand (teken); ~ -
handed, gul, vrygewig; ~ -**hand sketch**, ruwe skets;
vryehandskets, -tekening; ~ -**hearted**, vrygewig;
openhartig; ~ **hold**, vry erfpag, vryleen, allodiaal;
~ **holder**, besitter, eienaar; ~ **hold farm**, eiendoms=
plaas; ~ **issue**, gratis (kostelose) uitreiking; ~
kick, strafskop; ~ **lance**, vryskut(joernalis); ~ **lan=
cing**, vryskutwerk; ~ **length**, onbelaste lengte; ~
library, openbare biblioteek; ~ -**liver**, lekkerbek;
losbol; ~ **love**, vrye liefde; ~ **ly**, vry, vryuit; vrywil=
lig; graag; ryklik; geredelik; volop; ~ **man** (..**men**),
vryc, vryburger; ereburger; ~ **market**, vrye mark;
~ -**market system**, vryemarkstelsel; ~ **martin**, tras=
sie, hermafrodiet; F ~ **mason**, Vrymesselaar, boki y=
er (skertsend); F ~ **masonry**, Vrymesselary; kame=
raadskap; ~ **ness**, openhartigheid; vrypostigheid;
ongedwongenheid; vrymoedigheid; vrygewigheid;
~ **oil**, ekstra olie; ~ **pardon**, kwytskelding van
straf; ~ **pass**, vrykaartjie, vrypas; ~ **play**, vrye
loop (gang); ~ **quarters**, vrye inwoning; ~ -**range
eggs**, eiers van vryloophoenders.

frees'ia, freesia, kammetjie.

free: ~ **speech**, vryheid van spraak; vrye spraak; ~ -
speed, onbelaste spoed; ~ -**spoken**, rondut, rond=
borstig, vrymoedig; openhartig; ~ -**standing**, vry=
staande.

free: ~ **State**, Vrystaat; F ~ **stater**, Vrystater;
~ **stone**, lospit (vrug); arduin, hardsteen; ~ **style**,
vryslag (swem); ~ **thinker**, vrydenker, vrygees; ~
thinking, vrydenkery, vrygeestigheid; ~ **ticket**,
vrykaartjie; ~ **trade**, vryhandel; ~ -**trader**, vryhan=
delaar; ~ **translation**, vrye vertaling; ~ **travel**, vry
beweging; ~ **way**, snelweg; deurpad; ~ **wheel**, (n)
vrywiel, loswiel; (v) losloop; loswiel ry; ~ -**wheel
system**, vrywielstelsel; ~ **will**, (n) vrywilligheid;
vrye wil; (a) vrywillig, uit eie beweging.

freeze, (n) ryp; vors; (v) (**froze, frozen**), vries, bevries;
laat bevries; verkluim; ys, ril; ~ *one's BLOOD*, jou
bloed laat stol; jou lam skrik; ~ *to DEATH*, dood=
vries; ~ *ON to*, (jou) vasklamp aan; ~ *OUT*, weg=
werk, wegkyk ('n persoon); uitban, uitstoot; ~
WAGES, lone vaspen; *deep* ~ , diepvries(yskas).

freez'er, ysmasjien, vriesmasjien; vrieskas.

freez'ing, (n) bevriesing, verysing; (a) yskoud, ysig,
vriesend, vries=; ~ **agent**, vriesmiddel; ~ **appara=**

913

fret

tus, vriesapparaat; ~ -**chamber**, vrieskamer; ~
compartment, vriesvak(kie); ~ **level**, vrieshoogte;
~ -**machine**, ysmasjien; ~ -**mixture**, koudmakende
mengsel, vriesmengsel; ~ -**plant**, koelinrigting; ~ -
point, vriespunt.

freight, (n) vrag, (be)lading; vervoer; vragprys, vrag=
geld; (v) laai, bevrag; huur; ~ **aeroplane**, vragvlieg=
tuig; ~ **age**, lading, vrag, las; vragprys; skeepshuur;
~ **er**, versender, bevragter; vragskip, vragboot,
vragvaarder; vragvliegtuig; ~ **ing**, bevragting, be=
lading; ~ **shed**, vragloods; ~ **tariff**, vragtarief.

French, (n) Frans; (a) Frans; *take* ~ *leave*, wegloop,
dros; tussen vinger en neus vertrek, met die noor=
derson vertrek; ~ **bean**, snyboon; ~ **brandy**, frans=
brandewyn; ~ **curve**, tekenkromme; ~ **chalk**, kle=
remakerskryt; fyntalk, speksteen; ~ **drain**,
stapelriool; ~ **dressing**, Franse slaaisous; ~ **endive**,
witloof; ~ **fried**, diepgebraai; ~ **Hoek**, Fransch=
hoek; ~ **horn**, waldhoring; ~ **ifica'tion**, verfran=
sing; ~ **ify**, (..**fied**), verfrans; f ~ **ing**, sweepstok=
siekte; ~ **language**, Frans; ~ **man**, (..**men**), Frans=
man; ~ **muslin**, moeselien; ~ **polish**, (n) lakpoli=
toer, politoerocl; (v) lakpolitoer; ~ **polisher**,
lakpoleerder; ~ **scalloping**, Franse skulpwerk; ~
seam, rolsoom; ~ **white**, franswit; ~ **window**, oop=
slaanbare, oopslaanvenster; ~ **woman**, Franse
dame; ~ **y**, (n) (..**chies**), Fransman, Franse vrou;
ligtekooi; (a) Frans(er)ig.

frenet'ic, *kyk* **phrenetic**.

fren'um = fr(a)enum.

fren'zied, waansinnig, dol, rasend.

fren'zy, (n) (**frenzies**), waansin, kranksinnigheid; dol=
heid, dolsinnigheid, raserny, doldriftigheid; (v)
(**frenzied**), dol maak; *frenzied rage*, waansinnige
woede.

fre'quency, (..**cies**), (gedurige) herhaling, veelvuldig=
heid, menigvuldigheid; snelheid; frekwensie (elek.);
~ *of the pulse*, polssnelheid; ~ **control**, frekwensie=
reëling; frekwensierëelaar; ~ **modulation**, frekwen=
siemodulasie.

frequent', (v) dikwels besoek, boer by, baie omgaan
met.

fre'quent, (a) herhaaldlik, veelvuldig, dikwels,
gedurig.

frequent: ~ **a'tion**, drukke besoek, herhaalde om=
gang; ~ **ative**, (n) herhalingswoord, frekwentatief;
(a) herhalend, frekwentatief; ~ **ed**, baie besoek;
~ **er**, besoeker.

fre'quently, dikwels, herhaaldelik, baiemaal, veel,
veeltyds, heeldag; *LESS* ~ , nie so dikwels (baie)
nie; *MORE* ~ , meer dikwels.

fres'co, (n) (-**es**, -**s**), muurskildering, wandskildering,
fresko; *al* ~ , in die oop lug; (v) fresko skilder.

fresh, ~ van vroegte; stroomversnelling; aanwakkering;
in the ~ *of the morning*, douvoordag; (a) hard, styf
(wind); nuut, vars; fris, koel; ongesout (vleis); soet
(water); onervare, groen; astrant, opdringerig; *be=
gin a* ~ *CHAPTER*, 'n nuwe hoofstuk begin; *a* ~
COMPLEXION, 'n gesonde gelaatskleur; *DIF=
FICULTIES*, nuwe moeilikhede; *break* ~
GROUND, nuwe bane open; *KEEP* ~ , goed hou;
~ *MEAT*, vars vleis; *as* ~ *as PAINT*, springlewen=
dig; ~ *START*, nuwe begin; (adv) pas, net; ~
FROM, pas aangekom van; *GET* ~ *with a girl*,
vryhede neem met 'n nooi; ~ **air**, vars lug; ~ **arri=
val**, nuwe aankoms; nuwe aankomeling; ~ **breeze**,
fris bries; ~ **butter**, vars botter; ~ **chapter**, nuwe
hoofstuk; ~ **egg**, vars eier; ~ **en**, vervars, vernuwe;
ontsout; vars; verlewendig; opfris; verfris; aanwak=
ker; ~ **er**, sterk wind; groene, groentjie, nuweling.

fresh'et, vloedwater; stroom; oorstroming; ~ **te'**,
groentjie, nuweling.

fresh: ~ **horses**, vars perde, wisselspan; ~ **ly**, vars;
opnuut; fris; net, onlangs; ~ **man**, (..**men**), nuwe=
ling, novise; eerstejaarstudent, groene, groentjie;
~ **memory**, vars geheue; ~ **milk**, vars melk, soet
melk; ~ **ness**, varsheid, frisheid, koelheid; ~ **stu=
dent**, groene, groentjie; ~ **vegetables**, vars groente;
~ **water**, vars water; ~ -**water fish**, varswatervis,
riviervis; ~ **weather**, koel weer; ~ **wind**, fris wind.

fret[1], (n) lyswerk, ornament; saagwerk; (v) figure
saag; uitsaag (hout); versier (met snywerk).

fret², (n) afkarteling, wegvreting; skuring; ergernis; geknies, kniesery; *in a* ~, vererg; (v) **(-ted)**, vererg, pla, pieker, tob, doodknies, afmartel; knies, verknies, kwel; knor, mok; skuur, afslyt; vreet, verteer, skryn; knaag aan (toom); invreet; uitkalwe (grond); afvryf; kook (rivier); onstuimig beweeg; ~ *AWAY one's life*, jou doodtreur; ~ *and FUME*, raas en tier; ~ **ful**, ergerlik, knieserig, gemelik, prikkelbaar.

fret'saw, figuursaag, fretsaag.

frett'ing, (n) tobbery, gepieker, geknies; verknorsing; uitvreting; (a) tobberig.

fret'ty, lastig, prikkelbaar.

fret'work, fynsaagwerk, snywerk.

Freud'ian, (n) Freudiaan; (a) Freudiaans; ~**ism,** Freudianisme.

fri'able, bros, brokkel(r)ig; ~**ness,** brosheid.

fri'ar, monnik; *BLACK F*~, Dominikaner; ~ *MINOR,* minderbroer; *WHITE F*~, Karmeliet; ~'**s balsam,** terleton, kloosterbalsem, monnikebalsem; ~'**s cap,** monnikskap; akoniet, wolwekruid; ~'**s cowl,** monnikskap; ~'**s lantern,** dwaallig; ~ **y,** (..ries), monnikeklooster.

frib, naknipsel (wol).

frib'ble, (n) beuselaar; beuselary; (v) speel, beusel; ~ **r,** beuselaar, dwaas.

fric'andeau, (-x), braaivleis met sous, fricandeau.

fricassee', stoofvleis, frikassee.

fric'ative, (n) skuurklank, skuringsgeluid, frikatief; (a) skurend, skuur=, frikatief, spiranties.

fric'tion, wrywing, friksie; *angle of* ~, wrywings= hoek; ~ **area,** wrywingsvlak, wryfvlak; ~**al,** wry=wings=; ~*al DRAG*, wrywingsweerstand; ~*al PARTS,* wryfdele; ~ **block,** remblok; ~ **clutch,** wryfkoppelaar; ~ **drive,** wryfaandrywing; ~-**horsepower,** wrywingsperdekrag; ~**less,** wrywingsloos; wrywingsvry; ~ **plate,** wrywingsplaat; ~ **spark,** wryfvonk; ~ **spring,** wryfveer; ~ **surface,** wryfvlak; ~-**tight,** wryfvas; ~ **wheel,** wrywingswiel.

Frid'ay, Vrydag; *GOOD* ~, Goeie Vrydag; *ON* ~, Vrydags, Vrydae; ~ **evening,** Vrydagaand; ~ **morning,** Vrydagmôre, Vrydagoggend.

fridge, yskas, koelkas.

fried, gebraai; gebak; ~ *EGG*, spieëleier, gebakte eier; ~ *FISH,* gebraaide vis.

friend, vriend, vriendin; kennis, maat; *a* ~ *to ALL is a* ~ *to none,* allemansvriend is niemandsvriend; *BE* ~*s with,* bevriend wees met; *the BEST of* ~*s must part,* selfs die beste vriende gaan uiteindelik uitmekaar; *CIRCLE of* ~*s,* vriendekring; *a* ~ *at COURT,* 'n invloedryke vriend; 'n kruiwa; *a* ~ *at COURT makes the process short,* wie die naaste aan die vuur sit, word die warmste; *a* ~ *is never KNOWN till needed,* in die nood leer 'n mens jou vriende ken; *my LEARNED* ~, my geleerde vriend; *MAKE* ~*s,* maats maak; *a* ~ *in NEED,* 'n vriend in nood; *a* ~ *in NEED is a* ~ *indeed,* in die nood leer 'n mens jou vriende ken; ~**less,** verlate, alleen, sonder vriende; ~**liness,** vriendelikheid, minlikheid.

friend'ly, vriendelik, eie, vriendskaplik; bevriend; vriendskaps=; amikaal; *BE on* ~ *terms,* op vriendskaplike voet staan; ~ *MATCH,* vriendskaplike wedstryd; *perform a* ~ *OFFICE,* 'n vriendskapsdiens bewys.

friend'ship, vriendskap; *EXPRESSION of* ~, vriendskapsbetoon; *TIE of* ~; vriendskapsband; *TOKEN of* ~, vriendskapsbewys.

Frie'sian, Fries (dier).

Fries'land, (n) Friesland; Fries(bees), mofbees; (a) Fries; ~ **bull,** Friesbul; ~**er,** Friesbees.

frieze¹, duffel (materiaal).

frieze², stuk beeldhouwerk; fries (boukuns); friesrand (van plakpapier); ~ **moulding,** frieslys; ~ **rail,** friesreling.

frig'ate, fregatskip; ~ **bird,** fregatvoël, roofduiker *(Fregata magnificens).*

fright, (n) skrik; vrees; spook, voëlverskrikker; *have (be given) the* ~ *of one's LIFE,* jou byna dood skrik; jou uit lit skrik; *TAKE* ~ *at,* bang word vir; (v) skrikmaak.

fright'en, bangmaak, verskrik, skrikmaak; vrees aanjaag; ~ *AWAY,* afskrik; ~ *someone out of his WITS,* iem. die groot skrik op die lyf ja; ~**ed,** verskrik, bangerig; *be* ~*ed to death,* doodbang wees; ~**ing,** skrikaanja(g)end.

fright'ful, verskriklik, vreeslik, skriklik, skrikbarend, vervaarlik; afsigtelik; ~**ly,** vreeslik, verskriklik; bedroef; ~**ness,** vreeslikheid, vervaarlikheid; afsigtelikheid; skrikaanjaging.

fri'gid, yskoud; vormlik, styf; koud, koel, onhartlik, kil; vervelend; ~'**ity,** koudheid, kilheid; ~ **zone,** poolstreek.

frill, (n) valletjie; plooisel; kraag; (pl) fiemies, aanstellery; *full of* ~*s and FANCIES,* vol verbeeldings; vol kopstukke; *be FULL of* ~*s,* vol krulle wees; *WITHOUT* ~*s,* sonder tierlantyntjies; (v) plooi, valletjies maak; ~**ery,** valletjies, optooisel; ~**ing,** plooisel.

fringe, (n) fraiing; rand, soom; gordyntjiekop, haargordyntjie (op voorkop); gordyntjiekapsel; (v) met fraiings omsoom (afsit); omrand; uitrafel; ~ **benefits,** byvoordele.

fring'ing, soom, rand; fraiing; rafelwerk.

fripp'ery, rommel, tierlantyntjie(s), snuistery(e); opskik.

frisette', frisette, gordyntjie (van vals krulle).

friseur', kapper, barbier, haarsnyer.

Fris'ian, (n) Fries; (a) Fries.

frisk, (n) sprong, darteling; gier; (v) huppel, agteropskop, dartel, spring; iem. voel-voel (vir 'n wapen) ondersoek; visenteer.

frisk'et, frisket (druk.).

frisk: ~**iness,** dartelheid, uitbundigheid; ~**y,** dartel, vrolik; *be* ~*y,* springlewendig wees, na jou kwas skop.

frit, (n) smeltglas, frit; (v) **(-ted),** gloei.

frit'-fly, koringvlieg.

frith, bosryke streek; riviermond.

fritill'ary¹, (..ries), keiserskroon (lelie).

fritill'ary², (..ries), perlemoenvlinder.

fritt'er, (n) snippertjie, skyfie; verbrokkeling; poffertjie; vrugtepannekoekie; frituur; koekie; (v) (ver)snipper, in repies sny; brokkel; ~ *AWAY,* versnipper, verbrokkel; verbeusel, vermors, verspil; ~ *away one's CHANCES,* jou kanse verspeel.

friv'ol, beusel, verbeusel; ~ *away,* verbeusel, vermors.

frivolité', ogieswerk, knoopwerk, spoelwerk, frivolité.

frivol'ity, (..ties), beuselagtigheid; ligsinnigheid, wufheid; kinderagtigheid; beuselary.

friv'olous, kinderagtig; ligsinnig; wuf, oppervlakkig; beuselagtig, nietig, frivool; ~ *and vexatious,* beuselagtig en ergerlik (jur.); ~**ness,** oppervlakkigheid, ligsinnigheid, wuftheid.

frizz¹, (n) krulle; krulkop; kroeskop, kroeshare; (v) krul, kroes, friseer.

frizz², (v) sis (in pan), sputter.

frizz: ~**y,** kroes, krullerig; ~*y hair,* gekroeste hare.

frizz'le¹, (n) krulhare; (v) krul, friseer.

frizz'le², (v) sis, braai.

fro, terug; *to and* ~, heen en weer.

frock, monnikspy; japon, jurk, tabberd; kostuum; kleed; ~-**coat,** manel, gatjieponder.

Froe'belism, Froebelisme, kindertuinstelsel.

frog¹, straal (in perdehoef); muis (aan perdepoot).

frog², puntstuk (van spoorlyn); skroefgleuf (van skaaf); ploegyfr.

frog³, lis, hanger (vir sabel), knooplus (aan uniform).

frog⁴, verbandholte (by stene).

frog⁵, padda; *HUGE* ~, janblom; *have a* ~ *in the THROAT,* hees praat; 'n padda in die keel hê; ~-**cheese,** bobbejaansnuif; ~-**eater,** padda-eter (Fransman); ~-**fish,** seeduiwel.

frogged, met knoopplusse.

frog: ~**gy,** vol paddas; so koud soos 'n padda; ~-**hopper,** skuimbesie; ~-**man,** paddaman; ~-**march,** dra-mars; ~ **olympiad,** padda-olimpiade.

frog'-screw, stelskroef.

frog: ~-**spawn,** padda-eiers; ~-**stool,** paddastoel.

frol'ic, (n) vrolikheid, plesier, vermaak; skerts; plesiertjie; (v) **(-ked),** vrolik wees, grappe (pret) maak,

from 915 *frying*

jo(o)l, (jou) vermaak, dartel, baljaar; korswel, skerts; (a) vrolik, dartel, uitgelate; grapp(er)ig; ~ **some**, dartel, speelsiek, vrolik; ~ **someness**, vrolikheid, dartelheid, grapperigheid.

from, van, vandaan; uit, vanuit; af; na, volgens; op; ~ *ABOVE*, van bo; ~ *AFAR*, van ver; ~ *AMONG*, uit, tussen; *APART* ~, afgesien van; *AS* ~, met ingang van; ~ *his BEHAVIOUR*, te oordeel na sy gedrag; ~ *BELOW*, van onder; ~ *BENEATH*, van onder; ~ *BETWEEN*, tussen; ~ *a CHILD*, van jongs af; ~ *on HIGH*, van bo; *away* ~ *HOME*, weg v.d. huis af; ~ *MOUTH to mouth*, van mond tot mond; *OBTAINABLE* ~ *the printers*, verkrygbaar by die drukkers; *ORDER* ~ *the printers*, bestel by die drukkers; ~ *OUT of the bed*, vanuit die bed; v.d. bed af; *PAINT* ~ *nature*, na die natuur skilder; *PROTECT* ~, beskerm teen; *RECOVERABLE* ~, verhaalbaar op; *SUFFER* ~, ly aan; *TRANSLATED* ~ *French*, uit Frans vertaal; ~ *WHAT she says*, volgens wat sy sê.

frond, groen tak, varingblaar; uitloper; ~ **ed**, met uitlopers.

front, (n) voorkop, voorhoof; gelaat, uiterlik; gevegslinie, front; gewel; voorkant, bors (van hemp), los voorhempie; vals krulle; voorstuk, voorste gedeelte; onbeskaamdheid; *BRING to the* ~, vorentoe bring; die aandag vestig op; *CHANGE* ~, van front verander; *GO to the* ~, na die gevegslinie gaan; *HAVE the* ~, so astrant wees om; *IN* ~, voorop, vooraan; *IN* ~ *of*, voor; *COME to the* ~, op die voorgrond tree, *POPULAR* ~, populêre front; ~ *and REAR*, voor en agter; *RIGHT* ~, haar voor; *SHOW a bold* ~, jou manhaftig gedra; ~ *TO* ~, teenoor mekaar; (v) aan die voorkant versier; front maak; uitsien op; die hoof bied; teenoor staan; ~ *ed by a GARDEN*, met 'n tuin aan die voorkant; ~ *ed with STONE*, met die voorkant van klip; (a) voorste, eerste, voor-; ~ **age**, voorgewel, gewelbreedte; voorkant, front; fasade; ~ *SQUALL*, voorwind (lugv.).

fron'tal, (n) voorkant, voorgewel, altaardoek; kopband; (a) voorhoofs-; voor-, front-, frontaal; ~ **attack**, frontaanval; ~ **bone**, voorhoofsbeen; ~ **development**, kraagplooi (van skaap).

front: ~ **axle**, vooras; ~ **bench**, voorste bank; ~ **-bencher**, voorbanker; ~ **door**, voordeur; ~ **-drive**, voorwielaandrywing; ~ **elevation**, vooraansig, vooropstand; ~ **end**, voorkant; ~ **flasher**, voorste knipoog; ~ **fork**, voortang (ossewa); voorvurk (fiets); ~ **gable**, voorgewel; ~ **hub**, voorwielnaaf.

fron'tier, (n) (land)grens, grensskeiding; (a) grens-; ~ **guard**, grenswag; ~ **post**, grenspos.

fron'tiersman, (..men), grensbewoner; baanbreker.

fron'tier: ~ **spirit**, baanbrekersgees; ~ **town**, grensstad.

Fron'tignac, fronteljak, muskadelwyn; ~ **grapes**, fronteljakdruiwe.

fron'tispiece, gesig, bakkies; fransspies; voorgewel; titelblad; titelplaat; frontispies.

front: ~ **lamp**, voorlamp; ~ **less**, sonder front; onbeskaamd; ~ **leg**, voorpoot; ~ **let**, kopband; altaardoek; ~ **line**, voorlinie; frontlinie; ~ **page**, voorblad, hoofbladsy (van koerant); ~ **rank**, eerste gelid, voorste ry; ~ **room**, voorkamer; ~ **row**, voorste ry; ~ **seat**, voorgestoelte; ~ **side**, voorsy; ~ **squall**, voorwind; ~ **tooth**, voortand; ~ **tyre**, voorband; ~ **suspension**, voorvering; ~ **view**, vooraansig, frontaansig; ~ **wall**, voormuur; voorgewel; ~ **ward**, vorentoe; ~ **wheel**, voorwiel; ~ **-wheel drive**, voorwielaandrywing; ~ **width**, voorbaan; ~ **window**, voorvenster.

frost, (n) ryp; koudheid; mislukking; (v) bevries; ryp, doodryp; versier (koek); mat verf (glas); grys maak; ~ **-bitten**, bevries, bevrore, verkluim; ~ **-bound**, vasgeys; ~ **ed**, beskadig deur ryp; ~ *ed glass*, matglas; ysglas; ~ **-free**, rypvry; ~ **-hardy**, rypbestand; ~ **ily**, yskoud; uit die hoogte; ~ **iness**, koue, koudheid; ryperigheid; bevriesing; versiering; verglasing; ~ **seersel** (lekkers); bruinering; versiersel (koek); ~ **-nail**, ysspyker; ~ **-work**, ysblomme (op glas); versiering (van koek); matwerk (van silwer); ~ **y**, rypagtig; vriesend, koud; kil; onverskillig.

froth, (n) skuim; onsin, kaf; (v) bruis; skuim; ~ *at the mouth*, skuimbek; ~ **-blower**, biersuiper; ~ **iness**, skuimerigheid; ~ **ing**, skuiming; ~ **less**, sonder skuim; ~ **y**, skuimagtig; skuimend; oppervlakkig.

frou'-frou, geritsel, geruis (van 'n rok).

frow'ard, weerspannig.

frown, (n) frons, blik van misnoeë; (v) frons; kwaad (stuurs) kyk; ~ *AT*, suur aankyk; aanfrons; ~ *(UP)ON*, afkeur; suur aankyk; ~ **ing**, streng, somber, ontevrede; frons.

frowst, (n) bedompigheid; (v) broei (by die kaggel).

frowz'y, slordig, vuil; muf, bedompig.

froz'en, bevries, yskoud, verys; bevrore; styf; ~ *ASSETS*, bevrore bates; ~ *MEAT*, bevrore vleis; ~ *MONEY*, vasliggende geld; ~ *ZONE*, poolstreek.

fructif'erous, vrugdraend.

fructifica'tion, vrugvorming; bevrugting.

fruc'tiform, vrugvormig.

fruc'tify, (..fied), vrugte dra; vrugbaar maak; bevrug.

fruc'tose, vrugtesuiker, fruktose.

fruc'tuous, vrugdraend; vrugryk; vrugbaar.

frug'al, spaarsaam, matig, sober, suinig.

frugal'ity, **frug'alness**, spaarsaamheid, matigheid, soberheid, suinigheid.

frugif'erous, vrugdraend.

frugiv'orous, vrugetend.

fruit, (n) vrug; vrugte; resultaat, gevolg; voordeel; *BEAR* ~, vrugte dra; ~*s of EARTH*, vrugte v.d. aarde; *FIRST* ~*s*, eersteling; *FORBIDDEN* ~, verbode vrugte; *the* ~*s of INDUSTRY*, die opbrengs van industrie; *LIVE on* ~, van vrugte leef; *PLUCK the* ~, vrugte dra; ~ *in SEASON*, seisoensvrugte; (v) vrugte dra; vrugte laat dra; ~ **acid**, vrugtesuur; ~ **age**, vrugte; ~ **ar'ian**, vrugte-eter; ~ **-basket**, vrugtemandjie; ~ **-bearing**, vrugdraend; ~ **-cake**, vrugtekoek; ~ **-canning**, vrugte-inmaak; ~ **-chutney**, vrugteblatjang; ~ **cobbler**, vrugtepastei; ~ **cocktail**, vrugtekelkie; ~ **cordial**, vrugtedrank, ~ **-dict**, vrugtedieet; ~ **drink**, vrugtedrank; ~ **drop**, suurklontjie; ~ **-drying**, vrugtedroging; ~ **er**, vrugtekweker; vrugteboom; vrugteskip; ~ **erer**, vrugtehandelaar; vrugtewinkel; ~ **-farmer**, vrugteboer; ~ **feast**, vrugtefees; ~ **filling**, vrugtevulsel; ~ **-fly**, vrugtevlieg; ~ **-fork**, vrugtevurk(ie); ~ **ful**, vrugbaar; ~ **fulness**, vrugbaarheid; ~ **-germ**, vrugtekiem; ~ **-grove**, vrugteboord; ~ **-grower**, vrugtekweker; ~ **-growing**, vrugtekwekery.

frui'tion, genot, genieting; verwerkliking; rypwording.

fruit: ~ **jar**, vrugtefles; ~ **juice**, vrugtesap; ~ **-knife**, vrugtemes(sie); ~ **leather**, vrugtesmeer, vrugtameletjie; ~ **less**, sonder vrugte; vrugteloos, nutteloos; ~ **loft**, vrugtesolder; ~ **lunch**, vrugtemaaltyd; ~ **market**, vrugtemark; ~ **-packer**, vrugtepakker; ~ **puree**, vrugtemoes; ~ **rebate**, vrugtekorting; ~ **salad**, vrugteslaai; ~ **scale**, vrug(te)skub; ~ **season**, vrugtetyd; ~ **shop**, vrugtewinkel; ~ **show**, vrugtetentoonstelling; ~ **-spot**, vrugtevlek; ~ **squash**, vrugtekwas; ~ **stall**, vrugtestalletjie; ~ **-sugar**, vrugtesuiker, levulose; ~ **syrup**, vrugtestroop; ~ **-tart**, vrugtetert; ~ **-tree**, vrugteboom; ~ **whip**, vrugteskuim; ~ **y**, vrug-, vrugte-, smaaklik, pittig.

frum'enty, koringpap.

frump, slons, slordige vrou; ~ **ish**, ~ **y**, slordig, slonserig.

frustrate', verydel, omverwerp; uitoorlê; teleurstel; dwarsboom, frustreer

frustra'tion, verydeling; teleurstelling; frustrasie.

frus'tum, (-s, ..ta), keëlstomp, afgeknotte keël; ~ *of a sphere*, bolskyf.

tru'tan, froetang.

frutes'cent, struikagtig, struikvormig.

frut'ex, (frutices), struik, bossie.

frut'icose, struikagtig, bossieagtig.

fry[1], (n) (sing and pl) swerm, skool, trop; jong vissies; kleingoed; *small* ~, onbelangrike (niksbeduidende) mense; kleingoed, die kleinspan.

fry[2], (n) braaivleis; harslag; (v) (fried), braai, bak; ~ **er**, braaipan; bakpan; braaier; braaikuiken, braaihoender.

fry'ing, braai(ery); ~ **fat**, braaivet; ~ **-pan**, bakpan;

F sharp 916 *fume*

braaipan; *from the ~-pan into the fire*, van die wal in die sloot.
F' sharp, F-kruis.
fub'sy, vet, dik.
fuchs'ia, foksia, fuchsia.
fuch'sine, fuchsine, fuchsien.
fuch'site, fuchsiet.
fuc'us, (fuci), seegras.
fud'dle, (n) suipparty; roes, beskonkenheid; verwarring; (v) dronk word (maak); bedrink, suip; benewel; ~ **d,** dronkerig; benewel(d).
fud'dling, suipery.
fudd'y-duddy, (..ddies), remskoen, lamsak; (a) pap, slap.
fudge, (n) knoeiery; onsin, malligheid; geklets; (v) aanmekaar lap; knoei; saamflans; vervals; (interj) onsin! twak!
fu'el, (n) brandstof; petrol; vuurmaakgoed; nagekome berig; borsplaat, lekkergoed; *ADD* ~ *to the fire,* olie op die vuur gooi; *SOLID* ~, vaste brandstof; (v) (-led), brandstof inneem; van brandstof voorsien; vuurmaak, stook; ~ **capacity,** brandstofinhoud; ~ **chamber,** brandstofkamer; ~ **cock,** brandstofkraan; ~ **consumption,** brandstofverbruik; ~ **economizer,** brandstofbespaarder; ~ **economy,** brandstofbesparing; ~**-feed,** brandstofleiding; ~ **gauge,** brandstofmeter; ~ **injection,** brandstofinspuiting; ~ **oil,** brandstofolie; stookolie; ~ **pressure,** brandstofdruk; ~ **pump,** brandstofpomp; ~**-spray,** brandstofstuifsel; ~ **stamp,** brandstofseël; ~**-supply,** brandstoftoevoer; brandstofvoorraad; ~**-system,** brandstofstelsel; ~ **tank,** brandstoftenk; ~**-tanker,** brandstofwa; brandstofskip, olieskip.
fug, bedompigheid, mufheid; vuiligheid, stof; kamerwol; ~ **gy,** bedompig, muf.
fug'a = **fugue.**
fuga'cious, vlieënd; vlugtig, verganklik; verbygaande, vervliegend; ~**ness,** verganklikheid, kortstondigheid; vlugtigheid.
fuga'city, kortstondigheid, vlugtigheid.
fug'al, fuga=.
fugg'y, muf, bedompig; stowwerig.
fu'gitive, (n) vlugteling; voortvlugtige; wegloper; (a) (voort)vlugtig; verbygaande; weggeloop; swerwend; onvas (kleur); verganklik; kortstondig; ~ *dye,* onvaste kleurstof.
fu'gleman, (..men), vleuelman; leier, voorman.
fugue, (n) fuga; swerfsiekte; (v) 'n fuga komponeer; fuga(s) speel.
fug'uist, fugakomponis.
fu'ji silk, foedji-sy.
ful'crum, (..cra), draaipunt, stut; steunpunt; spilkop; (pl) steunorgaan (bot.).
fulfil', (-led), vervul; verwesenlik; uitvoer; volbring, volvoer; beantwoord aan; ~ **ler,** volbringer, voleinder; ~**ment,** vervulling, verwesenliking, volvoering, volbrenging, uitvoering.
ful'gency, luister; glans, skittering.
ful'gent, luisterryk; skitterend, glansend, blinkend.
ful'gurant, blitsend, bliksemend.
ful'gurate, blits, bliksem.
fulgura'tion, weerlig; skittering.
ful'gurite, bliksembuis, fulguriet (geol.).
fuli'ginous, roetagtig, donker.
full¹, (n) volheid; genoegsaamheid; volledigheid, hoogtepunt; *AT the* ~, op sy hoogtepunt; *IN* ~, ten volle; *TO the* ~, ten volle, heeltemal; (v) vul, vol maak; plooi; (a) vol, gevul; voltallig; volteken; vervul; volmaak; uitvoerig, volledig; ruim, oorvloedig; *turn to* ~ *ACCOUNT,* die volle gebruik maak van; ~ *AGE,* mondig; ~ *to the BRIM,* propvol; ~ *BROTHER,* eie broer; *be in* ~ *CRY,* in volle vaart agter iem. of iets wees; *his CUP is* ~, sy maat is vol; ~ *DETAILS,* volle besonderhede; ~ *in the FACE,* reg in die gesig; met 'n ronde (vet) gesig; ~ *of NONSENSE,* vol fratse; ~ *to OVERFLOWING,* tot oorlopens toe vol; propvol; kant en wal lê; *on* ~ *PAY,* met vol soldy, met volle betaling; ~ *of PLAY,* dartel, speels; *a* ~ *PULSE,* 'n kragtige pols; *at* ~ *SPEED,* in volle vaart; ~ *STEAM ahead,* met volle stoom vooruit; *a* ~ *STO=*

MACH, 'n vol maag; ~ *SUMMER,* hoogsomer; ~ *of VITALITY,* vol lewenskrag; ~ *of YEARS,* baie oud; ~ *of YEARS and honours,* oud en geëer; (adv) ten volle, ruim, baie, heeltemal, vol; *BE* ~, vol wees; *BE* ~ *of,* heeltemal vervul wees van; *BE* ~ *up,* vol wees; emosioneel wees; ~ *in the FACE,* reg in die gesig; *he who is* ~ *of HIMSELF is ever empty,* hy wat met homself vervul is, is 'n leë vat; *KNOW* ~ *well,* baie goed weet; ~ *MANY a,* meer as een; ~ *NIGH,* byna; *be* ~ *of ONESELF,* jou verbeel dat jy die koning (keiser) se hond se oom (neef) is; verwaand wees.
full², (v) vol (van laken).
full: ~**-back,** heelagter ~**-blood,** volbloed; ~**-blooded,** volbloedig; ~**-blown,** in volle bloei; heeltemal ontwikkel, uitgegroei; ~**-bodied,** lywig, swaar; ~**-bodied wine,** vol (lywige, pittige) wyn; ~**-bottomed (wig),** lang krulpruik, allongepruik; ~ **coat,** volle laag (verf); ~ **cream,** volvet; ~**-cream cheese,** volvet kaas.
full' dress, in galakleding; galatenue, groottenue; ~ *DEBATE,* formele debat; ~ *REHEARSAL,* algemene repetisie, eindrepetisie, kleedrepetisie; ~ *UNIFORM,* groot tenue.
full'er¹, (n) lakenvoller, bleiker.
full'er², (n) ritshamer, sethamer.
full'ering, rits; spykergroef.
full'er's earth, volaarde, vollersaarde; bleikpoeier.
full'ery, vollery.
full: ~**-faced,** met 'n ronde gesig; reg van voor; ~**-fashioned,** gepasweef; ~**-flavoured,** volgeurig; ~**-fledged,** vol vere, uitgegroei; volleerd; volwaardig, volslae; ~**-grown,** volwasse, uitgegroei, volgroeid; ~ **house,** huis vol; uitverkoop (teater).
full'ing, vollery; ~**-mill,** voelmeule.
full: ~**-length,** lewensgroot(te) (portret); volle lengte; *he fell* ~*-length on the ground,* hy het plat op die grond geval; ~ **load,** volle las, volle belasting, volle lading; vrag; ~ **marks,** vol(le) punte; ~ **moon,** volmaan; ~**-mouthed,** volbek=; dof, hol; luid; swaarklinkend; ~ **name,** volle naam; ~**ness,** volheid, volte; volkomenheid; ruimte (naaldw.); *in the* ~*ness of time,* die volheid v.d. tye; ~**-scale,** volslae, van volle omvang; ~**-service,** met volle diens; ~**-service garage,** voldiensmotorhawe; ~ **size,** volle grootte; ~ **speed,** in volle vaart; met groot snelheid, vinnig; ~ **stop,** punt; ~ **swing,** in volle gang, vinnig, heeltemal besig; ~**-throated,** uit volle bors; ~**-time,** heeltyds, voltyds; ~ **timer,** voltydse leerling, ~**-toothed,** volbek=.
full'y, volkome, ten volle, heeltemal; ~*-FASHION=ED,* snit volgens nuutste mode; ~ *LOADED,* volgelaai; ~ *MATURED,* volryp; ~ *PAID,* ten volle betaal, volgestort; ~ *paid-up shares,* volgestorte aandele.
ful'mar, stormvoël.
ful'minant, donderend, bliksemend; met snelle verloop (siekte); snelverlopend.
ful'minate, (n) fulminaat, knalsuursout; ~ *of mercury,* slagkwik; (v) donder, bliksem; ontplof, knal; te kere gaan, uitvaar (teen), fulmineer.
ful'minating, ontploffend, donderend, rasend; ~ **cap,** knaldoppie; ~ **gold,** dondergoud; knalgoud; ~ **mercury,** donderkwik, knalkwik; ~ **powder,** donderpoeier; ~ **silwer,** dondersilwer.
fulmina'tion, gedonder, ontploffing, knal; uitvaring, fulminasie.
ful'minatory, donderend, knallend; rasend, uitvarend.
ful'mine, donder, uitbliksem (digterlik).
fulmin'ic, knal=; ~ **acid,** knalsuur.
ful'ness, *kyk* **fullness.**
ful'some, grof, oordrewe; walglik, weersinwekkend; ~**ness,** grofheid, liederlikheid, oordrywing; walglikheid.
ful'vous, rooigeel, taankleurig.
fum'arole, fumarole, rookgat (van vulkaan).
fum'ble, friemel, frommel, sleg vat, misvat; peuter; voel, rondvat; ~ **r,** frommelaar; knoeier, onhandige mens.
fum'bling, gepeuter; onhandige gevroetel.
fume, (n) rook, damp, walm, uitwaseming; wierook;

woede, toorn; *in a* ~, briesend; hewig ontstoke; (v) rook; kook; berook, uitrook; ontsmet, fumigeer; bewierook; briesend maak; briesend wees; ~ **cupboard**, rookkas.
fum'igant, berokingsmiddel.
fum'igate, berook, deurrook, suiwer, fumigeer, ontsmet, uitrook.
fumiga'tion, ontsmetting, beroking, uitdamping, suiwering, fumigasie; ~ **fee**, berokingskoste.
fum'igator, ontsmettingsoond, ontsmettingstoestel; ontsmetter, beroker, fumigeerder.
fum'ing, rokend, dampend; woedend, rasend; *he is* ~, hy is rasend van woede (briesend; vuurwarm; hewig ontstoke).
fum'itory, aardrook, duiwelskerwel (plant).
fum'y, rokerig.
fun, skerts, pret, jool, korswel, tydverdryf; pretmakery; plesier, aardigheid; *now the* ~ *BEGINS*, nou gaan die poppe dans; *now there is GOING to be* ~, nou gaan die poppe dans; *FOR* ~, vir die grap; *GREAT* ~, baie plesier; *IN* ~, vir die grap; *LIKE* ~, dat dit gons; dat dit 'n naarheid is; *MAKE* ~ *of*, die gek skeer met iem.; die spot met iem. dryf; *NOT for* ~, nie vir die grap nie; *POKE* ~ *at*, vir die gek hou, die gek skeer met; *for the* ~ *of the THING*, vir die aardigheid.
funam'bulism, koorddansery.
funam'bulist, koorddanser.
func'tion, (n) verrigting, plegtigheid, bediening; beroep, amp, diens, pos, byeenkoms, fees, seremonie, geleentheid; funksie, ampsplig; rol, werking; (v) fungeer; funksioneer; werk, diens doen; ~ **al**, funksioneel; diens=; amps=; ~ *al disease*, bedryfsiekte; ~ **ary**, (..ries), funksionaris; amptenaar; beampte, ampsdraer.
func'tioning, (n) verrigting, werking, fungering; (a) werkend, fungerend.
func'tionless, sonder funksie, funksieloos.
fund, fonds, kapitaal; rykdom; voorraad; *IN* ~s, genoeg fondse (geld) he; *PUBLIC* ~s, openbare fondse; staatspapiere; *THE* ~s, staatspapiere, staatsfondse; (v) konsolideer, (in staatseffekte) belê; fundeer; versamel; ~*ed debt*, gevestigde skuld.
fun'dament, fondament; agterste.
fundamen'tal, (n) grondslag, grondbeginsel, basis; grondtoon; grondwaarheid; (a) hoof=, grond=, vernaamste, prinsipieel, grondig, grondliggend, wesenlik, oorspronklik, fundamenteel; *the* ~ *CAUSE*, die grondliggende oorsaak; ~ *PRINCIPLE*, grondbeginsel; ~ *RULE*, grondreël; ~ *TONE*, grondtoon; ~ **ism**, fundamentalisme; ~ **ist**, fundamentalis; ~ **ly**, prinsipieel, in die grond, in wese.
fundat'rix, (..trices), stammoeder.
fund: ~-**holder**, besitter van staatsfondse; ~**ing**, befondsing; ~-**raiser**, geldinsamelaar; ~-**raising**, geldinsameling.
fun'di, fundi, deskundige.
fun'dus, fundus (anat.).
tuneb'rial, *kyk* **funeral**, (a)
fun'eral, (n) begrafnis; lykstoet; *that is his* ~, dit is sy saak; (a) begrafnis=, graf=, doods=, lyk=; ~ **carriage**, lykwa; ~ **ceremony**, begrafnisplegtigheid; ~ **chapel**, begrafniskapel; ~ **contractor**, begrafnisondernemer, lykbesorger; ~ **expense**, begrafniskoste; ~ **furnisher**, begrafnisondernemer, lykbesorger; ~ **honours**, laaste eer; ~ **march**, treurmars; ~ **oration**, grafrede, lykrede; ~ **parlour**, roukamer; ~ **pile**, brandstapel; ~ **service**, lykdiens; ~ **urn**, lykbus; ~ **wail**, lykklag; ~ **wreath**, roukrans.
funer'eal, begrafnis=; treur=, lyk=, graf=; somber, droewig, treurig, naargeestig; ~ **voice**, grafstem.
fun'-fair, pretpark.
funga'ceous, swamagtig.
fun'gal, swamagtig, swam=; ~ **disease**, swamsiekte.
fun'gible, vervangbaar.
fun'gic, swam=; ~ **acid**, swamsuur.
fungicid'al, swamdodend.
fun'gicide, swamdoder, swamverdelger.
fun'giform, swamvormig.
fungiv'orous, swametend.
fun'goid, swamagtig.

fun'gous, sponsagtig; fungoïed, swamagtig, paddastoelagtig; verbygaande, kortstondig; ~ **trouble**, swamsiekte.
fun'gus, (..**gi**, -**es**), paddastoel, swam, skimmel, fungus; ~ **spore**, swamspoor.
fun'icle, draadjie, veseltjie; na(w)elstring; string.
funic'ular, kabel=, draad=, tou=, funikulêr; ~ **railway**, kabelspoorweg, tandratspoor.
funk, (n) vrees, angs; weifelaar, papbroek, bangbroek, lafaard; *be in a BLUE* ~, doodbang wees; lelik in die knyp sit; *THE* ~s, bewerasiesiekte; (v) bang wees; ontwyk; jou uitdraai; ~-**hole**, skuilplek; uitvlug; ~**y**, (n) bangbroek; (a) bang; papbroek=(er)ig.
fun'maker, pretmaker, grapmaker.
funn'el, tregter; skoorsteenpyp (van skip); ~-**shaped**, tregtervormig.
funn'iment, grap, mal streek.
funn'iness, snaaksheid, komieklikheid.
funn'y[1], (n) (**funnies**), smal bootjie (vir een persoon).
funn'y[2], (a) grapp(er)ig, snaaks, koddig; raar, aardig; ~-**bone**, elmboogbeentjie, kieliebeentjie, swernootjie, tinteltonnetjie, verneukbeentjie, einabeentjie; ~ **business**, spulletjies; bedrog, bedrieëry; ~ **man**, grapmaker.
fur, (n) diervel met sagte hare; pels, bont; bontmantel; bontkraag; aanslag, ketelsteen; aanpaksel, beslag (op tong); kim (op wyn); *make the* ~ *fly*, die vonke laat spat, die hare laat waai; (v) (-**red**), met bont uitvoer, met bont bekleë; aanpak, aanslaan (ketel); aanpaksel verwyder; beslaan (tong).
furb'elow, (n) geplooide strook (van rok), valletjie; tierlantyntjie; (v) optooi, opskik; stroke opsit.
furb'ish, opvrywe, oppoets, politoer, polys; ~ *up*, op=knap; ~**er**, poleerder, opvrywer.
fur: ~ **cap**, pelsmus; ~ **cape**, skouerpels.
furcate', (v) splits, verdeel; aftak; afdraai (pad).
furc'ate, **furc'ated**, (a) gevurk, gesplits, gesplete.
furca'tion, vertakking.
fur: ~ **cloak**, pelsmantel; ~ **coat**, bontjas, pelsjas; ~ **collar**, bontkraag; ~ **felt**, haarvilt.
fur'fur, skilfers, skobbe; ~**a'ceous**, skilferagtig; gekors, skubbig.
fur'ious, woes, waansinnig, woedend, verwoed, wild, rasend, briesend, doldriftig; *BE* ~ *with someone*, woedend kwaad wees vir iem., die hoenders in wees vir iem.; *FAST and* ~, oproerig; woes.
furl, oprol, opvou, inbind; plooi, inhaal; ~ *sails*, seile oprol (inhaal).
furl'ong, furlong (± 201 meter).
furl'ough, (n) (groot, lang) verlof; (v) verlof gee (toestaan).
furn'ace, (n) (vuur)oond, stookoond; vlamkas; smeltkroes; haard; fornuis; *tried in the* ~, deur die smeltkroes gegaan; (v) verhit; ~ **man**, smeltoondstoker; ~-**oil**, brandolie.
furn'ish, stoffeer, meubileer; voorsien; uitrus; verskaf, verstrek, besorg, lewer; ~**ed**, gestoffeer, ingerig; ~*ed house*, gemeubileerde huis; ~**er**, meubelmaker; meubileerder; leweransier; ~**ing**, verskaffing; meubilering; stoffering; ~ **ing fabric**, meubelstof; ~**ings**, meublement, toebehore.
furn'iture, huisraad, meubels, meublement, toerusting, toebehorens; inhoud; behang; *a piece of* ~, 'n meubelstuk; ~ **chintz**, meubelsits; ~ **factory**, meubelfabriek; ~ **firm**, meubelsaak; ~ **polish**, meubelwaks, meubelpolitoer; ~ **removal**, meubelvervoer; ~-**removal van**, meubelwa; ~ **store**, meubelwinkel; ~ **trade**, meubelhandel; ~ **van**, verhuiswa, meubelwa.
furor'e, furore, byval, opgang; gier; modegril.
furred, aangeslaan, aangepak; pels=, bont=.
fu'rrier, bontwerker; pelshandelaar, bonthandelaar; ~**y**, (..ries), bontwerk; velhandel; pelswerk; pelstery.
furr'ing, aanpaksel.
fu'rrow, (n) voor, sloot; grippie; rimpel; *DEAD* ~, strykvoor; *plough a LONELY* ~, 'n eensame paadjie bewandel; (v) vore trek, ploeg, deurploeg; rimpel; ~**ed**, gegroef; ~-**slice**, ploegwalletjie; ~-**weed**, kweekgras; ~-**wheel**, wurgwiel; ~**y**, sloterig.

furr'y, met bont gevoer; bont=; beslaan (tong), aangepak.
fur'stone, ketelsteen.
furth'er, (v) bevorder, ondersteun, behartig, aanhelp; ~ *one's AIMS*, jou doeleindes bevorder; (a, adv) verder, bowendien, voorts, vervolgens, buitendien; nader; *the* ~ *END*, die ander ent; *GO (a step)* ~, 'n stap verder gaan; ~ *INFORMATION*, meer (nadere) inligting; *till* ~ *NOTICE*, tot nader kennisgewing; *till* ~ *ORDERS*, tot nader bevele, tot later order; *I'll SEE you* ~ *first*, ek sien jou eerder op die verkeerde plek; *on the* ~ *SIDE*, aan die ander kant; ~ *TO*, met verdere verwysing na; ~ **ance**, bevordering, steun; ~ **er**, bevorderaar; begunstiger; ~ **ing**, behartiging; ~ **more**, boonop, verder, bowendien, daarenbowe, voorts; ~ **most**, verste, uiterste.
furth'est, verste, uiterste.
furt'ive, heimlik, skelm, slu, steels, onderduims, diefagtig; ~ **ly**, onderlangs, skelm(pies); ~ **ness**, sluheid, skelmheid, onderduimsheid.
fur: ~ **-trapper**, pelsjagter; ~ **-trimmed**, met bont gegarneer; ~ **trimming**, bontgarnering.
fur'uncle, bloedvin(t), pitsweer, steenpuis.
fur'uncular, fur'unculous, bloedvintagtig.
Fur'y¹, (..ries), Furie, Wraakgodin.
fur'y², (..ries), woede, raserny, drif, furie, waansin, grimmigheid, doldriftigheid, woestheid, verwoedheid, heftigheid; *in a* ~, rasend, woedend, die josie in; *LASH someone into a* ~, iem. woedend maak; *LIKE* ~, woes, rasend; soos blits.
furze, skerpioenkruid.
fus'cous, donker, somber.
fuse, (n) smeltdraadjie, veiligheidsdraadjie, sekering; *the* ~ *is BLOWN*, die smeltdraadjie het uitgebrand; *CAPPED* ~, doppielont; *the LIGHT has* ~ *d*, die lamp (sekering) het uitgebrand; (v) blus (van gloeilamp), ineensmelt, (ver)smelt; saamsmelt, verenig; uitbrand; van 'n smeltdraad voorsien; ~ **box**, sekeringskas; ~ **cap**, bruisdop; ~ **cartridge**, sekeringspatroon.
fusee'¹, wasvuurhoutjie.
fusee'², kettingspil, snekrat.
fuse'-head, lontdop.
fus'elage, romp, geraamte (vliegtuig), raamwerk.
fus'el oil, foeselolie.
fuse: ~ **-pin**, slagpen; ~ **-pliers**, lonttang; ~ **-plug**, sekeringsprop; ~ **-setting**, tempering ~ **-shell**, buisgranaat; ~ **-wire**, smeltdraad, veiligheidsdraad, sekeringsdraad.
fusibil'ity, smeltbaarheid.
fus'ible, smeltbaar; smelt=.
fus'iform, spilvormig, sigaarvormig.
fus'il, geweer, musket; ~ **ier'**, fusillier, musketier;
~ **lade'**, (n) geweervuur, salvo, fusillade; (v) fusilleer, doodskiet, platskiet; beskiet.
fu'sion, smelting, fusie; samesmelting; ineenvloeiing; versmelting; ~ **bomb**, smeltbom; ~ **heat**, smelthitte; ~ **ist**, koalisieman, smelter; ~ **point**, smeltpunt; ~ **welding**, smeltsweising;
fuss, (n) ophef, gedoente, gedoe, drukte, bohaai, omhaal, opskudding, rumoer, gewerskaf, werskaffery, bombarie; *kick up (make) a* ~, te kere gaan; 'n drukte maak; (v) drukte maak, omslag maak, oor kleinigheidjies lol; ~ **-free**, moeitevry; ~ **iness**, lollerigheid; omslagtigheid; ~ **-pot**, lolpot, neulpot, bemoeisieke; ~ **y**, woelerig; omslagtig; lollerig.
fust¹, (n) suilskag.
fust², (n) muf, skimmel; (v) muf, skimmel; (a) vermuf; sleg ruik.
fust'age, kuipwerk, vatwerk.
fus'tian¹, (n) bombasyn (stof).
fus'tian², (n) bombas, hoogdrawendheid; (a) hoogdrawend.
fus'tic, geelhout (van Wes-Indië) *(Chlorophora tinctoria)*; geel kleurstof, fustiek, fustine.
fus'tigate, slaan, looi, afransel.
fustiga'tion, pak slae, loesing.
fus'tiness, muwwerigheid, vunsigheid, dufheid.
fus'ty, muf, duf, vunsig; sleg; ~ *smell*, kelderlug.
futch'el(l), dwarshout (in perdewa).
fut'ile, nikswerd; kinderagtig; vergeefs, vrugteloos, ydel, ondoelmatig, futiel; ~ **ly**, vergeefs, vrugteloos.
futil'ity, niksbeduidendheid, ydelheid, vrugteloosheid, futiliteit, nutteloosheid; bakatel, kleinigheid.
futt'ock, buikstuk, oplanger (van skip).
fu'ture, (n) toekomende tyd; aanstaande (huweliksmaat); toekoms; vervolg; *DISTANT* ~, verre toekoms; *FOR the* ~, vir die toekoms; *IN* ~, in die toekoms; voortaan; *NEAR* ~, nabye toekoms; ~ *PERFECT*, volmaak toekomende tyd; *let the* ~ *TAKE care of itself*, kwel jou nie oor die dag van môre nie; (a) aanstaande, toekomstig; *the* ~ *LIFE*, die lewe hiernamaals; ~ *TENSE*, toekomende tyd; ~ **s market**, termynmark.
fu'turism, futurisme.
fu'turist, (n) futuris; (a) futuristies.
futur'ity, toekomstige gebeurtenis; toekoms, toekomstigheid; hiernamaals.
futuro'logist, toekoms(leer)kundige, futuroloog.
fuzz, dons; pluis; ~ **-ball**, stuifswam; ~ **iness**, wasigheid; ~ **y**, pluiserig; gerafel; donserig; kroeserig; wasig; ~ **y-wuzzy**, kroeskop.
fy(e)! = fie!
fyl'fot, hakekruis, swastika, fylfot.
fytte, vers; kanto; sang.

G

g, (gs, g's), g.
gab¹, (n) oog; nok (van masjien); keep; vurk, puntyster.
gab², (n) gebabbel, gekekkel; *stop your* ~, bly stil, hou jou mond (snater); (v) **(-bed)**, babbel, kekkel, klets.
gab'ardine = **gaberdine**.
gab'ble, (n) geklets; gesnater; (v) babbel, kekkel, afratel.
gab'bro, gabbro.
gab'bronite, gabbroniet.
gab'by, (sl.), praterig, kletserig.
gabelle', soutaksyns.
gab'erdine, oorkleed, oorjas; gabardine.
gab'fest, (sl.), geselsfees; geselsery, pratery.
gab'ion, skanskorf, skansmandjie; ~ **ade'**, borswering van skanskorwe, korfskans.
ga'ble, gewel, geweltop; ~ **d**, gegewel, met gewels; ~ **-end**, gewelspits; gewelmuur; puntgewel, wolwe-ent; ~ **-roof**, geweldak, saaldak; ~ **-window**, gewelvenster.

Gabon', Gaboon', Gabun', Gaboen.
gab'-string, neusyster; stangtoom.
gab'y, **(gabies)**, idioot, uilskuiken; sukkelaar.
gad¹, (n) staalwig, ysterpunt; splytwig, prikyster; graveernaald.
gad², (n): *he's always on the* ~, hy is altyd aan die rondflenter; (v) **(-ded)**, slenter, rondrentel; rondswerf; afdwaal; ~ *about*, rondslenter, rondloop.
gad!³ (interj) hemel! gits! *by* ~ *!* wragtie.
gad'about, slenteraar, rondloper, straatloper, uithuisige; flerrie.
Ga'dara, Gadara.
Ga'darene, (n) Gadarener; (a) Gadareens.
gad: ~ **ding**, rondswerwery, uithuisigheid; ~ **dishness**, uithuisigheid; ~ **fly**, perdevlieg, horsel.
gadg'et, katoeter; toestelletjie, dingesie; uitvinding, uitvindsel; ~ **ry**, geriefies; toestelle.
ga'dolinite, gadoliniet.
gadoli'nium, gadolinium.
gadroon', (n) godron; (v) godronneer.

gad'wall, varswatereend.
gad'zooks, genugtig!, liewe tyd!
Gael, (Skotse) Kelt.
Gael'ic, (n) Kelties (taal); (a) Kelties.
gaff¹, (n) ysterhaak; vishaak, haakstok; gaf(fel)seil (skip); (v) haak, spies.
gaff², (n): *blow the* ~, (ver)klik; met die hele mandjie patats voor die dag kom.
gaffe, blaps, flater.
gaff'er, opsigter, baas; agtervelder; voorman; ou=baas; paaier.
gaff: ~**-rigged,** toegerus met 'n gaffelseil; ~ **topsail,** gaf(fel)topseil.
gag, (n) prop, mondprop; grap; inlas (toneel); mond=klem, stang; leuen; sluiting (van parlement); *that's the old* ~, dis die ou leuen (grap); (v) (**-ged**), toe=stop, stilmaak; muilband, die mond snoer; smoor; vomeer; met 'n stang ry; kul; die woorde inlas (to=neel); die sluiting toepas (van parlement); ~**-bit,** knewelstang.
gag'a, mallerig; seniel; laf.
gage¹, (n) uitdaging; *throw down the* ~, die hand=skoen neergooi (as uitdaging); (v) wed.
gage², (n) pand, waarborg, (v) verpand.
gag'gle, trop ganse; klompie snaterende vroue; ge=snater; *the* ~ *of geese,* die gesnater van ganse; (v) snater, kekkel.
gag'-law, hou-jou-bek-wet.
gag'-snaffle, baktrens.
gai'ety, (..ties), vrolikheid, blymoedigheid, pret, ver=maaklikheid; opsmuk, vertoon.
gaillar'dia, kombersblom, katnaels, goudranonkel.
gall'y, vrolik, lewendig, opgewek.
gain¹, (n) drakeep (timmery).
gain², (n) wins, profyt, voordeel; baat; aanwins; voor=sprong; winsoogmerk; *no* ~*s without pains,* ge=braaide hoenders vlieg niemand in die mond nie; wie heuning wil eet, moet steke verdra; *incorpora=ted society not for* ~, ingelyfde vereniging sonder winsoogmerk; (v) wen (win); voordeel trek; verkry, verwerf; verdien; bereik; behaal; ~ *the DAY,* die oorwinning behaal; ~ *GROUND,* veld win; ~ *one's OBJECT,* sy doel bereik; ~ *ON,* wen op; ~ *on SOMEONE,* iem. begin inhaal; ~ *OVER,* oor=haal; ~ *TIME,* tyd win; ~ *the UPPER hand,* die oormag kry; ~ *WEIGHT,* swaarder word; in ge=wig toeneem; ~**er,** wenner; bevoordeelde; ~**ful,** voordelig, winsgewend; inhalig; ~**ing,** verwering, winning, (behaalde) wins.
gainsay', (..said), teenspreek, weerspreek, ontken; ~**er,** teenspreker, loënaar, ontkenner.
gait, gang, stap; beweging (perd)
gait'er, oorkous, slobkous, veerkous; kamas; binne=sool, lap (van motorband).
gal, meisie.
gal'a, fees, gala
gala'bia, kabaai.
ga'la costume, feesgewaad, galakostuum; gala=kleding.
galac'tic, melkweg=; melk=.
gal'actine, galaktine.
gal'actite, galaktiet.
galactom'eter, melkmeter.
galac'tophore, melkbuis.
galac'tose, galaktose, melksuiker.
gal'a day, feesdag, galadag.
gal'a dress = **gala costume.**
gala'go, (**-es**) ooraap, oormaki.
gal'antine, galantien, galantine, vleisrol.
galan'ty show, skimmespel, pantomime.
galate'a, galatea, gesteepte katoenstof.
Gal'atia, Galasië; ~ **n,** (n) Galasiër; (a) Galaties; ~ **ns,** Galasiërs; Galate (Bybelboek).
gal'axy, (..xies), melkweg; hemelstraat; skitterende versameling (geselskap); *the G* ~, die Melkweg.
gal'banum, galbanum, gomhars.
gale, sterk wind, stormwind; ~ **force,** stormsterkte; ~ **warning,** stormwaarskuwing.
gal'ea, galea, helm; ~**-te**(**d**), gehelm; helmvormig.
Gal'en, Galenus; dokter (skerts).
galen'a, gale'nite, loodglans, galeniet.
gale'nic, ..al, (a) galenies; (n) plantaardige medisyne.

Gali'cian, (n) Galiciër; (a) Galicies.
Galile'an, (n) Galileër; (a) Galilees.
Gal'ilee¹, Galilea.
gal'ilee², voorportaal (van kerk).
galima'tias, betekenislose gepraat, gerammel.
gal'ingale, galgant *(Alpinia galanga).*
gal'ipot, dennegom, wit harpuis.
galjoen', galjoen; *bastard* ~, snoekgaljoen.
gall¹, (n) gal; skaafplek; blaar; ergernis, kwelling; bit=terheid; *HAVE the* ~, die vermetelheid hê; *dip one's PEN in* ~, jou pen in gal doop; *it is so much* ~ *and WORMWOOD to him,* dis vir hom 'n bitte=re naarheid; dis gal en edik vir hom; (v) skaaf, skuur; verbitter; kwel; terg; vergal; verneder.
gall², (n) galneut; knop (by bome).
gall'ant, (n) minnaar, galant, hofmaker; *play the* ~, galant optree; (v) die hof maak, vry, flirt; vergesel, begelei; (a) dapper; sierlik; galant, fier, mooi; swie=rig, statig, smaakvol; ~**ry,** galanterie, hoflikheid, flinkheid; moed, kranigheid, dapperheid.
gal'late, gallaat.
gall: ~**-bladder,** galblaas; ~**-duct,** galbuisie.
gal'leas, gal'lias, galjas.
gall'con, galjoen (skip; vis); galjas.
gall'ery, (..**ries**), galery, tribune; kunsmuseum; gang; *OPEN* ~, balkon; *PLAY to the* ~, na effek strewe; *PLAYING to the* ~, effekbejag; ~ **girder,** galery=reling; ~ **play,** spogspel.
gall'et, klipsplinter; ~**ing,** splintstopwerk.
gall'ey, (**-s**) skeepskombuis; galei (boot); setplank, galei; ~ **boy,** koksjong, koksmaat; ~ **proof,** galei=proef, strookproef; ~**-slave,** galeislaaf; *work like a* ~*-slave,* jou afsloof, jou krom werk, soos 'n slaaf werk; ~ **worm,** oorkruiper.
gal'ley-west: *KNOCK* ~, skeef slaan; verslaan.
gall'-fly, galwesp.
galliam'bic, galliambies, versvoet met twee jambiese dimeters.
gall'ic acid, gallussuur.
Gall'ic, Gallies; ~ **an,** (n) Gallikaan, (a) Gallies; Gallikaans.
gall'ice, in Frans.
Gall'icism, Gallisisme.
gall'icize, verfrans.
galligas'kins, wye broek, sambalbroek.
gallimau'fry, (..**fries**), hutspot; mengelmoes, same=raapsel, ragout; bredie.
gallina'ceous, hoenderagtig, hoender=.
gall'ing, ergerlik, tergend; moorddadig, griewend, kwetsend.
gal(**l**)**'iot,** galjoot.
gal'linule: *lesser* ~, kleinkoningriethaan.
gal'liot, galjoot.
gall'ipot, salfpot; pilledraaier.
gall'ium, gallium.
gallivant', die hof maak; ronddrentel, rondflenter, rinkink.
gal'liwasp, Wes-Indiese akkedis.
gall'nut, galappel, galneut.
Galloman'ia, (oordrewe) Fransgesindheid, Galloma=nie; ~ **c,** (n) Fransgesinde; (a) Fransgesind.
gall'on, gallon, gelling (maat).
galloon', galon, omboorsel, boorlint.
gall'op, (n) galop; *AT a* ~, op 'n galop; *in FULL* ~, in vinnige galop; (v) galop, galoppeer; galpeer; ~ *ing CONSUMPTION,* galoptering, vlieënde te=ring; ~ *THROUGH,* deurjaag; ~ **ade',** galopdans; ~ **er,** galoppeerder; rapporttryer; ligte kanon.
Gallo'phil(**e**), (n) Fransgesinde, Gallofiel; (a) Fransgesind.
Gall'ophobe, (n) Fransehater; (a) Fransehatend.
Gall'ophobia, Fransevrees; Fransehaat, Gallofobie.
gallo-tan'nic acid, galneutolie.
gall'oway, ponie (van Galloway); Gallowaybees.
gall'ows, galg; *be born for the* ~, vir die galg (strop) grootword; ~**-bird,** galgaas, galgebrok; ~**-face,** galgetronie, galggesig, boewebakkies; ~ **humour,** galgehumor; ~**-tree,** galgpaal.
gall: ~ **sickness,** galsiekte; ~ **stone,** galsteen.
Gall'up poll, Gallupstemming, meningsopname.
galoot', lomperd.
gal'op, (n) galopdans; (v) die galop dans.

galore', in oorvloed, volop, soos bossies, by die vleet.
galosh', (-es), (rubber)oorskoen.
galumph', dartel, spring, bokspring.
galvan'ic, galvanies; ~ **electricity**, galvaniese elektrisiteit.
gal'vanism, galvanisme.
galvaniza'tion, galvanisasie, galvanisering.
gal'vanize, versink, galvaniseer; ~ *d IRON*, gegalvaniseerde yster; ~ *into LIFE*, deur 'n skok wakker maak; ~*d iron SHEET*, sinkplaat; ~*d WIRE*, bloudraad.
gal'vanizing, versinking, galvanisering.
galvanog'raphy, galvanografie.
galvanom'eter, galvanometer, stroommeter.
galvanom'etry, galvanometrie, stroommeting.
galvanoplas'ty, galvanoplastiek.
gal'vanoscope, galvanoskoop, stroomaanwyser.
gal'vanotypy, galvanotipie.
gam'ba, gamba; orrelregister; *viola da* ~, knieviool, viola da gamba.
gambade', (-s), **gambad'o**, (-es), perdesprong; malkopstreek; eskapade.
gam'bier, looistof, looiekstrak.
gam'bit, gambiet (skaakspel).
gam'ble, (n) dobbelary; waagstuk; (v) dobbel, (ver=)speel, verkwis; ~ *away*, verdobbel, verwed, verspeel; ~ **r**, speler, dobbelaar; ~ **some**, dobbelsiek, versot op dobbel.
gam'bling, (die) speel, gedobbel, dobbel(a)ry, spekulasie; ~ **debt**, speelskuld; ~**-den**, ~**-hell**, speelhol; dobbelnes, dobbelplek, dobbelsaal; ~**-house**, speelhuis, dobbelhuis; ~**-table**, speeltafel, dobbeltafel.
gamboge', geelgom.
gam'bol, (n) sprong, huppeling, bokkesprong; (v) (-led), spring, huppel, bokspring, baljaar, dartel, rinkink.
gam'brel, vleishaak; skamelhaak; skenkel (van perd).
game[1], (n) pot(jie), spelletjie, wedstryd; tydverdryf; wild, prooi, wildsvleis; skerts; skema; plan; *ABOUNDING in* ~, wildryk; *it is ALL in the* ~, dit vorm alles deel v.d. spel; *BIG* ~, grootwild; *the* ~ *is not worth the CANDLE*, die kool is die sous nie werd nie; ~ *of CARDS*, kaartspel; ~ *of CHANCE*, kansspel, waagspel; *play a DOUBLE* ~, vals speel; *DRAWN* ~, gelykopspel; *FAIR* ~, geoorloofde wild; *FORBIDDEN* ~, verbode wild; *GIVE the* ~ *away*, die saak verklap; *play a GOOD* ~, goed speel; *(royal)* ~ *of GOOSE*, gansbord, gansspel(etjie); *have the* ~ *in one's HANDS*, seker van die oorwinning wees; *HAVE a* ~, 'n potjie speel; ~ *of HAZARD*, gelukspel, kansspel; *MAKE* ~ *of someone*, die gek met iem. skeer; *PLAY the* ~, eerlik speel (handel); *PLAY a waiting* ~, 'n afwagtende houding aanneem; jou kans afwag; *play a POOR* ~, swak speel; ~ *of SKILL*, vernufspel; *STALK* ~, wild bekruip; *the* ~ *is UP*, die saak is verlore; *WHAT a* ~! pragtig! (v) speel, dobbel.
game[2], (a) klaar, strydvaardig, moedig, flink; veglustig; sportief; *BE* ~ *for*, aandurf; met iets saamgaan; *DIE* ~, sterf soos 'n man.
game[3], (a) lam, kruppel, mank.
game: ~ **animal**, wilddier; ~ **auction**, wildveiling; ~-**bag**, jagsak, bladsak; ~ **biltong**, wildsbiltong; ~ **bird**, wildvoël; ~-**cock**, veghaan; ~ **fish**, sportvis; ~ **fisherman**, grootvishengelaar; sportvisser; ~ **fishing**, sportvissery, grootvishengelary; ~-**fowl**, veghoender; ~ **keeper**, wildopsigter; boswagter; ~ **law**, jagwet, skietwet; ~ **licence**, jaglisensie, jagliksens; ~ **like**, wildagtig.
game: ~ **ly**, moedig, dapper; ~ **ness**, durf; gereedheid, bereidheid; sportiwiteit.
game: ~-**park**, wildtuin; wildpark; ~ **pie**, wildpastei; ~ **pit**, vangkuil; ~ **point**, wenpunt; potpunt; spelpunt; ~ **proof**, wildwerend; ~-**proof fence**, wildheining; ~ **ranger**, wildwagter; ~-**reserve**, wildreservaat, wildtuin; ~**sman**, onsportiewe deelnemer, sielkundespeler; ~**smanship**, onsportiwiteit; ~**smaster**, sportonderwyser; ~**some**, speels, speelsiek, dartel; ~ **soup**, wildsop; ~ **stalking**, wildjag; sluipjag; ~**ster**, dobbelaar, speler.
gametan'gium, gameetsakkie, =houer.

gamete', gameet, geslagsel, paarsel.
game'tophore, gametofoor, gameetdraer.
gamet'ophyte, geslagtelike plant, gametofiet.
gam'ing, (die) dobbel; ~-**debt**, speelskuld; ~-**house**, dobbelplek, speelhuis; ~-**table**, dobbeltafel, speeltafel.
gamm'a, gamma.
gammad'ion, swastika, hakekruis.
gamm'aglobulin, gammablobulien, gammaglobuline.
gamm'a radiation, gammabestraling.
gamm'a ray, gammastraal.
gamm'er, (ou) tannie, moedertjie.
gamm'on[1], (n) gerookte ham; (v) rook.
gamm'on[2], (n) kullery, foppery; (v) iets wysmaak, kul.
gamm'on[3], (v) vasbind, vassjor.
gamogen'esis, gamogenese, geslagtelike voortbrenging.
gamp, (slordige) tentsambreel.
gam'ut, musiekskaal, toonladder, gamut; omvang; *the whole* ~, die hele reeks.
gam'y[1], wildryk.
gam'y[2], dapper; bereid; adellik; met 'n geurtjie aan.
gan'der, mannetjiegans; idioot, stommerik.
gan'dy dancer, (sl.), spoorwerker.
gang, (n) bende, kliek; span, ploeg (werkers); stel; ~ *of ROBBERS*, rowerbende; ~ *of THIEVES*, diewebende; (v) gaan; ~ *agley*, misloop.
gang: ~ **board**, loopplank; ~ **boss**, ploegbaas; bendebaas, bendehoof, bendeleier.
gange, ('n vishoek) omwikkel, toedraai.
gang'er, opsigter; ploegbaas, baanmeester.
gang'land, boeewêreld; rampokkergebied.
gang'ling, lomp; langbeen=.
gang'lion[1], middelpunt.
gang'lion[2], (..lia), ganglion, peesknoop, senuweeknoop, middelknoop; ~**ated**, van senuweeknope voorsien.
ganglion'ic, senuweeknoop=.
gang: ~ **plank**, loopplank; ~-**plough**, tweevoorploeg; ~ **rape**, bendeverkragting.
gan'grel[1], rondloper.
gan'grel[2], swingel.
gang'rene, (n) gangreen, brand, (koue)vuur; nekrose; verrotting, afsterwing; (v) gangreen kry.
gang'renous, gangreneus, kouevuur=.
gang'-saw, raamsaag.
gang'ster, rampokker, bendelid; ~ **dom**, (die) rampokkers; ~**ism**, rampokkery.
gangue, afvalerts, gangsteen, ganggesteente; ~ **ore**, gangerts.
ga'nister, korrelkwarts, ganister.
gan'ja, dagga, marijuana.
gang'way, pad, deurgang; loopplank, valreep, afstap, trap, gangboord, (landings)brug; ~ *please*, gee pad asseblief; ~ **seat**, gangbank.
gann'et, malgas, seegans, seemeeu, basaangans, janvan-gent.
ga'noid, blink (visskub).
gan'try, (**gantries**), stellasie (vir vate); onderstel; ~ **crane**, bokkraan, portaalkraan; laaibrug.
Gan'ymede, Ganymedes; skinker, kelner; sodomieterksnaap.
gaol, (n) tronk, gevangenis; *be in* ~, vry losies hê; (v) opsluit, in die tronk sit; ~-**bird**, tronkvoël; ~**er**, tronkbewaarder, stokbewaarder, sipier, gevangebewaarder.
gap, bres, deurbraak; kloof, bergspleet, pas; skaar (in beitel); gaping, opening, gat, leemte, lakune, hiaat; *FILL (up) a* ~, 'n leemte aanvul; *STAND in the* ~, in die bres staan; *STOP a* ~, 'n gat stop; *TAKE the* ~, deurglip; ~ *of WING*, vlerkafstand.
gape, (n) opening, gaping, gaap; *the* ~*s*, gaapsiekte; opening; gaping; (v) oopstaan; oopreк; gaap; ~ *at*, aangaap; ~ **r**, (aan)gaper; smoeler (krieket); gaapvis.
gap: ~-**filler**, bladvulling; tydvulling; ~-**toothed**, haasbek; ~ **unit**, vonkbrugstuk.
ga'rage, (n) motorhawe; motorhuis, garage; (v) ('n motor) laat staan (bêre), in 'n garage (motorhuis) bring; ~ **man**, garagehouer.

ga'raging, stalling.
garb, (n) kleding, kleredrag; gewaad; (v) klee, uitdos, aantrek.
garb'age, afval, uitskot, rommel; vuiligheid, vuilis, vullis; ~ **bin,** vuilisblik, vullisblik; ~ **dump,** vuilgoedhoop, vuilishoop, vullishoop; ~ **man,** vuilisverwyderaar, vullisverwyderaar; ~ **truck,** vulliswa, vuilgoedwa.
gar'ble, verknoei, verhaspel, vermink; verkeerd voorstel.
garb'oard, gaarboord(gang), kielgang.
gardant', aansiende, gardant (her.).
gard'en, (n) tuin, hof; *LAYING out of a* ~, tuinaanleg; *everything in the* ~ *is rosy ONCE more,* die Kaap is weer Hollands; *everything in the* ~ *is ROSY,* dit gaan alles klopdisselboom; dit gaan alles voor die wind; *no* ~ *without WEEDS,* elke trop het sy swart skaap; (v) tuinmaak; (a) gewoon; ~ *variety,* gewone soort; ~ **bean,** tuinboontjie; ~**-bed,** tuinbedding; ~**-boy,** tuinhulp; ~**-bug,** plantluis, stinkbesie; ~ **centre,** tuin(bou)sentrum; ~ **city,** tuinstad; ~ **er,** tuinier, tuinman; ~ **flower,** tuinblom; ~**-fork,** tuinvurk; ~**-frame,** groeibak; ~ **gate,** tuinhek; ~ **hose,** tuinslang.
garden'ia, katjiepiering.
gard'ening, tuinbou; tuinmaak; ~ **glove,** tuinhandskoen; ~ **tools,** tuingereedskap.
gard'en: ~**-mould,** teelaarde, humus; ~ **party,** tuinfees; tuinparty; ~ **path,** tuinpad; *lead up the* ~ *path,* om die bos lei, mislei, kul, bedrieg; ~**-pea,** tuinertjie, dop-ertjie; ~**-pink,** grasangelier; ~ **planning,** tuinontwerp; ~**-plot,** stuk tuingrond; ~ **route,** tuinroete; ~ **seat,** tuinbank; ~**-shears,** snoeiskêr, tuinskêr, heiningskêr; ~ **snail,** tuinslak; ~ **spider,** tuinspinnekop; ~ **stuff,** tuingoed; tuinplante; ~ **tools,** tuingereedskap; ~ **tractor,** tuintrekker; ~ **village,** tuindorp; ~ **warbler,** tuinfluiter.
gare'fowl, alk.
gar'fish, geep.
gargan'tuan, reusagtig, kolossaal.
garg'et, keelsiekte (by vee); uierontsteking.
gar'gle, (n) gorreldrank, gorrelmiddel; spoeldrank; (v) gorrel.
garg'ling, gegorrel.
garg'oyle, spuier, geutspuit, drakekop.
garibal'di, garibaldibloes, garibaldibaadjie.
gar'ish, opsigtig, pronkerig; skel (van kleure).
garl'and, (n) blomkrans, guirlande, slinger, sierkrans; letterkrans; loofwerk; kraag; (v) bekrans, versier.
garl'ic, knoffel; ~**ky,** knoffelagtig.
garm'ent, (n) kleding, gewaad, kledingstuk; (v) aantrek, aanklee; ~**ed,** geklee; ~ **worker,** kleremaker, klerewerker.
garn, (interj.) ag nee!, loop nou!
garn'er, (n) skuur, pakhuis; (v) wegpak, bêre, versamel.
garn'et, granaatsteen; ~**-hinge,** T-skarnier; ~ **paper,** skuurpapier
garn'ish, (n) garneersel, versiersel, garnering, (v) garneer, stoffeer, versier; dagvaar (reg); op skuld beslag lê; ~ **ee,** beslagskuldenaar; ~ **ee' order,** bevel tot beslaglegging (op salaris); ~ **er,** versierder; ~**ment,** garnering, versiering; ~**-rail,** beslagreling.
garn'iture, garnituur, versiering, bybehorens, uitrusting, opskik.
gar'pike, *kyk* **garfish.**
ga'rret, solderkamer, dakkamertjie, vliering; ~ **eer',** solderbewoner; broodskrywer; ~ **staircase,** soldertrap; ~ **window,** soldervenster.
ga'rrick, leervis.
ga'rrison, (n) besetting, bemanning, garnisoen; (v) beset, beman; in garnisoen lê; ~ **life,** garnisoenlewe; ~ **town,** garnisoenstad.
ga'rron, botterkop (muil).
ga'rrot[1], see-eend, seeduiker, skeleend; brilduiker.
ga'rrot[2], knelverband.
gar(r)otte', (n) verwurging; wurgberowing; wurgtou; (v) wurg; wurgberoof; ~ **r,** wurger; wurgrower.
garrul'ity, spraaksaamheid, praatagtigheid, babbelsug, praterigheid.

ga'rrulous, praterig, praatsiek, spraaksaam; ~**ness** = **garrulity.**
gart'er, (n) kousband, rekker; *Knight of the G* ~, Ridder v.d. Kousband; (v) 'n kousband omsit; ~**-belt,** kousophouer; kousband; ~**-snake,** kousbandslang; ~ **stitch,** reksteek.
gas, (n) (**-es**), gas; petrol; bluf; *step on the* ~, vinniger ry; (v) (**-sed**), met gas verstik; met gas behandel (tandarts); grootpraat, klets, babbel; van gas voorsien; met gas besmet; ~ **attack,** gasaanval; ~ **bag,** gassak; lugskip, lugballon; blaaskaak, bluffer, windbuks, windorrel, windsak, windmaker, windlawaai; ~ **bracket,** gasarm; ~ **burner,** gasbrander; ~ **canister,** gashouer, gasfles; gasblikkie; ~ **chamber,** gaskamer; ~**-coal,** gaskole; ~**-coke,** kooks.
gasconade', (n) grootspraak, spoggery, windmakerigheid; (v) spog, bluf, grootpraat.
gas: ~ **consumption,** gasverbruik; petrolverbruik; ~ **constant,** gaskonstante; ~ **cooker,** gasstoof; ~ **cylinder,** gassilinder; ~ **decontamination,** gasontsmetting; ~**-detector,** gasverklikker; ~ **defence,** gasverdediging; ~ **economizer,** gasbespaarder; ~ **e'ity,** gasagtigheid; ~ **elier',** gaskroon; ~ **engine,** gasmotor; ~**eous,** gasagtig; ~ *eous vapour,* gasdamp; ~ **explosion,** gasontploffing; ~**-fitter,** gasaanleer; ~**-fitting,** gasaanleg; ~ **fixture,** gashouer; ~ **fumes,** gasdampe; ~ **gangrene,** gasgangreen.
gash, (n) (**-es**), wond, sny; hou; skeurgaping (geol.); (v) sny; 'n hou gee.
gas: ~**-heater,** gasverwarmer; ~ **helmet,** gasmasker; ~ **ifica'tion,** gasvorming, vergassing; verdamping; ~ **iform,** gasvormig; ~**ify,** (..**fied**), vergas, in gas verander; ~**-jet,** gaspit, gasvlam.
gas'ket, sloptou(werk); beslaglyn; voering; pakstuk, pakplaat, pakring; ~**-ring,** pakring; ~**-seat,** pakstukbedding.
gas'kin, broek, skenkel (perd).
gas: ~**-lamp,** gaslamp; ~**light,** gaspit, gaslig; ~ **main,** hoofleiding (gas); ~ **man,** gasfabrikant; ~ **mantle,** gloeikousie; ~ **mask,** gasmasker, ~ **meter,** gasmeter; *lie like a* ~*-meter,* soos 'n ketter lieg; ~ **ohol,** gasohol, alkohol-petrolmengsel; ~ **olene,** ~ **oline,** petrol; ~ **om'eter,** gashouer; ~ **oven,** gasoond.
gasp, (n) snak, hyging, moeilike asemhaling; *BE at one's last* ~, op sy uiterste lê; *the LAST* ~, doodsnik; (v) snik, snak, hyg; oop mond staan; ~ *for,* hyg na; uitblaas; ~**ing,** (n) gesnak; (a) hygend, snakkend; stom, verbaas.
gas: ~**-pipe,** gaspyp; ~ **plant,** gasfabriek; ~**-pliers,** gastang; ~**-pocket,** gasholte (sweis); ~ **poisoning,** gasvergiftiging; ~ **projector,** gaswerper; ~**-sed, gas**siek (persoon); met gas besmet; ~ **sing,** gasvergiftiging; gasbedwelming, begassing; gasverstikking; kook (battery); geswets, kletsery; grootpratery; ~ **stove,** gasstoof; ~**sy,** gasagtig, gasserig, gas-; gassiek; in gasvorm; praatsiek, windmakerig, spoggerig; ~**-tar,** koolteer; ~ **thermometer,** gastermometer.
gas't(e)ropod, buikpotige; ..**op'odous,** buikpotig.
gas'-thread, gasdraad.
gas'tric, gastries, maag-, buik-; *suffer from* ~ *trouble,* aan jou maag ly; ~ **fever,** maagkoors; ~ **haemorrhage,** maagbloeding; ~ **influenza,** maaggriep; ~ **juice,** maagsap; ~ **lavage,** maagspoeling; ~ **region,** maagstreek; ~ **ulcer,** maagsweer.
gastrit'is, maagontsteking, gastritis.
gastro-enterit'is, maag-en-dermontsteking; appelkoossiekte.
gastro-intes'tinal, maagderm-; ~ **tract,** maag-dermkanaal; spyskanaal.
gas'trolith, maagsteen, gastroliet.
gastro'logy, kookkuns, gastrologie.
gas'tronome, gastronoom, lekkerbek, smulpaap, likkebroer.
gastronom'ic(al), gastronomies, lekkerbekkig.
gastron'omist, gastronoom, lekkerbek, smulpaap.
gastron'omy, eetkuns, epikurisme, gastronomie, lekkerbekkery.
gas'tropod, (n) buikpotige; (a) buikpotig.
gas'troscope, maagspieël, gastroskoop.
gas'trospasm, maagkramp.

gastrotomy 922 *gemmation*

gastro'tomy, gastrotomie, maagoperasie.
gas: ~-**warfare,** gasoorlog; ~-**welding,** gassweising; ~ **works,** gasfabriek.
gat, (Am.), rewolwer.
gate, (n) hek, deur, ingang, poort; hekgeld, toegang; toeskouers; publiek; *creaking* ~*s hang long,* krakende waens hou die langste; (v) insluit; hok, hokstraf gee; ~ **crasher,** indringer; ongenooide gas; ~-**crashing,** indringery; ~-**end,** werkfrontkant (mynw.); ~-**house,** hekhuisie; ~ **keeper,** hekwagter, portier; ~ **leg(ged) table,** klaptafel; ~ **less,** sonder hek; ~ **post,** hekpaal; ~ **way,** poort, ingang.
Gath, Gat; *tell it not in* ~, verkondig dit nie in Gat nie.
gath'er, (n) rygplooi, intrekplooi; klont, stuk; (v) vergader, versamel, bymekaarbring, bymekaarsoek, in(gaar); aflei; verstaan; die bene optrek; plooi, ryg, inneem; byeenkom; opraap, oes, pluk, afpluk; saampak; oorneem, kry; ~ *BREATH,* asemskep; *CLOUDS* ~, wolke pak saam; ~ *DUST,* stof aantrek; *be* ~ *ed to one's FATHERS,* sterf; tot jou vadere versamel word; ~ *FLOWERS,* blomme pluk; ~ *HEAD,* swel, ryp word (sweer); groei, in krag toeneem; ~ *IN,* inhaal; oes; ~ *INFORMATION,* inligting inwin; ~ *STRENGTH,* krag kry; ~ *oneself TOGETHER,* die lendene omgord; jou gereed maak; ~ **er,** versamelaar, opgaarder; insamelaar; rimpelmasjien; ettergeswel; ~ **ing,** byeenkoms, vergadering, saamtrek; pitso, indaba; oes; kollekte; versameling, rygplooitjie; ~ **ing stitch,** inrygsteek; ~ **s,** rygplooitjies.
gatsom'eter, gatsometer, snelstrikmeter, snelheidsmeter.
gauche, links; onhandig, lomp; taktloos; ~ **rie',** lompheid, onhandigheid.
gaud, snuistery, klatergoud; sieraad, opskik, praal; (pl) feeste, vertonings; ~ **iness,** opgesmuktheid, opsigtigheid; ~ **y,** (n) (**gaudies),** fees(maal); reüniefees; (a) opgesmuk, opsigtig, pronkerig, bont, kakelbont.
gauff'er, *kyk* **goffer.**
gauge¹, (n) rimpel, frummelplooi; (v) rimpel, frommel, frummel.
gauge², (n) ykmaat, maat, standaard, kaliber; swaarte; dikte; spoorwydte, spoorbreedte; diepgang (van skip); stangpasser; maatstok; fynheidsgraad (van kouse); *NARROW* ~, smalspoor; *TAKE the* ~ *of,* skat; (v) yk, noukeurig meet; skat; iem. deursien; afmeet; peil; afpeil; ~ **able,** meetbaar, peilbaar; ~-**cock,** peilkraan; ~-**disc,** meterskyf; ~-**glass,** peilglas (loko.); ~ **length,** maatlengte; ~ **pin,** leipen; ~ **plate,** maatplaat; ~-**pointer,** meterwyser; ~ **r,** yker, ykmeester; meter; wynroeier; ~-**rod,** peilstok; ~ **saw,** stelsaag; ~-**tap,** peilkraan; ~ **washer,** wydtewaster; ~-**way,** landmetersketting; ~ **wheel,** stelwiel.
gau'ging¹, frummelwerk.
gau'ging², (die) yk; peil; meet, afmeet; aanmaak; gipsmenging (pleister); pasmaak (stene); ~-**board,** aanmaakblad; ~ **box,** maatkas; ~ **chain,** peilketting; ~ **flag,** meetvlag; ~ **hole,** leipengat; ~ **plaster,** gipspleister; ~ **rod,** peilstok; roeistok; ~ **weir,** meetsluis.
Gaul, Gallië (land); Galliër, Fransman.
gault, kleibedding (geol.).
gaulthe'ria, gaulteria, olieplant.
gaunt, hol, naar, aaklig; skraal, maer, vervalle, uitgeteer.
gaunt'let, pantserhandskoen; kaphandskoen; motorhandskoen; skaapstert, spitsroede; *MAKE someone run the* ~, iem. laat deurloop; *RUN the* ~, die spitsroede loop, skaapstert hardloop; deurloop; *TAKE up the* ~, die handskoen opneem; *THROW down the* ~, die handskoen toewerp, uitdaag.
gaunt'ness, maerte, skraalheid.
gaun'try = **gantry.**
gauze, gaas; dun mis (newel), waas; ~ **tape,** gaas; ~ **tissue,** gaasweefsel.
gauz'iness, waserigheid.
gauz'y, waserig, dynserig.
gav'el, voorsittershamer; afslaershamer; regter se hamer; ~ **lock,** breekyster.

ga'vial, gaviaal (reptiel).
gavotte', gavotte (dans, musiek).
gawk, (n) lomperd, lummel; (v): ~ *at,* aangaap; ~ **er,** aangaper; ~ **y,** lomp, verleë, onhandig, slungelagtig.
gay, (a) lewendig, vrolik, blymoedig, blygeestig; lustig; los, losbandig; veelkleurig, opsigtig; swierig; (n), (sl.), homoseksueel, homofiel; ~ **ness,** vrolikheid, lewendigheid; homoseksualiteit.
Ga'za, Gasa; ~ **land,** Gasaland.
gaza'nia, gazania, gousblom.
gaze, (n) aanstaring, (starende) blik; (v) aanstaar, aangaap, staroog, tuur, strak kyk; ~ *AFTER,* nastaar; ~ *AT,* aanstaar.
gaze'bo, (-s), uitkyktoring.
gazelle', gasel, gemsbok (Bybel).
gaz'er, aangaper, aanstaarder.
gazette', (n) koerant, nuusblad; staatskoerant; (v) aankondig, bekend maak; benoem; bankrot verklaar; proklameer; *be* ~ *d out,* jou ontslag kry.
gazetteer', aardrykskundige woordeboek; koerantskrywer, joernalis.
gaz'ing, aanstaring.
gaz'ogene, spuitwatertoestel.
gazpa'cho, gazpacho, koue Spaanse groentesop.
gazump', (sl.), swendel(ary); prysverhoging (ná ooreengekome prys).
gear, (n) tandrat; rat, versnelling; ratwerk; gereedskap, gerei, tuig; koppeling; uitrusting; tooi; *CHANGE* ~, oorskakel; ratte wissel; *CHANGEABLE* ~, veranderlike versnelling; *HIGH* ~, hoogste versnelling; *IN* ~, ingeskakel, gekoppel; aan die gang; in rat; *LOW* ~, laagste versnelling; *OUT of* ~, uit orde; uitgeskakel; *THROW out of* ~, los skakel; *be THROWN out of* ~, in die war wees; *in TOP* ~, in die hoogste versnelling; *everything is in TOP* ~, alles is in die boonste kerf; alles is in die hoogste versnelling; (v) inspan; aan die gang sit (masjien); inskakel; tandratte insit; aantrek; ~ **ing,** skakeling, koppeling; ~ **box,** versnellingsbak, ratkas; tandwielkas, wisselbak; ~-**casing,** ratomhulsel; kettingkas (fiets); ~-**housing,** rathulsel; ~ **ing,** versnelling; ratwerk, dryfwerk; hefboomfinansiering, leenkapitaalfinansiering; ~-**lever,** rathefboom, stelarm, versnellingshefboom; ~ **shift,** ratwissel(ing); ~-**shift lever,** wisselhefboom; ~ **wheel,** kamrat, tandrat.
geck'o, (-(e)s), akkedis, geitjie, gekko.
gee¹, (n) perd).
gee², **gee'-ho, gee'(h)up',** (interj) vort! vooruit! hop!
gee'-gee, perd(jie).
geese, *kyk* **goose.**
gee(-whiz')! allewêreld!
gee'zer, ou man, oukêrel.
Gehenn'a, Gehenna, hel.
Geig'er counter, geigertelbuis, geigerteller.
gei'sha, geisja.
Geis'sler tube, geisslerbuis.
geist, (Germ.), geist, gees.
gel, (n) jel; (v) verjel.
gelat'inate, in sjelei verander, gelatineer.
gel'atin(e), gelatien, gelatine.
gelat'inous, gelatienagtig, gelatineus, sjeleiagtig.
gela'tion, bevriesing; jelvorming (chem.).
geld, sny, kastreer, kapater, ontman; ~ *ed pig,* burg; ~ **er,** snyer, kastreerder; ~ **ing,** reun (perd); gekastreerde dier; (die) sny.
gel'id, yskoud; **gelid'ity, gel'idness,** ysige koue.
gel'ignite, gelignite.
gem¹, (n) lemoenpampoentjie.
gem², (n) edelsteen, edelgesteente; juweel, kleinood; briljant; (v) (**-med),** (met edelstene) versier.
gem' clip, skuifspeld.
gem' diamond, sierdiamant.
gem'inate, (v) verdubbel; in pare (twee-twee) rangskik; (a) dubbel; tweeling=; gepaar.
gemina'tion, verdubbeling, geminasie.
Gem'ini, die Tweeling, Gemini.
gemm'a, (blad)knop.
gemm'ate, (v) knoppe kry; deur knoppe voortplant; (a) met knoppe, bladknoppig.
gemma'tion, knopvorming, gemmasie.

gemmiferous 923 **genuflect**

gemmif'erous, knopdraend; ryk aan edelgesteentes.
gemmipar'ity, knopvorming, gemmiparie.
gemmip'arous, wat deur knoppe voortplant.
gemmol'ogist, juweelkenner, gemmoloog.
gemmol'ogy, juweelkunde, gemmologie.
gemm'ule, kiem; knoppie.
gemm'y, edelsteenagtig, edelsteen=.
gems'bok, gemsbok, gensbok.
gem' squash, lemoenpampoentjie.
gem'stone, edelsteen.
gemütlich, (Germ.), gemoedelik, vriendelik.
gen, inligting; ~ *up*, inligting verkry, op datum kom.
gen'darme, (-s), polisiesoldaat, gendarme.
gen'der[1], (n) geslag.
gen'der[2], (v) voortbring (digt.).
gen'derless, geslagloos.
gene, geen, erflikheidsbepaler, erffaktor.
genealo'gical, genealogies, stam=, geslagkundig; ~ **tree**, stamboom, geslagsboom, stamlys.
geneal'ogist, genealoog, geslagkundige.
geneal'ogy, (..gies), stamboom, afstamming, geslagsregister; genealogie, geslagkunde.
gen'era, genera.
gen'eral, (n) generaal (rang); die menigte; algemeenheid; *in* ~, in (oor) die algemeen; (v) aanvoer, bevel voer oor; (a) algemeen; gewoon; *the* ~ *PUBLIC*, die groot publiek, die gewone publiek; *the* ~ *RULE*, die algemene reël; *the* ~ *RUN of affairs*, die gewone loop van sake; *in* ~ *TERMS*, in algemene terme; *in a* ~ *WAY*, oor die algemeen; ~ **account**, hoofrekening; ~ **agent**, algemene agent; ~ **aircraft**, utiliteitsvliegtuig; ~ **ally**, oor die algemeen, in die reël, gewoonlik; ~ **average**, algemene awery; algemene gemiddelde; ~ **committee**, breë bestuur; ~ **dealer**, algemene handelaar; ~ **effect**, totale effek, algehele uitwerking; ~ **election**, algemene verkiesing; ~ **expenditure**, algemene uitgawe; ~ **headquarters**, groot hoofkwartier; ~ **hospital**, algemene hospitaal; ~**iss'imo**, (-s), opperbevelhebber; ~**ist**, generalis; ~'**lty**, algemeenheid; gemeenplaas; vaagheid; meerderheid; ~**iza'tion**, veralgemening, generalisasie; ~**ize**, algemeen maak, veralgemeen; saamvat, generaliseer; ~**ly**, gewoonlik, in die algemeen, in die reël, deurgaans; ~ **manager**, hoofbestuurder; ~ **meeting**, algemene vergadering; ~ *annual* ~ *meeting*, algemene jaarvergadering; ~ **office**, algemene kantoor; ~ **post office**, hoofposkantoor; ~ **overhaul**, algehele opknapping; ~ **practitioner**, algemene praktisyn, huisdokter; ~-**purpose**, utiliteits=; ~-**purpose aircraft**, utiliteitsvliegtuig; ~ **sales tax** *(GST)*, algemene verkoopbelasting *(AVB)*; ~**ship**, generaalskap, generaalsrang; veldheerstalent; krygskuns, strategie; aanvoering, leiding; takt; ~ **store**, algemene winkel.
gen'erate, teel, verwek, voortbring; voortplant; veroorsaak; opwek (elektrisiteit); ontwikkel (stoom, gas).
gen'erating station, elektriese sentrale, kragsentrale.
genera'tion, teling, voortbrenging; lid, geslag, nakomelingskap, generasie; ontwikkeling, opwekking (elektrisiteit); menseleeftyd; *the YOUNGER* ~, die jonger geslag; *unto the THIRD* ~, tot die derde geslag.
gen'erative, voortbrengend, telend, teel=, geslags=; vrugbaar; ~ **cell**, geslagsel; ~ **faculty**, teelkrag; ~ **instinct**, teeldrif; ~ **organ**, geslagsorgaan; ~ **power**, teelkrag.
gen'erator, voortbringer (elektrisiteit); ontwikkelaar, generator, opwektoestel; stoomketel; dinamo; ~ **armature**, ontwikkelaaranker; ~ **brush**, dinamoborsel; ~ **coupling**, dinamokoppeling; ~ **frame**, ontwikkelaarraam; ~ **output**, ontwikkelaarlewering; ~ **terminal**, ontwikkelaaraansluiter.
gene'ric, geslags=, generies; algemeen; ~ **name**, soortnaam.
generos'ity, grootmoedigheid, mildheid, edelmoedigheid, vrygewigheid, goedgeefsheid, gulheid, offervaardigheid.
ge'nerous, grootmoedig, edelmoedig, mild, goedgeefs, gul, offervaardig, vrygewig; vrugbaar; ruim(skoots); flink; vol, warm (kleur); *a* ~ *CONTRIBUTION*, 'n milde bydrae; *be* ~ *to a FAULT*,

oordrewe goedhartig wees; *GIVE* ~ *ly*, dra mild by; *a* ~ *SUPPLY*, 'n ruim voorraad.
Gen'esis, Genesis.
gen'esis, wording, genese, ontstaan, skepping; wordingsgeskiedenis.
gen'et, muskeljaatkat.
genet'ic, geneties, wordings=, oorerwings=; geslags=; ~**ist**, erflikheidsnavorser, genetikus; ~**s**, erflikheidsleer, genetika, wordingsleer.
genev'a[1], jenewer.
Genev'a[2], Genève; ~ *Convention*, Geneefse Konvensie; ~**n**, (n) burger van Genève; (a) Geneefs.
gen'ial[1], telend, voortplantings=; geslags=, huweliks=; lewendig, hartlik, vrolik, joviaal, gemoedelik; gesellig.
geni'al[2], ken=.
genial'ity, vernuftigheid; begaafdheid; vrolikheid, hartlikheid, jovialiteit.
genic'ulate(d), knievorming, gebuig, geknik.
gen'ie, (genii), gees, djin.
gen'ital, voortelend, geslags=; teel=; ~ **organs**, geslagsdele, skaamdele, genitaliëe.
genitiv'al, genitiefs=.
gen'itive, (n) genitief; (a) genitief=; ~ **case**, tweede naamval, genitief.
gen'ius[2], vernuf, talent, aanleg, aard, karakter, genialiteit; (-es, ..nii), beskermgees; gees; *EVIL* ~, bose gees; kwade gees; *PROTECTIVE* ~, (beskerm=) genie.
genn'y (**gennies**), *kyk* **jenny**.
Gen'oa, Genua.
gen'ocide, volksmoord, rassemoord; groepsmoord; menseslagting.
Genoese', (n, a) Genuees.
gen'otype, genotipe.
genre, genre, soort; ~-**painter**, genreskilder; ~-**painting**, genreskildery.
gent, meneer, heer.
genteel', deftig, elegant, modieus, beskaaf; kwasiebeskaaf, kastig wellewend (ironies); ~**ism**, eufemisme, verbloeming; ~**ness**, deftigheid, fatsoenlikheid.
gen'tian, gentiaan (blomplant).
gen'tile, (n) heiden; nie-Jood; *be delivered to the* ~ *s*, aan die heidene oorgelewer wees; (a) heidens, ongelowig; nie-Joods; ~ **dom**, Christenheid, nie Jode.
gentil'ity, beskaafdheid, fatsoenlikheid; goeie afkoms, stand; deftigheid, vernaamheid; *shabby* ~, armoedige deftigheid.
gen'tle, (n) maaieraas; (pl) hoë mense; (v) mak maak, dresseer (perd); (a) beskaaf; minsaam; sagsinnig, vriendelik; sag, teer; lig; aansienlik; mak (perd); matig; ~ *birth*, adellike afkoms; *the* ~ *CRAFT*, hengelkuns, hengelbedryf; ~ *READER*, welwillende leser; *the* ~ *SEX*, die skone geslag; *a* ~ *SLOPE*, 'n skotige afdraand; *a* ~ *TURN*, 'n wye draai; ~ *WIND*, 'n ligte wind; ~**folks**, deftige (vername) mense; ~**hood**, hoë afkoms; deftigheid, vernaamheid.
gen'tleman, (..men), goeie heer; fatsoenlike man; heer, gentleman; *the only* ~ *in a COMPANY of ladies*, maljan onder die hoenders; ~ *at LARGE*, gegoede heer; ~ *farmer*, hereboer; ~ *in waiting*, (diensdoende) kamerheer; ~**like**, fatsoenlik, beskaaf; deftig; ~**liness**, ordentlikheid, manierlikheid, opgevoedheid.
gen'tlemanly, beskaaf, fatsoenlik; ~ *APPEARANCE*, fatsoenlike uiterlike; *behave in a* ~ *WAY*, beleefd optree.
gen'tleman's: ~ **agreement**, ereooreenkoms, eerbare akkoord, boereooreenkoms; ~ **glove**, manshandskoen.
gen'tleness, sagsinnigheid, minsaamheid, sagtheid.
gen'tlewoman, (..men), (beskaafde) dame; edelvrou; ~**like**, ~**ly**, deftig, soos 'n dame; ~**liness**, fynheid van maniere.
gen'tly, vriendelik; suutjies; saggies; ~ **born**, van goeie (hoë) afkoms.
gen'to, jintoe.
gen'try, middelstand, fatsoenlike klas, middelklas.
gen'ual, knie=.
gen'uflect, die knie buig.

genuflec'tion, genufle'xion, kniebuiging, knieval.
gen'uine, eg, wettig, opreg, suiwer; reëel, waar; waaragtig, onvervals; deugdelik; natuurlik; *the* ~ *ARTICLE*, die regte ding; ~ *PARTS*, egte dele; ~ *REPENTANCE*, opregte berou; ~ **ness**, egtheid, onvervalstheid, waaragtigheid, opregtheid.
gen'us, (..**nera**), geslag, genus (biol.); soort, klas.
geobotan'ical, geobotanies.
geocen'tric, aardmiddelpuntig, geosentries.
geochem'istry, geochemie.
geochronol'ogy, geochronologie.
ge'ode, geode, kristalholte.
geodes'ic, geodesies.
geod'esy, landmeetkunde, aardmeting, geodesie.
geodet'ic, geodeties, landmeetkundig.
geodynam'ics, geodinamika.
geog'nosy, aardkunde, geognosie.
geog'rapher, aardrykskundige, geograaf.
geograph'ic(al), aardrykskundig, geografies; ~ **mile**, geografiese myl; ~ **north**, geografiese noorde.
geog'raphy, aardrykskunde, geografie; *COMMERCIAL* ~, handelsaardrykskunde; *ECONOMIC* ~, ekonomiese aardrykskunde; *MATHEMATICAL* ~, matematiese aardrykskunde; *PHYSICAL* ~, fisiese aardrykskunde; *POLITICAL* ~, politieke aardrykskunde.
ge'oid, geoïde.
geoid'al, geoïdaal.
geolo'gic(al), geologies, aardkundig; ~ **survey**, geologiese opname.
geol'ogist, geoloog, aardkundige.
geol'ogize, geologie beoefen, geologies ondersoek, geologiseer.
geol'ogy, aardkunde, geologie.
geomagnet'ics, aardmagnetisme.
ge'omancy, waarseëry.
geom'eter, meetkundige; landmeter, veldmeter; kruipruspe.
geomet'ric(al), meetkundig, geometries; ~ **drawing**, lyntekening; ~ **pen**, trekpen; ~ **progression**, meetkundige reeks; ~ **tortoise**, knoppiesdopskilpad.
geometri'cian, meetkundige.
geom'etry, meetkunde, geometrie; *PLANE* ~, vlakmeetkunde; *SOLID* ~, stereometrie.
geomorphol'ogy, geomorfologie.
geon'omy, geonomie.
geoph'agist, grondeter, geofaag.
geoph'agy, geofagie, grondlus, grondetery.
geophys'ic(al), geofisies; **G**~ **Year**, Geofisiese Jaar.
geophys'icist, geofisikus.
geophys'ics, geofisika.
ge'ophyte, geofiet.
geopon'ic, landboukundig (grappig).
geopon'ics, landboukunde.
George, Joris, Georg; *BY* ~! verduiwels! by my kool! *ST.* ~, Sint Joris.
georgette', georgette.
Geor'gian, (n) Georgiër; Georgies (taal); (a) Georgiaans; van die Georges.
geor'gic, (n) landelike gedig; (a) landbou=; landelik.
ge'osphere, geosfeer.
geostroph'ic, geostrofies.
ge'otherm, geoterm.
geotherm'al, geotermies.
geotrop'ical, geotropies.
geot'ropism, geotropisme.
geran'ium, malva, geranium.
gerbille', springhaasmuis.
ger'falcon, giervalk.
geriatri'cian, geriater, spesialis in ouderdomsiektes.
geriat'rics, geriatrie, studie van ouderdomsiektes.
germ, (n) kiem, oorsprong; (v) kiem, ontkiem.
Germ'an¹, (n) Duitser, Mof; Duits (taal); *HIGH* ~, Hoogduits; *LOW* ~, Platduits; *MIDDLE* ~, Middelduits; (a) Duits.
germ'an², vol, bloedeie; *cousin* ~, eie (volle) neef (niggie).
german'der, gamander, plant v.d. geslag *Teucrium*.
germane', verwant; ~ *to*, met betrekking tot.
Germ'an: ~ **flute,** dwarsfluit; ~ **gold**, klatergoud; ~ **'ic**, (n, a) Germaans; ~ **ism**, Germanisme; ~ **'ity**, Duitse karakter.

germ'ium, germanium.
Germ'an: ~ **ize,** verduits, germaniseer; ~ **jackplane**, skropskaaf; ~ **measles**, rooihond, Duitse masels; ~ **merino**, Vleismerino; ~ **oph'ilist**, Duitsgesinde; ~ **'ophobe**, anti-Duitsgesinde; ~ **sausage**, metwors; ~ **silver**, pleetsilwer, nieusilwer; ~ **text**, Gotiese letter; ~ **toys**, Neurenbergerspeelgoed; ~ **y**, Duitsland.
germ: ~ **-carrier,** kiemdraer; ~ **cell**, kiemsel.
germ'en, kiem, vrugbeginsel.
germicid'al, kiemdodend.
germ'icide, kiemdoder, ontsmettingsmiddel.
germ'inal, kiem=; in die kiem.
germ'inate, ontkiem, uitloop; opkom, ontspruit.
germina'tion, ontkieming; botting; kiemvorming.
germ'meal, kiemmeel.
germ'on, albakoor.
germ' plasm, kiemplasma.
germ'ule, kiemetjie.
ger'ontism, gerontisme.
gerontoc'racy, gerontokrasie, oumanneregering.
gerontol'ogist, gerontoloog, kenner van ouderdomsverskynsels.
gerontol'ogy, gerontologie, studie van ouderdomsverskynsels.
gerryman'der, (n) afbakeningsgeknoei; verkiesingsgeknoei; (v) oneerlik afbaken; ~ **er**, knoeier.
ge'rund, gerundium; ~ **-grinder**, skoolvos.
gerun'dial, gerundium=.
gerun'dive, gerundief.
gess'o, gips; gipsgrondlaag.
Gesta'po, Gestapo (Duitse Geheime Staatspolisie).
gesta'tion, dragtigheid (dier); swangerskap (mens); *period of* ~, dra(ag)tyd (dier); swangerskapsduur (mens).
gestator'ial, draag=; ~ **chair**, draagstoel (v.d. pous).
gestic'ulate, gebare maak, gestikuleer, beduie.
gesticula'tion, beduiery, gebarespel, gestikulasie; gebaar.
gestic'ulative, gestic'ulatory, gestikulerend, gebarend.
ges'ture, (n) gebaar, beweging; *make a* ~, 'n gebaar maak; (v) gebare maak, gestikuleer; deur gebare uitdruk.
gesund'heit, (Germ.), gesondheid, gesundheit.
get¹, (n) broeisel, kleintjies.
get², (v) (got, got(ten)), kry, verkry, bekom, verwerf, in die hande kry; verdien; gaan haal; begryp; verstaan; word; kul; hê; bring; sorg dat; gaan, beland; ~ *ABOUT*, rondgaan; ~ *ABROAD*, rugbaar word; ~ *ACROSS*, oorgaan; laat inslaan; aan die verstand bring; ~ *AHEAD*, vooruitkom; ~ *ALONG*, vooruitgaan, vorder; ~ *ALONG with it*, iets klaarkry; *get ALONG with someone*, oor die weg kom met iem.; met iem. klaarkom; ~ *an APPETITE*, eetlus kry; ~ *AT*, bykom, bereik; ~ *AT someone*, iem. beskimp (slegsê); ~ *AWAY*, wegkom; voertsek!; *no* ~ *ting AWAY from it*, daar nie kan verbykom nie; nie moontlik om te ontken (ontwyk) nie; *you can't* ~ *AWAY from*, jy kan nie daarvan wegkom nie (fig.); jy moet dit erken; *get AWAY with murder*, jou alles veroorloof; 'n onregmatige sukses behaal; ~ *BACK*, teruggaan; terugkry; ~ *BEATEN*, pak kry; ~ *out of BED on the wrong side*, met die verkeede been uit die bed kom; ~ *the BEST of*, oorwin, baasraak; ~ *the BETTER of someone*, die oorhand oor iem. kry; iem. droogsit; ~ *the BETTER of something*, iets onder die knie kry; ~ *down to BUSINESS*, by die kern kom; die hoofsaak behandel; ~ *BY*, op een of ander manier klaarkom; ~ *with CHILD*, swanger maak; ~ *into one's CLOTHES*, jou aantrek; ~ *a COLD*, koue vat; ~ *CRACKING*, aan die gang kom; ~ *out of one's DEPTH*, uit diep water raak; *DO you* ~ *it?*, snap jy dit?; ~ *it DONE*, iets laat doen; dit klaarkry; ~ *DONE with*, 'n einde maak aan; klaarmaak met; *it* ~*s one DOWN*, dit maak 'n mens mismoedig; ~ *DOWN*, afklim; na ondertoe gaan; ~ *DRUNK*, dronk word; ~ *GOING*, aan die gang kom; op dreef kom; voortgaan; weggaan; ~ *things GOING*, aan die gang sit; op tou sit; ~ *GOING!*, trap! skoert! kry jou ry!; ~ *your HAND in*, op stryk

geta 925 *gimp*

kom, gewoond raak; ~ *out of HAND,* hand-uit ruk; onregeerbaar word; ~ *into one's HEAD,* in die kop kry; na die kop styg; ~ *by HEART,* uit die kop (hoof) leer; ~ *HOLD of,* pak, gryp, beetkry; ~ *IN,* inklim, inkom; gekies word; inkry; ~ *off LIGHTLY,* 'n ligte straf (vonnis) kry; daar goedkoop van afkom; ~ *MARRIED,* trou, getroud raak; ~ *a MOVE on!,* opskud! roer jou!; ~ *on one's NERVES,* 'n mens senuweeagtig (mismoedig) maak; op die senuwees werk; ~ *NOWHERE,* g'n hond haaraf maak nie; ~ *OFF,* afklim; ontsnap; vrykom; wegspring; ~ *ON,* vooruitgaan; ~ *ON!,* loop! maak gou!; ~ *OUT,* uitlek; afklim; uitgaan, uitkom; uitkry (woorde); ~ *OUT!,* skoert! trap! maak dat jy wegkom!; ~ *OVER,* oorkom; aflê (pad); herstel (siekte); *be unable to get OVER something,* nie in staat om iets te bo te kom nie; *never mind, you'll soon get OVER it,* toe maar, jy sal dit gou baasraak; jy sal dit vergroei voor jy 'n meisie is; ~ *up a PLAY,* 'n toneelstuk gaan opvoer; ~ *into a RAGE,* woedend word; ~ *READY,* klaarmaak; ~ *RELIGION,* bekeer word; ~ *RID of,* kwytraak; ontslae raak van; ~ *ROUND,* beter word (sieke); rugbaar word (nuus); omkry; ~ *ROUND a person,* iem. ompraat; verbykom by iem.; ~ *under SAIL,* onder seil gaan; ~ *on one's SHOES,* jou skoene aankry; ~ *a START,* 'n voorsprong kry; ~ *STUCK,* vassit; *TELL someone where he* ~*s off,* iem. op sy plek sit; ~ *into a TEMPER,* woedend word; ~ *THROUGH,* aansluiting kry; in verbinding kom met; slaag; deurkry (wetsontwerp); ~ *THROUGH with,* klaar kry; ~ *TO,* bereik; ~ *TOGETHER,* bymekaarkom; bymekaarbring; ~ *UP,* opstaan; opklim; klaar maak; opmaak; op tou sit; opknap (opkry) (stoom); tot stand bring; ~ *under WAY,* wegkry; begin vaar; ~ *WELL,* beter word; ~ *on WELL with someone,* goed met iem. klaarkom; *they don't* ~ *on well together,* hulle sit nie langs een vuur nie; hulle eet nie uit een bak nie; ~ *in a WORD,* 'n woord tussenin kry; *he* ~*ting on in YEARS,* ouer word.

ge'ta, Japanse houtskoen, geta.
get-at'-able, genaakbaar, bekombaar, bereikbaar.
getaway', ontsnapping, vlug.
gett'er, verkryer, verskaffer; voortbringer; ~-up, organiseerder, reëlaar.
gett'ing, opbrings, voordeel, verdienste; kry; *there is no* ~ *AWAY from,* dis nou eenmaal so; jy kan daar nie verbykom nie; ~ *ON in years,* ouer word; ou kant toe staan.
get-up', opmaak; reëling, uitvoering; uitrusting; montering; vermomming.
ge'um, geum.
gew'gaw, prul, tierlantyntjie.
gey'ser, spuitbron; waterverwarmer; geiser.
Ghan'a, Ghana; **Ghanaian,** (n) Ghanees.
ghast'liness, spookagtigheid; aakligheid, afgryslikheid, afsigtelikheid.
ghast'ly, afgryslik, vreeslik, afsigtelik, verskriklik, aaklig, spookagtig; ysingwekkend, yslik; ~ *pale,* vreeslik bleek.
Ghent, Gent.
gherk'in, agurkie.
ghett'o, (-s), Jodebuurt, ghetto.
ghost, (n) spook, gees(verskyning), skim; *not the* ~ *of a CHANCE,* nie die geringste kans nie; *GIVE up the* ~, die gees gee; lepel in die dak steek; bokveld toe gaan; *the HOLY G* ~, die Heilige Gees; *LAY a* ~, 'n spook beswer; (v) spook; onder 'n ander persoon se naam skryf; ~**like,** spookagtig, skimagtig; verwilder; ~**liness,** spookagtigheid; ~**ly,** spookagtig; aaklig; geestelik; ~*ly apparition,* spookverskyning; ~ **story,** spookverhaal; ~ **town,** spookdorp; ~**word,** spookwoord; ~ **writer,** spookskrywer, skrywer onder 'n ander se naam.
ghoul, lykverslinder; grafskender; monster; ~**ish,** demonies; monsteragtig.
gi'ant, (n) reus; (a) reusagtig, reuse=; ~**ess,** (-es), reusin; ~**ism,** reusegroei; ~**like,** reusagtig; ~ **petrel,** reusestormvoël, nellie; ~**powder,** plofstof; ~ ('s)**stride,** sweefmeule; ~ **strides,** reusetreë, reuseskredes.

gib, teenspy; ~ *and cotter,* teen- en dwarsspy.
gibberell'ic acid, gibberellinesuur.
gibbere'llin, gibberelline, -ien.
gibb'er, (n) gebrabbel, brabbeltaal; (v) babbel, brabbel; snater.
gibb'erish, brabbeltaal, gebrabbel, koeterwaals, bargoens, wartaal, gebrou.
gibb'et, (n) galg; galgdood; galgpaal; (v) ophang; aan die kaak stel.
gibb'on, gibbon, langarmaap.
gibbos'ity, bulterigheid; uitpeuling, bolheid; bult.
gibb'ous, knopperig, bulterig, geboggel, bol.
gib'-cat, gesnyde kat.
gibe, (n) hoon, smaad, skimp(skeut), skimpwoord; (v) hoon, beskimp; ~**r,** bespotter, beskimper.
gib'ing, (n) skimpery; (a) skimpend; ~**ly,** spottend, honend, skimpenderwyse.
gib'lets, gansafval; hoenderafval, pluimveeafval; stukkiesvleis, kleinvleis.
gib'us, (-es), klaphoed, operahoed, klak.
gid, draaisiekte, dronksiekte.
gidd'iness, duiseligheid, aardigheid, swymel; ligsinnigheid.
gidd'y, (v) (..died), duiselig word (maak); (a, adv) duisellg, dronk(erig); duiselingwekkend, onbesonne, vlugtig, onnadenkend; ligsinnig; *BE* ~, duiselig wees, suisebol; *MAKE* ~, laat duisel; die kop op hol bring; *PLAY the* ~ *goat,* die gek skeer; ligsinnig wees; ~**-go-round,** mallemeule; ~**-headed,** sorgeloos; ~**-spaced,** waggelend.
gift, (n) geskenk, gawe, present, gif; donasie, skenking; begaafdheid; *have the* ~ *of the GAB,* goed van die tongriem gesny wees; nie op sy mond geval wees nie; *have IN one's* ~, beskik oor, te gee hê; (v) begiftig, skenk; ~**-book,** presentboek; boekgeskenk; ~**ed,** begaaf, talentvol; ~**edness,** begaafdheid, genialiteit; ~**-horse,** presentperd, gegewe perd; *one must not look a* ~*-horse in the mouth,* 'n gegewe perd moet 'n mens nie in die bek kyk nie; ~**ie,** vermoë, gawe; ~ **shop,** geskenkwinkel; ~ **token,** ~ **voucher,** geskenkkoepon.
gig¹, ligte karretjie; giek, sloep.
gig², harpoen, visspeer.
gigan'tic, reusagtig, reuse=, gigantie; ~ *FIGURE,* reusegestalte; ~ *STRUGGLE,* reusestryd; ~ *TASK,* reusetaak; **-ism,** gigantisme.
gigantom'achy, reusestryd.
gig'gle, (n) gegiggel; (v) ginnega(a)p; giggel; ~**r,** giggelaar; ~**s,** lagsiekte; gegiggel.
gig'-lamps, bril (spot).
gig'let, lagbek, lawwe meisie, giggelaarster.
gig'man, platburgerlike (hekrompe) persoon.
gigman'ity, platburgerlike stand.
gig'-mill, kaardmasjien; kaardery.
gig'olo, (-s), koppelaar; gigolo; beroepsdansmaat; betaalde vryer.
gig'ot sleeve, pofmou.
gigue, gigue.
Gilbert'ian, koddig, dwaas.
gild, verguld, verfraai; ~ *the pill,* die pil versuiker; ~**ed,** verguld; ~*ed youth,* ryk jongmense; ~**er,** vergulder; ~**ing,** vergulding, verguldsel.
gill¹, (n) kloof, bergstroom.
gill², (n) kwartpint.
gill³, (n) kieu (van 'n vis); lel (hoender); *rosy about the* ~**s,** blosend lyk; (v) kaak, skoonmaak.
gill'ie, aasjoggie; handlanger, agterryer.
gill'yflower, muurblom, vilet (min gebruik).
gilt¹, (n) jong sog.
gilt², (n) verguldsel; *take the* ~ *off the gingerbread,* van sy bekoring (aardigheid) beroof; (a) verguld; ~**-edged,** goudgerand, verguld op snee (lett.); doodveilig, uitstekend, eersteklas (beleggings); ~**-edged securities,** doodveilige sekuriteite, prima effekte; ~ **paper,** goudpapier.
gim'bal(s), kompasbeuel.
gim'crack, (n) kleinigheid, snuistery, prul; (a) prullerig, niksbeduidend.
gim'let, frikboor, swikboor, (hand)boor, fretboor.
gim'mer, jong ooi.
gimm'ick, kunsgreep; foefie, kunsie, truuk; dinges.
gimp, gimp, omboorsel; sydraad; kantdraad.

gin¹, jenewer.
gin², (n) valstrik, strik, val; katrol; pluismeul; windas; (v) **(-ned)**, in 'n strik vang; pluis, suiwer (katoen); ~-**block**, hysblok.
gin: ~ **bottle**, jenewerbottel; ~ **distiller**, jenewerbrander, jenewerstoker; ~ **distillery**, jenewerbrandery; ~ **drinker**, jenewerdrinker.
gin'ger, (n) gemmer; gemmerkleur; rooikop; fut, pit; ~ *shall be hot in the mouth*, die sug na plesier (liefde) is onsterflik; (v) met gemmer krui; lewendig maak, opwek; ('n perd) gemmer insteek; (a) rooiharig; ~ **ade'**, gemmerbier; ~ **ale**, gemmerlimonade, gemmerlim; ~ **beer**, gemmerbier; ~ **brandy**, gemmerbrandewyn.
gin'gerbread¹, (n) peperkoek; gemmerbrood.
gin'gerbread², (a) opsigtig, prullerig.
gin'ger essence, gemmeressens.
gin'gerly, versigtig; vieserig.
gin'ger: ~-**nut**, gemmerkoekie; ~-**race**, gemmerwortel; ~ **square**, dubbel gemmer (drankie); ~ **wine**, gemmerwyn; ~ **y**, gemmeragtig.
gingh'am, geruite (gestreepte) katoen; sambreel.
gingiv'al, tandvleis-.
gingivi'tis, tandvleisontsteking.
ging'lymus, (..mi), skarniergewrig.
gin' grog, jenewergrog.
gink, (sl.), man, kêrel, maat.
ginn'er, pluiser; ~ **y**, pluismeul.
ginn'ing, pluisery (katoen); ~ **machine**, pluismeule.
gin: ~-**palace**, spogkantien; ~-**shop**, drankwinkel.
gin'seng, ginseng, geneeskragtige plant.
gip'sy, (**gipsies**), Sigeuner; heiden; swartoog; heks; feeks; swerfvoël, rakker; ~ **bonnet**, groot kappie; ~ **dom**, Sigeunerdom; rondlopery; ~ **ish**, Sigeuneragtig; ~ **rose**, skurfkruid; ~ **table**, driepoottafeltjie; ~ **wagon**, woonwa.
giraffe', giraf, langnekkameel, kameelperd.
gi'randole, kroonkandelaar; son (van vuurwerk); oorsieraad; girandool; draaiende fontein (vuurwerk).
gi'rasol(e), vuuropaal, maansteen, girasol.
gird¹, (v) spot met.
gird², (v) omgord, ombind; insluit; aangord; omgeef, omring; ~ *one's LOINS*, jou lendene omgord; ~ *ON*, aangord; ~ *ONESELF*, die lendene omgord; klaarmaak; ~ *with POWER*, met mag beklee; ~ *ROUND*, ombind; ~**ed**, omgord; ~**er**, balk, dwarsbalk, steunbalk, draagbalk; lêer; ~**er beam**, dwarsbalk; ~**er bed**, lêerbedding, balkbedding; ~**er bridge**, leerbrug, balkbrug; ~**er-stay**, ankerplaat.
gir'dle¹, (n) roosterplaat.
gir'dle², (n) gord, gordel, lyfband; buikgord; ~ *of chastity*, kuisheidsgordel; (v) omgord; omsluit; insnyding maak (boom); ~-**belt**, buikriem.
gir'dle-cake, flappertjie, plaatkoekie.
gir'dle: ~-**joint**, ring; ~-**strap**, stoter.
girl, meisie, dogter; nooi, nôi; huishulp; *he is beginning to take an interest in* ~*s*, sy hakskene word al rooi; ~-**chaser**, meisiesgek; ~ **friend**, nooi, nôi, vriendin; **G**~ **Guide**, Girl Guide, Padvindster; ~**hood**, meisiesjare; meisies; ~ **ie**, nooi(en)tjie, meisietjie; ~ **ish**, skaam, meisieagtig; ~ **ishness**, meisieagtigheid; bedeesdheid; ~**s' choir**, meisieskoor; ~**s' high school**, hoër meisieskool; ~**s' school**, meisieskool.
gir'ly-girly, (oordrewe) meisieagtig.
gi'ro, giro(bank).
girt¹, (n) omvang, omtrek; (v) meet (omvang).
girt², (v) *kyk* **gird²**, (v).
girth, (n) buikgord; omtrek, omvang; borsmaat; (v) omgeef, omvat; 'n buikgord aansit; meet (omvang).
gist, kern, hoofsaak.
give, (n) (die) meegee; (v) (**gave, -n**), gee, verleen, oorgee; toegee; sedeer, skenk, lewer; meegee, insak; skiet (tou); oorhandig; slaak, laat hoor (sug); doen; toewens; toewys; aflê (getuienis); ~ *oneself AIRS*, jou aanstel; ~ *ATTENTION*, aandag skenk (gee); oplet; ~ *AWAY*, weggee (goed); uitlap, verklap (geheim); ~ *AWAY the show*, die aap uit die mou laat; met die hele mandjie patattas (patats) uitkom;

~ *oneself AWAY*, jou verraai; ~ *BACK*, teruggee; weergee; ~ *BATTLE*, slag lewer; ~ *BIRTH to*, die lewe skenk aan; ~ *a BLESSING*, seën; ~ *someone a BLOW*, iem. slaan (klap); ~ *away the BRIDE*, as bruidsvader optree; ~ *CHASE*, agternasit; ~ *a CRY*, skreeu; ~ *into CUSTODY*, in bewaring gee; ~ *one his DUE*, iem. gee wat hom toekom; ~ *EAR*, luister na; ~ *FORTH*, afgee; uit; versprei; rondstrooi; ~ *up the GHOST*, die gees gee; ~ *as GOOD as one gets*, in gelyke munt terugbetaal; ~ *GROUND*, wyk; *whoever HAS, to him shall be given*, aan wie het, sal gegee word; ~ *up HOPE*, die hoop laat vaar; ~ *an IMPRESSION*, die indruk wek; ~ *IN*, tou opgooi, opgee, toegee; onklaar raak (masjien); opdroog (water); inlewer; ~ *IT to someone (hot)*, iem. lelik inklim; iem. opkeil; iem. bloots ry; ~ *a LECTURE*, 'n lesing hou; ~ *the LIE to*, loënstraf; ~ *someone a LIFT*, iem. oplaai; ~ *up as LOST*, opgee as verlore; ~ *in MARRIAGE*, in huwelik gee; ~ *someone a bit of one's MIND*, iem. 'n uitbrander gee; iem. slegsê; ~ *NOTICE*, die huur opsê; iem. afdank; aansê; kennis gee; ~ *OFF*, afgee; ~ *OFFENCE*, aanstoot gee; ~ *OUT*, gee; uitdeel; te verstaan gee, bekend maak; uitstraal; voorgee; opraak (kos); ~ *OVER*, opgee, oorlewer; uitlewer; ~ *PLACE to*, plek maak vir; ~ *RISE to*, laat ontstaan; veroorsaak; ~ *away the SHOW*, die aap uit die mou laat; ~ *a SIGH*, 'n sug slaak; ~ *and SPEND and God will send*, wie geef wat hy heef, is waardig dat hy leef; *his STRENGTH will ~ out*, hy sal uitgeput raak; ~ *up the STRUGGLE*, die stryd gewonne gee; *to ~ a thing and TAKE a thing is to wear the devil's gold ring*, eers gegee en dan geneem, is erger as 'n dief gesteel; ~ *and TAKE*, gee en neem; ~ *THANKS*, dank betuig; ~ *a THOUGHT*, dink aan; ~ *TONGUE*, blaf; *he* ~*s TWICE who* ~*s in a trice*, wie gou gee, gee dubbel; tydige hulp is dubbele hulp; ~ *to UNDERSTAND*, te verstaan gee; ~ *it UP*, dit opgee; ~ *UP*, opgee; afstand doen; bedank; ~ *UP something*, iets laat vaar; van iets afstand doen; ~ *WAY*, wyk, beswyk; plek maak vir; padgee, uitwyk; toegee; verflou; omgee; ~ *the WORLD*, die wêreld sou wil gee; ~ *to the WORLD*, uitgee, beskikbaar stel.
giv'en, gegee; gegewe, bepaalde; verslaaf (aan); *whoever HAS, to him shall be* ~, aan wie het, sal gegee word; *MUCH* ~ *to*, 'n kind van, oorgegee aan; *be* ~ *OVER to*, verslaaf wees aan; *at a* ~ *TIME*, op 'n gegewe tyd; ~ **name**, doopnaam, voornaam.
giv'er, gewer, geër, skenker; trekker (wissel).
giv'ing, (die) gee.
gizz'ard, spiermaag, koumaag; krop; hoendermaag; *that sticks in his* ~, dit steek hom in die krop.
glab'rous, glad, kaal, onbehaard, sonder hare.
gla'cé, (n) glansstof; (v) glaseer; (a) (ge)glaseer; geglans; ~ **fruit**, geglaseerde vrugte; glansvrugte; ~ **icing**, glansversiering; ~ **kid**, glansleer.
gla'cial, bevries, ys-; gletser-; glasiaal; ~ **deposit**, gletserafsetting; ~ **period**, ystydperk.
gla'ciated, met ys bedek; bevries; geskuur (deur ys).
glacia'tion, bevriesing, ysvorming; gletservorming.
gla'cier, gletser; ~ **lake**, gletsermeer.
glaciol'ogy, gletserleer, gletserkunde, glasiologie.
gla'cis, helling, glooiing.
glad, bly, verheug, opgewek, opgeruimd, vrolik; *I shall be* ~ *to do it*, ek sal dit met genoeë doen; ~ *EYE*, knipogie; *give someone the* ~ *EYE*, vir iem. knik; ~ *NECK*, oop nek; ~ *RAGS*, kisklere; aanddrag; ~**den**, bly maak, verbly, verheug.
glade, oop plek (in 'n bos).
glad'iator, swaardvegter, gladiator.
gladiator'ial, gladiatories, swaardvegters-.
gladiol'us, (**-es**, ..**li**), swaardlelie, gladiolus, gladiool.
glad: ~**ly**, graag, met genoeë; bly, blymoedig; ~**ness**, blydskap, vrolikheid, opgewektheid; ~**some**, bly, vrolik.
Glad'stone (**bag**), reissak, valies.
glair, (n) eiwit, eiwitagtige stof; (v) eiwit aansmeer; ~**eous**, ~**y**, eiwitagtig, eiwithoudend; slymerig.
glam'orous, betowerend, toweragtig, verleidelik; ~**ness**, verleidelikheid.

glamour 927 *globule*

glam'our, (n) betowering, bekoring, begoëling; toor=
mag; verleidelikheid; kunsmatige glans; *cast a* ~
over, bekoor, betower; (v) betower, bekoor; ~ **girl,**
malmaakmeisie, prikkelpop.
glance¹, (n) glans.
glance², (n) oogopslag; skrams hou; (vlugtige) blik;
skynsel, flikkering; afkeerhou (krieket); *AT a* ~,
met een oogopslag; *at FIRST* ~, op die eerste ge=
sig; *a HURRIED* ~, skimp; (v) sydelings kyk, aan=
blik; afskram; vlugtig aanroer; flikker; skrams
raak; ~ *AT,* 'n blik werp, vinnig kyk na, skrams
raaksien; verwys na; ~ *OFF,* afskram; ~ *OVER,*
vlugtig deurkyk; ~ *UP,* opkyk; ~ **coal,** glanssteen=
kool, glanskole; ~ **cobalt,** kobaltiet; ~ **copper,**
koperglans.
glan'cingly, terloops, vlugtig; sydelings.
gland¹, klier; sel (bot.).
gland², drukstuk.
glan'dered, glan'derous, droesig, lydende aan droes.
glan'ders, droes, kwaaidroes.
glandif'erous, akkerdraend.
glan'diform, akkervormig; klieragtig.
gland: ~**-nut,** drukmoer; ~**-sleeve,** pakkingsbus,
drukhuls.
glan'dular, klieragtig, klier=; ~ **fever,** klierkoors.
glan'dule, kliertjie.
glan'dulous, klieragtig, klier=.
glare, (n) glans, skittering, glinstering, blikkering, ge=
blikker, flikkering; klatergoud, opsigtigheid; aan=
staring, woeste blik; felheid; (v) skitter, vonkel,
flikker, blikker, vas (woes) kyk; 'n vlammende blik
werp op; ~**-proof,** skynselwerend, dof.
gla'ring, vonkelend, skitterend; verblindend (lig),
brutaal, skandelik; skril, hard (kleure); flagrant,
opvallend (fout); skreeuend, fel (kleure); *in* ~
CONTRAST, in skrille teëstelling; ~ *HEAD=
LIGHTS,* skerp kopligte; ~ *INJUSTICE,* skreien=
de onreg; ~ *MISTAKE,* flater.
glar'y, verblindend; flikkerend; skreeuend.
glass, (n) glas; kelkie; ruit (venster); spieël; verkyker;
weerglas, barometer; lens; ruitglas, sandloper; so=
pie; **(-es),** bril; *ARMOURED* ~, pantserglas;
CLEAR as ~, glashelder; *GROUND* ~, geslypte
glas; *FOND of his* ~, lief vir sy sopie; *HAVE had a*
~ *too much,* aangeklam wees; *people who live in* ~
HOUSES should not throw stones, wie in glashuise
woon, moenie met klippe gooi nie; *settle it OVER a*
~, iets afdrink; dit afklink; *UNDER* ~, onder
glas; *WEAR* ~ *es,* bril, bril dra; (v) ruite insit; ver=
glaas; weerkaats; afspieël; van glas voorsien; ~
over, verglaas; (a) glas=; ~ **beads,** glaskrale; ~
beaker, glasbeker; ~ **bell,** stolp; ~**-beveller,**
glasslyper; ~**-blower,** glasblaser; ~ **cabinet,** ~
case, glaskas; ~ **chiller,** glasverkoeler; ~ **cloth,** af=
drooglap; ~**-culture,** broeikaskwekery; ~ **curtain,**
binnegordyn; ~**-cutter,** glassnyer; glasmakersdia=
mant; ~**-door,** glasdeur; ~**-dust,** glaspoeier; ~
eye, glasoog; ~ **fibre,** glasvesel; ~**-ful,** glasvol; ~
funnel, glastregter; ~**-furnace,** glasblasery; ~**-grin=
der,** glasslyper; glasblasery; glasfabriek; ~**-guard,**
afsluitruit; ~**-house,** broeikas; ~**-iness,** glasagtig=
heid; ~**-irrigator,** glasspuit; ~ **like,** soos glas, gla=
sig; ~**-lined,** met glasvoering; ~ **metal,** gesmelte
glas; ~**-painter,** glasverwer; ~ **pane,** glasruit; ~
paper, skuurpapier; ~ **plate,** hangplaatjie; ~ **roof,**
glasdak; ~**-stainer,** brandskilder; ~**-staining,**
brandskilderwerk; ~ **tile,** glasteël; ~ **ware,** glas=
werk; glasware; ~ **wool,** glasvesel, glaswol; ~**-
worker,** glaswerker; ~**-works,** glasfabriek.
glass'wort, loogkruid.
glass'y, glaserig, glasagtig; helder, deurskynend;
spieëlglad.
Glaub'er's salts, Glaubersout, natriumsulfaat.
glaucom'a, gloukoom, groenstaar.
glau'conite, groenaarde, gloukoniet.
glauc'ous, liggroen, seegroen; met 'n waslaag.
glaze, (n) glasuur, glanslaag (by keramiek); glans;
deurskynende dekverf; (v) van spieëls (glas) voor=
sien; verglaas; verglaas, glaseer (kos); agter glas sit;
glaserig word; erd; glad maak; polys; ~ **coat,** gla=
suurlaag (verf).
glazed, verglaas, glaserig, geglans; glansend; ~ **brick,**

glasuursteen; ~ **cabinet,** glaskas; ~ **earthenware,**
geglasuurde erdewerk; ~ **frost,** ysel; ~ **fruit,** glans=
vrugte; ~ **paper,** glanspapier; ~ **tile,** glasuurteël.
glaze'-kiln, verglaasoond.
glaz'er, verglaser; polyster; amarilskyf, polysskyf.
glaz'ier, glasmaker; ruitwerker; *is your father a* ~?,
groot lantern, weinig lig; ~ **'s knife,** stopmes; ~ **'s
lead,** vensterlood; ~ **'s putty,** stopverf.
glaz'ing, glasuur, verglaassel; (die) glad maak; bre=
king (oë); vensterglas; ~ **compound,** stopmengsel;
~**-furnace,** verglaasoond; ~ **rubber,** ruitrubber;
~**-sticks,** politoerhout; ~ **wheel,** polysskyf.
glaz'y, glaserig, glasagtig; blink.
gleam, (n) ligstraal, flikkerlig; glimp, flikkering,
straal; glans, skynsel; ~ *of hope,* 'n straaltjie hoop;
(v) straal, flikker, gloor, blink; ~ **ing,** stralend, flik=
kerend, glansend; ~ *ing white,* kraakwit.
glean, nalees; versamel; bymekaarmaak (are); ~ **er,**
versamelaar; aaropteller; ~ **ing,** insameling; (die)
optel, sprokkeling; nalesing.
glebe, grond, land.
glee, vrolikheid, blydskap; meerstemmige lied; ~ **ful,**
bly, vrolik, dartel; ~ **man, (. . men),** minstreel,
sanger.
gleet, vogafskeiding, etter; druiper; ~ **y,** etterlg.
glen, dal, laagte, vallei.
glib, beweeglik; glad, vlot; vloeiend; welbespraak; ~
TALK, slimpraatjies; *have a* ~ *TONGUE,* 'n glad=
de tong hê; goed v.d. tongriem gesny wees; ~ **ly,**
glad, vlot; los; ~ **ness,** gladheid, glyerigheid; welbe=
spraaktheid.
glide, (n) sweef; gly, sweefvlug; skuif; glissando
(mus); oorgangsklank; (v) gly, glip; sweef; kruip,
sluip; oorgaan; 'n sweefvlug maak, sweetvlieg; laat
gly; ~**-on road,** inglippad; ~ **path,** glybaan (lugv.);
~ **r,** glyer; sweeftuig, seilvliegtuig; glyvlieër; ~ **r fly=
ing,** sweef; ~ **r pilot,** sweefvlieër, swewer; ~ **r
troops,** sweefvlugtroepe.
glid'ing, gly; sweefvlieg, sweefvlieëry; ~ **angle,** gly=
hoek; ~ **certificate,** sweefsertifikaat; ~ **club,**
sweefklub; ~ **flight,** sweefvlug; ~ **licence,** sweef=
vlieglisensie; ~ **school,** sweef(vlieg)skool; - **site,**
sweef(vlieg)terrein; ~ **slope,** sweefhelling; ~ **speed,**
sweefsnelheid; ~ **turn,** sweef(vlieg)draai.
glim, lantern; kers; lig.
glimm'er, (n) flikkering, skemering, glinstering; (v)
flikker, glinster, gloor, skyn, glim; (a) flikkerend,
skynend; ~ **ing,** (n) skynsel, flikkering, glimp; flou
denkbeeld; *a* ~ *ing of hope,* 'n vleugie hoop.
glimpse, (n) ligstraal, skyn; vlugtige blik, glimp;
CATCH a ~ *of,* 'n vlugtige blik kry op; skrams
raaksien; *a* ~ *of the OBVIOUS,* 'n waarheid soos
'n koei; (v) gou (skrams) sien, met 'n skimp sien.
glint, (n) skynsel, glinstering; ligstraal; (v) blink, glin=
ster; skitter, flikker.
glissade', (n) afglyding (langs sneeuhelling), glissade;
glypad; (v) gly.
glissan'do, (It., mus.), glissando.
glis'ten, glis'ter, glinster, flikker.
glitch, (sl.), inkonking; wanfunksie.
glitt'er, (n) glans, glinstering, vonkeling; luister; (v)
blink, glinster, gloor, flikker, skitter; ~ **ing,** (n) ge=
skitter; (a) skitterend, blinkend, flikkerend.
gloam'ing, skemer(aand), skemerte.
gloat, lekker kry, jou verkneuter; ~ **ingly,** met duiwel=
se vreugde.
glob'al, globaal, wêreld=; ~ **ly,** globaal.
globe, (n) bol; wêreldbol, wêreldrond, aardbol, globe;
kom; glaskap (lamp); oogbol; gloeilamp; *CEL=
ESTIAL* ~, hemelbol; *TERRESTRIAL* ~, aard=
bol; (v) tot 'n bol maak. **artichoke,** artisjok; ~
cyathula, rondeklits; ~**-fish,** koeëlvis, egelvis; ~
lightning, bolblits; ~**-trotter,** wêreldreisiger; ~**-
valve,** bolklep.
globidio'sis, globidiose.
globigeri'na, globigerina.
glob'in, globien, globine.
glob'oid, glo'bose, bolvormig.
globos'ity, bolvormigheid.
glob'ous, glob'ular, bolvormig, bolrond.
glob'ule, klein bolletjie; pilletjie; ronde liggaampie;
druppel (by sweiswerk).

glob'ulin, globulien, globuline.
glock'enspiel, klokkespel (orkes), glockenspiel.
glom'erate, bolvormig, gebondel, koek=.
glomera'tion, op(een)hoping.
glom'erule, skynhofie (plantk.); vaatliggaampie (anat.).
gloom, (n) duisterheid, skemering; droefgeestigheid, naargeestigheid, swaarhoofdigheid, swaarmoedig= heid, somberheid, somberte; *throw a ~ over,* 'n waas van treurigheid gooi oor; (v) betrek; somber word; verdonker; neerslagtig kyk; ~**iness**, duister= heid; somberheid, droefgeestigheid; ~**y**, somber, droefgeestig, naargeestig, neerslagtig; betrokke, donker.
glor'ia, gloria, lofsang.
glorifica'tion, verheerliking, ophemeling.
glor'ify, (..fied), verheerlik, verhef; luister bysit, op= hemel.
glor'iole, stralekrans.
glorios'a, praglelie.
glor'ious, roemryk, deurlugtig, glansryk, glorieryk; heerlik, pragtig; goddelik; salig; getik, dronk.
glor'y, (n) roem, glorie, lof, trots; saligheid; strale= krans; heerlikheid; *BE in one's ~,* in sy (volle) glo= rie wees; *OLD G~,* die Amerikaanse vlag; *SEND to ~,* bokveld toe stuur; (v) (..ried), roem, trots wees, koning kraai; ~ *IN,* jou beroem op; ~ *OVER,* triomfeer oor; ~**-hole**, rommelplek; ~**ing= ly**, triomfantlik.
gloss[1], (n) glans, opheldering; skyn; (v) glans, ophel= der; glad vrywe, blink maak; ~ *over,* toesmeer, ver= doesel, vergoelik; 'n skyntjie gee, bemantel.
gloss[2], (n) wanvoorstelling, vals skyn; kanttekening, kommentaar; (v) glosseer, aantekeninge maak by; wegredeneer, verdraai.
gloss'al, tong=.
gloss: ~ **ar'ial**, verklarend; ~ **arist**, kommentator, glossariumskrywer, uitlêer; ~ **ary**, (..ries), glossa= rium; woordelys; ~ **a'tor**, kommentator, uitlêer; ~ **eme**, glosseem.
gloss'iness, glans, blinkheid.
glos'sing: ~ **board**, poetsplank(ie); ~ **iron**, poetsys= ter.
glossit'is, tongontsteking.
glossog'rapher, kommentator.
glossola'lia, talespraak, glossolalie.
glossol'ogy, woordverklaring; glossologie.
gloss'y, glansend, blink; ~ **magazine**, glanstydskrif; ~ **paint**, glansverf; ~ **print**, glansdruk; glansfoto; ~ **starling**, glansspreeu; ~ **wool**, glanswol.
glott'al, **glott'ic**, stemspleet=, stemband=, glottaal.
glott'is, stemspleet, glottis.
glove, (n) handskoen; *FIT like a ~,* pragtig pas; *be HAND in ~,* dik bevriend wees, kop in een mus wees; *HANDLE without ~s,* hard aanpak; *it is not to be HANDLED without ~s,* dis nie 'n kat om sonder handskoene aan te pak nie; *rule with an IRON hand in a velvet ~,* bedek met 'n ysterhand regeer; *with the ~s OFF,* op strydlustige wyse; met mening; *PUT on ~s,* baadjie uittrek; *TACKLE without ~s,* hard aanpak; *TAKE up the ~,* die handskoen opneem; *TAKE off the ~s,* die hand= skoen uittrek; *THROW down the ~,* die hand= skoen neergooi; (v) handskoene aantrek; van hand= skoene voorsien; ~ **box**, bêrehokkie, paneelkassie (in motor); ~ **compartment**, paneelkassie, oondjie; ~ **d**, gehandskoen, met handskoene aan; ~**-fight**, vuisgeveg, bokswedstryd; ~**-hook**, handskoenha= kie; ~ **puppet**, hand(skoen)pop; ~ **r**, handskoen= maker; ~**-stretcher**, vingerstok, handskoenrekker.
glow, (n) gloed, vuur; rooi kleur; (v) gloei, blaak, brand; ~ *with,* gloei van; ~ **bracelet**, hangkaatser.
glow'er, aanstaar, dreigend (boos) aankyk.
glow: ~ **ing**, gloeiend, vurig, blakend; ~**-lamp**, gloei= lamp; ~**-worm**, glimwurm, ligwurm.
gloxi'nia, gloxinia.
gloy, lym, kleefpasta (handelsnaam).
gloze, vlei; bemantel, vergoelik.
glu'cagon, glukagoon.
glu'cose, druiwesuiker, glukose.
glu'coside, glukosied, -ide.
glucosur'ia, glukosurie.

glue, (n) lym, gom; (v) vaslym, aanlym, vasplak; druk; ~ *ON,* vaslym; *be ~d to one's SEAT,* vasge= lak sit; ~**-boiler**, lymkoker; ~**-brush**, lymkwas; ~**ed**, vasgelak; ~**-pot**, lympot; ~**-priming**, lym= grondlaag; ~ **r**, lymer; ~**-sniffer**, gomsnuiwer; ~**- sniffing**, gomsnuif, gomsnuiwing; ~ **wash**, lymwa= ter; ~ **water**, lymwater; ~**y**, lymerig, klewerig; ~**yness**, klewerigheid, lymerigheid.
glum, somber, bedruk, droefgeestig, bek-af; *LOOK ~,* lyk asof die aasvoëls jou kos afgeneem het; *a ~ (mournful) SOUL,* 'n regte verdriet op note.
gluma'ceous = **glumose**.
glume, kafomhulsel, kafblaartjie, kelkkaffie, graan= doppie.
glum'ness, mismoedigheid, bedruktheid.
glumose', **glu'mous**, met kaffies.
glut, (n) oorvolheid, oorversadiging, oorvoering, oorvloed; *there is a ~ in the market,* die mark is oorvoer; (v) (**-ted**), oorlaai, oorvoer; volprop; swelg.
glu'tamate, glutamaat.
glut'en, kleefstof; graanlym, gluten.
glu'teus, boudspier, gluteus.
glu'tinate, saamkleef.
glut'inize, lym, saamvoeg.
glut'inous, klewerig, taai; lymerig.
glutt'ed, dik gevreet (dier); oorvoer (mark).
glutt'on, vraat, gulsigaard, aasvoël, vreetsak, gulsak, gulbek, skrok(ker), slokop, vreter; *a ~ for work,* 'n regte werkesel; ~ **ize**, vreet, gulsig eet; ~ **ous**, vrate= rig, gulsig, vraatsugtig; *eat ~ously,* vraterig eet; skrok; ~**y**, vraatsug; gulsigheid; swelgery.
gly'cerinate, met gliserien behandel.
gly'cerin(e), gliserien, gliserine; ~ *of tymol,* tiemie= gliserien.
gly'cerol, gliserol.
gly'cine, glisien, -ine.
gly'cocoll, glikokol.
glyc'ogen, dierstysel, glikogeen.
glyc'ol, glikol.
glyco'lysis, glikolise.
glycopro'tein, glikoproteïen, -ine.
glycosur'ia, glikosurie.
glyph, gleuf (argit.); glief (argeol.).
glyphogene', glifogeen.
glyph'ograph, glifograaf.
glyphog'raphy, glifografie.
glyp'tal, gliptal, alkiedhars.
glyp'tic, glipties; ~**s**, ..**tog'raphy**, steensnykuns, gliptiek.
glyp'todon, gliptodon.
glypto'graphy, gliptografie, edelsteengravure.
G'-man, Amerikaanse speurder.
gnarl: ~ **ed**, ~ **y**, kwasterig, knoesterig.
gnat, muggie; *STRAIN at ~s,* haarkloof, vit; *STRAIN at a ~ and swallow a camel,* 'n muggie uitsif, maar 'n kameel insluk.
gnath'ic, kaak=.
gnat: ~**-strainer**, muggiesifter, vitter; ~**-weight**, muggiegewig.
gnaw, knaag; wegknaag; (af)knabbel; ~ **er**, knaer, knaagdier; ~ **ing**, (n) geknaag, knaging; (a) kna= end.
gneiss, gneis.
gnome[1], aardgees, kabouter, dwergie, bergmannetjie, gnoom, kokkewiet, aardmannetjie.
gnome[2], leuse, sinspreuk, gnoom.
gnom'ic[1], gnomies, kabouter=, dwerg=.
gnom'ic[2], gnomies, spreukvormig.
gnom'ish, dwergagtig, dwerg=, kabouter=.
gnom'on, gnomon, sonwyserpen.
gnos'is, kennis van godsdienstige misterieë, gnosis.
gnos'tic, (n) gnostikus; (a) gnosties; ~**ism**, gnosti= sisme.
gnu, wildebees, ghnoe; *BLACK (white-tailed) ~,* swartwildebees; *BRINDLED ~,* blouwildebees.
go, (n) (die) gaan; wegspring; swang; voortvarend= heid; pit, go, fiksheid, energie, fluksheid, fut, vuur, besieling; puf; *ALL the ~,* hoog in die mode; *be FULL of ~,* vol vuur (fut) sit; *GIVE it a ~,* pro= beer dit; *HAVE a ~ at,* 'n slag probeer; onder han= de neem; *it was a NEAR ~,* dit het naelskraap ge=

gaan; *a NICE* ~, 'n groot grap; *ON the* ~, aan die gang; *it's NO* ~, dit help nie; dis alles verniet; *a RUM* ~, 'n snaakse affère; *from the WORD* "~", v.d. staanspoor af; (v) **(went, gone)**, gaan; verdwyn; geldig wees; ~ *ABOUT*, rondgaan; in omloop wees; ~ *ABOUT something*, iets aanpak; ~ *ABROAD*, oorsee gaan; gaan reis; ~ *AGAINST*, teëgaan; nie saamgaan nie met; ~ *AHEAD*, aangaan; vooruitgaan; ~ *it ALONE*, alleen te werk gaan; alleen die mas opkom; ~ *ALONG*, voortgaan; ~ *by APPEARANCES*, na die skyn oordeel; ~ *ASTRAY*, verdwaal; ~ *AT it*, iets aanval; ~ *AT one*, iem. onder hande neem; ~ *AWAY*, weggaan; siej»!; ~ *BACK*, teruggaan; agteruitgaan; ~ *BACK on*, nie nakom nie; jou onttrek aan; ~ *BAD*, bederf; ~ *BAIL*, borg staan; ~ *to the BAR*, advokaat word; ~ *BEFORE*, voorafgaan; *there* ~*es the BELL*, daar lui die klok; ~ *one BETTER*, verder gaan; oortref; ~ *BETWEEN*, tussenin kom; ~ *BEYOND*, oortref; ~ *BLIND*, blind word; ~ *by the BOARD*, oorboord wees; daarmee heen wees; ~ *BY*, verbygaan; *the CLOCK does not* ~, die klok loop nie; ~ *into DETAILS*, in besonderhede tree; ~ *to the DOGS*, na die hoenders gaan; ~ *well DOWN*, die goedkeuring wegdra; ~ *DOWN*, ondergaan (son); sak (water); sink (boot); te gronde gaan; ingang vind; ~ *DOWNHILL*, berg af gaan; agteruitgaan; ~ *EASY*, moenie jou haas nie; ~ *through ten EDITIONS*, 'n tiende druk beleef; ~ *down in his ESTIMATION*, in sy agting daal; ~ *in for an EXAMINATION*, eksamen doen (skryf); ~ *to EXPENSE*, koste maak (aangaan); ~ *to great EXPENSE*, groot koste aangaan; ~ *FAR*, ver reis; dit ver bring; ~ *too FAR*, die grens oorskry; te ver dryf; *as FAR as that* ~*es*, wat dit betref; ~ *FARTHER and fare worse*, beter soek en slegter kry; ~ *the way of all FLESH*, die weg van alle vlees gaan; ~ *FOR someone*, iem. inklim; iem. aanval; iem. te lyf gaan; lossteek; gaan haal; ~ *for the GOAL*, pyl reguit pale toe; ~ *HALVES*, gelykop deel; ~ *to one's HEART*, ter harte neem; ~ *for HIM*, pak hom aan; ~ *for the HOLE*, probeer die bal inslaan (gholf); ~ *on HORSEBACK*, te perd gaan; ~ *HUNGRY*, honger ly; sonder kos bly; ~ *IN for*, jou toelê op; inskryf vir; ~ *for a JOURNEY*, 'n reis onderneem; ~ *down on his KNEES*, op die knieë val; ~ *to LAW*, 'n hofsaak maak, na die hof gaan; ~ *to many LENGTHS*, na die uiterste gaan; *LET oneself* ~, alles in jou vermoë doen; gevoelens lug; jou die vrye teuels gee; *that* ~*es for very LITTLE*, dit beteken nie baie nie; ~ *MAD*, gek (mal) word; ~ *out of one's MIND*, gek word; ~ *into MOURNING*, rou; ~ *NAKED*, naak loop; ~ *by the NAME of*, deurgaan onder die naam van; ~ *NATIVE*, die lewensgewoontes van 'n onbeskaafde inboorling aanneem; ~ *NEAR*, nader kom; ~ *OFF*, weggaan; afgaan; ontplof (bom); wegspring; sterf; flou val; sleg (vrot) word; ~ *OFF well*, goed van stapel loop; ~ *ON*, verder gaan; voortgaan; voortduur; gebeur; 'n beurt kry; te kere gaan; jou gedra; ~ *ON!*, ag kom! jy meen dit nie!; ~ *OUT*, uitgaan; doodgaan (vuur, lig); uit die huis gaan; ~ *OVER*, oorgaan; deurgaan; ~ *into PARTICULARS*, in besonderhede gaan; ~ *to PIECES*, breek; versleg; verflenter; ~ *PLACES*, rondreis, besienswaardighede besoek; opgang maak; *it* ~*es to PROVE*, dit toon; ~ *RED*, bloos; ~ *ROUND*, agterom gaan; rondtrek; ronddraai; *enough to* ~ *ROUND*, genoeg vir almal; ~ *by the RULE*, 'n reël volg; *what he SAYS* ~*es*, sy woord is wet; *that* ~*es without SAYING*, dit spreek vanself; ~ *to SEED*, saad skiet; ~ *SHARES*, deel hê; 'n aandeel hê; ~ *to SLEEP*, gaan slaap; ~ *on the STAGE*, toneelspeler word; *the STORY* ~*es*, daar word vertel (gesê); ~ *STRAIGHT*, reguit gaan; koers hou; die regte weg bewandel; ~ *THROUGH*, deurgaan; deursoek; slaag; *as TIME* ~*es on*, in die loop v.d. jare; ~ *TOGETHER*, saamgaan; by mekaar pas; ~ *UNDER*, te gronde gaan; ~ *UNPUNISHED*, ongestraf bly; ~ *UP*, opgaan; ~ *one's own WAY*, jou eie gang gaan!; *WHO* ~*es there?*, wie loop daar? werda!; ~ *WEST*, na die weste gaan; doodgaan; na die maan gaan; ~ *WITH*, saamgaan met; ~ *WITHOUT*, sonder iets moet klaarkom; ~ *back on one's WORD*, sy woord terugtrek; ~ *WRONG*, 'n fout begaan; verkeerd doen; misloop, verkeerd loop.

goad, (n) prikkel, slaanding, sambok; (v) aanspoor, aandrywe, prikkel; ~ *him INTO*, hom aanspoor tot; ~ *ONWARD*, voortdrywe.

goaf(ing), dakpuin (mynb.).

go'-ahead, (a), vooruitstrewend, fluks, wakker; (n), verlof (om voort te gaan).

goal, grenspaal; doelpunt; eindpaal, doelwit; doel (voetbal); einddoel; *HAVE a* ~ *in view*, 'n doel voor oë hê; *KEEP* ~, die doel verdedig; *SCORE a* ~, 'n doel behaal; ~**-area**, doelgebied; ~**-average**, doelgemiddelde; ~**-circle**, doelkring; ~**-getter**, doelskieter; ~**ie**, ~**keeper**, doelverdediger; doelwagter; ~**-kick**, doelskop; ~**-line**, doellyn, doelstreep; ~**-mouth**, doelopening; bek; ~**-post**, doelpaal; ~**-shooter**, doelskopper.

goat, bok; *CASTRATED* ~, bokkapater; *GET someone's* ~, iem. kwaad (ergerlik) maak; iem. die hoenders in maak; *PLAY the giddy* ~, gekskeer; dwaas handel; malkop wees; ~**ee'**, bokbaardjie; ~**herd**, bokwagter; ~**ish**, bokagtig; ~**ling**, bokkie; ~**'s foot**, bokspoot; ~**'s meat**, bokvleis; ~**'s milk**, bokmelk; ~**skin**, bokvel; ~**sucker**, nagswaeltjie; ~**-willow**, waterwilg(er).

go-away' bird, kwêvoël, pêvoël.

gob¹, (n) slymbol; (v) **(-bed)**, spoeg.

gob², (n) (plat), matroos.

gob'ble¹, (n) slukskoot (gholf).

gob'ble², (v) gulsig eet, inlaai, wegslaan; ~ *up*, kafloop, verslind.

gob'ble³, (v) klok (soos 'n kalkoen).

gobb'ler¹, vraat, gulsigaard.

gobb'ler², kalkoenmannetjie.

gobb'le-stitch, springsteek.

gob'elin, gobelin, muurtapyt.

gobe'mouche, (-s), skinderbek, praatjiestrooier.

go'-between, tussenpersoon, bemiddelaar.

gob'let, (drink)beker, bokaal.

gob'lin, kabouter, gnoom, aardmannetjie; spook, spooksel.

go'-by, (die) verbygaan; *give the* ~, opsy sit; versmaad, negeer; uitstof.

gob'y, dikkop (vis).

go'-cart, stootwaentjie, stootkarretjie.

God¹, God, Opperwese; *ACT of* ~, natuurramp; Gods wil; oormag; *ALMIGHTY* ~, almagtige God; ~ *BLESS you*, mag God jou seën; *BY* ~, so waar as God; ~ *the FATHER, Son and Holy Ghost*, God die Vader, die Seun en die Heilige Gees; ~ *FORBID*, mag God dit verhoed; ~ *GRANT*, mag God gee; *after* ~*'s IMAGE*, na die beeld van God; *the LORD* ~, die Here God; *in the NAME of* ~, in Gods naam; *PLEASE* ~, as dit God behaag; *for* ~*'s SAKE*, om Gods wil; *THANK* ~, Goddank; *UNDER* ~, naas God; ~ *WILLING*, as God wil, met Gods hulp; *WITH* ~, met God; *WITHOUT* ~, Godloos; *know nothing about* ~ *and his WORD*, van God nóg sy gebod weet; *WOULD to* ~, mag God gee.

god², god, afgod; ~ *of DAY*, Phoebus; ~ *of FIRE*, Vulcanus; ~ *of HEAVEN*, Jupiter; ~ *of HELL*, Pluto; *in the LAP of the* ~*s*, in die skoot v.d. gode; ~ *of LOVE*, Cupido; *whom the* ~*s LOVE die young*, die liefling v.d. gode sterf jonk; *MAKE a* ~ *of*, 'n afgod maak van; ~ *of the SEA*, Neptunus; *a SIGHT for the* ~*s*, 'n verruklike (kostelike) gesig; *THE* ~*s*, die engelebak (skouburg); *a little TIN* ~, 'n regte godjie; ~ *of WAR*, oorlogsgod; ~ *of WINE*, Bacchus; ~ *of this WORLD*, die duiwel; *YE* ~*s!* goeie genugtig! ~**child**, peetkind; ~**daughter**, peetdogter; ~**dess**, **(-es)**, godin.

go'det, godet, klokstuk.

godetia, godetia.

godown', winkel, pakhuis.

god: ~**father**, (n) peetoom; (doop)getuie; (v) jou naam gee aan, peet staan vir; ~**-fearing**, godvresend; ~**-forsaken**, godverlate, ellendig, afgeleë.

God'-given, Godgegewe.

God'head¹: the ~, God.
god'head², godheid.
god: ~ **less,** goddeloos; ongelowig; ~ **like,** goddelik; ~ **liness,** godsvrug, vroomheid; ~ **ly,** godvrugtig, vroom; ~ **mother,** peettante; (doop)getuie; ~ **parent,** doopgetuie; peetouer.
God's'acre, kerkhof.
god: ~ **send,** uitkoms, uitredding; buitekansie, onverwagte geluk; ~ **ship,** godheid, goddelikheid; ~ **son,** peetseun; ~ **speed,** veels geluk; goeie reis; *bid one* ~ *speed,* iem. 'n goeie reis toewens; iem. sukses toewens; ~ **wards,** godwaarts.
god'wit, griet, grutto (voël).
go'er, loper, hardloper.
go'fer, wafel.
gof(f)'er, (n) plooiyster; stryktang; plooiing; (v) pyp, plooi; ~ **er,** plooier; ~ **ing-irons,** pypskêr; plooiyster; pypyster; stryktang.
go-gett'er, deurdrukker, deurdrywer, doring; *he is a* ~, hy kry wat hy wil hê.
gog'gle, die oë rek, aanstaar; skeel kyk; rol met die oë; uitpuil; ~ **eye,** puiloog; ~ **eyed,** met uitpuiloë.
gog'gles, stofbril, skermbril; oogklappe; dronksiekte, malkopsiekte (by skape).
gog'let, koelkan.
go'-go dancer, . . **girl,** wikkeldoedie.
go'ing, (n) (die) vertrek; gaan; treelengte (trappe); begaanbaarheid; ~ *s(-out) and COMINGS(-in),* doen en late; *GET* ~ *!* kry jou ry! trap! *GOOD* ~, vinnige reis; goeie pad; *the* ~ *is GOOD,* dit gaan voor die wind; *go while the* ~ *is GOOD,* die geleentheid aangryp; *make GOOD* ~, goeie vordering maak; *it is HARD* ~, dit gaan swaar; *KEEP* ~, aan die gang bly; *KEEP something* ~, iets aan die gang hou; *the* ~ *is ROUGH,* dit gaan wurg-wurg; (a) gaande; bestaande; *BE* ~ *to,* op die punt staan om; ~ *CONCERN,* lopende (gevestigde) saak; *one of the best FELLOWS* ~, een v.d. beste kêrels wat daar leef; *there is FISH* ~, daar is vis beskikbaar; ~, ~, *GONE,* vir die eerste, die tweede, die laaste maal; *are you* ~ *OUT?* gaan jy uit? *SET the engine* ~, sit die motor aan die gang; ~ *STRONG,* nog aan die gang; *one of the best THINGS* ~, een v.d. beste dinge wat bestaan; *things are* ~ *WELL,* sake vorder goed; ~ **-away dress,** reisrok, reiskostuum; ~ **s-on,** gedrag; kaskenades, gedoentes.
goi'tre, kropgeswel, skildkliervergroting.
goit'rous, skildklieragtig.
go'-kart, knortjor, renstel, snortjor.
gold, (n) goud; goudkleur; rykdom, geld; *all that GLITTERS is not* ~, skyn bedrieg; *as GOOD as* ~, so goed as kan kom; *OLD* ~, goudbruin; (a) goue, goud-; ~ **acquisitions,** goudaanwinste; ~ **alloy,** goudlegering, goudallooi; ~ **amalgam,** goudamalgaam; ~ **bar,** goudstaaf; ~ **-bearing,** goudhoudend; ~ **-beater,** goudslaer, goudslaner; ~ **-beater's skin,** goudvlies; ~ **bloc,** goudblok; ~ **bond,** goudobligasie; ~ **-bound,** ingelê in goud; ~ **braid,** goudkoord; ~ **brick,** goudstaaf; verneukery; ~ **brocade,** goudbrokaat; ~ **bronze,** goudbrons; ~ **-bug,** goudkoning; ~ **bullion,** staafgoud; ~ **bullion standard,** goudkernstandaard; ~ **chloride,** chloorgoud; ~ **circulation,** goudsirkulasie; ~ **circulation standard,** goudmuntstandaard; ~ **cloth,** goudlaken; G ~ **Coast,** Goudkus; ~ **coin,** goudmuntjie; ~ **-coloured,** goudkleurig; ~ **content,** goudgehalte; ~ **cover,** gouddekking; ~ **-digger,** goudgrawer; fortuinsoek(st)er; ~ **-diggings,** gouddelwery; ~ **-dust,** stofgoud; ~ **-dust plant,** goudmyn; gouemannetjie (*Alyssum saxatile*); ~ **dye,** goudkleurstof; ~ **-edged,** goudgerand, verguld op snee; ~ **embargo,** goudembargo.
gol'den, goue; gulde; verguld; goudgeel, goudkleurig; *worship the* ~ *calf,* die goue kalf aanbid; G ~ **Age,** Goue Eeu; ~ **anniversary,** goue jubileum; halfeeufees; ~ **brown,** goudbruin; ~ **calf,** goue kalf; ~ **dun,** goudvaal; ~ **eagle,** lammervanger; steenarend; G ~ **Fleece,** (die) Gulde Vlies; ~ **hamster,** goudhamster; ~ **handshake,** ontslagvergoeding, goue handdruk; ~ **key,** goue sleutel; ~ **mean,** (die) gulde middeweg; ~ **mole,** kruipmol(letjie); ~ **number,** goue nommer; ~ **opportunity,** ('n) gulde geleentheid; ~ **pudding,** strooppoeding; ~ **rain,** goudreën; ~ **rod,** goudroede; ~ **rule,** (die) gulde reël; ~ **syrup,** geelstroop; ~ **-voiced,** soetstemmig; ~ **wedding,** goue bruilof.
gold: ~ **-fever,** gouddors, goudkoors; ~ **field,** goudveld; ~ **finch,** geelvink; ~ **fish,** goudvis; ~ **-foil,** bladgoud.
gol'dilocks, botterblom.
gold: ~ **ingot,** goudstaaf; ~ **lace,** goudgalon, goudkoord; ~ **-leaf,** bladgoud; ~ **letters,** vergulde letters; ~ **loan,** goudlening; ~ **-lode,** goudaar; ~ **-medal,** goue medalje; ~ **-medallist,** houer van 'n goue medalje; ~ **-mine,** goudmyn; ~ **-miner,** (goud)mynwerker; ~ **-mining,** goudmynwese; ~ **-mining share,** goudmynaandeel; ~ **nugget,** goudklomp, goudklont; ~ **ore,** gouderts; ~ **outflow,** gouduitvloei; ~ **paint,** goudverf; ~ **parity,** goudpariteit; ~ **plate,** goudservies; ~ **-plated,** verguld; ~ **-reef,** goudrif; ~ **-rush,** goudstormloop; ~ **slimes,** goudslyk; ~ **smith,** goudsmid; ~ **standard,** goudstandaard; ~ **-strike,** goudontdekking; goudvonds; ~ **test,** goudproef; ~ **thread,** gouddraad; ~ **-tipped,** goudgepunt, met vergulde mondstuk (sigaret); ~ **tissue,** goudweefsel; ~ **-vein,** goudaar; ~ **weight,** goudskaaltjie; ~ **wire,** gouddraad; ~ **working,** goudbewerking; goudgrawing; goudmynbou; ~ **yield,** goudopbrengs.
golf, (n) gholf; (v) gholf speel; ~ **bag,** gholfsak; ~ **ball,** gholfbal; ~ **cart,** gholfkarretjie; ~ **championship,** gholfkampioenskap; ~ **-club,** gholfstok; gholfklub; ~ **club(house),** gholfklub(huis); ~ **course,** gholfbaan; ~ **er,** gholfspeler; ~ **-links,** gholfbaan; ~ **match,** gholfwedstryd; ~ **shoe,** gholfskoen; ~ **swing,** gholfswaai.
Gol'gotha, Golgota.
Goli'ath, Goliat; reus; ~ **beetle,** goliatkewer.
goll'iwog, paaiboelie; spookpop, nikkerpop.
gol'lop, sluk; groot sluk.
golly'! hede! hemel!
golup'tious, heerlik, hemels.
go'nad, gonade, teelklier.
gonadotro'p(h)ic, gonadotrofies, -tropies.
gona'gra, kniejig, gonagra.
gon'dola, gondel.
gondolier', gondelier.
gone, gegaan; weg; verlore; ~ *AWAY,* weg, vort; *BE* ~ *!* maak dat jy wegkom! trap! ~ *with CHILD,* swanger, in die ander tyd; ~ *in DRINK,* dronk; *he is FAR* ~, hy is baie dronk; sy einde is naby; *FEEL* ~ *-in,* afgemat voel; ~ *for GOOD,* vir goed weg; dis laaste sien v.d. blikkantien; *he is* ~ *ON her,* hy is beenaf op haar; *kyk* go (v).
gon'er: *he is a* ~, sy kerk is uit, dis klaarpraat met hom.
gon'falon, vaandel, banier; ~ **ier',** vaandeldraer.
gong, ghong.
gonid'ial, gonidiaal.
gonid'ium, gonidium.
goniom'eter, hoekmeter, goniometer.
goniom'etry, goniometrie, hoekmeting.
goni'tis, gonitis, kniegewrigontsteking.
gonorrhoe'a, druiper, gonorree.
good, (n) die goeie; welsyn; nut, voordeel; voorspoed, welvare; (pl) goedere, ware; *for* ~ *and ALL,* vir ewig en altyd; eens en vir altyd; *the* ~ *and the BAD,* die goeie en die slegte; *for* ~ *or BAD,* vir goed of vir kwaad; *only the* ~ *DIE young,* net goeie mense sterwe jonk; *what* ~ *will it DO?* watter nut sal dit hê? ~ *and EVIL,* goed en kwaad; *FOR his own* ~, in sy eie belang; *for* ~ *and ILL,* ten goede of ten kwade; *be up to NO* ~, kwajongstreke uithaal; *RETURN* ~ *for evil,* kwaad met goed vergeld; *all TO the* ~, ten goede; *TO the* ~, beter (ryker) daaraan toe wees; *WHAT'S the* ~ *?* wat help dit? wat baat dit? (a), (adv) (**better, best**), goed; goed gevorm; gaaf, deugsaam; vriendelik; vermaaklik; lekker; geskik; *AS* ~ *as,* so goed as; *be* ~ *AT something,* in iets uitmunt; *BE* ~, soet wees; *in his* ~ *BOOKS,* in 'n goeie blaadjie by hom; ~ *CHAP,* doring; *make* ~ *one's CLAIM,* bewys lewer; *as* ~ *as DEAD,* feitlik dood; ~ *DEBTS,* inbare skuld; *one* ~ *DEED deserves another,* as twee hande mekaar was, word

goodness 931 *gospel*

albei skoon; *it is* ~ *EATING*, dit smaak goed; *not* ~ *ENOUGH*, nie goed genoeg nie; nie die moeite werd nie; ~ *FAITH*, goeie trou; *of* ~ *FAMILY*, van goeie afkoms; *FAR from* ~, lank nie goed nie; *FOR* ~, vir altyd; ~ *FOR*, goed vir; *my* ~ *FRIEND*, my goeie vriend; *as* ~ *as GOLD*, so goed soos goud; ~ *GRACIOUS!* mastig! maskas! goeie genade! my goeie tyd! *be in* ~ *HEART*, goeie moed hê; ~ *HEAVENS*, mastig! maskas! goeie genade! my goeie tyd! *HOLD* ~, geld; *the rule HOLDS* ~, die reël is van toepassing; *meat KEEPS* ~, vleis bly vars; ~ *LAW*, geldige wet; *he is* ~ *for a LOAN*, hy sal jou seker met geld help; ~ *LOOKS*, mooi uiterlike; *MAKE* ~ *time*, vinnig reis; *MAKE* ~, vergoed (skade); aanvul (tekort); uitvoer (plan, belofte); slaag (sake); teregkom: nakom (belofte); bewys; regkom; *my* ~ *MAN*, my liewe man; *have a* ~ *MIND to*, geneig wees om; lus hê om; ~ *MONEY*, egte geld; *too MUCH of a* ~ *thing*, te erg; *be NO* ~, niks beteken nie; *for one's OWN* ~, vir jou eie beswil; *take in* ~ *PART*, goed opneem; *for* ~ *REASONS*, om gegronde redes; ~ *SENSE*, gesonde verstand; ~ *SOIL*, vrugbare aarde; *in* ~ *SPIRITS*, in opgewekte stemming; *TASTE* ~, lekker smaak; ~ *TASTE*, goeie smaak; ~ *THINGS of life*, aangenaamhede v.d. lewe; *too much of a* ~ *THING*, te erg; *have a* ~ *TIME*, 'n aangename (vrolike) tyd hê; *all in* ~ *TIME*, alles op die regte tyd; betyds; gepas, *nothing was TOO* ~ *for him*, vir hom was niks te goed nie; die wêreld was te koud vir hom om op te trap; *not TOO* ~ *and not too bad*, so goed soos dit onder omstandighede kan; *he is* ~ *for a TOUCH*, hy sal jou seker met geld help; *too* ~ *to be TRUE*, byna ongelooflik; *do a* ~ *TURN*, 'n diens bewys; *a* ~ *WHILE*, 'n hele ruk; *be as* ~ *as one's WORD*, jou belofte gestand doen; ~ *for YOU!* mooi skoot! skote Pretoors! ryperd! ~ **afternoon**, (goeie)middag; ~ **breeding**, wellewendheid, beskaafdheid; ~**bye'**, dit gaan jou goed, tot siens, vaarwel; *say* ~*bye*, vaarwel sê; dag sê; ~ **day**, (goeie)dag; ~ **evening**, goeienaand; ~-**fellowship**, kameraadskap; ~-**for-nothing**, misgewas, asjas, niksnuts, deugniet; **G**~ **Friday**, Goeie Vrydag; ~-**hearted**, goedhartig; ~ **humour**, goeie luim, opgeruimdheid; ~-**humoured**, opgeruimd, opgewek; ~**ish**, taamlik, nie alte sleg nie, goeierig, groterig (aantal); ~**liness**, beminlikheid, lieftalligheid, bevalligheid; ~-**looking**, mooi, knap; ~ **luck**, geluk; ~**ly**, goedig, beminlik, bevallig; uitmuntend; goedmoedig; gelukkig; ~ **man**, (ehr.), gesinshoof; ~ **manners**, goeie maniere; fatsoen; etiket; ~ **morning**, (goeie)môre; ~-**natured**, goedaardig; reggeaard; goedig; ~-**naturedness**, reggeaardheid; ~-**neighbourliness**, goeie buurskap.

good'ness, goedheid, vriendelikheid; geskiktheid; ~ *KNOWS*, dit mag joos weet; goeie (goeiste) weet; nugter weet; ~ *ME!* genugtig! gats! *for* ~ *'s SAKE*, in hemelsnaam, om Gods wil; *THANK* ~, goddank; *THROUGH the* ~ *of others*, met gunste en gawes; *since* ~ *knows WHEN*, van toeka se tyd af; *I WISH to* ~, ek wou in hemelsnaam.

good' night, goeienaand; nag.

goods, (pl) goedere, goed(jies), vraggoed; huisraad; ware; goederetrein; ~ *and CHATTELS*, hawe en goed; *DELIVER the* ~, 'n belofte nakom; aan die belofte voldoen; *he who GIVES away his* ~ *before he is dead, take a beetle and knock him on the head*, moenie jou uittrek voor jy gaan slaap nie; *all one's WORLDLY* ~, iem. se hebbe en houe; al sy aardse besittings; ~ **agent**, produkteagent; ~ **aircraft**, goederevliegtuig; ~ **lift**, goederehyser, goederehysbak; ~ **office**, goederekantoor; ~ **shed**, goedereloods; ~ **station**, goederestasie; ~ **traffic**, goederevervoer; ~ **train**, goederetrein; ~ **van**, bagasiewa; ~ **vehicle**, goederevoertuig; ~ **wagon**, goederetrok; ~ **yard**, goedereterrein.

good: ~-**tempered**, goedgehumeur(d); ~-**time girl**, flerrie, plesiersoekster; ~ **wife**, moeder, huisvrou; ~**will**, oorgawe, afstand; guns, goedgesindheid, welwillendheid, goedwilligheid, welgesindheid, toegeneentheid; klandisiewaarde, handelswaarde, klandisie, praktykwaarde; ~**y**, (n) lekkergoed; tannie, vroutjie (argaïes); (a) soetsappig; ~**y-goody**, (n) (..**dies**), skynheilige papbroek, sul, brawe Hendrik, heilige boontjie; (a) skynheilig, soetsappig, papbroekerig, stroopsoet.

goo'ey, klewerig, klouerig.

goof, (plat), dwaas, stommerik; ~**y**, dom, onnosel (plat).

goog'ly, (..**lies**), goëlbal (krieket).

goon, domkop; gehuurde bullebak.

goop, domkop.

goosan'der, duikergans.

goose, (**geese**), gans; uilskuiken, bobbejaan; (-**s**), parsyster (van 'n kleremaker); *A* ~, 'n uilskuiken, 'n bobbejaan; *not say BO to a* ~, nie ba of boe kan sê nie; *a wild* ~ *CHASE*, 'n mislukte onderneming; *COOK someone's* ~, iem. se kanse bederf; iem. se hoop verydel; *his* ~ *is COOKED*, dis klaar(praat) met hom; *kill the* ~ *that lays the golden EGGS*, die oorsprong van jou geluk vernietig; *a wild* ~ *never laid a tame EGG*, 'n randeier broei nooit 'n gesonde kuiken uit nie; *beware the geese when the FOX preaches!* as die vos die passie preek, boer, pas op vir jou ganse! *MOTHER* ~, Moeder Gans; *all his geese are SWANS*, sy eie goed is altyd beter as 'n ander s'n; hy meen dat sy uil 'n valk is; *everybody thinks his own geese are SWANS*, elke swart kraai dink sy eier is die witste; *WILD* ~, boomgans; ~-**barnacle**, eendemossel.

goose'berry, (..**berries**), appelliefie; *play* ~, derdemannetjie speel.

goose: ~-**bill**, gansbek; ~-**chase**, gansjag; *a wild* ~-*chase*, 'n wilde (nuttelose) soektog (agtervolging); ~-**egg**, ganseier; ~-**flesh**, gansvleis; *get* ~-*flesh*, hoendervel kry; ~-**foot**, ganspoot; gansvoet; ~-**grass**, brongras, ganserik; ~ **herd**, ganswagter; ~**like**, gansagtig; ~-**neck**, gansnek; swanehals (buis); ~-**quill**, gansveer; veerpen; ~-**rump**, hangkruis; ~-**skin**, gansvel; hoendervel (fig.); ~ **step**, paradepas, steekpas, hanepas; ~**y**, (n) gansie; uilskuiken; (a) gansagtig; dom.

go'pher[1], grondeekhoring.

go'pher[2], goferhout.

gor'ah, ghoera.

gorbli'mey, (vulg.), verdomp, verduiwels.

Gord'ian, Gordiaans; ingewikkeld; ~ **knot**, Gordiaanse knoop; *cut the* ~ *knot*, die Gordiaanse knoop deurhak (deurkap).

gore[1], (n) gestolde bloed; (v) stoot, gaffel; deurboor.

gore[2], (n) baan, geer; pant (rok); doekbaan (vliegtuig); (v) nouer maak; bane insit, geer; ~-**length**, doekbaanlengte.

gorge, (n) keel, strot; bergpas, ravyn, kloof; vretery, swelgery; (v) insluk, swelg, verslind, volprop; ~ *oneself*, jou oorvreet.

gor'geous, skitterend, pragtig, kostelik; oorlaai; ~**ness**, prag, heerlikheid; oorlading.

gor'get[1], halsstuk (van wapenrusting); halssnoer; halskraag; keelvlek.

gor'get[2], doktersmes.

gor'ging, ooretery; vretery; swelging.

gor'gon, skikgodin; gorgo; *the G*~*s*, die Gorgone.

gorgon'ian, verstenend, gorgoneagtig.

gorg'onize, laat versteen.

Gorgonzol'a, gorgonzola(kaas), Italiaanse vetkaas.

gorill'a, gorilla.

gorm'andize, gulsig eet, doodeet, skrok, swelg, vreet; ~**r**, gulsigaard, vraat, swelger.

gorm'andizing, swelgery.

gorm'less, dwaas, onnosel.

gorse, brem, skerpioenkruid.

gor'y, bloedig, bebloed.

gosh, gits! hede! *by* ~! allawêreld.

gos'hawk, swartsperwer.

Gosh'en, Gosen.

gos'ling, jong gans.

go-slow' strike, sloerstaking.

gos'pel, evangelie(woord); *ACCEPT everything as* ~, *REGARD (everything) as* ~, alles vir goeie munt aanneem; alles vir evangelie aanneem; iets heilig glo; ~**ler**, evangelieprediker; *hot* ~*ler*, ywerige prediker; rasende propagandis; ~ **message**,

evangelieboodskap; ~ **oath,** eed op die Bybel; ~ **truth,** evangelie(waarheid), heilige waarheid.
goss'amer, herfsdraad, spinnerak; fyn gaas (weefsel); ~ **ed,** uiters fyn, spinnerak=; ~**-like,** ragfyn; ~ **y** = **gossamered.**
goss'ip, (n) babbelaar, Antjie Taterat, kalfakter; gepraat, gebabbel; skinderpraatjies, (vroue)praatjies, pratery, gekeuwel; *be a* ~, los van mond wees; (v) babbel, gesels, stories vertel, skinder, klets; ~ **er,** ~**-monger,** kletskous, skinderbek; ~ **y,** babbelsiek, kletserig, loslippig.
gossoon', seun, kêreltjie.
got, *kyk* **get,** (v).
Goth, Goot; vandaal.
Goth'ic, (n) Goties (taal); Gotiese boukuns; (a) Goties; barbaars; ~**ism,** Gotiek; Gotiese taal; barbaarsheid; ~ **letter,** Gotiese letter, swart druk; ~ **window,** kruisraam.
go-to-meet'ing, kis=, Sondagse; ~ **clothes,** kisklere.
got'ta, (colloq.), het dit, het 'n; moet; ~ *go,* moet nou gaan.
gou'ache, gouache (dekverf; skilderwyse).
Goud'a (cheese), Goudse kaas, gouda(kaas).
gou'fing, fondamentversterking.
gouge, (n) guts(beitel); holbeitel; (v) guts, uitdiep, uitsteek, uithol; ~ **bit,** holboor, gutsboor.
gou'lash, ghoelasj, vleisbredie.
gourd, komkommer; kalbas; karkoer.
gourm'and, lekkerbek; smulpaap; vraat; gulsigaard; fynproewer; ~**ism,** lekkerbekkery; ~**ize,** gulsig eet.
gourm'et, fynproewer.
gout, jig, pootjie, podagra; vlek; (bloed)druppel; ~**iness,** jigtigheid; ~ **mixture,** jigmengsel; ~ **sufferer,** jiglyer.
gout'y, jigterig, jigagtig; ~ *PERSON,* jiglyer; ~ *PAINS,* jigpyne.
go'vern, regeer, beheers, bestuur; bedwing, lei; ~**able,** regeerbaar; gedwee; ~**ance,** beheer, leiding; bestuur; gedrag; ~**ess, (-es),** goewernante; ~**ing body,** beherende liggaam.
go'vernment, (n) regering, goewerment, (staats)bestuur, (staats)bewind, owerheid; leiding; beheersing; ~ *of a country,* landsregering; (a) regerings=, goewerments=, staats=; ~ **aid,** staatsondersteuning; ..**men'tal,** goewerments=, staats=; regerings=; ~ **assistance,** staatssteun; ~ **care,** staatsorg; ~ **circles,** regeringskringe; ~ **contribution,** staatsbydrae; ~ **despatch,** dienstelegram; ~ **enterprise,** staatsonderneming; ~ **expenditure,** staatsuitgawe; ~ **funds,** staatsgelde; ~ **gazette,** staatskoerant; ~ **help,** staatshulp; ~ **house,** goewerneurswoning; ~ **intervention,** regeringstussenkoms; ~ **loan,** staatslening; openbare lening; ~ **measure,** regeringsmaatreël; ~ **newspaper,** regeringsblad; ~ **notice,** regeringskennisgewing, goewermentskennisgewing; ~ **office,** regeringskantoor; regeringsamp; ~ **official,** regeringsamptenaar; staatsamptenaar; ~ **organ,** staatsblad; ~ **pension,** staatspensioen; ~ **policy,** regeringspolitiek; ~ **post,** regeringspos, staatsbetrekking; ~ **printing works,** staatsdrukkery; ~ **property,** staatseiendom; ~ **railways,** staatspoorweë; ~ **rebate,** staatskorting; ~ **school,** staatsskool; ~ **securities,** staatseffekte; ~**ship,** regeringskap; ~ **sugar,** goewermentsuiker; ~ **supervision,** staatstoesig; ~ **traffic,** staatsverkeer; ~ **translator,** staatsvertaler; ~ **troops,** regeringstroepe; ~ **warrant,** staatsorder.
go'vernor, goewerneur, regeerder, landvoog; bestuurder, bewindvoerder; baas; (spoed)reëlaar (masjien); ~ *of a BANK,* president van 'n bank; ~ *of a PRISON,* hoofsipier.
go'vernor-gen'eral, (governors-general), goewerneurgeneraal; ~**ship,** goewerneur-generaalskap.
go'vernorship, goewerneurskap.
go'vernor's wife, goewerneursvrou.
go-way' bird, kwêvoël, pêvoël.
go'wan, (Sk.), ma(r)griet, madeliefie.
gowk, koekoek; gek, idioot; lomperd.
gown, (n) toga; tabberd (vir vroue); mantel, talaar (Oosterse vors); kamerjas; (v) klee, die toga omhang; ~**ed,** in 'n toga; in 'n tabberd; ~**sman,** akademieburger, universiteitsman.

goy, nie-Jood, goi.
grab, (n) greep; (die) gryp; vangs; vanghaak, vangarm, grypkop; (v) **(-bed, -bed),** gryp, gap(s), skraap, beetpak; ~ **ber,** gierigaard; ~ **bing,** geskraap.
grab'ble, grabbel, gryp.
grab: ~ **bucket,** grypbak; ~ **crane,** grypkraan.
gra'ben, slenk.
grab: ~**-handle,** gryphandvatsel; ~**-sa'mple,** blinde monster.
grace, (n) genade, guns, goedertierenheid; grasie, bevalligheid, swier, bekoorlikheid, aanvalligheid, aantreklikheid; versiering; gunsbewys; gepastheid, fatsoen; voortreflikheid; pligsgevoel; vergifnis; dankgebed, tafelgebed; uitstel, respyt; triller (mus.); *ACT of* ~, genadebewys; amnestie; *be granted something as an ACT of* ~, iets uit vrye genade toegestaan word; *with a BAD* ~, teësinnig, met misnoeë; *BY* ~ *of,* danksy; *CREEP into someone's* ~*s,* by iem. witvoetjie soek; *a DAY'S* ~, een dag uitstel; *DAYS of* ~, respytdae, uitsteldae; *FALL from* ~, in ongenade verval; *a GIFT of* ~, 'n genadegif; *by the* ~ *of God,* deur Gods genade, by die grasie Gods; *GOOD* ~*s,* guns; *be in the GOOD* ~*s of,* in die goeie boeke staan van; *with a GOOD* ~, vriendelik; van harte; op hoflike wyse; *HAVE THE* ~ *to,* so fatsoenlik wees om; *with ILL* ~, teen heug en meug; ~ *at MEALS,* tafelgebed; *have no SAVING* ~, sonder enige verdienste wees; *SAY* ~, bid, dank (aan tafel); *THE Graces,* die Grasieë; *in the YEAR of* ~, in die jaar van ons Here; *YOUR* ~, U Hoogheid; (v) sier, bekoring verleen; vereer; pryk; ~ **cup,** afskeidsbeker; ~ **ful,** bekoorlik, sierlik, bevallig, grasieus; ~ **fulness,** bekoorlikheid, swier, sierlikheid, bevalligheid, grasie; ~ **less,** onbevallig, smaakloos; verdorwe, sleg, godvergete, goddeloos; lomp, brutaal; ~**-note,** triller, voorslag (mus.).
gra'cile, skraal, slank.
gra'cious, genadig, minsaam, bevallig; aangenaam; deugsaam; hoflik; *GOOD(NESS)* ~*!* o, liewe! *ME!* goeie hemel! my tyd! o, liewe! goeie genade! ~ *LIVING,* lewenskuns: deftige lewe; ~ **ly,** goedgunstig(lik); op bevallige wyse; ~ **ness,** goedgunstigheid; minsaamheid; bevalligheid.
gradate', gradeer; skakeer.
grada'tion, graad; klassifikasie, indeling; gradasie; skakering, gradering; opklimming; volgorde; ablaut.
grade, (n) graad; rang, trap, stand, klas; kwaliteit, gehalte; kruising; styging (baan); helling; *make the* ~, slaag, die paal haal; (v) indeel (vrugte), klassifiseer; gradeer; sorteer, rangskik; kruis (diere), deur kruising verbeter; waterpas maak; met verdrag laat styg; ~ **up,** verbeter, veredel; ~ **d,** gegradeer, gesorteer; opklimmend; geklassifiseer; ~ **level,** hellingshoogte; ~ **list,** ranglys; ~ **post,** hellingwyser; ~ **r,** skraper (pad); sorteerder, sorteermasjien; ~ **wheat,** graadkoring.
grad'ient, styging, helling (spoorweg); steilheid; steilte; val; opdraande; daling; hellingshoek; gradiënt; ~**-meter,** hellingmeter; ~ **post,** hellingwyser.
grad'ing, gradering; hellinggewing; afskuinsing; sortering; ~ **list,** ranglys; ~ **machine,** gradeermasjien; padskraper; ~ **truck,** skraperwa.
gradiom'etry, hellingmeting.
grad'ual, geleidelik, trapsgewyse; langsaam; ~ **acceleration,** geleidelike versnelling; ~ **ly,** langsamerhand, van liewerlee, geleidelik, stadigies, algaande, gaandeweg, trapsgewyse, allengs; ~ **ly** *sloping,* skotig afdraand; ~ **ness,** geleidelikheid.
grad'uand, gegradueerde, graduandus.
grad'uate, (n) gegradueerde; maatglas; (v) gradueer, promoveer; in grade indeel, gradeer, afdeel ('n instrument).
grad'uated, gegradueer (persoon); gegradeer; ~ **exercise(s),** opklimmende oefening(e); ~ **scale,** skaalverdeling; ~ **tax,** progressiewe belasting.
gradua'tion, geleidelike opklimming; promosie, graduasie; graadindeling; stap; gradering, kalibrering; ~ **ceremony,** gradeplegtigheid; ~ **day,** gradedag, promosiedag.

grad'uator, graadmeter, gradeerder; lynverdeler; stroomreëlaar.
Gr(a)e'cism, Grekisme, Gresisme, Griekse idioom.
Gr(a)e'cize, vergrieks.
Graec'o-, Grieks-; ~-**Roman**, Grieks-Romeins.
graffi'to, (..**fiti**), graffito; muurgekrap.
graft[1], (n) kuipery, politieke knoeiery; (v) knoei.
graft[2], (n) entstiggie, ent, oorentsel; weefseloorplanting (geneesk.); (v) ent; oorplant; spit.
graft[3], (n) spit; halfmaanvormige graaf.
graf'ter[1], kuiper, knoeier.
graf'ter[2], enter.
graft'ing, enting, entery; ~-**knife**, entmes; ~-**wax**, entwas.
Gra'hamstown, Grahamstad; ~ **wagon**, grahamstadter.
grail[1], graduaal.
grail[2], graal; *Holy G* ~, Heilige Graal.
grain[1], (n) graan; (graan)korrel; verfstof; grein; bietjie; draad (van hout); nerf (van leer); aar (marmer); eier (sywurm); weefsel; vleiskant (van leer); skarlakenrooi; aard, natuur; *ACROSS the* ~, teen die draad in; *it goes AGAINST THE* ~, dit gaan teen die draad in; dit stuit teen die bors; dit steek in die krop; *COARSE* ~, grof van draad; *DYE in* ~, deur die wol verf; *IN* ~, in sy binnenste; onverbeterlik; eg; *NOT a* ~ *of*, nie 'n greintjie van; *without a* ~ *of TRUTH*, sonder 'n sweempie waarheid; *WITH the* ~, regduads, met die draad; (v) korrel, korrelrig maak; versuiker (heuning); in die wol verf; nerf (vel); grein, vlam, marmer (hout); draadskilder.
grain[2], (n) mik; vurktand.
grain: ~ **bag**, streepsak; ~ **culture**, graanbou; ~ **district**, graandistrik; saaidistrik; ~**ed**, generf (vel); ru; gevlam, geaar (vleis); gemarmer (hout); ~*ed gunpowder*, korrelkruit; ~ **elevator**, graansuier, graansilo; ~ **elevator chute**, graansuierstortgeut; ~**er**, greineerder; houtskilder; marmerskilder; looimes; ~ **farmer**, graanboer, saaiboer; ~**ing**, (die) vlam, marmer, greineer, aring; draadskildering; korreling; versuikering (konfyt); afnerwing (leer); ~ **leather**, nerfleer; ~**less**, korrelloos; ~ **moisture-content**, graanvoggehalte.
grains, harpoen, vispies.
grain: ~ **section**, graanafdeling; ~-**sick**, bevange; ~-**side**, nerfkant; ~ **sorghum**, graansorghum; ~-**stack**, graanmied; ~ **stock**, graanvoorraad; ~-**sweepings**, graanafval; ~ **weavil**, kalander; ~ **wood**, greinhout; langshout; ~ **y**, korrelrig, geaar.
grain[2], (s) mik; vurktand.
grallator'ial, **gralla'tory**, steltpotig.
gram[1], perdevoer; dwerg-ertjie.
gram[2], gram (gewig); ~-**atom**, gramatoom; ~-**calorie**, gramkalorie.
gramina'ceous, **gramin'eous**, grasagtig, grasryk, gras-.
graminiv'orous, grasetend.
gramm'alogue, grammaloog, letterwoord, woordteken.
gramm'ar, spraakkuns, spraakleer, grammatika; *COMPARATIVE* ~, vergelykende grammatika; *HISTORICAL* ~, historiese grammatika; ~-**book**, taalboek; ~'**ian**, taalkundige; grammatikus.
grammat'ical, grammaties.
gramm'atist, taalkundige; vitter, taalindoena.
gram(me) = gram[2].
gram'ophone, grammofoon; ~ **record**, grammofoonplaat.
gram'pon, bergklimstewel, grampon.
gram'pus, noor(d)kaper, stormvis; blasende persoon; klaagpot.
granadill'a, granadilla, grenadella.
gran'ary, (..**ries**), graanskuur, koringskuur.
grand, (n) vleuelklavier; *do the* ~, die grootmeneer uithang; 'n toon aanslaan; jou verbeel; (a) groot; groots, belangrik, vernaam, verhewe, staatlik, weids; pragtig, mooi; waardig, deftig; kostelik; hoogspoggerig; *in* ~ *CONDITION*, in goeie toestand; so reg soos 'n roer; *the* ~ *RESULT*, die eindresultaat.
gran'dam, grootmoeder (dier).

gran'dam(e), ouma; ou vroutjie.
grand: ~-**aunt**, oudtante, groottante; ~ **child**, kleinkind; *have to take care of the* ~ *children too*, vir die nete ook sorg; *G* ~ *Cross*, grootkruis; ~ **dad**, oupa; ~ **daughter**, kleindogter; ~-**ducal**, groothertoglik; ~ **duchess**, (-es), groothertogin; ~ **duke**, groothertog; ~ **dukedom**, groothertogdom.
grandee', (Spaanse) edelman, grandee; vername man.
gran'deur, grootheid; grootsheid, staatlikheid, weidsheid; prag; vernaamheid.
grand'father, oupa, grootvader; ~ **chair**, grootvaderstoel, oupastoel; ~ **clock**, staanklok; ~ **y**, grootvaderlik.
grandil'oquence, grootpraterigheid, hoogdrawendheid.
grandil'oquent, hoogdrawend; grootpraterig, spoggerig, bombasties.
gran'diose, groots, grandioos, indrukwekkend; hoogdrawend.
grandios'ity, grootsheid, indrukwekkendheid; spoggerigheid.
grand: ~ **lodge**, grootlosie; ~ **ly**, uit die hoogte; pragtig; ~ **mal**, sware epilepsie; ~ **master**, grootmeester; ~ **mother**, ouma, grootmoeder; *try to teach your* ~ *mother to suck eggs*, jou ouma die paplepel wil leer vashou; ~ **nephew**, agterneef, kleinneef; ~ **ness**, grootheid; grootsheid; verhewenheid; ~ **niece**, kleinniggie, agterniggie; ~ **parents**, grootouers; ~ **piano**, vleuelklavier; ~ **sire** grootvader; voorvader; ~ **slam**, groot kap (kaartspel); taai, kap; ~ **son**, kleinseun; ~ **society**, hoë kringe; ~ **stand**, groot pawiljoen; hoofpawiljoen; ~ **total**, groot totaal, eindtotaal, uncle, oud-oom; *G* ~ *Vizier*, grootvisier.
grange, opstal, landhuis; boerdery; skuur.
gran'gerize, illustreer (met plate uit 'n ander boek geknip).
granif'erous, korreldraend, korrel-.
gran'iform, korrelrig, korrelvormig.
gran'ite, graniet; *disintegrated* ~, korrelgraniet.
granit'ic, **gran'itoid**, granietagtig.
graniv'orous, graanetend.
gran'nie, **grann'y**, (**grannies**), ouma, oumatjie; ~ **knot**, ouvrouknoop.
gran'olith, granoliet; ~ '**ic**, granolities.
grant, (n) vergunning, toekenning, skenking, verlening; handves, konsessie; bydrae, toelae, subsidie; oordrag (reg); (v) vergun, toeken, toestaan; verleen; skenk; oordra (reg); toegee, aanneem, inwillig; gevolg gee aan; *GOD* ~ *it*, mag God dit gee; *TAKE for* ~ *ed*, as vanselfsprekend beskou; ~ *ed THAT*, aangenome dat; *I* ~ *THAT it looks bad, but*, ek gee toe dat dit sleg lyk, maar...; ~ **able**, verleenbaar; vergunbaar; ~ **ed**, (a) toegegee; ~ **ed!** (interj) reg genoeg! aangenome! ~ **ee'**, konsessionaris; ontvanger, begiftigde; ~ **er'**, skenker, begiftiger, gewer; ~-**in-aid**, hulptoelae, subsidie; ~ **ing**, verlening.
gran'ular, korrelagtig, korrelrig.
gran'ulate, korrel, korrelrig word, granuleer; vergruis; gesond word, heel; ~ *d sugar*, korrelsuiker.
granula'tion, korreling, granulasie.
gran'ule, korreltjie.
gra'nulocyte, granulosiet, korrelsel.
granulome'tric, granulometries.
gran'ulous, korrelrig, korrelagtig.
gran'ulite, granuliet.
grape, druif; druiwekorrel; *BUNCH of* ~ *s*, druiwetros; *the* ~ *s are SOUR*, die druiwe is suur; ~ *s do not grow on THORNS*, mens pluk nie druiwe van distels nie; ~-**basket**, druiwemandjie; ~ **berry**, bobbejaandruif; ~-**box**, druiwekissie; ~-**brandy**, druiwebrandewyn; ~-**crusher**, druiwepers; ~ **cure**, druiwekuur; ~ **disease**, wingerdsiekte; ~ **export**, druiweuitvoer; ~ **fruit**, pomelo, bitterlemoen; ~-**gathering**, wynoes; ~-**grower**, druiweboer; ~-**harvest**, druiweoes; ~ **jam**, druiwekonfyt; ~ **juice**, druiwesap; ~ **mealy-bug**, druiwewitluis *(Pseudococcus maritimus)*; ~-**packer**, druiwepakker; ~ **scissors**, druiweskêr; ~ **season**, druiwetyd; ~-**shot**, kartets, skroot; ~-**shot bag**, skrootsak; ~-**shot gun**, skrootstuk, ~-**skin**, druiwedoppie; ~-**stone**,

druiwepit; ~**-sugar,** druiwesuiker, dekstrose; ~ **syrup,** moskonfyt; ~ **trade,** druiwehandel; ~**-treader,** druiwetrapper; ~ **variety,** druiwevariëteit; ~**-vine,** wingerdstok; *by the* ~, per riemtelegram; ~**-vinegar,** druiweasyn.
graph, (n) grafiek, grafiese voorstelling; kromme; hektograaf; (v) grafies voorstel; 'n kromme trek; ~ **eme,** grafeem; ~ **ic(al),** skilderend, aanskoulik, duidelik, lewendig; grafies; ~ *ic art,* grafiese kuns; ~ **style,** beeldende styl.
graph'ite, grafiet.
grapholog'ic, grafologies.
graphol'ogist, (hand)skrifkundige, grafoloog, handskrifontleder.
graphol'ogy, grafologie, handskrifkunde.
graphom'eter, hoekmeter.
graph'otype, grafotipie.
graph' paper, ruitjiespapier, grafiekpapier.
grap'nel, gryphaak, enterhaak; dreganker; werpanker.
grap'pa, afvalbrandewyn.
grap'ple, (n) gryphaak; dreghaak; greep; worsteling; (v) gryp, vasvat; worstel; omklem; aanpak; ~ *with,* worstel met; ~**-fork,** hooiklou; ~**-hook,** weerhaak; ~**-plant,** rankdoring, kloudoring; ~**-thorn,** duiwelsdoring.
grap'pling-hook, grap'pling-iron, enterhaak, gryphaak.
grap'tolite, graptoliet.
grap'y, druifagtig.
grasp, (n) (hand)greep; vashouplek; houvas; bereik; mag; bevatting, begrip, verstand; *BEYOND one's* ~, buite sy bereik; *WITHIN his* ~, binne sy bereik; (v) gryp, vasgryp, pak; bevat, begryp; omklem, vashou; najaag; ~ *the NETTLE,* gevaar (moeilikhede) moedig aanpak; ~ *an OPPORTUNITY,* 'n geleentheid aangryp; ~ **able,** begrypbaar; bereikbaar; ~ **er,** gryper; vashouer; begryper; ~ **ing,** grypend; inhalig, hebsugtig, grypsugtig.
grass, (n) (-es), gras, grassoort; weiveld; *BLADE of* ~, grashalm; *CUT the* ~ *from under one's feet,* die gras voor iem. se voete wegmaai; *GO to* ~, gaan wei; platval; *let no* ~ *GROW under one's feet,* nie gras oor iets laat groei nie; iets dadelik aanpak; *KEEP off the* ~, bly weg v.d. gras; *take LESS* ~, speel (hou) nouer (rolbal); *take MORE* ~, hou (speel) wyer (rolbal); *PUT to* ~, laat loop (perd); werkloos maak; pensioeneer; *SCENTED* ~, lemoengras; *SEND to* ~, platslaan; *the* ~ *is (seems) always greener on the other SIDE,* die gras is altyd die groenste aan die ander kant; *SOFT* ~, heuninggras, soetgras; *TURN out to* ~, laat loop (perd); werkloos maak; pensioeneer; (v) met grassooie toemaak; met gras beplant; laat bleik; platgooi, neertrek; laat wei; doodskiet; uittrek (vis); aan die daglig bring; ~**-bird,** grasvoël; ~ **border,** grasrand; ~ **box,** grashouer; grasvanger; ~**-cloth,** graslinne; ~ **cover,** grasbedekking; ~ **court,** grasbaan; ~**-cutter,** grassnyer; ~ **fire,** grasbrand, veldbrand; ~**-grown,** met gras begroei; ~ **hopper,** (veld)sprinkaan; ~**iness,** grasrykheid; grasagtigheid; ~ **land,** grasveld; ~ **less,** grasloos, sonder gras; ~**-linen,** graslinne; ~**-owl,** grasuil; ~**-parakeet,** budjie, grasparkiet; ~**-plot,** grasperk; grasveld; ~**-roots,** graswortels; *get down to the* ~*-roots,* nie baie diep gaan nie (mynw.); na die grondbeginsels gaan; tot die fundamentele feite deurdring; die kiesers; ~**-roots policy,** grondbeleid (politiek); ~ **snake,** grasslang; ringslang; ~ **veld,** grasveld; ~**-veld hookworm,** grasveldhaakwurm (*Bunostomum trigonocephalum*); ~**-veld merino,** grasveldmerino; ~ **whip,** grassekel, kapsekel; ~ **widow,** grasweduwee, onbestorwe weduwee; ~ **widower,** graswewenaar; ~ **y,** grasryk; grasgroen.
grate, (n) rooster; traliewerk; vuurherd; (v) van tralies voorsien; kras, kraak, knars; rasper; afmaak (mielies); *it* ~ *s (up) on the EAR,* dit klink onaangenaam; ~ *on the NERVES,* laat gril; ~ *the TEETH,* op die tande kners; ~**-area,** roosteroppervlak; ~ **carrier,** roosterstut; ~ **d,** getralie; gerasper; ~ *d cheese,* rasperkaas.

grate'ful, dankbaar, erkentlik; strelend; ~ *for,* dankbaar (erkentlik) vir; ~ **ly,** met dank; ~ **ness,** dankbaarheid, erkentlikheid.
grat'er, rasper.
grat'icule, meetnet.
gratifica'tion, bevrediging, voldoening; genoeë; genot, genieting; beloning, vergoeding, gratifikasie, toelae.
grat'ify, (..fied), bevredig, behaag, voldoening gee; verheug; beloon, vergoed; ~ **ing,** bevredigend, aangenaam, strelend.
gratin': *au* ~, gegratineer, au gratin.
grat'inate, gratineer.
grat'ing^1, (n) rooster(werk), traliewerk.
gra'ting^2, (a) krassend, knarsend, krakend.
grat'ing-bar, traliestaaf.
grat'ing voice, kraakstem.
gra'tis, gratis, vry, verniet.
grat'itude, dank, dankbaarheid, erkentenis, erkentlikheid.
gratu'itous, vrywillig; gratis, kosteloos; ongemotiveer(d), ongegrond, nodeloos, willekeurig, onnodig; ~ **lie,** onnodige leuen; ~**ly,** verniet; ongevraag.
gratu'ity, (..ties), geskenk, vrywillige gif, beloning; gratifikasie; fooi; lyfrente.
grat'ulatory, gelukwensend; ~ **letter,** gelukwensing(sbrief).
graunch, 'n knarsende geluid veroorsaak; beskadig (masjien).
gravam'en, (..**mina),** beswaar, grief; pit, kern, swaarpunt, hoofpunt, kernput (van aanklag); bewaarskrif, gravamen.
grave^1, (n) graf; *BEYOND the* ~, anderkant die graf; *DIG one's own* ~, jou eie graf grawe; *with one FOOT in the* ~, met een voet in die graf; *SINK into the* ~, ten grawe daal; *make someone TURN in his* ~, iem. in sy graf laat omdraai; *someone is WALKING over my* ~, iem. loop oor my graf; (v) **(-d,** or **-n),** graveer, grif, inbeitel.
grave^2, (v) skoon brand, skoonmaak (skip).
grave^3, (a) ernstig, bedenklik, gevaarlik, gewigtig; deftig, plegtig; swaar; stemmig; donker; diep; ~ *ACCENT,* swaar toonteken; gravisaksent; *a* ~ *ERROR,* 'n groot fout.
grave: ~**-clothes,** doodsklere; ~**-desecration,** grafskennis; ~ **digger,** grafmaker, grafgrawer.
grav'el, (n) growwe sand, gruis; niersteen, graweel (siekte); (v) **(-led),** gruis, begruis; dronkslaan, verleë maak; ~ **dump,** grondhoop, gruishoop; ~**ly,** gruiserig, gruis-; ~ **pit,** gruisgat; ~ **road,** gruispad; ~**-stone,** graweelsteen; ~ **walk,** gruispad, gruispaadjie.
gra've-mound, grafheuwel.
grav'en, gegrif, gesnede, gebeitel; ~ **image,** gesnede beeld.
gra'ver, graveur; radeernaald, graveernaald.
grave ~**-register,** grafboek; ~ **stone,** grafsteen; ~ **yard,** kerkhof, begraafplaas, godsakker; ~ **yard cough,** holklinkende hoes.
grav'id, swanger (mens); dragtig (dier), grootuier=.
gravim'eter, swaartemeter, gravimeter.
gravimet'ric, gravimetries.
grav'ing, snywerk; gravering.
grav'ing dock, droogdok.
grav'itate, graviteer; aangetrek word, neig; sak; oorhel; sif; ~ *towards,* oorhel, neig na.
gravita'tion, swaartekrag; aantrekkingskrag; neiging, oorhelling; die sif; *law of* ~, valwet; ~**al,** swaartekrag-, aantrekkingskrag-; ~ **feed,** valtoevoer.
grav'ity, swaarte, gewig; deftigheid, statigheid, gewigtigheid; plegtigheid, belangrikheid, stemmigheid; bedenklikheid, ernstigheid; erns; *CENTRE of* ~, swaartepunt; *FORCE of* ~, swaartekrag; *SPECIFIC* ~, soortlike gewig; ~**-catch,** valknip; ~ **fault,** afskuiwing; ~**-feed,** valtoevoer; ~ **irrigation,** leibesproeiing; ~ **metre,** swaartemeter, gravimeter; ~ **mixer,** valmenger; ~ **shot,** valgleuf; ~**-wheel,** skeprat; ~ **wind,** valwind.
gravure', *abbr. for* **photogravure,** fotogravure.
grav'y, (gravies), vleissous; ~ **beef,** sousvleis; ~-

boat, souskom, souspotjie; ~ **colouring,** souskleursel; ~**-ladle,** ~**-spoon,** souslepel.
gray, *kyk* **grey.**
gray'ling, vlagsalm.
graze¹, (n) skaafplek; skram(skoot); (v) skuur, skaaf; skram; skrams raak; afskram; afskuur, skryn; ~ *past,* rakelings verbygaan.
graze², (v) (be)wei; laat wei; graas.
gra'zier, veevetmaker, slagveeboer.
graz'ing, (n) (be)weiding; weiveld; (a) grasend, weidend; ~**-fee,** weigeld; ~**-ground,** weiveld; ~**-licence,** weilisensie; ~ **right,** weireg.
graz'ing-shot, skramskoot.
grease, (n) vet; ghries (vir wa, kar); olie, olierigheid, vetterigheid; vetwol; mok (aan perdepoot); *wool in the* ~, ongewaste wol; (v) smeer, insmeer, besmeer, olie; ~ *someone's PALM,* iem. omkoop; ~ *the WHEELS* (fig.), alles vlot laat loop (veral deur geld); *like* ~ *d lightning,* soos 'n vetgesmeerde blits; ~**-box,** smeerpot, ghriespot; ~**-cap,** ghrieskop; ~**-cup,** smeerdoppie, ghriespotjie; ~**-gun,** ghriesspuit, smeerspuit; ~ **heel,** mok(poot); ~ **less,** vetvry; ~ **monkey,** (sl.), werktuigkundige; ~**-nipple,** smeernippel; ~**-paint,** blanketsel; grimeersel; ~**-proof,** vetdig; ~**-proof bag,** vetvrysak; ~**-proof paper,** vetpapier; botterpapier; ~**r,** smeerder; stoker (skip); smeernippel; Mexikaan, Amerikaanse Spanjaard (neerh.); ~**-spot,** ~**-stain,** smeervlek, vetkol, vetvlek; ~**-trap,** vetvanger; ~**-wool,** vetwol.
greas'iness, vetterigheid, olierigheid, smerigheid.
greas'y, vetterig, olieagtig, olierig, smerig; vuil, salwend; mokkig; *a* ~ *fellow,* 'n teerputs; 'n teertou; ~ **heel,** mok(poot) (perd); ~ **pole,** vetgesmeerde paal; ~ **wool,** vetwol.
great, groot; tamaai; lang; beroemd, aansienlik, vernaam; bedrewe, handig; dik; oor-; *a* ~ *AGE,* 'n hoë ouderdom; ~ *est COMMON measure,* grootste gemene deler; *a* ~ *DEAL,* baie; *in* ~ *DETAIL,* tot in besonderhede; ~ *FRIENDS,* groot vriende; ~ *and GOOD are not the same,* hoe groter gees, hoe groter bees; ~ *est HAPPINESS for the* ~ *est number,* die grootste geluk vir die grootste aantal; *the* ~ *MAJORITY,* die groot meerderheid; *the* ~ *POWERS,* die groot moondhede; ~ *SCOTT!* my genugtig! allawêreld! *THAT'S* ~*!* pragtig! *THE* ~, die vername mense; *a* ~ *WHILE,* 'n lang ruk; ~ *WITH child,* swanger; ~ **age,** hoë ouderdom; ~**-aunt,** oud-tante, groottante; **the G**~ **Bear,** die Groot Beer; **G**~ **Britain,** Groot Brittanje; ~ **circle,** grootsirkel; ~ **coat,** warmjas, oorjas; **G**~ **Dane,** Deense hond; ~ **er flamingo,** grootflamink; ~**-grandchild,** agterkleinkind; ~**-granddaughter,** agterkleindogter; ~**-grandfather,** oorgrootvader, oupagrootjie; ~**-grandmother,** oorgrootmoeder, oumagrootjie; ~**-grandson,** agterkleinseun; ~**-hearted,** grootmoedig; moedig; ~ **house,** hoofhuis; groothuis; ~ **ly,** grootliks, baie, in hoë mate, ten seerste, ~ **ness,** grootte; grootheid, hoogheid; ~ **place,** hoofkraal; ~**-uncle,** oud-oom.
greave, beenplaat (van wapenrusting).
greaves, kaiings; afsaksel, vetmoer.
grebe, silwerduiker (voël); *crested* ~, kuifkopduiker.
Gre'cian, (n) Griek; (a) Grieks; ~ *nose,* Griekse neus.
Greece, Griekeland.
greed, lus, begeerte; begerigheid, gretigheid; inhaligheid, hebsug, grypsug; ~**ily,** gretig, gulsig; ~**iness,** gulsigheid, snoepheid, gretigheid; hebsug; ~**y,** gulsig; snoep; gretig, begerig, belus, grypsugtig; ~**y guts,** gulsigaard.
Greek, (n) Griek; Griekse taal; lid van die Griekse kerk; skelm; bedrieër; *when* ~ *MEETS* ~ *(a tug of war ensues),* wanneer die twee mekaar ontmoet, spat die vonke; dis bul teen bul; *this is* ~ *TO me,* dis Grieks vir my; (a) Grieks; *on the* ~ *calends,* in die jaar nul.
green, (n) groen, groenheid; grasveld, grasperk; (set)perk (gholf); fleur; groen stroop; (pl) moeskruid; groente; *do you see any (thing)* ~ *in my eye?* ek is oue as tien; (v) groen word; groen verf; vir die gek hou; (a, adv) groen (kleur); fris, bloeiend; vars; onryp; baar; onervare; *BE* ~, nat agter die ore wees; nog nie droog agter die ore wees nie; *he is not as* ~ *as he is CABBAGE looking,* hy is nie onder 'n uil uitgebroei nie; hy is nie so dom soos hy lyk nie; hy is nie so groen dat 'n koei hom sal vreet nie; *be* ~ *with ENVY,* die geelbaadjie aanhê; Jantjie wees; *the* ~ *EYE,* afguns; jaloesie; *not as* ~ *as one LOOKS,* nie onder 'n kalkoen uitgebroei nie; *keep* ~ *the MEMORY of,* in gedurige herinnering hou; *if that is done in the* ~ *TREE, what will be done in the dry?* as dit met groen hout gebeur, wat sal aan die dorre geskied? ~ **back,** Amerikaanse banknoot; ~ **bacon,** ongerookte spek; ~ **barley,** groenvoer; ~ **bean,** groenboontjie; ~**-bean bredie,** groenboontjiebredie; ~ **belt,** groen gordel; parkstrook; ~ **blowfly,** groenbrommer; ~ **book,** groenboek; ~ **brick,** rou steen; ~ **bug,** groenluis; ~ **bulbul,** bosvoël; ~ **cheese,** groen kaas; ~ **cloth,** groen laken; speeltafel; ~ **concrete,** vars beton; ~ **crop,** groenvoer; ~ **earth,** groenaarde; gloukoniet; ~**er,** nuweling; ~**ery,** groenigheid, loof, takke; ~ **eye,** jaloesie, afguns; ~ **fee,** baangeld; ~**-fig preserve,** groenvyekonfyt; ~ **finch,** groenvink; ~ **fingers,** groeihand; tuin(maak)aanleg; ~ **fly,** groen plantluis; ~ **fodder,** groenvoer; ~ **food,** groenvoer, groente; ~ **gage,** groenpruim; ~ **grocer,** groentehandelaar; ~ **ham,** ongekookte ham; ~ **hide,** nat vel; onbewerkte vel, rou vel.
green'horn, nuweling, groentjie; domkop; *NOT a* ~, vuisdik agter die ore; *STILL a* ~, nog nat agter die ore
green: ~ **house,** glasstoep; broeikas, kweekhuis; ~**ish,** groenagtig, groenerig; ~ **keeper,** baanopsigter; **G**~ **land,** Groenland; ~ **light,** groen lig; ~ **manure,** groenbemesting; ~ **manuring,** groenbemesting; ~ **mealie,** groenmielie; ~**ness,** groenheid; onrypheid; frisheid; ~ **pea,** dop-ertjie; groen-ertjie; ~ **pepper,** groenrissie; ~ **pigeon,** papegaaiduif; ~**-ranger,** (veld)opsigter; ~**-room,** artiestekamer, wagkamer, groenkamer (teater); ~ **s,** blaargroente; ~ **salad,** blaarslaai; ~ **scale,** groendopluis; ~ **shank,** groenpootruiter; ~ **shrike,** bokmakierie; ~ **sickness,** bleeksug; ~ **skin,** vars vel; ~ **some,** kiesspel (gholf); ~ **stall,** groentestalletjie; ~**-stick fracture,** buigbreuk; groenhoutbreuk; ~ **stone,** groensteen, dioriet; ~ **stuff,** groenigheid; groenvoer; groente; ~ **sward,** grasveld; ~ **table,** speeltafel; biljarttafel; ~ **tea,** groentee; ~ **vegetables,** blaargroente; ~ **vitriol,** groenvitriool, ystervitriool, ystersulfaat; ~ **wood,** bosveld, bosse; ~ **wound,** vars wond; ~**y,** groenerig, groenagtig.
greet, groet, begroet; *to* ~ *the eye,* aan die oog vertoon, sigbaar word; ~ **ings,** groetnis, groete.
gregar'ious, tropsgewys(e); gesellig; groep-, kudde-; ~ *ANIMAL,* kuddedier; ~ *INSTINCT,* kudde-instink, tropinstink; ~**ness,** gemeenskapsin; kuddegevoel.
grège, bruingrys; ~ **yarn,** ru-gare.
Gregor'ian, Gregoriaans.
greg'ory-powder, rabarberpoeier.
greige = **grège.**
grem'ial, biskopsvoorskoot.
grem'lin, tokkelossie, duiweltjie.
grenade', granaat.
grenadier', grenadier; **G**~ **Guards,** gardegrenadiere.
grenadill'a, grenadella, granadilla.
gren'adine¹, grenadien, grenadine; vleislappies ('n vleisgereg).
gren'adine², grenadien, grenadine, sy-en-wolstof.
grena'dine³, granaatstroop.
gressor'ial, lopend, loop-, stap-; ~ **bird,** loopvoël.
grew, *kyk* **grow.**
grey, (n) grys; grou; skimmel; (v) grys word, grys maak; (a) grys, grou; gespikkel, geskimmel; ~ *HORSE,* blouskimmel; *the* ~ *MARE is the better horse,* die vrou dra die broek; *TURN* ~, grys word; ~ **beard,** grysbaard, grysaard; ~ **cells,** harsings, brein, verstand; **G**~ **Friar,** Franciskaan, Franciskaner; ~**-haired,** grys; ~**-headed,** grys, gryskop-; ~ **heron,** bloureier.
grey'hound, windhond; ~**-racing,** hondewedrenne.
grey'ish, vaal(agtig), grou(erig), grysagtig, valerig.
grey: ~ **market,** grysmark; ~ **matter,** grysstof

(anat.); verstand, brein, harsings; ~ **ness**, grysheid, grouheid; ~ **rhebuck**, vaalribbok.
grey'wacke, grouwak.
grey'-wing partridge, bergpatrys.
grid, (n) rooster; skermrooster, dekrooster; tralie= (werk); sif (myn); bagasierak; motorhek; (a) ruit=.
grid'dle, (n) koekplaat, roosterplaat; (erts)sif; (v) rooster; sif; ~ **cake**, plaatkoekie, flappertjie.
gride, kners, knersend sny; deurboor, laat knars.
grid' gate, motorhek.
grid'iron, rooster; netwerk; raam; latsolder; voetbal= veld (Amerika); gridiron(voetbal).
grid: ~ **map**, ruitekaart; ~ **system**, ruitestelsel; ~ **zone**, ruitgebied.
grief, droefheid, droewenis, droefnis, wee(dom), hartseer, (siele)leed, verdriet, (siel)smart; kommer, sorg; krenking; *CAUSE someone* ~ , iem. leed aan= doen; *COME to* ~ , 'n ongeluk kry; misluk; strand; *DIE of* ~ , van hartseer sterf; ~**-stricken**, verslae, bedroef.
griev'ance, grief, verongelyking, beswaar, ergernis; *harbour a* ~ *against somebody*, 'n grief teen iem. hê; 'n wrok teen iem. koester; ~ **s committee**, griewekomitee.
grieve, grief, krenk; bedroef, smart (verdriet) aan= doen; treur; ~ *at (over)*, bedroef wees oor; ~ **d**, verontwaardig; bedroef.
griev'ing, doleansie.
griev'ous, griewend, bitter, smartlik; gevaarlik, be= denklik; drukkend; verdrietig, ernstig; ~**ly**, ern= stig; terdeë.
griff'(in)¹, nuweling, baar persoon.
griff'in², **griff'on**, griffioen, grypvoël.
griff'in³, wedrenwenk.
griff'on, Griffon (soort hond).
grig, kriekie; palinkie.
grill, (n) rooster; braaigereg, braaivleis; brand, bak; streng kruisvra; *MIXED* ~ , allegaartjie; ~ *to OR= DER*, roostervleis volgens bestelling; (v) braai, rooster; ~ **age**, rooster(werk).
grill(e), roosterwerk; sierrooster.
grill: ~ **ed meat**, braaivleis, geroosterde vleis; ~ **ed steak**, roosterbiefstuk; ~ **er**, rooster; roosteroond; ~ **ing pan**, roosterpan; ~**-room**, roosterlokaal; roosterrestourant, braairestourant.
grills, braaigeregte.
grilse, jong salm.
grim, grimmig; meedoënloos, onverbiddelik; bars, nors; afsigtelik; wreed; fel, hard, bar (klimaat); he= wig; afstotend, onvriendelik; dreigend; *hold on like* ~ *death*, op lewe en dood vasklou.
grimace', (n) grimas, gryns; skewebek; (v) gryns; ge= sigte trek, skewebek trek.
grimal'kin, feeks; ou kat.
grime, (n) vullis; roet; koolstof; (v) vuil maak, besoe= del, besmeer.
grim: ~**-faced**, nors; ~**ly**, onverbiddelik; nors; fel; hewig; ~**ness**, barsheid, norsheid.
grim'y, vuil, besmeer.
grin, (n) gryns, grynslag, glimlag; (v) **(-ned)**, gryns, grinnik, grimlag, meesmuil, tande laat sien; maak of jy lag; ~ *and BEAR it*, uithou; ~ *like a CHESHIRE cat*, soos 'n bobbejaan lag, ewig gryns.
grind, (n) gemaal; maal; geswoeg, geblok; *the DAILY* ~ , die daaglikse arbeid; *it's a REAL* ~ , dis 'n ge= swoeg; (v) **(ground)**, maal, vergruis, fynmaak; slyp (stomp snyding); swoeg, blok; skuur; kners; aan= slyp; afmaal; vernietig; onderdruk, uitmergel; kwel; draai (orrel); ~ *out a CURSE*, knarsetan= dend vloek; ~ *a DIAMOND*, 'n diamant slyp; ~ *DOWN*, fynmaal; onderdruk; ~ *into DUST*, tot stof vermaal; ~ *the FACES of the poor*, die armes onderdruk; ~ *at GREEK*, Grieks blok; ~ *to a HALT*, stadig tot stilstand kom; ~ *the TEETH*, die tande kners; ~ *in VALVES*, kleppe slyp; ~ **er**, (skêr)slyper; kiestand, baktand; boonste meul= steen; slypmasjien; verdrukker; blokker, swoeër; ~**ing**, (n) malery; slypery; (a) pynigend, nypend; afmalend; ~ **ing lathe**, slypbank; ~ **ing machine**, slypmasjien; ~ **ing paste**, slyppasta; ~ **ing powder**, slyppoeier; ~ **ing stone**, maalklip; ~ **ing wheel**, slyp=

skyf; ~**ings**, slypsels; ~ **mill**, slypmeul; ~**stone**, slypsteen; *keep one's nose to the* ~*stone*, hard werk.
grin'go, vreemdeling (in 'n Spaanssprekende land), gringo.
grip¹, (n) grippie, slootjie, voortjie.
grip², (n) handdruk, greep; vat, houvas; mag; mees= terskap; handvatsel; begrip; kramp; klem; haak; *CHANGE the* ~ , vervat; *COME to* ~ *s with*, hand= gemeen raak; aanpak; *HAVE a firm* ~ *on*, 'n sterk houvas hê op; *IN the* ~ *of*, in die kloue van; *LOSE one's* ~ , jou houvas verloor; (v) **(-ped)**, omknel, vasgryp; vasbyt (motorband); vat; (die aandag) boei.
gripe, (n) greep, vat; knaging; handvatsel; (pl) koliek, maagpyn; (v) gryp; knaag; pak; koliek veroorsaak; omvat, vasgryp; ~ **r**, gryper; vrek; afperser, uit= suier; ~**-water**, krampwater.
grip'ing, grypend; inhalig; knaend (pyn); kramp-.
grippe, griep, influensa.
gripp'ing, boeiend, pakkend.
Griq'ua, Griekwa; ~**land**, Griekwaland.
griq'ualandite, griekwalandiet.
grisai'lle, dekoratiewe skildering, grisaille.
gris'cent, asgrys.
griseoful'vin, griseofulvien, -ine, ringwurmantibio= tikum.
gris'eous, blougrys, pêrelgrys, liggrys.
grise'tte, grisette, Franse arbeidermeisie.
gris'kin, maer varkvleis.
gris'liness, afgryslikheid, aakligheid, vreeslikheid.
gris'ly, aaklig, afsigtelik, grieselig, afskuwelik.
grist¹, dikte (van tou).
grist², (maal)koring; *that BRINGS* ~ *to his mill*, dit is water op sy meul; *all is* ~ *that COMES to his mill*, vir hom is alles welkom; uit alles trek hy voordeel; ~**ing**, klantemaal.
gri'stle, kraakbeen.
gris'tly, kraakbeenagtig.
grit, (n) grint, sanderigheid, klipgruis, stof; pit; fut; durf; puf; (pl) growwe hawermeel; gruis, grutte; *have NO* ~ , geen pit hê nie; *have PLENTY of* ~ , hare op jou tande hê; (v) **(-ted)**, maal, knars, skuur; met stof bedek; ~ *one's teeth*, op jou tande byt; ~**s**, growwe meel; ~**stone**, growwe sandklip; ~= **tiness**, sanderigheid; ~**ty**, sanderig, korrelrig; pit= tig; gruiserig; ~**ty wool**, sandwol.
griz'zle, grens, neul, kerm.
griz'zled, grys, grou.
griz'zly, (. . lies), (n) roostersif; (Noord-Amerikaan= se) grysbeer; (a) gryserig, gryskleurig; valerig, grou, vaal; ~ **bear**, (Noord-Amerikaanse) grysbeer.
groan, (n) gekreun, versugting, gekerm, gesteun, sug; (v) kreun, steun, sug; weeklaag; ~**ing**, gesug, ge= kerm, gesteun.
groat, vierpenniestuk; *I don't care a* ~ , ek gee geen flenter om nie.
groats, (hawer)gort.
Grob'ian, lomperd; teerputs.
grob'man, seebrasem.
gro'cer, kruidenier; ~**y**, (. . ries), kruidenierswinkel; (pl) kruideniersware; kruidenierswinkel; ~ **y shop**, kruidenierswinkel.
grocete'ria, selfbedieningskruidenier.
grog, (n) g(h)rok; (v) g(h)rok drink; ~**-blossom**, jene= werneus, drankneus; ~**giness**, dronkenskap; ~ **gy**, geswa(w)el, aangeklam, slapperig, bewerig, dron= kerig.
grog'ram, grofgrein(materiaal).
grog'-shop, kantien, kroeg.
groin, lies; liesstuk; graatrib; gewelfkruis; ~ **arch**, kruisboog; ~ **vault**, kruisgewelf.
groom, (n) staljong; hofbeampte; bediende; bruide= gom; (v) oppas, bedien; skoonmaak, roskam (dier); *well* ~ *ed*, agtermekaar, netjies; ~**ing**, roskam= mery; versorging; *need* ~*ing*, afrigting (afronding) nodig hê.
grooms'man, strooijonker.
groove, (n) keep, groef, sponning, inkeping, indui= king; sleur; roetine; *ELONGATED* ~ , langskeep; *GET into a* ~ , die ou sleur volg; (v) uithol, ingroef, uitkeep, groef; ~ **angle**, groefhoek.

grooved, gegroef, ingekeep; omslag-; ~ **joint**, omslaglas; ~ **seam**, omslagnaat.
groove'-weld, groefsweislas.
groov'ing, (die) uithol, invreting, inkeping; (die) uitvreet; ~ **plane**, groefskaaf; ~ **saw**, groefsaag.
groov'y, gegroef, sleuragtig; (sl.), byderwets, baie goed.
grope, rondtas, omtas, voel, in die donker rondtas; ~ *for words*, na woorde soek; ~ **r**, voeler, rondsoeker.
grop'ing, rondtastend, rondsoekend, voelend; ~**ly**, soekend, voelend, voel-voel, op die tas.
gros'beak, appelvink.
gros'chen, groschen (munt).
gross¹, (n) (sing and pl), gros (getal); massa; *BY the* ~, by die gros, in die groot, op groot skaal; *DEALER in* ~, groothandelaar; *IN the* ~, globaal, oor die algemeen.
gross², (a) dik, grof, (p)lomp; ru-; bruto (gewig); groot; swaar; geil; vol, totaal; dig; onsmaaklik; *the* ~ *AMOUNT*, die totaal; *a* ~ *ERROR*, 'n growwe fout; ~ *HABITS*, walglike gewoontes; ~ **feeder**, gulsigaard; ~ **income**, bruto inkomste; ~ **national product**, bruto nasionale produk; ~**ness**, grofheid, onbeskoftheid; ~ **profit**, bruto wins; ~ **receipts**, bruto ontvangs; ~ **tonnage**, bruto tonnemaat; ~ **weight**, bruto gewig.
grot, grot (digt.).
grotesque', (n) grotesk (kunsstuk); (a) belaglik, snaaks, koddig, grotesk; ~**ness**, ..tes'querie, die groteske, groteskheid.
grott'o, (-es, -s), grot, spelonk.
grouch, (n) klaerigheid; knorrigheid; (-es), brompot, brombeer; (v) kla (gemeensaam).
ground, (n) grond; grondbeginsel; grondtoon; ondergrond, agtergrond; vloer; veld; terrein, land, erf; park; bodem, aarde; grondslag; grondkleur; grondlaag (verf); aardsluiting (elektr.); (pl) grondsop, besinksel, moer; terrein; ankerlatte; *ABOVE* ~, bo die grond; nog in lewe; *BREAK new* ~, aanvoor; pionierswerk doen; *BRING to the* ~, neertrek; onderkry; grond toe bring; *CHANGE one's* ~, van standpunt verander; *CLEAR the* ~ *for someone*, die weg vir iem. voorberei; *COVER much* ~, veel omvat; veel verrig kry; ver vorder; *CUT the* ~ *from under a person's feet*, die vaste grond onder iem. wegneem; die gras voor iem. se voete wegmaak; *FALL to the* ~, platval; in duie stort; *on FIRM* ~, op vaste grond; *FORBIDDEN* ~, verbode terrein; *GAIN* ~, veld wen; die oorhand kry; *GAIN* ~ *(up)on*, inhaal, *GIVE* ~, wyk; agteruitgaan; die veld ruim; *HOLD one's* ~, vasstaan; *LOSE* ~, veld verloor; *make up LOST* ~, verlore veld terugwin; *ON the* ~ *of*, op grond van; *ON these* ~*s*, om hierdie redes; uit die hoofde; *be on one's OWN* ~, jou op jou eie gebied bevind; *be on SAFE* ~, op vaste grond staan; *SHIFT one's* ~, van standpunt verander; *STAND one's* ~, vasstaan; *SUIT one down to the* ~, pas of dit geknip is; *on SURE* ~, op veilige grond; *TOUCH* ~, grond raak, grondvat; *YIELD* ~, wyk; (v) grond, grondves, bou, fundeer; strand (skip); met die aarde verbind (draad); op die grond loop; te lande kom; op die grond hou, belet om te vlieg (vliegtuig); op die grond sit; (a) gemaal, fyngeslyp; geaard (elek.); ~ **age**, haweg eld; ankergeld; ~ **air**, grondlug; ~ **angle**, waarnemingshoek; ~ **attack**, skeervlugaanval; ~**-attack aeroplane**, skeervliegtuig; ~**-attack flight**, skeervlugaanval; ~**-bait**, grondaas; ~ **beam**, fondamentbalk; ~ **beetle**, grondkewer; ~ **cable**, aardkabel; ~ **ance**, ashoogte; ~ **coat**, grondlaag (verf); ~ **colour**, grondverf; grondkleur; ~**-connection**, aarding, aardleiding (elek.); ~**-control**, vliegveldd iens; vliegveldpersoneel; ~ **cover**, grondbedekking; ~ **direction-finding station**, grondpeilstasie; ~**-duties**, gronddiens; ~ **ed**, gegrond; gestrand; *well-*~*ed in*, goed onderleg in; ~ **engineer**, grondingenieur; ~**er**, grondbal; ~ **facilities**, grondgeriewe; ~ **features**, terreinkenmerke; grondvorm (lugv.); ~ **floor**, grondvloer; onderste verdieping, benedeverdieping; begane grond; benedehuis; *GET in on the* ~ *floor*, oorspronklike aandele verkry; aan die begin inkom; eerste wees; *ON the* ~*floor*, gelykvloers; onder die eerstes wees; vroeg by die krip kom; in alle voorregte deel; ~ **frost**, grondryp; bevrore grond; ~ **game**, kleinwild; ~ **glass**, matglas; ~**-gudgeon**, modderkruiper; ~ **hornbill**, bromvoël; ~**ing**, basis, grondverf; fondering; ondergrond, grondslag; ~**-instruction**, grondonderrig; ~ **lead**, aardleiding; ~**less**, ongegrond; ~**lessness**, ongegrondheid; ~ **level**, grondhoogte, grondpeil; ~ **line**, grondlyn; ~ **ling**, kruipplant; grondel; filister, filistyn; ~ **man**, opsigter; baanwagter; ~ **mist**, grondmis, grondnewel; ~**-nut**, grondboontjie, kadjangboontjie; ~**-nut oil**, grondboontjiebotter; ~ **objective**, gronddoel; ~**-organization**, grondorganisasie; ~**-plan**, plattegrond, opset, grondplan; ~ **plate**, aardplaat (elek.); onderleer (spoor); ~**-rent**, grondhuur; ~**-robin**, katlagter, slangverklikker; ~**-room**, onderste kamer; ~ **sel**, fondament; drumpel; ~ **service**, gronddiens; ondervlak; draagrand (perdehoef); ~**-sheet**, grondseiltjie; ~**-sketch**, terreintekening; ~ **s'man**, vliegterreinwerker; (grond)opsigter; terreinopsigter; ~ **speed**, grondsnelheid; ~**-squirrel**, waaierstertmeerkat, erdmannetjie; ~ **staff**, grondpersoneel; ~ **support**, grondsteun; ~**-survey**, terreinopname; ~ **swell**, gronddeining; ~**-to-air missile (projectile)**, grondlugprojektiel; ~**-to-**~ **missile**, grondprojektiel; ~ **visibility**, grondsig; ~**-water**, grondwater; ~**-water level**, grondwatervlak; ~ **wind**, grondwind; ~ **wire**, aarddraad; ~ **work**, grondslag; grondwerk; ondergrond; hoofbestanddeel; ~**-worm**, reënwurm; ~**-yeast**, grondsop.
group, (n) groep; span; hoop, klomp; party; *in* ~*s*, groepsgewyse; (v) groepeer; ~**age**, groepering; groepvorming; ~ **area**, groepsgebied; ~ **building**, korfbehuising; ~**-captain**, groepskaptein; ~ **ed**, geskaar; ingedeel; gegroepeer; ~**ing**, groepering, rangskikking; ~ **insurance**, groepversekering; ~**-leader**, troepleier; troepleier; ~ **theory**, groepteorie; ~ **therapy**, groep(s)terapie.
grouse¹, (n) (sing and pl), korhoender.
grouse², (n) (-s), klag, grief; (v) kla, brom, murmureer, tjommel, grom, pruttel, mopper; ~**r**, brombeer, brommer, dwarskyker, brompot, tjommelaar, kermkous, ou klaagliedere.
grous'ing, gemopper, getjommel.
grout¹, (n) afsaksel; flodder, pleisterklei, pleisterkalk; (v) toepleister.
grout², (v) omvroetel (varke).
grout'er, skuifbalk; trappen.
grout'ing, bryvulling.
grove, lap bome, bos, boskasie; bossie.
grov'el, (-led), kruip, vroetel; *in the dust*, in die stof kruip; jou in die stof verneder; ~**ler**, kruiper; ~**ling**, kruiperig, laag.
grow, (grew, -n), groei; was (maan); toeneem; aanwas, groter word; laat groei; kweek, verbou, aankweek (gewasse); uitloop, ontstaan, voortkom, aangroei, voortbring; word; *ACCUSTOMED to*, gewoond word (raak) aan; ~ *a BEARD*, die baard laat groei; *the BOOK* ~*s on the reader*, die boek boei al hoe meer; ~ *out of one's CLOTHES*, uit jou klere groei; ~ *CROOKED*, vergroei, krom groei; ~ *DARK*, donker word; ~ *DIM*, dof word; ~ *out of a HABIT*, 'n gewoonte afwen; ~ *OBSOLETE*, verouder, uit die mode raak; ~ *ON one*, ingewortel raak; 'n vat op 'n mens kry; hoe langer hoe meer in die smaak val; ~ *OUT of*, voortspruit, ontstaan uit; ~ *RICH*, ryk word; ~ *TO*, aangroei tot; word; ~ *TOGETHER*, saamgroei; vasgroei; ~ *UP*, grootword, die sou n skoene ontgroei; ~ *VEG-ETABLES*, groente kweek; ~**er**, groeier (plant); kweker, verbouer, aankweker; boer; *a fast* ~*er*, 'n plant wat vinnig groei.
grow'ing, (n) kweek, aankweking; (a) groei-; ~ **boy**, groeiende seun; ~**-meal**, groeimeel; ~ **season**, groeiseisoen; ~**ly**, hoe langer hoe meer, meer en meer, toenemend.
growl, (n) geknor, gebrul, gebrom; (v) brom, grom, knor; ~**er**, brompot, grompot, knorpot; vierwielrytuig; ~**ery**, gegrom, brommery; privaat kamer; ~**ing**, geknor, brommery.
grown, begroei; groot, volwasse, opgegroei; ~**-up**, (n)

volwassene; (a) opgegroei, volwasse; ~-*ups first*, eers grootmense en dan langore; eers ou mense, dan langore; eers neus, dan bril.

growth, groei; gewas, geswel; aangroeiing; gesaaide; wasdom; ontwikkeling, vermeerdering, toeneming, aanwas; *FULL* ~, volle wasdom; ~ *of HAIR*, haargroei; ~ **fund**, groeifonds; ~ **industry**, groeinywerheid; ~ **point**, groeipunt; ~-**ring**, jaarring; ~ **share**, groeiaandeel.

groyne, pier, waterkering.

gro'zing iron, gruisyster.

grub, (n) wurm, ruspe; maaier; broodskrywer; slordige mens, teerputs; werkesel; eetgoed, kos; (v) (-**bed**), opgrawe, ontwortel; omspit; omvroetel; snuffel; graaf; ploeter, swoeg; kos gee; ~ **ber**, grawer, spitter; kruipbal (kr.); ~ **biness**, morsigheid, smerigheid; ~**bing hoe**, skoffelpik; ~**by**, vol maaiers; vuil, smerig; ~ **saw**, klipsaag; ~ **screw**, skroeftap; ~ **stake**, (sl.), kapitaalaandeel.

Grub' Street, (straat bewoon deur) broodskrywers, prulskrywers.

grudge, (n) wrok, hekel, haat, afguns, afgunstigheid; *BEAR a person a* ~, *HAVE a* ~ *against someone*, 'n wrok koester teen iem.; (v) beny, misgun; met lede oë aansien; ~ *oneself NOTHING*, jou niks ontsê nie; ~ *no PAINS*, geen moeite ontsien nie; ~ *the TIME*, die tyd nie gun nie.

grudg'ingly, met teensin, wangunstig, ongraag.

gru'el, (n) gortwater; pap; graanwater, dun graanpap; loesing; *GIVE a person his* ~, iem. van kant maak; iem. 'n loesing gee; *HAVE one's* ~, 'n loesing gee; (v) 'n loesing gee.

gru'elling, (n) loesing, kwaai pak; (a) moordend, uitputtend; *it was a* ~ *EXPERIENCE*, dit was 'n nare ondervinding; *he had a* ~ *TIME*, hy het baie swaar gekry; dit het lood gegaan.

grue'some, aaklig, grusaam, afsigtelik; ~**ness**, grusaamheid, afsigtelikheid, aakligheid.

gruff, stroef, stoets, bars, nors, stuurs, suur; ~**ish**, suurderig; norserig; ~**ness**, stuursheid, norsheid, barsheid, stroefheid.

grum'ble, (n) gebrom, geknor; gerommel; murmurering; gepruttel, mompeling; (v) mor, knor, brom, tjommel, grom, pruttel, mopper; ~ *and grouse*, brom en kla, mor en mopper; ~**r**, brompot, pruttelaar, grompot, iesegrim, dwarskyker, brommer, knorpot, tjommelaar, brombeer.

grum'bling, (n) geknor, gemopper, gemompel; gemor; getjommel; (a) klaerig, klaend, brommerig, pruttelrig; ~**ly**, pruttelend, brommend, klaend, klaerig.

grume, klont; fluim.

grumm'et, touoog, touring; valhelm; kabelbeslag; blokstrop; ~ **washer**, doekring.

grum'ous, klewerig; klonterig.

grump'iness, pruttelrigheid, norsheid.

grump'ish, grump'y, ontevrede, knorrig, brommerig, nors, pruttelrig.

Grun'dy: *Mrs.* ~, die kwaadsprekende wêreld; preutse mening; ~**ism**, fatsoen, konvensie; preutsheid.

grunt, (n) geknor; gegrom; (v) brom; knor; ~**er**, knorder; vark; knorhaan (vis); ~**ing**, geknor, gesteun; ~**ling**, varkie.

gru'yère, gruyère(kaas).

gryph'on = **griffin**.

G'-string, deurtrekker, stertriem, genadelappie; G-snaar.

guai'ac(um), guajak(hars).

gua'na, likkewaan.

guana'co, guanaco, wilde llama.

gui'anine, guanien, -ine.

gua'no, (-s), ghwano, guano, voëlmis; ~ **island**, guanoeiland.

gua'nyl, guaniel.

guar, guar (boontjie).

guarantee', (n) waarborg, garansie; onderpand, sekerheidstelling; vrywaring; borg, garandeerder; (v) waarborg, goedstaan, garandeer, borg staan vir, instaan vir; vrywaar teen; ~ **fund**, waarborgfonds; ~ **insurance**, herversekering; ~ **list**, waarborglys.

gua'rantor, borg; vrywaarder.

gua'ranty, (..ties), borgstelling; waarborg, garansie; ~ **fund**, waarborgfonds.

guard, (n) wag (by gebou); beskutting; kondukteur (trein); hoede; beskerming, bewaking; bewaker, wagter; skildwag, brandwag (soldate); borg (klep); skut, skerm(kap); (arm)bedekking; stootpaal; garde, lyfwag; stootplaat (swaard); beenbeskermer; beuel (aan sneller); *BE on* ~, wag staan; *BE on one's* ~, op sy hoede wees; *CATCH someone off his* ~, iem. onverhoeds betrap; ~ *of HONOUR*, erewag; *KEEP* ~, wag hou; *MOUNT* ~, die wag betrek; *OFF one's* ~, nie op jou hoede nie; *OFF* ~, onvoorbereid, onverhoeds; *the OLD* ~, die ou garde; *POST a* ~, 'n wag uitsit; *PUT someone off his* ~, iem. in slaap wieg; *RELIEVE* ~, die wag aflos; *TAKE* ~, reg staan; *TAKE someone off his* ~, iem. verras (oorrompel); (v) oppas; wag hou; bewaar; bewaak, beskerm, hom behoed teen; jou vrywaar (teen); beteuel; op sy hoede wees; dek; ~ *oneself against*, op jou hoede wees teen; jou in ag neem vir; ~-**boat**, patrolleerboot; ~ **book**, album; platboek; ~ **cell**, sluitsel; ~-**chain**, veiligheidsketting; nekketting; ~ **duty**, wagdiens; ~**ed**, behoedsaam, versigtig; bewaak; ~ **house**, wagkamer, waghuis.

guard'ian, voog (reg); kurator; bewaker, bewaarder; *joint* ~, medevoog; ~ **angel**, beskermengel, skutengel, bewaarengel; ~ **ship**, voogdy; voogdyskap; regentskap; hoede, bewaking, beskerming; ~ **spirit**, beskermengel.

guard: ~**less**, onbeskerm; ~-**plate**, skutplaat, skermplaat; ~-**pole**, skrampaal; ~-**post**, wagpos; ~-**rail**, reling, leuning; veiligheidstaaf (spoorw.); skermreling; ~ **room**, wagkamer, waghuis; detensiekamer, arrestantelokaal (mil.); ~-**ship**, wagskip; ~ **s'man**, gardeoffisier; ~-**stone**, skramklip; ~**'s van**, kondukteurswa.

Guarne'rius, Guarnerius(viool).

guarr'i, ghwarrie(boom).

gua'va, koejawel.

gub'bins, gemors; waardelose ding.

gubernator'ial, goewerneurs=.

gudg'eon, grondel (vis); lokaas; sukkelaar; skarnieroog; (roer)oog, ringhaak; pen, spil; ~-**pin**, suierpen (motor).

guel'der rose, sneeubal, balroos.

guerd'on, (n) (digt.) beloning, vergelding; (v) beloon.

Guern'sey, Guernsey(bees).

guer(r)ill'a, guerrilla, ongereelde oorlog; ongereelde vegter; ~ **war(fare)**, guerrillaoorlog, ongereelde oorlog.

guess, (n) gissing; raaiskoot; vermoede; *it is ANYBODY'S* ~, dit is hoogs onseker; *AT a* ~, vermoedelik; *BY* ~, op die oog; *EASY* ~, maklik om te raai; *by* ~ *and by GOD*, lukraak; *your* ~ *is as GOOD as mine*, ons weet dit albei ewe min; *HAVE a* ~, raai; *I* ~, (Amer.), ek is seker; ek glo; *MAKE a* ~, raai, gis; (v) gis, raai; skat; glo (Amer.); *how was I to* ~? ek kon dit nie ruik nie; hoe kon ek dit geweet het? ~**timate**, skatting, raaiskatting; ~**er**, raaier; ~ **work**, geraai, gissing, raaiery.

guest, gas, kuiergas; feesgenoot, aansitter, aangesetene; parasiet; ~ *of honour*, eregas; ~-**chamber**, vrykamer; ~ **conductor**, besoekende dirigent, gasdirigent; ~-**farm**, vakansieplaas, loseerplaas; ~-**house**, gastehuis; ~-**night**, introduksieaand; ontvangsaand; ~ **room**, vrykamer, spaarkamer, gastekamer; ~-**rope**, sleeptou; ~ **speaker**, geleentheidspreker, gasspreker; ~-**towel**, gastehanddoek.

guffaw', (n) skaterende lag, bulderlag, gebrul; (v) skaterlag, brul van die lag.

guid'able, bestuurbaar; volgsaam.

guid'ance, leiding; bestuur; rigsnoer.

guide, (n) gids; raadgewer, leidsman; geleier, reisgids; vraagbaak; wegwyser, padwyser, leiding, leidraad; leibalk, leiboom, leibaan (masjien); regulator, reguleerder; *vocational* ~, beroepsvoorligter; (v) die pad wys, lei; (be)stuur; raad gee, rondlei; ~-**block shoe**, leiblok; ~-**book**, reisgids; ~-**box**, leibus.

guid'ed, gerig, gelei; *be* ~ *BY*, gelei wees deur; jou laat lei deur; ~ *MISSILE*, geleide projektiel.

guide: ~-**dog**, geleidehond, gidshond; ~ **dot**, gidsstippel; ~**less**, sonder gids; sonder leiding; ~-**line**,

riglyn, leistreep; ~-**map,** gidskaart; ~-**pin,** leipen; ~-**plate,** leiplaat; ~-**post,** wegwyser, handwys(t)er; predikant; ~-**pulley,** leiskyf; ~-**rail,** leireling; keerstaaf; ~-**ring,** geleiring; ~-**rod,** leistang; ~-**rope,** sleepkabel; stuurlyn; tentlyn; ~-**screw,** geleiskroef; ~-**stone,** randsteen; ~ **way,** baan, spoor, groef; ~-**wheel,** leirat; ~-**wire,** leidraad.
guid'ing, leidend; ~ **star,** leister; ~ **stick,** skilderstok.
guid'on, vlaggie; banier, wimpel.
guild, gilde, vereniging.
guil'der, gulden, floryn.
guild'hall, gildehuis, stadhuis; *the G* ~, die Londense stadsaal.
guile, lis, slinksheid, arglistigheid; bedrog, valsheid, misleiding; ~**ful,** bedrieglik, listig, vals, misleidend; ~**less,** onskuldig, argeloos, eerlik.
guill'emot, duik(er)hoender.
guilloch'e, vlegversiering, guilloche.
guillotine', (n) guillotine, valbyl; (papier)snymasjien; sluiting, bekorting (van debatte); (v) onthoof, guillotineer; afsny; debatte bekort, die sluiting toepas; ~ **machine,** valbylmasjien.
guilt, skuld; (straf)skuldigheid; *ADMISSION of* ~, skulderkenning; *CONFESSION of* ~, skuldbekentenis; *lay the* ~ *at someone's DOOR,* iem. die skuld gee; ~**iness,** skuldigheid.
guilt'less, onskuldig; skuldeloos; ~**ness,** onskuld.
guil'ty, (straf)skuldig, strafwaardig; strafbaar; misdadig; *BE* ~ *of,* skuldig wees aan; *a* ~ *CONSCIENCE needs no accusers,* 'n slegte (skuldige) gewete verraai homself; *HAVE a* ~ *conscience,* 'n skuldige gewete hê; *PLEAD* ~, skuld beken, skuldig pleit; *VERDICT of* ~, skuldigbevinding.
Guin'ea, (n) Guinee; (a) Guinees.
guin'ea, ghienie; ~-**corn,** graansorghum; ~-**fowl,** tarentaal, drafhoender, wildehoender, poelpetaat; ~-**pig,** marmotjie (dier); geldmaker; 'proefkonyn; *be a* ~-*pig,* 'n proefkonyn wees.
guipure', guipure(kant).
guise, manier, voorkome; kleding; masker; *under (in) the* ~ *of,* onder die skyn (mom) van.
guitar', kitaar, ghitaar; ~**ist,** ~-**player,** kitaar-, ghitaarspeler.
Gujarat'i, Goedjarati (volk, taal).
gulch, kloof, donga, diep sloot.
gules, rooi, keel (heraldiek).
gulf, (n) golf, baai; draaikolk; kloof, afgrond; **G**~ **Stream,** Golfstroom; (v) verswelg; oorstroom.
gull¹, (n) seemeeu.
gull², (n) domkop, uilskuiken; (v) bedrieg, mislei, kul, fop; ~**er,** bedrieër, kuller.
gull'et, sluk; slukderm, keel; kloof, ravyn; *stick in one's* ~, jou dwars in die krop steek; ~**ing,** uitdieping.
gullibil'ity, liggelowigheid, onnoselheid.
gull'ible, liggelowig, onnosel, simpel; *he* ~, alles sluk; liggelowig wees.
gull'y¹, (n) **(gullies),** slagmes, slagtersmes.
gull'y², (n) **(gullies),** geut, grip, geul, afloop; versamelput, sinkput, riool(gat); donga, kloof; gangetjie (krieket); (v) (..**lied)** uithol, uitspoel, verspoel; ~-**drain,** rioolpyp; ~-**hole,** rioolgat; ~-**trap,** stankafsluiter.
gulos'ity, gulsigheid, vraatsug.
gulp, (n) sluk, teug; *at one* ~, in een sluk; (v) insluk, wegsluk; benoud wees; ~ *down,* afwurg, insluk, skrok, wegsluk.
gum¹, (n) (meestal mv.), tandvleis.
gum², (n) gom; gomboom, drag (van oë); (v) **(-med),** gom, vasplak; ~ *med paper,* gompapier, kleefpapier; (interj) *by* ~*! gits!* ~ **arabic,** Arabiese gom.
gum'boil, tandvleissweer, abses.
gum: ~ **boots,** oorskoene, rubberskoene; ~-**elastic,** gomlastiek; ~**miness,** taaiheid, klewerigheid; ~ **my,** klewerig, taai, gomagtig; geswel.
gum'my, tand(e)loos; ~ **sheep,** ou skaap.
gump'tion, (gemeens.) fut, pit; oorleg, gesonde verstand; ondernemingsgees; ~**less,** dom, onnosel.
gum' resin, gom(hars).
gum' ring, verhemeltering.
gum: ~ **shoe,** oorskoen; ~-**sniffing,** gomsnuif; ~-**tree,** gomboom; *up a* ~-*tree,* in die knyp, raad-op.

gun, geweer; kanon; (vuur)wapen, roer; stuk; spuit (vir smering); (pl) kanonne, geskut, vuurmonde, die artillerie; *BIG* ~, groot geweer (kanon); vername persoon, kokkedoor; *BLOW great* ~*s,* waai dat die klippe vlieg; *SON of a* ~, veragtelike vent, swernoot, smeerpoets; *SPIKE someone's* ~*s,* iem. se draad knip; *STICK to one's* ~*s,* op sy pos bly; voet by stuk hou; *SURE as a* ~, so seker as wat; ~-**barrel,** geweerloop; ~ **boat,** kanonneerbot; ~-**carriage,** kanonwa, affuit; ~-**case,** geweersak; ~-**cotton,** skietkatoen; ~-**crew,** stukbediening (leër); ~-**deck,** batterydek, geskutdek; ~-**dog,** jaghond; ~-**fight,** skietgeveg; ~-**fire,** kanonvuur, artillerievuur; ~ **fodder,** kanonvoer; ~-**founder,** geskutgieter; ~-**foundry,** geskutgietery; **gu'nite,** spuitsement; ~-**ladle,** laaiiepel; ~-**lock,** geweerslot; ~-**maker,** geweermaker, wapensmid; ~ **man,** vuurder, skieter; rampokker, gewapende rower; ~-**metal,** geskutmetaal, geskutbrons.
gunn'el¹ = **gunwale.**
gun'nel², bottervis.
gun: ~-**ner,** artilleris, kanonnier; (boord)skutter (vliegtuig); *kiss the* ~*ner's DAUGHTER,* afgeransel word; op 'n kanon oopgetrek word; *the* ~*ner to his LINSTOCK and the steerman to his helm,* skoenmaker, hou jou by jou lees; ~ **nery,** skietkuns, skietleer; kanonvuur, geweervuur; artilleriewetenskap; kanongietery; ~**nery-range,** artillerieskietbaan; boordskietbaan; ~**nery-school,** skietskool; ~**nery-spotter,** vuurleidingsvliegtuig; ~**ning,** skietery, jag.
gunn'y, goiing; ~ **bag,** ~ **sack,** goiingsak.
gun: ~-**park,** geskutwerf; ~-**pig,** kanonyster; ~-**pit,** geskutkuil; ~-**port,** geskutpoort; ~ **powder,** kruit, buskruit; *not to have invented* ~ *powder,* nie die buskruit uitgevind het nie; ~ **power,** artilleriesterkte; ~-**rack,** geweerrak; ~ **range,** skootafstand, draafstand; drag; ~-**rod,** laaistok; ~-**room,** geweerkamer; wapenkamer; ~-**runner,** geweermokkelaar; ~ **running,** geweersmokkelary.
gun'shot, geweerskoot; kanonskoot; *OUT of* ~, buite skoot; *WITHIN* ~, onder skoot.
gun: ~-**shy,** geweersku; ~-**shyness,** skootskuheid; ~-**sight,** visier; ~-**slide,** affuitslee; ~-**slinger,** skut; rower, rampokker; ~ **smith,** geweermaker; ~-**stick,** laaistok; ~-**stock,** geweerkolf; ~-**turret,** wapenkoepel.
gun'wale, ghonnel, dolboord; ~ **board,** ghonnelplank.
gup'py¹, guppie (vis).
guppy², duikboot.
gurgita'tion, borreling, maling.
gur'gle, (n) geklok; gemurmel; gegorrel; (v) gorrel; murmel; klok.
gurn'ard, gurn'et, knorhaan (vis).
gu'ru, ghoeroe; leermeester.
gush, (n) **(-es),** uitstroming, borreling; uitstorting, uitbarsting; vloed (vloeistof); oliespuitbron; dwepery; vlaag, bui; aanstellery; (v) guts; uitstroom, uitstort, oorborrel; baie (sterk) vloei; uitbars; laat stroom; aanstellerig wees, dweep; ~**er,** spuitende petroleumbron; dweper; ~**ing,** ~**y,** oorvloedig, stromend; oordrewe sentimenteel; aanstelleig.
guss'et, hoekverbinding, hoeksteun, plaatsteun; insetsel, okselstuk, hoeklappie, slipstrook; knoopplaat (vliegtuig); ~ **plate,** knoopplaat (brug); plaatanker (loko.); hoekplaat (meg.); ~-**stay,** hoeksteunplaat.
gust, (wind)vlaag, rukwind; stroom, vloed; *a* ~ *of smoke,* rookwolk.
gusta'tion, proewing, proe, proeëry, smaak.
gus'tative, smaak-, proe-.
gus'tatory, smaak-; ~ **nerve,** smaaksenuwee.
gust'iness, onstuimigheid, winderigheid.
gus'to, smaak; genot; ywer, vuur, animo.
gus'ty, stormagtig, buierig, onstuimig.
gut, (n) derm; (derm)snaar; engte; vernouing; seestraat; landengte; (pl) ingewande; fut, durf; *have no* ~ *s,* geen ruggraat (fut) hê nie; (v) **(-ted),** ingewande uithaal, vlek, skoonmaak; leegmaak, plunder; uitbrand (huis); vreet; opsomming maak (boek); ~**less,** lamsakkig, lafhartig; ~ **reaction,** natuurlike

gutta-percha 940 **hackle**

(onmiddellike) reaksie; ~ **scraper**, vioolkrasser, vioolsaer; ~-**string**, dermsnaar.
gutta-perch'a, guttapertsja, gomlastiek, rubber; ~ **tissue**, gomlastiekweefsel.
gutt'ate, gespikkel, gevlek.
gutta'tion, uitsweting.
gutt'er, (n) geut; voor; sloot; riool; suggeut; *from the* ~, van die straat; (v) uithol; vore of groewe maak; rioleer; stroom; afloop (kers); ~-**child**, ~-**imp**, straatkind; ~**ing**, afdrupsel; geute, geutwerk; groef; ~ **man**, ~-**merchant**, straatsmous; ~ **paper**, smeerblad; ~ **pipe**, geutpyp, dakpyp; ~ **press**, sensasiepers, smeerpers; geelpers; ~**snipe**, straatkind, straatjoggie; opraapsel; ~ **spout**, spuigat, spuier.
gut'tie, knoopderm, dermbeklemming.
gutt'le, gulsig eet, vreet; ~**r**, gulsigaard, vraat.
gutt'ural, (n) keelklank, gutturaal; (a) gutturaal; keel=; ~**ize**, gutturaliseer, met 'n keelklank uit= spreek.
gutt'y, (gutties), (gemeens.) rubberbal.
guy[1], (n) voëlverskrikker; gek; swaap; *be made a* ~ *of*, uitgelag word, vir die gek gehou word.
guy[2], (n) stuurtou, stuurketting; bultou; ankertou, stormlyn; tou, borgtou, veiligheidstou (tent); (v) span; bespot, die gek skeer met; as pop vertoon; ~-**rope**, stormlyn.
guz'zle, (op)suip; vreet; ~ *away*, verkwis, verbras; ~**r**, gulsigaard, vraat; suiplap.
gwyn'iad, witvleissalm.
gyle, brousel; gisbalie.
gym, (abbr.), springrok, springjurk, drilkostuum; gimnasium; gimnastieksaal.
gymkha'na, sportklub; sportfees, sportbyeenkoms; gimkana, perdesport; atletiekbaan.
gymna'sium, (-s, ..sia), gimnasium, gimnastiek= skool.
gym'nast, gimnas.
gymnas'tic, (n) gimnastiek; (a) gimnastiek=; gimnas= ties; ~ *costume (tunic)*, springrok; ~ **mattress**, springmatras; ~**s** gimnastiek.
gymnastrade' gimnastrade.

gymnos'ophist, gimnosoof, mistikus, askeet.
gymnos'ophy, gimnosofie.
gym'nosperm, gimnosperm, naaksadige.
gymnosperm'ous, naaksadig.
gym'nospore, gimnospoor.
gymnot'us, beefpaling, beefaal.
gymp, gimp; sydraad; omboorsel.
gyn, drievoethysblok.
gynaece'um, vroueverblyf; vroulike organe (van blom).
gynaecol'ogist, vrouearts, vrouedokter, ginekoloog.
gynaecol'ogy, ginekologie, kennis van vrouesiektes.
gynan'dromorph, dubbelslagtig, ginandromorf(ies).
gynan'drous, helmstylig, ginandries; dubbelslagtig, trassie=.
gynan'dry, helmstyligheid, ginandrie.
gynoc'racy, vroueregering, ginokrasie.
gyp's(e)ous, gipsagtig.
gypsif'erous, gipshoudend.
gypsoph'ila, krytblom, gipskruid.
gyp'sum, gips.
gyp'sy, *kyk* **gipsy**.
gyrate'[1], (v) ronddraai, wentel.
gyr'ate[2], (a) kringvormig, sirkelvormig.
gyra'tion, omwenteling, ronddraaiing, kringloop.
gyr'atory, draaiende, draai=; ~ **breaker**, walsbreker.
gyre, draai (digt.)
gyr'falcon = **gerfalcon**.
gy'ro compass, girokompas, tolkompas.
gy'rograph, girograaf, omwentelingsmeter.
gyr'omancy, giromansie, waarsêery.
gyr'ometer, toereteller, girometer.
gyr'oplane, (wind)meulvliegtuig, girovliegtuig, outo= giro.
gyr'oscope, giroskoop.
gyr'oscopic, giroskopies.
gyr'ose, golwend.
gyr'ostat, girostaat.
gyrostat'ic, girostaties; ~**s**, girostatika.
gy'rous, kringvormig.
gyves, (us. pl.), boeie, kluisters.

H

h, (hs, h's), h; *drop one's h's*, die h's nie uitspreek nie. **ha!** ha!
haarlemen'sis, haarlemmerolie.
habane'ra, habanera, Kubaanse dans.
habeas corp'us, habeas corpus (bevelskrif om 'n ge= vangene voor die hof te bring).
hab'erdasher, kramer; ~**y**, kramery, garing= en brandwinkel.
hab'ergeon, borsharnas.
hab'ile, handig, bekwaam, rats.
habil'iments, kleding, gewaad, mondering.
habil'itate, finansieer, finansier (myn); privaatdosent word (Eur.).
habilita'tion, habilitasie.
hab'it, (n) gewoonte, gewente, gebruik; sleur; sede; aanwensel; neiging; kleed, rykleed, gewaad; lig= gaamsgestel; py, ordekleed; geaardheid, hebbelik= heid; groeiwyse (plant); *BE in the* ~ *of*, gewoond wees om; *BY* ~, uit gewoonte; *FALL into the* ~ *of*, die gewoonte aanleer om; *from FORCE of* ~, uit pure gewoonte; *FORM a* ~, 'n gewoonte aanleer; *GET out of a* ~, 'n gewoonte afwen; 'n gewoonte afleer; *GROW into a* ~, 'n gewoonte word; ~ *of MIND*, denkwyse; ~ *becomes second NATURE*, die gewente maak die gewoonte; *TAKE to a* ~, 'n gewoonte aanleer; (v) klee(d); bewoon.
habitabil'ity, bewoonbaarheid.
hab'itable, bewoonbaar; ~**ness**, bewoonbaarheid.
hab'itant, bewoner, inwoner.
Hab'itant, Frans-Kanadees.
hab'itat, woonplek, verblyf; groeiplek, habitat (plan= te); houplek (diere).
habita'tion, woning, woonplek; bewoning.

hab'it-forming, verslawend, verslaaf=; ~ **drug**, verslaafmiddel.
habit'ual, gewoon, gewoonte=; gebruiklik, gewoon= lik; ~ *CRIMINAL*, gewoontemisdadiger; ~ *DRUNKARD*, gewoontedronkaard; ~ **ly**, gewoon= lik, uit gewoonte; ~ *ly unemployed*, gewoontewerk= lose.
habit'uate, gewend word, gewend raak, (aan)wen; ge= woond maak.
habitua'tion, gewenning.
hab'itude, gewoonte; aanwensel; hebbelikheid; ge= steldheid; geaardheid.
habit'ué, gereelde besoeker, vaste klant, habitué; stamgas; ~**'s table**, stamtafel.
habutai', habutai, Japanse sy (stof).
hachure', (n) arsering, arseerlyn; (v) arseer.
hacien'da, hacienda, (Spaanse) opstal.
hack[1], (n) knol, huurperd; broodskrywer, prulskry= wer; loonslaaf; (v) holrug ry, afgesaag maak.
hack[2], (n) stellasie.
hack[3], (n) kap, hou, pik; kapmes; skop; (v) kap, hou, inkerf; kug, hoes.
hack'ery, Indiese oskar.
hack'-file, mesvyl.
hack'ing; ~ **cough**, droë hoes; ~ **knife**, kapmes, hak= mes.
hac'kle[1], (n) kunsvlieg (as aas); vlashekel, ruwe sy; lang nekveer (haan); *enough to make one's* ~*s RISE*, genoeg om 'n mens se bloed te laat kook; *with his* ~*s UP*, bakleierig; kwaad; op sy agterpote; (v) skeur, stukkend breek; hekel (vlas); 'n kunsvlieg maak.
hack'le[2], (v) kerf, kap, vermink.

hack'ling, hekeling (vlas).
hack'-log, kapblok.
hack'ly, happerig, keperig, vol skare; hekelig.
Hack'ney, Hackney (perd).
hack'ney, (n) (-s), ryperd, huurperd, drawwer; huurling; huurrytuig; sloof; (v) verslyt, baie gebruik; holrug ry, afgesaag maak; ~ *something,* iets holrug (seerrug) ry; (a) huur=; ~ **coach,** huurrytuig; ~**ed,** afgesaag, alledaags, gemeenplasig.
hack: ~**-saw,** ystersaag, haksaag, metaalsaag; ~ **work,** broodskrywery; ~**writer,** broodskrywer, skribent.
had, *kyk* **have;** *he ~ BETTER go,* hy moet maar gaan; *he HAS been ~,* hy is gekul; *he has ~ it,* (sl.) sy doppie het geklap; dis klaar met hom; *he ~ RATHER go,* hy moet liewer gaan.
hadd'ock, skelvis; *bring a ~ to a paddock,* jou geld mors; deurbringerig wees.
hade, helling (van mynaar, ens.); afskuiwingshoek (geol.).
had'eda, hadida.
Had'es, onderwêreld, doderyk, skimmeryk, hel, Hades; *I'd rather see you in ~,* ek wou dat jy op Bloksberg sit.
hadj'i, hadjie.
hadom'eter, odometer.
ha'dron, hadron (fis.).
haecce'ity, ditheid; individualiteit.
h(a)em'al, bloed=.
h(a)eman'thus, bloedlelie, bloedblom.
h(a)em'aphobe, bloedsku.
h(a)emat'ic, (n) hematikum; bloedtonikum; (a) bloed=.
h(a)em'atin, hematien, hematine.
h(a)em'atite, hematiet, bloedsteen, rooiystersteen.
h(a)ematit'ic, hematiethoudend.
h(a)em'atocele, bloedsak, bloedgeswel.
h(a)ematog'enous, hematogeen.
h(a)emato'logy, hematologie, bloedkunde.
h(a)emato'ma, bloedblaas.
h(a)ematophob'ia, vrees vir bloed, bloedvrees.
h(a)ematur'ia, bloedwater, rooiwater, hematurie.
h(a)emoglob'in, bloedkleurstof, hemoglobien, hemoglobine.
h(a)ematox'ylin, bloedhout.
h(a)em'ocele, bloedliggaamsholte.
h(a)emophil'ia, hemofilie, erflike bloedsiekte, bloeiersiekte; ~**c,** bloeier.
h(a)emo'ptysis, bloedspuwing.
h(a)em'orrhage, bloeding, vloeiing, bloedstorting, *gastric ~,* maagbloeding.
h(a)em'orrhoids, aambeie, hemorroïdes.
h(a)emostat'ic, (n) bloedstelpende middel; (a) bloedstelpend, hemostaties.
haff, haf.
haf'nium, hafnium.
haft, (n) hef, handvatsel; steel; (v) 'n handvatsel aansit.
hag, (n) ou vrou, ou heks; ~ **fish,** slymprik, snotvis *(Heptatretus).*
hagg'ard, (n) valk; (a) verwilderd; maer en bleek, vervalle; afgerem, afgewerk.
hagg'is, harslag, longe, hart en lewer (van skaap, gekook soos wors in die maag van die dier), haggis.
hagg'ish, heksagtig, kwaadaardig; ~**ness,** kwaadaardigheid.
hag'gle, (n) knibbelary; rusie; (v) twis, stribbel; knibbel, afding; ~**r,** knibbelaar, afdinger; marskramer.
hagg'ling, geknibbel, gekwansel; gestribbel.
hag'iarchy, hagioc'racy, heilige regering, priesterregering.
hagiog'rapher, gewyde skrywer, hagiograaf.
hagiog'raphy, hagiografie, geskiedenis van heiliges.
hagiol'atry, aanbidding v.d. heiliges.
hagiol'ogy, lewensbeskrywing van heiliges, hagiologie.
hag'ridden, beheks.
Hague, 's-Gravenhage, Den Haag; *inhabitant of The ~,* Hagenaar.
ha ha¹, haha, gelag.
ha'-ha², diep sloot.
hai'ku, haikoe.

hail¹, (n) hael; (v) hael; laat neerdaal.
hail², (n) heilgroet, begroeting; aanroep; *within ~,* binne roepafstand; (v) begroet, welkom heet; roep; praai (skepe); ~ *FROM,* afkomstig wees van; ~ *as KING,* tot koning uitroep.
hail!³ (interj) heil!
hail: ~ **belt,** haelstreek; ~ **damage,** haelskade.
hail: ~ **fellow well met,** allemansvriend; ~**ing,** (n) begroeting; (a) afkomstig (van); ~*ing from X,* geboortig uit (afkomstig van) X.
hail: ~ **insurance,** haelversekering; ~ **shot,** haelskoot; skroot; ~ **shower,** haelbui; ~**stone,** haelkorrel; ~**storm,** haelstorm.
hair, haar; hare; *AGAINST the ~,* teen die draad in; *BOBBED ~,* polkahare; *BY a ~'s breadth,* ternouernood; op 'n haar na; *a ~ of the DOG that bit you,* 'n regmakertjie; *let DOWN the ~,* die hare laat hang; *GET into someone's ~,* iem. die olel gee; *not a ~ of his HEAD shall perish,* geen haar op sy kop sal gekrenk word nie; *KEEP one's ~ on,* bedaard bly; jou beheer; *PUT up the ~,* die hare opgemaak begin dra; bolla dra; *SPLIT ~s,* hareklool, it made his ~ *STAND on end,* dit het sy hare (te berge) laat rys; *TEAR out one's ~,* jou hare uittrek; *TO a ~,* presies, op 'n haar; *he did not TURN a ~,* hy het doodbedaard gebly; *WEALTH of ~,* haardos; ~ **ball,** haarbal, herkoutjie; ~**bow,** haarstrik(kie); ~**breadth,** haarbreedte; *by a ~'s breadth,* naelskraap; ternouernood; ~ **breadth escape,** noue ontkoming; ~**broom,** stofbesem; ~ **brush,** haarborsel, ~**bulb,** haarbol; ~ **clip,** haarknip; ~ **clippers,** haarknipper; ~**cloth,** harige stof; boetekleed; ~**cord,** haarkoord; ~ **curler,** haarkruller; ~ **cut:** *have a ~ cut,* jou hare laat sny; ~ **cutter,** haarsnyer; ~**do,** kapsel, haarstyl; ~ **dresser,** haarsnyer; haarkapper, friseur, coiffeur; ~ **dressing,** haarkappery; ~ **dressing saloon,** haarkapsalon; ~ **drier,** haardroër; ~ **dye,** haarkleurstof, haarverf; ~**ed,** harig; ~ **follicle,** haarsakkie, haarfollikel; ~**iness,** harigheid; ~ **knot,** bolla; ~**less,** sonder hare, haaraf, kaal; ~**-like,** haaragtig; ~ **line,** haarsnoer; ophaallyn (by skrywe); kruisdraad (lens); haarmerk (filatelie); haargrens (op voorkop); haarlyn, fynlyn; ~ **lotion,** haarwater; ~ **net,** haarnetjie; ~ **pad,** haarrol; ~ **piece,** pruik, haarstuk; ~ **pin,** haarnaald; ~ **pin bend,** dubbele draai, S-draai, skerp draai; ~**-raiser,** sensasieverhaal; ~**-raising,** drakerig, sensasioneel; skokkend, skrikwekkend; ~ **remover,** haarverwyderaar; ~ **restorer,** haar(groei)middel; ~ **ribbon,** haarlint, haarband; ~ **rinse,** haarwater, haarkleursel, haarspoelmiddel; ~**'s breadth,** haarbreedte; ~ **shirt,** boetehemp; ~ **slide,** haarskuifie; haarskikkertjie, ~**-splitter,** haarklower, muggiesifter, vitter, semelknoop; ~**-splitting,** muggiesiftery, haarklowery, vittery; ~ **spray,** haarsproei, haarsproeisel; ~ **spring,** spiraalveer, haarveer, onrusveer; ~ **stroke,** ophaallyn; ~ **style,** haardrag, kapsel; ~**-style parade,** kapselparade; ~ **stylist,** haarkapper, modis(te); ~ **tidy,** haarsakkie; ~ **tint,** haarkleursel; ~ **rigger,** haarsneller; ~ **wash,** haarwasmiddel; harewas; haarwater; ~**-waver,** haargolwer, haarkruller; ~ **worm,** draadwurm.
hair'y, harig, harerig, haaragtig; ~ **couch,** kwaggakweek; ~ **vetch,** sandwiek; ~ **worm,** harige wurm.
Hai'ti, Haïti.
Hait'ian, (n) Haïtiaan; Haïties (taal); (a) Haïtiaans, Haïties.
hake¹, stokvis.
hake², stellasie.
ha'kea, hakea, naaldbos.
hala'tion, sluier(ing), ligkringvorming.
hal'berd, hellebaard; ~**ier',** hellebaardier.
hal'cyon, (n) ysvoël; (a) klam, stil, rustig, vredig; ~ **days,** dae van rus en vrede.
hale¹, (arch.) (v) hys; sleep, sleur; trek.
hale², (a) gesond, fris, sterk; ~ *and hearty,* fris en gesond; perdfris, so fris soos 'n vis in die water.
half, (n) **(halves)** helfte; halwe; halfie; skakel (voetbal); semester (skool); ~ *AND ~,* om die helfte; half-om-half; *BETTER ~,* wederhelf, vrou; *the BETTER ~,* die beste helfte; *BY halves,* om die

helfte; *CRY halves,* die helfte eis; *DO nothing by halves,* alles deeglik doen; niks half doen nie; ~ *a DOZEN,* 'n halfdosyn; *GO halves,* om die helfte werk; gelykop deel; ~ *an HOUR,* 'n halfuur; *IN halves,* in twee gelyke dele; ~ *a LOAF,* 'n halwe brood; *a MILE and a* ~, anderhalfmyl; ~ *a MO= MENT,* net 'n oomblik; *NOT* ~, glad nie; inder= daad nie; *ONE and a* ~, anderhalf; ~ *PAST one,* halftwee; (a, adv) half; ~ *AS much,* half soveel; *not* ~ *as BAD,* glad nie sleg nie; ~**-a-crown,** halfkroon (25c); ~**-ape,** halfaap; ~**-aum,** halfaam; ~ **back,** skakel (rugby); ~**-baked,** halfgaar, onderkook, halfgebak; ~**-beam,** halfbalk; ~ **binding,** halfleer; ~ **blood,** baster, halfnaatjie; stiefbroer, stiefsuster; ~ **bond,** halfsteenverband; ~**-bound,** in halfleer= band; ~**-bred,** halfbeskaaf; baster=; ~**-breed,** half= naatjie, baster; ~**-brick,** halwe steen=; ~**-brick wall,** halfsteenmuur; ~**-brother,** halfbroer; ~**-cast(e),** (n) halfnaatjie, halfbloed; (a) baster=; ~**-cent,** half= sent, halwe sent; ~ **cock,** (n) rus; *AT* ~ *cock,* op rus; half oorgehaal; *GO off at* ~*-cock,* voorbarig wees; weens oorhaastigheid misluk; (v) half oor= haal; (a) half oorgehaal; ~**-cocked,** half oorgehaal; ~**-column,** halwe kolom; halfkolonne (mil.); ~**-conscious,** halfbewus; ~**-cooked,** halfgaar; ~**-dead,** halfdood; ~**-done,** halfgaar; halfklaar; ~**-door,** onderdeur; ~**-face,** van die kant, profiel; ~**-faced,** in profiel; ~**-grown,** halfwas, opgeskote; ~**-hearted,** onverskillig, weifelend, huiwerig, aar= selend; ~**-heartedness,** halfhartigheid, louheid; ~ **holiday,** vry middag; ~**-hose,** sokkies; ~**-hour,** halfuur; ~**-hourly,** om die halfuur, elke halfuur; van 'n halfuur; ~**-hunter,** oorlosie met 'n enkele kas; ~**-inch slice,** halfduimsny; ~**-jack,** halfbottel; ~**-length,** kniestuk; halflyf; ~**-line,** middellyn; ~ **ling,** penkop; ~**-mast,** halfstok; ~**-mast trou= sers,** kuitbroek; ~**-miler,** halfmylloper; ~ **moon,** halfmaan; ~ **moon spanner,** haaksleutel; ~**-mour= ning,** ligte rou, halfrou; ~**ness,** halfheid; ~ **pay,** halfsalaris; ~ **penny,** stuiwer, halfpennie; ~ **penny worth,** 'n stuiwer s'n; ~**-petticoat,** halfonderrok; ~**-price,** halwe prys; ~**-price day,** halfprysdag; ~**-round,** halfrond; ~**-round bit,** lepelboor; ~**-round file,** halfrondevyl; ~**-seas-over,** hoenderkop, aan= geklam, halfdronk; ~**-section,** maat; gade; halfdeursnee; ~**-sister,** halfsuster; ~ **slip,** half= onderrok; ~**-sole,** halfsool; ~ **sovereign,** tien sjie= lings; ~**-speed,** halwe snelheid; ~**-sphere,** halwe bol; ~**-starved,** uitgehonger; ~ **tide,** halfty; ~**-time,** rustyd, pouse; ~**-tint,** halftint; ~**-tone,** half= tint; halwe toon; outotipie; ~**-tone block,** outotipe, rasterblok; ~**-track,** met kruipbande; ~**-treble,** halflangbeen (hekel); ~**-truth,** halwe waarheid; ~**-volley,** skephou, lepelhou; ~ **way,** halfpad, half= weg; ~ **way house,** uitspanplek; verversingstasie; ~ **way line,** middellyn; ~**-wit:** *a* ~ *-wit,* 'n onnosele; ~**-witted,** onnosel, halfwys, simpel; ~**-worsted tis= sue,** sajetstowwe; ~**-worsted web,** sajetseil; ~**-wor= sted yarn,** sajet; ~**-yearly,** halfjaarliks.
hal'ibut, heilbot; ~**-liver oil,** heilbottraan.
halieut'ic, vis=; ~ **s,** visvangkuns, hengelkuns.
halitos'is, onwelriekende asem, halitose.
hal'itus, asem; wasem.
hall, (voor)portaal, vestibule; saal; aula; hal; huis; vergadersaal; ~ **attendant,** saalwagter.
hallelu'jah, halleluja.
hall'mark, (n) egtheidstempel; (v) waarmerk, stem= pel, yk; ~ **ed,** gewaarmerk; ~ **ing,** egstempeling, waarmerking.
hallo', (n) hallo, hello, begroeting; (v) hallo (hello) roep; (interj.) hallo!, hello!; ~**-girl,** telefoonmeisie.
halloo', (n) aanhitsing (van hond); geroep; (v) aan= hits, sa roep; roep, skree; *do not* ~ *till you are out of the wood,* tussen die lepel en die mond val die pap op die grond; moenie juig voor jy uit die gevaar is nie; (interj) sa!
hall'ow, heilig, wy; ~ **ed,** godgewy, geheilig; ~ *ed ground,* gewyde grond; H ~ **e'en',** Allerheiligeaand; H ~ **e'enmass,** Allerheiligefees.
hall: ~ **porter,** portier; ~ **stand,** gangkapstok, (hoede)standler.
hallu'cinate, begoël, in 'n sinsbegoëling bring.

hallucina'tion, sinsbedrog, oëverblindery, sinsbegoë= ling, dwaling, hallusinasie, waan; waanvoorstel= ling.
hallu'cinatory, waan=.
halm, *kyk* **haulm.**
hal'ma, halma ('n speletjie).
hal'o, (n) (**-es),** ligkrans, ligkring; heiligekrans, strale= krans; tepelkring; halo; (v) omstraal, met 'n strale= krans (halo) omgeef.
hal'ogen, halogeen.
hal'oid, soutagtig, sout=, haloïed.
hal'ophile, soutliewend, halofiel.
halo'phyte, soutplant, halofiet.
halt¹, (arch.) (n) mankstap; (v) mank loop; ~ *between two opinions,* op twee gedagtes hink; (a) mank, kreupel.
halt², (n) halt; halte (trein); stilstand; stilhouplek; *CALL a* ~, halt maak, laat stilstaan; *CALL a* ~ *to something,* 'n end aan iets maak; *COME to a* ~, tot stilstand kom; *MAKE a* ~, 'n oomblik stilstaan; (v) stilstaan; tot stilstand bring; halt maak; weifel; ~!, hanou!; ~, *who GOES there?,* werda!
hal'ter, (n) halter; strop, galgtou; (v) 'n halter aansit; ophang; belemmer; ~**-break,** touwys mak; ~ **chain,** halterketting; ~ **strap,** halterriem; *throw up one's* ~ *straps in DESPAIR,* die hande slap laat hang; moed opgee.
halt'ing, gehink; ~ **ly,** kruppel-kruppel; mank; weife= lend; staan-staan; ~**-place,** halte, staanplek.
halve, in twee deel, halveer; gelykop speel (gholf).
halv'ing, halvering.
hal'yard, vlagtou.
Ham¹, Gam; *the children of* ~, Gamsgeslag.
ham², (n) ham; dy; radioamateur; onbekwame (oner= vare) toneelspeler; *on his* ~ *s,* op sy hurke; (v) uit= send en opvang.
ham³, (n) dorp.
ham⁴, (v) raas, brul, te kere gaan.
hamadry'ad, (**-es, -s),** boomnimf; Indiese slang; Abes= siniese bobbejaan.
ham'burger, frikkadelbroodjie, hamburger.
ha'merkop, hamerkop.
hames, (pl) borsplaat; haam.
ham'-handed, lomp.
Ham'ite, Hamiet.
Hamit'ic, Hamities.
ham'let, dorpie, gehug.
hamm'er, (n) hamer; haan (geweer); *between the* ~ *and the ANVIL,* tussen hamer en aambeeld; *COME under the* ~, verkoop word; onder die ha= mer kom; *what they own will be PUT under the* ~, die klok sal agter hulle lui; *THROWING the* ~, hamergooi; *be at* ~ *and TONGS,* met alle mag werskaf; met volle mag dit uitspook; (v) hamer, slaan, moker; smee(d); plet; uitdink, versin; in= stamp; diskwalifiseer (op die Beurs); ~ *AWAY at,* aanhoudend aandring; ~ *DOWN,* inhamer; ~ *into one's HEAD,* instamp; ~ *it OUT of a person,* dit uit iem. slaan; ~ *OUT a plan,* 'n plan uitwerk; ~ **beam,** steekbalk, bindbalk; ~ **blow,** hamerslag; ~ **claw,** hamerklou; ~ **cloth,** bokleed (rytuig); ~ **dress,** kap; ~ **eye,** steelgat; ~ **face,** slaanvlak (van hamer); ~ **handle,** hamersteel; ~ **head,** hamerkop; hamerkophaai; hamerkopvoël; ~**head key,** vlin= derspy; ~ **head shark,** hammerkophaai; ~ **ing,** ge= klop; gehamer; afgedankste pak; diskwalifisering (op beurs); ~ **keyboard,** hamerklavier; ~ **lock,** ha= merslot (greep); ~ **man,** voorslaner; ~ **mill,** hamer= meul(e); ~ **smith,** ystersmid; ~ **stroke,** hamerslag; ~**-thrower,** hamergooier; ~ **toe,** hamertoon; ~**-tone finish,** tintklopafwerking.
hamm'ock, hangmat; ~ **chair,** seilstoel.
Ham'mond organ, Hammondorrel.
ham'per¹, (n) (sluit)mandjie; keldertjie (vir drank); geskenkpakkie.
ham'per², (v) bemoeilik, belemmer; hinder; verwar, verstrik; in die war bring; dwarsboom.
ham'shackle, kniehalter.
ham'ster, hamster.
ham'string, (n) dyspier (mens); kniesening (perd); (v) (**..strung** or **-ed),** verlam, die kniesening afkap; *be hamstrung,* verlam wees.

ha'mular, haakvormig.
ha'mulus, haakproses, hamulus.
hand, (n) hand (hoogtemaat); wyser (oorlosie); (hand)skrif; handtekening; hulp, werkkrag, werk=(s)man; manskap (vloot); sy, kant; kaarte, beurt (by kaartspel); bos (blare); hand (piesangs); skou=erstuk (vark); greep (geweer); applous; (pl) werklie=des; werkers; *ALL* ~ *s*, almal aan dek; almal; *ALL* ~ *s on deck*, elke man aan dek; *on ALL* ~ *s*, van alle kante; *ASK (for) a lady's* ~, 'n meisie om haar hand vra; *be AT* ~, voor die deur staan; op hand wees; *fall into BAD* ~ *s*, aan die heidene oorgelewer word; *be a BAD* ~ *at*, sleg wees in; nie die slag hê nie om; *BEAR a* ~, hand bysit; *with all* ~ *s on BOARD*, met man en muis; *BRING up by* ~, hans grootmaak; *BY* ~, met die hand; in hande; *CAP in* ~, nederig, met die hoed in die hand; *CHANGE* ~ *s*, van eienaar verwissel; in ander hande oorgaan; *CLASP* ~ *s*, mekaar die hand druk; *keep one's* ~ *s CLEAN*, 'n eerlike man bly; *with CLEAN* ~ *s*, eer=lik; onskuldig; *be CLOSE at* ~, naby wees; *COLD* ~ *s*, warm heart, koue hande, warme liefde; *COME to* ~, ter hand kom; *COMMIT (put) one's* ~ *to paper*, jou hand op papier sit; *a COOL* ~, 'n onge=ergde vent; *be a DAB* ~ *at figures*, knap (slim) met syfers wees; *go DOWN with all* ~ *s*, met man en muis vergaan; *DRAW out of* ~, uit die vrye hand teken; *on EITHER* ~, aan altwee kante; *with EMPTY* ~ *s*, met leë hande; *met 'n handvol vlieë; be unable to see one's* ~ *before one's FACE*, nie jou hand voor jou oë kan sien nie; *at FIRST* ~, uit die eerste hand; *FALL into the* ~ *s of*, in die hande val van; ~ *over FIST*, hand oor hand; vinnig; *with FOLDED* ~ *s*, met die hande in die skoot; *wait on someone* ~ *and FOOT*, op iem. se wenke vlieg; *al=low someone a FREE* ~, iem. vrye spel gee; *FROM* ~ *to* ~, van hand tot hand; *have one's* ~ *s FULL*, baie te doen hê; *GET out of* ~, onregeerbaar word; hand-uit ruk; *GET one's* ~ *in*, op stryk kom; op dreef kom; *GIVE one's* ~ *in marriage*, jou hand aan iem. skenk; *GIVE a* ~, 'n handjie help, 'n handjie bysit; *be* ~ *and GLOVE*, kop in een mus wees; *GO* ~ *in* ~ *with*, hand aan hand gaan met; *a GOOD* ~ *(at)*, knap; *he GOT a great* ~, hy is warm toegejuig; *HAVE a* ~ *in*, 'n aandeel in iets hê; 'n hand hê in; ~ *over HEAD*, halsoorkop; *offer one's* ~ *and HEART*, jou hart en hand aanbied; *with a HEAVY* ~, hardhandig; *be HEAVY on (in) the* ~, swaar op die hand wees, *extend a HELP=ING* ~, hulp aanbied; *with a HIGH* ~, uit die hoogte; *15* ~ *s HIGH*, 15 hand hoog; *HOLD* ~ *s*, hande vashou; *HOLD a good* ~ *(at cards)*, mooi kaarte hê; *HOLD one's* ~, jou hand terughou; 'n afwagtende houding aanneem; *IN* ~, in die hand; nog voorhande; *have something IN* ~, met iets be=sig wees; *take someone IN* ~, iem. onder hande neem; *have firmly IN* ~, volle beheer hê oor; *IN one's* ~ *s*, in jou sorg; *have one's* ~ *IN*, op stryk wees; *you must* ~ *it to HIM*, jy moet erken dat hy ...; *KEEP one's* ~ *in*, onderhou; *KEEP your* ~ *s to yourself*, hande tuis!; *KISS the* ~, die hoof buig; *go on* ~ *s and KNEES*, op die knieë gaan; na Ca=nossa gaan; *have one's* ~ *in one's LAP*, met die hande in die skoot sit; *put the LAST* ~ *to some=thing*, die laaste hand aan iets lê; *LAYING on of* ~ *s*, handeoplegging; *LAY* ~ *s on*, beetpak; die hand lê op; *the LEFT* ~ *does not know what the right* ~ *is doing*, die linkerhand weet nie wat die regterhand doen nie; *offer someone a LIMP* ~, iem. 'n slap hand gee; 'n slap pootjie gee; *LEND a* ~, 'n handjie bysit; 'n handjie help; *your LETTER to* ~, u brief ontvang; *the LONG* ~, die lang wy=ser; *MANY* ~ *s make light work*, baie hande maak ligte werk; baie honde is 'n haas se dood; *the MAT=TER in* ~, die onderhawige saak; *MONEY in* ~, geld in kas; *MOTION of the* ~, handgebaar; *at the* ~ *of a MURDERER*, deur die hand van 'n moor=denaar; *from* ~ *to MOUTH*, v.d hand in die tand; *put one's* ~ *to one's MOUTH*, jou hand op jou mond lê; *a NEW* ~, 'n nuweling; ~ *s OFF!*, hande tuis!, bly daar af!; *OFF one's* ~, van iem. se nek af; *OFFER one's* ~ *to someone*, jou hand aan iem.

bied; *be an OLD* ~, bedrewe wees; *an OLD* ~, 'n ou kalant; 'n ou rot; *ON* ~, voorradig; *ON all* ~ *s*, *ON every* ~, aan alle kante; van alle kante; *have something ON one's* ~ *s*, met iets opgeskeep sit; met iets bly sit; *on ONE* ~ . . . *on the other*, aan die een kant . . . aan die ander kant; *on the ONE* ~, ener=syds; aan die een kant; *on the OTHER* ~, aan die ander kant; *his* ~ *is OUT*, hy is van stryk af; ~ *OVER* ~, hand oor hand; vinnig; *for one's OWN* ~, vir jou eie voordeel; *PLAYING into someone's* ~ *s*, iem. se plan bevorder; in iem. se hand speel; *put one's* ~ *to the PLOUGH*, die hand aan die ploeg slaan; *stand about with one's* ~ *s in one's POC=KETS*, met die hande in die sakke staan; *be a POOR* ~ *at*, sleg wees in; nie die slag hê nie; *keep a PROTECTING* ~ *over someone*, die hand oor iem. hou; *PUT* ~ *to a document*, 'n dokument onderte=ken; *PUT in* ~, aan die gang sit; *RAISE one's* ~ *against another*, die hand teen iem. oplig; *have a pair of READY* ~ *s*, sy hande staan vir niks ver=keerd nie; *REAR by* ~, hans grootmaak; *REJECT out of* ~, sonder meer verwerp; *the* ~ *that ROCKS the cradle rules the world*, die hand wat die wieg skommel, regeer die wêreld; *under my* ~ *and SEAL*, onder my hand en seël; *at SECOND* ~, uit die tweede hand; *SELL something out of* ~, iets uit die hand verkoop; *SET one's* ~ *to a task*, jou hand aan iets slaan; *SHOW one's* ~, die kaarte oopl; *fall into the* ~ *s of STRANGERS*, in vreemde hande val; *STRENGTHEN someone's* ~, iem. tot krag=tiger optrede aanspoor; *not to STRETCH forth a* ~, geen hand uitsteek nie; *refuse to SULLY one's* ~ *s*, jou hande nie aan iets vuil wil maak nie; *TAKE one's life in one's* ~ *s*, jou lewe waag; *TAKE in* ~, ter hand neem; aanpak; *TELL out of* ~, uit die vuis sê; *THROW up one's* ~ *s in amazement*, die hande ineenslaan; *his* ~ *s are TIED*, sy hande is afgekap; *keep a TIGHT* ~ *on*, iem. aan die stang ry; ~ *TO* ~, van hand tot hand; *TRY one's* ~, probeer; *not to do a* ~ *'s TURN*, nie die minste po=ging aanwend nie; *UNDER his* ~, deur hom on=derteken; ~ *s UP!*, hensop! hande in die lug! *give someone a* ~ *UP*, iem. op die been help; iem. op=help; *get the UPPER* ~, die oorhand kry; iem. in die hok spit; *WASH ones* ~ *s of something*; die hande in onskuld was; niks met iets te doen wil hê nie; *one* ~ *WASHETH another (the other) and both the face*, as twee hande mekaar was, word hul=le altwee skoon; *have something WELL in* ~, goed onder bedwang hê; *WIN* ~ *s down*, fluit-fluit wen; *WITNESS the* ~ *of*, as getuie teken; *WRITE a fair* ~, 'n mooi hand skrywe; *the WORK in* ~, die werk wat tans gedoen word; (v) aangee, aanreik, oorhan=dig; met die hande bewerk; reef, inneem, vasmaak (seile); help; ~ *ABOUT*, ronddeel; ~ *into a CAR=RIAGE*, in 'n rytuig help; ~ *DOWN*, oorhandig; uitreik; ~ *IN*, indien, inlewer, oorhandig; voorlê; ~ *ON*, aangee; ~ *OUT*, uitdeel; bekend maak (nuus); ~ *OVER*, oorhandig, uitlewer; ter hand stel; afgee; ~ *ROUND*, rondgee, ronddeel, rond=dien; ~ *TO*, gee aan; ~ **ambulance**, wielbaar; ~ **attachment**, handvatsel; ~ **axe**, handbyl; ~ **bag**, handtassie; reistas, handkoffer; ~ **ball**, handbal; ~ **barrow**, stootwaentjie; ~ **basket**, handmandjie; ~ **-beaten**, handgedrewe; ~ **bill**, strooibiljet; ~ **book**, handboek, handleiding; wegwyser; ~ **bow**, handboog; ~ **-brace**, handomslag, omslag=boor; ~ **-brake**, handrem; ~ **-breadth**, handbreed=te; ~ **-canter**, kort galop; ~ **cart**, stootkarretjie; ~ **clasp**, handdruk; ~ **-compositor**, handsetter; ~ **-crafted**, handgemaak; ~ **cuff**, (n) handboei, (v) (vas)boei; ~ **-cut**, met die hand gesny; ~ **-dressing**, handbehandeling; handverband; ~ **-drill**, hand=boor; ~ **drive**, handaandrywing; ~ **drum**, hand=trom; ~ **-feed**, (n) handaansetting; (v) (. . **fed**), hans grootmaak, met die hand grootmaak; ~ **-fed calf**, hanskalf; ~ **-file**, handvyl; ~ **-firing**, handstoking (loko.); ~ **ful**, handvol; vuisvol; *the child is a* ~ *ful*, dis 'n lastige kind; ~ **-gallop**, kort galop; ~ **glass**, vergrootglas; handspieël; ~ **grasp**, houvas, hand=greep, handdruk; ~ **-grenade**, handgranaat; ~ **grip**, handdruk; greep; ~ **gun**, handgeweer; ~ **hammer**,

handhamer; ~ **hawk,** pleisterbord; ~ **hold,** houvas, vashouplek.

han'dicap, (n) voorgee, voorgif; agterstand; terugset=spel; voorgeehoue; voorgeespel; belemmering; *sea=led* ~, blinde voorgee; (v) **(-ped),** terugsit; belem=mer, bemoeilik; voorgee; kniehalter; ~ **ped person,** gestremde (persoon), belemmerde persoon; ~ **basis,** voorgeebasis; ~ **per,** voorgeër; ~ **race,** voor=geewedloop.

han'dicraft, handwerk, handearbeid; ambag; ~**sman,** handwerkman, ambagsman.

han'diness, handigheid, vlugheid, behendigheid.

han'diwork, handearbeid, handewerk.

han'dkerchief, sakdoek.

hand: ~**-knitted,** met die hand gebrei; ~**-labour,** han=dearbeid; ~**-lamb,** hanslam.

han'dle, (n) greep, handvatsel; hef (mes); hingsel (em=mer); stel; kruk; oor (koppie); knop; vat; stuur (ploeg)stert; *FLY off the* ~, woedend word; die jo=sie in raak; *MAKE a* ~ *of something,* iets as kap=stok gebruik; *a* ~ *to one's NAME,* 'n titel; (v) han=teer; behandel; betas, aanraak, bevoel; aanpak; onder hande neem; bedien (kanon); omgaan met; regeer, bestuur, beheer; handel drywe; van 'n hand=vatsel voorsien; *something or someone that cannot be* ~ *d without (or with velvet) gloves,* iets/iem. wat nie sonder handskoene aangepak moet word nie; ~**bar,** stuur (fiets); ~**bar moustache,** weglêsnor; ~**r,** hanteerder; afrigter; handvatselmaker; potte=bakker; pikeur.

hand: ~**less,** sonder hande; ~**-level,** handwaterpas; ~**-lever,** handhefboom; ~**line,** hand(vis)lyn.

han'dling, hantering; (be)handeling; ~ **appliance,** hanteertoestel; ~ **charge(s),** hanteerkoste.

hand: ~ **list,** naamlys; itemlys; ~**loom,** handgetou; ~ **lubrication,** handsmering; ~ **luggage,** hand=bagasie; ~**made,** met die hand gemaak; hand=werk=; geskep (papier); ~**maid(en),** diensmaagd; dienares; kamerbediende; ~**-me-down(s),** fabrieks=pak; ou klere; gebruikte klere; ~ **mill,** hand=meul(e); ~ **mirror,** handspieël; ~**-operated,** hand=; ~ **organ,** draaiorrel; ~**-out,** uitreiking (nuus); volgstuk; aalmoes; ~**-over,** oorhandiging; oor=drag; ~**-painted,** met die hand geskilder; ~**-picked,** uitgesoek; gekeur; uitgelese; ~**-picked men,** keur=korps; ~**-picked staff,** handgekeurde personeel; ~ **post,** padwyser; ~ **press,** handpers; ~ **print,** handafdruk; ~ **pump,** handpomp; ~**rail,** leuning, reling; ~**-raise,** hans grootmaak; ~**-reader,** hand=leser; ~**-reading,** handkykery, handlesery; ~ **rest,** handleuning, handstut; ~ **sander,** handskuurder; ~ **saw,** handsaag; ~ **screw,** handklem, hand=skroef; ~ **seat,** handstoel.

han(d)'sel, (n) handgif; voorsmaak (fig.); (v) **(-led),** inwy, vir die eerste maal gebruik; handgeld gee.

hand: ~**shake,** handdruk; *golden* ~ *shake,* rojale af=skeidsgeskenk; ~**shaking,** handgeëry; groetery; ~**-shape,** handvorm; ~ **signal,** handsein.

hand'some, aantreklik; mooi, fraai, bevallig; aansien=lik; ruim, groot, rojaal; hoflik, beleef; edel, groot=moedig; *DO the* ~ *thing by someone,* iem. vrygewig behandel; ~ *is as (that)* ~ *DOES,* 'n mens ken 'n boom aan sy vrugte; goed doen is mooier as goed lyk; *a* ~ *PRESENT,* 'n mooi (rojale, ruim) ge=skenk; ~**ly,** mooi, rojaal; ruim; ~**ness,** aantreklik=heid; mooiheid, fraaiheid, knapheid, aansienlik=heid; edelmoedigheid; rojaliteit.

hand: ~**-sorting,** handsortering; ~ **specimen,** hand=monster; ~**spike,** rigspaak, handspaak; koevoet, breekyster; ~**-spun yarn,** handspingare, -garing; ~ **stand,** handstand; ~**-starter,** handaansitter; ~**-strap,** handriem; ~**s-up,** hen(d)sop; ~**s-upper,** hen(d)sopper; ~ **syringe,** handspuit; ~ **to** ~ **fight(ing),** handgemeen; man-teen-mangeveg; ~ **to mouth,** v.d. hand in die tand; ~ *to mouth existence,* haglike (armoedige) bestaan; ~**-tooled,** met die hand gemaak; ~ **tools,** handgereedskap; ~ **towel,** handdoek; ~**-vice,** handskroef; ~ **work,** handear=beid, handwerk; ~**-worked gun,** handbedienings=kanon; ~ **wringing,** handegewring; ~ **writing,** handskrif; ~ **writing expert,** handskrifdeskundige; ~ **written,** handgeskrewe, met die hand geskryf.

han'dy, handig; behendig, vaardig; gemaklik, geskik; by die hand, byderhand; gerieflik; *come in* ~, goed te pas kom; ~**-dandy,** handraai (spel); ~ **man,** handlanger, algemene werksman, janregmaak, slimjan, nutsman, faktotum, hansie-my-kneg.

hang¹, (n) hang, helling; vertraging, opskorting; val (rok); rigting, neiging; *not CARE a* ~, geen flenter omgee nie; *GET the* ~ *of,* die slag kry, verstaan.

hang², (v) **(hung),** hang, ophang; plak, behang; **(-ed),** ophang; ~ *ABOUT,* ronddraal; hom êrens ophou; rondstaan; ~ *BACK,* weifel, aarsel; kop uittrek; ~ *everything on one's BACK,* alles aan jou lyf hang; ~ *in the BALANCE,* in die weegskaal hang; ~ *BE=HIND,* agterbly; ~ *DOWN,* afhang; ~ *FIRE,* kets (geweer); opskort; draal; sloer; *GO* ~, na die maan gaan; ~ *one's HEAD,* jou kop laat hang; *something is* ~ *ing over one's HEAD,* iets hang bo jou kop; *I'm* ~ *ed IF I do it,* ek sal dit vervlaks nie doen nie; ~ *IT!,* mastig! vervlaks!; ~ *upon someone's LIPS,* aan iem. se lippe hang; *a* ~ *ing MATTER,* 'n saak waar die doodstraf toegepas kan word; 'n halssaak; ~ *a MURDERER,* 'n moordenaar ophang; ~ *ON,* hang aan; vashou; aanbly, bly aan asb., wag 'n bietjie (foon); ~ *OUT,* uithang; woon; *thereby* ~ *s a TALE,* daaraan is 'n verhaal verbonde; ~ *by a THREAD,* aan 'n draadjie hang; *TIME* ~ *s heavy,* dit duur lank; ek verveel my; ~ *TOGETHER,* saamgaan; ~ *UP,* ophang; uitstel; ~ *YOU!,* stik! (interj) auk! verbrands! alle mensig!

hang'ar, hangar, vliegtuigloods; ~ **mechanic,** loods=werktuigkundige.

hang'dog, onderduimse verleë persoon; boef, galg=voël; *have a* ~ *look,* lyk soos 'n hond wat vet gesteel het; ~ **air (expression),** boewetronie; ~ **face,** galge=tronie.

hang'er, ophanger; haak, lis; beul; klerehanger, han=ger; dolk, jagmes; hangstang; ~ **bolt,** hangbout; ~**-on, (hangers-on),** aanhanger, volgeling; agter=ryer, trawant.

hang'-fire, (n) draalskoot; (v) draal.

hang'ing, (n) (die) (op)hang; behangsel, behang, muurtapyt; (pl) behangsel, draperie; (a) hangend; ~ **basket,** hangmandjie; ~ **bolt,** hangbout; ~ **brid=ge,** hangbrug; ~ **clock,** muurklok; ~ **committee,** keurkomitee; ~ **garden,** hangende tuin; ~ **glacier,** hanggletser; ~ **gutter,** hanggeut; ~ **hook,** hang=haak; ~ **judge,** ongenadige regter; ~ **lamp,** hang=lamp; ~ **link,** draagskakel (meg.); ~ **lip,** hanglip; ~ **matter,** hangende saak; halssaak; ~ **railway,** sweefspoor(weg); ~ **rock,** dakgesteente; ~ **roller,** spanskyf; ~ **sash,** skuifraam; ~ **scaffold,** hang=steier; ~ **steps,** vrydraende trappies; ~ **valley,** sweefdal; ~ **wall,** dak (myn); hangmuur.

hang: ~**-glide,** hangsweef; ~**-glider,** hangsweeftuig; hangswewer; ~**-glider pilot,** hangswewer; ~**-gli=ding,** hangsweef.

hang'man, beul, laksman; ~**'s noose,** strop, galgtou.

hang: ~**-out,** verblyf, houplek, skuilplek; ~ **over,** ka=ter, babalaas, dikkop, wingerdgriep.

hank, string; masband.

hank'er, snak (na), vurig verlang, hunker; ~ *after,* hunker na; ~ **ing,** (n) hunkering, verlange, begeer=te; ~ *ing after,* begeerte na; (a) verlangend.

hank'y, (..kies), sakdoek.

hank'y-panky, kunsie, foefie, goëlery; kullery; bedot=tery; hokus-pokus.

Han'over, Hanover (K.P.); Hannover (Duitsland).

Han'sard, Hansard, parlementsverslag; ~**ize,** met die Hansardverslag bewys, uit Hansard aan=haal.

Hanseat'ic, (n) Hansestaat; (a) Hanse=, Hanseaties; ~ **League,** Hanseverbond.

Han'se towns, Hansestede.

han'som (cab), huurrytuig, hansom.

hap, (n) lot, geluk; (v) toevallig gebeur.

haphaz'ard, (n) blote toeval; *at (by)* ~, op goeie ge=luk af, lukraak; (a) bloot toevallig; ~**ly,** by toeval, onverskillig, lukraak.

hap'less, ongelukkig.

haplog'raphy, haplografie.

hap'ly, miskien, moontlik.

hap'loid, (n) haploïde; (a) haploïed, enkelkernig.

ha"p'orth, vir 'n halfstuiwer; *spoil the ship for a ~ of tar,* uit suinigheid die boel bederf.

happ'en, gebeur, plaasvind, voorval, geskied, afspeel, voorkom; *I ~ to KNOW,* toevallig weet ek; *that will NEVER ~,* jy kan lank wag; *I ~ ed to NOTICE him,* toevallig het ek hom bemerk; *~ ON,* toevallig ontmoet; onverwags kry; teëkom; raakloop; *it so ~ ed THAT,* toe het dit gebeur dat; *THINGS are going to ~,* die poppe gaan nog dans; *~ing,* gebeurtenis, voorval.

happ'ily, gelukkig.

happ'iness, geluk, vreugde, blydskap.

happ'y, gelukkig; fleurig, monter; voorspoedig; tevrede, bly; salig; raak; *not be ~ ABOUT something,* nie lekker oor iets voel nie; *be ~ to ASSIST,* met genoeë help; *~ CHRISTMAS,* geseënde Kersfees; *~ LANDINGS!,* die beste! alles wat goed is!; *a ~ TURN of speech,* 'n raak gesegde.

happ'y-go-lucky, sorgloos, onbekommerd, onbesorg; lukraak, dons maar-op; *a ~ fellow,* 'n sieltjie sonder sorg.

Haps'burg, Habsburg.

hap'tophobia, vrees om aangeraak te word, haptofobie.

hara-ki'ri, hara-kiri, selfmoord (Japan).

harangue', (n) heftige rede; vurige toespraak; (v) toespreek, 'n opwekkende redevoering hou; opsweep.

ha'ras, perdestoetery.

ha'rass, kwel, pla, lastig val; bestook; terg; vermoei, afmat; *~ing,* tergend, kwellend; afmattend; *~ing fire,* kwelvuur; *~ment,* kwelling, teistering.

harb'inger, (n) voorbode, voorloper, boodskapper; kwartiermaker; *~ of spring,* lentebode; (v) aankondig, meld.

harb'our, (n) hawe; skuilplek; toevlugsoord; (v) herberg, skuilplek gee, heimlik huisves; koester, omdra, voed; veilige lêplek bied; skuil; *~ age,* hawe, skuilplek; toevlug; huisvesting, veilige ligging; *~-bar,* haweboom, hawedrumpel *~ board,* haweraad; *~ construction,* hawebou; *~ dues,* hawegeld; ankergeld; *~ engineer,* hawe-ingenieur; *~ entrance,* hawemond; hawetoegang; *~ less,* dakloos, sonder skuiling; *~-master,* hawemeester; *~ officer,* hawebeampte; *~-watch,* ankerwag.

hard, (n) vaste grond; dwangarbeid; harde strand; klipaanlêplek; *SOMETHING ~,* 'n hardigheid; *~ with ~ makes not the stone WALL,* twee harde stene maal nie; (a) hard, swaar, streng; verhard, hardvogtig; vas, stewig, stram, styf; grof, ru; skerp; suur (bier); sterk (drank); heftig, hewig; *BECOME ~,* hard word; *a ~ CASE,* 'n hopelose vent; *a ~ and FAST rule,* 'n vaste (bindende) reël; *a ~ FIGHT,* 'n hewige geveg; *~ of HEARING,* hardhorend; *be given ~ LABOUR,* hardepad kry; *RATHER ~,* hardérig, *~ TIMES,* kommervolle (moeilike) tye; *have a ~ TIME of it,* dit smoor kry; dit opdraand kry (hê); *he is in for a ~ TIME,* hy gaan nog les opsê; hy gaan nog stroppe draai; *he has known ~ TIMES,* hy het al harde bene (korsies) gekou; *earn something the ~ WAY,* iets swaar verdien; met moeite bereik; *a ~ WINTER,* 'n streng (kwaai) winter; *~ WORK,* swaar arbeid; (adv) hard, stewig; beswaarlik, met moeite; vlak; swaar, dugtig; *keep someone ~ AT it,* iem aan die gang hou; *~ to BELIEVE,* ongelooflik; *~ BESET,* dig omring; *be on the BIT,* taai in die bek wees; *~ BY,* naby; digby; *DIE ~,* 'n swaar dood sterf; *DRINK ~,* swaar drink; *~ and FAST,* onbuigsaam; *it GOES ~ with him,* dit gaan sleg met hom; *~ ON,* naby; *be ~ ON someone,* streng op iem. wees; *~ to PLEASE* moeilik om te bevredig; *~ PUT to,* swaar kry (leef); *be ~ PUT to it,* dit moeilik hê; noustrop trek; les opsê; dit hotagter hê; *RUN ~,* vinnig hardloop; *TRY ~,* hard probeer; *be ~ UP,* platsak (boomskraap) wees; *he is ~ UP for someone's help,* verleë wees om hulp van iem. se hulp; *~-bake,* amandeltameletjie; *~ ball,* harde bal; *~-bitten,* hardbekkig; taai; *~ board,* veselbord, hardebord; *~-boiled,* hardgekook (eier); hardvogtig; hardkoppig; *~ case,* deugniet, sondaar; onverbeterlike geval; *~ cash,* kontant(geld), klinkende munt; *~ cover(s),* hardeband(boek); *~ currency,* skaars betaalmiddel; *~ drinker,* strawwe drinker; *~-drinking,* lief vir die bottel; *~-earned,* suur verdien; *~ en,* hard maak; verhard, versteen; gewen; verstaal (fig.); bind (sement); vaster word (pryse).

hard'ened, gehard, gestaal; verhard, verstok; *a ~ sinner,* 'n ou sondaar.

hard'ener, verharder.

hard'ening, harding; *~ agent,* (ver)hardingsmiddel; *~ mixture,* (ver)hardingsmengsel; *~ solution,* (ver)hardingsoplossing.

har'der, (-s), harder.

hard: *~ facts,* harde (konkrete, vasstaande) feite; *~-favoured, ~-featured,* lelik, met harde gelaatstrekke; *~ fight,* harde (kwaai, skerp, hewige) geveg; *~-fisted,* met goeie vuiste; suinig; *~-fought,* kwaai bestrede; *~-handed,* hardhandig; *~-handedness,* hardhandigheid; *~-headed,* nugter, prakties; saaklik; *~-hearted,* hardvogtig, verhard; *~-heartedness,* hardvogtigheid; *~-hitting,* hewig, kragtig, hardhandig; *~ihood,* stoutmoedigheid, onversaagdheid; astrantheid; onbeskaamdheid; *~iness,* onversaagdheid, gehardheid, flinkheid, taaiheid; *~ish,* harderig; *~ labour,* hardepad, dwangarbeid; *~-labour prisoner,* dwangarbeider; *~ lines,* (11) jammerte, teenspoed; (interj) simpatie! jammer! *~ luck,* (n) teenspoed; (interj) simpatie! *~ ly,* nouliks, pas, ternouernood, nie eintlik nie, skaars; beswaarlik, met moeite; *~ ly ever,* byna nooit nie; *~-mouthed,* ru, grof; hardbekkig, taai in die bek (perd); *~ness,* hardheid; hardigheid; ongevoeligheid, *~ news,* harde (feitlike) nuus; *~-nosed,* nugter; hardekoejawel; *~ nut,* harde neut; hardekoejawel; *a ~ nut to crack,* 'n moeilike geval, 'n harde neut om te kraak; *~ pan,* dor(re)bank; *~-pressed,* kwaai agtervolg; verleë; noustrop trek; in die knyp; *~-sell,* aggressiewe verkoopmanskap; *~-set,* in die nood; bebroeid (eier); honger; met harde dop; *~ ship,* ontbering; moeilikheid; *~ solder,* harde soldeersel; *~ tack,* klinkers; *~ ware,* ysterware; apparaat, fisiese toerusting; apparatuur (rek.); *~ wareman,* handelaar in ysterware; *~ water,* harde water; *~-wearing,* sterk, onslytbaar, duursaam; *~-won,* suur verdien; *~ wood,* hardehout; *~ woods,* loofhoutsoorte, hardehoutsoorte; *~ work,* swaar (harde) werk; *~-working,* fluks, arbeidsaam.

hard'y, (n) (..dies), ysterstaaf; (a) sterk, taai, kragtig; gehard; *~ ANNUAL,* winterharde plant; steeds weerkerende vraagstuk (fig.); *HALF ~,* nie heeltemal teen koue bestand nie.

hare, haas; *first CATCH your ~,* moenie die vleis braai voordat die wildsbok geskiet is nie; *RUN with the ~ and hunt with the hounds,* blaf met die honde en huil met die wolwe; *if you run after TWO ~ s you will catch neither,* as jy op twee stoele tegelyk wil sit, kom jy op die grond te lande; *~ and hounds,* snipperjag; *~ bell,* lenteklokkie, grasklokkie; *~-brained,* onbesuis, onbesonne, wild, dol(sinnig); *~ lip,* haaslip, drielip.

har'em, harem, vrouverblyf; *~ skirt,* rokbroek; haremrok.

hare' pie, haaspastei.

hare's-foot, haaspoot; naelkruid.

ha'ricot, bredie, gestoofde (skaap)vleis; snyboontjie; *~ bean,* snyboontjie; slaaiboontjie.

hark, luister; *~ BACK,* teruggaan; terugroep; terugsnuffel; *~ BACK to,* terugkom op.

harl'equin, harlekyn, hanswors, nar; *~ ade,* grapmakery, harlekinade, narrespel.

harl'ot, (n) hoer; (v) hoer(eer); *~ ry,* hoerery ontug.

harm, (n) skade, kwaad, nadeel; *there is no ~ in ASKING,* vra is vry en weier daarby; *grievous BODILY ~,* ernstige letsel; *COME to ~,* kwaad oorkom; *there's NO ~ done,* daar is niks verlore nie; dis niks; *there's no ~ in TRYING,* al baat dit nie, dit skaad ook nie; *~ WATCH, ~ catch,* wie 'n put graaf vir 'n ander val self daarin; *be out of ~'s WAY,* buite gevaar wees; geen geleentheid vir kwaaddoen hê nie; (v) skade aandoen, beskadig, skaad, kwaad doen, benadeel; *not to ~ a fly,* geen vlieg enige kwaad aandoen nie.

harmatt'an, harmattan, warm stormwind.

harm: ~ **ful,** skadelik, nadelig; ~ **fulness,** skadelikheid; ~ **less,** onskadelik, skadeloos; onskuldig; ~ **lessness,** onskadelikheid; onskuld.

harmon'ic, welluidend, harmonies; ~ **a,** mondfluitjie, mondorreltjie, harmonika; ~ **curve,** sinuslyn; ~ **mean,** harmoniese gemiddelde; ~ **motion,** harmonies trillende beweging; ~ **progression,** harmoniese reeks; ~ **proportion,** harmoniese eweredigheid; ~ **s,** harmonieleer; ~ **tone,** harmoniese toon.

harmon'ious, harmonies; welluidend, harmonieus; eendragtelik, eendragtig; eensgesind; ~ **ness,** harmonie; welluidendheid; eensgesindheid.

harm'onist, harmonikus; musikus; toondigter; iem. wat parallelle lesings ondersoek, harmonis.

harmon'ium, (-s), harmonium, huisorrel, serfyn.

harm'onize, ooreenstem, saamklink, harmonieer; in ooreenstemming bring; harmoniseer (mus.); ~ **r,** harmonis, toondigter.

harmonom'eter, harmonometer.

harm'ony, (..nies), harmonie, welluidendheid; ooreenstemming; eensgesindheid, eendrag, eenstemmigheid; *theory of* ~, harmonieleer.

harn'ess, (n) tuig; harnas; wapenrusting; *DIE in* ~, in die tuig sterf; *GO in double* ~, getroud wees; *IN* ~, in die juk; in die tuig; aan die werk; (v) optuig, inspan; aanwend; ~ **-cask,** pekel(vleis)vaatjie; ~ **-horse,** tuigperd, karperd, trekperd; ~ **-maker,** tuiemaker; ~ **-room,** tuiekamer; ~ **-tub** = **harness-cask.**

harp, (n) harp; *hang one's* ~ *on the willow,* die lier aan die wilgerboom hang; (v) die harp bespeel, op die harp speel; ~ *on the same string,* dieselfde liedjie sing; op dieselfde aambeeld hamer; dieselfde ding herhaal; ~ **er,** ~ **ist,** harpspeler, harpenaar.

harpoon', (n) harpoen; (v) met 'n harpoen skiet, harpoeneer; ~ **er,** harpoenier; ~ **-gun,** harpoenkanon.

harp: ~ **-player,** harpenaar, harpspeler; harpspeelster; ~ **-playing,** harpspel.

harp'sichord, klavesimbel; ~ **ist,** klavesinis(te), klavesimbelspeler.

harp'y, (harpies), harpy; heks; uitsuier, vrek.

harq'uebus, (-es), haakbus, stutgeweer.

ha'rridan, ou heks, feeks.

ha'rrier¹, (n) plunderaar, verwoester, plaer; kuikendief; uilarend.

ha'rrier², (n) jaghond; afstandloper.

ha'rrier eagle, uilarend.

ha'rrow, (n) eg; *under the* ~, in benoudheid; (v) eg; folter, kwel, pynig.

ha'rrower, egger, êer; berower; ~ *of hell,* helberower.

ha'rrowing¹, (n) (die) eg.

ha'rrowing², (a) ergerlik, kwellend, folterend, hartverskeurend, martelend.

ha'rrow: ~ **perforation,** egtanding; ~ **pin,** egtand.

ha'rry, (v) **(harried),** pla, kwel, verontrus; verwoes, verniel, plunder; ruïneer.

harsh, ru; stroef, stug; skel, hard; nors, hardvogtig, onaangenaam, streng; vrank, wrang, guur (weer); bits(ig), skerp; *BE* ~, 'n swaar hand hê; ~ *WORDS,* harde woorde; ~ **ness,** hardheid, skelheid; ruheid; strengheid, skerpheid.

hars'let = **haslet.**

hart, takbok, hert.

hart'ebeest, hartbees; *LICHTENSTEIN'S* ~, vaalhartbees; *RED* ~, rooihartbees.

harts'horn, hertshoring; *spirits of* ~, ammoniakoplossing; vlugsout.

har'um-scarum, (n) malkop, maltrap; (a) holdersteboldèr, ligsinnig, onbesuis, halsoorkop.

harv'est, (n) oes; gewas; opbrengs; (v) oes; insamel; ~ **er,** oester; insamelaar, plukker; snymasjien, oesmasjien; ~ **er termite,** knipmier, stokkiesdraer, grasdraer *(Hodotermes mossambicus);* ~ **festival,** oesfees; ~ **home,** oesfees; ~ **ing,** oestery, oeswerk; ~ **man,** oester; oeswerker; ~ **moon,** oesmaan; ~ **mouse,** veldmuis; ~ **song,** oeslied; ~ **time,** oestyd.

has'-been, uitgediende; ou knol; iem. uit die ou doos.

hash, (n) fyngekapte vleis, dobbelsteentjies, hasjee; mengelmoes; opgewarmde kos; nagestoofde vleisstukkies; knoeiery; ~ *of DUCK,* eendhasjee; *MAKE a* ~ *of,* verknoei, bederf; *SETTLE a per-* son's ~, iem. kafloop; met iem. klaarspeel; (v) fynkap, in stukkies sny.

hash'eesh, hash'ish, dagga, hasjisj.

hash' house, koshuis.

has'let, (vark)karmenaadjie; (vark)harslag.

hasp, (n) grendel, werwel, knip; haak; oorslag; ~ *and staple,* kram en oorslag; (v) toemaak, sluit, grendel.

ha'ssle¹, (n) (-s), gesukkel, probleem, moeilikheid, gefoeter; herrie; stryery, gestry.

ha'ssle², (v) (-d), sukkel, foeter, probleme (moeilikhede) hê (kry); stry.

hass'ock, knielkussing; voetkussing; biesiemat; graspol.

has'tate, spiesvormig, speervormig, spies=.

haste, (n) haas, spoed; gehaastheid; vaart; *IN* ~, gou; haastig, in aller yl; *MAKE* ~, gou maak; jou roer; *MAKE* ~ *slowly,* haas jou langsaam; *MORE* ~ *less speed,* hoe meer haas, hoe minder spoed; ~ *makes WASTE,* haastige spoed is selde goed; (v) jou haas, gou maak.

ha'sten, yl; haastig (gou) maak, aanjaag; bespoedig, verhaas; ~ *AWAY,* wegstuif; ~ *FORWARD,* voortyl; ~ **ing,** verhaasting.

has'tily, haastig, gou.

has'tiness, drif, opvlieëndheid; haastigheid, gejaagdheid; ~ *of temper,* opvlieëndheid.

has'ty, haastig, heetgebaker, opvlieënd; snel, gejaag, vlugtig; driftig; ~ *climbers have sudden falls,* haastige spoed is selde goed; ~ **pudding,** blitspoeding.

hat, (n) hoed; kadot(jie); *don't wear a BROWN* ~ *in Friesland,* lands wys, lands eer; *knock into a COCKED* ~, iem. slaan dat hy sy ouma vir 'n eendvoël aansien; *EAT one's* ~, jou hoed opeet; *I'll EAT my* ~ *if it is not true,* ek is 'n boontjie as dit nie waar is nie; *come EAT one's* ~ *(if such should be the case),* jou hoed opeet (as dit so is); ~ *in HAND,* met die hoed in die hand kom; *HANG up one's* ~ *somewhere,* jou hoed êrens ophang; *that is where he is HANGING his* ~, sy rolplek is daar; ~ *s OFF!,* hoed af! *PASS (send) round the* ~, kollekteer; met die hoed rondgaan; *RED* ~, kardinaalshoed; *TAKE one's* ~ *and go,* jou hoed vat; *TAKE one's* ~ *off to someone,* jou hoed vir iem. afhaal; *TALK through one's* ~, grootpraat; kaf verkoop; deur sy nek praat; *you had better first THROW in your* ~, jy moet jou hoed eers ingooi; *TOSS one's* ~ *in the air,* jou hoed in die lug gooi; *TRIM a* ~, 'n hoed opmaak; *keep something UNDER one's* ~, iets dig hou; dit onder ons meisies hou; (v) **(-ted),** 'n hoed opsit; onder 'n hoed toemaak; ~ **band,** hoedband; ~ **block,** hoedevorm; hoedblok; ~ **box,** hoededoos; ~ **brim,** hoedrand; ~ **brush,** hoedeborsel.

hatch¹, (n) onderdeur; (skeeps)luik; ~ *es, CATCHES, matches and dispatches,* geboorte-, verlowings-, huweliks- en doodsberigte; *GO down the* ~, na die hoenders gaan.

hatch², (n) inlegging; arsering; (v) arseer, graveer, grif.

hatch³, (n) (-es), broeisel, broeiery; (v) uitbroei, uitkom (kuikens); smee, uitdink, beraam (plan).

hatch'-cleats, luikklappe.

hatch: ~ **er,** broeier; broeimasjien; samesweerder; ~ **ery,** (..ries), broeiplek; kwekery; broeihuis.

hatch'et, handbyltjie; *BURY the* ~, vrede maak; *DIG up the* ~, die strydbyl opgraaf; *TAKE up the* ~, die wapens opneem; *THROW the* ~, met spek skiet; *THROW the helve after the* ~, goeie geld agter slegtes aangooi; ~ **-face,** lang, skerpgetekende gesig, spits gesig; bylgesig; ~ **-stake,** beitelstaak.

hatch'ing, broeiery, (die) uitbroei; ~ **-house,** broeihuis; ~ **-pen,** broeihok; ~ **-oven,** broeioond.

hatch: ~ **ment,** wapenbord; roubord; ~ **way,** luikgat.

hate, (n) haat, afkeer; (v) haat, 'n hekel hê aan; *I* ~ *history,* ek het 'n hekel aan geskiedenis; ~ **d,** gehaat; ~ **ful,** haatdraend; haatlik; ~ **fulness,** haatlikheid; ~ **r,** hater.

hat: ~ **-guard,** hoedkoord; ~ **less,** kaalkop, sonder hoed; ~ **-maker,** hoedemaker; ~ **-peg,** kapstok; ~ **-pin,** hoedspeld; ~ **-press,** lakenpers; ~ **-rack,** kapstok.

hat'red, haat, wrok.

hat: ~ **-stand,** kapstok; ~ **ted,** met 'n hoed op; ~ **ter,**

hauberk 947 **head**

hoedemaker; hoedehandelaar; *mad as a* ~ *ter*, stapelgek; ~ **trick**, driekuns, driebalkuns; ~**-trimmer**, hoedemaker, hoedemaakster.
haub'erk, wapenrusting, maliekolder.
haugh, riviergrond.
haught'ily, uit die hoogte, verwaand.
haught'iness, hoogmoed(igheid), hooghartigheid, trots, aanmatiging.
haught'y, hoogmoedig, trots, hovaardig, hooghartig; *a* ~ *miss*, 'n ydeltuit.
haul, (n) trek, sleep; opbrengs, (vis)vangs; (v) trek, karwei, sleep; van koers verander (skip); ~ *ALONG*, aansjou; ~ *someone over the COALS*, iem. berispe; iem. laat verbykom; ~ *DOWN*, neerhaal, stryk (vlag); ~ *IN*, inbring; ~ *OUT*, uittrek, uitsleep; ~ *ROUND*, van koers verander; ~ *UP*, optrek, hys; ~ *upon the WIND*, na die wind seil.
haul'age, sleeploon; vervoer; hysweg; *endless* ~, aaneengeskakelde kabelvervoer; ~ **tractor**, sleeptrekker.
haul: ~**er**, trekker, sleper, hyser; ~**ier**, vervoerder, karweier; ~**ing**, (n) vervoer, transport; die sleep, slepery; (a) sleep-; ~**ing-gear**, hyswerktuig; ~**ing-iron**, sleephaak; ~**ing-rope**, sleeptou.
ha(u)lum, halm, stingel; stam; strooi.
haunch, (-es), dy; heup; boud; (pl) hurke; *SIT on one's* ~ *es*, op sy hurke sit; ~ *of VENISON*, wildsboud; ~ **bone**, heupbeen; ~**ing machine**, borstapmasjien; ~ **joint**, borstap.
haunt, (n) drukbesoekte plek; bymekaarkomplek; lêplek, boerplek (van wilde diere); (v) druk besoek, êrens boer; naloop; rondwaar; spook, kwel; ~ *someone's DOORSTEP*, iem. se drumpel platloop; op iem. se agterdeur lê; *a GHOST* ~ *s this place*, dit spook hier; *a* ~*ed HOUSE*, 'n spookhuis; *the IDEA* ~ *s me*, die gedagte is by my 'n obsessie; die gedagte laat my nie los nie; *don't* ~ *your NEIGHBOUR'S doorstep*, moenie dat jou buurman se honde vir jou blaf nie; *this PLACE is* ~*ed*, dit spook hier; ~**ing**, (n) spokery; (a) spokend, obsederend.
Hau'sa, Hausa.
haustell'um, (..lla), suigorgaan, slurp, suier, haustellum.
hausto'rium, (..ria), suigdraad, suigwortel, haustorium.
haut'boy, aarbei; *kyk* **oboe**.
haute couture', (F.), haute couture, hoogmode(makery).
haute cuisine', (F.), haute cuisine, hoëgraadkookkuns.
hauteur', hoogmoed, hooghartigheid.
haute relief, (F.), hoogrelief, -reliëf.
Havan'a, Havanna; havannasigaar; ~ **tobacco**, havannatabak.
have, (n) flousery; *the* ~ *s and the* ~ *-nots*, rykes en armes; (v) **(had)**, hê; besit; hou; ontvang; flous; *not to be having ANY*, nie wil saamspeel nie; ~ *another APPLE*, neem nog 'n appel; *the AYES* ~ *it*, die meerderheid is daarvoor; ~ *a BABY*, 'n kind kry; *he had BETTER go*, hy moet maar liewer gaan; *the BIBLE has it*, soos die Bybel sê; ~ *BREAKFAST*, ontbyt eet; ~ *a CARE!*, oppass!; ~ *no CARES*, kommerloos (onbesorg) wees; ~ *him COME*, sorg dat hy kom; ~ *the CONVERSATION to oneself*, alleen praat; ~ *DONE*, klaar kry; ophou; *I* ~ *no DOUBT*, ek twyfel nie daaraan nie; *I* ~ *it FROM him*, hy het my vertel; ~ *a GAME*, speel; ~ *at HEART*, op die hart dra; ~ *the IMPUDENCE to*, so astrant wees om; ~ *something IN one*, iets sit in jou bloed; *you haven't it IN you*, dit sit nie in jou broek nie; ~ *little LATIN*, 'n bietjie Latyn ken; *I would* ~ *you KNOW*, jy moet weet; ~ *and HOLD*, hê en hou; ~ *a LOOK at*, kyk na; *as LUCK would* ~ *it*, soos die toeval dit wou hê; *you* ~ *ME there*, nou het jy my; ~ *some MILK*, kry melk; ~ *in MIND*, in gedagte hê; ~ *ON*, aanhê, dra; ~ *it OUT*, dit uitspook; *RUMOUR has it*, hulle sê; *I regret to* ~ *to SAY*, dit spyt my om te moet sê; ~ *a TRY*, probeer; ~ *someone UP*, iem. voor die hof bring; *and WHAT* ~ *you*, ensovoorts; *some WILL* ~ *it*, party beweer.

have'lock, sondoek.
hav'en, hawe; toevlugsoord, skuilplek; ~ *of rest*, toevlugsoord.
ha'ver, (n), gebabbel, geklets; (v) babbel, klets.
hav'ersack, knapsak, bladsak; hawersak.
hav'ing(s), besitting, eiendom.
hav'oc, (n) verwoesting; *CRY* ~ *with*, die teken gee om te buit; *MAKE* ~ *of*, verwoesting aanrig onder; vreeslik te kere gaan met; *PLAY* ~ *with*, vreeslik huishou met; verwoesting aanrig onder; (v) **(-ked)**, verwoes; ruïneer, verniel.
haw¹, (n) knipvlies, wenkvlies, derde ooglid.
haw², (n) meidoring; heining; ingeslote ruimte.
haw³, (v) aarsel, hakkel; aanstellerig praat.
Hawai'i, Hawaii; ~ **an**, (n) Hawaiiër; (a) Hawaiïes.
haw'-haw', (n) aanstellerige pratery; skreeulag; (v) aanstellerig praat, skreeulag.
hawk¹, (n) pleisterplank.
hawk², (n) valk; bedrieër, swendelaar; *neither* ~ *nor BUZZARD*, nòg baas nòg Klaas; ~ *s will not pick* ~ *s' EYES out*, kraaie pik nie mekaar se oë uit nie; *know a* ~ *from a HANDSAW*, onderskeidingsvermoë hê.
hawk³, (v) smous, vent, verkoop; versprei; uitstrooi.
hawk⁴, (v) keel skoonmaak.
hawk: ~**-bill**, papegaaibek(tang); ~**-eagle**, hoenderjaer.
hawk'er¹, valkenier.
hawk'er², smous, venter, marskramer, straatverkoper; ~**'s licence**, marskramerslisensie.
hawk'-eyed, skerpsiende, met valkoë.
hawk'ing¹, smousery, ventery.
hawk'ing², valkejag.
hawk: ~**-moth**, stinks, pylstertmot; ~**-nose**, krom neus, haakneus; ~**-nosed**, met 'n arendsneus, kromneus-; ~**'s-bill turtle**, karetskilpad.
hawse, (anker)kluis; boeg; ~**-hole**, kluisgat; ~**r**, tou, sleepkabeltros; ~**r bend**, hieling.
haw'thorn, meidoring, haagdoring; *Mexican* ~, skaapvrug.
hay, (n) hooi; *take too much* ~ *on one's FORK*, te veel hooi op jou vurk neem; *between* ~ *and GRASS*, te groot vir 'n servet en te klein vir 'n tafeldoek; *MAKE* ~, hooi oopgooi (omkeer); *MAKE* ~ *of*, in verwarring bring; in die war stuur; *MAKE* ~ *while the sun shines*, die yster smee terwyl dit warm is; (v) hooi; van hooi voorsien; hooi maak; ~**-barn**, hooiskuur; ~**box**, hooikis, prutkissie; ~ **cart**, hooiwa; ~ **cock**, hooihopie, opper; ~ **crop**, hooigewas; ~ **fever**, hooikoors; ~**-fork**, hooivurk, gaffel; ~**-loft**, hooisolder; ~ **maker**, hooimasjien; hooier; swaaihou (boks); ~ **press**, hooipers; ~ **rack**, hooirak; ~ **rick**, ~ **stack**, hooimied; ~ **sweep**, laaihark.
hay'wire, deurmekaar, dol; *go* ~, deurmekaar raak.
haz'ard, (n) toeval, risiko, wisselvalligheid, gevaar; dobbelsteen; dobbelspel, kansspel; stopbal; hindernis (gholf); *at all* ~ *s*, op goeie geluk; laat dit kos wat dit wil; (v) waag, riskeer; op die spel sit; aan die hand doen; ~**ous**, onseker, gewaag, gevaarlik; ~**ousness**, onsekerheid, gewaagdheid, gevaarlikheid.
haze¹, (n) dynserigheid, waas, mis; onduidelikheid; benewelheid; (v) met 'n waas bedek, benewel.
haze², (v) terg, baasspeel (Amer.); doop, ontgroen (studentetaal).
haz'el, (n) haselaar, hasel(neut)boom, haselhout; (a) ligbruin; ~**-eyed**, met bruin oë; ~**-nut**, haselneut; ~**-worm**, blindwurm; ~ **wort**, mansoor.
haz'iness, wasigheid, dynserigheid, vaagheid; dofheid.
haz'y, dynserig, dampig, wasig, mistig, benewel(d); vaag; geswa(w)el, aangeklam.
H'-bomb, H-bom.
he, (n) mansmens; mannetjie; (pron) hy.
head, (n) hoof, kop; dop; beeldenaar, borsbeeld (op munt); verstand; kophare; kapsel; gewei (bok); aantal; knop; struik; bos (vlas); string (sy); stoomdruk (masjien); voorstewe (boot); kaap; myngang; brughoof, rubriek; koppenent (bed); kruin, top (berg); kap (van rytuig); prinsipaal (skool); hoofman, leier, bestuurder; skuim (bier); room (melk); krop (slaai); stuks (vee); posseël; bron, oorsprong

(fig.); bopunt (van stoet); *be at the* ~ *of AFFAIRS*, aan die hoof van sake staan; *make* ~ *AGAINST*, vorder teen; die hoof bied aan; *AT the* ~ *of*, aan die hoof van; *above the* ~ *s of the AUDIENCE*, te hoog vir die gehoor; ~ *of a BARREL*, deksel van 'n vat; *BE it on his own* ~, laat hom ly wat daarop volg; *the* ~ *of the BED*, die koppennent v.d. bed; *BOW one's* ~ *in submission*, die hoof buig; jou kop in die skoot lê; *BRING to a* ~, op 'n spits drywe; ~ *of CATTLE*, stuks vee; *COME to a* ~, oopgaan (sweer); tot 'n krisis kom; *keep a COOL* ~, jou kalm hou; *it COST him his* ~, dit het sy lewe gekos; *uneasy lies the* ~ *that wears a CROWN*, vir regeer= ders is daar min rus; wie regeer, is sy rus kwyt; *DRAG in by the* ~ *and ears*, iets by die hare insleep; *over* ~ *and EARS*, tot oor die ore; *FAIR* ~, wit= kop; *a* ~ *for FIGURES*, 'n kop vir syfers; ~ *first*, vooroor; *from* ~ *to FOOT*, van kop tot toon; *the* ~ *and FRONT of*, die kern van; *large* ~ *of GAME*, groot trop wild; *GATHER* ~, krag win; *GET into one's* ~, die idee kry; *GIVE someone his* ~, iem. sy kop laat volg; iem. sy gang laat gaan; *GO to one's* ~, na die kop gaan; *GO off one's* ~, gek word; ~ *of HAIR*, bos hare; *with HANGING* ~, met han= gende hoof; *HAVE a* ~ *on one's shoulders*, 'n kop op jou lyf hê; *HAVE a* ~ *for*, aanleg hê vir; ~ *over HEELS in love*, dolverlief; *turn* ~ *over HEELS*, bolmakiesie slaan; *HOLD one's* ~ *up*, die hoof hoog hou; moed hou; *give a HORSE its* ~, 'n perd die toom gee; *KEEP one's* ~, kop hou; *LAY their* ~*s together*, hulle koppe bymekaarsteek; *LAY down one's* ~ *in sleep*, die hoof neerlê; *at the* ~ *of the LIST*, bo-aan die lys; *LOSE one's* ~, die kluts kwytraak; jou kop verloor; onthoof word; *MAKE* ~, vooruitgaan; vorder; *so many* ~*s so many MINDS*, soveel hoofde soveel sinne; *be OFF one's* ~, nie al jou varkies in die hok hê nie; *go OFF one's* ~, van jou verstand raak; *an OLD* ~ *on young shoulders*, jonk van jare, maar oud van dae; *ON this* ~, op hierdie punt; *to do it ON one's* ~, iets fluit-fluit doen; *OVER one's* ~, oor 'n mens se kop; bokant jou vuurmaakplek; *bring something on one's OWN* ~, jou eie ongeluk veroorsaak; *PER* ~, per stuk; hoofdelik; *put a PRICE on someone's* ~, 'n prys op iem. se hoof stel; *PROMOTE over one's* ~, oor iem. anders heen aanstel; *PUT* ~*s together*, die koppe bymekaarsteek; *PUT something into one's* ~, iem. die gedagte laat kry; *PUT a thing out of one's* ~, die gedagte laat vaar; *RISE* ~ *and shoulders above*, 'n kop groter wees as; ~ *of a RIVER*, oorsprong van 'n rivier; ~*s are going to ROLL*, daar sal koppe waai; *RUN one's* ~ *against a stone wall*, met die kop teen die muur loop; *RUN someone's* ~ *from his shoulders*, 'n kop kleiner maak; *if that is so you may RUN my* ~ *from my shoulders*, as dit die geval is, laat ek my kop afkap; *have one's* ~ *SCREWED on the right way*, 'n goeie kop hê; *be* ~ *and SHOULDERS above others*, kop en skouers bo ander uitsteek; *threaten to have someone's* ~ *from his SHOULDERS*, iem. met die dood dreig; iem. die kop v.d. romp wil slaan; *have a SOUND* ~, 'n goeie kop hê; *the* ~ *of the STAIRS*, die bo-ent v.d. trap; *suffer from a SWOLLEN* ~, verwaand wees; *not to be able to make* ~ *or TAIL of a matter*, geen kop of stert van iets kan uitmaak nie; ~*s or TAILS*, kruis of munt; *TAKE into one's* ~, in die kop kry; *TALK someone's* ~ *off*, iem. se ore van sy kop praat; *TALLER by a* ~, 'n kop groter; *on THAT* ~, in daardie opsig; in daardie verband; *THREATEN to have someone's* ~, iem. dreig; ~ *and TROTTERS*, kop en pootjies; *TURN someone's* ~, iem. se kop op hol maak; *bring something UPON one's own* ~, jou iets op die hals haal; *keep one's* ~ *above WATER*, die kop bo water hou; *TWO* ~*s are better than one*, twee koppe is beter as een, al is een maar 'n skaapkop; *his* ~ *is in a WHIRL*, sy kop draai; sy kop is op hol; *WIN by a* ~, met 'n koplengte wen; ~*s I WIN, tails you lose*, alle voordeel is aan die een kant; (v) die kop afsny; knot (boom); 'n kop aan maak; bo-aan iets staan, eerste wees; van 'n opskrif voorsien; jou ontwikkel; aanvoer, lei (soldate); oortref; gerig wees na; koers vat na; laat koers neem; die hoof bied aan; optrek; afwend; met die kop stamp; ~ **BACK**, terugkeer; ~ **DOWN** *trees*, bome top; ~ **FOR**, in die rigting stuur van; ~ *the POLL*, die meeste stemme ver= werf; ~ **OFF**, afkeer; ~ *the TABLE*, aan die hoof v.d. tafel sit; (a) hoof=, vernaamste; ~**ache**, hoofpyn, kopseer; ~**ache powder**, hoofpynpoeier; ~**achy**, hoofpynerig; ~**band**, kopband; stryklint (boek); bestekband, kapitaalband (boek); ~ **beam**, kopbalk; ~ **board**, koppenent (bed); kopbord; kopplank; ~ **boy**, die eerste, leier, nommer een; primus, dux, hoofseun; hoofprefek; ~ **cheese**, hoofkaas; sult; ~ **clerk**, hoofklerk; ~ **cold**, kop= verkoue, neusverkoue; ~**-collar**, halter; ~ **commit= tee**, bestuur; hoofbestuur; hoofkomitee; ~ **con= stable**, hoofkonstabel; ~ **cover(ing)**, hoofbedek= king; ~**-dress**, hooftooisel, hoofbedekking; coiffu= re, haartooisel; ~ **ed**, wat aanvang met; getitel; met die hoof; ~ **er**, kopduik; kopsteen; aftakkas; ra= veelbak; ~**-footed**, kopvoetig; koppotig; ~**-fore= most**, kop vorentoe; halsoorkop; onbekook; ~ **gear**, hoofdeksel, hoofbedekking, hooftooisel; skagtoring (myn); toomtuig; ~ **girl**, hoofmeisie, prima; ~**hunter**, koppesneller; ~ **hunting**, koppe= snellery; ~**iness**, drif, koppigheid; ~**ing**, opskrif, hoof; gang; ~**ing course**, koplaag; ~**ing-joint**, kop= las (vloerplanke); ~**ing-tool**, naelyster; ~ **jamb**, bodrumpel; ~ **lamp**, koplig; ~**land**, wenakker; voorgeberge; kaap, landpunt; ~**less**, sonder kop; ~**light**, koplig; ~ **line**, (n) hoof, kop(reël), opskrif; raband (skip); (v) opskrifte (koppe) skryf; ~**liner**, opskrifskrywer; hoofpersoon; ~**long**, kop vooruit; blindelings, dolsinnig, onbesonne; ~ **man**, hoof= man, opperhoof, kaptein; ~ **master**, hoof(onder= wyser), skoolhoof, prinsipaal; ~ **measurement**, kopmaat; ~ **mistress**, hoofonderwyseres, prinsipa= le; ~**-money**, hoofgeld; ~ **most**, voorste; ~ **office**, hoofkantoor; hoofbestuur; ~ **official**, hoofampte= naar; ~**-on**, kop teen kop; tromp-op; ~**-on col= lision**, kop-teen-kopbotsing, frontbotsing; ~ **phone**, koptelefoon; kopstuk; ~ **piece**, kopstuk, mus, kap; verstand; titelprent; stormhoed; helm; kop; ~ **prefect**, hoofprefek; hoofseun; ~ **quarters**, hoofsetel, hoofkantoor, hoofkwartier; ~**-rail**, borsleuning; ~**-resistance**, voorweerstand; ~ **race**, toevoervoor; toevoersloot; ~**-rest**, kopstut; ~ **rhyme**, stafrym; ~ **room**, kopspasie, kopruimte; deurryhoogte; ~ **rope**, halterriem; togriem; ~ **sail**, boegseil; ~ **scarf**, kopdoek; ~**-scratching**, kop= krap(pery); ~ **sea**, stortsee, kopsee; ~**-shake**, kop= skudding; ~**s'man**, laksman, beul, skerpregter; ~ **spring**, hoofbron; ~ **stall**, kopstuk (van 'n toom); ~ **station**, hoofstasie; ~ **start**, voorsprong; ~**stock**, spilkop (van 'n draaibank); ~ **stone**, hoek= steen; grafsteen; ~**strong**, styfhoofdig, halsstarrig, balhorig, koppig, eiewys; *be* ~ *strong*, koppig wees; 'n harde kop hê; ~**strongness**, eiewysheid; ~ **stu= dent**, hoofstudent, primarius; klasleier; ~**-voice**, kopstem; ~ **waiter**, hoofkelner; ~**-waters**, boloop; ~ **way**, vooruitgang, vordering; vaart; boruimte; *make* ~ *way*, vooruitkom, vorder; ~ **wear**, hoofbe= dekking, kopbedekking; hoed; ~ **wind**, teenwind; ~ **word**, trefwoord, lemma; ~**-work**, hoofwerk, kopwerk; ~**y**, driftig; koppig (wyn).

heal, genees, heel, gesond maak (word); toegroei, dig= groei; ~**-all**, wondermiddel, panasee; ~ **er**, ge= sondmaker, heelmeester, dokter; ~**ing**, (n) gene= sing, gesondmaking; *the art of* ~*ing*, geneeskuns; (a) genesend; ~**ing power**, heelkrag, geneeskrag.

health, gesondheid, welstand; *DRINK the* ~ *of*, op die gesondheid drink van; *in GOOD* ~, in blaken= de gesondheid; *MINISTER of H* ~, Minister van Gesondheid; *a PICTURE of* ~, 'n toonbeeld van gesondheid; *PUBLIC* ~, volksgesondheid; *for* ~*'s SAKE*, gesondheidshalwe; *STATE of* ~, gesond= heidstoestand; ~ *is BETTER than WEALTH*, ge= sondheid is alles; *YOUR* ~ *! gesondheid!* ~ **certifi= cate**, gesondheidsertifikaat; ~ **committee**, gesond= heidskomitee; ~ **course**, gesondheidskursus; ~ **educator**, gesondheidsvoorligter; ~ **food**, gesond= heidskos, -voedsel; ~**ful**, gesond; heilsaam; ~**giving**, gesond; heilsaam; ~**iness**, gesondheid; ~-

heap 949 **heat**

officer, gesondheidsbeampte; ~ **resort**, gesondheidsoord; ~ **salts**, ligte purgeermiddel, gesondheidsout; ~ **service**, gesondheidsdiens; ~ **visitor**, siekebesoeker; ~**y**, fiks, gesond, fris; welvarend.

heap, (n) hoop; klomp; boel, stapel, menigte; ~*s of MONEY*, geld soos bossies; *STRUCK all of a* ~, dronkgeslaan, stom van verbasing; ~*s of TIME*, oorgenoeg tyd; (v) ophoop, opstapel; ~ *INSULTS upon his head*, hom lelik beledig; ~*ed SPOON*, opgehoopte lepel, lepel hoog vol; ~ *UP*, opstapel, ophoop.

hear, (heard), hoor; verhoor (gebed); luister na; verneem; aanhoor (regt.); ~*!* ~*!*, hoor! hoor!; ~ *FROM*, hoor van, berig kry oor; *MAKE oneself* ~*d*, jou hoorbaar maak; ~ *OF*, hoor van; berig kry oor; ~ *someone OUT*, iem. uithoor; *you WILL* ~ *(more) of this*, jy sal daarvoor moet deurloop; ~**er**, hoorder, toehoorder.

hear'ing, gehoor; verhoor (hofsaak); aanhoring; *DATE of* ~, aanhoordag; *DEFECTIVE* ~, swak gehoor, *be DULL of* ~, hardhorend wees; *give a FAIR* ~, geduldig luister na; onpartydig verhoor; *GIVE someone a* ~, iem. te woord staan; *HARD of* ~, hardhorend; *IN my* ~, sodat ek kon hoor; *IN the* ~ *of*, ten aanhore van; *OBTAIN a* ~, oudiënsie verkry; *be OUT of* ~, buite hoorbereik wees; *QUICK of* ~, fyn van gehoor; *WITHIN* ~, binne oorbereik; ~ **aid**, gehoortoestel; ~**-defective**, iem. met 'n gehoorgebrek, gehoorgebrekkige; ~ **distance**, gehoor(s)afstand.

heark'en, luister, hoor.

hear'say, hoorsê, praatjies, gerug; *from* ~, van hoorsê; ~ **evidence**, praatjies, gerugte; hoorsêgetuienis.

hearse, lykwa, doodswa, dodewa; doodbaar; ~ **cloth**, lykkleed; baarkleed.

heart, hart; gemoed; krag; siel; geneentheid, liefde; pit, kern, hoofsaak, binneste; moed, sterkte; (pl) hartens (kaartspel); *out of the ABUNDANCE of the* ~ *the mouth speaketh*, waar die hart van vol is, loop die mond van oor; *AFTER one's own* ~, so reg na jou hart; *with ALL my* ~, van ganser harte; *AT* ~, in sy hart; te moede; in die grond; *his* ~ *missed a BEAT*, sy hart het byna gaan staan; *his* ~ *sank into his BOOTS*, sy hart het in sy skoene gesink; sy moed het hom begewe; *from the BOTTOM (depth) of my* ~, van die grond van my hart; *BREAK someone's* ~, iem. se hart breek; *with a BROKEN* ~, met 'n gebroke hart; *BY* ~, uit die kop; van buite; *have a CHANGE of* ~, tot inkeer kom; *to one's* ~*'s CONTENT*, na hartelus, *indulge to one's* ~*'s CONTENT*, jou hart aan iets ophaal; *CRY one's* ~ *out*, jou doodhuil; warm trane stort; *it CUTS one to the* ~, dit maak 'n mens se hart seer; *my DEAR* ~, my skat (hartjie); *his* ~ *is DIVIDED*, sy hart is verdeel; *set one's* ~ *at EASE*, iem. gerus stel, *EAT one's* ~ *out*, jou doodtreur; *FAINT* ~ *never won fair lady*, wie nie waag nie sal nie wen nie; *not to FIND something in one's* ~, nie iets oor die hart kan kry nie; *put FRESH* ~ *into someone*, iem. 'n riem onder die hart steek; *with a GLAD* ~, blymoedig; *it GLADDENS one's* ~, dit doen 'n mens weldadig aan; *a* ~ *of GOLD*, 'n hart van goud; *be of GOOD* ~, vol goeie moed wees; *do one's* ~ *GOOD*, jou siel goed doen; *in GOOD* ~, vol goeie moed; *it does one's* ~ *GOOD*, dit doen weldadig aan; *that is something that does my* ~ *no GOOD*, dit sien ek nie graag nie; *take* ~ *of GRACE*, moed vat; *with* ~ *and HAND*, met moed en ywer; *HAVE at* ~, op die hart dra; *HAVE the* ~, die moed hê; *HAVE a* ~*!* wees nou billik! *not to HAVE the* ~, to do a thing, iets nie oor die hart kan kry nie; *part with something with a HEAVY* ~, iets swaar van jou hart laat gaan; *IN* ~, vol moed; *IN one's* ~ *of* ~*s*, in jou binneste; *KEEP* ~, moed hou; *have a KIND (warm)* ~, 'n goeie hart hê; *KNOW by* ~, van buite ken; uit die kop (hoof) ken; *LEARN by* ~, van buite ken; uit die kop ken; *LIE near one's* ~, na aan jou hart lê; *LOSE* ~, tou opgooi; moed verloor; *LOSE one's* ~, verlief raak; *the* ~ *of the MATTER*, die kern v.d. saak; *have one's* ~ *in one's MOUTH*, doodbang wees; *be NEAR one's* ~, jou na aan die hart lê; *have NO* ~,

geen hart hê nie; geen genade ken nie; ~*s of OAK*, manne met pit; *one's* ~ *goes OUT to*, jou hart gaan uit na; *OUT of* ~, neerslagtig, moedeloos; bek-af; *his* ~ *is in the right PLACE*, sy hart sit op die regte plek; *POUR out your* ~, jou hart uitstort; *PUT* ~ *into someone*, iem. 'n riem onder die hart steek; *SAD at* ~, treurig; *set one's* ~ *at REST*, iem. gerusstel; *SET one's* ~ *on something*, iets vurig begeer; *SICK at* ~, neerslagtig; *wear one's* ~ *on one's SLEEVE*, die hart op die mou dra; *every* ~ *has its own SORROW*, elke hart het sy smart; ~ *and SOUL*, hart en siel; *STEAL someone's* ~, iem. se hart steel; *have a* ~ *of stone*, 'n hart van steen hê; *TAKE* ~, moed skep; *TAKE to* ~, ter harte neem; ~ *TO* ~, openhartig, innig; ~*-to-*~ *TALK*, 'n openhartige gesprek; *what the* ~ *THINKS the mouth speaks*, waar die hart van vol is, loop die mond van oor; *TOUCH the* ~, die hart roer; *WIN the* ~ *of*, die hart wen van; *in the* ~ *of WINTER*, in die hartjie v.d. winter; ~ **ache**, hartseer, siel(e)smart; ~ **ailment**, hartgebrek; hartletsel; ~ **attack**, hartaanval; trombose(aanval); ~**beat**, hartslag, hartklop; ~**-blood**, harteblood, die lewe; ~ **break**, hartseer, gebrokenheid; ~**-breaking**, hartverskeurend; ~**-broken**, met 'n gebroke hart; ontroosbaar; ~ **burn**, sooibrand; pirose; suur; ~**-burning**, ergernis, afguns, ontstemming; ~ **chamber**, hartkamer; ~ **clot**, hart(bloed)klont; ~ **crack**, kernbars, -skeur; ~ **disease**, hartkwaal; hartsiekte.

heart'en, bemoedig, aanmoedig; moed skep; opfleur, opbeur, moed inpraat; ~**ed**, bemoedig, opgemonter.

heart: ~ **failure**, hartverlamming, hartversaking; ~**felt**, innig, diepgevoel, opreg, hartlik; ~**-free**, nie verlief nie; vry; ~**-girth**, hartgordel.

hearth, vuurherd, haardstede, haard, es; ~ *and home*, huis en haard; ~ **broom**, vuurherdbesem; ~ **brush**, haardborsel; ~**-plate**, skoorsteenplaat; ~**-rug**, haardkleedjie; ~**-steel furnace**, herdstaalhoogoond; ~ **stone**, haardsteen, kaggelsteen; skuursteen.

heart: ~**-hunger**, hunkering; ~**ily**, van harte; hartlik; *EAT* ~*ily*, smaaklik eet; ~*ily SICK of*, sat van; ~**iness**, innigheid, hartlikheid; ~ **land**, hartland; ~**less**, gevoelloos, hardvogtig, wreed; ~**lessness**, hardvogtigheid; ~**-lung machine**, hart-longmasjien; ~ **murmur**, hart(ge)ruis; ~ **muscle**, hartspier; ~ **pea**, hartvrug; ~ **rate**, hartklop; ~**-rending**, hartverskeurend; ~**-searching**, (n) selfondersoek; (a) deurvorsend; ~**'s-ease**, gesiggie; viooltjie.

heart: ~**-seizure**, hartverlamming; ~**-shake**, kernbars; ~**-shaped**, hartvormig; ~**sick**, diep bedroef, moedeloos, neerslagtig; ~ **sore**, hartseer; smart; ~ **sound**, hartklank; ~**-stirring**, hartroerend; ~**-strings**, hartsnare; ~ **stroke**, hartkramp; ~ **surgeon**, hartspesialis; ~**-throb**, hartklop; geliefde; nooi; kêrel; ~**-to-**~, openhartig; ~ **transplant(ation)**, hartoorplanting; ~ **trouble**, hartaandoening; ~ **valve**, hartklep; ~**-warming**, hartverwarmend; aandoenlik; verkwikkend; ~**-water**, hartwater; ~**-whole**, gesond van hart; vry, nie verlief nie; opreg, onvervals; ~**-wood**, kernhout; ~**y**, (n) (..**ties**), kêrel, matroos; atleet, sportman; (a) hartlik, vrolik, gesond, flink; volop; *hale and* ~*y*, fris en gesond.

heat, (n) hitte (vuur); warmte (van liggaam); verhitting; branderigheid, rooiheid; heftigheid; drif; hoogtepunt; bronstigheid, loopsheid, hitsigheid (diere); gloed; vuur; uitdunwedloop, uitdunning, voorwedstryd (sport); *COME on* ~, hittig (speels, bronstig) word; *a DEAD* ~, gelykop, 'n kop-aankopwedloop; *FINAL* ~, einduitdun(wedloop); *LATENT* ~, latente warmte; *in the* ~ *of the MOMENT*, in 'n oomblik van woede; *PRICKLY* ~, warmtejeuk, rooihond; *RED* ~, gloeihitte; *SPECIFIC* ~, soortlike hitte; *TURN on the* ~, die wêreld benoud maak; druk uitoefen op; *WHITE* ~, withitte; (v) warm maak (word); verhit; aanhits, ophits; ~ *up*, verwarm; opwarm; ~ **absorption**, hitteabsorpsie, hitteopneming, warmteabsorpsie, warmteopneming; ~ **barrier**, hitteglans; ~ **bump**, galbult; ~ **capacity**, warmtekapasiteit; ~ **con**=

duction, warmtegeleiding; ~ **conductivity,** warmte=
geleidingsvermoë; ~ **conductor,** warmtegeleier; ~
consumption, warmteverbruik; ~ **crack,** hittebars;
~ **cramp,** hittekramp; ~ **dissipation,** hitteafleiding;
~**ed,** warm, verhit; vurig, driftig; heftig; ~ **equiv‑**
alent, warmte-ekwivalent, hitte-ekwivalent, ~ **er,**
stoof, verwarmer; ~ **exhaustion,** hitte-uitputting;
~ **expansion,** warmte-uitsetting, hitte-uitsetting;
~ **gauge,** hittemeter.
heath, erika, heide; veld; *scented* ~, lekkerruikheide;
~‑**bell,** heideblom; ~ **cock,** korhaan.
heath'en, (n) heiden; ongelowige; *the* ~, die heidene;
(a) heidens; ~**dom,** heidendom; ~**ish,** heidens;
~**ism,** heidendom; ~**ize,** tot heiden maak (word);
verheiden; ~**ry,** heidendom.
hea'ther, hei(de), heideblom; heidekleur.
heath'y, heide‑, heideagtig, met hei(de) begroei.
heat' indicator, hitte(aan)wyser.
hea'ting, verwarming; verhitting; *central* ~, sentrale
verwarming; ~ **apparatus,** verwarmingsaanleg; ~
power, verwarmingsvermoë, verhittingsvermoë; ~
surface, verhittingsvlak; ~ **system,** verwarming=
stelsel.
heat: ~ **loss,** hitteverlies, warmteverlies; ~‑**meter,**
hitte(graad)meter; ~‑**proof,** hittevas; ~ **radiation,**
hittestraling; ~‑**range,** hittebereik; ~‑**rash,** hitte=
uitslag; rooihond; ~ **resistance,** hitteweerstand;
~‑**resistant,** hittewerend; ~‑**shield,** hitteskerm; ~‑
spot, somersproet; hittepuisie; ~‑**stroke,** sonsteek,
hittesteek; hitteberoerte; ~ **tolerance,** hitteweer=
stand; ~ **transmission,** warmte‑, hitteoordrag; ~‑
treated glass, warmte‑, hittegetemperde glas; ~
treatment, warmte‑, hittebehandeling; ~ **unit,**
warmte-eenheid; ~ **value,** hittewaarde (brand=
stowwe); verbrandingswarmte (skeik.); ~ **wave,**
hittegolf.
heave, (n) deining; opwelling; hyging; kortasemig=
heid; dekking, gaping (in myne); walging, kokhal=
sing (by naarheid); (pl) bevangenheid (perde); (v)
(‑d or **hove),** hef, ophef; hys; lig (anker); op en neer
gaan, dein; laat swel; opkom; ('n sug) slaak; snak
(na lug); trek; kokhals (by mislikheid); ~ *the AN=*
CHOR, die anker lig (hys); ~ *AT,* trek aan; ~
DOWN, neertrek; ~ *IN,* intol (anker, vis); ~
OUT, uithang; ~ *a SIGH,* 'n sug slaak; ~ *in*
SIGHT, in gesig kom, opdoem; ~ *TO,* bydraai; tot
staan bring; ~ *UP,* opgooi.
hea'ven, hemel; uitspansel; hemelstreek; (troon)he=
mel; *BY* ~! so wraggies! *it CRIES to* ~, dit skrei
ten hemel; *have* ~ *on EARTH,* hemel op aarde hê;
the ~*s may FALL* and *we may have lark-pie for*
supper, as die hemel val, is ons almal dood (het ons
almal blou musssies op); *GATE of* ~, hemelpoort;
GOOD ~*s!* liewe hemel! op die aarde! ~ *HELP*
you! die hemel bewaar jou! bewaar jou gebeente! *IN*
~, in die hemel; ~ *KNOWS,* goeiste weet; die Va=
der weet; *MOVE* ~ *and earth,* hemel en aarde be=
weeg; ~ *OF* ~*s,* die hoogste hemel; *for* ~ *'s SAKE!*
in hemelsnaam! *in the SEVENTH* ~, in die wolke;
in die sewende hemel; ~‑**born,** hemels, goddelik;
~‑**gate,** hemelpoort; ~ **liness,** hemelsgesindheid;
~**ly,** hemels, goddelik; hemel=; salig; bowemaans,
boweaards; ~*ly body,* hemelliggaam; ~‑**sent,** he=
mels; ~‑**stormer,** hemelbestormer; ~ **ward(s),** he=
melwaarts.
heave' offering, hefoffer.
hea'ver, ligter, losser; draaier.
heaves, bevangenheid (by perde).
hea'vily, swaar, kwaai, hard; hewig.
hea'viness, swaarte, gewig, swaarheid; swaarmoedig=
heid; traagheid.
hea'ving, gedein, ~‑**line,** werplyn.
Heaviside layer, Heavisidelaag.
hea'vy, swaar; gewigtig; swaarmoedig; lomp; druk=
kend; lomerig; slaperig; beswaard; vol, belaai;
hooglopend (see); grof; vervelend; vet (drukwerk);
~ *ARTILLERY,* swaar geskut; ~ *BREAD,* neer=
geslane brood; *a* ~ *CROP,* 'n groot oes; *a* ~
DRINKER, 'n kwaai drinker; *it was* ~ *GOING,* dit
het swaar gegaan; ~ *GUNS,* swaar geskut; *be* ~ *on*
the HAND, swaar op die hand wees; ~ *LAUN=*
DERING, die groot was; *LIE* ~ *on,* swaar druk op;

TIME hangs ~ *on his hands,* die tyd verveel hom;
speak with a ~ *TONGUE,* swaar van tong wees; ~
WITH, swanger van; ~ **artillery,** grofgeskut; ~‑
bodied: ~‑*bodied wine,* swaar versterkte wyn; ~‑
bottomed, swaarboom=; ~ **calibre,** grootkaliber,
swaarkaliber; ~‑**calibre gun,** grootkaliberkanon,
swaarkaliberkanon; ~ **cigar,** swaar sigaar; ~ **duty,**
vir swaar diens, swaardiens=; ~‑**duty tyre,** swaar=
diensband; ~‑**footed,** lomp; ~ **going,** swaarkry;
moeilike tyd (werk, probleem); ~ **gold,** grofgoud;
~‑**handed,** onhandig, lomp; ~‑**hearted,** bedroef,
bedruk, swaarmoedig; ~ **hydrogen,** swaarwater=
stof; ~ **industry,** swaar industrie; ~‑**laden,** swaar
gelaai; gedruk; ~‑**lidded,** slaperig, vaak; met swaar
ooglede; ~ **sleeper,** vaste slaper; ~ **smoker,** straw=
we roker; ~ **spar,** swaarspaat; ~ **traffic,** swaar
voertuie; druk verkeer; ~ **type,** vet letter; ~ **water,**
swaarwater; ~‑**weight,** swaargewig; ~ **wine,** swaar
wyn.
hebdom'adal, weekliks.
Heb'e, Hebe; kantienjuffrou, kantienmeisie, skinker.
hebephre'nia, hebefrenie, jeugkranksinnigheid.
heb'etate, verstomp, afstomp.
heb'etude, dwaasheid, domheid, onnoselheid.
he: ~‑**bird,** mannetjiesvoël; ~‑**goat,** bokram; ~‑
lamb, ramlam.
Hebra'ic, Hebreeus.
Heb'raism, Hebraïsme.
Heb'raist, Hebraïkus.
Heb'rides: *the INNER* ~, die Binne-Hebride; *the*
OUTER ~, die Buite-Hebride; *THE* ~, die Hebri=
de, die Hebridiese Eilande.
hec'atomb, hekatombe, slagting.
heck¹, vishek.
heck², hel; *BY* ~, verduiwels; *WHAT the* ~, wat die
(de) drommel.
he'ckelphone, baritonhobo.
hec'kle, hekel; uitslaan (vlas); skerp ondervra, kruis=
vra; ~**r,** hekelaar; ondervraer.
heck'ling, kwel=, kwellend; *a* ~ *question,* 'n kwel=
vraag.
hec'tare, hektaar.
hec'tic, (n) teringblos; teringlyer; teringkoors; (a)
hekties, koorsig, teringagtig; wild, woes; ~
COUGH, teringhoes; ~ *FEVER,* teringkoors; ~
FLUSH, teringkleur, teringblos.
hec'togram(me), hektogram.
hec'tograph, (n) hektograaf; (v) hektografeer.
hec'tolitre, hektoliter.
hec'tometre, hektometer.
Hec'tor, Hektor.
hec'tor, (n) ystervreter, baasspeler; blaaskaak; (v)
grootpraat, baasspeel; ~**ing,** (n) baasspelery; (a)
baasspelerig.
hed'dle, hewel, draadlus (weef); ~ **frame,** hewel=
raam.
hedge, (n) heg, laning; hinderpaal; dekking (wedden=
skap); *it does not grow on every* ~, dit word nie
agter elke bossie uitgeskop nie; (v) omhein; 'n hei=
ning plant; insluit, omring; uitvlugte soek; ontwy=
kend antwoord; albei kante wed; ~ *ABOUT,* toe=
kamp; ~ *IN,* inkamp; vaskeer; ~ *OFF,* afhok,
afkamp; ~‑**bill,** snoeimes; ~‑**clipper,** snoeiskêr; ~
hog, (rol)ystervark, krimpvark; dwarskop; ~‑
hopping, skeervlug; ~‑**knife,** snoeimes; ~‑**mar‑**
riage, geheime huwelik; ~‑**priest,** ongeletterde pre=
diker, haagprediker; ~**r,** heiningplanter; bont=
springer; ~ **row,** laning; heining; ~‑**shears,** hei=
ningskêr; ~ **sparrow,** mossie; ~ **tear,** winkelhaak;
~‑**writer,** prulskrywer.
hedg'ing, bontspringery, rondspringery.
hedon'ic, hedonisties, genotsugtig.
hed'onism, hedonisme, genotleer.
hed'onist, genotsugtige, hedonis; ..**nis'tic,** hedonis=
ties, genotsugtig.
hee'bie-jeebies, (sl.), bangheid, bevreesdheid, krie=
welkrappers.
heed, (n) aandag, sorg; hoede, oplettendheid, ag;
GIVE ~, oplet, aandag gee; *PAY* ~ *to,* ag slaan
op; luister na; *TAKE* ~ *of,* op die hoede wees vir;
oppas vir; *TAKE no* ~ *of something,* geen ag op iets
slaan nie; (v) oppas, ag gee, oplet; luister; ~**ful,**

oplettend; sorgvuldig; *be ~ful of*, ag slaan op; *~less*, onagsaam, onverskillig, ligvaardig; agteloos, sorgloos; onoplettend; *~ lessness*, ligvaardigheid.
hee'-haw', ie-a (gebalk van 'n esel), hieha.
heel¹, (n) hak, hiel (skoen); hakskeen; polvy; hoef (dier); agterstuk; hieling (v.d. mas); horingbal (perdehoef); hiel (geweer); *be AT someone's ~s*, op iem. se hakke wees; *BRING to ~*, mak maak; kleinkry; *be CARRIED with one's ~s foremost*, graf toe gedra word; *CLAP by the ~s*, in boeie slaan; *CLICK ~s*, die hakke aanslaan; *COME to ~*, agter die baas aanloop; jou onderwerp; *COOL one's ~s*, rondstaan; moet wag; *DIG in one's ~s*, vastrap; ysterklou in die grond slaan; *DOWN at (the) ~*, met halfgeslyte hakke; slordig; *FOLLOW on someone's ~, FOLLOW someone close at ~s*, op iem. se hakke bly; *KICK up one's ~s*, rondtrap; staan en wag; agteropskop; *LAY someone by the ~s*, iem. in boeie slaan; *MAKE someone take to his ~s*, iem. die hasepad laat kies; *be OUT at ~*, in armoedige toestand verkeer; *head OVER ~s*, halsoorkop; *SHOW a clean pair of ~s*, op loop sit; *TAKE to one's ~s*, die hasepad kies; op loop sit; *TREAD on someone's ~s*, iem. op die hiele volg; *TURN on one's ~s*, kortom draai; (v) hak aansit (skoen); spoor (haan); kiel (skip); dans; (uit)haak (voetbal); hak (gholf); *~ out*, uithaak.
heel², (n) oorhelling, krinking; (v) oorhel, krink.
heel: *~-and toe*, stap(wedstryd); *~ **ball***, skoenmakerspoets; gehaakte bal (rugby); *~ **bar***, polvystalletjie, polvyhoekie; *~ **bolt***, hielbout, hakbout; *~-bone*, skeenbeen; *~-chair*, hielstoel (wissels); *~-grip*, kousskut.
heel'ing¹, aansit van hakke; hakery; haakwerk (rugby).
heel'ing², oorhelling.
heel: *~-pad*, hielkussing; *~-piece*, polvystuk, hakstuk; end; *~ tap*, polvystuk, hakstuk; end, onderste (in 'n glas).
heft, (n) gewig; die oplig; (v) optel, oplig.
hef'ty, swaar, fris, sterk.
hegemon'ic, heersend, hegemonies.
hegem'ony, hegemonie, leierskap, leiding.
he'gira, he'jira, hegira, eksodus.
he'-goat, bokram.
hei'fer, vers; *~ in milk*, skotvers.
heigh? hê?
heigh'-ho, arrie! allawêreld! ag! so gaan dit!
height, hoogte; bult; verhewenheid; stand (van water); summum, toppunt; *AT its ~*, op sy hoogste; *~ of a BAROMETER*, barometerhoogte, -stand; *in the ~ of FASHION*, na (volgens) die jongste mode; *the ~ of FOLLY*, die toppunt van dwaasheid; *he drew himself to his FULL ~*, hy het hom in sy volle lengte opgerig; *the ~ of SUMMER*, die hartjie v.d. somer; *~ **computer***, hoogtemeter.
height'en, hoër maak; verhef; versterk, verhoog; kleur gee, opsmuk (verhaal).
height restriction, hoogtebeperking.
heil, (G.), heil.
hei'nous, verfoeilik, afskuwelik, snood, verskriklik, grusaam; *a ~ crime*, 'n snode misdaad; *~ness*, grusaamheid.
heir, erfgenaam; *BE ~ to*, erfgenaam wees van; *~ in the MALE (direct, ascending) line*, erfgenaam in die manlike (regte, opgaande) linie; *~ to the THRONE*, troonopvolger; *~ **apparent***, onbetwisbare erfgenaam, erfopvolger, regmatige troonopvolger; *~-at-law*, wettige erfgenaam; *~ **dom***, erfreg; erfenis; erfgenaamskap; *~ **ess***, (-es), erfgename, erfdogter; *~ **less***, sonder erfgenaam; *~ **loom***, erfstuk; familiestuk; *~ **presumptive***, vermoedelike opvolger; *~ **ship***, erfreg; erfenis; erfgenaamskap.
heist, (sl.), roof.
held, *kyk* **hold**, (v).
Hel'dentenor, heldetenoor, Wagnertenoor.
heli'acal, sonne=; met die son opkomende en ondergaande.
helian'thus, sonneblom.
hel'ical, spiraalvormig, spiraal=; skroefvormig; *~ curve*, skroeflyn; *~ gear*, skroefrat; *~ line*, skroeflyn; *~ spring*, spiraalveer; *~ stairs*, wenteltrap, slingertrap; *~ wheel*, skroefwiel.
hel'icite, penningsteen, helisiet.
helicit'ic, helisties.
hel'icoid, (n) skroefvlak, skroefvormige oppervlak; (a) skulpvormig, skroefvormig.
Hel'icon, Helikon, Sangberg.
hel'icopter, helikopter, hefskroefvliegtuig, windmeulvliegtuig.
helicotrem'a, wentelgaatjie.
hel'ictite, heliktiet.
Hel'igoland, Helgoland.
heliocen'tric, heliosentries.
hel'iochrome, kleurfoto.
hel'iochromy, kleurfotografie.
hel'iodor, heliodoor.
hel'iogram, heliogram.
hel'iograph, (n) heliograaf, seinspieël; (v) heliografeer; *~er*, heliografis.
heliograph'ic, heliografies.
heliog'raphy, heliografie, ligkoperdruk.
heliogravure', heliogravure.
heliolith'ic, heliolities.
heliom'eter, sonmeter, heliometer.
hel'iophyte, sonplant, heliofiet.
hel'ioscope, sonkyker, helioskoop.
helios'is, sonsteek, heliose; sonbrand (plantk.).
hel'iostat, heliostaat.
heliothe'rapy, helioterapie, sonliggenesing, sonbehandeling.
hel'iotrope, sonroerkertjie, sonnewende, heliotroop.
heliotrop'ic, heliotropies, ligsoekend.
heliot'ropism, heliotropisme, ligsoeking.
hel'iport, landingsblad (van helikopter), helihawe.
hel'ium, helium.
hel'ix, (helices), skroeflyn, spiraal(lyn); heliks; oorrand, oorskulprand; draadwinding; *double ~*, dubbele heliks; *~ angle*, helikshoek.
hell, hel; duisternis; speelhol, dobbelnes; *BEAT ~ out of*, 'n helse pak gee, uitlooi; *all ~ BROKE loose*, toe was die duiwel los; *COME ~ or high water*, buig of bars; *have ~ on EARTH*, hel op aarde hê; *GIVE a person ~*, iem. sonder genade (tot by oom Daantjie in die kalwerhok) opdons; *~ for LEATHER*, met geweldige vaart; *a ~ of a LIFE*, 'n hondelewe; *LIKE ~*, soos die duiwel; *a ~ of a NOISE*, 'n helse lawaai; *there was ~ to PLAY*, toe was die poppe aan die dans; *PLAY ~ with*, te kere gaan; *RAISE ~*, te kere gaan; *a ~ of a TIME*, 'n vreeslike lang tyd; 'n aaklige tyd; *TO ~ with it*, na die duiwel (die hel) daarmee.
hell-bent: *~ ON*, vasbeslote tot, *be ~ ON*, alles uithaal om.
hell: *~-born*, hels, duiwels; *~-box*, helbakkie (drukkery); *~-cat*, feeks, helleveeg; *~ **driver***, jaagduiwel.
hell'ebore, nieskruid; *FALSE ~*, basternieskruid; *GREEN ~*, vrankwortel.
Hell'ene, Helleen.
Hellen'ic, Helleens, Grieks.
Hell'enism, Hellenisme.
Hell'enist, Hellenis, kenner van Grieks.
Hell'enize, vergrieks.
hell: *~ fire*, helvuur, die groot vuur; *~ **hound***, helhond; duiwel; *~ ion*, hel, derduiwel; *~ish*, hels, boosaardig.
hel'lo, hallo.
hel'lo girl, (Amer.) telefoonmeisie, telefoonjuffrou.
helm¹, roer, helmstok, stuurrat; *BE at the ~ (of affairs)*, aan die roer van sake staan; *TAKE the ~*, die roer vat; die leisels in hande neem.
helm², helm; helmwolk.
hel'met, helm, kurkhoed; *~ed*, gehelm; *~ flower*, wolfswortel, wolwekruid, akoniet, monnikskap; *~ shrike*, helmlaksman; *~ spike*, helmspits.
hel'minth, wurmparasiet, ingewandswurm.
helminthia'sis, wurmsiekte, helmintiase.
helmin'thic, (n) wurmafdrywer; (a) wurmafdrywend.
hel'minthoid, wurmagtig; wurmvormig.
helminthol'ogist, helmintoloog.
helminthol'ogy, helmintologie.
helms'man, roerganger, stuurman; *~ship*, stuurkuns.

hel'ophyte, moerasplant, helofiet.
hel'ot, heloot; slaaf; ~ **ism,** slawerny; ~ **ry,** helotedom; slawerny.
help, (n) hulp, steun, bystand; helpster, helper; middel, raad; *there is NO* ~ *for it,* daar is niks aan te doen nie; *WITH the* ~ *of,* met behulp van; (v) help, steun, bysit, ondersteun; byspring, bystaan; rondien, bedien; bevorder; verhelp; ~ *ALONG,* voorthelp; *it CANNOT be* ~ *ed,* daar is niks aan te doen nie; *I COULD not* ~ *it,* ek kon daar niks aan doen nie; *so* ~ *me GOD,* so waarlik, help my God Almagtig; *GOD* ~ *s those who* ~ *themselves,* help jouself, dan het jou vriende jou lief; ~ *yourself to GRAVY,* kry sous; ~ *someone out of a HOLE,* iem. uit 'n moeilikheid help; *I could not* ~ *LAUGHING,* ek moes eenvoudig lag; ~ *ON,* bevorder, vooruithelp; ~ *OUT,* uit die moeilikheid help; bystaan, byspring; *don't REMAIN longer than you can* ~, moenie langer bly as wat nodig is nie; ~ **er,** hulp, helper; handlanger; ~ **ful,** behulpsaam; diensvaardig; nuttig; ~ **fulness,** hulpvaardigheid; diensvaardigheid; ~ **ing,** (n) skeppie, porsie; hulp; (a) helpend, behulpsaam; *hold out a* ~ *ing hand,* die helpende hand toesteek (reik); ~ **less,** hulpeloos; onbeholpe, magteloos; sonder hulp; hulpbehoewend; ~ **lessness,** hulpeloosheid, magteloosheid; ~ **mate,** ~ **meet,** lewensgesel, wederhelf.
hel'ter-skelter, (n) gedrang, harwar; (a) holderstebolder, halsoorkop, onbesuis.
helve, steel, handvatsel; *throw the* ~ *after the hatchet,* goeie geld agter slegte geld aan gooi; die laaste bietjie ook weggooi.
Helve'tia, Helvesië, Switserland; ~ **n,** Switsers.
hem¹, (n) soom; *FALSE* ~, stootkant; *WRAPPED* ~, soomnaat; sluitsoom; (v) **(-med),** omsoom, omboor; ~ *in,* insluit, omsingel.
hem², (v) keel skoonmaak, kug, hoes.
hem'atite = **h(a)ematite.**
hemeralop'ia, dagblindheid.
hemianop'sia, halfblindheid.
hemicrys'talline, halfkristallyn.
hemicy'clic, halfkransstandig, hemisiklies.
hemihe'dral, hemiëdries.
hemihe'dron, hemiëder.
hem'imorph, hemimorf; ~ **'ic,** hemimorf; ~ **'ism,** hemimorfie; ~ **'ite,** hemimorfiet.
hemiple'gia, verlamming aan die een kant, eensydige verlamming, hemiplegie.
Hemip'tera, Halfvleueliges, Halfvlerkiges.
hem'isphere, halfrond, hemisfeer.
hemisphe'ric(al), halfrond, hemisferies.
hem'istich, (-es), halfvers.
hem'-line, roksoom, voulyn van 'n soom.
hem'lock, skeerling, giftige kerwel.
hem: ~ **-marker,** soommerker; ~ **mer,** soomwerker; soomvoetjie (naaimasjien); ~ **ming,** soomwerk.
hem'orrhage = **haemorrhage.**
hem'orrhoids = **haemorrhoids.**
hemp, hennep; tou; galgtou; *wild* ~, dagga; ~ **en,** hennep=; ~ **-seed,** hennepsaad; ~ **-smoker,** daggaroker.
hem'stitch, (n) **(-es),** soomsteek; (v) met soomsteke naai.
hen, =wyfie, wyfie=; *it is not the* ~ *that cackles most that lays the largest EGG,* dis nie die koei wat die hardste bulk wat die meeste melk gee nie; ~ **-and-chickens,** sleutelblom.
hen'bane, dolkruid.
hen'-battery, lêbattery.
hence, hieruit, hiervandaan; daarom, bygevolg, derhalwe; *a fortnight* ~, oor veertien dae; ~ **forth',** ~ **for'ward,** voortaan, van nou af.
hench'man, (..**men),** dienaar, volgeling, trawant, lyfjong, handlanger, agterryer.
hen'-coop, hoenderhok, hoenderfuik.
hendec'agon, elfhoek, endekagoon.
hendecasyllab'ic, elflettergrepig.
hendi'adys, hendiadis.
hen: ~ **-harrier,** kuikendief; ~ **-house,** hoenderhok.
henn'a, henna.
hen: ~ **nery,** (..**ries),** hoenderhok; ~ **ny,** hennerig; ~ **ostrich,** volstruiswyfie; ~ **party,** damesparty;

~ **pecked,** onder die plak; *BE* ~ *pecked,* die rok dra; onder die besemstok staan; onder die pantoffel sit; onder die pantoffelregering staan; ~ *pecked HUSBAND,* man wat onder die plak sit; ~ **-roost,** hoenderstellasie, hoenderslaapplek; ~ **turkey,** kalkoenwyfie.
hepat'ic, lewer=; lewerkleurig; ~ **artery,** lewerslagaar; ~ **duct,** lewergalbuis; ~ **ulcer,** lewerabses; ~ **water,** swa(w)elwater.
hep'atite, lewersteen, hepatiet.
hepatit'is, lewerontsteking, hepatitis.
hep'tachord, sewesnarige musiekinstrument, heptakord.
hep'tad, sewetal.
hep'taglot, in sewe tale.
hep'tagon, sewehoek, heptagoon.
heptag'onal, sewehoekig, heptagonaal.
heptahe'dral, sewevlakkig, heptaëdries.
heptahed'ron, sewevlak, heptaëder.
hepta'meter, heptameter.
hep'tane, heptaan.
hep'tarchy, heptargie, sewehoofdige regering.
heptasyllab'ic, sewelettergrepig, heptasillabies.
Hep'tateuch, Heptateug (eerste sewe Bybelboeke).
her, haar; *I've never seen* ~ *EQUAL in cake-baking,* haar gelyke om koek te bak, het ek nog nie gekry nie; *she combs* ~ *HAIR,* sy kam haar hare.
her'ald, (n) voorloper, bode; heraldikus, wapenkundige; herout; (v) aankondig, uitroep; inlui; ~ **'ic,** heraldies, wapenkundig; ~ **ist,** wapenkundige, heraldikus; ~ **ry,** wapenkunde, heraldiek.
herb, kruid; bossie; ~ **a'ceous,** kruidagtig; bossieagtig; ~ *aceous border,* blomrand, randakker; ~ **age,** kruie; weiveld; weireg.
herb'al, (n) kruieboek; (a) kruie=; ~ *OINTMENT,* kruiesalf; ~ *REMEDY,* kruiemiddel; ~ **ism,** kruiekennis; ~ **ist,** kruiekenner; bossiedokter; handelaar in geneeskragtige kruie.
herb: ~ **ar'ium,** (..**ria, -s),** herbarium; kruieversameling; kruietuin; ~ **icide,** onkruiddoder; ~ **if'erous,** kruievoortbrengend; ~ **ivore,** planteter, herbivoor; ~ **iv'orous,** plantetend; ~ **orize,** kruie versamel, botaniseer; ~ **ous,** kruid=; vol plante; ~ **y,** vol kruie; kruierig.
Hercule'an, Herkulies; reuse=.
Her'cules, Herkules.
herd, (n) herder, (vee)wagter; trop, kudde; gespuis; *the COMMON (vulgar)* ~, die groot massa; *FOLLOW the* ~, saam met die swerm vlieg; *a LARGE* ~ *of game,* 'n groot trop wild; (v) vee oppas; saamhok; bymekaarkruip; ~ *TOGETHER,* saamhok, saamjaag; saamdrom; ~ *WITH,* aansluit by, saamboer; ~ **-book,** stamboek; ~ **boy,** veewagter; ~ **feeling,** kuddegees; ~ **instinct,** groepinstink; tropinstink, kuddegees; ~ **s'man,** veewagter; ~ **s'woman,** herderin.
here, hier, hierso; hiernatoe; *ABOUT* ~, hier ongeveer; hier in die buurt; ~ *you ARE!,* hier is dit! dit!; ~ *they ARE,* hier kom hulle; ~ *BELOW,* hier onder; *EVERY* ~ *and there,* hier en daar; *FROM* ~, hiervandaan; *FROM* ~ *to there,* van hier tot daar; *GET out of* ~, maak dat jy hier wegkom; ~ *GOES!,* ek begin, hoor! hier gaan hy!; ~ *'s your HEALTH!,* gesondheid! *LOOK* ~, kyk hier; *it is NEITHER* ~ *nor there,* nòg hier, nòg daar; dis nie ter sake nie; ~ *and NOW,* dadelik; op die daad; nou; ~ *and THERE,* hier en daar; ~, *THERE and everywhere,* hier, daar en oral; wyd en syd; rond en bont; ~ *TODAY and gone tomorrow,* vandag hier en môre daar; ~ *'s to YOU!,* op jou gesondheid!; ~ **about(s)',** hier omtrent; hier êrens in die buurt; hier rond, hierlangs; ~ **af'ter,** (n): *the* ~, die hiernamaals; (adv) hierna; na dese; later; ~ **at',** hierby, hierop; ~ **by',** hierdeur, hierby, hiermee; mits dese.
hereditabil'ity, erflikheid.
hered'itable, erfbaar, erflik.
heredit'ament, erfgoed.
hered'itary, erflik, oorerflik; oorgeërf, erf=; ~ **creed,** oorgeërfde geloof, erfgeloof; ~ **debt,** erfskuld; ~ **disease,** erfsiekte; ~ **enemy,** erfvyand; ~ **farm,** erfplaas; ~ **fief,** erfleen; ~ **portion,** erfdeel; ~ **prince,**

heredity — hibernation

erfprins; ~ **property**, stamgoed; ~ **right**, erfreg; ~ **sin**, erfsonde; ~ **tenure**, erfpag.
hered'ity, oorerwing; erflikheid, oorerflikheid; oorerwingsleer; *a victim of* ~, erflik belas wees; 'n slagoffer van erflikheid wees.
He'reford, Hereford(bees).
here: ~ **from'**, hiervandaan; ~ **in'**, hierin, hierby; ~ **inaf'ter**, hierna, verder; ~ **inbefore'**, hiertevore; ~ **of**, hiervan; ~ **on'**, hierop.
heres'iarch, aartsketter, ketterhoof.
he'resy, kettery, dwaalleer; *CHARGE with* ~, van kettery beskuldig; ~-**hunting**, ketterjag.
he'retic, ketter.
heret'ical, ketters, ketter=.
here: ~ **to'**, tot hier; hiertoe; hierby; ~ **tofore'**, hierintevore; tevore, eertyds; ~ **un'der**, hieronder; hierna; ~ **unto'**, hieraan; ~ **upon'**, hierop; hierna; ~ **with'**, hiermee; hierby, by dese; mits dese.
he'ritable, erfbaar, erflik, erfgeregtig.
he'ritage, he'ritance, erfenis, erfdeel, erfgoed.
he'ritor, erfgenaam.
he'ritrix, (her itrices), erfgename.
hermaph'rodite, (n) trassie, afrodiet, hermafrodiet; (a) tweeslagtig, hermafrodities, trassie=; dubbelslagtig.
hemaphrodit'ic, hermafrodities, tweeslagtig.
hermaph'roditism, tweeslagtigheid, dubbelslagtigheid, hermafroditisme.
hermeneut'ic, uitlegkundig, verklarend, hermeneuties; ~ s, Skrifverklaring, uitlegkunde, hermeneutiek.
hermet'ic, hermeties, lugdig, · **ally**, hermeties, lugdig; ~ *ally sealed*, hermeties gesluit.
herm'it, kluisenaar, hermiet; ~ **age**, kluis; kluisenaarshut; hermityk(wyn); ~ **crab**, kluisenaarkrap.
hern, *kyk* **heron**.
hern'ia, (-s, -e), breuk; hernia; *abdominal* ~, buikbreuk; ~ **l**, breuk=.
herniu'tomy, breukoperasie.
hern'(shaw), *kyk* **heron**.
her'o, (-es), held; halfgod; hoofpersoon; *the* ~ *of the DAY*, die held v.d. dag; *Heroes' DAY*, Heldedag (Oct. 10th, now called Kruger Day); ~ *'s WELCOME*, heldeontvangs.
Her'od, Herodes; *to out-* ~ ~, Herodes oortref.
Herod'ian, (n) Herodiaan; (a) Herodiaans.
hero'ic, heldhaftig, dapper, helde=; heroïes; hoogdrawend; ~ **age**, heldetyd; ~ **deed**, heldedaad; ~ **poem**, heldedig; ~ **verse**, heksameters (by Franse) vyfvoetige jambes; aleksandryne (in die Klassieke); ~ **s**, hoogdrawende taal; grootdoenery.
hero'ify, (..**fied**), tot 'n held maak.
he'roin, heroïen, heroïne.
he'roine, heldin.
he'roism, heldhaftigheid, heldemoed, heroïsme.
he'roize, tot held verhef; die held speel.
he'ron, reier; ~ **y**, reiernes.
her'o-worship, heldeverering.
herp'es, herpes, blasiesuitslag, koorsblare; omloop; ~ **zoster**, gordelroos, herpes zoster.
herpetol'ogist, herpetoloog.
herpetol'ogy, herpetologie.
her'ring, haring; *PICKLED* ~, pekelharing; *draw a RED* ~ *across the trail*, v.d. spoor bring; 'n haas opjaag; *SALT* ~, southaring; ~ **barrel**, haringvaatjie.
her'ring-bone, haringgraat; ~ **bandage**, visgraatverband (med.); ~ **bond**, visgraatverband (bouk.); ~ **gear**, hoektandrat; ~ **pattern**, visgraatpatroon; ~ **stitch**, visgraatsteek, heen-en-weersteek; ~ **tooth**, hoektand, pyltand.
her'ring: ~ **buss**, haringbuis; ~-**curer**, haringroker; ~ **fisher**, haringvanger; ~ **fishery**, haringvangs, haringvissery; ~ **fishing**, haringvangs; ~ **fleet**, haringvloot; ~ **net**, haringnet; ~-**packer**, haringpakker; ~-**pond**, (skerts.), die groot visdam; die Atlantiese Oseaan; ~ **season**, haringtyd; ~ **smack**, haringbootjie.
Herrn'huter, Hernhutter; ~ **knife**, herneutermes.
hers, hare; *that is* ~, dis hare, dis haar deel.
herse, drooggraam (vir velle); valpoort.
herself', haarself; syself; *BY* ~, sy alleen; *she is NOT*

~, sy voel nie lekker nie, sy is olik; *she SAW it* ~, sy het dit self gesien.
hertz, hertz (eenheid).
Hert'zogism, Hertzogisme.
hes'itancy, aarseling, weifeling, besluiteloosheid.
hesi'tant, aarselend, huiwerig; besluiteloos; *be* ~ *about*, huiwer om.
hes'itate, aarsel, weifel, draai, vassteek; *he who* ~ *s is lost*, wie aarsel, is verlore.
hes'itating, aarselend, weifelagtig, weifelend; ~ **ly**, skoorvoetend, ongraag.
hesita'tion, aarseling, weifeling, twyfeling, gedraai; hapering.
hes'itative, aarselend, weifelend.
Hesper'ian, Westelik, Westers, Hesperies.
Hes'perus, Hesperus, aandster.
hesperi'dium, hesperidium, oranjevrug.
He'ssian¹, (n) Hes; (a) Hessies.
he'ssian², growwe sakgoed; goiing; ~ **bag**, goiingsak.
hest, (arch.), bevel.
hetae'ra, hetere.
heteroblas'tic, heteroblasties.
het'eroclite, onreëlmatig verbuig.
het'erodox, onregsinnig, heterodoks; ~ **y**, onregsinnigheid, heterodoksie.
het'erodyne, (n) swewingstoestel, heterodine; (a) heterodien.
heterog'amous, heterogaam.
heterogene'ity, ongelyksoortigheid, vreemdsoortigheid; meerslagtigheid.
heterogen'eous, ongelyksoortig, heterogeen, vreemdsoortig; meerslagtig.
heterogen'esis, heterogenese.
heterogenet'ic, heterogeneties.
het'erogonism, heterogonie.
het'erogonous, heterogoon.
heteromorph'ic, heteromorf.
heteromorph'ism, heteromorfie.
heteron'omous, heteronoom.
het'eronym, heteroniem.
heteron'ymous, heteroniem.
heteron'omy, heteronomie.
heteropath'ic, heteropaties.
hetero'pathy, heteropatie.
heterosex'ual, teengeslagtelik; heteroseksueel.
heterosexual'ity, teengeslagtelike liefde; heteroseksualiteit.
het'erostyled, ongelykstylig.
heterostyl'ism, ongelykstyligheid.
heterotact'ic, heterotakties.
heterotax'is, heterotaksis.
heterozyg'ote, heterosigoot.
heterozyg'ous, heterosigoot.
het'man, hetman (aanvoerder van Kosakke).
heuris'tic, heuristies, ontdekkend.
hew, (-ed, -n or **-ed)**, kap, neervel; ~ *DOWN*, afkap; ~ *OFF*, afkap; ~ *OUT*, uitkap; ~ *to PIECES*, in stukke kap; ~ *one's WAY*, jou pad oopkap.
hew'er, kapper; ~ *s of wood and drawers of water*, houtkappers (houthakkers) en waterdraers (waterputters).
hex'ad, sestal.
hex'agon, seshoek, heksagoon; ~ **iron**, seskantyster; ~ **nut**, seskantmoer.
hexa'gonal, seshoekig, heksagonaal; ~ **connection**, seskantkoppeling.
hexahed'ral, sesvlakkig.
hexahed'ron, sesvlak, heksaëder.
hexam'eter, sesvoetige vers, heksameter.
hexamet'ric, sesvoetig, heksametries.
hex'apid, (n) sespoot; (a) sespotig.
Hex'ateuch, Heksateug.
hey! haai! hê?
hey'-day, vrolikheid; lentetyd; toppunt, glansperiode, fleur.
hi! haai!
hiat'us, (-s), gaping, opening, hiaat, leemte; breuk.
hibern'al, winter=.
hib'ernant, winterslaper.
hib'ernate, oorwinter, hiberneer; 'n winterslaap doen; doods bly, luilak.
hiberna'tion, oorwintering; winterslaap.

Hibern'ia, Hibernië, Ierland; ~ **n,** (n) Hibernïer, Ier; (a) Hibernies.
Hibern'icism, Ierse idioom, Hibernisme.
hibis'cus, vuurblom, heemswortel, hibiskus.
hic'cough, hicc'up, (n) hik; (v) hik.
hick'ory, Amerikaanse okkerneutboom; neuthout.
hidal'go, (-s), hidalgo, Spaanse edelman.
hidd'en, verborge, verhole, verskole, weggesteek; ~ *treasure,* verborge skat.
hide¹, (n) huid, vel; *DRESS a* ~, 'n vel looi; *SAVE one's* ~, jou lewe (bas) red; ~ *s and SKINS,* huide en velle.
hide², (n) skuilplek, wegkruipplek; (v) wegsteek, verberg; wegmoffel, wegstop; wegkruip, skuilgaan, jou skuil hou; verberg; ~ *AWAY,* wegkruip; ~ *FROM,* wegkruip vir; ~ *one's HEAD,* jou kop laat hang; jou doodskaam; ~ **-and-seek,** wegkruipertjie; ~ **bound,** styf in die vel, kleingeestig; stroef, bekrompe.
hid'eous, afskuwelik, afsigtelik; ~**ness,** afskuwelikheid, afsigtelikheid.
hide'-out, wegkruipplek, skuilplek.
hid'ing¹, pak, loesing, streepsuiker; *GET a* ~, 'n pak slae kry; *GIVE someone a* ~, iem. op sy baadjie gee; *the* ~ *of one's LIFE,* 'n afgedankste loesing; *there is a* ~ *in STORE for you,* jy kan maar jou lyf vetsmeer.
hid'ing², skuiling, wegkruip; *be in* ~, wegkruip.
hid'ing-place, skuilplek, skuiling, skuilhoek, wegkruipplek.
hidros'is, sweetafskeiding, hidrose.
hidrot'ic, (n) sweetmiddel, hidrotikum; (a) sweetdrywend.
hie, jou haas, rep.
hi'erarch, kerkvoog; aartsbiskop; hiërarg; ~ **'ic(al),** hiërargies; ~**y,** kerkregering; hiërargie.
hierat'ic, priesterlik; heilig, gewyd, hiëraties.
hieroc'racy, priesterregering, hiërargie.
hi'eroglyph, beeldskrif, hiëroglief; ~ **'ic,** hiëroglifies; ~**ics,** hiërogliewe.
hi'erograph, heilige inskripsie, hiërograaf.
hierol'atry, heiligeverering, heiligeaanbidding.
hi'erophant, opperpriester, hiërofant; ~ **'ic,** opperpriesterlik, hiërofanties.
hi'-fi, *kyk* **high-fidelity.**
hig'gle, afding, knibbel.
hig'gledy-pig'gledy, deurmekaar, onderstebo.
high, (n) die hoë; hoogtepunt, maksimum; *FROM on* ~, van bo; uit die hemel; *the* ~ *and the LOW,* hoog en laag; ryk en arm; *the MOST H* ~, die Allerhoogste; *ON* ~, in die hoë; in die hemel; (a, adv) hoog, verhewe; ryk, hooglopend; pikant, gekrui (grap); met 'n krakie, gekraak; adellik; sterk (vleis); kragtig, hewig; duur; vol; trots; hoogharig; ultra; opgewek, vrolik; erg; *BE* ~, die skoot hoog deur hê; *be* ~ *and DRY,* hoog en droog sit; *be in* ~ *FAVOUR,* hoog in die guns staan; *FEELING(S) ran* ~, gevoelens het hoog geloop; daar het groot bitterheid geheers; ~ *FINANCE,* hoë finansiewese; *don't FLY too* ~, moenie te hoog vlieg nie; *with a* ~ *HAND,* uit die hoogte; aanmatigend; *have* ~ *HOPES,* groot verwagtings koester; *on the* ~ *HORSE,* op sy perdjie; *LEAD a* ~ *life,* in hoë kringe beweeg; *be* ~ *on the LIST,* voorrang geniet; ~ *and LOW,* alle stande; oraal; ~ *and MIGHTY,* hoogharig, aanstellerig; *at* ~ *NOON,* reg op die middag; *PLAY* ~, hoog dobbel; *in* ~ *PLACES,* by hooggeplaastes; *on the* ~ *SEAS,* in volle see; *a* ~ *SEA,* 'n stormagtige see; 'n volle see; *SEEK* ~ *and low,* oral soek; *in* ~ *SPIRITS,* uitgelate, opgetoë, vrolik; *it is* ~ *TIME,* dis hoog tyd; *a* ~ *TIME,* 'n tyd van jolyt; 'n vrolike tyd; ~ *WORDS,* kwaai woorde; ~ **altar,** hoogaltaar; ~**-angle(d),** steilhoekig; ~**-backed,** hoërug=, met 'n hoë rug; ~ **ball,** whiskyen-sodadrank; ~**-blower,** blaserige perd; ~ **boot,** kapstewel; ~ **boy,** hoë laaikas; ~ **born,** hooggebore, van hoë afkoms; welgebore; ~ **brow,** geleerde, intellektueel; pedant; ~ **chair,** hoë stoel; ~ **change,** hoofomroep, môrebeurs; **H** ~ **Church,** Engelse (Hoog-) Kerk; ~**-class,** vernaam, eerste kwaliteit; ~ **colour,** blosende gelaatskleur; ~ **command,** opperbevel.

High: ~ **Commissioner,** hoë kommissaris; ~ **Court,** Hooggeregshof.
high: ~ **cost,** hoë koste; ~ **day,** hoogdag; ~**-density building (housing),** hoëdigtheidsbehuising, hoëdigtheidsbou; ~**er,** hoër, ~*er CRITICISM,* Bybelkritiek; *the* ~ *er up, the greater the FALL,* hoe hoër gevlieg, hoe harder geval; ~ **explosive,** brisant; ~**-explosive bomb,** brisantbom; ~**-falutin(g),** hoogdrawend, bombasties; ~ **fi(delity),** klanktrou, hoëtrou; louterklank; ~ **flown,** hoogdrawend, bombasties; ~**-flyer,** hoogvlieër; hardloper; ~**-flying,** hoogvlieënd; ambisieus; ~ **frequency,** hoë frekwensie; ~**-frequency modulation,** hoëfrekwensiemodulasie; ~**-gloss paint,** hoëglansverf; ~**-grade,** van hoë gehalte, eerstegraads; ~**-grade ore,** ryk erts; ~**-handed,** uit die hoogte; eiemagtig; ~**-handedly:** *do something* ~*-handedly,* iets uit die hoogte doen; ~**-handedness,** eiegeregtigheid; ~**-heeled,** hoëhak=; ~ **jump,** hoogspring; ~ **land(s),** hoogland, bergagtige land; **H** ~ **lander,** Hooglander, Bergskot; ~**-level,** hoogstaande; ~ **life,** die groot wêreld, die hoë (deftige) kringe; ~ **light,** (n) glanspunt, hoogtepunt; (v) sterk laat uitkom, na vore bring; ~ **lighter,** ~**-light pen,** glanspen, ligpen, markeerpen; ~ **limit,** bogrens; ~ **living,** weelderige lewe.
high'ly, hoogs, baie hoog; in hoë mate, uiters, seer, ten seerste; ~ *AMUSING,* hoogs vermaaklik; *COMMEND* ~, sterk aanbeveel; ~ *DESCENDED,* van hoë afkoms; ~ *PLEASED,* hoog in jou skik; ~ *SEASONED,* sterk gekruie; *SPEAK* ~ *of,* met baie lof praat oor; ~ *STRUNG,* oorgevoelig; hooggespanne.
high: ~ **mass,** hoogmis; ~ **meat,** sterk (adellike) vleis; ~**-minded,** edel, groothartig, grootmoedig, hoogstaande, idealisties; ~ **mindedness,** groothartigheid, edelmoedigheid; ~ **ness,** hoogheid (titel); hoogte; ~ **noon,** hoogmiddag; ~**-octane fuel,** hoëoktaanbrandstof; ~**-pitched,** hooggestem; verhewe; spits, steil (dak); ~**-placed,** hooggeplaas; ~**-powered,** kragtig.
high' pressure, hoë druk, hoogdruk; ~ **area,** hoog= (drukgebied); ~ **lubrication,** hoogdruksmering; ~ **salesmanship,** doeltreffende (kragtige) verkoopkuns.
high: ~**-priced,** duur, kosbaar; ~ **priest,** hoëpriester, owerpriester; ~**-priestly,** hoëpriesterlik; ~**-principled,** met hoë beginsels; ~**-ranking,** hooggeplaas; ~ **relief,** hoogreliëf; ~**-rise,** hoog; ~**-rise building,** toringgebou, hoogstyggebou; ~ **road,** grootpad, transportpad; ~ **school,** hoërskool, hoër skool; ~ **season,** volle seisoen; ~**-souled,** edeldenkend; ~**-sounding,** skelklinkend; verwaand.
high' speed, volle vaart; hoë spoed; ~ **aircraft,** snelvliegtuig; ~ **bomber,** snelbomwerper; ~ **steel,** snelstaal, sneldraaistaal; ~ **traffic,** snelverkeer.
high: ~**-spirited,** vol moed; fier, knap; ~**-stepper,** hoogdrawwer (perd); windmaker; hoogskopper (mens); ~**-stepping,** lewendig; spoggerig, windmakerig; hoogskoppend; ~**-strung,** hooggespanne, fynbesnaar, oorgevoelig.
hight, genoem(de), genaamd.
high tea, teemaaltyd.
high-tension, hoogspanning; ~ **cable,** hoogspanningskabel; ~ **current,** sterkstroom; ~ **supply unit,** anodespanningsapparaat; ~ **wire,** hoogspanningsdraad.
high: ~ **tide,** hoogwater; ~ **treason,** hoogverraad; majesteitskennis; **H** ~ **veld,** Hoëveld; ~ **voltage,** hoë spanning; ~**-voltage (current),** sterkstroom; ~ **water,** hoogwater, springvloed; ~**-water mark,** hoogpeil, hoogwatermerk; hoogtepunt.
high'way, grootpad, transportpad; seeweg; **dual** ~, dubbelpad; ~ **code,** padkode, ~ **robbery,** struikrowery; ~ **man,** struikrower.
high: ~**-wire artist,** koorddanser; ~ **words,** kwaai woorde, rusie.
hi'jack, kaap; ~**ing,** kaping, lugrowery; ~**er,** kaper.
hike, (n) plesierstap, staptoer; prysverhoging, prysstyging; (v) loop, voetslaan, stap; ~ **r,** plesierstapper, voetslaner, wandelaar, ryloper.

hik'ing, wandelsport, stap, voetslaan; ~-**tour**, staptoer, wandeltog.
hilar'ious, vrolik, opgeruimd; ~**ness**, vrolikheid, uitgelatenheid, uitbundigheid.
hilar'ity, opgeruimdheid, vrolikheid, laglus, hilariteit.
hill, (n) heuwel, bult, hoogte, koppie; hoop; *up ~ and down dale,* berg op en berg af; bult op en bult af; oor heg en steg; (v) ophoop; operd (ertappels); ~-**billy**, (..**lies**), agtervelder, bergbewoner; ~-**climbing test**, klimtoets; ~-**holder**, heuwelrem, steilrem; ~ **man**, bergbewoner.
hill'ock, koppie, bultjie.
hill: ~ **side**, hang, helling, skuinste; ~ **top**, heuweltop.
hill'y, heuwelagtig, bergagtig, bulterig.
hilt, (n) handvatsel, greep, hef; geves; *to the ~*, heeltemal, volkome, geheel en al, onweerspreeklik, afdoende; (v) van 'n hef voorsien.
hil'um, (..**la**), kiemvlekkie, oog (van boontjie); nael.
him, hom.
Himalay'as: *the ~*, die Himalaja.
himself', hom, homself, sig(self); *ALL by ~,* (hy, heeltemal) alleen; *he was NOT ~*, hy was nie heeltemal reg nie; hy was nie op sy stukke nie.
hind¹, (n) hinde, ooi.
hind², (n) lomperd; boerekneg; (a) agter=.
hind'er¹, (v) (ver)hinder, belet, skort, bemoeilik, pla, lastig val.
hin'der², (a) agterste, agter=.
Hin'di, Hindi.
hind: ~ **leg**, agterpoot, agterbeen; *talk the ~ leg off a donkey*, die ore van iem. se kop praat.
hind'most, agterste, verste; *the ~ dog may catch the hare*, agteros kom ook in die kraal.
Hin'doo, **Hindoosta'nee** *kyk* **Hindu, Hindustani.**
hind: ~ **part**, agterdeel; ~ **quarter**, agterkwart, agterdeel; (pl) agterste, agterdele.
hin'drance, hindernis, belemmering; *more of a ~ than a help,* 'n vyfde wiel aan die wa.
hind'sight, visier, wysheid agterna, agternaslimheid; trukennis.
Hin'du, (n) Hindoe; (a) Hindoes, Hindoe=.
Hin'duism, Hindoeïsme.
Hindustan', Hindoestan; ~**i**, (n) Hindoestaner; Hindoestani (taal); (a) Hindoestans.
hind wheel, agterwiel.
hinge, (n) skarnier; geleding; hingsel; spil; plakstrokie (filatelie); (v) met skarniere verbind; draai; afhang; buig; *the DECISION ~s on,* die beslissing draai om; ~*d SWITCH*, skarnierwissel; ~ **bolt**, skarnierbout; ~ **check**, skarnierkeep, ~ **joint**, skarnierlas; ~ **pin**, skarnierpen; ~ **screw**, skarnierskroef; ~ **valve**, skarnierklep.
hinn'y, (**hinnies**), (n) muiltjie, botterkop; (v) (**hinnied**, **hinnied**), runnik.
hint, (n) wenk; toespeling; sinspeling; sweem, aanduiding; skimp; *GIVE a ~,* 'n wenk gee; *TAKE the ~,* die wenk verstaan (aanvaar); (v) 'n wenk gee, aan die hand doen; aandui; te kenne gee; opper; ~ *at*, aanroer, aanstip; sinspeel op
hin'terland, agterland, binneland.
hip¹, (n) roosknop, roossaad.
hip², (n) swaarmoedigheid, hipokonders; (v) neerslagtig maak, druk.
hip³, (n) heup; hoekbalk; hoekspar; hoeknok, wolfhoek (van dak); hoekvlak (van trap); *HAVE someone on the ~,* iem. in jou mag hê; *SMITE ~ and thigh,* heup en skenkel slaan; sonder genade uitdelg; verslaan; ~-**bath**, sitbad; ~-**bone**, heupbeen; ~-**cavity**, heuppotjie, heupkom; ~-**disease**, heupsiekte; ~-**gout**, heupjig; ~-**joint**, heupgewrig; ~ **measurement**, heupmaat.
hipped¹, neerslagtig.
hipped², met heupe; ~ **end**, wolwe-ent, wolfent; ~ **roof**, skilddak; wolwedak
hipp'o, (-**s**), abbr. of **hippopotamus**.
hippocam'pus, (..**pi**), seeperdjie.
hip'-pocket, heupsak.
hipp'ocras, hippokras, kruiewyn, bruidstrane.
Hipp'ocrates, Hippokrates.
Hippocrat'ic, Hippokraties.
Hipp'ocrene, Hippokreen, hingstebron.

hipp'odrome, renbaan; sirkus.
hipp'ogriff, hipp'ogryph, gevleuelde perd, hippogrief.
hippopot'amus, (-**es**, ..**mi**), seekoei.
hip: ~-**purlin**, hoeknokkaplat; ~-**rafter**, hoekspar, hoekbeen; ~-**ridge**, (wolwe)hoeknok; ~-**roll**, hoeknokrol; ~ **roof**, skilddak, wolwedak, wolweentdak; ~-**shot**, lendelam.
hir'cine, bokagtig, bok=.
hire, (n) huur; loon, huurgeld; *for ~*, te huur; (v) huur; verhuur; ~ *out*, verhuur; ~ **d**, gehuur; ~ **ling**, huurling; huursoldaat; ~-**purchase**, koop op afbetaling, huurkoop; ~-**purchase system**, huurkoopstelsel; ~ **r**, huurder.
hirs'ute, ruig, harig.
hirun'dine, swa(w)elagtig.
his, sy, syne; *this is ~,* dit is syne.
Hispan'icism, Hispanisme, Spaanse idioom.
Hispan'o-, Spaans=.
his'pid, ruig, harig.
hiss, (n) (-**es**), gesis, geblaas; gejou; sisklank; gefluit; (v) sis; blaas; uitfluit; ~ *AT*, uitjou; ~ *OFF the stage*, van die verhoog af jou; wegfluit; ~ **er**, fluisteraar; sisser; ~ **ing**, (n) gesis; gefluit; geblaas; (a) sissend, uitfluitend.
hist! sjuut! sa!
histogen'esis, histogenese, ontstaan van weefsels.
histogenet'ic, histogeneties.
histog'eny, weefselvorming.
histolog'ic, histologies.
histol'ogist, histoloog.
histol'ogy, histologie, weefselleer.
histopathol'ogy, histopatologie.
histor'ian, geskiedskrywer, geskiedkundige, historikus.
histor'iated, versier, verlug.
histor'ic(al), geskiedkundig, histories; beroemd; ~ **atlas**, geskiedenisatlas, geskiedkundige atlas; ~ **novel**, historiese roman.
histori'city, historiese egtheid, historisiteit.
historiog'rapher, geskiedskrywer, historiograaf.
historiog'raphy, geskiedskrywing, historiografie.
historiol'ogy, geskiedkunde, historiologie.
his'tory, (..**ries**), geskiedenis; geskiedverhaal; verhaal, historie; *that is ANCIENT ~,* dit is ou nuus; *ANCIENT, medieval, modern ~,* ou, Middeleeuse, moderne geskiedenis; *MAKE ~,* geskiedenis maak; *NATURAL ~,* natuurkennis; ~ *REPEATS itself,* die geskiedenis herhaal hom; *a WOMAN with a ~,* 'n vrou met 'n verlede.
his'trion, toneelspeler; ~'**ic**, toneel=, toneelagtig; teatraal; huigelagtig; ~'**ics**, komedie; toneelkuns; aanstellery, oordrewenheid; ~ **ism**, toneelkuns; huigelary.
hit, (n) hou, slag; steek, raps; (vol)treffer; raakskoot; toeval; gelukkige set; suksesstuk, *a DIRECT ~,* 'n voltreffer; *IT is a ~,* dis 'n treffer; *MAKE a ~,* raak; inslaan; 'n slag slaan (sake); furore maak; *MAKE a ~ with someone,* indruk op iem. maak; groot byval vind by iem.; *the ~ of the SEASON,* die suksesstuk v.d. seisoen; *more by ~ than by WIT,* meer geluk as wysheid; (v) (**hit**), slaan, 'n hou gee, moker; raps; tref, raak (met skryfwerk); aanslaan; vind, teenkom; ~ *AT*, slaan na; ~ *BACK,* terugslaan; ~ *below the BELT,* onder die gordel slaan; oneerlik optree; ~ *out at the CRITICS,* die kritici aanval; ~ *someone when he is DOWN,* iem. 'n steek onder water gee; *be HARD ~,* swaar getref wees; ~ *IT,* raak, raak skiet; ~ *the MARK,* raak skiet; die doel bereik; ~ *and MISS,* lukraak; ~ *the NAIL on the head,* die spyker op die kop slaan; ~ *it OFF with each other,* met mekaar klaarkom; *be unable to ~ it OFF with someone,* nie met iem. kan klaarkom nie; nie met iem. kan stryk nie; nie saam om een vuur sit nie; nie (brand)hout van dieselfde tak breek nie; ~ *it OFF,* haarfyn nadoen; goed pas by; ~ *ON,* kry; uitdink; ~ *OUT,* uitval (skermkuns); met die vuis slaan; ~ *and RUN,* tref en trap, raak en ry; ~ *the TARGET,* die teiken (kol) raak skiet; ~ *UP,* lopies maak; ~ *UPON,* toevallig te binne skiet, uitdink; aantref, vind; ~ **and run accident**, tref-en trapongeluk, raak-en-ryongeluk; ~ **and run driver**, tref-en-trapbestuurder.

hitch, (n) (-es), lissie, haak; hink; haakplek, kinkel, hapering; ruk, stoot; belemmering, beletsel; *GO without a* ~, sonder haakplek vorder; *PASS off without a* ~, vlot van stapel loop; *THERE'S a* ~, daar's 'n haakplek; daar's 'n kinkel in die kabel; (v) haak; aanhaak; ruk; strompel; duimry; ~ *ON to*, vashaak aan, vasmaak; ~ *your wagon to a STAR*, hoog mik; ~ *UP*, opruk; vasmaak, vaswoel; ~-**hike**, ryloop, bedelry, duimry, duimgooi, soebatry; ~-**hiker**, duimryer, duimgooier, ryloper; ~-**hiking**, duimryery, rylopery; ~**ing-post**, vashaakpaal; koppelpaal.
hith'er, hiernatoe, hierheen; ~ *and thither*, heen en weer; kruis en dwars; ~ *to*, tot nog toe, tot op die oomblik; ~**ward**, hierheen, herwaarts.
Hit'lerism, Hitlerisme.
hitt'er, slaner; *a hard* ~, iem. wat hard (ver)slaan, verslaner, mokeraar.
hit'-parade, trefferparade.
hitt'ing, slanery; ~ *power*, slaankrag.
hive, (n) byekorf, heuningnes; byeswerm; (v) in 'n korf sit; 'n skuilplek verleen; opsamel, versamel; die neste opsoek; saamwoon, -huis; ~ *off*, 'n eie koers inslaan; ~ **r**, byeboer.
hives, huiduitslag.
ho! ho? o!
hoar, (n) ryp; grysheid; (a) wit, grys.
hoard, (n) (verborge) stapel, hoop, voorraad; omheining; spaargeld, skat; (v) opstapel; ophoop, opgaar, oppot, spaar; ~**er**, opgaarder, oppotter, versamelaar.
hoard'ing[1], opgaring, opsparing, oppotting.
hoard'ing[2], houtskutting, advertensiebord; ~ **display**, skuttingsreklame.
hoar' frost, ryp.
hoar'iness, grysheid, witheid.
hoarse, hees, skor; rou; ~**n**, hees word (maak); ~**ness**, heesheid, skorheid.
hoar'y, grys.
hoax, (n) grap, gekskeerdery, kullery, foppery; (v) kul, korswel, fop, 'n poets bak, om die bos lei; ~**er**, gekskeerder, fopper, kuller; ~**ing**, kullery, foppery.
hob, wurmfrees; pen (by spele); dikkopspyker.
hob'ble, (n) strompeling; hondedraffie; spanriem; blok; kluister; (v) mank loop, strompel, hink, hobbel; span (perde); kluister; in verleentheid bring.
hob'bledehoy, penkop; slungel, lummel; ~**ish**, penkopagtig.
hob'bler, mank mens, manke, strompelaar.
hob'ble skirt, strompelrok, hobbelrok.
hobb'y[1], **(hobbies)**, (boom)valk.
hobb'y[2], **(hobbies)**, stokperdjie, liefhebbery, tydverdryf; hobbelperd, skommelperd; ~-**horse**, hobbelperd; liefhebbery, stokperdjie; *ride one's* ~-*horse*, op jou stokperdjie ry.
hob'goblin, kaboutermannetjie; spook, paaiboelie.
hob'nail, skoenspyker, dikkopspyker; lomperd; ~**ed**, met dikkopspykers.
hob'-nob, **(-bed)**, saamdrink; vertroulik omgaan, saamboer; ~ *with*, omgaan met, maats wees met; gemeenskap hou met.
hob'o, **(-s)**, swerwer, landloper, boemelaar, rondloper.
hob'oism, rondlopery, boemelary.
Hob'son's choice: *it is* ~, daar is geen keuse nie.
hock[1], (n) Hochheimerwyn (droë wit wyn).
hock[2], (n) hakskeensening, hak(gewrig); sprongewrig; varkskenkel; (v) hakskeensenings afsny, verlam.
hock'ey, hokkie (spel).
hoc'us, **(-sed)**, gif ingooi, bedwelm; fop, kul, beetneem.
hoc'us-poc'us, (n) hokus-pokus, goëlery, kullery; (v) **(-sed)**, goël, kul, bedrieg; bedwelm.
hod, kleitrog, messelaarsbak.
hodge'podge, mengelmoes, hutspot, een-pot-in-die-ander, poespas, stamppot.
hodiern'al, huidig, hedendaags.
hod'man, handlanger; penlekker, pennelekker.
hod'ograph, hodograaf.
hodom'eter, afstandmeter, hodometer.

hoe, (n) skoffel(pik); (v) skoffel; grond losmaak.
hog, (n) vark, swyn; burgvark; padbuffel, motorbuffel; smeerlap; *DRIVE one's* ~**s** *to market*, balke saag; *what can one expect from a* ~ *but a GRUNT?* mens kan van 'n esel altyd 'n skop verwag; *rather my* ~ *HOME dirty than hog at all*, liewer vel en been as vel alleen; *to have brought one's* ~**s** *to a fine MARKET*, met skade en skande van iets afkom; *where the* ~**s** *are many the WASH is poor*, baie varke maak die spoeling dun; *go the WHOLE* ~, van A tot Z doen; geen halwe maatreël tref nie; (v) **(-ged)**, (maanhare) kort knip; kromrug maak (perd); jou toe-eien; ~**back**, varkrug; skerp bergrug; middelmannetjie (pad), maanhaar(paadjie); ~-**bristle**, varkhaar; ~ **casing**, varkderm(s).
hogg'et, tweetandskaap, jaaroud skaap, wissellam; (pl) lammerwol.
hogg'in, gesifte gruis.
hog'gish, varkagtig; beesagtig.
hog'manay, Oujaarsdag; geskenk, onthaal op Oujaarsdag.
hog: ~ **mane**, borselmaan, borselmaanhare; ~-**pen**, varkhok; ~ **('s)-back**, middelmannetjie (pad), maanhaar(paadjie); skerp bergrug; varkrug; ~ **'s bristle**, varkhaar.
hogs'head, okshoof.
hog: ~ **'s lard**, varkvet; ~ **'s meat**, swynekos; ~-**sty**, varkhok; ~-**tie**, (n) kniehalterknoop; maswerk (knoop), kniehalterslag; (v) kniehalterspan; ~-**wash**, varkkos, draf.
ho-ho', o-o, ho-ho.
ho'-hum, oninteressant, slaapwekkend.
hoi'polloi, gepeupel, plebs, hoipolloi.
hoist, (n) (die) ophys; ligter; hystoestel, hysbak, hyser; (v) hys, optrek (vlag); optel; ~ *with his own petard*, self in die put val wat jy vir 'n ander gegraaf het; in jou eie strik gevang word; ~**er**, hystoestel; ~**ing**, hysing; hyswerk; ~**ing chain**, hysketting; ~**ing drum**, hystrommel; ~**ing machine**, hysmasjien; ~ **rope**, hystou.
hoit'y-toit'y, (n) uitgelatenheid; (a) wild, uitgelate; opvlieënd; aanmatigend, verwaand, uit die hoogte; brommerig; (interj) allawêreld! stadig! kalm!
hok'ey-pok'ey, straatroomys; *kyk ook* **hocus-pocus**.
hok'um, bog twak.
hold, (n) vat, handvatsel; greep; houvas; invloed, mag; skuilplek; steun; ruim (skip); tronksel; gevangenis; *no* ~**s** *BARRED*, alles is toelaatbaar; *CATCH* ~ *of*, beetpak, beetgryp; *GET a* ~ *on somebody*, iem. in die hande kry; vat kry op iem.; *let GO one's* ~, loslaat; *HAVE no* ~ *on*, geen vat hê nie op; *KEEP* ~ *of*, vashou; *KEEP a* ~ *on oneself*, jou bedwing; *a* ~ *ON someone*, 'n houvas op iem.; (v) **(held)**, hou; besit; behou; huldig (beskouing); bevat, inhou; steun; boei (leser); inneem (plek); vier (dag); in besit hê, ophou, stilhou; deurgaan; volhou; aanhou (noot); teenhou; beklee (pos); verdedig (vesting); in besit bly van; daarop nahou; van mening wees; beskou; duur, geld; besig hou (aandag), vashou; bevrug word; geldig wees, van krag bly; ~ *something AGAINST someone*, iem. iets kwalik neem; ~ *ALOOF*, jou afsydig hou; ~ *BACK*, terughou, agterhou; ~ *to BAIL*, onder borgtog verbind; ~ *at BAY*, terughou; weerstand bied teen; ~ *one's BREATH*, die asem ophou; ~ *CHEAP*, geringag; ~ *in CONTEMPT*, minag; *the COURT held*, die hof het beslis; ~ *DEAR*, hoogskat, liefhê; ~ *them to a DRAW*, hulle gelykop laat speel; ~ *in ESTEEM*, hoogag; ~ *up as an EXAMPLE*, as voorbeeld voorhou; ~ *the FORT*, vasskop; in die bres staan; ~ *FORTH*, betoog; lostrek; *GET a* ~ *on somebody*, iem. beetkry; 'n vat op iem. kry; ~ *GOOD*, geldig wees; ~ *one's GROUND*, staande bly teen, vasstaan; ~ *one's HAND*, jou hand inhou; matig; *HAVE a* ~ *upon*, mag hê op; *HAVE a (strong)* ~ *on*, 'n houvas hê op; ~ *up one's HEAD*, die hoof hoog hou; moed hou; ~ *one's HEAD high*, jou trots hou; ~ *out HOPES*, hoop gee; ~ *your HORSES!* stadig oor die klippe! ~ *the LINE*, bly aan, wag 'n bietjie; ~ *your NOISE*, moenie so 'n lawaai maak nie; ~ *OFF*, op 'n afstand bly; wegbly; ~ *an OFFICE*, 'n

holding — home

pos beklee; ~ *ON*, aanhou; vashou, vasklou; ~ *an OPINION*, 'n mening daarop nahou; ~ *OUT*, uithou; volhou; *not to be able to* ~ *OUT much longer*, dit nie baie langer kan volhou nie; dit nie meer lank kan maak nie; ~ *OVER*, agterhou; uitstel; laat bly vir 'n volgende keer; oorhou; ~ *one's OWN*, jou man staan; jou handhaaf; *be unable to* ~ *one's OWN against someone*, nie teen iem. opgewasse wees nie; ~ *a good POSITION*, 'n goeie pos beklee; ~ *RESPONSIBLE for*, verantwoordelik hou vir; ~ *up to RIDICULE*, belaglik maak; ~ *in SUSPENSE*, in spanning hou; ~ *in SUSPENSION*, onopgelos hou; ~ *TO*, bly by; trou bly aan; ~ *TOGETHER*, bymekaarhou; byeenbly; ~ *one's TONGUE*, stilbly, jou mond hou; ~ *UP*, regop hou; steun; vertraag; aanhou; wegsteek; nie sak nie (melk); ~ *a VIEW*, van mening wees; ~ *WATER*, waterdig wees; steek hou; *if the WEATHER* ~ *s*, as die weer goed bly; ~ *WITH*, saamstem met; dit eens wees met; ~ **all**, stop-maar-in, reissak; ransel; ~ **back**, verhindering, beletsel, belemmering; ~ **er**, houer; besitter; bekleër (pos); huurder; draer; gryper; koker; glasie; ~ **fast**, houvas, greep; steun; kram; klemhaak.

hold'ing, eiendom, besit; hoewe; houvas; vat, (hand)greep; voorraad; ~ **action**, vaspenaksie; ~ **back**, terughouding; ~ **capacity**, laairuimte; ~ **company**, houermaatskappy; finansiële (beherende) maatskappy; ~ **ground**, ankergrond; ~ **pen**, vangkraal; vanghok.

hold'-up, aanhouding, roofaanval; belemmering, knelpunt; ophoping, knoop (in verkeer); vertraging; *this is a* ~ *!* jou geld of jou lewe!

hole, (n) gat, hok, pondok, opening; putjie (gholf); boring; moeilikheid; ertjie, et (tolspel); *BE in a* ~, in 'n penarie wees; in die knyp sit; *FULL of* ~ *s*, vol gate; gaatjiesrig; *it MAKES a* ~ *in one's pocket*, 'n mens se sak voel dit; *a square PEG in a round* ~, die verkeerde man op die verkeerde plek; *PICK* ~ *s in*, uitmekaar trek; stukkend kritiseer; *a POKY little* ~, 'n benoude plek; 'n gat van 'n plek; *PUT someone in a* ~, iem. in 'n moeilike posisie plaas; (v) 'n gat maak; uitgraaf; tonnel; inslaan (gholf); ingooi; in 'n gat jaag (diertjie); suikerriet plant; ~ *INTO*, deurbreek in; ~ *OUT*, 'n putjie voltooi (speel); ~ *OUT in four*, met vier houe in wees, putjie-vier maak; ~ *OUT in one*, putjie in een maak; ~ **putjie-en maak**; ~ **THROUGH**, deurbreek; ~ **-and-corner**, agterbaks, onderduims; ~ **-gauge**, kalibermaat; ~ **-in-one**, kolhou (gholf); ~ **-in-the-wall**; ~ *in-the-wall thieves*, diewe wat 'n gat in 'n muur maak; ~ **-proof**, stopvry, steekvas; ~ **-saw**, silindersaag; ~ **y**, vol gate, gaterig.

hol'iday, vakansie; *BE on* ~, met (op) vakansie wees; *GIVE a* ~, vakansie gee; vry gee; *GO on* ~, met vakansie gaan; *ON* ~, met vakansie; *TAKE a* ~, vakansie neem; ~ **course**, vakansiekursus; ~ **exodus**, vakansieuittog; ~ **maker**, plesiermaker; vakansieganger; ~ **mood**, vakansiestemming; ~ **reading**, vakansielektuur; ~ **resort**, vakansieoord, ~ **rush**, vakansiedrukte; ~ **season**, vakansietyd; ~ **spirits**, vakansiestemming; ~ **task**, vakansiewerk.

hol'iness, heiligheid.

hol'ing, eerste insnyding (myn); ~ *OUT*, 'n putjie speel (voltooi); ~ *THROUGH*, deurbraak.

hol'ism, holisme.

hol'ist, holis.

holis'tic, holisties.

holl'and[1], (gras)linne; *brown* ~, ongebleikte linne.

Holl'and[2], Holland; Nederland; ~ **er**, Hollander; ~ **s**, Hollandse jenewer, Schiedammer.

holl'andaise (sauce), vissous, hollandaise(sous).

Hol'lard street, aandelebeursstraat, geldmark.

hol'ler, (v), hard skree; (n) (harde) skreeu.

holl'o, haai! hallo!

holl'ow, (n) holte, holligheid; kom, dal, laagte; uitholling; *hold someone in the* ~ *of one's HAND*, iem. volkome in jou mag hê; in die holte van jou hand hê; *in the* ~ *of the NIGHT*, in die holste v.d. nag; (v) uithol, hol maak; hol word; (a) hol; leeg; uitgehol; ingesonke, ingevalle (wange); onopreg, vals; holklinkend; *beat* ~, uitstof; 'n groot pak gee; ~ -

back, holrug; ~ **brick**, holsteen; ~ **-cheeked**, met hol wange, holwang=; ~ **-chested**, met 'n ingevalle bors; ~ **chisel**, holbeitel; ~ **drill**, holboor; ~ **-eyed**, met hol oë, holoog=; ~ **ground**, hol geslyp; ~ **-hearted**, onopreg, ontrou, vals; ~ **ness**, holheid; voosheid; leegheid; onopregtheid, valsheid; holte; ~ **plane**, holskaaf; ~ **punch**, holpyp; ~ **rod**, naaf; ~ **screw**, busskroef; ~ **-sounding**, holklinkend; ~ **wall**, holmuur; ~ **ware**, vaatwerk, potte en panne; holware; ~ **wear**, holslytasie.

holl'y: huls; steekpalm; ~ **-fern**, steekpalm; ~ **hock**, stokroos; ~ **-oak**, steekpalm.

Hol'lywood, Hollywood, Amerikaanse filmbedryf; ~ **star**, Hollywoodster.

holm[1], riviereilandjie; moeras.

holm[2], steeneik.

hol'mium, holmium.

ho'locaust, brandoffer, groot offer; slagting.

Ho'locaust, slagting van die Jode deur die Nazi's, 1939-45.

hol'ocene, holoseen.

holocrys'talline, holokristallyn.

hol'ogram, hologram.

hol'ograph, holograaf, eiehandig geskrewe dokument; ~ **ic**, holografies, eiehandig geskrewe.

holohed'ral, volvlakkig, holoëdries.

holohed'ron, holoëder.

holohy'aline, holohialyn.

holophyt'ic, holofities.

holothur'ian, seekomkommer.

holozo'ic, holosoïes.

hol'ster, holster, pistoolsak.

holt, bos; bosbult; skuilplek, hol (van otter).

hol'us-bol'us, pens-en-pootjies, alles saam; meteens, in een slag.

Hol'y, Heilig; *the* ~ *CITY*, die Heilige Stad; *the* ~ *FATHER*, die Heilige Vader (die Pous); *the* ~ *GHOST (SPIRIT)*, die Heilige Gees; *the* ~ *GRAIL*, die Heilige Graal; *the* ~ *LAND*, die Heilige Land; *the* ~ *ONE, God*; ~ *ROMAN Empire*, Heilige Romeinse Ryk; ~ *SEE*, Heilige Stoel; ~ *WEEK*, die Paasweek; *the* ~ *WRIT*, die Heilige Skrif.

hol'y, (n) heilige; *the* ~ *OF holies*, die heilige der heilige; *a* ~ *OF holies*, 'n heiligdom; (a) heilig; gewyd; vroom; *SWEAR by all that is* ~, hoog en laag sweer.

hol'ystone, (n) sagte skuursteen; (v) met skuursteen bewerk.

hol'y: ~ **terror**: *a* ~ *terror*, 'n klein duiwel; ~ **war**, heilige oorlog; ~ **water**, wywater; ~ **year**, jubeljaar.

hom'age, eerbetoon, eerbetuiging, hulde, eerbewys; *do (pay, render)* ~ *to*, eer bewys aan.

Hom'burg (hat), homburg(hoed).

home, (n) tuiste, tuisplek; tehuis; woonplek; stigting; inrigting; gestig; verbeterhuis; geboortegrond; land, vaderland; verblyf, bof (balspel); *AT* ~, tuis; in die vaderland; *AT the* ~ *of*, by die huis van; *AT* ~ *in a subject*, goed tuis in 'n vak; *BE at* ~ *to*, iem. kan ontvang; *BRING something* ~ *to someone*, iem. iets aan die verstand bring; iem. iets laat verstaan; *BROKEN* ~, gebroke gesin; *CALL* ~, huis toe roep (bel); *a man's* ~ *is his CASTLE*, elkeen is baas op sy eie plaas (erf); *COME* ~, huis toe kom; *DRIVE* ~, huis toe ry; goed laat verstaan; *FEEL at* ~, tuis voel; *FOND of one's* ~, hokvas; *GO* ~, huis toe gaan; *a* ~ *from HOME*, 'n soete inval; *be at* ~ *IN*, tuis wees in; *LAST (LONG)* ~, die graf; *MAKE oneself at* ~, jou tuis maak; ~ *for old MEN*, oumannehuis; *I am NOT at* ~ *for him*, ek wil hom nie sien (ontvang) nie; *NOT at* ~, nie tuis nie; *there's no PLACE like* ~, oos wes, tuis bes; ~ *of REST*, rusoord; rushuis; *SAIL for* ~, die tuisreis aanvaar; *SEE* ~, tuis bring; *STAY at* ~, tuis bly; ~ *SWEET* ~, oos, wes, tuis bes; *TRAVEL* ~, terugreis; *nothing to WRITE* ~ *about*, baie oninteressant, vervelig; (v) huis toe gaan, terugkom (bv. 'n posduif); woon; huisves, 'n tehuis verskaf; aanpeil (vliegt.); (a) huis-, huislik; binnelands; op die man af, kragtig, raak; ~ **COMFORTS**, huislike geriewe; ~ *INDUSTRIES*, binnelandse nywerhede; huisvlyt; *a* ~ *QUESTION*, 'n vraag op die man

homeopathic 958 *honey*

af; *a ~ THRUST*, 'n raakskoot; *tell someone a ~ TRUTH*, iem. goed die waarheid vertel; iem. 'n kopskoot gee; (adv) huis toe; tuis, raak, op sy plek; deur en deur; *the ANCHOR comes ~*, die anker sleep; *BRING ~ to*, laat verstaan; aan die verstand bring; tuisbring; *bring a CHARGE ~ to someone*, iem. se skuld bewys; *STAY ~*, met Jan Tuisbly se karretjie ry; *the THRUST went ~*, die skoot was raak; **~ assistant**, tuishulp, huishulp; **~-baked**, tuisgebak, boere=; **~ base**, tuisbasis; **~-based**, tuis=; **~-bird**, huishen; *be a ~-bird*, hokvas wees; by die pappot bly; 'n huishen wees; **~-born**, aange= bore, inheems; in die moederland gebore; **~-bound**, op die tuisreis; **~-bred**, inheems; huislik, eenvoudig; onbeskaaf; onbedorwe; **~-brew**, tuis= gemaakte drank; **~-brewed beer**, tuisgemaakte bier; **~ builder**, huisbouer; **~ building**, huisbou, woningbou; **~ circle**, familiekring; **~ comforts**, huislike geriewe; **~-coming**, tuiskoms; **~ consump= tion**, tuisverbruik; binnelandse verbruik; vir binne= landse ore bedoel; **~ country**, tuisland, land van herkoms; **~ craft**, huisvlyt; **~ decoration**, huisver= siering; **~ defence**, tuisverdediging; landsverdedi= ging, binnelandse verdediging; **~-distilled**; **~-*dis= tilled brandy***, selfgestookte brandewyn; **~ district**, tuisdistrik; **~-doctor**, huisdokter; **~ economics**, huishoudkunde; **~-felt**, diepgevoel, innig; **~-freight**, retoervrag; **~-front**, tuisfront; **~-goer**, iem. wat huis toe gaan; raak slag, kopskoot; **~-grown**, inlands, in die eie land gekweek; **~ guard**, tuiswag; **~ journey**, tuisreis, terugreis; **~-keeping**, (n) huislikheid: (a) huislik; tuissittend; **~ land**, va= derland, moederland, tuisland; **~ land leader**, tuis= landleier; **~ language**, huistaal; **~ leave**, tuisverlof; **~ less**, (n) ontheemde; (a) sonder huis; sonder on= derdak; dakloos; **~ life**, huislike lewe; **~ liness**, huislikheid; alledaagsheid; eenvoudigheid, onaan= sienlikheid; lelikheid; **~-lover**, huishen; **~ ly**, ge= lykvloers, eenvoudig; huislik; boers; lelik; onaan= sienlik (vrou); **~-made**, eiegemaak, tuisgemaak, selfgemaak; binnelands; **~ match**, tuiswedstryd; **~ mission**, binnelandse sending; **~ movie**, huisrol= prent; selfvervaardigde rolprent; **~-nursing**, tuis= verpleging.

homeopath'ic, *kyk* **homoeophathic**.

home: **~ owner**, huiseienaar; **~ perm**, tuiskarteling; **~ port**, tuishawe.

Hom'er[1], Homerus, Homeros.
hom'er[2], posduif; boflopie.
home' remedy, boereraat.
Homer'ic, Homeries; **~ *LAUGHTER***, dawerende gelag; **~ *SIMILE***, Homeriese vergelyking.
home: **~ rule**, selfbestuur; **~ run**, boflopie; **~ shot**, raakskoot; **~ sick**: *be ~ sick*, heimwee hê; draad kou; **~ sickness**, heimwee; verlang(st)e; **~ side**, tuisspan; **~-site**, woonplek; **~ spun**, (n) tuisweef= stof; (a) selfgeweef, tuisgeweef; eenvoudig; **~ stead**, woonhuis, opstal; **~ straight**, **~ stretch**, pylvak; **~ thrust**, raakskoot (-hou); **~ team**, tuisspan; **~ town**, tuisdorp, tuisstad, woonplek; **~ thrust**, raak hou; **~ trade**, binnelandse handel; **~ truth**, harde waarheid; *tell someone some ~ truths*, iem. goed die waarheid vertel.
home'ward, huis toe, huiswaarts; **~ *BOUND***, op die tuisreis; **~ *JOURNEY***, tuisreis, terugrit; **~ *MARCH***, terugmars; **~ s**, huis toe.
home'work, huiswerk.
homicid'al, moorddadig, moordend, bloedig, moord=.
hom'icide, moord, manslag, doodslag; moordenaar, pleger van manslag; *culpable ~*, strafbare manslag.
homilet'ic, homileties, preek=; **~ s**, kanselwelspre= kendheid, homiletiek.
hom'ilist, homileet, kanselredenaar.
hom'ily, (homilies), preek, predikasie, kanselrede; ho= milie, boetpredikasie.
hom'ing, terugkeer, aanpeiling; **~ faculty**, **~ instinct**, aanpeilinstink, terugkominstink; **~ pigeon**, pos= duif; **~ station**, aanpeilstasie.
ho'minid, hominied, mensagtige wese.
ho'minoid, mensagtig.
hom'iny, mieliegruis; growwe mieliepap; **~ chop**, (fyn) mieliesemels; **~ grits**, mieliegruis, growwe mieliepap.
homocen'tric, met dieselfde sentrum, homosentries.
homoeopath'ic, hom(e)opaties.
homoeopath'y, hom(e)opatie.
homog'amous, gelykslagtig, homogaam.
homog'amy, gelykslagtigheid, homogamie.
homogene'ity, gelyksoortigheid, gelykslagtigheid, homogeniteit.
homogen'eous, gelyksoortig, gelykslagtig, homo= geen; egalig; eensoortig.
homogen'esis, homogenese.
homogenet'ic, homogeneties.
homogeniza'tion, homogenisering.
homog'enize, homogeniseer.
homo'geny, homogenie.
ho'mograft, homotransplantasie.
hom'ograph, homograaf.
homol'ogate, bekragtig, goedkeur.
homol'ogize, ooreenkomstig maak; ooreenkomstig wees; homologiseer.
homol'ogous, eweredig, ooreenstemmend, homo= loog, ooreenkomstig; gelyksoortig.
hom'ologue, homoloog.
homol'ogy, homologie, eweredigheid, ooreenstem= ming.
homomorph'ic, homomorf, gelykvormig.
homomorph'ous, homomorf.
hom'onym, gelykluidende woord, homoniem; **~ 'ic**, gelykluidend, homoniem.
homon'ymous, gelyknamig, homoniem.
homon'ymy, gelyknamigheid, homonimie.
hom'ophone, gelykluidende klank, homofoon.
homophon'ic, **homoph'onous**, gelykluidend, homo= foon.
homoph'ony, homofonie.
homop'terous, gelykvleuelig, gelykvlerkig.
homosex'ual, (n) homoseksueel; (a) homoseksueel; **~ ity**, homoseksualiteit.
homothet'ic, homoteties, gelykstandig.
hom'otype, homotipe.
homozyg'ote, homosigoot.
homozyg'ous, homosigoot.
homunc'(u)le, mensie, homunkulus, dwerg; fetus.
hom'y, huislik.
hone, (n) oliesteen, slypsteen; (v) slyp.
hon'est, eerlik, opreg, regskape; eerbaar, braaf, deug= saam, eersaam; eg, onvervals; *as ~ as DAY= LIGHT*, so eerlik soos die dag; *be ~ to a FAULT*, 'n Israeliet in wie daar geen bedrog is nie; doodeer= lik; **~ *INJUN!*** op my woord! **~ *to GOODNESS***, doodeerlik, eg; *turn (earn) an ~ PENNY*, 'n eerli= ke stuk brood verdien; **~ *WOMAN***, eerbare vrou; *make an ~ WOMAN of*, met 'n gevalle meisie trou; **~ ly**, regtig, eerlik; **~ to goodness**, opreg.
hon'esty, eerlikheid, opregtheid; eerbaarheid; braaf= heid, regskapenheid, deugsaamheid; reinheid; *in ALL ~*, in alle eer en deug; *~ is the BEST policy*, eerlikheid duur die langste; *he is ~ ITSELF*, hy is die eerlikheid self.
hon'ey, heuning; soetigheid; skatjie, hartjie; *~ is SWEET but the bee stings*, die by wat die lekker heuning maak, steek seer; *bees that have ~ in their mouths have stings in their TAILS*, heuning in die mond, gal in die hart; **~-badger**, ratel; **~-bag**, heu= ningsakkie; **~-bee**, werkby; **~-beer**, heuningbier; **~-bird**, heuningvoël; **~-bread**, johannesbrood; **~-cake**, heuningkoek.
hon'eycomb, (n) heuningkoek; gelykrigter; ruitjies= pens, netmaag (dier); (v) uitvreet, ondermyn, deur= graaf; **~ ed**, vol gate, gaterig; met selletjies; in alle rigtings deurboor (ondermyn); deurtrek, deurspek; **~ brick**, heuningkoeksteen; **~ weave**, wafelbin= ding; **~-stitch**, heuningkoeksteek; **~ stomach**, blompens.
hon'ey: **~ dew**, heuningdou; **~-eater**, suikerbekkie; **~ ed**, vol heuning; heuningsoet; sag, lief; *speak ~ ed words*, stroopsoet woorde gebruik; die heu= ningkwas gebruik; heuning in die mond dra; **~-extractor**, uitswaaimasjien; **~-flow**, heuningsa= meling, heuningoes; **~ gland**, heuningklier; **~-guide**, heuningvoëltjie, heuningwyser *(Indicato=*

ridae); ~**-lipped,** welbespraak; soetsappig; ~**-locust,** soetpeul *(Gleditsia triacanthos);* ~**moon,** (n) wit(te)broodsdae, huweliksreis; *the ~ moon is over, die piekniek is verby;* (v) wittebroodsdae deurbring; 'n huweliksreis maak; ~**mooners,** wittebroodspaar, pasgetroude paar; ~**-mouthed,** welbespraak; soetsappig, vleierig; ~**-pot,** heuningpot; hanepoot (druif); ~**-strainer,** heuningdeursyger; ~**suckle,** kanferfoelie, handskoentjies; ~**-sweet,** heuningsoet; ~**-sweet melon,** spanspek; ~**-tongued,** glad met die tong, salwend, welbespraak; ~**wort,** wasblom, waskruid.
honk, toeter; skreeu, snater.
hon'ky-tonk, (goedkoop) nagklub(danssaal); kantien; blikklavier (musiek) (Am.).
honorar'ium, (..**ria, -s),** honorarium, vergoeding.
hon'orary, honorêr, ere-; eervol; ~ **award,** eretoekenning; ~ **citizen,** ereburger; ~ **degree,** eregraad; ~ **doctorate,** eredoktorsgraad, eredoktoraat; ~ **member,** erelid; ~ **post,** ereamp, erebaantjie; ~ **president,** erevoorsitter; erepresident; ~ **secretary,** eresekretaris.
honorif'ic, (n) eretitel; beleefdheids(aanspreek)vorm; beleefheidswoord; (a) ere-, eervol; onderskeidend.
honor'is caus'a, honoris causa, ter wille van die eer, ere-.
hon'our, (n) eer, ere; agting, waardigheid; eerbaarheid, aansien; eergevoel; sieraad; eerbewys; onderskeiding; (pl) eerbewyse, onderskeidings, honneurs; telkaarte; *AFFAIR of ~,* eresaak; *be in ~ BOUND,* sedelik verplig wees om; aan sy eer verplig wees; ~ *BRIGHT,* op my erewoord; *CARRY away the ~s,* almal oortref; *CODE of ~,* erekode; *DEBT of ~,* ereskuld; *DO ~ to,* eer bewys aan; *DO the ~s,* die pligpleginge waarneem, die honneurs waarneem; *that DOES him ~,* dit strek hom tot eer; ~ *to whom ~ is DUE,* ere wie ere toekom; ~*s EVEN,* gelykop; *FUNERAL ~s,* laaste eer; *GUEST of ~,* eregas; *IN ~ of,* ter ere van; *IN his ~,* tot sy eer; *LAST ~s,* die laaste eer; *LEGION of ~,* legioen van eer; ~*s LIST,* lys van onderskeidings; *MAID of ~,* hofdame; *MATRON of ~,* eredame; *MILITARY ~s,* militêre eer; *PALM of ~,* erepalm; *a POINT of ~,* 'n eresaak; *POST of ~,* erepos; *an ~ to his PROFESSION,* 'n eer vir sy beroep; *be PUT on one's ~,* jou erewoord gee; *there is ~ among THIEVES,* diewe besteel mekaar nie; *UPON my ~,* op my erewoord; ~*s of WAR,* krygseer; *WITH ~s,* met lof, cum laude; *WORD of ~,* erewoord; *YOUR H~,* U Edele, Edelagbare; (v) eer, vereer; respekteer, hoogag; honoreer (wissel); gestand doen (woord).
hon'ourable, edel, eerwaardig, edelgestreng, (edel)agbaar; eervol; aansienlik, vernaam; eerlik, opreg; eersaam; ~ *DISCHARGE,* eervolle ontslag; *an ~ MAN,* 'n man van eer; *the ~ MEMBER,* die agbare lid; ~ *MENTION,* eervolle vermelding.
hon'our: ~**ably,** op eervolle manier, eervol; ~**s degree,** honneursgraad.
hooch, (sl.), rou drank; smokkeldrank; laegehaltedrank.
hood, (n) kap (van 'n toga, ens.); bakkop (slang); tent, kap (kar); enjinkap (motor); hoofdeksel, kappie; kleurserp; (v) van 'n kap voorsien; 'n kap omhang; omhul, bedek.
hood'ed, bedek; met 'n kap, kap-; ~ **cart,** kapkar, tentkar; ~ **chat,** skaapwagtertjie; ~ **cloak,** huik; ~ **crow,** bontkraai; ~ **snake,** kapelslang; ~ **wagon,** tentwa.
hood'ie, bontkraai.
hood'lum, straatboef; skurk; bullebak (Amer.).
hood'man-blind, blindemol(spel).
hood'-mould, kaplys, leksteen.
hoo'doo, (n) vloek, ongeluk, teenspoed, hoedoe; (v) teenspoedig maak, toor, beheks.
hood'stick, haakstok.
hood'wink, blinddoek; verskalk, mislei, verberg, bedrieg, fop; ~ *someone,* iem. om die bos lei; iem. vet om die oë smeer.
hood'y, (hoodies) = **hoodie.**
hoo'ey, (sl.), kaf, nonsies, nonsens, onsin.
hoof, (n) **(hooves, -s),** hoef; klou; poot; stuk vee; *under the ~,* vertrap; (v) loop, voetslaan; ~ *IT, PAD (beat) the ~,* stap; ~ *OUT,* uitskop; ~ *BEAT,* hoefslag, geklap (perdepote); ~**ed,** met hoewe, gehoef; ~**-mark,** spoor; ~**-ointment,** hoefsalf; ~**-pad,** aankapkussinkie; ~**-pick,** hoefsteker; ~ **wall,** horingwand.
hoo'ha, (colloq.), gedoente, opskudding, lawaai.
hook, (n) hoek; haak; hakie (vir klere); sekel; kram; hoekstoot (vuisgeveg); haakhou (gholf); vishaak; vishoek; snoeimes; draai, punt, bog; *ABOVE one's ~,* bokant sy vuurmaakplek; ~*s and EYES,* hakies en ogies; *by ~ or by CROOK,* al bars die bottel en al buig die fles; tot elke prys; op eerlike of oneerlike wyse; deur eerlike of oneerlike middele; *DROP off the ~s,* bokveld toe gaan; ~, *LINE and sinker,* volkome, heeltemal; *ON one's ~,* op eie houtjie; *STAPLE and ~,* haak en kram; (v) haak; aanhaak; inpalm, steel; skram (krieket); (uit)haak (voetbal); ~ *IN,* vashaak; inhaak; ~ *IT,* weghol; ~ *ON to,* aanhaak; ~ *UP,* aanhaak; verbind.
hook'ah, Turkse water(rook)pyp.
hook: ~**-bill,** kapmes; ~**-block,** haakblok; ~**-bolt,** hamerbout, haakbout; ~**-ed,** haak-, aangehaak; haakvormig, krom, gebuig; ~ *ed nose,* krom neus, haakneus; ~**er,** hoeker (visserskuit); haker (voetbal); ~**-grip,** haakgreep; ~**-knife,** snoeimes; ~**-nose,** haakneus, krom neus; ~**-rope,** haaktou; ~**-shaped,** haakvormig; ~**-spanner,** haaksleutel; ~**-stroke,** haakskoot; ~**-thorn,** haakdoring, swarthaak; ~**-up,** verbinding, konneksie; ~ **worm,** haakwurm; mynwurm; ~ **worm disease,** mynwurmsiekte; ~**y,** hakerig.
hool'igan, lawaaimaker; straatboef, skurk; (pl) skorrie-morrie, gespuis, rapalie; ~**ism,** lawaaimakery; straatbowery.
hoop, (n) hoepel; band, ring; beuel, kraag, beslag; hoepelrok; beuelnet; (v) met hoepels beslaan; hoepels omsit; omgeef; hyg, 'n hoe-hoe-geluid maak; optrek (kinkhoes); ~**er,** kuiper; hoepelmaker.
hoop'ing cough, kinkhoes.
hoop' iron, brandyster; hoepelyster.
hoop'-la, (n) waagspeletjie; (interj) hoepla!
hoop'oe, hoep-hoep.
hoop: ~ **skirt,** hoepelrok; ~**-stick,** hoepelstok, dakboog.
hooray', hoera.
hoose, longwurmsiekte.
hoo'segow, (sl.), tronk, tjoekie.
hoot, (n) geskreeu, gefluit, gejou; getoeter; gehoehoe; *I don't care two ~s,* ek gee geen flenter om nie; (v) skreeu, uitjou, uitfluit; hoe-hoe maak; toeter (motor); ~**enanny,** (colloq.), opskop; ~**er,** fluit; toeter; sirene; ~**er button,** toeterknop; ~**ing,** gejou; getoeter; gefluit; gehoe-hoe.
hoove, opblaassiekte, trommelsiekte.
hop¹, (n) hop, sprong, huppeling, skof (vir vliegtuig); informele dansparty, bokjol; *KEEP on the ~,* aan die gang hou; ~, *SKIP and jump,* driesprong; (v) (**-ped**), (op)spring, wip, hop, hup, huppel; dans; hink; op een been spring; oor iets spring; ~ *IT!* trap! loop! ~ *OFF,* afspring; ~ *the TWIG,* bokveld toe gaan.
hop², (n) hop; (pl) hop; (v) hop plant; ~ **beer,** hopbier; ~**-bind,** ~**-bine,** hoprank.
hop'-clover, akkerklawer *(Trifolium).*
hope, (n) hoop, verwagting; (pl) verwagtings; ~ *maketh not ASHAMED,* die hoop beskaam nie; *be BEYOND ~,* buite hoop wees; *have one's ~ BLIGHTED,* in jou verwagtings teleurgestel wees; *DEFERRED ~ maketh the heart sick,* uitgestelde hoop krenk die hart; *FORLORN ~,* ydele hoop; wanhopige onderneming; *GIVE up ~,* moed opgee; *you've GOT a ~!* jy lyk daarna! jy is laat! *IN ~s,* in verwagting; *you have NO ~ of success,* jy sal nooit slaag nie; *PAST ~,* hopeloos; (v) hoop; verwag; ~ *AGAINST ~,* aan die moontlike bly vashou; ~ *for the BEST,* op 'n gunstige afloop hoop; die beste hoop; ~ *FOR,* hoop op; ~**ful,** hoopvol, bemoedigend; veelbelowend; ~**less,** hopeloos; wanhopig; vrotsig; ~**lessness,** vrotsigheid, hopeloosheid.

hop: ~-**fly,** hopluis; ~-**garden,** hopveld; ~-**grower,** hopkweker.
hop'lite, hopliet.
Hop-o'-my-thumb', Klein Duimpie.
hopp'er¹, hopplukker.
hopp'er², springer; danser; tregter; stortkas; storthouer (staalw.); saadbak (planter); vulbak; voerbak; voetganger (sprinkaan); vlooi; ~-**beam,** stortgeutbalk; ~-**frame,** skotvensterraam; ~-**truck,** losser, storttrok, stortwa.
hop'-picker, hopplukker.
hop: ~-**pole,** ~-**prop,** hopstok.
hopp'le, (n) spanriem; (v) ('n perd) span.
hop'scotch, hinkspel, klippieskop, eenbeentjie; *play* ~, hinkel.
Hor'ace, Horatius.
hor'al, hor'ary, uur=.
Hora'tian, Horatiaans.
horde, horde, bende, trop, swerm.
hordeo'lum, staar; karkatjie.
hori'zon, (gesigs)einder, horison, kim; gesigskring; *on the DISTANT* ~, in die verskiet; *TRUE* ~, ware horison; *VISIBLE* ~, sigbare horison.
horizon'tal, (n) horisontale lyn; horisontale vlak; rekstok (gim.); (a) waterpas, plat; horisontaal; ~ **angle,** breedtehoek; ~ **bar,** rekstok; ~ '**ity,** horisontale stand, horisontaalheid.
hor'mone, hormoon.
horn, (n) horing (van dier); voelhoring (insek); drinkhoring; punt (van aambeeld); toeter (motor); herthoring; blaashoring; vleuel (leër); hoek, tak, arm (rivier); *on the* ~*s of a DILEMMA,* tussen twee vure; voor 'n dilemma; *DRAW in one's* ~*s,* in jou skulp kruip; die kop intrek; *come out at the little END of the* ~, aan die kortste end trek; *LOWER one's* ~, jou verneder; ~ *of PLENTY,* horing van oorvloed; *SHOW one's* ~, die duiwel in wees; (v) van horings voorsien; op die horings neem; met die horings steek, stoot; ~ *in,* indring, jou inmeng; (a) horing=; ~ **beak,** geep (vis); ~-**beetle,** bromkewer; ~**bill,** neushoringvoël, boskraai, horingbekvoël; ~-**blast,** horingsgeskal; ~ **blende,** horingblende; ~**blendite,** horingblendiet; ~-**blower,** horingspeler; ~ **book,** abc-boek; ~ **core,** horingpit.
horned, gehoring, horing=; horingsman=; ~ **cattle,** horingvee; ~ **ewe,** horingsmanooi; ~ **owl,** oortjiesuil, horinguil; ~ **viper,** horingsman(slang).
horn'er, horingblaser; horingbewerker, horingdraaier.
horn'et, perdeby, wesp; ~ **s' nest,** perdebynes, wespenes; *raise (bring) a* ~*s' nest about one's ears,* jou kop in 'n wespenes (byenes) steek; ~-**fly,** roofvlieg.
horn'fels, horingrots.
horn'-guards, draagpotvurk.
horn: ~**less,** poena, sonder horings, poenskop; ~ **pipe,** horingfluit; horrelpyp (dans); *make someone dance the* ~ *pipe,* iem. die horrelpyp laat dans; iem. laat riemspring; ~-**plate,** draagpotvurk; ~-**rimmed spectacles,** horingbril, uilbril; ~-**stone,** horingsteen; ~ **work,** horingwerk; ~ **wort,** horingblad; ~y, horingagtig, horing=; vereelt; *as* ~ *y as a toad,* so skurf soos 'n padda; ~ **y frog,** horingstraal (by 'n perd).
ho'rologe, uurwerk, oorlosie, horlosie.
horol'oger, uurwerker, oorlosiemaker.
horolog'ic, uurwerk=; uurwerkmakers=.
horol'ogy, uurwerkmakery, oorlosiemakery; tydmeetkunde, horologie.
horom'eter, tydmeter, horometer.
horo'metry, horometrie, tydmeting.
horop'ter, horopter.
ho'roscope, horoskoop; *cast a* ~, 'n horoskoop trek.
horos'copy, sterrewaarsêery, sterrewiggelary, horoskopie.
horren'dous, aaklig, afskuwelik.
ho'rrent, borsel(r)ig, regop.
ho'rrible, afskuwelik, vreeslik, aaklig; afgryslik, naar, verskriklik, yslik, gruwelik; ~**ness,** afskuwelikheid, afgryslikheid, aaklikheid, verskriklikheid, gruwelikheid.
ho'rribly, afskuwelik, vreeslik, aaklig.

ho'rrid, naar, afskuwelik; lelik; vreeslik; ~**ness,** afgryslikheid, afskuwelikheid; vreeslikheid.
horrif'ic, skrikbarend, ysingwekkend, afskuwekkend, afskuwelik, afgryslik.
ho'rrify, (. . fied), skrik aanjaag; skok, met ontsetting vervul; verskrik; ~**ing,** ysingwekkend.
horripila'tion, grille, hoendervleis, hoendervel
ho'rror, afsku, gruwel, aakligheid; afskuwelikheid, gruwelikheid, verskrikking, yslikheid; afkeer; huiwering; *CHAMBER of* ~ *s,* gruwelkamer; gruwelmuseum; *GIVE one the* ~ *s,* iem. stuipe op die lyf jaag; laat gril; *a PERFECT* ~, 'n regte ou draak; *THE* ~ *s,* delirium tremens, die horries, dronkmanswaansin; ~ **accident,** gruwelike (aaklige) ongeluk; ~ **film,** ~ **movie,** gruwelprent; ~-**stricken,** ~-**struck,** met afsku vervul, vol afgryse; geskok.
hors de combat', buite geveg, ongeskik.
hors-d'oeu'vre, (-s), snoepgereg, hors-d'oeuvre, voorgereg(gie), southappie.
horse, (n) perd; ruitery, kavallerie; ruiterregiment; hings; reun; perd (gim.); klemstuk (myn); muis (geol.); *BREAK in a* ~, 'n perd leer (tem); *CHANGE* ~ *s in midstream,* op die kritieke oomblik van plan verander; *a* ~ *of a different COLOUR,* 'n heeltemal ander saak; glad iets anders; ~ *s for COURSES,* die beste man vir die werk; *a DARK* ~, 'n onbekende perd; iem. van wie 'n mens nie baie weet nie; *flog a DEAD* ~, vergeefse werk doen; *EAT like a* ~, soos 'n wolf eet; *one must not look a GIFT* ~ *in the mouth,* moenie 'n gegewe perd in die bek kyk nie; *it's a GOOD* ~ *that never stumbles,* 'n perd met vier bene struikel, wat nog 'n mens met twee; *ride the HIGH* ~, 'n hoë toon aanslaan; *HOLD your* ~ *s!* bly kalm! *one man may LEAD a* ~ *to water, but fifty cannot make him drink,* met onwillige honde kan 'n mens nie hase vang nie; *LIGHT* ~, ligte kavallerie; *straight from the* ~'*s MOUTH,* uit die eerste hand; *that* ~ *won't RUN,* daardie vlieër gaan nie op nie; *one man may STEAL a* ~, *while another may not look over a hedge,* klein misdadigers het ysterkettings, groot diewe goue kettings; *as STRONG as a* ~, so sterk soos 'n os; so sterk soos 'n domkrag; *a* ~ *STUMBLES that has four legs,* 'n perd met vier bene struikel, wat wil sê 'n mens met twee; *SWOP (change)* ~ *s in midstream,* op die kritieke oomblik van plan verander; *TALK* ~ *s,* oor perde en wedrenne praat; *TO* ~! opklim! opsaal! *WHITE* ~ *s,* hoë, skuimende golwe; *WILD* ~ *s will not drag him away,* hy is nie met 'n stok te beweeg nie; *all lay load on a WILLING* ~, die gewillige perd moet die las dra; *ride a WILLING* ~ *to death,* misbruik maak van iem. se goedwil; *I'll WIN the* ~ *or lose the saddle,* dis buig of bars; dis daarop of daaronder; *WORK like a* ~, hard werk; *back the WRONG* ~, die verkeerde perd opsaal; jou misreken; (v) van perde voorsien; inspan; ry; op die rug dra, abba; dek, by die hings bring; ~-**apple,** perdevy; ~ **artillery,** berede artillerie; ~ **back:** *on* ~ *back,* te perd; ~ **back rounders,** ruiterbal; ~ **bean,** perdeboontjie, boerboontjie; ~-**blanket,** stalkombers, perdekombers; ~ **blinder,** oogklap; ~-**boat,** perdeskuit; ~ **box,** perdehok; perdetrok; ~-**brass,** tuieplaatjie; ~-**brasses,** tuiebeslag; ~-**breaker,** perdeafrigter, perdeleerder, perdetemmer; ~-**breed,** perderas; ~-**breeder,** perdeteler, perdeboer; ~-**brush,** perdeborsel; ~ **bully,** perdeduiwel; ~ **bush,** perdebos; ~ **cab,** ~-**cart,** perdekar; ~-**chestnut,** wilde kastaiing; ~ **cloth,** perdekombers; ~-**clothing,** perdetuig; ~ **collar,** borsplaat, haam; ~ **coper,** perdekoper; perdesmous; ~**d,** berede; ~-**dealer,** perdesmous, perdehandelaar; ~-**doctor,** perdedokter; ~-**draught,** perdetrekkrag; ~-**drawn vehicle,** perdevoertuig; ~-**drench,** perdemedisyne; ~ **droppings,** ~ **dung,** perdemis; ~ **fair,** perdevertoning; perdeverkoping; ~ **fig,** perdevy; ~ **fish,** perdevis; seeperdjie. ~-**flesh,** perdevleis; *judge of* ~-*flesh,* perdekenner; ~-**fly,** blindevlieg, steekvlieg; ~-**frutang,** perdefroetang; ~ **grass,** perdegras, rooisaadgras; ~ **guard,** ruiterwag; H ~ **Guards,** ruiterwag; ~ **hair,** perdehaar; ~-**hide,** perdevel; ~ **hoe,** skoffelmasjien; ~-**knacker,** perdeslagter; ~

latitudes, streek van windstiltes; ~-**laugh,** runniklag; ~-**leather,** perdeleer; ~-**leech,** bloedsuier; uitsuier; perdedokter; ~ **line,** spanlyn, perdelyn; stamlyn; ~ **lines,** perdestaanplek; stalle; ~-**lover,** perdeliefhebber; ~-**mackerel,** marsbanker; hakiesdraad; ~**man,** perderuiter; ~**manship,** ruiterkuns, (perd)rykuns; ~-**manure,** perdemis; ~-**marine,** walvisruiter; *tell that to the* ~*-marines,* maak dit aan jou ousus wys; vertel dit aan die swape; ~-**mastership,** perdebehandeling; ~**meat,** perdevleis; ~-**mill,** perdemeule; ~ **mould,** profielmaat; ~-**nail,** hoefspyker; ~ **opera,** cowboyfilm; ~**play,** ruwe spel, stoeiery; ~-**pond,** perdedam; ~**power,** perdekrag; ~-**race,** perdewedren; perdere(i)sies; ~-**radish,** peperwortel, ramenas; ~ **remedy,** perdemiddel; ~-**riding,** perdery; ~-**rug,** perdekombers; ~ **sense,** gesonde verstand.
horse'shoe, perdeyster, hoefyster; ~ **arch,** hoefysterboog; ~ **bend,** hoefdraai; ~ **crab,** koningkrap; ~ **magnet,** hoefmagneet; ~ **nail,** hoefspyker; ~**ing,** beslaan.
horse: ~'**s hoof,** perdehoef; ~ **show,** perdeskou; ~-**sickness,** perdesiekte; ~-**soldier,** kavalleris; ~-**standing,** perdestaanplek; ~-**statue,** ruiterstandbeeld; ~-**stealer,** perdedief; ~ **stud,** perdestoet(ery); ~ **sugar(-tree),** geelboom; ~-**tail,** perdestert; hermoes(kruie), dronkgras; ~ **wagon,** perdewa; ~-**track,** voetpad; ~-**trading,** perderuil; politieke gesmous, afdingery; ~-**trappings,** perdetuig; ~ **theft,** perdediefstal; ~**whip,** (n) karwats, rysweep; (v) **(-ped),** afransel, looi; ~**woman,** dameruiter, amasone.
hors'(e)y, jokkieagtig; perdagtig, perde-.
horst, horst.
horta'tion, vermaning, aansporing, aanmaning.
hort'ative, vermanend, aansporend.
hort'atory, aanmanend.
horten'sia, hortensia, hortensie, krismisroos.
horticul'tural, tuinboukundig, tuinbou-; ~ *EXHIBITION,* tuinboutoonstelling; ~ *SOCIETY,* tuinbouvereniging.
horticul'turist, tuinboukundige.
horto'logist, hortoloog.
horto'logy, hortologie.
hortus, hortus, tuin, ~ **siccus,** hortus siccus, droëplantversameling.
hosann'a, hosanna, lofsang.
hose, (n) kous; waterslang, tuinslang; gomlastiekpyp, rubberpyp; brandspuit; pyp; (v) van kouse voorsien; met 'n slang bespuit; ~ **down,** afspuit; ~ **clip,** slangklem; ~ **connection,** slangkoppeling; ~-**nozzle,** spuitkop; ~ **panty,** kousbroek; ~-**pipe,** tuinslang; spuitslang; waterslang; ~-**reel,** slangtol; ~ **top,** kaalvoetkous.
ho'sier, koushandelaar; handelaar in onderklere; ~**y,** wolgoed, gebreide goed, kouse en onderklere.
hos'pice, gashuis, tehuis, kloosterherberg.
hos'pitable, gasvry, herbergsaam.
hos'pital, hospitaal, siekehuis; ~**ism,** hospitaalwese.
hospital'ity, gasvryheid, herbergsaamheid.
hos'pital: ~ **carrier,** hospitaalskip; ~ **door,** hospitaaldeur; vlakdeur; ~ **fee,** hospitaalgeld; - **fever,** hospitaalkoors; -**izatlon,** hospitalisasie; -**ize,** hospitaliseer; ~'**ity,** gasvryheid; ~**(l)er,** hospitaalbroeder, -suster; **hospitaalkapelaan,** ~ **nurse,** hospitaalverpleegster; ~ **orderly,** hospitaalordonnans, -soldaat; ~ **ship,** hospitaalskip; ~ **train,** ambulanstrein; ~ **treatment,** hospitaalbehandeling; ~ **ward,** siekesaal.
hos'pitate, hospiteer.
host[1], trop; massa, swetterjoel, swerm, menigte; trop; *LORD of H*~*s,* die Heer der (v.d.) Leërskare; *a NUMEROUS* ~, 'n mag der menigte.
host[2], waard, herbergier, gasheer; voedster (plant); *reckon without one's* ~, nie rekening hou met jou gasheer nie.
host[3], hostie, oblaat.
hos'ta, hosta (plant).
hos'tage, gyselaar; pand.
hos'tel, hostel, losieshuis, tehuis, koshuis; herberg; ~ **board,** koshuisraad; ~**er,** kosganger; ~**ry, (..ries),** herberg, losieshuis.
hos'tess, (-es), gasvrou; hospita; waardin.
hos'tile, vyandig, sleggesind; vyandelik; strydig; ~ **forces,** vyandelike magte; ~ **intent,** vyandige opset; ~-**minded,** vyandiggesind; ~ **witness,** vyandige getuie.
hostil'ity, vyandigheid; **(..ties),** vyandelikhede.
hos'tler = **ostler.**
host' plant, gasheer(plant).
hosts, heerskare, leërskare, heir.
hot, (v) verhit; ~ **up,** verhit; (a, adv) warm, heet; vurig; heftig; driftig; skerp (kerrie); brandend (pyn); gretig; sterk (kruie); toornig; loops (dier); *it is nothing but* ~ *AIR,* dis alles pure wind; *emit* ~ *AIR,* grootpraat; wind maak (sonder stof); *sell like* ~ *CAKES,* soos soetkoek verkoop; *soon* ~, *soon COLD,* gou warm, gou afgekoel; ~ *under the COLLAR,* ontstig; ontsteld; *a* ~ *FAVOURITE,* 'n sterk gunsteling; *GIVE it a person* ~, iem. goed inpeper; *in* ~ *HASTE,* in vlieënde vaart; ~ *on his HEELS,* kort op sy hakke; *MAKE it* ~ *for someone,* die wêreld vir iem. te benoud maak; iem. die vuur na die skene lê; ~ *PACE,* groot vaart; *make a PLACE too* ~ *to hold a person,* die wêreld vir iem. te benoud maak; *in* ~ *PURSUIT,* op jag na; ~ *on the TRACKS of,* kort op die spoor van; *be in* ~ *WATER,* in die pekel sit; ~ **air,** warm lug; kafpraatjies, bog, onsin; ~-**air balloon,** warmlugballon; ~-**air duct,** warmlugbuis; ~-**air inlet,** warmlugtoevoer, -inlaat; ~ **and bothered,** warm, vervies, kwaad; ~ **and cold,** warm en koud; ~ **bed,** broeines, broeikas; groeibodem; ~ **belt,** warmgordel; ~-**bent,** warmgebuig; ~ **blood,** woede, drif, ~-**blooded,** warmbloedig; hartstogtelik; vurig; ~-**bloodedness,** warmbloedigheid, ~ **blush,** vurige blos; ~ **box,** warmloper; ~-**brained,** heethoofdig.
hotch'potch, hutspot, mengelmoes, mengsel; sameraapsel; een-pot-in-die-ander.
hot' cross bun, Paasbolletjie, kruisbolletjie.
hot'dog, worsbroodjie.
hotel', hotel; ~ **bill,** hotelrekening; ~ **board,** hotelraad; ~ **expenses,** hotelkoste; ~**ier',** hotelbaas; ~-**industry,** hotelbedryf, hotelwese; ~-**keeper,** hotelhouer; ~ **lounge,** hotelsitkamer; ~ **register,** hotelregister; ~ **tariff,** hoteltarief.
hot: ~ **foot,** vinnig, in aller yl; *run* ~ *foot,* vinnig hardloop; die knieë dra; ~ **frame,** broeikas; ~ **gospeller,** emosionele prediker; ~ **head,** heethoof, driftkop, vuurvreter; ~-**headed,** heethoofdig, (dol)driftig, kortgebaker; ~-**house,** broeikas, kweekhuis; ~**line,** blitslyn; ~**ly,** vurig, heftig, haastig, woedend; ~ **money,** vlugkapitaal; ~**ness,** warmte, hitte; ~ **news,** warm nuus, vars nuus, kraakvars nuus; ~ **pace,** snelpas; snelle vaart; ~ **pack,** warm omslag; warmwaterverband; ~ **pants,** sjoebroekie, knapbroekie; ~-**plate,** kookplaat, warmplaat, verwarmingsplaat; ~ **pot,** jagskottel; skaaphutspot; ~ **potato,** warmpatat; turksvy; ~ **press,** (n) lakenpers, gloeipers; (v) satineer (papier); glans; ~-**presser,** glanser, satineerder; ~ **pursuit,** hakkejag; dryfjag, ~ **rod,** hitstjor; ~ **scat,** elektriese stoel; brandstoel, warmstoel, besluitnemingsposisie; ~ **spell,** warm tydjie; ~-**spirited,** vurig, driftig; ~-**spot,** gevaarplek, gevaarkol; ~ **spring,** warmbad, warmbron; -**spur,** drifkop, waaghals; ~-**spurred,** driftig, onstuimig; ~ **stuff,** (n) windmakergoed; vrylustige persoon; (a) windmakerig; vrylustig; (interj) ryperd! ou haan! ou bul!; ~-**tempered,** driftig, opvlieënd, bitsig, kortgebaker.
hott'entot[1], hotno(tjie) (vis).
Hott'entot[2], (n) Hottentot; Hottentots (taal); (a) Hottentot-, Hottentots; ~ **dance,** hottentotsriel; ~'**s bread,** olifantspoot *(Testudinaria elephantipes);* ~'**s fig,** ghoena, perdevy *(Carpobrotus).*
hot tip, warm (vars) wenk; wenk uit die eerste hand.
hot wa'ter, warm water; moeilikheid; *get into* ~, in die pekel raak, in die knyp raak.
hot-water: ~ **bag,** warmwatersak; ~ **bottle,** warmwaterbottel; warmwaterfles; ~ **cylinder,** geiser, warmwatersilinder; badketel.
hot wave, hittegolf.
hough, (n) hakskeensening; spronggewrig; *see* **hock;** (v) die hakskeensening deurkap, verlam.

hound, (n) jaghond; *FOLLOW the* ~*s*, deelneem aan 'n jakkalsjag; *the H~ of HELL*, Kerberos; *THE* ~*s*, klomp jakkalshonde; (v) jag; vervolg; ~ *DOWN*, agternasit; ~ *OUT*, uit die diens dryf; ~**ing**, agtervolging, aanhitsing; vervolging.

hour, uur; (pl) getye; ure; *AFTER* ~ *s*, na kantoortyd; buitenstyds, na werktyd, na sluitingstyd; *at an EARLY* ~, vroeg; vroegtydig; *at the ELEVENTH* ~, ter elfder ure; *talk for* ~*s on END*, wêrelde aanmekaar praat; *in an EVIL* ~, op 'n verkeerde oomblik; ter kwader ure; *KEEP early* ~*s*, vroeg gaan slaap; *KEEP late* ~*s*, laat na bed gaan; *the MAN of the* ~, die man v.d. dag (oomblik); *the QUESTION of the* ~, die brandende saak; *the SMALL* ~*s*, na middernag; die vroeë ure; ~*s at a STRETCH*, ure aanmekaar; *his* ~ *has STRUCK*, sy (laaste) uur het geslaan; ~ **angle**, uurhoek; ~**book**, getydeboek; ~ **circle**, deklinasiesirkel, uursirkel; ~**-glass**, sandloper; eierkokertjie; uurglas; ~**-hand**, uurwyser.

hour'i, (-s), hoerie, houri, ewig jeugdige vrou.

hour: ~**-long**, uurlang(e); ~ **ly**, elke uur; al om die uur; ~**-plate**, wyserplaat; ~ **wage**, uurloon.

house, (n) huis, woning, woonhuis; herberg; klooster; parlementsgebou; skouburg; saal; die toeskouers, gehoor; geslag, stamhuis; firma, hok, kooi (diere); *H~ of ASSEMBLY*, Wetgewende Vergadering; *AT our* ~, by ons huis; *BRING down the* ~, uitbundige toejuiging uitlok; die gehoor in vervoering bring; ~ *of CALL*, bestelhuis; aanloopplek; besoekplek; ~ *of CARDS*, 'n kaartehuis; *collapse like a* ~ *of CARDS*, soos 'n kaartehuis inmekaartuimel; *H~ of COMMONS*, (Engelse) Laerhuis; ~ *of CORRECTION*, verbeterhuis; *no* ~ *but has its CROSS*, elke huis het sy kruis; ~ *of DETENTION*, huis van bewaring; *like a* ~ *on FIRE*, vinnig; soos die wind; soos vet; *FULL* ~, uitverkoop; vol saal; ~ *of GOD*, die huis v.d. Here, Godshuis, die kerk; *have neither* ~ *nor HOME*, geen onderkome hê nie; ~ *and HOME*, huis en haard; ~ *of ILL FAME*, ontughuis, bordeel; *KEEP one's* ~ *in order*, voor jou eie deur vee; *KEEP (to) the* ~, nie uitgaan nie; *KEEP open* ~, baie ontvang; op tafel hou; *a* ~ *to be LET for life or years, its rent is sorrow and its income tears*, huise is te kruise; *H~ of LORDS*, (Engelse) Hoërhuis; *no* ~ *without a MOUSE*, elke huis het sy kruis; *ON the* ~, verniet, 'n rondte deur die saak (eienaar, firma); *set one's* ~ *in ORDER*, jou eie sake in orde kry; *eat OUT of* ~ *and home*, rot en kaal eet; *H~ of PARLIAMENT*, parlementshuis; ~ *of PRAYER*, bedehuis; ~ *of REFUGE*, toevlugsoord; *H~ of REPRESENTATIVES*, Laerhuis, Volksraad; *the ROYAL* ~, die koninklike huis; *as SAFE as* ~*s*, so veilig soos die bank; *SET up* ~, 'n eie huishouding begin; *THE H* ~, die Beurs; ~ *TO* ~, van huis tot huis; *every* ~ *has its TRIALS*, elke huis het sy kruis; *throw the* ~ *out of the WINDOW*, die huis op horings neem; (v) huisves, onderbring, onder dak bring, huisvesting verleen; beveilig; bevestig; bêre; ~ **agent**, huisagent, eiendomsagent; ~ **agreement**, woningooreenkoms; ~ **arrest**, huisarres; ~ **bat**, dakvlermuis; ~ **boat**, woonboot; ~ **bound**, huisgebonde; ~ **breaker**, inbreker; afbreker; sloper; ~ **breaking**, huisbraak, inbraak; slopery; ~**-broken**, kamersindelik; kamerwys; ~ **bug**, weeluis; ~**-building**, huisbou; ~**-call**, huisbesoek; ~ **cleaner**, skoonmaker, skoonmaakster; ~**-cleaning**, huisskoonmaak; ~ **coat**, huisjas; huisbaadjie; ~ **craft**, huisvlyt, huishoudkunde; ~ **decorator**, dekorateur; ~ **detention**, huisarres; ~ **directory**, woninggids; ~**-dog**, huishond, waghond; ~**-door**, huisdeur, voordeur; ~ **expenses**, huisuitgawes; ~**-famine**, woningnood; ~ **father**, huisvader; ~**-fly**, huisvlieg; ~ **frock**, huisrok; ~**-full**, 'n huis vol.

house'hold, (n) gesin; huishouding; huishoue; *an unruly* ~, 'n huishouding van Jan Steen; (a) huishoudelik, huis ~; ~ **account**, huishoudelike rekening; ~ **affairs**, huislike sake; ~ **allowance**, huishoudelike toelae; ~ **effects**, huisraad; ~ **er**, gesinshoof; huiseienaar; ~ **expenses**, huisuitgawes; ~ **gods**, huisgode; ~ **linen**, huislinne; ~ **remedy**, huismiddel; ~

soap, gewone seep; ~ **tasks**, huislike pligte; ~ **troops**, lyfwag; ~ **word**, lyfspreuk; gemeenplaas; alombekende gesegde (benaming); *their names are* ~ *words*, almal ken hulle name; hulle name is op almal se lippe.

house: ~**-hunting**, huissoekery; ~ **journal**, huisblad, firmablad; ~ **keeper**, huishoudster; ~ **keeping**, huishouding, huishou; ~**-key**, huissleutel; ~ **leek**, huislook, donderkruid; ~ **less**, dakloos; ~**-linen**, huislinne, linnegoed; ~ **maid**, huishulp, werkmeisie; ~ **maid's knee**, kniewater, kruipknie, skropknie; ~ **magazine**, lyfblad, lyforgaan; vakblad; ~ **man**, inwonende arts, intern; proefarts; ~ **manship**, internskap; ~ **martin**, huisswa(w)el(tjie); ~**master**, huisonderwyser; huisvader; ~**-mate**, huisgenoot; ~**-money**, huishougeld; ~ **mother**, matrone.

house' organ¹, huisorrel.
house' organ², firmablad.

house: ~**-painter**, huisskilder; ~ **party**, gesamentlike loseerders, kuiergaste; huisparty(tjie); ~ **pest**, huisplaag; ~**-plant**, kamerplant; ~**-proud**, trots (gesteld) op die huis; ~ **refuse**, afval; ~**-rent**, huishuur; ~**-sitter**, huisoppasser, huiswagter; ~**-surgeon**, inwonende dokter; ~ **telephone**, binnetelefoon; ~**-to-**~, huis tot huis; ~**-top**, dak, nok; *proclaim from the* ~*-tops*, van die dakke verkondig; ~**-trained**, kamersindelik; kamerwys; ~ **warming**, inwyfees, huisinwyding, huisparty; ~ **wear**, huisklere; ~ **wife**, huisvrou; tuistesepper; naaisakkie; werksakkie; ~ **wifely**, huishoudelik; ~ **wifery**, huisbestuur; huishoudkunde; ~ **work**, huiswerk.

hous'ing, huisvesting, onderdak; behuising; benedemas (skip); inkeping; perdedeken; (om)hulsel (motor); ~ **board**, woningraad; ~ **cap**, (om)hulseldop; ~ **commission**, woningkommissie; ~ **famine**, woningnood; ~ **problem**, behuisingsvraagstuk; ~ **scheme**, behuisingsplan, behuisingskema.

hove, *kyk* **heave**, (v).

hov'el, (n) pondok, krot, strooihuis, hut; afdak; (v) (-l)ed), in 'n loods bêre; 'n skip berg.

hov'eller, ongediplomeerde loods; berger.

hov'en, opgeblaasdheid; trommelsiekte.

hov'er¹, kunsmoeder (pluimvee).

hov'er², (n) fladdering; weifeling, onsekerheid; (v) fladder; slinger; swewe; swerwe, heen en weer trek; ~ *about*, rondswerf; speel; ~ **craft**, skeertuig, sweeftuig, kussingtuig; ~ **fly**, sweefvlieg; ~**ing**, swewend.

how, (n) hoe; *THE* ~, die hoe; *the* ~ *and the WHY*, die hoe en die waarom; (adv) hoe; wat; waarom; waaraan; ~ *ABOUT?*, wat van?; *AND* ~!, (sl.) moenie praat nie; ~ *ARE you?*, hoe gaan dit?; ~ *COME?*, (Amer.) hoekom?; ~ *do you DO?*, bly om jou te ontmoet; hoe gaan dit; *HERE'S* ~!, (op jou) gesondheid!; ~ *IS it?*, hoekom? wat daarvan?! (kr.); ~ *MANY are there?*, is daar nie baie nie?; ~ *NOW?*, hoe is dit nou?; ~ *he SNORES!*, kan hy nie snork nie! ~ *SO?*, hoe so?; ~ *STUPID!*, hoe dwaas!; ~ *'s THAT!*, wat daarvan? uit of nie? hoe's daai? (krieket); ~ *are THINGS with you?*, hoe gaan dit?; ~ *THEN?*, hoe so?

howbe'it, nieteenstaande, hoe dit sy.

how' dah, olifantsaal.

how'-d'ye-do, affère, bogtery, neukery, lollery; *this is a fine* ~, dis nou 'n mooi grap (lollery, affère, spiets, bogtery).

how'ever, egter, maar, hoe dit sy, nogtans, hoewel, dog, ewewel.

how'itzer, houwitser.

howl, (n) gehuil, gebrul, geblêr, getjank; gil; (v) huil, tjank; gier; skreeu.

howl'er, huiler, tjanker, skree(u)balie; skreeuer; groot flater, stommiteit, bok; *commit a* ~, 'n bok skiet; 'n flater begaan.

howl'ing, (n) gegrens, getjank; (a) huilend, tjankend; skreiend, groot; *a* ~ *SHAME*, 'n skreiende skandaal; *a* ~ *WILDERNESS*, 'n verskriklike (huilende) woestyn, woesteny.

howsoev'er, hoe ook al, in elk geval.

hoy¹, (n) ligter, kusvaartuig.

hoy², (interj) haai!
hoyd'en, rabbedoe, wilde meisie; ~ish, wild, ongemanierd, luidrugtig, uitgelate.
hub¹, (colloq.), ou man, mannie.
hub², naaf (wiel); spil; middelpunt; doelwit; matrysstempel (drukk.); ~-band, naafband.
hub'ble-bubble, geborrel; gemompel; hookah, klein waterpyp (om uit te rook).
hub'-bolt, naafskroef.
hubb'ub, lawaai, rumoer, strawasie, bohaai, geraas, gedoe.
hubb'y, (hubbies), ou man (liefkosend), mannie.
hub: ~-cap, wieldop, naafbuskop, naafdop; ~-gland, naafdrukstuk.
hu'bris, hubris; ~'tic, hubristies, aanmatigend.
huck'aback, gansogies, vadoeklinne, handdoeklinne.
huc'kle, heup; boggel; ~-back, boggel; ~-backed, geboggel, boggelrug.
huc'kleberry, (..ries), bloubessie.
huc'kle-bone, heupbeen.
huck'ster, (n) smous, verkoper, venter; skurk; woekeraar; publisiteitsagent; (v) verkoop, rondsmous; vervals; ~ess, (-es), smousvrou; ~ing, smousery.
hud'dle, (n) hoop; bondel; oorhaasting; verwarring, warboel; *go into a* ~, koppe bymekaarsteek; (v) deurmekaarmaak, verwar; op 'n hoop gooi, konkel, knoei, bondel; opeendring; ~ *AROUND*, saamdring; ~ *INTO one's clothes*, jou klere aanpluk; ~ *TOGETHER*, bymekaarhok; ~ *UP*, inmekaarkrimp; haastig doen; in die doofpot stop; ~ *OVER*, verknoei, haastig saamflans; ~ *OVER the fire*, by die vuur buk; ~**d**, verward, deurmekaar.
hue¹, kleur, tint.
hue², geskreeu; aankondiging, alarmkreet; polisieblad; *a* ~ *and CRY*, 'n lawaai; 'n bohaai; *RAISE a* ~ *and cry*, skreeu-skreeu naloop; moord en brand skreeu.
hued, gekleur.
huff, (n) slegte bui, geraaktheid; nukkerigheid; *in a* ~, nukkerig, knorrig, kwaad; (v) opblaas; afjak, raas; aanstoot gee (neem); kwaad word; met minagting behandel; blaas (damspel); ~**iness**, aanmatiging; liggeraaktheid, knorrigheid; ~**ish**, ~**y**, knorrig, liggeraak.
hug, (n) omhelsing, omarming, omknelling; (v) (-ged), omhels, omarm; liefkoos; koester; ~ *a BELIEF*, jou aan 'n geloof vasklem; ~ *ONESELF*, jouself gelukwens; ~ *the SHORE*, naby die kus hou.
huge, baie groot, tamaai, kolossaal, reusagtig, vervaarlik; ~ *fellow*, groot (lomp) ou; ~**ly**, vreeslik, besonder; ~**ness**, reusagtigheid, kolossaalheid; ~**ous**, (grappig) besonder groot.
hugg'er-mugger, (n) geheimhouding, heimlikheid; deurmekaarspul, deurmekaarheid, warboel; (v) konkel, knoei, stilletjies doen; verberg; (a) geheim; verward.
hugg'ery, lekkery, witvoetjiesoekery.
Huguenot, (n) Hugenoot; (a) Hugenote-.
huh', hm!, hû!
hu'la, Hawaiiese dans.
hulk, (n) (skeeps)romp; pakskip; tronkskip; swaarlywige persoon; (v): ~ *up*, in omvang toeneem; ~**ing**, ~**y**, log, swaar, lomp.
hull, (n) romp (skip); dop, bas; peul; omhulsel; (v) skil, afdop; uitdop; stukkend skiet; ~ *ed BARLEY*, gort; ~ *ed RICE*, gedopte rys.
hullabaloo', gedoente, oproer, lawaai, geraas.
hullo(a)'! hallo! hello!; ~ *there!*, hêi!
hum', (n) gegons, gemompel, gebrom, geroesemoes; geneurie; (v) (-med), gons, brom; neurie; mompel; ~ *and HA(W)*, weifelend praat, huiwer, aarsel; *MAKE things* ~, lewe in die brouery bring; *THINGS are* ~*ming*, die mos begin werk; daar is lewe in die brouery.
hum², hm!, hum, hû.
hum'an, (n) mens, menslike wese; (a) menslik, mens-; *the* ~ *ELEMENT*, die menslike faktor; *have a (sound) KNOWLEDGE of* ~ *nature*, menskundig wees; *he is ONLY* ~, 'n mens is maar 'n mens; *the* ~ *VOICE*, die mensestem; *the* ~ *WORLD*, die mensewêreld; ~ **being**, mensekind, mens, skepsel.

humane', mensliewend, sag, goedhartig; humaan; ~ **killer**, dieredoder; genadedoder, pynlose doder; ~ **killing**, pynlose slagting; ~**ness**, mensliewendheid, humaniteit.
hum'an flesh, mensvleis.
Hum'anism, Humanisme.
hum'anism, menslikheid; humanisme.
hum'anist, mensekenner; humanis; ~**'ic**, humanisties.
humanitar'ian, (n) mensevriend; filantroop; (a) mensliewend; filantropies; ~**ism**, mensliewendheid.
human'ities, klassieke studies, geesteswetenskappe, humaniora.
human'ity, mensheid; mensliewendheid, menslikheid; mensdom; *what a specimen of* ~*!*, wat 'n stukkie mens!
humaniza'tion, beskawing, veredeling.
hum'anize, vermenslik, veredel, humaniseer.
hum'anizing, veredelend, humaniserend.
hum'ankind, mensdom.
hum'anly, menslik, menslikerwys(e); ~ *speaking*, menslikerwys gepraat (gesproke).
hum'an: ~ **material**, mensemateriaal; ~ **nature**, menslikheid, die menslike natuur; ~ **race**, die mensdom; ~ **relations**, menseverhoudinge; ~ **resources**, mensemateriaal, mensebromme, mannekrag; ~ **rights**, menseregte; ~ **science**, geesteswetenskap; lewenswetenskap.
hum'ble, (v) verootmoedig; verneder; verlaag; (a) nederig, beskeie, ootmoedig; onderdanig; *I beg you* ~ *PARDON*, ek vra u (nederig) om verskoning; *eat* ~ *PIE*, mooi (soet) broodjies bak; *your* ~ *SERVANT*, u dienswillige dienaar; ~-**bee**, waterdraer(by), hommel(by); ~-**minded**, nederig van gees; ~**ness**, nederigheid, ootmoed.
hum'bly, ootmoedig, nederig.
hum'bug, (n) (boere)bedrog, kullery; bog; aansteller; bedrieër, charlatan; bluf; (v) (-ged), kul, bedrieg, fop; ~**g'ery**, bedrieëry, kullery, foppery.
hum'drum, (n) eentonigheid, alledaagsheid, saaiheid; (v) (-med), die ou gangetjie loop, voortsukkel; (a) eentonig, alledaags, vervelend; ~ **way**, sleur.
hum'eral, skouer-, boarm-.
hum'erus, (..ri), boarmpyp, opperarmbeen, humerus.
hum'ic, humus-, humusryk; ~ **acid**, humussuur; ~ **coal**, humussteenkool.
hum'id, vogtig, nat, klam; ~**ifica'tion**, bevogtiging; ~**'ifier**, bevogtiger; ~**'ify**, bevogtig.
humid'ity, natheid, (lug)vogtigheid, klamheid, humiditeit.
humil'iate, verneder; verootmoedig; ~**d**, verneder, afgehaal.
humil'iating, vernederend.
humilia'tion, vernedering, verootmoediging.
humil'ity, nederigheid; ootmoed.
humm'el, poena-.
humm'er, gonser, brommer; neuriesanger.
humm'ing, (n) gegons, gezoem (bye); geneurie, gebrom; (a) murmelend, gonsend; bedrywig; ~-**bird**, kolibrie; ~-**top**, bromtol, gonstol.
humm'ock, bult, heuweltjie, hoogte; ysbultjie; ~**y**, bulterig.
hum'oral, vog; ~-**ism**, humoralisme.
humoresque', humoresk.
hum'orist, humoris; grapmaker; droogkomiek; ~'**ic**, humoristies.
hum'orous, humoristies; luimig, grappig, geestig; ~**ly**, grappenderwys.
hum'our¹, (n) luim, gril, bui; gemoedsgesteldheid, gemoedstemming; geaardheid; temperament, humeur; geestigheid; humor; vog; *AQUEOUS* ~, watervog (bv. in oog); *in a GOOD* ~, in 'n goeie bui; *be OUT of* ~, jou humeur verloor het; kwaad wees; *have a SENSE of* ~, 'n sin vir humor hê; *VITREOUS* ~, glasvog.
hum'our², (v) toegee aan, sy sin gee, paai, tevrede stel; jou skik na.
hum'oursome, humeurig, vol giere.
hum'ous, humusagtig.
hump, (n) boggel; skof (dier); bultjie, knoppie; *it*

humph! 964 *hutch*

GIVES me the ~, dit maak my vies; dit verveel my; **OVER** the ~, oor die ergste; (v) die rug hard maak (perd); geboggel maak; verveel; ~**back,** boggel; boggelrug; ~ **backed,** geboggel; ~ **back whale,** boggelwalvis; ~**ed,** boggelrig; bulterig; met 'n skof.
humph! hm!
humpty-dump'ty, (n) (..**ties),** diksak, vetsak; (a) vet.
hum'py, (n) (..**pies),** Australiese hut; (a) bulterig, geboggel.
hump'-yard, bultterrein, boggelterrein.
hum'us, teelaarde, humus.
Hun, Hun.
hunch, (n) (-es), bult; knop, boggel; homp (brood); voorgevoel, suspisie; (v) krom trek, optrek, buig; ~**back,** boggelrug; ~**backed,** geboggel.
hun'dred, honderd; *a* ~ *to one CHANCE,* hoogs onwaarskynlik; honderd teen een; *LONG (great)* ~, groot honderd; *a MAN in a* ~, 'n man honderd; *NOT a* ~ *miles off,* sommer naby; anderkant die bult; *a* ~ *and ONE,* honderd-en-een; *SOME* ~*s of men,* 'n paar honderd man; ~*s and THOU*=*SANDS,* versierlekkertjies, strooiversiersel; ~*s of THOUSANDS,* honderdduisende; ~ **fold,** honderdvoudig; ~**th,** honderdste; ~ **weight,** sentenaar.
hung, *kyk* **hang,** (v).
Hungar'ian, (n) Hongaar; Hongaars (taal); (a) Hongaars.
Hun'gary, Hongarye.
hung'er, (n) honger; begeerte, hunkering; ~ *is the best SAUCE,* honger is die beste kok; ~ *brings the WOLF from the woods,* honger is 'n skerp swaard; (v) honger ly; honger hê (kry); honger wees; verhonger; hunker, verlang na; *they must* ~ *in frost who will not work in heat,* wie nie werk nie, sal nie eet nie; wie nie saai nie, sal nie maai nie; ~**-bitten,** uitgehonger; ~**-blockade,** hongerblokkade; ~**ed,** hongerig, uitgehonger; ~**-march,** hongermars; ~ **pains,** hongerpyne; ~**-riot,** hongeropstootjie; ~**-strike,** hongerstaking, eetstaking; ~**-striker,** hongerstaker, kosweieraar.
hun'grily, hongerig; hunkerend.
hun'griness, honger.
hun'gry, hongerig, honger; begerig, hunkerend, lus; skraal (grond); *BE* ~, honger wees; *COME away* ~, droëbek tuiskom; ~ *DOGS will eat dirty pud*=*ding,* honger is 'n skerp swaard; *be* ~ *FOR,* lus vir, begerig wees na; *GET* ~, honger kry; *GO* ~, sonder kos bly; *be as* ~ *as a HUNTER,* so honger soos 'n wolf wees; so honger wees dat 'n mens 'n spyker se kop kan afbyt.
hunk, stuk, homp; klomp.
hunks, vrek, bloedsuier.
hunky-dor'y, eersteklas, uitstekend.
Hunn'ish, Hunne=, Huns.
hunt, (n) jag; jaggeselskap; jagveld; soektog; gesoek; *be out of the* ~, nie gereken word nie; nie saamtel nie; (v) jag; soek, snuffel; najaag, agtervolg, nasit; ~ *AFTER (for),* jag maak op; soek na; ~ *DOWN,* vaskeer; opspoor; ~ *OUT,* opspoor, opjaag; ~ *UP,* opsoek; opskarrel; ~ **ball,** jagtersdans; ~ **club,** jagklub; ~ **er,** jagter; skietperd, jagperd; soeker; dekseloorlosie.
hunt'ing, jag; slingering (masjien); *art of* ~, jagkuns; ~ **accident,** jagongeluk; ~ **box,** jaghuis; ~**-case,** dubbele kas (om 'n oorlosie); ~ **clothes,** jagklere; ~ **crop,** jagsweep, karwats; ~ **dog,** jaghond; wildehond; ~ **expedition,** jagtog; ~ **field,** jagveld; jagters; ~ **ground,** jagveld, skietveld; rolplek (fig.); ~ **horn,** jaghoring; ~ **knife,** herneutermes, jagmes, grootmes; ~ **lamp,** jaglamp; ~ **leopard,** jagluiperd; ~ **lodge,** jag(ters) huis; ~ **party,** jaggeselskap; jagparty; ~ **permit,** jaglisensie; ~ **season,** jagtyd, jagseisoen, skiettyd; ~ **spider,** ja(a)gspinnekop; ~ **story,** jagverhaal.
hunt'ress, (-es), jagteres; skietmerrie, jagmerrie.
hunts'man, (..**men),** jagter, jagopsigter.
hur'dle, (n) hek(kie); (v) hekkiesloop, hekkiespring; *it is but the FIRST* ~, dis maar die begin v.d. moeilikheid; *have TAKEN the first* ~, oor die eerste moeilikheid wees; ~**r,** hekmaker; hekkiespringer; ~**-race,** hekkiewedloop, hekkies.
hurd'y-gurdy, (..**dies),** draaiorrel, straatorrel.

hurl, (n) worp; (v) gooi, smyt, (in)slinger; ~ *ACCU*=*SATIONS at a person,* iem. beskuldigings na die hoof slinger; ~ *AWAY,* wegslinger, wegsmyt; ~ *DEFIANCE at,* uittart, uitdaag.
hurl'y-burl'y, lawaai, geraas, harlaboerla, opskudding.
hurley, (Ierse) hokkie(stok).
hurrah', hurray', (n) hoera, hoerê, jubelkreet; (v) hoera skreeu, juig; (interj) hoera! hoerê!
hu'rricane, orkaan; ~**-bird,** stormvoël, fregatvoël; ~ **deck,** promenadedek, stormdek; ~ **lamp,** stormlamp, stormlantern; ~ **light,** stormlamp; ~ **strength,** orkaansterkte.
hurr'ied, gejaag, haastig.
hu'rriedly, gejaag, haastig, ylings; sito-sito; *they CARRIED him* ~ *to hospital,* hulle het hom haastig na die hospitaal gedra; *he LEFT* ~, hy het haastig vertrek.
hu'rry, (n) haastigheid, haas, gejaagdheid, oorhaasting; *IN a* ~, haastig; *there is NO* ~, daar is geen haas by nie; (v) **(hurried),** jou haas, gou maak, opskud, wikkel, hardloop, voortmaak, haastig wees, yl; heenskeer; jakker; aanjaag, verhaas; oorhaas; ~ *ALONG,* jou voorthaas, aanyl, aanwikkel; ~ *AWAY,* haastig vertrek, wegsnel; *the FIRE BRI*=*GADE hurried to the scene,* die brandweer het hom na die toneel gehaas; *they* ~ *the INJURED to hos*=*pital,* hulle neem die beseerdes haastig hospitaal toe; ~ *ON one's clothes,* jou klere haastig aanpluk; ~ *ON,* aanjaag; ~ *UP,* gou maak; ~**-scurry,** (n) verwarring, groot haas, deurmekaar spul, deurmekaarheid; (a, adv) halsoorkop; ~**ing,** gewikkel; gejaag, gehaas; haas.
hurst, knoppie, sandbank; bos; bult.
hurt, (n) nadeel, skade; wond, seerplek, verwonding; (v) **(hurt),** seer maak; afknou; kwes, wond, beseer; hinder, foeter, grief, krenk; skaad, benadeel; *FEEL* ~, gekrenk voel; ~ *someone's FEELINGS,* iem. se gevoel krenk; iem. in die gesig vat; *GET* ~, jou beseer, seerkry; *IT* ~*s,* dit maak seer.
hurt'ful, skadelik, nadelig; ~**ness,** skadelikheid, nadeligheid.
hur'tle, stamp, ratel; smyt; gooi; aanval; kletter, dawer.
hurt'less, onskadelik; ongedeer(d).
hus'band, (n) man, eggenoot, gade, gemaal; (v) suinig werk met, spaarsaam omgaan met; besuinig; behou; versorg; trou; ~ *one's resources,* suinig met jou hulpmiddele (krag) werk; ~ **man,** (..**men),** boer, landbouer; ~**ry,** landbou, boerdery; huishoudkunde; landboukunde; spaarsaamheid; ~**'s brother,** swaer; ~**'s mother,** mansmoeder; ~**'s sister,** mansuster.
hush, (n) stilte; (v) stilmaak; laat bedaar; ~ *something up,* iets smoor; iets in die doofpot stop; (interj) sjuut! pst!
hush'aby, doedoe.
hush cloth, dempkleed.
hush'-hush, geheim, verhole; stilletjies.
hush: ~-money, omkoopgeld, afkoopgeld; ~**-ship,** oorlogskip wat in die geheim gebou is.
husk, (n) dop, peul; holster; vrughulsel; skil, bas; heesheid; longwurmsiekte; ~*s of mealies,* mielieblare; (v) uitdop (peulgewas); afskil; afblaar (mielies); ~**ed rice,** gedopte rys; ~**er,** uitdopper; dopmasjien, afmaakmasjien, afmaker.
hus'kiness, heesheid, skorheid.
hus'ky[1], (n) **(huskies),** Poolhond, Eskimohond, husky.
hus'ky[2], (a) dopperig; droog; taai, sterk; hees, skor.
hussar', husaar.
huss'y, **(hussies),** sloerie, flerrie, slegte vrou.
hus'tings, verkiesingsverhoog, eleksietribune, bokwa; verkiesingstryd.
hu'stle, (n) gedrang, gestoot; energie; *all was* ~ *and bustle,* alles was in rep en roer; (v) druk, stamp, stoot; deurmekaarskud; (uit)dring, jaag, gou maak; ~**r** spoker, woeler, aandrywer.
hus'wife, naaidosie, werksakkie.
hut, (n) strooihuis, pondok; hut; barak; (v) **(-ted),** in hutte woon; in 'n hut (barak) onder dak bring.
hutch, **(-es),** hok; huisie; kis, trog, bak.

hutment 965 *hypermetropic*

hut'ment, barak(ruimte); barakkekamp, huttekamp.
hut'pole, hutpaal; strooispaal.
hut' tax, hutbelasting, opgaaf.
huzza'! hoera! hoerê!
hy'acinth, naeltjie(blom), hiasint(blom); hiasint= (steen); ~ 'ine, hiasint=.
Hy'ades, die Hiade, die Reënsterre.
hy(a)en'a, *kyk* **hyena.**
hy'aline, (n) gladde seespieël; blou hemel; (a) glas=, glashelder, kristal=; deurskynend; kristalagtig.
hy'alite, hialiet, glasopaal; glassteen, lawaglas.
hyb'rid, (n) baster; kruising; basterwoord; hibried; (a) baster=, hibridies; ~ **form,** bastervorm; ~ **ism,** ver= bastering, kruising; ~ **iza'tion,** verbastering, krui= sing; ~ **ize,** (ver)baster, kruis; ~ **maize,** baster= mielie.
hyd'atid, waterblasie, blaaswurm, hidatide.
Hyd'ra, die Waterslang.
hyd'ra, waterslang; hidra; ~ **-headed,** veelkoppig.
hydran'gea, hortensia, hortensie, moeder-met-die= kindertjies (blom), krismisroos *(Hydrangea hor= tensia).*
hyd'rant, standpyp, standkraan, hidrant, brand= kraan.
hyd'rate, (n) hidraat; ~ *of lime,* gebluste kalk; (v) hidrateer.
hydra'tion, hidrasie, hidratasie, hidratering.
hydraul'ic, hidroulies, vloeistof=; ~ **brake,** hidrou= liese rem, vloeistofrem, olierem; ~ **engineer,** hi= drouliese ingenieur; ~ **engineering,** hidrouliese in= genieurswese; ~ **jack,** hidrouliese domkrag; ~ **press,** waterpers; ~ **ram,** waterram.
hydraul'ics, waterwerktuigkunde; hidroulika.
hydrio'dic, hidriodies.
hyd'ro, (-s), waterkuurinrigting.
hyd'ro=, water=, waterstof=, hidro=.
hydrocarb'on, koolwaterstof.
hydroceph'alous, waterhoofdig.
hydroceph'alus, waterhoof.
hydrochlor'ic acid, soutsuur, chloorwaterstofsuur.
hydrochlor'ide, hidrochloried, hidrochloride.
hydrocyan'ic acid, blousuur, siaanwaterstofsuur.
hydrodynam'ic, hidrodinamies; ~ **s,** waterwerktuig= kunde, hidrodinamika.
hydroelec'tric, hidro-elektries, hidroëlektries; ~ **power,** waterkrag, hidro-elektriese (hidroëlek= triese) krag.
hydroelectric'ity, waterkrag, hidro-elektrisiteit, hidroëlektrisiteit.
hydroextrac'tion, waterverwydering.
hydroextrac'tor, droogmasjien.
hydrofluor'ic acid, waterstoffluoriedsuur.
hy'drofoil, watervin; waterblad.
hy'drogen, waterstof, hidrogeen.
hydro'genate, hidreer, hidrogeneer.
hydrogena'tion, hidrering, hidrogenering.
hy'drogen: ~ **bomb,** waterstofbom; ~ **perox'ide,** wa= terstofperoksied, suurstofwater.
hy'drograph, hidrograaf.
hydrog'rapher, hidrograaf, seebeskrywer.
hydrograph'ic(al), hidrografies; ~ **map,** seekaart.
hydrog'raphy, waterbeskrywing, hidrografie.
hydrokinet'ics, hidrokinetika.
hyd'rolize, hidroliseer.
hydrolog'ic, waterkundig, hidrologies.
hydrol'ogy, waterkunde; waterleer, hidrologie.
hydrol'ysis, hidroliese watersplitsing.
hydromechan'ics, waterwerktuigkunde.
hydromat'ic, hidromaties.
hyd'romel, heuningwater; heuningdrank, heuningwyn.
hydrom'eter, vogmeter, watermeter, hidrometer.
hydromet'ric, hidrometries, watermeetkundig.
hydrom'etry, hidrometrie, watermeetkunde.
hyd'romorph'ic, hidromorf.
hydropath'ic, hidropaties, watergeneeskundig; ~ **es= tablishment,** inrigting vir waterkuur.
hydrop'athist, waterdokter, hidropaat.
hydrop'athy, watergeneeskunde, waterkuur, hidro= patie.
hy'drophane, wateropaal.
hyd'rophile, waterliewend; waterbewonend; water= bestuif.

hyd'rophobe, hidrofoob.
hydrophob'ia, watervrees, hidrofobie; hondsdolheid.
hyd'rophone, hidrofoon.
hyd'rophyl, waterliewend, wateropsuiend.
hyd'rophyte, waterplant, hidrofiet.
hydrophyt'ic, waterliewend.
hydrop'ic, watersugtig.
hyd'roplane, glyboot; watervliegtuig.
hydropon'ics, hidroponika, waterkweking, grond= lose verbouing.
hyd'ropsy, watersug, sugtigheid, hidropsie.
hyd'roscope, hidroskoop.
hyd'rosphere, hidrosfeer, wateromhulsel.
hydrostat'ic(al), hidrostaties.
hydrostat'ics, waterewewigsleer, hidrostatika.
hydrotech'nics, waterboukuns, hidrotegniek.
hydrotherapeut'ic, watergeneeskundig, hidrotera= peuties.
hydrothe'rapy, watergeneeskunde, hidroterapie.
hydrotrop'ic, vogkrommend, hidrotroop.
hydrotrop'ism, vogkromming, hidrotropie.
hyd'rous, waterig, waterhoudend.
hyd'rovane, (n) nooddryfvlak (watervliegtuig); hoog= tegoed (a) hoogte=.
hyen'a, hiëna, (strand)wolf; *BROWN* ~, strandwolf; *SPOTTED* ~, gevlekte hiëna; *STRIPED* ~, ge= streepte hiëna.
hy'etal, reën=; ~ **region,** reënstreek.
hy'etograph, reënkaart.
hyetog'raphy, reënkartering, hiëtografie.
hyetol'ogy, hiëtologie.
hyetom'eter, reënmeter.
hy'giene, gesondheidsleer, higiëne.
hygien'ic, higiënies, gesondheids=.
hygien'ist, higiënis.
hyg'rograph, higrograaf.
hygrol'ogy, vogtigheidsleer, higrologie.
hygrom'eter, vogmeter, higrometer.
hygromet'ric, higrometries, vogbepalend.
hygrom'etry, vogbepaling, higrometrie.
hyg'rophyte, moerasplant, higrofiet.
hyg'roscope, higroskoop, lugvogmeter.
hygroscop'ic, higroskopies, vogtrekkend.
hygros'copy, higroskopie.
hyl'ophyte, bosplant, hilofiet.
hylozo'ism, materialisme, hilosoïsme.
hylozo'ic, materialisties, hilosoïsties.
Hym'en¹, Hymen, huweliksgod.
hym'en², maagdevlies; ~ **e'al,** (n) bruilofslied; (a) huweliks=.
Hymenop'tera, Vliesvlerkiges, Vliesvleueliges.
hymenop'terous, vliesvlerkig, vliesvleuelig.
hymn, (n) gesang, kerklied, loflied, limne; (v) deur lofsange verheerlik, loof, lofsing; ~ **al,** (n) gesang= boek; (a) gesang=; ~ **-book,** gesangboek; ~ **ody,** ge= sangdigting; sang, himnodie; ~ **og'rapher,** gesang= digter; ~ **ol'ogy,** liedkuns, gesangkunde; kerklied.
hy'oid (bone), gaapbeen, tongbeen.
hyp, abbr. of **hypochondria;** *kyk ook* **hip.**
hypabyss'al, hipabissaal.
hypall'age, woordverwisseling, woordomspanning, hipallage.
hyperacid'ity, oorsuurheid, hiperasiditeit.
hyperaesthes'ia, oorgevoeligheid (van die vel), hiperestesie.
hyperaesthet'ic, oorgevoelig, hiperesteties.
hyperb'aton, woordomskikking, hiperbaton.
hyperb'ola, hiperbool (geom.).
hyperb'ole, hiperbool, oordrywing, grootspraak.
hyperbol'ic(al), hiperbolies, oordrewe.
hyperb'olism, hiperbolisme, oordrywing.
hyperbor'ean, (n) Noorderling; (a) uit die hoë noorde.
hypercorrect', hiperkorrek, oorkorrek; ~ **ness,** hiper= korrektheid, oorkorrektheid.
hypercrit'ic, muggiesifter, haarklower, vitter; ~ **al,** hiperkrities, oordrewe streng; ~ **ism,** hiperkritiek, haarklowery.
hyp'erite, hiperiet.
hyp'ermarket, hipermark.
hypermet'rical, hipermetries, met te veel versvoete.
hypermetrop'ia, hipermetropie, versiendheid.
hypermetrop'ic, versiende.

hypermod'ern, hipermodern.
hyperphys'ical, bo(we)natuurlik, hiperfisies.
hypersen'sitive, oorgevoelig.
hypersensitiv'ity, oorgevoeligheid.
hypertroph'ic, hipertrofies.
hyper'trophy, hipertrofie, sieklike vergroting (van 'n orgaan).
hyph'en, (n) koppelteken, strepie, verbindingsteken; rus, pouse; (v) koppel, met 'n koppelteken verbind; ~**ate(d),** ~**ed,** met 'n koppelteken verbind.
hypidiomorph'ic, halfeiervormig, hipidiomorfies.
hypidiomorph'ous, hipidiomorf.
hypnogen'esis, slaapverwekking, hipnogenese.
hypnogenet'ic, slaapwekkend.
hypnophob'ia, vrees om aan die slaap te raak.
hypnos'is, (..noses), hipnose, kunsmatige slaap.
hypnother'apy, hipnoterapie, slaapterapie.
hypnot'ic, (n) slaapdrank; gehipnotiseerde; (a) hipnoties, slaapwekkend.
hyp'notism, hipnotisme.
hyp'notist, hipnotiseur.
hyp'notize, hipnotiseer.
hypoacid'ity, suurgebrek.
hypocen'tre, hiposentrum, aardbewingshaard.
hypochon'dria, aanstellery, verbeelsiekte, hipochondrie, hipokonders, iepekonders; skeet; swaarmoedigheid.
hypochon'driac, (n) swaarmoedige persoon; hipochondris; (a) neerslagtig, aantreklik, hipochondries.
hypoc'risy, huigelary, skynheiligheid, geveinsdheid, femelary.
hyp'ocrite, huigelaar, skynheilige, geveinsde, pilaarbyter, veinsaard, femelaar, klipchristen.
hypocrit'ic(al), huigelagtig, geveins, dubbelhartig, skynheilig.
hypocrys'talline, hipokristallyn, deelkristallyn.
hyp'oderm, onderhuid, hipodermis; ~'**ic,** onderhuids, hipodermies; ~ *ic injection*, onderhuidse inspuiting; ~ *ic needle*, onderhuidse naald; ~ *ic syringe*, onderhuidse spuit.
hipoderm'is, onderhuid, hipodermis.
hypogas'tric, onderbuiks=.
hyp'ogene, hipogeen.
hypog'enous, onderstandig (plantk.); hipogeen (geol.).
hypog'yny, onderstandigheid, hipoginie.
hyp'oid gear, hiperboolrat, hipoïede rat.
hypos'tasis, (..tases), volbloedigheid; (goddelike) wese; grondslag; hipostase.
hypostat'ic, hipostaties; persoonlik.
hy'postyle, (a) suilesaal; (a) hipostiel.
hypot'enuse, hipotenusa, skuins sy.
hypoten'sion, lae bloeddruk.
hyp'othec, hipoteek, verband.
hypoth'ecary, hipoteek=, hipotekêr, verband=.
hypoth'ecate, verpand, verbind.
hypotheca'tion, verpanding, verhipotekering.
hypoth'ecator, verbandgewer.
hypotherm'al, hipotermaal, lou.
hypotherm'ia, diepvriesbehandeling (med.).
hypoth'esis, (..theses), veronderstelling, hipotese.
hypoth'esize, 'n hipotese opstel, veronderstel.
hypothe'tic(al), hipoteties, veronderstellend.
hypsom'eter, hoogtemeter, hipsometer.
hypsom'etry, hoogtemeting, hipsometrie.
hyra'ceum, dassiepis, klipsweet.
hyr'ax, (-es), dassie.
hys'on, groen Sjinese tee.
hyss'op, hisop.
hysterec'tomy, baarmoederuitsnyding, histerektomie.
hyster'ia, histerie.
hyster'ic(al), histeries.
hyster'ics, senuweeaanval; *BE in* ~, jou slap lag; *GO into* ~, dit op die senuwees kry; *HAVE* ~, jou 'n papie lag.
hys'teron pro'teron, histeron proteron, volgordeomkering, inversie.

I

i, (i's), i; *dot the i's and cross the t's,* die puntjie op die i sit.
I, ek; ekke (beklemtoon); ~ *FOR ONE,* wat my betref; *the great* ~ *AM,* die eie ek; ~ *SAY,* hoor 'n bietjie; ek sê.
i'amb, jambe.
iam'bic, (n) jambe; (a) jambies.
iam'bus, (-es, iambi), jambiese versvoet, jambe.
Iber'ia, Iberië; ~**n,** (n) Iberiër; Iberies (taal); (a) Iberies.
ib'ex, (-es), ibeks, Alpebok, Alpynse klipbok *(Capra hircus);* wilde bok *(Capra eigagrus).*
ibid'em, op dieselfde plek, aldaar, ibidem.
ib'is, (-es), ibis, Nylreier, skoorsteenveër; *BALD* ~, wildekalkoen; *SACRED* ~, heilige ibis, skoorsteenveër.
ice, (n) ys; koekversiering; roomys; *BREAK the* ~, die ys breek; *CUT no* ~, nie veel uitrig nie; geen hond haar-af maak nie; *DRY* ~, droë ys; *skate on THIN* ~, op dun ys skaats; iets gevaarliks onderneem; (v) laat verys; met ys bedek; in ys pak; ys vorm; verkil, laat verstyf; versuiker (koek); ~ ac= cretion, ysvorming; yspakking; **I** ~ **Age,** Ystyd; ~ **axe,** yspik; ~ **bag,** yssak; ~**-bank,** ysbank; ~ **bar= rier,** ysmuur; ~ **berg,** ysberg; ~ **blink,** ysrefleksie, ysblink; ~**-blue,** ysblou; ~**-boat,** ysskuit; ysboot; ysbreker; ~**-bound,** vasgeys, vasgevries; ~ **box,** yskas, koelkas; yshouer; ~**-breaker,** ysbreker; ~ **bucket,** ysemmer; ~**-cap,** ysdek, ysbedekking; ys= sak; ~**-chest,** yskas; ~**-cold,** yskoud; ~ **compress,** ysomslag; ~ **cornet,** roomyshoring; ~ **cream** roomys; ~ **cream cone,** roomyshoring; ~ **cream soda,** roomysbruisdrank, roomyssoda; ~ **cube,** ys= blokkie.
iced, bevries, afgekoel; geys; ~ **cake,** versierde koek;
~ **coffee,** yskoffie; verkilde koffie; ~ **lolly,** suig= ysie; ~ **melon,** verkilde spanspek; ~ **water,** ys= water.
ice: ~**-drift,** ysgang; ~ **factory,** ysfabriek; ~**-fall,** ys= neerslag; ysval; ~**-field,** ysveld; ysvlakte; ~**-float,** ~**-floe,** ysblok, ysskots; ~ **flower,** ysblom; ~**-foot,** ysrand; ~ **formation,** ysvorming; ~**-free,** ysvry; ~**-hockey,** yshokkie; ~**-hook,** yshaak; ~**-house,** yskelder.
Ice'land, Ysland; ~ **er,** Yslander; ~'**ic,** (n) Yslands (taal); (a) Yslands; ~ **poppy,** Yslandse papawer; ~ **spar,** dubbelspaat, Yslandspaat.
ice: ~ **man,** ysloper; baanveër; ysmaker; roomysma= ker; ~**-needle,** ysnaald; ~**-pack,** pakys; ~**-pick,** yspik, ysbreker; ~**-plant,** brakslaai, slaaibos, sout= slaai; ~**-plough,** ysploeg; ~ **pudding,** verysde poe= ding; ~**-rat,** ysrot; ~**-run,** sleebaan; ~ **s,** ysgeregte; ~**-sheet,** ysveld; ~**-stream,** ysgang; ~**-sucker,** ys= stokkie; ~**-wafer,** yswafel; ~**-water,** yswater; ~ **works,** ysfabriek.
Ich'abod, Ikabod.
ichneum'on, faraosrot, igneumon *(Herpestes);* ~ **fly,** sluipwesp.
ichnog'raphy, ignografie, plattegrondtekening.
ich'n(ol)ite, fossielvoetspoor.
ichnol'ogy, ignologie, studie van fossielvoetspore.
ich'or, godebloed; bloedwater, bloedvog, waterige wonduitvloeisel.
ichtyog'raphy, visbeskrywing, igtiografie.
ich'thyoid, visagtig.
ich'thyol, igtiol.
ich'thyolite, versteende vis, visfossiel.
ichthyolog'ic(al), viskundig, igtiologies.
ichthyol'ogist, viskundige, igtioloog.
ichthyol'ogy, kennis van visse, viskunde, igtiologie.

ichthyoph'agist, viseter, igtiofaag.
ichthyoph'agous, visetend.
ichthyosaur'us, visakkedis, igtiosourus.
i'cicle, yskeël, ysnaald.
i'cily, yskoud.
i'ciness, yskoudheid, ysigheid.
i'cing, ysvorming; yskors, suikerkors, versuikering; koekversiering; koekversiersel; ~ **sugar**, versiersuiker; ~ **syringe**, versierspuit; ~ **tube**, versierbuis.
ic'on, (-s), beeld, ikon.
icon'oclasm, beeldstorm; ikonoklasme.
icon'oclast, beeldstormer, ikonoklas.
iconoclas'tic, beeldstormend, ikonoklasties; ~ **riots**, beeldestorm.
iconog'rapher, tekenaar.
iconog'raphy, beeldbeskrywing, ikonografie; geïllustreerde werk.
iconol'ater, beeldedienaar.
iconol'atry, beeldediens.
iconol'ogy, ikonologie.
iconom'achy, beeldestormery.
icosahe'dral, twintigvlakkig, ikosaëdries.
icosahed'ron, twintigvlak, ikosaëder.
icositetrahed'ron, ikositetraëder.
icter'ic, (n) geelsuglyer; (a) geelsugtig.
ic'terus, geelsug; cholose (by plante).
ic'tus, (-es), klemtoon, toonheffing, iktus.
i'cy, ysagtig; yskoud, ys=.
ide¹, winde (soort vis).
ide², ide, idus; ~ **of March**, noodlotsdag (fig.).
ide'a, idee, denkbeeld; dunk, besef, benul; begrip, spesmaas, nosie; ontwerp, plan, opvatting; *what's the BIG* ~?, watter snertplan het jy nou weer?; *a BRIGHT* ~, 'n blink gedagte; *EXCHANGE of* ~ *s*, gedagtewisseling; *not the FAINTEST* ~, nie die minste benul nie; *be FULL of* ~ *s*, honderde planne hê; *HAVE an* ~, vermoed; dink, 'n spesmaas hê; *have a HIGH* ~ *of*, 'n hoë dunk hê van; *it IS an* ~, daar sit iets in; ~ *s are worth MONEY*, 'n plan is 'n boerdery; *I had NO* ~ *of doing it*, ek was hoegenaamd nie van plan om dit te doen nie; *MAN of* ~ *s*, vindingryke man; *THAT'S the* ~, dis die bedoeling; dis reg; *THE (very)* ~!, verbeel jou!; *have only a VAGUE* ~, die klok hoor lui, maar nie weet waar die klepel (bel) hang nie.
ide'a'd, ide'aed, vol planne, ryk aan idees.
ide'al, (n) ideaal; (a) ideaal; denkbeeldig; ideëel; voorbeeldig; ~ **ism**, idealisme; ~ **ist**, idealis; ~ **is'tic**, idealisties; ~ **ity**, idealiteit; die ideale; ~ **iza'tion**, idealisasie; ~ **ize**, idealiseer.
ide'ate, ideë vorm, uitdink.
idée fi'xe, idee fixe, obsessie, dominerende gedagte (denkbeeld).
id'em, idem, dieselfde.
iden'tical, identies, identiek, (die)selfde, einste; ~ *twins*, identiese (eenderse) tweeling.
iden'tifiable, herkenbaar; uitkenbaar.
identifica'tion, gelykstelling, vereenselwiging; aanwysing, bepaling, vasstelling; eiening, identifikasie; ~ **card**, identiteitskaart, ~ **certificate**, legitimasiebewys ~ **disc**, herkenningsplaatjie; ~ **parade**, uitkenparade, eieningsparade; ~ **plate**, nommerplaat.
iden'tify, (..fied), vereenselwig; aanwys, eien; bepaal; vasstel, identifiseer, uitken; herken; gelykstel; ~ *oneself with*, jou vereenselwig met.
iden'tity, (..ties), eenselwigheid, identiteit, persoonlikheid, individualiteit, gelykheid; *proof of* ~, identiteitsbewys; ~ **card**, persoonskaart, identiteitsbewys; ~ **disc**, identiteitskyf, kenplaatjie; ~ **document**, identiteitsdokument.
id'eogram, id'eograph, ideogram, begripteken.
ideograph'ic, ideografies.
ideog'raphy, ideografie, begriptekenskrif.
ideolog'ic, ideologies.
ideol'ogist, ideoloog; dweper.
i'deologue, ideoloog; teoretikus.
ideol'ogy, ideologie, begripsleer, ideëleer; dwepery.
ide'omotor, ideomotor.
ides, idus (15e Maart, Mei, Julie, Oktober, 13e van orige maande).

id'iocy, onnoselheid, stompsinnigheid, idiootheid, idiotery.
idio-elec'tric, bliksemstofhoudend, idioëlektries.
i'diolect, idiolek, individuele taalgebruik (taalvorm).
id'iom, spraakwending; tongval, dialek; idioom; idiomatiese uitdrukking, taaleie; spraakgebruik; *dictionary of* ~ *s*, idiotikon; ~ **at'ic**, idiomaties; eg.
idiomorph'ic, eievormig, idiomorf.
idiopath'ic, idiopaties.
idiop'athy, idiopatie.
idiosyn'crasy, (..sies), eienaardigheid, sonderlingheid, idiosinkrasie.
id'iot, onnosele, domkop, idioot, swaap, houtkop; ~ **'ic(al)**, dwaas, dom, onnosel, stompsinnig; onsinnig.
idiot'icon, idiomeversameling; idiotikon.
id'iotism, dwaasheid, onnoselheid, idiotisme; swaksinnigheid; onkunde.
i'dle, (v) lui wees, leeglê, niks doen, luier, beusel, lanterfanter, leegloop; vry loop, luier (motor); ~ *away*, verbeusel, mors, verluier, omdrentel; (a) lui, traag, niksdoende; ongegrond; leeg, vergeefs, nutteloos, ydel; werkloos, onbeset; uitgeskakel (rat); *BE* ~, leeglê; met die hande in die skoot sit; ~ *RUMOUR*, los gerug; ~ *TALK*, kafpraatjies; bogpraatjies; ~ *WORDS*, hol klanke.
i'dleness, luiheid, ledigheid; vrugteloosheid; ~ *is the DEVIL'S bolster*, ~ *is the root of all EVIL*, ledigheid is die duiwel se oorkussing; ~ *makes the WITS rust*, rus roes.
i'dler, luiaard, luilak, huisleër; leegloper, dagdief; ~ **shaft**, tussenratas (motor); ~ **wheel**, tussenrat.
i'dling, (n) (die) leegloop, niksdoenery; luiering (motor); (a) luierend; leegloperig.
i'dly, ledig, sonder om iets te doen.
id'ol, afgod; afgodsbeeld, aangebedene, skynbeeld; drekgod; *a clay* ~, 'n afgod van klei.
idol: ~ **'ater**, afgodsdienaar; vereerder; ~ **'atress, (-es)**, afgodsdienares; ~ **'atrous**, afgodies, heidens; ~ **'atry**, afgodsdiens, afgodery, beeldediens; vergoding, verering; ~ **iza'tion**, verafgoding.
id'olize, verafgod, verafgoed, vereer, aanbid; 'n afgod maak van; ~ **r**, verafgoder; vereerder.
idol'um, (..la), waan, dwaalbegrip; idee, voorstelling.
id'y(l), idille, herdersdig.
idyll'ic, idillies.
id'yllist, idilledigter.
if, (n) as; ~ *s and ands were POTS and pans*, as is verbrande hout; *WITHOUT any* ~ *s or ands*, sonder omweë; (conj) indien, as, so, ingeval; of; ~ *ANY*, as daar is; *AS* ~, asof; ~ *BUT*, as maar net; *he is forty* ~ *he is a DAY*, hy is geen dag jonger as veertig nie; *FEW* ~ *any*, weinig of geen; ~ *I had only KNOWN*, as ek maar net geweet het; ~ *NEED be*, desnoods; ~ *NOT*, so nie; ~ *SO*, so ja.
ifa'fa lily, ifafalelie.
ig'loo, Eskimohut, sneeuhut, igloe.
ig'neous, vuur=; vulkanies, vulkaan=, stol=, stollings=; ~ **complex**, stollingskompleks; ~ **rock**, stolrots, stollingsgesteente.
ignis fat'uus, (ignes fatui), dwaallig.
ignit'able, ontbrandbaar, brandbaar, ontvlambaar.
ignite', ontbrand, aan die brand raak (steek), ontvlam; ontsteek (motor); aansteek (vuur).
ignit'er, aansteker, ontsteker, lont; sunder (granaat); ~ **cord**, aansteekkoord.
igni'tion, ontbranding; ontsteking (motor); gloeiing; *ADVANCE the* ~, voorontsteking gee; *RETARD the* ~, naontsteking gee; *SPONTANEOUS* ~, selfontsteking; ~ **chamber**, ontstekingskamer, ontstekingskas, vlamkas; ~ **coil**, ontstekingsklos; ~ **control**, ontstekingsreëling; ~ **current**, ontstekingstroom; ~ **distributor**, vonkverdeler; ~ **key**, motorsleutel, aanskakelsleutel; ~ **point**, ontstekingspunt; vlampunt; ~ **system**, vonkstelsel; ontstekingstelsel; ~ **switch**, vonkskakelaar; ~ **timing**, vonkreëling, ~ **wire**, vonkdraad, verbindingsdraad.
igno'ble, laag, gemeen, onedel, veragtelik.
igno'bly, skandelik, op lae manier; ~ **born**, van geringe afkoms.

ignomin'ious, skandelik, veragtelik, laag, onterend, smadelik, oneervol.
ig'nominy, skande, oneer, smadelikheid.
ignoram'us, (-es), domkop, domoor, stommerik, weet-nie, onkundige.
ig'norance, onkunde, onwetendheid, onbekendheid; *where ~ is BLISS 'tis folly to be wise*, waar onkunde geluk bring, is wysheid dwaasheid; *as onkunde hom gelukkig maak, is hy 'n dwaas wat wys wil raak; he was LEFT in ~*, hy is onkundig gelaat.
ig'norant, onkundig, onwetend; onnosel; *~ of*, onbekend met; *~ly*, onwetend.
ignore', verbysien, ignoreer, doodswyg, misken, negeer; *~ a bill*, 'n aanklag verwerp.
igua'na, likkewaan, iguana.
iguan'odon, iguanodon.
ikeba'na, ikebana, Japanse blommerangskikking.
Ik'ey, (-s), Joodjie; heler; U.K.-student.
ila'la palm, ilalapalm *(Hyphoene crinita)*.
il'eal, kronkelderm-.
ilei'tis, kronkeldermontsteking, ileïtis.
il'eum, kronkelderm, ileum.
il'eus, dermknoop, dermafsluiting.
il'ex, (-es), steeneik; huls; ileks, waterhout.
il'iac, derm-; *~ artery*, dermslagaar; *~ bone*, dermbeen; *~ passion*, dermjig.
Il'iad: *the ~*, die Ilias.
Il'ium, Ilium, Troje.
il'ium, (ilia), heupbeen; dermbeen.
ilk, (n) klas, soort; *of THAT ~*, van dieselfde plek (naam); *THAT ~*, daardie soort (klas); (a) dieselfde.
ill, (n) kwaad; verdorwenheid; ramp, ongeluk; *the ~ s that flesh is heir to*, menslike kwale; (a) siek; ongesteld, kaduks; sleg; kwaad; kwaadwillig; *with ~ EFFECTS*, met slegte gevolge; *house of ~ FAME*, slegte huis, bordeel; *with an ~ GRACE*, nukkerig; *~ MANAGEMENT*, slegte beheer, gebrekkige bestuur; *take something in ~ PART*, iets kwalik neem; *do an ~ TURN to a person*, iem. 'n ondiens bewys; *~ WEEDS grow apace*, onkruid vergaan nie; *it's an ~ WIND that blows nobody good*, geen kwaad sonder baat; (adv) sleg, erg; kwalik; verkeerd; *it BECOMES him ~*, dit pas hom sleg; dit betaam hom nie; *be ~ at EASE*, nie op sy gemak wees nie; *SPEAK ~ of*, kwaadspreek van; *TAKE it ~*, dit kwalik neem; *TAKE (TAKEN) ~*, siek word; *THINK ~ of*, 'n slegte dunk hê van; *~ -advised*, onbedag, onberade; onverstandig, onbesonne, onwys; *~ -affected*, kwaadgesind, kwaadwillig.
illa'tion, gevolgtrekking.
illa'tive, gevolgtrekkend; redegewend.
ill: *~ -balanced*, onewewigtig; *~ -behaved*, onmanierlik, onbeskof; *~ blood*, kwaaivriendskap; *~ -bred*, ongemanierd, ru, onopgevoed; ongepoets; *~ breeding*, ongemanierdheid; *~ -conditioned*, beskadig; sleggeaard; *~ -conceived*, ondeurdag; *~ -considered*, onbedag, ondeurdag; onbekook; *~ -contrived*, onoordeelkundig; *~ -disposed*, kwaadgesind, kwaadwillig; *~ -doer*, oortreder, kwaaddoener; *~ -doers are ill-deemers*, soos die waard is, vertrou hy sy gaste; wie ander vervolg, staan self nie stil nie.
illeg'al, onwettig, wederregtelik, onregmatig, buitewetlik; *~ 'ity*, onwettigheid, onregmatigheid, wederregtelikheid; *~ ize*, onwettig maak.
illegibil'ity, onleesbaarheid, onduidelikheid.
illeg'ible, onleesbaar, onduidelik.
illegit'imacy, onwettigheid; onegtheid; ongeoorloofdheid.
illegit'imate, (n) buite-egtelike kind; (v) onwettig of oneg verklaar; (a) onwettig; ongeoorloof; oneg, baster-; buite-egtelik; *~ child*, buite-egtelike kind.
ill: *~ fame*, slegte naam; *~ -famed*, berug; *~ -fated*, ongelukkig, rampspoedig; *it is ~ -fated, daar sal geen seën op rus nie*; *~ -favoured*, lelik, mismaak; afstootlik; *~ feeling*, wrok, slegte gevoelens; *~ -fitting*, slodderig; *~ -gotten*, onregverdig verkry; *~ -gotten gains seldom prosper*, onregverdige goed gedy nie; *~ health*, sieklikheid, ongesondheid; *~ humour*, wrewelighed; *~ -humoured*, sleggehumeurd, wrewelig.

illib'eral, laag, onedel, kleingeestig, bekrompe; onvrysinnig; karig, stiefmoederlik.
illiberal'ity, onedelmoedigheid; suinigheid.
illi'cit, ongeoorloof, onwettig; *~ diamond buying*, onwettige diamanthandel.
illim'itable, onbegrens, grensloos.
illiq'uid, illikwied, illikied.
illiquid'ity, illikwiditeit, illikiditeit.
illit'eracy, ongeletterdheid, ongeleerdheid.
illit'erate, (n) analfabeet, ongeletterde; (a) ongeletterd, ongeleerd; onontwikkeld; onbelese; *~ ness*, ongeleerdheid.
ill: *~ -judged*, onbesonne, onberade; *~ -looking*, lelik, bedenklik; *~ luck*, teenspoed, ongeluk; *as ~ luck would have it*, soos die ongeluk dit wou hê; *~ -mannered*, ongemanierd, onwellewend; *~ -matched*, *~ -mated*, verkeerd gepaar, sleg passend; *~ nature*, sleggeaardheid, sleggehumeurdheid; *~ -natured*, kwaadaardig, boosaardig, sleggehumeurd; *~ ness*, siekte, ongesteldheid.
illog'ical, onlogies, onredelik.
ill: *~ omen*, voorspooksel, slegte voorteken; *~ -omened*, onheilspellend; rampspoedig; *~ -placed*, misplaas; *~ -pleased*, misnoeg, ontevrede; *~ -sorted*, deurmekaar, ongelyksoortig; *~ -starred*, onheilspellend, ongelukkig; *~ temper*, norsheid, *~ -tempered*, sleggeluim, sleggehumeurd, choleries; nors; *~ -timed*, ontydig; lastig; ongeleë; *~ -timed joke*, misplaaste (ontydige) grap; *~ -treat*, mishandel, sleg behandel.
illude', bedrieg; mislei.
illume', verlig; verhelder.
illum'inant, (n) verligtingsmiddel; (a) verligtend.
illum'inate, verlig, deurstraal, belig, bestraal, deurlig, illumineer; verduidelik; toelig; versier; opluister, beglans, begloor; verlug; *~ d ADDRESS*, verlugte (geïllumineerde) adres; *~ d MANUSCRIPT*, verlugte (geïllumineerde) handskrif (manuskrip); *~ d SIGN*, ligreklame; verligte uithangbord; neonlig, -advertensie.
illuminat'i, (n, pl) geheime genootskap (in 1776 gestig); verligte persone.
illum'inating, insigewend; verhelderend; verligtend.
illumina'tion, verligting, illuminasie; beligting (foto); versiering; luister; ligsterkte; openbaring; verlugting.
illum'inative, verligtend, leersaam; lig-, liggewend.
illum'inator, verligter; voorligter; liggewer; verlugter (ms.).
illum'ine, verlig, illumineer; verhelder; verlug.
ill: *~ usage*, slegte behandeling, mishandeling; *~ -use*, sleg behandel, mishandel.
illu'sion, sinsbedrog, illusie, hersenskim, (sins)begoëling, drogbeeld, spieëlbeeld, droombeeld; deursigtige tulle; *shatter someone's ~ s*, iem. uit die droom help; *~ ist*, illusionis; goëlaar.
illus'ive, illus'ory, bedrieglik; denkbeeldig.
ill'ustrate, ophelder, verduidelik, opluister, veraanskoulik; illustreer, verlug (boek); kenskets; *~ d*, verduidelik; geïllustreer, verlug; *~ d work*, geïllustreerde werk.
illustra'tion, opheldering; verlugting, illustrasie, prent, plaat; opluistering.
illustra'tive, ophelderend, verduidelikend; kensketsend.
ill'ustrator, toeligter, versierder; verlugter, illustreerder.
illus'trious, beroemd, vermaard, deurlugtig, skitterend, roemryk, hoog; *~ ness*, deurlugtigheid.
illuv'ium, inspoelgrond, illuvium.
ill: *~ will*, teensin; kwaadwilligheid; *~ -wisher*, kwaadgesinde.
Illyr'ia, Illirië; *~ n, (n)* Illiriër; (a) Illiries.
il'menite, ilmeniet.
im'age, (n) beeld; afbeelding, afbeeldsel, beeltenis; ewebeeld; toonbeeld; voorstelling; *the ~ of his COUNTRY has improved overseas*, die beeld van sy land het oorsee verbeter; *the very ~ of his FATHER*, die ewebeeld van sy vader, sy pa uitgeknip; (v) afbeeld, skilder, teken; voorstel; weerspieël, weergee, weerkaats; *~ breaker*, ikonoklas, beeldestormer; *~ -building*, beeldbouery, beeld-

imaginal 	 *impalpable*

skepping; ~ **ry,** afbeelding; verbeelding; beeld=
spraak; hersenskim; beeldwerk; beeldrykheid; ~
worship, beeldediens.
ima'ginal, imaginaal; beeldend; verbeeldend.
imag'inable, denkbaar.
ima'ginary, denkbeeldig, fiktief, ideëel; ~ *ailments,*
ingebeelde siekte, hipokonders, iepekonders, skete.
imagina'tion, verbeelding, voorstelling; verbeel=
dingskrag, voorstellingsvermoë.
imag'inative, vindingryk; verbeeldings=; ~ **faculty,**
~ **power,** verbeeldingskrag.
imag'ine, (jou) verbeel, dink, (jou) voorstel; 'n denk=
beeld vorm; waan; *JUST* ~*!,* bid jou aan! verbeel
jou! nou toe nou! dink net; *don't START imagining
things,* moenie voorspooksels maak nie.
i'magist, imagis.
imag'o, (imagines, -s), imago, volwasse insek.
imam', imam.
im'balance, wanbalans, gebrek aan ewewig.
im'becile, (n) swaksinnige, imbesiel; (a) swak; swak=
sinnig, geestelik swak, imbesiel.
imbecil'ity, swaksinnigheid, onnoselheid, imbesili=
teit; swakheid, onvermoë.
imbibe', opdrink, insuig, indrink.
imbibi'tion, indrinking, opneming, opsuiging.
im'bricate, (v) soos dakpanne oormekaar lê; (a) dak=
pansgewyse, skubsgewyse, oormekaarliggend.
imbrica'tion, dakpansgewyse ligging, oormekaar lig=
ging.
imbrog'lio, (-s), verwarring; imbroglio; (dramatiese)
verwikkeling, warboel.
imbrue': ~ *IN,* doop in; ~ *WITH,* bevlek.
imbrute', verdierlik, brutaliseer.
imbue', deurweek, deurtrek; drenk, vervul, inboesem,
inspireer (met); ~ *with,* vul met, besiel met.
imbu'a, imbuia(hout).
i'mide, imied, imide.
imitabil'ity, navolgbaarheid.
im'itable, navolgbaar.
im'itate, navolg, namaak, na-aap, naboots.
imita'tion, (n) navolging, namaaksel, nabootsing,
imitasie; (a) nagemaak, namaak; ~ *is the sincerest
form of flattery,* na-apery is vleiery; ~ **diamond,**
onegte diamant; ~ **lace,** nagemaakte kant; ~
leather, kunsleer; ~ **python(-skin),** nagemaakte lui=
slang(vel).
im'itative, na-apend, nabootsend; nagemaak; ~ *of,*
in navolging van; ~ **arts,** beeldende kunste.
im'itator, na-aper, nabootser, namaker, navolger, eg=
gomens.
immac'ulacy, onbevlektheid; vlekkeloosheid.
immac'ulate, rein, smet(te)loos, onbevlek, vlekloos;
onberispelik; ongevlek; **I** ~ **Conception,** Onbevlek=
te Ontvangenis; ~ **ness,** reinheid, vlekloosheid, on=
berispelikheid.
imm'anence, innerlikheid, immanensie; inwoning.
imm'anent, innerlik, inwonend, inherent, imma=
nent.
Imman'uel, Immanuel.
immater'ial, geestelik, onstoflik, stof(fe)loos; onbe=
langrik; onverskillig, *it IS* ~ *to me,* vir my is dit om
die ewe; *THAT'S* ~, dit maak nie saak nie; ~ **ism,**
immaterialisme; ~ **'ity,** onstoflikheid, onliggaam=
likheid; onbelangrikheid.
immature', groen, onvolgroei, onvolwasse; onbe=
kwaam (groente); ongeryp; ontydig; onryp; ~ **ly,**
ontydig, te vroeg; ~ **ness,** .. **tur'ity,** onrypheid; on=
tydigheid.
immeasurabil'ity, onmeetbaarheid, onmeetlikheid.
immea'surable, onmeetbaar, onmeetlik.
immed'iacy, onmiddellikheid.
immed'iate, direk, onmiddellik; dadelik, haastig, met
spoed; ~ **future,** onmiddellike (nabye) toekoms;
~ **ly,** dadelik, onmiddellik, op stel en sprong, su=
biet, sommer, terstond, op staande voet; ~ **ness,**
onmiddellikheid; ~ **past-president,** pas uitgetrede
president.
immemor'ial, onheuglik, eeue-oud; *from time* ~, van
onheuglike tye af; ~ **ly,** van onheuglike tye.
immense', onmeetlik, oneindig, onafsienbaar, baie
groot, enorm, kolossaal; ~ **ly,** ontsaglik; besonder;
~ **ness,** ontsaglikheid, onmeetlikheid.

immens'ity, onmeetlikheid, onbegrensdheid, ontsag=
likheid.
immensurabil'ity, onmeetbaarheid.
immen'surable, onmeetbaar.
immerge', immerse', (onder)dompel, insteek; laat
sink; ~ **d,** ondergedompel; weggeduik, onder
water.
immer'ser, dompelaar.
immer'sion, onderdompeling, (in)doping; immersie
(sterre); diepgang (skip); ~ **heater,** dompelverwar=
mer, dompelaar; ~ **rudder,** duikroer; ~ **tank,**
duiktenk.
immethod'ical, onmetodies, ongereeld.
imm'igrant, (n) landverhuiser, immigrant; (a) immi=
grerend, intrekkend.
imm'igrate, trek, verhuis, immigreer.
immigra'tion, verhuising, immigrasie.
imm'inence, nabyheid; dreiging.
imm'inent, aanstaande, dreigend; naby, naderende,
nakende, voor die deur staande; ~ *danger,* drei=
gende gevaar.
immiscibil'ity, onmengbaarheid.
immis'cible, onmengbaar.
immit'igable, onversagbaar, onvermurfbaar, onver=
soenlik.
immix'ture, vermenging; inmenging.
immob'ile, onbeweeglik, bewegingloos.
immobil'ity, onbeweeglikheid, immobiliteit.
immob'ilize, onbeweeglik maak; (troepe) immobiel
maak, buite geveg stel, lam lê, immobiliseer; vas=
hou; aan die omloop onttrek (geld).
immod'erate, onmatig, onredelik, mateloos, buiten=
sporig.
immodera'tion, onmatigheid, buitensporigheid, on=
redelikheid.
immod'est, onbeskeie; onbetaamlik, onfatsoenlik,
onkies, onkuis; ~ **y,** onbeskeidenheid; onbehoor=
likheid, onbetaamlikheid, onkiesheid.
imm'olate, (op)offer.
immola'tion, opoffering; offerande.
imm'olator, offeraar.
immor'al, onsedelik, onkuis, immoreel; sedeloos;
~ **'ity,** onsedelikheid, sedeloosheid; ontug; immo=
raliteit.
immort'al, onsterflik; onverganklik; *the* ~ *s,* die on=
sterflikes; ~ **'ity,** onsterflikheid; ~ **ize,** verewig, on=
sterflik maak.
immortelle', sewejaartjie, altydblommetjie, immor=
telle, strooiblom.
immovabil'ity, onbeweeglikheid, onbeweegbaarheid.
immov'able, (n) vaste besitting, vasstaande ding; (pl)
vaste eiendom, vasgoed; (a) onbeweeglik, onbe=
weegbaar, ongevoelig; vas, onroerend; onwrik=
baar, pal, onveranderlik, onversetlik; ~ **property,**
vaste eiendom; onroerende goed, vasgoed.
immune', vry van, immuun, onvatbaar (vir); gesout
(teen siekte), ~ *against disease,* onvatbaar vir siek=
te.
immun'ity, onvatbaarheid, souting; vrystelling, vry=
dom, vryheid; voorreg, onskendbaarheid, privile=
gie (diplomate).
immuniza'tion, onvatbaarmaking, immunisering.
imm'unize, immuun maak, immuniseer, sout.
immure', ommuur, omsluit; inmessel.
immutabil'ity, onveranderlikheid.
immut'able, onveranderlik.
imp, (n) kabouter; platjie, kwelgees, duiweltjie,
skelm, vabond, rakker, ondeug; (v) inplant (vere).
im'pact[1]**,** (n) skok, stamp; botsing; slag; aanslag; tref=
punt (projektiel); ~ *ON,* inwerking op; *POINT of*
~, trefpunt.
impact'[2]**,** (v) saampak, indryf; instamp; saampers.
impair', beskadig; verswak; verhinder, belemmer;
~ **ed,** beskadig, geknak; ~ **ment,** verswakking, be=
skadiging; benadeling.
impal'a, impala, rooibok; ~ **lily,** impalalelie *(Ade=
nium multiflorum, A. Swazicum).*
impale', deursteek, deurboor; ompaal; ~ **ment,** om=
paling, paalwerk; deurboring.
impalpabil'ity, onmerkbaarheid; fynheid; onvoel=
baarheid, ontasbaarheid.
impal'pable, ontasbaar, onvatbaar, onvoelbaar.

impalpably 970 *implicate*

impal'pably, ongemerk; ontasbaar.
impal'udism, moerassiekte.
impan'el, *kyk* **empanel**.
impa'radise, verruk; in 'n paradys verander.
impa'rity, ongelykheid.
impark', afkamp, omhein; in 'n park hou.
impart', meedeel, deelagtig maak, gee; ~ **a'tion**, meedeling.
impar'tial, onpartydig; ~ **'ity**, onpartydigheid, onbevangenheid; ~ **ly**, onpartydig.
impart'ible, onverdeelbaar.
impassabil'ity, ontoeganklikheid; onoorkoomlikheid; ondeurwaadbaarheid; onrybaarheid, onbegaanbaarheid.
impass'able, ontoeganklik; onpassabel, onrybaar, onbegaanbaar; ondeurwaadbaar; ~ **ness** = **impassability**.
impasse', doodloopstraat; dooie punt; benarde toestand, netelige posisie, impasse.
impassibil'ity, ongevoeligheid, onverskilligheid, onaandoenlikheid.
impass'ible, onaandoenlik, onaangedaan; ongevoelig, onvatbaar; ~ **ness** = **impassibility**.
impa'ssion, ontroer, aangryp, aanvuur, opwek; ~ **ed**, hartstogtelik, gepassioneerd, vurig.
impass'ive, ongevoelig, stomp; lydelik, onaandoenlik; ~ **ly**, drogies.
impassiv'ity, ongevoeligheid; lydelikheid; onverstoorbaarheid; onaandoenlikheid.
impaste', knee; toeplak; dik smeer; tot 'n deeg maak.
impas'to, dik kleuraanwending, impasto.
impa'tience, ongeduld; driftigheid.
impa'tient, ongeduldig; verlangend; driftig, moeilik; *be* ~ *FOR*, verlang na; *be* ~ *OF*, nie kan verdra nie.
impawn', verpand.
impeach', beskuldig, aankla; betwis, in twyfel trek; wraak (reg); ~ **able**, berispelik, aanklaagbaar; laakbaar; ~ **er**, beskuldiger, aanklaer; ~ **ment**, beskuldiging, aanklag; verdagmaking.
impeccabil'ity, sondeloosheid, onberispelikheid, volmaaktheid.
impecc'able, onfeilbaar; volmaak, onberispelik.
impecunios'ity, geldgebrek, onbemiddeldheid.
impecun'ious, arm, platsak, onbemiddeld.
imped'ance, skynweerstand, impedansie (elektr.).
impede', verhinder, bemoeilik, belemmer, vertraag, belet, teenhou.
imped'iment, hindernis, beletsel; hinderpaal; hapering, belemmering; ~ *of MARRIAGE*, huweliksbeletsel; ~ *in one's SPEECH*, spraakgebrek.
impedimen'ta, leërbagasie, laergoed.
impel', (-led), (aan)drywe, aanspoor, dring; voortstu; beweeg; ~ **lent**, (n) dryfkrag; aandrang, aansporing; (a) aansporend, aandrywend; ~ **ler**, looprat, dryfrat; voortdrywer, aanspoorder, dryfkrag.
impend', dreig, nader kom; bo die hoof swewe; op hande wees; voor die deur staan; ~ **ence**, dreiging; ~ **ing**, dreigend, naderend, aanstaande, op hande, nakende.
impenetrabil'ity, ondeurgrondelikheid; ondeurdringbaarheid.
impen'etrable, ondeurdringbaar, ondeurgrondelik; ongevoelig, onvatbaar, ontoeganklik.
impen'etrate, diep deurdring.
impen'itence, onboetvaardigheid, verstoktheid.
impen'itent, onboetvaardig, verstok.
impe'rative, (n) imperatief; (a) gebiedend; dringend; noodsaaklik; onafwysbaar, verplig; ~ *MOOD*, gebiedende wys(e), imperatief; ~ *NECESSITY*, dringende noodsaaklikheid; ~ **ness**, gebiedendheid.
imperat'or, keiser, imperator; ~ **'ial**, keiserlik, imperatories.
impercep'tible, on(be)merkbaar, onwaarneembaar; ~ **ness**, onmerkbaarheid, onwaarneembaarheid, onbespeurbaarheid.
impercip'ient, sonder waarnemingsvermoë, ongevoelig, bot.
imperf'ect, (n) imperfektum, onvoltooid verlede tyd; (a) onvolmaak, onvolkome; onvoltooid; ~ *tense*, onvoltooid verlede tyd, imperfektum; . . **fec'tion**, onvolmaaktheid, onvolkomenheid; gebrek, tekortkoming; ~ **ly**, onvolmaak; sleg, onduidelik.
imperf'orate, ongeperforeer, ongetand (filatelie); mondloos; nie deursteek nie, sonder opening; ~ *d stamp*, ongetande seël.
imper'ial, (n) imperiaalkoffer; imperiaalpapier; Napoleonsbaardjie, bokbaardjie, kenbaardjie; imperiaal (muntstuk); (a) keiserlik, imperiaal; keisers-; ryks-; verhewe; gebiedend; heerssugtig; heersers-; ~ **city**, rykstad; ~ **conference**, rykskonferensie; ~ **crown**, keiserskroon; ~ **gallon**, Britse gellingmaat; ~ **ism**, imperialisme; ~ **ist**, imperialis; ~ **is'tic**, imperialisties; ~ **preference**, ryksvoorkeur; ~ **section**, keisersnee; ~ **yellow**, keisersgeel.
impe'ril, (-led, -led), in gevaar bring.
imper'ious, heerssugtig, meesteragtig; gebiedend, dringend; ~ *NECESSITY*, gebiedende noodsaak; ~ *SPIRIT*, heerssug; ~ **ly**, gebiedenderwys; ~ **ness**, aanmatiging, heerssug, baasspelerigheid; noodsaaklikheid, drang.
imperishabil'ity, onverganklikheid; onbederfbaarheid, onbederflikheid.
impe'rishable, onverganklik; onbederfbaar, onbederflik (produkte).
impe'rium, imperium, oppermag, keiserryk.
imperm'anence, onbestendigheid, verganklikheid.
imperm'anent, onbestendig, onduursaam, tydelik.
impermeabil'ity, ondeurdringbaarheid.
imperm'eable, ondeurdringbaar, waterdig, syferdig.
impermissibil'ity, ontoelaatbaarheid.
impermiss'ible, ontoelaatbaar, ongeoorloof.
impers'onal, onpersoonlik; ~ **'ity**, onpersoonlikheid.
impers'onate, verpersoonlik; die rol speel van, vertolk; voorstel, jou uitgee vir.
impersona'tion, verpersoonliking, identiteitsbedrog; voorstelling, vertolking.
impers'onator, vertolker, voorsteller.
imperson'ify (. . fied), verpersoonlik, personifieer.
impert'inence, parmantigheid, brutaliteit, onbeskoftheid, astrantheid; onbeskaamdheid.
impert'inent, parmantig, brutaal; onbeskaamd, wys; onbeskof; vrypostig; ongerymd, onpas.
imperturbabil'ity, kalmte, onversteurbaarheid.
imperturb'able, onversteurbaar; koelbloedig.
imperv'ious, ontoeganklik; ondeurdringbaar, onvatbaar (vir); ~ **ness**, ondeurdringbaarheid, ontoeganklikheid.
impeti'go, puisie(s)uitslag, impetigo.
im'petrate, afsmeek, verkry.
im'petratory, versoekend, afsmekend.
impetuos'ity, drif, heftigheid, voortvarendheid.
impet'uous, onstuimig, heftig, voortvarend, onbesadig.
im'petus, (-es), beweegkrag, stoot, vaart; aandrif; bewegingsmoment; aandrang, stukrag; *give fresh* ~ *to*, 'n nuwe stoot gee aan.
im'pi, impie.
impi'ety, oneerbiedigheid; boosheid, goddeloosheid.
impinge', slaan, stoot, bots; ~ *on*, raak; inbreuk maak op; ~ **ment**, botsing, skok; inbreuk.
im'pious, goddeloos, oneerbiedig, ongodvrugtig.
im'pish, ondeund, platjieagtig, plaerig; ~ **ness**, ondeundheid, plaerigheid.
impit'eous, meedoënloos.
implacabil'ity, onversoenlikheid, onverbiddelikheid.
implac'able, onversoenlik, onverbiddelik.
implacen'tal, sonder nageboorte.
implant', inprent; saai, plant; ~ **a'tion**, inprenting; inplanting, planting.
implaus'ible, onaanneemlik.
impledge', verpand.
im'plement, (n) gereedskap; gebruiksvoorwerp, werktuig; hulpmiddel; (pl) uitrusting, gerei, benodigdhede; (v) uitvoer, volbring; toepas, uitvoering gee aan; implementeer; . . **ment'ing**, . . **ta'tion**, uitvoering, volbrenging, verwesenliking.
imple'tion, vulling.
im'plicate, (n) bedoeling; aangeduide ding; (v) deureenvleg; saamstrengel, verwikkel; betrek, inwikkel, insluit; meebring; veronderstel; ~ *someone in something*, iem. in iets betrek; ~ **d**, aandadig, medepligtig; handdadig; betrokke.

implication 971 improve

implica'tion, inwikkeling; gevolgtrekking; bybetekenis, insinuasie; implikasie, konsekwensie; *by* ~, stilswygend, by implikasie; indirek, onregstreeks.
im'plicative, insluitend, vanselfsprekend.
impli'cit, implisiet, stilswygend, vanselfsprekend; ingeslote; onvoorwaardelik; onuitgesproke; volslae, volkome; ~ *FAITH*, blinde (volkome) geloof; ~ *OBEDIENCE*, blinde gehoorsaamheid; ~ **ly**, blindelings; stilswyend; vanselfsprekend; volslae, volkome; *trust* ~ *ly*, blindweg vertrou; ~ **ness**, onvoorwaardelikheid; vanselfsprekendheid.
implied', daaronder begrepe, vanselfsprekend, stilswygend.
im'plode, inplof.
implora'tion, smeking, smeekbede.
implore', bid, smeek, afsmeek.
implor'ing(ly), smekend.
implo'sion, inploffing, implosie.
implos'ive, implosief.
imply', **(implied)**, bevat, behels, inhou, beteken; beduie, te kenne gee, insinueer, sinspeel op.
impol'der, inpolder.
impol'icy, onpolitieke set; onverstandige aksie; onwysheid, taktloosheid.
impolite', onbeleef, onwellewend, ongemanierd; onbeskof; ~ **ness**, onbeleefdheid, ongemanierdheid.
impol'itic, onversigtig, onverstandig, onoordeelkundig.
imponderabil'ia, abstrakte oorwegings, imponderabilia.
imponderabil'ity, onweegbaarheid, imponderabiliteit.
impo'nderable, onweegbaar; lig
impo'nderables, imponderabilia, onbepaalde invloede (faktore); onweegbare kleinighede.
impon'ent, (n) opleêr, voorskrywer; (a) opleênd, voorskrywend.
im'port, (n) invoer; inhoud; strekking, betekenis; dra(ag)krag; draagwydte; belang, gewig; (pl) invoerartikels; ~ *s and exports*, in- en uitvoer.
import', (v) invoer, importeer; beteken, inhou; uitdruk; bekend maak; van belang wees, raak; aandui (reg); ~ **abil'ity**, invoerbaarheid; ~ **able**, invoerbaar.
import'ance, belangrikheid, aansienlikheid, gewigtigheid; gewig; betekenis, aanbelang; *man of* ~, man van betekenis.
import'ant, belangrik, vernaam, swaarwigtig, noemenswaardig, gewigtig, betekenisvol, groot, saakryk.
im'port: ~ **a'tion**, invoer(ing); invoerartikel; ~ **control**, invoerbeheer; ~ **dues**, invoerreg; ~ **duty**, invoerreg, invoerbelasting; ~ **'er**, invoerder; ~ **goods**, invoergoedere; ~ **harbour**, invoerhawe; ~ **merchant**, invoerhandelaar; ~ **permit**, invoerpermit; ~ **premium**, invoerpremie; ~ **regulation**, invoerbepaling; ~ **restriction**, invoerbeperking; ~ **trade**, invoerhandel.
import'unate, lastig, ongeleë, opdringerig, dringend.
importune', lastig val, aandring, dringend versoek, opdruk.
Importun'ity, lastigheid, oorlas, opdringerigheid.
impos'able, oplêbaar.
impose', oplê; te laste lê; imponeer; strafwerk oplê; stel; vorms inslaan; skenk; laat deurgaan vir; bedrieg, kul; ~ *CONDITIONS*, voorwaardes stel; ~ *ON*, indruk maak op; wysmaak; ~ *LAWS*, wette oplê; ~ *UPON someone*, iem. iets op die mou speld; van iem. misbruik maak.
impos'ing, indrukwekkend, eerbiedwekkend, imponerend, imposant; bedrieglik; veeleisend.
imposi'tion, oplegging; bedrog, beetnemery; opgelegde las; strafwerk, taak; ~ *of HANDS*, handoplegging; ~ *of PUNISHMENT*, strafoplegging.
impossibil'ity, onmoontlikheid.
imposs'ible, onmoontlik, onbegonne; onuitstaanbaar; *ATTEMPT the* ~, water in 'n mandjie probeer dra; van 'n padda vere probeer pluk; *she IS* ~, met haar is geen huis te hou nie; ~ *of PERFORMANCE*, onuitvoerbaar.
im'post, belasting, impostlys (bouk.); draagsteen; draaglys; vrag, gewig (renbaan).

impos'tor, bedrieër, kuller, swendelaar.
impos'ture, bedrog, beetnemery, swendelary.
im'potence, im'potency, onmag, magteloosheid; onvermoë, impotensie.
im'potent, magteloos, impotent, onvermoënd; gebrekkig, hulpbehoewend.
impound', skut, opsluit; beslag lê op; opvang, opdam (water); ~ **age**, skutting; beslaglegging.
impov'erish, verarm; uitsuig; uitput; ~ **ment**, verarming; uitmergeling, uitputting.
impracticabil'ity, ondoenlikheid, onuitvoerbaarheid; ontoeganklikheid; onbegaanbaarheid; onregeerbaarheid.
imprac'ticable, onuitvoerbaar, ondoenlik; onbegaanbaar, ontoeganklik; onhandelbaar.
im'precate, verwens, vervloek; afsmeek.
impreca'tion, verwensing, vervloeking, vloek.
im'precatory, verwensend, vervloekend, vloek=.
impregnabil'ity, onneembaarheid.
impreg'nable, onneembaar, onverwinlik; onversetlik.
impreg'nate, (v) bevrug; beswanger; deurtrek, deurwerk, deurdrenk (met); vervul; vrugbaar maak; (a) beswanger; ~ *(d) with*, deurtrek van.
impregna'tion, bevrugting, beswangering; versadiging, deurtrekking, drenking.
impressar'io, (**-s**), impressario; konsertbestuurder; produksieleier.
imprescrip'tible, onverjaarbaar, onvervreembaar.
im'press, (n) stempel, merk, afdruk; motto, devies.
impress', (v) indruk; stempel; indruk maak; deurdring; in diens stel; met geweld werf (vir leër, vloot); ~ *FORCIBLY*, imponeer; ~ *something ON* u persoon, iem. iets inprent; iem. iets op die hart druk; ~ **ed**, beïndruk, geïmponeer; ~ *ed stamp*, ingedrukte seël; ~ **ibil'ity**, gevoeligheid, ontvanklikheid.
impress'ible, ontvanklik, gevoelig.
impress'ion, indruk; afdruk; druk; gevoel(ens); impressie, stempel; oplaag, uitgawe; nommer; invloed, uitwerking; *CREATE an* ~, indruk maak; *FORM an* ~, 'n indruk kry; *be UNDER the* ~, onder die indruk verkeer; ~ **abil'ity**, gevoeligheid, vatbaarheid; ~ **able**, gevoelig, vatbaar vir indrukke; ~ **ism**, impressionisme; ~ **ist**, impressionis; ~ **is'tic**, impressionisties.
impress'ive, indrukwekkend, eerbiedwekkend, imponerend; gevoelig; treffend; ~ **ness**, indrukwekkendheid, aangrypendheid; gewigtigheid; nadruklikheid.
impress'ment, vuur, erns.
im'prest, amptelike voorskot; ~ **system**, voorskotstelsel.
imprimat'ur, imprimatur, drukverlof.
Im print, (n) indruk; afdruk; merk; imprimatur; stempel, drukkerstempel, drukkersmerk; drukkersnaam.
imprint', (v) druk; stempel; inprent.
im'print block, naamblok.
impris'on, in die tronk gooi, opsluit.
impris'onment, gevangenisstraf, tronkstraf; gevangehouding, gevange(n)skap, gevangesetting, opsluiting, vry losies; *CIVIL* ~, ~ *for DEBT*, gyseling; *FALSE* ~, onwettige gevangesetting.
improbabil'ity, onwaarskynlikheid.
improb'able, onwaarskynlik.
improb'ity, oneerlikheid; slegtheid, boosheid.
impromp'tu, (n) improvisasie; (a, adv) uit die vuis, impromptu, ex tempore.
improp'er, onbehoorlik, ongepas, onoordentlik, onbetaamlik, gedurf; onkies, ongeskik; berug, sleg, oneg; onjuis, verkeerd; ~ *FRACTION*, onegte breuk; ~ *HOUSE*, huis van ontug; ~ *POSSESSION*, onregmatige besit; ~ **ly**, onbehoorlik; onfatsoenlik; ten onregte.
improp'riate, toe-eien; sekulariseer.
impropria'tion, toe-eiening; sekularisasie.
impropri'ety, onbehoorlikheid; onbetaamlikheid, onfatsoenlikheid; onjuistheid; ongepastheid.
improvabil'ity, vatbaarheid vir verbetering, verbeterbaarheid.
improv'able, vatbaar vir verbetering, verbeterbaar, bewerkbaar.
improve', verbeter; veredel; verhoog; bebou (grond);

gebruik maak van; vooruitgaan (pasiënt); ~ *one's* ACQUAINTANCE, nader kennis maak; ~ *upon* ACQUAINTANCE, in die guns val by nader kennismaking; ~ *in HEALTH*, beter (sterker) word; ~ *one's MIND*, jou kennis uitbrei; ~ *the OCCASION*, goeie gebruik van die geleentheid maak; *you can't ~ ON that*, daarop kan jy nie verbeter nie; ~**ment**, verbetering; veredeling; vordering; voordeel; stigting; vooruitgang (sieke); (pl) verbeterings; ~**r**, verbeteraar; ambagsgesel, vakleerling.

improv'idence, sorgloosheid; gebrek aan deursig; verkwisting; onopassendheid.

improv'ident, sorgloos, nalatig, onversigtig, verkwistend.

improv'ing, verbeterend; leersaam.

improvisa'tion, improvisasie.

improv'isator, improvisator.

im'provise, improviseer; uit die vuis lewer; ~**d**, uit die vuis uit, onvoorbereid; nood=, noodhulp=; ~**r**, improvisator.

imprud'ence, onversigtigheid, onbesonnenheid.

imprud'ent, onversigtig, onbedag, onbesonne.

im'pudence, onbeskaamdheid, skaamteloosheid; brutaliteit, domastrantheid.

im'pudent, onbeskaamd, skaamteloos; domastrant, brutaal, hanerig; ~ *person*, parmant.

impudi'city, skaamteloosheid; onbetaamlikheid.

impugn', bestry, weerspreek; aanval; in twyfel trek; ~ *someone's honour*, iem. in sy eer aantas; ~**able**, betwisbaar, weerlêbaar; ~**er**, bestryder, betwister; ~**ment**, weerlegging, bestryding, betwisting.

impu'issance, swakheid, magteloosheid, onvermoë.

impu'issant, magteloos, impotent, swak.

im'pulse, stoot, slag (hart); dryfkrag, (aan)drang, spoorslag; aandrif, aansporing, prikkel; opwelling; vaart; impuls; pols.

impul'sion, stoot; (aan)drang; aandrif, opwelling; stukrag, impulsie.

impul'sive, aandrywend, voortstuwend, voortvarend, impulsief; ~**ness**, voortvarendheid.

impun'ity, straflooshed; *with* ~, ongestraf, strafloos.

impure', onsuiwer, onedel; gemeng; onkuis; vuil.

impur'ity, (..**ties**), onsuiwerheid; onreinheid; onkuisheid; vuilheid.

imputabil'ity, toerekenbaarheid.

imput'able, te wyte, toerekenbaar.

imputa'tion, beskuldiging, betigting, aantyging; toerekening, aandigting, imputasie, toeskrywing, toedigting, telastelegging.

imput'ative, toegeskrewe; beskuldigend.

impute', wyt, toeskrywe; toereken, toedig, aanvryf, aantyg, die skuld gee van.

in (n): *the ~s and OUTS*, die kleinste besonderhede; *to want to know all the ~s and OUTS*, die naatjie v.d. kous wil weet; die fynste besonderhede wil weet; (a) binne; inwonend; (adv) binne, in, tuis; aan; ~ *ABSENTIA*, in sy/haar afwesigheid; by verstek; *you ARE ~ for it today*, vandag ry jy aan die pen; *the socialists ARE ~*, die sosialiste is aan die bewind; *BE ~ on something*, ingewyd wees; *BE ~*, tuis wees; ~ *BETWEEN*, tussenin; *the BOAT is ~*, die boot het aangekom; *BREED ~*, inteel; ~ *CAMERA*, agter geslote deure; *ENGAGE ~*, jou besig hou met; ~ *FOR it*, vas wees; *HELMETS are ~*, helmets is in die mode; *REJOICE ~*, jou verheug in; *KEEP ~ with*, op 'n vriendskaplike voet verkeer met; ~ *KIND*, in natura (betaling in goedere); ~ *LAW*, regtens, uit 'n regsoogpunt; *LOCK ~*, opsluit, insluit; *his PARTY is ~*, sy party het die meerderheid; *PUT ~*, insit; *RUB ~*, invryf, inpeper; *with the soft SIDE ~*, met die sagte kant na binne; (prep) in, by, op, met, aan; ~ *ABSENTIA*, in sy afwesigheid, in absentia; ~ *AFRIKAANS*, in (op) Afrikaans; ~ *the AFTERNOON*, agtermiddag, in die namiddag; ~ *ANSWER to*, in antwoord op; ~ *the BACKGROUND*, op die agtergrond; ~ *BEHALF of*, vir, ten behoewe van; *BELIEVE ~ God*, glo in God; ~ *any CASE*, in elk geval; ~ *this CASE*, in hierdie geval; ~ *CASH*, kontant; ~ *the COUNTRY*, in die binneland; op die platteland; ~ *CROSSING the river*, by die oorsteek (oorgaan) v.d. rivier; ~ *DEFENCE of*, ter verdediging van; ~ *the EVENING*, saans, in die aand; ~ *EXTENSO*, volledig, uitvoerig; ~ *EXTREMIS*, op sy uiterste; ~ *FACT*, om die waarheid te sê; feitlik; ~ *FACTO*, werklik; ~ *so FAR as*, in soverre as; ~ *FORMA*, in behoorlike vorm; *he HAS it ~ him*, dit sit in hom; ~ *HONOUR of*, ter ere van; *one ~ a HUNDRED*, een uit honderd; ~ *HUNDREDS*, in honderde; ~ *his IMAGE*, na sy beeld; ~ *INK*, met ink; ~ *ITSELF*, op sigself; *the LATEST ~ loudspeakers*, die nuutste wat luidsprekers betref; *as far as ~ me LIES*, sover ek kan; ~ *all LIKELIHOOD*, na alle waarskynlikheid; ~ *LIQUOR*, onder die invloed van drank; ~ *MEDIAS res*, in die midde van; ~ *MEMORIAM*, ter herinnering aan; ~ *MEMORY of*, ter nagedagtenis van; ~ *the MORNING*, soggens, smorens (smôrens); ~ *MOURNING*, in die rou; *there is NOTHING ~ it*, dis baie maklik; dis van geen belang nie; daar sit niks agter nie; *ONE ~ ten*, een op tien; ~ *forma PAUPERIS*, as 'n arm man; *PAY ~ cash*, kontant betaal; ~ *for a PENNY*, ~ *for a pound*, wie A sê, moet B sê; ~ *the PRESS*, in die pers; ~ *QUEST of*, op soek na; ~ *SEARCH of*, op soek na; ~ *SITU*, ter plaatse, op sy oorspronklike plek; ~ *SLIPPERS*, met pantoffels aan; ~ *the STREET*, op straat; *there is something ~ THAT*, daar is iets van waar; ~ *THAT*, daar; *one ~ a THOUSAND*, een uit 'n duisend; ~ *TIME*, met verloop van tyd; betyds; ~ *TOTO*, in sy geheel; ~ *TRANSIT*, onderweg; ~ *TRUTH*, inderdaad; om die waarheid te sê; ~ *this WAY*, op hierdie manier; ~ *WRITING*, op skrif, skriftelik.

inabil'ity, onbekwaamheid; onvermoë.

inaccessibil'ity, ontoeganklikheid; onbeklimbaarheid (berg); ongenaakbaarheid.

inaccess'ible, ontoeganklik, ongenaakbaar, onbereikbaar; onbeklimbaar (berg).

inacc'uracy, (..**cies**), onjuistheid, onnoukeurigheid.

inacc'urate(ly), onnoukeurig, verkeerd, onjuis.

inac'tion, werkloosheid, stilstand; traagheid, dadeloosheid, inaktiwiteit.

inac'tive, werkloos; dadeloos, traag, onwerksaam; ledig.

inactiv'ity, werkloosheid, ledigheid; dadeloosheid, traagheid, inaktiwiteit.

inadaptabil'ity, ongeskiktheid.

inadap'table, onbruikbaar, ongeskik.

inad'equacy, onvoldoendheid, ontoereikendheid; oneweredigheid.

inad'equate(ly), onvoldoende, ongenoegsaam, ontoereikend; oneweredig.

inadmissibil'ity, onaanneemlikheid; ontoelaatbaarheid.

inadmiss'ible, onaanneemlik; ontoelaatbaar.

inadvert'ence, **inadvert'ency**, onagsaamheid, onoplettendheid, onnadenkendheid, onbewustheid.

inadvert'ent, onagsaam, onoplettend, agteloos, onopsetlik, onbewus; ~**ly**, by vergissing, onbewus, onopsetlik.

inadvi'sable, nie raadsaam nie.

inalienabil'ity, onvervreembaarheid.

inal'ienable, onvervreembaar, onontvreembaar.

inalterabil'ity, onveranderlikheid, onveranderbaarheid.

inal'terable, onveranderlik, onveranderbaar.

inamorat'a, (-**s**) geliefde, minnares; ..**rat'o**, (-**s**), minnaar.

inane', (n) ledige ruimte, leegte; (a) doelloos, onbeduidend, sinloos, idioot, hol; leeg.

inan'imate, leweloos, onbesield.

inanima'tion, onbesieldheid, doodsheid, wesenloosheid.

inani'tion, leegheid, uitputting, kragteloosheid, swakheid, uittering.

inan'ity, sinloosheid; leegheid, ylheid; holheid, onbeduidendheid; sinlose opmerking; ..**ties**, banaliteite.

inappeas'able, onstilbaar, onbevredigbaar.

inappell'able, sonder hoër beroep.

inapp'etance, gebrek aan eetlus; lusteloosheid, onverskilligheid.

inapplicabil'ity, ontoepaslikheid, onaanwendbaarheid.

inapp'licable, ontoepaslik, ontoepasbaar, onbruikbaar, ongeskik, onaanwendbaar.
inapp'osite, ongepas, ongeskik, ondoelmatig, onvanpas.
inappre'ciable, onwaardeerbaar, onskatbaar; onmerkbaar; onbeduidend.
inapprecia'tion, gebrek aan waardering.
inappre'ciative, onwaarderend.
inapprehen'sible, onbegryplik, onverstaanbaar.
inapprehen'sion, gemis aan begrip.
inapproachabil'ity, ongenaakbaarheid; onbereikbaarheid.
inapproach'able, ongenaakbaar; ontoeganklik.
inapprop'riate, ongeskik, ondoelmatig, ongepas, onvanpas, ondienstig; ~ **ness,** ongeskiktheid, ondoelmatigheid, ongepastheid, ondienstigheid.
inapt', onbevoeg; ongeskik, ontoepaslik.
inap'titude, ongeskiktheid, onbekwaamheid.
inarch', afbuig; ketting-ent; vasent.
inartic'ulate, ongeleed, sonder litte; onduidelik, onverstaanbaar; stom, spraakloos; ~ **ness,** ..**la'tion,** spraakloosheid; gebrekkige artikulasie.
inartifi'cial, ongeskunstel(d); onartistiek, eenvoudig.
inartis'tic, onartistiek.
inasmuch' (as), aangesien; vir sover, omdat.
inatten'tion, onoplettendheid, agtelosigheid, onverskilligheid.
inatten'tive, onoplettend, onaandagtig, onagsaam, agteloos; ~ **ness,** onagsaamheid; onoplettendheid, onattentheid.
inaudibil'ity, onhoorbaarheid.
inaud'ible, onhoorbaar.
inaug'ural, intree=, inwydings=; openings=, stigtings=; ~ **address,** intreerede, openingsrede; ~ **ceremony,** inwyding(splegtigheid); ~ **flight,** eerste vlug; ~ **lecture,** intreelesing, intreerede; ~ **meeting,** stigtingsvergadering.
inaug'urate, inwy, inhuldig, inseën; open, plegtig in gebruik neem; installeer.
inaugura'tion, inwyding; ingebruikneming; inhuldiging; bevestiging; opening.
inaug'uratory, inougureel, openings=.
inauspi'cious, onheilspellend, ongunstig; ~ **ness,** ongunstigheid, onheilspellendheid.
in'board, binneboords.
in'born, aangebore, ingeskape; ingeteel.
in'bound, inkomend.
inbreathe', inblaas; inasem; inspireer.
in'bred, aangebore, ingeskape; ingeteel.
in'breed, (..bred), inteel.
in'breeding, inteelt.
Inc'a, Inka.
incalculabil'ity, onberekenbaarheid; ontelbaarheid.
incal'culable, onberekenbaar; ontelbaar; ~ **consequences,** onberekenbare gevolge.
incandesce', gloei; laat gloei.
incandes'cence, gloed, gloeihitte.
incandes'cent, gloeiend; liggewend; skitterend; ~ **lamp,** gloeilamp; ~ **light,** gloeilig; ~ **mantle,** gloeikousie.
incanta'tion, towerspreuk, betowering, beswering.
incapabil'ity, onbekwaamheid, onbevoegdheid, ongeskiktheid.
incap'able, onbekwaam, onbevoeg, eenvoudig; *DRUNK and* ~, dronk en onbekwaam; ~ *OF,* nie in staat nie tot (om).
incapa'cious, beperk, eng.
incapa'citate, onbekwaam maak, onbevoeg maak, onkapabel maak.
incapacita'tion, onbruikbaarmaking, onbevoegmaking.
incapa'city, onbekwaamheid; onbevoegdheid.
incar'cerate, in die tronk gooi, inkerker, opsluit, vaskluister.
incarcera'tion, inkerking, gevangesetting; beklemming.
incar'dinate, tot kardinaal verhef.
incardina'tion, inkardinasie.
incarn'adine, (n) vleiskleur; bloedkleur; inkarnaat; (v) bloedrooi kleur; (a) vleiskleurig, rooi.
incarn'ate, (v) beliggaam, verpersoonlik; (a) vleeslik, vleesgeworde, verliggaamlik, verpersoonlik; *the*

DEVIL ~, die verpersoonlikte duiwel, die baarlike duiwel; *GOD* ~, Godmens.
incarna'tion, vleeswording, menswording, inkarnasie, verpersoonliking, beliggaming.
incase', inpak, inwikkel.
incau'tious, onversigtig, onbedag.
incen'diarism, brandstigting, ophitsing, opruiing.
incen'diary, (n) (..ries), brandstigter; opruier, oproermaker; (a) brand=, brandstigtend; opruiend; ~ **bomb,** brandbom; ~ **grenade,** brandgranaat.
incensa'tion, bewieroking.
in'cense¹, (n) wierook; bewieroking; (v) bewierook; wierook brand; geurig maak.
incense'², (v) kwaad maak; terg; verbitter, erger, vertoorn.
in'cense boat, wierookskaal.
incen'sed, gebelg, woedend, smoorkwaad; *be* ~, smoorkwaad wees.
in'censory, (..ries), wierookvat.
incen'tive, (n) aansporing, spoorslag; prikkel, dryfveer; *serve as an* ~, as spoorslag dien; (a) aanmoedigend, aansporend, prikkelend; ~ **bonus,** aansporingsbonus, aanmoedigingsbonus; ~ **wage,** aansporingsloon.
incep'tion, begin, aanvang, ontstaan.
incep'tive, aanvangend, begin=, beginnend, aanvangs=.
incep'tor, aanvanger, beginner.
incert'itude, onsekerheid.
incess'ant(ly), onophoudelik, voortdurend, ewigdurend, onafgebroke, gedurig, aanhoudend.
incess'antness, onafgebrokenheid.
in'cest, bloedskande.
inces'tuous, bloedskendig.
inch, (n) (-s), duim; *BY* ~ *es,* stadig; ~ *BY* ~, voet vir voet; *EVERY* ~, deur en deur; *EVERY* ~ *a gentleman,* 'n pure man; *GIVE him an* ~ *and he will take an ell,* gee hom 'n pinkie en hy neem die hele hand; *MISS something by* ~ *es,* iets byna raak; iets net mis; *NOT an* ~, glad nie, nie 'n duimbreed nie; *TO an* ~, op 'n haar; *WITHIN an* ~, ampertjies; (v) voetjie vir voetjie (duim vir duim) beweeg; ~ **bar,** breekyster; ~ **-measure,** duimstok; ~ **-nail,** duimspyker.
in'choate, (v) begin, laat aanvang; (a) inchoatief, beginnend, aanvangs=; onontwikkel(d).
inchoa'tion, begin, aanvang.
incho'ative, inchoatief, aanvangend, aanvangs=.
inch: ~ **-pennyweight,** duim-pennyweight; ~ **-rule,** duimstok; ~ **-tape,** duimmaat.
in'cidence, (die) raak, tref; drukking; raakpunt, trefpunt; trefwydte; inval (wisk.); strekking, gebied, veld, sfeer; gevolgsomvang; omvang; voorkomssyfer; (druk)verdeling, vestiging (belasting); *ANGLE of* ~, invalshoek; *the* ~ *of a TAX,* die druk (trefwydte) van 'n belasting.
in'cident, (n) gebeurtenis, aangeleentheid, wedervaring, voorval; episode; bykomstigheid; *the* ~ *is closed,* die saak is afgehandel; (a) bykomstig, eie aan, toevallig; insidenteel (reg).
inciden'tal, (n) bykomstige omstandigheid; (pl) bykomende koste; (a) toevallig, onvoorsien, bykomend, insidenteel; ~ *CAUSE,* byoorsaak; ~ *EXPENSE,* onvoorsiene uitgawe; ~ *MUSIC,* agtergrondmusiek; ~ *REMARK,* obiter dictum, terloopse opmerking; ~ **ly,** terloops, tussen hakies, toevallig.
incin'erate, verbrand, veras.
incinera'tion, verbranding, lykverbranding, verassing.
incin'erator, verbrandingsoond.
incip'ience, begin, aanvang.
incip'ient, aanvangend, aanvangs=, begin=, opkomend, aanvanklik; ~ **hopper outbreaks,** opbouvoetgangerswerms; ~ **swarms (of locusts),** opbouswerms (sprinkane).
incise', insny, inkerf, graveer.
inci'sion, insnyding, snede; inkerwing, kerf; ~ **-knife,** lanset.
incis'ive, snydend; skerp, bits; kragtig; deurdringend; ~ **ness,** kragtigheid; skerpheid; raakheid; nadruklikheid.

incis'or, snytand.
inci'sure, insnyding; kerf.
incita'tion, aansporing, prikkel; opwekking, aanhit=
sing, opstokery.
incite', aanspoor, opsteek, opstook, aandryf, aan=
vuur, aansit, aanpor, opmaak, opsweep, oprui,
aanhits, aansweep; ~ **ment,** aansporing, prikkel;
aanhitsing, aandrywing, aanstoking, aanvuring;
~**r,** aanvuurder, aanjaer, aanblaser, aanporder,
opstoker, onrusstoker.
inciv'il, *kyk* **uncivil.**
incivil'ity, onbeleefdheid, ongemanierdheid, onhof=
likheid, buffelagtigheid.
in'civism, gebrek aan burgerdeug.
in'-clearing, klaringstukke.
inclem'ency, onbarmhartigheid, hardvogtigheid;
stormagtigheid, guurheid (weer).
inclem'ent, onbarmhartig; bar, ru, guur, stormagtig
(weer); wreed; ~ *weather,* ongure weer.
inclin'able, geneig, geneë, goedgesind, gunstig, met 'n
neiging tot.
inclina'tion, helling; buiging, nyging; neiging, gesind=
heid; gading, geneentheid, geneigdheid; lus, sin=
(nigheid); inklinasie; *ANGLE of* ~, hellingshoek;
FOLLOW one's own ~*s,* sy eie sin volg.
incline', (n) hang, helling, skuinste; opdraand; af=
draand, val; skuins skag (myn); (v) buig, neig, ge=
neig wees; (laat) afwyk; swenk; oorhang; oorhel; ~
TO, oorhel na; 'n neiging toon tot; ~ *TOWARDS
the view that,* geneig wees om te dink dat.
inclined', geneig; *BE* ~ *to,* geneig wees om; *FEEL* ~
for, lus hê vir; ~ **plane,** afdraande (hellende) vlak;
~ **roof,** skuins dak; ~ **shaft,** skuins skag, skuins
vervoerweg.
inclinom'eter, inklinometer, hellingmeter.
include', insluit, bevat, saamtel, omvat, meereken;
byreken; *not* ~*d,* nie daaronder begrepe nie, nie
inbegrepe nie.
includ'ing, met inbegrip van, inkluis, inbegrepe.
inclu'sion, insluiting, insluitsel.
inclu'sive, insluitend; ingeslote, inbegrepe, inklusief;
FROM the 3rd to the 7th ~, van die 3e tot en met
die 7e; *GST inclusive,* AVB ingesluit; ~ *OF,* bevat=
tend; ~ *TERMS,* prys waarby alles ingesluit (inbe=
grepe) is.
incog'nito, incognito, as onbekende.
incog'nizable, onkenbaar.
incog'nizance, onkenbaarheid, onbekendheid.
incog'nizant, onbekend (met); onbewus (van).
incoher'ence, incoher'ency, losheid, onsamehan=
gendheid; ongerymdheid.
incoher'ent, onsamehangend, los.
incohes'ive, nie klewerig nie, los.
incombustibil'ity, onbrandbaarheid.
incombus'tible, onbrandbaar.
in'come, inkomste, inkome; *be without an* ~, sonder
verdienste wees; *NATIONAL* ~, volksinkome;
~**r,** binnekomende; immigrant; intrekker; opvol=
ger; indringer; ~ **tax,** inkomstebelasting.
in'coming, (n) binnekoms, aankoms; intrede; (pl) in=
komste; (a) binnelopend (boot); aankomend, inko=
mend; opvolgend, nuwe; ~ *COMMITTEE,* nuwe
bestuur; ~ *TIDE,* opkomende gety.
incommensurabil'ity, onmeetbaarheid.
incommen'surable, onmeetbaar; nie te vergelyk
nie.
incommen'surate, onmeetbaar; oneweredig; buite
verhouding.
incommode', lastig val, hinder, verontrief, tot oorlas
wees.
incommod'ious, lastig, hinderlik; ongerieflik; be=
swaarlik.
incommunicabil'ity, onmeedeelbaarheid, onkommu=
nikeerbaarheid.
incommun'icable, onmeedeelbaar, onkommunikeer=
baar.
incom(m)unica'do, incommunicado; in afsondering.
incommun'icative, onmeedeelsaam, agterhoudend,
terughoudend; ~**ness,** onmeedeelsaamheid, swyg=
saamheid.
incommutabil'ity, onverwisselbaarheid; onverander=
likheid.

incommut'able, onveranderlik; onlosbaar; onverwis=
selbaar; ~**ness,** onverwisselbaarheid.
incomparabil'ity, weergaloosheid, onvergelyklik=
heid.
incom'parable, onvergelyklik, weergaloos, ongeëwe=
naar(d).
incompatibil'ity, onverenigbaarheid, strydigheid;
oneensgesindheid; ~ *of temper,* uiteenlopende
(teenstrydige) geaardheid.
incompat'ible, onbestaanbaar; onverenigbaar (met),
onverdraagsaam, nie by mekaar passend nie;
(teen)strydig; ~ *with,* strydig met.
incom'petence, incom'petency, onmag, onvermoë;
onbevoegdheid, onbekwaamheid, vrotsigheid.
incom'petent, onbevoeg, ongeskik, onbekwaam.
incomplete', onvolkome, onvolledig, onaf; ~ *com=
bustion,* gedeeltelike verbranding; ~**ness,** onvolko=
menheid, onvolledigheid.
incomprehensibil'ity, onbegryplikheid, onverstaan=
baarheid.
incomprehen'sible, onbegryplik, onverstaanbaar;
onbegrens.
incomprehen'sion, onbevatlikheid; onbegryplikheid.
incompressibil'ity, onsaamdrukbaarheid, onsaam=
persbaarheid.
incompress'ible, onsaamdrukbaar.
incomput'able, onberekenbaar.
inconceivabil'ity, onbegryplikheid, ondenkbaarheid.
inconceiv'able, ondenkbaar, onbegryplik, ongeloof=
lik.
inconclus'ive, nie afdoende nie, nie beslissend nie, on=
oortuigend; ~**ness,** onbeslistheid.
inconden'sable, onverdigbaar.
inconden'sed, onverdig.
incon'dite, sleg afgewerk; onsamehangend; lomp, ru.
inconform'ity, ongelykvormigheid; afwyking.
incon'gruence, inkongruensie.
incon'gruent, nie-ooreenstemmend.
incongru'ity, (..ties), ongepastheid, ongerymdheid,
wanverhouding, onverenigbaarheid.
incong'ruous, misplaas, ongepas, onbestaanbaar;
disparaat, ongerymd; onsamehangend, ongelyk=
matig, inkonsekwent; onverenigbaar (met); ~**ness,**
misplaastheid, ongepastheid; ongerymdheid.
inconsec'utive, inkonsekwent, ongeorden.
incon'sequence, onsamehangendheid, inkonsekwen=
sie.
incon'sequent, teenstrydig, inkonsekwent, onlogies;
onbelangrik.
inconsequen'tial, onbelangrik; teenstrydig, inkon=
sekwent.
incon'sequently, onlogies.
inconsid'erable, onbeduidend, gering, onaansienlik.
inconsid'erate, onbesonne, onbekook, agtelosig, on=
verskillig; onbedagsaam; onhoflik; ~**ness,** ..**a'=
tion,** onbesonnenheid, onbedagsaamheid; onhof=
likheid.
inconsis'tence, inconsis'tency, inkonsekwensie, teen=
strydigheid; onbestaanbaarheid; veranderlikheid,
wispelturigheid.
inconsis'tent, onbestaanbaar; teenstrydig; onverenig=
baar; ongerymd; inkonsekwent; wispelturig.
inconsolabil'ity, ontroosbaarheid.
inconsol'able, ontroosbaar.
incon'sonance, onverenigbaarheid; onwelluidend=
heid.
incon'sonant, onverenigbaar (met), teenstrydig
(met); onharmonieus.
inconspic'uous, onmerkbaar; onopvallend; skaars
sigbaar; onaansienlik; beskeie; ~**ness,** onopval=
lendheid.
incon'stancy, onbestendigheid, onstandvastigheid,
ongestadigheid, veranderlikheid, wispelturigheid,
wisselvalligheid.
incon'stant, onbestendig, ongedurig, veranderlik,
wispelturig, onstandvastig, wisselvallig.
inconsum'able, onverteerbaar; onverbruikbaar.
incontestabil'ity, onbetwisbaarheid, onweerlegbaar=
heid.
incontes'table, onbetwisbaar, onweerlêbaar, onteen=
seglik.
incon'tinence, incon'tinency, onmatigheid; ontugtig=

heid; bedwatering; onvermoë om in te hou; ~ *of speech*, praatsug, loslippigheid.
incon'tinent, onmatig, onbeheers, ongebonde; nie in staat om te bedwing (in te hou) nie; ~ **ly,** onmiddellik, dadelik.
incontroll'able, onbeheerbaar, onbedwingbaar.
inconvertibil'ity, onbetwisbaarheid, onweerlêbaarheid.
incontrovert'ible, onbetwisbaar, onomstootlik.
inconven'ience, (n) ongerief(likheid), oorlas, ongemak; *PUT to* ~, ongeleentheid veroorsaak, las aandoen; *SUFFER great* ~ *from,* groot ongerief ondervind van; (v) las aandoen, steur, geneer; ontrief.
inconven'ient, ongerieflik, lastig, ongeleë, ongeskik.
inconvertibil'ity, onverwisselbaarheid; onverruilbaarheid.
inconvert'ible, onverwisselbaar, onveranderlik; onverruilbaar, oninwisselbaar.
inconvincibil'ity, onoorreedbaarheid, onoortuigbaarheid.
inconvin'cible, onoortuigbaar, onoorreedbaar.
incorp'orate, (v) inlyf, verenig, inkorporeer; regspersoonlikheid verleen; stig, oprig (maatskappy); (a) verenig, ingelyf; beliggaam; ~ **d,** ingelyf; met regspersoonlikheid.
incorpora'tion, inlywing, opneming, inkorporasie; oprigting (maatskappy); vereniging; beliggaming.
incorpor'eal, onstoflik, onliggaamlik.
incorpore'ity, onstoflikheid, onliggaamlikheid.
incorrect', verkeerd, foutief, onjuis, onnoukeurig; ~ **ly,** ten onregte, verkeerdelik; ~ **ness,** onjuistheid, onnoukeurigheid.
incorrigibil'ity, onverbeterlikheid, onverbeterbaarheid; verstoktheid.
inco'rrigible, onverbeterlik, onverbeterbaar; verhard, verstok.
incorrod'ible, onaantasbaar.
incorrupt', onbedorwe; onomkoopbaar; ~ **ibil'ity,** onbederflikheid; onomkoopbaarheid; onverganklikheid; ~ **ible,** onomkoopbaar; onverganklik; eerlik; onbederflik.
incrass'ate, verdik, opgeswel.
in'crease, (n) vermeerdering, toeneming, toename, aangroeiing, aanwas, vergroting; verhoging; aanteel (vee); nakomelingskap; *on the* ~, aan die toeneem.
increase', (v) vermeerder, toeneem, verhoog, vergroot; aanwas; aanteel (vee); vooruitgaan; aangroei, aanswel, aanwakker (handel); ~ **d,** toenemend, groeiend, verhoog; ~ *d jurisdiction,* verhoogde strafbevoegdheid.
increas'ing(ly), meer en meer, toenemend.
incredibil'ity, ongelooflikheid; ongeloofbaarheid.
incred'ible, ongelooflik; ongeloofbaar, fabelagtig, fabuleus; ~ **ness** = **incredibility.**
incredul'ity, ongelowigheid.
incred'ulous, ongelowig.
in'crement, verhoging; inkrement; opslag, (waarde)vermeerdering; aanwas; differensiaal; *unearned* ~, toevallige waardevermeerdering; ~ '**al,** toenemend, differensiaal; verhogings=.
incrim'inate, betig, beskuldig, in 'n aanklag betrek, inkrimineer.
incrim'inating, beswarend; ~ *circumstances,* beswarende omstandighede.
incrimina'tion, inkriminasie; beskuldiging.
incrim'inatory, beskuldigend, inkriminerend.
incrust', incrus'tate, *kyk* **encrust.**
incrusta'tion, omkorsting; aankors(t)ing, oorkorsting, ketelsteen; aanpaksel; belegging, bekleding; roof (op wond), roofvorming.
in'cubate, broei; uitbroei; ontwikkel.
incuba'tion, uitbroeiing, inkubasie; ontwikkeling; *artificial* ~, kunsmatige uitbroeiing; ~ *period,* ontkiemingstyd (van 'n siekte).
in'cubator, broeimasjien; inkubator; broeikas; kweekmasjien; ~ **baby,** broeikasbaba.
in'cubus, (. . bi), swaar (neerdrukkende) las, nagmerrie, inkubus.
in'culcate, inprent, inskerp.
inculca'tion, inprenting, inskerping.

inculp'able, onskuldig, onberispelik.
in'culpate, beskuldig, betig, laak, in 'n aanklag betrek.
inculpa'tion, beskuldiging.
incul'patory, beskuldigend.
incult', onbebou; ru, onbeskof.
incum'bency, ligging; verpligting; predikantspos.
incum'bent, (n) predikant, geestelike; ampsbekleër; (a) opgelê as plig; toegevou, rustend; *it is* ~ *on you,* dis jou plig.
incum'brance, belemmering, beswaar.
incunab'ulum, (. . la), inkunabel, wieg(e)druk.
incur', (-red), op die hals haal, oploop; jou blootstel aan; ~ *DANGER,* gevaar loop; ~ *DEBT,* skuld maak; ~ *EXPENSES,* koste maak; ~ *a FINE,* 'n boete oploop.
incurabil'ity, ongeneeslikheid; ongeneesbaarheid.
incur'able, (n) ongeneeslike; (a) ongeneeslik, onheelbaar; ~ **ness,** ongeneeslikheid, onheelbaarheid.
incurios'ity, onverskilligheid, louheid, agtelosigheid, onopmerksaamheid.
incur'ious, agtelosig; nie nuuskierig nie; onverskillig, lou, onopmerksaam.
incur'sion, inval, strooptog; instroming.
incur'sive, invallend, binnedringend.
incurva'tion, kromming, bog, buiging.
incurve', (binnekant toe) buig.
in'cus, aambeeldbeentjie, inkus.
incuse', slaan, inhamer, stempel.
inda'ba, indaba, beraadslaging, vergadering; gedoente, moles.
indebt'ed, skuldig, verskuldig; verplig; *be* ~ *to,* verplig wees aan; dank verskuldig wees aan; ~ **ness,** verpligting; skuld.
inde'cency, onfatsoenlikheid, onwelvoeglikheid, onkiesheid, wanvoeglikheid; onsedelikheid; onwelvoeglike daad.
inde'cent, onbetaamlik; aanstootlik; onfatsoenlik, onordentlik, onkies; wanvoeglik, onwelvoeglik; onsedelik; ~ *ASSAULT,* onsedelike aanranding; ~ *EXPOSURE,* onwelvoeglike ontbloting; ~ *WOMAN,* drel; onsedelike vrou.
indecid'uous, bladhoudend, groenblywend, immergroen.
indeciph'erable, onleesbaar, onontsyferbaar.
indeci'sion, besluiteloosheid, weifelagtigheid.
indecis'ive, besluiteloos, onbeslis, onseker.
indeclin'able, onverbuigbaar.
indeclinabil'ity, onverbuigbaarheid.
indecompos'able, onontbindbaar, onskeibaar.
indecor'ous, onwelvoeglik, onbetaamlik; onsedig; ~ **ness,** onwelvoeglikheid, onbetaamlikheid, onsedigheid.
indecor'um, onwelvoeglikheid, onbetaamlikheid, onbehoorlikheid.
indeed', inderdaad, regtig, voorwaar, werklik; sowaar; ja-nee, ja; immers, feitlik, eintlik; weliswaar; ~ *AND* ~, werklik, regtig; *I shall be very GLAD* ~, ek sal regtig baie bly wees; *he is,* ~, *a REMARKABLE man,* hy is regtig (werklik waar) 'n merkwaardige man; *WHO is he,* ~?, wie is hy eintlik?
indefatigabil'ity, onvermoeibaarheid, rusteloosheid.
indefati'gable, onvermoeid, rusteloos, onverdrote.
indefeasibil'ity, onvervreembaarheid, onaantasbaarheid, onaanvegbaarheid.
indefeas'ible, onaantasbaar, onaanvegbaar, onvervreembaar.
indefectibil'ity, onverganklikheid.
indefec'tible, onverganklik; feilloos, onfeilbaar.
indefensibil'ity, onverdedigbaarheid.
indefen'sible, onverdedigbaar.
indefin'able, onverklaarbaar, onbepaalbaar, onomskryfbaar, vaag; ~ **ness,** onbepaaldheid, vaagheid.
indef'inite, onbepaald; onbegrens; vaag; onbeslis; ~ *article,* onbepaalde lidwoord; ~ **ly,** onbepaald, vir 'n onbepaalde tyd; ~ **ness,** onbepaaldheid; onbegrensdheid; onbeslistheid; ~ *pronoun,* onbepaalde voornaamwoord.
indehis'cent, nie oopspringend nie.
indelibil'ity, onuitwisbaarheid.

indel'ible, onuitwisbaar; ~ **ink**, merkink; ~ **pencil**, inkpotlood.
indel'icacy, onkiesheid, grofheid.
indel'icate, onkies, grof, onfyn.
indemnifica'tion, skadevergoeding, skadeloosstelling, vrywaring; genoegdoening.
indem'nify, (..fied), skadeloos stel, vergoed; vrywaar.
indem'nity, (..ties), skadeloosstelling, vergoeding; afkoopprys; vrywaring; amnestie; ~ **act**, vrywaringswet; ~ **form**, vrywaringsvorm; ~ **law**, vrywaringswet.
indemon'strable, onbewysbaar.
in'dent[1], (n) laagte, duik, holte.
indent'[2], (n) kerf, keep, intanding, uittanding; inham; insnyding; kontrak; formulier; bestelling; inspringende drukwerk; rekwisisie; (v) intand, induik, inkeep, uittand, uitkeep, inkerf; in reliëf stempel; beslag lê op; in duplo opmaak; bestel; inspring (van 'n reël by drukwerk); duik; indruk; inskryf, inboek, by kontrak verbind; ~ **a'tion**, uittanding, inkeping; saagwerk; kerf, sny; indruk, holte; ~ **clerk**, bestelklerk; ~ **ed**, geleed (kuslyn); ~ **er**, besteller; ~ **ion**, inspringing; ~ **officer**, besteloffisier.
inden'ture, (n) inboeking, leerkontrak; kontrak, verdrag; intanding; keep, insnyding, kerf; inspringende drukwerk; rekwisisie; (v) 'n kontrak aangaan, inboek; 'n holte maak in; ~ *d CLERK*, leerlingklerk; ~ *d LABOURERS*, kontrakarbeiders; ~ **ship**, leerjongskap.
indepen'dence, onafhanklikheid; selfstandigheid; privaat vermoë.
indepen'dency, onafhanklikheid; onafhanklike bestaan; (..cies), onafhanklike staat.
indepen'dent, (n) independent; onafhanklike; (a) onafhanklik, selfstandig; met eie middele van bestaan; *a person of* ~ *means*, 'n rentenier; ~ **ly**, selfstandig, onafhanklik.
indescribabil'ity, onbeskryflikheid.
indescrib'able, onbeskryflik; onbepaald, onduidelik.
indestructabil'ity, onverwoesbaarheid, onvernielbaarheid.
indestruc'tible, onvernielbaar, onverwoesbaar.
indeterm'inable, onbepaalbaar, nie uit te maak nie.
indeterm'inate, onbepaald, onseker; onbeslis; vryhandelend, vaag; lewenslank (straf); ~ **sentence**, onbepaalde vonnis.
indeterm'inateness, indetermina'tion, onbeslistheid; vaagheid; onbepaaldheid.
indeterm'inism, indeterminisme.
indeterm'inist, (n) indeterminis; (a) indeterministies.
in'dex, (n) (**indices**, **-es**), bladwyser; inhoudsopgawe; naamlys; register, klapper; indeks (ekon.); teken; tongetjie (skaal); eksponent (wisk.); aanwysing, aanduiding; indeks, verbodlys; wysvinger; wyser; *put on the* ~, op die indeks plaas, verbied; (v) van 'n bladwyser voorsien; wys, aanwys; op die indeks sit; ~ **card**, indekskaartjie; ~ **-card cabinet**, indekskaartjiekabinet; ~ **curve**, gidskromme; **I ~ Expurgatorius**, lys boeke deur die Rooms-Katolieke kerk verbied; ~ **finger**, voorvinger, wysvinger; ~ **map**, sleutelkaart; ~ **number**, indeksgetal, indekssyfer; kengetal.
In'dia, Indië; *Further* ~, Agter-Indië; ~ **man**, (Oos-)Indiëvaarder.
In'dian, (n) Indiër; Asiër; Indiaan, Rooihuid (Amer.); *Red* ~, Rooihuid, Indiaan; (a) Indies; Indiaans; ~ **club**, knots; ~ **corn**, mielies; ~ **file**, gansemars; *in* ~ *file*, die een agter die ander; ~ **fire**, Bengaalse vuur; ~ **hemp**, dagga; ~ **ink**, (Oos-)Indiese ink; ~ **lilac**, sering; ~ **manna**, boermanna; ~ **meal**, mieliemeel; ~ **Ocean**, Indiese Oseaan; ~ **pink**, grasangelier; ~ **saffron**, borrie; ~ **summer**, opslagsomer, (Noord-Amerikaanse) nasomer; ~ **tea**, Indiese tee; ~ **weed**, tabak; ~ **yellow**, Oos-Indiese geel.
In'dia: ~ **paper**, dundrukpapier; ~ **rubber**, gomlastiek, rubber, gummi; uitveër.
in'dicate, aanwys, wys, aandui, uitdui, te kenne gee; aantoon; aangee; ~ *d horsepower*, aangewee perdekrag.
indica'tion, aanwysing, aanduiding, teken.
indic'ative, (n) aantonende wys(e); (a) aanwysend,

aantonend; *be* ~ *of*, wys op, dui op; ~ **mood**, aantonende wys(e).
in'dicator, aangeër; wyser, rigtingwyser; aanwyser, aantoner; nommerbord; wyspennetjie; meter; verklikker; ~ **diagram**, arbeidsdiagram.
indict', formeel beskuldig, in staat van beskuldiging stel, aankla, vervolg; ~ **able**, strafbaar, vervolgbaar; ~ **ion**, indiksie; ~ **ment**, aanklag; akte van beskuldiging, skriftelike beskuldiging.
In'dies: *the* ~, Indië; *East* ~, Oos-Indië; *West* ~, Wes-Indië.
indiff'erence, onverskilligheid, louheid; onbeduidendheid; afsydigheid; *a matter of* ~, 'n saak van min betekenis.
indiff'erent, onverskillig; agtelosig; indifferent (elek.); onbevooroordeeld; taamlik, middelmatig, so-so, dunnetjies, nie te danig nie, onbeduidend; slegterig, swakkerig; *he is in* ~ *health*, sy gesondheid is swak; ~ **ism**, (godsdienstige) onverskilligheid; ~ **ist**, onverskillige.
in'digence, armoede, onvermoë, gebrek, nooddruf, behoeftigheid, hulpbehoewendheid.
in'digene, inboorling.
indig'enous, inheems, inlands.
in'digent, (brand)arm, minvermoënd, hulpbehoewend, doodarm, nooddruftig, onvermoënd, behoeftig, armoedig, berooid; *be* ~, arm wees, van die oostewind lewe.
indiges'ted, onverteer; onverwerk; ongeorden, vormloos.
indigestibil'ity, onverteerbaarheid.
indigest'ible, onverteerbaar; ongenietbaar.
indiges'tion, slegte spysvertering, indigestie.
indiges'tive, lydende aan slegte spysvertering (indigestie).
indig'nant, verontwaardig, verbolge; ~ **ly**, met verontwaardiging, verontwaardig.
indigna'tion, verontwaardiging, verbolgenheid; ~ **meeting**, protesvergadering.
indig'nity, (..ties), hoon, smaad, belediging.
in'digo, (-s), indigo; ~ **blue**, indigoblou; ~ **plant**, indigoplant; ~ **t'ic**, indigo-; ~ **white**, kleurlose indigo, indigowit.
indirect', indirek, onregstreeks, middellik; onopreg; ~ **evidence**, afgeleide (indirekte) bewys; ~ **ly**, onregstreeks; ~ **ion**, ~ **ness**, indirektheid; oneerlikheid, slinksheid; ~ **lighting**, indirekte verligting; ~ **object**, indirekte voorwerp; ~ **speech**, indirekte rede; ~ **tax**, onregstreekse belasting.
indiscern'ible, onbespeurbaar, onwaarneembaar; onderskeibaar.
indiscerp'tible, onskeibaar, ondeelbaar; onvernielbaar.
indiscipli'nable, onhandelbaar, tugteloos, onbuigbaar; ondissiplineerbaar.
indis'cipline, tugteloosheid, gebrek aan dissipline.
indiscreet', onverstandig, onbeskeie, onbesonne; *he made an* ~ *remark*, hy het sy mond verbygepraat.
indis'crete, ongeskei, onverdeel.
indiscre'tion, onverstandigheid, onbesonnenheid, onbeskeidenheid, indiskresie.
indiscrim'inate, deurmekaar; voor die voet, sonder onderskeid, onoordeelkundig; ~ **ly**, deurmekaar, voor die voet, blindelings, in die wilde; ~ **ness**, verwarring, gebrek aan onderskeiding, onoordeelkundigheid.
indiscrim'inating, sonder onderskeid, onoordeelkundig, blind.
indiscrimina'tion = **indiscriminateness**.
indispensabil'ity, noodsaaklikheid, onmisbaarheid; onvermydelikheid.
indispen'sable, onontbeerlik, onmisbaar, noodsaaklik; *be* ~, broodnodig wees; ~ **ness**, onmisbaarheid, onontbeerlikheid.
indispose', ongunstig stem; ontstem; ongesteld maak; ongeskik maak; onvatbaar maak; ~ **d**, ongunstig gestem; siek, oeserig, onwel; afkerig, ongeneë; *he is* ~ *d to AGREE*, hy is nie geneig om saam te stem nie; *they are* ~ *d TOWARDS the idea*, hulle is teen die idee.
indisposi'tion, ongesteldheid; onwelwillendheid, ongeneentheid; afkerigheid.

indisputabil'ity, onbetwisbaarheid.
indis'putable, onbetwisbaar, onaanvegbaar, onloën=
baar.
indisput'ably, beslis, onteenseglik.
indissolubil'ity, onoplosbaarheid; onverbreekbaar=
heid.
indissol'uble, indissolv'able, onoplosbaar; onskei=
baar, onontbindbaar; onverbeekbaar.
indistinct', onduidelik; dof, vaag; verward; ~ **ive,**
sonder besondere kenmerke; ~ **ly,** vaag, onduide=
lik; ~ **ness,** onduidelikheid, verwardheid.
indisting'uishable, onsigbaar, nie te onderskei nie,
onwaarneembaar; ~ **ness,** onwaarneembaarheid.
indite', opstel, ontwerp, neerskryf; ~ **r,** opsteller,
skrywer.
in'dium, indium.
indivertibil'ity, onafwendbaarheid, onkeerbaarheid.
indivert'ible, onkeerbaar, onafwendbaar.
individ'ual, (n) indiwidu, persoon, eenling, enkeling;
(a) indiwidueel, persoonlik, eieselwig; afsonderlik;
eienaardig; ~ **ism,** indiwidualisme; ~ **ist,** indiwidu=
alis; ~ **is'tic,** indiwidualisties; ~ **'ity,** indiwiduali=
teit, selfstandigheid, persoonlikheid, eiendomlik=
heid, karakter; ~ **iza'tion,** indiwidualisasie; ~ **ize,**
onderskei; indiwidualiseer, afsonderlik beskou;
~ **ly,** persoonlik, indiwidueel, afsonderlik, apart.
individ'uate, indiwidualiseer, onderskei; afsonder.
indivisibil'ity, ondeelbaarheid.
indivis'ible, ondeelbaar.
In'do-China, Agter-Indië, Indo-Sjina, Indo-China.
In'do-Chinese, Indo-Sjinees, Indo-Chinees.
indo'cile, onleersaam, onhandelbaar, ongeseglik.
indocil'ity, onleersaamheid, ongeseglikheid, onhan=
delbaarheid.
indoc'trinate, onderwys, leer, onderrig, indoktrineer
(met).
indoctrina'tion, onderwysing, lering, beïnvloeding;
inpompery, indoktrinering, indoktrinasie.
In'do-European, (n) Indo-Europeaan, Indo-Euro=
peër; (a) Indo-Europees, Aries.
In'do-Germanic, Indo-Germaans, Oergermaans,
Aries.
in'dolence, luiheid, gemaksug, lamlendigheid, laks=
heid, vadsigheid, traagheid.
in'dolent, lui, traag, vadsig, laks, lamlendig.
Indol'ogy, Indologie.
indomitabil'ity, ontembaarheid; onoorwinlikheid.
indom'itable, ontembaar, ontoombaar; onbedwing=
baar, onoorwinlik.
Indones'ia, Indonesië; ~ **n,** (n) Indonesiër; (a) In=
donesies.
in'door, in die huis, binne, huislik; huis=, kamer=; ~
game, kamerspeletjie, huisspeletjie; ~ **s,** binne, bin=
nenshuis; ~ **work,** huiswerk.
indorsa'tion, endossement, tekening.
indorse', *kyk* endorse.
indorsee', geëndosseerde.
in'draft, in'draught, trek; instroming.
in'drawn, ingetrek, ingehou.
indub'itable, ontwyfelbaar; ~ **ness,** ontwyfelbaar=
heid.
Induce', beweeg, oorhaal; veroorsaak; opwek; aanlei=
ding gee tot, aanlei; aflei, besluit; oorbring; noop;
oorhaal; induseer (tegn.); ~ **ment,** aanleiding, be=
weegrede, dryfveer, lokmiddel, prikkel; bron, oor=
saak.
induct', orden, bevestig; inseën; installeer (ampsbe=
kleër); in 'n amp bevestig (predikant); inwy, bekend
maak met; ~ **ile,** onsmeedbaar; onhandelbaar.
induc'tion, installasie; inlaat; induksie; inseëning, be=
vestiging, ordening (geestelike); invoering; aanvoe=
ring (van feite); gevolgtrekking; veroorsaking; ~
coil, induksieklos; ~ **compass,** induksiekompas; ~
current, induksiestroom; ~ **sermon,** intreepreek; ~
stroke, inlaatslag; ~ **system,** inlaatstelsel.
induct'ive, induktief, afleidend; aanleidend; in=
leidend.
inductiv'ity, induksievermoë.
induc'tor, induktor; bevestiger, installeerder.
indulge', toegee, toestaan, inwillig, bevredig; verwen;
jou oorgee aan; begunstig met; koester; ~ *a
HOPE,* hoop koester; ~ *IN,* jou oorgee aan; jou

die weelde veroorloof; ~ *one's PASSIONS,* jou
luste botvier.
indul'gence, toegeeflikheid, inskiklikheid; bevredi=
ging; weelde, genoeë, uitspanning; guns; vergifnis,
aflaat (R.K.); uitstel; ~ **money,** aflaatgeld.
indul'gent, toegewend, toegeeflik, inskiklik; goed=
gunstig, goedig.
indult', dispensasie, genadebrief, indult.
indun'a, indoena; impieleier.
in'durate, verhard, verstok maak; verstok word; vas=
wortel.
indura'tion, verstoktheid; verharding.
indus'trial, (n) industrieel, nyweraar; industriewer=
ker; (a) industrieel, nywerheids=; ~ **age,** nywer=
heidseeu; ~ **area,** nywerheidsgebied; ~ **art,** kuns=
nywerheid; ~ **bank,** nywerheidsbank; ~
chemistry, bedryfschemie; ~ **conflict,** industriële
botsing; ~ **consultant,** nywerheidsraadgewer; ~
council, nywerheidsraad; ~ **dermatitis,** nywer=
heidsdermatitis; ~ **diamond,** nywerheidsdiamant;
~ **disease,** nywerheidsiekte; ~ **dispute,** arbeidsges=
kil; ~ **exhibition,** nywerheidstentoonstelling;
~ **ism,** industrialisme, nywerheidswese; ~ **ist,**
industrieel, fabrikant, nyweraar; ~ **iza'tion,** indus=
trialisasie, ontwikkeling van nywerhede; ~ **ize,** in=
dustrialiseer; ~ **peace,** industriële vrede; ~ **re=
lations,** arbeidsbetrekkinge, bedryfsverhoudinge;
~ **research,** industriële navorsing; ~ **revolution,** in=
dustriële rewolusie; ~ **school,** industrieskool, ny=
werheidskool, ambagskool; ~ **site,** nywerheidster=
rein; ~ **strife,** industriële stryd (botsing).
indus'trious, werksaam, fluks, vlytig, arbeidsaam,
ywerig, noes, naarstig; ~ **ly,** ywerig, vlytig; ~ **ness,**
vlytigheid, werksaamheid, flukscheid.
in'dustry, vlyt, fluksheid, ywer, werkywer, werk=
saamheid; (..**ries),** bedryfswese; nywerheid, indus=
trie.
indwell', bewoon, inwoon; ~ **er,** inwoner.
ineb'riant, bedwelmend, dronkmakend.
ineb'riate, (n) dronkaard, dronklap, beskonkene; (v)
dronk maak; (a) dronk, beskonke; ~ **d,** beskonke,
dronk; ~ **reformatory,** dronkaardsasiel.
inebria'tion, inebri'ety, dronkenskap, dranksug.
inedibil'ity, oneetbaarheid.
ined'ible, oneetbaar.
ined'ited, onuitgegee; ongewysig uitgee.
ineffabil'ity, onuitspreeklikheid, onsegbaarheid.
ineff'able, onuitspreeklik, onsegbaar.
ineffaceabil'ity, onuitwisbaarheid.
ineffa'ceable, onuitwisbaar.
ineffec'tive, vrugteloos, vergeefs; ondoeltreffend;
sonder uitwerking; onbekwaam; ~ **ly,** vrugteloos,
tevergeefs; ~ **ness,** vrugteloosheid, vergeefsheid,
ondoeltreffendheid.
ineffec'tual, nutteloos, ondoelmatig, vrugteloos, ver=
geefs; *prove* ~, mislik; vergeefs wees; ~ **ness,** vrug=
teloosheid, ondoeltreffendheid.
ineffica'cious, ondoeltreffend, vrugteloos, onafdoen=
de; ~ **ly,** vrugteloos, ondoeltreffend.
ineff'icacy, kragteloosheid, vrugteloosheid; ondoel=
treffendheid.
ineffi'ciency, onbekwaamheid, ondoeltreffendheid,
vrotsigheid, vrugteloosheid.
ineffi'cient, ongeskik, onbruikbaar; onbekwaam;
vrotsig; ondoeltreffend.
inelas'tic, onveerkragtig, nie soepel nie; onelasties;
star.
inelasti'city, onveerkragtigheid
inel'egance, inel'egancy, onbevalligheid, onsierlik=
heid.
inel'egant, onbevallig, smaakloos, onsierlik, onele=
gant.
ineligibil'ity, onverkiesbaarheid, onraadsaamheid,
ongeradenheid.
inel'igible, onverkiesbaar; onraadsaam, ongerade.
inel'oquence, onwelsprekendheid.
inel'oquent, onwelsprekend.
ineluc'table, onontkombaar, onvermybaar, onaf=
wendbaar.
inept', onbekwaam, ongeskik; ongepas; ongerymd;
onsinnig, dwaas; ~ **itude,** ~ **ness,** onbekwaamheid;
ongepastheid; dwaasheid; ongerymdheid.

ineq'uable, ongelyk.
inequal'ity, ongelykheid; oneffenheid; verskil.
inequilat'eral, ongelyksydig.
ineq'uitable, onbillik, onredelik, onregverdig.
ineq'uity, onbillikheid, onregverdigheid.
inerad'icable, onuitroeibaar.
inerrabil'ity, onfeilbaarheid.
ine'rrable, onfeilbaar.
inert', lui, loom, bewegingloos, traag.
iner'tia, traagheid, bewegingloosheid, inersie; traagheidsvermoë; *MOMENT of* ~, traagheidsmoment; *PERMANENCY of* ~, traagheidswerking; ~ **radius,** traagheidstraal.
inert'ness, luiheid, loomheid, traagheid.
inescap'able, onontkombaar.
inessen'tial, onnodig, onbelangrik, onessensieel, onwesenlik.
ines'timable, onskatbaar, onberekenbaar.
inevitabil'ity, onvermydelikheid, onafwendbaarheid.
inev'itable, onvermydelik, noodwendig, onontkombaar; ~ **ness,** onvermydelikheid, noodwendigheid.
inev'itably, onvermydelik, noodwendig.
inexact', onnoukeurig, agteloos; onjuis; ~ **itude,** ~ **ness,** onnoukeurigheid, onjuistheid.
inexchange'able, oninwisselbaar; onomruilbaar.
inexcit'able, onvatbaar vir aandoening.
inexcusabil'ity, onvergeeflikheid, onverskoonbaarheid.
inexcus'able, onvergeeflik, onverskoonbaar.
inexec'utable, onuitvoerbaar.
inexer'tion, werkloosheid; onbeweeglikheid, passiefheid.
inexhaustibil'ity, onuitputlikheid; onvermoeidheid.
inexhaus'tible, onuitputlik; onvermoeid.
inexhaus'tive, onuitputlik.
inexorabil'ity, onverbiddelikheid.
inex'orable, onverbiddelik, onvermurfbaar; ~ **ness,** onverbiddelikheid.
inexpec'tant, niks verwagtend; onverwagtend, onvermoedend.
inexped'iency, ongeskiktheid, ondienstigheid; onraadsaamheid.
inexped'ient, ondienstig, ongeskik; onraadsaam.
inexpen'sive, goedkoop, billik; ~ **ness,** billikheid.
inexper'ience, onervarenheid, onbedrewenheid, ongeoefendheid; ~ **d,** onervare, onbedrewe.
inex'pert, onbedrewe, onsaakkundig, onervare, ondeskundig; ~ **ness,** ondeskundigheid.
inex'piable, nie goed te maak nie; onversoenlik.
inexplicabil'ity, onverklaarbaarheid.
inex'plicable, onverklaarbaar, onuitlegbaar.
inexpli'cit, onduidelik; onuitgesproke.
inexplos'ive, onontplofbaar.
inexpress'ible, onuitspreeklik.
inexpress'ive, sonder uitdrukking, uitdrukkingloos.
inexpugn'able, onoorwinlik, onneembaar.
inexten'sible, onrekbaar.
in exten'so, (L.), in extenso, uitgerek, ten volle.
inexterm'inable, onuitroeibaar.
inexting'uishable, onuitblusbaar; onlesbaar.
in extrem'is, in 'n uiterste toestand; sterwend.
inex'tricable, onoplosbaar, onontwarbaar; onontkombaar.
inex'tricably, onontwarbaar.
infall'ibilism, onfeilbaarheid.
infallibil'ity, onfeilbaarheid; sekerheid, stelligheid.
infall'ible, onfeilbaar; seker.
in'famize, tot skande maak, onteer.
in'famous, skandelik, verfoeilik; berug; eerloos.
in'famy, skande(likheid), eerloosheid, skanddaad, laagheid.
in'fancy, suigelingskap; kindheid; kleutertyd; vroegste jeug; minderjarigheid, onmondigheid; aanvang.
in'fant, (n) klein kind, suigeling, minderjarige, onmondige; ~ *-mortality rate,* suigelingsterfsyfer; (a) klein, jong, jeugdig; kinder=.
infan'ta, infante.
in'fant: ~ **christening,** kinderdoop; ~ **hood,** kindheid.
infan'ticidal, kindermoord=.
infan'ticide, kindermoord; kindermoordenaar.
in'fantile, kinderlik, kinder=; kinderagtig; ~ **paralysis,** kinderverlamming, polio(miëlitis).

infan'tilism, infantilisme.
in'fantine = **infantile.**
in'fant prodigy, wonderkind.
in'fantry, infanterie; voetvolk; ~ **battalion,** infanteriebataljon; ~ **brigade,** infanteriebrigade; ~ **man,** voetganger, infanteris; ~ **patrol,** infanteriepatrollie; ~ **training,** infanterieleer, infanterieopleiding; ~ **weapon,** infanteriewapen.
in'fant-school, kleinkinderskool, kleuterskool.
in'farct, infark, prop, afgestorwe weefsel; ~ **ion,** infarksie, propvorming, weefselafsterwing.
in'fauna, infauna, seebodemdiere.
infat'uate, versot maak, verdwaas; ~ **d,** versot, verslaaf, verdwaas; verlief; *become* ~ *d with,* dol verlief wees op; versot wees op.
infatua'tion, versotheid, dwaasheid; bevlieging; verdwasing, verdwaasdheid; verliefdheid.
infeasibil'ity, ondoenlikheid; onuitvoerbaarheid.
infeas'ible, ondoenlik, onuitvoerbaar.
infect', besmet, aansteek; bederf; verpes; aantas, inwerk op; ~ **ed,** verpes; besmet, aangesteek; *become* ~ *ed,* besmet raak, aangesteek wees; ~ **ion,** besmetting, aansteking, infeksie, aantasting; *period of* ~ *tion,* aansteektyd.
infec'tious, besmetlik, aansteeklik; ~ **abortion,** besmetlike misgeboorte; ~ **disease,** aansteeklike (besmetlike) siekte; ~ **matter,** smetstof; ~ **ness,** aansteeklikheid, besmetlikheid; ~ **sterility,** besmetlike onvrugbaarheid.
infec'tive, aansteeklik; verpestend; ~ **ness,** aansteeklikheid; besmetlikheid.
infecund'ity, onvrugbaarheid.
infeli'citous, ongelukkig.
infeli'city, ongeluk, ellende, rampspoed; ongelukkigheid.
infer', (-red), aflei, 'n gevolgtrekking maak; ~ **able,** afleibaar.
in'ference, gevolgtrekking, deduksie; bybetekenis; *draw* ~ *s,* gevolgtrekkings maak.
inferen'tial, afleibaar; afgelei.
infer'ior, (n) ondergeskikte, mindere; (a) laer, minder, onderhorig, ondergeskik; minderwaardig; onderstandig (plant); onder die lyn (reël) gedruk (letter); ~ TO *his brother,* die mindere van sy broer; *be* ~ *TO,* ondergeskik wees aan; nie so goed wees nie; onderdoen vir; ~ **character,** laaggedrukte letterteken (bv. H_2); ~ **court,** laerhof.
inferior'ity, ondergeskiktheid; minder(waardig)heid; *feeling of* ~, minderwaardigheidsgevoel; ~ **complex,** minderwaardigheidskompleks.
infern'al, hels, duiwels; verfoeilik; ~ **machine,** helse masjien.
infern'o, (-s), inferno, hel, vuurpoel.
infer'rable, *kyk* **inferable.**
infert'ile, onvrugbaar.
infertil'ity, onvrugbaarheid.
infest', kwel, verontrus; onveilig maak; verpes, teister; vervuil; ~ **a'tion,** teistering, onveiligmaking; vervuiling, besmetting, plaag; ~ **ed,** verpes; vervuil; ~ *ed with,* vergewe van, wemel van.
infib'ulate, vasgespe.
infibula'tion, vasgesping.
in'fidel, (n) ongelowige; (a) ongelowig.
infidel'ity, ongeloof; ontrou, ongetrouheid; *conjugal* ~, huweliksontrou.
in'field, werfgrond; ploegland; binneveld (krieket).
in'fighting, binnegeveg; binnestryd.
infil'trate, intrek, insypel, insyg, insyfer, deurdring, infiltreer.
infiltra'tion, insypeling, insyging; deurdringing, deursyfering, insyfering, infiltrasie.
in'filtrator, infiltreerder, ïnsypelaar.
in'finite, (n) oneindigheid; (die) Oneindige; (a) eindeloos, oneindig, grensloos; onbegrens; ~ **ly,** oneindig; ~ **ness,** oneindigheid, eindeloosheid.
infinites'imal, oneindig klein, infinitesimaal.
infinitiv'al, infinitiefs=.
infin'itive, (n) infinitief, onbepaalde wys(e); (a) oneindig, eindeloos; ~ **mood,** onbepaalde wys(e).
infin'itude, oneindigheid, onbegrensdheid, eindeloosheid.

infin'ity, eindeloosheid, oneindigheid; *to* ~, tot die oneindige.
infirm', swak; gebrekkig; onvas; weifelend, onseker; ~ **ar'ian**, siekebesorger; ~ **ary**, (..**ries**), siekehuis, hospitaal; ~ **ity**, swakheid; swakte; gebrekkigheid; gebrek.
in fix¹ (n) invoegsel (gram.).
infix',² (v) inprent; invoeg; inlas; vestig.
inflame', verhit, ontsteek; aanstook, aanvuur, aan= hits; ontvlam, ontbrand; laat brand; aanwakker; ontstoke raak; inflammasie kry; ~ *d wound*, ont= steekte wond.
inflammabil'ity, ontvlambaarheid.
inflamm'able, vlambaar, brandbaar, ontvlambaar; hartstogtelik.
inflamm'ables, vlamstof, brandbare stof.
inflamma'tion, ontsteking, inflammasie; ontvlam= ming.
inflamm'atory, verhittend; ontstekend; opruiend, aanhitsend; prikkelend.
inflat'able, opblaasbaar.
inflate', opblaas, oppomp; opswel; opjaag, opdryf (pryse); opgeblaas maak; inflasioneer (geld); ~ **d**, opgeblaas, opgeblase (fig.); opgepomp; geswolle, hoogdrawend (taal); opgejaag, opgedrewe (pryse).
infla'tion, opblasing; (die) oppomp; inflasie; opdry= wing (pryse); opgeblasenheid; ~ **ary**, inflasionis= ties; ~ *ary spiral*, inflasionistiese kringloop.
inflat'or, pomp.
inflect', buig; krom; flekteer, verbuig (spraakk.); mo= duleer; ~ **ed**, verboë.
inflec'tion, buiging, kromming; buigingsuitgang; mo= dulasie; verbuiging (gram.); ~ **point**, buigpunt.
inflec'tive, buigbaar; verbuigbaar.
inflexibil'ity, onbuigbaarheid; onversetlikheid.
inflex'ible, onbuigsaam; onversetlik; onveranderlik; ~ *honesty*, onkreukbaarheid.
infle'xion, buiging; fleksie; ~ **al**, buigings=.
inflict', oplê (straf); toebring (wond); lastig val met; ~ **ion**, oplegging; kwelling, marteling, straf.
inflores'cence, blomstand; bloeiwyse; bloei.
in'flow, instroming, invloeiing; toevloed.
in'fluence, (n) invloed, gesag; inwerking; *BE under the* ~ *of*, onder die invloed van; *HAVE* ~ *with*, invloed hê by; *HAVE* ~ *on (with)*, invloed hê op; *HAVE a good* ~ *on*, 'n goeie invloed uitoefen op; *USE one's* ~, jou invloed laat geld; (v) beïnvloed, inwerk, invloed hê op.
in'fluent, (n) syrivier, sytak; (a) invloeiend.
influen'tial, invloedryk, gesaghebbend, vermoënd.
influen'za, influensa, griep; ~ **l**, grieperig.
in'flux, instroming, invloeiing; toevloed, toevoer; ~ **control**, instromingsbeheer.
infold', *kyk* **enfold**.
inform', meedeel, berig, verwittig, laat weet; besiel, vervul; onderrig, inlig; aandra, verklik, vertel; aan= kondig, aansê; ~ *AGAINST*, aangee, aankla; ~ *OF*, in kennis stel met; ~ *WITH*, vervul met, deur= dring van.
inform'al, informeel, gewoon; ongegeneerd, gemoe= delik; sonder seremonies; onreëlmatig; ~ **ly**, infor= meel; ~ **'ity**, informaliteit; ongereeldheid.
inform'ant, informant, segsman, beriggewer; aan= klaer; mededeler.
informa'tion, informasie, berig, verwittiging, aangif= te; inligting, gegewens; voorligting; kennis; aan= klag, beskuldiging; mededeling; aangewing (reg); *FOR the* ~ *of*, vir die (ter) inligting van, tot narig van; *for YOUR* ~, vir u inligting; *for GENERAL* ~, vir algemene kennisname; ~ **bureau**, inligtings= kantoor; ~ **officer**, voorligtingsbeampte; inlig= tingsbeampte; ~ **service**, voorligtingsdiens; inlig= tingsdiens.
informa'tive, inform'atory, leersaam; inligtend.
informed', op hoogte, goed ingelig; saakkundig; *keep one* ~, iem. op hoogte hou.
inform'er, aanbringer; aangeër, beriggewer, segsman; nuusdraer; aanklaer; *common* ~, aanbrenger, ver= klikker.
inform'ing, leersaam.
in'fra, infra, benede; ~ *dig(nitatem)*, infra dig(nita= tem), benede iem. se waardigheid.

infrac'tion, breuk, verbreking, skennis, oortreding.
infrangibil'ity, onbreekbaarheid, onskendbaarheid.
infran'gible, onbreekbaar.
in'fra-red, infrarooi.
infrastruc'ture, infrastruktuur.
infreq'uency, seldsaamheid.
infreq'uent, seldsaam; ~ **ly**, selde.
infringe', oortree, oorskry; vergryp, verkrag; ver= breek, inbreuk maak op; ~ *the rules*, die reëls nie nakom nie; ~ **d**, geskonde; ~ **ment**, skending, in= breuk, oortreding, verbreking; vergryp, verkrag= ting.
infruc'tuous, onvrugbaar; vrugteloos.
infundib'ular, tregtervormig.
infur'iate, vertoorn, woedend maak; ~ **d**, woedend, rasend; *be* ~ *d*, woedend wees; die ongeluk in wees.
infuse', ingiet, ingee, inblaas; besiel; (laat) trek (kof= fie); 'n infusie maak.
infusibil'ity, onoplosbaarheid; onsmeltbaarheid.
infus'ible, onsmeltbaar; onoplosbaar.
infu'sion, ingieting; inspuiting; trekking, aftreksel; in= gewing; bymenging.
infusor'ia, infusorieë, infusiediertjies, afgietseldier= tjies; ~ **l**, afgietsel=, infusie=; ~ **n**, (n) infusiediertjie; (a) = **infusorial**.
in'gathering, insameling, oes.
ingem'inate, herhaal.
ingen'ious, vernuftig, skrander, geniaal, geesryk, ta= lentvol, ingenieus, vindingryk, sinryk; ~ **ness**, vin= dingrykheid, vernuf.
ingenu'ity, vernuf(tigheid), vindingrykheid, oulik= heid, skranderheid, sinrykheid.
ingen'uous, opreg, ongekunsteld, openhartig, onge= veins, naïef; - **ness**, ongekunsteldheid, openhartig= heid, naïefheid, naïwiteit.
ingest', opneem, inbring; ~ **ion**, opneming, inbren= ging; voedselinname.
in'gle, haardvuur; vuurherd; ~ **nook**, ~ **side**, hoekie van die vuurherd, haardhoekie.
inglor'ious, onbekend; roemloos; skandelik, ~ **ness**, skande; roemloosheid.
in'going, (n) ingang; (a) ingaande.
ing'ot, (metaal)staaf, baar; gietblok; goudstaaf; ~ **iron**, vloeiyster; ~ **mould**, gietvorm; ~ **steel**, vloei= staal.
ingraft', inent, inprent, inskerp.
ingrain', (v) in die wol verf; (a) deur die wol geverf; ingewortel; ~ **ed**, ingewortel; verstok; deur die wol geverf.
ingra'tiate, in die guns bring; ~ *oneself*, jou bemind maak; jou indring, inkruip.
ingra'tiating, innemend, beminlik; indringerig, in= kruiperig.
ingratia'tion, gunsverwerwing.
ingrat'itude, ondank(baarheid).
ingraves'cent, verergerend (med.).
ingred'ient, bestanddeel, aanmaakgoed, ingrediënt; (pl) bestanddele, aanmaakgoed.
in'gress, toegang, intrede, ingang.
in'growing, ingegroei; ingroeiend.
in'growth, ingroeisel.
ing'uinal, lies=.
ingulf', *kyk* **engulf**.
ingur'gitate, verswelg, insluk.
ingurgita'tion, inslukking, verswelging.
inhab'it, bewoon, woon in; ~ **able**, bewoonbaar; ~ **ancy**, bewoning; ~ **ant**, bewoner (van 'n stad of huis); inwoner (van 'n land); ~ **a'tion**, bewoning.
inhal'ant, inasemingsmiddel.
inhala'tion, inaseming, inhalasie.
inhale', inasem, intrek; ~ **r**, inasemtoestel, respira= tor.
inharmon'ic, onwelluidend, onharmonies.
inharmon'ious, onwelluidend, onharmonies, wanlui= dend.
inhere', saamhang, berus, verbonde wees, aankleef, inherent wees.
inher'ence, onafskeidelikheid, samehang, aanklewing.
inher'ent, onafskeidelik, ingebore, eie (aan), inherent; *it is* ~ *in our nature*, dit sit in ons bloed.
inhe'rit, (-ed), erwe, oorerwe; ~ **abil'ity**, erflikheid, oorerfbaarheid; ~ **able**, erflik, oorerfbaar.

inhe'rit: (~ ed), geërf, oorgeërf, aangeërf; ~ or, erfgenaam; ~ ress, (-es), ~ rix, (..trices), vroulike erfgenaam.
inhe'ritance, erfenis, erfgoed, erfporsie, aanbesterwing; oorerwing; ~ never ascends, erfgeld is swerfgeld; ~ tax, suksessiebelasting.
inhe'sion, samehang, inherensie.
inhib'it, verbied, belet; teenhou, verhinder; inhibeer.
inhibi'tion, verbod; stuiting; skorsing; remming, onderdrukking, beletting, verhindering; inhibisie.
inhib'itory, belettend, verbiedend, remmend, verbods=.
inhos'pitable, ongasvry; onherbergsaam; ~ ness, ..tal'ity, ongasvryheid; onherbergsaamheid.
in'-house, intern; ~ training, interne opleiding.
inhum'an, onmenslik, wreed, barbaars.
inhumane', onmensliewend, inhumaan.
inhuman'ity, onmenslikheid.
inhuma'tion, begrawing, teraardebestelling.
inhume', begrawe, ter aarde bestel.
inim'ical, vyandelik, vyandig; nadelig, skadelik.
inimitabil'ity, onnavolgbaarheid.
inim'itable, onnavolgbaar; onverbeterlik; ~ ness, onnavolgbaarheid.
iniq'uitous, onregverdig, onbillik; boos, snood, sondig.
iniq'uity, (..ties), onregverdigheid, onbillikheid; snoodheid; sondigheid, sonde.
ini'tial, (n) voorletter, beginletter; (pl) voorletters; naamsyfer; (v) (-led), met voorletters teken, parafeer; (a) eerste, begin=; aanvangs=; ~ ly, aanvanklik, in die begin.
ini'tiate, (n) ingewyde; nuweling; (v) begin, aanvang, onderneem; doop, (in)sout, ontgroen; inlei, inwy; ~ d, ingewy.
initia'tion, inwyding; begin; ontgroening, inisiasie; ~ committee, doopkomitee; ~ school, inisiasieskool, bergskool.
ini'tiative, (n) eerste stap, begin, inisiatief, voortou; ondernemingsgees; *HAVE the* ~, die leiding hê; *TAKE the* ~, die leiding neem; (a) aanvangend, aanvangs=.
ini'tiatory, inwydings=; eerste, inleidend, inwydend.
inject', inspuit.
injec'tion, inspuiting, injeksie; *intravenous* ~, aarinspuiting; *subcutaneous* ~, onderhuidse inspuiting.
injec'tor, inspuiter; spuit.
injudi'cious, onoordeelkundig, onverstandig; ~ ness, onoordeelkundigheid, onverstandigheid.
injunc'tion, bevel, opdrag; geregtelike verbod (bevel).
in'jure, beskadig, seermaak, skaad; kwes; wond; benadeel, krenk; beledig, aantas; onreg aandoen; ~ d, beseer; verongelyk, beledig, ~ *d party,* benadeelde persoon.
injur'ious, skadelik, nadelig, verderflik; beledigend, krenkend.
in'jury, (..ries), besering, kwetsing, kwetsuur; skade, nadeel; wond, seerplek, letsel; benadeling, verongelyking.
injus'tice, onregverdigheid, verongelyking, onreg; *do someone an* ~, iem. 'n onreg aandoen, iem. verongelyk (veronreg).
ink, (n) ink; (v) met ink merk; met ink besmeer; ~ *IN (over),* met ink bedek; ~ *OUT,* met ink onleesbaar maak; *SLING* ~ *at someone,* op iem. lostrek; iem. met ink beswadder; ~ -**bag,** inkblaas; ~ -**ball,** inkbal; ~ -**berry bush,** inkbessiebos *(Cestrum laevigatum);* ~ **blot,** klad; ~ -**blot test,** Rorschachtoets, inkkladtoets; ~ -**bottle,** inkbottel; inkpot; ~ -**bush,** inkbos *(Suaeda);* ~ **dabber,** inkkussing; ~ **drawing,** pentekening; ~ **er,** inkrol; ~ -**eraser,** inkuitveër; ~ -**fish,** inkvis *(Cephalopoda);* seekat; ~ -**fountain,** inkbak; ~ -**horn,** inkhoring; ~ **iness,** swartheid; ~ **ing,** swartmaak.
ink'ling, aanduiding, idee, vermoede; snuf, wenk; *get an* ~, die lug kry (van); 'n snuf in die neus kry.
ink: ~ -**pad,** inkkussing; ~ -**powder,** inkpoeier; ~ -**slinger,** broodskrywer, koerantkrabbelaar; ~ -**spot,** inkkol; ~ -**stain,** inkvlek; ~ **stand,** inkpot; ~ -**table,** inktafel; ~ -**tippler,** inkwellusteling; ~ -**trough,** inkbak; ~ -**well,** inkpot; ~ **y,** inkagtig, so swart soos ink.

in'laid, ingelê; ~ **work,** (in)legwerk.
in'land, (n) binneland, onderveld; (a) binnelands; (adv) landwaarts; ~ **duty,** aksyns; ~ **er,** binnelander, ondervelder; ~ **navigation,** binneskeepvaart; ~ **port,** binnehawe; ~ **revenue,** belastinginkomste; ~ **revenue office,** belastingkantoor; ~ **sea,** binnesee; ~ **town,** stad in die binneland.
in'-laws, aangetroude familie, skoonfamilie.
in'lay, (n) inlegsel, inlêwerk, houtmosaïek; inslag.
inlay', (v) (..laid), inlê, oplê; inlaat; opsit (tegn.).
in'layer, maker van inlêwerk.
in'lay work, inlegwerk.
in'let, inham, baai; ingang; insetsel; inlaat (motor); ~ -**pipe,** toevoerpyp; ~ **valve,** inlaatklep; insuigklep.
in'lying, binne(lands) geleë.
in'mate, inwoner; bewoner; huisgenoot; (pl) huismense.
in'most, binneste; geheimste.
inn, herberg.
in'nards, binnegoed, afval.
innate', aangebore, ingeskape; ~ **ness,** ingeskapenheid, aangeborenheid.
innav'igable, onbevaarbaar.
inn'er, (n) binnekring; binnekringskoot; (a) innerlik, inwendig; geheim; intiem; *FORTIFY the* ~ *man,* die inwendige mens versterk; *the* ~ *MAN,* die inwendige mens; ~ **harbour,** binnehawe; ~ **lining,** binnevoering; ~ **most,** binneste; ~ **office,** privaat kantoor; ~ **sole,** binnesool; ~ -**spring mattress,** binneveermatras, veermatras.
innerv'ate, die senuwees span; van senukrag voorsien; tot aktiwiteit prikkel.
innerva'tion, senuweeprikkeling; senuwerking.
inn'ings, speelbeurt, slaanbeurt, kolfbeurt (krieket); regeringsperiode; kans; *FIRST* ~, eerste beurt; *to have had a LONG* ~, lank gelewe (gedien) het.
inn'keeper, herbergier, hotelbaas, waard.
inn'keeping, herberghouery, hotelhouery.
inn'ocence, onskuld; eenvoudigheid, argeloosheid; *INJURED* ~, die verdrukte onskuld; *PROTEST his* ~, sy onskuld betuig.
inn'ocent, (n) onskuldige; *the massacre of the* ~ *s,* kindermoord; die slagting van wetsontwerpe; (a) onskuldig; skuldeloos; argeloos; *as* ~ *as a BABE (lamb),* so onskuldig soos 'n lam; ~ *OF,* onskuldig aan; *PRETEND to be quite* ~, maak of jy doodonskuldig is; jou doodluiters hou.
innocu'ity, onskadelikheid.
innoc'uous, onskadelik; ~ **ness,** onskadelikheid.
innom'inate, naamloos, onnoembaar; ~ **bone,** heupbeen.
inn'ovate, nuwighede invoer, veranderinge aanbring.
innova'tion, invoering van nuwighede; nuwigheid; verandering.
inn'ovator, invoerder van nuwighede.
inno'xious, onskadelik; ~ **ness,** onskadelikheid.
innuen'do, (n) (-es), toespeling, sinspeling, skimp, innuendo; (v) insinueer, sinspeel op, skimp.
innum'erable, ontelbaar, onafsienbaar (menigte).
innutri'tious, onvoedsaam.
inobserv'ance, veronagsaming, verwaarlosing; agtelosigheid; nie-nakoming.
inobserv'ant, agteloos, onoplettend; *be very* ~, teen sy neus vaskyk.
inoccupa'tion, werkloosheid.
inoc'ulant, entstof.
inoc'ulate, okuleer; inent, fluit; ~ *d shoot,* inlêerloot.
inocula'tion, okulasie, inenting.
inoc'ulative, inentings=.
inoc'ulator, okuleerder; enter.
inod'orous, reukloos, sonder reuk.
inoffen'sive, onskadelik, onskuldig; onaanstootlik; argeloos; ~ **ness,** onskadelikheid; onaanstootlikheid.
inoffi'cious, amptenloos, werkloos, kragteloos; ongedienstig.
inop'erable, nie opereerbaar nie, onopereerbaar.
inop'erative, werkloos; sonder uitwerking; nie in werking nie, nie van krag nie; buite werking.
inopp'ortune, ongeleë, onvanpas, ontydig; ~ **ness,** ontydigheid, ongeleentheid.

inordinate 981 *insomnia*

inord'inate, ongereeld; buitensporig, bowemate, oordrewe; onmatig; wanordelik; ~ ly, buitengewoon, oormatig.
inorgan'ic, anorganies; onbesiel; onbewerktuig; ~ chemistry, anorganiese skeikunde.
inorganiza'tion, gebrek aan organisasie.
inornate', onopgesmuk, onversier.
inos'culate, ineenloop, inmond, saamvoeg, oorgaan in; ~ d, ineenlopend, saamgevoeg.
inoscula'tion, immonding, saamvoeging, vereniging.
in'-patient, inwonende pasiënt, binnepasiënt.
in'pouring, invloeiing.
in'put, toevoer; lading; ingang; inset; ingevoerde hoeveelheid.
inq'uest, ondersoek; lykskouing.
inqui'etude, ongerustheid; onrustigheid.
in'quilines, gasdiere.
inquire', vra, informeer; ondersoek; navors; verneem, navraag doen; ~ *ABOUT,* navraag doen omtrent; ~ *AFTER,* vra na, verneem na; ~ *FOR,* vra na; ~ *INTO,* ondersoek; ~ *OF,* inligting inwin oor; ~ *WITHIN,* vra hier; ~ r, vraer; ondersoeker.
inqui'ring, ondersoekend, vorsend.
inquir'y, (..ries), navraag, ondersoek, enquête; navorsing; (pl) navrae, inligting; *COURT of* ~, hof van ondersoek; *MAKE ..ries,* navraag doen; inligting inwin; *WRIT of* ~, bevelskrif tot ondersoek; ..ries office, ~ office, inligtingskantoor, informasieburo, navraagkantoor.
inquisi'tion, ondersoek; inkwisisie.
inquis'itive, nuuskierig; uitvraerig, ondersoekend; benieud, vraagsugtig, weetgierig, vraagsiek; ~ ness, nuuskierigheid; weetgierigheid.
inquis'itor, ondersoeker, naspeurder; regter van ondersoek; inkwisiteur; ~ 'ial, streng ondersoekend, inkwisitoriaal.
inquis'itress, (-es), inkwisitrise; ondervraagster.
inquo'rate, sonder 'n kworum.
in'road, inval, strooptog; inbreuk; *make* ~ *s on,* inbreuk maak op.
in'rush, binnestroming, instroming, toevloed; ~ ing, binnestromend.
insal'ivate, met speeksel meng.
insalub'rious, ongesond.
insalub'rity, ongesondheid.
insane', kranksinnig, waansinnig, stapelgek, mal; ~ asylum, kranksinnigegestig.
insan'itary, ongesond, onsanitêr, onhigiënies.
insan'ity, kranksinnigheid, verstandsverbystering, waansin; *religious* ~, godsdienswaansin.
insatiabil'ity, onversadelikheid, onversadigbaarheid.
insa'tiable, onversadelik, onversadigbaar.
insa'tiate, onversadigbaar, onversadig.
inscribe', inskrywe; van 'n opskrif voorsien; opdra; inprent, graveer; ~ d, met inskrif; ~ *d stock,* aandele op naam.
inscrip'tion, inskrywing; opskrif, titel; opdrag; inskripsie (op iets); onderskrif, byskrif.
inscrip'tional, inscrip'tive, as opskrif, opskrif-, ingeskrewe.
inscrutabil'ity, ondeurgrondelikheid, onnaspeurlikheid.
inscrut'able, onnaspeurlik, ondeurgrondelik.
in'seam, binnesoom.
in-sea'son, (n, a), binneseisoen(s).
in'sect, insek, gogga; ~ a'rium, (..ria), insektarium; ~-control, insekbestryding.
insec'ticide, (n) insekmiddel, insektegif, insektedoder; (a) insekdodend.
insec'tion, inkerwing.
insectiv'ora, insekte-eters.
insectiv'orous, insektetend.
insectol'ogy, insektologie, insektekunde, entomologie.
in'sect-powder, insekpoeier.
insecure', onveilig; onseker; *built on* ~ *foundations,* op los sand gebou; ~ ly, onseker; onveilig.
insecur'ity, onveiligheid; onsekerheid.
in'selberg, eilandberg.
insem'inate, saai; inprent; bevrug, besaad, insemineer.
insemina'tion, saai; bevrugting, inseminasie; *artificial* ~, kunsmatige bevrugting (inseminasie).

insen'sate, onsinnig; gevoelloos, ongevoelig.
insensibil'ity, ongevoeligheid; bewusteloosheid, anestesie, floute; onverskilligheid; onmerkbaarheid.
insen'sible, ongevoelig; onbewus; bewusteloos, flou; onverskillig; onmerkbaar.
insen'sitive, ongevoelig; dood; ~ ness, ongevoeligheid.
insen'tient, gevoelloos, onbesield.
inseparabil'ity, onskei(d)baarheid; onafskeidelikheid.
insep'arable, onskei(d)baar; onafskeidelik.
insert', invoeg, inlas; opneem; plaas (in 'n blad).
inser'tion, invoeging, inlassing, tussensetsel; opname, plasing; sierinsetsel, binnewerk (naaldw.); aanhegting.
in'set, (n) bylae, byblad, byvoegsel; byportret, inlas; bykaart; inlegsel.
inset', (v) (inset or **-ted),** inlas, invoeg, opplak; ~ map, bykaart; ~ photo(graph), inlasfoto.
inshore', naby die kus; ~ fishery, kusvissery.
in'side, (n) binnekant, binnesy, binneste; inwendige; muurkant; binnegoed, ingewande; *know something* ~ *out,* iets deur en deur ken; iets van hoek tot kant ken; ~ *OUT,* die binneste buite; *TURN* ~ *out,* binnestebuite keer; (a) binne-; binneste; (adv) binne, binne-in; (prep) binne; ~ *of a week,* binne 'n week; ~ callipers, binnepasser; ~ cover, binneomslag; ~ information, privaat inligting; ~ job, binnediefstal, binnemisdaad; ~ left, links binne; ~ pocket, binnesak; ~ r, ingewyde.
insid'ious, verraderlik, arglistig, slu; kruipend, inkruiperig, sluipend; ~ ness, verraderlikheid, arglistigheid; inkruiperigheid.
in'sight, insig, begrip, deursig; blik.
insig'nia, (n, pl) onderskeidingstekens, ordetekens, insignia.
insignif'icance, onbeduidendheid, onbelangrikheid, onaansienlikheid, nietigheid.
insignif'icant, niksbeduidend, gering, nietig, onbetekenend, onbelangrik, onaansienlik.
insincere', onopreg, huigelagtig, vals.
insince'rity, onopregtheid, valsheid, huigelagtigheid.
insin'uate, inwerk, inwurm; ingang verskaf; sinspeel, insinueer, te kenne gee; ~ *oneself into,* jou indring by, jou na binne werk.
insin'uating, insinuerend, sinspelend; vleierig, indringend; inpalmend, innemend.
insinua'tion, sinspeling, skimp, steek, toespeling, inblasing, verdagmaking, insinuasie; inwerking; kronkeling; innemendheid.
insin'uative, inpalmend, innemend; insinuerend.
insin'uator, vleier; indringer.
insip'id, smaakloos, flou, laf; geesteloos, soetsappig, stuitig; wateragtig.
insip'idness, insipid'ity, smaakloosheid, flouheid, lafheid; geesteloosheid; soutloosheid, soetsappigheid, stuitigheid; wateragtigheid.
insip'ience, onverstandigheid.
insist', aanhou, daarop aandring, daarop staan; met nadruk beweer; volhou; volhard by; ~ *on,* volhard by, bly by, volhou; - ence, ~ ency, volharding, aandrang; ~ ent, aanhoudend; opdringend, opdringerig, aandringerig, dwingerig; ~ ently, met klem, met aandrang, knaend.
insobri'ety, onmatigheid; dronkenskap.
insola'tion, sonsteek; sonbad, besonning, sonbestraling.
in'sole, binnesool.
in'solence, onbeskaamdheid, onbeskoftheid, astrantheid, brutaliteit.
in'solent, onbeskaamd, parmantig, brutaal, astrant, onbeskof.
insolubil'ity, onoplosbaarheid.
insol'uble, onoplosbaar; ~ matter, onoplosbare bestanddele.
insol'vency, (..cies), brankrotskap, insolvensie.
insol'vent, (n) insolvente persoon, bankrotspeler, bankroetier; (a) bankrot, insolvent; *be* ~, bankrot wees; die langslewende erf niks; ~ estate, bankrot boedel; ~ laws, wette oor bankrotskap.
insom'nia, slaaploosheid, insomnia.

insomuch', vir sover (as); aangesien; in soverre; ~ *that*, in so 'n mate dat.
insouc'iance, onverskilligheid, sorgeloosheid.
insouc'iant, onverskillig, sorgeloos.
inspan', **(-ned)**, inspan, aanhaak; bespan.
inspect', ondersoek, inspekteer, besigtig, in oënskou neem, nagaan.
inspec'tion, inspeksie, ondersoek; insae; toesig; ~ **circuit**, inspeksiekring; ~ **cover**, inspeksiedeksel; ~ **fuse**, blitslont; ~ **lamp**, soeklamp, inspeksielamp.
inspec'tor, inspekteur; opsiener; visitator; ~ *of weights and measures*, yker; ~ **ate**, inspektoraat; inspekteurskap; inspeksieafdeling; ~ **'ial**, inspeksie=, inspekteurs=; ~ **ship**, inspekteurskap; ~ **ess**, **(-es)**, inspektrise.
inspira'tion, inaseming; inboeseming, besieling, inspirasie; aanblasing; begeestering; ingewing; ~ **al**, inspirerend; inspiratories; ~ **ist**, gelower aan godelike ingewing (bv. van die Bybel).
in'spirator, inasemingtoestel, inspirator.
inspir'atory, inasemings=, asemhalings=.
inspire', inasem; inboesem, bemoedig, besiel, begeester; ingee, vervul, inspireer, aanvuur; ~ **d**, ingegewe, geïnspireer; besielend; ~ **r**, aanmoediger, besieler, inspireerder.
inspir'ing, sielverheffend, besielend, bemoedigend.
inspir'it, besiel, opwek, moed gee.
inspiss'ate, verdik; dik word, stol.
inspissa'tion, verdikking, stolling.
instabil'ity, onbestendigheid, ongestadigheid, wankelmoedigheid; veranderlikheid, onstabiliteit.
install', installeer; bevestig; insit, aanbring, aanlê; inrig, vestig; ~ *oneself*, jou inrig, jou vestig.
installa'tion, installasie, bevestiging; oprigting, inrigting; aanleg; vestiging; *cost of* ~ , aanlêkoste.
install'er, insteller; oprigter.
instal'ment, paaiement; storting; aflewering; termyn; gedeelte; bevestiging, installasie; *IN* ~ *s*, in paaiemente; *PAY in* ~ *s*, paaiementsgewyse betaal; ~ **system**, paaiementstelsel.
in'stance, **(n)** voorbeeld, geval; aandrang, versoek; instansie; *AT the* ~ *of*, op aandrang van; *in the FIRST* ~ , ten eerste, in die eerste plek; *FOR* ~ , byvoorbeeld; *in THIS* ~ , in hierdie geval; **(v)** siteer, aanhaal, aanvoer, voorbeelde gee.
in'stancy, drang, dringendheid.
in'stant, **(n)** oomblik; *ON the* ~ ; *this* ~ , oombliklik; **(a, adv)** onmiddellik, dadelik, kits=; hierdie maand, die 15e deser.
instantan'eous, oombliklik, moment=; ~ *EXPOSURE*, momentopname; ~ *SHUTTING*, momentsluiting.
instantan'eously, onmiddellik; *killed* ~ , op slag dood.
in'stant coffee, kitskoffie.
instan'ter, oombliklik, op die daad.
in'stantly, oombliklik, dadelik, op die daad.
in'stant informa'tion, kitsinligting.
instate', plaas, aanstel; installeer.
instaura'tion, vernuwing, herstel.
instead', in plaas daarvan, as plaasvervanger, as alternatief; ~ *of*, in plaas van, pleks van, in die plek van.
in'step, grootboog, wreef, middelvoet, voetrug, voetboog.
in'stigate, aanhits, aanspoor, opstook, aanstig, aanpor, aansit, ophits.
instiga'tion, aanhitsing, aanporring, aandrywing, aandrif, opruiing, aanstoking, aansetting, opstokery, ophitsing, aansporing, aanstigting; *at the* ~ *of*, op aandrang (aansporing) van.
in'stigator, aanstigter, aanstoker, opstoker, opruier, ophitser, aanblaser, aandrywer, aanporder, aansitter, aanlêer (van 'n skelm plan).
instil(l)', (..**lled**), inboesem, inprent, besiel met; induppel; bybring.
instilla'tion, **instil'ment**, inboeseming, inprenting; induppeling.
in'stinct, **(n)** instink, natuurdrif, aandrif.
instinct', **(a)** vervul van, besiel deur; ~ **ive**, onwillekeurig, instinktief, instinkmatig, spontaan.

in'stitute, **(n)** instelling; instituut; **(pl)** institute; **(v)** instel; stig, inrig; begin; aanstel; ~ *COMPARISONS*, vergelykings maak; ~ *an INQUIRY*, 'n ondersoek instel; ~ *legal PROCEEDINGS against*, geregtelike stappe doen teen.
institu'tion, instelling; gestig, inrigting; stigting; vaste gewoonte; bepaling, institusie; ~ **al**, ingestel, vasgestel; genootskaps=, stigtings=; ~ **ary**, intree=, bevestigings=.
instit'utive, stigtings=.
in'stitutor, stigter; insteller.
instruct', onderwys gee, oplei, leer, onderrig; voorskryf; instrueer; opdra, las gee, gelas; ~ **ion**, onderwys, onderrig, les; bevel, instruksie; voorskrif, opdrag; leerrede; ~ **ed**, opgedra; meegedeel; gelas; ~ **ional**, opvoedings=, onderwys=; leer=; ~ **ive**, leersaam, instruktief, leerryk; ~ **iveness**, leersaamheid; ~ **or**, leermeester, instrukteur; ~ **ress**, **(-es)**, instruktrise; onderwyseres.
in'strument, **(n)** instrument, werktuig; speeltuig; dokument, oorkonde; middel; *negotiable* ~ , verhandelbare dokument; **(v)** instrumenteer.
instrumen'tal, werktuiglik; instrumentaal; diensbaar, bevorderlik, behulpsaam; handdadig, aandadig; *be* ~ *IN*, meewerk tot; *be* ~ *TO*, saamwerk aan, bydra tot; ~ **ist**, instrumentalis, bespeler van 'n instrument; ~ **'ity**, medewerking, toedoen; werktuig, middel; *by the* ~ *ity of*, met behulp van.
instrumenta'tion, instrumentering; gebruik van instrumente.
in'strument: ~ board, instrumentplaat, instrumentpaneel; ~ **room**, toestelsaal, apparaatkamer.
insubord'inate, weerspannig, ongehoorsaam.
insubordina'tion, weerspannigheid, verset, insubordinasie.
insubstan'tial, onwesenlik; swak.
insuff'erable, onverdraaglik, onuitstaanbaar.
insuffi'ciency, ontoereikendheid, ongenoegsaamheid; onbekwaamheid; gebrek.
insuffi'cient, ontoereikend, ongenoegsaam, onvoldoende; ~ **ly**, te min, onvoldoende.
in'sufflate, inblaas.
insuffla'tion, inblasing.
in'sufflator, inblaasinstrument, bestuiwer.
in'sular, eiland=; eilandvormig; bekrompe, eng, insuliêr; ~ **ism**, insulariteit; eienaardigheid van 'n eiland; bekrompenheid; ~ **'ity**, bekrompenheid; afsondering, insulariteit.
in'sulate, afsonder, isoleer; tot 'n eiland maak; ~ *d brush*, geïsoleerde borsel.
in'sulating, isoleer=, isolerend; ~ **brick**, isoleersteen; ~ **material**, isoleerstof; ~ **tape**, isoleerband.
insula'tion, afsondering, isolasie, afgesonderdheid; isolering.
in'sulator, isolator, isoleerder, nie-geleier.
in'sulin, insulien, insuline.
in'sult, **(n)** belediging, beskimping, smaad, affrontasie; *add* ~ *to injury*, iem. benadeel en boonop beledig.
insult', **(v)** beledig, te na kom, afhaal; beskimp, smaad, hoon; ~ **ing**, krenkend, beledigend, smadelik.
insuperabil'ity, onoorkoomlikheid, onoorkombaarheid.
insup'erable, onoorkoomlik, onoorkombaar.
insupport'able, ondraaglik; onuitstaanbaar.
insurabil'ity, versekerbaarheid.
insur'able, versekerbaar.
insur'ance, versekering, assuransie; *CONDITIONS of* ~ , versekeringsvoorwaardes; *COST of* ~ , versekeringskoste; *THIRD party* ~ , derdeversekering; ~ **agent**, (lewens)versekeringsagent, assuransieagent; ~ **broker**, versekeraar, assuradeur; ~ **company**, versekeringsmaatskappy; ~ **fund**, versekeringsfonds; ~ **office**, assuransiekantoor; ~ **policy**, assuransiepolis, versekeringspolis; ~ **premium**, versekeringspremie; ~ **ticket**, versekeringskaartjie.
insur'ant, versekerde.
insure', verseker, verassureer; ~ **d**, **(n)** versekerde, geassureerde; **(a)** verseker; verassureer; ~ **r**, versekeraar, assuradeur.

insur'gence, insur'gency, oproer, opstand.
insur'gent, (n) oproerling, oproermaker, opstandeling, rebel; (a) oproerig, opstandig; woelig.
insurmountabil'ity, onoorkoomlikheid, onoorkombaarheid.
insurmoun'table, onoorkoomlik, onoorkombaar.
insurrec'tion, opstand, oproer, muitery, volksoproer; ~**al,** ~**ary,** oproerig, opstandig; ~**ist,** oproerling, rebel.
insusceptibil'ity, onvatbaarheid.
insuscep'tible, ongevoelig, onvatbaar, onontvanklik.
intact', ongeskonde, ongerep, intak, onaangeroer; ~**ness,** intaktheid, ongeskondenheid.
inta'gliated, uitgesny.
inta'glio, (s) (-s), verdiepte beeldwerk; snywerk; diepdruk; steen met verdiepte (ingesnyde) beeld; intaglio; (v) verdiep graveer; verdiep druk; ~ **printing,** diepdruk.
in'take, instroming, inloop; opneming, opvangplek; inlaat; vernouing; ~**-airway,** intrekluggang; ~ **manifold,** insuigverdeelpyp; ~ **pipe,** inlaatpyp; ~ **section,** ontvangsafdeling; ~ **stroke,** suigslag; ~ **valve,** inlaatklep.
intangibil'ity, ontasbaarheid.
intan'gible, onvoelbaar; ontasbaar.
intar'sia, intarsia, houtinlegwerk; gekleurde breiwerk.
in'teger, heel getal, heeltal, geheel.
in'tegral, (n) integraal; (a) heel, volledig, ongeskonde; onafskeidbaar, integraal, integrerend; ~ **calculus,** integraalrekening; ~**iza'tion,** integralisasie.
in'tegrant, integrerend.
in'tegrate, (v) volledig maak, tot 'n geheel verenig; inskakel; (a) geheel, ongeskonde.
in'tegrating, integrerend.
integra'tion, integrasie, vervolmaking; inskakeling; ~**ist,** integrasionis (in die politiek).
integ'rity, volledigheid, ongeskondenheid; opregtheid; egtheid; suiwerheid; onkreukbaarheid, braafheid, regskapenheid, eerlikheid.
integ'ument, vlies, vel, (dek)huid, dop, omkleedsel, bedeksel; eiervel; ~ **'ary,** vliesagtig, vlies=.
in'tellect, verstand, vernuf, intellek, gees.
intellec'tion, begrip, bevatting, verstand.
intellect'ive, verstandelik, begrips=.
intellec'tual, (n) intellektueel; (a) verstandelik, intellektueel; geestelik; geestes=, verstands=; ~ **work,** kopwerk; ~**ism,** intellektualisme, oorskatting van die rede; ~**ist,** intellektualis; ~**iza'tion,** intellektualisering; ~**ize,** intellektualiseer.
intell'igence, begrip, verstand, intelligensie, vernuf; oordeel; berig; narig, verwittiging, inligting, tyding, nuus; verstandigheid, skranderheid; *latest* ~, jongste berigte; ~ **corps,** inligtingskorps; ~ **department,** departement van inligting; ~ **office,** inligtingsburo; informasieburo; inligtingskantoor; ~ **officer,** inligtingsoffisier; inligtingsbeampte; ~ **post,** inligtingspos; ~ **quotient,** intelligensiekwosiënt, ~**t,** nuusaanbringer; spioen; ~ **report,** inligtingsberig; ~ **section,** inligtingsafdeling; ~ **service,** inligtingsdiens; ~ **ship,** spioenskip, verkenningskip; ~ **summary,** inligtingsresumé; ~ **test,** verstandsmeting, intelligensietoets.
intell'igent, verstandig, intelligent, skrander, slim, vlug van begrip.
intelligen'tial, verstandelik, verstandig, verstands=.
intelligent'sia, ..**zia,** intelligentsia, intellektuele leiers.
intelligibil'ity, verstaanbaarheid, bevatlikheid.
intell'igible, verstaanbaar, begryplik.
intem'perance, onmatigheid, dranklustigheid; onbesadigdheid, oordaad.
intem'perate, onmatig, oordadig; dranklustig; ~ **ly,** onmatig, buitensporig; ~**ness,** onmatigheid, oordaad; dranklustigheid.
intend', van plan wees, voornemens wees; voorhê; bedoel, meen, wil; *we* ~ *to go,* ons is voornemens (van plan, van voorneme) om te gaan.
inten'dant, opsigter, bestuurder.
inten'ded, (n) aanstaande; (a) bestem, gemeen(de), voorgenome; opsetlik, bedoel; *his* ~ *BRIDE,* sy aanstaande; ~ *JOURNEY,* voorgenome reis; *he is* ~ *for the MINISTRY,* hy is vir predikant bestem; *WAS this* ~ ?, is dit opsetlik bedoel?
inten'ding, aanstaande, aankomende; ~ *buyer,* voornemende (moontlike) koper, kooplustige..
intend'ment, bedoeling, sin.
intense', hewig, kragtig, diep, intens, fel, strak; (in)gespanne; ~**ly,** geweldig, baie, in hoë mate; ~**ness,** hewigheid, intensiteit, krag.
intensifica'tion, versterking, intensifikasie, verhoging, toeneming.
inten'sified, verhoog, verdiep, versterk, vererger.
inten'sifier, versterker.
inten'sify, (..**fied**), versterk, verhoog, verdiep, vererger, kragtiger maak, intensiveer.
inten'sion, spanning; gespannenheid; intensiteit, krag, intensie.
inten'sitive, duratief.
inten'sity, (..**ties**), hewigheid, krag, felheid, intensiteit; ~ *of CURRENT,* stroomsterkte; ~ *of WORK,* arbeidsintensiteit.
inten'sive, (n) intensief (gram.); (a) kragtig; intensief; intens; versterkend; gespanne; ~ **agriculture,** intensiewe landbou; ~ **bombardment,** gekonsentreerde bombardement; ~ *care unit,* waakeenheid, (intensiewe) sorgeenheid.
intent', (n) oogmerk, bedoeling, plan, opset; *to all* ~ *s and purposes,* in alle opsigte; in werklikheid; vir alle praktiese doeleindes; (a) aandagtig, gespanne, verdiep in, vervul van, gretig, opmerksaam; ~ *upon MISCHIEF,* daarop uit om kwaad te doen; ~ *on his READING,* verdiep besig om te lees; ~ *upon his WORK,* ywerig besig met sy werk.
inten'tion, voorneme, doel, plan, bedoeling, oogmerk; inspanning; ~**al,** opsetlik, voorbedag, moedswillig, ekspres, aspris, voorgenome; ~**ally,** opsetlik, ekspres, aspris.
intent'ly, gespanne, strak, aandagtig.
intent'ness, inspanning; gespannenheid; ywer; vasbeslotenheid.
inter'¹, (v) (**-red**), begrawe, bysit.
in'ter², (prep) tussen, onder; ~ *alia,* onder ander(e).
in'teract¹, (n) pouse; tussenspel, tussenbedryf.
interact'², (v) op mekaar inwerk, op mekaar reageer; ~**ion,** wisselwerking.
interall'ied, intergeallieerde.
interblend', (**-ed,** or ..**blent**), meng, vermeng.
interbreed', (..**bred**), kruis, verbaster, kruisteel.
interc'alary, ingevoeg, tussengevoeg, ingeskuif, ingelas; ~ **day,** skrikkeldag; ~ **year,** skrikkeljaar.
interc'alate, inskuif, inlas, tussenvoeg.
intercala'tion, invoeging, inlassing, tussenvoeging, inskakeling; tussenlaag.
intercede', pleit, bemiddel, tussenbei(de) kom; ~ *for someone with,* iem. se voorspraak wees; ~**r,** voorspraak.
intercell'ular, tussen die selle, intersellulêr.
intercept', onderskep, ondervang, opvang; teenhou, belemmer; afsny; ~**ion,** onderskepping, ondervanging; afsnyding; versperring, belemmering, ~ **lon flight,** onderskepvlug; ~**ive,** onderskeppend, belemmerend; ~ **or,** onderskepper; onderskepvliegtuig; ~ **or flight,** onderskepvlug.
interces'sion, bemiddeling, voorspraak, middelaarswerk, tussenkoms; voorbidding, voorbede; ~ **service,** biduur.
intercess'or, middelaar, voorspraak; voorbidder; ~**y,** bemiddelend.
in'terchange¹, (n) wisseling; (verkeers)wisselaar; ruilhandel, verkeer; afwisseling; (om)ruiling, vervanging.
interchange'², (v) (uit)wissel, (om)ruil, vervang; afwissel; (ver)wissel; ~**abil'ity,** verwisselbaarheid; ~**able,** verwisselbaar, (om)ruilbaar, uitwisselbaar.
intercolle'giate, interkollegiaal.
intercolon'ial, interkoloniaal.
in'tercom, binnetelefoon, interkom.
intercommun'al, interkommunaal.
intercommun'icate, onderling gemeenskap hê, met mekaar verkeer, met mekaar in verband staan.
intercommunica'tion, interkommunikasie; onderlinge kommunikasie, verkeer, gedagtewisseling, gemeenskap.

intercommunion 984 *intermingle*

intercommun'ion, verkeer, omgang; onderlinge betrekking.
intercommun'ity, gemeenskaplikheid, gemeenskaplike besit.
in'tercom system, interkom(stelsel).
interconnect', onderling verbind; ~**ion,** onderlinge verbinding.
intercontinent'al, interkontinentaal; ~ **missile,** ruimteprojektiel; interkontinentale missiel.
intercos'tal, tussen die ribbes, tussenribs, interkostaal; ~ **muscle,** tussenribspier, interkostale spier.
in'tercourse, omgang, verkeer, gemeenskap; *sexual* ~, geslagsgemeenskap.
intercropp'ing, tussenverbouing.
intercross', (mekaar) kruis.
intercu'rrent, tussenkomend, ongereeld, afwisselend; ~ **pulse,** ongereelde pols.
in'tercut, snywisseling (film).
interdenomina'tional, interkerklik, tussenkerklik.
interdent'al, tussentands, interdentaal.
interdepartmen'tal, interdepartementeel.
interdepend', van mekaar afhang; saamhang; ~**ence,** onderlinge afhanklikheid; ~**ent,** onderling afhanklik.
in'terdict, (n) verbod; interdik (reg); skorsing.
interdict', (v) verbied; skors.
interdic'tion, verbod; interdik (reg); ontsegging; banvonnis.
interdict'ory, verbods=, verbiedend.
in'terest, (n) belang; aandeel; voordeel; eiebelang; invloed; interesse, belangstelling; rente; (pl) belange; *AT* ~, op rente; *the BANKING* ~, die bankiers; *COMPOUND* ~, samegestelde rente; *HAVE an* ~ *in,* belang hê by; 'n aandeel hê in; *HAVE* ~*s in,* belange hê in; *IN his* ~ *(s),* in sy voordeel; *IN the* ~ *(s) of,* in belang van; ten behoewe van; *the LANDED* ~, die grondeienaars; *have LOST* ~ *in,* belangstelling verloor hê in; *the MONEYED* ~, die geldmense; *OF* ~, van belang, interessant; ~ *ONESELF in,* belang stel in; *look after one's OWN* ~*s,* na jou eie belange omsien; *RATE of* ~, rentevoet; *SIMPLE* ~, enkelvoudige rente; *TAKE an* ~ *in,* belang stel in; *it is to YOUR* ~, dit is in jou belang; *WITH* ~, met rente; *let someone have something back WITH* ~, iem. iets met rente laat terugkry; *WITHOUT* ~, renteloos, sonder rente; (v) belang stel, interesseer; die belange raak van; woeker; ~ *ONESELF in (on) behalf of,* jou interesseer vir; ~ **account,** renterekening; ~**-bearing,** rentegewend, rentedraend; ~ **burden,** rentelas; ~ **date,** rentedatum.
in'terested, belangstellend; geboeid; belanghebbend; ~ *IN,* betrokke by; geïnteresseer in; ~ *PARTY,* belanghebbende party.
in'terest: ~**-free,** rentevry; ~**ing,** wetenswaardig, interessant, belangwekkend; ~ *ing condition,* verwagtend (moeder); ~ **rate,** rentekoers; ~ **table,** rentetabel.
in'terface, raakvlak.
interfa'cing, (stywe) tussenvoering.
interfere', (jou) bemoei (met), jou inmeng (in); dwarsboom; ingryp, tussenbei(de) tree; aanslaan, aankap (perd); steurend inwerk, benadeel.
interfer'ence, bemoeiing, inmenging; interferensie (radio); botsing; steuring; inwerking; aankap (perd).
interfer'ing, bemoeiend, bemoeisiek; steurend, belemmerend.
interfero'meter, interferometer, golfmeter.
interfe'ron, interferon.
interflu'ent, inmekaarstromend, -vloeiend.
interfol'iated, deurskote (boek); tussenblarig (plant).
interfuse', saamsmelt, vermeng; deurgiet.
intergovernment'al, tussenregerings.
intergrown', deurgroei, vergroei; deurmekaargegroei.
in'tergrowth, deurgroeiing, vergroeiing; deurmekaargroeiing.
in'terim, (n) tussentyd; interim; *in the* ~, intussen; (a) tussentyds; voorlopig, interim; ~ **dividend,** tussentydse dividend; ~ **report,** voorlopige verslag.
inter'ior, (n) binneland, agterland; die binneste; binnekant, interieur; (a) binne=; binnelands; binnehuis=; inwendig, innerlik, interieur; ~ **angle,** binnehoek; ~ **decoration,** binnehuisversiering; ~ **decorator,** binnehuisversierder; binneargitek; ~ **monologue,** alleenspraak, interne monoloog.
interja'cent, tussen=; tussenliggend, tussengeleë.
interjac'ulate, tussenin gooi; uitroep.
interjac'ulatory, as tussenwerpsel geuit, tussenwerpsel=; ~ **prayer,** skietgebed.
interject', tussenin gooi; uitroep; in die midde bring; opmerk.
interjec'tion, tussenwerpsel; uitroep, opmerking; ~**al,** tussengevoeg, tussengegooi; uitroep=; ~*al sentence,* uitroepsin.
interjec'tor, tussenwerper.
interlace', deurmekaarvleg; deurvleg; inmekaargryp; deurmekaarstrengel; ~**d,** deurvleg.
interla'cing, deureenstrengeling; deurvlegting; vlegwerk.
interlard', deurspek; opstop; ~**ed,** deurspek; opgestop.
interlead'ing, tussen=; ~ **door,** tussendeur; ~ **rooms,** verbonde kamers.
in'terleaf, (wit) tussenblad.
interleave', deurskiet.
interleaved', deurskote; ~ **book,** ~ **copy,** deurskote boek (eksemplaar); ~ **page,** tussenblad; ~ **sheet,** tussenblad.
interline', invoeg, tussen die reëls skryf; interlinieer.
interlin'ear, tussen die reëls, interliniêr.
interlinea'tion, tussenreël; tussenskrywing, tussengeskrewene.
interlin'ing, binnevoering.
interlink', onderling verbind, aaneenskakel.
interlock', inmekaarsluit, inmekaarpas, inmekaarhaak; grendel, afsluit; ~**ed,** gegrendel.
interlock'ing, grendeling; ~ **apparatus,** grendeltoestel; ~ **directorates,** aaneengeskakelde direkteurskappe.
interlocu'tion, gesprek; samespraak.
interloc'utor, medespreker, deelnemer (aan 'n gesprek); ondervraer.
interlocu'tory, tussen=; gesprek=; ~ **judgment (order),** tussenvonnis; ~ **proceedings,** tussenproses.
interlope', indring; onderkruip.
in'terloper, onderkruiper; knoeier; indringer.
in'terlude, pouse; tussenspel, tussenbedryf, klug.
interlun'ar, donkermaans.
interluna'tion, tydperk van donkermaan.
interma'rriage, ondertrouery, huwelik onder mekaar, oor-en-weertrouery.
interma'rry, (..rried), ondertrou, oor en weer trou, onder mekaar trou, introu.
intermaxill'ary, (n) tussenkaaksbeen; (a) tussenkaaks.
intermed'dle, (jou) inmeng in, (jou) bemoei met; ~**r,** bemoeier, laspos, bemoeial.
intermed'ial, tussenkomend; ~ **planet,** tussenplaneet; ~ **year,** tussenjaar.
intermed'iary, (n) (..ries), skakel, tussenpersoon, bemiddelaar; bemiddeling, tussenkoms; tussenvorm; (a) tussen=, tussenliggend.
intermed'iate, (n) oorgang, tussenvorm; (v) as tussenpersoon optree; bemiddel; (a) tussen=, tussenkomend, middelbaar; intermediêr; oorgangs=; ~ **boat,** tussenboot; ~ **class,** tussenklas; ~ **colour,** tussenkleur; ~ **gear,** tweede versnelling; ~ **host,** tussengasheer; ~ **period,** oorgangstyd, tussentyd; ~ **port,** tussenhawe; ~ **service,** middelkerk (halfpad tussen twee Nagmaalvierings); ~ **shaft,** tussenas; ~ **stage,** tussenstadium.
intermedia'tion, tussenkoms, bemiddeling.
intermed'iator, bemiddelaar, tussenpersoon; ~**y,** bemiddelend.
intermed'ium, (..dia, -s), medium, tussenstof.
inter'ment, begrafnis, teraardebestelling.
interme'zzo, (..zi, -s), intermezzo, tussenspel.
intermigra'tion, landverhuising oor en weer, intermigrasie.
interminabil'ity, eindeloosheid.
interm'inable, oneindig, eindeloos.
interming'le, meng, vermeng.

intermi'ssion, tussenpose, onderbreking, verposing; *without* ~, sonder ophou, onafgebroke.
intermit', (**-ted**), afbreek, ophou, staak, rus; ~ **tence,** onderbreking; tussenpose.
intermitt'ent, afwisselend, onderbroke, met tussenposes; ~ **fever,** anderdaagse koors.
intermix', deurmekaar maak, meng; ~ **ture,** vermenging; mengsel.
in'tern, (n) inwonende geneesheer, intern; (v) interneer.
intern'al, inwendig; binne-; innerlik; binnelands; intern; *for* ~ *use,* om in te neem; ~ **auditor,** interne ouditeur; ~ **brake,** binnerem; ~ **check,** interne kontrole (verifikasie); ~ **combustion,** binneverbranding, binnebrand-; ~ **-combustion engine,** binnebrandmotor; ~ **control,** interne beheer (toesig); ~ **ear,** binneoor; ~ **evidence,** inwendige getuienis; ~ **expanding,** inwendig uitsittend; ~ **gasket,** binnepakstuk; ~ **matters,** huishoudelike sake; ~ **student,** inwonende (interne) student; ~ **waterway,** binnewater.
interna'tional, (n) internasionale speler; (a) internasionaal; ~ **boundary,** internasionale grens; ~ **contest,** internasionale wedstryd, toetswedstryd; ~ **dateline,** internasionale datumgrens; ~**ism,** internasionalisme; ~**ist,** internasionalis; ~**iza'tion,** internasionalisering, internasionalisasie; ~**ize,** internasionaal maak, internasionaliseer; ~ **language,** internasionale taal; ~ **law,** internasionale reg, volkereg; **I**~ **Monetary Fund,** Internasionale Monetêre Fonds (IMF).
interne'cine, moordend, moorddadig, verwoestend; ~ **war,** verdelgingsoorlog.
internee', geïnterneerde.
intern'ment, internering; **- authorities,** interneringsoutoriteite; ~ **camp,** interneringskamp.
internode', stingellit, tussenknoop, lit.
in'ternship, internskap.
internun'cio, internunsius, pouslike ambassadeur.
interocean'ic, tussenoseanies.
interos'culate, meng; as skakel dien.
interpage', deurskiet (blaaie in 'n boek).
interparliamen'tary, interparlementêr.
interp'ellate, interpelleer, ondervra.
interpella'tion, interpellasie, ondervraging.
interpellat'or, ondervraer, interpellant.
interpen'etrate, heeltemal deurdring; mekaar deurdring.
interpenetra'tion, deurdringing.
interplan'etary, interplanetêr; ~ **aviation,** heelalvaart.
in'terplay, tussenspel; wisselwerking, onderlinge inwerking; heen-en-weerspel.
interplead'er, tussenpleitgeding.
In'terpol, Interpol.
interp'olate, inskuiwe, tussenvoeg, interpoleer, inlas.
interpola'tion, inlassing, interpolasie, inskuiwing, invoeging, ~ *of the Scriptures,* Skrifvervalsing.
interp'olator, interpolator.
interpose', tussen sit; tussen skuif; in die rede val; tussenbeide kom; jou inmeng in; uitwei; in die midde bring.
interposi'tion, tussenkoms, bemoeiing, bemiddeling; tussenvoeging, tussenplasing; invoegsel.
interp'ret, tolk; verklaar, uitlê, vertolk; weergee; lees (foto); ~**able,** verklaarbaar, vertolkbaar, vir uitleg vatbaar; ~**a'tion,** verklaring, vertolking, uitleg; ~**ative,** uitleggend, verklarend; ~**er,** tolk; uitlêer, vetolker; leser (foto); skrifuitleer; ~**ress,** (**-es**), vertolkster; vrouetolk.
interprovin'cial, interprovinsiaal.
interpunc'tion, interpunksie, punktuasie.
interpunc'tuate, leestekens aanbring, punktueer.
interra'cial, tussen rasse, veelrassig.
interreg'num, (..**na, -s**), interregnum, tussenregering; tussentydperk.
interrela'tion, onderlinge verhouding, wedersydse betrekking.
inte'rrogate, ondervra, (uit)vra, verhoor.
interroga'tion, ondervraging, ondersoek; vraag; ~ **mark,** vraagteken.
interrog'ative, (n) vraende voornaamwoord, interrogatief; (a) vraend, vraag-; ~**ly,** vraenderwys(e).
inte'rrogator, ondervraer, vraer.
interrog'atory, (n) (..**ries**), vraag; vraelys; ondervraging; (a) vraend.
interrupt', steur; in die rede val; hinder, onderbreek, afbreek; afsny; ~**ed,** onderbroke; ~ *ed perforation,* roltanding; ~**er,** onderbreker, in-die-redevaller, steurder; stroombreker; onderbrekingsnok; ~**ible,** onderbreekbaar.
interrup'tion, onderbreking, verbreking, steuring; *without* ~, sonder ophou, onafgebroke.
interrup'tive, onderbrekend, steurend.
in'ter-school, tussenskools, skole-.
intersect', deursny, deurkruis, sny; ~**ing,** sny-; ~**ion,** (deur)snyding; snypunt; deursnede; kruispunt, kruising; *flat-grade* ~*ion,* vlakkruising.
in'terspace, (n) tussenruimte; tussenspasie; (v) deur 'n tussenruimte skei, interspasieer.
intersperse', strooi, rondstrooi, saai; aangenaam wissel; deurspek.
intersper'sion, deurmenging, rondstrooiing.
in'terstate, tussen state.
interstell'ar, tussen sterre.
inters'tice, tussenruimte, opening.
intersti'tial, tussen-, met tussenruimtes.
intertrib'al, tussen die stamme; ~ **warfare,** stamoorloë.
intertrop'ical, tussen die keerkringe.
intertwine', deurvleg, deurstrengel; ineenstrengel, verwar.
inter-univers'ity, interuniversiteits-, interuniversitêr.
inter-urb'an, tussenstedelik.
in'terval, ruspose, pouse, tussenpose, rustyd, tussenruimte, tussentyd; afstand, toonafstand; interval; *at* ~*s,* so nou en dan, by tussenpose; dikwels, telkens.
intervar'sity, (n) (..**ties**), intervarsitie, interuniversiteitswedstryd, interuniversiteitskragmeting; (a) interuniversiteits-.
intervene', tussenin kom; steur; lê tussen; tussenbeide kom (tree); ingryp.
interven'ient, interven'ing, tussenkomend.
interven'tion, tussenkoms, bemiddeling, ingryping, intervensie; ~**ist,** intervensionis.
in'terview, (n) onderhoud, (pers)gesprek; vraaggesprek; (v) ondervra, uitvra, uithoor, formeel besoek; 'n onderhoud hê; ~**er,** ondervraer, verslaggewer; ~**ing officer,** ondervra-amptenaar, ondervragingsamptenaar.
intervoc'al, intervokalies.
intervolve', deurmekaarstrengel.
interweave', (..**wove,** ..**woven**), deurmekaar weef, deurstrengel, verweef, ineenvleg, deurweef.
interwind', (..**wound**), deurmekaarvleg.
interwo'ven, deurweef, deureengevleg.
intes'tacy, testamentloosheid.
intes'tate, (n) oorledene sonder testament, intestaat; (a) sonder testament, intestaat; *by versterf.*
intes'tinal, ingewands-, derm-; ~ **tube,** dermkanaal; ~ **worm,** ingewandswurm.
intes'tine¹, (n) derm; (pl) ingewande, binnegoed, derms; (a) inwendig; *LARGE* ~, dikderm; *SMALL* ~, dunderm.
intes'tine², (a) binnelands (van oorloë); inwendig.
in'timacy, (..**cies**), vertroulikheid, gemeensaamheid, eieheid, danigheid, intimiteit; (vleeslike) gemeenskap.
in'timate¹, (n) boesemvriend(in); vertroueling(e); (a) vertroulik, intiem, eie, danig, gemeensaam; inwendig; innig, diepgaande, grondig; *BE* ~ *with,* vertroulik omgaan met; geslagsgemeenskap hê met; ~ *FRIENDSHIP,* intieme vriendskap; ~ *KNOWLEDGE,* intieme kennis.
in'timate², (v) te kenne gee, aandui, meedeel, laat deurskemer, laat verstaan.
in'timately, innig, vertroulik; intiem.
intima'tion, kennisgewing, aankondiging; aanduiding, wenk.
intim'idate, bang maak; vrees aanjaag, intimideer; ~ *into,* deur vrees bring tot.

intimidation 986 *invent*

intimida'tion, afskrikking, vreesaanjaging, bangmakery.
intim'idator, skrikaanjaer, bangmaker; ~y, vreesaanjaend.
intim'ity, innigheid; heimlikheid, intimiteit.
intitula'tion, titel, betiteling.
intit'uled, betitel (wet).
in'to, in, tot; ~ *the BARGAIN,* boonop; op die koop toe; *COME* ~ *the house,* kom binne; kom in die huis; *COME* ~ *property,* erf; *GET* ~ *trouble,* in die moeilikheid raak; *INQUIRE* ~, ondersoek instel na; *MARRY* ~ *a family,* deur huwelik in 'n familie kom; *far* ~ *the NIGHT,* tot laat in die nag; *TRANSLATE* ~, vertaal in.
in'toed, met die tone binnekant toe.
intol'erable, ondraaglik, onduldbaar, onuitstaanbaar; ~ness, onuitstaanbaarheid, ondraaglikheid.
intol'erance, onverdraagsaamheid.
intol'erant, onverdraagsaam; *be* ~ *of,* nie kan verdra nie.
in'tonate, *kyk* **intone.**
intona'tion, aanhef; toonaangewing; intonasie, stembuiging.
intone', insit, intoneer; aanhef, laat hoor; sing-sing opsê.
intox'icant, (n) bedwelmende middel; dwelmmiddel; sterk drank; (a) dronkmakend; bedwelmend.
intox'icate, dronk maak, bedwelm; ~d, aangeskote, dronk, beskonke; bedwelm; *be* ~*d,* dronk wees; die skoot hoog deur hê; hoog aan wees; die straat meet; geswa(w)el wees.
intox'icating, dronkmakend; bedwelmend.
intox'ication, dronkenskap, bedwelming, roes.
in'tra, binne.
intracell'ular, binnesellig, intraselluêr.
intracer'ebral, binneharsing=.
intractabil'ity, onhandelbaarheid, balsturigheid, ongeseglikheid, weerbarstigheid, halsstarrigheid.
intrac'table, onhandelbaar, weerspannig, balsturig, ongeseglik, balhorig, weerbarstig, halsstarrig.
intrad'os, binnewelf (myn); intrados, binnewelwing.
intramur'al, binnemuurs, intern, binne die mure.
intramus'cular, binnespiers.
intrans'igence, onversoenlikheid.
intran'sigent, onversoenlik, koppig.
intrans'itive, (n) onoorganklike werkwoord; (a) onoorganklik.
intransmiss'ible, onoordraagbaar.
intranspar'ency, ondeursigtigheid.
intranspar'ent, ondeursigtig.
in'trant, nuwe lid, nuweling.
intraven'ous, binneaars; ~ *injection,* aarinspuiting.
intrench', *kyk* **entrench.**
intrep'id, onverskrokke, moedig, onversaag; ~'ity, onverskrokkenheid, onbevreesdheid, onversaagdheid.
in'tricacy, (..cies), ingewikkeldheid; verwikkeling, moeilikheid, warnet.
in'tricate, ingewikkeld, verward, moeilik.
intrig(u)ant', intrigant, konkelaar; ~e, konkelaarster.
intrigue', (n) intrige, kuipery, draadtrekkery, gekonkel; vryery, amouretjie; (v) konkel, kuip, knoei, bak en brou; intrigeer, nuuskierig maak; ~*d by,* bekoor deur, nuuskierig gemaak deur; ~r, intrigant, konkelaar, draadtrekker.
intrigu'ing, (n) gekonkel, gekuip, gemodder; (a) interessant, belangwekkend; *an* ~ *item of news,* 'n belangwekkende brokkie nuus.
intrin'sic, inwendig, innerlik; wesenlik, eg, essensieel, intrinsiek; ~ *value,* intrinsieke waarde.
intrins'ically, intrinsiek, op sigself.
introduce', invoer, inlei, inbring; indien (wetsontwerp); aanbring, invoeg; bekend maak (persoon); voorstel, introduseer; ~ *a BILL,* 'n wetsontwerp indien; ~ *a LADY,* 'n dame voorstel; ~ *a TOPIC,* 'n onderwerp ter sprake bring; ~r, voorsteller; inleier; indiener.
introduc'tion, inleiding; voorspel; voorstelling, introduksie (van mense); aanloop (toespraak); invoering, ingebruikneming, inbrenging; toepassing; *letter of* ~, aanbevelingsbrief.
introduc'tory, inleidend.
intro'it, introïtus (R.K.).
intromis'sion, toelating; inbrenging.
intromit', (-ted), invoeg, inlaat, toelaat.
introspect', jouself ondersoek, die eie gemoed beskou, die blik binnekant toe slaan; ~ion, selfondersoek, innerlike selfwaarneming, selfbespieëling, introspeksie; ~ive, selfondersoekend, selfbespieëlend.
introver'sion, inkering, introversie.
in'trovert, (n) eenselwige, introvert; (a) eenselwig, introvert, na binne gekeer.
introvert', (v) intrek, tot jouself inkeer; ~ed, ingekeer, eenselwig.
intrude', indring, inpers; lastig val; opdring, inbreuk maak; steur; ~ *ON someone's privacy,* iemand se privaatheid versteur; ~ *UPON,* jou opdring aan; ongeleë kom; versteur; ~r, indringer; opdringer, inkruiper.
intru'sion, indringing; opdringing; inbreuk; steurnis, steuring; intrusie (geol.); ingroeiing (plant.).
intrus'ive, indringend; opdringerig; orig; binnedringend; intrusief (geol.); ~ **rock,** intrusiegesteente.
in'tuit, by intuïsie ken.
intui'tion, intuïsie; ingewing.
intu'itive, intuïtief, by ingewing.
intumes'cence, geswel, swelling; geswollenheid.
intumes'cent, opswellend.
intussuscep'tion, opneming, vertering; knoopderm, derminstulping.
inunc'tion, insmering.
in'undate, onder water sit, oorstroom; oorstelp.
inunda'tion, oorstroming, vloed, onderwatersetting, watersnood, watervloed; oorstelping.
inurbane', onbeleef, onhoflik.
inurban'ity, onhoflikheid, onbeleefdheid.
inure', gewoon word, gewen, wen (aan); oefen; in werking tree, van krag word (wet); ~**ment,** gewoonwording, gewenning; gehardheid; inwerkingtreding.
inurn', in 'n lykbus wegsit.
inut'ile, nutteloos.
inutil'ity, nutteloosheid.
invade', inval, aanval, binneval; indring; binnedring (geol.); oorval; inbreuk maak op; aanrand, skend; ~r, invaller, indringer; aanvaller; aanrander; inbreukmaker.
in'valid[1]**,** (n) sieke, invalide; (a) swak, siek, invalide.
invalid'[2]**,** (v) siek maak; op die siekelys plaas; ongeskik maak vir aktiewe diens; *be* ~*ed out of the army,* weens siekte uit die leër ontslaan word.
inval'id[3]**,** (a) ongeldig, nie van krag nie.
inval'idate, kragteloos (nietig) maak, vernietig, ontsenu; ongeldig verklaar.
invalida'tion, ongeldigverklaring; ontsenuwing; vernietiging (vonnis).
in'valid: ~ **chair,** rolstoel, siekestoel; ~ **cup,** tuitkoppie; ~ **diet,** siekedieet; ~ **food,** siekekos; ~ **table,** bedtafeltjie; ~**ism,** sieklikheid, liggaamswakte.
invalid'ity, swakheid, kragteloosheid; sieklikheid; ongeldigheid.
inval'uable, onskatbaar, met geen goud te betaal nie.
in'var, nikkelstaal.
invariabil'ity, onveranderlikheid.
invar'iable, onveranderlik, standvastig; konstant (wisk.); ~**ness,** onveranderlikheid.
invar'iably, sonder uitsondering, onder alle omstandighede, onveranderlik.
inva'sion, inval, aanval, oorvalling; aanranding, indringing; strooptog.
invas'ive, invallend, invals=, aanvallend; aanrandend.
invec'tive, skeldwoord, skimprede, skimptaal, smaadrede, bitter verwyt.
inveigh', heftig uitvaar, uitskel, slegmaak, fulmineer; verwyt.
invei'gle, (ver)lok, aanlok, verlei, meesleep; *ALLOW oneself to be* ~*d,* jou laat omkonkel; ~ *OUT of,* afrokkel; ~**ment,** verleiding, verlokking; ~r, aanlokker.
invent', uitvind; bedink, uitdink, versin, verdig; uit die lug gryp; ~**ion,** uitvinding; versinsel; vinding, vindingrykheid; verdigting; ~**ive,** vindingryk;

~**iveness,** vindingrykheid; ~**or,** uitvinder; versinner.
in'ventory, (n) (..**ries**), lys, inventaris; boedellys, boedelbeskrywing; **(v)** (..**ried**), inventariseer; 'n lys opmaak van.
inven'tress, (-es), uitvindster; versinster.
invera'city, ongeloofwaardigheid.
in'verse, (n) die omgekeerde; **(a)** omgekeerd; ~ **proportion,** ~ **ratio,** omgekeerde verhouding.
inverse'ly, omgekeerd.
inver'sion, omkering, omsetting; woordomsetting.
inver'sive, omkerend.
in'vert¹, (n) omgekeerde boog; boom (van pyp); homoseksueel; invertsuiker; **(a)** omgekeer(d); homoseksueel.
invert'², (v) omkeer, omsit, op sy kop sit.
invert'ebrate, (n) ongewerwelde dier; swakkeling, papbroek; **(a)** ongewerwel; pap, ruggraatloos.
invert'ed, omgekeer, omgedraai; ~ *ARCH,* omgekeerde boog; ~ *COMMAS,* aanhalingstekens; ~ *FLIGHT,* rugvlug; *in* ~ *ORDER,* in omgekeerde orde; ~ **pleat,** springplooi.
invest', beklee, omhul; mag verleen; insluit, beset, omsingel; vassit, belê (geld), investeer (geld); skenk, gee; bevestig; ~ *ed with MEANING,* vol betekenis; ~ *with POWERS,* met bevoegdhede beklee.
inves'tigate, ondersoek, (uit)snuffel, naspeur, napluis, bestudeer, navors; ~ *into,* ondersoek instel na.
investiga'tion, ondersoek, naspeuring, nasporing, navorsing, enquête.
inves'tigator, ondersoeker, uitvorser, navorser; ~**y,** ondersoekings=, ondersoekend.
inves'titure, investituur; installering, ordening; omhanging, huldiging, bekleding.
invest'ment, kleding; omhulsel; bekleding; investituur; plasing; (geld)belegging, investering; insluiting, omsingeling; *make an* ~, geld belê (vassit).
inves'tor, belêer, belegger.
invet'eracy, ingeworteldheid, hardnekkigheid.
invet'erate, verstok, hardnekkig, ingewortel; ingekanker.
invid'ious, haatlik; haatwekkend; aanstootlik; onbenydenswaardig; netelig; ~**ness,** aanstootlikheid; partydigheid; onbenybaarheid.
invi'gilate, toesig hou oor, oppas.
invigila'tion, toesig.
invi'gilator, opsiener.
invig'orate, versterk; besiel; krag gee.
invig'orating, versterkend; opwekkend; besielend.
invigora'tion, versterking, krag; besieling.
invig'orative, versterkend; besielend.
invig'orator, versterkingsmiddel; besieler
invincibil'ity, onoorwinlikheid; onoorkoomlikheid.
invin'cible, onoorwinlik; onoorkoomlik.
inviolabil'ity, onskendbaarheid, onaantasbaarheid.
invi'olable, onskendbaar, onaantasbaar.
invi'olacy, onskendbaarheid; ongeskondenheid.
invi'olate, ongerep, ongeskonde; gewyd.
invisibil'ity, onsigbaarheid.
invis'ible, onsigbaar, onsienlik; *the CHURCH* ~, die onsigbare kerk; *THE I*~, die Onsienlike; ~ **export,** onsigbare uitvoer; ~ **ink,** geheimink; simpatieiese ink; ~ **mender,** fynstopper; ~ **mending,** fynstopwerk, kunsstop; ~**ness,** onsigbaarheid.
invita'tion, uitnodiging; beroep; *a standing* ~, 'n vaste uitnodiging.
invit'atory, uitnodigend; uitlokkend.
invite', (n) uitnodiging; **(v)** uitnooi, nooi, sket; aanlok, uitlok; versoek om; ~ *QUESTIONS,* geleentheid vir vrae gee; ~ *TENDERS,* inskrywings vra; ~ *TROUBLE,* moeilikheid soek; *not WAIT to be* ~ *d,* jou nie laat nooi nie.
invit'ing, aanloklik, uitlokkend; uitnodigend.
in vi'tro, in vitro, in 'n proefbuis, buite die liggaam.
in vi'vo, in vivo, in die liggaam.
invoca'tion, aanroeping, smeekbede, inroeping; afsmeking; beswering, towerformulier.
invoc'atory, aanroepend, aanroepings=.
in'voice, (n) faktuur, geleibrief; **(v)** op die faktuur sit, faktureer; ~ **book,** faktuurboek.

invoke', aanroep; afsmeek, inroep; oproep; ~ *the aid of the Almighty,* die hulp van die Almagtige afsmeek.
in'volucre, omhulsel (plantk.); omwindsel (anat.).
invol'untarily, teen wil en dank; vanself, onwillekeurig.
invol'untariness, onwillekeurigheid; onopsetlikheid.
invol'untary, onwillekeurig; teen wil en dank, onvrywillig.
in'volute, (v) ineendraai, ineenrol; **(a)** ingewikkel(d); ingedraai; ineensluitend; spiraalvormig.
involu'tion, inwikkeling; ingewikkeldheid; inkrulling; inrolling; verskrompeling; magsverheffing (wisk.).
involve', indraai, inrol, inwikkel; omvat, insluit; meesleep, meebring; ingewikkeld maak; betrek in, insleep; tot gevolg hê; draai, kronkel; raak, betref; in hom sluit; wikkel; ~**d,** moeilik, ingewikkel(d); daarin betrokke; *the PERSON* ~ *d,* die betrokke persoon; *an* ~ *d SENTENCE,* 'n ingewikkelde sin; ~ **ment,** betrokkenheid; verwikkeling; ingewikkeldheid; geldelike moeilikheid, skuld; moeilikhede.
invol'ving, wikkeling.
invulnerabil'ity, onkwesbaarheid.
invul'nerable, onkwesbaar.
in'ward, (a) inwendig; innerlik; binnensmonds; (adv) binnewaarts, inwaarts; die land in; in die binneland; ~**ly,** inwendig; van naby; innerlik; binnensmonds; ~**ness,** inwendigheid; innerlike betekenis; innerlikheid.
in'wards, (n) binnegoed, ingewande; **(adv)** na binne, binnewaarts, inwendig, innerlik.
inweave', (..**wove,** ..**woven**), deurweef, deurvleg, invleg.
inwov'en, ingeweef, deurgevleg.
inwrought', deurvleg; deurwerk; ingelê; ingeweef.
inyal'a, grys bosbok, injala(bok).
i'odic, jodium=, jood=; ~ **acid,** jodiumsuur.
i'odine, jodium, jood; ~ **tincture,** jodiumtinktuur.
iodiza'tion, jodering.
i'odize, jodeer, met jodium behandel.
io'doform, jodoform.
i'olite, ioliet, cordieriet.
i'on, ioon.
Ion'ia, Ionië.
Ion'ian, (n) Ioniër; **(a)** Ionies.
Ion'ic¹, Ionies.
ion'ic², ioon=, ionies.
ioniza'tion, ionisering.
io'nosphere, ionosfeer.
iot'a, jota; ~**cism,** jotasisme.
IOU, (skuld)bewys; skuldbekentenis.
ipecacuan'ha, braakwortel, ipekakuana; ~ **wine,** wynvomitief, braakwyn, vermeerwortelwyn.
ipse dixit, ipse dixit, dogmatiese bewering.
ipsiss'ima verb'a, ipsissima verba, die einste woorde.
ip'so fac'to, ipso facto, deur die feit self, vanselfsprekend.
Irak', Iraq', Irak, Mesopotamië.
Iraki, Iraqi, (n) Irak; Irakies (taal); **(a)** Iraaks.
Iran, Iran, Persië; ~**ian, (n)** Iraniër; Iraans (taal).
irascibil'ity, oplopendheid, opvlieëndheid, driftigheid, liggeraaktheid.
iras'cible, driftig, opvlieënd, oplopend, liggeraak, kortgebonde.
irate', kwaad, woedend, toornig.
ire, kwaadheid, gramskap, toorn, woede; ~**ful,** toornig, woedend.
Ire'land, Ierland, Eire.
iren'ic(al), irenies, vredeliewend.
iren'icism, ireniese rigting.
iren'icist, ireniese persoon.
irida'ceous, lelie=, lelieagtig.
irides'cence, kleurspeling, reënbooggeling.
irides'cent, skitterend, reënboogkleurig.
irid'ium, iridium.
ir'is, (irises) iris, reënboogvlieg (oog); reënboog; iris, (pl) lisblom.
Ir'ish, (n) Iers; *the* ~, die Iere; **(a)** Iers; *an* ~ *rise,* salarisvermindering; ~ **Free State,** Ierse Vrystaat; ~ **man,** (..**men**) Ier; ~ **stew,** gestoofde vleis-en-ertappels, vleis-en-groentebredie.

irit'is, reënboogvliesontsteking.
irk, verveel; vermoei; kwel; ~ **some**, vervelig; ergerlik, lastig; verdrietlik.
i'ron, (n) yster; strykyster; brandyster; harpoen; yster(stok) (gholf); soldeerbout; ~ *in BARS*, staalyster; *CAST* ~, gietyster, gegote yster, potyster; *CORRUGATED* ~, gegolfde yster, golfyster; *the* ~ *HORSE*, die swart merrie; *a MAN of* ~, 'n harde man; *have too MANY* ~ *s in the fire*, te veel hooi op die vurk hê; *PUT in* ~ *s*, in boeie slaan; *a ROD of* ~, 'n ysterroede; *rule with an* ~ *rod*, met 'n ystervuis regeer; *the* ~ *has entered his SOUL*, sy lewe is vergal; *STRIKE while the* ~ *is hot*, smee die yster terwyl dit warm is; ~ *and steel WORKS*, yster-en-staalfabriek; *WROUGHT* ~, smeedyster; (v) stryk; met yster beslaan; beslaan (perd); boei; kettings aansit; ~ *out*, uit die weg ruim; uitstryk; (a) yster=, van yster; ysteragtig; **I** ~ **Age**, Ystertyd= (perk); ~ **bar**, ysterstaaf; stuk yster; ~ **beam**, ysterbalk; ~ **-bound**, ysterhard; deur rotse ingesluit; met ysters beslaan; onbuigsaam; rotsagtig; ~ **building**, sinkgebou; ~ **chest**, brandkas; ~ **clad**, (n) slagbodem, pantserskip; (a) gepantser; ~ **-colour(ed)**, ysterkleur(ig); ~ **constitution**, ystergestel; sterk gestel; **I** ~ **Cross**, Ysterkruis; ~ **curtain**, ystergordyn; ~ **discipline**, ysterdissipline, streng dissipline; ~ **ed**, gepers; ~ **fence**, ysterheining; ~ **fillings**, ystervylsel; ~ **fist**, ystervuis; ~ **-fisted**, suinig, vrekkig; ~ **forge**, ystersmedery; ~ **-founder**, ystergieter, ystersmelter; ~ **foundry**, ystersmeltery; ~ **-grey**, ysterkleurig; ~ **-grey horse**, ysterskimmel (perd); ~ **-handed**, met ysterhand; ~ **hat**, staalhelm; ~ **-hearted**, hardvogtig; ~ **-heater**, strykbout; ~ **holder**, vatlap; ~ **horse**, ysterperd; fiets; lokomotief.
iron'ic(al), ironies, spottend.
i'roning, strykwerk; strykgoed; ~ **blanket**, strykkombers; ~ **board**, strykplank; ~ **cloth**, strykdeken; ~ **room**, strykkamer.
ir'onist, ironiese persoon; ironis, ironikus.
i'ron: ~ **like**, ysteragtig, yster-; ~ **lode**, ysteraar; ~ **lung**, ysterlong; ~ **master**, ysterfabrikant; ~ **mill**, ysterplettery; ~ **mine**, ystermyn; ~ **monger**, ysterhandelaar; ~ **mongery**, ysterware; ~ **mould**, (n) ysterroes; (v) vol roesvlekke word; ~ **ore**, ystererts, spieëlerts; ~ **oxide**, ysteroksied; ~ **pan**, ysterpan; ~ **plane**, ysterskaaf; ~ **pyrites**, ysterpiriet, ysterkies; ~ **ration**, noodrantsoen; ~ **roof**, ysterdak; sinkdak; ~ **-shod**, met ysters beslaan; **I** ~ **-sides**, Cromwell se soldate; ystervreters, dapper kêrels; ~ **smith**, grofsmid; ~ **stone**, ysterklip; ~ **ware**, ysterware; ~ **wire**, ysterdraad; ~ **wood**, ysterhout; ~ **work**, ysterwerk; ~ **works**, ystergietery; ysterfabriek.
ir'ony¹, (n) ironie, spot.
ir'ony², (n) (..nies), ysteralbaster; ghoen; (a) ysteragtig, ysterhoudend.
Ir'oquois, Irokees.
irrad'iance, straling, glans.
irrad'iant, stralend, skitterend, glansend.
irrad'iate, uitstraal, deurstraal, bestraal, verlig, ophelder; (om)straal.
irradia'tion, uitstraling; stralekrans; straling; verligting.
irra'tional, onredelik, irrasioneel, onbillik; dwaas; redeloos; onmeetbaar, irrasionaal (wisk.); ~ **'ity**, onredelikheid; redeloosheid.
irrebutt'able, onweerlegbaar.
irreclaim'able, onverbeterlik; onherstelbaar; verstok; onherwinbaar.
irrec'ognizable, onherkenbaar.
irreconcilabil'ity, onversoenlikheid; onverenigbaarheid.
irrec'oncilable, (n) onversoenlike; (a) onversoenlik; onverenigbaar.
irrec'onciled, onversoen(d).
irrecov'erable, onherstelbaar; oninvorderbaar, oninbaar (skuld); onherkrygbaar; ~ *debts*, oninvorderbare skulde; ~ **ness**, onverhaalbaarheid.
irrecus'able, onontwykbaar; onafwysbaar, onwraakbaar (reg).
irredeemabil'ity, onaflosbaarheid; onherstelbaarheid.

irredeem'able, onredbaar, reddeloos; onafkoopbaar, onaflosbaar (obligasie); onherstelbaar, onverbeterlik; ~ *debenture*, onaflosbare obligasie; oninwisselbare papiergeld.
irredent'ism, irredentisme.
irredent'ist, (n) irredentis; (a) irredenties.
irreducibil'ity, onverminderbaarheid; onherleibaarheid.
irredu'cible, onherleibaar; onverminderbaar, onverkleinbaar (wisk.); nie onderdrukbaar nie; ~ *minimum*, onverminderbare minimum.
irref'ragable, onbetwisbaar, onweerlegbaar.
irrefran'gible, onskendbaar, onbreekbaar; onbuigbaar (straal).
irrefutabil'ity, onweerlegbaarheid, onomstootlikheid.
irref'utable, onweerlegbaar, onomstootlik, sonneklaar.
irreg'ular, (n) ongereelde; (pl) ongereelde troepe; (a) ongereeld; onreëlmatig; ongeoorloof; wanordelik; ~ **army**, volksleër, ongereelde leër; ~ **'ity**, ongereeldheid; anomalie; onreëlmatigheid.
irrel'ative, met geen betrekking op nie, nie toepaslik nie, onvanpas; nie verwant nie, onverwant.
irrel'evancy, ontoepaslikheid, onsaaklikheid.
irrel'evant, ontoepaslik, nie ter sake nie.
irreli'gion, ongodsdienstigheid; godsdienstloosheid.
irreli'gious, ongodsdienstig; godsdiensloos.
irremed'iable, onherstelbaar; ongeneeslik; onverbeterbaar.
irremiss'ible, onvergeeflik; bindend.
irremo'vable, onverplaasbaar, onverwyderbaar.
irreparabil'ity, onherstelbaarheid.
irrep'arable, onherstelbaar.
irreplace'able, onvervangbaar.
irrepress'ible, onbedwingbaar; onweerhoubaar.
irreproachabil'ity, onberispelikheid.
irreproach'able, onberispelik, onbesproke; ~ **ness**, onbesprokenheid.
irresistibil'ity, onweerstaanbaarheid.
irresis'tible, onweerstaanbaar; bekoorlik; verleidelik.
irres'olute, besluiteloos, willoos, weifelmoedig, wankelmoedig; ~ **ness**, onbeslistheid, besluiteloosheid, wankelmoedigheid.
irresolu'tion, besluiteloosheid, willoosheid, wankelmoedigheid, weifelmoedigheid.
irresol'vable, onoplosbaar.
irrespec'tive, niks ontsiende nie; ~ *OF*, afgesien van, ongeag; ~ *of PERSONS*, sonder aansien van persoon (des persoons).
irresponsibil'ity, onverantwoordelikheid; ontoerekenbaarheid.
irrespon'sible, onverantwoordelik; ontoerekenbaar.
irrespon'sive, onsimpatiek, ongevoelig, stug, onontvanklik; ~ **ness**, ongevoeligheid.
irreten'tive, swak (geheue); nie vashoudend nie; wat urine nie kan inhou nie.
irretrac'eable, onherroeplik.
irretrievabil'ity, onherkrygbaarheid; onherstelbaarheid.
irretriev'able, onherstelbaar; onherroeplik; onherkrygbaar, onredbaar.
irretriev'ably, onherstelbaar; ~ *lost*, onherroeplik verlore.
irrev'erence, oneerbiedigheid.
irrev'erent, oneerbiedig.
irrevers'ible, onomstootlik; onveranderlik; onomkeerbaar; onherroeplik.
irrevocabil'ity, onherroeplikheid.
irrev'ocable, onherroeplik; *it is* ~, daar val nie aan te torring nie.
i'rrigable, besproeibaar.
i'rrigate, besproei, natlei, bevloei, bewater, irrigeer.
irriga'tion, besproeiing, bevloeiing, bevogtiging, irrigasie; *water for* ~, leiwater, besproeiingswater; ~ **dam**, besproeiingsdam; **I** ~ **Department**, Departement van Besproeiing; ~ **canal**, besproeiingskanaal; ~ **scheme**, besproeiingskema; ~ **settlement**, damnedersetting, besproeiingnedersetting; ~ **water**, leiwater, besproeiingswater; ~ **works**, irrigasiewerke, besproeiingswerke.
i'rrigator, besproeier; sproeier.

irritability 989 *iterative*

irritabil'ity, prikkelbaarheid, dwarsheid, (lig)geraaktheid, kwasterigheid, oorgevoeligheid, iewerigheid.
i'rritable, prikkelbaar, liggeraak, oorgevoelig, omgekrap, iewerig, kwasterig, kortgebaker, wrewelig.
i'rritancy[1], prikkelende eienskap; prikkelbaarheid; geprikkeldheid.
i'rritancy[2], vernietiging (reg); kragteloosheid.
i'rritant, (n) prikkelmiddel, prikkelstof; prikkelgas; (a) prikkelend, irriterend; ~ **poison**, prikkelgif.
i'rritate[1], vernietig, te niet doen (reg).
i'rritate[2], vererg, prikkel, verbitter, irriteer, versondig; *you* ~ *me BEYOND words (measure)*, jy prikkel my in hoë mate, jy gee my die olel; ~ *a PERSON*, iem. vererg; ~ **d**, geprikkel; vererg, versondig.
irr'itating, prikkelend, irriterend, ontstemmend.
irrita'tion, verbittering, prikkeling; ergernis; verergdheid, wrewel; branderigheid.
i'rritative, prikkelend, irriterend.
irrup'tion, inval; inbraak; irrupsie.
irrup'tive, invallend, indringend.
is, is; *kyk* **be**.
Isabell'a, Isabella; glipdruif, glippertjie.
isagog'ic, inleidend, isagogies; ~ **s**, isagogick.
Isai'ah, Jesaja.
i'satin, isatien, isatine.
isch(a)e'mia, ischemie, iskemie, plaaslike bloedloosheid.
ischiad'ic, ischiat'ic, heup=.
is'chium, (..ia), sitbeen, iskium.
isentro'pic, isentropies, isentroop.
Ish'mael, Ismael.
Ish'maelite, Ismaeliet.
is'inglass, vislym, waterglas; mika.
Is'lam, Mohammedanisme, Islam; ~ **ic**, Mohammedaans, Islamities, Slams; ~ **ite**, Islamiet, Slamaier.
is'land, (n) eiland; (v) tot eiland maak; met eilande besaai; isoleer; (a) eiland=; ~ **-dotted**, met eilande besaai; ~ **empire**, eilandryk; ~ **er**, eilandbewoner; ~ **platform**, eilandplatform; ~ **-strewn**, ~ **-studded** = **island-dotted**.
isle, eiland.
isl'et, eilandjie.
i'sm, isme, teorie, leer.
is'n't, abbr. of **is not**, is nie.
is'obar, isobaar, isobarometriese lyn, lyn van gelyke druk; ~ **'ic**, isobaries, isobarometries.
isochromat'ic, gelykkleurig, isochromaties.
isochron'al, isoch'ronous, isochronies, gelyktydig, van gelyke duur.
is'ochrone, (n) isochroon; (a) isochroon.
iso'chronism, isochronisme, gelyktydigheid.
isoclin'ic, isoklien=, isoklinies; ~ **al**, isoklien=, isoklinaal; ~ **lines**, isokliene; ~ **map**, isokliniese kaart.
isodynam'ic, isodinamies.
is'ogloss, isoglos.
is'ogon, isogoon; ~ **'ic**, gelykhoekig, isogonies.
is'olate, afsonder, afhok, isoleer; ~ **d**, afgesonder, eensaam, afgeslote, geskei, afsonderlik, opsigselfstaande, geïsoleer, alleenstaande.
is'olating switch, skeiskakelaar.
isola'tion, afsondering, isolement, isolasie; *in splendid* ~, heeltemal alleen; op sy eentjie; ~ **camp**, isolasiekamp; ~ **hospital**, afsonderingshospitaal; ~ **ward**, afsonderingsaal.
isola'tionism, isolasionisme.
isola'tionist, isolasionis.
is'olator, isolator.
isome'ric, isomeries.
isomet'ric(al), isometries.
iso'metry, isometrie.
Is'omorph, isomorf, gelykvormig.
isomor'phism, gelykvormigheid, isomorfisme.
isomorph'ous, isomorf, van gelyke vorm.
ison'omy, wetsgelykheid.
is'ophone, isofoon.
is'opod, ringkreef, isopode.
Isop'tera, Isoptera, Termiete.
isos'celes, gelykbenig; ~ **triangle**, gelykbenige driehoek.
is'otherm, isoterm; ~ **'al**, isoterm=.

isoton'ic, isotonies.
is'otope, isotoop.
isotop'ic, isotopies.
isotrop'ic, isotropies.
is'otropism, isotropisme.
I-spy', wegkruipertjie, aspaai.
Is'rael, Israel; ~ **i**, (n) Israeli; (a) Israelies; ~ **ite**, Israeliet; ~ **i'tic**, ~ **i'tish**, Israelities.
is'suable, uitreikbaar.
iss'uance, uitgifte, uitreiking.
iss'ue, (n) uitgang; uitslag, afloop; uitgawe, edisie (boek); uitgifte (banknote); uitreiking; oplaag, nommer (koerant); uitkoms, uitmonding (rivier); uitstroming (water); nakomelingskap, nakroos, nageslag, afstamming; resultaat; uitvaardiging, uitdeling; (geskil)punt, saak, strydvraag; uiting; uittog; opbrengs (reg); voortbrengsel; uitskrywing, emissie (lening); *BE at* ~, betwis word; *BRING to an* ~, uitmaak; *FORCE the* ~, alles wil maak en breek; sake forseer; *JOIN* ~, die stryd aanbind (met); die saak begin; in geding tree; *MAKE an* ~ *of*, 'n geskilpunt maak van; *without MALE* ~, sonder manlike afstamming; *the POINT at* ~, die geskilpunt; *PRICE of* ~, emissieprys; *RAISE an* ~, 'n saak in bespreking bring; *SPECIAL* ~, feesnommer; *on THAT* ~, op daardie punt; (v) uitgee; voortkom, ontspruit, te voorskyn kom; uitstroom (water); uitgaan, ontsnap (gas); uitreik; afstam, voortspruit; afloop; uitloop; afkom; afgee; uitstuur; in omloop bring (geld); uitvaardig (dekreet); ~ *FORTH*, na buite kom, voortkom; ~ *FROM*, voortkom uit; ~ *IN*, uitloop op; ~ *less*, kinderloos; sonder resultaat; ~ **r**, uitgewer, uitreiker, uitvaardiger; ~ **voucher**, uitreikbewys.
Is'tanbul, Istanboel, Konstantinopel.
isth'mian, landengte=, ismies; lopende deur (van, behorende tot) 'n landengte.
isth'mus, (-es), landengte, ismus.
is'tle, vesel.
it, (pron) dit; hy; *AS* ~ *is*, tog al; *FACE* ~, die gevolge dra; *GIVE* ~ *him!* dons hom op! *who IS* ~? wie is dit? *that IS just* ~, net die regte ding, *that's JUST* ~! presies; *LORD* ~ *over him*, oor hom baasspeel; *OF* ~, daarvan; ~ *is all OVER*, dis gedaan; *the PITY of* ~ *is*, die ongeluk is; ~ *is SAID*, dit word gesê; daar word beweer; ~ *SAYS in the Book*, daar staan in die Bybel; ~ *SNOWS*, dit kapok (sneeu); *WALK* ~, voetslaan; *WITH* ~, daarmee.
Ital'ian, (n) Italiaan, Italianer; Italiaans (taal); (a) Italiaans; ~ **iron**, plooiyster; ~ **writing**, lopende skrif, kursiefskrif.
Ital'ic, Italies.
ital'ic, (n) kursiewe letter; (pl) skuins (kursiewe) druk; *IN* ~ *s*, kursief; *the* ~ *s are MINE*, ek kursiveer; (a) kursief, skuins; ~ **ize**, kursiveer.
It'aly, Italië.
itch, (n) jeuking; skurfsiekte, lekkerkrap, (lekker)jeuk, uitslag; hunkering, sug; (v) jeuk, wriemel; hunker; *his fingers* ~ *to*, sy hand jeuk om; ~ **iness**, joukerigheid; ~ **ing**, (n) jeuking, jeukte; lus; (a) jeukend, jeukerig; *have an* ~ *ing palm*, inhalig wees; maklik omkoopbaar wees; ~ **mite**, brandsiektemyt, skurftemyt; ~ **y**, jeukerig.
it'em, (n) item, punt; nommer (program); besonderheid; pos (rekening); artikel; berig (in koerant); *the next* ~ *on the programme*, die volgende nommer op die program; (v) aanteken, 'n nota maak, noteer; (adv) verder, ook; net so ~ **ize**, spesifiseer.
itin'eracy, itin'erancy, rondtrekkery; rondreis; reisplan.
itin'erant, (n) rondstapper; (a) rondreisend, rondtrekkend, swerwend; ~ **post**, rondreispos, rondrypos.
itin'erary, (n) (..ries), reisgids; reisplan; reisbeskrywing; (a) reisend, rondtrekkend, swerwend, reis=.
itin'erate, rondreis, rondtrek.
it'erance, it'erancy, herhaling.
it'erant, herhalend.
it'erate, herhaal.
itera'tion, herhaling.
it'erative, herhalings=; iteratief (gram.).

its, van hom, sy; daarvan.
itself', self; jouself; homself; *BY* ~, alleen; *IN* ~, op= sigself; *OF* ~, vanself; *she was RUDENESS* ~, sy was die onbeskoftheid self.
it'sy-bit'sy, it'ty-bit'ty, (colloq.), klein, fyntjies, piepklein.
iv'ied, met klimop begroei.
iv'ory, (n) ivoor, elpebeen, olifantstand; (..**ries**), dob= belsteen; biljartbal; *black* ~, ebbehout; swart sla= we; (a) ivoor-, van ivoor; ~ **black**, ivoorswart, beenswart; ~-**coloured**, ivoorkleurig; ~-**dealer**, ivoorhandelaar; ~-**head**, ivoordruk; ~ **like**, ivoor= agtig; ~-**nut**, ivoorneut; ~ **paper**, ivoorpapier; ~- **smooth**, ivoorglad; ~ **tower**, ivore toring, ivoorto= ring; ~-**turner**, kunsdraaier, ivoordraaier; ~ **ware**, ivoorwerk; ~ **white**, ivoorwit; ~ **work**, ivoorwerk; ~ **yellow**, ivoorgeel.
iv'y, (**ivies**), klimop; ~-**leaved**, met klimopvormige blare; ~-**mantled**, met klimop begroei.
ix'ia, (k(a)lossie, ixia.
i'zard, Pirenese gemsbok.
i'zzard, die letter Z.

J

j (js, **j's**), j.
jab, (n) (stamp)hou; por; steek; (v) (**-bed**), por; steek; stoot.
jabb'er, (n) gebabbel, gekekkel; gesnater; (v) babbel, kekkel, snater, brabbel; ~ **er**, babbelkous, kekkel= bek; ~ **ing**, brabbeltaal; gebabbel; ~ **wocky**, jab= berwocky, nonsenspratery, sinlose taalgebruik.
jabot', jabot, strook, plooisel, kanttooisel.
jacaran'da, jakaranda(boom) *(Jacaranda acutifo= lia).*
ja'cinth, hiasint.
jack¹, geus, vlag; seinvlag.
jack², (arch.) soldatebaadjie; karba.
jack³, (n) mannetjie (dier); matroos; ruiter; domkrag (vir oplig van voertuig); saagbok; werkman, kneg; windas; vysel; skildersteier; hamer; hefboom; jong snoek; witte(tjie) (rolbal); stopkontak (elek.); boer (kaartspel); ~ *of CLUBS*, klawerboer; ~ *of DIA= MONDS*, ruitensboer; ~ *of HEARTS*, hartens= boer; *every MAN* ~, elke lewende siel; ~ *of SPA= DES*, skoppensboer; ~ *of TRUMPS*, troefboer; (v) opdraai; opdomkrag; verniel; ~ *up*, opgee ('n poging, ens.).
Jack⁴, Jan; ~ *FROST*, die ryp; ~ *'s as GOOD as his master*, Klaas is die gelyke van sy baas; *a good* ~ *makes a good JILL*, soos die man is, so die vrou; *every* ~ *has his JILL*, elke pot kry sy deksel; al is 'n pot nog so skeef, hy kry 'n deksel; ~ *KETCH*, die laksman; ~ *among the MAIDS*, 'n liefling v.d. da= mes; ~ *in OFFICE*, verwaande amptenaartjie; *be= fore you could say* ~ *ROBINSON*, voor jy mes kon sê; ~ *of all TRADES*, 'n klein jukskeitjie met 'n groot kop; ~ *of all TRADES, master of none*, twaalf ambagte, dertien ongelukke.
jack'-a-dandy, (..**dies**), modegek, fat.
jack'al, jakkals; handlanger; ~ *s never go empty*, 'n vlieënde kraai het altyd wat; ~ **buzzard**, jakkals= valk; ~-**proof fence**, jakkalsheining, jakkalsdraad; ~-**proof fencing**, jakkalsdraad.
jac'ana, langtoon.
jack'anapes, na-aper; uilskuiken; bluffer.
jack'-arch, stukboog.
jack'aroo, nuweling, groene, groentjie.
jack: ~ **ass**, donkiehings, eselhings; domkop; ~ **boot**, kapstewel; ~ **catch**, slotgreep; ~ **daw**, kerkkraai; ~ **ass penguin**, brilpikkewyn.
jack'et, (n) baadjie; py; jakkie, jekker(t); omhulsel; mantel; skil (van ertappels); pels, vel; omslag (boek); *DUST his* ~, sy baadjie vir hom afstof; *boil POTATOES in their* ~ *s*, ertappels met die skil kook; (v) beklee, omhul; klop, slaan; ~ **ed**, beklee; met 'n baadjie aan; ~ *ed cylinder*, mantelsilinder; ~ **potatoes**, ongeskilde ertappels (aartappels).
jack: ~-**flag**, geus, vlag; ~-**fruit**, jakka(vrug) *(Arto= carpus integrifolia);* ~ **hammer**, boorhamer, hamerboor, klopboor; ~-**in-office**, (opgeblase) klerk; ~-**in-the-box**, kaartmannetjie; *a real* ~-*in= the-box*, 'n regte kaartmannetjie; ~-**knife**, groot knipmes; herneutermes; ~-**line**, lyn; ~ **mackerel**, marsbanker; ~-**o'-lantern**, dwaallig; ~ **plane**, bankskaaf, blokskaaf, voorloper(skaaf); ~ **pot**, prysgeld; boerpot (kaartspel); *hit the* ~ *pot*, 'n groot slag slaan; ~-**pudding**, hansworst, nar; ~ **rab=**

bit, prêriehaas; ~-**rafter**, kortspar; ~-**saw**, (hand=) kloofsaag, treksaag, mootsaag; ~ **screw**, skroef= domkrag; ~ **shaft**, tussenas; ~ **snipe**, klein snip; ~-**staff**, vlagstok; ~ **tar**, pikbroek, janmaat; ~- **towel**, rolhanddoek; ~-**tree**, broodboom.
Jac'ob, Jakob.
Jacobe'an, Jakobeaans.
Jac'obin, (n) Jakobyn; Dominikaner; (a) Jakobyns.
Jac'obite, Jakobiet.
Jac'ob's: ~ **ladder**, touleer; Jakobsleer; speerkruid; ~ **staff**, pelgrimstaf, degenstok; graadboog.
jac'onet, jakonet.
Jac'quard, Jacquard; ~ **loom**, jacquardgetou.
jacta'tion, spoggery.
jactita'tion, woelery (van 'n sieke), koorswoeling; spiertrekking, senuweetrekking; valse voorwendsel (reg); ~ *of marriage*, voorwendsel van met iem. ge= troud te wees.
jac'ulator, spuitvis; werper.
jade¹, (n) nefriet, niersteen, bittersteen, bylsteen; jaspis.
jade², (n) ou uitgeputte perd, ou knol; vroumens, feeks; slet; (v) vermoei, uitput, afjakker; ~ **d**, moeg, afgemat, vermoeid, afgeslof, afgebeul; ~ **ite**, ja= deiet.
jae'ger, jaeger(baadjie).
Jaf'fa orange, jaffalemoen.
jaffle, jafel.
jag, (n) kerf; tand; keep, insnyding (bot.); vrag; (v) (**-ged**), tand, kerf; inkeep; ~ **ged**, getand, puntig; gekartel; ru, skerp; vol skare, ingekeep; ~ **ger**, ge= tande wieletjie; tandbeitel; steekbeitel.
jagg'ery, ruwe palmsuiker.
jag: ~ **ging**, inkerwing; uittanding; uitkeping; ~ **ging iron**, tandbeitel; ~ **gy**, skerp; gekerf; vol skare.
jag'uar, jaguar, S-Amer. luiperd *(Felis onca).*
Jah, Jehova, Jah(h).
jail, gaol, (n) tronk, gevangenis; (v) in die tronk sit; ~-**bird**, tronkvoël, tronkboef; ~-**break**, ontsnap= ping; ~-**breaker**, ontsnapte gevangene; ~ **er**, si= pier, gevangebewaarder, tronkbewaarder; ~ **eress**, (**-es**), tronkbewaarster; ~ **fever**, hospitaalkoors, vlektifus, luiskoors.
Jakar'ta, Djakarta.
jake, (sl.), eg, in orde.
jakes, (sl.), latrine, kleinhuisie.
jal'ap, jalap.
jalop(p)'y, rammelkas, tjorrie.
jal'ousie, sonblinding, hortjie, jalousie.
jam¹, (n) fynkonfyt, jem; *money for* ~, volop geld.
jam², (n) gedrang; ophoping, klemming; verkeer= stremming, verstopping, verkeersknoop; klomp; *be in a* ~, in die knyp wees; (v) (**-med**), klem, plat druk, vasklem, vasknel; vassit; versper (pad); saamdring, pers, druk; smoor (radio); *BE* ~ *med*, vassit; ~ *on the BRAKES*, die rem(me) aanslaan.
Jamaic'a, Jamaika; ~, **n**, (n) Jamaikaan; (a) Jamai= kaans; ~ **ginger**, jamaikagemmer; ~ **pepper**, won= derpeper.
jamb, wang (van deur); binnedeurkosyn; wangbekle= ding; kaggelwand.
jamboree', fuif, drinkgelag, fees; saamtrek, same= koms, laer, uitkampery, jamboree.

jam'bos, jamboes.
jamb: ~ **post,** deurstyl; ~ **shaft,** wangsuil; ~ **stone,** wangklip.
jam'-dish, konfytpotjie.
James, Jakobus, Koos.
jam'-jar, konfytfles.
jammed, propvol; vasgesteek, vasgeklem.
ja'mming, (n) knelling; storing (elek.); (a) knellend; ~**-station,** steursender.
jam' nut, sluitmoer.
jam'-packed, propvol.
jam: ~**-pot,** konfytpotjie, jempot; ~**-roll,** konfytrol; ~ **tart,** konfyttertjie; ~ **tomato,** peertamatie, konfyttamatie; ~ **turnover,** toe konfyttertjie.
jane, (sl.), vrou, meisie aster.
ja'ngle, (n) gekrys, geharwar; gerammel, lawaai; gekrys; rusie, gekyf; (v) krys; raas; rusie maak, twis; versteur, ontstem.
ja'ngling, (n) gerammel, geraas; (a) rammelend.
jan'issary = **janizary.**
jan'itor, deurwagter; portier, pedel; opsigter.
jan'izary, janitsaar.
jan'kers, (sl.), (militêre) straf.
Jan'senism, Jansenisme.
Jan'uary, Januarie.
jan'us-faced, met 'n janusgesig.
Jap, (n) Japanner, Japannees; (a) Japans.
japan'[1], (n) lak; metaallak; lakwerk; Japanse porselein; (v) (**-ned**), vernis, japanneer; verlak.
Japan'[2], (n) Japan; (a) Japannees; ~ **ese,** (n) Japannees, Japanner; Japannees (taal); (a) Japannees, Japans; ~ **ize,** verjapans.
japan: ~ **lacquer,** japanlak; ~ **ned goods,** lakwerk; ~ **ned leather,** lakleer; ~ **ner,** verlakker.
jape, (n) poets, grap; (v) gekskeer, 'n grap maak, skerts.
Japon'ic, Japannees, Japans.
japon'ica, japonika; kamelia (Camellia japonica); Japanse blomkweper.
jar[1], (n) kruik, fles, pot.
jar[2], (n): on (the, a) ~, op 'n skrefie.
jar[3], (n) onenigheid; geratel, knarsgeluid, geknars, trilling, skudding, skok; rusie; wanklank; a nasty ~, 'n lelike stamp; 'n wanklank; (v) (**-red**), knars, pyn aandoen; ratel, tril; vals laat klink, dissoneer; skok; in botsing kom; rusie maak, kibbel; kras, skuur; laat tril; stukkend stamp; ~ (up) on the NERVES, op die senuwees werk; laat seerkry; onaangenaam aandoen; ~ WITH, bots met; indruis teen.
jardinière'[1], blomstander, jardinière.
jardinière'[2], groentesop; jardinière (gereg); a la ~, met groentegarnering.
jarg'on[1], jargoon', kleurlose sirkoon.
jarg'on[2], brabbeltaal, koeterwaals, kombuistaal, wartaal, potjieslatyn; jargon; ~ **ize,** brabbel.
jarl, jarl, (Noorse) hoofman.
ja'rrah, jarra, Australiese mahonie(hout) (Eucalyptus marginata).
jar' ring[1], bottelring, flesring.
jarr'ing[2], (n) trilling (masjien); (a) trillend, knarsend; a ~ NOTE, 'n wangeluid; STRIKE a ~ note, 'n wanklank veroorsaak.
jar'vey, (**-s**) huurkoetsier.
jas'ey, (**-s**) pruik.
jas'min(e), jasmyn.
jas'per, jaspis; ~ **y,** jaspisagtig.
jaun'dice, (n) geelsug; afguns, nyd; blue ~, blousug; (v) geelsug laat kry; afgunstig maak; ~ **d,** geelsugtig; borriegeel; bevooroordeeld, afgunstig.
jaunt, (n) uitstappie, plesierrit; on the ~, op die swier; (v) 'n uitstappie maak; ~ **iness,** swierig, lugtig; lewendig; parmantig.
Ja'va, Java; ~ **nese',** (n) Javaan; Javaans (taal); (a) Javaans; ~ **coffee,** Javakoffie; ~ **sparrow,** rysvoël.
jav'elin, werpspies; throwing the ~, spiesgooi; ~ **man,** speerdraer, spiesdraer; ~ **throw,** spiesgooi.
Javelle'(water), javelwater.
jaw, (n) kakebeen; gepraat, geklets; bek (tang); klou (gereedskap); mond, bek; gepreek; (pl) klou, knyper, bek (tang); brutaliteit; the ~s of DEATH, die kake v.d. dood; HOLD your ~, hou jou mond

(snater); (v) babbel, klets; preek, skreeu; ~**-bone,** kakebeen; ~**-breaker,** moeilike woord, tongknoper; ~ **clutch,** blokkoppeling; kloukoppelaar; ~ **crusher,** knypbreker; ~**ing:** give someone a ~ing, iem. 'n skrobbering gee; ~ **spanner,** beksleutel; ~**-tooth,** maaltand, kiestand; ~ **vice,** skroef.
jay, gaai; kletskous; ~**-walker,** bontloper, gansloper, straatgans; ~**-walking,** bontlopery, ganslopery.
jazz, (n) jazz; nonsens; (v) jazz, op jazzmusiek dans; (a) opsigtig, skreeuerig; and all that ~, en al daai jazz (kaf, nonsies); ~ **band,** jazzorkes; ~ **man,** jazzspeler; ~ **y,** raserig, lawaaierig, skreeuerig.
jeal'ous, jaloers, naywerig, afgunstig, ywersugtig, jannie, kannie-koenie; BE ~, jaloers wees; langoog wees; jantjie wees; Jannie se baadjie aanhê; BE ~ of, jaloers wees op; view someone with a ~ EYE, jaloers op iem. wees; ~ of his HONOUR, gesteld wees op sy eer; MAKE someone ~, iem. jaloers maak; ~ of his NAME, gesteld op sy goeie naam; ~**y,** jaloesie, naywer, afguns(tigheid); besorgdheid; professional ~**y,** broodnyd; professionele jaloesie, beroepsjaloesie.
jean, keperstof, gekeperde katoenstof; (pl) kuitbroek; jeans, jannas, klinknaelbroek; denim(broek).
jeep, jeep.
jeer, (n) spot, beskimping; (v) hoon, beskimp, spot, uitlag, uitkoggel; ~ at, bespot, uitjou.
jeer'ing, (n) beskimping, gespot, bespotting; (a) skimpig; spottend; ~ **ly,** spottend(erwys), honend.
jeer(s), katrol.
jeg, geweerkaliber.
Jehov'ah, Jehova; ~ **Witnesses,** Jehovasgetuies, Russelliete.
Je'hu, Jehu; woeste koetsier.
jejune', leeg, nugter (maag); skraal, maer; dor (land); ~ **ness,** maerheid, skraalheid; dorheid.
jejun'um, nugterderm, jejunum.
jell, (v), stol, verstyf, styf word.
jellaba, djellaba, kapmantel (Arabies).
jell'ied, jellieagtig.
jell'y, (n) (**jellies**), jellie, jelei, selei; beat (in) to a ~, pap slaan; (v) (**jellied**), dik word; laat styf word; ~**-bag,** deursygsakkie, filtreersak; ~**-bean,** jellieboontjie; ~**-crystals,** jelliekristalle; ~**-fish,** (see) kwal; jellievis, drilvis; ~**-like,** jellieagtig, jellierig; ~ **mould,** jellievorm, jelliebakkie; ~**-powder,** jelliepoeier.
jemi'ma, rekkerskoen; geknoopte das.
jemm'y[1], (**jemmies**), koevoet, breekyster; inbraakyster.
jemm'y[2], (**jemmies**), gebraaide skaapkop.
jenn'et, Spaanse perdjie, genet.
jenn'y, (**jennies**), donkiemerrie; loopkraan; winterkoninkie (voël); ~**-ass,** eselmerrie; ~ **callipers,** kweepasser; ~ **wheel,** wielkatrol; ~ **winch,** handlaaiboom; ~ **wren,** winterkoninkie.
jeo'pardize, in gevaar bring.
jeo'pardous, gevaarlik.
jeo'pardy, gevaar; be in ~, op die spel wees; in gevaar wees.
jequi'rity, mienie-mienie; ~ **bean,** mienie-mienie(boontjie).
jerbo'a, oortjiespringmuis, woestynmuis (Dipodidae); jerboa.
jeremi'ad, jeremiade, klaaglied.
Jeremi'ah, Jeremia.
Je'richo, Jericho; GO to ~! loop na jou grootjie! loop na die maan! he can GO to ~, hy kan na die maan vlieg; SEND someone to ~, iem. na sy verstand laat gaan.
jerk, (n) ruk, stoot, skok, stamp; senuweetrekking; wrik; snedige uitval; skobbejak, niksnut(s); BRING him up with a ~, hom tot besinning bring (regruk); PHYSICAL ~s, gimnastiekoefeninge, liggaamsoefening(e); (v) stoot, draai, skud, wrik, ruk; ~ **ily,** met rukke en stote, rukkerig.
jerk'in, jekker, (leer)baadjie.
jerk: ~ **iness,** rukkerigheid, stamperigheid; ~ **y,** hortend, rukkend, stotend.
jerobo'am, jerobeam.
jerook', jeroek, jeroep.
jeropig'o, jeropiko.

Je'rry¹, (Jerries), Duitser.
jer'ry², (jerries), koos, kamerpot; knipmasjien; bierkroeg; ~**-builder,** knoeibouer; ~**-building,** knoeigebou; knoeibouery; ~**-built,** sleg gebou; wankelrig, lendelam.
Jers'ey¹, Jersey(bees).
jers'ey², (-s), trui, jersie.
Jerus'alem, Jerusalem; *GO to* ~*!* loop na die hoenders! *the HEAVENLY* ~, die hemelse Jerusalem; *a NEW* ~, 'n nuwe Jerusalem.
jess, pootband.
jess'amine, jasmyn.
jest, (n) skerts, grap, gekheid, korswel; *IN* ~, uit korswel, vir die grap; *full MANY a* ~ *is spoken in earnest,* baie grappies is ernstig bedoel; (v) jil, gekskeer, skerts, 'n grap maak, korswel; bespot; ~**book,** grappeboek; ~**er,** nar; grapmaker.
jest'ing, (n) gekskeerdery, gekker(n)y, jillery; (a) jillerig; ~ *APART,* alle gekheid op 'n stokkie; *no* ~ *MATTER,* nie iets om oor te lag nie; ~**ly,** skertsend, grappig, gekskerend.
Jes'uit, Jesuïet; ~**'ic(al),** Jesuïties; ~**ism,** Jesuïtisme; ~**ry,** Jesuïetemoraal; ~**'s bark,** kinabas.
Je'sus, Jesus.
jet¹, (n) git; (a) git=.
jet², (n) straal; pit; vlam; tuit, pyp; bek; straler (vliegtuig); sproeier (vergasser); staalskroef; spuit (masjien); ~ *of water,* waterstraal; (v) **(-ted),** uitskiet, uitspuit, straal; ~ **aeroplane,** straler, straalvliegtuig; ~ **age,** straaleeu; ~ **aircraft,** straler, straalvliegtuig.
jet'black, gitswart, pikswart; ~ *horse,* pikswart perd, gitswart perd.
jet: ~ **engine,** straalmotor; ~ **fighter,** straalvegter, straaljaer, -jagter; ~ **lag,** stralervermoeidheid, reistamheid, reismoegheid; ~ **liner,** straal(passasiers)vliegtuig; ~ **pipe,** straalpyp; ~ **plane,** straler, straalvliegtuig; ~**-propelled,** straalaangedrewe; ~ **propulsion,** straalaandrywing; ~ **pump,** straalpomp.
jet'sam, strandgoed, wrakgoed, opdrifsel(s), afdryfsel(s).
jet' set, stralerkliek, stralerjakkeraars.
jett'age, aanlêgeld.
jett'ison, (n) oorboordwerping; (v) oorboord gooi, jonas; ~ **valve,** stortklep.
jet' trotter, straalreisiger; stralerjakkeraar.
jett'y¹, (n) **(jetties),** landingshoof, hawehoof, kaai, seehoof; pier; aanlêplek.
jett'y², (a) gitagtig.
Jew¹, (n) Jood; ~*s and GENTILES alike,* Jode en nie-Jode (heidene); *TELL that to the* ~*s,* maak dit aan jou grootjie wys; *UNBELIEVING* ~, ongelowige persoon; ongelowige Thomas.
jew², (v) toetrek, kul, verneuk.
Jew: ~**-baiter,** Jodevervolger; ~**-baiting,** Jodevervolging.
jew'el, (n) juweel, kleinood; steen (in oorlosie); edelsteen; *a* ~ *of a girl,* 'n pêrel van 'n meisie; (v) **(-led),** met juwele tooi (versier); van stene voorsien (oorlosie); ~**-box,** ~**-case,** juwelekissie; ~**ler,** juwelier; ~**(le)ry,** juwele, juwelierware; ~**ling,** juweelsetwerk, steensetwerk.
Jew: ~**ess, (-es),** Jodin, ~**ish,** Joods; ~**ry,** Jodebuurt; Jodedom; ~**'s harp,** trompie.
Je'zebel, skaamtelose vrou, jesebel.
jib¹, (n) fok(seil); (v) **(-bed),** verlê (seil).
jib², (n) kraanbalk; arm (van hyskraan); (v) **(-bed),** omdraai.
jib³, (n) steeksheid; steeks perd; (v) **(-bed),** steeks wees (perd); rusteloos wees; ~ *at,* steeks wees vir; afkerig wees van; wegskram van; ~**ber,** steeks perd; vassteker.
jib: ~**-boom,** kluifhout; ~**-door,** blinde deur; ~**-sail,** kluiwer(seil).
jiff'(y), (colloq.) oomblik, rukkie, kits; *HALF a* ~*; IN a* ~, in 'n kits, een-twee-drie; *do something IN a* ~, in tien tellings iets doen; in 'n japtrap doen.
jig, (n) horrelpyp; lewendige deuntjie; wipsif; lepel (vis); setstuk (masj.); (v) **(-ged),** die horrelpyp dans; spring, huppel, skommel, wiegel; sif; op en neer wip; set (masj.).

jigg'er¹, sandvlooi.
jigg'er², (n) ertssif; biljartbok, langkop; heupjas, halfjas; agterseil; pottebakkerskyf; kopiehouer; (v): *well, I'll be* ~ *ed!* nou is ek dronkgeslaan!
jigg'er-flee, sandvlooi.
jigg'er-mast, agtermas.
jiggery-pok'ery, agterbakse konkelary, geknoei, intrige.
jig'gle, wieg; heen en weer trek, skud.
jig'saw, rondsaag, figuursaag, uitsnysaag; ~ **puzzle,** legkaart; inlegspel.
jilt, (n) flirt, koket; (v) in die pad steek, laat loop, afsê.
Jim Crow¹, (derog.), Neger.
jim'-crow², spoorbuier.
jim'-jams', ritteltits, bewerasie; horries.
jimm'y = jemmy.
jimp, skraal, maer.
jin'gle, (n) gerinkink; gerammel, gerinkel, geraas, lawaai; rymelary, klinkklank; (v) rinkink; raas, klink, rinkel, rammel; rym; ~ **bell,** veerklokkie; ~**jangle,** klinkklank; ~**r,** rammelaar.
jin'gling, geklingel.
jing'o, (-es), jingo, chauvinis; *by* ~*!* by my siks! by my kool! ~**ism,** jingoïsme; ~**is'tic,** jingoïsties, chauvinisties; ~ **paper,** jingoblad; ~ **party,** jingoparty.
jink, (n) sprong; ontduiking; draai, wending; gerinkel; *high* ~*s,* luidrugtige vermaak, baljaardery; (v) rinkel (geld); vinnig beweeg; wegduik; fop, kul; pret maak.
jinn, jinnee', bose gees, djin.
jinrick'sha, jinrik'sha, riksja.
jinx, (colloq.), vloek, onheil; towery.
jit'ter, bewe, rittel; (pl) senuweeagtigheid, senuwees; *GET the* ~*s,* dit op die senuwees kry; *HAVE the* ~*s,* die ritteltit(s) kry; ~**bug,** (n) ritteldanser; (v) ritteldans.
jiu-jitsu' = ju-jitsu.
jive, (n) ritteldans; (v) ritteldans; ~ **session,** ritteldans.
Job¹, Job; *the patience of* ~ *and the wisdom of Solomon,* Job se geduld en Salomo se wysheid.
job², (n) werk, betrekking, karweitjie; werkstuk, taak; pos; spekulasie; smoutwerk (drukkery); saak; baantjie; knoeiery; *a BAD* ~, 'n beroerde affère; *a DIFFICULT* ~, 'n moeilike taak; *DO one's* ~, jou plig doen; *DO a good* ~, goeie werk lewer; *GET on with the* ~, aan die werk spring; *GIVE up as a bad* ~, laat vaar; *a GOOD* ~, 'n goeie saak; *GOOD* ~! mooi so! goed so! *KNOW one's* ~, sy vak verstaan; *MAKE the best of a bad* ~, jou na iets skik; *MAKE a good* ~ *of it,* iets tot welslae bring; *ODD* ~*s,* los werkies; allerhande karweitjies; *ON the* ~, besig, wakker; ~*s for PALS,* baantjies vir boeties; *a ROTTEN* ~, 'n hondebaantjie; *a SOFT* ~, 'n lekker baantjie; (v) **(-bed),** werkies verrig; verhuur; spekuleer; agentwerk doen; handel in effekte; makelaarswerk doen; knoei.
job³, (n) steek; ruk (van perd se bek); (v) **(-bed),** por, steek; ruk (v.d. perd se bek).
job' analysis, posontleding, werkontleding, taakontleding.
joba'tion, sedepreek, (uit)brander.
job'ber, los werknemer; stukwerker; spekulant; efektehandelaar; konkelaar, knoeier; smoutdrukker.
jobb'ernowl, domkop, klipkop, uilskuiken.
jobb'ery, knoeiwerk, geknoei; los werkies.
jobb'ing, makelaarswerk, spekuleerwerk; spekulasie; geknoei; smoutwerk (drukkery); werkery; stukwerk; ~ **compositor,** smoutsetter; ~ **gardener,** los tuinman; ~ **hand,** stukwerker; ~ **house,** drukkery; ~ **printer,** smoutdrukker; ~ **work,** smoutwerk.
job: ~**-card,** werkkaart; ~**-carriage,** huurrytuig; ~**clerk,** werkopsigter; ~**-coachman,** huurkoetsier; ~ **description,** posbeskrywing; ~ **enrichment,** werkverryking; ~ **evaluation,** posevaluering; ~**-goods,** ongereelde goed; ~ **horse,** huurperd; ~**-hunter,** werksoeker; baantjiesoeker; ampjagter; ~**-hunting,** werksoekery; baantjiesjaery; ~**less,** werkloos; ~ **lot,** rommelspul; (reeks) restante; ~ **master,** rytuigverhuurder; stalhouer; ~**-office,** smoutdrukkery; ~ **opportunity,** werk(s)geleentheid; ~**-printer,** smoutdrukker; ~ **reservation,** werkafbake=

ning; ~ **seeker**, werksoeker; baantjiesoeker; ~ **specification**, posspesifikasie; ~ **work**, stukwerk; ~ **worker**, stukwerker.
Job's: ~ **comforter**, Jobstrooster, swak trooster; ~ **news**, Jobstyding.
jocket'te, vrouejokkie.
jock'ey[1], (n) (-s), jokkie, reisiesjaer; ruiter; snuiter; vent.
jock'ey[2], (v) wegstamp, wegstoot; kul, bedrieg, uitoorlê; ~ *a person AWAY*, iem. uitwerk; ~ *IN*, inwerk; inkry; ~ *INTO*, listig inbring; ~ *OUT of*, afhandig maak, fop uit; ~ *for a POSITION*, ander probeer uitoorlê.
jock'ey: ~ **cap**, jokkiepet; ~ **club**, wedrenklub; ~ **ism**, rykuns; ~ **pulley**, leikatrol; ~ **strap**, liesband; ~ **wheel**, spanwiel.
jock'o, (-s), sjimpansee; aap, kees.
jock'-strap, deurtrekker, liesband.
jocose', grapp(er)ig, snaaks, boertig.
jocose'ness, **joco'sity**, grapp(er)igheid.
joc'ular, grapperig, grappig, boertig, snaaks; ~ **'ity**, grappigheid, snaaksheid, boertigheid; ~ **ly**, spelenderwyse, grappenderwyse.
joc'und, vrolik, opgewek, bly; ~ **'ity**, blyheid, vrolikheid.
jodhpurs', jodpoer, rybroek.
jo'ey, (-s), kangaroetjie; jong dier.
jog, (n) stamp, stoot; pretdraf, pretloop; sukkeldraffie; (v) (-ged), skud; stoot, stamp; draf; stap-hardloop; ~ *ABOUT*, omsukkel; ~ *ALONG*, voortsukkel; aantjokker; op 'n sukkeldraffie aangaan; nog op die ou trant gaan; ~ *the MEMORY*, die geheue optrns; iem. aan iets herinner; ~ **ger**, pretloper, pretdrawwer; ~ **ging association**, pretdrafvereniging.
jogg'le[1], (n) geskud; sukkeldraffie; (v) skommel; skud.
jogg'le[2], (n) vertanding; inkeping; hol-en-dolvoeg; (v) inkeep; joggel; ~ **joint**, joggelvoeg; hol-en-dolvoeg.
jog'trot, sukkeldraffie; skilpaddraffie, drafstap, sleurgang; sukkelgang; *be going at a* ~, op 'n sukkeldraffie gaan.
Johan'nisberger, Johannisberger, witwyn.
John, Jan; ~ *BULL*, die Engelsman, Engeland; ~ *CITIZEN*, Jan Burger; ~ *COMPANY*, Jan Kompanjie.
johnn'y, (. .nnies), kêrel, vent, japie, snuiter.
joie de vivre, (F.), joie de vivre, lewenslus, lewensvreugde.
join, (n) voeg, las, naat, verbinding; koppeling; verbindingslyn; (v) verenig, verbind, saamvoeg, aaneensluit, dig (pype); byeenvoeg, aaneenvoeg; aanlas, aaneenlas; paar aan; saammaak, meedoen; jou aansluit by, jou voeg by; grens aan; uitloop in; toetree tot; ~ *BATTLE*, slaags raak; ~ *a CHURCH*, lidmaat word; by 'n kerk aansluit; ~ *FORCES*, saamspan, saamwerk; ~ *in the FUN*, aan die pret meedoen; ~ *HANDS*, die hande vou; die hande in mekaar lê; mekaar die hand gee; gemene saak maak met; ~ *IN*, saammaak; inval; ~ *IN a song*, saamsing; ~ *ISSUE*, die stryd aanknoop; ~ *ON to*, aansluit; ~ *the RANKS*, aansluit (by die weermag); *the Caledon RIVER* ~ *s the Orange River*, die Caledonrivier loop in die Grootrivierin ; ~ *a SHIP*, aan boord gaan; ~ *TO*, las aan; vasmaak aan; ~ *UP*, aansluit; ~ *WITH*, saammaak; aansluit by.
join'der, samevoeging, vereniging.
join'er[1], hen(d)sopper; verraaier.
join'er[2], skrynwerker, houtwerker; ~ **s' bench**, skrynwerkersbank, houtwerkbank; ~ **'s gauge**, kruishout; ~ **'s glue**, houtlym; ~ **'s putty**, stophars; ~ **'s saw**, voegsaag; ~ **y**, skrynwerk, houtwerk; skrynwerkwinkel, houtwerkwinkel.
joint, (n) gewrig, geleding; skarnier; vleisstuk; voeg, naat; verbinding; aanknopingspunt; dwarspleet, skeur, naat (geol.); lit; ring, beuel; *FLEXIBLE* ~, draaikoppeling; ~ *and several LIABILITY*, gesamentlike en afsonderlike aanspreeklikheid; *OUT of* ~, uit lit; uit die voeë; *PUT out of* ~, uit die voeë geruk word; *UNIVERSAL* ~, kruiskoppeling,

kardankoppeling; (v) **(joint)**, saamvoeg; las, verbind; verdeel; stukkend sny (vleis); voeg; digmaak; (a) verenig, gesamentlik, mede-; *on* ~ *ACCOUNT*, vir gesamentlike rekening; *in our* ~ *NAMES*, in naam van ons almal; ~ **account**, gesamentlike rekening; deelrekening; ~ **action**, gesamentlike optrede; ~ **author**, medeskrywer, medeouteur; ~ **bolt**, lasbout; ~ **committee**, gesamentlike komitee; ~ **coupling**, skarnierkoppeling; ~ **creditor**, medeskuldeiser; ~ **debtor**, medeskuldenaar; ~ **ed**, met litte; ~ *ed cactus*, litjieskaktus; ~ **er**, blokskaaf; voegtroffel; voegspyker; lasser; voegyster; ~ **estate**, gemeenskaplike boedel; gemeenskap van goedere; ~ **file**, skarniervyl; ~ **gout**, gewrigsrumatiek; ~ **heir**, mede-erfgenaam; ~ **ing**, naatvorming, kliewing; laswerk; ~ **ing plane**, blokskaaf; ~ **ing rule**, rigplank; ~ **less**, ongeleed; voegloos.
joint'ly, gesamentlik; ~ *LIABLE*, medeaanspreeklik; ~ *and SEVERALLY*, gesamentlik en afsonderlik.
joint: **J** ~ **Matriculation Board**, Gemeenskaplike Matrikulasieraad; ~ **owner**, mede-eienaar; ~ **plate**, lasplaat; voegplaat; ~ **rule**, vouduimstok; voegreihout; ~ **screw**, lasskroef; ~ **sovereign**, medeheerser; ~ **stock**, gemeenskaplike kapitaal; ~**-stock company**, aandelemaatskappy; ~ **stool**, voustoel; ~ **system**, naatstelsel; ~ **tenancy**, gesamentlike huur; ~ **tenant**, medehuurder.
join'ture, (n) weduweegoed; (v) weduweegoed nalaat.
joint' washer, voegwasher.
joist, (n) dwarsbalk, stutbalk, vloerbalk; (v) van balke voorsien; ~ **ing**, balklaag, dwarsbalke.
joke, (n) grap, skerts, kwinkslag; ui, frats, gekheid, spiets, aardigheid; *AS a* ~, vir die grap; *CRACK a* ~, 'n grap verkoop; 'n grap maak; *a jolly GOOD* ~, 'n goeie grap; 'n grap en 'n half; *IN a* ~, uit korswel, vir die grap; *it is NO* ~, dis nie 'n kleinigheid nie; dit is erns; *the* ~ *is ON you*, die grap is ten koste van jou; *PLAY a practical* ~ *on someone*, iem. 'n poets bak; *STAND a* ~, skerts verdra, he *can TAKE a* ~, hy kan 'n grap verstaan; 'n grap bring hom nie van koers nie; (v) grappe maak, skerts; gekskeer, jil, pla, speel; ~ **r**, grappemaker, skertser; asjas, vent, kêrel; speelman, piet (kaartspel).
jok'ing, (n) grapmakery; gekker(n)y, gejil, jil(lery); ~ *APART*, alle gekheid op 'n stokkie; in alle erns; *he was ONLY* ~, hy het sommer gespeel; hy het dit nie ernstig bedoel nie; *YOU'RE* ~, jy speel; ~ **ly**, speel-speel, vir die grap.
jok'y, grapperig.
jollifica'tion, vrolikheid, pret, plesierigheid.
joll'ify, (. .fied), pret maak; fuif; feesvier.
joll'iness, **joll'ity**, vrolikheid, joligheid, speelsheid, feestelikheid.
joll'y, vrolik, plesierig, joviaal; jollie; lekker, aangeklam; *a* ~ *DOG*, 'n plesierige ou, 'n vrolike Frans; *I felt a* ~ *FOOL*, ek het 'n mooi gek gevoel; ek het my dood geskaam; *a* ~ *GOOD fellow*, 'n lekker kêrel; *you will* ~ *well HAVE to*, jy sal eenvoudig moet; *a* ~ *PARTY*, 'n vrolike partytjie; ~ *ROGER*, seerowervlag; *I should* ~ *well THINK so*, ek sou so dink.
joll'y(-boat), jol.
joll'y-jumper, ritstuig, huppeltuig.
jolt, (n) hort, stoot, stamp, skok; (v) stamp, stoot; laat skud.
jolt'erhead, domoor, domkop.
jolt: ~ **ing**, (n) geskommel; (a) hortend, stamperig; ~ **y** = **jolting** (a).
Jon'ah, Jona; *a regular* ~, 'n regte Jona.
jon'athan, Jonatanappel; *Brother* ~, Broer Jonatan; die Verenigde State.
jon'gleur, swerwende musikant; jongleur.
jonq'uil, sonkieltjie, geel narsing, jonkuil *(Narcissus jonquilla)*; ~ **colour**, liggeel.
Jord'an[1], Jordaan.
jord'an[2], uil, pot, koos.
jor'um, groot beker, kom; pons; hele klomp.
Jos'eph[1], Josef; kuis man.
jos'eph[2], damesrykleed.

josh, (sl.), (n), grappie; (v) gekskeer, pla; ~ **er,** grapmaker, gekskeerder.
jos'kin, plaasjapie, tor.
joss, josie, Chinese afgod; ~ **er,** dwaas, asjas, uilskuiken; ~ **-house,** Chinese tempel; ~ **-stick,** wierookstokkie.
jo'stle, (n) stamp, geworstel; botsing; gedrang; (v) verdring, teen mekaar stamp, stoot, bots; dring; worstel, stoei; ~ *one's way,* met sy skouers 'n pad maak.
jo'stling, (n) stampery; (a) stampend.
jot¹, (n) jota, kleinigheid; *NOT a* ~, nie 'n jota nie; *not ONE* ~ *or tittle,* nie 'n jota of tittel nie.
jot², (v) **(-ted),** aanteken, opteken, aanstip; ~ *down,* aanteken, aanstip; ~ **ter,** notaboekie, aantekeningboekie; ~ **ting,** aantekening, nota.
joule, joule.
jounce, bons, skud, stamp.
journ'al, dagboek, joernaal; tydskrif; dagblad; ashals, kussingblok; ~ **bearing,** draaglaer; ~ **box,** draagpot, asnaaf; ~ **ese'**, koeranttaal; ~ **ism,** joernalistiek, koerantskrywery, die pers; ~ **ist,** koerantskrywer, dagbladskrywer, joernalis; ~ **is'tic,** joernalisties, nuusblad=, koerant=.
journ'ey, (n) **(-s),** (land)reis, tog; *have GONE on one's last* ~, die laaste skof afgelê het; *MAKE (take, go) on a* ~, op reis gaan; *a* ~ *THROUGH the whole country,* 'n landreis; *TWO days'* ~, twee dagreise; (v) reis, 'n reis maak; ~ **-book,** reisbeskrywing; ~ **ed,** bereis.
jour'neyman, (..men), dagloner, werksman; handwerkgesel, handlanger, huurling; vakman, ambagsman.
jour'neywork, dagwerk, loonwerk.
joust, (n) toernooi, steekspel; (v) 'n toernooi hou; 'n lans breek; 'n tweegeveg aanknoop.
Jove, Jupiter; *by* ~ *!* mensig! mapstieks!
jov'ial, vrolik, plesierig, opgeruimd, joviaal; ~ **'ity,** vrolikheid, blygeestigheid, opgewektheid, jovialiteit, opgeruimdheid.
Jov'ian, Jupiteragtig, soos Jupiter.
jowl, wang; kakebeen, kaak; kop; krop; onderken; keelvel; viskop; keelgang; skêr (perd); *cheek by* ~, wang teen wang, intiem, sy aan sy; ~ **ed,** met hangwange; ~ **er,** hanglipjaghond; ~ **wool,** kenwol, wangwol.
joy, (n) blydskap, genoeë, vreugde, verheuging; bron van vreugde; genot; *no* ~ *without ANNOY,* wie heuning uithaal, moet steke verwag; *one's* ~ *and DELIGHT,* iem. se lus en lewe; *it GIVES me* ~, dit doen my genoeë, dit verheug my; ~ *of LIVING,* lewensvreugde; *SIGN of* ~, vreugdeteken; *SONG of* ~, vreugdelied; *WISH someone* ~ *of something,* iem. met iets gelukwens; *TEAR of* ~, vreugdetraan; *WISH someone* ~, iem. gelukwens; (v) jou verheug, jou verbly; ~ **-bells,** vreugdeklokke; ~ **flight,** plesiervlug; ~ **ful,** vrolik, verheug, vreugdevol, bly(hartig); ~ **fully,** met vreugde, bly; ~ **fulness,** blydskap, blyhartigheid, vrolikheid; ~ **less,** vreugdeloos; ~ **ous,** genotvol; vrolik; verblydend; ~ **ride,** plesierit, plesiertog; ~ **rider,** plesierryer; ~ **stick,** stuurstok, stuurarm; ~ **wheel,** pretwiel, swaaiwiel.
jub'ate, maanhaar=.
jub'ilance, gejubel, verrukking.
jub'ilant, juigend, jubelend.
Jubilate', lofsang (psalm 100).
jub'ilate, jubel, juig.
jubila'tion, gejubel, gejuig; juigtoon, jubeltoon.
jub'ilee, jubileum; jubelfees; jubeljaar; gejubel, gejuig; *silver* ~, silwerjubileum; ~ **issue,** feesuitgawe; ~ **stamp,** feeseël; ~ **year,** jubeljaar.
Judae'a, *kyk* Judea.
Juda'ic, Joods.
Jud'aism, Judaïsme; Jodedom.
Jud'aize, verjoods.
jud'as¹, loergaatjie, kykgaatjie.
Jud'as², Judas, verraaier; ~ **beard,** Judasbaard, rooi baard; ~ **-coloured,** rooi; ~ **kiss,** Judaskus, verraaierskus; ~ **-tree,** judasboom *(Cercis siliquastrum).*
jud'cock, watersnip.

jud'der, (v.), sidder, tril; (n.), siddering, trilling.
Jude'a, Judea; ~ **n,** (n) Judeër; (a) Judees.
judge, (n) regter; skepen (hist.); deskundige, kenner, beoordelaar, keurder, skeidsregter; rigter (Bybel); *be a* ~ *in one's own CAUSE,* jou eie regter wees; *as GOD is my* ~, so waar as God; (v) oordeel; vonnis, beslis; beoordeel; ag, beskou; regspreek; 'n oordeel vorm; ~ *by APPEARANCES,* na die uiterlike oordeel; iem. voor die kop, maar nie in die krop sien nie; ~ *BY,* oordeel volgens; ~ *the DISTANCE,* die afstand skat; *do not* ~ *OTHERS by yourself,* as jy self agter die deur staan, moet jy 'n ander nie daar soek nie; ~ **-made law,** regbankreg.
judgema'tical, skerpsinnig, oordeelkundig.
judg(e)ment, oordeel; vonnis, uitspraak; opinie; berekening, skatting; beoordeling; godsoordeel; (pl) oordeelvellings; *against your own BETTER* ~, teen jou eie beterwete in; *DAY of* ~, oordeelsdag; *GIVE* ~, uitspraak gee; *IN my* ~, volgens (na) my mening; *the LAST J* ~, die Laaste Oordeel; *PASS* ~, oordeel vel; *PRONOUNCE* ~ *on,* die vonnis vel; uitspraak doen; *SIT in* ~ *on,* oordeel vel oor; ~ **-day,** oordeelsdag; ~ **debt,** vonnisskuld; ~ **hall,** geregsaal; ~ **seat,** regterstoel, vierskaar.
judge' president, regter-president.
Judg'es, Rigters.
judge'ship, regterskap.
judg'ing, (n) beoordeling; ~ *from (by),* te oordeel na; (a) keur=; ~ **committee,** keurkomitee.
jud'icable, onderworpe aan die jurisdiksie.
jud'icative, oordelend; ~ **faculty,** oordeelvermoë.
jud'icatory, (n) regspleging; regbank; (a) regs=, regterlik; geregtelik.
jud'icature, regspleging, justisie, regspraak; regtersamp; regbank; regterlike mag.
judi'cial, geregtelik; regterlik; oordeelkundig; ~ **committee,** regterlike kommissie; ~ **management,** geregtelike bestuur; ~ **murder,** geregtelike moord; ~ **order,** hofbevel; ~ **sale,** eksekusieverkoping, verkoop in eksekusie; ~ **separation,** geregtelike (eg)skeiding.
judi'ciary, (n) die regters; regterlike mag; (a) geregtelik; regs=.
judi'cious, verstandig, oordeelkundig, skerpsinnig, weloorwoë; ~ **ness,** wysheid, verstandigheid.
ju'do, judo; ~ **ka,** judoka.
jug¹, (n) kan, kruik; karaf; beker; wasbeker; tronk.
jug², (v) **(-ged),** stoof, stowe (vleis); ~ *ged hare,* gestoofde haas, hasepeper.
jug³, (v) **(-ged),** sing (soos 'n nagtegaal).
jug'al, jukbeen=.
jug'ate, in pare, paar-paar.
Ju'gendstil, Jugendstil (kunsrigting).
jug'ful, beker(vol).
Jugg'ernaut, Jagannat, Indiese afgod; Molog van selfopoffering.
jugg'ins, uilskuiken, domkop.
jug'gle, (n) goëlery; kullery; (v) goël, oë verblind, tower; kul, bedrieg; ~ *AWAY,* wegtoor; ~ *with FACTS,* feite verdraai; ~ *OUT of,* uitoorlê, afrokke; ~ **r,** goëlaar, towenaar; bedrieër; ~ **ry,** goëlery, gegoël; bedrieëry.
jug'gling, gegoël.
jug'lene, jugleen.
Jug'oslav, (n) Joego-Slaaf; (a) Joego-Slawies.
Jugosla'via, Joego-Slawië, Suid-Slawië.
jug'ular, (n) slagaar, nekslagaar; (a) nek=, hals=; ~ **gland,** halsklier; ~ **vein,** nekslagaar.
jug'ulate, keel afsny, doodmaak; smoor.
juice, sap, vog; *stew in one's own* ~, in jou eie sous gaar kook; ~ **extractor,** sapperser; ~ **less,** saploos, droog.
jui'ciness, sappigheid; malsheid.
jui'cy, sapperig, sappig; mals, smaaklik; nat (weer).
ju-jit'su, joejitsoe.
ju'jube, jujube(bessie) *(Zizyphus jujuba);* joepjoep (lekker).
juke'-box, blêrkas, speelkas.
juk'skei, jukskei; ~ **club,** jukskeilaer; ~ **league,** jukskeiliga; ~ **play,** jukskeispel.
jul'ep, medisynestroop, julep.

Julian 995 *Justinian*

Jul'ian, (n) Julianus; (a) Juliaans; ~ **calendar,** Juliaanse tydrekening.
Jul'ich, Gulik.
julien'ne, groentesop, julienne.
July', Julie; *DURBAN* ~, ~ *HANDICAP,* Durbanse Juliewedren.
jum'ble[1], (n) verwarring; allegaartjie, poespas, sameraapsel, deurmekaarspul, mengelmoes; geskud.
jum'ble[2]: ~ **sale,** rommelverkoping; ~ **shop,** rommelwinkel.
jum'bo, lomperd, diksak, kolos, wolsak; ~ **jet,** makrostraler.
jump, (n) sprong, spring; skielike styging; gaping; (pl) springnommers; *ALL of a* ~, baie senuweeagtig; *AT a* ~, met een sprong; *FROM the* ~, uit die staanspoor; *GIVE a* ~, spring; skielik skrik; *HAVE the* ~ *s,* die bewerasie hê; *HIGH* ~, hoogspring; *KEEP on the* ~, nie met rus laat nie; opdreun; *LONG* ~, verspring; *ON the* ~, aan die gang; (v) spring, opspring; skrikmaak; styg, opgaan (pryse); spring oor; bedrieg; steel; oorslaan (bladsy); ~ *AT something,* iets gretig aanneem; iets aangryp; ~ *one's BAIL,* jou borgtog verbeur; met die noorderson vertrek; ~ *into one's CLOTHES,* jou klere vinnig aanpluk; ~ *to a CONCLUSION,* 'n alte haastige gevolgtrekking maak; ~ *the COUNTRY,* uit die land vlug; ~ *a FENCE,* oor 'n draad (heining) spring; ~ *IN,* inspring; ~ *for JOY,* van vreugde opspring; ~ *the traffic LIGHTS,* oor die verkeersligte ry; ~ *a LINE,* 'n reël oorslaan; ~ *the PISTOL (gun),* te haastig wees; te gou wegspring; die sein voorspring; ~ *at a PROPOSAL,* 'n voorstel gretig aanvaar; ~ *the RAILS,* ontspoor; ~ *ROUND,* omspring; ~ *a SHIP,* van 'n skip wegloop; ~ *out of one's SKIN,* uit jou vel spring; ~ *down someone's THROAT,* teen iem. uitvaar; ~ *a TRAIN,* 'n trein steel; ~ *UPON,* te lyf gaan; bespring; ~ **drill,** slagboor, stampboor.
jum'per[1], (oor)bloes, (oor)bloese; kiel (matroos).
jum'per[2], springer; rotsboor, stampboor; voetganger(sprinkaan); ~ **drill,** slagboor; ~ **man,** boorman.
jumpiness, senuweeagtigheid; skrikkerigheid; beweërigheid.
jum'ping, springend; ~ **bean,** springboontjie; ~ **hare,** springhaas; ~ **jack,** akrobatiese nar, kaartmannetjie; ~ -**off place,** wegspringplek; stygplek; vastrapplek; ~ **pole,** springstok, polsstok; ~ **sheet,** springlaken.
jump: ~ **jet,** sprongstraler, springstraler; ~ **lead,** (oor)brugkabel, (oor)brugdraad; ~ -**off,** afspring (plek), afspring (punt); ~ **seat,** skuifsitplek, skuifstoel.
jum'py, skrikkerig; senuweeagtig.
junca'ceous, biesieagtig.
jun'cous, vol biesies.
junc'tion, verbinding; vereniging; las; saamvloeiing, sameloop, ineenvloeiing (riviere); kruispunt, aansluiting, knoop (spoorweg); ~ **box,** aansluitkas; koppelkas; ~ **call,** koppel(lyn)oproep; ~ **railway,** verbindingspoor, aansluitingspoorweg; ~ **valve,** aansluitklep.
junc'ture, vereniging; verbinding, aansluiting, las; naat, voeg, tydsgewrig, krisis, tydstip; *at this* ~, op hierdie tydstip.
June, Junie.
jung'le, oerwoud, bos; ruigte, bosruigte, wildernis; warboel; ~ **fever,** moeraskoors; ~ **gym,** wouterklouter, klimraam; ~ **hat,** veldhoed, boshoed; ~ **kit,** bostoerusting.
jun'ior, (n) junior, mindere, jongere; laagste in rang, jongste in diensjare; *he is my* ~, hy is my junior, hy is jonger as ek; hy staan onder my; (a) jonger, junior; ~ **clerk,** onderklerk; ~ **'ity,** juniorskap; ~ **officer,** junior offisier; die laagste in rang teenwoordig; ~ **partner,** jongste vennoot, junior vennoot.
jun'iper, jeneverstruik; ~ **berry,** jeneverbessie; ~ **bush,** jenewerbossie; ~ **tree,** jenewerboom.
junk[1], (n) jonk (Sjinese boot).
junk[2], (n) uitgerafelde tou; brok, groot stuk; rommel; soutvleis; walvisspek; (v) in stukke kap; verdeel; ~ -**dealer,** rommelwinkelier; ~ **dump,** rommelhoop.

junk'er, jonker, junker.
junk'et, (n) soet dikmelk, stremmelk; eetparty, piekniek, fuif; (v) onthaal, feesvier, smul; ~ **ing,** fuiwery.
junk' food, gemorskos, ongesonde kos.
jun'kie, jun'ky, dwelmslaaf, verslaafde.
junk: ~ **mail,** rommelpos; ~ **ring,** drukring; ~ **shop,** rommelwinkel; ~ **yard,** rommelwerf.
Jun'o, Juno.
Junoesque', Junoagtig.
jun'ta, jun'to, (-s), junta, party, kliek, faksie.
Ju'piter, Jupiter.
Ju'ra, Jura(formasie).
jur'al, regs-, wetlik.
Jurass'ic, Jurassies.
jurid'ical, geregtelik, juridies.
jur'is consult', regsgeleerde, juris.
jurisdic'tion, regsgebied, ampsgebied, jurisdiksie; regsbevoegdheid; *CIVIL* ~, siviele regsbevoegdheid; *CRIMINAL* ~, strafbevoegdheid.
jurisprud'ence, regsgeleerdheid, jurisprudensie, regsleer, wetsgeleerdheid.
jurisprud'ent, (n) regsgeleerde; (a) regsgeleerd.
jur'ist, juris, regsgeleerde, regswetenskaplike, wetkenner, ~ **'ic(al),** juristies, regsgeleerd.
jur'or, gesworene, jurielid.
jur'y[1], (n) **(juries),** jurie; *GRAND* ~, groot jurie; *PETTY* ~, klein jurie; *TRIAL by* ~, verhoor met 'n jurie.
ju'ry[2], (a) nood-.
jur'y: ~ **box,** juriebank; ~ **man,** jurielid.
jur'y: ~ **mast,** noodmas; ~ **rudder,** noodroer.
jur'y woman, vroulike jurielid.
just, (a) regverdig, billik, onpartydig, welverdiend, juis, presies; (adv) net, so-ewe, flus(sies), presies; effens, effentjies; ~ *AS,* net soos, nes, gelykerwys; *it is* ~ *AS well,* dit is ook maar goed; *I* ~ *could not BEAR it any longer,* ek kon dit nou eenmaal nie meer verdra (duld) nie; ~ *FANCY!* verbeel jou! dink net! ~ *IMAGINE!* verbeel jou! dink net! *that's* ~ *it!* presies! daar het jy dit nou! ~ *a LINE,* net 'n paar reëls (woorde); ~ *a MOMENT!* net 'n oomblik! wag 'n bietjie! ~ *NOW,* netnou, so-ewe, so pas; ~ *one O'CLOCK,* op die kop eenuur; ~ *POSSIBLE,* net moontlik; ~ *RIGHT,* doodreg; ~ *SO!* presies!; ~ *SPLENDID!* eenvoudig skitterend! ~ *THEN,* net toe; ~ *THERE,* net daar; ~ *as WELL,* net so goed; ~ *WHEN,* met dat; net toe; *not* ~ *YET,* nie nou al nie, vir eers nie.
jus'tice, geregtigheid; regverdigheid; justisie, regspleging; regter; billikheid; onpartydigheid; *ADMINISTER* ~, regspreek; *ADMINISTRATION of* ~, regsbedeling; *in ALL* ~, in alle billikheid; *BRING to* ~, straf laat ondergaan; *with COMPLETE* ~, met die volste reg; *COURT of* ~, geregshof; *DEPARTMENT of J* ~, Departement van Justisie; *DO* ~ *to,* reg laat geskied aan; eer aandoen; *DO oneself* ~, jou met ere van jou taak kwyt; *IN* ~, van regsweë; in billikheid teenoor; *MINISTER of J* ~, Minister van Justisie; *a (grave) MISCARRIAGE of* ~, 'n (growwe) regtelike dwaling; ~ *of the PEACE,* vrederegter; *Mr. JUSTICE Q,* regter Q; *SECRETARY of J* ~, Sekretaris van Justisie; ~ **hall,** (ge)regsaal; ~ **ship,** regterskap.
justi'ciable, beregbaar.
justi'ciary, (n) (..ries), regspreker; (a) regs-.
justifiabil'ity, verdedigbaarheid, verskoonbaarheid.
jus'tifiable, verdedigbaar; verskoonbaar; ~ **homicide,** straflose manslag.
jus'tifiably, tereg.
justifica'tion, regverdiging, verantwoording, regverdigmaking; wettiging.
jus'tificative, jus'tificatory, regverdigend, verskonend, regverdigings-.
jus'tified, geregverdig, gelyk, gegrond; *your FEARS were* ~, jou vrees was gegrond; *you were QUITE* ~ *in,* jy het volkome gelyk gehad om.
jus'tifier, verdediger; vryspreker.
jus'tify, (..fied), regverdig, verdedig, goedpraat, wettig, verantwoord; bewaarheid; bewys; aanvul, justeer (drukkuns); *justified in* .., geregtig om.
Justin'ian, (n) Justinianus; (a) Justiniaans.

just'ly, regverdig, billik; tereg, met reg.
just'ness, regverdigheid, billikheid; juistheid, noukeurigheid; gegrondheid.
jut, (n) uitsteeksel, oorhangende deel; (v) (-ted), uitsteek, (voor)uitspring.
Jute[1], Jut.
jute[2], growwe sakgoed, goiing, jute.
Jut'land, Jutland.
Juv'enal, Juvenalis.
juvenes'cence, jeugdigheid, jonkheid.
juvenes'cent, jeugdig; verjongend.
juv'enile, (n) jongeling, jong mens, jeugdige; (a) jong;
jeugdig; jeug=; *J~ Advisory Board,* Jeugraad; *J~ Affairs Board,* Jeugraad; ~ **court,** kinderhof; ~ **delinquency,** jeugmisdaad, jeugmisdadigheid; ~ **delinquent,** jeugoortreder; ~ **lead,** jeughoofrol; kinderhoofrol; ~ **literature,** jeuglektuur; ~ **offence,** jeugoortreding, jeugmisdryf; ~ **offender,** jeugmisdadiger; ~ **rally,** jeugsaamtrek.
juvenil'ia, juvenilia, jeugwerke; jeuggeskrifte.
juvinil'ity, jeugdigheid, jonkheid.
juxtapose', langs mekaar plaas.
juxtaposi'tion, nabyheid; naasmekaarstelling, jukstaposisie.

K

k, (ks, k's), k.
Ka'aba = Caaba.
kaa'ma, hartbees.
kab'bala = cabbala.
kabeljou', kabeljou.
kabob(s)', sosaties; kabob, kebab.
kabu'ki, kaboeki.
kaf(f)'ir, kaffer (tans vero. en neerh.); **kaffer-** word nog egter in sekere samestellings, gewoonlik planten diername, sonder enige neerhalende bedoelings gebruik; ~ **circus,** S.A. mynaandelemark; ~ **basket,** seroet; ~**-bread tree,** kafferbroodboom *(Encephalartos);* ~ **corn,** graansorghum; ~ **melon,** kafferwaatlemoen; ~ **millet,** kaffermanna *(Pennisetum typhoides);* ~ **pox,** kafferpokke, alastrim; ~**s,** Suid-Afrikaanse goudaandele; ~ **sheeting,** kafferlakengoed, kafferbaai; ~ **sorrel,** kaffersuring; ~ **tree,** kafferboom *(Erythrina Caffra);* ~ **watermelon,** kafferwaatlemoen *(Colocynthis citrullus).*
Kaffrar'ia, Kaffrarië; ~**n,** Kaffraries.
kaf'tan, kaftan.
kail, *kyk* **kale.**
kain'it(e), kaïniet.
kai'ser, keiser; **K**~**ism,** Duitse imperialisme; **K**~**ist,** Duitse imperialis; ~**ship,** keiserskap.
kakistoc'racy, kakistokrasie (regering deur die slegstes).
kala-a'zar, kala-asar, kala-azar.
Kalahar'i, Kalahari.
kale, boerkool, krulkool; koolsop.
kaleid'oscope, kaleidoskoop.
kaleidoscop'ic, kaleidoskopies.
kale'yard, groentetuin.
kali, kali.
Kal'muck, Kalmuk; Kalmuks (taal).
ka'long, kalong, vlieënde hond.
kamas'si, kamassie(hout).
kame, kame (geol.)
kamika'ze, (Jap.), kamikaze; kamikazevliegtuig; kamikazevlieënier.
kangaroo', kangaroe; ~ **bear,** koalabeer; ~ **rat,** buidelrot; ~ **closure,** behandeling van enkele amendemente met uitsluiting van ander; ~ **court,** boendoehof, boshof, skynhof; ~ **justice,** boendoegereg, bosgereg, skyngereg.
kan'nip, bobbejaankos, kannip.
kanot' grass, kanotgras *(Flagellaria guineensis).*
Kan'tian, (n) Kantiaan; (a) Kantiaans.
ka'olin, porseleinaarde, kaolien, kleiaarde.
ka'on, kaon (fis.).
kapell'meister, (G.), kapelmeester.
ka'pok, kapok; ~**-bird,** kapokvoëltjie.
kap'pa, kappa.
kaput', (slang), poot-uit, kapot.
Ka'rakul, Karakoel.
kara'te, karate.
karm'a, karma, lot.
Karoo', Karoo; *the GREAT* ~, die Groot Karoo; *the LITTLE* ~, die Klein Karoo.
kaross', (-es), karos.
karee', karee(boom) *(Rhus).*
kar'ri, karri *(Eucalyptus diversicolor).*

Kashmir', Kasjmir; ~**i,** Kasjmiri (taal; indiwidu); ~**ian,** (n) Kasjmiri; (a) Kasjmirs.
katabol'ic, katabolies, afbouend.
katab'olism, katabolisme.
katamorph'ism, katamorfisme.
kat'el, (wa)katel.
kat'ydid, langhoringsprinkaan.
kaur'i pine, kauriden *(Piper methysticum);* kawa= (drank).
ka'va, kawa.
kavass', Turkse bediende, konstabel.
kay'ak, kajak, Eskimobootjie.
ke'a, groot papegaai.
keck, hik, kokhals, braak; ~ *at,* walg van.
ked, skaapluis, skaapvlieg.
kedge, (n) werpanker; (v) verhaal, versleep (skip); ~ **anchor,** werpanker.
kedg'eree, kitsery.
keel[1], (n) koleskuit.
keel[2], (n) kiel; naat, rand; skip, vaartuig; *on an EVEN* ~, in ewewig; gelykmatig; *be on an EVEN* ~, dit gaan klopdisselboom; *keep on an EVEN* ~, in ewewig hou; *a FALSE* ~, 'n los kiel; *FLOAT* ~ *up,* onderstebo dryf; *LAY down a* ~, die kiel lê; (v) kiel; omgooi; omval, omslaan; ~ *over,* omslaan; om= kantel; ~**age,** kielgeld; ~ **boat,** kielboot; ~ **box,** kielbak; ~**ed,** gekiel; ~**er,** skuitaanvoerder; ~**- haul,** kielhaal; ~**less,** kielloos; ~**son** = kelser.
keen[1], (n) Ierse klaaglied, treurlied; (v) weeklaag.
keen[2], (a) skerp; vlymend; belangstellend; ywerig, gretig; happig; bytend, (skerp)snydend, deurdringend; hewig, lewendig, vurig, skrander, skerpsinnig; *be* ~ *ABOUT something,* baie sin in iets hê; dol oor iets wees; ~ *DESIRE,* vurige verlange; ~ *on DOING something,* vurig verlang om iets te doen; ~ *INTEREST,* lewendige belangstelling; *as* ~ *as MUSTARD,* uiters entoesiasties; ~ *ON,* versot op; tuk op; ~ *SIGHT,* skerp gesig; ~ *SMELL,* fyn reuk; *not VERY* ~, glad nie geesdriftig nie; ~**-edged,** skerp; ~**-eyed,** skerp van gesig; ~**ly,** vurig; skerp; diep, besonder; ~**ness,** skerpheid, skerpte; vurigheid; lewendigheid; gretigheid, happigheid; belangstelling; ~**-scented,** skerp van reuk; ~**-witted,** geestig, gevat, slim, skrander, skerpsinnig.
keep, (n) bewaring, sorg, hoede; onderhoud; toesig; slottoring, vestingtoring, kasteeltoring; losies; voedsel, kos; *EARN one's* ~, in jou eie onderhoud voorsien; jou kos en klere verdien; *EARN its* ~, die koste dek; *FOR* ~*s,* om te hou; *PLAY for* ~*s,* in erns speel; (v) (kept), hou; oppas, bewaar, behoed, bêre; onderhou ('n persoon); jou hou aan; vier; nakom, in ag neem; aanhou, in voorraad hê (goedere); bly in (kamer); ophou; voortgaan, aangaan met; goed bly (vleis); ~ *ACCOUNTS,* boekhou; ~ *ALIVE,* aan die lewe bly; in die lewe hou; ~ *up APPEARANCES,* die skyn bewaar; ~ *an APPOINTMENT,* 'n afspraak hou; ~ *AT,* aanhou met; volhard; ~ *AWAY,* weghou, afhou; ~ *BACK,* terughou, weerhou; onderdruk; ~ *one's BALANCE,* jou ewewig bewaar; ~ *the BALL rolling,* die saak aan die gang hou; ~ *(to) one's BED,*

in die bed bly, die bed hou; ~ *BODY and soul together*, siel en liggaam aanmekaarhou; ~ *BOOKS*, boekhou; ~ *CLEAR*, uit die pad bly; ~ *someone in clothes*, iem. van klere voorsien; ~ *COMING*, aanhou kom; ~ *COMPANY*, geselskap hou; ~ *one's COUNSEL*, jou mond hou; ~ *COOL*, koel hou (bly); kalm bly; ~ *COUNT*, tel; telling hou; ~ *one's COUNTENANCE*, 'n ernstige gesig bewaar; ~ *up COURAGE*, moed hou; ~ *DARK*, geheim hou; ~ *a DIARY*, 'n dagboek hou; ~ *one's DISTANCE*, op 'n afstand bly; ~ *DOWN*, bedwing, in toom hou; onderdruk; ~ *one's END up*, jou man staan; jou deel bydra; ~ *EXPENSES down*, uitgawes beperk; ~ *FAITH*, woord hou; ~ *one's FEET*, op die voete bly; ~ *the FIELD*, die slagveld behou; ~ *FIT*, fiks bly; ~ *FROM*, afhou; jou onthou van; ~ *GARRISON*, in garnisoen bly; *GOD* ~ *you*, mag God jou bewaar; ~ *someone GOING*, iem. aan die gang hou; ~ *something GOING*, iets aan die gang hou; iets gaande hou; iets in stand hou; ~ *one's GROUND*, jou terrein behou; standhou; ~ *someone GUESSING*, iem. in die duister hou; ~ *your HAIR on!*, moenie kwaad word nie!; ~ *in HAND*, beheers; ~ *out of HARM'S way*, uit die gevaar bly (hou); ~ *in good HEALTH*, gesond bly, ~ *late HOURS*, laat opbly; ~ *open HOUSE*, gasvry wees; ~ *HOUSE*, huishou; ~ *IN*, inhou; laat skoolsit, op skool hou; in toom hou; ~ *down INSECTS*, insekte bedwing; ~ *up with the JONESES*, graag in tel wees; byhou by die bure; ~ *within the LAW*, binne die perke v.d. wet bly; ~ *to the LEFT*, links hou; ~ *a LOOK-OUT*, wag hou; *the MEAT won't* ~, die vleis sal bederf; ~ *in MIND*, daaraan dink; in gedagte hou; voor oë hou; onthou; ~ *MOVING*, aan die gang bly; aanstap; ~ *OFF*, v.d. lyf hou; ~ *OFF the grass!*, bly v.d. gras af; ~ *ON*, bly vashou; ~ *it ON*, hou dit aan; ~ *OUT*, buite hou; buite bly; ~ *PACE with*, bybly; op hoogte bly; ~ *PEACE*, die vrede bewaar; ~ *the POT boiling*, die pot aan die kook hou; ~ *a PROMISE*, 'n belofte nakom; ~ *in REPAIR*, onderhou; in stand hou, ~ *to one's ROOM*, in die kamer bly; ~ *the SADDLE*, in die saal bly; ~ *SAYING*, gedurig sê; ~ *a SECRET*, 'n geheim bewaar; *better* ~ *now than SEEK anon*, liewer aldag wat as een dag sat; ~ *SHOP*, 'n winkel hou; ~ *SILENCE*, stilbly; ~ *SOME till more come*, moenie ou skoene weggooi voor jy nuwes het nie; moenie die vulletjie se rug afry voordat jy die groot perd het nie; moenie vuil water weggooi voor jy skones het nie; ~ *up one's SPIRITS*, moed hou; ~ *STEP*, in die pas bly; ~ *STRAIGHT*, op die regte pad bly; ~ *one's TEMPER*, kalm bly; ~ *TIME*, die maat hou; goed loop (oorlosie); ~ *TO*, jou hou aan; bly by; ~ *TOGETHER*, bymekaarhou; bymekaar bly; ~ *in TOUCH with*, in voeling bly met; ~ *TRACK of*, die spoor volg van; ~ *UNDER*, teenhou; onderdruk, bedwing; ~ *UP*, ophou; wakker bly; onderhou; volhou; ~ *UP with*, byhou; ~ *it UP*, aanhou; aan die gang hou, hou so aan; ~ *a person WAITING*, iem. laat wag; ~ *WATCH*, die wag hou; ~ *out of the WAY*, uit die pad bly; ~ *WELL*, gesond bly; goed bly, goed hou; ~ *to the WIND*, bo die wind hou.

keep'er, bewaarder, bewaker, wagter, versorger, opsigter; jagopsigter; veiligheidsring; goedhouer, varsblyer; sipier; lis, sluitknip; anker (van magneet); doelwagter; *K*~ *of the ARCHIVES*, argivaris; *am I my BROTHER'S* ~ ?, is ek my broer se hoeder?; *K* ~ *of the PRIVY Seal*, Bewaarder van die Geheime Seël (Eng.); ~ **pin**, borgpen, sluitpen; ~ **screw**, borgskroef.

keep'ing, (n) hoede, bewaring; onderhoud; ooreenstemming; verhouding; kos; *IN his* ~, onder sy hoede; *NOT be in* ~, uit die toon val; *OUT of* ~ *with*, nie strook nie met; ~ *PROPERTIES (QUALITIES)*, duursaamheid, goedhouvermoë; ~ *of RECORDS*, rekordhouding; *in SAFE* ~, in veilige bewaring; *in* ~ *WITH*, in ooreenstemming met; (a) goedhou=.

keep: ~ **-net**, hounet (hengelterm); ~ **-plate**, sluitplaat; ~ **sake**, herinnering, aandenking, gedagtenis.

Kees'hond, Keeshond.
keeve, kuip, brouvat, vat; wasvat (myn).
keg, vaatjie.
Kei'-apple, keiappel, dingaansappel(koos) *(Doryalis caffra)*.
kelp, kelp, ruwe soda, assoda, loogas.
kel'pie¹, Australiese Skaaphond.
kel'pie², **kel'py**, (..pies), watergees.
kel'son, kolsem.
Kelt = **Celt**.
ke'lvin, kelvin.
kemp, uitkamsel; steekhaar, steekhaarwol; ~ **y**, vol steekhare; ~ *y wool*, steekhaarwol.
ken¹, (n) gesigskring; oog, blik; bereik (verstand); waarneming; *BEYOND one's* ~, bokant iem. se vuurmaakplek; *OUT of* ~, nie meer te sien nie; *WITHIN* ~, in sig.
ken², (v) ken; weet; herken.
ke'naf, kenaf, veselplant.
ken'nel¹, (n) straatsloot, voor.
ken'nel², (n) dierehawe, dierehotel; hondehok; jaghond; telery; hok, krot; (v) **(-led)**, in 'n hok hou; bêre; ~ **-dog**, hokhond; ~ **-raker**, rommelraper, papieropteller.
kenos'is, kenosis, aflegging, lediging.
kenot'ic, kenoties; ~ **ism**, kenotisisme.
kenotron', kenotron.
Ken'tish, Kents; ~ **cousins**, ver familie; ~ **crow**, bontkraai; ~ **fire**, langdurige toejuiging.
kent'ledge, ballasyster.
Kentu'cky grass, swenkgras.
Ke'nya, Kenia.
kep'i, **kép'i**, Franse militêre pet, kepi.
keps, hysbakruste, hyshokruste.
kept, onderhou; gehou; *a* ~ *woman*, maitresse; *kyk* **keep**, (v).
keram'ic = **ceramic**.
kerati'asis, verhoorning; horingstof, keratiase.
ke'ratin, kerateni, keratine.
keratiniza'tion, verhoorning.
ker'atinize, verhoring.
keratit'is, horingvliesontsteking, keratitis.
keratom'a, horingsuil, keratoom.
ke'ratose, (n) keratose; (a) horingagtig.
kerau'nometer, keraunometer, weerligmeter.
kerb, sypaadjie, randsteen; straatrand; *on the* ~, op straat; ~ **cock**, straatkraan; ~ **ing**, beranding; randstene; ~ **stone**, randsteen.
kerch'ief, kopdoek; (sak)doek.
kerf, kerf, insnyding, keep.
kerm'es, kermes, skildluis; karmoesyn.
kermes'se, kermes(se).
ker'mis, kermis.
kern'el, pit, kern; *he that will eat the* ~ *must break the nut*, jy moet jou inspan om sukses te behaal; eers inspan en dan sukses.
ke'rosene, paraffien, lampolie, keroseen.
ke'rrie, kierie.
kers'ey, karsaai.
kers'eymere, kasjmier.
kes'trel, toringvalk; rooivalk; *lesser* ~, kleinrooivalk.
ketch, **(-es)**, kaag.
ketch'up, tamatiesous, kruiesous, ketjap.
ketogen'esis, ketogenese.
ketogen'ic, ketogeen.
ket'one, ketoon.
keto'sis, ketose.
ket'tle, ketel; *a pretty* ~ *of fish*, 'n mooi spul; 'n mooi affêre; ~ **drum**, keteltrom, pouk; ~ **drummer**, trompslaner, tamboerslaner; ~ **maker**, ketelmaker.
kev'el, kruithout (skip); ~ **hammer**, klipkappershamer.
kew'pie, kupido'tjie, selluoïdepop.
kex, droë stingel.
key, (n) **(-s)**, sleutel; toets, klawer (klavier); toonaard; toon(soort) (musiek); pen, wig; sleutelpunt; spie; sluitsteen; balkband (bouwerk); seingewer; vertaling (uit bv. Latyn); antwoordboek (somme); tros gevleuelde saad; slot (geweer); *in ANOTHER* ~, op 'n ander toon; *GET (have) the* ~ *of the street*, uitgesluit wees; *GOLDEN (silver)* ~, omkoop=

geld; *under LOCK and* ~, agter slot en grendel; *OFF* ~, vals; *in the SAME* ~, in dieselfde trant; (v) sluit; vaswig; span (snare); stem (klavier); opdryf (masjien); ~ *up,* stem (musiekinstrument); die standaard verhoog; opwek; opskroef, aanhits, aan=dryf; (a) belangrik, sleutel=; ~**-basket,** sleutel=mandjie; ~**-bearer,** sleuteldraer; ~**-bed,** spygleuf, wigholte; ~**-bit,** sleutelbaard; ~**board,** toetsbord, manuaal, klawerbord; skakelbord; ~**board cover,** klavieropertjie; ~ **bolt,** hamerbout; ~**-bone,** sleutelbeen; ~**-bugle,** klepbeuel; ~ **container,** sleutel=houer; ~**-clog,** sleutelplankie; ~**ed,** met toetse; ~ **figure,** sleutelfiguur; ~**hole,** sleutelgat; ~**hole-cover,** sleutelgatplaatjie; ~**hole-saw,** steeksaag, spitssaag, skropsaag; ~**-hook,** sleutelhaak; ~ **industry,** sleutelnywerheid, sleutelbedryf, grond=bedryf; ~**ing,** kleinwerk, wigwerk; ~**less,** sonder sleutel; ~ **man,** sleutelfiguur; ~ **map,** hoofkaart, grondkaart; ~**-money,** sleutelgeld, sleuteldeposito; ~ **move,** sleutelset (skaak); ~**note,** grondtoon; ~**note address,** hoofrede; ~ **piece,** sluitstuk; ~**-pin,** spy; ~**-pipe,** sleutelpyp ~**-plan,** sleutelplan; ~**-plate,** stamplaat; beslag; ~ **position,** sleutelposi-sie; ~**-rack,** sleutelbord; ~**-ring,** sleutelring; ~**-screw,** skroefsleutel; ~ **seat,** penholte; ~**-spanner,** moersleutel; ~ **stone,** sluitsteen; hoeksteen; ~ **way,** spygleuf; spygroef; penholte; ~**-web,** sleutelbaard; ~**word,** slagwoord, sleutelwoord, trefwoord.
kha'ki, (n) kakie (stof, kleur); (a) kakiekleurig; ~**-bush,** kakiebos; ~**-coloured,** kakiekleurig; ~ **shirt,** kakiehemp; ~ **trousers,** kakiebroek; ~**-weed,** kakiebos.
khal'ifa, etc. = **caliph,** ens.
khan[1], goewerneur, vors, prins, khan.
khan[2], herberg, karavansera(i).
khan'ate, khanaat.
Khartoum', Khartoem.
khedive', onderkoning, khedive.
kib'ble[1], (n) hysemmer.
kib'ble[2], (v) grof maal; ~**r,** breker.
kibbutz', **(-im),** kibboets, gemeenskapsplaas.
kibe, (swerende) winterhakskeen; *gall (tread on) a person's* ~*s,* iem. te na kom.
ki'bosh, onsin, kaf; *put the* ~ *on,* 'n end maak aan.
kick, (n) skop (perd, geweer); skok; teensin, beswaar, verset; skopper; holte (bottel); krag, pit; (pl) skop=pens (albasterspel); *have a good DEAL of* ~ *left,* sy gô is nog lank nie uit nie; oud maar nog nie koud nie; *GET the* ~, ontslaan word; *GET a* ~ *out of,* behae skep in; *receive more* ~*s than HALFPEN-CE,* meer slae as kos kry; *a* ~ *in the PANTS,* 'n skop onder die agterstel; *more* ~*s than THANKS,* meer stank as dank; (v) skop; jou versit; ~ *ACROSS,* dwars skop; ~ *AGAINST something,* beswaar teen iets maak; in opstand teen iets kom; ~ *AT,* skop na; skop teen; in opstand kom teen; ~ *the BUCKET,* bokveld toe gaan; lepel in die dak steek; ~ *DOWNSTAIRS,* die trap afsmyt; ~ *up a DUST,* lawaai maak; ~ *one's HEELS,* lank moet wag; ~ *up one's HEELS,* agteropskop; na sy kwas skop; ~ *IN,* inskop; lepel in die dak steek; ~ *OFF,* afskop; uitskop (skoene); ~ *OUT,* uitsmyt, uit=skop; ~ *OVER,* oorskop; ~ *against the PRICKS,* die versene teen die prikkels slaan; ~ *up a ROW,* lawaai maak; raas, rusie maak; ~ *over the TRA-CES,* uit die band spring; onklaar trap (raak); ~ *UPSTAIRS,* met 'n pos paai; ~**-back,** hewige reaksie, terugstoot; gunsloon; ~**er,** skopper; skop=perige perd; dwarsskop; ~**ing,** geskop; skopwerk; ~**-off,** inskop; afskop; beginskop; ~**-plate,** skut=plaat; ~**-pleat,** stapplooi.
kick'shaw, kleinigheid; beuselary; snuistery; spoggery.
kick'-starter, trapaansitter.
kid[1], (n) boklam; bokvel; sagte leer, glacé, bokleer; kind, snuiter; (pl) jongspan; *a mere* ~, 'n pure (bog)kind; (v) **(-ded),** lam.
kid[2], (v) **(-ded),** vir die gek hou, gekskeer; kul, fop, bedrieg; *don't* ~ *him,* moet hom nie kul nie.
kid'dish, kinderagtig; dartel.

kid'ding, kullery, foppery, flousery.
kid'dle, fuik, visweer, viswal.
kidd'y, (kiddies), boklammetjie; snuiter, kêreltjie, ventjie, kleintjie, tjokkertjie.
kid' glove, leerhandskoen, glacéhandskoen; *handle with* ~*s,* baie versigtig behandel; sag behandel; ~ **treatment,** sagte behandeling.
kid'ling, klein bokkie.
kid'nap, **(-ped),** wegvoer, ontvoer, steel ('n kind); skaak; ~**per,** ontvoerder, skaker, mensdief, kin=derdief; ~**ping,** ontvoering, skaking, menseroof, wegvoering.
kid'ney, (**-s**), nier; aard, soort, slag; *of the right* ~, van die regte soort; ~ **basin,** vangbakkie; ~ **bean,** sny=boontjie; boerboontjie; ~ **disease,** nierkwaal; ~**-form,** ~**-shaped,** niervormig; ~**-stone,** niersteen, nefriet; ~ **suet,** niervet.
kie'selguhr, infusorieëaarde, kieselgoer, diatomeë=aarde.
Kiku'yu, Kikoejoe; **K**~ **grass,** kikoejoe(gras).
kil'derkin, vaatjie.
kill, (n) doodmaak; slagting; jagopbrengs, dooie dier; doodgemaakte dier; *in at the* ~, aanwesig by die end; (v) doodmaak, om die lewe bring, doodkry, doodslaan; afmaak; slag; vermoor, vernietig; ver=ongeluk (wetsontwerp); ~ *a BALL,* 'n bal teenhou; 'n bal 'n mokerhou toedien; ~ *two BIRDS with one stone,* twee vlieë met een klap slaan; *a case of* ~ *or CURE,* daarop of daaronder; *DRESSED to* ~, fyn uitgevat; ~ *with KINDNESS,* met vriendelikheid oorweldig; *LAUGH fit to* ~ *oneself,* jou doodlag; ~ *OFF,* afmaak; laat doodgaan; uitroei; ~ *TIME,* die tyd verdryf; ~**-devil,** draaiaas; ~**ed,** geval, ge=sneuwel; gedood; *be* ~*ed in battle,* sneuwel; ~**er,** doodmaker; moordenaar; slagter; mensvreter (leeu, haai); ~**ing,** (n) doding, doodmaak; moord; doodslag, slagting; (a) dodelik, moordend; hartver=skeurend; noodlottig; oorweldigend, onweerstaan=baar; ~**joy,** spelbederwer, suurpruim; ~**-time,** tyd=verdryf, tydkorting.
kiln, oond, steenoond; ~**-dry,** (..**dried**), kunsmatig droog, in 'n oond droog; ~**-drying,** oonddroging; ~**-hole,** bek van 'n oond.
kil'o, **(-s),** *abbr. of* **kilogramme, kilometre,** kilo.
kil'ocycle, kiloperiode.
kil'ogram(me), kilogram.
kil'olitre, kiloliter.
kil'ometer, kil'ometre, kilometer.
kil'owatt, kilowatt.
kilt, (n) Skotse rokkie; (v) opgord, opneem; plooi; ~**ed,** geplooi; met 'n Skotse rokkie aan; ~**ie,** rok=soldaat; Skot, Bergskot.
kim'berlite, blougrond, kimberliet.
kimon'o, **(-s),** kimono.
kin, (n) familie, bloedverwant, maagskap; *he has nei-ther KITH nor* ~, hy het nòg kind nòg kraai; *NEXT of* ~, naasbestaande; (a): ~ *to,* familie van, verwant aan.
kinch, **(-es),** lissie met 'n skuifknoop.
kin'chin, kind; ~ **lay,** kinderbesteling.
kin'cob, goudbrokaat.
kind[1], (n) soort; genre; geslag; aard, natuur; ge=aardheid, aanleg; *AFTER its* ~, in sy soort; *ALL* ~*s of,* allerhande soorte; *the BEST of its* ~, die beste in sy soort; *EVERY* ~ *of people,* allerhande soorte mense; *a* ~ *of GENTLEMAN,* 'n soort me=neer; *HUMAN* ~, die mensdom; *NOTHING of the* ~*!,* niks daarvan nie!; *OF a* ~, nie v.d. beste nie; *PAY in* ~, in natura (goedere) betaal; *RECEIVE in* ~, in goedere (natura) ontvang; *REPAY (pay back) in* ~, in gelyke munt betaal; *SOMETHING of the* ~, iets v.d. aard; *THIS* ~ *of thing,* hierdie soort ding; *TWO of a* ~, twee van dieselfde soort; *of TWO* ~*s,* tweërlei; *WHAT* ~ *of?,* watter soort?
kind[2], (a) vriendelik, minsaam; lief, goed(hartig); wel=willend, liefdevol, beminlik; goedig, goeierig; *BE so* ~ *as to,* wees so vriendelik om; ~ *to a FAULT,* eintlik sleg van goeiigheid; *with* ~ *REGARDS,* met vriendelike groete.
kin'dergarten, kindertuin, kindergarten, kleuter=skool, kleinkinderskool.

kind'-hearted, goedhartig, gemoedelik; ~ness, goedhartigheid, goedaardigheid.

kin'dle, aansteek; aanstook, laat ontvlam; aan die brand raak, vuur vat; verlewendig, aanhits; *don't ~ the fire*, moenie die vuur aanblaas nie; moenie die gevoelens gaande maak nie.

kind'liness, vriendelikheid, welwillendheid, goedhartigheid.

kind'ling, (die) aanblaas, brand; vuurmaakhoutjies, fynhout, fyn houtjies; (pl) aanmaakhout.

kind'ly, (a) goedhartig, goedaardig; sag, vriendelik, aangenaam; (adv) goedgunstiglik; *TAKE ~ to*, ingenome wees met; ~ *TELL him*, wees so goed om hom te sê.

kind'ness, vriendelikheid; weldaad, welwillendheid, vriendskapsdiens; geneentheid, goedgesindheid, goeiigheid, goedheid.

kin'dred, (n) verwantskap; familie, bloedverwante; (a) verwant; gelyksoortig; aanverwant; ~ *soul*, geesverwant.

kine, (old pl of **cow**), koeie.

kin'ema, *kyk* **cinema.**

kinemat'ic, kinematies; ~s, bewegingsleer, kinematika

kinemat'ograph, etc., *kyk* **cinematograph**, ens.

kinet'ic, kineties, bewegings-, bewegend; ~ **energy**, draaiingsenergie; ~ **phenomenon**, bewegingsverskynsel; ~s, bewegingsleer, kinetiek; ~ **theory**, kinetiese teorie.

kine'sics, kinese.

king, (n) koning, vors; heer (by kaarte); koning (by skaak); dam (damspel), ~ *of the BEASTS*, koning v.d. diere; ~'s *BLUE*, koningsblou; *not to CALL the ~ your uncle*, te ryk vir die koning wees; ~ *of CLUBS*, klawerheer; ~'s *COUNSEL*, koningsadvokaat, ryksadvokaat; ~ *of DIAMONDS*, ruitensheer; ~'s *ENGLISH*, Standaardengels; ~'s *EVIDENCE*, kroongetuie; ~'s *EVIL*, koningseer, skrofulose, kliertuberkulose; ~ *of HEARTS*, hartensheer; *K ~ OF ~'s*, Koning v.d. konings; ~'s *PEG*, sjampanje en brandewyn; ~ *of SPADES*, skoppensheer; ~'s *SPEECH*, troonrede; ~ *of TRUMPS*, troefheer; *the ~ can do no WRONG*, die koning is onskendbaar; ~'s *YELLOW*, koningsgeel; ~**-at-arms**, wapenkoning; ~**bolt**, hoofbout; ~**craft**, regeerkuns, staatkunde; ~**cup**, botterblom.

king'dom, koninkryk; *ANIMAL (vegetable, mineral) ~*, diereryk (planteryk, mineraleryk); ~ *COME*, die hiernamaals; *send someone to ~ COME*, iem. na die ander wêreld help; ~ *of HEAVEN*, die Koninkryk v.d. Hemele.

king: ~ **fish**, koningmakriel; ~**fisher**, visvanger; ysvoël; ~**hood**, koningskap; ~**less**, koningloos; ~**let**, koninkie; ~**like**, koninklik, vorstelik; ~**liness**, koninklikheid; ~**ling**, koninkie, bogkoning; ~**ly**, koninklik, vorstelik; ~ **penguin**, koningpikkewyn; ~ **pin**, skamelbout, krinkspil; ~**post**, hoofstyl (van dak); ~**ship**, koningskap; ~**size**, ekstra grootte; ~ **truss**, hoofstylkap; ~**-wood**, vioolboomhout, tulphout.

kink, (n) kinkel; nuk, gril, eienaardigheid; kunsgreep; *moral ~*, sedelike afwyking; (v) 'n slag maak, kink; ~**y**, vol kinkels, kinkelrig; vol nukke.

kin: ~**less**, sonder verwante; ~'s**folk**, familie, verwante; ~**ship**, stamverwantskap, bloedverwantskap; ~**s'man**, stamverwant, bloedverwant, nabestaande, familielid; ~**s'woman**, bloedverwante, vroulike familielid.

kiosk', kiosk; winkeltjie, kraampie, stalletjie, hoekie; tuinhuisie.

klp¹, kalfsvel, vel van 'n jong dier, kalfsleer.

kip², losieshuis; bed, kooi.

kipp'er, (n) mannetjiesalm; gerookte haring, kipper; (v) sout en rook; ~*ed herring*, gerookte haring, kipper; bokkem, bokkom.

kirk, kerk; *the nearer the ~ the farther from God*, hoe nader aan Rome, hoe slegter Christen; ~ **session**, kerkraadsvergadering; ~**yard**, kerkhof.

kirsch'(wasser), (G.), kersiebrandewyn.

kis'met, noodlot, fatum, kismet.

kiss, (n) (-es), soen, kus; ligte aanraking, klots (biljart); *BLOW a ~*, 'n kushandjie gee, 'n handkus gooi; jou onderwerp; *the ~ of JUDAS*, 'n Judaskus; *LOUD ~*, smak; (v) soen, kus; lig aanraak, klots (biljart); ~ *AWAY*, wegsoen; ~ *the BOOK*, op die Bybel sweer; ~ *the DUST*, in die stof byt; jou in die stof verneder; ~ *and be FRIENDS*, dit afsoen; ~ *GOODBYE*, 'n afskeidsoen gee; *you can ~ him GOODBYE*, dis die laaste sien v.d. blikkantien; ~ *GOODNIGHT*, 'n nagsoen gee; ~ *the GROUND*, op jou gesig val; ~ *one's HAND to*, iem. 'n kushandjie toewuif; ~ *the ROD*, jou deemoedig aan straf onderwerp; ~**able**, om te soen; soenbaar; ~**-curl**, oorkrulletjie, koketkrulletjie, spoeglok; ~**er**, soener; ~**ing**, gesoen, soenery; ~**ing-crust**, sagte korsie; ~**ing-gate**, draaihek; ~**in-the-ring**, 'n speletjie; ~**-me-at-the-garden-gate**, hoe-langer-hoe-liewer *(Sacifraga umbrosa)*; ~**-me-quick**, kappie; voorkopkrul; ~**proof**, soenvas, soenbestand.

kist, kis.

kit¹, katjie.

kit², klein viooltjie.

kit³, knapsak, ransel; gereedskap; uitrusting, mondering; reisbenodigdhede; balie, kuip, houtmelkemmer, vaatjie; vismandjie; ~**bag**, paksak, knapsak, ransel; uitrustingsak; gereedskapsak; ~**box**, gereedskapskis.

kit'-cat (portrait), bolyfportret.

kitch'en, kombuis; ~**-boy**, kombuisbediende, kombuisjong; ~ **broom**, kombuisbesem; ~ **dresser**, kombuiskas; ~ **Dutch**, Kombuishollands; ~ **equipment**, kombuisuitrusting; ~ **English**, Kombuisengels; ~**er**, stoof; kok (klooster); groot stoof.

kitchenette', kombuisie, minikombuis; popkombuis.

kitch'en: ~ garden, groentetuin; ~**-girl**, kombuishulp; ~**-knave**, kombuisjong; ~ **ladle**, potlepel; ~ **language**, kombuistaal; ~ **Latin**, potjieslatyn; ~**maid**, kombuishulp; ~ **midden**, afvalhoop; ~ **physic**, versterkende kos; ~ **range**, stoof; ~ **salt**, kombuissout; ~ **saw**, vleissaag; ~ **shower**: *give a ~ shower*, bruidskombuis hou; ~ **sink**, opwasbak; ~ **spoon**, potlepel; ~**-stuff**, groente; kombuisbenodigdhede; ~ **tea**, kombuistee, bruidskombuis; ~ **utensils**, kombuisgereedskap; ~ **ware**, kombuiswa re; -gerei; -goed.

kite, (n) vlieër; kuikendief; inhalige mens; skoorsteenwissel; *fly a ~*, 'n proefballon oplaat opgaan; (v) sweef; oplaat; skoorsteenwissels trek; ~ **balloon**, kabelballon; ~**-flier**, vlieëroplater; wisselruiter; ~**-flying**, (die) oplaat van 'n vlieër ('n proefballon); probeerslag; wisselruitery.

kith, vriende, bekendes, kennisse; ~ *and KIN*, vriende en na(as)bestaandes; *have neither ~ nor KIN*, kind nog kraai hê; nóg vriende nóg familie hê; *one's OWN ~ and kin*, jou eie vlees en bloed.

kitsch, kitsch, waardelose (onegte) kuns.

kitt'en, (n) katjie; flerrie; (v) katjies kry; ~**ish**, speels, dartel.

kltt'iwake, drietonige seemeeu.

kit'tle, kielierig; moeilik, lastig; gewaag, gevaarlik; ~ *cattle*, moeilike mense.

kitt'y¹, (kitties), katjie, kietsie.

kitt'y², pot (geld); kontantgeld, kontantlaai.

kitt'y³, (kitties), witte(tjie) (rolbal).

Ki'wi, Kiwi, Nieu-Seelander; lid van Nieu-Seelandse sportspan.

ki'wi, kiwi; ~ **fruit**, kiwivrug.

klax'on, motortoeter.

kleptoman'ia, steelmanie, steelsug, kleptomanie; ~**c**, kleptomaan, steelsieke; -cal, kleptomanies.

klieg (light), kollig; klieglig, flits(lig)

klip'springer, klipspringer.

kloof, (-s), kloof.

knack, slag, handigheid, behendigheid, kuns; gewoonte, hebbelikheid; *GET THE ~ of*, die slag kry, op dreef kom met; *HAVE the ~ of doing something*, die slag hê om iets te doen.

knack'er, perdeslagter; sloper; ~'s **yard**, perdeslagtery; ~**y**, perdeslagtery.

knack'ish, knack'y, handig, behendig.

knag, kwas, knoes; ~**gy**, knoesterig, kwasterig.

knap¹, (n) bultjie, verhewenheid.
knap², (v) **(-ped)**, breek, stukkend slaan; afknak; ~ **per** klipbreker.
knap'sack, bladsak, knapsak.
knar, kwas, knoets; ~**red**, knoesterig, kwasterig.
knave, skurk, skelm, skobbejak; boer (kaarte); ska= vuit; *there is no pack of CARDS without a* ~, elke trop het sy swart skaap; ~ *of CLUBS*, klawerboer; ~ *of DIAMONDS*, ruitensboer; *ONCE a* ~ *always a* ~, wie een maal steel, is altyd 'n dief; ~ *of SPADES*, skoppensboer; ~ *of TRUMPS*, troef= boer.
knav'ery, skelmery, bedrieëry, skavuitstreek; *a piece of* ~, 'n skurkestreek.
knav'ish, skurkagtig, skelmagtig; ~ *trick*, skurk= streek; ~**ness**, skurkagtigheid, skelmagtigheid.
knead, knee (knie); kleitrap; brei (klei); ~*ed in the same trough*, van dieselfde stoffasie; ~**able**, knie= baar; ~**er**, knieër; **kniemasjien;** ~**ing**, (die) knie, geknie, knieëry; ~**ing-trough**, knieskottel, knie= bak, kniekom.
knee, (n) knie; kniestuk; kromhout (tegn.); *BE on one's* ~*s to*, gekniel wees voor; *BEATEN to one's* ~*s*, totaal verslaan; *BEND (bow) the* ~, die knie buig; *BRING someone to his* ~*s*, icm. platslaan; iem. kleinkry; *GO down on one's* ~*s*, op die knieë val; *on the* ~*s of the GODS*, in die skoot v.d. gode; *OFFER a* ~ *to*, op die knieë neem; *PUT (take) across one's* ~, oor die knie (skoot) trek; *have WEAK* ~*s*, 'n papbroek wees; (v) op die knieë val; knieë kry (van 'n broek); met die knie aanraak; ~**action**, knievering; ~**band**, knieverband; ~**bone**, knieskyf; ~**boot**, kapstewel, waterstewel; ~**breeches**, kniebroek; ~**cap**, knieskyf; knieskut (by voetbal); ~**d**, met knieë; ~**deep**, kniediep, tot aan die knieë; ~**guard**, knieskut; ~**halter**, knie= halter; ~**halter marks**, kniehaltermerke; ~**high**, kniehoog; ~**joint**, kniegewrig.
knee, (knelt), kniel, op die knieë val; ~ *DOWN*, neer= kniel; ~ *TO*, kniel voor; ~**er**, knieler; kniekus= sing.
kneel'ing, kniel; ~**chair**, bidbankie; ~**cushion**, knielkussing; ~**mat**, knielmat.
knee: ~**pan**, knieskyf; ~**piece**, kniestuk; kromhout; ~**riem**, spantou; ~**shaped**, knievormig; ~**sprin= ging**, knievering; ~**strap**, spantou; ~**timber**, kromhout; ~**tribute**, knieval.
knell, (n) doodsklok; gelui; *RING the* ~ *of*, uitlui; *his* ~ *has been RUNG*, sy laaste uur het geslaan; (v) lui; die doodsklok lui; aankondig.
knelt, *kyk* **kneel**.
knew, *kyk* **know**, (v).
knick'erbocker(s), gespebroek, kniebroek, pofbroek, sakbroek.
knick'ers, kniebroek; vrouebroek.
knick'-knack, snuistery, tierlantyntjie; (pl) goedjies; ~**ery**, snuisterye; ~**ish**, prullerig.
knife, (n) (knives), mes; lem; *BEFORE one can say* ~, in 'n kits; *HAVE one's* ~ *into someone*, 'n wrok koester teen iem; op iem. pik; *PLAY a good* ~ *and fork*, 'n goeie mondslag slaan; lekker weglê; *have a* ~ *at someone's THROAT*, die mes op iem. se keel sit; *WAR to the* ~, stryd op lewe en dood; (v) met 'n mes steek, sny; met 'n mes verf aanbring; ~**blade**, lem; ~**board**, slypplank, mesplank; ~**boy**, messkoonmaker; ~**cleaner**, mespoetser, skoon= maakmasjien; ~**edge**, snykant; meskant (tegn.); ~**grinder**, messlyper; ~**haft**, meshef; ~**handle**, meshef; ~**point**, mespunt; ~**polish**, slyppoeier; ~**powder**, mespoeier; ~**r**, soolafwerker; ~**rest**, meslêer; ~**sharpener**, slypstaal, messlyper; ~**sheath**, messkede, messak; ~**tray**, messebak.
knif'ing, messtekery.
knight, (n) ridder; perd (skaakspel); ~ *BACHELOR*, ridder; ~ *BARONET*, baronet; *K*~ *of the BATH*, Ridder v.d. Badsorde; ~ *of the BRUSH*, ridder v.d. palet; ~ *COMMANDER*, ridder-komman= deur; ~ *ERRANT*, dwalende (swerwende) ridder; swerfridder; *K*~ *of the GARTER*, Ridder v.d. Kousband; ~ *of the HAMMER*, smid; ~ *HOSPI= TALLER*, hospitaalridder; gashuisprediker; *K*~ *of MALTA*, Johannesridder; ~ *of the NEEDLE (thimble)*, kleremaker, elleridder; ~ *of the PESTLE*, apteker; ~ *of the POST*, vals getuie; ~ *of the QUILL*, ridder v.d. pen; ~ *of the ROAD*, padrower; *K*~ *of the ROUND Table*, Ridder v.d. Tafelronde; *K*~ *of the RUEFUL countenance*, Rid= der v.d. Droewige Figuur; ~ *of the STICK*, letter= setter; ~ *of the YARDSTICK*, elleridder, klerema= ker; ~**age**, ridderskap; ~**errantry**, swerfridder= skap; ~**hood**, ridderskap; ridderorde; *order of* ~*hood*, ridderorde, lintjie; ~**liness**, ridderlikheid; ~**ly**, ridderlik; ~**service**, ridderdiens; ~**ship**, rid= derskap.
knit, **(-ted** or **knit)**, brei; saamvleg, verenig; saamtrek, frons; saamvoeg; jou nou verenig; ~ *the BROWS*, die winkbroue frons; die voorhoof rimpel; ~ *UP*, toebrei, toeknoop; verbind; tot 'n end bring, saam= vat, sluit; ~ **carpet**, baantapyt; ~ **cloth**, ~ **fabric**, breistof; ~**goods**, breiware; ~ **stocking**, gebreide kous; ~**ter**, breier; breimasjien.
knitt'ing, breigoed, breiwerk; gebrei; ~**bag**, breisak; ~**basket**, breimandjie; ~**case**, breinaaldekoker; ~**class**, breiklas; ~**cotton**, breigaring; ~**lesson**, breiles; **machine**, breimasjien; ~**needle**, brei= naald; ~**pattern**, breipatroon, ~**pin**, breipen; ~**sheath**, breipenskede; ~ **stitch**, breisteek; ~ **wool**, breiwol; ~ **work**, breiwerk; ~ **yarn**, breigaring; be= slaglyn (see).
knit'tle, toetreklyntjie (van tabaksak), ryglyntjie.
knit'wear, gebreide klere; breigoed.
knob, (n); knoets, knobbel; bult; klont; harspan, klapperdop; (v) **(-bed)**, knoppe maak; bulte gee; ~**bed**, kwasterig, knoes(t)erig, knopperig; ~**ble**, klein knoppie; bultjie; ~**bly**, ~**by**, knopperig; bul= terig; knoes(t)erig; ~ **bolt**, knopgrendel; ~**kerrie**, knopkierie; ~ **latch**, veerknopslot; ~**stick**, kierie, knots; onderkruiper; ~ **thorn**, knoppiesdoring *(Acacia nigrescens)*; ~**wood**, perdepram.
knock, (n) klop; aanklop (deur); stamp; klap, raps, slag; beurt (krieket); *there is a* ~, daar word ge= klop; *RECEIVE a hard* ~, 'n taai klap kry; *TAKE a* ~, 'n neerlaag ly; (v) slaan; klop (aan deur, in enjin); bons, stamp, stoot, klap; ~ *ABOUT*, rond= slenter, rondtrek; rondslinger; opdons; *be* ~*ed ABOUT*, baie te ly hê; pimpel en pers geslaan wees; ~ *AGAINST*, die kop stamp teen; slaan teen; ~ *AT*, aanklop; ~ *BACK*, na binne slaan; wegslaan; ~ *the BOTTOM out of*, in duie laat val; ~ *on the DOOR*, aan die deur klop; ~ *DOWN*, platslaan; toeslaan (op vendusie); neerslaan; omry; vermin= der; ~ *DOWN with a feather*, omblaas; ~ *someone into a cocked HAT*, iem. slaan dat sy ouma hom vir 'n eendvoël aansien; ~ *something on the HEAD*, iets die nekslag gee; ~ *one's HEAD*, die kop stamp; ~ *INTO*, inhamer; inslaan; ~ *INTO someone*, jou teen iem. vasloop; iem. raakloop; ~ *someone into the MIDDLE of next week*, iem. slaan dat hy opslae maak; iem. slaan dat hy ouma vir 'n eendvoël aansien; ~ *OFF 10c*, 10c afslaan; ~ *OFF work*, ophou werk; uitskei; ~ *his head OFF*, iem. lelik te lyf gaan; ~ *ON*, aanslaan (by rugby); ~ *OUT*, ver= slaan; 'n uitklophou gee, uitslaan; *be* ~*ed OVER*, omgery word; ~ *OVER*, omslaan; omry; ~ *to PIECES*, stukkend slaan; ~ *someone SIDE= WAYS*, iem. van sy stukke bring; ~ *SPOTS off someone*, iem. opdons (kafloop); ~ *TOGETHER*, aanmekaartimmer; ~ *UP*, haastig reël; 'n hoë tel= ling maak (krieket); iem. uit die bed jaag; uitput, poot-uit raak; swanger maak; *be* ~*ed UP*, kwaai toegetakel wees; poot-uit wees; ~ *someone into the middle of next WEEK*, iem. slaan dat hy opslae maak; ~**about**, (n) lawaaitoneel; (a) ru, wild, luid= rugtig; ~*about clothes*, slenterdrag, informele drag; ~**down**, uitklop=; ongemonteer (motors); ~**down blow**, uitklophou, nekslag; ~**down price**, reserweprys, minimumprys; ~**er**, klopper; ~**ing**, geklop; ~**ing-off time**, uitskeityd; ~**kneed**, met x-bene, met aankapknieë; swak; ~**knees**, x-bene, aankapknieë; ~**on**, aanslaan.
knock'-out, niksnuts; vegparty; knoeivandisie; knoeikoper; uitklophou; ~ **argument**, dooddoe= ner; ~ **blow**, uitklophou; ~ **competition**, uitval=

knoll

kompetisie, uitklopkompetisie; ~ **cup**, uitklopbeker.
knoll¹, hopie, knop, bultjie.
knoll², gelui.
knot, (n) knoop; strik; kwas; string; knoop (seemyl); blomfiguur; senuweeknoop; moeilikheid; wrong, bolla (hare); knoe(t)s, knobbel; bult; klont; groep, bende; *CUT the* ~, die knoop deurkap (deurhak); *cut the GORDIAN* ~, die Gordiaanse knoop deurhak; *tie a* ~ *in one's HANDKERCHIEF*, 'n knoop in die sakdoek maak; *TIE the* ~, die huwelik bevestig; *get oneself TIED into a* ~, jou laat vastrek; jou vasloop; jou in moeilikheid laat wikkel; *UNDO a* ~, 'n knoop losmaak; *UNRAVEL a* ~, 'n knoop ontwar; (v) (-ted), (aanmekaar)knoop; strik; vasbind; verbind; vasknoop; frons, saamtrek; verwikkel; ~ *a bow*, 'n strik knoop; ~**-grass**, varkgras, duisendknoop; ~**ted**, verward; geknoop, gekinkel; knoes(t)erig, knopperig; ~ *ted brows*, gefronste wenkbroue; ~**ting**, (die) knoop; knoopwerk; ~**ty**, geknoop; moeilik, lastig; ingewikkeld; netelig; kwasterig, gekwas, geknoes; *a* ~*ty point*, 'n moeilike saak; ~**-weed**, varkgras, duisendknoop; ~**work**, knoopwerk.
knout, (n) knoets; (v) met 'n knoets slaan.
know, (n) weet, wete; *be in the* ~, ingelig wees; (v) (**knew, -n**), weet; ken; verstaan; onderskei; herken; beken (vrou); ~ *ABOUT something*, van iets weet; ~ *ABSOLUTELY nothing of a thing*, soveel van iets weet as 'n kat van saffraan; *you'll* ~ *ALL about it*, jy sal dit hotagter kry; *for ALL one* ~ *s*, so wat jy kan; *for ALL you* ~, moontlik; *BEFORE you* ~ *where you are*, voor jy jou kom kry; ~ *BETTER than to*, verstandig genoeg wees om te; *you* ~ *BETTER*, jy weet van beter; ~ *BY*, herken aan; ~ *CARNALLY*, geslagsgemeenskap hê met; ~ *for CERTAIN*, seker weet; *COME to* ~, te wete kom; leer ken; ervaar; *not to* ~ *whether one is COMING or going*, nie hot of haar weet nie; ~ *exactly with whom you are DEALING*, weet watter vleis jy in die kuip het; ~ *for a FACT*, seker weet; *GET to* ~, leer ken; ~ *GOOD from evil*, goed van kwaad onderskei; *I'll HAVE you* ~, dit kan jy my glo; dit moet jy mooi verstaan; ~ *by HEART*, van buite ken; uit die hoof ken; *you'd LIKE to* ~, *wouldn't you?*, dis vir my om te weet en vir jou om uit te vind; *not* ~ *one's own MIND*, self nie weet wat jy wil hê nie; ~ *by NAME*, by naam ken; *NOT that I* ~ *of*, nie wat ek van weet nie; ~ *the ROPES*, die geklap v.d. sweep ken; *RUN all you* ~, hardloop so wat jy kan; ~ *by SIGHT*, van sien ken; ~ *a THING or two*, ouer as twaalf wees; nie 'n pampoen wees nie; ~ *WHAT is what*, ouer as tien wees; weet hoe die ding inmekaarsit; ~ *WHICH is which*, uitmekaar ken; ~ *a WOMAN*, 'n vrou beken; ~ **able**, te ken, kenbaar; weetbaar; ~**ableness**, kenbaarheid; weetbaarheid; ~**-all**, alweter, veelweter; *be a* ~*-all*, maak of jy die wysheid in pag het; ~**-how**, vaardigheid, kundigheid, slag, kenkundigheid, kenvaardigheid.
know'ing, (n) kennis, ken; wete; bekendheid; *there is no* ~, 'n mens kan nooit weet nie, (a) verstandig; kundig, vernuftig, bedrewe; slim, geslepe, uitgeslape; oulik; opsetlik, voorbedagtelik, willens en wetens, bewus; veelbetekenend; ~**ly**, op veelseggende manier, veelbetekenend; *insult someone* ~*ly*, iem. met opset beledig.
knowl'edge, kennis, kunde; wete; wetenskap; voorkennis; bekendheid; bewussyn; medewete; *COME to one's* ~, te wete kom; ter ore kom; *that is COMMON* ~, dis algemeen bekend; *to the BEST of my* ~, sover ek weet; na my beste wete; *FIRST-HAND* ~, eerstehandse kennis; *IN the* ~ *that*, in die bewussyn dat; ~ *is POWER*, kennis is mag; *WITHIN his* ~, aan hom bekend; *WITHOUT my* ~, buite my wete; sonder my medewete; sonder dat ek geweet het; *with a WORKING* ~ *of*, met 'n gang-

bare kennis van; redelik tuis wees in; ~ **able**, verstandig; kundig, goed ingelig.
known, bekend; *BECOME* ~, bekend raak; ~ *FOR*, bekend vir; *MAKE* ~, bekend maak; *WELL* ~, goed bekend.
know'-nothing, weet-nie, domkop, uilskuiken, domoor.
knuc'kle, (n) kneukel; hak, sprong, skenkel; knik (van skarnier); *NEAR the* ~, op die randjie van onwelvoeglikheid; *RAP someone over the* ~*s*, iem. op die vingers tik; (v) met die kneukels slaan; met albasters op kneukels skiet; ~ *down (under)*, toegee, swig, jou onderwerp; ~**bone**, kneukel, hotnotjie; ~**duster**, boksyster, vuisyster; ~**-joint**, vurkgewrig, kneukelgewrig; skarnierverbinding; knaklas (van dak); knik (rewolwer).
knurl, knoes; knop; knobbel; kartelrand; misvormde mens; ~**ed**, knopperig, knoes(t)erig; gekartel.
knur(r), knoes, knop; houtbal.
knut, jongkêrel; fat; *kyk ook* **nut**.
koa'la, koalabeer, buidelbeer.
kob', kabeljou.
kob'old, kabouter, myngees.
koe'doe = **koodoo**.
Koh'-i-noor, Koh-i-noor (Indiese diamant).
kohl, fyn antimoon.
kohlra'bi, raapkool.
koi'ne, koine; gemeenskaplike taal; omgangstaal.
kol'anut, *kyk* **cola-nut**.
kolkhoz', kolchos, kollektiewe plaas in Rusland.
kon'imeter, stofmeter, konimeter.
koo'doo, koedoe.
ku'peck, *kyk* **copeck**.
kop'je, kopp'ie, koppie.
Kor'an, Koran; ~**'ic**, Koraans, van die Koran.
Kore'an, (n) Koreaan; Koreaans (taal); (a) Koreaans.
kor'i bustard, gompou.
kor'ra, korra.
kosh'er, kosjer; ~ **meat**, kosjervleis.
kowtow', (n) diep buiging, voetval, salaam; (v) diep buig, salaam; vlei, kruip.
koum'iss, perdemelkdrank, koemis.
kourb'ash, **(-es)**, sambok, karwats; kats.
kraal, (n) kraal; (v) in 'n kraal jaag.
kraft, kraftpapier.
krait, krait (slang).
kra'ken, kraken, seemonster.
krans, krans.
krem'lin, kremlin; *the K* ~, die Kremlin; die Russiese regering.
krill, kril.
kris, kris, dolk.
Krish'na, Krisjna.
kro'na, kroon.
kron'e, kroon.
kromes'ky, kromeskie.
krum(m)horn, (G.), kromhoring.
kru'puk, kroepoek.
kryp'ton, kripton.
ku'da, katonkel, kuda.
kud'os, roem, eer, kudos.
ku'du = **koodoo**.
Ku' Klux-Klan', Ku-Klux-Klan.
kukumakran'ka, koekemakranka.
kul'ak, (-i), koelak.
kumm'el, kummel.
kum'quat, koemkwat.
kung fu, koeng foe, Chinese karate.
Kurd, Koerd; ~**ish**, (n) Koerdies (taal); (a) Koerdies; ~**istan**, Koerdistan.
kur'per, kurper *(Tilapia)*.
kus'tingsbrief, kustingsbrief, verkoperverband.
Kuwait', **Kuweit'**, Koewcit.
kwash'iorkor, kwasjiorkor.
ky'anize, kianiseer.
kym'ograph, kimograaf.
Ky'rie (ele'ison), Kyrie (eleison).
kythos'is, kitose.

L

l, (ls, l's), l.
la, la.
laag'er, (n) laer; **(v)** laer trek; ~ **commandant,** laerkommandant; ~ **ed,** gelaer.
lab = laboratory.
lab'arum, (..ra), labarum; banier, vaandel.
lab'dacism = lambdacism.
labefac'tion, verval, agteruitgang; verswakking; instorting.
lab'el, (n) kaartjie, etiket, adreskaart, strokie; druplys (bouk.); **(v) (-led),** merk; klassifiseer; etiketteer, 'n kaartjie aansit, adresseer; bestempel; van 'n druplys voorsien; ~ **clip,** etiketklem.
label'lum, (..la), lip (plantk.); eindlip (insek).
lab'ial, (n) lipklank, lipletter, labiaal; **(a)** labiaal, lipvormig, lip-; ~ **ism,** labialisme; ~ **iza'tion,** labialisering; ~ **ize,** labialiseer.
lab'iate, gelip, lipvormig; lipblommig.
lab'ile, onstandvastig, labiel, wankelbaar.
labil'ity, wankelbaarheid, onvastheid.
lab'iodental, liptand=, labiodentaal.
laborato'rial, laboratorium=.
labo'ratory, (..ries), laboratorium, werkplek.
labor'ious, werksaam, arbeidsaam; moeilik, beswaarlik, moeisaam; ~ *ATTEMPT,* sukkelpoging; ~ *WORK,* sukkelwerk; tydrowende werk; ~ **ly,** moeisaam; ~ **ness,** werksaamheid, arbeidsaamheid, noestheid; moeisaamheid.
lab'our, (n) arbeid, werk; taak; moeite; inspanning; arbeiders, werkers; barenswee; arbeiderstand; mannekrag, arbeidskrag, werkskrag; ~ *ENNOBLES,* arbeid adel; *FIELD of* ~, arbeidsveld; *HARD* ~, dwangarbeid, hardepad; *a* ~ *of HERCULES,* 'n reusetaak; *IN* ~, in barensnood; *LOST* ~, vergeefse moeite; *it is* ~ *LOST,* dit is botter aan die galg gesmeer; *a* ~ *of LOVE,* 'n liefdeswerk; *MINISTER of* ~, Minister van Arbeid; ~ *WARMS, sloth harms,* werk maak sterk; **(v)** werk, arbei; swoeg; uitwerk; verkeer, ly; bewerk, bebou (grond); tot stand probeer bring; ~ *under great DIFFICULTIES,* met groot moeilikhede te kampe hê; ~ *under a MISAPPREHENSION,* in 'n dwaling verkeer; ~ *under a MISTAKE,* in 'n dwaling verkeer; ~ *a POINT,* lank uitwei oor iets; nader ingaan op 'n punt; ~ **colony,** arbeidskolonie; ~ **costs,** arbeidskoste; **L**~ **Day,** Arbeidsdag; ~ **differential,** arbeidskostedifferensiaal; ~ **dispute,** arbeidsgeskil; ~ **ed,** bewerk; styf, gekunsteld(e); swaar, moeilik; breedvoerig uitgewerk.
lab'ourer, dagloner, werk(s)man; arbeider; *SKILLED (unskilled)* ~, bedrewe (onbedrewe) arbeider; *the* ~ *is WORTHY of his hire,* die arbeider is sy loon werd; ~ **'s cottage (dwelling),** arbeidershuisie; ~ **'s ticket,** arbeiderskaartjie.
Lab'our Exchange, Arbeidsburo.
lab'our gang, werkspan, span arbeiders.
lab'ouring, arbeidend; ~ *CLASSES,* arbeidende stand, werkerstand; ~ *MAN,* arbeider.
lab'our-intensive, arbeid-intensief.
Lab'ourite, Arbeider.
lab'our: ~ **market,** arbeidsmark; ~ **organization,** arbeidsorganisasie; ~ **pains,** barenswee; **L**~ **Party,** Arbeidersparty; ~ **registry,** arbeidsburo; ~ **relations,** arbeidsbetrekkinge, bedryfsverhoudinge; ~ **room,** kraamkamer; ~ **-saving, (n)** arbeidsbesparing; **(a)** arbeidsbesparend; ~ **service,** arbeidsdiens; ~ **some,** moeilik, swaar; ~ **supply,** arbeidstoevoer; ~ **turnover,** arbeidsomset; ~ **union,** werkvereniging; vakbond, vakunie.
lab'ret, lipversiering, lipversiersel.
la'brum, labrum, (bo)lip.
laburn'um, goureën, laburnum.
lab'yrinth, doolhof, warnet, labirint.
labyrin'thian, verward, ingewikkeld.
labyrin'thic, soos 'n doolhof, verward, duister, ingewikkeld.
labyrin'thiform, labirintvormig.
labyrin'thine, soos 'n doolhof, verward, duister, ingewikkeld, labirinties.
lac, lak, 100 000 ropye.

lacc'olite, lakkoliet.
lace, (n) kant; (ryg)band, boordlint; galon; snoer; skoenriem, veter; skeutjie (drank); *not fit to tie (unloose) someone's* ~ *s (latchet),* nie werd om iem. se skoenriem los te maak nie; **(v)** ryg, toeryg, vasryg (skoen); vasmaak; inpen; omboor, borduur, galonneer (kledingstuk); afransel; sterk drank byvoeg; ~ *one's FINGERS,* die vingers inmekaar vleg (sluit); ~ *IN,* inryg; ~ *UP,* vasryg, toeryg; ~ **bobbin,** kantklos; ~ **-boot,** rygskoen, oprygstewel; ~ **border,** kantboorsel; ~ **box,** kantdoos; ~ **collar,** kantkraag; ~ **cushion,** kantkussing; ~ **d,** geryg; met alkohol versterk; ~ *d shoe,* rygskoen.
Lacedaemon'ian, (n) Lacedemoniër; **(a)** Lacedemonies.
lace: ~ **edging,** randkantjie; ~ **embroidery,** kantborduurwerk; ~ **insertion,** kantinsetsel; ~ **inset,** kantinsetsel; ~ **-maker,** kantmaker; ~ **man,** kantverkoper; kantwerker; ~ **-paper,** kantpapier; ~ **-pillow,** kantkussing.
la'cerate, skeur, verskeur; bedroef; ~ **d,** geskeur.
lacera'tion, skeur, verskeuring; wond.
lacert'a, groen akkedis.
lacer'tian, lacert'ine, akkedisagtig, akkedis=.
lace: ~ **-shoe,** rygskoen; ~ **shop,** kantwinkel; ~ **stitch,** kantsteek; ~ **trimming,** kantbelegsel; ~ **-up boot (shoe),** rygstewel, rygskoen; ~ **-winged,** netvlerkig; ~ **-wing fly,** gaasvlieg; ~ **woman,** kantverkoopster; kantwerkster; ~ **work,** kantwerk.
lachena'lia, lachenalia, viooltjie, kalossie.
lach'es, strafbare nalatigheid, versuim.
lach'rymal, (n) traanbeen; (pl) traanorgane; huilbui; traanflessie; **(a)** traan=; ~ **bag,** traansak; ~ **duct,** traanbuis; ~ **gland,** traanklier.
lachryma'tion, storting van trane, traanafskeiding, tranevloed.
lach'rymatory, (n) (..ries), traanflessie; **(a)** traan=, traanverwekkend; ~ **bomb,** traanbom.
lach'rymose, traanstortend, huilerig, tranerig, droewig.
la'cing, veter; ryglyn; (die) vasmaak; toeryg; boorsel (aan klere); toevoegsel; afranseling; skeutjie (drank); ~ **bond,** vlegverband; ~ **dropper,** vlegspar.
lack, (n) gebrek, skorting, gemis, behoefte; *FOR* ~ *of,* uit (weens) gebrek aan: ~ *of SPACE,* gebrek aan ruimte; **(v)** gebrek hê; ontbreek, skort, skeel, derwe, mis, kortkom, makeer, ontbeer; *BE* ~ *ing in,* mank gaan aan; te kort skiet in; ~ *WISDOM,* verstand kortkom, ontbreek aan verstand.
lackadais'ical, sentimenteel, gemaak treurig, geaffekteer(d); smagtend; onverskillig.
lackaday'! helaas!
lack'er = lacquer.
lack'ey, (n) (-s), agterryer, livreikneg, lakei; **(v)** as lakei dien; slaafs dien.
lack'-lustre, glansloos, dof.
lacon'ic, bondig, kernagtig, lakoniek.
lacon'icism, lac'onism, lakonisme, bondigheid, kernagtigheid.
lacq'uer, (n) lak, vernis, lakvernis; lakwerk; **(v)** verlak; vernis; ~ *up,* toelak; ~ **ed,** verlak; ~ *ed ware,* lakwerk; ~ **er,** verlakker; vernisser.
lacq'uey = lackey.
lac'rim-, lac'rym- = lachrym-.
lacrosse', lacrosse.
lac'tase, laktase.
lac'tate, (n) melksuursout, laktaat; **(v)** melk afskei; laat drink, soog.
lacta'tion, melkvorming, melkafskeiding; soging; soogtyd, laktasie; ~ **period,** melkduur, soogtyd, melkvloeitydperk.
lac'teal, (n) lakteaal, chylvat, limfvat; **(a)** melkhoudend, melk=; ~ **duct,** melkbuis; ~ **fever,** melkkoors; ~ **gland,** melkklier; ~ **s,** melkvate; ~ **vein,** melkaar; ~ **vessel,** melkvat.
lac'teous, melkerig, melk=.
lactes'cence, melkerigheid; melksap.
lactes'cent, melkagtig, melk=, melkerig; melkhoudend; melkafskeidend.

lac'tic, melk=; ~ **acid,** melksuur; ~ **fermentation,** suurword van melk; ~ **sugar,** melksuiker.
lactif'erous, melkafskeidend, melk=; ~ **duct,** melkaar, melkbuis.
lactom'eter, melkmeter, laktometer.
lac'toscope, laktoskoop.
lactose', melksuiker, laktose.
lacun'a, (-e, -s), gaping, hiaat, lakune, leemte; kuiltjie; ~**l,** ~**r(y),** vol gate, met gapings; sponsagtig.
lacus'trian, paalbewoner.
lacus'trine, paal=, meer=; ~ **age (period),** paalwoningtydperk; ~ **dwelling,** paalwoning.
lac' varnish, lakvernis.
lad, seun, jongeling, knaap, kêreltjie.
lada'num, ladanum.
ladd'er, (n) leer; *CLIMB the social* ~, the maatskaplike leer bestyg; *have one's FOOT on the* ~, jou voet in die stiebeuel hê; *GO into* ~*s,* lostrek, uitrafel, leer (kous); *KICK down the* ~ *by which one has climbed,* sy vriende nie meer wil ken nie; *reach the TOP of the* ~, die hoogste sport bereik; (v) lostrek, leer (kous); ~**-dredge,** baggermasjien; ~**ed,** geleer (kous); ~**less,** steekvas; ~**-post,** leerstyl; ~**-rope,** valreep; ~**-rung,** leersport; ~**-shell,** wenteltrap, draaitrap; ~**-side,** leerstyl; ~**-stitch,** dwarssteek; ~ **tournament,** klimtoernooi, stygtoernooi; ~**-truck,** leerwa.
ladd'ie, seun, kêreltjie, mannetjie, joggie, jongie.
lade, (-d, -n), laai, bevrag; ~**n,** belaai, bevrag.
la-di-da', (n) windbuks, aansteller; aanstellerigheid; (a) aanstellerig, windmakerig, la-di-da.
la'dies, vroue, dames; ~' **club,** damesklub, vroueklub; ~' **choir,** dameskoor, vrouekoor; ~' **doubles,** vrouedubbelspel.
lad'ified = **ladyfied.**
lad'ify = **ladyfy.**
lad'ing, lading, vrag; *bill of* ~, vragbrief; ~**-port,** ladingshawe.
la'dle, (n) potlepel, soplepel; laailepel; skeplepel; skepbak (waterwiel); smeltlepel, gietpan; (v) opskep; skep, oorskep; ~ *out,* uitskep; ~**-ful,** lepelvol, skeppie.
lad'y, (ladies), dame, vrou; beminde, nooi; wyfie; teef (hond); lady (titel); *L*~ *BOUNTIFUL,* weldoende fee; *ladies' CHOIR,* dameskoor; *ladies' DOUBLES,* damesdubbelspel; *ladies and GENTLEMEN,* dames en here; ~ *of the HOUSE,* huisvrou, vrou v.d. huis; *LITTLE* ~, dametjie; *OUR L*~, ons Liewe Vrou; *PAINTED* ~, pypie; *ladies' SINGLES,* damesenkelspel; *STOUT* ~, soustannie; ~ *of easy VIRTUE,* 'n vrou van los sedes; *YOUNG* ~, jong dame; nooi; ~ **author,** skryfster; ~ **amateur,** damesamateur; ~**bird,** skilpadjie, liewenheersbesie; *L*~**-chapel,** Mariakapel; ~ **clerk,** vroulike klerk, vroueklerk, damesklerk; ~**-clock,** ~**-cow** = **ladybird;** ~ **companion,** geselskapsdame; *L*~ **Day,** Mariaboodskap; ~ **doctor,** dokter, vrouedokter, damesdokter; ~ **dog,** teef; ~ **employer,** werkgeefster; ~**-fern,** wyflesvaring, ~**fied,** damesagtig; ~ **finger,** lady finger (soort piesang); ~ **friend,** vriendin; ~ **fy,** (**fied,** , **fied),** 'n dame maak van; "lady" noem; ~ **help,** hulp in die huishouding; ~ **hood,** dameskap; ~ **inspector,** inspektrise; ~**-in-waiting,** hofdame; ~**ish,** soos 'n dame, damesagtig; ~**-killer,** Don Juan, hartveroweraar; liefling v.d. dames; ~**like,** damesagtig, goed gemanierd, vroulik, fyn, beskaaf; kies; ~**-love,** liefste, hartlam, geliefde, beminde nooi; ~ **mayor,** burgemeesteres; ~'s **companion,** dameswerksakkie; ~'s **finger,** suikerbroodvinger; lady finger;; woudklawer; ~'s **heart grass,** klokkiesgras; ~'s **jacket,** damesjas; ~ **ship,** mevrou; titel van "lady"; ~'s**-maid,** kamenier, lyfbediende; ~'s **man,** meisiesgek; damesvriend; ~'s **shoe,** dameskoen; ~'s **mount,** damesperd; ~ **superintendent,** direktrise; ~ **teacher,** onderwyseres; ~ **warden,** prinsipale.
laev'ulose, *kyk* **levulose.**
lag¹, (n) nakomer, agterblyer; vertraging (tegn.); (v) **(-ged),** agterbly, draai, talm, sloer; agternakom; nayl; ~ *behind,* agterbly, uitsak.
lag², (sl.), (n) dwangarbeider, boef; (v) **(-ged),** dwangarbeid laat verrig; deporteer.

lag³, (n) silindermantel, bekleding (tegn.); (v) **(-ged),** beklee, toedraai; isoleer (stoomketel).
la'gan, redgoed.
la'ger, lager; ~ **beer,** lagerbier.
lagg'ard, (n) luiaard, draaier, agterblyer, draler; *be no* ~, nie 'n lui haar op sy kop hê nie; (a) lui, stadig, traag.
lagg'er = **laggard,** (n).
lagg'ing¹, (n) latbekleding, bekleding(shout); stutwerk.
lagg'ing², (n) draaiery; (a) agterblywend, dralend.
lagg'ing³, (n) (sl.), tronkstraf.
lagoon', strandmeer, lagune.
lagophthal'mia, lagoftalmie, haasoog.
lagune' = **lagoon.**
la'ic, (n) leek; (a) leke=, wêreldlik; ~**iza'tion,** sekularisasie; ~**ize,** sekulariseer.
laid, gelê; ~ *up,* in die bed, siek; uit die vaart (skip); *kyk* **lay;** (v): *eggs* ~, legsel; ~ **paper,** geribde papier; waterlynpapier.
lain, *kyk* **lie²,** (v).
lair, (n) lêplek, boerplek; afdak; grond; (v) boer, hou, lê; stal toe gaan; ~ **age,** lêplek.
laird, grondbesitter, landheer (Sk.).
laissez'-aller, laissez-aller, laat-maar-loop, donsmaar-op, agterlosigheid, gemaksug; ongedwongenheid.
laissez faire', laissez-faire, dons-maar-op; nie-inmenging, nonintervensie.
la'ity, lekedom, die leke.
lake¹, lakverf; karmosynbruin.
lake², meer, pan; *the L*~ *Country,* die Merestreek; ~ **dweller,** paalbewoner; ~ **dwelling,** paalwoning; ~ **land,** meerdistrik; ~ **let,** klein meertjie, pannetjie; ~ **poet,** digter uit die Meredistrik; ~ **scape,** meergesig; pangesig; *L*~ **School,** Engelse digterskool (Wordsworth, ens.); ~ **settlement,** paaldorp.
lakh, lak.
lak'y, ryk aan mere.
lalla'tion, lambdasisme, spraakgebrek (vervanging van **r** deur **l**).
lam, (-med), uitwiks, uitlooi.
la'ma¹, = **llama.**
la'ma², lama (Boeddhistiese priester); *L*~**ism,** Lamaïsme; *L*~**ist,** Lamaïs; ~'**sery,** (..**ries),** lamaklooster.
lamb, (n) lam; lamvleis, skaapvleis; *GOD tempers the wind to the shorn* ~, as die lam geskeer is, sorg God vir 'n warm windjie; *L*~ *of GOD,* die Lam van God; *IN* ~, grootuier; *be led like a* ~ *to SLAUGHTER,* soos 'n lam na die slagplek gelei word; (v) lam; laat lam.
lambaste', uitlooi, slae gee.
lambast'ing, loesing, drag slae.
lamb: ~ **chop,** lamskarmenaadjie; ~ **cutlet,** lamskotelet.
lamb'da, lambda, Griekse letter λ; ~**cism** — **lallation.**
lamb'doid, lambdoid'al, lambdavormig.
lamb'-dysentry, bloedpens.
lamb'ency, (die) lek (vlam); straal; glinstering, geestigheid.
lam'bent, lekkend, spelend; glinsterend, stralend.
lamb'ing, (die) lam; ~ **season,** lamtyd.
lamb: ~ **kin,** lammetjie; ~ **like,** sag, soos 'n lam; ~**-pen,** lammerhok; ~**-pie,** lampastei.
lam'brequin, helmkleed; draperie.
lamb: ~'s **fry,** gebraaide skaaplewer; ~ **skin,** lamsvel; ~'s**-tails,** katjies, bloeisel (populierboom, ens.); ~'s**-wool,** lammerwol; ~ **yield,** lammeroes.
lamé', (n) lamé.
lame, (n) manke; (v) kruppel maak, vermink, verlam; (a) mank, kruppel, kreupel; gebrekkig; onvoldoende; hortend (maat); *a* ~ *EXCUSE,* 'n flou verskoning; *GO* ~, kruppel loop; ~ *IN one leg,* mank aan die een been; ~**d,** verlam.
lamell'a, (-e), dun blaartjie; skilfer; plaatjie; lagie; ~**r,** ..**m'ellate(d),** skilferig, bladvormig, plaatvormig.
lamelli'branch, (n) mossel; (a) mosselagtig.
lamelli'form, plaatvormig.
lamell'ose, skilferig; bladvormig; plaatvormig.
lame'ness, mankheid, kruppelheid, gebreklikheid; verlamming, lamsiekte, lam(mig)heid.

lament', (n) weeklag, jammerklag; treursang; (v) weeklaag, jammer; jeremieer, beween, beklaag, betreur, bejammer; ~**able**, beklaaglik, erbarmlik, betreurenswaardig, bejammerenswaardig, jammerlik, power; ~**ableness**, powerheid.
lamenta'tion, weeklag, jammerklag, wening, gekryt, geklaag, gejeremieer, gejammer, gekerm; treurtoon; treurlied; *the L~s of Jeremiah*, die Klaagliedere van Jeremia.
lament'ed, betreur, beklaag.
lament'ing, gejammer.
lamett'a, dun, onegte goud- of silwerdraad.
lam'ia, (-e), bose gees, heks, towenares, towerheks.
lam'ina, (-e), dun plaatjie, lagie, blaadjie; metaalstrook; blaarskyf; ~**r**, skilferig, laag-; ~**te**, (v) plat maak, plat slaan, uitklop, plet, lamineer, lamelleer; met plaatjies belê; (a) skilferig, plaat-; ~**ted**, plaatvormig, laagvormig; opgelê, gefineer, gelamineer; ~**ted** *SPRING*, bladveer; ~**ted** *WOOD*, lamelhout, fineerhout; ~**'tion**, laagvorming; laminering, lamellering.
laminit'is, hoefontsteking; bevangenheid; borsseer.
lam'inose = **laminar**.
Lamm'as, St. Pietersdag, oesfees; *at latter ~*, wanneer die perde horings kry; in die jaar nul.
lamm'ergeyer, lammergier (Europa); *African ~*, lammervanger.
lamp, (n) lamp; lig; *ALADDIN'S ~*, towerlamp; *it SMELLS of the ~*, na die lamp ruik; (v) skyn; van lampe voorsien.
lam'pas¹, keelontsteking (by perde).
lam'pas², lampassy, geblomde sy.
lamp: ~**black**, lampswartsel, roet; ~**-burner**, (lamp)brander; ~**-chimney**, lampglas; ~**factory**, lampfabriek; ~**-glass**, lampglas.
lam'pion, illumineerglasie, lampion.
lamp: ~**less**, lamploos; ~**light**, lamplig; ~**lighter**, lampopsteker; ~**-maker**, lampmaker.
lampoon', (n) skimpskrif, skandskrif, smaadskrif, smaalskrif; (v) hekel, 'n skimpskrif skrywe; ~**er**, pamfletskrywer, hekelaar.
lamp' post, lanternpaal, lamppaal.
lam'prey, (-s), prikvis, negeoog, lamprei.
lamp: ~**shade**, lampkap; ~**-signal**, lampsein, ligsein; ~**-socket**, lamphouer; ~**-wick**, lamppit.
lance, (n) lans; harpoen; *break a ~ FOR someone*, 'n lansie vir iem. breek; *with ~ in REST*, met gevelde lans; *break a ~ WITH*, met iem. argumenteer; (v) met 'n lans deursteek; werp, gooi; oopsny (sweer); met 'n lanset oopmaak; ~**-corporal**, onderkorporaal; ~**-flag**, vlaggie; ~**-head**, lanspunt.
lan'ceolate, lansvormig; lansetvormig.
lan'cer, lansier, lansruiter; (pl) lansiers (dans).
lance: ~**-sergeant**, ondersersant; ~**-shaped**, lansvormig.
lan'cet, vlym, lanset, lanseermes, steekmes; ~**-arch**, spitsboog; ~**ed**, spitsboog-; ~**-fish**, lansetvis.
lance'-thrust, lanssteek.
lan'cet light, **lan'cet window**, spitsboogvenster.
lan'cinating, stekend, skerp (pyn).
land, (n) land, grond; landstreek; grondbesit; landerye; *BACK to the ~*, terug na die grond; *BY ~*, oor land; *CULTIVATED ~*, landerye, bewerkte grond; *FALLOW ~*, braakland; *the L~ of the LEAL*, die hemel; *see how the ~ LIES*, kyk hoe sake staan; poolshoogte neem; *~ of the LIVING*, land v.d. lewendes; *MAKE ~*, land sien; by land aangaan; *MINISTER of L~s*, Minister van Lande; *NATIVE ~*, geboorteland; *ON ~*, aan wal; *the PROMISED ~*, die beloofde land; (v) land, aanland; aan land sit, aflaai, los, ontskeep (passasiers); val, grondvat; wen; gaan sit, neerstryk; aan land stap; bring (moeilikheid); laat land; vang, uittrek (vis); kry; neerstryk (voël, vliegtuig); *~ a BET*, 'n weddenskap wen; *~ a BLOW*, iem. 'n hou gee; *~ in DIFFICULTIES*, in moeilikhede beland (bring); *~ ON*, beland op; *~ agent*, eiendomsagent; rentmeester; *~ animal*, landdier.
lan'dau, landauer; ~**let(te)'**, landaulet.
land: ~**bank**, landbank, landboubank; ~**-baron**, grondbaron, plaasbaron, groot grondbesitter; ~-**breeze**, landwind; ~**-crab**, landkrap; ~**-drain**, sugriool; ~**drost**, landdros; ~**drost's residence**, drosdy.
lan'ded, grond-, grondbesittend; geland; totaal (koste); *~ with*, opgeskeep met iets; ~**aristocracy**, landadel; *~ cost*, koste aan wal; *~ estate*, grondbesit; *~ gentleman*, hereboer; *~ gentry*, hereboere; *~ interest*, grondbesitters; *~ nobility*, landadel; *~ price*, prys aan wal; *~ property*, grondbesit, landeiendom; *~ proprietor*, landbesitter.
land: ~**-engine**, landketel; ~**fall**, grondafskuiwing; nadering van land; ~**-force**, landmag; ~**-forces**, landleër; ~**-girl**, plaaswerkster; ~**-grabber**, grondwolf; ~**grave**, landgraaf; ~**graviate**, landgraafskap; ~**gravine**, landgravin; ~**holder**, grondeienaar; ~**-hunger**, grondhonger, landhonger.
lan'ding, (n) landing, aanlanding; oorloop (op 'n trap); bordes, trapportaal, oorgang (trap); aanlêplek, steier (boot); *FORCED ~*, noodlanding; *MAKE a ~*, aan land gaan; (a) landings-; *~ apron*, landingsblad; ~**-area**, landingsterrein; ~**-beacon**, ~**-beam**, aanvliegbaken; ~**-bridge**, landingsbrug; ~**-charges**, lossingskoste; ~**-craft**, landingsvaartuig; ~**-enterprise**, landingsonderneming; ~**-forces**, landingstroepe; ~**-gear**, onderstel (vliegtuig); ~**-ground**, landingsveld; ~**-light**, landingslig; ~**-net**, skepnet; ~**-party**, landingsdivisie; ~**-place**, platform; landingsplek; ~**-stage**, aanlêsteier, landingshoof; ~**-strip**, landingsbaan, aanloopbaan.
land: ~**-jobber**, grondspekulant; ~**-labour**, landsdiens; ~**lady**, eienares; waardin, losieshuishoudster; ~**-line**, oorlandse telegraaflyn, landlyn; ~**-locked**, deur land ingesluit; ~**lord**, huisbaas; baas, grondeienaar; waard, hotelhouer; ~**lubber**, landrot, landloper; ~**mark**, baken, grenspaal; koersbaken, landteken, landkenning, terreinbaken (lugvaart); mylpaal, keerpunt; ~**-measure**, landmaat; ~**mine**, landmyn; ~**o'cracy**, die grondbesitters; ~**owner**, grondbesitter, landbesitter, landheer; ~**ownership**, (groot) grondbesit.
Land'race, Landras(vark).
land: ~**rail**, kwartelkoning; ~**-rat**, landrot; ~**reclamation**, grondherwinning; ~**-rent**, landpag, landhuur, grondhuur; ~**-reeve**, onderrentmeester; ~**-roller**, kluitbreker.
land'scape, landskap; ~**-architect**, tuinargitek, terreinargitek; ~**-architecture**, parkaanleg, tuinbeplanner; ~**d**, uitgelê; ontwerp; *~d garden*, uitgelegde tuin, ontwerpte tuin; ~**-designer**, landskapargitek; terreinbeplanner; ~**-gardener**, tuinargitek; ~**-gardening**, tuinargitektuur; ~**-painter**, landskapskilder.
land: *L~s Commission*, Landraad; ~**-service**, landtroepe; landdiens; ~**-shark**, grondwolf; matrooskuller; ~**-side**, landsy; hoef(ie) (aan ploeg); ~**slice**, grondsooi; ~**slide**, aardverskuiwing, afskuiwing, grondverskuiwing, bergstorting; politieke omkeer; ~**slip**, aardstorting, grondstorting, grondverskuiwing; ~**s'man**, landrot; ~**-steward**, rentmeester; ~**-surveying**, landmeting; ~**-surveyor**, landmeter; ~**-swell**, kusdeining; ~**-tax**, grondbelasting; *~ tenure*, pagstelsel; *~ tortoise*, landskilpad; ~**ward(s)**, landwaarts; ~**-wind**, landwind.
lane, pad; laan, steeg (in straatname); nou straatjie; deurgang; vaargeul; (verkeers)baan; *BLIND ~*, doodloopstraatjie; *it is a LONG ~ that has no turning*, aan alles kom 'n end; *RIGHT-HAND ~*, regterbaan; *SPEED-CHANGE ~*, spoedwisselbaan; *demarcated TRAFFIC ~*, afgemerkte verkeersbaan.
lang syne', (Skots en net in die gedig), lank gelede, vanmelewe se dae, "die goeie oue tyd".
lang'uage, taal, spraak; *use BAD ~*, vloek; uitskel; *CORRUPTION of ~*, taalbederf; *~ of the COUNTRY*, landstaal; *DEAD ~*, dooie taal; *~ of FLOWERS*, blomtaal; *HISTORY of ~*, taalgeskiedenis; *MASTERY of ~*, taalbeheersing; *POVERTY of ~*, taalarmoede; *SIMPLIFICATION of ~*, taalvereenvoudiging; *use STRONG ~*, jou heftig uitdruk; *~ boundary*, taalgrens; *~ caviller*, taalvitter; *~ congress*, taalkongres; *~ examination*, taaleksamen; *~ farm*, taalplaas; *~ laboratory*, spraaklaboratorium, taallaboratorium, taalprakti-

kum; ~-**master**, taalonderwyser; ~-**medium question**, voertaalvraagstuk; ~ **movement**, taalbeweging; ~ **problem**, taalkwessie; ~ **sense**, taalgevoel; ~ **study**, taalstudie.
lang'uid, swak, kwynend; lusteloos, lui, dooierig, loom; slap, traag (mark); langsaam, stadig; ~**ness**, lusteloosheid, dooierigheid; lomerigheid; traagheid (mark).
lang'uish, (ver)kwyn, wegkwyn, agteruitgaan, sukkel, treur; verslap, verswak; versmag; ~ *for*, smag na; ~**ing**, smagtend; kwynend; ~**ingly**, kwynend; smagtend; ~**ment**, kwyning; verflouing, verslapping; versmagting; gesmag; minnesmart.
lang'uor, swakheid, matheid, lusteloosheid, moegheid; loomheid; liefdesverlange, teerheid; slapte; drukkendheid; ~**ous**, kwynend; loom, moeg, afgemat, lusteloos; smagtend; drukkend.
lan'iary, (n) (..ries), skeurtand, slagtand; (a) slagtand=, skeur=.
lanif'erous, lani'gerous, wollerig, woldraend.
lank, skraal, maer, spigtig, slank; rank; sluik, steil (hare); ~-**haired**, steilharig, sluikharig; ~**ness**, skraalheid, slankheid, rankheid; steilheid; ~y = **lank**.
lann'er, lann'eret, lann'er falcon, edelvalk.
lan'olin, wolvet, lanolien, lanoline.
lans'quenet, lanskneg; lanskenet (spel).
lan'tern, lantern; lampion; *CHINESE* ~, lampion; *DARK* ~, diewelantern; *MAGIC* ~, towerlantern; ~-**fly**, glimwurm, vuurvlieg; ~-**jawed**, met ingevalle wange; ~-**lecture**, lesing met ligbeelde; ~-**post**, lanternpaal; ~-**slide**, lanternplaatjie; ~-**wheel**, lanternrat, dryfrat.
lan'thorn, lantern.
lanug'inous, wollerig, donserig.
lan'yard, aftrektou (kanon); skouerkoord, skouerband, draagriem; riem (pistool); ~ **knot**, slurpknoop.
Lao'coon, Laokoön.
Laodice'a, Laodicea; ~**n**, (n) Laodiceër; (a) Laodicees; lou, onverskillig.
lap¹, (n) klap (saal); oorlel; pant; skoot; *DROP into the ~ of*, in die skoot val van; *you must not expect things to FALL in your ~*, moenie verwag dat gebraaide hoenders in jou mond sal vlieg nie; *in the ~ of the GODS*, in die skoot v.d. gode; *LAY something in someone's ~*, iem. iets in die skoot werp; (v) toevou, omvou; opvou; inwikkel, omslaan; omwikkel, omhul, omgeef; laat dek; oorsteek; ~*ped in LUXURY*, van weelde omgewe.
lap², (n) voeg; las; rondte (sport); konka; *last* ~, laaste rondte.
lap³, (n) slyper, polysskyf, slypskyf; (v) polys, slyp.
lap⁴, (n) opslurping; gekabbel, kabbeling (water); vloeibare voedsel, slap kos; (v) oplek, slurp, slobber; spoel, kabbel (water); ~ *something up*, jou verlustig in; jou te goed doen aan iets.
lap' dog, skoothondjie, juffershondjie.
lapel', lapel, kraagomslag.
lap'ful, skootvol.
lap'icide, graveur, steensnyer.
lap'idary, (n) (..ries), steensnyer, graveur; (a) steensnyers=; in klip gebeitel, lapidêr; ~ *style*, bondige (kernagtige) styl.
lap'idate, stenig.
lapida'tion, steniging.
lapidifica'tion, verstening.
lapid'ify, (..fied), versteen.
lap'is: ~ *infernalis*, helsteen, silwernitraat; ~ *lazuli*, lapis lazuli, lasuursteen; ~ *pumex*, puimsteen.
lap; ~ **joint**, oorslaglas, blinde las; ~-**jointed seam**, oorslagnaat.
Lap'land, Lapland; ~**er**, Lap(lander).
Lapp, (n) Lap(lander); Lap(land)s (taal); (a) Laplands.
lapp'er¹, vouer; suiper.
lapp'er², polyster, slyper.
lapp'et, strook, pant; oorlel; lapel; slotplaatjie; afhangende lint.
lapp'ing, geklots (van water).
Lapp'ish, Laplands, Laps.
Lappon'ian, (n) Lap(land)s (taal); (a) Laplands, Laps.

lap' record, baanrekord.
lap'sable, vervalbaar.
lapse, (n) verloop(tyd); verval; feil, misslag, vergissing; misstap; afdwaling, versaking; val, daling; opskorting; loop; verbygang; ~ *of an ACT*, buitenwerkingstelling van 'n wet; ~ *of GOOD manners*, vergryp teen goeie maniere; ~ *of MEMORY*, vergissing (deur vergeetagtigheid); *SOCIAL* ~, vergryp teen goeie maniere; ~ *of TIME*, tydsverloop; (v) verval (kontrak; voorstel); dwaal, glip; verbygaan, afloop; verloop; ~ *INTO*, verval tot; ~ *FROM*, afwyking van; ~**d**, verloop; verval.
lap'stone, klopsteen.
lap' strap, skootriem.
lap'sus, (-us), vergissing, fout; ~ *calami*, skryffout; ~ *linguae*, verspreking, spreekfout.
Laput'an, (n) inwoner van Laputa; (a) van Laputa; hersenskimmig, visionêr.
lap: ~-**weld**, oormekaarlas, laplas, oorslagsweislas; ~**wing**, kiewiet; ~-**work**, mekaar dekkende werksaamhede.
lar¹, (-es), Romeinse huisgod; (pl) huisgode, lares.
lar², (-s), Birmaanse aap, gibbon.
larb'oard, bakboord.
lar'cener, lar'cenist, dief.
lar'cenous, stelerig, diefagtig.
lar'ceny, (..nies), diefstal, stelery; *petty* ~, diefstal van kleinighede.
larch, (-es), lorkeboom.
lard, (n) varkvet; (v) deurspek; met spek stop, lardeer.
larda'ceous, vetterig, spekagtig.
lard'er, spens, provisiekamer; vetvark.
lard'ing, lardeer, deurspek; ~-**bacon**, lardeerspek; ~-**needle**, ~-**pin**, lardeernaald, stopnaald.
lard'on, lardoon', stopspek; spekrepie.
lard'y, vetterig, spekkerig, vet.
lard'y-dard'y, gemaak, aanstellerig.
lar'es, huisgode; ~ *et penates*, persoonlike besittings; die tuiste.
large (n): *AT* ~, oor (in) die algemeen; op vrye voet; uitvoerig; rondswerwend; *BE at* ~, op vrye voet wees; *BY and* ~, oor (in) die algemeen; *a GENTLEMAN at* ~, 'n groot meneer; 'n ryk man sonder beroep; *IN* ~, in die groot, op groot skaal; *the PUBLIC at* ~, die groot publiek; (a) groot; breed, wyd; ruim, oorvloedig, swaar; veelomvattend, omvangryk; pronkerig, spoggerig; *as* ~ *as LIFE*, lewensgroot; in lewende lywe; ~ *of LIMB*, grof gebou; *on a* ~ *SCALE*, op groot skaal; ~-**bodied**, groot van lyf; ~-**boned**, benig, grof; ~-**hearted**, edelmoedig, grootmoedig; ~-**heartedness**, grootmoedigheid, groothartigheid; ~-**limbed**, grof gebou; ~**ly**, grootliks, in groot mate, grotendeels; ruimskoots; hoofsaaklik; ~-**minded**, ruim van blik, edelmoedig; ~**ness**, grootte; ruimte; breedte.
lar'gess(e), geskenk, aalmoes; mildheid.
lar'gish, groterig, nogal groot.
larg'o, largo (mus.).
la'riat, lasso, vangtou, vangriem.
lark¹, (n) leeurik, lewerkie; *be up with the* ~, douvoordag opstaan; vroeg uit die vere wees.
lark², (n) grap; gekskeerdery; *for a* ~, vir die grap; (v) grappe verkoop, streke uithaal, pla; ~**er**, pretmaker, grapmaker; ~**ish**, ~**some**, grappig, vrolik.
lark'spur, ridderspoor.
lark'y, jolig, vrolik, ondeund.
la'rrikin, rondloper, lawaaimaker, vabond, rabbedoe; ~**ism**, baldadigheid.
la'rrup, afransel, skerp hekel.
larv'a, (-e), larwe, maaier; ~**l**, larwe-; ~ **stage**, larwetoestand, larwestadium.
larv'icide, larwegif.
larvip'arous, wat larwes voortbring.
laryn'geal, laryn'gic, strottehoof-, keel-.
laryngit'is, keelontsteking, laringitis.
laryngol'ogist, keelarts.
laryng'oscope, keelspieël, laringoskoop.
laryngot'omy, keeloperasie, laringotomie.
la'rynx, (larynges), strottehoof, larinks.
Las'car, Laskaar (Indiese matroos).
lasciv'ious, wellustig, wulps; ~**ness**, ontugtigheid, wulpsheid, venusdiens.

la'ser, laser; ~ **beam,** ~ **ray,** laserstraal.
lash, (n) (-es), raps, haal, sweepslag; tugtiging; sweep, plak, gesel(roede); ooghaar; satire; voorslag; oog (sweep); *let someone FEEL the* ~, iem. onder die voorslag kry; *be UNDER the* ~, onder die plak sit; (v) slaan, striem, gesel, onder die sambok steek; skop (perd); beuk, slaan teen (golwe); hekel, bespot; vasbind; sjor; ~ *AT*, slaan na; ~ *DOWN*, vasbind; ~ *oneself into a FURY*, jou tot raserny opsweep; ~ *INTO*, opsweep; ~ *OUT*, agteropskop; uit die band spring; lossteek, hard slaan; ~ *TOGETHER*, aanmekaarbind; ~ *someone with the TONGUE*, iem. onder jou tong laat deurloop; ~**er,** bindtou; koptou; oorloop; binder; damwal; slaner; ~**ing,** bindsel, bindtou; vasknopery, vasmakery; slanery; woeling (bouk.); ~**ing chain,** bindketting; ~**ing hook,** woelhaak.
las'pring, jong salm.
lasque, sleggevormde diamant.
lass, (-es), lass'ie (-s), meisie, nooi, nôi, juffertjie.
Las'sa fever, Lassakoors.
lass'itude, vermoeidheid, lusteloosheid, moegheid, afgematheid, lomerigheid.
lasso', (n) (-s), vangriem, gooitou, lasso; (v) met 'n tou vang, 'n vangriem om die nek gooi.
last¹, (n) lees (vir skoen); *cobber, stick to your* ~, skoenmaker, hou jou by jou lees.
last², (n) las (gewigsmaat).
last³, (n) uithouvermoë, weerstandsvermoë.
last⁴, (n) laaste; duur; end; *AT* ~, eindelik, ten laaste; *BREATHE one's* ~, die laaste asem uitblaas; *the* ~ *shall be FIRST and the first* ~, baie laastes sal die eerstes wees; *we shall never HEAR the* ~ *of it*, ons sal nooit die end daarvan hoor nie; ~ *but not LEAST*, les bes; die laaste maar nie die minste nie; *at LONG* ~, op die ou end; eindelik; *LOOK one's* ~, vir die laaste maal kyk; *TILL the* ~, tot op die laaste; *TO the (very)* ~, tot op die laaste; tot die end; tot die allerlaaste; (v) duur; voortduur, aanhou; goed bly, goed hou (kos); uithou; voldoende wees; ~ *a LIFETIME*, 'n leeftyd hou; *he cannot* ~ *LONG*, hy kan dit nie lank maak nie; ~ *a MONTH*, 'n maand duur (hou); *the* ~ *but ONE*, tweede laaste, voorlaaste, op een na die laaste; ~ *OUT*, langer aanhou; (a) laaste, verlede, vergange; uiterste; jongslede; *the* ~ *AGONIES*, die laaste stuiptrekkings; *the* ~ *DAY*, die oordeelsdag; *of the* ~ *IMPORTANCE*, v.d. uiterste belang; *on its* ~ *LEGS*, op sy uiterste; *have a* ~ *LOOK*, 'n laaste maal kyk; *the* ~ *MILE is the longest*, die laaste loodjies weeg die swaarste; *at the* ~ *MINUTE*, op die laaste oomblik; ~ *MONDAY*, verlede Maandag; ~ *NIGHT*, gisteraand; verlede nag; ~ *POST*, laaste taptoe; *it is the* ~ *STRAW that breaks the camel's back*, die laaste strooi breek die kameel se rug; *the* ~ *THROES*, die doodstryd; *for the* ~ *TIME*, vir oulaas; ~ *WEEK*, verlede week; *the* ~ *WORD in*, die allerbeste, die allernuutste; (adv) laas; eindelik; ~**-comer,** heksluiter; ~**ing,** (n) duiwelsterk (stof); kalmink; duursaamheid; (a) durend, durabel, duursaam, blywend, bestendig; ~*ing several days*, meerdaags; ~**ingly,** vir altyd, blywend; ~**ly,** uiteindelik, ten laaste, laastelik, vergange.
last'-maker, leesmaker.
latch, (n) (-es), klink, (duim)knip; nagslot; *on (off) the* ~, op (van) die knip; (v) op die knip sit.
latch'et, skoenriem, veter.
latch'ing, lym.
latch'key, nagslotsleutel; huissleutel; knipsleutel.
late, (a) laat; wyle, oorlede, saliger; ver gevorder; vroeër, voormalig; jongste, pas afgelope; ~ *BLIGHT*, laatroes; ~ *FEE*, laatgeld; lêgeld; *at a* ~ *HOUR*, laat in die dag (aand); *KEEP* ~ *hours*, laat na bed gaan en laat opstaan; *the* ~ *KING*, die oorlede koning; ~ *POST*, laatpos, napos; *the* ~ *PREMIER*, die gewese (wyle) eerste minister; ~ *RISER*, laatslaper; *of* ~ *YEARS*, in die laaste jare; (adv) laat; te laat; onlangs, vroeër, voorheen, kort gelede; *AS* ~ *as 1900*, tot in 1900; *BE* ~, laat kom (wees); *BETTER* ~ *than never*, liewer laat as nooit; *it is too* ~ *in the DAY*, dit is al te laat; *it is rather* ~ *in the DAY*, dis effens laat; dis taamlik laat; *too* ~ *for one's own FUNERAL*, te laat vir sy eie begrafnis; *an HOUR* ~, 'n uur te laat; *it is never too* ~ *to LEARN*, 'n mens is nooit te oud om te leer nie; *OF* ~, in die laaste tyd; *too* ~ *for TEARS*, te laat om te huil, te laat vir trane; ~**-comer,** laatkommer.
lateen' sail, latynseil.
la'te-flowerer, nabloeier, laatbloeier.
late'ly, onlangs, kort gelede, pas, vergange; laastelik.
lat'en, laat word.
lat'ency, verborgenheid; latente krag, latentheid.
late'ness, laatheid; vergevorderdheid; *the* ~ *of the hour*, die laat uur.
lat'ent, verborge; latent, slapend, sluimerend; ~ **heat,** latente warmte.
lat'er, later; naderhand; *SEE you* ~, tot siens; *SOONER or* ~, vroeër of later.
lat'eral, (n) sytak; syspruit; (a) sydelings, sy=; ~ **branch,** sytak; ~ **control,** dwarskontrole, -bestuur; ~**ly,** sywaarts; ~ **movement,** sywaartse beweging; ~ **road,** sypad; ~ **root,** sywortel; ~ **stability,** dwarsstabiliteit.
Lat'eran, (n) Lateraan; (a) Lateraans.
lat'erite, ouklip, lateriet.
lat'est, laaste, jongste, nuutste; *AT the* ~, uiterlik; op sy (die) laaste; *the* ~ *FASHION*, die nuutste mode; *have you HEARD the* ~? het jy die jongste grap gehoor? *the* ~ *NEWS*, die jongste nuus; *THE* ~, die nuutste; *THURSDAY at the* ~, Donderdag op sy laaste; *WHAT'S the* ~? wat is die nuus? wat sê Horak?
lat'ex, melksap, lateks, rubbermelk.
lath, (n) lat; deklat; latwerk; *as thin as a* ~, so maer soos 'n kraai, brandmaer, rietskraal; (v) latte spyker aan, van latwerk voorsien.
lathe, draaibank; draaiskyf; ~**-carrier,** meenemer; ~**-dog,** draaibankklou, meenemer.
lath'er, (n) seepskuim; seepsop; skuim (van perd); *a GOOD* ~ *is half the shave*, 'n goeie begin sit voordeel in; *RIDE a horse into a* ~, 'n perd ry dat die skuim op hom staan; (v) inseep; in seepsop was; skuim; met skuim bedek raak; afransel.
lathe'-work, draaibankwerk.
la'thi, bamboesstok, knuppel.
lath'ing, latwerk.
lath'like, maer, skraal.
lath'-work, latwerk, rasterwerk.
la'thy, van latte gemaak; maer, rietskraal.
laticif'erous, melksaphoudend.
laticos'tate, met breë ribbes.
latiden'tate, met breë tande.
latifol'iate, met breë blare, breedblarig.
La'tin, (n) Latyn; *classical* ~, klassieke Latyn; (a) Latyns, Romeins; ~ *NATIONS*, Romaanse volke; ~ *QUARTER*, Latynse kwartier; ~**ism,** Latynse spreekwyse, Latinisme; ~**ist,** Latinis; ~**'ity,** Latynse styl; Latiniteit; ~**iza'tion,** verlatynsing; ~**ize,** verlatyns, Latiniseer, Latynse idiome invoer; ~ **races,** Latynse rasse.
lat'ish, laterig, taamlik laat.
lat'itude, poolshoogte; breedte; (speel)ruimte, speling, vryheid; omvang; *CIRCLE of* ~, breedtesirkel; *DEGREE of* ~, breedtegraad; *the* ~ *at NOON*, middagbreedte; *PARALLEL of* ~, hoogtesirkel; *TOO much* ~, te groot speling; *WORK the* ~, poolshoogte neem.
latitu'dinal, breedte=; ~ **incline,** dwarsstelling.
latitudinar'ian, (n) vrydenker; (a) vrysinnig, ruim, breed, liberaal; ~**ism,** vrysinnigheid, vrydenkery.
latitud'inous, vrysinnig.
latrine', latrine, kleinhuisie, gemakhuisie, privaat, kasteeltjie, klooster.
latt'en, latoen, geelkoper; tinplaat.
latt'er, laasgenoemde; laaste; *the* ~ *DAYS*, die eindtyd; ~ *END*, slot; agterste; uiteinde, dood; *the FORMER and the* ~, eersgenoemde en laasgenoemde; *THE* ~, hierdie, (die) laasgenoemde; ~**day,** modern, hedendaags; *L*~*-day Saints*, Mormone; ~ **grass,** nagras; ~**ly,** onlangs, in die laaste tyd; ~**math,** nagras; *L*~ **Rain,** Spade Reën.
latt'ice, (n) traliewerk, latwerk, hortjies; (v) met latwerk betimmer; vleg; ~ **bridge,** traliebrug; ~**d,** ge=

tralie, van traliewerk voorsien; ~ **pew,** kerkbank met traliewerk; ~ **truss,** skoorbalk; ~ **window,** tralievenster; venster met ruitjies in lood; ~ **-work, lat't'icing,** traliewerk, rasterwerk.

Lat'via, Letland; ~ **n,** (n) Let; Letties (taal); (a) Letties.

laud, (n) lof; lofsang; (v) loof, prys, verheerlik, roem, ophemel; ~ *to the skies,* hemelhoog prys; tot die hemel verhef; ~ **able,** prysenswaardig, lofwaardig; gesond, bevredigend.

laud'anum, loudanum.

lauda'tion, lof, lofspraak.

laud'ative, lowend, prysend.

laud'atory, prysend, lowend; *in* ~ *terms,* vol lof.

laud'ed, geprese.

laud'er, pryser, lower.

laud'ing, bewieroking; verheerliking.

lauds, vroegmis, laude.

laugh, (n) lag; gelag; *GET the* ~ *of someone,* iem. uitlag; *a HEARTY* ~, 'n vrolike lag; *JOIN in the* ~, saamlag; *LOUD* ~, skamperlag; *have the* ~ *on one's SIDE,* die laggers aan jou kant hê; (v) lag; ~ *at,* lag oor (vir, om); ~ *AT him,* hom uitlag; ~ *AWAY,* weglag; *he* ~ *s BEST who* ~ *s LAST,* die laaste lag die lekkerste; ~ *out of COURT,* belaglik maak; ~ *DOWN,* so lag dat iem. moet stilbly; ~ *in the FACE of,* uitlag; uittart; ~ *and grow FAT,* lag en bly gesond; *he who* ~ *s FRIDAY, will weep on Sunday,* van vrolikheid kom olikheid; *I'll* ~ *my HEAD off,* ek sal my 'n papie lag; ~ *him INTO it,* hom deur lag bring tot; ~ *MERRILY,* hartlik lag; ~ *on the wrong SIDE of one's mouth,* met 'n suur gesig lag; ~ *OFF,* jou lag-lag van iets afmaak; ~ *to ONESELF,* in jouself lag; ~ *OUT aloud,* hard lag; ~ *to SCORN,* bespot, uitlag; ~ *oneself SICK,* jou siek lag; ~ *up one's SLEEVE,* in jou vuis lag; ~ *and the WORLD laughs with you (cry and you cry alone),* as jy lag, lag ander saam (as jy treur, treur jy alleen); ~ *on the WRONG side of one's face,* met 'n suur gesig lag; lag soos 'n boer wat tandpyn het; ~ **able,** belaglik, bespotlik; lagwekkend, snaaks, grappig; ~ **er,** lagger; lemoenduifie.

laugh'ing, (n) lag(gery); gelag; *burst out* ~, (dit) uitskater; (a) lag-lag, laggend, lag=; *no* ~ *matter,* nie iets om oor te lag nie; ~ **-dove,** lemoenduif; ~ **fac'ulty,** lagvermoë; ~ **-gas,** laggas; ~ **hyena,** gevlekte hiëna; ~ **ly,** lag-lag, laggend; ~ **-stock,** belaglike voorwerp, voorwerp van bespotting; 'n uil onder die kraaie.

laugh'ter, gelag, geproes, laggery; *JOIN in the* ~, saamlag; *ROAR with* ~, skater; ~ **-loving,** laggerig, vrolik, laglustig.

launch¹, (n) (-es), barkas, sloep; plesierboot.

launch², (n) (die) van stapel loop, tewaterlating; helling; (v) van stapel laat loop, te water laat (boot); gooi; slinger, werp; jou stort in, aanpak; losbars; op tou sit (aanval); lanseer (vuurpyl); van wal steek; ~ *an ATTACK on,* 'n aanval rig teen; ~ *INTO,* begin, instuur; ~ *a LOAN,* 'n lening uitskryf, ~ *OUT,* uitbrei, onderneem; uitbars, van wal steek; ~ *a SHIP,* 'n skip te water laat; ~ **er,** tewaterlater; lanseerder.

launch'ing, tewaterlating; lansering (vuurpyl); ~ **cradle,** slee, wieg; ~ **gear,** lanseertoestel; ~ **pad,** lanseerkussing; ~ **platform,** lanseerplatform, lanseerstelling; ~ **ramp,** lanseerhelling; ~ **site,** lanseerbaan; ~ **tube,** lanseerbuis; ~ **way,** afloopbedding.

laun'der, (n) kuip; wasbak; geut, spoelvoor; (v) was (en stryk); ~ **er,** wasser; ~ **ette,** selfbedienwassery.

laun'dress, (-es), wasvrou; skoonmaakster.

laun'dry, (..dries), washuis, wassery; wasgoed, was; ~ **-bag,** wasgoedsak; ~ **blue,** blousel; ~ **-board,** wasplank; ~ **-list,** waslys; ~ **man,** wasser; wasserywerker; bleiker; ~ **-tub,** wasbalie; ~ **unit,** wassery (wa); ~ **woman,** wasvrou; wasserywerkster; ~ **work,** was- en strykwerk; waskunde.

lau'reate, (n) hofdigter; (v) louer, bekroon, vereer; (a) gelouer(d), bekroon(d), vereer(d), geëer(d); ~ **ship,** hofdigterskap.

laurea'tion, bekransing.

lau'rel, (n) lourier; louer-, lourierkrans; *LOOK to one's* ~ *s,* sorg om op die voorpunt te bly; *REAP* ~ *s,* roem verwerf; *REST on one's* ~ *s,* op jou louere rus; (v) **(-led),** louer, met louere kroon; ~ **led,** gelouer, bekroon; ~ **-tree,** lourierboom; ~ **wreath,** louer-, lourierkrans.

la'va, lawa; *torrent of* ~, lawastroom.

lavab'o, (-s), lavabo, rituele handewassing; wasbak, waskom.

la'va: ~ **cone,** lawakeël; ~ **flow,** lawastroom.

lava'tion, wassing, reiniging.

lavator'ial, was=.

lav'atory, (..ries), waskamer, toiletkamer, wasvertrek, wasgeleentheid; ~ **brush,** latrineborsel; ~ **pan,** gemakpan; ~ **paper,** toiletpapier.

lave, bad, was; bespoel, besproei; skep; ~ **ment,** inspuiting, lawement, klisma.

lav'ender, (n) laventel; ruikende salie; laventelbossie; laventelblomkleur; lig lila; *lay up in* ~, sorgvuldig bewaar, op sterkwater sit; (v) laventel opgooi; in laventel pak; (a) laventel=; laventelkleurig; ~ **water,** laventelwater.

lav'er¹, ereprys (wier).

lav'er², waskom, wasbak; spoelwaentjie; doopwater; doopvont.

lav'erock, lewerkie, leeurik.

lav'ic, lawa-agtig, lawa=.

lav'ish, (v) verkwis, verspil; volop uitdeel; (a) kwistig, spilsiek, verkwistend; volop, oorvloedig, rojaal; ~ **er,** verkwister; ~ **ly,** met milde hand, kwistig; ~ **ment,** verkwisting, verspilling; uitstorting; ~ **ness,** rojaalheid, kwistigheid.

law, (n) wet; reggeleerdheid; reg(stelsel); regsgeding, proses; justisie; reglement, statuut; reël; *ACCORDING to* ~, regtens; *AGAINST the* ~, strydig met die wet, onwettig, teen die wet; ~ *of ARMS,* krygsreg; *be AT* ~, in 'n hofsaak betrokke wees; proses deer; ~ *of AVERAGES,* wet van gemiddeldes; *BAD in* ~, regtens ongegrond; *BE at* ~, 'n hofsaak hê; *BY* ~, volgens die wet; regtens; van regsweë; ~ *of CAUSALITY,* ~ *of CAUSATION,* wet van oorsake en gevolg; *CIVIL* ~, burgerlike reg; *COMMERCIAL* ~, handelsreg; *COMMON* ~, gewoontereg; *CONSTITUTIONAL* ~, staatsreg; ~ *of CONTRACTS,* kontraktereg; ~ *of the COUNTRY,* landsreg; ~ *of CRIMINAL procedure,* strafprosesreg; *CUSTOMARY* ~, gewoontereg; ~ *of DIMINISHING returns,* wet van afnemende opbrengs; ~ *of EVIDENCE,* bewysleer; ~ *of EXCHANGE,* wisselreg; ~ *of EXTRADITION,* uitleweringsreg; *GIVE the* ~ *to,* jou wil deurvoer; *GO to* ~, hof toe gaan, prosedeer; ~ *of GRAVITY,* wet van swaartekrag; *take the* ~ *into one's own HANDS,* die reg in jou eie hande neem; eie reg gebruik, eiemagtig optree; op eie verantwoordelikheid handel; *HAVE the* ~ *of someone,* iem. geregtelik vervolg; 'n hofsaak teen iem. maak; *IN* ~, volgens die wet; *INCORPORATED L~ Society,* Prokureursorde; ~ *of INCREASING returns,* wet van toenemende opbrengs; *INTERNATIONAL* ~, volkereg; ~ *of the JUNGLE,* vuisreg, reg v.d. sterkste; *KEEP* ~ *and order,* wet en gesag (orde) handhaaf; ~ *of the LAND,* landswette; *LAY down the* ~, die wet voorskryf; *new LORDS, new* ~ *s,* nuwe meesters, nuwe wette; *MARTIAL* ~, krygswet; ~ *of the MEDES and Persians,* 'n wet v.d. Mede en Perse; *MERCANTILE* ~, *MERCHANT* ~, handelsreg; *MOSAIC* ~, Mosaïese wet; ~ *s of MOTION,* (Newton se drie) bewegingswette; ~ *of NATURE,* natuurwet; ~ *of NATIONS,* volkereg; *NATURAL* ~, natuurreg; *NECESSITY knows no* ~, nood breek wet; *be a* ~ *unto ONESELF,* jou eie gang gaan; jou niks laat voorskryf nie; jou aan niks steur nie; ~ *and ORDER,* wet en orde; *maintain* ~ *and ORDER,* wet en orde (gesag) handhaaf; ~ *s of the PENDULUM,* slingerwette; ~ *of PERSONS,* persoonlike reg; *PRACTISE* ~, 'n regspraktyk uitoefen; in die regte praktiseer; *PRIVATE* ~, privaatreg; ~ *of PROCEDURE,* prosesreg; *READ* ~, in die regte studeer; *ROMAN DUTCH* ~, Romeins-Hollandse reg, privaatreg; *STUDY* ~, in die regte studeer; ~ *of SETTLEMENT,* suksessiewet; *TAKE some=*

lawn 1008 *lead*

one to ~, iem. voor die hof daag; *UNDER a* ~, volgens 'n wet; ~*s of WAR,* oorlogswette; *the WORST of* ~ *is that one suit breeds twenty,* prosedeer oor 'n baadjie en hou jou broek klaar vir die onkoste; (interj) maggies! ~-**abiding,** onderdanig, ordeliewend, wetsgehoorsaam; wetsgetrou(e); ~-**adviser,** regsadviseur; ~-**agent,** wetsagent; ~-**binding,** liggeel leerband; ~-**book,** wetboek; regsboek; ~**breaker,** wetverbreker; wetsoortreder; ~-**breaking,** wetsverkragting; wetskennis; ~ **case,** hofsaak; ~ **costs,** geregskoste, hofkoste; oordragkoste; ~ **court,** geregshof, geregsaal, regbank; ~**ful,** wettig, wetlik, regmatig, geoorloof; ~**fully,** wettiglik; ~**fulness,** wettigheid; regmatigheid; ~-**giver,** wetgewer; ~-**giving,** wetgewend; ~ **Latin,** advokatelatyn, potjieslatyn; ~**less,** wetteloos; onordelik; losbandig; ~**lessness,** verwildering, losbandigheid, wetteloosheid; ~**maker,** wetgewer; ~**making,** (n) wetgewing; (a) wetgewend; ~-**monger,** (regsver)= knoeier.
lawn¹, (n) batis, gaas, kamerdoek.
lawn², (n) grasperk; grasveld; ~-**mower,** (gras)= maaier, grassnyer, grassnymasjien.
lawn' sieve, doeksif.
lawn: ~-**sprinkler,** grasproeier; ~ **tennis,** tennis.
law: ~-**officer,** regsamptenaar, regsdienaar; ~ **report,** hofverslag; ~ **society,** wetsvereniging; prokureursorde; ~-**stationer,** verkoper van skryfbehoef= tes vir geregshowe; kopieerder van regsdokumente; ~ **student,** student in die regte; ~**suit,** hofsaak, proses, regsgeding; ~ **term,** regsterm; sittings= termyn; ~-**writer,** kopieerder van aktes; juridiese skrywer, regskrywer, regsouteur.
law'yer, juris, regsgeleerde, regspraktisyn, wetken= ner.
lax¹, (n) Sweedse salm.
lax², (a) slap, ongespanne, los; laks; slordig, nalatig; loslywig; ~**a'tion,** maagwerking, laksering; ~**ative,** (n) lakseermiddel, aperitief, afvoermiddel, purgasie; (a) lakserend, purgerend, purgeer=, lak= seer=; ~**ity,** ~**ness,** losheid, slapheid; laksheid, onverskilligheid.
lay¹, (n) lied, gesang, gedig.
lay², (v) (**laid**), lê (eier, hoeksteen); platslaan, neer= slaan; begraaf; aflê; insit; wed; rig, mik (geweer); indien (klag); ten laste lê, toeskryf aan; beraam (plan); oplê (kleure); neersit, neerlê; besweer (gees); set (letters); oorlê; voorlê; neergooi; les, stil (dors); draai (lyn); laat bedaar; aanmaak, aanlê (vuur); aangaan; dek (tafel); ~ *ABOUT one,* sambok inlê; om jou heen slaan; ~ *at ANCHOR,* voor anker lê; ~ *ASIDE,* opsy lê; aflê; bêre; ~ *BARE,* aan die lig bring; blootlê; ~ *BEFORE,* voorlê aan; ~ *a BET,* 'n weddenskap aangaan (maak); ~ *BRICKS,* messel; ~ *BY,* aflê; bêre, weglê; spaar; ~ *a CHARGE,* 'n aanklag indien; ~ *CLAIM to,* eis, aanspraak maak op; ~ *the CLOTH,* die tafel dek; ~ *under a COMMAND,* opdra; ~ *under CONTRIBUTION,* 'n bydrae hef van; ~ *out a CORPSE,* 'n lyk aflê; ~ *DAMAGES,* skadevergoeding vasstel; ~ *at the DOOR of,* beskuldig van; toedig; *the regulations* ~ *DOWN,* die regulasies bepaal; ~ *DOWN,* neerlê; vasstel (reëls); neervly; op stapel sit (boot); ~ *the DUST,* die stof laat neerslaan; ~ *EYES on,* die oë slaan op; ~ *FAST,* vassit; ~ *one's FINGER upon,* die vinger lê op; ~ *the FIRE,* die vuur aanpak; ~ *out a GARDEN,* 'n tuin aanlê; ~ *a GHOST,* 'n spook beswer; *be laid up with GOUT,* in die bed met jig; ~ *one's HANDS on,* die hand aan iets slaan; *I cannot* ~ *my HAND on it,* ek kan dit nie kry nie; ~ *HEADS together,* die koppe bymekaar= steek; ~ *down one's HEAD,* die kop neerlê; *I'd* ~ *my HEAD on the (a) block,* ek sal my kop op 'n blok sit; ~ *by the HEELS,* vang; ~ *HOLD of,* in hande kry; ~ *HOUNDS on the scent,* honde op die spoor bring; ~ *IN,* versamel, bymekaar maak; ~ *INTO someone,* iem. te lyf gaan; iem. inpeper; ~ *IT on,* oordryf; ~ *down a KEEL,* die kiel lê; ~ *down LAND to teff,* 'n land onder tef sit; ~ *on the LASH,* onder die sweep steek; ~ *down the LAW,* die wet voorskryf; ~ *down one's LIFE,* jou lewe neerlê (veil hê); ~ *LOW,* in die stof verneder; in die stof loop;

~ *under a NECESSITY,* noodsaak; ~ *under an OBLIGATION to one,* aan jou verplig; ~ *OFF a workman,* 'n werkman tydelik werkloos stel; ~ *ON,* oplê (boete); water aanlê; aanskaf; die lat ge= bruik; slae toedien; heftig aanval; ~ *OPEN,* bloot= lê; blootstel; ~ *oneself OUT,* sy bes doen; ~ *OUT,* aanlê (draad); uitlê; ooplê (goed), afsteek (kamp); vier (anker); afpen (pad); vaslê (rigting); uitgee; aflê, uitlê (lyk); ~ *someone OUT,* iem. katswink slaan; ~ *OVER,* bedek; ~ *a PLACE,* 'n plek dek; ~ *a PLAN,* 'n plan ontwerp; ~ *a PLOT,* saam= sweer; ~ *to REST,* ter ruste lê; ter aarde bestel; ~ *in RUINS,* in puin lê; ~ *down a RULE,* 'n reël vas= stel (neerlê); *the SCENE is laid in Pretoria,* die stuk speel in Pretoria; ~ *SIEGE,* beleër; die beleg slaan voor; ~ *SNARES,* strikke span (stel); ~ *it on THICK,* baie oordryf; die heuningkwas gebruik; *those who have plenty of butter can* ~ *it on THICK,* wie dit breed het, kan dit breed uithang; ~ *a SUIT,* 'n aksie instel; ~ *the TABLE,* tafel dek; ~ *a TRAP,* 'n val (strik) stel; ~ *UP,* bêre, spaar; afskaf; bedlêerig wees; uit die vaart neem (skip); ~ *something UP for a rainy day,* 'n appeltjie vir die dors bêre; ~ *a WAGER,* wed; ~ *WASTE,* verwoes; ~ *under WATER,* onder water sit; ~ *on WATER,* water aanlê.
lay' brother, lekebroer.
lay'-by, spaargeld; bêrekoop, bêrekopie.
lay' clerk, leek.
lay'er, (n) laag; aflêer, loot (plant); lêhoender; inlêer; oesterbed; leerlooierskuip; rigter (geweer); rigka= nonnier; bed (myne); ~ *of AMALGAM,* amal= gaamlaag; ~ *of DUST,* stoflaag; ~ *of EARTH,* grondlaag; *a GOOD (bad)* ~, 'n goeie (slegte) lêer; *IN* ~*s,* gelaag(d), laagsgewys(e); ~ *ON* ~, laags= gewys(e); (v) aflê, inlêers maak; gaan lê (graan); met 'n laag bedek; ~**ed,** in lae; ~**cake,** laagkoek; ~**on,** inlêer; ~**out,** lykbesorger.
layette', kinderuitrusting, baba-uitrusting, baba-uit= set, luiermandjie.
lay' figure, ledepop; nul, onbelangrike persoon.
lay' gear, byrat.
lay'ing, (die) lê; rig (geweer); legsel; laag; ~ *on of hands,* handoplegging; ~ **hen,** lêhoender, lêhen; ~ **house,** lêhuis; ~ **meal,** lêmeel; ~-**meal pellets,** lê= (meel)korrels; ~ **strain,** lêras; ~ **tools,** messelge= reedskap.
lay'man, leek; oningewyde.
lay'-out, aanleg; uitrusting, benodigdhede; uitleg.
lay: ~ **preacher,** ~ **reader,** lekeprediker; ~ **preacher's service,** leesbeurt.
lay' shaft, tussenas.
lay' sister, lekesuster.
lay'stall, hoop afval, vuilgoedhoop.
lazaret', (-os), lazarett'o, (-s), kwarantynhuis; lasaret.
laze, luier, niks doen nie, lanterfanter; ~ *ABOUT,* rondlê; ~ *AWAY,* verluier.
laz'ily, lui-lui.
laz'iness, luiheid, traagheid, vadsigheid.
laz'uli, lasuursteen.
laz'ulite, blouspaat, lasuursteen, lasuliet, blousteen.
laz'y, lui, gemaksugtig, traag, vadsig; *BE* ~, luier; *BORN* ~, moeg gebore; *be EXTREMELY* ~, moeg gebore wees; ~ *folk take the most PAINS,* 'n luiaard dra hom dood, maar hy loop nie twee maal nie; ~**bones,** luiaard, lamsak, dooierd, dagdief, lui= sak, luilak; ~ **shark,** luihaai.
lea, grasveld, weiland, vlakte; ruiland.
leach, (n) (-es), loogvat; (v) uitloog; uitspoel, was; deursyg; ~-**tub,** loogvat; ~**y,** poreus.
lead¹, (n) lood; peilood, dieplood; seëlood; interlinie (drukwerk); koeël; (pl) looddak; loodjies (ruite); *basic* ~ *ACETATE,* loodasetaat; *BLACK* ~, pot= lood; *COVER with* ~, verlood; *HARDENED* ~, hardlood; *as HEAVY as* ~, loodswaar; *IN* ~, in lood gevat; *OUNCE of* ~, loodkoeël; *RED* ~, loodmenie; *SWING the* ~, siekte voorwend; lui= lak; diens versuim; jou lyf wegsteek; *WHITE* ~, loodwit; (v) met lood swaar maak; in lood vat (glas); interlinieer (drukwerk); met lood bedek; aanpak, vuil word (geweerloop); ~ *out,* spasieer; interlinieer; (a) lood=.

lead², (n) leiding; aanvoering; voorbeeld; voorsprong; eerste plek; vaarweg (skip); hoofrol; hondetou; mynaar; wenk, hulp; geleiding, leidraad (elek.); voortou (sport); voorspeel (kaart); *FOLLOW someone's* ~, iem. volg; *GET a* ~, 'n voorsprong kry; *GIVE a* ~, leiding gee; *men of LIGHT and* ~*ing*, geleerde mense; *ON a* ~, aan 'n tou; *PLAY the* ~, die hoofrol vertolk; *RETURN the* ~, dieselfde kleur terugspeel; *SECOND* ~, die tweede rol; *TAKE the* ~, die voortou neem; die leiding neem; (v) **(led)**, lei; aanvoer; voor wees; voorgaan; voorloop, voorwerk; bring tot; die leiding neem; uitkom, voorspeel (kaart); dirigeer (orkes); ~ *ALONG*, voortlei; ~ *to the ALTAR*, na die (huweliks)altaar voer; ~ *ASTRAY*, op 'n dwaalspoor bring; ~ *AWAY*, wegvoer; ~ *to BATTLE*, aanvoer; ~ *CAPTIVE*, gevanklik wegvoer; ~ *to CONFUSION*, verwarring veroorsaak (stig); ~ *the CONVERSATION*, leiding aan die gesprek gee; ~ *the DANCE*, voordans; ~ *someone a DANCE*, die wêreld vir iem. moeilik maak; ~ *a DOG'S life*, 'n hondelewe hê; ~ *a DOUBLE life*, 'n dubbele bestaan voer; ~ *EVIDENCE*, getuienis aanvoer; ~ *the FASHION*, die mode aangee; ~ *the FIELD*, die leiding neem; ~ *IN*, inlei; ~ *someone a LIFE*, iem. die lewe suur maak; ~ *the LIST*, die lys open; ~ *by the NOSE*, aan die neus lei; ~ *NOWHERE*, tot niks lei nie; ~ *ON*, verder lei; ~ *ONE to expect*, iem. onder die indruk bring; ~ *a PLEASANT life*, aangenaam lewe; ~ *in PRAYER*, in gebed voorgaan; ~ *a QUIET life*, stil lewe; ~ *TO*, lei tot; ~ *UP to*, voer tot; ~ *the WAY*, voorgaan; die pad wys; ~**able**, geseglik, leibaar
lead: ~ **acetate**, loodasetaat; ~ **bullion**, staaflood; ~ **colic**, loodkoliek; ~ **colour**, loodkleur; ~**coloured**, loodkleurig; baftablou; ~ **coat**, loodlaag; ~**-covered**, met lood bedek; ~ **ed**, in lood gevat; gespasieer (drukwerk).
lead'en, lood-; loodswaar; drukkend; log, lomp; loodgrys; *with* ~ *feet*, met lood in die skoene; ~**-footed**, met lood in die skoene; ~**-hearted**, ongevoelig; ~**ness**, botheid, ongevoeligheid.
lea'der, leier, voorman, leidsman, aanvoerder; voorbok, voorperd (by kwaad); voorryer (perderuiters); hoofartikel (koerant); vooros (span); touleier; voorloper, gidsaartjie, leier (geol.); dirigent (van orkes); eerste viool (orkes); uitloper; hoofrat (boekdr.); ~**ette'**, subartikel, kort hoofartikel; ~**-head**, geutbak; ~**-less**, sonder leier; ~ **ship**, leiding, aanvoering, leierskap; *under the* ~*ship of*, onder leiding van; ~**-writer**, skrywer van hoofartikels.
lead: ~**-foil**, bladlood; ~**-fouling**, loodaanslag; ~ **fuse**, loodsekering; ~**-glance**, loodglans; looderts; ~ **glass**, loodglas; ~ **glaze**, loodglasuur.
lead'ing¹, (n) loodwerk; loodwerk; loodvernis.
lead'ing², (n) (ge)leiding, aanvoering; (a) leidend, aanvoerend; vernaamste, eerste, toonaangewend, vooraanstaande, hoof-; ~ **article**, hoofartikel; ~ **case**, sleutelsuitspraak; ~ **counsel**, eerste (vernaamste) advokaat; ~ **elder**, leierouderling; ~ **hand**, voorman; ~ **horse**, voorperd; ~ **judgement**, hoofuitspraak; ~ **lady**, eerste speelster, ~ **light**, bakenlig, leilig; voorperd; ~ **man**, eerste speler; ~ **question**, rigtinggewende vraag, wenkvraag; vraag wat die antwoord aandui; ~ **rating**, baasseeman; baasseemansgraad; ~**-rein**, toom, leiriem; ~ **residents**, notabeles; ~ **seaman**, baasseeman; ~**-strings**, leiband; *be in* ~*-strings*, aan 'n toutjie gelei word; aan 'n leiband wees.
lead: ~**-line**, loodlyn; ~ **mine**, loodmyn; ~ **ore**, looderts; ~ **palsy**, loodverlamming; ~ **pencil**, potlood; ~ **pipe**, loodpyp; ~**-poisoning**, loodvergiftiging, saturnisme; ~**sman**, (diep)loder; peiler; ~ **spar**, loodspaat; ~**-tree**, hardekool; ~ **wood**, hardekool, loodhout *(Combretum imberbe)*; ~**-work**, loodmakerswerk; ~**-works**, loodsmeltery; ~ **y**, loodagtig.
leaf, (n) (**leaves**), blad (van boek); blaar (van boom); insteekblad, skuifblad (tafel); velletjie (papier); (pl) gebladerte (boom); ~ *of BACKSIGHT*, visierklep; *BURST into* ~, blare kry; *IN* ~, met blare, uitgeloop; *TAKE a* ~ *out of someone's book*, iem. tot voorbeeld neem; *TURN over a new* ~, 'n nuwe lewe begin; die ou mens aflê; (v) blare kry, uitloop; ~ *through a book*, 'n boek deurblaai; ~ **age**, blare; loofwerk; ~**-blight**, blaarbrand, blaarsiekte; ~ **blister**, blaarskilfer; ~ **brass**, bladkoper; ~ **bridge**, ophaalbrug; ~ **bud**, blaarknop; ~ **canopy**, blaardak; ~ **crinkle**, blaarkroes; ~ **crown**, blaarkroon; ~**-cutter**, bladvreter; ~**-eater**, blaarvreter; ~ **ed**, met blare; ~ **fall**, val van die blare; ~ **fat**, bladvet, reusel; ~ **form**, blaarvorm; ~ **gold**, bladgoud; ~**-green**, bladgroen; ~**iness**, blaarrykheid; ~ **insect**, wandelende blaar; ~**-lard**, uitgebraaide bladvet (reusel); ~ **less**, blaarloos; ~ **let**, blaartjie (boom); blaadjie (boek); strooibiljet; ~ **lettuce**, blaarslaai; ~ **louse**, bladluis; ~ **metal**, bladmetaal, verfoeliesel; ~ **mould**, blaargrond; ~ **scorch**, bladskroei, bladbrand; ~**-shaped**, blaarvormig; ~ **silver**, bladsilwer; ~**-spot**, blaarvlek; *angular* ~ *spot*, hoekvlek, hoekige blaarvlek; ~ **stalk**, bladsteel, blaarsteel; ~ **table**, klaptafel; uittrektafel; ~ **tobacco**, blaartabak; ~ **tube**, blaarbuisie; ~ **y**, blaarryk, beblaar; ~ *y vegetables*, blaargroente.
league¹, (n) drie myl.
league², (n) verbond, bond; eedgenootskap; liga (ook sport); *BE in* ~ *against*, saamspan teen; *BE in* ~ *with*, kop in een mus wees met; *L* ~ *of NATIONS*, Volke(re)bond; (v) 'n verbond sluit; ~ **log**, puntelys.
league'-long, myl lange; myle lank.
league' match, ligawedstryd.
leag'uer¹, (n) bondgenoot; laer, kamp; (v) laer trek; beleër.
leag'uer², (n) lêer (wynmaat).
leak, (n) lek, lekplek; lekkasie; *PLUG a* ~, 'n lekplek toestop; *SPRING a* ~, 'n lek kry; (v) lek; ~ *out*, uitlek; rugbaar word; ~ **age**, lekkasie, lek(plek); vermindering; ~ **age water**, lekwater; ~ **ing**, lekkery, lek; ~ **ing heart**, lekhart; ~**-proof**, lekvas, lekvry.
leak'y, lekkerig; praatsiek, praterig; ~ *CONDITION*, ondigtheid; ~ *VALVE*, lekklep.
leal, trou, lojaal.
lean¹, (n) maer vleis; (a) maer (vleis); skraal (mens); onvrugbaar (grond); ~ *CUTS*, maer snitte; ~ *MIXTURE*, swak mengsel; *as* ~ *as a RAKE*, so maer soos 'n kraai; *be having a* ~ *TIME of it*, dit maar skraps hê; ~ *YEARS*, maer jare.
lean², (n) oorhelling, helling, skuinste; *have a* ~ *to the left*, na die linkerkant oorhel; (v) (**-ed** or **-t**), leun, steun; oorhel, oorhang; buig; laat leun; geneig wees; ~ *AGAINST*, aanleun teen; ~ *BACK*, agteroorleun; ~ *FORWARD*, vooroor leun; ~ *ON*, steun op, ~ *OVER*, oorhel, oorhang; ~ *OVER backward*, uit jou pad gaan (fig.).
lean: ~**-faced**, met maer gesig; ~**-fleshed**, maer.
lean'ing, (n) oorhelling; neiging; *have a* ~ *to the left*, na die linkerkant oorhel; (a) leunend, oorhellend, skeef.
lean'ness, maerheid, maerte, skraalheid; onvrugbaarheid.
leant, *kyk* **lean**, (v).
lean'-to, afdak, abbageboutjie.
lean'-witted, dom; dwaas.
leap, (n) sprong, vaart; spring; val (rivier); *AT a* ~, met een sprong; *by* ~ *s and BOUNDS*, hand oor hand; met lang hale; *a* ~ *in the DARK*, 'n sprong in die duister; (v) (**-t** or **-ed**), spring; opspring; huppel; oorspring; flikker; laat spring; ~ *AT*, bespring, spring na; *his HEART leapt*, sy hart het van vreugde opgespring; *LOOK before you* ~, besin eer jy begin; ~ *to MIND*, byval, te binne skiet; ~ *into the SADDLE*, in die saal spring; *nearly* ~ *out of one's SKIN*, amper uit jou vel spring; ~**-day**, skrikkeldag, 29 Februarie; ~ **er**, springer; ~**-frog**, hasieoor; ~**-ing-pole**, polsstok; ~ **t**, *kyk* **leap**, (v); ~**-year**, skrikkeljaar; ~**-year dance**, skrikkeldans; ~**-year's day**, skrikkeldag.
learn, (**-t** or **-ed**), leer, aanleer; verneem; hoor; *it is GOOD to* ~ *at other men's cost*, dit baat mens om uit ander se skade en skande wys te word; *to* ~ *the HARD way*, duur leergeld betaal; *I HAVE yet to* ~ *that ...*, ek het nog nooit gehoor dat ...; ~ *by*

learned 1010 *leeway*

HEART, uit die hoof leer, van buite leer; ~ *by ROTE*, soos 'n papegaai leer.
learn'ed, geleerd; *my* ~ *FRIEND*, my geleerde vriend; *a* ~ *MAN*, 'n geleerde; ~ *SOCIETY*, vereniging van geleerdes; *be VERY* ~, geleerd wees; baie letters geëet hê.
learn: ~ **er**, leerling, beginner, leerder; ~ **er's licence**, leerlinglisensie.
learn'ing, (die) leer; geleerdheid; wetenskap; *a MAN of* ~, 'n geleerde man; *MUCH* ~ *doth make thee mad*, jou geleerdheid bring jou tot raserny; *the NEW L* ~, die Renaissance.
learn'er miner, leerlingmynwerker.
leas'able, verhuurbaar.
lease[1], (n) inslag (wewery).
lease[2], (n) huurkontrak; pag; pagbrief; huurtyd; verhuring; huur; bruikhuur; *take a new* ~ *of LIFE*, nuwe moed skep; nuwe lewe kry; *LONG* ~, langtermynhuur; *PERIOD of* ~, pagtyd; *PUT out to* ~, verhuur; *SHORT* ~, korttermynhuur; *TAKE on* ~, huur; *TERMS of* ~, (ver)huurvoorwaardes; (v) verhuur, uithuur, verpag; huur, pag; ~**hold**, huurbesit, huurpag (huise); bruikhuur (motors); ~*hold lot*, huurperseel; ~**holder**, huurder; bruikhuurder; huurpaghouer; ~**hold stand**, huurstandplaas; ~**-lend**, huurleen, bruikleen.
leash, (n) **(-es)**, koppelriem, tou, band; drietal (jag); *HOLD in* ~, in die mag hê; in bedwang hou; *ON* ~, aan 'n tou; *SLIP the* ~, loskom; uit die band spring; (v) bind, saamkoppel, vaskoppel, aankoppel.
leas'ing, verpagting; huur; bruikhuur.
least, (n) die minste; ~ *of ALL*, die allerminste; *AT* ~, ten minste, minstens; *AT the* ~, op sy (die) minste; *BE the* ~, die minste wees; *NOT in the* ~, glad nie; nie in die minste nie; op verre na nie; heeltemal nie; *to SAY the* ~ *of it*, op sy (die) sagste uitgedruk; ~ *SAID soonest mended*, hoe minder daarvan gesê word, hoe beter; (a, adv) kleinste, minste, geringste; ~ *COMMON denominator*, kleinste gemene noemer (deler); ~ *COMMON multiple*, kleinste gemene veelvoud; *LINE of* ~ *resistance*, die maklikste weg; ~**ways**, ~**wise**, ten minste.
leat, meulstroom, watervoor.
leath'er, (n) leer, oorleer; leerwerk; voetbal; (pl) kamaste; *run HELL for* ~, hardloop dat jy oople; *nothing LIKE* ~, eie goed is beste goed; *LOSE* ~, jou deurry; (v) met leer oortrek; uitlooi, afransel; ~ **apron**, leervoorskoot, skootvel; ~**-back**, leerskilpad; ~ **belt**, dryfriem; ~ **binding**, leerband; ~ **cloth**, weefleer; ~**-dresser**, leerbewerker; ~**ette'**, kunsleer; ~**-head**, domkop; ~ **industry**, leernywerheid; ~**ing**, loesing, afranseling; *give someone a* ~*ing*, iem. 'n loesing gee; ~**-lunged**, met sterk longe; ~**-merchant**, leerkoper; ~**n**, van leer, leer-; ~**oid**, katoenpapier; ~ **parings**, leersnippers; ~ **punch**, gustang; ~ **upholstery**, leerbekleding; ~ **washer**, leerring, leerwaster; ~**work**, leergoed, leerwerk; ~**y**, taai, leeragtig, leer-; seningrig.
leave[1], (n) verlof; verloftyd; vergunning; ~ *of AB= SENCE*, verlof; *APPLICATION for* ~, verlofaanvraag; *ASK* ~, verlof vra; *BEG* ~, verlof vra; *I BEG* ~ *to inform you*, ek neem die vryheid om u mee te deel; *BY your* ~, met u verlof; *CANCEL all* ~, alle verlof intrek; *EXTENSION of* ~, verlofsverlenging; *take FRENCH* ~, wegloop; *GET* ~, verlof kry; *GIVE (grant)* ~, verlof gee; ~ *to IN= TRODUCE*, verlof tot indiening; *without as MUCH as a 'by (with) your* ~, sommer sonder komplimente, sonder om eers toestemming te vra; *OBTAIN* ~, verlof kry; *ON* ~, met verlof; *PER= SON on* ~, verlofganger; *TAKE* ~, afskeid neem; met verlof gaan.
leave[2], (v) **(left)**, laat staan; verlaat; wegtrek; agterlaat, nalaat; skoert, vertrek, afreis; ophou; laat (oor)bly; weggaan; stet (drukkerstekens); laat lê; ~ *ABOUT*, laat rondlê; ~ *nothing to ACCIDENT*, niks aan die toeval oorlaat nie; ~ *ALONE*, met rus laat; ~ *BEHIND*, agterlaat, laat agterbly; nalaat; ~ *his CARD*, sy kaartjie afgee; ~ *someone to his FATE*, iem. aan sy lot oorlaat; *two FROM four* ~ *s two*, twee van vier laat twee; ~ *the GROUND*, opstyg; *left on HAND*, oorhê; ~ *in the LURCH*, in die steek laat; ~ *it to ME*, laat dit aan my oor; ~ *MUCH to be desired*, veel te wense oorlaat; ~ *OFF*, ophou met; 'n end kry; ~ *a matter OPEN*, 'n saak onbeslis laat; ~ *OUT*, uitlaat, weglaat; verbygaan; ~ *OVER*, oorhou; oorlaat; laat bly; laat oorskiet; ~ *the RAILS*, ontspoor; ~ *the ROAD*, v.d. pad af loop; ~ *SEVERELY alone*, glad nie aanraak nie; ~ *a bad TASTE in the mouth*, 'n slegte smaak nalaat; *TAKE it or* ~ *it*, neem dit of laat dit staan; ~ *it at THAT*, laat dit daarby; ~ *UN= DONE*, ongedaan laat; ~ *UNSAID*, ongesê laat bly; ~ *WELL alone*, bemoei jou nie daarmee nie; alle verandering is nie verbetering nie; ~ *WORD*, 'n boodskap laat staan; *I* ~ *YOU to it*, ek laat jou maar voortgaan; *I* ~ *it to YOU*, ek laat dit aan jou oor.
leave'-breaker, verlofbreker.
leaved, geblaar.
leav'en, (n) suurdeeg; (v) laat rys, insuur; deurtrek; ~**ing agent**, gismiddel.
leave: ~ **pass**, verlofpas; ~ **privileges**, verlofvoorregte; ~ **regulation**, verlofregulasie, verlofsbepaling.
leaves, *kyk* **leaf**, (n).
leave'-taking, afskeid, groetery.
leav'ing-certificate, eindsertifikaat.
leav'ings, oorblyfsel, oorskiet, afval, res.
Lebanese', (n, a) Libanees.
Leb'anon, Libanon.
le'bensraum, (G.), lewensruimte, lebensraum.
lech'er, wellusteling; ontugtige; ~**ous**, wellustig, ontugtig; ~**y**, wellus, onkuisheid, ontug.
lech'we, basterwaterbok *(Onotragus leche)*.
le'cithin, lesitien, lesitine.
lec'tern, koorlessenaar, knaap, standertjie.
lec'tion, lesing; les.
lec'ture, (n) lesing, voorlesing; kollege, klas; berisping, skrobbering, strafpredikasie, vermaning; sermoen, boetpredikasie; *DELIVER (give) a* ~, 'n voordrag hou; 'n lesing gee; *READ someone a* ~, iem. berispe; iem. die les lees; (v) les gee, kollege gee, doseer; 'n lesing hou; vermaan, die les lees; ~**r**, lektor; dosent; referent; spreker; ~**r guide**, lektorgids; ~ **room**, lesingsaal, klaskamer; ~**ship**, lektoraat.
lec'turess, **(-es)**, lektrise; spreekster.
lec'turing post, doseerpos.
led, *kyk* **lead**[2], (v).
led' captain, parasiet, klaploper.
le'derhosen, (G.), leerbroek, lederhosen.
ledge, bank, rif, rand; (rots)lys; bergrand; rug; ertslaag.
ledg'er, grootboek (boekh.); dwarsbalk; plat grafsteen; ~**-bait**, lêaas; ~ **clerk**, grootboekhouer, grootboekklerk; ~**-hook**, stelhoek; ~**-line**, stellyn.
led' horse, handperd, pakperd.
lee, ly(kant); beskutting; *under the* ~ *of*, onder beskutting van; aan die lykant van; ~ **anchor**, lyanker; ~**-board**, lyboord; ~ **brace**, lybras.
leech[1], (n) **(-es)**, bloedsuier; *cling like a* ~, klou soos 'n neet.
leech[2], (n) **(-es)**, (arch.), arts, geneesheer, dokter.
leech[3], (n) **(-es)**, lyk (van 'n seil).
Lee-En'field (rifle), Lee-Enfield(geweer).
leek, prei; *eat (swallow) the* ~, jou eie woorde insluk; ~ **soup**, preisop.
Lee-Met'ford (rifle), Lee-Metford(geweer), lemetford.
leer[1], (n) koeloond.
leer[2], (n) sydelingse blik, lonk; gryns; (v) skuins kyk, loer; verlief kyk; aangluur; lonk; gryns.
lee' rail, leuning v.d. windkant af.
leer'fish, leervis.
leer'y, (sl.), uitgeslape, geslepe.
lees, moer, besinksel, afsaksel, grondsop, droesem; *DRINK (drain) to the* ~, tot die laaste druppel uitdrink; ~ *of WINE*, wynmoer.
lee: ~ **shore**, lywal, sluiphawe, laerwal; ~ **side**, lyboord, lykant; ~ **tide**, gety aan die lykant; ~ **ward**, onder die wind, lywaarts; *L* ~ *ward Islands*, Eilande onder die Wind, Benedewindse Eilande.
lee'way, (die) afdrywe; *GIVE ample* ~, uit die pad

left 1011 *lend*

gaan; ruimte gee; *MAKE up* ~, die agterstand inhaal.
left¹, (n) linkerhand; linkerhou; linkerkant; *KEEP to the* ~, hou links; *NEW L* ~, Nuwe Linksgesindes; *ON the* ~, links; *TO the* ~, links; na links; (a) links, linker=; oor, orig; hot (dier); *the* ~ *HAND shall not know what the right one does,* die linkerhand moenie weet wat die regterhand doen nie; *MARRY with the* ~ *hand,* morganaties trou; *THE L* ~, die Linksgesindes; (adv) links, aan die linkerkant; ~ *and RIGHT,* links en regs; ~ *TURN!* links om! ~ *WHEEL!* links swenk!
left², p.p. of **leave:** *GET* ~ *(behind),* agterbly; agteraan kom; *be* ~ *in the LURCH,* in die steek gelaat wees.
left: ~ **ear,** linkeroor; ~ **eye,** linkeroog.
left' hand, linkerhand; ~ **drive,** linkerstuur; ~ **screw,** linkse skroef; ~ **thread,** linkse draad.
left'-handed, links; onhandig, lomp; ~ *COMPLIMENT,* dubbelsinnige kompliment; ~ *MARRIAGE,* morganatiese huwelik.
left'-hander, linkshandige, hotklou; linkerhou; *be a* ~, links wees.
left: ~ **hind,** links agter; hot agter; ~ **ish,** linksgesind; ~ **ism,** linksgesindheid; ~ **ist,** (n) linksgesinde; (a) linksgesind.
left: ~ **-off,** gedra, ou (klere); ~ **-over,** oorblyfsel, oorskiet; ~ **-overs,** oorskietkos.
left: ~ **shoulder,** linkerskouer; ~ **side,** linkerkant; linkersy; ~ **ward,** na links; ~ **wing,** linkervleuel.
leg, (n) been; poot (van dier, stoel); boud (vleis); pyp (van broek); stut, paal, tak, bykant (kricket); skof, trajek (reis); *BE on one's* ~ *s,* die woord voer; *FIND one's* ~ *s,* staan; tuis raak; *GET on one's* ~ *s,* opstaan; *GIVE someone a* ~ *up,* iem. help; hand bysit; *HAVE the* ~ *s of,* vinniger gaan as; *get on one's HIND* ~ *s,* op sy agterbene gaan staan; *KEEP one's* ~ *s,* op sy bene bly; ~ *of LAMB,* lamsboud, skaapboud; *on one's LAST* ~ *s,* op sy uiterste; poot-uit; *LONG* ~, langby; *MOVE one's* ~ *s,* jou knieë dra; ~ *of MUTTON,* skaapboud; *ON one's* ~ *s,* op die been; op eie bene; aan die woord, *PULL someone's* ~, met iem. die gek skeer; met iem. 'n lopie neem; *SET someone on his* ~ *s,* iem. op die been help; *SHAKE a* ~! roer jou riete! *SHORT* ~, kortby; *SHOW a* ~! roer jou riete! roer jou angel! *have no* ~ *to STAND on,* geen gegronde rede hê nie; heeltemal verkeerd wees; *STAND on one's own* ~ *s,* op jou eie bene staan; *STRETCH one's* ~ *s,* jou bene versit; jou litte losmaak; *TAKE to one's* ~ *s,* die rieme neerlê (bère); *TO* ~, na die bykant (krieket); ~ *of VEAL,* kalfsboud; ~ *of VENISON,* wildsboud; ~ *before WICKET,* been voor paaltjie; (v): ~ *it,* voetslaan; hardloop.
leg'acy, (..cies), legaat, erflating, erfenis, nalatenskap; ~ **duty,** suksessiereg.
leg'al, wetlik, regsgeldig, (ge)regtelik, wettig; regs=, regskundig; ~ **advice,** regsadvies; ~ **adviser,** regsadviseur; ~ **aid,** regshulp; ~ **aid bureau,** regshulpburo; ~ **authority,** regsmag; ~ **claim,** wettige eis, regsvordering; ~ **compulsion,** regsdwang; ~ **consequences,** regsgevolge; ~ **deposit,** pliglewering; ~ **disability,** regsonbevoegdheid; ~ **dispute,** regsgeskil; ~ **duty,** regsverpligting; ~ **expenses,** regskoste; ~ **fare,** vasgestelde tarief; ~ **force,** regskrag; ~ **formality,** regsformaliteit; ~ **ground,** regsgrond; ~ **interest,** regsbelang; ~ **ism,** wettiesheid; wetsvering, werkheiligheid; ~ **ist,** werkheilige (R.K.); ~ **'ity,** wettigheid, legaliteit; egtheid, wetlikheid, geldigheid; ~ **iza'tion,** wettiging, legalisasie; ~ **ize,** wettig; eg, wettig; ~ *ly invalid,* regsongeldig; ~ **opinion,** regsadvies, *take* ~ *opinion,* regsadvies inwin; ~ **point,** regspunt; ~ **position,** regsposisie; ~ **practice,** regspraktyk; ~ **practitioner,** regsprak= tisyn; ~ **principle,** regsbeginsel; ~ **procedure,** regsprosedure; ~ **proceedings,** regsgeding, geregtelike stappe; ~ **provision,** regsbepaling; ~ **question,** regskwessie; ~ **remedy,** regsmiddel; ~ **representative,** regsverteenwoordiger; ~ **studies,** regstudie; ~ **tender,** wettige betaalmiddel; ~ **terminology,** regsvaktaal, -terminologie; ~ **title,** regstitel.
leg'ate¹, (n) legaat, gesant; *papal* ~, pouslike legaat.

legate'², (v) nalaat, bemaak, legateer.
legatee', legataris, erfgenaam.
leg'atine, legaat=.
lega'tion, gesantskap, legasie; sending.
lega'to, gedrae, legato (musiek).
legat'or, erflater.
leg'-bail, wegloop, ontsnap; *give* ~, jou uit die voete maak.
leg: ~ **ball,** bybreekbal; ~ **-bone,** skeenbeen, maermerrie; ~ **break,** bybreek; ~ **bye,** byloslopie.
le'gend, legende, sage, oorlewering; legende, byskrif (kaart); onderskrif, opskrif, randskrif (munte); ~ **ary,** (n) (..ries), legendeboek; (a) fabelagtig, legendaries.
legerdemain', goëlery, goëltoer, handigheid; bedrog.
legged, met bene, been=.
legg'iness, langbenigheid.
legg'ing(s), kamas(te).
leg: ~ **-glide,** bygly; ~ **-guard,** beenskut; (pl) beenskerms; ~ **gy,** met lang bene, langbeen=; ~ **-hit,** byslag; ~ **-hold,** beengreep; ~ **-hooking game,** hakkekrukke.
leghorn', Leghorn(hoender); strooihoed.
legibil'ity, leesbaarheid.
le'gible, leesbaar, duidelik.
le'gion, legioen; legio; *L* ~ *of HONOUR,* Legioen van Eer; *my NAME is L* ~, Legio is my naam; *their SUPPORTERS are* ~, hulle ondersteuners is legio; ~ **ary,** (n) (..ries), legioensoldaat; (a) legioen=.
leg'iron, voetboei; beenyster (vir 'n gebreklike).
leg'islate, wette maak, wetgee.
legisla'tion, wetgewing, wette.
le'gislative, wetgewend; *L* ~ *ASSEMBLY,* Wetgewende Vergadering, Volksraad; *L* ~ *COUNCIL,* Wetgewende Raad; ~ *POWER,* wetgewende mag.
le'gislator, wetgewer.
le'gislature, wetgewende mag; wetgewing; wetgewer.
le'gist, wetgeleerde, regsgeleerde.
legit'imacy, wettigheid; egtheid.
legit'imate, (v) wettig, eg verklaar, legitimeer; (a) wettig, eg; gewettig; erken, normaal; *the* ~ *drama,* die erkende drama.
legitima'tion, wettigverklaring, legitimasie.
legit'imist, legitimis.
legit'imize, wettig (eg) verklaar.
leg: ~ **-less,** sonder bene, afbeen=; ~ **let,** beentjie; beenring; ~ **-of-mutton sleeve,** skaapboudmou; ~ **parade,** beenvertoning; ~ **-piece,** plat bilstuk; ~ **-puller,** terggees, gekskeerder; ~ **-pulling,** tergery, plaery; ~ **punch,** vingerdeurslag; ~ **-rest,** beenbankie; ~ **room,** beweegruimte; ~ **side,** beenkant; ~ **stump,** bypaaltjie; ~ **theory,** bykantboulwerk; ~ **-up,** hulp, steun.
leguan', likkewaan.
leg'ume, legum'en, peulvrug, peulgewas.
legum'inous, peul=, peulvrugdraend.
lei'sure, ledige tyd, vrye tyd; gemak; *AT one's* ~, op sy gemak; vry; *AWAIT someone's* ~, wag tot iem. tyd het; *BE at* ~, niks te doen hê nie; onbeset wees; *UTILIZATION of* ~, vryetydsbesteding; ~ **d,** met baie tyd; *the* ~ *d class,* die renteniers, die stand met min werk; ~ **ly,** (a) stadig, tydsaam, langsaam; (adv) stadig, langsaam, op sy gemak, tydsaam; ~ **wear,** ontspanningsdrag.
leit'motif, hooftema, leimotief, leitmotif.
lemm'ing, lemming, bergmuis.
lem'on, (n) suurlemoen; suurlemoenboom; sitroenkleur; (a) sitroengeel; sitroenkleurig; ~ **ade',** limonade; ~ **-barley water,** suurlemoen-gortwater; ~ **-coloured,** sitroengeel; ~ **curd,** suurlemoensmeer; ~ **dove,** lemoenduif; ~ **drop,** suurtjie; ~ **essence,** suurlemoengeursel; ~ **flavouring,** suurlemoengeur; ~ **juice,** suurlemoensap; ~ **oil,** sitroenolie; ~ **peel,** suurlemoenskil; ~ **squash,** suurlemoendrank, -kwas, water met suurlemoensap; ~ **-squeezer,** (suur)lemoendrukker, lemoenpers; ~ **syrup,** suurlemoenstroop; ~ **tree,** suurlemoenboom; ~ **-wood,** lemoenhout, borriehout; ~ **-yellow,** sitroenkleurig, sitroengeel.
lem'ur, lemur, vosaap, halfaap, maki.
lem'ures, geeste van afgestorwenes.
lend, (lent), leen; uitleen; voorskiet; gee, skenk, ver=

lending   1012   letter

leen; ~ *ASSISTANCE,* hulp verleen; ~ *an EAR,* die oor leen; luister; ~ *a HAND,* 'n handjie bysit; ~ *ONESELF to,* jou leen tot; ~ *OUT,* uitleen; ~ *TO,* leen aan; ~**er,** lener, uitlener; geldskieter.

len'ding, (die) leen, lenery; ~ **library,** leesbiblioteek, (uit)leenbiblioteek.

length, lengte; duur; afstand; grootte; entjie (tou), stuk; *go to ANY* ~ *s,* niks ontsien nie; *AT* ~ , eindelik; uitvoerig, voluit; *at ARMS'* ~ , op armlengte; *FULL* ~ , lank uit, lewensgroot; *GO to great (all)* ~ *s,* alles in jou vermoë doen; *GO to the* ~ *of asserting that,* so ver gaan om te beweer; *at GREAT(ER)* ~ , uitvoerig(er); *KEEP someone at arm's* ~ , iem. op 'n afstand hou; *at SOME* ~ , taamlik uitvoerig; *a* ~ *of STRING,* 'n stuk tou; *THROUGHOUT the* ~ *and breadth of the district,* deur die hele distrik; *some* ~ *of TIME,* 'n taamlike tyd; *one's WHOLE* ~ , in sy volle lengte; *WIN by a* ~ , met 'n lengte wen.

leng'then, langer maak, verleng; rek; langer word; ~**ing,** verlenging, rekking.

length'ways, length'wise, in die lengte.

leng'thy, lang; langdurig; langdradig, omslagtig.

len'ience, len'iency, sagtheid; toegewendheid.

len'ient, versagtend; toegewend, toegeeflik, genadig; sag, sagsinnig.

Len'inism, Leninisme.

len'itive, (n) pynstillende middel; (a) versagtend, lenigend.

len'ity, sagtheid, sagsinnigheid, sagmoedigheid.

len'o, katoengaas, leno.

lens, (-es), lens; ~**ed,** met 'n lens; ~**-grinding,** (die) slyp van 'n lens; ~ **screen,** lenskap.

Lent¹, (n) die Vaste, Vastyd.

lent², (v) *kyk* **lend.**

Len'ten, vas-, vaste-; skraal, maer; ~ **face,** droewige gesig; ~ **fare,** skraal kos (sonder vleis).

len'ticel, lentisel, asemopening.

len'ticle, lens, lensvormige laag.

lentic'ular, lensvormig; dubbelbol.

len'ticule, lensie.

len'tiform = **lenticular.**

lentig'inous, met sproete, sproeterig.

lenti'go, (-es), somersproet, bruinvlek.

len'til, lensie; ~**-cream soup,** lensieroomsop; ~ **flour,** lensiemeel.

lentis'cus, len'tisk, mastikboom.

len'titude, stadigheid, langsaamheid, traagheid, luiheid.

len'toid, lensvormig.

Le'o, (die) Leeu (sterrebeeld).

le'onine, leeuagtig, leeu=.

Le'onine, Leonies; ~ **verse,** Leoniese vers.

leo'pard, luiperd; Afrikaanse tier; *the* ~ *cannot change its spots,* 'n jakkals verander van hare, maar nie van streke nie; ~**ess, (-es),** luiperdwyfie; ~ **tortoise,** bergskilpad.

le'otard, leotard.

lep'er, melaatse, lepralyer; verworpene; ~**-asylum,** ~**-hospital,** ~**-house,** ~**-institute,** lasaret, leprosegestig.

lepi'dolite, lepidoliet.

lepidop'ter, dagvlinder.

Lepidop'tera, Skubvleueliges; ~**l,** skubvlerkig.

lepidop'terous, met skubvlerke, skubvleuelig.

le'porine, haasagtig.

leprechaun', Ierse fee; kabouter; aardmannetjie.

leprosa'rium, leprosegestig.

lepros'is, leprose (sitrus).

lep'rosy, melaatsheid, lepra, lasarus.

lep'rous, melaats.

lep'ton, lepton.

lep'tospirosis, leptospirose.

Les'bian, (n) Lesbiër; Lesbies (taal); (a) Lesbies; ~**ism,** Lesbinisme.

lese-maj'esty, majesteitskennis, lèse-majesté.

le'sion, beskadiging, kneusing, letsel, skade, benadeling.

Lesoth'o, Lesotho.

less, (n) minder; *NONE* the ~ , nietemin; *THE* ~ , hoe minder; (a) minder, kleiner, geringer; *I could not CARE* ~ , (slang), ek gee geen flenter om nie; ~

than *FAIR,* glad nie billik nie; *FOR* ~ , goedkoper; *NO* ~ *a person than,* niemand minder nie as; *in* ~ *than no TIME,* in 'n kits; (adv) minder; ~ *KNOWN,* minder bekend; (prep) min; *five* ~ *four,* vyf min vier.

lessee', huurder; pagter.

less'en, verminder; lenig; kleineer.

less'er, minder, kleiner; *L* ~ *ASIA,* Klein-Asië; *the* ~ *of (the) two EVILS,* die minste v.d. twee euwels; *the* ~ *LIGHTS,* die mindere gode; *the L* ~ *PROPHETS,* die Klein Profete; *the* ~ *must make WAY for the greater,* as meerderman kom, moet minderman wyk.

less'on, (n) les, oefening; Bybellesing, leesgedeelte; vermaning; *DURING* ~ *s,* gedurende die onderwys; *READ someone a* ~ , iem. oor die kole haal; iem. die leviete voorlees; iem. berispe; *TEACH someone a* ~ , iem. 'n les leer; (v) onderrig, leer; vermaan, kapittel.

less'or, verhuurder, verpagter.

lest, sodat . . . nie, uit vrees dat; ~ *we forget,* sodat ons nie vergeet nie.

let¹, (n) beletsel, verhindering; *without* ~ *or hindrance,* onbelemmerd, onverhinderd; (v) verhinder, belet.

let², (n) toestaan; verhuur; plekbespreking; (v) **(let, let),** laat; verhuur (gebou); toestaan, toelaat; ~ *ALONE,* jou nie bemoei nie met; laat staan; daar gelate; ~ *it BE,* laat dit maar staan; ~ *BLOOD,* bloedlaat; ~ *someone DOWN,* iem. in die steek laat; teleurstel; ~ *DOWN one's hair,* die hare losmaak; losbreek; ~ *FALL,* laat val; ~ *GO,* loslaat; vergeet; jou nie inhou nie; ~ *oneself GO,* vrye loop aan jou gevoel gee; jou gevoelens lug; jou oorgee; ~ *someone HAVE it,* iem. bestraf; op iem. lostrek; ~ *IN,* laat inkom; inlas; insleep; ~ *IN for,* op die hals haal; ~ *someone IN for something,* iem. in die moeilikheid bring; *not know what one is* ~ *ting oneself IN for,* nie weet waarin jy jou begewe nie; ~ *INTO,* inlaat, toelaat tot; aanbring in; bekend maak met; inlig omtrent; bestorm; ~ *KNOW,* laat weet; ~ *LOOSE,* loslaat; ~ *OFF,* loslaat; vrylaat; afblaas, uitlaat (stoom); laat val; vrystel van (straf); kwytskeld (oortreder); afskiet (geweer); ~ *OUT,* in pag gee; laat uitgaan; verhuur; verklap; lostrek; ~ *something OUT,* iets uitblaker; iets verklap; ~ *OUT a dress,* 'n rok groter maak; ~ *that PASS,* neem geen notisie daarvan nie; *TO* ~ , te huur; *not to* ~ *UP,* nie slap laat hang nie; *without* ~ *ting UP,* een stryk deur; ~ *WELL alone,* jy moet jou nie daarmee bemoei nie; ~**able,** verhuurbaar.

leth'al, dodelik, doods=; ~ *CHAMBER,* verstikkingstoestel, gaskamer, stikkamer; ~ *GAS,* dodelike gas.

lethar'gic, loom, slaperig; lusteloos, sufferig; slaapwekkend.

leth'argy, slaperigheid; slaapsiekte; koma; letargie, sufheid, botheid, ongevoeligheid.

Leth'e, die Lethe, doodsrivier; vergetelheid.

let'-off, ontkoming.

Lett, Let.

lett'er¹, (n) verhuurder.

lett'er², (n) letter; sendbrief, brief; (pl) lettere; ~ *s of ACCREDITATION,* geloofsbriewe; ~ *s of ADMINISTRATION,* briewe van administrasie; ~ *of ADVICE,* adviesbrief; ~ *of ALLOTMENT,* toekenningsbrief; ~ *of APPLICATION,* aansoekbrief (vir 'n betrekking); aanvraagbrief (aandele); ~ *of ATTORNEY,* volmag, prokurasie; ~ *of AUTHORITY,* magtigingsbrief; *BLACK* ~ , vet letter; Gotiese letter; *BY* ~ , per brief; skriftelik; *CAPITAL* ~ , hoofletter; ~ *of CONDOLENCE,* brief van roubeklag; ~ *of CREDENCE,* geloofsbrief; ~ *of CREDIT,* kredietbrief; *a DEAD* ~ , 'n dooie letter; 'n onbestelbare brief; ~ *of DEMAND,* aanmaning; aanskrywing; *written in* ~ *s of GOLD,* in goue letters geskryf; *INFERIOR* ~ , laaggedrukte letter (bv. C$_n$); ~ *of INTENT,* voornemensbrief; ~ *of INTRODUCTION,* bekendstellingsbrief, introduksiebrief; *the* ~ *KILLETH but the spirit giveth life,* die letter maak dood, maar die gees maak lewend; *LATE* ~ *s,* napos, laatpos; *according*

Lettic   1013   *liar*

to the ~ *of the LAW*, na die letter v.d. wet; *MAN of* ~*s*, geleerde; letterkundige; *OPEN* ~, oop (ope) brief (nie toegeplak nie); ope brief (in koerant); ~*s PATENT*, oktrooibriewe; ~ *of RECOMMEN-DATION*, aanbevelingsbrief; *in* ~ *and in SPIRIT*, na die letter en gees; *STICK to the* ~, aan die letter hou; *SUPERIOR* ~, hooggedrukte letter (2ª); (v) letter, nommer, merk; die titel gee; ~ **bag**, brieweˍsak; ~ **balance**, brieweskaal, briefweër; ~ **basket**, briewemandjie; ~-**book**, brieweboek; ~-**bound**, lettervas, gebonde aan die letter; ~-**box**, (-es), brieˍwebus; ~-**card**, briefkaart; ~-**carrier**, briewebeˍsteller; ~ **case**, briewetas; ~ **ed**, geletter, genomˍmer; geleerd; ~**ette**', briefie; ~-**face**, letterbeeld; ~-**file**, inryer, briefleêr, lias; ~-**folder**, voubeen; ~-**founder**, lettergieter; ~ **foundry**, lettergietery; ~-**head**, ~-**heading**, briefhoof; ~ **ing**, merk, letter; letterwerk; rugtitel; ~ **ing tool**, titelstempel; ~-**lock**, letterslot; ~-**paper**, briefpapier; ~-**perfect**, rolvas (toneelspeler); ~-**post**, briefpos; ~ **press**, drukwerk, byskrif, gedrukte teks; hoogdruk; koˍpieerpers; papiergewig; ~ **press printing machine**, drukpers, drukmasjien; ~-**rack**, briewerakkie; ~-**riddle**, letterraaisel; ~ **scales**, briefskaal; ~-**wood**, letterhout; ~-**worship**, letteraanbidding, letterˍknegtery; ~-**writer**, briefskrywer; brieweboek.
Lett'ic, Letties.
lett'ing, (die) verhuur, verhuring.
Lett'ish, (n, a) Lets, Letties.
Lott'land, Letland.
Letton'ia, Letland; ~**n**, (n, a) Letties.
lett'uce, blaarslaai; ~ **bed**, slaaiakkertjie; ~ **salad**, groen slaai.
leu'coblast, leukoblas(t), witselkiem, onvolwasse leukosiet.
leuc'ocyte, leukosiet, witbloedliggaampie, witbloedˍsel.
leuco'ma, leukoom, witvlek, witstaar.
leucop'athy, leukopatie, albinisme.
leucorrhoe'a, witvloed.
leu'cotome, leukotoom.
leuco'tomy, leukotomie.
leuk(a)em'ia, bloedkanker, leukemie.
leuk(a)cm'ic, witbloedig, leukemies.
lev, (-s), lev (Bulgaarse muntstuk).
Levant'¹, (n) Levant; (a) Levantyns.
levant'², (v) weglooop, trap.
Levant'er¹, Levantyn; sterk oostewind (Middellandˍse See).
levant'er², weglooper.
Levan'tine, (n) Levantyn; levantine (sy); (a) Levantyns.
levat'or, hefspier.
lev'ee, byeenkoms, oggendresepsie; ongeboude riˍvierwal; oewerwal, afsluitdam (Amer.).
lev'el, (n) waterpas; paslood; (hoogste) stand; verdieˍping (myn); peil; gelykte; vlak; *ABOVE one's* ~, bokant jou vuurmaakplek; *BE on a* ~ *with*, op een lyn staan met; gelykstaan met; *at DIPLOMATIC* ~, langs diplomatieke weg; *FIND one's* ~, jou (staan)plek vind, *on the HIGHEST* ~, op die hoogste vlak; *ON the* ~, doodeerlik; *ON a* ~, op een lyn; *on the SAME* ~, op dieselfde vlak; op gelyˍke voet; *at TOP* ~, op die hoogste vlak; (v) **(-led)**, gelykmaak; sloop; waterpas maak; korrelvat, aanˍgooi, rig, aanlê (geweer); op peil bring; ~ *AT*, mik op, korrelvat na; ~ *a CHARGE at*, iem. van iets beskuldig; ~ *CRITICISM against*, kritiek uitoefen op; ~ *DOWN*, gelykmaak; ~ *with the GROUND*, met die grond gelykmaak; ~ *OFF*, gelykmaak; staˍdiger gaan, verslap; ~ *UP*, opvul, gelykmaak; (a, adv) gelyk; waterpas; horisontaal; gelykmatig; efˍfen, egaal, effe, egalig; *do one's* ~ *BEST*, jou uiterˍste bes doen; *DRAW* ~ *with*, gelyk kom met; *GET* ~ *with*, afreken met; *a* ~ *HEAD*, 'n helder kop; *KEEP* ~ *with*, byhou; *a* ~ *SPOONFUL*,'n gelykˍvol lepel; ~ **crossing**, (spoor)oorweg, oorgang; ~-**crossing gate**, spoor(weg)hek; ~-**headed**, bedaard, koel, verstandig; ewewigtig, besadig; *remain* ~-*headed*, die kop koel hou; ~**(l)er**, gelykmaker; nivelleerder (masjien); grondstryker; ~**(-lifting) valve**, opligklep.

lev'elling, effening, slegting; gelykmaking; (die) waterˍpas maak, waterpassing; normalisering; nivellering; (die) mik; ~ **board**, korrelplank; ~ **instrument**, waterpasinstrument; nivelleerder; ~ **machine**, grondstryker; ~ **point**, gelykmaker, gelykbringˍpunt; ~ **screw**, stelskroef; ~ **system**, gelykmakende stelsel, nivelleerstelsel.
lev'elness, gelykheid, effenheid, egaligheid.
lev'er, (n) hefboom; stelarm; ligter; (v) met 'n ligter verskuif; ~ **age**, hefboomwerking; hefboomkrag; mag, invloed; ~ **bracket**, hefboomsteun.
lev'eret, jong hasie.
lev'er: ~ **guide**, stelarmgeleiding; ~ **pivot**, hefboomˍas; ~ **rod**, hefboomstang; ~ **switch**, hefboomuitˍskakelaar; ~ **watch**, ankeroorlosie.
lev'iable, hefbaar, invorderbaar, inbaar.
levi'athan, (n) leviatan; knewel; reuseskip; (a) kolosˍsaal, reusagtig, leviatans=.
lev'igate, fyn maak, fyn vryf; fyn skuur; glad maak.
leviga'tion, fynvrywing; gladmaking.
lev'in, bliksemstraal, blits.
lev'irate, leviraat, swaershuwelik.
lev'itate, laat drywe; sweef.
levita'tion, drywing; sweving; *power of* ~, sweefˍvermoë.
Lev'ite, Leviet; priester.
Levit'ical, Levities; priesterlik.
Levit'icus, Levitikus.
lev'ity, ligtheid, ligsinnigheid, wuftheid, wispelturigˍheid.
le'volose, **lev'ulose**, levulose.
lev'y, (n) **(lovies)**, heffing, inning; ligting (mil.); werˍwing; *a* ~ *on capital*, kapitaalheffing; (v) **(levied)**, hef; oproep, werf; invorder (geld); oplê; ~ *an ARMY*, 'n leër op die been bring; ~ *BLACKMAIL*, geld afpers; ~ *a FINE*, boete oplê (hef); ~ *MONEY*, geld invorder; ~ *WAR upon*, oorlog voer teen; ~ **fund**, heffingsfonds.
lewd, ontugtig, wellustig, onkuis, hitsig, wulps; ~ **ness**, wulpsheid, wellus, ontugtigheid.
le'wis, wolf (tap); grypyster, gryphaak; ~ **bolt**, wolfsˍbout.
le'wisite, lewisiet, gifgas.
lex'ical, leksikaal, van (betreffende) die leksikon.
lexicog'rapher, leksikograaf, woordeboekskrywer, woordeboekmaker.
lexicograph'ic(al), leksikografies, woordeboek=.
lexicog'raphy, leksikografie, woordeboekmakery.
lexicol'ogist, leksikoloog.
lexicol'ogy, leksikologie.
lex'icon, woordeboek, leksikon.
ley, grasland, grasveld, rusland; herstelgewas; rusoes; ~ **crop**, rusoes.
Ley'den, Leiden; ~ **jar**, Leidse fles.
liabil'ity, (..ties), verantwoordelikheid; onderhewigˍheid, aanspreeklikheid, verpligting; vatbaarheid; (pl) skulde, geldelike verpligtings, passiva; *BE a* ~ *to*, 'n blok aan die been wees vir; *CONTINGENT* ~, voortvloeiende verpligting; ~ *for DAMAGES*, skadepligtigheid; *LIMITED* ~, beperkte verantˍwoordelikheid; *LIMITED* ~ *company*, maatskapˍpy met beperkte aanspreeklikheid; *MEET one's liabilities*, jou geldelike verpligtings nakom; ~ *to SERVICE*, dienspligtigheid.
li'able, verantwoordelik; vatbaar; aanspreeklik; verˍplig, onderworpe; onderhewig; *BE* ~ *to doubt*, aan twyfel onderhewig wees; ~ *for DAMAGES*, skadeˍpligtig; ~ *to DANGER*, aan gevaar blootgestel; ~ *for DUTY*, onderhewig aan belasting; *be* ~ *to ERR*, geneig wees om 'n fout te begaan; ~ *to HAPPEN*, gebeurlik; *HOLD* ~, verantwoordelik hou; ~ *to military SERVICE*, dienspligtig.
liai'se, skakel, lieer (ong.).
liais'on, (ongeoorloofde) liefdesverhouding; verbinˍding (tussen leërs); skakeling, skakelwerk; ~ **comˍmittee**, skakelkomitee; ~ **duties**, skakeldiens; ~ **fire**, skakelvuur; ~ **officer**, skakeloffisier, verbinˍdingsoffisier; ~ **plane**, skakelvliegtuig; ~ **post**, skakelpos; ~ **service**, skakeldiens.
lia'na, liane', liaan, klimop, slingerplant.
li'ar, leuenaar, spekskieter; ~*s should have good me-*

mories, leuenaars moet oor goeie geheues beskik; wie leuens vertel, moet goed kan onthou.
li'as, leiagtige kalkklip, lias.
li'bate, 'n plengoffer bring.
liba'tion, die pleng, plengoffer, drankoffer; drink=gelag.
lib'el, (n) laster; bespotting, hoon, verguising; spot=skrif, paskwil, skimpskrif, skandskrif, lasterskrif, smaadskrif, skendskrif; (v) **(-led)** belaster, be=skimp, beklad, verguis; ~ **ler,** spotskrifskrywer; (be)lasteraar; ~ **lous,** lasterlik, eerrowend; ~ *lous language,* skendtaal, lasterlike taal.
lib'eral, (n) liberaal; vrysinnige; verligte; *L* ~, Libe=raal (partylid); (a) mild, goedgeefs, vrygewig, libe=raal; gul; vry, vrysinnig; oorvloedig, ruim; onbe=krompe, onbevooroordeeld; verlig; *the* ~ *ARTS*, die vrye kunste; *a* ~ *DISCOUNT*, 'n ruim afslag; *a* ~ *EDUCATION*, 'n veelsydige opleiding; ~ *HELP*, groot hulp; *L* ~ *PARTY*, Liberale Party; ~ *ism,* liberalisme; ~ **ist,** liberalis; ~ **is'tic,** liberalis=ties; ~ **'ity,** mildheid, goedgeefsheid, vrygewigheid; onbekrompenheid, vrysinnigheid; ~ **iza'tion,** libe=ralisering; ~ **ize,** vrysinnig maak, liberaal wees; ~ **-minded,** liberaal gesind, vrysinnig, ruimhartig.
lib'erate, bevry, vrymaak; vrylaat; ontwikkel; loslaat; uitskakel (elek.).
libera'tion, bevryding, invryheidstelling, vrylating, verlossing, vrymaking; uitskakeling (elek.); *war of* ~, vryheidsoorlog; ~ **ist,** vrymaker.
lib'erator, bevryder.
Liber'ia, Liberië; ~ **n,** (n) Liberiër; (a) Liberies.
libertar'ian, (n) aanhanger v.d. leer v.d. vrye wil, li=bertyn; (a) gelowend aan die leer v.d. vrye wil; *the* ~ *doctrine,* die leer v.d. vrye wil; ~ **ism,** leer v.d. vrye wil; ~ **ist,** voorstander v.d. leer v.d. vrye wil; vryheidsman.
libert'icide, (n) vryheidsmoord; vryheidsmoorde=naar; (a) vryheidmoordend.
li'bertinage, losbandigheid.
li'bertine, (n) libertyn, vrygees, vrydenker; ligmis, los=bol, pierewaaier; (a) libertyns, vrydenkend; losban=dig.
lib'ertinism, vrydenkery; losbandigheid.
lib'erty, (..**ties**), vryheid; *AT* ~, vry, in vryheid; *you ARE at* ~ *to,* dit staan jou vry om; *CAP of* ~, vryheidsmus; *CIVIL liberties,* burgerlike vryhede; ~ *of CONSCIENCE*, gewetensvryheid; *DEPRI=VATION of* ~, vryheidsberowing; *FLAG of* ~, vryheidsvlag, vryheidsvaan; *HAVE the* ~ *of,* die gebruik hê van; *LEAN* ~ *is better than fat slavery,* liewer klein heer as groot kneg; ~ *of the PRESS,* persvryheid; *SET at* ~, op vrye voet stel; *SPIRIT of* ~, vryheidsin; *TAKE liberties,* jou vryhede ver=oorloof; ~ **-cap,** vryheidsmus; ~ **hall,** maak-soos-jy-lekker-kry-plek; ~ **-loving,** vryheidliewend; ~ **pole,** vryheidsboom.
libid'inous, wellustig, wulps.
libid'o, libido, geslagsbegeerte, geslagsdrif; lewens=drang, lewensdrif.
Lib'ra¹, Libra, die Weegskaal (sterrebeeld).
lib'ra², (-e), (Romeinse) pond, libra.
librar'ian, bibliotekaris; ~ **ship,** bibliotekarispos; bi=blioteekwese; bibliotekarisskap.
lib'rary, (..**ries**), biblioteek, boekery; ~ **authority,** biblioteekowerheid; ~ **book,** biblioteekboek; ~ **official,** biblioteekbeampte; ~ **organizer,** biblio=teekorganiseerder; ~ **scheme,** biblioteekskema; ~ **science,** biblioteekleer, biblioteekkunde; ~ **service,** biblioteekdiens; biblioteekwese; ~ **ship,** biblioteek=amp.
librate', weeg, in ewewig wees, balanseer, skommel.
libra'tion, ewewig, balans; skommeling; librasie.
librett'ist, librettoskrywer, librettis.
librett'o, (..**retti**), operateks, libretto.
Lib'ya, Libië; ~ **n,** (n) Libiër; (a) Libies.
lice, *kyk* **louse.**
li'cence¹, (n) lisensie; verlof, vergunning, vryheid; ser=tifikaat, patent; losbandigheid; sedeloosheid; *MARRY by special* ~, met spesiale lisensie trou; *SPECIAL* ~, dispensasie.
li'cence², (v) toelaat, vergun, lisensieer; ~ **d,** gelisen=sieer(d); erken; ~ *d VICTUALLER,* drankhande=laar, drankverkoper; ~ *d VICTUALLING,* drank=handel.
li'cence: ~ **fee,** lisensiegeld; ~ **-holder,** lisensiehouer; rybewysraampie.
li'cense = licence, (v)
licensee', lisensiehouer, gelisensieerde; drankhande=laar.
li'censer, lisensieverlener; ~ *of the press,* perssensor.
li'censing, lisensieverlening; lisensiëring; ~ **act,** drankwet; ~ **authority,** lisensieowerheid; *L* ~ **Board,** Lisensieraad; *L* ~ **Court,** Lisensiehof.
lice'ntiate, lisensiaat.
licen'tious, losbandig, bandeloos, los, ongebonde; wellustig, wulps; ~ **ness,** losbandigheid, bande=loosheid; wellustigheid.
lich, lyk; liggaam.
li'chen, korsmos, ligeen; douwurm; ~ **ed,** bemos; ~ **ol'ogy,** moskunde; ~ **ous,** mos=, mosagtig.
lich: ~ **-gate,** kerkhofportaal; ~ **-house,** lykhuis; ~ **-owl,** kerkuil.
li'chi, li'tchi, lietsjie, Chinese pruim.
li'cit, geoorloof, wettig.
lick, (n) lek, lekgoed; lekplek (vir diere); harde hou; *at FULL* ~, in volle vaart; soos die wind; *a* ~ *and a PROMISE,* 'n vegie met die waslap (stoflap); *give someone a* ~ *with the rough side of one's TONGUE,* iem. 'n veeg uit die pan gee; (v) lek, oplek; aflek; afransel, afros; 'n pak (slae) toedien; hardloop, nael; ~ *AT,* lek aan; ~ *one's CHOPS (lips),* lippe aflek; jou tande slyp; ~ *CLEAN,* skoon lek; ~ *the DUST,* in die stof byt; ~ *one's FINGERS,* jou vingers aflek; *that* ~ *s ME,* dit slaan my dronk; ~ *OFF,* aflek; ~ *into SHAPE,* vorm gee aan; reg=maak; ~ *a person's SHOES,* iem. lek; iem. laag vlei; ~ *UP,* oplek; ~ *one's WOUNDS,* jou wonde lek; ~ **er,** lekker; ~ **erish,** ~ **erous,** kieskeurig, lek=kerbekkig; begerig, wellustig, wulps; ~ **ing,** gelek; 'n pak (slae); siepsop-en-braaiboud; ~ **spittle,** krui=per, lekker, witvoetjiesoeker.
lic'orice, *kyk* **liquorice.**
lic'tor, lictor, byldraer.
lid, deksel; ooglid; *with the* ~ *OFF,* met die sluier gelig; soos dit werklik is; *that puts the* ~ *ON it,* dis darem te erg; die kroon op alles sit; alles oortref; ~ **ded,** met 'n deksel; met oogleede; ~ **less,** sonder deksel; slapeloos, waaksaam; sonder oogleede; ~ **-lock,** dekselslot.
li'do, lido, baaistrand, swemoord.
lie¹, (n) leuen, kluitjie; *ACT a* ~, leuenagtig handel; kul sonder om iets te sê; *GIVE the* ~ *to,* weer=spreek; loënstraf; die onwaarheid blootlê; *though a* ~ *is well dressed it is ever overcome,* al loop 'n leuen nog so snel, die waarheid agterhaal dit wel; ~ *s by the SCORE,* lieg dat 'n mens dit met 'n stok kan voel; *give the* ~ *to a STORY,* 'n leuen weerlê; *give someone the* ~ *in the THROAT,* iem. van leuentaal beskuldig; *TELL a* ~, lieg; *a WHITE* ~, 'n nood=leuen; *a* ~ *has a short WING,* al is die leuen nog so snel, die waarheid agterhaal dit wel; (v) lieg; stories vertel, jok; ~ *AWAY one's reputation,* jou reputa=sie deur lieg kwytraak; ~ *like a GASMETER,* lieg of dit gedruk staan; ~ *someone out of his MONEY,* iem. uit sy geld lieg; ~ *oneself OUT of,* jou losliegs; ~ *like a TROOPER,* erger lieg as 'n donkie kan skop; lieg soos 'n tandetrekker.
lie², (n) ligging; lêplek; *the* ~ *of the land,* die stand van sake; hoe die wind waai; (v) **(lay, lain),** lê, rus; jou bevind; in garnisoen lê; toelaatbaar wees (reg); ~ *ABOUT,* rondlê; *an ACTION* ~ *s,* dit is aksiona=bel; ~ *in AMBUSH,* voorlê, in hinderlaag lê; ~ *BACK,* agteroorleun; ~ *under a CHARGE of,* be=skuldig wees van; ~ *DOWN,* plat lê; gaan lê; jou neervly; ~ *DEAD,* dood lê, vier stewels in die lug lê; ~ *in DUST,* in puin lê; bouvallig wees; ~ *near one's HEART,* 'n voorwerp van kommer wees; ~ *IN,* in die kraam wees; *as far as IN me* ~ *s,* sover ek daartoe in staat is; *find out how the LAND* ~ *s,* die kat uit die boom kyk; ~ *LOW,* plat lê; jou tyd afwag; wegkruip; siek wees; ~ *at the MERCY of,* afhang v.d. genade van; *the boat* ~ *s OFF Durban,* die skip lê voor anker naby Durban; ~ *ON,* lê op, rus op; ~ *OPEN to,* blootstaan aan; ~ *OVER,* bly

lê; oorbly; uitgestel word; *the REMEDY* ~*s in*, die redmiddel moet gesoek word in; ~ *at the ROOT of*, ten grondslag lê aan; ~ *in RUINS*, in puin lê; vervalle (bouvallig) wees; ~ *in STATE*, op 'n praalbed lê; *it* ~*s on the SURFACE*, dit lê voor die hand; ~ *TO*, bydraai; ~ *UNDER*, gebuk gaan onder; ~ *UP*, dok (skip); uitrus, in die bed lê; ~ *in WAIT*, voorlê; op die loer lê; ~ *WITH*, slaap by; *if it* ~*s WITH me*, as dit in my vermoë lê; *it* ~*s WITH you*, dit hang van jou af; ~**-abed**, luilak, laatslaper.

lied (lieder), (G.), kunslied.

lie'-detector, leuen(ver)klikker.

lief, graag; *I would as* ~, ek sou net so lief.

Liege¹, Luik.

liege², (n) leenheer; koning, vors; vasal; (a) leenpligtig; leen=; ~ **lady**, leenvrou; ~ **lord**, leenheer, vors; ~ **man**, leenman, vasal; volgeling.

lien'¹, retensiereg, pandreg; verband; beladingskuld.

li'en², milt: ~*i'tis*, miltontsteking.

lierne, bindrib; ~ **vault**, stergewelf.

Lierre, Lier.

lieu, plaas, plek; *in* ~ *of*, in plaas van, in die plek van, pleks van.

licuten'ancy, luitenantskap, luitenantsrang.

lieuten'ant, luitenant; ~**-colonel**, luitenant-kolonel; ~**-commander**, luitenant-kommandeur; ~**-general**, luitenant-generaal; ~**-governor**, luitenant-goewerneur.

life, (lives); lewe; lewensduur (voertuig); draagduur (klere); duursaamheid; bruikbaarheidsduur (lening); duur (myn); bestaan, lewenswyse; lewensbeskrywing; naakstudie; lewendigheid, lewenskrag; *ALL my* ~, my hele lewe; my lewe lank; *make an ATTEMPT on someone's* ~, 'n aanslag op iem. se lewe maak; ~ *is not too BAD*, dit gaan leefbaar; *BREATH of* ~, lewensasem; *BRING to* ~, bybring; in die lewe roep; *BUZZ of* ~, lewensgewoel; *set one's* ~ *on a CHANCE*, jou lewe waag; *the CHANCE of one's* ~, die beste kans van sy lewe; *bear a CHARMED* ~, onkwesbaar wees; *COME to* ~, lewendig word; jou roer; *COURSE of* ~, lewensloop; *for DEAR* ~, uit alle mag; *between* ~ *and DEATH*, tussen lewe en dood; *a matter of* ~ *and DEATH*, 'n saak van lewe of dood; *DRAWN from* ~, na die lewe geteken; uit die lewe; *ENTER* ~, sy loopbaan begin; *ESCAPE with* ~, met die lewe daarvan afkom; ~ *EVERLASTING*, die ewige lewe; *EXPECTATION of* ~, lewensverwagting; vermoedelike lewensduur; *I cannot FOR the* ~ *of me*, ek kan om die dood nie; met die beste wil v.d. wêreld kan ek nie; *FOR* ~, lewenslank; vir die lewe; *FULL of* ~, springlewendig; *the FUTURE* ~, die hiernamaals; *take your* ~ *into your own HANDS*, jou lewe waag; *while there is* ~ *there is HOPE*, solank daar lewe is, is daar hoop; *HUMAN* ~, mensclewens; *as LARGE as* ~, lewensgroot; in lewende lywe; *LAY down one's* ~, jou lewe neerlê; *a new LEASE of* ~, 'n nuwe lewensduur; *LENGTH of* ~, lewensduur; ~ *and LIMB*, lyf en lewe; *LOSE one's* ~, die lewe inskiet; *with no LOSS of* ~, sonder verlies van menselewens; ~ *of a MOTOR*, lewensduur van 'n motor; *NOTHING in* ~, hoegenaamd niks; *not ON your* ~! nooit! *PORTRAY to the* ~, na die lewe teken; *PSYCHIC* ~, sielelewe; *lead a QUIET* ~, 'n stil lewe lei; *RUN for dear* ~, uit alle mag hardloop; *SEE* ~, die lewe leer ken; *SIGN of* ~, lewensteken; *the* ~ *and SOUL*, die siel van; *not to be SURE of one's* ~, jou lewe nie seker wees nie; *TAKE one's* ~, jou hand aan jou eie lewe slaan; *TAKE a* ~, iem. die lewe ontneem; *TAKEN from* ~, uit die lewe gegryp; na die lewe geteken; *his* ~ *hangs by a THREAD*, sy lewe hang aan 'n draadjie; *THROUGHOUT* ~, lewenslank; *TO the* ~, sprekend gelyk; *TREE of* ~, lewensboom; *at this TIME of* ~, op hierdie leeftyd; *be on TRIAL for one's* ~, tereg staan weens 'n halsmisdaad; *TRUE to* ~, lewensgetrou; *UPON my* ~, by my siel; *WRETCHED* ~, hondelewe; ~**-and-death**, *-and-death struggle*, stryd op lewe en dood; ~ **annuity**, lyfrente; ~ **assurance**, lewensversekering; ~ **belt**, reddingsgordel; ~**-blood**, lewensbloed, lewe, siel; ~ **boat**, reddingsboot; ~ **buoy**, reddingsboei, reddingsgordel; ~**-changing**, lewensverandering; ~**-class**, figuurtekening, modeltekening, klas met lewende model; ~ **cycle**, lewenskring; ~ **drawing**, teken na die lewe; ~ **expectancy**, lewensverwagting; lewensduur; ~**-force**, lewenskrag; lewensdrang; ~**-form**, lewensvorm; ~**-giving**, kraggewend; besielend, opwekkend; ~**-guard**, lyfwag; ~ **history**, lewensbeskrywing, lewensgeskiedenis; ~ **insurance**, lewensversekering; ~ **interest**, lewensreg, vruggebruik; ~**-jacket**, reddingsbaadjie; ~ **less**, leweloos, sielloos; dooierig; ~ **lessness**, dooierigheid; ~ **like**, na die lewe; ~ **line**, reddingstou; lewenstreep; ~ **long**, lewenslank; ~**-member**, lewenslid; ~**-office**, versekeringskantoor; ~ **policy**, lewensversekeringspolis; ~**-preserver**, reddingstoestel; ~ **r**, iem. met lewenslange gevangenisstraf; ~**-raft**, reddingsvlot; ~ **rent**, vruggebruik, usufructus; ~**-renter**, iem. in besit van 'n lyfrente; ~**-saver**, menseredder, lewensredder.

life'-saving, (n) reddingswerk; (a) reddings-; ~ **appliance**, reddingstoestel; ~ **company**, reddingsmaatskappy.

life: ~ **sentence**, lewenslange gevangenisstraf; ~**-size**, lewensgrootte; ~**-sized**, lewensgroot; ~**-span**, lewensduur; ~**-spring**, lewensbron; ~**-story**, lewensgeskiedenis; ~**-string**, lewensdraad; ~**-struggle**, lewenstryd; ~**-table**, sterftetabel.

life'time, lewensduur, duurtyd; leeftyd; *the CHANCE of a* ~, 'n kans wat 'n mens nooit weer sal kry nie; *it will LAST a* ~, dit sal lewenslank hou.

life: ~**-weary**, lewensmoeg; ~**-work**, lewenswerk, lewenstaak.

lift, (n) opheffing, opligting; verhoging, stoot; vuurverlegging (mil.); vrag; hefvermoë, draagweerstand; hysbak, hystoestel; bultjie; draagkrag (vliegtuig); hefvermoë, stygkrag; *GET a* ~, opgelaai word; met geleentheid kom; *GIVE a* ~, iem. laat saamry, iem. oplaai; iem. help; (v) optel, oplig, oprig; (op)hef; verhef (stem); optrek, opklaar (wolke); kromtrek (vloer); steel; iem. oplaai, saamneem, uithaal (ertappels); opsteek (hand); opwek, opblaas; opgaan; ~ *DOWN*, aftel; *not* ~ *a FINGER (hand)*, geen poging aanwend nie; geen vinger verroer nie; *a FOG* ~*s*, 'n mis trek op; ~ *a HAND against*, 'n hand oplig teen; ~ *up one's HEAD*, die kop oplig; ~ *OFF*, aftel; ~ *UP*, ophef; verhef; ~ *up one's VOICE*, jou stem verhef; ~**-bridge**, ophaalbrug; ~**-capacity**, dravermoë; ~ **club**, saamryklub; ~ **er**, ligter; heffer; haak; opligter; dief; lugbal (kr.); uithaler (van o.a. ertappels).

lift'ing, hef-; ~ **bracket**, hefarm; ~ **bridge**, hefbrug; ~ **crane**, hyskraan; ~**-hook**, hefhaak; ~ **jack**, domkrag; ~ **power**, hefvermoë; stygkrag; ~ **pump**, hefpomp; ~ **screw**, uitnemer; ~ **truck**, hefwa; ~ **wire**, hefhaak.

lift: ~**-lock**, ophaalsluis; ~**man**, hysbediende.

lig'ament, gewrigsband, verband; bindspier, ligament.

ligate', afbind, verbind.

liga'tion, afbinding, toebinding.

lig'ature, (n) verband, draad, bindsel; afbinding, knoop; koppelteken, verbindingsteken, koppelletter; (v) afbind, verbind.

lig'er, leeutier, tierleeu.

light¹, (n) lig, beligting; glans, verligting; daglig, hemellig; vuur, vuurhoutjie; vuurtoring; *ACCORDING to one's* ~*s*, na die lig wat 'n mens besit; *AT first* ~, met dagbreek; *it cannot BEAR the* ~ *of day*, dis oneerlik (onderduims); *to present in the BEST* ~, in die beste lig stel; *BRING to* ~, aan die lig bring; *COME to* ~, aan die lig kom; voor die dag kom; *see the* ~ *of DAY*, die lewenslig aanskou; *view in a DUBIOUS* ~, baie twyfelagtig beskou; *the* ~ *of my EYES*, die lig van my oë; *in a GOOD* ~, in die beste plooie; *HIDE one's* ~ *under a bushel*, jou lig onder 'n koringmaat verberg; *IN the* ~ *of the facts*, in hierdie lig gesien; *LAY* ~, lig en skaduwee aanbring; *men of* ~ *and LEADING*, leidende geeste; ~*s OUT!* ligte uit! *SEE the* ~, die lewenslig aanskou; iets verstaan; *let something SEE the* ~, iets uitgee; iets publiseer; iets laat verskyn;

he is beginning to SEE the ~, daar gaan vir hom 'n lig op; *SHED (throw)* ~ *on*, lig werp op; *STAND in someone's* ~, in iem. se lig staan; *not to be able to STAND the* ~ *of day*, die lig nie kan verdra nie; nadere ondersoek nie kan deurstaan nie; *STAND in one's own* ~, in jou eie lig staan; jou eie kanse bederwe; *you are STANDING in my* ~, groot lantern, weinig lig; *STRIKE a* ~, lig maak, 'n vuurhoutjie trek; *THROW a flood of* ~ *on*, 'n helder lig laat val op; *VIEW in the* ~ *of what has happened*, van agteraf beskou; (v) (**-ed** or **lit**), lig; verlig; aansteek, ontsteek, opsteek (vuur); trek; blink, straal; aan die brand raak, vuur vat; belig; voorlig; ~ *someone ON his way*, iem. voorlig; ~ *UP*, opheder; opsteek (pyp); ~ *the WAY*, voorlig; (a) lig; helder; blond (hare).

light², (v) neerkom, afkom; afklim; beland; te lande kom; ~ *(up)on*, kom tot; gaan sit op (voël); raakloop, teen die lyf loop, teëkom; (a) maklik; bros; los (sedes); ligsinnig; lighartig; gou, vlug; onstandvastig; onbesorg; *have* ~ *FINGERS*, lang vingers hê; ~ *of FOOT*, rats; *a* ~ *SLEEPER*, 'n ligte slaper; (adv) lig; los; ~ *BAY*, ligbruin; *MAKE* ~ *of*, gering ag; *TRAVEL* ~, met min bagasie reis; ~**-armed**, liggewapen; ~ **artillery**, ligte geskut.

light: ~**-ball**, ligkoeël; ~ **beacon**, ligbaken; ~**-bearer**, fakkeldraer.

light: ~ **blue**, ligblou; ~**-bodied**: ~*-bodied wine*, ligte wyn; ~ **brown**, ligbruin.

light'-buoy, ligboei.

light: ~ **cavalry**, ligte ruitery; ~ **concrete**, ligte beton; ~ **delivery van**, bakkie, ligte afleweringswa.

light'en¹, ophelder, verlig, flikker, gloei; weerlig, bliksem.

light'en², ligter maak; ligter word; uitlaai; opvrolik, opbeur.

light'er¹, opsteker, aansteker, aanbrandsteker.

light'er², ligter(skip).

light: ~ **erage**, oorlaaiing in 'n ligter; ligtergeld; ~**erman**, ligterman, skuitvoerder; ~ **fabric**, dun stof; ~**-fingered**, langvingerig, skelm.

light'-flash, ligflits; ligflikkering.

light: ~**-footed**, gou, rats, vinnig; ~**-handed**, sag; taktvol; ~**-headed**, ligsinnig, lighoofdig; ylhoofdig; ~**-hearted**, lughartig, vrolik, opgewek; ~ **heavyweight**, ligswaargewig; ~**-heeled**, vinnig, gou; ~ **horse**, ligte ruitery.

light'house, vuurtoring; ~ **keeper**, vuurtoringwagter.

light' infantry, ligte voetgangers, ligte infanterie.

light'ing, opsteek, aansteek; beligting; verligting; ~ **fittings**, lamptoebehore; ligtoebehore; ~ **plant**, liginstallasie, verligtingsaanleg; ~**-switch**, ligknippie, ligskakelaar.

light'ish¹, ligterig, nie heeltemal donker nie.

light'ish², ligterig, nie danig swaar nie.

light'ly, lugtig; lig, saggies; maklik; ligsinnig; ligweg; ~ *COME*, ~ *go*, so gewonne, so geronne; *his LEARNING sits* ~ *upon him*, hy maak geen vertoon van sy geleerdheid nie.

light: ~**-minded**, ligsinnig; ~**ness**, helderheid; ligsinnigheid; maklikheid; ~*ness of heart*, opgeruimdheid.

light'ning, weerlig, hemelvuur, blits; *LIKE* ~, soos die blits; *QUICK as* ~, blitsig; *RUN like greased* ~, soos 'n makgemaakte (vetgesmeerde) blits loop; *with* ~ *SPEED*, blitssnel; ~ **bug**, vuurvlieg(ie); ~ **calculator**, blitsrekenaar, snelrekenaar; ~ **conductor**, weerligafleier, bliksemafleier; ~ **cooker**, snelkoker; ~ **flash**, bliksemstraal; ~**-like**, blitsig; ~**-proof**, blitsvry; ~**-rod**, bliksemafleier; ~ **speed**, bliksemsnelheid; ~ **storm**, elektriese storm; ~ **strike**, blitsstaking, skielike staking; ~ **stroke**, bliksemslag.

light'-o'-love, flerrie, ligtekooi.

light' opera, operette; musiekspel.

light'-plant, liginstallasie.

lights, longe (van diere), harslag.

light: ~**-sensitive**, liggevoelig; ~ **ship**, ligskip.

light'-skirts, ligtekooi, flerrie.

light' socket, ligmof, ligsok.

light: ~**some**, lig, helder; opgewek, vrolik, lewendig; vinnig, rats; ~**-spirited**, opgewek.

light: ~**-tight**, ligdig; ~**-unit**, ligeenheid; ~**-wave**, liggolf.

light'weight, liggewig; onbeduidende persoon, nul; ~ **fabric**, ligte (dun) materiaal (stof).

light'wood, vuurmaakhout.

light'-year, ligjaar.

lig'neous, hout=, houtagtig.

lignifica'tion, houtvorming.

lig'nified, verhout.

lig'niform, houtvormig.

lig'nify, (..fied), verhout, tot hout word.

lignine', houtstof, lignien, lignine.

lig'nite, bruinkool, ligniet, houtsteen.

lignum vit'ae, pokhout, guajakhout.

lig'ulate, tongvormig.

lig'ule, tongetjie.

Ligur'ia, Ligurië; ~**n**, (n) Liguriër; Liguries (taal); (a) Liguries.

lik'able, beminlik, aangenaam, gaaf.

like, (n) gelyke, ewebeeld; (pl) voorliefde; ~ *ATTRACTS* ~, soort soek soort; *his* ~*s and DISLIKES*, sy simpatieë en antipatieë; *EVERY* ~ *is not the same*, aal is geen paling nie; *the* ~*s of HIM*, sy soort; *HIS* ~*s*, sy gelyke; *did you ever hear the* ~ *OF it?* het jy al ooit so iets gehoor? ~ *PRODUCES* ~, eenderse oorsake het eenderse gevolge; die appel val nie ver v.d. boom nie; ~ *SEEKS* ~, soort soek soort; *THE* ~, iets dergeliks; sulkes; (v) hou van, aanstaan, beval; behae skep in; graag wil, lus hê vir; *not to* ~ *something one BIT*, niks daarvan hou nie; *I DON'T* ~ *that*, ek hou nie daarvan nie, dit beval my nie; *FEEL* ~, lus voel; *HOW do you* ~ *that?* hoe vind jy dit? hoe pruim (rook) daardie twak vir jou? *IF you* ~, as jy wil; *to* ~ *it or LUMP it*, dit eenvoudig moet verdra; *whether you* ~ *it or NOT*, of jy daarvan hou of nie; *she RATHER* ~*s him*, sy hou nogal van hom; *I SHOULD* ~ *to see*, ek sou graag wou sien; *I* ~ *THAT!* dis 'n mooi grap! (a, adv) gelyk; soos; eenders, gelykend; ooreenkomstig, dergelik; *AS* ~ *as not*, hoogs waarskynlik; ~ *BLAZES*, dat dit gons; *DO as you* ~, maak soos jy wil; *not anything* ~ *so well DONE*, glad nie so goed gedoen nie; ~ *FATHER*, ~ *son*, die appel val nie ver v.d. boom nie; *I don't FEEL* ~ *it*, ek het geen lus daarvoor nie; *nothing* ~ *so GOOD*, lank nie so goed nie; *IN* ~ *manner*, op dieselfde manier; *LOOK* ~, lyk na; ~ *MASTER*, ~ *man*, so heer, so kneg; *there is NOTHING* ~ *it*, daar is niks beter nie; *AS* ~ *as two PEAS*, soos twee druppels water; ~ *a SHOT*, onmiddellik; *THAT'S just* ~ *you*, dis nou wat 'n mens van jou kan verwag; *WHAT is he* ~*?* hoe lyk hy? *WHOM is he* ~*?* op wie lyk hy? *a WRITER* ~ *you*, 'n skrywer soos jy; (prep, conj) soos.

like'lihood, waarskynlikheid; *in all* ~, na alle waarskynlikheid.

like'ly, waarskynlik, vermoedelik; geskik; aangenaam; aanneemlik (storie); *AS* ~ *as not*, heel moontlik; *NOT* ~, nie waarskynlik nie; *VERY (most)* ~, heel waarskynlik.

like'minded, van dieselfde gevoelens, eensgesind, eendersdenkend, gelykgesind.

lik'en, vergelyk.

like'ness, gelykenis; gedaante; uiterlik(e); gelykheid; portret, ewebeeld; *take a* ~ *of*, 'n portret laat maak van.

like'-sided, gelykbenig.

like'wise, eweneens; desgelyks; net so; so, insgelyks, eweso; ~ *present*, medeaanwesig, ook aanwesig.

lik'ing, lus, behae, sin(nigheid), skik, smaak; welgevalle, gading, geneentheid; ingenomenheid; *DEVELOP a* ~ *for*, begin hou van, liefkry; *HAVE a* ~ *for*, hou van; *NOT to my* ~, nie na my smaak nie; *TAKE a* ~ *to someone*, tot iem. aangetrokke voel.

lil'ac, (n) sering(blom), seringstruik; (a) pers, lila, sering=.

lilangen'i, (mv. **emalengeni**), lilangeni (Swazilandse munteenheid).

lilia'ceous, lelieagtig.

Lille, Rysel.
Lillipu'tian, (n) lilliputter; dwerg; (a) lilliputterig; dwergagtig.
lilt (n) vrolike deuntjie; kadans, ritme; (v) ronddans, vrolik sing; ~ **ing,** sangerig.
lil'y, (n) **(lilies),** lelie; (a) lelie=, lelieagtig; *PAINT the* ~, wat mooi is nog mooier wil maak; ~ *of the VALLEY,* lelie-der-dale, dallelie; *WILD* ~, wilde lelie; ~ **bulb,** leliebol; ~ **-iron,** harpoen; ~ **-livered,** lafhartig, papbroekerig; ~ **-shaped,** lelievormig; ~ **-white,** leliewit, spierwit.
li'ma bean, limaboontjie, goewerneursboontjie.
lima'ceous, slakagtig.
limb¹, (n) rand; verdeelde skaal, limbus.
limb², (n) lit; been; arm; tak; deel; kruisarm; uitloper (berg); vleuel (gebou); ~ *of the DEVIL,* duiwelskind, skobbejak; ~ *of the LAW,* konstabel; *be OUT on a* ~, in 'n moeilike posisie wees; *SOUND in wind and* ~, gesond van lyf en lede; (v) uitmekaar skeur.
limb'ate, met gekleurde rand (plantk.).
limbed, met ledemate.
lim'ber¹, (n) voorwa, voorstel (van 'n kanonwa); loosgat; (v) aanhaak; ~ *up,* die voorstel (voorwa) inhaak.
lim'ber², (v) buigsaam maak; ~ *up,* litte losmaak; (a) buigsaam, lenig.
lim'ber: ~ **-box,** ~ **-chest,** ammunisiekis.
limb'less, sonder ledemate.
lim'bo, (-s), voorgeborgte, voorhemel, voorhel, limbus; limbo; tronk; *relegate to the* ~ *of forgotten things,* in die vergeetboek raak.
limbs, ledemate.
Lim'burger, Limburger(kaas).
lime¹, (n) lemmetjie, suurlemoen.
lime², (n) linde(boom).
lime³, (n) kalk; voëlent, (voël)lym; dief; (v) voëlent smeer aan; vang; kalk gooi op; in kalk laat lê; met kalk bemes; kalk, wit; ~ **-brush,** witkwas; ~ **-burner,** kalkbrander; ~ **-burning,** kalkbrandery; ~ **-cast,** kalkbedekking; ~ **concrete,** kalkbeton; ~ **content,** kalkgehalte; ~ **deposit,** kalklaag; kalkafsetting; kalkaanpaksel (in ketel); ~ **feldspar,** kalkveldspaat.
lime'-flower, lindeblom.
lime'-juice, suurlemoensap, sitroensap.
lime-kiln, (kalk)brandery, kalkoond.
lime'light, kalklig; *be IN the* ~, die aandag trek; op die voorgrond wees; in die kalklig wees; *SEEK the* ~, publisiteit soek; *STEP into the* ~, op die voorgrond tree; *THRUST oneself into the* ~, jou op die voorgrond dring.
lim'en, drumpel, limen.
lime'-pit, kalkgat.
lim'erick, bogrympie, vyfreëlige (onsin)rympie, limerick, limeriek.
lime: ~ **-rock,** kalkbank; ~ **-slaking,** (die) blus van kalk; ~ **stone,** kalkklip; ~ **sulphur,** kalkswael.
lime' tree¹, suurlemoenboom.
lime'-tree², lindeboom; *avenue of* ~ *s,* lindelaan.
lime: ~ **-wash,** (n) witkalk; (v) wit; ~ **water,** kalkwater.
lime'wood, lindehout.
lim'it, (n) grens; perk; limiet, grenslyn; beperking; eindpaal; toppunt; ~ *of ELASTICITY,* elastisiteitsgrens; ~ *of ERROR,* foutgrens, toegestane afwyking; *GO the* ~, tot die uiterstes gaan; *GO beyond all* ~ *s,* alle perke oorsky, *there IS a* ~ *to everything,* alles het sy grense; *SET a* ~ *to,* 'n grens stel aan; *SHE is the* ~, sy gaan te ver; *THAT'S the* ~, dis darem te erg; *TO the* ~, tot die alleruiterste; *everything WITHIN* ~, alles binne perke; *WITHOUT* ~, onbegrens, onbeperk; (v) begrens, bepaal, afperk; beperk; vasstel; ~ **able,** begrensbaar, beperkbaar; ~ **ar'ian,** aanhanger v.d. leer van beperkte verlossing; ~ **ary,** beperk, grens=; begrensend.
limita'tion, beperking; inperking; begrensing, afperking; bepaling; verjaringstermyn; ~ *of ACTIONS,* verjaring van aksies; *KNOW one's* ~ *s,* jou eie beperkings ken.
lim'it: ~ **ative,** beperkend; ~ **ditch,** heiningsloot.
lim'ited, beperk; ~ *ACCESS,* beperkte toegang; ~ *EDITION,* beperkte uitgawe; ~ *LIABILITY company,* maatskappy met beperkte aanspreeklikheid; ~ *MONARCHY,* beperkte monargie.
lim'itless, grensloos, onbeperk.
lim'itrophe, aangrensend, grens=.
limn, skilder, teken; ~ **er,** skilder, tekenaar.
limnol'ogy, limnologie, meerkunde.
li'monite, limoniet, moerasyster.
limousine', limousine.
limp¹, (n) mankheid; (die) mank loop; *HAVE a* ~, *WALK with a* ~, mank loop; (v) mank wees, mank loop, hink.
limp², (a) lenig, slap, buigsaam; *be* ~ *with laughter,* slap wees v.d. lag; ~ **cover,** sagte (slap) band.
lim'per, kreupele.
lim'pet, klipmossel; *stick like a* ~, klou soos 'n neet.
lim'pid, helder, deursigtig.
limpid'ity, lim'pidness, helderheid, deursigtigheid.
limp'ing, mank, kruppel.
limp'ness, slapp(er)igheid.
lim'y, kalkagtig, kalk=; klewerig.
lin'age, aantal gedrukte reëls.
linar'ia, weeskindertjies.
linch'-pin, (wa)luns, lunspen.
lin'ctus, hoesstroop, leksap.
lin'den, linde(boom); ~ **bark,** lindebas.
line¹, (n) reël (wisk.); lyn, draad, koord; waslyn; reël (wat geskryf is); reëltjie, briefie; snoer; vislyn; rigsnoer; spoor (trein); ry, reeks; versreël; vak, artikel, ware, besigheid; streep; grens; geslag; strafreël; tou; ewenaar; linie (militêr); stoomvaartlyn; gelid; soort, rigting; afstamming, bloedlyn (diere); (pl) belyning; ~ *of ACTION,* koers, gedragslyn; *ALL along the* ~, langs die hele linie; dwarsdeur; *ALONG the* ~ *s,* op hierdie grondslag; in hierdie rigting; ~ *of AUTHORITY,* lyngesag; ~ *of BATTLE,* slagorde; *BE in* ~ *for,* in aanmerking kom vir; *BEHIND the* ~ *s,* agter die front; *read BETWEEN the* ~ *s,* tussen die reëls lees; *BRING in* ~ *with,* in ooreenstemming bring met; *BRING into* ~, oorhaal om saam te werk; *in the BOOK* ~, in die boekevak; ~ *of COMMUNICATION,* verbindingslyn; ~ *of CONDUCT,* gedragslyn; *CROSS the* ~, die linie passeer; ~ *of CURVATURE,* krommingslyn; ~ *of DEMARCATION,* skeidslyn, grenslyn; ~ *of DIP,* hellingslyn; *DRAW the* ~, die grens trek; *DRAW up into* ~, in slagorde opstel; *DOWN the* ~, met die lyn; langs die lyn af; *DROP me a* ~, skryf vir my 'n briefie; *FALL (come) into* ~, in gelid gaan staan; aantree; ooreenstem met; akkoord gaan met; ~ *of FIRE,* skootslyn; *take a FIRM* ~, ferm optree; *GIVE somebody* ~ *enough,* iem. die nodige vryheid gee; *GIVE* ~, die lyn laat skiet; die lyn vier; *come of a GOOD* ~, van goeie afkoms wees; *HARD* ~ *s!* simpatie! dis jammer! *IN a* ~ *with,* op een lyn met; *it is not IN one's* ~, dis nie iets vir jou nie; dit lê nie op jou weg nie; dit lê buite jou gebied (vak); ~ *of INCIDENCE,* invalslyn; ~ *of INTERSECTION,* snylyn; ~ *of LIFE,* lewenstreep; ~ *of MARCH,* marsweg, marsroete; *a NEW* ~, 'n nuwe soort artikel; 'n nuwe rigting; *OFF the* ~, ontspoor; *ON these* ~ *s,* op hierdie manier; volgens hierdie beginsels; *on his OWN* ~, op sy eie manier; ~ *of RESISTANCE,* weerstandslyn; ~ *of least RESISTANCE,* die maklikste weg; ~ *of RETREAT,* terugtoglyn, aftoglyn; *by RULE and* ~, haarfyn; *on the SAME* ~ *s,* op dieselfde manier; *SHIP of the* ~, linieskip; ~ *of SIGHT,* gesigslyn; riglyn; *on SIMILAR* ~ *s,* op gelyke manier; ~ *and STAFF,* lyn en staf; *STAND in* ~, toustaan; *STRIKE out a new* ~, 'n nuwe rigting inslaan; die bakens versit; ~ *of SUPPLY,* aanvoerlyn; *TAKE the* ~, die houding aanneem; ~ *of THOUGHT,* gedagtegang; ~ *UPON* ~, reël vir reël; ~ *of VISION,* gesigslyn, ooglyn; *WRITE* ~ *s,* strafreëls skryf; (v) afteken; lyne trek; in gelid stel; uitstraat (pad), groef, rimpel, beset, onderstreep, linieer; deurtrek; skets; grens aan; ~ *IN,* skets; omlyn; ~ *OFF,* afskei; ~ *OUT,* ontwerp; lynstaan (rugby); ~ *THROUGH,* deurtrek; ~ *UP,* opstel; in lyn bring, haaks maak; in rye gaan staan, in gelid bring.

line², (v) uitvoer, voering insit; volprop (maag); spek (beurs); ~ *one's POCKET*, jou sakke vul; jou beurs spek; ~ *one's STOMACH*, jou maag vul.
line³, (v) dek, paar (teef).
lin'eage, geslag, afkoms, stamboom; afstammelinge.
lin'eal, reglynig, lynvormig, lyn=; lengte=; lynreg, direk; ~ **descendant**, regstreekse afstammeling, direkte afstammeling; ~ **measure**, lengtemaat.
lin'eament, gelaatstrek, wesenstrek, trek.
lin'ear, lynvormig; lyn=, lineêr; lengte=; ~ **accelerator**, lineêre versneller; ~ **dimension**, lengtemaat; ~ **drawing**, lyntekene; ~ **equation**, eerstemagsvergelyking; ~ **expansion**, lengte-uitsetting; ~ **foot**, lengtevoet; ~ **measure**, lengtemaat; ~ **perspective**, lynperspektief.
lin'eate, gelyn, gelinieer(d).
linea'tion, liniëring.
line: ~-**block**, lyncliché, lynblok; ~-**breeding**, lynteelt; ~-**conductor**, lyngeleier; ~ **d**, gelyn, gelinieer; gegroef; *a face ~ d with*, met rimpels, vol plooie; 'n gesig gegroef deur; ~-**drawing**, pentekening; ~-**engraving**, lyngravure, streepgravering; ~ **fish**, lynvis; bankvis; ~ **fisherman**, lynvisser; ~-**fishing**, lynvissery; ~-**keeper**, lyninspekteur, baanwagter; ~ **level**, hangwaterpas.
lin'en, (n) linne; linnegoed; *wash one's dirty ~ in public*, 'n privaat geskil in die publiek uitveg; (a) linne=; ~ **basket**, wasgoedmandjie; ~ **cupboard**, linnekas; ~-**draper**, linnehandelaar; ~ **fold**, met plooipanele; ~-**fold moulding**, orrelfries; ~ **goods**, linne(ware); ~-**merchant**, groothandelaar in linne; ~ **press**, linnekas; ~ **shower**, bruidslinneparty; ~ **thread**, rugare; ~-**weaver**, linnewewer.
line'-of-battle ship, linieskip.
line: ~ **operator**, telefonis; lynbediener; ~ **peg**, lynpen, afsteekpen; ~ **perforation**, lyntanding.
lin'er¹, voering; bekleding.
lin'er², linieskip; lynskip, lynboot, pasasiersboot; linievliegtuig; liniesoldaat; linieerder; broodskrywer; ~ **company**, stoomvaartmaatskappy.
line: ~ **regiment**, linieregiment; ~ **shaft**, hoofdryfas.
lines'man, liniesoldaat; lynopsigter; vlagman, grensregter; lynwerker; baanwagter, lynwagter (sport).
line: ~ **spectrum**, lynspektrum; ~ **tapper**, afluisteraar (op foon); ~-**tapping**, afluistery.
ling¹, leng (vis).
ling², heide.
ling'er, draai, draal, sloer, versuim, vertoef, talm, sy bestaan rek; sukkel, kwyn; lank uitbly, op hom laat wag; ~ *AWAY one's time*, die tyd verbeusel; *he ~ ed for a MONTH after the operation*, hy het vir 'n maand na die operasie voortgekwyn; ~ *ON*, voortsleep; ~ *OVER one's meal*, lank aan tafel sit; ~ **er**, talmer, draaier, drentelkous.
lin'gerie, linnegoed; fyn onderklere.
ling'ering, (n) getalm, gedraai; kwyning; (a) talmend, dralend, langsaam; slepend, kwynend; *a ~ DISEASE*, 'n langdurige (slepende) siekte; ~ *DEATH*, langsame dood; *a ~ LOOK*, 'n blik wat nie kan skei nie.
ling'o, (-es), vreemde taal, klastaal, koeterwaals, plat taal, patois, brabbeltaal.
lingua franc'a, mengeltaal, lingua franca.
ling'ual, (n) tongletter; (a) tong=; taal=; ~ **artery**, tongslagaar; ~ **bone**, tongbeen; ~ **gland**, tongklier; ~ **muscle**, tongspier; ~ **nerve**, tongsenuwee.
ling'uiform, tongvormig.
ling'uist, taalkenner, taalkundige, taalgeleerde, linguis.
linguis'tic, taalkundig, taal=, linguisties; ~ **s**, taalwetenskap, linguistiek.
ling'ulate, tongvormig.
ling'y, met heide begroei.
lin'iment, smeersel, salf, smeergoed, smeermiddel.
lin'ing¹, voering; bekleding.
lin'ing², liniëring; merking (tennisbaan); belyning.
link¹, (n) toorts, fakkel.
link², (n) skakel; skakelman (mil.); string; binding (skeik.); mouskakel, mansjetknoop; (v) (aaneen=) skakel, verbind, aaneensnoer, aaneenkoppel, vaskoppel; inhaak; ~ *HANDS with*, aansluit by, saamhang met; ~ *ON*, aanhaak; aansluit by; ~ *TOGETHER*, aaneensluit; verbind; ~ *UP*, verbind; ~ *UP with*, aansluit by; saamhang met; ~ **age**, verbinding, aaneenskakeling; ~-**chain**, skakelketting; ~-**committee**, skakelkomitee; ~ **ed**, gekoppel; verbonde; ~ *ed ARMS*, arm-in-arm, ingehaak; ~ *ed HORSES*, gekoppelde perde; ~ **ing**, aaneenhegting; ~ **ing-up**, vereniging, samesmelting; ~ **man**, fakkeldraer; ~-**pin**, kettingbout; ~-**plate**, skakelverbinding; ~ **road**, skakelpad.
links, (n, pl) gholfbaan.
link: ~ **spanner**, pypstang; ~-**up**, verbinding.
linn, waterval; seekoeigat; afgrond.
Linn(a)e'an, van Linnaeus.
linn'et, vlasvink, groenvink.
lin'ocut, linoleumsnee.
linol'eum, linoleum; ~-**block print**, linoleumdruk; ~ **cut**, lino(leum)snee; ~ **ed**, met linoleum bedek.
lin'otype, linotipe, setmasjien (handelsnaam); ~ **r**, masjiensetter.
lin'seed, lynsaad; ~ **cake**, lynkoek; ~ **meal**, lynmeel; ~ **oil**, lynolie; *boiled (raw) ~ oil*, gaar (rou) lynolie; ~ **poultice**, lynsaadpap; ~ **tea**, lynsaadaftreksel.
lin'sey-wool'sey, linnewol, halfwolstof, wolkatoen, tierentyn.
lin'stock, lontstok.
lint, pluksel; gaas, verbandlinne.
lin'tel, latei.
lint'ers, katoenpluis.
lin'y, vol strepe, streperig; lyn=; gerimpel, gegroef, geplooi.
li'on, leeu; beroemde persoon, beroemdheid; *right in the ~ 's MOUTH*, reg in die leeu se bek; *SHOW the ~ s*, besienswaardighede wys; *SMALL ~*, leeutjie; *TWIST the ~ 's tail*, die Britse leeu terg; *there is a ~ in the WAY*, daar dreig gevaar; ~ **ess**, (-es), leeuwyfie, leeuin; ~-**hearted**, manmoedig, heldhaftig; ~-**hunt**, leeujag; ~-**hunter**, leeujagter; naloper van beroemde persone; ~ **ize**, 'n besoeker ophemel; verafgo(o)d; die besienswaardighede wys; ~-**like**, leeuagtig; ~-**monkey**, syaap; ~ **'s den**, leeukuil; ~ **'s-foot**, edelweiss; ~ **'s share**, leeueaandeel; ~ **'s skin**, leeuvel; ~-**tamer**, leeutemmer.
lip, (n) rand; *BITE one's ~*, op jou lip byt; *CURL one's ~*, jou lip optrek; *ESCAPE one's ~ s*, onbedagsaam laat uitglip; *FROM his own ~ s*, uit sy eie mond; *HANG the ~*, die kop laat hang; *HANG on someone's ~ s*, aan iem. se lippe hang; *LICK one's ~ s*, die lippe aflek; jou tande slyp; *LOWER ~*, onderlip; *be ON everybody's ~ s*, op almal se lippe wees; *not to allow food to PASS one's ~ s*, nie jou mond aan iets sit nie; *nothing has PASSED his ~ s*, hy het nog niks oor sy lippe gehad nie; *keep one's ~ s SEALED*, niks sê nie; *SMACK one's ~ s*, met die lippe smak; *keep a STIFF upper ~*, moed hou; styfhoofdig wees; *UPPER ~*, bolip; *none of YOUR ~!*, geen parmantigheid nie!; (v) **(-ped)**, die lippe sit aan; soen; uit; 'n rand vorm; hoeke uit die rand van iets breek; ~ **ase**, lipase; ~-**Christian**, naam-Christen; ~-**deep**, bolangs, onopreg; oppervlakkig; ~-**devotion**, skynvroomheid, lippabiddig; ~-**homage**, lippediens; ~ **id(e)**, lipied, lipide; ~-**language**, liptaal; ~ **less**, sonder lippe, liploos; ~ **let**, lippie.
lip'ocele, vetbreuk.
lipo'ma, vetgewas, lipoom.
lip'oid, lipoïde.
lipomatos'is, vetsug.
lip: ~ **ped**, gelip, lipvormig; ~-**reading**, liplesery, (die) lees v.d. lippe; ~ **salve**, lipsalf; vleiery; ~-**service**, lippediens; ~-**shaped**, lipvormig; ~ **stick**, lipstif(fie); ~-**worship**, lippediens, lipaanbidding.
Lipp'izzaner, Lippizzaner.
liquate', smelt; suiwer; afdryf; afskei, uitskei; uitsmelt.
liqua'tion, smelting; uitsyging; ontmenging; afdrywing.
liquefac'tion, (ver)smelting, vloeibaarmaking.
liq'uefiable, smeltbaar.
liq'uefy, (..fied), (ver)smelt, vloeibaar maak.
liques'cent, vloeibaarwordend, smeltend.
liqueur', soetsopie, likeur; ~ **brandy**, likeurbrandewyn; ~ **chocolates**, likeursjokolade; ~ **distillery**,

liquid 1019 *little*

likeurstokery; ~**-glass**, likeurglasie; ~**-frame**, ~**-stand**, likeurstelletjie.
liq'uid, (n) vloeistof; vloeiende letter; (pl) vloeibare kos; (a) vloeibaar; helder, deurskynend; vloeiend, sagvloeiend; onvas, los, lik(w)ied (bates); ~ **air**, vloeibare lug; ~ **ate**, vereffen, likwideer; afwikkel; ophelder, besleg.
liquida'tion, afrekening; afwikkeling, vereffening, likwidasie; ~ *of DEBT*, skulddelging; *GO into* ~, gelikwideer word; ~ **account**, likwidasierekening; ~ **costs**, likwidasiekoste; ~ **order**, likwidasiebevel; ~ **sale**, likwidasie-uitverkoop.
liq'uid capital, likiede (likwiede) kapitaal, vlottende kapitaal.
liq'uidator, likwidateur, likwideerder.
liq'uid: ~ **egg**, vloeibare eier; ~ **fuel**, vloeibare brandstof; ~ **funds**, likiede (likwiede) fondse; ~ **gas**, vloeibare gas; ~ **'ity**, vloeibaarheid; lik(w)iditeit (bates); ~**ize**, vloeibaar maak; versap; ~ **manure**, miswater; ~**izer**, vloeibaarmaker; sapmeul; versapper, versaptoestel; ~ **measure**, vogmaat; ~**ness**, vloeibaarheid; ~ **ounce**, vloeistofons; ~ **paraffin**, aptekersparaffien, drinkparaffien; ~ **resources**, lik(w)iede middele; ~ **soap**, vloeiseep; ~ **starch**, vloeistysel; ~ **veneer**, vloeivernis, meubelvernis, fineerpolitoer.
liq'uor, (n) vog, vloeistof; drank, sterk drank; *ILLICIT sale of* ~, onwettige drankverkoop; *IN* ~, beskonke, dronk, besope; *SPIRITUOUS* ~, geesryke drank; *the WORSE for* ~, dronk, besope, beskonke, hoenderkop; (v) met vet smeer; week, natmaak.
liq'uorice, soethout, drop; droplekker(s); ~ **allsorts**, droplekkers, reënboogklokkers; **pills**, droppille.
liq'uor: ~**ish**, versot op drank; ~ **law**, drankwet; ~ **licence**, dranklisensie; drankvergunning; ~**-runner**, dranksmokkelaar; ~**-running**, dranksmokkelary; ~ **shop**, drankwinkel; ~ **trade**, ~ **traffic**, drankhandel, drankverkoop.
lir'a, lire, (-s), lira (munt).
Lis'bon, Lissabor.
Lisbon'ian, (n) Lissabonner; (a) Lissabons.
Lisle, (n) Rysel; (a) Rysels.
lisle: ~ **glove**, garinghandskoen; ~ **stocking**, katoenkous; ~ **thread**, katoengaring.
lisp, (n) gelispel; gestamel; (v) lispel; met die tong stoot, sleeptong praat; ~**ing**, lispelend; krom.
liss'om(e), lenig, slap, rats, buigsaam; ~**ness**, lenigheid, buigsaamheid, ratsheid.
list¹, (n) oorhelling (skip); neiging, begeerte; (v) oorhang, oorhel; slagsy maak; *the ship* ~*ed to one side*, die skip het na een kant oorgehel.
list², (n) lys; selfkant; togband; band; rand; katalogus; naamlys, rol; rugstreep, aalstreep (dier); (pl) strydperk; *ACTIVE* ~, aktiewe lys; *on the BLACK* ~, op die swart lys; *ENTER the* ~*s*, in die strydperk tree; *FREE* ~, vrye lys; *be HIGH on the* ~, voorrang geniet; ~ *of NAMES*, naamlys; *ON the* ~, op die lys; *be on the RETIRED* ~, gepensioeneer wees; (v) opskrywe; oplerd (mielies); 'n band aanwerk; noteer, kwoteer (aandele); lys; 'n lys maak van; ~ *the door*, 'n deur van 'n togband voorsien.
list³, (v) *kyk* **listen**.
list⁴, (v) sin hê; wil; lus hê; *the wind bloweth where it* ~*eth*, die wind waai waarheen hy wil.
list'ed¹, oorgehel.
lis'ted², gesoom; gestreep; op die amptelike lys genoteer, gekwoteer (aandele); op 'n lys geplaas, gelys; *not* ~ *in the CATALOGUE*, nie op die (prys)lys nie; ~ *COMMUNIST*, gelyste Kommunis; ~ *COMPANY*, genoteerde maatskappy; ~ *HOTEL*, aanbevole hotel; ~ *PERSONS*, gelyste persone; ~ *SECURITIES*, genoteerde aandele.
lis'ten, luister, toehoor; ~ *very ATTENTIVELY to someone*, aan iem. se lippe hang; ~ *CLOSELY*, aandagtig luister; *who do not* ~ *will be made to FEEL*, wie nie hoor nie, moet voel; ~ *IN*, inluister; toeluister; ~ **er**, luisteraar, toehoorder; ~ **er-in, (listeners-in)**, (in)luisteraar; luistervink.
lis'tening, luister; ~**-apparatus**, luistertoestel; ~**-frequency**, luisterfrekwensie; ~**-gallery**, hoorgang;

luistergang; ~**-in apparatus**, afluistertoestel; ~**-post**, luisterpos; ~**-system**, luisterstroombaan; ~**-tender**, luisterwa.
lis'tening-in jack, luistervink.
lis'terine, listerien, listerine (handelsnaam).
lis'terize, antisepties behandel.
listerello'sis, listerellose.
lis'ter plough, operdploeg.
list'ing¹, (n) oorhelling; (a) oorhellend (skip).
list'ing², (n) notering, kwotasie; lysting.
list'less, lusteloos; doodgeryp (fig.), dooierig, pap, onverskillig; ~**ness**, dooierigheid, onlus(tigheid), lusteloosheid.
list' price, katalogusprys.
lit, *kyk* **light¹**, (v).
lit'any, **(litanies)**, litanie.
lit'chi, lietsjie.
lit'eracy, geletterdheid, lees- en skryfkundigheid.
lit'eral, (n) drukfout; (a) letterlik, letter-, woordelik; ~ **error**, letterfout; ~ **equation**, lettervergelyking; ~**ism**, letterlike uitlegging; letterlikheid; letterknegtery; ~**ist**, letterkneg, literalis; ~**ize**, letterlik beskou; ~**ly**, letterlik.
lit'erary, geletterd; letterkundig, literêr; ~ **hack**, broodskrywer, prulskrywer; ~ **history**, geskiedenis van die letterkunde; ~ **talent**, letterkundige aanleg.
lit'erate, (n) geletterde; (a) geletterd; beskaaf.
literat'i, geleerdes, geletterdes, literati.
literat'im, letterlik.
lit'erator, letterkundige, literator.
lit'erature, letterkunde, literatuur, lettere; leesstof; *light* ~, ligte leesstof.
lith'arge, loodglit, geellood.
lithe, buigsaam, slap, lenig; ~**ness**, buigsaamheid, lenigheid, slapheid; ~**some**, buigsaam, lenig, slap.
li'thia, steenloogsout, litine, litien; litiase (med.).
lithi'asis, steenvorming, steensiekte, litiase.
lith'ic, steenagtig, steen-, graweel-; ~ **acid**, steensuur.
lith'ium, litium.
lithoch'romy, steenkleurdruk.
lith'ograph, (n) steendrukplaat, litografie; steendruk; (v) steendruk, litografeer.
lithog'rapher, steendrukker, litograaf.
lithograph'ic, litografies, steendrukkers-.
lithog'raphy, steendrukkuns, litografie.
litholog'ical, litologies.
lithol'ogy, steenkunde, litologie.
litho'lysis, litolise.
lith'oscope, litoskoop.
lith'osphere, litosfeer, (vaste) aardkors.
lithot'omist, steensnyer.
lithot'omy, steensnykuns, litotomie.
Lithuan'ia, Litaue; ~**n**, (n) Litauer; Litaus (taal); (a) Litaus.
Lithuan'ic, Litaus.
lit'igant, (n) gedingvoerder, prosedeerder; (a) prosederend, gedingvoerend.
lit'igate, prosedeer, hof toe gaan, 'n geding voer, 'n saak maak, litigeer.
litiga'tion, proses, regsgeding, saak, gedingvoering, litigasie.
liti'gious, pleitsiek; twissiek, rusieagtig.
lit'mus, lakmoes; ~ **paper**, lakmoespapier.
lit'otes, litotes.
lit're, liter.
litt'er, (n) drag, werpsel, nes kleintjies; draagbaar; skropgoed (hoenders); kooigoed, strooi (in 'n stal); warboel, wanorde, rommel; afval, asvel; *BE in* ~, dragtig wees; *a* ~ *of PIGS*, 'n werpsel varkies; (v) van strooi voorsien; kooi maak, kooigoed opgooi; rondstrooi, oorhoop gooi; openhoop; deurmekaar lê; omkrap, 'n warboel maak van; deurmekaar maak; werp, jong (diere); ~**ed**, rommel(r)ig, deurmekaar; ~*ed with BOOKS*, bestrooi met boeke; ~*ed with PAPERS*, besaai met papiere; ~**bug**, morsjors; ~**ing**, strooiing; rommelstrooiing; ~**y**, rommel(r)ig, deurmekaar.
lit'tle, (n) iets, rapsie, bietjie, weinig, min; *A* ~, 'n bietjie; ~ *if ANY*, feitlik niks; ~ *if ANYTHING*, weinig of niks; ~ *BY* ~, stadig, langsamerhand, trapsgewyse; *EVERY* ~ *helps*, alle bietjies help; *FOR a* ~, 'n rukkie; *IN* ~, in die klein; *MAKE*

littoral   *loaf*

a ~ *go a long way,* ver kom met 'n klein bietjie; *many a* ~ *makes a MICKLE,* alle bietjies help; ~ *or NONE,* min (bietjie) of niks; *NOT a* ~, nie min nie; ~ *or NOTHING,* skaars iets; *VERY* ~, bloedmin; (a) klein; min, weinig, luttel; gering, onaansienlik; kleingeestig; *L* ~ *BEAR,* die Klein BEER; ~ *FINGER,* pinkie; *the L* ~ *KAROO,* die Klein Karoo; ~ *MAN,* mannetjie; kêreltjie; ~ *MONEY,* 'n bietjie geld; *the* ~ *ONE,* die kleintjie; ~ *PEOPLE,* die kleingoed; die feë; *L* ~ *RUSSIA,* Klein-Rusland; ~ *TOE,* kleintoontjie; *WAIT a* ~ *while,* wag 'n bietjie; wag 'n rukkie; *a* ~ *WAY,* 'n entjie; (adv) min, weinig; geleidelik; ~ *-KNOWN,* minder bekend; *he* ~ *KNOWS that,* min weet hy dat; ~ *MORE,* bietjie meer; *TOO* ~, te min; ~ *-known,* min bekend; onbekend; ~ *-minded,* bekrompe, kleinsielig; ~ **ness,** kleinheid, geringheid; kleinsieligheid.

litt'oral, (n) kusgebied, strandgebied, kusstrook; (a) kus=, strand=.

litur'gical, liturgies.

liturgi'cian, liturg.

litur'gist, liturg.

lit'urgy, (. .gies), liturgie.

liv'able, bewoonbaar; gaaf; draaglik; gesellig.

live¹, (v) lewe, bestaan; woon, bly; hou (dier); ~ *to a great AGE,* 'n hoë ouderdom bereik; ~ *on AIR,* v.d. wind lewe; *man shall not* ~ *by BREAD alone,* die mens sal van brood alleen nie lewe nie; ~ *BY,* lewe van; ~ *a DOUBLE life,* twee rolle in die lewe speel; ~ *DOWN,* te bowe kom; ~ *IN,* woon in; inwoon; ~ *and LEARN,* 'n mens is nooit te oud om te leer nie; ~ *and LET* ~, leef en laat leef; ~ *a LIE,* huigel, veins; ~ *one's LIFE,* jou uitleef; ~ *on LOVE and fresh air,* van liefde en koue water lewe; ~ *ON,* teer op; bly lewe; ~ *OUT,* buite woon; deurkom; ~ *up to one's PROMISE,* jou belofte gestand doen; ~ *on one's REPUTATION,* op jou roem teer; ~ *up to one's REPUTATION,* sy naam eer aandoen; ~ *to SEE,* belewe; ~ *down SLANDER,* deur 'n vleklose lewe laster loënstraf; ~ *in a SMALL way,* eenvoudig en stil lewe; ~ *out a STORM,* 'n storm deurstaan; ~ *THROUGH,* deurmaak, deurlewe; ~ *TOGETHER,* saamwoon; ~ *UP to,* lewe ooreenkomstig; ~ *UPON,* leef van; ~ *WELL,* in weelde leef, 'n goeie lewe lei; ~ *WITH,* leef met, saamwoon met.

live², (a) lewendig; lewend; gloeiend, brandend (kole); suiwer (lug); onontplof (bom); vars (stoom); gelaai, onder stroom (elek.); bewegend, dryfbaar; *a* ~ *ISSUE,* 'n brandende vraag; *he is a* ~ *WIRE,* hy is 'n ondernemende (wakker) kêrel; 'n voorslag; ~ **axle,** draaias; ~ **bait,** lewende aas; ~ **bomb,** onontplofde bom; gewapende bom; ~ **broadcast,** direkte uitsending; ~ **cartridge,** ongebruikte patroon; ~ **coal,** gloeiende kole; ~ **grenade,** brisantgranaat.

live'lihood, broodwinning, bestaansmiddel, lewensonderhoud, bestaan; *earn (make) a* ~, sy brood verdien.

live'liness, lewendigheid, wakkerheid, vrolikheid, roerigheid, hupsheid; beweeglikheid.

live'long, heel; lewenslank; *the* ~ *day,* die hele liewe dag, die godganselike dag.

live'ly, lewendig, opgeruimd, monter, hups, vief, fleurig, viewerig; sprekend, treffend (portret); skuimend (drank); moeilik, hotagter, roerig, druk (sake); *a* ~ *DESCRIPTION,* 'n lewendige beskrywing; *MAKE it* ~ *for,* die wêreld moeilik (warm) maak vir; *we hade a* ~ *TIME during the siege,* gedurende die beleg het ons dit hotagter gehad.

liv'en: ~ *up,* opvrolik, opbeur, verlewendig.

liv'er¹, lewende; *a FAST* ~, 'n losbol; *a GOOD* ~, 'n deugsame persoon; *LONGEST* ~, langslewende.

liv'er², lewer; *DRY* ~, droë lewer; *be LILY-* ~ *ed,* lafhartig wees; *PREPARED* ~, haksel; ~ **abscess,** lewersweer; ~ **-coloured,** lewerkleurig; ~ **complaint,** lewerkwaal; ~ **fluke,** lewerslak; ~ **-hearted,** lafhartig.

liv'eried, in livrei.

liv'er: ~ **ish,** met die lewer gepla, lewersugtig; ~ **oil,** lewertraan; ~ **paste,** lewersmeer; ~ **patty,** lewerkoekie; ~ **pill,** galpil; ~ **polony,** lewerwors.

Liverpud'lian, (n) inwoner van Liverpool; (a) Liverpolitaans.

liv'er: ~ **salts,** lewersout; ~ **sausage,** lewerwors; ~ **-spot,** lewervlek; ~ **-stone,** lewersteen; ~ **wort,** lewerkruid; lewermos.

liv'ery¹, (n) (. .ries), livrei; ampsgewaad; mondering, kleredrag.

liv'ery², (a) lewer=; met die lewer gepla; taai (grond).

liv'ery: ~ **coat,** livreibaadjie; ~ **company,** gilde; ~**man,** livreibediende, livreikneg; ~ **stable,** huurstal.

live'stock, lewende hawe, vee; ~ **sale,** veevendusie.

live: ~ **weight,** lewende gewig; ~ **wire,** 'n draad onder stroom; 'n persoon soos 'n voorslag; 'n pure man.

liv'id, blou, loodblou; doodsbleek, bestorwe, lykkleurig; *be* ~, woedend wees; die josie in wees; die herrie in wees; ~ **colour,** lykkleur; ~ **'ity,** loodkleur; doodsbleekheid.

liv'ing, (n) bestaan, broodwinning; lewensonderhoud; lewenswyse, lewe; standplaas (predikant); *COST of* ~, lewenskoste; *FOR a* ~, vir die kos; vir 'n bestaan; *GOOD* ~, weelderige lewe; *JOY of* ~, lewensvreugde; *the LAND of the* ~, die land v.d. lewendes; *MAKE a* ~, 'n bestaan vind; jou brood verdien; *THE* ~, die lewendes; *WAY of* ~, lewenswyse; (a) lewend, bedrywend; lewendig; sprekend; stromend; gloeiend; *a* ~ *LANGUAGE,* 'n lewende taal; *a* ~ *LIKENESS,* 'n sprekende gelykenis; *no MAN* ~, niemand nie, geen man ter wêreld nie; geen sterfling; *within* ~ *MEMORY,* binne menseheugenis; *every* ~ *SOUL,* elke lewende siel; ~ **-habits,** lewensgewoontes; ~ **-in,** inwonend; ~ **-in servant,** inwonende bediende; ~ **-out,** uitwoon=; ~ **-out allowance,** uitwoontoelae; ~ **-room,** woonkamer; ~ **space,** leefruimte, woonruimte; ~ **-wage,** bestaanbare loon; ~ **-wagon,** woonwa; ~ **water,** fonteinwater.

Livon'ia, Lyfland; ~ **n,** (n) Lyflander; Lyflands (taal); (a) Lyflands.

Liv'y, Livius.

lixiv'ial, loogagtig; uitgeloog.

lixiv'iate, uitloog; uitwas; uittrek.

lixivia'tion, (die) uitloog, uitloging.

lixiv'ium, loog.

liz'ard, akkedis; ~ **buzzard,** akkedisvanger.

lla'ma, lama, skaapkameel; lamawol.

lla'no, (-s), grasvlakte, llano.

lo! kyk! ~ *and behold,* so waarlik; kyk en aanskou.

loach, moddervis, modderkruiper.

load, (n) vrag; drag; lading; las, belading, belasting (masj.); dra(ag)krag; gewig; (pl) vragte; hope; *DEAD* ~, dooi(e)gewig, dooi(e)las; *a* ~ *OFF one's shoulders,* 'n las v.d. hart; *a* ~ *ON one's CONSCIENCE,* 'n las op sy gemoed; 'n las op die hart; ~ *of SINS,* sondelas; (v) oplaai; laai; belaai; inneem; belas, swaarder maak, beswaar; verhoog (premie); vervals; oorlaai; oorstelp; dik oplê (verf); lood aansit; ~ *d with,* oorlaai met; gebuk onder; ~ **capacity,** laaivermoë; ~ **-carrier,** lasdraer; ~ **-displacement,** dieepgang van 'n gelaaide skip; ~ **-distribution,** lasverdeling; ~ **-draught,** diepgang van 'n gelaaide skip.

load'ed, gelaai; ~ *CANE (stick),* 'n stok met 'n loodknop; ~ *DICE,* vals dobbelstene; ~ *WINE,* gedokterde (versterkte) wyn; ~ *WORDS,* gelaaide woorde.

load'er, laaier; laaigaaf.

load'ing, (die) laai; vrag, lading; verhoging (premie); ~ **bay,** laaivak; ~ **berth,** laaiplek; ~ **bin,** laaibak; ~ **board,** laaiplank; ~ **box,** laaikis; ~ **capacity,** laaivermoë; ~ **charges,** laaigeld, laaikoste; ~ **date,** laaidatum; ~ **facilities,** laaigeriewe; ~ **hatch,** laailuik; ~ **hole,** laaigat; ~ **movement,** laaibeweging; ~ **pen,** laaikraal; ~ **place,** laaiplek; ~ **platform,** laaiplatform; ~ **port,** laaihawe; ~ **ramp,** laaibrug; ~ **space,** laairuimte; ~ **stage,** laaisteier; ~ **zone,** laaigebied.

load: ~ **line,** laslyn; ~ **mark,** diepgangsmerk; ~ **sheet,** ladingstaat; ~ **s'man,** loods.

load'star, *kyk* **lodestar.**

load'stone, magneet.

loaf¹, (n) **(loaves),** brood; kop (kool); *a* ~ *of BREAD,*

loaf
'n brood; *BROWN* ~, growwe (bruin) brood; *HALF a* ~ *is better than no bread at all*, 'n halwe eier is beter as 'n leë dop; krummels is ook brood; *WHITE* ~, wit brood.

loaf², (n) leeglê, leeglopery; *on the* ~, aan die rondloop; (v) leegloop, luier, slenter, lanterfanter; ~ *about*, rondloop, leegloop.

loaf' cheese, broodkaas.

loaf: ~ **er**, leegloper, niksdoener, padloper, stompiesoeker, slenteraar, rondloper; lieplapper; ~ **ing**, niksdoenery, leegleery.

loaf' sugar, klontjiesuiker, blokkiesuiker.

loam, (n) leem; klei (vir stene); (v) pleister; ~ **y**, leemagtig; klei-, kleierig.

loan, (n) lening; geldlening; lenery; ~ *for CONSUMPTION*, verbruikleen; *CONTRACT a* ~, 'n lening sluit; *CONVERT a* ~, 'n lening omsit; *GRANT a* ~, 'n lening toestaan; *HAVE on* ~, in bruikleen hê; *ON* ~, te leen; geleen; *PUT out to* ~, uitleen; (v) (uit)leen; ~ **able**, leenbaar; ~ **account**, leningsrekening; ~ **bank**, leenbank, voorskotbank; ~ **-collection**, leenversameling, versameling in bruikleen; ~ **ee'**, lener; ~ **er**, uitlener; ~ **-estimate**, leningsbegroting; ~ **expenditure**, leningsuitgawe; ~ **-farm**, leenplaas, leningsplaas; ~ **form**, leenvorm; ~ **-funds**, leningsfondse; ~ **indent**, bruikleenbestelling; ~ **-money**, geleende geld; ~ **-office**, voorskotbank; leenkantoor; ~ **programme**, leningsprogram; ~ **-register**, leenboek; ~ **shark**, woekeraar, woekerwinsmaker; ~ **stock**, leningseffekte; ~ **translation**, leenvertaling, calque; ~ **word**, leenwoord.

lo(a)th, wars, afkerig, onwillig; ongeneë; ~ *to GO*, nie lus om te gaan nie; *NOTHING* ~, gewillig.

loathe, verfoei, walg van, verafsku.

loath'ing, (n) weersin, walg(ing), afkeer, verafskuwing; (a) walgend, verfoeilik.

loath'ly, loath'some, walgend, weersinwekkend, verfoeilik, afsigtelik; galsterig.

loaves, *kyk* **loaf** (n).

lob, (n) lughou, hoogslag; lugbal (tennis); onderhandse bal; lummel; (v) **(-bed)**, hoog slaan; gooi, rol; oor iem. se kop slaan; 'n lughou slaan (tennis); lomp beweeg, voortsukkel; afknot (boom).

lob'ate, lobbig, gelob; lobvormig.

loba'tion, lobbigheid; lob; lobvorming.

lobb'y, (n) **(lobbies)**, wandelgang (parlement); voorportaal, voorhal; drukgroep, pressiegroep; koukus(groep); *haunt the* ~, parlementslede probeer beïnvloed; (v) **(lobbied)**, in die wandelgange boer; parlementslede probeer beïnvloed; ~ **correspondent**, parlementêre medewerker; ~ **ist**, wandelgangpolitikus, steunwerwer.

lobe, lob; ~ **d**, gelob; ~ **less**, sonder lobbe.

lobel'ia, lobelia.

loblol'ly, gortpap; pap kos; ~ **boy**, ~ **man**, dokters-handlanger.

lobol'a, (n) lobola, bruidsprys; (v) lobola (betaal), die bruidsprys betaal.

lobot'omy, lobotomie.

lob'scouse, hutspot, matroosbredie.

lob'ster, kreef; ~ **bisque**, dik kreefsop; ~ **claw**, kreefknyper; ~ **coral**, kreefkuit; ~ **-eyed**, jakopeweroog; ~ **-pot**, krewefuik, kreefmandjie; ~ **salad**, kreefslaai; ~ **soup**, kreefsop.

lob'ular, gelob; lobvormig.

lob'ule, saadhuisie; lelletjie.

lob'worm, erdwurm.

loc'al, (n) plaaslike trein; plaaslike persoon, plaaslike bewoner, inwoner; kroeg, kantien; plaaslike nuus; plaaslike eksamen; (a) plaaslik, lokaal, streek-; ~ **anaesthesia**, plaaslike verdowing; ~ **authority**, plaaslike owerheid; ~ **charges**, plaasverlies (bankw.); ~ **colour**, plaaslike kleur, lokale kleur.

locale', plek, toneel, lokaliteit.

loc'al: ~ **government**, plaaslike bestuur; ~ **industries**, inheemse nywerheid; ~ **inhabitant**, plaaslike bewoner.

loc'alism, voorliefde vir 'n plek; plaaslike uitdrukking, gewoonte, ens.; streekuitdrukking; lokalisme; bekrompenheid.

local'ity, **(..ties)**, omtrek, oord; lokaliteit, plek; ligging; steunpunt (mil.); ~ **plan**, liggingsplan.

localiza'tion, lokalisasie, plaasbepaling.

loc'alize, tot een plek beperk; naspoor, vasstel, bepaal, lokaliseer.

loc'al: ~ **ly**, plaaslik, op dié plek, alhier, hier te lande; ~ **name**, pleknaam; streeknaam; ~ **option**, plaaslike keuse; ~ **organ**, ~ **paper**, plaaslike blad; ~ **sense**, pleksin; ~ **stamp**, streekseël; ~ **time**, plaaslike tyd; ~ **value**, plekwaarde.

locate', plaas; aanwys; die plek aanwys; lokaliseer; stel, tuisbring; die grens bepaal; vestig, vasstel; vind (vyand); *be* ~ *d*, lê, geleë wees.

loca'tion, lokasie; aanwysing; aanduiding (water); plek, ligging; plekbepaling, plekaanwysing; opsporing; opstelling; *on* ~ (film), op die terrein (lokaliteit); ~ **plan**, liggingsplan.

loc'ative, (n) lokatief, plekaanduidende naamval; (a) lokatief, plekaanduidend.

loch, meer, loch.

lock¹, (n) krul, lok (hare).

lock², (n) slot (aan deur); geweerslot; opeenhoping, gedrang; sluitplaat; klem (stoei); klos (skaap); sluis (water); slot(voorspeler); (pl) loks (wol); *under* ~ *and KEY*, agter slot en grendel; ~, *STOCK and barrel*, romp en stomp; soos dit reil en seil; alles inbegrepe; die hele boel; (v) sluit, toesluit; opsluit; klem (stoei); insluit; afsluit; vasmaak, vassit; inmekaargryp; omsluit; van 'n sluis voorsien; vasgryp; ~ *AWAY*, wegsluit; ~ *up CAPITAL in*, kapitaal vaslê in; ~ *HORNS*, die horings inmekaarhaak; ~ *IN*, opsluit; ~ *OUT*, buitesluit, uitsluit; ~ *the STABLE when the steed is stolen*, die put demp nadat die kalf verdrink het, te laat voorsorg tref; ~ *UP*, wegsluit, toesluit; vaslê; ~ **able**, sluitbaar; ~ **age**, sluisgeld; sluiswerk; skutgeld; ~ **bolt**, sluitgrendel; ~ **-box**, posbus; ~ **-bridge**, slotbrug; ~ **-catch**, slotknip; ~ **-cavity**, slotopening (spoorweg); ~ **-chain**, remketting; ~ **-chamber**, sluiskolk; sas; ~ **-dues**, sluisgeld.

locked, slotvas; op slot; ~ *CONTROLS*, vasgesette stuur; ~ *in SLEEP*, vas aand die slaap; ~ *WATER*, stilstaande water.

lock'er, laaitjie; berekas; (sluit)kis, sluitkas; toesluiter; *have a shot in the* ~, nog 'n pyl op die boog hê.

lock'et, hangertjie, medaljon; sluitband (mil.).

lock: ~ **-fast**, op slot, goed gesluit; ~ **-gate**, sluisdeur; ~ **-hatch**, **(-es)**, sluisskuif; ~ **indicator**, slotwyser.

lock'ing, (n) sluiting; ineengryping; (a) sluit-; ~ **-catch**, sluittoestel; ~ **cock**, sluitkraan; ~ **-gear**, grendelapparaat; ~ **-nut**, sluitmoer; ~ **-pin**, sluitpen; ~ **-plate**, sluitplaat; ~ **-screw**, sluitskroef; ~ **-spring**, sluitveer; ~ **-tray**, grendelbak, ~ **-tube**, sluitbuis.

lock: tetanus, klem in die kaak, ~ **jaw**, (kaak)klem, kaakkramp, styfkramp; ~ **-keeper**, sluiswagter; ~ **master**, sluiswagter; ~ **-nut**, (op)sluitmoer, klemmoer; ~ **-out**, uitsluiting; ~ **-paddle**, skuif, ~ **plate**, borgplaat; ~ **-rail**, slotreling; ~ **-ring**, borgring; ~ **-saw**, steeksaag; ~ **-shaft**, slotas; ~ **-sman**, sluiswagter; ~ **-smith**, slotmaker; ~ **-stitch**, slotsteek, kettingsteek; ~ **-up**, sluitingstyd; vaslegging; opsluitplek; gevangenis, tronk; sel; *be in the* ~ **-up**, agter slot en grendel wees; ~ **-up garage**, sluitgarage.

lo'co, (Lat.): ~ *CITATO*, ter aangehaalde plaatse; op die aangehaalde plek; *INSPECTION in* ~, ondersoek ter plaatse; *in* ~ *PARENTIS*, in die plek v.d. ouer.

locomob'ile, (n) lokomobiel; (a) selfbewegend.

locomo'tion, (voort)beweging, plaasverandering; verplasing; ~ **allowance**, vervoertoelae.

loc'omotive, lokomotief; (a) bewegend, bewegings-; ~ **engine**, lokomotief; vuurwa; ~ **organs**, bewegingsorgane; ~ **power**, beweegkrag.

loc'omotor, (n) bewegende persoon; bewegende masjien; (a) bewegings-; ~ **ataxy**, rugmurgtering; ~ **y**, bewegings-, bewegend.

lo'culus, **(..li)**, sel; hokkie.

locum-ten'ency, plaasvervanging, waarneming; waarnemende pos.

locum ten'ens, plaasvervanger, plaasbekleër, locum tenens.

loc'us, (loci), lokus, meetkundige plek.
loc'ust, treksprinkaan; kassiaboom; ~ **bird,** sprinkaanvoël; ~ **menace,** sprinkaanbedreiging; ~ **officer,** sprinkaanbeampte; ~ **plague,** sprinkaanplaag; ~ **poison,** sprinkaangif; ~ **-wood,** sprinkaanbos.
locu'tion, spreekwyse, uitdrukking.
loc'utory, (..ries), spreekkamer, ontvangkamer.
lode, afvoerkanaal, sugsloot; mynaar, ertsaar; ertsliggaam, ertsgang.
lode'star, poolster, noordster, leidster.
lode'stone, magneet.
lodge, (n) hut, huisie; jaghuis; portierhuis; woning; verblyf; boerplek; lêplek; pondokkie (Indiaan); losie (Vrymesselaars); wynhok; (v) huisves, herberg, loseer; neerlê; plek verskaf; deponeer (geld); inlewer, indien (klag); plaas; laat neerkom; inwoon; vassit; plat lê, plat waai, gaan lê; neerslaan (koring); opspoor (wild); ~ *an APPEAL,* appèl aanteken, in hoër beroep gaan; *a BULLET ~d in his brain,* 'n koeël het in sy harsings vasgesit; ~ *a COMPLAINT,* 'n klag indien; ~ *a DOCUMENT,* 'n stuk inlewer (indien); ~ *NOTICE,* kennis gee; ~ *an OBJECTION,* 'n beswaar opper; *POWER ~d with,* mag berustend by; ~ *WITH,* woon by; indien by; laat bly by; ~**-box,** baanwagtershuisie; ~**-gate,** inryhek; ~**-keeper,** oppasser, portier; ~**ment** = **lodgment;** ~**r,** loseerder, kamerhuurder.
lodg'ing, losies, huisvesting, inwoning; indiening, inlewering (bedanking); onderkome, woonplek; (pl) huurkamers; *BOARD and ~,* kos en inwoning; *LIVE in ~s,* op kamers woon; ~**-allowance,** verblyftoelae; ~**-fee,** indieningsgeld; ~**-house,** huurkamerhuis, losieshuis.
lodg'ment, huisvesting, onderdak; verblyf; ophoping; deposito (reg); inlewering (dokumente); *make (find) a ~,* vaste voet kry.
loess, löss, loess.
loft, (n) solder; solderkamer; galery; ligskuinste, ligvermoë (gholf); duiwehok; orrelkoor; (v) ('n gholfbal) lig; 'n lugskoot slaan (krieket); ~**er,** ligter; ~**ily,** hoog; uit die hoogte; ~**iness,** hoogheid; hooghartigheid, hoogmoed; verhewenheid; ~**-ladder,** solderleer; ~**-window,** soldervenster; ~**y,** verhewe, hoog; hooghartig, fier, trots; donserig (wol).
log[1], (n) logaritme.
log[2], (n) blok (hout); opgawe, staat; puntelys (sport); dagboek; log (snelheidsmeter); logboek; skeepsjoernaal; *HAVE no ~s to roll,* geen selfsugtige bedoelings hê nie; *HEAVE (throw) the ~,* die log uitgooi; *ROLL my ~ and I'll roll yours,* as jy my saak bevorder, bevorder ek joue; *SLEEP like a ~,* soos 'n klip slaap; (v) **(-ged),** opskryf, aanteken (in logboek); in blokke saag; die opgetekende afstand aflê; beboet.
log'anberry, (..ries), loganbessie.
lo'gan stone, wipklip, skommelklip
log'arithm, logaritme.
logari'thmic(al), logaritmies; ~ **table,** logaritmetafel.
log: ~**-book,** logboek; skeepsjoernaal, seejoernaal; dagboek; skooljoernaal; logaritmetafel; ~ **cabin,** blokhuis; ~ **canoe,** boomkano; ~**ged,** vol water; onbeweeglik, stilstaande; opgeskrywe, aangeteken.
logg'erhead, domoor, lummel, domkop; *be at ~s,* soos kat en hond wees; oorhoop lê met mekaar; haaks wees met iem.
logg'ia, (-s), loggia, oop galery, arkade.
log'house, log'hut, blokhuis.
lo'gic, logika, redeneerkuns, redeneerkunde; ~**al,** beredeneerd, logies; ~**al'ity,** die logiese.
logi'cian, logikus.
lo'gion, logion.
logist'ic, logisties.
logis'tical, logisties.
logis'tics, logistiek.
log'-line, loglyn.
log'man, houtkapper.
lo'go, logo, letternaam, naambeeld.
log'ogram, logogram.
logog'rapher, logograaf.
log'ogriph, logogrief, woordraaisel.
logom'achy, woordestryd, haaklowery.

logopaed'ic, logopedies; ~**s,** logopedika, logopediek.
logoped'ist, spraakterapeut, logopedis.
log'os, logos; die woord.
lo'gotype, logo(tipe), skakelletter, letternaam, naambeeld.
log'-rolling, wedersydse ophemeling, rugkrappery.
log'wood, blouhout, gifhout.
loin, lende(stuk); (pl) lendene; *GIRD up the ~s,* die lendene omgord; ~ *of MUTTON,* skaaplende; ~**-cloth,** lendekleed; ~ **chop,** lendekarmenaadjie; ~**-strap,** kruisriem; lendedoek.
loit'er, draai, draal, talm, drentel, rondslenter, sloer, leuter; ~ *AROUND the premises,* op die werf ronddrentel; ~ *the time AWAY,* die tyd verbeusel (mors); ~ *with INTENT,* rondsluip om in te breek; ~**er,** draaier, talmer, draaikous, draler, drentelkous, drelkous, slenteraar, leegloper; ~**ing,** (n) draaiery, getalm, gedraal; dagdiewery; (a) dralend, talmend, draaierig.
loll, lusteloos lê; laat uithang; slap neerhang; laat leun; ~ *about,* rondhang.
Loll'ard, Lollard.
loll'ipop, suikerpop, suikerstafie; borssuiker; (pl) lekkers, lekkergoed.
loll'op, lui lê; loom beweeg; rondslinger.
Lom'bard, (n) Lombardiër; (a) Lombardies.
Lombard'ic, Lombardies.
Lom'bard Street, (die) Londense bankstraat; geldmark; *all ~ to a China orange,* 'n skat teenoor 'n bakatel; tien teen een.
Lom'bardy, Lombardye; ~ **poplar,** Lombardiese populier.
loment'(um), litpeul, gelede peul, lomentum.
Lon'don, Londen; ~**er,** Londenaar; ~**ism,** Londense eienaardigheid; ~ **ivy,** Londense rook; ~ **particular,** Londense mis.
lone, eensaam, verlate; *PLAY a ~ hand,* 'n sterk hand alleen speel (kaartspel); sonder bondgenote optree; alleen optree; ~ *WOLF,* alleenloper, eenspaaier; ~**liness,** eensaamheid, enigheid, eensaamte, verlatenheid; ~**ly,** eensaam, allenig, afgesonder, verlate; ~**r,** alleenloper; ~**some,** eensaam, verlate.
long[1], (n) lang tyd; *BEFORE ~,* eer v.d. dae, eerlank; *IN ~s,* in lang broek; *NOT for ~,* nie lank nie; *that is the ~ and the SHORT of it,* dit is al; dit is alles; om kort te gaan; *it will not TAKE ~,* dit sal nie lank duur nie; (a) lang (lank); geruim, langdurig; vervelend; *he has a ~ ARM,* sy mag (invloed) reik ver; *a ~ BEER,* 'n groot glas bier; *not by a ~ CHALK,* lank nie, glad nie; *the DAY is ~,* die dag is lank; *have a ~ HEAD,* nie onder 'n kalkoen uitgebroei nie; *it is a ~ LANE that has no turning,* aan alles kom 'n end; *the ~ arm of the LAW,* die lang arm v.d. gereg; *have a ~ MEMORY,* 'n goeie geheue hê; *NEVER is a ~ word,* nooit is baie lank; *a ~ PURSE,* 'n vol beursie; *in the ~ RUN,* op die lange duur; ~ *SERVICE,* langdurige diens; *of ~ STANDING,* oud; van ou datum; *make a ~ STORY short,* om kort te gaan; *it will TAKE a ~ time,* dit het baie tyd nodig; *have a ~ TONGUE,* 'n lang tong hê; *take a ~ VIEW,* in die toekoms kyk; (adv) lang (lank), lankal; *don't be too ~ ABOUT it,* maak 'n bietjie gou; ~ *AGO,* lankal, vanmelewe, lank gelede; *AS ~ as,* solank as; *AT its ~est,* op sy langste; *don't BE ~,* moenie lank wegbly nie; *BEFORE ~,* gou, netnou; *it's as ~ as it is BROAD,* dit is om die ewe; *all DAY ~,* die hele dag; *ERE ~,* eerlank, een v.d. dae; *as ~ as I LIVE,* solank ek leef; *NO ~er,* nie langer nie; *he is NOT ~ for this world,* hy sal dit nie meer lank maak nie; *SO ~!* tot siens!
long[2], (v) verlang, hunker (na); ~ *for the hour,* snak na die uur.
long'ago, lank gelede; *the ~,* die verre verlede.
longanim'ity, lankmoedigheid.
longan'imous, lankmoedig.
long' bill[1], langsigwissel.
long'-bill[2], langbekvoël.
long: ~ **boat,** sloep; ~ **bone,** pypbeen; ~**bow,** lang boog; *draw the ~bow,* met spek skiet; ~**-breathed,** lank van asem; ~ **cloth,** fynlinne; ~**-clothes,** lang babaklere; ~**-dated,** op langsig; ~**-dated bill,** langsigwissel.

long' distance, lang afstand; ~ **bomber,** langafstandsbomwerper; ~ **call,** hooflynoproep; ~ **flight,** langafstandsvlug; ~ **traffic,** langafstandsverkeer.

long: ~ **division,** lang deling; ~ **dozen,** dertien; ~**drawn,** lank gerek, ellelang; ~**-eared,** langoor-; ~**-enduring,** lank staande, oud.

long'er, langer; *the* ~ *the BETTER,* hoe langer, hoe beter; *NO* ~, nie meer nie.

long'est, langste; *at* ~, op sy langste; ~ **liver,** langslewende.

longev'al, langlewend.

longev'ity, lang lewe, hoë ouderdom.

long: ~**-faced,** met 'n lang gesig; ~ **finger,** middelvinger; ~**hand,** gewone skrif.

long' head: *have a* ~, uitgeslape wees; ~**ed,** langhoofdig; langskedelig; verstandig, uitgeslape; ~**edness,** langskedeligheid; slimheid; skerpsinnigheid.

long' hundred, 120.

long'ing, (n) verlange, hunkering; (a) verlangend, smagtend.

lon'giped, langvoetig.

longipenn'ate, met lang vlerke, lank gevlerk.

longiros'tral, langbek-.

long'ish, taamlik lank, langerig.

lon'gitude, geografiese lengte; *CIRCLE of* ~, middaglyn, meridiaan; *DEGREE of* ~, lengtegraad.

longitud'inal, in die lengte, lengte-, sy-; oorlangs; ~ **axis,** lengteas; ~ **clinometer,** langshellingmeter; ~ **muscle,** lengtespier, oorlangse spier; ~ **seam,** langsaar; ~ **section,** langs(deur)snee.

long: ~ **jump,** verspring; ~ **leave,** langverlof; ~ **leg,** diepby; ~**-legged,** langbenig, langbeen-; ~**-legs,** langbeenspinnekop; ~**-lived,** langlewend; langdurig; ~**-livedness,** langlewendheid; ~ **measure,** lengtemaat; ~**-necked,** langnek-; ~ **odds,** ongelyk wedenskap, ver kanse; ~ **off,** diepweg; ~ **on,** ver-by; ~ **paper,** wissels op lang termyn; ~**-playing record,** langspeelplaat; ~ **premium,** hoë premie; ~ **price,** volle prys; ~ **primer,** klein romein (letter); ~ **range,** verdraend; ~**-range gun,** verdraende geskut; ~**-range fighter,** jagkruiser; ~**s,** lang broek; ~ **saw,** kuilsaag; ~**-shanked,** langbeen-, langbenig; ~**shore,** aan die kus, kus-; ~**shoreman,** dokwerker, stuwadoor; ~ **shot,** skoot van ver; groot afstand; waagstuk; *not by a* ~ *shot,* verreweg nie; ~**-sighted,** versiende; slim; ~**-sighted bill,** wissel op lang termyn; ~**-sightedness,** versiendheid; ~**-spun,** langdradig; gerek; ~**-standing,** oud; langdurig; ~**-stapled,** met lang drade, langdraad-; ~ **stop,** veragter (krieket); ~**-suffering,** (n) lankmoedigheid; (a) lankmoedig; ~**-tail,** langstert-; ~**-tailed tit,** langstert; ~**-term,** langdurig; op lang termyn; ~**-term loan,** langtermynlening; ~**-term policy,** toekomsbeleid; ~**-term prisoner,** gevangene met 'n lang vonnis; ~ **ton,** Engelse ton (2 240 lb.); ~ **tongue,** lastertong; ~**-tongued,** praterig, praatsiek; ~**wall,** strookbou (myn); ~**wall mining,** strookmynbou; ~ **wave,** lang golflengte; ~**-wave station,** langgolfstasie; ~**ways,** in die lengte; ~**-winded,** vervelend; omslagtig, gerek; langasem-; *BE* ~*-winded,* by die Kaap omdraai; lank van draad wees; nie amen kan sê nie; *a* ~*-winded PERSON,* 'n langasemkriek; 'n langasemsprinkaan; ~**-windedness,** gerektheid; wydlopigheid; ~ **wise,** in die lengte.

loo, (n) lanterlu; privaat, WC, kleinhuisie; (v) lanterlu speel.

loob'y, (loobies), lummel, lomperd, gek.

loof'ah, luffa(spons.).

look, (n) voorkome, voorkoms; blik; aanblik; kykie; gesig; gelaat; uitdrukking; aanskyn; (pl) voorkome, gesig; wese; *give someone a BLACK* ~, iem. kwaad aankyk; *just FOR the* ~ *of the thing,* net vir die skyn; *GOOD* ~*s,* mooi uiterlik; *her GOOD* ~*s,* haar mooiheid; *HAVE a* ~ *at,* kyk na; *I don't LIKE the* ~ *of it,* dit beval my nie; *the NEW* ~, die nuwe voorkoms; *TAKE a* ~, 'n kykie neem; *by the* ~ *of THINGS,* soos dit wil voorkom; soos sake daar uitsien; (v) kyk; sien; aanskou; deur die gelaatsuitdrukking te kenne gee; nakyk; oplet, oppas; bekyk; uitkyk; daar uitsien; ~ *ABOUT,* rondkyk;

~ *ABOUT one,* jou oë oophou; ~ *AFTER,* nastaar; ~ *AFTER something,* na iets kyk; iets oppas; iets versorg; ~ *AFTER oneself,* jou man kan staan; na jouself kyk; ~ *one's AGE,* so oud lyk soos jy is; ~ *AHEAD,* vooruitsien, vooruitkyk; ~ *ALIVE!* maak gou! roer jou riete! lyk soos jy is; ~ *AWAY,* wegkyk; ~ *BACK,* terugkyk, terugblik; omkyk; *he has never* ~*ed BACK,* daar was by hom nog nooit enige naberou nie; hy het steeds vorentoe gebeur; ~ *BEHIND,* omkyk; ~ *one's BEST,* sy mooiste lyk; op sy voordeligste daar uitsien; ~ *BLANK,* beteuterd lyk; ~ *on the BRIGHT side,* hou die blink kant bo; ~ *DAGGERS,* kyk of jy kan moor; *you* ~ *like DOING it!* jy lyk 'n mooi eend! jy lyk 'n mooi aap! ~ *DOWN,* afkyk; die oë neerslaan; ~ *DOWN on,* neersien op; ~ *one in the FACE,* iem. in die oë kyk; ~ *FIT,* daar gesond (fiks) uitsien; ~ *FOR,* soek na; verwag; let op; ~ *FOR it,* daarna soek; daarna maak; ~ *FORWARD to,* uitsien na; ~ *HERE!* kyk hier! ~ *IN on someone,* by iem. aangaan; by iem. inloer; by iem. 'n draai gooi; ~ *IN quickly at,* êrens inloer; êrens 'n kooltjie vuur gaan haal; ~ *after one's INTERESTS,* jou belange behartig; ~ *INTO,* kyk in; ondersoek instel; ~ *one's LAST,* 'n laaste blik werp op; ~ *before you LEAP,* besin eer jy begin; ~ *LIKE,* lyk na; *you* ~ *LIKE it!* jy lyk 'n mooi bobbejaan! ~ *to your MANNERS,* dink aan jou gedrag; *will NOT* ~ *at,* nie eers daarna wil kyk nie; ~ *ON,* toekyk; ~ *OUT,* uitkyk; oppas; ~ *OUT for,* soek na; verwag; ~ *OVER,* nasien, nagaan, bekyk; deurkyk; deur die vingers sien; ~ *someone OVER from head to foot,* iem. van kop tot tone opneem; ~ *the PART,* 'n goeie lyf hê vir; ~ *after a PRACTICE,* 'n praktyk waarneem; ~ *ROUND,* omkyk; kyk hoe dit staan; ~ *SHARP!* roer jou! maak gou! ~ *SMALL,* verleë lyk; klein voel; ~ *to someone for SUPPORT,* op iem. se steun reken; ~ *THROUGH,* deurkyk; deursien; *I must have my car* ~*ed TO,* ek moet my motor goed laat nagaan; ~ *TO it that the door is locked,* sorg dat die deur gesluit is; ~ *for TROUBLE,* moeilikheid soek; ~ *TWICE at his money,* 'n sent twee maal omkeer; ~ *UP,* opkyk; opsoek, naslaan; besoek; beter word; ~ *UP to someone,* na iem. opsien; ~ *a person UP and down,* iem. van kop tot tone bekyk; *you* ~ *WELL,* jy sien daar goed uit; *well,* ~ *WHO'S here!* dit gaan seker reën; *the WINDOW* ~*s north,* die venster kyk op die noorde uit.

look'er, kyker; *a good-*~, 'n mooi mens; ~**-on', (lookers-on),** toeskouer.

look'-in, kant; kykie.

look'ing, (die) kyk, voorkoms; ~**-glass, (-es),** spieël.

look'-out, uitkyk; uitkykpos (mil.); vooruitsig; nitsig; *it is a BAD* ~ *for him,* sy vooruitsigte is glad nie gunstig nie; *that is HIS* ~, dis sy eie saak; *KEEP a good* ~, goed uitkyk; *be ON the* ~, op die uitkyk wees; brandwag staan; *ON the* ~ *for,* op die uitkyk na; ~ **post,** uitkykpos.

look'-see, inspeksie, kyk.

loom¹, (n) rooinekduiker.

loom², (n) weeftoestel, weefgetou; handvatsel (van 'n roeispaan).

loom³, (n) opdoem; (v) opdoem, opskemer; ~ *AHEAD,* opdoem; ~ *LARGE,* 'n vername plek inneem; ~**ing,** opdoeming.

loon¹, lummel, domkop, vent, uilskuiken, leegloper.

loon², ysduiker.

loon'y, (n) **(loonies),** mal mens; (a) mallerig, dwaas, getik.

loop, (n) lussie, strop; hingsel, oog (tou); haak (saag); trensie, garingoog; bog; kykgat, oogstuk (toom); agteroorslaanvlug; uitwykspoor; (v) 'n lussie of ogie maak; met 'n vangstok vang; met 'n lus vang, agteroorslaan; ~ *the* ~, agteroorslaanvlieg, bolmakiesie vlieg, kringduikel.

looped: ~ *FABRIC,* lusstof; ~ *PILE,* luspool; ~ *WEFT,* inslaglus.

loop'hole, (n) skietgat; skuiwergat; kykgat, gaatjie; luggat (skip); uitweg, uitvlug; *keep a* ~ *open,* 'n agterdeur oophou; (v) van kykgate voorsien; uitvlugte soek.

loop: ~ **knot,** lusknoop; ~ **lace,** galon; ~**-line,** oog-

loose

lyn, ringlyn, verbindingslyn; uitwykspoor; ~ -**road**, uitwykpad; ~ -**step**, beueltrap; ~ -**stitch**, lussteek; ~ -**stitched bar**, trensie; ~ **y**, vol bogte.

loose, (n) losspel (rugby); uitdrukking; *GIVE (a)* ~ *to one's feelings*, uitdrukking gee aan jou gevoelens; *IN the* ~, in die losspel; los (graan); *LIVE on the* ~, losbandig lewe; *ON the* ~, aan die boemel, losbandig; (v) losmaak; bevry; onthef; aftrek, skiet; die anker lig; slap laat hang; ~ *HOLD*, loslaat; ~ *OFF*, los(laat); (a) los, vry; onsamehangend; slap (perig); ruim; loslywig; slordig, agteloos, onnoukeurig, vaag; bros, krummelrig (grond); ~ *BO(W)ELS*, loslywigheid; *be at a* ~ *END*, ledig, sonder vaste werk; *with a* ~ *REIN*, met slap leisels; *have a* ~ *TONGUE*, loslippig wees; (adv) los; *BREAK* ~, losbreek; *GET* ~, loskom; *LET* ~, loslaat, vrylaat; *SET* ~, vrylaat, in vryheid stel; ~ -**box**, hok wat los staan; ~ **cash**, los geld; ~ **ends**, onafgerondheid; ~ **fish**, losbol; ~ -**fitting**, los passend; ~ **forward**, losvoorspeler; ~ -**leaf**, losblad=; ~ -**leaf diary**, losbladdagboek; ~ -**leaf system**, ringbandstelsel; ~ -**limbed**, lenig; ~ -**lipped**, loslippig; ~ **ly**, lossies; ~ -**minded**, ligsinnig; ~ **n**, losmaak; los word; laat verslap, laat skiet; ~ **ness**, losheid; slapheid; buitensporigheid; loslywigheid; losbandigheid; laksheid; ~ **play**, losspel; ~ **scrum**, losskrum; ~ **sleeve**, wye mou; ~ -**stone peach**, lospitperske; ~ -**tongued**, loslippig; ~ **woman**, ligte vrou, ligtekooi.

loos'ish, losserig.

loot, (n) roof, buit; (v) buit, roof, plunder; ~ **er**, plunderaar, buitmaker.

lop¹, (n) takkies, snoeihout; (v) **(-ped)**, snoei, afknip, knot, (af)top (boom); ~ *AT*, kap na; ~ *AWAY*, wegkap; ~ *OFF*, afknot.

lop², (n) hangoorkonyn; (v) laat hang; afhang, slap hang, neerhang; talm; rondslenter.

lop³, (n) deining, geklots (water); (v) klots (water).

lope, (n) lang haal; (v) lang hale gee.

lop: ~ -**ear**, hangoorkonyn; ~ -**eared**, ~ -**ears**, met hangende ore, hangoor=, hangore=.

lop: ~ **per**, snoeier; kês (melk); ~ **pings**, snoeihout, snoeisels; ~ **ping-shears**, snoeiskêr.

lopp'y¹, slap, hangend, hangoor=.

lopp'y², deinend, klotsend (water).

lop'-sided, skeef, windskeef; oorhangend, eensydig, onewewigtig; ~ **ness**, skeefte, skeefheid; oorhang; onewewigtigheid.

loqua'cious, spraaksaam, babbelsiek, babbelsugtig, praatsiek; ~ **ness**, **loqua'city**, spraaksaamheid, woordrykheid, babbelsug.

loq'uat, lukwart; lukwartboom.

lor! magtie! heiden!

Lord¹ Here, Heer; ~ *BLESS me!* goeie genugtig! *the* ~ *'s DAY*, die dag v.d. Here, Sondag; *the* ~ *GOD*, die Here God, God die Heer; *the* ~ *of HOSTS*, die Here der Leërskare; *the* ~ *KNOWS who*, die hemel weet wie; ~, *have MERCY*, Heer, ontferm U; mag die Here ons genadig wees; *the* ~ *'s PRAYER*, die Onse Vader, die gebed v.d. Here; *the* ~ *'s SUPPER*, die Heilige Nagmaal; *the* ~ *'s TABLE*, die Nagmaalstafel; *THE* ~, die Here (Heer); *in the YEAR of our* ~, in die jaar van ons Here.

lord², (n) heer, meester; baas; gebieder; lord (titel); *the L* ~ *s of the ADMIRALTY*, die admiraliteit; ~ *s of CREATION*, here v.d. skepping; *as DRUNK as a* ~, smoordronk; *HOUSE of L* ~ *s*, die Engelse Hoërhuis; ~ *s and LADIES*, dames en here; gevlekte aronskelk; *LIKE a* ~, soos 'n grootmeneer; ~ *of the MANOR*, grondeienaar; ~ *and MASTER*, heer en meester; *MY L* ~, edelagbare; *L* ~ *s SPIRITUAL*, die geestelike lede; *SWEAR like a* ~, vloek soos 'n matroos; *L* ~ *s TEMPORAL*, die wêreldlike lede; *TREAT like a* ~, vorstelik onthaal; (v) kommandeer, baasspeel; tot lord verhef; ~ *it over*, baasspeel oor, kommandeer.

Lord: ~ **Chamberlain**, Lord-Kamerheer; ~ **Chancellor**, Lord-Kanselier; ~ **Chief Justice**, Hoofregter (Br.); ~ **Lieutenant**, onderkoning.

lord: ~ **liness**, trotsheid; deftigheid, vernaamheid; ~ **ling**, lordjie, meneertjie; ~ **ly**, lordagtig, trots, hoogmoedig, heerssugtig; edel, vernaam; *in a* ~ *ly manner*, heeragtig; *L* ~ *Mayor*, stadsburgemeester (Eng.).

lordos'is, lordose, holrug.

Lord: ~ **Privy Seal**, Geheime Seëlbewaarder (in Brittanje); ~ **s Seventeen**, Here Sewentien.

lord'ship, lordskap; heerskappy; *HIS L* ~ *ship*, sy lordskap; *YOUR L* ~ *ship*, u lordskap.

lore¹, kennis, kunde.

lore², lel, bel (voëls).

lorgnette', toneelkyker; lornjet.

lo'rica, pantserhemp, skild.

lo'ricate, gepantser.

lo'riot, wielewaal (voël).

lor'is, (-es), lori, apie.

lorn, verlate, verlore; eensaam.

Lorraine', Lotharinge; ~ **r**, Lotharinger.

lo'rry, (lorries), vragmotor, vragwa, lorrie.

lor'y, (lories), loerie, troupand.

lose, (lost), verloor; weggooi; kwytraak; verbeur, verspeel; mis, misloop; uitval (in 'n verkiesing); nie haal nie (trein); laat verloor; agterloop (oorlosie); ~ *a BABY*, 'n babatjie verloor; 'n miskraam hê; ~ *one's BALANCE*, jou ewewig verloor; ~ *a CHANCE*, 'n kans laat verbygaan, 'n geleentheid misloop; ~ *COLOUR*, bleek word, verbleek; ~ *CONCIOUSNESS*, flou word; ~ *CONTACT with*, uit die oog verloor; ~ *CONTROL of oneself*, jou selfbeheersing verloor; ~ *FLESH*, afval, maer word; ~ *GROUND*, veld verloor, agteruitgaan; ~ *one's HEAD*, kop verloor, die kluts kwytraak; *don't* ~ *HEART*, moed hou; moenie by die pokke gaan neersit nie; ~ *one's HEART*, sy hart verloor; verlief raak; ~ *one's LIFE*, die lewe verloor; ~ *one's MIND*, die verstand verloor; swaksinnig word; ~ *one's NERVE*, bang word; ~ *ONESELF*, verdwaal; ~ *ONESELF in*, verward raak in; opgaan in; ~ *PATIENCE*, jou geduld verloor; ~ *one's RAG*, jou herkoutjie kwyt wees; smoorkwaad word; die hoenders in word; ~ *SIGHT of*, iets uit die oog verloor; ~ *one's TEMPER*, kwaad word; ~ *one's THREAD*, die kluts kwytraak; afdwaal; ~ *TOUCH*, voeling verloor; ~ *the happy TOUCH*, jou slag verloor; ~ *one's TRAIN*, die trein nie haal nie, die trein mis; ~ *one's WAY*, verdwaal; ~ *WEIGHT*, afval, gewig verloor.

los'er, verloorder; *a BAD* ~, iem. wat nie kan verdra om te verloor nie; *BE a* ~ *by*, êrens by verloor; *COME off the* ~, aan die kortste end trek; *a GOOD* ~, iem. wat hom dit nie aantrek wanneer hy verloor nie, 'n goeie verloorder.

los'ing, (n) (die) verloor; verlies; (a) verlorend, verliesend; hopeloos; *they are fighting a* ~ *BATTLE*, hulle is aan die verloorkant; *a* ~ *GAME*, 'n hopelose spel; *they cannot play a* ~ *GAME*, hulle word kwaad wanneer hulle verloor; ~ *SIDE*, verloorkant.

loss, verlies; derwing; skade(pos); ondergang; nadeel; *never to be at a* ~ *for an ANSWER*, nooit om 'n antwoord verleë wees nie; altyd klaar wees met 'n antwoord; *BE at a* ~, buite raad wees; geen raad weet nie; verleë wees; met die hand in die hare sit; in die middel v.d. wêreld wees; *CUT one's* ~ *es*, die verlies maar dra; *one man's* ~ *is another man's GAIN*, die een se dood is die ander se brood; ~ *of MEMORY*, geheueverlies, amnesie; *SELL at a* ~, met verlies verkoop; *with* ~ *and SHAME*, met skade en skande; ~ *of TIME*, tydverlies; *the car was a TOTAL* ~, die motor was 'n voslae wrak.

lost, verlore, na sy grootjie, geskore; verdwaal; versonke; *ALL is not* ~ *that is delayed*, uitstel is geen afstel nie; *BE* ~, verlore wees; verdwaal wees; omkom; ~ *CAUSE*, verlore saak; *EVERYTHING is* ~, alles is na die maan; *GET* ~, verdwaal; verlore raak; maak dat jy wegkom; *the MOTION was* ~, die voorstel is verwerp; *the SHIP was* ~, die skip het vergaan; ~ *SOUL*, verlore siel; ~ *in THOUGHT*, in gedagtes verdiep; *that is* ~ *(UP)ON him*, dis botter aan die galg gesmeer; dis bokant sy vuurmaakplek; ~ **motion**, dooiegang; ~ **property**, vermiste goedere; ~ -**property office**, kantoor vir vermiste goedere.

lot, (n) lot; aandeel; lewenslot; perseel, stuk grond;

loth

party; hoeveelheid, bossie, hoop; klomp, swetter=
joel, spul; *a BAD* ~, 'n skurk; 'n gemene vent; *BY*
~, deur loting, deur die lot; *CAST* ~ *s*, loot; die lot
laat beslis; *DRAW* ~ *s*, lootjies trek; *FALL to the*
~ *of*, te beurt val; *it did not FALL to his* ~, dit was
nie vir hom weggelê nie; dit was hom nie beskore
nie; *HAVE a* ~ *to say*, baie te sê hê; baie note op
sy psalm hê; *IN* ~ *s*, by hopies; *it is MY* ~, die lot is
my beskore; *a* ~ *of MONEY*, geld soos bossies; *a*
~ *OF*, baie, volop; *have no PART nor* ~ *in*, geen
aandeel hê nie in; *THAT* ~, daardie spul; *THE* ~,
alles saam; die hele boel; *THINK a* ~ *of*, 'n hoë
dunk hê van; ~ *s of TIME*, volop tyd; *THROW in
one's* ~ *with*, jou lot inwerp met; jou skaar aan die
kant van; *the WHOLE* ~, die hele boel; die hele
spul; (v) **(-ted)**, toewys, toebedeel; in stukke ver=
deel; ~ **out**, in erwe verdeel; in klompies verdeel.
loth, *kyk* **loath**.
lo'tion, water, wasmiddel; vloeimiddel; huidwater,
velmiddel; kromhoutsap.
lott'ery, (..ries), lotery; **L**~ **Act**, Loterywet; ~ **loan**,
premielening; ~ **office**, loterykantoor; ~ **ticket**,
loterykaartjie.
lott'o, lotto (spel).
lot'us, (-es), lotusblom; lotusplant; ~**-eater**, lotus=
eter, lewensgenieter, dromer; ~**-eating**, (n) gemak=
sugtige dromery, dagdromery; (a) gemaksugtig.
lo'tus land, luilekkerland, lotosland; *live in* ~, 'n lui=
lekker bestaan voer.
loud, (a) luid, hard; opsigtig, skreeuend (kleure); uit=
gelate, luidrugtig, lawaaierig; *- colours*, skreeuen=
de kloure; (adv) hardop, luid, luidkeels; ~ **en**, har=
der word; ~**ish**, taamlik hard; ~**ly**, hard;
~**-mouthed**, luidrugtig; grootpraterig; ~**ness**, luid=
rugtigheid, hardheid, uitgelatenheid; opsigtigheid;
~**speaker**, luidspreker; ~**-spoken**, luidrugtig; ~**-
voiced**, met harde stem.
lough, meer.
lou'is, lou'is-d'or, louis, louis-d'or (20 frank).
lounge, (n) slentery, drentelry; slentergang; tyd=
verdryf; rusbank; luierstoel; woonkamer (huis), sit=
kamer; geselskapsaal; lekkerhoekie; (v) slenter,
drentel; luier; ~ *ABOUT*, rondluier; ~ *AWAY
one's time*, jou tyd vermors; ~ **chair**, luierstoel, lê=
stoel; ~ **coat**, drabaadjie; ~ **r**, rondleêr, rond=
draaier, slenteraar; ~ **suit**, dra(ag)pak, dagpak; ~
suite, sitkamerstel.
loung'ing, gedrentel, geslenter; rondlêery.
loupe, (diamant)vergrootglas, loep.
lour, (n) nors gesig, dreigende blik; dreigende weer;
(v) dreig, saampak (wolke); nors lyk, frons; *kyk ook*
lower.
lou'rie, loerie; *grey* ~, kwêvoël, pêvoël.
lour'y, wolkerig; donker, dreigend; nors.
louse, (lice), luis.
lous'iness, luisigheid; gemeenheid; walglikheid.
lous'y, vol luise; laag, gemeen; armsalig, beroerd; dik
van (geld, ens.).
lout, drommel, vent, takhaar, (gom)tor, lierjy, slun=
gel, ghwar, lummel; ~**ish**, onhandig, lummelagtig,
torrerig.
Louvain', Leuven.
louv'er, louv're, rookgat, luggat, ventilasieskreef;
hortjie(venster); ~ **blind**, hortjieblinding; ~ **win=
dow**, hortjievenster.
louv'ered, met hortjies.
lo'vable, lieftallig, beminlik, beminnenswaardig;
~**ness**, liefheid, beminlikheid.
lo'vage, lavas (plant) *(Levisticum)*.
love, (n) liefde; minne, geneentheid; beminde, lief=
ling, skat, hartjie; liefdegod; mingenot; stroop, nul
(tennis); *live on* ~ *and fresh AIR*, van liefde en koue
water leef; ~ *ALL*, almal nul; ~ *to ALL*, hartlike
groete aan almal; *ARDOUR of* ~, minnegloed; ~
in a COTTAGE, huwelik met onvoldoende midde=
le; ~ *is BLIND*, die liefde is blind; *FALL in* ~,
verlief raak; *FIRE of* ~, minnevuur; *FIRST* ~ *ne=
ver dies*, ou liefde roes nie; *FLAME of* ~, minne=
koors, minnevlam; *FOR the* ~ *of somebody*, om
iem. se ontwil; *FOR* ~, uit liefde; nie vir geld nie;
for the ~ *of GOD*, om Godswil; *IN* ~, verlief,
been-af; *LABOUR of* ~, liefdewerk; ~ *laughs at*

low

LOCKSMITHS, die liefde maak altyd 'n plan; lief=
de gebruik lis; *there is no* ~ *LOST between them*,
hulle sit nie langs een vuur nie; *MAKE* ~ *to*, die hof
maak, vry na, vlerksleep by; *a MARRIAGE for* ~,
'n huwelik uit liefde; *for the* ~ *of MIKE (Pete)*, om
liefdeswil; ~ *of MONEY*, geldgierigheid; *not to be
had for* ~ *or MONEY*, vir geen geld of goeie woor=
de te kry nie; *live on MOONSHINE and* ~, van
liefde en koue water leef; *don't be off with the OLD*
~ *before you are on with the new*, moenie ou skoene
weggooi voor jy nuwes het nie; *OLD* ~ *never dies*,
ou liefde roes nie; *OUT of* ~, uit liefde; *PLAY for*
~, om die keiser se baard speel; ~ *makes the world
go ROUND*, alles draai om die liefde; *SEND one's*
~, groete laat weet; ~ *at first SIGHT*, liefde op die
eerste gesig; *the course of TRUE* ~ *never did run
smooth*, by geliefdes moet daar verskil van mening
verwag word; ware liefde moet hinderpale verwag;
all's fair in ~ *and WAR*, in liefdesake is alles geoor=
loof; ~ *will find a WAY*, liefde maak altyd 'n plan;
liefde soek lis; (v) liefhê, bemin; baie hou van; ~ *to
DO something*, iets uiters graag doen; ~ *me*, ~ *my
DOG*, wie A sê, moet ook B sê; wie my liefhet, moet
alles op die koop toe neem; ~ *me LITTLE*, ~ *me
long*, al is die liefde min, laat dit blywend wees; *I
SHOULD* ~ *to come*, ek sou graag wil kom; *I* ~
THAT! dis 'n mooi grap! ~**d**, gelief; bemind; ~ **d
ones**, dierbares; ~ **affair**, liefdesgeskiedenis, min=
narytjie, liefdesaak; ~**-apple**, tamatie; ~ **bean**,
mienie-mienie; ~**-begotten**, buite-egtelik; ~**-bird**,
parkiet, dwergpapegaai; *a pair of* ~**-birds**, 'n ver=
liefde paartjie; ~**-charm**, liefdesamulet; ~**-child**,
buite-egtelike kind; ~**-crossed**, ongelukkig in die
liefde; ~**-feast**, liefdemaal; ~ **game**, stroop-, nul=
pot; ~**-god**, liefdegodjie, kupie; ~**-grass**, klitsgras
('n *Setaria*-soort); oulandgras *(Eragrostis)*; ~**-in-
a-mist**, vinkelblom, duiwel-in-die-bos, juffertjie-in-
die-groen *(Nigella damascena)*; ~**-knot**, liefde=
knoop; ~ **less**, onbemin; liefdeloos; ~**-letter**,
minnebrief; vrybrief; ~**-lies-bleeding**, rooi kat=
stert; amarant; nooienslok; ~**-life**, liefdeslewe;
~**liness**, lieflikheid, aanminlikheid, aanvalligheid,
beminlikheid; skattigheid; ~**lock**, oorlok, spoeg=
lok; ~**lorn**, deur die minnaar verlaat, alleen;
smoorverlief; ~**ly**, lieflik, beminlik, aanminlik,
aanvallig, skattig, beeldig, mooi; heerlik, baie lek=
ker; *everything in the garden was* ~*ly*, dit was alles
maanskyn en rosegeur; ~**-making**, vryery, hof=
makery, vryasie; ~**-match**, huwelik uit liefde; ~**-
philtre**, minnedrank, doepa; ~**-pledge**, minnepand;
~**-potion** = **love-philtre**; ~ **r**, minnaar, beminde,
jongetjie, vryer, liefhebber, kêrel, snaar, ghantang;
(pl) verliefde paar; ~ **r's-knot**, duiwelsnaaigaring,
warkruid; ~ **rs' talk**, minnepraatjies; ~ **seat**, opsit=
bankie; ~ **set**, nulstel, stroopstel; ~**-shaft**, Lief=
despyl, minnepyl; ~ **sick**, smoorverlief, minsiek,
doodverlief; ~ **sickness**, smoorverliefdheid; ~**'s
lament**, ~**-song**, minnedig, minnesang; ~**-story**,
liefdesgeskiedenis, liefdesverhaal; ~ **suit**, huwelik=
saansoek; ~**-token**, liefdesgeskenk, liefdepand.
lov'ey, hartjie, liefie.
lo'ving, (n) liefhê; vryery; (a) toegeneë; liefhebbend;
teer; hartlik, liefderyk; *in* ~ *memory*, in liefdevolle
herinnering; ~**-cup**, vriendskapsbeker; ~**-kind=
ness**, goedertierenheid, liefde, goedheid; ~ **kiss**,
liefdesoen; ~**ness**, teerheid, hartlikheid, liefderyk=
heid.
low[1], (n) gebulk, (v) bulk, loei.
low[2], (n) laagdrukgebied, depressiegebied, laagte=
punt; (a) laag; gemeen; minderwaardig; nederig;
klein, min; swak; plat, laag uitgesny (rok); dood=
diep (buiging); diep ter neergedronk, neerslagtig; on=
voldoende, gering; *a* ~ *BOW*, 'n diep buiging; *a* ~
DRESS, 'n laag uitgesnyde (gedekolleteerde) rok;
have a ~ *OPINION of*, 'n lae dunk hê van; *at a* ~
RATE, teen 'n lae prys; *in* ~ *SPIRITS*, neerslagtig;
a ~ *VOICE*, 'n sagte stem; *be in* ~ *WATER*, in
moeilikheid verkeer; aan laer wal, in geldnood;
(adv) sag; laag; *BE* ~, laag staan; ~ *DOWN*, laag
(af); *FEEL* ~, neerslagtig voel; *LAY* ~, platloop;
neervel; *LIE* ~, doodlê; sy tyd afwag; stilbly; *RUN*
~, opraak; *SPEAK (talk)* ~, sag praat; *TACKLE*

~, laagvat; ~ **birth**, lae geboorte; ~-**born**, van lae geboorte; ~ **boy**, lae laaikas; ~-**bred**, van lae afkoms; onopgevoed, onbeskaaf; ~ **brow**, (n) domkop, sufferd; filistyn; (a) verstaanbaar, maklik vir die massa; ~-**browed**, met lae voorkop; oorhangend; ~-**caste**, van 'n lae kaste; L~ **Church**, Evangeliese seksie v.d. Engelse Kerk; ~-**class**, gemeen, van lae klas; minderwaardig; ~ **comedy**, klugspel; ~**cost**, goedkoop; ~ **country**, laeveld; *the Low Countries*, die Nederlande; ~-**crowned**, met lae bol; ~-**density building**, laedigtheidsbehuising; ~ **diet**, skraal dieet; ~-**down**, (Amer.) (a) veragtelik; (n) inligting, nuus, besonderhede.
low'er, (v) laat sak, neerlaat (boot); verlaag; afdraai; buig, buk; neerslaan (rook); laer word; verminder, verneder; verdun (vloeistof); neerhaal, stryk (vlag); ~ *the COLOURS*, die vlag stryk; ~ *one's EYES*, die oë neerslaan; ~ *one's GUARD*, die waaksaamheid verslap; ~ *ONESELF*, jou verlaag; ~ *one's VOICE*, sagter praat; (a) laer; swakker; minder; geringer; onder-; ~ *CHAMBER*, tweede kamer; *the* ~ *DECK*, die minderes, die bemanning; *the L* ~ *HOUSE*, die Laerhuis; *the* ~ *REGIONS*, die onderwêreld; *with* ~*ed SIGHTS*, met plat visier; *the* ~ *WORLD*, die onderwêreld; ~ *case*, onderkas; ~ **class(es)**, (die) mindere stand(e); ~ **deck**, benededek; L~ **Egypt**, Onder-Egipte, Benede-Egipte; ~**ing**, neerlating; ~**most**, laagste, onderste; ~ **orders**, (die) mindere stand.
low'est, onderste, laagste; kleinste; ~ *common FACTOR*, kleinste gemene deler; ~ *common MULTIPLE*, kleinste gemene veelvoud.
low: ~-**fat diet**, vetarm dieet; ~ **gear**, laagste (eerste) versnelling (rat); L~ **German**, Nederduits, Platduits; ~-**grade**, van minder gehalte, swakgraads, laegraads; ~-**laid**, begrawe; ~ **land**, laagland; L~**lander**, Laaglander; L~ **Latin**, Middeleeuse Latyn; ~ **level**, lae vlak; ~-**level attack**, skeervlugaanval; ~-**level bridge**, laagwaterbrug; ~ **liness**, geringheid; nederigheid; ~-**lived**, 'n gewone lewe leidend; ~**ly**, gering, nederig, ootmoedig; ~*ly born*, laaggebore; ~-**lying land**, laagland; ~-**minded**, laag, gemeen, onedel; ~**ness**, laagheid; geringheid; swakheid; gemeenheid; ~-**pitched**, laag gestem; sag; ~ **point**, laagtepunt; ~ **pressure**, lae druk; lae spanning (elektr.); ~-**pressure area**, laagdrukgebied; ~-**priced**, goedkoop; ~-**rated**, geminag; ~-**salt diet**, soutarm dieet; ~-**spirited**, neerslagtig, terneergedruk; ~ **storey**, benedeverdieping; L~ **Sunday**, Sondag na Paasfees; ~ **tide**, laagwater; L~**veld**, Laeveld; ~-**voiced**, met sagte stem; ~ **water**, laagwater; *in* ~ *water*, in die moeilikheid; ~-**water level**, laagwaterstand; ~-**water mark**, laagwaterlyn; ~-**wing monoplane**, laagdekker.
lo'xodrome, loxodrom'ic, (n) streeklyn; loksodroom; (a) skuinsseilend.
lo'xostylis, teerhoutboom.
loy'al, getrou, lojaal; ~ *and faithful*, hou en trou; ~**ism**, lojalisme; ~**ist**, (n) lojalis, staatsgesinde, getroue onderdaan; (a) lojalisties; ~**ly**, lojaal; ~**ty**, getrouheid, lojaliteit, trou.
loz'enge, tabletjie; suigpil; ruit (figuur); ~**d**, ruitvormig, geruit; ~-**moulding**, versiering met ruitvormige panele; ruitjieslys; ~-**shaped**, ruitvormig.
lubb'er, lomperd, lummel, tor, stumper, gaip, slungel; ~**like**, ~**ly**, lomp, log, lummelagtig; ~**'s line**, stuurstreep.
lub'ricant, (n) masjienolie, smeerolie; (a) gladmakend, smerend.
lub'ricate, smeer, olie; *lubricating oil*, masjienolie, smeerolie.
lubrica'tion, (die) olie, smeer, smering.
lub'ricator, smeerder; smeersel, smeermiddel; smeerpot, oliekannetjie.
lubri'cious, glibberig, glad; wellustig, wulps.
lubri'city, gladheid, glibberigheid; ongestadigheid, onsekerheid; ontugtigheid, wellustigheid.
lub'ricous = **lubricious**.
lubritor'ium, smeerkamer.
Luc'as, Lukas.
luce, varswatersnoek.

lu'cency, helderheid, glans.
lu'cent, blinkend, skynend; helder, deurskynend.
Lucerne'¹, Luzern.
lucern(e)², lusern, klawer; *bale of* ~, lusernbaal; ~ **camp**, lusernkamp; ~ **crop**, lusernoes; ~ **meal**, lusernmeel.
Lu'cian, Lucianus.
lu'cid, helder, duidelik; deurskynend, deursigtig; blinkend; ~ *intervals*, helder oomblikke; **..cid'ity**, ~**ness**, skittering, blinkheid; duidelikheid, deursigtigheid; helderheid.
Lu'cifer, Lucifer, Satan.
lu'cifer, vuurhoutjie.
Lucifer'ian, satans; trots.
lucif'ugous, ligsku.
luck, geluk; toeval; fortuin; *BAD* ~, teenspoed; ongeluk; *BAD* ~! simpatie! *BE in* ~, geluk hê; *BETTER* ~ *next time*, die kans kan keer; *the worse* ~ *now, the BETTER next time*, nou ongelukkig, later gelukkig; *BY* ~, by toeval; *have the* ~ *of a CHINAMAN*, die geluk loop hom onderstebo; *he has the* ~ *of the DEVIL*, *he has the DEVIL'S own* ~, die geluk loop hom onderstebo; *be DOWN on one's* ~, daar sleg aan toe wees; in die moeilikheid wees; *FOR* ~, om voorspoedig te maak; *GOOD* ~, geluk; geluksdag; *GOOD* ~! sukses! die beste! alle heil! *as* ~ *would HAVE it*, toevallig; soos die toeval dit wou hê; *HAVE no* ~, teenspoedig wees; *ILL* ~, teenspoed; *his* ~ *is IN*, hy is voorspoedig; hy is gelukkig; hy tref dit gelukkig; *more by* ~ *than good JUDGMENT*, dit was meer geluk as wysheid; *his* ~ *is OUT*, hy is ongelukkig; die geluk loop hom teë; *PIECE of* ~, gelukskoot; geluksslag; *that was SHEER* ~, dit was pure geluk; *more* ~ *than SKILL*, meer geluk as wysheid; *TRY one's* ~, probeer; jou geluk beproef; *the* ~ *may TURN*, die fortuin kan verander; *be in* ~*'s WAY*, dit gelukkig tref; *WORSE* ~, ongelukkig; ~**ily**, gelukkig(erwyse); ~**iness**, geluk; ~**less**, ongelukkig; ~-**money**, gelukgeld; ~-**penny**, gelukspennie.
luck'y, gelukkig; *a* ~ *DOG (beggar)*, 'n gelukvoël; 'n gelukskind; *a* ~ *HIT*, 'n groot geluk; 'n gelukskoot; *you may thank your* ~ *STARS*, jy kan van geluk praat; ~-**bag**, loterysak, verrassingsak; ~ **bean**, mienie-mienie; ~ **dip**, donkervat, grabbelsak, verrassingsak; ~ **dog**, geluksvoël; gelukskind; ~ **guess**, goeie raaiskoot; ~ **packet**, gelukspakkie, verrassingspakkie; ~ **shot**, gelukskoot.
luc'rative, voordelig, winsgewend, renderend.
luc're, wins, voordeel; *filthy* ~, vuil gewin, aardse slyk, geld.
Lucre'tius, Lucretius.
luc'ubrate, in die nag werk; oorpeinsings opskryf.
lucubra'tion, nagstudie, nagwerk; geleerde verhandeling.
luc'ubrator, nagwerker.
luc'ulent, duidelik, glansend; oortuigend.
Lucull'us, Lucullus.
lud'icrous, belaglik, bespotlik, lagwekkend; ~**ness**, lagwekker'heid.
lud'o, ludo(spel).
lu'es, pes, plaag; vuilsiekte, sifilis.
luff, (n) loef, loefkant; (v) na die wind draai; die loef afsteek.
lug¹, (n) seewurm.
lug², (n) loggerseil.
lug³, (n) oor; hingsel; uitsteeksel; pen, lang stok; klou (masj.).
lug⁴, (n) pluk; (v) (**-ged**), sleep; sjou, trek; ~ *AT*, trek aan; ~ *IN*, bysleep; insleep; ~-**box**, plukkis, maatkissie.
luge, ysslee.
lugg'age, bagasie, passasiersgoed; ~ **carrier**, bagasierak, bagasiedraer, karet; ~ **department**, bagasieafdeling; ~ **label**, adreskaart (vir die bagasie), etiket; ~ **office**, bagasiekantoor; ~ **porter**, kruier, bagasiedraer; ~ **rack**, bagasierak; ~ **receipt**, bagasiebewys; ~ **room**, bagasiekantoor; ~ **slip**, bagasiebiljet; ~ **ticket**, bagasiekaartjie; ~ **train**, bagasietrein; ~ **van**, bagasiewa.
lugg'er, logger; *once aboard the* ~ *and the girl is mine*, as die bruid in die skuit is, is die mooi praatjies uit.

lug: ~-**mark,** merk; ~-**sail,** loggerseil.
lugub'rious, somber, treurig, luguber; ~**ness,** somberheid, treurigheid.
lug'worm, seewurm.
Luke, Lukas.
luke'warm, lou; louwarm; onverskillig, halfhartig.
lull, (n) sussing; stilling; stilte; rus, bedaring, verposing, stilstand; windstilte; *the ~ before the storm,* die stilte voor die storm; (v) kalmeer, laat bedaar; aan die slaap wieg; gaan lê; ~ *someone to sleep,* iem. aan die slaap sus.
lull'aby, (n) (..**bies),** slaapliedjie, slaapdeuntjie, wiegeliedjie; (v) (..**bied),** aan die slaap sing.
lumba'ginous, jigagtig, jigtig.
lumbag'o, (-s), lendejig, spit, spit-in-die-rug.
lum'bar, van die lende, lumbaal, lende=; ~ **punction,** lumbale punksie; ~ **region,** lendestreek; ~ **vertebra,** lendewerwel.
lum'ber, (n) spul, rommel, prulle; timmerhout; orige vet; (v) weggooi, deurmekaar neergooi; vol prop; met rommel bedek; opstapel; swaar beweeg, ongemaklik wees; kap (hout); ~ **camp,** houtkapperskamp; ~**er,** boswerker, houtkapper; ~**ing,** houtkappery; skoonkap (van bome); ~**jack,** houtkapper; ~-**jacket,** bosbaadjie, toeritsbaadjie, ritsbaadjie; ~**man,** houtkapper; ~-**mill,** saagmeul(e); ~-**miller,** saagmeulenaar; ~-**room,** rommelkamer, pakkamer.
lum'brical, wurmagtig, wurmvormig.
lum'en, lumen, ligeenheid; buisholte (anat.); selholte (anat.).
lum'inary, (..**ries),** ligpunt, hemelliggaam; notabele.
lumina'tion, verligting.
lumines'cent, ligtend.
luminif'erous, liggewend.
luminos'ity, ligsterkte, glans, skittering.
lum'inous, liggewend, skitterend, glim=, glimmend; stralend, glansend; helder; ~ **backsight,** glimvisier; ~ **circle,** ligkring; ~ **dial,** glimwyserplaat; ~ **foresight,** ligkorrel; ~ **paint,** glimverf; ~ **signal,** ligsein.
lumm'e, magtie!
lum'mox, (colloq.), lommerd, lomperd, lomp mens.
lump[1] (n) stuk, klont, bonk (modder), brok; prop (in keel); knop, bult; hoop; lummel; *IN a ~,* alles saam; as geheel; deur die bank; *a ~ of SUGAR,* 'n suikerklontjie; *a ~ in the THROAT,* 'n knop in die keel; (v) bymekaargooi, saamgooi; klompe vorm; 'n massa vorm; saamsmelt; ~ *DOWN,* neerplak; ~ *TOGETHER,* saamgooi; (a): *a ~ sum,* 'n ronde som.
lump[2], (v) ontevrede wees oor; dit verdra; *just have to ~ it,* dit eenvoudig moet verdra.
lum'penproletariat, (G.), laer klasse, oningeligte massa, lumpenproletariat.
lump: ~**er,** laaier, dokwerker; ~**iness,** klonterigheid; ~**ing,** (a) groot, stewig; (n), saamgooi(ing); ophoping; ~**ish,** lomp, swaar; loom; traag, dom, onbenullig; ~ **sugar,** klontjiesuiker; ~**y,** klonterig, stukkerig, knopperig; onstuimig; ~**y skin disease,** knop(pies)velsiekte.
lun'acy, kranksinnigheid, waansin(nigheid).
lun'ar, van die maan, maans=; ~ **caustic,** helsteen, silwernitraat; ~ **cycle,** maansirkel; ~ **eclipse,** maansverduistering; ~ **ian,** maanbewoner; ~ **month,** maanmaand; ~ **rainbow,** maanreënboog; ~ **year,** maanjaar.
lun'ate, (half)maanvormig; halfmaan=.
lun'atic, (n) kranksinnige, waansinnige, mal mens, maansieke; *rave like a ~, soos 'n besetene te kere gaan;* (a) maansiek, mal, kranksinnig; gek; *the ~ fringe,* die ekstremistiese buitekring; die mal rand; ~ **asylum,** kranksinnigegestig, malhuis.
luna'tion, maansomloop.
lunch, (-es), (n) middagete, noenmaal, koue maal; (v) die middagete gebruik; eet.
lun'cheon, noenmaal, middagmaal.
lunch: ~-**hour,** etensuur; ~-**room,** eetplek, (snel)restourant; ~-**set,** noenmaalstel.
lune, halfmaan; boltweehoek.
lunette', lunet, brilskans; plat oorlosieglas; oogklap; halfmaanvenster.

lung, long; ~-**book,** boeklong; ~ **complaint,** longaandoening; ~-**disease,** longsiekte.
lunge[1], (n) lonsriem; (v) laat lons (perd).
lunge[2], (n) uitval; stoot; sprong; skopgraaf; (v) uitval; stoot; steek; skop; ~ *out,* uitval, 'n uitval maak; skop (perd).
lung: ~**ed,** met longe; ~-**fish,** longvis; ~-**lozenge,** borsklontjie; ~-**sickness,** longsiekte; ~ **worm,** longwurm; ~ **wort,** longkruid.
luniso'lar, son-en-maan=, lunisolêr.
lun'kah, lankaseroet.
lun'ula, (-e), naelmaantjie.
lun'ulate, halfmaanvormig.
lup'in(e), (n) wolfsboontjie, lupine, lupien.
lup'ine, (a) wolf=, wolfagtig.
lup'inous, lupine=, lupien=.
lup'ous, lupusagtig.
lup'us, lupus, veltering.
lur, beestrompet, lur.
lurch[1] (n): *leave in the ~,* in die steek laat.
lurch[2], (n) **(-es),** ruk, swaai, slingerbeweging; (v) swaai, slinger, steier; ~**er,** loerder, speurder, spioen; opligter, dief, skelm; jaghond.
lure, (n) lokaas, verlokking; (v) aanlok, weglok; ~ *AWAY,* weglok, wegrokkel; ~ *INTO,* verlok tot; ~ *ON,* aanlok, verlok.
lur'id, luguber, somber, donker, onheilspellend, aaklig; bruingeel (vuur); *cast (throw) a ~ LIGHT on,* 'n somber lig gooi op; ~ *PAST,* duistere verlede; ~**ness,** aakligheid, donkerheid.
lurk, (n): *on the ~,* op die loer; aan die spioen; (v) loer, op die loer lê; wegkruip, skuil(gaan); verskuil wees; ~ *about,* omsluip; ~**er,** spioen, loerder.
lurk'ing, loerend; ~-**hole,** ~-**place,** skuilplek, loerplek.
lu'scious, lekker, sappig, soet (vrugte); oorsoet, oordrewe; oorlaai (styl); ~**ness,** oorsoetheid; aanloklikheid.
lush[1], (n) lawaaiwater, kromhoutsap; drinkparty; (v) drink, drank gee.
lush[2], (a) weelderig; sappig; ~**ness,** weelderigheid; sappigheid.
lush'y, hoog aan, dronk.
lust, (n) wellus, vleeslike lus, begeerte, belustheid, sinlikheid; sug, begeerlikheid; ~ *for BLOOD,* bloeddors; ~ *for CONQUEST,* veroweringsug; ~ *for GAIN,* gewinsug; ~ *of LIFE,* lewenslus; ~ *of MONEY,* geldsug; ~ *for POWER,* magswellus; ~ *for TERRITORY,* landhonger; ~ *for WAR,* oorlogsug; (v) sterk begeer, dors na; ~ *after,* vurig verlang; ~**ful,** wellustig, belustig; sinlik; begerig; ~**ihood,** krag; knapheid, gesondheid; stewigheid, flinkheid; ~**ily,** kragtig, lewendig; uit alle mag; ~**iness,** krag, flinkheid; gesondheid; stewigheid.
lus'tral, suiwerings=, reinigings=; ~ **water,** wywater.
lustrate', reinig, suiwer.
lustra'tion, suiwering, reiniging.
lus'tre, (n) glans; luister; skittering; roem, glorie, ligkroon, kroonlugter, kroonkandelaar; lustrum; *add ~ to,* luister bysit; luister verleen aan; (v) glans gee, blink maak; ~ **cloth,** glansstof; ~**less,** glansloos, dof.
lus'trine, glanssy.
lus'trous, glansryk; luisterryk; roemryk; skitterend; ~**ness,** skittering, glans.
lus'trum, (..tra, -s), lustrum, vyfjaartydperk.
lus'ty, lustig, kragtig, gesond; kloek, ferm, stewig; swaargebou, sterk.
lu't(an)ist, luitspeler.
lute[1], (n) stopverf, klei; (v) toesmeer, lugdig maak.
lute[2], (n) luit; (v) op die luit speel; *a rift in the ~,* 'n krakie in die luit.
lu'teous, oranjegeel.
lute'-pin, luitskroef.
lute'-string[1], luitsnaar.
lute'-string[2], glanssy.
lute'tium, lute'cium, lutesium.
Lu'theran, (n) Lutheraan; (a) Luthers; ~**ism,** Lutheranisme; ~**ize,** tot die Lutheranisme bekeer.
lu'thern, dakvenster.

lu'thier, luitmaker.
lu'ting, kleefdeeg.
lut'ist, luitspeler.
lux, lux, ligeenheid.
lux'ate, ontwrig, verrek, verstuit.
luxa'tion, ontwrigting, verrekking, verstuiting.
luxe: *EDITION de* ~, praguitgawe, luukse-uitgawe, bibliofiele uitgawe; *de* ~ *MODEL,* luuksemodel.
luxur'iance, oorvloed, weelderigheid, weligheid.
luxur'iant, welig, weelderig; oorvloedig, oordadig; geil; bloemryk (styl).
luxur'iate, weelderig groei; lekker lewe.
luxur'ious, weelderig, geil, oordadig; wellustig.
lux'ury, (..ries), (n) weelde, weelderigheid; pragliewendheid; lekkerny, kosbaarheid; oordaad, luukse; (pl) weeldeartikels; *ALLOW oneself the* ~, jou die weelde veroorloof; *grow up in the LAP of* ~, in Abraham se skoot grootword; (a) weelde-, luukse-; ~ **train,** luuksetrein.
ly'canthrope, weerwolf.
lycan'thropy, weerwolfswaansin.
Lyce'um, Lyceum; ~ *of Aristotle,* Aristoteles se Lyceum.
ly'copod, lycopod'ium, wolfsklou, likopodium.
lydd'ite, liddiet.
Lyd'ian, (n) Lidiër; (a) Lidies; ~ **stone,** toetssteen, lidiet, swart jaspis.
lyd'ite, toetssteen, lidiet, swart jaspis.

lye, (n, v) loog; ~**-bush,** ganna(bos), brakbos(sie), loogbos; ~**-tub,** loogvat.
ly'ing¹, (n) gelieg, liegery, leuenagtigheid; (a) leuenagtig, liegend; *kyk* **lie¹.**
ly'ing², (n) (die) lê; lêplek; *take a thing* ~ *down,* iets gedwee ondergaan; *kyk* **lie².**
ly'ing-in, kraambed, bevalling; ~ **chamber,** kraamkamer; ~ **hospital,** kraaminrigting; ~ **woman,** kraamvrou.
lyme'-grass, duingras, sandhawer, seehawer.
lymph, bloedwater, limf; ~ **at'ic,** (n) limfvat; (a) limfaties, limf-; ~ *atic gland,* limfklier; ~ **ocyte,** limfsel, limfosiet; ~ **oid,** limf-; ~ **oid tissue,** limfweefsel; ~ **ous,** limf-; ~ **y,** limfagtig.
lynce'an, met rooikatoë, skerpsiende.
lynch, (n) lynch; (v) lynch; ~ **law,** lynchwet.
lynx, (-es), rooikat; ~**-eyed,** oplettend, waaksaam, met rooikatoë.
Ly'ons, Lyon.
Lyr'a, die Lier (ster).
lyr'ate, liervormig.
lyre, lier; ~**-bird,** liervoël; ~**-shaped,** liervormig.
ly'ric, (n) liriese gedig; liriek; (pl) liriese poësie, liriek; (a) liries; ~ **al,** liries; ~ **ism,** liriek, lirisisme, lirisme; liriese vlug; ~**-ist,** lirikus; ~ **poem,** liriese gedig, lierdig, liersang; ~ **poet,** lierdigter, lirikus.
lyr'ist, lierspeler.
lythe, koolvis.
lyth'rum, katstert, bloedkruid.

M

m, (ms, m's), m.
ma, ma.
ma'm, nooi; mevrou.
maar, vulkaankrater, maar.
maas'banker, marsbanker.
mac¹, seun (in Skotse en Ierse name).
mac² = **mac(k)intosh,** reënjas.
maca'bre, dode-, aaklig, grieselig; *danse* ~, dodedans, danse macabre.
macac'o, (-s), makaakaap *(Lemur macaco);* vosaap, maki.
macad'am, macadam, klipgruis.
macad'am: ~ **iza'tion,** macadamisering; ~ **ize,** macadamiseer, 'n pad bestraat met klipgruis; gruis; ~ **road,** gruispad.
macada'mia, macadamia; ~ **nut,** macadamianeut.
maca'que, uilaap, kuifaap, makaak(aap).
macaron'i, macaroni; fat, windmaker; mengelmoes.
macaron'ic, (n) mengelmoes (gedigte); (a) macaronies.
macaron'i cheese, (gereg van) macaroni en kaas.
macaroon', makrol(letjie), bitterkoekie, amandelkoekie.
macass'ar, makassar; ~ **oil,** makassarolie.
macaw'¹, arapapegaai.
macaw'², waterpalm; ~ **berry,** palmkool.
macc'abaw, makubasnuif.
Maccabe'an, Makkabees.
Maccabees'. Makkabeërs.
macc'aboy, makubasnuif.
ma'cchia, fynbos, macchia.
mace¹, foelie.
mace², staf, knots; septer, roede; kierie; ~**-bearer,** stafdraer, roededraer.
ma'cédoine, (F), macédoine, vrugteslaai; husareslaai.
Ma'cedon, Macedon'ia, Macedonië.
Macedon'ian, (n) Macedoniër; (a) Macedonies.
ma'cerate, kwel; pynig; kasty; laat week, pap maak; laat vermaer, uitteer; masereer.
macera'tion, kwelling, kastyding; (die) papmaak, deurweking; uittering; maserering.
machan', jagplatform.
mache'te, kapmes, machete.
Machiavell'i, Machiavelli; ~ **an,** Machiavelliaans; dubbelhartig, arglistig; ~ **sm,** Machiavellisme;

~ **st,** (n) Machiavellis; (a) Machiavellisties, Machiavelliaans.
machic'olate, met kantele; van werpgate voorsien; gekanteel(d).
machin'able, verwerkbaar.
mach'inate, beraam, planne maak; ontwerp; konkel, intrigeer.
machina'tion, sameswering, kuipery, konkelary, intrige.
mach'inator, intrigant, sameswerder.
machine', (n) masjien, werktuig, toestel, apparaat; fiets, rywiel; politieke organisasie; (v) met 'n masjien bewerk of maak; ~**-die,** masjienvorm; ~ **drawing,** werktuigtekening; masjientekening; ~ **drill,** kragboor; ~ **factory,** masjienfabriek; ~**-finished,** masjinaal afgewerk; ~**-fitter,** monteur, passer.
machine-gun, (n) masjiengewer; (v) (**-ned),** onder masjiengeweerkoeëls steek; ~ **ner,** masjiengeweerskutter; ~ **nest,** masjiengeweernes.
machine: ~ **hand,** masjienbediener; ~**-knitted,** masjinaal gebrei; ~**-made,** fabriekmatig, fabrieks-, masjinaal gemaak; ~**-made paper,** masjienpapier; ~**-minded,** met voorliefde (aanleg) vir masjinerie; ~**-minder,** masjienbediener; ~**-minding,** masjienbediening; ~ **oil,** masjienolie; ~ **room,** masjienkamer; ~**-ruler,** linieermasjien.
machi'nery, masjinerie; meganiek; inrigting; bonatuurlike magte in toneelstuk of verhaal; ~ *of government,* regeringsmasjien; landsbestuur.
machine': ~ **shop,** masjienwinkel; ~ **stitch,** masjiensteek; ~ **tools,** masjiengereedskap, masjienwerktuie; ~**-work,** fabriekswerk, masjienwerk.
machi'ning, masjienwerk, masjinale bewerking, masjienafwerking.
machi'nist, masjinis; masjienmaker; naaister; masjienwerker.
machis'mo, (Sp.), machismo, moed, viriliteit.
ma'cho, (Sp.), macho, viriele man.
Mach: Mach; ~ **number,** Machgetal; ~ **meter,** Machmeter; ~ **one,** etc., Mach een, ens.
mack'erel, makriel; *as mute as a* ~, so stom soos 'n vis; ~ **clouds,** vlieswolkies, skaapwolkies; ~ **shark,** haringhaai; ~ **sky,** lug met vlieswolkies (skaapwolkies) bedek.
mac(k)'intosh, (-es), reënjas.

mac'kle, misdruk, dubbeldruk, deurdruk.
ma'cle, holspaat.
macra'mé, macramé, knoopwerk.
macrocephal'ic, langhoofdig, grootkoppig.
mac'roclimate, makroklimaat.
mac'rocosm, heelal, makrokosmos.
mac'ron, lengteteken, makron.
mac'ronucleus, makronukleus, makrokern, grootkern.
mac'ropod, met lang bene, langbeen=.
macrop'terus, langvleuelig.
macroscop'ic, sigbaar vir die blote oog, makroskopies.
mac'rospore, makrospoor (dierk.); megaspoor (plantk.).
mac'ula, (-e), vlek, sproet; ~r, gevlek.
mac'ulate, bevlek, smet; ~d, bont; bevlek.
macula'tion, bevlekking; vlekverdeling; vlek.
mac'ule, vlek; misdruk, dubbeldruk, deurdruk.
mad, (v) mal wees, mal maak; *the ~ding crowd*, die wêreldse gewoel; (a, adv) mal, gek, kransinnig; rasend; bedol, sot; speeklos; sinneloos; dol (op, van); *~ ABOUT*, versot op; *~ AT*, kwaad vir; *GO ~*, gek word; *~ as a HATTER (a March hare)*, stapelgek; in die bol gepik; *~ with JOY*, dol van vreugde; *LIKE ~*, woedend, soos 'n rasende; *~ ON*, versot (dol) op, gek na; *a ~ PERSON*, 'n mal mens; *RAVING ~*, stapelgek; *YOU'RE ~!* jou verstand!
Madagas'can, (n) Malgas; (a) Malgassies, Madagassies.
Madagas'car, Madagaskar; ~'ian, Madagassies, Malgassies.
mad'am, mevrou; juffrou; madam (ongunstig).
mad'ame, (mesdames), mevrou; juffrou; madame.
madapoll'am, madapolam.
mad'cap, malkop, maltrap, gek.
madd'en, mal maak, woedend maak; dol word; ~ing, genoeg om 'n mens mal te maak; *the ~ing crowd*, die wêreldse (jagende) gewoel.
madd'er, krapwortel, meekrap.
made, gemaak; aangelê; kunsmatig; ~*up in BUNDLES*, in pakke; *a ~ DISH*, 'n opgewarmde gereg; *he HAS ~ it*, sy kop is deur; *a ~ MAN*, 'n man met pitte, 'n welgestelde man; ~*-up SET* (tennis), gereëlde stel; *a ~-up STORY*, 'n voorbedagte leuen; 'n versinsel; *~ UP*, gemaak, versonne; vermom; opgemaak; *~ WORD*, uitgedinkte woord.
Madeir'a, Madeira, Madeirawyn; ~ cake, Madeirakoek; ~ chair, Madeirastoel.
mademoiselle', (mesdemoiselles), mademoiselle, juffrou.
mad: ~house, malhuis, dolhuis, gekkehuis, groendakkies; ~ly, mal; soos 'n besetene; *~ly in love*, tot oor die ore verlief; ~man, gek, kransinnige, waansinnige; ~ness, malheid, gekheid, sinneloosheid, dol(lig)heid, sotheid, gekkewerk, waansin(nigheid).
Madonn'a, Moedermaagd, Madonna; Mariabeeld; ~ lily, madonnalelie.
mad'repore, sterkoraal.
ma'drier, swaar balk (plank).
mad'rigal, madrigaal.
Madrilen'ian, (n) Madrileen; (a) Madrileens.
Maecen'as, Maecenas, Mesenas, kunsbeskermer.
mael'strom, maalstroom, draaikolk.
maen'ad, menade, bacchante.
maes'tro, (. . stri), meester, komponis, dirigent.
Mae West, (ophlaasbare) reddingsgordel.
ma'fia, mafia, georganiseerde misdaad.
mafio'so, mafialid, mafioso.
mag¹, stuiwer; babbelkous; magneto=.
mag² = magazine, tydskrif.
magazine', tydskrif; pakhuis, loods; wapenmagasyn; patroonhouer; kruitkamer; magasyn (geweer); ~ catch, magasynknip; ~ gun, repeteergeweer, magasyngeweer; ~ lamp, veiligheidslamp; ~ man, magasynwerker; ~ rifle, magasyngeweer.
Mag'deburg, Maagdenburg.
Magel'lan, Magellaan; *Straits of ~*, Straat van Magellaan.
mage, magiër, towenaar.

magen'ta, persrooi (verf), magenta.
magg'ot, maaier, wurm, draaiwurm; gril, nuk (fig.); (pl) onsuiwer; ~y, vol maaiers (onsuiwer); nukkerig, vol giere.
ma'gi, (sing. **magus**), magiërs, magi, wyses.
Ma'gian, (n) Magiër; towe(r)naar; (a) Magiër=, Magies.
ma'gic, (n) towerkuns, duiwelskunstenary; toordery, toorkrag; betowering; *BLACK ~*, swartkuns; *as if BY ~*, soos by towerslag; *WHITE ~*, goëlary; (a) toweragtig, tower=; betowerend; ~ art, towerkuns; ~ article, toorgoed; ~ circle, towerkring; ~ flute, towerfluit; ~ herb, toorkruid; ~.i'cian, towe(r)naar; ~ image, toorbeeld; ~ lantern, towerlantern; ~ potion, toordrank; ~ power, toorkrag; ~ sign, toorteken; ~ touch, towerslag; ~ sound, towerklank; ~ stick, toorhoutjie; ~ word, toorwoord, towerwoord; ~ wand, towerstaf.
magister'ial, magistraats=, landdros=; meesteragtig; gebiedend, heersend; ~ district, landdrosdistrik.
ma'gistracy, (. . cies), magistratuur, magistraatskap; magistraatsdistrik, landdrosdistrik; landdroskantoor, magistraatskantoor; drosdy.
magis'tral, gebiedend; magistraal; gesaghebbend; meester=.
ma'gistrate, landdros, magistraat; ~'s court, hof, magistraatskantoor, landdroshof; ~'s office, landdroskantoor, magistraatskantoor; ~'s residence, residensie, magistraatshuis, drosdy.
ma'gistrature, magistratuur.
mag'ma, (-s, -ta), magma; mengsel; salf; ~t'ic, magmaties, magma=.
Mag'na Chart'a, Magna Carta (1215).
magnanim'ity, grootmoedigheid, edelmoedigheid, sielegrootheid.
magnan'imous, grootmoedig, edelmoedig.
mag'nate, magnaat; grootgeldbesitter, geldman, kapitalis.
magne'sia, magnesia, bitteraarde; *sulphate of ~*, Engelse sout; ~n, magnesiumbevattend, magnesies.
mag'nesite, magnesiet.
magnes'ium, magnesium; ~ light, magnesiumlig; ~ sulphate, Engelse sout, magnesiumsulfaat.
mag'net, magneet.
magnet'ic, magneties; vol aantrekkingskrag; ~al, magneties; ~ field, (aard)magnetiese veld, magneetveld; ~ mine, magnetiese myn; ~ needle, magneetnaald; ~ north, magnetiese noorde, kompasnoorde; ~ ore, magneetyster; ~ pole, magnetiese pool; ~ pyrite, magneetsteen; ~s, magnetisme.
mag'netism, magnetisme; aantrekkingskrag; *ANIMAL ~*, dierlike magnetisme; *TERRESTRIAL ~*, aardmagnetisme.
mag'netite, magnetiet, magnetyster, magneetsteen.
magnetiza'tion, magnetisering.
mag'netize, magnetiseer; aantrek; ~r, magnetiseerder.
magnet'o, (-s), ontstekingsmagneet, magneet; ~-chemistry, magnetochemie; ~-electricity, magnetiese elektrisiteit; ~-ignition, magneetontsteking; ~ m'eter, magnetiese kragmeter, magnetometer.
magnif'ic(al), groots.
magnif'icat, lofsang van Maria, magnificat.
magnifica'tion, vergroting; verheerliking.
magnif'icence, heerlikheid, prag, luister, praal.
magnif'icent, pragtig, luisterryk; verhewe, manjifiek.
magnif'ico, (-es), groot meneer, Venesiaanse edelman, magnifico.
mag'nifier, vergrootglas; versterker (elektrisiteit); vergroter.
mag'nity, (. . fied), vergroot; verheerlik; ophemel; oordryf.
mag'nifying: ~ glass, vergrootglas, loep; *put something under the ~ glass*, onder die vergrootglas sit; *iets onder die loep neem*; ~ power, vergrotingsvermoë.
magnil'oquence, grootsprakigheid, hoogdrawendheid, bombasme.
magnil'oquent, bombasties, grootsprakig, hoogdrawend.
mag'nitude, grootte, omvang; belangrikheid; grootheid; betekenis.

magnol'ia, magnolia, tulpboom, tulpblom.
mag'num, magnum(fles); dubbele fles; groot glas; ~ *opus*, meesterwerk, hoofwerk, magnum opus.
Ma'gog, Magog; reus.
mag'pie, ekster; babbelkous; tweede kring, middel=kring; drietjie (skyf), middelskoot (skyf).
mag'us, (. . gi), magiër, wyse; *the (three) Magi*, die (drie) Wyses uit die Ooste.
Mag'yar, (n) Magjaar, Hongaar; Magjaars (taal); (a) Magjaars, Hongaars; ~ **sleeve**, aaneenmou, Hon=gaarse mou.
maharaj'a(h), maharadja, Indiese prins.
maharan'ee, maharan'i, maharani.
mahat'ma, mahatma, Boeddhistiese geestelike leier.
Mahd'i, Mahdi; Mohammedaanse leier.
mah'-jong(g)', mah-jong.
mahl'stick, *kyk* **maulstick**.
mahog'any, (n) mahoniehout; eettafel; (a) mahonie=.
Mahom'et, *kyk* **Mohammed**.
mahout', olifantdrywer, olifantjong, kornak, mahout.
mahrad'ja, *kyk* **maharaja(h)**.
Mahratt'a, Mahratta ('n Hindoeras).
maid, meisie, maagd; diensmeisie; vroulike bediende; ~ *of HONOUR*, hofdame; *there are MORE ~s than MALKIN and more men than Michael*, hulle is nie handvol nie, maar landvol; *OLD ~,* oujong=nooi; *OLD ~s' children and bachelors' wives are the best trained,* die beste touleier sit op die voorbok; die beste boer woon in die stad; die beste stuurman staan aan wal; *a WHISTLING ~, a crowing hen, is neither fit for God nor men,* meisies wat fluit, word die deur uitgesmyt en 'n hoenderhen wat kraai, word die nek omgedraai; **~-of-all-work**, diensmei=sie-alleen, alleenwerkster.
maid'en, (n) meisie, nooi, maagd; leë boulbeurt; (a) maagdelik; ongetroud; eerste (toespraak, reis, ens.); ~ **assize**, handskoensitting; ~ **aunt**, onge=troude tante; ~ **century**, eerste honderdtal; ~ **ef=fort**, eerste poging; ~ **engagement**, vuurdoop; ~ **flight**, eerste vlug; ~**hair**, fynblaarvaring, vroue=haarvaring; ~**head**, ~**hood**, maagdelikheid, maag=dom; himen; ~**ish**, maagdelik, sedig, rein; ~**liness**, maagdelikheid; ~**ly**, maagdelik, sedig, kuis; ~ **name**, nooiensvan; meisiesnaam; ~ **over**, leë boul=beurt; ~ **speech**, intreetoespraak, eerstelingtoe=spraak, nuwelingtoespraak; ~ **stakes**, wedstryd (pryse) vir jong reisiesperde; ~ **sword**, ongebruikte swaard; ~ **voyage**, eerste seereis.
maid's cap, bediendekappie.
maid' servant, diensmeisie; huishulp.
maieut'ic, majeuties, verloskundig; Sokraties; ~s, majeutiek, verloskunde; die Sokratiese metode.
mai'gre¹, (n) ombervis.
mai'gre², (a) vetvry, skraal (voedsel).
mail¹, (n) pantser, harnas; *COAT of ~,* maliehemp, maliekolder; *play at ~,* malie; *RING of ~,* malie; (v) bepantser.
mail², (n) pos; briewesak; poskar; postrein; malie (spel); (v) pos, per pos stuur; ~**able**, per pos ver=voerbaar; versendbaar; ~ **advise**, posberigte; ~ **aircraft**, posvliegtuig; ~ **bag**, possak; ~ **bat**, malie=kolf; ~ **boat**, passasierskip, posboot; ~ **box**, brie=webus, posbus; ~ **carrier**, posdraer; ~**cart**, poskar.
mail'-clad, geharnas, gepantser.
mail: ~ **clerk**, posamptenaar; ~ **coach**, poskar; pos=koets; ~ **day**, posdag.
mailed, geharnas, gepantser; *the ~ fist,* gewapende mag, gepantserde vuis, ysterhande, wapengeweld.
mail: ~**ing list**, poslys; ~ **order**, posbestelling; ~-**order house**, posbestellingsaak; ~ **packet**, pos=stoomboot; ~ **plane**, posvliegtuig; ~-**runner**, pos=draer; ~ **service**, posdiens; ~ **steamer**, posboot; ~ **train**, passasierstrein; postrein; ~-**van**, pos=rytuig.
maillot', (F.), maillot, danspak.
maim, (n) verminking; (v) vermink; skend; ~**ed**, (n) (die) verminkte(s); (a) afgeknot; vermink; ~**edness**, verminktheid.
main¹, (n) hanegeveg.
main², (n) see, oseaan; hoofdeel; hoofpyp; hooflei=ding; hoofkabel; krag, geweld; vernaamste deel; *IN the ~*, in hoofsaak; oor die algemeen; in die reël; in die geheel; *with MIGHT and ~*, uit alle mag; met mag en krag; *TURN off at the ~*, die hoofkraan sluit; (a) vernaamste, grootste; hoof=; *with an EYE on the ~ chance,* nie om die hondjie nie, maar om die halsbandjie; *the ~ FEATURE,* die hoofvorm; die hoofkenmerk; *the ~ FORCE,* die hoofmag; *by ~ FORCE,* met krag en mag; *the ~ POINT,* die hoofargument (hoofsaak); *the ~ SEA,* die oop see; ~ **beam**, hoofbalk; ~-**beam track**, hoofrigstraal; ~ **bearing**, hooflaer; ~ **blade**, hoofblad; ~ **body**, hoofmag; ~ **brace**, groot bras; *splice the ~-brace,* 'n dubbel dop steek; in die kan kyk; ~ **building**, hoofgebou; ~ **cause**, hoofoorsaak; ~ **course**, groot seil; ~ **deck**, hoofdek; ~ **drive**, hooftonnel; ~ **entrance**, hoofingang; ~ **feature**, hoofkenmerk; ~ **girder**, hoofbalk; hoofleer; ~ **guard**, hoofwag; ~ **haulage**, hoofvervoerweg; ~ **jet**, hoofsproeier; ~**land**, vasteland; *on the ~ land,* op die vaste wal; ~ **ledger**, hoofgrootboek; ~ **line**, hooflyn; ~**ly**, hoofsaaklik, grotendeels, vernaamlik; ~**mast**, grootmas; ~ **pipe**, hoofpyp; ~ **plane**, hoofdraag=vlak; ~ **prize**, borgtog; ~ **resistance**, hoofweer=stand; ~ **rigging**, hoofwant; ~ **road**, hoofweg, grootpad; ~ **rod**, dryfstang; ~ **root**, penwortel; ~**sail**, grootseil; ~**s filter**, anti storingsfilter; ~ **shaft**, krukas; hoofdryfas (masj.); hoofskag (myn); ~ **sheet**, grootskroot; ~ **shroud**, grootwant; ~**spring**, slagveer; hoofmotief, dryfveer; dryfkrag; ~**stay**, grootstag; staatmaker, steunpilaar; ~ **street**, hoofstraat; voorstraat; ~ **switch**, hoof=skakelaar.
maintain', in stand hou, handhaaf; betoog, beweer; onderhou (kinders); volhou; versorg; steun; voer (briefwisseling); ophou (stand); behou (militêr); ~ *one's GROUND,* pal staan, stand hou; ~ *ONE=SELF,* jou onderhou; ~**able**, houbaar; verdedig=baar.
maintain'er, behouer; versorger; verdediger; hand=hawer; ~**s' league**, handhawersbond.
main'tenance, onderhoud, instandhouding, versor=ging; handhawing; verdediging; ~ **camp**, onder=houdskamp; ~ **costs**, onderhoudskoste; ~ **order**, bevel tot onderhoud.
main'top, grootmars; ~ **gallant**, grootbram; ~ **mast**, grootmarssteng; ~ **sail**, grootmarsseil.
main yard, grootra.
maio'lica = **majolica**.
maison(n)ette', huisie, woninkie; (stel) huurkamers, woonstel; skakelhuis.
maî'tre, meester; ~ *de BALLET,* balletmeester; ~ *d'HOTEL,* hofmeester; hotelbestuurder; hoof=kelner.
maize, mielies; mieliegeel (kleur); ~ **flour**, mielie=blom; ~ **grits**, mieliegruis.
maizek'o, maizeko (geregistreerde handelsmerk vir mieliemeelblom).
maizen'a, maizena (geregistreerde handelsnaam vir mieliemeelblom).
maize: ~ **oil**, mielieolie; ~ **porridge**, mieliepap; ~-**sheller**, mielieafmaker; ~-**stalk borer**, mieliestam=ruspe.
majes'tic, majestueus, groots, statig, verhewe, vorstelik.
maj'esty, groot(s)heid, verhewenheid; (. . ties), majes=teit; *His (Her, Your) M~*, Sy (Haar, U), Majesteit.
Majlis', Persiese parlement, Madjlis.
majol'ica, majolika.
maj'or¹, (n) majoor (rang).
maj'or², (n) mondige; majeur (mus.); (a) mondig; gro=ter, vernamer, meerder; hoof=; *A ~,* A-majeur; *the M ~ Prophets,* die Groot Profete; ~ **arc**, groot=boog; ~ **axis**, hoofas, grootas; langas; ~ **change**, belangrike verandering; ~ **course**, hoofkursus.
maj'or: ~-**domo**, (-s), hofmeester; major domo; ~-**general**, generaal-majoor.
maj'or industries, hoofindustrieë.
maj'ority¹, majoorskap, majoorsrang.
major'ity², (. . ties), meerderheid; gros, merendeel; meerderjarigheid, mondigheid; *ABSOLUTE ~,* volstrekte meerderheid; *ATTAIN one's ~,* meer=derjarig word; *JOIN the ~,* die weg van alle vlees

gaan; jou by die meerderheid skaar; *the ~ of the PEOPLE*, die meerderheid v.d. volk; *a SWEEPING ~*, 'n oorweldigende meerderheid; *THE ~*, die groot massa; *the ~ of VOTES*, die meerderheid van stemme; ~ **decision**, meerderheidsbesluit; ~ **party**, meerderheidsparty; ~ **report**, meerderheidsverslag; ~ **rule**, meerderheidsregering; ~ **verdict**, meerderheidsbesluit; ~ **vote**, meerderheidstem.

maj'or: ~ **offence**, ernstige misdaad; ~ **operation**, ernstige operasie; ~ **overhaul**, totale opknapping; ~ **part**, hoofrol; hoofaandeel; ~ **planets**, groter planete; ~ **repairs**, belangrike (groot) herstelwerk; ~ **road**, grootpad, hoofpad, hoofweg; ~ **scale**, groot skaal.

maj'orship, majoorskap.

maj'or: ~ **subject**, hoofvak; ~ **suit**, hoofkleur (kaartspel); ~ **surgery**, groot operasie; ~ **third**, groot terts.

majus'cule, hoofletter, majuskel.

make, (n) vorm; gedaante; snit (klere); maaksel, fabrikaat (voertuig); soort, aard, karakter; bou; *a MAN of his ~*, 'n man van sy soort; *be ON the ~*, probeer wins maak; daarop uit wees om geld te maak; (v) **(made)**, maak, vervaardig; doen; verrig, aangaan (ooreenkoms); voorsien in; uitskryf (tjek); sluit (vrede); bereik (bed); begaan (fout); hou (toespraak); dwing, forseer; voorgee; opmaak (bed); voer (oorlog); verdien (geld); ~ *out an ACCOUNT*, 'n rekening uitskryf; ~ *AFTER one*, iem. vervolg (agternasit); ~ *AGAINST*, pleit teen; ~ *AMENDS for*, jou verontskuldig weens; vergoed; ~ *AS if*, maak asof; voorgee dat; ~ *AVAILABLE to*, beskikbaar stel aan; ~ *AWAY with something*, van iets ontslae raak; ~ *BEDS*, bedde opmaak; ~ *a BEE-LINE for*, afpyl op; ~ *BELIEVE*, maak asof; wysmaak; ~ *the BEST of*, iets vir lief neem; ~ *the BEST of a bad job*, jou na iets skik; iets vir lief neem; ploeg met die osse wat jy het; *I ~ BOLD to say*, ek verstout my om te sê; ~ *one's BOW*, jou buiging maak; buigend afskeid neem; ~ *and BREAK*, maak en breek; ~ *a CALL*, 'n besoek aflê; telefoneer, 'n oproep deursit; ~ *the CARDS*, die kaarte was (skommel); ~ *out a CASE*, 'n saak bewys; 'n saak stel; ~ *CERTAIN of*, jou vergewis van; ~ *CERTAIN that*, vasstel dat; verseker dat; ~ *a COMPLAINT*, kla; 'n klag indien; ~ *a CONFESSION*, 'n bekentenis aflê; ~ *a CONTRACT*, 'n kontrak sluit; *I COULD not ~ it*, ek kon dit nie regkry nie; ~ *a CROSS*, 'n kruisie trek; ~ *a DASH for*, afpyl op; storm na; ~ *DO with*, klaarkom met; ploeg met die ossies wat jy het; roei met die rieme wat jy het; ~ *an EFFORT*, 'n poging aanwend; ~ *ENEMIES*, vyande maak; ~ *one's ESCAPE*, ontsnap, wegkom; ~ *an EXAMPLE, of*, tot voorbeeld stel; ~ *a FIRE*, vuur maak (aanlê); ~ *a FOOL of*, belaglik maak; vir die gek hou; ~ *FOR*, aangaan; koers hou na; bydra tot; mik na; lei tot; pleit vir; pyl na; ~ *FREE with*, vryhede neem met; ~ *FRIENDS*, vriende maak; ~ *FUN (game) of*, gekskeer met; uitlag; ~ *GOOD*, vergoed (skade), opmaak; jou belofte nakom; vooruitgaan; suksesvol wees; *the prisoner would ~ GOOD*, die gevangene sou 'n nuwe blaadjie omslaan; ~ *GOOD one's loss*, opmaak vir jou verlies; die skade inhaal; ~ *the GRADE*, die paal haal; die mas opkom; ~ *up lost GROUND*, verlore veld wen; skade inhaal; ~ *the HARBOUR*, die hawe binnevaar (binneloop); ~ *HASTE*, gou maak; jou haas; ~ *the HEADLINES*, baie aandag trek; ~ *HEADWAY*, vooruitgaan; vorder; *HOW do you ~ that out?*, hoe kom jy daaraan? hoe verklaar jy dit?; ~ *INTO*, verander in; ~ *IT just in time*, dit net haal; ~ *KNOWN*, bekend maak; ~ *LIGHT of*, min waarde heg aan; onderskat (moeilikheid); minag (siekte); ~ *LITTLE of*, gering ag; min waarde heg aan; ~ *up LOST time*, verlore tyd inhaal; ~ *LOVE*, die hof maak; vry; ~ *or MAR*, goedmaak of verknoei; maak of breek; ~ *one's MARK*, naam maak; presteer; *he ~ s a good MEAL*, hy eet goed; ~ *a MESS of*, sake verknoei; ~ *MERRY*, pret maak; ~ *up one's MIND*, 'n besluit neem; voorneem; tot 'n besluit kom; ~ *MISCHIEF*, kwaad stig, kattekwaad

aanrig; ~ *MONEY*, geld verdien; ~ *the MOST of*, die meeste voordeel probeer trek uit; ~ *the MOST of one's talents*, met jou talente woeker; ~ *a MOVE*, roer; vertrek; ~ *MUCH of something*, baie waarde heg aan iets; baie gewig heg aan iets; ~ *MUCH of someone*, 'n ophef van iem. maak; iem. op die hande dra; 'n ophef maak van; ~ *NOTHING of*, gering ag; ~ *an OATH*, 'n eed aflê (sweer, doen); *not to know what to ~ OF it*, nie weet wat om daarvan te maak nie; ~ *OFF*, wegloop; ~ *an OFFER*, 'n aanbod doen; ~ *OUT*, ontdek; voorgee; verklaar; bewys lewer; uitmaak, onderskei (skrif, vlag); voorstel; uitskryf (rekening); *I could never ~ him OUT*, ek kon nooit uit hom wys word nie; ek kon hom nooit verstaan nie; ~ *OUT a list*, 'n lys opmaak; ~ *OVER*, oordoen; oordra (eiendom); ~ *up a PAPER*, 'n koerant opmaak; ~ *PAYMENT*, betaal; ~ *a PAYMENT*, 'n paaiement betaal; 'n storting doen; ~ *PEACE*, vrede sluit; ~ *a PILE*, 'n fortuin maak; ~ *a POINT*, 'n belangrike aspek van 'n saak aanhaal; 'n punt beredeneer; 'n rede (argument) aanvoer; ~ *up a PRESCRIPTION*, 'n voorskrif klaarmaak; ~ *a PROMISE*, 'n belofte doen (aflê); ~ *up a QUARREL*, versoen raak; weer goeie vriende word; ~ *oneself SCARCE*, jou uit die voete maak: ~ *SHIFT with*, klaarkom met; ~ *SHORT work of*, kort proses maak met; ~ *a SPEECH*, 'n toespraak hou (aflê steek); ~ *a STAND*, vastrap, standhou; ~ *a STATEMENT*, 'n verklaring doen; ~ *up a STORY*, 'n verhaal versin; ~ *SURE of*, verseker, sorg dat; jou vergewis; ~ *good TIME*, 'n afstand in kort tyd aflê; met 'n goeie vaart gaan; ~ *one's TOILET*, sy toilet maak; ~ *TRACKS for*, oople na; *TWICE seven ~ s fourteen*, twee maal sewe is veertien; ~ *UP*, vol maak; inhaal (skade); goedmaak; vorm; uit sy duim suig; voltallig maak; aanvul; opmaak (lys); versin (verhaal); blanket, grimeer (gesig); verklee; aanmaak; saamstel (trein); ~ *UP a set*, 'n span (viertal) vorm; ~ *UP for*, vergoeding doen; ~ *UP to*, witvoetjie soek by; ~ *a VOYAGE*, 'n seereis doen (maak); ~ *WAR*, oorlog voer; ~ *WATER*, lek (boot); water laat; ~ *one's WAY*, jou weg baan; die mas opkom; vooruitkom in die wêreld; ~ *WAY for*, padgee vir; ~ *-believe*, (n) verbeelding; wysmakery, aanstellery; komedie; smoesie, voorwendsel; (a) kastig, voorgewend; onwerklik; oneg; ~**r**, maker; fabrikant; skepper; ~**shift**, (n) redmiddel, hulpmiddel, noodhulp; lapwerk, middeltjie; surrogaat; (a) nood=, tydelik; ~**-up**, aankleding, vermomming, grimering; versinsel; uitvoering; samestelling; opmaak (drukwerk); *mental ~-up*, geestelike samestelling; ~**weight**, toegif; noodhulp; stoplap; aanvulling; teenwig.

ma'ki, maki, vosaap, lemur.

mak'ing, maaksel; maak, aanmaak; wording; *IN the ~*, in wording; *he HAS the ~s of an artist*, hy het kunstenaarsaanleg; daar skuil 'n kunstenaar in hom; *of his OWN ~*, sy eie skuld; deur homself bewerk; *THE ~ of him*, wat hom bo-op gehelp het; wat hom sukses besorg het.

mak'ings, verdienste, profyt; aanleg, kwaliteite.

mako, mako, blouhaai.

Mal'abar, (n), Malabar (streek): Malbaar (persoon); (a) Malabaars.

Malacc'a, Malakka.

Mal'achi, Maleagi.

mal'achite, malagiet, ~ **kingfisher**, kuifkopvisvanger; ~ **sunbird**, jangroentjie.

ma'lacoderm, malakodermies, sagtevel=.

malaco'logy, weekdierkunde, malakologie.

mal'adjusted, sleg aangepas.

maladjust'ment, wanaanpassing; swak reëling.

maladministra'tion, wanbestuur, wanbeheer.

mal'adroit, onhandig, onbeholpe, links, lomp; ~ **ness**, onhandigheid, lompheid.

mal'ady, **(maladies)**, siekte, kwaal.

mala fid'e, te kwade trou, mala fide; ~ *possessor*, onregmatige besitter.

Mal'aga, Malaga; Malagawyn.

Malagas'y, (n) Malagassies (taal); Malgas; (a) Malgassies.

malaise 1032 man

malaise', (n) onbehaaglike gevoel; (die) onwel voel, ongesteldheid; slapte, malaise; (a) onbehaaglik.
Ma'lamute, Ma'lemute, Eskimohond, Malemoet, Poolhond.
mal'anders, beenskurfte.
mal'apert, (n) onbeskaamde, wysneus; (a) onbeskaamd, brutaal.
mal'aprop(ism), verkeerde gebruik van 'n moeilike woord, verminking van 'n moeilike woord, malapropisme.
malapropos', (n) ongeskikte gesegde; (a) onvanpas; ongeskik; ongeleë; ontydig.
mal'ar, (n) kaak, kakebeen; (a) kaak=, kakebeen=.
malar'ia, malaria, moeraskoors; ~ **l,** ~ **n,** ..**rious,** malaries, malaria=, koors=.
malar'key, (sl.), nonsens, nonsies, kaf.
mala'thion, malation.
Mal'awi, (n) Malawi (land); Malawiër (persoon); (a) Malawies.
Mal'awian, Malawies.
Malay', (n) Maleier, Slamaier; Maleis (taal); (a) Maleis, Slams.
Malay'a, Maleia.
Malaya'lam, Mal(a)baars, Malajalam.
Malay'an, Maleis.
mal'conduct, wangedrag, wanbeheer.
malconforma'tion, wanverhouding, misvorming.
mal'content, (n) ontevredene; (a) ontevrede; ~ **ed,** ontevrede, misnoeg.
mal de mer, (F.), mal de mer, seesiekte, naarheid.
mal'distribution, wanverdeling, swak verdeling.
male, (n) man; mannetjie; mansmens; manspersoon; (a) manlik; mannetjies=; mans=; ~ **bend,** buigstuk met skroefdraad; ~ **branch,** swaardsy.
maledic'tion, verwensing, vervloeking, vloek.
maledic'tory, vervloekend, verwensend.
mal'efactor, kwaaddoener, boosdoener, misdadiger.
malef'ic, kwaadaardig, boos, skadelik.
malef'icence, boosaardigheid, kwaadaardigheid.
malef'icent, verderflik, onheilstigtend, misdadig.
male' heir, stamhouer, manlike erfgenaam.
Malei'a, Maleia.
male: ~ **and female bond,** buigstok met moer en skroefdraad; ~ **and female callipers (parts, socket),** ineenpassende dele; ~ **issue,** manlike afstammeling; ~ **line,** manlike linie; ~ **nurse,** verpleër; ~ **rhyme,** staande (manlike) rym; ~ **role,** mansrol; ~ **secretary,** sekretaris; ~ **thread,** skroefdraad; ~ **voice,** manstem; ~ **(-voice) choir,** mannekoor.
malev'olence, kwaadwilligheid, boosaardigheid.
malev'olent, kwaadwillig, boosaardig, skadelik.
malfeas'ance, ampsoortreding, ampsmisdryf; wanbedryf, onwettige handeling.
malforma'tion, misvorming, wanskapenheid.
malformed', misvorm, wanskape, mismaak.
malgov'ernment, wanbestuur.
mal'ic, appel=; ~ **acid,** appelsuur.
mal'ice, arglistigheid, boosaardigheid, haatlikheid, kwaadwilligheid; haatdraendheid, haat, vyandskap; plaagsug, bose opset (reg); baldadigheid, geniepsigheid; with ~ *AFORETHOUGHT*, met opset, met voorbedagte rade; *BEAR* ~ *to(wards)*, 'n wrok koester teen; *OUT of* ~, kwaadwillig; uit wrok; *with* ~ *PREPENSE*, met opset, met voorbedagte rade.
mali'cious, sleg, boosaardig; haatdraend, haatlik; baldadig; kwaadwillig; opsetlik, voorbedag; ~ *desertion*, kwaadwillige verlating; ~ **ly,** moedswillig; ~ **ness,** geniepsigheid; *kyk* **malice.**
malign', (v) kwaadspreek, beskinder, belaster beswadder, beklad; (a) verderflik, skadelik; kwaadaardig.
malig'nancy, kwaadaardigheid (siekte); boosaardigheid; verderflikheid.
malig'nant, kwaadaardig; boos; kwaadgesind; boosaardig; aansteeklik; verderflik; ~ *tumour*, kwaadaardige geswel.
malign'er, kwaadwillige; lasteraar, kwaadspreker.
malig'nity, boosaardigheid; kwaadaardigheid (siekte); vyandskap, haat.
Malines', Mechelen.
malin'ger, siekte voorwend, simuleer, jou siek aanstel; ~ **er,** iem. wat siekte voorwend, simulant; ~ **ing,** voorwend van siekte; skoolsiekte, simulasie; *be* ~ *ing,* skynsiek wees.
ma'lism, malisme.
mal'ison, vervloeking, verwensing.
mall, maliebaan; kolfbaan; winkelbaan, winkellaan; wandelplek, wandellaan; mokerhamer.
mall'ard, wilde-eend; wildemannetjieseend.
malleabil'ity, smee(d)baarheid, rekbaarheid, pletbaarheid.
mall'eable, smee(d)baar; pletbaar; buigsaam, gedwee; ~ **iron,** smeeyster.
mall'eate, smee, uitklop.
mall'emuck, malmok.
mall'et, houthamer, slaghamer, blokhamer, klopper, beukhamer; ~ **shark,** hamerkophaai.
mall'eus, (..llei), hamer (in die oor), gehoorbeentjie.
mall'ow, kiesieblaar, malva.
malm, kalkagtige leem.
malmais'on, malmaison(angelier).
malm'sey, malvesy(wyn).
malnutri'tion, ondervoeding; wanvoeding.
malocclu'sion, wanpassing.
malod'orous, slegruikend, stinkend; onwelriekend; ~ **ness,** onwelriekendheid.
malod'our, slegte reuk, stank.
malprac'tice, verkeerde behandeling; oortreding, wanpraktyk; wandaad, wangedrag.
malpresenta'tion, abnormale ligging (bevalling).
malt, (n) mout; (v) mout; (a) mout=; ~ *ed milk*, moutmelk.
Mal'ta, Malta; ~ **fever,** Maltakoors, febris recurrens, brucellose.
malt' dust, moutafval.
Maltese', (n) Malteser; Maltees (taal); (a) Maltees; ~ **cross,** Maltese kruis; ~ **dog,** Maltese hond; ~ **knight,** Maltese ridder.
malt' extract, moutekstrak.
mal'tha, bergteer.
malt'-house, moutery.
Malthus'ian, (n) Malthusiaan, volgeling van Malthus; (a) Malthusiaans; ~ **ism,** Malthusianisme.
malt: ~ **ing,** moutery; ~ **ing barley,** brouersgars, moutgars; ~ **kiln,** moutoond; ~ **liquor,** moutdrank, bier.
mal'tose, maltose, moutsuiker.
maltreat', mishandel, sleg behandel; ~ **ment,** mishandeling.
malt: ~ **spirits,** graanbrandewyn; ~ **ster,** mouter, moutwerker; ~ **sugar,** moutsuiker; ~ **vinegar,** moutasyn; ~ **-worm,** dronklap; ~ **y,** moutagtig.
malversa'tion, (geld)verduistering; misbruik van vertroue; malversasie, wanbeheer.
malvoisie', malvesy(wyn).
mam'ba, mamba, beesbyter, makoppa.
mam'bo, mambo, S.-Amer. dans.
Mam'eluke, Mameluk; slaaf (by Mohammedane).
mamill'a, (-e), tepel; speen; ~ **ry,** tepelvormig, tepel=.
mam'illate(d), getepel, tepelvormig.
mamill'iform, tepelvormig, tepel=.
mam(m)a'¹, mamma.
mamma'², (-e), bors; uier; ~ **l,** soogdier; ~ **l'ia,** soogdiere, mammalia; ~ **l'ian,** (n) soogdier; (a) soogdier=; ~ **l'ogy,** soogdierkunde; ~ **ry,** bors=, melk=; ~ **ary gland,** melkklier.
mam'mitis, melkklierontsteking.
mammif'erous, getepel, met tepels.
Mamm'on, Mammon, geldduiwel, geldgod, goudduiwel; *serve* ~, Mammon dien.
mam'mon, rykdom; ~ **ism,** mammonisme, geldvereering; ~ **ist,** geldvergoeder.
mamm'oth, (n) mammoet; gevaarte; (a) kolossaal, reusagtig, reuse=.
mamm'y, (mammies), mammie, moedertjie.
man, (n) **(men),** man, mansmens; eggenoot; werkkrag, arbeider; skepsel, mens; stuk (damspel); persoon; bediende; soldaat; manskap; keersy van 'n munt; ~ *of ACTION*, 'n man v.d. daad; ~ *of AFFAIRS*, sakeman; ~ *ALIVE!* kragtie! mastag! *AS a* ~, as man; as mens; *BE one's own* ~, jou eie baas wees; by jou volle verstand wees; *BETWEEN* ~ *and* ~, tussen mense onderling; tussen twee perso=

manacle 1033 *manicure*

ne; ~ *BY* ~, man vir man; ~ *of DESTINY*, geroe= pene; voorbestemde man; *he is* ~ *ENOUGH to*, hy is mans genoeg om; *come to* ~ *'s ESTATE*, die manlike leeftyd bereik; 'n man word; *EVERY* ~ *for himself*, elkeen vir homself; ~ *of FAMILY*, iem. van goeie familie; ~ *FOR* ~, man vir man; ~ *FRI= DAY*, handlanger; slaaf; *a* ~ *of GOD*, man van God; geestelike; *HER* ~, haar man; haar minnaar; *every INCH a* ~, 'n pure man; *every* ~ *JACK*, elkeen sonder uitsondering; *KNOW your* ~, weet met wie jy te doen het; *no* ~ *'s LAND*, niemands= land (tussen loopgrawe); *to the LAST* ~, tot die laaste man; ~ *of LETTERS*, geleerde; *MAKE a* ~ *of someone*, 'n man van iem. maak; *a MAN'S* ~, 'n flinke kêrel; *a MARKED* ~, iem. op wie gelet word; iem. wat dopgehou word; ~ *of MEANS*, be= middelde man; *a* ~ *in a MILLION*, 'n man dui= send; *so many men, so many MINDS*, soveel hoof= de, soveel sinne; ~ *in the MOON*, die man in die maan; *know as much about something as the* ~ *in the MOON*, soveel van iets weet as die man in die maan; so min van iets weet as 'n aap van godsdiens; ~ *or MOUSE*, man of muis; *put on the NEW* ~, die ou mens affê; *the OLD* ~, die ou Adam; die oukêrel; *as ONE* ~, soos een man; *a* ~ *of PEACE*, 'n man van vrede; *PER* ~, per kop; *PLAY the* ~, jou soos 'n man kwyt (gedra); ~ *of PROPERTY*, grondeienaar; ~ *PROPOSES, God disposes*, die mens wik, maar God beskik; ~ *of SENSE*, ver= standige man; *the M* ~ *of SORROWS*, die Man van Smarte; *a* ~ *of STANDING*, 'n man van aan= sien; ~ *of STRAW*, strooipop; *the* ~ *in the STREET*, die gewone man; ~ *of SUBSTANCE*, vermoënde man; *a* ~ *in a THOUSAND*, 'n pure man; 'n man duisend; *TO a* ~, tot die laaste man; ~ *TO* ~, van aangesig tot aangesig; *TODAY a* ~, *tomorrow a mouse*, vandag baas, môre klaas; ~ *about TOWN*, slenteraar; pierewaaier; man in so= siale kringe; ~ *of the TOWN*, losbol; *the VERY* ~, net die regte man; die einste man; *WHAT a* ~! ou tier! *a WHITE* ~, 'n Blanke; ~ *and WIFE*, man en vrou; *they are now* ~ *and WIFE*, hulle is getroud; hulle het hulle skapies in een trop gejaag; ~, *WO= MAN and child*, man en maagd; *a* ~ *of his WORD*, 'n man van sy woord; *he is not a* ~ *of his WORD*, sy aand= en môrepraatjies kom nie ooreen nie; *a* ~ *of the WORLD*, 'n man v.d. wêreld; 'n wêreldwyse; ~ *of all WORK*, handlanger; *I'm YOUR* ~, ek neem jou aanbod aan; (v) **(-ned)**, beman, beset; moed in= praat; ~ **oneself**, jou verman; moed skep; (a) mans=, manlik.
man'acle, (n) handboei; (v) boei.
man'age, bestuur; regeer; beheer, hanteer; lei; baas= raak, behartig, behandel; regkry, regkom, klaar= kom; bedissel; beredder (boedel); *he CAN* ~, hy sal klaarkom; ~ *a PERSON*, iem. die baas wees; met iem. regkom; ~ **abil'ity**, handelbaarheid; regeer= baarheid; ~ **able**, handelbaar; regeerbaar.
man'aged, beheer; gelei; ~ *CURRENCY*, beheerde geldstelsel; ~ *ECONOMY*, beheerde ekonomie.
man'age= ment, bestuur, direksie, leiding, bestu= ring, administrasie; lis, handigheid, oorleg; ~ **ment by objectives** (MBO), doelwitbestuur; ~ **ment com= mittee**, bestuurskomitee; ~ **r**, bestuurder; direk= teur; beheerder; baas, hoof; ~ **ress, (-es)**, bestuur= deres, leidster, direktrise, hoof.
manager'ial, bestuurs=, direksie=.
man'agership, bestuurderskap, leiding, beheer; ad= ministrasie; direkteurskap.
man'aging, besturend, beherend; prakties, oorleg= gend, spaarsaam; baasspelerig; ~ **board**, direksie, bestuursraad; ~ **director**, besturende direkteur.
man'-ape, mensaap.
man-at-arms', (men-at-arms), krygsman, soldaat.
manatee', lamantyn, manatee.
man' cage, hyshok.
Man'chester, Manchester; ~ **goods**, katoengoedere, katoenstowwe.
man'-child, seunskind.
Manchur'ia, Mantsjoerye; ~ **n**, (n) Mantsjoeryer; (a) Mantsjoerys.
man'ciple, hofmeester; provisiekoper (kollege).

mandament', mandement; ~ *of spoliation*, mande= ment van spolie.
mandam'us, bevelskrif, mandamus.
mand'arin, mandaryn; ~ **collar**, mandarynkraag; ~ **duck**, mandaryneend.
man'darin(e), nartjie; nartjielikeur.
man'datary, (..ries), mandataris, gevolmagtigde; mandaathouer.
man'date, (n) bevel; lasbrief, bevelskrif; volmag; las= gewing, opdrag; mandaat.
mandate', (v) onder mandaat bring; ~ **d territory**, mandaatgebied.
man'datory, (n) (..ries), lashebber, lasnemer, gelas= tigde, gevolmagtigde; (a) bevelend, gebiedend, ver= pligtend; ~ **power**, mandataris, mandaatland; ~ **territory**, mandaatgebied.
man'dible, onderkakebeen; voorkaak, bokaak (van insek).
mandib'ular, kakebeen=.
mandol'a, mandola.
man'dolin(e), mandolien, mandoline.
man'dolinist, mandolienspeler.
mandor'a = **mandola**.
mandrag'ora, man'drake, alruin (narkotiese plant), mandragora.
man'drel, man'dril, doring, horing (van aambeeld); spil; drewel (mynwerkers)pik.
man'drill, mandril (bobbejaan), woudduiwel.
man'ducate, kou, eet.
manduca'tion, kou(ery), etery.
man'ducatory, kou=, koubaar, eetbaar.
mane, maanhaar, manie.
man'-eater, menseter, mensvreter; mensvreterleeu; byter; ~ **shark**, mensvreterhaai.
maned, met maanhare.
manège', ryskool; rykuns.
man'es, skimme, manes.
man'ful, moedig, dapper, manhaftig; ~ **ness**, dapper= heid, manmoedigheid.
mang'anate, manganaat
mang'anese, mangaan, bruinsteen; glasblaserseep; ~ **bronze**, mangaanbrons; ~ **ore**, mangaanerts; ~ **steel**, mangaanstaal.
mangane'sian, mangan'ic, mangaan=.
manganif'erous, mangaan=, mangaanhoudend.
mange, skurfte, brandsiekte.
mang'el(-wurzel), mangelwortel.
man'ger, krip, trog, voerbak.
man'giness, skurfagtigheid; gemeenheid.
man'gle[1], (n) mangel, wringmasjien; (v) uitwring, mangel.
man'gle[2], (v) kap, vermink, verskeur; verknoei, rad= braak (woorde); ~ **d**, vermink.
man'gler[1], verminker.
man'gler[2], mangelaar; vleismeul.
man'go, (-es), mango, draadperske, veselperske; mangoboom.
mang'old(-wurzel), mangelwortel.
mang'onel, blyde, werpgeskut.
mang'osteen, mangostan.
man'go-tree, mangoboom.
mang'rove, wortelboom, mangrove.
man'gy, skurfagtig; armoedig, armsalig; veragtelik, gemeen.
man'handle, mishandel, toetakel, karnuffel, afknou; (deur mensekrag) beweeg, hanteer, sleep.
man: ~ **-hater**, mannehater; mensehater; ~ **hole**, mangat, kykput, skouput, inspeksiegat, inklimgat, werkgat; ~ **hole cover**, werkgatdeksel, kykputdek= sel; ~ **hood**, manlikheid; manlike jare; manlike staat; manlike bevolking; menslikheid; dapperheid, moed; ~ **hood suffrage**, mannekiesreg; ~ **-hour**, manuur.
manhat'tan, manhattan (mengeldrankie).
man'ia, manie, waansin, raserny; hartstog; sug, gier.
man'iac, (n) maniak, besetene, waansinnige; (a) waansinnig; ~ **al**, waansinnig, gek.
man'ic, manies; ~ **-depressive**, manies-depressief.
Manich(a)e'an, (n) Manicheër; (b) Manichees.
Man'ich(a)eism, Manicheïsme.
Manichee', Manicheër.
man'icure, (n) manikuur, manikuris, handversorger;

naelpoetsery, handversorging; naelversorging; (v) manikuur, hande en naels versorg; ~ **scissors**, naelskêrtjie; ~ **set**, manikuurstel, naelstel.
man'icuring, manikuur, naelversorging.
man'icurist, naelpoetser, manikuris.
man'ifest, (n) manifes; vraaglys; (v) bekend maak, voor die dag bring; laat blyk, toon, bewys, manifesteer; (a) (oor)duidelik, openbaar, blykbaar, klaarblyklik.
manifesta'tion, openbaring; betoging; manifestasie; betoon.
man'ifestly, klaarblyklik.
manifes'to, (-s), manifes.
man'ifold, (n) verdeelpyp (motor); kopie; blaarpens, derde maag (sekere diere); (v) vermenigvuldig, op 'n duplikator afrol; (a) baie, menigvuldig; veelsoortig; ~**er**, kopieerder; afrolmasjien; ~ **paper**, kopieerpapier; ~ **valve**, verdelingsklep.
man'ikin, mannetjie, dwerg; model, pop.
manill'a¹, armring.
manill'a², manilla(sigaar); ~ **paper**, manillapapier; ~ **tobacco**, manillatabak.
manille', nel (kaartspel).
man'ioc, maniok(meel), kassawe, broodwortel.
man'iple, manipel, manipulus.
manip'ulate, behandel, hanteer, bewerk; knoei; manipuleer, kunsmatig beïnvloed (mark).
manipula'tion, behandeling, bewerking; hantering; manipulasie; knoeiery; belasting; *of easy* ~, maklik hanteerbaar.
manip'ulative, manipulerend; hanterend.
manip'ulator, behandelaar, hanteerder; seingewer; knoeier, manipuleerder.
ma'nitou, goeie gees; bose gees; manitoe.
man: ~ **kind**, mensdom, mensheid; die mense; die manne; ~ **like**, manlik, soos 'n man; mannetjiesagtig; menslik; ~ **liness**, manlikheid; dapperheid, moed; ~ **ly**, manlik; manmoedig; moedig, kloek, dapper; ~ **made**, fabrieks-, gefabriseer, mensgemaak, kunsmatig; ~ **milliner**, hoedemaker; peuteraar; verwyfde man.
mann'a, manna; hemeldou; ~ **grass**, kanariegas, kruipgras.
manned, beman.
mann'equin, mannekyn; model, klerepop; ~ **parade**, modeparade.
mann'er, manier; gewoonte; wyse; soort; styl; trant; (pl) sedes; *AFTER a* ~, so op 'n manier, nie alte goed nie; *ALL* ~ *of people*, allerhande soorte mense; *to the* ~ *BORN*, uitgeknip vir; voorbeskik vir; ~*s and CUSTOMS*, sedes en gewoontes; *no* ~ *of DOUBT*, nie die minste twyfel nie; *GOOD* ~*s*, goeie maniere; *IN a* ~, in 'n sekere sin; *in LIKE* ~, op dieselfde manier; ~*s maketh MAN*, goeie (beskaafde) gedrag is alles; *it is NO* ~ *to*, dit is nie mooi nie om; *in a* ~ *of SPEAKING*, om so te sê; by wyse van spreke; ~ *of SPEECH*, praatmanier; *TEACH one* ~*s and customs*, iem. maniere leer; *in THIS* ~, op dié manier; *WHAT* ~ *of*? watter soort? ~**ed**, gemanierd; gekunsteld; gemaniëreerd, aanstellerig; *badly* ~*ed*, onmanierlik, sleggemanierd, agter die bossies opgegroei; ~**ism**, gemaaktheid, gemaniëreerdheid, gesogtheid; affektasie; aanwensel, gewoonte; ~**ist**, gekunstelde persoon; ~**less**, onbeskof, ongemanierd; ~**liness**, beleefdheid, gemanierdheid; ~**ly**, beleef, gemanierd, manierlik.
mann'ish, managtig; mannetjiesagtig; lomp; ~**ness**, managtigheid; onhandigheid; mannetjiesagtigheid.
mann'ite (sugar), mannasuiker.
manoeuvrabil'ity, beheerbaarheid, maneuvreerbaarheid, wendbaarheid, regeerbaarheid.
manoeu'vrable, maneuvreerbaar, wendbaar, regeerbaar, beheerbaar.
manoeu'vre, (n) maneuver, krygsoefening; kunsgreep; listige plan; slim plan; (v) maneuvreer; bedissel, lis gebruik, intrigeer; hanteer; ~ *INTO*, op handige (listige) wyse bring tot; ~ *oneself OUT of a situation*, jou op handige wyse uitdraai.
manoeu'vring, maneuvrering, maneuvreerdery.
man'-of-war, (men-of-war), oorlogskip, slagskip, slagbodem.

manom'eter, manometer, drukmeter.
manomet'ric, manometries.
man'or, landgoed; riddergoed; kasteel; *lord of the* ~, grondheer, landheer; ~ **house**, ridderslot, kasteel; landhuis; ~ **'ial**, ridder=, landheerlik.
man'-pack, rugpak.
man'power, strydkragte, leërsterkte; werkkragte, arbeidskragte, mannekrag; volkskragte; ~ **development**, mannekragontwikkeling.
man'-rope, valreep.
man'sard, mansarde(dak), solderkamer.
manse, pastorie (Presbiteriaans).
man'servant, kneg, bediende.
man: ~**'s' hand**, manshand; ~**'s' height**, manshoogte.
man'sion, herehuis, deftige woning; gebou; ~ **house**, woonhuis; landheerswoning.
man: ~**-skip**, hysbak vir mense; ~**slaughter**, manslag, doodslag; ~**slayer**, moordenaar.
man: ~**'s shirt**, manshemp; ~ **stealer**, menserower, ontvoerder; ~**'s trousers**, mansbroek.
man'suetude, sagmoedigheid, sagaardigheid.
man'ta, manta, rog; ~ **ray**, manta(rog).
man'tel, skoorsteenmantel; ~**piece**, skoorsteenmantel; kaggelrak; ~**shelf**, skoorsteenrak, kaggelrak.
man'tic, mantiek.
mantill'a, sluier, mantilla.
man'tis, (..tes), hotnotsgot, mantis.
mantiss'a, mantisse, aanwyser.
man'tle, (n) mantel; dekmantel; omhulsel; gloeikousie, lampkousie; *his* ~ *has fallen upon his FRIEND'S shoulders*, sy mantel het op sy vriend se skouers geval; *don the* ~ *of a PROPHET*, die profetemantel omhang; (v) bedek; hul; na die wange styg; gloei; bloos; skuim; ~ **cavity**, mantelholte; ~ **cloth**, mantelstof; ~**t**, manteltjie; stormdak; koeëlskerm.
man'trap, voetangel, val.
man'tua, los mantel, mantua.
man'ual, (n) voorskrif, handleiding, handboek; leidraad; klavier, toetsbord; manuaal (orrel); (a) met die hand, hande=; ~ **alphabet**, vingeralfabet; ~ **arts**, kunshandwerk; ~ **control**, handbeheer, handkontrole; handreëling; ~ **exchange**, handsentrale; ~ **instruction**, onderrig in handearbeid; ~ **labour**, handearbeid; ~ **labourer**, handwerker; ~**ly**, met die hand; ~ **sign**, handtekening, ~ **training**, ambagsopleiding.
manu'brial, handvatsel=, hingsel=.
manu'brium, hingsel, handvatsel.
manufac'tory, (..ries), fabriek, werkwinkel.
manufac'ture, (n) fabrikasie, vervaardiging; maaksel; aanmaak; fabrikaat; (v) vervardig, fabriseer; bedink; ~**d**, fabriekmatig, fabrieks=; ~**d goods**, fabrieksware; ~**r**, fabrikant, fabriseerder, vervaardiger.
manufac'turing, (n) fabrikasie, vervaardiging; (a) fabriserend; ~ **chemist**, fabriserende apteker, fabrikantapteker; ~ **industry**, fabriekswese; ~ **town**, fabriekstad.
manumi'ssion, vrylating (van slawe), manumissie.
manumit', (-ted), vrymaak, vrylaat.
manure', (n) mis; (v) mis gee, bemes; ~ **heap**, mishoop; ~ **spreader**, misstrooier.
manur'ial, bemestings=.
manu'ring, bemesting.
man'uscript, (n) handskrif, manuskrip; (a) in manuskrip, met die hand geskrewe.
Manx, van die eiland Man; ~ **cat**, Manse kat, stompstertkat; ~**man**, Maneilander.
ma'ny, (n) die menigte; *a GOOD* ~, baie; *a GREAT* ~, baie; (a) baie, veel; *as* ~ *AGAIN*, weer net soveel; *for* ~ *a DAY*, al lank; ~ *a MAN*, menigeen; baie; ~ *a ONE*, menigeen; baie; ~ *THANKS*, hartlik dank, baie dankie; ~ *a TIME*, baiemaal; veel; *be one TOO* ~ *for someone else*, een te veel wees; iem. se tier wees; *TWICE as* ~, twee maal soveel; ~**-angled**, veelhoekig; ~**-coloured**, veelkleurig, bont; ~**-headed**, veelhoofdig; ~ **plies**, blaarpens; ~**-sided**, veelkantig, veelsydig; ingewikkeld; ~ **times**, menigmaal, baie.
Maor'i, (n) Maori; (a) Maori=.
map, (n) (land)kaart; plattegrond; *OFF the* ~, afge-

maple

leë; onbereikbaar; *ON the* ~, van belang; *PUT on the* ~, bekend maak; bekendheid verwerf vir; *TRACE a* ~, 'n kaart oortrek; (v) (**-ped**), teken; karteer, in kaart bring; afbeeld; ~ **out**, 'n plan ont= werp van; indeel; uitstippel.
ma'ple, esdoring; ahorn(boom); *Canadian* ~, Kana= dese ahorn; ~**-leaf**, ahornblaar; ~**-sugar**, ahorn= suiker; ~**-syrup**, ahornstroop.
map: ~**-maker**, (land)kaartmaker, kaartekenaar, kartograaf; ~**-making**, kartografie.
mapp'ing, kartering; kartografie; ~**-office**, topogra= fiese inrigting.
map: ~**-projection**, kaartprojeksie; ~**-reading**, kaart= lees.
maquette', maket, ontwerpmodel.
maquillage', (F.), grimering.
mar, (**-red**), bederwe, beskadig; skend, ontsier; vergal; *make or* ~, maak of breek.
ma'rabou, maraboe, adjudantvoël; maraboevere.
ma'rabout, maraboet; maraboetgraf.
mara'ca, marakka, maranka.
maraschi'no, (**-s**), maraschino(likeur), maraskyn.
maras'mus, uittering, verval (liggaam).
ma'rathon, (n) marathon; (a) marathon=, langgerek, langasem=; ~ **race**, marathonwedloop; ~ **runner**, langafstandloper, marathonloper.
maraud', plunder, stroop, buit; ~**er**, plunderaar, ro= wer, buiter; ~**ing**, (n) buitery, plundering; (a) plun= derend, rowend, buit=; stroop=; ~**ing band**, stroop= bende.
mar'ble, (n) marmer, albaster; (pl) albasters; marmer= beelde; *talk as if one has a* ~ *in one's mouth*, praat of jy pap in jou mond het; (v) marmer; gevlam maak; (a) marmer=; ~ **bust**, marmerborsbeeld; ~**-colour**, marmerkleur; ~**d**, gemarmer, gevlek, ge= vlam; deurspek, deurwas (vleis); ~**-edged**, gemar= mer op snee; ~**-hearted**, hardvogtig, gevoelloos; ~**like**, marmeragtig; ~ **paper**, marmerpapier; ~ **quarry**, marmergroef; ~ **ray**, pylstert; ~ **slab**, mar= merblad; ~ **statue**, marmerbeeld; ~ **stone**, mar= mersteen; ~ **top**, marmerblad; ~**-topped**, met 'n marmerblad; ~**-work**, marmerwerk.
marb'ling, (die) marmer, marmering; gemarmerde vleis; marmerstruktuur; ~ **effect**, marmereffek.
marb'ly, marmeragtig, gemarmer.
marc, vrugtemoer.
mar'casite, markasiet, swa(w)elkies.
marca'to, (It., mus.), marcato, met nadruk.
marcel', (F.), marcel; ~ **wave**, marcelkapsel.
marces'cence, verwelking.
marces'cent, verwelkend, verleppend.
March[1], Maart; *as MAD as a* ~ *hare*, stapelgek; *the MONTH of* ~, Maartmaand.
march[2], (n) (**-es**), grens; *the* ~**es**, die grense; (v) grens aan; ~ **with**, grens aan.
march[3], (n) (**-es**), mars, tog, skof; loop, gang, voort= gang; pas, tred; *DEAD* ~, treurmars, dodemars; *FORCED* ~, geforseerde mars; *ON the* ~, op mars; *STEAL a* ~ *on*, iem. voorspring; iem. 'n vlieg afvang; *the* ~ *of TIME*, die verloop van tyd; (v) marsjeer, trek; opruk; stap; ~ *AGAINST*, op= trek (opruk) teen; ~ *AWAY*, wegmarsjeer; ~ *OFF*, afmarsjeer; laat afmarsjeer; ~ *ON*, voort= marsjeer, aanruk; ~ *OUT*, uittrek; ~ *PAST*, defi= leer, verbymarsjeer; ~ *WITH*, gelyke tred hou met; ~**er**, marsjeerder.
march'ing, (n) (die) marsjeer; (a) mars=; marsjerend, marsjeer=; ~ **column**, marskolonne, voetkolonne; ~ **kit**, veldtenue; velduitrusting, marstenue; ~ **or= ders**, marsorders; marsbevel; *give someone* ~ *or= ders*, lem. in die pad steek; iem. die trekpas (blou= pas) gee.
mar'chioness, (**-es**), markiesin.
march'pane, marsepein.
march: ~ **route**, marsweg; ~ **past**, defileermars, défi= lé; ~ **time**, marstyd.
marc'id, verlep, verwelk.
marcon'igram, radiogram, marconigram, draadlose telegram.
marcon'i operator, marconis, radiotelegrafis.
Mardi Gras', (F.), mardi gras, karnaval.
mare, merrie(perd); *the GREY* ~ *is the better horse*,

marital

die vrou dra die broek; *find a* ~ *'s NEST*, jou oor 'n dooie mossie verheug; ~**'s milk**, perdemelk; ~**'s tail**, perdestert; lang veerwolk.
marem'ma, (It.), maremma, ongesonde (moeras)= streek.
mar'feast, spelbederwer.
marg'arine, kunsbotter, margarien, margarine.
marg'ay, tierkat (Suid-Amerika).
marg[1], rand.
marg[2] = **margarine**; kunsbotter, margarine.
mar'gin, (n) rand, kant; kantlyn, marge, kantruimte; soom, grens, skeiding; surplus, wins; dekking (beurs); speling, speelruimte; *ECONOMIC* ~, be= taalbaarheidsgrens, winsmarge; ~ *of ERROR*, speelruimte vir foute; foutgrens; *LEAVE a* ~, 'n bietjie speelruimte laat staan; *by a NARROW* ~, skrap(pie)s; ampertjies; op 'n haar na; met 'n klein verskil; *as PER* ~, volgens kanttekening; *small* ~ *of PROFIT*, 'n klein voordeeltjie; ~ *of SAFETY*, veiligheidsgrens; *SELL on* ~, op marge verkoop; (v) van kanttekeninge voorsien; dek (beurs); 'n sur= plus stort; 'n rand laat.
marg'inal, rand=; grens=, aan die kant, marginaal, kant=, ~ **case**, grensgeval; ~ **cost**, grenskoste; ~ **line**, kantlyn; ~ **mine**, grensmyn, myn wat skaars die koste dek; ~ **note**, kanttekening; ~ **number**, kantnommer; ~ **pair**, kantpaar, kanttweetal; ~ **seat**, onveilige setel, grenssetel; ~ **value**, grens= waarde; ~ **zone**, randstreek.
marginal'ia, marginalia, kantaantekeninge, kantte= keninge.
mar'ginate, van 'n rand voorsien; ~**d**, met 'n rand, gerand.
mar'gin line, kantlyn.
marg'ravate, markgraafskap.
marg'rave, markgraaf.
marg'ravine, markgravin.
marg'uerite, margriet.
Mari'a, Maria; *black* ~, vangwa.
ma'riage de con'venance, huwelik uit belang, bereke= ningshuwelik.
Mar'ian, Maria=, van Maria.
mar'igold, gousblom; afrikaner; ~**-window**, wiel= venster.
marihua'na, **marijua'na**, marijuanu *(Nicotiana glau= ca)*, dagga.
marim'ba, marimba.
mari'na, marina, waterdorp, wateraanleg.
marinade', **marinate'**, (n) gekruide asynsous; gemari= neerde vis (vleis); marineersous, marinade; (v) ma= rineer, inlê; ~**d**, gemarineer(d); *marinated fish*, in= gelegde vis.
marine', (n) vloot, marine; seesoldaat, vlootsoldaat; seestuk; *DEAD* ~**s**, dooie hotnotjies; leë bottels; *TELL that to the* ~**s**, dit kan jy aan die ape vertel; dit kan jy vir die bobbejane gaan wysmaak; gaan vertel dit aan die hoenders; maak dit aan jou groo= tjie wys; dié kaf kan jy op 'n ander mark gaan ver= koop; (a) see=; marine=; skeeps=; kus=; ~ **barometer**, skeepsbarometer; ~ **biology**, seebiologie; ~ **blue**, marineblou; seeblou; ~ **boiler**, skeepsketel; ~ **cable**, seekabel; ~ **cadet**, adelbors; ~ **climate**, see= klimaat; ~ **corps**, marinekorps; ~ **deposit**, seebo= demafsetting; ~ **drive**, kusryweg, kuspad; ~ **en= gine**, skeepsmasjien; ~ **engineer**, skeepsmasjinis; skeepsingenieur, skeepsboukundige ingenieur; ~ **engineering**, skeepsboukunde; ~ **fitter**, skeeps= monteur; ~ **insurance**, seeversekering; ~ **law**, see= reg; ~ **light**, seevaartlig; ~ **militia**, seesoldate; ~ **painter**, seeskilder; ~ **phosphorescence**, blinkwater; ~ **plant**, seeplant; ~ **rainbow**, seereënboog.
mar'iner, matroos, seevaarder, seeman; ~**'s compass**, skeepskompas, seekompas.
marine': ~ **store**, seepakhuis; skeepswinkel; ~ **stores**, skeepsvoorraad; ~ **superintendent**, walkaptein.
Mariol'atry, Maria-aanbidding, Mariaverering.
marionette', marionet, pop.
ma'rish, (n) (**-es**), moeras; (a) moerasagtig.
ma'rital, egtelik, huweliks=, maritaal; ~ **power**, hu= weliksmag, maritale mag; ~ **privileges**, huweliks= regte; ~ **separation**, egskeiding; ~ **state**, ~ **status**, huwelikstaat.

ma'ritime, maritiem; see=, strand=, kus=; aan die see geleë; **M~ Alps,** See-Alpe; **~ climate,** seeklimaat; **~ commerce,** seehandel; **~ country,** seevarende land; **~ insurance,** seeversekering; **~ law,** skeeps=reg, seereg; **~ power,** seemoondheid; **~ province,** seegewes; **~ station,** skeepsvaartstasie.

marj'oram, moederkruid, marjolein.

Mark¹, Markus.

mark², (n) mark (munteenheid).

mark³, (n) merk, moet; punt (eksamen); teken; krui=sie; doel, mikpunt; merkteken, blyk; kenmerk; sy=fer; peil, hoogtemerk; watermerk; vlek, litteken; stempel (afdruk); stigma; wegspringplek; eindpaal; aantekening; skoonvang (rugby); vadem (diepte); **~** *of AFFECTION,* liefdeblyk; *BAD* **~,** skande=punt; *BELOW* **~,** benede die peil; *BESIDE the* **~,** heeltemal mis; totaal verkeerd; nie ter sake nie; **~** *of DISTINCTION,* onderskeidingsteken; *FIND the* **~,** die doel tref; **~** *of GRATITUDE,* blyk van erkentlikheid; *HIT the* **~,** raakskiet; sy doel bereik; die spyker op die kop slaan; *that HIT the* **~,** dit was 'n raakskoot; dit was 'n kopskoot; **~** *of HOMAGE,* huldeblyk; *KEEP something up to the* **~,** iets op peil hou; *LEAVE one's* **~,** sy invloed laat voel; *MAKE one's* **~,** sy spore verdien; naam maak; jou onderskei; *a MAN of* **~,** 'n man van betekenis (naam); *MISS the* **~,** die kol mis skiet; die bal misslaan; nie inslaan nie; *ON your* **~**s, op die streep; op julle merke; *ON the* **~,** ter sake; *be QUICK off the* **~,** vinnig wegspring; **~** *of RE=SPECT,* eerbetoon; *be UP to the* **~,** aan die eise voldoen; *not UP to the* **~,** benede die peil; *be WIDE of the* **~,** ver verkeerd wees; *WITHIN the* **~,** sonder oordrywing; (v) merk, stempel, teken; aandui; te kenne gee; opmerk; ag gee op, let op, aanteken; laat merk; punte gee; nasien; oplet; **~** *DOWN,* in prys verlaag; aanteken; *to* **~** *an EVENT,* ter ere van 'n gebeurtenis; **~** *with a hot IRON,* brandmerk; *that* **~**s *the MAN,* dit teken die man; **~** *the OCCASION,* die geleentheid vier; **~** *OFF,* afbaken; afgrens; afpen; afmerk; **~** *OUT,* aanwys; bestem; onderskei; afbaken; **~** *TIME,* die pas markeer; **~** *UP,* hoër prys; **~** *my WORDS,* let op my woorde; **~-book,** punteboekie, syferboekie; **~-down,** prysverlaging; **~ ed,** gevlek (klere); duide=lik; opvallend; sterk, geprononseer; *a* **~** *ed DIF=FERENCE,* 'n duidelike verskil; *a* **~** *ed MAN,* iem. wat in die oog gehou word; 'n verdagte; **~ edly,** opvallend; sterk.

mark'er, merker, opskrywer; markeur (biljart); teller, tellinghouer (gholf; skiet); boekmerk; stempelaar; merkyster; baken; merk(teken); **~ beacon,** (hoof=) merkbaken; **~ buoy,** merkboei.

mark'et, (n), mark; bemarking; aanvraag, debiet, af=trek; afsetgebied; ertjie (tolspel); *bring the eggs (hogs) to a BAD* **~,** met die kous oor die kop tuis kom; *BE in the* **~,** te koop wees; *BLACK* **~,** smok=kelhandel; swart mark; *CLERK of the* **~,** mark=meester; *COME into the* **~,** te koop aangebied word; op die mark kom; *MAKE a* **~** *for,* 'n mark skep vir; *NO* **~** *for,* geen aanvraag nie om; *NOT in the* **~,** nie in die handel nie; nie te koop nie; *in the OPEN* **~,** op die oop mark; *PUT on the* **~,** in die openbaar verkoop; te koop aanbied; *find a READY* **~** *for,* 'n groot aanvraag geniet; 'n gerede (goeie) aftrek (debiet) vir; (v) koop; verkoop; be=mark, op die mark bring; **~ able,** verkoopbaar, af=setbaar, vir die mark geskik; **~** *able securities,* ver=handelbare effekte; **~ agent,** markagent; **~ booth,** markstalletjie; **~-day,** markdag; **~ dues,** mark=geld; **~-garden,** groentetuin; **~-gardener,** groente=boer, groentekweker; **~-gardening,** groenteboer=dery; **~ hall,** markgebou; **~ ing,** bemarking; verkoop; **~ ing table,** markpryslys; **~-master,** markmeester; **~-place,** mark(plein); **~-porter,** markbediende; **~ price,** markprys; **~ regulations,** markregulasies; **~ report,** markberig; markver=slag; handelsberig; **~ research,** marknavorsing; **~ square,** markplein; **~ stall,** markstalletjie; **~ value,** markwaarde.

mark'ing, merk; merkteken; nasien (eksamenboeke); tekening; afbakening; (pl) tekening, aftekening;

merke (patroon); **~-gauge,** kruishout; **~-ink,** let=terink, merkink; **~-iron,** brandyster; **~-knife,** trekpen, merkmes; **~-target,** aanwysbord.

mark'-sheet, merkblad, puntelys.

marks'man, (..men), skerpskutter, fynskut; **~ ship,** skietkuns, skerpskutterskuns, fynskietkuns.

mark'-up, prysverhoging; winsgrens, winsruimte.

marl¹, (n) vrugbare kleigrond, mergel; (v) met mergel bemes.

marl², marlyn(stof).

mar'lin, marlyn (vissoort).

marl'ine, marlyn; **~-spike, mar'lin-spike,** marlpriem.

marm'alade, marmelade; lemoenkonfyt.

marm'ite, kookpot, kookskottel.

mar'molite, marmoliet.

marmor'eal, marmeragtig, marmer=.

marm'orize, marmeriseer.

marm'oset, klouapie, syapie.

marm'ot, marmotjie.

ma'rocain, marokyn (klerestof).

Ma'ronite, (n) Maroniet; (a) Maronities.

maroon'¹, (n) Bosneger, Bergneger.

maroòn'², (n) karmosynrooi, bruinrooi, wynrooi; karmynrooi, donkerrooi; klapper, vuurpyl.

maroon'³, (n) agtergelate persoon; (v) (op 'n onbe=woonde eiland of kus) agterlaat; rondslenter, rond=swerf.

mar'plot, planbederwer, spelbederwer.

marque, kaperskip; *letter(s) of* **~,** kaperbrief.

marquee', markiestent, offisierstent, groot veld=tent.

marq'uess, (-es), markies.

marq'ueterie, marq'uetry, inlegwerk.

marq'uis, (-es), markies; **~ ate,** markisaat.

mar'ram, sandhawer.

ma'rriage, huwelik; bruilof, huweliksvoltrekking, eg=(verbintenis); nou verbinding; *ASK in* **~,** ten hu=welik vra; *BY* **~,** aangetroud; *CIVIL* **~,** burgerli=ke huwelik; *COMPANIONATE* **~,** huwelik in kameraadskap; proefhuwelik; *CONSUMMATED* **~,** voltooide huwelik; **~** *of CONVENIENCE,* hu=welik uit berekening; *DISSOLVE a* **~,** 'n huwelik ontbind; *GIVE in* **~,** uithuwelik; **~** *s are made in HEAVEN,* 'n huwelik is voorbeskik; **~** *is a LOT=TERY,* trou is nie perdekoop nie; *one* **~** *MAKES many,* van 'n bruilof kom 'n bruilof; *PROMISE of* **~,** troubelofte; **~** *by PROXY,* huwelik met die handskoen; *TAKE in* **~,** trou; **~ able,** troubaar, hubaar, manbaar; **~ ableness,** troubaarheid, hu=baarheid, manbaarheid; **~ articles,** huweliksvoor=waardes; **~ bed,** huweliksbed; **~ bond,** huweliks=band; **~ broker,** huweliksmakelaar; **~ ceremony,** huweliksbevestiging; **~ certificate,** trousertifikaat, huweliksertifikaat; **~ contract,** huweliksvoorwaar=des, huwelikskontrak; **~ day,** troudag, huweliks=dag; **~ feast,** huweliksfees, bruilof; **~ gift,** trou=present; **~ guidance,** huweliksvoorligting; **~ knot,** huweliksband; **~ licence,** huweliklisensie, trouli=sensie; **~ lines,** huweliksakte, troubewys; **~ market,** huweliksmark; **~ officer,** huweliksbevesti=ger; huweliksbeampte; **~ outfit,** bruidsuitset; **~ partner,** lewensmaat; gade, eggenoot, eggenote; **~ partners,** huweliksgenote; **~ pledge,** troupand; **~ portion,** bruidskat; **~ record,** register, trouregis=ter; **~ ring,** trouring; **~ service,** huweliksdiens; **~ settlement,** huweliksooreenkoms, huweliksbema=king; huweliksbevoordeling; **~ song,** bruilofslied; **~ vow,** huweliksgelofte, trougelofte.

ma'rried, getroud, gekerk; huweliks=; *BE* **~,** getroud wees; *GET* **~,** in die huwelik tree, velletjies byme=kaargooi; **~ life,** huweliksewe; **~ person,** getroude persoon; **~ quarters,** kwartier vir getroudes; **~ state,** huweliksstaat, egtelike staat.

marron glacé, (F.), marron glacé, versuikerde kas=taiing(s).

ma'rrow, murg; pit; krag; *in the* **~** *of one's BONES,* in hart en niere; *CHILLED to the* **~,** deur en deur koud; *PIERCE (penetrate) to the* **~,** deur murg (merg) en been dring; *SPINAL* **~,** rugmurg; **~ bone,** murgbeen; (pl) knieë; *he brought him to his* **~** *bones,* hy het hom op sy knieë gebring; **~ cavity,** murgholte; **~-fat,** murgvet; **~ less,** sonder murg;

swak; papbroekerig; ~-**spoon**, murglepel; ~**y**, murgryk; kragtig; pittig, kernagtig.

ma'rry, (married), trou, hu, in die eg tree; in die huwelik verbind; koppel, verbind; ~ *BELOW one's station*, onder jou stand trou; ~ *in HASTE, repent at leisure*, gou getrou, lank berou; ~ *INTO*, introu; ~ *MONEY*, 'n ryk vrou (man) trou; ~ *OFF*, aan die man bring; ~ *by PROXY*, met die handskoen trou; met volmag trou; *be SURE before you ~ of a house wherein to tarry*, eers die koutjie, dan die vroutjie.

ma'rrying, trou(ery); *not the ~ sort*, geen mens vir trou nie; ~ **income**, inkomste waarop 'n man kan trou.

Marseillaise', Marseillaise (Franse volkslied).

Marseilles', Marseille (Frankryk); Marseilles (O.V.S.).

marsh, (-es), moeras.

marsh'al, (n) maarskalk; seremoniemeester; aanvoerder; balju; veldbeampte; **(v) (-led)**, rangskik, orden, monster, opstel; aanvoer; gelei; ~ **ler**, rangskikker; aanvoerder; ~ **ling**, rangskikking, opstelling (treine); ~ **ling yard**, opstel(lings)werf, opstel(lings)terrein; ~ **ship**, maarskalkskap, maarskalksrang.

marsh: ~ **fever**, moeraskoors; malaria; ~ **fire**, dwaallig; ~ **gas**, moerasgas; ~ **harrier**, vleivalk; ~ **iness**, drassigheid, moerassigheid, deurslagtigheid; ~ **mallow**, malvalekker, sponslekker; ~ **owl**, vlei-uil; ~ **y**, deurslagtig, moerassig, drassig.

marsup'ial, (n) buideldier; (a) buidel-, buideldraend.

mart, (n) mark; verkoopplek, vendusielokaal; wêreldmark, (v) verhandel, verkoop.

martell'o, (-s), ronde kustoring, kusfort, martello.

mart'en, marter; marterbont.

mar'tensite, martensiet.

mar'text, teksbederwer.

Mar'tial¹, (n) Martialis (digter).

Mar'tial², (a) van Mars.

mar'tial³, (a) krygshaftig, strydbaar, krygs-, dapper; oorlogs-; marsiaal; ~ **eagle**, breëkoparend *(Polemaetus bellicosus)*; ~ **law**, krygswet, Martjie Louw; ~ **music**, krygsmusiek.

Mar'tian, (n) Marsbewoner; (a) van Mars.

mart'in, (huis)swaeltjie.

martinet', martinet, drilmeester, tugmeester; haantjie, vuurvreter; ~ **ism**, vuurvretery, haantjieagtigheid.

mart'ingale, springteuel(s) (perde); dubbele inset (dobbelary); onderstag (skip).

marti'ni, martini (skemerkelkie).

Martin'ni-Henry rifle, martini-henry(geweer)

mart'let, (muur)swaeltjie.

mart'yr, (n) martelaar; martelares; *be a ~ to GOUT*, 'n slagoffer van jig wees; *MAKE a ~ of oneself*, jou opoffer; 'n martelaar wil wees; (v) martel, folter; die marteldood laat sterf; ~ **dom**, martelaarskap; marteldood, marteling; *crown of ~ dom*, martelaarskroon; ~ **ize**, 'n martelaar maak van; 'n slagoffer van jouself maak; ~ **ol'atry**, martelaarsaanbidding, martelaarsverering; ~ **ol'ogy**, (..gies), martelaarsgeskiedenis, martelaarsboek; ~ **'s blood**, martelaarsbloed; ~ **'s crown**, martelaarskroon; ~ **'s death**, marteldood; ~ **y**, (..ries), martelaarskerk, martirium.

marul'a, maroela(boom) *(Sclerocarya caffra)*; ~ **nut**, maroelaneut.

marv'el, (n) wonder; verbasing, verwondering; *a ~ of CHEAPNESS*, spotgoedkoop; *the ~ of it IS that*, die wonderlikste daarvan is dat; *a ~ of NEATNESS*, 'n wonder van netheid; (v) **(-led)**, verwonder, verbaas wees (oor); ~ **lous**, wonderlik, verbasend, wonderbaar(lik); ~ **lousness**, wonderlikheid.

Marx'ian, (n) Marxis; (a) Marxisties.

Marx'ism, Marxisme.

Marx'ist, Marxis, volgeling van Marx.

Ma'ry, Maria, Marie; *statue of ~*, Mariabeeld; ~ **'s-tears**, mariastrane.

marz'ipan, marsepein.

masa'la, masala (spesery).

mascar'a, maskara.

mas'cle, ruitvormige stuk; oop ruit (her.); malie.

mas'con, maskon.

mas'cot, gelukbringer, gelukspop(pie).

mas'culine, manlik; kragtig, sterk, fors; mannetjiesagtig, onvroulik; staande (rym); ~ **ending**, beklemtoonde slot; ~ **gender**, manlike geslag; ~ **name**, mansnaam; ~ **rhyme**, manlike (staande) rym.

masculin'ity, manlikheid.

mas'er, maser, maserstraal.

mash¹, (n) (-es), mengsel; mengelmoes; kapokaartappels, fyn aartappels; meelkos; beminde; *DRY ~*, droë mengsel; *WET ~*, nat mengsel; (v) fyn stamp, fynmaak, meng.

mash², (v) verlief maak; *whom is he ~ ing?* na wie vry hy?

mashed, gestamp; fyngemaak; ~ *potatoes*, kapokaartappels, kapokertappels.

mash'er¹, fynmaker.

mash'er², hartveroweraar, doring.

mash'-hammer, stamphamer, gruishamer.

mash'ie, vyfyster (gholf); ~ **niblick**, seweyster (gholf).

Mashon'a, Masjona; ~ **land**, Masjonaland.

mash: ~ **-tub**, broeikuip; ~ **y**, papperig.

ma'sjid, moskee, masied.

mask, (n) masker; vermomming, mombakkies; skerm; gemaskerde; voorwendsel; *PULL off, (pluck) the ~ from*, die masker van iem. afruk; *THROW off the ~*, die masker afwerp; *UNDER the ~ of*, onder die masker (mom) van; (v) maskeer, vermom; verklee; bedek, bemantel; jou voordoen; ~ **ed**, vermom, gemasker; ~ *ed ball*, gemaskerde bal, maskerbal; ~ **er**, gemaskerde (persoon); ~ **ing**, maskering, vermomming; bedekking, plakcol; ~ **ing sauce**, deksous.

mas'lin¹, messing (metaal).

mas'lin², (tweedeklas) meelblom.

mas'ochism, masochisme.

mas'ochist, masochis.

masochis'tic, masochisties.

Mas'on¹, Vrymesselaar.

mas'on², (n) klipkapper; messelaar; (v) messel; ~ **bee**, malkopby.

Mason'ic, Vrymesselaars-; ~ **emblems**, Vrymesselaarstekens; ~ **lodge**, Vrymesselaarslosie.

Mas'onry¹, Vrymesselary.

mas'onry², (klip)messelwerk; ~ **arch**, klipboog; ~ **wall**, klipmuur.

mas'on: ~ **spider**, messelspinnekop; ~ **wasp**, messelwesp; ~ **-work**, (klip)messelwerk.

masque, maskerade; maskerspel; ~ **r**, gemaskerde (persoon).

masquerade', (n) maskerade; vermomming; (v) vermom; vermom rondloop; jou uitgee vir, deurgaan vir, jou voordoen as, huigel.

mass¹, mis (R.K.); *AT ~*, by die mis; *ATTEND ~*, na die mis gaan; *CELEBRATE ~*, die mis opdra; *HEAR ~*, die mis hoor; *HIGH ~*, hoogmis; singende mis; *LOW ~*, stil mis; *SAY ~*, die mis lees.

mass², (n) **(-es)**, massa, groot klomp; hoeveelheid, trop, menigte; massa (gewig); *the GREAT ~ of*, die meeste; die menigte, die groot meerderheid, die massa, die volk; *IN ~*, in massa, en masse; *IN the ~*, oor die algemeen; voor die voet; (v) vergader, versamel, groepeer, ophoop, konsentreer; ~ *ed bands*, verenigde musiekkorpse.

mass'acre, (n) bloedbad, (mense)slagting, moordery, uitmoording; *the ~ of St. Bartholomew*, Bartholomeüsnag; (v) uitmoor, doodmaak, 'n slagting aanrig.

massage', (n) massage, masseerdery, massering, vryfkuns; (v) masseer, vrywe; ~ **parlour**, masseersalon; ~ **r**, masseerder, masseur.

massag'ing, massering.

massag'ist, masseerder, masseur, vrywer.

mass' attack, massa-aanval.

mass'book, misboek.

mass: ~ **buying**, massa-aankope; massa-aankoop; ~ **consumption**, massaverbruik; ~ **distribution**, massaverspreiding; ~ **ed**, in massa; opgehoop.

mass'é, massé(stoot), masseerstoot (biljart).

masseur', masseur, vrywer, masseerder.

masseuse', masseuse, masseerster, vryfster.

mass' grave, massagraf.

mass'icot, loodgeel, koningsgeel.
mass'if, massief.
mass'iness, swaarheid, massiwiteit.
mass'ive, massief, massaal, dig, swaar, omvangryk; solied, ongelaag; ~**ness,** massiwiteit.
mass: ~ **market,** massamark; ~ **media,** massamedia, massamediums; ~ **meeting,** massavergadering; ~ **meter,** massameter; ~-**produced,** in massa geproduseer; ~ **production,** massaproduksie; ~ **suggestion,** massasuggestie.
mass: ~ **stipend,** misaalmoes; ~ **vestments,** misgewaad.
mass'y, massief, swaar, solied.
mast¹, (n) akkers, neute; varkkos.
mast², (n) mas; *serve (sail) before the* ~, gewone matroos wees; (v) mas; die mas op stuur (as straf); van 'n mas voorsien, bemas; ~-**beam,** seilbalk; ~**ed,** van 'n mas voorsien, bemas.
ma'staba, mastaba; Egiptiese graf; klipbank.
ma'ster, (n) meester; baas; skipper, gesagvoerder, kaptein (skip); weesheer; werkgewer; onderwyser; jong(e)heer; huisvader; bobaas; gesinshoof, huisheer; magister (akademiese titel); ~ *of AFRIKAANS,* kenner van Afrikaans; *M*~ *of ARTS,* Magister Artium (M.A.); *a* ~ *AT something,* 'n meester in iets; *BE* ~ *of,* baas wees van; beskik oor; *we can't BOTH be* ~ *here,* ek meneer en jy meneer, wie sal dan die wa moet smeer? *the* ~ *'s eye makes the CATTLE thrive,* ver van jou goed, naby jou skade; ~ *of CEREMONIES,* seremoniemeester; *while* ~ *s DINE fools sing,* die here eet en gekke sing; *ENGLISH* ~, Engelse onderwyser, Engelsonderwyser; *EVERYBODY'S* ~, die meerdere van almal; *the* ~ *'s EYE makes the horse fat,* ver van jou goed, naby jou skade; ~ *of one's FATE,* beskikker oor eie lot; *m*~ *of the HOUNDS,* jagmeester; ~ *of the HOUSE,* huisheer; *early* ~, *soon (long) KNAVE,* vandag baas, môre klaas; *M*~ *'s Liability ACT,* Ongevallewet; *LIKE* ~ *like man,* so die heer, so die kneg; ~ *of the art of LYING,* baasleuenaar, meester van; *MAKE oneself* ~ *of,* jou meester maak van; ~*s and MEN,* werkgewers en werknemers; *M*~ *of the MINT,* muntmeester; *NEW* ~*s, new laws,* nuwe here, nuwe wette; *an OLD* ~, 'n ou meester; *be one's OWN* ~, jou eie baas wees; ~ *PETER,* die jongeheer Petrus; *M*~ *of the ROBE,* kamerheer; *M*~ *of the ROLLS,* eerste argivaris; *M*~ *of SCIENCE,* Magister Scientiae (M. Sc.); ~ *and SERVANT,* baas en kneg; *first* ~ *then SLAVE,* eers baas en dan klaas; *be a* ~ *of a SUBJECT,* 'n vak beheers; ~ *of the SUPREME COURT,* weesheer; *be a* ~ *of one's TRADE,* jou vak meester wees; *no man can serve TWO* ~*s,* niemand kan twee here dien nie; (v) oormeester, oorwin, baasraak; meester word; tem, in bedwang hou; beheer; (taal) aanleer; baas wees oor; (a) hoof-; ~-**at-arms,** provoosgeweldige, skeepsprovoos; ~ **baker,** bakkersbaas, meesterbakker; ~ **bedroom,** hoofslaapkamer; ~-**brain,** groot leier, leidende gees; voorbok, grootkop; ~ **builder,** meesterbouer, boumeester, boubaas; ~ **butcher,** baasslagter, slagtersbaas; ~ **card,** gids-, hoofkaart; baaskaart; ~ **carpenter,** baastimmerman; ~ **clock,** hoofklok; ~ **compass,** moederkompas, kontrolekompas; ~ **cook,** hoofkok, meesterkok; ~ **die,** stamsnyblok, matryssnyblok; ~ **dom,** heerskappy; gesag; ~**ful,** meesterlik; meesteragtig; despoties, baasspelerig; ~ **gauge,** ykmaat; ~ **gunner,** hoofkanonnier; ~-**hand,** meesterhand; ~ **hood,** meesterskap; ~-**key,** dieweseutel, loper; ~ **less,** onbeheer, sonder baas; ~**liness,** meesterlikheid; ~ **link,** lasskakel; koppelskakel; ~ **ly,** meesterlik, kunstig, vaardig; ~ **mariner,** seekaptein, skipper; ~ **mason,** baasmesselaar; boumeester; meester (Vrymesselaars); ~ **mind,** buitengewone gees, grootkop, leier; ~**piece,** meesterstuk; ~ **pilot,** hoofvlieër; ~ **plan,** sleutelplan, baasplan; ~ **plate,** stamplaat; ~ **printer,** drukkersbaas; ~ **race,** heerseras; ~**'s degree,** magistergraad; ~ **ship,** meesterskap; onderwyserspos; meesterstuk; ~ **spirit,** genie, voortreflike gees; ~ **spring,** hoofveer; hoofmotief; ~**'s ticket,** kapteinsdiploma; ~-**stroke,** meesterwerk; geniale set; meesterstuk; pragstuk; ~ **switch,** hoofskakelaar; ~ **tailor,** kleremakersbaas, meesterkleremaker; ~ **theme,** hooftema; ~ **treaty,** algemene verdrag.
mas'tery, meesterskap, (opper)heerskappy, beheer; oorhand; bedrewenheid; ~ *of the AIR,* lugheerskappy; *he HAS a* ~ *of the subject,* hy is die onderwerp volkome meester; *OBTAIN the* ~ *of,* die oorhand kry oor.
mast: ~**head,** mastop; kopstuk (tydskrif, koerant); ~-**hoop,** masband.
mas'tic, mastiek(boom); steenlym, mastiekgom.
mas'ticable, koubaar.
mas'ticate, kou; maal, fynmaak.
mastica'tion, kou; kouery, mastikasie.
mas'ticator, die tande; kakebeen; kouer; vleismeul; fynmaker.
mas'ticatory, (n) (..ries), koumiddel; (a) kou-.
ma'stiff, slagtershond, bulbyter.
mastit'is, uierontsteking, mastitis, blou-uier.
mast: ~ **less,** sonder mas; ~-**tackle,** sytakel.
mas'todon, mastodon; ~'**tic,** mastodonties.
mas'toid, (n) mastoïde; (a) tepelvormig, mastoïed; ~**bone,** agteroorbeen.
mas'turbate, selfbevlekking pleeg, masturbeer.
masturba'tion, selfbevlekking, masturbasie.
mas'turbator, selfbevlekker, onanis, masturbeerder.
mat¹, (n) mat; verwarde massa; (v) **(-ted),** met matte bedek; deurmekaarvleg, verwar; mat (stoel); ~*ted HAIR,* deurmekaar hare, gekoekte hare; ~*ted SOIL,* gekoekte grond.
mat², (v) mat (dof) maak, matteer; (a) mat, dof.
Matabel'e, Matebele; ~-**flower,** rooiblom.
mat'ador, matador, stiervegter, bulvegter.
match¹, (n) (-es), vuurhoutjie; lont; pit (kers); *SAVE a* ~ *and buy a farm,* wie spaar, vergaar; *STRIKE a* ~, 'n vuurhoutjie trek.
match², (n) (-es), wedstryd; paar, huwelik; gelyke, portuur, eweknie, weerga; *be ANOTHER'S* ~, iem. oortref; iem. se baas wees; *BE a* ~ *for,* opgewasse wees teen; *be a GOOD* ~, goed by mekaar pas; 'n goeie party wees; *he HAS no* ~, sy maters is klein dood; *MAKE a* ~, 'n huwelik tot stand bring; *MEET one's* ~, jou portuur kry; *acknowledge that one has MET one's* ~, erken dat jy jou meerdere gekry het; *MORE than a* ~ *for,* meer as opgewasse teen; *be NO* ~ *for,* geen portuur wees nie vir; nie opgewasse nie teen; te lig in die broek wees vir; *he has NO* ~, sy maters is klein dood; *we shall never SEE his* ~, ons sal sy gelyke nooit sien nie; *SOMEONE'S* ~, iem. se moses; iem. se tier; (v) bymekaargooi; paar; pas, uitsoek; die gelyke kry van; teen mekaar opgewasse wees, ewenaar; teenoor mekaar stel; laat trou; 'n huwelik aangaan; aanpas; *this colour is HARD to* ~, dis moeilik om 'n kleur te kry wat hierby pas; *a HAT to* ~, 'n bypassende hoed; ~ *ONESELF against someone,* jou met iem. meet; *with SILK to* ~, met daarby passende sy; *can you* ~ *THAT?* kan jy dit nadoen? ~**able,** passend; vergelykbaar.
match: ~**board,** dunhout; ~-**box,** vuurhoutjiedosie.
matched: *be EVENLY* ~, teen mekaar opgewasse wees; ~ *IMPEDANCE,* aangepaste teenstand; *NOT to be* ~, weergaloos, onvergelyklik; ~ *SAMPLES,* gepaarde monsters; *be WELL* ~, goed by mekaar pas.
match: ~**ing,** (n) aanpassing; (a) harmoniërend, bypassend, soortgelyk; ~**less,** weergaloos, ongeewenaard, voorbeeldeloos, onvergelyklik.
match'lock, snaphaan.
match'-maker¹, vuurhoutjiemaker.
match'maker², koppelaar; promotor (sport).
match'making, huweliksmakelary, koppelary; promosie (sport).
match'-plane, ploegskaaf.
match'-play, putjiespel (gholf).
match: ~-**stand,** vuurhoutjiestandertjie; ~-**stick,** vuurhoutjie; *have legs like* ~-*sticks,* spykerbeentjies hê, sigaretbeentjies hê; ~ **wood,** hout vir vuurhoutjies; *make* ~ *wood of,* fyn en flenters breek, versplinter, kafloop.
mate¹, (n) (skaak)mat; *FOOL'S* ~, narremat, gekke-

mat; *give* ~, mat gee (skaak); (v) skaakmat sit; (a) skaakmat.
mate², (n) maat, kameraad, gesel, vriend; mannetjie; wyfie; gade; stuurman (boot); helper, hulp; *first* ~, opperstuurman; (v) maats maak, omgaan (met); paar, trou; ~**d,** gepaard; ~**less,** sonder maat, ongepaard.
mat'elot, matroos.
ma'telote, (F.), matelote, visgereg.
mat'er, moeder; *ALMA* ~, alma mater; *DURA* ~, dekvlies; *PIA* ~, binnevlies, voedvlies; ~ *FAMILIAS,* mater familias, vrouehoof (huishouding).
mater'ial, (n) materiaal, boustof; stof, klerasiestof, goed; (pl) boustowwe; (a) stoflik, materieel; liggaamlik; wesenlik, belangrik, beduidend, ter sake, saakmakend; gewigtig; *have a* ~ *BEARING on,* wesenlike betrekking hê op; *a* ~ *DIFFERENCE,* 'n wesenlike onderskeid; ~ *WELL-BEING,* stoflike welvaart; ~ *to one's WELFARE,* van groot belang vir 'n mens se welsyn; ~ **ism,** stofaanbidding, materialisme; ~**ist,** materialis; ~**is'tic,** stoflik, materialisties; . .**ial'ity,** (. .**ties),** stoflikheid; materialiteit; belangrikheid; (pl) stoflike dinge; **iza'tion,** verstofliking, versinliking; verwesenliking; ~**ize,** verwesenlik, verwerklik; verstoflik; 'n stoflike gedaante laat aanneem (spiritisme); iets oplewer; *it did not* ~*ize,* daar het niks van gekom nie; ~**ly,** stoflik; belangrik; aanmerklik, in hoofsaak.
mate'ria medica, materia medica, helende middele.
materiel', middele, materiaal.
matern'al, moederlik; moeder=; ~ **aunt,** tante aan (van) moederskant; ~ **benefit,** uitkering by bevalling; ~ **bliss,** moederweelde, moedergeluk; ~ **love,** moederliefde; ~ **portion,** moedersdeel, moedersporsie.
matern'ity, moederskap; moederlikheid; ~ **gown,** kraamrok; ~ **grant,** kraamtoelae; ~ **home,** ~ **hospital,** kraaminrigting; ~ **nurse,** kraamverpleegster; ~ **ward,** kraamafdeling; ~ **wear,** kraamdrag, ooievaarsdrag.
mat'(e)y, (n) maat; ou maat; (a) boetieagtig, familiêr, gesellig, maatsmakerig.
mat' glass, matglas.
mat' grass, borselgras.
math(s), wiskunde, matesis.
mathemat'ical, matematies, wiskundig.
mathemati'cian, wiskundige, matematikus.
mathemat'ics, wiskunde, matesis; *APPLIED* ~, toegepaste wiskunde; *PURE* ~, suiwer wiskunde.
Ma'tie, Matie.
mat'in, more=, more=, oggend=
mat'inee, middagvoorstelling, matinee; ~ **coat,** babamantel; ~ **idol,** toneelafgod, toneelheld(in); ~ **jacket,** bababaadjie.
mat'ing, paring, ~**-ground,** broeiplek; ~ **season,** paartyd.
mat'ins, vroeë oggenddiens, vroeë mette.
mat'man, stoeier.
mat'-painted, mat geskilder.
mat' paper, mat papier.
mat'rass, (-es), kolf(glas), distilleerkolf.
mat'riarch, matriarg, stammoeder, aartsmoeder; ~**'al,** matriargaal, ~**y,** matriargaat.
matric', matriek, matrikulasie.
mat'ricidal, moedermoord=.
mat'ricide, moedermoord; moedermoordenaar.
matric'ulant, matrikulant.
matric'ulate, matrikuleer; as universiteitstudent toelaat.
matricula'tion, matrikulasie; inskrywing; *Joint M* ~ *Board,* Gesamentlike Matrikulasieraad, M examination, matrikulasie-eksamen; ~ **results,** matrikulasie-uitslae.
matrilin'eal, matrilin'ear, in die vroulike linie, matrilineaal, matrilineêr.
matrimon'ial, huweliks=, egtelik; ~ **agency,** huweliksburo; ~ **agent,** huweliksbemiddelaar, huwelikshandelaar; ~ **court,** huwelikshof; ~ **duties,** huwelikspligte; ~ **market,** huweliksmark; ~ **yoke,** huweliksjuk.
mat'rimony, huwelik, eg; huwelikstaat; *enter into* ~, jou in die eg begewe, in die huwelik tree.

mat'rix, (. .**trices),** baarmoeder; matrys; (giet)vorm (masjinerie); kweekplek, skoot (fig.); moedergesteente, matriks, grondmassa, tussenmassa (geol.); ~ **die,** matryssnyblok; ~ **stone,** matrikssteen.
mat'ron, (getroude) vrou; middeljarige dame; huismoeder; matrone; ~**al** = **matronly;** ~**hood,** matroneskap; ~**ly,** matrone=; deftig, statig; huisvroulik; ~**-of-honour, (-s-of-honour),** eredame; ~**ship,** matroneskap; huismoederlikheid.
matt, dof, mat.
matt'amore, onderaardse pakhuis (woonhuis).
matte, swa(w)elmetaal, sulfidemengsel; ~ **copper,** rusteenkoper, swartkoper, swa(w)elmetaal.
matt'er, (n) stof, substansie, materie; ding, geval, saak, kwessie; vuilis; voorwerp, onderwerp; som; aangeleentheid; gewig; sug, etter; kopie (druk.); *relating to the* ~ *CONCERNED,* in verband met die betrokke saak; *a* ~ *of COURSE,* 'n vanselfsprekende saak; *as a* ~ *of COURTESY,* beleefdheidshalwe; *a* ~ *of FACT,* 'n feit; *as a* ~ *of FACT,* om die waarheid te sê; *FOR that* ~, wat dit betref; *GREY* ~, harsings, verstand; *no GREAT* ~, nie van baie betekenis nie; *a HANGING* ~, 'n saak waaroor iem. opgehang kan word; *a* ~ *of IMPORTANCE,* 'n gewigtige (vername) saak; *IN the* ~ *of,* insake, wat betref; *a* ~ *of INDIFFERENCE,* 'n saak van min betekenis; *as a* ~ *of INTEREST,* interessantheidshalwe; *no LAUGHING* ~, nie 'n kleinigheid nie; niet iets om oor te lag nie; *a* ~ *of LIFE and death,* 'n lewenskwessie; *a* ~ *of MONEY,* 'n geldkwessie; *NO* ~ *what,* ongeag wat; *there is NOTHING the* ~ *with him,* hy makeer niks; *POSTAL* ~, posstukke; *PRINTED* ~, drukwerk; *a* ~ *of five RAND,* 'n sommetjie van vyf rand, *us a* ~ *of ROUTINE,* in die gewone loop van sake; *if I have any SAY in the* ~, as dit aan my lê; *in a* ~ *of SECONDS,* in 'n paar sekondes; *that is how the* ~ *STANDS,* so staan sake; *for THAT* ~, wat dit betref; *a* ~ *of TIME,* 'n kwessie van tyd; *WHAT is the* ~*?* wat makeer? (v) van belang wees, van betekenis wees, saak maak; etter; *it does not* ~ *ABOUT me,* moenie jou oor my bekommer nie; *it does NOT* ~, dit maak nie saak nie; dit kom daar nie op aan nie; dit maak geen verskil nie; *it does not* ~ *TO me,* dit kan my nie skeel nie; ~**ful,** saakryk, pittig; ~**-of-course,** natuurlik, vanselfsprekend; ~**-of-fact,** saaklik; prosaïes, droog, nugter; ~**y,** etterend, etterig.
Ma'tthew, Mattheüs, Matteus.
matt'ing, mat; matwerk; saamkoeking.
matt'ock, houweel, bylpik.
matt'ress, (-es), matras; ~ **case,** matrasoortreksel; ~ **needle,** matrasnaald; ~ **stitch,** matrassteek
mat'urate, ryp word; laat ryp word.
matura'tion, rypwording, rypheid; veroudering (wyn); ettering.
matur'ative, ettervormende middel.
mature', (v) ryp word; ryp maak; verouder; verval (wissel); opeisbaar word (polis); (a) ryp, beleë (wyn); jarig; geryp; bekwaam (vrugte); uitgegroei (dier); voldrae; vervalle (wissel); *after* ~ *consideration,* na rype beraad; ~**d,** ryp; geryp; volgroei; beleë (wyn); vervalle (reg); ~*d policy,* uitkeerbare polis.
mature'ness, rypheid; beleënheid.
matur'ing, ryping, rypwording.
matur'ity, rypheid; bekwaamheid (vrugte); beleënheid (wyn); vervaldag (wissel, tjek); opeisbaarheid; volwassenheid; *AT* ~, op die vervaldag; *REACH* ~, tot rypheid kom.
matut'inal, môre=, more=, vroeg.
mat'y = **mat(e)y.**
matz'o, matso.
maud, (geruite) reisdeken.
maud'lin, sentimenteel, liggeroer, oorgevoelig, stroperig; huilerig-dronk.
maul, (n) moker, slaanhamer, breekhamer, stoeiery; (v) slaan, kneus, moker; afmaak, aan stukke skeur; lelik byt; mishandel, toetakel; skerp kritiseer.
maul'ey, poot, klou, vuis.
maul'stick, skilderstok, leunstokkie.
Mau'-Mau', Mau-Mau.

maun'der, mompel, prewel; sanik, neul; ~**er,** brompot.
maun'dy, voetwassing; uitdeling; ~ **money,** aalmoes; M ~ **Thursday,** Wit Donderdag.
Mauri'tian, (n) Mauritiaan; (a) Mauritiaans.
Mau'ser, mauser.
mausole'um, (-s, ..lea), praalgraf, mausoleum.
mauve, ligpers, mauve, malvapers.
mav'erick, (n) ongebrande bees; dwarstrekker, juskeibreker, hardekop; (v) wegdwaal, wegraak; wegbreek; (a) ongewoon; dwarstrekkerig; buitenissig, eksoties.
mav'is, sanglyster.
mauvour'neen, skatjie, liefling.
maw, pens, maag; swemblaas; krop (voël).
mawk'ish, walglik; sentimenteel; oorgevoelig; stroperig; wee, naar; ~**ness,** sentimentaliteit; walglikheid, stroperigheid.
maw'seed, maansaad, papawersaad.
maw'worm, ingewandswurm, spoelwurm.
max'i, (n) maksi; (a) maksi=.
maxill'a, (-e), bokakebeen, bokaak, maksil; onderkaak (insek); ~**ry,** (n) bokaak; (a) kaak=, kakebeen=, maksillêr.
max'im¹, maxim.
max'im², grondreël, stelreël; leuse, (kern)spreuk; spreekwoord.
max'imal, maksimaal; ~**ist,** maksimalis.
max'imize, maksimaliseer, maksimeer, vermeerder, vergroot.
max'imum, (n) (..ma, -s), maksimum; ~ *and minimum thermometer,* maksimum-en-minimumtermometer; (a) hoogste, top=, maksimaal, maksimum=; ~ **height,** maksimumhoogte; ~ **speed,** topspoed, topsnelheid.
May¹, Mei; bloeityd, lente.
may², (n) meisie, nooi (digterlik).
may³, (v) **(might),** mag; kan; *BE that as it* ~, hoe dit ook sy; laat dit wees soos dit wil; *it* ~ *BE so,* dit kan so wees; *COME what* ~, wat ook al mag gebeur; *IF I* ~, as ek mag; *he* ~ *LOSE his way,* hy kan verdwaal; *you might have SAID so,* jy kon dit darem gesê het; miskien het jy dit gesê; *it* ~ *or it* ~ *not be TRUE,* miskien is dit waar, miskien ook nie; *it* ~ *WELL be that . . .,* heel moontlik is dit . . .
Ma'ya, Maja.
may'be, miskien, moontlik, dalk.
May: ~**-bug,** meikewer; **m**~**-bush,** meidoring, meiblom; ~ **Day,** le Mei, Meidag; ~**-day celebrations,** Meiviering; **m**~**flower,** meidoring, meiblom; ~**fly,** eendagsvlieg, kokerjuffer.
may'hap, moontlik, allig.
may'hem, verminking (reg); lyfgeweld; oproer.
May: ~**-lily,** lelie-van-dale; ~ **meeting,** Meibyeenkoms.
mayonnaise', mayonnaise, slaaisous; ~ **relish,** mayonnaisesmeer.
may'or, burgemeester.
may'oral, burgemeesters=, burgemeesterlik; ~ **chain,** burgemeestersketting; ~ **reception,** burgemeestersonthaal; M ~ **Sunday,** Burgemeestersondag; ~**ty,** burgemeesterskap.
may'or: ~**-ess, (-es),** burgemeestersvrou; ~**ess' at-home,** ontvangs v.d. burgemeestersvrou; ~ **ship,** burgemeesterskap; ~**'s parlour,** burgemeesterskamer.
may: ~ **pole,** meipaal, meiboom; M~ **Queen,** Meikoningin.
mazarine', donkerblou, diepblou.
maze, (n) doolhof, labirint; warnet; kronkelgang; verleentheid; warboel; (v) verbyster, verwar.
maz'er, houtbreker.
maz'iness, verwardheid.
mazurk'a, masurka.
maz'y, vol kronkelpaadjies; verward, soos 'n doolhof.
me, my; ek; *AH* ~! *o my!* ~ *and MINE,* my goed en bloed; *POOR* ~! arme ek!
mea cul'pa, (L.), mea culpa, dit is my fout.
mead¹, heuningdrank, karie, mede.
mead², weiland.
mead'ow, weiveld, wei, grasland; ~**-clover,** rooi klawer; ~**-land,** weiland; ~**-mouse,** veldmuis; ~ **pipit,** kwikstertjie; ~**y,** vol weilande; weiveld=.
mea'gre, maer, skraal; armsalig, skamel; dor; *a* ~ *income,* 'n skraal inkomste; ~**ly,** skraal; ~**ness,** maerte, maerheid, skraalheid, skamelheid; onvrugbaarheid.
meal¹, (n) meel; *unsifted* ~, boermeel.
meal², (n) (eet)maal, maaltyd, ete; etery; kos; *AT* ~*s* aan tafel; by die maaltyd; *MAKE a* ~ *of,* eet; (v) eet.
meal'ie, mielie; *CRUSHED* ~*s,* (mielie)gruis; *GREEN* ~, groenmielie; ~ **beard,** mieliebaard; ~**-borer,** mielieruspe(r); ~ **bread,** mieliebrood; ~ **cob,** mieliestronk; mieliekop; ~ **ear,** mieliekop; ~ **farmer,** mielieboer; ~ **field,** mielieland; ~ **grain,** mieliepit; ~ **grits,** mieliegruis; ~ **harvest,** mielieoes; ~ **heath,** mielieheide; ~ **leaf,** mielieblaar; ~ **meal,** mieliemeel; ~ **porridge,** mieliepap; ~ **rice,** mielierys, (mielie)gruis; ~ **seed,** mieliepit; mieliesaad; ~ **stalk,** mieliestronk; ~ **worm,** mieliewurm.
meal'iness, melerigheid, meelagtigheid.
meal' interval, etenspouse, etensonderbreking.
meal'man, meelhandelaar.
meal: ~ **planning,** maaltydbeplanning; ~ **time,** etenstyd; ~ **tray,** eteskinkbord.
meal' worm, meelwurm.
meal'y, meelagtig; melerig; krummelrig; bleek; vlekkerig; ~**-bug,** wolluis, witluis; ~**-mouthed,** soetsappig, stroperig; papbroekerig; verleë.
mean¹, (n) middel, middelmaat; gemiddelde; middelterm (wisk.); (pl) bron, drakrag, fonds, middel; hulpmiddel; vermoë; *by ALL* ~*s,* alte seker, bepaald; *not by ANY* ~*s,* glad nie; onder geen omstandighede nie; *BEYOND his* ~*s,* bokant sy vermoë; meer as wat hy vermag; *BY this* ~*s,* op hierdie manier; *BY* ~*s of,* deur middel van; *EM-PLOY* ~*s,* 'n middel aanwend; *by FAIR* ~*s or foul,* op eerlike of oneerlike wyse; *the GOLDEN (happy)* ~, die gulde middeweg; *LIVE beyond one's* ~*s,* bo jou inkomste lewe; *a MAN of* ~*s,* 'n bemiddelde man; *by NO* ~*s,* glad nie; *STRIKE the happy* ~, 'n middeweg vind; *devise WAYS and* ~*s,* middele beraam, raad verskaf; *WITHIN our* ~*s,* binne ons vermoë; *it is not WITHIN my* ~*s,* dit val buite my mag.
mean², (v) **(meant),** meen, bedoel; beteken; van plan wees; bestem; *he* ~*t no HARM,* hy het dit goed bedoel; *I* ~ *to SAY,* ek bedoel; ~ *WELL by (towards) one,* dit goed bedoel met iem.; *WHAT do you* ~? wat bedoel jy?
mean³, (a) gemiddeld; middelmatig; tussen=, middel=; ~ *DISTANCE,* gemiddelde afstand.
mean⁴, (a) gemeen, laag(hartig), smerig, skurkagtig, snood, onedel, skunnig, vuig, sleg; suinig; ~ *BEHAVIOUR,* lae gedrag; *of* ~ *BIRTH,* van lae afkoms; *FEEL* ~, jou skaam; *no* ~ *SCHOLAR,* 'n geleerde van naam; ~**-born,** van lae afkoms.
mean'der, (n) meander, kronkeling, kronkel; slingering; (pl) kronkelpaaie; doolhof; (v) kronkel, meander; slinger; ronddool; ~**ing,** omswerwing; gekronkel, kronkeling.
mean'drine, meanderend, vol kronkelinge, kronkelslinger=.
mean'drous, kronkelend, vol bogte.
mea'nie, mea'ny, gemene vent.
mean'ing, (n) betekenis, sin; plan, bedoeling; *with* ~, beslis; nadruklik; (a) veelbetekenend, betekenisvol; *a* ~ *look,* 'n veelseggende blik; ~**ful,** veelseggend, betekenisvol, sinvol, sinryk, wesensvol; ~**fulness,** betekenisvolheid; wesensvolheid, sinrykheid; ~**less,** sonder betekenis; niksseggend, betekenisloos; onbeduidend, sinloos, sinledig; ~**lessness,** sinloosheid, sinledigheid; ~**ly,** veelbetekenend, betekenisvol; opsetlik.
mean'ly, gering, min; geringskattend; gemeen; *think* ~ *of,* 'n lae dunk hê van.
mean'ness, gemeenheid, laag(hartig)heid, gemeniteit, vuigheid, smerigheid, smeerlappery, snoodheid.
means, middel(e); *by ALL* ~, sekerlik; *by* ~ *of a LADDER,* met (deur middel van) 'n leer; *his SOLE* ~ *of livelihood,* sy enigste bestaansmiddel; ~ **test,** middeletoets;

mean'-spirited, kruiperig, laag, gemeen; lafhartig; van lae inbors.
mean'time, (n) tussentyd; *FOR the* ~, voorlopig; *IN the* ~, intussen; (adv) intussen, solank, ondertussen, middelerwyl; nietemin, nogtans.
mean'while, (n) intussen; (adv) intussen, ondertussen; nogtans, nietemin.
meany = meanie.
mea'sled, vol masels, uitgeslaan, masel=.
mea'sles, masels; *German* ~, rooihond, rubella, Duitse masels.
meas'ly, vol masels, masel=; armsalig, miserabel; *a ~ little sum of money*, bespotlike klein sommetjie geld.
mea'surable, (af)meetbaar; afsienbaar.
mea'sure, (n) maat (musiek); maatstaf, maatreël; maatemmer; digmaat; afmeting, omvang, hoeveelheid; wetsontwerp; formasie (geol.); *there is a ~ in ALL things*, alles het sy maat; *BEYOND* ~, bowemate, buitemate; *a CHAIN'S weakest link is the ~ of its strength*, 'n ketting is nooit sterker as sy swakste skakel nie; *CUBIC* ~, kubieke maat; *DESPERATE* ~, wanhoopsmaatreël; *DRY* ~, maat vir droë ware; ~ *FOR* ~, leer om leer; *FULL* ~, volle maat; *for GOOD* ~, op die koop toe; *in GREAT* ~, in hoë mate; *GREATEST common* ~, grootste gemene deler; *HAVE the* ~ *of someone*, weet waartoe iem. in staat is; weet wat jy aan iem. het; *IN A* ~, in seker(e) mate; *LINEAR* ~, lengtemaat; *MADE to* ~, op maat gemaak; *a ~ OF*, 'n sekere mate van, *SQUARE* ~, vierkantmaat; *TAKE* ~ *s*, maatreëls tref; *TAKE someone's* ~, iem. takseer; iem. aan die tand voel; *TREAD a* ~, dans; *WITHIN* ~, redelikerwyse; (v) meet, maat neem, afpas, afmerk; afloop (atletiekbaan); skat, begroot; met die oog meet; takseer; goed bekyk; bedra; ~ *someone with one's EYES*, iem van kop tot tone besigtig; ~ *one's LENGTH*, plat val; op die grond neerslaan; ~ *OFF*, afmeet; ~ *ONESELF against another*, kragte meet met; *SET* ~ *s to*, paal en perk stel aan; ~ *by two STANDARDS*, met twee mate meet; ~ *SWORDS with*, die swaard kruis met; ~ *UP*, opmeet; *as you* ~ *so WILL it be* ~ *d unto you*, met die maat waarmee jy meet, sal jy weer gemeet word; ~ *one's WORDS*, jou woorde wik en weeg; ~ **d**, afgemeet; weldeurdag; ~ *d MILE*, afgemete myl; *in* ~ *d TONES*, op afgemete toon; ~ **less**, onmeetlik; mateloos.
mea'surement, maat; (af)meting; ~ *GOODS*, goed waarvoor vrag na die grootte betaal word; *INSIDE (outside)* ~, binnemaat (buitemaat).
mea'surer, meter, maatnemer.
mea'suring, (n) (die) maat neem, afmeting; (a) maat=, meet=; ~**-chain**, meetketting, landmetersketting; ~**-cup**, maatkoppie; ~**-glass**, maatglas; ~**-line**, maatlyn, meetlyn; ~**-rod**, meetstok, meetroede; ~**-scoop**, maatgrafie, ~**-tape**, meetlint, maatband.
meat, vleis; kos; maaltyd; prooi, *AFTER* ~, na ete; *BE at* ~, aan tafel wees; *BEFORE* ~, voor ete; ~ *and DRINK*, ete en drinke; *that is* ~ *and DRINK to him*, dis net so in sy kraal; *as full as an EGG is of* ~, propvol; *GRACE before* ~, tafelgebed; *MINCED* ~, gemaalde vleis, maalvleis; *one man's* ~ *is another man's POISON*, die een se dood is die ander se brood; *SALT(ED)* ~, soutvleis; *STRONG* ~, swaar kos; ~ **axe**, vleisbyltjie; ~ **ball**, frikkadel; ~ **bat**, vleisklopper; ~ **biscuit**, vleisbeskuit; ~ **block**, vleisblok.
meat' board[1], vleisplank.
Meat' Board[1], Vleisraad.
meat: ~ **breed**, vleisras; ~ **chopper**, vleisbyltjie; ~ **course**, vleisgereg; ~ **cover**, vleisdeksel, koevertuur; ~ **dish**, vleisskottel; vleisgereg; ~**-eating**, vleisetend; ~ **extract**, vleisekstrak; ~ **fly**, brommer; ~**-hook**, vleishaak; ~ **inspector**, vleisinspekteur, vleiskeurder; ~ **juice**, vleissap; ~ **less**, vleisloos; ~ **loaf**, vleisbrood; ~ **maggot**, vleismaaier; ~ **mallet**, vleishamer; ~ **market**, vleismark; ~ **meal**, vleismeel; ~**-offering**, spysoffer; ~ **packer**, vleisinmaker; ~ **paste**, vleissmeer; ~ **patty**, frikkadel; vleispasteitjie, vleiskoekie; ~ **pie**, vleispastei; ~ **plate**, platbord; ~ **roll**, vleisrol; ~ **safe**, vleiskas,

vlieëkas; ~ **salesman**, vleishandelaar; ~ **screen**, vlieëdeksel; ~ **skewer**, vleispen; ~ **slicer**, vleissnyer; ~ **stock**, vleisaftreksel; ~ **tenderizer**, vleissagmaker, vleisbeuker.
meat'us, (~, -es), buis, kanaal; opening.
meat'y, goed in die vleis; kragtig; vleisagtig; pittig, kernagtig.
Mecc'a, Mekka, heilige plek; mekka; kweekplek (fig.).
mechan'ic, werktuigkundige, meganikus; handwerksman, ambagsman.
mechan'ical, masjinaal, werktuiglik, werktuigkundig, masjien=, fabriekmatig, meganies; outomaties; ~ **draughtsman**, masjientekenaar; ~ **drawing**, lyntekene, masjientekene; ~ **engineer**, werktuigkundige ingenieur; ~ **engineering**, masjienbou, werktuigkunde; meganiese (werktuigkundige) ingenieurswese; ~ **excavator**, graafmasjien, hapmasjien; ~ **horse**, voorhaker, voorspanmotor; abbatrekker; ~ **jack**, masjiendomkrag; ~ **loader**, laaimasjien; ~ **ly**, meganies; sonder nadink; ~ **mixture**, mengsel; ~ **motor**, skakelmotor; ~ **ness**, werktuiglikheid; ~ **piano**, pianola; ~ **power**, meganiese krag; ~ **scraper**, skraapmasjien; ~ **science**, werktuigkunde; ~ **shovel**, hapmasjien; ~ **transport**, motordiens; motorvoertuig; motorvervoer, motorverkeer; ~ **unit**, werktuigkundige eenheid; ~ **workshop**, masjienwerkplaas; motorwerkswinkel.
mechani'cian, werktuigkundige, meganikus.
mechan'ics, werktuigkunde, masjienleer; meganika.
mech'anism, meganiek, meganisme; bou; masjinerie; toestel; meganistiese filosofie.
mech'anist, masjienbouer, tegnikus.
mechaniza'tion, meganisering, meganisasie.
mech'anize, meganiseer; ~ **d**, gemeganiseer(d).
Mech'lin, Mechelen; ~ **lace**, Mechelse kant.
mecon'ic: ~ **acid**, papawersuur, mekonsuur.
meco'nium, mekonium, babafeses.
med'al, gedenkpenning; medalje; *COMMEMORATIVE* ~, gedenkpenning; *the REVERSE (obverse) of the* ~, die keersy (voorsy) van die medalje; die ander kant v.d. saak; ~ **led**, vol medaljes; ~**l'ic**, medalje=; ~ **lion**, medaljon; gedenkpenning; ~**'lion portrait**, medaljonportret; ~ **list**, muntkenner; stempelsnyer, medaljesnyer; medalleur; bekroonde student; medaljehouer; ~ **lurgy**, penninggraveerkuns; ~ **play**, slagspel, houespel (gholf); ~ **round**, slagspelronde.
med'dle, jou bemoei (met), jou inlaat (met), torring aan, jou neus steek in; *DON'T* ~ *with it*, moenie daaraan torring (daaraan peuter) nie; ~ *WITH*, jou afgee met; jou inmeng met.
med'dler, loller, lolpot, bemoeial.
med'dlesome, bemoeisiek, orig; ~ **ness**, bemoeigees, bemoeisug.
med'dling, (n) inmenging; (a) = **meddlesome**.
Mede, Mediër; ~ **s**, Mede; *law of the* ~ *s and Persians*, 'n wet van Mede en Perse.
Med'ia[1], Medië
med'ia[2], (-e), media, stemhebbende ploɔief.
med'ia[3], (die) media, (die) massakommunikasiemedia (-middele).
Medi(a)ev'al, Middeleeus; ~ **farce**, sotternie; ~ **ism**, die gees van die Middeleeue, navolging van die Middeleeue; ~ **ist**, kenner (vereerder) van die Middeleeue.
med'ial, middel=; tussen=; gemiddeld; ~ **consonant**, tussenmedeklinker, -konsonant.
Med'ian[1], (n) Mediër; (a) Medies.
med'ian[2], (n) mediaan, middellyn; middelwaarde; (a) tussen=; middel=; mediaan=; ~ **line**, mediaan(lyn).
med'iant, middeltoon, mediant.
mediastin'um, (..na), middelvlies.
med'iate, (v) bemiddel, bemiddelend optree, tussenbei(de) kom; bewerk; ~ *BETWEEN two disputants*, bemiddel tussen twee rusiemakers; ~ *IN a dispute*, bemiddelend optree in 'n geskil; bemiddel; (a) middellik; ~ **ly**, middellik.
media'tion, bemiddeling, tussenkoms, voorspraak; tussenspraak, middelaarswerk.
me'diative, bemiddelend.
mediatiza'tion, mediatisasie, inlywing.

med'iatize, annekseer, mediatiseer, inlyf.
med'iator, (be)middelaar; voorspraak; ~ **'ial**, bemiddelend; ~**ship**, middelaarskap.
med'iatory, bemiddelend.
med'iatress, (-es), **med'iatrix**, (..trices), bemiddelaarster.
me'dic, dokter, medikus; mediese student.
me'dic(k), lusern, klawer.
med'icable, geneesbaar, geneeslik.
med'ical, (n) mediese student; (a) medies, geneeskundig; ~ *INSPECTOR of schools*, mediese skoolinspekteur, skooldokter; ~ *OFFICER of health*, stadsgeneesheer; geneeskundige beampte; ~ **adviser**, mediese (geneeskundige) adviseur; ~ **aid**, mediese (geneeskundige) hulp (bystand); ~ **aid society**, siekehulpvereniging; ~ **attendance**, mediese behandeling; ~ **benefit society**, mediese hulpvereniging, siekefonds, siektebystandsvereniging; ~ **book**, doktersboek; ~ **certificate**, doktersertifikaat, mediese sertifikaat; ~ **corps**, mediese diens; mediese korps; ~ **cross-vein**, middelste dwarsaar; ~ **examination**, mediese ondersoek; geneeskundige ondersoek; mediese eksamen; ~ **jurisprudence**, geregtelike geneeskunde, regsgeneeskunde; ~ **missionary**, sendingdokter; ~ **officer**, mediese offisier; ~ *officer of health*, gesondheidsbeampte; ~ **expenses**, doktersgeld, dokterskoste; ~ **fee**, doktersgeld; ~ **inspection**, mediese keuring; ~ **jurisprudence**, regsgeneeskunde, geregtelike geneeskunde, mediese reg; ~ **man**, dokter, medikus; ~ **pannier**, dokterskis; verbandmandjie; ~ **practitioner**, geneeskundige, arts, dokter, mediese praktisyn, geneesheer; ~ **profession**, beroep van dokter, mediese professie; ~ **report**, mediese verslag; ~ **school**, mediese skool; ~ **science**, geneeskunde; ~ **staff**, geneeskundige personeel; hospitaalpersoneel; geneeskundige staf (mil.); ~ **student**, mediese student, student in die medisyne; ~ **superintendent**, mediese direkteur, geneesheer-direkteur; ~ **training**, mediese (geneeskundige) opleiding; ~ **treatment**, doktersbehandeling, geneeskundige behandeling.
med'ically, medies; ~ **unfit**, liggaamlik (medies) ongeskik.
medic'ament, geneesmiddel, medikament.
med'icaster, kwal(salwer).
med'icate, geneeskundig behandel, dokter; geneeskundig toeberei.
med'icated, geneeskundig berei; geneeskragtig; ~ **coffee**, gesondheidskoffie; ~ **cotton-wool**, verbandwatte; ~ **lint**, verbandpluksel; ~ **paper**, sanitêre papier; ~ **soap**, geneeskragtige (medisinale) seep; ~ **water**, geneeskragtige (medisinale) water.
medica'tion, geneeskundige behandeling; geneeskundige bereiding.
med'icative, genesend.
Medice'an, van die Medici.
medi'cinal, geneeskragtig, genesend, medisinaal; ~ **herbs**, geneeskragtige kruie; ~**ly**, geneeskragtig; ~ **spring**, geneeskragtige bron.
med'icine, (n) medisyne, geneesmiddel; geneeskunde; toorgoed; *there is NO ~ against death*, vir die dood groei daar geen kruid nie; *STUDY ~* , in die medisyne studeer; *TAKE ~* , medisyne drink; *TAKE one's ~* , deur 'n suur appel byt; die pil sluk; (v) dokter, medisyne toedien; ~ **ball**, gimnastiekbal, medisynebal; ~ **bottle**, medisynefles(sie); ~ **chest**, medisynekassie, huisapteek, medisynetrommel; ~-**man**, toordokter; ~ **murder**, medisynemoord.
med'ico, (n) (-s), dokter, medikus, eskulaap; (a) medies=; ~-**botanical**, medies-botanies; ~-**legal**, regsgeneeskundig.
mediev'al = **medi(a)eval**.
med'iocre, middelmatig.
medioc'rity, (..ties), middelmatigheid.
med'itate, (oor)peins, oordink, oorweeg, nadink; planne maak, planne beraam.
medita'tion, oordenking, gemymer, gepeins, (oor)peinsing, nabetragting, meditasie.
med'itative, peinsend, nadenkend.
med'itator, peinser, denker.
mediterran'ean, middellands.

Mediterran'ean, (n): *the ~* , die Middellandse See; (a) Mediterraan, Mediterreens; ~ **climate**, Middellandse Seeklimaat, Mediterreense klimaat; ~ **race**, Mediterrane ras; ~ **Sea**, Middellandse See.
med'ium, (n) (..**dia, -s**), middel; medium; voertaal; tussenkoms; tussenstof, mengstof; gemiddelde; middelmaat; tussenpersoon; bindmiddel; tussensoort; middelgehalte (vee); *AT a ~* , gemiddeld; ~ *of EXCHANGE*, ruilmiddel; *THROUGH the ~ of*, deur bemiddeling (middel) van; (a) middelmatig; gemiddeld, middelslag=, deursnee=.
mediumis'tic, mediumisties, medium=.
med'ium: ~ **length**, gemiddelde lengte; ~ **price**, middelprys; ~-**sized**, middelmatig, taamlik, van middelbare grootte, halfslag=; ~-*sized apple*, halfslagappel; ~ **sweet**, mediumsoet, halfsoet, effens soet.
med'lar, mispel(boom).
med'ley, (n) (-s), allegaartjie, mengelmoes, deurmekaarspul, sneesvraggie, sameraapsel, mengeling; potpourri; (v) meng, deurmekaar maak; (a) gemeng, bont, deurmekaar.
Medoc', Medoc, rooi Boergondiese wyn.
medull'a, murg; pit; ~ **oblongata**, verlengde rugmurg; ~**ry**, murg=, murgagtig; ~**ry cavity**, murgholte; ~**ry ray**, murgstraal.
medull'in, murgstof.
Medus'a^1, Medusa.
medus'a^2, (-e, -s), jellievis, kwal; ~**'s head**, hondebos.
meed, beloning, loon, prys.
meek, sagmoedig, sagsinnig, nederig, ootmoedig, deemoedig, beskeie, gedwee; *as ~ as a LAMB*, so sag soos 'n lam; ~ *and MILD*, sagmoedig en gedwee; ~**ness**, sagsinnigheid, nederigheid, ootmoed, deemoed(igheid); ~-**spirited**, sagsinnig, sagmoedig.
meer'kat, meerkat.
meer'schaum, meerskuim.
meet, (n) byeenkoms; jaggeselskap; vergaderplek; (v) **(met)**, ontmoet; raakloop, teëkom, aantref; afhaal (by stasie); bymekaarkom, byeenkom; voldoen aan, bevredig; nakom, inwillig; mekaar sny (lyne); bestry; die hoof bied; voorsien; saamkom met; tref; ~ *with an ACCIDENT*, 'n ongeluk oorkom (kry); ~ *AGAIN*, weer sien; (mekaar) weer ontmoet; ~ *with APPROVAL*, die goedkeuring wegdra; *it ~s the CASE*, dis voldoende; dit voldoen aan die eise; ~ *one's DEATH*, sy dood vind; ~ *on EQUAL terms*, op gelyke voet mekaar ontmoet; ~ *EXPENSES*, onkoste dek; ~ *the EYE*, sigbaar word; in die oog kyk; *more is meant than ~s the EYE (EAR)*, daar steek meer agter as 'n mens sou dink; ~ *HALFWAY*, tegemoetkom; ~ *one's LIABILITIES*, jou verpligtings nakom; ~ *with a LOSS*, 'n verlies ly; ~ *the MARKET*, aan die aanvraag voldoen; ~ *OBJECTIONS*, besware weerlê; ~ *a PAYMENT*, 'n betaling voldoen; *PLEASED to ~ you*, bly om kennis te maak, bly u te ken(ne); ~ *PRICES*, meeding teen die prys; ~ *REQUIREMENTS*, aan die vereistes voldoen; ~ *with a REVERSE*, 'n teenslag kry; ~ *at the STATION*, by die stasie afhaal (ontmoet); ~ *TROUBLES halfway*, moeilikhede vooruitloop; ~ *all someone's WANTS*, in al iem. se behoeftes voorsien; (a) gepas, paslik, passend, geskik.
meet'ing, vergadering, byeenkoms; ontmoeting; samekoms; godsdiensoefening; wedstryd; kennismaking; *call a ~* , 'n vergadering belê; ~-**house**, bedehuis, kerk; vergadersaal; ~-**place**, versamelplek; vergaderplek.
megacephal'ic, groothoofdig, grootkoppig.
megaceph'aly, grootskedeligheid, grootkoppigheid.
meg'acycle, megaperiode.
me'gahertz, megahertz.
megalith'ic, gekenmerk deur groot klippe, megalities.
megaloman'ia, grootheidswaansin.
megalo'polis, megalopolis, reusestad, groot grootstad.
meg'aphone, (n) skeepsroeper, megafoon, spreektrompet, hardroeper; (v) deur 'n spreektrompet roep.
meg'ascope, megaskoop.
megascop'ic, megaskopies.

meg'aspore, megaspoor (bot.); makrospoor (dierk.).
megass(e)', uitgeperste suikerriet, bagasse ampas.
meg'aton, megaton.
meg'awatt, megawatt.
megg'er, isolasiemeter.
meg'ohm, megohm (elekt).
meg'rim¹, (skeel)hoofpyn, migraine; gril, luim; (pl) swaarmoedigheid; duiseligheid.
me'grim², flonder, platvis.
mei'nie, (arch.), familie; skare.
meio'sis, reduksiedeling, meiosis, meiose.
Meis'tersinger, (G.), meestersanger, Meistersinger.
melanchol'ia, swaarmoedigheid, droefgeestigheid, melancholie.
melanchol'ic, (n) swaarmoedige, melancholikus; (a) melancholiek, naargeestig.
mel'ancholy, (n) swaarmoedigheid, melancholie, naargeestigheid, somberheid, droefgeestigheid; swartgalligheid, weemoed, weemoedigheid; (a) swaarmoedig; droefgeestig, droewig; melancholies, neerslagtig, somber, swartgallig.
Melane'sia, Melanesië; ~**n**, (n) Melanesiër; (a) Melanesies.
melange', mengsel; melange; warboel.
me'lanin, melanien, melanine.
mel'anism, melanisme, donkerheid van kleur.
melanis'tic, melanisties.
mel'anite, melaniet.
melanos'is, melanose, swartsug.
mel'anous, donker, brunet=.
mel'ba finch, melbasyoie.
Mel'ba toast, dun roosterbrood, melbaroosterbrood.
mel'chite, melkiet.
mêlée', deurmekaar geveg; deurmekaar geworstel, deurmekaar gestoei, skermutseling, mêlée, gevegs= warreling.
melibe'an song, beurtsang.
mel'ic, sang=.
mel'ilite, meliliet.
mel'ilot, heuningklawer; plant v.d. geslag *Melilotus*
mel'inite, meliniet.
mel'iorate, versag, verbeter, beter word.
meliora'tion, verbetering, veredeling.
mel'iorative, verbeterend, versagtend, melioratief.
mel'iorism, meliorisme.
mel'iorist, melioris.
melior'ity, groter voortreflikheid.
melis'ma, melodiese musiek (wysie), melisma.
mellif'erous, heuningvoortbringend, heuninggewend.
mellif'luence, soetvloeiendheid.
mellif'luent, **mellif'luous**, soetvloeiend; heuningsoet.
melliph'agous, heuningetend.
mell'ite, heuningsteen, melliet.
mell'ow, (v) ryp word; sag maak; laat oud word, laat lê (wyn); versag; temper; (a) ryp, mals, soet, sappig; mollig; sag, vol, geryp, met die jare versag; beleë (drank); lekkerlyf, vrolik; getik, ~ *AGE*, ryp leeftyd; ~ *CIGAR*, ligte sigaar; ~ *WINE*, ou wyn, beleë wyn; mollige wyn; (adv) sag, saf; soet; vrolik; *be* ~ , sag wees; ~**ness**, sagtheid, malsheid; ryp= heid, beleënheid; ~**y**, sag, soet.
melod'eon, **melod'ion**, serafyn(orrel).
melod'ic, melodies, welluidend; ~**s**, melodieleer.
melod'ious, welluidend, soetvloeiend, skoonklin= kend, sangryk, melodies, sangerig; ~**ness**, soet= vloeiendheid, welluidendheid, sangrykheid.
mel'odist, sanger; liederkomponis.
mel'odize, 'n melodie maak; welluidend maak; meng.
melodra'ma, spektakelstuk, melodrama; ~**t'ic**, me= lodramaties; ~**tist**, skrywer van 'n melodrama; ~**tize**, tot 'n melodrama maak.
mel'ody, (. . **dies**), melodie, sangwysie, wysie; welluidendheid.
meloman'ia, versotheid op melodie, melomanie; ~**c**, melomaan.
mel'on, spanspek; *SWEET* ~ , spanspek; *WILD* ~ , kafferwaatlemoen; ~**-cutting**, buitverdeling.
melt, (n) smeltsel; gesmelte metaal; (v) (**-ed** or **molten**), smelt; versag; verteder, roer; oplos, verdwyn; ver= meng tot; ontdooi; ~ *AWAY*, wegsmelt; ~ *DOWN*, smelt; uitbraai; ~ *in the MOUTH*, in die mond smelt; ~ *into TEARS*, in trane wegsmelt; ~**er**, smelter.
mel'ting, (n) smelt(ing); vertedering; (a) smeltend; roerend, vertederend, smagtend; ~ *MOMENT*, aandoenlike oomblik; smeltkoekie; *in a* ~ *MOOD*, in 'n sagte luim; ~ **crucible**, smeltkroes; ~**-down**, omsmelting; (ver)smelting; ~**-furnace**, smeltoond; ~**-heat**, smelthitte; ~**-house**, smeltery; ~**-point**, smeltpunt; ~**-pot**, smeltkroes; *be in the* ~**-pot**, deur die smeltkroes gaan.
mel'ton, melton(stof).
mem'ber, lid (vereniging); lidmaat (kerk); deel, stuk, onderdeel; afgevaardigde; liggaamsdeel; ledemaat; *HONORARY* ~ , erelid; ~ *NATIONS*, lidlande (van V.V.O.); ~ *of PARLIAMENT*, parlements= lid; *the UNRULY* ~ , die onbedwingbare lid; die tong; ~ **body**, lidliggaam; ~ **church**, lidkerk; ~ **country**, lidland; ~**ed**, met lidmate; ~**ship**, lid= maatskap, ledetal; ~**ship card**, lidmaatskapkaart; ~**ship list**, ledelys; ~**ship fee**, ledegeld; toetredings= geld, intreegeld; ~ **state**, ledestaat, lidstaat.
membrana'ceous, vliesagtig.
mem'brane, vlies, weefsel; vel; perkamentblad.
membran'(e)ous, vlieserig, vliesagtig.
membrum viri'le, (L.), penis, membrum virile.
memen'to, (**-(e)s**), herinnering, memento, aanden= king; ~ *mori*, onthou (bedink) dat jy moet sterf.
mem'o, abbr. of **memorandum**.
mem'oir, gedenkskrif; verhandeling; (pl) lewens= beskrywing, memoires.
memorabil'ia, gedenkwaardighede, memorabilia.
memorabil'ity, gedenkwaardigheid, heuglikheid.
mem'orable, heuglik, gedenkwaardig; ~**ness** = **memorability**.
memoran'dum, (**-s**, . . **da**), memorandum; aanteke= ning; berig; ~ *of association*, akte van oprigting; ~ **book**, aantekeningboek; sakboekie; dagboek.
memor'ial, (n) gedenkstuk; gedenkteken; memorie; versoekskrif, adres, petisie; herinnering, gedagtenis, nota, aantekening; (pl) gedenkstukke; (a) gedenk=; gedagtenis=, herinnerings=, herdenkings=; ~ **cere= mony**, herdenkingsfees; ~ **day**, gedenkdag; ~**ist**, petisionaris; skrywer van gedenkskrifte; ~**ize**, 'n memorie indien; petisioneer; herdenk, vier; ~ **ser= vice**, gedenkdiens; ~ **tablet**, gedenksteen; gedenk= plaat.
memoria tech'nica, (L.), geheuehulp, memoria technica.
mem'orize, memoriseer, uit die hoof leer, van buite leer; te boek stel.
mem'ory, (. . **ries**), geheue; aandenking, nagedagte= nis; herinnering; *BLESSED (happy)* ~ , saliger ge= dagtenis; *CALL to* ~ , jou te binne roep; *COMMIT to* ~ , van buite leer, uit die hoof leer; *my* ~ *is playing me FALSE*, my geheue begin my parte speel; *IN* ~ *of*, ter gedagtenis aan (van); *KEEP in* ~ , in die gedagte hou; *within LIVING* ~ , sinds (sedert) menseheugenis; *have a LONG* ~ , 'n goeie geheue hê; *PLAY from* ~ , uit die hoof (kop) speel; *REPEAT from* ~ , uit die hoof opsê; *SACRED to the* ~ *of*, gewy aan die nagedagtenis van; *have a SHORT* ~ , kort van gedagte wees; *STAMP some= thing in one's* ~ , iets in jou oor knoop; *WITHIN the* ~ *of man*, sover die mense kan onthou, sinds menseheugenis; ~ **aid**, eselsbrug, geheuebrug; ~ **training**, geheue-oefening; geheueleer; ~ **work**, geheuewerk.
mem'sahib, memsahib, getroude Europese vrou.
men, mans; mense, werkers; manne (soldate); *so many* ~ , *so many minds*, soveel hoofde, soveel sinne; ~ *only*, slegs mans; *kyk* **man**, (n).
men'ace, (n) (be)dreiging, dreigement; (v) (be)dreig; ~**r**, bedreiger.
men'acing, dreigend, onheilspellend.
ménage', huishouding, bestuur (van 'n huis, ens.); menasie.
mena'gerie, diereversameling, menagerie; dieretuin.
menar'che, menarg, eerste menstruasie.
mend, (n) stopplek, lapplek, reparasie; lasplek; *on the* ~ , aan die beterhand; op weg om gesond te word; (v) heelmaak, lap, regmaak, opknap, verstel, repa= reer; verbeter; beter word (sieke); skerp maak; stop

mendacious 1044 merciful

(kouse); las; ~ *or END*, verbeter of afskaf; ~ *the FIRE*, sit brandgoed op die vuur; *it is never too LATE to* ~, dit is nooit te laat om iets reg te maak nie; dit is nooit te laat om 'n beter weg in te slaan nie; ~ *one's MANNERS*, jou maniere verbeter; ~ *one's PACE*, gou maak, jou pas versnel, aanstap; ~ *one's WAYS*, jou lewe verbeter; ~ **able**, verbeterbaar; lapbaar; herstelbaar.
menda'cious, leuenagtig, vals.
menda'city, leuenagtigheid, valsheid, leuen.
mendele'vium, mendelevium.
Mendel'ian, (n) Mendeliaan; (a) Mendeliaans.
Men'delism, Mendelisme.
mend'er, heelmaker; hersteller; stopper; *invisible* ~, fynstopper.
mend'icancy, bedelary; armoede.
men'dicant, (n) bedelaar; bedelmonnik; (a) bedelend; bedelaars=; bedel=; ~ **friar**, bedelmonnik; ~ **order**, bedelorde.
mendi'city, bedelary; die bedelaars.
mend'ing, verbetering; (die) heelmaak; verstelgoed; verstelwerk, herstelwerk; reparasie; stopwol; lapen stopwerk; *invisible* ~, fynstopwerk; ~ **basket**, stopmandjie.
mendo'zite, mendoziet.
men'folk, mans, mansmense.
menhad'en, Amerikaanse marsbanker *(Breevoortia tyrannus)*.
men'hir, suil, menhir (argeologie).
men'ial, (n) bediende, diensbode, kneg, ondergeskikte; (a) diensbaar; slaafs; ondergeskik; laag, gering; onterend, gemeen.
Men'in, Mene.
menin'geal, harsingvlies=.
meningit'is, harsingvliesontsteking, meningitis; *CEREBRAL* ~, harsingvliesontsteking; *SPINAL* ~, rugmurgvliesontsteking.
men'inx, (meninges), harsingvlies(e), meninks.
menis'cus, (..ci), meniskus, halfmaanlens.
Men'nonism, Mennonisme.
Menn'onite, (n) Doopsgesinde, Mennoniet; (a) Doopsgesind, Mennonities.
menol'ogy, (Griekse) heilige kalender, menologie.
men'opause, lewensoorgang, menopouse.
meno'rah, menora, sewearmkandelaar.
menorrha'gia, vloeiing, oormatige bloeding, menorragie.
men'sal[1], maandeliks.
men'sal[2], tafel=.
men's: ~ **clothes**, mansklere; ~ **doubles**, mansdubbelspel.
men'ses, menstruasie, maandstonde.
Men'shevik, Mensjewiek.
Men'shevist, (n) Mensjewis; (a) Mensjewisties.
mens rea, (L., jur.), mens rea, misdadige voorneme (handeling).
men's: ~ **singles**, mansenkelspel; ~ **shoes**, manskoene.
men'strual, maandeliks; menstruasie=, menstruaal.
mens'truate, menstrueer, maandsiek wees.
menstrua'tion, maandstonde, menstruasie, maandsiekte, verandering.
men'struous = **menstrual**.
men'struum, (..strua), oplosmiddel, oplossende middel, menstruüm.
mensurabil'ity, meetbaarheid.
men'surable, meetbaar, begrens; met vaste tyd.
men'sural, meet=, maat=; met vaste ritme.
men'surate, meet, afmeet.
mensura'tion, meting, opmeting, uitmeting, meet, meetkuns.
men's' wear, mansdrag; manslere.
men'tal[1], (n) swaksinnige; (a) geestelik, verstandelik; geestes=, mentaal.
men'tal[2], (a) ken=, v.d. ken.
men'tal: ~ **agony**, sielsangs, sielepyn, sielskwelling; ~ **arithmetic**, hoofrekene; ~ **condition**, geestesgesteldheid; ~ **confusion**, begripsverwarring; ~ **defect**, geestesgebrek; ~ **defective**, swaksinnige; ~ **deficiency**, swaksinnigheid; ~ **derangement**, geestesverwarring, sielsiekte; ~ **disease**, sielsiekte; ~ **distress**, sielsverdriet; ~ **experience**, geestelike ervaring, sielservaring; ~ **faculties**, geesvermoëns; ~ **gymnastics**, harsinggimnastiek; ~ **healer**, geestelike geneser; ~ **healing**, geestelike genesing; ~ **health**, geestesgesondheid; ~ **hospital**, kranksinnigegestig, sielsieke-inrigting; ~ **hygiene**, geestes= higiëne; ~ **indisposition**, geestesongesteldheid; ~ **institution**, sielsiekegestig; ~ **ism**, mentalisme; ~ '**ity**, geestesgesteldheid; verstand; geeskrag; mentaliteit.
men'tally, geestelik, verstandelik; uit die hoof; by jouself; ~ *DEFICIENT*, swaksinnig, geestelik minderwaardig; ~ *DERANGED*, sielsiek; ~ *ILL*, sielsiek; ~ *RETARDED*, vertraag.
men'tal: ~ **patient**, sielsieke; ~ **power**, geeskrag; ~ **prayer**, stil gebed; ~ **reading**, stillees; ~ **reservation**, heimlike voorbehoud; ~ **state**, geestestoestand; ~ **test**, verstandstoets; ~ **work**, kopwerk, dinkwerk.
menta'tion, geestestoestand; geesteswerksaamheid.
men'thol, mentol.
men'thyl, mentiel.
men'tion, (n) (ver)melding, aanroering, gewag; *AT the* ~ *of*, by vermelding van; *HONOURABLE* ~, eervolle vermelding; *MAKE no* ~ *of*, geen melding maak nie van; *WORTHY of* ~, vermeldenswaardig; (v) (ver)meld, noem; rep, gewag; maak van, aanroer; aangee; ~*ed in DISPATCHES*, eervol vermeld; *DON'T* ~ *it!*, tot u diens!, nie te dankie nie!; *please DON'T* ~ *it*, moet asseblief nie daarvan melding maak nie; *NOT to* ~, wat nog te sê; laat staan; *not WORTH* ~*ing*, nie die moeite werd nie; ~ **able**, noemenswaardig, meldenswaardig.
men'tor, raadgewer, mentor, gids; ~**ship**, mentorskap.
men'u, spyskaart, spyslys, menu.
Mephistophele'an = **Mephistophelian**.
Mephistoph'eles, Mefistofeles.
Mephistophel'ian, Mefistofelies, Satanies, duiwels, verleidend.
mephit'ic, stinkend, verpestend.
mephit'is, verpestende uitwaseming, mefitis.
meph'itism, verpesting van die lug.
mer'cantile, handels=, koopmans=, kommersieel, merkantiel; baatsugtig; ~ **arithmetic**, handelsreken(e); ~ **code**, handelswetboek; ~ **law**, handelsreg; ~ **marine**, handelsvloot, handelskeepvaart; ~ **pursuits**, handelsonderneming(s); ~ **school**, handelskool; ~ **system**, handelstelsel; ~ **theory**, merkantiele teorie; ~ **town**, handelstad.
merc'antilism, handelsgees, merkantilisme.
merc'antilist, merkantilis.
mercap'tan, merkaptaan.
Mercat'or's projection, Mercator se projeksie.
mer'cenariness, winssug, geldbejag.
mer'cenary, (n) (..ries), huursoldaat; huurling; (a) omkoopbaar, veil; gehuur; baatsugtig, inhalig; ~ **arm**, huurleër; ~ **marriage**, huwelik om geld; ~ **troops**, huurtroepe.
mer'cer, tekstielhandelaar, handelaar in sy- en wolstowwe; ~**ize**, materiaal berei vir die verf, merceri= seer; ~**ized**, gemerceriseer; ~**ized cotton**, garekant; namaaksy; ~**y**, (die) handel in sy- en wolstof, weefstofhandel; tekstielware.
merch'andise, (n) (negosie)goed, (handels)ware, koopware; verkoop; (v) verhandel, handel dryf; ~**r**, handelaar.
merch'andizing, (die) handeldrywe, verkoop; verkoopkuns; bevoorrading.
merch'ant, (n) winkelier, handelaar, koopman; (a) handels=, koopmans=; ~ **able**, verhandelbaar, verkoopbaar; ~ **bank**, aksepbank; ~ **cruiser**, koopvaartkruiser; ~ **flag**, koopvaardyvlag, handelsvlag; ~ **fleet**, handelsvloot, koopvaardyvloot; ~**man**, koopvaardyskip, handelskip, handelsvaartuig; ~ **marine**, handelsvloot; ~ **navy** = **merchant fleet**; ~ **prince**, handelsvors, handelsprins; ~**ry**, handel; ~**seaman**, matroos op 'n handelskip; ~ **service**, handelsvloot; handelsdiens; ~-**tailor**, handelaarsnyer; ~ **warfare**, handelsoorlog.
mer'ciful, genadig, barmhartig, mededoënd, medelydend; ~**ly**, genadiglik; ~**ness**, mededoëndheid, barmhartigheid.

mer'ciless, onbarmhartig, meedoënloos, ongenadig, wreed, hard; ~ **ness**, wreedheid, hardheid.
mer'colized wax, merkolwas.
mercur'ial¹, (n) kwikmiddel; (a) kwiksilweragtig; kwiksilwer=; lewendig; veranderlik.
Mercur'ial², (a) Mercurius=.
mercur'ial: ~ **barometer**, kwikbarometer, bakbarometer; ~ **disposition**, lewendige geaardheid, kwiksilweragtige temperament; ~**ism**, kwikvergiftiging; ~ **'ity**, lewendigheid; veranderlikheid; ~**ize**, met kwiksilwer behandel; ~ **ointment**, kwiksalf, ruitersalf; ~ **thermometer**, kwiktermometer.
mercur'ian, kwikhoudend.
mercur'ic, kwiksilweragtig, kwik=; kwikhoudend; lewendig; ~ *compounds*, kwikverbindings.
merc'urize, kwik byvoeg.
Merc'ury¹, Mercurius; bode; gids.
merc'ury², kwiksilwer, kwik; lewendigheid; ~ **barometer**, bakbarometer, kwikbarometer; ~ **fulminate**, slagkwik; ~ **ointment**, kwiksalf; ~ **vapour**, kwikdamp.
mer'cy, (..cies), genade, genadigheid, barmhartigheid; vergif(fe)nis; seën; geluk; ontferming; *be AT the ~ of*, aan die genade oorgelewer wees van; *BEG for ~*, om genade smeek; *HAVE ~ upon us*, wees ons genadig; ontferm u oor ons; *for ~ 's SAKE*, om Godswil; *SISTER of ~*, suster van barmhartigheid, liefdesuster; *left to the TENDER mercies of*, oorgelaat aan die willekeur van; *THANKFUL for small mercies*, dankbaar vir klein gunstes, vir geringe seëninge dankbaar wees; *THAT is a ~*, dis 'n geluk (seën); *THROWN on someone's ~*, aan iem. se genade oorgelewer; *WORK of ~*, werk van barmhartigheid; ~**-seat**, versoendeksel, genadetroon.
mere¹, (n) meer; vlei.
mere², (n) grens(paal).
mere³, (a, adv) eenvoudig, enkel, louter, suiwer, bloot, maar net; *by the ~st CHANCE*, net deur toeval; *a ~ CHILD*, 'n pure kind; 'n bogkind; *the ~ FACT*, die blote feit; ~**ly**, alleen, maar, slegs, net, blootweg, enkel.
meretri'cious, ontugtig, hoeragtig, verlokkend; opsigtig, opvallend; bedrieglik, skoonskynend, voorgewend, vals; ~ **ness**, hoeragtigheid, ontugtigheid; onegtheid, opsigtigheid.
mergan'ser, duikergans.
merge, indompel, (laat) sink; ondergaan, versink; (in= een)smelt; *BE ~d in*, opgaan in; ~ *INTO the traffic stream*, by die verkeerstroom aansluit.
mer'ger, saamsmelting (van maatskappye), fusie.
mer'icarp, deelvruggie.
merid'ian, (n) middaglyn, meridiaan; middaghoogte; hoogtepunt, toppunt; peil; middagsirkel, lengtesirkel; ~ *of the globe*, kopermeridiaan; (a) hoogste, middag=; hoogte=; ~ **altitude**, middaghoogte, meridiaanshoogte.
merid'ional, (n) suiderling; (a) suidelik, meridionaal, middag=; ~ **distance**, lengteverskil; ~ **'ity**, suidwaartse ligging (rigting), meridionaliteit.
meri'fic, wonderbaarlik, verbasingwekkend.
meringue', meringue, skuimpie, skuimkoekie; ~ **top**, skuimkop.
meri'no, (-s), merino(skaap), mof; ~ **sheep**, merinoskaap, mofskaap; ~ **wool**, merinowol.
me'ristem, meristeem, teelweefsel.
me'rit, (n) verdienste; waarde, verdienstelikheid, voortreflikheid; meriete; eer; *ACCORDING to ~*, volgens verdienste; *the ~s of a CASE*, die wesenlike waarde (meriete) van 'n saak; *the ~s and DEMERITS*, die voor en teen; *someone of GREAT ~*, iem. van groot verdienste; *MAKE a ~ of necessity*, v.d. nood 'n deug maak; *have NO ~*, sonder verdienste wees; *NOT without ~*, nie onverdienstelik nie; *ON its (own) ~s*, op sigself, op eie meriete; *ORDER of M~*, Orde van Verdienste; *the painting is WITHOUT ~*, die skilderstuk is waardeloos; (v) werd wees, verdien; aanspraak hê op; *more than is ~ed*, bo verdienste; ~**-certificate**, kaart van goeie gedrag; ~**ed**, welverdiend.
merito'cracy, meritokrasie.
merito'rious, verdienstelik; ~ *service*, voortreflike diens; ~ **ness**, verdienstelikheid, lofwaardigheid.

mer'it rating, prestasieloon; verdienstebepaling; merietegradering.
merle, merel.
merl'in, merlyn, steenvalk.
merl'ing, wyting (vis).
merl'on, merloen.
merm'aid, meermin, waternooi(e)ntjie, seevrou.
merm'an, (..men), meerman.
mero'tomy, kliewing, merotomie.
Merovin'gian, (n) Merowinger; (a) Merowingies.
me'rrily, vrolik, opgeruimd, plesierig, lekker.
me'rriment, vrolikheid, plesier(igheid), pret, opgeruimdheid.
me'rriness, vrolikheid, plesierigheid.
me'rry, vrolik, plesierig, spelerig, lewendig; getik, lekker; *BE ~*, lekker wees; *a ~ CHRISTMAS*, 'n geseënde Kersfees; *as ~ as a CRICKET (grig)*, *as ~ as the DAY is long*, so vrolik soos 'n voël in die lug; *~ is the FEAST-MAKING till we come to the reckoning*, na vrolikheid kom olikheid; *MAKE ~*, vrolik wees, pret maak, feesvier; *make ~ WITH*, die gek skeer met; ~ **andrew**, grapmaker, hanswors; ~**-go-round**, mallemeule; ~**-maker**, pierewaaier, plesiermaker; ~**-making**, fees, vrolikheid, pretmakery; fuif, feesvreugde, gejol; ~ **thought**, geluksbeentjie.
me'sa, mesa, tafelland(skap); tafelberg.
mésall'iance, mésalliance (huwelik benede iem. se stand).
mescal', meskal (*Lophophora williamsii)*; ~ **button**, meskalknopie.
mescal'ine, meskalien, meskaline.
mesdames, *kyk* **madame**.
meseems', dit lyk my.
mesembryan'themum, vygie.
mesence'phalon, middelharsings, middelbrein.
mesente'ric, tot die dermvlies behorende, mesenteries, dermband=.
mesenterit'is, dermvliesontsteking, mesenteritis.
mes'entery, dermvlies, dermskeil, mesenterium.
mesh, (n) (-es), netwerk, oog, maas; strik, val; skakel= (rat); *size of ~*, maaswydte; (v) in 'n net vang; inskakel, inmekaargryp, ingryp (ratte); pas; inkam; verstrik; knoop; ~ **connection**, driehoekskakeling; ~ **paper**, netpapier; ~ **stockings**, maaskouse; ~ **weave**, maasbinding; driehoekskakeling; ~ **wire**, maasdraad; ~ **work**, netwerk; ~**y**, vol gate; geknoop.
mes'ial, middel=.
mesme'ric, mesmeries.
mes'merism, mesmerisme, hipnose; hipnotiese toestand.
mes'merist, mesmeris, hipnotiseur.
mes'merize, mesmeriseer, hipnotiseer; betower.
mesne, tussenkomend, tussen=; ~ **lord**, onderleenheer, agterleenheer; ~ **process**, tussenproses; ~ **tenure**, agterleen.
me'soblast, mesoblas(t).
me'socarp, mesokarp, middelvrugwandlaag.
mesolith'ic, mesolities.
mes'ophyll, bladmoes, blaarmoes.
Mesopotam'ia, Mesopotamië; ~**n**, (n) Mesopotamiër; (a) Mesopotamies.
mesosom'a, middelstuk.
me'sosphere, mesosfeer.
me'son, meson.
Mesozo'ic, Mesosoïes.
mes'quite, mesquite, meskiet, muskiet(boom) *(Nahuati mizquiti)*.
mess, (n) gereg, gemeenskaplike tafel; wanorde, janboel, grouspul, gebrou, deurmekaar spul; smeerboel, rommel; vuilgoed; vuilheid; spyse, voedsel; bak (op skip); menasie (op land of by die leër); *GET oneself into a ~*, jou allerhande moeilikhede op die hals haal; *MAKE a ~ of things*, sake verknoei; *a ~ of POTTAGE*, 'n bord lensiesop; (v) mors; saameet; voer; knoei; verknoei; verwar; besmeer; ~ *ABOUT*, rondvroetel; foeter met; rondpeuter; ~ *UP*, bederf; besmeer; in die war bring; verknoei; ~ *WITH*, saameet met; lol met; ~ **account**, menasierekening.
mess'age, (n) boodskap, berig; *BEAR a ~*, 'n bood=

skap bring; *GO on a* ~, 'n boodskap doen; (v) be=
rig, 'n boodskap oorsein, laat weet.
mess: ~ **boy,** bakseun; ~ **book,** menasieboek (op
land); bakboek (op skip); ~ **cook,** bakskok (skip);
~ **deck,** baksdek, bak; ~ **dress,** tafeltenue.
mess'enger, boodskapper; loopjong; afgesant, koe=
rier; rapportganger; haaltou; ~ *of the court,* ge=
regsbode; ~ **boy,** telegrambesteller; loopjong,
boodskapseun; ~ **pigeon,** posduif; ~ **service,**
bodediens.
mess'er, morsjors, morspot.
Messi'ah, Messias.
Messian'ic, Messiaans.
messieurs', menere, here.
mess'ing, tafelgeleentheid (op land); bakgeleentheid
(op skip); tafelgeld, menasiegeld; ~ **allowance,** ta=
felgeld, voedseltoelae.
mess: ~ **jacket,** tafelbaadjie, tafeluniform; ~ **kit,** ta=
feltenue; ~**mate,** tafelmaat, tafelgenoot (op land);
bakmaat (op skip); ~ **orderly,** menasiesoldaat, me=
nasieordonnans (op land); bakseun (op skip); ~
room, eetsaal, menasie.
Messrs., Menere; firma; ~ *A and B,* die firma A en B;
mnre. A en B, die here A en B.
mess: ~ **rules,** menasiereglement; ~ **table,** eettafel,
menasietafel (op land); baktafel (op skip); ~ **tent,**
eettent (op land); baktent (op skip); ~ **tin,** eetblik.
mess'uage, opstal, huis met erf en buitegeboue.
mess'-up, verwarde toestand; flater, warboel, ge=
mors; *things are now in a proper* ~, nou is dit 'n
regte gemors.
mess'y, morsig, smerig; wanordelik.
mesti'zo, (-s), halfbloed, mesties, mestizo.
metabol'ic, stofwisselend, metabolies.
metab'olism, stofwisseling, metabolisme.
metab'olize, verwerk; metaboliseer.
metacarp'al, (n) middelhandbeen; (a) middelhand=.
metacarp'us, middelhand, metacarpus.
met'age, (die) weeg; weegloon; meting; meetgeld.
metagen'esis, metagenese, generasiewisseling.
met'al, (n) metaal; brons, geskutmetaal; steengruis;
verharding, verhardsel; kunsbaan; skeepsgeskut;
(pl) spoorstawe; treinspoor; *BASE* ~, onedele me=
taal; *LEAVE the* ~*s,* ontspoor; *PRECIOUS* ~,
edele metaal; (v) **(-led),** beklee (skip); pad uitlê; ver=
hard; metalliseer; metaal ingiet; ~*led road,* klip=
gruispad; (a) metaal=; ~ **coating,** metaallaag; ~ **fa=
tigue,** metaaluitputting; ~**-filament lamp,** metaal=
draadlamp.
me'ta language, metataal.
metall'ic, metaalagtig, metaal=, metallies; ~ **alloy,**
metaallegering; ~ **currency,** goud- of silwergeld; ~
fouling, metaalvuil; ~ **lustre,** metaalglans; ~ **pack=
ing,** metaalpakking; ~ **poisoning,** metaalvergifti=
ging; ~ **sound,** metaalklank; ~ **vein,** metaalaar; ~
voice, metaalstem; ~ **water,** mineraalwater.
met'al: ~ **lif'erous,** metaalhoudend; ~**l'iform,** me=
taalagtig; ~**line,** metaal=, metaalagtig; ~**line wa=
ter,** mineraalwater; ~**ling,** verharding; ~**lism,** me=
tallisme; ~**list,** metaalwerker; *gold (silver)* ~*list,*
voorstander van die goudstandaard (silwerstan=
daard); ~**iza'tion,** metallisasie, metallisering;
~**lize,** metalliseer (van hout); vulkaniseer (gomlas=
tiek); ~**log'raphy,** metaalbeskrywing; ~**loid,** (n)
metalloïed, metalloïde, halfmetaal; (a) metaalag=
tig; ~**lur'gic,** metallurgies; ~**l'urgist,** metaalbewer=
ker, metaalkenner; metallurgis; ~**l'urgy,** metaal=
kennis; metallurgie; ~ **mirror,** metaalspieël; ~
rolling-mill, plettery; ~ **rule,** metaalduimstok; ~
saw, metaalsaag, ystersaag; ~ **sheet,** metaalplaat;
~ **ware,** metaalware; ~ **wire,** metaaldraad; ~
work, metaalwerk; ~ **worker,** metaalwerker.
metamorph'ic, metamorfies, metamorf.
metamorph'ism, gedaanteverandering, metamorfis=
me, metamorfose.
metamorph'ose, omskep, (van gedaante) verander,
metamorfoseer.
metamorph'osis, (..ses), gedaanteverandering, vorm=
verandering, metamorfose; *undergo a* ~, van ge=
daante verander; 'n gedaanteverwisseling onder=
gaan.
met'aphor, metafoor; beeldspraak, ~**'ic(al),** figuur=

lik, oordragtelik, metafories; ~**'ically,** figuurlik,
metafories.
met'aphrase, (n) woordelike vertaling; (v) woordelik
vertaal.
metaphys'ical, metafisies; bonatuurlik.
metaphysi'cian, metafisikus.
metaphys'ics, metafisika.
met'aplasm, metaplasma.
metapol'itics, metapolitiek, abstrakte politiek.
metas'tasis, (..tases), stofwisseling; metastase; vorm=
verandering.
metatars'al, (n) voetwortel; (a) voetwortel=.
metatars'us, middelvoet.
metath'esis, metatesis, letteromsetting, klank=
omsetting.
metazo'an, metasoön.
mete, (n) maat; grens; baken; maatstaf; (v) meet, uit=
meet; *JUSTICE was* ~*d out,* volle reg is gedoen; ~
OUT, uitdeel, toedien; *TREATMENT* ~*d out to
someone,* behandeling wat iem. ten deel geval het.
metempsychos'is, sielsverhuising, metempsigose.
met'eor, vallende ster, skietster; meteoor; lug=
verskynsel; dwaallig.
meteor'ic, meteooragtig, meteories, skitterend, ver=
blindend; bliksemsnel; ~ *CAREER,* skitterende
loopbaan; ~ *SHOWER,* sterrereën; ~ *STONE,*
meteoorklip.
met'eor: ~**ite,** meteoorsteen, meteoriet; ~**ogram,**
meteorogram; ~**ograph,** meteorograaf; ~**oid,** me=
teoroïed, vallende ster; ~**olite,** meteoorsteen, me=
teoroliet.
meteorolog'ical, weerkundig, meteorologies; ~ **bur=
eau,** ~ **office,** weerburo; ~ **report,** weerberig; ~
station, weerstasie, weerkundige stasie.
meteorol'ogist, weerkundige, meteoroloog.
meteorol'ogy, weerkunde, meteorologie.
met'er, (n) meter; meetapparaat; (v) meet; ~ **age,** me=
ting; meetloon; meterlesing; ~**ed:** ~*ed calls,* getel=
de oproepe; ~ **girl,** metermeisie, boetebessie; ~ **in=
spector,** meterinspekteur; ~ **maid,** boetebessie, me=
terjuf, metermeisie; ~**-reader,** meteropnemer, me=
terleser; ~**-reading,** meterstand.
meth'ane, moerasgas, metaan.
methinks', (..thought), dit lyk my, soos dit my lyk
(voorkom); ek dink.
meth'od, metode, manier, wyse; leerwyse, werkwyse;
reëlmaat, sisteem, stelsel; *there is* ~ *in his madness,*
hy is nie so gek as wat hy lyk nie; ~ *of APPROXI=
MATION,* benaderingsmetode; ~ *of CON=
STRUCTION,* boumetode; ~ *of OBSERVA=
TION,* waarnemingsmetode.
method'ic(al), metodies, sistematies, stelselmatig.
method'ics, metodiek.
Meth'odist, Metodisme.
Meth'odist, (n) Metodis; (a) Metodisties; ~ **Church,**
Metodistekerk.
Methodis'tic, Metodisties.
methodis'tic, metodisties.
meth'odize, metodies orden, rangskik.
methodolog'ical, metodologies.
methodol'ogy, metodeleer, metodiek, metodologie.
Methu'selah, Metusalem; *as old as* ~, so oud soos
Metusalem.
meth'yl, metiel (skeik.); ~ **alcohol,** houtgees, metiel=
alkohol.
meth'ylate, met metiel meng; ~*d spirits,* brand=
spiritus.
me'tic, metoikos, vreemdeling.
metic'ulous, oorangsvallig, besonder nougeset, bene=
pe, peuterig-presies; ~**ness,** puntene(u)righeid,
nougesetheid.
métier', beroep, metier.
me'tif, metief, kwartbloed.
mét'is, halfbloed, mesties.
me'tol, metol.
meton'ic, maan=; ~ **cycle,** maansirkel.
metonym'ic(al), metonimies.
me'tonym, metoniem.
meton'ymy, metonimie, oornoeming, naamwisseling.
me'tope, metoop.
me'tre¹, versmaat, digmaat, metrum.
me'tre², meter (lengtemaat).

met'ric, metriek.
met'rical, metries, in verse; ~ *art*, metriek.
met'rically[1]**,** metries, in verse.
met'rically[2]**,** metries, volgens die metrieke stelsel.
me'tricate, metriseer.
metrica'tion, metrisering.
met'ricize, metriseer.
met'ricks, versleer, metriek.
met'ric: ~ **system,** metrieke (tiendelige) stelsel; ~ **ton,** skeepston.
metri'tis, metritis, baarmoederontsteking.
met'rograph, metrograaf.
metrolog'ical, metrologies.
metrol'ogist, metroloog.
metrol'ogy, metrologie, maat-en-gewigsleer.
met'ronome, metronoom, takmeter.
metronom'ic, metronoom=, metronomies.
metron'omy, metronomie, takmeting.
metrop'olis, (-es) hoofstad, moederstad, metropool, wêreldstad, metropolis, grootstad.
metropol'itan, (n) metropolitaan; aartsbiskop; stedeling; (a) hoofstedelik; metropolitaans; aartsbiskoplik; ~ **area,** stadsgebied, metropolitaanse gebied.
metropol'itanate, aartsbisdom.
metropol'itan: ~ **church,** hoofkerk; ~ **city,** metropool, metropolis.
metrorrha'gia, metrorragie, baarmoederbloeiing.
met'tle, ywer, moed; fut, vuur, gees, energie; *BE on one's* ~, op jou stukke wees; *HORSE of* ~, vurige perd; *a MAN of* ~, 'n pure man, 'n staatmaker; *PUT a person on his* ~, iem. laat wys wat hy kan doen; *SHOW one's* ~, wys uit watter hout jy gesny is; jou uiterste bes doen; *TRY a person's* ~, sien wat 'n man kan doen; iem. al sy kragte laat inspan; ~ **d,** ~ **some,** vurig, ywerig, driftig.
Meuse, Maas.
mew[1]**,** (n) valkhok; (v) toesluit, in die hok sit.
mew[2]**,** (n) gemiaau; (v) miaau.
mew[3]**,** (n) meeu.
mewl, kerm, kreun, grens; ~ **er,** skreeulelik; grensbalie; ~ **ing,** grensery.
mews, stel stalle, stalling, stal.
Mex'ican, (n) Mexikaan; (a) Mexikaans; ~ **aloe,** garingboom; ~ **hawthorn,** skaapvrug; ~ **marigold,** stinkkakiebos(sie) *(Tagetis minuta);* ~ **poppy,** bloudissel, blouduiwel, steekbossie *(Argenone mexicana).*
Mex'ico, Mexiko.
me'zzanine, tussenverdieping; verdieping onder die toneel; ~ **floor,** tussenvloer.
me'zzo, mezzo=, half=, tussen=; ~ **soprano,** mezzosopraan; ~ **tint,** (n) mezzotint; swartkuns; (v) in mezzotint graveer.
mi, mi (musiek).
miaow', (n, v), miaau.
mi'asm, (-s), mias'ma, (-ta, -s), miasma, smetstof.
miasmat'ic, malariaagtig, miasmaties.
miaul', miaau.
mic'a, mika, glimmer.
mica'ceous, mikaägtig, glimmeragtig, glinsterend.
Mic'ah, Miga.
mic'anite, mikaniet.
mic'a plate, mikaplaat.
mice, *kyk* **mouse.**
Mich'aelmas, die fees van St. Michiel; ~ **holiday(s),** Septembervakansie (Eng.).
mic'key, mic'ky: *take the* ~ *(out of)*, sonder respek behandel.
Mic'key (Finn), mickey finn, sterk alkoholiese drankie (met verdowingsmiddel in), slaapdrank(ie).
mic'kle, (n) grootheid; grootte; *many a* ~ *makes a muckle*, alle bietjies help; elke dag 'n draadjie is 'n hempsmou in 'n jaar; baie kleintjies baar 'n grote; (a) baie groot.
mic'robe, mikrobe.
microb'ial, mikrobies.
microb'ic, mikrobies; vol mikrobes.
microbiolog'ical, mikrobiologies.
microbio'logist, mikrobiologies.
microbio'logy, mikrobiologie.
microcephal'ic, kleinhoofdig, kleinskedelig.
microceph'alous, kleinhoofdig, kleinskedelig.

microchem'istry, mikrochemie.
mic'rocosm, die wêreld in die klein, mikrokosmos; die mens.
microcos'mic, mikrokosmies, klein; ~ **salt,** fosforsout.
mic'rocrith, mikrokriet.
mic'rofilm, (n) mikrofilm; (v) 'n mikrofilm maak; op mikrofilm opneem, vermikrofilm, mikroverfilm.
microgran'ite, mikrograniet.
mic'rolite[1]**, mic'rolith,** mikroliet.
mic'rolite[2]**,** muggievliegtuig, mikrovliegtuig.
microlog'ic, mikrologies.
microl'ogist, mikroloog.
microl'ogy, mikrologie; haarklowery.
microm'eter, mikrometer; ~ **calipers,** diktepasser.
micromet'ric, mikrometries.
microm'etry, mikrometrie.
mic'ro-midget car, dwergmotor, muggiemotor, minimotor.
mic'ron, mikron.
micronu'cleus, mikrokern, mikronukleus.
micro-or'ganism, mikro-organisme, mikroörganisme.
mic'rophone, geluidversterker, mikrofoon.
microphot'ograph, (n) mikrofoto; (v) mikrofotografeer.
microphotog'raphy, mikrofotografie.
mic'roscope, mikroskoop, vergrootglas.
microscop'ic, mikroskopies.
micros'copist, mikroskopis, mikroskoopgebruiker.
micros'copy, mikroskopie.
mic'rospore, mikrospoor.
mic'rotome, mikrotoom.
microt'omy, mikrotomie.
mic'rowave, mikrogolf; ~ **oven,** mikrogolfoond.
micrur'gy, mikrurgie, selmanipulasie.
micturi'tion, urienlosing, urinering; pissiekte.
mid, (a) middel=, middelste; *in* ~ *-AIR*, tussen hemel en aarde; *in* ~ *-WINTER*, in die hartjie (middel) v.d. winter.
Mid'as, Midas.
mid'brain, middelharsings.
mid'day, (n) middag; *at* ~, op die middaguur; (a) middag=; ~ **meal,** middagete.
midd'en, vuilgoedhoop, afvalhoop, ashoop.
Mid'dle: (a) *the* ~ *AGES*, die Middeleeue; *the* ~ *EAST*, die Midde(l)-Ooste; ~ *ENGLISH*, Middelengels; ~ *High GERMAN*, Middelhoogduits; *the* ~ *LANDS*, die Middellande (Kaapland); Middel-Engeland; ~ *STONE Age*, Middelsteentydperk; *the* ~ *WEST*, die Midde(l)-Weste.
mid'dle, (n) middel; tussentyd; middellyf; middelweg, middelpunt; *in the* ~ *of*, in die middel van; (v) in die middel sit; vou; verdeel, die middel kry; inskiet (voetbal); (a) middelste, middel=; tussen=; middelmatig; ~ **age,** middelbare leeftyd; ~ **-aged,** van middelbare leeftyd, middeljarig; ~ **bearing,** middellaer; ~ **class,** middelklas, burgerstand; ~ **course,** middeweg, middelloop; ~ **cut,** middelmoot; ~ **deck,** midde(l)dek; ~ **ear,** middeloor; ~ **finger,** middelvinger, langeraad, langman; ~ **-income group,** middelinkomstegroep; ~ **life,** middelbare leeftyd; ~ **man,** middelman, agent; tussenpersoon, tussenhandelaar; ~ **most,** middelste; ~ **-of-the-road policy,** middelkoers, tussenbeleid; ~ **price,** gemiddelde prys; ~ **-rate,** middelmatig; ~ **sea,** volle see; ~ **-sized,** van middelbare grootte; middelgroot; ~ **slice,** middelmoot; **M** ~ **veld,** Middelveld; ~ **watch,** hondewag; ~ **way,** midde(l)weg; ~ **weight,** middelgewig; ~ **weight boxing champion,** middelgewigbokskampioen.
mid'dling, (n) tussenlaag; (pl) griesmeel, growwe meel; middelslag; (a) middelmatig, redelik, skaflik; (adv) taamlik; so-so.
midd'y, (middies), adelbors, seekadet.
midge, muskiet, muggie; warmassie, brandassie; dwerg.
midg'et, dwergie; ~ **car,** dwergmotor, muggiemotor, minimotor; ~ **golf,** miniatuurgholf, minigholf; ~ **submarine,** dwergduikboot, miniduikboot; ~ **-weight,** dwerggewig.
mid: ~ **-heaven,** boonste hemel; hemellyn; ~ **-hour,** middag.

mi'di, (n), midi; (a) midi=.

mid: ~-**iron**, tussenyster (gholf); ~ **land**, (n) binne=land, middelland; (a) binnelands; ~-**lent**, halfvaste; ~ **most**, middelste; ~ **night**, (n) middernag, pikdonker(heid); (a) middernagtelik, middernag=; pikdonker; ~ **night feast**, nagtelike fees; *burn the* ~ *night oil*, tot diep in die nag studeer; ~ **night sun**, middernagson; ~-**ocean**: *in* ~-*ocean*, op die oop see; ~-**off**, halfweg (krieket); ~-**on**, halfby; ~ **rib**, dunrib, middelrib; ~ **riff**, middelrif; mantelvlies, diafragma; ~ **shipman**, (..**men**), seekadet, adelbors, vlagjonker; ~ **ship(s)**, midskeeps.

midst, (n) middel; *in OUR* ~, in ons midde; *in THE* ~ *of*, te midde van; (prep) te midde van.

mid: ~ **stream**: *in* ~ *stream*, in die middel van die stroom; ~ **summer**, hartjie v.d. somer; **M** ~ **summer day**, St. Jan(dag); ~ **summer madness**, die toppunt van malligheid; ~-**watch**, spookwag; ~ **way**, halfpad; ~ **wicket**, middelbaan.

mid'wife, (..**wives**), kraamverpleegster, ouvrou, vroedvrou; ~ **ry**, verloskunde.

mid'winter, middel v.d. winter.

mien, voorkome, uitsig; houding; gelaat, gesig.

miff, (n) rusietjie; slegte luim; (v) verdrietig wees; kwaad maak; ~ **y**, liggeraak.

might[1], (n) mag; geweld; vermoë; *with* ~ *and MAIN*, uit alle mag; met man en mag; dat dit so kraak; ~ *is RIGHT*, mag is reg.

might[2], (v, pret.), mog; sou; mag; *you* ~ *as well CLOSE the door*, jy kan gerus die deur toemaak; *I* ~ *have KNOWN this would happen*, ek kon geweet het dat dit sou gebeur; *you* ~ *have TOLD me*, jy kon my darem gesê het; *and WHO* ~ *this gentleman be?*, en wie is dié meneer kastig?; *and WELL he* ~ *be afraid*, hy het rede om bang te wees.

might: ~-**have-beens**, wat kon gewees het; ~ **ily**, magtig, geweldig; groot, kolossaal; ~ **iness**, magtigheid; hoogheid.

might'y, magtig, sterk, geweldig, kolossaal; groot, wonderlik; *he thinks himself a* ~ *CLEVER fellow*, hy verbeel hom dat hy danig slim is; *HIGH and* ~, hoog verhewe; ~ *WORKS*, wonderwerke.

migmat'ic, migmaties.

mig'matite, migmatiet.

mig'non, klein en fyn, keurig.

mignonette', reseda; resedakleur; mignonette(kant).

migraine', skeelhoofpyn, migraine, senuweehoofpyn.

mig'rant, (n) trekvoël, swerfvoël; verhuiser; swerwer; (a) rondswerwend, trek=, trekkend, verhuisend, nomadies.

migrate', verhuis, trek, swerwe.

mig'rating, trek=, nomadies.

migra'tion, verhuising, trek, migrasie; ~ *of people*, volksverhuising.

mi'grator, trekker; trekvoël.

mig'ratory, swerwend, trek=; ~ **bird**, trekvoël; ~ **labour**, trekarbeid; ~ **locust**, treksprinkaan; ~ **route**, trekroete.

Mika'do, Mikado.

Mike[1] (*abbr. of* **Michael**): *for the love of* ~, in hemelsnaam.

mike[2], (n) mikrofoon.

mike[3] (n): *on the* ~, aan rondslenter; (v) leeglê, rondslenter, lyf wegsteek, luier.

mil, duisend; een duisendste; milliliter.

mila'dy, adellike dame, meesteres, milady.

Milan', Milaan; ~ **ese'**, (n, a) Milanees.

milch, melk=; ~ **cow**, melkkoei; ~ **goat**, melkbok.

mild, mild, soel, sag; koel; sagsinnig, vriendelik; goedaardig, goedig; lig (siekte; rookgoed); sagwerkend (medisyne); kalm, onskuldig; *DRAW it* ~, moenie so vergroot nie; stadig oor die klippe; sak, Sarel!; *as* ~ *as MILK*, so mak soos 'n lam; ~ **attack**, ligte aanval; ~ **cigar**, ligte sigaar; ~ **climate**, sagte klimaat; ~ **dose**, matige dosis; ~ **en**, versag, sag maak.

mil'dew, (n) skimmel(siekte); witroes; brand (koring); meeldou; aanslag; dufheid; muf; (v) beskimmel, muf; ~ **ed**, beskimmel, aangeslaan; ~ **y**, bederf, beskimmel(d), muf.

mild: ~ **ly**, sag; lig; *he was only* ~ *ly ANNOYED*, hy was net effens kwaad; *to PUT it* ~ *ly*, op sy sagste gesê; ~-**flavoured**, lig gegeur; ~-**mannered**, sagsinnig; ~ **ness**, mildheid, sagtheid, vriendelikheid; ligtheid; goedaardigheid; ~-**spirited**, sagaardig; ~ **steel**, sagte staal, vloeistaal, weekstaal; ~ **weather**, aangename weer; ~ **winter**, sagte winter.

mile, myl; ~ *AFTER* ~, myl na myl; ~ *s AHEAD*, ver voor; ~ *s AWAY*, myle ver; *GEOGRAPHICAL* ~, geografiese myl; *many* ~ *s in LENGTH*, myle lank; *NAUTICAL* ~, seemyl; *it STICKS out a* ~, 'n blinde kan dit met 'n stok voel; ~ **age**, mylafstand; mylgeld; ~ **age allowance**, myltoelae; ~ **age scale**, mylskaal; ~-**hunter**, mylvreter; ~-**mark**, mylpaal; ~-**post**, mylpaal; ~ **r**, mylhardloper.

Mile'sian[1], (n) Milesiër, Mileter; (a) Milesies, Mileties.

Mile'sian[2], (n) Ier; (a) Iers.

mile'stone, mylpaal.

mil'foil, duisendblad.

miliar'ia, hittepuisies.

mil'iary, giers=; korrelrig; ~ **fever**, sweetkoors; ~ **tuberculosis**, galoptering.

milieu', milieu, omgewing.

mil'itancy, strydlus, strydbaarheid, militantheid.

mil'itant, vegtend, strydend, militant; *the Church* ~, die strydende kerk.

mil'itarism, militarisme.

mil'itarist, (n) militaris; (a) militaristies; ~ '**ic**, militaristies.

mil'itarize, militariseer.

mil'itary, (n) die soldate, die militêre; militêre diens; (a) militêr, landsmag=; oorlogs=, krygs=; krygshaftig; ~ **academy**, krygsakademie, militêre akademie; ~ **aircraft**, militêre vliegtuig; ~ **attaché**, militêre attaché; ~ **band**, musiekkorps; ~ **chest**, krygskas; ~ **college**, militêre kollege, krygskool; ~ **commander**, militêre bevelvoerder; ~ **court**, krygshof; ~ **discipline**, krygstug; ~ **drill**, parade; ~ **duty**, diensplig; ~ **engineer**, genie-offisier; geniesoldaat; ~ **engineering**, genie; ~ **engineering school**, genieskool; ~ **fever**, maagkoors; ~ **force**, krygsmag, militêre mag; ~ **history**, krygsgeskiedenis; ~ **honours**, militêre eer, krygsmanseer; ~ **intelligence**, militêre inligting; militêre inligtingsdiens; ~ **language**, krygstaal; ~ **law**, krygswet; leërwet; ~ **operation**, krygsverrigting; ~ **police**, militêre polisie; ~ **saddle**, militêre saal; ~ **science**, krygswetenskap, krygswese; ~ **service**, krygsdiens, militêre diens; ~ **stores**, krygsvoorraad, krygsbehoeftes; ~ **surgeon**, offisiersgeneeskundige; ~ **terminology**, krygstaal; ~ **tribunal**, militêre regbank.

mil'itate, veg, oorlog maak; strydig wees met; in die pad staan; ~ *against*, weerspreek; pleit teen.

mili'tia, burgermag, burgerlike verdedigingsmag, milisie; ~ **force**, milisiemag; ~ **man**, landweerman, burgersoldaat; ~ **system**, milisiestelsel, landweerstelsel.

milk, (n) melk; *that is* ~ *for BABES*, dis kinderspeletjies; *BE in* ~, melk gee; *that accounts for the* ~ *in the COCOANUT*, dit verklaar alles; *CONDENSED* ~, blikkiesmelk, gekondenseerde melk; *COW in* ~, koei wat melk gee; *EVAPORATED* ~, gekonsentreerde melk; ~ *is a wholesome FOOD*, melk is voedsaam; *FRESH* ~, soetmelk, varsmelk; *come HOME with the* ~, in die vroeë môre-ure tuis kom; ~ *and HONEY*, melk en heuning; ~ *of human KINDNESS*, mensliewendheid; ~ *of LIME*, kalkmelk; ~ *of MAGNESIA*, magnesiamelk; *imbibe something with one's MOTHER'S* ~, met die moedermelk indrink; *NOT in* ~, droog; *POWDERED* ~, melkpoeier; *SKIMMED* ~, afgeroomde melk; *it's no use crying over SPILT* ~, gedane sake het geen keer nie; *SUGAR of* ~, melksuiker; *SWEET* ~, varsmelk, soetmelk; (v) melk; ~ *the BULL*, bloed uit 'n klip tap; veer van 'n skilpad pluk; ~ *someone DRY*, iem. droog suig; ~ *the RAM*, dassie aan sy stert optel; ~-**abscess**, klont in die bors; ~-**and-water**, water-en-melkagtig, pap, flou; ~ **bar**, melksalon, melkbuffet, melkskinkery, melkhoekie, kattekroeg, melksjokolade; ~-**blue**, opaalblou; ~-**boiler**, melkkoker; ~ **bottle**, melkbottel; ~ **boy**, melkaflewerraar; ~ **bucket**, melkem=

milking   1049   *mind*

mer; ~-**bush,** melkbos; ~ **can,** melkkan; ~ **cart,** melkkar; ~ **chocolate,** melksjokolade; ~ **diet,** melkdieet; ~ **duct,** melkleier; ~**er,** melker; melk=koei; ~ **factory,** melkfabriek; ~ **farm,** melkboer=dery; ~ **feeding,** melkvoeding; ~ **fever,** melkkoors; ~ **food,** melkkos; ~ **gauge,** melkmeter; ~ **glass,** melkglas; matglas; ~**iness,** melkagtigheid; week=heid, papheid.

milk'ing, (die) melk; ~ **machine,** melkmasjien; ~-**stool,** melkstoeltjie; ~ **cow,** melkkoei; ~ **strap,** spantou; ~ **time,** melktyd.

milk: ~ **jug,** melkbeker; ~-**leg,** kraambeen; ~-**liver**=**ed,** lafhartig, papbroek(er)ig; ~ **lounge,** melksalon; ~**maid,** melkmeisie, melkster; ~**maid's stool,** melkstoeltjie; ~**man,** melkjong; melkverkoper, melkboer; ~-**molar,** melkkies, wisselkies; ~ **pail,** melkemmer, dopemmer; ~ **powder,** poeiermelk; ~-**pox,** amaas; ~ **pudding,** melkpoeding; ~ **reten**=**tion,** wegsteek (van melk deur koei); ~ **room,** melk=kamer; ~ **shake,** bruismelk, roomysmelk, skuim=melk.

milk'sop, papbroek, moederskindjie, papklaas, meid, valsbaard; *he is a* ~, hy is ook net man omdat hy broek dra.

milk: ~ **soup,** melkkos; ~ **strainer,** melksif; ~ **sugar,** melksuiker, laktose; ~ **tart,** melktert; ~ **thistle,** sy=dissel; ~-**tooth,** melktand, wisseltand, muistand; ~ **teeth,** muistandjies, muistande, wisseltande; ~ **van,** melkwa, melkkar; ~-**white,** spierwit; ~**wood,** melkhout; ~**wort,** kruisblom; melkkruid.

milk'y, melkagtig; soetsappig; ~ *QUARTZ,* melk=kwarts; ~ *THISTLE,* sydissel; *the M* ~ *WAY,* die Melkweg, die Hemelstraat.

mill[1], (n) 1,000e deel van 'n dollar.

mill[2], (n) meul(e); fabriek; masjien; frees; walsmasjien (staalfabriek); maalmasjien; spinnery (wol, ka=toen); vuisgeveg; *GO through the* ~, deur die smelt=kroes gaan; *though the* ~ *s of GOD grind slowly, yet they grind exceeding small,* die straf van God kom nie gou nie, maar hy kom seker; *the* ~ *cannot GRIND with the water that is past,* wat verby is, is verby; *PUT through the* ~, laat swaar kry; *have been THROUGH the* ~, ervaring hê, 'n leerskool deurloop hê; (v) maal; stempel; kartel (munte); klits, klop (sjokoladedrank); ronddraai (vee); boks, stamp, slaan; frees (metaal); vol (tekstielgoed); ~ *about,* rondmaal; ~**able,** maalbaar; ~-**bin,** bun=ker; ~**board,** bordpapier; tekenkarton; ~-**cog,** rat=tand; ~-**dam,** meuldam; ~-**dust,** meulstof.

milled, gemaal; ~ *EDGE,* kartelrand; ~ *HEAD,* kar=telkop, keperkop; ~ *NUT,* kartelmoer.

mill' effluent, afvalwater.

millenar'ian, (n) chilias, gelower in die duisendjarige ryk; (a) duisendjarig; chiliasties, van die duisendja=rige ryk.

mill'enary, (n) (..ries), duisendtal, duisend jaar; dui=sendste verjaarsdag; iem. wat die millennium ver=wag; (a) duisendjarig.

millenn'ial, duisendjarig; langdurig.

millenn'ium, duisendjarige ryk; millennium; vrede=tydperk.

mill'epede, duisendpoot.

mill'er, meulenaar; meulenaarmot.

mill'erite, nikkelkies, haarkies, milleriet.

miller's thumb, harnasmannetjie (vis).

milles'imal, (n) duisendste (deel); (a) duisenddelig.

mill'et, manna; giers *(Panicum miliacum); JAPANE*=*SE* ~, Japannese manna; *RED* ~, rooimanna.

mill: ~-**gearing,** dryfwerk; ~-**girl,** fabriekwerkster; ~ **hand,** meulwerker; fabrieksw̃erker; ~-**head,** bo=water; ~-**hopper,** meultregter; ~-**house,** meulhuis; meule.

mill'iard, miljard.

mill'igramme, milligram.

mill'ilitre, milliliter.

mill'imetre, millimeter.

mill'iner, hoedemaker, hoedemaakster, modiste; ~ **'s knot,** hoedeknoopsteek.

mill'inery, hoedemakery; hoedeafdeling; modewin=kel; modeware; ~ **department,** hoedeafdeling; modeafdeling.

mill'ing, (die) maal; malery; karteling (munt); wals=werk (smeltery); vergruising; ~ **mill,** fresery (erts); frees; ~ **cutter,** frees; ~ **machine,** freesmasjien, kartelmasjien.

mill'ion, miljoen; *a man in a* ~, 'n man honderd; ~**aire',** miljoenêr; geldkoning; ~**th,** miljoenste.

mil'lipede = **millepede.**

mill: ~-**owner,** meuleienaar; fabrikant; ~-**pond,** meul=dam; **M** ~ **Pond,** Atlantiese Oseaan; ~-**race,** water=voor, meulvoor; ~ **sheet,** fabrieksvel; ~-**sluice,** meulsluis; ~-**spun,** masjinaal gespin.

mill'stone, meulsteen; *a* ~ *round one's NECK,* 'n meulsteen om die nek; *have a* ~ *round one's NECK,* 'n ketting (klip) om jou nek hê; *the NETHER* ~, 'n harde mens; iem. met 'n harde hart; *SEE far into a* ~, deur 'n muur kan sien (ironies); besonder skerp=sinnig wees; *between the UPPER and nether* ~, tus=sen twee meulstene; *WEEP* ~ *s,* droë trane huil.

mill: ~-**stream,** meulstroom; ~-**sweepings,** meulaf=val; ~-**tail,** uitstromende meulwater; ~ **test,** meul=toets; maaltoets; ~ **waste,** fabrieksafval; ~-**wheel,** meulrat; ~-**work,** saagmeulwerk; walswerk; ~ **wright,** meulbouer, meulmaker; freser, freeswer=ker; masjienmonteur.

milord', milord, heer.

mil'reis, milreis.

milt, (n) milt; viskuit, hom (van visse); (v) bevrug; ~**er,** hommer.

Milton'ian, Milton'ic, Miltoniaans.

mim'bar, mimbar, moskeekansel.

mi'me, (n) gebarespel, mimiek; hanswors, grap=maker; gebaremaker; na-aper; (v) mimeer, gebare maak; speel, naboots, na-aap.

mim'eograph, (n) mimeograaf; (v) kopieer, mimeo=grafeer.

mim'er, toneelspeler; na-aper.

mimes'is, na-aping, nabootsing.

mimet'ic, nabootsend, nageaap; aanpassend.

mim'ic, (n) na-aper; mimikus; koggelaar, nabootser; (v) (-ked), (uit)koggel; namaak, naboots, na-aap; (a) mimies; nabootsend, na-apend, voorgewend, skyn=; ~ **art,** mimiek, gebarekuns; ~ **ker,** na-aper, nabootser; ~ **ry,** na-apery; mimiek; aanpassing by die omgewing (diere); ~ **s,** gebarekuns; ~ **warfare,** spieëlgeveg.

mim'iny-pim'iny, gemaak, oordrewe verfyn(d).

mimo'sa, mimosa; doringboom.

mi'mulus, mimulus, aapblom.

min'a[1], (-e), mina (Griekse gewig en muntstuk).

min'a[2], (-s), Indiese spreeu.

mina'cious, dreigend.

mina'city, bedreiging.

minar', vuurtoring, torinkie.

min'aret, minaret.

min'atory, dreigend.

mince, (n) gemaalde vleis, maalvleis; (v) maal, fyn=kap; bewimpel, vergoelik, verbloem; gemaak praat; gemaak loop, trippel; ~ *the MATTER,* die saak bewimpel; *do not* ~ *your WORDS,* moenie draai nie; Hollands met iem praat; geen blad voor die mond neem nie; *he did not* ~ *his WORDS,* hy het ronduit gepraat; (a) fyngekap, gemaal.

mince'meat, frikkadel; gemaalde vleis, maalvleis; *make* ~ *of,* kafloop, kleingeld maak van; ontsenu (argument).

minced, gemaal, fyngekap; ~ **meat,** frikkadel; ge=maalde vleis, maalvleis.

mince: ~ **pie,** vleispastei; Kerspasteitjie; ~ **r,** vleis=meul(e), vleismasjien.

min'cing, (n) malery; (a) gemaak; geaffekteer; trippe=lend; ~**ly,** gemaak, geaffekteer; ~-**machine,** vleis=meul(e).

mind, (n) siel, gees, gemoed; verstand; sin, mening; herinnering, gedagte; wil, lus; gevoelens, neiging; gesindheid; doel, voornemens; *ABSENCE of* ~, afgetrokkenheid; *a man AFTER my* ~, 'n man na my hart; *at the BACK of one's* ~, agter in die kop; *BEAR (keep) in* ~, onthou; in gedagte hou; *give someone a BIT of one's* ~, iem. goed die waarheid vertel; iem. se kop was; *in* ~ *and BODY,* na siel en liggaam; *BRING to* ~, jou herinner; *CALL to* ~, jou herinner, dink aan; iets voor die gees roep; *CHANGE one's* ~, van plan verander; *the* ~ *'s*

EYE, die sielsoog; *bearing in* ~ *the FACTS*, gelet op die feite; *FOLLOW one's* ~, jou eie kop volg; *GIVE one's* ~ *to*, aandag skenk aan; *have HALF a* ~ *to*, amper lus voel om; *HAVE in* ~, voor oë hê; in gedagte hê; *HAVE a good* ~ *to*, baie lus hê om; *KNOW one's own* ~, weet wat jy wil hê; *LOSE one's* ~, jou verstand verloor; *MAKE up one's* ~, besluit, jou voorneem; ~ *over MATTER*, die gees oor die stoflike; *someone's* ~ *MISGIVES him*, iem. begin twyfel; *to MY* ~, vir my; volgens my opvatting; *NOT in one's right* ~, nie by sy positiewe nie; *a great weight OFF my* ~, 'n groot las van my hart; *have something ON one's* ~, iets op die hart hê; *be of ONE* ~, van dieselfde mening wees; dieselfde opvatting hê (huldig); een van sin wees; *with an OPEN* ~, onbevange; *OUT of one's* ~, nie al sy varkies in die hok hê nie; sy verstand kwyt wees; *have a* ~ *of one's OWN*, weet wat jy wil hê; *give someone a PIECE of one's* ~, iem. goed die waarheid vertel; *possess PRESENCE of* ~, teenwoordigheid van gees besit; *PUT one in* ~ *of*, 'n mens herinner aan; *be in one's RIGHT* ~, by sy volle verstand wees; *SET one's* ~ *on*, voornemens wees; sy kop staan soontoe; *out of SIGHT, out of* ~, uit die oog, uit die hart; *SPEAK one's* ~, ronduit praat; jou hart lug (gee); vir jou mening uitkom; *SPRING to one's* ~, voor die gees kom; *great* ~ *s THINK alike*, groot geeste dink altyd dieselfde; *TIME out of* ~, sedert onheuglike tye; *TO my* ~, na my mening; *be in TWO* ~ *s about something*, op twee gedagtes hink; *of UNSOUND* ~, nie by sy volle verstand nie; met gekrenkte geesvermoëns; (v) sorg (vir); oppas, oplet; omgee (vir); steur (aan); (jou) herinner; bedink; *never* ~ *ABOUT*, bekommer jou nie daaroor nie; ~ *your ARM*, pas op vir jou arm; ~ *your own BUSINESS*, bemoei jou met jou eie sake; ~ *a CHILD*, 'n kind oppas; *I DON'T* ~, ek gee nie om nie; ek het geen beswaar nie; ~ *the HOUSE*, die huis oppas; *NEVER* ~ *!* dis niks nie! toe maar! *NEVER* ~ *what people say*, moenie jou steur aan wat die mense sê nie; ~ *one's P's and Q's*, op jou telle pas; oppas; in jou pasoppens wees; ~ *the STEP*, pas op vir die trappie; ~ *one's STEP*, uiters versigtig wees; *would you* ~ *TELLING me?* sou u my asb. kan sê? *WOULD you* ~ *?* gee jy om? wil jy asb.? ~ *YOU*, jy moet weet; sien jy; let wel.
mind'ed, gesind, geneig; *BE* ~ *to*, van plan wees om, lus hê om; *MECHANICALLY* ~, meganies aangelê.
mind: ~ **er**, oppasser, versorger; bediener (van masjien); ~ **ful**, gedagtig; oplettend; versigtig; ~ *ful of*, gedagtig aan; ~ **fulness**, oplettendheid; versigtigheid; ~ **less**, geesteloos, dom; onverskillig, agteloos, onoplettend; ~ *less of*, sonder om te dink aan; ~ **-projection**, telepatie; ~ **-reader**, gedagteleser; ~ **-reading**, gedagtelesery.
mine¹, (n) myn; bron (fig.); *CHAMBER of M* ~ *s*, Kamer van Mynwese; *DEPARTMENT of* ~ *s*, Departement van Mynwese; *be is a* ~ *of INFORMATION*, hy is 'n vraagbaak; *MINISTER of M* ~ *s*, Minister van Mynwese; *SCHOOL of M* ~ *s*, Skool vir Mynwese; (v) delf, grawe; ontgin; ondermyn; opblaas; myne lê.
mine², (pron) myne, van my; *it is no AFFAIR of* ~, dit is nie my saak nie; *a FRIEND of* ~, 'n vriend van my; ~ *and THINE*, myn en dyn; *he does not distinguish between* ~ *and THINE*, sy besef van myn en dyn is gebrekkig.
mine: ~ **able**, ontginbaar; ~ **blockade**, mynversperring; ~ **captain**, mynopsigter, mynkaptein; ~ **chamber**, mynkamer; ~ **crater**, mynkrater, myntregter; ~ **-dragging**, mynveëry; ~ **dump**, mynhoop; ~ **entrance**, mynportaal; ~ **field**, mynveld; ~ **gas**, myngas; ~ **lamp**, mynlamp; ~ **layer**, mynlêer; ~ **-laying**, mynlêery; ~ **manager**, mynbestuurder; ~ **official**, mynbeampte; ~ **overseer**, mynopsigter; ~ **owner**, mynbaas; ~ **plan**, mynkaart; ~ **plant**, myninrigting; mynmasjinerie; ~ **prop**, mynstut; ~ **r**, mynwerker; delwer; mynlêer.
min'eral, (n) mineraal, delfstof; mineraalwater, spuitwater, koeldrank; *rich in* ~ *s*, delfstofryk; (a) mineraal*;* delfstof*;* ~ **bed**, mineraallaag; ~ **coal**, steenkool; ~ **compounds**, mineraalverbindings; ~ **deficiency**, mineraaltekort; ~ **deposit**, mineraalafsetting; ~ **iza'tion**, mineralisering; ~ **ize**, vererts, mineraliseer; ~ **kingdom**, mineraleryk, delfstowweryk; ~ **nutrition**, mineraalvoeding.
mineralog'ical, delfstofkundig.
mineral'ogist, delfstofkundige, mineraloog.
mineral'ogy, delfstofkunde, mineralogie.
min'eral: ~ **oil**, mineraalolie, aardolie; ~ **pipe**, ertspyp; ~ **resources**, delfstofbronne; ~ **right**, mineraalreg; ~ **salt**, minerale sout; ~ **spring**, mineraalbron; ~ **water**, mineraalwater, bruiswater, spuitwater.
min'er: ~ **'s dial**, mynkompas; ~ **'s lamp**, mynlamp; ~ **'s phthis'is**, myntering; ~ **s' strike**, mynstaking; ~ **s' union**, mynwerkersbond.
Minerv'a, Minerva.
mine: ~ **shaft**, mynskag; ~ **-surveying**, mynopmeting; ~ **surveyor**, mynopmeter; ~ **sweeper**, mynveër; ~ **-thrower**, mynwerper; ~ **timber**, mynhout; mynstut.
minestro'ne, minestrone, dik groentesop.
min'ever, witbont, eekhoringbont, hermelyn.
mine'worker, mynwerker; ~ **s' union**, mynwerkersbond.
ming'le, meng, vermeng, deurmekaar maak; aansluit by; ~ *with the crowd*, deur die skare opgeneem word, by die skare aansluit.
ming'y, suinig, vrek(ker)ig.
min'i-, mini-.
min'iate, verlug, illumineer (manuskrip).
min'iature, (n) miniatuur; miniatuurportret; miniatuurskildery; (v) in die klein voorstel; in miniatuur skilder; (a) klein; miniatuur*;* ~ **cartridge**, miniatuurpatroon; ~ **clinic**, miniatuurkliniek; ~ **painter**, miniatuurskilder; ~ **portrait**, miniatuurportret; ~ **rifle**, miniatuurgeweer; ~ **stamp**, miniatuurseël.
miniaturiza'tion, verdwerging, miniaturisasie.
min'ibus, (-es), minibus.
min'i: ~ **car**, mini, muggiemotor, dwergmotor, minimotor; ~ **dress**, mini(rok).
min'ify, (..fied), verklein; geringskat.
min'igolf, minigholf.
min'ikin, (n) kleintjie; liefling; (a) baie klein; geaffekteer(d), gemaak.
min'im, (n) klein bietjie; druppel; dwerg; halwe noot (mus.); (a) miniem; ~ **al**, minimaal, baie klein, miniem; ~ **iza'tion**, verkleining, veragting; minimisering, minimalisering; ~ **ize**, minimaliseer, minimiseer, verklein; gering ag, verkleineer, verag; ~ **izer**, verkleineerder, pessimis.
min'imum, (n) (..nima), minste, minimum; (a) kleinste; minimum*;* ~ **PRICE**, minimumprys; ~ **WAGE (pay)**, minimumloon.
min'imus, (..mi), jongste, kleinste, tropsluitertjie, heksluitertjie.
min'ing, mynbou, mynwerk; mynwese; lê van myne; ~ **activities**, mynwerksaamhede; ~ **area**, myngebied; ~ **-camp**, mynkamp; ~ **case**, Hollandse raam; ~ **commissioner**, mynkommissaris; ~ **company**, mynmaatskappy; ~ **district**, myndistrik; ~ **engineer**, myningenieur; ~ **industry**, mynbedryf; ~ **lease**, mynhuur, mynpag; ~ **magnate**, mynmagnaat; ~ **pump**, mynpomp; ~ **right**, mynreg; ~ **share**, mynaandeel; ~ **title**, mynreg.
min'ikini, minikini.
min'ion, gunsteling; volgeling; mignon(letter); ~ *s of FORTUNE*, gunstelinge v.d. fortuin; ~ *s of the LAW*, geregsdienaars.
min'i: ~ **skirt**, minirok; ~ **steak**, miniskyf, minibiefstuk.
min'ister, (n) minister; staatsdienaar; bedienaar; predikant; gesant.
Min'ister: ~ *of AGRICULTURE*, Minister van Landbou; ~ *of DEFENCE*, Minister van Verdediging; ~ *of FINANCE*, Minister van Finansies; ~ *of FOREIGN Affairs*, Minister van Buitelandse Sake; ~ *of FORESTRY*, Minister van Bosbou; ~ *of HEALTH*, Minister van Gesondheid; ~ *of JUSTICE*, Minister van Justisie; ~ *of Mines*, Minister van Mynwese.
min'ister plenipotentiary, gevolmagtigde minister.

Min'ister: ~ *of POSTS and Telegraphs*, Minister van Posterye; *PRIME* ~, Eerste Minister; ~ *of PUBLIC Works*, Minister van Openbare Werke.
min'ister: ~ *of religion*, predikant.
min'ister: ~ *of SPORT*, Minister van Sport; ~ *of TOURISM*, Minister van Toerisme; ~ *of TRANSPORT*, Minister van Vervoer; ~ *of WATER Affairs*, Minister van Waterwese.
min'ister, (v) bedien, verskaf, versorg, gee; hulp verleen; diens verrig; ~ *TO*, bevorderlik aan; ~ *UNTO*, bedien, behulpsaam wees; ~ *to the WANTS of*, sorg vir, voorsien in die behoeftes van, bydra tot.
minister'ial, amptelik; ministerieel; geestelik; dienend; ~ **benches**, regeringsbanke; ~ **council**, ministerraad; ~**ist**, ministerialis, regeringsondersteuner, regeringsman.
min'istering, dienend, gedienstig; *a ~ angel*, 'n gedienstige gees; 'n behulpsame persoon.
min'istrant, (n) dienaar; (a) dienend.
ministra'tion, diens; bediening; bearbeiding; toediening; uitoefening, medewerking; ~**s**, geestelike bystand.
min'istry, (..tries), ministerie; ministerskap; ampsverrigting; bediening, predikamp, predikantskap; tussenkoms, medewerking; beroep; besigheid; *enter the* ~, predikant word.
min'ium, menie, rooimenie.
min'iver, witbont, eekhoringbont, hermelyn.
mink, nerts.
minn'esinger, minnesanger.
minn'ow, witvissie.
Min'or¹, (-s), Minoriet, Minderbroer.
min'or², (n) onmondige; kleinere, mindere; mineur (musiek); minor (log.); *that is a* ~, dis nou minder; (a) onmondig, minderjarig; ondergeskik, bykomend; van laer rang; mineur (mus.); van minder belang, gering, minder belangrik; tweederangs; *A* ~, A-mol, A mineur; *ASIA M*~, Klein-Asië; *that is of* ~ *IMPORTANCE*, dit is van minder belang; *in a* ~ *KEY*, in mineur; op klaende toon; *SMITH* ~, die jong Smith; ~ **arc**, kleinboog; ~ **axis**, neweas, kort as, klein as.
Minorc'a, Minorka: ~ **fowl**, Minorkahoender.
min'or: ~ **chord**, molakkoord; ~ **damage**, geringe skade; ~ **detail**, bykomstigheid.
Min'orite, Minderbroer, Minoriet.
minor'ity, (..ties), onmondigheid, minderjarigheid; minderheid; ~ **report**, minderheidsverslag; ~ **vote**, minderheidstem.
min'or: ~ **operation**, klein operasie; ~ **planet**, kleiner planeet; ~ **poems**, kleiner gedigte; ~ **poet**, mindere digter; ~ **prophets**, Klein Profete; ~ **road**, sekondêre pad; ~ **subject**, byvak; ~ **third**, kleinterts.
Min'otaur, Minotaurus.
min'ster, munster, hoofkerk, kloosterkerk, domkerk, katedraal.
min'strel, minstreel, minnesanger, jongleur, troebadoer, speelman; *Negro* ~**s**, Negersangers; ~**sy**, minnesangerskuns; die minnesangers; balladeversameling.
mint¹, kruisement.
mint², (n) munt (gebou); werkplek; bron (fig.); groot som, boel; *a* ~ *of money*, 'n hoop (skat) geld; (v) munt, munt slaan, aanmunt; beraam; ~ *MONEY*, geld munt; geld soos water verdien; ~ *MONEY out of something*, 'n skat geld uit iets slaan; (a) eersteklas, puik, splinternuut; posvars, muntvars (seël); ~ *condition (state)*, splinternuut, volmaak, ongevlek; ~ **age**, munt, gemunte geld, muntloon; muntreg; stempel.
mint' drops, peperment.
mint'er, munter.
mint' julep, kruisementdrankie.
mint: ~ **mark**, muntteken; ~-**master**, muntmeester.
mint' sauce, kruisementsous.
min'uend, aftrektal.
minuet', menuet.
min'us, min, minus; sonder; waardeloos; negatief; ~ *his HAT*, sonder sy hoed; *he came from the gaming-table* ~ *all his MONEY*, hy het al sy geld by die dobbeltafel verloor; *a* ~ *QUANTITY*, 'n negatiewe hoeveelheid; *he fled* ~ *his SHOES*, hy het gevlug sonder sy skoene aan.
minus'cule, (n) klein letter; minuskel; (a) klein, gering.
min'us sign, minusteken.
min'ute¹, (n) minuut; oomblik; brief, skrywe, diensbrief; memorandum; (pl) notule; memorandum; *the* ~ *he ARRIVES*, net wanneer hy kom; sodra hy kom; *I won't BE a* ~, ek kom nou-nou; *ENTER in the* ~**s**, in die notule aanteken; *FOR the* ~, op daardie oomblik; *IN the* ~**s**, in die notule; *JUST a* ~, (wag) net 'n oomblikkie; *a MATTER of* ~**s**, dit was net enkele minute; *PUNCTUAL to the* ~, presies op tyd; *READ and confirm the* ~**s**, die notule lees en goedkeur; *THAT* ~, op daardie oomblik; *THE* ~ *that*, op die oomblik dat; *THIS* ~, dadelik; *TO the* ~, op die minuut; (v) die tyd in minute aanteken; notuleer, opteken; 'n konsep maak van.
minute'², (a) baie klein, haarklein, nietig, gering; haarfyn, noukeurig.
min'ute: ~-**book**, notuleboek; ~-**glass**, sandglas; ~-**gun**, minuutskote; ~-**hand**, minuutwyser.
min'utely¹, elke minuut, minuutsgewys.
minute'ly², omstandig, noukeurig, haarfyn.
minute'ness, kleinheid; presiesheid; omstandigheid.
min'ute steak, kitsskyf, kitsbiefstuk.
minu'tiae, besonderhede, kleinighede, minutiae.
minx, maltrap; snip, rissie, geitjie.
Mi'ocene, Mioseen.
mio'sis, myo'sis, miose, kykervernouing.
mir, mir, dorpsgemeenskap.
mirabelle, mirabel, pruimboom.
mirabile dictu, (L.), mirabile dictu, wonderlik om te sê (vertel).
mir'acle, wonder, wonderwerk, wonderdaad, mirakel; *FAITH works* ~**s**, die geloof doen wonderwerke; ~ *OF* ~**s**, wonder bo wonder; *WORK* ~**s**, wondere verrig; ~-**man**, wonderdoener (gunstig); ~-**monger**, wonderdoener, wonderverrigter (ongunstig); ~ **play**, mirakelspel; ~-**worker**, wonderdoener, wonderverrigter (gunstig).
mirac'ulous, wonderlik, wonderdadig, wonderbaarlik; bonatuurlik; ~**ly**, wonderlik, wonderbaarlik, buitengewoon; ~*ly good*, wonderbaarlik goed; ~**ness**, wonderbaarlikheid; bonatuurlikheid.
mirador', mirador.
mirage', lugspieëling, newelbeeld, mirage, opgeefsel; bedrog, sinsbegoëling.
mire, (n) modder, slib; vuilgoed, vuiligheid; *drag through the* ~, deur die modder sleep (sleur); (v) bemodder, besoedel; in die modder sak; in die modder laat vas.
mirif'ic, wonderverrigtend; wonderlik, wonderbaarlik.
mir'iness, modderigheid, vuilheid.
mir'liton, mirliton.
mi'rror, (n) spieël; toonbeeld; (v) weerkaats, weerspieël; afspieël; ~*ed SIDEBOARD*, spieëlbuffet; ~ **image**, spieëlbeeld; ~-**iron**, mangaanyster, spieëlyster; ~-**print**, spieëldruk; ~ **surface**, spieëlvlak; ~-**writing** spieëlskrif.
mirth, opgeruimdheid, pret, plesier; ~**ful**, opgeruimd, vrolik, plesierig; ~**fulness**, vrolikheid, plesierigheid, opgeruimdheid; ~**less**, droefgeestig, treurig.
mir'y, modderig, bemodder(d); vuil, laag.
mir'za, vors, Persiese eretitel.
misaccepta'tion, verkeerde begrip.
misaddress', verkeerd adresseer.
misadven'ture, ongeluk, teenspoed.
misadvise', verkeerde raad gee; ~**d**, bedroë.
misalign'ment, wansporing (wiele).
misalli'ance, ongelyke verbintenis, mésalliance.
misall'ied, verkeerd verenig.
mis'anthrope, mensehater, misantroop.
misanthrop'ic, misantropies, mensehatend.
misan'thropist, mensehater, misantroop.
misan'thropy, mensehaat, misantropie.
misapplica'tion, misbruik; verkeerde toepassing, wantoepassing; wanbesteding.
misapply', (..plied), verkeerd toepas; misbruik, wanbestee.

misappre'ciate, onderskat, verkeerd waardeer.
misapprecia'tion, onderskatting, miskenning.
misapprehend', misverstaan, verkeerd verstaan.
misapprehen'sion, misverstand; wanbegrip.
misapprop'riate, wederregtelik toe-eien; misbruik; ontvreem.
misappropria'tion, onwettige toe-eiening, verduistering; wanbeheer; ontvreemding.
misarrange', verkeerd rangskik; ~ment, verkeerde rangskikking.
misbecome', (..came, ..come), sleg pas, nie betaam nie.
misbecom'ing, ongepas, onvoegsaam, onbetaamlik.
misbefitt'ing, onvoegsaam.
misbegott'en, oneg, sleg, baster=.
misbehave', jou sleg gedra, verbrou; ~ oneself, oor die tou trap; ~d, onbeskof, ongemanierd.
misbehav'iour, wangedrag.
misbelief', ongeloof, wangeloof; dwaalleer.
misbelieve', dwaal, verkeerd glo; ~r, dwaler, ongelowige.
misbeseem', nie pas nie, onpassend wees.
miscal'culate, misreken, verreken, verkeerd reken.
miscalcula'tion, misrekening, rekenfout, verkeerde berekening.
miscall', verkeerd noem (roep); uitskel.
misca'rriage, mislukking, dwaling, misslag; verlore gaan (brief); miskraam; ~ of justice, geregtelike dwaling, regsdwaling.
misca'rry, (..carried), misluk, in duie val (stort), verongeluk, faal; 'n miskraam kry; verlore gaan (brief); in verkeerde hande kom.
miscast', verkeerd bereken; in 'n verkeerde (ongepaste) rol plaas (toneelspeler); ~ing, verkeerde opteling; verkeerde (slegte) keuse.
miscegena'tion, rasvermenging, verbastering.
miscellan'ea, mengelwerk; allerlei.
miscellan'eous, gemeng, deurmekaar; oraloor; veelsydig; diverse; ~ness, verskeidenheid; veelsydigheid; ~ poems, mengelgedigte.
miscell'anist, skrywer van mengelwerk.
miscell'any, (..nies), mengeling; mengelwerk; boek met mengelwerk.
mischance', ongeluk, ongeval; by ~, per ongeluk.
mis'chief, kwaad, onheil; nadeel; streke, kattekwaad, goddeloosheid, ondeundheid; nadeligheid; boosaardigheid; onheilstigter, rusverstoorder; there is ~ BREWING (afoot), daar broei iets; teen die son= weer in die lug; CAUSE ~, kwaad doen; DO ~, kwaad doen; be FULL of ~, vol streke wees; GET up to ~, kattekwaad aanvang; he that ~ HATCH= ETH ~ catcheth, graaf jy 'n kuil vir 'n ander, dan val jy daar self in; Satan finds some ~ still for IDLE hands to do, ledigheid is die duiwel se oorkussing; KEEP out of ~, uit die moeilikheid bly; LEAD into ~, tot kwaad verlei; MAKE ~, kattekwaad uit= haal; kwaad stig; he who ~ MAKETH, ~ taketh, wie 'n put vir 'n ander graaf, val daar self in; out of PURE ~, moedswillig; uit pure onnutsigheid; the ~ OF it is, die ongeluk is; SOW ~, kwaad stig; he is UP to ~, hy voer iets in die skild; kwaad stook; ~-loving, ondeund; ~-maker, kwaadstoker, stokebrand, beroerder, onheilstigter; ~-making, kwaadstigting, kwaadstokery; ~-monger, kwaadstoker, onheilstigter.
mis'chievous, ondeund, niksnutsig, goddeloos, moedswillig; skadelik, verkeerd; nadelig; ~ness, ondeundheid, moedswilligheid, gruwelikheid, stoutigheid.
miscibil'ity, mengbaarheid.
mis'cible, (ver)mengbaar.
miscite', verkeerd aanhaal (siteer).
miscomprehend', misverstaan.
miscomprehen'sion, misverstand.
misconceive', misverstaan, verkeerd opvat.
misconcep'tion, wanopvatting, verkeerde opvatting, misverstand, dwaalbegrip, wanbegrip, misvatting.
miscon'duct, (n) wangedrag; wanbeheer; owerspel.
misconduct', (v) jou sleg gedra; sleg bestuur; owerspel pleeg; ~ oneself, jou sleg gedra.
misconjec'ture, verkeerde gissing.
misconstruc'tion, verkeerde uitleg, misvatting.

misconstrue', verkeerd uitlê, verkeerd opvat.
miscontent'ed, ontevrede, misnoeg.
miscoun'sel, slegte raad gee.
miscount', (n) verkeerde telling; (v) mistel, verkeerd optel; verkeerd vertel.
mis'creant, (n) ellendeling, onmens, snoodaard, skurk; ongelowige; (a) afskuwelik, gemeen, laag, ellendig; ongelowig.
miscreat'ed, misvorm, wanskape.
miscred'it, wantrou.
miscue', misstoot (biljart).
misdate', verkeerd dateer.
misdeal', (n) fout; verkeerd uitgee (kaarte); misdeling; (v) (..dealt), (kaarte) verkeerd uitgee; misdeel.
misdeed', misdaad, verkeerde daad, vergryp, wandaad.
misdeem', verkeerd beoordeel; verkeerd hou vir; ten onregte dink.
misdemean', jou sleg gedra; ~ant, boosdoener, misdadiger; ~our, wangedrag; misdaad, misdryf.
misdirect', verkeerd bedui; op 'n dwaalspoor bring, in verkeerde rigting lei; verkeerd adresseer; ~ion, verkeerde aanduiding, verkeerde inligting; verkeerde adres; wanbeleid.
misdo', (..did, ..done), kwaad doen, onreg doen; ~er, oortreder, boosdoener; ~ing, vergryp, misdaad, wandaad.
misdoubt', wantrou, verdink; betwyfel.
mise en scène', toneelskikking, mise en scène.
misemploy', verkeerd toepas, misbruik; ~ment, misbruik, verkeerde gebruik.
misen'ter, verkeerd boek, verkeerd inskryf.
misen'try, (..tries), verkeerde inskrywing, verkeerde boeking.
mis'er, (aarts)gierigaard, vrek, geldwolf, skraalhans, oppotter.
mis'erable, ellendig, miserabel, beroerd, deerlik, erbarmlik, (gods)jammerlik, sielig, rampsalig, naar, ongelukkig, armsalig, veragtelik; aaklig; ~ fellow, treurige vent, miskruier; ~ness, ellendigheid, naarheid; aakligheid; rampsaligheid.
mis'erably, ellendig.
miserer'e, boetpsalm (Ps. 51), miserere.
mise'ricord, misericord.
mis'erliness, vrekkigheid, suinigheid.
mis'erly, vrekkig, vreksuinig, (geld)gierig, skraapsugtig, inhalig, snoep; be ~, vrekkig wees.
mis'ery, (..ries), ellende, jammer, naarheid; misère; make someone's life a ~, iem. se lewe suur maak.
misesteem', (n) minagting, onderskatting; (v) minag, geringskat.
misfeas'ance, oortreding, vergryp, misbruik van bevoegdheid, magsmisbruik.
misfire', (n) ketsskoot, weiering; weieraar (patroon); oorslaan (motor); (v) kets, weier; oorslaan (motor).
misfir'ing, ketsing.
mis'fit, (n) sleg passende kledingstuk, ens.; mislukkeling; a social ~, iem. wat nie pas in die samelewing nie; 'n wanaangepaste; (v) (-ted), sleg pas (sit).
misform', misvorm; ~a'tion, misvorming; mismaaktheid, wanskapenheid; ~ed, wanskape, misvorm, mismaak.
misfort'une, ongeluk; BY ~, per ongeluk; ~s never COME singly, 'n ongeluk kom nooit alleen nie.
misgive', (..gave, -n), betwyfel; met angs vervul; bedenkings hê.
misgiv'ing, twyfel, argwaan; angstige voorgevoel; bekommernis, besorgdheid; have ~s, beswaard voel.
misgott'en, onregverdig verkry.
misgov'ern, sleg bestuur; ~ment, wanbestuur, wanbeheer.
misguid'ance, verkeerde leiding; misleiding.
misguide', verkeerd lei; mislei; ~d, mislei, onbesonne; verblind; dwaas, onverstandig.
mishan'dle, verkeerd aanpak; sleg behandel.
mishand'ling, verkeerde hantering; mishandeling.
mishap', ongeluk, ongeval.
mishear', (..heard), verkeerd hoor, sleg opvang.
mis'hit, (n) misslag, mishou; (v) (~), misslaan, mis.
mish'mash, mengelmoes, warboel, deurmekaarspul.
Mishna(h), Misjna.

misinfer', (-red), verkeerd aflei.
misinform', verkeerd inlig; ~**a'tion**, verkeerde inligting.
misinstruct', verkeerd onderrig.
misintell'igence, verkeerde inligting, vals berig, riemtelegram.
misinterp'ret, verkeerd uitlê; ~**a'tion**, verkeerde uitleg, misduiding, wanvertolking.
misjoin', verkeerd verbind.
misjudge', verkeerd beoordeel; veroordeel; verkeerd bereken.
misjudg(e)'ment, verkeerde beoordeling; verkeerde berekening.
miskick', misskop.
mislaid', verlê, weg.
mislay', (..laid), verlê; verkeerd bêre, op 'n verkeerde plek bêre.
mislead', (..led), mislei, kul; verlei; ~**er**, misleier; ~**ing**, misleidend.
mislike', (n) (arch.), mishae, afkeer, weersin; (v) mishae hê in.
misman'age, verkeerd beheer, sleg aanpak; verkeerd behandel; ~**ment**, wanbeheer, wanbestuur, wanbeleid; verkeerde optrede; *culpable* ~*ment*, strafbare wanbestuur.
mismatch', (n) verkeerde paring; wanaanpassing; verkeerde huwelik; (v) verkeerd paar.
mismat'ed, verkeerd saamgevoeg (gepaar), onpaar.
mismea'sure, verkeerd meet; verkeerd oordeel; ~**ment**, verkeerde maat.
misname', verkeerd noem.
misnom'er, verkeerde benaming; naamfout; verkeerde naam.
misog'amist, huweliksghater, misogamis.
misog'amy, afkeer van die huwelik of huwelikstaat, misogamie.
misog'ynist, vrouehater, misoginis.
misog'yny, vrouehaat, misoginie.
mispersuade', verkeerd aanraai.
mis'pickel, arseenkies, arseenpiriet.
misplace', misplaas; verlê; ~**ment**, misplasing; verlegging.
misprint', (n) drukfout; foutdruk (seël); (v) verkeerd druk.
mispri'sion[1], veragting.
mispri'sion[2], ampsversuim, wangedrag; nalatigheid; miskenning; ~ *of treason (felony)*, versuim om hoogverraad (misdaad) te openbaar.
misprize', onderskat; verag; misken.
mispronounce', verkeerd uitspreek.
mispronuncia'tion, verkeerde uitspraak.
mispropor'tion, wanverhouding.
misquota'tion, verkeerde aanhaling (sitaat).
misquote', verkeerde aanhaal.
misrate', verkeerd bereken.
misread', (~), verkeerd lees; verkeerd uitlê.
misreck'on, verkeerd reken, misreken, verreken.
misremem'ber, jou nie reg herinner nie.
misreport', verkeerd rapporteer.
misrepresent', verkeerd voorstel; verdraai; ~**a'tion**, wanvoorstelling; verdraaiing.
misrule', (n) wanbestuur; oproer; slegte regering; (v) verkeerd bestuur, sleg regeer.
miss[1], (n) (-es), mejuffrou; nooi; kleinnoi, kleinnôi, meisie; *the M ~ es Smith*, die (me)juffroue (dames) Smith.
miss[2], (n) misstoot; mishou, misskoot; gemis; *FEEL the ~ of*, verleë wees oor; *GIVE it a ~*, laat dit staan; vermy dit; *a ~ is as GOOD as a mile*, amper is nie stamper nie, mis is mis; amper is honderd myl van Amsterdam; *a NEAR ~*, byna raakskoot; byna misskoot; *there is NO ~ of*, niemand is eintlik verleë nie; (v) mis, nie raak nie; oorslaan; derwe, misloop; mis stoot, mis skiet; mis vang; kets (geweer); mis slaan; uitlaat; ~ *the BUS*, die bus verpas (mis); die bus nie haal nie; na die maal kom; *have ~ ed the BOAT*, agter die net visvang; neusie verby wees; ~ *a CHANCE*, 'n kans laat verbygaan; ~ *EACH other*, mekaar misloop; ~ *FIRE*, kets, weier; misloop, misluk; ~ *one's FOOTING*, mistrap; gly; ~ *the MARK*, mis skiet; *it NEVER ~ es*, dit mis nie; ~ *an OPPORTUNITY*, 'n geleentheid verby laat gaan; ~ *OUT*, uitlaat, oorslaan; ~ *the POINT*, die kern nie begryp nie; ~ *one's ROAD*, verdwaal; ~ *one's STEP*, gly; ~ *a TRAIN*, 'n trein verpas; 'n trein nie haal nie; ~ *one's WAY*, verdwaal.
miss'al, misboek, missaal.
missend', (..sent), aan 'n verkeerde adres stuur.
misshape', verkeerd vorm, wanstaltig maak.
misshap'en, mismaak, gedrogtelik, misvorm, wanskape, wanstaltig; ~**ness**, wanstaltigheid, mismaaktheid.
miss'ile, projektiel; werptuig; gooiing; missiel.
miss'ing, verlore; ontbrekend; vermis, op soek, weg; *BE ~*, vermis word; *the ~ LINK*, die ontbrekende skakel; ~ *PERSON*, vermiste.
mi'ssion, sending; tog; opdrag, missie (R.K.); lewenstaak, roeping; gesantskap; sendinghuis, sendingstasie; ~**ary**, (n) (..ries), sendeling; afgesant; (a) sending-; ~ *ary society*, sendinggenootskap; ~-**box**, sendingbussie; ~ **church**, sendingkerk; ~**er**, sendeling; ~ **festival**, sendingfees; ~ **field**, sendingveld; ~ **school**, sendingskool; ~ **station**, sendingstasie, sendingpos; ~ **work**, sendingwerk.
miss'is — **missus**.
miss'ish, juffertjiesagtig, nufferig; sentimenteel, vol fiemies.
miss'ive, brief, missive; sendbrief.
misspell', (..spelt or -ed), verkeerd spel; ~**ing**, verkeerde spelling.
misspend', (..spent), verkeerd bestee.
misstate', verkeerd voorstel; verdraai; ~**ment**, verkeerde voorstelling, verdraaiing.
misstep', (n) misstap, verkeerde stap; (v) (-ped), misstrap, 'n misstap doen.
miss'us, mevrou, nooi; vrou; miesies; *kyk* **mistress**.
miss'y, (missies), juffroutjie, nooientjie, nonnie.
mist, (n) mis, newel; mistige weer; sluier, waas; *BE in a ~*, aan die dwaal wees; *SCOTCH ~*, motreën, vaarlandsdou; (v) motreën; newelig word, benewel.
mistak'able, vatbaar vir verkeerde uitleg, onduidelik, misverstaanbaar.
mistake', (n) fout, vergissing, dwaling, flater, glips, blaps, glip (van pen), misgreep, abuis; *BY ~*, per abuis; *MAKE a ~*, 'n fout begaan; *not to MAKE the same ~ twice*, jou nie twee maal aan dieselfde klip stamp nie; *and NO ~*, absoluut seker; ongetwyfeld; *make NO ~ about this*, wees gewaarsku; *a PROFOUND ~*, 'n groot fout; *WISE men learn by other men's ~ s, fools by their own*, wie hom aan 'n ander spieël, spieël hom sag; (v) (..took, -n), jou vergis, verkeerd verstaan, misverstaan; dit mis hê, dwaal; ~ *FOR*, aansien vir; *there is NO mistaking*, jy kan jou nie vergis nie.
mistak'en, verkeerd; onjuis, fout(ief); misplaas; misluk; *I was ~ ABOUT her age*, ek het my vergis omtrent haar ouderdom; *you ARE ~*, jy het dit mis; jy vergis jou; *BE ~*, dit mis hê; *BE ~ for a spy*, aangesien word vir 'n spioen; ~ *IDENTITY*, persoonsvergissing; *I was ~ IN him*, ek het my met hom vergis; ~ *NOTION*, dwaalbegrip; ~**ly**, by vergissing, ten onregte, verkeerdelik.
misteach', (..taught), verkeerd leer, verkeerd onderrig.
mis'ter, (n) meneer, heer; baas; (v) meneer noem.
misterm', verkeerd noem.
mist'ful, newelagtig, mistig.
mistime', op die verkeerde oomblik sê of doen; die tyd verkeerd bereken; ~**d**, misplaas, ongepas, onvanpas; ontydig.
mistim'ing, misplaastheid; ontydigheid; verkeerde tydsberekening.
mist'iness, mistigheid, newelagtigheid; wasigheid, onhelderheid.
misti'tle, verkeerd betitel.
mis'tletoe, mistel, voëlent; maretak.
mist'like, newelagtig.
mis'tral, mistral.
mistranslate', verkeerd vertaal.
mistransla'tion, verkeerde vertaling.
mistreat', mishandel.
mis'tress, (-es), mevrou; minnares, bysit, maitresse,

mistrial 1054 mock

bywyf; meesteres, nooi, ounooi; onderwyseres; ge= biedster; *BE* ~ *of,* baas wees van; *the* ~ *of the HOUSE,* die huisvrou.
mistri'al, wanverhoor.
mistrust', (n) wantroue, verdenking; agterdog; (v) wantrou, verdink; ~ **ful,** agterdogtig, wantrouig; ~ **fulness,** wantroue, agterdog.
mistry', (..**tried**), ten onregte verhoor.
mistune', ontstem, verkeerd stem.
mist'y, mistig; newelagtig; wasig, dyns(er)ig; vaag, onduidelik; *a* ~ *idea,* 'n vae idee.
misunderstand', (..**stood**), misverstaan, verkeerd verstaan; ~ **ing,** misverstand, geskil, onenigheid.
misus'age, mishandeling; misbruik; verkeerde ge= bruik.
misuse', (n) misbruik; verkeerde gebruik; mishande= ling; (v) misbruik; mishandel.
miswrite', (..**wrote**, ..**written**), verkeerd skryf, ver= skryf.
mite, miet (insek); fluweelgogga; kleinigheid; klein kindjie; duit, penning; *a* ~ *of a CHILD,* 'n kindjie; 'n kleintjie; 'n tjokkertjie; *CONTRIBUTE (offer) one's* ~, jou steentjie bydra; *NOT a* ~, glad nie; *the WIDOW'S* ~, die weduwee se penning.
mithrid'atize, mitridatiseer.
mit'igant, versagtend, lenigend.
mit'igate, versag, lenig, verlig, stil; temper; matig, tot bedaring bring; ~ *PAIN,* pyn verlig; ~ *PUNISH= MENT,* straf ligter maak; *mitigating CIRCUM= STANCES,* versagtende omstandighede.
mitiga'tion, versagting, leniging, verligting; *IN* ~ *of,* vir (ter) versagting van; ~ *of PUNISHMENT,* strafvermindering.
mit'igative, versagtend, lenigend.
mit'igatory, versagtend.
mitos'is, (..**ses**), mitose, seldeling.
mitrailleur', snelvuurskutter.
mitrailleuse', mitrailleuse, (verouderde) snelvuurge= weer.
mit'ral, mytervormig; ~ **valve,** myterklep.
mi'tre, (n) biskopshoed, myter; verstek, hoek van 45°; (v) die myter opsit; verstek, reghoekig voeg; ~ *a corner,* 'n hoek verstek, 'n verstekhoek maak; ~ **angle,** verstekhoek; ~ **arch,** verstekboog; ~ **bevel,** verstekhaak; ~ **box,** verstekbak; ~**d,** gemyter, tot biskop verhef; in verstek bewerk; ~*d corner,* ver= stekhoek; ~*d moulding,* versteklys; ~ **gear,** ver= stekrat; ~ **joint,** verstekvoeg; ~ **plane,** verstek= skaaf; ~ **saw,** versteksaag; ~ **square,** verstekhaak.
mi'treform, mytervormig.
mitt, mitt'en, (hand)mof(fie); duimhandskoen; *GET the mitten,* 'n bloutjie loop; uitgeskop word; die trekpas kry; *HANDLE something without mittens,* iets sonder handskoene aanpak.
mitt'imus, opsluitbevel; afdanking; *get one's* ~, ont= slag kry, afgedank word.
mit'y, vol miet.
mix, (n) mengsel; aanmaaksel; (v) meng, vermeng, deurmekaar maak; berei, aanmaak; omgaan met, hom meng met; *I have* ~*ed AMONG all classes,* ek het met mense van allerlei slag omgegaan; ~ *a DRINK,* 'n drankie meng; *she won't* ~ *IN with the other guests,* sy sal nie mooi pas by die ander gaste nie; ~ *IT,* vuisslaan, baklei; *don't* ~ *your META= PHORS,* moenie jou metafore deurmekaar ge= bruik nie; ~ *in SOCIETY,* onder die mense kom; omgaan met mense; ~ *UP,* verwar; meng; *become* ~*ed UP in something,* gewikkel raak in iets; *they don't* ~ *WELL,* hulle kom nie goed met mekaar klaar nie; ~ *WITH,* meng met; omgaan met; ~**able,** mengbaar; ~**crystal,** mengkristal.
mixed, gemeng; deurmekaar; aangemaak; *BE* ~ *up,* deurmekaar (onthuts) wees; *be* ~ *up WITH,* ge= wikkel wees in, betrokke wees in; ~ **bag,** mengel= moes, allegaartjie; ~ **bathing,** gemengde baaiery; ~ **blessing,** halwe seën; ~ **doubles,** gemengde dub= belspel; ~ **gril,** allegaartjie; ~ **marriage,** gemengde huwelik; ~ **merchandise,** sneesvraggie; ~ **pickles,** suurtjies, atjar; ~ **race,** gemengde ras; ~ **spice,** ge= mengde speserye.
mix'er, menger; mengmasjien; *a BAD* ~, 'n eenloper, 'n alleenloper; iem. wat nie maklik in die omgang is

nie, 'n eenspaaier; *be a GOOD* ~, maklik in die omgang wees.
mix'ing, vermenging; ~**-basin,** ~**-bowl,** mengbak; ~**-drum,** mengtrommel; ~**-fan,** mengwaaier; ~ **faucet,** mengkraan; ~**-trough,** mengbak.
mix'ture, vermenging; mengsel; mikstuur; drankie; aanmaaksel; ~**-indicator,** mengselmeter.
mix'-up, warboel, verwarring, deurmekaarspul.
Miz'pa, Mispa; ~ **ring,** Misparing.
miz(z)'en, besaan; ~**-mast,** agtermas; besaanmas; ~**- sail,** besaanseil; ~ **topsail,** kruismarsseil; ~ **yard,** kruisra.
miz'zle¹, (n) motreën, stofreën; (v) motreën.
miz'zle², (v) weghol, trap.
miz'zly, motreënagtig.
mnemon'ic, (n) geheuerympie; (a) mnemonies; ge= heue=; ~**s,** geheueleer, mnemoniek.
mnemotechnique', mnemotegniek.
mnemotech'ny, geheueleer.
mo, *abbr. of* **moment;** *half a* ~, wag 'n bietjie.
mo'a, moa.
Mo'abite, (n) Moabiet; Moabities (taal); (a) Moa= bities.
moan, (n) gekerm, gesteun; jammerklag, weeklag; ge= kreun; (v) kerm, steun, weeklaag; betreur, bejam= mer; ~ *AND groan,* steen en been kla; ~ *with PAIN,* kerm van pyn; ~**ful,** jammerend, droewig, treurig; ~**ing,** (n) gekerm, gesteun, gejammer; (a) klaend, kermend.
moat, (n) sloot, grag; (v) met 'n grag omring.
mob, (n) gepeupel, gespuis; bende, trop; menigte, volkshoop; (v) (**-bed**), mishandel, molesteer, toeta= kel, iem. lastig val; saamstroom; ~ *someone,* op iem. toesak; ~ **bish,** oproerig; grof, laag.
mob'-cap, floddermus, mopmus.
mob'ile, beweeglik, lig, mobiel; vlug, lewendig, veran= derlik; reisend, vlieënd; gemotoriseer; marsvaardig (soldate); ~ **canteen,** (veld)winkel op wiele, reisen= de (veld)winkel; verversingswa; ~ **capital,** vlotten= de kapitaal; ~ **crane,** loopkraan; ~ **division,** ligte divisie; gemotoriseerde divisie; ~ **face,** beweeglike gesig; ~ **market,** mobiele (reisende) mark; ~ **pa= trol,** vlieënde patrollie; ~ **post-office,** mobiele pos= kantoor; ~ **troops,** ligte troepe: ~ **warfare,** bewe= gingsoorlog.
mobi'liary, betreffende roerende goed.
mobil'ity, beweeglikheid, mobiliteit; veranderlikheid.
mobiliza'tion, mobilisasie; ~ **order,** mobilisasiebe= vel; ~ **plan,** mobilisasieplan.
mob'ilize, mobiliseer; losmaak, verkry (kapitaal).
Mö'bius strip, möbiusstrook.
mob' law, gespuisreg, rampokkerregering.
moboc'racy, mob' rule, gepeupelheerskappy, ram= pokkerregering, oglokrasie.
mobo'la plum, grysboom.
mocc'asin, mokassin, Indiaanse skoen, Indiane= skoen.
Mo'cha¹, mokkasteen; mosagaat.
mo'cha² (coffee), mokka(koffie).
mock, (n) bespotting; namaaksel; *make a* ~ *of,* be= spot; (v) bspot, uitkoggel; die spot dryf met, (a) na= gemaak, oneg; skyn=, kamma=, kwasie=; ~ **cream,** nagemaakte room, foproom, kammaroom; ~**er,** spotter, skimper, spotvoël; bedrieër; ~**ery,** spot= (sug), uitkoggelry, tergery, beskimping, gehoon, bespotting, skimp(ery), skimptaal, spotterny; na= bootsing; skynvertoon; ~ **fight,** spieëlgeveg, skyn= geveg; ~**-heroic,** (n) komies-heroïese gedig; (a) ko= mies-heroïes.
mock'ing, (n) tergery, spot; ~ *is catching,* spotter kry sy loon; spotter se huis brand af; (a) spottend, ho= nend, skimperig, spotagtig; ~**-bird,** piet-my-vrou; spotvoël; ~ **chat,** dassiebergwagter; dassievoël; ~ **laugh,** simplag, spotlag; ~**ly,** spottend(erwyse).
mock: ~ **moon,** bymaan; ~ **parliament,** skynparle= ment; ~ **pocket,** fopsak; ~ **poem,** spotgedig; ~ **prophet,** valse profeet; ~ **sun,** byson; ~ **trial,** ver= hoorspel, skynverhoor, skynhof(saak); ~ **turtle soup,** nagemaakte skilpadsop, kammaskilpadsop; ~**-up,** lewensgroot model; ~ **velvet,** market, tryp= ferweel; ~ **venison,** kammawildsvleis.

**mod, **(a), modern; (n) moderne tiener(groep).
mod'al, modaal; ~ **'ity,** modaliteit.
mode, metode, manier, vorm, gewoonte, gebruik; modus; toon(skaal), toonaard (musiek); mode; *ALL the* ~, die nuutste mode; erg in die mode; ~ *of FIGHTING,* vegwyse; *in MINOR* ~, mineurtoon; ~ *of ORIGIN,* ontstaanswyse; ~ *of PAYMENT,* betaalwyse.
mod'el, (n) model, voorbeeld; voorbeeldigheid; ontwerp; ewebeeld; patroon, vorm, toonbeeld; skildersmodel; *he IS the* ~ *of,* hy is die ewebeeld van; *ON the* ~ *of,* na die model van; (v) (**-led**), vorm; modelleer; boetseer; as model optree; as mannekyn optree; ~ *after,* skoei op die lees van; (a) model=, uitsoek=; voorbeeldig; ~**-drawing,** modeltekening; ~**ler,** vormer; modelleerder; boetseerder.
mod'elling, modelleerwerk, boetseerwerk; modelleerkuns; ~**-board,** modelleerplank; ~**-clay,** boetseerklei; ~**-wax,** boetseerwas.
mod'el: ~**-maker,** modelmaker; ~ **pupil,** voorbeeldige leerling; ~**-room,** modelkamer; ~ **train,** speelgoedtrein(tjie).
mo'dem, modulasie en demodulasie, modem.
mod'ena, donkerpers.
moderam'en, moderatuur, moderamen.
mod'erate, (n) gematigde; (v) modereer (eksamen); matig, versag; wysig; kalmeer; (laat) bedaar; afkoel; beteuel; (a) matig, skaflik, middelmatig; besadig, gematig, getemper; *man of* ~ *means,* 'n man van gemiddelde inkomste; (adv) taamlik, redelik; ~**ly,** matig, redelik; ~*ly GOOD,* skaflik, redelik; ~*ly PRUNED,* matig gesnoei; ~**ness,** matigheid; middelmatigheid.
modera'tion, matigheid, gematigdheid, besadigdheid, selfbeheersing; *IN* ~, met mate, matig; *LACK of* ~, mateloosheid.
modera'to, taamlik vinnig, moderato.
mod'erator, moderator (kerk, eksamen); bemiddelaar, arbiter; moderateur; ~ **lamp,** moderateurlamp; ~ **ship,** moderatorskap.
mod'ern, (n) (die) moderne; (die) nuwere; *the* ~*s,* die modernes; die nuweres; (a) modern, nieumodies, nuwerwets; ~ *times,* die nuwe tyd; ~ **Dutch,** Nieu-Nederlands; ~ **history,** nuwe (moderne) geskiedenis; ~**ism,** modernisme; ~**ist,** (n) modernis, nieuligter; (a) modernisties; ~**'ity,** moderniteit, nuwerwetsheid; ~**iza'tion,** modernisering, modernisasie; ~**ize,** moderniseer; ~ **language,** moderne taal; ~**ness,** nuwerwetsheid, moderniteit.
mod'est, beskeie, stemmig, sedig, ingetoë, kuis; fatsoenlik; matig; *on a* ~ *scale,* op beskeie voet; ~**y,** ingetoënheid, beskeidenheid; sedigheid; stemmigheid; eerbaarheid; skaamte.
modi'city, geringheid.
mod'icum, bietjie, greintjie, weinig; *a* ~ *of good,* 'n bietjie goed.
mod'ifiable, wysigbaar, veranderbaar.
modifica'tion, wysiging, verandering; beperking; matiging, versagting.
mod'ified, gewysig; gematig.
mod'ifier, wysiger.
mod'ify, (..**fied**), wysig, verander; matig, beperk, versag; bepaal (gram.).
modill'ion, modiljon.
mod'ish, modies, na die mode; modieus; ~**ness,** modesug.
modiste', modiste, modemaakster.
mod'ular, modulêr.
mod'ulate, stel, reguleer; moduleer, temper.
modula'tion, buiging, reëling; modulasie; ~ *of the voice,* stembuiging.
mod'ulator, maatslaner, toonaangeër, modulator.
mod'ule, eenheidsmaat, maatstaf; modulus, eenheid, module.
mod'ulus, (..**li**), modulus, module.
mod'us, modus; manier, wyse; ~ *OPERANDI,* werkwyse, metode; ~ *VIVENDI,* voorlopige skikking.
Mogul', (n) Mongool; Mogol; *Great* ~, Grootmogol; (a) Mongools.
mogul', magnaat, outokraat, grootbaas.
mo'hair, angorahaar, (sy)bokhaar.

Mohamm'ed, Mohammed; ~**an,** (n) Mohammedaan, Slamaier; (a) Mohammedaans, Islams; ~**anism,** Mohammedanisme, Islam; ~**anize,** islamiseer.
Mo'hawk, Mohawkindiaan.
Mo'hican, (n) Mohikaner; (a) Mohikaans.
mo'hole, mohole *(geol.).*
moho'li lemur, (Senegalese) nagapie.
mo'hur, mohur.
moi'ety, helfte; gedeelte, deel.
moil, (n) swaar werk; handkoevoet; rotsbeitel; (v) swoeg, slaaf; ~ *and toil,* swoeg en slaaf; jou malle moer (maai) af sukkel.
moist, klam, natterig, vogtig; reënerig; (sm)etterig (seer); ~**en,** deurweek; natmaak, aanklam, bevogtig; ~ *en one's throat,* jou keel natmaak; 'n dop(pie) steek; ~**ened,** aangeklam, aangeslaan; ~**ness,** natigheid, vogtigheid, klamheid.
mois'ture, vog, klammigheid; voggehalte, vogtigheid, nattigheid; ~ **content,** voggehalte; ~**-proof,** vogdig; ~**-proofing,** vogdigting.
moke, esel; ou (swak) rydier; uilskuiken.
mo'ko, moko, bakteriese vervelsiekte.
mol'ar¹, (n) kiestand, maaltand, agtertand: (a) maal=, malend; kies=, maaltand=.
mol'ar², (a) gewig=, massa=, molêr.
molass'es, melasse, beesstroop.
Moldave', Moldawiër.
Moldav'ia, Moldawië; ~**n,** Moldawies.
mole¹, (n) moesie, moedervlek, huidvlek.
mole², (n) pier, dwarswal; dyk; hawehoof, seehoof, seebreker, golfbreker.
mole³, (n) mol (dier); molskyn, molvel (materiaal); *as BLIND as a* ~, so blind soos 'n mol; *GULDEN* ~, kruipmol; ~**-cast,** molshoop; ~**-cricket,** waterkriek, molkriek.
molec'ular, molekulêr; ~ **weight,** molekulêre gewig.
mol'ecule, stofdeeltjie, molekule.
mole: ~**-eyed,** bysiende, kortsigtig; ~**heap,** ~**hill,** molshoop; ~**-hole,** molsgat; ~**-rat,** grysmol.
mole'skin, molvel (materiaal); molskyn.
mole'-snake, molslang.
molest', pla, hinder, lol met, molesteer, moveer, lastig val; ~**a'tion,** oorlas, kwelling, plaery, belediging, molestasie; ~**er,** molesteerder, plaer.
mole: ~**-track,** molgang; ~**-trap,** molval.
Mol'inism, Molinisme.
moll, ligtekooi; morrie, bendelid se geselline.
moll'ifiable, vermurfbaar.
mollifica'tion, versagting, vermurwing, vertedering.
moll'ifier, versagter, versagtende middel.
moll'ify, (..**fied**), versag, vermurf, verlig, verteder.
moll'usc, weekdier; ..**us'can,** weekdier=.
moll'y, (**mollies**), verwyfde man, papbroek; ~**cod'dle,** (n) papbroek; (v) (ver)troetel, verwen, piep.
mollymauk', mollymawk', malmokkie.
Mol'och¹, Molog.
mol'och², mologakkedis.
mol'ten, gesmelt; gegiet, gogote; ~ **image,** gegote beeld; ~ **image(s),** afgodsbeeld(e); ~ **lead,** gesmelte lood; ~ **metal,** gesmelte metaal.
Molten'o disease, krampsiekte (by vee).
Molucc'as, (die) Molukke, Speseryeilande.
mol'y, wilde knoffel.
molyb'denite, molibdeniet, molibdeenglans.
molyb'dite, molibdiet.
mom'ent, oomblik, rukkie, bietjie, wyl(e); kits; oogwenk, moment; gewig, belang; bewegingshoeveelheid; *a* ~ *AGO,* so pas, so-ewe, vanêffe; *at ANY* ~, elke oomblik; *AT the* ~, op die oomblik, juis nou; *FOR the* ~, vir die oomblik; ~ *of FORCE,* kragmoment; *of GREAT* ~, van groot belang; *HALF a mo(ment),* net 'n oomblikkie; wag 'n bietjie; *IN a* ~, in 'n kits; ~ *of INERTIA,* traagheidsmoment; *JUST a* ~, wag so 'n bietjie, wag 'n oomblikkie; *at the LAST* ~, op die nippertjie; die laaste oomblik; *MEN of* ~, vername manne; *MEN of the* ~, manne van die dag; *NOT for a* ~ *did I suspect him,* nooit ofte nimmer het ek hom verdink nie; *at a* ~ *'s*

NOTICE, dadelik, gou; ~ *of RESISTANCE*, weerstandsmoment; *THIS* ~, oombliklik; net; kort gelede; *TIMED to the* ~, presies op tyd; net presies; ~ *of TORSION*, torsiemoment; *the* ~ *of TRUTH*, die ontnugtering; die gewaarwording; *the VERY* ~, net toe; die einste oomblik; dadelik wanneer; *WAIT until the last* ~, tot die laaste oomblik wag; *I WON'T be a* ~, ek kom nou-nou; ek is nou-nou klaar; ~**arily**, elke oomblik; oombliklik; (vir) 'n oomblik; ~**ariness**, kortstondigheid, ~**ary**, oombliklik; vlugtig, kortstondig, verbygaande; ~**ly**, elke oomblik; van oomblik tot oomblik; enige tyd.
momen'tous, gewigtig, belangrik; ~**ness**, belangrikheid, gewigtigheid.
momen'tum, (..ta), moment, bewegingshoeveelheid; aandrang; snelheid; vaart, dryfkrag, stootkrag.
Mom'us, Momus; *a son (disciple) of* ~, spotvoël; vitter; grapmaker.
mon'ac(h)al, monnike-, klooster-.
mon'achism, kloosterlewe; monnikegees; monnikstand, kloosterwese, kloosterlewe.
mon'ad, (n) monade; ondeelbare bestanddeel; eenvoudige element; kragpunt; infusiediertjie; (a) eenwaardig; monadies.
monadelph'ous, eenbroederig.
monad'ic, monadies.
monan'drian, monan'drous, eenmannig; eenhelmig, eenmeeldradig.
monan'dry, monandrie, eenhelmigheid; huwelik met een man.
monan'thous, eenblommig.
mon'arch, alleenheerser, monarg; vors; ~ **'al**, monargies, vorstelik; ~ **'ic(al)**, monargaal, koningsgesind; eenhoofdig (regering); ~**ism**, monargisme, koningsgesindheid; ~**ist**, (n) monargis, koningsgesinde; (a) koningsgesind; ~**y**, (..chies), eenhoofdige regering, alleenheerskappy; monargie; koninkryk.
monaster'ial, klooster-; monnike-.
mon'astery, (..ries), monnikeklooster, manneklooster.
monas'tic, (n) kloosterling, monnik; (a) klooster-; monnik-; ~ **frock**, monnikskleed, monnikspy; ~**ism**, kloosterlewe; kloosterwese, monnikewese; ~ **life**, monnikelewe; ~ **order**, monnikeorde; ~ **state**, monnikestand; ~ **vow**, kloostergelofte.
monatom'ic, eenatomies, monatomies (molekule).
mondaine', mondaine; wêreldse (ydele) vrou.
Mon'day, Maandag; *blue* ~, blou Maandag; ~**ish**, Maandagsiek, met 'n bloumaandagse gevoel.
mon'dial, wêreldwyd.
mo'netary, geldelik, finansieel, monetêr, geld-, munt-; ~ **fund**, geldfonds; ~ **policy**, muntpolitiek; ~ **system**, muntstelsel; ~ **unit**, munteenheid; ~ **value**, geldwaarde.
monetiza'tion, (die) munt, standaardiseer van geld.
mo'netize, aanmunt; munt, tot betaalmiddel maak.
mo'ney, (n) (-s), geld; munt; betaalmiddel; duimkruid; fonds, rykdom; ~ *of ACCOUNT*, rekenmunt; ~ *BEGETS* ~, waar geld is, wil geld wees; geld soek geld; die water loop altyd see toe; *more* ~ *than BRAINS*, meer geld as verstand; *have* ~ *to BURN*, geld soos bossies hê; *the* ~ *BURNS in his pocket*, die geld brand sy sak; *COIN* ~, geld soos water verdien; ~ *DOWN*, botter by die vis; *not EVERYBODY'S* ~, nie vir elkeen van eenderse waarde nie; ~ *GALORE*, geld soos bossies; *throw GOOD* ~ *after bad*, goeie geld na slegte geld gooi; *his* ~ *burns a HOLE in his pocket*, sy geld pla hom; die geld brand sy sak; *there is* ~ *IN that*, daar steek geld in; *be IN the* ~, goed daarin sit; ~ *for JAM*, maklik verdiende geld; geld verniet; ~ *and KINDNESS will open all gates*, met geld en goeie woorde kry mens alles gedaan; *not to be had for LOVE or* ~, nie vir geld of goeie (mooi) woorde te kry nie; *I am not MADE of* ~, geld groei nie op my rug nie; *MAKE* ~, (baie) geld verdien; ~ *makes the MARE go round*, geld is die siel v.d. handel; vir geld kan 'n mens die duiwel laat dans; *MARRY* ~, 'n vrou (man) met geld trou; *ready* ~ *is ready MEDICINE*, geld wat stom is, maak reg wat krom is; geld wat geel is, maak reg wat skeel is; *MUCK and* ~ *go together*, geld wat sleg is, maak krom wat reg is; *for MY* ~, as ek moet kies; na my mening; na my wens; na my smaak; ~ *is no OBJECT*, geld is van minder belang; dit sal nie op geld aankom nie; *beauty is potent, but* ~ *is OMNIPOTENT*, geld wat stom is, maak reg wat krom is; geld wat geel is, maak reg wat skeel is; *be OUT of* ~, platsak wees; *PUT one's* ~ *on*, wed op; *READY* ~, kontant; *ROLL in* ~, in geld swem; ~ *is ROUND and rolls away*, geld moet rol; *if* ~ *be not thy SERVANT, it will be thy master*, as jy geld jou nie laat dien nie, sal hy jou regeer; *make* ~ *SPIN*, geld laat rol; ~ *TALKS*, geld wat stom is, maak reg wat krom is; *THROW away one's* ~, met geld smyt; *TIME is* ~, tyd is geld; ~ *does not grow on TREES*, geld groei nie op 'n mens se rug nie; ~ *is lost for WANT of* ~, geld maak geld; ~ *makes the WORLD go round*, geld is die siel van die handel; *not for all the* ~ *in the WORLD*, vir geen geld ter wêreld nie; *get one's* ~ *'s WORTH*, waarde vir jou geld kry; (v) aanmunt; van geld voorsien; tot geld maak; ~**-agent**, geldwisselaar; ~**-bag**, geldsak; ~**-bill**, belastingwetsontwerp; ~**-box**, spaarpot, spaarbussie; ~**-broker**, geldmakelaar; geldwisselaar; ~**-business**, geldhandel; ~**-cares**, geldsorge; ~**-changer**, geldwisselaar; ~**ed**, bemiddeld, geldkragtig, gegoed; geld-; ~**-grabber**, ~**-grubber**, geldwolf, skraper; ~**-lender**, geldskieter, gelduitlener; ~ **less**, arm, sonder geld; ~**-making**, (n) geldmakery; (a) winsgewend; ~**-market**, geldmark, geldhandel; ~ **matters**, geldsake; ~ **order**, poswissel; ~**-proof**, onomkoopbaar; ~ **rate**, geldkoers; ~**-spinner**, geldmaker; gelukspinnekop; ~**'s-worth**, volle waarde; ~**-trade**, geldhandel; ~ **wort**, penningkruid.
mo'nger, (n) handelaar, winkelier; (v) handel.
Mong'ol[1], (n) Mongool; Mongools (taal); (a) Mongools.
mong'ol[2], swaksinnige, mongool.
Mongol'ia, Mongolië.
Mongol'ian, (n) Mongool; Mongools (taal); (a) Mongools.
mongol'ianism, mon'golism, mongolisme.
mon'goose, (-s), muishond; igneumon (Indië).
mo'ngrel, baster; opraapsel; basterhond, brak; ~**iza'tion**, verbastering; ~**ize**, verbaster.
mon'ial, middelstyl (venster).
mon'ied = **moneyed**.
monil'iform, soos 'n halssnoer, halssnoervormig.
mon'ism, monisme.
mon'ist, monis.
monis'tic, monisties.
moni'tion, waarskuwing, vermaning; dagvaarding.
mon'itive, vermanend.
mon'itor, (n) vermaner; klasleier (skool); monitor (boot); vermaning; waarskuwing; pantserskip; luisterinrigting (vir vuurpyleksperimente): (v) opvang, kontroleer; ~ **'ial**, vermanend; waarskuwend; ~**y**, (n) (..ries), maanbrief; (a) vermanend; waarskuwend.
mon'itress, (-es), vermaner (vroulik); klasleidster.
monk, monnik; mynlont; drukkersklad; ~**dom**, monnikedom; ~**ery**, (..ries), monnikestand, monnikeorde; monnikeklooster; monnikelewe; (pl) monnikepraktyke.
mo'nkey, (n) (-s), aap; heiblok; straatstamper, ramblok; waterkruik; *GET one's* ~ *up*, kwaad word; *MAKE a* ~ *out of someone*, iem. vir die gek hou; *PLAY the* ~, die gek skeer; *PUT your* ~ *up*, jou vererg; *TRY* ~ *business*, streke uithaal; ~ *'s WEDDING*, die jakkalse trou; *YOU* ~! jou klein aapstert! (v) bobbejaanstreke uithaal, dwaas handel; na-aap, uitkoggel; ~ *about with*, speel met, peuter met; ~**-bird**, kakelaar; ~**-bread**, aapbrood, kremetartvrug; ~**-bread tree**, kremetartboom, baobab; ~**-face**, apetronie; ~**-fish**, doodskop; ~**-flower**, maskerblom; ~**-gland**, aapklier; ~**-house**, aaptuin; ~**ism**, aapnatuur; aapstreke; ~**-jacket**, matroosbaadjie; ~**-nut**, grondboontjie; ~ **orange**, klapper-

(boom); ~-puzzle, voëltjie-kan-nie-sit-nie, bobbejaanverdriet *(Araucaria imbricata)*; veelkeusige vraag; ~-rope, bobbejaantou; ~-spanner = monkey-wrench; ~-trick, bobbejaanstreek; ~-wrench, skroefhamer, skroefsleutel, bobbejaanbek, duiwelsbek; *throw a ~-wrench into the works*, 'n stok in die wiel steek.
monk: ~ **hood**, monnikskap; monnikedom; ~ **ish**, monnikagtig, monnike=; ~ *ish work*, monnikewerk; ~ **ishness**, monnikagtigheid; ~ **'s bench**, banktafel; ~ **'s frock**, monnikskleed; ~ **'s-hood**, wilde ridderspoor; monnikskap; wolfswortel; ~ **'s Latin**, Middeleeuse Latyn, Monnikelatyn.
monobas'ic, eenbasies.
monocarp'ic, eenmaalbloeiend.
monocell'ular, eensellig.
monoceph'alous, eenhoofdig, monosefaal.
mon'ochord, monochordium, eensnarige toestel (teleg.).
monochro'ic, eenkleurig, monochroïes.
monochromat'ic, eenkleurig, monochroom.
monochro'matism, monochromatisme, kleurblindheid.
mon'ochrome, (n) eenkleurige skildery, monochroom; (a) eenkleurig, monochroom.
mon'ocle, oogglas, monokel.
mon'ocline, monoklien, monoklinaal, enkelplooi.
monoclin'ic, monoklien.
monocli'nous, tweeslagtig
mon'ocoloured, eenkleurig.
mon'ocoque, skulpromp; ~ **construction,** skulpbou.
monocotyled'on, (-es), eensaadlobbige plant, monokotiel; ~ **ous,** een(saad)lobbig, monokotiel.
monoc'racy, eenhoofdige regering, monokrasie.
mon'ocrat, alleenheerser.
monoc'ular, eenoog=, eenogig.
mon'nculture, monokultuur.
mon'ocycle, monofiets.
monocy'clic, monosiklies; eenjarig.
monodac'tylous, eenvingerig, eentonig, monodaktiel.
mon'odrama, dramatiese alleenspraak, monodrama; ~ **t'ic,** monodramaties.
mon'ody, (..dies), treurdig; monodie, alleensang.
monoe'cious, eenhuisig (bot.); hermafrodities.
monog'amist, monogamis.
monog'amous, monogamisties, monogaam, eenwywig.
monog'amy, eenwywery, monogamie, enkelvoudige huwelik.
monogen'esis, monogenese.
mon'oglot, (n) eentalige; (a) eentalig.
mon'ogram, naamsyfer, monogram.
mon'ograph, monografie; ~ **og'rapher,** monografieskrywer, monografis; ~ **ic,** monografies; ~ **og'raphy,** monografie.
mono'gynous, eenstylig; eenwywig.
mono'gyny, eenwywery.
mon'olith, suil uit een klip, monoliet; ~ **'ic,** monolities.
mon'ologue, alleenspraak, monoloog.
monoman'ia, monomanie; ~ **c,** (n, a) monomaan.
monoman'iacal, monomaan.
monomet'allism, monometallisme.
monomet'allist, monometallis.
monom'ial, (n) monomium, eenterm; (a) monomiaal, eentermig.
monomorph'ic, monomorph'ous, monomorf, eenvormig.
monop'athy, monopatie.
monopet'alous, eenbladig, eenblarig, monopetaal.
mon'ophase, eenfasig.
mon'ophthong, eenklank, monoftong.
monophylet'ic, eenstammig.
monophyll'ous, eenbladig, eenblarig.
mon'oplane, eendekker, enkeldekker.
monop'olist, (n) alleenhandelaar, houer van 'n monopolie, monopolis; (a) monopolisties.
monopoliza'tion, monopolisasie.
monop'olize, monopoliseer, die alleenhandel besit; iets heeltemal vir jouself hou; ~ **r,** monopolis.

monop'oly, (..lies), alleenhandel, monopolie.
monopol'ylogue, voorstelling waarby een speler verskillende rolle vertolk.
monopsych'ism, monopsigisme.
monopsych'ite, monopsigiet.
monop'teral, eenvlerkig; eenvinnig.
monop'tic, eenogig.
monopyrene'ous, eenpittig.
mon'orail, eenspoor(trein).
monorgan'ic, monorganies.
mon'ospar, eenleer=; ~ **construction,** eenleerbou; ~ **wing,** eenleervlerk.
monosperm'al, monosperm'ic, monosperm'ous, eensadig.
monosyllab'ic, eenlettergrepig, monosillabies.
monosyll'able, eenlettergrepige woord, monosillabe; *speak in ~s,* kortaf praat, net ja en nee sê.
monothal'amous, eenkamerig.
mon'otheism, monoteïsme, geloof in een God.
mon'otheist, (n) monoteïs; (a) monoteïsties.
monotheis'tic, monoteïsties.
mon'otint, eenkleurige skildery, monotint.
mon'otone, (n) eentoon; eentonigheid; (v) op een toon sing (voordra); eentonig praat; (a) eentonig, vervelend, monotoon.
monot'onous, eentonig, eenselwig; vervelend; geesdodend.
monot'ony, eentonigheid, eenselwigheid; vervelendheid, verveling.
mo'notreme, monotreem, kloaakdier.
monotrop'ic, eenvormig, monotroop.
monotrop'ism, eenvormigheid.
mon'otropy, monotropie.
mon'otype, monotipe (setmasjien) (handelsnaam).
Mon'roe doctrine, Mon'roeism, Monroeleer.
Mons, Bergen.
monseigneur', (messeigneurs), monseigneur (my heer).
monsieur', (messieurs), meneer.
monsignor'(e), (-i), monseignor.
monsoon', passaatwind; moeson; reënseisoen.
mon'ster, (n) monster, gedierte, dierasie, gevaarte, misbaksel, gedrog; wangedrog; *delicious ~,* mielievrug, geraamteplant; (a) monsteragtig, reusagtig; ~ **meeting,** massavergadering; ~ **petition,** monsterpetisie, reusepetisie.
mon'strance, monstrans.
monstros'ity, (..ties), gedrog(telikheid), onding, monster; monsteragtigheid; wangedrog.
mon'strous, monsteragtig, wanskape, afskuwelik, gedrogtelik, afgryslik; vreeslik; ~ **ly,** monsteragtig, verskriklik, ~ **ness,** monsteragtigheid, afskuwelikheid, gedrogtelikheid; afgryslikheid.
mon'tane, berg=, bergagtig.
montan'ic, bergagtig.
montbre'tia, montbretia.
mon'te, monte.
Monteneg'rin, (n) Montenegryn; (a) Montenegryns.
Monteneg'ro, Montenegro.
Montessor'i system, Montessoristelsel.
month, maand; ~ *AFTER ~,* maand na maand; ~ *BY ~,* maande agtereen; *this DAY ~,* vandag oor 'n maand; *a ~ of SUNDAYS,* 'n eindelose tyd; *THIS ~,* hierdie maand; ~ **ling,** maandoud dier.
month'ly, (n) (..lies), maandblad; (pl) maandstonde, menstruasie; (a) maandeliks, maand=; ~ **magazine,** maandblad; ~ **meeting,** maandelikse vergadering; ~ **order,** maandorder; ~ **pay,** maandgeld; ~ **report,** maandverslag; ~ **returns,** maandstaat; ~ **statement,** maandverslag; ~ **rose,** maandroos; ~ **ticket,** maandkaartjie; ~ **wages,** maandloon.
monticel'lite, monticelliet.
mon'ticle, mon'ticule, bultjie, hoogtetjie.
mon'ument, monument, gedenkteken, gedenksteen; grafsteen.
monument'al, monumentaal; kolossaal, groots; gedenk=, monument=; ~ **fountain,** monumentfontein; ~ **mason,** grafsteenmaker.
mon'zonite, monzoniet.

moo, bulk, loei.
mooch, (n) rondloper, bedelaar; (v) steel; rondslenter; luier, klaploop; ~ **er,** slenteraar, klaploper, rondloper; goudief.
moo'cha, stertriem.
mood, stemming, luim; humeur; bui, gestemdheid; wyse, modus (gram.); *he is in a very BAD* ~, hy is in 'n slegte bui; 'n vlieg het oor sy neus geloop; *in a GOOD* ~, in 'n goeie bui; *IN the* ~, in die stemming; *INDICATIVE* ~, aantonende wys(e); *SUBJUNCTIVE* ~, aanvoegende wys(e); ~ **iness,** humeurigheid, buierigheid, nukkerigheid; swaarmoedigheid; ~ **y,** buierig, humeurig, knorrig, nukkerig, nors, stuurs; swaarmoedig.
moo'lah, (sl.), geld, malie.
moon, (n) maan; maand (poëties); *ARTIFICIAL* ~, kunsmaan; *once in a BLUE* ~, omtrent nooit, baie selde, elke skrikkeljaar; *never mind, daddy will BRING you the* ~, toe maar, more bak Ma koekies; *CRY for the* ~, die onmoontlike begeer; *FULL* ~, volmaan; *there IS a* ~, dis ligte maan; *MAKE a person believe that the* ~ *is made of green cheese,* iem. knolle vir sitroene verkoop; *the MAN in the* ~, die man in die maan; *NEW* ~, nuwemaan; *there is NO* ~, dis donkermaan; *have as many PHASES as the* ~, so veranderlik soos die maan wees; *REACH for the* ~, aan die maan wil vat; *WISH a person over the* ~, iem. na die maan wens; (v) droom; rondslenter; ~ *ABOUT,* rondluier; ~ *AROUND,* met jou siel onder jou arm rondloop, ronddwaal; ~ **beam,** maanstraal; ~ **-blind,** nagblind; ~ **-blindness,** maanblindheid; ~ **-buggy,** maanbesie, maanbakkie; ~ **calf,** gedrog, misgeboorte; uilskuiken; ~ **-craft,** maantuig; ~ **er,** dromer, suffer; ~ **-eyed,** bysiende; ~ **-faced,** met 'n ronde gesig; ~ **-fish,** maanvis; ~ **-flight,** maanvlug; ~ **flower,** margriet; maanblom; ~ **-landing,** maanlanding; ~ **less,** donker(maan), sonder maan; *a* ~ *less night,* donkermaan, 'n donker aand.
moon'light, maanlig; *a* ~ *NIGHT,* 'n maanligaand; ~ *and ROSES,* rosegeur en maneskyn; ~ **er,** nagtrekker; ~ **lighting,** nagwerk.
moon: ~ **lit,** maanlig=, deur die maan verlig; ~ **probe,** maanreis; maanruimtevaart; ~ **rise,** maansopgang; ~ **set,** maansondergang.
moon'shee, *kyk* **munshi.**
moon: ~ **shine,** maanskyn; onsin, kaf, bog; smokkeldrank (Amerk.); *that's all* ~ *shine,* dis pure bog; ~ **shiner,** dranksmokkelaar; ~ **shiny,** deur die maan beskyn, maanlig=; onsinnig; ~ **spot,** maanvlek; ~ **stone,** maansteen, wateropaal; ~ **struck,** maansiek, mal, met die maan gepla; sentimenteel; *be* ~ *struck,* getik wees; deur lotjie getik wees; deur die maan gepla wees; ~ **traveller,** maanreisiger; ~ **-watch,** maanwag; ~ **-watcher,** maanwagter; ~ **wort,** maanvaring; ~ **y,** maan=, maanvormig; maansiek; getik; dronk; ~ **-year,** maanjaar.
Moor¹, Moor.
moor², (n) heide, heiveld; vlei, moeras.
moor³, (v) (vas)meer, vasmaak, aanlê, (vas)anker; ~ **age,** ankerplek, aanlêplek.
moor: ~ **cock,** bleshoender(mannetjie) (S.A.); ~ **hen,** waterhoender.
moor'ing, (die) vasmeer; (pl) ankerplek, aanlêplek; ankerketting, meertoue; *the ship BROKE her* ~ *s,* die skip se ankertoue het gebreek; *DRIVEN from the* ~, losgeraak het; *LIE at the* ~ *s,* (vas)gemeer lê; ~ **-area,** ankerplek, meervlak; ~ **-buoy,** meerboei; ~ **-cable,** meerkabel; ~ **-mast,** aanlêmas, meermas, ankermas; lêplek (van skepe), ankerplek; ~ **-pin,** meerpen; ~ **-place,** meerplek, lêplek; ~ **-post,** meerpaal.
Moor'ish¹, Moors.
moor'ish², heiagtig; nat, vleiagtig, moerassig.
moor'land, heideveld; vlei, moeras.
moor: ~ **pin,** meerpen; ~ **ring,** meerring, kaairing; ~ **rope,** meertou.
moose, Amerikaanse eland.
moot, (n) vergadering; debat; (v) opper, ter sprake bring; bespreek, debatteer; *first* ~ *ed,* vir die eerste keer ter sprake gebring; (a) betwisbaar; *a* ~ *point,*

'n ope vraag; ~ **case,** geskilpunt, onuitgemaakte saak.
mop¹, (n) poetsbesem, klosbesem; vryflap, vryfdoek, stokdweil, (stof)dweil; boskasie (fig.); (v) **(-ped),** afvee, dweil, opvryf; insluk; ~ *UP,* opvee; insluk; opvang; uit die weg ruim; ~ *the floor WITH somebody,* iem. kafloop.
mop², (n) grimas, skewebek; (v) skewebek trek; ~ *and mow,* skewebek trek.
mopan'i, mopanie *(Copaifera mopane);* ~ **worm,** mopaniewurm.
mop'-board, spatlys.
mope, (n) druiloor, knieser; (v) droom, suf; jou verknies; neerslagtig wees, druil; ~ *AWAY,* versuf; ~ *oneself to DEATH,* jou doodknies; ~ *one's HEART OUT,* jou verknies (doodknies).
mo'ped, kragfiets, bromfiets.
mop: ~ **head,** bossiekop; dweilkop; ~ **headed,** bossiekop=.
mop'ing, druilend, druilerig; neerslagtig; suf.
mop'ish, knieserig, druilerig; verdrietig, swaarmoedig; ~ **ness,** swaarmoedigheid; knieserigheid.
mopp'et, meisie, skattebol.
mopp'ing-up, opruiming.
mops, Mopshond(jie).
mop' stick, opvryfstok, dweilstok; sukkelaar.
mop'y, druilerig, knieserig.
moquette', moket, trypferweel.
mor, mor, suurhumus; **mor(r)a,** mor(r)a, vingerraaispel.
moraine', gletserpuin, moreen.
mor'al, (n) moraal; sedeles; *his* ~ *s LEAVE much to be desired,* sy sedelike gedrag laat veel te wense oor; *POINT a* ~, 'n sedeles laat uitkom; (a) sedelik, moreel; sede-; moraal-; geestelik; *it is a* ~ *certainty,* dit is so goed as seker; ~ **ascendancy,** sedelike oorwig; ~ **courage,** sedelike moed; ~ **depravity,** sedeverbastering, sedeverwording, sedeontaarding.
morale', moed, volharding (in moeilikhede), veggees, selfvertroue; die moreel (van 'n leër).
mor'al: ~ **force,** sedelike krag; ~ **ism,** sug tot moralis= seer; sedeprekery; moralisme; ~ **ist,** sedepreker, moralis, strafprediker.
moral'ity, (..ties), sedelikheid; sedeleer; sedelike gedrag; sinnespel; ~ **play,** moraliteit(spel); sinnespel.
mor'al: ~ **iza'tion,** moralisasie; ~ **ize,** sedelesse gee, moraliseer, sedelik verbeter; ~ **izer,** sedemeester, sedepreker; ~ **law,** sedewet; ~ **lecture,** sedepreek; sedewet; ~ **obligation,** sedelike verpligting; ~ **philosophy,** sedekunde; ~ **rearmament,** geestelike (sedelike) herbewapening; ~ **sense,** sedelikheidsgevoel; ~ **support,** sedelike bystand; ~ **theology,** moraalteologie, sedeleer; ~ **victory,** morele oorwinning.
morass', (-es), moeras; ~ **y,** moerasagtig, vleierig.
mor'at, moerbeidrank.
morator'ium, (..ria), moratorium, wettige uitstel van betaling.
Morav'ia, Morawië.
Morav'ian, (n) Morawiër, Herrnhutter; (a) Morawies; ~ **Brotherhood,** Morawiese Broederskap.
mor'bid, sieklik; ongesond; morbied; ~ **anatomy,** patologiese anatomie; ~ **depression,** sieklike neerslagtigheid; ~ **'ity = morbidness;** ~ **matter,** siektestof; ~ **ness,** sieklikheid; ongesondheid; morbiditeit.
morbif'ic, siekte=, siekteveroorsakend; ~ **matter,** siektestof.
morbill'ous, masel=, maselagtig.
morda'cious, bytend; skerp.
morda'city, bytendheid.
mord'ant, (n) etssuur, bytstof; hegmiddel; (v) beits (by weefstowwe); (a) bytend, snydend, skerp; beits.
more, meer; nog, groter; ~ *AND* ~, steeds meer; hoe langer hoe meer; meer en meer; *the* ~ *the BETTER,* hoe meer, hoe beter; *little* ~ *than a CHILD,* nog byna 'n kind; *there is* ~ *than meets*

moreen   1059   **mortise**

the *EYE*, daar skuil iets agter; *a FEW or* ~, 'n stuk of wat; *he IS no* ~, hy is dood; ~ *or LESS*, naasteby, min of meer; *that is* ~ *LIKE it!* so moet dit wees! *MANY* ~, nog baie meer; *the* ~ *the MERRIER*, hoe meer siele, hoe meer vreugde; *so MUCH the* ~, soveel te meer; *so MUCH* ~, baie meer; *NEVER* ~, nooit weer nie; *NEITHER* ~ *nor less*, presies soveel; *NO* ~, nie meer nie; *NO* ~ *did I*, ek ewemin; ek ook nie; *NOT* ~ *than that*, nie meer as dit nie; *ONCE* ~, nog 'n keer; *ten OR* ~, 'n stuk of tien; ~ *is the PITY*, des te jammerder; ~ *to the PURPOSE*, doelmatiger; *I hope to SEE* ~ *of you*, ek vertrou dat ons mekaar weer sal ontmoet; *the* ~ *SO*, (des) te meer; *SOME* ~, nog meer; *SOMETHING* ~, iets meer, nog iets; ~ *THAN*, meer as; ~ *than THAT*, nog meer; buitendien, boonop; *THE* ~, hoe meer; *THREE* ~, nog drie; *WHAT is* ~, wat meer is; buitendien.
moreen', woldamas, moreen.
morel'[1], swart nastergal.
morel'[2], morielje, sampioen.
morell'o, (-es), morel (kersie).
moreov'er, bowendien, daarenbowe, verder, buitendien, te meer, voorts, wyders.
Mores'que[1], (n) Moorse styl; (a) Moors.
moresque'[2], (n, a) arabesk.
morganat'ic, morganaties; ~ **marriage**, morganatiese huwelik.
morg'en, morg; ~-**foot**, morgvoet.
morgue[1], lykhuis, identifiseerplek (van lyke); dodehuis.
morgue[2], hoogmoed, trotse houding.
mo'ribund, (n) sterwende, sieltogende; (a) doodsiek, sterwend.
mo'rion, stormhoed.
Moris'co, (n) Moorse dans; (a) Moors.
Morm'on, Mormoon; ~**ism**, Mormonisme; ~**ite**, Mormoon.
morn, môre, more, môrestond, oggend, voormiddag; *from* ~ *till eve*, van die oggend tot die aand.
mor'nay, kaassous, mornay.
morn'ing, (n) more, môre, oggend, voormiddag; môrestond; ~! more! môre! *FIRST thing in the* ~, soggens heel eerste; *GOOD* ~, goeiemôre; more; *the* ~ *HOUR has gold in the mouth*, die môrestond het goud in die mond; *IN the* ~, in die môre; *the* ~ *after the NIGHT before*, olikheid na vrolikheid; *OF a* ~, in die môre, smôrens; *ONE* ~, op 'n sekere môre; *THIS* ~, vanmôre; *TOMORROW* ~, môreoggend; ~ **call**, môrebesoek; ~ **coat**, pantbaadjie; ~ **draught**, môreglasie; oggenddrankie; ~ **dress**, oggendrok, huisrok; oggendpak; oggenddrag; ~ **glory**, (..ries), purperwinde, eendagmooi (blom); ~ **gown**, kamerjapon, kamerjas; oggendrok; ~ **gun**, môreskoot; **M** ~ **land**, Môreland, die Ooste; ~ **mass**, vroegmis; ~ **paper**, oggendblad; ~ **performance**, oggendvertoning; kindervertoning, matinee; ~ **prayer**, oggendgebed; ~ **prayers**, oggendgodsdiens; ~ -**room**, huiskamer, woonkamer; ~ **service**, môrediens; ~ **sickness**, mislikheid (met swangerskap); ~ **star**, môrester; ~ **task**, môretaak; ~ **tea**, oggendtee; ~ **tide**, oggendstond; ~ **watch**, môrewag, rooidagwag.
morn'ward, teen die môre; na die ooste.
Morocc'an, (n) Marokkaan; (a) Marokkaans.
Morocc'o[1], Marokko.
morocc'o[2], marokyn(leer); ~ **paper**, saffiaanpapier.
mor'on, moron, swaksinnige.
moron'ic, swaksinnig, moronies.
mor'onism, swaksinnigheid, moronisme.
morose', stuurs, swartgallig, swaartillend, gemelik, stug, nors; ~**ness**, gemelikheid, knorrigheid, swaartillendheid.
morph, morf (taalk.).
Morphe'an, Morpheus=; slaap=.
mor'pheme, morfeem (taalk.).
Morph'eus, Morpheus; die slaap; *in the arms of* ~, in die arms van Morpheus.
morph'ia, **morph'ine**, morfien, morfine; ~ **syringe**, morfinespuit(jie).

morph'inism, morfinisme, verslaafdheid aan morfien.
morph'inist, morfinis.
morphinoman'iac, morfinis.
morphoge'nesis, morfogenese.
morphog'raphy, morfografie.
morpholog'ical, morfologies.
morphol'ogy, vormleer, morfologie.
morphon'omy, morfonomie.
morpho'sis, morfose, vormingswyse.
morp'ion, platluis.
mor'ris: ~ **chair**, russtoel, luierstoel; ~ **dance**, Moorse dans, morrisdans, narredans; ~ **pike**, Moorse piek.
mo'rrow, môre; *on the* ~, die volgende dag.
morse[1], walrus.
Morse[2], morsetoestel; morsealfabet; ~ **alphabet**, morsealfabet; ~ **code**, morsekode, morseskrif; ~ **flag**, morsevlag.
mors'el, stukkie, happie, krummel, brokkie, mondvol.
Morse: ~ **signal**, morsesein; ~ **telegraph**, morsetoestel.
mort[1], horinggeskal (om dood van takbok aan te kondig).
mort[2], salm in derde jaar.
mort[3], menigte, boel.
mort'al, sterfling, sterweling; (a) sterflik; stoflik, eindig; dodelik; vreeslik; ewig; vervelend; menslik; ~ *BLOW*, 'n dodelike slag; *for two* ~ *HOURS*, vir twee vervelende uur; *be in a* ~ *HURRY*, vreeslik haastig wees; *no* ~ *POWER*, geen mag ter wêreld nie; *PUT off the* ~ *and put on immortality*, die tydelike met die ewige verwissel; *a* ~ *SHAME*, 'n ewige skande; *any* ~ *THING*, net wat jy wil; ~ **agony**, doodsangs; ~ **combat**, stryd op lewe en dood; ~ **enemy**, doodsvyand; ~ **hour**, sterfuur; ~ **hurry**, vlieënde haas.
mortal'ity, sterflikheid; sterfte, dodetal; vrekte (diere); sterftesyfer; ~ **rate**, sterftesyfer; ~ **table**, sterftetabel.
mort'ally, dodelik; sterflik; ~ *AFRAID*, doodbang; ~ *OFFENDED*, dodelik beledig; ~ *WOUNDED*, dodelik gewond.
mort'alness, dodelikheid.
mort'al: ~ **remains**, stoflike oorskot; ~ **shame**, ewige skande; ~ **sin**, hoofsonde, doodsonde; ~ **wound**, dodelike wond.
mor'tar[1], mortier (kanon); vuurpyltoestel.
mor'tar[2], vysel.
mor'tar[3], (n) dagha; messelkalk, messelklei; bindsel; *BRICKS and* ~, geboue; *PESTLE and* ~, stamper en vysel; (v) pleister; ~-**battery**, mortierbattery; ~ **board**, pleisterplank; studentbaret; ~ **bomb**, mortierbom; ~ **box**, vyselbak; mortierkis; ~ -**carrier**, mortierkar; ~ **droppings**, afvalklei; ~-**emplacement**, mortierstand; ~-**gunner**, mortieris; ~ **mill**, kalkmeul, kleimeul; ~-**mixer**, kleimenger.
mort'gage, (n) verband, hipoteek, kusting; *GIVE in* ~, verpand; *LEND on* ~, op verband leen; (v) verband opneem, verband beswaar; verbind, verpand; ~ **bank**, hipoteekbank; ~ **bond**, verband, verbandakte, hipoteek; pandbrief; akte van skepekennis; ~ **d**, verpand, onder verband; *a house* ~*d with a building society*, 'n huis onder bouverenigingverband; *a mortaged property*, 'n verbande eiendom; ~ **deed**, verbandakte; ~**e'**, verbandhouer, hipoteekhouer; ~ **loan**, verbandlening; ~**r**, **mort'gagor**, verbandgewer.
mort'ice = **mortise**.
morti'cian, lykbesorger, begrafnisondernemer.
mortifica'tion, kwelling, verdriet; selfverloening, selfkastyding, doding; deemoediging; vernedering, gekrenktheid; kouevuur, gangreen, versterwing (siekte).
mort'ified, gekrenk, beledig.
mort'ify, (..fied), (die vlees) dood(maak); kwel, krenk, beledig, beskaam; tugtig, kasty; kouevuur (gangreen) kry.
mort'ise, (n) tapgat, voeggat; insteekslot; *HAUNCHED* ~ *and tenon*, skoftap-en-gat; *SHOULDERED* ~ *and tenon*, skouertap-en-gat; ~ *and*

mortmain 1060 *moujik*

TENON joint, tap-en-gatvoeg; (v) tap, inlaat, invoeg, aanmekaarvoeg; ~ **bolt,** opsluitpen; insteekgrendel; ~ **chisel,** kantbeitel, steekbeitel, tapbeitel; ~ **cleaner,** opruimbeitel; ~ **gauge,** dubbel(pen)kruishout, tapkruishout; ~ **lock,** inlaatslot, tapslot; ~ **machine,** tapgatboor, tapboormasjien, tapmasjien.
mort'main, (eiendom in die) dooie hand.
mort'uary, (n) (..ries), lykhuis, dodehuis; (a) dode=, sterf=, graf=; begrafnis=.
moru'la, moerbei (med.); maroela.
Mosa'ic¹, Mosaïes.
mosa'ic², (n) mosaïek; (v) met mosaïek inlê; (a) mosaïek=; ~ **work,** mosaïek(werk).
Mosarab'ic, Mosarabies.
mosasaur'us, mosasouriër, mosasourus.
mos'chate, muskusagtig.
moschatel', muskusplant.
Mos'covite, Moskowiet.
Mos'cow, Moskou.
moselle', moeselwyn.
mo'sey, (sl.), aanslenter, luier, voortslenter.
Moshesh', Mosjesj.
mos'konfyt, moskonfyt.
Mos'lem, (n) Mohammedaan, Islamiet, Slamaier; (a) Mohammedaans, Islamities, Slams; ~ **ism,** Mohammedanisme, die Islam.
mosque, moskee, masied.
mosqui'to, (-es), muskiet; ~-**armament,** bewapening teen torpedo's; ~-**bite,** muskietbyt; ~-**craft,** vinnige oorlogsbote; ~-**lotion,** muskietolie; ~-**net,** muskietnet; ~-**proof,** muskietvry; ~-**proof gauze,** muskietgaas; ~**weight,** muskietgewig.
moss, (n) mos; moeras; turf, mos; *a rolling stone gathers no* ~, 'n swerwer bly 'n derwer; (v) bemos, met mos bedek.
moss'banker, moss'bunker, marsbanker.
moss: ~-**clad,** ~-**covered,** ~-**grown,** bemos, met mos begroei; ~-**iness,** mossigheid; ~-**litter,** strooisel; ~-**rose,** mosroos; ~ **y,** bemos, mosagtig.
mos'so, (It., mus.), mosso, vinnig.
most, (a) meeste; uiterste; grootste; ~ *of the DAY,* die grootste deel v.d. dag; *MAKE the* ~ *of,* die meeste voordeel trek uit; die beste gebruik maak van; uitbuit; woeker met; *for the* ~ *PART,* meestendeels, grotendeels; ~ *PEOPLE,* die meeste mense; ~ *TIMES,* meestal, gewoonlik; ~ *of the TIME,* meestal, gewoonlik; ~ *of US,* die meeste van ons; (adv) mees, baie, hoogs, uiters, aller=, besonders; *AT (the)* ~, hoogstens; ~ *CERTAINLY,* alte seker; *the M* ~ *HIGH,* die Allerhoogste; *SIX at the* ~, uiters ses; ~-**favoured nation,** mees begunstigde nasie; ~ **learned,** hoogsgeleerd; ~ **ly,** meestendeels, meestal, hoofsaaklik, deurgaans, vernaamlik.
mote, stoffie, stofdeeltjie; kleinigheid; splinter; *the* ~ *in another's EYE,* die splinter in 'n ander se oog; *see the* ~ *in another's EYE and forget the beam in one's own,* die splinter in 'n ander se oog sien, maar die balk in jou eie vergeet.
motel', motel.
motet', motet.
moth, mot; nagvlinder; ligte vliegtuig; ~ **ball,** motgifballetjie; ~-**eaten,** deur motte gevreet; verouderd.
mo'ther¹, (n) moer, droesem.
mo'ther², (n) moeder, ma; huismoeder; abdis (klooster); moer (van 'n dier); kunsmoeder; *M* ~ *CAREY'S chickens,* stormvoëls; *at the* ~ *'s KNEE,* aan moeder se knie; *every* ~ *'s SON,* iedereen sonder uitsondering; (v) die lewe gee; aanhaal, vroetroetel; versorg, moeder speel oor, bemoeder; (a) moeder=; *M* ~ **Church,** moederkerk; ~ **city,** moederstad; ~ **country,** vaderland; ~**craft,** moederkunde; ~ **die,** stamstempel, stamblok; ~ **earth,** moeder aarde; ~**hood,** moederskap; ~**ing,** moedersorg; liefkosing; ~-**in-law,** skoonmoeder; ~-**in-law's tongue,** sansevieria, slangvel (plant); ~ **land,** vaderland; ~ **language,** moedertaal; ~-**lay-the-table,** moedersepoppie; ~**less,** moederloos; ~**liness,** moederlikheid; ~ **liquor,** moederloog; ~ **lode,** hoofertsliggaam; ~-**love,** moederliefde; ~ **ly,** moederlik;

~-**naked,** poedelnakend; ~-**of-pearl,** perlemoer; ~-**right,** moederreg, matriargaat; ~ **rock,** moedergesteente; ~ **'s boy,** ma se witbroodjie; *M* ~ **'s Day,** Moedersdag; ~ **'s help,** kindermeisie; ~ **ship,** moederskip; ~ **'s lap,** moederskoot; ~-**spot,** moedervlek, moesie; ~ **superior,** moederowerste; ~-**to-be,** aanstaande moeder; ~ **tongue,** moedertaal; grondtaal; ~-**tongue education,** moedertaalonderwys; ~ **wit,** gesonde verstand.
mo'thery, moeragtig; moerderig.
moth: ~-**hole,** motgaatjie; ~-**killer,** mottekruid; ~-**proof,** motvry; ~-**proofing,** motwerende maatreëls; motwering; ~-**resisting,** motwerend; ~ **y,** deur motte gevreet; vol motte.
motif', motief, hoofidee.
mot'ile, beweeglik.
motil'ity, beweeglikheid.
mo'tion, (n) beweging; mosie, voorstel; aansoek; stoelgang; handbeweging; werk (masjien); ~ *of CENSURE,* mosie van afkeuring; ~ *of CONDOLENCE,* mosie van roubeklag (deelneming); *a* ~ *of CONFIDENCE,* 'n mosie van vertroue; *IN* ~, aan die gang; *the* ~ *was LOST,* die voorstel is verwerp; *a* ~ *of NO CONFIDENCE,* 'n mosie van wantroue; *NOTICE of* ~, kennisgewing van voorstel; *PUT a* ~, 'n voorstel tot stemming bring; *SET in* ~, aan die gang sit, in beweging bring; *SLOW* ~, stadige aksie; ~ *of SYMPATHY,* mosie van deelneming; *UNOPPOSED* ~, onbestrede voorstel; (v) wink, 'n wenk gee; 'n teken gee; 'n beweging maak om ...; ~**less,** botstil, onbeweeglik, bewegingloos; ~ **picture,** rolprent, film; ~ **pictures,** die rolprentwêreld; bioskoop, fliek; ~ **shaft,** bewegingsas; ~ **sickness,** rysiekte.
mot'ivate, motiveer, beweeg.
motiva'tion, aandrywing, motivering.
mot'ive, (n) beweegrede, motief, aanleiding, beweegrond, dryfveer; (v) beweeg, aandrywe tot (a) bewegend; beweeg=; dryf=; ~ **force,** beweegkrag, motief, dryfkrag; ~**less,** doelloos; ongemotiveerd; ~ **power** = **motive force.**
motiv'ity, beweegkrag.
mot'ley, (n) deurmekaarspul; mengelmoes; narrepak; (a) bont, gemeng, deurmekaar, kakelbont, veelkleurig; vreemdsoortig; *a* ~ *crowd,* 'n bontspan.
mot'or, (n) motor; beweegkrag; dryfkrag; (v) (in 'n motor) ry; (a) bewegend, motories; dryf=; ~ **ambulance,** motorambulans; ~ **bandit,** motordief; ~ **bicycle,** ~ **bike,** motorrywiel, motorfiets; ~ **boat,** motorboot; ~ **breakdown,** motorweiering; ~ **bus,** (motor)bus; ~**cade,** motorstoet, motoroptog, motorkade; ~-**car,** motor; ~-**coat,** stofjas; ~-**cycle,** motorfiets; ~-**cyclist,** motorfietsryer; ~-**drome,** motorrenbaan; ~ **engine,** motormasjien, -enjin; ~ **fuel,** petrol, brandstof; motorolie; ~ **gate,** ~ **grid,** roosterhek, motorhek; ~ **horn,** toeter; ~ **'ial,** beweeg=, bewegende, motories; ~ **impulse,** bewegingsprikkel; ~**ing,** gemotor, motor ry; ~**ist,** motoris, motorbestuurder, motorryer; ~**iza'tion,** motorisasie; ~**ize,** motoriseer; ~**ized,** gemotoriseer; ~ **launch,** motorboot; ~ **lead,** motorleiding; ~ **lorry,** vragmotor, motorwa; ~ **man,** bestuurder (van 'n trem); ~ **nerves,** bewegingsenuwees; ~ **road,** motorpad; ~ **scooter,** bromponie; ~ **ship,** motorskip; ~ **spirit,** petrol, motorbrandstof; ~ **transport,** motorvervoer; ~ **truck,** vragmotor; tuig; ~ **veil,** motorsluier; ~ **vessel,** motorvaartuig; ~ **way,** snelweg, motorpad, motorweg; deurpad.
mot'ory, bewegend, bewegings=, motories; ~ **muscle,** trekspier.
motte, motte, kasteelterrein.
mot'tle, (n) vlek, kol; (v) vlek, marmer, skakeer; streep.
mot'tled, bont, gemarmer, gestreep, gestippel; ~ **glass,** duikiesglas; ~ **iron,** gevlekte yster; ~ **paper,** bontpapier; ~ **soap,** spikkelseep, blouseep.
mott'o, (-es), leuse, sinspreuk, motto, devies, kernspreuk, byskrif, leenspreuk; ~ **kiss,** vrylekker, leeslekker, skryflekker.
mouff'lon, bergskaap, moeflon.
mou'jik, *kyk* **mujik.**

mould — mouth

mould¹, (n) gedaante; karakter; roes(vlek); skimmel, stuifaarde; skimmelbesmetting; grond, teelaarde; *contract* ~, beskimmel word; (v) skimmel word.

mould², (n) vorm; matrys; gietvorm; sjabloon; vormgereg; stempel; model, tangvorm; *CAST in the same* ~, in dieselfde vorm (ge)giet; op dieselfde lees (ge)skoei; *MAN of* ~, sterflike mens; (v) vorm; giet; knee, formeer, modelleer, boetseer; vervorm; skep, ontwerp.

mould'able, vormbaar; kneebaar.

mould: ~**-board**, rysterplank, rysterplaat (ploeg); strykplank; ~**-board plough**, rysterplaatploeg.

mould'-culture, skimmelkultuur.

mould'ed, gevorm; gegiet; ~ **door**, gelyste deur; ~ **gutter**, gevormde geut; ~ **pudding**, vormpoeding; ~ **shot**, vormhael.

moul'der¹, (n) vormer, formeerder, vormsnyer, modelgieter, vormgieter.

moul'der², (v) verbrokkel, verrot, vermolm, stik; vergaan, afbrokkel.

moul'diness, skimmelagtigheid, vunsigheid, mufheid.

moul'ding, lyswerk; lys; fries; formering; ~**-board**, knieplank; strykbord, vormplank; ~**-clay**, vormklei; ~**-frame**, vormraam, gietraam; ~**-machine**, vormmasjien; lysmasjien; ~**-plane**, lysskaaf.

moul'dy, beskimmel, geskimmel, skimmelig, vermuf; vunsig; verouderd, ouderwets; vervelend, onnosel (plat); *BECOME* ~, verskimmel; ~ *BREAD*, skimmelbrood; *it's a* ~ *IDEA*, dis 'n onnosele idee; ~ *SPOT*, skimmelvlek

moult, (n) verwering (pluimvee); verharing (diere); vervelling (slange); (v) verveer (hoender); verhaar (perd); vervel (slang); ~ **er**, verveerder; ~ **ing**, ververing; vervelling; ~ *ing time*, verveertyd; verhaartyd; verveltyd.

mound¹, (n) ryksappel.

mound², (n) hoop, heuweltjie; bolwerk; wal, skans; (v) omwal; ophoop.

mount¹, (n) raam, omlysting, montering (portret); beslag, montuur; montering, montasie; affuit (kanon); ryperd.

mount², (n) berg, heuwel, kop; *the M* ~ *of OLIVES*, die Olyfberg; *the SERMON on the M* ~, die Bergrede; (v) opklim, bestyg; opgaan; optrek; oploop (skuld); insit; opplak (foto); opslaan (blok); monteer, set (diamant); voer (kanon); uitsit (wag); opstel (kanon); beklim (bres); betrek (loopgrawe); ~ *a BREACH*, in die bres spring; ~ *ed in GOLD*, in goud gevat; ~ *GUARD*, wag staan (opstel, uitsit); ~ *a GUN*, 'n kanon opstel; ~ *a HORSE*, 'n perd opklim; ~ **able**, (be)klimbaar, bestygbaar; ~ *able kerbs*, skuins randstene.

moun'tain, berg, kop; *if the* ~ *won't come to MOHAMMED*, Mohammed *must go to the* ~, as die berg nie na Mohammed wil kom nie, moet Mohammed na die berg gaan; *MAKE a* ~ *of something*, 'n berg van iets maak; *make a* ~ *of a MOLEHILL*, van 'n muggie (vlooi) 'n olifant maak; ~ *brought forth a MOUSE*, die berg het 'n muis gebaar; *MOVE* ~ *s*, berge versit; ~ *of VENUS*, venusheuwel, skaamheuwel; *a* ~ *of WORK*, werk soos bossies; ~ **air**, berglug; ~ **artillery**, bergeskut, bergartillerie; ~ **ash**, lysterbesboom; ~ **canary**, bergkanarie; ~ **cat**, poema; ~ **cave**, berggrot; ~ **chain**, bergreeks, bergketting; ~ **chat**, bergwagter; ~ **cork**, bergkurk; ~ **crest**, bergkruin; ~ **crystal**, bergkristal; ~ **dew**, (Skotse) whisky; onwettig gestookte whisky; ~ **eer'**, bergbewoner; bergklimmer; ~ **eer'ing**, bergklim; ~ **fortress**, bergvesting; ~**-green**, malagiet; ~ **gun**, bergkanon; ~ **hare**, kolhaas; ~ **heath**, besembossie; ~**-high**, berghoog; ~ **lion**, bergleeu, poema; ~ **ous**, bergagtig; ~ **pass**, bergpas; poort; ~ **railway**, bergspoorweg; ~ **range**, bergketting; ~ **ridge**, bergkam, bergrug; ~ **rose**, bergroos, skaamblom *(Protea rosacea)*; ~ **sickness**, bergsiekte; ~ **slide**, bergstorting, bergverskuiwing; ~ **slope**, berghang; ~ **syringa**, bergsering, slaphout *(Kirkia wilmsii)*; ~ **torrent**, bergstroom; ~ **tortoise**, bergskilpad; ~ **troops**, bergtroepe; ~ **view**, berggesig; ~ **war(fare)**, bergoorlog(voering).

moun'tebank, (n) kwaksalwer, boer(e)verneuker, charlatan; (v) verneuk, bedrieg; (a) kwaksalwer-.

moun'ted, berede, gesete, rydend; ruiter-, te perd, perde-; opgeklim; uitgesit (wag); opgestel (affuit); gemonteer (juweel); opgeplak (foto); beslaan, met beslag; ~ **attack**, ruiteraanval; ~ **brigade**, berede brigade; ~ **guard**, ruiterwag; ~ **patrol**, ruiterpatrollie; ~ **police**, berede polisie; ~**-riflemen guard**, ruiterwag; ~ **rifles**, berede skutters; ~ **service**, berede diens; ~ **tactics**, ruitertaktiek; ~ **troops**, perderuiters; ~ **unit**, berede eenheid.

moun'ter, monteur.

moun'ting, (die) opklim; beslag, montuur, montering; (pl) onderdele; ~ *s of a gun*, geweerbeslag; ~ **board**, monteerkarton; ~ **paper**, monteerpapier; ~ **tissue**, kristalkleefpapier.

mourn, rou, treur; betreur; beween; ~ *for a FRIEND*, in die rou oor 'n vriend; ~ *a person's LOSS*, iem. se heengaan betreur; ~ **er**, roudraer, treurende; ~ **ful**, treurig, droewig; verdrietig; ~ **fulness**, treurigheid, droewigheid.

mourn'ing, rou; rougoed, rouklere; droefheid, smart; getreur; *DEEP* ~, swaar rou; *one of his EYES is* ~, hy het 'n blou oog; *GO into* ~, in die rou gaan; *HALF* ~, ligte rou; *IN* ~, in die rou; *his NAILS are in* ~, hy rou vir dooie katte; *OUT of* ~, uit die rou; ~**-band**, rouband; ~**-border**, rourand; ~ **bride**, hen-en-kuikentjies, speldekussing; ~**-coach**, roukoets; ~**-paper**, roupapier; ~**-suit**, roupak.

mous(s)aka, moesaka.

mouse, (n) **(mice)**, muis; blouoog; bangbroek; venstergewig; (v) muise vang; snuffel, rondsluip; ~ *about*, rondsnuffel, rondsoek; ~**-bird**, muisvoël; ~**-colour**, vaal, muiskleur, vaal muiskleur; ~**-coloured**, muiskleurig, vaal; ~**-dung**, muiskeutels; ~**-eaten**, deur muise gevreet; ~**-grey**, muisvaal; ~**-hole**, muisgat; ~**-like**, muisagtig; ~**-piece**, muis (in beesboud); ~**-proof**, muisvry, muisdig; ~**-proofing**, muisdigting; ~ **r**, muisvanger; ~**-trap**, muisval; slagystertjie.

mous'ing, muisvangery.

mouseline', moeselien, moeseline; neteldoek.

mousse, (F.), mousse, kloproomgereg; mosgroen.

moustache', snorbaard, snor; ~**d**, met snorbaard.

mous'y, vol muise; muisagtig.

mouth, (n) mond; snater; eet-en-drink, bek; snoet; inloop, monding (rivier); uitloop; opening; *out of the* ~ *of BABES and sucklings*, uit die mond van kinders sal 'n mens die waarheid verneem; ~ *like a CAVERN*, 'n mond soos 'n wawiel; *be DOWN in the* ~, neerslagtig wees; bek-af wees; lyk of die hoenders jou kos afgeneem het; *he is in EVERYBODY'S* ~, almal praat van hom; *GIVE* ~, blaf; *live from HAND to* ~, van die hand in die tand lewe; *the horse has a HARD* ~, die perd is taai in die bek; *his HEART was in his* ~, sy hart het in sy keel geklop; *KEEP your* ~ *shut*, hou jou mond; *MAKE a* ~, skewebek trek; *with ONE* ~, uit een mond; *not to OPEN one's* ~, jou mond nie oopmaak nie; *OUT of his own* ~, met sy eie woorde; *PASS from* ~ *to* ~, van mond tot mond gaan; ~ *of a RIVER*, riviermond; *SHUT one's* ~, die mond hou; *it sounds STRANGE in your* ~, dit klink vreemd uit jou mond; *make one's* ~ *WATER*, jou mond laat water; jou laat watertand; *by WORD of* ~, mondeling; *take the WORDS out of another's* ~, die woorde uit iem. se mond neem; *laugh on the WRONG side of one's* ~, verleë lag; lag soos iem. wat tandpyn het; *make a WRY* ~, 'n suur gesig trek; (v) hard skreeu; gemaak praat; hap, kou; proe aan; skewebek trek; ('n perd se bek) brei; ~ **cavity**, mondholte; ~ **ed**, met 'n mond, mond-; *hard* ~ *ed*, taai in die bek; ~ **er**, grootprater; ~**-filling**, bombasties, geswolle; ~ **fissure**, mondspleet; ~ **ful**, hap, sluk, teug (water); mondvol; ~**-glass**, mondspieël; ~**-harp**, trompie; ~**-organ**, mondfluitjie, bekfluitjie; ~ **piece**, mondstuk; spreekbuis (telefoon); spreektrompet; woordvoerder; *somebody's* ~ *piece*, iem. se spreekbuis (woordvoerder, mondstuk) wees; ~-**wash,** mondwassing; mondspoeling, mondwatertjie, mondspoelmiddel; ~**y,** hoogdrawend; lawaaierig; grootpraterig; vuilbekkig.

mou'ton, skaappels, skaapvel.

movabil'ity, beweegbaarheid, beweeglikheid.

mo'vable, (n) iets beweegbaars, iets los; (pl) losgoed, roerende goedere; (a) beweegbaar, beweeglik; roerend; verplaasbaar, los; ~ **feast,** veranderlike feesdag; ~ **kidney,** wandelende nier; ~**ness,** beweeglikheid, beweegbaarheid; ~ **ordnance,** verplaasbare geskut; ~ **property,** roerende goed, losgoed; ~ **type,** los letter.

move, (n) beweging; set; stoot, skuifbeurt (in spel); stap, maatreël; verhuising; *a BAD* ~, 'n fout; 'n onverstandige ding; *BE on the* ~, in beweging wees; op die trekpad wees; *GET a* ~ *on!* maak gou! roer jou riete! *a GOOD* ~, 'n verstandige stap; *KEEP on the* ~, in beweging hou; *MAKE a* ~, 'n set maak, skuiwe; jou roer; aanstalte maak; *YOUR* ~ *next,* dis nou jou beurt; (v) beweeg, wrik, roer (voorwerp); ontroer, oorhaal; trek, vervoer; voorstel (mosie), 'n mosie indien; verhuis, wegtrek (uit buurt); stoot; 'n set maak (spel); buig; stappe doen; verplaas, versit, skuif; optrek, gaan, marsjeer; aandoen; aandrywe; ~ *ALONG,* wikkel; ~ *someone to ANGER,* iem. kwaad maak; ~ *AWAY,* wegtrek; *the BOWELS* ~, die maag werk; ~ *HEAVEN and earth,* hemel en aarde beweeg; ~ *into a HOUSE,* in 'n huis intrek; ~ *IN,* intrek; ~ *INTO,* intrek; ~ *OFF,* weggaan; ~ *ON,* aanloop; vort! ~ *OUT,* verhuis; trek! *a OVER,* opskuif; *the SPIRIT* ~*s me,* ek voel my gedronge; ~ *to TEARS,* tot trane beweeg; ~**able** = **movable;** ~**d,** geroer, bewoë, aangedaan; ~**less,** bewegingloos.

move'ment, beweging; verplasing; ontwikkeling; maatreël, stap; gang; meganiek; aandrang; opwelling; tempo, ritme; omset; stoelgang; ~ *of the BOWELS,* stoelgang, opelyf; *a DOWNWARD* ~, 'n daling; *HIS* ~ *s,* sy doen en late; *an UPWARD* ~, 'n styging; ~ **control,** bewegingsreëling; ~ **order,** marsbevel.

mo'ver, voorsteller, indiener (van 'n mosie); beweger; trekker; dryfkrag; dryfveer, aanstoker.

mo'vie, bioskoop, fliek; ~ **fan,** fliekvlooi; ~ **star,** filmster, rolprentster; ~ **theatre,** bioskoop; ~ **tone,** klankfilm.

mo'ving, (n) trekkery, verhuising; (a) roerend, treffend, aangrypend; aandoenlik; beweeg-; dryf-; *FAST-*~, vinnig bewegend (bv. verkeer); *KEEP* ~*!* stap aan! aanstap! *SLOW-*~, stadig bewegend (bv. verkeer); *he gave a very* ~ *SPEECH,* hy het 'n roerende toespraak gelewer; ~ **day,** verhuisdag, trekdag; ~ **force,** dryfkrag; ~**ly,** roerend, treffend, gevoelvol, aandoenlik; ~ **pictures,** bioskoop, rolprent; ~ **power,** beweegkrag; ~ **spirit,** die siel van iets; ~ **staircase,** roltrap; ~ **target,** bewegende skyf; ~**-van,** verhuiswa.

mow[1], (n) skewemond, grimas; *HOLD your* ~ *s!* hou jou bek! *MOPS and* ~ *s,* lelike gesigte; (v) skewebek trek.

mow[2], (n) hooimied; gemaaide; (v) (-ed, -n), (af)maai; hooi maak; ~ *the enemy down,* die vyand in die pan hak (afmaai); ~**burnt,** gestik, gebroei; ~**er,** maaier; snymasjien; kragmes; grasmasjien; ~**ing,** (n) maai, snyery; (a) maai-; ~**ing-machine,** snymasjien.

mox'a, moxa, byvoetwol (middel teen jig).

mo'xie, (sl.), krag, energie; waagmoed, waaghalsigheid.

moy'a, vulkaanmodder.

Mozambic'an, (n) Mosambieker; (a) Mosambieks.

Mozambique', Mosambiek.

much, baie, erg, seer, veel; *as* ~ *AGAIN,* nog soveel; *as* ~ *AS,* soveel as; *AS* ~, net soveel; ~ *BETTER,* baie beter; *a BIT* ~, darem te erg; effens te veel; *not so* ~ *as a CENT,* nie eers 'n sent nie; *DO* ~ *to,* baie daartoe bydra om; *FAR too* ~, oordrewe, baie; *so* ~ *FOR that,* daarmee is dit afgehandel; *so* ~ *FOR him,* dit wat hom betref; *it is too* ~ *of a GOOD thing,* wat te erg is, is te erg; *HOW* ~*?* hoeveel? ~ *the LARGEST town,* verreweg die grootste stad; *MAKE* ~ *of,* 'n ophef maak van; hoogag; ~ *will have MORE,* hoe meer iemand het, hoe meer wil hy hê; *it is so* ~ *NONSENSE,* dis alles pure kaf; *he is NOT* ~ *of a singer,* hy is nie 'n danige sanger nie; *NOT* ~ *of a writer,* nie eintlik 'n skrywer nie; *NOTHING* ~, nie veel snaaks nie; niks besonders nie; *with* ~ *REGRET,* met groot leedwese; ~ *the SAME,* omtrent (vrywel, ongeveer) dieselfde; *as* ~ *as to SAY,* asof hy wou sê; *SO* ~ *for that,* dis afgehandel; *so* ~ *SO that,* soseer dat; *I THOUGHT as* ~*!* net soos ek gedink het! *you can have TOO* ~ *of a good thing,* jy kan te veel van 'n ding hê; *be TOO* ~ *for someone,* iem. oor wees; te veel vir iem. wees; *TOO* ~ *is too* ~, wat te erg is, is te erg; *that was TOO* ~ *for me,* dit was vir my te erg; *it is not UP to* ~, dis niks besonders nie; dit beteken nie veel nie; *he is not UP to* ~, hy beteken maar min; ~ *the WORST,* verreweg die slegste; ~**-beloved,** seergeliefde; ~**ly,** erg, seer (plat); ~**-married,** al dikwels getroud; verwyf; ~**ness,** veelheid, grootheid; ~ *OF a* ~*ness,* omtrent dieselfde; vinkel en koljander; *TOO* ~ *of a* ~*ness,* ten enemale te veel.

mu'cic acid, slymsuur.

mu'cid, slymerig; skimmelrig.

mucif'ic, slymafskeidend.

mu'ciform, slymerig.

mu'cilage, gom; slym.

mucila'ginous, slymerig; gomagtig; ~ **gland,** slymklier.

mucip'arous, slymafskeidend.

muck, (n) mis; vuilis; bog; gemeenheid; gemors; aardse slyk; *make a* ~ *of,* verknoei; (v) bemes; bederf; vuil maak, bemors; rondslenter; rinkink; ~ *ABOUT,* rondpeuter; rondslenter; ~ *UP,* verbrou, verknoei; ~**-bin,** vuilgoedblik, vuilgoedbak; ~**-cart,** vuilgoedkar, askar; ~**-carter,** askarryer.

muck'er, ruwe persoon; vriend, maat; swaar val; *COME a* ~, baken steek, val.

muck: ~**-fork,** misvurk; ~**-heap,** ~**-hill,** mishoop; ~**iness,** smerigheid, vuilheid.

muc'kle, baie, veel; *kyk* **mickle.**

muck: ~**-rake,** mishark; smeerpoets; ~**-raking,** gevroetel, moddergooiery; ~**worm,** miswurm; vrek, gierigaard; ~**y,** smerig, vuil; gemeen, laag.

mucos'ity, slymerigheid, slym.

muc'ous, slymerig; slym(agtig), slym-; ~ **gland,** slymklier; ~ **membrane,** slymvlies; ~**ness,** slymagtigheid, slymerigheid; ~ **secretion,** slymafskeiding.

muc'ro, punt; ~**nate(d),** gepunt.

muc'us, slym, snot, fleim, bel, mukus.

mud, modder, slib; slyk; vuilgoed; *as CLEAR as* ~, so helder soos modder; *DRAG through the* ~, deur die modder sleep; *FLING* ~ *at,* met modder gooi, beklad; *his NAME is* ~, hy het sy naam weggesnyt; *STICK in the* ~, vasval, vassit; *THROW* ~ *at,* met modder gooi, beswadder; ~**-bath,** modderbad; ~**boat,** baggerskuit; ~**diness,** modderigheid, slibberigheid.

mud'dle, (n) verwarring; deurmekaarspul, warboel, knoeiwerk, janboel, brousel, brouspul, dikkedensie; *MAKE a* ~ *of,* verknoei; *IN a* ~, in die war; (v) verwar, troebel maak; (ver)knoei, verbrou; deurmekaarmaak, vertroebel, benewel; dronk maak; ~ *ALONG,* voortsukkel; ~ *THROUGH,* deursukkel; ~**d,** deurmekaar, verfoes; ~**-head,** domkop, warkop; ~**-headed,** suf, verward, deurmekaar, benewel(d); ~**r,** knoeier; sukkelaar.

mud: ~**-dredger,** baggermasjien; (v) ~**dy,** (..died,) bemodder; vertroebel; verwar; (a) ~**dy,** modderig, slykerig, troebel, morsig; onduidelik, verward, deurmekaar; dof; ~ **drum,** slyktrommel; ~**-fever,** mok; ~**-fish,** moddervis; ~**-flat,** modderbank; ~ **floor,** kleivloer; ~ **hole,** moddergat; ~ **hut,** kleihut; ~ **lark,** (n) straatseun; vuilgoedman; gemodder; (v) in die modder speel; ~**pack,** kleimasker; ~ **pie,** modderkoekie; ~ **pump,** modderpomp; ~ **rush,** moddervloed; ~ **scraper,** voetskraper; ~ **shield,** modderskerm; ~ **skipper,** klimvis; ~**-slinging,** moddergooiery; bekladding; ~**-stained,** vol mod-

der, modderig; ~ **stone,** moddersteen; ~ **wall,** kleimuur.
mue'sli, muesli.
muezz'in, gebedsroeper, muezzin, moëddzin, bilal.
muff¹, (n) mof.
muff², (n) lomperd, sukkelaar, stumper(d), domkop; misslag; prulwerk, mislukking; misvang (krieket); handruiker; (v) mis, mis vang; onhandig wees; verknoei, bederf.
muffetee', polsmof.
muff'in, roosterkoekie, plaatkoekie; muffin; ~ **eer',** suikerstrooier; ~**-faced,** met wesenlose gesig; bleekneus=; uitdrukkingloos; ~**-pan,** muffinpan.
muf'fle¹, (n) bolip, snuit (van diere).
muf'fle², (n) doek; moffie; dwanghandskoen; moffeloond; demper; moffel (van oond); lysonderlaag (bouk.); (v) inwikkel, toedraai; omfloers (trom); die mond toebind; demp; mompel; ~ **d,** toegemaak; gedemp; ~ *d DRUM,* omfloerste trom; ~ *d VOICE,* gedempte stem; ~ **furnace,** ~ **kiln,** moffeloond; ~ **r,** serp; sluier; (geluid)demper, knalpot (masj.); bokshandskoen.
muf'ti, gewone drag, burgerdrag, burgerkleding; Turkse priester, mufti; *IN* ~, in burgerdrag; *RETURN to* ~, die soldaterok uittrek.
mug¹, (n) kommetjie, beker, koppie; drank; dronk.
mug², (n) bakkies, snoet, gevreet; smoel, snater, bek (mens); domkop; swaap, sukkelaar; blokker; *CUT a, skewebek trek; a* ~ *'s GAME,* 'n gek spulletjie; (v) (**-ged),** volprop; skewebek trek; opmaak; blok; ~ *up Latin,* Latyn blok.
mug, (v) wurgroof, aanrand, beroof.
mugg'er, krokodil; blokker; wurgrower.
mugg'ing, wurgroof, aanranding, berowing.
mugg'ins, domino; kaartspel; dwaas, uilskuiken.
mugg'y, drukkend, bedompig; benoud, broeierig, swoel.
mug'wump, grootmeneer, groot kokkedoor; onafhanklike; draadsitter (in politiek).
muid, mud.
mu'jik, moesjiek (Russiese boer).
mulatt'o, (n) **(-es),** baster, halfnaatjie, mulat; (a) baster=; geelbruin.
mul'berry, (..**rries),** moerbei; **M**~ **dock,** oorlogsdok; ~**-tree,** moerbeiboom.
mulch, (n) grondkombers, deklaag; bladaarde; molm; (v) (met bladaarde) toemaak, bedek; ~ **ing,** stoppelbewerking.
mulct, (n) geldboete; (v) straf, beboet; ~ *IN,* beboet met; ~ *OF,* beroof van.
mule¹, muiltjie, uitskoppantoffel.
mule², muil; styfkop, onnosel, dommerik; dwarstrekker; baster; fynspinmasjien; ~**-drawn,** deur muile getrek, muil=; ~**-driver,** muildrywer; ~**-headed,** koppig; ~ **jenny,** fynspinmasjien.
Mule'-operation, Mule-operasie (skape).
mule: ~**-kick,** muilskop; volstruisskop (stoei); ~**-mark,** muilstreep; ~ **team,** muilspan; ~ **teer',** muildrywer; ~**-track,** ruiterpaadjie.
mulieb'rity, vroulikheid; verwyfdheid.
mulieros'ity, gekheid na vroue.
mul'ish, muilagtig; koppig; *be* ~, *so steeks soos 'n muil wees;* ~**ness,** eselagtigheid; koppigheid.
mull¹, (n) dun moeselien; neteldoek; (v) kruie; warm maak; ~ *ed wine,* warm gekruide wyn, kandeel.
mull², (n) snuifdoos.
mull³, (n) molm; verwarring, mislukking; geknoei; (v) verwar, verknoei; 'n gemors maak van; mis; omboor (naaldwerk); ~ *a pass,* 'n bal mis vat.
mull'a(h), molla.
mull'ein, koningskruid, fakkelkruid.
mull'er, wynketel; vryfsteen; maalklip.
mull'et, harder (seevis); kalwerkop (varswatervis); mul; *grey, LESSER* ~, harder; *RED* ~, seebarbeel.
mul'ligan, mulligan, bredie.
mulligatawn'y, (Indiese) kerriesop.
mull'grubs, maagpyn, koliek; slegte humeur.
mull'ing, randomboorsel.

mull'ion, (n) raamstyl, tussenstyl, vensterroei, middelstyl (venster); (v) vensterroeie insit.
mull'ock, puin; gewaste grond; bog; vuilgoed.
mulse, heuningwyn.
multang'ular, veelhoekig.
multe'ity, veelvuldigheid.
multicell'ular, veelsellig.
multicip'ital, veelhoofdig.
mul'ticoloured, veelkleurig, bont.
mul'ti-engined, meermotorig.
multifar'ious, veelsoortig, velerlei, allerhande; ~ **ness,** veelvuldigheid, veelsoortigheid.
multiflor'ous, met baie blomme, veelblommig.
mul'tifold, veelvuldig, veelsoortig.
mul'tiform, veelvormig; ~ **'ity,** veelvormigheid; verskeidenheid, veelsoortigheid.
multi'grade, meergraad=; ~ **oil,** meergraadolie.
mul'tilane, meerbanig.
multilat'eral, veelsydig.
multilin'gual, veeltalig.
multimillionaire', multimiljoenêr.
multinom'ial, veelterm.
multinom'inal, veelnamig.
multip'arous, veelbarend.
multipart'ite, veeldelig.
mul'tiped(e), (n) duisendpoot; (a) veelvoetig.
mul'tiphase, veelfasig, meerfasig.
mul'tiplane, meerdekker.
mul'tiple, (n) veelvoud; *least common* ~, kleinste gemene veelvoud; (a) veelvoudig, veeltallig, baie; ~ **call,** meervoudige oproep; ~**-choice questions,** veelkeusige vrae, veelkeusevrae; ~ **injuries,** veelvuldige beserings; ~ **switch,** parallelskakelaar.
mul'tiplex, veelvoudig, veelsoortig, veeltallig.
mul'tipliable, vermenigvuldigbaar.
multiplicand', vermenigvuldigtal.
multiplica'tion, vermenigvuldiging; ~ **sign,** vermenigvuldigingsteken; ~ **sum,** vermenigvuldigingsom; ~ **table,** tafel van vermenigvuldiging.
mul'tiplicative, (n) herhalingsgetal; (b) vermenigvuldigend.
mul'tiplicator, vermenigvuldiger.
multipli'city, veelheid, menigvuldigheid.
mul'tiplier, vermenigvuldiger; multiplikator, versterker.
mul'tiply, (..**plied),** vermenigvuldig, maal; voortteel, vermeerder; toeneem; ~**ing coil,** versterkingspoel; ~ **ing glass,** vermenigvuldigingspieël.
multip'otent, veelvermoënd.
mul'tipurpose, meerdoel=, meerdoelig.
mul'tiracial, veelrassig.
multira'cialism, veelrassigheid.
mul'tispeed, meergang=; ~ **machine,** meergangmasjien.
mul'tistage, meertrappig; ~ **rocket,** meerstukvuurpyl.
multisyllab'ic, meerlettergrepig.
multisyll'able, meerlettergrepige woord.
mul'titude, menigte, skare, massa, swetterjoel, 'n duisternis; veelheid, talrykheid; *cover a* ~ *of sins,* 'n menigte gebreke bedek.
multitud'inous, menigvuldig, talryk; veeltallig, eindeloos.
multival'ence, veelwaardigheid, meerwaardigheid.
multival'ent, veelwaardig, meerwaardig.
mul'tivalve, (n) veelkleppige dier; (a) veelkleppig.
multivoc'al, dubbelsinnig.
multoc'ular, veelogig.
multung'ulate, veelhoewig.
mul'ture, maalgeld.
mum¹, (n) mombier.
mum², (n) mamma, moedertjie, mams.
mum³, (v) **(-med),** in 'n pantomine speel; (a) swygend, stil; *BE* ~, hou jou mond; nie 'n woord sê nie; *KEEP* ~, nie 'n woord sê nie; *KEEP it* ~, dit stilhou; ~*'s the WORD,* vertel niks nie; bly stil; hou jou mond.
mum'ble, (n) gemompel; (v) mompel, mummel; (af)prewel; ~ **r,** mompelaar, prewelaar.
mum'bling, (n) geprewel; gemompel; (a) mompelend, onduidelik, ~ **ly,** binnensmonds.

mumbo-jumbo 1064 *music*

mum'bo-jum'bo, hokuspokus, leë ritueel; wartaal; nuttelose afgod; paaiboelie.
mum'chance, stom, swygend; *PLAY* ~, die mond hou; *SIT* ~, met die mond vol tande sit.
mumm'er, vermomde, gemaskerde; ~**y,** vermomming, maskerade.
mummifica'tion, balseming; mummifikasie.
mumm'ify, (..**fied),** balsem; mummieagtig word; opdroog, mummifiseer.
mumm'y¹, (**mummies**), mummie; bruin entwas; *beat to a* ~, pap slaan.
mumm'y², (**mummies**), mammie, moedertjie, mams.
mump¹, (rond)bedel; bedrieg, kul.
mump², pruil; mompel; gryns; 'n skynheilige gesig trek; ~**ish,** verdrietig; pruilend.
mumps, pampoentjies; knorrige bui.
munch, hoorbaar kou, (op)knabbel, vreet, oppeusel; ~**ing,** geknabbel, gekou.
mun'dane, wêrelds, aards, ondermaans, wêreld=; ~**ness,** wêreldsheid.
mung'o, pluiswol; herwonne wol.
mun'goose, (-s) = **mongoose.**
Mun'ich, München.
muni'cipal, munisipaal, dorps=, stedelik, stads=; ~ **council,** dorpsraad; stadsraad; ~ **election,** munisipale verkiesing; ~ **government,** munisipale bestuur; ~'**ity,** (..**ties**), munisipaliteit, stadsraad; ~**ize,** onder munisipale beheer bring; ~ **law,** munisipale regulasie; ~**ly,** munisipaal; ~ **rates;** munisipale belasting; ~ **tax,** munisipale belasting; ~ **valuation,** munisipale waardering.
munif'icence, milddadigheid, vrygewigheid, goedheid; *by the* ~ *of,* deur die vrygewigheid van.
munif'icent, milddadig, vrygewig.
mun'iment, versterking, vesting; oorkonde, akte; ~ **deed,** eiendomsbewys; ~ **room,** argief.
muni'tion, (n) krygsvoorraad, krygsbehoeftes; (am)munisie; (pl) krygstuig; (v) van ammunisie voorsien; ~ **trade,** ammunisiehandel; ~ **train,** ammunisietrein; ~ **wagon,** ammunisiewa; ~**-worker,** ammunisiemaker; ammunisiewerker; ~**-works,** ammunisiefabriek.
munn'ion, *kyk* **mullion.**
mun'shi, tolk; taalgeleerde; sekretaris (Indië).
mun'tin, tussenstyl (by deur).
munt'jac, muntjak (Asiatiese takbok).
mur'age, muurbelasting.
mur'al, (n) muurskildering; muurskildery; (a) muur=; ~ **decoration,** muurversiering; ~ **paint,** muurverf; ~ **painter,** muurskilder; ~ **painting,** muurskildery.
murd'er, (n) moord; *get AWAY with* ~, enigiets kan regkry; jou alles veroorloof; jou verdiende loon vryspring; *COMMIT* ~, moord pleeg (begaan); *CRY blue* ~, moord en brand skree; *the* ~ *is OUT,* die geheim is verklap; *be SHEER* ~, niks anders as 'n foltering wees nie; *WILFUL* ~, moord met voorbedagte rade; ~ *WILL out,* 'n moord kom altyd uit; (v) vermoor; moor; vermink, radbraak, verknoei; *I COULD* ~ *him,* ek kon hom stenig; ~ *one's LANGUAGE,* jou taal radbraak; ~ **ed,** vermoor; ~*ed person,* vermoorde; ~ **er,** moordenaar, vermoorder; ~ **ess,** (**-es**), moordenares; ~ **ing,** vermoording.
murd'erous, moorddadig, wreed; ~ *ASSAULT,* moordaanslag; ~ *IMPLEMENT,* moordtuig; ~ *WEAPON,* moordwapen.
mure, opsluit; ommuur.
mur'ex, (**-es,** ..**rices**), purperslak.
mur'iate, chloried, chloride; ~ *of soda,* kombuissout.
muriat'ic, sout=; ~ **acid,** soutsuur.
mur'icate(d), skerp, stekerig.
mur'ine, muis=.
murk, (n) somberheid; duisterheid; (a) duister, dreigend; ~**iness,** duisterheid, donkerheid; ~**y,** duister, donker; morsig.
murm'ur, (n) gemurmel, gemompel; gebrom, geruis, gesuis; gemopper, gemor; *not to UTTER as much as a* ~, sonder om te hik of te kik; sonder te kwi(e)k of te kwa(a)k; *WITHOUT a* ~, sonder om te hik of te kik; (v) murmel, lispel; ruis, suis; mompel, mor, murmureer; ~ *AGAINST a proposal,* teen 'n voorstel mor; ~ *AT having to go home,* murmureer omdat huis toe gegaan moet word; ~**er,** murmureerder; ~**ing,** (n) gemurmel; gemor; (a) mompelend; ~**ous,** murmelend; ruisend; morrend.
mu'rrain, veepes; *a* ~ *on you!* kry die pes!
mu'rrey, (n) purperrooi, moerbeikleur; (a) moerbeikleurig, moerbeirooi.
mu'rrhine, murrinies; ~ **glass,** vloeispaatglas.
muscadel', muscat', muscatel', muskadel (=druiwe, =wyn).
mu'scle, (n) spier; spierweefsel; spierkrag; *without moving a* ~, sonder om 'n spier te vertrek; (v): ~ **in,** indring, inbars; ~**-bound,** met stywe spiere; ~**-bundle,** spierbundel; ~**-cramp,** spierkramp; ~ **d,** gespier(d); ~ **fibre,** spiervesel; ~ **less,** spierloos.
mu'scoid, mosagtig.
muscol'ogy, moskunde, briologie.
muscova'do, ongesuiwerde suiker, moskovado, bruinsuiker.
Mus'covite¹, (n) Moskowiet; Rus; (a) van Moskou; Russies.
mus'covite², (n) wit glimmer, muskowiet, mika.
Mus'covy, Moskowië, Rusland; ~ **drake,** makoumannetjie; ~ **duck,** makou(wyfie); ~ **glass,** mika, muskowiet; ~ **leather,** Russiese leer.
mus'cular, gespierd; spier=; sterk; ~ **fatigue,** spieraf=matting; ~'**ity,** spierkrag, gespierdheid; ~ **fascicle,** spierbundel; ~ **movement,** spierbeweging; ~ **pains,** spierpyn; ~ **paralysis,** spierverlamming; ~ **rheumatism,** spierrumatiek; ~ **spasm,** spierkramp; ~ **stiffness,** spierstyfheid; ~ **strength,** spierkrag; ~ **system,** spierstelsel; ~ **tissue,** spierweefsel; ~ **twitch,** spiertrekking; ~ **wall,** spierwand.
mus'culature, spierstelsel.
muse¹, (n) sanggod(in), muse; *the M*~*s,* die Muses.
muse², (v) peins, mymer, diep dink; ~ **on,** bepeins, mymer oor; ~**r,** peinser; dromer.
musette', (klein) doedelsak; herderswysie; landelike dans; orrelregister.
muse'um, (**-s,** ..**sea**), museum; ~ **piece,** museumstuk.
mush¹, pap; moes, bry.
mush², sambreel; huurkoetsier.
mush'iness, papperigheid; soetsappigheid.
mush'room, (n) paddastoel; sampioen; duiwelskos, slangkos; parvenu; sambreel; *spring up like* ~ *s,* soos paddastoele verrys; (v) paddastoele soek; platslaan (koeël); soos paddastoele groei; ~ **company,** swendelmaatskappy; ~ **valve,** skildklep.
mush'y, papperig; week, slap.
mus'ic, musiek, toonkuns; *ART of* ~, musiekkuns; *CLASSICAL* ~, klassieke musiek; *FACE the* ~, moeilikhede onder die oë sien; opdaag om verantwoording te doen; *HAVE* ~, musiek maak; *MAKE (play)* ~, musiek maak; *RECORDED* ~, platemusiek; *SACRED* ~, koraalmusiek, gewyde musiek; *SCHOOL of* ~, musiekskool; *SET to* ~, op musiek set, toonset.
mus'ical, (n) sangspel; musiekblyspel; (a) musikaal, welluidend; musiek=; met (op) musiek; ~ **art,** musiekkuns; ~ **box,** musiekoutomaat; speeldoos; ~ **chairs,** stoeldans; ~ **comedy,** operette; musiekblyspel; ~ **composer,** komponis; ~ **critic,** musiekkritikus.
musicale', musiekaand, konsert.
mus'ical: ~ **evening,** musiekaand; ~ **glasses,** glasharmonika; ~ **instrument,** musiekinstrument; ~ **item,** musieknommer; ~'**ity,** musikaliteit, musikale aanleg; ~**ness,** musikale aanleg; welluidendheid; ~ **performance,** musiekuitvoering; ~ **recital,** musiekuitvoering; ~ **ride,** kavalleriedans; ~ **salute,** musieksaluut; ~ **score,** musiekpartituur; ~ **sketch,** toneelstuk met musiek; ~ **world,** musiekwêreld.
mus'ic: ~ **book,** musiekboek; ~ **cabinet,** musiekkassie; ~ **carrier,** ~ **case,** musieksak; ~ **critic,** musiekkritikus; ~ **drama,** musiekdrama; ~**-hall,** konsertsaal; variététeater; ~**-hall artist,** variétéarties.

musi'cian, musikus, toonkunstenaar, musikant.
mus'ic-hall entertainment, verskeidenheidskonsert.
mus'ic: ~ lesson, musiekles; ~ lover, musiekliefhebber; ~-mad, verslaaf aan musiek; ~ master, musiekonderwyser; ~ mistress, musiekonderwyseres.
musicolog'ical, musikologies.
musico'logist, musikoloog.
musicol'ogy, musikologie.
mus'ic: ~ paper, notepapier, musiekpapier; ~-room, musiekkamer; konsertsaal; ~ shop, musiekwinkel; ~ stand, musiekstander; musiektent; ~-stool, klavierstoel; ~-teacher, musiekonderwyser(es).
mus'ing, (n) gemymer, gepeins; (a) mymerend, peinsend, dromerig.
musk, (n) muskus; muskusgeur; muskusdier; muskusplant; (v) met muskus parfumeer; ~-apple, muskadelappel; ~-beaver, muskusrot; muskusrotbont; ~-cat, muskeljaatkat; ~-deer, muskushert; ~-duck, makou.
musk'et, roer, geweer; ~-ball, geweerkoeël; ~-barrel, geweerloop; ~-bearer, wapendraer; ~ eer', musketier; ~-proof, koeëlvry, bestand teen koeëls; ~-rest, geweerstandertjie.
musk'etry, skietkuns; geweervuur; muskette; infanterie; ~ drill, skietoefening; ~ school, infanterieskietskool; ~ training, (infanterie)skietopleiding.
musk'et-shot, geweerskoot.
musk: ~ iness, muskusgeur; ~-melon, spanspek; ~-ox, muskusos; ~-plant, muskusplant; ~-plum, muskadelpruim ~-rat, bisamrot, muskusrot; ~-rose, muskusroos; ~-tree, muskusboom; ~-wood, muskushout; ~ y, muskusagtig, muskus=.
Mus'lim, kyk Moslem.
mus'lin, kamerdoek; neteldoek; moeselien; BIT of ~, vrou, meisie; PRINTED ~, doerias; ~ et', growwe neteldoek.
musophob'ia, vrees vir muise.
mus'quash, bisamrot, muskusrot; bont van muskusrot.
mus'rol(e), neusriem; neusband.
muss, (Amer.) (n) verwarde toestand, herrie, klapparty, warboel, rusie; (v) vuil maak; kreukel; deurmekaar maak.
mussal', toorts; toortsdraer.
muss'el, mossel; ~ bed, mosselbank; ~ cracker, poenskop, biskop (vis); ~ shell, mosselskulp.
Mus(s)ulman, (-s), Mohammedaan, Muselman, Islamiet.
muss'y, vuil; verward; gekreukel(d).
must¹, (n) skimmel, kim; (v) (-ed), kim, skimmel word.
must², (n) mos; jong wyn.
must³, (n) bronstigheid, hittigheid; raserny; (a) bronstig, hittig; rasend, dol (olifant).
must⁴, (n) noodsaaklikheid; verpligting; it is a ~, dit moet; ~ is a KING'S word, moet is dwang (en huil is kindergesang); (v) (must), moet; verplig wees; mag; if you ~ KNOW, as jy dan wil weet; he ~ have KNOWN it, hy moet dit geweet het; you ~ NOT, jy moenie.
mus'tang, mustang, wilde perd (Amer.)
mus'tard, mosterd; bielie, doring (fig.); he was ~ when it came to FIGHTING, hy was 'n doring om te baklei; ~ after MEAT, mosterd na die maal; ~ blister, mosterdblaar, mosterdblasie; ~ gas, mosterdgas; ~-oil, mosterdolie; ~-pickles, mosterdatjar; ~ plaster, mosterdpap; ~ pot, mosterdpotjie; ~ poultice, mosterdpap; ~ seed, mosterdsaad; ~ spoon, mosterdlepeltjie.
must'-bun, mosbolletjie.
mus'teline, weselagtig; rooibruin.
mus'ter, (n) monstering; wapenskouing; inspeksie; byeenkoms, versameling; in FULL ~, voltallig; PASS ~, die toets deurstaan; die revue passeer; it will not PASS ~, dit kan nie die toets deurstaan nie; dit kan nie deur die beuel nie; there was a STRONG ~, baie het opgekom; (v) monster, oproep; versamel; onder die wapens kom; indeel; ~ an ARMY, 'n leër op die been bring; ~ up COUR=

AGE, moed bymekaarmaak; moed versamel (skep); ~ up a SMILE, met moeite glimlag; ~ STRENGTH, al die kragte inspan; ~-book, monsterrol; ~-place, monsterplek; ~-roll, monsterrol.
mus'tiness, skimmel; dufheid, vermuftheid, vunsigheid, mufheid; sufheid.
must: ~-roll, mosbolletjie; ~-rusk, mosbeskuit; ~ syrup, moskonfyt; ~-vat, mosbalie.
mus'ty, (ver)muf, beskimmel, skimmelagtig; muf; suf; verouderd; vunsig; ~ old BOOKS, vermufte ou boeke; ~ BREAD, muwwe brood; GROW ~, vermuf.
must' yeast, mossuurdeeg.
mutabil'ity, veranderlikheid, onbestendigheid, wispelturigheid.
mut'able, veranderlik, onbestendig, wispelturig, ongestadig.
mutate', verander, muteer.
muta'tion, verandering, afwyking; mutasie (biol.); umlaut, klankverwisseling; stemverandering (van seun); ~ism, mutasieleer.
mutatis mutan'dis, mutatis mutandis, met die nodige veranderings.
mutch, laphoed.
mute¹, (n) voëlmis; (v) mis.
mute², (n) stom mens, stomme; muta, stom letter; toondemper, sourdine (musiek); figurant; toeskouer; grafbidder; (v) demp; (a) stom; sprakeloos, swygend; toonloos; stemloos; woordeloos; in ~ ADORATION, in stille aanbidding; ~ d LIGHT, gedempte lig, ~d STRINGS, gedempte snare; ~ consonant, stemlose eksplosief, klapper; ~ ly, stil, swygend; ~ ness, stomheid, sprakeloosheid, stille swygendheid; stemloosheid.
mu'ti, medisyne, toorgoed.
mut'ilate, vermink, skend; mutileer; ~ a language, 'n taal radbraak; 'n taal mors; ~d, geradbraak.
mutila'tion, verminking, skending.
mut'ilator, verminker.
mutineer', (n) muiter, oproerling, oproermaker; (v) opstaan, muit, tot muitery oorgaan, rebelleer.
mut'ing, demping, ~ circuit, dempkring.
mut'inous, oproerig, muitsiek, muitsugtig, opstandig.
mut'iny, (n) (..nies), muitery, oproer; foment ~, tot muitery opstook; (v) (..nied), opstaan, muit, rebelleer.
mut'ism, mutisme, stomheid; stilte.
mut'ograph, (n) mutograaf; (v) mutograveer.
mut'oscope, mutoskoop.
mutoscop'ic, mutoskopies.
mutt'er, (n) gemompel, geprewel, gebrom; (v) mompel; (af)prewel; brom, brabbel, binnensmonds praat; ~ er, mompelaar; murmureerder; ~ ing, gemompel, geprewel, geprewel, gestamel.
mutt'on, skaapvleis; skaap; as DEAD as ~, so dood soos 'n mossie; ~ dressed as LAMB, 'n ouerige vrou wat soos 'n jong meisie aantrek; LEG of ~, skaapboud; RETURN to one's ~ s, op die onderwerp terugkom; ~ breed, vleisras, ~ bredic, skaapvleisbredie; ~ chitterlings, skaapvetderm; ~ chop, ~ cutlet, skaapribbetjie, skaapkarmenaadjie; ~-fat, skaapvet; ~-fisted, lomp; ~-head, skaapkop, domkop; ~y, skaapvleis=, skaapvleisagtig.
mut'ual, onderling; wedersyds; wederkerig; gemeenskaplik; ~ ADMIRATION, wedersydse bewondering; ~ AFFECTION, wedersydse liefde; ~ BENEFIT Society, onderlinge hulpvereniging; ~ CONSENT, wedersydse toestemming; ~ FRIEND, gemeenskaplike vriend; ~ FUND, groofonds; ~ INSURANCE company, onderlinge versekeringsmaatskappy; ~ LOVE, wedersydse liefde; on ~ TERMS, op gelyke voorwaardes; ~ WILL, gesamentlike testament.
mu'tualism, mutualisme.
mutual'ity, onderlingheid; wederkerigheid.
mut'ually, onderling, oor en weer, van weerskante.
muu'-muu, Hawaiiese rok, muu-muu.
muzz, suf maak, benewel; ~iness, sufheid; vaagheid.
muz'zle, (n) snoet, bek; loop, tromp, monding, mondstuk (geweer); muilband (bees); muilkorf (hond); (v) muilband (dier); (be)snuffel; stryk (seil);

muzzy stil maak; ~ *the PRESS*, die pers muilband; ~ *SOMEONE*, iem. die swye oplê; iem. muilband; iem. die mond snoer; ~**-cover**, loopdeksel; ~**-loader**, voorlaaier, doppiesgeweer, doppiesroer; ~**-loading**, voorlaai=; ~**-loading gun**, voorlaaierge=weer; olifantroer; ~**-plug**, monddeksel; ~**-protec-tor**, trompbeskermer; ~**r**, opstopper, hou op die mond; ~ **velocity**, aanvangsnelheid.

muzz'y, benewel(d), suf; verstrooid; hoenderkop.

my, my; *OH* ~*!* o my hede! goeie genade! ~ *WORD, don't do that!* genugtig, moenie dit doen nie!

myal'gia, spierpyn, mialgie.

mycel'ium, swamvlok, miselium.

mycolog'ic, swamkundig, mikologies.

mycol'ogist, swamkundige, mikoloog.

mycol'ogy, swamkunde, mikologie.

mycot'ic, swam=, mikoties.

mydri'asis, midriase, kykerbeweeglikheid.

myelit'is, rugmurgontsteking, miëlitis.

my'eloid, murgagtig, murg=.

myl'onite, miloniet.

my'na(h), Indiese spreeu.

myn'heer, Hollander; meneer.

myn'pacht, mynpag.

myocar'diac, hartspier=.

myocardit'is, hartspierontsteking.

myocard'ium, hartspier.

my'ograph, miograaf.

myog'raphy, spierbeskrywing, miografie.

myolog'ic(al), spierkundig, miologies.

myo'logist, spierkundige, mioloog.

myol'ogy, spierkunde, miologie.

myol'omy, anatomie van die spiere; spierdeursny=ding.

my'ope, bysiende persoon.

myop'ia, bysiendheid, miopie.

myop'ic, bysiende, miopies, stiksienig.

my'opy, bysiendheid, miopie.

myosit'is, spierontsteking, miositis.

my'osote, myosot'is, vergeet-my-nietjie, miosotis.

my'riad, (n) tienduisendtal, swerms, miriade; (a) on=telbaar, talloos.

my'riapod, (n) duisendpoot; (a) veelpotig.

myrm'idon, handlanger, volgeling; huurling; ~ *of the law*, geregsdienaar; beulskneg.

myrrh, mirre; ~'**ic**, mirre=.

myr'tle, mirte; mirtegroen; ~**-grove**, mirtebos; ~**-wreath**, mirtekrans.

myself', ek self, myself; *I AM not (do not feel)* ~ , ek voel nie lekker nie; ek voel nie reg op my stukke nie; *I ASK* ~, ek vra my af; *BY* ~, ek alleen; *I DID it* ~, ek het dit self gedoen; *FOR* ~, *I*, wat my betref; *I HURT* ~, ek het my seergemaak; *I KNOW* ~, ek ken myself; *I SHAVE* ~, ek skeer my.

mysophob'ia, vrees vir vuilis (besmetting).

mys'tagogue, misterievertolker, mistagoog.

myster'ious, geheimsinnig, geheimenisvol, raaisel=agtig, spookagtig, misterieus, verborge, duister; ~**ness**, geheimsinnigheid, verborgenheid.

mys'tery, (..ries), geheim(enis), duisterheid, miste=rie, raaisel, verborgenheid, sakrament, misterie=spel; *make a* ~ *of something*, iets geheim hou; ~ **play**, misteriespel; ~ **tart**, raaiseltert.

mys'tic, mistikus.

mys'tic(al), misties; mistiek, sinnebeeldig, geheimsin=nig, duister.

mys'ticism, mistiek; mistisisme.

mystifica'tion, mistifikasie, kullery, foppery.

mys'tify, (..fied), kul, fop, mislei; in geheimsinnig=heid hul.

mysti'que, mistieke kultus; waas van verering; mis=tiekheid, geheimsinnigheid.

myth, mite, sage, fabel; bedenksel; ~'**ic(al)**, mities, fabelagtig, fabel=; ~ **maker**, miteskrywer; ~**og'ra-pher**, miteskrywer; ~**og'raphy**, mitografie; ~ **olo-gic(al)**, mitologies; fabelagtig; ~**ol'ogist**, mito=loog; ~ **ol'ogize**, mitologiseer; ~**ol'ogy**, mitologie, godeleer; fabelleer, fabelkunde.

mythopo'et, mitedigter.

my'thos, myth'us, mite; fabel.

myt'iloid, mosselagtig, mossel=.

myx'oma, miksoom, slymgewas.

myxomatos'is, miksomatose.

myxomycete', slymswam.

N

n, (ns, n's), n; *little* ~, n'etjie.

naar'tjie, nartjie.

nab[1], (n) kaap, uitsteeksel; sluitraampie (van slot); grendelkeep.

nab[2], **(-bed)**, vang; betrap, arresteer, inpik.

nab'ob, nabob; kapitalis, rykaard.

Nabo'th: ~'s *vineyard*, Nabot se wingerd.

nac'arat, helder oranjerooi.

nacelle', gondel.

na'cre, perlemoen; ~**-coloured**, perlemoenkleurig; ~ **ous, nac'rous**, perlemoenagtig, perlemoen=.

nad'ir, voetpunt, laagste punt, nadir.

naev'us, moesie, moedervlek.

nag[1], (n) ponie, knol, bossiekop.

nag[2], (v) **(-ged)**, pla, sar, seur, treiter, lastig val; sanik; neul, lol, vererg, vit, pes, karring (aan iem.); ~ *at SOMEONE*, aan iem. torring; *STOP* ~ *ging*, moe=nie aanhou torring (neul, sanik) nie.

naga'na, nagana, vliegsiekte, tripanosomiase.

nag: ~**ger**, klaer, treiteraar, terger; neulpot, neul=kous, vitter; ~ **ging**, (n) vittery, geneul, neulery; ge=torring, dwingery; gekanker, gekarring; gesanik; gevit; (a) lollerig, vitterig, neulerig, dwingerig; kyf=agtig; ~**gy**, plaerig; vitterig.

na'iad, waternimf, najade, riviergodin; naaldekoker=nimf; fonteinkruid.

nail, (n) spyker; nael (vinger); *it adds a* ~ *to his COF-FIN*, dis 'n spyker in sy doodkis; *DRIVE in a* ~, 'n spyker inslaan; *as HARD as* ~ *s*, kliphard, onge=voelig; in goeie kondisie; *hit the* ~ *on the HEAD*, die spyker op die kop slaan; *that hit the* ~ *on the HEAD*, dit was 'n raakskoot; *drive the* ~ *HOME*, die saak tot 'n spoedige end bring; *I'll PARE your* ~ *s*, ek sal jou vlerke knip; *PAY on the* ~, op die dag betaal; *as RIGHT AS* ~ *s*, so reg soos 'n roer; *with TOOTH and* ~, met hand en tand; *as TOUGH as* ~ *s*, so taai soos 'n ratel; (v) inspyker, vasspyker, nael; inslaan; kluister, bind; betrap, vang; ~ *ed to his CHAIR*, aan sy stoel genael; ~ *one's COLOURS to the mast*, veg sonder ophou of oorgee; ~*ed to the CROSS*, aan die kruis gespyker; ~ *DOWN*, toespyker, vasspyker; bind (fig.); ~ *a LIE*, 'n leuen aan die kaak stel; ~ *UP*, toespyker; ~**-biter**, naelbyter; ~**-box**, spykerbak; ~**-brush**, naelborsel; ~**-claw**, spykerklou; ~**-cleaner**, nael=skoonmaakmiddel; ~**-crayon**, naelpotlood; ~**-cutter**, naelknipper; ~**er**, spykermaker; spyker=smid; doring (fig.); ~**ery**, (..ries), spykermakery, spykerfabriek; ~ **extractor**, spykertang, spyker=trekker; ~**-file**, naelvyl(tjie); ~**-hammer**, klouha=mer; ~**-head**, spykerkop; ~**-headed characters**, spykerskrif; ~**-head rust**, leprose (sitrus): ~**-hole**, spykergat.

nail'ing, (plat) pragtig, uitmuntend; ~ *good*, (ge=selst.) regtig goed, uitmuntend; ~ **block**, spyker=blok; ~ **strip**, spykerlat.

nail: ~**-nippers**, spykertang; spykerknipper; nael=knipper (manikuur); ~**-polish**, naelpoets, nael=smeer, naellak, naelverf; ~**-puller**, spykertrekker; ~**-punch**, spykerdrywer, spykerpons; ~ **scissors**, naelskêr; ~**-shaped**, spykervormig; ~ **smith**, spy=kersmid; ~**-stick**, naelstokkie; ~**-trimmer**, nael=skêrtjie, naelknipper.

nain'sook, nansoek.

naive / narrow

naive', naïve', naïef, kinderlik, ongekunsteld.
naï'veté, naiv'ety, naïwiteit, ongekunsteldheid, eenvoudigheid, kinderlikheid.
nak'ed, nakend, naak, kaal; onbeskut, weerloos, blootgestel; onverbloem(d); bloot (oog); blank (swaard); oop, ongeïsoleer (draad); *DELIVERED* ~ *to one's enemies*, weerloos aan jou vyande oorgelewer; *with the* ~ *EYE*, met die blote oog; *a* ~ *LIGHT*, 'n oop lig; 'n onbeskermde lig; *STARK* ~, poedelnakend; *STRIP* ~, kaal uittrek; *the* ~ *TRUTH*, die naakte (blote) waarheid; ~**ness**, naaktheid, kaalheid; ~ **wire**, ongeïsoleerde draad.
nak'er, keteltrom.
Nam'a, Nama.
Namaq'ua, Namakwa; ~ **daisy**, Namakwalandse gousblom (madeliefie); ~ **dove**, namakwaduif; ~ **partridge**, ~ **sandgrouse**, namakwapatrys, kelkiewyn.
nam'by-pam'by, (n) sentimentaliteit, sentimentele praatjies; *a* ~, soetsappige vent; ou stroop; (a) sentimenteel, soetsappig; geaffekteer(d); popagtig.
name, (n) naam; benaming; roem; *APPEAR below someone's* ~, onder iem. se naam verskyn; *ASK for something by* ~, uitdruklik na iets vra; *BECOME a* ~, beroemd word; *BUY in another's* ~, op iem. anders se naam koop; *BY* ~, met (by) name; *CALL* ~*s*, uitskel; beswadder; *CHRISTIAN* ~, voornaam; *in the* ~ *of my FATHER*, namens my vader; *FIRST* ~, voornaam; *GIVE it a* ~, wat sal dit wees? *GIVE someone's* ~, iem. aanmeld; *GO by the* ~, the naam dra; *take GOD'S* ~ *in vain*, Gods naam ydellik gebruik; *a GOOD* ~ *is better than riches (precious ointment)*, 'n goeie naam is beter as skatte; *HAVE to one's* ~, besit; *HAVE a* ~ *for*, bekend wees vir; die reputasie hê van; *have a* ~ *for HONESTY*, bekend vir sy eerlikheid; *IN* ~, in naam; *IN the* ~ *of*, in naam van; *what's IN a* ~? wat beteken 'n naam? *KEEP one's good* ~, jou naam hooghou; *KEEP one's* ~ *on the books*, jou naam op die boeke laat bly; *KNOW by* ~, van naam ken, *LEAVE one's* ~, jou kaartjie afgee; *MAKE a* ~, naam maak; *MENTION by* ~, met name noem; *PASS by the* ~ *of*, deurgaan onder die naam van; *PERSONS of* ~, mense van naam; *a PRINCE in* ~ *only*, net in naam 'n prins; *PROTECT one's* ~, jou naam hooghou; *PUT down one's* ~, jou naam opskryf; *PUT his* ~ *down as member*, skryf hom in as lid; *in the* ~ *of the QUEEN*, in die naam van die koningin; *his* ~ *was taken off the ROLL*, sy naam is geskrap; hy is geskrap; *TAKE one's* ~ *off the books*, jou naam laat skrap; (v) noem, naam gee; benoem; opnoem; vermeld; betitel; heet; ~ *AFTER*, vernoem na; ~ *a DAY*, 'n dag bepaal vir; *not to be* ~*d the same DAY*, nie in dieselfde asem te noem nie; ~ *a PRICE*, 'n prys maak; *the SHIP was* ~*d by the director's wife*, die skip is deur die direkteur se vrou gedoop; ~*d by the SPEAKER*, deur die Speaker tot orde geroep; ~ **able**, noembaar; ~ **-board**, naambord; ~ **-calling**, geswets; beledigende taalgebruik; ~ **-child**, genant, naamdraer; ~ **d**, getitel; ~ **-day**, naamdag; ~ **-dropping**, naamspoggery, benoeming, te koop loop met (beroemde) name; ~ **-index**, naamwyser; ~ **less**, naamloos, anoniem, sonder naam, onbeduidend, onbekend; onuitspreeklik; walglik, onnoembaar; *one who shall be* ~ *less*, iem. wie se naam ek nie sal noem nie; ~ **ly**, naamlik, te wete, by name, met name; ~ **-part**, titelrol; ~ **-plate**, naambordjie; naamplaat; ~ **r**, naamgewer; ~ **sake**, genant, naamgenoot; vangenoot; mieta.
nam'ing, naamgewing, noeming; benaming; benoeming.
namptissiment', handvulling.
Namur', Namen.
nan'cy-boy, verwyfde kêrel, moffie.
nan'ism, dwergagtigheid, nanisme.
nankeen', nanking, geel katoenstof; ~**s**, ~ **(trousers)**, katoenbroek, nankingbroek.
nann'y, (nannies), kindermeisie, kinderjuffrou; bokooi; ~ **-goat**, bokooi.
na'os, naos, binnetempel.

nap¹, (n) nop, pluis (klere); dons (vrugte); *the* ~ *of the green*, die nop v.d. setperk; grasneiging: (v) **(-ped)**, van pluis voorsien.
nap², nap(oleon) (kaartspel); *GO* ~, alles waag; *hold the* ~ *HAND*, die hoogste troewe in die hand hê.
nap³, ('n) dutjie, sluimering, slapie, siësta; *take a* ~, 'n dutjie vat, 'n uiltjie knip; (v) **(-ped)**, dut, sluimer.
nap(p)a, napaleer.
nape, nekrug, agternek, norra.
na'palm, napalm, brandbom.
nap'ery, tafellinne, tafelgoed.
naph'tha, nafta, bergteer.
naph'thalene, naftaleen, mottegif; ~ **balls**, naftaleenballe; ~ **flakes**, naftaleenskilfers, naftaleenvlokkies.
Na'pier: ~ **grass**, Napiergras; ~**'s fodder**, olifantsgras.
nap'iform, raapvormig.
nap'kin, servet; doek, luier; *lay up talents in a* ~, talente in 'n sweetdoek bêre; ~ **ing**, servetgoed, tafellinne; doekgoed; ~ **-ring**, servetring; ~ **-service**, luierdiens.
Na'ples, Napels; ~ *yellow*, napelsgeel.
nap'less, kaal, sonder haartjies, afgeslyt.
napol'eon, napoleon (geldstuk; kaartspel); kapstewel.
Napoleon'ic, Napoleonties.
napoo', op, gedaan, uitgeput, pê, klaarpraat; verdwyn.
napp'er¹, ligte slaper.
napp'er², pluiser; pluismasjien.
napp'er³, klapperdop.
nap'ping¹, (n) pluising.
nap'ping², (a) vaak, sluimerend; *catch one* ~, iem. aan die slaap kry; iem. onverhoeds betrap.
napp'y¹, (n) (nappies), luier.
napp'y², (a) wollerig; kroes; pluiserig.
napp'y³, (a) skuimend (drank); bedwelmend; aangeklam.
na'pu, dwerghert.
narc'ism, narciss'ism, selfaanbidding, selfliefde, narcisme, narcissisme.
narciss'ist, narc'Ist, narcis.
narcissist'ic, narcist'ic, narcisties.
narciss'us, (-es, ..cissi), narsing.
narc'olepsy, vaaksuk, narkolepsie.
narcos'is, narkose, verdowing, bedwelmingstoestand.
narcot'ic, (n) slaapmiddel; verdowingsmiddel; (a) narkoties, verdowend.
narc'otine, narkotien, narkotine.
narc'otism, narkose, slaapsug.
narc'otist, persoon verslaaf aan verdowende middels; narkotiseur.
narcotiza'tion, verdowing, narkotisering.
narc'otize, onder narkose bring, wegmaak, narkotiseer, verdoof.
nard, nardus; ~ **ine**, nardus-.
na'res, neusgate.
nar'ghile, nargile, water(rook)pyp.
na'rina trogon, bosloerie.
na'rine, neus-.
nar'is, (nares), neusgat.
nark, (n) lokvink, verklikker, spioen; (v) spioeneer (boewetaal); verklik.
narrate', vertel, verhaal.
narra'tion, vertelling, verhaal; verslag; relaas.
na'rrative, (n) verhaal, vertelling; (a) verhalend, vertellend; ~ *art*, vertelkuns.
narrato'logy, narratologie, vertelkunde.
narrat'or, verhaler, verteller, narrator.
narrat'ress, (-es), vertelster.
na'rrow, (n) engte; (v) vernou, vereng, beperk, inkrimp, kleiner maak; ~ *DOWN*, verminder; *it* ~*s DOWN to*, dit kom hierop neer; ~ *one's EYES*, jou oë op 'n skrefie trek; ~ *down SUSPICION*, verdagte persone uitdun; (a) nou, smal, eng; beknop (ruimte); deurdringend, noukeurig; kleingeestig, bekrompe; ~ *BRIDGE*, smal (nou) brug; ~ *ENTRANCE*, nou ingang; *have a* ~ *ESCAPE*, 'n noue ontkoming hê; ternouernood ontkom (ontsnap); ~ *GOODS*, band en lint; *a* ~ *INQUIRY*, 'n noukeurige ondersoek; *a* ~ *MAJORITY*, 'n klein

meerderheid; *the ~ SEAS*, die see-engtes; *in the ~est SENSE*, in die beperkste sin; *~ VIEWS*, bekrompe idees; *the ~ WAY*, die smal pad, die noue weg; **~-brimmed**, met smal rand, smalrand=; **~-chested**, smalborstig; **~ er**, vernouer, verenger; **~ front**, smal front; **~ gauge**, smalspoor; **~-gauge railway**, smalspoorweg; **~-gauge road**, smalbaanpad; **~ing**, vernouing, inkrimping; **~ ish**, nouerig; smallerig; **~ ly**, ternuernood, skrap(pie)s, so hittete, amper; deurdringend, noukeurig; **~-minded**, kleingeestig, eng(hartig), bekrompe; **~-mind'edness**, kleingeestigheid, eensydigheid, enghartigheid, bekrompenheid; **~ ness**, smalte; nouheid; engheid, bekrompenheid.

nar'thex, (-es), portaal, voorhal.

na'ry, niks; g'n (geen) enkele.

nas'al, (n) nasaal, neusletter; neusklank; neusstuk; (a) nasaal, neus=; **~ attachments**, neusverband; **~ bone**, neusbeen; **~ catarrh**, neuskatar; **~ cavity**, neusholte; **~ douche**, neusbad; **~ fumes**, neusontsmettingsmiddel; **~ horn**, neushoring.

nasal'is, neusaap.

nasal'ity, neusgeluid, nasaliteit.

nas'al: **~iza'tion**, nasalering; **~ize**, nasaleer, deur die neus uitspreek; **~ letter**, neusletter; **~ ly**, deur die neus; **~ peak**, neuspunt; **~ sound**, neusklank, nasale klank.

nas'cency, ontstaan, oorsprong, geboorte.

nas'cent, groeiend, wordend, in wording, ontwikkelend, opkomend; aangebore word.

nascut'i, neushorings.

nasopha'rynx, nasofarinks, neus-en-keelholte.

nas'tiness, narigheid, vieslikheid, liederlikheid, goorheid, walglikheid, onaangenaamheid; nydigheid; aakligheid.

nastur'tium, kappertjie, moederkappie; Oos-Indiese kers; bronkors.

nas'ty, onbeskof, naar, aaklig, onaardig, grieselig, vies; walglik, goor, vuil, smerig, liederlik; gemeen; *a ~ COLD*, 'n nare verkoue; *a ~ FEELING*, nare gevoel; *a ~ FELLOW*, 'n onaangename vent; *a ~ ONE*, 'n harde slag; 'n taai klap; *TURN ~*, onaangenaam word; aggressief raak; *~ WEATHER*, slegte weer.

Nat, Nat, Nasionalis.

Natal'¹, (n) Natal.

nat'al², (a) boud=.

nat'al³, (a) geboorte=; *his ~ shore*, die kus waar hy gebore is; **~ day**, verjaarsdag; **~ hour**, geboorteuur.

Natal'ian, (n) Nataller; (a) Natals.

natal'ity, geboortesyfer; geboorte.

nat'al muscle, boudspier.

nat'ant, drywend, swemmend.

nata'tion, swemkuns.

natator'ial, swem=, swemmend.

natato'rium, (binnenshuise) swembad, natatorium.

nat'atory, swem=; **~ bladder**, swemblaas.

natch, (sl.), natuurlik.

nat'es, boude, sitvlak.

nath(e)'less, nietemin, desnieteenstaande.

natimortal'ity, doodgeboortesyfer.

na'tion, volk, nasie; moondheid; *building of a ~*, volksbou, nasiebou.

na'tional, (n) burger, landgenoot; (pl) landgenote (in die vreemde); onderdane, burgers; (a) nasionaal; vaderlands, volks=, staats=; **~ air**, volkswysie; **~ anthem**, volkslied; **~ army**, volksleër; **~ assembly**, volksvergadering; **~ bank**, nasionale bank, volksbank; **~ budget**, staatsbegroting; **~ character**, volkskarakter; landaard; **~ church**, staatskerk; volkskerk; **~ consciousness**, volksbewussyn; **~ convention**, nasionale konvensie; **~ dance**, volksdans; **~ debt**, staatskuld; **~ defence**, landsverdediging; **~ disease**, volksiekte; **~ dress**, volksdrag; **~ drink**, volksdrank; **~ economy**, volkshuishouding; **~ emergency**, volksnood, landsnood; **~ executive**, hoofbestuur; **~ existence**, volksbestaan; **~ festival**, volksfees; **~ flag**, landsvlag; **~ funeral**, staatsbegrafnis; **~ health**, volksgesondheid; **~ honour**, nasie-eer; **~ income**, volksinkomste, volksinkome; **~ interest**, landsbelang; **~ism**, nasionalisme; nasionaliteitsgevoel; **N~ism**, Nasionalisme; **~ist**, nasionalis; **N~ist**, Nasionalis; **~is'tic**, nasionalisties; **~'ity**, (..ties), nasionaliteit; volkskarakter; *mark of ~ity*, nasionaliteitskenmerk; **~iza'tion**, nasionalisasie, onteiening; naasting; naturalisasie; **~ize**, nasionaliseer; naas; onteien; **~ language**, volkstaal; landstaal; **~ ledger**, grootboek; **~ ly**, vir die hele volk; oor die hele land; **~ monument**, nasionale monument, volksmonument; **~ newspaper**, nasionale koerant; **~ park**, nasionale park; **~ pest**, landsplaag; **~ poet**, volksdigter; **~ pride**, nasietrots; **~ reserve**, nasionale reservaat; nasionale reserwe(fonds); **~ revenue**, staatsontvangste, =inkomste; **~ road**, nasionale pad; **~ school**, volkskool; **~ scout**, hanskakie; **~ security**, landsveiligheid; **~ service**, weerplig, konskripsiediens, weermagsdiens; **~ socialism**, nasionaal-sosialisme; **~ spirit**, volksiel, volksgees, nasiegees; **~ treasury**, landskas; **~ unity**, volkseenheid; **~ volunteer**, nasionale vrywilliger; **~ welfare**, nasieheil; volkswelsyn; **~ well-being**, volkswelsyn.

na'tion: **~-building**, nasiebou; **~hood**, samehorigheid as nasie; nasieskap; **~ wide**, landswyd; nasionaal; *a ~wide campaign*, 'n landswye veldtog.

nat'ive, (n) inboorling; inlander; boorling; (a) aangebore; oorspronklik; geboorte=; eie; inheems; gedeë, natuurlik, vry (element); *GO ~*, soos 'n veldmens leef; *~ to the SOIL*, in die land gebore; inheems; **~-born**, inlands; inheems; **~ city**, geboortestad; **~ country**, vaderland; **~dom**, inheemsheid; **~ flower**, inheemse blom; **~ land**, vaderland, moederland; **~ language**, moedertaal; **~ mineral**, gedeë mineraal; **~ paper**, growwe papier; **~ plant**, inheemse plant; **~ soil**, geboortegrond; **~ son**, geboorteseun, eie seun; **~ tree**, inheemse boom; **~ wit**, natuurlike gevatheid, spitsvondigheid.

nat'ivism, leer van aangebore begrippe, nativisme.

nativ'ity, geboorte, natiwiteit; herkoms; afkoms; geboorte van Jesus, Maria of Johannes die Doper; horoskoop; **~ ode**, geboortesang; **N~play**, Kersspel.

Natol'ia, Anatolië.

nat'rium, natrium.

nat'rolite, natroliet.

nat'ron, loogsout, natron, wassoda.

natt'er, vit, kerm; **~er**, brompot, vitter; **~ing**, gevit, gekerm.

natt'erjack, (Britse) streeppadda.

natt'iness, keurigheid, netheid, fynheid.

natt'y, keurig, netjies, fyn.

nat'ural, (n) wit klawer; herstellingsteken (mus.); natuurmens; idioot; (in)boorling; (a) natuurlik; eie; aangebore; vriendelik, menslik; buite-egtelik (kind); ongesog, ongedwonge, natuur=; *it COMES ~ to him*, dit is maklik vir hom; dit is sy geaardheid; *man in his ~ STATE*, natuurmens; **~ beauty**, natuurskoon; natuurlike skoonheid; **~-born**, van natuur; deur geboorte; **~ bridge**, rotsbrug; **~ child**, buite-egtelike kind; **~ classification**, natuurlike klassifikasie; **~ colour**, natuurkleur, natuurlike kleur; **~ cover**, natuurlike dekking; **~ death**, natuurlike dood; **~ disaster**, natuurramp; **~ food**, natuurlike kos (voedsel); **~ fortification**, natuurvesting; **~ gas**, aardgas; **~ history**, natuurstudie, natuurleer; **~ism**, natuurstaat; naturalisme; **~ist**, naturalis, aanhanger v.d. naturalisme; natuurkundige navorser, natuurondersoeker, naturalis; **~is'tic**, naturalisties; **~iza'tion**, naturalisasie, inburgering, verlening van burgerreg; **~ize**, naturaliseer; jou inburger; jou akklimatiseer; natuurondersoeke doen; **~ language**, natuurlike taal (teenoor *kunstaal*); **~ law**, natuurreg; **~ life**, lewensduur; **~ ly**, natuurlik; uiteraard, van nature; op natuurlike wyse; **~ man**, natuurmens; natuurlike mens; **~ness**, ongesogtheid, natuurlikheid; **~ oil**, aardolie; **~ order**, natuurorde; **~ phenomenon**, natuurverskynsel; **~ philosophy**, natuurfilosofie; natuurleer; **~ religion**, natuurlike godsdiens; **~ resistance**, natuurlike weerstand; **~ resources**, natuurlike hulpbronne; **~ science**, natuurwetenskap; natuurleer; **~ selection**, natuurlike seleksie; **~ slope**, natuurlike helling; **~ state**, natuurstaat; **~ the-**

ology, natuurlike teologie; ~ **world**, sigbare wêreld; ~ **year**, sonjaar.

na'ture, natuur; karakter, aard, wese, geaardheid, gemoedsaard; gesteldheid; inbors; soort; *AGAINST* ~, teen die natuur, teennatuurlik, onnatuurlik; *BACK to* ~, terug na die natuur; *BY* ~, van nature; uiteraard; *CALL of* ~, die eise v.d. natuur; *from the* ~ *of the CASE*, uit die aard v.d. saak; *CHILD of* ~, natuurkind; ~ *of a COUNTRY*, landsgeaardheid; *COURSE OF* ~, loop v.d. natuur; *in the COURSE of* ~, in die gewone loop van sake; *pay one's DEBT to* ~, jou tol aan die natuur betaal, sterwe; *DRAW from* ~, na die natuur teken; *you cannot fly in the FACE of* ~, 'n mens kan 'n koei die bulk nie belet nie; *FREAK of* ~, monstrositeit; speling v.d. natuur, natuurfrats; *FROM* ~, na die natuur; *FROM its very* ~, uit die aard v.d. saak; *in* ~ *'s GARB*, in Adamspak; *GOOD* ~, goeie geaardheid; *HUMAN* ~, die menslike natuur; *IN the* ~ *of the case*, uit die aard v.d. saak; *LOVE of* ~, natuurliefde; ~ *passes NURTURE*, ~ *is above NURTURE*, die natuur is sterker as die leer; *OPERATION of* ~, natuurwerking; *PAINT from* ~, na die natuur skilder; *the PARTY will be in the* ~ *of*, die party(tjie) sal die vorm aanneem van; *POWERS of* ~, natuurmagte; ~ *is the best PHYSICIAN*, die natuur is die beste geneesheer (dokter); *PROTECTION of* ~, natuurbeskerming; *a SECOND* ~, 'n tweede natuur; *anything in the* ~ *of SYMPATHY*, alles wat lyk na meegevoel; *in the* ~ *of THINGS*, uit die aard v.d. saak; *TRUE to* ~, natuurgetrou; ~ **conservation**, natuurbewaring; ~ **cure**, natuurgenesing; ~**d**, geaard, gehumeur(d); van geaardheid; ~**-lover**, natuurliefhebber; ~ **power**, natuurkrag; ~ **product**, natuurproduk; ~ **reserve**, natuurreservaat; ~ **study**, natuurstudie, natuurkennis; ~ **worship**, natuuraanbidding; ~ **worshipper**, natuuraanbidder.

nat'urism, naturisme, natuuraanbidding; naaklopery, nudisme.

nat'urist, natuurnavolger; naakloper, nudis.

nat'uropath(ist), natuurgeneser, naturopaat.

naught, (n) niks, nul; *COME to* ~, op niks uitloop, misluk; *SET at* ~, in die wind slaan; (a) nikswerd, waardeloos, sleg.

naught'ily, ondeund, stout.

naught'iness, ondeundheid, stout(ig)heid; goddeloosheid, kattekwaad.

naughts' and crosses, soort kinderspel.

naught'y, ondeund, stout, goddeloos; ~ **boy**, ~ **child**, bengel, rakker, karnallie, stout seun (kind).

nau'plius, nouplius, skaaldierlarwe.

naus'ea, mislikheid, naarheid, naarwording, seesiekte; walging; *AD* ~ *m*, tot vervelens toe; *INDUCE* ~, walging opwek; *SUFFER from* ~, seesiek wees.

naus'eate, mislik word, naar word; walg van; walging opwek; ~**d**, naar.

naus'eating, walgingwekkend, walglik, afskuwelik.

naus'eous, vol walging; mislik; ~**ness**, walglikheid, mislikheid.

nautch, Indiese dans(vertoning); ~**-girl**, Indiese danseres.

naut'ical, see=, skeeps=; seevaart=, seevaartkundig; ~ **almanac**, seemansalmanak; ~ **art**, seevaartkunde; ~ **chart**, seekaart; ~ **compass**, skeepskompas; ~ **knot**, knoop; ~ **language**, seemanstaal; ~ **man**, seevaarder; ~ **matters**, seesake; ~ **mile**, seemyl; ~ **table**, seevaarttafel; ~ **term**, seeterm, skeepsterm.

naut'ilus, nouplius, seilslak.

nav'al, see=, skeeps=, vloot=, marine=; ~ **action**, seegeveg; ~ **aeroplane**, marinevliegtuig; ~ **affairs**, vlootsake; marinewese; ~ **air component**, marinelugmag; ~ **air force**, vlootlugmag; ~ **architect**, skeepsontwerper, skeepsboukundige, skeepsboumeester; ~ **architecture**, skeepsbou; ~ **artillery**, marineartillerie; ~ **aviation**, vlootlugvaart; ~ **aviation base**, vlootlugbasis; ~ **base**, vlootsteunpunt, vlootbasis; ~ **battery**, vlootgeskut; ~ **battle**, seeslag; ~ **cadet**, adelbors; ~ **chaplain**, vlootprediker; ~ **college**, marineskool; ~ **communication**, seeverbinding; seeverbindingsdiens; ~ **construction**, vlootbou; marinekonstruksie; ~ **dockyard**, skeeps=

werf; ~ **engagement**, seegeveg; ~ **flyer**, marinevlieënier; ~ **force**, seemag, seestrydmagte; ~ **gun**, skeepskanon; ~ **hospital**, vloothospitaal, marinehospitaal; ~**ism**, marinisme; ~ **league**, vlootliga; ~ **lieutenant**, vlootluitenant (S.A.); luitenant-tersee; ~ **marine**, koopvaardyvloot; ~ **matters**, vlootaangeleenthede; ~ **mine**, seemyn; ~ **officer**, seeoffisier; ~ **operation**, vlootoperasie; ~ **ordinance**, skeepsgeskut; ~ **patrol**, seepatrollie; ~ **policy**, vlootbeleid; ~ **port**, oorlogshawe; ~ **power**, seemoondheid; ~ **practice**, vlootoefening; ~ **programme**, vlootprogram; ~ **review**, vlootskou; ~ **school**, seevaartskool; ~ **service**, seediens; ~ **squadron**, vlooteskader; ~ **staff**, marinestaf; vlootpersoneel; ~ **station**, marinestasie; ~ **stores**, skeepsvoorrade, skeepsbehoeftes; skeepsmagasyn; ~ **strength**, vlootsterkte; ~ **term**, skeepsterm; ~ **unit**, vlooteenheid; ~ **victory**, oorwinning op see; ~ **war**, seeoorlog; ~ **yard**, marinewerf.

na'varin, lamskottel.

nave[1], skip (van kerk).

nave[2], naaf (van wiel); ~**-bolt**, naafbout; ~**-hole**, naafgat.

nav'el, nawel, nael=; ~ **orange**, nawellemoen; ~ **rupture**, naelbreuk; ~**-string**, naelstring; ~ **wort**, naelkruid, benediktekruid.

nave'-ring, naafband.

nav'icert, vaarvergunning, vaarsertifikaat.

navic'ular, bootvormig, skuitvormig; ~ **bone**, skuitvormige beentjie, skuitjiebeen.

navigabil'ity, bevaarbaarheid (water); bestuurbaarheid (vaartuig).

nav'igable, bevaarbaar (water); bestuurbaar (vaartuig); *in a* ~ *condition*, seewaardig.

nav'igate, vaar; bevaar; bestuur; navigeer; ~ *by the compass*, op die kompas stuur.

naviga'ting officer, stuurman, navigasieoffisier.

naviga'tion, skeepvaart, navigasie; lugvaart; *AERIAL* ~, lugskeepvaart; *COMMERCIAL* ~, koopvaardy, *INLAND* ~, binnevaart; ~ **al**, navigasie=; ~ **light**, vaarlig, navigasielig

nav'igator, seevaarder, seeman; koerspeiler, navigator (lugv.); navigasieoffisier; *Prince Henry the N* ~, prins Hendrik die Seevaarder.

navv'y, (**navvies**) werksman, dokwerker, slootgrawer; (pl) doodtrappers (skoene).

nav'y, (**navies**), seemag, vloot, marine; *IN the* ~, in die vloot; *MERCANTILE (merchant)* ~, handelsvloot, koopvaardyvloot; ~ **blue**, marineblou, vlootblou; ~ **cut**, tamaryn; ~ **department**, departement van marine; *N* ~ **League**, Vlootbond; ~ **list**, offisierslys; marinelys; ~ **office**, admiraliteit; ~ **yard**, marinewerf.

nawab', nabob; goewerneur.

nay, (n) nee; weiering; (adv) nee, wat meer is.

Nazarene', (n) Nasarener; (a) Nasareens.

Naz'areth, Nasaret; *can any good thing come out of* ~*?* kan daar uit Nasaret iets goeds kom?

Naz'arite, Nasireër.

naze, kaap, voorgebergte, landpunt.

Naz'i, Nazi; ~**ism**, Naziisme, Nazisme.

Nean'derthal: ~ **man**, Neanderdalmens.

neap, (n) dooigety, dooie ty; (a) aflopend, laag, dood.

Neapol'itan, (n) Napolitaan; (a) Napolitaans; Napels.

neap' tide, dooigety, laaggety.

near, (v) naderkom, nader, naby kom; (a) na(by), nabygeleë; naburig; suinig; nouverwant; dierbaar; intiem; links, hot= (in span); *on* ~ *er ACQUAINTANCE*, by nader kennismaking; *the N* ~ *EAST*, die Nabye Ooste; *FAR and* ~, wyd en syd; ~ *FRIEND*, intieme vriend; *the* ~ *FUTURE*, die nabye toekoms; *it was a* ~ *GUESS*, dis amper raak geraai; *the* ~ *HORSE*, die hotperd, die linkerperd; ~ *LEADER*, hotvoordier; *a* ~ *RELATIVE*, 'n bloedverwant; *it was a* ~ *THING*, dit was so hittete; dit het maar min geskeel; (adv) naby, digby, by, aan; ~ *BY*, naby, digby; *one* ~ *and DEAR*, 'n dierbare nabestaande; *DRAW* ~, nader(kom); *from FAR and* ~, van heinde en ver; *this matter lies* ~ *to my HEART*, die saak gaan my ter harte; (prep) by, naby, na-aan; ~ *the END*, teen die end; ~ *at*

HAND, naby; ~ the KNUCKLE(bone), op die kantjie (randjie) van onwelvoeglikheid; gewaag; ~ the MARK, naby; ~ by, langsaan, naby.

near'est, naaste; our ~ and DEAREST, ons dierbares; ~ FIGURE, naaste syfer; ~ GUESS, naaste gissing; ~ RELATIVE, naaste bloedverwant.

near'ly, amper, byna, bykans; circa; haas; half en half; innig; not ~ so rich, glad nie so ryk nie.

near: ~-miss, amperraakskoot; ampermisskoot; ~ ness, nabyheid; intimiteit; nou verwantskap; ~-shore, bylandig; ~ side, linkerkant, hotkant; ~-sighted, bysiende; ~-sightedness, bysiendheid.

neat¹, (n) grootvee; bees.

neat², (a) netjies, aankant, sindelik; skoon; ongemeng, skoon (drank); ordelik, sierlik, keurig; noukeurig; handig; take LIQUOR~, drank skoon drink; be as ~ as a new PIN, deur 'n ring getrek kan word; so blink soos 'n nuwe sikspens wees; a ~ STYLE, 'n goed versorgde styl; ~ WHISKEY, skoon whisky.

neat'en, afrond, afwerk.

neath, (poet.), benede, onder.

neat'-handed, rats, handig, gou, behendig.

neat'-herd, beeswagter.

neat'ly, netjies, sindelik; behendig, knap; keurig; ~ done, knap gedaan.

neat'ness, netheid, sindelikheid; knapheid; behendigheid.

neat: ~'s-foot, beespoot; ~'s-foot oil, kloutjiesolie; ~'s-leather, beesleer; ~'s-tongue, beestong.

neb, snawel, bek (voël); tuit, neus (ketel); klep; punt (pen).

neb'bish, (colloq.) onderdanig.

neb'ula, (-e), nebula, newelvlek, newelster (sterrek.); vlekkie op die horingvlies, pêrel (op oog); ~ r, newel=; wolk=; newelagtig, newelig; ~ r theory, newelteorie.

neb'ulize, benewel; verstuif; ~ r, stuifsproeier, verstuiwer.

nebulos'ity, newelagtigheid; wolkerigheid (fig.).

neb'ulous, newelagtig, vaag, wolkerig (fig.); ~ ness, newelagtigheid, wolkerigheid; ~ star, newelster.

ne'buly, gegolf (her.).

ne'cessarily, noodwendig; noodsaaklik(erwyse).

ne'cessary, (n) (..ries), benodigdheid; vereiste; necessaries of life, lewensbehoeftes, lewensbenodigdhede; (a) nodig, noodsaaklik; noodwendig; onvermydelik; FOOD is ~ to life, voedsel is noodsaaklik vir die lewe; ~ for the PURPOSE, noodsaaklik vir die doel.

necessitar'ian, (n) determinis; (a) deterministies; ~ ism, determinisme.

necess'itate, noodsaaklik maak; noodsaak, dwing.

necess'itous, behoeftig, noodlydend, berooid.

necess'ity, (..ties), noodsaaklikheid, noodwendigheid, nood, onvermydelikheid; nooddruf; benodigdheid, behoefte; behoeftigheid; an ABSOLUTE ~, 'n gebiedende noodsaaklikheid; the BARE necessities, die blote noodsaaklikhede; FROM ~, uit nood; ~ knows no LAW, nood breek wet; armoede leer bene kou; ~ is the MOTHER of invention, nood leer bid; NO ~ for, nie nodig nie; OF ~, noodwendig, noodsaaklikerwys; OUT of ~, uit nood; of PRIMARY ~, hoogs noodsaaklik; be UNDER a ~ of earning a living, genoodsaak wees om 'n bestaan te maak; make a VIRTUE of ~, van die nood 'n deug maak.

neck, (n) nek, hals; pas, engte (berg); nek(stuk) (vleis); landengte; see-engte; halsstuk (van tabberd); onbeskaamdheid; ~ AND ~, kop en kop; kop aan kop; BOW one's ~, jou nek buig; ~ and CROP, huid en haar; pens en pootjies; come down ~ and CROP, pens en pootjies val; have ~ ENOUGH for anything, onbeskaamd genoeg om enigiets te waag; FALL on someone's ~, iem. om die hals val; GET it in the ~, 'n skrobbering kry; dit hotagter kry; HARDEN the ~, die hart verhard; steeks word; HAVE the ~, die vermetelheid hê; ~ or NOTHING, daarop of daaronder; op lewe en dood; roekeloos; RIDE ~ or nothing, in dolle vaart ry; RISK one's ~, jou lewe waag; SAVE one's ~, met jou lewe daarvan afkom; STICK one's ~ out, jou blootstel aan; jou aan iets waag; STIFFEN one's ~, steeks word; a STIFF ~, 'n stywe nek; TALK through one's ~, kaf praat; TREAD on the ~ of, die voet op die nek sit; WIN by a ~, met 'n nek wen; break the ~ of a WORK, oor die hond se stert wees; die grootste deel v.d. werk agter die rug hê; (v) omhels; vry; nekomdraai; ~-band, halsband; halsriem; ~-bar, draaghout; ~ bone, nekbeen; ~ chain, nekketting; halsketting; ~ cloth, halsdoek; ~ erchief, halsdoek, serp; ~ ing, vryery; ~ lace, halskettinkie; halssnoer; ~ let, halskettinkie; ~ line, halslyn; ~-ornament, halssierraad; ~-piece, draagriem (tuig); halsstuk; ~-rope, halstou; ~ strap, draagband; nekriem; ~-tie, strikkie, das; ~ vein, nekaar; ~ ware, boordjies en dasse.

necrol'ogist, skrywer van 'n nekrologie, nekroloog.

necrol'ogy, (..gies), sterftelys, nekrologie, doodsberig; lewensberig.

nec'romancer, towe(r)naar, swartkunstenaar, geestebesweerder.

nec'romancy, towerkuns, towery, swartkuns.

necroman'tic, beswering=, tower=.

necropha'gia, aasvretery.

necroph'agous, lykvretend, aasvretend.

necrophil'ia, necro'philism, necro'phily, nekrofilie.

necrophob'ia, vrees vir lyke, nekrofobie.

necrop'olis, (-es), dodestad, begraafplaas, nekropolis.

nec'ropsy, lykskouing, nekropsie.

necroscop'ic, rakende 'n lykskouing, nekroskopies.

necros'copy, lykskouing, nekroskopie.

necrose', afsterf, versterf.

necros'is, beeneter, beenvreter; nekrose, afsterwing; versterwing; kouevuur.

necrot'ic, afgestorwe, nekroties.

nec'tar, nektar, godedrank; ~'eal, ~'ean, ~'eous, nektaragtig, soos nektar; ~ gland, heuningklier; ~-guide, heuningmerk; ~ if'erous, heuningsaphoudend.

nec'tarine, kaalperske, nektarien.

nec'tary, (..ries), heuningsakkie, nektarium; heuningpotjie (blom).

ne'e, gebore (van 'n getroude vrou); Mrs. X, ~ Y, mev. X, gebore Y.

need, (n) nood; nodigheid, noodsaaklikheid; gebrek, behoefte, nooddruf; AT ~, in geval van nood; if ~ BE, in geval van nood; as dit nodig is; in ~ of CARE, sorgbehoewend; in CASE of ~, in geval van nood; the ~ FOR, die behoefte aan; no ~ FOR alarm, geen rede om ontsteld te raak nie; a FRIEND in ~ is a friend indeed, in die nood leer 'n mens jou vriende ken; HAVE ~ of your advice, jou raad nodig hê; when the ~ is HIGHEST, help is nighest, as die nood die hoogste is, is die redding naby; in the HOUR of ~, as die nood druk; IN his ~, in sy ellende; ~ s MUST when the devil drives, dit moet as die nood druk; there is NO ~ to, ons (be)hoef nie; SUFFER ~, behoeftig wees; STAND in ~ of, nodig hê; in TIME of ~, as die nood druk; be in URGENT ~ of, dringend nodig hê; (v) behoef, nodig hê; makeer; gebrek ly; you ~ not DO it, jy hoef dit nie te doen nie; it ~ s to be DONE, dit moet gedoen word; he ~ s KNOWING, 'n mens moet hom ken; he ~ s to REMEMBER this, hy behoort dit te onthou.

need'ful, (n) die nodige; do the ~, die nodige verrig; (a) nodig, noodsaaklik; the one thing ~, die een noodsaaklike ding; ~ ness, noodsaaklikheid.

need'iness, behoeftigheid.

nee'dle, (n) naald; magneetnaald, wyser; obelisk; ergernis; slagpen (vuurwapen); from a ~ to an ANCHOR, van 'n naald tot 'n koevoet; LOOK for a ~ in a haystack, 'n naald in 'n hooimied soek; 'n hopelose taak aanpak; onbegonne werk verrig; on PINS and ~ s, op hete kole; as SHARP as a ~, uiters skerpsinnig; (v) naai, deurboor; prikkel, erger; 'n weg baan; ~ bath, fyn stortbad, straalbad, naaldbad; ~ beam, steekbalk; ~-book, naaldeboekie; ~-case, naaldekoker; ~ chisel, naaldbeitel; ~ clamp, naaldklem; ~ craft, naaiwerk; ~ file, naaldvyl; ~-fish, naaldvis; ~-gun, naaldgeweer; ~ holder, naaldekoker; ~ instrument, naaldetele=

needless — **nephritis**

graaf; ~ **lace**, hekelkantwerk, naaldkant; ~**-point**, naaldpunt; ~**'s eye**, oog van 'n naald.
need′less, onnodig, nodeloos; ~**ness**, nodeloosheid.
nee′dle: ~**-shaped**, naaldvormig; ~**-threader**, garinginsteker; ~ **valve**, naaldklep; ~**woman**, naaister; ~**work**, naaldwerk, handwerk; naaigoed; *fancy* ~*work*, kunsnaaldwerk; ~**work lesson**, naaldwerkles.
need′ments, behoeftes, benodigdhede.
needs, (n) nooddruf, behoeftes; (adv) noodsaaklik; *he must* ~ *DO it*, hy kan nie anders nie; *he* ~ *must GO*, hy moet met alle geweld gaan; *he* ~ *must HAVE his coupons*, hy wil met alle geweld sy koepons hê.
need′y, behoeftig, arm, hulpbehoewend.
ne'er, nooit; ~**-do-well**, niksnuts, askoek, aslêer; lieplapper; asjas, asgat, deugniet.
nefar′ious, afskuwelik, skandelik, misdadig, goddeloos; ~**ness**, afskuwelikheid, skandelikheid, misdadigheid, gruwelikheid.
negate′, ontken, loën, weerspreek.
nega′tion, ontkenning; weiering; loëning, negasie; ~**ist**, ontkenner.
neg′ative, (n) ontkenning; weiering; negatiewe pool; min(us)teken; negatief (fotog.); *answer in the* ~, nee sê, ontkennend antwoord; (v) ontken; afstem, verwerp; weerspreek; ongedaan maak, neutraliseer; ~ *a motion*, 'n mosie (voorstel) verwerp; (a) ontkennend; afwysend; negatief; weierend; *give a* ~ *reply*, ontkennend antwoord, nee sê; ~ **electricity**, negatiewe elektrisiteit; ~ **quantity**, negatiewe hoeveelheid; ~ **report**, negatiewe berig, ~ **sign**, min(us)teken; ~ **vote**, teenstem.
neg′ativism, negativisme.
neg′atron, negatron.
neglect′, (n) verwaarlosing; nalatigheid; nalating, versuim; ~ *of DUTY*, pligsversuim; *FALL into* ~, verwaarloos raak; *FROM* ~, uit nalatigheid; *TO the* ~ *of*, met verwaarlosing van; (v) verwaarloos, verontagsaam, nalaat, versuim, verbygaan; ~**ed**, verwaarloos, versuim, nagelaat, versaak; verroes; ~**ed genius**, miskende genie; ~**edness**, verwaarlosing; ~**ful**, nalatig, agtelosig; *be* ~*ful of*, verwaarloos, verontagsaam.
nég′ligé, môrerok, négligé; *in* ~, in huisdrag.
neg′ligence, nalatigheid, agtelosigheid, verontagsaming, versuim, onagsaamheid.
neg′ligible, verwaarloosbaar; nietig, onbeduidend; *a* ~ *quantity*, 'n nietige (onbeduidende) hoeveelheid; *he is a* ~ *quantity*, hy is 'n nul.
negotiabil′ity, verhandelbaarheid, wisselbaarheid; begaanbaarheid (pad).
nego′tiable, verhandelbaar, wisselbaar; rybaar, begaanbaar (pad); deurwaadbaar, deurgaanbaar (rivier); ~ *INSTRUMENT*, verhandelbare dokument; *law of* ~ *INSTRUMENTS*, wisselreg.
nego′tiate, handel drywe, verhandel; verdiskonteer (wissel); deurdruk, deursit; onderhandel; deurstaan; behartig; tot stand bring, bewerk, sluit; plaas ('n lening); ~ *a BILL*, 'n wissel verhandel; ~ *a DIFFICULTY*, 'n moeilikheid baasraak; ~ *a FENCE*, oor 'n heining spring; ~ *FOR*, onderhandel vir; ~ *ON an issue*, oor 'n kwessie onderhandel; ~ *a RIVER*, 'n rivier oorsteek; ~ *WITH a person*, met iem. onderhandel.
negotia′tion, handel; onderhandeling; omset; totstandbrenging; verhandeling, verdiskontering (wissel); *CARRY on* ~*s with*, onderhandel met; *OPEN* ~*s*, onderhandelinge aanknoop.
nego′tiator, onderhandelaar; verhandelaar.
negotia′trix, (..trices), onderhandelaarster.
Neg′ress, (-es), Negerin.
Negrill′o, (-s), Dwergneger.
Negri′to, Negrito.
negritude, negritude, Negerheid.
Neg′ro, (-es), Neger; N~ **blood**, Negerbloed; ~ **dance**, Negerdans.
Negroid′, Negeragtig, negroïed.
Neg′ro: ~ **language**, Negertaal; ~ **minstrel**, Negersanger.
neg′rophil(e), negroph′ilist, negrofiel.
negrophob′ia, Negervrees.

Neg′ro: ~ **population**, Negerbevolking; ~ **slave**, Negerslaaf; ~ **traffic**, Negerhandel; ~ **type**, Negertipe; ~ **woman**, Negervrou.
Neg′us[1], (hist.), Negus (van Abessinië).
neg′us[2], warm gekruide wyn, kandeelwyn.
neigh, (n) gerunnik, gehinnik; (v) runnik, hinnik.
neigh′bour, (n) buurman, buurvrou; (ewe)naaste; *DUTY to one's* ~, naasteplig; *NEXT-DOOR* ~*s*, naaste bure; (v) grens aan; naby woon; ~ *upon*, grens aan; (a) naburig, aangrensend.
neigh′bourhood, (ge)buurt(e), buurtskap; nabyheid, nabuurskap, omtrek; *in the* ~ *of*, in die buurt van; omtrent, om en by.
neigh′bour: ~**ing**, naburig, aangrensend, omliggend; ~**liness**, goeie buurskap; hulpvaardigheid; ~**ly**, soos goeie bure, vriendskaplik, behulpsaam; ~**ship**, buurskap.
neigh′ing, gerunnik, gehinnik.
neith′er, (pron) geen van twee nie; (adv) ewemin, ook nie, nòg; ~ ... *NOR*, nòg ... nòg, nie ... nie; *that's* ~ *here NOR there*, dit maak hoegenaamd geen saak nie; dit is van geen betekenis nie; dit het geen betrekking hierop nie.
nek′ton, nekton.
nell′y[1]: *swallow that story? Not on your* ~*!* daardie storie glo? So nimmer as te nooit!
nell′y[2], (nellies), reusestormvoël.
nel′son, nelson(greep).
ne′matocyst, nematosis(t).
nem′atode, spoelwurm, aalwurm, aaltjie, nematode, rondewurm.
nem′butal, nembutal (handelsnaam).
ne′mertine, platwurm, nemertien, snoerwurm.
neme′sia, moederskoentjies (blom).
Nem′esis, Nemesis, wraakgodin.
nem′esis, wraak, vergelding.
nen′ta, nenta, krimpsiek(te); ~ **bush**, nentabos(sie).
nen′uphar, waterlelie.
Neo-Cal′vinist, Neo-Calvinis.
Neo-Chris′tian, Neo-Christen.
neoclass′ical, neoklassiek.
neoclass′icism, neoklassisisme.
neoclass′icist, neoklassisis.
ne′ogene, neogeen.
neogen′esis, nuutwording, nuwe geboorte.
Neolith′ic, (n) Neolitikum; (a) Neolities, van die Jonger Steentydperk.
neolo′gian, neologies.
neol′ogism, nuwe woord, nieuvorming, neologisme.
neol′ogist, woordsmeder, neoloog.
neol′ogy, neologie, invoering van nuwe woorde, ens.
Neo-Malthu′sian, (n) Neo-Malthusiaan; (a) Neo-Malthusiaans.
Neo-Malthus′ianism, Neo-Malthusianisme.
ne′on, neon; ~ **light**, neonlig; ~ **lighting**, neonverligting; ~ **sign**, neonteken, neonreklame; ~ **tube**, neonbuis.
ne′onate, neonaat, pasgebore kind.
neonto′logy, neontologie.
neophob′ia, vrees vir nuwe dinge, neofobie.
ne′ophyte, neofiet, beginner; pasbekeerde; nuweling.
ne′oplasm, neoplasma, nieugroei, nuutgroei(sel).
neoplas′tic, nuutgevorm (vleis in wond).
Neo-Platon′ic, Neo-Platonies.
neo-repub′lican, neorepublikein.
neote′ric, (n) moderne skrywer; (a) nuwerwets, modern, hedendaags.
neozo′ic, neosoïes.
Nepal′i, (n) Nepalees (taal); Nepali (inwoner); (a) Nepalees.
nepen′the(s), towerdrank, vergetelheidsdrank; bekerplant.
neph′alism, afskaffing.
neph′alist, afskaffer.
nephelo′meter, troebelheidsmeter, nefelometer.
nepho′logy, wolkeleer, nefologie.
ne′phew, neef, broerskind, susterskind.
nephral′gia, nierpyn.
neph′ric, nier=.
neph′rite, niersteen, nefriet, jade.
nephrit′ic, (n) niermiddel; (a) nier=, nefrites.
nephrit′is, nierontsteking, nefritis.

neph'roid, niervormig.
neph'rolith, niersteen.
nephrol'ogy, nierbeskrywing, nefrologie.
nephro'pathy, nierkwaal, nefropatie.
nephro'sis, nieraandoening, nefrose.
nephrot'omy, nieroperasie, nefrotomie.
nep'otism, begunstiging, nepotisme, voortrekkery.
Nep'tune, Neptunus.
neptu'nium, neptunium.
nerd, (sl.), slimmerd, slimkous.
Ner'eid, seenimf, Nereïde.
nerin'e, voëlkloutjie (blom), nerina.
nerit'ic, nerities.
Ner'o, Nero; wreedaard.
nero anti'co, nero antico, swartmarmer.
ner'oli, lemoenbloeiselolie; *oil of* ~, lemoenbloeiselolie.
Neron'ian, Neronies, van Nero.
nerv'al, senuwee=, nervaal.
nerv'ate, generf, gerib (blare).
nerva'tion, nerwatuur, bladaarstelsel.
nerve, (n) senu(wee), (senu)pees; (blad)aar (plantk.); spierkrag; moed, durf, geeskrag; nerf (plantk.); (pl) senuwees; *be ALL* ~*s,* die ene senuwees wees; *he is a BUNDLE of* ~*s,* hy is 'n senuweebol (senuweeorrel); ~*s on EDGE,* senuwees op hol; *FIT of* ~*s,* senuweetoeval; *GET on one's* ~*s,* op jou senuwees kry; *GET it on a person's* ~*s,* iem. senuweeagtig maak; op iem. se senuwees werk; iem. se geduld laat opraak; *HAVE the* ~ *to,* die onbeskaamdheid hê om; *HAVE no* ~*s,* maklik skrik; *HAVE the* ~ *for something (to do something),* die moed hê om iets te doen; *STRAIN every* ~, alle kragte inspan; elke spier span; ou kragte uithaal; *a WAR of* ~*s,* 'n senuweeoorlog; (v) krag gee, sterk maak; bemoedig, staal; ~ *oneself,* die stoute skoene aantrek; jou verman, jou moed byeenskraap; ~-**bundle,** senu(wee)bundel; ~ **cell,** senu(wee)sel; ~ **centre,** senu(wee)sentrum; ~ **cord,** senu(wee)string; ~ **disease,** senu(wee)siekte; ~ **fibre,** senu(wee)draad, =vesel; ~ **ganglion,** senu(wee)knoop; ~-**knot,** senu(wee)knoop; ~ **less,** kragteloos, swak, pap; senuloos, sonder senuwees; ontsenu; ~ **pain,** senu(wee)pyn; ~ **patient,** senu(wee)lyer; ~-**racking,** senu(wee)kwellend, veeleisend; ~ **specialist,** senuarts, senuspesialis; ~-**sufferer,** senu(wee)lyer; ~ **tissue,** senu(wee)weefsel; ~ **tonic,** senu(wee)versterker.
nerv'ine, (n) kalmerende middel, senu(wee)versterker; (a) senuwee=.
nervose', generf.
nervos'ity, senuweeagtigheid.
nerv'ous, senuweeagtig; skrikkerig; ~ *of DOING something,* skrikkerig om iets te doen; *too* ~ *to SAY anything,* te opgewonde om iets te sê; die herkoutjie spring in sy keel; *a* ~ *WRECK,* 'n senu(wee)wrak; ~ **affection,** senu(wee)aandoening; ~ **attack,** senu(wee)aanval; ~ **breakdown,** senu(wee)toeval, senu(wee)instorting; ~ **collapse,** senu(wee)insinking; senu(wee)-instorting; ~ **complaint,** senu(wee)aandoening; ~ **debility,** senu(wee)swakte; ~ **disease,** ~ **disorder,** senu(wee)siekte; ~ **disturbance,** senu(wee)storing; ~ **fever,** senu(wee)siekte; ~ **fit,** senu(wee)toeval; ~ **headache,** senu(wee)hoofpyn; ~**ness,** senu(wee)agtigheid; ~ **shock,** senu(wee)skok; ~ **sufferer,** senu(wee)lyer; ~ **system,** senu(wee)stelsel; ~ **twitch,** senu(wee)trekking.
nerv'ure, middelnerf, hoofnerf; nerwatuur; rib, vleuelnerf (insek).
nerv'y, sterk, kragtig; parmantig, vermetel; senu(wee)agtig.
nesc'ience, onwetendheid.
nesc'ient, onwetend, onkundig.
ness, (-es), voorgebergte, landtong, kaap.
nest, (n) nes; *FEATHER one's* ~, jou verryk; goeie sake doen; *FOUL (befoul) one's* ~, jou nes bevuil; *it's an ill bird that FOULS its own* ~, 'n mens moenie jou eie nes bevuil nie; ~ *of ROBBERS,* rowersnes; ~ *of SAWS,* saagstel; ~ *of TABLES,* inskuiftafeltjies, pastafeltjies; hen-en-kuikens; mimitafeltjies; (v) nes maak; neste uithaal; ~-**box,** neskassie; ~-**down,** nesdons, nesvere; ~-**egg,** neseier; spaargeld.

nest'ing, nesmakery; ~ **season,** broeityd.
ne'stle, nestel, vly; nes skop; lekker lê, jou tuis maak; ~ *CLOSE to,* aankruip teen; jou aanvly teen; ~ *DOWN,* nes skop.
ne'stling, (n) nesvoël, neskuiken; skuiling, nesteling; (a) vertroetelend, omhelsend; ~ **bird,** nesvoël.
Nes'tor, Nestor; wyse raadgewer; ~'**ian,** (n) Nestoriaan; (a) Nestoriaans.
net^1, (n) net; strik; korf (korfbal); spinnerak; netstof; *AT the* ~, by die net (tennis); *AT the* ~*s,* in die nette (krieket); (v) **(-ted),** hekel, brei; knoop (net); in 'n net vang.
net^2, (v) **(-ted),** netto opbring, skoon verdien; (a) netto, skoon, suiwer; ~ *PROFITS,* suiwer (netto) wins; *the* ~ *RESULT,* die slotsom.
net: ~**ball,** netbal; ~ **cloth,** toudoek; ~-**cotton,** netkatoen; ~ **embroidery,** netborduurwerk; netborduursel.
neth'er: *the* ~ *WORLD,* die onderwêreld; *this* ~ *WORLD,* die ondermaanse; ~ **garments,** broek; ~ **jaw,** onderkaak.
Neth'erlander, Nederlander.
Neth'erlandish, Nederlands.
Neth'erlandism, Neerlandisme.
Neth'erlands, (n) Nederland, die Nederlande; (a) Nederlands.
ne'thermost, onderste, laagste.
net: ~-**layer,** netlêer (skip); ~-**like,** netvormig.
net' loss, netto verlies.
net: ~-**maker,** netmaker; ~ **play,** netspel; ~-**pole,** netpaal.
net'suke, netske, gordelknoop.
nett, *kyk* **net^2.**
nett'er, netvisser; netmaker.
nett'ing, netwerk, gaas; knoopwerk; ogiesdraad, sifdraad; ~-**needle,** netvlegnaald; ~ **wire,** ogiesdraad, sifdraad.
net'tle, (n) brandnetel, brandnekel; *grasp the* ~, die bul by die horings pak; gevaar moedig aanpak; (v) kwaad maak, prikkel, vererg; met netels slaan; *be* ~*d,* beledig, geraak, gepikeer; ~ **rash,** netelroos, brandjeuk, galbult, bort.
net': ~-**veined,** netvormig.
net' weight, netgewig; netto gewig.
net'work, netwerk, net.
neur'al, senu(wee)=.
neural'gia, sinkings, gesigspyn, senu(wee)pyn, neuralgie; ~-**cure,** sinkingskuur; ~-**mixture,** sinkingsmengsel.
neural'gic, senu(wee)=, neuralgies.
neurasthen'ia, senu(wee)swakte, neurastenie.
neurasthen'ic, (n) senu(wee)lyer, neurastenikus; (a) senu(wee)siek, senu(wee)swak, neurastenies.
neura'tion, aarstelsel.
neura'xon, senu(wee)assilinder.
neurine', neurine.
neurit'ic, neurities.
neurit'is, senu(wee)ontsteking, neuritis.
neurolog'ical, senu(wee)=, neurologies.
neurol'ogist, neuroloog, senu(wee)arts.
neurol'ogy, senu(wee)siekteleer, neurologie.
neur'on, neuron, senu(wee)sel.
neur'opath, senu(wee)lyer, neuropaat; ~'**ic,** neuropaties, senusiek.
neurophysio'logy, neurofisiologie.
Neurop'tera, Netvlerkiges, Neuroptera.
neuros'is, senu(wee)siekte, neurose.
neur'osurgeon, neurochirurg.
neur'osurgery, neurochirurgie.
neurot'ic, (n) senu(wee)middel; senu(wee)pasiënt, senu(wee)lyer; (a) senu(wee)=, senu(wee)agtig; senu(wee)siek, neuroties; ~ **complaint,** ~ **disease,** senu(wee)kwaal, senu(wee)aandoening.
neut'er, (n) onsydige geslag, neutrum; geslaglose; (a) onsydig, neutraal; geslagloos.
neut'ral, (n) neutrale, onsydige (skip, staat); onpartydige (persoon); uitgeskakelde posisie, neutraal, neutrale stand (motor); (a) neutraal, onpartydig, onsydig, afsydig; uitgeskakel (motor); *in* ~, in rus (neutraal) (motor); ~ **equilibrium,** labiele ewewig; ~ **gear,** neutrale stand; ~**ist,** voorstander van neutraliteit; ~'**ity,** onsydigheid, neutraliteit; ~**iza'**

neutrino / **nice**

tion, neutralisasie; neutraalverklaring; opheffing; ~**ize,** onsydig maak, neutraliseer; ophef; ~*ize each other*, mekaar balanseer; teen mekaar opweeg; mekaar neutraliseer; ~ **tint,** neutrale kleur.
neutri'no, neutrino.
neu'tron, neutron, ~ **bomb,** neutronbom; ~ **star,** pulsar.
névé, korrelsneeu, névé.
nev'er, nooit, nimmer; *BE he* ~ *so smart,* al is hy ook hoe slim; ~ *say DIE,* "kannie" is dood; aanhouer wen; ~ *you FEAR,* wees maar nie bang nie; *it is* ~ *too LATE to mend,* dit is nooit te laat om te verbeter nie; ~ *on your LIFE!* nog nooit! ~ *MIND,* dit maak g'n saak nie; ag, toe maar; ~ *MIND what other people say,* moenie jou aan ander mense se praatjies steur nie; *I can scarcely afford this house,* ~ *MIND a bigger one,* ek kan hierdie huis skaars bekostig, moenie nog praat van 'n groter een nie; ~ *is a MONTH of Sundays,* so nooit as te nimmer; ~ *so MUCH as,* nie eers nie; *were he* ~ *so RICH,* al was hy ook nog so ryk; *don't SAY I'll* ~ *drink of this water how dirty so ever it be,* mens moet nooit sê: Fonteintjie, ek sal nooit weer uit jou drink nie; *you've* ~ *SOLD that horse!* jy het tog seker nie daardie perd verkoop nie! *WELL, I* ~*!* my liewe tyd! daar het jy dit! nou toe nou! dis 'n mooi grap! praat v.d. ding! ~ *a WORD,* nie 'n enkele woord nie; geen stomme woord nie; ~ *is a long WORD,* nooit is 'n groot woord; ~**-ceasing,** onophoudelik, onafgebroke; ~**-dying,** onsterflik; ~**-ending,** oneindig, eindeloos; ~**-fading,** onverwelkbaar, onverwelklik; kleurvas (klerestof); ~**-failing,** onfeilbaar; onbedrieglik; ~ **more,** nooit meer nie, nimmermeer, nooit weer nie.
nev'er-never: *the* ~ *COUNTRY,* gramadoelas; kammaland; *ON the* ~, tot in die oneindige.
nev'er: ~**theless,** (des)nieteenstaande, ewe(n)wel, desondanks, nietemin, tog; ~**-to-be-forgotten,** onvergeetlik, gedenkwaardig.
new, (a) nuut; onervare, baar; onbekend; vars; ~ *to the BUSINESS,* nog baar; nog nie op hoogte van sake nie; *turn over a* ~ *LEAF,* 'n nuwe begin maak, *it LOOKS like* ~, dit lyk of dit nuut is; *put on the* ~ *MAN,* die ou mens aflê; *that's NOT* ~ *to me,* dis niks nuuts vir my nie; *there is NOTHING* ~ *under the sun,* daar is niks nuuts onder die son nie; *that is a* ~ *ONE!* dit is iets nuuts! *SOMETHING* ~, 'n nuwigheid; *a* ~ *STUDENT,* 'n groentjie (groene); *The N* ~ *WORLD,* die Nuwe Wêreld; (adv) pas, onlangs; opnuut; ~ **birth,** wedergeboorte; ~**-born,** pasgebore; ~ **bread,** vars brood; ~**-build,** (~**-built**), herbou, vernuwe; ~**-built,** pas gebou; herbou
New'castle, Newcastle; *carry coals to* ~, water na die see dra; ~ **disease,** Newcastlesiekte.
new'comer, nuweling, inkomeling, bykomeling, aankomeling; groentjie.
new'el, spil, knop (trapleuning), trapstyl.
New Eng'lander, Nieu-Engelander.
new: ~**-fangled,** nuwerwets; ~**-fashioned,** nieuwmodies, nuwerwets, byderwets; ~ **formation,** nieuvorming, nuutvorming, neologisme.
Newfound'land, New'toundland, Newfoundland; ~ **dog,** Newfoundlandse hond.
New Guin'ea, Nieu-Guinee.
New: *the* ~ *Hebrides,* die Nuwe Hebride; ~ **Holland,** Nieu-Holland.
new: ~**ish,** amper nuut, nuwerig; ~**-laid,** pasgelê, kekkelvars; **N** ~ **Left,** Nieu-Linkses, Nuutlinkses, New Left; ~ **look,** nuwe voorkoms; ~**ly,** nuut; onlangs; ~**-made,** net gemaak; vars (koffie); ~**-married,** pas getroud; ~ **moon,** donkermaan, nuwemaan; ~**ness,** nuutheid, nuwigheid; ~ **potatoes,** jong aartappel(tjie)s; ~ **rich,** parvenu, nuutryke(s); *the* ~ *rich,* die pas rykes.
news, nuus, tyding, berig; mare; *ill* ~ *FLIES apace,* slegte nuus trek vinnig; *GOOD* ~, goeie nuus; *no* ~ *GOOD* ~, geen tyding goeie tyding; *GREAT* ~, 'n verrassing; *I HEARD it in the* ~, ek het dit oor die nuus gehoor; *that is NO* ~, dit is ou nuus; *a PIECE of* ~, 'n nuusbrokkie; *that's* ~ *TO me,* ek weet daar nog niks van nie; ~**-agency,** nuusagentskap; ~**-agent,** nuusagent, koerantverkoper, koeranthandelaar; ~ **black-out,** nuusverbod; ~**-boy,** koerantseun; koerantjoggie. ~**-cable,** perskabelgram; ~ **cast,** nuusuitsending; (radio)nuusberig; ~ **caster,** nuusleser.
New Scot'land, New Scotland (in Tvl.).
news: ~ **coverage,** nuusdekking; ~**-editor,** nuusredakteur; ~**-flash,** flitsberig; ~ **gathering,** beriggewing; ~ **hound,** nuusjagter; ~**-hungry,** gretig na nuus; ~**-item,** nuusberig; ~**-letter,** nuusbrief; ~ **man,** verslaggewer, beriggewer; ~ **monger,** nuusverspreier, nuusdraer, nuuskramer.
news'paper, koerant, nuusblad; *chain of* ~*s*, netselsel van koerante; ~ **clippings,** koerantuitknipsels; ~ **man,** koerantskrywer, joernalis; ~ **woman,** joernaliste, koerantskryfster.
news: ~ **print,** koerantpapier; ~ **reader,** nuusleser; ~**-reel,** nuusfilm; ~ **report,** nuusberig, (nuus)verslag; ~**-room,** nuuskantoor; nagkantoor; leessaal; ~**-service,** persburo; ~ **sheet,** nuusblaadjie.
New South Wales, Nieu-Suid-Wallis.
New'speak, Newspeak.
news: ~**-stand,** koerantstalletjie, koerantkraam; ~ **value,** nuuswaarde; ~**-vendor,** koerantverkoper; ~ **worthiness,** nuuswaarde, belangwekkendheid, ~ **worthy,** belangwekkend; ~**-writer,** koerantskrywer, joernalis, beriggewer; ~**y,** vol nuus, interessant.
New Test'ament: *the* ~, die Nuwe Testament.
newt, paddavis; watersal(a)mander.
new'ton, newton.
new wave, nuwe golf; nieuroman.
New World: *the* ~, die Nuwe Wêreld.
New Year, Nuwejaar; ~*'s day,* Nuwejaarsdag; ~*'s eve,* Oujaarsaand.
New York', New York.
New Zea'land, Nieu-Seeland; ~ **er,** Nieu-Seelander.
ne'xal, neksaal.
next, (n) volgende; ~ *of KIN,* naaste bloedverwant; ~ *PLEASE,* volgende asseblief; (a) (eers)volgende, eerskomend, aanstaande; naaste, langsaan; *BE* ~, die volgende wees; ~ *DAY,* die volgende dag; ~ *DOOR,* langsaan, hiernaas; *the lady* ~ *DOOR,* die dame hier langsaan; ~ *to NOTHING,* so goed as niks; ~ *SUNDAY,* volgende Sondag, aanstaande Sondag; ~ *TIME,* die volgende keer; (adv) daarna, vervolgens; ~ *TO,* langs(aan), naas; *in* ~ *TO no time,* in 'n japtrap; *WHAT* ~? wat gaan nog gebeur? (prep) langsaan, naasaan; ~ *to one's skin,* op die blote lyf.
next'-best, tweede beste, op een na die beste.
next' door, langsaan, hiernaas; ~ *to DISHONESTY,* baie naby oneerlikheid; ~ *to a FOOL,* driekwart gek; ~ **neighbour,** naaste buurman.
nex'us, verbinding; band; skakel; neksus.
Nga'mi: *Luke* ~, die Ngamimeer; ~**land,** Ngamiland.
ni'acin, niasien, niasine.
nib, (n) pen; penpunt; tand, punt (gereedskap); spits; (v) (**-bed**), aanpunt; 'n punt aansit.
nib'ble, (n) geknaag, gepeusel; (v) knaag; knabbel (vis); peusel; vit; ~ *at,* knabbel aan; ~**r,** knabbelaar; vitter (fig.).
nib'bling, geknabbel; gepeusel; vittery.
nib'lick, kuilstok, sandyster (gholf).
nibs: *his* ~, (sl.), sy hoogedele (spottend).
nic(c)'olite, nikkoliet.
Nice, Nizza, Nice.
nice, lekker, aangenaam; snoesig, aardig; gaaf, gawerig, lief (persoon); keurig, verfyn; skerp (sintuig); nougeset, kieskeurig; fyn, netelig, ingewikkeld (vraagstuk); oulik; *you ARE a* ~ *one!* jy is 'n mooi een! jy is 'n mooie! *a* ~ *DISTINCTION,* 'n fyn onderskeid; *a* ~ *EXPERIMENT,* 'n moeilike proefneming; *a* ~ *GIRL,* 'n gawe meisie; *a* ~ *JOB,* 'n lekker werkie; *a* ~ *MESS,* 'n mooi gemors; *that's NOT* ~ *of you,* dis nie mooi van jou nie; *a* ~ *POINT,* 'n treffer; *a* ~ *QUESTION,* 'n netelige vraagstuk; ~ *and WARM,* lekker warm; ~ *WORK!* mooi so! ~**-looking,** mooi; ~**ly,** mooi; netjies; *he is doing* ~*ly,* dit gaan goed met hom;

~**ness**, lekkerheid, aangenaamheid; keurigheid; liefheid, vriendelikheid.
ni'cety, (..ties), fynheid, fraaiigheid; noukeurigheid; kieskeurigheid; lekkerny; fyn onderskeiding, finesse; *to a* ~, presies, uiters noukeurig.
niche, nis; hoekie, plekkie; *a* ~ *in the temple of fame*, 'n plek in die heldegalery.
nick, (n) nerf, keep; stippie; skaar (in 'n lem); *OLD N*~, die duiwel, Haantjie Pik; *in the very* ~ *of TIME*, net op die regte tyd; op die tippie; op die nippertjie; net betyds; *arrive in the* ~ *of TIME*, kom of jy geroep is; net op die regte tyd aankom; (v) inkerf, inkeep; juis tref; fop, kul; goed paar (diere).
nick'el, (n) nikkel; (v) (**-led**), vernikkel; ~ **alloy**, nikkellegering; ~ **coin**, nikkelmunt(stuk); ~**if'erous**, nikkelhoudend; ~**o'deon**, blêrkas; ~**-plate**, vernikkel; ~**-plated**, vernikkel; ~**-plating**, vernikkeling; ~ **pyrites**, nikkelkies; ~ **silver**, nieusilwer, nikkelsilwer; ~ **steel**, nikkelstaal.
ni'ck-nack, *kyk* **knick-knack**.
nick'name, (n) bynaam; skel(d)naam, spotnaam; (v) 'n bynaam gee; ~**d**, bygenaamd, met die bynaam.
ni'col prism, nicolprisma.
nico'tian, (n) roker; (a) tabak(s)=.
nic'otine, nikotien, nikotine; pypolie.
nicotin'ic: ~ **acid**, nikotinesuur, nikotiensuur.
nic'otinism, nikotienvergiftiging.
nic'otinize, met nikotien vergiftig.
nic'tate, nic'titate, oë knip.
nic'tating (nic'titating) membrane, knipvlies, derde ooglid.
nidamen'tal, nidamentaal.
nid(d)'ering, (n) lafaard, gemene vent; (a) laaghartig, gemeen.
nid'dle-nod'dle, (v) kopspeel; knik, knikkebol; waggel; (a) knikkend; kopspelend; waggelend.
nide, broeisel fisante (ganse).
nidi'ficate, nes bou, nes maak.
nidifica'tion, nesbou(ery).
nid'-nod, (-ded), gedurig knik, kopspeel, skuddebol.
nid'orous, onwelriekend; bederf.
nid'us, (-es, ..di), nes; broeines; besmettingshaard; nidus.
niece, nig(gie), susterskind *of* broerskind.
niello, niëllo.
niff, (sl.), (v) sleg ruik, stink; (n.), slegte reuk, stank.
nif'ty, fynuitgevat, agtermekaar, soos 'n nuwe sikspens; slim.
Niger'ia, Nigerië; ~**n**, (n) Nigeriër; (a) Nigeries.
nigg'ard, (n) gierigaard, skraalhans, vrek; (a) vrekkig, inhalig, suinig; ~**liness**, gierigheid, inhaligheid, vrekkigheid.
nigg'ardly, stiefmoederlik, skraaltjies; gierig, inhalig, suinig, vrekkig, krenterig; ~ *with his MONEY*, vrekkig met sy geld; ~ *of his PRAISE*, suinig met sy lof.
nigg'er, (derog.), Neger; *a* ~ *in the woodpile*, die sondaar, die oorsaak v.d. kwaad; ~**-ball**, toorballetjie; nikkerbol; ~**-brown**, donkerbruin; ~**-curls**, peperkrulle (karakoelvel).
nig'gle, peuter, beusel, sukkel, bekriebel.
nig'gling, (n) gepeuter, beuselary; peuterwerk; vittery; (a) beuselagtig; vitterig; peuterig.
nigh, naby, byna; *draw* ~, nader kom; ~**ness**, nabyheid.
night, nag; aand; *ALL* ~, die hele nag; *AT* ~ *we sleep*, snags slaap ons; *as BLACK (dark) as the* ~, so donker soos die nag; *BY* ~, snags; *burglars work BY* ~, inbrekers werk snags; *under COVER of* ~, in die donker; ~ *and DAY*, dag en nag; *what is done by* ~ *appears by DAY*, wat in die donker gedoen word, word in die lig openbaar; *GOOD* ~, goeienag; *LAST* ~, gisteraand; *LATE at* ~, laat in die nag; *MAKE a* ~ *of it*, laat deurloop dag toe; ~ *OUT*, vrye aand; *PASS the* ~, oornag, die nag deurbring; *STAY the* ~, die nag oorbly, oornag; *all THROUGH the* ~, die hele nag; *TRAVEL over* ~, reis gedurende die nag; *TURN* ~ *into day*, v.d. nag 'n dag maak; ~**-accommodation**, nagherberg; ~**-adder**, nagadder; ~**-attack**, nagaanval; ~ **atti**=re, nagklere; ~**-bell**, nagklok(kie); ~**-bird**, nag=
voël; naguil, nagvlinder (mens), nagwolf; ~**-blind**, nagblind; ~**-blindness**, nagblindheid; ~ **bomber**, nagbomwerper; ~**-brawler**, rusverstoorder; ~**-call**, nagoproep; ~ **cap**, slaapmus, nagmus; nagsopie, aandsopie, aandsnapsie; ~**-cart**, nagwa; ~ **cellar**, nagkroeg; ~**-chair**, stilletjie; ~**-class**, aandklas; ~**-clothes**, nagklere, slaapklere; ~**-club**, nagklub; ~**-cream**, nagpommade; ~**-dress**, naghemp; nagrok; ~**-duty**, nagdiens; ~ **editor**, nagredakteur; ~**-fall**, skemerdonker, aandskemering; ~ **fighter**, nagjagter; ~ **flight**, nagvlug; ~**-flower**, aandblom; ~**-fly**, mot; ~**-gear**, naggoed; ~**-gown**, naghemp, nagjurk, nagjapon; ~**-guard**, nagwag; ~**-hag**, nagmerrie; ~**-hawk**, bokmelker, nagvalk(ie); nagwolf, nagvlinder (mens); ~ **heron**, nagreier.
ni'ghtie, (colloq.), naghemp, nagjurk, nagrok.
night'ingale, nagtegaal; *voice of a* ~, nagtegaalstem.
night: ~ **jar**, naguil; nagswael; ~ **jump**, nagsprong; ~ **landing**, naglanding; ~ **life**, naglewe; ~**-light**, naglig; ~ **lighting**, nagverligting; ~**-long**, die hele nag; ~ **ly**, (a) nagtelik, snags; (adv) elke aand; elke nag; ~ **march**, nagmars; ~ **mare**, nagmerrie; ~**-moth**, nagmot, uiltjie; ~**-nurse**, nagverpleegster, nagsuster; ~**-piece**, nagstuk, nagskildery; ~**-porter**, nagkruier; nagportier; ~**-quarters**, nagverblyf; slaapplek; ~**-round**, nagronde (patrollie); ~ **school**, aandskool; ~ **service**, nagdiens; ~ **shade**, nastergal; ~ **shelter**, nagskuiling; ~ **shift**, nagskof; ~**-shirt**, naghemp; ~**-soil**, nagvuil, fekalieë; ~**-stand**, bedkassie; ~**-study**, lukubrasie; ~**-suit**, slaappak; ~**-tender**, nagbediener; ~**-time**, aand, nag; ~**-time photography**, nagopname; ~ **vision**, donkersien; ~**-walker**, slaapwandelaar; vabond; prostituut, straatvrou; ~**-watch**, nagwag; ~**-watchman**, nagwagter; nagwaker; ~**-wind**, nagwind; ~**-work**, nagwerk; ~**y**, (..ties), nagjurk, naghemp.
nigres'cence, donkerheid, swartheid.
nigres'cent, swartagtig, swarterig.
nig'ritude, swartheid.
nig'romancy, nigromansie.
ni'hilism, nihilisme.
ni'hilist, nihilis; ~ **ic**, nihilisties.
ni'hility, nietigheid, niks; nulliteit; onbestaanbaarheid.
nil, niks, nul; ~ **desperandum**, moenie tou opgooi nie, hou moed.
Nile, (die) Nyl; *the Blue* ~, die Blou Nyl; *the WHITE* ~, die Wit Nyl.
nil'gai, nilgai, bloubul *(Boselaphus tragocamelus).*
Nilom'eter, Nylmeter.
Nil'ot, Niloot, Nylstreekbewoner; ~ **ic**, Nyl=, van die Nyl.
nim'ble, lenig, vinnig, snel, vlug, rats; handig; *as* ~ *as a squirrel*, soos 'n voorslag wees; so rats soos 'n apie wees; ~**-fingered**, vingervlug; ~**-footed**, snelvoetig, rats, ligvoet(s); ~ **ness**, ratsheid, vinnigheid, vlugheid, lenigheid; ~**-witted**, vlug (van gees), gevat.
nimbo-stratus, nimbostratus, reënwolk.
nim'bus, (..bi), nimbus; reënwolk; stralekrans, ligkrans, oureool, heiligekrans.
nimi'ety, oormaat, oortolligheid, oordaad.
nim'iny-pim'iny, gemaak-fyn, aanstellerig, vol fiemies.
Nim'rod, Nimrod; groot jagter, nimrod.
nin'compoop, lummel, drommel, bog, idioot, asjas, 'n man van toet, oliekoek.
nine, (n) nege; *DRESSED to the* ~**s**, piekfyn aangetrek; fyn uitgevat; ~ *O'CLOCK*, negeuur; *POSSESSION is* ~ *points of the law*, salig is die besitters; *THE N*~, die nege Muses; ~ *TIMES out of ten*, nege uit elke tien keer; ~ *of TRUMPS*, nel; *we WERE* ~, ons was nege; daar was nege van ons; ~**-day's WONDER**, 'n kortstondige nuwigheid; ~ **fold**, (n) negevoud; (a) negevoudig; ~ **pence**, sewe en 'n half sent, nege pennies, vierskelling; ~ **pins**, keëls; *be knocked down like* ~ **pins**, soos keëls onderstebo gegooi word; ~ **teen'**, negentien; ~ **teenth'**, negentiende; *the* ~ *teenth hole*, klubgebou; kroeg, oog; ~**-tenths**, nege-tiendes; ~ **tieth**, negentigste; ~ **ty**, negentig; *the nineties*, die negentigerjare.

ninn'y, (ninnies), uilskuiken, domkop, bog, sukkelaar.
ni'non, ninon.
ninth, negende, neënde; ~**ly,** in die negende plek, ten negende.
nio'bium, niobium.
nip¹, (n) halfie; halfbotteltjie, kleintjie, nip; snapsie, regmakertjie, skrikmakertjie; (v) **(-ped),** klein slukkies gee, nip.
nip², (n) knyp; byt; skimpskoot; steek; knak (in draad); *there is a* ~ *in the air,* die luggie is skerp; (v) **(-ped),** byt; knyp; steek; knou; ~ *in the BUD,* in die kiem smoor; ~*ped by FROST,* doodgeryp; ~ *IN,* inwip, inglip; wegglip, uitglip.
nipp'er, knyper; spotter; knapie, seuntjie, snuiter; snytand (van 'n perd); (pl) knyptang; knypers, draadskêr; knypbril.
nipp'ing, knypend; skerp, snydend, sarkasties, bytend.
nip'ple, tepel (mens); tiet; speen (dier); koppie; nippel (geweer); aansluitstuk; spuitgaatjie ~**-shield,** tepelbeskermer.
Nipp'on, Nippon, Japan; ~'**ian,** Nipponies, Nippoñees, Japans.
nipp'y, bytend, bits, skerp; gou, rats, vinnig.
nirva'na, nirwana (Boeddhistiese geluksaligheid).
nis'i: *decree (rule)* ~, bevel nisi, voorwaardelike egskeidingsvonnis.
Nis'sen hut, nissenhut, tonnelhut.
nit, neet; *the world's biggest* ~, die grootste skaap (haas) in die wêreld; ~**-picking,** foutsoekery, foutvindery, muggiesiftery.
ni'tery, (sl.), nagklub.
ni'tid, helder, skynend.
nit'rate, (n) nitraat, salpetersuursout; ~ *of LIME,* kalksalpeter; ~ *of SILVER,* silwernitraat; ~ *of SODA,* natriumnitraat, chilisalpeter.
nitrate', (v) nitreer, met salpetersuur behandel.
nitra'tion, nitrasie.
ni'tre, salpeter.
nit'ric, salpeter-; ~ **acid,** salpetersuur.
ni'tride, nitried, nitride.
nitrifica'tion, salpetervorming, nitrifikasie.
nit'rify, (..fied), nitrifiseer.
ni'trile, nitriel.
nit'rite, nitriet.
nitrocell'ulose, nitrosellulose.
nitrogel'atine, nitrogelatien.
nit'rogen, stikstof, nitrogeen; ~ **cycle,** stikstofsiklus; ~ **compound,** stikstofverbinding, ~ **fixation,** stikstofbinding; ~ **narcosis,** stikstofbedwelming.
nitrog'enous, stikstofhoudend; stikstof-; ~ **manure,** stikstofbemesting.
nitrogly'cerin(e), nitrogliserien, nitrogliserine.
nit'rous, salpeteragtig; ~ **acid,** salpetersuur; ~ **fumes,** nitrosedampe; ~ **oxide,** laggas.
nitty-grit'ty, (sl.), basiese feite, grondfeite.
nit'wit, domkop, swaap.
nix¹, niks.
nix², niks, manlike watergees; ~**ie,** vroulike watergees; nikse.
njug'o-bean, bambarragrondboontjie, duif-ertjie, duiwe-ertjie, grond-ertjie *(Voandzeia subterranea).*
no, (n) weiering, nee; teenstem; *I will not take* ~ *for an ANSWER,* ek wil van geen weiering hoor nie; *the* ~*es HAVE it,* die voorstel is verwerp; *a PLAIN* ~, 'n besliste nee; *THE* ~*es,* teenstemme; (a) geen, g'n; ~ *BALL,* foutbal; *a vote of* ~ *CONFIDENCE,* 'n mosie van wantroue; ~ *DATE,* ongedateer; ~ *DUMPING,* afvalgooi verbied, storting verbode, geen stortplek; ~ *END of trouble,* baie moeite (moeilikheid); ~ *ENTRY,* geen toegang (nie); ~ *EXTRAS,* alles inbegrepe; *it's* ~ *GO,* daar kan niks gedoen word nie; ~ *LUCK,* geen geluk nie; ~ *MAN,* geen mens; papbroek; ~ *MAN'S land,* niemandsland; *by* ~ *MEANS,* in geen geval nie, glad nie, hoegenaamd nie; *there was* ~ *MISTAKING what he meant,* sy bedoeling was baie duidelik; ~ *ONE,* niemand; ~ *PARKING,* geen parkering (nie); *to* ~ *PURPOSE,* tevergeefs; ~ *SIDE,* die end (rugby); ~ *SMOKING,* rook verbode; ~ *THOROUGHFARE,* geen deurgang (nie); deurgang verbied; *in* ~ *TIME,* in 'n oogwenk, gou; ~ *TRUMPS,* geen troewe nie; *of* ~ *USE,* van geen waarde nie; ~ *U-TURN,* geen U-draai (nie); ~ *WHERE,* nêrens; ~ *WHIT,* glad nie; *in* ~ *WISE,* hoegenaamd nie; (adv) nee; niks; ~ *BETTER than before,* niks beter as tevore nie; ~ *sooner said than DONE,* so gesê, so gedaan; *she fancies herself* ~ *END,* sy verbeel haar wat wonders; ~ *MORE,* nie meer nie; ~ *THANKS!* nee, dankie!
No'ah, Noag; *in the days of* ~, toe Tafelberg nog 'n vulletjie was; ~**'s ark,** die Ark.
nob¹, (n) knop; kop, klapperdop; hoë meneer; *quite a* ~, 'n hele Piet.
nob², (v) **(-bed),** 'n opstopper gee.
no'-ball, foutbal (kr.).
nob'ble, peuter, doepa, dokter (van reisiesperd); bewerk; omkoop; kul; vang; ~**r,** bedrieër; omkoper; kuller.
nobb'y, piekfyn, windmakerig.
nobe'lium, nobelium.
Nobel' prize, Nobelprys.
nobil'iary, adellik, adel-.
nobil'ity, adel, adellikheid, adelstand, adeldom; edele; edelheid; ~ *of MIND,* sieleadel; *THE* ~, die adel.
no'ble, (n) edelman; *bring a* ~ *to sixpence,* 'n fortuin deurbring; (a) adellik; edelgebore; edel; grootmoedig; groots; aansienlik; *the* ~ *science,* die bokskuns; ~**-hearted,** edel; ~ **lady,** edelvrou; ~**man,** edelman; edele; ~ **metals,** edele metale; ~**-minded,** grootmoedig, fier, edeldenkend; ~**-mindedness,** grootmoedigheid, grootharligheid, edelmoedigheid; ~**ness,** edelheid, adellikheid, grootheid.
nobless'e, adel, edelheid; ~ **oblige,** 'n voorreg bring verantwoordelikheid mee.
no'blewoman, edelvrou, adellike dame.
no'bly, edel, edelmoedig; ~ *BORN,* van adellike geboorte (afkoms); *he bore his TROUBLES* ~, hy het sy moeilikhede edelmoedig gedra.
no'body, niemand; *it is* ~*'s BUSINESS,* dit gaan niemand aan nie; *he is* ~*'s FOOL,* hy is geen swaap nie; *a MERE* ~, 'n nul; ~ *in PARTICULAR,* niemand besonders nie.
no'cent, nadelig, skadelik.
nock, (n) keep, inkeping, kerf; nok (seil); (v) op die boog sit.
no-claim'(s) bonus, geeneisbonus.
noctam'bulant, slaapwandelend.
noctam'bulism, slaapwandeling, somnambulisme.
noctam'bulist, slaapwandelaar.
noctiflor'ous, nagbloeiend.
nocti'vagant, nocti'vagous, snags swerwend (dwalend).
Noctu'idae, nagmotte, nagvlieënde motte.
noc'tule, (groot soort) vlermuis.
noctur'nal, (n) nagdier; (a) nagtelik, nag-.
noc'turne, nokturne, naglied; nagstuk (skildery); naggesang (R.K.).
noc'uous, skadelik; giftig.
nod, (n) (kop)knik; wenk (wink); *GIVE a* ~, toeknik; *be GIVEN the* ~, goedkeuring kry; die jawoord kry; *send a child to the LAND of N*~, 'n kind droomland toe stuur; *a* ~ *is as good as a WINK,* 'n goeie verstaander (begryper) het 'n halwe woord nodig; *a* ~ *is as good as a WINK to a blind horse,* dit help nie om vir 'n blinde te knik nie; vir 'n dom mens het 'n wenk geen betekenis nie; (v) **(-ded),** knik; wenk; insluimer; visvang (fig.); ~ *APPROBATION,* goedkeurend knik; ~ *AT,* toeknik; ~ *one's HEAD,* met die kop knik; *HOMER sometimes* ~*s,* Homerus dut ook soms; *SIT and* ~, sit en visvang, sit en slaap.
nod'al, knoop-; knooppunt-.
nod'ding, knikkend; *have a* ~ *acquaintance,* van sien ken; op 'n afstand ken.
nod'dle, (n) kop; kok; 'n klapperdop; (v) knik; kopspeel.
nodd'y¹, (n) **(noddies),** domkop, uilskuiken, stommerik.
nodd'y², (a) vaak, slaperig.
node, kwas, knoes (in hout); nodus; knoop; knoop punt; stingelknoop; jigknobbel.

nod'ical, litterig.
nodose', kwasterig, knoesterig (hout); knopperig.
nodos'ity, knoesterigheid, kwasterigheid.
nod'ous, litterig; vol knope, geknoop.
nod'ular, klonterig; knollerig, knolvormig; knobbelrig, knopperig; knoestig, kwasterig, knoppies=; litterig; ~ **worm**, knoppieswurm.
nod'ule, knoppie, knobbeltjie, klontjie; knolletjie (van plant).
nod'us, (nodi), nodus, knooppunt, knoop; verwikkeling.
Noel', Kersfees.
noet'ic, (n) verstandsleer, noëtiek; **(a)** geestelik, verstands=, verstandelik, intellektueel, noëties.
nog¹, (n) sterk bier.
nog², (n) houtspyker; houtprop, tap; (v) **(-ged)**, vasspyker; tap.
nogg'in, beker, kroesie, kommetjie.
no'-go', mislukking; *it is a* ~, ons het ons vasgeloop.
no'-go gauge, kanniemaat, pasniemaat.
no'-good, (n) onnut, niksnut; **(a)** nikswerd.
Noh, No, Noh(drama).
no'how, glad nie.
noil, wolafval, uitkamsel.
noise, (n) geraas, lawaai, rumoer, gedruis, herrie, gedoe, gedoente, gerinkink; gerug, geruis; getier, orasie; geluid; (ge)ruis; steuring; *BIG* ~, meneer Grootlawaai; *a* ~ *to rouse the DEAD*, 'n lawaai v.d. ander wêreld; *HOLD your* ~, hou op met raas; *MAKE much* ~, baljaar; *MAKE a* ~, lawaai maak; *make a* ~ *in the WORLD*, opspraak verwek; aandag trek; (v) raas; rondstrooi; versprei, uitbasuin; ~ *it abroad*, iets rugbaar maak; ~**less**, stil, geluidloos, geruisloos; ~**lessly**, stil, soetjies, doekvoet; ~**lessness**, stilte, geluidloosheid; ~**maker**, lawaaimaker; ~**-proof**, klankdig, geluiddig.
nois'iness, luidrugtigheid, lawaai.
nois'ome, nadelig, ongesond; walglik; hinderlik; ~**ness**, walglikheid; nadeligheid; ongesondheid.
nois'y, luidrugtig, rumoerig; skreeuend (kleure).
nolens vol'ens, teen wil en dank.
nom'ad, (n) swerwer, nomade; **(a)** swerwend, rondtrekkend, nomadies.
nomad'ic, nomadies, rondtrekkend, swerwend; ~ **tribe**, herderstam, nomadiese stam.
nom'adism, trekkerslewe, nomadisme.
nom'adize, omswerf, rondswerf.
nom: ~ *de GUERRE*, skuilnaam; ~ *de PLUME*, skuilnaam, skryfnaam, pennaam, nom de plume.
nom'en, (nomina), naamwoord, nomen.
nom'enclator, naamgewer; naamafroeper.
nom'enclature, naamlys; benaming; vaktaal, terminologie; nomenklatuur.
nom'inal, in naam, nominaal; naamwoordelik (gram.); *a* ~ *rent*, 'n uiters lae huur; ~ **amount**, nominale bedrag; ~ **definition**, woordverklaring; ~**ism**, nominalisme; ~**ist**, nominalis; ~**ly**, in naam; ~ **partner**, vennoot in naam; ~ **price**, nominale prys; ~ **roll**, appèl nominaal; ~**-roll book**, naamboek; ~ **share**, aandeel op naam; ~ **value**, nominale waarde, pariwaarde.
nom'inate, benoem, nomineer; vasstel, aanwys, bepaal; kandidaat stel; ~ *as a CANDIDATE*, as kandidaat benoem; ~ *a DATE*, 'n datum vasstel; ~ *for a POSITION*, vir 'n amp voordra; ~ *to a POST*, in 'n pos benoem.
nomina'tion, benoeming, nominasie, kandidaatstelling; voordrag; aanwysing; *put in a* ~, 'n kandidaat stel; ~ **day**, benoemingsdag, nominasiedag; ~ **meeting**, benoemingsvergadering; ~ **roll**, groslys.
nominativ'al, nominatief.
nom'inative, (n) nominatief, eerste naamval; **(a)** wat benoem word, nominatief; ~ **case**, eerste naamval, nominatief.
nom'inator, noemer (wisk.); benoemer; voorsteller.
nominee', benoemde; genoemde; voorgestelde, genomineerde; ~ **company**, genomineerde maatskappy.
no'mogram, nomogram.
nomograph'ic, nomografies.
nomog'raphy, nomografie.
nomol'ogy, nomologie.

nomothe'tic, nomoteties, wetgewend.
non-, nie-.
non-accep'tance, nie-aanname, weiering.
non-accum'ulative, nie-oplopend.
non-ac'tive, non-aktief.
non-activ'ity, non-aktiwiteit.
non'age, minderjarigheid, onmondigheid.
nonagenar'ian, (n) negentigjarige; **(a)** negentigjarig.
non-aggress'ion, nie-aanvals=; ~ **pact**, nie-aanvalsverdrag.
non'agon, negehoek; ..**ag'onal**, negehoekig.
non-alcohol'ic, alkoholvry, nie-bedwelmend.
non-aligned', onverbonde.
non-alignment', onverbondenheid; afsydigheid.
non-appear'ance, nie-verskyning, ontstentenis, wegbly.
non-arriv'al, (die) nie-aankoms, wegbly.
non'ary, (n) negetal; **(a)** negetallig.
non-attend'ance, (die) wegbly, nie-verskyning, afwesigheid, nie-bywoning.
non-believ'er, ongelowige.
non-bellig'erent, nie-oorlogvoerend.
nonce: *for the* ~, vir hierdie keer; ~**-word**, geleentheidswoord.
non'chalance, traak-(my-)nieagtigheid, nonchalance, nonchalantheid, ongeërgdheid.
non'chalant, onverskillig, nonchalant, traak-(my-)nieagtig, staan of hy geld in die bank het, ongeërg.
non-com'batant, (n) nie-vegter, nie-stryder; **(a)** nie-strydend, nie-vegtend.
non-combust'ible, onbrandbaar.
non-commis'sioned: ~ *officer*, onderoffisier.
non-committ'al, nie-bindend, nieseggend, ontwykend, onbeslis; ~ *answer*, ontwykende antwoord.
non-com'parable, onvergelykbaar.
non-compli'ance, nalatigheid; weiering.
non-conduc'ting, nie-geleidend.
non-conduc'tor, slegte geleier, nie-geleier.
nonconform'ing, afwykend; afgeskeie.
nonconform'ism, nonkonformisme.
nonconform'ist, (n) afgeskeidene, nonkonformis; **(a)** afgeskei, nonkonformisties.
nonconform'ity, nie-ooreenstemming, afwyking, nonkonformiteit; afgeskeidenheid.
non-conta'gious, nie-aansteeklik.
non-corros'ive, nie-bytend, nie-vretend.
non-creas'ing, kreukelvry.
non-deliv'ery, nie-(af)lewering.
non'descript, (n) doodgewone persoon of ding; baster, tweeslagtige wese; **(a)** onklassifiseerbaar, onbeduidend, vreemdsoortig, onbestemd.
none, (pron) geneen, niemand; niks; ~ *at ALL*, glad niks; ~ *of your BUSINESS*, nie jou saak nie; ~ *of your IMPUDENCE*, hou jou astrantheid vir jouself; ~ *OTHER than*, niemand (niks) anders nie as; ~ *of THIS*, niks hiervan nie; *I'll have* ~ *of THAT*, nie van (met) iets gedien wees nie; **(a)** niks, geen; (adv) niks; ~ *the BETTER*, niks beter nie; ~ *of the CLEAREST*, nie van die helderste nie; ~ *too FOND of*, nie danig lief nie vir; ~ *too HIGH*, niks te veel (hoog) nie; ~ *the LESS*, nietemin; ~ *too SOON*, glad nie te gou nie; *be* ~ *the WISER*, nog net so in die duister wees; ~ *the WORSE*, glad nie slegter af nie.
non-effec'tive, sonder uitwerking, oneffektief.
non-elec'tion, nie-verkiesing.
non-elec'tric, nie-elektries.
nonen'tity, (..ties), nieteling, nonentiteit; onding; 'n Jan Salie; 'n groot nul; ambraal, man van toet.
nones, none (5e of 7e van maand).
none'-so-pretty, porseleinblom.
non-essen'tial, (n) nie-noodsaaklike; **(pl)** bykomstighede; **(a)** nie-noodsaaklik, misbaar.
none'such, weergaloos, sonder weerga.
non'-event, mislukking, nie-gebeurtenis.
non-exis'tence, nie-bestaan.
non-exis'tent, nie-bestaande.
non-explos'ive, (n) nie-ontplofbare stof, plofvrye stof; **(a)** onontplofbaar, nie-ontplofbaar, plofvry, plofvas.
non-fer'rous, nie-ysterhoudend.
non-fic'tion, vakliteratuur, nie-fiksie, feiteboeke.

non-fight'ing vehicle, transportvoertuig.
non-fig'urative, nie-figuratief.
non-fulfil'ment, nie-vervulling; nie-nakoming.
non-incen'diary, nie-brandstigtend.
non-infec'tious, nie-besmetlik.
non-inflam'mable, onontvlambaar.
non-inflamm'atory, nie-ontvlambaar.
non-interfer'ence, nie-tussenkoms, non-intervensie.
non-interven'tion, non-intervensie, afsydigheid.
non-intox'icant, (n) alkoholvrye drank; (a) nie-bedwelmend, alkoholvry.
non-i'ron, strykvry.
non'ius, nonius.
non-lum'inous, nie-liggewend.
non-mem'ber, nie-lid.
non-met'al, nie-metaal; ~ 'lic, nie-metallies, nie-metaal=.
non-mig'ratory bird, standvoël.
non-nego'tiable, onverhandelbaar.
non-obed'ience, ongehoorsaamheid.
non-observ'ance, nie-nakoming, veron(t)agsaming.
non-organ'ic, nie-organies, anorganies.
nonpareil', (n) pêreldrukletter; (a) onvergelyklik.
non-part'isan, onpartydig.
non-par'ty, partyloos.
non-pay'ing, nie-betalend (gas); nie-winsgewend.
non-pay'ment, wanbetaling, nie-betaling.
non-perform'ance, nie-uitvoering; nie-nalewing, nie-nakoming.
non'-person, nie-persoon; vergetene; onerkende (persoon).
non' playing, nie spelend; - captain, nie spelende kaptein.
nonplus', (n) verleentheid; raaisel; (v) (ood), verleë maak, verbluf, oorbluf; in die war bring; ~ sed, verleë, beteuterd, verslae, verboureerd; be ~ sed, verleë (beteuterd) wees.
non-pow'er tools, handgereedskap.
non-produc'tion, nie-voortbrenging; nie-produksie.
non-product'ive, onproduktief; ~ capital, dooie kapitaal; ~ ness, onproduktiwiteit.
non-prof'it, sonder voordele, sonder winsoogmerke; a ~ concern, 'n saak sonder winsbejag.
non-prolifera'tion, nie-vermeerdering (bv. kernwapens); ~ treaty, (kern)sperverdrag.
non-recov'erable, onverhaalbaar, oninbaar; ~ debt, onverhaalbare (dooie) skuld.
non-representa'tional, nie-beeldend, abstrak.
non-res'idence, afwesigheid, nie-inwoning.
non-res'ident, (n) uitwonende; buitelander; (a) uitwonend, ekstern; buitelands; ~'s interest, nie-inwonersbelang.
non-resis'tance, onderworpenheid, gehoorsaamheid, lydelikheid.
non-return', nie-terugkeer.
non-return'able, houbaar.
non'sense, onsin, kaf, malligheid, nonsies, dwaasheid, wilde wolhaarpraatjies, draadwerk, bogpraatjies, gekkepraatjies, gekheid, apekool; it is ALL ~, dis alles pure kaf; dit is alles onsin; ARRANT (absolute) ~, klinkklare onsin; he is FULL of ~, hy is vol nukke (fiemies); that is SHEER ~, dis pure bog; STAND no ~, nie met jou laat speel nie; geen gekskeerdery toelaat nie; ~ verse, onsinrympie, onsinvers.
nonsen'sical, onsinnig, gek, mal, sot, verspot.
nonsensical'ity, onsinnigheid, dwaasheid, gekheid.
non-sex'ual, geslagloos.
non-shrink'able, krimpvry.
non-skid', antigly=, slipvry, glyvas; ~ surface, antiglyloopvlak, glyvry opporvlak; tyre, glyvaste band.
non-smo'ker, nie-roker.
non-smo'king, nie-rokend.
non-sol'vency, bankrotskap.
non-spar'ing, veeleisend, meedoënloos.
non-splint'ering, splintervry.
non'-stop, deurlopend, deurgaande, nie-stilhoudend; ononderbroke; ~ dance, langasemdans; ~ flight, deurvlug, ononderbroke vlug; ~ train, deurgaande trein, sneltrein.
non-submiss'ive, nie-onderworpe.

non-subscrib'er, nie-intekenaar.
non-success', mislukking.
non'such = nonesuch.
non'suit, (n) ontsegging van 'n eis; (v) 'n eis ontsê.
non-tech'nical, nie-tegnies.
non-un'ionist, (n) ongeorganiseerde arbeider; (a) ongeorganiseer.
non-us'er, nie-gebruiker.
non-vi'olence, geweldloosheid.
non-vi'olent, geweldloos.
non-vol'atile, nie-vlugtig.
noo'dle¹, dwaas, domkop, uilskuiken.
noo'dle², snysel; noedel.
nook, hoek; uithoek; gesellige hoekie; in every ~ and cranny, in alle hoekies en gaatjies; ~ y, vol hoeke.
noon, middag; twaalfuur; middaghoogte; ~ day, middag; ~ tide, middag; hoogtepunt.
noose, (n) lissie, strik; strop; have one's NECK in the ~, 'n strop om die nek hê; PUT (run) one's head in a ~, jou kop in 'n strop steek; (v) knoop; vasstrik; vang.
nop'al, nopalplant, (Amerikaanse) kaktus.
nope, (sl.), nee.
nor, ook nie, nóg, en ewemin; I haven't the MONEY ~ yet the time, ek het nóg die geld nóg die tyd; NEITHER John ~ I, nóg Jan, nòg ek.
Nor'dic, (n) Nordiër, (a) Nordies.
Norf'olk: ~ jacket, los baadjie, norfolkbaadjie; ~ pine, Norfolkden(neboom).
nor'ite, noriet.
norit'ic, norities.
nor'land, noorderland, noorde.
norm, norm, standaard; ~ s of conduct, gedragsnorme.
norm'al, (n) gemiddelde; loodregte; normaal; normale, gewone; (a) normaal; ~ charge, gewone lading (tarief), gebruikslading; ~ college, opleidingskollege, normaalskool; ~ fault, afskuiwing (geol.); ~ 'ity, normaliteit; ~ iza'tion, normalisasie; gelykmaking; ~ ize, normaliseer; gelyk maak; ~ ly, reëlmatig, gewoonlik; gewoonweg, normaalweg; ~ pressure, normaaldruk.
Norm'an, (n) Normandiër; (a) Normandies; ~ dy, Normandië.
norm'ative, normatief.
normati'vity, normatiwiteit.
Norn, Norne.
Norse, (n) Noors (taal); (a) Noors; ~ land, Noorweë; ~ man, Noorman; Noor.
north, (n) (die) noorde; noordewind; THE N ~, die Noorde; to THE ~, noord van; (a) noord(e), noordelik; (adv) noordwaarts; noordelik; DUE ~, reg noord, ~ OF, noord van; ten noorde van; ~ bound, noordwaarts; ~ coast, noordkus; ~-east, noordoos; ~-easterly, noordoostelik; ~-eastern, noordoostelik; N ~-east Passage, Noordoostelike Deurvaart; ~ end, noordeinde; ~ erly, noordelik.
north'ern, (n) noorderling; (a) noordelik, noord=; ~ er, noorderling; N ~ Hemisphere, die Noordelike Halfrond; ~ lights, noorderlig; ~ most, noordelikste.
north: ~ ing, die vaar in noordelike rigting; noord-deklinasie; N ~ land, Noorderland; ~ latitude, noorderbreedte; ~ light, noorderlig; ~ line, noordlyn; N ~ man, Noorman; ~ most, noordelikste; ~-east', noordnoordoos; ~-~-west, noordnoordwes; N ~ Pole, Noordpool; N ~ Star, Poolster; ~ ward(s), noordwaarts; ~-west, (n) noordweste; (a) noordwestelik; (a) noordwes; N ~ west Passage, Noordwestelike Deurvaart; ~-wester, noordwestewind; ~-westerly, noordweste=lik; ~-western, noordwestelik; the ~ western Cape, die Noordweste, Noordwes-Kaapland; ~ wind, noordewind.
Nor'way, Noorweë.
Norwe'gian, (n) Noor, Noorweër; Noors (taal); (a) Noors, Noorweegs.
nor'wester, noordwestewind; sterk dop; matrooshoed.
nose, (n) neus; reuk, ruik; tuit (van ketel); nek; punt (torpedo); boeg (skip); walk under one's ~ in the AIR, met die neus in die lug loop; BITE someone's

~ off, iem. toesnou; have one's ~ in one's BOOKS, met jou neus in die boeke sit; COUNT ~s, koppe tel; CUT off one's ~ to spite one's face, wie sy neus skend, skend sy aangesig; FOLLOW one's ~, agter jou neus aanloop; keep a ~ in FRONT, net-net voor bly; not to see what's in FRONT of your very ~, 'n pampoenbril ophê; he cannot see FURTHER than his ~, hy kan nie verder sien as sy neus lank is nie; have a GOOD ~, 'n fyn neus hê; hold someone's ~ to the GRINDSTONE, iem. hard laat werk; HOLD one's ~, die neus toeknyp; put someone's ~ out of JOINT, iem. uitoorlê; KEEP one's ~ out of other people's business, jou neus uit ander mense se sake hou; LEAD by the ~, aan die neus lei; blindelings laat volg; make a LONG ~, iem. uitkoggel; vir iem. skewebek trek; LOOK down one's ~ at someone, (minagtend) op iem. neersien; not LOOK beyond one's ~, nie verder kyk as jou neus lank is nie; LOOK down one's ~, skeef aankyk; met misnoeë betrag; make someone PAY through the ~, iem. die vel oor die ore trek; PLAIN as the ~ on your face, volkome duidelik; POKE one's ~ into, sy neus insteek; POKE one's ~ into another's business, jou neus in ander mense se sake steek; PUT someone's ~ out of joint, iem. uitoorlê; iem. se planne in die war stuur; RUB ~s, gemeensaam omgaan met; TAKE something from under someone's very ~, iets voor iem. se neus wegneem; not to SEE further than one's ~, nie verder kyk as wat jou neus lank is nie; TALK through one's ~, deur die neus praat; TURN up one's ~, jou neus optrek; UNDER his ~, vlak voor hom; lie UNDER one's very ~, onder jou neus lê; fail to see what is UNDER one's ~, siende blind wees; WIN by a ~, met 'n neuslengte wen; net-net die paal haal; (v) ruik; snuffel; ~ ABOUT, rondsnuffel; ~ AFTER, soek na; ~ AROUND, rondsnuffel; ~ AT, besnuffel; ~ OUT, uitsnuffel; ~ one's WAY into, stadig indring; ~-ape, neusaap; ~bag, voersak, hawersak, beksak; ~band, neusriem, bekstuk; ~-bit, lepelboor; ~-bleeding, neusbloeding; ~-cap, monddeksel; neuskap; kop (torpedo); ~dive, (n) (neus)duik, duikvlug; (v) 'n neusduik maak; ~-drop, neusdruppel; nosey: a ~ parker, 'n nuuskierige agie; 'n bemoeial; ~-flute, neusfluit; ~-gas, neusgas; ~-gay, ruiker; ~-glasses, knypbril; ~-hole, neusgat; ~less, sonder neus; ~less monkey, neusaap; ~-nippers, knypbril; ~-piece, neusstuk; tuit; neusriem; ~ r, teenwind, teëwind; ~ rag, sakdoek; ~ ring, neusring; ~ speculum, neusspieël; ~ warmer, neuswarmmaker, kortsteelpyp, baardbrander; ~ y, (n) grootneus; agie; (a) kyk nosy.
nosog'raphy, nosografie, siektebeskrywing.
nosol'ogy, siekteleer, nosologie.
noson'omy, nosonomie.
nos'otaxy, nosotaksie.
nostal'gia, heimwee, nostalgie.
nostal'gic, met heimwee, verlangend, nostalgies.
nos'tril, neusgat.
nos'trum, (-s), kwak(salwers)middel; geheime middel, geheimmiddel.
nos'y, met 'n groot neus, grootneus=; stinkend; geurig; nuuskierig; a n ~ parker, 'n nuuskierige agie; 'n bemoeial.
not, nie; ~ at ALL, glad nie, (h)aikôna; ~ ANY, geen; ~ half BAD, nogal goed; ~ a BIT (of it), nie in die minste nie; ~ by a very long CHALK, glad nie; did you enjoy yourself? ~ HALF, het jy dit geniet? Ja, geweldig!; I hope ~, ek hoop nie dat . . .; ~ in the LEAST, nie in die minste nie; glad nie; ~ LESS than, minstens; op sy (die) minste; ~ a LITTLE, taamlik baie; ~ for a MOMENT, geen oomblik nie; ~ a PATCH ON, baie slegter as; I THINK ~, ek glo nie; ~ for YEARS, nie in jare nie; eers oor jare; ~ YET, nog nie.
nota ben'e, nota bene, let wel.
notabil'ia, merkwaardighede, notabilia.
notabil'ity, merkwaardigheid; beroemdheid, aansienlikheid; notabiliteit.
not'able, (n) hooggeplaaste (persoon), notabele, (a) merkwaardig; vernaam, aansienlik; belangrik; aanmerklik; opmerklik; Jan Celliers is ~ AS one of our first poets, Jan Celliers is belangrik as een van ons eerste digters; the Paarl is ~ FOR its wine, die Paarl is beroemd vir sy wyne.
not'ably, merkbaar; belangrik; insonderheid.
notar'ial, notarieel; ~ deed, notariële akte.
notar'iate, notarisskap, notariaat.
not'ary, (. . ries), notaris; ~ public, notaris; ~'s clerk, notarisklerk; ~ship, notariaat, notarisskap; ~'s profession, notarisamp.
notate', aanteken, noteer.
nota'tion, aantekening, notasie; notering, noteskrif; skryfwyse; scale of ~, talstelsel, tellestelsel.
notch, (n) (-es), merkkepie; kerf (ook in salaris); groef, sluitkeep; snytjie; skaar (in mes); vergaarteken (naaldw.); ~ of BACKSIGHT, visierklep; be taken DOWN a ~ or two, 'n toon laer leer sing; the TOP ~, die boonste kerf; (v) kerf, (in)keep; opskryf, aanteken; uitkerf, uitkeep; ~ points, punte aanteken; ~ing, kerfstelsel (salaris); ~y, vol kepe.
note, (n) aantekening, glos, nota; noot (musiek); klawer, toets (klavier); merk, teken; merkteken; toon; banknoot; betekenis, aansien; notisie; an AUTHOR of ~, 'n skrywer van naam; CIRCULAR ~, omsendbrief; COMPARE ~s, bevindinge vergelyk; CHANGE one's ~, 'n noot laer sing; DIPLOMATIC ~, diplomatieke nota; strike a DISCORDANT ~, 'n wanklank laat hoor; ~ of EXCLAMATION, uitroepteken; ~ of HAND, promesse, bewys; begin on too HIGH a ~, iets te hoog insit; ~ of INTERROGATION, vraagteken; hold (sustain) a ~ LONGER than necessary, 'n noot onnodig rek; 'n noot rek soos 'n voorslagriempie; MAKE ~s, aantekeninge maak; a MAN of ~, 'n man van aansien; make a MENTAL ~ of it, dit in jou oor knoop; OF ~, van belang; as PER ~, volgens nota; strike the RIGHT ~, die regte toon tref; ~ of SALE, verkoopnota; TAKE ~ of, let op, kennis neem van, nota neem van; WORTHY of ~, van belang om te weet; strike the WRONG ~, 'n wanklank tref; (v) aanteken; opskrywe; opmerk (gunstig); aanmerk (ongunstig); kennis neem van, oplet; noteer; annoteer, van aantekeninge voorsien; ~ an APPEAL, appèl aanteken; ~ a BILL, 'n wissel noteer; ~ DOWN, aanteken; ~book, sakboekie; aantekeningboek; ~d, aangeteken; beroemd, vermaard, welbekend; ~ issue, note-uitgifte; ~ paper, briefpapier, skryfpapier; ~worthy, merkwaardig, opmerkenswaardig.
no'thing, niks; prul; nul; ~ at ALL, glad niks nie; ~ BUT, niks as; COME to ~, misluk; op niks uitloop nie; he is ~ if not CRITICAL, hy is oordrewe krities; ~ DAUNTED, glad nie verskrik nie; glad nie van stryk nie; have ~ to DO with something, jou nie met iets ophou nie; niks met iets te doen hê nie; have ~ further to DO with someone, niks verder met iem. te doen wil hê nie; ~ DOING, daar is niks te doen nie; jy is laat; FOR ~, verniet; tevergeefs; ~ FOR ~, niks verniet nie; niks vir niks (en baie min vir 'n tiekie); thank you FOR ~, dank jou die duiwel; there is ~ FOR it but to . . ., daar is geen ander uitweg nie as; there is ~ IN it, daar is geen woord van waarheid in nie; dis van geen belang nie; dit is maklik; there is ~ IN him, daar sit niks in hom nie; ~ near so LARGE, nie half so groot nie; ~ LESS than, niks minder nie as; ~ LIKE so good, lank nie so goed nie; ~ LIKE so severe, nie half so streng nie; there is ~ quite LIKE it, niks kom daarby nie; the LITTLE ~s of life, die kleinighede v.d. lewe; MAKE ~ of, lig reken; geen swarigheid sien nie; I could MAKE ~ of it, ek kon daar geen tou aan vasknoop nie; ek kon daar niks uit wys word nie; I MAKE ~ of it, niks daarvan verstaan nie; niks daaruit wys word nie; iets as 'n kleinigheid beskou; she is ~ to ME, ek het niks met haar te doen nie; MEAN ~ to, niks beteken nie; van geen belang of waarde wees nie; a MERE ~, iets onbeduidends; 'n nul; NEXT to ~, so goed as niks; buy (sell) something for NEXT to ~, iets vir 'n appel en 'n ei koop (verkoop); he that ~ QUESTIONETH nothing learneth, wie nie vrae vra nie, word niks wyser nie; wie nie in twyfel trek nie, léer niks nie; ~ SEEK, ~ find, wie nie soek nie, kry nie; ~ to SPEAK of, nie

die moeite werd om oor te praat nie; *talk (whisper) SOFT (sweet)* ~*s,* komplimentjies maak; soet woordjies sê; *THANKS for* ~, dankie sê vir niks; dank jou die duiwel; *there is* ~ *TO it,* daar is niks aan nie; ~ *like TRYING,* aanhouer wen; probeer is die beste geweer; ~ *VENTURE* ~ *gain,* wie nie waag nie, sal nie wen nie.

no'thingness, nietigheid; waardeloosheid; niks; *fade into* ~, in die niet verdwyn.

nothingar'ian, godloënaar.

not'ice, (n) kennis; kennisgewing, bekendmaking, verwittiging; opsegging (van huur); aankondiging, aansegging; berig; aandag, opmerksaamheid, oplettendheid; waarskuwing; ~ *of ASSESSMENT,* aanslagbiljet; *AT* ~, met opsegging; *BENEATH one's* ~, sy aandag nie werd nie; *BRING to someone's* ~, onder iem. se aandag bring; *COME to one's* ~, onder die oë kom; ~ *CONVENING a meeting,* vergaderingskennisgewing; ~ *of DISCHARGE,* ontslagbrief; *ESCAPE* ~, onopgemerk bly; *until FURTHER* ~, tot nader kennisgewing; *for GENERAL* ~, tot algemene kennis; *GIVE* ~, kennis gee; iem. afdank; huur opsê; *JUDICIAL* ~, geregtelike kennisgewing; *at a MOMENT'S* ~, op staande voet; oombliklik; *he given a MONTH'S* ~, 'n maand kennis kry; *give* ~ *of (a) MOTION,* kennis gee van 'n voorstel; *SERVE* ~ *on someone,* iem. in kennis stel; *at SHORT* ~, op kort termyn; *SIT up and take* ~, belangstelling toon; *TAKE* ~ *of,* ag slaan op; ~ *of WITHDRAWAL,* kennisgewing van opsegging; (v) opmerk, gewaar(word), (be)speur, bemerk; oplet; opteken, aanteel, bespreek, vermeld, aankondig; ag slaan op, waarneem; aansê; notisie neem van; huur (diens) opsê; ~ **able,** merkbaar; opvallend, merkwaardig; ~ **-board,** aanplakbord.

not'ifiable, aanmeldbaar, aangeebaar, rapporteerbaar; ~ *disease,* aanmeldbare siekte.

notifica'tion, bekendmaking, kennisgewing; aanskrywing; aankondiging; aansegging; aanmelding; aangifte (siekte).

not'ify, (..fied), kennis gee, meedeel, berig, verwittig, bekend maak, aankondig; aanskryf; aanmeld, aangee (siekte).

no'tion, denkbeeld, idee; spesmaas; nosie, begrip; opvatting, benul, besef; gedagte, voorstelling; *that is the COMMON* ~, dis die algemene opvatting; *HAVE no* ~ *of,* glad nie 'n idee hê nie van; nie die vaagste benul hê nie; ~ **al,** denkbeeldig, begrips=; ~ *al verb,* begripswerkwoord.

no'tochord, vrugrugmurg.

notori'ety, (..ties), algemene bekendheid, rugbaarheid, befaamdheid; berugtheid (ongunstig); bekende persoon.

notor'ious, oorbekend, rugbaar, befaamd; berug (persoon); welbekend (feit); ~ *FOR,* berug wees (vir, om); *as* ~ *as a PARIAH (pye) dog,* bekend soos die bont hond; *he is a* ~ *THIEF,* hy is 'n berugte dief; ~ **ly,** soos elkeen weet; ~ **ness,** algemene bekendheid; berugtheid.

notwithstand'ing, nieteenstaande, nietemin, ondanks, trots, ten spyte van, tog, in weerwil van, egter, darem; ~ *this,* ten spyte hiervan, desnieteenstaande.

noug'at, noga, nougat.

nought, niks; nul; *it all CAME to* ~, dit het op niks uitgeloop; die hele saak was 'n misoes; *COME to* ~, verongeluk; op niks uitloop nie; ~ *s and CROSSES,* meul(spel); nulletjies-en-kruisies; *SET at* ~, in die wind slaan.

nou'menon, noumenon.

noun, (selfstandige) naamwoord, nomen, substantief.

nou'rish, voed; koester; aanmoedig, aanwakker, aankweek; ~ *the HOPE that,* die hoop koester dat; ~ *a TRADITION,* 'n tradisie huldig; ~ **able,** voedbaar; ~ **er,** voeder, kweker; ~ **ing,** (n) spysiging; koestering; (a) voedsaam, voedend; ~ **ment,** voedsel, voeding.

nous, nous, verstand; helderheid, snuggerheid, intellek, vernuf.

nou'veau riché, (F.), nouveau riche, nieuryke(s), nuutryke(s), parvenu('s).

nou'velle vague, (F.) nouvelle vague, nuwe golf, nuwe tendens (bv. film, roman).

nov'a, nova, nuwe ster.

novate', vernuwe (skuld).

nova'tion, skuldvernuwing.

nov'el, (n) roman; ~ *with a purpose,* strekkingsroman, tendensroman; (a) nuut; ongekend; modern; eienaardig, vreemd; *a* ~ *FEELING,* 'n vreemde gevoel; *it is a* ~ *IDEA,* dit is 'n eienaardige (besondere, nuwe) idee; ~ **ette'**, novelle; ~ **ist,** romanskrywer, romansier; ~ **is'tic,** romanagtig, roman=; ~ **ize,** tot 'n roman verwerk; ~ **la,** novelle; kort roman; ~ **reader,** romanleser; ~ **ty,** (..ties), nuwigheid; iets nuuts; nuwe artikel, feesartikel, fantasieartikel; nuutheid; (pl) fantasieware; ~ **writer,** romanskrywer.

Novem'ber, November.

noven'a, noveen (R.K.).

novenn'ial, negejaarliks.

noverc'al, stiefmoederlik.

nov'ice, nuweling; noviet, novise (R.K.); beginner, groentjie, penkop.

novi'ciate, novi'tiate, novisiaat; proeftyd, leertyd, groentyd; nuweling.

no'vocaine, novocaine, narkosemiddel (handelsnaam).

now, (n) hede, teenswoordige; (adv) nou; tans, teenswoordig; ~ *and AGAIN,* af en toe; *BEFORE* ~, vroeër; *BUT* ~, maar nou; nog onlangs; 'n rukkie gelede; *BY* ~, teen hierdie tyd; nou; *DID he* ~*?,* het hy regtig; *EVERY* ~ *and then,* telkens; *FROM* ~ *on,* in die toekoms, hiervandaan; *HERE and* ~, hier en nou; tans; *JUST* ~, netnou; ~ *or NEVER,* nou of nooit; *NOT* ~, nie nou nie; ~ *REALLY!,* ag nee!; ~ *THAT,* noudat; ~ *THEN,* toe nou; komaan!; ~ *and THEN,* nou en dan; af en toe; *TILL* ~, tot nou toe; *UP to* ~, tot dusver; (conj) nou(dat).

now'adays, teenswoordig, deesdae, heden ten dage, hedendaags.

no'way(s), no'wise, glad (en geheel) nie, op geen wyse nie.

no'where, nêrens, niewers; *APPEAR from* ~, skielik (onverwags) opdaag; uit die niet verskyn; *BE* ~, ver agterbly; nie meetel nie; nie in tel wees nie; heeltemal uitval; nêrens wees; *GET* ~, niks bereik nie; *HAVE* ~ *to go,* nie weet waarheen nie; geen heenkome hê nie; ~ *NEAR,* glad nie naby nie; heeltemal mis.

no'wither, nêrens heen.

no'wise, geensins, glad nie, hoegenaamd nie.

nowt, (dial.), niks.

no'xious, skadelik; verderflik; ~ **gas,** gifgas; ~ **ness,** skadelikheid; verderflikheid; ~ **weeds,** skadelike onkruid.

noyade', (F.) noyade, teregstelling deur verdrinking.

noy'au, (F.) brandewynlikeur, noyau.

noz'zle, neus, tuit; straalpyp, sproeipyp (slang); spuitkop, stuifkop (sproeier); mondstuk.

nth: *that was my* ~ *CHANCE,* dit was my hoeveelste kans; *to the* ~ *DEGREE,* tot die nde mag.

nuance', (n) nuanse, skakering; (v) nuanseer.

nub, nub'ble, knoppie; klontjie; kluitjie; kern (van saak).

nub'bin, dwergmieliekop.

Nub'ia, Nubië; ~ **n,** (n) Nubiër; (a) Nubies.

nubif'erous, wolkebrengend.

nub'ile, hubaar, troubaar.

nubil'ity, hubaarheid, troubaarheid.

nu'cha, nekkuil, nekholte; ~ **l,** nek=, nekkuil=.

nucif'erous, neut=, neutdraend.

nu'ciform, neutvormig.

nuc'lear, kern=; nukleêr; kernfisies; ~ **age,** kerneeu, kerntydperk; ~ **body,** kernliggaampie; ~ **charge,** kernlading; ~ **chemistry,** kernchemie; ~ **division,** kerndeling; ~ **energy,** kernenergie; ~ **fall-out,** kernas; ~ **family,** gesin, kerngesin; ~ **fission,** kernsplyting; ~ **fusion,** kernfusie; ~ **membrane,** kernmembraan, kernvlies; ~ **physicist,** kernfisikus; ~ **physics,** kernfisika; ~ **power,** kernkrag; ~ **-powered,** met kernkrag, met kernkrag aangedryf, kernaangedrewe; ~ **-powered submarine,** kern(krag)=

nucleate

duikboot; ~ **reaction,** kernreaksie; ~ **reactor,** kernreaktor; ~ **war,** kernoorlog; ~ **warfare,** kernoorlogvoering; ~ **weapon,** kernwapen.
nuc'leate, om 'n kern saamtrek; ~**d,** met 'n kern.
nucleo'lus, (..li), kiemvlek; kernliggaampie.
nucleon'ics, kernwetenskap.
nu'cleoside, nukleosied, -ide.
nu'cleotide, nukleotied, -ide.
nuc'leus, (..clei), kern, pit, nukleus; middelpunt, kiem; kop (komeet); ~ **garrison,** kernbesetting; ~ **house,** kernhuis.
nu'clide, nuklied, -ide.
nuda'tion, ontbloting.
nudaure'lia, pouoogmot; krismiswurm, taaiboswurm.
nude, (n) (die) naakte; naakfiguur; naakskildery; naakbeeld; *IN the* ~, naak; *STUDIES from the* ~, studies v.d. naakmodel; (a) kaal, naak, bloot; vleiskleurig; ~ *CONTRACT,* naakte ooreenkoms; ~ *PROHIBITION,* blote verbod; ~ *STOCKING,* vleiskleurige kous; ~**ness,** naaktheid.
nudge, (n, v) stamp, stoot, pomp.
nud'ism, nudisme, naaklopery.
nud'ist, naakloper, kaalloper, nudis; ~ **colony,** naakloperkolonie, nudistekolonie; ~ **cult,** kaalbaskultus.
nud'ity, (..ties), naaktheid; naakte figuur; naakstudie.
nu'gae, kleinighede.
nug'atory, beuselagtig, niksbeduidend, nietig; waardeloos.
nug'gar, platboomskuit.
nugg'et, klomp (ruwe goud); klont, stuk.
nuis'ance, oorlas; stoornis, plaag, ergernis; laspos; *BE a* ~, las gee; lastig (vervelig) wees; *COMMIT no* ~, verontreiniging verbode; *a COMMON* ~, 'n algemene oorlas; *DOMESTIC* ~, huiskruis; *MAKE a* ~ *of oneself,* tot oorlas wees; *a PRIVATE* ~, 'n kruis; *a REGULAR* ~, 'n ware laspos; ~ **value,** oorlasbetekenis, plafaktor, lolfaktor, steurfaktor.
nuke, (sl), kernbom, kerntoestel.
null, nikswerd, nietig; kragteloos; ongeldig; onbekend; ~ *and void,* kragteloos, ongeldig, van nul en gener waarde; ~**ifica'tion,** ongeldigverklaring, nietigverklaring; verydeling, vernietiging; ~**ifier,** vernietiger; ~**ify,** (..**fied**), vernietig, ongeldig verklaar; verydel; ~**ify all attempts,** alle pogings verydel; ~**ity,** ongeldigheid, nietigheid, waardeloosheid; onbenulligheid; holheid; ~ **position,** nulstand.
numb, (v) laat verkluim; verstyf, verdoof; doodlê (jou arm); ~ *ed feeling,* 'n gevoel van verdowing; (a) gevoelloos, verkluim, dom (weens koue), verstyf; *fingers* ~ *with COLD,* verkluimde vingers; *a mind* ~ *to GRIEF,* 'n gemoed gevoelloos vir smart.
num'ber, (n) nommer; getal; aantal, party, klomp; aflewering (blad); man (militêr); *BACK* ~, ou aflewering; remskoen (fig.); *ENEMY* ~ *one,* hoofvyand; *by FORCE of* ~*s,* deur oormag; *in GREAT* ~*s,* in groot getalle; *IN* ~*s,* in aantal; ~ *of INHABITANTS,* aantal inwoners; sieletal (kerk); *in LARGE* ~*s,* in groot getalle; *not OF our* ~, nie uit ons kring (geledere) nie; ~ *ONE,* ek (self); eerste luitenant ter see; *ONE of our* ~, een van ons; *take care of* ~ *ONE,* net vir jouself sorg; *SERIES of* ~*s,* nommerreeks; *THEORY of* ~*s,* getalleleer; *TIMES without* ~, tallose male (kere); *TO the* ~ *of,* soveel as; *an UNLUCKY* ~, 'n ongeluksgetal; *his* ~ *is UP,* dis klaar(praat) met hom; dit is doppie in die emmer met hom; *WITHOUT* ~, sonder tal; *get the WRONG* ~, verkeerd aangesluit word (telefoon); *WRONG* ~, verkeerde getal; verkeerde nommer; (v) nommer; tel, reken; bedra; laat nommer (by dril); ~ *AMONG,* tel onder; ~ *OFF,* nommer; ~-**chart,** telskaal; ~ **ed,** getel; geletter; genommer; ~**ing,** telling, tel=; ~**ing machine,** telmasjien; ~**ing-stamp,** nommerstempel; ~ **less,** tallos, baie, ontelbaar; ~-**plate,** nommerplaat; ~-**reference,** nommerverwysing.
Num'bers, Numeri.
num'bles, ingewande (van 'n bok), harslag.

numb'ness, styfheid, verstywing, verdowing; gevoelloosheid.
numb'skull = **numskull.**
numerabil'ity, telbaarheid.
num'erable, telbaar.
num'eral, (n) telwoord; syfer; *Roman* ~*s,* Romeinse syfers; (a) getal=, nommer=; ~ **adjective,** telwoord; ~ **system,** telstelsel.
num'erate, opsom, tel.
numera'tion, telling, opsomming, berekening; getalstelsel; ~ **table,** rekentafel.
num'erative, tellend, tel; ~ **system,** telstelsel.
num'erator, teller.
numer'ic = **numerical.**
numer'ical, numeriek, getal=; ~ *COEFFICIENT,* getallekoëffisiënt; ~ *FACTOR,* getallefaktor; ~ *ORDER,* numerieke orde; ~ *STRENGTH,* getalsterkte; ~*ly STRONGER,* getalsterker; ~ *SUPERIORITY,* groter getalsterkte, oormag; ~ *VALUE,* getalwaarde.
numer'ic: ~ **frame,** rekenmasjien.
numerol'ogy, getalleleer, numerologie.
num'erous, talryk; baie, oorvloedig, groot; tal van; *a* ~ *FAMILY,* 'n groot huisgesin; *receive* ~ *INVITATIONS,* baie uitnodigings ontvang; ~**ness,** menigvuldigheid, talrykheid.
Numid'ia, Numidië; ~**n,** (n) Numidiër; (a) Numidies.
num'inous, bonatuurlik, misterieus; bewus v.d. godelike; met 'n beroep op die hoëre in skoonheidsgevoel, numineus.
numismat'ic, numismaties, munt=, penning=; ~ **cabinet,** muntkabinet; ~**s,** penningkunde, numismatiek, muntkunde.
numis'matist, muntkenner, muntkundige, numismatikus.
numismatog'raphy, numismatografie.
numismatol'ogy, numismatologie, penningkunde.
numm'ary, numm'ulary, munt=, geld=, met geld handelend.
num'mulite, nummuliet, skyfskulp.
num'nah, saalkleedjie.
num'-num, noem-noem (*Carissa arduina*).
num'skull, uilskuiken, dwaas, bobbejaan, swaap, domkop.
nun, non; nonnetjie (duif).
nu'natak, nunatak, rotspiek.
nun'-buoy, tolboei, puntboei.
nun'ciature, nunsiatuur, pouslike gesantskap.
nun'cio, (-s), nuntius, pouslike gesant.
nunc'upate, 'n mondelinge testament maak, mondeling verklaar.
nuncupa'tion, mondelinge testament.
nunc'upative, nuncu'patory, mondeling.
nun: ~ **hood,** nonnestaat, nonskap; ~**like,** nonagtig; ~**nery,** (..ries), nonneklooster, susterhuis, vroueklooster; ~**nish,** nonagtig; ~**'s cloth,** fyn vlagdoek; ~**'s veil,** nonnesluier; ~**'s veiling,** kamerdoek.
nuph'ar, geel waterlelie.
nup'tial, huweliks=, bruilofs=; *by ante* ~ *contract,* op huweliksvoorwaardes; ~ **benediction,** huweliksinseëning; ~ **ceremony,** trouplegtigheid; ~ **day,** troudag; ~ **flight,** paringsvlug; ~ **tie,** huweliksband; ~**s,** builof, troufees, huweliksfees; trouplegtigheid.
Nur'emburg, Neurenberg.
nurse, (n) verpleegster; plegie, suster (aanspreekvorm); oppasser, kindermeisie; même, kinderjuffrou; baker; werkby; werkmier; skutboom; kweker; *DRY* ~, kindermeisie; *PUT (out) to* ~, by 'n oppasser uitbestee; *WET* ~, soogvrou; (v) verpleeg, oppas; koester, grootmaak; soog; kweek (plante); suinig beheer; versorg; ~ *ALONG,* troetel; ~ *one's CONSTITUENCY,* jou kiesers tot vriende hou; ~ *a GRIEVANCE,* 'n grief koester; ~ *one in (through) an ILLNESS,* iem. gedurende 'n siekte verpleeg; ~ *a SECRET,* 'n geheim sorgvuldig bewaar; ~ *one's STRENGTH,* jou kragte bewaar; ~-**cell,** voedingsel; ~-**child,** pleegkind; ~-**father,** pleegvader; ~-**girl,** kindermeisie; kinderoppasster.
nurs(e)'ling, voedsterling, troetelkind; saailing (plant).

nurse 1081 **obedient**

nurse: ~-**maid,** kindermeisie; kinderoppaster; ~**pond,** dammetjie vir visteelt.
nurs'ery, (..ries), kinderkamer; kwekery (plante); kweekdam (visse); kweekplek; ~ **chair,** kinderstoel; ~ **class,** kleuterklas; ~ **education,** kleuteronderwys; ~-**gardener,** plantkweker; ~ **governess,** kinderjuffrou; ~-**maid,** kindermeisie; ~ **man,** (blom)kweker, (boom)kweker; ~-**plant,** stiggie, steggie; ~ **rhyme,** kinderversie, kinderrympie, paaidiggie; ~ **school,** kleuterskool; ~-**school teacher,** kleuteronderwyseres; ~ **tale,** sprokie, kinderverhaaltjie.
nurse: ~'s **home,** verpleegsterstehuis; ~ **tree,** kweekboom.
nurs'ing, (n) (die) oppas, verpleging; (a) verplegend; ~ **bottle,** kinderbottel, pypkan, bababottel; ~ **council,** verpleegstersraad; ~ **father,** pleegvader; ~ **home,** verpleeginrigting; ~ **mother,** pleegmoeder; sogende moeder; ~ **service,** verpleegdiens; ~ **sister,** verpleegster, suster.
nur'ture, (n) voeding; voedsel, kos; aankweking; opvoeding; versorging; *nature and* ~, (die) aangeborene en (die) aangeleerde; aanleg en opvoeding; (v) opvoed; grootmaak; aankweek; koester.
nut, neut; moertjie (van 'n skroef); modegek; windmaker, fat; klapperdop, malkop, mal vent (groeptaal); (pl) neutkole, duimkole; *BE* ~ *s, BE off one's* ~, gek wees; getik wees; van lotjie getik wees; *BE* ~ *s on,* gek wees na; mal wees oor; *BE* ~ *s at tennis,* 'n uithaler tennisspeler wees; *be DEAD* ~ *s on,* baie versot wees op, *he who would EAT the* ~ *must crack the shell,* wie nie werk nie, sal nie eet nie; *a HARD* ~ *to crack,* 'n moeilike taak; 'n harde koejawel; *NOT for* ~ *s,* vir geen geld ter wêreld nie; *OFF his* ~, getik wees; *he's a REAL* ~, hy is 'n regte karnallie; *as SOUND (sweet) as a* ~, baie gesond (heilsaam); *a TOUGH* ~, 'n harde koejawel.
nut'ant, knikkend; verwelk, neerhangend.
nut'ate, knik; slap hang, verwelk.
nuta'tion, knikking; asskommeling, asskudding (sterr.)
nut: ~-**brown,** kastaiingbruin; ~-**coal,** neutkool; ~ **crackers,** neutkraker; ~-**gall,** galappel; ~-**grass,** uintjie *(Moraea edulis);* steentjieskweek; ~-**key,** skroefsleutel.
nut'meg, (muskaat)neut; ~-**grater,** neutskraper; ~-**oil,** muskaatolie; ~-**tree,** muskaatboom.
nut' oil, neutolie.
nut'ria, moerasbewer, nutria.
nut'rient, (n) voedingstof; voedselbestanddeel; (a) voedsaam, voedend.
nut'riment, kos, voedsel; ~ '**al,** voedsaam.
nutri'tion, kos, voedsel, voeding; *science of* ~, voedingsleer; ~ **al,** voedings-; ~ *al value,* voedingswaarde; ~ **expert,** voedingsdeskundige; ~ **ist,** voedingkundige.
nutri'tious, voedsaam; ~ **matter,** voedingstof; ~ **ness,** voedsaamheid; ~ **plant,** voedingsplant.
nut'ritive, (n) voedingsmiddel, kos; (a) voedsaam, voedend; ~ **ness,** voedsaamheid; ~ **ratio,** voedingsverhouding; ~ **value,** voedingswaarde.
nut'-screw, stelskroef.
nut'-sedge, uintjie *(Moraea edulis).*
nut'shell, neutdop; neutedop (fig.); *IN a* ~, baie beknop; in 'n neutedop; in 'n paar woorde; *a NOVEL in a* ~, 'n roman in kort bestek.
nut: ~-**tapper,** moersnyer; ~ **ter,** neutplukker; ~ **ting:** *go* ~ *ting,* gaan neute pluk; ~-**tree,** neutboom; ~ **ty,** vol neute, neut-, neutagtig; korrelrig (grond); verlief, been-af; gek, getik (groept.); ~-**weevil,** neutmiet.
nux vom'ica, braakneut, opbringneut.
nuz'zle, (be)snuffel; vly, koester, aankruip teen.
nya'la, njala, basterkoedoe.
Nyas'aland, (hist.) Njassaland, Malawi.
nyct'alope, nagblinde.
nyctalop'ia, nagblindheid.
nyctalop'ic, nagblind.
nyctaphob'ia, vrees vir die donker, niktafobie.
nyl'on, nylon.
nymph, nimf; papie (van 'n mot); ~ **ish,** ~ **like,** nimfagtig, soos 'n nimf; ~ **olep'sy,** waansinnige ekstase, nimfolepsie; ~ **oman'ia,** mansiekte, nimfomanie; ~ **oma'niac, (n)** mansieke, nimfomaan; (a) mansiek, nimfomaan.
nystag'mus, nistagmus.

O

o¹, (os, o's, oes), o, nul (in getalle); *FIVE* ~, *six,* vyf, nul, ses; *LITTLE* ~, o'tjie.
O!², (interj) O!
o'³, = of.
oaf, (-s, oaves), uilskuiken, idioot; wisselkind; gebreklike kind; tor, lomperd; ~ **ish,** onnosel, torrerig, lomp, ~ **ishness,** onnoselheid; lompheid.
oak, (n) eik, akkerboom; eikehout; (a) eike-, van eikehout; ~-**apple,** galappel; ~ **avenue,** eikelaan; ~ **bark,** eikebas; ~ **beam,** eikebalk; ~ **branch,** eiketak; ~ **en,** eike-, van eikehout; ~ **forest,** eikebos; ~-**gall,** galneut; ~-**graining,** eikaring; eikehoutkleur; ~-**leaf,** akkerblaar; ~-**leather,** swamme op ou eike; ~ **let,** ~ **ling,** eikeboompie; ~ **mould,** eikeblaarhumus; ~-**tree,** eikeboom, akkerboom.
oak'um, gepluisde tou; toupluksel; *pick* ~, tou pluis; ~-**picker,** toupluiser; ~-**picking,** toupluisery; pluiswerk.
oak'-wood, eikehout; eikebos.
oar, (n) roeispaan, roeiriem; roeier; *have an* ~ *in every man's BOAT,* jou neus oral insteek; bemoeisiek wees; *a GOOD* ~, 'n goeie roeier; *PLY the* ~ *s,* kragtig aanroei; *PULL an* ~, roei; *PUT in one's* ~, jou bemoei met; *REST on one's* ~ *s,* op jou louere rus; *TUG at the* ~, die tou styf trek; jou inspan; *you must always shove in YOUR* ~, jy wil altyd 'n duit in die armbeurs gooi; (v) roei.
oars'man, (..men), roeier; ~ **ship,** roeikuns.
oa'sis, (oases), oase.
oast, moutoond; hoopoond; droogoond.
oat, hawerkorrel; *kyk* **oats.**
oat: ~-**cake,** hawerkoek; ~ **en,** hawer-.
oath, (n) eed; affidavit; vloek; ~ *of ABJURATION,* afsweringseed; *ADMINISTER an* ~, die eed afneem; ~ *of ALLEGIANCE,* eed van getrouheid; verbondseed; *BE on (under)* ~, beëdig wees; ~ *of OFFICE,* ampseed; *ON* ~, onder eed; *PUT someone on* ~, iem. die eed laat sweer; *TAKE someone on* ~, iem. die eed laat sweer; *TAKE a solemn* ~, 'n heilige eed sweer; 'n heilige eed aflê; *UPON my* ~, op my woord; ~-**breaking,** meineed; (v) sweer; 'n eed afneem, laat sweer; vloek.
oat: ~-**hay,** hawerhooi; ~-**malt,** hawermout; ~ **meal,** hawermeel.
oath'-taker, eedaflêer.
oats, hawer; hawermeel; *FEEL one's* ~, jou aanstel, grootdoenerig wees; *ROLLED* ~, hawermout; *WILD* ~, wildehawer; *sow one's WILD* ~, jeugsondes begaan; *he has sown his WILD* ~, sy wilde hare het uitgeval.
obbliga'to, obligaat, obbligato.
obduc'tion, lykskouing.
ob'duracy, koppigheid, hardnekkigheid, verstoktheid, verhardheid.
ob'durate, koppig, hardnekkig, verstok, verhard.
obdura'tion, verharding.
obed'ience, gehoorsaamheid; *IN* ~ *to,* in gehoorsaamheid aan; ooreenkomstig; *PASSIVE* ~, lydelike gehoorsaamheid; ~ *is better than SACRIFICE,* gehoorsaamheid is beter as offerande.
obed'ient, gehoorsaam, gesêglik, dienswillig; *your* ~

obeisance   1082   *observation*

servant, u dienswillige dienaar; ~ **ly,** gehoorsaam; *yours* ~ *ly,* dienswillig die uwe.
obeis'ance, diep buiging; voetval; hulde; *make an* ~, 'n buiging maak.
ob'elisk, gedenknaald, obelisk, (ere)suil.
obese', vet, dik, swaarlywig.
obes'ity, vetheid, swaarlywigheid, gesetheid.
obey', gehoorsaam, luister na, gehoor gee aan, gevolg gee aan; ~ **ance,** gehoorsaamheid.
ob'fuscate, verduister; verbyster; benewel; ~ **d,** benewel, verbluf.
obfusca'tion, verduistering, verbystering.
ob'iit, (hy, sy is) oorlede, obiit.
ob'it, gedenkdiens.
ob'iter, terloops; ~ *dictum,* terloopse opmerking, obiter dictum.
obit'uary, (n) (..ries), doodberig; kennisgewing van 'n sterfgeval; lewensbeskrywing, nekroloog; (a) dood(s)=, sterf=; ~ **notice,** doodsberig.
ob'ject, (n) voorwerp; bedoeling, plan; doel, oogmerk, doelwit; *be the* ~ *of someone's AFFECTION,* iem. se trekpleister wees; ~ *of LUXURY,* luuksevoorwerp; weeldeartikel; *MAKE it one's* ~, jou iets ten doel stel; ~ *MATTER,* hoofsaak, onderwerp; *MONEY is no* ~, geld is bysaak; *SALARY no* ~, op salaris sal minder gelet word; *SERVE no* ~ *but,* geen ander doel hê nie as.
object', (v) beswaar maak, objekteer, 'n teenwerping maak; *it was* ~ *ed AGAINST the proposal that . . .,* teen die voorstel is beswaar aangeteken omdat . . .; ~ *to,* beswaar maak teen; wraak (reg).
ob'ject: ~ **-ball,** mikbal, slaanbal (biljart); ~ **-glass,** objektieflens, voorwerplens, objektiefglas.
objectifica'tion, objektivering.
objec'tify, (..fied), objektiveer, beliggaam.
objec'tion, beswaar, bedenking, swarigheid, teenwerping, aanmerking, objeksie; *CONSCIENTIOUS* ~, gewetensbeswaar; *DISALLOW an* ~, 'n beswaar afwys; *MUTTER* ~ *s,* teëpruttel; *OVERRULE an* ~, 'n beswaar v.d. hand wys; *RAISE* ~ *s,* besware opper (opwerp); swarigheid maak; ~ **able,** laakbaar, onaanneembaar, verwerplik, stuitend, betwisbaar, aanstootlik; afkeurenswaardig.
objec'tive, (n) objektief; voorwerpnaamval; doel, teiken, mikpunt; (a) voorwerplik, objektief, saaklik; ~ **case,** voorwerpsnaamval, vierde naamval; ~ **ly,** objektief; doodnugter; ~ **ness,** objektiwiteit.
objectiv'ity, objektiwiteit.
ob'ject: ~ **-lens,** objektief, objektiefglas, objektieflens; ~ **-less,** doelloos, onbestemd; ~ **-lesson,** aanskouingsles; sprekende voorbeeld; ~ **'or,** beswaarmaker, teenstander; *conscientious* ~ *or,* iem. met gemoedsbeswaar, diensweieraar; gewetensbeswaarde; ~ **-teaching,** aanskouingsonderwys.
objet d'art, (F.), objet d'art, kunsvoorwerp.
objura'tion, beswering.
objure', beëindig, besweer.
ob'jurgate, verwyt, berispe; 'n skrobbering gee, bestraf.
objurga'tion, verwyt, berisping; vermaning.
ob'jurgatory, verwytend, berispend.
ob'late¹, (n) oblaat, geestelike.
oblate'², (a) afgeplat (aan die pole).
obla'tion, offerande; offering, offergawe; gawe, skenking.
oblecta'tion, welbehae.
ob'ligate, verbind, verplig.
obliga'tion, verpligting; gehoudenheid, plig; verband; skuldbrief, obligasie; *PLACE someone under an* ~, iem. aan jou verplig; *be UNDER an* ~ *to,* verplig wees aan (om); dank verskuldig wees aan; *WITHOUT* ~, sonder verpligting.
ob'ligator, skuldenaar.
oblig'atory, verpligtend; (ver)bindend.
oblige', verplig; 'n diens bewys; dwing, noodsaak; *an ANSWER will* ~, antwoord asseblief; ~ *with a SONG,* 'n lied ten beste gee; *WILL you* ~ *me?* wil u my 'n diens bewys?
obliged', genoop; ~ *to DO it,* verplig om dit te doen; *FEEL* ~ *to,* gedronge (verplig) voel om; *be MUCH* ~, baie dankbaar wees.

obligee', obligasiehouer; skuldeiser.
obli'ging, diensvaardig, gedienstig; hups, vriendelik, voorkomend, beleef, hulpvaardig, tegemoetkomend; ~ **ness,** diensvaardigheid, voorkomendheid; hulpvaardigheid, tegemoetkomendheid.
oblique', (v) skuins opmarsjeer; (a) skeef, skuins; afwykend, indirek; sydelings; ~ **angle,** skewe hoek; ~ **-angled,** skeefhoekig; ~ **case,** verboë naamval; ~ **fault,** skuins verskuiwing; ~ **fire,** skuinsvuur; ~ **ly,** skuins; ~ *ly opposite,* skuinsoor; ~ **ness** = **obliquity;** ~ **oration,** indirekte rede; ~ **photograph,** skuins opname; ~ **plane,** hellende vlak; ~ **reference,** toespeling; ~ **wind,** skuinswind.
obliq'uity, skuinsheid; afwyking; verkeerdheid.
oblit'erate, doodvee; uitwis, uitkrap, vernietig; afstempel; doodverf; ~ *from one's memory,* uit die geheue wis.
oblitera'tion, uitwissing; deurhaling; vernietiging.
obliv'ion, vergetelheid; *FALL into* ~, in die vergeetboek raak; in vergetelheid raak; *allow to FALL into* ~, aan die vergetelheid prysgee; *RESCUE from* ~, aan die vergetelheid ontruk; *SINK into* ~, in die vergetelheid raak.
obliv'ious, vergeetagtig; onbewus; ~ *of,* onbewus van; sonder inagneming van.
ob'long, (n) langwerpige figuur; langwerpige stuk; (a) langwerpig; ~ **ated,** verleng; ~ **ness,** langwerpigheid.
ob'loquy, (..quies), verwyt, laster, hoon, smaad, oneer, skande; *CAST* ~ *upon,* belaster; *FALL into* ~, in slegte reuk kom.
obmutes'cence, hardnekkige stilswye.
obmutes'cent, koppig swygend.
obno'xious, skadelik; stuitend, nadelig; aanstootlik; haatlik; ~ **ness,** aanstootlikheid; haatlikheid.
obnub'ilate, verduister, benewel.
obnubila'tion, verduistering, beneweling.
ob'oe, hobo.
ob'oist, hobospeler, hoboïs.
ob'ol(us), obool.
obscene', sedeloos, onkuis, liederlik, smerig, skurf, dubbelsinnig (grap), gemeen, vuil; ~ **ness, obscen'ity,** vuilheid, onkuisheid, liederlikheid, dubbelsinnigheid, onbetaamlikheid, onwelvoeglikheid.
obscur'ant, domper, remskoen (fig.); ~ **ism** dompersug, obskurantisme, remskoenpolitiek, verkramptheid; ~ **ist,** (n) domper; duisterling, vyand van verligting, verkrampte, remskoen; (a) bekrompe, remskoen=, domperagtig.
obscura'tion, verdonkering, verduistering.
obscure', (v) verdonker, verduister; onduidelik maak; in die skaduwee stel, oorskadu; verberg, die uitsig belemmer; ~ *the sea from view,* die uitsig op die see belemmer; (a) duister; onbekend; donker, benewel, onduidelik; nederig; verborge, obskuur; ~ *BIRTH,* geringe afkoms; *LIVE* ~ *ly,* teruggetrokke woon; *the MEANING is still* ~ *to me,* die betekenis bly vir my duister; *an* ~ *PERSON,* 'n onbekende beroemdheid; 'n onbekende, nonentiteit; ~ **d,** verduister; oorskadu; verberg; ~ **d glass,** matglas.
obscur'ity, duisterheid, duisternis, donkerheid; onduidelikheid; onbekendheid, onbekende (beroemdheid); *LIVE in* ~, stil lewe, teruggetrek lewe; *RETIRE into* ~, jou uit die openbare lewe terugtrek.
ob'secrate, smeek, bid.
obsecra'tion, smeking, smeekbede.
obseq'uial, lyk=, begrafnis=.
ob'sequies, begrafnis, lykdiens.
obseq'uious, slaafs, kruiperig; gedwee, onderworpe, onderdanig; oorgedienstig; ~ **ness,** (oor)gedienstigheid; kruiperigheid; onderworpenheid.
observ'able, waarneembaar, bespeurbaar; opmerklik.
observ'ance, waarneming, viering, onderhouding; eerbiediging, nalewing; voorskrif.
observ'ant, oplettend, opmerksaam; *be* ~ *of,* oplet, gesteld wees op.
observa'tion, opmerking; waarneming; opvolging; viering; *GIFT of* ~, opmerkingsgawe; *KEEP under*

observatory   1083   *occupy*

~, onder toesig hou; *POWERS of* ~, waarnemingsvermoë, opmerkingsvermoë; ~ **al**, waarnemings=; ~ **aircraft**, waarnemingsvliegtuig; ~ **area**, waarnemingsgebied; ~ **balloon**, waarnemingsballon; ~ **car**, uitkykwa; ~ **hole**, kykgaatjie; ~ **point**, uitkykpunt; ~ **post**, uitkykpos; ~ **slit**, kykgleuf; ~ **turret**, uitkyktoring.
observ'atory, (..ries), sterrewag, observatorium; weerwag.
observe', bemerk, sien, betrag, gadeslaan, waarneem; aanmerk; noteer; nakom; vier, hou (Sondag); bewaar; dophou; in ag neem; ~ *an ANNIVERSARY*, 'n gedenkdag vier; ~ *the LAW*, die wet naleef; ~ *SILENCE*, stilbly, die stilswye bewaar.
observ'er, opmerker; waarnemer (ook lugdiens).
observ'ing(ly), waarnemend, oplettend.
obsess', agtervolg; kwel, nie los nie; ~**ed**, besete; ~*ed with (by)*, besete word deur; vol wees van; behep wees met; ~**ion**, obsessie, kwelgedagte, voortdurende kwelling, dwangvoorstelling; ~**ive**, kwellend, drukkend.
obsid'ian, lawaglas.
obsid'ional, beleërings=.
obsolesce', verouder.
obsoles'cence, veroudering.
obsoles'cent, verouderend, aan die verouder, in onbruik raak; verwordend.
ob'solete, verouder, in onbruik; ouderwets; *become* ~, verouder, uitgedien raak.
ob'stacle, hinderpaal, struikelblok, beletsel, verhindering, belemmering; ~-**race**, sukkelwedloop, hindernisswedloop.
obstet'ric, verloskundig, obstetries; ~ **al**, verloskundig, obstetries.
obstetri'cian, verloskundige, obstetrikus.
obstet'rics, verloskunde, obstetrie; kraamverpleging.
ob'stinacy, (..cies), (hard)koppigheid, eiewysheid, eiesinnigheid, hardnekkigheid, (styf)hoofdigheid, halsstarrigheid, balsturigheid, weerspannigheid, weerstrewigheid.
ob'stinate, koppig, balsturig, hardnekkig, verbete, obstinaat, dikkoppig, eiesinnig, (hard)hoofdig, styfkoppig; wys; weerspannig, weerstrewig, steeks.
obstipa'tion, verstopping.
obstrep'erous, woelig, luidrugtig, lawaaierig; parmantig, opstandig, weerbarstig, weerspannig; ~**ness**, luidrugtigheid, gerinkink, lawaai; weerspannigheid.
obstruct', verhinder, dwarsboom, belemmer, verstop; versper; teenhou; ~ *the police*, die polisie dwarsboom; ~**ed**, belemmerd, verhinderd; ~**ionism**, dwarsboming; ~**ionist**, obstruksievoerder, dwarsdrywer; remskoen; dwarstrekker; ~**ive**, (n) dwarstrekker, dwarsdrywer; (a) belemmerend, obstruktief; dwarstrekkerig; versperrend; ~ **or**, dwarsdrywer, versperrer; versperring.
ob'struent, (n) stoppende middel; obstruent; (a) hinderend; stoppend.
obtain', verkry, verwerf, bekom, behaal, erlang, aanskaf; aan iets kom; in gebruik wees, bestaan; heers, van krag wees; geld (regte), vigeer (wette); *may BE* ~*ed from*, verkrygbaar by, ~ *an OPTION on*, 'n opsie kry op; die voorkeur kry van; ~**able**, verkrygbaar; ~**ing**: *now* ~*ing*, tans gebruiklik; in swang; ~**ment**, verkryging, verwerwing.
obtrude', opdring, lastig val; ~ *one's opinion on (upon) a friend*, jou mening aan 'n vriend opdring; ~**r**, opdringer, indringer.
obtrunc'ate, van die top beroof, afknot, top.
obtru'sion, opdringing; opdringerigheid; indringerigheid.
obtrus'ive, lastig; indringerig; opdringerig.
obtund', stomp maak, afstomp; verdoof; ~**ent**, (n) verdowende middel; (a) verdowend.
ob'turate, toemaak, toestop.
obtura'tion, toestopping, afsluiting.
ob'turator, afsluiting, sluitspier, afsluiter; verstopper.
obtuse', stomp, stoets; bot, dof, suf, onnosel; ~**angle**, stoets hoek, stomp hoek; ~-**angled**, stomphoekig; ~**ness**, stompheid; domheid, botheid.
ob'verse, (n) voorkant; bokant; regte kant (mate-

riaal); ander kant, keersy, omgekeerde; (a) omgekeer; teenoorgestel(d); ~**ly**, omgekeerd.
obver'sion, omkering.
obvert', omkeer, omdraai.
ob'viate, verhelp, voorkom; wegruim, pad maak, afwend, verwyder, wegneem; uitskakel; verhoed, vermy; *to* ~ *misunderstanding*, om misverstand te voorkom.
obvia'tion, voorkoming; wegruiming.
ob'vious, duidelik, klaarblyklik, handtastelik; aangewese; vanselfsprekend; *a GLIMPSE of the* ~, 'n waarheid soos 'n koei; *it IS* ~ *that*, dit spreek vanself dat; dit lê voor die hand dat; ~**ly**, klaarblyklik; ~**ness**, duidelikheid, vanselfsprekendheid.
ocari'na, okarina.
occa'sion, (n) geleentheid; okkasie; aanleiding, rede; oorsaak; behoefte, noodsaaklikheid; *when the* ~ *DEMANDS it*, as die omstandighede dit vereis; *at the EARLIEST* ~, by die eerste geleentheid; *GIVE* ~ *to*, aanleiding gee tot; *GO about one's lawful* ~*s*, jou met jou eie sake besig hou; *HAVE* ~ *for*, nodig hê vir; *an* ~ *of IMPORTANCE*, 'n belangrike geleentheid; *IMPROVE the* ~, 'n sedepreek oor iets lewer; *an* ~ *for MERRYMAKING*, 'n geleentheid vir pretmakery; *there is NO* ~ *to*..., daar is geen rede om...; *ON* ~, soms, somtyds; as dit nodig is; *ON this* ~, met die geleentheid; *on the* ~ *OF*, by geleentheid van; *RISE to the* ~, jou uitstekend kwyt; jou man staan; bereken wees vir die taak; teen iets opgewasse wees; *TAKE* ~ *to*, die geleentheid aangryp om; *UPON* ~, soms; by geleentheid; as dit nodig is; (v) veroorsaak, teweeg gebring; aanleiding gee tot.
occa'sional, toevallig; nou en dan, af en toe, geleentheids=; ~ **chair**, los stoel; ~ **expenses**, los uitgawes; ~ **help**, noodhulp; ~ **leave**, geleentheidsverlof; ~ **speaker**, geleentheidspreker; ~ **speech**, geleentheidstoespraak; ~ **table**, los tafel; ~**ly**, nou en dan, by wyle, dan en wan, af en toe.
Oc'cident, (die) Weste, Aandland.
Occiden'tal, (n) Westerling; (a) Westers.
occiden'tal, westelik.
occip'ital, van die agterkop, agterhoofs=.
oc'ciput, agterhoof, agterkop.
occlude', sluit, toestop; opneem; verstop; absorbeer, opsuig (gas).
occlu'sion, toesluiting, toestopping; absorpsie, opname (gas).
occlus'ive, (n) plosief, klapper, eksplosief; (a) okklusief, plosief.
occult'¹, (n): *SCIENCE of the* ~, okkultisme; *THE* ~, die verborgene, die okkulte; (a) geheim, verborge, okkult, geheimsinnig, onbekend; *the* ~ *sciences*, die swart kuns, die geheime wetenskappe.
occult'², (v) verberg; verduister; okkulteer (sterrek.); ~**a'tion**, verberging; sterbedekking, okkultasie (sterrek.), verduistering; ~**ing**, flikker=, wisselend; ~*ing light*, flikkerlig.
occult'ism, okkultisme, studie v.d. geheime wetenskappe.
occult'ist, okkultis, student v.d. geheime wetenskappe.
occ'upancy, inbesitneming; bewoning; besetting.
occ'upant, besitter; bewoner; huurder; insittende, opvarende (in voertuig); *the* ~ *of a post*, die bekleër van 'n pos.
occupa'tion, beroep, ambag, besigheid, werkkring; besetting (stad); beset; *ARMY of* ~, besettingsleër; *BE in* ~ *of*, beset hou; *BY* ~, van beroep; *by* ~ *he is a SHOEMAKER*, van beroep is hy skoenmaker.
occupa'tional, beroeps=; ~ **centre**, sentrum vir arbeidsterapie; ~ **disease**, bedryfsiekte; ~ **hazard**, beroepsrisiko; bedryfsrisiko; ~ **therapy**, arbeidsterapie; beroepsterapie; ~ **training**, beroepsopleiding.
occupa'tion: ~ **centre**, werkplek vir werkloses; ~ **forces**, besettingstroepe.
occ'upied, besig, onledig; beset; bewoon; *my time is fully* ~ *by my work*, my werk hou my heeltyds besig.
occ'upier, bewoner, huurder, besitter.
occ'upy, (..pied), beset; in besit neem; besig hou; be-

trek (huis); bewoon, gebruik; beklee (betrekking); inneem, in beslag neem; *BE occupied with*, besig wees met; ~ *the BENCH*, op die regbank sit; ~ *a POST*, 'n amp beklee; ~ *a THRONE*, op 'n troon sit; ~ *one's TIME by reading*, jou tyd gebruik om te lees; ~ *a TOWN*, 'n dorp beset; ~ *oneself WITH a novel*, jou besig hou met 'n roman.

occur', (-red), voorkom; byval, inval; voorval, gebeur, plaasvind, wedervaar; aangetref word; *it* ~*s to ME*, dit lyk vir my, dit wil my voorkom; ~ *to SOMEONE that*, by iem. opkom dat.

occu'rrence, voorval, gebeurtenis; verskynsel; wedervaring, wedervare; voorkoms, aanwesigheid (minerale); evenement; *it is of frequent* ~, dit kom herhaaldelik voor; ~ **book**, voorvalleboek.

o'cean, oseaan, wêreldsee; ~ *of life*, lewensee; ~ **arium**, seemuseum; ~ **bed**, seebodem; ~ **current**, seestroom; ~ **-going**, seevarend (land); ~ **greyhound**, snelvaarder.

Ocean'ia, Oseanië, die Suidsee-eilande.

ocean'ic, van die see, oseaan=, oseanies; ~ **deep**, diepseeslenk.

Oce'anid, (-(e)s), Oseanide, seenimf.

o'cean: ~ **lane**, seeroete; ~ **liner**, lynboot, passasiersboot; ~ **mail service**, seeposdiens; ~ **og'rapher**, seebeskrywer, oseanograaf; ~ **og'raphy**, seebeskrywing, oseanografie; ~ **ol'ogy**, oseanologie; ~ **wave**, oseaangolf, seegolf.

o'cellate(d), met oogvormige vlekke, oogvormig; kollerig.

ocel'lus, osel, enkelvoudige oog, puntoog.

o'celot, (Suid-Amerikaanse) luiperd, panterkat.

ochloc'racy, oglokrasie, gepeupelheerskappy.

och'locrat, oglokraat, volksmenner.

och're, oker, geelbruin; bergaarde, geelklei; *RED* ~, rooiklei; *YELLOW* ~, geeloker.

och'r(e)ous, och'ry, okeragtig, oker=.

o'clock', op die klok; *he KNOWS what* ~ *it is*, hy weet sy weetjie; *NINE* ~, negeuur; *ONE* ~, een uur; *SEVEN* ~, seweuur; *TEN* ~, tienuur.

oc'tachord, (n) toonskaal van agt note; agtsnarige lier; (a) agtsnarig; agttonig.

oc'tagon, agthoek, oktogoon; ..**tag'onal**, agthoekig, oktogonaal.

octahed'ral, agtkantig, agtsydig, agtvlakkig, oktaëdries.

octahed'ron, agtvlak, agtkantige figuur, oktaëder.

octam'eter, agtvoetige vers, oktameter.

octan'drous, agthelmig, oktandries.

oc'tane, oktaan; ~ **number**, oktaanwaarde, oktaangetal.

octang'ular, agthoekig.

oc'tant, oktant.

oc'tave, oktaaf, agttal; agtdaagse fees; ~ **flute**, piccolo, oktaaffluit.

Octav'ian, Octavianus, Oktavianus.

octav'o, oktavo(formaat), oktaaf(formaat).

octenn'ial, agtjarig; agtjaarliks.

octet(te)', oktet (mus.); oktaaf (vers).

octingenten'ary, (..ries), 800ste gedenkfees, agteeufees.

Octob'er, Oktober.

octocenten'ary, (..ries), *kyk* **octingentenary**.

octode'cimo, octodecimo(formaat).

octogenar'ian, (n) tagtigjarige; (a) tagtigjarig.

oc'tonal, oct'onary, agttallig.

octopet'alous, agtblarig.

oc'topod, agtpotig, agtvoetig.

oc'topus, (-es, **octopodes**), seekat, veelarm, agtarmige poliep, oktopus, platkop.

octosyllab'ic, agtlettergrepig, oktosillabies.

octosyll'able, agtlettergrepige woord, oktosillabe.

oc'troi, oktrooi.

oc'tuple, (n) agtvoud; (v) veragtvoudig; (a) agtvoudig.

oc'ular, (n) oogglas; (a) oog=, okulêr; gesigs=; ~ **witness**, ooggetuie.

oc'ulist, oogdokter, oogheelkundige, okulis.

od, vermeende natuurkrag, magnetiese krag.

od'alisque, Oosterse slavin, odalisk.

odd, snaaks, koddig, sonderling, eksentriek, potsierlik, raar, vreemd, vreemdsoortig; onewe, onpaar; ongelyk; *in an* ~ *CORNER*, in 'n verlore hoekie; ~ *in one's DRESS*, snaaks aangetrek; ~ *and EVEN*, gelyk en ongelyk; paar en onpaar; *FIFTY* ~, 'n rapsie oor vyftig, ruim vyftig, effens oor vyftig; *an* ~ *GLOVE*, 'n onpas handskoen; ~ *JOBS*, peuselwerkies, los werkies; ~ *LOTS*, restante, oorskietsels, oorskietklompies; *the* ~ *MAN*, die orige kêrel; ~ *MAN out*, die derdemannetjie; ~ *MOMENTS*, ledige (verlore) oomblikke, snipperoomblikke; ~ *NUMBER*, ongelyke getal; los eksemplaar; *the* ~ *THING is*, die snaaksste is; *at* ~ *TIMES*, so nou en dan; *the* ~ *TRICK*, die wennende trek; ~ **-coloured**, agaatbont; ~ **ish**, snaaks, komieklik.

odd'ity, (..**ties**), sonderlingheid, koddigheid, potsierlikheid, rarigheid, eienaardigheid, vreemdsoortigheid, snaaksigheid, snaakse affêre, koddige gebeurtenis; snaakse vent.

odd: ~ **-jobber**, ~ **-job man**, handlanger, faktotum, hansie-my-kneg; ~ **-looking**, snaaks, koddig, komieklik.

odd'ly, snaaks, koddig; ~ *ENOUGH*, snaaks genoeg; ~ *FAMILIAR*, sonderling bekend.

odd'ments, allerhande dinge, stukkies en brokkies, oorskietsels, restant.

odd'ness, koddigheid, eienaardigheid.

odds, onewenheid, ongelykheid; verskil; onenigheid; oormag, meerderheid; kans; wedsyfer; wedvoorwaardes; voorgif, voordeel; *by ALL* ~, verreweg; *the* ~ *ARE*, die moontlikheid bestaan; *BE at* ~ *with one another*, met mekaar oorhoop lê; dit nie met mekaar eens wees nie; haaks met mekaar wees; ~ *and ENDS*, ditjies en datjies; goetertjies; stukkies en brokkies; *the* ~ *are EVEN*, hulle is ewe vinnig (sterk); die kanse is gelyk; *the* ~ *are in his FAVOUR*, die voordeel is aan sy kant; *FIGHT against* ~, teen die oormag stry; *GIVE* ~ *of five to one*, vyf teen een wed; *an* ~ *-on HORSE*, 'n perd waarop swaar gewed word; *lay LONG* ~, 'n ongelyke weddenskap aangaan; *MAKE* ~ *even*, dinge gelykmaak; *that MAKES no* ~, *it is NO* ~, dit maak geen verskil nie; ~ *ON*, met goeie wenkanse; *OVER the* ~, onwaarskynlik; *SET at* ~, teen mekaar opmaak; *at SHORT* ~, met geringe kanse; *the* ~ *are on his SIDE*, die voordeel is aan sy kant; *TAKE the* ~, die weddenskap aanneem; *WHAT are (what's) the* ~? watter saak (verskil) maak dit? *WHAT'S the* ~ *that* . . .? hoe waarskynlik is dit . . .? *WITHIN the* ~, waarskynlik.

odd'-toed, meerhoewig.

ode, ode.

ode'um, (**odea, -s**), odeon.

Od'in, Wodan.

od'ious, haatlik, verfoeilik, afskuwelik, walglik; ~ **ness**, haatlikheid, afskuwelikheid.

od'ist, odedigter.

od'ium, haat; afkeer, afsku; veragting; blaam.

odom'eter, afstandsmeter, meetwiel, mylmeter, odometer.

odontal'gia, od'ontalgy, tandpyn, odontalgie.

odon'tic, (n) tandmiddel; (a) tand=.

odontog'raphy, tandbeskrywing, odontografie.

odon'toid, tand=.

odontol'ogy, tandkunde, tandleer, odontologie.

odorif'erant, reukstof.

odorif'erous, od'orous, geurig, welriekend.

od'our, geur, reuk; reukwerk; slegte reuk; *be in BAD* ~ *with*, in 'n slegte reuk staan by; *be in GOOD* ~, goed aangeskrewe staan by; *in the* ~ *of SANCTITY*, in reuk van heiligheid; ~ **less**, reukloos.

Od'yssey, Odyssee, Odussee; swerftog.

oecumen'ical, algemeen, universeel, ekumenies.

oedem'a, watergeswel, watersug, edeem.

oedem'atose, oedem'atous, watersugtig, edemies.

oedem'ic, edemies.

Oed'ipus, Oedipus; ~ **complex**, Oedipuskompleks.

oenolog'ic, enologies.

oenolog'ical, wynkundig, enologies.

oenol'ogist, wynkundige, enoloog.

oenol'ogy, wynkunde, enologie.

o'er, *kyk* **over**.

oesopha'geal, slukderm=.

oesoph'agus, (..gi, -es), slukderm, rooiderm.
oes'trual, bronstig, hittig; ~ **period,** bronstyd.
oestrua'tion, bronstigheid, hittigheid.
oes'trum, oes'trus, oestrus, bronstyd; bronstigheid; bronssiklus.
of, van; uit; aan; deur; op; in; ~ *AGE*, meerderjarig, mondig; *come* ~ *AGE*, mondig word; *she* ~ *ALL people*, en dit nogal sy; dat dit nou juis sy moet wees; *BOY* ~ *us*, ons albei; *BOY* ~ *ten*, seun van tien (jaar); *CARE* ~, sorg vir; per adres; *be* ~ *good CHEER*, vrolik en hoopvol wees; *the CITY* ~ *Bloemfontein,* die stad Bloemfontein; *CUP* ~ *tea*, koppie tee; *DIE* ~, sterf van; ~ *an EVENING*, in die aand; op 'n aand; *all* ~ *a HEAP*, alles tesaam; skielik; *die* ~ *HUNGER*, van honger doodgaan; ~ *IT*, daarvan; ~ *ITSELF*, vanself; ~ *LATE*, in die laaste tyd; *LIST* ~ *books*, lys (van) boeke; ~ *NECESSITY*, noodsaaklikerwys; ~ *ONESELF*, vanself; ~ *OLD*, vanouds, vanmelewe; ~ *RECENT months*, in die laaste maande; ~ *a SORT*, van minderwaardige gehalte; *all* ~ *a SUDDEN*, meteens, skielik; *there were TEN* ~ *them,* hulle was (met hulle) tien; ~ *all THINGS,* bo alles; *that* ~ *all THINGS!* reken dit; en dit nogal! ~ *THAT*, daarvan; ~ *THIS*, hiervan; ~ *WHICH,* waarvan; ~ *WHOM,* van wie.
off, (v) in die steek laat; (a) ander; regter=, haar=; afgeskakel; afgestel, gekanselleer; onjuis; sleg; galsterig; suur; *on the* ~ *CHANCE*, met die geringe hoop; met die minste kans; *be* ~ *COLOUR*, ongesteld wees; nie op jou stukke wees nie; nie in goeie kondisie wees nie; van stryk (slag) wees; dag wanneer 'n mens siekerig is; ~ *DAY*, vrye dag; *the* ~ *FORELEG,* die regtervoorbeen; *this pork is GOING* ~, hierdie varkvleis is al sleg; *the* ~ *HORSE*, die haarperd; *the* ~ *LEADER*, die haarvoordier; ~ *MOMENTS*, slegte humeur (stemming); ~ *PARADE*, paradevry; ~ *POSITION*, afgeskakelde stand; *the SALAD is* ~ *(the menu)*, die slaai is gedaan; *the* ~ *SIDE of a ship*, die seekant van 'n skip; *the* ~ *SIDE,* aan die ander kant; (adv) af, weg; ver vandaan; van; *the BARGAIN is* ~, die koop is uit; *BE* ~! maak dat jy wegkom! trap! *BE* ~, vertrek, wegspring; *be BETTER* ~, dit beter hê; *BREAK* ~, ophou; *BUY* ~, afkoop; *COME* ~ *it!* sak Sarel; *have a DAY* ~, 'n vrye dag hê; *FALL* ~, afval (van ryding); agteruitgaan; *GET* ~, wegkom; afklim; vry (na); *GO* ~, weggaan; bewusteloos word; afgaan; agteruitgaan; ~ *you GO!* trap! *BE* ~ *one's HEAD*, van sy verstand af wees; *LEAVE* ~, laat staan; *MAKE* ~, wegloop; ~ *and ON*, af en toe; so nou en dan; *STAND* ~! staan agteruit! *TAKE* ~, afneem, wegneem; opstyg; vlieg; *THEY'RE* ~! daar gaan hulle! *be WELL* ~, dit goed hê; daar goed in sit; ~ *WHITE*, ligbeige; halfwit; ~ *with YOU!* weg is jy! trap! (prep) van; ~ *one's own BAT*, op eie houtjie; ~ *the BEATEN track,* weg v.d. gewoel; weg v.d. gewone; ~ *CALAIS*, op die hoogte van Calais; ~ *the CUFF,* uit die vuis; ~ *DUTY*, vry; van diens; dienstvry; *the matter is* ~ *my HANDS*, ek is v.d. las ontslae; *fall* ~ *a LADDER*, van 'n leer afval; ~ *the LATCH*, nie op knip nie; ~ *the MAP,* vergelee, onbelangrik (plekkie); *get* ~ *the MARK*, wegspring, begin; *clothes* ~ *the PEG,* klaargemaakte winkelklere; *eat* ~ *a PLATE*, uit 'n bord eet; ~ *the RAILS,* v.d. spoor af, ontspoor; ~ *the RECORD*, onoffisieel; vertroulik; ~ *the REEL*, sommer, meteens; ononderbroke; ~ *the ROAD,* v.d. pad; verdwaal; ~ *the STAGE*, agter die skerms; *a STREET* ~ *Pretorius Street*, 'n dwarsstraat uit Pretoriusstraat; *go* ~ *the TOP*, kwaad word; *speak* ~ *the TOP*, oppervlakkig praat.
off'al, oorskiet; afval; uitskotstukkies en -brokkies; ~ **wheat**, tweedeklas koring.
off: ~ **chance,** moontlikheid; geringe kans; ~ **colour**, olik, ongesteld; van stryk; *be* ~ *colour*, nie lekker voel nie; ~ **-consumption**, buiteverbruik; ~ **-course**, buitebaan; ~ **-course totalizator**, buitebaantotalisator; ~ **-cut**, afknipsel; afvalstuk.
offence', oortreding, misstap, vergryp, delik (reg), wanbedryf, misdryf; aanstoot, ergernis, onstigting, belediging; struikelblok; aanval; *woe to that man by whom the* ~ *COMETH*, wee hom deur wie die ergernis kom; *COMMIT an* ~, 'n oortreding begaan; *GIVE* ~, aanstoot gee; beledig; *no* ~ *was MEANT*, so kwaad was dit nie bedoel nie; neem my dit nie kwalik nie; *QUICK to take* ~, liggeraak wees; gou op jou perdjie wees; *TAKE* ~ *at*, aanstoot neem aan; ~ **less**, onskuldig, weerloos.
offend', beledig, vererg, te na kom, aanstoot gee, ontstig; krenk; 'n vergryp pleeg, oortree; skend; ~ **ed**, beledig, kwaad, gepikeer, gesteur; *BE* ~ *ed at,* beledig voel deur; *EASILY* ~ *ed*, gou op sy perdjie, liggeraak.
offend'er, belediger; oortreder; sondaar; misdadiger; *JUVENILE* ~, jeugmisdadiger; *an OLD* ~, 'n ou sondaar; *PRINCIPAL* ~, hoofskuldige.
offend'ing, beledigend, aanstootlik.
offen'sive, (n) aanval, offensief; *be ON the* ~, aanvallenderwys(e) te werk gaan; aanvallend optree; *TAKE the* ~, aanval; (a) beledigend, aanstootlik, ergerlik, kwetsend; walglik; stuitig; aanvallend, aanvals=, offensief; onaangenaam, vies (reuk); galsterig (smaak); ~ *and DEFENSIVE league*, aanvallende en verdedigende verbond; ~ *LANGUAGE*, beledigende taal; ~ *SMELL*, slegte (onaangename) reuk; ~ *TRADE*, hinderlike bedryf; ~ *WAR*, aanvalsoorlog; ~ **ness**, aanstootlikheid; onaangenaamheid.
off'er, (n) aanbod, aanbieding; bod (vendusie); voorstel; aanpresentasie; huweliksaansoek; *MAKE me an* ~, gee my 'n bod; *MAKE an* ~ *of something to*, iem. iets aanbied; *ON* ~, te koop; verkrygbaar, (v) aanbied; aanpresenteer; bied; offer; bereid wees; opper; ~ *an APOLOGY*, apologie aanteken; ekskuus vra; verskoning maak; ~ *BATTLE*, uitdaag om te veg; ~ *COMMENTS*, kommentaar lewer; ~ *CRITICISM,* kritiek uitoefen; ~ *ed FOR re-election*, weer verkiesbaar; ~ *a LIBATION*, pleng; *whenever an OCCASION* ~ *ed,* so dikwels daar 'n geleentheid was, ~ *an OPINION*, 'n mening uitspreek; *as OPPORTUNITY* ~ *s*, wanneer die geleentheid hom voordoen; ~ *a PLEA*, pleit; 'n pleit opper; ~ *up a PRAYER*, bid; ~ *a PRIZE*, 'n prys uitloof; ~ *for SALE*, te koop aanbied; ~ *a SUGGESTION,* 'n wenk aan die hand doen; ~ **er**, aanbieder; ~ **ing**, offerande; aanbieding; *floral* ~ *ing*, blomstuk, blommehulde.
off'ertory, (..ries), offergebed; offerande, offertorium; kollekte.
offhand', (a) kortaf, ongeërg, onbeleef; (adv) kortaf, onbeleef, ongegeneer(d); op staande voet, onvoorberei; ~ **ed**, ongeerg; onbeleef, kortaf; ~ **edness**, ongeërgdheid, onbeleefdheid, kortafheid.
off'-hours, vrye ure, vrye tyd.
off'ice, kantoor; amp, diens, bediening; taak, plig; begrafnisdiens; betrekking; vriendelikheid; *AT the* ~, op kantoor; *BE in* ~, op die kussings sit; aan die roer wees; *COME into* ~, aan die bewind kom; *FRIENDLY* ~, vriendskapsdiens; *offer one's GOOD* ~ *s*, jou bemiddeling aanbied; *HIGH in* ~, hooggeplaas; *HOLD* ~, 'n amp beklee; sitting hê; in die saal wees; *be IN* ~, 'n pos beklee; *his KIND* ~ *s,* sy vriendelike bemiddeling; *LEAVE* ~, aftree; uit diens tree; *be OUT of* ~, nie meer aan die bewind nie; *PERFORM the last* ~ *s to*, die laaste eer bewys aan; ~ *of PROFIT*, besoldigde amp; *RETIRE from* ~, jou amp neerlê; *TAKE* ~, 'n pos (amp) aanvaar; *TERM of* ~, ampstermyn; ~ **accommodation**, kantoorruimte; ~ **-bearer**, amptenaar, beampte, ampsbekleër; ~ **boy**, kantoorseun; kantoorjongetjie; ~ **building**, kantoorgebou; ~ **clerk**, kantoorklerk; ~ **desk**, skryftafel; ~ **equipment**, kantoorbehoeftes, kantoortoerusting; ~ **hours**, kantoorure; ~ **-hunter**, baantjiejaer, baantjiesoeker; ~ **practice**, kantoorbedryf.
off'icer, (n) offisier; amptenaar, beampte, konstabel; bestuurslid; ~ *in CHARGE*, verantwoordelike offisier; ~ *COMMANDING*, bevelvoerder; verantwoordelike offisier; ~ *on DUTY*, diensdoende offisier; *MEDICAL* ~ *of health*, gesondheidsbeampte, stadsgeneesheer; (v) van offisiere voorsien; die be

vel voer; aanvoer; ~-**in-charge,** verantwoordelike amptenaar.
off'ice: ~ **requisites,** kantoorbehoeftes, kantoortoerusting; ~ **routine,** kantoorroetine.
off'icership, offisiersrang; offisierskap.
off'icers' mess, offisierstafel, offisiersmenasie.
off'ice: ~-**seeker,** baantjiesjaer, baantjiesoeker; ~-**seeking,** baantjiesoekery; ~ **supplies,** kantoorbehoeftes, kantoortoerusting; ~ **time,** kantoortyd; ~ **work,** kantoorwerk.
offi'cial, (n) beampte, amptenaar; (a) amptelik, amps=, offisieel; ~ **action,** ampshandeling; ~ **allowance,** ampstoelae; ~ **business,** amptelike briefwisseling; ampsake, dienssake; ~**dom,** amptenaarswêreld; burokrasie; ~ **duties,** ampspligte.
offi'cialese', amptenaretaal, kanselarystyl.
offi'cial: ~ **gazette,** staatskoerant; ampsblad; ~**ism,** amptenaarswêreld, burokrasie; ~**ize,** burokratiseer; ~ **journey,** ampsreis; ~ **language,** offisiële (amptelike) taal; ~ **letter,** amptelike brief, diensbrief; ~**ly,** amptelik; van goewermentsweë; ampshalwe; ~ **residence,** ampswoning; ~ **secret,** ampsgeheim; ~ **title,** ampstitel; ~ **visit,** ampsbesoek; ~ **year,** diensjaar.
offi'ciant, dienswaarnemer.
offi'ciate, 'n diens lei; 'n pos beklee; optree; preek; ~ **as,** fungeer as, optree as.
offi'ciating, diensdoende; ~ **priest,** altaardienaar.
offi'ciator, voorganger.
offi'cinal, geneeskragtig; voorradig.
offi'cious, gedienstig, oorgedienstig, oorbeleef; indringerig, bemoeisiek; offisieus, halfamptelik; ~**ness,** bemoeisug; gedienstigheid, oorbeleefdheid.
off'ing, (die) oop see; verskiet; *BE in the* ~, op hande wees; naby wees; *there is something IN the* ~, daar is iets op til; daar is iets aan die kom; *IN the* ~, voor die boeg; op die horison.
off'ish, neusoptrekkerig, ongesellig.
off: ~-**issue,** bysaak; ~ **leader,** haarvoor (dier); ~-**licence,** buitelisensie, drankwinkellisensie; ~-**load,** aflaai; uitlaai; ~-**print,** afdruk, oordruk; ~-**ramp,** afrit; ~-**saddle,** afsaal; ~-**sales,** buiteverkope; ~-**scourings,** afskuursel; uitvaagsel; afval; ~-**season,** slap tyd, buiteseisoen, buitentyds.
off'set, (n) teenrekening; spruit, loot; kontras; uitloper (van berg); loodlyn (driehoeksmeting); suier; begin; teenwig; draai (in pyp); ordinaat (landm.); vergoeding; vlakdruk; (v) (~), voorsien in, goedmaak; teenoormekaar stel; opweeg teen; verplaas (geol.); ~ **press,** litopers, vlakdrukpers; ~ **printing,** rubberdruk; vlakdruk; ~ **tunnel,** dwarstonnel.
off: ~ **shoot,** uitspruitsel, tak, loot, suier, spruit; telg; uitloper, tong (geol.); ~ **shore,** naby die kus, aflandig; ~ **shore ore berth,** aflandige ertslaaiplek; ~ **shore wind,** landwind; ~ **side,** onkant, aan die verkeerde kant; wegkant; ander kant; haarkant; oneerlik; ~-**side wheel,** regterwiel; ~ **spring,** kroos, nakomelingskap, afstamming; aanteel (diere); vrug, voortbrengsel, resultaat; ~-**street,** (n) systraat; (a) buitenstraats; ~-**street parking,** buitenstraatse parkering; ~ **stump,** wegpaaltjie; ~ **time,** vrye tyd; ~ **wheeler,** haaragter dier; ~-**white,** naaswit, amperwit.
oft, (digt.), dikwels, baiekeer, menigwerf.
o'ften, dikwels, baiemaal, baiekeer; *MORE* ~ *than not,* in die reël, gewoonlik; *as* ~ *as NOT,* dikwels, nie selde nie; *QUITE* ~, sommer baie.
oft'-times, baiemaal, dikwels.
ogee', ogief, ojief; ~ **arch,** ogiefboog; ~ **moulding,** ogieflys, vloeilys; ~ **plane,** lysskaaf.
ogiv'al, spitsboogvormig, ogivaal; ~ **arch,** Gotiese boog, spitsboog, ogiefboog.
og'ive, ogief, kruisboog, spitsboog.
o'gle, (n) lonk, oogknip; verliefde blik; (v) toelonk, wink, aangluur, begluur; aanlonk, verliefderig kyk; ~**r,** toelonker, knikker, begluurder.
og'ling, gelonk.
Og'pu, Ogpoe.
o'gre, paaiboelie, skrikbeeld, bullebak.
o'gr(e)ish, paaiboelieagtig, skrikaanjaend.
o(h)! o! ag! og! ~ *dear!,* foeitog!
ohm, ohm; ~ **meter,** ohmmeter.

oho'! o so! o ho! wê!
oid'ium, witroes.
oil, (n) olie; ~ *of ALMONDS,* amandelolie; *BRING* ~ *to fire,* olie op die vlamme gooi; ~ *of CLOVES,* naeltjieolie; *CRUDE* ~, ru-olie; *IN* ~ *(s),* in olieverf; ~ *of LAVENDER,* salieolie, laventelolie; *LUBRICATING* ~, smeerolie; *MINERAL* ~, smeerolie; *burn the MIDNIGHT* ~, tot laat in die nag studeer; *NATURAL* ~, petroleum, aardolie; *PAINT in* ~ *s,* in olieverf skilder; *POUR* ~ *on the fire,* olie op die vlamme gooi; *PUT* ~ *to the fire,* olie op die vuur gooi; die gemoedere weer gaande maak; ~ *of ROSES,* roosolie; *STRIKE* ~, 'n oliebron ontdek; 'n fortuin maak: 'n gelukslag kry; ~ *of VITRIOL,* swa(w)elsuur; *like* ~ *and VINEGAR,* soos dag en nag; soos vuur en water; *pour* ~ *on the troubled WATERS,* olie op die golwe (water) gooi; die gemoedere tot bedaring bring; ~ *will not mix with WATER,* olie en water meng nie; ~ *of WINTERGREEN,* wintergroenolie; (v) olie, smeer; tot olie maak; olie inneem; olie word; in olie lê; ~ *someone's PALM,* iem. omkoop; iem. duimkruid gee; ~ *one's TONGUE,* mooi broodjies bak; ~ *the WHEELS,* die wiele smeer; sake glad laat loop; ~-**atomizer,** olieverstuiwer; ~-**bag,** oliesak; vetklier; ~-**bath,** oliebad; ~-**bean,** sojaboontjie; ~-**bearing,** oliehoudend; ~-**box,** oliepot; ~-**brake,** oliedrukrem; ~-**burner,** oliebrander; oliestookskip; oliestookketel; ~**cake,** oliekoek, lynsaadkoek; ~**can,** oliekan; ~**cloth,** oliekleedjie; ~-**coat,** oliebaadjie; ~-**cock,** oliekraan; ~-**colour,** olieverf; ~ **company,** oliemaatskappy; ~ **consumption,** olieverbruik; ~-**container,** oliekan; ~-**cooler,** oliekoeler; ~-**cup,** oliepot; ~ **drum,** oliekonka; ~**ed,** gesmeer, geolie; geswael, dronk; ~*ed SILK,* gewaterde sy; *be WELL* ~*ed,* goed aangeklam wees; ~ **engine,** oliemotor; ~**er,** oliekan; oliesmeer, smeerder; olieboot; ~-**feed,** olietoevoer; ~-**field,** olieveld; ~ **film,** olielaag; olievlies; ~-**filter,** oliesuiweraar, oliefilter; ~-**fired,** met olie gestook; ~-**flare,** oliefakkel; ~-**fuel,** stookolie; ~-**gauge,** olieaanwyser, oliemeter; ~-**gland,** vetklier; oliekannetjie (hoender); ~-**gun,** oliespuit; ~-**heater,** olieverwarmer; oliekagel; ~**iness,** olieagtigheid; ~-**jar,** oliekruik; ~-**lamp,** olielamp; ~-**less,** sonder olie; ~ **level,** oliepeil, oliestand; ~-**level indicator,** oliewyser; ~ **lubrication,** oliesmering; ~ **man,** oliehandelaar; ~-**measure,** oliemaat; ~-**mill,** oliemeul; ~-**nut,** oliehoudende neut; ~-**paint,** olieverf; ~ **painting,** olieverfskildery; *she is no* ~ *painting,* sy is geen skoonheid nie; ~-**palm,** oliepalm; ~-**pan,** oliebak; ~ **paper,** oliepapier; ~-**pipeline,** oliepyplyn; ~-**press,** oliepers; ~-**pressure,** oliedruk; ~-**proof,** oliedig, oliebestand, olievry; ~-**pump,** oliepomp; ~ **refinery,** olieraffinadery; ~-**rich,** ryk aan olie; ~**s,** olieverf; oliepak; olies; ~-**seed,** oliesaad; ~-**shale,** olieskalie, olieklip; ~ **skin,** oliejas; waskoek; ~ **skin clothing,** oliekIere; ~ **skin cover,** oliekleedjie, oliedeken; ~ **skin fabric,** oliekleed; ~ **skins,** oliepak; ~-**spring,** oliebron; ~-**squirt,** oliespuitjie; ~ **stain,** olievlek, oliekol; ~-**steamer,** olieboot; ~-**stock,** olieflessie, oliedosie; ~ **stone,** oliesteen; slypsteen; ~-**stove,** paraffienstoof; ~ **strainer,** oliesif; ~-**sump,** oliebak; ~-**tank,** olietenk; ~-**tanker,** (olie)tenkskip; ~ **trap,** olievanger; ~ **vapour,** oliedamp; ~-**well,** oliebron; olieboorgat; ~**y,** olieagtig, vet, olierig; glad, salwend.
oint'ment, salf, smeergoed, smeersel.
oka'pi, okapi, boskameelperd.
o'kay, (n) goedkeuring; *give one the* ~, iets goedkeur; (v) goedkeur; ~ *a proposal,* 'n voorstel goedkeur; (interj) reg, in orde, O.K.
okey-do'key, (sl.), reg, in orde, oukei, O.K., doodreg.
old, (n) oue; *OF* ~, vanmelewe; vanouds; *PEOPLE of* ~, vanmelewe se mense; *a SONG of* ~, 'n lied van vanmelewe; (a, adv) oud, ou; slim, geslepe; ouderwets; afgeleef, bejaard; *the* ~ *ADAM,* die ou Adam, die ou mens; *an* ~ *BACHELOR,* 'n oujongkêrel; ~ *BEFORE one's time,* oud voor jou tyd; *an* ~ *BIRD,* 'n ou kalant; ~ *CHAP (boy, fellow, man),* ou kêrel; *the* ~ *COUNTRY,* die moederland, Engeland; *in DAYS of* ~, in die

olden 1087 *on*

ou dae; *she is an* ~ *FORTY*, sy lyk ouer as veertig; ~ *GIRL*, ou vrou (tante); *be an* ~ *HAND at some=thing*, gekonfyt wees in; baie ondervinding van iets hê; *as* ~ *as the HILLS*, so oud soos die Kaapse wapad; uit Noag se ark; *one is never too* ~ *to LEARN*, 'n mens is nooit te oud om te leer nie; ~ *MAID*, oujongnooi; ~ *MAN*, grysaard, ou man; ~ *MAN of the sea*, inkubus; ~ *PEOPLE*, ou men=se; *in any* ~ *PLACE*, net waar jy wil; *an* ~ *SALT*, 'n pikbroek; *any* ~ *THING*, net wat voorkom; *the good* ~ *TIMES*, die goeie ou tyd; ~ *WIVES' tale*, ouwyweverhaal, ouvroustorie; ~ *WOMAN*, ou vrou; papbroek; ~ *in YEARS*, oud in jare; ~ *and YOUNG*, oud en jonk; ~ **age**, die ouderdom; ou=dag; ~ *age has its infirmities*, die ouderdom kom met gebreke; ~-**age home**, ouetehuis; ~-**age pen=sion**, ouderdomspensioen; ~ **blue**, ou porselein; ~ **boy**, oud-leerling; ~-**boys' union**, oud-leerling-bond; ~-**clothesman**, ouklerekoper, voddekoper.

ol'den, (v) verouder; oud word, agteruitgaan; oud maak; (a) oud, vanmelewe, vroeër; *in* ~ *times*, in die ou tyd.

old: ~-**established**, oud, lank gevestig; ~-**fangled**, ~-**fashioned**, ouderwets, outyds, oubakke; oudmo=dies; ~-**fogeyism**, oumensagtigheid; ~ **girl**, oud-meisie (-leerling); O~ **Glory**, Old Glory, die Amerikaanse vlag; ~ **gold**, ougoud; ~**ish**, ouerig, oudagtig; ~ **lag**, tronkvoël; ~**maid**, oujongnooi; ~-**maidish**, oujongnooiagtig; ~ **man**, (sl.), pa, ou-toppie, ou man; ~-**man saltbush**, oumansoutbos; ~ **men's home**, oumannetehuis; ~ **ness**, oudheid, ouderdom; ouderwetsheid; O~ **Nick**, die duiwel; ~ **people's home**, ouetehuis; ~ **stager**, grysaard, ringkop; ~**ster**, ou man, nie vandag se kind nie; ~ **student**, oud-student; O~ **Testament**, Ou Testa=ment; ~-**time**, outyds; ~-**time recipe**, outydse re=sep; ~-**timer**, ou ingesetene; ringkop; ~-**woman=ish**, ouvrouagtig; O~ **World**, die Ou Wêreld; O~ **Year**, Oujaar; O~ **Year's night**, Oujaarsnag.

olea'ginous, olieagtig, vetterig.

olean'der, oleander, selonsroos.

oleas'ter, wildeolyfboom.

olefi'ant, olievormend.

ole'ic: ~ *acid*, oliesuur.

ol'ein, oleïne.

ol'eograph, oleograaf; ..**og'raphy**, oleografie.

oleomarg'arine, kunsbotter, oleomargarien, oleo=margarine.

oleom'eter, oliemeter, oleometer.

o'leum, oleum; olie; swa(w)elsuur.

olfac'tion, reuksin.

olfac'tories, reukorgane.

olfac'tory, (n) reukorgaan; (a) reuk=; ~ **nerve**, reuk-senuwee; ~ **organ**, reukorgaan; ~ **sense**, reuksin.

olib'anum, wierookhars.

olib'enite, olyferts.

ol'id, stink; galsterig.

ol'igarch, oligarg, lid van 'n oligargie; ~'**ic(al)**, oli-gargies; ~**y**, (..**chies**), oligargie.

ol'igocene, oligoseen.

oligo'polist, oligopolis.

oligopol'ogy, oligopolie.

oligop'oly, oligopolie (in die handel).

ol'io, mengelmoes, mengsel; bredie; hutspot; pot=pourri.

oliva'ceous, olyfkleurig, olyfgroen.

ol'ivary, olyfvormig, ovaal.

ol'ive, (n) olyf; olyfboom; *the Mount of O*~*s*, dic Olyfberg; (a) olyfkleurig; ~ **branch**, olyftak; (pl) telg, spruit, kinders; *hold out the* ~ *branch*, 'n olyf-tak aanbied; 'n vredespoging aanwend; ~-**colour**, olyfkleur; ~-**grove**, olyfbos.

oliv'enite, olyferts, oliveniet.

ol'ive: ~ **oil**, olyfolie; ~-**press**, olyfpers; ~-**shaped**, olyfvormig, ~-**tree**, olyfboom; *wild* ~-*tree*, wilde-olyfboom, olienhoutboom; ~-**wood**, oliewenhout, olienhout; ~ **wreath**, olyfkrans.

ol'iver, voethamer.

o'livet, olyfboord; naamaakpêrel; ovale knoop.

ol'ivine, olivien, chrisoliet.

olla podri'da, mengelmoes, mengsel; bredie; pot=pourri.

Olymp'ia, Olimpië.

Olym'piad, Olimpiade; Olimpiese Spele.

Olym'pian, (n) bewoner van Olimpus; (a) Olimpies.

Olym'pic, Olimpies; ~ **games**, Olimpiese spele; ~**s**, Olimpiese spele.

Olymp'us, Olimpus.

omas'um, blaarpens, boekpens.

om'bre, omberspel.

ombrom'eter, reënmeter.

om'budsman, (..**men**), bemiddelaar, onderhande=laar, volkskommissaris, ombudsman.

om'ega, omega, end.

om'elet(te), omelet; *you cannot make an* ~ *without breaking eggs*, 'n mens kan nie vuis maak sonder 'n hand nie; die koste kom voor die winste.

om'en, (n) voorteken, voorbode; *bad (ill)* ~, voor-spooksel; (v) voorspel; aankondig; voorbode wees.

omen'tal hernia, **omen'tocele**, netbreuk.

omen'tum, (..**ta**), netvet, buiknet.

om'inous, onheilspellend, dreigend, ongunstig, veeg.

omiss'ible, weglaatbaar.

omi'ssion, uitlating, weglating; nalatigheid; agtelo=sigheid, versuim; *REPAIR an* ~, 'n fout goedmaak (regmaak); *SINS of* ~ *and commission*, sondes van versuim en bedryf.

omis'sive, weglatend; onvolledig.

omit', (-**ted**), weglaat, oorslaan, uitlaat; versuim; ver-waarloos.

omit'tance, weglating; ~ *is no quittance*, uitstel is nog nie afstel nie.

om'nibus, (-**es**), (omni)bus; ~ **act**, ~ **bill**, rommel-wetsontwerp, versamelwet; ~ **book**, versamelboek, dundrukboek; ~ **edition**, dundrukuitgawe, omni=busuitgawe; ~ **resolution**, omvattende besluit; ~ **service**, omnibusdiens; ~ **toast**, heildronk op die hele bruidsgroep; ~ **train**, boemeltrein.

omnifar'ious, allerhande, verskillend, veelsoortig.

omni'genous, veelsoortig.

omnip'otence, almag, alvermoë.

omnip'otent, almagtig, alvermoënd; *the O*~, die Al=magtige.

omnipres'ence, alomteenwoordigheid.

omnipres'ent, alomteenwoordig.

omni'science, alwetendheid.

omni'scient, alwetend.

omnium gath'erum, deurmekaarspul, mengelmoes.

omni'vidence, alsiendheid.

om'nivore, allesverslinder, omnivoor.

omniv'orous, allesverslindend, allesetend, omni=voor=; ~ *animal*, omnivoor, allesverslinder.

om'oplate, skouerblad.

omphal'ic, na(w)el=.

om'phalocele, na(w)elbreuk.

om'phalos, middelpunt; na(w)el.

omphalo'tomy, naelstringsnyding, omfalotomie.

on, (a) aangedraai, aangeskakel; aan die beurt; *what is* ~ *in the BIOSCOPE*, wat word in die bioskoop vertoon (gewys)?; ~-*CONSUMPTION*, binnever-bruik; ~-*LICENCE*, binnelisensie; *the* ~ *SIDE*, die bykant (beenkant); (adv) aan, deur, op, verder, voorwaarts; ~ *AND* ~, aanhoudend; *well* ~ *in APRIL*, 'n hele entjie in April; *the CASE is* ~, die saak word verhoor; *from that DAY* ~, van dié dag af; *FARTHER* ~, verder vorentoe; verder weg; *the GAS is* ~, die gas is oop; *GO* ~, gaan verder; *be GONE* ~, gesteld wees op; versot wees op; *HAVE* ~, aanhê; *be KEEN* ~, gesteld wees op; versot wees op; *OFF and* ~, nou en dan; ~ *and OFF*, af en toe; *not to know whether one is* ~ *or OFF*, nie weet hoe jy daaraan toe is nie; *be* ~ *to a PERSON*, iem. verdink; iem. dophou; *the PLAY is* ~ *tonight*, die toneelstuk word vanaand opgevoer; *far* ~ *in the SEASON*, laat in die seisoen; *and SO* ~, enso-voorts; *she TURNED her back* ~ *him*, sy het hom die rug gekeer; *WHAT'S* ~ *here?*, wat is hier aan die gang?; ~ *with the WORK!*, hou aan werk! (prep) op, in, aan, te, by, oor, met, van, om; ~ *ACCOUNT*, op rekening; ~ *ACCOUNT of*, omre-de, as gevolg van; ~ *no ACCOUNT*, hoegenaamd nie; ~ *APPRO*, op sig; ~ *ARRIVING (arrival)*, by (my) aankoms; ~ *an AVERAGE*, gemiddeld; ~ *or BEFORE*, voor of op; ~ *BOARD*, aan boord;

~ *the BORDER*, op die grens; *have something ~ the BRAIN*, gedurig deur iets gekwel (gepla) word; ~ *BUSINESS*, vir sake; ~ *CALL*, ter beskikking; ~ *CONDITION*, op voorwaarde; *DEBATE ~ foreign affairs*, debat oor buitelandse sake; ~ *DECK*, op die dek; ~ *DELIVERY*, by aflewering; ~ *DEPARTURE*, by vertrek; ~ *the DOT of one o'clock*, presies om eenuur; *be ~ DUTY*, diens doen (hê); werk; *look like nothing ~ EARTH*, daar aaklig uitsien; ~ *FIRE*, aan die brand; ~ *FOOT*, te voet; ~ *FULL pay*, met volle betaling; *be ~ the GO*, aan die gang (doenig) wees; ~ *GUARD*, op wag; *be ~ one's GUARD*, op jou hoede wees; ~ *HALF pay*, met halwe betaling; ~ *all HANDS*, van alkante; ~ *HIGH*, in die hoogte; omhoog; ~ *HOLIDAY*, met vakansie; ~ *my (word of) HONOUR*, op my erewoord; *be ~ one's HONOUR*, op jou erewoord gesteld wees; ~ *HORSEBACK*, te perd; *it's ~ the HOUSE*, dis gratis; ~ *the INSTANT*, op die daad; onmiddellik; ~ *a JOURNEY*, op reis; ~ *the LEFT*, links; ~ *LINE*, op (aan) lyn, ingeskakel, verbind (rekenaar by 'n hoofrekenaar); ~ *LOAN*, geleen; in bruikleen; ~ *the LOOK-OUT*, op die uitkyk; ~ *the MAKE*, uit winsbejag; *MARCH ~ a city*, teen 'n stad opruk; *the next round is ~ ME*, ek betaal die volgende ronde; ~ *MERIT*, na verdienste; ~ *the MINUTE*, op die minuut; ~ *such OCCASIONS*, by sulke geleenthede; ~ *PARADE*, op parade; ~ *PENALTY of*, op straf van; ~ *PENSION*, met pensioen; *win ~ POINTS*, met punte wen; ~ *POSITION*, aangeskakelde stand; aanstand (elektr.); ~ *PRINCIPLE*, uit beginsel; ~ *PROBATION*, op proef, op parool; ~ *PURPOSE*, opsetlik; ~ *the QUIET*, skelmpies; ~ *RECEIPT*, by ontvangs; ~ *my RETURN*, by my terugkeer; ~ *the RIGHT*, regs; ~ *the RUN*, op die vlug; voortvlugtig; ~ *a large SCALE*, op groot skaal; ~ *the SEA*, aan die see; ~ *active SERVICE*, in aktiewe diens, te velde, op diens; ~ *the SHORE*, op die strand; ~ *the SLY*, stilletjies, skelm, agteraf; ~ *the STAFF*, by die personeel; ~ *SUNDAY*, op Sondag; *talk ~ a SUBJECT*, oor 'n onderwerp praat; ~ *TIME*, betyds; *have someone ~ TOAST*, die gek skeer met iem; *be ~ one's TOES*, wakker wees; ~ *the UNDERSTANDING*, met dien verstande; *be ~ a VISIT*, op besoek wees; *declare WAR ~*, oorlog verklaar teen; *wage WAR ~*, oorlog voer teen; ~ *the WING*, vlieënd, in die vlieg; in die vlug.

on'ager, (-s, onagri), wilde esel (donkie), onager.
on'anism, selfbevlekking, onanie, masturbasie.
on'anist, selfbevlekker, masturbeerder.
once, (n) een keer; *FOR ~ he behaved himself*; hierdie keer het hy hom gedra; *THIS ~*, hierdie keer; (a) vroeër; eertyds; (adv) een keer (spesifiek); eendag, eenslag, eenkeer; eens, eenmaal; ~ *AGAIN*, nog een maal; ~ *and AGAIN*, af en toe; nou en dan; ~ *(and) for ALL*, vir goed, finaal; *ALL at ~*, skielik, plotseling; *AT ~*, terstond, dadelik, onmiddellik; ~ *in a BLUE moon*, baie selde; ~ *MORE*, nog 'n keer; ~ *upon a TIME*, eenmaal; ~ *or TWICE*, een of twee maal; ~ *bitten, TWICE shy*, 'n esel stamp hom nie twee maal teen dieselfde klip nie; ~ *in a WAY (while)*, so nou en dan; 'n enkele maal; (conj) sodra, as; ~ *he finds out*, sodra hy uitvind.
once'-over, vlugtige blik; vinnige ondersoek; *give something the ~*, die oog vinnig oor iets laat gaan.
oncoge'nic, onco'genous, onkogeen, onkogenies, geswasvormend.
onco'logy, onkologie, gewasleer, gewaskunde.
on'coming, (n) nadering; (a) naderend, aanstaande.
on'-consumption, binnegebruik.
on'-cost, bokoste, algemene koste.
one, (n) een; *what A ~ he is!*, wat 'n eienaardige mens is hy nie; ~ *AFTER another*, een-een; die een na die ander; ~ *and ALL*, almal saam; soos een man; die laaste een; *ALL in ~*, in een stuk; *be ALL ~ to*, eenders wees; om die ewe wees; *it is ALL ~*, dis alles eenders; ~ *with ANOTHER*, deur die bank, gemiddeld; *BE at ~*, dit eens wees; saamstem; versoen wees; *BECOME ~*, saamsmelt; een word; *go ~ BETTER*, oortroef; meer waag; *is no BET-*

TER than the other, dis vinkel en koljander, die een is soos die ander; die een is nie beter as die ander nie; *COME ~s and twos*, een-een en twee-twee kom; *COME at ~*, kom om eenuur; *they had ~ over the EIGHT*, die skoot hoog deur hê; *EVERY ~*, elkeen; *the EVIL ~*, die duiwel; *give a person ~ in the EYE*, iem. 'n hou op die oog gee (slaan); *I FOR ~*, wat my betref; *FOR ~ thing*, om maar een voorbeeld te noem; *the GREAT ~s*, die grotes; die groot ooms; *a KNOWING ~*, 'n ou kalant; *to be about to be MADE ~*, die skapies bymekaar gaan jaag; die velletjies bymekaar gaan gooi; *MAKE ~*, een wees; jou by die ander aansluit; *MANY a ~*, baie; *he is ~ too MANY for me*, hy is my moses; hy is my oor; *that was ~ too MANY for him*, dit was bokant sy vuurmaakplek; dit was meer as hy kon uitstaan; *that was a NASTY ~*, dit was 'n harde (geniepsige) hou; *NUMBER ~*, die eie ek; die eerste; *the ONLY ~ of its kind*, die enigste van sy soort; enig in sy soort; *in ~s and TWOS*, een-een en twee-twee; ~ *for the ROAD*, 'n glasie op die valreep, loopdop; *TEN to ~*, tien teen een; hoogs onwaarskynlik; *be ~ UP on*, 'n voorsprong op iem. hê; iem. voor wees; *in the YEAR ~*, in die jaar nul; (pron) 'n mens, een; ~ *ANOTHER*, mekaar; ~ *after ANOTHER*, die een na die ander; *DEAR ~*, liefste, beminde; ~ *in the EYE*, 'n slag op die oog; *the LITTLE ~s*, die kleintjies, die kleinspan; ~ *may easily LOSE ~'s way*, mens kan maklik verdwaal; *like ~ MAD*, soos 'n besetene; ~ *MORE*, nog een; *you're a NICE ~!*, jy is 'n mooie!; ~ *or OTHER*, die een of ander; (a) een; enigste; ~ *DAY*, eenmaal, eendag; ~ *BY ~*, een-een, een vir een; ~ *JOHN*, 'n seker(e) Jan; ~ *and a HALF*, anderhalf, een-en-'n-half; ~ *HOUR*, een uur; *as ~ MAN*, almal, almal sonder uitsondering; soos een man; ~ *MAN ~ vote*, een man, een stem; *be ~ too MANY for someone*, iem. baasraak; iem. oor wees; ~ *man's MEAT is another man's poison*, die een se dood is die ander se brood; *for ~ REASON and (or) another*, om meer as een rede; *at ~ TIME*, 'n tyd lank; tegelykertyd; ~ *at a TIME*, een-een; ~ *or TWO people*, 'n stuk of wat mense, 'n paar mense; *my ~ WISH*, my enigste wens; *the ~ and only WAY*, die enigste manier; *not ~ WORD*, geen enkele woord nie; ~ **act**, eenbedryf; ~**-act play**, eenakter, eenbedryf; ~**-armed**, eenarmig, met een arm; ~**-day**, eendaags; ~**-day lily**, daglelie; ~**-eyed**, eenogig, eenoog=, met een oog; ~ **fold**, enkelvoudig; ~**-footed**, met een voet; ~**-handed**, met een hand; ~**-hoofed**, eenhoewig.
one'-horse, (a) eenperd=; armoedig, armsalig; *a ~ SHOW*, nie veel snaaks nie; 'n armsalige gedoente; *a ~ TOWN*, 'n stil dorpie; 'n slaapdorp(ie).
oneirocrit'ic, droomuitlêer.
oneirol'ogy, droomuitlegkunde.
oneir'omancy, droomuitleg(ging).
one: ~**-leaved**, eenbladig; ~**-legged**, eenbeen=, eenbenig, eenvoetig; met een been; ongelyk; ~**-man**, (a) eenmans=; eenpersoons=; ~**-man school**, eenmanskool; ~ **ness**, eenheid; samestemming; onveranderlikheid.
one'-party, eenparty=; ~ **state**, eenpartystaat; ~ **system**, eenpartystelsel.
one: ~**-piece**, (a) uit een stuk; ~**-pounder**, pompom, eenponder; eenpondnoot.
on'er, een (by kennetjie); een (lopie by krieket); doring (fig.); opstopper; vervlaekste leuen; *he GOT a ~ on the jaw*, hy het 'n opstopper gekry; *a ~ at RUNNING*, 'n baashardloper.
on'erous, swaar, drukkend; ~**ness**, gewig, las, druk, swaarte.
one'-seater, eensitplekmotor; eensitplekvliegtuig.
oneself', homself, haarself, jouself; sig(self); *BESIDE ~ with rage*, dol van woede; *BY ~*, alleen; *KEEP to ~*, eenkant bly; hy nie met ander omgaan nie; *OF ~*, vanself; *THINK to ~*, by jouself dink.
one: ~**-sided**, eensydig; partydig; bekrompe; ~**-sidedness**, eensydigheid; partydigheid; ~**-step**, stapdans; ~**-storeyed**, eenverdieping=, met een verdieping; ~**-stringed**, eensnarig; ~**-time**, (a) eertyds, voormalig.

one'-track mind: have a ~, jou op een ding blind staar.
one-way, (a) eenrigting=; ~ **road**, eenrigtingpad; ~ **traffic**, eenrigtingverkeer; ~ **street**, eenrigting=straat.
on'flow, toevloed, stroom.
on'going, (n) voortgang; gebeurtenis; (pl) uitspat=tings; gedrag, bedrywighede, dinge; (a) voortgaan=de.
on'ion, (n) ui(e); *BED of* ~ *s*, uieakkertjie, uiebed=ding; *KNOW one's* ~ *s*, uitgeslape wees; jou kaarte ken; *OFF one's* ~, gek, dol; *sliced and PICKLED* ~ *s*, ajuin; (v) 'n ui aansmeer; met 'n ui vrywe; ~ **flavour**, uiesmaak; ~ **leaves**, uielof; ~ **like**, uieag=tig; ~ **salad**, uieslaai; ~ **sauce**, uiesous; ~-**shaped**, uivormig; ~ **smell**, uielug; ~ -**soup**, uiesop; ~ -**stew**, uiebredie; ~ **y**, uieagtig.
on'looker, toeskouer, aankyker, omstander, aan=skouer.
on'ly, (a) enig, enigste; *an* ~ *CHILD*, 'n enigste kind; *my one and* ~ *HOPE*, my enigste hoop; *the* ~ *one of its KIND*, die enigste van sy soort; *the* ~ *THING we can do is*, al wat ons kan doen, is; (adv) enigste, alleen, slegs, enkel, pas, maar net; *not* ~ *but ALSO*, nie alleen nie . . . maar ook; *it is* ~ *FAIR to say*, billikheidshalwe moet gesê word; ~ *too GLAD*, maar alte bly; *it is* ~ *HUMAN*, dis maar menslik; ~ *JUST*, so pas, nou net; *MEMBERS* ~, net lede; ~ *THINK*, dink net; *it is* ~ *RIGHT*, dis nie meer as reg nie; ~ *YESTERDAY*, nog gister; (conj) al=leen, eers, maar, as; *he is a capable worker*, ~ . . ., hy is 'n bekwame werker, maar . . .; ~ -**begotten**, eniggebore.
onomast'ics, naamkunde, onomastiek.
onomast'ical, naamkundig, onomasties.
onomatopoe'ia, klanknabootsing, onomatopee.
onomatopoe'ic, onomatopoet'ic, klanknabootsend, onomatopeïes.
on-ramp, (n) oprit (verkeer).
on'rush, stormloop, opmars, aanval.
on'set, aanval, begin.
on'-side, bykant; speelkant; ~ **drive**, bykantdryf=hou.
on'slaught, aanval, bestorming, stormloop.
on-stage, op die verhoog, sigbaar (vir die toeskouers).
on-the-spot', ter plaatse.
on'to, op, na, tot, by.
ontogen'esis, ontwikkelingsgeskiedenis, ontogenese.
ontogenet'ic, ontogeneties.
ontog'eny, ontogenie.
ontolog'ic(al), ontologies.
ontol'ogy, ontologie, wesensleer, synsleer.
on'us, (onera), (bewys)las; verpligting; verantwoorde=likheid, onus; ~ *PROBANDI*, bewyslas; ~ *of PROOF*, bewyslas.
on'ward, voorwaarts.
on'ward(s), voorwaarts, verder, vooruit, voort.
on'yx, (-es), oniks.
o'ocyst, oösist.
o'ocyte, oösiet, oereier.
oo'dles, oorvloed, volop, hope; ~ *of money*, geld soos bossies.
oof, (sl.), geld, blik; ~ -**bird**, goudmyn; miljoenêr; ~ **y**, skatryk.
ooh! alla! o!
o'olite, oöliet, kuitsteen, eiersteen.
o'olith, oölietkorrel.
oolog'ic(al), eierkundig, oölogies.
ool'ogist, eierkundige, oöloog.
ool'ogy, eierkunde, oölogie.
oo'long, oelong(tee).
oom'pah, oempa; ~ **band**, oempaorkes.
oomph, (sl.), geslagsbekoring, aantreklikheid.
oops! aitsa!
o'osperm, bevrugte eier(sel), oösperm.
ooze, (n) slib, slik, modder; afsaksel, slyk; (v) (uit)sy=pel, syfer, syg, lek; *his courage* ~ *d AWAY*, sy moed het in sy skoene gesink; *he* ~ *d CHARM*, hy het oorgeloop van vriendelikheid; ~ *OUT*, uitsak, deursyfer.
ooz'iness, modderigheid.
ooz'y, modderig.

opa'city, donkerheid, duisterheid; ondeurskynend=heid, ondeursigtigheid; domheid; dekvermoë.
op'al, opaal; ~ **esce'**, kleure versprei; ~ **es'cence**, opa=lisering, opaalglans; ~ **es'cent**, ~ **ine**, opaalglan=send, opaalagtig, opaal=; ~ **glass**, opaalglas.
opaque', (n) donkerheid, duisternis; (a) ondeursky=nend; onduidelik; donker; dom; ~ **ness** = **opacity**.
op'en, (n) die oop veld; ope lug; ruimte; *BRING into the* ~, openbaar; *COME into the* ~, te voorskyn tree; openlik optree; *in THE* ~, in die oop lug, on=der die blote hemel; (v) oopmaak (brief); oopkry (blik); inlei (onderwerp); oopgaan; oopstel; begin; blootlê; oprig; inwy (gebou); open, uitkom (kamer op stoep); verruim; ~ *on to a BALCONY*, op 'n balkon uitkom; ~ *the BALL*, die bal open; 'n saak aan die gang sit; die bal aan die rol sit; *I will BE quite* ~ *with you*, ek sal jou heeltemal openhartig behandel; ~ *the BOWELS*, opelyf laat kry; *BURST* ~, oopbeur; oopbreek; oopbars; *CUT* ~, oopsny; ~ *the DOOR to*, die deur oopmaak vir; die geleentheid skep vir; ~ -**ended** *QUESTION*, vry=antwoordvraag; ~ *someone's EYES*, iem. se oë oopmaak; ~ *a FILE on*, 'n lêer oor iets aanlê; ~ *FIRE*, losbrand, begin skiet; *LIE* ~, oop en bloot lê; ~ *the MIND to*, die gemoed oopstel vir, ~ *u MINE*, 'n myn ontgin; ~ *OUT*, oopmaak; oop=gaan; uitsprei; ontwikkel; *the stranger began to* ~ *OUT*, die vreemdeling het begin ontdooi; ~ *a SHOP*, 'n winkel begin (open); *THROW* ~, oop=stel; oopgooi; ~ *UP*, oopmaak; toeganklik maak; ~ *UP the possibility*, die moontlikheid skep; (a) oop, openhartig, rondborstig; openlik; blootgestel; vatbaar, ontvanklik; ~ *ARREST*, kamerarres; ~ *to CONVICTION*, vir oortuiging vatbaar; *In* ~ *COURT*, in openbare sitting; *keep* ~ *DOORS*, gasvry wees; baie ontvang; ~ *to DOUBT*, aan twy=fel onderhewig; *an* ~ *ENEMY*, 'n verklaarde vy=and; *an* ~ *HAND*, 'n oop (vrygewige) hand; *keep* ~ *HOUSE*, gasvry wees; *LAY oneself* ~ *to criti=cism*, jou blootstel aan kritiek; *in the* ~ *MARKET*, op die oop mark; *with an* ~ *MIND*, met onbevoor=oordeelde gemoed; *have an* ~ *MIND*, onbevoor=oordeel wees; ontvanklik wees vir nuwe begrippe; ~ *MINE*, oop myn; ~ *MINING*, dagbou; *in* ~ *ORDER*, versprei opgestel; *an* ~ *QUESTION*, 'n onuitgemaakte saak; 'n onbesliste punt; 'n ope vraag; ~ *SEA*, volle (oop) see; *an* ~ *SECRET*, 'n openbare geheim; ~ *SIGHT*, oop visier; ~ *TO abuse*, vatbaar vir misbruik; ~ *TO the public*, oop vir die publiek; *I am* ~ *to SUGGESTIONS*, ek ont=vang graag wenke; ~ *VERDICT*, onbesliste uit=spraak; ~ **able**, oopmaakbaar; ~ **air**, buitelug; ~ -**air meeting**, opelugvergadering; ~ -**air theatre**, buitelugteater; ~ -**armed**, met ope arms; ~ **cast**, oop, dagbou= (myn); ~ **cast workings**, dagmyn, oop delfplek; ~ -**circuit television**, oopbaanelevi=sie; ~ **city**, oop (onverskanste) stad; ~ **country**, onbeboude landskap; platteland; oop grond(ge=bied); ~ **court**, ope hof; ~ **day**, opedag; ~ -**eared**, met oop ore; ~ -**ended**, oop, sonder beperking(s); ~ **er**, inleier (debat); oopmaker; openingskolwer; ~ -**eyed**, waaksaam; met oop oë; ~ -**handed**, mild, vrygewig, rojaal, skeutig, liberaal; ~ -**handedness**, mildheid, skeutigheid, vrygewigheid; ~ **harmony**, oop harmonie; ~ -**hearted**, openhartig; ~ -**hearted=ness**, openhartigheid; ~ -**heart operation**, opehart=operasie; ~ -**hearth process**, opeherdproses; ~ **ice**, oop ys (seevaart).
op'ening, (n) opening; spasie; gat; begin; inleiding; kans; geleentheid; inwyding; vakature; *have an* ~ *for an apprentice*, 'n leerjonge kan plaas; (a) aan=vangs=, openings=, inleidings=, eerste; purgerend (medisyne); ~ *CEREMONY*, openingsplegtig=heid; ~ *LINES*, aanhef; ~ *PARAGRAPH*, begin=paragraaf; ~ *SPEECH*, openingsrede; ~ **bats=man**, openingskolwer (kr.).
op'en: ~ **letter**, ope brief; ~ **ly**, openlik; openbaar; openhartig, rondborstig, onverbloemd; ~ **market**, ope (vrye) mark; ~ -**minded**, onbevooroordeeld, onbevange; ontvanklik.
op'en-mouthed, oopmond, met oop mond; dronkge=slaan; *LISTEN* ~, oopmond luister; *LOOK on* ~,

jou vergaap aan; *he STARED* ~, sy mond het oopgehang.

op'en: ~**-neck(ed) shirt,** oop hemp; ~ **ness,** openhartigheid; oopheid; ~ **order,** oop orde (mil.); ~ **plan,** oop kantoor(plan); ~ **prison,** oop gevangenis (tronk); ~ **question,** ope vraag; ~ **sandwich,** sny brood; ~ **sea,** oop see; ~ **season,** ope (jag)seisoen; ~ **shelf,** oop rak; ~ **shop,** oop winkel; oop; ~ **society,** oop maatskapy; ~ **space,** oop ruimte; ~ **weave,** gaatjiesweefwerk; ~**-work,** gaatjieswerk, oopwerk.

op'era, opera; operagebou; *COMIC* ~, komiese opera; *GRAND* ~, opera; *PERFORM an* ~, 'n opera uitvoer; *SING in* ~, in operas sing; ~**-cloak,** aandmantel; ~**-dancer,** baletdanser(es); ~**-glasses,** toneelkyker; ~**-hat,** klapkeil, gibus; ~**-house,** operagebou; ~**-singer,** operasinger.

op'erable, opereerbaar.

o'perand, operandus.

op'erate, werk, fungeer; opereer, sny (pasiënt); uitwerking hê; bewerk; teweegbring, veroorsaak; bestuur; hanteer, bedien (masjien); eksploiteer; in werking tree; werk met; reël; ~ *an ACCOUNT,* op 'n rekening werk; ~ *d BY,* gedryf deur; ~ *ON,* opereer op.

operat'ic, operaägtig, opera-.

op'erating, werkend; opererend; ~ **clause,** inwerkingtredingsklousule; *the* ~ *clause of a bill,* die artikel wat die inwerkingtreding van 'n wetsontwerp bepaal; ~ **costs,** bedryfskoste; ~ **crew,** bedryfsbemanning; ~ **gear,** dryfmeganiek; ~ **loss,** bedryfsverlies; ~ **room,** snykamer, operasiekamer; ~ **table,** snytafel, operasietafel; ~ **theatre,** operasiesaal, teater.

opera'tion, werking; bewerking; proses; krygsverrigting, onderneming, maneuver (mil.); verrigting; bediening; eksploitasie; operasie; *BE in* ~, in werking wees; *COME into* ~, in werking tree; *IN* ~, in werking; *PERFORM an* ~, 'n operasie doen; *PUT into* ~, in werking stel; aan die gang sit; *UNLAWFUL* ~, onwettige operasie; ~**al,** operasie-; bedryfs-; gevegs-, stryd-; werkings-, operatief; ~ **area,** gevegsveld, operasieveld; ~ **centre,** operasiesentrale, operasiesentrum.

op'erative, (n) arbeider, ambagsman, werk(s)man; werktuigkundige; (a) werkend, werksaam, aan die werk, arbeidend, operatief; werkdadig, doeltreffend; prakties; snykundig; meganies; *become* ~, in werking tree; van krag word.

op'erator, werker; ondernemer; eksploitant; hanteerder; beheerder; operateur, instrumentseiner; telegrafis; telefonis; bediener; operator.

op'eratrix, (..trices), operatrise.

operc'ulum, (..la), kieudeksel, deksel.

operett'a, operette; sangspel.

op'erose, bedrywig, ywerig, fluks; vermoeiend, swaar.

ophid'ian, (n) slang; (a) slangagtig.

ophidophob'ia, vrees vir slange.

ophid'ium, slangvis.

ophiol'atry, slangaanbidding.

ophiol'ogy, ofiologie.

ophiomorph'ous, slangvormig.

O'phir, Ofir.

o'phite, ofiet, serpentyn(marmer).

oph'ites, slangaanbidders; slangdienaars.

ophthal'mia, oogontsteking, oogsiekte, oftalmie.

ophthal'mic, (n) oogmiddel; (a) oog-, oftalmies; ~ **clinic,** oogkliniek; ~ **remedy,** oogmiddel; ~ **surgeon,** oogarts, oogkundige.

ophthalmol'ogy, oogheelkunde.

ophthal'moscope, oogspieël, oftalmoskoop.

opthalmos'copy, oftalmoskopie, ondersoek met die oogspieël.

op'iate, (n) slaapmiddel; pynstiller; opiaat; opiumpreparaat; (v) met opium meng; (a) slaapwekkend; pynstillend, verdowend.

opine', van mening wees, meen, dink, veronderstel.

opin'ion, mening, gevoel, sienswyse; denkbeeld; goeddunke; denkwyse, gedagte, opinie; advies, oordeel; dunk; *DIFFERENCE of* ~, meningsverskil; ~ *is DIVIDED,* die gevoelens is verdeeld; *HAVE a good* ~ *of,* baie dink van; *have a HIGH* ~ *of,* 'n hoë dunk hê van; *IN my* ~, volgens my mening; myns insiens; *LEGAL* ~, regsadvies; *a MATTER of* ~, 'n kwestieuse saak; 'n saak waaroor menings uiteenloop; *be OF the* ~, van mening wees; die sienswyse huldig; *PUBLIC* ~, die openbare mening; *STICK to one's* ~, by jou standpunt bly; *there can be no TWO* ~ *s about it,* daaroor bestaan geen twyfel nie.

opin'ionated, opin'ionative, koppig, eiewys, eiesinnig, styfhoofdig, waanwys.

opin'ion: ~ **former,** meningvormer, gedagtevormer; ~**ist,** dwarskop; ~ **poll,** meningopname, meningpeiling, opiniepeiling.

opisom'eter, kromlynmeter, opisometer.

op'ium, opium; *CONSUMPTION of* ~, opiumverbruik; *STATE CONTROL of* ~*-production,* opiumregie; *TINCTURE of* ~, opiumtinktuur; ~ **den,** opiumhol; ~**-eater,** opiumeter; ~ **extract,** opiumekstrak; ~ **farm,** opiumpag; ~ **pipe,** opiumpyp; ~ **smoker,** opiumroker; ~**-smuggler,** opiumsmokkelaar; ~ **trade,** opiumhandel.

opodel'doc, seepsmeergoed, opodeldok.

opo'panax, opopanaks, gomhars; ~ **tree,** gomboom.

oposs'um, buidelrot, opossum.

opp'idan, (n) stedeling, stadsbewoner; (a) stads-, stedelik.

opp'ilate, verstop.

oppila'tion, verstopping.

oppon'ent, (n) teenstander, wederparty, opponent; bestryder; (a) teenstrydend, teenwerkend; strydig, vyandig.

opp'ortune, geleë, tydig; gunstig, geskik; van pas; ~**ly,** op die regte tyd; ~**ness,** geskiktheid.

opportun'ism, opportunisme.

opportun'ist, opportunis.

opportunist'ic, opportunisties.

opportun'ity, (..ties), geleentheid; kans; *AFFORD an* ~, 'n geleentheid bied; *AVAIL oneself of the* ~, die geleentheid gebruik; *HAVE the* ~, die geleentheid kry; ~ *MAKES the thief,* die geleentheid maak die geneentheid; *SEIZE the* ~ *to,* die geleentheid aangryp om; *as* ~ *SERVES,* by geleentheid; *let the* ~ *SLIP through one's fingers,* die kans laat verbyglip (verbygaan); *TAKE the* ~, die geleentheid gebruik.

oppose', bestry, weerstaan, weerstreef, teenwerk, opponeer; teenoor stel; jou versit teen; ~ *d ELECTION,* bestrede verkiesing; *FIRMLY* ~ *d to,* sterk gekant teen; *as* ~ *d TO,* teenoor; ~ **r,** teenstander, opponent, bestryder; verdediger.

opp'osite, (n) teenoorgestelde, teendeel; ~ *s ATTRACT (take to) each other,* uiterstes trek mekaar aan; (a) teen(oor)gestel(d), teenoorgeleë, teenoormekaarstaande, teen-; *in the* ~ *CASE,* in die teenoorgekeerde geval; *in* ~ *DIRECTIONS,* in teenoorgestelde rigtings; *the* ~ *PARTY,* die teenparty; *the* ~ *SEX,* die ander geslag; *the* ~ *SIDE,* die oorkant, anderkant; (adv) oorkant, anderkant; (prep) (daar)teenoor, regoor; anderkant; *nearly* ~ *the post office,* skuins teenoor die poskantoor; ~ **angle,** oorstaande hoek; ~ **bank,** oorkantste wal; ~ **number,** teenspeler; teenhanger; kollega; ~ **page,** teenoorstaande bladsy; ~ **sign,** teengestelde teken.

opposi'tion, teenstand, opposisie, verset, weerstand, weerstrewing; teenparty; teenstelling; *BE in (the)* ~, tot die opposisie behoort; *in the FACE of all* ~, ten spyte van alle teenstand; teen alle teenstand in; *IN* ~ *to,* in stryd met; *LEADER of the* ~, opposisieleier; *MEET with no* ~, geen teenstand kry nie; *SET up in* ~ *to,* mededingend optree teen; *SPIRIT of* ~, opposisiegees; *in SPITE of* ~, ten spyte van teenstand; ~ **ist,** (n) opposisielid; (a) opposisie-; ~ **paper,** opposisieblad; ~ **sign,** teengestelde teken; ~ **team,** teenspan; ~ **vote,** opposisiestem.

oppos'itive, weerbarstig, dwarstrekkerig, weerstrewig.

oppress', onderdruk, (ver)druk, beklem, benou, beswaar; ~ **ed,** (n) verdrukte; *the* ~, die verdruktes; (a) benoud, terneergedruk; verdruk; ~ *ed with the heat,* beklem deur die hitte; ~ **ion,** onderdrukking, verdrukking; benoudheid, beklemming, beklemd-

heid, beswaring; *feeling of* ~*ion*, bedrukte gevoel; ~**ive**, onderdrukkend, (ver)drukkend; benouend, drukkend; lastig; swoel; ~**iveness**, druk; swoelheid, swoelte; ~**or**, onderdrukker, verdrukker, tiran, geweldenaar.
opprob'rious, veragtelik, smadelik; beledigend, skimpend, smalend; ~**ness**, veragtelikheid.
opprob'rium, skande, oneer, smaad.
oppugn', bestry, aanval; in twyfel trek; weerlê; ~**ance**, ~**ancy**, teenstand, stryd, vyandigheid; ~**ant**, strydig.
op'simath, opsimaat, iem. wat laat eers leer; ~**y**, opsimatie, laatbloei (student, geleerde).
op'sonin, opsonien, -ine.
opt, 'n keuse uitoefen, kies; ~ *FOR*, verkies; ~ *OUT of*, jou onttrek aan.
op'tative, (n) optatief; (a) wensend, optatief; ~ **mood**, wensende wyse, optatiewe wyse.
op'tic, (n) lens; oog; optika; (a) gesigs-, opties, oog-; ~**al**, opties, gesigs-; ~*al illusion*, gesigsbedrog; ~ **angle**, gesigshoek; ~ **delusion**, oëverblindery; ~**ian**, brilmaker, optisiën, optikus; ~ **nerve**, oogsenuwee; ~**s**, gesigskunde, optika.
op'timal, beste, gunstigste, optimaal.
op'timism, optimisme.
op'timist, optimis; ..**mis'tic**, optimisties, hoopvol.
op'timization, optmisering, optimalisering.
op'timize, optimiseer, optimaliseer.
op'timum, (n) optimum; (a) beste, optimaal.
op'tion, opsie, keuse, voorkeur; verkoopreg; verkiesing; reg van keuse; *AT my* ~, na my keuse; *the* ~ *of a FINE*, boetekeuse; *HAVE no* ~ *but*, niks anders te doen staan nie as; *HAVE an* ~ *between German and mathematics*, 'n keuse hê tussen Duits en wiskunde; *an* ~ *on a HOUSE*, 'n opsie op 'n huis; *LOCAL* ~, plaaslike keuse; ~**al**, opsioneel, na keuse, nie-verpligtend, fakultatief; ~*al subject*, keusevak.
optom'eter, optometer, gesigsmeter.
optom'etrist, gesigskundige, optometris.
optom'etry, gesigskunde, optometrie.
op'tophone, optofoon.
op'ulence, rykdom, welgesteldheid; oorvloed, weelde.
op'ulent, ryk, oorvloedig, weelderig; welgesteld.
opun'tia, opuntia, turksvy.
op'us, (opera), opus; musiekstuk; werk; *magnum* ~, groot werk, vernaamste werk, magnum opus.
opus'cule, (-s), **opus'culum**, (..la), werkie.
or¹, (n) goud (her.).
or², (conj) of; anders; *he is an AGENT* ~ *something*, hy is 'n agent of so iets; *a DAY* ~ *so*, 'n dag of wat; *a DAY* ~ *two*, twee of drie dae; ~ *ELSE*, of anders; *EITHER* . . . ~, of . . . of; *VERY sensible*; ~ *is it?* baie verstandig; of is dit so?
o'racle, godspraak, orakel; vraagbaak; *work the* ~, agter die skerms werk, konkel.
orac'ular, dubbelsinnig, duister, geheimsinnig, raaiselagtig, orakelagtig.
o'racy, vloeiende spraakvermoë, redenaarsvermoë, welsprekendheid.
or'al, mondeling; mond-; oraal; ~ **administration**, mondelike toediening; ~ **cavity**, mondholte; ~ **confession**, oorbieg, ~ **examination**, mondelinge eksamen; ~**ly**, mondelik; mondeling; oraal.
o'range, (n) lemoen, soetlemoen; oranjekleur; *HOUSE of O* ~, Huis van Oranje; ~*s and LEMONS*, aljander (deurkruipspeletjie); *SQUEEZE the* ~, droog tap; die pit uithaal; (a) oranjegeel, oranje; ~**ade'**, lemoendrank; ~ **aphis**, lemoenluis; ~ **bitters**, oranjebitter; ~-**blossom**, lemoenbloeisel; ~-**coloured**, lemoenkleurig; ~ **creeper**, oranje klimop; ~ **crush**, lemoensap; ~ **favour**, oranjestrikkie, ~ **fin**, forel; ~ **flavour**, lemoengeur; **O** ~ **Free State**, Oranje-Vrystaat; ~ **grove**, lemoenboord; **O** ~ **ism**, Oranjegesindheid; **O** ~ **ist**, (n) Oranjeman; (a) Oranjegesind; **O** ~ **man**, Oranjeman; ~ **juice**, lemoensap; **O** ~ **Nassau**, Oranje-Nassau; ~ **oil**, lemoenolie; ~ **orchard**, lemoenboord; ~ **peel**, lemoenskil; ~ **ry**, (..ries), oranjerie; ~ **squash**, lemoendrank; **O** ~ **squeezer**, lemoenpers; ~ **stick**, lemoenstokkie; ~ **syrup**, lemoenstroop; ~-**throated longclaw**, kalkoentjie; ~ **tree**, lemoenboom; ~-**wood**, lemoenhout.

or'angist, lemoenkweker.
orang'-outang', orang-oetang.
orate', 'n redevoering hou, oreer.
ora'tion, rede(voering), toespraak, orasie.
or'ator, spreker, redenaar, redevoerder, orator; ~'**ical**, oratories, redenaars-.
orator'io, (-s), oratorium.
o'ratory¹, welsprekendheid, redenaarskuns; retoriek.
o'ratory², (..ries), kapel, bidkamer, bidplek, bidvertrek, oratorium.
o'ratress, (-es), redenaarster, spreekster.
orb, (n) bol, sfeer; loopbaan; kring; oog(appel); hemelliggaam; ryksappel; *celestial* ~*s*, hemelbolle; (v) omsluit; rond maak; in 'n kring beweeg; ~**ed**, rond, sirkelvormig; ~**ic'ular**, rond, bolvormig; sirkelrond, sirkelvormig; ~*icular muscle*, kringspier.
orb'it, (n) oogholte; loopkring; wentelbaan, baan (van hemelliggaam); *go into* ~, in 'n baan beweeg; (v) wentel (in 'n baan); omsirkel; ~**al**, baan-; oog- (biol.); ~*al bomb*, wentelbom.
orc, stormvis; (see)monster; ork.
orch'ard, boord, vrugteboord, boomgaard; ~**ing**, vrugtebou, vrugtekwekery; ~**ist**, vrugtekweker.
orches'tic, dans-; ~**s**, danskuns, orkestiek.
or'chestra, orkes.
orches'tral, orkes-, orkestraal; ~ **music**, orkesmusiek.
or'chestra: ~ **pit**, orkesruimte; orkesput; ~ **score**, orkespartituur; ~ **well**, orkesruimte, orkesbak.
or'chestrate, orkestreer, vir 'n orkes rangskik (musiek).
orchestra'tion, orkestrasie.
orchestri'na, orkestrion.
or'chid, **or'chis**, orgidee, bakkiesblom.
orchida'ceous, orgideeagtig.
orch'idist, orgideekweker; orgideeliefhebber.
orchil(la), verfmos, lakmoes.
orchit'is, balontsteking, orgitis, kalbassies.
or'cin(ol), orsinol.
ordain', orden, bevestig; wy, inseën; ordineer, instel; bepaal, voorskryf; bestel, bestem, verorden; ~**ment**, inseëning, ordening; beskikking, bestiering.
ordeal', beproewing; toets; godsgerig; vuurproef; ~ *by FIRE*, vuurproef; *SURVIVE the* ~, die vuurproef deurstaan.
ord'er, (n) orde (ontwikkelingsleer); orde, reëlmaat; order; bestelling; bevel, aanseëging, opdrag; reeks, rang, stand, klas; rangorde; dekorasie, orde(teken); ordening, skikking; toestand, staat; voorskrif; *ADDITIONAL* ~, nabestelling; *AT his* ~*s*, op sy bevel; ~ *of BATTLE*, slagorde; *BY* ~, op las; *BY* ~ *of*, in opdrag van; op las van; *CALL to* ~, tot die orde roep; *the old* ~ *CHANGETH*, ander tye, ander sedes; ~ *of CONDUCT*, gedragsorde, gedragskode; *an* ~ *in COUNCIL*, 'n koninklike besluit; ~ *of COURT*, hofbevel; *DAILY* ~ *s*, dagbevel; ~ *of the DAY*, agenda; die orde van die dag; *be the* ~ *of the DAY*, skering en inslag vorm; aan die orde v.d. dag wees; *under DOCTOR'S* ~ *s*, onder doktersbehandeling; *until FURTHER* ~*s*, tot nadere beskikking; voorlopig; *GIVE the* ~*s*, bevele gee; die lakens uitdeel; *GIVE an* ~, 'n bevel gee, las gee; 'n bestelling plaas; *GIVE* ~*s for*, bestel; *in GOOD* ~, in goeie toestand; agtermekaar; heel; in die haak; *of the HIGHEST* ~, v.d. allerbeste; die uitnemendste; *take HOLY* ~*s*, 'n geestelike word; *IN* ~, agter mekaar, in volgorde; in die haak; in orde, pluis; *IN* ~ *that*, sodat, opdat; *IN* ~ *to marry*, om te kan trou; *IN (holy)* ~*s*, geordende geestelike; *ISSUE an* ~, 'n bevel uitvaardig (uitreik); *KEEP in* ~, aan kant hou; skoon hou; die orde bewaar; in bedwang hou; ~ *of KNIGHTHOOD*, ridderorde; *that is a LARGE* ~, dis nie 'n kleinigheid nie; *MADE to* ~, op maat gemaak; passend; *in* ~ *of MERIT*, in volgorde van verdienste; *the NATURAL* ~ *of things*, die natuurlike gang van sake (volgorde); *NOT in* ~, buiten orde; *OF the* ~ *of*, om en by; *it is ON* ~, dit is bestel; *act ON* ~*s*, bevele uitvoer; *OUT of* ~, in wanorde, onklaar, stukkend; *PLACE an* ~, bestel; *on a POINT of* ~, op 'n punt van orde; *POSTAL* ~, posorder; ~ *of PRECE-*

orderly   1092   *ornamental*

DENCE, voorranglys; *PUT in* ~ , regmaak; in orde bring; aan kant maak; *RESTORE* ~ , die orde her=stel; *STANDING* ~ *s,* reglement van orde; *TAKE* ~ *s,* bestellings neem; bevele volg; *TAKE things in* ~ , iets puntsgewyse behandel; iets sistematies be=handel; *that is a TALL* ~ , dis 'n bietjie kras; dis geen kleinigheid nie; dis 'n bietjie dik vir 'n daalder; *it is in the* ~ *of THINGS,* dit vorm skering en in=slag; *in* ~ *TO,* om, ten einde; *UNDER* ~ , met op=drag; *be UNDER* ~ *s,* bevel hê; onder bevel staan; *in WORKING* ~ , in goeie orde; (v) gelas, gebied, sê, beveel; opdra; voorskryf; bestel (goed); reël (sake), orden; verordineer, bepaal; baasspeel oor; ~ *ABOUT,* rondkommandeer; baasspeel oor; *I won't be* ~ *ed ABOUT,* ek laat my nie kommandeer nie; ~ *ARMS!* sit af geweer! ~ *AROUND,* hiet en gebied; ~ *FROM,* bestel van; *GOD has* ~ *ed,* God het dit verordineer; ~ *HOME,* gelas (beveel) om huis toe te gaan; ~ *OUT,* uitjaag; ~ *someone RIGHT and left,* iem. hiet en gebied; ~-**book,** be=stelboek; orderboek (mil.); ~-**clerk,** bestelklerk; orderklerk (mil.); ~-**form,** bestelvorm; ~ **ing,** (die) bestel; reëling; skikking; bestelling; ~ **less,** deurme=kaar, wanordelik; ~ **liness,** ordelikheid; gereeld=heid, reëlmatigheid.

ord'erly, (n) (. . **lies),** oppasser, lyfdienaar; ordonnans (mil.); (a) ordelik, aan kant; gereeld; geordend; or=deliewend; ~ **bin,** vuilgoedblik; ~ **book,** ordon=nansboek; diensboek; ~ **man,** ordonnans; ~ **offi=cer,** ordonnansoffisier; ~ **room,** kantoor; ~ **ser=geant,** onderadjudant.

ord'er: ~-**mark,** ordemerk; ~-**office,** bestelkantoor; ~-**paper,** agenda, dagorde, ordelys; ~-**word,** pa=rool.

ord'inal, (n) rangtelwoord; (a) rangskikkend; ~ **num=ber,** ranggetal.

ord'inance, reglement, ordinansie; verordening, voorskrif; kerklike gebruik; ordonnansie.

ord'inand, proponent; wydeling (R.K.).

ord'inarily, gewoonlik, in die reël.

ord'inary, (n) (. . **ries),** biskop; ordinaris; *PHYSI=CIAN in* ~ , lyfarts; *something OUT of the* ~ , iets ongewoons (buitengewoons); (a) (dood)gewoon, gebruiklik; middelmatig, ordinêr; alledaags; ~ **debts,** lopende skulde; boekskulde; ~ **seaman,** lig=matroos.

ord'inate, (n) ordinaat; (v) koördineer; (a) gereeld, reëlmatig.

ordina'tion, wyding, ordening, inseëning; rangskik=king, klassifikasie; bestel, besluit, bepaling.

ordinee', pas geordende.

ord'nance, geskut, veldgeskut, artillerie; *HEAVY* ~ , grofgeskut; *PIECE of* ~ , veldstuk, kanon; ~ **ammunition,** geskutammunisie; ~ **factory,** geskut=fabriek, artilleriewerkplaas, kanongietery; ~ **ma=chinery,** krygsmasjinerie; ~ **map,** stafkaart; ~ **stores,** krygsbehoeftes; ~ **survey,** topografiese op=name; triangulasie; ~ **yard,** artilleriepark, geskut=werf.

ord'ure, mis, uitwerpsels; vuiligheid; vuil taal.

ore, erts.

or'ead, bergnimf.

ore: ~-**bearer,** ertsdraer; ~-**bearing,** ertshoudend; ~ **bed,** ertslaag; ~ **body,** ertsliggaam; ~ **box,** ertskas; ~ **chamber,** ertskamer; ~ **chute,** ertsglybaan; ~ **crusher,** ertsmeul.

orec'tic, lus=, begeerte=.

ore: ~ **deposit,** ertslaag, ertsafsetting; ~ **dressing,** ertsbereiding; ~ **furnace,** ertsoond.

orega'no, marjolein; orego.

or'eide, kunsgoud.

oreo'graphy, oreo'logy, or(e)ografie, or(e)ologie.

ore: ~-**passes,** ertsglybaan; ~ **pipe,** ertspyp; ~ **poc=ket,** ertskol, ertsnes; ~ **reserve,** ertsreserwe; ~ **shoot,** ertsstrook; stortbaan, ertsgeut.

orf, vuilbek(siekte).

org'an, orgaan; orrel (mus.); werktuig; mondstuk; tydskrif, blad; ~ *of MOTION,* bewegingsorgaan; ~ *of SCENT,* reukorgaan; ~ *of SENSE,* sintuig; ~ *s of SPEECH,* spraakorgane; ~-**bellows,** orrel=blaasbalk; ~-**blower,** orreltrapper; ~-**builder,** orrelmaker.

org'andie, organdie.

organe'lle, organel, selorgaan(tjie).

org'an-grind'er, orreldraaier.

organ'ic, organies; ~ **chemistry,** organiese skeikunde (chemie); ~ **disease,** organiese kwaal; ~ **remains,** organiese oorblyfsels.

org'anism, organisme.

org'anist, orrelis, orrelspeler.

org'anizable, organiseerbaar.

organiza'tion, inrigting, organisasie, samestelling, reëling; ~ **al,** organisatories.

org'anize, organiseer, reël, inrig; ~ **d,** georgani=seer(d); ~ **r,** organiseerder, organisator.

org'anizing, reëling(s)=, organiserend; organisatories; ~ **committee,** reëlingskomitee; ~ **secretary,** orga=niserende sekretaris.

org'an-loft, orrelgalery, orrelkoor.

org'an music, orrelmusiek.

organog'raphy, organografie.

organolep'tic, organolepties.

organol'ogy, organologie.

org'anon, organum, instrument van die gedagte; sa=mestel van reëls.

organothe'rapy, organoterapie.

org'an: ~-**piano,** piano-orrel; ~-**pipe,** orrelpyp; ~-**playing,** orrelspel; ~ **recital,** orreluitvoering, orrel=konsert; ~-**stop,** register (van 'n orrel); ~-**tone,** or=reltoon; ~ **transplanta'tion,** orgaanoorplanting; ~-**treader,** orreltrapper; ~-**tuner,** orrelstemmer.

org'anum = **organon.**

or'ganzine, orgasynsy.

org'asm, geprikkelde toestand, opwinding; woede; orgasme.

or'geat, amandelmelk.

orgias'tic, bandeloos, orgie=.

or'gy, (orgies), swelgparty, drinkparty, suipparty, brasparty, orgie, swelgery.

o'ribi, oribi, oorbietjie.

or'iel, spitsboogvenster.

Or'ient, (n) (die) Ooste; (a) Oosters.

or'ient, (n) ooste; glanspêrel; dageraad; (a) oostelik; skitterend, glansend, stralend.

or'ient, (v) oriënteer; na die ooste draai; die ligging bepaal, plek bepaal; opstel; ~ **eering,** padvindery, oriënteerkuns.

Orien'tal, (n) Oosterling; (a) Oosters; ~ **ism,** Ooster=se gewoonte; kennis van Oosterse gebruike; Oriën=talisme; ~ **ist,** Oriëntalis.

or'ientate = **orient,** (v).

orienta'tion, oriëntering; plekbepaling, liggingsbepa=ling.

o'rifice, opening, gaatjie, mond.

o'riflamme, oriflamme.

origa'mi, origami, papiervoukuns.

o'rigan, orig'anum, wilde moederkruid, marjolein.

o'rigin, oorsprong, ontstaan, begin, bron, bakermat, herkoms; afkoms; wording; oorsaak.

ori'ginal, (n) oertipe, (die) oorspronklike; sonderlin=ge mens, eksentrieke persoon; (a) oorspronklik, origineel, eerste; ~ **capital,** stamkapitaal; ~ **'ity,** oorspronklikheid; ~ **language,** oertaal; ~ **ly,** oor=spronklik, in die begin, aanvanklik, van huis uit; ~ **sin,** erfsonde; ~ **text,** grondteks, oerteks.

ori'ginate, ontstaan, sy oorsprong neem, voortspruit, afkomstig wees; begin; ontkiem; voortbring.

origina'tion, oorsprong, afkoms, ontstaan, wording, begin.

ori'ginative, skeppend, voortbrengend.

ori'ginator, skepper, verwekker, ontwerper, vader, bewerker, veroorsaker.

orinas'al, met mondneusklank, orinasaal.

or'iole, wielewaal, geelspreeu.

Ori'on, Orion.

o'rison, gebed.

Ork'neys, die Orkadiese Eilande, die Orkade.

orl'op, oorloopdek, laagste dek, koeibrug.

orm'olu, goudbrons, mosaïekgoud, verfgoud.

orn'ament, (n) sieraad, versiersel, versiering, or=nament; (pl) tierlantyntjies, fieterjasies; (v) versier, tooi, opsier, versier, ornamenteer, mooimaak, verfraai.

ornamen'tal, sierlik, versierend; fraai, ornamenteel, dekoratief; ~ **art,** sierkuns, ornamentiek; ~ **letter=**

ornamentation   1093   **ostrich**

ing, sierskrif; ~ **painter,** dekorasieskilder; ~ **tree,** sierboom; ~ **writing,** sierskrif.
ornamenta'tion, versiering, ornamentiek.
ornate', versierd, sierlik; beeldryk; bloemryk, retories (styl); ~**ness,** oorladenheid; beeldrykheid; bloemrykheid.
or'nery, (colloq.), swak, van swak gehalte; ru, ongeskik.
ornith'ic, voël=.
orn'ithoid, voëlagtig.
ornitholog'ical, voëlkundig, ornitologies.
ornithol'ogist, voëlkenner, ornitoloog.
ornithol'ogy, voëlbeskrywing, voëlkunde, ornitologie.
ornith'omancy, voëlwiggelary.
ornithop'ter, klapvliegtuig.
ornithorhyn'chus, eendbekdier, platipus.
ornithos'copy, voëlwaarneming, ornitoskopie.
orogen'esis, bergvorming, gebergtevorming.
orogen'ic, orogeen, orogeneties.
orograph'ic, orografies.
orog'raphy, bergbeskrywing, orografie.
or'oide, kunsgoud.
orolog'ical, orologies, gebergte=.
oro'logy, orologie, gebergteleer.
or'otund, deftig; gewigtig, geswolle, hoogdrawend; ~**'ity,** geswollenheid, hoogdrawendheid.
orph'an, (n) weeskind; (v) ouerloos maak (wees), verwees, wees maak; (a) wees=, ouerloos, verwees; ~ **age,** weeshuis, weesinrigting; ouerloosheid, verweesdheid; ~ **calf,** hanskalf; **O** ~ **Chamber,** weeskamer; ~ **ed,** wees, ouerloos; ~ *ed child,* weeskind; ~ **hood,** ouerloosheid, verweesdheid; ~ **lamb,** hanslam; ~ **master,** weesheer; ~ **s' fund,** weesfonds.
Orph'eus, Orfeus, Orpheus.
Orph'ic, Orfies; meeslepend, soetvloeiend, welluidend.
orph'rey, rand van goudborduursel.
orp'iment, operment.
orp'in, geelverfstof.
orp'ine, smeerwortel.
Orp'ington, Orpington (hoender).
o'rrery, (orreries), klein planetarium.
o'rris¹, goudgalon; silwergalon.
o'rris², Florentynse irisblom; ~**-root,** iriswortel.
ors'on, ruwe en dapper kêrel.
orthocen'tre, hoogtesnypunt.
orthocen'tric, ortosentries.
orthocepha'lic, ortosefaal, ortokefaal.
orthochromat'ic, kleurgevoelig, ortochromaties.
orth'oclase, ortoklaas.
orthodont'ia, ortodonte.
orthodon'tics, gebitsregulering, ortodonsie.
orth'odox, regsinnig, gereformeerd, ortodoks; eg, waar, solied, ouderwets, konvensioneel; wetties; *the O* ~ *Church,* die Grieks-Ortodokse Kerk; ~**y,** regsinnigheid, ortodoksie.
orthoep'ic, uitspraak=, ortoëpies.
ortho'epy, uitspraakleer, ortoëpie.
orthogen'esis, ortogenese.
orth'ogon, reghoek; ..**g'onal,** rekhoekig.
orthog'rapher, spellingkundige, ortograaf.
orthograph'ic(al), ortografies, spelling=, spel=; ~ **er= ror,** spelfout; ~ **mark,** skrifteken; ~ **rule,** spelreël.
orthog'raphy, spelling(stelsel), ortografie; spellingleer, spelkuns, spelwyse.
orthop(a)ed'ic, ortopedies; ~**s,** ortopedie; ~ **surgeon,** ortopedis.
orthop(a)ed'ist, ortopediese dokter, ortopedis.
orth'op(a)edy, ortopedie.
orthop'ter, orthop'teran, ortopter, regvlerkige.
Orthop'tera, Regvlerkiges, Orthoptera.
ortho'tropism, ortho'tropy, ortotropie, regopstandigheid.
ort'olan, ortolaan.
orts, afvalstukkies, oorskiet.
Orvieto, Orvieto(wyn), witwyn.
o'ryx, (-es), gemsbok, gensbok.
Os'car, Oscar(toekenning) (rolprentkuns).
os'cillate, slinger, swaai, ossilleer, skommel; weifel.
os'cillating, weifelend; slingerend.

oscilla'tion, trilling, slingering, skommeling, geslinger, swaai, ossillasie; weifeling.
os'cillator, stroombreker, ossillator, wisselaar; ~**y,** (n) trillingskring; (a) slingerend, skommelend; weifelend; trillend.
oscill'ograph, ossillograaf.
oscil'loscope, ossilloskoop.
os'citancy, gaap; vaakheid.
os'citate, gaap.
os'cular, mond=, soen=.
os'culate, soen; oskuleer (wisk.); in noue aanraking met mekaar kom.
oscula'tion, soen; soenery; noue aanraking; oskulasie.
os'culatory, soen=.
os'cule, klein opening; mondjie.
os'culum, oskulum, mondopening.
o'sier, katwilger, waterwilger; wilgerlat; ~**-bed,** wilgerbossie; ~**-bottle,** mandjiebottel, karba; ~**-work,** mandjiewerk.
Osi'ris, Osiris.
osmirid'ium, osmiridium.
os'mium, osmium.
osmol'ogy, osmologie.
osmom'eter, osmometer.
osmom'etry, osmometrie.
os'mose, osmos'is, osmose.
osmot'ic, osmoties.
osmun'da, os'mund-royal, osmunda.
os'prey, (-s), visvalk *(Pandion haliaëtus);* egretpluim.
oss'ein, beenweefsel, osseïen, osseïne.
oss'elet, beentjie, skedelbeen.
oss'eous, beenagtig, been=.
oss'icle, beentjie.
ossif'erous, beenbevattend.
ossifica'tion, beenvorming, verbening, ossifikasie; verharding.
oss'ified, verbeen; verhard, verstok, verstar.
oss'ifrage, visarend.
oss'ify, (..**fied),** in been verander, verbeen; ongevoelig word, verhard.
ossiv'orous, beenetend.
oss'uary, (..**ries),** knekelhuis, beenderhuis, bene-urn, beenhoop; ~ **urn,** bene-urn.
ostei'tis, beenontsteking, osteïtis.
Os'tend, Oostende.
ostensibil'ity, oënskynlikheid, duidelikheid.
osten'sibly, soos voorgegee word; oënskynlik, kastig, konsuis, sogenaamd.
osten'sory, (..**ries),** monstrans.
ostenta'tion, vertoon, pronkery, (ge)pronk, praal= (sug), pralery, spoggerigheid, windmakerigheid, aanstellery.
ostenta'tious, ydel, opsigtig, praalsiek, aanstellerig, praalsugtig, windmakerig, spoggerig, pronkerig, blufferig; ~**ly,** op 'n ooglopende manier; ~**ness,** ydelheid, praalsug, windmakerigheid, pronksug.
osteoarthri'tis, been-en-gewrigsontsteking, osteoartritis.
osteogen'esis, beenvorming, beenontwikkeling, osteogenese.
osteog'rapher, beenbeskrywer, osteograaf.
osteog'raphy, beenbeskrywing, osteografie.
osteolog'ic, beenkundig, osteologies.
osteol'ogist, beenkundige, osteoloog.
osteol'ogy, beenderleer, beenkunde, osteologie.
os'teopath, beensetter, osteopaat.
osteopath'ic, osteopaties.
osteo'pathy, beensettery, osteopatie.
osteosarcom'a, beenkanker.
ostina'to, (It., mus.), ostinato, herhalend; *basso* ~, *basso ostinato.*
ostit'is, beenontsteking, ostitus.
os'tler, staljong, perdekneg.
os'tracism, verbanning, ostrasisme, uitsluiting; skerwegerig (hist.).
os'tracize, verban, uitsluit, ostraseer, verstoot.
os'tracon, ostrakon.
os'treiculture, oesterteelt.
ostreoph'agist, oestereter.
os'trich, (-es), volstruis; *he has the digestion (stomach) of an* ~, hy het 'n volstruismaag; ~

Ostrogoth camp, volstruiskamp; ~ **egg**, volstruiseier; ~ **farmer**, volstruisboer; ~ **farming**, volstruisboerdery; ~ **feather**, volstruisveer; ~ **leather**, volstruisleer; ~ **plume**, volstruisveer; ~ **policy**, volstruispolitiek.

Os'trogoth, Oos-Goot; ~**ic**, Oos-Goties.

otal'gia, otal'gy, oorpyn.

o'ther, (n, pron, a, adv) ander; anders; *AMONG* ~ *things*, onder andere; *the* ~ *DAY*, onlangs, kort gelede, nou die dag; *EACH* ~, mekaar; ~ *things being EQUAL*, alles gelyk synde; *EVERY* ~ *day*, al om die ander dag; *and a FEW* ~, en nog 'n paar; *on the* ~ *HAND*, aan die ander kant; daarteenoor, daarenteen; *NONE* ~ *than*, niemand anders nie as; *the* ~ *PLACE*, die ander plek; die hel; ~ *RANKS*, mindere; *SOMEHOW or* ~, op die een of ander manier; *SOMEONE or* ~, die een of ander; *SOME TIME or* ~, een v.d. mooi dae; *SOMEWHERE or* ~, iewers, êrens; ~ *THAN*, behalwe; *some TIME or* ~, eendag; een v.d. mooi dae; *the TWO* ~ *s*, die ander twee; *the* ~ *WORLD*, die hiernamaals; ~**ness**, andersheid, verskil.

o'thers, ander(e).

o'therwise, anders, andersins, origens; ~ *not BAD*, origens nie sleg nie; *what could he DO* ~? wat kon hy anders doen? ~ *ENGAGED*, met iets anders besig; met ander planne; *KNOW* ~, beter weet; ~ *MINDED*, van ander gevoele, andersdenkend; *his SINCERITY or* ~, sy opregtheid of onopregtheid; ~ *THAN*, buiten, behalwe; ~**-minded**, andersdenkend.

o'ther-worldliness, nie-aardsgesindheid; bonatuurlikheid.

o'ther-worldly, nie-aardsgesind; boweaards.

otiat'ria, oorsiektes.

otiat'rics, oorheelkunde.

ot'ic, oor-.

o'tiose, lui; leeglêerig; nutteloos, ydel, oorbodig; ~**ness**, luiheid; ledigheid; nutteloosheid.

otit'is, oorontsteking, otitis; ~ **media**, middeloorontsteking, otitis media.

otog'raphy, otografie, oorbeskrywing.

otolaryngo'logy, otolaringologie.

o'tolith, otoliet, oorsteen.

otol'ogist, oorheelkundige, otoloog.

otol'ogy, oorheelkunde, otologie.

ot'olite, ot'olith, ewewigsbeentjie, oorsteentjie, gehoorsteentjie, otoliet.

otolog'ical, oorheelkundig, otologies.

oto'pathy, oorsiekte, otopatie.

ot'ophone, gehoortoestel, otofoon.

otosclero'sis, oorverkalking, otosklerose.

ot'oscope, oorspieël, otoskoop.

ottava ri'ma, ottava rima, agtreëlige vers.

ott'er, otter; ~**-flower**, otterblom.

ott'o, *kyk* attar.

Ott'oman¹, (n) (..men), Turk, Ottoman; (a) Turks, Ottomaans, Ottomanies.

ott'oman², (n) (-s), ottoman, sofa.

oubliette', kerker met valdeur, oubliette.

ought¹, (n) nul.

ought², (v) behoort, moet; *you* ~ *to DO it*, jy behoort dit te doen; *he* ~ *to KNOW*, hy behoort dit te weet; *he* ~ *to have SAID it*, hy moes dit gesê het; hy behoort dit te gesê het.

oui'ja (-board), ouija, spiritistiese bord.

ounce¹, bergpanter, sneeuluiperd.

ounce², ons (gewig); ~ *FINE*, fyn ons; *FIVE* ~ *s*, vyf ons; *an* ~ *of PREVENTION is worth a pound of cure*, voorkoming is beter as genesing.

our, ons (onse); *O* ~ *FATHER*, Onse Vader; *O* ~ *LADY*, Onse Liewe Vrou.

ou'rebi, oorbietjie, oribie.

ours, ons s'n, ons; *he likes* ~ *BETTER*, hy hou meer van ons s'n; *it is not* ~ *to COMMAND*, dis nie vir ons om te beveel nie; *it is* ~ *to OBEY*, dis ons plig om te gehoorsaam.

ourself', (..**selves**), ons, onsself; *BY* ~, net ons alleen; *we ourselves will SEE to it*, ons sal self daarvoor sorg.

ou'sel, *kyk* ouzel.

oust, uitdrywe; verdring; uitsit, afvry; uitwip, uitlig;

uit die besit stoot; uitwerk; ~ *someone from a position*, iem. uit 'n pos uitwerk; ~**er**, uitdrywer; ~**ing**, uitsetting, berowing.

out: (n); *the ins and* ~ *s*, die fyne v.d. saak; die naatjie van die kous; (v) uitsmyt; *his opponents tried to* ~ *him*, sy teënstanders het hom probeer uitsmyt uit sy pos; uitklop (boks); (a) weg van huis; groot, buitengewoon; (adv) uit; dood (vuur); weg; bekend; ~ *and ABOUT*, op die been; ~ *of ACTION*, buite werking; buite geveg; ~ *of ALIGNMENT*, verkeerd gespoor; uit die lyn; ~ *AND* ~, deur en deur; *I've put my ARM* ~, ek het my arm uit lit geruk; ~ *and AWAY*, verreweg; ~ *of BALANCE*, uit die ewewig; *BE* ~ *to*, van plan wees om; ~ *of BOUNDS*, verbode; oor die grens (gholf); ~ *of BREAD*, sonder brood; ~ *of BREATH*, uitasem; ~ *of CASH*, platsak; *feel left* ~ *in the COLD*, uitgesluit wees; verontagsaam voel; ~ *of COMMISSION*, buite werking (diens); ~ *of the CONTEXT*, buite die verband; ~ *of CONTROL*, onregeerbaar; ~ *of DATE*, verouderd, uit die mode; *a DAY* ~, 'n vrye dag; ~**-of-DOORS**, buitekant, in die oop lug; ~**-at-ELBOW**, in behoeftige omstandighede; *not FAR* ~, nie ver verkeerd nie; ~ *of FASHION* uit die mode; *FEEL* ~ *of it*, uit jou plek voel; uitgesluit wees; *the FIRE is* ~, die vuur is dood; ~ *of FOCUS*, sleg ingestel; uit fokus; ~ *of GEAR*, uit die haak; neutraal (motor), uit die rat, uitgeskakel; *GO all* ~, alle kragte inspan; *HAVE it* ~, dit uitspook; ~ *of HEALTH*, ongesteld; ~ *of HEART*, moedeloos; ~ *HERE*, hier buite; ~ *and HOME*, uit en tuis; *the INVITATIONS are* ~, die uitnodigings is uitgestuur; ~ *of KEEPING with*, strydig met; *his LUCK is* ~, die geluk is teen hom; *MOTHER is* ~, moeder is nie tuis nie; ~ *of his MIND*, van sy verstand; ~ *for MONEY*, met die doel om geld te maak; ~ *OF*, buitekant; van; uit; ~ *of OFFICE*, sonder betrekking; nie aan die bewind nie; ~ *of ORDER*, buite orde; buite werking; ~ *of PLACE*, ongewens, onnodig, onvanpas; ~ *of PRINT*, uit druk; onverkrygbaar, uitverkoop; ~ *of PROPORTION*, buite verhouding; *PUT oneself* ~, baie moeite doen, jou inspan; ~ *of RANGE*, buite skoot; buite trefafstand; ~ *of one's REACH*, buite bereik; *in SEASON and* ~, te pas en te onpas; ~**-of-SEASON**, buitentyds; buiteseisoens; ~ *of SIGHT*, ~ *of mind*, uit die oog, uit die hart; ~ *of SORTS*, nie gesond nie, kroeserig; ~ *of SPITE*, uit nydigheid; ~ *of STEP*, uit die pas; ~ *to SWINDLE people*, met die doel om mense te bedrieg; ~; *of TEMPER*, uit sy humeur; ~ *THERE*, daarso; *TIMES* ~ *of number*, talle kere; *TIRED* ~, doodmoeg, uitgeput; ~ *of TOWN*, uitstedig; *be* ~ *for TROUBLE*, moeilikheid soek; ~ *of TRUE*, nie suiwer nie; ~ *of TUNE*, van die wysie af; ontstemd; *on the VOYAGE* ~, op die uitreis; ~**-of-the-WAY**, uit die pad; buitengewoon; verafgeleë, onbereikbaar; ~ *of WEDLOCK*, buite-egtelik, buite die huwelik; ~ *WITH him!* weg met hom! ~ *of the WOOD*, oor die ergste moeilikheid; oor die hond se stert; *the WORKERS are* ~, die arbeiders het gestaak; (prep) uit, buite.

out-act', beter speel (as), oortref.

out-and-out', deur en deur; volslae; aarts-; *an* ~ *scoundrel*, 'n aartsskelm; ~**er**, doring, ryperd, ramkat, bulperd; ekstremis.

out-ar'gue, doodredeneer.

out-at-el'bows, armoedig.

out'back, agterveld, boendoe, gramadoelas.

outbal'ance, swaarder weeg.

outbid', (~ or ..**bade**, ~ or **-den**), hoër bied, oorbie; oortref.

out'board, buiteboord-; ~ **motor**, aanhangmotor, buiteboordmotor; ~**s**, buiteboords.

out'bound, op die uitreis.

outbox', oorrompel; oortref.

out'break, uitbreking, uitbarsting; opstand.

out'building, bygebou, buitegebou.

out'burst, uitbarsting, losbarsting, uitval.

out'cast, (n) balling, swerweling; verstoteling, verskoppeling; (a) uitgeworpe; diep gesink, verstoot, dakloos.

**outclass', **oortref, oorskadu, ver agter laat, totaal verslaan.
out'clearing, sending ter verrekening.
out'come, uitslag, resultaat, gevolg, uitvloeisel.
out'crop, (n) dagsoom (geol.); opduiksel; resultaat; opbrings; (v) **(-ped),** uitslaan, aan die dag kom.
out'cry, geskreeu, geroep, lawaai; protes.
outdare', tart, trotseer; meer durf as.
outdat'ed, verouderd; uit die mode.
outdis'tance, verbyloop, agterlaat, uithardloop, verbygaan, verbystreef, disnis loop.
outdo', (..did, -ne), oortref, baasraak.
out'door, buite=; buitelug=; ~ **exercise,** oefening in die buitelug; ~ **game,** opelugspel; ~ **inspector,** buitebeampte; ~ **life,** lewe in die buitelug; buitelewe; ~ **officer,** buitebeampte; ~**s,** (n) buitelug; (adv) buitenshuis, in die buitelug.
out'er, buite=, uiterste, buitenste; ~ **darkness,** buitenste duisternis; ~ **flank,** buiteflank; ~ **garments,** boklere; ~ **man,** die uiterlike; ~**most,** buitenste, uiterste; ~ **port,** buitehawe; ~ **race (ball-bearing),** buitering; ~ **space,** die buitenste ruim; ~ **world:** *the* ~ *world,* die buitewêreld.
outface', verleë maak, die oë laat neerslaan, trotseer.
out'fall, uitloop, monding.
out'field, buiteveld (krieket); *in the* ~, op die grens.
outfight', (..fought), wen, verslaan, oortref, uitstof.
out'fit, (n) uitrusting; uitset; benodigdhede; (v) **(-ted),** uitrus, toerus; ~**ter,** uitruster; leweransier (van uitrusting); ~**ting,** klerehandel.
outflank', omtrek, omflank; uitoorlê.
out'flow, uitloop; uitstroming; uitvloeiing.
outfly', (..flew, ..flown), vinniger vlieg as.
outgen'eral, oortref in krygsbekwaamheid; uitoorlê.
out'go, (n) uitgawes, onkoste; uitvloeiing; uitgang.
outgo', (v) (..gone), oortref; gouer gaan.
out'going, (n) uitgaan; einde; (pl) uitgawes, onkoste; (a) vertrekkend; aftredend; uitgaande, heen=; ~ **cable,** heenkabel.
outgrow', (..grew, -n), uitgroei; vergroei; te groot word vir (klere), ontgroei.
out'growth, uitwas; resultaat; uitvloeisel; loot, uitgroeisel.
outgun', (-ned), (geskut) tot swye bring; oortref.
out-Herod': ~ *Herod,* in wreedheid oortref.
out'house, buitegebou.
out'ing, uitstappie, toggie, kuier, ekskursie.
outjock'ey, uitoorlê; uitstof, oortref.
out'lander, vreemdeling, uitlander, buitelander.
outland'ish, vreemd, uitlands, uitheems.
outlast', oorleef, langer duur as.
out'law, (n) voëlvryverklaarde; balling; (v) buite die wet stel; voëlvry verklaar; ~**ry,** voëlvryverklaring.
out'lay, uitgawe, (on)koste.
out'let, uitweg; uitgang; opening, uitmonding (masj.); mond (rivier); afvoerkanaal; afsetgebied (handel); uitloop; afvoerpyp; ~ **pipe,** dampyp; ~ **valve,** uitlaatklep.
out'lier, los deel; uitloper; los lap.
out'line, (n) skets, omtrek; belyning, omlyning; *in BROAD* ~, in breë trekke; *IN* ~, in hooftrekke; *THE* ~*s,* die hoofpunte; (v) skets, teken; met enkele lyne teken, die hooflyne aangee, uitstippel; ~ *a plan,* 'n plan in breë trekke voorlê; ~**d,** omlyn; *broadly* ~*d,* in groot lyne; ~ **map,** oorsigkaart; ~ **plan,** breë (algemene) plan; ~ **stitch,** randsteek.
outlive', oorleef; langer leef as; *not* ~ *the night,* die dag nie haal nie.
out'look, vooruitsig; kyk; uitsig; *BE on the* ~, uitkyk na; ~ *on LIFE,* kyk op die lewe, lewensopvatting, lewensbeskouing.
out'lying, ver, afgeleë.
outmanoeuv're, uitoorlê, die loef afsteek, uitmaneuvreer, verskalk.
outmarch', vinniger marsjeer as.
outmatch', oortref.
outmod'ed, uit die mode, oudmodies, verouderd.
out'most, buitenste, uiterste.
outnum'ber, oortref in getal, talryker wees as; *be* ~ *ed,* in die minderheid wees, teen 'n oormag veg.
out'-of-doors, buitenshuis, buite=.

out-of-fash'ion, wat uit die mode is; uit die mode, oudmodies.
out-of-pock'et: ~ *expenses,* kontantuigawes, klein uitgawes.
out-of-sea'son, buiteseisoen(s).
out-of-the-way', afgeleë; ongewoon; ~ *place,* uithoek.
out'-of-work, (n) werklose; (a) sonder werk, werkloos.
outpace', uithardloop, verbyhardloop, voorbly.
out'-parish, buiteparogie.
out'-patient, buitepasiënt.
out'-pensioner, uitwonende, invalide.
outplay', oortref, uitstof.
outpoint', op punte wen.
out'-porch, voorportaal.
out'-port, buitehawe.
out'post, voorpos, voorpunt, buitepos; brandwag; ~ **duties,** voorposdiens; ~ **picket,** brandwag; ~ **troops,** voorpostroepe.
out'pouring, uitstorting, ontboeseming; uitstroming.
out'put, opbrings, produksie, uitset; vermoë (van masjien); afvoer (elektr.).
out'rage, (n) vergryp; belediging; aanranding, verkragting; wandaad, euweldaad, gewelddadigheid, skanddaad, wanbedryf; smaad; (v) aanrand, verkrag; vergryp; beledig, skend.
outra'geous, beledigend; gewelddadig, woes; skandelik, skandalig; vreeslik; verregaande.
outrange', verder skiet as.
outrank', oortref in rang, 'n hoër rang beklee.
outre', (F.), eksentriek, eienaardig.
outreach', oortref, verder reik as.
outride', (..rode, ..ridden), verbyry; vinniger ry as; ~**r,** voorryer, agterryer, los ruiter; losperd.
out'rigger, loefbalk, papegaaistok (skip); uithouer (masjien); arm, hysbalk.
out'right, (a) direk; rondborstig, ronduit, onomwonde; volkome; openlik; ~ *purchase,* aankoop ineens; (adv) meteens, op slag; heeltemal, volkome; *KILL* ~, op slag doodmaak; *LAUGH* ~, hard lag.
outriv'al, (-led), in die skaduwee stel, wen, oortref, verbysteek, verbystreef.
out'room, buitekamer.
outrun', (..ran, ..run), uithardloop, verbyhardloop; verder gaan as; verbystreef; ~ *one's INCOME,* te groot leef; *your TONGUE* ~*s your discretion,* jy sê meer as wat jy kan verantwoord.
out'rush, uitstroming.
outsail', verbyseil.
out'sentry, (..tries), voorpos.
out'set, begin, aanvang; *at (from) the* ~, dadelik, van die begin, uit die staanspoor.
outshine', (..shone), in glans oortref, uitblink; oortref.
out'side, (n) buitekant; uiterlik, uiterste; *FROM the* ~, van buite; *a KILOMETRE at the* ~, uiters 'n kilometer, op sy (die) meeste 'n kilometer; *ON the* ~, buite; *TEN at the* ~, hoogstens tien, (v) na buite! voertsek! (a) buite=, buitenste; uiterste; ~ *BODY,* buite-instansie; ~ *CHANCE,* geringe kans; ~ *DOOR,* buitedeur; ~ *KITCHEN,* buitekombuis; ~ *LEFT,* linksbuite; ~ *MEASUREMENT,* buitemaat; ~ *PLAYER,* buitespeler; ~ *PRICES,* uiterste (hoogste) pryse; *the* ~ *PUBLIC,* die buitestaanders; ~ *RIGHT,* regsbuite; ~ *WORLD,* buitewêreld; (adv) daarbuite, buitekant, buitekant toe; (prep) buite, buitekant; afgesien van, buiten; ~*-in,* binneste buite; ~**r,** vreemde, oningewyde, buitestaander, buiteparty, buiteman; buiteperd, vreemde perd (wedren).
out'size, ekstramaat, buitemaat; groot vrouegrootte; *extra* ~, ekstragroot vrouegrootte.
out'skirts, grens; buitewyke; kante; voorpunt.
outsmart', kul, uitoorlê.
out'sorts, uitskotwol.
out'span, (n) uitspanning, uitspanplek; (v) **(-ned),** uitspan.
out'spoken, openhartig, reguit, ronduit, vrymoedig, rondborstig, opreg; onomwonde; ~**ness,** rondborstigheid, openhartigheid, vrymoedigheid.
outstan'ding, uitstekend, uitblinkend, hoogstaande,

outstare vernaam, belangrik, opmerklik, voortreflik, puik, treffend, markant; opvallend; onbetaal(d), uit= staande (skulde); ~ *DEBTS*, uitstaande skulde; ~ *FOR his speeches*, 'n uitblinker as redenaar; ~ *IN ability*, van voortreflike bekwaamheid; *an* ~ *SCHOLAR*, 'n skitterende geleerde.
outstare', die oë laat neerslaan, onbeskof aankyk.
out'-station, buitepos.
outstay', langer bly as, te lank bly; ~ *the TIME*, oor jou tyd bly; ~ *your WELCOME*, te lank bly; vir jou gasheer 'n oorlas word.
out'stretch, ~**ed**, uitgestrek, uitgespan.
outstrip', (-ped), wen, verbyhardloop; verbystrewe; uitloop; ~ *another*, uitblink bo; verbystrewe.
outtalk', doodpraat; oorbluf.
outtrump', oortroef.
out'turn, opbrengs.
outvie', oortref.
outvote', oorstem; doodstem, afstem.
outwalk', vinniger loop; iem. gedaan loop.
out'ward, (n) uiterlik; (a) uiterlik, uitwendig, buite= kant; na die buitekant; *the* ~ *MAN*, die uiterlike; ~ *POLICY*, uitwaartse beleid; (adv) na die buite= kant; *clear* ~,'n skip uitklaar; ~ **angle**, buitehoek; ~**-bound**, uitgaande, op die uitreis; ~ **flight**, heen= vlug; ~ **form**, voorkome, die uiterlike; ~ **journey**, heenreis, uitreis; ~ **mail**, uitgaande pos; ~ **man**, die uitwendige mens; ~**ness**, uiterlikheid, opper= vlakkigheid; objektiwiteit; belangstelling in uiter= likhede; ~**s**, na die buitekant, buitekant toe, uit= waarts.
outwear', (..wore, ..worn), gedaan dra; langer dra as.
outweigh', swaarder weeg as, oortref.
outwit', (-ted), verskalk, doodsit, uitoorlê, te slim wees vir; fop, kul.
out'work[1], (n) buitewerk (van fort).
outwork'[2], (v) meer werk as, iem. gedaan werk.
ou'zel, lyster.
ou'zo, ouzo.
ov'al, (n) ovaal; krieketveld; (a) ovaal, eierrond.
Ovam'bo, (-s), Ovambo.
ovar'ial, ovar'ian, tot 'n eierstok behorend, eierstok=.
ovariot'omy, wegneming van die eierstok, ovarioto= mie.
ov'arism, ovarisme.
ovarit'is, ovaritis, eierstokontsteking.
ovar'ium, (..ria), eierstok.
ov'ary, (..ries), eierstok; vrugbeginsel (bot.).
ov'ate, eiervormig, ovaal; ~ *oblong*, langwerpig ovaal.
ova'tion, hulde, ovasie, toejuiging.
o'ven, oond, kooktoestel; *no man will another in the* ~ *seek, except that himself have been there*, as jy agter die deur staan, soek jy 'n ander ook daar; ~ **roast**, (n) oondbraaistuk; ~**-roast**, (v) oondbraai.
ov'er, (n) boulbeurt, oorbeurt (krieket); *maiden* ~, leë boulbeurt; (adv) oor; omver, onderstebo, om; opnuut; ~ *AGAIN*, nog 'n keer; ~ *AGAINST*, teenoor; in teenstelling met; *ALL* ~, oral; tot in die kleinste besonderheid; *it is ALL* ~ *with him*, dis klaarpraat met hom; *that is John ALL* ~, dis net wat ek van Jan verwag het; ~ *AND* ~, keer op keer, herhaaldelik, oor en oor; *ASK someone* ~, iem. uitnooi; *BLOW* ~, omwaai; oorwaai; *not* ~ *CLEVER*, nie danig slim nie; *DO it all* ~, alles oordoen; *it is* ~ *and DONE with*, dis uit en gedaan; *the quarrel is* ~ *and DONE with*, die ou rusie is nou finaal uit die wêreld; *HAND* ~, oorhandig; *MAKE* ~, oormaak, skenk; *READ this passage* ~, lees die stuk oor; *RUN* ~ *to buy ice cream*, oorhardloop om roomys te koop; *TURN* ~ *by a bicycle*, met 'n fiets raakry; ~ *THERE*, daarso; *ten TIMES* ~, 'n tien keer, tiendubbel; *TURN* ~ *a page*, omblaai; *not* ~ *WELL*, nie danig gesond nie; ~ *to YOU*, dis jou beurt; neem jy oor; (prep) oor; bo-op; oorkant; by; uit; aan; ~ *and ABOVE*, boonop, bowendien, buitendien; bo en behalwe; *ALL* ~ *India*, oor die hele Indië; ~ *a GLASS of wine*, by 'n glasie wyn; ~ *HEAD and ears*, tot oor die ore; ~ *his HEAD*, bui= te hom om; bokant sy vuurmaakplek; *head* ~ *heels*, halsoorkop; ~ *one's NAME*, bokant iem. se naam; *SIXTY and* ~, oor sestig; *SLEEP* ~ *a mat= ter*, oor 'n saak nadink (slaap); ~ *SUPPER*, gedu= rende die aandete; ~ *the TELEPHONE*, oor die telefoon; ~ *TO you!* dis nou jou beurt; *all the WORLD* ~, die hele wêreld deur.
over-abound', alte oorvloedig wees, oorvloed hê van.
over-abun'dance, oorvloed, oorvloedigheid.
over-abun'dant, meer as volop, oorvolop.
over-accent'uate, oorbeklemtoon.
overact' oordryf.
over-act'ive, ooraktief.
ov'erall, (n) oorpak; oorrok; (pl) oorbroek, oorpak, werkpak; morsjurk (kind); (a) totaal; algemeen; al= geheel; ~ *CARPET*, volvloertapyt; ~ *DIA= METER*, buitemiddellyn; ~ *DIMENSION*, totale maat; ~ *FIGURE*, totaalsyfer; ~ *LENGTH*, to= tale lengte; ~ *MEASURE*, bruto maat; ~ *SIZE*, totale grootte; ~ *SPAN*, sweefwydte (brug); ~ *SUIT*, oorpak; (adv) geheel en al, oral.
over-anxi'ety, te groot besorgdheid, oorbesorgdheid; oorbegerigheid.
over-an'xious, alte besorg; alte begerig.
overarch', oorwelf.
over'-arm, oorhands; ~ **bowling**, oorhandse boul= werk; ~ **stroke**, boarmslag.
overawe', ontsag inboesem, in ontsag hou, imponeer, oorbluf, oorduiwel.
overbal'ance, (n) oorgewig; onewewigtigheid; (v) meer weeg; oorhel; die ewewig verloor; omkantel, omslaan.
overbank', te veel (laat) oorhel, te veel (laat) kantel.
overbear', (..bore, ..borne), onderdruk, onderwerp; omvergooi; oortref; oorweldig, oorrompel; ~**ing**, aanmatigend, trots, hoogmoedig, heerssugtig, baasspelerig; *be* ~ *ing*, 'n hoë hart hê.
overbid', (~ or ..bade, ~ or -den), te veel bie; meer bied as, oorbie.
overblown', te ver uitgekom; uitgebloei, uitgeblom.
ov'erboard, oorboord; *throw* ~, oorboord gooi.
overboil', te lank kook; oorkook.
overbold', alte vrymoedig, vermetel.
ov'erboot, oorstewel.
ov'erbridge, (n) bobrug; lugbrug, oorbrug.
overbridge', (v) oorbrug.
ov'erbright, te helder; te knap.
overbrim', (-med), oorloop.
overbuild', (..built), te dig bebou; te veel bou.
overburd'en, (n) deklaag, oordekking, dekterrein; bo= laag; (v) oorlaai; ooreis; ~**ing**, oorlading.
overbus'y, baie besig.
overbuy', (..bought), te veel koop; jou vaskoop.
overcall', hoër bie (kaarte); ~ *one's hand*, oorbie.
overcapitaliza'tion, oorkapitalisasie.
overcap'italize, oorkapitaliseer, die kapitaal te hoog maak.
over-care'ful, oorsekuur, te versigtig, oorvsigtig.
overca'rry, (..ried), te ver ry (dra, vervoer).
overcast', (v) (~), bewolk, verduister; omkap (naald= werk); (a) bewolk, toegetrek, betrokke; ~**ing**, om= kapsteek; ~ **seam**, oorhandsgewerkte naat.
over-cau'tion, oorversigtigheid.
over-cau'tious, te versigtig, oorvsigtig.
ov'ercharge, (n) oorbelasting; oorvraging, oorvorde= ring, oordrewe prys; te swaar lading; strafport.
overcharge', (v) te hoog reken; afset, te veel laat be= taal, uitsuig; oorlaai; oorvra.
overcloud', bewolk, benewel.
ov'ercoat, jas, warm jas, winterjas; ~**ing**, jasgoed, jasstof.
overcome', (v) (..came, ~), oormeester, platloop, oorkom, baasraak; (a) verslae, oorstelp, aange= daan; ~ *BY grief*, deur smart oorstelp; ~ *WITH emotion*, deur ontroering aangegryp (oormeester).
over-con'fidence, te groot vertroue, vermetelheid, as= trantheid, oormoedigheid.
over-con'fident, te seker, astrant, oormoedig.
overcook', doodkook, te lank kook.
overcooked', te lank gekook.
over-cred'ulous, (alte) liggelowig.
overcrop', (-ped), saaigrond uitput, roofbou pleeg; ~**ping**, roofbou.
overcrow', triomfeer oor, kraai oor.

overcrowd', oorlaai, te vol laai; oorvol maak; oorbevolk; ~ **ed**, oorvol; oorbevolk; oorlaai; ~ **ing**, oorlading; oorbevolking.
overcrust', met 'n kors bedek.
over-cur'ious, te nuuskierig.
over-dar'ing, te waaghalsig.
overdevel'op, oorontwikkel; ~ **ment**, oorontwikkeling.
overdo', (..did, -ne), oordryf, te buite gaan; te ver dryf; te gaar maak; *don't* ~ *it*, moenie jou ooreis nie; moenie jou te veel vermoei nie.
overdone', oorgaar, te gaar; oorwerk, uitgeput; oordrewe; oorlaai.
ov'erdose, (n) oordosis.
overdose', (v) te groot dosis ingee.
ov'erdraft, oortrokke bankrekening, oortrekking; bankskuld.
overdraw', (..drew, -n), oortrek (bankrekening); 'n oordrewe beskrywing gee, alte lewendig skilder.
ov'erdress, (n) oorkleed; bokleed; borok.
overdress', (v) opsigtig aantrek; ~ **ed**, te opsigtig geklee.
ov'erdrive¹, (n) snelrat, spoedrat.
overdrive'², (v) oorwerk, ooreis; flou ry; te ver (hard) slaan.
overdue', agterstallig; vervalle; te laat, oor die tyd; *be* ~, uitbly; agterstallig wees; ~ **bill**, vervalle wissel.
over-eag'er, oorgretig, oorywerig, te voortvarend; ~ **ness**, oorgretigheid.
overeat', (..ate, -en), ooreet.
over-ed'ucated, oorbeskaaf(d).
over-emphat'ic, alte nadruklik.
over-em'phasize, oorbeklemtoon.
over-enthusias'tic, oorywerig, dweepagtig.
overes'timate, (n) oorskatting; (v) oorskat, te hoog skat.
over-excite', prikkel, baie opwek; ~ **d**, te opgewek, te opgewonde; ~ **ment**, ooropgewondenheid, oorspanning.
over-exert', te veel inspan; oorspan; ~ **ion**, oorspanning.
over-expose', te lank belig,oorbelig.
over-expo'sure, oorbeligting; oorontbloting.
ov'erfall, (n) onstuimige see (water); oorloop; (pl) bankgolwe.
overfall', (v) (..fell), val oor (op), oorval; aanval.
over-famil'iar, oorgemeensaam, vrypostig.
over-fatigue', oorvermoeidheid, oormoegheid; ~ **d**, oorvermoeid, doodmoeg.
overfeed', (..fed), te veel voer; volstop.
overfish', te veel vis; leeg vis.
o'verflight, oorvlug.
o'verflow, (n) oorloop; uitloop; oorstroming; (a) ekstra, orig; ~ *meeting*, ekstra vergadering.
overflow', (v) oorstroom.
overflow'ing, (n) oorvolheid, oorvloed; oorstroming; *full to* ~, oorlopend vol, tot oorlopens toe vol; boordevol; (a) stampvol, boordensvol.
ov'erflow: ~ **meeting**, byvergadering, ekstra vergadering; ~ **pipe**, oorlooppyp, morspyp; ~ **valve**, morsklep.
overfly', (..flew, ..flown), vlieg oor; verder vlieg.
o'verfond, te lief vir, alte versot op.
over-free', vatterig, vrypostig, astrant.
ov'erfreight, (n) te swaar vrag, oorvrag.
overfreight', (v) oorlaai.
over-friend'ly, danig, oorvriendelik; inkruiperig.
overfull', stampvol, oorvol.
o'vergarment, bokleed.
over-gen'erous, oordadig; ooredelmoedig.
over-gov'ern, oorreguleer, oorbestuur.
overgraze', oorbewei; ~ **d**, oorbewei.
overgraz'ing, oorbeweiding.
ov'erground, bokant die grond.
overgrow', (..grew, -n), begroei, toegroei, oorgroei; te vinnig groei; ~ **n**, toegegroei, bedek, begroei; verwilderd.
ov'ergrowth, te weelderige groei; uitwas.
ov'erhand, oorhands; ~ *BOWLING*, oorhandse boulwerk; ~ *KNOT*, gewone knoop, oorhandse knoop.
over-han'dle, te veel gebruik.

ov'erhand stitch, oorhandse steek.
ov'erhang, (n) oorhangende deel, oorsteeksel; oorhelling.
overhang', (v) (..hung), oorhang, uitsteek; bedreig; oorsteek; ~ **ing**, oorhang; ~ **rock**, hangklip.
ov'er-happy, oorgelukkig.
over-has'ty, oorhaastig.
ov'erhaul, (n) opknapping, deeglike ondersoek.
overhaul', (v) goed nakyk, noukeurig ondersoek, nasien, repareer, herstel (masjien); opknap.
ov'erhead, (n) algemene koste; (a) bolug=, bogronds; oorhoofs; (adv) bokant die hoof, in die lug; ~ **aerial**, lugantenne; ~ **bridge**, lugbrug, bobrug; ~ **charges (expenses)**, bokoste; indirekte koste, algemene koste, bykomende koste; ~ **flight**, oorvlug; ~ **irrigation**, sprinkelbesproeiing; ~ **projector**, truprojektor; ~ **railway**, lugspoor; ~ **rope**, lugtou; ~ **s**, bokoste; ~ **traveller**, loopkraan; ~ **valve**, kopklep; ~ **wires**, luggeleiding, lugdrade.
overhear', (-d), afluister, opvang; toevallig hoor; ~ **d**, afgeluister; *you might be* ~ *d*, mure het ore.
overheat', te veel verhit, oorverhit; ~ **ing**, oorverhitting; warm word (geweer, masjien).
overhung', oorhang, behang.
over-indulge', te veel toegee; verwen, jou oorcct, onmatig wees.
over-indulg'ence, onmatigheid; te groot toegeeflikheid, verwenning.
over-indulg'ent, te toegeeflik.
ov'er-irrigation, oormatige besproeiing.
over-iss'ue, (n) te groot uitgifte; (v) te veel in omloop bring.
overjoy', verruk; ~ **ed'**, alte bly, in die wolke, verruk, opgetoë, sielsverheug.
over-keen', oorywerig; ~ **ness**, oorywer(igheid).
over-lab'our, oorwerk; te sorgvuldig bewerk.
overland', oor land; ~ **journey**, landreis; ~ **mail**, landpos; ~ **route**, landroete, landweg.
ov'erlap, (n) oorvleueling, uitvalgrond, oorvleuelde stuk; dakpanligging; oordekking.
overlap', (v) (-ped), oormekaar val, gedeeltelik bedek; uitsteek oor, groter wees as; oorvleuel; ~ **ping**, oorvleueling, oormekaargryping; oorslag; oorvalling, gedeeltelike dekking; verdubbeling, duplikasie.
over-lav'ish, alte kwistig, te volop.
ov'erlay, (n) tafelkleedjie, dekkleedjie, deken; bomatras; deklaag (filatelie); ~ **work**, belegwerk.
overlay', (v) (..laid), bedek, lê oor; belê (houtwerk).
overleaf', op die anderkant v.d. blad, aan die ommesy, anderkant; *turn* ~, blaai om.
overleap', (..lept or -ed), oorspring, spring oor; uitlaat.
ov'crlcather, oorleer, boleer.
overlie', (..lay, ..lain), lê op, bedek; smoor; doodlê, versmoor; ~ *a child*, 'n kind doodlê (versmoor).
overlive', oorleef, langer lewe as.
ov'erload, te swaar vrag; oorlading.
overload', te swaar laai, oorlaai; ~ **ing**, oorlading; oorbelasting.
overlook', oor die hoof sien, verbysien, deur die vingers sien; oorsien; miskyk; uitkyk op (bv. die see); toesig hou; ~ **er**, opsigter.
ov'erlord, opper(leen)heer.
over-loud', hardop; te hard.
ov'erman, voorman, ploegbaas; skeidsregter.
over-mann'ed, met te veel bemanning, oorbeman.
ov'ermantel, skoorsteenmantel; skoorsteenspieël.
over-man'y, (glad) te veel, te baie.
over-mast'ed, met te hoë (swaar) maste.
overmas'ter, oormeester, oorwin, baasraak.
ov'ermatch, (n) meerdere, bobaas.
overmatch', (v) oortref, oorwin, baas wees.
overmea'sure, toegif, oormaat.
ov'ermitten, oormof.
overmuch', te veel.
over-nice', te lekker; te kieskeurig, te puntenerig.
overnight', (adv) die vorige nag, gedurende die nag; snags; skielik, ineens; *remain* ~, oornag.
ov'ernight, (a) van die vorige aand; ~ **bag**, nagtas; ~ **guest**, slaapgas; ~ **stay**, oornagting.
over-offi'cious, te gedienstig, oorgedienstig.
over-optimis'tic, te optimisties.

ov'erpass, (-es), lugbrug, oorbrug; oorpad, bopad.
overpass', oortref, verbygaan; oorsteek, oorgaan; verbysteek; oortree; oor die hoof sien.
overpay', (..paid), te veel betaal; 'n hoë loon gee; ~**ment,** teveelbetaling, oorbetaling, oorbesteding.
over-peo'pled, oorbevolk.
overpersuade', ompraat, oorreed.
overpitch', te ver gooi; oordryf.
overplay', oordryf; ~ *one's hand,* te veel waag; die spel te ver voer.
ov'erplus, te veel; oorskot, surplus.
over-polite', oorbeleef.
over-pop'ulated, oorbevolk.
over-popula'tion, oorbevolking.
overpow'er, oorweldig, oorstelp, oorman, oormeester; ~**ing,** (n) oormeestering; (a) onweerstaanbaar; oorstelpend.
overpraise', (n) oordrewe lof; (v) te veel prys; ophemel, opvysel.
over-pre'ssure, te groot druk, oorlading, oordruk.
ov'erprint, (n) opdruk, oordruk.
overprint', (v) oordruk, bo-oor druk; 'n donker afdruk maak (fot.); deur opdruk aanbring, opdruk.
over-produce', te veel produseer.
ov'er-production, oorproduksie.
ov'erproof, bokant die normale sterkte beproef, van meer as gewone sterkte (alkohol).
overrate', te hoog skat, oorskat.
overreach', agterhaal; vang, inhaal; bedrieg; jou verrek; aanslaan, aankap (perd); ~ *oneself,* jou verrek; te ver gaan; jou doel verbystrewe.
overread', (~), te veel lees.
over-refine', te suiwer maak; ~**d',** oorbeskaaf.
override', (..rode, ..ridden), oorry, afmat; laat plat trap; vernietig; jou nie steur nie aan; ter syde stel; flou ry; tot niet maak, vernietig; te bowe kom.
overri'ding, oorheersend; ~ *FACTOR,* oorheersende faktor; ~ *JURISDICTION,* meerdere regsbevoegdheid; ~ *PRINCIPLE,* deurslaggewende beginsel.
overripe', oorryp, doodryp, papryp.
overrule', oorstem; verwerp (voorstel); ongeldig verklaar; tot niet maak; v.d. hand wys (beswaar); baasspeel; ~ *an OBJECTION,* 'n beswaar verwerp; 'n beswaar v.d. hand wys; ~ *a PLEA,* 'n pleit van die hand wys.
overrul'ing, oppermagtig, allesbeheersend.
ov'errun[1], (n) kraaines (visvang).
overrun'[2], (v) (..**ran,** ~), oorstroom; plat loop; oorrompel; oorry; oordek, wemel van (onkruid, ens.); ~ *a COUNTRY,* 'n land oorrompel; *a house* ~ *with IVY,* 'n huis oortrek met klimop; *a cellar* ~ *with MICE,* 'n kelder wat van muise wemel; ~ *ONESELF,* jou kragte met hardloop ooreis; ~ *with WEEDS,* vervuil van onkruid.
over-scrup'ulous, alte nougeset.
oversea(s)', (adv) oorsee; na (in) die buiteland.
overseas', (a) oorsees; ~ *post,* oorsese pos.
oversee', (..saw, -n), oorsien; die toesig hê oor.
ov'erseer, opsigter, opsiener, fabrieksopsigter.
oversell', (..sold), meer verkoop as 'n mens kan lewer, te veel verkoop.
over-sen'sitive, oorgevoelig.
oversew', oorhands werk.
oversexed', oorseksueel, seksbehep, speuls, katools.
overshad'ow, beskut; oorskadu, oortref; ~ *another,* iem. in die skaduwee stel.
ov'ershoe, oorskoen.
overshoot', (..shot), verbyskiet; te ver skiet; oorheen skiet; mis; verbyloop; ~ *the MARK,* die doel verbyskiet; ~ *ONESELF,* jou mond verbypraat; te ver gaan, oordryf.
ov'ershot, (n) boslag; (a) boslag-; mis; oordrewe; ~ **wheel,** boslagwaterwiel.
ov'erside, (n) hoogste kant; (a) oorboord, oor die kant.
ov'ersight, vergissing, onoplettendheid, fout, nalatigheid, versuim; toesig.
oversimplifica'tion, oorvereenvoudiging.
oversim'plify, (..fied), oorvereenvoudig.
ov'ersize, (n) bomaat, bogrootte; (a) ~**d,** bonormaal, oorgroot.

ov'erskirt, oorrok, borok.
ov'erslaugh, (mil.), oorslag; ontheffing van gewone pligte; passering.
oversleep', (..slept), jou verslaap, te lank slaap.
ov'ersleeve, morsmou, oormou.
oversmoke', te veel rook.
over-soon', alte gou.
overspan', (-ned), oorspan.
overspend', (..spent), te veel geld uitgee, spandabel wees.
overspent', oorspanne, afgemat.
ov'erspill, (n) (die) gemorste, oortollige; oorloop; oorbevolking.
overspill', (v) (..**spilt** or **-ed),** oorkook; oorloop.
overspread', (~), oorsprei, oordek, besaai.
overstaff', te sterk beman; oorbeman; ~**ed,** met 'n te groot personeel, oorbeset.
overstate', oordryf; te hoog opgee; oorbeklemtoon; ~**ment,** oordrywing; oorbeklemtoning.
overstay', langer bly as, te lank bly.
overstep', (-ped), oorstap, oorskry, te buite gaan; ~ *all BOUNDS,* alle perke te buite gaan; ~ *the MARK,* te ver gaan; oor die tou trap; ~ **ping,** oorskryding (perke).
over-stim'ulate, oorprikkel.
ov'erstock, (n) te groot voorraad; oorvoorraad.
overstock', (v) oorlaai, oorhoop; te groot voorraad hê; te veel vee aanhou; ~ *a FARM,* te veel vee op 'n plaas hou; ~ *the MARKET,* die mark oorvoer; ~**ing,** oorinkoop; oorbeweiding.
ov'erstrain, (n) oorspanning; verrekking.
overstrain', (v) oorspan; verrek; ooreis; laat doodtrek (perd); oordrywe; ~ *oneself,* jou verrek.
overstress', te sterk beklemtoon, oorbeklemtoon.
overstrewn', oorstrooi, oordek.
ov'erstrung[1], (a) oormekaar gespan; kruissnarig (piano).
overstrung'[2], (a) oorspanne, oorprikkel(d) (senuwees).
oversubscribe', oorteken, volteken, oorskryf (lening).
oversubscrip'tion, oortekening, oorinskrywing.
oversupply', (n) oorvoering; (v) (..**lied),** te goed voorsien, oorvoer.
ov'ert, openbaar, duidelik, openlik; uiterlik.
overtake', (..took, -n), inhaal, agterhaal; verbysteek; oorval; ~ *ARREARS,* agterstand bywerk; ~ *n by a CATASTROPHE,* deur 'n ramp getref; ~*n in DRINK,* beskonke, hoenderkop.
overtak'ing, verbysteek; *no* ~, nie verbysteek nie.
overtask', te veel werk oplê, ooreis, te veel verg van, oorlaai.
overtax', te swaar belas, oorbelas; ooreis; ~**a'tion,** oorbelasting.
ov'erthrow, (n) ondergang, val, neerlaag; verbygooi, oorgooi (krieket).
overthrow', (v) (..threw, -n), omgooi, omverwerp; laat val, tot 'n val bring, oorwin; omvergooi; oorgooi.
ov'erthrust, oorskuiwing.
ov'ertime[1], (n) oorwerk, oorure, oortyd(diens).
overtime'[2], (v) oorbelig.
ov'ertime[3], (adv): *work* ~, oortyd werk, oorwerk doen; ~**-pay,** betaling vir oortyddiens.
overtire', te veel vermoei; ~**d,** oorvermoeid, afgemat, uitgeput; ~**d'ness,** oorvermoeidheid, afmatting.
ov'ertone[1], (n) botoon; te donker kleur.
overtone'[2], (v) oorstem; te donker maak (foto).
overtop', (-ped), uitsteek bokant; oortref.
overtop'ple, (laat) omslaan; omverwerp.
overtrade', oor(ver)handel.
overtrad'ing, oorhandel(drywing).
overtrain', ooroefen.
overtrump', oortroef, aftroef, hoër troef.
ov'erture, voorstel; opening, inleiding; aanbieding tot onderhandeling; eerste stappe; uitnodiging; ouverture, voorspel (musiek); *MAKE* ~ *s to,* toenadering soek by; ~ *s of PEACE,* voorstelle tot vredesonderhandeling.
ov'erturn, (n) omkering; mislukking; rewolusie.
overturn', (v) onderstebo keer, omslaan; tot 'n val bring, verslaan, omverwerp; onderstebo gooi; omdans.

overval'ue, te hoog skat (waardeer); oorwaardeer.
ov'erwear, (n) oorklere, oorkleding.
overwear', (v) (..wore, ..worn), uitslyt; uitgroei.
overwea'ry, oorvermoeid.
overween'ing, trots, hoogmoedig, verwaand, verwate; aanmatigend, baasspelerig.
ov'erweight, (n) oorgewig; oorwig; te groot gewig; (a) te swaar, oorgewig≠; ~ **luggage**, oorgewigbagasie.
overweight', (v) oorlaai; oorbelas; ~**ed**, te swaar gelaai.
overwhelm', oorstelp, oorweldig, oorman, oorrompel; ~**ing**, (n) oorstelping; (a) oorstelpend, oorweldigend, verpletterend.
ov'erwind, (n) oorhysing; ooropwinding (kabel).
overwind', (v) (..wound), te styf opwen; oorhys.
overwin'ter, oorwinter.
overwise', te slim.
ov'erword, titel, opskrif; refrein.
ov'erwork, (n) ekstra werk, oorwerk; te groot inspanning.
overwork', (v) oorwerk, te veel (laat) werk, met werk oorlaai, uitput; ~ *an idea*, 'n idee te ver uitspin; ~**ed**, afgewerk, oorwerk; ~*ed phrase*, holrug geryde (afgesaagde) uitdrukking.
overworn', uitgeput, afgemat; afgesaag; afgedra.
overwound', te styf opgewen; oorhys.
overwrought', oorspanne, opgewonde; oorlaai; te fyn uitgewerk.
over-zea'lous, alte ywerig, oorywerig.
ov'icell, eiersel.
ovic'ular, eier≠.
Ov'id, Ovidius.
ov'iduct, eierleier.
ov'iform, eiervormig.
ov'ine, skaapagtig, skaap≠.
ovip'arous, eierlëend; ~ *animal*, ovipaar.
ovipos'it, eiers lê; ..**si'tion**, eierlegging; ~**or**, lêboor, eierboor.
ov'Isac, eiersak.
ov'oid, eiervormig.
ovol'ogy, ovologie.
ov'ular, ovulêr.
ov'ulary, kiemsel≠.
ov'ulate, ovuleer.
ovula'tion, eieruitstoting, ovulasie.
ov'ule, kiemsel, onbevrugte eiertjie, eierkiem; saadknop (bot.).
ov'ulite, fossieleier.
ov'um, (ova), eier; vroulike kiem, ovum.
owe, skuld, verskuldig wees; te danke hê (gunstig); te wyte hê (ongunstig); *I ~ it to my FAMILY*, ek is dit aan my gesin verskuldig; ~ *FIFTEEN*, min vyftien (tennis); ~ *someone a GRUDGE*, 'n wrok teen iem. koester; *I ~ not any MAN*, ek skuld niemand iets nie; ~ *MONEY to someone*, geld aan iem. skuld; *I ~ him MUCH*, ek is baie aan hom verskuldig; *he ~ s his SUCCESS to his teachers*, hy het sy welslae aan sy onderwysers te danke.
ow'ing, (a) skuldig, onbetaal, verskuldig, uitstaande (skulde); (prep) weens; as gevolg van, danksy; ~ *TO*, ten gevolge van, danksy; ~ *TO an outbreak of measels*, weens 'n uitbreking van masels; ~ *TO rising costs*, ten gevolge van stygende koste.
owl, uil; uilskuiken; ~**-beak**, uilbek; ~**ery**, boerplek van uile; ~**et**, uiltjie; ~**-eyed**, met uiloë; ~**ish**, uilagtig; ~**-light**, skemering, skemer(te); ~**-like**, uilagtig.
own¹, (v) besit; erken, toegee; eien; ~ *to a FAULT*, 'n fout erken; ~ *UP*, beken, opbieg; ~ *UP to a mistake*, erken dat jy 'n fout begaan het; ~ *oneself in the WRONG*, ongelyk beken.
own², (a) eie; *of one's ~ ACCORD*, uit eie beweging; *hold one's ~ AGAINST*, jou handhaaf teen; *get one's ~ BACK*, wraak neem; ~ *BROTHER*, volle broer; *his ~ BUSINESS*, sy eie saak; *a CHARM of its ~*, 'n eienaardige (besondere) bekoring; *COME into one's ~*, in die besit van sy eiendom gestel word; *COME to one's ~*, tot jou reg kom; na waarde erken word; *she COOKS her ~ meals*, sy kook self; *through no FAULT of his ~*, sonder eie toedoen; *GET one's ~ back*, iem. met gelyke munt betaal; wraak neem op iem.; *HOLD one's ~*, jou man staan; *be one's ~ MAN*, jou eie baas wees; *know one's ~ MIND*, weet wat jy wil hê; *he has NOTHING of his ~*, hy het self niks; *ON his ~*, op eie houtjie; onafhanklik; *be ON one's ~*, op jou eentjie wees; *START on one's ~*, vir eie rekening iets begin; *my ~ SWEETHEART*, my eie (liefste) skat; *his TIME is his ~*, hy beskik oor sy eie tyd; *I want this for my VERY ~*, ek wil dit vir my alleen hê; *have it all one's ~ WAY*, jou eie sin kan volg; jou gang kan gaan.
own'er, eienaar, besitter, baas; eienares; *at ~'s risk*, op eie risiko; ~**-builder**, eienaarbouer; ~**-driven**, deur die eienaar bestuur; ~**-driver**, eienaarbestuurder; ~**-farmer**, eienaarboer; ~**less**, sonder eienaar, onbeheer, sonder baas; ~**ship**, eiendomsreg, besit; ~ *ship of land*, landbesit.
ox, (-en), os; *the black ~ has TRODDEN on his foot*, die ongeluk het hom getref; *YOUNG ~*, ossie, tollie.
oxal'ic, oksaal≠, suringsuurhoudend; ~ **acid**, oksaalsuur, suringsuur.
ox'alis, wildesuring.
ox: ~**-bow**, boogjuk; rivierdraai, meander; ~**-bow lake**, meandermeer, rivierkronkelmeer; ~**-cart**, oskar; ~**er**, beesdraad; ~**-eye**, osoog, margriet (blom), gansblom; ~**-eyed**, met groot oë; ~**-fence**, beesdraad.
Ox'ford bags, sambalbroek, sakbroek, fladderbroek, wye broek.
ox: ~**-gall**, beesgal; ~**-head**, oskop; domkop; ~**-heart**, beeshart; ~**herd**, beeswagter; ~**hide**, beesvel, osvel.
ox'ident, oksideermiddel
ox'idate, oksideer.
oxida'tion, oksidering, oksidasie, suurstofopname.
ox'ide, oksied, okside, suurstofverbinding; ~ *of iron*, ysteroksied.
ox'idize, oksideer.
ox'idizing, oksidasie≠; oksiderend; ~ **agent**, oksideermiddel; ~ **flame**, oksideervlam; ~ **reaction**, oksiderende reaksie.
Oxon'ian, (n) Oxfordstudent; Oxfordgeleerde, (a) Oxfords, van Oxford.
ox: ~**-pecker**, renostervoël; ~**-pluck**, beesharslag; ~**-stall**, osstal; ~ **tail**, osstert, beesstert; ~**-tail soup**, beesstertsop; ~**-team**, osspan.
ox'ter, armholte, oksel.
ox: ~**-tongue**, beestong; ~**-tripe**, beespens; ~**-wagon**, osşewa; ~**-whip**, ossweep, groot sweep.
oxy-acet'ylene, oksiasetileen; ~ **blowpipe**, sweispyp; ~ **welding**, (die) las met 'n oksiasetileenvlam.
ox'ygen, suurstof; ~ **apparatus**, suurstoftoestel.
ox'ygenate, met suurstof verbind, oksideer; ~**d**, suurstofhoudend.
ox'ygen: ~ **cylinder**, suurstofsilinder; ~**ize** = **oxygenate**; ~ **lance**, suurstofsnypyp; ~ **mask**, suurstofmasker; ~**ous**, suurstofhoudend.
oxy-hyd'rogen, knalgas.
oxymor'on, oksimoron.
ox'ytone, woord met die klem op die laaste lettergreep, oksitonon.
oxy-sacc'harum, asynsuiker.
oyes'! o yes'! oyez'! stilte! luister!
oys'ter, oester; *as close as an ~*, so dig soos 'n pot (oester); ~**-bank**, oesterbank; ~**-basket**, oestermandjie; ~**-bed**, oesterbed; ~**-boat**, oesterskuit; ~**-catcher**, oestervanger; ~**-culture**, oesterkwekery; oesterteelt; ~**-culturist**, oesterkweker; ~**-farm**, oesterkwekery; ~**-fisher**, oestervisser; ~**-fishery**, oestervissery; ~**-gatherer**, oestervisser; ~**-knife**, oestermes; ~ **patty**, oesterpastei; ~**-plant**, hawerwortel; ~**-poisoning**, oestervergifting; ~**-preserve**, oesterpark; ~**-shell**, oesterskulp.
ozo'cerite, **ozok'erite**, paraffienwas, osokeriet.
oz'one, osoon.
ozoni'ferous, osoonhoudend.
ozon'ic, osoonagtig, osoon≠.
oz'onize, met osoon versadig, osoniseer; ~**r**, osoonapparaat, osoniseertoestel.
ozonom'eter, osoonmeter.

P

p, (ps, p's), p; *LITTLE* ~ , p'tjie; *MIND one's P's and Q's,* op jou telle pas; in jou pasoppens bly.
pa, pa.
Paarl, Paarl; *AT* ~ , in die Paarl; *OF* ~ , Paarls; ~ **ite,** Paarliet; ~ **wine,** Paarlse wyn.
pab'ulary, voedsaam, voedsel=.
pab'ulum, voedsel; *mental* ~ , geestesvoedsel.
pace, (n) tree, pas, stap, skrede; gang (perd); tred; tempo; vaart, snelheid; *EVEN* ~ , egalige marstempo; *GO the* ~ , vinnig loop; losbandig lewe; *go at a GREAT* ~ , met groot snelheid beweeg; *(at) a HOT* ~ , baie vinnig; *KEEP* ~ *with,* tred hou met; byhou by; *the* ~ *of the OX,* die stap van die os; *PUT through his* ~ *s,* sy passies laat maak; iem. laat toon wat hy kan doen; *QUICK* ~ , versnelde pas; *SET the* ~ , die maat (pas) aangee; *SHOW one's* ~*s,* toon wat jy kan doen; jou passies maak; *at a SLOW* ~ , stadig; *STEADY* ~ , matige marstempo; (v) stap; aftree (afstand); trippel, 'n pas loop (perd); die pas aangee (wedrenne); ~ **bowler,** snelbouler; ~**-maker,** gangmaker; ~**-making,** gangmakery; ~**r,** voetganger, stapper; gangloper (perd); ~**-setter,** gangmaker, pasaangeër.
pa'cha, *kyk* **pasha.**
pach'yderm, dikvel, dikhuid; dikvellige mens; ~**'atous,** dikvellig; ongevoelig.
pachyderm'ia, dikvelligheid, dikhuidigheid, pagidermie.
pacif'ic, vreedsaam, stil; *P* ~ *Ocean,* Stille Oseaan; Groot Oseaan; *South P* ~ *Ocean,* Stille Suidsee; ~**a'tion,** versoening, bedaring; stilling; vredestigting, pasifikasie; ~ **atory,** vredestigtend, bedarend, sussend, versoenend.
pacif'icism, pa'cifism, vredeliewendheid, pasifisme.
pacif'icist, pa'cifist, vredesvoorstander, pasifis.
pa'cifier, vredestigter, kalmeerder; trooster.
pa'cify, (..fied), vrede maak, stilmaak, laat bedaar, kalmeer, paai.
pac'ing, gangmakery; stap; afgemete stap.
pack, (n) pak, bondel; baal; pakket; klomp; rugsak; pakdier; vrag; rotsopvulling (myn); trop (honde); bende; pakys; voorhoede (rugby); *a* ~ *of CARDS,* 'n pak (stel) kaarte; *HOT* ~ , warm omslag; *a* ~ *of HOUNDS,* 'n trop honde; *a* ~ *of LIES,* 'n boel leuens; *a* ~ *of ROGUES,* 'n klomp skurke; (v) pak; inpak, verpak; inmaak (groente), dig opmekaar pak (klippe); vas teen mekaar druk; volstop, volprop, laai, partydig saamstel (jurie; parlement); ~ *AWAY,* wegpak; ~ *a JURY,* 'n jurie volstop; ~ *someone OFF,* iem. wegstuur; iem. in die pad steek; ~ *UP,* inpak (gereedskap); trap, maak dat jy wegkom; ~ *on all SAILS,* alle seile bysit; ~ *one's THINGS,* jou matte oprol; vertrek.
pack'age, (n) pakket; pakkasie, verpakking; pakkie; pakloon; (v) verpak; ~ **deal,** alomvattende reëling, allesinsluitende akkoord; bondelkoop; pakketooreenkoms; ~ **transaction,** bondelkoop; pakkettransaksie (-koop).
pack: ~**-animal,** pakdier, lasdier; ~**-cloth,** paklinne; ~**-donkey,** pakdonkie; ~**-drill,** pakdril; *no names no* ~*-drill,* geen naam, geen straf.
packed, gepak; stampvol, propvol; ~ *to CAPACITY,* stampvol; daar was nie meer plek vir 'n muis nie; *a* ~ *HALL,* 'n stampvol saal.
pack'er, pakker; pakmasjien, verpakker; inmaker.
pack'et, pakkie, pakket, doos; boot; ~ **boat,** posboot; pakketboot.
pack: ~**horse,** pakperd; ~**-ice,** pakys.
pack'ing, (die) inpak; verpak; verpakking; digtingsmiddel; pakking (meganika); opvulling, vulling (in myn); paksel; *SEND someone* ~ , iem. wegjaag; iem. in die pad steek; *be SENT* ~ , die trekpas kry; in die pad gesteek word; ~**-awl,** paknaald, pak-els; ~**-case,** pakkis; ~**-cellar,** pakkelder; ~ **house,** pakhuis; ~**-material,** pakgoed, verpakkingsmateriaal; ~**-needle,** paknaald, seilnaald; ~**-paper,** pakpapier; ~**-press,** pakpers; ~**-room,** pakkamer; ~**-shed,** pakhuis; ~**-sheet,** paklinne, pakdoek; nat omslag; ~**-thread,** pakgaring; ~ **yard,** pakkery; pakwerf.

pack: ~**-leader,** voorste pakdier; ~ **man,** smous, pakkiesdraer; ~**-mule,** pakmuil, pakesel; ~**-needle,** seilnaald; ~**-ox,** pakos; ~**-saddle,** paksaal; ~**-saddlery,** paktuig; ~**-set,** paktoestel; ~**thread,** seilgaring, pakgaring; ~**-train,** ry pakdiere; ~**-transport,** vervoer met pakdiere, lasdiervervoer.
pact, verdrag, verbond, ooreenkoms.
pad¹, (sl) pad; struikrowery; trippelaar, pasganger (perd); *gentleman of the* ~ , struikrower; (v) loop, stap; stadig gaan; ~ *the HOOF,* ~ *IT,* met dapper en stapper gaan.
pad², (n) kussinkie; skryfblok; poot; saaltjie; beenskut (krieket); voetsool; opvulsel, opstopsel (by klere); hef; (v) (**-ded**), opvul; beklee; volstop; uitvoer, watteer (klere); ~**ded,** gevul, opgestop; ~*ded room (cell),* uitgevoerde kamer, isoleerkamer; ~**ding,** opstopping; vulsel, stopsel; vulwerk, bladvulling; pakking; (woord)omslagtigheid, gegorrel.
pad'dle¹, (n) roeispaan; skepspaan, skepbak, pagaai; roeiery; (v) losroei, pagaai; ~ *one's own canoe,* op eie wieke dryf; jouself red; op eie bene staan; self sien dat jy regkom.
pad'dle², (v) plas, pootbaai, pootjiebaai; waggel, valval loop.
pad'dle: ~**-ball,** spaanbal; ~ **boat,** ratboot, wiel= (stoom)boot; ~**-box,** ratkas.
pad'dler¹, pagaaier, los roeier; wiel(stoom)boot.
pad'dler², plasser, pootbaaier.
pad'dle: ~**-ski,** handroei, skiroei, plankski; ~**-steamer,** ratboot, wielstoomboot; ~**-wheel,** skeprat.
pad'dling, plassery; ~ **pool,** plasdam.
padd'ock, kamp; kraal; perk, renbaanperk.
Padd'y¹, (Paddies), Ier.
padd'y², rys; padie; ~**-rice,** doprys.
padd'y(whack), boosheid, slegte bui; klap.
pad'lock, (n) hangslot; (v) toesluit.
pad'-nag, trippelaar, pasganger.
pad're, veldprediker, kapelaan.
pad'-saw, skropsaag.
pad'stone, draagsteen.
pae'an, segelied, triomflied, jubelsang, danklied; segekreet, loflied.
p(a)ed'erasty, sodomie, pederastie.
p(a)ediatri'cian, p(a)ediat'rist, kinderdokter, kinderarts, pediater.
pa(e)dia'trics, kindergeneeskunde, pediatrie.
pa(e)dia'trist, kinderarts.
p(a)edobap'tism, kinderdoop.
pa(e)dolog'ical, pedologies.
pa(e)dol'ogist, kinderkenner, pedoloog.
pa(e)dol'ogy, kinderstudie, pedologie.
pag'an, (n) heiden; (a) heidens; ~**ism,** heidendom, paganisme; ~**ist,** heiden, paganis; ~**is'tic,** heidens, paganisties; ~**ize,** tot heiden maak.
page¹, (n) bode, boodskapper, skildknaap; edelknaap; livrekneg, page, hoteljoggie; sleepdraertjie; hofknapie (by troue); (v) laat roep, oproep.
page², (n) bladsy, pagina; *from the FIRST* ~ *to the last,* v.d. begin tot die end; *TURN a* ~ , omblaai; (v) pagineer, bladsye nommer; ~ *through,* deurblaai.
pa'geant, praalvertoon, skouspel, optog, historiese (allegoriese) vertoning; ~**ry,** praal, prag, skynvertoon.
page'(boy), page, hoteljoggie; sleepdraertjie; boodskappertjie; hofknapie (by troue).
page' proof, bladsyproef, paginaproef.
pa'ginal, pa'ginary, bladsy=.
pa'ginate, pagineer, bladsye nommer.
pagina'tion, bladsynommering, paginering.
pagod'a pagode, tempel.
pah! ga! ba!
paid, betaal, voldaan; loontrekkend; ~ *in ADVANCE,* vooruitbetaal; *PUT* ~ *to,* 'n end maak aan; ~ **leave,** betaalde verlof, verlof met salaris; ~**-on,** teenkrediet.
paid'-up, (op)betaal; ~**-capital,** gestorte kapitaal; ~ **policy,** opbetaalde polis; ~**-share,** volgestorte aandeel.
pail, emmer, dopemmer.
paillasse', strooimatras.

paillette — palliatory

paillette', pailjet; blinker(tjie).
pail'ful, emmervol; *two* ~*s of milk*, twee emmers melk.
pain, (n) pyn; smart, leed; weedom, wee; kommer; straf; (pl) moeite, inspanning; barensweë; *BE in* ~, pyn ly; *on* ~ *of DEATH*, op doodstraf, op straffe des doods; *FOR one's* ~*s*, vir sy moeite; *no* ~*s no GAINS; no GAINS without* ~*s*, sonder moeite kry 'n mens niks; wie heuning uithaal, moet steke ver= wag; *GIVE* ~, seermaak; *he was at GREAT* ~*s to*, hy het hom baie moeite getroos om; *be a* ~ *in the NECK to someone*, 'n doring in iem. se vlees wees; *that gives me a* ~ *in the NECK*, dit gee my 'n pyn op my naarheid; ~*s and PENALTIES*, strawwe; *after PLEASURE comes the* ~, na vrolikheid kom olik= heid; *SHARP* ~, skrynende pyn; *SPARE no* ~*s*, g'n moeite ontsien nie; *SUFFER* ~, pyn ly; *TAKE* ~*s over*, baie moeite doen; *UNDER* ~ *of*, op straf van; (v) seermaak, pyn, pynig; kwel; bedroef, smart veroorsaak; ~**-expeller**, pynverdrywer; ~**ful**, pyn= lik, seer; smartlik; snerpend, skrynerig; ~**fulness**, pynlikheid, smartlikheid; skrynerigheid; ~**-killer**, pynstiller; ~**less**, pynloos; ~**lessness**, pynloosheid; smarteloosheid.
pains'taking, werksaam, nougeset, sorgsaam; ywerig, fluks, vlytig; presies, deeglik.
paint, (n) verf; grimeersel, blanketsel (vir gesig); *as FRESH AS* ~, springlewendig; gloednuut, vonkel= nuut; *the SMELL of* ~, verfreuk; (v) verf; skilder; aanstryk; blanket, grimeer; afbeeld, afskilder; ~ *BLACK*, swart maak; ~ *the LILY*, iets wat vol= maak is, probeer verbeter; iets mooier voorstel as wat dit is; ~*ed in OILS*, in olieverf; ~ *OUT*, oor= skilder; *SHE* ~*s*, sy verf; sy skilder; ~ *the TOWN red*, die dorp (stad) op horings neem; ~**-box**, verf= doos; ~**-brush**, verfkwas; skilderpenseel; Maart= blom, rooikwas, misryblom; ~**-dealer**, verfhande= laar.
paint'ed, geverf; geskilder; gevlek; *not as BLACK as it is* ~, nie so erg soos dit voorgestel word nie; ~ **glass**, skilderglas; ~ **lady**, katjietee; distelvlinder; ~ **snipe**, goudsnip.
paint'er¹, vanglyn, werplyn, vangtou: *cut the* ~, 'n skeiding bewerkstellig; jou los sny; jou eie pad gaan.
paint'er², verwer, skilder; kunsskilder; ~'**s canvas**, skilderslinne; ~'**s colic**, loodkoliek; ~'**s easel**, skil= deresel; ~'**s putty**, stopverf.
paint: ~ **factory**, verffabriek; ~ **gold**, nerfgoud; ~ **gun**, verfspuit; ~ **ing**, skildery, skilderstuk, doek; skilderwerk; skilderkuns; ~**-pan**, verfpot; ~**-rag**, verflap; ~**ress**, skilderes; ~**-shop**, verfwinkel; ~ **spray**, verfspuit; ~**-work**, verfwerk, skilderwerk; ~**y**, vol verf, bemors.
pair, (n) paar; ~ *of BELLOWS*, blaasbalk; ~ *of BI= NOCULARS*, verkyker; *a CARRIAGE and* ~, 'n rytuig met twee perde; ~ *of COMPASSES*, passer; *IN* ~*s*, twee-twee, paarsgewys; ~ *of PINCERS*, knyptang; ~ *of SCISSORS*, skêr; *a* ~ *of SHOES*, 'n paar skoene; *that is another* ~ *of SHOES (boots)*, dit is heeltemal 'n ander saak; ~ *of SPEC= TACLES*, bril; ~ *of TROUSERS*, broek; (v) paar; saampas, saamvoeg, verenig; twee-twee bymekaar= voeg; ~ *off*, twee-twee bymekaarvoeg; afpaar (par= lementslede); ~**-off**, afparing; paarstelsel.
pair'ing, paring; ~**-off**, afparing (parlementslede); ~ **sea'son**, paartyd.
paja'mas, *kyk* **pyjamas**.
Pakistan', Pakistan; ~**i**, (n) Pakistani; (a) Pakistans.
pal, (n) maat, makker; boetie; *jobs for* ~*s*, baantjies vir boeties; (v) (**-led**) maats maak, omgaan (met); ~ *up*, maats maak.
pal'ace, paleis; *P* ~ *of Justice*, Paleis van Justisie; *P* ~ *of Peace*, Vredespaleis.
pal'adin, paladyn, ridder.
pal(a)eobot'any, paleobotanie.
pal(a)eog'rapher, paleograaf.
pal(a)eograph'ic, paleografies.
pal(a)eog'raphy, paleografie.
pal(a)eolith, paleoliet; ~**ic**, paleolities, uit die vroegste Steentydperk.
pal(a)eol'ogy, oudheidkunde, paleologie.

pal(a)eontolog'ic, paleontologies.
pal(a)eontol'ogist, paleontoloog.
pal(a)eontol'ogy, paleontologie.
Pal(a)eozo'ic, (n) Paleosoïkum.
pal(a)eozo'ic, (a) paleosoïes.
pal(a)eozool'ogy, paleosoölogie.
pal(a)es'tra, worstelperk; gimnastiekskool.
pal'ampore, spreisis.
palankeen', **palanquin'**, draagstoel, palankyn.
palatabil'ity, smaaklikheid.
pal'atable, lekker, smaaklik.
pal'atal, (n) verhemeltemedeklinker, palatale mede= klinker; (a) palataal, verhemelte=; ~**iza'tion**, pala= talisasie; ~**ize**, palataliseer.
pal'ate, verhemelte, gehemelte; smaak; *BONY (hard)* ~, harde verhemelte; *CLEFT* ~, gesplete verhemelte; *have a DELICATE* ~, 'n fyn tong hê; *NOT to my* ~, nie na my smaak nie; *SOFT* ~, sagte verhemelte.
pala'tial, paleis=, soos 'n paleis; vorstelik, groots, pragtig.
palat'inate, paltsgraafskap; *the P* ~, die Palts.
Pal'atine¹, die Palatyn; ~ *hill*, die Palatynse heuwel.
pal'atine², (n) verhemeltebeen; (a) verhemelte=.
pal'atine³, (n) pelskraag.
pal'atine⁴, (a) tot die keiserlike hof behorend, palts= graaflik; *count* ~, paltsgraaf.
pal'atogram, palatogram.
palatog'raphy, palatografie.
pala'ver, (n) konferensie, bespreking, onderhoud; pa= lawer; gesnater, geklets; gevlei; affêre; (v) praat, babbel, klets; flikflooi, vlei; boopreek, onderhandel.
pale¹, (n) paal, balk; grens; spar; *outside the CIVIC* ~, buite die maatskappy; *without the* ~ *of CIVI= LIZATION*, buite die grense v.d. beskawing; *with= in the* ~ *of the LAW*, binne die perke v.d. wet.
pale², (v) bleek word, verbleek; bleek maak; verdof, dof word; (a) bleek; lig (kleur); dof; vaal, vaalagtig, flets, flou, mat; *GROW* ~, verbleek, bleek word; *as* ~ *as a SHEET*, asvaal; ~ **ale**, wit bier; ~**-face**, bleekgesig, bleekneus; ~**-faced**, bleek; ~**-hearted**, lafhartig; ~**ness**, bleekheid, fletsheid.
Pal'estine, Palestina.
Palestin'ian, (n) Palestyn; (a) Palestyns.
pales'tra = **pal(a)estra**.
pal'etot, oorjas; paletot.
pal'ette, palet, verfbord; *set the* ~, die kleure op die palet bring; ~**-knife**, tempermes, paletmes.
pal'frey, (**-s**), damesryperd.
pal'impsest, palimpses.
pal'indrome, letterkeer, palindroom, keervers; ..**dro= m'ic**, letterkeer=, palindromies.
pal'ing¹, rasterwerk, skutting, paalheining.
pal'ing², verbleking, verkleuring.
palingen'esis, wedergeboorte, palingenese.
pal'inode, herroeping, palinodie, teensang.
pal'inodist, teensangdigter, palinodis.
palisade', (n) paalwerk, skutting, staakheining, sta= ketsel, palissade; skanspaal; (v) omhein, ompaal, palissadeer, verskans; ~ **tissue**, palissadeweefsel.
palisad'ing, palissadering.
palisan'der, palissander(hout).
pal'ish, blekerig, bleekagtig, valerig.
pall, (n) doodskleed, lykkleed; (staatsie)mantel; slui= er; (v) smaakloos word, sy aantreklikheid verloor, verflou; walg; *it* ~*s on one*, 'n mens word daar sat van.
pallad'ium, (..**dia**), pleganker, waarborg, bolwerk; palladium (metaal).
pall'bearer, slip(pe)draer.
pall'et, strooimatras, veldbed; palet, pottebak= kerskyf; windklep (orrel), draagplaat; hegstrook, laaiplank (vir vrag); ~**iza'tion**, stapeling.
pall'iasse, strooimatras.
pall'iate, versag, verlig; lenig, vergoelik, verontskul= dig, verbloem, bemantel, bewimpel.
pallia'tion, versagting, verligting; verbloeming, ver= goeliking, bemanteling.
pall'iative, (n) palliatief, versagtingsmiddel, nood= hulp; (a) versagtend, tydelik verligtend; verbloe= mend; ~ *measure*, lapwerk.
pall'iatory = **palliative**, (a).

pall'id, bleek, doodbleek, asvaal; ~**ness,** bleekheid.
pall'ium, (-s, ..llia), pallium, opperkleed (v.d. ou Grieke); skouermantel (van 'n aartsbiskop); mantel (weekdiere).
pall'or, bleekheid.
pall'y, maats, bevriend, vriendskaplik; *be* ~ *with,* maats wees met.
palm, (n) palm (hand); palm(boom); lengtemaat; klou (anker); tak (takbokhoring); segepalm; *BEAR the* ~, die prys wegdra; *GREASE someone's* ~, iem. omkoop; *YIELD the* ~, die veld ruim; (v) inpalm, hanteer; streel, bevoel; in die hand wegsteek; omkoop; kul; ~ *something off on someone,* aan iem. iets afsmeer; iem. iets wysmaak; ~**a'ceous,** palmagtig; ~**ar,** palm=; ~**ary,** voortreflik, uitstekend, uitnemend; ~**ate,** handvormig; met swemvliese; ~**-branch,** palmtak; ~**-butter,** palmbotter; ~**er,** professionele pelgrim; palmiet; ruspe; kunsvlieg; ~**ette,** palmversiersel, palmet; ~**ett'o, (-s),** dwergpalm; ~**-grease,** omkoopgeld; ~**-greasing,** omkopery; ~**-house,** palmhuis; ~**if'erous,** palmdraend.
pal'miped(e), (n) swemvoël; (a) met swemvliese, swempotig.
palm'ist, handkyker, handwaarseër; ~**ry,** handlesery, handkykery.
pal'mitine, palmitien, palmitine.
palm: ~**-kernel,** palmpit; ~**-leaf,** palmblaar; ~**-oil,** palmolie; duimkruid, omkoopgeld; ~**-reader,** handleser; handkyker; ~**-stand,** blomstander, palmstander; ~**-stay,** bladanker; **P** ~ **Sunday,** Palmsondag; ~**-tree,** palmboom; ~ **wine,** palmwyn.
pa'lmy, palmagtig, palmryk; voorspoedig, skitterend, roemryk; ~ *days,* gulde dae, bloeitydperk.
palmyr'a, waaierpalm.
Palomin'o, (-s), Palomino(perd).
palp, voeler, voelspriet, voelhoring, taster, tasorgaan.
palpabil'ity, tasbaarheid, voelbaarheid.
pal'pable, voelbaar, tasbaar, handtastelik; duidelik, waarneembaar; *a* ~ *lie,* 'n tasbare leuen.
palp'atory, betastend, betastings=.
pal'pably, voelbaar; duidelik.
pal'pate, (v) voel, betas; (a) met tasorgane.
palpa'tion, betasting, bevoeling.
pal'pebral, ooglid=, van die ooglede, palpebraal.
palpebra'tion, oogknippery, palpebrasie.
pal'piform, in die vorm van voelhorings.
palpi'gerous, voelhoringsdraend, met voelhorings.
pal'pitate, klop, tril, pols, bons.
palpita'tion, hartklopping, trilling, polsslag.
pal'pus, (..**pi**) = **palp.**
pa'lsgrave, paltsgraaf.
pa'lsgravine, paltsgravin.
pal'sied, verlam.
pal'sy, (n) beroerte, lamheid, verlamming; (v) (..**sied**), verlam.
pa'lter, uitvlugte soek; speel met; knoei; knibbel; peuter.
pa'ltriness, nietigheid, armsaligheid; laagheid, ellendigheid, veragtelikheid.
pa'ltry, klein, miserabel, nietig; bogterig, onbetekenend; waardeloos, armsalig; erbarmlik, ellendig; ~ *writer,* prulskrywer.
palud'al, palud'inous, moeras=, vlei=; malaria=.
pal'udism, moerassiekte.
pal'y, blekerig.
pam, klawerboer.
pam'pa, pampa, vlakte; ~**s-grass,** pampasgras.
pam'per, piep, (ver)troetel, bederf, verwen; ~**ed,** vertroetel; ~**ing,** gepiep.
pamper'o, (-s), pampero(wind).
pamph'let, pamflet, brosjure, vlugskrif; ~**eer',** (n) vlugskrifskrywer, brosjureskrywer, pamfletskrywer; (v) pamflette skryf.
Pan¹, (n) Pan.
pan², (n) pan; *from the frying-* ~ *into the FIRE,* v.d. wal in die sloot; *a FLASH in the* ~, 'n onbeduidende saak; (v) (**-ned**), was, win (sout); gaarmaak (in 'n pan); ~ *OUT,* was (goud); ~ *out WELL,* goed uitval, slaag.
Pan-³, (a) Al-, Pan-.

panace'a, panasee, wondermiddel, geneesal, al(heil)=middel.
panache', veerbos, helmpluim; spoggerigheid, windmakerigheid, panache.
pana'da, broodpap, panade.
Pan-Afr'ican, Pan-Afrikaans, Al-Afrikaans; ~**ism,** Pan-Afrikanisme; ~**ist,** Pan-Afrikanis.
Pan'ama, Panama; ~ **canal,** Panamakanaal.
pan'ama, panamahoed.
Pan-Ame'rican, Pan-Amerikaans, Al-Amerikaans; ~**ism,** Pan-Amerikanisme.
pan'ary, broodagtig, brood=.
panatel'la, panatella.
pan'cake, (n) pannekoek; *as flat as a* ~, so plat soos 'n pannekoek; (v) laat deursak; platval; ~ **landing,** deursaklanding, vallanding.
panchromat'ic, panchromaties.
pancra'tium, pankratium, vuis-en-worstelwedstryd.
panc'reas, alvleisklier, pankreas, buikspeekselklier.
pancreat'ic, pankreaties, alvleis=, pankreas=; ~ **juice,** alvleiskliersap, pankreassap.
panc'reatin, pankreatien, pankreatine.
pan'da, panda, bamboesbeer.
pan'dects, pandekte, (volledige) wetteversameling.
pande'mic, (n) pandemie; (a) pandemies, algemeen.
pandemon'ium, hel; pandemonium, helse lawaai.
pan'der, (n) koppelaar; handlanger; (v) koppelaar wees; koppel; lae luste bevorder; ~ *to the public taste,* probeer om die smaak v.d. publiek te behaag; toegee aan die smaak v.d. publiek; ~ **age,** koppelary; ~**er,** koppelaar; handlanger; ~**ess, (-es),** koppelaarster; ~**ism,** koppeling.
pan'dit, *kyk* **pundit.**
pan'door = **pandour.**
pandor'a¹, pandore', pandoor (soort luit).
Pandor'a², Pandora; ~**'s box,** doos van Pandora.
pan'dour, pandoer.
pane, (venster)ruit; paneel (deur); vak; pant; ~**-glass,** ruitglas.
panegy'ric, lofrede; loftuiting, ~**al,** prysend, ophemelend, loftuitend.
panegy'rist, lofredenaar, loftuiter.
pan'egyrize, hoog prys, 'n lofrede hou, lof toeswaai, uitbundig prys, ophemel.
pan'el, (n) paneel; vak; naamlys, naamrol van jurie; ploeg, span (wetenskaplikes); saalkussing; paneelsaal; rooster (van dokters); tussensetsel; baan, strook (van rok); (v) (**-led**), panele aansit; op die lys sit; opsaal; van stroke voorsien; ~**-awl,** kussingels; ~**-beater,** duik(uit)klopper, plaatwerker, koetswerker, bultklopper; ~ **board,** skakelbord; paneelbord; ~ **box,** sekeringskas(sie); ~**-gardening,** mosaïekwerk (in tuine); ~ **inspection,** paneelinspeksie; ~ **ling,** beskot, lambrisering, paneelwerk; ~**-picture,** paneeltjie; ~ **plane,** paneelskaaf; ~**-saw,** paneelsaag; ~ **van,** paneelwa; ~**-work,** paneelwerk.
pang, angs, benoudheid, steek; foltering pyniging, wee, smart; ~*s of CONSCIENCE,* gewetenswroeging; ~*s of DEATH,* doodstuipe; ~*s of HUNGER,* knaende honger; ~*s of PARTURITION,* barensweë; ~*s of REMORSE,* knaende wroeging.
pang'a, kapmes, panga.
Pan-Germ'an, (n) Pan-Germanis; Al-Duitser; (a) Al-Duits; Pan-Germaans; ~**ism,** Pan-Germanisme.
pangol'in, ietermagô, pangolien.
pan'handle, (n) pansteel; smal strook land; (v) bedel; ~ **erf,** pypsteelerf.
pan'ic¹, (n) vingergras, panikgras.
pan'ic², (n) plotselinge skrik, paniek; (v) op loop sit, vlug; (a) panies; ~**-bolt,** noodgrendel; ~ **gas,** paniekgas; ~**ky,** paniekerig, verskrik, beangs.
pan'icle, pluim; ~**d,** gepluim.
pan'ic: ~**-monger,** alarmis, skrikaanjaer; ~**-stricken,** verbouereerd, deur skrik bevange, paniekerig.
panifica'tion, broodbakkery.
panjan'drum, Grootmogol (spottitel), panjandrum.
pann'age, varkkos, akkers; weiveld vir varke; weigeld, masreg.
pann'ier, mandjie, draagmandjie (vir lasdiere); rokhoepel, panier.
pann'ikin, pannetjie, (blik)kommetjie.
pann'ings, panwasse, panspoelings.

panoplied   1103   *paradisic(al)*

pan'oplied, in volle wapenrusting, geharnas.
pan'oply, (..plies), volledige wapenuitrusting; wa= pentrofee.
panop'ticon, koepelgevangenis; tentoonstelling van nuwighede; panoptikum.
panora'ma, panorama, vergesig.
panoram'ic, panoramies; ~ *view*, breë uitsig.
pan' pipes, panfluit.
Pan-Ru'ssian, Pan-Russies, Al-Russies.
Pan-Sla'vic, Panslawies, Alslawies.
Pan-Sla'vism, Panslawisme.
Pan-Slav'ist, Panslawis.
pan'sy, (pansies), gesiggie (blom); ~ **boy**, meisieag= tige seun, moffie, verwyfde man.
pant, (n) hyging, gehyg; klopping; (v) hyg, snak; ver= lang; kortasem wees; ~ *for (from)*, hunker na, snak na.
pantalet(te)s', lang damesbroek, pantalet.
pantaloon', broek, pantalon; hanswors; ~ery, hans= worstery.
pantech'nicon, meubelmagasyn, meubelpakhuis; ~ **van**, huiswa, meubelwa, verhuiswa.
pan'theism, panteïsme, algodedom.
pan'theist, panteïs; ~'ic, panteïsties.
pan'theon, panteon, eretempel; godedom, godewê= reld.
pan'ther, panter; luiperd; ~ess, (-es), luiperdwyfie; panterwyfie; ~ine, luiperd=; panter=.
pan'tie, knapbroekie, damesbroekie.
pan'tihose, kousbroek, broek(ie)kous.
pan'tile, dakpan.
pant'ing, (n) gehyg; (a) hygend.
pantisoc'racy, kommunistiese ideaalstaat, pantiso= krasie.
pan'tograph, pantograaf, tekeninstrument, tekenaap.
pan'tomime, (n) gebarespel, pantomime; (v) deur ge= barespel voorstel, mimeer.
pantomim'ic, pantomimies; ~ry, pantomimiek.
pantomim'ist, pantomimis, gebarespeler.
pantophob'ia, vrees vir alles, pantofobie.
pan'try, (pantries), spens, spyskamer, ~ **shelf**, spens= rak.
pants, onderbroek; broek; *be CAUGHT with one's ~s down*, onverwags in die verleentheid gebring word; *a KICK in the ~*, 'n skop onder die sitvlak.
pan'ty, (panties), damesbroekie; *scanty* ~, amper= broekie; ~ **girdle**, gordelbroekie; ~ **hose**, ~**stock= ing**, kousbroek, broek(ie)kous.
pan'zer, (n) pantsermotor; (a) pantser=, gepantser=.
pap¹, moes, papperige kos, pap.
pap², tepel.
papa', pa(pa), pappie; ta.
pap'acy, pousdom, pouslike mag.
pap'al, pouslik, paaps; *the P~ State*, die Kerklike Staat; ~**ism**, pousgesindheid; ~**ist**, (n) pousgesin= de; (a) paapsgesind.
papat'so, papatso
papav'eric acid, papawersuur
papav'erous, papaweragtig.
papaw', papay'a, papaja.
pap'er, (n) papier; koerant; opstel, verhandeling; ek= samenstel, vraestel; agenda; papiergeld; wissel; lys; plakpapier; sakkie; (pl) dokumente, paperasse, (staat)stukke; getuigskrifte; *be BETTER on ~*, teoreties beter wees; in teorie beter wees; *COM= MIT to ~*, op skrif stel; swart op wit sit; *GET into the ~s*, in die koerante kom; *ON ~*, op skrif; op papier; *READ a ~*, 'n koerant lees; 'n lesing hou; ~ *never REFUSES ink*, papier is geduldig; *SEND in one's ~s*, jou getuigskrifte instuur; jou ontslag indien; *SET a ~*, eksamenvrae stel; *not WORTH the ~ it is written on*, van nul en gener waarde; (v) (uit)plak, behang (huis); in papier toedraai (wik= kel); van papier voorsien; (a) papier=; ~ **back**, inge= naaide boek; sagteband(boek); papierband; ~-**bag**, kardoes, papiersakkie; ~-**board**, karton; ~-**boy**, koerantseun; ~-**case**, papierhuls; skryf= map; ~-**chase**, snipperjag; ~-**clip**, papierknyper; skuifspeld; ~ **collar**, papierboordjie; ~ **cover**, om= slag; ~ **credit**, wisselkrediet; ~ **cup**, papiervorm= pie; ~ **currency**, papiergeld; ~-**cutter**, snymasjien; papierskêr, papiermes; ~-**fastener**, papierknyper=

tjie; ~ **flower**, papierblom; ~ **folder**, voubeen; pa= piervouer; ~ **gold**, papiergoud; ~-**hanger**, plak= ker, behanger; ~-**hanging**, muurplakwerk; be= hangsel, plakpapier; ~-**knife**, briewemes, papiermes; voubeen; ~-**maker**, papierfabrikant; ~ **manufacturer**, papierfabrikant; ~-**mill**, papier= fabriek; ~ **money**, papiergeld, banknote; ~ **nap= kin**, papierluier; ~ **pattern**, knippatroon; ~ **pellet**, papierprop(pie); ~-**reed**, papirus; ~ **serviette**, pa= pierservet; ~ **shavings**, papierwol; ~-**stainer**, (prul)skrywer; plakpapierfabrikant; penlekker; ~ **towel**, papierhanddoek; ~ **trade**, papierhandel; ~ **tree**, papierboom; ~ **war(fare)**, koeranteoorlog; polemiek; ~-**weight**, papierdrukker; papiergewig (boks); ~ **y**, papieragtig.
papier mâché', papierdeeg, papierpap, papiermâché.
papiliona'ceous, skoe(n)lapperagtig, vlinderagtig, skoe(n)lapper=.
papill'a, (-e), tepel, papil; ~**ry**, tepelvormig, tepel=.
pap'illate, tepelvormig.
papill'on, skoenlapper; papillon; speelgoedhond.
pap'illote, papillot.
Papin's diges'ter, Papiniaanse pot.
pap'ism, pousdom, papery.
pap'ist, (n) Rooms-Katoliek, pousgesinde; (a) Rooms, pousgesind, papisties, paaps.
papis'tic(al), papisties, pousgesind, paaps.
pap'istry, pousgesindheid, Rooms-Katolisisme, Roomsheid.
papoose', rooihuidkind; kindjie.
pappose', van saadwol voorsien.
papp'us, saadwol, saadpluis, vrugpluis
papp'y, sag, papperig
pap'rika, paprika, (Hongaarse) rissie.
pap'ula, (-e), pap'ule, (-s), puisie, papil, knoppie.
pap'ular, pap'ulate, knobbel=, knobbelagtig.
papyra'ceous, papier=, papieragtig; papierdun.
papyro'logy, papirologie.
papyr'us, (..piri), papirus.
par¹, (n) pari, gelykheid; gemiddelde; *ABOVE ~*, bo= kant pari; *AT ~*, teen (op) pari; a pari; *BELOW ~*, onderkant pari; onder die gemiddelde; olik; *ON a ~ with*, gelykstaande met; gelyk (op een lyn) staan met; *UP to ~*, fris en gesond.
par², (n) abbr. of **paragraph**.
par³, (prep) by; ~ *EXCELLENCE*, by uitnemend= heid; ~ *EXAMPLE*, byvoorbeeld.
parabio'sis, parabiose.
pa'rable, gelykenis, parabel.
parab'ola, parabool; kegelsnede, keëlsnede.
parabol'ic(al), parabolies; soos 'n gelykenis.
para'boloid, (n) paraboloïde; (a) paraboloïdaal.
parace'tamol, parasetamol, pynpil.
parach'ronism, parachronisme, tydfout.
pa'rachute, (n) valskerm, parasjuut; (v) (met 'n val= skerm) afspring; *be ~ d*, met 'n valskerm neergelaat word; ~ **descent**, valskermdaling; ~-**harness**, val= skermtuig; ~ **jump**, valskermsprong; ~ **kite**, val= skermvlieër; ~ **tank**, slurptenk, tregtertenk; ~ **troops**, valskermtroepe.
pa'rachutist, valskermspringer; valskermsoldaat.
pa'raclete, parakleet, voorspraak, bemiddelaar, trooster; *the P~*, (die) Heilige Gees, die Parakleet.
parade', (n) parade, vertoon, pronkery, optog; wa= penskouing; plein, wandelplek; paradeterrein; ap= pèl (mil.); *MAKE a ~ of*, pronk met; *OFF ~*, para= devry; *ON ~*, op parade; (v) ekserseer, oefen; parade laat hou, inspekteer, laat marsjeer, para= deer; pronk met, uitkraam, te koop loop met; ~ *the streets*, deur die strate trek; ~ **ground**, parade= terrein, eksersisieveld, eksersisieterrein; ~ **march**, parademars; ~ **square**, paradeplein; ~ **station**, aantreeplek.
paradid'dle, tromgeroffel.
pa'radigm, voorbeeld; paradigma; ~**at'ic**, paradig= maties.
paradisa'ic(al), paradysagtig
pa'radise, paradys; lushof; hemel(hof); dierepark; ~ **apple**, paradysappel; ~ **flycatcher**, paradysvlieë= vanger *(Tchitrea plumbeiceps)*; ~ **widow-bird**, pa= radysvink *(Steganura paradisea)*.
paradis'ic(al), paradysagtig.

pa'rados, parados, rugskerm, rugweer.
pa'radox, (-es), paradoks, skynbare teenstrydigheid; wonderspreuk; ~**ical,** paradoksaal.
pa'raffin, paraffien, lampolie; ~ **oil,** paraffien(olie), lampolie; ~ **pump,** oliepomp; ~ **stove,** paraffienstoof, oliestoof; ;~ **tin,** paraffienblik; ~ **wax,** paraffienwas.
paragen'esis, paragenese.
parago'ge, paragoge, agteraanvoeging.
parago'gic, paragogies.
pa'ragon, (n) model, toonbeeld; voorbeeld; paragon (diamant van meer as 100 karaat); (v) (poëties) vergelyk; ewenaar.
pa'ragram, paragram, woordspeling.
pa'ragraph, (n) paragraaf; nuusberig; (v) paragrafeer, in paragrawe verdeel; in die koerant skrywe, 'n kort beriggie skryf oor; ~**er,** paragrafeerder; ~**'ic,** paragraaf=, in paragrawe; ~**ing,** paragrafering; ~**ist,** koerantskrywer.
Pa'raguay, Paraguay; ~**an,** (n) Paraguaan, (a) Paraguaans.
pa'rakeet, parkiet.
pa'rakite, valskermvlieër.
paral(e)ip'sis, paralipsis.
parallac'tic, parallakties.
pa'rallax, parallaks.
pa'rallel, (n) parallel; ewewydige lyn; gelyke, weerga; vergelyking, ooreenkoms; *the CASE has no* ~, dit is 'n uitsonderingsgeval; dit het geen gelyke nie; *DRAW a* ~ *between,* 'n vergelyking tref tussen; ~ *of LATITUDE,* breedtesirkel; *WITHOUT* ~, sonder weerga; (v) naas mekaar stel, ewenaar; 'n tweede voorbeeld aanhaal van; ewewydig loop; vergelyk; (a) parallel, ewewydig; ooreenstemmend; ~ *TO,* ewewydig met (aan); *one line is* ~ *TO (with) the other,* een lyn is parallel met die ander; *this street runs* ~ *WITH Church Street,* hierdie straat loop parallel met Kerkstraat; ~ **bars,** brug (by gimnastiek); ~**ep'iped,** parallelepipedum; ~**ism,** ooreenkoms, parallelisme, vergelyking; ~ **medium,** (n) paralelle voertaal, (a) parallelmedium=; ~ **motion,** ewewydige beweging; ~**'ogram,** parallelogram; ~*ogram of forces,* kragteparallelogram; ~ **ruler,** parallelle liniaal.
paralog'ical, onlogies.
paral'ogism, drogrede, vals gevolgtrekking, vals sluitrede.
paralysa'tion, verlamming.
pa'ralyse, verlam, lam lê; met lamheid slaan; magteloos maak.
paral'ysis, verlamming; lamsiekte; lamheid, beroerte; magteloosheid; *FACIAL* ~ gesigsverlamming; *INFANTILE* ~, kinderverlamming, polio(miëlitis).
paralyt'ic, (n) lamme, verlamde, paralitikus, geraakte; (a) verlam, geraak, paralities; ~ **attack,** ~ **seizure,** ~ **stroke,** (aanval van) beroerte; ~ **tick,** lambosluis.
paramagnet'ic, paramagneties.
paramag'netism, paramagnetisme.
param'eter, parameter.
paramil'itary, paramilitêr.
paramne'sia, paramnesie.
pa'ramount, hoogste, vernaamste, opperste, opper=; oorwegend; oorheersend; *BE* ~ *to,* van groter belang wees as; *of* ~ *IMPORTANCE,* van oorwegende belang; *a reason* ~ *TO all others,* 'n rede wat alle ander redes oortref; ~ **chief,** hoofkaptein, opperhoof; ~**cy,** superioriteit, oorwig, oorwegende belang; baasskap, oppergesag; ~ **power,** heersende moondheid; grootmoondheid.
pa'ramour, minnaar; minnares, bysit, liefie.
paranoe'a, paranoi'a, grootheidswaan(sin), paranoia, vervolgingswaansin.
paranoi'ac, (n) paranoïkus; (a) paranoïes.
pa'ranut, paraneut.
pa'ranymph, paranimf, helper, ondersteuner.
pa'rapet, borswering, parapet; leunmuurtjie; ~**ed,** met borswering.
pa'raph, (n) paraaf; krul (by naamtekening); (v) parafeer.
paraphernal'ia, toebehoorsels, uitrusting, parafernalia; mondering; rommel.

pa'raphrase, (n) parafrase, omskrywing; (v) parafraseer, omskryf.
paraphras'tic(al), omskrywend.
para'physis, parafise.
parapleg'ia, paraplegie.
parapleg'ic, (n) parapleeg, paraplegielyer; (a) paraplekties.
parapsychol'ogist, parapsigoloog.
parapsychol'ogy, parapsigologie.
pa'rarock, paragesteente.
paraselen'e, bynaam.
pa'rasite, parasiet; woekerplant; tafelskuimer, klaploper, rugryer.
parasit'ic(al), parasities, parasietagtig, woekerend.
parasit'icide, parasietgif, middel teen parasiete.
pa'rasitism, parasitisme, woekering.
pa'rasitize, parasiteer; woeker, op koste van ander leef.
parasitol'ogy, parasitologie.
par'asol, sambreel, sonskerm, parasol; ~ **tree,** kiepersol, sambreelboom.
parasympathet'ic, parasimpaties.
parasyn'thesis, parasintese.
paratax'is, neweskikking, parataksis.
parathes'is, neweskikking.
parathi'on, paration.
parathyr'oid, byskildklier.
par'atroop, par'atrooper, valskermsoldaat; ~**s,** valskermtroepe.
paraty'phoid, paratifus.
pa'ravane, paravaan, mynbyter.
parb'oil, gedeeltelik kook; half afkook; te warm maak.
parb'uckle, (n) roltou, skrooitou; (v) met 'n tou rol, skrooi, laat sak.
Par'cae, (die) Skikgodinne.
par'cel, (n) pak(kie), pakket; stuk, deel; party, aantal; ~*-BLIND,* half blind; *BY* ~*s,* by gedeeltes; *a* ~ *of DIAMONDS,* 'n pakkie diamante; *PART and* ~ *of,* 'n integrerende (onmisbare) deel van; *good things are done up in SMALL* ~*s,* in die kleinste potjies bewaar mens die beste salf; (v) **(-led),** verdeel; inpak; seildoek omdraai; ~ *out,* uitdeel; ~ **carrier,** bagasiedraer; ~ **delivery,** afleweringsdiens; ~ **ling,** verdeling; ~ **office,** bestelkantoor, pakkieskantoor; ~ **post,** pakkiespos, pakketpos; ~ **rate,** tarief vir pakkiesgoed; ~**'s services,** besteldiens.
par'cenary, mede-erfgenaamskap.
par'cener, mede-erfgenaam.
parch, opdroë, verseng; verskroei, verdor; rooster, braai.
parched, (ver)droog, verskroei; *BECOME* ~, uitdroog; ~ *LIPS,* droë lippe; ~ *with THIRST,* versmag van dors.
parch'ing, verskroeiend, versmagtend.
parch'ment, perkament; ~ **paper,** perkamentpapier; ~**y,** perkamentagtig.
pard[1]**,** panter, luiperd.
pard[2]**,** (sl.), maat; pêl.
pard'on, (n) (skuld)vergifnis, kwytskelding, genade; grasie; pardon, amnestie, begenadiging; aflaat (R.K.); ekskuus; *I BEG your* ~, ekskuus; neem my nie kwalik nie; *GENERAL* ~, amnestie; (v) vergewe, kwytskeld, vergifnis skenk; begenadig (gevangene); verskoon, ekskuseer, deur die vingers sien; ~ *ME,* neem my nie kwalik nie; ekskuus; ~ *a person for an OFFENCE,* iem. 'n oortreding vergewe; ~ **able,** vergeeflik, verskoonbaar; ~**er,** aflaatverkoper.
pare, (af)skil, wegsny, afsny, afskaaf; snoei; besnoei; besny; verminder; ~ *AWAY,* afsny, afknip; ~ *someone's NAILS,* iem. se naels knip; iem. kortwiek; ~ *to the QUICK,* tot op die lewe sny.
parego'ric, (n) pynstillende middel, pynstiller, paregorie; kalmeermiddel; (a) pynstillend; kalmerend.
paren'chyma, selweefsel, parenchiem.
par'ent, (n) ouer; vader, moeder; bron, oorsprong; *ask your* ~*s' CONSENT,* ouers vra (om te trou); *our FIRST* ~*s,* ons stamouers; (a) moeder=; oorspronklik; ~ **age,** afkoms, geboorte; geslag.
paren'tal, ouerlik; vaderlik; ouer=; ~ *HOME,* ouerhuis; ~ *JOY,* ouervreugde.

par'ent: ~ **bird,** moedervoël; ~ **body,** moederliggaam; ~ **cell,** moedersel; ~ **company,** moedermaatskappy.
paren'thesis, (..**ses),** parentese, tussensin; hakie; *in parentheses,* tussen hakies.
paren'thesize, tussen hakies plaas; in 'n tussensin vermeld.
parenthet'ical, tussen hakies, parenteties; ~ **clause,** tussensin; ~**ly,** terloops, tussen hakies.
par'ent: ~ **hood,** ouerskap; ~**less,** ouerloos; ~ **metal,** basismetaal; ~ **organization,** moederorganisasie; ~ **rock,** moedergesteente; ~**s-in-law,** skoonouers; ~**ship,** ouerskap; ~ **stock,** onderstam; ~-**tea'cher association,** ouer-onderwysersvereniging; ~ **tree,** moederboom; ~ **unit,** stameenheid.
par'er, dunskiller; snoeier; skilmes; skilmasjien; hoefmes.
pa'resis, gedeeltelike verlamming, spierverlamming, parese.
par e'xcellence, by uitstek, by uitnemendheid.
parfait', parfait.
par'get, (n) (sier)pleister, pleisterwerk; (v) pleister; ~**er,** (sier)pleisteraar; ~**ing,** (sier)pleistering; (sier)pleister.
parhel'ion, parhelium, byson.
par'i: ~ *passu,* op gelyke voet, pari passu.
par'iah, paria, uitgeworpene, verstoteling, uitwerpeling, verskoppeling; *as notorious as a* ~, so bekend as die bont hond; ~ **dog,** rondloperhond, swerfhond, pariahond; *as notorious as a* ~ *dog,* so bekend soos die bont hond.
par'ian, fyn soort wit porselein.
pari'etal, tot 'n muur behorend, muur-, wand-, wandstandig, pariëtaal; ~ **bone,** wandbeen.
par'ing, skil; bas; die sny; (pl) afsnysel, skaafsel; skille; ~ **chisel,** gladbeitel, polysyster; ~-**knife,** hoefmes; halfmes; skilmes; ~-**machine,** steekmasjien, groefmasjien.
Pa'ris, Parys; ~ *BLUE,* parysblou; ~ *GREEN,* parysgroen; *PLASTER of* ~, gips.
pa'rish, (-es), gemeente, parogie; ~ **church,** parogiekerk; ~ **clerk,** koster; ~ **council,** dorpsraad; ~ **hall,** kerksaal; ~ **'ioner,** gemeentelid, lidmaat, parogiaan; ~ **priest,** dorpsgeestelike; pastoor; ~ **pump politics,** kleinlike, vitterige politiek; ~ **register,** kerkregister; ~ **relief,** ondersteuning, diakonie, onderhoud (deur die gemeente); ~ **work,** herderlike werksaamhede.
Pari'sian, (n) Parysenaar; Parisienne, Paryse vrou; (a) Paryse.
Parisienne', Paryse vrou, Parisienne.
parisyllab'ic, met dieselfde getal lettergrepe, parisillabies, gelyklettergrepig.
pa'rity, gelykheid, (munt)pariteit; pari; waardeverhouding; ~-**price,** pariteitskoers.
park, (n) park; wildtuin; (v) ompaal; versamel; laat staan, parkeer (motor); omhein; ~ *a motor-car,* 'n motor parkeer; ~**ed,** geparkeer; ~**er,** parkeerder.
park'in, hawermeelkoek.
park'ing, parkering; *no* ~, geen staanplek, geen parkeerplek, parkeer verbode; ~ **allowance,** parkeertoegewing, ~ **area,** (motor)staanplek, parkeergebied, parkeerterrein, parkeerruimte; ~ **attendant,** parkeerbeampte; ~ **bay,** staanplek, parkeerplek; ~-**fee,** parkeergeld; ~ **ground,** (motor)staanplek, parkeerplek; ~-**light,** parkeerlig; ~-**meter,** parkeermeter; ~ **regulation,** parkeerregulasie; ~ **site,** parkeerterrein; ~ **space,** parkeerplek, parkeerruimte; ~ **sticker,** parkeerbewys; ~ **time,** parkeertyd.
park: ~-**keeper,** parkopsigter, ~**y,** parkagtig.
parl'ance, manier van praat; taal, spraak(gebruik); *in COMMON* ~, in die alledaagse taal; *in LEGAL* ~, in die regstaal.
parlementaire', witvlagdraer, onderhandelaar.
parl'ey, (n) (-s), (mond)gesprek, onderhandeling; onderhoud; (v) praat, onderhandel.
parl'iament, parlement, volksraad; *HOUSES of* ~, parlementsgebou; *MEMBER of* ~, parlementslid, volksraadslid; *SESSION of* ~, parlementsitting; ~**ar'ian,** parlementariër, redenaar; parlementsgesinde.

parliamen'tary, parlements-, parlementêr; fatsoenlik; ~ **agent,** parlementêre prokureur; ~ **election,** parlementsverkiesing; ~ **secretary,** onderminister (in Eng.).
parl'our, sitkamer, voorkamer, ontvangkamer; drinkkamer; salon; ateljee; ~ **boarder,** inwonende kosleerling; ~-**clock,** huisklok, sitkamerklok; ~ **game,** geselskapspel; ~ **joke,** skoon grap; ~ **maid,** binnehulp; kamermeisie; ~ **music,** kamermusiek.
parl'ous, (a) gevaarlik; lastig; oulik, geslepe; (adv) erg, vreeslik.
Parmesan', Parmesaans; ~ **cheese,** parmakaas, parmesaan(kaas).
Parnass'us, Parnassus; *aspire to* ~, Parnassus bestyg.
paroch'ial, parogiaal; gemeente-; kleingeestig, bekrompe; ~**ism,** kleingeestigheid; engheid, bekrompenheid; kleinburgerlikheid; ~ **relief,** armesorg.
pa'rodist, parodieskrywer, parodis.
pa'rody, (n) (..**dies),** parodie, spotdig; bespotting; (v) (..**died),** parodeer, travesteer.
parole', herkenningswoord; parool, erewoord; wagwoord; *released on* ~, op parool vrygelaat; op sy erewoord losgelaat.
paronomas'ia, woordspeling, paronomasia.
par'onym, gelykluidende (verwante) woord, paroniem.
paron'ymous, paronimies, stamverwant.
pa'roquet, parkiet.
parot'id, (n) oorspeekselklier, oorspoegklier; (a) naby die oor; oor(speeksel)klier-; ~ **gland,** oorspeekselklier.
parotit'is, oorspeekselklierontsteking, pampoentjies.
pa'roxysm, hewige aanval (siekte), vlaag, paroksisme; ~**al,** hewig, in vlae; stuipagtig.
parq'uet, (n) parketvloer; ingelegde vloer, blokkiesvloer; (v) 'n parketvloer insit, parketteer; ~ **floor,** blokkiesvloer.
parq'uetry, parketvloer; parketwerk.
par(r), jong salm.
par' rate, pariteitskoers.
parricid'al, vadermoord-, vadermoordenaars-.
pa'rricide, vadermoord; vadermoordenaar; landverraaier; landverraad.
pa'rrot, (n) papegaai; na-aper; (v) namaak; napraat; nababbel, na-aap; ~ **cry,** papegaaikreet; ~-**fashion,** soos 'n papegaai, papegaaiagtig, ~-**fish,** bastergaljoen, papegaaivis; ~-**like,** papegaaiagtig; ~**ry,** na-apery, nabootsing; ~ **talk,** napratery.
pa'rry, (n) parering, afwering; (v) **(parried),** afkeer, afweer, pareer; ontwyk; ~ *and thrust,* pareer en uitval.
parse, (woorde) ontleed.
pars'ec, parsek (3¼ ligjaar).
Parsee', (n) vuuraanbidder, Pars; Oud-Persies (taal); (a) Oud-Persies.
parsimon'ious, karig, suinig, gierig; - **ness,** suinigheid, gierigheid.
pars'imony, spaarsaamheid, suinigheid, gierigheid.
pars'ing, (woord)ontleding.
pars'ley, pietersielie.
pars'nip, witwortel.
pars'on, predikant, dominee, geestelike; ~ **age,** pastorie; ~ **crow,** witborskraai, bontkraai; ~**ic(al),** predikantagtig, domineeagtig; ~**'s nose,** stuitjie (van pluimvee).
part, (n) deel, gedeelte; aandeel; rol; stuk, part; streek; stem (musiek); party; onderdeel (masjien); plig; (pl) bekwaamhede, gawes, talente; skaamdele; *take in BAD* ~, sleg opneem; *the BEST* ~ *of it was,* die mooiste van die saak was; *for the BEST* ~ *of an hour,* amper 'n uur lank; *DO one's* ~, jou plig doen; *it is* ~ *of the GAME,* dit hoort daarby; *take in GOOD* ~, vir goeie munt aanneem; goed opneem; *HAVE a* ~ *in,* aandeel hê in; *IN* ~, deels; *IN* ~ *s,* in aflewerings; hier en daar; *have neither* ~ *nor LOT in,* part nòg deel hê aan; *LOOK the* ~, 'n mooi lyf hê vir; lyk of hy vir iets uitgeknip is; *a MAN of many* ~ *s,* 'n bekwame (veelsydige) man; 'n klein jukskeitjie met 'n groot kop; *for the MOST* ~, hoofsaaklik; grotendeels; *for MY* ~, wat my betref; *ON the* ~ *of,* ten behoewe van; deur iem.; *be*

partake   1106   *pass*

~ *and PARCEL of,* 'n integrerende (onafskeidelike) deel uitmaak van; ~ *nor PARCEL,* part nòg deel; *PLAY a* ~, 'n rol speel; *PLAY a leading* ~, die hoofrol speel; *the PRIVY* ~ *s,* die geslagsdele; ~ *of SPEECH,* woordsoort; *TAKE somebody's* ~, iem. se kant kies; *TAKE* ~ *in,* deelneem aan; *in THESE* ~ *s,* in hierdie streke; *it is not my* ~ *TO,* dit lê nie op my weg nie om; ~ *of the WAY,* 'n end; (v) deel, verdeel; afstand doen; skei; afbreek; uiteengaan, uitmekaargaan; afskeid neem van; ~ *COMPANY,* vanmekaar gaan; ~ *the best of FRIENDS,* as goeie vriende skei; ~ *FROM,* skei van; ~ *one's HAIR in the middle,* 'n paadjie in die middel kam; *the WIRE* ~ *ed,* die draad het gebreek; ~ *WITH,* afstand doen van; afskeid neem van; ~ **able,** (a) deelbaar, skeibaar; (adv) gedeeltelik.

partake', **(partook, -n),** deelneem; deelhê aan; deel in; geniet, gebruik, nuttig, eet (maaltyd); *his attitude* ~ *s of INSOLENCE,* daar is iets parmantigs in sy houding; ~ *OF,* eet; deel hê aan; ~**r,** deelhebber, deelgenoot.

part'-author, medeskrywer, medeouteur; medewerker.

parterre', blomperk; parterre, bak (teater).

parthenogen'esis, partenogenese, ongeslagtelike voortplanting.

Par'thenon, Parthenon.

par'tial, gedeeltelik; partydig, eensydig, bevooroordeel(d); *be* ~ *to,* baie hou van; voortrek; partydig wees vir; ~ **eclipse,** gedeeltelike verduistering; ~**ism,** partydigheid; ~**'ity,** vooringenomenheid, partydigheid; eensydigheid, voorliefde; ~ **turn,** gedeeltelike wending (draai); ~ **vacuum,** gedeeltelike vakuum.

part'ible, verdeelbaar.

parti'cipant, (n) deelnemer, deelhebber, deelgenoot; (a) deelnemend.

parti'cipate, deelneem aan, deel hê in (aan); *ENTITLED to* ~, deelgeregtig; ~ *IN,* deel in; deel hê in (aan).

partic'ipating, (wins)delend; ~ **bond,** deelverband(stelsel); ~ **share,** winsdelende aandeel.

participa'tion, deelneming; deelhebberskap; deelname.

parti'cipator, deelnemer, deelhebber, deelgenoot.

particip'ial, deelwoordelik, partisipeel.

parti'ciple, deelwoord, partisipium.

part'icle, deeltjie; greintjie; sprankie; partikel; *not a* ~ *of,* glad niks (nie).

part'icoloured, bont, veelkleurig.

parti'cular, (n) besonderheid; *one CASE in* ~, een saak in die besonder; *ENTER into* ~ *s,* in besonderhede tree; ~ *s to FOLLOW,* besonderhede volg; *FURTHER* ~ *s,* nadere besonderhede; *GIVE full* ~ *s,* verstrek volledige besonderhede; *IN* ~ *s,* in besonderhede; *he is NOBODY in* ~, hy is niks besonders nie; (a, adv) presies; kieskeurig, puntenerig; besonder; noukeurig, spesiaal; buitengewoon, merkwaardig; bepaalde (persoon); *BE* ~, kieskeurig wees; *BE* ~ *about one's diet,* baie kieskeurig met jou ete wees; *a* ~ *FRIEND,* 'n besonder goeie vriend; *for no* ~ *REASON,* om geen besondere rede nie; *TAKE* ~ *trouble,* besonder baie (veel) moeite doen; ~**ism,** partikularisme; ~**ist,** (n) partikularis; (a) partikularisties; ~**ist'ic,** partikularisties; ..**ar'ity,** (..**ties),** besonderheid, eienaardigheid; ~**ize,** in besonderhede tree, spesifiseer, in die besonder vermeld; ~**ly,** besonderlik, veral, by uitstek, met name; *not* ~ *ly pleased,* maar matig tevrede; nie juis tevrede nie.

part'ing, (n) afskeid; deling; skeiding; paadjie (in die hare); skeidingsrots, tussengesteente (geol.); kliewing; *AT* ~, by die vertrek; *COME to the* ~ *of the ways,* op die tweesprong kom; by die uitdraaipad kom; by die kruispad kom; (a) afskeids=, vaarwel=; ~ **breath,** laaste asemtog; ~ **cup,** afskeidsdronk; ~**-kiss,** afskeidskus; ~**-plate,** skeiplaat; ~ **shot,** laaste skoot; ~**-song,** afskeidslied; ~**-washer,** skeiwasser; ~**-word,** afskeidswoord.

part'isan¹, (n) hellebaard, kort piek.

part'isan², (n) partygenoot, partyganger, aanhanger, volgeling, voorstander; guerrillastryder, opstan= deling; (a) partydig; ~**ship,** partyskap, partydigheid.

part'ite, gedeel, gesplete.

parti'tion, (n) deling, verdeling; afdeling; afskorting, afskot, beskot, tussenskot, skeidsmuur; partituur (musiek); (v) deel, verdeel, afskei; afskort; ~ *off,* afskort; ~ **treaty,** verdelingsverdrag; ~ **wall,** skeidsmuur.

part'itive, verdelend, verdelings=; ~ **genitive,** partitiewe genitief, verdelingsgenitief, deelsgenitief.

partizan' = **partisan.**

part'ly, gedeeltelik, deels, eensdeels, ten dele, eenkant; ~ *worn,* halfslyt.

part'-music, meerstemmige musiek.

part'ner, (n) maat, gesel; (deel)genoot, deelhebber; firmant, vennoot (sake); eggenoot; speelmaat, medespeler, teenspeler (toneel); *ACTIVE* ~, werkende vennoot; *DORMANT* ~, stille vennoot; *SILENT* ~, stemlose (stille) vennoot; *SLEEPING* ~, slaapmaat; stille vennoot; (v) die maat (vennoot) wees van; saamspeel; verbind.

part'nership, vennootskap; deelgenootskap; *ARTICLES of* ~, vennootskapsakte; *DEED of* ~, akte van vennootskap; *ENTER into (contract a)* ~ *with,* vennoot word van.

part: ~**-owner,** deelhebber; mede-eienaar; ~**-pay,** waggeld.

part'-payment, gedeeltelike (af)betaling; paaiement; *in* ~, in (ter) afbetaling.

part'ridge, patrys; ~ **breast,** patrysbors; kanniedood *(Aloe variegata);* ~ **egg,** patryseier.

part: ~**-singing,** meerstemmige sang; ~**-song,** veelstemmige (meerstemmige) lied; ~**-time,** deeltyds.

partur'ient, barend, voortbrengend.

parturi'tion, bevalling, baring.

part'-worn, halfslyt.

part'y, (..**ties),** party; geselskap; gesellige aand, geselligheid; aanhang; gevolg; *BE a* ~ *to,* deelneem aan; medepligtig wees aan; betrokke wees by; *BECOME a* ~ *to,* deelneem aan; *the* ~ *CONCERNED,* die betrokke persoon; ~ *to a CONTRACT,* deelhebber in 'n kontrak; ~ *to a CRIME,* medepligtige; *be OF the* ~, tot die geselskap behoort; *be a* ~ *to a SUIT,* party wees in 'n geding; *a THIRD* ~, 'n derde persoon; ~ **affiliation,** partyverband; ~ **allegiance,** partyverband; ~**-coloured,** veelkleurig, bont; ~ **congress,** partykongres; ~ **cry,** partyleuse; ~ **discipline,** partytug; ~ **funds,** partyfondse; ~ **gown,** aandrok; ~ **interest,** partybelang; ~ **issue,** partykwessie; ~ **line,** groeplyn, gemeenskaplike lyn, plaaslyn; *the* ~ *line,* die partybeleid; ~ **man,** partyaanhanger, partyman; ~ **nomination,** partybenoeming; ~ **organization,** partyorganisasie; ~ **platform,** partyprogram; ~ **politics,** partypolitiek; ~ **press,** partypers; ~ **rally,** partydag, stryddag; ~ **spirit,** partygees; faksiegees; pret; ~ **vote,** partystemming; ~ **wall,** gemeenskaplike muur, tussenmuur, skeidsmuur; ~ **whip,** partysweep.

par' value, parikoers, pariwaarde.

parv'enu, parvenu, nuweling.

pas'cal, pascal, drukeenheid.

pasch'a, pasga (Joods); Pase; ~**l,** paas=.

pa'sha, pasja.

pasquinade', paskwil, smaadskrif, skotskrif.

pass¹, (n) nek, bergpas; deurgang; *HOLD the* ~, die nek hou; *SELL the* ~, verraad pleeg.

pass², (n) paspoort, pas; (die) slaag (by eksamen); gewone graad; verlofpas; stoot (in 'n spel); kritieke toestand, moeilike toestand; handgreep; aangee (voetbal); skermstoot; *BE on* ~, 'n verlofpas hê; *BRING to* ~, veroorsaak; *COME to* ~, gebeur; *COME to a bad* ~, 'n lelike wending neem; *the* ~ *that things have COME to,* die wending wat sake geneem het; die toestand van sake; *a FREE* ~, vrye toegang; vrykaartjie; *MAKE a* ~ *at a girl,* by 'n meisie aanlê; *things have come to a PRETTY* ~, sake het 'n lelike wending geneem; *have things come to SUCH a* ~? het sake so 'n wending geneem? is dit so laat?

pass³, (v) verbygaan; omgaan; oorgaan (pyn); wissel; weggaan; passeer (kaartspel); uitspraak doen, vel

(vonnis); voldoen, goedgekeur word; oorsteek (straat); sterf, heengaan; oortref; slyt, deurbring (tyd); reik; aangee (voetbal); verloop; slaag, diplomeer; deurkom, aflê (eksamen); deurstaan (toets); aanneem; deurgaan; ~ *AWAY*, verbygaan; verdwyn; sterf; ~ *a BILL*, 'n wetsontwerp aanneem; ~ *a BOND*, 'n verband passeer; ~ *all BOUNDS*, alle perke te buite gaan; ~ *BY*, verbygaan; nie raaksien nie; ~ *base COIN*, vals geld in omloop bring; *it* ~*es all COMPREHENSION*, dit gaan alle verstand te bowe; ~ *CURRENT*, algemeen aanvaar word; oral van gepraat word; ~ *with DISTINCTION*, met onderskeiding slaag; ~ *a DIVIDEND*, nie 'n dividend betaal nie; *the DOCTOR has* ~*ed me*, die dokter het my goedgekeur; ~ *DOWN*, deurgee, aangee; ~ *an EXAMINATION*, in 'n eksamen slaag, 'n eksamen deurkom; 'n eksamen aflê; ~ *one's EYE over*, die oog laat gaan oor; ~ *FOR an honest person*, deurgaan vir 'n eerlike persoon; ~ *one's HAND over*, die hand stryk oor; ~ *with HONOURS*, met lof slaag; ~ *INTO*, oorgaan in (na, tot); ~ *JUDGMENT on*, 'n oordeel vel oor; *LET that* ~, praat nie meer daaroor nie; *that MAY* ~, dit kan gaan, ~ *with MERIT*, goed slaag; ~ *by the NAME of*, bekend wees as; deurgaan onder die naam van; ~ *the NIGHT*, die nag deurbring; ~ *oneself OFF as*, jou voordoen as; ~ *OFF without a hitch*, goed afloop; ~ *OFF well*, goed van stapel (laat) loop; ~ *ON*, aangee; deurgee; sterf, heengaan; verder gaan; oorvertel, verder vertel; ~ *OUT*, uitgee, aangee (rugby); flou val; doodgaan; ~ *OVER*, heengaan, sterf; weglaat; verbygaan; oorslaan; ~ *OVER something*, oor iets heenstap; ~ *REMARKS upon*, aanmerkings maak oor; ~ *the REVIEW*, die revue laat passeer; ~ *a ROPE round*, 'n tou slaan om; ~ *ROUND*, uitdeel; rondgee; ~ *SENTENCE on*, 'n oordeel uitspreek oor; ~ *SENTENCE of death*, die doodvonnis uitspreek; ~ *out of SIGHT*, verdwyn; *SUFFER to* ~, deurlaat; laat verbygaan; ~ *the SUGAR*, die suiker aangee; ~ *a TEST*, in 'n eksamen slaag; 'n toets deurstaan; ~ *THROUGH*, deurmaak, ondervind; deurgaan; ~ *the TIME of day*, groet; 'n praatjie aanknoop; in die verbygaan klets; ~ *TRANSFER*, transport gee; ~ *WATER*, water, urineer.
pa'ssable, gangbaar, draaglik; begaanbaar, berybaar (pad); taamlik, skaflik; *his KNOWLEDGE is* ~, hy het taamlik kennis van; *the ROAD is* ~, die pad is begaanbaar; ~**ness,** begaanbaarheid; gangbaarheid.
pass'ably, taamlik, gangbaar, nie te sleg nie.
pass'age¹, (n) gang, deurlaat, steeg, deurloop; deurgang, deurweg, deurvaart (skip); deurtog (rivier); deurrit, deurreis (land); reisgeld; passasie (uit 'n boek; per boot); aanneming (wet); ~ *of (at) ARMS*, woordestryd, woordetwis; *BIRDS of* ~, trekvoëls; *RIGHT of* ~, reg van oorgang; ~ *of TIME*, verloop van tyd; *WORK one's* ~, vir jou oortog (passaat) werk; jou oortog (passaat) verdien.
pass'age², (v) skuins (laat) loop; oorsteek; met woorde skerm.
pass'age: ~**-accommodation,** bootgeleentheid; ~**-money,** passasiegeld, reisgeld; ~**-way,** deurloop.
pas'sant, passant (her.); *en* ~, en passant (skaak).
pass: ~ **book,** bankboek; pasboek; bewysboek; ~**-check,** uitgangskaart.
pass'enger, passasier; opvarende; meeloper (beseerde speler); reisiger, insittende; ~**-aircraft,** passasiersvliegtuig; ~**-carriage,** passasierswa; ~**-coach,** passasierswa; ~**-lift,** personehyser, hysbak; ~**-list,** passasierslys; ~**-luggage,** passasiersgoed; bagasie; ~ **ship,** passasierskip; ~**-steamer,** passasiersboot; ~**-traffic,** personeverkeer, passasiersverkeer; ~**-train,** passasierstrein, personetrein.
pass'er, geslaagde; verbyganger; keurder; ~**-by, (passers-by),** verbyganger.
passibil'ity, gevoeligheid, vatbaarheid.
pass'ible, lydsaam, vatbaar, ontvanklik, gevoelig.
passiflor'a, passieblom.
pass'im, oral; deurgaans, passim.
passim'eter, passimeter, kaartjieoutomaat.

pa'ssing, (n) verbygaan; verloop; aanneem; heengaan, afsterwe, dood; aangee(beweging) (rugby); slaag; *a* ~ *BOUT*, 'n aangeebeweging; *IN* ~, terloops; in die verbygaan; (a) verbygaande, kortstondig, tydelik; eksaminerend; voortreflik, uitstekend, in hoë mate; kortstondig, terloops; *a* ~ *FANCY*, tydelike verliefdheid (gril); ~ *REFERENCE*, terloopse verwysing; ~ *RICH*, skatryk; ~ *SHOT*, verbyhou; veeg; ~ *SHOWERS*, los buie; ~ *THOUGHT*, opwellende gedagte; ~**-bell,** doodsklok; ~**-note,** oorgangsnoot; ~**-out,** voltooiing, afsluiting (van kursus); floute; afsterwe; ~**-out parade,** voorstellingsparade.
Pa'ssion, Passie, Lydensgeskiedenis.
pa'ssion, hartstog, drif; toorn; vlaag van hartstog; liefde(gloed); voorliefde; lyding; *FLY into a* ~, woedend word; *IN a* ~, kwaad, woedend; driftig; *PUT someone into a* ~, iem. woedend maak; *have a* ~ *for RUGBY*, 'n hartstogtelike liefhebber van rugby wees; *give WAY to* ~, jou deur drif laat meesleep.
pa'ssional¹, (n) passionaal, heilige-en-martelareboek.
pa'ssional², (a) hartstogtelik.
pa'ssionate, hartstogtelik, driftig, heethoofdig, oplvieënd; ~**ness,** driftigheid.
pa'ssion: ~**-flower,** passieblom, kruisblom, granadillablom; ~**-fruit,** granadilla, grenadella; ~**less,** koel, bedaard, kalm; onhartstogtelik, hartstogloos; ~**-play,** passiespel; *P* ~ *Sunday*, Passiesondag; *P* ~ *tide*, die Lydenstyd; *P* ~ *Week*, Lydensweek, Passieweek.
pass'ive, (n) lydende vorm, passief; (a) lydend; lydelik; passief; willoos; onderdanig; ~ **debt,** rentelose skuld; ~**ly,** lydelik; ~**ness,** lydelikheid; ~ **obedience,** lydelike gehoorsaamheid; ~ **resistance,** lydelike verset; ~ **verb,** lydende (passiewe) werkwoord; ~ **voice,** lydende vorm, passief.
passiv'ity, lydelikheid.
pass: ~ **key,** loper, diewesleutel; ~**-law,** paswet; ~**-list,** lys van geslaagdes; ~ **office,** paskantoor; ~**-out,** terugkomkaartjie; uitgangskaartjie.
Pass'over, Joodse Paasfees.
pass: ~ **port,** paspoort; vrybrief; ~ **word,** wagwoord, parool.
past, (n) verlede; die gebeurde; *ENQUIRE into someone's* ~, iem. se seel lig; navraag na iem. se verlede (geskiedenis) doen; *LAY bare a man's* ~, iem. se doopseel lig; *the* ~ *and PRESENT*, die hede en verlede; *RAKE up the* ~, ou koeie uit die sloot haal; *THE* ~, die verlede; *a WOMAN with a* ~, 'n vrou met 'n (minder gunstige) verlede; (a) verby; verlede, vergange; afgelope, oud-, vorige, eertyds, gewese, voormalig; *the* ~ *CENTURY*, die vorige eeu; ~ *CURE*, ~ *care*, geen genesing, geen versorging; ~ *HOPE*, hopeloos, buite hoop; ~ *PARTICIPLE*, verlede deelwoord; ~ *STUDENT*, oud-student; ~ *TENSE*, verlede tyd; *THINGS* ~ *cannot be recalled*, gedane sake het geen keer; *for a YEAR* ~, sedert 'n jaar gelede.
past², (adv) verby; (prep) oor, verby; langs; ~ *BEARING*, dit kan nie meer verdra word nie; ~ *COMPREHENSION*, onbegryplik; *it is* ~ *CRYING for*, dit help nie om daaroor te huil nie; *HALF* ~ *two*, halfdrie; ~ *MARRYING*, te oud om te trou; ~ *PRAYING for*, reddeloos verlore; daar is geen salf meer aan te smeer nie; ~ *RECOGNITION*, onherkenbaar; ~ *RECOVERY*, onherstelbaar.
paste¹, (n) lym, gom, pap; plaksel, plakstysel; pasta (tande); smeersel; deeg; vals edelgesteente, kunssteen.
paste², (v) plak, vasplak, opplak; (sl.) uittrap, slaan; ~ *on*, opplak, vasplak.
paste: ~ **board,** (n) bordpapier; speelkaart; namaaksel; deegplank; visitekaartjie; (a) goedkoop, sleg, nagemaak; ~**-brush,** papkwas, lymkwas, gomkwas; ~**-grain,** nagemaakte marokyn(leer).
pas'tel, pastel, papierkryt; ~**ling,** pastel(lering); pasltelwerk; ~ **list,** pasteltekenaar; ~ **shade,** pastelkleur.
paste'-pot, lympot.
pas'tern, koot (van perd).
paste'-up, plaksel.
pasteuriza'tion, pasteurisasie.

pas'teurize, pasteuriseer.
pa'stil, pastille', pastil, tablet, klontjie, pil.
past'ime, tydverdryf, tydkorting, ontspanning; spel.
past'ing¹, (die) plak.
past'ing², vuisslanery; uittrappery.
past' master, meester, volleerde, doring, bobaas.
pastra'mi, pastrami, gerookte beesvleis.
pa'stor, pastor, predikant, herder; pastoor (veral R.K.).
pa'storal, (n) herdersdig; herderspel; pastorale; (a) herderlik, pastoraal; landelik, herders=; ~ 'e, pastorale; ~ ist, veeboer; ~ letter, herderlike brief; ~ play, herderspel; ~ poem, herdersdig; ~ staff, herderstaf; ~ visit, huisbesoek.
pa'storate, predikantskap, herdersamp; priesterstand.
pa'storless, herderloos, sonder leraar.
pa'storship, herdersamp, pastoorskap.
pas'try, (..tries), tertdeeg, pasteideeg; tertgebak; deeg; siergebak, soetgebak; ~-board, rolplank, deegplank; ~-brush, deegkwassie; smeerkwassie; ~ cook, tertbakker; pasteibakker; ~-cutter, deegwieletjie; deegafdrukker, deegsnyer; ~ pincer, deegkartelaar; ~-roll(er), deegroller, tertroller.
pa'sturage, weiland, gras, weiding; (v) laat wei; wei; ~ ground, ~ land, weiveld.
pas'ty, (n) (..tries), (vleis)pastei; (a) deegagtig; week, papperig; oneg (van edelgesteentes); bleek (gesig).
Pat¹, (bynaam vir) Ier.
pat², (n) tikkie, kloppie, sagte geluid; klontjie, stukkie (botter); a ~ of butter, 'n klontjie botter; (v) (-ted), tik, klop; platstryk; streel, aai, paai; ~ oneself on the BACK, jouself 'n pluimpie gee; ~ on the HEAD, oor die kop streel; ~ his SHOULDER, hom op die skouer klop; (a) geskik, toepaslik; vlot, vaardig; oppervlakkig; a ~ quotation, 'n toepaslike aanhaling; (adv) van pas, raak, net geskik, net mooi, toepaslik; KNOW ~ off, iets op sy duimpie ken; SAY ~ off, glad opsê; STAND ~, onversetlik staan; TELL something ~, iets soos 'n rympie opsê; op 'n rympie lieg; ~-a-cake, handjiesklap (kinderrympie).
Patagon'ia, Patagonië; ~n, (n) Patagoniër; (a) Patagonies.
patch, (n) (-es), lap; kol; stukkie, strook; vlek; skoonheidspleister; a BAD ~ of road, 'n slegte stuk pad; not a ~ ON, kan nie kers vashou nie vir; kom nie naby nie; haal daar nie by nie; PUT a ~ on, 'n lap opsit; the RAIN fell in ~es, dit het kol-kol gereën; STRIKE a bad ~, van stryk wees; ongelukkig wees; (v) lap, heelmaak; a ~ed up PEACE, 'n haastig gemaakte (gelapte) vrede; ~ UP, lap; saamflans; skik (rusie); haastig inmekaarknoei (aanmekaarplak); ~ed TROUSERS, gelapte broek; ~-budding, plakokulering; ~ er, lapper; knoeier; ~ ery, lapwerk; knoeiwerk; ~ ing, lapwerk; rubberlap; plakstrook.
patch'ouli, patchouli.
patch: ~-pocket, oppgestikte sak; ~-word, stoplap, stopwoord; ~ work, lapwerk, knoeiwerk; ~ work quilt, lappiesdeken (-kombers); ~ y, gelap, in kolle, kollerig, vlekkerig; sporadies, wisselvallig, ongelyk.
pate, kop, harspan, klapperdop.
pât'é, patee; ~ de foie gras, ganslewerpatee.
patell'a, knieskyf, patella; offerpannetjie.
patell'ar, patell'ate, skottelvormig.
pat'en, pateen, hostiebord; vaas; pan.
pat'ent, (n) patent, oktrooi; APPLY for a ~, patent aanvra; GRANT a ~, patent verleen; ~ PENDING, patent toegesê; TAKE out a ~, 'n patent neem op; (v) patenteer, oktrooieer, 'n patent (oktrooi) uitneem; (a) uitstekend, gepatenteer, openbaar; duidelik, vanselfsprekend; voortreflik; ~ agent, patentagent, patentbesorger; ~ed, gepatenteer; ~ ee', patenthouer, gepatenteerde; ~ leather, blinkleer, glansleer, verlakte leer, lakleer; ~ ly, klaarblyklik; ~ medicine, huismiddel, patente medisyne; ~ office, patent(e)kantoor; ~ remedy, patente middel; ~ right, patent(e)reg; ~-roll, patenteregister.

pat'er, oubaas, oukêrel; ~familias, vader, hoof van die gesin, huisvader, paterfamilias.
patern'al, vaderlik, vader=; van vaderskant; ~ism, vaderlike sorg, paternalisme; ~ist, (n) paternalis; (a) paternalisties; ~ portion, vadersgoed.
patern'ity, vaderskap; outeurskap; bron, oorsaak.
paternos'ter¹, Onse Vader, paternoster; rosekrans.
paternos'ter², vislyn met 'n gewig, setlyn.
path, pad, weg; baan; BREAK a ~, 'n weg baan; DEVIATE from the ~ of virtue, v.d. deugsame pad afwyk; ~ of LIFE, lewensweg; ~ of a PROJECTILE, projektielbaan.
pathet'ic, aandoenlik, pateties, (siel)roerend, gevoelvol; ~ al, aandoenlik, pateties, roerend; ~s, patetiese taal (gevoelens).
path'finder, padvinder; baanbreker, pionier.
path'less, sonder pad, ongebaan(d).
pathogen'esis, pathog'eny, siekteontstaan, patogenese.
pathogen'ic, patogeen.
pathog'raphy, siektebeskrywing, patografie.
patholog'ic(al), patologies.
pathol'ogist, siektekenner, patoloog.
pathol'ogy, patologie, siekteleer.
path'os, gevoel, patos, aandoenlikheid.
path'way, (voet)pad, paadjie; baan.
pa'tience, geduld, lydsaamheid; lankmoedigheid; volharding; geduldspel, kaartspel vir een persoon, patience, solitaire; EXERCISE ~, geduld beoefen; HAVE ~, wees geduldig; geduld hê (gebruik); HAVE ~ in adversity, geduld beoefen in teenspoed; the ~ of JOB and the wisdom of Solomon, Job se geduld en Salomo se wysheid; I am OUT of ~, my geduld is op; ~ is a VIRTUE, geduld oorwin alles; have no ~ WITH, geen geduld hê nie met; nie kan verdra nie.
pa'tient, (n) pasiënt, lyer, sieke; (a) geduldig; gelate, lydsaam, toegewend; volhardend; onvermoeid; BE ~ of, geduldig dra; be ~ with a CHILD, geduldig wees met 'n kind; ~ as JOB, so geduldig soos Job.
pat'ina, roeslaag, verweringslaag, patyn, patina.
patina'tion, patinering, patina.
pa'tio, (-s), binnehof, patio.
pat'riarch, aartsvader, patriarg; ~ 'al, aartsvaderlik, patriargaal; ~ate, patriargaat; ~ism, partriargisme, aartsvaderlike regering; ~ y, patriargale regeringsvorm, patriargie.
patri'cian, (n) patrisiër; (a) patrisies.
pat'ricide, vadermoord; vadermoordenaar.
patricid'al, vadermoord=.
patrilin'eal, patrilin'ear, van vaderskant, patrilineêr, patriliniaal.
patrimon'ial, geërf, deur erfreg verkry, patrimoniaal.
pat'rimony, (..nies), vaderlike erfdeel, erfgoed, patrimonium.
pat'riot, vaderlander, patriot; ~ 'ic, patrioties, vaderlandsliewend; ~ism, vaderlandsliefde, patriotisme.
patris'tic(al), kerkvaderlik, patristies.
patrist'ics, patristiek.
patrol', (n) patrollie; rondte; span; on ~, op patrollie; (v) (-led), patrolleer, die rondte doen; ~ action, patrolliewerk; patrolliebotsing; ~ boat, patrollieboot; ~ man, patrolleerder; konstabel; ~-plane, patrollievliegtuig; ~ wagon, vangwa.
patrol'ogy, patrologie.
pat'ron, (n) beskermheer, skutsheer; patroon, beskermheilige; begunstiger, donateur; gesagvoerder; klant; gereelde besoeker; (pl) klandisie; (a) beskermend; beskerm=; ~ age, beskerming; begunstiging; beskermheerskap; ondersteuning, aanloop; klandisie; steun; under the distinguished ~ age of, onder die beskerming van; ~ ess, (-es), beskermvrou, beskermheilige, skutsvrou; ~ize, begunstig, ondersteun; jou klandisie gee; neerbuigend behandel; ~ize someone, iem. uit die hoogte behandel; ~izing, beskermend; uit die hoogte, neerbuigend; ~ saint, skutpatroon, beskermheilige, skutsheilige.
patronym'ic, (n) patroniem, familienaam, vadersnaam; (a) vader=, familie=, patronimies.
patt'en, oorskoen, klomp; sneeuskoen.
patt'er¹, (n) gepraat, gebabbel, gesnater; afgerammel=

patter / peace

de taal; geheime vaktaal; (v) babbel, snater; aframmel, kekkel.

patt'er², (n) gekletter, geklater; getrappel; (v) kletter; ratel, rammel, klater; trippel, trappel; ~**ing,** gekletter, geklik.

patt'ern, (n) patroon, model; voorbeeld, toonbeeld; monster; staaltjie; *a* ~ *father,* 'n modelvader; (v) volgens patroon maak; modelleer, fatsoeneer; met 'n patroon bewerk; ~ *after (on),* namaak; ~**-book,** patroonboek, modeboek; ~**-drawer,** patroontekenaar; ~**ing,** (die) modelleer; ~**-maker,** patroonmaker; modelmaker; ~ **wife,** modelvrou.

patt'y, (patties), pasteitjie; frikkadelletjie; koekie; ~**-cake,** pasteitjie; ~**-cake pan,** kolwyntjiepan; ~ **pan,** kolwyntjiepan.

pat'ulous, uitgesprei, uitstaande; wyd oop.

pau'city, skaarste, geringheid, skaarsheid; gebrek; kleinheid in aantal; ~ *of labour,* gebrek aan werkkragte.

Paul, Paul; Paulus (apostel); *St.* ~ *'s Cathedral,* die St. Pauluskatedraal; ~ **Jones,** 'n wisseldans; Paul Jones; ~ **Pry,** nuuskierige agie, snuffelaar, snuffelgraag.

Paul'ine, Paulinies.

Paul'inism, Paulinisme.

paunch, (n) **(-es),** pens; dikbuik, spekbuik, buik; buidelsak (by diere); (v) die ingewande uithaal; ~**-bellied,** buikig, boepens=; ~**-belly,** dikpens; ~**y,** buikig.

paup'er, (n) arme, arm mens, armlastige, behoeftige, pouper; *a* ~, 'n kaal jakkals; 'n armlastige; (a) arme=; ~ **funeral,** armebegrafnis.

paup'eris: *sue in forma* ~, kosteloos prosedeer.

paup'er: ~**ism,** armoede, behoeftigheid, armlastigheid, verarming, pouperisme; ~**ize,** verarm, arm maak, tot die bedelstaf bring; ~ **suit,** armmansgeding.

pause, (n) pouse, verposing, ruspoos, ruspose, pose, poos, tussenpoos, tussenpose; pousering; rustyd; orrelpunt (mus,); sesuur (poësie); gedagtestreep; *give* ~ *to his plans,* iem. se planne in die wiele ry; (v) rus; wag, ophou, pouseer; weifel, jou bedink; ~ *over the details,* stilstaan by die besonderhede.

pav'age, straatbelasting; bestrating, plaveisel.

pave, plavei, bevloer, (be)straat, uitlê; ~ *the way for,* die weg baan vir; ~**d,** uitgelê, geplavei, bestraat, gestraat.

pave'ment, sypaadjie; plaveisel, voetstraatjie; vloer (geol.); ~ **artist,** sypadtekenaar, straatskilder.

pav'er, straatmaker; uitstrater; straatsteen, plaveiklip; ~ **stone,** straatsteen, plaveiklip.

pavil'ion, pawiljoen; tent.

pav'ing, plaveisel; bestrating; ~ **beetle,** straatstamper; ~**-block,** plaveiblok; ~**-flag,** straatteël; ~**-stone,** straatsteen, plaveiklip; ~**-tile,** vloerteël.

pav'io(u)r, straatmaker; plaveiklip; stamper.

pav'onine, pouagtig, pou=.

paw, (n) poot, klou; poot (slegte handskrif); (v) krap; skop, kap (met 'n poot); lomp hanteer; betas; ~ *a girl,* 'n meisie betas; ~**ing,** gekap; gekrap; lompe hantering; *a dog* ~*ing at the door,* 'n hond wat aan die deur krap.

pawk'iness, geslepenheid, slimheid; skalksheid.

pawk'y, slim; listig; oulik; skalks.

pawl, pal, ligterhout met ratte, pal; ~ **cog,** sperratand; ~**-spindle,** palas.

pawn¹, (n) pion; werktuig.

pawn², (n) pand; *GIVE in* ~, in pand gee; *TAKE out of* ~, inlos; (v) verpand; in pand gee; ~ **able,** verpandbaar; ~ **broker,** pandjieshouer, pandjiesbaas; ~**-broking,** pandhouery; ~**ee',** pandhouer; ~**er,** verpander, pandgewer; ~**ing,** verpanding; ~ **shop,** pandjieshuis, lommerd; ~**-ticket,** pandbewys.

paw'paw, *kyk* **papaw.**

pay¹, (n) betaling, loon, soldy, gasie; werkloon, traktement, salariëring, besoldiging; *a holiday on FULL* ~, 'n vakansie met behoud van loon; *IN the* ~ *of,* in die diens van; (v) **(paid),** betaal, vergoed, voldoen, afreken met; beloon, salarieer; vergeld; boet, vereffen; aflê (besoek); die moeite loon, voordelig wees; beantwoord; uitkeer; winsgewend wees; ~ *into an ACCOUNT,* op 'n rekening stort; ~ *on ACCOUNT,* op afbetaling stort; ~ *ATTENTION,* aandag skenk; ~ *AWAY,* uitbetaal; ~ *BACK,* terugbetaal; uitkeer; laat boet; ~ *into a BANK,* in 'n bank deponeer; ~ *BEFOREHAND was never well served,* vooruit betaal is dubbel betaal; *the BUSINESS does not* ~, dis geen winsgewende saak nie; ~ *by CHEQUE,* per tjek betaal; ~ *him back in his own COIN,* hom met gelyke munt betaal; ~ *someone a COMPLIMENT,* iem. 'n kompliment maak; ~ *COURT,* die hof maak; ~ *DEARLY for,* swaar boet vir; ~ *(cash) DOWN,* kontant betaal; ~ *as you EARN,* lopende betaalstelsel; deurlopend betaal; ~ *FOR,* betaal vir; ~ *into a FUND,* inbetaal in 'n fonds; ~ *as you GO,* deurlopend betaal; ~ *HONOUR,* hulde bring; ~ *IN,* stort, deponeer; ~ *on the NAIL,* kontant betaal; botter by die vis; ~ *through the NOSE,* te veel betaal; jou die vel oor die ore laat trek; *it does NOT* ~, dit loon nie die moeite nie; ~ *OFF,* afbetaal; afdank; ~ *OUT,* uitbetaal; afkoop; laat skiet, uitvier (tou); vergeld; ~ *the PIPER,* die gelag betaal; ~ *the PRICE,* boet vir; ~ *one's RESPECTS,* jou opwagting maak; *he will* ~ *for THIS,* hy sal daarvoor boet; ~ *UP,* betaal; opdok; ~ *a VISIT,* 'n besoek aflê; ~ *one's WAY,* geen skuld maak nie; nie in skuld raak nie.

pay², (v) met teer (pik) smeer (seeterm).

payabil'ity, betaalbaarheid; winsgewendheid, rendabiliteit.

pay'able, betaalbaar; winsgewend, lonend, betalend; ~ *AFTER 90 days,* op langsig betaalbaar; *BILL* ~, skuldwissel.

pay: ~**-as-you-earn,** (PAYE), lopende betaalstelsel (LBS); ~**-bill,** betaallys; ~**-book,** soldyboekie; ~**-box,** loket, kaartjieskantoor; ~**-clerk,** loonklerk; ~**-corps,** betaaldiens; ~**-day,** betaaldag; ~ **ee',** ontvanger; persoon aan wie betaal word; ~ **envelope,** loonkoevert; ~**er,** betaler.

pay'ing, lonend, betalend; winsgewend; ~ **guest,** betalende gas, loseerder; ~**-in,** storting; ~ **load,** betalende vrag.

pay: ~**-limit,** rendeergrens; ~**-list,** betaalstaat, betaalrol; ~ **load,** lonende vrag; ~ **master,** betaalmeester; ~ **master general,** betaalmeester-generaal.

pay'ment, betaling, voldoening, delging, aansuiwering; loon; vergelding; ~ *in ADVANCE,* vooruitbetaling; *DEFERRED* ~, agterskot; nabetaling; *IN* ~ *of,* ter afbetaling van; *MAKE a* ~, betaal; ~ *by RESULTS,* vergoeding volgens prestasie.

pay: ~**-office,** betaalkantoor; ~ **ore,** lonende erts; ~**-out,** uitbetaling; ~**-packet,** loonkoevert; ~**-roll,** ~**-sheet,** betaalstaat, betaalrol; traktementstaat; ~ **shoot,** loonstrook; ~ **warrant,** betalingsmandaat.

pea, ertjie, akkerertjie; (pl) *ook* gruissteenkool; *GREEN* ~, dopertjie; *as LIKE as two* ~*s,* soos twee druppels water op mekaar lyk; op 'n haar eenders lyk; sprekend op mekaar lyk; *SWEET* ~ *s,* pronkertjies, blomertjies, sierertjies.

peace, vrede; rus, kalmte; eendrag; stilte; ~! stilte! *APOSTLE of* ~, vredesapostel; *ARMED* ~, gewapende vrede; ~ *be his ASHES,* sy as(se) rus in vrede; *mag sy as in vrede rus; AT* ~, in vrede; *BREACH of the* ~, vredebreuk; *BREAK the* ~, die rus versteur; *DISTURBER of the* ~, vredesteurder; *DOVE of* ~, vredesduif; *not to HAVE a moment's* ~, geen rus of duur hê nie; *HOLD one's* ~, stilbly; ~ *with HONOUR,* eervolle vrede; *JUSTICE of the* ~, vrederegter; *KEEP the* ~, die vrede bewaar; *he cannot KEEP his* ~, hy kan nie die vrede bewaar nie; hy kan nie sy rus hou nie; *LEAVE someone in* ~, iem. met vrede laat; *LIVE at* ~ *with one's neighbours,* in vrede woon; *MAKE* ~, vrede sluit; 'n versoening tot stand bring; ~ *of MIND,* gemoedsrus, sielevrede, gerustheid; *PIPE of* ~, vredespyp; ~ *makes PLENTY,* uit vrede kom oorvloed; ~ *at any PRICE,* vrede teen elke prys; *PRINCE of* ~, Vredevors; *may he REST in* ~, mag hy in vrede rus; ~ **able,** vreedsaam, vredeliewend; ~ **ableness,** vredeliewendheid; ~**-breaker,** rusiemaker, rusversteurder; ~**-breaking,** rusversteuring; ~ **conference,** vredeskonferensie; ~**-delegate,** vredesafgevaardigde; ~**-establishment;** vre=

desterkte; ~ **footing**, vredesvoet; ~**ful**, vreedsaam, rustig, gerus; vredig; vredeliewend; ~**fulness**, vreedsaamheid; rustigheid; ~**less**, rusteloos, woelig; ~**-loving**, vredeliewend; ~**maker**, vredestigter, vredemaker; ~**-movement**, vredesbeweging; ~**-offer**, vredesaanbod; ~**-offering**, soenoffer; vredeoffer; olyftak; ~**-officer**, polisiedienaar, konstabel; ~ **pipe**, vredespyp; ~**-proclamation**, vredesafkondiging; ~**-training**, vredesopleiding; ~**-treaty**, vredesverdrag.

peach[1], (n) (-es), perske; perskeboom; skoonheid, aantreklike nooi; *a* ~ *of a girl*, 'n juweel van 'n meisie; 'n beeld van 'n nooi; ~ **aphis**, perskeluis; ~ **blossom**, perskebloeisel; ~ **brandy**, perskebrandewyn; ~**-coloured**, perskekleurig; ~ **down**, perskedons, perskehare.

peach[2], (v) verklap, klik, verraai; ~ *upon*, verklik.

pea'-chick, poukuiken.

peach: ~ **jam**, perskekonfyt; ~**-leaf**, perskeblaar; ~**-leaf curl**, perskekrulbaar; ~ **Melba**, Melbaperske; ~**-stone**, perskepit; ~**-tree**, perskeboom; ~ **y**, perskeagtig; perskekleurig.

pea'-coal, ertjiesteenkool.

pea'cock, (n) (-s, peafowl), pou; *as proud as a* ~, so trots soos 'n pou; (v) trots stap, pronkerig loop; ~**-butterfly**, dagpouoog; ~**-fish**, pouoog(vis); ~**ish**, ~**-like**, pouagtig; ~**-moth**, pouoogmot; ~ **pheasant**, spieëlpou.

pea: ~**-flour**, ertjiemeel; ~ **fowl**, pou; ~ **hen**, pouwyfie.

pea'-jacket, jekker(t), matroosbaadjie.

peak[1], (n) punt, bergpunt, bergtop, spits; top, piek; ~ *of CAP*, pettuit; *REACH its* ~, die hoogtepunt bereik.

peak[2], (v) regop sit (seil); ~ *the oars*, die rieme opsteek.

peak[3], (v) kwyn, vergaan, sieklik lyk; ~ *and pine*, kwyn, agteruitgaan.

peak'ed, gepunt, puntig; spits, skerp; ~ *CAP*, pet; ~ *HAT*, punthoed.

peak: ~ **hour**, spitsuur; ~**-load**, spitslading; ~ **period**, spitstyd, drukste (besigste) tyd; ~ **price**, topprys, hoogste prys; ~ **traffic**, spitsverkeer; ~ **voltage**, topspanning.

peak'y, skerp, spits.

peal, (n) klokgelui; galm; slag, knal, donderslag; salvo, geratel, sarsie; klokkespel; gedawer; ~ *of BELLS*, stel klokke; ~ *of LAUGHTER*, skaterlag; *RING a* ~, die klokke lui; ~ *of THUNDER*, donderslag; (v) lui, weergalm; ratel, (weer)klink, rammel (donder); ~ *forth*, laat hoor; luid lui.

pea'nut, grondboontjie, apeneutjie, Angola-ertjie; ~ **brittle**, grondboontjielekker; ~ **butter**, grondboontjiebotter; ~ **oil**, grondboontjieolie; ~ **sheller**, grondboontjiedopper.

pea'-pod, ertjiepeul.

pear, peer; ~**-drop**, peersuurtjie; peervormige hangertjie.

pearl, (n) pêrel; ~ *of great PRICE*, pêrel van groot waarde; *cast* ~*s before SWINE*, pêrels voor die swyne gooi; (v) bepêrel; met pêrels versier; na pêrels vis; (a) pêrel=; ~ **ash**, pêrelas; ~ **barley**, pêrelgort; ~**-bed**, pêrelbank; ~ **button**, perlemoenknoop; ~**-coloured**, pêrelkleurig; ~**-disease**, pêrelsiekte; ~**-diver**, pêrelvisser, pêrelduiker; ~**ed**, bepêrel(d); ~**-eyed**, met 'n oogpêrel (vlek op die oog); ~**-fisher**, pêrelduiker, pêrelvisser; ~**-fishery**, pêrelvissery; ~**-grey**, pêrelgrys; ~ **hen**, tarentaalwyfie; ~**ies**, draers van 'n perlemoenkostuum; ~**-like**, pêrelagtig; ~**-moss**, pêrelmos; ~**-mussel**, pêrelmossel; ~**-oyster**, pêreloester; ~**-powder**, pêrelwit; ~ **rope**, pêrelsnoer; ~**-shell**, perlemoen; ~**-studded**, met pêrels beset, bepêrel; ~**-white**, pêrelwit; ~ **y**, (n) (..**lies**), draer van 'n perlemoenkostuum; (a) pêrelagtig, bepêrel(d); ~ *y gate*, hemelpoort.

pear: ~**-scab**, peerbrand; ~**-shaped**, peervormig; ~**-slug**, peerslak; ~**-switch**, skakelpeer; ~**-tree**, peerboom; ~**-wood**, witpeerhout.

peas, ertjie(steen)kool.

pea'sant, boer, landbouer; plattelander; ~ **boy**, boerseun; ~ **girl**, boeremeisie; ~ **ly**, boers; ~ **ry**, boeremense, boerestand, buitemense; ~ **wife**, boerevrou.

pease, ertjies.

pea: ~**-shell**, ertjiepeul, ertjiedop; ~ **shooter**, blaasroertjie, blaaspyp; ~ **soup**, ertjiesop, snert; ~**-souper**, dik (digte) mis; rookmis; ~**-soupy**, dik, dig.

peat turf, moerasturf, veen; ~**-bed**, ~ **bog**, turfmoeras, turflaagte, turfgrond; ~**-cutter**, turfsteker; ~**-litter**, turfstrooisel; ~**-moor** = **peatbog**; ~**moss**, veengrond; ~ **y**, turfagtig; turfryk.

pea'-valve, koeëlklep.

peb'ble, spoelklippie; kieselsteen; bergkristalsteentjie; *she is not the only* ~ *on the beach*, meisies is nie handvol nie maar landvol; ~**-bed**, spoelkliplaag; ~**-crystal**, bergkristal; ~ **d**, **peb'bly**, vol klippies.

peb'ble finish, spoelklipafwerking.

pecan', pekan(boom); ~ **nut**, pekanneut.

peccabil'ity, sondigheid.

pecc'able, sondig.

peccadill'o, (-es), kleinsonde, sondetjie, pekelsonde, peccadillo.

pecc'ancy, sondigheid, slegtheid; sonde, vergryp.

pecc'ant, sondig, skuldig; sieklik, bedorwe.

pecc'ary, (..**ries**), pekari, muskusvark.

peccav'i, peccavi, ek het gesondig; skuldbekentenis; *cry* ~, skuld beken.

pêche Mel'ba, Melbaperske.

peck[1], (n) peck (2 gelling); *a* ~ *of DIRT*, 'n vrag vuilgoed; *a* ~ *of TROUBLES*, 'n hoop moeilikhede.

peck[2], (n) pik; vlugtige soen; *be OFF one's* ~, geen eetlus hê nie; ~ *and PERCH*, kos en inwoning; bed en brood; (v) pik, oppik; ~ *at*, met lang tande eet; vit.

peck'er, pikker; vitter; *keep one's* ~ *up*, moed hou.

peck'ish, hongerig; vitterig.

pec'ten, kam.

pec'tic, pekties; ~ **acid**, pektinesuur, pektiensuur.

pec'tin, plantjellie, pektine, pektien.

pec'tinate, kamvormig.

pec'toral, (n) borsmiddel; borsstuk; borsspier; (a) bors=, pektoraal; ~ **fin**, borsvin; ~ **muscle**, borsspier.

pec'tose, pektose.

pec'ulate, geld verduister.

pecula'tion, verduistering (van geld); ontvreemding.

pec'ulator, (geld)verduisteraar.

pecu'liar, (n) persoonlike eiendom; uitsluitende reg; (a) besonder, eienaardig; buitengewoon, vreemd, snaaks; persoonlik, eie; eiendomlik; seldsaam; ~ *CHARACTER*, eiesoortigheid; eienaardige karakter; ~ *to ONESELF*, eiesoortig; ~ *PEOPLE*, die uitverkore volk; eienaardige mense; ~ *TO*, eie aan.

peculia'rity, (..**ties**), eienaardigheid, besonderheid, vreemdheid, hebbelikheid, kenmerkende eienskap, eiendomlikheid; seldsaamheid.

pecul'iarly, besonder(lik); persoonlik; *it AFFECTS me* ~, dit raak my persoonlik; ~ *ANNOYING*, besonder ergerlik (lastig).

pecun'iary, geld=, geldelik, finansieel; ~ *AFFAIRS*, geldsake; ~ *AID*, geldelike hulp (steun); *in* ~ *DIFFICULTIES*, in geldelike moeilikheid.

pedagog'ic(al), opvoedkundig, pedagogies.

pedagog'ics, pedagogie, opvoedkunde.

pedagog'ism, pedagogisme; skoolmeesteragtigheid.

ped'agogue, skoolmeester, opvoeder, pedagoog.

ped'agogy, opvoedkunde, pedagogie.

ped'al, (n) pedaal; trapper; orrelpunt; *soft (loud)* ~, sagte (harde) pedaal; (v) (-**led**), die pedaal gebruik; trap; fiets; *to soft-*~, demp, versag; (a) voet=; hoef=; ~ **bone**, hoefbeen; ~ **brake**, traprem; ~ **curve**, voetpuntkromme; ~ **cycle**, trapfiets; ~ **disc**, voetskyf; ~ **extremities**, voete; ~ **gland**, voetklier; ~ **note**, aangehoue toon, pedaaltoon.

pe'dant, pedant, beterweter, wysneus; skoolvos; doktrinêr; ~ **'ic**, waanwys, pedanties, skoolmeesteragtig; verwaand; ~ **ry**, (..**tries**), pedanterie, verwaandheid, wysneusigheid, beterwetery, houterigheid, skoolwysheid, geleerddoenery.

ped'ate, met voete, gevoet.

ped'dle, smous, met negosie rondry, bondel dra, rondvent, vent; beusel; rondtrek; ~ **r** = **pedlar**.

ped'dling, beuselagtig, onbetekenend.

ped'estal, (n) voetstuk; verhoog, stander, stoel; *place (set) someone on a* ~, iem. op 'n voetstuk plaas;

pedestrian 1111 **penalty**

iem. vereer; (v) **(-led)**, op 'n voetstuk plaas, van 'n voetstuk voorsien; ~ **lamp,** staanlamp.
pedes'trian, (n) voetganger, stapper; (a) voet=, voet= ganger=; gewoon, alledaags, prosaïes, platvloers; ~ **crossing,** oorgang vir voetgangers, voetoorweg; ~ **island,** vlugheuwel; ~ **ism,** loopsport; alledaags= heid, laag-by-die-grondsheid, platvloersheid; ~ **traffic,** voetgangerverkeer.
ped'icel, blomsteel, stingeltjie.
ped'icellate, gesteel, met 'n steel.
pedic'ular, pedic'ulous, vol luise, luisig; luis=.
ped'icure, (n) liddoringsnyer, pedikuur; (v) die voete behandel.
ped'igree, (n) stamboom, geslagregister, geslagslys; afstamming, afkoms; stamboek; (a) stamboek=, ras=; ~ **cattle,** stamboekvee, rasvee; ~ **d,** met 'n stamboom; ~ **dog,** rashond; ~ **fowl,** rashoender; ~ **horse,** rasperd.
ped'iment, kroonlys, kroonstuk, fronton.
pe'dipalp, skerpioenspinnekop, kaaktaster.
ped'lar, smous, bondeldraer, (straat)venter, kramer; ~ **of gossip,** skinderbek; ~**y,** smousware; smou= sery.
pedolog'ic, pedologies.
pedol'ogist, pedoloog.
pedol'ogy, bodemkunde, grondkunde, pedologie.
pedom'eter, treëmeter, pedometer.
pedunc'le, (blom)stingel, (blom)steel; ~**d,** gesteel(d).
pedunc'ular, blomsteel=, steel=.
pedunc'ulate, met 'n steel.
pek, plassie maak, water, piepie.
peck, loer, kyk; ~ **a-boo,** kiekeboe; koekeloerstyl.
peel¹, (n) toring.
peel², (n) bakkersgraaf, bakkerskop, oondskop.
peel³, (n) skil; dop; *candied* ~, versuikerde skil, suka= de; (v) (af)skil; afdop; bas afmaak, skilfer; vervel (slang); uittrek; gelyk wees, portuurs wees (rolbal); ~ *OFF,* afskil; afskilfer, verskilfer; ~ *OFF one's clothes,* jou klere afpluk.
peel'er¹, skiller; skilmasjien; skilmes.
peel'er², konstabel.
peël: ~**ings,** skille; ~ **trap,** skilvanger.
peen, pen (van hamer); ~**-hammer,** penhamer; klip= kaphamer; ~**-tool,** righamer, penhamer.
pep¹, (n) gepiep; (v) piep (kuiken).
peep², (n) blik, kykie; ~ *of DAWN,* dagbreek, dag= lumier; *HAVE a* ~ *at,* iets vlugtig bekyk; (v) loer, gluur; ~ *AT,* afloer, loer na; ~ *over someone's SHOULDER,* in iem. se kaarte kyk; ~**er,** loerder; ~**-hole,** kykgaatjie, loergaatjie, venstertjie; ~**ing,** loerdery, afloerdery; *no* ~ *ing!,* moenie loer nie!; die wat loer, kry niks; ~*ing TOM,* loerder; ~**-show,** kykkas, kykspel; ~ **sight,** guatjievisier.
peer¹, (n) edelman; gelyke, eweknie, portuur; weerga, synsgelyke; *without* ~, sonder weerga (gelyke); (v) gelykstaan met; ewenaar; in die adelstand verhef; ~ **group,** portuurgroep; ~ **rating,** portuurgrade= ring.
peer², (v) (na)loer, tuur, kyk
peer'age, adelstand, adel, adelbock; *be raised to the* ~, in (tot) die adelstand verhef word.
peer'ess, (-es), edelvrou.
peer'ing, getuur, geloer.
peer'less, weergaloos, ongeëwenaard, sonder gelyke.
peeved, vererg, ontevrede, gekrenk.
peev'ish, nors, stuurs, dwars, nurks, suur; krieuwelrig; prikkelbaar, geraak, gemelik; ~**ness,** norsheid, stuursheid, wrewelligheid, geraaktheid, gemelik= heid, dwarsheid, nukkerigheid.
pee'wit, kiewiet.
peg, (n) (tent)pen; piket; kapstok; skroef; paaltjie (krieket); spy, spie; wasgoedknyper; *BRING some= one down a* ~ *or two,* iem. se stertvere uittrek; iem. 'n toontjie laer laat sing; *not find a* ~ *to fit the HOLE,* daar nie 'n mou aan kan pas nie; *a ROUND* ~ *in a square hole,* die verkeerde persoon op die verkeerde plek, *a SUIT off the* ~, 'n pak v.d. rak; *TAKE down a* ~ *or two,* 'n toontjie laer laat sing; (v) **(-ged),** vasslaan; afpen (kleim); stoot; har= poeneer (walvis); gooi na; blok; sterf; vaspen (pry= se); ~ *AWAY,* ploeter, aansukkel; volhard, vol= hou; ~ *out a CLAIM,* 'n kleim afsteek; ~ *DOWN,*

beperk tot; ~ *OUT,* afpen, lepel in die dak steek; bokveld toe gaan; ~ *down PRICES,* die pryse vas= pen; ~ *at one's WORK,* swoeg.
peg'amoid, kunsleer (handelsnaam).
Peg'asus, Pegasus.
peg: ~**-awl,** penels; ~**-board,** gaatjiesbord, spyker= bord; ~**-drum,** dorstrommel; ~**ging,** afpenning; vaspenning; ~**ging act,** vaspenwet; ~**-leg,** hout= been; ~**-ladder,** eenstylleer.
peg'matite, pegmatiet.
peg'matoid, pegmatoïed.
peg'-stake, merkpen.
peg'-top, priktol, kaptol.
pej'orative, (n) pejoratief; (a) verkleinerend; pejora= tief, ongunstig.
pek'in, peking(sy).
Pek'ing, Peking; ~ **duck,** Pekingeend; ~ **man,** Pekingmens.
Pekin(g)ese', Pekinees.
pek'oe, pekkotee.
pel'age, hare; pels; wol.
Pela'gian¹, (n) Pelagiaan; (a) Pelagiaans.
pela'gian², (n) seebewoner, pelagiese dier; (a) see=.
pela'gic, pelagies, pelageen, diepsee=; ~ *fish,* pelagie= se vis, diepseevis.
pel'agite, pelagiet, mangaankool.
pelargon'ium, pelargonium, geranium, malva.
pel'erine, pelerien(mantel), skouermantel.
pelf, geld, pitte, aardse slyk, blik.
pel'ican, pelikaan; tang, haak.
pelisse', bontmantel, pelsmantel; boestroentjie.
pelit'ic, kleihoudend, kleidraend, pelities.
pellag'ra, pellagra, Italiaanse melaatsheid.
pelleliza'ion, pellelisasie.
pel'letize, pelleliseer.
pell'et, (n) koeëltjie; korrel; proppie; haelkorrel; pas= til; pilletjie; (v) beskiet.
pell'icle, velletjie, vliesie.
pell'-mell, (n) warboel, verwarring; (a) deurmekaar, in wanorde, holderstebolder; (adv) onderstebo, deurmekaar; halsoorkop.
pellu'cid, deurskynend; helder; ~**'ity,** deurskynend= heid; helderheid.
pel'met, (gordyn)kap.
Peloponne'sian, (n) Peloponnesiër; (a) Peloponne= sies.
Peloponnes'us, Peloponnesus, Peloponnesos.
pelor'us, peilskyf.
pelt¹, (n) vel; pels, bontvel; vag.
pelt², (n) gooiery; *at full* ~, in volle vaart; (v) gooi; neerkletter; koeël; ~ *with questions,* met vrae be= stook.
pel'tate, skildvormig.
pelt'er, gooier.
pelt'erer, velhandelaar.
pelt: ~**-monger,** velkoper; ~ **ry,** (..**tries),** vel; velle en huide; peltery, bontwerk.
pel'vic, bekken=; ~ **cavity,** bekkenholte; ~ **girdle,** bekkengordel; ~ **peritonitis,** bekkenvliesontste= king.
pelvi'meter, pelvimeter.
pel'vis, (pelves), bekken, pelvis; nierbekken.
Pem'broke, Pembroke, ~ **table,** klaptafel.
pemm'ican, biltongkoek, pemmikan; opsomming (fig.).
pen¹, (n) pen; stif; ~*s may blot but they cannot BLUSH,* papier is geduldig; *DRAW your* ~ *through,* met die pen deurhaal; deurstreep; *wield a FACILE* ~, 'n vaardige (welversnede) pen hê; *LIVE by one's* ~, van jou pen lewe; *STROKE of the* ~, pennestreep; *TAKE up one's* ~, na die pen gryp; (v) skrywe; neerpen.
pen², (n) hok (vir hoenders); kraal; kampie; broei= toom (pluimvee); wyfieswaan; (v) **(-ned),** opsluit; inja, in die hok ja.
pen'al, straf=, strafregtelik; strafbaar; ~ **clause,** straf= bepaling; ~ **code,** strafreg; ~ **colony,** strafkolonie; ~**ize,** straf, beboet; penaliseer; benadeel; ~ **law,** strafwet; ~ **reform,** strafhervorming; ~ **servitude,** hardepad, dwangarbeid; ~ **settlement,** strafkolo= nie.
pen'alty, (..ties), straf, boete, strafvoltrekking; *the*

penance 1112 *pentagon*

EXTREME ~, doodstraf; *UNDER* ~ *of*, op straf van; ~ **clause**, strafbeding, strafbepaling; ~ **corner**, strafhoek; ~ **drill**, strafoefening; ~ **drop**, strafskepskop; ~ **goal**, strafdrie, strafdoel; ~ **kick**, strafskop; ~ **stamp**, boeteseël; ~ **stroke**, strafhou; ~ **throw**, strafgooi, strafworp.

pen'ance, (n) boetedoening, boete, straf; (v) straf, boete laat doen.

penat'es, huisgode, penate.

pen'-case, penkoker.

pence, pennies, dubbeltjies; *take care of the* ~, let op die kleintjies; wees spaarsaam met die klein uitgawes.

pen'chant, neiging, geneigdheid.

pen'cil, (n) potlood; griffel; ~ *of LIGHT*, ligstreep; *PUT one's* ~ *through something*, 'n streep deur iets trek; ~ *of RAYS*, straalbundel, ligbundel; (v) (-led), teken; opskryf; ~ -**bait**, pypmossel; ~ -**box**, ~ -**case**, potlooddoos; griffeldoos; ~ -**compasses**, potloodpasser; ~ -**drawing**, potloodtekening; ~ **iform**, penseelvormig; ~ -**sharpener**, potloodskerpmaker; ~ **skirt**, regaf rok, nousluitende (noupassende) rok; ~ -**sketch**, potloodskets.

pen'-craft, skryfkuns.

pend, laat oorstaan, laat hang.

pen'dant, (n) hanger(tjie), hangornament; pendant; wimpel, vlaggie; gaskroon; teenhanger; (a) hangend, hang, oorhangend; hangende, onbeslis.

pen'dency, onsekerheid; *during the* ~ *of the matter*, terwyl die saak nog hangende is.

pen'dent = **pendant**; ~ **'ive**, hanggewelf.

pend'ing, (a) hangende; onbeslis; onafgehandel; in afwagting; *patent* ~, patent toegestaan; (prep) hangende; gedurende; in afwagting van; *the AFFAIR is* ~, die saak is hangende; ~ *the DECISION*, hangende die beslissing; ~ *the MEETING*, gedurende die vergadering; ~ *the NEGOTIATIONS*, terwyl die onderhandelinge aan die gang is; ~ *the REPLY*, in afwagting v.d. antwoord; ~ *his RETURN*, in afwagting van sy terugkoms; totdat hy terugkom; ~ *the TRIAL*, hangende die verhoor.

pendrag'on, vors (by die ou Britte).

pen'-driver, penlekker.

pend'ulant, neerhangend; slingerend.

pen'dulate, slinger; weifel, op twee gedagtes hink.

pen'duline, hangend; ~ **tit**, kapokvoëltjie.

pen'dulous, hangende, hang; swewend; weifelend; ~ *lip*, hanglip.

pend'ulum, (-s), slinger; *the swing of the* ~, die skommeling v.d. slinger; ~ **clock**, slingeruurwerk; ~ **magnet**, slingermagneet; ~ -**proof**, slingerproef; ~ **rod**, slingerstang; ~ **saw**, hangsaag; ~ **tit**, kapokvoël; ~ **weight**, slingergewig.

penetrabil'ity, deurdringbaarheid, deurgrondelikheid.

pen'etrable, deurdringbaar; toeganklik.

penetral'ia, binneste heiligdom.

pen'etrant, deurdringend; skerpsinnig.

pen'etrate, binnedring, deurboor, deurbreek, deurdring; deurgrond, inlewe; deursien, agterkom.

pen'etrating, deurdringend, skerp; skerpsinnig; *a* ~ *analysis*, 'n indringende ontleding.

penetra'tion, deurdringing, indringing; deurbraak; sterkte (van 'n lens); skerpsinnigheid, speursin, deursig; *LACK of* ~, gebrek aan deurdringingsvermoë; *POINT of* ~, indringingspunt.

pen'etrative, deurdringend, deurdringings, skerp; skerpsinnig.

pen: ~ -**feather**, slagpen; ~ -**friend**, penvriend; briefmaat, pennemaat.

peng'uin, pikkewyn; ~ -**egg**, pikkewyneier.

pen'holder, penhouer.

pen'ial, penis, van die penis.

penicill'in, penisillien, penisilline.

penin'sula, skiereiland; ~ **r**, (n) skiereilandbewoner; (a) van 'n skiereiland, skiereilands; ~ **te**, in 'n skiereiland verander.

pen'is, (penes), penis; peester (diere).

pen'itence, boetvaardigheid, berou.

pen'itent, (n) boeteling, boetvaardige, biegteling; (a) boetvaardig, berouvol, berouhebbend.

peniten'tial, berouvol, boetvaardig; boet; ~ **robe**, boetekleed; ~ **psalm**, boetpsalm; ~ **tears**, trane van berou.

peniten'tiary, (n) (..ries), verbeteringsgestig, verbeterhuis, tughuis; (a) boete, tug; boetvaardig.

pen: ~ **knife**, sakmes, knipmes; pennemes; ~ **man**, (..men), skoonskrywer; outeur; ~ **manship**, skoonskrif; skryfkuns; skryfwyse; ~ -**name**, skuilnaam, pennenaam.

penn'ant, wimpel, vlaggie.

penn'ate, gevleuel, met vlerke.

pennif'erous, veerdraend.

penn'iform, veervormig.

penn'iless, arm, behoeftig, platsak; ~ **ness**, armoede.

Pen'nine, Pennies; ~ **Alps**, Penniese Alpe; ~ **Mountains**, Penniese Gebergte.

penn'on, banier, wimpel, vlag, vaantjie.

penn'orth = **pennyworth**.

penn'y, (**pence, pennies**), (hist.), pennie, dubbeltjie, oulap, duit; *turn up like a BAD* ~, onwelkom wees; *not have a* ~ *to BLESS oneself with*, geen duit besit nie; *spend every* ~ *on CLOTHES*, alles in klere steek; *the* ~ *has DROPPED*, daar gaan 'n lig op; *turn an HONEST* ~, 'n stukkie brood verdien; *he who will not keep a* ~ *shall never have many*, wie die kleine nie eer nie, is die grote nie werd nie; ~ *and* ~ *LAID up will be many*, baie kleintjies maak 'n grote; *LOOK after the pennies and the pounds will look after themselves*, wees spaarsaam in die kleine; *MAKE a pretty* ~, baie geld verdien; *NOT a* ~, geen dooie duit nie; ~ *PLAIN and twopence coloured*, blinkerige bog; *in for a* ~, *in for a POUND*, wie A sê, moet ook B sê; *it costs a PRETTY* ~, dit kos nogal iets; dit kos 'n mooi sommetjie; *a* ~ *SAVED is a* ~ *gained*, as jy iets spaar, dan het jy iets; *a* ~ *for your THOUGHTS*, waaroor peins jy? waaraan dink jy? *TURN the* ~ *to profit*, jou geld winsgewend aanwend; ~ *WISE and pound foolish*, verkeerd (agterstevoor) suinig; suinig in kleinighede en roekeloos in groot dinge; *not a* ~ *the WISER*, niks wyser nie; *WITHOUT a* ~ *to this name*, brandarm, kaal; ~ -**a-liner**, broodskrywer, skribent; ~ **dreadful**, ~ **horrible**, goedkoop prikkelroman, dubbeltjiesroman, sensasieroman; (pl) prikkellektuur; ~ -**pinching**, vrekkerig; ~ **post**, penniepos; ~ **royal**, kruisement(drank); ~ **stamp**, pennieposeël; ~ **weight**, pennyweight (24 grein); ~ **whistle**, kwêlafluit; ~ **wise**, verkeerd suinig, agterstevoor suinig; ~ **wort**, waternawel; ~ **worth**, vir 'n dubbeltjie, 'n oulap s'n; *not a* ~*worth of GOOD*, niks werd nie; *a* ~*worth of SWEETS*, 'n pennie se lekkers, lekkers vir 'n pennie.

penolog'ic, penologies.

penol'ogist, penoloog.

penol'ogy, penologie.

pen: ~ -**picture**, penskets; ~ -**pusher**, penlekker, klerk.

pen'sile, hangend, slingerend.

pen'sion, (n) pensioen; jaargeld; losieshuis, pension; *OLD-AGE* ~, ouderdomspensioen; *RETIRE on* ~, met pensioen aftree; (v) pensioeneer, pensioen toeken; *op pensioen stel*; ~ *off*, pensioeneer; ~ **able**, geregtig op 'n pensioen; pensioendraend; ~ **ary**, (n) (..ries), gepensioeneerde, pensioentrekker, pensionaris; (a) pensioens; gepensioeneer; ~ **ed**, gepensioeneer(d); ~ **er**, pensioentrekker, pensioenaris, gepensioeneerde; ~ **fund**, pensioenfonds; ~ **insurance**, pensioenversekering; ~ **money**, pensioengeld; P ~ **s Act**, Pensioenwet; ~ **scheme**, pensioenskema.

pen'sive, peinsend; droefgeestig, swaarmoedig; ~ **ness**, gepeins; droefgeestigheid.

penste'mon = **penstemon**.

pen'stock, sluisdeur.

pent, opgesluit; ~ **up**, verbete; ingehoue, opgekrop.

pen'tachord, vyfsnarige musiekinstrument, pentakord; reeks van vyf note.

pen'tacle, towerfiguur, pentagram.

pen'tad, vyftal.

pentadac'tyl, vyfvingerige (vyftonige) dier; ~ **ous**, vyfvingerig; vyftonig.

pen'tagon, vyfhoek; pentagoon; *the P* ~, die Pentagon (hoofkwartier v.d. V.S.A. se verdedigingsde

partement); ..**ag'onal**, vyfhoekig, vyfsydig, pentagonaal.
pent'agram, vyfhoekige ster, pentagram.
pentahed'ral, vyfsydig, vyfkantig, pentaëdries.
pentahed'ron, reëlmatige vyfkant, pentaëder.
pentam'eter, pentameter, vyfvoetige versreël.
pentapet'alous, vyfbladig.
pen'tarch, vyfman, pentarg; ~y, vyfmanskap, pentargie.
pentasperm'ous, vyfsadig.
Pen'tateuch, Pentateug.
pentath'lon, vyfkamp, pentatlon (ry, skiet, skerm, swem, hardloop).
pentav'alent, vyfwaardig.
Pen'tecost, Pinkster.
Pentecos'tal, Pinkster=.
pen'-thorn, pendoring.
pent'house, afdak; skutting, skerm (dak); bygebou; dakwoning, dakhuis; dakwoonstel; woonstelwoning, woonstelhuis; skuur.
pentimen'to, pentimento, herverskyning (skildery).
pen'tode, pentode.
pen'-tray, penbakkie.
pent'-roof, afdak; skuinsdak.
pentstem'on, skildblom.
penul't(imate), (n) voorlaaste lettergreep; (a) voorlaaste.
penum'bra, halfskaduwee, byskaduwee; ~l, halfdonker.
penur'ious, karig, armoedig, behoeftig; gierig, vrekkig, inhalig; suinig; ~**ness**, armoede, behoeftigheid; inhaligheid.
pen'ury, behoeftigheid, gebrek, armoede, broodsgebrek, geldgebrek, armoedigheid.
pen'wiper, penafveër, penwisser.
pe'on, oppasser, polisiedienaar, bode; dagloner; infanteris, voetganger (soldaat); ~**age**, daglonerskap.
pe'ony (peonies), pinksterroos, pioen.
peo'ple, (n) mense, persone; volk, nasie; publiek; *he of ALL* ~, juis hy; *the CHOSEN* ~, die uitverkore volk; *COLOURED* ~, Bruinmense; *the FRENCH* ~, die Franse volk; *OLD* ~, senior burgers; ou mense; *OLD* ~ *'s HOME*, tehuis vir senior burgers; ouetehuis; *one's OWN* ~, mens se bloedverwante; jou eie mense; ~ *SAY*, dit word vertel; die mense sê; *THE* ~, die mense, die volk; die publiek; *a WARLIKE* ~, 'n krygshaftige (militaristiese) volk; *YOUNG* ~, die jongspan; (v) bevolk; *a thickly* ~*d country*, 'n digbevolkte land; ~**'s court**, volkshof; ~**'s front**, volksfront; ~**'s quarter**, volksbuurt; ~**'s republic**, volksrepubliek.
pep, (n) lewe, fut, gô, pit; *give someone a* ~ *talk*, iem. moed inpraat; (v): ~ *up*, warm maak; opwek, versterk.
peperi'no, peperino, poreuse vulkaanrots.
pep'lum, (..**pla, -s**), peplum.
pepp'er, (n) peper; (v) peper, peper ingooi, inpeper; bestook, bombardeer; afransel, looi (fig.); ~ *someone*, iem. laat deurloop; iem. onder die lood steek; ~ **and salt (material)**, swart en wit, peper-en-sout= (kleur); ~**-box**, peperpotjie, peperbus, ~**-castor**, peperpotjie, peperbus; ~ **corn**, peperkorrel; ~ **ing**: *give someone a* ~*ing*, iem. bestook; ~**-mill**, pepermeul.
pepp'ermint, pepermint; ~ **cream**, roompeperment; ~ **crisp**, sjokoladepeperment; ~ **liqueur**, pepermentlikeur, jangroentjie, groenmamba.
pepp'er: ~**-pot**, peperbus; gekruide kos; peperkos; ~**-tree**, peperboom; ~ **wort**, peperwortel; ~**y**, peperagtig; gepeper; skerp; prikkelend; bitsig, opvlieënd.
pep'pill, opwekpil, opkikker(pil).
pepp'y, lewendig, vol lewe; pittig.
pep'sin, pepsien, pepsine.
pep'tic, spysverterend; pepties; maag=; ~**s**, spysverteringsorgane; *the* ~*s*, die spysverteringsorgane; ~ **ulcer**, maagseer.
pep'tone, peptoon.
pep'tonize, peptoniseer.
per, per, deur, deur middel van; ~ *ANNUM*, jaarliks, per jaar; ~ *CAPITA*, per capita, per kop, per per=

soon; ~ *CENT*, persent, per honderd; ~ *CONTRA*, aan die ander kant; ~ *DIEM*, per dag; ~ *HIMSELF*, eiehandig; ~ *SE*, juis, per se; *send* ~ *POST*, per pos (oor die pos) stuur; *as* ~ *USUAL*, soos gewoonlik.
per'acid, oorsuur.
peracute', perakuut.
peradven'ture, miskien, moontlik, by toeval.
peram'bulate, rondloop, rondwandel, rondtrek; afloop.
perambula'tion, rondgang, rondwandeling; uitgestrektheid; omtrek; inspeksie.
peram'bulator, kinderwaentjie; meetwiel; ~**y**, rondtrekkend.
peraton'a, horingsuil.
percale', katoenbatis, perkal.
perceiv'able, waarneembaar, bemerkbaar, begryplik.
perceive', waarneem, bemerk, bespeur, gewaarword, begryp, gewaar; observeer, ontwaar.
perceiv'ing, skerpsiende; skerp; waarnemend; skrander, skerpsinnig.
percen'tage, persentasie; persentsgewys(e); *on a* ~ *BASIS*, persentsgewys(e); *BY* ~*s*, persentsgewys(e); ~ **error**, persentasiefout.
per'cept, die waarneembare; waargenomene; waarneming.
perceptibil'ity, waarneembaarheid, merkbaarheid, aanskoulikheid.
percep'tible, waarneembaar, merkbaar, duidelik, aanskoulik.
percep'tion, waarneming, persepsie, besef, gevoel; invordering; insig, begrip, inning, ontvangs, toe eiening (reg).
percep'tive, opmerksaam; waarnemings=, gewaarwordings=; ~ **faculty**, waarnemingsvermoë.
percept'iveness, perceptiv'ity, waarnemingsvermoë, insig.
percept'ual, waarnemings=, perseptueel.
perch¹, (n) baars (vis).
perch², (n) (-es), (dwars)stokkie (in 'n voëlkou); slaapstok (hoender); sitplek; veilige plek; roede (5½ jrt.); langwa (voertuig); *HOP* the ~, bokveld toe gaan; *KNOCK off one's* ~, uitstof; kafloop; *the bird TAKES its* ~, die voël stryk neer (gaan sit); (v) op 'n stok sit (hoender); neerstryk (voël); hoog en droog sit; ~ *ed on a hill*, op 'n koppie geleë; ~**er**, takslaper, voël wat op 'n tak slaap.
perchance', miskien, dalk, altemit.
Per'cheron, Percheron (perd).
perchlor'ate, perchloraat.
perch'-pole, langwa.
percip'ience, gewaarwording, waarneming, skerpsinnigheid, deursig.
percip'ient, (n) gewaarwordende wese; iem. wat telepaties waarneem; waarnemer; (a) gewaarwordend, waarnemend, onderskeidend; insigryk, skerpsiende.
per'colate, deursyfer, filtreer, deursypel; (deur)syg.
percola'tion, deursyfering, deursypeling, filtrasie.
per'colator, sypelkan, sypelaar, filtreerkan; filter; filtreermasjien; siffie.
percuss', hard slaan, klop, perkuteer.
percu'ssion, slagwerk; skok; slag; botsing, perkussie; beklopping; *instrument of* ~, slaginstrument; ~ **band**, slagorkes; ~ **bomb**, skokbom; ~ **cap**, geweerdoppie; skietdoppie, slagdoppie; ~ **charge**, skoklading; ~ **drill**, stampboor; ~ **fire**, skokvuur; ~ **fuse**, skokbuis; ~ **igniter**, skokontsteker; ~ **ignition**, slaghamerontsteking; ~ **ist**, slagwerkspeler, slagwerker; ~ **lock**, perkussieslot; ~ **mine**, trapmyn; ~ **needle**, skoknaald; ~ **primer**, slaghoofdjie, slagdoppie; ~ **rifle**, perkussiegeweer; ~ **tube**, slagpypie, skokbuis.
percuss'ive, (n) slaginstrument; (pl) slagwerk(instrumente); (a) slag=, skok=.
percutan'eous, deur die vel.
perdi'tion, verderf, verderfnis, verdoemenis; *the ROAD to* ~, die weg na die verderf; *TO* ~, na die duiwel.
perdu(e)', verskuil, in hinderlaag; *lie* ~, in hinderlaag lê.
perdurabil'ity, duursaamheid, ewigdurendheid.

perdur'able, langdurig; duursaam; blywend; ewig.
pe'regrinate, swerf, reis, rondreis.
peregrina'tion, reis, swerftog, omswerwing, tog.
pe'regrin(e), (n) swerfvalk; (a) vreemd, uitheems, ingevoer; ~ **falcon,** swerfvalk.
perempt', verbeur; ~**ion,** verbeuring van appèlreg.
peremp'torily, gebiedend, op gebiedende wyse; *he was* ~ *dismissed,* hy is op staande voet afgedank.
peremp'toriness, bepaaldheid; beslistheid; noodsaaklikheid.
peremp'tory, gebiedend, bevelend, meesteragtig; dringend, beslissend; ~ *command,* gebod, gebiedende bevel; magspreuk.
perenn'ial, (n) deurbloeier, oorblywende (meerjarige) plant; (a) oorjarig, meerjarig, aanhoudend, altyddurend, veeljarig, deurgroeiend, voortdurend, altydgroeiend; standhoudend, permanent (water); ~ **plant,** (oor)blywende (oorstaande, oorjarige, meerjarige, deurgroeiende) plant; ~ **spring,** standhoudende fontein; ~ **stream,** standhoudende water (stroom, rivier, loop).
perf'ect, (n) voltooid teenwoordige tyd, perfektum; (a) volmaak, volkome, perfek, eksieperfeksie; ~ *in his MANNERS,* met volmaakte maniere; ~ *NONSENSE,* klinkklare onsin; *PRACTICE makes* ~, al doende leer 'n mens; *be a* ~ *STRANGER,* 'n volslae vreemdeling wees; heeltemal vreemd wees.
perfect', (v) volmaak, vervolmaak; voltooi; voleindig; volvoer; verbeter; ~ *oneself in the art of oratory,* 'n volmaakte redenaar probeer word.
perfectibil'ity, volmaakbaarheid, vatbaarheid vir verbetering.
perfec'tible, volmaakbaar.
perfec'tion, volmaaktheid, volkomenheid, vervolmaking; perfeksie; voortreflikheid; *BRING to* ~, tot volkomenheid bring; *DO something to* ~, iets voortreflik doen; *TO* ~, volmaak; ~**ism,** perfeksionisme; ~**ist,** (n) perfeksionis; (a) perfeksionisties.
perfec'tive, perfektief.
perferv'id, gloedvol, vurig.
perfid'ious, troueloos, verraderlik, vals, meinedig, valshartig; ~**ness,** troueloosheid, valsheid.
perf'idy, troueloosheid, verraderlikheid, troubreuk, ontrou, valsheid, valshartigheid, verraad.
perf'orate, deurboor, deurprik, deurknip, gaatjies maak; perforeer; tand (seëls); ~*d plate,* sifplaat.
perfora'tion, deurboring, deurknipping; gaatjie, perforasie; tanding.
perf'orator, boor, knipper, perforeermasjien.
perforce', met geweld, noodsaaklikerwyse, noodgedwonge, uit nood; *by* ~, deur geweld.
perform', uitvoer, vervul, volbring, volvoer, doen, waarneem; nakom, maak, verrig, optree, voordra, speel, vertoon, ten gehore bring; ~ *a BALLET,* 'n ballet uitvoer; ~ *a COMPOSITION,* 'n stuk uitvoer; ~ *a DUTY,* 'n plig nakom; ~ *a FUNCTION,* 'n funksie waarneem; ~ *an OBLIGATION,* 'n verpligting nakom; ~ *a PLAY,* 'n toneelstuk opvoer; ~**able,** uitvoerbaar; opvoerbaar, speelbaar.
perform'ance, uitvoering; verrigting, daad; prestasie; volvoering, vervulling; vertoning, spel, voorstelling; werkverrigting (motor); ~ *of work,* werkverrigting.
perform'er, speler; voordraer; sanger; volbringer, volvoerder; vertoner; bakleier (boks); ~**'s licentiate,** voordraerslisentiaat.
perform'ing, (n) uitvoering; nakoming; (a) afgerig, gedresseer; ~ *ANIMAL,* gedresseerde (afgerigte) dier; ~ *ARTS,* uitvoerende kunste; ~ *RIGHT,* reg van vertoning (opvoering); opvoerreg.
perfum'atory, welriekend.
perf'ume, (n) geur, reuk, reukwerk, parfuim; lavantel; (v) welriekend maak, deurgeur, parfumeer; ~**d,** geurig, welriekend, geparfumeer(d).
perfum'er, parfumeur; ~**y,** (..ries), parfumerie, reukwerk.
perf'ume sprinkler, reukwaterspuit.
perfunc'toriness, sleurdiens, oppervlakkigheid; agtelosigheid, slordigheid.
perfunc'tory, agtelosig, slordig, meganies, sonder toewyding; vlugtig, oppervlakkig.

perfuse', natspat, besprinkel; begiet; deurgiet; deurdrenk; deursyfer; deurstraal.
perfu'sion, besprinkeling; begieting; deurgieting; deursyfering; deurstraling.
pergamen'eous, perkamentagtig, perkament=.
perg'ola, prieel.
perhaps', miskien, dalk, straks, strakkies, altemit, wellig; omtrent.
per'i^1**,** (n) (-s), engel, gees, fee.
per'i^2**,** (pref) om, rond, buite, peri=.
pe'rianth, blombekleedsel, blomdek.
pe'riapt, behoedmiddel, amulet.
pericard'iac, pericard'ial, hartvlies=, hartsak=.
pericardit'is, hartsakontsteking, perikarditis.
pericard'ium, hartsak.
pe'ricarp, saadvlies; saadvat; vrugwand; ~ **'ial,** saadvlies=, perikarpies.
peri'cope, perikoop, leesstuk.
pericran'ium, kopbeenvlies, skedelvlies.
pe'ricycle, perisikel, perikambium.
pe'riderm, kurkhuid.
pe'ridot, olivien, peridoot.
pe'rigee, naaste stand van 'n hemelliggaam by die aarde, perigeum.
pe'rigone, perigoon (dierk.); blomdek, perigonium (plant.).
perig'ynous, omstandig, perigien.
perig'yny, omstandigheid, periginie.
perihel'ion, naaste stand van 'n hemelliggaam aan die son, perihelium.
pe'ril, (n) gevaar; risiko; *AT your* ~, op eie verantwoordelikheid; *the BLACK* ~, die swart gevaar; *in* ~ *of DROWNING,* met gevaar van verdrinking; *in* ~ *of one's LIFE,* in lewensgevaar; *at one's OWN* ~, op eie risiko; ~*s of the SEA,* seegevare; (v) **(-led),** in gevaar stel; aan gevaar blootstel; ~**ous,** gevaarlik, haglik, gewaag.
perim'eter, omtrek, perimeter, grenslyn, buitelyn, buitekant; *on the* ~, aan die buiterand; ~ **camp,** laerkamp; ~ **fence,** buiteheining, grensheining.
perine'al, boudnaat=, bilnaat=.
perine'um, boudnaat, bilnaat, perineum; dam (by perd).
per'iod, tydperk, tydvak, termyn, periode; volsin; omlooptyd (planeet); lesuur; punt, rus; maandstonde; ~ *of MOTION,* duur van beweging; ~ *in OFFICE,* diensperiode; *PUT a* ~ *to,* 'n end maak aan; ~ *under REVIEW,* onderhawige tydperk; ~ *of SERVICE,* dienstermyn; ~ *of VALIDITY,* geldigheidsduur; ~ *of VIBRATION,* trillingstyd; ~ **doll,** pop in historiese drag; ~ **furniture,** stylmeubels; ~ **piece,** geskiedenisstuk; ~ **play,** kostuumstuk.
period'ic^1**:** ~ *ACID,* perjoodsuur; ~ *LAW,* periodieke wet; ~ *LEASE,* termynhuur; ~ *TABLE,* periodieke tabel.
period'ic^2**,** periodiek, gereeld terugkerend; periodies; ~**al,** (n) tydskrif, periodiek; (a) gereeld, periodiek; ~**ally,** van tyd tot tyd, periodiek.
periodi'city, gereelde terugkeer, periodisiteit.
per'iods, maandstondes.
perios'teum, beenvlies.
periostit'is, beenvliesontsteking.
peripatet'ic, (n) wandelaar, rondstapper, peripatetikus; voetganger; (a) peripateties, rondtrekkend.
peripetei'a, perip'ety, peripetie, ommekeer.
periph'eral, perifeer, omtrek=; rand=; ~ **area,** randgebied.
periph'ery, omtrek, periferie; buitekant.
periph'rasis, (..ses), omskrywing, perifrase.
periphras'tic, omskrywend, perifrasties; ~ **conjugation,** omskrywende vervoeging.
pe'riplus, omseiling.
peri'pteral, omsuil.
pe'riscope, periskoop.
periscop'ic, periskopies.
pe'rish, vergaan, omkom, doodgaan; tenietgaan, ondergaan; bederf; *the ROPE was* ~*ed,* die tou was vergaan; ~ *the THOUGHT,* dit sy verre van my; jy kan maar gaan slaap; ~**ed,** dood, omgekom; vergaan, vrot; ~*ed with cold,* verkluim, half dood van die kou(e).

pe′rishable, verganklik; bederfbaar, aan bederf on=derhewig; ~ *product*, bederfbare produk; ~*s* be=derfbare produkte, goed wat sleg kan word.
pe′risperm, saadeiwit, kiemwit.
peristal′sis, peristalsis, peristalse, dermbeweging.
peristal′tic, peristalties, kronkelend, dermbeweging=.
peristreph′ic, ronddraaiend.
pe′ristyle, suilery, suilegang.
periton(a)e′al, buikvlies=, peritoneaal; ~ *CAVITY*, buikholte; ~ *LAYER*, buikvlieslaag.
peritonit′is, buikvliesontsteking, peritonitis.
pe′ri-urban, buitestedelik, omstedelik.
pe′riwig, pruik; ~**ged**, gepruik.
pe′riwinkle, alikreukel; maagdeblom; maagdepalm; katoog.
perj′ure: ~ *oneself*, meineed pleeg, vals sweer; ~**d**, meinedig; ~**r**, meinedige, eedbreker.
perjur′ious, meinedig.
perj′ury, meineed, woordbreuk, eedbreuk; *commit* ~, meineed pleeg.
perk, parmantig wees, neus in die wind steek; brutaal kyk; ~ *the EARS*, die ore spits; ~ *UP*, mooi maak, optooi; meer lewendig word; ~**y**, parmantig, as=trant, brutaal, snipperig; ~*y girl*, 'n snip van 'n meisie.
perks, byverdienste, ekstra verdienste, ekstra(tjies).
perl′ite, perliet.
perl′on, perlon.
perlustra′tion, besigtiging, monstering.
perm, (n) vaste golwing, duurgolf (hare); (v) laat golf.
perm′afrost, ysgrond, permavries(grond).
perm′anence, perm′anency, duur, voortduring, duursaamheid, bestendigheid, permanensie.
perm′anent, blywend, duursaam, bestendig, voortu=rend, staande, standhoudend, permanent; ~ **ad=dress**, vaste adres; ~ **appointment**, vaste aanstel=ling; ~ **colour**, vaste kleur; ~ **establishment**, vaste diensstaat; ~ **force**, staande mag; ~ **joint**, duursa=me las; ~**ly**, permanent, blywend, vas; ~ **rank**, vaste rang; ~ **staff**, vaste (permanente) personeel; ~ **teeth**, blywende tande; ~ **wave**, vaste haargolf, vaste karteling, vasgolf; ~ **way**, vaste baan, spoor=baan, aardebaan (van spoorweg).
permang′anate, permanganaat; ~ *of potash*, kalium=permanganaat.
permeabil′ity, deurdringbaarheid, deurlaatbaarheid.
perm′eable, deurdringbaar, deurlaatbaar, deurtrek=baar.
per′meance, deurdringing, magnetiese deurdrin=gingsvermoë.
perm′eate, deurdring, deurtrek, deursyfer.
permea′tion, deurdringing, deurdringendheid.
Perm′ian, (n) Perm; (a) Permies.
permissibil′ity, toelaatbaarheid, vergunbaarheid, verskoonbaarheid.
permiss′ible, toelaatbaar, vergunbaar, geoorloof; ~ **error**, foutgrens; ~ **load**, veilige vrag.
permi′ssion, verlof, toelating, toestemming, vergun=ning, veroorlowing, permissie; *by your* ~, met u verlof.
permiss′ive, veroorlowend, vergunnend, toestem=mend, toegeeflik, toeskietlik, permissief; ~ *society*, permissiewe maatskappy; ~**ness**, toegeeflikheid, toeskietlikheid, permissiwiteit.
perm′it, (n) permit, verlof(brief), geleibrief, vrybrief, pas.
permit′, (v) (-ted), toelaat, toestaan, vergun, veroor=loof, duld, gedoë, permitteer; ~*ted AREA*, bebou=bare gebied; streek met vergunning; *this* ~*s of no DELAY*, dit kan geen uitstel duld nie; *SMOKING is not* ~*ted*, rook word nie toegelaat nie; *WEA=THER* ~*ting*, as die weer gunstig is; ~*tance*, ver=lof, vergunning, veroorlowing.
permut′able, verwisselbaar.
permuta′tion, verwisseling, omsetting, klankverskui=wing, permutasie; rangskikking; groepering; kom=binasie.
permutat′or, stroomwender, stroomwisselaar, gelyk=rigter.
permute′, verwissel, omsit.
perni′cious, skadelik, verderflik, verpestend, dodelik, kwaadaardig, heilloos, pernisieus; ~ **anaemia**, kwaadaardige bloedarmoede; ~**ness**, skadelik=heid, verderflikheid; ~ **scale**, verderflike dopluis.
pernick′ety, peuterig; kieskeurig, puntene(u)rig.
pernocta′tion, nagwaak.
pe′rorate, peroreer, 'n toespraak afsluit.
perora′tion, slot (van 'n toespraak), slotrede, perora=sie.
perox′ide, peroksied, perokside.
perpend′, oorweeg, bedink.
perp′end(er), kraagsteen, sluitsteen.
perpendic′ular, (n) loodlyn; loodregte stand; *DRAW a* ~ *to*, 'n loodlyn trek op; *let FALL a* ~, 'n loodlyn neerlaat; *OUT of* ~, uit die lood; (a) pen=regop, vertikaal, loodreg; regstandig; staande; ~ *LINE*, loodlyn; ~ *WRITING*, loodregte (steil) skrif.
perpendicular′ity, loodregte stand.
perp′etrate, bedrywe, begaan, pleeg, besondig.
perpetra′tion, volvoering, pleging, (die) pleeg, be=gaan, aanrigting.
perp′etrator, skuldige, bedrywer, dader, aanrigter.
perpet′ual, onophoudelik, (ewig)durend; lewenslang; onaflosbaar; ~**ly**, ewig en altyd; ~ **motion**, ewig=durende beweging, perpetuum mobile; ~ **screw**, skroef sonder end.
perpet′uate, verewig, bestendig, aan die vergetelheid ontruk, in stand hou.
perpetua′tion, verewiging, bestendiging, instandhou=ding.
perpetu′ity, bestendigheid; ewige duur, ewigheid; ewigdurendheid; *in (to, for)* ~, vir ewig en altyd.
perplex′, verwar, in verwarring bring, verbyster, inge=wikkeld maak, verboureeer; verleë maak; ~**ed**, verward, ontsteld; verlee, beteuterd, bedrommeld, verslae; verboureerd; ~**ity**, (..ties), verwarring, verleentheid, benepenheid, bedremmeldheid, be=teuterdheid.
perq′uisite, fooi; uitsluitende reg; byverdienste, ek=stratjie; (pl) emolumente, voordele, voorregte.
Per′rier (water), Perrierwater.
pe′rron, stoep, perron.
pe′rry, peerwyn, peerdrank.
perscruta′tion, deeglike ondersoek.
perse, donkerblou, grysblou.
per se, (L), per se, op sigself genome (geneem), in=trinsiek.
pers′ecute, vervolg, lastig val, kwel, pla.
persecu′tion,′ vervolging; ~ **mania**, vervolgings=waansin.
pers′ecutor, vervolger.
pers′ecutrix, (..trices), vervolgster.
persever′ance, volharding, deursettingsvermoë, aan=houvermoe; ~ *will be rewarded*, aanhou(er) wen.
persever′ant, volhardend, volhoudend.
persevere′, volhard, deurbyt, vastrap, aanhou, vol=hou, deursit; ~ *IN a task*, volhou met 'n taak; ~ *WITH a child*, volhard met 'n kind; ~**r**, aanhouer.
persever′ing, volhardend, aanhoudend, standvastig.
Per′sia, Persië.
Per′sian, (n) Pers; Persies (taal); (a) Persies; ~ **carpet**, Persiese mat; ~ **cat**, Persiese kat; ~ **lamb**, Persiese lam; karakoelpels; ~ **powder**, insektepoeier; ~ **sheep**, Persiese skaap; ~ **wheel**, bakklespomp, ket=tingpomp.
pers′iflage, spot, onsin, jillery, persiflage.
persimm′on, tamatiepruim, dadelpruim, persimmon.
persist′, aanhou, volhard, deurbyt, deurdruk, deur=drywe, deursit; bly by, volhou; bly voortbestaan; ~ *in one's folly*, volhard met jou dwaasheid; ~**ence**, ~**ency**, volharding, aanhouding; hardnek=kigheid; deurdrywery, deursettingsvermoë; voort=bestaan; nawerking (gas); ~**ent**, volhardend; aan=houdend, hardnekkig; nawerkend; ~**er**, deurdruk=ker, volharder, volhouer.
pers′on, persoon, mens; persoonlikheid, iemand; voorkoms, postuur; ~ *under ARREST*, gearres=teerde; ~ *on BOARD*, opvarende; ~ *in COM=MAND*, gesagvoerder, bevelvoerder; ~ *in CUS=TODY*, bewaarde; *LEGAL* ~, regspersoon; *a* ~ *of NOTE*, iem. van naam; iem. van aansien; *in one's OWN* ~, in eie per=soon; *the* ~ *in QUESTION*, die betrokke persoon;

without REGARD to ~s, sonder aansien des persoons; *without RESPECT of* ~s, sonder aansien van persoon; ~ *under SENTENCE*, veroordeelde; *SOME* ~ *or other*, iemand; ~ *TRIED*, verhoorde; ~ *UNDER sentence*, veroordeelde; *WHITE* ~, blanke, witman; ~ **able**, aanvallig, knap van uiterlik, aansienlik; ~ **age**, persoon; rol (toneelstuk).

pers'onal, (n) persoonsberig; persoonlike voornaamwoord; (pl) persoonlike eiendom; (a) persoonlik, eie, self; *for* ~ *gain*, uit eie belang; ~ **appearance**, verskyning in eie persoon; voorkoms; ~ **column**, personekolom; ~ **contact**, (liggaamlike) aanraking; ~ **description**, persoonsbeskrywing; ~ **effects**, roerende goedere; personalia; ~ **estate**, roerende goed; ~ **'ia**, personalia, persoonlike berigte; ~ **'ity**, (..**ties**), individualiteit, selfheid, persoonlikheid; *legal* ~ *ity*, regspersoonlikheid; ~ **ization**, verpersoonliking; ~ **ize**, verpersoonlik; ~ **ly**, persoonlik, in persoon; ~ *ly I am quite satisfied*, self is ek heeltemal tevrede; ~ **physician**, lyfarts; ~ **property**, roerende goed; ~ **servant**, lyfbediende; ~ **share**, aandeel op naam; ~ **tax**, persoonsbelasting; ~ **ty**, (..**ties**), persoonlike besit; ~ **violence**, lyfsgeweld.

pers'onate, voorstel; die rol speel van, optree as; jou uitgee vir, jou voordoen as, personeer.

persona'tion, voorstelling; rolvervulling, uitbeelding; persoonsbedrog, (die) optree (as 'n ander), personasie.

pers'onator, iem. wat in 'n ander se plek optree; iem. wat hom uitgee vir 'n ander.

personifica'tion, verpersoonliking, persoonsverbeelding, personifikasie.

person'ify, (..**fied**), verpersoonlik, personifieer; *innocence personified*, die onskuld in eie persoon.

personnel', personeel, staf; manne; troepe.

perspec'tive, (n) perspektief; perpektieftekening; verskiet; vergesig, uitsig, vooruitsig; deursig; (a) perspektiwies.

per'spex, perspeks.

perspica'cious, skerpsinnig, skrander, skerpsiende.

perspica'city, skerpsiendheid, skerpsinnigheid, skranderheid.

perspicu'ity, duidelikheid, helderheid.

perspic'uous, duidelik, helder.

perspir'able, uitsweetbaar; *the* ~ *point*, die sweetpunt.

perspira'tion, sweet, (die) uitsweet, uitwaseming; perspirasie; ~ **mark**, sweetvlek.

perspir'ative, (n) sweetmiddel; (a) uitwasemend; sweet=.

perspir'atory, sweet=.

perspire', sweet, perspireer, uitsweet, uitwasem, transpireer.

persuadabil'ity, oorreedbaarheid, oortuigbaarheid.

persuad'able, vatbaar vir oortuiging, oorreedbaar, oortuigbaar.

persuade', oorhaal, ompraat, beweeg, oorreed, oortuig; *BE* ~ *d of*, oortuig wees van; *I CANNOT* ~ *myself that* . . ., ek kan nie glo dat . . . nie; ~ *FROM (against)*, afraai; ~ *INTO*, oorhaal tot; ~ **r**, oorreder, oorhaler.

persuasibil'ity, oorreedbaarheid.

persuas'ible, oorreedbaar.

persua'sion, oorhaling, omprating, oorreding, oortuiging, geloof, gesindheid, gesindte; *ART of* ~, oorredingskuns; *of FRENCH* ~, van Franse nasionaliteit; *of the MALE* ~, van die manlike geslag; *OPEN to* ~, oorreedbaar, vatbaar vir oortuiging; *POWER of* ~, oorredingskrag.

persuas'ive, (n) oorredingsmiddel; (a) oorhalend, ompratend, oorredend; oorredings=; ~ **ness**, oorredingskrag; ~ **power**, oorredingskrag.

pert, vrypostig, wysneusig, astrant, snipperig.

pertain', behoort, deel wees (van); ~ *to*, behoort by; betrekking hê op, slaan op.

pertina'cious, hardnekkig, halsstarrig, eiesinnig, koppig; volhardend, vashoudend.

pertina'ciousness, **pertina'city**, hardnekkigheid, halsstarrigheid, koppigheid; volharding.

pert'inence, **pert'inency**, geskiktheid, gepastheid, saaklikheid, pertinensie.

pert'inent, geskik, gepas, toepaslik, voegsaam, saaklik, ter sake, doeltreffend, pertinent; ~ *to the question*, verbandhoudend met die saak.

pert'ness, vrypostigheid, wysneusigheid, onbeskaamdheid, snipperigheid.

perturb', versteur, verstoor, verontrus; in die war bring; ~ *ed AT the suggestion*, geskok deur die wenk; ~ *ed BY the rumours*, verontrus deur gerugte; ~ **ance**, ~ **a'tion**, versteuring, storing, beroering, onrus, verontrusting; ~ **ative**, steurend; ~ **er**, versteurder, verontruster.

pertused', deurboor, vol gate.

pertuss'is, kinkhoes.

Peru', Peru.

peruke', pruik.

peru'sal, deurlesing, noukeurige deurlees; ondersoek.

peruse', deurlees, noukeurig lees, nalees; deursien, deurkyk, deurloop; ondersoek; ~ **r**, leser; ondersoeker.

Peruv'ian, (n) Peruaan; (a) Peruaans; ~ **bark**, kinabas.

pervade', deurdring, vervul, deurtrek.

perva'sion, deurdringing, deurdringendheid.

pervas'ive, deurtrekkend, deurdringend.

perverse', verkeerd; hardnekkig; eiewys; dwars, befoeterd; onnatuurlik; verdorwe, sleg, pervers; onredelik, onhandelbaar; ~ **ness**, verkeerdheid; hardnekkigheid; dwarsheid; onredelikheid; ondankbaarheid, dwarstrekkery, dwarstrekkerigheid.

perver'sion, verdraaiing; verleiding, verdorwenheid, afvalligheid, verwording, perversie.

pervers'ity, (..**ties**), hardnekkigheid, onhandelbaarheid; verkeerdheid; verdorwenheid, slegtheid, perversiteit.

pervers'ive, verderflik; omkerend; *be* ~ *of*, geheel omkeer, onderstebo gooi.

perv'ert, (n) afvallige; afwykende; verdorwene, ontaarde.

pervert', (v) verdraai; verlei; omkeer, misbruik, bederf; verderf; afvallig maak; 'n verkeerde wending gee; ~ **ed**, verdraaid, verkeerd; verdorwe; ~ **er**, verdraaier; verleier; ~ **ible**, verdraaibaar; verleibaar.

perv'ious, deurdringbaar; vatbaar; toeganklik; ~ **ness**, deurdringbaarheid; toeganklikheid.

pese'ta, peseta (Spaanse muntstuk).

pes'kiness, beroerdheid; lastigheid.

pes'ky, beroerd; vervelend, lastig.

pe'so, (-s), peso (Suid-Amerikaanse muntstuk).

pess'ary, (..**ries**), (baar)moederkrans, baarmoederring; steekpil, setpil.

pess'imism, pessimisme; swartgallige lewensbeskouing, swaarmoedigheid, swaartillendheid, swaarhoofdigheid.

pess'imist, pessimis, swartgallige.

pessimis'tic, pessimisties, swartgallig, swaartillend.

pest, pes; plaag; neulkous, kwelgees, nare mens; kwelling; *BE a* ~, 'n kwelgees wees; 'n blindevlieg wees; *a TROUBLESOME* ~, 'n seurkous; 'n nare mens.

pes'ter, pla, lastig val, treiter, vervolg, neul, verpes, foeter; ~ *SOMEBODY for something*, aan iem. se kop maal oor iets; ~ *one ABOUT a matter*, iem. gedurig lastig val oor 'n saak; ~ *one FOR money*, neul oor geld by iem.; ~ **er**, kwelgees, plaaggees.

pest: ~-**house**, peshuis, peshospitaal; ~**icide**, plaagdoder, plaagmiddel; ~**if'erous**, verderflik; verpestend, skadelik.

pes'tilence, pessiekte, pestilensie.

pes'tilent, pesagtig; verderflik; skadelik; lastig, verpestend.

pestilen'tial, pesagtig, verpestend; besmetlik, aansteeklik; verderflik, pes=; ~ **air**, peslug; ~ **pox**, pespokke.

pe'stle, (n) stamper; (v) stamp, fynmaak, fynstamp.

pestol'ogy, pestologie.

pet[1], (n) slegte bui, kwaadheid; *get into a* ~, boos word.

pet[2], (n) gunsteling, liefling; hansdier, troeteldier, lieflingsdier; (v) (-**ted**), (ver)troetel, liefkoos, verwen, streel; (a) geliefde, hans=, troetel=, lieflings=; *one's* ~ *aversion*, jou doodsteek; die doring in jou vlees.

pet'al, blomblaar, kroonblaar; ~**iform**, kroonblaarvormig; ~(**l**)**ed**, met blomblare, met kroonblare;

pet animal / **phenocryst**

~oid, blomblaaragtig, kroonblaaragtig; ~ous, met blomblare, met kroonblare.
pet' animal, troeteldier.
petard', springbus, kruitbom, klapper, voetsoeker; *be hoist with his own* ~, 'n put vir 'n ander grawe en daar self in val.
pet' calf, hanskalf.
pet'-cock, aftapkraan, deurblaaskraan.
pet' dog, skoothondjie; lieflingshond.
Pet'er¹, Petrus; Pieter; *St.* ~ *'s CHURCH,* die St. Pieterskerk; *rob* ~ *to pay PAUL,* bo afsny om onder aan te las; een gat maak om 'n ander te vul; skuld maak om skuld te betaal.
pet'er², (v) opraak; ~ *out,* doodloop, tot 'n end kom, op niks uitloop, doodgaan.
Pet'er-penny, Pieterspenning.
Pet'er's finfoot, watertrapper.
pet'ersham, koordband.
pet'iolar, blaarstingel=.
pet'iolate, met 'n stingel.
pet'iole, blaarstingel, bladstingel.
petit', (masc.), **petite',** (fem.), klein, tingerig, fyn; ~ *BOURGEOIS,* kleinburgerlike persoon; ~ *POINT,* tentsteek.
peti'tion, (n) smeekskrif, versoekskrif, beswaarskrif, smeekbede, memorie, petisie; *make a* ~, 'n versoekskrif indien; (v) smeek; versoek; 'n versoekskrif indien, petisioneer; ~ *AGAINST a return,* protes aanteken teen 'n verkiesing; ~ *the AUTHORITIES,* 'n versoekskrif tot die outoriteite rig; ~**ary,** smekend, versoekend, versoek=; ~**er,** eiser, versoeker, petisionaris.
pet: ~ **lamb,** hanslam; ~ **name,** lieflingsnaam, troetelnaam, roepnaam; vleinaam.
Pet'rarch, Petrarca.
pet'rel, stormvoël; *stormy* ~, stormvoël; rusverstoorder.
petrifac'tion, verstening, petrifikasie.
pet'rifiable, versteenbaar.
pet'rified, versteen; verhard, lam geskrik.
pet'rify, (..fied), versteen, in steen verander, petrifiseer; verstar; styf word, verhard.
petrochem'ical, (n) petrochemikalie; (a) petrochemies.
petrochem'istry, petrochemie.
petrogen'esis, petrogenese.
pet'roglyph, petroglief; rotsgravure; rotsinskripsie.
petrog'rapher, petrograaf.
petrograph'ic, petrografies, gesteente=.
petrog'raphy, gesteenteleer, petrografie.
pet'rol, (n) petrol; (v) petrol ingooi, van petrol voorsien; petrol inneem; ~ **attendant,** petroljoggie; ~ **bomb,** petrolbom; ~ **consumption,** petrolverbruik; ~ **coupon,** petrolkoepon; ~**-controller,** petrolkontroleur; ~**-driven,** petrolaangedrewe; ~ **dump,** petrolopslagplek; ~ **engine,** petrolenjin; petrolmasjien; ~ **eum,** petroleum, aardolie, steenolie, ~ **feed,** petroltoevoer; ~ **filter,** petrolsuiweraar, petrolfilter, petrolfiltreerder, petrolsif, ~ **gauge,** petrolmeter; ~ **'ic,** petrol=; petroleum=; ~**og'ical,** petrologies; ~ **'ogist,** petroloog; ~**l'ogy,** petrologie; steenkunde; gesteenteleer; ~ **pump,** petrolpomp; ~ **station,** vulstasie; ~ **supply,** petrolaanvoer; petrolvoorraad; petrollewering; ~ **tank,** petroltenk; ~ **tanker,** petroltenkwa; petrolskip.
pet'ronel, ruiterpistool.
pet'rous, steenagtig, rotsagtig.
pet' shop, troeteldierwinkel, arkmark.
pet'tichaps, tuinfluiter (voël).
pett'icoat, onderrok; vrou; *when he was still IN* ~ *s,* van sy kinderdae af; toe hy nog 'n snuiter was; *be under* ~ *RULE,* onder die pantoffel sit; ~**-commando,** kappiekommando; ~**ed,** met 'n onderrok aan ~ **government,** vroueregering; ~ **heath,** onderrokheide; ~ **influence,** vroulike invloed; ~**-ridden,** onder die pantoffel; ~**-string,** rokband.
pett'ifog, (-ged), kulsakies aanneem, konkel; knoei; redetwis; kibbel; ~ **ger,** knoeier; beunhaas; regsverdraaier; boereverneuker, boerebedrieër; skelm prokureur; ~**gery,** regsverdraaiing; haarklowery, knoeiery; ~**ging,** (n) haarklowery; (a) peuterig, kleingeestig, knoei=, vitterig.

pett'iness, kleinheid, nietigheid, beuselagtigheid; kleinsielgheid, bekrompenheid, kleingeestigheid.
pett'ing, (die) liefkoos, liefkosery, vertroeteling; vryery; ~ **party,** vryparty.
pett'ish, knorrig, liggeraak, kortgebonde, nurks, nors, stuurs.
pett'itoes, varkpootjies.
pet'to: *in* ~, in petto; op die hart; in die geheim.
pett'y, klein, gering, nietig, onbetekenend, onbeduidend, triviaal, benepe; kleinsielig, bekrompe; onder=; ~ **cash,** kleinkas; los geld; ~ **dealer,** skarrelaar; ~ **expenses,** klein onkoste; ~ **larceny,** eenvoudige diefstal; ~**-minded,** kleingeestig; ~ **officer,** onderoffisier; ~ **theft,** diefstal van kleinighede.
pet'ulance, pet'ulancy, prikkelbaarheid, liggeraaktheid, lastigheid, brutaliteit; moedswil.
pet'ulant, prikkelbaar, kriewelrig, lastig, ontevrede, gemelik, brutaal.
petun'ia, petunia.
pew, (n) kerkbank; gestoelte; (v) kerkbanke maak, van kerkbanke voorsien; ~ **age,** bankgeld, bankhuur.
pe'wit, kiewiet.
pew' rent, bankgeld, bankhuur.
pew'ter, piouter; tinkan; tingoed; ~**er,** piouterwerker.
pha'eton, ligte koets, faëton.
phag'ocyte, fagosiet, vreetsel.
phagocyt'ic, fagosities, fagositêr.
phal'ange, falanks; vingerbeentjie; toonbeentjie.
phalan'ger, vlieënde eekhoring; koets-koets, koes-koes.
phal'anstery, gemeenskaplike woonhuise.
phal'anx, (-es, ..langes), falanks, vingerbeentjie; toonbeentjie; kootjie; bundel meeldrade.
phalarope, fraiingpoot(voël).
phall'ic, fallies; penis=.
phall'ism, fallisme.
phall'us, (phalli), fallus, manlike lid, koker.
phanerog'amous, sigbaar bloeiend.
phan'tasm, hersenskim, gesigsbedrog, visioen; droombeeld; (gees)verskyning; ~ **agor'ia,** fantasmagorie, droombeeld, skimmespel; ..**tas'mal,** fantasties, spookagtig.
phan'tast, fantas.
phan'tasy = fantasy.
phan'tom, spook, verskyning, spooksel, spookbeeld, spookgestalte; spieëlbeeld, newelbeeld, fantoom; hersenskim, droombeeld; ~ **at'ic,** spookagtig, hersenskimmig; ~ **ship,** spookskip; ~ **view,** deurskynaansig.
Phar'aoh, Farao.
Pharisa'ic, Fariseïes (sekte).
pharisa'ical, farisees, skynheilig, huigelagtig.
Pha'risaism, Fariseïsme.
pha'risaism, skynheiligheid, fariseïsme.
Phar'isee, Fariseër.
pha'risee, fariseër, huigelaar, femelaar.
pharmaceut'ic(al), artsenykundig, farmaseuties; ~ **chemist,** apteker, farmaseut.
pharmaceut'ics, artsenybereikunde, farmasie.
pharmaceut'ist, artsenybereider, apteker, farmaseut.
pharm'acist, apteker, farmaseut.
pharmacolog'ical, artsenykundig, farmakologies.
pharmacol'ogist, artsenykundige, farmakoloog.
pharmacol'ogy, artsenykunde, artsenyleer, farmakologie, geneesmiddelleer.
pharmacopoe'ia, artsenykersboek, farmakopee.
pharm'acy, (..cies), apteek; artsenybereikunde, farmasie, geneesmiddelbereiding; ~ **board,** aptekersraad.
phar'os, vuurtoring, ligbaken; skeepslantern.
pharyn'geal, behorende tot die keelholte, keelholte=.
pharyngit'is, ontsteking van die keelholte, keelontsteking, faringitis.
pha'rynx, (-es, ..ryngs), keelholte, farinks.
phase, stadium; toestand; voorkome, verskynsel; fase, skyngestalte; *IN* ~, gelykfasig; ~ *of the MOON,* maangestalte; *OUT of* ~, ongelykfasig.
phas'ing, fasering.
phea'sant, fisant; ~**-egg,** fisanteier; ~ **ry,** fisantehok.
phena'cetin, fenasetien, fenasetine.
phen'ocryst, fenokris, eersteling.

phen'ol, karbolsuur, fenol.
phenol'ogy, fenologie.
phenom'enal, wonderlik, buitengewoon, merkwaar=
dig, fenomenaal.
phenomenolog'ical, fenomenologies.
phenomenol'ogy, fenomenologie.
phenom'enon, (..**mena**), verskynsel, natuurverskyn=
sel, wonder, wondermens, fenomeen.
phe'notype, fenotipe.
phen'yl, feniel.
phew! ba! sies! ga! poe!
phi, pi.
phi'al, botteltjie, flessie, fiool.
philan'der, (n) flirt; vryer; vryerige kêrel; vryery; (v)
flirt, skarrel, koketteer, meisies agternaloop; ~ **er,**
flirt, skarrelaar, vrouegek.
philanthrop'ic, mensliewend, filantropies.
philan'thropism, mensliewendheid, filantropie.
philan'thropist, filantroop, mensevriend.
philan'thropize, mensliewendheid betoon, weldoen.
philan'thropy, mensliewendheid, menseliefde, filan=
tropie.
philatel'ic, filatelies, posseëlversameling=; **p~ so=
ciety,** vereniging van posseëlversamelaars, filatelie=
vereniging.
philat'elist, posseëlversamelaar, filatelis.
philat'ely, (die) versamel van posseëls, posseëlkunde,
filatelie.
philharmon'ic, (n) musiekliefhebber; (a) musieklie=
wend, filharmonies; ~ *orchestra,* filharmoniese
orkes.
phil'hellene, (n) vriend van die Grieke, filhelleen; (a)
filhelleens, Grieksgesind.
Philhel'lenism, Filhellenisme, Grieksgesindheid.
Philipp'ians, Filippense (Bybelboek).
philipp'ic, filippika, hekelrede, skerp redevoering.
philippi'na, philippine', filippien, filippyn.
Phil'ippine, Filippyns.
Phil'ippines, (die) Filippynse Eilande, die Filippyne.
phil'ister, materialis, filister; filistyn.
Phil'istine, (n) Filistyn; (a) Filistyns.
phili'stine, (n) filistyn, materialis; onkunssinnige per=
soon, filister; (a) kultuurloos, filistyns, materialis=
ties; bekrompe.
phil'istinism, bekrompenheid, kultuurloosheid, ge=
brek aan kunssin.
phillum'enist, lusiferis, versamelaar van vuurhoutjie-
etikette.
phillum'eny, lusiferisme.
philoc'alist, skoonheidsliefhebber.
philog'yny, verwyfdheid.
philolog'ic(al), filologies.
philol'ogist, filoloog.
philol'ogy, filologie.
phil'omath, liefhebber van kennis, filomaat.
philom'athy, liefde vir kennis, filomatie.
Phil'omel, Philomel'a, nagtegaal, filomeel.
philoprogen'iture, teellustig; lief vir jou kinders.
philos'opher, wysgeer, filosoof, denker; wêreldwyse;
~ **'s stone,** steen van die wyse.
philosoph'ic(al), wysgerig, filosofies; wêreldwys.
philos'ophize, filosofeer, bespieël; teoretiseer.
philos'ophy, wysbegeerte, filosofie; wêreldwysheid;
~ *of LIFE,* lewensfilosofie; *MENTAL* ~, metafi=
sika; *MORAL* ~, etiek; *NATURAL* ~, natuurwe=
tenskap.
philotech'nic(al), kunsliewend.
phil'ter, phil'tre, minnedrank, liefdesdrank.
phiz, tronie, gesig, bakkies, gevreet.
phlebit'is, aarontsteking, flebitis.
phlebog'raphy, aarbeskrywing, flebografie.
phleb'orrhage, aarbreuk.
phlebosclero'sis, aarverharding, aarverkalking.
phlebothrombo'sis, aarverstopping.
phlebot'omize, bloedlaat, aarlaat.
phlebot'omy, bloedlating.
phlegm, slym, roggel, fleim; onverskilligheid, traagheid,
flegma; ~ **at'ic,** onverskillig, flegmaties, ongevoelig,
koel; slymagtig; ~-**expelling,** slymafdrywend.
phleg'mon, bindweefselontsteking; sweer.
phlegm'y, slymerig, slym=.
phlo'em, binnebas, basweefsel, floëem.

phlogis'tic, verbrandings=, flogisties.
phlogis'ton, flogiston.
phlo'gopite, flogopiet.
phlog'oscope, flogoskoop.
phlox, floksie, vlamblom.
phob'ia, sieklike vrees, fobie.
phob'ic, fobies.
phoc'a, rob, seehond.
Phoeni'cia, Fenisië.
Phoeni'cian, (n) Fenisiër; (a) Fenisies.
phoen'ix, feniks.
phon, foon (fisika), fon.
phon'ate, verklank, stem voortbring.
phone, (n) telefoon; klank, foon; (v) telefoneer, (op)=
bel, oplui.
phon'eme, foneem.
phonen'doscope, fonendoskoop.
phone'-tapping, afluistering.
phonet'ic, foneties.
phoneti'cian, fonetikus.
phonet'ics, fonetiek, klankleer.
phon'etism, klankvoorstelling, fonetisme.
phon'etist, fonetikus.
phon'ey, (sl.), vals, verdag, oneg, bedrieglik.
phon'ic, klank=, fonies; ~ **method,** klankmetode; ~ **s,**
fonetiek, klankleer; geluidskeer, fonetika.
phon'ofilm, praatrolprent, fonofilm.
phon'ogram, fonogram.
phon'ograph, fonograaf, grammafoon.
phonograph'ic(al), fonografies.
phonog'raphy, fonografie.
phonolog'ic(al), fonologies.
phonol'ogist, fonoloog.
phonol'ogy, klankleer, fonologie.
phonom'eter, fonometer, klankmeter.
pho'non, fonon.
phon'oscope, fonoskoop.
phonotique', fonoteek.
pho'ny = **phoney.**
phoo'ey, twak, kaf.
phor'mium, formium.
phorom'eter, forometer.
phos'gene, fosgeen.
phos'phate, fosfaat; ~ **rock,** rotsfosfaat.
phos'phene, fosfeen.
phos'phide, fosfied, -ide.
phos'phite, fosfiet.
phosphon'ic acid, fosfoonsuur.
phospho'nium, fosfonium.
phos'phor, fosfor.
phos'phorate, met fosfor verbind.
phosphoresce', glim, lig, fosforesseer; ~ **nce,** glim=
ming, gloeiing, fosforessensie; ~ **nt,** ligtend, blin=
kend, skynend, fosforesserend.
phosphor'ic, fosfories, gloeiend, fosfor=; ~ **acid,**
fosforsuur.
phos'phorite, fosforiet.
phosphor'oscope, fosforoskoop.
phos'phorous, fosfor=, fosforagtig.
phos'phorus, fosfor.
phoss'y: ~ *jaw,* kakebeenontsteking.
pho'tic, lig=, foties.
phot'ism, fotisme.
phot'o, (-s), abbr. of **photograph;** foto(grafie), portret;
~ **album,** fotoalbum; ~ **chem'ical,** fotochemies;
~ **chemistry,** fotoskeikunde, fotochemie;
~ **chromy,** kleurfotografie; ~ **composition,** foto=
komposisie; ~ **conductivity,** fotogeleiding; ~
copier, fotokopieerder; ~ **copy,** (n) fotokopie; (v)
fotokopieer; ~ **diode,** fotodiode; ~ **-electric,** foto=
elektries; ~-**engrave',** foto-ets; ~ **-engraver,** foto=
etser; ~ **-engraving,** fotogravure; foto-etswerk; ~ **-
finish,** wenpaalfoto, fotobeslissing; ~ **-finish
camera,** fotobeslissingskamera; ~ **gen'ic,** fotogeen;
liggewend; fotogeniek; ~ **-geology,** fotogeologie;
~ **gram,** fotogram; ~ **gram'meter,** fotogrammeter;
~ **gramme'tric,** fotogrammetries; ~ **gram'metry,**
fotogrammetrie.
phot'ograph, (n) portret, foto; (v) afneem, fotogra=
feer; *OBLIQUE* ~, skuinsopname; *VERTICAL*
~, loodregte opname; ~ **album,** fotoalbum; por=
tretalbum.

photog'rapher, afnemer, fotograaf.
photograph'ic, fotografies; ~ **copy,** (n) fotokopie; (v) fotokopieer; ~ **map,** fotografiese landkaart; ~ **studio,** fotografiese ateljee; ~ **survey,** fotogrammetrie; ~ **surveyor,** fotokarteerder.
photog'raphy, fotografie.
photogravure', fotogravure, rasterdiepdruk.
photo-library, fototeek.
photolith'ograph, fotolitografie, ligsteendruk; ~ **er,** fotolitograaf.
photolithograph'ic, fotolitografies.
photolithog'raphy, ligsteendrukkuns, fotolitografie.
photol'ogy, fotologie, ligkunde.
phot'omap, (n) fotokaart; (v) fotokarteer.
photom'eter, ligmeter, fotometer.
photomet'ric, fotometries.
photom'etry, meting van die ligsterkte, fotometrie.
photomic'rogram, photomic'rograph, mikrofoto.
photomicro'graphy, mikrofotografie.
photo-mul'tiplier tube, fotoverveelvoudbuis.
phot'on, ligdeeltjie, foton.
pho'to-offset (-printing), fotvlakdruk.
phot'ophobe, (n) ligskuwe; (a) ligsku, fotofoob.
photophob'ia, ligskuheid, dagskuheid, fotofobie.
phot'ophone, fotofoon, ligtelefoon.
phot'oplay, rolprentdrama.
phot'oprint, lig(af)druk, fotokopie.
photosens'itive, liggevoelig.
phot'osphere, ligkring, fotosfeer.
phot'ostat, fotostaat; fotostaatafdruk, fotostatiese afdruk; ~ **copy,** fotostaatafdruk, fotostatiese afdruk.
photostat'ic, fotostaties, ~ **copy,** fotostaat(afdruk).
photosyn'thesis, fotosintese.
photosynthet'ic, fotosinteties.
phototax'ic, fototakties.
phototax'is, fototaksis.
phototeleg'raphy, fototelegrafie.
phototheo'dolite, fotogrammeter.
phototherapeut'ics, fototerapie, ligterapie.
photother'apist, fototerapeut, ligterapeut.
photother'apy, fototerapie, ligterapie, ligbehandeling.
phototrop'ic, fototroop.
phot'otropism, ligkromming, fototropie.
phot'otype, ligdrukbeeld, ligdrukkuns, fototipie.
phototyp'ic, fototipies.
phot'otypy, fototipie, ligdruk.
photovolta'ic, fotovoltaïes.
phrase, (n) uitdrukking, segswyse; maatmotief (musiek); frase, sinsdeel; spraakwending, spreekwyse; (v) fraseer, in frases indeel; in woorde uitdruk, bewoord, beskryf; *a well ~d speech,* 'n goed gefraseerde toespraak; ~ **-book,** idiomeboek, boek met idiomatiese uitdrukkings; ~ **-monger,** praatjiesmaker, fraseur; ~ **ogram,** fraseogram; ~ **ol'ogy,** woordkeuse, skryftrant, fraseologie, uitdrukkingswyse.
phras'ing, frasering, bewoording.
phra'try, fratrie; stamverdeling (volkek.).
phreat'ic, ondergronds; ~ *water,* grondwater.
phrenet'ic, freneties; kranksinnig, mal, rasend; fanatiek, fanaties.
phren'ic, mantelvliese, middelrif=.
phrenit'is, waansin, frenesie.
phrenolog'ic, frenologies, skedelkundig.
phrenol'ogist, frenoloog, skedelkundige.
phrenol'ogy, skedelleer, skedelkunde, frenologie.
Phry'gia, Frigië; ~ **n,** (n) Frigiër; Frigies (taal); (a) Frigies.
phthal'lic, ftaal=; ~ **acid,** ftaalsuur.
phthis'ic(al), teringagtig.
phthis'is, myntering, longtering.
phut, plaps, klap; *go ~,* breek; inmekaarstort.
phycol'ogy, wierkunde, fikologie.
phylac'tery, (..ries), amulet; gebedsriem; gedenkseel; relikwiekassie (R.K.); filakterie.
phyle'tic, afstammings=, fileties.
phyllogenet'ic, blaarvormend, fillogeneties.
phyl'lophagous, blaarvretend, fillofaag.
phyllotac'tical, fillotakties.
phyllotax'is, phyllotax'y, blaarstand.
phyllox'era, druifluis, filloksera.

phylogen'esis, filogenie, filogenese.
phylogenet'ic, filogeneties.
phylog'eny, filogenie, filogenese, stamgeskiedenis.
phyl'um, filum, hoofgroep, stam.
physiat'ric, fisiatries.
physiatri'cian, natuurgeneser, fisiater.
physiat'rics, fisiatrie, natuurgeneeskunde.
phys'ic, (n) geneeskunde; geneesmiddel; ~ *use,* medisynegebruike; (v) **(-ked),** medisyne gee; dokter.
phys'ical, natuurkundig, fisies; liggaamlik, fisiek; ~ **characteristic,** fisiese eienskap; ~ **astronomy,** fisiese sterrekunde; ~ **chemistry,** fisiese skeikunde (chemie); ~ **condition,** liggaamsgesteldheid; ~ **culture,** liggaamsopvoeding, heilgimnastiek; ~ **culturist,** heilgimnas; ~ **defective,** liggaamlik gebrekkige; ~ **education,** liggaamlike opvoeding; ~ **energy,** liggaamskrag; ~ **exercise,** liggaamsoefening; ~ **features,** terreingesteldheid; ~ **force,** natuurkrag; ~ **geography,** fisiese aardrykskunde (geografie); ~ **jerks,** liggaamsoefeninge; ~ **ly,** fisies, natuurkundig; liggaamlik, fisiek; ~ *ly impossible,* fisiek (fisies) onmoontlik; ~ **science,** natuurkunde, fisika; ~ **strength,** liggaamskrag; ~ **training,** liggaamsontwikkeling, liggaamskultuur; ~ **-training instructor,** liggaamskultuurinstrukteur, instrukteur in liggaamskultuur.
physi'cian, dokter, geneesheer, geneeskundige, eskulaap; ~, *heal thyself,* medisynmeester, genees jouself; ~ **-in-ordinary,** lyfarts.
phys'icist, natuurkundige, fisikus.
phys'icky, medisyneagtig.
phys'ics, natuurkunde, fisika.
physio'cracy, fisiokrasie.
phys'iocrat, fisiokraat.
physiocrat'ic, fisiokraties.
physiognom'ic(al), gelaatkundig, fisionomies.
physiogn'omist, gelaatkundige.
physiogn'omy, gesig, voorkome; gelaatkunde, fisionomie.
physiograph'ic, fisiografies.
physiog'raphy, natuurbeskrywing, fisiografie.
physiolog'ic(al), fisiologies.
physiol'ogist, fisioloog.
physiol'ogy, fisiologie, natuurleer.
physiotherapeut'ic, fisioterapeuties.
physiotherapeut'ics, fisioterapie.
physiothe'rapist, fisioterapeut.
physiothe'rapy, fisioterapie; *occupational ~,* beroepsterapie.
physique', liggaamsbou, liggaamsgestel.
phytobiol'ogy, plantebiologie, fitobiologie.
phytogen'esis, planteteelt, fitogenese.
phytog'eny, planteteelt, fitogenese.
phytogeog'raphy, plantegeografie, fitogeografie.
phytog'raphy, plantebeskrywing, fitografie.
phytol'ogy, plantkunde, planteleer, fitologie.
phy'ton, fiton.
phy'toparasite, woekerplant, plantparasiet, fitoparasiet.
phytopathol'ogy, plantsiektekunde, fitopatologie.
phytoph'agous, plantetend.
phytosa'nitary, fitosanitêr.
phytot'omy, plantanatomie.
phytoto'xic, fitotoksies.
pi, pi.
piac'ular, versoenend.
piaffe', drafstap.
pia mat'er, sagte (harsing)vlies, pia mater.
pianette', pianet.
piani'no, (-s), pianino.
pi'anism, klaviertegniek.
pi'anist, pianis, klavierspeler.
pianiste', klavierspelster, pianiste.
pianis'tic, pianisties.
pian'o¹, (-s), piano, klavier; *grand ~,* vleuelklavier.
pia'no², (a, adv) piano, sag (mus.).
pian'o: ~ **accompaniment,** klavierbegeleiding; ~ **-accordion,** trekklavier; ~ **concert,** klavieruitvoering, pianokonsert; ~ **fort'e** piano; ~ **l'a,** pianola; ~ **player,** klavierspeler; ~ **-playing,** pianospel, klavierspel; ~ **recital,** pianouitvoering, klavieruitvoe=

ring; ~ **stool,** musiekstoel, pianostoel; ~ **teacher,** klavieronderwyser(es); ~ **tuner,** klavierstemmer.
piassa'va, piassawa, palmvesel.
pias'ter, pias'tre, piaster.
piazz'a, plein; piazza; stoep, veranda.
pib'roch, doedelsakmelodie, krygsmars op die doedelsak.
pic'a¹, pika, mediaanletter, twaalfpuntletter.
pic'a², pika, verworde eetlus.
pic'ador, berede stiervegter, pikador.
Pic'ardy, Pikardië.
picaresque', pikaresk, skelm=; ~ **novel,** skelmroman.
picaroon', (n) rower; seerower; vrybuiter, kaperskip; (v) vrybuit, plunder, beroof.
picayune', nietige geldjie, oortjie; bog, bogding.
picc'alilli, atjar, mosterdsuurtjies, piccalilli.
picc'aninny, (n) (.. nnies), kind; klonkie, piekanien; (a) klein.
picc'olo, (-s), piccolo (fluit).
pick¹, (n) keuse; beste; *the ~ of the BASKET (BUNCH),* die neusie v.d. salm; die uitsoek, die room; *HAVE one's ~,* die keuse hê; (v) kies; uitsoek; *~ and CHOOSE,* sorgvuldig uitsoek; *you can't ~ and CHOOSE,* jy kan nie uitsoekerig wees nie; *~ OUT,* uitkies, uitsoek; *~ one's WORDS,* jou woorde met sorg kies.
pick², (n) pik, kielhouer; tandestokkie; steeksleutel, slotoopsteker; (v) pik; pluk; afeet, afkluif (been); peusel, skoonmaak; sorteer; stook, skoonmaak (tande); oopsteek (slot); aanwys; *~ an ACQUAINTANCE with,* kennis maak met; *~ a BONE,* 'n been afeet (afkluif); *have a BONE to ~,* 'n appeltjie te skil hê; *~ someone's BRAINS,* van iem. anders se kennis gebruik maak; *~ up COURAGE,* moed skep; *~ up FLESH,* gewig aansit; groei; *~ FLOWERS,* blomme pluk; *~ at FOOD,* langtand eet; *~ up a HABIT,* 'n gewoonte aanleer; *~ HOLES in,* aanmerkings maak op; *~ up a LANGUAGE,* 'n taal deur omgang leer; *~ up a LIVELIHOOD,* aan die kos kom; jou brood verdien; met moeite 'n bestaan maak; *~ a LOCK,* 'n slot oopsteek; *~ OFF,* afpluk; *~ ON,* uitsoek; die kop was, bestraf, berispe, kapittel; *why ~ ON me?* waarom dit op my uithaal? *~ OUT,* inklim; *~ up PASSENGERS,* passasiers oplaai; *~ to PIECES,* uitmekaar maak; vanmekaar skeur; kritiseer, afkam (fig.); *~ POCKETS,* uit die sakke steel; sakke rol; *~ a QUARREL with,* rusie soek met; *~ up the STEP,* in die pas kom; *~ UP,* oppik; opraap; optel; oplaai, opneem; leer, opdoen; oplig (poot); oprol (kabel); opmaak (berig); toeneem (in gewig); verbeter (sake); *~ UP Moscow,* Moskou opvang; *~ oneself UP,* weer orent kom; *~ someone UP,* toevallig met iem. kennis maak; *~ up WOOD,* hout bymekaarmaak.
pick'-a-back, abba=, op die rug; ~ **plane,** abbavliegtuig.
pic'karninny = **piccaninny.**
pick'ax(e), (n) pik, kielhouer, kielpik; (v) pik, met 'n pik werk.
picked, gepluk; skoongemaak; uitgesoek; *~ MEN,* 'n keurbende; *~ SOLDIERS,* uitgesoekte soldate, keursoldate.
pic'kelhaube, (Ger.), pickelhaube, stekelhelm.
pick'er, plukker; pikker, kapper; opraper, opteller (lappe); plukmasjien.
pick'erel, jong snoek.
pick'et, (n) paal; pas; piket, wagpos, buitepos, brandwag, staakwag; (v) omhein met pale; plaas; stasioneer, posteer, op wag stel (soldate); veranker, vasmaak; ~ **duties,** (brand)wagdiens.
pick'eting, (n) stasionering; bewaking; (a) anker=; ~ **-pin,** ankerpen; ~ **-rope,** ankertou.
pick'-handle, piksteel.
pick'ing, (die) pluk, plukkery; *FOR the ~ and choosing,* te kus en te keur; *WITHOUT ~ and choosing,* voor die voet; ~ **s,** voordele; oorskiet, krummels, oorblyfsels, opraapsel.
pic'kle, (n) moeilikheid; stouterd, bengel, ondeug; pekel; suurbad; (pl) piekels, atjar, suurtjies; *in a FINE (NICE) ~,* in die knyp; *many a ~ makes a MICKLE,* baie kleintjies maak 'n grote; (v) inlê, inmaak, insout; insult; afbyt, skoonbyt (met sure), in 'n suurbad steek.
pic'kled, ingelê; gesout; dronk; ~ **beans,** sultbone; ~ **fish,** ingelegde vis; ~ **herring,** pekelharing; ~ **mealies,** mielieatjar, mieliesuurtjies; ~ **meat,** pekelvleis; tasal; ~ **onions,** piekels, suuruie; ~ **pork,** sout varkvleis; ~ **rib,** soutribbetjie; ~ **vegetables,** groenteatjar, suurtjies, piekelgroente.
pic'kle: ~ **-fork,** suurvurk, atjarvurk; ~ **-jar,** atjarfles; ~ **-pump,** pekelpomp.
pick'ling, inmaak, inlê (in asyn).
pick'lock, slotoopsteker, slothaak, steeksleutel; inbreker; diewesleutel.
pick'-me-up, sopie, regrukker, hartversterker, regmakertjie, skrikmakertjie.
pick'pocket, sakkeroller, goudief.
pick'some, kieskeurig, puntenerig.
pick'-up, gramradio; platespeler; herstel, verbetering; versnelvermoë; toevallige kennis; ~ **sticks,** optelstokkies; ~ **van,** bakkie; vangwa; patrolliewa.
pick'wick, goedkoop sigaar, stinkstok.
pic'nic, (n) piekniek, veldparty(tjie); maklike taak; *it is no ~,* dit is 'n moeilike taak; (v) **(-ked),** piekniek hou; ~ **-basket,** piekniekmandjie; ~ **-dance,** piekniekdans; ~ **hamper,** piekniekmandjie; ~ **ker,** pieknieker, piekniekhouer; ~ **ky,** piekniekagtig; ~ **-spot,** piekniekplek, terrein.
picot', (-s), bogie, puntjie (in rand); ~ **-edging,** picotrand, picotsoom, bogierand, puntjiesoom.
picotee', spikkelangelier.
pic'rate, pikraat, pikrinesuursout.
pic'ric, pikrien=, pikrine=; ~ **acid,** pikriensuur, pikrinesuur.
pic'rite, pikriet.
Pict, Pikt.
pic'togram, pic'tograph, piktogram, beeldskrif; rotsskildering.
pictog'raphy, beeldskrif, piktografie.
pictor'ial, (n) geïllustreerde tydskrif; (a) skilderagtig; afgebeeld, geïllustreer, prent=; ~ **advertisement,** geïllustreerde advertensie; ~ **art,** skilderkuns; ~ **Bible,** prentebybel; ~ **glass,** beskilderde glaswerk; ~ **view,** prentebeeld.
pic'ture, (n) prent; skildery, skilderstuk; afbeelding; ewebeeld; beskrywing; tafereel; toonbeeld; beligganing; rolprent, fliek; *BE in the ~,* meetel; *COME into the ~,* op die toneel kom; *DRAW a ~ of,* 'n prent(jie) teken van; 'n tafereel ophang van; *a ~ of a GIRL,* in beeld van 'n meisie; *a ~ of HEALTH,* 'n toonbeeld van gesondheid; *IN the ~,* in tel; goed op hoogte; van belang; *be OUT of the ~,* nie meetel nie; *she is as PRETTY as a ~,* sy is 'n beeld van 'n mens; *PUT one in the ~,* iem. op hoogte van sake bring; iem. inlig; *the other SIDE of the ~,* die keersy v.d. penning; *THE ~ s,* die bioskoop (fliek); *the VERY ~,* 'n beeld van; (v) beskrywe, afbeeld, voorstel; *~ to oneself,* jou voorstel; ~ **-beading,** kraalportretlys; ~ **-book,** prenteboek; ~ **-card,** prentkaart; ~ **-cord,** skilderytou; ~ **-dealer,** kunshandelaar; ~ **-frame,** skilderyraam, portretraam; ~ **-gallery,** skilderymuseum, kunsmuseum; kunssaal; kunsgalery; ~ **-goer,** fliekganger, bioskoopbesoeker; ~ **hat,** breërandhoed; ~ **-house,** ~ **-palace,** fliek, bioskoop; ~ **-language,** beeldskrif; ~ **-play,** rolprent; ~ **postcard,** prentposkaart; ~ **-poster,** reklamebiljet, (aan)plakbiljet, reklameplaat; ~ **-puzzle,** prentraaisel; ~ **-rail,** portretlys, prentlys; ~ **-shop,** kunshandel.
picturesque', skilderagtig, pittoresk; ~ **ness,** skilderagtigheid.
pic'ture: ~ **telegraphy,** fototelegrafie; ~ **window,** uitsigvenster, landskapvenster; ~ **-writing,** beeldskrif, piktografie.
pi'cul, pikol, Chinese gewigseenheid.
pid'dle, water, piepie, fluit, plassie maak; peuter, peusel; ~ **r,** peuteraar; (klein) seuntjie.
pidg'in, werk, taak; pidgin; ~ **English,** Pidginengels.
pie¹, (n) ekster (voël).
pie², (n) chaos, verwarring; *MAKE ~ of,* in die war stuur; (v) deurmekaar gooi (setsel).
pie³, (n) een twaalfde anna (muntstuk).
pie⁴, (n) pastei; tert; grafiekkoek; *a CUT of the ~,* 'n

sny v.d. tert; aandeel in die begroting (van die fondse); *EAT humble* ~, 'n toontjie laer sing; *have a FINGER in the* ~, in iets betrokke wees.
pieb'ald, swartbont, swartlap.
piece, (n) stuk; hap, brok(kie); deel; entjie; munt; kanon, geweer; rol; musiekstuk, skilderstuk; (pl) afvalwol, stukwol; afvalvleis, stukkiesvleis; *a man who is ALL of a* ~, 'n man uit een stuk; *BY the* ~, by die stuk; ~ *BY* ~, stuk vir stuk; *a* ~ *of CAKE*, 'n stuk koek; so maklik soos nog iets; doodmaklik; *COME to* ~*s*, breek; stukkend raak; *GO to* ~*s*, stukkend raak; versleg; na die haaie gaan; *a* ~ *of IMPUDENCE*, brutaliteit; *IN* ~*s*, stukkend; *give someone a* ~ *of one's MIND*, iem. lelik die waarheid vertel; iem. skrobbeer; ~ *of MUSIC*, musiekstuk; ~ *of NEWS*, nuusberig(gie); *she is a NICE* ~ *(of goods)*, sy is 'n gawe nooi(entjie); ~ *of NONSENSE*, onsinnigheid, verspottigheid; *OF a* ~, van dieselfde soort; *of ONE* ~, uit een stuk; *PER* ~, per stuk; *the* ~ *s fall into PLACE*, dit sluit soos 'n bus; *PULL to* ~*s*, stukkend trek; *a QUEER* ~ *of humanity*, 'n snaakse entjie (stukkie) mens; *SAVE the* ~*s*, red wat daar te red is; *SAY one's* ~, jou sê sê; *a* ~ *of STRING*, 'n toutjie, 'n stukkie lyn; *TAKE to* ~ *s*, uitmekaarmaak; (v) 'n stuk insit; lap; saamvoeg; las; ~ *IN*, invoeg; ~ *ON to*, vasheg aan; ~ *OUT*, aanvul; verleng; ~ *TOGETHER*, saamvoeg, aanmekaarsit; ~**-goods**, stukgoed(ere); ~**less**, uit een stuk; ~**meal**, stuksgewys(e); met stukkies en brokkies; ~**r**, lapper; ~**-wages**, stukloon; work, stukwerk; ~**-work wage**, taakloon; ~**-worker**, stukwerker.
pièce de résistance, (F.), pièce de résistance, hoofdis, hoofitem.
pie chart, sirkelkaart, pasteikaart.
pie'crust, pasteikors(ie); *promises are like* ~, beloftes is waardeloos.
pied-à-terre, (F.), pied-à-terre, tydelike kwartier; toevlugsoord.
pied, bont, geskakeer(d), gespikkel(d); *the P* ~ *Piper of Hamelin*, die Rottevanger van Hamelin; ~ *crow*, witborskraai, bontkraai.
pie'-dish, pasteiskottel.
pied': ~ **kingfisher,** bontvisvanger; ~ **mont,** piedmont, voetheuwelstreek; ~ **starling,** witgatspreeu.
pie: ~**-eyed,** dronk, pap, poegaai; ~**-face,** lelike vent.
pie'man, pasteibakker; koekverkoper.
pier, hawehoof, seehoof, seebreker, wandelhoof, landingsplek, aanlêplek, landingshoof, pier; beer (in rivier); pilaar, pyler (brug); steunstuk; ~ **age,** piergeld, lêgeld, hawegeld
pierce, deursteek, deurboor, deurdring; 'n gat steek in; ~ **able,** deurboorbaar; ~ **r,** boor, priem; lapper; angel; lêboor.
pier'cing, deurdringend, skerp; ~ **COLD,** deurdringende koue; *a* ~ **CRY,** 'n skril geroep; *a* ~ *VOICE*, 'n sketterstem; ~ *WIT*, skerp geestigheid; ~**-pin,** sifonspeld; ~**-saw,** steeksaag.
pier: ~ **dues,** lêgeld, hawegeld; ~**-glass,** penantspieël; ~**-head,** waterdam; pierkop.
pier'id, witjie (skoenlapper).
pierrette', pierrette.
pi'errot, pierrot, nar, hanswors.
pier'-table, penanttafel.
pier' toll, lêgeld, hawegeld.
pietà, (It.), piëta.
pi'etas, piëtas, eerbied.
pi'etism, piëtisme; kweselary; oordrewe vroomheid.
pi'etist, piëtis; kwesel; vrome.
pietis'tic, piëtisties; kweselagtig.
pi'ety, vroomheid, piëteit, devosie, godsvrug, godvrugtigheid, godvresendheid.
piezochem'istry, piësochemie.
piezo-electric'ity, piësoëlektrisiteit.
piezom'eter, drukmeter, drukkingsmeter, piësometer.
pif'fle, (n) bog, onsin; kafpraatjies, twakpraatjies, bogpraatjies, vrouepraatjies, beuselpraat, gê; (v) kafpraatjies verkoop; peuter; ~ **r,** peuteraar; bogprater.
pif'fling, bogterig, peuterig; nikswerd.
pig, (n) vark, ot(jie), swyn, varkvleis; gietstaaf, metaalblok, gieteling; huisie, skyfie (van lemoen); gulsigaard; smeerlap; *be DRIVING* ~ *s*, balke saag; *as FAT as a* ~, so vet soos 'n vark; *when* ~ *s FLY*, as die perde horings kry; *MAKE a* ~ *of oneself*, jou soos 'n vark gedra; *bring one's* ~ *s to a fine (pretty, the wrong) MARKET*, jou kop stamp; jou rieme styfloop; ~ *s MIGHT fly*, wonders kan nog altyd gebeur; *buy a* ~ *in a POKE*, 'n kat in die sak koop; *SQUEAL like a* ~, soos 'n maer vark skree; *have the WRONG* ~ *by the ear*, die verkeerde een in hande hê; *the YOUNG* ~ *grunts like the old sow*, soos die oue songe, so piepe de jonge; (v) **(-ged),** kleintjies kry, jong; saamhok; ~**-breeder,** varkboer; ~**-bristle,** varkhaar.
pi'geon, (n) duif; swaap; *pluck a* ~, 'n dwaas beroof; (v) fop, kaal pluk; ~**-breast,** hoenderborst; ~ **clock,** wedvlugoorlosie; ~ **eer,** posduiweversorger; ~**-fancier,** duiweboer, duiweteler; ~**-flying,** duiwesport; ~**-hearted,** lafhartig; bang, skrikkerig; ~**-hole,** (n) duiwenessie; nessie, hokkie, vak(kie), loket (van lessenaar); (v) in 'n hokkie sit, bêre; uitstel, op die lange baan skuif, in die vergeetboek skryf; in gedagte hou; ~**-house,** ~**-loft,** duiwehok; ~ **pair,** paar duiwe; *a* ~ *pair*, 'n seuntjie en dogtertjie; ~**-pea,** duiweboontjie, dalboontjie *(Caljanus indicus)*; ~**-pie,** duiwepastei; ~**-post,** duiwepos; ~ **race,** duiwewedvlug; ~**ry, (..ries),** duiwehok; ~**'s egg,** duifeier, duiwe-eier; ~**-service,** duiwepos; ~**-shooting,** duiwejag; ~**'s milk,** duiwemelk; *go and buy* ~ *'s milk*, gaan pluk skilpadvere; ~**-toed,** met tone wat binnekant toe staan; ~**-toed person,** toontrapper
pig; ~**-eyed,** met varkoë; ~**-farmer,** varkboer; ~**gery, (..ries),** varkhok, varkboerdery; smeerboel; ~**gish,** vark-, varkagtig; vuil, smerig; koppig; ~**gishness,** varkagtigheid; smerigheid; koppigheid; ~**gy,** varkie, otjie; ~**headed,** dom; eiesinnig, dwars, eiewys; koppig, styfhoofdig; *a* ~ *headed person*, 'n hardekop; 'n dwarskop; ~**headedness,** eiesinnigheid, eiewysheid; koppigheid; domheid; ~**-iron,** ruyster; ~**-lead,** gietlood, ruloed; ~**let,** ~**ling,** varkie; ~**-lily,** aronsklerk, varkoor, varkblom, varklelie; ~**ling,** varkie; ~ **measles,** varkmasels.
pig'ment, kleur, verfstof, pigment; ~**-cell,** kleursel, verfstofsel.
pig'my = pygmy.
pig: ~**-nose,** varkneus, snoet; ~**'s ear,** varkoor; ~**'s fry,** gebraaide varklewer; ~ **skin,** varkvel; varkleer; ~ **stick,** wildevarkjag; ~ **sticker,** wildevarkjagter; ~**'s seilnasal;** steekpen; ~ **sticking,** wildevarkjag; ~**'s trotters,** varkpootjies; ~**'s trough,** varktrog; ~**'s sty, varkhok,** *have grown up in a* ~ *sty*, in 'n varkhok grootgeword; ~ **tail,** varkstert; stertvlegsel; pruikstert; ~ **wash,** skottelgoedwater, spoeling; ~ **weed,** misbredie *(Amaranthus paniculatus)*; gansvoet.
pi'-jaw, (n) sedepreek; (v) 'n sedepreek hou.
pi'ka, pika (soort konyn).
pike¹, (n) tolhek, tol
pike², (n) spies, lans, pick; bergspits; varswatersnoek *(Esox lusius)*; (v) deursteek (met spies); ~ **d,** puntig; ~**-dog,** hondshaai; ~ **let,** jong snoek; teekoek; plaatkoekie.
pike'man¹, tolman, tolbaas.
pike'man², piekdraer.
pike'staff, lansstok; *as plain as a* ~, glashelder, 'n waarheid soos 'n koei.
pilaff', pilaf
pilas'ter, pilaster.
Pil'ate, Pilatus.
pilau', **pilaw'** = pilaff.
pilch, luierbroekie
pil'chard, sardyn(tjie); pelser.
pil'cher, broekie.
pile¹, (n) aambei.
pile², (n) wol, pluis, donsies, nop, pool.
pile³, (n) hoop, massa, stapel; stapel geld, fortuin; suil (elektr.); piramide; geboukompleks, fabriek, groot gebou; *ATOMIC* ~, atoomsuil, kernsuil; *GALVANIC* ~, galvaniese suil; *MAKE one's* ~, jou fortuin maak; *VOLTAIC* ~, voltasuil; (v) opstapel, ophoop; ~ *ARMS*, geweers koppel; ~ *on*

the AGONY, iets invryf; ~ *DRUMS*, tromme opstapel; ~ *INTO*, inklim; ~ *it ON*, iets oordryf; iets dik oplê; ~ *WORK on a person*, iem. met werk oorlaai.

pile⁴, (n) pyler (brug); heipaal; balk, paal; (v) pale inslaan; (in)hei; ~**-ate,** hoedvormig; ~**-bridge,** paalbrug.

pile′-carpet, pooltapyt.

pile: ~**-driver,** heiblok; heier, heimasjien; ~**-driving,** heiwerk; ~**-dwelling,** paalwoning; ~**-engine,** heimasjien.

pile′-fabric, poolstof.

pile: ~**-hammer,** heihamer; ~**-house,** paalwoning.

pile′-pier, juk (van brug).

pile′-proof, poolvas.

pile′root, kafferwortel.

piles, aambeie; *suffer from ~s*, aan aambeie ly.

pi′leus, (bot.), pileus, sambreeltop.

pile′-weave, poolbinding.

pile: ~**-work,** paalwerk; ~**-worm,** paalwurm.

pil′fer, steel, wegkaap, wegmoffel, wegroof, ontfutsel; ~ **age,** diefstal, stelery; ~**er,** dief, steler; ~**ing,** stelery, diewery; ~**-proof,** peutervry, diefvry.

pilgar′lic, kaalkop; sukkelaar.

pil′grim, (n) pelgrim; bedevaartganger; (v) op 'n pelgrimstog gaan; ~ **age,** (n) pelgrimsreis; pelgrimstog, bedevaart; (v) 'n pelgrimsreis onderneem; ~**-basket,** rietreismandjie; **P**~ **Fathers,** Pelgrimvaders; ~**'s staff,** pelgrimstaf.

pilif′erous, harig, behaard; ~ *layer*, wortelhaarlaag.

pil′iform, haarvormig, haaragtig.

pil′ing, heiwerk.

pill¹, (n) pil; koeël; bal; *a BITTER* ~, 'n bitter pil; *a ~ to cure an EARTHQUAKE*, 'n ondoeltreffende maatreël; *bitter ~s have wholesome EFFECTS*, bitter in die mond maak die maag gesond; (v) pille ingee; oorwin; verslaan.

pill², (v) plunder, beroof.

pill′age, (n) roof, plundering, berowing, buit; (v) roof, plunder, uitplunder; ~**r,** rower, buiter, stroper, plunderaar.

pill′ar, (n) pilaar; suil, stut; steunpilaar; *a ~ of FIRE*, vuurkolom; ~ *of a GATE*, hekpaal; *send someone from ~ to POST*, iem. van Pontius na Pilatus stuur; iem. v.d. kassie na die muur stuur; iem. van puntjie na pooltjie stuur; iem. van babo na bibo stuur; iem. hot en haar stuur; ~ *of SOCIETY*, steunpilaar v.d. maatskappy; (v) steun, stut; ~**-box,** briewebus; ~**-box red,** bloedrooi; ~ **lamp,** staanlamp.

pill′box, pil(le)doos; pildooshoedjie; veldbunker; ystervark.

pill′ion, vrouesaal; kussing; agtersaal (motorfiets); ~**-rider,** agterryer; ~ **seat,** agtersaal.

pill′iwinks, duimskroef.

pill′-monger, pildraaier.

pill′ory, (n) (..ries), skandpaal; kaak; *put into the ~*, aan die kaak stel; (v) (..ried), aan die kaak stel.

pill′ow, (n) kussing, peul; asblokvoering (masjien); *CONSULT with one's ~*, *take COUNSEL of one's ~*, oor iets slaap; (v) kussing, op 'n kussing laat rus; ~**-case,** kussingsloop; ~**-fight,** kussinggeveg; ~**-lace,** kloskant; ~ **lava,** kussinglawa; ~ **sham,** fopsloop; ~**-slip,** kussingsloop; ~**y,** sag; soos 'n kussing.

pill: ~**-roller,** pilledraaier; ~**-worm,** duisendpoot; ~**wort,** pilvaring.

pil′ose, harig, behaar.

pilos′ity, harigheid.

pil′ot, (n) gids; lugskipper; loods, stuurman (see); loodsboot; bestuurder; vlieënier, vlieër; *automatic ~*, stuuroutomaat; (v) lei; loods (see); die pad wys; bestuur (vliegtuig); ~ *into port*, die hawe binneloods; ~ **age,** loodsgeld; vliegtuigbesturing; loodskunde; loodsdiens; ~ **balloon,** gidsballon, proefballon; ~ **boat,** loodsboot; ~ **bomb,** peilbom; ~**-bread,** skeepsbeskuit; ~**-bridge,** kommandobrug; ~**-car,** gidsmotor; ~ **cutter,** loodskotter; ~ **drill,** voorloperboor; ~ **engine,** voorspanlokomotief, rangeerlokomotief; ~ **experiment,** loodsproef (-eksperiment), voorloperproef; ~**-fish,** loodsvis; ~**-house,** stuurhuis; ~**ing,** besturing; ~ **jack,**

loodsvlag; ~**-jacket,** jekker(t); ~ **jet,** voorsproeier; ~ **lamp,** kliklamp; ~**less,** sonder loods, onbeman; ~**less aircraft,** onbemande vliegtuig; ~ **light,** waarskuwingslig; ~**-line,** werplyn; ~ **parachute,** uittrekvalskerm; ~ **plant,** gidsaanleg, proefinstallasie, voorloperinstallasie; ~ **project,** proefprojek; ~ **registration,** proefregistrasie; ~**'s cabin,** stuurkajuit; ~**'s certificate,** vliegbewys; loodsbewys; ~**'s licence,** loodslisensie; vliegvergunning; ~**'s seat,** stuurstoel; ~**'s test,** vliegtoets; vlieërstoets; ~**'s wings,** vlieërskenteken, vleuels; ~ **train,** voortrein; ~**-whale,** loodswalvis; ~ **wheel,** skokwiel; loodswiel.

pil′ous = **pilose.**

pil′ular, pilvormig; pilagtig; nietig.

pil′ule, pilletjie.

pil′ulous = **pilular.**

Pils(e)ner, pilsener(bier).

pimen′to, piment, wonderpeper, jamaikapeper.

pimien′to, soetpeper, pimiënto.

pimp, (n) souteneur, koppelaar; (v) koppel.

pim′pernel, pimpernel, muurkruid, blouselblommetjie.

pim′ping, klein, nietig; sieklik.

pim′ple, puisie; ~**d, pim′ply,** vol puisies, puisieagtig.

pin, (n) speld; pen, tap; wig, spy, spie; luns; skroef (by musiekinstrumente); naelvlies (oog); bout; stif, klink; vlag, pen (gholf); *not to CARE a ~*, geen flenter omgee nie; *one could have heard a ~ DROP*, jy kon 'n speld hoor val; *be as LIKE as two ~s*, soos twee druppels water op mekaar lyk; *as NEAT as a new ~*, so blink soos 'n splinternuwe sikspens; *be on ~s and NEEDLES*, op hete kole sit; *I have ~s and NEEDLES in my foot*, my voet slaap; *QUICK on one's ~s*, rats op jou bene; (v) **(-ned),** vassteek, vasprik, vasspeld; opsluit; ~ *someone DOWN*, iem. bind aan; iem. aan sy belofte hou; ~ *something DOWN to a person*, die dader aanwys; ~ *one's FAITH on someone*, 'n mens se hoop op iem. stel; staatmaak op iem.; ~ *one's HOPES on*, jou hoop vestig op; ~ *ON*, vasspeld; ~ *TOGETHER*, vassteek; ~ *UP*, vasspeld; opspeld; ~ *against the WALL*, teen die muur druk; teen die muur vassteek.

pin′acoid, pinakoïed.

pin′afore, voorskoot; ~ **dress,** voorskootrok.

pinas′ter, seeden(neboom), pinaster.

pin: ~**-ball machine,** spykertafel; dobbeloutomaat; ~**-bit,** penboor; ~**-box,** speldebakkie, speldedoos; ~**-case,** speldekoker; ~**-check,** speldgeruit.

pince′-nez, knypbril.

pin′cers, knyptang; tangetjie; knypers (krap).

pincette′, pinset.

pinch, (n) **(-es),** knyp; nood, verleentheid; knypie (snuif); snuifie; *AT a ~*, as die nood druk; *if it COMES to the ~*, as dit tot die uiterste kom; *FEEL the ~*, in die nood wees; *a ~ of SALT*, 'n knypie sout; *take something with a ~ of SALT*, iets met 'n korreltjie sout neem; ~ *of SNUFF*, snuifie, knypie snuif; (v) knyp, knel; kwel, pynig; suinig wees; afpers; steel, vaslê, skaai, gap(s); vang, arresteer; ~ *on FOOD*, op kos besuinig; ~ *and PARE*, ~ *and SCRAPE*, raap en skraap; *that is where the SHOE ~es*, daar lê die knoop; *no one but the wearer knows where the SHOE ~es*, 'n ander man se briewe is duister om te lees.

pinch′-bar, breekyster, stootkoevoet.

pinch′beck, (n) pinsbek; namaaksel; (a) oneg, vals.

pinch′-cock, klemkraan.

pinch′ed, geknyp; gekwel; gesteel; suinig; *in ~ CIRCUMSTANCES*, in armoedige omstandighede; ~ *with COLD*, verkluim; ~ *HORNS*, knyphorings.

pinch′er, knyper; steler.

pinch′penny, (n) gierigaard; (a) suinig, gierig.

pin′-curl, skulpkrul.

pin′cushion, speldekussing; hen-en-kuikentjies, skurfkruid; (pl) luisies *(Leucospermun nutans)*.

pin′da, grondboontjie, pindaneut.

Pinda′ric, (n) Pindariese ode; (a) Pindaries.

pine, (n) pyn, den; masboom; pynappel.

pine, (v) kwyn; versmag; ~ *AWAY*, wegkwyn; ~ *to*

DEATH, doodtreur; ~ *FOR (after)*, hunker na, smag na; versmag; snak na.
pin'eal, pynappelvormig, dennebolvormig; keëlvormig; ~ **gland**, pynappelklier, harsingklier, epifise.
pine: ~ **apple**, pynappel; ~-**beetle**, denneskeerder; ~ **beauty**, ~ **carpet**, dennemot; ~-**clad**, met dennebome oortrek; ~-**cone**, dennebol; ~-**grove**, dennebos; ~ **marten**, dennemarter; ~-**needle**, dennenaald; ~ **ry**, (..ries), pynappelplaas; denneplantasie; ~-**seed**, dennepit; ~ **timber**, dennehout, greinhout; ~-**tree**, denneboom, pynboom.
pine'tum, denneaanplanting, dennebos.
pine'-wood, dennehout, greinhout; mashout.
pin'-feather, onontwikkelde veer.
pin'fold, (n) skut; (v) in die skut hou.
ping, (n) fluitende geluid, gegons; gepingel (motor); (v) skreeu, huil, gons; pingel (motor).
ping'pong, (n) tafeltennis, pingpong; (v) tafeltennis (pingpong) speel.
pin'guid, olierig, vetterig.
pin: ~-**head**, speldekop; uilskuiken; ~-**hole**, speldegaatjie; lunsgat (voertuig); ~-**hole camera**, gaatjiekamera, speldeprikkamera, stenopeïese kamera.
pin'ic, denne=; ~ **acid**, dennesuur.
pin'ing, (n) verlangste, verlange, hunkering, smagting, versmagting; wegtering, wegkwyning; verknorsing; (a) smagtend, verlangend, hunkerend.
pin'ion¹, (n) vlerk, vleuel, vleuelpunt, wiek; slagpen; (v) vasmaak; boei, kortwiek, die vlerke knip.
pin'ion², (n) rondsel; kleinrat (motor); dryfrat, dryfwiel; ~-**case**, rondselhuis; ~-**shaft**, rondselas; dryfas.
pink¹, (n) jong salm.
pink², (n) pink, vissersboot.
pink³, (n) ontstekingsklop, klop (motor); (v) klop, pingel (motor).
pink⁴, (n) grasangelier; skarlaken; jakkalsjagter; die beste; *in the ~ of CONDITION*, perdfris, in uitstekende kondisie; *the ~ of ELEGANCE*, die toonbeeld van eleganse; *in the very ~ of FASHION*, na die allerjongste mode.
pink⁵, (v) steek; deurboor; wond; prik; met gaatjies versier; opsier, uitdos.
pink⁶, (v) loer met half toe oë; die oë knip; (a) half toe (oë).
pink disease, rooskleursiekte, pienksiekte.
pink'-eyed, met ontsteekte oë, rooioog=.
pin'kie, pinkie.
pink'ing¹, (n) klopping; pingel(ing).
pink'ing², (a) uittand=; ~ **scissors**, ~ **shears**, kartelskêr, uittandskêr.
pink'ko, (sl.), linksgesinde, pienke.
Pink'ster, Pinkster.
pink'-sterned, met smal agterstewe.
pink'y¹, (n) (..kies), vissersbootjie.
pink'y², (a) roos=, rôse, vleiskleurig, pienk; linksgesind.
pin' money, sakgeld.
pinn'a, oorskulp; vin; veer.
pinn'ace, sloep, pinas.
pinn'acle, (n) top, toppunt, punt, trans; toring; (v) torinkies opsit; bekroon; die toppunt wees van.
pinn'ate, geveer; getak; gevin.
pinn'iform, vinvormig; veervormig.
pin'nigrade, **pin'niped**, vinpotig, vinvoetig.
pinn'iped, met vinpote.
pin'nula, **pin'nule**, spilletjie.
pinn'y, (**pinnies**), kindervoorskootjie.
pin: ~-**oak**, moeraseik, naaldeik; ~ **ochl'e**, pinochle (kaartspel); ~ **o'le**, mieliemeel; **piñon**, piñon, neutden; ~-**perforation**, priktanding; ~-**point**, (n) spel=depuntstippel; (v) haarfyn aanwys; die plek aanwys van; ~ **prick**, (n) speldeprik; aanstoot; (v) steek (met 'n speld); aanstoot gee; ~-**stripe**, potloodstrepie.
pint, pint.
pin'-table, spykertafel, dobbeltafel.
pinta'do, (-s), tarentaal, poelpetaat, drafhoender, pintado.
pin' tail, pylstert.
pint' bottle, pintmaat, pintbottel.

pin'tle, pen, bout; roerhaak; sleephaak; skarnier= haak; ~-**plate**, oogbeslag; kussingplaat.
pint: ~ **measure**, pintmaat; **pin'to**, pinto, bont perd, skilderperd; ~ **pot**, pintpot; ~-**sized**, klein.
pin'-tuck, haaropnaaisel.
pin'-up, kalendermeisie, knipportret; ~ **girl**, plakpoppie, kalendermeisie, prikkelpop; ~ **lamp**, muurlamp.
pin'y, vol dennebome; denneagtig, denne=.
piolet', (F.), piolet, ysbyl.
pi'on, pion (fis.).
pioneer', (n) pionier, baanbreker, wegbereider, voortrekker; padmaker; (v) pionierswerk doen, die weg berei, die pad oopmaak, die eerste aanpak; ~ **corps**, pionierkorps; ~ **ing**, baanbrekerswerk; ~ **spirit**, pioniersgees; ~ **work**, baanbrekerswerk, pionierswerk.
pi'ous, vroom, godvrugtig, devoot, hemelsgesind; ~ *FRAUD*, bedrog met 'n goeie doel; ~ *WISH*, vrome wens; ~-**minded**, met 'n vroom gemoed; ~ **ness**, vroomheid.
pip¹, (n) piep (hoendersiekte); nukkerigheid, neerslagtigheid; *you GIVE me the ~*, jy gee my die piep (olel); *be GIVEN the ~*, die piep kry; *HAVE the ~*, die piep hê.
pip², (n) pitjie.
pip³, (n) gepiep; (v) (-**ped**), piep.
pip⁴, (n) blokkie (kaarte, ens.).
pip⁵, (n) rangster (offisier).
pip⁶, (v) (-**ped**), oes, kafloop; raak skiet; die loef afsteek; ~ *out*, sterf, bokveld toe gaan.
pi'pa, pipa (soort padda).
pip'age, pypleiding; petrolpyp.
pi'pal, pipal, Indiese vyeboom; banjan.
pipe, (n) pyp; dagon; fluit; buis; orrelpyp; geluid; stop (tabak); omboorsel, bies (klere); oog (op dobbelsteen); gefluit; (pl) doedelsakke; *DANCE to another's ~*, na iem. se pype dans; *FILL a ~*, 'n pyp stop; *LIGHT a ~*, 'n pyp opsteek; *the ~ of PEACE*, die vredespyp; *smoke the ~ of PEACE*, vreedsaam (in vrede) verkeer; *PUT that in your and smoke it*, dit kan jy in jou sak steek; *SMOKE a ~*, 'n pyp rook; (v) op 'n fluit speel; pype lê; van pype voorsien; huil, sing; omboor (met 'n koordjie); deur 'n koekspuit druk; skree, hard praat; ~ *DOWN*, ontslaan; 'n toontjie laer sing; minder lawaai maak; ~ *one's EYE*, huil; ~ *UP*, begin speel; ~ **band**, doedelsakkorps, pypkorps; ~ **bend**, pypbuigstuk; ~-**bowl**, pypkop; ~ **clay**, pypgrond, pypaarde; ~-**cleaner**, (pyp)deursteker, pypskoonmaker; ~-**clip**, pypklem; ~-**cover**, pypdoppie; ~-**cutter**, pypsnyer; ~ **dream**, lugkasteel; wensdroom; dromery; droombeeld, hersenskim; opiumdroom; ~-**factory**, pypfabriek; ~-**fish**, naaldvis; ~-**fitter**, pypwerker; ~-**ful**, stop; ~-**gourd**, pypkalbas; ~-**hammer**, pyphamer; ~-**head**, pypkop; ~-**layer**, pyplêer; ~ **laying**, lê van pype; ~ **line**, pyplyn; informasiekanaal, inligtingskanaal; ~ **major**, doedelsakmajoor; ~ **man**, pypwerker; ~-**oil**, pypolie; ~-**organ**, pyporrel; ~-**picker**, pypuitpluiser.
pip em'ma, (colloq., mil.), namiddag.
pip'er, fluitspeler, doedelsakspeler; lokhond; vis; opiumskuimer; *PAY the ~*, die gelag betaal; *he who PAYS the ~ calls the tune*, wie betaal, mag sy sin volg; *the PIED P~ of Hamelin*, die Rottevanger van Hamelen.
pipe: -**rack**, pyprakkie; ~ **ridine**, piperedien, -ine; ~-**stem**, pypsteel; ~ **thread**, pypskroefdraad; ~-**to-bacco**, pyptabak; ~-**tree**, seringboom.
pipette', suigbuis, pipet.
pipe: ~-**union**, pypkoppeling; ~-**wrench**, pypsleutel, bobbejaan, kraaibek, pyptang.
pip'ing, (n) pypleiding; gefluit; omboorsel, bies, koord; pyp; buisversiering, buisversiersel (op koek); (a) fluitend; ~ *HOT*, vuurwarm; sissend warm; *the ~ TIMES of peace*, die aangename vredestyd.
pipistrel(le)', vlermuisie, pipistrel.
pip'it, koestertjie, vlakvoël(tjie).
pip'kin, potjie, pannetjie.
pipp'in, pippeling, rooiappel, dessertappel.
pip'squeak, nul, veragtelike persoon, bog.

pi′quancy, skerpheid (van smaak), die pikante, pikantheid, prikkeling, pittigheid.
pi′qué, pikee.
pique, (n) wrok, wrewel, gebelgdheid, hekel, twis; gepikeerdheid, spytigheid; piket(spel); *in a fit of* ~, in 'n ergerlike bui; (v) beledig, prikkel, pikeer, erger, krenk; ~ *oneself on,* jou beroem op; ~ **d,** gepikeer; gekrenk, gesteur; *be* ~ *d,* geraak (kwaad) wees.
piquet′, piket (kaartspel).
piqueur′, pikeur.
pir′acy, (..**cies**), seerowery, seeroof, seeskuimery; letterdiewery; roof; nadruk.
pira′gua, piragua, kano (van uitgeholde boomstam).
piran′ha, piranha.
pir′ate, (n) seerower, seeskuimer, vrybuiter; nadrukker; letterdief; rower; (v) roof; seeroof pleeg; nadruk; *a* ~ *d edition,* roofdruk; 'n onwettige nadruk; ~ **listener,** roofluisteraar; ~**-ship,** roofskip; ~**'s nest,** sluiphawe; ~ **taxi,** kaperhuurmotor, ₌taxi.
pirat′ic(al), seerowend, seerowers₌; nagedruk.
pirn, garingklos.
piripir′i, piri-piri.
pirogue′, *kyk* **piragua.**
piroplasmo′sis, piroplasmose.
pirouette′, (n) koorddansersdraai, pirouette; (v) pirouetteer.
pis′cary, visreg; viswater.
piscator′ial, pis′catory, vis₌; vissers₌.
Pis′ces, die Visse (sterrebeeld).
pis′ciculture, visteelt, visboerdery.
pis′ciculturist, visteler, visboer.
pisci′na, (-e, -s), visdam; Romeinse swemdam.
pis′cine, (n) swembad; (a) vis₌.
pisciv′orous, visetend.
pis′é, vasgestampte klei; ~ *de terre,* vasgestampte klei.
pish! ba! sies! foei!
pishogue′, towery.
pis′iform, ertjievormig.
pis′mire, mier (beessiekte).
pis′olite, ertjiesteen, pisoliet.
piss, (vulg.), (n) pis; water; urine; (v) water; pis; urineer.
pissoir′, (F.), pissoir, urinaal, urinoir.
pista′chio, pistasie(neut), groenamandel, pimperneut; ~ **nut,** pistasie(neut), pimperneut, groenamandel.
pis′til, stamper (blom); ~**la′ceous,** stamper₌; ~ **late,** met 'n stamper; ~ **lif′erous,** stamperdraend.
pis′tol, (n) pistool; *hold a* ~ *to someone's head,* iem. met die dood dreig; (v) **(-led),** met 'n pistool skiet; ~**-case,** pistoolsak.
pistole′, pistool (geldstuk) (hist.).
pis′tol: ~**-packing,** pistooldraend; ~**-pocket,** pistoolsak; ~**-point:** *at* ~**-***point,* met die pistool voor die bors.
pis′ton, suier; klep; ~ **area,** suieroppervlakte; ~**-clearance,** vryslag van suier; ~**-cover,** suierdeksel; ~ **displacement,** silinderinhoud; ~ **engine,** suiermotor, suierenjin; ~**-head,** suierkop; ~**-lift,** suierstoot; ~**-nut,** suiermoer; ~**-pin,** suierpen; ~ **ring,** suierring; ~**-rod,** suierstang; pompstang; ~**-slap,** suierwikkeling, suierwaggel; suierklap; ~**-spring,** suierveer; ~**-stroke,** suierslag; ~**-valve,** suierklep; ~**-wall,** suierwand.
pit, (n) put, kuil, gat; graf; leembank; koolmyn; mynskag, bek (myn); bak, parterre (skouburg); afgrond; herstelkuil, kuip, pertrolstasie (motorwedrenne); *the BOTTOMLESS* ~, die hel; *DIG a* ~ *for someone,* 'n put vir iem. grawe; ~ *of the STOMACH,* maagholte, krop van die maag; (v) **(-ted),** uithol, uitgrawe; inkuil; ophits; merk (van pokke); stel, stig; uithol (vrugte); ~ *one's strength against,* teen mekaar stel, laat baklei, kragte meet met.
pit′-(a)-pat, doef-doef, tikketak, triptrap, rikketik.
pitch[1]**,** (n) pik; *as BLACK as* ~, *as DARK as* ~, so donker soos die nag; *they that toucheth* ~ *shall be DEFILED therewith,* wie met pik omgaan, word daarmee besmet; wie met roet speel, word swart; (v) met pik smeer, teer.
pitch[2]**,** (n) **(-es),** booghou (gholf); tandafstand (rat); hoogte, toppunt; toonhoogte (musiek); helling; skuinste; hellingshoek; spoed (skroef); steek; galop (perd); rigting (hoefyster); stamp, duik (skip); staanplek; (krieket)baan; spasiëring (skroef); *FLY at too high a* ~, hoër vlieg as jou vlerke lank is; *at too HIGH a* ~, op 'n te hoë noot; *to the HIGHEST* ~, tot die hoogste punt; ~ *of a roof,* die skuinste van 'n dak; ~ *of a SAW,* tandhoek; (v) slinger (tent) opslaan; inplant; gooi, smyt; kampeer; hei (blok); duik, skommel, stamp (skip); galop (perd); beklee (helling); bestraat (wal); rig (hoefyster); grondvat (gholf); op toonhoogte bring, stem; val, omslaan; inklim; ~ *CAMP,* kamp opslaan; ~ *on one's HEAD,* hard op jou kop val; ~ *IN,* fluks aanpak; ~ *INTO someone,* iem. inklim (invlieg); ~ *INTO one another,* mekaar inklim; mekaar in die hare vlieg; *he* ~ *d his VOICE high,* hy het sy stem verhef; ~ *WICKETS,* paaltjies inslaan.
pitch′-and-toss, muntstukspeletjie; *play* ~, dobbel.
pitch′-black, pikswart.
pitch′blende, uraanpik(erts), pikblende.
pitch′-circle, steeksirkel.
pitched: *a* ~ *BATTLE,* 'n gereelde (vaste) veldslag; *our EXPECTATIONS were* ~ *too high,* ons verwagtings was te hoog gespanne.
pitch′-dark, pikdonker; ~**ness,** pikdonker.
pit′ched battle, gereelde (vaste) (veld)slag.
pit′ched roof, staandak, kapdak.
pitch′er[1]**,** (straat)venter; straatklip; (bal)gooier (bv. bofbal).
pitch′er[2]**,** (water)kruik; kan; *little* ~*s have long EARS,* klein muisies het groot ore; *the* ~ *goes so often to the WELL that it comes home broken,* die kruik gaan na die water tot dit breek; *let the* ~ *go to the WELL once too often,* om die kers vlieg tot jy daarin val; ~**-plant,** bekerplant.
pitch: ~ **fork,** (n), gaffel, hooivurk; (v) met 'n gaffel gooi; inkruiwa, inabba, instoot (in 'n pos); ~**ing,** galop, geskommel (boot); ~**-line,** steeklyn; ~**-pine,** pikden; ~**-pipe,** stemfluit(jie); ~**-sea,** stampsee.
pitch: ~ **stone,** piksteen; ~ **thread,** pikdraad.
pitch′-tone, grondtoon.
pitch′-wheel, tandrat.
pitch′y, pik₌, pikagtig; pikdonker.
pit′-coal, myn(steen)kool.
pit′eous, jammerlik, erbarmlik, treurig, ellendig; ~**ness,** jammerlikheid, ellendigheid, treurigheid.
pit′fall, vanggat, valkuil, wolfskuil; valstrik.
pith, (n) kern, pit; murg; krag; sterkte; siel; pittigheid, belangrikheid; wit (van 'n lemoen); *in* ~ *and marrow,* in hart en niere; (v) die murg afsteek; die pit uithaal.
pit′head, mynskag, mynbek, myningang.
pithecan′thrope, aapmens, pitekantroop.
pithec′oid, aap₌, aapagtig.
pith: ~ **helmet,** pithelm; ~**iness,** pittigheid, kernagtigheid; ~**less,** kragteloos, futloos, sonder pit; ~**y,** pittig, kernagtig, kragtig.
pit′-hole, pokgaatjie.
pit′iable, (gods)jammerlik, beklaenswaardig, deernisvaardig, betreurenswaardig, bedroewend, stom, erbarmlik, armsalig; ~**ness,** beklaenswaardigheid, armsaligheid, erbarmlikheid.
pit′iful, medelydend, droewig, treurig, jammerlik, armsalig, sielig, deerniswekkend, deerlik.
pit′iless, onbarmhartig, meedoënloos, onmeedoënd; ~**ness,** onbarmhartigheid, meedoënloosheid, hardvogtigheid.
pit: ~ **man,** mynwerker; koppelstang; ~**on′,** piton, rotspen; ~**-prop,** mynstut; ~ **sand,** putsand; ~**-saw,** kuilsaag, boomsaag; ~ **side,** by 'n mynskag, steengroef, ens.; ~ **silo,** voerkuil, kuilgat.
pit′so, (-s), pitso.
pitt′ance, armoedige bestaan; klein salaris; bietjie, liefdegawe; *a MERE* ~, 'n bedroef klein bietjie; *a MISERABLE* ~, 'n bedroef klein bietjie; 'n miserabele klein bietjie.
pitt′ed, pokdalig; mottig (sandsteen); ~ *with smallpox,* pokdalig; ~ **valve,** ingevrete klep.
pitt′er-patt′er, (n) getrippel, getrappel, rikketik; (v) trippel, trappel.
pitt′ing, invreting, vertering, uitvreting; pokdaligheid.

pittospo'rum, pittosporum, kasuur.
pitu'itary, slymagtig, slymerig, slym=; slymafskei=
dend, pituïtêr; ~ **fever,** slymkoors; ~ **gland,** slym=
klier, pituïtêre klier.
pitu'itous = **pituitary.**
pit: ~ **water,** skagwater; ~**-work,** mynwerk.
pit'y, (n) **(pities),** medelye, jammer, erbarming, deer=
nis; *it is a GREAT* ~, dit is alte jammer; *HAVE* ~
for, medelye hê met; *HAVE* ~ *on,* genadig wees;
MORE'S the ~, des te erger; wat erger is; *OUT of*
~, uit jammerte; *for* ~ *'s SAKE,* uit jammerte; om
hemelswil; in hemelsnaam; *TAKE* ~ *on,* medelye
hê met; *it is a THOUSAND pities,* dit is alte jam=
mer; *WHAT a* ~*!* hoe jammer! (v) **(pitied),** medelye
hê, bekla(ag), bejammer; ~**ing,** medelydend.
pityri'asis, pitiriase, semeluitslag.
piv'ot, (n) (draai)spil, draaipunt; skakel (sport); (v)
om 'n spil draai; laat draai; draai, krink, skarnier
(gholf).
piv'otal, vernaamste, hoof=; draaiend; ~ **axis,** spilas,
draaias; ~ **fault,** spilbreuk; ~ **industry,** sleutel=
bedryf; ~ **question,** hoofsaak, kernsaak.
piv'ot: ~ **bridge,** draaibrug; ~ **centre,** draaibord;
~ **ed,** draaibaar bevestig; ~ **joint,** spilgewrig; ~-
pin, spiltap; ~ **plate,** spilplaat, skamelplaat.
pi'xil(l)ated, verward; mal; dronk.
pix'y, (pixies), towerfee, kabouter.
piz'za, (It.), pizza; ~ **(pie),** pizza(pastei).
pizzeri'a, (It.), pizzeria, pizzaplek.
pizzica'to, (It mus.), pizzicato.
piz'zle, roede, peester (diere); koker (perd).
placabil'ity, vergewensgesindheid, versoenbaarheid.
plac'able, versoenbaar, inskiklik, vergewensgesind.
plac'ard, (n) plakkaat, aanplakbiljet; (v) aanplak,
met aanplakbiljette bedek, adverteer.
placate', bevredig; versoen; gunstig stem, paai.
placa'tory, versoenend, paaiend.
place, (n) plek, plaas; oord, keerstraat, keerom (by
straatname); ruimte; instansie, woonplek; plaas=
hou (tennis); rang, stand; pos; betrekking, posisie,
amp; desimaal (rekenk.); ~ *of AMUSEMENT,*
vermaaklikheidsplek; ~ *of ASSEMBLY,* versa=
melplek, plek van samekoms; *AT* ~ *s,* hier en daar;
CHANGE ~ *s,* plekke omruil; *CLARENDON* ~,
Clarendonoord, -keerstraat, -keerom; *to six DECI=
MAL* ~ *s,* tot ses desimale; ~ *of DETENTION,*
huis van bewaring; gevangenis; aanklagkantoor;
~ *of EMPLOYMENT,* werkplek; *in the FIRST*
~, in die eerste plek, ten eerste; *GIVE* ~ *to,* plek
maak vir; *GO* ~ *s,* rondreis; uitgaan; *HOLD in* ~,
op sy plek hou; *IN* ~, op sy plek; geskik vir; *IN*
of, in plaas van; ~ *s of INTEREST,* interessante
plekke; *KNOW one's* ~, jou
plek ken; weet waar jy staan; *LAY another* ~, dek
nog 'n plek; *MAKE* ~, plek maak; *it is not MY* ~,
dis nie my plig nie; dit lê nie op my weg nie, *feel*
OUT of ~, jou nie op jou plek voel nie; *OUT of* ~,
nie op sy plek nie; ongeskik, misplaas; onvanpas;
all OVER the ~, oral; *PRIDE of* ~, die ereplek,
PUT yourself in my ~, stel jou in my plek; ~ *of*
SAFETY, veilige plek; plek van bewaring; *TEACH*
someone his ~, iem. op sy plek sit; *a* ~ *in the SUN,*
'n plek in die son; *TAKE* ~, plaasvind, gebeur;
TAKE the ~ *of,* die plek inneem van; vervang; ~
of WORSHIP, kerk, bedehuis; (v) plaas, neersit;
aanstel; verkoop; belê (geld); tuisbring (fig.); 'n be=
trekking besorg; gee (bestelling); stel (rugby); ~
under ARREST, aanhou, arresteer; ~ *the BALL,*
die bal plaas (tennis); die bal stel (rugby); *I CAN=*
NOT ~ *him,* ek kan hom nie eien nie; ek weet nie
wat ek van hom moet dink nie; ~ *CONFIDENCE*
in, vertroue stel in; ~ *in CUSTODY,* in bewaring
stel; ~ *on END,* regop sit; ~ *on the MARKET,* in
die handel bring; ~ *an ORDER,* bestel; ~ *OUT,*
uitbestee; ~ *SHARES,* aandele privaat plaas;
UNABLE to ~ *someone,* iem. nie kan eien nie; ~ *a*
VALUE upon, waarde heg aan; ~ *somebody in the*
WRONG, iem. in die ongelyk stel.
place'bo, (-es, -s), placebo, troosmedisyne, fopme=
disyne; aangebed vir die dooie(s) (R.K.).
place: ~**-brick,** misgebakte steen; ~**-holder,** ampte=
naar, ampsbekleder, plekhouer; ~**-hunter,** baan=

tjiesoeker; ~**-kick,** stelskop; ~**-kicker,** stelskop=
per; ~ **less,** sonder plek; sonder betrekking, werk=
loos; onbegrens; swerwend; ~ **man,** boetie, baan=
tjiehouer; ~**-mat,** tafelmatjie; ~**ment,** plasing;
uitplasing; ~ **name,** pleknaam, plaasnaam, topo=
niem.
placen'ta, (-e), nageboorte, moederkoek, plasenta;
saadkoek; vuilgoed; ~**l,** nageboorte, moeder=
koek=.
pla'cer, steller (rugby); plaser; mineraalgrond, goud=
afsetting; goudwassery; ~ **diamond,** spoeldiamant;
~ **mining,** spoelwassery.
place'-seeker, baantjiesoeker.
pla'ce-setting, gedekte plek; plek(eet)gerei.
pla'cid, kalm; sag, vreedsaam; rustig; bedaard.
placid'ity, pla'cidness, onbewoënheid, rustigheid,
vreedsaamheid; stilte, kalmte.
pla'cing, plasing.
plack'et, roksak; slip; ~**-fastener,** drukknopie; ~-
hole, slipgat, slip.
pla'coid, plaatvormig.
plafond', plafon.
plage, (see)strand.
pla'giarism, plagiaat, letterdiewery, letterdiefstal, let=
terkundige diefstal, kunsroof.
pla'giarist, letterdief, plagiaris; kunsrower.
pla'giarize, oorskryf, letterdiewery pleeg.
pla'gioclase, plagioklaas.
plague, (n) plaag, ramp; pes, pestilensie; *BUBONIC*
~, builepes; *the* ~ *s of EGYPT,* die plae van Egip=
te; *INJECT with* ~, verpes; (v) met 'n pessiekte
besoek; kwel, pla; versondig, lastig val, vervolg; *be*
~ *d with,* vergewe wees van; oortrek wees van; ~-
blotch, pesblaar; ~**-fighting,** pesbestryding; ~
germ, peskiem; ~ **hospital,** peshospitaal; ~**-mark,**
pesmerk; pesteken; ~ **patient,** peslyer.
plag'uer, kweller, plaer.
plague: ~ **regulation,** pesregulasie; ~ **some,** lastig,
hinderlik, kwellend; ~**-sore,** pesbuil; ~**-spot,** pes=
buil; pesvlek; skandvlek; broeines; ~ **virus,** pesstof.
pla'gu(e)y, (a) lastig, ondraaglik, ellendig, geweldig,
verduiwels; (adv) baie, erg.
plaice, skol (vis).
plaid, Skotse geruit; geruitmantel; reisdeken.
plain[1], (n) (gras)vlakte; vlak; (a) eenvoudig, duidelik,
verstaanbaar; onopgesmuk, onversier, ongekleur,
onbewerk; alledaags, lelik (persoon); plat, gelyk=
vloers; effe; glad; gewoon; regs; *in* ~ *CLOTHES,*
in burgerklere, in gewone klere; *a* ~ *FACE,* 'n on=
aantreklike gesig; *a* ~ *GIRL,* 'n doodgewone (alle=
daagse) meisie; ~ *LANGUAGE,* eenvoudige taal;
the ~ *MAN,* die gewone man; *it is* ~ *MURDER,*
dis niks anders as moord nie; ~ *NEEDLEWORK,*
gewone naaldwerk; *a* ~ *NO,* 'n besliste ontken=
ning; *it is as* ~ *as the NOSE on one's face,* dit staan
soos 'n paal bo water; *as* ~ *as a PIKESTAFF,* soos
'n paal bo water; ~ *SILLY,* sommer net dom;
TELL someone the ~ *truth,* iem. padlangs die
waarheid vertel; *in* ~ *TERMS,* ronduit; eenvoudig
gesels; *the* ~ *TRUTH,* die naakte waarheid; (adv)
klaarblyklik, duidelik; ~ *BAD luck,* blote teen=
spoed; *knit* ~ *and PURL,* regs en aweregs brei;
be ~ *WITH,* geen doekies omdraai nie; reguit
praat.
plain[2], (v) kla, beween.
plain: ~**-bodied,** gladdelyf=; ~ **cake,** eenvoudige
koek; ~ **cigarettes,** sigaret sonder kurk; ~ **clothes,**
burgerdrag; ~ **concrete,** ongewapende beton; ~
cooking, gewone kokery; ~ **dealer,** eerlike mens; ~
dealing, (n) opregtheid, eerlikheid; (a) eerlik, opreg;
~ **living,** eenvoudige lewenswyse.
plain'ly, duidelik; eenvoudig, gewoonweg; rondbors=
tig; klaarblyklik; *PUT it* ~, eenvoudig sê; ~
SILLY, klaarblyklik dom (verspot).
plain: ~ **ness,** duidelikheid; eenvoudig(heid); ~ **sail=**
ing, maklik, doodeenvoudig; ~ **sewing,** nuttige
naaldwerk; ~**s'man, (..men),** vlaktebewoner; ~-
song, koraalgesang; ~ **speaking,** openhartigheid,
opregtheid; ~**-spoken,** rondborstig, eerlik.
plaint, klag; aanklag; klaaglied.
plain'tiff, klaer, eiser (eiseres); aanklaer; aanlêer.
plain'tive, klaend, klaag=; ~ **ness,** klaaglikheid.

plain: ~ **washer,** gewone drukring (waster); ~ **wire,** gladde draad; ~ **work,** nuttige handwerk.

plait, (n) haarstring, haarvlegsel; plooi, vou; (v) (aaneen)vleg; plooi, vou; ~ *round,* omvleg; ~ **er,** vlegter; plooier, vouer; ~ **ing,** strengeling; (die) vleg.

plan, (n) plan; opset; voorneme, bedoeling, toeleg; ontwerp, kaart, skets, tekening; bestektekening, bouplan, plattegrond; metode, sisteem; aanleg; *ACCORDING to* ~, volgens plan; ~ *of ACTION,* plan van aksie (optrede); *the BEST* ~, die beste plan; ~ *of CAMPAIGN,* krygsplan; *CHANGE one's* ~, van plan verander; ~ *of DEFENCE,* verdedigingsplan; *the* ~ *FELL through,* die plan het in duie geval(misluk); *MAKE a* ~, 'n plan maak (beraam); ~ *of SITE,* situasietekening; liggingskaart; terreinplan; (v) (**-ned**), 'n plan maak; ontwerp; inrig; bedink, prakseer; in skets bring, teken; vooraf reël; aanlê; ~ *a CURRICULUM,* 'n leerplan ontwerp; ~ *OUT,* ontwerp; beplan; uitkom.

plan'ar, vlak=; ~ **element,** vlakelement.

plana'rian, platwurm.

plana'tion, vlaktevorming.

plan'chet, muntplaatjie.

planchette', plansjet; meettafel; plankie (van spiritiste).

plane[1], (n) plataan(boom).

plane[2], (n) skaaf (gereedskap); (v) skaaf, skawe; ~ *down,* wegskawe, afskawe.

plane[3], (n) (draag)vlak; gelykte, trap, hoogte, niveau; vliegtuig; *on a HIGHER* ~, op 'n hoër vlak; ~ *of PROJECTION,* projeksievlak; ~ *of REFRACTION,* brekingsvlak; *on the SAME* ~, in dieselfde sfeer; op dieselfde niveau (vlak); (a) vlak, plat.

plane[4], (v) oor die water skeer; vlieg.

plane' angle, vlakhoek.

plane: ~ **bit,** ~ **blade,** skaafyster, skaafblad.

plane: ~ **chart,** kaart na die projeksie van Mercator; vlakkaart; ~ **figure,** plat figuur; ~ **geometry,** vlakmeetkunde, planimetrie.

plane'-iron, skaafmes, skaafbeitel.

plane'-load, vliegtuigvrag.

plan'er, skaaf; skawer, skaafmasjien, gladmaker; ~ **tool,** skaafbeitel.

plane: ~ **sailing,** vlakseil; ~ **surface,** plat vlak; ~ **table,** meettafel.

plan'et, planeet, dwaalster; kasuifel (kleed); *secondary* ~ *s,* satelliete; ~ **ar'ium,** (-s, ..ria), planetarium.

plan'etary, planeet=, planetêr; dwalend, dolend; aards; ~ **gear,** planeetrat; ~ **motion,** planeetloop; ~ **system,** planeetstelsel, sonnestelsel.

plan'etoid, planetoïed, planetoïde, asteroïed, asteroïde; ~ **al,** planetoïdaal.

plane'-tree, plataanboom.

plan'et-stricken, plan'et-struck, verbysterd, ontsteld.

plan'et-wheel, planeetrat.

plan'gent, luidklinkend, klotsend; klaend.

planim'eter, (opper)vlaktemeter, planimeter.

planimet'ric(al), planimetries; ~ **map,** plat kaart.

planim'etry, vlakmeetkunde, vlaktemeting, planimetrie.

plan'ing, (die) skaaf; ~ **-bench,** skaafbank; ~ **-hammer,** planeerhamer; ~ **-knife,** skraapstaal; ~ **-machine,** skaafmasjien.

plan'ish, planeer; polys; gelykmaak, glad maak; plet, uitklop (plaat); ~ **er,** poleerder; pletter.

plan'ishing, uitkloppery; planeerwerk; ~ **hammer,** planeerhamer; ~ **tool,** duikklopper.

plan'isphere, planisfeer, hemelkaart.

plank, (n) plank; beginsel (politiek); verkiesingsleuse; *a* ~ *in their ELECTION platform,* 'n beginsel in hulle verkiesingsprogram; *make someone WALK the* ~, iem. se voete spoel; (v) planke lê, 'n vloer insit, beplank, met planke beklee; neersit; ~ *DOWN,* neergooi; aftel; opdok; ~ *ONESELF down,* gaan sit, neerplof; ~ **ing,** plankwerk; onderdek.

plank'ton, plankton.

plan: ~ **less,** sonder plan, planloos; ~ **ned,** onderworpe, vooruitberaam, beoog; volgens plan, planmatig; ~ **ner,** ontwerper, uitdinker; planmaker.

plann'ing, ontwerp; oorleg; voorbereiding; beraming; beplanning; ~ **council,** planneraad; ~ **section,** ontwerpafdeling.

plano: ~ **conc'ave,** plathol, planokonkaaf; ~ **con'vex,** platbol, planokonveks; ~ **'meter,** planometer.

plant, (n) plant, gewas; masjinerie, bedryfsuitrusting, installasie, inrigting; fabriek; materiaal, uitrusting, skelmstuk, swendelary; houding; bêreplek; onderskuiwing; *IN* ~, aan die groei; *LOSE* ~, doodgaan (plant); *MISS* ~, nie opkom nie (plant); (v) plant; beplant (grond); aanlê; opstel; vestig (kolonie); sout (myn); plaas; posteer ('n wag); toedien ('n hou); wegsteek, heel (gesteelde goed); iets skelm neersit; skelmstreke bedink; aan sy lot oorlaat; ~ *a GARDEN with flowers,* blomme in 'n tuin plant; 'n tuin met blomme beplant; ~ *something ON someone,* iem. iets in die skoene skuif; iem. iets aansmeer; ~ *OUT,* verplant; ~ **able,** plantbaar.

plan'tain[1], piesang; plantaan.

plan'tain[2], weeblaar.

plan'tar, voetsool=; ~ **arch,** voetsoolboog.

planta'tion, plantasie; volksplanting, kolonie.

plant: ~ **-cane,** jong suikerriet; ~ **cell,** plantsel; ~ **disease,** plantsiekte; ~ **er,** planter; landbouer; ~ **fibre,** plantvesel.

plant'igrade, (n) soolloper, platvoetloper, soolganger; (a) soolganger=.

plant'ing, plantery; ~ **ground,** plantgrond; oesterbank, oesterbed; ~ **season,** planttyd.

plant: ~ **less,** sonder plante; ~ **let,** plantjie; ~ **life,** plantelewe; plantegroei; ~ **-louse,** blomluis, plantluis; ~ **-marker,** plantnaambordjie; ~ **pathol'ogy,** plantsiektekunde.

plant'ule, plantkiem.

plaque, plaat, beskilderde bord, plaket.

plaquette', plaket.

plash[1], (n) (-es), moeras; plas; gespat; (v) plas, spat.

plash[2], (v) saamvleg, deurvleg.

plash'y, plassend, spattend.

plasm, plasma.

plas'ma, plasma, bloedwei; groenkwarts; ~ **t'ic,** plasmaagtig; vormgewend.

plasmo'dium, plasmodium.

plasmo'lysis, plasmolise.

pla'ster, (n) pleister; pleisterkalk; gips; *ADHESIVE* ~, hegpleister; ~ *of PARIS,* gebrande gips; gips= (meel); (v) pleister, stukadoor; pleister opsit; belaai; besmeer; bekalk; met gips behandel; ~ *with PRAISE,* met lof oorlaai; ~ *THICK, some will STICK,* as dit dik aangeplak word, sal daarvan bly sit; ~ **board,** pleisterbord; ~ **bust,** gipsborsbeeld; ~ **cast,** gipsmodel; gipsafdruk; ~ **coat,** pleisterlaag; ~ **er,** pleisteraar, stukadoor; ~ **figure,** gipsbeeld; ~ **image,** gipsbeeld; ~ **ing,** pleistering; pleisterwerk, stukadoorwerk; ~ **ing-plank,** pleisterplank; ~ **ing-trowel,** pleistertroffel; ~ **mould,** gipsvorm; ~ **setting,** gipsverband; ~ **stucco,** stukadoorspleister; ~ **-work,** pleisterwerk; ~ **y,** gipsagtig.

plas'tic, (n) beeldende kuns; plastiek; (a) beeldend, vormbaar, plasties; plastiek=; ~ **arts,** beeldende kunste; ~ **clay,** besteerklei; modelleerklei; pottebakkersklei; potklei; ~ **fabric,** plastiekstof; ~ **foam,** skuimplastiek, skuimrubber.

plas'ticine, kunsklei, boetseerklei (geregistreerde handelsnaam).

plastic'ity, plastisiteit, vormbaarheid.

plas'ticizer, plastiseermiddel.

plas'tics, plastika; kunshars; plastiek; plastiese chirurgie.

plas'tic: ~ **surgeon,** plastiese chirurg; ~ **surgery,** plastiese chirurgie; ~ **ware,** plastiekware.

plas'tid, plastied, -ide.

plas'tron, borsplaat, borsstuk, borsie, plastron; onderdop (skilpad).

plat[1], (n) lappie grond.

plat[2], (n) vlegstrooi; (v) (**-ted**), vleg.

plat[3], (n) 'n bord kos.

plat'an, (Oosterse) plataan.

plate, (n) bord; plaat; bordvol (kos); naamplaat; kollektebord; kunstande; breekgoed; plateerware, tafelsilwer; silwerwerk; goudwerk; pleetwerk; me=

plateau taalwerk; beker; plaatwedren, prys (reisies); balkplaat, muurbalk; *DENTAL* ~, (plaat met) kunstande; *PERFORATED* ~, voegplaat; *a* ~ *SERVICE*, 'n silwerservies; (v) versilwer; plateer; verguld; vertin; pantser (skip); met metaalplate bedek; van nommerplaatjies voorsien; ~ *d silver*, silwerplaat; ~ **armour**, harnas, pantserplaat.

plateau', (-s, -x), plato, gelykte, tafelland; plat dameshoed.

plate: ~**-cloth**, bordedoek; ~**-error**, plaatfout; ~**ful**, bordvol; ~**-gauge**, diktemeter; ~**glass**, spieëlglas; ~ **iron**, plaatsnyer; ~**layer**, spoorwegwerker, baanwerker, spoorlêer, ploegwerker, baanmeester; ~**laying**, spoorlegging; ~**let**, plaatjie, bloedplaatjie; ~**-maker**, plaatwerker; ~**-mark**, keurmerk.

plat'en, druktafel, degel; roller (tikmasjien); ~**-man**, degeldrukker; ~ **press**, degelpers.

plate: ~**-powder**, skuurpoeier, silwerpoeier, metaalpoeier; ~**r**, versilweraar, vergulder; plaatwerker; ~**-rack**, borderak; ~**-shears**, blikskêr; ~**-spring**, platveer; ~**-table**, meetbord; ~**-warmer**, bordverwarmer.

plat'form, (n) verhoog, spreekgestoelte, platform, tribune, podium; perron; politieke program, beleid, standpunt, opvatting; buik (van wa); (v) op 'n verhoog sit; 'n toespraak hou; ~**-balance**, weegbrug; ~**-board**, buikplank; ~ **committee**, beleidskomitee; ~**-scale**, weegbrug, baskule; ~**-ticket**, platformkaartjie.

plat'ina, platina.

plat'ing, silwerlaag, goudlaag; pantserbedekking; ~ **work**, plaatwerk.

platinif'erous, platinahoudend.

plat'inize, met platina bedek, platineer.

plat'inoid, platina-, platinoïed, platinoïde.

plat'inum, platinum, platina, witgoud; ~**-bearing**, platinahoudend; ~ **blonde**, withaarnooi, vrou met platinablonde hare, platinablondine; ~**-plate**, platineer; ~**-plated**, geplatineer; ~ **wire**, platinadraad.

plat'itude, platheid, gemeenplaas, algemeenheid, banaliteit, onbeduidendheid.

platitudinar'ian, (n) verkoper van banaliteite; (a) banaal, alledaags, gemeenplasig.

platitud'inize, gemeenplase uit.

Platon'ic, platonies; ~ **love**, platoniese liefde; ~ **year**, platoniese jaar (± 26 000 jaar).

Plat'onism, Platonisme.

platoon', peloton, seksie; ~ **drill**, pelotondril; ~ **firing**, pelotonskiet, pelotonvuur; ~ **formation**, pelotonopstelling.

plat'teland, (Afr.), platteland.

platt'en = **platen**.

platt'er, platbord, vlakbord, plat skottel; vleisskottel; *hand on a* ~, op 'n skinkbord aanbied.

plat'y, bord-, bordagtig, soos 'n bord.

platycephal'ic, breedhoofdig.

plat'ypus, eendbekdier.

plat'yr(r)hine, **platyr(r)hin'ous**, breedneusig.

plau'dit, applous; goedkeuring.

plaud'itory, prysend, toejuigend.

plaud'it(s), toejuiging, applous, handgeklap.

plausibil'ity, aanneemlikheid.

plaus'ible, aanneemlik, innemend, skoonskynend, skoonklinkend, plousibel; ~**ness** = **plausibility**.

play, (n) spel; vermaak; (toneel)stuk; speelruimte, speling; *AT* ~, aan die speel; *the BALL is in* ~, die bal is in spel; *BRING into* ~, aanwend; *CALL all one's influence into* ~, al jou invloed laat geld; *it is CHILD'S* ~, dis maklik; ~ *of COLOURS*, kleurespel; *COME into* ~, in die spel kom; *FOUL* ~, vals spel; *FULL of* ~, vrolik, dartel; *in FULL* ~, in volle werking; *allow FULL* ~ *to*, die vrye teuels gee aan; *GIVE* ~ *to*, op die voorgrond stel; *GO to a* ~, na 'n opvoering gaan; *as GOOD as a* ~, vermaaklik; *something said IN* ~, iets vir die grap gesê; *MAKE a great* ~ *of*, baie ophef maak van; *PUT into* ~, in beweging sit; ~ *of WORDS*, woordspeling; (v) speel; baljaar; bespeel (musiekinstrument); korswel; rats hanteer; laat speel; uithaal ('n grap); vertoon, opvoer (stuk); spuit (fontein); ~ *ABOUT*, rondjakker; rondspeel; ~ *ALONG with*, saamspeel met; ~ *AT ball*, met 'n bal speel; ~ *AWAY one's chances*, jou kanse verspeel; ~ *AWAY one's money*, jou geld uitdobbel; ~ *BACK*, oorspeel; terugspeel; ~ *BALL*, met 'n bal speel; saamspeel, saamwerk; ~ *the BALL, not the man*, speel met die bal, nie teen die man nie; ~ *CARDS*, kaartspeel; *he* ~ *ed his CARDS well*, hy het goed gebruik gemaak van sy kanse; ~ *the DEUCE with*, vreeslik huishou met; ~ *the DEVIL*, iets verrinneweer; ~ *DOGS*, op honde wed; ~ *DOWN*, minder belangrik laat voorkom; verkleineer; ~ *DUCKS and drakes with*, verkwistend werk met; ~ *by EAR*, op gehoor speel; optree na gelang jy vasstel wat die beste is om te doen; op gevoel afgaan; ~ *FAIR*, eerlik optree; *if my memory does not* ~ *me FALSE*, as my geheue my nie bedrieg nie; *a person who* ~ *s FAST and loose*, 'n onbetroubare (onverantwoordelike) persoon; ~ *on a person's FEELINGS*, iem. se gevoelens uitbuit; ~ *second FIDDLE*, tweede viool speel; ~ *a FISH*, 'n vis laat uitspook; ~ *the FOOL*, die gek skeer; ~ *to the GALLERY*, iets doen (sê) om die guns v.d. massa te wen; ~ *the GAME*, eerlik wees; eerlik handel; ~ *at GARDENING*, kamma tuinmaak; ~ *the GUNS on*, die kanonne laat speel op; ~ *into each other's HANDS*, in mekaar se kaarte speel; ~ *into someone's HANDS*, iem. se planne bevorder; in iem. se kaarte speel; *that is* ~ *ing right into his HANDS*, dis water op sy meul; ~ *the HORSES*, op perde wed; ~ *with an IDEA*, droom oor 'n plan; ~ *IN*, inspeel; ~ *a JOKE on someone*, iem. 'n poets bak; ~ *KEEPS*, hou-hou speel; ~ *a good KNIFE and fork*, lekker weglê; ~ *(the) LEAD*, die hoofrol speel; ~ *the LINE*, 'n lyn laat skiet en intrek; ~ *a LOSING game*, stadig maar seker die onderspit delf; ~ *for LOVE*, vir die keiser se baard speel; nie vir geld speel nie; ~ *OFF one against the other*, teen mekaar uitspeel; ~ *ON*, bespeel; aanhou speel; *he is* ~ *ed OUT*, sy blus is uit; hy is kapot; *be* ~ *ed OUT*, afgerem wees; uitgedien wees; ~ *the MARKET*, spekuleer; ~ *a PART*, 'n rol speel; ~ *the PIANO*, klavier speel; ~ *POSSUM*, voorgee dat jy siek is; ~ *SAFE*, elke fout uitsluit, heeltemal seker wees; versigtig optree; ~ *one's strongest SUIT*, die beste kaarte eerste speel; ~ *for TIME*, die uitslag (afloop) vertraag; tyd probeer wen; ~ *a TRICK on someone*, iem. 'n poets bak; iem. 'n kool stowe; ~ *TRICKS with*, iem. 'n poets bak; iem. 'n streep trek; ~ *TRUANT*, stokkies draai; *TWO can* ~ *at the game*, slaan is twee man se werk; ~ *UP*, lol; neul; lastig wees; ~ *UP to*, flikflooi, vlei; in iem. se kaarte speel; ~ *WATER on a fire*, water op 'n vuur rig; ~ *upon WORDS*, 'n woordspeling maak; ~**able**, speelbaar; bespeelbaar; ~**-acting**, toneelspeel; aanstellerigheid; ~**-actor**, toneelspeler, akteur; ~ **bill**, aanplakbiljet; program; ~**-book**, boek met toneelstukke; ~**boy**, losbol, swierbol, pierewaaier, joljantjie, pretmaker, plesiersoeker; ~**-day**, speeldag, vakansiedag; ~**-debt**, speelskuld; ~**er**, speler; toneelspeler; ~**er-piano**, pianola, outomatiese piano; ~**fellow**, speelmaat, speelgenoot; ~**ful**, spelerig, dartel, speels; ~**fully**, speelsgewys; speels, nie ernstig nie; ~**fulness**, spelerigheid; speelsheid; ~**goer**, skouburgbesoeker; teaterganger; ~**-going**, skouburgbesoek; teaterbesoek; ~**ground**, speelterrein, speelplek; ruimte; ~**-hour**, speeluur; ~**house**, skouburg, teater.

play'ing, (n) (die) speel; (a) speel-; ~ **area**, speelgebied; ~**-ball**, speelbal; ~**-cards**, handkaarte, speelkaarte; ~**-field**, speelveld; speelplek.

play: ~**-let**, toneelstukkie; ~ **mate**, speelmaat; speelgenoot; ~**-night**, speelaand, ~ **off**, uitspeelwedstryd; ~**-pen**, speelhok; ~**-reading**, toneellesing, rollesing; ~ **room**, speelkamer; ~**-suit**, speelpak; ~ **thing**, speelding speelbal; (pl) speelgoed; ~ **time**, speeltyd, pouse; ~ **wright**, dramaturg, dramakrywer; ~**-writer**, dramaskrywer; ~**-writing**, dramaskryf.

pla'za, stadsplein, plaza.

plea, pleidooi, pleit, smeekbede; verdediging; verontskuldiging; verweerskrif; ~ *of GUILTY*, pleit van skuldig; *ON* ~ *that*, onder voorwendsel dat.

pleach, deurvleg, ineenstrengel.

plead, pleit, smeek, soebat, 'n pleidooi hou; bepleit; jou beroep op; jou verontskuldig; verdedig; ~ *one's BRIEF well*, jou saak goed verdedig; ~ *someone's CAUSE*, iem. se saak bepleit; ~ *to a CHARGE*, op 'n aanklag pleit; ~ *FOR someone*, vir iem. pleit; ~ *GUILTY*, skuldig pleit; skuld beken; ~ *not GUILTY*, skuld ontken; onskuldig pleit; *he could only* ~ *IGNORANCE*, sy enigste verontskuldiging was onkunde; ~ *for all one is WORTH*, lelik soebat; ~ **able**, verdedigbaar, regsgeldig; ~ **er**, pleiter, pleitbesorger; ~ **ing**, (n) pleidooi; (die) pleit; (a) smekend, pleitend; ~ **ings**, pleitstukke.

plea'sant, aangenaam; prettig, genoeglik; innemend, vriendelik; opgeruimd, lekker; *make* ~, veraangenaam; ~ **ly**, aangenaam; prettig; ~ **ness**, aangenaamheid, plesierigheid, prettigheid, genoeglikheid; ~ **ry**, (..tries), skerts, vrolikheid, grappigheid, geestigheid, luimigheid, aardigheid; gekheid.

please, beval, behaag, belief; aanstaan, genoeë doen; ~! asseblief! *AS you* ~, soos jy (u) wil; ~ *COPY*, kopieer, asb.; *DO as you* ~, maak soos jy lekker kry; ~ *DO*, ja, asb.; toe dan tog; ~ *DON'T*, moenie, asseblief nie; ~ *GOD*, as dit God behaag; *may it* ~ *your HONOUR*, met U Edele se verlof; *IF you* ~, asseblief; ~ *take NOTICE that*, neem asb. kennis dat; ~ *TURN over*, blaai om, asb.; ~ *YOURSELF*, maak soos jy wil; volg jou eie sin.

pleased, ingenome, tevrede, bly, (wel)behaaglik, verheug; *BE* ~ *with*, ingenome wees met; in jou skik wees met; ~ *at being CHOSEN*, verheug omdat jy gekies is; ~ *as a DOG with two tails*, in jou noppies wees; ~ *by FLATTERY*, gestreel deur vleitaal; ~ *to MEET you*, aangename kennis(making); *as* ~ *as PUNCH*, hoog in jou skik; in jou noppies; *I SHALL be* ~ *to* . . ., dit sal vir my aangenaam wees om . . .; ek sal graag . . .

pleas'ing, aangenaam, welgevallig, innemend; smaakvol; ~ *ways*, innemende maniere.

plea'surable, aangenaam, genoeglik, prettig, vermaaklik; ~ **ness**, aangenaamheid, genoeglikheid, prettigheid.

plea'sure, (n) genot, vermaak, pret, genoeë, plesier; wens, begeerte; welgevalle, skik, welbehae; singenot; *AT* ~, na verkiesing; na willekeur; na goeddunke; *we request the* ~ *of the COMPANY of*, ons het die genoeë om . . . uit te nooi na; *DO me the* ~ *of*, doen my die genoeë om; *FIND* ~ *in helping others*, plesier daarin vind om ander te help; *it IS a* ~, dit is vir my 'n genoeë; *a MAN of* ~, 'n losbol; *MALICIOUS* ~, leedvermaak; *the* ~ *is MINE*, dit was 'n plesier; *no* ~ *without PAIN*, vandag vro= lik, môre olik; na lag kom huil; ~ *s are like POPPIES spread, you seize the flower, its bloom is shed*, plesier is nes 'n jong komkommer, as jy hom pluk, verlep hy sommer; *at the PRESIDENT'S* ~, solank dit die President behaag; *TAKE* ~ *in*, behae skep in; *TAKE one's* ~, jou vermaak; *THIRST for* ~, genotsug; *WITH* ~, met genoeë; graag; (v) genoeë doen, voldoen aan; plesier, behae skep, behaag; ~ **-boat**, plesierboot; ~ **-cruise**, plesiervaart, plesierreis; ~ **-drive**, plesierrit; ~ **fair**, kermis; ~ **-garden**, park; ~ **-ground**, speelterrein, speelpark, pretpark; ~ **-lover**, genotsoeker; ~ **-loving**, pretliewend; ~ **resort**, plesieroord; ~ **-seeker**, plesiersoeker, plesierreisiger; ~ **-seeking**, genotsug; ~ **train**, plesiertrein; ~ **-trip**, plesiertoggie; ~ **yacht**, plesierjag.

pleat, (n) plooi, plooisel, vou; (v) plooie maak, plooi, vou; ~ *ed skirt*, plooirok.

plebei'an, (n) burger, plebejer; (a) burgerlik; plebejies; laag, gemeen.

pleb'iscite, volkstemming, referendum, plebissiet; *take a* ~, 'n volkstemming (referendum) hou.

plebs, (sl.) gepeupel, skorriemorrie, janrap en sy maat, plebs.

plec'trum, (..tra), plektrum, krappertjie.

pledge, (n) pand, onderpand; borgtog; heildronk; belofte; *DEED of* ~, pandakte; *GIVE in* ~, in pand gee; *HOLD in* ~, in pand hou; *LEAVE in* ~, in pand gee; *PUT in* ~, verpand; *REDEEM one's* ~, jou pand inlos; *RIGHT to* ~, verpandingsreg; *under* ~ *of secrecy*, onder belofte van geheimhouding; *TAKE the* ~, afskaffer word; *TAKE out of* ~, los; *UNREDEEMED* ~ *s*, oningeloste pande; (v) verpand, in pand gee; die gesondheid drink van; ~ **able**, verpandbaar; ~ **d**, verpand, toegesê.

pledgee', pandhouer.
pledg'er, pandgeër, verpander.
pledg'et, plukselverband.
Plei'ad, Sewester, Pleiade; groep van sewe (skitteren= de persone of dinge); ~ **es**, Sewegesternte, Pleiade.
Pleis'tocene, (n, a) Pleistoseen.
plen'ary, volkome, onbeperk; voltallig, vol (vergadering); volledig; ~ **indulgence**, volle aflaat; ~ **meeting**, voltallige vergadering; ~ **powers**, volmag; ~ **session**, volle sitting.
plenipoten'tiarize, as gevolmagtigde optree.
plenipoten'tiary, (n) (..ries), gevolmagtigde; (a) gevolmagtig.
plen'ish, vul, vol maak.
plen'itude, oorvloed, volheid.
plen'teous, oorvloedig, volop; ~ **ness**, oorvloed.
plen'tiful, oorvloedig, volop, ruim, talryk.
plen'ty, (n) oorvloed; hele boel, hoop; *IN* ~, volop, oorvloedig; ~ *MORE chances*, nog volop kanse; *in* ~ *of TIME*, goed op tyd; *in TIME of* ~, in tyd van oorvloed; ~ *of TIME*, volop tyd; (a) genoeg, oorvloedig.
plen'um, volledige sitting, voltallige vergadering; volheid.
pleochro'ic, pleochroïes, rigtingsveelkleurig.
pleomor'phic, pleomorfies, veelvormig.
ple'onasm, oortolligheid (van woorde), pleonasme.
pleonas'tic, pleonasties.
plero'me, pleroom.
plesiosau'rus, plesiosourus.
pleth'ora, volbloedigheid; oorvloed, oorvolheid, oormaat; *a* ~ *of words*, 'n stroom woorde.
plethor'ic, volbloedig, bloedryk; oorvloedig, vol, oorlaai.
pleur'a, borsvlies, longvlies.
pleur'al, borsvlies=, longvlies=, ~ **cavity**, borsholte; ~ **pneumonia**, long= en longvliesontsteking.
pleur'isy, borsvliesontsteking, pleuritis.
pleuropneumon'ia, long= en longvliesontsteking.
ple'xiglass, perspeks, pleksiglas.
ple'xor, perkussiehamertjie, pleksor.
plex'us, senuweevleg, netwerk, vlegsel; *solar* ~, sonnevleg.
pliabil'ity, buigsaamheid, plooibaarheid.
pli'able, buigsaam, buigbaar, lenig; plooibaar; volg= saam, meegaande; voubaar; soepel; smedig.
pli'ancy, lenigheid, buigsaamheid, handelbaarheid, volgsaamheid; toegewendheid, inskiklikheid.
pli'ant, lenig, soepel; handelbaar, inskiklik, plooi= baar; gedwee, toeskietlik, smedig; ~ **ness**, lenig= heid, handelbaarheid, gedweeheid, inskiklikheid.
plic'a, (-e), huidplooi; ~ **te(d)**, gevou; geplooi.
plica'tion, vouing; plooiing.
pli'ers, draadtang; knyptang; **locking** ~, kloutang, klemtang.
plight[1], (n) gesteldheid, toestand; *in a perilous (sorry)* ~, in 'n benarde (treurige) toestand.
plight[2], (n) belofte, verbintenis; (v) belowe; ~ *one's FAITH (word)*, jou woord gee; ~ *one's TROTH*, jou woord gee; verloof raak; ~ **ing**, troubelofte.
plim'soll, seilskoen.
Plim'soll line, plimsollmerk, laslyn, diepgangsmerk.
plinth, dekblad; plint, voetlys.
Plin'y, Plinius.
Pli'ocene, (n, a) Plioseen.
plissé, (n), plissé; (a) gepliseer(d).
plod, (n) gesloof, gesukkel, geswoeg; (v) (-ded), swoeg, ploeter, voortsukkel, doodsukkel; ~ *ALONG*, voortsukkel, aanpiekel; ~ *one's WAY*, moeisaam jou weg gaan; ~ **der**, slower, swoeër, blokker, werkesel, ploeteraar, sukkelaar; ~ **ding**, gesukkel, geswoeg; ~ **dingly**, sukkelrig.
ploi'dy, ploïdie, chromosoomaantal.
plonk[1], neerplof; neerplak.
plonk[2], (sl.), goedkoop wyn.
plop, (n) plons; (v) (-ped), plons; (adv) pardoems, ploems.

plo'sion, ploffing (fonet.).
plos'ive, (n) klapper, plofklank, eksplosief; (a) eksplosief.
plot, (n) sameswering, samespanning, komplot; verwikkelingsplan, intrige, knoop (van 'n roman); perseel, kleinhoewe, landbouhoewe, klein plasie; erf; plot; (v) **(-ted),** saamsweer, intrigeer; ontwerp, beraam; skets, teken, in kaart bring, karteer, traseer; ~ *AGAINST,* 'n sameswering smee teen; ~ *TOGETHER,* saamspan; ~ **coverage,** erfdekking, terreindekking; ~ **ter,** ontwerper; samesweerder, intrigant; meetdriehoek; karteerder (persoon).
plott'ing, geknoei, samewering, toutrekkery; ontwerp, beraming; skets, tekening; trasering, uitstipping; ~ **instrument,** meetdriehoek; ~ **scale,** verkleinde skaal, herleidingstafel; ~ **table,** batterybord.
plough, (n) ploeg; *put one's HAND to the* ~, die hand aan die ploeg slaan; *land UNDER the* ~, ploeglande); (v) ploeg, omploeg; braak; (deur)klief; voortswoeg; druip, laat sak (in eksamen); ~ *BACK,* terugploeg; (in die saak) belê; ~ *through a BOOK,* deur 'n boek worstel; ~ *an EXAMINATION,* druip in 'n eksamen; onderdeur wees, *I EXPECT to be* ~ *ed,* ek verwag om te sak (dop); ~ *with another man's HEIFER,* met 'n ander se kalf ploeg; ~ *a lonely FURROW,* alleen staan; man alleen veg; eensaam deur die lewe gaan; ~ *IN,* inploeg, onderploeg; ~ *OUT,* uitploeg; ~ *the SANDS,* water in 'n mandjie aandra; ~ *THROUGH,* deurworstel; ~ *UP,* omploeg, ombraak; ~ **able,** ploegbaar; ~**beam,** ploegbalk; ~**-boy,** touleier; plaasseun; ~ **breast,** strykbord, rysterplaat; ~ **ed,** geploeg (land); gesak (eksamen); ~**-handle,** ploegstert; ~**ing,** ploeëry, ploegwerk; ~**ing season,** ploegtyd; ~**-iron,** ploegskaar; ~**-land,** ploegland; beboubare grond; ~**man,** ploeër; ~**-ox,** ploegos; ~**-plane,** verdiepskaaf; ~**share,** ploegskaar; ~**-sole,** ploegbank; ~**-tail,** ploegstert.
plo'ver, kiewiet; *live like a* ~, van liefde en koue water lewe.
ploy, gedoente, gewerskaf; werk.
pluck, (n) (waag)moed, durf, kloekheid; ruk; sak (eksamen); harslag (dier); (v) ruk, pluk; vere afpluk; laat sak, dop (eksamen); bedrieg, kul, kaal maak; ~ *AT,* trek aan; ~ *AWAY,* wegruk; ~ *up COURAGE (spirits, heart),* moed skep; ~ *LAURELS,* louere behaal; ~ *a PIGEON,* iem. bedrieg; ~ *a STUDENT,* 'n student laat sak; ~**y,** moedig, dapper.
plug, (n) prop; tap, pen, stop; spy, spie; vonkprop (motor); pluisie, kokertjie; pruimpie (tabak); (tand)stopsel, plombeersel; (kontak)sok, stopkontak, kragprop, steker (elektr.); trektou (in gemak); ~ *of a pump,* suier van 'n pomp; (v) **(-ged),** stop, toestop; digmaak, toeprop, opprop, prop insteek (elektr.); plombeer, stop (tand); tap; inslaan; ruim; swoeg, in vuishou gee; in die oor trommel (lied); ~ *AWAY at something,* vasberade volhou met 'n poging; met iets aanhou sukkel; ~ *a HOLE,* 'n gat toestop; ~ *IN,* inprop; ~ *SOMETHING,* iets gedurig adverteer; ~ **basin,** vaste wasbak; ~**-connection,** stopkontak; ~**ging,** ruimwerk; vulling; ~**hole,** propgat; ~ **box,** kontakkas; ~**-point,** vonkpunt; ~ **switch,** propskakelaar; ~**-in stove,** inpropstoof; ~**-in telephone,** inproptelefoon; ~ **tap,** propkraan; ~**-wire,** vonkpropdraad.
plum, pruim; groot fortuin; beste deel; vet baantjie.
plu'mage, vere, pluimasie.
plumassier', handelaar in siervere, pluimbereider.
plumb, (n) paslood, skietlood, dieplood; *out of* ~, uit die lood; (v) peil, sondeer; loodreg stel, waterpas maak; (a) loodreg, vertikaal, regop; sekuur; presies, beslis.
plumbago, grafiet, potlood.
plumb: ~**-bob,** dieplood, peillood, werplood; ~ **centre,** doodwaterpas; ~ **crazy,** stapelgek; ~**eous,** loodagtig, lood-; ~**er,** loodgieter; ~**ery,** loodgietery.
plumb: ~**ic,** loodhoudend, lood-; ~ **acid,** loodsuur; ~ **acetate,** loodsuiker.
plumb: ~**if'erous,** loodhoudend; ~**ing,** loodgieters-werk, soldeerwerk; sondering; ~**ism,** loodvergiftiging; ~ **level,** waterpas; ~**-line,** loodlyn, skietlood, riglyn; ~ **nonsense,** klinkklare onsin; ~**-rule,** paslood.

plum: ~ **cake,** rosyntjiekoek, vrugtekoek; ~**cot,** appelkoospruim; ~ **duff,** doekpoeding, ketelkoek, Jan-in-die-sak.
plume, (n) pluim, veer; veerbos; pluimbos; *strut about in borrowed* ~*s,* met anderman se vere pronk; (v) van vere voorsien; pronk, jou in geleende vere steek; pluk; die vere glad stryk; ~ *oneself on something,* jou op iets beroem; ~ **alum,** pluimaluin; ~**less,** sonder vere; pluimloos; ~**let,** pluimpie; ~**like,** veervormig, veeragtig.
plum'iped, met veerpote, veerpoot-.
plum'-jam, pruimkonfyt.
plum'mer-block, boklaer, staanlaer.
plumm'et, (n) peillood, dieplood, skietlood, meetlood; las; (v) peil; met 'n dieplood vasvang; neerstort.
plumm'y, pruimagtig, vol pruime, pruim-; voortreflik, begeerlik.
plu'mose, veeragtig, gepluim, geveer, pluimagtig, veervormig.
plumos'ity, geveerdheid.
plu'mous = **plumose.**
plump¹, (n) plons, plof; (v) neerval, neerplof; alle stemme aan een kandidaat gee; ~ *DOWN,* neerplof; ~ *FOR a candidate,* soos een man vir 'n kandidaat stem; alle stemme op een kandidaat konsentreer; (adv) pardoems; botweg, reguit, onomwonde, *ANSWER with a* ~ *no,* botweg weier; *he fell* ~ *into the TRAP,* hy het reguit in die val geloop.
plump², (v) sag (vet) maak; vet (dik) word; (a) vet, dik, spekvet, blinkvet; geset, mollig; *as* ~ *as a partridge,* moddervet, rondvet.
plump'er¹, pruimpie, wangprop.
plump'er², plons; growwe leuen; stemmer vir net een kandidaat.
plump'ing, saamhoping, konsentrasie (stemme).
plump: ~**ish,** vet, dikkerig; ~**ness,** vetheid, dikheid, gesetheid; welgedaanheid.
plum: ~ **pudding,** rosyntjiepoeding, doekpoeding, waterbul, Jan-in-die-sak; ~**-pudding stone,** poedingklip; ~ **tomato,** pruimtamatie; ~**-tree,** pruimboom.
plu'mule, blaartjie; veertjie, donsie.
plu'my, met vere, veer-; sag.
plun'der, (n) buit, roof, plundering; (v) buit, (be)rowe, plunder; ~**age,** buit, roof; ~**er,** plunderaar, berower, buiter.
plunge, (n) indompeling; duik; val; breking (golf); waagstuk, *ABOUT to take the* ~, trouplanne hê, al begin nes skop; *TAKE the* ~, die sprong waag; (v) indompel, onderdompel; (in)duik; plons; stort; deurdring; vorentoe spring; spekuleer, dobbel; ~ *into a CONTROVERSY,* jou in 'n strydvraag werp; ~ *into DARKNESS,* in duisternis dompel; ~ *DOWN,* neerstort; ~ *HEADLONG into danger,* jou in die gevaar stort; ~ *IN,* inspring; ~ *INTO,* jou dompel in; ~ *after a PERSON,* iem. agternaspring; ~ *into a ROOM,* 'n kamer binnestorm; ~ *someone into RUIN,* iem. in die ongeluk stort; ~*d in THOUGHT,* in gedagtes verdiep; ~ *into WAR,* met 'n oorlog begin; ~**-bath,** diep swembad; ~ **battery,** dompelbattery; ~**r,** duiker; dompelaar, suier (pomp); dobbelaar, spekulant; koker (skip); drukker; plunjer; skuiwer' ~**r-lock,** plunjerslot.
plun'ging: ~ **fire,** boorvuur; ~ **neckline,** lae halslyn; ~ **shot,** boorskoot.
plunk, (n) plof; getokkel; (v) laat plof; tokkel; ~ *down,* neersmyt.
plu'perfect, voltooid verlede tyd, plusquamperfectum.
plu'ral, (n) meervoud; (a) meervoudig; ~**ism,** pluralisme; ~**ist,** pluralis; geestelike met meer as een besoldigde amp.
plural'ity, menigte; meerderheid; pluraliteit, meervoudigheid; veelheid, talrykheid; ~ *of husbands,* veelmannery.
plur'alize, meervoudig maak.
plur'al marriage, veelwywery, poligamie.

plus, (n) plus(teken); (a) ekstra; positief (elektr.); (prep) meer, plus, daarby; ~ *or minus*, plusminus, plus of minus; ~**-fours**, kniebroek, kardoesbroek, sakbroek, pofbroek.
plush, fluweel, pluche.
plus: ~ **player**, plusspeler; ~ **sign**, plusteken.
plu'tarchy, plutoc'racy, plutokrasie, geldheerskappy, geldadel.
plu'tocrat, plutokraat, kapitalis, geldkoning, geldbaas; magnaat; ~ **'ic**, plutokraties.
plutol'atry, geldaanbidding.
pluton'ian, pluton'ic, plutonies; diepte=; *plutonic rock*, dieptegesteente.
plu'tonism, plutonisme.
plu'tonist, plutonis.
pluton'ium, plutonium.
pluton'omy, staatshuishoudkunde, plutonomie.
plu'vial, (n) priesterkleed, pluviale; (a) reënagtig, reën=; vogtig.
pluv'iograph, registrerende reënmeter, reënskrywer, pluviograaf.
pluviom'eter, reënmeter, pluviometer.
plu'vious, reënagtig, reën=.
ply, (n) **(plies)**, kronkel, vou, plooi; draad (wol); laag (hout); neiging; (v) **(plied)**, uitoefen (beroep); behartig; gebruik, hanteer; voer; oorlaai; lastig val; bestorm met; bestook (met vrae); laveer; bevaar (die see); ~ *BETWEEN*, gereeld vaar (ry) tussen; ~ *the BOTTLE*, die bottel goed aanspreek; ~ *with FOOD*, met kos volstop; ~ *for HIRE*, teen huur ry; ~ *the OARS*, kragtig roei; ~ *with QUESTIONS*, met vrae bestorm (bestook); ~ *a TRADE*, 'n beroep uitoefen; ~ *the WHIP*, die lat inlê.
Plym'outh, Plymouth; ~ **Brethren**, Darbiste, Calvinistiese Broedergemeente; ~ **Rock**, koekoek(hoender).
ply'wood, laaghout, plakhout.
pneumat'ic, (n) lugband; (a) lug=, wind=, pneumaties, lugdruk=; ~ **brake**, lugrem; ~ **dispatch tube**, lugdrukpospyp; ~ **drill**, klopboor, lugklopboor, hamerboor, lugboor; ~ **hammer**, lughamer; ~ **hoist**, lughyser; ~ **post**, lugdrukpos; ~ **pressure**, lugdruk; ~ **pump**, lugpomp; ~ **s**, lugkunde, pneumatika, pneumatiek; ~ **tyre**, lugband.
pneumatol'ogy, geesteleer, pneumatologie.
pneumatol'ysis, pneumatolise.
pneumococ'cus, (..cocci), pneumokokkus.
pneumoconios'is, pneumokoniose.
pneumon'ia, longontsteking, pneumonie.
pneumon'ic, (n) longmiddel; (a) van die longe; longontstekings=; ~ **plague**, longpes.
po, (kamer)uil, nagpot.
poach[1], (eier) sonder dop kook, kaal kook, posjeer; ~ *ed egg*, kalfsoog, kaaleier, watereier, geposjeerde eier.
poach[2], vertrap; modderig maak; deurslagtig word; stroop, wild steel; skaai, steel (tennis); ~ *on a person's preserves*, onder iem. se duiwe skiet; in iem. se kraal kom; ~ **er**, wilddief; steler, stroper, skaaier; ~ **ing**, wildstelery, stropery; stelery.
poch'ard, bruineend.
pochet'te, (koevert)handsak, pochette.
pock, pokkie.
pock'et, (n) sak (van klere); (mark)sakkie; beurs; holte, diepte; lugknik; kol, ertsholte; nes (militêr; diamante); *it is BEYOND my* ~, ek kan dit nie bekostig nie; *DIP into one's* ~, jou hand diep in jou sak steek; *EMPTY* ~, platsak; *put one's HAND in one's* ~, geld spandeer; *HAVE someone in your* ~, iem. in jou sak hê; *she has him in HER* ~, sy kan hom om haar vinger draai; sy het hom in die sak; *it makes a HOLE in one's* ~, 'n mens se sak voel dit; *I am five cents IN* ~, ek het vyf sent in my sak; *it helps to LINE one's* ~, dit bring jou iets in die sak; ~ *of ORE*, ertsholte; *be OUT of* ~, platsak wees; *put your PRIDE in your* ~, sluk maar jou trots; (v) in die sak steek; wegbêre; jou toe-eien; sluk ('n belediging); onderdruk (gevoel); stop (biljart); ~ *an INSULT*, 'n belediging sluk; ~ *SOMETHING*, iets in jou sak steek; ~ **almanac**, sakalmanak; ~ **battleship**, dwergslagskip; ~**-book**, sakboek; sakportefeulje; ~ **comb**, sakkammetjie; ~ **dictionary**, sakwoordeboek; ~ **edition**, sakuitgawe; ~ **expenses**, klein uitgawes; ~ **flap**, sakklap; ~**ful**, sakvol; ~ **glass**, sakspieëltjie; ~ **handkerchief**, sakdoek; ~**-hole**, sakopening; ~ **ing**, sakstof; verkropping; ~**-knife**, sakmes; ~**-money**, sakgeld; ~ **patriot**, sakpatriot; ~**-picking**, goudiewery, sakkerollery; ~**-piece**, gelukmunt; ~**-pistol**, sakpistool; ~**-size**, sakformaat; sakgrootte; ~**-sized**, klein; sakgrootte=, sak=; ~**-wallet**, sakportefeulje, notebeursie.
pock: ~**-mark**, pokmerk; ~**-marked**, pokdalig, mottig; ~**-wood**, pokhout; ~ **y**, pokdalig.
pococuran'te, onverskillig(e).
pod, (n) dop, peul, huls; (v) uitdop; peule dra.
podag'ra, jig, pootjie, voetjig, podagra.
pod'agral, podag'ric, pod'agrous, jigtig, podagreus.
podd'ed, peul=; welgesteld.
podge, vaatjiebuik, dikkerd, potjierol, vetsak.
podg'y, dik, vet.
podi'atrist, voetheelkundige.
podi'atry, voetheelkunde, podiatrie.
pod'ium, (podia), podium, verhoog.
podom'eter, hoefmeter.
pod'sol, pod'zol, podsol.
po'em, gedig, vers.
po'esy, digkuns, poësie.
po'et, digter, poëet; sanger, lirikus; ~ **as'ter**, rymelaar, versiemaker, pruldigter; poëtaster; ~ **ess**, (-es), digteres.
poet'ic, digterlik, poëties; ~ **licence**, digterlike vryheid; ~ **al** = **poetic**; ~ **ize**, poëtiseer; besing; ~ **s**, poëtika, verskuns.
poet laur'eate, hofdigter.
po'etry, digkuns, poësie; sang; *write* ~, dig, verse maak.
po'go (stick), stelt.
pogono'tomy, baardskeerdery.
pogrom', pogrom, bloedbad, Jodemoord.
poign'ancy, skerpheid; pynlikheid.
poign'ant, skerp, vlymend, stekerig, pynlik, smartlik; bytend; ~ *sorrow*, skrynende smart.
poincia'na, poinciana, koraalboom.
poinsett'ia, poinsettia, karlienblom.
point, (n) punt; onderwerp, kwessie; stippel; desimaalpunt; tip; landpunt; (lees)teken; plek; spits= (man) (patrollie) steek (skermkuns); tydstip; kenmerk, eienskap; doel; kompasstreek; puntigheid; wenk; stif; (pl) wissel(punt) (spoorweg); *agree on ALL* ~ **s**, in alle opsigte ooreenstem; *at ALL* ~ **s**, oral; ~ *of ATTACK*, aanvalspunt; *be quite BESIDE the* ~, nie ter sake wees nie; ~ *BY* ~, puntsgewys; *CARRY one's* ~, jou doel bereik; jou in sou kry; *a CASE in* ~, 'n toepaslike geval; *COME to a* ~, in een punt uitloop; tot 'n hoogtepunt kom; *COME to the* ~, tot die kern van die saak kom; *when it COMES to the* ~, op stuk van sake; as dit daarop aankom; ~ **s** *of the COMPASS*, kompasstreke, windstreke; ~ *of CONTACT*, raakpunt, kontakpunt; ~ **s** *and CROSSINGS*, wissels en kruisings; *at the* ~ *of DEATH*, op sterwe; ~ *of DEPARTURE*, beginpunt; vertrekpunt; ~ *of DIFFERENCE*, verskilpunt; *in* ~ *of FACT*, feitlik; in werklikheid; op stuk van sake; *not put too FINE a* ~ *upon it*, nie doekies omdraai nie; *the FINER* ~ **s**, die fyner puntjies; ~ *of FRICTION*, wrywingspunt; *GAIN a* ~, jou slag slaan; 'n punt aanteken; ~ *de GAZE*, gaaskant; *GIVE* ~ **s**, voorgee, 'n voorsprong gee; punte gee; *he can GIVE you* ~ **s**, hy kan jou iets leer; *you HAVE a* ~ *there*, jy het gelyk; jy noem 'n sterk beswaar; ~ *of HONOUR*, eresaak; ~ *of INTERSECTION*, snypunt; ~ *at ISSUE*, geskilpunt; *that is JUST the* ~, net waaroor dit neerkom; *LACK* ~, flou (laf) wees (bv. 'n grap); ~ *of LAW*, regsvraag; *MAKE a* ~ *of*, nie nalaat nie om; jou daarop toelê om; *MAKE one's* ~, jou bewering bewys; *MAKE a* ~, 'n argument aanvoer; *MISS the* ~, nie snap waaroor dit gaan nie; *a NICE* ~, 'n goeie punt; *there's NO* ~ *in your asking*, dit help nie om te vra nie; *I was ON the* ~ *of telephoning you*, ek wou jou net telefoneer; *be ON the* ~ *of*, op die punt staan om; *a* ~ *of ORDER*, 'n punt van orde; *POSSESSION is nine* ~ **s** *of the law*, salig is die besitters; *PRESS the* ~, op iets

aandring; *the* ~ *in QUESTION*, die saak waarom dit gaan; *RAISE a* ~, 'n vraag opwerp; ~ *of no RETURN*, punt waar geen terugkeer meer moontlik is nie; veiligheidskeerpunt; *he did not SEE the* ~ *of the joke*, hy het die grap nie begryp nie; *SEE someone else's* ~, iem. anders se opvatting (saak) begryp; *SEE the* ~, begryp waarom dit gaan; *that is a SORE* ~ *with him*, dis 'n teer saak; *STAND upon* ~ *s*, puntene(u)rig wees; *there is no* ~ *in STAYING any longer*, dit het geen sin om langer te bly nie; *STRETCH a* ~, dit wyer laat strek; dit nie so nou neem nie; *his STRONG* ~, sy krag lê daarin; hy munt daarin uit; *THAT is just the* ~, daar kom dit op neer (aan); *at this* ~ *in TIME*, op hierdie tydstip; *TO the* ~, ter sake; *TURN the* ~ *s*, die wissel omlê; *wander from* ~ *TO* ~, uitwei (dwaal) van een punt na die ander; *UP to a* ~, tot op sekere hoogte; *URGE the* ~, daar sterk op aandring; ~ *of VIEW*, gesigspunt; standpunt, oogpunt; *have a* ~ *of VIEW*, 'n mening huldig; *WIN on* ~ *s*, met punte wen; (v) skerp (spits) maak; wys, dui; aanpunt; instryk, voeg (messelwerk); rig, mik, aanlê (geweer); prik; aanwys (jaghond); ~ *AT*, met die vinger wys na; ~ *a FINGER of scorn at someone*, iem. met die vinger nawys; ~ *a MORAL*, 'n sedeles puntig uitdruk; ~ *OUT*, aanwys; aantoon; ~ *a PISTOL at*, aanlê op, rig op, korrel na; ~ *a SPEECH with illustrations*, 'n toespraak met voorbeelde toelig; ~ *TO*, aanwys, wys na (op); aanstip; die aandag vestig op; *the evidence* ~ *s TO murder*, die getuienis dui op moord; ~ *UP differences*, verskille beklemtoon; verskille laat uitkom.
point'-blank, tromp-op, op die man af; reguit, bot-af, botweg; *let someone HAVE it* ~, iem. tromp-op loop; iem. kaalkop aanval; *REFUSE* ~, botweg weier; ~ *FIRE (shot, range)*, tromp-op skiet.
point'-duty, verkeersdiens (paaie); wisselwagdiens (spoorweë)
point'ed, spits, skerp; geestig, gevat; puntig; ~ *BEARD*, spitsbaard; ~ *BULLET*, spitskoeël; ~ *DRILL*, puntboor; ~ *HAMMER*, punthamer, spitshamer; ~ **ly**, puntig; stip, reguit; geestig; ~**ness**, spitsheid; geestigheid.
point'er, wyser, voorvinger; Patryshond; wenk, vingerwysing; (aan)wysstok; naald; wisselwagter (spoorweë); aanwyser; etsnaald; ~**s**, twee sterre wat na die Suiderkruis wys; wysers.
point'illism, pointillisme.
point'illist, (n) pointillis; (a) pointillisties.
point'ing, voegwerk, voegstryking (messelwerk); voegvulling (teëls); prikking; aanduiding; punktuasie; kop (sweer); ~ **hammer**, prikhamer; ~ **trowel**, voegtroffel.
point: ~ **lace**, naaldkant; ~ **less**, sinloos, betekenisloos; stomp, sonder punt; geesteloos; flou, onbeduidend; nul; sonder telling; ~ *less draw*, nul-nulspel; ~ **register**, punteregister.
points'man, (..men), wisselwagter (spoorweë); verkeerswagter (paaie).
point: ~ **system**, puntstelsel; ~**to-point**, reguit; ~-*to-point race*, 'n reguit wedren.
poise, (n) ewewig; gewig; houding; gemoedsewewig; selfversekerdheid; kalmte, selfbeheersing; statigheid; regte houding; swewende toestand; onsekerheid; (v) weeg, wik; in ewewig hou, balanseer; reghou; hang, sweef; ~**d**, selfversekerd; in ewewig, statig, staatlik; gebalanseerd.
pois'on, (n) gif, vergif; *irritant* ~, prikkel(ver)gif; (v) vergiftig, vergewe; verpes; bederf; vergal, verbitter; ~ **bait**, gifaas, lokgif; ~ **bladder**, gifsakkie; ~ **cup**, gifbeker; ~**ed**, vergif, gif-; ~*ed ARROW*, gifpyl; ~*ed CUP*, gifbeker; ~**er**, vergiftiger; gifmoordenaar, -moordenares; ~**fang**, giftand; ~ **gas**, gifgas; ~**-gland**, gifklier.
pois'oning, vergiftiging.
pois'onous, (pred) giftig, vergiftig; verderflik; ~**ness**, giftigheid; verderflikheid.
pois'on: ~ **pen**, lasterskrywer; ~ **pill**, gifpil.
poke¹, (n) sak.
poke², (n) stoot, stamp; tuit (van 'n hoed); klep (van 'n pet); (v) stoot, stamp; steek; roer, (op)por, pook (vuur); ~ *ABOUT*, rondsnuffel; ~ *the FIRE*, die

vuur oppor; ~ *FUN at*, gekskeer met; *walk with one's HEAD* ~*d forward*, vooroor loop; ~ *one's NOSE into*, jou neus steek in; ~ *someone in the RIBS*, iem. in die ribbes pomp; ~**-bonnet**, tuitkappie.
pok'er¹, (n) poker(spel).
po'ker², vuuryster, stookyster, vuurhaak, pook(yster); *as STIFF as a* ~, stokstyf; *have SWALLOWED a* ~, 'n laaistok ingesluk hê; ~**-drawer**, brandskilder; ~**-drawing**, brandskildery; ~**-face**, ongevoelige (nikssegende) blik; ~**-work**, brandwerk.
pok'y, beknop, hokkerig; bekrompe; armoedig; peuterig.
Po'lack, (derog.), Polak, Pool.
Pol'and, Pole.
pol'ar, pool-; polêr; direk teenooorgesteld; ~ **air**, poollug; ~ **bear**, ysbeer, poolbeer; P~ **Circle**, Poolsirkel; P~ **Countries**, Poollande; P~ **Expedition**, Poolekspedisie; P~ **Explorer**, Poolreisiger; ~**igraph'ic**, polarigrafies; ~**i'meter**, polarimeter; ~**iscope**, polarimeter, polariskoop; ~**'ity**, polariteit; ~**iza'tion**, polarisasie; *plane of* ~ *ization*, polarisasievlak; ~**ize**, polariseer; ~ **light**, noorderlig; ~ **number**, valensiegetal, polêre getal; ~**o'graphy**, polarografie; P~ **region**, Poolstreek; p~**star**, poolster.
pol'der, (n) polder; *dike of a* ~, polderdyk; (v) (in)polder; ~ **board**, polderbestuur; ~**ing**, (in)poldering; ~ **land**, polderland.
Pole¹, Pool.
pole², (n) pool; *be* ~*s APART*, hemelsbreed verskil; soos dag en nag verskil, *ELEVATION of the* ~, *poolshoogte; GEOGRAPHIC* ~, ware pool.
pole³, (n) paal, stok, spar; disselboom (kar), roede (55 jrt.); *not to be TOUCHED with a ten-foot* ~, so vuil dat jy dit nie met 'n tang kan aanraak nie; *UP the* ~, in 'n moeilikheid; swanger; sleg, vrot; (v) pale inplant, van pale voorsien; vooruitstoot (met 'n paal), boom; ~**-axe**, (n) byl; enterbyl (skip); strydbyl; slagtersbyl, (v) met 'n byl neerslaan; ~**-bar**, disselboom.
pole'cat, (dikster t)muishond; stinkdier.
pole: ~**-chain**, borsketting, disselboomketting; ~**-climber**, paalklimmer; klimyster; ~**-horse**, agterperd; ~**-jumper**, paalspringer, polsstokspringer; ~**-jump(ing)**, polsstokspring, paalspring; ~**-lug**, disselboomkram.
polem'ic, (n) twisgeskryf, polemiek, pennestryd; (a) polemies; ~**ist**, polemikus; ~**s**, polemiek.
pol'emist, polemikus.
pol'emize, polemiseer, polemiek voer.
polen'ta, polenta, mieliepap.
pole: ~**-pin**, disselboombout, ~**-prop**, disselboomstut; ~**-sitter**, paalsitter; ~**-sitting**, paalsittery; P~**-star**, Poolster; ~**-strap**, borsriem; ~**-thread**, pooldraad; ~**-vault**, (n, v) paalspring.
police', (n) polisie; (v) van polisie voorsien; onder polisietoesig bring; die orde handhaaf; *properly* ~ *d*, onder behoorlike polisietoesig; ~ **barracks**, polisiekwartiere; ~ **commissioner**, kommissaris van polisie; ~**-constable**, konstabel; diender (vero.); ~**-court**, landdroshof; ~ **dog**, speurhond, polisiehond; ~**-drive**, klopjag; ~ **force**, polisiemag; ~ **law**, polisiewet; ~ **man**, konstabel, polisieman; ~**-officer**, polisiebeampte, konstabel; polisieoffisier; ~ **raid**, polisieklopjag; ~ **state**, polisiestaat; ~ **station**, polisiekantoor; ~ **supervision**, polisietoesig; ~**-trap**, lokval, polisieval; lokvink (persoon); ~ **watch**, polisiewag; ~**woman**, vroulike konstabel, polisievrou.
policlin'ic, buiteafdeling, polikliniek.
pol'icy¹, (..cies), staatkunde, staatsbeleid; gedragslyn, politiek; oorleg, beleid; handigheid; ~ *of equal RIGHTS*, gelykstellingsbeleid; *STATEMENT of* ~, beleidsverklaring; ~ **makers**, beleidbepalers, beleidvormers.
pol'icy², (..cies), polis; *take out a* ~, 'n polis uitneem; ~**-holder**, polishouer.
pol'io(myelit'is), kinderverlamming, polio(miëlitis).
Pol'ish¹, Pools; ~ *Corridor*, Poolse Korridor.
pol'ish², (n) waks, politoer; glans, skyn; verfyning; beskawing; (v) polys, (af)poets, blink maak; (op)vry-

we, poleer, skoonmaak; blink skuur; beskaaf, ver=
fyn; ~ *GLASS*, glas slyp; ~ *OFF*, kafloop, klaar=
speel; verslind (kos); ~ *OFF a task*, gou met 'n
werk klaarspeel; ~ *UP*, blink maak, skoonmaak;
verbeter, opknap.
pol'ished, geslyp; welgemanierd, beskaaf; gepolys, ge=
politoer; gepoleer; blink; *a* ~ *DIAMOND*, 'n ge=
slypte diamant; ~ *MANNERS*, beskaafde manie=
re; ~ *RICE*, witrys; ~ *WOOD*, gepoleerde hout.
pol'isher, poleerder, politoerder (werktuig); polyster,
poetser; slyper (diamant); poetsmiddel.
pol'ishing, polyswerk; polering; beskawing; ~ **brush,**
skoenborsel; ~ **cloth,** vryflap; ~ **iron,** verglansys=
ter; ~ **machine,** poleermasjien; slypmasjien; ~-
mill, slypmeul; ~ **mop,** poleerlap, poetsdweil; ~
powder, polyspoeier; ~ **rag,** vryflap; ~ **stone,** po=
leersteen; ~ **wax,** vryfwaks; politoer(waks); ~
wheel, poleerskyf.
po'litburo, politburo.
polite', beleef, beskaaf, verfynd, vriendelik, hoflik,
galant, welopgevoed; poliets; ~ **ness,** beleefdheid,
beskawing, manierlikheid, vriendelikheid; poliets=
heid.
polites'se, (formele) beleefdheid.
pol'itic, slim, geslepe, slu; verstandig; poliets; poli=
tiek; *the body* ~, die staatsgemeenskap.
polit'ical, staatkundig, staats=, politiek; polities; ~
allegiance, staatsverband; ~ **boundary,** landsgrens;
~ **criminal,** staatsmisdadiger, politieke misdadiger
(oortreder); ~ **economist,** staatkundige, ~ **econo=
my,** staatkunde; ~ **offence,** staatsmisdaad, politie=
ke oortreding; ~ **ly,** op staatkundige gebied; in
staatkundige opsig; polities; ~ **party,** politieke
party; ~ **philosophy,** staatsfilosofie; ~ **prisoner,**
staatsgevangene; politieke gevangene; ~ **science,**
staatswetenskap, staatsleer; ~ **system,** staatsinrig=
ting, politieke stelsel; staatsbestel.
politi'cian, politikus.
polit'icize, politiseer, aan politiek deelneem.
poli'tico, (Sp.), politikus.
pol'itics, politiek; staatkunde, staatsleer.
pol'ity, (..**ties),** staatsreëling, staatsbewind; rege=
ringsvorm.
polk, die polka dans.
pol'ka, polka; ~ **dot,** kolletjiespatroon; ~-**mazurka,**
polkamasurka.
poll¹, (n) papegaai.
poll², (n) poena, poenskop; (v) top, snoei, afknot
(boom); afknyp; afsaag (horings); (a) poenskop=.
poll³, (n) agterhoof, harspan, skedel; agterkop (perd);
stembus; stemming, stemmery; stemlys, kieserslys;
verkiesing; meningsopname; *AT the* ~ *s*, by die
stembus; *DECLARE the* ~, die uitslag bekend
maak; *DEMAND a* ~, 'n stemming eis; *GO to the*
~ *(s)*, gaan stem; *there is a HEAVY* ~, daar is
goed gestem; *be (returned) at the TOP of the* ~, die
meeste stemme op jou verenig; (v) stem; stemme
opneem, stemme kry.
pol'lack, pol'lock, pollak (kabeljou).
poll'ard, (n) knotboom; knothout; poena, poenskop
(dier); semelmeel, fynsemels; (v) knot, top, snoei;
~-**willow,** knotwilger.
poll: ~-**beast,** poena, poenskop; ~-**cattle,** poenskop=
beeste; ~-**cow,** poenskopkoei.
poll'en, (n) stuifmeel, blomstof, blompoeier; (v) be=
stuif, met stuifmeel bedek; ~-**cell,** stuifmeelsel;
helmhok; ~-**grain,** stuifmeelkorrel; ~ **ize,** met
stuifmeel bevrug; ~-**tube,** stuifmeelbuis.
poll'-excise, hoofaksyns.
poll'inate, bevrug, bestuif.
pollina'tion, bevrugting, bestuiwing.
poll'ing, stemmery, stemming; (die) snoei; ~ **booth,**
stemhokkie, stemburo; ~ **clerk,** stemopnemer; ~
day, stemdag; ~ **district,** stemdistrik; ~ **officer,**
stemopnemer, stembeampte; ~ **place,** ~ **station,**
stemkantoor, stemplek.
pollin'ical, stuifmeel=.
pollinif'erous, stuifmeelvormend.
poll'oi: *hoi* ~, hoi polloi, gepeupel, Jan Rap en sy
maat.
poll' parrot, wyfiepapegaai; kletskous, naprater.
poll: ~-**pick,** hamerpik; ~-**tax,** hoofbelasting.

pollute', besoedel, verontreinig, bevlek, vuil maak.
pollu'tion, besoedeling, verontreiniging, bevlekking.
poll'y, (pollies), papegaai.
pol'o, polo; ~ **jersey,** polotrui.
polonaise', polonaise; polonys (japon).
po'lo: ~ **neck,** polonek, rolhals; ~ **match,** polowed=
stryd.
polon'ium, polonium.
polon'y, (..**nies),** polonie.
po'lo pony, poloponie, poloperd.
pol'tergeist, kwelgees, poltergeist.
poltroon', lafaard, papbroek, bangbroek; ~ **ery,** laf=
hartigheid, bangheid, papbroekigheid.
pol'y=, veel=.
polyadel'phous, veelbroederig.
polyan'drist, vrou met meer as een man.
polyan'drous, veelmannig; veelhelmig (bot.).
polyan'dry, veelmannery; veelhelmigheid (bot.).
polyan'thus, sleutelblom, primula.
pol'yarchy, veelhoofdige regering, poliargie.
polychromat'ic, veelkleurig.
pol'ychrome, (n) veelkleurigheid, polichromie; (v)
polichromeer; (a) veelkleurig, polichroom.
pol'ychromy, beeldversiering, polichromie.
polyclin'ic, polikliniek.
polyes'ter, poliëster.
polyg'amist, poligamis, veelwywer.
polyg'amous, met meer as een vrou, veelwywery=, po=
ligaam; meerslagtig (bot.).
polyg'amy, veelwywery, poligamie.
poly genous, veelsoortig, meerslagtig.
poly'geny, meerslagtigheid.
pol'yglot, (n) veeltalige (persoon), poliglot; (a) veelta=
lig, poliglotties.
pol'ygon, veelhoek, poligoon.
polyg'onal, veelhoekig.
polyg'onum, duisendknoop, litjiesgras.
pol'ygraph, poligraaf, veelskrywer; kopieermasjien.
polyg'raphist, veelskrywer, poligraaf.
polyg'raphy, veelskrywery, poligrafie.
poly gynous, veelwywig; veelstylig (bot.); poligien
(dierk.).
polyg'yny, veelwywery; poliginie.
polyhe'dral, veelvlakkig, poliëdries.
polyhed'ron, veelvlak, poliëder.
polyhis'tor, pol'ymath, veelweter, polimaat.
pol'ymer, polimeer.
pol'ymerize, polimeriseer.
poly'merous, veeltallig, polimeer.
pol'ymorph, polimorf.
polymorph'ic, polymorph'ous, veelvormig, polimorf.
polymorph'ism, veelvormigheid, polimorfie.
Polyne'sia, Polinesië.
Polyne'sian, (n) Polinesiër; (a) Polinesies.
pol'yp(e), poliep.
polypet'alous, veelblombladig, polipetaal.
polyph'agous, polifaag, veelvretend; vraatsugtig.
polyphon'ic, meerstemmig, polifonies.
poly'phony, veelstemmigheid, polifonie.
polyphyll'ous, veelbladig.
polyplas'tic, veelvormig.
pol'ypod, veelvoetig, veelpotig; ~ **y,** veelpotigheid,
veelvoetigheid.
pol'ypous, veelarmig.
pol'ypus, (..**pi),** poliep, veelarm; uitwas.
polysperm'al, veelsadig.
pol'ystyle, (n) polistyl; (a) veelsuilig.
polysyllab'ic, veellettergrepig, polisillabies.
polysyllab'able, veellettergrepie (polisillabiese) woord.
polysyn'deton, polisindeton.
polysynthet'ic, polisinteties.
polytech'nic, (n) politegniese skool; ambagskool; (a)
politegnies; ~**s,** politegniek.
pol'ytheism, veelgodery, politeïsme.
pol'ytheist, politeïs, aanhanger van veelgoedery.
polytheis'tic, politeïsties.
pol'ythene, politeen.
polyung'ulate, meerhoewig.
pom'ace, visafval; appelmoes.
poma'ceous, appel=.
pomade', (n) pommade, haarolie, haarsalf, (v) pom=
madeer, smeer.

poman'der, reukbal.
pomat'um = **pomade**, (n).
pome, appelvrug; metaalbal.
pome'granate, granaat.
pom'elo, (-s), pomelo, bitterlemoen.
Pomeran'ia, Pommere; ~ **n**, (n) Pommer; (a) Pom=
    mers; ~ *n dog*, Pommerhond, Spitshond.
pom'iculture, vrugtekwekery.
pom'iform, appelvormig.
pomm'el, (n) (swaard)knop; saalboomknop; (v)
    (-led), moker, stamp.
pomolog'ical, vrugtekundig, pomologies.
pomol'ogist, vrugtekundige, pomoloog.
pomol'ogy, vrugtekunde, pomologie.
Pomon'a, Pomona, vrugtegodin.
pomp, prag, praal; praalvertoon; plegstatigheid,
    staatsie; ~ *and ceremony*, prag en praal.
pom'padour, pompadour (haarstyl; snit).
Pompe'ian, (n) Pompeiaan, Pompejaan; (a) Pompei=
    aans, Pompejaans.
Pompei'i, Pompeii, Pompeji.
pom'pelmoes(e), pampelmoes.
Pom'pey, Pompeius.
pom'pier ladder, brandleer.
pom'-pom[1], pompom, masjiengeweer, maxim.
pom'-pom[2], pompom(dahlia).
pom'pon, kwassie, strikkie.
pompos'ity, verwaandheid, praalsug; hoogdrawend=
    heid; geswollenheid, gewigtigdoenery.
pom'pous, praalsugtig, luisterryk; verwaand, groot=
    doenerig, hoogdrawend, geswolle; ~ **ness** = **pom=
    posity**.
pon'cho, poncho.
pond, (n) dam, vywer; (v) opdam, dam; ~ **age**, op=
    damming.
pon'der, peins, dink; oorweeg, besin; mymer; ~
    (over) a question, nadink oor 'n vraag, 'n vraag
    oordink; ~ **abil'ity**, oorweegbaarheid; ~ **able**, oor=
    weegbaar.
ponderos'ity, swaarte, gewig, swaarwigtigheid; om=
    slagtigheid.
pon'derous, swaar, gewigtig; swaarwigtig; lomp; om=
    slagtig, vervelend; ~ **ness** = **ponderosity**.
Pon'do, Pondo, ~ **land**, Pondoland.
pone, Indiaanse mieliebrood.
pongee, ongebleikte Sjinese sy, pongee.
pon'go, mensaap.
pon'iard, (n) dolk, ponjaard; (v) ponjaardeer, met 'n
    dolk steek.
pont', pont.
pon'tac, pontak.
Pon'tic Sea, Swart See.
pon'tifex, (..fices), hoëpriester; biskop; pous.
pon'tiff, hoëpriester; pous; biskop.
pontif'ical, hoëpriesterlik; pontifikaal; pouslik; bis=
    koplik; *the P~ State*, die Kerklike Staat.
pontif'icate, pontifikaat; opperpriesterskap; pouslike
    waardigheid.
pon'tify, (..fied), jou onfeilbaar hou, die rol van pous
    speel.
Pont'ine[1]: ~ **Marshes**, die Pontynse Moerasse.
pont'ine[2]: ~ **artery**, brugslagaar.
pontoneer', pontonnier, pontwerker.
pontoon', (n) ponton; pontonbrug; pontondok, dryf=
    dok; (v) 'n pontonbrug bou; ~ **bridge**, ponton=
    brug; ~ **corps**, pontonnierskorps; ~ **train**, ponton=
    trein.
pon'y, **(ponies)**, ponie, bossiekop; ~-**tail**, perdestert;
    poniestert (haarstyl); ~ **trap**, karretjie.
poo'dle, (n) Poedel; (v) knip, skeer (hond); ~-**faker**,
    meisiesgek.
poof(ter), homoseksueel, poefter, moffie.
pooh! bog! kaf!
Pooh-Bah', groot kokkedoor, grootmeneer.
pooh-pooh', die neus optrek vir, met minagting be=
    handel.
poo'ka, kabouter.
poo'koo, rooi waterbok.
pool[1], (n) poel, dammetjie; vywer; kuil; swembad; (v)
    graaf.
pool[2], (n) trust, ring, sindikaat; pot, potgeld, inset,
    speelgeld; poel; (v) saamgooi, saambring, gemene

beurs maak, kombineer, kapitaal bymekaarsit,
saammaak, saamwaag; poel; gesamentlik uitvoer;
winste deel.
pool'ing, saamvoeging, saamstorting; winsdeling.
pool' system, bankstelsel, potstelsel; poelstelsel.
poop, (n) agterdek, agterstewe; ellendeling; niksnuts;
    haas, skaap, onbenullige vent; (v) mis (slaan)
    (gholf).
poor, (n) armes, arm mense; *the ~ in SPIRIT*, die
    armes van gees; *the ~ are always with US*, die ar=
    mes is altyd by ons; (a) arm, behoeftig, berooid,
    armoedig, haweloos; power, skamel; skraal, dor;
    armsalig, ongelukkig; minderwaardig; beskeie, ne=
    derig; prullerig; gering; floutjies, flou (grap); ver=
    boep (dier); ~ *APPETITE*, slegte eetlus; ~ *AT=
    TENDANCE*, swak opkoms; ~ *as a CHURCH
    MOUSE*, straatarm; *a ~ CONSOLATION*, 'n
    skrale troos; oëtroos; ~ *CREATURE (devil)*,
    arme vent; ~ *EXCUSE*, flou ekskuus; ~ *FEL=
    LOW*, arme drommel; *HAVE a ~ opinion of*, nie
    veel dink nie van; *in ~ HEALTH*, nie heeltemal
    gesond nie, sieklik; *it's a ~ HEART that never re=
    joices*, net suurknolle lag nooit; *in my ~
    OPINION*, na my beskeie mening; ~ *in QUA=
    LITY* van 'n swak gehalte; *a ~ SECOND*, tweede,
    maar ver agter die eerste; ~ *VISIBILITY*, slegte
    sig; ~-**box**, armbus; ~-**house**, armhuis; **P~-law**,
    Armewet; ~ **ly**, siek(lik), ongesteld; armsalig, ellen=
    dig, arm; gemeen; sleg; skrappies, skraps, skrap=
    sies, smalletjies; *be ~ ly off*, dit nie ruim hê nie;
    ~**ness**, armoede; skraalheid, skraalte; minderwaar=
    digheid; ~-**rate**, armebelasting; ~-**relief**, armever=
    sorging; ~-**spirited**, lafhartig, papbroek(er)ig; ~
    whites, armblankes.
pop[1], (n) volkskonsert; popkonsert; (a) pop=, populêr.
pop[2], (n) pappie.
pop[3], (n) knal, slag, plof; kol, merk; bruisdrank; (v)
    (-ped), skiet, knal, klap; verpand; plotseling ver=
    skyn; ~ *AT*, skiet na; ~ *DOWN*, neersmyt; neer=
    val; ~ *one's HEAD out*, jou kop uitsteek; ~ *IN*,
    inwip, 'n oomblikkie kuier; ~ *INTO bed*, in die bed
    spring (wip); ~ *the KETTLE on*, gou die ketel op=
    sit; ~ *OFF*, uit die weg ruim; doodgaan; ~ *a
    QUESTION*, 'n vraag opwerp; ~ *the QUES=
    TION*, die jawoord vra; ~ *ROUND to the shop*,
    gou winkel toe gaan; ~ *UP*, opduik; (interj) ker=
    plaks! poef!; ~**corn**, springmielies, kiepiemielies.
pope[1], Russiese priester.
pope[2], pous; ~**dom**, pousdom; ~**hood**, pousskap;
    ~**ry**, pousgesindheid; papistery; ~**'s nose**, stuitjie
    (van hoender).
pop: ~ **eye**, uitpeuloog, puiloog; ~-**eyed**, met uitpui=
    lende oë; ~ **gun**, propgeweertjie; speelgeweertjie;
    ~-**hole**, pafgat.
pop'injay, papegaai; grootprater, grootbek, wind=
    buks.
pop'ish, pouslik, paaps, Rooms.
pop'lar, populier' ~-**grove**, populierbos; ~-**tree**, po=
    pulier(boom); ~-**wood**, populierhout.
pop'lin, popelien.
popli'teal, waai=.
pop: ~ **music**, popmusiek; ~ **orchestra**, poporkes.
popp'et, blok; skattebol, skatlam, meisiemens; skag=
    toring; ~-**head**, hyswerk (van myn); ~-**valve**,
    stootklep.
popp'ied, vol papawers, papawer=.
popp'ing, geknal; ~ **crease**, kolfstreep (kr.).
pop'ple, (n) geklots, geborrel; (v) kabbel, klots, bor=
    rel.
popp'y, **(poppies)**, papawer; *Iceland ~*, Yslandse pa=
    pawer; ~**cock**, bog, kaf; *it's all ~cock*, dis kaf, dis
    bogpraatjies; dis larie.
pop'-shop, pandjieshuis.
pop' singer, popsanger.
pop'sy(-wopsy), skatlief, hartlam.
pop'ulace, bevolking; menigte, gepeupel, gespuis,
    plebs, skorriemorrie.
pop'ular, populêr, bemind, gewild, mode=, gesog; ge=
    woon, algemeen; volks=; verstaanbaar, eenvoudig;
    ~ *with*, bemind by; ~ **art**, volkskuns; ~ **belief**,
    volksgeloof; ~ **concert**, volkskonsert; ~ **custom**,
    volksgewoonte; ~ **enlightenment**, volksvoorlig=

populate

ting; ~ **error,** algemene fout; volksdwaling; ~ **etymology,** volksetimologie; ~ **fallacy,** algemene dwaling; ~ **favour,** volksguns; ~ **'ity,** populariteit, volksguns, gewildheid; ~**iza'tion,** popularisasie; ~**ize,** populariseer, bekend maak; ~**ly,** algemeen, onder die volk, populêr; ~*ly known as,* algemeen bekend as; ~ **myth,** volksmite; ~ **song,** volksliedjie; populêre liedjie; ~ **tradition,** volksoorlewering; ~ **vote,** volkstem; ~ **word,** modewoord.
pop'ulate, bevolk.
popula'tion, bevolking, inwoners; ~ **census,** volkstelling; ~ **explosion,** bevolkingsontploffing; ~ **register,** bevolkingsregister.
pop'ulous, volkryk, dig bevolk; ~**ness,** volkrykheid.
porb'eagle, haringhaai.
por'cate, geriffel, met riwwe.
por'celain, porselein; ~ **clay,** porseleinaarde, kaolien; ~ **dish,** porseleinskottel; ~ **factory,** porseleinfabriek; ~**ize,** in porselein verander; ~ **lacquer,** porseleinlak; ~**ware,** porseleinware.
porcellan'eous, porcell'anous, porselein=, porselein= agtig.
porch, (-es), (voor)portaal, portiek.
por'cine, vark=, varkagtig.
porc'upine, ystervark; ~ **quill,** ystervarkpen.
pore¹, (n) sweetgaatjie, porie.
pore², (v) tuur, aandagtig kyk; bepeins, diep dink; ~ *one's EYES out,* jou oë gedaan lees, jou blind lees; ~ *OVER,* verdiep wees in; aandagtig oorweeg; goed bestudeer.
pore'-bearing fungus, gaatjieswam *(Polyporaceae).*
porg'y, (..**gies),** steenbrasem.
por'iform, soos 'n porie, porie=.
por'ing, getuur.
pork, varkvleis; ~**-butcher,** varkslagter; ~**-butchery,** varkslagtery; ~ **chop,** varkkarmenaadjie; ~ **cutlet,** varkribbetjie; ~**er,** vleisvark, voervark; ~ **fat,** lardeervet, varkvet; ~**ling,** speenvark(ie); ~**-measels,** varkmasels; ~ **pie,** varkpastei; ~**-pie hat,** plat hoed (vir mans); ~ **rind,** swoerd; ~ **sausage,** varkwors; ~**-wood,** spekhout; ~**y,** vet; vark=, varkagtig.
pornog'rapher, pornograaf.
pornograph'ic, pornografies.
pornog'raphy, pornografie.
poros'ity, poreusheid.
por'ous, poreus.
porph'yrite, porfiriet.
porphyrit'ic, porfier bevattend, porfiries, porfier=.
porph'yry, porfier; porfirie.
porp'oise, seevark, bruinvis, tornyn.
porrect', uitstrek; ~**ed,** uitgestrek.
po'rridge, pap; *keep one's breath to cool one's* ~, liewers stilbly; jou raad vir jouself hou; ~ **bowl,** papbord.
po'rringer, kommetjie, bakkie; diepbord.
port¹, (n) poort(wyn).
port², (n) houding; voorkome, voorkoms.
port³, (n) bakboord; *ON the* ~ *side,* aan bakboord; *PUT the helm to* ~, die roer na bakboord (links) gooi; (v) na bakboord stuur.
port⁴, (n) hawe; hawestad; ingang, poort; ~ *of CALL,* aanlêhawe, aanloophawe; ~ *of DEPARTURE,* afvaarhawe; ~ *of EMBARKATION,* inskeephawe; ~ *of EXPORT,* uitvoerhawe; *FREE* ~, vrye hawe; *IN* ~, in die hawe; ~ *of LADING,* laaihawe; *PUT in at a* ~, 'n hawe binneloop; ~ *of REFUGE,* vrye hawe; *any* ~ *in a STORM,* alles is welkom in geval van nood.
port⁵, (v) (wapen, geweer) skuins teen die lyf hou.
portabil'ity, draagbaarheid; verplaasbaarheid.
port'able, draagbaar; vervoerbaar; verplaasbaar; ~ **forge,** veldblaasbalk; ~ **radio,** draradio; ~ **telephone,** veldtelefoon; ~**s,** roerende goed.
port' admiral, hawekommandant.
port'age, (n) dra(ag)loon; (die) vervoer; (v) dra, vervoer.
por'tal, deur; poort; ingang; ~ **gate,** portaalhek; ~ **vein,** poortaar.
port'ative, draagbaar, vervoerbaar; draag=.
port: ~**-bar,** hawebank; ~ **business,** hawebedryf; ~ **captain,** hawekaptein; ~ **charges,** hawegeld;

positive

~**cull'is, (-es),** valpoort; ~ **doctor,** hawedokter; ~ **dues,** hawegeld.
porte-cochère, (F.), dekingang, porte cochère.
Porte: *The Sublime (Ottoman)* ~, die Verhewe Porte (Turkse Regering).
portend', voorspel, bedui, aankondig, beteken.
port'ent, voorteken; wonder.
porten'tous, gewigtig; veelbetekenend; onheilspellend; ~**ness,** onheilspellendheid; gewigtigheid; veelbetekenendheid.
port'er¹, portier, deurwagter.
port'er², kruier, pakdraer, pakkiesdraer, draer (spoorweg); porterbier; ~**age,** dra(ag)loon, kruiersloon; ~**house,** bierhuis; ~**house steak,** lendebiefstuk.
port' facilities, hawegeriewe, hawegeleentheid; haweinrigtings.
portfol'io, (-s), portefeulje; ministerspos; aandeleportefeulje; tas, sak; *Minister without P* ~, Minister sonder Portefeulje.
port'hole, geskutpoort; patryspoort, kajuitvenster.
port'ico, (-s), voorportaal, portiek, oordekte suilegang.
portière', deurgordyn.
por'tion, (n) deel, porsie, gedeelte; aandeel; erfdeel; (v) (ver)deel, uitdeel; 'n bruidskat gee; ~ *out,* uitdeel; ~**less,** sonder bruidskat; onterf.
Port Jack'son, geelboom, goudwilger, Port Jacksonboom *(Acacia cyanophylla).*
Port'land cement, portlandsement.
port: ~ **last,** dolboord; ~**-lid,** deur van 'n geskutpoort; ~ **light,** bakboordlig.
port'liness, swaarlywigheid; welgedaanheid; deftigheid, statigheid.
port'ly, swaarlywig, vet, dik; deftig, statig.
portman'teau, (-s, -x), handsak, reistas, handkoffer, valies, portmanteau.
portola'no, portolano
port'rait, portret; beeld, skildering; ~ **hook,** portrethakie; ~**ist,** portretskilder; ~ **painter,** portretskilder; ~**ure,** portret, afbeelding; skildering; portretkuns.
portray', afbeeld, skilder, uitteken, portretteer; beskrywe; ~**al,** beskrywing; afbeelding, skildering; ~**er,** skrywer, beskrywer; skilder.
port'reeve, (hist.), burgemeester; onderburgemeester.
port' regulations, hawereglement.
port'ress, (-es), portierster.
Port'ugal, Portugal.
Portuguese', (n) Portugees; (a) Portugees; ~ **man-of-war,** Portugese oorlogskip; bloublasie, bloukwint.
por'y, poreus.
pose, (n) houding, pose; aanstellery; (v) poseer, figureer; 'n houding aanneem; uitkom (dominospel); verleë maak, vasvra, lastige vrae stel; uithang; deurgaan vir; ~ *AS,* jou voordoen as; jou uitgee vir; ~ *for a PHOTO,* poseer vir 'n foto; ~**r,** strikvraag; raaisel; aansteller.
posh, swierig, deftig.
pos'ing, posering; aanstellery.
pos'it, as feit aanneem, postuleer.
posi'tion, (n) toestand; posisie; stand, stelling, ligging; houding; rang, status, staat; betrekking, pos, amp; *ADOPT (assume) a* ~, 'n houding aanneem; ~ *of AFFAIRS,* die stand van sake; die toestand; ~ *of EQUILIBRIUM,* ewewigstand; *FINANCIAL* ~, geldelike omstandighede; *GEOGRAPHICAL* ~, geografiese ligging; *of HIGH* ~, hooggeplaas; *IN* ~, in sy plek, reg; *be in NO* ~ *to,* nie by magte om; *NOT in a* ~ *to,* nie by magte nie om; nie in staat nie om; *OUT of* ~, nie op sy plek nie; ~ *of REST,* russtand; *TAKE up a* ~, 'n standpunt inneem; *TAKE a* ~, 'n stelling inneem (verower); ~ *of TRUST,* vertrouenspos; (v) plaas, opstel; die plek bepaal van.
posi'tional, wat 'n posisie betref; stelling=, posisioneel, posisie=; ~ *PLAY,* posisionele spel; ~ *WARFARE,* stellingoorlog.
posi'tion: ~**ed:** *well* ~*ed,* goed geplaas; goed geleë; ~**ing,** plasing; plekbepaling.
pos'itive, (n) positief (fotografie); werklikheid; stellende trap (gram.); *two Sir P* ~*s can scarce meet*

without a skirmish, twee harde stene maal nie; (a) bevestigend, positief; pertinent, stellig, bepaald, vas, beslis, uitdruklik; seker; *BE ~ that,* stellig meen dat . . .; ~ *PROOF,* 'n stellige (positiewe) bewys; *be QUITE ~,* volkome seker (positief) wees, doodseker wees; ~ **degree,** stellende trap; ~ **electricity,** positiewe elektrisiteit; ~ **philosophy,** positivistiese wysbegeerte; positivisme; ~ **proof,** positiewe bewys; ~ **quantity,** positiewe getal; ~ **sign,** plusteken; ~ **ly,** stellig, beslis, seker; positief; ~**ness,** sekerheid, stelligheid, versekerdheid, beslistheid.
pos'itivism, positivisme.
pos'itivist, positivis; ~ **'ic,** positivisties.
pos'itron, positron, positief gelaaide elektron.
poso'logy, posologie.
poss'e, agtervolgingsgroep, kommando, posse.
possess', besit, hê; bemagtig, jou meester maak van; beheers; geniet; vervul; ~ *oneself,* jou beheers.
possess'ed, besete, gepla, gekwel; ~ *by a DEVIL,* deur 'n duiwel besete; *what ~ him to DO such a thing?,* wat het hom besiel (makeer) om so iets te doen?; *be ~ with an IDEA,* vervul wees van 'n denkbeeld; besete deur 'n gedagte; *LIKE one ~,* soos 'n besetene.
posse'ssion, besitting, besit, eiendom; besetenheid; beheersing; *BE in ~ of,* besit; *with IMMEDIATE ~,* om dadelik aanvaar te word; met onmiddellike inbesitneming; *IN the ~ of,* in besit van; ~ *is nine POINTS of the law,* lig is hê, maar kry is die kuns; salig is die besitters; *TAKE ~ of,* besit neem van; *TAKE ~ of one's own,* neem wat jou is.
possess'ive, (n) besitlike voornaamwoord; tweede naamval; (a) besitlik; besittend; possessief; ~ **case,** tweede naamval; ~ **pronoun,** besitlike voornaamwoord; ~ **ness,** besitlikheid.
possess'or, besitter, eienaar; ~**y,** besit-, besittend.
possibil'ity, (..**ties),** moontlikheid, gebeurlikheid; *she cannot by any ~ DO it,* sy kan dit onmoontlik doen; *there IS a ~ that,* daar bestaan 'n moontlikheid dat; *within the RANGE of ~,* dis moontlik.
poss'ible, (n) maksimum; voltal; hoogste aantal punte; uiterste; (pl) moontlikes; (a) moontlik, gebeurlik; uitvoerbaar; denklik; doenlik; eventueel; *DO all that is ~,* doen wat in jou vermoë is; *EVERYTHING ~,* al wat moontlik is; *IF ~,* indien moontlik; *MAKE ~,* moontlik maak; *only one ~ MAN among them,* net een geskikte man onder hulle; *the ONLY ~ man,* die enigste geskikte man.
poss'ibly, moontlik, miskien, straks, dalk.
poss'um, buidelrot; *play ~,* jou dood hou; siekte voorwend.
post¹, (n) stut, paal, styl (deur); stander, pilaar, (mynb.); (v) aanplak; bekend maak.
post², (n) pos; posisie, betrekking; wag; fort; poskantoor; poswese, posdiens; pospapier; standplaas; *AT his ~,* op sy pos; *BY ~,* per pos; *FILL a ~,* 'n pos vul; ~ *of HONOUR,* erepos; *the LAST ~,* die laaste pos; die laaste taptoe; *MINISTER of P~s and Telegraphs,* Minister van Pos- en Telegraafwese; *by RETURN of ~,* per kerende pos; *RIDE ~,* die pos ry; vinnig ry; (v) pos; oorboek; stasioneer, op wag sit, posteer; vinnig ry, jaag; byhou; *BE well ~ ed,* goed op hoogte wees; ~ *an ENTRY,* 'n pos boek; *KEEP ~ed,* op hoogte hou; *a LEDGER duly ~ed up,* 'n grootboek behoorlik bygehou; ~ *OUT,* uitwys; ~ *a SENTINEL,* 'n wag plaas, ~ *a SHIP,* aankondig dat 'n skip vermis word; ~ *UP,* opplak; iem. goed op hoogte van sake hou.
post³-, na-.
post'age, posgeld, frankeerkoste; vrag; *additional ~,* strafport; ~ **due,** posgeld verskuldig; ~ **-due stamp,** boeteseël; ~ **paid,** porto (posgeld) betaal; ~ **prepaid,** posgeld vooruitbetaal; ~ **rate,** postarief; ~ **stamp,** posseël.
post'-abdomen, agterbuik.
post'agram, telegrambrief.
pos'tal, pos-; ~ **article,** posstuk; ~ **connection,** posverbinding; ~ **guide,** posgids; ~ **messenger,** posbode; ~ **note,** posbewys; ~ **official,** posbeampte; ~ **order,** posorder; ~ **parcel,** pospakket; ~ **rate,** postarief; ~ **service,** posdiens; ~ **system,** poswese; ~

tariff, postarief; ~ **traffic,** posverkeer; ~ **train,** postrein; ~ **union,** posunie; ~ **unit,** poseenheid.
post'-bag, possak, briewesak.
post'-bellum, (van) na die oorlog.
post: ~ **-box,** posbus; ~ **-boy,** briewebesteller, posbode; ~ **card,** poskaart; ~ **-cart,** poskar; ~ **-car(t) driver,** posryer; ~ **-chaise,** poskar; ~ **code,** poskode.
post'-date, (n) later datum.
post-date', (v) vooruit dateer, later dateer, postdateer; ~ **d,** later gedateer, vooruit gedateer; ~ *d cheque,* vooruit gedateerde tjek.
post'-day, posdag.
post-diluv'ian, (n) mens van na die sondvloed, postdiluviaan; (a) (van) na die sondvloed, postdiluviaans.
posteen', posteen, skaapveljas.
post-en'try, laat inskrywing; later boeking.
pos'ter, vertoonbord; aanplakbiljet, plakkaat; aanplakker; *illustrated ~,* prentplakkaat.
poste restante', poste restante.
poster'ior, (n) agterstel; agterent; (a) later; agterste; ~**s,** agterste, agterent.
poste'rity, nageslag, nakomelingskap.
pos'tern, (n) agterdeur, geheime ingang, agterpoort, sydeur; (a) agter-.
post'-fix, (n) (-es), agtervoegsel.
post-fix', (v) (letters) byvoeg aan die end; agtervoeg.
post'-free, posvry, franko, gefrankeer(d).
post-gla'cial, (van) na die Ystyd.
post-grad'uate, (n) gegradueerde; (a) nagraads.
post-haste, in aller yl, met groot haas.
post'hole digger, gatgrawer.
post: ~ **-horn,** posbeuel; ~ **-horse,** posperd.
post'humous, (kind) na die dood van sy vader gebore; nadoods, postuum; ~ *CHILD,* nakind; ~ *WRITINGS,* nagelate werke; ~ **ly,** na die dood, postuum.
posti'che, postiche, vals haartooisel.
pos'til, kanttekening, kommentaar.
postil(l)'ion, voorryer, postiljon.
post-impressionism, postimpressionisme.
post-impress'ionist, (n) postimpressionis; (a) postimpressionisties.
post'ing, (die) pos; indeling, plasing; inskrywing, inboeking; ~ **-bill,** aanplakbiljet; ~ **-box,** posbus, briewebus.
post'lude, naspel.
post: ~ **man,** posbode, briewebesteller; ~ **mark,** (n) posmerk, posstempel, afstempeling; (v) stempel; ~ **marked,** gestempel; ~ **master,** posmeester; ~ **master-general,** (~ **masters-general),** posmeester-generaal; ~ **mastership,** posmeesterskap.
post-matricula'tion, na-matrikulasie-.
post'-mature, oortydig.
post-millen'nialism, post-millennialisme.
post'mistress, (-es), posmeesteres.
post-mort'em, (n) lykskouing, post mortem; nabetragting; (a) na die dood, nadoods; ~ *examination,* lykskouing (mense); nadoodse ondersoek.
post-natal, na die geboorte; ~ *care,* kraaminasorg.
post-nup'tial, na die huwelik; ~ *debts,* nahuwelikse skulde.
post: ~ **office,** poskantoor; ~ **-office box,** (pos)bus; ~ **-office order,** posorder; ~ **-office savings bank,** posspaarbank.
post'-operative, na 'n operasie.
post'-paid, gefrankeer(d), posgeld betaal.
postpon'able, verskuifbaar, kan uitgestel word.
postpone', uitstel, verskuiwe, verdaag, opskort; *MEETING ~ d to next month,* vergadering uitgestel tot volgende maand; ~ **ment,** uitstel, verskuiwing, opskorting.
postpon'ing, uitstel, gesloer.
postposi'tion, agtersetsel; agtersetting.
postpran'dial, na die maaltyd, tafel-; ~ **speech,** tafelrede.
post'script, naskrif, byskrif.
pos'tulancy, kandidaatskap, postulantskap.
pos'tulant, sollisitant, kandidaat, postulant.
pos'tulate, (n) postulaat, veronderstelling; hipotese; aksioma; (v) veronderstel, sonder bewys aanneem, postuleer, vooropstel; eis, aanspraak maak op.

postula'tion, veronderstelling; versoek; eis.
pos'ture, (n) houding, postuur; stand, toestand; (v) plaas; poseer; 'n houding gee (aanneem); ~-**dance,** houdingsdans; ~-**maker,** akrobaat; slangmens; ~-**master,** kallistenieonderwyser.
post'-war, na die oorlog, na-oorlogs.
pos'y, (posies), ruiker; ringversie.
pot, (n) pot; kan; blompot; kamerpot, nagpot; stormhoed; silwervaas; *keep the* ~ *BOILING,* die pot aan die kook hou; sorg dat die skoorsteen rook; *that can't keep the* ~ *BOILING,* daar sal die skoorsteen nie van rook nie; *there is DEATH in the* ~, die dood skuil in die pot; dis 'n dooie boel; *GO to* ~, gaan na die hoenders; heeltemal verwaarloos raak; *the* ~ *calls the KETTLE black,* die pot verwyt die ketel; *have KISSED the* ~, het die potte gelek; ~ *s of MONEY,* baie geld; geld soos bossies; *PUT on a lot of* ~, pronk; 'n aanstellerige houding aanneem; *SHOOT for the* ~, wild skiet om self te gebruik; vir die pot skiet; (v) **(-ted),** inmaak, inlê; oppot; in 'n pot plant; stop (biljart); neerskiet, omkap; gryp; ~ *AT,* skiet na; ~ *OUT,* verpot.
potabil'ity, drinkbaarheid.
pot'able, drinkbaar; ~**ness,** drinkbaarheid; ~**s,** drank, drinkgoed.
potam'ic, rivier=.
potamog'raphy, rivierbeskrywing, potamografie.
potamol'ogy, rivierkunde, potamologie.
pot'ash, potas, kali, kalium.
potass'ium, kalium.
pota'tion, drinkparty, (die) drink, suip; drinkgelag, drinkparty.
potat'o, (-es), ertappel, aartappel; *a HOT* ~, 'n netelige kwessie, 'n turksvy; *drop something like a HOT* ~, iets soos 'n warm patat(ta) los; ~ *es in JACKETS,* ongeskilde ertappels; *MASHED* ~ *es,* kapokertappels; *speak with a hot* ~ *in one's MOUTH,* praat of jy warm pap in jou mond het; *that's QUITE a* ~, dis net die ding; *think SMALL* ~ *es of something,* niks van iets dink nie; iets as onbeduidend beskou; ~ **beetle,** coloradokewer; ~ **blight,** ertappelroes; ~ **chips,** ertappelskyfies; ~ **disease,** ertappelsiekte, vrotpootjie; ~ **famine,** ertappelskaarste; ~ **flour,** ertappelmeel; ~ **foliage,** ertappellowwe; ~ **fritter,** ertappelpoffertjie; ~ **lifter,** ertappeluithaler; ~-**masher,** fynmaker; ~ **peel,** ertappelskil; ~ **peeler,** ertappelskiller; ~ **puff,** ertappelbolletjie; ~-**rot,** ertappelsiekte, vrotpootjie; ~ **salad,** ertappelslaai; ~ **stew,** ertappelbredie.
pot: ~-**barley,** nie-uitgedopte gars; ~-**bellied,** dikbuikig; ~-**belly,** halfaampie, dikbuik, bierbuik, vaatjiebuik, boepens; ~-**black,** potswartsel; ~-**boiler,** broodskrywer; geskrif om den brode; ~-**boy,** kelner, kroegbediende; ~-**clay,** potklei; ~-**companion,** drinkmaat, drinkebroer.
pot'ency, mag, vermoë, krag, sterkte.
pot'ent, magtig, kragtig, sterk, koppig; *a* ~ *brew,* 'n kragtige (sterk) brousel.
pot'entate, potentaat, vors, heerser, maghebber.
poten'tial, (n) potensiaal, vermoë; moontlikheid; (a) gebeurlik, moontlik, latent, potensieel; ~ **buyers,** moontlike kopers; ~ **difference,** potensiaalverskil; ~ **energy,** potensiële energie; ~ **'ity,** (..ties), potensialiteit; moontlikheid, gebeurlikheid; ontwikkelingsmoontlikheid.
pot: ~-**fire,** soldeervuur; kuilvuur; ~ **handle,** pothingsel.
poth'er, (n) rumoer, geraas, gehaspel, lawaai; wolk, rookwolk, stofwolk; *make a* ~, 'n bohaai maak; (v) raas, lawaai opskop; 'n bohaai maak, kabaal maak.
pot: ~-**herb,** kruiegroente; ~-**holder,** vatlap, potlap; ~-**hole,** slaggat (in pad); rotsholte, kolkgat, maalgat (geol.); ~-**hook,** hanepoot; pothingsel; ~-**house,** bierhuis, kantien; ~-**hunter,** platskieter; potjagter; prysjagter; eersoeker; ~-**hunting,** jag vir die pot; eersoekery; prysjag.
po'tion, drank; dosis; gifdrank.
pot: ~ **ladle,** potlepel; ~ **lid,** potdeksel; ~ **luck,** wat die pot verskaf; *take* ~ *luck with us,* vir lief neem wat by ons te ete is; tevrede wees met wat die pot verskaf; ~-**money,** inlêgeld.

poto'meter, potometer.
pot' plant, potplant, stoepplant.
pot-pourri', potpourri, allerleitjies, mengelmoes; gedroogde blare en speserye.
pot: ~ **sherd,** potskerf; ~ **roast,** (n) potbraaistuk; (v) potbraai; ~-**shot,** potskoot; tromp-op skoot; ~-**still,** stookketel.
pott'age, sop, pap; *a MESS of* ~, 'n skottel lensies; *SELL for a mess of* ~, vir 'n skottel lensiesop verkoop.
pott'ed, ingemaak; ~ *MEAT,* ingemaakte vleis, blikkiesvleis; ~ *PLANT,* potplant.
pott'er¹, (n) pottebakker.
pott'er², (v) prutsel, peusel, peuter; knoei; sukkel; ~ *ABOUT,* knoeiwerkies verrig, doelloos peuter; rondskarrel; ~ *AWAY,* verbeusel, vermors; ~**er,** peuteraar; ~**ing,** gesukkel; peuselwerk.
pott'er: ~'**s clay,** potklei; ~'**s field,** begraafplek vir armes; ~'**s wheel,** pottebakkerskyf; ~**y,** (..ries), pottebakkery; erdewerk; pottebakkerswinkel.
pot'ting shed, tuinskuurtjie.
po'ttle, vrugtemandjie.
pot: ~**ty,** beuselagtig, nietig, niksbeduidend, bog; mal; ~-**valiant,** drankdapper; ~ **valour,** drankmoed, brandewynmoed; ~ **valve,** potklep.
pouch, (n) **(-es),** sak, tabakssak; beurs; patroonsak; buidel (dier); krop (voël); (v) insluk, opsluk; in die sak steek, jou toe-eien; 'n fooi gee; opbol.
poudrette', poeiermis.
pouffe, rol vals hare; sitkussing, poef.
poulp(e), seekat.
poult, kalkoenkuiken; kuiken (van pluimvee).
poul'terer, pluimveehandelaar, poelier.
poul'tice, (n) pap; (v) pap opsit.
poul'try, pluimvee; gevoëlte; ~-**farmer,** pluimveeboer; eierboer; ~-**farming,** pluimveeboerdery; ~-**food,** pluimveevoer, hoendervoer; ~-**house,** hoenderhuis; ~-**rearing,** pluimveeteelt, hoenderteelt; ~-**run,** pluimveekamp(ie); ~-**yard,** hoenderkamp(ie), hoenderhok.
pounce¹, (n) klou, poot; aanval; (v) aanval, neerskiet op; gryp; ~ *upon,* neerskiet op, neerval op.
pounce², (n) strooisand; houtskoolpoeier; (v) bestrooi (poeier); ~-**box,** sandstrooier.
poun'cet-box, reukdosie.
pound¹, (n) pond (gewig; geld); ~ *for* ~ *BASIS,* pond-vir-pond-basis; *want one's* ~ *of FLESH,* wil hê wat jou toekom; ~ *STERLING,* pond sterling.
pound², (n) skut (diere); (v) skut (diere).
pound³, (v) vergruis, stamp, (ver)maal, fynstamp; afkamp; oorspring; slaan, moker, beuk (golwe); bestook, papslaan; bombardeer, beskiet; klop (vleis); ~ *to pieces,* fyngoed maak.
pound'age¹, kommissie per pond; pondgeld.
pound'age², skutgeld.
pound'-cake, pondkoek.
pound'er¹, ponder.
pound'er², stamper; vysel.
pound'ing, gebeuk; beskieting; ~ **mill,** stampmeul.
pound: ~ **keeper,** skutmeester; ~ **mark,** skutmerk; ~ **master,** skutmeester; ~ **money,** skutgeld; ~ **notice,** skutberig; ~ **sale,** skutverkoping.
pour, (n) stortbui; gietsel; (v) giet, uitstort (metaal); inskink (drinkgoed); stortreën, sous, in strome neerkom; ~ *FORTH,* uitgooi; uitstort; ~ *out one's HEART,* jou hart uitstort; ~ *IN,* inskink, ingooi; instroom; *MONEY came* ~ *ing in,* geld het ingestroom; ~ *OFF,* skink; afgiet; ~ *OUT,* uitstort; inskink; ~ *OUT the tea,* tee (in)skink; *the STREAM* ~ *s itself into the sea,* die stroom loop in die see; ~ *out WINE,* wyn (in)skink; ~ **er,** inskinker; gieter.
pour'ing, (n) gieting; skinking; (a) gietend, stortend; (in)skinkend; *it was* ~, dit het gereën dat dit giet; die reën het gestort; ~ *BATTER,* gietbeslag; ~ *CHUTE,* gietgeut; ~ *CUSTARD,* vlasous; ~ *RAIN,* stortreën; ~ *SAUCE,* dun sous.
poussin', braaikuiken.
pout¹, (n) wyting; paling.
pout², (n) suur gesig, dik mond; (die) pruil; *be in the* ~ *s,* pruil; (v) suur gesig trek, pruil, mok; tuit, die

poverty — **prank**

lippe vooruitsteek; ~**er**, pruiler, pruilmond; dik= bek; kropduif; ~**ing**, (n) tuiting; (a) pruilerig.

pov'erty, armoede, armoedigheid; skraalte; skamel= heid, powerheid; behoefte, gebrek; skaarste; *when ~ comes in at the DOOR, love flies out of the win= dow*, as die armoede by die voordeur inkom, gaan die liefde by die agterdeur uit; *REDUCE to ~*, tot armoede bring; ~ *is not a SHAME, but the being ashamed of it is*, armoede is geen skande nie; ~- **stricken**, armoedig, arm.

powd'er, (n) poeier; kruit (vir skiet); stof; *AC= CUSTOMED to the smell of ~*, dikwels in die vuur gewees; *keep your ~ DRY*, hou jou kruit droog; *FOOD for ~*, kanonvleis; ~ *and SHOT*, kruit en lood; *not to have SMELT ~*, nog nie kruit geruik het nie; *WASTE one's ~ and shot*, jou kruit verspil; *not WORTH ~ and shot*, nie 'n skoot kruit werd nie; (v) (be)poeier; fynstamp, fynmaal; ~**-barrel**, kruitvat; ~**-blast**, kruitslag; ~**-blue**, blousel; lig= blou; ~**-box**, poeierdoos; kruitdoos; ~**-cart**, kruit= wa; ~**-charge**, kruitlading; ~**-chest**, kruitkis; ~- **compact**, poeierdosie; ~**-down**, donsvere.

powd'ered, poeier=; gepoeier; fyngemaak, -**cork**, kurkmeel; ~ **milk**, melkpoeier; droëmelk; ~ **soap**, seeppoeier.

powd'er: ~**-flask**, ~**-horn**, kruithoring; ~**-magazine**, kruitmagasyn; ~**-mill**, kruitfabriek; ~**-mine**, kruitmyn; ~**-puff**, poeierkwas; ~**-room**, kruitka= mer; damesruskamer, kleedkamer, opknapkamer; ~**-works**, buskruitfabriek, ~y, poeierig, poeierag= tig, gepoeier, poeiervormig.

pow'er, (n) mag, krag; gesag, invloed; (at beide)ver= moë, drywing (werktuigk.); sterkte (lens); bevoegd= heid (liggaam); magpunt (hefboom); bekwaam= heid; mag (wisk.); elektriese krag; *ABUSE of ~*, magsmisbruik; ~ *of ATTORNEY*, volmag, proku= rasie; *the ~s that BE*, die owerheid; die gestelde mag; *BEYOND my ~*, bokant my mag, buite my mag; *COME into ~*, aan die bewind kom; *DIS= TRIBUTION of ~s*, verdeling van magte; *more ~ to your ELBOW*, alle sukses; goed so; ~ *of EX= PRESSION*, uitdrukkingskrag; *the GREAT ~s*, die groot moondhede; *HAVE ~ over*, mag hê oor; *those IN ~*, die maghebbendes; *IN one's ~*, in iem. se mag; ~ *of LIFE and death*, halsreg; *LUST for ~*, magswellus; *MERCIFUL ~s!* goeie hemel! *a ~ of MONEY*, 'n mag van geld; *NAVAL ~*, seemag; seemoondheid; *under one's OWN ~*, met eie krag; *the PARTY in ~*, die regerende party; *a ~ of PEOPLE*, 'n mag der menigte; *RAISE to the nth ~*, tot die n^e mag verhef; ~ *of RESISTANCE*, weerstandsvermoë; *be RETURNED to ~*, (weer) aan die bewind kom; *a SEA ~*, 'n seemoondheid; *UNDER her own ~*, onder eie stoom; ~ *of VETO*, vetoreg; ~ *and WEIGHT*, krag en las; ~ *of WORK*, werkkrag; (v) aandryf; krag opwek; ('n voertuig) van krag voorsien; ~ **boat**, motorboot, ~ **brake**, kragrem; ~ **cable**, kragkabel; ~ **con= sumption**, kragverbruik; ~ **drill**, kragboor; ~- **drunk**, magsdronk, vol magswellus; ~ **failure**, kragonderbreking; ~**-flight**, motorvlug; ~**ful**, magtig, kragtig, sterk, stoer, fors; vermoënd; in= vloedryk; ~**fulness**, mag, sterkte, krag; invloedryk= heid; ~ **head**, kragkop; ~**-house**, kragsentrale; ma= sjienkamer; ~**-hungry**, honger na mag; ~ **lathe**, kragdraaibank; ~**-less**, magteloos, hulpeloos; krag= teloos; impotent; ~**-lessness**, magteloosheid; ~ **line**, kragleiding; ~ **loom**, weefmasjien; ~ **main**, hoof(krag)leiding; ~ **mill**, stoommeul; weeffa= briek; ~**-operator**, kragskrop, kragwerktuig; ~- **paraffin**, kragparaffien; ~**-plant**, elektriese kragin= stallasie; kragsentrale, kragbron; ~ **plug**, stopkontak, kragprop; ~ **point**, kragpunt; ~ **poli= tics**, magspolitiek; ~ **press**, stoomdrukpers; ~- **rating**, drywingsvermoë; ~**-saw**, kragsaag; ~- **scraper**, kragskrop; ~**-station**, kragsentrale, (elektriese) sentrale; ~ **supply**, kragtoevoer; ~- **tools**, masjiengereedskap; ~ **transmission**, krag= oorbrenging; ~ **unit**, krageenheid; kragvoerder; ~ **valve**, kragklep.

pow'wow, powwow', Indiaanse towenaar; indaba; konferensie van offisiere.

pox, pokke, pokkies; sifilis.

practicabil'ity, uitvoerbaarheid, doenlikheid, moontlikheid.

prac'ticable, uitvoerbaar, doenlik, bruikbaar; be= gaanbaar; bevaarbaar, rybaar.

prac'tical, prakties, werkdadig, daadliewend; werk= lik, doelmatig; *play a ~ joke on someone*, iem. 'n poets bak; ~ **class**, praktiese klas; ~ **engineer**, werktuigkundige; ~ **examination**, praktiese eksa= men; ..**cal'ity**, werklikheid; daadliewendheid; praktiesheid; ~**ly**, prakties, feitlik, so te sê, nage= noeg; ~ **test**, praktiese toets.

prac'tice, praktyk; uitoefening; oefening, gebruik; ge= woonte; toepassing; prosedure; lis; *BE in ~*, prak= tiseer; goed geoefen wees (sport); *CORRUPT ~s*, wanpraktyke; *IN ~*, in die praktyk; *don't MAKE a ~ of it*, moenie daar 'n gewoonte van maak nie; *be OUT of ~*, van stryk wees; ~ *makes PERFECT*, al doende leer 'n mens; oefening baar kuns; *an ounce of ~ is worth a pound of PRECEPT*, een ons praktyk is beter as 'n pond teorie; *PUT into ~*, toepas, in praktyk bring; *SHADY ~s*, twyfelagtige praktyke; *SHARP ~*, knoeiery; skelmery; onder= duimsheid; ~**-ball**, oefenbal; ~**-bomb**, oefenbom; ~ **drill**, driloefening; oefendril; ~**-flight**, oefen= vlug; ~**-ground**, skietbaan, oefenveld; ~**-jump**, oe= fensprong; ~**-records**, skietregister, skietstaat; ~- **school**, skietskool; leerskool; ~**-shell**, oefengra= naat; ~**-target**, skyf; ~ **teacher**, kwekelingonder= wyser(es).

practi'cian, praktikus, man v.d. praktyk.

prac'tise, oefen; verrig; beoefen; uitoefen; praktiseer; toepas, uitvoer, in praktyk bring; instudeer (lied); ~ *what you PREACH*, laat jou woorde en dade ooreenstem; ~ *a PROFESSION*, 'n beroep uit= oefen; ~**d**, geoefen, bedrewe, ervare.

prac'tising, (n) oefening; (a) praktiserend; oefen=; ~- **ground**, oefenveld.

practi'tioner, praktisyn; beoefenaar; *GENERAL ~*, geneesheer, dokter, algemene praktisyn; *LEGAL ~*, regspraktisyn; *MEDICAL ~*, mediese prakti= syn, dokter.

praet'or, owerheidspersoon (by die Romeine), pretor.

praetor'ian, (n) pretoriaan; (a) pretoriaans.

pragmat'ic, pragmaties; dogmaties; bemoeisiek; ~**al**, eiewys, dogmaties; ~ **sanction**, onherroeplike be= sluit van 'n vors, pragmatiese sanksie.

prag'matism, pragmatisme.

prag'matist, pragmatis.

Prague, Praag.

prair'ie, grasvlakte, prerie; ~ **chicken**, prêriehoender; ~ **dog**, prêriehond; ~ **fire**, prêriebrand; ~ **grass**, prêriegras; ~ **schooner**, tentwa; ~ **wolf**, prêriewolf.

praise, (n) lof, roem, eer; lofspraak, loftuiting; *BEYOND all ~*, bokant alle lof verhewe; *DAMN with faint ~*, deur matige lof veroordeel; *GIVE high ~ to*, iem. groot lof toeswaai; ~ *be to GOD*, die Here sy dank; *be LOUD in one's ~*, hoog roem, baie prys; *SING the ~ of*, die lof verkondig van; die loftrompet steek oor; *SING his own ~s*, sy eie lof verkondig; *SONG of ~*, lofgesang; (v) loof, prys, roem, verheerlik, die lof verkondig van, ophemel, opvysel; ~ *a fair DAY at night*, 'n mens moenie die dag voor die aand prys nie; ~ *day at night, and LIFE at the end*, prys die dag nooit voor twaalfuur in die nag nie; ~ *the LORD*, die Here loof; ~- **singer**, lofsanger; ~**-singing**, loftuiting; ~**worthi= ness**, prysenswaardigheid, loflikheid; ~ **worthy**, loflik, prysenswaardig.

pra'line, suikeramandel, praline.

pram^1, kinderwaentjie, stootwaentjie.

pram^2, **praam**, platboomskuit.

prance, (n) bokspring; kopspeel (perd); (v) spring, bokspring, steier; windmakerig stap; sekelnek stap, pronk.

pran'dial, maaltyd=, maal=.

prank, (n) streek, grap, poets, kaskenade, gruwel= stuk, petalje, kaperjol; *be FULL of ~s*, vol streke wees; *PLAY ~s (up)on someone*, iem. 'n poets bak; (v) pronk; optooi, uitdos, versier; spog; flik= ker.

prate, (n) gepraat, gebabbel, gesanik; ~ *is* ~, *it's money buys land,* praatjies vul geen gaatjies nie; (v) praat, babbel, snater, leuter; ~ **r**, babbelaar, klets= kous.

prat'incole, klein sprinkaanvoël.

prat'ing, (n) (die) gebabbel; (a) praterig, kekkelend.

prat'ique, verlof tot handelsverkeer; *admit to* ~, die kwarantyn (van 'n skip) ophef.

prat'tle, (n) gesnater, kindergebabbel; (v) babbel (soos 'n kind), snater, aframmel; oor koeitjies en kalfies praat; ~**r**, babbelaar.

pratt'ling, gebabbel, gesnater.

prav'ity, bedorwenheid, slegtheid.

prawn, steurgarnaal, krewel.

prax'is, gebruik, praktiese toepassing; voorbeeld; steloefeninge.

pray, bid; smeek; versoek; ~ *be CAREFUL,* pas tog op; ~ *be QUIET,* wees asseblief stil; ~ *TELL me,* sê my asseblief.

pray'er[1], (n) bidder.

prayer'[2], (n) gebed; bede, versoek, smeking, versug= ting; (pl) godsdiensoefening; *FAMILY* ~*s,* huis= godsdiens; *LEAD in* ~, in gebed voorgaan; *the LORD'S P*~, die Onse Vader; *OFFER* ~*s,* gods= diens hou; *SAY one's* ~*s,* bid; *you can SAY your* ~*s,* jy kan maar jou testament maak; *he SAYS more than his* ~*s,* sy aand- en môrepraatjies stem (kom) nie ooreen nie; ~**-bead**, bidkraal; ~**-book**, gebedeboek; ~**ful**, smekend, biddend; ~**-leader**, voorbidder; ~**less**, biddeloos; ~**-meeting**, biduur; ~**-mill**, bidwiel; ~**-rug**, bidmatjie; ~**-shawl**, ge= bedsmantel; ~**-wheel**, bidwiel.

pray'ing, (n) gebid, biddery; *he is past* ~ *for,* aan hom is geen salf te smeer nie; (a) biddend; ~ **insect,** ~ **mantis,** hotnotsgot.

pre-ab'domen, voorbuik.

preach, (n) preek; (v) preek; verkondig; voorstaan, bevorder; ~ *to a CONGREGATION,* vir 'n ge= meente preek; ~ *to DEAF ears,* vir dowes preek; ~ *DOWN,* afkeur, afbreek, slegmaak; ~ *the GOS= PEL,* die Evangelie verkondig; ~ *on a SUBJECT,* vir 'n gemeente preek; ~ *UP,* ophemel; lof toe= swaai; ~**er**, predikant; prediker; ~**ership**, preek= amp.

preach'ify, (..fied), sedepreke hou, moraliseer, preek.

preach'iness, prekerigheid.

preach'ing, prediking; gepreek, prekery.

preach'ment, sedeprekery, gepreek.

preach'y, preekagtig, prekerig, domineeagtig.

pre-acquaint', vooraf bekend stel; ~**ance**, vooraf= gaande bekendstelling.

pre-Adam'ic, (v) voor Adam se tyd.

pre-A'damite, (n) pre-Adamiet; (a) pre-Adamities.

preadmon'ish, vooraf waarsku.

preadmoni'tion, voorafgaande waarskuwing; voor= wete.

preadoles'cence, preadolessensie.

pream'ble, (n) inleiding, voorrede; aanloop; aanhef; (v) van 'n leiding voorsien, inlei.

pream'plifier, voorversterker.

preappoint', vooraf aanstel.

preapprehen'sion, vooroordeel.

preappren'ticeship, vooropleiding van vakleerlinge.

prearrange', vooraf reël (skik); ~**ment**, voorafgaan= de reëling.

preb'end, prebende; ~**ary**, (..ries), diensdoende domheer.

precar'ious, onseker, twyfelagtig; wisselvallig; haglik, gevaarlik, bedenklik (siekte), prekêr; ~ *EXIS= TENCE,* sukkelbestaan; *the* ~ *LIFE of a soldier,* die gevaarvolle lewe van 'n soldaat; *a* ~ *LIVING,* 'n wisselvallige bestaan: 'n sukkelbestaan; *a* ~ *POSITION,* 'n wisselvallige betrekking; 'n gevaar= like posisie; ~**ness**, onsekerheid, twyfelagtigheid; wisselvalligheid; haglikheid, bedenklikheid.

pre'cast, (v) (~), vooraf giet; (a) vooraf gegiet.

prec'atory, versoekend, biddend, smeek=; ~ *words,* versoek.

precau'tion, voorsorg, voorbehoedmiddel, voorsorg= maatreël; ~**ary**, waarskuwend, voorsorg=; ~*ary measure,* voorsorgmaatreël; veiligheidsmaatreël.

precau'tious, omsigtig, behoedsaam, versigtig.

precede', voorafgaan, voorgaan; die voorrang hê.

prec'edence, voorrang, prioriteit, voorkeur; *GIVE* ~ *to someone,* vir iem. terugstaan; iem. voorrang ver= leen; *ORDER of* ~, voorranglys; *TAKE* ~ *of,* die voorrang hê bo.

prec'edent[1], (n) voorbeeld, presedent; *CREATE a* ~, 'n presedent stel; *WITHOUT* ~, sonder weerga, ongeëwenaard.

preced'ent[2], (a) voorafgaande, voorgaande.

preced'ing, vorige, voorafgaande.

pre'censorship, presensuur, vooraf sensuur.

precent', voorsing; ~**or**, voorsinger, koorleier; ~**or= ship,** voorsingersamp.

pre'cept, voorskrif, bevel; lering, stelreël; bevelskrif, lasbrief.

precep'tive, bevelend, gebiedend, voorgeskrewe; le= rend.

precep'tor, onderwyser, meester; ~**y**, (n) (..ries), bedehuis; seminarium; (a) met voorskrifte.

prece'ssion, presessie; voorrang.

pre-Christ'ian, voorchristelik.

pre'cinct, grenslyn; gebied; buitenste omtrek; *the* ~ *s of,* die omgewing van.

precios'ity, presieusheid, oordrewe gemaaktheid, ge= sogtheid, aanstellerigheid.

pre'cious, (a) kosbaar, kostelik; edel (gesteente); voortreflik, dierbaar; presieus, gesog, gemaak (styl); *my* ~ *child,* my dierbare kind; (adv.) ver= vlaks, drommels; ~ *FEW people,* bedroef min mense; *take* ~ *GOOD care of something,* drommels goed vir iets sorg; *there is* ~ *LITTLE left,* daar is uiters min oor; ~ **metals,** edele metale; ~ **ness,** kos= telikheid; kosbaarheid; gesogtheid; ~ **stone,** edel= steen.

pre'cipice, afgrond, steilte, krans.

precip'itance, **precip'itancy**, oorhaasting, ooryling; onbesonnenheid, voorbarigheid.

precip'itant, (n) neerslagmiddel, besinkmiddel; (a) presipiterend.

precip'itate, (n) presipitaat, neerslag; (v) (laat) neer= slaan, besink, presipiteer; gou maak; verhaas, oor= haas, bespoedig; ~ *MATTERS,* sake verhaas; *it served to* ~ *his RUIN,* dit het sy ondergang ver= haas.

precipita'tion, oorhaasting; haastigheid; neerslag, besinking; neerstorting; verhaasting, bespoediging; ontketening; *act with* ~, oorhastig te werk gaan.

precip'itator, oorhaaster; neerslagmiddel; besinker, presipiteerder (geol.); bewerker, presipiteerma= sjien, presipitator.

precip'itous, steil, oorhaastig; ~**ness**, oorhaastig= heid; steilte, valskerpte.

pré'cis, précis, oorsig, uittreksel, same= vatting, kort inhoud, kort begrip; ~**-writer**, same= vatter, opsommer.

precise', noukeurig, presies; stip, sekuur, strik, nou= geset; saaklik; *at that* ~ *moment,* presies op daardie oomblik; ~ **ly,** presies; juistement; ~ **ness,** noukeu= righeid, nougesetheid, presiesheid; juistheid.

preci'sian, femelaar, Jantjie Sekuur, gewetensmens.

preci'sion, noukeurigheid, akkuraatheid, netheid, stiptheid, striktheid, sekuurheid, presiesheid, juist= heid; ~ **bombing,** presisiebombardering, -bomwer= ping; ~ **engineer,** fynwerker; ~ **fire,** presisievuur; ~ **fitter,** fynmonteur; ~ **grinder,** fynslyper; ~ **in= struments,** ~ **tools,** fyngereedskap; presisiewerk= tuie; ~ **sight,** fynvisier; ~ **turner,** fyndraaier; ~ **work,** presisiewerk.

preclude', uitsluit; verhinder; voorkom, belet; *so as to* ~ *all doubt,* om alle twyfel uit te sluit.

preclu'sion, uitsluiting; voorkoming.

preclus'ive, uitsluitend; verhinderend.

preco'cious, vroegryp, voorlik, ouderwets; astrant, oulik, snipperig, vrypostig; mondig.

preco'ciousness, **preco'city**, vroegrypheid, voorlik= heid; vrypostigheid, oulikheid.

precogni'tion, voorkennis; voorlopige ondersoek.

preconceive', vooraf opvat; vooraf vorm; vooraf uit= dink; ~ **d,** vooropgeset; *a* ~ *d opinion,* 'n vooropge= sette mening.

preconcep'tion, vooroordeel, vooropgesette mening.

preconcert', vooraf beraam, afspreek.
precondemn', vooraf veroordeel; ~ **a'tion**, voorafveroordeling.
precondi'tion, (n) vereiste, voorwaarde; (v) vooraf as voorwaarde stel; vooraf berei.
preconsid'er, vooraf oorweeg.
precontract', vooraf ooreenkom.
pre'-cook, halfgaar kook.
pre'-cool, voorkoel.
pre-cool'ing, voorkoeling; ~ **store**, voorkoelkamer.
precurs'ive, voorafgaande.
precurs'or, voorloper; voorbode; ~ **y**, voorafgaande, voorlopig, inleidend.
preda'cious, roof=, roofgierig, roofsugtig.
predate', vroeër dateer, te vroeg dateer.
pred'ator, roofdier; plunderaar, rower; roofvyand.
pred'atory, roofsugtig, roof=; ~ *ANIMAL*, roofdier; ~ *BIRD*, roofvoël; ~ *RAIDS*, strooptogte.
predecease', (n) vroeëre dood, vooroorlye; (v) eerder sterf; ~ **d**, vooroorledene.
pred'ecessor, voorganger; voorvader; ~ *in title*, regsvoorganger.
predell'a, altaarstuk, predella.
predestinar'ian, persoon wat aan voorbeskikking glo, predestinasiër.
predes'tinate, voorbeskik, uitverkies, voorbestem, predestineer; ~ **d**, voorbeskik, voorbestem, uitgekies, uitverkore, gepredestineer.
predestina'tion, voorbeskikking, uitverkiesing, voorbestemming, predestinasie.
predes'tine, voorbestem, voorbeskik, vooraf bepaal, uitverkies, gepredestineer.
predeterm'inable, vooraf bepaalbaar.
predeterm'inate, vooraf bepaal, predestineer.
predetermina'tion, voorbeskikking; voorbestemming; vooraf gemaakte besluit.
predeterm'ine, vooruit bepaal, voorbeskik, vooraf bepaal.
pred'ial, (n) slaaf, lyfeiene; (a) landelik, land=; ~ **servitude**, grondservituut, erfdiensbaarheid, saaklike servituut.
predicabil'ity, bevestigheid, bepaalbaarheid, voorspelbaarheid; prediseerbaarheid.
pred'icable, (n) hoedanigheid, kenmerk; (a) bepaalbaar; beweerbaar; voorspelbaar; prediseerbaar.
predic'ably, soos verwag (voorspel) kon word.
predic'ament, klas, geval, kategorie; moeilike toestand, predikament; *be in a* ~, in die knyp sit.
predicamen'tal, kategories.
pred'icant, predikant; prediker.
pred'icate, (n) gesegde, predikaat; eienskap, karaktertrek; (v) bevestig, verseker; beweer.
predica'tion, bewering, bevestiging, uiting.
predic'ative, predikatief, bevestigend.
pred'icatlve, prieek=, prekerig
predict', voorspel, voorsê; wiggel (water); ~ **able**, voorspelbaar, voorsienbaar; ~ **ion**, voorspelling; voorsegging; ~ **ive**, voorspellend; ~ **or**, voorspeller.
predikant', predikant.
predilec'tion, voorliefde, voorkeur, partydigheid.
predispose', voorberei, geneig maak; vatbaar maak, ontvanklik maak, predisponeer; ~ **d**, vooringenome; *be* ~ *d to*, geneig wees om; vatbaar (ontvanklik) vir.
predisposi'tion, vatbaarheid, ontvanklikheid, voorbereiding, aanleg, predisposisie.
predom'inance, oorheersing, oormag, oorhand.
predom'inant, oorheersend, oorwegend, predominerend, ~ **ly**, oorwegend, hoofsaaklik.
predom'inate, die oorhand hê; oorheers, domineer; in die meerderheid wees, sterk verteenwoordig wees, predomineer.
predom'inating, allesbeheersend, allesoorheersend.
predomina'tion, oorhand; oorheersing.
predoom', vooraf veroordeel; voorbestem.
pre-elect', vooraf kies; ~ **ed**, vooraf gekies; ~ **ion**, voorafverkiesing.
pre-em'inence, uitnemendheid, voorrang, voortreflikheid.
pre-em'inent, voortreflik, uitstekend, uitmuntend, uitblinkend; ~ *AMONGST musicians*, uitblinkend tussen musici; ~ *IN surgery*, voortreflik in chirurgie; ~ **ly**, by uitstek, by uitnemendheid.
pre-empt', vooruit koop, 'n opsie verkry oor; iem. voorkoop; 'n afsluitbod maak (kaartspel); ~ **ion**, voorkoop, opsie; *right of* ~ *ion*, reg van voorkoop; ~ **ive**, afsluitend, afsluit=; aanvalsvoorkomend; ~ *ive bid*, afsluitbod (kaartspel).
preen, glad stryk (vere met snawel); tooi; ~ *oneself*, jou mooi maak, jou fyn uitvat.
pre-engage', vooraf bespreek; vooraf verbind; ~ **ment**, voorbespreking; voorafgaande indiensneming.
preen' gland, oliepotjie (hoender); oliekannetjie (voël).
pre-estab'lish, vooraf bepaal, vooruit reël; ~ **ment**, voorafgaande bepaling; vooraf reëling.
pre-es'timate, (n) vooruitskatting; (v) vooruit skat.
pre-examina'tion, voorafgaande ondersoek.
pre-examine', vooraf ondersoek.
pre-exist', vooraf bestaan; ~ **ence**, voorbestaan; ~ **ent**, vooraf bestaande.
pref'ab, opslaanhuis, monteerhuis, voorafvervaardigde huis (gebou).
prefab'ricate, voorafvervaardig, opslaan.
prefab'ricated, voorafvervaardig, opslaan=; ~ **building**, opslaangebou; montasiebou; ~ **house**, opslaanhuis; monteerhuis, montasiehuis.
prefabrica'tion, voorafvervaardiging; prefabrikasie; opslaanwerk.
pref'ace, (n) voorrede, voorwoord, inleiding; (v) inlei; van 'n voorrede voorsien; ~ *with*, vooraf laat gaan deur.
pref'atory, inleidend, voorafgaande.
pref'ect, prefek; klasleier; ~ *of police*, polisiepretek; ~ **or'ial**, prefektoraal; ~ **ure**, prefektuur.
prefer', (-red), verkies, voorkeur gee aan, liewer hê, beter vind, meer hou van, prefereer; bevorder; verhef; indien; aanhangig maak; ~ *a CHARGE*, 'n klag indien; ~ *a CLAIM*, 'n eis instel; *he* ~ *s to LEAVE it alone*, hy verkies om dit te laat staan; ~ *to an OFFICE*, tot 'n amp bevorder; ~ *a REQUEST*, 'n versoek voordra; ~ *a STATEMENT*, 'n verklaring indien; ~ *TEA to coffee*, tee bo koffie verkies; ~ *TO*, verkies bo.
pref'erable, verkieslik; ~ *to*, verkieslik bo.
pref'erably, by voorkeur, liewers, liefs.
pref'erence, voorkeur, voorliefde; preferensie (handel); voorkeurreg; bevoorregting; *BY* ~, by voorkeur; *HAVE a* ~, die voorrang hê; *HAVE a* ~ *for green*, 'n voorliefde vir groen hê; *IN* ~ *to*, liewer as; ~ **bond**, prioriteitsobligasie; ~ **share**, voorkeuraandeel, preferente aandeel.
pre'ferent, preferent; ~ **share**, voorkeuraandeel, preferente aandeel.
preferen'tial, begunstigend, voorkeur=, preferent; bevoorreg; prioriteits=; ~ *charge against the ESTATE*, preferente vordering teen die boedel; ~ **debt**, prioriteitskuld; ~ **duty**, voorkeurtarief; ~ **rate**, voorkeurtarief; ~ **shares**, voorkeuraandele; ~ **tariff**, voorkeurtarief.
prefer'ment, verhoging, bevordering.
preferr'ed, voorkeur=, preferent; ~ **share**, voorkeuraandeel, preferente aandeel.
prefigura'tion, voorafgaande voorstelling; prototipe; afskaduwing.
prefig'ure, voorberei; as voorbeeld stel; voorspel.
pref'ix, (n) (-es), voorvoegsel, prefiks.
prefix', (v) voorvoeg, vooraan heg; as inleiding plaas voor; ~ **ion**, voorplasing, voor(aan)voeging.
preform', vooraf vorm.
preg'nable, inneembaar, verowerbaar; aantasbaar, wondbaar.
preg'nancy, swangerskap (mense); dragtigheid (diere); gewigtigheid, betekenisvolheid; vrugbaarheid, vindingrykheid, veelseggendheid; ~ **-disease**, domsiekte (skape).
preg'nant, swanger, in die ander tyd (mense); onklaar; bevrug, dragtig, beset, gedek (dier); grootuier (bees); oortuigend, dwingend; betekenisvol, veelseggend; vrugbaar, pregnant; *a* ~ *SILENCE*, 'n veelseggende (betekenisvolle) stilte; *a* ~ *STATEMENT*, 'n veelseggende uitspraak; ~ *WITH*, vol van, ryk aan (gevolge), pregnant.

pregusta'tion, voorproef, voorsmaak.
preheat', voorverhit; ~ing, voorverhitting.
prehen'sible, grypbaar.
prehen'sile, geskik om mee te gryp, gryp=; ~ **tail,** grypstert.
prehen'sion, (die) pak, (die) gryp; begrip, bevatting.
prehistor'ic, voorhistories, prehistories.
prehis'tory, voorgeskiedenis.
pre-igni'tion, voorontsteking.
prejudge', vooruit veroordeel; voorbarig oordeel.
prejudg(e)'ment, vooroordeel, voorbarige oordeel.
prej'udice, (n) vooroordeel, partydigheid, vooringe= nomenheid; nadeel, benadeling (reg), skade; ~ *AGAINST,* vooroordeel teen; *TO the* ~ *of,* tot ska= de van; ten nadele van; *WITHOUT* ~, sonder voorbehoud; *WITHOUT* ~ *to,* alle regte voor= behou; onbevooroordeeld; (v) bevooroordeeld maak; benadeel, skadelik wees, kwaad doen; ~d, vooringenome; bevooroordeeld; ~*d AGAINST,* vooringenome teen; ~*d in FAVOUR of,* vooringe= nome met.
prejudi'cial, bevooroordeeld; skadelik, nadelig; *BE* ~ *to,* afbreuk doen aan; ~ *TO,* ten nadele van.
pre-knowl'edge, voorkennis.
prel'acy, (..cies), prelaatskap; biskoplike regering; die hoë geestelikheid.
prelapsar'ian, van voor die sondeval.
prel'ate, prelaat, kerkvors.
prela'tess, (-es), abdis, priores; vrou van 'n prelaat (grappig).
prelat'ic, kerkvorstelik.
prel'atism, biskoplike kerkregering.
prel'atize, onder biskoplike beheer bring.
prel'ature, prelaatamp; die prelate.
prelect', redevoering (lesing) hou; ~**ion,** lesing; open= bare les; ~**or,** voorleser, lektor.
preliba'tion, voorsmaak, voorproef.
prelim'inary, (n) (..ries), inleiding, voorlopige maat= reël, voorafgaande reëling, voorbereiding; (a) inlei= dend, voorbereidend, voorlopig, voorafgaande, preliminêr; ~ **examination,** voorlopige ondersoek; voorondersoek (reg); voorbereidende eksamen; ~ **punishment,** voorarres; ~ **training,** vooropleiding.
prel'ude, (n) inleiding; voorspel, preludium; (v) prelu= deer; insit, begin, inlei, vooraf laat gaan, 'n inlei= ding vorm.
prelus'ive, prelus'ory, inleidend, as voorspel.
premar'ital, voorhuweliks, premaritaal.
prem'ature, ontydig, voorbarig; oorhaastig; vroeg= ryp; ~ *birth,* ~ *confinement,* ontydige bevalling.
premature'ness, prematur'ity, vroegrypheid; voor= barigheid; ontydigheid; oorhaastigheid.
premed'itate, bepeins, oordink, vooraf oorlê; ~d, voorbedag; ~*d murder,* moord met voorbedagte rade (gepleeg).
premedita'tion, voorbedagtheid, voorafgaande oor= leg, opset; *with* ~, met voorbedagte rade.
pre'mier, (n) eerste minister, premier; (a) eerste, ver= naamste, belangrikste, beste.
première', eerste opvoering, première.
prem'iership, eersteministerskap, premierskap.
prem'ise, (n) voorafgaande stelling, basis, premis; (pl) huis en erf, perseel, erf, gebou; die voorgaande; *BY these* ~*s,* op grond hiervan; *ON the* ~*s,* op die plek, ter plaatse.
premise', (v) vooropstel, as premis stel, vooraf laat gaan.
prem'iss = **premise,** (n).
prem'ium, premie; prys, beloning; waarde bokant pari; leergeld; toegif; opgeld; *AT a* ~, bokant pari; *BE at a* ~, hoog staan; 'n sterk aanvraag geniet; hoog op prys wees; *this will PUT a* ~ *on fraud,* dit sal 'n premie stel op bedrog; dit sal bedrog aanmoe= dig; *SELL* at a ~, met wins verkoop; ~ **bond,** pre= mieobligasie; premielening; ~ **loan,** premielening; ~ **rate,** versekeringstarief; ~ **system,** premiestel= sel.
pre'-mix, (n) voormengsel; (v) vooraf meng.
pre-mix'ture, voormengsel.
premol'ar, voorkies.
premon'ish, waarsku.
premoni'tion, waarskuwing, voorgevoel; voorteken.

premon'itory, waarskuwend.
prenat'al, van voor die geboorte.
preno'tion, voordenkbeeld.
pren'tice, abbr. of **apprentice,** vakleerling, leerjonge; ~ **poetry,** sukkelvers; ~**ship,** vakleerlingskap.
prenup'tial, voorhuweliks; ~ **contract,** huweliks= voorwaardekontrak.
preocc'upancy, vroeëre inbesitneming.
preoccupa'tion, afgetrokkenheid, verstrooidheid; vroeëre besit; vooringenomenheid; besorgdheid.
preocc'upied, afgetrokke, in gedagtes versonke, inge= dagte; ~ *with family cares,* in beslag geneem deur gesinsorge.
preocc'upy, (..pied), vroeër beset; in beslag neem; (die gedagte) heeltemal besig hou.
preordain', vooruit bepaal, vooraf beskik, voorbe= skik.
preordina'tion, voorafgaande bepaling; vroeëre be= sluit.
prep, (sl), huiswerk (vir skool).
pre-pack'age, klaar verpak.
pre-pack'aging, klaarverpakking.
prepaid', posvry, vooruitbetaal, vragvry, gefran= keer(d), franko.
prepara'tion, voorbereiding; voorbereidsel, gereed= making, aanstalte; huiswerk; preparaat; bereiding; bewerking; instudering; (pl) toebereidsels, voorbe= reidsels, aanstaltes; *in* ~ *FOR,* as voorbereiding vir; *IN* ~, in voorbereiding.
prepa'rative, (n) voorbereidsel; (a) voorbereidend; *BE* ~ *to,* as voorbereiding dien tot; ~ *TO,* têr voorbereiding van.
prepa'ratory, voorbereidend, voorbereidings=; inlei= dend, voorlopig; ~ *to his going,* voordat hy gaan; ~ **class,** voorbereidingsklas; ~ **course,** voorberei= dingskursus; ~ **examination,** voorbereidende eksa= men; ~ **school,** voorbereidingskool; ~ **study,** voorstudie; ~ **work,** voorarbeid.
prepare', voorberei, klaarmaak, gereed maak; oplei; berei; bewerk; ~ *a LESSON,* 'n les voorberei; ~ *a MEAL,* 'n maaltyd klaarmaak; ~ *ONESELF for,* jou voorberei vir, jou gereed maak om, jou lyf reg= hou vir; ~ *the WAY,* die weg voorberei.
prepared', klaar, paraat, gereed; gewapend; ingerig; *BE* ~, gereed (voorbereid) wees; ~ *to DO some= thing,* bereid (gereed) om iets te doen; ~ **milk food,** bereide melkkos; ~ **mustard,** aangemaakte mos= terd; ~**ness,** gereedheid, paraatheid, voorbereid= heid; bereidwilligheid.
prepar'er, voorbereider; opmaker, bereider.
prepay', (..paid), vooruitbetaal; frankeer; ~**able,** vooruitbetaalbaar; ~**ment,** voorafbetaling, voor= uitbetaling; frankering.
prepense', voorbedag, opsetlik, moedswillig; *MA= LICE* ~, bose opset; *of MALICE* ~, met voorbe= dagte rade.
preplace'ment, voorplasing.
prepon'derance, prepon'derancy, oorwig; oorhand; ~ *(in point) of NUMBERS,* groter getalsterkte; *be in* ~ *OVER,* in getal oortref.
prepon'derant, oorwegend; ~**ly,** oorwegend, hoof= saaklik.
prepon'derate, swaarder weeg, oortref, oorwegend wees, oorheers; die deurslag gee; die getal oortref; ~ *over,* sterker (talryker, groter, belangriker) wees as.
prepon'derating, oorwegend.
preposi'tion, voorsetsel; ~**al,** voorsetsel=.
prepos'itive, voorgevoeg, voorop geplaas.
prepossess', voorinneem, beïnvloed; vooraf in besit neem; ~**ing,** innemend, aantreklik; ~**ion,** vroeëre besit; vooroordeel; vooringenomenheid; ~**or,** vroeëre besitter.
prepos'terous, ongerymd, verkeerd, bespotlik, onsin= nig, dwaas; ~**ness,** ongerymdheid, dwaasheid.
prepot'ency, oorwig, oormag; prepotensie, erfdwang (biol.).
prepot'ent, oormagtig; invloedryk, veelvermoënd; prepotent (biol.).
prepran'dial, voorete=.
prep'uce, voorhuid.
Pre-Raph'aelite, (n) Pre-Rafaeliet; (a) Pre-Rafaelities.

prereq'uisite, (n) eerste vereiste, noodsaaklike vereiste; (a) vooraf vereis, noodsaaklik.
pre'-rinse, vooraf spoel, voorspoel.
prerog'ative, (n) voorreg, privilegie, prerogatief; *EXERCISE a ~,* 'n prerogatief uitoefen; *ROYAL ~,* prerogatief v. d. koning; (a) met voorrang.
pres'age, (n) voorgevoel, voorbode, voorteken; voorspelling.
presage', (v) voorspel, aankondig, 'n voorgevoel hê van; voorsê; ~**ful,** profeties, voorspellend.
pres'byope, versiende (persoon), presbioop.
presbyop'ia, versiendheid, presbiopie.
presbyop'ic, versiende, presbioop.
pres'byter, ouderling, presbiter; priester.
presbyter'ial, presbiteriaal.
Presbyter'ian, (n) Presbiteriaan; (a) Presbiteriaans; ~**ism,** Presbiterianisme; presbiteriaanse stelsel van kerkregering.
pres'bytery, (..ries), heiligdom, presbiterie; priesterwoning; pastorie.
pre'-school, voorskools; ~ *child,* voorskoolse kind.
pre'science, voorkennis, voorwetendheid, voorwetenskap; voorgevoel.
pre'scient, voorwetend, vooruitsiende; met die helm gebore.
prescind', afsny, afsonder.
prescribe', voorskrywe; behandel; voorskrifte gee; stel; ~**d,** voorgeskrewe; verjaar (vonnis, skuld); ~*d book,* eksamenboek, voorgeskrewe boek.
pres'cript, (n) voorskrif, bevel; (a) voorgeskrewe.
prescrip'tible, wat voorgeskryf mag word.
prescrip'tion, voorskrif, proskripsie, bevel; resep; verjaring; (die) voorskryf; gewoontereg; *MAKE up a ~,* 'n resep toeberei; *NEGATIVE ~,* beperkte verjaring; *POSITIVE ~,* reg deur verjaring.
prescrip'tive, verjaar, deur lang gebruik verkry; voorskrywend; ~ *PERIOD,* verjaringstermyn; ~ *RIGHT,* verjaringsreg.
pres'ence, teenwoordigheid, bysyn, aanwesigheid; houding, voorkome; persoonlikheid; *IN the ~ of,* in bysyn van; voor; ten owerstaan (oorstaan) van; *IN my ~,* in my teenwoordigheid; ~ *of MIND,* teenwoordigheid van gees; *a man of NOBLE ~,* 'n man van edele gestalte (voorkoms); ~**-chamber,** ~**-room,** oudiënsiesaal.
pres'ent, (n) present, geskenk; die teenwoordige, die hede, die huidige dag; teenwoordige (tyd); *AT ~,* op die oomblik, tans; *FOR the ~,* vir die oomblik; voorlopig; *MAKE one a ~ of something,* iem. iets present gee; *by THESE ~s,* hierdeur; *UP to the ~,* tot datum, tot die huidige tyd; (a) teenwoordig, aanwesig; onderhawig; onmiddellik; huidig; *ALL ~,* almal teenwoordig; *she is ALWAYS ~,* sy maker nooit; *in the ~ CASE,* in die onderhawige geval, *in the ~ CIRCUMSTANCES,* in die huidige omstandighede; ~ *COMPANY excepted (excluded),* die aanwesiges uitgesonder; *at the ~ DAY,* deesdae, teenswoordig; ~ *DAY fashions,* hedendaagse modes; *at the ~ MOMENT,* op die oomblik; ~ *TENSE,* teenwoordige tyd; *at the ~ TIME,* tans, vandag; ~ *VALUE,* kontantwaarde, toonwaarde.
present', (v) aanbied, skenk, present gee; indien, voorlê (voorstel); voorstel, aandien (persoon); bied; voordra (vir betrekking); presenteer (geweer); wend, (toe)keer; voorhou; uitreik (pryse); wys; op= voer (toneelstuk); aanbeveel; ~ *ARMS,* die geweer presenteer; ~ *a CASE,* 'n saak stel; ~ *a CHEQUE,* 'n tjek aanbied; ~ *at COURT,* aan die hof voorstel; ~ *ONESELF,* jou aanmeld; *when an OPPORTUNITY ~s itself,* wanneer die geleentheid hom voordoen; ~ *a PLAY,* 'n toneelstuk opvoer; *this POSSIBILITY ~ed itself to me,* hierdie moontlikheid het hom aan my voorgedoen; ~ *PRIZES,* pryse uitdeel.
presen'table, vertoonbaar, presentabel, fatsoenlik; *make oneself ~,* jou opknap.
presenta'tion, voorstelling; aanbieding; oorhandiging; inkleding (van feite); indiening, vertoning; presentasie; *MAKE a ~ of,* aanbied; *ON ~,* by aanbieding; ~ *of PRIZES,* prysuitdeling; ~ **copy,** presenteksemplaar; ~ **sword,** ereswaard.

presen'tative, met reg van voordrag; aanskouings=, voorstellings=.
presentee', voorgestelde; voorgedraene; begiftigde, ontvanger van 'n geskenk.
presen'ter, gewer, skenker; voorsteller.
presen'tient, voorvoelend, met 'n voorgevoel.
presen'timent, voorgevoel.
pres'ently, netnou, aanstons, strakkies, oor 'n rukkie, straks, weldra.
present'ment, aanbieding; voorstelling, indiening; verklaring; inkleding.
preserv'able, wat bewaar (goed gehou) kan word.
preserva'tion, bewaring; behoud, redding; instandhouding; preservasie, preservering; (die) inmaak; (die) inlê; *FOR the ~ of,* tot behoud van; vir die bewaring van; ~ *of LIFE,* lewensbeskerming, lyfsbehoud; *in a good STATE of ~,* in 'n goeie toe= stand; ~**ist,** bewaarder; bewaringsbewuste; voorstander van bewaring; behoudsman.
preserv'ative, (n) bederfwerende middel, preserveer= middel; (a) behoed=, voorbehoedend; behoud=.
preserve', (n) ingelegde vrugte; konserf, stukkonfyt, heelkonfyt; heiligdom; dieretuin, wildpark; visdam; (pl) ingelegde eetware, gepreserveerde resepsel; (v) bewaar, behoed, beskerm, onderhou, in stand hou, handhaaf; preserveer, inlê, inmaak, berei, verduursaam.
preserved', ingelê (ingelegde); behou, in stand gehou; veilig gehou; bewaar; *they were ~ from DEATH,* hulle is van die dood gered; ~ *GINGER,* gemmer= konfyt; ~ *MEAT,* blikkiesvleis; *she is very WELL ~,* sy dra haar jare goed.
preserve'-pot, inmaakpot.
preserv'er, bewaarder, behoeder; inmaker; bederfwerende middel.
preserv'ing, bewaring; (die) inmaak; ~**-jar,** inmaak= fles.
pre-shrunk': ~ *material,* vooraf gekrimpte stof, voorkrimpstof.
preside', voorsit, presideer, die voorsitterskap beklee; die leiding hê; ~ *AT the organ,* die orrel bespeel; ~*d BY,* onder voorsitterskap (leiding) van; ~ *OVER,* presideer; die baas speel oor; ~ *OVER (at) a meeting,* voorsit op 'n vergadering; 'n vergadering lei.
pres'idency, (..cies), presidentskap; voorsitterskap; presidentshuis.
pres'ident, staatspresident; president, voorsitter; *honorary ~,* erevoorsitter; ~ **elect,** aangewese president; ~**ess, (-es),** presidente; voorsitster; ~ **for life,** lewenslange president.
presiden'tial, presidents=, voorsitters=, presidensieel; ~ **candidate,** kandidaat vir die presidentskap; ~ **election,** presidentsverkiesing; ~ **residence,** presidentswoning; ~ **sash,** (staats)presidentserp.
pres'identship, presidentskap.
presid'ial, presidiaal; voorsitters=, presidents=, voor= sittend.
presid'iary, (n) besetting, wag; (a) besettings=, garnisoens=.
presi'ding, voorsittend; ~ **officer,** voorsittende be= ampte.
press, (n) (-es), pers, drukpers; perswese; drukkery; pers(kas); drukte, menigte, gedrang; gejaagdheid, haas; druk; klerekas; *CORRECT the ~,* drukproe= we nasien; *CORRECTOR of the ~,* proefleser; *GO to ~,* ter perse gaan; *as we GO to the ~,* by die ter perse gaan; *IN the ~,* in die pers, word gedruk, ter perse; *LIBERTY of the ~,* persvryheid; *READY for the ~,* persklaar; *SEE through the ~,* vir die druk besorg; *SEND to the ~,* na die pers stuur; (v) pers, druk, prang; pars (druiwe); dring; aanspoor, haastig maak, aanpor; bestook; platdruk; dwing, forseer, aandring; aftrek (sneller); ~ *for an answer,* aandring op 'n antwoord; ~ *one's ADVANTAGE,* gebruik maak van 'n behaalde voordeel; ~ *the BUTTON,* op die knoppie druk; ~ *a CHARGE,* deurgaan met 'n aanklag; ~ *a CLAIM,* op 'n eis aandring; ~ *a person to DO something,* by iem. aandring om iets te doen; ~ *FORWARD,* vooruit= beur; ~ *HOME an advantage,* 'n voordeel uitbuit; ~ *for an INQUIRY,* op 'n ondersoek aandring; ~

MATTERS to extremes, sake tot die uiterste dryf; ~ *ON*, voortdring; vooruitbeur; ~ *something ON (UPON) someone*, iets op iem. afdwing (forseer); ~ *OUT*, uitdruk; ~ *the QUESTION*, aandring op 'n saak; ~ *SOMEONE hard*, iem. opdruk; *TIME* ~ *es*, die tyd word kort; ~ *UPON*, aandring op; ~ *the URGENCY of a matter on the authorities*, die dringendheid van 'n saak by die owerheid beklemtoon; ~ **agency**, persburo; ~ **agent**, advertensieagent; ~ **board**, persbord; ~**-box**, pershuisie, persbank; ~ **bureau**, persburo; ~**-button**, drukknop(pie); ~ **cable**, perskabelgram; ~ **campaign**, perskampanje; ~ **censor**, perssensor; ~ **censorship**, perssensuur; ~ **comment**, perskommentaar; ~ **copy**, afdruk; perskopie; ~ **cutting**, koerantuitknipsel.
press'ed, gedruk, benoud; *be* ~ *for BUSINESS*, min werk (sake) hê; *HARD* ~, in die knyp; *be* ~ *for TIME*, min tyd hê; ~ *YEAST*, koekiesuurdeeg.
press: ~ **er**, perser; drukker; ~**er foot**, drukvoetjie (van masjien); ~ **gallery**, persgalery; ~ **gang**, persgroep.
press'ing, dringend; dreigend; *since you ARE so* ~, aangesien julle (jy) so daarop aandring; ~ *DANGER*, dreigende gevaar; *a* ~ *INVITATION*, 'n dringende uitnodiging; ~ **block**, persblok; ~ **cloth**, parslap; ~**-iron**, parsyster.
press: ~ **law**, perswet; ~**man**, joernalis, persman, koerantskrywer; persbeampte; ~ **magnate**, koerantmagnaat; ~ **mark**, boekstempel; ~**-money**, handgeld; ~ **notice**, persaankondiging; ~ **pass**, perskaart; ~ **photographer**, persfotograaf; ~ **proof**, masjienproef; ~ **propaganda**, perspropaganda; ~ **reader**, proefleser; ~ **release**, amptelike persverklaring, persmededeling; ~ **report**, persberig, persverslag; ~ **representative**, persverteenwoordiger; ~ **review**, persoorsig; ~ **room**, perskamer, perslokaal; ~**-stud**, drukknoop, drukkertjie.
pre'ssure, druk; (aan)drang, dringendheid; drukking, pressie; drukspanning; drukte; *ATMOSPHERIC* ~, lugdruk; *BRING* ~ *to bear upon*, druk uitoefen op; *DO something under* ~, iets haastig doen; iets onder dwang doen; *at FULL* ~, met volle krag; *HIGH* ~, hoogdruk; *at HIGH* ~, kragtig; flink; *INITIAL* ~, begindruk; *SIGN a document under* ~, gedwing word om 'n dokument te teken; ~ *on SPACE*, plaasgebrek; *be UNDER* ~, noustrop trek; onderhewig aan druk wees; *owing to* ~ *of WORK*, a.g.v. te veel werk; weens drukke werksaamhede; ~ **boiler**, stoomdrukketel; drukkoker; ~ **bomb**, bodemdrukmeter; ~ **burst**, drukskeur, drukbars; ~ **cabin**, drukkajuit; ~ **cooker**, stoomkoker, drukkoker, drukkastrol, snelkoker; ~ **face**, drukvlak; ~**-feed**, druktoevoer; ~ **flake**, drukskilfer; ~ **gauge**, drukmeter; ~ **group**, drukgroep; ~ **lamp**, druklamp; ~ **lead**, drukleiding; ~ **lubrication**, druksmering; ~ **oil**, drukolie; ~ **point**, drukpunt; ~ **pump**, drukpomp; ~ **ring**, drukring; ~ **spring**, drukveer; ~ **steam**, drukstoom; ~ **stove**, drukstoof, pompstofie; ~ **stress**, drukspanning; ~ **welding**, druksweising.
pressuriza'tion, drukreëling.
pre'ssurize, die lug(druk) reël; ~**d**, druk, haastig, woelig, gejaag.
press: ~ **switch**, drukskakelaar; ~ **work**, perswerk; drukwerk.
pres'ter, priester.
prestidigita'tion, goëlery, kulkuns.
prestidig'itator, goëlaar, kulkunstenaar.
prestige', invloed; prestige, aansien, oorwig, ontsag.
prestig'ious, invloedryk; goëlend.
pres'to, gou, vinnig; *hey* ~! siedaar!
prestress', voorspan, vooraf span; ~*ed CONCRETE*, voorgespanne beton; ~*ed reinforced CONCRETE*, gewapende spanbeton; ~**ing**, voorspanning.
presum'able, vermoedelik.
presum'ably, glo, vermoedelik.
presume', vermoed, beskou, veronderstel, bevroed; aanneem; waag; *may I* ~ *to ASK*? mag ek so vry wees om te vra? ~*d KILLED*, as dood beskou; ~ *(UP)ON*, misbruik maak van.

presum'ing, verwaand, ingebeeld, aanmatigend; ~ *that*, veronderstel (aangenome) dat.
presump'tion, vermoede, veronderstelling; verwaandheid, verwatenheid, aanmatiging, oormoed, waanwysheid, onbeskaamdheid; voorbarigheid; *ACT on the* ~, v.d. veronderstelling uitgaan; ~ *of DEATH*, veronderstelling van dood; ~ *of LAW*, regsvermoede; *ON the* ~ *that . . .*, op vermoede dat . . .
presump'tive, waarskynlik, vermoedelik; aanwysend; ~ *EVIDENCE*, vermoedelike (waarskynlike) getuienis; *HEIR* ~, vermoedelike troonopvolger.
presump'tuous, aanmatigend, voorbarig, oormoedig; ingebeeld, verwaand, astrant, waanwys; ~**ness**, voorbarigheid, verwaandheid, waanwysheid.
presuppose', (voor)onderstel, aanneem.
presupposi'tion, onderstelling, vooronderstelling.
presurmise', argwaan, vermoede.
pre'-tax profit, voorbelaste wins, wins voor belasting.
pretence', voorwendsel, skyn, veinsing; aanspraak; *by FALSE* ~*s*, onder valse voorwendsels; *MAKE no* ~ *to*, nie aanspraak maak nie op; *MAKE a* ~ *of crying*, maak of jy huil; kastig huil; *ON* ~ *of*, onder voorwendsel van; *on the SLIGHTEST* ~, by (met) die geringste aanleiding; *UNDER the* ~ *of*, onder voorwendsel van.
pretend', voorwend, voorgee, veins, fingeer; beweer, kastig maak asof, die skyn aanneem van; aanspraak maak op; ~ *ILLNESS*, siekte voorwend; *he does not* ~ *to be a SCHOLAR*, hy gee nie voor dat hy 'n student is nie; ~ *TO*, aanspraak maak op; ~**ed**, voorgegewe, sogenaamd, voorgewend, gewaand, skyn=; kastig, kwasie=; ~**er**, pretendent, aanspraakmaker; huigelaar; ~**ing**, aanmatigend; huigelagtig; pretensieus, kamtig, sogenaamd.
preten'sion, voorwendsel; aanspraak.
preten'tious, aanmatigend; pronkerig, pretensieus; ~**ness**, aanmatiging; pronkerigheid, pretensieusheid.
preterhum'an, bo(we)menslik.
pret'erit(e), verlede tyd, preteritum.
preteri'tion, veronagsaming, weglating.
pretermi'ssion, weglating, uitlating, (die) weglaat.
pretermit', (-ted), verbygaan, oorslaan, veronagsaam, weglaat; oorslaan.
preternat'ural, buitengewoon; bonatuurlik; ~**ness**, bonatuurlikheid.
pret'ext, (n) voorwendsel, ekskuus, smoesie; *on the SLIGHTEST* ~, by die geringste voorwendsel; *UNDER the* ~ *of*, onder die skyn van; kastig om; *a* ~ *for a VISIT*, 'n ekskuus om te kuier.
pretext', (v) voorwend, voorgee.
pret'or, *kyk* **praetor**.
Pretor'ian, (n) Pretorianer; (a) Pretoriase, Pretoriaans.
prettifica'tion, mooimakery.
pre'ttify, (. . fied), mooimaak, mooi voorstel.
pre'ttily, mooi, netjies, fraai.
pre'ttiness, mooiheid, fraaiheid, liefheid; hupsheid; gesogtheid, mooiigheid.
pre'tty, (n) mooi dingetjie, mooi meisie; mooie; skoonveld (gholf); *fill my GLASS up to the* ~, vul my glas tot by die kerkraampies; *MY* ~, my skat; (a) mooi, lief, bevallig, snoesig; hups; *MAKE a* ~ *mess of*, 'n gemors maak van; *cost a* ~ *SUM*, 'n mooi sommetjie kos; (adv) taamlik, vrywel; *find it* ~ *HARD*, dit nogal moeilik vind; ~ *MUCH the same*, ongeveer dieselfde; *be SITTING* ~, daar goed in sit; jou oor niks verder hoef te kwel nie; ~ *SURE*, taamlik seker; ~ *WELL completed*, so goed as klaar (voltooi); ~**ish**, mooierig, nogal mooi; ~**ism**, gesogtheid; ~**-pre'tty**, (n) snuisterye; tierlantyntjies; (adv) oordrewe mooi (lief), gesog.
pret'zel, gevlegte kaasstrooitjie, soutkrakeling, pretzel, southappie.
prevail', heers, in swang wees, van krag wees; die oorhand kry; seëvier; algemeen wees; *allow JUSTICE to* ~; *let JUSTICE* ~, reg laat geskied; ~ *ON someone*, iem. ompraat, oorhaal, oorreed; *TRUTH will* ~ *over*, die waarheid sal (oor die leuen) seë=

vier; *if favourable WEATHER* ~ s, as die weer gunstig bly; ~ **ing**, heersend (wind); algemeen.
prev'alence, prev'alency, oorhand, oorwig; (die) heers, voorkoms; algemeenheid.
pre'valent, oorwegend; heersend (siekte); algemeen.
preva'ricate, uitvlugte soek, dubbelsinnig praat, bontspring, rondspring, jakkalsdraaie maak, die waarheid verdraai (ontwyk), ontwykend antwoord.
prevarica'tion(s), uitvlugsoekery; dubbelsinnigheid, jakkalsdraaie, slimpraatjies, jokkery, bontpratery, slimstories, uitvlug; ontwykende antwoord(e).
preva'ricator, uitvlugsoeker, draaier, jokker, bontprater.
preven'ient, voorafgaande, vorige.
prevent', belet, verhinder, voorkom, verhoed; afweer (siekte); voorkeer, weer; keer; ~ *one from DOING something,* iem. verhinder om iets te doen; ~ *an EVIL,* kwaad verhoed; ~ *a FIRE,* 'n brand voorkom; ~ *the RAIN from coming in,* keer dat die reën inkom; ~ **abil'ity,** vermybaarheid; voorkombaarheid; ~ **able,** voorkombaar; vermybaar; ~ **ative,** (n) voorbehoedmiddel; (a) belettend, verhinderend, voorkomend, preventief, voorsorgs-; ~ **er,** beletter, voorkomer.
preven'tion, voorkoming, verhindering; verhoeding, (af)wering; ~ *is better than cure,* voorkoming is beter as genesing; voorsorg voorkom nasorg.
preven'tive, (n) voorbehoedmiddel, preventief; *a* ~ *against malaria,* 'n voorbehoedmiddel teen malaria; (a) voorkomend, verhinderend, voorbehoed-, voorsorg-; ~ **arrest,** voorkomende hegtenis; ~ **detention,** voorkomende aanhouding; ~ **measure,** voorsorgmaatreël; voorbehoedmiddel; ~ **medicine,** voorkomende geneeskunde; ~ **officer,** bewakingsbeampte.
pre'view, (n) voorbesigtiging; voorvertoning; voorbeskouing; (v) vooraf sien (besigtig, kyk).
prev'ious, (a) voorafgaande, vroeër, vorige; voorbarig; ~ *conviction,* vorige veroordeling; (adv) voor; ~ *TO,* voor; *a little TOO* ~, 'n hietjie voorbarig; ~ **ly,** vantevore, vooraf, vroeër, voorheen; ~ **ness,** voorbarigheid.
previse', vooruitsien, voorspel; aankondig.
previ'sion, (die) vooruitsien; die gawe om te voorsien.
pre'-war, (van) voor die oorlog, vooroorlogs.
prey, (n) prooi; buit, roof; slagoffer; *FALL a* ~ *to,* 'n slagoffer word van; *BIRD of* ~, roofvoël; (v) roof, plunder, aas; loer; ~ *ON one's friends,* aas op jou vriende; ~ *ON the mind,* knaag aan die gemoed.
Pri'am, Priamus.
pria'pic, fallies.
pri'apism, priapisme.
price, (n) prys; waarde; *ADVANCE in* ~, prysstyging, prysverhoging; *at ANY* ~, teen enige prys; tot elke prys; *AT the* ~, teen die prys; tot elke prys, *BEYOND* ~, onskatbaar; onbetaalbaar; *CURRENT* ~ *(s),* lopende (gangbare) prys(e); *a DROP in* ~, 'n prysdaling; *what has that to do with the* ~ *of EGGS?* hoe raak dit die saak? *EVERY man has his* ~, daar is niemand wat nie omgekoop kan word nie; ~ *of ISSUE,* uitgifteskoers; ~ *of MONEY,* rentekoers; *NAME one's (own)* ~, jou eie prys maak; *PUT a* ~ *on someone's head,* 'n prys op iem. se kop sit; *at a REDUCED* ~, teen 'n verminderde prys; *a RISE in* ~, 'n prysstyging, 'n prysverhoging; *SET a* ~ *on someone's head,* iem voëlvry verklaar; *WHAT is the* ~? wat kos dit? *WITHOUT a* ~, nie vir geld te koop nie, onbetaalbaar; (v) die prys vasstel, prys gee; waardeer; die prys vra; ~ *oneself out of the market,* die prys onmoontlik duur maak; ~ **-book,** pryslys, katalogus; ~ **ceiling,** prysplafon, prystop, pryshoogte; ~ **class,** prysklas; ~ **control,** prysbeheer; ~ **current,** prys koerant; ~ **cutter,** pryssnoeier; ~ **cutting,** prysbesnoeiing, prysvermindering, prysverlaging; onderkruipery; ~ **fixing,** prysvasstelling; ~ **index,** prysindeks; ~ **less,** onbetaalbaar, onskatbaar; ~ **less joke,** kostelike grap; ~ **level,** pryspeil; ~ **-limit,** prysgrens; ~ **-list,** pryslys, ~ **-mark,** pryskaartjie; ~ **quotation,** prysnotering; pryskwotasie; ~ **range,**

prysbeweging; prysreeks; ~ **ring,** pryskartel; ~ **tag,** pryskaartjie.
prick, (n) steek; prikkel, doring; gaatjie; wroeging, knaging; ~ *s of CONSCIENCE,* gewetensknaging, gewetenswroeging; *KICK against the* ~ *s,* teen die prikkels skop; teenstribbel; (v) steek, prik; deursteek, priem, 'n gaatjie steek; aanspoor; spits; knaag; uitplant; ~ *the BUBBLE,* iets (iem.) aan die kaak stel; ~ *up the EARS,* die ore spits; ~ *OFF,* uitstippel; ~ *OUT,* uitplant; ~ **er,** punt; prikkel, stif, priem, els, steekding; vuurhaak (spoorweg); (oop)steker(tjie), prikker.
prick'et, spiesbok, spieshert; kerssteek, steekblaker.
prick'ing, (die) steek; bekrapping (van pleister).
pric'kle, (n) prikkel, doring, stekel, dorinkie; pen; (v) steek, prikkel.
prick'liness, doringrigheid, stekelagtigheid, stekeligheid; jeukerigheid.
prick'ly, stekerig, doringrig, doring-, prikkelend, stekelig; jeukerig; ~ **heat,** hitteuitslag; ~ **pear,** turksvy.
pride, (n) trots, hoogmoed, hovaardy; fierheid, hooghartigheid; trop (leeus); *BURSTING with* ~, baie trots; ~ *comes before a FALL,* ~ *will have a FALL,* hoogmoed kom voor die val; *his FATHER'S* ~ *(and joy),* sy vader se oogappel; ~ *of FRENCH HOEK,* Trots van Franschhoek; *GIVE* ~ *of place,* die voorrang gee; die hoogste plek toeken; ~ *of INDIA,* skubliesroos; ~ *of DE KAAP,* vlam-van-die-vlakte *(Bauhinia galpinii);* ~ *of LIONS,* 'n leeutrop; *a PEACOCK in his* ~, 'n pronkende pou; ~ *of PURSE,* geldtrots; *SWOLLEN with* ~, opgeblase van hoogmoed; ~ *of TABLE MOUNTAIN,* hakkiesblom, rooi disa; *TAKE* ~ *in,* trots wees op; jou eer stel in; *TAKE* ~ *of place,* die voorrang geniet; *YIELD* ~ *of place,* die ereplek afstaan aan; die voorrang gee aan; (v) trots wees, hoogmoedig wees, jou verhef; ~ *oneself on,* jou beroem op; ~ **ful,** trots, hoogmoedig; ~ **fulness,** trots.
prie-dieu', bidstoeltjie, bidbank, knielbank.
pri'er, snuffelaar, spioen.
priest, (n) priester; leviet, tempeldienaar; geestelike, pastoor; houthamer; ~ *in charge,* diensdoende priester; (v) tot priester wy; ~ **craft,** priesterlis; priesterbeleid; ~ **ess, (-es),** priesterees; ~ **hood,** priesterskap; ~ **-in-the-pulpit,** varkblom, geelpiet-in-die-manteljas; ~ **like,** ~ **ly,** priesterlik; ~ **-ridden,** deur priesters geregeer; onder die plak v.d. priesters.
prig, (n) pedant, wysneus, verwaande persoon; dief; (v) **(-ged),** steel, ontfutsel; ~ **gery,** pedantheid; ~ **gish,** ingebeeld, eiewys, verwaand, pedanties; ~ **gishness,** ~ **gism,** eiewysheid, verwaandheid, wysneusigheid, aanstellery, pedanterie.
prim, (v) **(-med),** die mond op 'n sedige plooi trek, sedig lyk; (a) styf, sedig, gekunsteld, vormlik; geaffekteerd, jufferagtig, preuts, presies, netjies; ~ *and proper,* ewe sedig, danig sedig.
pri'ma, eerste, vernaamste, prima; ~ *BALLERINA,* hoofdanseres, prima ballerina; ~ *DONNA,* prima donna; ~ *FACIE,* op die eerste gesig; op die oog; prima facie (*reg*).
prim'acy, (..cies), opperkerkvoogdy, primaatskap, voorrang, voortreflikheid.
prim'age, vragpremie.
prim'al, eerste, vernaamste, oer-, grond-, hoof-.
prim'arily, voor alles, in die eerste plek, vernaamlik, hoofsaaklik.
prim'ary, (n) **(..ries),** première planeet; slagpen (voël, hoender); première kleur; hoofsaak; laerskool; benoemingsverkiesing (V.S.A.); (pl) vlerkvere; (a) aanvanklik; laer, eerste; primêr (onderwys); hoof-; vroegste, oorspronklik, grond-; ~ **axis,** hoofas; ~ **cause,** aanleidende (première) oorsaak; ~ **charge,** hooflading; ~ **colour,** grondkleur; ~ **education,** laer onderwys; ~ **evidence,** eerstehandse getuienis; ~ **feather,** slagpen; ~ **importance,** hoogste belang; ~ **meeting,** benoemingsvergadering; ~ **pupil,** laerskoolleerling; ~ **role,** hoofrol; ~ **school,** laerskool, laer skool; première skool; ~ **-school teacher,** laerskoolonderwyser(es); ~ **shaft,** hoofas.

prim'ate, aartsbiskop; primaat; ~**ship,** primaatskap.
primave'ra, primavera.
prime, (n) begin, eerste tyd; aanvangstadium; bloeityd, lente, fleur; priemgetal; *be in the* ~ *of life,* in die bloei v.d. lewe wees; (v) in die grondverf sit; grondeer; opkook (stoomketel); 'n grondlaag gee; voorvoer; afrig, onderrig; laai, kruit op die pan gooi; ontsteek, (slagdoppie, sunder) aanbring; oorlaai met drank; insuur; blare afbreek (tabak); inpomp (kennis); aan die gang sit; inspuit (motor); ~ *a witness,* 'n getuie voorsê; (a) eerste, vernaamste, primêr, oorspronklik; fleur=; prima, eersteklas, uitstekend; *in* ~ *CONDITION,* in 'n eersteklas kondisie; *a* ~ *CONDITION is that,* 'n grondvoorwaarde is dat; *of* ~ *QUALITY,* puik; van prima kwaliteit; ~ **cattle,** eersteklas (prima) beeste; ~ **cost,** inkoopprys; direkte koste; ~ **meridian,** nul=meridiaan; ~ **minister,** eerste minister, premier; ~ **ministership,** eersteministerskap, premierskap; ~ **mover,** oorspronklike beweegkrag; hoofkragbron, hoofaandryfmasjien; leier, aanstigter, aanstoker; ~ **number,** priemgetal, ondeelbare getal; ~ **object,** vernaamste oogmerk, hoofdoel.
prim'er, eerste leesboek, abc-boek; ab-jab; inleiding; drukletter; ontstekingsmiddel, ontsteker, doppie, sunder; ruimnaald; grondlaag, grondverf; gebedeboek; inspuitpomp; voorvoerder; *GREAT* ~, agt=tienpuntletter; *LONG* ~, tienpuntletter; ~-**cartridge,** doppiepatroon.
prime' rib, prima rib.
prime'ro, primero (kaartspel).
primev'al, oer=, oeroud, oorspronklik, uit die voortyd, eerste (inwoners); ~ **forest,** oerwoud; ~ **race,** oervolk.
primigra'vida, primigravida, eersswangere.
prim'ing, pankruit; inpomping (van kennis); grondverf; opkoking; inspuit; voorskrif, opdrag; aanwakkering; opkook (stoomketel); *the* ~ *of the tides,* vervroeging van die gety; ~ **cap,** slaghoedjie; ~ **coat,** grondlaag; ~ **colour,** grondkleur; ~-**gear,** inspuittoestel; ~ **hole,** sundgat; ~-**iron,** ruimnaald; ~ **paint,** grondverf; ~-**powder,** slagkruit; ~-**pump,** inspuitpomp; ~-**wire,** ruimnaald.
primip'ara, primipara, eersbarende.
primipar'ity, eerste swangerskap.
primip'arious, eersbarend, vir die eerste keer barend.
prim'itive, (n) primitief; primitiewe mens; (a) oorspronklik, primitief, vroegste, allereerste; eenvoudig, rudimentêr; oer=; ~ **ness,** eenvoud, eenvoudigheid; primitiwiteit; ~ **man,** die oermens; ~ **rocks,** oergesteentes.
primitiv'ity, primitiwiteit.
prim'ness, sedigheid, vormlikheid, preutsheid; netheid.
prim'o, eerste.
primogen'ital, oorspronklik, eerste gebore.
primogen'itor, stamvader, voorvader.
primogen'iture, eersgeboortereg, majoraat.
primord'ial, oorspronklik, eerste, primordiaal, oer=; fundamenteel; oudste; ~ **cell,** oersel; ~ **leaf,** oorgangsblaar; ~ **tissue,** grondweefsel.
primor'dium, primordium, beginpunt, oervorm, oorsprong.
primp = **prink.**
prim'rose, sleutelblom, primula; *the* ~ *PATH,* die pad van plesier en singenot; die breë pad (weg); *TREAD the* ~ *path,* die breë weg bewandel.
prim'ula, primula, sleutelblom.
prince, prins, koningseun; vors; ~ *of the BLOOD,* prins van den bloede; *P*~ *CHARMING,* die Toweprins; ~ *of DARKNESS,* vors van die duisternis, Satan; *he is a* ~ *among MEN,* hy is 'n baie goeie man; *P*~ *of PEACE,* Vredevors; *P*~ *of WALES,* Prins van Wallis; ~ **consort,** prins-gemaal; ~**dom,** prinsdom; vorstedom; ~**hood,** vorsterang; ~**like,** vorstelik; ~**ling,** prinsie; ~**ly,** vorstelik; luisterryk, skitterend; ~ **regent,** prins-regent; regerende prins; ~ **royal,** kroonprins; ~'**s feather,** katstert (plant); ~'**s metal,** prinsmetaal.
prin'cess, (-es), prinses, koningsdogter; vorstin; ~ *royal,* koninklike prinses.

prin'cipal, (n) hoof, hoofonderwyser, prinsipaal; rektor (universiteit); kapitaal, hoofsom (geld); direkteur; lasgewer, prinsipaal (van 'n agent), maggeër (reg); hoofbalk (gebou); *only* ~*s will be DEALT with,* van tussenpersone word geen notisie geneem nie; ~ *of a SCHOOL,* prinsipaal, hoofonderwyser; ~ *of a UNIVERSITY,* rektor van 'n universiteit; (a) vernaamste, oorwegend; gewigtigste; belangrikste, hoof=; ~ **beam,** hoofbalk; ~ **clause,** hoofsin; ontvangsin; ~ **clerk,** eerste klerk; ~ **feature,** hoofkenmerk, vernaamste kenmerk; ~'**ity,** prinsdom, vorstedom; vorstelike waardigheid; ~**ly,** hoofsaaklik, veral, grotendeels; ~ **offender,** hoofskuldige; ~ **parade,** hoofparade; ~ **parts,** hoofdele (v.d. werkwoord); ~ **post,** hoofstyl, dakstyl; ~ **rafter,** kapbeen; ~ **sentence,** hoofsin; ~**ship,** prinsipaalskap, hoofskap; ~ **trait,** hooftrek.
prin'ciple, beginsel; grondslag; prinsipe; grondbeginsel; *ACCEPT something in* ~, iets in beginsel aanvaar; *ACT up to one's* ~*s,* handel volgens 'n mens se beginsels; *APPROVE in* ~, in beginsel aanvaar (goedkeur); *IN* ~, in beginsel; *a MAN of* ~*s,* 'n man met vaste beginsels; *a MATTER of* ~, 'n beginselsaak; *man of NO* ~*s,* 'n beginsellose man; *ON* ~, uit beginsel; *TRUE to one's* ~*s,* beginselvas; *WITHOUT* ~, beginselloos; ~**d,** met vaste beginsels, beginselvas.
prink, opskik, uitdos, mooimaak, optooi; die vere glad stryk; ~**ing,** optooiery, mooimakery, uitdossery.
print, (n) merk, spoor; edisie, druk; drukskrif; prent; plaat; vorm, stempel; blad; gedrukte katoenstof, sis; *APPEAR in* ~, in druk verskyn; *GERMAN* ~, Gotiese druk(letter); *IN* ~, gedruk, in druk; *LARGE* ~, groot druk; *OUT of* ~, uit druk; *RUSH into* ~, te gou 'n brief aan 'n koerant skryf; werk te gou laat druk (publiseer); *SMALL* ~, klein (fyn) letter (druk); (v); druk; afdruk; merk, stempel; uitgee, publiseer; in drukletter(s) skryf; in=prent; ~ *on the mind,* op die gemoed druk, in die geheue prent; ~**able,** drukbaar, publiseerbaar; ~-**drier,** droogmasjien (fotogr.); ~ **dress,** sisrok; ka=toenrok.
print'ed, afgedruk; bedruk; gestempel; gepubliseer (boek); ~ **calico,** Duitse sis; ~ **card,** gedrukte kaartjie; ~ **linoleum,** bedrukte linoleum; ~ **material,** bedrukte stof (materiaal); ~ **matter,** druk=werk; ~ **page** *(of type area),* bladspieël; ~ **paper,** bedrukte papier; ~ **word,** die gedrukte woord.
prin'ter, drukker; ~'**s devil,** drukkersduiwel; ~'**s error,** drukfout, erratum; ~'**s galley,** setgalei; ~'**s imprint,** monogram; drukkersmerk; ~'**s ink,** drukink; ~'**s mark,** monogram; drukkersmerk; ~'**s pie,** ingevalle setsel; ~'**s proof,** drukproef; ~'**s reader,** proefleser.
print'hand, drukletter(skrif).
prin'ting, druk; drukkuns; drukwerk; uitgawe, oplaag; *faint* ~, matdruk; ~ **box,** afdrukkas; ~ **cylinder,** druksilinder; ~ **error,** drukfout; ~ **expenses,** drukkoste; ~ **form,** drukvorm; ~ **frame,** kopieerpers, drukraam; ~ **house,** drukkery; ~ **ink,** drukink; ~ **machine,** drukpers; snelpers; ~ **office,** drukkery; ~ **paper,** drukpapier; ~ **plate,** drukplaat; ~ **press,** drukpers; ~ **set,** drukstelletjie; ~ **surface,** bladspieël, drukspieël; ~ **type,** drukletter; lettervorm; ~ **works,** drukkery.
print: ~-**off,** afdruk; ~-**out** *(computer),* drukstuk; ~ **script,** blokskrif; ~-**seller,** prentehandelaar; ~-**shop,** prentewinkel; ~-**trimmer,** prentoptooier; ~-**works,** fabriek waar katoenstof gedruk word.
pri'or, (n) prior, kloostervoog; (a) vroeër, eerder; voor, voorafgaande; *have a* ~ *engagement,* reeds 'n afspraak hê; (adv) vroeër, voor; ~ *to my arrival,* voor my aankoms; ~**ate,** prioraat; ~ **claim,** ouer eis (reg); voorgaande eis (reg); ~**ess, (-es),** priores.
prio'rity, (..ties), voorrang, voorkeur, prioriteit; voorkeurreg; ~ *of BIRTH,* eersgeboorte; *have a* ~ *CLAIM,* ouer regte hê; *CREDITORS by* ~, bevoorregte skuldeisers; *GIVE one thing* ~ *to (over) another,* iets voorrang bo 'n ander saak verleen; *you must get your ..ties in ORDER,* jy moet besluit wat die belangrikste is; jy moet jou prioriteite regkry.

pri'or lien, eerste verband.
pri'orship, prioraat, priorwaardigheid.
pri'ory, (..ries), priory, klooster.
prise, (n) hefboom; breekyster; (v) oopbreek, oopmaak.
prism, prisma; ~ **at'ic,** prismaties; ~ *atic glasses,* prismakyker.
pris'on, (n) tronk, gevangenis; (v) opsluit, in die tronk sit; *BE in* ~ , in die tronk wees, tussen vier mure sit; *BREAK out of* ~ , uit die tronk ontsnap; *DEPARTMENT of P* ~ *s,* Departement van Gevangeniswese; *PUT into* ~ , in die tronk sit; ~ **bars,** tronktralies; ~ **-break,** ontsnapping uit die tronk; ~ **breaker,** ontsnapte bandiet; voortvlugtige; ~ **camp,** gevangeniskamp, gevangenekamp; ~ **cell,** tronksel; ~ **editor,** sitredakteur.
pris'oner, gevangene, prisonier; bandiet; ~ *at the BAR,* (die) aangeklaagde; ~ *of STATE,* politieke gevangene; *TAKE* ~ , gevange neem; ~ *of WAR,* krygsgevangene; ~ **'s friend,** prisoniersvriend.
pris'on: ~ **officer,** sipier; ~ **term,** straftyd; ~ **van,** tronkwa; ~ **warder,** tronkbewaarder, sipier; ~ **yard,** tronkbinneplaas.
pris'tine, oorspronklik, vroeër, eerste, ou, eertyds, jeug=; ~ *glory,* ou glorie, eertydse glorie.
pri'thee, ek vra u; asseblief.
priv'acy, geheimhouding; heimlikheid; afsondering, eensaamheid, privaatheid, stilte; *in* ~ , privaat, afgesonder.
priv'ate, (n) gewone soldaat, weerman, manskap; (pl) (ook) skaamdele, geslagsdele; *in* ~ , in die geheim; in stilte; onder vier oë; agter geslote deure; (a) privaat, besloto; persoonlik; partikulier; vertroulik, geheim; gereserveer, afgesonder; *a* ~ *AFFAIR,* 'n onderonsie; 'n private saak; *a* ~ *ASSEMBLY,* 'n geslote byeenkoms; ~ *BAG,* privaat sak; *in* ~ *CLOTHES,* in burgerklere, in gewone klere; ~ *and CONFIDENTIAL,* streng vertroulik; *a* ~ *CONVERSATION,* 'n vertroulike gesprek; *for his own* ~ *ENDS,* vir sy eie persoonlike doel(eindes); *KEEP* ~ , stilhou; *have* ~ *MEANS,* privaat middele hê; *a* ~ *OPINION,* 'n persoonlike (private) opinie; ~ **bill,** privaatwetsontwerp, wetsontwerp deur 'n gewone lid ingedien; ~ **box,** (pos)bus; ~ **coach,** privaatpassasierswa; ~ **company,** privaatmaatskappy; familievennootskap; ~ **entrance,** aparte ingang.
privateer', (n) kaper; kaperskip; (v) kaap; ~ **ing,** kapery, kaapvaart; ~ **s'man,** kaapvaarder.
priv'ate: ~ **examination,** privaateksamen; ~ **hotel,** ongelisensieerde (droë) hotel, losieshuis, privaathotel; ~ **house,** woonhuis; ~ **individual,** partikulier, gewone mens; ~ **information,** vertroulike inligting; ~ **law,** privaatreg; ~ **lesson,** privaatles; ~ **ly,** heimlik, privaat, alleen; op eie koste; in stilte; onder vier oë; ~ **opinion,** persoonlike mening; ~ **ownership,** privaatbesit; ~ **parts,** skaamdele, geslagsdele; ~ **property,** privaatbesit; ~ **road,** privaatpad; ~ **sale,** onderhandse verkoping; ~ **school,** (..skole), privaatskool; ~ **secretary,** privaatsekretaris, private sekretaris; privaatsekretaresse; ~ **siding,** privaatlyn; ~ **soldier,** gewone soldaat, weerman; ~ **tender,** onderhandse inskrywing; ~ **view,** voorbesigtiging; persoonlike sienswyse.
priva'tion, berowing; ontbering, gebrek, derwing.
pri'vative, ontkennend, berowend, privatief.
priv'et, liguster.
priv'ilege, (n) voorreg; vrywaring; guns, privilegie; (v) bevoorreg; vrystel; magtig; ~ *from,* vrygestel van; ~ **d,** bevoorreg; beskerm.
priv'ily, in die geheim.
priv'ity, medewete; geheime verstandhouding; wetlike verhouding.
priv'y, (n) **(privies),** gemak(huisie), privaat, sekreet, kleinhuisie, kasteeltjie, klooster; (a) heimlik, geheim; verborge; *be* ~ *to,* ingewy wees; kennis dra van; *P* ~ **Council,** Geheime Raad; *P* ~ **Counsellor,** lid van die Geheime Raad; ~ **parts,** geslagsdele; ~ **purse,** siviele lys; ~ **seal,** geheimseël.
prize¹, (n) hefboom; (v) oopmaak, oopbreek.
prize², (n) buit; prysskip; *make a* ~ *of a ship,* 'n skip buit (prys maak); (v) buit maak (skip).

prize³, (n) (ere)prys, beloning; *DISTRIBUTION of* ~ *s,* prysuitdeling; *OFFER a* ~ , 'n prys uitloof; *WIN a* ~ , 'n prys wen (kry); (v) waardeer, op prys stel; ~ *liberty more than life,* vryheid hoër ag as die lewe; (a) prys=, bekroonde; *a* ~ *d possession,* 'n hooggewaardeerde besitting; ~ **-book,** boekprys; ~ **competition,** prysraaisel, pryswedstryd.
prize'-court, pryshof, prysgerig.
prize: ~ **-day,** ~ **distribution,** prysuitdeling; ~ **essay,** prysverhandeling, bekroonde verhandeling; ~ **-fight,** professionele bokswedstryd, vuisgeveg; ~ **-fighter,** beroepsbokser; bokser, vuisvegter; ~ **-fighting,** beroepsboks; vuisvegtery; ~ **-giving,** prysuitdeling; ~ **judge,** prysregter.
prize'-law, seebuitreg.
prize: ~ **man,** pryswenner; ~ **-medal,** prysmedalje; ~ **-meeting,** prysskiet; ~ **-money,** prysgeld; ~ **poem,** bekroonde gedig; ~ **question,** prysvraag; ~ **-ring,** bokskryt; plek van mededinging.
prize'-ship, prysskip.
prize: ~ **subject,** prysvraag; ~ **-winner,** pryswenner, bekroonde.
pro¹, *abbr. of* **professional,** (n) **(-s),** beroepspeler.
pro², (prep) voor; vir; ~ *s and CONS,* voor en teë; ~ *DEO,* pro Deo, kosteloos; ~ *FORMA,* vir die vorm; ~ *FORMA invoice,* pro forma-faktuur; ~ *RATA,* na verhouding, eweredig; ~ *TEMPORE (tem),* tydelik, voorlopig; waarnemend.
pro-Afrikaans', Afrikaansgesind.
prob'abilism, probabilisme, waarskynlikheidsleer.
probabil'ity, (..ties), waarskynlikheid; gebeurliklikheid; *in ALL* ~ , na alle waarskynlikheid; *there is NO* ~ *of,* dit is baie onwaarskynlik dat; *THEORY of probabilities,* waarskynlikheidsrekening, kansrekening.
prob'able, waarskynlik, denklik.
prob'ably, vermoedelik, waarskynlik, allig; *most* ~ , hoogs waarskynlik.
pro'band, proband.
pro'bang, keelstokkie, probang.
prob'ate, regterlike verifikasie van 'n testament; ~ **duty,** suksessiereg, boedelbelasting.
proba'tion, proeftyd; ondersoek; voorwaardelike vrystelling; *ON* ~ , op proef; *PERIOD of* ~ , proeftyd; ~ **al,** ~ **ary,** proef=; ~ **er,** aspirant; kweekling; leerling op proef, proeweling; leerlingverpleegster; voorwaardelik veroordeelde; ~ **officer,** proefbeampte, reklasseringsbeampte; ~ **sermon,** proefpreek.
prob'ative, op proef, proef=; bewys=.
probe, (n) wondyster; sonde, sondeeryster, peilstif; noukeurige ondersoek; (v) ondersoek, peil; sondeer (wond); ~ *to the BOTTOM,* grondig ondersoek; ~ *INTO,* (noulettend) ondersoek; ~ **-scissors,** wondskêr.
prob'ing, sondering; ~ **-bar,** peilyster, soekyster.
pro'bit, probit.
prob'ity, eerlikheid, regskapenheid, onkreukbaarheid, deug, deugsaamheid, opregtheid.
prob'lem, probleem, vraagstuk; raaisel; opgawe, som; *study of* ~ *s,* problematiek; ~ **at'ic,** twyfelagtig; onuitgemaak, problematies; ~ **ist,** problematikus; ~ **-solving centre,** dinkfabriek.
pro-Boer', (n) Boerevriend; (a) Boergesind, pro-Boer(s).
proboscid'ean, (n) slurpdier; (a) slurpdier=.
probos'cis, (..cides), suigmond, (heuning)slurp, suigsnawel; snuit, neus; ~ **monkey,** neusaap.
pro-Brit'ish, Britsgesind.
proced'ure, handelwyse, werkwyse, metode, prosedure; *LAW of* ~ , prosesreg; *LEGAL* ~ , regspraktyk.
proceed', aangaan, voortgaan, verder gaan, deurgaan, vervolg; te werk gaan, handel; voortsit, verder gaan; in reg optree; oorgaan; ~ *AGAINST,* 'n aksie instel teen; ~ *FROM,* voortkom uit; ~ *ON one's way,* jou weg vervolg; ~ *TO,* oorgaan tot; jou begewe na; ~ **ing,** handelwyse, handeling, gedragslyn; (pl) handelinge; verslae; verrigtinge; *institute (take) legal* ~ *ings against,* 'n hofsaak maak teen, geregtelike stappe doen, 'n vervolging instel, vervolg.
pro'ceeds, opbrings, wins.

pro'cess, (n) (-es), voortgang; loop, verloop; handelwyse; bereidingswyse; regsgeding, proses; dagvaarding; verlengstuk; uitwas; *BE in* ~, aan die gang wees; *CIVIL* ~, siviele saak; *in* ~ *of CONSTRUCTION*, in aanbou; *serve a* ~ *on*, dagvaar; *in* ~ *of TIME*, met verloop van tyd; (v) prosedeer, 'n aksie instel; kos inlê (inmaak); (tekening) reproduseer; verwerk.
process', (v) in optog loop.
pro'cess: ~ **block,** cliché; ~ **camera,** reproduksiekamera; ~ **engraver,** clichémaker, sinkograaf; ~ **engraving,** clichémakery, sinkografie; ~**ing,** verwerking.
proce'ssion, (n) optog, prosessie, stoet; staatsie; reeks; *funeral* ~, lykstoet; (v) 'n stoet vorm; ~**al,** (n) prosessiegesang, prosessielied; (a) prosessie=; ~**ary,** prosessie=; ~**ist,** deelnemer aan 'n prosessie.
pro'cess: ~ **or,** verwerker; ~ **printing,** driekleuredruk.
pro'chronism, voordatering, prochronisme.
proc'idence, versakking, uitsakking.
proclaim', afkondig, aankondig, bekend maak, uitroep; proklameer; stempel; ~ *something from the HOUSETOPS*, iets v.d. dakke verkondig; iets uitbasuin; iets aan die groot klok hang; ~ *MARTIAL law,* krygswet afkondig; ~ *a REPUBLIC*, 'n republiek uitroep; ~**er,** afkondiger, uitroeper.
proclama'tion, afkondiging, proklamasie; uitroeping; aankondiging, verklaring.
proclit'ic, (n) proklitiese woord; (a) proklities.
procliv'ity, (..ties), oorhelling; neiging; ~ *to*, neiging tot.
procliv'ous, oorhellend, geneig.
procon'sul, prokonsul, landvoog; ~ **ar,** prokonsulêr; ~**ate,** prokonsulaat; ~**ship,** prokonsulskap.
procras'tinate, uitstel, verskuiwe; talm, draal, draai, sloer.
procrastina'tion, uitstel; getalm; ~ *is the thief of time*, van uitstel kom afstel.
procras'tinator, uitsteller; draler.
proc'reate, voortbring, teel, verwek.
procrea'tion, voortbrenging, teling, verwekking, voortplanting, prokreasie.
proc'reative, voortbrengend, voorttelend; voortplantings=; ~ **faculty,** teelkrag, voortplantingsvermoë; ~**ness,** teelkrag, voortplantingsvermoë; ~ **power,** teelkrag.
proc'reator, voortbrenger, verwekker, voortplanter.
Procrus'tean, na eenvormigheid strewend deur geweld; ~ **bed,** Prokrustesbed.
Procrust'es, Prokrustes; *stretch something on the bed of* ~, deur geweld probeer eenders maak; deur geweld na eenvormigheid strewe.
proc'tor, saakgelastigde, saakwaarnemer; tugmeester; prokurasiehouer; ~**ship,** saakwaarnemerskap.
proc'toscope, proktoskoop.
procum'bent, vooroor(leënd), uitgestrek, plat.
procurabil'ity, verkry(g)baarheid.
procur'able, verkry(g)baar.
procura'tion, verskaffing; koppelary (vir ontug); volmag, prokurasie, magtiging; *by* ~, by volmag; ~ **fee,** ~ **money,** makelaarsloon.
proc'urator, gevolmagtigde, saakgelastigde; prokurator; agent; ~**ship,** agentskap, staat van gevolmagtigde.
procure', verkry, verskaf, besorg, kry; bewerk; koppel (vir ontug); ~**ment,** verskaffing, verkryging; bemiddeling; koppeling (vir ontug); ~**r,** verskaffer, besorger; koppelaar (vir ontug).
procur'ess, (-es), koppelaarster.
procur'ing, verkryging; koppelary (vir ontug).
procurva'tion, vooroorbuiging.
prod, (n) stoot, por; pen; steek, prikkel; priem; els; (v) (-ded), steek, stoot, prik; prikkel; aanpor; ~ **der,** prikstok, porstok; *electrical* ~ *der*, elektriese porstok.
prodeli'sion, prodelisie, vokaalelisie.
prod'igal, (n) verkwister, deurbringer; (a) verkwistend, deurbringerig, spandabel, spandabelrig; spilsiek; roekeloos, verlore; ~ *OF*, rojaal met; *the P* ~ *SON*, die Verlore Seun; ~**'ity,** verkwisting, roekeloosheid, spandabelheid, spilsug, kwistigheid; vrygewigheid; ~**ize,** verkwis, deurbring, verspil.
prodigios'ity, (..ties), wondermens.
prodi'gious, kolossaal, enorm, ontsaglik, verskriklik; wonderbaarlik, ongehoord; ~**ness,** verskriklikheid, ontsaglikheid; wonderbaarlikheid.
prod'igy, (..gies), wonder; seldsaamheid; wondermens; iets wonderbaarliks; ~ *of nature,* natuurwonder.
prod'rome, prodroom, inleiding, voorlopige verhandeling; voorloper, voorbode, voorteken.
prod'uce, (n) voortbrengsel; produkte, oes; naturalieë; opbrengs, produksie; resultaat.
produce', (v) voortbring, oplewer, genereer, fabriseer, produseer; voor die dag haal, te voorskyn bring, toon, vertoon; opvoer op die toneel bring; verleng; teweegbring, veroorsaak; aanvoer; lewer; ~ *d by the AUTHOR*, onder leiding (regie) v.d. skrywer; ~ *a DOCUMENT*, 'n dokument voorlê; ~ *EVIDENCE*, bewys lewer; ~ *a GUN*, 'n rewolwer uitpluk; ~ *a LINE TO* (geom.), 'n lyn verleng tot (meetk.); ~ *a PLAY*, 'n toneelstuk opvoer; ~ *PROOF,* bewys lewer; ~ *a SENSATION,* 'n opskudding veroorsaak; ~ *WITNESSES,* getuies bring.
prod'uce: ~ **dealer,** produktehandelaar; ~ **exchange,** koopmansbeurs; produktebeurs; ~ **market,** produktemark.
produ'cer, nywereaar, produsent; opvoerder, afrigter; regisseur, spelleier, spelleidster, regisseuse; ontwerper; uitgewer; vervaardiger, produksieleier (van rolprent); ~**'s price,** produsenteprys.
prod'uce trade, produktehandel.
producibil'ity, vertoonbaarheid, produseerbaarheid.
produ'cible, vertoonbaar.
prod'uct, opbrings, produk, voortbrengsel; gevolg, resultaat; (pl) ware, goedere.
produc'tion, voortbrenging; gewrog; produksie; winning; voortbrengsel; voorlegging; opvoering (toneelstuk); verlenging (van 'n lyn); oorlegging (van dokument); vervaardiging; lewering (van bewys); *CAPACITY of* ~, produksiekapasiteit; *COST of* ~, produksiekoste; *EXCESS of* ~, produksieoorskot; *IN* ~, word vervaardig; *ON* ~ *of*, op vertoon van; ~ **line,** produksiebaan; monteerband; ~ **rate,** produksietempo.
produc'tive, voortbrengend, produktief; vrugbaar; *of great annoyance,* die oorsaak van baie ergernis; ~ **capacity,** produktiwiteit, produksievermoë; ~**ness,** ~**ti'vity,** produktiwiteit, vrugbaarheid.
pro'em, voorrede, voorwoord, proloog; voorspel.
proem'ial, inleidend.
pro-Eng'lish, pro-Engels, Engelsgesind, Rooi.
profana'tion, ontheiliging, ontwyding, skending, profanasie.
profane', (v) ontheilig, skend; misbruik; ontwy, profaneer; (a) ontheiligend, ongewyd; goddeloos, godslasterlik; profaan; ~ **history,** ongewyde geskiedenis; ~ **language,** vloekwoorde; ~ **writer,** ongewyde skrywer; ~**r,** ontwyer, ontheiliger, skender; misbruiker.
profan'ity, heiligskennis, godslastering, goddeloosheid, profaniteit, onheiligheid; vloekwoorde, gevloek.
profess', bely, erken; verseker; betuig; beweer; voorgee, aanspraak maak op; beoefen, les gee, kollege gee; ~ *to be,* jou voordoen as; ~**ed,** erkende, verklaarde; beroeps=; voorgewend; ~**edly,** erkend; oënskynlik, soos beweer word; openlik; sogenaamd, kastig.
profe'ssion, beroep, vak; bedryf, professie; geloof, belydenis; bekentenis; gelofteaflegging; betuiging; *BY* ~, van beroep; *PRACTICE a* ~, 'n beroep uitoefen; *THE* ~ *s,* die geleerde beroepe.
profe'ssional, (n) vakman; beroepspeler; beroepsmens; (a) beroeps=, professioneel, vak=; ~ **conduct,** beroepsgedrag; eerbare gedrag; ~ **honour,** beroepseer; ~**ism,** beroepseienaardigheid; beroepsport, professionalisme; ~ **jealousy,** broodnyd, beroepsjaloesie; ~ **liar,** gewoonteleuenaar; ~**ly,** beroepshalwe; professioneel; ~ **man,** vakman; ~ **officer,** vakkundige amptenaar (beampte); ~

player, beroepspeler, professionele speler; ~ **politician,** beroepspolitikus; ~ **rugby,** geldrugby, vertoonrugby; ~ **school,** vakskool; ~ **secret,** ampsgeheim; ~ **training,** vakopleiding; ~ **woman,** sakevrou.
profess'or, professor, hoogleraar; belyer; ~ *of English in the University of Pretoria*, hoogleraar in Engels aan die Universiteit van Pretoria; ~**ate,** professoraat.
professor'ial, professoraal.
professor'iate, professorpersoneel.
profess'orship, professoraat, professorskap, leerstoel.
proff'er, (n) aanbod; (v) aanbied, toesteek; ~ *one's hand*, iem. jou hand toesteek; ~**er,** aanbieder.
profi'ciency, bedrewenheid, bekwaamheid; vaardigheid, kundigheid; vordering; ~ **allowance,** bedrewenheidstoelae; ~ **certificate,** bevoegdheidsertifikaat; ~ **pay,** vaardigheidstoelae.
profi'cient, (n) vergevorderde, meester; (a) bedrewe, volleerd, vaardig, bekwaam; knap; ~ *IN mathematics*, knap in wiskunde; ~ *at SPORT*, bedrewe in sport; ~ *WITH*, handig met.
prof'ile, (n) profiel, butelyn (van die gesig); vertikale deursnee; (v) in profiel teken; profileer; ~ **drag,** profielweerstand; ~ **drawing,** profieltekening.
prof'ilist, silhoeëttekenaar; profilis.
prof'it, (n) wins, gewin, profyt, voordeel; verdienste; nut; rendement, voordeligheid; *DERIVE* ~ *from*, nut trek uit; ~ *and LOSS*, wins en verlies; ~ *and LOSS account*, wins-en-verliesrekening; *MAKE a* ~ *on goods*, wins maak op goedere; *MARGIN of* ~, winsgrens; *small* ~*s and quick RETURNS*, klein wins, groot omset; *SELL at a* ~, met wins verkoop; *make a* ~ *by SELLING at the right moment*, wins maak deur op die regte tyd te verkoop; *YIELD a* ~, wins afwerp; (v) wins maak; baat, van nut wees; voordeel trek uit, profiteer; uitwin; ~ *BY*, munt slaan uit; ~ *from EXPERIENCE*, voordeel trek uit ondervinding; ~**abil'ity,** voordeligheid, winsgewendheid; ~**able,** winsgewend, voordelig; ~**ableness,** voordeligheid, voordeel; ~**ably,** voordelig; nuttig; met vrug; ~ **balance,** winssaldo; ~**-earning,** winsgewend; ~**eer',** (n) woekerwinsmaker, gewinsoeker, woekeraar, oorwinsmaker, winsjagter; (v) profiteer; oorwins maak; oorlogswins maak; ~**eer'ing,** woekerwins, winsbejag, geldmakery; ~**less,** onvoordelig; nutteloos; ~**-maker,** winsmaker; ~ **motive,** winsoogmerk; ~**-seeker,** winsjagter; ~**-seeking,** winsbejag; ~**-sharing,** winsdeling; ~**-taking,** winsneming.
prof'ligacy, losbandigheid, sedeloosheid; verkwisting.
prof'ligate, (n) losbandige, losbol; verkwister; sedelose persoon; (a) losbandig, sedeloos; roekeloos, verkwistend.
profound', diep, diepsinnig, grondig, diepgaande, diepdinkend; innig, deerlik; *a* ~ *BOW*, 'n diep buiging; ~ *GRIEF*, groot smart; ~ *IGNORANCE*, volslae onkunde; *take a* ~ *INTEREST in*, diep (sterk) belangstel in; *a* ~ *MISTAKE*, 'n groot fout; ~ *RELIEF*, heerlike verligting; ~ *SLEEP*, diepe slaap; ~**ly,** diep, grondig, deur en deur.
profound'ness, profun'dity, diepdinkendheid, diepte; diepsinnigheid; grondigheid; innigheid; diepgang.
profuse', kwistig, oordadig; verkwistend; mild; oorvloedig, volop; ~ *in apologies*, met volop verskonings.
profuse'ness, profu'sion, kwistigheid, oorvloed, oorvloedigheid; verkwisting; oordaad, weelde; *in profusion*, in oorvloed; by die vleet.
prog, padkos.
Prog, lid van die Progressiewe Party, Prog.
progen'erate, voortplant, voortteel.
progen'itive, voortbrengend, voortplantend, teel=.
progen'itor, voorvader, voorsaat; (pl) stamouers.
progen'itress, (-es), stammoeder.
progen'iture, nakomelingskap, nageslag; verwekking.
prog'eny, nageslag, nakomelingskap, nasate, nakroos; gevolg; voortbrengsel; ~**-test,** nageslagtoets.

pro-Germ'an, Duitsgesind, pro-Duits.
proges'terone, progesteroon.
proglot'tis, proglottis.
prognath'ic, prognath'ous, met vooruitstekende (onder)kakebeen; vooruitstekend, prognaat.
prog'nathism, prognatisme.
prognos'is, (..noses), prognose (med.); voorspelling; vooruitsig.
prognos'tic, (n) voorteken; voorspelling; siekteverskynsel; (a) voorspellend; aanduidend; prognosties; ~**ate,** voorspel; dui op; ~**a'tion,** voorspelling; voorteken; ~**ator,** voorspeller, profeet; ~**atory,** voorspellend.
prog'ram(me), (n) program; ~ *of action*, program van aksie (optrede); (v) 'n program opstel; uitwerk; aankondig; programmeer; ~ **music,** programmusiek.
prog'ramming, bestuurkunde; programmering.
prog'ress, (n) vordering, vooruitgang; verloop (siekte); lewensloop; vaart; gang; reis; ontwikkelingsgang; voortgang; *be in ACTIVE* ~, in volle gang wees; *BE in* ~, aan die gang wees; *IN* ~, aan die gang; *REPORT* ~, vooruitgang (vordering) rapporteer; *the* ~ *of SCIENCE*, die vordering (vooruitgang) v.d. wetenskap; ~ *towards a SOLUTION*, vordering om 'n oplossing te vind.
progress', (v) vooruitgaan, vorder, opskiet.
progre'ssion, voortgang; vordering; opklimming, opklimmende reeks; progressie; *ARITHMETICAL* ~, rekenkundige reeks; *GEOMETRICAL* ~, meetkundige reeks; ~**al,** vooruitgaande, vorderend.
progre'ssionist, voorstander van vooruitgang, progressief, progressionis.
progress'ive, (n) progressief; vooruitstrewende persoon; (a) vooruit, progressief, opklimmend, vooruitgaande, vooruitstrewend; toenemend; *a* ~ *age*, 'n eeu van vooruitgang; ~ **disease,** voortskrydende siekte; ~**ly,** aanhoudend; in toenemende mate; progressief; ~ **nation,** vooruitstrewende volk; ~**ness,** vooruitstrewendheid, progressiwiteit; ~ **number,** volgnommer; **P** ~ **Party,** Progressiewe Party.
prohib'it, belet, verbied; ~*ed IMMIGRANT*, verbode immigrant; ~ *SCHOOLBOYS from smoking*, skoliere verbied om te rook; *TALKING* ~*ed*, moenie praat nie; hier word nie gepraat nie.
prohibi'tion, verbod, afskaffing, drankverbod, prohibisie; ~**ist,** (n) afskaffer, prohibisionis; (a) afskaffend, prohibisionisties.
prohib'itive, prohib'itory, verbiedend; buitensporig hoog, prohibitief, onbetaalbaar (pryse); ~ **duties,** beskermende regte; ~ **price,** afskrikkende (te hoë) prys; ~ **taxes,** beskermde invoerregte; te hoë belasting; ~ **terms,** onaanneemlike voorwaardes.
prohib'itor, verbieder.
proj'ect, (n) plan, ontwerp, skema, projek.
project', (v) ontwerp, beraam; slinger, uitskiet (skaal); (voor)uitsteek, uitloop, projekteer; werp (lig); in projeksie bring; uitspring, 'n projeksioteke= ning maak; ~ *a beam of light onto*, 'n ligstraal werp op; ~*ed*, voorgenome.
project'ile, (n) projektiel; bom; werptuig; (a) uitwerpend, slingerend; skiet=; ~ **force,** dryfkrag.
project'ing, uitstekend, uitstaande; ~ **lantern,** projeksielamp.
projec'tion, ontwerp; projeksie; (die) uitgooi; (die) uitsteek; punt, uitsteeksel; verlenging; ~**-drawing,** projeksietekening; ~**ist,** projeksiemaker; projeksionis; projekteerder.
projec'tive, projekterend, projeksie=.
projec'tion: ~ **level,** projeksievlak; ~ **line,** projektor.
projec'tor, ontwerper, planmaker, beramer; skynwerper; projeksielamp, projektor; projektielwerper; soeklig.
proj'ect school, projekskool.
prolapse', (n) breuk, afsakking, uitsakking, versakking; (v) neerval; uitglip, uitsak.
prol'ate, baie versprei, uitgestrek, verleng.
prola'tive, prolatief (gram).
prole, (colloq.), proletariër.
pro'leg, buikpoot, vals poot.

prolegomenon 1148 *pronounced*

prolegom'enon, (..**mena**), inleiding, inleidende beskouinge; prolegomena; ..**m'enous**, inleidend.
prolep'sis, prolepsis, antisipasie.
prolep'tic, proleptis, antisiperend.
proletar'ian, (n) proletariër, proleet; (a) proletaries; ~ **ism**, proletariaat; proletariese toestand.
proletar'iat, arbeidersklasse, loonarbeiders, werkersklas, proletariaat; gepeupel, Jan Rap en sy maat; die arm klasse.
prol'etary, (n) proletariër; (a) proletaries.
prol'icide, kindermoord.
prolif'erate, groei; vervuil, woeker; vorm; vermenigvuldig.
prolifera'tion, vervuiling, woekering; groei; selvorming.
prolif'ic, vrugbaar; oorvloedig.
prolifi'city, voortteling; oorvloedigheid; vrugbaarheid.
proli'gerous, voortbrengend.
prol'ix, langdradig, breedsprakig, omslagtig, wydlopig; vervelig; ~'**ity**, wydlopigheid, langdradigheid, breedsprakigheid, omslagtigheid.
prol'ocutor, woordvoerder; voorsitter; ~ **ship**, voorsitterskap.
prol'ogue, (n) voorrede, voorwoord; voorspel, proloog; *the* ~ *to a play*, die proloog van 'n toneelstuk; (v) inlei, van 'n inleiding voorsien.
prolong', verleng, rek; ~ **a'tion**, verlenging, uitstel; ~**ed**, langdurig; ~**er**, verlenger.
prolu'sion, voorspel, poging, proewe.
promenade', (n) wandelpad, promenade; (v) op en neer wandel; spoggerig rondstap; wandel, loop; ~ **concert**, promenadekonsert; ~ **deck**, wandeldek; ~**r**, wandelaar.
prome'thazine, prometasien, -ine.
Prometh'eus, Promet(h)eus.
prome'thium, prometium.
prom'inence, prom'inency, uitstekendheid, vernaamheid, belangrikheid; onderskeiding; beroemdheid; verhewenheid; bult; uitsteeksel; punt; *BRING INTO* ~, op die voorgrond bring; *COME into* ~, op die voorgrond kom; *GIVE* ~ *to*, voorrang verleen; op die voorgrond bring.
prom'inent, uitstekend, vooraanstaande, opmerklik, treffend, vernaam, prominent, belangrik, opvallend, in-die-oog-lopend; verhewe; *a* ~ *place*, 'n vername plek.
promiscu'ity, deureenmenging, verwarring; vrye geslagtelike omgang, promiskuïteit.
promis'cuous, gemeng; verward; toevallig, ongeërg; promiskueus; ~ *BATHING*, gemengde baaiery; ~ *MASSACRE*, wilde slagting; ~**ly**, deurmekaar, sonder onderskeid, voor die voet; toevallig; promiskueus; ~**ness** = **promiscuity**.
prom'ise, (n) belofte, toesegging; verbintenis; verwagting, hoop; jawoord; *a* ~ *is BINDING*, belofte maak skuld (wie daarop wag is gekuld); *BREAK a* ~, 'n belofte nie nakom nie; ~ *is DEBT*, belofte maak skuld; *the bride is gotten, the* ~ *s FORGOTTEN*, die bruid is in die skuit, nou is die mooipraatjies uit; *HOLD a person to his* ~, iem. aan sy belofte hou; *a* ~ *IS a* ~, belofte maak skuld; *give* ~ *of*, beloof; *KEEP one's* ~, jou belofte nakom; *MAKE a* ~, 'n belofte aflê (doen); ~ *of MARRIAGE*, troubelofte; *OF* ~, veelbelowend; ~ *s and PIECRUSTS are made to be broken*, belofte maak skuld, maar wie daarop wag, is gekuld; *SHOW* ~, belowend lyk, baie beloof; (v) belowe, toesê; 'n belofte doen; laat verwag, hoop gee op; aanleg hê; *I* ~ *you it will be DIFFICULT*, ek kan jou verseker dit sal moeilik wees; *I* ~ *you it will not be EASY*, ek verseker jou dit sal nie maklik wees nie; *it* ~ *s to be a FINE day*, dit lyk na 'n mooi dag; *the P* ~ *d LAND*, die Beloofde Land; ~ *the MOON*, goue berge beloof; ~ *WELL*, die beste verwagtings wek; ~**breaker**, woordbreker; ~**-breaking**, woordbreuk; ~**e'**, ontvanger van 'n belofte; skuldeiser; ~**r**, belower.
prom'ising, (veel)belowend; *a* ~ *beginning*, 'n goeie begin.
pro'misor, belower; skuldenaar; promissor, promessegeër.

prom'issory, belowend; ~ **note**, skuldbewys, promesse.
prom'ontory, (..**ries**), voorgebergte, kaap, landpunt; uitsteeksel (anat.).
promote', bevorder, in rang verhoog, promoveer; aanmoedig; begunstig, bevoordeel, in die hand werk; oorsit; op tou sit, organiseer; oprig (maatskappy); bespoedig; adverteer; *BE* ~ *d*, promosie maak, verhoging kry; ~ *a BILL*, 'n wetsontwerp steun; ~ *a COMPANY*, 'n maatskappy oprig; ~ *the INTERESTS of*, die belange bevorder van; ~ **r**, voorstander, bevorderaar; oprigter (maatskappy); promotor (universiteit); ~**r's shares**, oprigtersaandele.
promo'tion, bevordering, promosie, verheffing, verhoging; ~ *by SENIORITY*, bevordering volgens diensjare; *TRANSFER on* ~, met bevordering verplaas; ~ **al**, bevorderend; ~ **ceremony**, promosieplegtigheid; ~ **dinner**, promosiedinee; ~ **list**, promosielys.
promot'ive, bevorderlik, gunstig.
prompt, (n) vervaldatum, betalingstermyn; (v) aanspoor, aanhits, drywe; influister, voorpraat; voorsê, souffleer (by toneelspel); inblaas, besiel; aanleiding gee; *what* ~ *ed you?* wat het jou besiel? (a) stip, vaardig; vlug, snel, pront, geredelik, onmiddellik; kontant; *a* ~ *ANSWER*, 'n vaardige antwoord; *for* ~ *CASH*, kontant op die plek; ~ *to the HOUR*, stip op tyd; ~ *to OBEY*, gou om te gehoorsaam; ~ *PAYMENT*, kontantbetaling; ~**-book**, souffleursboek; ~**-box**, souffleurshokkie, voorsêershokkie; ~**er**, voorsêer, souffleur, souffleuse.
promp'ting, (die) voorsê; ingewing, aandrang; aanhitsing; (pl) ingewing; stem; ~ *s of CONSCIENCE*, die stem v.d. gewete; *the* ~ *s of his HEART*, die ingewing van sy hart.
prompt'itude, vaardigheid, stiptheid, vlugheid, snelheid, prontheid.
prompt'ly, stip, spoedig, onmiddellik; fluks, pront.
prompt'ness = **promptitude**.
promp'tuary, (..**ries**), bêreplek, magasyn, pakhuis.
promp'ture, inblasing, voorsegging.
prom'ulgate, bekend maak, openbaar maak, afkondig, verkondig; uitvaardig, promulgeer; ~ *a secret*, 'n geheim bekend maak.
promulga'tion, afkondiging, verkondiging; uitvaardiging, promulgasie; bekendmaking.
prom'ulgator, verkondiger, openbaarmaker, uitvaardiger, afkondiger.
prona'os, pronaos, tempelhal.
pron'ate, (v) binnetoe buig; plat neersit; (a) gebuig.
prona'tion, binnewaartse draaiing (buiging), pronasie.
prone, vooroor, plat, uitgestrek; afdraand; gebuig; geneig; ~ *to ANGER*, opvlieënd; *FALL* ~ *before*, neerval voor; ~ *to LIE*, geneig om te lieg; lêerig; ~ *TO*, geneig tot; onderhewig aan; ~ *POSITION*, liggende (lêende) houding; ~**ness**, neiging, geneigdheid, sug, aanleg; (die) lê.
prong, (n) (hooi)vurk; tand(eg); gaffel; (v) omspit, steek; ~**-buck**, gaffelbok. ~**ed**, getand; gevurk.
pronom'inal, voornaamwoordelik, pronominaal.
pro'noun, voornaamwoord, pronomen; *DEMONSTRATIVE* ~, aanwysende voornaamwoord; *INDEFINITE* ~, onbepaalde voornaamwoord; *INTERROGATIVE* ~, vraende voornaamwoord; *PERSONAL* ~, persoonlike voornaamwoord; *POSSESSIVE* ~, besitlike voornaamwoord; *RELATIVE* ~, betreklike voornaamwoord.
pronounce', uitspreek; uit(er); verklaar, uitspraak doen; *the COURT* ~ *d for the firm*, die hof het uitspraak ten gunste van die firma gegee; ~ *ON a matter*, 'n mening oor 'n saak uitspreek; ~ *SENTENCE of death*, die doodvonnis uitspreek; ~ **able**, uitspreekbaar.
pronounced', beslis, duidelik, duidelik kenbaar; onbetwisbaar, klaarblyklik, sterk, sprekend; ~ *FEATURES*, skerp gelaatstrekke; ~ *IMPROVEMENT*, 'n merkbare verbetering; *the word is* ~ *THUS*, die woord word só uitgespreek; *have* ~ *VIEWS*, besliste menings daarop nahou.

pronounce'ment, uitdruklike verklaring; uitspraak; *make a ~,* 'n verklaring doen.
pronoun'cing, uitspraak=; ~ **dictionary,** uitspraak=woordeboek.
pron'to, pront, dadelik, gou (Amer.).
pronuncia'tion, uitspraak.
pronun'ciative, verklarend.
proof, (n) bewys, bewysgrond, stawing; blyk; proef, drukproef; sterktegraad, gehalte (drank); *BRING to the ~,* op die proef stel; *BURDEN of ~,* bewyslas; *~ to the CONTRARY,* teenbewys; *~ of DEBT,* skuldvordering; *IN ~ of,* as bewys van; *OVER ~,* bo proef; *PRODUCE ~ in support of,* bewys(e) ter stawing aanvoer; *the ~ of the PUDDING is in the eating,* die gehalte van iets kan alleen vasgestel word nadat dit op die proef gestel is; ondervinding is die beste leermeester; probeer is die beste geweer; *REVISE the ~s,* die drukproewe nagaan; *STAND the ~,* die proef deurstaan; *UNDER ~,* onder proef; (v) waterdig maak; bestand maak teen; (a) bestand, beproef; proefhoudend; dig; ondeurdringbaar; ~ **against temptation,** bestand teen versoeking; **~-range,** patroontoetsbaan; **~-reader,** proefleser; **~-reading,** proeflees, proeflesing; **~-sheet,** drukproef; proefvel, proetblad; letterproef; ~ **spirit,** toetsalkohol; ~ **strength,** proefsterkte.
prop¹, (n) stut, steun, paal, staf, pilaar; steunsel; stutpaal (omheining); ondersteuner, steunpilaar, staatmaker; (v) **(-ped),** steun, stut, skraag, stu; ~ **up,** onderskraag, stut.
prop², (n) *kyk* **propeller.**
prop³, (n) *kyk* **property.**
prop⁴, (n) *kyk* **proposition.**
propaedeut'ic, voortbereidend, propedeuties; ~**s,** propedeutika.
prop'agable, propageerbaar.
propagan'da, propaganda.
propagan'dist, propagandis; bekeerling; sendeling.
propagandis'tic, propagandisties.
propagan'dize, propaganda maak.
prop'agate, voortplant; verbrei, versprei, uitdra, propageer.
propaga'tion, voortplanting; verspreiding, verbreiding.
prop'agative, voortplantings=, voortplantend.
prop'agator, voortplanter; propageerder, verspreier, verbreider.
propane', propaan.
propel', **(-led),** (voort)drywe, beweeg, vooruitstoot, voortbeweeg.
propel'lent, (n) drytkrag; dryfmiddel; (a) drywend, dryf=; ~ **charge,** dryflading, ~ **gas,** dryfgas.
propell'er, drywer; skroef (stoomboot); voortstuwer (torpedo); (lug)skroef (vliegtuig); ~ **blade,** skroefblad; ~ **engine,** skroefmasjien; ~ **hub,** skroefnaaf; ~ **pencil,** skuifpotlood, draaipotlood; **~-post,** skroefstewe; ~ **propulsion,** skroefaandrywing; skroefvoortstuwing; ~ **shaft,** skroefas, (aan)dryfas.
propell'ing, drywend, dryf=; ~ **agent,** dryfmiddel; ~ **force,** dryfkrag; ~ **rod,** dryfstang; ~ **pencil,** skuifpotlood, draaipotlood.
propense', geneig.
propen'sity, (..ties), neiging, geneigdheid; sug, voorliefde; ~ *for (towards),* neiging tot.
prop'er, eie; besonder; behoorlik; welvoeglik, fatsoenlik, geoorloof, goed, gevoeglik, ordentlik; eintlik; geskik; reg, gepas, betaamlik; voeglik, voegsaam; aangewese; nodig; *ARABIA ~,* die eintlike Arabië; *the CITY ~,* die eintlike stad; *~ DISTANCE,* gevegsafstand (in skermkuns); *it was a ~ FIGHT,* dit was 'n regte bakleiery; *LITERATURE ~,* werklike letterkunde; *it is NOT the ~ thing to do,* dit pas nie; dis onbetaamlik; *in the ~ SENSE of the word,* in die werklike betekenis v.d. woord; *THINK ~,* goedkeur, as welvoeglik beskou; *a ~ THRASHING,* 'n gedugte pak slae; *the ~ TIME,* die regte (geskikte) tyd; *the ~ WAY,* die regte manier; ~ **fraction,** egte breuk.
prop'erly, eintlik; behoorlik, fatsoenlik; absoluut; na regte, tereg; *you have MESSED things up ~ now,* nou het jy behoorlik 'n gemors van sake gemaak; ~ *SPEAKING,* eintlik gesê.
prop'er name, eienaam.
prop'ertied, besittend, vermoënd.
prop'erty, (..ties), eienskap; eiendom, besitting, goed; vermoë; eiendomsreg; (huis en) erf; (pl) toneelbenodigdhede, (toneel)rekwisiete; eienskappe; *FIXED ~,* onroerende eiendom; vasgoed; *FUNDED ~,* vermoë; *IMMOVABLE ~,* vasgoed, vaste (onroerende) eiendom; *LANDED ~,* vaste eiendom; *a MAN of ~,* 'n grondbesitter; *MOVABLE ~,* losgoed, roerende goed; *~ in POSSESSION,* ingekoopte eiendom (bouver.); *REAL ~,* onroerende besitting; *the ~ ties of SODIUM,* die eienskappe van natrium; ~**less,** besitloos; ~ **letter,** toneelbrief; ~**man,** rekwisietemeester; toneelbaas; ~ **market,** eiendomsmark; ~ **master,** toneelbaas; ~ **owner,** eiendomsbesitter; ~ **tax,** eiendomsbelasting, grondbelasting.
proph'ecy, (..cies), profesie, voorspelling, waarsegging, voorsegging; godspraak; *MAKE a ~,* 'n voorspelling doen (maak); profeteer; *the ~ came TRUE,* die voorspelling is bewaarheid.
proph'esier, profeet.
proph'esy, (..sied), voorspel, profeteer, voorsê.
proph'et, profeet, godsman, voorspeller; ~ *of DOOM,* onheilsprofeet; *a ~ has no HONOUR in his own country,* 'n profeet word nie in sy eie land geëer nie; *the MINOR P~s,* die Klein Profete; *SAUL among the ~s,* Saul onder die profete; ~**ess,** **(-es),** profetes.
prophet'ic(al), profeties; ~ *eye,* sienersoog, siendersblik.
prophylac'tic, (n) voorbehoedmiddel, profilaktikum; (a) voorbehoedend, profilakties.
prophylax'is, profilakse, voorbehoeding.
propinq'uity, (bloed)verwantskap; nabyheid; ooreenkoms.
propio'nic acid, propioonsuur.
propi'tiable, versoenbaar; versoenlik.
propi'tiate, versoen, gunstig stem, tevrede stem; paai.
propitia'tion, versoening, soenoffer.
propi'tiator, versoener; ~**y,** (n) genadetroon; (a) versoenend, soen=; ~*y sacrifice,* soenoffer.
propi'tious, genadig, gunstig; vergewend; ~**ness,** genade, guns; vergewensgesindheid; goedgesindheid.
prop'lasm, gietvorm, gietmodel, matrys.
prop'olis, propolis, maagdewas, stopwas, byewas.
propon'ent, (n) voorsteller; voorstander; (a) voorstellend.
propor'tion, (n) eweredigheid, proporsie, verhouding; deel, gedeelte; (pl) afmetings; *BEAR ~ to,* in verhouding staan tot; ~ *BETWEEN,* verhouding tussen; *IN ~,* na verhouding; *IN ~ to,* na gelang van; in verhouding tot; *IN ~ as,* namate; *IN the ~ of,* in die verhouding van; *INVERSE ~,* omgekeerde eweredigheid; *OUT of all ~,* heeltemal uit proporsie; buite alle verhouding; *the RULE of ~,* die reël van drie; *SENSE of ~,* sin vir verhoudings; *SIMPLE ~,* enkelvoudige eweredigheid; (v) afmeet; eweredig maak, in verhouding stel.
propor'tional, (n) eweredige; (a) eweredig, ewematig, proporsioneel; verhoudings=; ~ *COMPASSES,* verhoudingspasser; ~ *ERROR,* betreklike fout; ~ *MEAN,* middeleweredige; ~ *REPRESENTATION,* proporsionele verteenwoordiging; ~ *SCALE,* verhoudingskaal; ~ *THIRD,* derde eweredige; ~**'ity,** eweredigheid; ~**ly,** eweredig; na verhouding, na eweredigheid; persentsgewyse.
propor'tionate, (v) eweredig maak; (a) eweredig, proporsioneel; ~**ly,** eweredig; ~**ness** = **proportionality.**
propor'tionless, oneweredig.
propor'tion scale, verhoudingskaal.
propo'sal, voorstel, aanbod, aanbieding; liefdesverklaring, huweliksaansoek, huweliksaanbod; *make a ~,* 'n voorstel doen.
propose', voorstel, aanbied, proponeer; van voorneme wees, van plan wees; vra, 'n huweliksvoorstel doen; voortbring; ~ *to a GIRL,* die hand van 'n meisie vra; ~ *the HEALTH of,* 'n heildronk instel op; *MAN ~s, God disposes,* die mens wik, maar

proposition 1150 *protection*

God beskik; ~ *a TOAST,* 'n heildronk instel; ~**d**, voorgestel, voorgenome; ~**r**, voorsteller; indiener.

proposi'tion, voorstel; aanbod, proposisie; stelling, probleem; saak; *a BUSINESS* ~, 'n handelsonderneming; *MAKE a* ~, 'n voorstel doen; *a MINING* ~, 'n mynonderneming; *a PAYING* ~, 'n lonende handelsonderneming; *a STIFF* ~, 'n moeilike saak.

propound', voorstel, opgee, voorlê; aanbied; ~**er**, voorsteller, voorlêer.

propri'etary, (n) (..ries), eiendomsreg; besit, besitterskap; (a) eiendoms=, eienaars=, besit=; patent=, gepatenteer; patentregtelik; *the* ~ *classes,* die besittende klasse; ~ **account**, eienaarsrekening; ~ **article**, artikel deur patent beskerm, gepatenteerde artikel; ~ **company**, eiendomsmaatskappy, private (partikuliere) maatskappy; ~ **interest**, eienaarsbelang; ~ **medicine**, patente medisyne; ~ **name**, handelsnaam; ~ **right**, eiendomsreg; ~ **school**, privaatskool.

propri'etor, eienaar, besitter; ~**'s capital**, aandelekapitaal; ~**ship**, besitterskap.

propri'etress, (-es), eienares, besitster.

propri'ety, fatsoenlikheid, welvoeglikheid, voegsaamheid; gepastheid, behoorlikheid, (ge)voegligheid; juistheid; *a BREACH of* ~, in stryd met die welvoeglikheid; ~ *of LANGUAGE,* juiste woordkeuse; *the PROPRIETIES,* die welvoeglikheid, die goeie vorm, die dekorum.

props, *abbr. for* **properties**, toneelbenodigdhede, (toneel)rekwisiete.

prop'-stick, disselboomstut.

propto'sis, proptose, uitpeuling (oog).

propul'sion voortdrywing, voortstuwing; stukrag, dryfkrag; (die) drywe.

propul'sive, propul'sory, voortdrywend, stuwend, aandrywend, dryf=.

propyl', propiel.

Propylae'a: *the* ~, die Propulaia.

propylae'um, (..laea), tempelingang.

pro'pylene, propileen.

proroga'tion, verdaging, opskorting, prorogering; ~ *of Parliament,* verdaging (prorogering) van die Parlement.

prorogue', verdaag, uitstel, opskort, prorogeer, sluit.

pro-Rus'sian, Russiesgesind, pro-Russies.

prosa'ic, prosaïes, alledaags; prosa=; ondigterlik.

pros'aist, prosaskrywer, prosaïs; prosaïese mens.

proscen'ium, (..nia), proscenium, voortoneel.

proscribe', buite die wet stel; verbeurd verklaar; verban; voëlvry verklaar; verbied.

proscrip'tion, verbanning; voëlvryverklaring; verwerping.

proscrip'tive, verbannend; voëlvryverklarend; tiranniek.

prose, (n) prosa; die prosaïese, die alledaagse; (v) in prosa vertel; in prosa oorbring; vervelend praat (skryf), sanik; (a) prosa=; prosaïes, alledaags.

prosect', lyke ontleed; ~**or**, prosektor.

pros'ecutable, vervolgbaar.

pros'ecute, geregtelik vervolg; voortsit; uitoefen; ~ *a person for LIBEL,* iem. weens laster vervolg; ~ *one's STUDIES,* jou studie voortsit; *TRESPASSERS will be* ~*d,* oortreders sal vervolg word.

pros'ecuting counsel, advokaat vir die vervolging.

prosecu'tion, vervolging, prosekusie; voortsetting; uitoefening (beroep).

pros'ecutor, aanklaer; voortsetter, *public* ~, openbare (publieke) aanklaer, staatsaanklaer.

pros'ecutrix, (..trices), aanklaagster.

pros'elyte, (n) bekeerling, proseliet; (v) bekeer, 'n proseliet maak van.

pros'elytism, proselytiza'tion, proselietmakery; bekeringsywer.

pros'elytize, bekeer, proseliete maak; ~**r**, proselietmaker, bekeerder.

prosen'chyma, prosenchiem.

pros'er, prosaskrywer; vervelende verhaler.

prose: ~ **poem**, prosagedig; ~ **poet**, prosadigter; ~ **poetry**, prosadigkuns; ~ **writer**, prosaskrywer; ~ **writing**, prosa.

pros'ify, (..fied), in prosa oorbring; prosa skryf.

pros'iness, verveling; verveligheid.

pro'sings, vervelende produkte.

prosit', prosit, gesondheid.

prosod'ic, prosodies.

pros'odist, prosodis.

pros'ody, prosodie, versleer.

proso'pis, prosopis(boom).

prosopo'graphy, prosopografie, persoonsbeskrywing.

prosopopoe'ia, prosopopee, persoonsverbeelding.

pros'pect, (n) vooruitsig, vergesig, uitsig; verwagting; moontlike klant (koper); toekomstige klant; kandidaat (vir versekering); proposisie, mynproposisie; *BE a* ~, 'n moontlike klant wees; 'n moontlike wees; *his* ~*s are BLEAK,* sy kanse is maar skraal; *HAVE nothing in* ~, niks verwag nie; *HOLD out the* ~ *of something,* iets in die vooruitsig stel; ~ *of SUCCESS,* kans op sukses.

prospect', (v) prospekteer; ondersoek, soek; ~ *FOR,* soek na; prospekteer na.

pros'pect adit, prospekteertonnel.

prospect'ing, prospektering; prospekteerdery.

prospect'ive, aanstaande, toekomstige; voornemende; waarskynlike, te wagte; aspirant=; ~ **bridegroom**, aanstaande bruidegom; ~ **buyer**, gegadigde; voornemende koper; ~ **customer**, moontlike klant; ~**ly**, vooruitwerkend; ~ **measure**, voorgenome maatreël; ~ **professor**, toekomstige professor; ~ **teacher**, aspirant-onderwyser.

prospect'or, prospekteerder, prospektor; ~**'s licence**, prospekteerlisensie.

pros'pect: ~ **pit**, prospekteergat; ~ **shaft**, prospekteerskag; ~ **trench**, prospekteersloot, soeksloot.

prospec'tus, (-es), prospektus; intekenbiljet.

pros'per, bloei, voorspoedig wees; floreer, vooruitgaan, (ge)dy, goed gaan; seën.

prospe'rity, voorspoed, bloei, welvaart, vooruitgang; heil, seën.

pros'perous, voorspoedig; gelukkig; welvarend, bloeiend; glad verhaar (fig.); ~**ness** = **prosperity**.

pross'er tool, uitdywerktuig.

prostagla'ndin, prostaglandien, -ine.

pros'tate, (n) voorstanderklier, prostaat; (a) prostaties; ~ **gland**, voorstanderklier, prostaat.

pros'thesis, kunsmatige liggaamsdeel, prostese; voorvoeging; protesis (gram.).

prosthet'ic, prosteties.

pros'titute, (n) hoer, sedelose vrou, prostituee, prostituut, straat vrou, straatslet, publieke vrou, ligtekooi, jentoe; jintoe; (v) onteer; skend, ontug bedrywe, prostitueer; misbruik, vir 'n eerlose doel veil hê.

prostitu'tion, ontering, ontwyding; ontug, hoerery, prostitusie.

pros'trate, (v) neerwerp, eerbiedig buig; verneder; heeltemal verwoes; gedaan maak; ~ *oneself,* neerkniel, jou in die stof buig; (a) uitgestrek; neergebuig; plat; uitgeput; gekniel, verneder; *BE* ~, plat lê; *FALL* ~, op jou gesig val; *LAY* ~, neerslaan; plat lê; *LIE* ~, plat op die grond lê.

prostra'tion, diepe vernedering, neerbuiging, neerknieling, voetval; uitputting; verslaen(t)heid; *nervous* ~, senu(wee)swakte, senu(wee)toeval.

pros'tyle, (n) suilegang, portiek, prostyl; (a) met 'n portiek, prostiel.

pros'y, prosaïes, nugter, vervelend, alledaags, platvloers.

protag'onism, pleitbesorging.

protag'onist, hoofpersoon, leier, voorman; protagonis; woordvoerder, voorvegter; hoofspeler; teenspeler.

pro'tamine, protamien, -ine.

pro tan'to, (L), pro tanto, in dié mate, tot sover.

prot'asis, (..tases), voorwaardelike bysin, protasis.

prot'ea, suikerbos, protea.

Protea'ceae, Proteaceae.

prot'ean, veranderlik, proteaans, proteusagtig.

protect', beskerm, behoed, bewaar, beskut, beveilig; verdedig; vrywaar, protegeer; honoreer, dek ('n wissel); ~ *FROM,* beskerm teen; ~ *oneself against LOSS by fire,* jou teen brandskade beskerm; ~**ed**, beskerm, beskut, beveilig, verdedig; geharnas.

protec'tion, beskerming, beveiliging, beskutting; be=

protective 1151 *provision*

gunstiging, proteksie, vrywaring; vrygeleide, paspoort; ~ **ism,** proteksionisme; ~ **ist,** (n) proteksionis; (a) proteksionisties, beskermend; ~ **plate,** skermplaat; ~ **rail,** (be)skermreling.
protec'tive, beskermend, beskuttend; ~ **clothing,** beskermende klere, skutklere; ~ **coating,** beskermende laag; ~ **custody,** beskermende bewaring; ~ **duties,** beskermende regte; veiligheidsdiens; ~ **fire,** gordynvuur; ~ **food,** verrykte voedsel; ~ **measure,** veiligheidsmaatreël; ~ **paper,** skutpapier, dekpapier; ~ **screen,** skerm; ~ **wire,** draadversperring.
protec'tor, beskermer, beskermheer; handhawer; regent; ~ **ate,** protektoraat; ~ **ship,** protektoraat; beskermheerskap; ~**y,** (..**ries**), weeshuis, opvoedingsinrigting (R.K.).
protec'tress, (-es), beskermster, beskermvrou, skutsvrou.
prot'égé, beskermling, protégé.
pro'teïd, proteïed, proteïde.
pro'teïform, veranderlik, proteusagtig.
prot'ein, proteïen, proteïne, eiwit(stof).
pro tem (pore), tydelik; waarnemend.
proteo'lysis, proteolise.
proteoly'tic, proteolitles.
prot'est, (n) protes, verset, teëspraak; teenverklaring; AS a ~, by wyse van protes; ENTER a ~ against, verset (protes) aanteken teen; IN ~, uit protes; NOTE of ~, protesnota; UNDER ~, onder protes, teen jou sin.
protest', (v) beswaar maak, protesteer; betuig, jou touniť; proter aanteken teen; plegtig verklaar; ~ AGAINST, protesteer teen; ~ one's INNO= CENCE, jou onskuld betulg.
Prot'estant, (n) Protestant; (a) Protestants.
protes'tant, (a) protesterend.
Prot'estantism, Protestantisme.
protesta'tion, versekering; protes; verklaring; verset, protestasie; betuiging.
protes'ter, beswaarmaker, protesteerder.
prot'est meeting, protesvergadering.
prothalam'ion, (-s), prothala'mium, (..mia), bruilofslied.
prothal'lium, prothal'lus, protallus, voorkiem.
proth'esis, voorvoeging, protesis (gram.); altaartafel.
prothet'ic, voorgevoeg, proteties.
prot(h)ono'tary, protonotarius.
prot'ocol, (n) protokol; oorkonde; (v) **(-led),** 'n protokol opstel; op die protokol plaas.
protegen'ic, primêr.
prot'oman, protoman, brandbestryder (in myne).
pro'tomartyr, eerste martelaar
prot'on, proton.
prot'oplasm, protoplasma; ~ **'ic,** protoplasmies, protoplasmaties.
prot'oplast, oermens, eerste mens; model; protoplas; -**'ic,** ocr², model⁻.
prot'o-team, protospan, brandbestryderspan.
prot'otype, grondbeeld, eerste voorbeeld, prototipe.
protozo'a, oerslymdiertjies, protosoa, laagste diersoorte; ~ **l,** protosoön⁻.
protozoo'logy, protosoölogie.
protozo'on, protosoön, oerslymdiertjie.
protract', uitstel; verleng; rek; op skaal teken; ~ **ed,** langdurig, gerek; ~ **ed struggle,** langdurige stryd (worsteling); ~ **edness,** (uit)gerektheid; ~ **ile,** (uit)rekbaar; verlengbaar; ~ **ion,** uitstel; verlenging; (die) rek, uitrekking; tekening volgens skaal; ~ **ive,** verlengend; rekkend; ~ **or,** graadboog, graadmeter; hoekmeter; strekspier, strekpees, streksening.
protrude', uitsteek, vooruitsteek, vooruitstaan, uitpuil; papers ~ from his pocket, papiere steek by sy sak uit.
protrud'ing, uitstekend; ~ eyes, uitpeuloë, jakopeweroë.
protru'sion, vorstoting; uitsteking, uitsteeksel; bank (rots).
protrus'ive, vorstotend; vooruitstekend; opdringerig.
protub'erance, geswel, uitwas; uitpeuling, uitpuiling; bult; knop, uitsteeksel.
protub'erant, vooruitstekend, uitspringend, uitpuilend, uitpuil=; ~ **eyes,** (uit)puiloë, uitpeuloë.

protub'erate, swel, uitpuil, uitpeul, uitgroei.
proud, trots, hoogmoedig; fier, eergevoelig; styf, statig; pragtig; hovaardig, hoohartig; groots; BE very ~, van die hondjie gebyt wees; too ~ to BEG, te hoogmoedig om te bedel; you DO me ~, jy doen my 'n te groot eer aan; DO oneself ~, jou die weelde veroorloof; DO someone ~, iem. op rojale wyse onthaal; as ~ as LUCIFER (as a peacock, as Punch), so trots soos 'n pou; NOTHING to be ~ about (of), niks om oor te spog nie; ~ OF your country, trots op jou land; his ~est POSSESSION, sy trotsste (mees gewaardeerde) besitting; a ~ SIGHT, 'n gesig waarop 'n mens trots kan wees; ~ **flesh,** wildvleis; woekervleis (by wond); ~**-hearted,** trots, hoogmoedig; ~ **ish,** trotserig; ~**-spirited,** hoogartig, met 'n trotse gees.
prov'able, bewysbaar; ~ **ness,** bewysbaarheid.
prove, bewys; proef lewer; goedmaak; beproef, op die proef stel, probeer; voorreken; verifieer; inskiet (geweer); ~ BREAD, brood laat rys; ~ a CLAIM, 'n eis bewys; the EXCEPTION ~s the rule, die uitsondering bewys die reël; a ~d FACT, 'n bewese feit; it ~d to be FALSE, dit het vals geblyk; NOT ~n, nie bewys nie; a ~n REMEDY, 'n beproefde middel; ~ all THINGS and hold fast that which is good, ondersoek alle dinge en behou die goeie; ~ to be TRUE, bewaarheid word; ~ a WILL, 'n testament verifieer; ~ someone WRONG, iem. in die ongelyk stel; ~ YOURSELF, wys wat jy kan doen; ~**able,** bewysbaar.
prov'ed, bewese (feit); beproef (vriend).
prov'en, bewese; beproef.
prov'enance, herkoms, oorsprong.
prov'ender, voer; voedsel, kos.
proven'ience, herkoms, oorsprong.
prov'erb, spreekwoord, spreuk; the Book of P~s, die Spreuke van Salomo.
proverb'ial, spreekwoordelik; a mule is ~ly stubborn, 'n muil se (hard)koppigheid is spreekwoordelik; ~ **ism,** spreekwoordelike uitdrukking, ~ **ist,** spreekwoordemaker.
prov'iant, proviand.
provide', verskaf, voorsien, lewer; sorg vir; bepaal, neerlê, voorskryf; maatreëls neem teen; ~ AGAINST the drought, voorsorgmaatreëls tref teen die droogte; ~ AGAINST a rainy day, 'n appeltjie vir die dors bewaar; BE ~d for, al die nodige hê; the CHILD is ~d for, vir die kind se toekoms is gesorg; ~ FOR one's family, sorg vir jou gesin; the LAW ~s, die wet bepaal; ~ for ONESELF, jou eie potjie krap; ~ for SHRINKAGE, rekening hou met krimp; ~ WITH, voorsien van, verstrek.
provid'ed, mits, met dien verstande, op voorwaarde dat, as; voorsien (van); ~ all is SAFE, op voorwaarde dat alles veilig is; ~ THAT, op voorwaarde dat; met dien verstande.
prov'idence, voorsienigheid; voorsorg, voorsiening; Divine P ~, die Goddelike Voorsienigheid.
prov'ident, versigtig, sorgvuldig; sorgend; spaarsaam; ~ **bank,** spaarbank; ~ **fund,** voorsorgfonds, spaarfonds.
providen'tial, beskik deur die Voorsienigheid, wonderbaarlik; gelukkig; toevallig; it was ~, dit was 'n bestiering.
prov'ident society, voorsorgfonds, bystandsfonds.
provid'er, besorger; leweransier, verskaffer; versorger; universal ~, algemene handelaar.
prov'ince, provinsie; afdeling; gewes, vak, gebied, werkkring; not within my ~, buitekant my vak.
provin'cial, (n) plattelander, provinsiebewoner; (a) provinsiaal; gewestelik; bekrompe, nougeset; ~ **ism,** provinsialisme; gewestelike eienaardigheid; ~ **ist,** (n) provinsialis; (a) provinsialisties; ~ **'ity,** provinsialiteit; bekrompenheid.
prov'ing, waarmaking; toets; bewys; ~ **flight,** toetsvlug; ~**-ground,** toetsterrein; ~ **run,** toetsvaart.
provi'sion, (n) voorsiening, voorsorg; voorraad; bepaling; (pl) lewensmiddele, provisie, mondvoorraad, eetware, leeftog, proviand; AFTER ~ for, na aftrek van; na voorsiening vir; ~s of a LAW, bepalings van 'n wet; MAKE ~ for, voorsiening maak vir; UNDER the ~s of, kragtens, ooreenkomstig;

(v) van lewensmiddele voorsien, proviandeer; ~ **al,** voorlopig; provisioneel; ~ *al sentence,* voorlopige vonnis, namptissement; ~ **clerk,** voorraadklerk; ~ **cupboard,** spenskas; voorraadkas; ~ **dealer,** handelaar in eetware, provisiehandelaar; ~**ment,** proviandering; ~ **merchant,** verkoper van lewens= middele, provisiehandelaar; ~ **ship,** proviandskip.

provis'o, (-s), bepaling, voorbehoudsbepaling, voor= waarde, voorbeding, stipulasie; *there IS a* ~, daar is 'n voorwaarde by; *PUT in a* ~, 'n voorbehoud maak; *WITH a* ~, onder voorwaarde; *WITH the* ~ *that,* met dien verstande dat; mits; onder voor= behoud dat; behoudens.

provis'or, versorger; kerkvoog; vader; ~**y,** voor= waardelik, voorlopig, provisioneel.

provoca'tion, terging, belediging, uitdaging, uitlok= king; aanleiding, provokasie; ~ *of a CRIME,* uit= lokking van 'n misdaad; *GUILTY under* ~, skuldig op rede; *without the LEAST* ~, sonder die minste aanleiding; *under SEVERE* ~, onder sterk provo= kasie; weens uittarting; *on the SLIGHTEST* ~, by die geringste aanleiding.

provo'cative, (n) provokasie(middel), aanleidende oorsaak; uitdaging; (a) prikkelend; tartend, uitda= gend; uitlokkend; *be* ~ *of,* uitlok, aanleiding gee tot.

provoke', terg; prikkel, aanhits, aanleiding gee; bele= dig; (uit)tart; uitlok; vererg; verwek; uitdaag, pro= vokeer; ~ *a person to ANGER,* iem. tot woede prikkel; *this* ~ *d my INDIGNATION,* dit het my verontwaardig gemaak; ~**r,** belediger, terger, uit= tarter.

provok'ing, tergend, ergerlik, tartend, ergerniswek= kend, uitdagend.

prov'ost, opsiener, provoos; ~ **marshal,** hoofpro= voos; ~ **sergeant,** sersant-provoos.

prow, voorstewe, boeg, neus (van skip).

prow'ess, moed, dapperheid, heldemoed, manhaftig= heid; vaardigheid.

prowl, (n) rooftog, swerftog; *on the* ~, op roof uit; (v) loer op buit; rondsluip, soek na prooi; ~ *round,* omsluip; rondsluip; ~**er,** swerwer; stroper, rond= sluiper.

prox'imal, naaste, proksimaal.

prox'imate, naby; naaste, onmiddellik; *the* ~ *cause,* die onmiddellike oorsaak.

proxim'ity, nabyheid; ~ *of blood,* bloedverwant= skap.

prox'imo, aanstaande (maand); naaste.

prox'y, (proxies), volmag, prokurasie; gevolmagtig= de, volmaghebber, gelastigde, sekundus; *MARRY by* ~, met die handskoen trou; *STAND* ~ *for another,* volmag hê vir 'n ander; *VOTE by* ~, met volmag stem; ~ **bride,** handskoenbruid; ~ **mar= riage,** handskoenhuwelik.

prude, preutse mens; preutse vrou; skynsedige meisie, nuffie.

pru'dence, versigtigheid, bedagsaamheid; verstandig= heid, wysheid; skaamte; ~ *is the best part of valour,* versigtigheid is die moeder van wysheid.

pru'dent, versigtig; verstandig, wys; beleidvol.

pruden'tial, verstandig, beleidvol; ~**s,** versigtigheids= maatreëls.

pru'dery, preutsheid, skynvroomheid, aanstellerig= heid.

pru'dish, preuts, skynsedig, aanstellerig, nuffig; ~**ness,** preutsheid, skynsedigheid, aanstellerig= heid.

prune¹, (n) gedroogde pruim; pruimedant; donker= rooi (kleur).

prune², (v) snoei; besnoei; top; ~**d,** afgeknot; gesnoei.

prunell'a¹, prunella (wolstof).

prunell'a², keelsiekte, seerkeel; ~ **salt,** prunel= sout.

prunell'o, (-s), prunel(lo), pruimedant.

prun'er, snoeier; snoeiskêr.

prun'ing, (die) snoei, snoeiery; ~**-hook,** ~**-knife,** snoeimes; ~**-shears,** snoeiskêr.

prur'ience, prur'iency, jeuking, jeukerigheid; vleesli= ke begeerte, wulpsheid, wellus.

prur'ient, jeukend; verlangend, wulps, wellustig.

pruri'ginous, jeukend, jeukerig.

prurig'o, prurit'us, jeuksiekte, jeukerige uitslag, jeuk= bulte, gejeuk.

Pru'ssia, Pruise.

Pru'ssian, (n) Pruis; (a) Pruisies; ~ **binding,** tresband; ~ **blue,** berlynsblou, pruisiesblou.

pruss'ic: ~ **acid,** pruisiessuur, blousuur, hidrosiaan= suur; ~ **poisoning,** geilsiekte, blousuurvergiftiging.

pry¹, (pried), oopmaak, oopbreek.

pry², (pried), snuffel; tuur, nuuskierig kyk; loer; spioeneer; ~ *ABOUT,* rondsnuffel; ~ *INTO,* die neus insteek, napluis; ~**ing,** snuffelend, nuuskie= rig, loer=.

psalm, psalm; ~**-book,** psalmboek; ~**ist,** psalmdig= ter.

psalm'odist, psalmdigter.

psalm'odize, psalmodieer; psalmsing.

psalm'ody, psalmgesang.

psal'ter, psalmboek.

psalter'ium, blaarpens; lier (van harsings).

psal'tery, (..ries), lier, siter.

psephol'ogy, psefologie, sistematiese studie van ver= kiesings, verkiesingstudie.

pseud'o=, vals, oneg; kamma, sogenaamd, half=, pseudo=.

pseud'omorph, pseudomorf.

pseudomorph'ism, pseudomorfisme.

pseudomorph'ous, pseudomorf.

pseud'onym, skuilnaam, pennaam, pseudoniem.

pseudon'ymous, pseudoniem, onder 'n skuilnaam ge= skrywe, anoniem.

pseudopo'dium, skynvoet.

pseudopreg'nancy, skynswangerskap.

pseudostem', skynstam, pseudostam.

pshaw! foei! sies! ag!

psitt'acine, papegaaiagtig, papegaai=.

psittacos'is, papegaaisiekte, psittakose.

pso'cid, houtluis.

psor'a, skurfte.

psori'asis, psoriase.

psor'ic, (n) skurfmiddel; (a) skurf=.

Psych'e¹, Psyche, Psuchê.

psych'e², psige, siel, gees.

psychede'lic, psigedelies, ekstaties, waan=, hallusina= sie=, bont, wild.

psychiat'ric(al), psigiatries.

psychi'atrist, psigiater, senuspesialis.

psychi'atry, senusiekteleer, psigiatrie.

psych'ic, (n) spiritistiese medium; (a) psigies, sielkun= dig, siels=; ~ *al research,* okkultisme; ~**s,** sielkun= dige navorsing.

psychoan'alyse, psigoanaliseer.

psychoanal'ysis, psigoanalise, dieptesielkunde, diep= tepsigologie.

psychoan'alyst, psigoanalis.

psychoanalyt'ic, psigoanalities.

psychogen'ic, sielkundig, psigogeen.

psychogen'esis, psigogenese.

psych'ogram, psigogram.

psych'ograph, psigograaf.

psycholog'ical, sielkundig, psigologies.

psychol'ogist, psigoloog, sielkundige.

psychol'ogy, sielkunde, psigologie.

psych'omancy, geestebeswering, towerkuns.

psychomat'ic, psigomaties.

psychom'eter, psigometer.

psychomet'ric, psigometries.

psychom'etry, psigometrie.

psy'chomotor(ic), psigomotories.

psych'opath, sielsieke, psigopaat; ~**'ic,** sielsiek, psi= gopaties; ~**ist,** senuarts, psigiater; ~**ol'ogy,** psigo= patologie.

psychop'athy, psigopatie, sielsiekte; behandeling van sielsiekes.

psychopharmacol'ogy, psigofarmakologie.

psychos'is, psigose.

psychosomat'ic, psigosomaties.

psychother'apy, psigoterapie.

psychot'ic, (n) psigoot; (a) sielsiek, psigoties.

psychotech'nics, psigotegniek.

psyl'la, psilla.

psyll'ium seed, psilliumsaad.

ptarm'igan, sneeuhoender.

pteridol'ogist, varingkundige.
pteridol'ogy, bestudering van varings, varingkunde.
ptisan', garswater, gortwater.
Ptolema'ic, Ptolemeïes.
Ptol'emy, Ptolemeus, Ptolemaios.
ptom'aine, lykgif, ptomaïne; ~ **poisoning,** voedselvergiftiging.
pty'alism, spoegafskeiding, speekselvloed.
pub, kantien, kroeg, drankhuis, oog, tappery; ~-**crawler,** kroegkruiper, kroegloper; ~-**crawling,** kroeglopery; ~-**loafer,** kroegvlieg.
pub'erty, geslagsrypheid, manbaarheid, hubaarheid, puberteit.
pub'es, skaamstreek; skaambeen; geslagshare, skaamhare.
pubes'cence, manbaarwording, geslagsrypheid; donshaar(tjies) (bot.).
pubes'cent, manbaar, geslagsryp(wordend); donsharig, sagharig, donserig (bot.).
pub'ic, skaam=; ~ **bone,** skaambeen; ~ **hair,** skaamhare; ~ **region,** skaamstreek.
pub'is, (pubes), skaambeen.
pub'lic, (n) publiek; *IN* ~, in die publiek; in die openbaar; *the* ~ *at LARGE,* die groot publiek; *MEMBERS of the* ~, lede v.d. publiek; *the READING* ~, die lesende publiek; (a) openbaar, publiek; algemeen; lands=, staats=, volk(s)=; *at* ~ *COST,* op regeringskoste; *by* ~ *DEMAND,* op aandrang v.d. publiek; *be in the* ~ *EYE,* algemene aandag trek; *the* ~ *INTEREST,* die openbare belang; die landsbelang; *give* ~ *UTTERANCE,* in die openbaar uitspreek; ~ **accounts,** staatsrekeninge; ~ **address system,** luidsprekerstelsel; ~ **administration,** openbare administrasie, landsbestuur; ~ **affairs,** staatsake.
pub'lican, kroeghouer, kantienman; tollenaar.
publica'tion, uitgawe; openbaarmaking, bekendmaking; geskrif, verskyning, publikasie; ~ *of banns,* afkondiging van gebooie; ~ **day,** verskyningsdag.
pub'lic: ~ **company,** publieke maatskappy; ~ **debt,** staatskuld, landskuld; ~ **debt commissioner,** staatskuldkommissaris; ~ **enemy,** openbare vyand; volksvyand; ~ **funds,** staatsgeld; ~ **health,** volksgesondheid; ~ **holiday,** openbare vakansiedag; ~ **house,** herberg; kantien; ~ **interest,** volksbelang; die openbare belang; ~**ist,** skrywer oor die volkereg; dagbladskrywer, joernalis; publisis.
publi'city, bekendheid, openbaarheid, rugbaarheid, publisiteit; ~ **agent,** publisiteitsagent, reklamemaker; ~ **association,** reklamevereniging; ~ **manager,** reklamebestuurder; ~ **stunt,** reklamesensasie, reklametoetie.
pub'licize, bekend maak, publisiteit gee aan, rugbaar maak.
pub'lic: ~ **lands,** staatsgrond; ~ **law,** publieke reg; ~ **liability,** publieke aanspreeklikheid; ~ **life,** openbare lewe; ~ **mind,** openbare mening; ~ **nuisance,** openbare oorlas, landsplaag; ~ **opinion,** die openbare mening; ~ **property,** staatseiendom; ~ **prosecutor,** staatsaanklaer; ~ **relations,** openbare betrekkinge; skakeldiens; ~ **relations officer,** skakelbeampte; ~ **road,** openbare pad; ~ **resort,** ontspanningsoord; ~ **sale,** openbare veiling; ~ **school,** openbare skool; ~ **servant,** staatsamptenaar; ~ **service,** staatsdiens; ~ **speaking,** redenaarskuns; ~ **spirit,** burgersin; ~**-spirited,** vol ywer vir die algemene welsyn, met burgersin; ~ **welfare,** openbare welsyn; ~ **worship,** erediens.
pub'lish, openbaar maak; uitgee, publiseer (boek); aankondig; afkondig; plaas; bekend maak; ~ *the BANNS of marriage,* huweliksgeboöe afkondig; ~ *in SERIAL form,* in aflewerings uitgee; ~**able,** geskik vir publikasie.
pub'lisher, uitgewer; *firm of* ~ *s,* uitgewersfirma; ~'**s imprint,** uitgewersmerk; ~'**s reader,** boekkeurder; perskiaarmaker; ~'**s trade list,** fondslys.
pub'lishing, uitgewery; (die) uitgee; ~ **business,** ~ **company,** ~ **house,** uitgewersaak, uitgewery, uitgewersmaatskappy.
pub' loafer, kroegvlieg.
puce, rooibruin, donkerbruin, persbruin.
puck[1], kaboutermannetjie, elf; stouterd.

puck[2], rubberskyf (vir yshokkie).
puck[3], miltvuur.
puck'a, eg, vas, blywend; agtermekaar.
puck'er, (n) kreukel, rimpel, plooi; (v) kreukel, plooi; frons; ~**ed,** geplooi, gekreukel(d); gerimpel(d); ge= frons; ~*ed brow,* gefronste voorhoof; ~**ing,** rimpeling; plooiing; ~**y,** vol voue.
puck'ish, ondeund, tergerig; ~**ness,** tergerigheid, ondeundheid.
pud, kinderhandjie; voorpoot.
pud'ding, nagereg, poeding; bloedwors; skuurkabel; *BLACK* ~, bloedwors; *get more PRAISE than* ~, meer lof as loon kry; *YORKSHIRE* ~, deegtoespys, yorkshirepoeding; ~**-basin,** poedingbak; ~-**bowl,** poedingbakkie; ~**-face,** volmaangesig; ~**-head,** domkop; ~**-heart,** lafaard; ~**-mould,** poedingvorm; ~**-pie,** pastei; ~**-sleeve,** pofmou; ~**-stone,** ouklip.
pud'dle, (n) poel, dammetjie, plas(sie); gemors, warboel; vulklei; (v) troebel maak, mors; pleister; ruyster bewerk, poedel (yster); toeslaan (grond); vasstamp; plas; aanklam.
pudd'ly, modderig, morsig, vuil.
pud'ency, skaamte, eerbaarheid, ingetoënheid, beskeidenheid.
puden'da, skaamdele.
pudge, diksak, dikkerd, vaatjie.
pud'gy, vet, dik.
pud'ic, skaam=.
pudi'city, eerbaarheid, kuisheid.
pud'sy, vet, dik.
pu'erile, kinderagtig, puerlel, beuselagtig.
pu'erilism, puerilisme.
pueril'ity, (..ties), kinderagtigheid.
puerp'eral, barens=, kraam=; ~ **fever,** kraamkoors.
puerper'ium, puer'pery, kraambed, kraamtyd (mense); kalftyd; vultyd; lamtyd.
puff, (n) geblaas; rukwind; skuif, haal, trek (aan 'n pyp); rookwolkie, damp; bluf; poeierkwas; poffertjie; ophemelende resensie, reklame, oordrewe aanbeveling; pof; *give a few* ~ *s,* 'n paar skuiwe trek; (v) blaas, hyg, puf, pof; opswel; pronk, spog; adverteer, ophemel, aanprys; trek aan, skuif (pyp); ~ *AWAY,* wegblaas; ~ *AWAY vigorously,* groot skuiwe trek; *BE* ~*fed,* uitasem wees; ~ *up one's CHEST,* jou bors uitstoot; *HUFF and* ~, hyg en blaas; ~ *OUT,* uitblaas; ~ *and PANT,* hyg en blaas; ~ *at one's PIPE,* aan jou pyp trek; ~ *UP somebody or something,* iem. (iets) opvysel; ~**-adder,** pofadder; ~**-ball,** duiwelsnuif, stuifswam; ~**-cake,** poffertjie; ~**-creams,** roomkoekies.
puffed, opgeblaas; uitasem; spring=; gepofte; *BE* ~, uitasem wees; *be* ~ *up with PRIDE,* opgeblase wees van hoogmoed; ~ *SLEEVE,* pofmou; ~ *WHEAT,* springkoring, pofkoring.
puff: ~**er,** windmaker, grootprater, spogger; reklamemaker; opjaer (vendusie); ~**ery,** plooisel; grootpratery; reklamemakery.
puff'in, papegaaiduiker.
puff'iness, winderigheid, opgeblasenheid; swaarlywigheid; geswollenheid; ~ *under the eyes,* sakke onder die oë.
puff'ing, (n) gehyg; reklamemakery; (a) blasend; ~**-pig,** bruinvis.
puff: ~ **paste,** skilfertertdeeg; ~ **pastry,** blaarkors, blaartertdeeg; skilferkors; ~**-sleeve,** pofmou.
puff'y, opgeblaas, geswel; winderig; bombasties; swaarlywig; uitasem.
pug[1], (n) steenklei; (v) **(-ged),** kleitrap, klei maak; die solder opvul met saagsels.
pug[2], (n) dierespoor, (v) **(-ged),** spoorsny.
pug[3], (n) Mopshond(jie), kabouter, rangeerlokomotiefie; hoofbediende; ~**-face,** plat gesiggie, mopsgesig; ~**-nose,** stompneus, mopsneus; ~**-nosed,** stompneus=.
pugg'(a)ree, alabama, hoedwindsel, helmband.
pugh! foei! aag!
pu'gilism, vuisvegtery, boks(ery).
pu'gilist, vuisvegter, bokser; ~'**ic,** vuisvegter=, boks=.
pug'-mill, kniemasjien, kleimeul, rondomtalie.
pugna'cious, strydlustig, twissoekerig, bakleierig; byterig (dier); militant; ~ **ant,** malmier; ~**ness,** pug=

na'city, strydlustigheid, twissoekerigheid, bakleierigheid.
pug'-nose, stompneus; platneus.
puisn'e, jonger, klein; later; van laer rang; ~ **judge,** junior strafregter, ondergeskikte regter.
puiss'ance, mag, invloed, gesag.
puiss'ant, magtig, invloedryk.
puke, (n) braking, opgooiery; (v) braak, vomeer, opgooi.
pukk'a(h), *kyk* **pucka.**
pul'chritude, skoonheid; mooiheid, aantreklikheid.
pule, kreun, steun, piep, tjank, grens, huil.
pul'ing, (n) getjank, gegrens, grensery; (a) skreeuend, huilend, tjankerig, pieperig.
pull, (n) ruk, trek, pluk; strookproef, galeiproef; groot sluk; trekker; handvatsel; roeitoggie; voorsprong, voordeel; haaromhou, trekhou (gholf); skuif (rook); *a ~ of BRANDY,* 'n sluk brandewyn; *HAVE the ~ of (over) someone,* 'n voorsprong op iem. hê; *a LONG ~,* 'n kwaai ent; 'n lang tog; *TAKE long ~s,* groot skuiwe trek; *have a ~ WITH someone,* invloed hê by iem.; (v) trek, ruk, pluk; roei; haarom slaan, trek (gholf); *~ ABOUT,* rondtrek; *~ ASUNDER,* stukkend skeur; *~ AT,* trek aan; *~ in one's BELT,* suinig lewe; *~ the long BOW,* oordryf, vergroot; leuens vertel; *~ DEVIL, pull baker,* elke man vir homself; laat elkeen sien en kom klaar; *~ DOWN,* afbreek; *it is easier to ~ DOWN than to build,* afbreek is makliker as opbou; *~ EARS,* ore trek; *~ FACES,* gesigte trek; skewebek trek; *~ a long FACE,* 'n lang gesig trek; *~ a FAST one over a person,* iem. fop; *~ed HEN,* geplukte hoender; *~ IN,* inhou; (die stasie) inkom; intrek; *~ someone's LEG,* iem. vir die gek hou; 'n lopie met iem. neem; *~ a MUSCLE,* 'n spier verrek; *~ OFF a fine stroke of business,* 'n goeie slag slaan; goeie sake doen; *~ a thing OFF,* 'n goeie slag slaan; die pyp rook; *~ ON one's clothes,* jou klere aanpluk; *~ OUT,* uittrek; wegtrek; jou onttrek; retireer; *~ OVER,* omtrek; *~ to PIECES,* stukkend trek; afbrekende kritiek uitoefen; *~ someone to PIECES,* iem. stukkend trek; iem. uitmekaar trek; oor iem. uitpak; *~ at his PIPE,* aan sy pyp suig; *~ PROOFS,* proewe trek; *~ one's PUNCHES,* jou inhou; *~ a REVOLVER,* 'n rewolwer uitpluk; *~ ROUND,* weer regkom, bo-op kom; herstel; *~ up SHARP,* in jou vier spore vassteek; *~ someone up SHORT,* iem. tot besinning bring; iem. regruk; *~ up one's SOCKS,* jou roer; jou regruk; *~ STRINGS,* drade (toutjies) trek; *~ THROUGH,* weer regkom; deurkom; dit maak; *he has ~led THROUGH,* sy kop is deur; *~ TIGHT,* styf trek, sjor; *~ oneself TOGETHER,* jou regruk; die beste been voorsit; herstel; *if we all ~ TOGETHER,* as ons almal saamwerk; *be UNABLE to ~ together,* nie met mekaar kan klaarkom nie; *~ UP,* optrek, intoom; stilhou; uittrek, uitpluk; op sy plek sit; *~ UP short,* iem. berispe; iem. teregwys; iem. in die bek ruk; *~ up WEEDS,* onkruid uitroei (uittrek); *~ one's WEIGHT,* met volle krag roei; jou deel doen; alle kragte inspan; *~ the WOOL over someone's eyes,* sand in iem. se oë strooi; *~-back,* struikelblok, remskoen; *~er,* trekker, plukker; aantrekkingskrag.
pu'llet, hennetjie.
pu'lley, (n) (-s), katrol; riemskyf, bandwiel; (v) van 'n katrol voorsien; met 'n katrol hys; *~-block,* katrolblok, takel; *~ system,* katrolkoppeling.
pu'lling, getrek, gesjor.
Pu'llman car, slaapsalon, slaapwa (op trein).
pull: *~-over,* (oortrek)trui; *~-rod,* trekstang; *~-through,* deurtrekker, wisser; stertriem; trekstang.
pull'ulate, uitkom, uitspruit, groei, bot; ontwikkel, ontkiem.
pullula'tion, ontkieming; knopvorming; wemeling.
pull'wire, haler; trekdraad.
pul'monary, long=; *~ artery,* longslagaar; *~ consumption,* longtering; *~ disease,* longsiekte; *~ inflammation,* longontsteking; *~ vein,* longaar.
pul'monate, met longe.
pulmon'ic, (n) longlyer; longmiddel; (a) long=; *~ circulation,* klein bloedsomloop.

pulp, (n) murg; pap, pulp; moes; sagte massa; vleisgedeelte (vrugte); *beat to a ~,* papslaan; (v) fynmaak, pap maak; verpulp; in pap verander, maal, tot pap kook; sag word; *~er,* pulpmasjien; *~iness,* vlesigheid; papheid.
pu'lpit, preekstoel, kansel; *~eer,* (n) beroepsprediker; (v) preek; *~ eloquence,* kanselwelsprekendheid; *~ language,* kanseltaal; *~ orator,* kanselredenaar; *~ oratory,* kanselwelsprekendheid; *~ style,* kanselstyl, preekstyl.
pulp: *~ literature,* prulskrywery; *~ magazine,* prultydskrif.
pulp'-mill, papmeul, pulpmeul.
pulp'ous, papperig, sag.
pulp'-wood, dennepap; houtpap.
pulp'y, sag, papperig, vlesig; *~ kidney,* bloednier.
pulsate', klop, slaan; tril.
pul'satile, kloppend, slag=.
pulsa'tion, klopping; (pols)slag; trilling, pulsasie.
pulsat'or, klopper, pulsator; *~y,* kloppend, klop=.
pulse¹, (n) peulvrug.
pulse², (n) pols, polsslag; slagaar; trilling; (im)puls; *FEEL someone's ~,* iem. se pols voel; iem. pols; voel hoe iem. se pols klop; *a LOW ~,* 'n swak pols; (v) klop, slaan; tril; pulseer; ritmies slaan; *~-beat,* polsslag; *~less,* sonder pols; *~ rate,* polsslag.
pulsim'eter, polsmeter.
pulsom'eter, pulsometer.
pulta'ceous, papperig, sag.
pulveriza'tion, fynstamping, vergruising; vermorseling; vermaling, verpoeiering; vernietiging.
pul'verize, tot poeier maak (stamp); vergruis; vermorsel, verpoeier, fynmaak, fynstamp; vernietig; tot gruis word; *~d,* vergruis, verpoeier, fyn; *~r,* vergruiser, poeiermeul; verstuiwer.
pul'verous, pulve'rulent, fyn, poeieragtig; bros, krummelrig; bepoeier.
pul'vinate(d), kussingvormig (bot.); duigvormig.
pum'a, bergleeu, poema.
pum'ice, (n) puimsteen, sponssteen; (v) met puimsteen vrywe.
pumi'ceous, puimsteenagtig.
pum'ice: *~ powder,* puimsteenpoeier; *~-stone,* puimsteen.
pumm'el, (-led), met die vuis slaan, moker.
pump¹, (n) dansskoen.
pump², (n) pomp; uithoorder; (die) uitvra; (v) pomp; oppomp; leegpomp; uitvra; uithoor; uitasem raak; plotseling styg en daal; *~ DRY,* leeg pomp; *~ SOMEONE,* iem. uitvra; *~ SOMEONE full of lies,* iem. vol leuens stop; *~ attendant,* pompbediende; *~ balance,* pompswingel; *~ barrel,* pompsilinder; pompromp; *~ brake,* pomprem, =briek; *~ casing,* pompbuis; *~ cistern,* pompbak; *~ connection,* pompbuisie; *~ delivery,* pompvermoë; *~ dredger,* sandsuier; *~er,* pomper; pomp.
pum'pernickel, pumpernickel, pompernikkel, rogbrood.
pump: *~ gasket,* pomppakking; *~ gear,* pomptoestel; *~-handle,* pompslinger; *~ head,* pompkop; *~-house,* pomphuis; *~ing,* (n) (die) pomp; (a) pomp=; *~ing-station,* pompstasie.
pump'kin, pampoen; *~ fritter,* pampoenkoekie, pampoenpoffertjie.
pump: *~ man,* pompwerker; pompwagter; *~ plunger,* pompplunjer, pompdompelaar; *~ rod,* pompstang; *~-room,* pompkamer; drinksaal; *~ spear,* pompstang; *~ station,* pompstasie; *~-station man,* pompmasjinis; *~ trolley,* pomptrollie; *~ valve,* pompklep; *~ wright,* pompmaker; pompwerker.
pun¹, (n) woordspeling; (v) (-ned), woordspelings maak.
pun², (v) (-ned), vasstamp.
punch¹, (n) vrugtebole, pons (drank).
punch², (n) sterk trekperd.
punch³, (n) (-es), vuisslag, opstopper, hou; deurslag; knyptang; holpypie, knipper; stempel; hansworsdiksak; *DEAL out ~es right and left,* regs en links rondes uitdeel; *P~ and JUDY show,* poppekas; *as PLAIN as ~,* glashelder, so duidelik as wat; *as PLEASED as P~,* hoog in jou skik; (v) slaan, moker, stamp; knip; deurdruk; deurslaan; ogies maak

punch-bowl   **Puritan**

in, perforeer; ~ *OUT,* uitslaan, uitdryf; uitstamp; ~ *TICKETS,* kaartjies knip; ~ *ed WORK,* perfo= reerwerk; ~ **-ball,** boksbal, slaanbal; ~ **-bar,** deur= slagyster.
punch'-bowl, ponskom.
punch' card, ponskaart.
punch'-drunk, ylhoofdig, benewel(d), duiselig; deur die wind; vuisvoos; ~ **enness,** beneweldheid, duise= ligheid; vuisvoosheid.
pun'cheon¹, groot vat (84 gelling – 382 liter).
pun'cheon², stut; ~ **-prop,** dwarsstut.
punch'er, ponser; vuisslaner; veedrywer.
Punchinell'o, (-s), hanswors; diksak.
punch'ing, (n) gaatjiesteek; slanery; ponswerk; (a) deurslag=; ~ **bag,** slaansak; ~ **bear,** handponsma= sjien; ~ **machine,** deurslagmasjien; ~ **needle,** pons= naald; ~ **pliers,** holpyptang; ~ **power,** slaankrag; ~ **tool,** deurslag, pons.
punch' plier, gaatjieknipper.
punch'y, kort en dik.
punc'tate, gepunt; gestippel, bont.
punc'tiform, soos 'n punt, puntvormig.
punctil'io, (-s), oordrewe vormlikheid, pynlike nou= gesetheid.
punctil'ious, oordrewe nougeset, puntenc(u)rig, ~ **ness,** nougesetheid; puntene(u)righeid.
punc'tual, stip, nougeset, presies; nougeset; *BE* ~, presies op tyd wees; ~ *with his BILLS,* presies wees met sy rekeninge.
punctual'ity, stiptheid, nougesetheid, presiesheid.
punc'tuate, leestekens insit, punktueer; onderstreep (fig.); beklemtoon; krag bysit; onderbreek, inter= pungeer; *a speech ~ d with cheers,* 'n toespraak on= derbreek deur toejuigings.
punctua'tion, punktuasie, leestekens, interpunksie; ~ **mark,** leesteken.
punc'tum, (..ta), punt, kolletjie.
punctura'tion, punktuur.
punc'ture, (n) lek(plek); gaatjie, prik; *HAVE a ~,* 'n lek kry; *MEND a ~,* 'n lek heelmaak; (v) prik, stukkend maak; 'n lek kry; ~ *someone's pride,* iem. op sy neus laat kyk; ~ **-proof,** lekvry.
pun'dit, kenner (van die Indiese wysheid), geleerde, gesaghebbende.
pun'gency, skerpheid; bitterheid; bytendheid, bitsig= heid.
pun'gent, skerp, deurdringend, pikant, bytend, prik= kelend; vinnig, bitsig.
Pun'ic, Punies; ~ **faith,** trouelcosheid; ~ **Wars,** Pu= niese Oorloë.
pun'ish, straf, kasty, deurloop; toetakel, afransel; ~ **able,** strafbaar (persoon); strafwaardig (daad).
pun'ishment, straf; strafwerk; strafvoltrekking; tug; boete; *AS a ~,* by wyse van straf; *AWARD ~,* straf oplê; *on ~ of DEATH,* op straf v.d. dood; *EXECUTE ~,* straf uitvoer; *INFLICT ~,* straf toedien; *POWER of ~,* strafbevoegdheid; *TAKE ~,* straf kry; gekasty word; ~ **book,** strafregister.
pun'itive, straffend, straf=; ~ **expedition,** strafekspe= disie; ~ **measure,** strafmaatreël.
Pun'jab, Pandjab.
punk, (n) vrot hout; kaf, bog, onsin, snert; swam (a) beroerd, sleg, vrot.
punk'a(h), waaier.
punk'y, swammig.
punn'er, stamper; woordspeler.
punn'et, (vrugte)kardoesie, klein mandjie.
pun'ster, woordspeler, maker van woordspelinge.
punt¹, (n) lugskop, hoogskop; (v) hoog skop.
punt², (n) wedder; speler; (v) wed; vir geld speel.
punt³, (n) pont, pontskuit, platboomskuit; (v) oor= vaar; vooruitstoot; boom (skuit), punter.
punt'er¹, skopper.
punt'er², beroepswedder; spekulant.
pun'ter³, bomer; visser; jagter.
punt: ~ **-gun,** eendegeweer; ~ **man,** eendejagter; ~ **- pole,** vaarstok, punterstok.
pun'y, klein, pieperig, swak, tingerig; onbedui= dend.
pup, (n) jong hondjie; *a CONCEITED ~,* 'n ver= waande snuiter; *IN ~,* dragtig; *SELL someone a ~,* iem. kul; iem. in die nek kyk; *when the WORLD was but a ~,* toe Tafelberg 'n vulletjie was; (v) (-ped), hondjies kry; jong.
pup'a, (-e), papie; ~ **l,** papie=; ~ **te,** verpop, in 'n papie verander; ~ **tion,** verpopping.
pup'il, leerling, skolier; onmondige; pleegkind; kyker; pupil, oogappel; ~ **(l)age,** minderjarigheid, on= mondigheid; leertyd; ~ **(l)ary,** oogappel=; minder= jarig; ~ **(l)ize,** leer, onderrig; ~ **-pilot,** leerlingvlieër; ~ **-teacher,** leerlingonderwyser, kwekelingonder= wyser.
pupp'et, speelpop, handpop, draadpop, marionet; strooipop; werktuig, speelbal, figurant; ~ **govern= ment,** marionetteregering; ~ **-man,** marionetspeler; ~ **-play,** poppespel; ~ **ry,** poppespel; skynvertoon; poppekastery; ~ **-show,** poppekas, poppespel; ma= rionet(te)spel; ~ **state,** vasalstaat, popstaat; mini= staat; ~ **-valve,** stootklep.
pupp'y, (puppies), jong hond; snuiter, bog, snoes= haan; ~ **-biscuits,** hondebeskuit; ~ **-dog,** jong hond; ~ **fat,** jeugvet; ~ **-headed,** kinderagtig; on= nosel; ~ **ism,** lawwigheid; verwaandheid, aanstelle= ry; ~ **love,** kalwerliefde.
purb'lind, (v) halfblind maak, verblind, benewel; (a) bysiende, halfblind; kortsigtig.
purch'asable, te koop, verkrygbaar.
purch'ase, (n) koop, aankoop; oorname; aanskaf= fing, verwerwing; spil; hefkrag; hefinrigting; hou= vas, vastrapplek, vatplek; kragtakel; *BY ~,* deur aankoop; *DEED of ~,* koopbrief; *MAKE ~ s,* in= kope (inkopies) doen; *there was not the slightest ~ on the ROCK-FACE,* daar was geen vastrapplek (vatplek) op die rotswand nie; *his life is not WORTH an hour's ~,* hy sal nog skaars 'n uur lewe; (v) koop; verwerf, aanskaf; optrek, optel, op= lig; ~ *one's discharge,* jou uitkoop; ~ **block,** takel= blok; ~ **deed,** koopbrief, koopakte; ~ **money,** koopprys, koopskat; ~ **price,** inkoopprys, koop= prys; koopsom; ~ **r,** (aan)koper, klant; ~ **sample,** koopmonster; ~ **tax,** koopbelasting.
purch'asing power, koopkrag.
purd'ah, skermgordyn; afsondering.
pure, (n) reine; *to the ~ all things are ~,* vir die reine is alles rein; (a, adv) suiwer, rein, kuis, onbevlek; onvervals, ongemeng; louter, puur, fyn (goud); eg; ~ *COINCIDENCE,* blote toeval; *IGNORANCE ~ and simple,* skone onkunde; ~ *NONSENSE,* pure onsin; ~ *WHITE,* suiwer wit; ~ **-blooded,** volbloed=, raseg; ~ **-bred,** opreg, volbloed, raseg, rassuiwer.
pur'ee, puree, moes.
pure: ~ **honey,** slingerheuning; ~ **ly,** rein, louter; en= kel, alleen; ~ **mathematics,** suiwer wiskunde, ~ **ness,** reinheid, egtheid.
pur'fle, (n) geborduurde rand; borduurkant; sier= rand; (v) versier, omsoom, omboor.
purga'tion, suiwering; purgasie; loutering.
purg'ative, (n) suiweringsmiddel; purgeermiddel; purgasie; (a) suiwerend, afdrywend, purgerend; purgeer=, laksatief; reinigend.
purgator'ial, tot die vaevuur behorend, vaevuur=.
purg'atory, (n) vaevuur; (a) suiwerend, reinigend.
purge, (n) suiwering, reiniging; purgeermiddel; (v) suiwer; reinig, lakseer, purgeer, afdryf; ~ *some= thing of impurities,* iets van onsuiwerhede reinig; ~ **r,** reiniger.
purg'ing, suiwering; laksering; ~ **nut,** purgeerneut.
purifica'tion, suiwering, reiniging; ~ **plant,** suiwe= ringstoestel, -installasie.
pur'ificative, suiwerend, reinigend.
pur'ificator, kelkdoekie.
pur'ificatory, suiwerings=, reinigings=.
pur'ifier, suiweraar, reiniger, skoonmaker; suiwe= ringsmiddel.
pur'ify, (..fied), suiwer, reinig, louter, skoonmaak; ~ *from (of) impurities,* van onsuiwerhede reinig; ~ **ing agent,** suiweringsmiddel; ~ **ing process,** sui= weringsproses.
Pur'im, Purimfees.
pur'ism, taalsuiwering; purisme.
pur'ist, taalsuiweraar; puris; taalpartikularis.
puris'tic, puristies; taalsuiwerend.
Pur'itan, (n) Puritein; (a) Puriteins.

Puritan'ic(al), Puriteins.
Pur'itanism, Puritanisme.
pur'ity, suiwerheid, reinheid, vlekkeloosheid; kuisheid.
purl¹, (n) val, tuimeling; (v) val, omtuimel; onderstebo gooi.
purl², (n) kabbeling, gemurmel; (a) kabbel, murmel (water).
purl³, (n) jenewerbier.
purl⁴, (n) gestikte rand; boorsel; borduurdraad; aweregse breiwerk; (v) stik; borduur; omboor; aweregs brei; (a) aweregs; *plain and* ~, regs en aweregs.
purl'er, bolmakiesiehou; tuimeling; *come (take) a* ~, neerslaan; neertuimel; aftuimel.
purl'ieu, (-s), omtrek, grens; (pl) agterbuurte; buitewyke, -kant.
purl'in, kaplat, onderbalk, hanebalk, dwarsbalk, gording.
purl'ing¹, kabbel.
purl'ing², aweregse breiwerk.
pur'loin, steel, ontfutsel, wegroof, wegkaap; ~**er,** steler, dief.
pur'ple, (n) pers, purper, purperkleur; purper gewaad; kardinaalskleed; koninklike waardigheid; *BORN in the* ~, van koninklike bloed; *be RAISED to the* ~, tot kardinaal verhef word; (v) pers word; purper kleur; (a) purperkleurig, pers; ~ **emperor,** pouoog(skoenlapper); ~ **fever,** purperkoors; ~ **fish,** purperslak; ~ **grunter,** knorhaan (vis); ~ **patch,** purperkol; mooiskrywery; ~ **sin,** doodsonde.
purp'lish, purperagtig, persagtig.
pur'port, (n) sin, betekenis, bedoeling, inhoud, strekking.
purport', (v) inhou, omvat, behels; voorgee, beweer; bedoel; *an article that* ~ *s to express public opinion,* 'n artikel wat kastig die openbare mening sou weergee.
purp'ose, (n) voorneme, plan, doel, oogmerk, bedoeling; *ACHIEVE one's* ~, jou doel bereik; *ANSWER the* ~, aan die doel beantwoord; *FOR the* ~ *of,* met die doel om; *FULL of* ~, vasbereade; doelgerig; *GENERAL* ~*s,* algemene doeleindes; *serve a GOOD* ~, van groot nut wees; *to LITTLE* ~, met min sukses; met geen sukses nie; *to NO* ~, tevergeefs; *for NO other* ~ *than,* met geen ander doel nie as; *NOVEL with a* ~, tendensroman, strekkingsroman; *OF* ~, met voorbedagte rade; *ON* ~, opsetlik, ekspres; met voorbedagte rade; met opset; *for all PRACTICAL* ~*s,* prakties; *SERVE no* ~, tot niks lei nie; van geen nut wees nie; *to SOME* ~, met 'n (sekere) mate van sukses; *SUIT someone's* ~, in iem. se kraam pas; *for THAT* ~, met daardie doel; *TO the* ~, ter sake; *for WHAT* ~?, waarom?; *WIDE off the* ~, ver verkeerd; (v) bedoel, beoog; van plan wees, voornemens wees; ~**ful,** doelgerig, vasberade, doelbewus; ~**fulness,** doelgerigtheid, vasberadenheid, doelbewustheid; ~**less,** doelloos; vrugteloos; ~**ly,** opsetlik, met opset, ekspres; ~**-made,** spesiaal gemaak; ~ **novel,** tendensroman, strekkingsroman.
purp'osive, met 'n doel, doelbewus.
purp'ura, huidbloeding; purperslak.
purpur'eal, purper=, skarlaken=.
purpur'ic, purper=, skarlaken=; ~ **acid,** purpersuur.
purp'urin, purpurine, purpurien, meekrappurper.
purr, (n) gespin (van katte); snork; gesnor; (v) spin (kat); snor (masjien); ~**ing,** gespin (van katte); geronk (van masjien); gesnor.
purse, (n) beurs(ie); skatkis, middele, som geld; buidel (bv. van kangaroe); vegprys; beurs; *GIVE a* ~, 'n prys uitloof; *have a HEAVY* ~, daar goed in sit; *have a LIGHT* ~, platsak wees; *a LONG* ~, 'n beurs vol geld; 'n vet beurs; *the PUBLIC* ~, die skatkis; *you cannot make a silk* ~ *out of a SOW'S ear,* jy kan van 'n skilpad (padda) nie vere pluk nie; (v) in die beursie steek; die mond saamtrek; frons, rimpel, plooi; ~**-bearer,** tesourier, penningmeester; kassier (kerk); ~**-crab,** buidelkreef; ~**-cutter,** sakkeroller; ~**ful,** beursvol; ~**-net,** saknet; ~**-pride,** geldtrots; ~**-proud,** opgeblase van geldtrots; ~**r,** betaalmeester; ~**rette',** reiswaardin, skeeps=

waardin; ~**-seine,** saknet, visnet; ~**-seining,** saknetvissery.
purse'-string, koord van 'n beurs; *HOLD the* ~*s,* oor die beurs beskik; *LOOSEN one's* ~*s,* die hand in die sak steek; *TIGHTEN the* ~*s,* spaarsaam wees.
purs'lane, postelein.
pursu'able, vervolgbaar; nastreefbaar.
pursu'ance, nastrewing, voortsetting, nakoming, uitvoering; *in* ~ *of,* na aanleiding van, volgens, ooreenkomstig, kragtens.
pursu'ant, ingevolge, ooreenkomstig.
pursue', vervolg, agtervolg, agternasit, ja(ag); voortsit; volg, najaag (plesier); nastrewe (doel); in toepassing bring (plan, metode); verder ingaan op ('n onderwerp); beoefen, voortsit (studie); uitoefen (beroep); ~ *a course of CONDUCT,* 'n gedragslyn volg; ~ *an OBJECT,* 'n doel nastrewe; ~ *a PROFESSION,* 'n beroep uitoefen; ~ *SOMEONE closely,* iem. op die hakke sit; ~ *one's STUDIES,* jou studie voortsit; ~**r,** vervolger; najaer; ~**rs and pursued,** die vervolgers en vervolgdes.
pursuit', vervolging; najaging, jag; uitoefening; nastrewing; (pl) werksaamhede, arbeid, besigheid; *in CLOSE* ~ *of the enemy,* op die vyand se hakke; *IN* ~ *of the enemy,* op die vyand se hakke; ~ *of KNOWLEDGE,* die strewe na kennis; *the* ~ *of RICHES,* die jag na rykdom; ~ **aircraft,** jagvliegtuig; ~ **bomber,** jagbomwerper; ~ **plane,** jagvliegtuig; ~ **squadron,** jageskader.
purs'uivant, volgeling, dienaar.
purs'y¹, kort en dik; opgeblaas; kortasem.
purs'y², geplooi; sakkerig; *a* ~ *mouth,* 'n geplooide mond.
purt'enance, harslag; binnegoed.
pur'ulence, pur'ulency, ettering, etterigheid.
pur'ulent, etterend, etterig, etteragtig.
purvey', lewer, verskaf, verstrek; ~ *for,* van lewensmiddele voorsien; ~**ance,** verskaffing, versorging, voorsiening, lewering; proviandering.
purvey'or, verskaffer, leweransier; ~ *to their majesties (to the royal household),* hofleweransier.
purv'iew, inhoud, strekking; gesteldheid; gesigskring; omvang, bestek; bepalinge (van 'n wet).
pus, etter, vuilis, vuilgoed, drag, sug (uit wond).
push, (n) (-es) stamp, stoot, druk; ambisie, eersugtige energie; pit, volharding, fiksheid, deursettingsvermoë, kragsinspanning; gedrang, mensemenigte; kritieke oomblik, nood, moeilikheid, knyp; stukrag; offensief; set; drukknop (elek.); biljartstoot; *AT a* ~, in een slag; in geval van nood; *the BIG* ~, die groot offensief; *when it COMES to the* ~, wanneer dit daarop aankom; in geval van nood; *GET the* ~, ontslaan word; jou ontslag kry; afgedank word; in die pad gesteek word; *GIVE someone a* ~, iem. 'n stoot vorentoe gee; (v) stamp, druk, stoot, du, stu; skuif; bevorder; bespoedig, verhaas; aanhelp, voorthelp; (aan)dring; ~ *ABOUT,* rondstoot; aanstoot; ~ *AROUND,* rondstoot; hiet en gebied; ~ *an ARTICLE,* propaganda vir 'n artikel maak; ~ *ASIDE,* verdring; ~ *AWAY,* wegstoot; ~ *BACK,* terugstoot; ~ *one's CLAIM,* vashou aan jou eis; ~ *DOWN,* afstoot, afdruk; ~ *FORWARD,* voortstoot; voortgaan; vooruitskuif (troepe); ~ *someone HARD,* iem. opkeil; *be* ~*ed for MONEY,* opgeskroef word; ~ *OFF,* afstoot, wegstoot; vertrek, trap; ~ *ON with the work,* deurdruk (aanstoot) met die werk; ~ *an unpleasant job ON someone else,* 'n onaangename taak op iem. anders skuiwe; ~ *ON,* voortstoot; voorthelp; aangaan; vorder; ~ *OUT,* uitdruk, wegdruk; ~ *for PAYMENT,* aandring op betaling; ~ *out ROOTS,* wortelskiet; ~ *THROUGH,* deursit; deurdrywe; be ~*ed for TIME,* min tyd hê; ~ *UP,* opskuif, opstoot; ~ *a VESSEL,* 'n skip te vinnig laat loop; ~ *one's WAY,* deurdruk; jou indring; ~ **ball,** stootbal; ~**-bell,** drukklokkie; ~**-bike,** trapfiets; ~**-button,** drukknoppie; ~**-button war,** drukknopoorlog; ~**-cart,** handkar, stootwaentjie; ~**-chair,** invalidestoel; ~**er,** stoter; aandrywer; drukker; knop; afstoter; opdringer; deurdrukker; stootskroef (vliegtuig); ~**ful,** ondernemend, vooruitstrewend; voortvarend; indringerig; ~**ing,** (n) gestoot, stotery; (a)

pusillanimity / **put**

ondernemend; volhardend; voortvarend; indringerig; *be* ~*ing*, indringerig wees; oorambisieus wees; vol selfvertroue wees; ~**-over try**, oorstootdrie; ~ **pin**, duimspykertjie; ~**-rod**, stootstang; ~**-shot**, stamphou, stampskoot; ~**-stroke**, deurstoot; drukstoot; ~ **tap**, drukkraan.
pusillanim'ity, kleinmoedigheid, lafhartigheid; kleinsieligheid.
pusillan'imous, kleinmoedig, lafhartig, lamsakkerig; kleinsielig, papbroek(er)ig, skroomhartig, versaag; ~**ness** = **pusillanimity**.
puss, kat; haas; tier; meisie; *P* ~ *in Boots*, die Gelaarsde Kat; *a SLY* ~, 'n geslepe meisie(mens).
pu'ssy, (n) (**pussies**), kietsie, kat(jie); wilgerkatjie; ~**cat**, katjie; ~**foot**, (n) afskaffer; (v) saggies loop; skelm besoek; (a) met sagte pote; ~**-footed**, sagvoetig, sagpotig; heimlik; ~ **willow**, katwilger.
pus'tular, puisierig, vol puisies.
pus'tulate, blare (puisies) vorm.
pus'tule, puisie; blaartjie; vratjie.
pust'ulous, vol puisies.
put, (n) gooi; stoot (gewig); drang, dwang, opsie; (v) (**put**), sit, neersit, stel, plaas; stoot; steek; sê; uitdruk; ~ *ABOUT*, laat omdraai; die stewe wend; lastig val, ongerief veroorsaak; ~ *ACROSS*, na die oorkant roei; ~ *it ACROSS*, iets oortuigend oordra (voorstel); ~ *it ACROSS someone*, iem. in die nek kyk; ~ *out of ACTION*, buite geveg stel; ~ *on AIRS*, jou aanstel; ~ *in an APPEARANCE*, opdaag, jou verskyning maak; ~ *ASHORE*, ontskeep; land; ~ *it AT*, skat; ~ *AWAY*, bêre, wegsit, spaar (geld); opeet, wegslaan (kos); ~ *BACK*, agteruitsit; weer op sy plek sit; vertraag, uitstel; ~ *one's BACK into it*, hande uit die mou steek; ~ *somebody's BACK up*, iem. die hoenders in maak; ~ *up BANNS*, gebooie afkondig; ~ *to BED*, in die bed sit; ~ *down in BLACK and white*, swart op wit sit, neerskryf; ~ *the BLAME on someone*, die skuld op iem. pak; ~ *BY*, opsysit (geld); ontwyk ('n vraag); bêre, wegsit; ~ *in CHAINS*, in boeie slaan; ~ *in a CLAIM*, 'n eis indien; ~ *a CHECK on*, teenhou, beteuel; *CLEARLY* ~, duidelik gestel; ~ *a CLOCK on*, 'n klok vorentoe sit; ~ *out to CONTRACT*, aanbestee; ~ *out of COUNTENANCE*, van sy stukke bring; verleë maak; ~ *the DAMAGE at R250*, die skade op R250 skat; ~ *to DEATH*, teregstel, doodmaak; ~ *up a DEFENCE*, jou verdedig; ~ *DOWN*, neersit, neertel (geld); ~ *DOWN for*, skat op; beskou as; *do not* ~ *it DOWN to negligence*, skryf dit nie aan nalatigheid toe nie; *you can* ~ *me DOWN for* R1, ek sal R1 bydra; ~ *it DOWN to my account*, debiteer my rekening daarmee; ~ *one's best FACE on*, jou aangenaam voordoen; ~ *up a FIGHT*, teenstand bied; ~ *on FLESH*, swaarder word, bykom; ~ *to FLIGHT*, op die vlug jaag; *he did not* ~ *a FOOT wrong*, hy het geen enkele fout gemaak nie; ~ *one's FOOT down*, beslis optree; streng verbied; ~ *FORTH*, uitsteek; uitvaardig; ~ *FORTH leaves*, uitloop, blare kry; ~ *FORWARD*, voortbring; indien; opper, verkondig, aankom met; ~ *into GEAR*, inskakel (motor); ~ *out to GRASS*, die halter afhaal; ~ *up one's HAIR*, die hare opsteek; bolla dra; ~ *out one's HAND*, die hand uitsteek; ~ *in HAND*, ter hand neem; aanpak; *be HARD* ~ *to it*, dit benoud (moeilik) hê; broekskeur gaan; ~ *their HEADS together*, die koppe bymekaarsteek; ~ *money on a HORSE*, op 'n perd wed; ~ *up at an HOTEL*, oorbly in 'n hotel; ~ *IN*, insit, inlas; plant; aanstel; binneloop (skip); aanvra; ~ *IN for a post*, aansoek doen om 'n betrekking; ~ *IN candidates for an examination*, kandidate vir 'n eksamen inskryf; ~ *someone across one's KNEE*, iem. oor die knie trek; ~ *into LATIN*, vertaal in Latyn; ~ *in for LEAVE*, (om) verlof vra; ~ *the LID on a plan*, 'n plan verydel; ~ *on the MARKET*, in die handel bring; ~ *it MILD(LY)*, dit sag uitdruk; iets op sy sagste stel; ~ *in MIND of*, herinner aan; ~ *someone out of his MISERY*, 'n einde aan iem. se lyding maak; ~ *into MONEY*, in geld omsit; ~ *MONEY into an undertaking*, geld in 'n onderneming steek; ~ *up the MONEY*, die geld voorskiet; ~ *MONEY out at interest*, geld op rente

sit; ~ *a MOTION*, 'n voorstel in behandeling bring; 'n voorstel tot stemming bring; ~ *one's NAME to a document*, 'n dokument onderteken; ~ *up for the NIGHT*, onderdak verskaf; vir 'n nag laat loseer; losies kry; ~ *in a NUTSHELL*, in 'n paar woorde stel; ~ *under an OBLIGATION*, onder 'n verpligting stel; ~ *a murderer under OBSERVATION*, 'n moordenaar onder waarneming stel; ~ *OFF*, uitstel; op die lange baan skuif; afskeep; ontwyk, afsit; tydelik werkloos stel; ~ *someone OFF altogether*, iem. heeltemal van stryk (van sy stukke) bring; by iem. afkeer inboesem; ~ *someone OFF with fair words*, iem. met 'n kluitjie in die riet stuur; *never* ~ *OFF till tomorrow what you can do today*, stel nie uit tot môre wat jy vandag nog kan besôre; *that will not* ~ *me OFF from doing what I think right*, dit sal my nie belet om te doen wat ek as reg beskou nie; ~ *ON*, jou aanstel; aanstellerig wees; gemaak wees; ~ *it ON*, oordryf; te veel vra; *he is* ~*ting ON*, hy stel hom aan; hy wend voor; ~ *in ORDER*, in orde bring; regmaak; ~ *on ORDER*, bestel; ~ *oneself OUT*, jou inspan; besonder baie (veel) moeite doen; ~ *someone OUT*, iem. bewusteloos maak; iem. lastig val; ongerief veroorsaak; van die wysie bring; ~ *OUT*, belê (geld); bewusteloos maak; doodmaak, doodblaas (kers); afskakel, afknip (elektriese lig); uitgee; uitsteek; uit lid raak, verstuit; uitbou; steur, ongerief veroorsaak, deurmekaarmaak; vererg; omkrap; van sy stukke bring; uitvaar; ~ *PAID to someone's chances*, iem. se kanse verydel; ~ *to PAINS*, moeite veroorsaak; ~ *in the PAPER*, publiseer, in die koerant sit; ~ *into a PASSION*, briesend (woedend) maak; ~ *that in your PIPE and smoke it!* smeer dit op jou brood! ~ *someone in his PLACE*, iem. op sy plek sit; ~ *it in your POCKET*, steek dit in jou sak; ~ *in at a PORT*, 'n hawe aandoen; ~ *PRICES up*, pryse verhoog (opslaan); ~ *in PRINT*, in druk gee; ~ *in PRISON*, in die gevangenis sit; ~ *there for a PURPOSE*, vir 'n doel daar geplaas; ~ *RIGHT*, ~ *to RIGHT*, regmaak, regsit; ~ *a RUMOUR about*, 'n gerug versprei; ~ *up for SALE*, opveil, vir verkoop aanbied; ~ *to SCHOOL*, in die (op) skool sit; ~ *out to SEA*, die see invaar; die see kies; uitseil; ~ *someone in the SHADE*, iem. in die skadu(wee) stel; ~ *down a SHAFT*, 'n skag grawe; ~ *to SHAME*, beskaamd maak; ~ *into SHAPE*, 'n goeie vorm gee; ~ *the SHOT*, gewigstoot; ~ *on SIDE*, 'n aanstellerige houding aanneem; ~ *on one SIDE*, eenkant sit; ~ *on SPECTACLES*, 'n bril opsit; ~ *on the STAGE*, op die toneel bring; ~ *STOP to*, 'n end maak aan; ~ *forth all one's STRENGTH*, al jou kragte inspan; *STAY* ~, onbeweeglik bly, ~ *forward a SUGGESTION*, iets aan die hand doen; ~ *to the SWORD*, platkap, neersabel; ~ *THROUGH*, deursteek; laat doen; deursit (telefoonproep); ~ *me THROUGH to number* 100, skakel my deur na nommer 100; sluit my aan met nommer 100; ~ *TO*, laat dek (diere); ~ *something TO someone*, iets vir oorweging aan iem. voorlê; ~ *TOGETHER*, bymekaarsit, saamvoeg, saamstel; ~ *to the TORCH*, aan die brand steek; ~ *oneself to much TROUBLE*, baie moeite doen; ~ *UP*, opmaak (hare); opsteek (hand); verhoog, opslaan (prys); opstel; bou; optrek; onderdak verskaf; knoei, onderduims werk; ~ *UP with something*, iets verdra (duld); iets maar vir lief neem; ~ *UP a candidate*, 'n kandidaat stel (nomineer); *he was* ~ *UP to do it*, hy is opgesteek om dit te doen; ~ *UP at*, tuisgaan by; ~ *UP for the night*, oornag; *have to* ~ *UP with someone or something*, met iets of iem. opgeskeep sit; *he is easily* ~ *UPON*, hy laat hom maklik kul; iem. iets wysmaak; sand in iem. se oë strooi; ~ *to good USE*, goeie gebruik maak van; ~ *in(to) USE*, in gebruik neem; ~ *to VOTE*, tot stemming bring; ~ *out of the WAY*, ontslae raak van; uit die weg ruim; doodmaak; ~ *on WEIGHT*, swaarder word; ~ *the WIND up someone*, iem. die skrik op die lyf jaag; *please* ~ *me WISE*, gee my die regte inligting, asb.; ~ *to WORK*, aan die werk sit; ~ *in a WORD*, ook 'n woordjie te sê kry (hê); ~ *in a WORD for me*, 'n goeie woordjie doen vir my; ~

into WORDS, in woorde uitdruk; ~ *in WRITING*, dit op skrif stel; *I* ~ *it to YOU*, ek stel dit aan jou; ek vra jou; ~ **and call option**, dubbele opsie; ~ **and take**, gee-en-neem.
put'ative, vermeen(d), veronderstel(d), gewaan(d); ~ **father**, vermoedelike vader.
put'lock, put'log, steierbalk, hangpaal, korteling; ~ **hole**, steiergat, skuiwergat, kortelinggat; ~ **rope**, steiertou.
put'-off, uitstel; uitvlug, ontwyking.
put'-on, mooidoenery, aanstellings.
putred'inous, verrot, stinkend.
putrefac'tion, verrotting; vrotheid, ontbinding, sepsis.
putrefac'tive, verrottend; verrottings=.
put'refy, (..fied), verrot, vrot, ontbind, vergaan, bederf; ontaard; sweer.
putres'cence, rotting, verrotting, rotheid.
putres'cent, rottend, verrottend, vrot.
putres'cible, gedeeltelik verrot, bederfbaar, aan verrotting onderhewig.
put'rid, verrot, vrot; bederwe, bedorwe; smetterig; stink; ontaard.
putrid'ity, (ver)rotting, vrotheid; smetterigheid.
putsch, putsch, blitsopstand.
putt, (n) sethou; (v) set (gholf).
putt'ee, beenband; kamasband.
putt'er, setstok, setyster; setter.
putt'ing, setwerk; plasing; ~ *the HAMMER*, hamergooi; ~ *the SHOT*, gewigstoot; ~**-green**, setperk; ~**-iron**, setstok, setyster.
putt'-putt, set-set.
putt'y, (n) stopverf; (v) (**puttied**), met stopverf toesmeer; ~**-face**, deeggesig; ~ **knife**, glasmakersmes; ~ **plaster**, fynpleister.
put'-up: *a* ~ *job*, 'n knoeiery.
puz'zle, (n) raaisel, enigma; verleentheid; moeilikheid, dilemma; vraagstuk; legkaart; geduldspel, sukkelspel; *Chinese* ~, Sjinese (Chinese) raaisel (toestel); (v) in die war bring, verleë maak; in verleentheid bring; verbyster, hoofbrekens gee; ~ *ABOUT*, ~ *OVER*, tob oor, jou kop breek oor; ~ *OUT*, oplos, uitpluis; uitpieker; ~**d**, verward, deurmekaar, verleë, beteuterd; ~**-headed**, verward, deurmekaar; ~**-lock**, letterslot; ~ **ment**, verwarring, verleentheid; ~ **picture**, soekprentjie; ~**r**, lastige kwessie, turksvy.
pyaem'ia, etterige bloedvergiftiging, piëmie.
pycnom'eter, digtheidsmeter, piknometer.
pyeli'tis, piëlitis.
pyg'mean, dwerg=, dwergagtig, ~ **race**, dwergvolk.
pyg'my, (n) (..mies), dwerg, pigmee; nieteling, nonentiteit; (a) dwerg=, dwergagtig.
pyja'ma, pajama; ~ **jacket**, pajamabaadjie; ~ **trousers**, pajamabroek.
pyja'mas, slaapklere, slaappak, nagpak, pajamas.

pyl'on, poort, ingang; spantoring; ankermas; baldakyn; heilpaal.
pyogen'ic, ettervormend.
pyorrhoe'a, tandvleissiekte, piorree.
pyo'sis, ettering.
pyr'al, brandstapel=.
py'ramid, piramide.
pyram'idal, piramidaal, piramidevormig; kolossaal.
pyre, brandstapel.
Py'renees, Pireneë.
pyreth'rum, bertramkruid, vuurplant, kwylwortel, piretrum.
pyret'ic, (n) koorsmiddel; (a) koorsig; koors=; koorswekkend.
pyrex'ia, koorstoestand, pireksie; ~**l**, koorsagtig.
pyrheliom'eter, warmtemeter, pirheliometer.
py'riform, peervormig.
pyrit'es, piriet, swawelkies.
pyrit'ic(al), pyr'itous, piriet=.
pyr'o=, warmte=, vuur=, piro=.
pyrogen'esis, pirogenese.
pyrogenet'ic, pirogeneties, koorswekkend; warmtewekkend.
pyro'genous, pirogeen.
pyrog'raphy, brandwerk, pirografie.
pyrol'atry, vuuraanbidding, pirolatrie.
pyrolig'neous acid, houtasyn.
pyromagnet'ic, piromagneties.
pyroman'ia, piromanie, brandstigtingsmanie; ~**c**, piromaan, brandstigter.
pyrom'eter, hittemeter, vuurmeter, pirometer.
pyrom'etry, hittemeting, pirometrie.
pyr'one, piroon.
pyronom'ics, hittekunde.
pyr'ope, piroop.
pyr'oscope, piroskoop.
pyros'is, suur, branding in die maag.
pyrotech'nic, (n) vuurwerk; (a) vuurwerk=, piroteg= nies; ~ **al**, pirotegnies; ~**s**, vuurwerkkuns, pirotegniek.
pyrotech'nist, vuurwerkmaker.
pyr'otechny, vuurmakerskuns, pirotegniek.
pyrot'ic, (n) brandmiddel; (a) bytend, brandend.
Py'rrhic, soos van Pyrrhus; ~ **victory**, Pyrrhusoorwinning, skynoorwinning.
Py'rrhonism, twyfelsug, skeptisisme, Pyrrhonisme.
Py'rrhonist, skeptikus, twyfelaar.
Pythagore'an, (n) volgeling van Pit(h)agoras; (a) Pit(h)agories.
pyth'on¹, luislang, piton.
pyth'on², waarseggende gees; waarsêer.
python'ic, profeties, voorspellend.
pyth'on skin, luislangvel.
pyx, (n) monstrans; muntkissie; (v) keur (munte).
pyx'is, kissie, dosie; juweelkissie.

Q

q, (qs, q's), q; *little* ~, q'tjie.
Q'-boat, vermomde (verkapte) oorlogskip, Q-boot.
qua, in die hoedanigheid van, as.
quack¹, (n) gekwaak; (v) kwaak.
quack², (n) kwaksalwer, beunhaas, wonderdokter; charlatan; (v) kwaksalwer; opvysel, ophemel; (a) kwaksalwers=; ~ **cure**, wonderkuur; ~ **doctor**, kwak(salwer); ~**ery**, kwaksalwery; ~**ish**, kwaksalweragtig; ~ **medicine**, kwaksalwersmiddel; ~**salver**, kwak(salwer).
quad, *abbr. of* quadrangle, binneplaas, binneplein.
quadragenar'ian, (n) veertigjarige; (a) veertigjarig.
Quadrages'ima, Vaste, Vastyd; ~**l**, Vaste=, veertigdaags.
quad'rangle, vierkant, vierhoek; binneplaas, binnehof, binneplein.
quadrang'ular, vierkantig; vierhoekig.

qua'drant, kwadrant, hoekmeter; tandboog; meetskyf; kwartsirkel.
quandran'tal, kwadrant=, regsydig.
quad'raplegic, kwadrapleeg.
qua'drat, kwadraat.
qua'drate, (n) vierkant, kwadraat; (v) ooreenbring, ooreenstem; kwadreer, kwadrateer.
quadrat'ic, (n) vierkantsvergelyking; vierkant; (a) vierkants=, tweedemags=, kwadraties; ~ **equation**, vierkantsvergelyking; ~**s**, leer van vierkantsvergelykings.
qua'drature, kwadratuur.
quadrenn'ial, vierjarig; vierjaarliks.
qua'dric, van die tweede graad.
quadricell'ular, viersellig.
qua'dricorn, quadricorn'ous, met vier horings.
qua'drified, vierspletig.
qua'drifoil, vierbladig.

quadrigem'inous, viervoudig.
quadrilat'eral, (n) vierhoek, viersydige figuur; (a) vierkantig, viersydig.
quadriling'ual, viertalig.
quadrille', (n) kadriel; (v) 'n kadriel dans; ~ **paper,** ruitpapier.
quadrill'ion, kwadriljoen.
quadrilob'ate, vierlobbig.
quadriloc'ular, viersellig; vierhokkig.
quadrinom'ial, viertermig.
quadripart'ite, vierdelig.
quadriphyll'ous, vierbladig.
quadrisyllab'ic, vierlettergrepig, viersillabies.
quadrisyll'able, vierlettergrepige woord.
quadrival'ent, vierwaardig.
quadrival'vular, vierkleppig.
quadriv'ium, quadrivium.
quadroon', baster, kwadroon.
quadruman'a, diere met vier hande.
qua'drumane, vierhandig.
quadru'manous, vierhandig.
qua'druped, (n) viervoetige dier; (a) viervoetig.
qua'druplane, vierdekker.
qua'druple, (n) viervoud; (v) verviervoudig; (a) viervoudig; *Q~ ALLIANCE,* die Viervoudige Verbond; *~ RHYTHM (time),* vierkwartmaat; *~ TREBLE,* vierslagsteek.
qua'druplet, viertal; vierling; vierpersoonsfiets; (pl) vierling.
qua'druplex, viervoudig.
quadrup'licate, (n) viervoudige afskrif; (v) verviervoudig; (a) viervoudig.
quadruplica'tion, verviervoudiging.
quads, *abbr.,* vierling.
quadrupli'city, viervoudigheid.
quaes'tor, tesourier, kwestor, betaalmeester; ~**ship,** kwestuur.
quaff, (n) groot sluk; (v) drink, vinnig wegslaan; ~ **er,** drinker, swelger.
quag, moeras, deurslag.
quagg'a, kwagga.
quagg'y, moerassig, modderig, deurslagtig.
quag'mire, modderpoel; valsplek, drilgrond, deurslag.
quail¹, (n) kwartel.
quail², (v) moedeloos word; bang word; terugdeins; *make someone ~,* iem. vrees aanjaag.
quail: ~**-call,** ~**-pipe,** lokfluitjie, kwartelslag.
quaint, snaaks, sonderling; eienaardig, vreemdsoortig, raar; ouderwets; ~**ness,** snaaksheid, grilligheid, vreemdsoortigheid.
quake, (n) bewing, siddering, skudding, trilling; (v) bewe, tril, skud, ril.
Quak'er, Kwaker; *a ~ 's meeting,* 'n swygsame byeenkoms (geselskap); ~**ish,** Kwakeragtig; ~**ism,** leer van die Kwakers, Kwakerleer.
quak'ing, (n) bewing, siddering, skudding, trilling; (a) bewend, sidderend, skuddend; ~ **bog,** drilmoeras; ~**-grass,** bewertjies.
quak'y, bewerig, trillerig; skuddend.
qua'lifiable, omskryfbaar, kwalifiseerbaar.
qualifica'tion, bevoegdheid; bekwaamheid, vereiste, kwalifikasie; beperking; wysiging; eienskap, hoedanigheid; *ELECTORAL ~s,* kiesvereistes; *HAVE the necessary ~s,* die nodige bevoegdheid hê; *the STATEMENT needs ~,* die verklaring moet gekwalifiseer word.
qua'lificative, qua'lificatory, beperkend; wysigend, kwalifiserend.
qua'lified, bevoeg, bekwaam, geskik, gekwalifiseer; geregtig; gewysig; ~ *PRIVILEGE,* beperkte bevoorregting; ~ *SHOT,* bekwame skut.
qua'lifier, beperkende toevoeging; restriksie; toelatingswedstryd.
qua'lify, (..fied), bevoeg maak, bekwaam maak, kwalifiseer; wysig; matig, versag; betitel, noem, aandui; eed aflê; beperk; flou maak (deur water); aanmeng; in aanmerking kom; *an ADJECTIVE qualifies a noun,* 'n byvoeglike naamwoord bepaal 'n selfstandige naamwoord; ~ *in MEDICINE,* as dokter kwalifiseer; ~ *ONESELF for,* jou bekwaam vir; ~ *for a PENSION,* voldoen aan die vereistes vir 'n pensioen; ~ *a STATEMENT,* 'n bewering kwalifiseer; ~**ing examination,** eindeksamen; graadeksamen; ~**ing round,** kwalifiserende ronde.
qua'litative, kwalitatief.
qua'lity, (..ties), gehalte, kwaliteit; hoedanigheid, eienskap, kenmerk; aard, inbors; aanleg; stand; deug; *HAVE ~,* van goeie gehalte wees; *of HIGH ~,* van uitstekende gehalte; *PEOPLE of ~,* hoë lui; *POOR ~,* swak gehalte; ~ *matters more than QUANTITY,* dit kom meer aan op gehalte as op hoeveelheid; kwaliteit bo kwantiteit; *give a TASTE of one's ~,* wys wat jy kan doen; ~ *of a VOICE,* die toonkleur van 'n stem; ~ **article,** kwaliteitsartikel.
qualm, naarheid, mislikheid; gewetenswroeging; angsgevoel; twyfel; ~*s of conscience,* gewetenswroeging; ~**ish,** mislik, naar; flou; ~**ishness,** mislikheid, weeheid.
quan'dary, (..ries), verleentheid; moeilikheid; verknorsing; *be in a ~,* in die knyp sit.
quant, stootstok.
quantifica'tion, hoeveelheidsbepaling, kwantifisering.
qua'ntify, (..fied), die hoeveelheid bepaal, kwantifiseer.
qua'ntitative, qua'ntitive, kwantitatief.
qua'ntity, (..ties), hoeveelheid, kwantiteit; menigte; grootheid (wisk.); *in ANY ~,* baie; *BILL of quantities,* hoeveelheidslys; *in LARGE quantities,* in groot hoeveelhede; by die groot maat; *a NEGLIGIBLE ~,* wat buite rekening gelaat kan word; *QUALITY matters more than ~,* kwaliteit tel meer as kwantiteit; *an UNKNOWN ~,* 'n onbekende hoeveelheid; 'n onbekende grootheid (wisk. en fig.); ~**-billing,** opmaak van 'n hoeveelheidslys; ~**-mark,** lengteteken (vokale); ~ **surveying,** bourekene, bourekenkunde, bestekopmaking; ~ **surveyor,** bourekenaar, materiaalberekenaar, bestekopmaker.
qua'ntum, (..ta), hoeveelheid, bedrag, omvang; ~ **theory,** kwantumteorie.
qua'rantine, (n) kwarantyn, isolering, afsondering; *place in ~,* onder kwarantyn plaas; toesit; (v) onder kwarantyn stel, isoleer, afsonder.
qua'rrel¹, (n) vierkantige (diamantvormige) glas; ruit (teël); pyl.
qua'rrel², (n) twis, rusie, onenigheid, geskil, vete; geding; *FIGHT his ~ for someone,* vir iem. opkom; *a GOOD ~,* 'n regverdige saak; *I HAVE no ~ with him,* ek het niks teen hom nie; *PICK a ~,* rusie soek; *it takes TWO to make a ~,* twee is nodig om rusie te maak; *have no ~ WITH a person,* niks teen iem. hê nie; (v) **(-led),** twis, rusie maak; dwarstrek; skoor; ~ *with one's BREAD and butter,* wie se brood 'n mens eet, dié se woord 'n mens spreek; rusie maak met jou baas; jou eie belang misken; *nobody can ~ WITH that,* daar is niks teen in te bring nie; ~**ler,** rusiesoeker, rusiemaker; ~**ling,** stryery, gestry, gerusie, gestruwel; ~**some,** twissiek, rusiemakerig, bakleierig, geitjierig; ~**someness,** skoorsoekery, twissoekery.
qua'rry¹, (n) **(quarries),** vierkantige (diamantvormige) glas.
qua'rry², (n) **(quarries),** slagoffer, prooi; wild; (v) **(quarried),** naspoor, agtervolg, opspoor.
qua'rry³, (n) **(quarries),** steengroef; klipgat, gruisgat; (v) **(quarried),** uitgrawe; klippe breek; ~**ing,** klipgroefwerk; ~**man,** klipbreker; klipgroefwerker.
qua'rry: ~ **stone,** breekklip; ~ **tile,** kleiteël.
quart, kwart (2 pinte); *get (put) a ~ into a pint pot,* die onmoontlike probeer.
quar'tan, (n) vierdaagse koors; vierde deel; (a) vierdaags; ~ *fever,* vierdaagse koors.
quar'ter, (n) kwartier; huisie (van lemoen); vierde deel, kwart; kwartaal; 8 boesel; ¼ vadem; hoek (waaruit wind waai); buurt, buurte, wyk; genade, pardon; sygedeelte (hoefyster); agterdeel; (pl) kwartiere (van soldate); kruis (van perd); *from ALL ~s,* van alkante; *APPEAL to higher ~s,* jou op 'n hoër gesag beroep; *ASK (cry) for ~,* om genade smeek; *a BAD ~ of an hour,* 'n benoude kwartiertjie; *at CLOSE ~s,* van naby, tromp-op;

quartern   1160   *question*

in CLOSE ~s, in geslote kolonne; *FIRST* ~, eerste kwartier (maan); vrykwartier (her.); *no help FROM that* ~, geen hulp van daardie kant nie; *GIVE no* ~, geen kwartier gee nie; geen genade toon nie; *no* ~ *s to be GIVEN*, geen genade sal betoon word nie; *from a GOOD* ~, uit goeie bron; *in HIGH* ~s, in hoë kringe; *the HIGHEST* ~s, die hoogste kringe; ~ *of an HOUR*, kwartier; *LAST* ~, laaste kwartier (maan); *OCCUPY* ~ s, kwartiere betrek; *a* ~ *PAST four*, kwart oor vier; *PREPARE* ~s, kwartiere inrig; ~ *of a QUIRE*, katern; *RECEIVE no* ~, geen genade ontvang nie; *ROOMY* ~ s, 'n ruim vertrek; *TAKE up one's* ~ s, jou intrek neem; *the WIND blows from all* ~ s, die wind waai van alle kante af; *does the WIND blow from that* ~? is dit hoe die wind waai? *know from what* ~ *the WIND is blowing*, weet uit watter hoek die wind waai; *see what* ~ *the WIND is in*, kyk uit watter hoek die wind waai; (v) in vier verdeel, vierendeel; (in)kwartier; onderbring; in kwarte (stukke) sny; *draw and* ~, vierendeel; ~ **age**, kwartaalgeld, driemaandelikse loon; ~ **-bell**, klok wat om die kwartier slaan; ~ **-bred**, 'n kwart opreg; ~ **-day**, betaaldag; ~ **-deck**, agterdek, kwartdek; ~ **ed**, gekwartier, gekwartileer; ~ **-evil**, sponssiekte; ~ **-final**, kwarteindronde; ~ **-guard**, voorwag; ~ **ing**, verdeling in vier; leëring, inkwartiering (soldate); kwartering; (die) voor die wind seil; (pl) gevierendeelde hout; ~ **loaf**, kwartbrood; ~ **ly**, (n) (. . **lies**), kwartaalblad; (a) driemaandeliks, kwartaal=; (adv) kwartaalsgewyse, kwartaalliks, elke drie maande; ~ *ly RETURNS*, kwartaalstate; ~ *ly TEST*, kwartaaltoets; ~ **master**, kwartiermeester, betaalmeester, intendant; ~ **mile**, kwartmyl; ~ **-miler**, kwartmylloper.

quart'ern, kwart, vierde deel; kwartmaat; ~ '**ary**, kwarternêr.

quarter'nion, kwaternion.

quar'ter: ~ **-piece**, hak(skeen) van skoen; ~ '**s allowance**, woningtoelae; ~ **session**, driemaandelikse sitting; ~ **staff**, skermstok, lang stok; ~ **-strain**, kruising; ~ **-tone**, kwarttoon; ~ **-turn**, kwartwending; ~ **-wheel**, kwartswenk(ing).

quartet(te)', kwartet, viertal.

quar'to, (-s), kwarto; kwartyn (boekformaat).

quartz, kwarts; *MILKY* ~, melkkwarts; *SMOKY* ~, rookkwarts; ~ **-blow**, kwartsswelling; ~ **-crusher**, kwartsstamper; ~ **if'erous**, kwartshoudend; ~ **ite**, kwartsiet; ~ **lamp**, kwartslamp; ~ **-mill** = quartzcrusher; ~ **ose**, ~ **ous**, kwartsbevattend; ~ **porphyry**, kwartsporfier; ~ **vein**, kwartsaar; ~ **y**, kwartsagtig.

quash, verpletter; verbrysel; nietig verklaar, vernietig; onderdruk, 'n end maak aan.

quas'i=, kwasie=, kamtig, kastig, kwansuis; ~ **-deaf**, Oos-Indies doof; ~ **-religious**, kwasiegodsdienstig; ~ **-usufruct**, oneintlike vruggebruik.

Quasimo'do Sun'day, eerste Sondag na Pase.

quass'ia, bitterhout, kwassiehout.

quatercenten'ary, vierde eeufees, vierhonderdste herdenkingsdag.

Quatern'ary, (n) Kwartêr; (a) Kwartêr (geol.).

quatern'ary, (n) viertal; vier; (a) vierdelig.

quatern'ion, getal vier; vierlettergrepige woord; katern.

quatern'ity, viertal, viereenheid.

quat'orzain, veertienreëlige vers, onreëlmatige sonnet.

quat'rain, vierreëlige vers, kwatryn.

quav'er, (n) ag(t)ste noot; triller; (v) tril, trillers maak, vibreer; ~ **y**, bewerig, trillerig.

quay, hawehoof, kaai, wal; ~ **age**, kaaigeld; kaairuimte; ~ **dues**, ~ **rent**, kaaigeld.

quean, kween; slegte vrou, slet.

queas'iness, mislikheid; walglikheid; kieskeurigheid.

queas'y, mislik; walglik; kieskeurig, puntene(u)rig.

queen, (n) koningin; vrou (kaart); koningin, dame (skaak); homoseksueel; *Q* ~ *of the ADRIATIC*, Venesië; *Q* ~ *Anne is DEAD*, dis ou nuus; ~ *of CLUBS*, klawervrou; ~ *of DIAMONDS*, ruitensvrou; ~ *of HEARTS*, hartevrou; ~ *of SPADES*, skoppensvrou; ~ *of TRUMPS*, troefvrou; (v) koningin speel; tot koningin maak; as koningin heers; ~ *it over the others*, baasspeel oor al die ander; ~ **-bee**, bykoningin, moederby; ~ **-bee jelly**, byemelk; koninginjellie; ~ **consort**, vrou v.d. regerende vors; ~ **dowager**, koningin-weduwee; ~ **hood**, koninginskap; ~ **ing**, (die) koningin speel; (die) inbring v.d. koninginby; ~ **liness**, vorstelike houding; ~ **ly**, soos 'n koningin, vorstelik; ~ **mother**, koninginmoeder; ~ **-post**, hangstyl; ~ **regent**, koningin-regentes; *Q* ~ '*s Birthday*, Koninginsverjaardag; ~ '**s carriage**, gevangeniswa; ~ '**s counsel**, ryksadvokaat, koninginadvokaat (Q.C.); ~ '**s evidence**, staatsgetuie; ~ '**s gambit**, dameruiter; ~ '**s messenger**, koninklike koerier; ~ '**s metal**, wit silwer; ~ '**swarehouse**, (Eng.), staatspakhuis; ~ '**s weather**, sonskynweer.

queer, (n) homoseksueel, moffie, poefter; (v) verbrou, bederwe; ~ *someone's pitch*, iem. se saak bederwe (verbrou); (a, adv) snaaks, wonderlik, aardig (arig), naar, potsierlik, wee (gevoel), vreemd, sonderling, eksentriek; duiselig; verdag; gek; *a* ~ *BIRD*, 'n snaakse vent; *FEEL* ~, naar voel; *be in Q* ~ *STREET*, in die verknorsing wees; ~ **ish**, taamlik snaaks, snaakserig; ~ **ness**, snaaksheid, sonderlingheid, wonderlikheid, wechheid, vreemdheid, sonderbaarheid; homoseksualiteit.

que'lea, *kyk* **red-billed finch**.

quell, demp, bedwing, onderdruk; ~ *a revolt*, 'n opstand onderdruk; ~ **er**, onderdrukker.

quench, blus, uitdoof; les (dors); bekoel; demp, onderdruk; laat ophou; die mond snoer, laat stilbly; ~ *thirst*, dors les, dors verslaan; ~ **able**, dempbaar; lesbaar; blusbaar; ~ **er**, blusser; demper; doppie, sopie, drankie; ~ **ing**, stilling; lessing; demping; ~ **less**, onlesbaar; onblusbaar; ~ **lessness**, onlesbaarheid; onblusbaarheid.

querimon'ious, klaend, ontevrede, jammerend.

quer'ist, vraer; ondersoeker.

quern, handmeul.

que'rulous, klaerig, klaagsiek, iesegrimmig, brommerig, ontevrede; ~ **ness**, ontevredenheid, iesegrimmigheid, klaerigheid.

quer'y, (n) (. . **ries**), vraag; vraagteken; kapsie; wraking; vraagpunt; ouditeursnota; ~ , *did he say that?* ek sou graag wil weet of hy dit gesê het; (v) (. . **ried**), vra, betwyfel, bevraagteken, 'n vraagteken sit by; in twyfel trek; navraag doen; wraak; ~ *an assertion*, 'n bewering in twyfel trek.

quest, (n) soektog; ondersoek, aansoek; nasporing, najaging; *BE in* ~ *of*, soek na; *a* ~ *for hidden TREASURE*, 'n soektog na verborge skatte; (v) vra, soek; ~ **er**, speurhond.

ques'tion, (n) vraag; vraagstuk, kwessie; punt van behandeling; ondersoek, strydpunt, twyfel; *BEG the* ~, iets as bewys aanneem wat nog bewys moet word; *BESIDE the* ~, buite die orde; nie ter sake nie; *BEYOND* ~, sonder twyfel, ongetwyfeld; *CALL in* ~, betwyfel; in twyfel trek; *COME into* ~, ter sprake kom; van praktiese belang wees; ~ *of FACT*, saaklike kwessie; kwessie van feite; *the subject IN* ~, die onderhawige saak; die saak onder bespreking; *INVITE* ~ *s*, geleentheid gee vir vrae; *a* ~ *of LAW*, 'n regspunt; *LEADING* ~, suggestiewe vraag, sêvraag; *ask no* ~ *s and you'll hear no LIES*, van nuuskierigheid is die tronk vol; ~ *of LIFE and death*, lewensvraag; *the MATTER in* ~, die saak onder bespreking; *it is a* ~ *of MONEY*, dit is 'n geldkwessie; *there is NO* ~ *about it*, daar is geen twyfel aan nie; *OUT of the* ~, buite die kwessie; heeltemal onmoontlik, ondoenlik; *the POINT in* ~, die onderhawige saak; *PUT to the* ~, onder verhoor neem; *PUT the* ~, die debat sluit en laat stem; 'n meisie vra; *RAISE a* ~, 'n vraag opper; *THAT is the* ~, dit is die vraag; *a* ~ *of TIME*, 'n saak van tyd; *WITHOUT* ~, sonder twyfel; sonder teëpraat; (v) vra; ondervra; betwyfel, in twyfel trek; beswaar maak teen; *it cannot be* ~ *ed*, dit is seker; ~ **able**, twyfelagtig, betwyfelbaar, betwisbaar, dubieus; ~ **ableness**, twyfelagtigheid; verdagtheid; ~ **er**, ondervraer, vraer; ~ **ing**, ondervraging; betwyfeling; ~ **ingly**, vraend; ~ **less**, ongetwyfeld; ~ **mark**, vraagteken; ~ **-master**, vraesteller; ~ **naire'**,

queue 1161 **quite**

queue, rondskrywe, vraelys, vraagbrief, questionnaire; ~-**time**, vraetyd; rondvraag.
queue, (n) vlegsel; ry, rits, tou (mense); stert; *form a* ~, toustaan; (v) toustaan, in 'n ry staan; ~ *up*, toustaan, in 'n ry staan; ~-**jumper**, indrukker, toubuffel; ~**r**, toustaner.
quib'ble, (n) spitsvondigheid; woordspeling; dubbelsinnigheid; ontwyking; woordestryd; (v) spitsvondig wees, haarklowe; uitvlugte soek; vit; *nobody can* ~ *about that*, daar val nie aan te torring nie; ~**r**, haarklower; vitter.
quib'bling, haarklowery, woordsiftery; vittery.
quick, (n) lewendige vleis; lewe; lewende persoon; *BE something to the* ~, iets in murg en been wees; *BITE one's nails to the* ~, die naels tot op die vleis byt; *CUT to the* ~, tot die lewende vleis sny; diep gegrief wees; tot in die siel tref; *the* ~ *and the DEAD*, die lewendes en die dooies; *the INSULT stung him to the* ~, die belediging het hom in die siel geraak; *TOUCH one on the* ~, 'n teer (gevoelige) plek raak; (a, adv) lewendig, fiks; vinnig, gou, haastig, fluks, geswind, gewiks; gevat; rats; snel; *BE* ~ *about it*, maak gou; roer jou; ~ *with CHILD*, ver gevorderde swangerskap; *a* ~ *EAR*, 'n fyn gehoor; *a* ~ *EYE*, 'n skerp oog; ~ *at FIGURES*, vinnig met syfers; ~ *of FOOT*, vinnig op die been; rats op die voete; ~ *to LEARN*, gou om te leer; *as* ~ *as LIGHTNING*, bliksemsnel; ~ *in one's MOVEMENTS*, rats op die voete; *have a* ~ *ONE*, gou 'n kleintjie (drankie) maak; ~ *to take OFFENCE*, opvlieënd, liggeraak; kort van draad; ~ *of SCENT*, met 'n fyn neus; - *of TEMPER*, gou kwaad; liggeraak; ~ *to UNDERSTAND*, vlug van begrip; ~ *WITS*, gevat wees; ~-**bread**, snelbroodjie; ~-**cooking**, gougaar.
quicken, verlewendig, versnel, aanspoor, opwek; besiel, nuwe lewe gee; aanwakker; lewendig word; ~ *the pace*, die pas versnel; ~**ing,** verlewendiging; opwekking, herlewing.
quick: ~-**eyed,** skerpsiende, skerp van oog; ~ **fire,** (n) snelvuur; (a) vinnig; ~-**firing,** snelvuurkanon; ~-**freeze,** snelvries; ~-**freezing,** snelbevriesing; ~-**frozen,** snelbevries, snelbevrore; ~-**grass,** kweek; ~ **lime,** bytkalk, ongebluste kalk; ~-**loading,** snellaai-; ~-**loading gun,** snellaaier, ~**ly,** vinnig, gou, haastig, sito-sito; ~ *ly come*, ~ *ly go*, so gewonne, so geronne; ~ **march,** gewone marspas; versnelde pas; ~-**mix cake,** kitskoek; ~**ness,** vlugheid, snelheid; ~ **release,** sliphaak; ~ **sand,** welsand, dryfsand; ~-**scented,** fyn van reuk; ~-**sighted,** skerp van sig; skerpsiende; ~ **silver,** (n) kwiksilwer, (v) versoele, ~ **silver action,** blitsoptrede; ~ **step,** snelpasdans; vastrap; ~ **step,** versnelde pas; ~-**tempered,** opvlieend, kortgebaker(d), driftig, kort van draad; ~-**witted,** gou van begrip, gevat, skerpsinnig, byderhand, by-die-hand, slagvaardig.
quid[1], tabakpruimpie, slaaitjie.
quid[2], (pl **quid**), pond (Britse geld).
quid'ist, pruimer.
quidd'ity, (..**ties**), wesenlikheid; kleinigheid; spitsvondigheid, haarklowery.
quid'nunc, nuuskierige agie, nuusdraer, skinderbek, vraagal.
quid pro quo', quid pro quo; teenprestasie, vergoeding, kompensasie; leer om leer.
quiesce', stilbly; ~**nce,** berusting; kalmte, bedaardheid, stilte.
quies'cent, rustig, kalm, bedaard; rustend; ~ *state*, rustoestand.
qui'et, (n) rus, vrede; kalmte, bedaardheid; *DO something on the* ~, iets skelm doen; iets om die hoekie doen; *ON the* ~, stilletjies, skelm; *PEACE and* ~, rus en vrede; *RESTORE* ~, die rus herstel; (v) laat bedaar, kalmeer, gerus stel; bedaar; stilmaak; ~ *down*, kalmeer; (a, adv), rustig, gerus, stil, bedaard, vredig; stilswy(g)end; mak (perd); stemmig (klere); ~ *HORSE*, mak perd; *as* ~ *as a MOUSE*, so stil soos 'n muis (in 'n kalbas); *KEEP* ~, stilbly; iets stilhou; ~ **en,** *kyk.* **quiet,** (v); ~ **ism,** kwiëtisme; berusting; onderwerping; ~ **ist,** kwiëtis, aanhanger van die kwiëtisme; onderwerpe persoon; ~ **ly,** stil, bedaard, eenvoudig; stilletjies, stilweg, soetjies; ~ **ness, qui'etude,** rustigheid, stilte, bedaardheid, kalmte, stemmigheid; ~-**spoken,** sagmoedig.
quiet'us, volkome rus; kwytskelding; dood, uitvaart; doodsteek.
quiff, haarkrul (teen voorhoof geplak), spoeglok.
quill[1], (n) slagpen, skag; skryfpen; pyp, fluit (mus); tandestokkie; (ystervark)pen; spoel.
quill[2], (v) fyn plooi; om 'n spoel draai.
quill: ~-**covers,** dekvere; ~-**driver,** penlekker, klerk; ~ **et,** kwinkslag, spitsvondigheid, woordspeling; ~-**feather,** slagpen.
quill'ing, fyn plooisel, dubbele plooi.
quill'-wort, biesievaring.
quilt, (n) sprei, donskombers, veerkombers, (gestikte) deken; deurnaaiwerk; (v) stik, watteer, deurwerk; bymekaarflans; (sl), uitlooi; ~**ing,** (deur)stikwerk, deurnaaiwerk.
quin'ary, vyfdelig, vyfledig, vyftallig.
quince, kweper; kweperboom; ~ **jam,** kweperkonfyt.
quincenten'ary, (n) (..**ries**), vyfde eeufees, vyfhonderdjarige fees; (a) vyfhonderdjarig.
quince' stick, kweperlat.
quindec'agon, vyftienhoek.
quingenten'ary, (n) vyfde eeufees, vyfhonderdjarige fees; (a) vyfhonderdjarig.
quinine', kina, kinine, kinien; ~-**bush,** pienangbossie.
quinquagenar'ian, (n) vyftigjarige (persoon); (a) vyftigjarig.
Quinquages'ima, Sondag voor die Vaste.
quinquang'ular, vyfhoekig.
quinquefol'iate, vyfbladig.
quinquelat'eral, vyfsydig.
quinqueloc'ular, vyfsellig.
quinquenn'ial, vyfjarig; vyfjaarliks.
quinquenn'ium, vyfjarige tydperk, lustrum.
quinquepart'ite, vyfdelig, vyfledig.
quins = **quintuplets.**
quin'sy, keelsweer, wurggeswel.
quint, kwint.
quin'tain, steekpaal, steekpaalspel.
quin'tal, sentenaar (100 lb., 112 lb., 100 kilogram).
quin'tan, (n) vyfdaagse koors; (a) vyfdaags.
quintess'ence, kwintessens, kern, beliggaming.
quintett(e)', kwintet; vyftal.
Quintil'ian, Quintilianus.
quintill'ion, kwintiljoen.
quin'tuple, (n) vyfvoud; (pl) vyfling; (v) met vyf vermenigvuldig, vervyfvoudig; (a) vyfvoudig.
quin'tuplet, vyfling; vyftal.
quintuplica'tion, vervyfvoudiging.
quin'zaine, vyftienreëlige vers.
quip, (n) skimpskoot, skimpskeut; (kwink)slag, geestigheid, spitsvondigheid, raakhou; (v) (**-ped**), beskimp; gevat antwoord, grap.
qui'pu, knoopskrif.
quire, boek, papier (24 vel), katern.
Qui'rinal, Quirinaal, Kwirinaal.
quirk, uitvlug; krul (handskrif); lopie (mus.); lysgroef (bouk.); kwinkslag, spitsvondigheid, leerlingvlieë; nier; grap, steek; ~ **bead,** groeflys.
quirl, botterkruller.
quirt, rysweep, karwats.
quis'ling, quisling, verraaier.
quit, (v) (**-ted**), verlaat; ontslaan; kwiteer; oorlaat; loslaat; vergeld; kwytskeld; opgee, laat vaar; vertrek; terugbetaal; ophou; *give NOTICE to* ~, die huur opsê; ~ *the RANKS*, uit die gelid tree; ~ *SCORES*, afreken met; *death* ~ *s all SCORES*, die dood besleg alle geskille; ~ *the SERVICE*, die diens verlaat; *he* ~ *ted himself WELL*, hy het hom goed van sy taak gekwyt; ~ *WORK*, die werk neerlê; (a) ontslae van, vry, los; *be well* ~ *of*, gelukkig ontslae wees van.
quitch'-grass, kweekgras.
quit'claim, (n) afstanddoening; (v) afstand doen van.
quite, heeltemal, glad, totaal, volkome, (ge)heel, gansegaar, ganselik, absoluut; ~ *ANOTHER matter*, glad 'n ander saak; *BE* ~ *by oneself*, stokalleen wees; ~ *one of the BEST*, seker een v.d. beste; ~ *a JOURNEY*, 'n hele reis; *I* ~ *LIKE him*, ek hou bepaald van hom; ~ *a NICE few*, heelparty; ~

OFTEN, heel dikwels; sommer baie; ~ *POSSIBLE*, bes moontlik; *it is not* ~ *PROPER*, dit hoort nie so nie; ~ *SO*, presies; reg-reg; ~ *the THING*, die nuutste mode; die ware Jakob; ~ *SOMETIME*, 'n hele ruk; ~ *TOO bad*, bepaald te erg; *it is* ~ *WARM*, dis taamlik warm; ~ *a WHILE*, 'n hele rukkie.
quit'rent, erfpag, rekonie, rekognie; ~ **farm**, leningsplaas; ~ **tenure**, erfpag.
quits, gelyk, kiets; *we ARE* ~ *now*, nou is ons kiets; *CRY* ~, sê ons is kiets; kiets wees; *DOUBLE or* ~, twee keer soveel of niks; *I SHALL be* ~ *with you yet*, ek sal nog met jou afreken.
quitt'ance, kwytskelding; kwitansie; betaling; voldoening; *omittance is no* ~, uitstel van betaling is nog nie kwytskelding nie.
quitt'er, touopgooier.
quiv'er, (n) (pyl)koker; ritseling; trilling; *a* ~ *FULL of children*, 'n hele tros kinders; *IN a* ~, sidderend; *have another SHAFT left in one's* ~, nog 'n pyl in jou koker hê; nog 'n plan hê; ~**-grass**, bewertjies; ~**ing**, (n) ritseling; trilling; (a) trillend, bewend, bewerig.
qui vive', wakkerheid; *be on the* ~, wakker loop (wees); op jou hoede wees.
Quix'ote: *Don* ~, Don Quixote.
quixot'ic, buitensporig, avontuurlik, donquichotterig.
quix'otism, quix'otry, donquichotterie.
quiz, (n) grap, poets, spotterny; eksentrieke persoon, voëlverskrikker, spotvoël; vasvraery; vasvra(wedstryd); (v) (**-zed**), uitvra; vir die gek hou, bespot, belaglik maak; spottend aankyk; ~**-master**, vraesteller, vasvraer; ~**zical**, grappig, tergerig, skalks, platjiesrig; ~**zing-glass**, monokel, oogglas.
quod, (n) tjoekie, tronk; *in* ~, agter die tralies; (v) (**-ded**), in die tjoekie stop.
quod'libet, spitsvondigheid, woordspeling; potpourri (mus.).
quoin, (n) buitehoek (van muur); hoeksteen, hoekklip; keil, wig, stelwig; (v) keil, wig; ~ **stone**, hoekklip.
quoit, (n) (werp)skyf, gooiskyf; gooiring; platring; (pl) ringgooi; (v) skyfgooi, ringgooi.
quon'dam, voormalig, vroeër.
quor'um, kworum.
quot'a, aandeel, kwota; *electoral* ~, kiesdeler.
quotabil'ity, geskiktheid om aangehaal te word, siteerbaarheid.
quot'able, geskik om aangehaal te word, siteerbaar.
quota'tion, aanhaling, sitaat; notering, prysopgawe; koers; ~ *of prices*, prysnotering; ~**-marks**, aanhalingstekens.
quote, (n) aanhaling; aanhalingsteken; (v) aanhaal; kwoteer; siteer; prys opgee, noteer; ~ *from the BIBLE*, aanhaal uit die Bybel; ~ *CHAPTER and verse*, man en perd noem; ~ *in FULL*, die geheel aanhaal; *in REPLY please* ~, in antwoord meld asseblief.
quoth, het gesê.
quotid'ian, (n) alledaagse koors; (a) daagliks; beuselagtig.
quo'tient, uitkoms (van 'n deelsom); kwosiënt.
quot'ing, notering; kwotasie (pryse); aanhaling (woorde).

R

r, (rs, r's), r; *LITTLE* ~, r'etjie; *ROLL one's* ~ *'s*, bry; die r pront uitspreek.
rab, mengstok.
rabb'et, (n) sponning, voegnaat, groef; (v) inmekaarvoeg; 'n sponning maak; ~ **joint**, bossing; sponninglas; ~**-plane**, sponningskaaf.
rabb'i, rabb'in, rabbi, rabbyn.
rabbin'ic(al), rabbyns.
rabb'inism, rabbinisme, rabbynse leer.
rabb'it, (n) konyn; konynpels; makou, beginner (sport); *PRODUCE a* ~ *from the hat*, iets uit die mou skud; (v) konyne jag; ~**-hutch**, konynhok; ~ **punch**, nekhou, nekkap; ~ **stew**, gestoofde konynvleis.
rab'ble¹, oondstok, oondskraper, oondhark.
rab'ble², gespuis, gepeupel, sameraapsel; plebs, rapalje, uitskot, skorriemorrie, hoipolloi; ~**ment**, lawaai, rumoer.
rab'bler, roerstang.
rab'ble: ~**-rouser**, opruier, volksmenner, demagoog; ~**-rousing**, (n) opruiery, opruiing, volksmennery; (a) opruiend, opswepend.
rab'id, mal, woes, onstuimig, rasend; ~**ness**, woestheid, dolheid.
rab'ies, hondsdolheid.
raccoon', wasbeer *(Procyoninus)*.
race¹, (n) gemmer(wortel).
race², (n) ras; (volk)stam, geslag, afkoms; *the HUMAN* ~, die menslike geslag; *of NOBLE* ~, van edele afkoms; *MIXTURE of* ~*s*, rassevermenging; *SCIENCE of* ~, rassekunde.
race³, (n) wedloop, re(i)sies, (wed)ren; snelle vaart; loopbaan; baan (van son); gang (vir diere); (pl) wedrenne, re(i)sies; ~ *against time*, wedloop met die tyd; (v) re(i)sies jaag; hardloop, ren, jaag; vinnig (laat) loop; ~ *a bill through*, 'n wetsontwerp deurjaag; ~**-boat**, wedstrydboot, renboot, re(i)siesboot; ~**-card**, wedrenprogram.
race'-conscious, rasbewus; ~**ness**, rasbewussyn, rasgevoel.
race'course, renbaan, re(i)siesbaan.
race'-ginger, gemmerwortel.
race: ~ **goer**, wedrenganger; ~ **ground**, renbaan.
race'-hatred, rassehaat.
race'horse, renperd, re(i)siesperd.
racema'tion, trosvorming.
raceme', (blom)tros.
race'-meeting, wedrenne, re(i)sies.
racem'ic acid, druiwesuur.
racemi'ferous, trosdraend.
race'-mixture, rassevermenging.
racemiza'tion, rasemisasie, rasemisering.
ra'cemose, trosvormig.
race organizer, wedrenorganiseerder.
race'-problem, rassevraagstuk.
ra'cer, hardloper; jaer; re(i)siesperd; renmotor; snelfiets; jaagvlieër; sweepslag.
race: ~ **relations**, rassebetrekkinge; ~ **suicide**, rasseselfmoord; ~ **superiority**, rassewaan.
race'-track, renbaan, re(i)siesbaan.
race'way, meulstroom, toevoersloot.
Ra'chel, Ragel.
rachi'tic, ragities.
rachit'is, Engelse siekte, ragitis.
ra'cial, ras=, rasse=; stam=; ~ **affairs**, ras(se)aangeleenthede; ~ **feeling**, rasgevoel; ~ **group**, rasgroep; ~ **hatred**, rassehaat; ~**ism**, rassehaat; ~**ist**, rassehater; ~ **policy**, rassebeleid; ~ **prejudice**, rassevooroordeel; ~ **problem**, rassevraagstuk; ~ **purity**, rassuiwerheid; ~ **relations**, rasseverhoudings; ~ **scene**, rassegebied; rassemoles; ~ **separation**, rasseskeiding; ~ **theory**, rasseleer.
ra'ciness, lewendigheid, geestigheid, pikantheid, pittigheid.
ra'cing, (n) reisiesjaery, rensport; (die) hardloop, hardlopery; (a) jaag=, ren=; ~ **ace**, renkampioen; jaagduiwel; ~ **boat**, renboot, spoedboot, jaagboot; ~ **car**, renmotor; ~ **driver**, motorjaer; ~ **pigeon**, renduif; ~ **pilot**, jaagvlieër; ~ **stable**, renperdstal.
rac'ism, rasseleer, rassisme.
rac'ist, (n) rassis; (a) rassisties.

rack¹, (n) drywende wolke; ondergang; *go to ~ and ruin*, heeltemal te gronde gaan.
rack², (n) gang, pas, telgang, trippelgang (perd); (v) stryk, trippel, 'n gang loop.
rack³, (n) pynbank; rak; rooster (masj.); tandrat; arak (drank); kapstok; geweerrak; tandstang; *be ON the ~* , in groot spanning verkeer; *PUT on the ~*, op die pynbank sit; tot die uiterste inspan; (v) folter, pynig, op die pynbank sit, martel; afpers; uitput; *~ one's BRAINS over*, jou hoof breek oor; *~ed with PAIN*, gefolter deur pyn.
rack⁴, (v) oortap, aftap (wyn).
rack'er¹, folteraar; afperser.
rack'er², trippelaar (perd).
rack'et¹, (n) raket; (pl) raketspel.
rack'et², (n) geraas, lawaai, rumoer; spektakel, vrolikheid; slim plan; moeilikheid; drukte, beweging; 'n groot party; afpersbende; swendelary; *stand the ~*, die gevolge dra; die gelag betaal; die lawaai uithou; (v) vrolik lewe; baljaar, lawaai maak; **~eer'**, afperser; misdadiger; **~eer'ing**, afpersery, afpersing.
rack'et-press, raketpers.
rack'ety, rondjakkerig, woelig; lawaaierig.
rack'ing, (n) foltering; *it led to a ~ of brains*, dit het kopkrap gekos; (a) folterend, martelend; uitputtend; *~ cough*, folterende hoes; *~ headache*, 'n folterende hoofpyn.
rack: *~ pinion*, tandstangrondsel; *~-nut*, tandstangmoer.
rack' punch, arakpons.
rack'-railway, tandratspoorweg.
rack'-rent, hoë huur, woekerhuur; *~er*, woekerhuurder, woekerhuurbaas.
rack: *~-saw*, wyetandsaag; *~ system*, tandratstelsel; *~-wheel*, tandrat, kamrat.
raconteur', verteller, raconteur.
rac'quet, raket.
ra'cy, sterk, geurig (wyn); pittig; pikant; oorspronklik, lewendig, geestig; raseg; *~ of the SOIL*, raseg, karakteristiek; *~ STYLE*, pittige styl.
rad'ar, radar, radionasporing; radioplekbepaling; *~ operator*, radaroperateur.
rad'dle, (n) rooi klei, rooi oker, rooisel; (v) rooi verf, rooi smeer.
rad'ial, straalvormig; straal-; radiaal; *~ artery*, polsslagaar; *~ backsight*, straalvisier; *~ bone*, spaakbeen; *~ engine*, stermotor; *~ line*, straallyn; *~ saw*, hangsaag; *~ shake*, straalbars; *~ vein*, polsaar.
rad'ian, straalhoek, straalboog.
rad'iance, **rad'iancy**, glansrykheid, skittering, luister, prag.
rad'iant, (n) uitstralingspunt; (a) glansryk; glinsterend, skitterend; stralend; luistervol; *~ with joy (happiness)*, stralend van geluk; *~ energy*, stralingsenergie; *~ health*, blakende gesondheid; *~ heat*, uitstralingshitte.
rad'iate, (v) uitstraal; afstraal; versprei; glinster; skitter; *~ happiness*, van vreugde straal; (a) straalvormig, straal-; gestraal.
rad'iating, uitstraling, *~ point*, uitstralingspunt; *~ power*, uitstralingsvermoë; *~ theory*, uitstralingsteorie.
radia'tion, uitstraling, straling, bestraling, radiasie (med.); *~ of heat*, warmtestraling; *~ meter*, stralingsmeter.
rad'iator, straalverspreier; verwarmingstoestel, (straal)verwarmer, straalkaggel, radiator; verkoeler (motor); seinantenne; *~-apron*, verkoelersbeslag; *~-cap*, verkoelerdop, verkoelerkop; *~-cock*, aftapkraan; *~-connection*, verkoelerslang; *~-grid*, verkoelerrooster; *~-hose*, verkoelerslang; *~-shell*, verkoelerhulsel; *~-tank*, verkoelertenk; *~-tube*, verkoelerbuis.
rad'ical, (n) grondwoord, stamwoord; wortel; radikaal (skeik.); grondstof; (a) oorspronklik; wortel-; radikaal; prinsipieel, fundamenteel, ingewortel; afdoende, volkome; *it was a ~ CHANGE*, dit was 'n radikale verandering; *he made some ~ REFORMS*, hy het 'n aantal drastiese veranderings teweeggebring; *~ error*, prinsipiële fout; *~ idea*, grondgedagte; fundamentele gedagte; *~ism*, radikalisme; *~ly*, radikaal, in die grond, totaal; *~ quantity*, wortelgrootheid; *~ sign*, wortelteken; *~ vowel*, stamklinker; *~ word*, grondwoord.
rad'icate, (v) laat wortelskiet; (a) ingewortel.
radica'tion, worteling, wortelstand.
rad'icle, wortelkiem, worteltjie.
rad'io, (n) (-s), radio; radiotelefonie, radiotelegrafie; omroep, radiodiens, draadloos (vero.); (v) uitsaai, uitsend, sein; *~ a picture*, beeldsend.
radioac'tive, radioaktief, uitstralend; *~ debris*, radioaktiewe puin; *~ dust*, radioaktiewe stof; *~ fallout*, radioaktiewe neerslag; *~ rain*, radioaktiewe reën; *~ snow*, radioaktiewe sneeu.
radioactiv'ity, radioaktiwiteit.
rad'io: *~ beacon*, radiobaken; *~ beam*, radiokoerslyn; *~ bearing*, radiopeiling; *~ communication*, radiooorverbinding; radioberig; radiokommunikasie; *~ control*, radiobesturing, radiobeheer; radioleiding; *~ conversation*, radiogesprek; *~ direction-beacon*, radiorigtingsbaken; *~ direction-finder*, radiopeiler; *~ drama*, hoorspel, radiodrama; *~ engineer*, radiowerktuigkundige; *~ gram*, radiogram, marconigram; *~ graph*, (n) radiograaf, röntgenogram, X-straalfoto, röntgenfoto; (v) radiografeer.
radiog'rapher, radiografis.
radiog'raphy, radiografie.
rad'io ham, radioamateur.
radio is'otope, radio-isotoop.
rad'io-loca'tion, radionasporing, radio-ontdekking; radioaanwysing, radiolokasie.
radiolog'ic, radiologies.
radiol'ogist, radioloog.
radiol'ogy, radiologie.
radio mechan'ic, radiowerktuigkundige.
radiom'eter, radiometer.
radiophon'ic, radiofonies.
radioph'ony, radiofonie.
rad'io: *~ play*, hoorspel; *~ quiz*, radiovasvra(wedstryd); *~ scope*, radioskoop.
radio'scopy, radioskopie, straalondersoek.
rad'io: *~ script*, radioteks; *~-script writer*, radioskrywer; *~-sender*, radiosender; *~ service*, radiodiens; *~ silence*, radiostilte; *~ station*, radiostasie; *~-technics*, radiotegniek; *~ tel'egram*, radiotelegram; *~-telegraph*, (n) radiotelegraaf; (v) radiotelegrafeer; *~ teleg'raphy*, radiotelegrafie; *~-teleph'ony*, radiotelefonie; *~-telescope*, radioteleskoop; *~-the'rapy*, radioterapie; *~-transmission*, radiosending; *~-transmitter*, radiosender; *~ tri'cian*, radiotegnikus.
rad'ish, (-es), radys; *black ~*, ramenas.
rad'ium, radium; *~ the'rapy*, radiumterapie; *~ treatment*, radiumbehandeling.
rad'ius, (..dii), straal, radius; speekbeen, spaakbeen (arm); bereik; *~ of ACTION*, vliegbereik; vaarbereik (skepe); rybereik (voertuie); seinbereik; operasiebereik (geveg); bestek, omvang; *~ of CURVATURE*, krommingstraal; *WITHIN a ~ of 3 kilometres*, binne 'n omtrek van 3 kilometer; *~ bar*, trekstang; *~ corner*, rondehoek; *~ post*, straalwyser; *~ vector*, voerstraal.
rad'ix, (radices), wortel; grondgetal.
rad'on, radon.
raff, *kyk* **riff-raff**.
raff'ia, raffia, raffiavesel; *~ work*, raffiawerk.
raff'ish, onterend, losbandig, onfatsoenlik.
raf'fle¹, (n) vuilgoed, rommel, afval.
raf'fle², (n) verloting, lotery, uitloting; (v) uitloot, verloot; *~r*, dobbelaar.
raf'fling, uitloting; *~-board*, draaibord.
raff' net, treknet.
raft, (n) vlot; dryfhout; (v) op 'n vlot vaar (vervoer); dryf; *~-bridge*, vlotbrug.
ra'fter, (n) kap, (hane)balk, spanrib, dakspar, kapspar; ribbetjie (skip); *PRINCIPAL ~*, kapbeen, staanbalk; *make the ~s RING*, die lug laat dawer; (v) van dakspare voorsien; *~ plate*, muurplaat; *~ table*, kapskaal.
rafts'man, (..men), vlotter.
rag¹, (n) leidakpan; laagklip.
rag², (n) vod, lomp, flard, toiing, flenter, lor, lap, va-

doek; (pl) lompe; *not a* ~ *to one's BACK*, nie 'n draad klere nie; *BOIL to* ~*s*, fynkook; *not a* ~ *of CLOTHING*, geen draad klere nie; *not a* ~ *of EVIDENCE*, geen greintjie bewys nie; *the LOCAL* ~, die plaaslike koerant(jie); *LOOSE one's* ~, die hoenders in word; *not to have a* ~ *ON*, geen draad aan die lyf hê nie; *from* ~ *s to RICHES*, van lompe tot luukse, van armoede tot rykdom.

rag³, (n) jool; (v) **(-ged)**, lawaai maak; terg; jool (hou); op horings neem; in rep en roer bring; ~ *someone*, iem. se siel uittrek.

rag'amuffin, skobbejak, skurk, smeerlap, flenterkous, skooier, skollie, flenterkind.

rag'-and-bone man, voddekoper.

rag'-bolt, steenbout, takbout, hakkelbout.

rag: ~ **book**, lapboek; ~**-dealer**, voddekoper; ~ **doll**, lappop.

rage, (n) woede, gramskap; raserny; hartstog, begeerte; manie, gier, mode; besieling; *ALL the* ~, hoog in die mode; die nuutste mode; *be CONSUMED with* ~, woedend wees; die herrie (josie) in wees; *the* ~ *for building*, die bouwoede; *the* ~ *for COLLECTION*, die versamelmanie; *HAVE a* ~ *for*, 'n manie hê vir; versot wees op; *be IN a* ~, woedend wees; die herrie (josie) in wees; *the* ~ *of the STORM*, die woede v.d. storm; (v) woed, regeer (siekte); raas, te kere gaan, uitvaar, bulder, woes wees; ~ *ON*, voortwoed; ~ *itself OUT*, uitraas.

rag: ~ **fair**, voddemark; rommelverkoping; ~**-gatherer**, vodderaper.

ragg'ed, toiingrig, verflenter, flenterig, haweloos; ruig, ongelyk; gerafel; knoesterig; slordig; *live on the* ~ *END of nothing*, te min om van te leef en te veel om van dood te gaan; ~ *PLAY*, los spel; ~ **handle**, gekeepte handvatsel; ~**ness**, haweloosheid; ~ **robin**, koekoekblom.

ragg'ing, onordelikheid, wanorde; treitering; gekskeerdery; spotterny; *give someone a* ~, iem. se siel uittrek.

ra'ging, woedend; woes.

rag'lan, raglanjas; ~ **sleeve**, raglanmou; ~**-sleeve pattern**, raglanpatroon.

rag'-man, (..**men**), voddekoper.

ragout', ragout; ~ *of mutton*, skaapvleisragout.

rag: ~ **paper**, lompepapier; ~**-picker**, lapopteller, vodderaper; voddesmous; ~ **review**, toiingsparade; ~**-sorter**, voddesorteerder; ~ **stall**, lorrekraam; ~ **tag**, skorriemorrie; ~ *tag and bobtail*, Jan Rap en sy maat, gepeupel.

rag'time, ragtime; sinkopasie, gesinkopeerde musiek; lied (dans) in gesinkopeerde maat.

rag'trade, voddehandel; (skerts.) klerehandel.

rag'-wheel, kamrat.

rag'-work, ruwe messelwerk.

rag'wort, kruiskruid.

raid, (n) strooptog, rooftog; aanval, inval; kaapvaart; plundering; razzia, klopjag (polisie); ~ *on a BUILDING*, klopjag op 'n gebou; ~ *on CRIMINALS*, klopjag op misdadigers; (v) 'n inval maak; plunder, roof; 'n klopjag onderneem; kaap (op see); ~**er**, stroper, invaller; plunderaar; aanvaller; kaperskip, kaapvaarder, kaper; ~ **ing expedition**, strooptog; ~**ing party**, stropersbende.

rail¹, (n) ral; *Cape* ~, riethaantjie.

rail², (n) riggel; leuning; reling (wa); spoorstaaf; lys, boom, dwarsbalk; sport (van stoel); *BY* ~, per trein; per spoor; *LEAVE the* ~*s*, ontspoor; *be OFF the* ~*s*, v.d. spoor wees; die spoor byster wees; *RUN (go) off the* ~*s*, ontspoor; op 'n verkeerde pad raak; buite beheer raak; die spoor byster raak; (v) per spoor stuur; met traliewerk toemaak; ~ *in*, omraster, afkamp, afsluit.

rail³, (v) spot, smaal, skinder, persifleer; uitvaar; ~ *against (at) one's fate*, teen jou lot uitvaar.

rail: ~ **age**, vervoer, spoorwegkoste; spoorvrag; ~**-bender**, gogga; ~**-bond**, lasverbinding; ~**-bus**, spoorbus; ~**-car**, spoorbus; ~**-connection**, spoorverbinding; ~ **drift**, dryfyster.

rail'er, skimper, smaler.

rail: ~ **fence**, paalheining; ~**-flange**, spoorstaafflens; ~ **gauge**, baanwydte, spoormaat; ~**head**, spoorwegeindpunt, spoorwegterminus.

rail'ing¹, (n) tralie, leuning; reling, reiling; afrastering.

rail'ing², (n) skimp, spot; (a) smalend.

rail'lery, spotterny, skerts, plaery.

rail: ~**-joint**, spoorlas; ~**-layer**, spoorlêer; ~ **level**, spoorhoogte; ~ **mill**, fabriek vir spoorstawe; ~**-motor**, spoorwegmotor; ~**-motor** service, spoorwegmotordiens; ~ **road**, spoorweg, spoorbaan; ~**-skid**, gly-yster; ~**-tongs**, spoortang; ~**-trolley**, spoormotor; ~**-track**, spoorbaan; ~ **warrant**, vrykaartjie; spoorwegmagsbrief, spoorwegorder.

rail'way, spoorweg; treinspoor; *ELEVATED* ~, lugspoor; ~ **accident**, spoorwegongeluk; **R** ~ **Act**, Spoorwegwet; ~ **administration**, spoorwegadministrasie; ~ **bridge**, spoorwegbrug; ~ **carriage**, spoorwegrytuig, treinwa, spoorwa; ~ **charges**, spoorvrag; ~ **communication**, spoorwegverbinding; ~ **company**, spoorwegmaatskapy; ~ **compartment**, kompartement; ~ **connection**, treinverbinding, spoorverbinding; ~ **construction**, spoor(weg)bou, spoorwegaanleg; ~ **crossing**, (spoor)oorweg; ~ **disaster**, spoorwegramp; ~ **doctor**, spoorwegdokter; ~ **earnings**, spoorweginkomste; ~ **embankment**, spoor(weg)wal; ~ **employee**, spoorbeampte; ~ **engine**, lokomotief; ~ **engineer**, spoorwegingenieur; ~ **extension**, spoorweguitbreiding; ~ **guard**, spoorwegkondukteur; ~ **guide**, spoorboek, spoorweggids; ~ **halt**, spoorweghalte; ~ **journey**, treinreis; ~ **junction**, spoorwegaansluiting, spoorwegknoop; ~ **line**, spoorlyn; ~ **man**, spoorwegbeampte; ~ **map**, spoorwegkaart; ~ **official**, spoorwegbeampte; ~ **plant**, spoorwegplek; spoorweginrigting; ~ **property**, spoorwegeiendom; ~ **quarters**, spoorweghuis; ~ **rates**, spoorwegtariewe; ~ **reading matter**, treinlektuur; ~ **refreshment room**, stasieversversingskamer; ~ **revenue**, spoorweginkomste; ~ **section**, baanvak; ~ **servant**, spoorwegdienaar; ~ **service**, spoorwegdiens; ~ **sleeper**, dwarslêer, spoorlêer; ~ **smash**, spoor(weg)ongeluk; treinbotsing, -ongeluk; ~ **staff**, spoorwegpersoneel; ~ **station**, (spoorweg)stasie; ~ **stock**, spoorwegmateriaal; ~ **switch**, spoorwegwissel; ~ **system**, spoorwegstelsel; spoorwegnet; ~ **ticket**, treinkaartjie; ~ **timetable**, treingids; ~ **track**, spoorbaan; ~ **traffic**, spoor(weg)verkeer; ~ **train**, trein; ~ **transport**, spoorvervoer; ~ **tunnel**, spoorwegtonnel; ~ **warrant**, spoorwegorder, spoorwegmandaat, vrykaartjie, spoorwegmagsbrief; ~ **workshop**, spoorwegwerkswinkel; ~ **yard**, spoorwegwerf.

rail' wheel, spoorwegwiel.

raim'ent, kleding, gewaad, dos.

rain, (n) reën, reent; *a* ~ *of ASHES*, 'n asreën; *COME* ~, *come shine*, in lief en leed; *FINE* ~, stofreën; ~ *before seven, fine at ELEVEN*, 'n vroeë môrereën is soos 'n ou vrou se wals; *RIGHT as* ~, so reg soos 'n roer; *in* ~ *or SHINE*, onder alle omstandighede; *a SHOWER of* ~, 'n reënvlaag, 'n reënbui; ~ *and SUNSHINE at the same time*, jakkalstrouweer; *UNSEASONAL* ~, ontydige reën; (v) reën, reent; sous; laat reën, laat neerdaal; ~ *BLESSINGS upon*, met seëninge oorlaai; *it* ~ *ed CATS and dogs*, dit het strome gereën; *it* ~ *ed LETTERS*, briewe het ingestroom; *it never* ~*s but it POURS*, 'n ongeluk kom nooit alleen nie; ~**-belt**, reëngordel; ~**bird**, reënvoël; vleiloerie; ~**bow**, reënboog; *in all colours of the* ~ *bow*, in al die kleure v.d. reënboog; ~**bow trout**, skimmelforel; ~**chart**, reënkaart; ~**-cloud**, reënwolk; ~**-coat**, reënjas; ~ **drop**, reëndruppel; ~ **fall**, reënval; ~ **forest**, reënwoud; reënbos; ~**-frog**, janblom; ~**-gauge**, reënmeter, udometer; ~**-glass**, barometer, weerglas; ~**iness**, reënerigheid; ~ **less**, droog; ~ **maker**, reënmaker, reënbesweerder; ~**-making**, reënmakery; ~ **proof**, waterdig, reëndig; ~**-storm**, storm, bui; ~**-swept**, aan reën blootgestel; ~**-tight**, reëndig; ~ **water**, reënwater; ~**-water head**, geutbak; ~ **worm**, reënwurm.

rain'y, reënagtig; reënerig, onweers-; ~ *DAY*, reëndag; *SAVE for a* ~ *day*, 'n appeltjie vir die dors bewaar; vir die oudag opsy sit; ~ *SEASON*, reëntyd; ~ *WEATHER*, reënweer, pannekoekweer.

raise, (n) styging, styggang (in myn); verhoging, opslag (van salaris); opdraande; (v) optel, oplig; laat regop staan; regop sit; oprig (gebou); verhoog; versamel, insamel; opslaan (oë); bou, opbou; teel (diere); kweek (plante); grootmaak, grootbring (kinders); aanleiding gee tot; veroorsaak; aanhef ('n kreet); verwek (opstand); oproep (gees); hys (vlag); opper, aanvoer (beswaar); verhef (stem); bevorder (amptenaar, ens.); inbring, opwerp ('n kwessie); werf, hef (troepe); op die been bring (mag); opklap (visier); lig; ophef (beleg); ~ *the ALARM*, alarm blaas; ~ *an ARMY*, 'n leër op die been bring; ~ *a BLISTER*, 'n blaar trek; ~ *a BLOCKADE*, 'n blokkade ophef (verbreek); ~ *BREAD*, brood laat rys; ~ *CAIN*, 'n spektakel aanvang; moeilikheid maak; ~ *CATTLE*, vee teel; ~ *a CRY*, 'n geskreeu aanhef; ~ *the DEAD*, die dooies laat opstaan; ~ *from the DEAD*, uit die dode opwek; ~ *DOUBT*, twyfel wek; ~ *(the) DUST*, stof maak; ~ *a DUST*, 'n gedoente veroorsaak; die waarheid bewimpel; ~ *the ELBOW*, die elmboog lig, sterk drank gebruik; ~ *one's EYES*, die oë ophef; opkyk; ~ *a FIRE*, brand stig; ~ *FUNDS*, geld insamel; ~ *a GHOST*, 'n gees oproep; ~ *one's HAT*, die hoed afneem; ~ *HEAVEN and earth*, hemel en aarde beweeg; ~ *a LAUGH*, die mense laat lag; ~ *a LOAN*, 'n lening aangaan; ~ *MONEY*, geld inskry, geld opneem; ~ *an OBJECTION*, beswaar maak; ~ *to the PEERAGE*, tot die adelstand verhef; ~ *a POINT*, 'n vraag opwerp; ~ *a QUARREL*, 'n twis veroorsaak; ~ *a QUESTION*, 'n vraag opwerp; ~ *the ROOF*, 'n helse lawaai maak; ~ *old SCORES*, ou koeie uit die sloot haal; ~ *a SIEGE*, 'n beleg opbreek; ~ *one's ophef*; ~ *SIGHTS*, die visier hoër stel; ~ *one's SIGHTS*, hoog mik; ~ *STEAM*, stoom opwek; ~ *the TEMPERATURE of a room*, 'n kamer warmer maak, die hittegraad in 'n kamer verhoog; ~ *VEGETABLES*, groente kweek; ~ *your VOICE against*, jou stem verhef teen; ~ *WHEAT*, koring verbou; ~ *the WIND*, op een of ander manier geld loskry.
raised, opgehewe; verhoog; reliëf-; ~ *FURROW*, moelvoor; ~ *LETTERS*, verhewe letters, letters in reliëf; ~ *MOULDING*, verhewe lys; *in a* ~ *VOICE*, met verheffing van stem; hard; ~ *WORK*, dryfwerk, gedrewe werk.
rais'er, oprigter; stigter (maatskappy); teler (vee); kweker, verbouer (gesaaides); heffer.
rais'in, rosyn(tjie); *stalked* ~ *s*, trosrosyne; ~ **-blanc,** raisin-blanc; ~ **bread,** rosyntjiebrood; ~ **-bush,** rosyntjiebos.
rais'ing, verhoging, opheffing; opneming (van geld); ~ **-fee,** leningskommissie, heffingsloon; ~ **hammer,** versinkhamer, dryfhamer.
rait = **ret.**
ra'ja(h), radja (Indiese prins).
rake¹, (n) losbol, ligmis, swierbol, pierewaaier, immorele mens.
rake², (n) helling, skuinste; hellingsvlak; (v) oorhel, oorhang; skuins staan; ~ *d floor*, hellende vloer.
rake³, (n) hark; vuurhark; *as thin as a* ~, so maer soos 'n kraai; (v) hark, bymekaarskraap; (op)rakel; versamel; deursoek; bestryk; ~ *up DEAD issues*, ou koeie uit die sloot haal; ~ *by FIRE*, met vuur bestryk; ~ *out a FIRE*, 'n vuur doodmaak; ~ *up old GRIEVANCES*, ou koeie uit die sloot haal; ~ *up the PAST*, ou koeie uit die sloot haal; ~ *OUT*, uitrakel; ~ **hell,** losbol, ligmis; ~ **-off,** kommissie, deel (van wins); buitaandeel, oneerlike winsaandeel; ~ **r,** rakelyster (bakkery); krapyster (smedery); harker, harkmasjien; ~ **'s progress,** verkwistery, pierewaaiery.
rak'ing¹, (n) bestryking; (a) harkend; bestrykend.
rak'ing², (a) hellend, skuins.
rak'ing course, skuins laag.
rak'ing fire, strykvuur, kamvuur, enfileervuur.
rak'ings, opgeharkte stukkies.
rak'ing shore, leunstut, skuins laag.
rak'ish¹, snelvarend; kaperagtig; swierig; rank.
rak'ish², buitensporig, losbandig.
rak'ishness¹, losbandigheid.
rak'ishness², swierigheid.
rall'y¹, (n) **(rallies),** saamtrek, byeenbrenging, byeenkoms; hereniging; stryddag; (die) opknap, herstel; beterskap; verbetering; sarsie (tennis); houe(ver)wisseling; tydren, sterrit (motors); (v) **(rallied),** versamel, herenig, verenig; herstel; bykom, verfris; moed inpraat; 'n sarsie maak; (langdurig) houe wissel (tennis); ~ *round*, te hulp snel.
rall'y², (v) **(rallied),** pla, terg, vir die gek hou; ~ *a person on something*, iem. terg oor iets.
rall'ying point, vergaderplek; ontmoetingspunt.
ram, (n) ram (dier); stormram (wapen); straatstamper; heiblok (vir pale); hidrouliese pers; drukpompplunjer; (v) **(-med),** hei, inslaan (paal); (vas)stamp; ram (skip); instop, inprop; ~ *AGAINST*, stamp teen; ~ *CLOTHES into a bag*, klere in 'n sak stop; ~ *DOWN*, neerstamp, vasstamp, instamp; ~ *facts HOME*, feite aan die verstand bring; ~ *LATIN into boys*, Latyn in seuns inpomp; ~ *something down one's THROAT*, iets in iem. se keel afdruk.
ram'al, tak-.
Ra'madan, Ramadan.
ram'ble, (n) uitstappie; staptog; swerftog; wandeling; (v) omswerf, rondloop, ronddool; afdwaal, v.d. hak op die tak spring, bontpraat, onsamehangend praat; ~ *about*, omdool, ronddool; ~ **r,** rankroos; klimplant; rondswerwer, ronddoler.
ram'bling, (n) rondswerwing, swerwery; (a) swerwend; slingerend; onsamehangend; slinger-, klim-, rankend; onreëlmatig (gebou); ~ **house,** kasarm.
rambunc'tious, wild, weerbarstig; rumoerig.
ram'ekin, eier-en-kaasgereg.
ram'eous, tak-.
ram'equin, kyk **ramekin.**
ramifica'tion, vertakking.
ram'iform, takvormig.
ram'ify, (..fied), vertak, takke gee; laat vertak.
ram'-jet, stustraal; ~ *aircraft*, stustraler, stustraalvliegtuig.
ramm'er, laaistok (geweer); heiblok, stamper; aansitter (geskut); ram.
ramm'ish, ramm'y, bokagtig, onwelriekend, stinkend; gemeen.
ramose', vol takke, vertak, getak.
ramp¹, (n) bedrog, swendelary; (v) swendel; afpers.
ramp², (n) klimming; hang; opdraand; oprit (garage); laaibrug; *OFF-* ~, afrit; *ON-* ~, oprit; (v) spring, klouter; steier, op die agterpote staan (perd); te kere gaan, uitgelate wees; ~ *and rage*, alles maak en breek.
rampage', (n) dolheid, uitgelatenheid, luidrugtigheid; *BE on the* ~, uitgelate wees, woes te kere gaan; *GO on the* ~, rumoer; (v) soos 'n gek rondspring; baljaar.
rampa'geous, woes, luidrugtig, skreeuerig.
ramp'ancy, voortwoekering; toeneming; buitensporigheid, uitgelatenheid.
ramp'ant, klaar om te spring; steierend, klimmend; uitgelate; welig, geil; heersend; toenemend; aan die orde v.d. dag, algemeen; woekerend; *BRIBERY was* ~, omkopery was algemeen; *LION* ~, klimmende leeu (her.); ~ *arch*, klimmende boog, klimboog.
ramp'art, (n) skans, (vesting)wal, bolwerk, borswering; (v) verskans, omwal.
ramp'ion, raponsie.
ram'-pump, slagpomp, rampomp.
ram'rod, laaistok; *as straight as a* ~, so regop soos 'n kers.
ram'shackle, bouvallig, lendelam, vervalle, lutterig; ~ *BUILDING*, kasarm; ~ *CAR*, tjorrie.
ram'ulose, ram'ulous, met baie klein takkies.
ran, *kyk* **run.**
rance, bont marmer.
ranch, (n) **(-es),** veeplaas, beesboerdery, groot beesplaas; wildplaas; (v) met grootvee boer; met wild boer; ~ **er,** veeboer; ~ **ing,** beesboerdery; veeboerdery; wildboerdery; ~ **ing country,** beeswêreld.
ran'cid, suur, rens; galsterig (botter); goor.
rancid'ity, ran'cidness, galsterigheid.
ranc'orous, kwaadaardig, wrewelig, haatdraend.

ranc'our, wrok, haat, haatdraendheid, wrewel(igheid); *bear* ~, 'n wrok koester.
rand, rant; rand geldeenheid; *the R* ~, die Witwatersrand, die Rand.
randan'¹, roeiboot.
randan'², drinkpartytjie.
ran'dem, (n) drieperdrytuig; (adv) met drie perde.
ran'dom, (n) toeval, geluk; *AT* ~, sonder berekening, op goeie geluk; wildweg, blindweg, lukraak, sonder uitsoek; *TALK at* ~, kaf verkoop; (a) toevallig, willekeurig; onreëlmatig; ewekansig; ~ *ERROR*, ewekansige fout, dwaalfout; ~ *MASONRY*, ongelaagde messelwerk; ~ *SAMPLE*, ewekansige steekproef; ~ *SHOT*, skoot op goeie geluk, 'n blinde skoot; ~ *TEST*, steekproef, toevaltoets; ~ *THOUGHTS*, los gedagtes; *a* ~ *WALL*, muur van stene van verskillende grootte.
ran'dy, skreeuerig, woes; wellustig, loops (dier).
ran'ee, rani; Hindoekoningin.
rang, *kyk* **ring.**
range, (n) ry, reeks; speling, speelruimte; skietbaan; rooster; gesigskring; klas; uitgestrektheid; kaggel, stoof, kookplek; bergreeks; weiveld, weiding; terrein; drag, koeëlafstand, sendbereik (radio); skootafstand, dra(ag)wydte, trefwydte, dra(ag)krag (stem; kanon); bereik (kanon; gholf); kabellengte; rigting, lyn; gebied, veld; omvang, sfeer; meetgrens; deining, verskeidenheid (gereedskap, goedere); skaalwydte; *at CLOSE* ~, tromp-op, op kort afstand; *EFFECTIVE* ~, uitwerkingsafstand, trefafstand; *FIND the* ~, die afstand bepaal; inskiet; ~ *of FLIGHT*, vlieglengte; *GET the* ~, die afstand soek; *KEEP out of* ~, buite skoot bly; buite bereik bly; *the* ~ *of his KNOWLEDGE*, die omvang van sy kennis; ~ *of MOUNTAINS*, bergreeks; *OUT of* ~, buite bereik (v.d. geskut); buite hoorafstand; *Russian is OUT of my* ~, Russies is buitekant my gebied; ~ *of PERCEPTION*, gesigskring; ~ *of READING*, belesenheid; *the* ~ *of TEMPERATURE*, die verskil tussen hoogste en laagste temperatuur; *give free* ~ *to one's THOUGHTS*, jou gedagtes die vrye loop gee; ~ *of VISION*, gesigsveld, waarnemingsveld, waarnemingskring; *the* ~ *of a VOICE*, die omvang (register) van 'n stem; *WITHIN* ~, onder skoot, binne bereik; *have WITHIN* ~ *or shot*, onder skoot kry; binne trefafstand kry; (v) in 'n ry sit, rangskik; uitstrek; ronddwaal; vaar; bestryk (kanon); jou plaas aan die sy van; dra (geweer); aftas (radio); varieer; skaar; opstel; ~ *FROM 5 to 10*, wissel van 5 tot 10; ~ *over a KILOMETRE*, oor 'n kilometer strek; ~ *oneself on the SIDE of*, jou skaar aan die kant van; ~ *with the great WRITERS*, 'n plek onder die groot skrywers inneem; ~**-finder**, afstandmeter, afstandsoeker (kamera); ~ **masonry**, gelaagde messelwerk; ~ **practice**, skyfskietoefening.
ran'ger, boswagter, veldwagter; speurhond; rondloper, swerwer.
rang'ing, omswerwing; aftasting (radio).
rang'y, skraal; bergagtig; ruim.
ran'ine, paddaägtig.
rank¹, (n) rang, ry, gelid; stand; staat; staanplek (voertuig); (pl) manskappe (leër); offisiere (vloot); *BREAK* ~*s*, die gelid verbreek; *CLOSE the* ~*s*, die geledere sluit; *the* ~ *and FASHION*, die hoë kringe; *the* ~ *and FILE*, die minderes; die gewone soldate; die klomp; Piet, Paul en Klaas; *the FRONT* ~, die voorste ry; *be INFERIOR in* ~, in rang kom na; *fall INTO* ~, aantree; *JOIN the* ~*s*, diens neem, soldaat word; *KEEP* ~, in die gelid bly; ~ *in LIFE*, posisie, maatskaplike rang; ~ *of OFFICER*, offisiersrang; *OTHER* ~*s*, manskappe; *PEOPLE of all* ~*s*, mense van alle stande; *PERSONS of* ~, mense van hoë rang; *RISE from the* ~*s*, van onder af opkom; *hold a SUPERIOR* ~ *to*, 'n hoër rang beklee as; *TAKE* ~ *with*, gelyk staan met; *THE* ~*s*, alle soldate; die geledere; (v) rangskik, skik, skat; indeel; in orde stel, in gelid stel; sy plek hê, 'n plek inneem; 'n rang hê; ~ *AFTER someone*, iem. in rang volg; ~ *AMONG*, hoort onder; ~ *WITH*, op een lyn stel met, gelykstaan met (aan).

rank², (a) geil, welig; rens, galsterig (botter); wulps; eg, puur; ~ *FRAUD*, gemene bedrieëry; ~ *NONSENSE*, pure (klinkklare) onsin; ~ *OUTSIDER*, randeier; ~ *TREASON*, gemene verraad.
rank: ~**er**, rangskikker; manskap, gewone sodaat; ~**ing**, (n) rangskikking; *list of* ~*ings*, ranglys; (a) hooggeplaas; senior; ~ *ing official*, hooggeplaaste amptenaar.
ran'kle, ontsteek, sleg word (sere); knaag; met 'n wrok vervul, verbitter; ~ *in one's HEART (mind, soul)*, die hart (gemoed, siel) met 'n wrok vervul; *an INJUSTICE which* ~ *s with him*, 'n onreg wat hom verbitter.
rank'ness, geilheid, weligheid; galsterigheid; wulpsheid.
ran'sack, (uit)plunder, afstroop; deursnuffel, deursoek; ~**ing**, plundering, afstroping; deursnuffeling, deursoeking.
ran'som, (n) losgeld, losprys, soengeld, afkoopsom; loslating, bevryding; rantsoen; brandskatting; *HOLD to* ~, 'n losgeld vra vir; *not for a KING'S* ~, nie vir 'n plaas se prys nie; nie vir 'n koning se skat nie; (v) vrykoop, verlos, bevry, afkoop; ~**er**, bevry(d)er.
rant, (n) grootspraak; woordepraal, bombas; (v) grootpraat, spog; opskep; hoogdrawend praat; uitvaar; ~**er**, grootprater; straatskreeuer; ~**ing**, (n) skreëry, skreeuery; (a) skreërig, skreeuerig.
ranunc'ulus, (-es, ..li), ranonkel.
rap¹, (n) tik, slag, klop; *GIVE a* ~ *on the KNUCKLES*, op die vingers tik; *the one who TAKES the* ~, die kind v.d. rekening; *TAKE the* ~, die verantwoordelikheid aanvaar; (v) **(-ped)**, slaan, tik, klop; uitblaker, uitflap; ~ *at the DOOR*, aan die deur klop; ~ *someone on the KNUCKLES*, iem. op die vingers tik; ~ *OUT instructions*, instruksies (bevele) afbyt (kragtig uitspreek).
rap², (n) die minste, duit; *I don't care a* ~, ek gee geen flenter om nie; *not WORTH a* ~, niks werd nie.
rapa'ceous, raapvormig.
rapa'cious, roofgierig, roofsugtig, roofagtig, gulsig, hebsugtig.
rapa'ciousness, rapa'city, roofsug, skraapsug, gierigheid, hebsug.
rape¹, (n) druiwedoppe.
rape², (n) verkragting, ontering; wegvoering; roof; (v) onteer, verkrag; wegvoer.
rape³, (n) raap, koolraap; ~**-cake**, raapkoek; ~**-oil**, raapolie.
rap'er, verkragter, onteerder.
rape'-seed, raapsaad.
rap'id, (n) stroomversnelling, skietstroom; *shoot a* ~, oor 'n stroomversnelling gaan; (a) gou, snel, rats, fluks, geswind, vinnig; ~ **fire**, snelvuur; ~**-firing**, snelvurend; ~**-firing gun**, snelvuurkanon; ~**ly**, vinnig, gou.
rap'idness, rapid'ity, snelheid, vinnigheid.
rap'ier, rapier; ~**-fish**, swaardvis.
rap'ine, plundering, roof.
rappee', rapé (snuif).
rapp'er, klopper; spiritis.
rapport', verhouding, verband, verbinding; mededeling; ooreenkoms; voeling; rapport; *en (in)* ~, in noue voeling.
rapporteur', referent.
rapproche'ment, toenadering (veral tussen state).
rapscall'ion, skelm, skurk, skobbejak.
rapt, opgetoë, verruk; meegesleep, weggevoer; versonke, gespanne; ~ *in ADMIRATION*, weggesleep deur bewondering; *LISTEN with* ~ *attention*, met gespanne aandag luister.
rap'tor, (-es), ontvoerder; roofvoël.
raptor'ial, (n) roofvoël; (a) roof-; roofvoël-.
rap'ture, (siels)verrukking, vervoering, ekstase, opgetoënheid, geesverrukking, geesvervoering; *be in* ~*s*, verruk wees; in die wolke wees.
rap'turous, verruk, opgetoë, wegslepend, verruklik.
rare¹, half gaar (vleis); sag gekook (eier).
rare², seldsaam, skaars; dun, yl; ongewoon; besonder, voortreflik, pragtig; *a* ~ *EVENT*, 'n seldsame gebeurtenis; ~ *FUN*, besondere vrolikheid; *a* ~ *GOOD sign*, 'n buitengewoon goeie teken; *a* ~

JOKE, 'n kostelike grap; *on* ~ *OCCASIONS*, selde, so af en toe; *a* ~ *SIGHT*, iets buitengewoons.
rare'bit: *Welsh* ~ *(rabbit)*, roosterbrood met kaassous.
rare earths, seldsame aardmetale.
rar'ee-show, kykkas; kykspel.
rarefac'tion, rarefica'tion, verdunning.
rare: ~**fied,** yl, (ver)dun; ~ **fy,** (..**fied**), verdun, yler maak; verfyn; veredel; ~ **gas,** edelgas; ~**ly,** selde, seldsaam; ~ **meat,** halfgaar vleis; ~**ness,** seldsaamheid, rariteit, skaarsheid; ylheid, dunheid; ~ **ripe,** vroegryp.
rar'ity = **rareness.**
ras'cal, (n) skurk, skelm, vabond, karnallie, skavuit, derduiwel, deugniet, skobbejak, hondsvot, rakker, blikslaer, maaifoedie, vloek, blikhouer; *you lucky* ~, jou geluksvoël; (a) laag, gemeen, skurkagtig; *the* ~ *rout,* die gepeupel; ~**dom,** gepeupel, gespuis.
rascal'ity, skurkstreek, skurkagtigheid.
ra'scally, skurkagtig, skelmagtig.
rase, *kyk* **raze.**
rash, (n) (huid)uitslag; *get a* ~, uitslaan; (a) haastig, onbedagsaam, voortvarend, onbesonne, ligvaardig, uitsinnig, dolsinnig, onbekook, roekeloos; voorbarig, ondeurdag, ooryld, vermetel.
rash'er, reep (spek); sny (ham).
rash'ly, blindweg.
rash'ness, onbedagsaamheid, voortvarendheid, vermetelheid, dolsinnigheid, uitsinnigheid; onbesuisdheid, onbesonnenheid, oormoedigheid.
rasp, (n) rasper; (v) rasper, skraap; kras; afskraap, laat gril; jrriteer; *a* ~*ing SOUND,* 'n krassende geluid; *a* ~*ing VOICE,* 'n krassende stem, 'n krassstem.
rasp'berry, (..**rries**), framboos; *give someone a* ~, iem. uitkoggel of hoon; ~ **bush,** framboosstruik; ~ **syrup,** framboosstroop.
rasp: ~**er,** rasper, krapper; ~**ing file,** raspervyl; ~**y,** krassend, hees.
ra'sure, gekrap, geskaaf, geskram.
rat, (n) rot; onderkruiper; oorloper, droster; ~ *s desert a sinking SHIP,* die ontroues vlug altyd eerste; ~ *S!* bog! kaf! dis ongelooflik! *SMELL a* ~, lont ruik; *caught like a* ~ *in a TRAP,* vas soos 'n muis in 'n kalbas; (v) (**-ted**), oorloop, onderkruip, onder die loon werk; muise (rotte) vang; (weg)dros; ~ *on someone,* ontrou word teenoor iem.
rat'able, belasbaar, belastingpligtig, waardeerbaar; skatpligtig, skatbaar; ~**ness,** belasbaarheid, belastingpligtigheid.
ratafi'a, ratafia, amandellikeur; amandelkoekie.
rat'al, belasbare bedrag; waardebepaling, valuasie, waardering, skatting.
rataplan', (n) rataplan, getrommel; (v) (**-ned**), trommel, tamboer slaan.
rat: ~**-bite,** rotbyt; ~**-burrow,** muisgat; rottegat; ~**-catcher,** rotvanger.
ratch, ratch'et, tandskyf, slagrat, palwerk, sperrat, palrat; ratel(boor); ~**-brace,** ratelomslag; ~**-drill,** ratelboor; ~ **wheel,** palrat; ~ **wrench,** ratel(moer)sleutel.
rate¹, (n) waarde, prys; belasting; syns; maatstaf, verhouding, graad; tarief; snelheid, tempo; koers, voet; eiendomsbelasting; *at ANY* ~, in alle (elk) geval; *AT the* ~ *of,* met 'n vaart van; met 'n snelheid van; teen die koers van; ~ *of CLIMB,* stygsnelheid; ~ *of DEPOSITION,* neerslagsnelheid; ~ *of DISCOUNT,* diskonto; ~ *of EXCHANGE,* wisselkoers; ~ *of FIRE,* vuurtempo; *at a GREAT* ~, met 'n vinnige vaart; *at a HIGH* ~, teen 'n hoë prys; ~ *of INTEREST,* rentekoers, rentevoet; *the* ~ *for the JOB,* loon na werk; *at a LOW percentage* ~, teen lae rente; ~ *of MORTALITY,* sterftesyfer; ~ *of PAY,* salaris; ~ *s and TAXES,* plaaslike en algemene belasting, eiendomme en landsbelasting; ~ *of TAXATION,* belastingvoet; *at THAT* ~, op daardie manier; *at THIS* ~, op hierdie manier; teen hierdie koers; ~ *of WAGES,* loonskaal; (v) bereken, takseer, die waarde bepaal, skat, waardeer; belas; beskou, reken; vrot (muf) word (hooi); *I do not* ~ *his ability high,* ek skat sy bekwaamheid nie hoog nie; ek slaan hom nie hoog aan nie.

rate², (v) uitvaar, uitskel, afjak.
rate'-cutting, verlaging van tariewe.
rat'ed, bereken; beskou; ontwerp-; ~ *CAPACITY,* ontwerpvermoë; ~ *CURRENT,* ontwerpstroom; ~ *LOAD,* ontwerpbelasting.
ra'tel, ratel.
rate'payer, belastingbetaler; ~**s' association,** belastingbetalersvereniging.
rates' equalization fund, tariewereserwefonds.
rathe, vroegtydig, vroegryp (poëties).
ra'ther, (adv) liewer(s), eerder, eer; meer, veel meer; taamlik; alte seker, nogal, danig; enigsins, bietjie; baster; ~! (interj) alte seker! graag! ~ *EARLY,* taamlik ('n bietjie) vroeg; *it was* ~ *GOOD,* dit was nogal goed; ~ *LESS,* bietjie minder; ~ *MORE so,* nog 'n graadjie erger; *he would MUCH* ~ *not go,* hy sou veel liewer nie gaan nie; *I had* ~ *NOT,* ek wou liewer nie; *OR* ~, beter gesê; ~ *PRETTY,* mooierig; ~ *SHY,* skuwerig, skamerig; ~ *THAN,* eerder as om.
ratifica'tion, bekragtiging, goedkeuring, ratifikasie.
rat'ifier, bekragtiger.
rat'ify, (..**fied**), bekragtig, goedkeur sanksioneer; ratifiseer.
rat'ing¹, uitbrander, skrobbering, afjak, teregwysing.
rat'ing², aanslag; skatting; taksering, waardering; rang, klas; mindere (matroos); vermoë (ingenieurswese); sterkte, krag (motor); graad, stand; ~ **scale,** merieteskaal.
ra'tio, (-s), verhouding; ratio, grond; *in the* ~ *of 1 to 5,* in die verhouding 1 tot 5.
ratio'cinate, 'n gevolgtrekking maak, logies redeneer.
ratiocina'tion, gevolgtrekking, konklusie, bewysvoering.
ra'tion, (n) porsie, rantsoen; (pl) kos, rantsoen; *on full* ~ *s,* op volle rantsoen; (v) rantsoeneer, op rantsoen stel; 'n rantsoen gee.
ra'tional, (n) wortelgetal (wisk.,); verstandelik begaafde wese; (a) redelik, rasioneel, met rede begaaf, verstandig; beredeneer(d); ~ **number,** meetbare getal.
rational'e, opgaaf van redes, logiese grond, beredeneerde opgaaf; rationale.
ra'tionalism, rasionalisme; redelike godsdiens.
rationalist, rasionalis.
rationalis'tic, rasionalisties.
rational'ity, redelikheid, verstandelikheid; dinkvermoë.
rationaliza'tion, rasionalisasie; sanering (ekon.).
ra'tionalize, verstandelik verklaar, rasionaliseer; ~**r,** saneerder; rasionaliseerder.
ra'tion: ~ **bag,** proviandsak; ~ **book,** rantsoenboek.
ra'tioning, rantsoenering.
rat'lin(e)s, rat'lings, weeflyne (op skip); touleer.
ratoon', (n) uitloopsel, spruit, opslag (van suikerriet, katoen, ens.); (v) uitloop, opslaan.
rat: ~ **plague,** rottepes; ~ **poison,** rottegif; ~ **proof,** rotdig; ~ **race,** dolle gejaag, gedrang; ~**-run,** deur rotte verpes; ~ **s' bane,** rottekruid, muisgif; ~**-tail,** rotstert.
rat(t)an', spaansriet, rottang, bamboes.
ratteen', ratyn (wolstof).
ratt'en, sabotasie pleeg, saboteer; ~**er,** saboteur; ~**ing,** sabotasie.
ratt'er, muisvanger; droster.
rattinet', fyn ratyn.
rat'tle, (n) ratel; (ge)ratel, gerammel, geroggel; geklets, gebabbel; babbelkous; rammelaar (speelgoed); *an AGREEABLE* ~, 'n gesellige babbelkous; *THE* ~*s,* kroep; (v) ratel, kletter, rammel; klets, aframmel; irriteer, van stryk bring (sport); roggel; ~ *up the ANCHOR,* die anker optrek; ~ *AWAY,* aanhou babbel; aanhou kletter; daarop los rammel; ~ *OFF,* aframmel, opdreun; afbabbel; ~ *the SABRE,* die swaard rammel; met oorlog dreig; ~**-bag,** ~**-box,** ratelkous; ~ **bone,** klaphoutjie; ~**-brained,** leeghoofdig; ~**-bush,** stywesiektebossie; ~**d,** omgekrap; *get* ~ *d,* kwaad word; ~**-headed,** ~**-pated,** ylhoofdig, onbesonne, luidrugtig; ~**r,** ratelaar; ratel, ratelslang; iets uitstekends; ~ **snake,** ratelslang; ~ **trap,** (n) rammelkas; (a) lendelam; ~ **traps,** tierlantyntjies, snuisterye.

rat'tling, (n) geratel, geraas; (a) ratelend; uitstekend, deksels goed; vinnig: *a ~ good PACE,* 'n vinnige gang; *have a ~ good TIME,* dit besonder geniet.

rat: *~-trap,* rotval; *~ ty,* waardeloos; gemeen, lelik; liggeraak, iesegrimmig, katterig, prikkelbaar; rotagtig.

rau'city, heesheid, rouheid, skorheid.

rauc'ous, hees, skor; *~ness,* heesheid, skorheid.

raught'y = **rorty.**

rav'age, (n) verwoesting, plundering, skade; *~s of time,* die tand v.d. tyd; (v) verniel, verwoes, plunder; *~ r,* verwoester, plunderaar.

rav'aging, (n) verwoesting; ontering; (a) verwoestend, plunderend.

rave¹, (n) reling (wa).

rave², (n) geraas, rasery; loftuiting; (v) deurmekaar praat; yl, raas, uitvaar, raaskal, uitbulder, skeld; dweep met, die lof besing, in verrukking raak oor; *~ ABOUT a pop singer,* dweep met 'n popsanger; *~ about an INJUSTICE,* uitvaar oor 'n onreg; *~ AT a person,* teen iem. uitvaar; *~ itself OUT,* uitwoed, uitraas.

rav'el, (n) verwarring, knoop; rafel; (v) **(-led),** uitrafel, ontwar; verwar, deurmekaar maak; *~ out,* uitrafel, ontwar.

rav'elin, ravelyn.

rav'ellings, uitgerafelde tou(e).

rav'en¹, (n) raaf, kraai; (a) pikswart; *~ locks,* swart lokke.

rav'en², (v) verslind, roof; opsluk; opvreet; *~er,* rower, plunderaar.

rav'enous, roofsugtig, roofgierig, verslindend; vraatsugtig; uitgehonger; *~ly hungry,* so honger soos 'n wolf; *~ness,* uitgehongerdheid.

rav'in, buit, roof.

ravine', kloof, bergkloof, ravyn, skeur.

rav'ing, (n) yling; dwepery, gedweep; geraaskal; (a) rasend, mal; *~ mad,* stapelgek.

rav'ish, ontroof; verkrag, onteer; bekoor, betower, verruk; *~er,* rower, ontvoerder, skaker; vrouseskender, verkragter; *~ing,* (n) verkragting, ontering; (a) betowerend, verruklik; *~ment,* ontrowing; verkragting; skaking; verrukking; *~ment of maidens,* maagderoof.

raw, (n) rou plek; koudheid; *touch someone on the ~,* 'n teer plek aanraak; iem. op sy seer tas; (v) skawe, skrynerig maak, rou maak; (a) ru; rou, ongekook; guur (weer); dom; baar, onbedrewe (mens); onbekook; seer; onvermeng; onverwerk, onbewerk; *BE quite ~,* heeltemal rou wees; heeltemal baar wees; *~ with CHILBLAINS,* met winterhande; *he has had rather a ~ DEAL,* hy is baie onregverdig behandel; *a ~ ENGLISHMAN,* 'n rou Engelsman; *a ~ TASTE,* 'n wrede (rou) smaak; *~-boned,* brandmaer; *~ brick,* rou steen; *~ coffee,* ongebrande koffie; *~ edge,* ruwe kant; rafelkant; *~hide,* rouvel, ongebreide vel; *~hide hammer,* rouvelhamer; *~hide thong,* rou riem; *~ish,* rouerig; *~ linseed oil,* rou lynolie; *~ material,* grondstof; *~ness,* rouheid; baarheid; *~ products,* grondstowwe; *~ recruit,* baar rekruut; *~ score,* ruwe telling; *~ silk,* ongespinde sy; *~ sugar,* swart suiker; *~ taste,* wrede smaak; *~weather,* gure weer.

ray¹, (n) pylstert(vis), rog.

ray², (n) straal; strepie; rigstreep (kaart); *a ~ of HOPE,* 'n straal van hoop; *a ~ of SUNSHINE,* 'n sonstraal; 'n sonnetjie; (v) straal, uitstraal, strale skiet; *~-grass,* Engelse roggras; *~less,* donker.

ray'on, rayon, kunssy.

ray' therapy, bestraling, straleterapie.

raze, uitkrap; sloop, afbreek, met die grond gelykmaak, sleg; skawe, krap; kras; *~d to the ground,* met die grond gelykgemaak; geen steen op die ander laat nie.

raz'ing, slegting, gelykmaking, afbreking.

raz'or, (n) skeermes; (v) skeer; *~-back,* spitsrug; spitsrug(walvis), rugvinwalvis; *~-bill,* alk; *~-blade,* skeerlemmetjie, skeermesleem; *~ clam,* potloodaas *(Solen capensis);* *~-cut,* (n) skeerwond; (v) skeerknip; *~-edge,* skerp kant; netelige posisie; *be on the ~-edge,* in 'n haglike posisie wees; in die noute wees; *~-edged,* vlymskerp; *~-grinder,* skeer=

messlyper; *~-sharp,* vlymskerp; *~-strop,* skeermesriem, slypriem.

raz'ure, deurkrapping, uitkrapping.

razz'ia, rooftog, razzia.

raz'zle(-daz'zle), gewoel, opgewondenheid; drinkparty; *on the ~,* aan die boemel, aan die swier.

re¹, (n) re (mus.).

re², (prep) na aanleiding van, met betrekking tot, insake.

reabsorb', weer opsuig, weer absorbeer, reabsorbeer.

reabsorp'tion, reabsorpsie, weeropsuiging.

reaccept'ance, heraanvaarding.

reach, (n) **(-es),** bereik; omvang, uitgestrektheid; grens; boloop (van rivier); armlengte (boks); *ABOVE my ~,* bokant my bereik; bokant my vuurmaakplek; *BEYOND my ~,* buite my bereik; *the LOWER ~es,* die benedeloop; *OUT OF ~,* buite bereik; *the UPPER ~es,* die boloop; *WITHIN ~ of the city,* binne bereik v.d. stad; (v) aanreik, bereik, bykom, haal; aangee; uitsteek; uitstrek; reik (sport); dra (stem); by die wind seil; opgooi, opbring; *~ an AGREEMENT,* tot ooreenstemming raak, ooreenkom; *the coat ~ed DOWN to his feet,* die jas het tot op sy voete gehang; *~ing DOWNWARD,* (neer)buiging; *~ FOR,* probeer om te bereik; *~ forward to an IDEAL,* strewe na 'n ideaal; *the LAW ~es it,* dit val binne bereik v.d. wet; *he ~ed for his MATCHES,* hy het hom uitgestrek om sy vuurhoutjies by te kom; *NEWS has ~ed us,* die nuus het ons bereik; *~ OUT,* uitstrek, uitsteek; *~ one's READERS,* jou lesers boei; *~ SAFETY,* in veiligheid kom; *~able,* bereikbaar; *~-me-down,* klaargekoop; klaargemaak.

re-act', weer opvoer, weer speel.

react', terugwerk, reageer; *~ to,* reageer op.

react'ion, terugwerking, weeromslag, weeromstuit; uitwerking, reaksie; *~ to,* reaksie op; *~ary,* (n) **(..ries),** opstandeling, reaksionêr; (a) opstandig, reaksionêr.

react': *~ivate,* reaktiveer; *~iva'tion,* reaktivering; *~ive,* reagerend, gevoelig; *~or,* reaktor; reaksiesuil, reaksietoring; reaksiespoel, reaksievat.

read, *(~),* lees (boek); raai, gis; vertolk; verklaar; uitlê; studeer; lesing hou; aflees (van 'n instrument); *~ AGAIN,* oorlees, herlees; *~ ALOUD,* voorlees; hardop lees; *~ BACK,* voorlees; *~ for the BAR,* in die regte studeer; *~ the CLOCK,* kyk hoe laat dit is; *~ a DREAM,* 'n droom uitlê; *EAGERNESS to ~,* leeslus; *~ for an EXAMINATION,* vir 'n eksamen studeer; *~ the FUTURE,* die toekoms voorspel; *~ the GREEN,* die neiging v.d. setperk skat (gholf); *~ a person's HAND,* iem. se hand lees; *~ INTO,* aflei; meer lees as wat daar geskrywe staan; *~ LAW,* in die regte studeer; *~ a LECTURE,* 'n lesing hou; *~ someone a LESSON,* iem. die leviete voorlees; *~ between the LINES,* tussen die reëls lees; *~ LIPS,* lip lees; *~ MUSIC,* van die blad speel; *~ ON,* aanhou lees; *~ OUT,* aflees; *~ OVER,* deurlees, oorlees; *~ a PAPER on,* 'n voorlesing (referaat) hou oor; *~ for the PRESS,* proewe nasien; *the SENTENCE ~s thus,* die sin lui so; *~ to SLEEP,* aan die slaap lees; *~ up a SUBJECT,* 'n onderwerp bestudeer; *~ TEA-LEAVES,* die toekoms lees in teeblare; *~ a THERMOMETER,* die stand van 'n termometer lees; *~ THROUGH,* deurlees; *~ TO a person,* vir iem. (voor)lees; *~ UP,* jou inwerk in; naslaan; *~ the WRITING on the wall,* die skrif teen die muur lees; 'n waarskuwing vir die toekoms in die tekens v.d. tyd sien.

read, (p.p.) gelees; *TAKEN as ~,* as gelees beskou; *WELL ~,* belese; *WIDELY ~,* veelbelese (persoon); veelgelese (boek).

read: *~abil'ity,* leesbaarheid; *~able,* leesbaar; lesenswaardig, interessant.

readdress', agternastuur; readresseer, heradresseer.

read'er, leser; voorleser; leesboek; persleser, keurder; reviseur; lektor, dosent; *~ advertisement,* leesstofadvertensie; *~-plate,* wyserplaat; *~ ship,* lektoraat; leserskring.

rea'dily, geredelik, dadelik, maklik; graag.

rea'diness, bereidwilligheid, gewilligheid; gereedheid; vlugheid, prontheid, vaardigheid; *~ for BATTLE,*

strydvaardigheid, slagvaardigheid; *HOLD in* ~, gereedhou; ~ *in JUDGEMENT*, oordeelvaardigheid; ~ *of MIND (wit)*, teenwoordigheid van gees; *in* ~ *for the WINTER*, ter voorbereiding vir die winter.

read'ing, (n) (die) lees, lesery; voorlesing, lesing; belesenheid; leesstof, lektuur; aanwysing, meting, stand (van termometer); verklaring, vertolking, interpretasie; opvatting; *first* ~ *of a BILL*, eerste lesing van 'n wetsontwerp; *DULL* ~, vervelende lektuur; *what is your* ~ *of the FACTS?* hoe vertolk jy die feite? *FOND of* ~, leesgraag; *LIGHT* ~, ligte lektuur, ontspanningslektuur; *MANNER of* ~, leeswyse; *METHOD of* ~, leesmetode; *a man of WIDE* ~, 'n belese man; (a) lesend; lees=; ~**-book**, leesboek; ~**-club**, leesgeselskap, leesunie; leesklub; ~**-desk**, lessenaar; ~**-glass**, vergrootglas; ~**-glasses**, leesbril; ~**-hour**, leesuur; ~**-lamp**, studeerlamp; leeslamp; ~ **knowledge**, leeskennis; ~ **matter**, lektuur, leesstof; ~**-room**, leeskamer, leessaal; ~**-table**, leestafel; ~**-time**, leestyd.

readjourn', weer verdaag, weer uitstel; ~ **ment**, herhaalde uitstel.

readjust', herstel, weer regmaak; verstel; weer stel; ~**ment**, herstelling; verstelling; herskikking.

readmis'sion, weertoelating.

readmit', (-ted), weer toelaat; ~**tance**, weertoelating, hertoelating; heropname.

readopt', weer aanneem.

readorn', weer versier; ~**ment**, herversiering.

readvance', weer opruk, weer voorwaarts beweeg; weer voorskiet (geld).

rea'dy, (n) gereedheid; *AT the* ~, oorgehaal; *bring a RIFLE to the* ~, 'n geweer in aanslag bring; (v) gereedmaak; (a, adv) klaar, bereid, gereed, gewillig, vaardig; pront, geredelik, bereidwillig; gestewel en gespoor, volvaardig; gou, vinnig; by die hand; onmiddellik; kontant; ~ *for ACTION*, slaggereed; *BE* ~, gereed wees; *too* ~ *to BELIEVE the worst of someone*, alte bereid om die ergste van iem. te glo; ~ *CASH*, kontant (geld); ~ *to DEPART*, reisvaardig, op die punt om te vertrek; *GET* ~, maak jou klaar; *he is* ~ *with his HANDS*, hy is 'n handige werksman; *MAKE* ~, gereedmaak; ~ *to MARCH*, marsvaardig; ~ *MONEY down*, botter by die vis; ~ *PAYMENT*, kontant; *a* ~ *PEN*, 'n vaardige pen; ~ *for PICKING*, bekwaam (vrugte); ~ *to PLEASE*, voorkomend; ~ *SALE*, vinnige verkoop; ~ *to START*, reisvaardig; ~, *STEADY*, *go!* een, twee, drie! klaarstaan, weg! op julle merke, gereed, gaan! ~**-made**, pasklaar; klaargemaak; klaargekoop; ~**-mixed paint**, aangemaakte verf; ~ **money**, kontant; ~ **reckoner**, kitsrekenaar, blitsrekenaar, vlugrekenaar; ~**-to-drink**, drinkgereed; ~**-to-eat**, klaargaar; ~**-to-use**, gebruiksklaar; ~**-to-wear** = **ready-made**; ~**-witted**, gevat.

reaffirm', opnuut bekragtig, herbevestig; ~**a'tion**, herbevestiging.

reaffo'rest, weer bebos, herbebos; ~**a'tion**, herbebossing, weerbebossing.

rea'gency, reageervermoë, reaksievermoë; reageerproses.

rea'gent, reageermiddel, reagens.

reaggrava'tion, laaste vermaning.

re'al¹, (n) reaal (ou Spaanse muntstuk).

re'al², (a) wesenlik, regtig, waarlik, waar, eintlik, feitlik, effektief, werklik, reëel; eg; *a* ~ *FRIEND*, 'n opregte vriend; ~ *GROSS domestic product*, reële bruto binnelandse produk; *in* ~ *LIFE*, in die werklikheid; *the* ~ *MACKAY*, die ware Jakob; *that is* ~ *MONEY*, dit is klinkende munt; *the* ~ *PRESENCE*, die werklike teenwoordigheid; *the* ~ *THING*, die regte ding; die ware Jakob; ~ *hard WORK*, regtig harde werk; ~ **estate**, vaste eiendom; ~**-estate agent**, eiendomsagent.

real'gar, realgar, rooi swa(w)elarseen.

realign', hergroepeer, herskik; ~**ment**, herskikking.

re'alism, realisme.

re'alist, realis.

realist'ic, realisties; aanskoulik; *BE* ~, realisties wees; *MAKE* ~, veraanskoulik.

real'ity, (..ties), werklikheid, wesenlikheid; feitlikheid; waarheid; doodsaak; realiteit; *BECOME a* ~, werklikheid word; *IN* ~, in werklikheid, waarlik, werklik.

realiza'tion, verwesenliking, verwerkliking, totstandkoming; besef; realisering, realisasie; tegeldemaking, geldmaking.

re'alize, verwesenlik, verwerklik, realiseer; besef; tot geld maak; werklik maak; opbring, haal; likwideer (boedel); ~ *ONESELF*, jou individualiteit tot sy volle reg laat kom; ~ *a PRICE*, 'n prys behaal.

realli'ance, hernieude verbond.

re-ally', (reallied) weer verbind, weer verenig.

re'ally, regtig, inderdaad, darem, gerus, eintlik, rêrig, sowaar, reg-reg, werklik, waarlik, wraggieswaar, waaragtig; trouens; ~ *and truly*, waarlik waar.

realm, ryk, koninkryk; gebied; *the* ~ *of FANCY*, die ryk van verbeelding; ~ *of SHADES*, skaduryk.

re'alty, vaste eiendom, vasgoed.

ream¹, (n) riem (papier).

ream², (v) ruim, wyer maak; uithol (vrugte).

ream'er, ruimnaald; ruimer; ~ **bit**, ruimboor, ruimer.

rean'imate, weer besiel; laat herleef.

reanima'tion, besieling; herlewing.

reannex', weer aanheg, herannekseer; ~**a'tion**, weeraanhegting, heranneksasie.

reap, (af)oes; maai; pluk; insamel; wen; ~ *ADVANTAGE from*, voordeel trek uit; ~ *the FRUITS of*, die vrugte pluk (inoes) van; ~ *the benefit of another's LABOUR*, ~ *where one has not SOWN*, maai waar jy nie gesaai het nie; ~ *what one has SOWN*, maai wat 'n mens gesaai het; ~**er**, maaier; oester; snymasjien

reap'ing, (die) oes, oestery, oeswerk; ~**-hook**, sekel, sens, ~**-machine**, snymasjien, maaimasjien; selfbinder; ~**-time**, oestyd.

reappear', weer verskyn, herverskyn; ~**ance**, weerverskyning, herverskyning.

reapply', (..plied), opnuut aanwend; weer aansoek doen.

reappoint', herbenoem, weer aanstel; ~**ment**, herbenoeming.

reappor'tion, weer indeel; herverdeel; ~**ment**, herindeling; herverdeling.

reapprais'al, herwaardering.

reappraise', herwaardeer.

rear¹, (n) agterhoede; agterpunt; agtergrond; agterkant; stert; *AT the* ~ *of*, agter; *ATTACK in the* ~, in die rug aanval; *BRING up the* ~, die agterhoede vorm; agteraan kom; *COVER the* ~, die rug dek; *FAR in the* ~, heeltemal agteraan; *GO to the* ~, agtertoe gaan; *be IN the* ~, agteraan kom; *IN the* ~, in die agterhoede; agteraan; in die rug; *in the* ~ *OF*, agter, agteraan; *PROTECT the* ~, die rug beveilig; *SEND to the* ~, agtertoe stuur; *TAKE the enemy in the* ~, die vyand in die rug aanval; (a) agter=, agterste.

rear², (v) kweek, grootmaak, grootbring; oprig; opvoed, opkweek; oplei; vorm; steier, op sy agterpote staan (perd); verbou (plante); teel, aanteel (diere); ~ *CATTLE*, beeste teel; ~ *CHILDREN*, kinders grootmaak.

rear: ~**-admiral**, skout-by-nag, skoutadmiraal (S.A.); ~ **arch**, agterboom (van saal); ~ **attack**, rugaanval; ~ **axle**, agteras; ~ **bearing**, agterlaer; ~ **brake**, agterrem; ~**guard**, agterhoede; ~**guard action**, agterhoedegeveg; ~**-gunner**, stertskutter; ~ **lamp**, agterlamp, agterste lamp; ~ **leg**, agterpoot; ~ **light**, agterlamp, agterlig; ~ **line**, agterste gelid.

rearm', weer bewapen, herbewapen; ~**ament**, ~**ing**, herbewapening.

rear'most, agterste.

rear'mouse, (..mice), vlermuis.

rearrange', verander, omskik, verskik, verstel, anders rangskik; ~**ment**, verandering, omskikking.

rearrest', (n) herarrestasie; (v) weer gevange neem.

rear: ~ **rank**, agterste gelid; ~ **spring**, agterveer; ~ **view**, agteraansig; ~**-view mirror**, ~**-vision mirror**, agteruitkykspieël, terugkykspieël, truspieël(tjie); ~ **ward**, (n) agterhoede; (a) agterste; ~ **wards**, agterwaarts; ~ **wheel**, agterwiel; ~**-wheel drive**, agterwielaandrywing; ~ **wind**, rugwind, meewind.

reascend', weer beklim; weer opstyg.
reas'on, (n) rede, verstand; redelikheid, billikheid; oorsaak, dryfveer, grond; *AGAINST* ~, strydig met die rede; *for no APPARENT* ~, vir spek en boontjies; *BY* ~ *of*, weens; ten gevolge van; uit hoofde van; *FOR this* ~, hierom, om hierdie rede; *GIVE* ~ *to*, aanleiding gee tot; *GIVE* ~ *for*, motiveer; *with GOOD* ~, met reg, tereg; *for* ~*s of HEALTH*, om gesondheidsredes; *HEAR* ~, na rede luister; *IN* ~, billik, redelik; billikerwyse; *KEEP one's* ~, by jou verstand bly; *LISTEN to* ~, na rede luister; *not to LISTEN to* ~, jou nie laat gesê nie; *LOSE one's* ~, jou verstand kwytraak; *he will NOT listen to* ~, daar val nie met hom te praat nie; *OPEN to* ~, vatbaar vir oortuiging; *OUT of all* ~, heeltemal onbillik; buitensporig; *REGAIN one's* ~, weer by jou verstand kom; *there is* ~ *in what you SAY*, daar sit waarheid in wat jy sê; *I can't SEE the* ~ *of it*, ek vind dit onverklaarbaar; *for SOME* ~, om die een of ander rede; *SPEAK* ~, verstandig praat; *it STANDS to* ~, dit spreek vanself; *WITHIN* ~, billik, redelik; *everything WITHIN* ~, alles binne perke; *WITHOUT* ~, sonder oorsaak; *that is the* ~ *WHY*, daarom; *a WOMAN'S* ~, vrouelogika; (v) redeneer; praat; beredeneer, bespreek; oorweeg; ~ *AWAY*, wegsyfer, wegredeneer; ~ *someone INTO something*, iem. oorhaal om iets te doen: ~ *it OUT*, dit uitredeneer; ~ *WITH a person about (on) a subject*, met iem. oor 'n onderwerp redeneer; ~**able**, redelik, billik; leefbaar; skiklik; verstandig; ~**ableness**, billikheid, skiklikheid, redelikheid; ~**ably**, billikerwys, redelikerwys; tereg; ~*ably GOOD*, redelik goed; *TALK* ~*ably*, verstandig praat; ~**ed**, beredeneer(d); ~**er**, redeneerder; denker; ~**ing**, beredenering; redenasie, redenering; *there is no* ~*ing with him*, met hom kan 'n mens nie redeneer nie; ~**less**, redeloos, verstandeloos.
reassem'ble, weer vergader, weer bymekaarmaak; weer inmekaarsit.
reassert', weer verklaar; ~**ion**, herhaalde verklaring.
reassess', weer vasstel, weer bepaal, herskat; ~**ment**, herskatting, herwaardering.
reassign', weer toewys.
reassume', terugneem; weer aanvaar, weer begin, hervat.
reassump'tion, weeraanneming; hervatting.
reassur'ance, gerusstelling; herversekering.
reassure', opnuut verseker; gerusstel; *reassuring news*, gerusstellende nuus.
reattach', opnuut verbind (aanbind); weer in beslag neem; ~**ment**, herverbinding; herinbeslagneming.
reattempt', weer probeer.
reawake', herontwaak; ~**ning**, herontwaking.
rebake', oorbak.
rebap'tism, wederdoop, herdoop.
rebaptize' herdoop; verdoop.
reb'ate, (n) vermindering, korting, rabat, afslag.
rebate', (v) kort, verminder, afslaan; ~**ment**, vermindering, korting.
reb'ate-voucher, kortingsbewys.
reb'el, (n) oproerling, rebel, opstandeling, muiter; (a) opstandig, rebels, rebelle=
rebel', (v) (-led), rebelleer, opstaan, muit; ~**lion**, opstand, rebellie, sedisie; ~**lious**, oproerig, weerspannig, onregeerbaar, opstandig, rebels, sedisieus; *he is* ~*lious*, hy is opstandig; hy is hard in die bek; ~**liousness**, oproerigheid, opstandigheid.
rebell'ow, hard weerklink (poëties).
rebind', (..bound), weer bind.
re'birth, we(d)ergeboorte.
rebloom', weer blom.
rebore', naboor.
rebor'ing, naboring.
reborn', weergebore, herskape.
rebound', (n) terugstuiting, terugslag, weeromslag, weeromstuit; *catch on the* ~, na 'n teleurstelling probeer oorhaal; (v) opslaan, terugstuit, afstuit, terugspring, terugslaan, weeromstuit; ~**ing shot**, opslagskoot.
rebroad'cast, (n) heruitsending; (v) heruitsaai.
rebuff', (n) afjak; affront; terugstoting, teenstand, weiering, afstoting; belemmering, teenslag; *meet with a* ~, 'n terugslag ondervind; (v) terugstoot, afwys, afjak.
rebuild', (..**built**), herbou, herstel, verbou; ~**er**, herbouer, hersteller; ~**ing**, weeropbou, heropbou.
rebuke', (n) berisping, brander, teregwysing; (v) berispe, teregwys, skrobbeer, snou, bestraf, voorkry, afklim op, beknor, inklim, uittrap; ~ *a PERSON*, iem. die leviete voorlees; iem. op sy nommer sit; *BE* ~*d*, geroskam word, haarlaat; ~**ful**, berispend, bitter; ~**r**, berisper.
rebulli'tion, opkoking, opborreling.
rebu'rial, herbegrafnis.
rebu'ry, (**reburied**), opnuut begrawe, herbegrawe.
reb'us, rebus.
rebut', (-**ted**), terugslaan; weerlê; repliseer; ~**tal**, weerlegging, repliek, dupliek; ~**ter**, tweede dupliek.
recal'citrance, verset, weerstand, weerbarstigheid, weerstrewigheid, weerspannigheid.
recal'citrant, (n) weerspannige; (a) teenstrewend, weerspannig, weerbarstig, balsturig.
recal'citrate, teenstribbel, teenspartel, weerspannig wees.
recalibra'tion, heryking.
recall', (n) intrekking, herroeping (woorde); terugroeping (personeel); *BEYOND* ~, onherroeplik; *LETTERS of* ~, briewe van terugroeping (gesant); (v) herroep; terugneem (hou); terugvorder; terugdink, laat dink aan, in die geheue roep; terugtrek, terugroep, rappel (wet); opsê; ~ *to MIND*, byval; herinner; ~ *MEMORIES*, herinneringe ophaal; ~**able**, herroepbaar.
recant', herroep, intrek; terugtrek; ~**a'tion**, herroeping; terugtrekking.
recap', (-**ped**), versool.
recapit'ulate, kortliks herhaal, saamvat, opsom, rekapituleer.
recapitula'tion, herhaling, samevatting, opsomming.
recapit'ulatory, rekapitulerend, herhalend.
recap'tion, herneming, terugname.
recap'tor, heroweraar, hernemer.
recap'ture, (n) herowering, herneming; (v) herower; weer gevange neem.
recarb'on, nuwe koolelektrodes insit.
recast', (n) omgieting, omwerking, verwerking; (v) (**recast**), opnuut giet; verander, wysig; vervorm, omwerk.
recede', wyk, terugtrek, terugwyk; sak, terugloop; aan 'n vroeër besitter weer afstaan.
reced'ing, afgaande; teruggaande; ~ **tide**, afgaande gety.
receipt', (n) ontvangs; ontvangsbewys; bewys, voldaan, kwitansie; (pl) inkomste, ontvangste; *ACKNOWLEDGE the* ~ *of*, die ontvangs erken van; *CLEAN* ~, afdoende ontvangsbewys; *FULL* ~, finale kwitansie; *be IN* ~ *of*, ontvang hê; gekry hê; *ON* ~, by ontvangs; *SHORT* ~, onvolledige ontvangs; (v) voldaan teken; 'n ontvangsbewys gee, kwiteer; ~ *ed bill*, voldane rekening; ~ **book**, kwitansieboek; ~ **stamp**, kwitansieseël; ~ **voucher**, ontvangsbewys.
receiv'able, ontvangbaar, aanneemlik; invorderbaar; *bill* ~, baatwissel.
receive', ontvang, in ontvangs neem, aanneem; verwelkom, onthaal; opvang (uitsending); kry; ondervind; opneem, toelaat; heel (gesteelde goed).
received': ~ *into the CHURCH*, aangeneem as lidmaat; ~ *PAYMENT*, voldaan; *TENDERS will be* ~ *until*, inskrywings word ingewag tot; *for VALUE* ~, vir waarde ontvang.
receiv'er, ontvanger; ontvangtoestel; horing, (ge=) hoorbuis (telef.); terugslaner (tennis); heler (van gesteelde goed); kurator; opvangbak; ~ *of REVENUE*, ontvanger van inkomste, Jan Taks, belastinggaarder; *the* ~ *is as bad as the THIEF*, die heler is so goed as die steler.
receiv'ing, ontvangs; inning; heling (gesteelde goed); *be on the* ~ *end*, aan die kortste end wees; die spit moet afbyt; ~ **set**, ontvangtoestel; ~ **ship**, wagskip.
re'cency, onlangsheid, nuutheid, resentheid.

recen'sion, hersiening; lys; hersiene uitgawe.
re'cent, nuut, vars, jonk, onlangs, resent, kort gelede, pas gelede; *MOST* ~, jongste; *a* ~ *WOUND,* 'n vars wond; *a* ~ *WRITER,* 'n resente skrywer; *of* ~ *YEARS,* in die laaste jare; ~ **ly,** onlangs, kort gelede, resent; anderdag; *more* ~ *ly,* baie onlangs; taamlik resent.
recep'tacle, vergaarbak; houer; skuilplek; heuningkelk, blombodem (bot.); steeksok (elek.).
receptibil'ity, ontvangbaarheid; ontvanklikheid.
recep'tible, ontvangbaar; ontvanklik.
recep'tion, ontvangs; radio-ontvangs; onthaal, resepsie; verwelkoming; aanvaarding; ontvangstoonbank; *CORDIAL* ~, hartlike ontvangs; *GIVE a* ~, 'n onthaal gee; *the* ~ *of stolen GOODS,* die heling van gesteelde goed; *a WARM* ~, 'n hartlike ontvangs; ~ **hall,** ontvangsaal; ~ **ist,** ontvangsklerk (hotel); ontvangsdame (dokter); ~ **-order,** opnemingsbevel; ~ **room,** ontvangsaal, ontvangskamer, voorkamer.
recep'tive, ontvanklik, vatbaar; ~ **faculty,** opnemingsvermoë; ~ **ness,** ontvanklikheid, vatbaarheid.
receptiv'ity, opnemingsvermoë, ontvanklikheid, vatbaarheid.
recep'tor, ontvanger; opnemer; reseptor.
recess', (n) terugtrekking; diepdruk; (-es), skuilplek; nis, alkoof, hoek; pouse; vakansie, reses; groef; uitsnyding, holte, leplek, gleuf; uitboring; induiking; inham; uitkeping; versinking; *GO in* ~, op reses gaan; ~ *es of the HEART,* die diepste skuilhoeke v.d. hart; (v) uitsny, wegsny, uithol, uitgleuf, uitboor; induik; op reses gaan; inlaat, versink
recessed', uitgehol; ~ *ARCH,* spanningboog, ~ *JOINT,* diepvoeg; ~ *SWITCH,* vlakskakelaar.
recess'ing tool, versinkbeitel.
rece'ssion, terugtreding; agteruitgang, teruggang; handelslapte, resessie (handel); afstand; ~ **al,** (n) slotgesang; (a) reses=; slot=; teruggaande; ~ **al hymn,** slotgesang.
recess'ive, teruggaande, terugwykend, resessief.
recharge', opnuut aanval; opnuut beskuldig; herlaai (elek.), weer laai; hervul.
rechart'er, opnuut huur, opnuut bevrag.
recheck', weer nasien, kontroleer.
recherch'é, vergesog; uitgesoek, fyn.
rechri'sten, herdoop; ~ **ing,** herdoping.
recidiva'tion, nuwe aanval.
recid'ivism, terugvalling, residivisme.
recid'ivist, residivis, terugvaller (in misdaad).
re'cipe, resep; voorskrif; ~ **book,** reseptebook.
recip'ient, (n) ontvanger, aannemer; (a) ontvangend, opnemend.
recip'rocal, wederkerig, wedersyds; ~ **action,** wisselwerking; ~ **friendship,** wedersydse vriendskap; ~ **love,** wedersydse liefde; ~ **ness,** wederkerigheid; ~ **proportion,** omgekeerde eweredigheid; ~ **visit,** teenbesoek.
recip'rocate, wederkerig handel; wissel; met gelyke munt betaal; iets terugdoen; vergeld; beantwoord; 'n weerdiens bewys; heen en weer beweeg.
recip'rocating: ~ **pump,** suierpomp; ~ **table,** skudtafel.
reciproca'tion, heen-en-weerbeweging; beantwoording; (uit)wisseling; vergelding.
recipro'city, beantwoording, wisselwerking, wederkerigheid, wederkerige daad, resiprositeit.
recit'al, verhaal, vertelling; voorlesing; voordrag; musiekaand; uitvoering (musiek); opsomming, aanhef (akte); *give a* ~, 'n uitvoering gee.
recita'tion, resitasie, voordrag; opsomming.
recitative', (n) resitatief; (a) verhalend.
recite', opsê; voordra, deklameer, resiteer; vermeld; ~ **r,** voordraer, deklamator; voordragversameling, voordragbundel.
reck, omgee, jou bekommer; *he LITTLE* ~ *s,* dit kan hom weinig skeel; ~ *OF,* omgee, traak.
reck'less, roekeloos, onverskillig, onversigtig, waaghalsig, onbesuis, ongereen, ligvaardig, oormoedig, gedagteloos; ~ *of CONSEQUENCES,* onverskillig omtrent die gevolge; *he is* ~ *of DANGER,* hy steur hom niks aan gevaar nie; ~ *DEED,* waag=

stuk; ~ *DRIVING,* roekelose bestuur; *a* ~ *FELLOW,* 'n waaghalsige vent; ~ **ness,** roekeloosheid, sorgeloosheid, waaghalsigheid, oormoed, onbesonnenheid, onbesuisdheid, onverskilligheid.
reck'on, reken, tel, skat, glo, meen, dink; gereken word; ~ *AMONG,* tel onder; ~ *BY,* reken met; ~ *without his HOST,* nie met die gasheer rekening hou nie; *HOW do you* ~ *him up?* wat dink jy van hom? hoe verstaan jy hom? ~ *ON,* staatmaak op; *he is* ~ *ed one of the best PLAYERS,* hy word as een van die beste spelers beskou; ~ *UP,* optel, uitreken; ~ *UPON,* reken op; ~ *WITH,* rekening hou met.
reck'oner, rekenaar.
reck'oning, berekening; gissing; tydrekening; *BE out in one's* ~, die tel kwytraak, verkeerd wees; *CALL someone to a* ~ *for his past sins,* iem. vir oud en nuut straf; *DAY of* ~, dag van vergelding; *LEAVE out of* ~, buite rekening laat; *MERRY is the feasting till we come to the* ~, die knoop sit aan die end v.d. tou; *be OUT in one's* ~, jou misgis; misreken.
reclaim', (n) herroeping; *past (beyond)* ~, onherroeplik verlore; (v) herroep, terugeis; terugbring; hervorm; beskaaf, verbeter; drooglê, droogmaak, herwin (grond), inpolder, demp; terugkry; ~ **able,** opeisbaar, terugvorderbaar; ~ **ant,** teenparty.
reclaim'ed, teruggevorder; ~ *LAND,* drooggelegde gebied; ~ *OIL,* herwonne olie; ~ *WASTE,* herwonne poetskatoen.
reclaim'er, nawinner; herwinner.
reclaim'ing, nawinning; drooglegging; herwinning; ~ *of land,* landwinning.
reclama'tion, herwinning, terugvordering, terugroeping, winning, aanwinning; protes; opeising; verbetering; bekering; ontginning; drooglegging, (die) droogmaak (grond), inpoldering.
ré'clame, reklame.
reclassifica'tion, herindeling, herklassifikasie.
reclass'ify, (..**fied**) herindeel, herklassifiseer.
rcc'linate, neergebuig, afhangend.
recline', leun, agteroor lê, rus; staatmaak op.
reclin'ing chair, verstelbare leuningstoel, lêstoel.
reclose', opnuut sluit.
reclothe', opnuut klee.
recluse', (n) kluisenaar; (a) afgesonder, eensaam; ~ **ness,** afsondering.
reclu'sion, afsondering, eensaamheid.
reclus'ive, eensaam, teruggetrokke.
recoat', oorskilder, weer verf; weer klee.
recogni'tion, herkenning; erkenning, waardering; erkentlikheid; *IN* ~ *of,* ter erkenning van (vir); *changed OUT of all* ~, onherkenbaar (baie) verander; *RECEIVE* ~, erkenning geniet.
rec'ognizable, herkenbaar.
recog'nizance, erkenning, verbintenis, verklaring; skuldbekentenis; borgtog; *BIND over under* ~, onder sekerheidstelling (borgtog) verbind; *ON his own* ~, op eie borgakte.
rec'ognize, herken, eien ('n persoon); erken; besef, insien (waarheid); *I* ~ *d the HANDWRITING as that of my mother,* ek het die handskrif as dié van my moeder erken; ~ *as HEIR,* as erfgenaam erken; ~ **r,** herkenner; erkenner.
recoil', (n) terugsprong; terugslag; terugloop (kanon); skop (geweer); weeromslag, weeromstuit; (v) terugspring, terugdeins; terugloop; weeromstuit; skop (geweer); ~ *on themselves,* op hulleself weer neerkom; ~ **-absorber,** terugslagbreker, ~ **-reducer,** skokbreker.
recoin', oormunt, hermunt, ommunt; ~ **age,** hermunting; ~ **ing,** ommunting.
recollect'¹, weer versamel.
recollect'², herinner; ~ *oneself,* jou beheers; tot nadenking kom.
recollec'tion, herinnering, geheue; besinning; hersameling; *to the BEST of my* ~, vir sover ek weet (onthou); *NOT to my* ~, nie sover ek kan onthou nie.
recol'onize, weer koloniseer.
recombina'tion, herverbinding.
recombine', weer verbind, weer saamvoeg.
recommence', weer begin, hervat; ~ **ment,** hervatting.

recommend 1172 recreation

recommend', aanbeveel; aanprys; aanraai; aanpreek, rekommandeer; ~ *a BOOK*, 'n boek aanbeveel; ~ *ONESELF*, jou aanbeveel; *the PAINTING has nothing to ~ it*, die skilderstuk is onverdienstelik (swak); ~ *for a POST*, vir 'n betrekking aanbeveel; ~ *for PROMOTION*, vir bevordering aanbeveel; ~ *as a TEACHER*, as onderwyser aanbeveel; ~ **able**, aanbevelenswaardig.

recommenda'tion, aanbeveling; rekommendasie; *LETTER of* ~, aanbevelingsbrief; *with a ~ for MERCY*, met 'n aanbeveling vir genade; *ON the ~ of*, op aanbeveling van.

recommend'atory, aanbevelend, aanbevelings=.

recommend'ed, aanbeveel, aanbevole; *HIGHLY* ~, hoogs aanbeveel; ~ *HOTEL*, aanbevole (aanbeveelde) hotel.

recommit', (-ted), opnuut opdra; terugverwys; weer begaan; ~ **ment**, hernude opdrag; terugverwysing; hergevangesetting; ~ **t'al**, terugverwysing; hergevangesetting.

recommun'icate, weer meedeel; weer in verbinding tree.

rec'ompense, (n) beloning; (weder)vergelding; skadeloosstelling; *in ~ for*, as vergoeding vir; (v) beloon, vergoed; skadeloos stel.

recompose', weer saamstel; weer komponeer; gerusstel.

recomposi'tion, herstelling; nuwe samestelling.

rec'oncilable, versoenbaar; verenigbaar; bestaanbaar.

rec'oncile, (met mekaar) versoen; bylê ('n twis); ooreenbring, laat ooreenstem (rekeninge); verenig; *BE ~ d to*, jou skik in, berus in; ~ *FACTS with each other*, feite met mekaar ooreenbring (rym); ~ *oneself to one's FATE*, jou in jou lot skik; ~ **d**, versoen (met); geskik; *be ~ d*, versoen wees; ~ **ment**, versoening, bylegging; ~ **r**, versoener.

reconcilia'tion, versoening; ooreenbringing, hereniging; rekonsiliasie; vergelyking (boekhou).

reconcil'iatory, versoenend, versoenings=.

reconcil'ing, versoenend.

recondensa'tion, herverdigting, herkondensasie.

recondense', weer verdig, herkondenseer.

rec'ondite, geheim, verborge, diepsinnig, duister, weinig bekend; ~ **ness**, geheimsinnigheid, duisterheid.

recondi'tion, herstel, repareer, vernuwe, opknap; ~ **ed**, hernieu, vernieu, opgeknap; *a ~ ed car*, 'n opgeknapte motor; ~ **ing**, opknapping, vernuwing.

reconduct', teruglei; ~ **ion**, terugleiding.

reconfirm', opnuut bevestig.

reconn'aissance, verkenning, verspieding; spioentog; spioenasie; ~ **aircraft**, verkenningsvliegtuig, verkenner; ~ **duties**, verkenningsdiens; ~ **flight**, verkenningsvlug; ~ **plane**, verkenningsvliegtuig, verkenner.

reconnoi'tre, (n) verkenning; (v) verken, verspied, spioen.

reconnoi'tring, verkenning; ~ **army**, verkenningsleër; ~ **expedition**, verkenningstog; ~ **service**, verkenningsdiens.

reconq'uer, herower, herwin.

reconq'uest, herowering, herwinning.

recon'secrate, opnuut wy, herwy.

reconsecra'tion, hernieude wyding, herwyding.

reconsid'er, weer oorweeg, opnuut in oorweging neem; ~ **a'tion**, heroorweging.

reconsign'ment, terugsending.

recon'stitute, opnuut saamstel.

reconstitu'tion, hersamestelling.

reconstruct', hervorm, opnuut bou, ombou, saneer; opnuut saamstel, rekonstrueer; ~ **ion**, herbou, weeroprigting, ombou; rekonstruksie.

reconvene', weer byeenroep; weer vergader.

reconven'tion, teeneis; *plaintiff in ~*, teeneiser.

reconver'sion, herbekering; terugskakeling; heromsetting.

recon'vert, (n) herbekeerde.

reconvert', (v) herbekeer; terugskakel; weer omsit.

reconvey', terug(ver)voer; terug oordra.

rec'ord, (n) verslag; register; dokument, rekord; strafregister; staat; beskeid; (grammofoon)plaat; aantekening; gedenkskrif, gedenkteken; loopbaan, geskiedenis; dossier; boeking, inskrywing; (pl) argief; annale, stukke; *have a BAD ~*, baie op jou kerfstok hê; *BEAR ~ of*, getuie wees van; getuig van; *BEAT the ~*, die rekord slaan; *a BLOT on one's ~*, 'n klad op jou goeie naam; *the only CASE on ~*, die enigste geval bekend; *a CLEAN ~*, 'n skoon verlede; *with a CRIMINAL ~*, met 'n kriminele rekord, met veroordelings; *FOR the ~*, vir notulering as feite; vir rekorddoeleindes; om dit reg te stel; *HOLD the ~*, die rekord hou; *KEEP a ~ of*, aanteken, opskrywe; rekord (aantekening) hou van; *KEEP the ~ straight*, by die feite bly; *KEEPER of the ~s*, argivaris; *KEEPING of ~s*, rekordhouding; *OFF the ~*, onoffisieel, nie-amptelik; *ON ~*, amptelik bekend; aangeteken; *the greatest ON ~*, die grootste waarvan die geskiedenis vertel; *PUBLIC ~s*, staatsargief; *PUT on ~*, boekstaaf; op rekord plaas.

record', (v) opteken, aanteken, notuleer, opgee, noteer; inskryf; vermeld; registreer; herinner; ~ *ed MUSIC*, platemusiek; ~ *one's VOTE*, jou stem uitbring.

rec'ord: ~ **book**, verslagboek; register; ~ **cabinet**, platekabinet; ~ **card**, kontrolekaart, aantekenkaart; registerkaart; ~ **clerk**, verslagklerk, argiefklerk; registerklerk; ~ **collection**, plateversameling; ~ **collector**, plateversamelaar, plateliefhebber, diskofiel.

record'er, argivaris; griffier; notulehouer; optekenaar; historikus; registreertoestel; opvangtoestel.

rec'ord flight, rekordvlug.

record'ing, opname; ~ **instrument**, registreertoestel; ~ **machine**, opneemtoestel; ~ **tape**, klankband; ~ **telegraph**, druktelegraaf, skryftelegraaf.

rec'ord: ~ **librarian**, diskotekaris; ~ **library**, diskoteek; ~ **office**, argief; ~ **player**, platespeler, plaatspeler; ~ **room**, argief; opbergkamer; ~ **s clerk**, leerklerk, argiefklerk; ~ **s office**, registrasiekantoor; ~ **time**, rekordtyd.

recount'¹, (n) oortelling, natelling; (v) oortel.

recount'², (v) verhaal, vertel.

recoup', inhou; skadeloos stel; verhaal, terugvorder; aftrek; vergoed; ~ **losses**, skade inhaal, verliese verhaal; ~ **ment**, skadeloosstelling; vergoeding; verhaling.

recourse', toevlug; regres, verhaal; verhelp(ing); *HAVE ~ to*, jou toevlug neem tot; *there is NO ~*, daar is geen verhaal op nie; *RIGHT of ~*, regresreg.

reco'ver¹, (n) herstel; (v) herkry; terugkry, terugvind, terugwin, herwin; herower; verhaal, langs geregtelike weg verkry; skadevergoeding kry; weer inhaal; herstel, aansterk, gesond word; bykom (bewustelose); red; weer bereik; win (mynbou); ~ *one's BREATH*, weer asem kry; ~ *CONSCIOUSNESS*, weer bykom; ~ *DAMAGES*, skadevergoeding kry; ~ *one's FEET (legs)*, weer op die been kom; ~ *one's HEALTH*, jou gesondheid terugkry (herwin); ~ *one's SENSES*, weer tot besinning kom; ~ *lost TIME*, verlore tyd inhaal.

re-co'ver², (v) oortrek, weer beklee; weer toemaak.

reco'verable, herkrygbaar; terugvorderbaar, invorderbaar; verhaalbaar, inbaar; ~ *ADVANCE*, verhaalbare voorskot; ~ *FROM*, reg van verhaal op; ~ *at LAW*, in regte te verhaal.

reco'verer, herwinner; redder; winner (mynbou).

reco'very, terugkryging, winning; beredering; berging; herstel(ling), genesing; terugvordering; herkryging, verhaal (reg); standsherstel (vliegtuig); *BEYOND ~*, onherstelbaar; ongeneeslik; reddeloos, buite hoop; *make a COMPLETE ~*, volkome herstel; *PAST ~*, onherstelbaar; ongeneeslik; reddeloos, buite hoop; ~ **account**, dekkingsrekening; ~ **gear**, hystoestel; ~ **shot**, herstelskoot.

rec'reancy, lafhartigheid; afvalligheid.

rec'reant, (n) lafaard; afvallige; (a) lafhartig, afvallig.

recreate'¹, (v) herskep, omskep.

rec'reate², (v) vermaak; ontspan, ontspanning neem; jou verlustig, verkwik.

recrea'tion, herskepping; vermaak, ontspanning; spel, tydverdryf; rekreasie; geestelike opfrissing; ~ **al**, ontspannings=; ~ **grounds**, sportterrein, ont-

spanningsterrein; ~ **hall**, ontspanningslokaal, ontspanningsaal.
rec'reative, ontspannend; opwekkend; vermaaklik; herskeppend.
rec'rement, uitwerpsel, skuim, afval; afskeiding.
recrim'inate, wederkerig beskuldig; 'n teenbeskuldiging inbring.
recrimina'tion, teenbeskuldiging, teenklag; (pl) verwyte.
recrim'inator, teenbeskuldiger.
recross', weer oorgaan.
recrudesce', weer uitbreek; herleef; ~ **nce**, weeruitbreking; heroplewing; oplewing, oplaaiing, verergering.
recruit', (n) rekruut; nuweling; (v) (aan)werf, rekruteer; aanvul; opknap, versterk, herstel; ~ *one's strength*, jou kragte herwin; ~ **er**, werwer.
recruit'ing, werwing, rekrutering; ~ **-depot**, werwingsdepot; ~ **money**, werfgeld; ~ **office**, werwingskantoor; ~ **officer**, werwingsoffisier; werwingsamptenaar; werfoffisier.
recruit'ment, herstel, versterking; rekrutering.
recrystalliza'tion, herkristallisasie.
recrys'tallize, herkristalliseer.
rec'tal, rektaal, endelderm=, nersderm=, rektum=; ~ *feeding*, rektale voeding; ~ **pipe**, rektumspuit, rektumpyp.
rec'tangle, reghoek.
rectang'ular, reghoekig.
rec'tifiable, verbeterbaar, vatbaar vir verbetering, herstelbaar.
rectifica'tion, verbetering, verhelping (foute); ontwringing (foto); herstelling, rektifikasie; tweede distillasie (drank); gelykrigting (radio).
rec'tifier, verbeteraar; oorhaler; ruimer, ruimhoutjie; gelykrigter (radio); rektifikator (skeik.).
rec'tify, (..**fied**), verbeter; verhelp; regstel, regmaak, in orde bring; uit die weg ruim, reghelp; suiwer, distilleer; louter; ruim, groter maak; ontwring (foto); gelykrig (radio); pasmaak (koeël).
rectilin'eal, rectilin'ear, reglynig.
rec'titude, regskapenheid, opregtheid, onkreukbaarheid; juistheid, korrektheid.
rec'tor, rektor, prinsipaal (universiteit); predikant; ~ *ate* = rectorship; ~ **al**, ~ '**ial**, rektoraal; ~ **ship**, rektoraat, rektorskap; leraarskap (kerk); ~ **y**, (..**ries**), pastorie; rektorswoning.
rec'trix (..**trices**), stertveer.
rec'tum, (..**ta**), endelderm, nersderm, fondament, rektum.
recul'tivate, herbou; weer verbou.
recum'bency, leënde (leunende) houding.
recum'bent, leunend, rustend, liggend; ~ *on (against)*, liggende op, leunende op; ~ **fold**, liggende plooi.
recup'erate, herstel, beter word, kragte herwin, aansterk, herkry, opknap.
recupera'tion, herstel, herkryging (gesondheid).
recup'erative, (n) versterkende middel; (a) herstellings=, herstellend, versterkend; ~ **capacity**, herstel(lings)vermoë; ~ **leave**, herstelverlof; ~ **power**, herstel(lings)vermoë.
recur', (**-red**), terugkom, weerkeer; herhaal); byval, voor die gees kom; repeteer; ~ *to the MEMORY*, te binne skiet; ~ **rence**, terugkeer, herhaling; ~ *rent fever*, wederkerende koors; ~ **ring**, weer gebeur; repeterend (wisk.); ~ *ring DECIMAL*, repeterende breuk; ~ *ring FRACTION*, repeterende breuk.
recurv'ate, teruggebuig; ombuiging.
recurv'ature, terugbuiging; ombuiging.
recurve', terugbuig; ombuig.
rec'usance, rec'usancy, hardnekkige weiering, weerbarstigheid.
rec'usant, (n) weieraar; weerspannige; (a) afwysend; weierend; opstandig.
recusa'tion, wraking, onttrekking (deur regsbeoefenaar); weiering.
recuse', verwerp, beswaar maak; onttrek, rekuseer, wraak (reg); *the judge* ~ *d himself*, die (regter) het hom onttrek (gewraak).

recut', (~), versny; hergraveer.
Red, (n) Kommunis, Rooie; (a) Kommunisties; Russies; *the* ~ *ARMY*, die Russiese leër; *the* ~ *CROSS*, die Rooi Kruis; *the* ~ *Cross Society*, die Rooi Kruisvereniging; *the* ~ *FLAG*, die Rooi Vlag; *the* ~ *SEA*, die Rooi See.
red, (n) rooiheid; rooie; rooi kleur; rooi bal; *be in the* ~, oortrek (oortrokke) wees; (v) rooi wees; rooi maak; bloos; (a) rooi; ~ *with ANGER*, woedend kwaad; *he hasn't a* ~ *cent*, hy besit geen bloue duit nie; *he doesn't care a* ~ *CENT*, hy gee geen flenter om nie; *DARK* ~, donkerrooi; *become* ~ *in the FACE*, rooi word; bloos; *GROW* ~, bloos; rooi word; *see the* ~ *LIGHT*, gevaar sien; *PAINT the town* ~, aan 'n fuif in die dorp deelneem; *it is like a* ~ *RAG to a bull*, dit werk op hom soos 'n rooi lap op 'n bul; *SEE* ~, woedend word; jou bloedig vererg; ~ *as a TURKEY COCK*, so rooi soos 'n kalkoenmannetjie; ~ *and WHITE*, rooibont.
redact', redigeer, persklaar maak; ~ **ion**, redaksie; nuwe uitgawe; (die) redigeer.
red: ~ **admiral**, admiraalskoenlapper; ~ **ambercane**, soetriet.
redan', borswering.
red: ~ **bait**, rooiaas; ~ **-billed finch (quelea)**, rooibekvink; ~ **-bill teal**, rooibekeend; ~ **-billed hoopoe**, rooibekkakelaar; ~ **blood corpuscle**, rooi bloedligaampie; ~ **bolus**, rooibolus; ~ **book**, staatsalmanak; adelboek; ~ **breast**, rooiborsie; ~ **-breasted wryneck**, draaihals; ~ **buck**, impala, rooibok; ~ **-bush tea**, rooibostee; ~ **cabbage**, rooikool; ~ **-cheeked**, met rooi wange, rooiwangig; ~ **clay**, rooi (diepsee)klei; ~ **clover**, rooiklawer; ~ **coat**, rooibaadjie; ~ **currant**, rooi aalbes; ~ **deer**, edelhert; ~ **den**, rooi maak, rooi kleur; rooi word; bloos; ~ **disa**, rooidisa, bakkiesblom; ~ **dish**, rooierig.
reddi'tion, teruggawe, uitlewering.
red'dle, (n) rooikryt, rooioker; (v) rooi smeer.
red'-duck, smee-eendjie.
redec'orate, weer versier, herversier.
reded'icate, weer toewy, opnuut toewy.
rededica'tion, hertoewyding.
redeem', terugkoop; loskoop, afkoop, vrykoop; van sonde verlos, red; vervul, nakom; aflos, inlos, amortiseer, delg (skuld); boet, vergoed, goedmaak kompenseer; ~ *a DEBT*, 'n skuld delg; ~ *a PLEDGE*, 'n pand aflos; ~ *a PROMISE*, jou woord gestand doen; ~ **able**, aflosbaar, inlosbaar; te herstel.
Redeem'er, Verlosser, Heiland.
redeem'er, losser.
redeem'ing, verlossend; ~ **blood**, soenbloed; ~ **death**, soendood; ~ **feature**, goeie hoedanigheid, goeie eienskap, ligpunt.
redelib'erate, heroorweeg.
redeliv'er, weer bevry; teruggee; weer aflewer; weer oorbring; ~ **y**, teruggawe; herbevryding; herafflewering; ~ **y charges**, herafleweringskoste.
redemand', terugvorder, terugeis.
redemp'tion, verlossing, bevryding; afkoping, (in)lossing, vrykoping; delging, aflossing; *EQUITY of* ~, inlossingsreg; *be PAST* ~, reddeloos verlore wees; aan hom is geen salf te smeer nie; ~ **fund**, delgingsfonds, amortisasiefonds.
redemp'tive, afkopend, verlossend.
redemp'tory, verlossings=; ~ **price**, losprys.
red en'sign, (Britse) koopvaardyvlag.
redescend', weer na onderto gaan, weer afdaal.
redesign', herontwerp.
redes'ignate, hernoem.
red: ~ **-eyed**, met rooi oë; ~ **-eyed pochard**, bruineend; ~ **fire**, Bengaalse vuur.
red' gum¹, rooi bloekom.
red' gum², spru.
red: ~ **-haired**, met rooi hare, rooihaar=; ~ **-handed**, op heter daad; *be caught* ~ *-handed*, op heter daad betrap word; ~ **hare**, rooihaas; ~ **hartebeest**, rooihartbees; ~ **hat**, kardinaalshoed; ~ **head**, rooikop; ~ **heat**, rooihitte, gloeihitte.
red herring, bokkem; *DRAW a* ~ *across the track*, die aandag van 'n saak aflei; *neither FISH, flesh nor good* ~, vis nog vlees.

red-hot 1174 reel oven

red-hot, rooigloeiend, gloeiend warm; *make* ~, hits; ~ **poker,** vuurpyl.
Red' Indian, Rooihuid, Indiaan.
redin'tegrate, herstel, vernuwe, die eenheid herstel.
redintegra'tion, herstelling, vernuwing.
redirect', agternastuur, aanstuur, nastuur, nasend, heradresseer; ~**ion,** aansturing, nasending.
redisco'ver, weer ontdek, herontdek; ~**y,** herontdek= king.
redistil', (-led), oorstook; ~**la'tion,** oorstoking.
redistrib'ute, opnuut uitdeel, herverdeel.
redistribu'tion, herindeling, redistribusie.
redivide', herverdeel, weer indeel.
redivi'sion, herverdeling.
rediviv'us, herrys, herrese, redivivus.
red: ~ **ivory,** rooihout, rooi-ivoor *(Phyllogeiton zey= heri);* ~ **jackal,** rooijakkals; ~ **keel,** rooigrond; ~**-knobbed coot,** bleshoender; ~ **lead,** rooiminie, rooilood; ~**-letter,** gedenkwaardig, besonder; ~*- letter day,* gedenkwaardige dag, geluksdag; ~ **light,** rooi lig; *see the* ~ *light,* gevaar sien, onraad merk; ~**-light district,** ongure buurt, bordeelbuurt; ~ **meat,** rooivleis; ~ **mungoose,** rooimuishond; ~*- necked frankolin,* rooikeelfisant; ~**ness** rooiheid, rooiigheid.
red'olence, geurigheid, geur, welriekendheid.
red'olent, welriekend, geurig; *be* ~ *of,* ruik na; vervul wees met die geur van; die herinnering wek aan.
redou'ble, verdubbel, vermeerder, aangroei, toe= neem; herhaal; redoebleer (kaartspel).
redoubt', skans, versterking, vesting; ~**able,** gedug, gevrees; vreeslik.
redound', terugstuit, terugkeer; strek tot, bydra tot; uitloop op; voortvloei; *the BENEFITS that* ~ *to us,* die voordele wat vir ons daaruit voortvloei; ~ *to the CREDIT of,* tot eer strek van.
red' pepper, Spaanse peper; rissiepeper, rooipeper.
Red' Poll, Rooipoenskop(bees).
redraft', (n) nuwe ontwerp; omwerking; retoerwissel; (v) opnuut wissel; herontwerp; omwerk, weer op= stel, herformuleer.
redraw', (..drew, -n), oorteken; opnuut trek; ~**n,** oorgeteken.
redress'¹, (v) weer aantrek.
redress'², (n) herstel(ling); verhaal; verhelp(ing); ver= goeding; (v) herstel, verhelp, regmaak, verbeter, vergoed; ~**ment,** herstel.
Red' Riding Hood, Rooikappie.
red: ~ **roan,** rooiskimmel; ~ **roman,** rooiroman; ~ **scale,** rooi dopluis.
Red'skin, Rooihuid, Indiaan.
red: ~ **spider,** rooispinnekop; ~ **steenbras,** rooisteen= bras; ~ **stumpnose,** rooistompneus; ~ **tab,** rooilus; ~ **tape,** rooi lint (lett.); rompslomp (fig.); burokra= sie, amptelike omslagtigheid, amptenary; ~**-ta= pery,** burokrasie, amptenary, rompslomp; ~**-ta= pey,** amptelik, omslagtig; ~**-tapism,** burokrasie, amptenary, rompslomp; ~**-tapist,** burokraat; ~ **terror'(ism),** (rooi) skrikbewind.
reduce', herlei, reduseer (wisk.); verminder, afmerk, afkom (prys); inkrimp, verklein; verkort; onder= werp (vyand); kleinkry; bedwing; verdun; verlaag, degradeer, terugsit (in rang) verower, inneem (ves= ting); ligter maak, vermaer, verslank, afbring (ge= wig); ~ *to ASHES,* in die as lê; ~ *to BEGGARY,* tot die bedelstaf bring; *in* ~*d circumstances,* ar= moedig, behoeftig; ~ *to a common denominator,* gelyknamig maak; ~*d to DESPAIR,* tot wanhoop gedryf; ~ *the ESTABLISHMENT,* die personeel verminder; ~ *by FAMINE,* uithonger; ~ *to POV= ERTY,* verarm, tot armoede bring; ~ *to POW= DER,* fynmaal; ~ *one's POWER,* die mag inkort; ~*d PRICES,* verminderde pryse; ~ *to the RANKS,* degradeer; ~*d RATE,* verlaagde tarief; *in a* ~*d STATE,* swak; ~ *to SUBMISSION,* tot on= derwerping dwing; ~ *to TEARS,* laat huil; ~**ment,** herleiding; vermindering; onderwerping; ~**r,** ver= loopsok; afswakker; reduseerder.
redu'cible, herleibaar; verkleinbaar.
redu'cing: ~ **agent,** reduksiemiddel, reduseermid= del; ~ **compass,** reduksiepasser, herleidingspasser; ~ **flame,** reduseervlam; ~ **furnace,** reduksieoond;

~ **socket,** verloopsok; ~ **valve,** drukverligtings= klep.
reduc'tion, herleiding (wisk.); terugbrenging; verla= ging (berekening); beperking; korting, afslag (han= del); reduksie (skeik.); terugsetting (reg); verminde= ring, afname; onderwerping; inkrimping, inkor= ting; degradering (in rang); verswakking (fot.); *AT a* ~, teen 'n verminderde prys; ~ *in PRICES,* prys= vermindering, prysverlaging; *TABLE OF* ~, her= leidingstafel; ~ *of WAGES,* loonsvermindering; ~ **worker,** reduksiewerker; ~ **works,** reduksiewerk= plaas; smeltoond.
reduc'tive, verminderend.
redun'dance, redun'dancy, oortolligheid, oorbodig= heid; oorvloed, oordaad.
redun'dant, oortollig; oorvloedig, weelderig.
redup'licate, verdubbel; reduplisser (gram.).
reduplica'tion, verdubbeling, herhaling; redupli= kasie.
redup'licative, verdubbelend; redupliserend.
red: ~**-water,** rooiwater (by dier); bilharziase (by mens); ~ **weed,** varkgras, papawer; ~**wing,** koper= wiek; ~ **wing partridge,** rooivlerkpatrys; ~**-winged starling,** rooivlerkspreeu.
reeb'ok, = **rhebok.**
re-ech'o, (n) weerkaatsing; naklank; (v) weergalm, weerkaats, naklink; herhaal.
reed, (n) fluitjiesriet, riet; matjiesgoed; biesie; fluitjie; wewerskam; balein; tongetjie (in orrel); (pl) riete, fluitjiesriet; biesies; *a BROKEN* ~, 'n geknakte riet; *COMMON* ~, fluitjiesriet; *LEAN on a* ~, op 'n swakkeling staatmaak; *SPANISH* ~, spaans= riet; *a* ~ *shaken by the WIND,* 'n riet wat deur die wind beweeg word; (v) met riete dek; 'n rietjie insit; ~ **babbler,** rietvink; ~ **buck,** rietbok; ~ **cormorant,** rietduiker; ~**ed,** met riet begroei; ~ **fence,** riet= skerm; ~ **fescue,** vleigras; ~ **grass,** rietgras; ~*- hen,* riethaantjie; ~ **hut,** matjieshuis.
re-ed'ify, (..fied), herbou, weer opbou.
reed: ~**-pipe,** rietfluit; tongstem (orrel); ~**-plane,** rif= felskaaf; ~ **screen,** rietskerm; ~**-warbler,** parkiet; rietsanger, rietvink; ~**y,** rieterig, vol riet; krassend; swak, skraal, tingerig.
re-ed'ucate, heropvoed.
re-educa'tion, heropvoeding.
reef¹, (n) reef; (v) reef, die seile inbind.
reef², (n) rif; klipbank, rotslaag; *basal* ~, voetrif, ba= saalrif; ~**-cutter,** rifsaag, rifsnyer.
reef'er¹, rewer (van seile); platknoop; oorknoop= baadjie.
reef'er², rifwerker.
reef' gold, rifgoud, aargoud.
reef: ~**ing,** (die) reef; ~**-knot,** platknoop, kruis= knoop.
reef' packing, rifopvulling.
reef' point, spanpunt.
reef' width, rifdikte.
reek, (n) wasem, damp, rook; walm; stank; (v) rook, walm; damp, wasem; sleg ruik, stink; *the hall* ~*ed of tobacco smoke,* die saal het gestink van tabak= rook; ~**y,** rokerig, berook, swart.
reel¹, (n) riel (dans); wankelende gang, slingerbewe= ging; *DANCE a* ~, askoek slaan; *RIGHT off the* ~, een streep deur; (v) waggel, wankel; duisel, dui= selig word; slinger, swaai, aanslinger (dronkaard); warrel, dwarrel; 'n riel dans; ~ *ALONG,* aanslin= ger; ~ *to and FRO,* heen en weer slinger; *my HEAD* ~*s,* my kop draai, ek word duiselig.
reel², (n) rolletjie; spoel, rol; garetolletjie, klos; dwar= rel; katrolstok (hengel); *(straight) off the* ~, vinnig na mekaar, sonder aarseling; (v) opdraai, oprol, opwen; ~ *off a LINE,* 'n tou afrol (laat afloop); ~ *something OFF,* iets soos 'n rympie opsê; iets af= rammel; ~ *off POETRY,* poësie aframmel; ~ *OUT,* afrol, vier.
re-elect', herkies; ~**ion,** herkiesing.
re-el'igible, herkiesbaar, weer verkiesbaar.
reel'ing¹, slingering; *be* ~ *with DRINK,* twee rye spo= re loop; die straat meet; *he IS* ~, die wêreld draai met hom.
reel'ing², (die) opdraai, opdraaiing.
reel oven, haspeloond.

re-embark', weer inskeep, herinskeep; ~ **a'tion**, weerinskeping, herinskeping; ~ **a'tion leave**, inskepingsverlof.
re-emerge', weer verskyn, herverskyn, weer te voorskyn kom; ~ **nce**, herverskyning.
re-enact', weer vasstel; ~ **ment**, hervasstelling.
re-enforce', weer deurdryf; weer van krag maak.
re-engage', opnuut verbind; diens vernuwe, opnuut in diens neem, weer in diens neem; opnuut slaags raak; ~ **ment**, diensvernuwing, nuwe dienstermyn.
re-enlist', opnuut inskryf; opnuut in diens neem; ~ **ment**, herinskrywing; hernieude indiensneming.
re-en'ter, weer binnekom; herinskryf.
re-en'trance, weerintreding.
re-en'trant, (n) inspringende hoek; (a) inspringend.
re-en'try, herinskrywing; weerintreding; *card of* ~, trekkaart, slagkaart.
re-erect', weer opbou, heropbou; ~ **ion**, weeropbouing, heropbouing.
re-estab'lish, herstel, weer oprig; ~ **ment**, herstel=(ling), weeroprigting.
reeve[1], (n) wyfiekemphaan.
reeve[2], (n) skout; opsigter; balju.
reeve[3], (v) (rove or -d), inskeer (skeepsterm); steek deur; vasbind; jou deurwerk.
re-examina'tion, hereksamen; nuwe ondersoek, herondervraging.
re-exam'ine, weer ondersoek; herkeur; hereksamineer; herondervra.
re-exchange', (n) omwisseling; herwisseling; uitwisseling; (v) omwissel; omspan; herwissel.
re-ex'port, (n) heruitvoer.
re-export', (v) weer uitvoer; ~ **a'tion**, heruitvoer.
ref, *abbr. of* **referee**, (n) skeidsregter (by sport); (v) as skeidsregter optree.
refash'ion, omvorm, omwerk; ~ **ing**, omvorming, omwerking.
refa'sten, verbind.
refec'tion, verversing; tussenmaaltyd, ligte maaltyd.
refec'tory, (..ries), eetsaal, refter, eetkamer.
refer', (-red), verwys; sinspeel op, betrekking hê op; melding maak van; refereer; toeskryf aan; voorlê aan, onderwerp aan; jou beroep op; ~ *BACK*, terugverwys; ~ *to a BOOK*, 'n boek naslaan; na 'n boek verwys; *the BOOK* ~ *red to*, die genoemde boek; ~ *to a DICTIONARY*, 'n woordeboek raadpleeg; ~ *to DRAWER*, verwys na trekker; *EASY to* ~, maklik om na te slaan; *I* ~ *myself to your GENEROSITY*, ek beroep my op u goedhartigheid; ~ *a MATTER to*, 'n saak verwys na; *the PERSON* ~ *red to*, die betrokkene; ~ *TO*, verwys na, slaan op, betrekking hê op; ~ *him TO me*, verwys hom na my; ~ *to one's WATCH*, 'n mens se oorlosie raadpleeg.
ref'erable, verwysbaar na; toe te skryf aan; terug te bring tot.
referee', (n) skeidsregter; (v) skeidsregter wees; as skeidsregter optree; ~ **ing**, skeidsregterswerk.
ref'erence, verwysing, referte; sinspeling; melding, gewag; referensie (handel); getuigskrif, verband, betrekking; uitspraak, beslissing; raadpleging, (die) naslaan; verwysteken; bewysplaas; *BEAR* ~ *to*, betrekking hê op; *BOOK of* ~, naslaanboek, vraagboek; *for EASY* ~, om maklik te kan naslaan; *for FUTURE* ~, vir toekomstige gebruik; *HAVE* ~ *to*, betrekking hê op; *IN* ~ *to*, met verwysing na; met toespeling op; *MAKE no* ~ *to*, nie verwys nie na; *have NO* ~ *to*, nie slaan nie op; geen betrekking hê nie op; *ON* ~ *to*, by die naslaan van; *for* ~ *s PLEASE apply to*, wend u om inligting asseblief tot; *TERMS of* ~, opdrag; *WITH* ~ *to*, met betrekking tot; met verwysing na (u brief), met referte tot; ~ **book**, naslaanboek; ~ **library**, naslaanbiblioteek; ~ **number**, verwys(ings)nommer.
referen'dary, (..ries), referendaris.
referen'dum, (..da), referendum, volkstemming.
referen'tial, verwysings-; ~ *meaning*, verwysingsbetekenis.
refer'ring, verwysing; betrekking; ~ *to*, na aanleiding van, met betrekking tot.
refill', (n) nuwe vulling, hervulling; vervanger; nuwe battery, potlood, ens.

refill', (v) opnuut vul, weer vol maak, byvul.
refine', verfyn, beskawe; veredel; louter, suiwer, raffineer (suiker); afdrywe (goud); uitpluis; spitsvondig wees; fineer, affineer (metale); ~ *on a statement*, oor 'n verklaring uitwei.
refined', gesuiwer, geraffineer; (ver)fyn, beskaaf; *a* ~ *accent*, 'n deftige uitspraak; ~ **cruelty**, geraffineerde (verfynde) wreedheid; ~ **gold**, geaffineerde goud; ~ **iron**, louteryster; ~ **manners**, beskaafde maniere; ~ **morals**, verfynde sedes; ~ **steel**, loutersstaal; ~ **sugar**, geraffineerde suiker.
refine': ~ **ment**, verfyning; beskawing, veredeling; loutering, suiwering; geaardheid, raffinement; ~ **r**, verfyner; louteraar; suiweraar, raffinadeur; affineerder (van metale); ~ **ry**, (..ries), raffinadery; suiweringsfabriek; affineerdery (metale).
refin'ing: ~ **furnace**, gaaroond; ~ **works**, raffinadery (suiker); affineerdery (metale).
refit', (n) herstel, reparasie; vernuwing; (v) (-ted), herstel, repareer; opnuut uitrus; weer aanpas.
reflect', weerkaats, afstraal, afspieël, weerspieël; nadink, wik, oorpeins, besin, oorweeg; reflekteer; terugwerp; afwyk; ongunstig uitlaat, onaangename opmerkings maak; sinspeel op; ~ *ABOUT*, oordink; ~ *CREDIT on*, tot eer strek; ~ *upon one's good FORTUNE*, oor jou voorspoed nadink; ~ *UPON*, blaam werp op, in 'n ongunstige lig plaas; nadink oor.
reflect'ed, weerkaats, gereflekteer, afgespieël; ~ **angle**, hoek van terugkaatsing; ~ **glory**, ontleende luister; ~ **lustre**, ontleende luister; ~ **ray**, gebreekte straal.
reflec'ting paper, glimpapier.
reflec'tion, weerkaatsing, weerspieëling, afskynsel, afspieëling; straalbreking; spieëlbeelddenke; nabetragting, oordenking, besinning, bedenking, refleksie; afkeuring, verdagmakery, blaam, verwyt; haat-like toespeling; *ANGLE of* ~, uitvalshoek; *CAST a* ~ *upon*, skimp op; blaam werp op; verdag maak; ~ *on someone's INTELLIGENCE*, geringskatting van iem. se verstand; ~ *of LIGHT*, ligweerkaatsing; *ON* ~, by nader oorweging.
reflec'tive, weerkaatsend, weerspieëlend; peinsend, nadenkend, bespieëlend; wederkerend; ~ **index**, brekingsindeks.
reflec'tor, straalbreker; reflektor, skynwerper; weerkaatser; trukaatser; ~ **strip**, glimlig, glimstrook.
ref'lex, (n) (-es) weerkaatste beeld; afspieëling, weerspieëling; afstraling, weerkaatsing; refleksbeweging; (a) teruggekaats; refleks-; selfbespieëlend, ondersoekend, introspektief; ~ **action**, refleksbeweging; - **angle**, inspringende hoek; ~ **arc**, omkeerboog, refleksboog.
reflexibil'ity, weerkaatsbaarheid.
reflex'ible, weerkaatsbaar.
reflex'ive, (n) refleksief; (a) terugsiende; wederkerend, refleksief; ~ **verb**, wederkerende werkwoord, refleksief.
ref'lex reflector, straalkaatser.
refloat' weer vlot maak.
reflou'rish, herbloei.
reflow', terugvloei.
ref'luence, ref'luency, terugvloeiing.
ref'luent, terugvloeiend.
ref'lux, terugvloeiing, eb; ~ **condenser**, terugvloeikoeler; ~ **valve**, terugslagklep.
refold', weer vou; hervou.
refo'rest, herbebos.
reform'[1], (n) hervorming, verbetering; beterskap; (v) hervorm, verbeter, reformeer.
reform'[2], (v) weer vorm, opnuut vorm; ~ **a'tion**, hervorming, reformasie; *the Reformation*, die Hervorming; ~ **'ative**, hervormend; verbeterend, verbeterings-; ~ **'atory**, (n) (..ries), verbeterskool, verbeteringsgestig, verbeterhuis; (a) hervormend; verbeterings-; ~ **ed**, hervormd, gereformeerd; *R* ~ *ed Church*, Hervormde Kerk; Gereformeerde Kerk; ~ **er**, hervormer; **R** ~ **er**, Hervormer; ~ **ist**, (n) hervormingsinde; (a) hervormingsgesind.
refortifica'tion, hernude versterking.
refort'ify, (..fied), opnuut versterk.
refound', weer stig, herstig.

refract', breek (ligstraal); ~ **able**, breekbaar.
refract'ion, straalbreking; breking; *ANGLE of* ~, brekingshoek; ~ *OF LIGHT*, ligbreking; ~**ist**, gesigkundige.
refract': ~ **ive**, (straal)brekend; brekings=; ~ *ive index*, brekingsindeks; ~ **or**, refraktor; dioptriese kyker; ~ **oriness**, vuurvastheid, vuurbestendigheid; weerspannigheid, weerbarstigheid.
refract'ory, (n) vuurvaste artikel, vuurvaste stof, vuurvaste ware; (a) weerspannig, eiesinnig, hardnekkig, onhandelbaar, balhorig, weerbarstig; vuurvas, vuurbestand; *the CHILD is* ~ *with me*, die kind trotseer my; ~ *PERIOD*, onvatbare periode.
ref'ragable, weerlegbaar.
refrain'[1], (n) refrein.
refrain'[2], (v) beteuel, bedwing, terughou, inhou; ~ *FROM*, nalaat, jou onthou van (drank); ~ *FROM doing something*, jou weerhou daarvan om iets te doen.
refrangibil'ity, breekbaarheid.
refran'gible, breekbaar.
refresh', verfris, verkwik, laaf; verkoel; ~ *the INNER man*, die inwendige mens versterk; ~ *one's KNOWLEDGE*, jou kennis opknap; ~ *one's MEMORY*, die geheue opfris; ~ **er**, opknappertjie, opfrisser, verkwikker; versterkinkie; ekstratjie; ~ **er course**, opknappertjie; opknap(pings)kursus, herhalingskursus, stoomkursus, opfrissingskursus; lenteskool; ~ **ing**, (n) opfrissing; (a) verfrissend, verkwikkend, verkoelend.
refresh'ment, verversing, lawing, opfrissing, verkwikking; (pl) verversings; versnaperinge; ~ **room**, verversingskamer, verversingsplek; ~ **stall**, verversingskraampie.
refri'gerant, (n) verkoelende middel, verkoelmiddel; (a) verkoelend.
refri'gerate, verkoel, koel maak, ys; ~ *d MEAT*, bevrore vleis; ~ *d SHIP*, koelskip.
refri'gerating, koel=, koelend; ~ **chamber**, koelkamer; ~ **hold**, koelruim; ~ **plant**, koelinstallasie.
refrigera'tion, koeling; koeltegniek.
refrig'erative, koelend.
refri'gerator, koelkas; koelkamer, afkoeler; koelvat; ~ **y**, (n) (. . **ries**), vrieskamer; kondensator; koelkamer; (a) verkoelend.
reft, beroof; *kyk* **reave**.
refu'el, (-led), brandstof inneem; bunker; ~ **ling**, brandstofinname; bunkering; ~ **ling station**, vulstasie.
ref'uge, (n) toevlug, skuilplek, beskerming, toevlugsoord, heenkome; toeverlaat; vryplaas, wykplaas; *CITY of* ~, vrystad; *HOUSE of* ~, tehuis vir dakloses; *TAKE* ~ *in*, jou toevlug neem tot; (v) beskerm; (jou) toevlug soek.
refugee', vlugteling, uitgewekene; ~ **camp**, vlugtelingekamp ~ **-capital**, vlugkapitaal.
reful'gence, reful'gency, glansrykheid, glans, luister, skittering.
reful'gent, glinsterend, glansryk.
refund', (n) terugbetaling; (v) terugbetaal, teruggee, vergoed; ~ **book**, terugbetalingsboek.
refurb'ish, opnuut polys; opknap; opkalfater.
return'ish, nuut meubileer; hermeubileer.
refus'able, afwysbaar.
refus'al, weiering, afwysing; verwerping; opsie, keuse; *FIRST* ~, opsie; *a FLAT* ~, 'n besliste weiering; *GIVE the* ~ *of*, 'n opsie hê (gee) op; *MEET with a* ~, afgewys word; *TAKE no* ~, geen weiering aanneem nie.
ref'use[1], (n) afval, oorskiet, vuilgoed; uitskot, skuim; vuilis; (a) vuilgoed=, vuil; waardeloos.
refuse'[2], (v) weier, afslaan, van die hand wys, afwys, wegwys, bedank, verwerp; inhou; *BE* ~ *d*, afgewys word, 'n weiering kry; ~ *a CALL*, vir 'n oproep bedank; *what one* ~ *s one LOSES*, wat jy bedank, is jy kwyt; ~ *ONESELF something*, jou iets ontsê; ~ *a PERSON something*, iem. iets weier; ~ *POINTBLANK*, botweg weier.
ref'use: ~ **bin**, vuilgoedblik, vuilisblik; ~ **chute**, vuilgoedgeut, vuilisgeut; ~ **consumer**, vuilgoedoond; ~ **dump**, ashoop, vuilisoond; ~ **heap**, vuilishoop; ~ **iron**, ou-yster.

refus'er, weieraar.
ref'use tin, vuilgoedblik, vuilisblik, vullisbak.
refutabil'ity, weerlêbaarheid.
ref'utable, weerlêbaar.
refuta'tion, weerlegging; ontsenuwing.
refute', weerlê; ontsenu; teenspreek; ~ **r**, weerlêer; teenargument.
regain', herwin, terugkry; weer bereik; ~ *CONSCIOUSNESS*, die bewussyn herwin; bykom; ~ *one's FEET*, weer op die been kom.
reg'al, koninklik, vorstelik.
regale', (n) gasmaal, onthaal; (v) onthaal, trakteer, vergas; ~ *with*, trakteer op; ~ **ment**, onthaal.
regal'ia, koninklike waardigheidstekens; ampsierade; kroonsierade; *in full* ~, in volle ornaat.
regal'ity, koninklike waardigheid, koningskap; koninkryk; koninklike voorreg.
regard', (n) agting, ontsag, eerbied; opsig; verband, betrekking; aandag; (pl) groete; *having* ~ *to all the CIRCUMSTANCES*, met inagneming van al die omstandighede; *KIND* ~ *s to*, groete aan; *have NO* ~ *for others*, jou nie aan ander (se gevoelens, gerief) steur nie; *OUT of* ~ *for*, met die oog op, ten opsigte van; *PAY* ~ *to*, rekening hou met, let op; *in THIS* ~, in hierdie opsig; *WITH* ~ *to*, met betrekking tot, nopens, ten aansien van, ten opsigte van; *WITHOUT* ~ *to (for)*, sonder om jou te bekommer oor; (v) beskou, gadeslaan, ag; betref; in aanmerking neem; omgee; *he does not* ~ *my ADVICE*, hy slaan geen ag op my raad nie; *AS* ~ *s myself*, wat my betref; *AS* ~ *s this*, wat dit betref; ~ *someone with SUSPICION*, iem. met agterdog beskou; ~ *something as WRONG*, iets as verkeerd beskou.
regard'ant, omsienend, omsiende; oplettend.
regard'ful, oplettend, opmerksaam; *be* ~ *of*, let op, in die oog hou, eerbiedig; sorg vir.
regard'ing, aangaande, met betrekking tot, betreffende, nopens, belangende; ~ *this*, wat dit betref.
regard'less, onoplettend, onagsaam; ~ *of EXPENSE*, sonder om koste te bespaar; geen koste ontsien nie; ~ *OF*, onverskillig vir.
regath'er, weer versamel; weer bymekaarkom.
regatt'a, roeiwedstryd, seilwedstryd, regatta.
regauge', heryk.
regelate', aanmekaarvries.
regela'tion, aaneenvriesing.
re'gency, (. . **cies**), regentskap; ~ **council**, regentskapsraad.
regen'eracy, wedergeboorte, herlewing.
regen'erate, (v) laat herleef, herskep, tot nuwe lewe bring, regenereer; (a) wedergebore.
regenera'tion, wedergeboorte; herlewing, verjonging, regenerasie, vernuwing; weefselherstel.
regen'erative, vernuwend, herlewend, herskeppend.
regen'erator, weeropwekker, herskepper; warmteversamelaar; regeneratoroond; ~ **y** = **regenerative**.
regen'esis, vernuwing, wedergeboorte.
re'gent, (n) regent; vors, bewindhebber; *Queen R* ~, koningin-regentes; (a) heersend, regerend; ~ **ess**, (-es), regentes; ~ **ship**, regentskap.
regerm'inate, weer ontkiem.
re'gicide, koningsmoord; koningsmoordenaar.
regime', regering, bestuur, regime, regeringstelsel; *under the old* ~, onder die ou stelsel.
re'gimen, leefreël; dieet; huishouding, regimen; stelsel; regering; *under* ~, op dieet.
re'giment, (n) regiment; (v) orden; dissiplineer; reglementeer.
regimen'tal, regiments=; reglementêr; ~ **band**, regimentsorkes; ~ **clothes**, regimentsuniform; ~ **colours**, regimentsvaandel; ~ **commander**, regimentsbevelvoerder; ~ **cook**, regimentskok; ~ **crest**, regimentswapen; ~ **duties**, regimentsdiens, troepdiens; regimentswagte; ~ **front**, regimentsfront; ~ **headquarters**, regimentshoofkwartier; ~ **number**, soldatenommer; ~ **officer**, regimentsoffisier; troepoffisier; frontoffisier; ~ **orders**, regimentsbevele, regimentsorders; ~ **paymaster**, regimentsbetaalmeester; ~ **s**, uniform, mondering; ~ **tailor**, regimentskleremaker.
regimenta'tion, organisasie, reglementering; dissiplinering; indeling.

re'gion, streek; landstreek, gewes, gebied; oord; sfeer; *the ~ of the HEART,* die hartstreek; *IN the ~ of,* in die omgewing van; in dié geweste; *IN the ~ of* R100, omtrent R100; *the LOWER (NETHER) ~s,* die onderwêreld; *the UPPER ~s,* die hemel.

re'gional, streek=, gewestelik; ~ **authority,** streek= owerheid; ~ **committee,** streekkomitee; ~ **court,** streekhof; ~ **development,** streekontwikkeling; ~**ly,** streeksgewys(e); ~ **magistrate,** streekland= dros; ~ **metamorphism,** streekmetamorfose; ~ **news,** streeknuus; ~ **office,** streekkantoor; ~ **plan= ning,** streekbeplanning; streekindeling; ~ **represen= tative,** streekverteenwoordiger.

re'gister, (n) register; rol, lys, kieserslys; skuif, plaat (van 'n pyp); kontroletoestel; orrelregister; inskry= wingsboek; kasregister; vreemdelingeboek; ~ *of ATTENDANCE,* presensielys; *BE on the ~,* op die rol staan; *KEEP a ~ of,* 'n lys hou van; ~ *of VO= TERS,* kieserslys; (v) registreer, inskryf; aanteken; staan op; (aan)wys; indruk maak op; begryp word; ~ *100 DEGREES,* 100 grade aanwys; ~ *FEAR,* vrees verraai; ~ *a HIT,* raak skiet; ~ *a LETTER,* 'n brief laat aanteken (registreer); *the NAME simply didn't ~ with me,* die naam het geen indruk op my gemaak nie; ~ *a PROTEST,* 'n protes aan= teken (indien); ~ *as STUDENT,* jou as student laat inskryf; ~ *a VOW,* 'n eed aflê, plegtig beloof.

re'gistered, geregistreer, aangeteken; ~ *in the name of the BANK,* staan op naam v.d. bank; ~ *BONDS,* aandele; ~ *as a COMMERCIAL bank,* as handelsbank geregistreer; ~ *at the G.P.O. as a newspaper,* by die poswese as nuusblad geregi= streer; ~ *HOLDER,* ingeskrewe aandeelhouer; ~ *LETTER,* aangetekende (geregistreerde) brief; ~ *OFFICE,* geregistreerde kantoor; *by ~ POST,* per aangetekende (geregistreerde) pos; ~ *SHARE= HOLDER,* ingeskrewe aandeelhouer; ~ *TON= NAGE,* registertonnemaat.

re'gister: ~ **office,** registrasiekantoor; ~ **ther= mometer,** selfregistrerende termometer; ~ **ton,** re= gisterton.

re'gistrar, registrateur (universiteit, aktekantoor); griffier (reg); ~ *of the COURT,* griffier; ~ *of DEEDS,* registrateur van aktes; ~**ship,** registra= teurskap; griffierskap.

registra'tion, registrasie, inskrywing; aantekening (brief); ~ **certificate,** registrasiebewys; ~ **fee,** in= skrywingsgeld; aantekenkoste (pos); ~ **form,** in= skrywingsvorm; ~ **letter,** registrasieletter; registra= siebrief; ~ **mark,** inskrywingsmerk; ~ **number,** in= skrywingsnommer.

re'gistry, (..tries), inskrywing; registrasie, register; registrasiekantoor; huurkantoor; ~ *of shipping,* skeepsregister; ~ **office,** registrasiekantoor.

reg'let, spaan (drukkery); voegloodgroef; plat lysie, vlak lysie; skeilys.

reg'nal, regerings=; ~ **day,** verjaarsdag v.d. troon= bestyging.

reg'nancy, regering, heerskappy.

reg'nant, regerend, heersend.

regorge', opbring; vomeer; weer uitbraak; terugvloei, terugstroom.

regrade', hergradeer.

regrad'ing, hergradering.

regraft', weer ent.

regrant', (n) hernude vergunning; hervergunning; (v) weer verleen.

regrate', opkoop.

reg'ress, (n) terugkeer, teruggang.

regress', (v) teruggaan; agteruitgaan; ~**ion,** terug= keer, teruggang, agteruitgang, regressie; ~**ive,** te= rugkerend, teruggaande, regressief.

regret', (n) berou, verdriet, leedwese; spyt; hartseer; *EXPRESS ~,* spyt te kenne gee; *FEEL ~ at leav= ing my home town,* met droefheid my tuisdorp ver= laat; *HEAR with ~,* met leedwese verneem; *a MATTER of ~,* iets wat te betreur is; *TO my ~,* tot my leedwese; *VIEW with ~,* iets met lede oë aanskou; (v) **(-ted),** spyt wees, betreur; treur oor; *you'll LIVE to ~ it,* dit sal jou nog berou; jy sal dit nog betreur; *I ~ to SAY,* dit spyt my om te sê; ~**ful,** berouvol, bedroef; ~**table,** betreurenswaar=

dig; ~**tably,** jammer genoeg; ~**ted,** betreur; *the error is ~ted,* ons is spyt oor die fout.

regroup', hergroepeer, herindeel; ~**ing,** hergroepe= ring.

regrowth', opslag, hergroei.

reg'ulable, reguleerbaar.

reg'ular, (n) ordegeestelike; vaste werkman; vaste klant (besoeker); (pl) gereelde troepe; (a) gereeld; gestadig; stip; vas, reëlmatig; gelykmatig; trou (le= ser); eg; formeel; staande (troepe); *a ~ BATTLE,* 'n formele geveg; *a ~ FOOL,* 'n regte esel; *a ~ NUISANCE,* 'n ware laspos; ~ **army,** staande mag, beroepsleër; ~ **customers,** vaste klante; ~ **forces,** beroepsoldate, aktiewe strydmagte; ~ **hours,** vaste ure; ~'**ity,** reëlmatigheid, gereeldheid, reëlmaat; ~**iza'tion,** regularisering; ~**ize,** reëlma= tig maak, wettig; ~ **physician,** vaste dokter; ~ **sal= ary,** vaste salaris; ~ **troops** = **regular forces.**

reg'ulate, reël, rangskik; reguleer, regstel; reglemen= teer; ~ *by statute,* by wet bepaal.

reg'ulating, stel; reël, reëling; ~ **cell,** reëlsel; ~ **screw,** stelskroef.

regula'tion, reëling; voorskrif; bepaling, verordening, regulasie; reglement; (pl) diensreëling; ~ **al= lowance,** rantsoen; ~ **boots,** modelstewels; diens= stewels; ~ **fare,** vasgestelde tarief; ~ **issue,** voorge= skrewe uitrusting.

reg'ulative, reëlend, reëlings=, regulerend.

reg'ulator, reëlaar; inrigter; balans; slinger (aan uur= werk); afsluiter (loko.); regulator.

reg'ulus, rumetaal; rusteen; metaalkorrel.

regur'gitate, terugwerp, uitspuug, teruggee, uit= braak; terugvloei.

regurgita'tion, terugwerping; uitbraking; terugvloei= ing.

rehabil'itate, herstel, rehabiliteer.

rehabilita'tion, herstelling, rehabilitasie;. eerher= stel.

rehash', (n) opwarming; opgewarmde kos; geherkou; (v) opwarm; weer opdis; ~ *an old story,* ou kos opwarm; weer ou kos opdis.

rehear', (-d), weer verhoor; herverhoor; ~**ing,** tweede ondersoek; revisie; herverhoor.

rehears'al, herhaling; repetisie; *the play is in ~,* die toneelstuk word gerepeteer.

reheat', opwarm (kos).

rehearse', herhaal, repeteer; opsom.

rehouse', weer 'n huis gee, hervestig; na 'n beter huis verplaas.

rehous'ing scheme, hervestigingskema.

Reich'stag, Ryksdag; Reichstag (Duitse parlement) (hist.).

reign, (n) regering; bestuur; bewind; *DURING the ~ of,* onder die regering (bewind) van; ~ *of TER= ROR,* skrikbewind; (v) regeer, heers.

reignite', weer aan die brand steek; herontsteek.

reillum'inate, weer verlig.

reimbod'y, (..died), opnuut inlywe.

reimburse', terugbetaal, vergoed; ~**ment,** vergoe= ding, terugbetaling.

reim'port, (n) weer ingevoerde (heringevoerde) ar= tikel.

reimport', (v) weer invoer, herinvoer.

reimporta'tion, herinvoer.

reimpose', weer oplê.

reimposi'tion, weeroplegging.

reimpre'ssion, herdruk.

reimpris'on, weer in die gevangenis sit.

rein, (n) leisel (tuig); teuel (toom); *ASSUME the ~s of government,* die bewind aanvaar; *DRAW ~,* stil= hou, inhou; *DROP the ~s,* die teuels neerlê; *give FREE ~ to one's imagination (thoughts),* vrye spel aan jou verbeelding (gedagtes) gee; *assume the ~s of GOVERNMENT,* die bewind aanvaar; *have the ~s firmly in HAND,* vas in die saal sit; die leisels stewig in jou hande hê; *GIVE ~ to,* die vrye loop gee aan; *GIVE the horses the ~s,* die perde die teuels gee; *HOLD the ~s,* die leisels hou; *KEEP on a tight ~,* streng in toom hou; *PULL in the ~s,* die teuels (leisels) stywer trek; *keep a SLACK ~ on,* die teuels (leisels) slap laat hang; *TAKE the ~s,* die bestuur in jou hande neem; *hold a TIGHT ~ over,*

streng in toom hou; (v) leisels hou; in toom hou, beteuel.
reincarn'ate, reïnkarneer, weer vlees word.
reincarna'tion, reïnkarnasie, vleesworing.
reincorp'orate, weer inlyf, herinlyf.
reincorpora'tion, herinlywing.
rein'deer, rendier.
reinfect', opnuut besmet, weer aansteek.
reinforce', (n) versterking; wapening; (v) versterk; wapen; ~ *an ARGUMENT,* nuwe bewyse aan= voer; ~ *d CONCRETE,* gewapende beton; ~ *d CONSTRUCTION,* versterkte konstruksie; ~ *a FORTRESS,* 'n vesting versterk; ~ **ment,** verster= king, wapening; wapeningsmateriaal.
reinfor'cing, versterking; wapening; ~ **plate,** ver= sterkplaat; ~ **steel,** betonstaal.
reinform', weer in kennis stel, weer meld.
reinhab'it, weer bewoon, herbewoon.
reins, niere; lende.
reinsert', weer invoeg, weer inlas, weer plaas; ~**ion,** herplasing.
reinspire', opnuut besiel.
reinstall', weer aanstel, herbenoem.
reinstate', herstel; terugneem; terugplaas; ~ **ment,** herstel; herindiensneming.
reinstruct', weer onderrig; weer gelas.
reinsur'ance, hersersekering.
reinsure', herverseker.
rein'tegrate, hernuwe, herstel.
reintegra'tion, herstel.
reinter', herbegrawe; ~**ment,** herbegrafnis.
reintroduce', weer invoer.
reintroduc'tion, herinvoering.
reinvest', weer beklee; hervestig; opnuut belê, herbe= lê, weer uitsit.
reinves'tigate, weer (opnuut) ondersoek.
reinvestiga'tion, heronderoek.
reinvest'ment, herbelegging; herbekleding.
reinvig'orate, opnuut besiel, weer versterk.
reiss'ue, (n) heruitreiking; nuwe uitgawe; (v) weer uitgee.
reit'erate, herhaal.
reitera'tion, herhaling.
reit'erative, (n) reduplikasie, iteratief; (a) herhalend, herhalings=, iteratief, redupliserend.
rej'ect, (n) afgekeurde; (pl) uitskot, afgekeurde goed.
reject', (v) verwerp; afslaan, afwys, van die hand wys; wegwys; afstem (voorstel); wraak (regter); ver= stoot; weier; uitgooi; opbring, opgooi, vomeer; te= rugwys; uitmonster (soldate); ~ *an APPEAL,* 'n appèl v.d. hand wys; ~ *a CANDIDATE,* 'n kandi= daat afwys; ~ *a DOCTRINE,* 'n leer verwerp; ~ *a REQUEST,* 'n versoek weier; ~ *a RESOL= UTION,* 'n mosie verwerp; ~ *one THING for (in favour of) another,* een ding vir 'n ander verwerp; ~**able,** verwerplik.
rejectamen'ta, uitskot, afval; uitwerpsels; uitspoel= goed, strandgoed.
rejec'tion, verwerping; afwysing; uitmonstering (sol= date); afstemming (voorstel).
rejec'tive, verwerpend.
rejoice', verheug wees, juig; bly wees; bly maak; *BE ~ d at (by),* verheug wees oor; ~ *the HEART,* vreugde gee; ~ *IN good health,* jou verheug in goeie gesondheid; ~ *over a VICTORY,* oor 'n oorwin= ning juig.
rejoi'cing(s), vreugdebetoon, feesvreugde, feestelik= heid, gejuig.
rejoin', weer verbind; weer saamvoeg; antwoord; du= pliek lewer; dupliseer (reg); weer bykom, weer aan= sluit; ~ **der,** antwoord, weerwoord; dupliek (reg).
rejoint', weer saamvoeg, opnuut voeg.
reju'venate, verjong, weer jonk maak.
rejuvena'tion, verjonging.
rejuvenesce', verjong, die lewenskragte herkry.
rejuvenes'cence, verjonging.
rejuv'enize = rejuvenate.
rekin'dle, weer aansteek, weer laat ontvlam; opnuut aanwakker.
relapse, (n) weerinstorting, insinking, terugslag (na 'n siekte); terugval; aanmaning (bv. perdesiekte); (v) weer instort, terugval; ~ *into silence,* weer swyg.

relaps'ing fever, weerkerende (terugkerende) koors, spirillekoors; aanmaningskoors.
relate', vertel, berig, verhaal; in verband staan met; in verband bring; ~ *one FACT with another,* een feit met 'n ander in verband bring; *this ~ s only to SCHOLARS,* dit het alleen betrekking op skoliere; ~ *TO,* in verband bring met; vertel aan; ~**d,** ver= want, familie van; *CLOSELY ~ d,* naverwant; ~ *d to my FRIEND,* familie van my vriend.
relat'ing: ~ *to,* in verband met.
rela'tion, betrekking, verhouding; verwantskap; bloedverwant, nabestaande, (na)verwant; verhaal, berig, vermelding; verband; (pl) maagskap; bloed= verwante; *BEAR no ~ to,* geen betrekking hê nie op; buite alle verhouding staan tot; *COMMER= CIAL ~ s,* handelsbetrekkinge; *the ~ of one FACT with another,* die verhouding van een feit met 'n ander; *FINANCIAL ~ s,* finansiële betrekkinge; *IN ~ to,* met betrekking tot; ~ *s by MARRIAGE,* aangetroude familie, skoonfamilie; *he is NO ~ of mine (to me),* hy is glad nie familie van my nie; *OUT of all ~ to,* geen verband hê nie met; *POOR ~ s,* arm familie; *have SEXUAL ~ s,* geslagtelike gemeenskap hê; *the ~ s are STRAINED,* die ver= houding is gespanne; *the ~ between WAGES and costs,* die verband tussen lone en koste; ~ **ship,** ver= wantskap; verhouding; naverwantskap, verwant= skapsbetrekking.
rel'ative, (n) (bloed)verwant, nabestaande, familielid; betreklike voornaamwoord; (pl) familie; (a) be= treklik, relatief; betrokke; *the FACTS ~ to the matter,* die feite met betrekking tot (in verband met) die saak; *the ~ POSITION,* die onderlinge ligging; ~ *TO,* met betrekking tot; ~ **humidity,** lugvoggehalte; ~**ly,** betreklik; ~**ness = relativity;** ~ **pronoun,** betreklike (relatiewe) voornaam= woord.
relativ'ity, betreklikheid, relatiwiteit; *theory of ~,* relatiwiteitsteorie.
relat'or, verteller, verhaler.
relax', verslap, verflou; laat skiet, losmaak; ontspan; versag, matig, verlig; minder streng opvat; ~ *one's ATTENTION,* jou aandag laat verslap; ~ *in one's DUTY,* jou plig minder streng opvat; *FEEL ~ ed,* ontspanne voel; ~ *from one's WORK,* 'n bietjie ontspan; ~ **ant,** lakseermiddel; ~ **a'tion,** versag= ting; verslapping; verposing.
relay'¹, (n) aflosspan; voorspanning, ploeg; wissel= plek; heruitsending (radio); narigting (geweer); oordraer (elek.); relê; *in ~ s,* aflosgewyse; (v) aflos; afwissel; deur nuwe(s) vervang; heruitsaai.
re-lay'², (..laid), weer lê, herlê; teruglê.
relay': ~**post,** aflospos; ~ **race,** afloswedstryd; spanwedloop; ~ **station,** heruitsaaistasie.
release', (n) bevryding, vrylating, invryheidstelling, verlossing, loslating; ontslag (van gevangene); ont= heffing, oordrag; ontspanning (veer); kwytskelding (skuld); ontslag (eksekuteur); lossing (uit opslag= plek); beskikbaarstelling (dokumente); uitlating (stoom); vertoning (film); *a NEW ~,* 'n nuwe (plaat)opname; *ORDER for ~,* bevel tot vrylating; (v) loslaat; vrygee; vrylaat; vrystel; verlos; ontslaan (gevangene); beskikbaar stel; ophef (druk); ont= span (veer); die eerste keer vertoon; openbaar maak; afstel; oordra; onthef, bevry; ~ *d AREA,* oopgestelde gebied; ~ *from CUSTODY,* uit bewa= ring ontslaan; ~ *from DUTY,* van diens vrystel; aflos; ~ *a FILM,* 'n rolprent vir algemene verto= ning vrystel; ~ *a PRISONER,* 'n gevangene vry= laat; ~ **cord,** treklyn; lostou; ~ **lever,** loshefboom; ~ **wire,** toegewer; losdraad.
releas'ing lever, loshefboom.
rel'egate, verban; verwys na, relegeer; verplaas; ~ *a player to the third team,* 'n speler na die 3e span afskuif.
relega'tion, verbanning; verwydering; verwysing; verplasing; terugsetting.
relent', swig, toegee, versag; week word; bedaar, sag= ter gestem word; ~**ing,** (n) toegewendheid; (a) toe= gewend; ~**less,** onversetlik, onverbiddelik, mee= doënloos; ~**lessness,** onversetlikheid, onverbidde= likheid, meedoënloosheid.

relet', (~), weer verhuur; ~**ting**, weerverhuring.
rel'evance, rel'evancy, toepaslikheid; verband; betrekking; saaklikheid.
rel'evant, toepaslik, ter sake, desbetreffend, van pas, saaklik, verbandhoudend, relevant; *the documents ~ to the case*, die dokumente wat op die saak betrekking het.
reliabil'ity, deeglikheid, betroubaarheid, soliditeit; ~ **competition**, betroubaarheidswedstryd; ~ **trial**, betroubaarheidstoets.
reli'able, vertroubaar, getrou; deeglik; betroubaar; gesaghebbend; vertrouenswaardig; solied; ~**ness** = **reliability**.
reli'ably, op betroubare wyse; *be ~ informed*, uit goeie bron verneem.
reli'ance, vertroue, fidusie; *my ~ is upon GOD*, my vertroue is op God; *HAVE ~ in, PLACE ~ upon*, vertroue hê in.
rel'ic, oorblyfsel; reliek, relikwie (godsd.); aandenking; relik; oorblyfsel; (pl) stoflike oorskot; oorblyfsels.
rel'ict, weduwee; loskop, losberg; erosiestuk.
relief', verligting, verademing, herademing; opluging; versagting; ondersteuning, onderstand, hulp; versterking; ontset (beleërde plek); skof (by werk); aflossingstroepe; ontsettingstroepe; aflossing (wag); reliëf, skerp aftekening; ~ *someone from ANXIETY*, iem. sy angs verlos; *APPLY for ~*, om onderstand vra; *bring out in BOLD ~*, duidelik laat uitkom; *GIVE ~*, onderstand verleen; ~ *of the GUARD*, aflossing v.d. wag; ~ *of MAFEKING*, die ontset van Mafeking; *get ~ from PAIN*, verligting van pyn kry; *STAND out in ~*, sprekend uitkom, skerp afgeteken wees; *by WAY of ~*, by wyse van afwisseling; ~ **fund**, noodlenigingsfonds, bystandsfonds; ~ **map**, reliëfkaart; ~ **scale**, tegemoetkomingskaal; ~ **train**, hulptrein; ~ **works**, onderstandswerke.
relieve', verlig, versag, ondersteun; aflos; gerusstel; opbeur, help, ontset (beleërde plek); onthef, ontslaan (uit pos); afwissel; laat uitkom, laat afsteek; ontlas; *I FEEL ~d*, ek voel opgelug; ~ *one's FEELINGS*, jou hart lug; ~ *the GUARD*, die wag aflos; ~ *NATURE*, sy behoefte doen; jou ontlas; ~ *someone of his OFFICE*, iem. ontslaan; ~*d of RESPONSIBILITY*, vry van verantwoordelikheid; ~ *a person of his WEALTH*, iem. se besittings steel; ~**r**, verligter; aflosser; bevryder, ontsetter.
reliev'ing, verligtend; aflos=; ~ **arch**, draboog; ~ **army**, ontsettingsleër; ~ **guard**, aflossende wag; ~ **minister**, konsulent; ~ **officer**, armeversorger; ~ **staff**, aflospersoneel.
relight', weer opsteek.
relig'ion, godsdiens, geloof; *ENTER into ~*, in 'n klooster gaan; *GET ~*, bekeerd raak; *MAKE a ~ of something*, iets aanbid; iets as 'n heilige plig beskou; *MINISTER of ~*, leraar, predikant; *WAR of ~*, godsdiensoorlog; ~**er**, kloosterling; vrome; ~**ism**, oordrewe godsdienswyer, kweselary; ~**ist**, godsdienswyeraar, dweper; ~**ize**, godsdienstig maak; bekeer.
reli'giose, oordrewe godsdienstig, skynheilig.
religios'ity, godsdiensdwepery.
reli'gious, (n) kloosterling; geestelike; (a) godsdienstig, godvresend, vroom, religieus; nougeset; ~ **ceremony**, godsdienstige plegtigheid; ~ **denomination**, kerkgenootskap; ~ **instruction**, godsdiensonderwys; ~ **liberty**, godsdiensvryheid; ~**ly**, godsdienstig; stip, getrou, angsvallig; ~**ness**, godsdienstigheid, vroomheid; ~ **war**, godsdiensoorlog.
reline', die voering vervang; herbeklee.
relinq'ulsh, laat staan, laat vaar, opgee, afsien van, loslaat; ~ *a CLAIM*, afsien van 'n eis; ~ *a COMMAND*, die bevel neerlê; ~**ment**, verlating; afstand; loslating.
rel'iquary, (..ries), relikwieëkassie, reliekkas.
rel'ish, (n) smaak; bysmakie, tikkie; versnapering, smaaklike toespys; voorsmaak; suurtjie; kruiesous; *EAT with ~*, met smaak eet; *GIVE ~ to*, die smaak verhoog van; *HAVE no ~ for*, geen behae skep nie in; geen smaak hê nie vir; *with LITTLE ~*, met lang tande; *it LOSES in ~*, sy aardigheid verdwyn;

READ with ~, met lus lees; (v) smaaklik maak; in die smaak val; behae skep in; geniet van, lekker vind, smul; goedkeur; ~ *to the FULL*, die grootste behae skep in; ~ *OF*, smaak na; ~ *the PROSPECT*, vooruitsien na; ~**able**, smaaklik, genietbaar.
relive', herleef, weer opleef; oorleef.
reload', oorlaai; weer laai, herlaai; ~**ing charges**, herlaaikoste.
reloca'tion, huurverlenging, herplasing.
relu'cent, skitterend, helder.
reluc'tance, reluc'tancy, teensin, teensinnigheid; teenstand, onwilligheid, huiwerigheid.
reluc'tant, weerstrewig, teensinnig, met teensin, ongraag, onwillig; ~**ly**, teensinnig, onwillig, skoorvoetend, ongraag, langtand.
relume', relum'ine, weer aansteek; weer ophelder.
rely', (..lied), vertrou op, reken op; jou verlaat op, staatmaak op, bou op; *you may ~ upon it*, jy kan daarop reken.
remade', omgewerk.
remain', (n) oorblyfsel; ruïne; (pl) stoflike oorskot; oorblyfsels, oorskiet; nagelate werke; res; ~ *BEHIND*, agterbly; ~ *to DINNER*, bly vir ete; *all that ~s to him of his INHERITANCE*, al wat hy oorgehou het van sy erfporsie; *it ~s to be PROVED*, dit moet nog bewys word; *that ~s to be SEEN*, dit moet nog bewys word; dit staan nog te besien; ~**der**, oorblyfsel, oorskot, oorskiet, res, restant; ~**der theorem**, restestelling; ~**ing**, (n) (die) res; oorblywing; (a) oor, orig; ~**ing portion**, restant, resterende gedeelte.
remake', (..made), oormaak, omwerk, weer maak.
reman', (-ned), opnuut beman; herbeman; opnuut beset.
remand', (n) uitstel; terugsending; *GRANT a ~*, uitstel verleen; *he is UNDER ~*, sy saak is uitgestel; (v) terugstuur (na die gevangenis); terugroep; ('n saak) uitstel; ~ *on BAIL*, op borgtog vrylaat; ~ *in CUSTODY*, gevange hou; weer laat vang; ~ *for TRIAL*, ter strafsitting verwys.
rem'anent, blywend, voortdurend.
remark'¹, (v) oormerk, weer merk.
remark'², (n) aanmerking (ongunstig); opmerking (gunstig); bedenking; *worthy of ~*, opmerkenswaardig, merkwaardig, opmerklik, (v) aanmerk (ongunstig); opmerk (gunstig); ~ *on*, 'n opmerking maak oor; ~**able**, merkwaardig, opmerklik, opvallend, buitengewoon, frappant.
rema'rriage, tweede huwelik, hertroue.
rema'rry, (..ried), hertrou.
remas'ticate, herkou.
remea'sure, weer meet, hermeet.
reme'diable, herstelbaar, geneeslik.
reme'dial, helend, genesend; geneesbaar; heilsaam; ~ *EDUCATION*, remediërende (verhelpende) onderwys, *take ~ MEASURES*, verbeterings aan die hand doen; ~ **exercises**, ~ **gymnastics**, heilgimnastiek.
rem'edied, verholpe.
rem'ediless, ongeneeslik, onherstelbaar.
rem'edy, (n) (..dies), geneesmiddel, middeltjie, remedie; herstel; baat; verhaal, verhelp(ing); *the ~ of ABUSES*, die verwydering van misbruike; *it is BEYOND ~*, dis onherstelbaar; die kalf is verdrink; *there is a ~ for everything but DEATH*, vir die dood groei daar geen kruid nie; *DESPERATE diseases must have desperate remedies*, ernstige toestande eis drastiese maatreëls; *HAVE a ~ against*, 'n verhaal hê op; *there is NO ~ but*, daar is geen ander middel nie as; (v) (..died), genees; help, regmaak, verbeter, herstel, verhelp.
remelt', oorsmelt, omsmelt.
remem'ber, jou herinner; dink aan, gedenk; byval, onthou; *it will be ~ed AGAINST you*, dit sal teen jou aangeteken staan; *he will be ~ed as the AUTHOR of*, sy naam sal voortleef as die skrywer van; *BE it ~ed*, laat dit onthou word; dink daaraan; *BE ~ed*, voortleef; *I DON'T ~*, ek herinner my dit nie; ~ *ME*, dink aan my; gedenk my; ~ *ME to your friends*, sê groete aan jou vriende; *I don't ~ having MET him*, ek kan my nie herinner dat ek

hom ontmoet het nie; ~ *ONESELF*, jou bedink; *if I* ~ *RIGHTLY*, as ek my nie vergis nie; as ek dit wel het; ~ *the SABBATH DAY*, dink aan die Sabbatdag; ~ *to SAY*, dink daaraan om te sê; *he* ~*ed his friend in his WILL*, hy het in sy testament aan sy vriend gedink.
remem'brance, herinnering, geheue; herdenking; aandenking; gedagtenis, nagedagtenis; (pl) groete, komplimente; *DAY of* ~, gedenkdag; *IN* ~ *of*, ter gedagtenis aan; *it PUTS me in* ~ *of*, dit herinner my aan; ~ **book**, gedenkboek; ~**r**, aandenking; herinnering.
re'mex, (remiges), vlerkveer.
remind', herinner, help onthou, indagtig maak (aan); ~ *someone OF*, iem. help onthou; iem. laat dink aan; *THAT* ~ *s me*, dit laat my dink; dit herinner my; ~**er**, aanmaning; wenk; waarskuwing; herinnering; *a GENTLE* ~*er*, 'n vriendelike wenk; *GIVE someone a* ~, iem. 'n wenk gee; ~**ful**, herinneringwekkend, herinnerend.
reminisce', herinneringe ophaal, reminisseer.
reminis'cence, herinnering, reminissensie.
reminis'cent, herinnerend, reminisserend; *be* ~ *of*, jou laat (terug)dink aan.
remint', hermunt.
remise'¹, (n) remise, koetshuis.
remise'², (n) teruggawe; (v) teruggee, opgee, afstand doen van.
remiss', nalatig, onverskillig, sorgeloos, agtelosig, traag, slap; ~ *in one's duties*, jou pligte versuim.
remiss'ible, vergeeflik; toegeeflik.
remi'ssion, vergifnis; kwytskelding, skuldvergif(fe)nis; afname, vermindering; verslapping, verflouing; *the* ~ *of the DEATH sentence*, die versagting v.d. doodstraf; ~ *of SINS*, vergewing van sondes.
remit', (-ted), vergewe; terugstuur, terugverwys, remitteer; terugkeer; terugbetaal; versag, verminder (straf); skenk; oorstuur, oorsend, oorlewer; oormaak; afneem, verslap; uitstel; ~ *a CASE to a magistrate*, 'n saak na 'n landdros terugverwys; *never* ~ *one's EFFORTS to succeed*, nooit in jou pogings om sukses te behaal, verslap nie; ~ *a FINE*, 'n boete verminder; ~ *MONEY*, geld stuur; ~ *by RETURN of post*, per kerende pos terugstuur; ~ *RIGHTS*, afstand doen van regte; ~**ment**, kwytskelding; vergifnis; ~**tal**, vergifnis; kwytskelding; oormaking, oorsending.
remitt'ance, betaling, oormaking, geldsending, remise; oorgemaakte bedrag; ~**man**, toelaagtrekker, toelaagontvanger; leegleer.
remittee', ontvanger (van oorgemaakte geld).
remitt'ent, afnemend, verminderend; op- en afgaande (koors).
remitt'er, vergewer; afsender, oormaker, remittent.
remix', weer meng, oormeng.
rem'nant, (n) res; stuk, oorblyfsel, oorskiet, brokkie; (res)lappie, oorskietstuk, restant; stert; (a) oorgeblewe; ~ **day**, stukdag, lappiesdag; ~ **sale**, restanteverkoping, oorskietverkoping.
remod'el, (-led), opnuut modelleer; vervorm, omwerk, bewerk; hermodelleer.
remoll'ient, versagtend.
remon'etize, (munt) weer in omloop bring; weer aanmunt.
remon'strance, vertoog; vermaning; protes; beswaarskrif, remonstransie.
Remon'strant, (n) Remonstrant; (a) Remonstrants.
remon'strant, (n) protesteerder; (a) vertoënd, teenwerpend, protesterend.
remon'strate, betoog, aanvoer, onder die oog bring; teregwys, vermaan; beswaar maak, jou versit; protesteer, remonstreer; ~ *against a COURSE*, beswaar maak teen 'n beleid; ~ *with a PERSON*, iem. teregwys.
remonstra'tion, remonstrasie.
remon'strator, betoër, beswaarmaker.
rem'ora, suigvis; belemmering.
remorse', (gewetens)wroeging, selfverwyt, berou; *in* ~ *for the GRIEF caused*, uit berou oor die veroorsaakte smart; ~ *always comes too LATE*, berou is 'n goeie ding, maar kom altyd te laat; *feel* ~ *for*

one's MISDEEDS, berou hê oor 'n mens se wandade; ~ *is the POISON of life*, naberou is galberou (swaar berou); ~**ful**, berouvol; ~**less**, onbarmhartig, meedoënloos, hardvogtig; ~**lessness**, onbarmhartigheid, hardvogtigheid.
remote', ver, veraf, afgeleë, verwyderd, afgesonderd, gering, min, flou; *make a* ~ *ALLUSION to*, ver langs sinspeel op; *our* ~ *ANCESTORS*, ons voorouers uit die ver verlede; ~ *ANTIQUITY*, die gryse oudheid; ~ *CAUSE*, verwyderde oorsaak; *a* ~ *CHANCE*, 'n geringe moontlikheid; *a* ~ *CORNER*, 'n uithoek; ~ *CONSEQUENCES*, ver verwyderde gevolge; *in the not too* ~ *FUTURE*, in die nabye toekoms; *not the* ~*st IDEA*, nie die flouste benul nie; *a* ~ *KINSMAN*, 'n verre verwant; *in* ~ *PARTS*, in afgeleë streke; *a* ~ *RESEMBLANCE*, 'n flou gelykenis; ~ *from the SUBJECT*, glad nie in verband met die onderwerp nie; ~ **control**, afstandsbediening, afstandsbeheer; ~**ly**, ver, veraf, indirek; ~**ness**, verte, afgeleënheid; afgesonderdheid.
remould', opnuut giet; vernuwe, vervorm; omwerk (fig.); hervorm.
rem'ount, (n) perdevoorsiening, vars perd, remonte(perd) (militêr); nuwe omlysting.
remount', (v) weer opklim, weer beklim; van perde voorsien; remonteer; weer omlys (skildery).
rem'ount commission, remontekommissie.
removabil'ity, verplaasbaarheid.
remov'able, afneembaar, verwyderbaar, los; verplaasbaar; afsitbaar.
remov'al, verwydering, wegruiming, uitlating; verplasing; verhuising; afsetting; ~ **contractor**, verhuiskontrakteur; ~ **expenses**, verhuiskoste; ~ **van**, toewa, verhuiswa, meubelwa.
remove', (n) verwydering; bevordering; gereg; verplasing; verhuising; graad, stap, trap; *one* ~ *from*, een trap van; (v) verwyder; uithaal (vlek); verplaas, verskuiwe, oorkarwei (meubels); ontslae raak van; afdank, afsit; ~ *to a new ADDRESS*, verhuis na 'n nuwe adres; ~ *the CLOTH*, afdek; ~ *FROM Aberdeen to Pretoria*, van Aberdeen na Pretoria trek (verhuis); ~ *one's HAT*, jou hoed afhaal; ~ *MOUNTAINS*, berge versit; ~ *from OFFICE*, afsit; ~ *one's OVERCOAT*, jou jas uittrek; ~ *from SCHOOL*, uit die skool haal; ~**d**, verwyder(d); afgeleë; *a COUSIN once* ~*d*, 'n neef (niggie) in die eerste graad, 'n kleinneef; *SOUP* ~*d by fish*, sop gevolg deur vis; ~**r**, verhuiser.
remov'ing, wegruiming; verwydering; verplasing; ~-**van**, verhuiswa.
remun'erable, te beloon, te vergeld.
remun'erate, beloon, vergoed; betaal, vereffen.
remunera'tion, beloning, vergoeding, betaling.
remun'erative, remun'eratory, belonend, vergoedend; betalend, lonend, winsgewend voordelig.
remun'erativeness, lonendheid, voordeligheid.
remus'ter, herindeel, anders indeel.
Renaiss'ance¹, (n) Renaissance; (a) Renaissancisties.
renaiss'ance², herlewing.
Renaissanc'ist, Renaissancis.
ren'al, nier-; ~ **calculus**, niersteen; ~ **colic**, nierkoliek; ~ **disease**, niersiekte.
rename', herdoop, hernoem.
renam'ing, vernoeming, naamsverandering.
renas'cence, wedergeboorte; herlewing, oplewing.
renas'cent, herlewend, oplewend.
rencon'tre, rencoun'ter, (n) ontmoeting; botsing, skermutseling; (v) ontmoet; bots, skermutsel.
rend, (rent), vanmekaar skeur, verskeur; ontruk, uitruk; ~ *ASUNDER*, losskeur; in twee skeur; ~ *one's CLOTHES*, jou klere skeur; ~ *one's HAIR*, jou hare uit die kop trek.
ren'der, lewer; oorgee; oorsit, vertaal; aanbied; opgee; weergee, vertolk, ten gehore bring (musiekstuk); maak; oplewer, gee; suiwer, uitsmelt (vet); pleister; teruggee, vergeld; bewys (diens); ~ *an ACCOUNT*, verslag doen; 'n rekening lewer; *ACCOUNT* ~*ed*, gelewerde rekening; ~ *ASSISTANCE*, hulp verleen; ~ *FAT*, vet uitbraai; ~ *GOOD for evil*, kwaad met goed vergeld; ~ *HARMLESS*, onskadelik maak; ~ *INTO French*,

rendezvous

in Frans vertaal; ~ *a piece of MUSIC*, 'n musiekstuk speel (vertolk); ~ *ONESELF up*, jou oorgee; ~ *OUT*, vet uitbraai; ~ *a PART*, 'n rol vertolk; ~ *PLASTER*, pleister beraap; ~ *a SERVICE*, 'n diens bewys; ~ *THANKS*, dank betuig; ~**ing**, oorgewing; lewering; vertaling; vertolking (stuk), weergawe; verlening; bepleistering; beraping (bouk.); ~**ing coat**, raaplaag.

ren'dezvous, (n) (sing en pl), vergaderplek, bymekaarkomplek; rendezvous, versamelplek; werfkantoor (mil.); (v) saamkom, vergader, bymekaarkom.

rend'ing, verskeuring.

rendi'tion, oorgawe, uitlewering; weergawe, vertolking (musiek).

ren'egade, (n) renegaat, afvallige; droster, hendsopper; (v) afvallig word, oorloop.

rene(g)ue', kleur versaak.

renew', vernuwe, vernieu, hernuwe, hernieu; herhaal; hervat; laat herleef; heelmaak, repareer; verjong; ~ *the ATTACK*, die aanval hervat; ~ *a CORRESPONDENCE*, 'n briefwisseling hervat; ~**able**, hernieubaar, hernubaar, vernieubaar; verlengbaar (wissel); ~**al**, vernuwing; vervanging; hernuwing; ~**ed**, verleng; ~**er**, vernuwer.

ren'iform, niervormig.

renit'ent, veerkragtig; weerspannig.

renn'et, stremsel, stremstof; lebekstrak; renetappel; ~ **bag**, vetmaag; ~ **curd**, dikmelkkaas.

renounce', verloën, versaak, opgee, laat staan; afstand doen van; vaarwel sê; verwerp, afsweer; ~ *FRIENDSHIP*, vriendskapsbande verbreek; ~ *the WORLD*, die wêreld vaarwel sê; jou v.d. wêreld onttrek; ~**ment**, verloëning; versaking; afstanddoening; ~**r**, versaker.

ren'ovate, opknap; vernuwe; regmaak, herstel, repareer, versien.

renova'tion, vernuwing; opknapping; reparasie, versiening.

ren'ovator, vernuwer; opknapper; versiener.

renown', beroemdheid, vermaardheid; roem, faam; *of* ~, vermaard; ~**ed**, beroemd, vermaard, gevierd; ~*ed for COURAGE*, beroemd om sy moed; ~*ed throughout the WORLD*, deur die hele wêreld beroemd.

rent¹, (n) skeur; bars; opening.

rent², (n) huur, pag; (v) huur, pag; verhuur, verpag; ~**abil'ity**, opbringsvermoë, rendabiliteit; ~**able**, huurbaar; verhuurbaar; ~ **allowance**, vergoeding van huisgun toelae; ~ **charge**, (erf)pag; ~ **collector**, huurinvorderaar; ~ **day**, betaaldag; ~**er**, huurder, pagter; ~**-free**, pagvry, huurvry; verniet, kosteloos; ~ **roll**, rentebook.

rent'al, huur, pag; huurgeld, ~ **earning**, huurtrekkend; ~ **free**, huurvry; ~ **rights**, erfpag; ~ **value**, huurwaarde.

renum'erate, optel, opsom.

renuncia'tion, afswering, versaking; afstand; selfverloëning.

reobtain', herkry.

reoccupa'tion, weerinneming, hernieude bewoning; herbesetting.

reocc'upy, (..pied), weer beset; weer intrek neem in.

reop'en, heropen; weer opbring; weer oopgaan; weer begin; ~**ing**, heropening.

reorganiza'tion, reorganisasie; herskikking, hergroepering, herindeling; herorganisasie; sanering.

reorg'anize, herskik, hergroepeer; reorganiseer; saneer; herorganiseer.

reor'ientate, reoriënteer.

reorienta'tion, reoriëntasie.

rep¹, losbol.

rep², geribde stof; ~ **paper**, geriffelde papier.

repaint', (n) oorgeverfde voorwerp (bv. 'n gholfbal); (v) weer verf, oorverf.

repair'¹, (n) skuilplek; (v) vlug; gaan na; ~ *to*, jou begeef na.

repair'², (n) herstel(ling), reparasie; *in BAD* ~, sleg onderhou; *BEYOND* ~, nie meer te herstel nie; *OUT of* ~, in verval; uit orde, stukkend; *UNDER* ~, in reparasie; dit word gerepareer; (v) repareer, herstel, heelmaak, vergoed (skade); goedmaak (fout); ~ **depot**, hersteldepot; ~**er**, hersteller;

~**man**, hersteller, heelmaker; ~ **outfit**, hersteldoos, hersteluitrusting, reparasieuitrusting; ~ **park**, ~ **(work)shop**, herstelwerkplek, herstelwinkel.

repap'er, oorplak, weer plak, herplak.

reparabil'ity, herstelbaarheid.

rep'arable, herstelbaar.

repara'tion, herstelling, reparasie; voldoening, genoegdoening; skadeloosstelling, vergoeding; eerherstel; *make* ~ *for*, die skade herstel; weer goedmaak; ~ **payment**, herstelbetaling.

repartee', (n) gevatte antwoord; gevatheid; *quick at* ~, slagvaardig, gevat; (v) 'n gevatte antwoord gee.

reparti'tion, herverdeling, herindeling.

repass', weer verbygaan, weer oortrek.

repast', maaltyd.

repatch', oorlap.

repat'riate, repatrieer.

repatria'tion, repatriasie.

repay', (repaid), terugbetaal; vergoed; inlos; beloon, vergeld; ~ *a CALL (visit)*, 'n besoek beantwoord; ~ *a DEBT*, 'n skuld aansuiwer (betaal); ~**able**, terugbetaalbaar; ~**ment**, terugbetaling; vergoeding; *on* ~**ment**, teen terugbetaling.

repeal', (n) herroeping, intrekking; afskaffing; (v) herroep, terugtrek, ophef, afskaf; ~**abil'ity**, herroeplikheid; ~**able**, herroeplik, herroepbaar.

repeat', (n) herhaling, herhalingsteken (musiek); toegif; nabestelling; (v) herhaal, repeteer, oordoen; herkou; hervat; nasê; oorvertel, oorbrief (storie); ~ *oneself*, jou herhaal; dieselfde oor en oor vertel; ~**able**, herhaalbaar; ~**edly**, herhaaldelik, oor en oor, aljimmers; ~**er**, herhaler; herhaaltoetser; opsêer; repetisieoorlosie, periode, repeteergeweer; repeteerseintoestel.

repeat'ing, (n) herhaling; (a) herhalend, repeterend, repeteer-; herhalend; ~ **coil**, oordraspoel; ~ **decimal**, repeterende breuk; ~ **rifle**, repeteergeweer; ~ **watch**, repetisieoorlosie.

repeat: ~ **inspection**, tweede inspeksie; ~ **order**, nabestelling; ~ **performance**, tweede opvoering; heropvoering; ~ **sign**, herhaalsein.

repel', (-led), terugdrywe, verslaan; afweer, terugslaan, afslaan; weerstaan; afstoot; ~ *an ATTACK*, 'n aanval afslaan; ~ *a BLOW*, 'n slag afweer; ~ *an OFFER*, 'n aanbod weier; ~ *TEMPTATION*, versoeking weerstaan.

repel'lent, (n) afweermiddel, afstotende middel; (a) afwerend; afstotlik, stuitig; terugstotend; terugdrywend; *it is* ~ *to me*, dit stuit my teen die bors.

repent'¹, (v) spyt wees; berou hê; *I* ~ *my KINDNESS*, ek is spyt oor my vriendelikheid; *you will* ~ *OF this*, dit sal jou berou.

rep'ent², (a) rank-, rankend.

repent'ance, berou; ~ *COMES too late*, berou kom te laat; ~ *for what one has DONE*, berou oor jou dade; ~ *of one's SINS*, berou oor jou sondes.

repent'ant, (n) boetvaardige; (a) berouvol, berouhebbend, boetvaardig.

repeo'ple, weer bevolk, herbevolk.

repercu'ssion, weerkaatsing; terugslag; repercussie, reaksie, gevolg, nasleep; *cause* ~ *s on*, opslae maak, 'n nasleep hê.

repercuss'ive, terugkaatsend.

rep'ertoire, repertoire.

rep'ertory, (..ries), register, bladwyser; versameling; repertorium, repertoire; ~ *of useful knowledge*, skat van nuttige kennis; ~ **company**, vaste toneelgeselskap; ~ **theatre**, repertoriumteater, repertoireteater.

reperuse', weer deurlees, herlees.

re'petend, refrein; repetent, repeterende breuk.

repeti'tion, herhaling, repetisie; ewebeeld, kopie; *in* ~ *of*, met herhaling van.

repeti'tious, **repet'itive**, herhalend; eentonig.

rephras'ing, herbewoording.

repine', ontevrede wees, murmureer, kla; knies.

repin'ing, (n) geklae, gemor; (a) ontevrede; ~**ly**, morrend, klaend.

replace', terugsit, herplaas; opvolg, vervang; die plek inneem van; vergoed; *he CANNOT be* ~ *d*, hy kan nie vervang word nie; ~ *damaged PARTS with*

replait — **republican**

new, beskadigde onderdele deur nuwes vervang; ~ **able**, ~ **ment**, vervanging; vervanger; verplasing; vernuwing; (pl) vervangstukke; vervangingstroepe; ~ **ment value**, vervangingswaarde; ~ **r**, vervanger; hersteller (wissels).
replait', weer vleg, hervleg.
replant', verplant; weer plant, oorplant; inboet; ~ **ing**, oorplanting.
rep'lay, (n) oorspeelwedstryd, herhaalwedstryd.
replay', (v) oorspeel, herspeel.
replen'ish, aanvul; vol maak; ~ **with**, vol maak met; ~ **ed**, volgemaak; aangevul; ~ **er**, aanvuller; ~ **ment**, aanvulling; (die) volmaak.
replete', vol; oorvol; goed voorsien van; ~ **with**, sat van; tot versadigens vol van.
reple'tion, volheid; oorvolheid; oorlading, oorversadiging.
replev'in, opheffing (van beslag), bevelskrif tot opheffing van beslag; lossing.
replev'isor, opheffer; losser.
replev'y, (..vied), beslag ophef; los.
rep'lica, replika; tweede eksemplaar; kopie; weergawe; ewebeeld (fig.); herhaling (mus.); ~ **te**, teruggevou; ~ **'tion**, antwoord, repliek; reproduksie, navolging; herhaling.
replunge', weer inspring; weer insteek.
reply', (n) (**replies**), antwoord; repliek; *IN* ~ *to*, in antwoord op; *MAKE no* ~, geen antwoord gee nie; nie antwoord nie; *a POOR* ~, 'n swak antwoord; *by WAY of* ~, in antwoord; *WRITE in* ~, terugskryf; (v) (**replied**), antwoord, terugskryf; repliseer; ~ *to a DEBATE*, repliek lewer; ~ *to a LETTER*, 'n brief beantwoord; ~ **card**, antwoordkaartjie; ~ **paid**, antwoord betaal; ~ **-paid envelope**, antwoordbetaalde koevert, frankeerkoevert; ~ **-paid telegram**, vooruitbetaalde telegram, antwoordbetaaltelegram.
repol'ish, opnuut polys, oppoets, weer blink maak, oorvrywe.
report', (n) berig, tyding; mare; verslag, rapport; gerug, skoot, knal; aangewing, aanmelding; *BRING out a* ~, 'n verslag uitbring (lewer); *FROM* ~, van hoorsê; *the* ~ *GOES*, daar word vertel; die gerug lui; *of GOOD* ~, met 'n goeie reputasie; *the* ~ *of GUNS*, die geknal van geweers; die gebulder van kanonne; *MAKE A* ~, 'n verslag saamstel (opstel); ~ *of a RIFLE*, die geknal van 'n geweer; *he is by ~ an able SCIENTIST*, volgens berigte is hy 'n bekwame wetenskaplike; (v) berig, vermeld, vertel; verslag gee, rapporteer; knal (geweer); verklae, aangee; ~ *AGAINST*, ongunstig rapporteer teen; ~ *BACK*, verslag uitbring; ~ *for DUTY*, jou vir diens aanmeld; *it IS* ~ *ed*, daar word gesê, hulle sê, die gerug lui; ~ *a MEETING*, verslag doen van 'n vergadering; *he was* ~ *ed MISSING*, hy is as vermis gemeld; ~ *ON*, rapporteer oor, verslag doen van; ~ *ONESELF*, jou aanmeld; ~ *s for the PAPERS*, hy doen verslag vir die koerante; ~ *PROGRESS*, vooruitgang (vordering) meld; *they* ~ *ed him TO to his employer*, hulle het hom by sy werkgewer aangekla; ~ **able**, meldbaar, rapporteerbaar; ~ **age**, beriggewing, verslaggewing; ~ **er**, verslaggewer, beriggewer; rapporteur; stenograaf; ~ **ers' gallery**, perstribune, persgalery; ~ **ing**, verslaggewery; beriggewing.
repose', (n) rus, verposing; kalmte, stilte; slaap; *ANGLE of* ~, natuurlike helling; *he LACKS* ~, hy het nie rus vir sy siel nie; (v) gerus wees, vertrou op; uitrus, laat rus, rus geniet; ~ *CONFIDENCE in a person*, vertroue stel in 'n persoon; ~ *ON the bed*, op die bed uitrus; ~ *TRUST in*, vertrou op; ~ **ful**, rustig, kalm.
repos'itory, (..ries), bewaarplaas, depot, pakhuis; kolleksie; rusplek; bron; vertroueling.
repossess', weer in besit neem, terugneem; ~ **ed car**, teruggeneemde motor (kar); ~ **ion**, herbesitneming, weerinbesitneming, terugneming.
repot', (**-ted**), verpot.
repp, *kyk* **rep**.
reprehend', berispe, betig, blameer, skrobbeer.
reprehen'sible, berispelik, laakbaar; ~ **ness**, laakbaarheid, berispelikheid.

reprehen'sion, berisping, skrobbering; skuld, blaam.
reprehen'sive, berispend; laakbaar.
represent', voorstel; verteenwoordig; afbeeld; voorgee, beweer, aanvoer, voorhou; ~ *a CONSTITUENCY in Parliament*, 'n kiesafdeling in die Parlement verteenwoordig; ~ *on the COUNCIL*, verteenwoordig in die raad; *NOT* ~ *ed*, onverteenwoordig; onverdedig (reg); ~ *ONESELF as*, jou uitgee vir; *that PICTURE* ~ *s heaven*, daardie prent stel die hemel voor; ~ **able**, wat voorgestel kan word; ~ **a'tion**, voorstelling; uiteensetting; verteenwoordiging; vertoog; aandrang; opvoering; *make* ~ *ations to*, vertoë rig tot.
represent'ative, (n) verteenwoordiger; saakgelastigde; (a) verteenwoordigend; tipies, tekenend, kenmerkend; *BE* ~ *of*, tipies van; verteenwoordigend van; ~ *COMMITTEE*, skakelkomitee; verteenwoordigende raad; ~ *GOVERNMENT*, verteenwoordigende bestuur; ~ *TARGET*, skaalskyf.
repress', onderdruk; inhou, in toom hou, beteuel, teëgaan, bedwing, tot onderwerping bring; ~ **abil'ity**, bedwingbaarheid; ~ **able**, bedwingbaar; ~ **er**, onderdrukker.
repre'ss: ~ **ion**, onderdrukking, beteueling; bedwang; ~ **ive**, onderdrukkend, beteuelend, bedwingend; ~ *ive measure*, dwangmaatreël.
reprieve', (n) uitstel; opskorting; invryheidstelling, grasie, begenadiging; *grant a* ~, begenadig; (v) uitstel, opskort (vonnis).
rep'rimand, (n) berisping, teregwysing, bestrawwing, brander, skrobbering; (v) berispe, teregwys, bestraf, skrobbeer, opkeil, voorkry, deurloop, uitvreet.
re'print, (n) herdruk; afdruk, oordruk.
reprint', (v) herdruk; 'n nuwe afdruk maak; ~ **ed**, herdruk.
repris'al, (weer)vergelding, weerwraak; *LETTER of* ~, kaperbrief; *MAKE* ~ *s*, weerwraak neem.
reprise', herneming; hervatting; herhaling (mus.).
reproach', (n) (**-es**), verwyt; skande, oneer, smaad; blaam; berisping; *ABOVE* ~, bo verwyt; bo verdenking; skoon; *ABSTAIN from* ~, nie verwyte maak nie; *BE a* ~ *to*, tot oneer strek; *BEYOND* ~, bo verwyt; bo verdenking; skoon; *CAST* ~ *on*, afbreuk doen aan; tot oneer strek van; *HEAP* ~ *es on someone*, iem. verwyte toeslinger; *TERM of* ~, skimpwoord; *it is a* ~ *TO us*, dit strek ons tot oneer; *WORD of* ~, verwyt; berisping, smaadwoord; (v) verwyt, beskuldig van; berispe; tot oneer strek; ~ *a person with DISHONESTY*, iem. van oneerlikheid beskuldig; ~ *oneself WITH*, jouself verwyt oor; ~ **able**, laakbaar, berispelik; ~ **ful**, verwytend; skandelik, oneervol; ~ **less**, onberispelik, vlekloos.
rep'robate, (n) verworpeling, verdoemeling, ellendeling, verstokte sondaar; (v) verwerp; verdoem, veroordeel; (a) verworpe, sleg, goddeloos.
reproba'tion, verwerping; verdoeming; afkeuring.
reproduce', weer voortbring; weergee; vermenigvuldig; voortplant; namaak, naskilder, kopieer; reproduseer; ~ **r**, voortbrenger; reproduseerder; weergewer (radio).
reproduc'tion, reproduksie, weergawe; voortplanting, vermenigvuldiging; kopie.
reproduc'tive, telend, voortplantings-; voortbringend, reproduktief; ~ **cell**, voortplantingsel; ~ **gland**, voortplantingsklier; ~ **organ**, geslagsorgaan, voortplantingsorgaan; ~ **power**, voortplantingsvermoë, teelkrag.
reproof', berisping, bestrawwing, teregwysing, standjie, strafpredikasie, skrobbering; verwyt.
reprov'able, berispelik.
reprove', berispe, bestraf, teregwys, uitbesem; verwyt; ~ **r**, verwyter; bestrawwer, strafprediker.
reps, *kyk* **rep**.
rep'tant, kruipend.
rep'tile, (n) kruipende gedierte, reptiel; veragtelike kruiper; (a) kruipend; laag, veragtelik, kruiperig.
Reptil'ia, Reptilia (kruipende diere).
reptil'ian, (n) kruipende dier; (a) kruipend.
repub'lic, republiek; ~ *of letters*, republiek v.d. lettere; ryk v.d. boeke.
repub'lican, (n) republikein; (a) republikeins; ~ **ism**,

republikanisme; ~ize, republikeins maak; in 'n republiek omskep.
republica'tion, nuwe uitgawe, herdruk.
repub'lish, weer uitgee, heruitgee.
repud'iate, verwerp, afwys; weier; verstoot; loën, ontken, verloën.
repudia'tion, verstoting; weiering; ontkenning; loëning, verloëning; verwerping.
repudia'tor, verstoter; ontkenner.
repugn', weerstreef, weerstaan, stuit; teensin opwek.
repug'nance, teensin, teenspraak, afkeer, weersin; ~ *against,* afkeer (afsku) van, weersin (teensin) in.
repug'nant, afkerig, weerstrewig, weerspannig; onverenigbaar, teenstrydig; weersinwekkend, walglik, stuitend, afstootlik.
repull'ulate, weer bot, weer uitloop; vervat.
repulse', (n) terugstoting; teenstand, terugslag; weiering; *meet with a* ~, teruggeslaan word; 'n weierende antwoord kry; (v) terugstoot, terugdrywe, terugslaan, afslaan; weier.
repul'sion, terugstoting; weiering; weersin, afkeer.
repul'sive, terugstotend; walglik, obseen, weersinwekkend; ~**ness,** walglikheid, afstootlikheid, obseniteit.
repurch'ase, (n) terugkoop; (v) weer koop, terugkoop.
repur'ify, (..fied), weer suiwer.
reputabil'ity, agtenswaardigheid, fatsoenlikheid, eervolheid.
rep'utable, geag, geëer, eervol, fatsoenlik, agtenswaardig, solied.
reputa'tion, goeie naam, agting, eer, aansien, reputasie; *a BAD* ~, 'n slegte naam; *he has a* ~ *FOR,* hy het die naam van; *have a GREAT* ~, 'n groot naam hê; *be HIGH in* ~, hoog in aansien wees; *KEEP up one's* ~, jou naam ophou; *KNOW by* ~, deur gerugte ken; *a MAN of* ~, iem. van naam.
repute', (n) naam, roem, aansien, reputasie; eer; faam; *be in BAD* ~, 'n slegte naam hê; *BY* ~, volgens gerugte; na bewering; *in COMMON* ~, volgens die algemene opvatting; *he is held in HIGH* ~, hy staan hoog aangeskrewe; hy staan in hoë aansien; *of ILL* ~, met 'n slegte naam; *a MAN of* ~, 'n man met 'n goeie naam; 'n man van naam; (v) reken; voorgee; ag, beskou; *he is* ~*d to be the best preacher,* hy word as die beste prediker beskou.
reput'ed, beweerde, voorgegee, sogenaamd, vermeende; aangeskrewe; *his* ~ *FATHER,* sy vermeende vader.
reput'edly, na bewering; volgens reputasie; *he is* ~ *a good shot,* hy het die naam van 'n goeie skut.
request', (n) versoek; vraag; bede; versoekskrif; *AT his* ~, op sy versoek; *BY* ~, op versoek; *DIRECT a* ~ *to,* vra, 'n versoek rig aan; *IN great* ~, gesog, in groot aanvraag; *MAKE a* ~, 'n versoek doen; *ON* ~, op aanvraag; (v) versoek, vra; aanvraag doen om; ~ **form,** aansoekvorm.
requick'en, nuwe lewe gee, verlewendig, laat opleef (herlewe).
re'quiem, rus; sielmis, lyksang, requiem.
require', eis, vorder, (af)verg; nodig hê; vereis; *two things* ~ *to be EXPLAINED,* twee dinge moet uitgelê word; *it* ~*d all his INFLUENCE to,* al sy invloed was nodig om; *INFORMATION is* ~*d from you,* inligting word van jou verlang; *this is all we* ~ *to KNOW,* dit is al wat ons moet weet; *the LAW* ~ *s of you,* die wet vereis van jou; *a TYPIST is* ~*d,* 'n tikster word benodig; *WHAT do you* ~ *of him?* wat wil jy van hom hê? wat verlang jy van hom? watter bevoegdhede verlang jy van hom?
required', gevra, verlang; ~ *HORSEPOWER,* benodigde perdekrag; ~ *READING,* voorgeskrewe lektuur (leeswerk); *the THING* ~, die benodigde.
require'ment, vereiste, eis; benodigdheid, behoefte; ~*s of an act,* voorskrifte van 'n wet.
req'uisite, (n) vereiste; benodigdheid; (pl) toebehore(ns), toebehoorsels; ~ *for success,* 'n vereiste vir welslae; (a) vereis, benodig; nodig.
requisi'tion, (n) vordering; aanvraag, eis; oproep; rekwisisie; aansoek; kommandeerbrief; (v) opvorder, opeis, 'n beroep doen op; 'n rekwisisie uitskryf;

versoek; aanvra; kommandeer; ~**ing,** kommandering.
requit'al, (weer)vergelding; beloning; wraak; *in* ~, as beloning; uit wraak.
requite', vergeld, beloon; weerwraak neem op; ~ *like for like,* met gelyke munt betaal; ~**r,** vergelder.
rerail'ment, hersporing.
reread', (~), herlees, weer lees; ~**ing,** herlesing.
rere'dos, altaarskerm; agterwand.
rere'gister, herregistreer.
reregistra'tion, herregistrasie, herinskrywing.
reroute, verlê; omlê.
rerout'ing, verlegging.
resad'dle, weer opsaal.
resail', terugseil, weer seil.
resale', weerverkoop.
re'schedule, herskeduleer; weer indeel, herindeel; ..*ling plan,* herskeduleringsplan.
rescind', herroep, intrek; afskaf, ophef; vernietig; ~**able,** intrekbaar, herroepbaar.
resci'ssion, vernietiging; intrekking; afskaffing.
resciss'ory, afskaffend, opheffings=.
re'script, edik, dekreet; kopie, afskrif, reskrip.
rescrip'tion, reskripsie, skriftelike antwoord.
res'cue, (n) bevryding, redding; hulp; verlossing; *come to the* ~, te hulp kom; (v) red, bevry; te hulp kom; verlos, ontset; ~ **home,** reddingshuis; ~ **party,** reddingspan, reddingsgeselskap; ~**r,** redder, verlosser; ~ **train,** hulptrein.
reseal', herverseël; ~**ing,** lap; herverseëling.
research', (n) ondersoek, nasporing; navorsing; *FIELD of* ~, ondersoekgebied; *MAKE* ~*es into the causes of juvenile delinquency,* navorsing doen oor die oorsake van jeugmisdaad; (v) navors, navorsingswerk doen; ondersoek, naspoor; ~ *in MEDICINE,* navorsing op geneeskundige gebied; ~ **aeroplane,** navorsingsvliegtuig; ~ **award,** navorsingstoekenning; ~**er,** ondersoeker, navorser; ~ **fellowship,** navorsingsbeurs; ~ **programme,** navorsingsprogram; ~ **scientist,** wetenskaplike navorser; ~ **student,** navorsingstudent; ~ **work,** navorsing(swerk); ondersoekwerk; bronnestudie.
reseat', weer plaas; van nuwe sitplekke voorsien; weer gaan sit; 'n nuwe boom (sitplek) insit (broek); hermat (stoel).
resect', gedeeltelik verwyder, wegsny; ~**ion,** verwydering, inpeiling, insnyding.
resed'a, reseda.
reseek', (..sought), opnuut soek.
reseize', weer bemagtig, herneem, weer in besit neem.
resei'zure, (her)bemagtiging.
resell', (..sold), weer verkoop, herverkoop.
resem'blance, ooreenkoms, gelykenis; afbeelding; *BEAR a* ~ *to,* lyk na; ~ *to another THING,* ooreenkoms met iets anders.
resem'blant, ooreenkomstig.
resem'ble, lyk na, ooreenkom, trek na, 'n ooreenkoms hê met.
resem'bling, gelykend op.
resend', (..sent), weer stuur.
resent' kwalik neem, beledig voel; geraak wees oor; ~ *strongly,* sterk afkeur; 'n groot weersin hê in; ~**ful,** liggeraak, gevoelig; wrewelig; haatdraend; gebelg, gegrief; ~**fulness,** wreweligheid; liggeraaktheid, gevoeligheid; haatdraendheid; ~**ment,** wrok, haatdraendheid; wrewel, wreweling; gekrenktheid, gegriefdheid.
reserva'tion, voorbehoud, reserwe, agterhoudendheid; bewaring; bespreking; reservasie, reservering; *with a* ~, onder (met) voorbehoud.
reserve', (n) voorbehoud; noodvoorraad; ingetoënheid, selfbedwang, terughoudendheid, eenselwigheid, gereserveerdheid; beskeidenheid, ingetoënheid; reserweprys; reserwe, reserwevoorraad; reservaat; wildtuin, diereeltuin; (pl) reserwevoorraad; reserwetroepe; *ACCEPT without* ~, sonder voorbehoud aanneem; onvoorwaardelik aanneem; *with ALL* ~, met die nodige voorbehoud; *IN* ~, in voorraad; *INNER* ~*s,* innerlike reserwe; ~ *of OFFICERS,* offisiersreserwe; *SECRET* ~*s,* geheime reserwes; *THE* ~*s,* reserwetroepe; *under USUAL* ~, onder gewone voorbehoud; *WITHOUT* ~,

reserve sonder voorbehoud; (v) voorbehou; agterhou, reserveer, bewaar; bestem; opskort; bespreek (sitplek); ~ *a DANCE*, 'n dans oophou (bespreek); ~ *JUDGEMENT*, 'n oordeel opskort; uitspraak voorbehou (reg); ~ *for a special PURPOSE*, bespreek vir 'n besondere doel.

reserve': ~ **bank,** reserwebank; ~ **capital,** reserwekapitaal.

reserved', agterhoudend, ingetoë, geslote; bespreek, gereserveer (plek); toe; *have a* ~ *NATURE*, terughoudend van aard wees; ~ *SEATS*, bespreekte sitplekke; ~**ly,** ingetoë, op terughoudende wyse.

reserve': ~ **fund,** reserwefonds; ~ **list,** reserwelys; ~ **price,** reserweprys; ~ **stock,** reserwevoorraad.

reserv'ist, reservis; reserwespeler.

res'ervoir, reservoir, opgaardam; dam; bewaarplek; vergaarbak opgaarbak.

reset', (~), verberg; inboet (saad); opnuut insit; weer skerp maak; weer styf word; herset, oorset.

reset'tle, hervestig, weer vestig; weer in orde bring, herstel; ~**ment,** hervestiging.

reship', (-ped), weer inskeep, verskeep; oorlaai; ~**ment,** weerinskeping; verskeping; oorlaaiing.

reshuf'fle, weer skud, weer skommel; anders verdeel; verskuif, omruil; hervorm (kabinet).

reside', woon, verblyf hou; setel; berus; uithang; ~ *AT*, woon op; ~ *IN*, woon in; *the POWER* ~ *s in*, die mag berus by.

res'idence, woonplek; setel; inwoning; woning, verblyf, residensie; *BE in* ~, inwonend wees; inwoon (onderwyser, student); *BOARD and* ~, kos en inwoning; *HAVE one's* ~ *at (in),* woon op; *TAKE up one's* ~, jou (metterwoon) vestig.

res'idency, (..cies), drosdy (hist.); landdroswoning, residensie, magistraatswoning.

res'ident, (n) bewoner, inwoner, ingesetene; loseerder; (a) woonagtig; inwonend; resident-; ~ **ambassador,** gewone gesant; ~ **bird,** standvoël; ~ **doctor,** inwonende geneesheer.

residen'tial, woon-, huis-; verblyf-; inwonend; ~ **address,** woonadres, huisadres; ~ **allowance,** huistoelae; ~ **area,** woonwyk, woongebied, deftige buurt; ~ **building,** woongebou; ~ **permit,** verblyfvergunning; ~ **qualification,** woonbevoegdheid; ~ **quarter,** woonwyk.

residen'tiary, met ampswoning; woonagtig, inwonend.

res'ident: ~ **magistrate,** resident-magistraat; resident-landdros; ~ **master,** huisvader; ~ **member,** inwonende lid; ~ **physician,** inwonende geneesheer; ~ **population,** vaste bevolking.

resid'er, bewoner, verblyfhouer.

resid'ing, wonend.

resid'ual, (n) res; oorblyfsel; byproduk; (a) oorgebly, agtergeblewe, oorblywend; ~ **effect,** nawerking; ~ **product,** afvalproduk; ~ **stress,** naspanning.

resid'uary, (n) erfgenaam; (a) orig, oorblywend.

res'idue, oorblyfsel, oorskiet, restant; besinksel; oorskot, res, saldo.

resid'uum, oorskiet; besinksel, afsaksel, residu; uitvaagsel, skuim.

re'sign¹, oorteken, weer teken.

resign'², afstaan; opgee, neerlê, bedank, aftree, (jou) ontslag neem; afstand doen van ('n eis); jou onderwerp aan; berus in; jou neerlê by; ~ *as CHAIRMAN*, as voorsitter bedank; ~ *ONESELF to*, jou onderwerp aan; jou getroos met; ~ *ONESELF to one's destiny (fate)*, in jou lot berus; ~ *from a POST*, vir 'n pos bedank: 'n amp neerlê.

resigna'tion, gelatenheid, berusting; neerlegging; oorgawe; bedanking, ontslag; *HAND in one's* ~, jou ontslag indien, jou bedanking instuur; *LETTER of* ~, bedankingsbrief.

resigned', gelate, onderworpe, berustend.

resile', terugspring, veerkragtig wees; ~ *from*, terugtree uit ('n ooreenkoms).

resil'ience, resil'iency, terugspringing; veerkrag, elastisiteit.

resil'ient, terugspringend; veerkragtig, elasties.

res'in, (n) gom, hars; harpuis; (v) met harpuis bestryk; ~ **a'ceous,** = **resinous;** ~ **-bush,** harpuisbos; ~ **if'erous,** harsvoortbrengend; ~ **iform,** harsagtig;

~ **ous,** gomagtig, harsagtig; ~ *ous electricity*, negatiewe elektrisiteit; ~ **ousness,** gomagtigheid, harsagtigheid; ~**y** = **resinous.**

resipis'cence, inkeer, berou; beter insig.

resist', weerstaan, uithou; jou verset teen, weerstand bied, weerstreef, jou teësit; bestand wees teen, nie toegee nie aan; *he cannot* ~ *a JOKE*, hy kan nie nalaat om 'n grap te maak nie; ~ *TEMPTATION*, versoeking weerstaan.

resis'tance, weerstand, teenstand; verset, weerstrewing; afwering; versetpleging; *ACTIVE* ~, gewelddadige verset; ~ *of the AIR*, lugweerstand; ~ *to DROUGHT*, bestandheid teen droogte; ~ *of HEAT*, hittevastheid; *take the LINE of least* ~, die maklikste weg volg; die afdraande pad kies; ~ *with* ~, weerstand ondervind; *OFFER* ~, weerstand bied; *PASSIVE* ~, lydelike verset; ~ *to SHOCK*, skokvastheid; ~ **coil,** weerstandspoel; ~ **fighter,** versetstryder; ~ **level,** weerstandspeil; ~ **movement,** versetbeweging, weerstandsbeweging; ~ **test,** weerstandstoets.

resist': ~**ant,** weerstandbiedend; bestand; ~*ant to*, bestand teen; ~**er,** weerstandbieder; versetpleger; ~**ibil'ity,** weerstaanbaarheid; weerstandsvermoë; ~**ible,** weerstaanbaar; ~**ive,** weerstandbiedend; ~**iv'ity,** weerstandsvermoë; soortlike geleidingsvermoë; ~**less,** onweerstaanbaar.

resite', verskuif.

resol'der, weer soldeer, hersoldeer.

resole', versool.

resol'ing, versool, versoolwerk.

reso'luble, oplosbaar; ontleedbaar.

res'olute, vasberade, onverskrokke, deurtastend, onversaag; ~ *in one's DESIRE*, vasberade in jou verlange; ~ *of PURPOSE*, vasberade om jou doel te bereik; ~**ly,** op onverskrokke manier, vasberade; ~**ness,** vasberadenheid, deurtastendheid, beslistheid.

resolu'tion, besluit, beslissing, resolusie; standvastigheid, vasberadenheid; oplossing; voorneme; ontleding, ontbinding; ~ *of an EQUATION*, oplossing van 'n vergelyking; ~ *of FORCES*, ontbinding van kragte; *FORM a* ~, 'n voorneme opvat; *make GOOD* ~*s*, goeie voornemens hê; *a* ~ *was PASSED*, 'n besluit is aangeneem; *PROPOSE a* ~, 'n mosie voorstel; ~*s of the SYNOD*, Acta Synodi, handelinge v.d. sinode; ~**s committee,** agendakomitee.

res'olutive, (n) oplosmiddel; (a) oplossend; herleibaar.

resolvabil'ity, oplosbaarheid; herleibaarheid.

resol'vable, oplosbaar; herleibaar; ~**ness** = **resolvability.**

resolve', (n) besluit; voorneme; *keep one's* ~, by jou besluit bly; (v) besluit, beslis; 'n besluit neem, voorneem; ontbind, oplos, ontleed; 'n oplossing vind; *BE* ~ *d*, vasbeslote wees om; ~ *a CRISIS*, 'n krisis oplos; ~ *DIFFERENCES*, geskille bylê; *all DOUBTS were* ~ *d*, alle twyfel is weggeneem; ~ *FORCES*, kragte ontbind; *the HOUSE* ~ *d itself into committee*, die raad het in komitee gegaan.

resolv'ed, vasberade, vasbeslote; voornemens; ~**ness,** vasberadenheid.

resol'vent, oplosmiddel.

resolv'er, oplosser.

res'onance, res'onancy, weerklank, gehorigheid (huis), resonansie; ~ **box,** klankkas.

res'onant, weerklinkend, resonerend; *be* ~ *with*, weerklink van.

res'onator, resonator; klankbord; klankkas.

resorb', weer absorbeer, herabsorbeer.

resorb'ence, reso'rption, resorpsie, heroplossing, weeroplossing, opslurping.

resort'¹, (n) sameloop, samekoms; oord, bymekaarkomplek; toevlugsoord; hulpmiddel, redmiddel; *LAST* ~, laaste toevlug; as uiterste middel; ~ *of THIEVES*, diewenes; (v) gaan, jou toevlug neem tot; jou begewe na; ~ *to force*, geweld gebruik, toevlug tot geweld neem.

resort'², (v) weer sorteer, oorsorteer, hersorteer.

resound'¹, weer laat klink; weer klink.

resound'², galm, weerklink, nagalm, weergalm; skal;

resource

uitbasuin; *the hall ~ed with applause*, die saal het weergalm van applous; **~ing**, (n) gedawer; (a) gehorig; weerklinkend; klinkend; *a ~ victory*, 'n klinkende oorwinning.

resource', hulpbron, hulpmiddel; redmiddel, toevlug; vindingrykheid; (pl) hulpbronne; geldmiddele; talente; *at the END of one's ~s*, ten einde raad; raadop; *FULL of ~*, vol planne: vindingryk; *a MAN of ~*, 'n vindingryke man; *NATURAL ~s*, natuurlike hulpbronne; *READING was his chief ~*, lees was sy vernaamste tydverdryf; *he was THROWN on his own ~s*, hy moes homself maar red; *WITHOUT ~*, reddeloos; **~ful**, slim, vindingryk; **~fulness**, vindingrykheid; **~less**, radeloos, sonder middele, hulpeloos; **~lessness**, radeloosheid, hulpeloosheid.

resow', (-ed, -n or -ed), weer saai.

respect', (n) eerbied, aansien, ontsag, agting; eerbiedigheid, eerbiediging, eer; opsig; (pl) groete, komplimente; *in ALL ~s*, in alle opsigte; *in EVERY ~*, in alle opsigte; *GIVE my ~s to*, groete laat weet; *with GREAT ~*, met alle agting; *HAVE a ~ for*, eerbied hê vir; *HAVE ~ to*, betrekking hê op; *have a HEALTHY ~ for*, groot ontsag hê vir; *HOLD in ~*, respekteer; *HOLD someone in ~*, iem. hoogag; *IN ~ of*, met betrekking tot; ten opsigte van; *PAY one's ~ to someone*, by iem. jou opwagting maak; *PAY the last ~s*, die laaste eer bewys; *SEND one's ~s*, groete laat weet; *SHOW ~ to*, eerbied betoon aan; *in SOME ~s*, in sommige opsigte; *WITH ~ to*, met betrekking tot; ten opsigte van; ten aansien van; *WITHOUT ~ of persons*, sonder aansien van persoon (des persoons); (v) eerbiedig, hoogag; ontsien; respekteer; betref; betrekking hê (op); *you must ~ my age*, jy moet my ouderdom ontsien; **~abil'ity**, agbaarheid; soliditeit; fatsoen, aansien; deftige persoon, agtenswaardige mens; **~able**, agtenswaardig, agbaar, eerbiedwaardig; deftig, fatsoenlik; eersaam, aansienlik; *a ~able amount*, 'n aansienlike bedrag; **~ably**, fatsoenlik; netjies; **~ed**, geëer, geag, gesien; **~er**, eerbiediger, iem. wat eerbiedig (eer betoon); aannemer; *he is no ~er of persons*, hy is geen aannemer van die persoon nie; **~ful**, eerbiedig; **~fully**, eerbiedig, beleef; *yours ~fully*, u dienswillige dienaar; **~fulness**, eerbied; **~ing**, (n) eerbiediging, agting; (prep) aangaande, betreffende, oor.

respect'ive, betreklik, respektief; onderskeie, eie, besonder; *in their ~ places*, elkeen op sy eie plek; **~ly**, onderskeidelik, respektiewelik.

respell', herspel, oorspel.

respira'tion, asemhaling, respirasie.

res'pirator, gasmasker; respirator; *~ mask*, gasmasker.

res'piratory, asemhalings-; *~ bag*, asemsak; *~ organ*, asemhalingsorgaan; *~ system*, asemhalingstelsel.

respire', asemhaal, asem skep; uitasem; inasem.

respiro'meter, asemmeter, respirometer.

res'pite, (n) uitstel, respyt; verademing, rus; opskorting; *a ~ from one's work*, 'n verposing, rustydjie; (v) uitstel, verdaag, opskort, skors; verligting gee; betaling terughou; **~ days**, respytdae, uitsteldae.

resplen'dence, resplen'dency, glans; luister.

resplen'dent, luisterryk, glansryk, skitterend, glansend.

respond'¹, (n) stut.

respond'², (n) beurtsang, teensang; (v) antwoord, beantwoord, reageer, gehoor gee aan, vatbaar wees vir; *he does not ~ to KINDNESS*, hy reageer nie op vriendelikheid nie: *~ to a TOAST*, op 'n heildronk antwoord; *~ to TREATMENT*, reageer op behandeling; **~ent**, (n) verweerder, gedaagde, respondent; (a) beantwoordend; *be ~ent to*, gehoor gee aan; reageer op.

response', antwoord; gedrag; weerklank (fig.); responsorium, beurtsang; *IN ~ to*, as antwoord op; *MAKE no ~*, geen antwoord gee nie; *meet with a READY ~*, onmiddellik weerklank vind; *SHOW no ~ to treatment*, geen reaksie op die behandeling toon nie; *in ~ to a SUMMONS*, ingevolge 'n dagvaarding.

responsibil'ity, (..ties), verantwoordelikheid, aanspreeklikheid; taak; *FREE of ~*, sonder verantwoordelikheid; *EVERYBODY'S ~ is nobody's ~*, allemansgoed is niemandsgoed; *it IS his ~*, dit is vir sy rekening; hy is daarmee belas; *he is a MAN without any responsibilities*, hy is sonder verbintenisse (verantwoordelikhede); *ON his own ~*, op eie verantwoordelikheid; *RELEASE on his own ~*, op eie verantwoordelikheid vrylaat; *SENSE of ~*, verantwoordelikheidsgevoel; *TAKE ~ for*, vir jou eie verantwoordelikheid neem.

respon'sible, verantwoordelik, aanspreeklik; vertroubaar, deeglik; *~ FOR*, verantwoordelik vir; belas met; *~ GOVERNMENT*, verantwoordelike bestuur; *NOT to be ~ for one's actions*, nie verantwoordelik vir jou dade nie; ontoerekenbaar; *~ TO*, verantwoordelik aan.

respon'sive, antwoordend; simpatiek, deelnemend; *be ~ to*, reageer op, antwoord op; **~ness**, meegevoel, simpatie.

responsory, (..ries), teensang, beurtsang, responsorium, responsorie.

rest¹, (n) oorskiet, oorskot, res (voedsel); die orige; *and all the ~ of it*, en wat dies meer sy; (v) oorskiet, oorbly.

rest², (n) rus; verposing; rustigheid, kalmte; doodslaap; ruspunt; rusteken (musiek); rukkie; drievoet; bok (biljart); leunspaan; kussingblok; reservefonds; *AMONG the ~*, onder andere; *ANGLE of ~*, natuurlike helling; *AT ~*, rustig, stil; in rus; *BE at ~*, rus hê; bedaard wees; uit die wêreld (dood) wees; *COME to ~*, tot rus kom; tot stilstand kom; *DAY of ~*, rusdag; *ENJOY a ~*, rus; 'n ruspouse geniet; *pass into ETERNAL ~*, die ewige rus ingaan; *as FOR the ~*, origens; *GIVE your men a ~*, laat jou mense rus; *GO to ~*, gaan rus; gaan slaap; *GONE to his ~*, sy ewige rus ingegaan; *HAVE a ~*, rus; 'n ruspouse geniet; *LAY to ~*, ter ruste lê, begrawe; *~ breeds RUST*, rus roes; *SEEK one's ~*, jou ter ruste begeef; *SET a person's mind at ~*, iem. gerusstel; *TAKE a ~*, gaan rus; *WITHOUT ~*, sonder rus; *a ~ from WORK*, rus na arbeid; (v) rus; slaap; steun, leun; berus op; laat rus; *~ ASSURED*, wees gerus; *the matter CANNOT ~ there*, die saak kan nie daarby gelaat word nie; *~ one's ELBOW on the table*, met jou elmboog op die tafel leun; *~ on the EVIDENCE of one person*, berus op die getuienis van een persoon; *~ in GOD*, in die Here rus; *let the MATTER ~*, laat die saak rus; dit daarby laat; *~ your MEN*, laat jou mense rus; *~ ONESELF*, uitrus; *God ~ his SOUL*, mag sy siel in vrede rus; *WELL ~ed*, goed uitgerus; *it ~s WITH you*, dit hang van jou af; jy moet besluit.

restart', opnuut aan die gang sit; weer begin.

restate', herhaal, heraankondig, herkonstateer; **~ment**, herhaling; heraankondiging.

res'taurant, restourant, restaurant, eetsaal.

restaurateur', restouranthouer, restouranteienaar.

rest: *~-block*, draagblok; *~-camp*, ruskamp; *~-cure*, ruskuur; *~ful*, rustig, stil, rusgewend; *~fulness*, rustigheid, stilte; *~ home*, rushuis; *~ house*, herberg; *~ing*, rustend, uitrustend; *~ing-place*, rusplek.

restip'ulate, opnuut bepaal.

res'titute, teruggee, vergoed; herstel (huweliksregte).

restitu'tion, teruggawe, restitusie; vergoeding, skadeloosstelling; herstel, restitusie; *~ of CONJUGAL rights*, herstel van huweliksregte; *MAKE ~*, die skade vergoed; 'n onreg goedmaak; restitueer; *~ order*, bevel tot herstel van huweliksregte.

res'tive, koppig, eiewys, weerspannig; ongeduldig; woelig, kriewelrig; steeks (perd); **~ness**, koppigheid; woeligheid; steeksheid.

rest'less, rusteloos, woelig; gejaag, onrustig; slapeloos; **~ness**, rusteloosheid, woeligheid; slapeloosheid.

restock', weer van voorrade voorsien; weer van vee voorsien.

restor'able, herstelbaar.

restora'tion, teruggawe; herstel(ling), restourasie (gebou); weeroprigting; weerinvoering.

restor'ative, (n) versterkende middel, laafdrank, ge-

nesende middel; (a) versterkend; herstellend, herstel=.
restore', teruggee; herstel; restoureer, vernuwe (ou gebou); terugbring, terugsit; genees; opnuut bêre; ~ *CONFIDENCE*, vertroue herwin; ~ *to FAVOUR*, in die guns herstel; ~*d to HEALTH*, herstel; ~ *to LIFE*, weer laat lewe; ~ *to the THRONE*, op die troon herstel; ~ **r**, hersteller; wederoprigter; restoureerder.
restrain', bedwing, beteuel; beperk; weerhou, in toom, inhou; ~ *from*, weerhou van; ~ **abil'ity**, bedwingbaarheid; ~ **able**, bedwingbaar; beperkbaar; ~**ed**, ingetoë.
restraint', bedwang, beperking, weerhouding; teuel; selfbeheersing, selfbedwang, intoming; mag, kontrole; opsluiting; terughoudendheid, ingetoënheid; *BE under* ~, onder bedwang wees; in hegtenis gehou word; *EXERCISE* ~ *in drink*, matig drink; *be under NO* ~, heeltemal vry wees; *PLACE* ~ *on expenditure*, uitgawes beperk; *WITH* ~, ingehoue; *WITHOUT* ~, onbeperk; onbeheers; heeltemal vry.
restrict', beperk, begrens, bepaal; inperk.
restric'tion, beperking, bepaling; voorbehoud; inperking, restriksie; *PLACE* ~*s on*, beperkings oplê aan; *WITHOUT* ~, sonder voorbehoud (beperking).
restring', (..**strung**), herbesnaar; ~**ing**, herbesnaring.
restrict'ive, beperkend; bepalend.
restrin'gent, saamtrekkend.
rest' room, ruskamer.
resubject', opnuut onderwerp, heronderwerp.
result', (n) gevolg; uitslag, resultaat; slotsom, afloop, effek, end; voortvloeisel, uitvloeisel; vrug; uitkoms (som); *AS a* ~ *of*, ten gevolge van, as gevolg van; *PAYMENT by* ~*s*, beloning na prestasie; *WITHOUT* ~, tevergeefs; (v) volg, ontstaan, voortvloei, voortspruit, uitvloei, voortkom, gedy; lei (tot), uitloop (op); *the ACCIDENT* ~*ed in the death of two persons*, die ongeluk het die dood van twee persone veroorsaak; *DEATH* ~*ed from an overdose of drugs*, die oorsaak v.d. dood was 'n oordosis van verdowingsmiddels; ~ *FROM*, voortkom uit; ~**ant**, (n) resultante; resultaat; gevolg; (a) gevolglik, daaruit voortvloeiend, as gevolg; ~*ant from*, voortkom uit.
resume', herneem; hervat; herkry; weer inneem; weer aanneem; verval; terugneem; saamvat, resumeer; weer voortgaan, vervolg; ~ *a CONVERSATION*, 'n gesprek weer aanknoop; *the HOUSE* ~*d its labours*, die Parlement het sy werksaamhede hervat; ~ *one's PIPE*, weer begin rook; ~ *one's SEAT*, gaan sit; ~ *one's WORK*, jou werk hervat.
rés ́umé, (n) kort samevatting, opsomming, résumé, oorsig; (v) opsom, saamvat.
resumm'on, weer dagvaar; ~**s**, nuwe dagvaarding.
resump'tion, hervatting; herneming.
resump'tive, hernemend; hervattend.
resup'inate, omgekeer, onderstebo.
resur'face, 'n blad vernuwe, hervlak; weer bo kom.
resurf'acing, bladvernuwing, hervlakking; terugkoms na die oppervlak (duikboot).
resurge', herrys, weer opstaan.
resurg'ence, herrysing, weeropstanding, herrysenis.
resurg'ent, (n) opstandeling; (a) (weer) opstaande.
resurrect', opgrawe; opwek; oprakel; weer opstaan, herrys.
resurrec'tion, wederopstanding, herrysenis, opwekking; ~ **man**, lykdief; ~ **pie**, oorskietpastei; opgewarmde kos; ~**ist**, lykdief.
resurv'ey, (n) nuwe besigtiging; heropmeting.
resurvey', (v) nasien; weer opmeet.
resus ́citate, opwek, laat herlewe; bybring; oprakel.
resuscita'tion, opwekking, herlewing; herstel; by= brenging; ~ **ward**, bybringsaal.
resus ́citative, herlewend.
resus ́citator, herlewer; opwekkingsmiddel; opwekker; asemhalingsmasjien.
ret, week (vlas); vrot, stik, muf word (hooi).
reta'ble, retabel, agterstuk.

ret'ail, (n) kleinhandel; *sell by* ~, by die klein maat verkoop; (a, adv) by die klein maat, kleinhandel=.
retail', (v) by die klein maat verkoop; omstandig vertel; ~ *something for what it is worth*, iets vir dieself= de prys verkoop.
ret'ail: ~ **business**, kleinhandel; ~ **dealer**, ~**er**, kleinhandelaar; ~ **price**, kleinhandelsprys; ~-**price maintenance**, prysbinding; ~ **shop**, winkel; kleinhandelaar; ~ **trade**, kleinhandel; ~ **trader**, kleinhandelaar.
retain', hou, behou; in diens hou; huur; teenhou, terughou, onthou; bespreek (advokaat); wegsteek (melk); binnehou, inhou (kos); ~**er**, volgeling, aanhanger; bediende; retensie; sluitpen (geweer); bindgeld, honorarium (advokaat).
retain'ing, (n) teenhouding, agterhouding; (a) teenhoudend, agterhoudend; ~ **bolt**, klembout; ~ **catch**, keerknip; ~ **dam**, studam, keerdam; ~ **fee**, retensiegeld, retensiehonorarium, vaste honorarium, bindgeld; ~ **flange**, keerflens; ~ **pay**, waggeld; ~ **pin**, klemskroef, sluitskroef; ~ **wall**, dwarswal, steunmuur, keermuur.
retake', (n) heropname; (v) (..**took, -n**), herower; terugneem, herneem; weer opneem.
retal'iate, vergeld, terugbetaal; weerwraak neem, met gelyke munt betaal.
retalia'tion, weervergelding, wraakneming, weerwraak, wraak.
retal'iative, **retal'iatory**, terugbetalend, vergeldings=.
retard', (n) vertraging; (v) vertraag, uitstel, teenhou, ophou; agteruitsit; belemmer; strem; ~**a'tion**, vertraging; belemmering; uitstel; agterlikheid; stremming; ~**ative**, ~**atory**, belemmerend; vertragend.
retard'ed, agterlik; ~ *CHILDREN*, vertraagde kinders; ~ *EXPLOSION*, na-ontploffing; ~ *IGNI= TION*, vertraagde ontsteking.
retard'ment, vertraging.
retch, kokhals, braakbewegings maak.
retell', (..**told**), opnuut vertel, weer vertel.
reten'tion, terughouding; teenhouding; onthouvermoë; behoud; aanhouding; instandhouding; wegsteek (van melk); retensiereg; *right of* ~, retensiereg; ~ **money**, bindgeld, retensiegeld.
reten'tive, terughoudend; vashoudend, behoudend; *BE* ~ *of*, vashou aan, bewaar; *have a* ~ *MEMORY*, 'n sterk geheue hê; ~**ness**, vashoudendheid.
retentiv'ity, inhouvermoë.
retest', herkeur; ~**ing**, herkeuring.
rethink', (..**thought**), opnuut deurdink.
rethread', weer ryg; 'n skroefdraad nasny.
re'tiary, (..**ries**), sterwebspinnekop.
ret'icence, stilswygendheid, terughoudendheid; verswyging; geslotenheid, gereserveerdheid.
ret'icent, agterhoudend, geslote, swygsaam, gereserveer.
ret'icle, kruisdraad.
retic'ular, netvormig; ingewikkeld.
retic'ulate, (v) netvormig verdeel; (a) netvormig.
reticula'tion, netwerk; benetting; netvorming.
ret'icule, (dames)werksakkie.
retic'ulum, (..**la**), blaarpens, kleinpensie, ruitjiespens, blompens, netmaag; netwerk.
ret'iform, netvormig.
ret'ina, netvlies (van die oog), retina; ~**l**, netvlies=; ~**l pigment**, netvlieskleurstof.
retinit'is, netvliesontsteking, retinitis.
ret'inue, gevolg, stoet, trein.
retire', (n) aftog; *sound the* ~, die aftog blaas; (v) terugtrek; jou ontslag neem; aftree, uit diens tree; gaan rentenier; terugneem, retireer, terugwyk; wyk; uit sake gaan, stil gaan lewe; gaan slaap; weg= gaan, jou verwyder; jou onttrek; ~ *from the ARMY*, uit die leër tree; ~ *to BED*, na bed gaan; ~ *from BUSINESS*, uit sake gaan; ~ *before an ENEMY*, voor 'n vyand terugtrek; *the LADIES* ~*d*, die dames het hulle verwyder; ~ *into ONE= SELF*, tot jouself inkeer; eenselwig wees; ~ *on a PENSION*, jou pensioen neem, met pensioen aftree; ~ *from PRACTICE*, die praktyk neerlê; ~ *from PUBLIC life*, jou aan die openbare lewe onttrek.

retired', stil, afgetrokke; oud-, gewese; afgesonder, afgeleë; gepensioeneer; ~ *FARMER*, rustende boer; *a* ~ *GENTLEMAN*, 'n rentenier; 'n afgetredene; *place on the* ~ *LIST*, op pensioen sit (stel); ~ *PAY*, pensioen, russoldy.

retire'ment, uittreding; terugtreding, terugtrekking; verwydering; afsondering; aftog; ontslag; uitdienstreding, pensioenering; rusplek; *live in* ~, stil lewe; ~ **annuity**, uittredingsannuïteit, aftreelyfrente.

retir'ing, (n) uitdienstreding; verwydering; (a) terugtredend; stil, teruggetrokke, ingetoë (persoon); ~ **age**, ouderdomsgrens, leeftydsgrens; ~ **pension**, aftreepensioen; ~ **room**, ruskamer; toiletkamer; privaat.

retort'¹, (n) vinnige (gevatte) antwoord; teenwerping; (v) teenwerp, vinnig (gevat) antwoord gee.

retort'², (n) retort, kolfglas, kromhals, kromnek; (v) suiwer (in 'n retort); ~ **ed**, omgebuig; afgewend; ~ **ion**, ombuiging; vergelding, weerwraak.

retouch', (n) bywerking; (v) weer aanraak; bywerk, retoesjeer (foto).

retrace', weer oortrek; naspeur; volg; teruggaan; ~ *one's steps*, teruggaan (op jou spore); ~ **able**, naspeurbaar, wat gevolg kan word.

retract', terugtrek, herroep, intrek, iets terugneem; terugkrabbel; ~ **able**, intrekbaar; herroepbaar; ~ **able undercarriage**, intrekbare onderstel; ~ **ile**, intrekbaar; ~ **ion**, terugtrekking; intrekking, terugname; herroeping; ~ **or**, terugtrekker; terugtrekkende spier; herroeper.

retrans'fer, (n) hertransport; heroorplasing; (v) hertransporteer; heroorplaas.

retranslate', weer vertaal, hervertaal.

retransmit', (-ted), hersend.

re'tread, (n) versoolde band.

retread', (v) versool.

retreat'¹, (n) skuilplek; aftog, terugwyking; afsondering; terugtog; rusplek, toevlugsoord; gestig; asiel; vlagstryking; aandsinjaal; *BEAT a* ~, die aftog blaas; die stryd gewonne gee; *COVER the* ~, die terugtog dek; *in FULL* ~, in volle aftog; *make GOOD one's* ~, daarin slaag om weg te kom; die terugtog verseker; ~ *for INEBRIATES*, gestig vir dranksugtiges (dronkaards); *SOUND the* ~, die aftog blaas; (v) terugtrek, (terug)wyk, retireer, duinkerk.

retreat'², (v) (~), weer behandel.

retrench', besnoei, inkort, inkrimp, besuinig; verskans; afdank; ~ **ment**, besnoeiing, inkorting, besuiniging; verskansing; afdanking.

retri'al, herverhoor.

retribu'tion, (weer)vergelding, wraak; vergoeding, beloning.

retrib'utive, vergeldend, wraak=, vergeldings=.

retriev'able, herstelbaar; herkrybaar.

retriev'al, herstel; (die) terugkry; ~ *of information*, ontsluiting van inligting.

retrieve', (n) herstel; *beyond* ~, onherstelbaar; (v) herstel; terugkry, herwin; red; opspoor; weer goedmaak; - *a BATTLE*, 'n veldslag herwin; ~ *one's CHARACTER*, jou karakter herwin; ~ *one's FORTUNE*, jou fortuin herstel; ~ *a LOSS*, 'n verlies weer goedmaak; ~ *the SITUATION*, die posisie red; ~ **r**, aanbringer; apporteerhond; apporteur.

retroact', terugwerk; ~ **ion**, terugwerkende krag, terugwerking; ~ **ive**, terugwerkend.

ret'rocede¹, terugtree; wyk.

retrocede'², weer afstaan (grondgebied).

retroce'ssion, terugtreding, terugwyking; weerstand.

retrograda'tion, agteruitgang; terugtrekking; ontaarding.

ret'rograde, (n) gedegenereerde, ontaarde; (v) terugwyk, agteruitgaan; ontaard, versleg; (a) teruggaande, agterwaarts; retrograde; ontaardend, versleg= tend; ~ **dictionary**, retrograde woordeboek.

retrogress', agteruitgaan; versleg, ontaard; ~ **ion**, agteruitgang, teruggang; ontaarding, verslegting; terugstelling; ~ **ive**, agteruitgaande; ontaardend.

retrorse', teruggedraai, teruggebuig; ondertoe gebuig.

ret'rospect, terugblik, oorsig; *in* ~, van agter beskou, retrospektief.

retrospec'tion, terugblik; (die) terugsien, terugkyk; retrospeksie.

retrospec'tive, terugblikkend; terugwerkend, retrospektief; *with* ~ *effect*, met terugwerkende krag.

ret'rovert, terugdraai; terugkeer.

retrude', terugstamp.

retry', (retried), herverhoor.

rett'ing, week, weking (vlas), roting; verrotting (strooi); ~ **tank**, weektenk, rotingsbak.

return'¹, (n) terugkeer, tuiskoms; terugkoms; teruggawe; voordeel, rendement, wins (sake); opgawe, staat; statistiek, verslag; terugreis; retoer(kaartjie); terugsending; beloning; opbrings; antwoord; verkiesing; (pl) omsetstate, rapporte; opgawes; *BIG* ~ *s*, *small profits*, groot omset, klein winste; *BY* ~, per omgaande (per kerende) pos; *EMPTY* ~ *s*, leë houers; *GET nothing in* ~, niks daarvoor kry nie; *many HAPPY* ~ *s*, veels geluk; nog baie jare; *IN* ~ *for*, in ruil vir; as erkenning; *the* ~ *s were LARGE*, groot winste is gemaak; *ON their* ~, by hulle terugkoms; *POINT of no* ~, punt van geen terugkeer nie; veiligheidskeerpunt; *by* ~ *of POST*, per kerende pos; per omgaande; *small PROFITS and quick* ~ *s*, klein profyte en vinnige omset; *RENDER a* ~, 'n opgawe maak; (v) teruggaan, terugkeer, terugkom; terugstuur, besorg; vergeld; antwoord, beantwoord; terugwerp; kies, verkies (parlement); terugslaan, terugspeel (sport); ~ *an ANSWER*, antwoord; ~ *to the ATTACK*, die aanval hernuwe; ~ *a BALL*, 'n bal terugslaan; ~ *a BLOW*, terugslaan; ~ *the COMPLIMENT*, in (met) gelyke munt terugbetaal; ook komplimenteer; ~ *to DUST*, tot stof terugkeer; ~ *EVIL for evil*, kwaad met kwaad vergeld; ~ *a GREETING*, teruggroet; ~ *HOME*, tuiskom; ~ *the LEAD*, terugspeel; in dieselfde kleur naspeel; ~ *LIKE for like*, met (in) gelyke munt betaal; ~ *to one's MUTTONS*, op die onderwerp (saak) terugkom; ~ *a PROFIT*, wins oplewer; ~ *a SALUTE*, terugsalueer; *the MEMBER was* ~ *ed*, die lid is gekies; ~ *to a SUBJECT*, op 'n onderwerp terugkom; ~ *THANKS*, bedank; dank (na ete); ~ *a VERDICT*, uitspraak doen, vonnis vel; ~ *a VISIT*, 'n teenbesoek aflê.

return'², (v) weer draai.

return'able, terug te stuur, nie-behoubaar; *the rule is* - *tomorrow*, môre is die keerdag v.d. bevel.

return': ~ **bout**, herontmoeting; ~ **cable**, terugkabel; ~ **cargo**, retoerlading, retoervrag; ~ **commission**, retoerkommissie; ~ **crease**, retoerlyn; ~ **day**, keerdag (van hofbevel); ~ **fight**, teenwedstryd, herontmoeting(swedstryd); ~ **flight**, terugvlug; ~ **ing**, (die) terugkeer; ~ **ing officer**, stemopnemer; terugsender (pos); ~ **journey**, terugreis, retoerreis; ~ **match**, teenwedstryd, weeromspel; ~ **pipe**, terugloop pyp; ~ **portion**, retoergedeelte; ~ **stroke**, terugslag; ~ **ticket**, retoerkaartjie; ~ **visit**, teenbesoek; ~ **voucher**, terugstuurbewys.

retuse', baie stomp, breedpuntig.

retype', oortik.

reun'ion, hereniging, reünie.

reunite', herenig, versoen; weer bymekaarkom.

reuse', (n) weergebruik, hergebruik; (v) weer gebruik.

rev, (n) *abbr. for* **revolution**, omwenteling, toer; (v) (-ved), draai; laat draai; ~ *up an engine*, 'n motor vinnig laat loop; die toeretal vermeerder.

revac'cinate, herent, oorent.

revaccina'tion, oorenting, herenting.

revalen'ta, lensie-en-garsmeel, revalenta.

reval'idate, herbekragtig.

revaloriza'tion, waardeverhoging, herwaardering, koersverhoging.

reval'orize, herwaardeer.

revalua'tion, herskatting, nuwe skatting, herwaardering.

reval'ue, opnuut skat, oorskat.

reveal', openbaar, bekend maak, onthul, blootlê; ontdek; vertoon; verraai; ~ *oneself as*, jou ontpop as; ~ **er**, openbaarmaker; verraaier; ~ **ing**, (n) openbaring; (a) openbarend.

reveil'le, reveille, ontwaking; wekroep, beuelblaas (vir opstaan).

rev'el, (n) straatgeraas; pretmakery; fuif, luidrugtige

revelation 1188 *revolution*

fees, drinkparty; uitgelatenheid, luidrugtigheid; (v) (**-led**), rumoer (maak); rinkink, fuif; pret maak, uitgelate wees; swelg, bras, slampamper; ~ *in,* jou verlustig in; geniet van; jou vermei in.

revela'tion, openbaring, onthulling, openbaarmaking; *Book of R*~*s,* Openbaring; ~ **al,** openbarend, onthullend.

rev'eller, losbol; pretmaker; slampamper, fuiwer, pierewaaier, nagloper, ligmis.

rev'elling, geboemel, verlustiging.

rev'elry, luidrugtige feesvreugde; brassery; joligheid, pretmakery; swelgery, swelgparty; luidrugtigheid.

reven'dicate, terugeis, opvorder.

revendica'tion, terugeising, opvordering.

revenge', (n) wraak, wraakneming; wraaksug; *HAVE one's* ~, wraak neem; *IN* ~ *for,* uit wraak oor; ~ *is SWEET,* die wraak is soet; (v) wreek; wraak neem; ~ **ful,** wraakgierig, wraaksugtig, haatdraend; ~**fulness,** wraakgierigheid, wraaksug, haatdraendheid; ~ **r,** wreker.

rev'enue, inkomste; ~ **account,** inkomsterekening; ~ **office,** inkomstekantoor, belastingkantoor; ~ **officer,** belastingbeampte; ~ **stamp,** inkomsteseël, belastingseël; ~ **return,** inkomsteopgawe.

reverb'erant, weerkaatsend; weergalmend, weerklinkend.

reverb'erate, terugkaats; weergalm, weerklink.

reverb'erating furnace (kiln), reverbereeroond, vlamoond.

reverbera'tion, galm; trilling; weerklank, nagalm; terugkaatsing.

reverb'erative, weergalmend; weerkaatsend.

reverb'erator, terugkaatser, reflektor; ~**y,** (n) (**..ries**), reverbereeroond, heetoond, vlamoond; (a) weerkaatsend; weergalmend; ~*y furnace,* vlamoond, reverbereeroond.

revere', eer; hoogag; eerbiedig, vereer.

rev'erence, (n) eerbied, hoogagting, verering, ontsag, buiging; *HIS R*~, sy eerwaarde; *HOLD in* ~, eer; ~ *of OLD customs,* eerbied vir ou gebruike; *PAY* ~, eer betoon; ~ *for SACRED things,* ontsag vir wat heilig is; *YOUR R*~, u eerwaarde; (v) eerbied bewys, eerbiedig, vereer.

rev'erend, (n) dominee, eerwaarde; (a) eerwaardig, eerwaarde; *R*~ *X,* dominee (ds.) X, eerwaarde (eerw.) *X; Right R*~, hoogeerwaarde.

rev'erent, reveren'tial, eerbiedig.

rev'erie, mymering, gemymer; dromery, gepeins; hersenskim; *lost in* ~, in gepeins versink.

revers', (sing and pl) lapel, omslag; revers; ~ **collar,** omslaankraag, lapelkraag.

revers'al, herroeping; wysiging; omkering, omsetting, vernietiging (reg).

reverse', (n) keersy, agterkant, weersy, verkeerde kant; (die) omgekeerde, teenoorgestelde, teendeel; teenspoed; neerlaag; agteruitrat, trurat, truversnelling (motor); terugsetting; *FORTUNE'S* ~*s,* teenspoed, teëvallers; *IN* ~, omgekeerd; in trurat; *it is JUST the* ~, dit is net (heeltemal) die teenoorgestelde; *PUT in* ~, in trurat sit; agteruitskakel; *SUFFER a* ~, 'n neerlaag ly; (v) omkeer, omdraai, onderstebo draai; wysig; omskakel, omset, omsit (masjien); tru (motor), agteruitry; verander; hotom(dans); terugboek; herroep, intrek (uitspraak); ~ *ARMS!* keer geweer! ~ *a JUDGMENT,* 'n uitspraak nietig verklaar; (a) omgekeerd, teenoorgestel(d), teengesteld; *in the* ~ *direction,* in die teenoorgestelde rigting; ~ **block,** negatiefblok; ~ **clutch,** trukoppelaar; ~ **current,** teenstroom.

reversed' omgekeerd; verkeerd; *with* ~ *ARMS,* met gekeerde geweer; ~ *FAULT,* opskuiwing; ~ *IMPRESSION,* agterstevoorafdruk.

reverse': ~ **fire,** rugvuur; ~ **gear,** trurat, truversnelling; ~ **light,** trulig; ~ **ly,** omgekeerd, aan die ander kant; ~ **pass,** terugaangee; ~**r,** stroomwisselaar, omskakelaar; ~ **side,** keersy, agterkant; ~ **switch,** omskakelaar; ~ **valve,** lugklep.

reversibil'ity, dubbelkantigheid; omsetbaarheid; omkeerbaarheid; herroepbaarheid.

revers'ible, omkeerbaar, dubbelkantig (mat); omsetbaar; herroepbaar; omstelbaar; ~ **carpet,** dubbelkantige tapyt; ~ **coat,** omkeerjas, omkeerbare jas.

revers'ing, (n) tru; omstelling; (a) omkerend; omstellend; ~ **engine,** ~ **gear,** omsetmasjien, omsteller (skip); ~ **lever,** omkeerhefboom, omstelarm; ~ **motion,** omkeerbeweging; ~ **shaft,** omsetas.

rever'sion, omkering; terugkering; atavisme (biol.); terugvalling; ~ *to type,* atavisme; ~**ary,** terugkomend; terugvallend; atavisties (biol.).

revert', (n) herbekeerde; (v) omkeer; terugkeer; terugval; *the ESTATE will* ~ *to,* die eiendom sal terugval na; ~ *to the RANKS,* tot mindere rang verlaag (word); ~ *to a SUBJECT,* terugkom op 'n onderwerp; ~**ible,** terugkerend, terugvallend.

revet', (-ted), bestraat; beklee, bemantel (vesting); ~**ment,** bekleding(smuur); steunmuur, keermuur.

revi'ctual, (-led), herproviandeer, opnuut proviandeer.

review', (n) oorsig; boekbeoordeling, boekbespreking; resensie; tydskrif; parade, wapenskouing, revue; hersiening; *PASS in* ~, parade laat maak, die revue passeer; *the PERIOD under* ~, die onderhawige tydvak; *the YEAR under* ~, die jaar onder beskouing, die verslagjaar; (v) nasien, hersien; beoordeel; resenseer, aankondig (boek); monster, inspekteer, laat paradeer (troepe); terugblik op; ~ *and rescind,* herroep; ~**able,** hersienbaar; ~ **dress,** groot tenue; ~ **er,** beoordelaar; resensent.

revile', (be)skimp, uitskel, smaal, verguis, smaad, slegmaak; ~**ment,** smaad, geskimp, beskimping; ~**r,** smader, beskimper.

revin'dicate, terugeis; terugvorder; weer regverdig.

revindica'tion, terugvordering, regverdiging.

revis'al, hersiening.

revise', (n) hersiening, revisie; hersiene uitgawe; (v) hersien, nasien, verbeter, verwerk, revideer; wysig; ~**r,** hersiener, verbeteraar, reviseur.

revi'sion, hersiening, bewerking, revisie; ~ *of punishment,* strafhersiening; ~**al,** hersienings-, revisie-; ~ **court,** hersieningshof.

revi'sionist, (n) revisionis; (a) revisionisties.

revis'it, weer besoek.

revis'ory, hersienings-, revisie-.

revit'alize, nuwe lewe inblaas.

reviv'al, herlewing, oplewing; opwekking; herstel, weeropbloei, renaissance; verlewendiging; heropvoering (toneelstuk); ~**ism,** opwekkingsbeweging; ~**ist,** opwekkingsprediker; ~ **meeting,** ~ **service,** opwekkingsdiens.

revive', herlewe, weer oplewe, opbloei; opfris, opwek; weer aanwakker, laat herleef; verlewendig; bykom; bykry, bybring; weer aan die gang sit; oprakel; vernuwe; weer opvoer; ~ *old differences,* ou koeie uit die sloot haal; ~**r,** opwekker; versterkinkie, opknappertjie.

revivifica'tion, weeropwekking; herlewing.

reviv'ify, (**..fied**), verlewendig, weer aanwakker, weer laat opleef; suiwer berei (skeik.); ~**ing,** verfrissend, versterkend.

revis'cence, herlewing, oplewing.

revis'cent, herlewend.

reviv'or, hervatting van 'n regsaak (na die dood v.d. prosederende).

rev'ocable, herroepbaar, intrekbaar.

revoca'tion, herroeping, intrekking.

revoke', (n) renons (kaartspel); *beyond* ~, onherroeplik; (v) herroep, intrek; vernietig; kleur versaak, nie kleur beken nie (kaartspel), renonseer; ~**d,** herroep, ingetrek; versaak; ~**ment,** herroeping.

revolt', (n) opstand, verset, oproer, rebellie; walging; *in* ~, in opstand; (v) opstaan, in opstand kom, rebelleer; oproerig word; afvallig word; laat walg, met afkeer vervul; ~ *at,* jou walg vir; ~**ed,** oproerig, in opstand; ~**er,** oproerling, rebel, opstandeling; ~**ing,** rebels, opstandig, oproerig; walglik, stuitlik, weersinwekkend.

rev'olute, teruggerol.

revolu'tion, rewolusie, (staats)omwenteling; kringloop, omkeer; wenteling; omdraaiing, toer (masjien); slag; *number of* ~*s,* toeretal; ~**ary,** (n) (**..aries**), opstandige, rewolusionêr; opstandeling, oproerling; (a) rewolusionêr, opstandig; ~ **counter,** toereteller; ~**ism,** rewolusionisme; ~**ist,** op-

roerling, rewolusionêr; ~ **ize**, omkeer, verandering bring, 'n omwenteling (rewolusie) teweegbring.
revolve', ronddraai, (om)wentel, draai; oordink, oorweeg; ~ *on an AXLE*, op 'n as draai; *its MOONS* ~ *round Jupiter*, sy mane draai om Jupiter.
revol'ver, rewolwer.
revol'ving, draai=, draaiend; draaibaar; ~ **axle**, draaias; ~ **book-stand**, draaiboekrak; ~ **chair**, draaistoel; ~ **credit**, afloskrediet, wentelkrediet, selfaanvullende (lopende) krediet; ~ **disc**, draaiskyf; ~ **door**, draaideur; ~ **drum**, draaitrommel; ~ **light**, draailig; ~ **mirror**, draaispieël; ~ **screen**, trommelsif, draaisif; ~ **stage**, draaiverhoog; ~ **table**, draaitafel; ~ **target**, draaiskyf; ~ **turret**, draaitoring; ~ **wind**, dwarrelwind.
revue', revue; musiekkomedie.
revul'sion, omkeer (van gevoel), omslag, reaksie; terugwerping; afleiding.
revul'sive, (n) afleimiddel; (a) afleidend, afdrywend, afdrywings=.
reward', (n) beloning, vergoeding, gasie, loon; *AS a* ~ *for, IN* ~ *for*, ter beloning vir; *DUE* ~ , verdiende loon; *he GOT his* ~ , hy het sy verdiende loon gekry; (v) beloon, vergoed; vergeld; ~ *kindness with ingratitude*, stank vir dank kry.
rewarding, lonend, betalend; ~ *EXPERIENCE*, lonende ondervinding; ~ *TASK*, dankbare taak.
reweigh', oorweeg.
rewin', (..won), terugwen, herwin.
rewind', (n) herwikkeling; (v) (..wound), weer opwen.
rewire', herbedraad.
rewir'ing, herbedrading.
reword', anders stel, herformuleer, anders uitdruk.
rewrite', (..wrote, ..written), oorskryf, omwerk; herskryf.
Rey'nard, Reinaard, Jakkals.
rezone', herindeel (in streke).
rezon'ing, herindeling.
rhab'domancer, wateraanwyser.
rhab'domancy, wateraanwysing, watersoekery (met wiggelroede).
rhap'sode, rapsodis.
rhapsod'ic(al), rapsodies.
rhap'sodist, rapsodis.
rhap'sodize, rapsodies voordra; rapsodieë skryf; opgeskroef en onsamehangend praat.
rhap'sody, (..dies), rapsodie.
rhe'bok, ribbok; *GREY* ~ , vaalribbok; *RED* ~ , rooiribbok.
Rhen'ish, (n) Rynwyn; (a) Rynlands, Ryns.
rhe'ocord, weerstandsmeter.
rhe'sus, resus (Indiese aap); ~ **factor**, resusfaktor.
rhet'or, redenaar, retor; ~ **ic**, retoriek; retorika; welsprekendheid; rederykerskuns; ~ **'ical**, retories; welsprekend; hoogdrawend; ~ **i'cian**, redenaar, retor; rederyker; dosent in welsprekendheid; retorikus.
rheum, verkoue; slymafskeiding; katar; (pl) rumatiese pyne.
rheumat'ic, (n) rumatieklyer; (a) rumaties; ~ *FEVER*, rumatiekkoors; sinkingskoors; ~ *PAINS*, sinkings; rumatiek.
rheum': ~ **atism**, rumatiek; ~ **atoid**, reumaties, rumatiekagtig; ~ **y**, vogtig; tranerig; ~ *y eyes*, drupoë.
rhin'al, neus=.
Rhine, (die) Ryn; ~ **wine**, Rynwyn; ~ **lander**, Rynlander.
rhine'stone, rynsteen.
rhini'tis, neusontsteking.
rhin'o, (-s), *abbr. of* **rhino'ceros**, (-es), renoster; *BLACK* ~ , swartrenoster; *WHITE* ~ , witrenoster; ~ **bird**, renostervoel.
rhinol'ogy, neusheelkunde, rinologie.
rhinoplas'tic, neusplastiek.
rhin'oplasty, neusplastiek.
rhin'oscope, neusspieël, rinoskoop.
rhinos'copy, neusondersoek, rinoskopie.
rhiz'ome, wortelstok.
rhizomorph'us, wortelvormig.
rhizoph'agous, worteletend.
rhiz'opod, gaatjiesdier, risopode.

Rhode Isl'and Red, Rhode-Eilandhoender.
Rhode'sia, (hist.), Rhodesië; ~ **n**, (n) Rhodesiër; (a) Rhodesies; ~ *n ridgeback (dog)*, Leeuhond, Pronkrughond, Rifrughond.
rhod'ium, rodium(hout); rodium (metaal).
rhododen'dron, alperoos, rododendron.
rhomb, ruit, rombus; ~ **ic**, ruitvormig; ~ **ohed'ral**, sesruitig; ~ **ohed'ron**, sesruit, sesruitige liggaam, romboëder; ~ **oid**, (n) langwerpige ruit, romboïed, romboïde; (a) ruitvormig, romboïed=, romboïdaal; ~ **oid'al**, ruitvormig, romboïdaal; ~ **us**, (-es, rhombi), ruit, rombus.
Rhone, Rhône.
rhu'barb, rabarber; ~ **plant**, rabarberplant, rabarberstoel; ~ **preserve**, rabarberkonfyt; ~ **syrup**, rabarberstroop.
rhumb, windstreek; kompasstreek; ~ **card**, windroos; ~ **line**, loksodromiese lyn, loksodroom.
rhyme, (n) rym; rympie, vers; rymwoord; *DOUBLE* ~ , vroulike (slepende) rym; *END* ~ , endrym; *FEMALE* ~ , vroulike (slepende) rym; *FEMININE* ~ , vroulike (slepende) rym; *final* ~ , endrym; *IN* ~ , in (op) rym; *MALE* ~ , manlike (staande) rym; *MASCULINE* ~ , manlike (staande) rym ; *for no* ~ *or REASON*, sonder betekenis, sonder rede of grond; sonder die minste rede; *SINGLE* ~ , manlike (staande) rym; (v) rym, dig; laat rym; ~ *with*, rym met (op); ~ **d**, berym; ~ *d verse*, berymde verse; ~ **less**, rymloos; ~ *less verse*, rymlose verse; ~ **r**, ~ **ster**, rymelaar.
rhym'ing, gerymel.
rhym'ist, rymer, rymelaar.
rhy'thm, ritme, maat; ~ **ic(al)**, ritmies.
ri'ant, vrolik, laggend, bly, riant.
rib, (n) rib, ribbetjie; ribbebeen; ribstuk; middelnerf (van blaar); speek (sambreel); rif (in breiwerk); vrou; *you can COUNT his* ~ *s*, jy kan sy ribbetjies tel; *DIVIDING* ~ , verdeelrib; *FLAT* ~ , platrib; *FLOATING* ~ , sweefrib; ~ *of MUTTON*, skaapribbetjie; (v) (-bed), riffel; van ribbetjies voorsien; banke ploeg; terg, die gek skeer; ~ *someone unmercifully*, iem. se siel uittrek.
rib'ald, (n) lasteraar, vuilbek; (a) liederlik, vieslik, smerig, vuil, vuilbekkig; godslasterlik; ~ **ry**, liederlike taal.
rib' band, lat, spar.
ribbed, geriffel; generf; gerib; ~ **fabric**, ribstof; ~ **glass**, riffelglas; ~ **paper**, geriffelde papier; ~ **steel**, geribde staal.
ribb'ing[1], geriffelde werk, riffelstrook.
ribb'ing[2], tergery, treitering.
ribb'on, lint, band; strook; (pl) leisels; *OBTAIN a* ~ *of honour*, 'n lintjie kry; *TEAR to* ~ *s*, in flenters skeur; ~ **building**, strookbou; ~ **cake**, lintkoek; ~ **development**, strookbou, streepbou, lintbebouing; ~ **embroidery**, lintborduurwerk; ~ **fish**, lintvis; ~ **-grass**, lintgras; ~ **-like**, lintvormig, lintagtig; ~ **road**, tweespoorpad, dubbelbaanpad; ~ **saw**, bandsaag; ~ **-weaver**, lintwerker, lintwewer; ~ **wire**, lintdraad; ~ **worm**, lintwurm.
rib: ~ **-chop**, ribkarmenaadjie; ~ **cord**, ribkoord; ~ **less**, sonder ribbes; glad; ~ **steak**, ribfilet; ~ **-stitch**, ribsteek.
rice, rys; *GRAIN of* ~ , ryskorrel; ~ *with RAISINS*, rosyntjierys; *YELLOW* ~ , borrierys; ~ **bird**, rysvoël; ~ **crop**, rysoes; ~ **culture**, rysverbouing, ryskultuur; ~ **-dumpling**, ryskluitjie; ~ **field**, rysland, rysveld; ~ **-flour**, ~ **-meal**, rysmeel; ~ **-measure**, rysmaat; ~ **milk**, rysbry; ~ **-mill**, rysmeul; ~ **paper**, ryspapier; ~ **plantation**, rysland; ~ **porridge**, ryspap, rys(te)bry; ~ **pudding**, ryspoeding; ~ **soup**, ryssop; ~ **starch**, rysstysel; ~ **table**, rystafel; ~ **-water**, ryswater; ~ **-weevil**, ryswurm, ryskalander; ~ **wine**, ryswyn.
rich, (n) rykes; *the* ~ *and the POOR*, die rykes en die armes; *THE* ~ , die rykes, ryk mense; (a) ryk, welgesteld, vermoënd, bemiddeld, gefortuneer; kosbaar; vrugbaar; vet (grond); oorvloedig; swaar (dieet); kragtig, voedsaam, magtig (voedsel); vol (stem); warm (kleur); kostelik, goed ('n grap); ~ *in vitamines*, vitamienryk; ~ **clay**, vet klei; ~ **en**, verryk; ryker word; ~ **es**, rykdom; ~ **food**, kragtige

(ryk) kos; ~ **lime**, vetkalk; ~**ly**, ryklik, ruim=
skoots; dubbel en dwars; ~*ly rewarded*, dubbel en
dwars vergoed; ~ **mixture**, ryk mengsel; ~**ness**,
rykdom; prag; oorvloed; ~ **rhyme**, dubbelrym.
Rich'ter scale, Richterskaal.
rick¹, (n) verrekking; (v) verrek; *kyk* **wrick**.
rick², (n) mied; (v) mied pak; ~**er**, miedpakker;
steierpaaltjie.
rick'etiness, mankoliekigheid, slapheid.
rick'ets, Engelse siekte, ragitis.
rick'ety, slap, lendelam, lutterig; mankoliek(ig); ragi=
ties; *a* ~ *chair,* 'n lendelam stoel.
rick'sha(w), riksja.
rick'-yard, voerkamp.
ric'ochet, (n) opslag; opslagskoot, wegskramskoot;
(v) **(-(t)ed)**, opslaan, wegskram, opslag maak, af=
kets, wegspring.
ric'tus, gaap; mondwydte; mondopening.
rid, **(-ded** or **rid)**, bevry, ontslaan, verlos; opruim, ver=
wyder; *BE* ~ *of*, kwyt wees van; bevry wees van;
GET ~ *of*, ontslae raak van; iets kwytraak.
rid'able, rybaar.
ridd'ance, bevryding, verlossing; *a GOOD* ~ , 'n ware
oplugting; *GOOD* ~*!* dankie tog! dankie bly!
ridd'en, gery; ~ *by fears*, met vrees bevange.
rid'dle¹, (n) growwe sif, sandsif; graansif; (v) (uit)sif;
vol gate maak, deurboor, deursif; ~ *with BUL=
LETS*, met skote deursif; ~*d with DISEASE*, vrot
v.d. siekte.
rid'dle², (n) raaisel; *he is a* ~ *that I cannot read*, ek
kan hom glad nie verstaan nie; (v) raaiselagtig
praat; raai, oplos; oorval (met vrae); uitrakel.
ridd'ling, raaiselagtig.
ride, (n) rit, toggie, toer, rytoertjie; ryperd; berede re=
krute; rypad; *give a child a* ~ *on one's BACK*, 'n
kind abba, 'n kind op jou rug laat ry; *GIVE a* ~,
oplaai; laat ry; *GO for a* ~, gaan uitry; *TAKE
someone for a* ~ , iem. kul; iem. om die bos lei; 'n
lopie met iem. neem; iem. van kant maak; (v) **(rode,
ridden)**, ry, bery; laat ry; ~ *ABOUT*, rondry; ~ *at
ANCHOR*, voor anker lê; ~ *a CHILD on one's
back*, 'n kind abba, 'n kind op jou rug laat ry; ~ *to
DEATH*, doodry; holrug ry; ~ *DOUBLE*, twee op
een perd ry; agter mekaar ry; ~ *DOWN*, inhaal;
doodry; onderstebo ry; ~ *for a FALL*, wild (woes)
ry; roekeloos wees; moeilikheid soek; ~ *a FORD*,
te perd 'n drif deurgaan; ~ *someone HARD*, iem.
met spore ry; ~ *one's HOBBY HORSE*, jou stok=
perdjie ry; ~ *a HORSE down*, 'n perd flou ry
(jaag); ~ *to HOUNDS*, op 'n jakkalsjag gaan; *LET
it* ~ , dit maar so laat; dit daarby laat; ~ *a RACE*,
deelneem aan 'n wedren; ~ *ROUGHSHOD over*,
hardhandig optree; heeltemal verontagsaam; iem.
se gevoelens nie ontsien nie; ~ *out a STORM*, vei=
lig deur 'n storm kom; die storm afry; ~ *the
WIND*, op die wind seil; ~ *a WINNER* ('n perde=
wedren) wen.
rid'er, ruiter; meetkundige probleem (vraagstuk);
ryer, beryer; byvoeging, bygevoegde klousule;
~**less**, ruiterloos; ~ **weight**, bygewig.
ridge, (n) rug; vors, nok (van 'n dak); rif, kam, berg=
rug, rant; maanhaar (in 'n pad); hart (van 'n omge=
ploegde akker); bult; pronk (springbok); (v) vore
ploeg, walle gooi; rimpel; in beddings plant; van 'n
nok voorsien; operd (ertappels); ~**back**, Rifrug=
(hond), Pronkrug; ~ **capping**, nokdekking.
rid'gel, **ridge'ling**, klophings; klopram.
ridge: ~**-piece**, nokbalk; ~**-plate**, nokplaat; ~**-pole**,
nokpaal, vorsbalk; ~ **purlin**, noklat; ~**r**, operd=
ploeg; ~ **rafter**, ruiterbalk; ~**-roof**, geweldak,
saaldak; ~**-tile**, vorspan, nokpan; ~**-tree**, nok=
balk; ~ **turret**, noktorinkie, dakruiter, nokdek=
king.
ridg'ing, (die) operd; vorsbedekking, nokdekking,
(dak).
ridg'y, nokvormig; bergagtig; gerimpel, geriffel; ~
country, ranteveld, rüensveld.
rid'icule, (n) belaglikheid; spot, bespotting; *CAST* ~
upon, belaglik maak; *HOLD up to* ~ , belaglik
maak; *IN* ~ , spottend; *POUR* ~ *on*, belaglik
maak; *SUBJECT to* ~ , belaglik maak; (v) belaglik
maak, uitlag, bespot; ~**r**, spotter.

ridic'ulous, belaglik, verspot, bespotlik; dol; ~**ness**,
belaglikheid, verspotheid, bespotlikheid; dolheid.
rid'ing¹, (n) afdeling, distrik.
rid'ing², (die) ry; ryery; rykuns; rypad; *be* ~ *high*, op
die kruin van voorspoed wees; ~ **animal**, rydier;
~**-bit**, rystang; ~**-boot**, rylaars, rystewel; ~**-
breeches**, rybroek; ~**-crop**, rysweep, karwats; ~**-
glove**, ryhandskoen; ~**-habit**, rykostuum; ~**-hood**,
rymantel; ~**-light**, ankerlig; ~**-master**, ryinstruk=
teur, pikeur; ~**-rein**, teuel; ~**-school**, ryskool; ~**-
whip**, rysweep, karwats.
ridott'o, dans-en-musiekparty, ridotto.
rife, oorvloedig, algemeen, vol van, heersend; *BE* ~ ,
algemeen wees, baie voorkom; *REPORTS are* ~ ,
RUMOUR is ~ , die gerugte gaan oral rond.
Riff'ian, (n) Riffyn; Riffbewoner; (a) Riffyns.
rif'fle, (n) riffel (mynw.); gleufdeler; (v) riffel
(mynw.); ~**r**, groefvyl, hobbelvyl; verdeler.
riff'-raff, gepeupel, uitskot, Jan Rap en sy maat, die
Kretie en die Pletie, uitvaagsels, skorriemorrie,
hoipolloi.
Riffs = **Riffians**.
Riff' tribe, Riffstam.
ri'fle, (n) geweer, roer; *MOUNTED* ~*s*, berede skut=
ters; *do* ~ *PRACTICE*, teikenskiet; *with* ~
RESTED, dooierus; (v) 'n geweerloop groef; skiet;
plunder, buitmaak, steel, wegroof; ~**-barrel**, ge=
weerloop; ~**-bucket**, kolfsak; ~**-butt**, geweerkolf;
~**-clip**, geweerknyper; ~**-club**, skietvereniging; ~
commando, skietkommando; ~**-corps**, skutters=
korps; ~**-fire**, geweervuur; ~**-gallery**, skietbaan;
~ **man**, skerpskutter; skut; ~**-pit**, skuilplek; ~
practice, skietoefening; ~**r**, rower, plunderaar; ~**-
range**, skietbaan; skietafstand; ~**-shooting**, skiet=
oefening; ~**-shot**, geweerskoot; ~**-sling**, geweer=
band.
rift, (n) skeur, bars, spleet; onenigheid; *a* ~ *in the lute*,
die eerste krakie (bv. in 'n vriendskap); die eerste
teken van onenigheid; nie alles pluis nie; (v) ~**-saw**,
kloofsaag, stersaag; ~**-sawn**, gevierendeel (hout);
R~ **Valley**, Slenkdal; **R**~ **Valley fever**, Slenkdal=
koors.
rig¹, (n) klophings.
rig², (n) grap, poets; skelmstreek, bedrog; (v) ~ *the
market*, die mark bewerk; kul, bedrieg; knoei met,
manipuleer (mark).
rig³, (n) kostuum, uitrusting; tuigasie, touwerk; boor=
toring; (v) **(-ged)**, aantrek, opmaak; optakel, op=
tuig; uitrus, toerus; opsit, oprig; ~ *OUT*, uitdos;
uitrus; ~*ged out in the latest STYLE*, uitgedos vol=
gens die nuutste mode; ~ *UP* aanmekaartimmer;
saamflans; ~ *UP a shelter*, 'n skuiling opslaan.
rigg'er¹, raammonteur; (op)takelaar; touwerker.
rigg'er², manipuleerder (v.d. mark); swendelaar.
rigg'ing¹, kullery, knoeiery; manipulasie (v.d. mark),
bewerking.
rigg'ing², touwerk, tuigasie (van 'n skip), want; raam=
werkmontasie; optooiing, uitrusting; ~**-wire**,
raamwerkdraad.
rigg'ot, klophings.
right, (n) reg; aanspraak; regverdigheid, billikheid;
regterhand; regterkant; (pl) regte; ~ *of AD=
MISSION*, reg van toegang; ~ *of APPEAL*, reg
van appèl; *AT the* ~ , regs; *BE in the* ~ , gelyk hê,
reg wees; *BY* ~*(s)*, eintlik; van regsweë; *BY* ~ *of*,
kragtens, op grond van, uit krag van; *the* ~ *s of the
CASE*, die ware toedrag van sake; *a DUCHESS in
her own* ~ , 'n hertogin deur geboorte; *EXERCISE
a* ~ , 'n reg uitoefen; *FORFEIT one's* ~*(s)*, jou
reg(te) verbeur; *HAVE a* ~ *to*, die reg hê om; *IN its
own* ~ , op sigself; *KEEP to the* ~ , regs hou;
MIGHT is ~ , mag is reg; *MR. R*~, die ware
Jakob; *have NO* ~ *to something*, geen aanspraak
op iets kan maak nie; ~ *of OCCUPATION*, woon=
reg; besitreg; *ON the* ~ , aan die regterkant; *in one's
OWN* ~ , uit eie reg; uit sigself; op eie gesag; ~ *of
OWNERSHIP*, eiendomsreg; ~ *of PASSAGE*,
deurgang; *let* ~ *PREVAIL*, reg laat geskied; *PUT
to* ~*s*, regmaak; aan kant maak; *RESERVE the* ~
to, die reg voorbehou om; *all* ~*s RESERVED*, alle
regte is voorbehou; nadruk is verbied; *TURN about
to the* ~ , haarom draai; ~ *of WAY*, deurgangsreg,

padserwituut, ryreg; reg om voor te ry, ryvoorrang, voorrit; *WITHIN one's* ~*s*, binne jou reg; *the* ~ *and WRONG*, die goeie en verkeerde (kwade); (v) regsit, in orde bring; oprig, orent (regop) laat staan; verbeter; regmaak; ~ *ONESELF*, jou ewewig her= kry; jou herstel; *the SHIP* ~*ed itself*, die skip het weer reg gaan lê; (a) regter=; haar= (dier in span); regsgesind, reg, billik, juis, regskape, regverdig; aangewese; *ALL* ~, mooi; in orde; reg so; orraait (geselst.); *at* ~ *ANGLES*, reghoekig; ~ *you ARE*, mooi, reg so, in orde; *DO the* ~ *thing*, jou plig doen; *be someone's* ~ *HAND*, iem. se regterhand wees; *not* ~ *in one's HEAD*, 'n streep hê; getik wees; *the* ~ *MAN*, die ware Jakob; *be in one's* ~ *MIND*, by jou volle verstand wees; *as* ~ *as RAIN*, so reg soos 'n roer; ~ *SIDE*, haarkant; ~ *SIDE up*, met die regterkant bo; *on the* ~ *SIDE of forty*, nog nie veertig jaar nie: *as* ~ *as a TRIVET*, so reg soos 'n roer; *the* ~ *WAY*, die regte manier; die regte pad; ~ *and WRONG*, reg en verkeerd; (adv) pre= sies; reg, gelyk; regs; regte; ~ *ABOUT*, regs om; ~ *ACROSS*, dwarsoor; ~ *AHEAD*, reg voor; reg vooruit; ~ *ALONG*, reg vorentoe; *turn* ~ *AROUND*, heeltemal omdraai; ~ *AWAY*, dade= lik; *BUY* ~ *and left*, los en vas koop; *COME* ~, regkom; *COME* ~ *in!* kom binne! *DO* ~, regver= dig handel; *DO someone* ~, iem. reg laat weder= vaar; *EYES* ~*!* oë regs! ~ *in FRONT*, heel voor; ~ *GLAD*, regtig bly; *GO* ~ *at*, reguit gaan na; ~ *HERE*, (net) hier, hierso; *KNOW* ~ *well*, baie goed weet; *LEFT and* ~, links en regs; hot en haar; *make promises* ~ *and LEFT*, beloftes aan talle mense maak; ~ *in the MIDDLE*, heeltemal in die middel; *it is no MORE than* ~, dis nie meer as billik nie; ~ *NOW*, dadelik; op die oomblik; ~ *OH!* goed! reg so! afgespreek! ~ *to the POINT*, reg op die doel af; *PUT a person* ~, iem. in die gelyk stel; *PUT* ~, regmaak; reghelp; verbeter; in die reine bring; *if I REMEMBER* ~, as ek dit reg het; *SAY* ~ *out*, sonder omweë sê; reguit praat; *SEE someone* ~, vir iem. sorg; *it SERVES you* ~, dis jou verdiende loon; *THAT's* ~, presies, ~ *about*, regs om; *send someone to the* ~*-about(s)*, iem. in die pad steek; iem. wegjaag.

right′ about turn: *do a* ~, regsomkeer maak.

right: ~ **angle**, regte hoek; ~**-angled**, reghoekig, haaks; ~**-down**, deur en deur; ~ **en**, regmaak, reg= ruk; regkom; ~**eous**, regverdig, regskape, billik; ~**eousness**, regskapenheid, billikheid; ~ **eye**, reg= teroog; ~**ful**, regmatig; regverdig; wettig; *the* ~*ful owner*, die wettige eienaar; ~**fulness**, regverdig= heid, regmatigheid.

right: ~ **hand**, regterhand; regter=, regterkantse; *someone's* ~ *hand*, iem. se regterhand; ~**-drive**, regterstuur; ~**ed**, regs, met die regterkant ~**er**, slag met die regterhand; iem. wat regs is.

right: ~ **hearted**, goedhartig, regskape, ~**-ho!** afge= sproke! mooi! goed! ~ **hook**, regterhaakhou; ~**ist**, (n) regsgesinde, konserwatief; verkrampte; (a) regs= gesind, konserwatief, verkramp, (v) (regs)loos; ~**lessness**, regteloosheid; ~**-lined**, reglynig; ~**ly**, tereg, presies, juis; regverdig; behoorlik; ~*ly or wrongly*, tereg of ten onregte; ~**-minded**, welden= kend, reggeaard; ~**ness**, juistheid, gepastheid; ~ **side**, regterkant; ~**-sided**, regs; ~**-thinking**, reg= denkend; ~ **through**, dwarsdeur; ~**ward**, regs.

ri′gid, styf, streng, rigied, onbuigbaar; strak, stroef, star; (ver)stram, stug; wetties; stip; ~ *DIS= CIPLINE*, strenge tug; ~ *STAY*, vaste anker.

rigid′ity, styfheid, stramheid; strengheid; starheid, strammigheid, styfte; onbuigsaamheid; stiptheid.

rig′lessness, afgetakeldheid.

rig′marole, (n) kafpraatjies, kaf, onsin, kletsery, on= samehangende geklets; (a) onsamehangend.

rig′or, koorsrilling, bewerasie; ~ *mortis*, rigor mortis, lykverstywing, lykstywigheid, styfheid v.d. dood; ~**ism**, strengheid; ~**ist**, rigoris, iem. wat streng in die leer is; ~**ous**, streng, gestreng, straf, onbuig= saam; stip; ~**ousness**, strengheid, onbuigsaamheid.

rig′our, strengheid, gestrengheid, hardheid; stiptheid, nougesetheid; *the full* ~ *of the law*, die uiterste strengheid v.d. wet.

rig′-out, uitrusting; pluiens; opskik; *that* ~ *does not suit her*, daardie uitrusting pas haar nie.

rile, boos maak, die josie in maak, irriteer.

rill, spruitjie, lopie, beek.

rim, (n) rand, lys; kant; velling (wiel); (v) **(-med)**, om= rand, omlys; 'n velling insit; ~ **brake**, vellingrem.

rime[1], (n) spleet.

rime[2], (n) *kyk* **rhyme**; rym.

rime[3], (n) ryp; (v) met ryp bedek.

rime[4], (n) sport (van 'n leer).

rim: ~**-lining**, vellingvoering; ~**-lock**, oplegslot.

rim′ose, rim′ous, vol barste, gebars.

rim′ple, (n, v) rimpel.

rim: ~**-tool**, vellingtrekker; ~**-wedge**, vellingkloutjie.

rim′y, vol geryp, vol ryp.

rind, (n) skil; bas; kors; (v) afskil; bas afmaak.

rin′derpest, runderpes.

ring[1], (n) ring; kring, sirkel; kartel, kombinasie; boks= kuns; kryt, boksstrydperk; beroepswedders; *AN= NUAL* ~, jaarring; ~ *of BIT*, stangring; *BLOW* ~*s*, kringe blaas; *MAKE* ~*s round a person*, iem. ver oortref; baie vinniger wees; *MILLED* ~, kar= telring; *RUN* ~*s round*, iem. ver oortref; iem. uit= stof; *THE* ~, boks, vuisvegtery; beroepswedders; *TRAINED to the* ~, as bokser opgelei; vir die sir= kus opgelei; (v) **(-ed)**, 'n ring aansit; in 'n kring loop; aan skywe (ringe) sny; ~ *round*, 'n kring maak om.

ring[2], (n) toon, klank, gerinkel, gelui; geluid; klokke= spel; *give the BELL a* ~, lui die klokkie; *have a FAMILIAR* ~, bekend klink; *there IS a* ~, daar word gebel, die telefoon lui, (v) **(rang, rung)**, lui, bel (klokkie, foon); 'n oproep deursit; weerklink, weer= galm (geluid); laat lui; ~ *BACK*, terugbel; *it* ~*s a BELL*, dit laat my aan iets dink; dit herinner my aan iets; ~ *the CHANGES*, iets gedurig ophaal; telkens veranderinge aanbring; ~ *a COIN*, 'n muntstuk laat klink; ~ *the CURTAIN down*, lui om die skerm te laat sak; *the gordyn laat sak*; ~ *in one's EARS*, in jou ore weerklink; ~ *FALSE*, vals klink; ~ *IN the new year*, die nuwe jaar inlui; ~ *OFF*, aflui, afbel; ~ *OUT*, weerklink; uitlui; ~ *up a SALE*, 'n verkoop aanteken (registreer); ~ *for TEA*, bel om tee te bestel; ~ *TRUE*, eg klink; ~ *UP*, (op)bel; ~ *WITH*, weerklink van.

ring: ~**-a-rosy**, patertjie-langs-die-kant; ~**-bark**, rin= geleer; ~**-barking**, ringelering; ~**-bolt**, ringbout; ~**-bone**, ringbeen; ~**-cartilage**, ringvormige kraak= been; ~**-craft**, krytkennis, boksvernuf; ~**-dove**, ringduif; ~**ed**, gering; ring=; ~**ed bird**, geringde voël; ~**ed cobra**, spoegslang, bakkop; ~**ed plover**, ringnekkiewiet.

ring′er[1], (klok)luier; gholfbedrieër; bedrieër; vals perd.

ring′er[2], ringer, ringelaar; bobaas.

ring: ~**-fenced**, rondomheining; ~**-finger**, ringvin= ger, naaspink, fielafooi; ~**-gauge**, ringmaat.

ring′ing, (n) gelui, gebel (telef.); gebeier, gebom (klok); gebengel; gesuis (in ore), (a) klinkend, weer= galmend; ~ *CHEERS*, luide toejuiging; ~ *DE= NUNCIATION*, klinkende veroordeling.

ring: ~**-leader**, belhamel, voorbok, voorperd; rad= draaier; leier; ~**-let**, ringetjie; krulletjie; ~**leted**, ge= krul; ~**-mail**, maliekolder; ~**-man**, beroepswedder; ringvinger; ~**-necked snake**, rinkhals(slang); ~**-pad**, ringkussinkie; ~**-plate**, oogplaat; ~ **road**, sir= kelpad, kringpad; singel; ~**-shaped**, ringvormig; ~ **side**, krytkant; ~**-sight**, ringvisier, ringkorrel; ~**-spanner**, ringskroefsleutel, toebek(moer)sleutel; ~**-streaked**, met ringe geteken, gering; ~ **worm**, douwurm, omloop.

rink, (n) baan; rolskaatsbaan; ysbaan; volspan (rol= bal); (v) rolskaats; ~ **championship**, spankampi= oenskap; ~ **er**, rolskaatser.

rinse, (n) spoelsel; (mond)spoeling; haarkleurmiddel; *give a* ~, uitspoel, afspoel; (v) uitspoel, deurspoel, omspoel, skoon spoel; kleur (hare); ~ *out*, uit= spoel.

rins′ing, uitspoeling; ~ **water**, spoelwater.

ri′ot, (n) rusverstoring; (volks)oproer, oploop, op= stootjie, muitery; luidrugtigheid, uitgelatenheid; uitspatting; (pl) onluste, wanordelikhede; *read the*

R~ *ACT,* 'n laaste waarskuwing gee; die leviete voorlees; ~ *of COLOUR,* bont kleurepag; *let one's FANCY run* ~, jou verbeelding die vrye teuels gee; *RUN* ~, hand-uit ruk; te kere gaan; amok maak; uit die band spring; wild groei; *it WAS a* ~, dit was 'n hele affêre; (v) rus verstoor (versteur); oproer maak; oproerig word; wild lewe, uitspat; die teuel gee; ~**er,** oproerling, rusverstoorder, oproermaker; ~**ing,** oproer; ~**ous,** rusverstorend, oproerig, wanordelik, losbandig; woelerig, woelsiek; bandeloos; ~**ousness,** oproerigheid, wanordelikheid; bandeloosheid; ~**ry,** oproerigheid; losbandigheid; ~ **squad,** oproerafdeling; ~ **stave,** knuppel, baton.

rip¹, (n) losbol; skurk; niksnuts; knol (perd); *he is an old* ~, hy is 'n ou kalant.

rip², (n) skeur, bars; sny; spykerhaak; onstuimige water; (v) **(-ped),** oopskeur, ryt; oopsny; lostorring; losgaan, lostrek; kloof; jaag; ~ *APART,* uitmekaar skeur; *LET her* ~, gee hom vet; laat hom teen volle snelheid loop (motor); ~ *OFF,* aftrek, afpluk, afskeur; verneukery; ~ *OPEN,* oopskeur; ~ *OUT,* uitpluk; ~ *up old QUARRELS,* ou koeie uit die sloot grawe; ~ *UP,* opskeur; uitpluk; opgrawe.

ripar'ian, (n) oewerbewoner; (a) oewer-; ~ **land,** oewergrond; ~ **owner,** oewereienaar; ~ **rights,** oewerregte.

rip'-cord, sluitdraad; trektou, trekkoord (van valskerm).

ripe, (n) ryp; *the* ~ *and the green,* ryp en groen; (a) ryp; oud; beleë (kaas, wyn); bekwaam (groente); *soon* ~, *soon rotten,* vroeg ryp, vroeg rot; ~ **age,** hoë ouderdom; ~**n,** ryp word; ryp maak; ~**ness,** rypheid; vergevorderdheid; ~**-rot,** rypvrot, rypverrotting.

riposte, (n) vinnige (gevatte) anwoord; terugsteek (skermkuns); (v) skerp antwoord; 'n terugstoot gee (skerm).

ripp'er, oopskeurder, oopsnyer; torringmes; (ligte) tandploeg, korsbreker, skeurploeg; gawe nooi; haan, doring, ramkat, bulperd.

ripp'ing, (n) (die) oopsny, oopskeuring; (a) oopskeurend; uitstekend, gaaf, aangenaam, verruklik; *they are* ~ *good FRIENDS,* hulle is wonderlike vriende; *we had a* ~ *TIME,* ons het 'n piekfyn tyd gehad; ~ **bar,** breekyster; ~ **chisel,** steekbeitel, breekbeitel; ~ **saw,** skulpsaag, kloofsaag; ~ **tool,** breekbeitel.

rip'ple¹, (n) vlasrepel, vlaskam; (v) repel (vlas).

rip'ple², (n) kabbeling, gekabbel; rimpel; rimpelmerk; golwing; *a* ~ *of laughter,* 'n gegiggel; (v) kabbel, golf; rimpel, riffel; ~**-mark,** riffel (op strand); golfmerk, riffelmerk (geol.).

ripp'ling, gekabbel; ~ *LOCKS,* golwende hare; ~ *WATER,* kabbelende water.

ripp'ly, rimpelend, rimpelrig.

rip'-roaring, uitgelate, uitbundig, lawaaierig.

rip' saw, kloofsaag, skulpsaag.

rise, (n) styging, opgang; opkoms; promosie; opslag; verhoging (salaris); opdraand; verhewenheid; bult, steilte, hoogte; opklimming; rysing; styggang (mynbou); *ASK for a* ~, 'n verhoging vra; *a BLIND* ~, 'n blinde bult; ~ *and FALL of ground,* terreindeining; *GIVE* ~ *to,* aanleiding gee tot; daartoe lei; *be ON the* ~, aan die styg wees; *PRICES are on the* ~, pryse is aan die styg; *the RIVER takes its* ~ *in,* die rivier ontspring in; *a* ~ *in SALARY,* salarisverhoging, opslag van salaris; *not a SIGN of* ~, die vis het glad nie gebyt nie; *TAKE a* ~ *out of someone,* met iem. die gek skeer; iem. vir die gek hou; iem. versondig; (v) **(rose, -n),** rys (brood); opstaan; regop staan; in opstand kom; opgaan; opvlieg, styg; vooruitkom; toeneem; opkom (son, wind); uitsteek; uitkom; ontspring, begin (spruit); uiteengaan; gis (bier); ~ *ABOVE it,* iets te bowe kom; ~ *ABOVE,* uitstyg bokant; bo iets verhewe wees; ~ *AGAIN (from the dead),* uit die dode opstaan; ~ *AGAINST,* in opstand kom teen; ~ *in ARMS,* die wapens opneem; ~ *from the ASHES,* uit die as verrys; ~ *to the BAIT,* byt aan; jou laat versondig; *the BREAD will not* ~, die brood wil nie rys nie; ~ *from the DEAD,* uit die dode opstaan; *the DOUGH will not* ~, die deeg wil nie rys nie; ~

FROM, opstaan uit; ~ *to GREATNESS,* beroemd word; vermaard word; ~ *from NOTHING,* van niks iets word; ~ *to the OCCASION,* teen die moeilikheid opgewasse wees; bereken wees vir die taak; ~ *to a point of ORDER,* op 'n punt van orde praat (beswaar maak); ~ *to POWER,* mag kry; ~ *in PRICE,* duurder word; styg in prys; ~ *from the RANKS,* van onder af opkom; *my STOMACH* ~ *s at it,* ek walg daarvan; *the SUN* ~ *s,* die son kom op; ~ *from the TABLE,* van tafel opstaan; ~ *TO,* styg tot; jou verhef tot; *the WIND will* ~, die wind sal opkom; ~ *in the WORLD,* opgang maak; vooruitkom in die wêreld.

ris'en, verrese; herrese, gerese; *the* ~ *Saviour,* die verrese Heiland.

ris'er, opstaner; treehoogte; stootbord (trap); stygleiding (pyp); *an early* ~, iem. wat vroeg opstaan, vroegopstaner.

risibil'ity, lagwekkendheid; laglus.

ris'ible, lagwekkend, lag-; laggerig; belaglik; ~ **muscles,** ~ **nerves,** laglspiere.

ris'ing, (n) opstand, oproer; opgang, opstyging; opstanding, opwekking; geswel; verdaging (hof); opdraand, bult; (a) rysend; opgaande, opkomend; wassend (maan); stygend; *the* ~ *GENERATION,* die opkomende geslag; *his HORSE is* ~ *six,* die perd word ses; ~ **ground,** opdraand, stygende terrein, bult, hoogte; ~ **novelist,** opkomende romanskrywer; ~ **tide,** opkomende (stygende) gety.

risk, (n) gevaar; waagstuk, risiko; durf; *AT the* ~ *of,* op gevaar af van; *a BAD* ~, 'n waagstuk; *BEAR the* ~, die risiko dra; *at BUYER'S* ~, op risiko v.d. koper; *a GOOD* ~, 'n mens kan dit waag; *at the* ~ *of his LIFE,* met lewensgevaar; *at OWNER'S* ~, op eienaarsrisiko; *the* ~ *PASSES,* die risiko gaan oor; *RUN a* ~, gevaar loop; *TAKE* ~ *s,* waag; (v) waag, riskeer; in die weegskaal stel; in gevaar bring; op die spel sit; ~ *one's LIFE,* jou lewe waag; ~ *ON,* waag aan; ~**-capital,** ondernemingskapitaal, risikokapitaal, waagkapitaal; ~ **cover,** risikodekking; ~**er,** waaghals; ~**y,** riskant, gewaag, gevaarlik, haglik, gedurf, bedenklik; ~*y loan,* riskante lening.

risor'ial, lagwekkend, lag-; ~ **muscle,** lagspier.

risqué', gewaag, gedurf.

riss'ole, frikkadel; krummelfrikkadel, deegfrikkadel.

rite, godsdienstige plegtigheid, ritus; seremonie; *BURIAL* ~ *s, the LAST* ~ *s,* begrafnisplegtigheid.

rit'ual, (n) kerklike instelling, ritueel; rituaal; (a) rituuel; ~**ism,** ritualisme; ~**ist,** ritualis; ~**is'tic,** ritualisties; ~ **murder,** rituele moord (doodslag), medisynemoord.

riv'al, (n) mededinger; medeminnaar; weerga; *there is no* ~ *TO Shakespeare,* Shakespeare het geen gelyke nie; *WITHOUT a* ~, sonder weerga; (v) **(-led),** meeding, wedywer; konkurreer, probeer ewenaar; (a) mededingend, wedywerend; teen-; *a* ~ *CANDIDATE,* 'n teenkandidaat; ~ *SHOPS,* mededingende winkels; ~**ry, (..ries),** ~**ship,** mededinging, wedywer, naywer, konkurrensie.

rive, (-d, -n), splits, kloof; vanmekaarskeur.

riv'er, rivier; stroom; *sell others down the* ~, ander verraai; ander in die steek laat; ~**ain,** (n) oewerbewoner; (a) oewer-; ~**-bank,** rivierwal, rivieroewer; ~ **basin,** stroomgebied; ~**-bed,** rivierbedding; ~**-craft,** riviervaartuie; ~**-diggings,** rivierdelwery; ~ **dweller,** oewerbewoner; ~**-god,** riviergod; ~ **head,** fontein; ~**-horse,** seekoei, nylperd; ~ **ine,** oewer-; rivier-; ~ **mouth,** riviermond; ~ **sand,** riviersand; ~ **side,** rivieroewer; ~ **soil,** riviergrond, spoelgrond; ~ **system,** rivierstelsel; ~ **tortoise,** waterskilpad; ~ **water,** rivierwater.

riv'et, (n) klamp, kram; omklinkspyker, klinknael; (v) vasklink, saamklink, vaskalmp; boei; ~ *the ATTENTION,* die aandag boei; ~ *one's EYES on,* die oë gedurig gerig hou op; stip kyk na; ~*ed to the GROUND,* aan die grond genael; ~*ed JOINT,* klinklas; ~**-angler,** klinkgatboor; ~**er,** klinkhamer, klinkmasjien; naelklinker, klinkwerker; ~**-head,** klinknaelkop; ~**-hole,** klinkgat; ~**ing,** klinkwerk; ~**ing hammer,** klinkhamer, ~**ing machine,**

rivière 1193 *rocket*

klinkmasjien; ~-**punch,** klinknaeldeurslag; ~-**tongs,** klinknaeltang; ~-**weld,** naelsweislas.
riv'**ière,** juwelehalsband.
riv'**ing knife,** kloofyster.
riv'**ulet,** riviertjie, spruit, lopie.
rix' **dollar,** riksdaalder.
roach[1], **(-es),** gilling (skeepsterm).
roach[2], **(-es),** kakkerlak.
roach[3], **(-es),** karp; ~-**backed,** met 'n karprug, boggelrug.
road, pad, weg; vaal streep; rede, ankerplek; *BY* ~, oor land; pad langs, met die pad; *GENTLEMAN of the* ~, struikrower; *GO on the* ~, handelsreisiger word; *HIGH* ~, grootpad, transportpad; *the* ~ *to HELL is paved with good intentions,* die pad na die hel is met goeie voornemens geplavei; *the car HOLDS the* ~ *well,* die motor is padvas; *be LONG on the* ~, 'n lang tyd op die pad wees; *ONE for the* ~, 'n glasie op die valreep; loopdop; *ON the* ~, op weg, op die pad; *be on the* ~ *to RECOVERY,* aan die beterhand wees; *the ROYAL* ~ *to,* die hoofweg na; die koninklike weg na; *the* ~ *to RUIN,* die pad na die verderf; *RULES of the* ~, verkeersreëls; *RULE of the* ~, uitwykreël; *TAKE the* ~, in die pad val; die vaal streep kies; ~ **accident,** padongeluk; ~-**barrier,** versperring; ~-**bearer,** dekbalk; ~-**bed,** baanblad; ~-**block,** padversperring, padblokkade; voorstaandiens; ~ **board,** padraad; ~-**book,** padgids; ~-**breaker,** padbreker; ~-**bridge,** wabrug; ~-**building,** padbou; ~ **clearance,** ashoogte; ~-**construction,** padbou, padaanleg; ~ **courtesy,** padhoflikheid; ~-**crater,** padkrater; ~ **crossing,** padoorgang; ~-**deviation** padverlegging; ~ **engineer,** padingenieur, padboukundige; ~ **engineering,** padboukunde; ~ **fork,** vurk, padvertakking, tweesprong; ~ **fund,** padboufonds; ~ **gang,** padwerkersploeg; ~-**grader,** padskraper; ~ **head,** eindpunt van 'n pad; ~**hog,** motorbuffel, padbuffel, mylvreter, snelheidsduiwel, ryduiwel; ~**house,** herberg; inrykafee, padkafee; ~-**indicator,** padwyser; ~-**inspector,** weginspekteur; ~-**junction,** padknoop; ~ **locomotive,** lokomobiel; ~ **maintenance,** padonderhoud; ~**man,** padmaker; ~ **map,** padkaart; ~-**metal,** padverharding, padgruis; ~ **motor service,** padmotordiens; ~ **network,** padnet; ~-**plough,** padploeg; ~-**reconnaissance,** padverkenning; ~-**repairs,** padherstelwerk; ~-**report,** padverslag; ~-**roller,** padroller, padwals; ~ **runner,** pretdrawwer; ~ **running,** pretdraf; ~ **scraper,** padskraper; ~-**sense,** padinstink, padsin, padvernuf, ryverstand; ~-**sentry,** padwag; ~-**service,** paddiens; ~ **side,** (n) die kant v.d. pad; (a) langs die pad, pad-; ~ **sign,** padwyser, predikant; ~-**space,** padruimte; ~ **spy,** padspioen; ~**stead,** ankerplek, rede; ~**ster,** rywiel; ervare reisiger; ryperd; gekerkde skip; tweepersoonstoermotor; ~-**stud,** straatknop; ~ **surface,** padblad, padoppervlak; ~-**surfacing,** paddekmateriaal; ~ **tanker,** tenkwa; ~-**tax,** padbelasting; ~ **traffic,** padverkeer; ~-**traffic sign,** padverkeersteken; ~-**transport,** padvervoer; ~-**wagon,** wa; ~ **way,** ryweg, rylaan, rypad; ~-**worker,** padmaker; ~ **worthiness,** padwaardigheid, geskiktheid vir die pad; ~**worthy,** geskik vir die pad, padwaardig; in staat om te reis.
roam, dwaal, omdool, rondwerwe, (rond)dool; ~ **er,** swerwer; ~**ing,** gedwaal, divagasie.
roan[1], (n) skaappleer, basaanleer.
roan[2], (n) stippelaar, (rooi)skimmel(perd); rooiskilder(bees); (a) rooigrys, rooiskimmel; *BAY* ~, rooiskimmel, bruinskimmel; *BLUE* ~, blouskimmel; *RED* ~, bruinskimmel, rooiskimmel; ~ **antelope,** bastergemsbok, bastergensbok; bastereland.
roar, (n) gebrul; gebulder, geraas; dreun(ing), gebruis, geloei (storm); geskater (van mense); ~ *(s) of APPLAUSE,* stormagtige toejuiging; ~ *of GUNS,* kanongebulder; *SET up a* ~, begin brul; ~ *of the WAVES,* gedreun v.d. golwe; (v) brul; bulder; raas, dreun, donder; dawer, druis, bruis (wind); skater(lag); ~ *like a BULL,* soos 'n bees brul; ~ *DOWN,* oorskreeu; ~ *oneself HOARSE,* jou hees skreeu (brul); ~ *with LAUGHTER,* skater v.d. lag; ~**er,** bruller.

roar'ing, (n) gebrul; gedonder; gebulder; (a) brullend; bulderend; luidrugtig; uitstekend; *a* ~ *FIRE,* 'n knetterende vuur; *the* ~ *FORTIES,* die stormagtige see tussen 40° en 50° N.Br.; *a* ~ *GAME,* 'n lewendige wedstryd; *in* ~ *HEALTH,* in blakende gesondheid; *a* ~ *SUCCESS,* 'n uitmuntende sukses; *have a* ~ *TIME,* lekker verjaar; dolle pret hê; *a* ~ *TRADE,* 'n lewendige handel; geld maak soos bossies; ~ **drunk,** smoordronk; ~ **sand,** brulsand.
roast, (n) braaistuk, braaivleis; (v) braai; bak; rooster, brand (koffie); pla, die spot dryf met; *rule the* ~, baasspeel; (a) gebraai, braai-; ~ **beef,** gebraaide beesvleis; ~ **chicken,** gebraaide hoender; braaikuiken; ~**ed,** gebraai, gebak (kos); gebrand (koffie); ~**ed coffee,** gebrande koffie; ~**er,** braaier, braaioond; koffiebrander; braaivark; braaihoender; ~ **game,** wildbraad.
roast'ing, braaiery, die braai; *give someone a* ~, iem. roskam; iem. laat deurloop; ~ **jack,** spitbraaier; ~ **time,** braaityd.
roast' lamb, gebraaide lamsvleis.
rob, (-bed), rowe, steel; besteel; wegroof; plunder; ~**ber,** (struik)rower; dief; ~**bery, (..ries),** rowery, diefstal, diewery.
robe, (n) tabberd; toga, mantel; kleed, jurk, gewaad; (pl.) ampsgewaad; *GENTLEMEN of the* ~, registers en advokate; *MASTER of the* ~*s,* kamerheer; ~*s of OFFICE,* ampstoga, ampsgewaad; ~*s of STATE,* praalgewaad; (v) beklee, aantrek, aanklee.
rob'in, janfrederik, wipstert; ~-**chat,** janfrederik.
rob'ing, (die) aantrek; ~ **room,** ampskleedkamer; aantrekkamer.
Robin Hood': *many talk of* ~ *who never shot with his bow,* die haan kraai baie harder as die hen wat die eier gelê het.
robin red'breast, rooiborsie.
robinsonade', robinsonade.
rob'orant, (n) versterkmiddel; (a) versterkend, versterk-.
rob'ot, robot; masjienmens; verkeersein, verkeersoutomaat; verkeerslig; ~ **ahead,** robot voor.
rob'urite, roburiet.
robust', sterk, gespierd, flink, fors, kragtig, frisgebou, robuus; *in* ~ *health,* blakend gesond; ~**ious,** verwaand, rumoerig, lawaaierig, woes; ~**ness,** krag, gespierdheid, forsheid, fiksheid, robuustheid.
roc, rok (reusefabelvoël); ~*'s egg,* iets fabelagtigs.
roch'et, rokelyn, roket, rochet, koorhemp.
rock, (n) rots, kliprots; *R* ~ *of AGES,* Rots v.d. Eeue; *BUILT on the* ~, op vaste fondament gebou; *a DRINK on the* ~*s,* skoon drankie met ys; *stand as FIRM as a* ~, so vas soos 'n rotssteen staan; *LEDGE of* ~, rotslys; *be ON the* ~*s,* in die knyp sit; geldgebrek ly; *RUN onto the* ~*s,* skipbreuk ly; *THE R*~, die Rots van Gibraltar; *this is the* ~ *you'll SPLIT on,* dit is die rots wat jou gaan laat skipbreuk ly; dit is die rots waarteen jy jou te pletter gaan loop; (v) skud, skommel, hobbel; laat skud, wieg, slinger, wiegel; wankel, waggel; wikkel (gholf); ~ *with LAUGHTER,* skud v.d. lag; ~ *and ROLL,* ruk en pluk; ~ *to SLEEP,* aan die slaap wieg; ~ **alum,** aluinsteen; ~ **ammonia,** ammoniumkarbonaat, vlugsout; ~ **and roll',** ruk-en-rol (dans); ~-**bed,** rotsbodem; ~ **bottom,** (n) rotsbodem, rotsgrond; *strike* ~ *bottom,* die allerlaagste punt bereik; (a) die allerlaagste; ~ *bottom prices,* die allerlaagste pryse; ~-**bound,** deur rotse ingesluit; ~-**breaker,** rotsbreker; ~-**burst,** rotsbarsting; ~ **cod,** koningklip; ~-**cork,** bergkurk; ~-**crystal,** bergkristal; ~-**drill,** klipboor, diamantboor; ~-**dump,** rotshoop; ~-**engraving,** rotsgravure.
rock'er, wiegster; wiegpoot, skommelaar (wieg); tuimelaar, skommelaar (mynb.); rystoel, hobbelperd, skommelstoel; wasmasjien (vir grond); *be off one's* ~, 'n krakie hê; getik wees.
rock'ery, (..ries), rotstuin, kliptuin.
rock'et[1], (n) damasblom.
rock'et[2], (n) vuurpyl; *go up like the* ~ *and come down like the stick,* hoog vlieg en laag val; (v) met vuurpyle beskiet; in die hoogte skiet (pryse); ~-

propelled aircraft, vuurpylvliegtuig; ~ **cannon**, vuurpylkanon; ~ **launcher**, vuurpyllanseerder; ~**-mould**, vuurpylstok; ~**-projectile**, vuurpyl; ~ **projector**, vuurpylwerper; ~**-propelled**, vuurpylaangedrewe.

rock: ~**-face**, bergwand; breekvlak (in myn); ~**-fall**, rotsstorting; ~ **fill**, rotvulling; ~**-fish**, skerpioenvis; ~**-garden**, rotstuin; ~ **hammer**, kliphamer; ~**-hare**, kolhaas, rooihaas; ~**-hewn**, uit rots (klip) gekap; ~ **hoist**, rotshysmasjien; ~**-hopper**, geelkuifpikkewyn; ~ **iness**, rotsagtigheid.

rock'ing, (n) wiegeling; wikkeling; (a) skommelrig; wiegend; ~**-chair**, skommelstoel, rystoel; ~**-grate**, skommelrooster, skudrooster; ~**-horse**, hobbelperd, skommelperd; ~**-horse motion**, skommel-(perd)beweging; ~ **screen**, skommelsif; ~ **stone**, wieqklip.

rock: ~ **kestrel**, kransvalk; ~**-ladder**, bergleer; ~**like**, rotsvas; ~**-lobster**, Afrikaanse kreef; seekreef; ~**-martin**, kransswa(w)el(tjie); ~**-oil**, steenolie, petroleum, aardolie; ~**-painting**, rotsskildery; ~ **phosphate**, rotsfosfaat; ~**-pigeon**, bosduif, kransduif; ~**-plant**, rotsplant; ~**-rabbit**, (klip)dassie; ~**-rose**, sonroos; ~**-salt**, klipsout; ~**-shaft**, rotsskag; ~ **shelter**, rotsskuiling; ~**-silk**, bergvlas; ~**-slide**, bergstorting, rotsafskuiwing; ~ **sulphur**, rotsswa(w)el; ~ **wall**, klipmuur, rotsmuur; ~**-wool**, bergvlas; ~**-work**, rotswerk; kliptuin; grotwerk; ~ **y**, rotsagtig; klipperig; klipsteenhard; bewerig; slap; ~**y bed**, nabank; ~**y outcrop**, klipbank.

rococ'o, rococo (styl); ouderwets, verouderd.

rod, roede; staf; meetroede; stok; stang, staaf; stiffie; rottang; *make a* ~ *for one's own BACK*, jouself moeilikheid op die hals haal; *BLACK R*~, ampswag v.d. Senaat; Draer v.d. Swart Roede (Eng.); ~ *of CORRECTION*, tugroede, geselroede; *have a GO at the* ~, gaan visvang; *KISS the* ~, jou gedwee aan straf onderwerp; *have a* ~ *in PICKLE for someone*, nog met iem. wil afreken; vir iem. oorgehaal sit; 'n appeltjie met iem. te skil hê; *RULE with a* ~ *of iron*, met 'n ystervuis regeer; *SPARE the* ~ *and spoil the child*, wie die roede spaar, bederf die kind; *WIELD the* ~, die septer swaai.

rode, *kyk* **ride**, (v).

rod'ent, (n) knaagdier; (a) knaag-, knaend.

roden'tial, knaagdier-, tot die knaagdiere behorend.

ro'dent-proof, rotdig.

rode'o, (-s), rodeo, die bymekaarmaak van wilde perde (of beeste); ruiteryvertoning (deur baasruiters); vertoning deur motorfietsryers.

rod: ~**-fishing**, stokvisvangs; ~ **iron**, staafyster, stangyster.

rod'man, visvanger (met 'n stok).

rod'omont, grootprater, pronker, spogter; ~ **ade'**, (n) pronkery, grootpratery, spoggery; (v) bluf, grootpraat, spog; (a) spoggerig, windmaker-.

rod: ~**-punch**, steeldeurslag; ~**-shaped**, staafvormig.

roe[1], viskuit, viseiertjies.

roe[2], takbokooi; ree; ~ **buck**, gemsbok (Bybel).

roga'tion, litanie v.d. heiliges; Rogate; *R*~ *DAYS*, die drie dae voor Hemelvaart; *R*~ *WEEK*, Hemelvaartsweek.

rogue, (n) skurk, skelm, karnallie, boef, skobbejak, skavuit, swernoot; platjie, guit; derduiwel, abjater, vabond; uilspieël; tingerige plant; *a* ~ *through and through*, 'n uiterste karnallie (vabond); (v) skurkstreke uithaal, bedrieg; swak plante uittrek; ~ **elephant**, dwalerolifant, eenloperolifant; ronkedoor; ~**ry**, skurkestreek, skelmagtigheid, skelmery, boewestreek, boefagtigheid, slenterslag, skurkagtigheid, skavuitstreek; skalksheid; ~**s' gallery**, skurkemuseum; ~**s' Latin**, bargoens, diewetaal.

rog'uish, skurkagtig, skelmagtig; boefagtig; guitig, skalks, ondeund; ~**-ness**, skelmagtigheid, boewestreek, skurkery, boewery; ondeundheid, guitigheid.

rois'ter, luidrugtig pret maak, raas; ~ **er**, grootprater, lawaaimaker; ~ **ing**, luidrugtig, lawaaierig, uitbundig.

Ro'land, *a* ~ *for an Oliver*, leer om leer.

role, rol (in toneelstuk); funksie, taak; ~**-play**, rolvertolking.

roll, (n) rol; naamlys, register; silinder; broodrolletjie; gerol, gerommel, geroffel; wal, bank; deining, golwing; (die) slinger (skip); wrong (hare); (pl) argief; *CALL the* ~, die presensielys opmaak; ~ *of DRUMS*, tromgeroffel; ~ *of HONOUR*, lys van gesneuweldes; ererol; ~ *of MEMBERSHIP*, ledelys; *PUT on the* ~*s*, inskryf; ~ *of a SHIP*, slingering van 'n skip; *STRIKE a solicitor off the* ~*s*, 'n prokureur v.d. rol skrap; (v) rol; oprol; inrol; wals (staal); laat rol; draai (pille); dreun; roffel (mil.); skommel, slinger (skip); ~ *ALONG*, voortrol; ~ *AWAY*, wegrol; skraap; ~ *BY*, verbyrol; ~ *a CIGARETTE*, 'n sigaret draai; ~ *DOWN*, afrol; ~ *one's EYES*, met die oë rol; ~ *IN*, inrol; ~ *in MONEY*, geld soos water hê; in weelde baai; hard v.d. geld wees; ~ *ON*, aanhou rol; ~ *OUT*, laat rol; plet, uitrol (metaal); ooprol; ~ *OVER*, omrol; ~ *and PITCH*, slinger en stamp (skip); ~ *one's R'S*, bry; die r pront uitspreek; ~ *up one's SLEEVES*, moue oprol; ~ *UP*, oprol; verskyn, te voorskyn kom, opdaag; ~ *in WEALTH*, geld soos water hê; in weelde baai; ~ *of WIRE*, rol draad, draadrol; ~ **bandage**, rolverband; ~**-call**, rollesing, appèl (mil.); presensielys neem; ~ **collar**, rolkraag.

rolled, gerol, rol-; gewals (yster); geplet (staal); opgerol; ~ *into one*, ineengerol; in een persoon verenig; ~ **bacon**, gerolde spekvleis; ~ **bar**, gewalste staaf; ~ **beef**, rolstuk, rollende rollade; ~ **gold**, oorgeblaasde goud, goudpleet; ~ **ham**, rolham; ~ **hem**, boorselsoom; ~ **meat**, rolvleis; ~ **oats**, hawermout; ~ **rib**, rolrib; ~ **sirloin of beef**, beeslenderol; ~ **steel**, gewalste staal; ~ **tobacco**, roltabak; ~ **tongue**, roltong; ~ **wafer**, oblietjie.

roll'er, rol; roller; rolsteen; tuimelaar (duif); troupant (voël); rolstok, leirol; wals (staal); deining, groot golf; ~ **bandage**, rolverband; ~**-bearing**, rollaer; ~ **blind**, rolblinding; ~ **coaster**, wipwaentjie; ~ **engine**, padroller; ~ **flaw**, roldefek; ~**-mark**, (n) rolmerk; (v) rolmerk; ~ **mill**, walsmeule, pletmeule; ~ **milling**, pletmalery; ~ **pin**, leirolpen; ~**-post mark**, rolposmerk; ~ **shutter**, rolluik; ~ **skate**, (n) rolskaats; ~**-skate**, (v) rolskaats; ~**-skating**, rolskaats; ~ **towel**, rolhanddoek; ~ **wheel**, rolwieletjie.

roll' fire, roffelvuur.

roll'ick, (n) plesier, fuif, uitgelatenheid; (v) dartel, woel, speel, baljaar, fuif; ~ *about*, rondjakker; ~**ing**, (n) baljaardery; (a) dartel, uitgelate.

roll'ing, (n) gerol; golwing; (a) golwend, rollend; *a* ~ *STONE*, iem. van twaalf ambagte en dertien ongelukke; ~ **door**, skuifdeur; ~ **hills**, golwende heuwels; ~**-machine**, walsmasjien, pletmasjien; ~**-mill**, rolmeul, walsmeul, pletmeule, plettery; ~ **motion**, rolbeweging; ~**-pin**, rolstok, deegroller; ~**-press**, rolpers; ~ **stock**, rollende materiaal.

roll'-top desk, rolluiklessenaar.

rol'y-pol'y, (n) rolpoeding; roltert; vetsak, diksak; (a) vet, dik; poffertjie-.

Roman, (n) Romein; romein (drukletter); (a) Romeins; Rooms (kerk); *the Holy* ~ *Empire*, die Heilige Roomeinse Ryk; ~ **Catholic**, Rooms-Katoliek.

Romance'[1], (n) Romaanse taal; (a) Romaans.

romance'[2], (n) romanse; verdigting; (ridder)roman; versinsel; romantiek; liefdesverhouding; liefdesverhaal; (v) romantiese verhale opdis; leuens opdis; fantaseer, spekskiet; ~ **r**, romansier, romanskrywer; spekskieter.

Rom'an: ~ **character**, gewone (Latynse) letter; ~**-Dutch**, Romeins-Hollands; ~**esque'**, -'ic, Romaans; ~**ish**, Rooms; Roomsgesind; Rooms-Katoliek; ~**ize**, latiniseer, verromeins; in romeinse letters oorbring; Rooms maak; Rooms word.

rom'an letter, romeinse letter.

Rom'an nose, arendsneus, hawiksneus, kromneus.

roman'tic, (n) romantikus; (a) romanties; fantasties, avontuurlik; *the R*~ *Movement*, die Romantiek; ~ **al**, romansk; ~ **ism**, romantiek; ~ **ist**, romantikus; ~ **ize**, romantiseer.

rom'an type, gewone drukletter, romein.

Rom'any, (n) Sigeuner; (a) Sigeuns, Sigeunertaal.

Rome, Rome; die Romeinse Ryk; die Roomse kerk;

~ *was not BUILT in a day,* Rome is nie in een dag gebou nie; môre is nog 'n dag; *when in* ~, *DO as the Romans do,* jou na die gebruike v.d. land skik; lands wys, lands eer; *'tis ill sitting in* ~ *and striving with the POPE,* wie se brood 'n mens eet, die se woord 'n mens spreek; *all ROADS lead to* ~, alle paaie gaan na Rome.

Rom'ic, Sweet se fonetiese skryfwyse, Romic.

Rom'ish, Rooms.

romp, (n) gedartel, gespeel, stoeiery; rabbedoe; wilde meisie; (v) stoei, rondspring, jakker, baljaar, ravot; ~ *HOME,* maklik eerste kom; fluit-fluit wen; ~ *PAST,* verbysnel; ~**er,** baljaarder; ~**er(s),** kruippakkie; ~**ing,** (n) gespeel, stoeiery, gerinkink; (a) stoeisiek, speels; ~**ish,** ~**y,** uitgelate, dartel.

ronda'vel, rondawel.

ron'deau, ron'del, rondeel, rondeau; keerdig; refrein.

ron'eo, (n) (-s), roneo; (v) afrol, roneo (geregistreerde handelsnaam).

rönt'genize, röntgen, deurlig.

rönt'genogram, X-straalfoto, röntgenfoto.

rönt'genograph, (n) X-straalfoto, röntgenfoto; (v) röntgen, deurlig; ..**no'graphy,** röntgenografie.

röntgeno'scopy, röntgenoskopie.

Rönt'gen rays, röntgenstrale, X-strale

röntgen ther'apy, röntgenterapie, straalterapie.

rood, roede (lengtemaat); kruisbeeld; ~**-loft,** kruisgalery; ~**-screen,** koorhek.

roof, (n) dak; verhemelte (mond), gehemelte; gewelf; kap; *FLAT* ~, platdak; *FLAT-* ~ *ed house,* platdakhuis; *a* ~ *of FOLIAGE,* 'n blaredak; *have a* ~ *over one's HEAD,* 'n dak oor jou kop hê; *not to have a over one's HEAD,* nie 'n dak oor jou kop he nie; geen onderdak hê nie; ~ *of the MOUTH,* verhemelte; *PROVIDE a* ~, 'n dak voorsien; *RAISE the* ~, 'n yslike lawaai maak; 'n lawaai v.d. ander wêreld opskop; *THATCHED* ~, rietdak, grasdak; *TILED* ~, teëldak; *WET the* ~, dakfees hou; dak natmaak; (v) 'n dak opsit, onder dak bring; ~ *in,* bedek, onder dak bring; ~ **age,** dakwerk, dakbedekking; ~ **batten,** deklat; ~ **beam,** hanebalk, dakbalk; ~**-clutcher,** dakvink; ~ **door,** dakdeur; ~ **er,** dakwerker; ~ **frame,** daktimmerasie; ~ **garden,** daktuin; ~ **gutter,** dakgeut.

roof'ing, dakmateriaal; dakwerk, dakbedekking; dek; ~ **felt,** dakvilt; ~ **shingle,** dakspaan; ~ **rafter,** dakspar, kapspar.

roof: ~ **slate,** daklei; ~ **tile,** dakpan; ~ **lamp,** daklamp; ~**-less,** dakloos, sonder dak; ~ **let,** dakkie; ~**-light,** daklig; ~**-pendant,** dakhanger; ~**-plate,** dakplaat; ~**-principal,** dakkap, dakstoel; ~**-rail,** dakreling; ~**-ridge,** vors; ~ **sheeting,** dakplate ~ **stick,** dakboog, dakrib, ~ **support,** dakstut; ~**-tie,** -hanebalk, ~**-tile,** dakspan; dakbint; ~**-tiler,** pandekker; ~**-tree,** nokbalk; ~**-truss,** dakkap, dakstoel; ~ **wetting,** dakfees, daknatmaak(seremonie).

rook¹, (n) kasteel, toring (skaak); (v) rokeer.

rook², (n) kraai; bedrieër, oneerlike speler; (v) bedrieg, oneerlik speel; te veel laat betaal, afpers; ~ *someone,* geld van iem. attroggel; iem. te veel laat betaal; ~**er,** bedrieër, oneerlike speler; ~**ery,** (..ries), kraaines; diewenes; broeiplek; agterbuurte; bordeel.

rook'ie, rouriem, groentjie, beginner, nuweling.

room, (n) kamer, vertrek; plek, ruimte; geleentheid; aanleiding, rede; *I'd rather have his* ~ *than his COMPANY,* ek sien hom liewers gaan as kom; *no* ~ *for DOUBT,* sonder die minste twyfel; *GIVE* ~ *to,* plek maak vir; *there is always* ~ *for a GOOD one,* daar kom baie mak skape in 'n kraal; ~ *for IMPROVEMENT,* ruimte vir verbetering; dit kan beter; *MAKE* ~, plek maak; padgee; *NO* ~ *for dispute,* onbetwisbaar; *there is always PLENTY of* ~ *at the top,* talent is daar genoeg; *have no* ~ *to TURN,* jou nie kan draai nie; *no* ~ *to SWING a cat,* baie min ruimte; (v) 'n kamer bewoon; ~ *with,* 'n kamer deel met; ~**ful,** kamervol; ~**iness,** ruimheid; wydheid; ~ **mate,** kamermaat, kammie; ~ **orderly,** kamerwag; ~ **service,** kamerbediening; ~ **temperature,** kamertemperatuur; ~**y,** ruim, groot.

roop, heesheid; ~**y,** hees.

roost, (n) slaapplek, stok, steier, slaapstok; stellasie; *AT* ~, op stok; *GO to* ~, gaan slaap; op stok gaan; *RULE the* ~, haantjie die voorste wees, baasspeel; (v) sit en slaap (hoender); gaan slaap, die nag deurbring; *your chickens come home to* ~, jou sonde vind jou; ~**er,** haan.

root¹, (n) wortel (boom); oorsprong; oorsaak; bron; stam; grondtoon; *AT the* ~, in die grond; in die kern; *lay AXE to the* ~, iets se bestaan bedreig; *BE at the* ~ *of,* ten grondslag lê van; *get rid of something* ~ *and BRANCH,* iets met wortel en tak uitroei; *CUBE* ~, kubieke wortel; *the* ~ *of all EVIL,* die wortel van alle kwaad; *GET (GO) to the* ~ *of the matter,* tot die kern v.d. saak deurdring; *HAVE its* ~ *in,* spruit uit; *PULL up by the* ~ *s,* met wortel en tak uitroei; *SHAKE something to its* ~ *s,* iets tot sy fondament laat skud; *SQUARE* ~, vierkantswortel; *STRIKE at the* ~ *of,* die wortel tref; *the idea STRUCK* ~, die idee het wortel geskiet; *TAKE* ~, groei, wortel skiet; posvat (fig.); (v) wortel skiet; ingewortel wees, vaswortel; inprent; ~*ed to the GROUND,* vasgenael aan die grond; ~ *OUT,* uitroei, uitdelg; ~ *UP,* omvroetel.

root², (v) vroetel; ~ *ABOUT,* omvroetel; ~ *OUT,* uitsnuffel; ~ *UP,* omvroetel.

root: ~**-bound,** vasgewortel; ~**-cap,** wortelmussie; ~ **cause,** grondoorsaak; ~ **crop,** wortelgewas; ~**ed,** ingewortel, vasgewortel, diep, vasgenael; *be* ~ *ed to,* vasgenael wees; ~**-edge,** wortelrand; ~**-end,** wortelpunt; ~**er,** (swaar) tandploeg; toejuiger, ondersteuner; ~ **extraction,** worteltrekking.

root'le, vroetel, omvroetel, omwoel

root: ~**-hair,** wortelhaar; ~**-knot,** wortelknoop; ~ **less,** sonder wortels, wortelloos; ~**let,** worteltjie; ~**-opening,** wortelopening; ~ **rot,** vrotpootjie; ~ **sign,** wortelteken; ~**-stock,** wortelstok; onderstam; ~ **system,** wortelstelsel; ~ **vegetables,** wortelgroente; ~ **vowel,** stamvokaal; ~**y,** vol wortels.

rope, (n) tou, lyn; *come to the END of one's* ~, jou rieme styfloop; *GIVE someone plenty of* ~, iem. alle vryheid van beweging gee; iem. vrye spel (skiet) gee; *GIVE someone enough* ~ *to hang himself,* iem. vryheid van beweging laat om sy eie ongeluk te bewerk; *on the HIGH* ~ *s,* uitgelate; hoogmoedig; kwaad; *KNOW the* ~ *s,* touwys wees; goed op hoogte van sake wees; *a* ~ *of PEARLS,* 'n snoer pêrels; *PUT someone up to the* ~ *s,* iem. goed touwys maak; *make* ~ *s of SAND,* vrugtelose arbeid verrig; *like a* ~ *of SAND,* soos droë sand aanmekaar hang; *SHOW someone the* ~ *s,* iem. touwys maak, iem. inlig; *STRAIN at the* ~, die tou styf trek; *be sentenced to THE* ~, tot die strop veroordeel word; *THROW the* ~ *in after the bucket,* die laaste bietjie ook weggooi; (v) vasmaak, vasbind; aanmekaar ryg; draderig word (brood); inhou; vang (perd); met 'n tou vang; omspan; in 'n onderneming kry; binnehaal; ~*d ARENA,* touafskorting; ~ *IN helpers,* oorhaal om te help, inspan; *vir 'n saak werk;* mense in 'n saak betrek; ~ *UP,* vasbind; ~**-bridge,** toubrug; ~ **dancer,** koorddanser; ~**-dancing,** koorddansery; ~**-drill,** lynoefening; ~**-ladder,** touleer; ~ **maker,** toudraaier; ~ **railway,** kabelspoor; ~**ry,** toudraaiery; ~**-walk,** lynbaan; ~**-walker,** koorddanser; ~ **way,** kabelspoor; ~**-yarn,** kaalgaar(tou), kaaltou.

rop'iness, draderigheid; leng (in brood); touagtigheid.

rop'y, touagtig; draderig; *the BREAD is* ~, die brood trek drade; ~ *BREAD,* draderige brood; lengbrood.

roq'uet, wegskram, skrams raak.

ro'ric, dourig, dou-.

rorq'ual, vinvis, rugvinwalvis.

rort'y, heerlik, aangenaam, lekker.

ros'ace, rosetvenster; roosvenster.

rosa'ceous, roosagtig; rosetvormig, roosvormig.

rosar'ian, rooskweker.

rosar'ium, (..ria), roostuin.

ros'ary, (..ries), rosekrans, paternoster; roostuin.

rose¹, (n) roos (plant); rooskleur; roset; roos (siekte); broes, gieterkop, sproeier (van gieter); *life is not a BED of* ~ *s,* dis nie altyd net sonskyn nie; die lewe is

nie net rosegeur en maanskyn nie; *lie on a BED of* ~*s*; op rose loop; *the* ~ *s in her CHEEKS*, die rose op haar wange; *CLIMBING* ~, rankroos; *GATHER life's* ~ *s*, die lewe geniet; ~ *of JERICHO*, Jerigoroos; *MOONLIGHT and* ~ *s*, rosegeur en maneskyn; *OIL of* ~*s*, roosolie; *their PATH is not strewn with* ~*s*, hulle pad is nie met rose bestrooi nie; *SCENT of* ~ *s*, roosgeur, rosegeur; ~ *of SHARON*, roos van Saron; *no* ~ *without a THORN*, geen roos sonder dorings nie; *a* ~ *among THORNS*, 'n roos tussen die dorings; *UNDER the* ~, in die geheim; onder ons meisies; sub rosa; (a) rooskleurig, roserooi, pienk.
rose², (v) *kyk* **rise**.
rose' apple, jamboes.
ros'eate, rooskleurig; vol rose.
rose: ~**-bay**, oleander; asalea; ~**-bit,** sinkboor; ~**-bowl,** roosbak; ~**-bud,** roosknop; ~**-bug,** roosluis; ~**-bush,** roosstruik, roosboom; ~**-colour,** rooskleur; ~**-coloured,** rooskleurig; *see life through* ~ *-coloured spectacles*, die lewe v.d. ligte kant sien; ~ **copper,** gaarkoper; ~**-cutting,** roossteggie; ~ **diamond,** rosetsteen; ~**-drop,** oorbelletjie; roosuitslag; ~**-head,** sproeier, broes; ~ **hedge,** rooslaning; ~**-hued,** met roostint; ~**-leaf,** roosblaar; ~ **madder,** donkerrooi; ~**-mallow,** strokroos.
rose'mary, (. . ries), roosmaryn.
rose'ola, roosuitslag.
rose: ~**-oil,** roosolie; ~**-pink,** roos, rooskleurig; ~ **quartz,** rooskwarts; ~**-rash,** roosuitslag; ~**-red,** roosrooi; ~**-slip,** roosstiggie; ~**-tree,** roosboom.
rosette', roset, kokarde.
rose: ~**-water,** rooswater; ~ **window,** rosetvenster, roosvenster; ~ **wood,** rooshout, palissanderhout.
ros'in, (n) hars, harpuis; (v) met harpuis smeer.
Rosinan'te, Rosinante, knol.
ros'iness, rooskleurigheid, blosendheid.
ros'iny, harsagtig, harpuisagtig, hars=.
ros'ter, rooster; lys.
ros'tral, bek=, snawelagtig; snawelvormig.
rostrat'ed, gesnawel(d).
ros'triform, snawelagtig.
ros'trum, (. . tra, -s), snawel, bek; spreekgestoelte; rostrum.
ros'y, rooskleurig; roosagtig; blosend, bloesend; roos=; ~**-cheeked,** met rooi wange; ~**-faced lovebird,** rooiwangparkiet; ~**-fingered,** roosvingerig.
rot, (n) verrotting, vrotheid; ontbinding; lewersiekte (by skape); kaf, onsin, gewawel, snert; *it's ALL* ~, dis alles pure kaf; *DRY* ~, droëvrot (by plante); molm (by hout); *the* ~ *SET in,* alles het verslep; *TALK* ~, twak (kaf) verkoop; *TOMMY* ~, kaf, onsin, bog; (v) **(-ted),** vrot, verrot; sleg word, bederwe; verkwyn, wegteer; terg, pla; *it* ~ *ted AWAY*, dit het verrot (vrot geword); ~ *OFF*, afvrot.
rot'a, lys, rooster, rota; ~**cism,** rotasisme.
Rotar'ian, Rotariër.
Rot'ary¹, Rotariërbeweging, Rotary.
rot'ary², (n) rotasiemasjien; (a) ronddraaiend; rondgaande; rotasie=, draai=.
Rot'ary Club, Rotariërklub.
rot'ary: ~ **crane,** draaikraan; ~ **cultivator,** woeleg; ~ **current,** draaistroom; ~ **cutter,** swaaielsmyner; ~ **engine,** draaimotor; ~ **hoe,** wielskoffel, kapeg, roltandeg.
Rot'ary International, Rotary Internasionaal.
rot'ary: ~ **motion,** draaibeweging; ~ **pan,** draaipan; ~ **plough,** kapploeg; ~ **press,** rolpers, rotasiepers; ~ **printing,** rotasiedruk; ~ **pump,** draaipomp; ~ **valve,** draaiklep.
rotate', ronddraai, draai; omdraai, wentel, roteer; (laat) afwissel; ~ *crops,* wisselbou toepas.
rotat'able, draaibaar.
rotat'ing, draai=, draaiend, roterend; ~ **beacon,** draaibaken; ~ **current,** draaistroom; ~ **door,** draaideur; ~ **drum,** draaitrommel, draaiende trommel (silinder); ~ **engine,** draaimotor.
rota'tion, ronddraaiing, wenteling, gewentel, rotasie; volgorde; afwisseling; omlooptyd; *ANGLE of* ~, draaiingshoek; *AXIS of* ~, omwentelingsas; *BY* ~, om die beurt; ~ *of CROPS*, wisselbou; *DIRECTION of* ~, draairigting; *PLANE of* ~, omwentelingsvlak; *TIME of* ~, omwentelingstyd.
rota'tional, draaiend; beurtelings, afwisselend, wissel=; ~ *CROPPING*, wisselboustelsel; ~ *GRAZING,* wisselweiding.
rota'tion number, volgnommer.
rot'ative, draaiend; afwisselend.
rotat'or, ronddraaier; omdraaier; draaispier.
rot'atory, ronddraaiend, wentelend, roterend, draai=; afwisselend; ~ **motion,** draaibeweging, ronddraaiende beweging; ~ **mower,** swaaielmgrassnyer.
rote, sleur, gewoonte; roetine; *BY* ~, van buite, uit die kop; *DO by* ~, sleurwerk doen; masjinaal doen; *KNOW by* ~, uit die hoof ken; *LEARN by* ~, soos 'n papegaai leer; iets soos 'n rympie leer.
rot'gut, withond, drank van swak gehalte.
rot'ifer, raderdiertjie.
rot'iform, wielvormig.
rot'ograph, diepdruk, rotograaf; ~ '**ic,** rotografies.
rotogravure', diepdruk, rotagravure.
rot'or, rotor; draaivlerk; ~**-boat,** rotorboot, Flettnerskip.
rot'ovator, rolskoffel.
rott'en, vrot, vergaan, bederf, vrotsig, ellendig, miserabel, sleg; vervelend; beroerd; ~ *to the CORE*, deur en deur bedorwe (vrot); *there is something* ~ *in the state of DENMARK*, sake is nie pluis nie; *it is* ~ *LUCK*, dis regtig 'n jammerte; *it is WORSE than* ~, dis sleg verby; ~**ly,** ellendig, beroerd; ~ **ness,** vrotheid, verrotting, bederf, verdorwenheid, rotheid; slegtigheid.
rott'er, lamsak, vrotterd, niksnut(s), deugniet.
rotund', rond, gerond; omvangryk; klankvol, klinkend; plomp, vet; ~ **a,** rotonde, koepelgebou, uitkykkoepel; ~**ity,** rondheid.
rou'ble, roebel.
rou'é, losbol.
rouge, (n) rooisel, (rooi) blanketsel, rouge; rooie, rewolusionêr; rooi poetspoeier; (v) blanket, rooi verf.
rough, (n) ruwe (rowwe) kêrel, skurk; ruwe (rowwe) skets; ruwe grond; ruigte, sukkelveld, rof, ruveld (gholf); hobbelagtigheid; *IN the* ~, onafgewerk; in die ruveld (rof) (gholf); *the* ~ *s and SMOOTHS of life*, die soet en suur v.d. lewe; voor= en teenspoed; *take the* ~ *with the SMOOTH*, dit neem soos dit val; *over* ~ *and SMOOTH*, oor grof en glad; *that is TRUE in the* ~, dit is oor die algemeen waar; *a* ~ *and TUMBLE*, 'n wilde worsteling; (v) ru maak; touwys maak; 'n ruwe skets maak; hard behandel; ~ *IT*, jou ongemak getroos; dit neem soos jy dit kry; ~ *OUT a plan*, 'n ruwe skets maak; ~ *UP*, hard aanpak; (a, adv) ru, grof, rof, hard; ruig; onefffe, hobbelagtig (pad); onafgewerk; onstuimig, wild, stormagtig (see); onmanierlik, woes, hardhandig; globaal; *CUT up* ~, uitvaar (teen); te kere gaan; *make a* ~ *ESTIMATE*, by benadering skat; *as* ~ *as a GRATE*, so skurf soos 'n padda; *make a* ~ *GUESS*, naaste(n)by skat; *I gave him a LICK with the* ~ *er side of my tongue*, ek het sy kop gewas; ek het hom terdeë ingeklim; ~ *LUCK*, teenspoed; ~ *MANNERS*, onbeskaafde maniere; *it is* ~ *ON them*, dit is 'n terugslag vir hulle; ~ *PLAY*, ruwe spel; *a* ~ *RIDER*, 'n perdeduiwel; 'n baasruiter; ~ *SEA*, stormagtige see; *the* ~ *er SEX*, die sterk geslag; *have a* ~ *TIME*, swaarkry; dit hotagter kry; ~ *and TUMBLE*, woes; wild; deurmekaar; ~ **age,** growwigheid; growwe voedsel, veselstof; ruvoer (vee); ~**-and-ready,** ru, grof; ondeurdag; ongeërg, ongegeneerd; onafgerond, onafgewerk; ~**-and-tumble,** (n) geveg, wilde worsteling; (a) verward, deurmekaar, wild, ongereeld, woes; ~ **book,** kladboek; ~ **cast,** (n) ruwe skets; grintspat(pleister); ruwe pleisterkalk; (v) (~), ru skets; aansmeer; rofkas, grintspat; (a) onafgewerk, lomp; ~ **coat,** eerste laag; raaplaag (pleistering); nuwe pels; ~ **copy,** klad; ~ **diamond,** ongeslypte (ruwe) diamant; 'n deugsame maar onbeskaafde man; ~ **draft,** ontwerp, klad; ~**-draw,** (. . drew, -n), ru skets; ~**-dried,** winddroog; ~**-dry,** (. . dried), ongestryk opmaak (wasgoed); ~**en,** ru maak; ~ **estimate,** ruwe skatting; ~ **file,** snelvyl, growwe vyl; ~ **going,** moeilike tog; *it was* ~ *going*, dit het swaar gegaan;

~**-ground**, grof gemaal; ~**-hew, (-ed, -n)**, ru bekap; roffel, 'n ruwe model maak van; ~**-hewer**, voorkapper; ~**-hewn**, ru, ongepolys, grof; ~**ing-reamer**, voorruimer; ~**ly**, naasteby, min of meer, ruweg, sowat, globaal; ~ *ly speaking*, globaal geneem; ~ **music**, ketelmusiek; ~**neck**, ruwe kêrel; ~**ness**, ruheid, oneffenheid, ongelykheid; hardhandigheid; ~ **plan**, sketsplan, ruwe skets; ~**-plane**, afroffel; ~ **play**, ruwe spel; ~ **proof**, eerste (vuil) proef; ~**-rider**, perdetemmer; perdeduiwel; baasruiter; pikeur; ~**-sawn**, ru gesaag; ~**shod**, skerp beslaan; *ride* ~ *shod over*, baasspeel oor; nie ontsien nie; verontagsaam; ~ **sketch**, ruwe (rowwe) skets; ~ **time:** *have a* ~ *time*, swaar kry; ~**-spoken**, grof, ru van mond; ~ **wine**, vrank wyn; ~ **work**, growwe werk; ~**-wrought**, grof bewerk, onafgewerk.
roulade', toonroller, lopie, roulade.
rouleau', **(-s, -x)**, rolletjie (bv. van goue muntstukke).
roulette', wieletjie; roulette (dobbelspel).
Rouman'ia, Roemenië; ~**n**, (n) Roemeniër; Roemeens (taal); (a) Roemeens.
round, (n) kring; bol; omloop; omgang; roetine; rondreis; rondte (om 'n sportbaan); rondgang (van wagte); ronde (in sportnommers); rondedans; sport (van leer); sny (brood); rondjie; patroon (geweer); granaat, bom, skoot, laag; (pl) stuksteenkool; *ten* ~ *s of AMMUNITION*, tien patrone; ~ *of APPLAUSE*, handgeklap; *a* ~ *of CHEERS*, toejuiging; *the DAILY* ~, daaglikse arbeid; *DO the* ~ *s*, die rondte van vader Cloete doen; *a* ~ *of DRINKS*, 'n rondjie; *GO on one's* ~ *s*, die rondte doen; *a* ~ *of GOLF*, 'n rondte gholf, 'n gholfspel; *HAVE a* ~, 'n potjie speel; *MAKE one's* ~ *s*, die rondte doen; *MAKE a* ~ *of the rooms*, die kamers deurgaan; *TWO* ~ *s of TOAST*, twee snye geroosterde brood; (v) rond maak; afrond; omring; omseil; insluit; inkluister; ~ *the CAPE*, die Kaap omseil; ~ *OFF*, afrond; ~ *ON someone*, iem. invlieg; ~ *OUT*, aanvul, voller maak; afrond; ~ *UP*, bymekaarmaak, aankeer; gevange neem; (a) rond, sirkelvormig, kringvormig; gerond; rondborstig, openhartig; welluidend, vol (klank), ~ *BEEF*, boudvleis; ~ *COAL*, stukkool, blokkool; *a* ~ *DANCE*, 'n rondedans; *a* ~ *DOZEN*, 'n volle (ronde) dosyn; *in* ~ *FIGURES*, in globale (ronde) syfers; *a* ~ *LIE*, 'n onverbloemde leuen; *in good* ~ *TERMS*, onbewimpeld(e); *at a* ~ *TROT*, op 'n vinnige draf; *a* ~ *VOICE*, 'n vol stem; (adv) om; rondom; in die rondte; ~ *ABOUT*, rondom; ~ *ABOUT 10c*, omtrent 10c; *ALL* ~, oral, in alle opsigte; ~ *AND* ~, om en om; *BE* ~ *with*, openhartig wees; reguit praat; *BRING* ~, ombring; bybring; (icm.) omhaal; *COME* ~, besoek; van opvatting verander; *GET* ~ *someone*, iem. afrokkel; by iem. flikflooi; *GO* ~, omgaan, draai; genoeg wees; *HAND* ~, rondgee; *LOOK* ~, omkyk; *SHOW* ~, rondneem; *go* ~ *the SUN to meet the moon*, 'n groot ompad ry (loop); *TALK* ~, oorreed, ompraat; *go a long WAY* ~, 'n groot draai loop; *all the YEAR* ~, die hele jaar deur; (prep) rondom, ~ *the BEND*, van lotjie getik; ~ *the CORNER*, om die hoek; sommer hier; *GO* ~ *the back*, agterom gaan; ~ *these PARTS*, hierlangs; ~ *TEN o'clock*, omstreeks tienuur.
round'about, (n) ompad, omweg, sirkelpad; omskrywing; draaimeul; rondedans; (a) omlopend; omskrywend; wydlopig, omslagtig; *a* ~ *WAY*, 'n omweg (ompad); ~ *WAYS*, jakkalsdraaie; *choose a* ~ *WAY*, by die Kaap draai.
round'ed, gerond, afgerond; ~ *spoonful*, hoogvol lepel.
roun'del, skildjie; rondedans; medalje; rondeau.
roun'delay, liedjie met refrein; voëlsang; rondedans.
roun'ders, honkbal.
round: ~ **flight**, rondvlug; ~ **hand**, rondskrif; ~**-head**, rondekop; ~**ing**, ronding; ~**ing machine**, afrondmasjien; ~**ing plane**, rondskaaf; ~**ish**, rondering, rondagtig; ~**ly**, rond, sirkelvormig; kortaf, ronduit, botweg, vierkant, onbewimpeld; ~**ness**, rondheid; volheid; ~ **oath**, lelike vloek; ~ **plane**, rondskaaf; ~ **seam**, rondenaat; ~ **shot**, ronde kanonkoeël; ~**-shouldered**, met krom skouers;

~**sman**, rondbringer (van brood, ens.); ~ **style**, vloeiende styl; ~ **sum**, ronde som; **R** ~ **table**, Tafelronde; ~**-table conference**, tafelronde; ~ **trip**, rondreis; rondvaart; ~ **turn**, hele slag; ~**-up**, (die) bymekaarmaak, omsingeling; klopjag; ~ **worm**, rondewurm.
roup, hoenderverkoue, hoenderwitseerkeel.
rouse, (n) opwekking, reveille; (v) wek, wakker maak; wakker word, ontwaak; aanspoor, aanblaas, aanpor; oproep, opjaag; ~ *to ANGER*, kwaad (woedend) maak; ~ *ONESELF*, jou wakker skud; jou regruk; ~ *PASSIONS*, hartstogte wek; ~ *UP*, wakker skud; ~**r**, (op)wekker; growwe leuen; merkwaardigheid.
rous'ing, (n) aanporring; (a) opwekkend, besielend; kolossaal, groot; dawerend, donderend.
rout[1], (n) oproer, gedrang, twis; wanordelike bende; aandparty; algemene vlug, verwarde terugtog; verpletterende neerlaag; *put to* ~, op die vlug jaag; (v) op die vlug jaag, oorwin, in verwarring laat vlug.
rout[2], (v) vroetel, uitdiep; ~ *out of bed*, uit die bed jaag.
route, (n) pad, weg, koers, roete; *EN* ~, op pad; ~ *of MARCH*, marsweg; (v) versend; van wegwysers voorsien; ~**-book**, reisboek; ~**-indicator**, roeteaanwyser; ~**-map**, roetekaart; ~**-march**, afstandsmars, marsoefening.
rout'er plane, verdiepskaaf.
routine', (n) sleur, gewoonte, roetine; (a) roetine-, gereeld; ~ **call**, vaste (gereelde) besoek.
rout'ing[1], roetebepaling; versending.
rout'ing[2], verdiepwerk; ~ **plane**, rondskaaf, verdiepskaaf.
routin'ist, sleurganger.
rove, (n) omswerwing; *be on the* ~, rondswerf; (v) rondswerwe, ronddool, swalk; ~**r**, swerwer; losspeler (rugby); seerower, seeskuimer; voorspinner; *shoot at* ~ *rs*, voor die vuis skiet.
rov'ing, (n) omswerwing, ronddoling; (a) dwalend, dolend, swerwend; *be given a* ~ *COMMISSION*, volmag kry om oral rond te reis; *a* ~ *SHOT*, 'n verdwaalde koeel; ~ **commission**, uitgebreide opdrag; ~ **correspondent**, reisende verslaggewer; ~ **disposition**, ongestadige geaardheid; ~ **envoy**, reisende gesant; ~ **eye**, dwalende oog; ~ **life**, swerwerslewe.
row[1], (n) geraas, rumoer, rusie, relletjie, spektakel, spokery, herrie, standjie, struweling, twis; *GET into a* ~, in die moeilikheid kom; *HAVE a* ~ *with a person about (over) something*, rusie maak met iem. oor iets; *KICK up a* ~, lawaai maak, bombarie opskop, (v) lawaai maak, 'n skrobbering gee.
row[2], (n) reeks; ry; *a hard (long)* ~ *to HOE*, 'n moeilike taak; *IN* ~ *s*, in rye; *STAND in a* ~, op 'n ry staan; ~ *UPON* ~, bankvas.
row[3], (n) roeitog; (v) roei; ~ *AWAY*, wegroei; ~ *DOWN*, inhaal; ~ *OUT*, moeg roei; ~ *OUT to sea*, uitroei (see toe); ~ *TO the shore*, na die wal roei; ~**-boat**, roeiboot.
rowd'iness, lawaaierigheid, rumoerigheid, wanordelikheid.
rowd'y, (n) (. **dies**), lawaaimaker, raasbek, herriemaker, woesteling; (a) rumoerig, lawaaierig; ~**-dowdy**, lawaaierig, rumoerig; ~**ish**, lawaaierig; ~**ism**, ruheid; baldadigheid, wanordelikheid, herrie.
row'el, (n) spoorwieletjie, spoorratjie; (v) (**-led**), met die spore steek, die spore gee.
row'er, roeier.
row' galley, (roei)galei.
row'ing[1], (n) lawaai, geraas, rasery.
row'ing[2], (n) (die) roei; (a) roei-; ~ **boat**, roeiboot; ~ **club**, roeiklub; ~ **match**, roeiwedstryd.
row'lock, roeimik, dolpen, roeiklamp, roeidol.
roy'al, koninklik, vorstelik; edel, rojaal, uitstekend: *BATTLE* ~, titaniese stryd; *a* ~ *BREEZE*, 'n sterk wind; *the* ~ *ROAD*, die koninklike weg; *there is no* ~ *ROAD to learning*, geleerdheid tel 'n mens nie sommer op nie; *in* ~ *SPIRITS*, in uitstekende stemming; *be having a* ~ *TIME*, 'n aangename tyd hê; verjaar; ~ **blue**, koningsblou; ~ **circle**, voorgalery, voorbalkon; ~ **cypher**, koninklike paraaf; ~

family, koninklike familie; ~ **flush,** die vyf erekaarte van een kleur; ~ **game,** beskermde wild; ~ **house,** vorstehuis; ~ **icing,** harde versiersel; ~**ist,** (n) rojalis; (a) koningsgesind; ~ **jelly,** prinsesselei; ~ **ly,** koninklik, vorstelik, rojaal; ~ **mast,** kroonsteng; ~ **octavo,** groot oktawo; ~ **paper,** rojaalpapier; ~ **road,** maklike weg; koninklike weg; ~ **sail,** kroonseil; ~ **tiger,** Indiese tier; ~ **ty,** (..**ties),** koningskap; majesteit; die koninklike familie; outeursaandeel, skrywersaandeel, eienaarsreg; honorarium, aandeel in opbrengs, vrugreg; huurtol; (pl) vorstelike persone; koninklike (voor)reg; huurtol; ~ **warrant,** koninklike bevelskrif; ~ **water,** koningswater.
rub, (n) (die) vrywe; moeilikheid, hinderpaal, knoop; vrywing; wederwaardigheid; *GIVE something a* ~, iets opvryf (oppoets); *GIVE someone a* ~, iem. voor stok kry; *the* ~ *of the GREEN,* belemmering, tussenkoms (gholf); die toeval op die baan; *THERE'S the* ~, daar sit die knoop; daar lê die ding (moeilikheid); *the* ~*s and WORRIES of life,* die moeilikhede en kwellinge v.d. lewe; (v) **(-bed),** vrywe, uitvrywe, invrywe; afvee; skuur; polys, poets, blink maak; skawe; ~ *ALONG,* oor die weg kom; klaarkom; ~ *off the CORNERS,* die skerp kante afslyt; ~ *DOWN,* afvrywe, droogvryf; skoonvryf; ~ *one's EYES,* jou oë (uit)vryf; ~ *one's HANDS,* die hande vrywe; ~ *it IN,* invrywe; inpeper; dit onder die neus vryf; dit op iem. se brood smeer; ~ *it INTO someone,* iem. iets goed onder die neus vryf; ~ *NOSES,* groet; ~ *someone's NOSE in something,* iem. iets onder die neus smeer; ~ *OFF,* afvrywe; ~ *OUT,* uitvryf; uitwis; doodmaak; ~ *SHOULDERS with,* in aanraking kom met; ~ *UP,* opvrywe, blink maak; deurmekaar maak; opfris (geheue); ~ *UP one's French,* jou kennis van Frans opfris; ~ *someone up the WRONG way,* iem. verkeerd aanpak; op iem. se senuwees werk; iem. vererg.
rub'-a-dub (n) getrommel, geroffel; (v) **(-bed),** trommel.
rubbed, gevrywe, gevryf; ~ *surface,* gevryfde vlak.
rubb'er¹, reeks (spele); *play a* ~, 'n potjie speel.
rubb'er², rubber, gomlastiek; uitveër, wisser; polyster; masseur; radeerder; vryflap; ~ **adhesive plaster,** rubberkloupleister; ~**-crab,** buidelkreef; ~ **dinghy,** gomlastiekbootjie; ~ **hose,** tuinslang; ~**ize,** met gomlastiek behandel; ~ **plantation,** rubberplantasie, rubberaanplanting; ~ **solution,** rubberlym; ~ **stamp,** (druk)stempel, rubberstempel.
rubb'ing, skuur; vrywe; vrywing; ~**-down,** afvrywing, afskuring; ~ **plate,** skuurplaat; ~ **post,** skuurpaal; ~ **stone,** skuurklip.
rubb'ish, (n) vuilgoed, vuilis, vullis; puin; afval; onsin, kafpraatjies, twak; prulwerk; *DEPOSIT (dump) no* ~ *here,* moenie vuilgoed hier gooi nie; *OH (what)* ~! kaf! onsin! bog! *TALK* ~, kaf praat; (a) kaf-; ~ **bin,** asblik, vuilisblik; ~ **dump,** afvalhoop; ~ **heap,** ashoop; *relegate to the* ~ *heap,* iets op die ashoop gooi; ~ **removal,** vullisverwydering; ~**y,** prullerig; vol kaf (onsin); twakkerig.
rub'ble, puin, gruis, klipafval; ruklip; afbraak; ~ **stone,** gruisklip; klip wat deur water afgeslyt is; ~ **concrete,** rukklipbeton; ~ **masonry,** ongelaagde ruklip.
rubb'ly, vol klippe, puinagtig.
rube, plaasjapie, pampoenkop.
rubefa'cient, (n) rooimaakmiddel; (a) rooimakend; prikkelend.
rubefac'tion, rooimaking; huidprikkeling.
ru'befy, (..**fied),** rooi maak.
rubell'a, Duitse masels, rooihond.
rube'ola, masels.
rubes'cence, rooiheid.
rubes'cent, rooiagtig; blosend.
ru'bicelle, ligte robyn, rubicella.
Ru'bicon: *cross the* ~, die Rubikon oorsteek; die teerling werp; die beslissende stap doen.
ru'bicund, rooierig, blosend; ~'**ity,** rooiheid.
rubid'ium, rubidium.
ru'bied, (poëties vir) robynrooi.
ru'bify = **rubefy.**

rubi'ginous, rooibruin, roeskleurig.
ru'bious, robynrooi, robynkleurig.
ru'bric, rubriek, afdeling; opskrif; ~**al,** liturgies, ritueel; ~**ate,** met rooi merk; in rubrieke verdeel.
rub'-stone, slypsteen.
ru'by, (n) **(rubies),** robyn; rooi puisie; robynkleur; rooi wyn; klein drukletter; *ABOVE rubies,* kosbaarder as robyne; *her PRICE is far above rubies,* haar waarde is ver meer as korale; (v) **(rubied),** rooi kleur; (a) robynrooi, robynkleurig.
ruche, plooisel.
ruck¹, (n) kreukel, plooi; (v) kreukel, plooi, vou.
ruck², (n) massa, trop, hoop, klomp; stapel; mied; trapskrum (rugby); *the* ~, die groot hoop (in 'n wedren); die massa; (v) saamdrom, saampak; 'n trapskrum vorm.
ruc'kle¹, (n) geroggel, gereutel; (v) roggel.
ruc'kle², (n) kreukel, plooi; (v) kreukel, plooi, vou.
ruck'sack, rugsak, knapsak, bladsak, ransel.
ructa'tion, oprisping.
ruc'tion, herrie, lawaai, rumoer; rusie, twis, oproer; *there will be* ~*s,* dit sal onaangenaamheid afgee (veroorsaak); daar sal 'n herrie wees.
rud'der, roer, stuur, rigtingsroer (vliegtuig); *who won't be ruled by the* ~ *must be ruled by the rock,* wie nie hoor nie, moet voel; ~**-head,** roerkoning; ~**less,** sonder roer, stuurloos.
ruddi'ness, rooiheid, blosende kleur.
rud'dle, (n) rooigrond, rooiaarde; rooisel; (v) rooi merk.
rudd'ock, rooiborsie.
rudd'y, (v) **(ruddied),** rooi word, bloos; rooi kleur; (a) rooi, rooierig; blosend, bloesend.
rude, ru, grof; onbeskaaf, primitief, onbeleef; woes, hardhandig; onhebbelik; onsag; lomp, onbeskof, ongepoets, onverfynd; *BE* ~ *to someone,* onbeskof wees teenoor iem.; *it was* ~ *of you to INTERRUPT the lady,* dit was onbeleef van jou om die dame in die rede te val; ~ *HEALTH,* blakende gesondheid; ~ *PASSIONS,* onbeteuelde hartstog; ~ *SHOCK,* hewige skok; ~**ness,** ruheid; onbeleefdheid.
ru'diment, grondslag, beginsel; rudiment, halfontwikkelde orgaan; oorblyfsel; (pl) eerste beginsels, grondbeginsels, grondslae; ~'**ary,** elementêr; aanvangs-, rudimentêr.
rue¹, (n) wynruit.
rue², (n) berou, droefheid; (v) betreur, berou hê oor; beklaag; *you will* ~ *it (the day),* dit sal jou nog berou; jy sal die dag betreur; ~**-bargain,** roukoop; ~**ful,** treurig, droewig, verdrietig; ~**fulness,** treurigheid, droewigheid, verdrietigheid.
rue-raddy, (..**dies),** skouertrektou.
rufes'cent, rooierig.
ruff¹, (n) troef; (v) troef.
ruff², (n) plooi, geplooide kraag, halskraag; kraagduif, ringnekduif; kemphaan, strandloper; (v) plooi; frommel, kreukel.
ruffed¹, getroef.
ruffed², gekraag.
ruff'ian, (n) booswig, boef, woesteling, woestaard, skurk; (a) gemeen, skurkagtig, woes, beesagtig; ~**ism,** skurkery, woestheid.
ruf'fle, (n) plooi, valletjie; rimpeling; worsteling; verwarring; twis, rusie; roffel (op tamboer); (v) frommel, plooi, kreukel; in die war bring, deurmekaarmaak; vererg, ontstem; verwaand wees; ~ *someone's FEATHERS,* iem. kwaad maak; ~*d HAIR,* deurmekaar hare; *he is NEVER* ~*d,* hy is nooit ontstem(d) (vererg) nie; ~ *SOMEONE,* iem. oorstuurs maak; ~**r,** inplooivoetjie (naaimasjien); plooier.
ru'fous, rooibruin; rossig.
rug, (n) reisdeken, reiskombers; vloerkleedjie, vloermat; (v) beklee.
ru'gate, gerimpel, gegolf; geplooi.
rug'by, rugby; ~ **authorities,** rugbybase; ~ **fan,** rugbyentoesias; ~ **football,** rugbyvoetbal; ~ **ground,** rugbyveld; ~ **league,** rugbyliga; ~ **match,** rugbywedstryd; ~ **player,** rugbyspeler; ~ **shorts,** rugbybroekie; ~ **union,** rugbyunie.
rugg'ed, ru; hobbelrig, oneffe, ongelyk; grof, sterk; gerimpel; hard, onwelluidend; nors, streng; lomp,

onbeskaaf; stoer; kragtig; ~ness, grofheid; lompheid; stoerheid; ongelykheid; oneffenheid.
rugg'er, rugby.
rug'-making, matmaak, matmakery.
rugose', rimpel(r)ig, gerimpel, gegolf.
rugos'ity, rimpel(r)igheid; rimpeling.
ru'gous = rugose.
rug' strap, kombersriem.
ru'in, (n) bouval, puinhoop, ruïne, murasie; ondergang, verval, vernietiging, verderf; (pl) bouval, murasie, ruïne; *be bringing ABOUT one's own* ~, jou eie ondergang bewerk; *bring ABOUT someone's* ~, iem. se val bewerk; *that will BE the* ~ *of us,* dit sal ons ondergang wees; *BRING to* ~, in die ongeluk stort, ruïneer; *FALL into* ~, in puin val; *GO to rack and* ~, na die maan (te gronde) gaan; *IN* ~*s,* in puin; *LIE in* ~ *s,* in puin wees; (v) verwoes, verniel, ruïneer; in die verderf stort; onteer, tot 'n val bring; neerstort, instort; verslons (klere); ~ *oneself,* jou eie ondergang bewerk; ~**a'tion,** verwoesting, ondergang, vernieling, rinnewasie, ruïnasie; ~**er,** bederwer, verwoester; ~**ous,** verderflik, nadelig; vervalle, bouvallig; ~ *ous price,* 'n moordende prys; ~**ousness,** verderflikheid; vervallenheid; bouvalligheid.
rule, (n) reël, stelreël; voorskrif; verordening; bepaling; maatstaf; bestuur, bewind, gesag, regering; lewensreël; liniaal, maatstok, duimstok; uitspraak (reg); ~ *of ACTION,* gedragslyn; *AS a* ~, in die reël, gewoonlik; *BY* ~ volgens die reël; ~ *of CONDUCT,* gedragslyn; rigsnoer; *in CONFLICT with the* ~ *s,* teen die reels; ~ *of EVIDENCE,* bewysreël; ~ *s of the GAME,* reëls v.d. spel; *as a GENERAL* ~, oor (in) die algemeen; *the GOLDEN* ~, die gulde reël; *HARD and fast* ~ *s,* vaste reëls; ~ *of LAW,* regsorde; (beginsel van) regsoewereiniteit, regswaarbog van persoonlike vryheid; *LEGAL* ~, regsreël; *work by* ~ *and LINE,* met matematiese noukeurigheid werk; *MAKE a* ~ *to,* 'n reël daarvan maak om; ~ *NISI,* bevel nisi; ~ *s of PROCEDURE,* reglement van orde; ~*s and REGULATIONS,* reglement; ~ *of the ROAD,* uitwykreël; ryreël; verkeersreël; ~ *the ROOST,* die lakens uitdeel; *a STANDING* ~, 'n vaste reël; *the STANDING* ~ *s and orders,* die reglement van orde; ~ *of THREE,* reël van drie; ~ *of THUMB,* praktiese metode; *UNDER British* ~, onder Britse bewind; *WITHIN the* ~*s,* ooreenkomstig die reglement; *WITHIN the* ~ *s of the game,* binne die reëls van die spel; *WORK to* ~, stadig werk; streng volgens reëls v.d. vakunie werk; (v) regeer, heers; bestuur; uitmaak; linieer, 'n lyn trek; ~ *out of COURT,* v.d. hand wys; wraak; *public OPINION* ~ *s that,* die openbare mening bepaal dat; ~ *something OUT,* iets buite rekening laat; iets uitskakel; deurstreep; ~ *out of ORDER,* buite die orde verklaar; *the same PRICES* ~ *as yesterday,* pryse is dieselfde as gister.
ruled, gelinieer; gereel; *that is* ~ *OUT,* dit is uitgesluit; ~ *PAPER,* gelinieerde papier; *PRICES* ~ *high,* die pryse was hoog.
ru'ler, heerser, heerseres (vrou), regeerder, gebieder, gebiedster (vrou); liniaal, duimstok, lynhoutjie.
ru'ling, (n) heersing, bevinding (van hof); liniëring, lyntrekking; beslissing, uitspraak; (a) regerend, heersend; geldend; ~ **classes,** heersende klasse; ~ **machine,** linieermasjien; ~ **passion,** allesoorheersende hartstog; ~ **pen,** trekpen; ~ **price,** markprys, heersende prys; ~ **wind,** heersende wind.
rum¹, (n) rum.
rum², (a) snaaks, vreemd.
Ruman'ia, Roemenië; ~**n,** (n) Roemeen; Roemeens (taal); (a) Roemeens.
rum'ba rumba.
rum'ble, (n) gerommel, gedruis, geratel; agterbak; (v) rommel; ratel, dawer; dreun; ~**r,** poetstrommel; ~ **seat,** kattebak, agterbak; ~**-tumble,** rammelkas; gerammel.
rum'bling, (n) gerommel, gedruis; gegrom; (a) rommelend.
rumbus'tious, luidrugtig, lawaaierig, rumoerig; wild.

ru'men, grootpens.
ru'minant, (n) herkouer; (a) herkouend; peinsend.
ru'minate, herkou; diep dink, broei (oor), oordink; ~ *upon,* broei oor, diep dink oor.
rumina'tion, herkouing; bepeinsing, oorpeinsing.
ru'minative, peinsend, nadenkend; herkouend.
rumm'age, (n) rommel; gesnuffel, gesoek; (v) (deur)snuffel, deursoek, napluis; (uit)vroetel, omvroetel; omroer; omkrap; woel, rommel; skarrel; ~ *up, (out),* uitsnuffel, opdiep; ~**r,** snuffelaar; ~ **sale,** rommelverkoping.
rumm'aging, deursnuffeling, geskarrel, gesnuffel; deursoeking.
rumm'er, roemer, wynglas.
rumm'y¹, (n) kaartspel, rummy.
rumm'y², (a) snaaks, sonderling.
rum'our, (n) gerug, riemtelegram; mare; sprake; *a* ~ *GOES,* die mense sê; daar gaan 'n gerug; ~ *HAS it,* volgens gerug; die mense sê; daar gaan 'n gerug rond; *HEAR a* ~ *that,* 'n voëltjie hoor fluit dat; *there IS a* ~, daar gaan 'n gerug rond; (v) as gerug versprei; uitstrooi, rondstrooi, rondvertel; *it is* ~*ed,* die mense sê; daar gaan 'n gerug rond; ~**-monger,** skinderbek, verspreier van praatjies; ~**-mongering,** nuusdraery, skindery.
rump, kruis; stuitjie; agterste deel, agterste; kruisstuk (vleis); oorskot; restant; ~ **bone,** stuitjiebeen; ~ **cutlet,** kruiskotelet.
rum'ple, (n) vou, kreukel; (v) rimpel, kreukel, vou, (ver)frommel, verfronsel.
rump'less, stompstert.
rump' steak, kruisstuk, kruisskyf.
rum'pus, spektakel, rumoer, rusie, kabaal; *cause a* ~, 'n bohaai veroorsaak.
rum'-runner, dranksmokkelaar; smokkelskip.
run, (n) lopie (krieket); bestorming; aanvraag, toeloop (na winkel); aanloop, galop; wedloop; ren; tog (skip); opeenvolging; lopie, spruitjie; loopplank; vrye toegang; vaart; toggie, ritjie, uitstappie; kampie, weiveld; hoenderkampie; tipe; deining (see); reeks (van tydskrif); skool (visse); leer (in kouse); luggang (myn); stoot (biljart); *AT a* ~, op 'n drafje; *there was a* ~ *on the BANK,* die bank is bestorm; *the BOOK had a considerable* ~, daar is 'n aansienlike vraag na die boek; *it was a CLOSE* ~, dit was so hittete; *the COMMON* ~ *of men,* die gewone mens; *let him HAVE his* ~, laat hom sy gang gaan; *have the* ~ *of a HOUSE,* vrye toegang tot 'n huis hê; *a LONG* ~, groot gewildheid; sterk aanvraag; *a LONG* ~ *of office,* 'n lang reeks diensjare; *in the LONG* ~, op die lange duur; *MAKE a* ~ *for,* weghardloop, vlug; ~ *of the MILL,* die gemiddelde; *have a* ~ *for one's MONEY,* waarde vir jou geld kry; the ~ *OF (the house),* die vrye gebruik (v.d. huis); *ON the* ~, op die vlug; aan die gang; nie rustig nie; ~ *ON something,* 'n groot aanvraag (toeloop); *the general* ~ *of THINGS,* die algemene loop van sake; *a* ~ *of rainy WEATHER,* onafgebroke reënerige weer; (v) **(ran, run),** loop, hardloop, hol; draf; vloei (ink, water); deurbreek (blokkade); afloop (kers); stroom (water); smelt; laat loop (bus); stryk (vingers); laat skiet; dryf, bestuur (saak); agtervolg; smokkel (goedere); klim, kruip (plant); geldig wees (huur); wegloop, vaar, seil, stoom (skip); skif (melk); lek; oorloop; etter (seer); meeding; najaag; vervolg; ryg; stel (kandidaat); trek, steek; hê (rekening); vervloei (kleure); lê (kabel); ~ *ABOUT,* rondloop; ~ *an ACCOUNT,* 'n rekening hê; ~ *up ACCOUNTS,* rekeninge laat oploop; ~ *ACROSS,* toevallig ontmoet; raakloop; ~ *AFTER,* agternaloop, najaag, nahardloop, nahol; ~ *AGAINST,* bots met; ~ *AGROUND,* strand; ~ *AMUCK,* amok maak; ~ *ASHORE,* laat strand; ~ *AT,* aanval; afstorm op; ~ *AWAY,* wegloop, dros; spaander, die hakskene lig, heensnel; wegloop met 'n ander se vrou; *the BEER ran out,* die bier het opgeraak; ~ *up BILLS,* skuld maak; *a BILL* ~ *s,* 'n wissel loop; ~ *in the BLOOD,* in die bloed wees; ~ *a CANDIDATE,* 'n kandidaat stel; *my CAR* ~ *s on diesel oil,* my motor loop met dieselolie; ~ *a CHANCE of,* 'n kans hê om; *have* ~ *out of CIGARETTES,* die sigarette het

opgeraak; ~ *CIRCLES round someone*, iem. ver oortref; ~ *a person CLOSE*, op iem. se hakke wees; hom byna ewenaar; *the illness must ~ its COURSE*, die siekte moet sy gang gaan; *things must ~ their COURSE*, sake moet hulle gang gaan; ~ *a person for DAMAGES*, iem. om skadevergoeding vervolg; ~ *into DEBT*, in die skuld raak; ~ *away from a DIFFICULTY*, 'n moeilikheid ontduik; ~ *into DIFFICULTIES*, moeilikheid ondervind (teëkom); ~ *DOWN*, omloop; afloop (oorlosie); opspoor (deur polisie); uitput, verswak; doodjaag; slegmaak; afbreek; *I feel ~ DOWN*, ek voel afgewerk (uitgeput, afgerem); *my watch has ~ DOWN*, my oorlosie is afgeloop; ~ *a friend DOWN behind his back*, 'n vriend agter sy rug beskinder; ~ *DRY*, droogloop; vasbrand; ~ *to EARTH*, in 'n gat jaag; na 'n lang soektog ontdek (fig.); ~ *into EDITIONS*, uitgawes beleef: *don't ~ the ENGINE in a closed garage*, moenie die masjien in 'n toe motorhuis laat loop nie; ~ *into ERROR*, in foute verval; *EXPECTATIONS ~ high*, die verwagtings is hoog gestem; ~ *one's EYES along*, jou oë laat gly oor; ~ *one's EYE down the page*, die bladsy vinnig deurgaan; *it ~ s in the FAMILY*, dis 'n familietrek; ~ *FAST*, vinnig hardloop; *FEELING ~ s high*, daar is groot opgewondenheid; *I've been ~ off my FEET today*, ek was die ganse dag aan die gang (in die weer); ~ *one's FINGERS over*, die vingers laat gly oor; ~ *FOUL of*, bots met; ~ *the GAUNTLET*, deur die spitsroede loop; skaapstert loop; ~ *GOODS*, goed smokkel; ~ *one's fingers through one's HAIR*, die vingers deur die hare stryk; ~ *one's HEAD up against a stone wall*, jou kop teen 'n muur stamp; ~ *HIGH*, hoog loop; ~ *HOT*, warmloop; ~ *with the hare and HUNT with the hounds*, met twee monde praat; ~ *away with an IDEA*, jouself iets wysmaak; jou alte gou verbeel; op hol raak oor 'n idee; ~ *IN*, loswerk, insluit; inry (motor); in hegtenis neem; inhardloop; ~ *INTO each other*, in mekaar vasry, bots met; teen mekaar vasloop; mekaar ontmoet; ~ *for dear LIFE*, hardloop of jou lewe daarvan afhang; loop vir die vale; ~ *for one's LIFE*, uit alle mag hardloop; ~ *LOOSE*, losloop; vir kwaadgeïd rondloop; ~ *LOW*, opraak, min word; ~ *MESSAGES*, boodskappe dra; ~ *a MOTOR*, 'n motor aanhou; ~ *OFF*, tap; laat afloop; weghardloop; ~ *for OFFICE*, kandidaat wees; ~ *ON*, voortgaan; een stryk deur praat; ~ *OUT*, afloop; opraak (voorraad); uitloop (plant); uithardloop (krieket); volbring; deurbring (geld); ~ *OVER*, oorloop, oorvloei; vlugtig beskou; ~ *OVER a child*, 'n kind onderstebo ry; ~ *one's PEN through*, jou pen trek deur; *the PLAY ran two weeks*, die stuk is twee weke agtereen gespeel; *as POLITICS ~*, soos dit met politiek gesteld is; soos dit met politiek gaan; *he who ~s may READ*, so klaar soos die dag; ~ *RIOT*, losbandig word; tot bandeloosheid oorslaan; ~ *the RISK*, die risiko loop; ~ *SECOND*, tweede kom; ~ *to SEED*, saadskiet; ~ *into seven figures*, in die sewe syfers loop; ~ *a SHOP*, 'n winkel bestuur; ~ *SHORT*, kortkom, opraak; ~ *the SHOW*, baas wees; die lakens uitdeel; *the STORY ~ s*, die verhaal gaan; ~ *SMOOTHLY*, sag loop (masjien); glad loop (saak, motor); gladweg hardloop (atleet); ~ *a friend to the STATION*, 'n vriend per motor stasie toe neem; ~ *the TAP for a few minutes*, die kraan 'n paar minute laat loop; ~ *a TEMPERATURE*, koors hê; ~ *in a THIEF*, 'n dief agtervolg; ~ *THROUGH*, deursteek, deurboor; verkwis; ~ *THROUGH a report*, 'n verslag vlugtig deurkyk; ~ *TOGETHER*, saam hardloop; inmekaarloop; vervloei (kleure); ~ *into TROUBLE*, in die moeilikheid raak; *the TUNE ~ s in my head*, die deuntjie draai in my kop; ~ *TRUE to form*, konsekwent wees; ~ *UP*, oploop; laat optrek; opskiet; opjaag; opdryf (prys); hys, optrek (vlag); in posisie bring; ~ *UP against*, op die lyf loop; ~ *into bad WEATHER*, ongunstige weer teëkom; ~ *WILD*, wild word; ~ *like WILDFIRE*, soos 'n lopende vuur versprei; ~ *like the WIND*, so vinnig soos die wind hardloop.

run'about, (n) swerwer; kruipplant; ligte motor, toermotor; (a) rondswerwend.
run'agate, (arch.), landloper; renegaat; vlugteling; droster.
run'-and-fell seam, platnaat.
run'away, (n) wegloper, droster; (a) weghardlopend; op hol; gevlug, weggeloop; ~ *MARRIAGE*, skelm trouery; ~ *VICTORY*, reuseoorwinning; oorrompeling; verpletterende oorwinning; *score a ~ VICTORY*, 'n reuseoorwinning behaal; baie ver wen; speel-speel wen; die teenstanders oorrompel (kafloop).
run'cible spoon, lepelvurk.
run'-down, (n) verslapping; (a) verval; afgewerk, afgerem, uitgeput.
rune, rune(skrif); geheimsinnigheid.
rung[1], sport (van 'n leer); *to have reached the topmost ~*, die hoogste sport bereik het.
rung[2], (v) *kyk* **ring**.
ru'nic, (n) runeskrif; (a) rune=, runies; ~ **alphabet,** runealfabet; ~ **letter,** rune; ~ **writing,** runeskrif.
run'let, stroompie; vaatjie.
runn'el, riviertjie, spruit; geut.
runn'er, loper, boodskapper, hardloper; agent; rank= (plant), klimplant; blokkadebreker; smokkelaar; draaiende meulsteen; skuifknoop; leibalk, leiboom, leiding; gangtapyt, loper; loopvoël; tafeloper; ~ **bean,** rankboon; ~ **guide,** katrolbaan; ~ **rail,** leireling.
runn'er-up, mededinger; opjaer; naaswenner; ~ **position,** tweede plek, naaswennerposisie.
runn'ing, (n) (die) loop, (die) hardloop, gehol, geren, hardlopery; (die) stroom; klein rygsteek; *be IN the ~*, in aanmerking kom; *MAKE the ~*, die maat aangee; *be OUT of the ~*, geen kans hê nie; nie in aanmerking kom nie; *TAKE up the ~*, die voortou neem; *everything is ~ SMOOTHLY*, dit gaan maklik; dit gaan klopdisselboom; dit loop op rollertjies; (a) stromend, lopend (water); kruipend, slingerend (van plante); agtereenvolgend; deurlopend (kommentaar); gebruiks=; *three DAYS ~*, drie dae agtermekaar; *the FISH are ~*, die vis loop; *three TIMES ~*, drie keer na mekaar; ~ **account,** lopende rekening; ~**-board,** trapplank, treeplank, syplank; ~ **button,** skuifknoop; ~ **commentary,** deurlopende kommentaar; ~ **debts,** lopende skulde; ~ **expenses,** daaglikse uitgawes; bedryfskoste; ~ **fight,** terugtoggeveg; ~ **file,** aanhoudende vuur; ~ **foot,** strekkende voet; ~ **fuse,** snellont; ~ **hand,** lopende skrif; ~ **head,** kolomtitel; ~ **headline,** kolomhoof; ~ **hours,** loopure; ~ **joint,** streklas; ~ **knot,** los knoop, skuifknoop; ~ **order:** *in ~ order*, in werkende toestand; ~ **period,** looptyd; ~ **repair,** handherstelwerk; ~ **sore,** lopende seer; ~ **staff,** treinpersoneel; ~ **stitch,** voorsteek, rygsteek; ~ **time,** looptyd; ~ **title,** kolomtitel.
run'off, afloop.
run'-of-the-mill, gemiddeld, alledaags.
run'-of-the-mine ore, onbehandelde erts.
runt, dwerg; misgewas; uitskot, pieperige diertjie; (groot) Spaanse duif.
run'-up, laagslag (gholf); aanloop.
run'way, stroombed (rivier); rolbaan, aanloopbaan (vliegtuie); groef; sponning.
rupee', ropy, roepee.
rupes'tral, rots=, rotsbewonend; ~ **plant,** rotsplant, muurplant.
rupes'trian, rots=; op rots gegrif.
rup'ture, (n) breuk; skeuring; deurbraak; splitsing; (v) breek; verbreek; 'n breuk kry; ~**d,** gebreek; met 'n breuk; ~*d muscle*, geskeurde spier.
rur'al, plattelands, landelik; ~ **bank,** landboukrediétbank; ~ **charm,** landelike skoonheid, landelikheid; ~ **district,** buitedistrik; (pl) platteland; ~ **economist,** landhuishoudkundige; ~ **economy,** landhuishoudkunde; ~ **education,** landbouonderwys; ~**ist,** plattelander; ~**'ity,** landelikheid; ~**ize,** plattelands maak (word); ~ **servitute,** landelike servituut; ~ **tenement,** landelike erf.
ruse, lis, krygslis; oëverblindery.
rush[1], (n) (-es), biesie; palmiet, papkuil; *not worth a ~*, geen duit werd nie; (v) mat ('n stoel).

rush², (n) bestorming, stormloop; toeloop; haas, vaart; geraas, gedruis; drukte; (**-es**), snelle beweging; *there was a* ~ *on the BANK,* die beleggers het die bank bestorm; *MAKE a* ~ *for,* storm; lostrek op; (v) hardloop, storm, bestorm, stormloop; stuiwe; voortsnel, jaag, snel; haastig maak; onmiddellik stuur; oorrompel, verras; foeter; ~ *AFTER,* agternasnel, nael; ~ *AROUND,* rondval; ~ *AT,* bestorm; lostrek op; ~ *AWAY,* weghol; *BE* ~ *ed,* gejaagd wees; met te min tyd; ~ *a BILL through,* 'n wetsontwerp deurjaag; *DON'T* ~ *me,* moenie my aanja nie; ~ *DOWN,* afstorm; afwaai; afstort; ~ *to EXTREMES,* van die een na die ander uiterste spring; *FOOLS* ~ *in where angels fear to tread,* 'n dwaas storm waar 'n wyse huiwer; dwase sal injaag waar engele dit nie eers waag nie; ~ *IN,* insnel, instorm; ~ *MATTERS,* oorhaastig te werk gaan; ~ *ON,* voortsnel; ~ *OUT,* uitstorm; uitstort; sterk uitvloei; ~ *PAST,* verbysnel; ~ *a PERSON,* iem. oorval; ~ *into PRINT,* oorhaastig pers toe gaan; oorhaastig laat druk; *the enemy* ~ *ed the TOWN,* die vyand het die stad oorrompel.
rush'-bottom, met 'n matsitting; ~ **carpet,** biesiesmat.
rush: ~**er,** bestormer; ~**-hour,** spitsuur, besige uur; ~**ing,** (n) gebruis; stormloop; (a) stormend; bruisend; ~ **job,** spoedwerk.
rush' light, nagkers, nagpitjie.
rush' order, spoedbestelling.
rush'y, vol biesies, biesie-.
rusk, (boere)beskuit.
Russ'ellism, Russellisme.
Russ'ellite, (n) Russelliet; (a) Russellities.
russ'et, rooibruin, rossig.
Ru'ssia, Rusland; ~ **leather,** jugleer; ~**n,** (n) Rus; Russies (taal); (a) Russies; ~**n boot,** Russiese stewel, Russiese skoen; ~**nize,** russifiseer.
Russifica'tion, russifikasie.
Ru'ssophil(e), Russiesgesinde.
Ru'ssophobe, Rus(se)hater.
Russophob'ia, Rus(se)haat, Rus(se)vrees.
rust, (n) roes; verroesting; (v) roes; verroes; agteruitgaan; laat roes; ~**-colour,** roeskleur; ~**-eaten,** verroes.
rus'tic, (n) boer, landbewoner; plaasjapie; takhaar; (a) landelik, plattelands; onbedorwe, eenvoudig; ongemanierd, boers, lomp; rustiek; ~**alness,** eenvoud; lompheid; boersheid; ~ **ate,** op die land lewe; landelik maak; wegstuur, skors, tydelik wegjaag; ~**a'tion,** landlewe; buiteverblyf; skorsing (student).
rusti'city, landelikheid; eenvoud, ongekunsteldheid; lompheid, boersheid.
rust'iness, roeserigheid, verroesting.
rust'ing, verroesting.
ru'stle, (n) geritsel, geruis; (v) ritsel, ruis, suis, suisel, soef (wind); vinnig loop; roof, veediefstal pleeg; ~**r,** veedief.
rust'less, roesvry.
ru'stling, (n) geritsel, geruis; gefluister, gelispel (blare); veeroof, veediefstal; (a) ritselend, ruisend.
rust: ~**-proof,** (v) roesvry maak; (a) roesvry; ~ **prevention,** roeswering; ~**-red,** roesrooi; ~**-resistant,** ~**-resisting,** roeswerend; ~ **solvent,** roesoplosmiddel; ~ **spot,** ~ **stain,** roesvlek.
rust'y¹, galsterig, ranserig.
rust'y², roeserig, roesagtig, verroes; ouderwets; krassend; stram; *my German is getting* ~, my Duits gaan agteruit.
rut¹, (n) bronstyd, geurtyd, hittigheid; (v) (**-ted**), brons wees, loops wees, hittig wees; jags wees.
rut², waspoor, wielspoor, uitgeryde spoor, groef, voor; sleur, roetine; *BE in a* ~, die ou sleur volg; in 'n sleur wees; *GET into a* ~, vasroes; in 'n groef raak; *in the SAME old* ~, in dieselfde ou sleur.
ruth, (arch.), medelye, verdriet, smart.
ruth: ~**ful,** meewarig, medelydend; ~**less,** onbarmhartig, meedoënloos, wreed, genadeloos; ~**lessness,** genadeloosheid, onmeedoë.
Ruthen'ia, Roetenië; ~**n,** (n) Roeteen; Roeteens (taal); (a) Roeteens.
rutt'ing, brons(tig), hitsig, hittig, loops; jags; ~ **season,** ~ **time,** bronstyd, geurtyd, teeltyd, paartyd; jagstyd.
rutt'ish, hittig, brons(tig); ~**ness,** bronstigheid, hittigheid, speelsheid; jagsheid.
rutt'y¹, vol spore.
rutt'y², loops, brons(tig), hittig, hitsig, jags.
rye, rog; ~ **bread,** rogbrood; ~**-grass,** roggras; ~ **meal,** rogmeel.
Rys'wick, Rijswijk.

S

s, (**ss, s's**), s; *little* ~, s'ie.
Sabae'an, (n) Sabeër; Sabees (taal); (a) Sabees.
Sab'aism, sterreverering, sterrediens.
Sab'aist, sterredienaar.
Sab'aoth, Sebaot; *the Lord* ~, die Here Sebaot.
Sabbatar'ian, (n) Sabbatariër; (a) Sabbataries.
Sabbatar'ianism, Sabbatarisme.
sabb'ath, Sabbat, rusdag; *BREAK the* ~, die Sabbat ontheilig; *KEEP the* ~, die Sabbat heilig; ~**-breaker,** Sabatskender; ~**-day,** Sabbatdag; ~**-day's journey,** Sabbatsreis; *it is but a* ~*-day's journey,* dit is maar 'n sabbatsreis; dis maar 'n kort entjie; ~**-keeper,** Sabbathouer; ~**-keeping,** Sabbatsheiliging.
sabbat'ical, Sabbats-; ~ **year,** sabbatsjaar.
sabb'atize, die Sabbat vier.
Sab'ian, (n) Sabiër; sterreaanbidder; (a) Sabies; ~**ism,** Sabisme.
Sab'ine, (n) Sabyn; (a) Sabyns.
sa'ble¹, (n) sabel (dier; bont).
sa'ble², (n) swart; donker kleur; (a) donker; swart; ~ **antelope,** swartwitpens(bok).
sab'ot, klomp, blokskoen, houtskoen; klomp (van projektiel).
sab'otage, (n) sabotasie; (v) saboteer; rysmier, ondergrawe.
sab'oteur, saboteur.
sa'bre, (n) sabel; (v) neersabel, met 'n sabel wond; ~**tache,** sabelsak; ~**-toothed tiger,** sabeltandtier.
sabulos'ity, sanderigheid.
sab'ulous, sanderig, sand-, korrel(r)ig.
sac, sak; ~**cate,** sakvormig.
saccha'ric, suiker-; ~ **acid,** suikersuur.
saccharif'erous, suikerhoudend; suikervoortbrengend.
sacc'harify, (..**fied**), versuiker, in suiker verander.
sacc'harin(e), (n) sakkarine, sakkarien, saggarine, saggarien, suringsuiker; (a) suikeragtig, suiker-; ~ **combination,** suikerverbinding.
saccharom'eter, suikermeter, saggarometer, suikerpennetjie.
sac'charose, rietsuiker, sakrose, sukrose.
sac'ciform, sakvormig, buidelvormig.
sacc'ulate, sakvormig.
sacc'ule, sakkie.
sa'cerdocy, priesterskap; priesterstelsel.
sa'cerdotage, priesterheerskappy; priestergees.
sacerdot'al, priesterlik, priester-; ~ **dress,** priestergewaad; ~**ism,** priestergees; priesterlike aanmatiging, priesterheerskappy.
sa'chet, sachet, sasjet, reukkussinkie, reuksakkie.
sack¹, (n) plundering, verwoesting; (v) plunder, verwoes.
sack², (n) sak; *GET the* ~, ontslaan word; *GIVE the*

~, in die pad steek; (v) wegstuur, ontslaan, in die pad steek, wegjaag, afsê; in sakke gooi.
sack'age, plundering.
sack'but, skuiftrompet, skuiftromboon.
sack: ~ **cloth**, sakgoed, saklinne; *in* ~ *cloth and ashes*, in sak en as; ~ **dress**, sakrok.
sack'er, plunderaar.
sack'ing¹, plundering, verwoesting.
sack'ing², sakmateriaal, sakgoed; paklinne; afsetting, afdanking.
sack'less, onskuldig; swaksinnig.
sack'-race, sakwedloop, sakreisies.
sac'ral, (n) kruiswerwel; (a) heilig; sakraal; ~ **bone**, kruisbeen, heiligbeen; ~ **region**, kruisbeenstreek; ~ **vessel**, heilige vat; ~ **vertebra**, kruiswerwel, heiligbeenwerwel.
sac'rament, sakrament; ~ **'al**, sakramenteel, heilig, gewyd; offer-; ~ *al DEATH*, offerdood; ~ *al WINE*, Nagmaalswyn, Avondmaalswyn.
sacrar'ium, (..ria), sacrarium.
sac'red, heilig; gewyd, geheilig; geestelik, kerk-; onskendbaar; ~ *FROM*, gevrywaar van; *HOLD* ~, heilig ag; ~ *to the MEMORY of*, gewy aan die nagedagtenis van; ~ **concert**, gewyde konsert, konsert van gewyde musiek; ~ **duty**, heilige plig; ~ **history**, gewyde geskiedenis; ~**ness**, heiligheid.
sac'rifice, (n) offer, offerande; opoffering, verlies; *AT a* ~, met groot verlies; *AT the* ~ *of*, ten koste van; *MAKE the supreme (great, last)* ~, jou lewe opoffer, sterwe, die hoogste offer bring; (v) offer, opoffer; afstaan; ~**r**, offeraar.
sacrifi'cial, offer-, offerings-; ~ **altar**, offeraltaar; ~ **animal**, offerdier; ~ **banquet**, offermaal; ~ **ceremony**, offerplegtigheid; ~ **cup**, offerbeker; ~ **dress**, offerkleed; ~**knife**, offermes; ~ **service**, offerdiens.
sac'rilege, heiligskennis, ontheiliging; kerkroof.
sacrile'gious, heiligskennend, skendig, godtergend; ~**ness**, heiligskennis, ontheiliging.
sacrile'gist, ontheiliger, ontwyder, heiligskenner.
sac'ring bell, misbel.
sac'rist(a), koster, sakristein; ..risty, (..ties), sakristie, kleedkamer.
sac'rosanct, heilig, onskendbaar, onaantasbaar; ~ **'ity**, onskendbaarheid, heiligheid.
sac'rum, (..cra), heiligbeen, kruisbeen.
sad, treurig, droewig, verdrietig, (be)droef, deerlik, somber; onverbeterlik; ~ *BREAD*, neergeslane brood, kluitjiebrood; *a* ~ *CAKE*, 'n ongerysde koek; *a* ~ *COWARD*, 'n groot lafaard; *a* ~ *DOG*, 'n treurige vent; *in* ~ *EARNEST*, in volle erns; *FEEL* ~ *about something*, treurig voel oor iets; *he writes* ~ *STUFF*, hy is 'n prulskrywer; *THAT'S* ~, dis betreurenswaardig; ~**den**, treurig maak, bedroef; somber stem.
sad'dle, (n) saal (vir perd); stut; bergrug; lendestuk, rugstuk; rugstring (vleis); dakvors; pypklem, beuel; nek (geol.); glystuk (meg.); *GET into the* ~, in die saal raak (klim); *IN the* ~, in die saal; aan die bewind; ~ *of MUTTON*, skaaprug, lendestuk; *REMAIN in the* ~, in die saal bly; *SET the* ~ *on the right horse*, die skuldige blameer; die geskikste persoon die las laat dra; *SET the* ~ *on the wrong horse*, die skuld op die verkeerde persoon pak; die verkeerde persoon blameer; *SIT firmly in the* ~, vas in die saal sit; (v) opsaal (perd); belas, opskeep; oplê; *BE* ~*d with*, opgeskeep sit met; met die gebakte pere sit; met iets geskore sit; ~ *someone with the RESPONSIBILITY*, die verantwoordelikheid op iem. skuif; ~ *someone WITH something*, iem. iets op die nek skuif; ~**back**, saalrug; wigstuk; holrug; saalvormige bergrug, plooirug (geol.); manteelmeeu; ~**backed**, met 'n holrug, holrug-; ~ **back jackal**, saalrugjakkals; ~ **bag**, saalsak; ~ **bill stork**, saalbekooievaar; ~ **bow**, saalknop; ~ **burr**, saaldroes; ~-**cloth**, saalkleedjie; *ornamental* ~-*cloth*, skabrak; ~-**cushion**, saalkussing; ~ **fast**, saalvas; ~-**flap**, saalklap; ~-**galled**, deurgery, deur die saal geskaaf; seerrug-; ~-**girth**, buikgord; ~-**horse**, ryperd; *American* ~-*horse*, (Amerikaanse) saalperd; ~ **joint**, rugvoeg; ~-**lap**, saalklap; ~-**mark**, saalmerk; ~ **pillar**, saalstang; ~-**pommel**, saalknop;

~**r**, saalmaker, tuiemaker; ~ **roof**, saaldak, geweldak; ~**r's hammer**, saalmakershamer, klophamer; ~**ry**, (..ries), saalmakery; saalmakersartikels; ~-**seat**, saalsitvlak; ~-**shaped**, saalvormig; ~-**soap**, saalseep; ~-**sore**, (n) saalseer, skaafplek; blikners (plat); (a) deurgery, blikners (plat); ~-**spring**, saalveer; ~ **stone**, topsteen; ~-**tree**, saalboom; saalbok, saalgeraamte.
Sadduce'an, Saddusees.
Sadd'ucee, Sadduseër; ~**ism**, Sadduseïsme.
sad'-hearted, treurig, droewig.
sad'-iron, strykyster, parsyster.
sa'dism, sadisme.
sa'dist, sadis; ~'**ic**, sadisties.
sad'ly, droewig, treurig.
sad'ness, droefheid, treurigheid, treurnis, droefnis, droewenis, getreur, verdrietigheid, weedom; ~ *and gladness succeed each other*, na reën kom sonskyn.
safa'ri, (n) safari, jagtog; (v) op safari gaan.
safe, (n) brandkas, kluis, geldkis; vlieëkas, koskas; (a) veilig, gevaarloos, seker, geborge; ongedeerd; ~ *from ATTACK*, veilig teen aanval; *BE a* ~ *first*, seker wees v.d. eerste plek; *a* ~ *BET*, 'n veilige weddenskap; *ERR on the* ~ *side*, baie versigtig wees; ~ *FROM*, beveilig teen; *KEEP something* ~, iets bewaar, iets veilig hou; *in* ~ *KEEPING*, in veilige bewaring; *it is* ~ *to SAY*, 'n mens kan met sekerheid sê; *to be on the* ~ *SIDE*, om heeltemal seker te wees; ~ *and SOUND*, heeltemal veilig; veilig en onbeskadig; ~ *STRESS*, veilige spanning; *the WAY to be* ~ *is never to feel secure*, versigtigheid is die moeder van die wysheid; ~ **buster**, brandkasbreker; ~ **conduct**, vrygeleide; *with* ~ *conduct*, onder vrygeleide; ~ **convoy**, vrygeleide; ~ **custody**, versekerde bewaring (persone); veilige bewaring (goed); ~ **deposit**, brandkas; (loket)kluis; ~**guard**, (n) beskerming, vrygeleide; beveiliging; waarborg, vrywaring; bewaking; voorsorg; (v) beskerm, vrywaar (teen), beveilig, waarborg; verseker, sekureer; ~**keeping**, bewaring; hoede; ~**ly**, veilig, ongedeerd; gerus; ~**ness**, veiligheid; ~ **return**, veilige terugkeer, behoue terugkeer.
safe'ty, veiligheid; gerustheid; sekerheid; ongevaarlikheid; sekering (elektr.); *seek* ~ *in FLIGHT*, jou heil in vlug soek; *IN* ~, in veiligheid; *there is* ~ *in NUMBERS*, as 'n mens tussen baie is, voel jy veiliger; *PLAY for* ~, die kat uit die boom kyk; versigtig speel; versigtig te werk gaan; geen risiko neem nie; *REACH* ~, in veiligheid kom; *for* ~ *SAKE*, veiligheidshalwe; *SET at* ~, veilig stel; *WITH* ~, sonder gevaar; ~ **appliance**, veiligheidstoestel; ~-**belt**, veiligheidsgordel; reddingsgordel; veiligheidstreek; ~-**bolt**, rus (van geweerslot); knip (van deur); ~-**brake**, noodrem; ~-**buoy**, reddingsboei; ~-**cage**, veiligheidskooi; ~-**catch**, veiligheidsverbinding; veiligheidsknip; *on the* ~-*catch*, in rus (geweer); ~-**chain**, nagketting; noodketting; ~-**clutch**, veiligheidskoppeling; ~ **curtain**, brandskerm; ~ **device**, beveiliger, beveiligingstoestel; ~ **exit**, nooduitgang; ~ **fuse**, smeltdraad, sekering; veiligheidslont; ~ **glass**, veiligheidsglas; ~-**guard**, noodremhouer; beskermer; ~ **island**, vlugheuwel; ~ **lamp**, veiligheidslamp; ~ **lead**, smeltprop; ~ **limit**, veiligheidsgrens; ~-**line**, veiligheidsgrens; ~-**link**, koppelskakel; ~-**lock**, nagslot; rus (geweerslot); ~-**loop**, veiligheidspoor; ~ **match**, (veiligheids)vuurhoutjie, vonkvrye vuurhoutjie; ~ **net**, veiligheidsnet; ~-**nut**, veiligheidsmoer, borgmoer; ~ **paper**, veiligheidspapier; ~-**pin**, knipspeld, haakspeld; ~ **precaution**, veiligheidsmaatreël; ~ **rail**, skutreling; ~ **razor**, (veiligheid)skeermes; slotlem; ~ **signal**, veiligheidsein; ~ **specifications**, veiligheidspesifikasies; ~ **speed**, veilige snelheid; ~ **switch**, veiligheidskakelaar; ~-**valve**, veiligheidsklep; *sit on the* ~-*valve*, 'n onderdrukkingsbeleid volg; geen uiting van gevoelens of menings toelaat nie; ~ **zone**, vlugstreek, vlugheuwel.
saff'ian, marokynleer, saffiaan.
saff'lower, wilde saffraan, bastersaffraan.
saff'ron, (n) saffraan; saffraankleur; (v) met saffraan kleur; (a) saffraankleurig, saffraangeel, geelrooi; ~

milk, slemp; ~ **pear**, saffraanpeer; ~ **y**, saffraankleurig, saffraangeel.
sag, (n) deursakking; versakking; insakking; afsakking; verslapping; daling; (v) **(-ged)**, uitsak, deursak, afsak, slap hang, hang, sak, versak; verslap; oorhel; insak, insink; afdryf; daal.
sa'ga, sage, legende; saga.
saga'cious, skerpsinnig, skrander, slim; ~ **ness**, skerpsinnigheid, skranderheid.
saga'city, skranderheid, skerpsinnigheid, slimheid.
sage¹, (n) wysgeer, wyse; (a) verstandig, slim, wys.
sage², (n) salie (plant); ~**-bush**, wildeals; ~ **tea**, salietee.
sag: ~ **ging**, uitsakking, deursakking; afsakking; daling; ~ **gy**, hangerig, bakkerig.
sag'ittal, pyl=; pylvormig.
Sagittar'ius, die Boogskutter.
sa'gittary, (n) (..ries), skutter; (a) pylvormig; pyl=.
sa'gittate(d), pylvormig, sagittaal.
sagit'tiform, pylvormig.
sag'o, sago; ~ **pudding**, sagopoeding, paddaeiers (poeding).
sa'gy, salieagtig, salie=.
Sahar'a, Sahara.
sah'ib, sahib, menee, meester.
said, genoem, gemeld; *more easily* ~ *than DONE*, baie myle lê tussen doen en sê; *after all is* ~ *and DONE*, per slot van rekening; *you have* ~ *IT!* so moet 'n bek (mond) praat! *there is MUCH to be* ~ *for him*, daar kan baie ten gunste van hom gesê word; *he is* ~ *to be RICH*, hy is glo ryk; *no SOONER* ~ *than done, so gesê, so gedaan; kyk* **say**, (v)
sail, lengteduin.
saig'a, steppebok.
sail, (n) seil; skip; seiltoggie; *five DAYS* ~, vyf dae met die skip; *a FLEET of thirty* ~, 'n vloot van dertig skepe; *in FULL* ~, met volle seile; *GET* ~ *on*, seil maak; *GO for a* ~, 'n seiltoggie maak; *HOIST all* ~ *s*, alle seile bysit; *LOOSE* ~, die seile span; *MAKE* ~, meer seil bysit; *MAKE* ~ *for*, onder seil gaan na; *SET* ~ *for*, onder seil gaan na; *SHORTEN* ~, seil verminder; *STRIKE* ~, seil stryk; jou onderwerp; *TAKE in* ~, seil minder maak; jou matig; *TRIM one's* ~ *s to the wind*, die seile na die wind hang; die mantel na die wind draai; *UNDER* ~, onder seil; *take the WIND out of someone's* ~ *s*, iem. die loef afsteek; (v) vaar, uitseil; laat seil; gly; statig loop; ~ *ALONG*, voortseil, voortvaar; ~ *CLOSE to the wind*, skerp by die wind vaar; amper die wet oortree; ~ *under FALSE colours*, onder valse vlag vaar; ~ *INTO*, binneseil, binnevaar; bevlieg; ~ *the SEA*, die see bevaar; ~ *THROUGH*, deurseil; maklik deurkom; ~ **able**, bevaarbaar; ~ **arm**, meulroede; ~**-axle**, meulas; ~**-cloth**, seildoek; seiltent; ~ **er**, seiler, seilskip; ~ **fish**, seilvis.
sail'ing, (die) seil; afvaart; *it's all plain* ~, dit gaan vanself, dit gaan voor die wind; ~**-list**, (af)vaartrooster; ~**-master**, skipper; ~ **orders**, afvaartbevele; ~**-vessel**, seilskip.
sail' loft, seilmakery.
sail'or, matroos; seeman; skepeling, varensgesel; *a bad* ~, iem. wat maklik seesiekte kry; ~ **blouse**, matroosbloes; ~ **blue**, matroosblou; ~**-boy**, matroos, janmaat; ~ **collar**, matroeskraag; ~ **hat**, matrooshoed; ~ **ing**, matrooswerk; ~ **man**, matroos; ~**'s dance**, matroosdans; ~**'s dress**, matroosdrag; ~**'s home**, seemanshuis; ~**'s knot**, seemansknoop; ~**'s smock**, py; ~**'s song**, matrooslied; ~**'s trousers**, matroosbroek; ~ **suit**, matroospakkie; ~**'s-work**, matrooswerk; ~ **top**, matrooskraag.
sail: ~ **plane**, sweeftuig; ~ **plane pilot**, sweefvlieër; ~ **planing**, sweefvlieëry, sweefvlieg; ~**-yard**, ra; ~**-yarn**, seilgare.
sain'foin, sporrie, spurrie.
saint, (n) heilige, vrome; gesaligde; sint; sant; *PLAY the* ~, die vrome uithang; jou vroom voordoen; *YOUNG* ~ *s, old sinners*, heilig in die jeug, duiwels in die ouderdom; (v) heilig; heilig verklaar; (a) heilig, geheilig; vroom; salig; **S**~ **Anthony's fire**, (bel)roos; **S**~ **Bernard**, Sint Bernardhond; ~**ed**, heilig, salig, vroom; **S**~ **Elmo's fire**, Sint Elmsvuur; **S**~ **George's Day**, Sint Jorisdag; **S**~ **Germain**, Sint Germain; ~**hood**, heiligheid; **S**~ **Joseph's lily**, Sint Joseflelie; **S**~ **Laurence River**, Sint Laurencerivier; ~**like**, heilig; vroom; ~**liness**, heiligheid; vroomheid; ~**ly**, heilig; vroom; ~**'s'-day**, heiligedag; ~**ship**, heiligheid; **S**~ **Vitus's Dance**, (senuwee)trekkings, Sint Vitusdans.
sakabu'la, flap, sakaboela.
sake: *just for the* ~ *of APPEARANCES*, net vir die skyn; *for the* ~ *of CLEARNESS*, duidelikheidshalwe; *for CONSCIENCE'S* ~, om die gewete; *for the* ~ *of CONVENIENCE*, gerieflikheidshalwe; *FOR both our* ~ *s*, ter wille van ons albei; *for GOD'S* ~, in hemelsnaam; *for GOODNESS'* ~, *for MERCY'S* ~, in hemelsnaam; *for the* ~ *of*, ter wille van, ten behoewe van; *for the* ~ *of PEACE*, ter wille v.d. liewe vrede, in vredesnaam; *for YOUR* ~, om jou ontwil, om uwentwil.
sa'ke, rysbier; ryswyn; sake.
sa'ki, saki (aap).
sal, sout.
salaam', (n) plegtige groet, salaam; (v) plegtig groet, salaam.
sal'able, *kyk* **saleable**.
sala'cious, wellustig, wulps, ontugtig.
sala'ciousness, **sala'city**, wellus, wulpsheid.
sal'ad, slaai; ~**-bowl**, slaaibak; ~ **course**, slaaigang; ~**-days**, onervare jeug; ~ **dish**, slaaiskottel; slaaigereg; ~**-dressing**, slaaisous; ~**-oil**, slaaiolie; ~**-servers**, slaailepel-en-vurk; ~**-spoon**, slaailepel.
sal'amander, sal(a)mander; vuurgees; vuurvreter.
sala'mi, salami (sterkgekruide Italiaanse wors).
salaman'drine, salamanderagtig, salamander=.
salammon'iac, salmiak, vlugsout, ammoniumchloried.
sal'angane, salangaan.
salar'iat, salariaat, salaristrekkers.
sal'aried, loontrekkend, besoldig, gesalarieer.
sal'ary, (n) (..ries), salaris, loon, besoldiging, traktement, gasie; *with FULL* ~, met behoud van salaris; met volle salaris; *WITH a* ~ *of*, met 'n salaris van; (v) (..ried), besoldig, salarieer; ~ **expenditure**, salarisuitgawes; ~ **rate**, ~ **scale**, salarisskaal.
sale, verkoop; (uit)verkoping, prysfees; uitverkoop; afset; vendusie, veiling; debiet; *AGREEMENT of* ~, koopbrief; *CONDITIONS of* ~, verkoopvoorwaardes; veilvoorwaardes; *CONTRACT of* ~, koopkontrak; *DAY of* ~, verkoopdag; *DEED of* ~, verkoopakte; ~ *in EXECUTION*, eksekusieverkoping, baljuverkoping, baljuvendusie; *FOR* ~, te koop; *OFFER for* ~, te koop aanbied; *ON* ~, te koop; *PUBLIC* ~, openbare verkoping; *PUT up for* ~, te koop aanbied, opveil; *meet with (find) a READY* ~, goed verkoop; ~ **abil'ity**, verkoopbaarheid; ~ **able**, verkoopbaar; ~ **and lease back**, koop-en-verhuur; verkoop-en-huur; ~ **counter**, toonbank; ~ **price**, verkooprys; ~**-ring**, kring van verkopers; ~**-room**, verkooplokaal; vendusielokaal; ~ **s' book**, verkoopboek; ~ **s' department**, verkoopafdeling.
sales: ~ **girl**, winkelmeisie, verkoopjuffrou; ~ **lady**, verkoopster; ~ **man**, (..men), verkoper; verkoopsverteenwoordiger; handelaar; winkelbediende; ~ **manship**, verkoopkuns, verkoopbedryf; ~ **promotion**, verkoopbevordering, afsetbevordering, verkoopsreklame; ~ **representative**, verkoopsverteenwoordiger; handelsverteenwoordiger; fabrieksverteenwoordiger; ~ **resistance**, verkoopsweerstand; ~ **talk**, verkoopspraatjie; ~ **tax**, verkoopbelasting; omsetbelasting; ~ **team**, handelspan; verkoopspan; ~ **volume**, afset; ~ **woman**, (..men), verkoopster.
Sal'ic¹, Salies.
sal'ic², salies.
Sal'ic law, Saliese wet.
sal'icyl, salisiel; ~ **'ic acid**, salisielsuur.
sal'ience, uitspringende hoek; opvallendheid.
sal'ient, (n) uitloper, uitspringer; uitspringende hoek; (a) vooruitspringend; opvallend; treffend, markant, in die oog lopend; ~ **angle**, spitshoek; ~ **feature**, hooftrek, vernaamste punt; ~ **point**, hoofpunt.

salif'erous, southoudend.
salim'eter, soutmeter.
salin'a, soutpan, soutfontein, soutbron.
salina'tion, versouting; verbrakking.
sal'ine, (n) saline; sout; soutpan, soutbron; soutmakery; soutpurgasie; (a) sout, southoudend; soutagtig, souterig; ~ **deposit**, soutneerslag; ~ **solution**, soutoplossing; ~ **spring**, soutbron.
salinif'erous, southoudend.
salin'ity, soutgehalte; southeid.
saliniza'tion, versouting.
sal'inize, versout.
salinom'eter, salinometer, soutmeter.
saliv'a, spoeg, spuug, speeksel.
sal'ivant, (n) speekseldryfmiddel; (a) speekseldrywend.
sal'ivary, speeksel=; ~ **gland**, speekselklier.
sal'ivate, kwyl; laat kwyl.
saliva'tion, kwyling, speekselafskeiding.
sall'et, stormhoed.
sall'ow[1], (n) waterwilger; dwergwilger.
sall'ow[2], (n) vaal (bleek) kleur; (v) bleek wees, vaal word; (a) bleek; blas; vaal; soel; sieklik bleek; ~**ness**, bleekheid; soelheid.
sall'y[1], (n) (**sallies**), klokslag.
sall'y[2], (n) (**sallies**), uitstappie; uitval; vlaag; bevlieging; boutade; kwinkslag, geestige set; *DIVERSIONARY* ~, skynuitval; *MAKE a* ~, 'n uitval doen; *WITTY* ~, geestige inval; (v) (**sallied**), 'n uitval maak, uitstorm, uittrek; ~ *forth*, uitgaan, uitstap; ~**-port** uitvalpoort.
salmagun'di, salmagundi (vleis-vis-eiergereg); mengelmoes, tjou-tjou, deurmekaarspul.
sal'mi, salmi, wildsvleisbredie, voëlpastei.
salm'on (n) salm; *CAPE* ~, geelbek; *KIPPERED* ~, gerookte salm, bokkem; (a) salmkleurig; ~ **colour**, salmkleur; ~**-coloured**, salmkleurig; ~**-fishing**, salmvissery; ~ **net**, salmnet; ~ **peel**, jong salm; ~ **pink**, salmkleur; ~**-rearing**, salmteelt; ~ **steak**, (gebakte) salmmootjie; ~ **trout**, salmforel.
sal'on, salon; *literary* ~, literêre salon.
saloon', saal, salon; gelagkamer, kantien; salonrytuig; ~**-car**, toe motor; ~**-carriage**, salonwa; ~**-keeper**, kantienman; ~ **rifle**, .22-geweer.
sal'pinx, buis van Eustachius.
sal'sify, hawerwortel.
salt, (n) sout; silt; seerob, matroos; geestigheid; vernuf; (pl) Engelse sout; *ABOVE the* ~, aan die boent v.d. tafel; *ATTIC* ~, verfynde humor, Attiese sout; reuksout; *BASIC* ~, basiese sout; *to have eaten a BUSHEL of* ~ *with someone*, 'n sak sout met iem. opgeëet het; *COMMON* ~, gewone (tafel)sout; *he is the* ~ *of the EARTH*, hy is een van die beste; hy is 'n witman; *EAT* ~ *with a person*, iem. se gas wees; *IN* ~, ingesout; ~ *s of LEMON*, soutsuur; *not MADE of* ~, nie van suiker gemaak nie; *an OLD* ~, 'n ervare seeman, 'n seerob; *stand like a PILLAR of* ~, soos 'n soutpilaar staan; *take something with a PINCH of* ~, iets met 'n knypie (korreltjie) sout neem; *SPIRIT of* ~, soutsuur; *put* ~ *on a bird's TAIL*, sout op 'n voël se stert gooi; *TAKE with a grain of* ~, nie te letterlik opvat nie; *to WANT* ~, sout nodig hê; *WORTH one's* ~, jou sout werd; *rub* ~ *in the WOUNDS*, sout in die wonde vryf; (v) sout; insout; pekel; insult; ~ *an ACCOUNT*, 'n rekening sluit; ~ *the BOOKS*, ontvangste vervals; ~ *a MINE*, 'n myn sout; ~ *down MONEY*, geld opgaar; ~ *SAMPLES*, monsters sout; (a) sout; gesout; pekel; bitter; gekrui; *as* ~ *as LOT'S wife*, so sout soos brem; *a* ~ *RIB of mutton*, 'n soutribbetjie.
sal'tant, springend (her.); dansend.
salta'tion, dans; dansery; springery; sprong.
sal'tatory, springend.
salt: ~**-bag**, soutsak; ~**-box**, soutvaatjie, soutbak; ~**-briquette**, soutbriket; ~**-bush**, vaalbos, soutbos; ~**-cat**, soutklont (as lokaas vir duiwe); ~**-cellar**, soutvaatjie, soutpotjie; ~**-content**, soutgehalte; ~**-duty**, soutaksyns; ~**-ed**, gesout, immuun; beproef; *a* ~*ed HORSE*, 'n gesoute perd; ~*ed PEANUTS*, sout grondbone; ~**er**, southandelaar; insouter; ~**ern**, soutmakery; soutpan; ~**ery**, soutmakery;

vissoutery; ~**-farmer**, soutmaker; ~**-fish**, soutvis; ~**-herring**, southaring.
sal'tigrade, (n) springspinnekop; (a) springend, spring=.
salt: ~**iness**, souterigheid, siltigheid; ~**ing**, insouting; ~**ish**, soutagtig, brak; ~**-junk**, (gedroogde) soutvleis; ~ **lake**, soutmeer; ~ **less**, soutloos, laf, onsmaaklik; ~**-lick**, soutlek (vir vee); soutplek, brakplek; ~**-maker**, soutmaker; ~**-making**, soutmakery; ~**-marsh**, soutmoeras; ~ **meat**, soutvleis; ~**-mine**, soutmyn; ~ **monopoly**, soutmonopolie; ~ **ness**, southeid; ~**-pan**, soutpan.
saltpe'tre, salpeter; *CHILE* ~, chilisalpeter, natriumnitraat; *GERMAN* ~, ammoniumnitraat; *PURIFIED* ~, soutsteenskuim; ~ **rot**, salpeteruitslag (op mure).
salt: ~**-pit**, soutmyn; ~ **refinery**, soutraffinadery; ~ **snacks**, southappies; ~**-spoon**, soutlepeltjie; ~ **stratum**, soutlaag; ~**-trade**, southandel; ~ **water**, soutwater; ~**-well**, soutbron; ~**-works**, soutmakery, soutsiedery; ~**y**, souterig, brak; ~ *y taste*, soutsmaak.
salu'brious, gesond, heilsaam; ~**ness**, **salu'brity**, heilsaamheid, gesondheid.
sal'utariness, heilsaamheid, gesondheid.
sal'utary, heilsaam, weldadig, gesond.
saluta'tion, groet; begroeting; briefaanhef.
sal'utatory, begroetend, begroetings=.
salute', (n) saluut, groet, begroeting; saluutskote, salvo; hulde; *COME to the* ~, die saluut gee; *FIRE a* ~, saluutskote afvuur; *GIVE the* ~, die saluut gee; *RETURN a* ~, die saluut beantwoord; *STAND at the* ~, in die posisie staan om te salueer; *TAKE the* ~, die saluut beantwoord (waarneem); (v) groet, begroet, salueer, aanslaan; huldig; ereskote afskiet; ~ **r**, iem. wat salueer.
salut'ing, salueer; ~ **base**, salueerlyn; ~ **flag**, defileervlag; ~ **point**, salueerpunt.
salvabil'ity, bergbaarheid; redbaarheid.
sal'vable, bergbaar; redbaar.
sal'vage, (n) berging; bergloon; wrakgoed, strandgoed; (v) berg; red; herwin; ~ **boat**, bergingsboot; ~ **fee**, berggeld; ~ **money**, bergloon; ~ **officer**, bergingsoffisier; ~ **plant**, bergingsgereedskap; ~ **unit**, bergingseenheid; ~ **train**, hulptrein; ~ **work**, bergingswerk.
sal'vaging, berging.
salva'tion, saligheid, redding, heil, verlossing; behoud; behoudenis; *BE the* ~ *of*, die behoud wees van; *his* ~ *DEPENDS on it*, sy saligheid hang daarvan af; *DESIROUS of* ~, heilbegerig; *FIND* ~, bekeer word; tot bekering kom; *WORK out one's own* ~, jou eie saligheid uitwerk; jou eie redding bewerk.
Salva'tion: ~ **Army**, Heilsleër, ~**ist**, Heilsoldaat.
salve, (n) salf, smeergoed, smeersel; balsem; (v) salf, insmeer; heel; versag, genees; red; berg, ophaal; sus (gewete); ~ *one's conscience*, jou gewete sus.
sal'ver, skinkbord, presenteerblad; heler; redder; geneser.
sal'via, salie, pragsalie.
sal'vo, (-(e)s), salvo, sarsie; verontskuldiging, uitvlug; voorbehoud; ~ *es of APPLAUSE*, dawerende toejuigings; *a* ~ *of BOMBS*, 'n sarsie bomme.
sal volat'ile, vlugsout.
sal'vor, berger; redder; bergingskip.
Sam, Sam; *STAND* ~, trakteer; *UPON my* ~, by my kool, by my siks.
Sama'ria, Samaria.
Sama'ritan, (n) Samaritaan; *a good* ~, 'n barmhartige Samaritaan; (a) Samaritaans.
sam'ba, samba.
sam'bo, (-es, -s), basterneger.
same, (die)selfde; einste; eenders; eentonig; genoemde; *it is ALL the* ~ *to me*, dis vir my so lank as wat dit breed is; vir my is dit om 't ewe; *ALL the* ~, almal eenders; almaskie; nietemin; tog; *I went ALL the* ~, ek het tog gegaan; ~ *HERE!* ook so! *JUST the* ~, nietemin, tog; *MUCH the* ~, ongeveer dieselfde; *ONE and the* ~, presies dieselfde; *THE* ~, idem, dieselfde; *at the* ~ *TIME*, tegelykertyd, terselfdertyd; tog; *the VERY* ~, presies

dieselfde; die einste; *in the* ~ *WAY*, op dieselfde manier.
same'-day service, eendagdiens.
sam'el, half gebak (steen).
same'ness, gelykheid, eendersheid, eenvormigheid; eentonigheid.
samfold tractor set paper, vouperforasiepapier.
Sam'ian, (n) Samiër; (a) Samies.
sam'ite, sameet.
sam'let, jong salm.
Samm'y¹, (Sammies), Indiër.
samm'y², (sammies), halfklik (in gholf).
Sam'nite, (n) Samniet; Samnities (taal): (a) Samnities.
Samo'a, Samoa; ~ **n,** (n) Samoaan; (a) Samoaans.
samovar', samowar.
samp, stampmielies, gestampte mielies.
sam'pan, sampan (Sjinese bootjie).
sam'phire, seevinkel.
sa'mple, (n) monster; steekproef; staaltjie; voorbeeld; eksemplaar; *a COMPLETE range of* ~ *s,* 'n volledige stel monsters; ~ *s not for SALE,* monsters sonder waarde; (v) monsters haal uit; monsters neem (geol.); keur, probeer; proe; staaltjies gee van; tot voorbeeld dien; ~ **-book,** monsterboek; ~ **-boy,** monsterjong, monsterbediende; ~ **-card,** monsterkaart; ~ **-case,** monsterkis; ~ **-order,** proefbestelling; ~ **-post,** monsterpos; ~ **r,** borduurlap; letterlap; leerlap(pie); monsternemer, toetser; steker (kaas); ~ **-room,** uitstalkamer, monsterkamer; ~ **-spoon,** proeflepel; ~ **-tin,** monsterblik.
sa'mpling, monsterneming.
Sam'son, Simson.
Sam'uel, Samuel.
sam'urai, (sing. and pl.) samoerai.
san'able, geneesbaar.
san'ative, geneeskragtig, heilsaam, genesend; ~ **ness,** geneeskrag.
sanator'ium, (..ria), sanatorium, geneesinrigting.
san'atory, genesend, geneeskragtig
sanctifica'tion, wyding, heiliging, heiligmaking.
sanc'tified, heilig, vroom, geheilig.
sanc'tifier, heiligmaker.
sanc'tify, (..fied), heilig, heilig maak; wy; regverdig; *the end sanctifies the means,* die doel heilig die middele.
sanctimon'ious, skynheilig, huigelagtig, skynvroom; *BE* ~, skynheilig wees; ~ *MIEN,* Sondagsgesig; ~ **ness, sanctim'ony,** skynheiligheid.
sanc'tion, (n) bekragtiging, bevestiging, goedkeuring; toestemming; waarborg; strafmaatreël, sanksie; *APPLY* ~ *s against a country,* sanksies teen 'n land toepas, *GIVE one's* ~ *to,* jou goedkeuring heg aan, *WITHHOLD one's* ~ *from,* jou goedkeuring weerhou van; (v) bekragtig, goedkeur.
sanc'titude, heiligheid.
sanc'tity, heiligheid, geheiligdheid, onskendbaarheid; reinheid.
sanc'tuary, (..ries), heiligdom; vryplaas, toevlugsoord, allerheiligste; geslote jagtyd; *seek (take)* ~, 'n skuilplek soek.
sanc'tum, (-s), privaat vertrek; (..ta), gewyde binnevertrek; ~ **sanctorum,** heiligdom (in 'n Joodse tempel); studeerkamer.
sanc'tus bell, misbel.
sand, (n) sand; sandbank; sandgrond; (pl) sandstreek, sandoewer; strand; sandbank; sand(korrels); *BUILD on* ~, op sand bou; *BUILT on* ~, op sand gebou; *NUMBERLESS as the* ~ *s,* soos sand aan die see; *a ROPE of* ~, 'n vrot tou; *the* ~ *s of TIME are running out,* die tyd word kort; (v) versand; met sand meng; met sand skuur; onder sand begrawe; met sand bestrooi.
san'dal¹, (n) sandelhout.
san'dal², (n) sandaal; (v) sandale aantrek; ~ **led,** met sandale aan.
san'dalwood, sandelhout.
sand: ~ **-apple,** goorappel; grysappel; ~ **bag,** (n) sandsak; (v) **(-ged),** sandsakke pak; met 'n sandsak slaan; ~ **bagger,** iem. wat met 'n sandsak slaan; ~ **bank,** sandbank; sandplaat; ~ **-bar,** sandbank; skoorwal (myn); ~ **-bath,** sandbad; ~ **-bed,** sandbedding; sandbodem; ~ **-beetle,** sandvlooi; ~ **-blast,** sandstraal; sandspuit; sandstuiwing; ~ **-blast machine,** sandblaastoestel; ~ **-blaster,** sandblaser; ~ **-box,** sandkis; sandkoker; ~ **-blind,** bysiende; ~ **-boy,** sandvlooi; *as happy as a* ~ *boy,* doodgelukkig; ~ **-cart,** sandkar; ~ **castle,** sandkasteel; ~ **crack,** horingskeur; bars (in klou van 'n perd); ~ **-drift,** sandheuwel; sandstuiwing; ~ **-dune,** sandduin; ~ **-eel,** smelt (soort vis); ~ **er,** sandstrooier; ~ **erling,** strandlopertjie (voël); ~ **filling,** sandopvulling; ~ **flea,** sandvlooi; ~ **-fly,** sandvlieg; ~ **-glass,** sandloper, eierkokertjie, uurglas; ~ **-goggles,** sandbril; ~ **-grouse,** sandpatrys; ~ **gulley,** sandvanger.
san'dhi, sandhi.
sand: ~ **-hill,** sandduin, sandbult; ~ **-hopper,** sandspringer; ~ **iness,** sanderigheid; ~ **ing,** afskuur, afskuring; bestrooiing met sand; ~ **ing belt,** skuurband; ~ **ing drum,** skuurtrommel; ~ **-leaf,** sandblad (tabak); ~ **man,** Klaas Vakie; *the* ~ *man is coming,* Klaas Vakie gaan hom vang; Klaas Vakie gaan sand in sy oë strooi; ~ **-martin,** oewerswaeltjie; ~ **-mole,** sandmol, duinmol; ~ **paper,** (n) skuurpapier; (v) met skuurpapier vrywe; ~ **piper,** strandloper (voëltjie); ~ **-pit,** sandgat, sandkuil, sandgroef; ~ **-plover,** strandlopertjie; ~ **-shark,** sandhaai, vioolhaai, vioolvis, sandkruiper; ~ **-shoe,** strandskoen; ~ **-snake,** sandslang; ~ **stone,** sandklip, sandsteen; ~ **storm,** sandstorm, stofstorm; ~ **trap,** sandvanger; ~ **-viper,** sandadder.
sand'wich, (n) (-es), toebroodjie; (v) inskuif, tussenin sit, invoeg, insluit; ~ **cake,** tweelaagkoek; ~ **man,** plakkaatdraer; ~ **relish,** mayonnaisesmeer; ~ **spread,** toebroodjiesmeer, broodsmeer, groentesmeer.
Sand'y¹, Skot.
sand'y², (n) **(sandies),** rooikop; (a) sanderig, sandagtig; rooierig; hoogblond (kleur); ~ **country,** sandveld; ~ **hair,** rooierige hare; ~ **path,** sandpad; ~ **plain,** sandvlakte; ~ **soil,** sandgrond; ~ **stretch,** sandplaat.
sane, gesond (van verstand); verstandig; gematig; ~ **ness,** verstandigheid; gematigdheid.
sangaree', kruiewyn.
sang-froid', onverskilligheid, koelheid, bedaardheid, koudheid, selfbeheersing.
sangrail', sangreal', heilige graal.
sanguif'erous, bloedhoudend.
sanguifica'tion, bloedvorming.
sanguin'arily, bloedig, met baie bloedvergieting.
sang'uinary, bloeddorstig, moorddadig, moordgierig; bloedig; wreed.
sang'uine, (n) rooi kryt; rooikryttekening; (a) bloedryk, hartstogtelik, vurig, hoopvol, sanguinies; ~ *of one's chances of success,* vol hoop om te slaag.
sanguin'eous, sanguinies; bloedryk, volbloedig; bloedrooi; bloed=
San'hedrin, Sanhedrin, Joodse Raad.
san'icle, heelkruid.
san'idin, ysspaat.
san'ies, bloed-etter.
san'ify, (..fied), saneer, skoonmaak; gesond maak.
sanitar'ian, (n) sanitariër; (a) higiënies.
san'itary, sanitêr, gesondheids=; higiënies, gesond, heilsaam; ~ **condition,** higiëniese toestand; ~ **engineer,** gesondheidsbeampte; ~ **fittings,** sanitêre toebehore; ~ **inspector,** gesondheidsinspekteur; ~ **lane,** nagsteeg; ~ **officer,** gesondheidsbeampte; ~ **paper,** toiletpapier; ~ **napkin,** ~ **pad,** sanitêre doekie, maanddoek; ~ **regulation,** gesondheidsregulasie; ~ **service,** reinigingsdiens, gesondheidsdiens; ~ **towel,** sanitêre doekie, maanddoek; ~ **ware,** sanitêre ware.
san'itate, higiënies versorg, higiënies verbeter.
sanita'tion, toepassing van gesondheidsmaatreëls; verbetering van gesondheidstoestand, sanitasie; sanering.
san'ity, gesondheid (van verstand), geestesgesondheid; gematigdheid, verstandigheid.
sank, *kyk* **sink,** (v).
sans, sonder.
San'scrit, *kyk* **Sanskrit.**
sansculotte', sansculotte, uiterste rewolusionêr.

sansculott'erie, uiterste nasionalisme, chauvinisme.
sansculott'ic, (n) ruwe persoon, voëlverskrikker; (a) rewolusionêr.
sansculott'ism, uiterste nasionalisme, jingoïsme, chauvinisme.
sansevier'ia, slangvel, helpen, sambok(bos)plant.
San'skrit, (n) Sanskrit, Oud-Indiese taal; (a) Sanskri= ties; ~ **ist,** Sanskritis.
Santa Claus', Vader Krismis, Kersvader; Sinter= klaas.
sap[1]**,** (n) blokker, boekwurm; dwaas; moeilike taak; (v) **(-ped),** swoeg, blok.
sap[2]**,** (n) loopgraaf, ingrawing; ondermyning; (v) sap= peer, loopgrawe maak; ondermyn, ondergraaf; uit= kalwe (water); sloop.
sap[3]**,** (n) sap (sop), vog; lewensap; lewenskrag; (v) **(-ped),** tap; droogmaak; verswak (krag); sloop; ~ *the energy of,* die krag ondermyn van.
sap'an-wood, sapanhout.
sap'-green, sapgroen.
sap'id, smaaklik, geurig; ~**'ity,** smaaklikheid, geurigheid.
sap'ience, wysheid; waanwysheid, eiewysheid.
sap'ient, slim; eiewys, waanwys.
sap: ~ **less,** droog, dor; uitgeput; ~**ling,** jong boom= pie; jongkêrel, opgeskote seun; jong wind= hond.
sapona'ceous, seepagtig, seep=; glad, glibberig.
saponifica'tion, verseping.
saponifi'able, verseepbaar.
sap'onite, seepklip; seepsteen; saponiet.
sap'or, smaak, geur; ~**if'ic,** smaakgewend.
sapp'er, sappeur, myngrawer, skansgrawer.
sapph'ire, saffier.
sapph'irine, saffierblou, saffier=.
sap: ~ **piness,** sappigheid; ~ **py,** sappig.
sap'rophyte, rottingskimmel, saprofiet.
saprophyt'ic, saprofities.
sap'rophytism, saprofitisme.
sap: ~**-rot,** vermolming; ~ **wood,** spinthout, spin= hout.
sar, seebrasem.
sa'raband, sarabande.
Sa'racen, (n) Saraseen; (a) Saraseens; ~**'ic,** Sara= seens; ~ **tank,** Saracentenk.
sarc'asm, sarkasme, bytende spot, stekelagtigheid.
sarcas'tic, sarkasties, spottend, stekelig, spotsiek, spotterig.
sar'cenet, voeringsy, sarsenetsy.
sarc'ode, sarkode, protoplasma.
sarc'oid, vleisagtig.
sarc'oline, vleiskleurig.
sarco'ma, kwaadaardige gewas, sarkoom.
sarcoph'agous, vleisetend.
sarcoph'agus, (..gi), sarkofaag.
sarc'ophile, vleisetende dier.
sarcos'is, vleisvorming.
sarcot'ic, vleisvormend.
sarc'ous, vol vleis, vleis=, spierweefsel=, spier=.
sardine', sardientjie.
Sardin'ia, Sardinië; ~ **n,** (n) Sardiniër; (a) Sardinies.
sardon'ic, sardonies, bitter, smadelik, grynsend; ~ *laugh,* grynslag.
sard'onyx, sardoniks.
sargass'o, (-es, -s), sargasso (seewier); S~ **Sea,** Sar= gassosee, Wiersee.
sa'ri, sari (van Hindoevroue).
sarm'entose, sarmen'tous, met takke soos ranke.
sarong', sarong.
sarsaparill'a, sarsaparilla.
sars'enet, voeringsy, sarsenetsy.
sartor'ial, kleremakers=.
sash[1]**,** (n) **(-es),** lyfband, serp, gord, seintuur; ~ *of office,* ampserp; (v) 'n serp ombind.
sash[2]**,** (n) **(-es),** vensterraam, skuifraam; (v) van ruite voorsien.
sash' bolt, raamgrendel.
sash' buckle, bandgespe.
sash: ~**-cord,** raamtou; ~**-door,** glasdeur; ~**- fastener,** raamhaak, raamknip; ~ **frame,** venster= raam; ~ **handle,** raamligter; ~**-lead,** raamlood, vensterlood; ~**-line,** raamtou; ~**-plane,** kosyn= skaaf; ~**-pocket,** skuifraamkoker; ~**-weight,** raamgewig; ~**-window,** skuifraamvenster.
sas'saby, (..bies), tsessebe(bok), basterhartbees.
sass'afras, sassafras; ~ **oil,** sassafrasolie.
sat, *kyk* **sit.**
Sat'an, Satan; duiwel; ~ *finds some MISCHIEF still for idle hand to do,* ledigheid is die duiwel se oorkus= sing; ~ *quoting SCRIPTURE,* ~ *rebuking SIN,* die vos wat die passie preek.
satan'ic(al), satanies, duiwels, hels.
Sata'nism[1]**,** Satanisme.
sat'anism[2]**,** duiwelstreke, duiwelse neiginge; duiwel= agtigheid.
satch'el, sakkie, boeksak, tas.
sate, versadig, oorlaai, walg; ~ *oneself with drink,* jou stomdronk drink.
sateen', satinet, satynsy, wolsatyn.
sate'less, onversadigbaar (poëties).
sat'ellite, satelliet; byplaneet; volgeling, trawant; wagter; ~ **country,** satelliet(land); ~ **launching,** sa= tellietlansering; ~**-launching pad,** satellietlanseer= blad; ~ **state,** satellietstaat; ~**-launching station,** satellietlanseerstasie; ~ **town,** satellietdorp.
sat'elloid, satelloïde, satelloïed.
sa'tiable, versadigbaar, bevredigbaar.
sa'tiate, versadig, bevredig, sat maak; ~ **d,** sat (vir), (oor)versadig, bevredig; dik, dikgevreet (dier).
satia'tion, versadiging; oorvoldaanheid.
sati'ety, volheid; dikheid; (oor)versadigheid, be= koms, satheid; geblaseerdheid; *to* ~, tot walgens toe.
sat'in, (n) satyn; (v) met satyn uitvoer; satineer; (a) satyn=; ~**-bird,** atlasvoël; ~ **et',** ~ **ette',** satinet; ~ **finish,** satynafwerking, satynglans; ~**-moth,** atlas= mot; ~ **paper,** satynpapier, atlaspapier; ~ **shoe,** satynskoen; ~**-spar,** atlasspaat; ~**-stitch,** satyn= steek; ~**-weaver,** satynwewer; ~**-wood,** satynhout, atlashout; ~ **y,** satynagtig.
sat'ire, satire, spotskrif, hekelskrif, skimpdig, spot= dig.
satir'ic(al), satiries, spottend, hekelend, spotsiek.
sat'irist, hekeldigter, satirikus, hekelaar, spotdigter, skimpdigter.
sat'irize, hekel, satiriseer, spot met.
satisfac'tion, voldoening, voldaanheid, genoegdoe= ning, bevrediging; genoeë; betaling; bekoms; *CAU= SE for* ~, rede vir tevredenheid; *FIND* ~ *in,* vol= doening vind in; *GIVE* ~, voldoen, genoeë gee; *it is a GREAT* ~ *to me,* dit gee my groot genoeë; *IN* ~ *of,* ter voldoening aan; *MAKE* ~, betaling doen; goedmaak; *RECEIVE* ~, bevredig word; *TO the* ~ *of,* tot bevrediging van.
satisfac'torily, bevredigend.
satisfac'tory, bevredigend; voldoende; genoegsaam; ~ **explanation,** bevredigende verklaring; ~ **proof,** genoegsame bewys; ~ **result,** bevredigende uitslag.
sat'isfiable, bevredigbaar.
sat'isfied, tevrede, versadig; bevredig, voldaan.
sat'isfy, (..fied), bevredig, voldoen, tevrede stel; ver= sadig; gerusstel; ~ *the DOCTOR,* medies goedge= keur word; ~ *the EXAMINERS,* slaag in 'n eksa= men; ~ *one's HUNGER,* jou honger stil; ~ *an OBJECTION,* 'n beswaar tegemoetkom; ~ *ONE= SELF,* jou oortuig; ~ *the REQUIREMENTS,* aan die eise voldoen; ~ *one's THIRST,* jou dors les; *I am satisfied of the TRUTH of his story,* hy het my oortuig v.d. waarheid van sy verhaal.
sat'rap, satraap; ~ **y,** satraapskap, satrapie.
sat'suma plum, bloedpruim, satsumapruim.
sat'urable, deurweekbaar, deurtrekbaar, versadig= baar.
sat'urate, versadig, vul, (deur)drenk, deurtrek, deur= week, satureer; ~ **d,** deurtrek; versadig, deurvoed.
satura'tion, versadiging; deurtrekking, deurweking; ~ **point,** versadigingspunt.
Sat'urday, Saterdag; *on* ~ *s,* Saterdae, Saterdags.
Sat'urn, Saturnus.
saturnal'ia, (pl) uitspattinge, buitensporighede; drinkpartye, saturnalieë; ~ **n,** saturnalies, onge= bonde, teuelloos, liederlik, losbandig, dol, uitspat= tig.
Saturn'ian, (n) bewoner van Saturnus; (a) Saturnies.

sat'urnine, swaarmoedig, flegmaties, somber; lood=; aan loodvergiftiging lydend; ~ **disease,** loodvergif= tiging.
sat'urnism, loodvergiftiging.
sat'yr, sater, bosgod; wellusteling; ~ **i'asis,** buitenge= wone wellus (by mans), wellussiekte.
saty'ric, saters=.
sauce, (n) sous; pikantheid; onbeskaamdheid, bru= taalheid, brutaliteit; *what's* ~ *for the GOOSE is* ~ *for the gander,* as dit vir die een geld, geld dit ook vir die ander; *NONE of your* ~*!* moenie jou so bru= taal hou nie! *PIQUANT* ~, pikante sous; *SERVE with the same* ~, met gelyke munt betaal; (v) sous; kruie; brutaliseer, astrant wees; ~**-boat,** souskom= metjie, souspotjie; ~**box,** parmant, brutale vent, astrante persoon; ~ **ladle,** souslepel; ~**pan,** kas= trol, pot.
sau'cer, piering.
saucer'ian, pieringvaarder, insittende van 'n vlieënde piering.
sauce'-tureen, souskom.
sau'cily, brutaal; lewendig, piekfyn; vrypostig.
sau'ciness, parmantigheid, brutaalheid, brutaliteit; voorbarigheid.
sau'cy, onbeskaamd, parmantig, brutaal; voorbarig; piekfyn; *BE* ~, astrant (parmantig) wees; *a* ~ *MISS,* 'n snip.
Saud, Saoed.
Saud'i Arabia, Saoedi-Arabië.
sauer'kraut, suurkool, sauerkraut.
Saul, Saul; *is* ~ *also among the prophets?* is Saul ook onder die profete?
saun'ter, (n) drentelpas, slentergang; slenterdans; (v) slenter, drentel, kuier, slinger; *into,* inslenter; ~**er,** drentelaar, slenteraar.
saur'ian, (n) akkedis(dier), souriër; (a) akkedis=, sou= ries, souriër=.
saurisch'ian, souriskiër.
sau'sage, wors; *GERMAN* ~, metwors; *SMALL* ~, worsie; ~**-casing,** worsderm; ~**-filler,** worshorin= kie, worsstopper; worsvulstof; ~**-grinder,** ~**-ma= chine,** worsmasjien; ~ **r,** worsvark; ~ **roll,** worsrol= letjie; ~ **seasoning,** worskruisel; ~**-shaped,** worsvormig; ~**-skins,** worsderms; ~**-tree,** wors= boom, komkommerboom.
sav'able, redbaar.
sav'age, (n) barbaar, onbeskaafde; woestaard, wreed= aard; robbedoe; (v) byt, toetakel; beseer; verskeur; mishandel; (a) wild, woes, barbaars, heidens; vals; wreed, boosaardig, rasend; ~**dom,** wilde staat; die wildes; ~**-looking,** verwilder(d); ~**ness,** barbaars= heid, wreedheid, woestheid; ~**ry,** woestheid, wreedheid.
savann'a(h), savanne, grasvlakte.
sav'ant, geleerde.
save, (n) keerslag; redding; (v) red, verlos; salig maak; spaar, bêre, wegsit, bymekaarmaak; bewaar, be= hoed; ~ *APPEARANCES,* die skyn red; ~ *one's BREATH,* stilbly; ~ *someone from DEATH,* iem. v.d. dood red; ~ *a person from DROWNING,* iem. van verdrinking red; ~ *FACE,* die aansien red; ~ *FOR,* spaar vir; ~ *a GOAL,* 'n doel verhoed (voor= kom); *GOD* ~ *the queen,* God behoede die konin= gin; ~ *MONEY,* geld oppot (spaar); ~ *the PIECES,* red wat nog te red is; ~ *for a RAINY day,* 'n appeltjie vir die dors bewaar; ~ *the SITU= ATION,* die situasie red; ~ *one's SKIN,* jou bas red; ~ *TIME,* tyd uitwin; ~ *oneself the TROU= BLE,* jou die moeite spaar; (prep) behalwe, uitge= sonder, behoudens; ~ *FOR,* afgesien van; met die uitsondering van; *the LAST* ~ *one,* die voorlaaste; (conj) behalwe, tensy.
saved, (a) gered; gespaar; ~*-up capital,* spaarkapi= taal; (interj) gered! *well* ~*!* mooi skoot!
sav'er, redder; spaarder (van geld).
sav'in, seweboom.
sav'ing, (n) besparing; redding, verlossing, behoud; voorbehoud, uitsondering; winning; (pl) spaargeld, spaarsente, spaarduitjies, spaarpenninge; (a) spaarsaam; reddend; saligmakend; *a* ~ *CLAUSE,* 'n voorbehoudsbepaling; *his only* ~ *GRACE,* sy enigste voortreflikheid; (prep) behalwe, behou=

dens, met uitsondering van; ~ *FOR,* behalwe dan; ~ *your PRESENCE,* met u verlof; ~ *your REV= ERENCE,* met alle respek vir u Eerwaarde.
sav'ings: ~ **account,** spaarrekening; ~ **bank,** spaar= bank; ~**-bank book,** spaarboekie, inlegboek; ~ **certificate,** spaarsertifikaat; ~ **fund,** spaarfonds; ~ **levy,** spaarheffing.
Sav'iour, Heiland, Saligmaker, Redder, Verlosser.
sav'iour, redder.
sav'ory, boontjiekruid.
sav'our, (n) smaak; geur, aroma; smaaklikheid; reuk; (v) proe, ruik, laat dink aan; ~ *OF,* ruik na; laat dink aan; ~ *WELL,* lekker smaak, behaag; ~**= iness,** geur, smaaklikheid; ~**less,** smaakloos; ~**y,** (n) (..ries), soutigheid, southappie, soutnagereg= gie; (a) smaaklik, geurig, soutig; gekrui.
Savoy'¹, Savoje.
savoy'², savojekool.
savv'y, (n) (sl.) verstand; benul; (v) verstaan, begryp.
saw¹, (n) gesegde, spreuk.
saw², (n) saag; (v) **(-ed, -n),** saag.
saw³, (v) *kyk* **see.**
saw: ~**-back,** saagrug; ~**-bench,** saagbank; ~**-bill,** saagbek; ~**-blade,** saagblad; ~**-block,** saagblok; ~**-bones,** snydokter; ~**-how,** saagboog; ~**-cut,** saagkerf.
saw'der: *soft* ~, vleiery, komplimente.
saw: ~**-die,** setyster; saagsetter; ~**-doctor,** saag= hersteller; ~**dust,** saagsel; *let the* ~*dust out of a person,* iem. se ware karakter openbaar; ~**dust ring,** kryt; arena (sirkus); ~**-edged,** met saagrand; ~**-file,** saagvyl; ~**fish,** saagvis; ~**-fly,** saagwesp; ~**-frame,** saagraam; ~**-horse,** saagbok.
saw'ing, gesaag; ~ **block,** saagleier; ~ **machine,** saag= masjien.
saw: ~**like,** saagagtig; ~**mill,** saagmeul; ~**-pit,** saag= kuil; ~**-set,** tandsetter, saagsteller; ~**-shark,** saag= bekhaai; ~**-toothed,** getand; ~**-toothed roof,** saag= dak; ~**-trestle,** saagbok.
saw'-wort, wou (plant).
saw'yer, saer; drywende boomstam.
saxe¹, fotografiese papier.
Saxe², Sakse; ~ **blue,** saksiesblou.
sax'horn, saxbeuel.
sax'ifrage, klipbreker (plant).
Sax'on, (n) Sakser; Engelsman; Saksies (taal); (a) Saksies; Angel-Saksies; ~ **blue,** saksiesblou.
Sax'ony, Sakse; *Lower* ~, Neder-Sakse.
sax'ophone, saxofoon.
sax'ophonist, saxofoonblaser.
say, (n) mening, sê; gesegde, bewering; seggenskap; *have ALL the* ~, alles te sê hê; *have the GREATEST* ~, die grootste seggenskap hê; *HAVE a* ~, ook 'n woordjie te sê hê; *I HAVE a* ~ *in the matter,* ek het seggenskap in die saak; *LET him have his* ~, laat hom klaar praat (uitpraat); ~ *ONE'S* ~, jou hart uitpraat; (v) **(said),** sê, vertel; beweer; opsê; *you can* ~ *that AGAIN!* dit kan jy gerus sê! so moet 'n bek praat! *it* ~*s in the BIBLE,* dit staan in die Bybel, *I really COULDN'T* ~, om die waarheid te sê, moet ek lieg; *have a great DEAL to* ~ *about,* die mond vol hê van; *never* ~ *DIE,* moenie moed opgee nie; *in what we* ~*s and DOES,* in iem. se doen en late; *you DON'T* ~ *so!* a nee a! ag nee! wil jy glo? praat v.d. ding! ~ *in EVIDENCE,* getuig; ~ *GOODBYE,* dagsê; vaarwel sê; ~ *GOOD-NIGHT,* nagsê; ~ *GRACE,* bid (voor ete); *before one can* ~ *KNIFE,* in 'n kits; *to* ~ *the LEAST of it,* om die minste daarvan te sê; ~ *one's LESSON,* jou les opsê; ~ *what one LIKES,* sê wat jy wil; ~ *MASS,* die mis lees; *if I MAY* ~ *so,* as ek dit mag sê, *have MUCH to* ~, baie te sê hê; *baie note op sy sang hê, it* ~*s MUCH for,* dit pleit vir; *I'LL* ~ *that MUCH for him,* dit moet ek hom ter ere nagee; *it* ~*s MUCH for him,* dit spreek boekde= le vir hom; *there is MUCH to be said for him,* daar kan baie ten gunste van hom gesê word; *I have MUCH to* ~, baie te sê hê; baie note op jou gesang hê; *what did you* ~ *his NAME was?* hoe is sy naam nou weer? *to* ~ *someone NAY,* vir iem. nee sê; ~ *more than is NECESSARY,* meer sê as wat nodig is; jou mond verbrand; ~ *NO more about the matter,*

sê niks verder oor die saak nie; maak daar nou maar geen praatjies oor nie; ~ *NO*, weier, nee sê; *to* ~ *NO to someone*, vir iem. nee sê; *there is NOTHING to be said for it*, daar is niks voor te sê nie; ~ *OVER*, herhaal; ~ *one's PIECE*, jou bydrae lewer; jou sê sê; *SHALL we* ~, laat ons maar sê; *SO to* ~, as't ware; *no SOONER said than done*, so gesê, so gedaan; *THAT is to* ~, dit wil sê; *THEY* ~, dit word vertel; ~ *TWENTY*, stel dit maar op twintig; *you may WELL* ~ *so*, dit kan jy wel sê; *WHAT do you* ~ *to a walk?* hoe sal dit wees as ons gaan loop? ~ *WHEN!* hoeveel? *just* ~ *the WORD*, sê net ja; *have a good WORD to* ~ *for*, 'n goeie woordjie doen vir; *YOU'VE said it!* so moet 'n mond (bek) praat.
sayet'te, sajet.
say'ing, gesegde, spreekwoord; sê; *AS the* ~ *goes,* soos die spreekwoord lui; *it is COMMON* ~, elk= een sê dit; dit is 'n gemeenplaas; ~ *and DOING are two different things,* baie myle lê tussen doen en sê; *his* ~*s and DOINGS,* sy doen en late; *there is NO* ~ *who it was,* dis uiters moeilik om te sê wie dit was; *it goes WITHOUT* ~, dit spreek vanself; dit lê voor die hand.
scab, (n) kors, roof (seer); skurfte; brandsiekte (klein= vee); onderkruiper (staking); skurwigheid; (v) **(-bed),** 'n rofie vorm.
scabb'ard, skede.
scabb'iness, brandsiekte; skurfte.
scabb'y, vol brandsiekte, brandsiek; skurf.
scab'ies, skurfte, skurfsiekte, jeuksiekte, help-my-krap, lekkerjeuk, lekkerkrap.
scab'-inspector, brandsiekte-inspekteur.
scab'ious¹, (n) speldekussinkie, duifkruid (blom).
scab'ious², (a) skurf.
scab: ~ -law, brandsiektewet; ~ **-mite,** brandsiek= temyt; skurfmyt; ~ **-regulations,** brandsiektereg= ulasies.
scab'rous, skurf; ru, ongelyk; delikaat, netelig (on= derwerp, saak); onwelvoeglik, skunnig; ~ **ness,** ru= heid; las; geswaagdheid, onwelvoeglikheid.
scad, horsmakriel.
scaff'old, (n) steier, stellasie; skavot; (v) skraag, steun; van 'n steier voorsien, 'n steier opstel; ~ **board,** steierplank; ~ **ing,** steierwerk, steiers; stella= sie; ~ **ing beam,** steierbalk; ~ **ing pole,** steierpaal.
scagliol'a, skagliola, imitasieklip.
scal'able, beklimbaar.
scal'ar, (n) skalaar; (a) skalêr.
scala'riform, trapvormig, leervormig.
scal'awag, *kyk* **scallawag.**
scald¹, (n) skald, oud-Noorse digter.
scald², (n) skroeiwond, brandwond (deur vloeistof); (v) skroei; brand (met vloeistof); opkook; uitkook; warm maak; ~ **-head,** skurfkop.
scald'ing (n) verskroeiing; (a) skroeiend, ver= skroeiend, brandend, gloeiend; ~ *HOT,* gloeiend warm; ~ *TEARS,* brandende trane.
scale¹, (n) weegskaal; *HOLD the* ~ *s,* die oordeel vel; *HOLD the* ~ *s even,* met 'n gelyke maat meet; on= partydig wees; *PAIR of* ~ *s,* (weeg)skaal; *throw the SWORD into the* ~ *s,* die oorlog laat beslis; *TIP the* ~ *s,* die deurslag gee; *TURN the* ~ *(s),* die deurslag gee; (v) weeg.
scale², (n) stelsel; maatstaf; skaal; toonladder, toon= skaal (musiek); scala; ~ *of CHARGES,* tarief; *CONSTRUCT to* ~, op skaal vervaardig; *DRAW to* ~, op skaal teken; *on a LARGE* ~, grootskaals; ~ *of NOTATION,* telstelsel; *SOCIAL* ~, maat= skaplike leer; ~ *of WAGES,* loonskaal; (v) opklim, beklim, beklouter; volgens skaal teken; ~ *DOWN,* na verhouding verlaag; ~ *UP,* groter maak, ver= hoog.
scale³, (n) skub (van vis); skilfer; doplus; lagie, dop; tandsteen; ketelsteen; *ARMOURED* ~, harde doplus; *the* ~ *s FELL from his eyes,* die skille het van sy oë geval; *RED* ~, rooi doplus; *SOFT* ~, sagte doplus; (v) skubbe afkrap; afskilfer; uitdop; ketelsteen verwyder; ~ *a GUN,* 'n kanon uitgloei; ~ *OFF,* afskilfer; *PERNICIOUS* ~, verderflike doplus; *RUSTY* ~, roesdoplus; ~ **armour,** ge= skubde pantser.

scale'-beam, weegbrug.
scale'-board, skaalplankie.
sca'lecide, doplusdoder.
scal'ed, geskub, skub=.
scale' division, skaalverdeling.
scale: ~ **-insect,** skildluis, doplus, dopdiertjie, skaal= insek; ~ **less,** sonder skubbe; ~ **model,** skaalmodel; ~ **-model boat,** skaalmodelboot; ~ **-model boating,** skaalmodelbootvaart.
scalene', ongelyksydig; ~ **triangle,** ongelyksydige driehoek.
scal'er¹, klimmer.
scal'er², skraper.
scal'iness, skubberigheid, skubagtigheid; skilferig= heid, skilferagtigheid.
scal'ing¹, beklimming; gradering.
scal'ing², afskraping; afskilfering.
scal'ing hammer, bikhamer.
scal'ing ladder, stormleer; brandleer.
scal'ing tool, bikbeitel.
scall, skurfte; *DRY* ~, jeuksiekte; *WET* ~, ekseem.
scall'awag, vabond; niksnuts; prulbees, verpotte dier (bees).
scall'ion, salot.
scall'op, (n) kammossel; skulp; skulpwerk, uitskul= ping; (v) uitskulp, uitpunt, festoen; in die skulp kook; ~ **ed,** uitgetand, uitgeskulp; ~ **ed edge,** skulprand; ~ **ing,** skulpwerk; ~ **-shell,** mantel= skulp; ~ **stitch,** skulpsteek.
scall'ywag, vabond; niksnuts; prulbees, verpotte dier (bees).
scalp, (n) kopvel; *out for* ~ *s,* slagoffers soek; (v) die kopvel afslag, skalpeer; kwaai kritiseer.
scal'pel, ontleedmes, skalpel, skalpeermes.
scalp: ~ **er,** skalpeerder; ~ **-hunt,** koppesnel; ~ **-hunter,** koppesneller; ~ **ing knife,** skalpeermes; ~ **massage,** kopmassering.
scal'priform, beitelvormig.
scal'y, skilferig, skilferagtig; skubberig; geskub; ~ **ant-eater,** ietermagô; ~ **-winged,** skubvlerkig.
scamp, (n) skelm, skurk, kwajong, vabond, skobbe= jak; platjie, karnallie; abjater; (v) knoei, afskeep; ~ *one's work,* halwe werk doen; jou werk af= skeep.
scam'per, (n) haastige vlug; draf; *take a* ~ *through a reference book,* 'n naslaanwerk vlugtig deurlees; (v) weghol, hardloop, galop; vlug; ~ *ABOUT,* rond= hardloop, dartel; ~ *OFF (away),* weghol.
scan, (-ned), skandeer (verse); noukeurig ondersoek, beskou; aftas (radar, televisie).
scan'dal, skandaal, skande; aanstoot; laster, skin= dery, kwaadpraat, lasterpraatjies; *a* ~ *to his PRO= FESSION,* 'n skande vir sy beroep; *give RISE to* ~, opspraak verwek; ~ **ize,** laster, skandaliseer; beledig; opspraak verwek; ergernis verwek, ontstig; ~ **monger,** skinderbek, lastertong, kwaadspreker; ~ **mongering,** ~ **mongery,** kwaadsprekery, skinde= ry.
scan'dalous, skandelik, lasterlik, skandalig, aan= stootlik, skandaleus; ~ *act (deed),* skanddaad; ~ **ness,** skandelikheid, lasterlikheid, skandaligheid, aanstootlikheid.
scan'dent, klimmend.
Scandinav'ia, Skandinawië; ~ **n,** (n) Skandinawiër; (a) Skandinawies.
scan: ~ **ner,** bekyker; skandeerder; ~ **ning,** bespie= ding; beskouing; skansie; ~ **ning lens,** bespiedings= lens.
scan'sion, skandering, skansie.
scansor'es, klimvoëls.
scansor'ial, klimmend, klim=; ~ **bird,** klimvoël; ~ **foot,** klimpoot.
scant, (v) inkrimp; bekrimp, verminder; (a) skraal; karig, gering, armoedig; ~ *of BREATH,* kort= asem; *with* ~ *COURTESY,* met min beleefdheid; *do* ~ *JUSTICE to,* nie genoeg reg laat wedervaar nie; *with* ~ *SUCCESS,* met min sukses; ~ **ies,** am= perbroekie; ~ **ily,** karig, skaars, armoedig, dun, ef= fentjies, skraaltjies; ~ *ily dressed,* met min klere aan; armoedig aangetrek; ~ **iness,** karigheid, ge= ringheid, skaarsheid.
scan'tle, verbrokkel.

scant'ling, stukkie, klein bietjie; staaltjie; afmeting; kleinhout; langklip.
scan'ty, karig, skraal, dun, gering, min, onvoldoende, skriel, skaars; ~ *of hair*, met min hare; ~**-panty**, amperbroekie.
scape, (n) steel; skag (van 'n pilaar); vlug (van suil); (v) (archaic) ontsnap.
scape'goat, sondebok.
scape'grace, deugniet, onnut.
scaphand'er, swemgordel; duikerpak.
scaph'oid, skuitvormig (been).
scap'ula, (-e), skouerblad, bladbeen; ~ **r**, (n) skouer=verband; skouerkleed, skapulier; rugveer (van 'n voël); (a) v.d. skouerblad, skouerblad=.
scap'ulary, skouerkleed, skapulier.
scar[1], (n) krans, steilte.
scar[2], (n) litteken, merk; skraap; *not achieved without* ~ *s*, nie sonder klereskeur nie; (v) **(-red)**, toegaan (seer); 'n litteken vorm.
sca'rab, skarabee; kewer, miskruier.
sca'ramouch, (-es), skelm, grootprater, bluffer.
scarce, skaars; skraps; seldsaam; *make oneself* ~, sorg dat jy wegkom, trap; ~ **resources**, skaars hulpbronne.
scarce'ly, nouliks, skaars, skrappies, skraps, skrap=sies, beswaarlik, ternouernood; ~ *ANYONE*, byna niemand; ~ *ANYTHING*, byna niks; ~ *EVER*, byna nooit; *she is* ~ *TEN years old*, sy is skaars tien jaar oud; *I* ~ *THINK so*, ek dink dit amper nie.
scarce'ness, skaarsheid; seldsaamheid.
scarc'ity, skaarsheid, skrapsheid; skaarste, gebrek.
scare, (n) paniek, skrik, vrees; (v) skrikmaak, afskrik, bang maak; ~ *away*, wegjaag, verwilder; ~**crow**, voëlverskrikker; skrikbeeld; geraamte (fig.); *look like a* ~*crow*, soos 'n voëlverskrikker lyk; lyk soos een wat met die nagtrein gekom het.
scare: ~**-heading**, ~**-headlines**, sensasieopskrif (in koerant); ~**monger**, onrussaaier, alarmis; ~**mongering**, onrussaaiery; ~ **story**, bangmaak=praatjie, -storie.
scared, bang, lugtig, bevrees; *BE* ~ *of*, bang wees vir; ~ *to DEATH*, doodbang; ~ *STIFF*, lam ge=skrik.
scarf[1], (n) las, naat; (v) saamvoeg, las; afskuins.
scarf[2], (n) **(scarves)**, halsdoek, serp; (v) 'n serp omsit; omsluier, omfloers; ~**-knot**, halsknoop; ~**-pin**, dasspeld; ~**-ring**, serpring.
scarf'skin, opperhuid.
scarf'wise, dwars, skuins.
scarifica'tion, insnyding, kerwing; hekeling.
sca'rificator, snepper, skraapmes.
sca'rifier, snepper; bladbreker, korsbreker, skeur=ploeg; meseg, padeg.
sca'rify, (..fied), kerf (bas); eg, loswerk, losmaak; kwel, hekel.
scar'ious, droog; dun; draderig.
scarlati'na, rooivonk, skarlakenkoors.
scarl'et, (n) skarlakenrooi; skarlakenkleed; (a) skar=lakenrooi, skarlakens; ~ **bean**, pronkboon; ~ **fever**, skarlakenkoors, rooivonk; ~ **hat**, kardi=naalshoek; ~ **runner**, pronkboon, sierboontjie; ~ **woman**, sedelose vrou.
scarp, (n) steilte, helling; (v) skuins maak, eskarpeer; ~**ed**, steil, skuins; ~*ed plain*, bankeveld.
scar'us, papegaaivis.
scar'y, bang, skrikkerig; vreesaanjaend.
scathe, (n) letsel; *without* ~, onbeskadig, ongedeerd, sonder letsel; (v) benadeel, beskadig, kwes, beseer; ~**ful**, kwetsend, nadelig; ~**less**, ongedeerd.
scath'ing, vernietigend, verpletterend, skerp, sny=dend, vlymend; ~ *sarcasm*, vlymende sarkasme.
scatolog'ical, skatologies.
scatol'ogy, skatologie.
scatt'er, (n) spreiding, verspreiding; (v) uitstrooi, uit=saai; verstrooi, versprei; wegspat, uiteenspat; uit=mekaarjaag, uitmekaardryf, uiteendryf, verdrywe; verydel (hoop); ~**-brain**, warhoof, warkop; ~**-brained**, deurmekaar, warhoofdig; ~**ed**, verspreid, verstrooid; onreëlmatig; ~*ed instances*, sporadiese gevalle; ~*ed showers*, verspreide (reën)buie; ~*ed thunderstorms*, verspreide donderstorms; ~ **er**, ver=strooier; ~**ing**, (n) (ver)strooiing, verspreiding; *a* ~*ing of*, 'n handjievol; (a) verstrooiend.
scaur, steil krans.
scav'enge, reinig, skoonmaak; strate vee; aas vreet; afvalgas uitlaat (motor).
scav'enger, straatveër; aasvoël; opruimer, aaskewer; reinigingsmiddel; ~**-beetle**, miskruier; ~ **hunt**, aasjag; ~**-oil**, gebruikte olie; ~ **party**, aasparty; ~**-pump**, afsuigpomp; ~ **vulture**, aasvoël.
scav'engery, scav'enging, reiniging, skoonmaak, skoonmakery.
scenar'io, (-s), scenario, draaiboek; ~**-writer**, draai=boekskrywer.
scen'arist, draaiboekskrywer.
scene, toneel, tafereel; skerm; skouspel; spektakel; scène, standjie, woordewisseling; *BEHIND* the ~ *s*, agter die skerms; *CHANGE of* ~, verandering van toneel; *CREATE a* ~, molesie maak, lawaai maak; *the* ~ *is LAID in*, die stuk speel in; *don't MAKE a* ~, moenie 'n lawaai (scène) maak nie; *that's not MY* ~, ek is nie tuis daar nie; dis nie my terrein (gebied) nie; *QUIT the* ~, v.d. toneel verdwyn, sterwe; *the SECOND* ~ *of Act 4*, die tweede toneel van die vierde bedryf; *the SETTING of the* ~ *is*, die stuk speel in; ~**-painter**, toneelskilder, dekorasie=skilder, toneeldekorateur; ~**-painting**, dekorskil=dering; ~**ry**, toneel, toneeldekorasie; natuurto=nele, natuurskoon; dekor; ~**-shifter**, (toneel)masji=nis, toneelhulp, toneelhandlanger.
scen'ic, toneel=; skilderagtig; landskap=, natuur=skoon=; dramaties, teatraal; ~ **drive**, uitsigpad, na=tuurpad, uitkykpad; ~ **railway**, uitkykspoor, pa=noramaspoor.
scenograph'ic, in perspektief.
scenog'raphy, perspektieftekening; toneelskilder=kuns.
scent, (n) geur, reuk; reuksin; spoor; reukwerk, par=fuum, laventel, odeur; *this FLOWER has no* ~, hierdie blom ruik nie; *FOLLOW the* ~, die spoor volg; *LOSE the* ~, die spoor byster raak; *PUT one off the* ~, iem. v.d. spoor bring; *on the RIGHT* ~, op die regte spoor; (v) ruik, in die neus kry, die reuk kry van; ontdek; parfumeer; ~ *GAME*, wild ruik; die spoor kry; ~ *OUT*, uitsnuffel; ~ *TREACH=ERY*, verraad vermoed; ~**-bag**, reukklier; reuk=sakkie; ~**-bottle**, reukflessie, laventelflessie; ~**-box**, reukdosie; ~**ed**, gegeur, lekkerruik=; ~*ed CIGARETTE*, geparfumeerde sigaret; ~*ed HEATH*, lekkerruikheide; ~**-gland**, reukklier, ruikklier; ~**less**, reukloos; ~**-organ**, reukorgaan; ~**-spray**, laventelspuitjie.
scep'sis, twyfel, ongeloof.
scep'tic, (n) twyfelaar; (a) twyfelsiek, twyfelsugtig, ongelowig; ~ **al**, skepties, ongelowig, twyfelend, twyfelsugtig; ~ *al of (about) the success*, skepties omtrent die welslae; ~**ism**, ongeloof, twyfelsug, twyfelary, skeptisisme.
scep'tre, septer; *wield the* ~, die septer swaai; ~**d**, vorstelik; ~**less**, septerloos.
scha'denfreude, leedvermaak, schadenfreude.
sched'ule, (n) lys, tabel, opgaaf, inventaris; bylae, skedule, staat; diensreëling; *AHEAD of* ~, vroeg; *BEHIND* ~, agter, *UP to* ~, op tyd; (v) op die lys plaas; 'n staat maak van; as bylae voeg by.
sched'uled, vasgestel(d), bepaald; ~ *AREA*, aange=wese (vasgestelde) gebied; ~ *to LEAVE at*, vasge=stel om te vertrek om (trein); ~ *SERVICE*, ge=reelde diens; *at the* ~ *TIME*, op die vasgestelde tyd.
Scheldt, Schelde.
schem'a, (-ta), skema; ~**t'ic**, skematies ~**tist**, ske=matis, sketser; konkelaar, knoeier; ~**tize**, skemati=seer.
scheme, (n) skema, plan, intrige, ontwerp, skets; oog=merk; *CONTRIVE a* ~, 'n plan ontwerp; ~ *of AS=SISTANCE*, hulpskema; ~ *of THINGS*, wêreld=beeld; ~ *of WORK*, leerplan; werkplan; (v) konkel, knoei, intrigeer; planne maak; ~ **r**, planmaker; knoeier, konkelaar, intrigant.
schem'ing, (n) geïntrigeer, konkelry, gemodder, tou=trekkery; (a) vol planne; beramend; intrigerend.
Schiedam', Schiedammer (jenewer).

schipp'erke, Skippertjie, Skipperke.
schism, (af)skeur(ing); verdeeldheid; skisma; ~ **at'ic**, (n) dwarstrekker, skeurder, skeurmaker; (a) skeur= makend, verdelend; ~ **atist**, skismatikus, skeurder.
schist, leisteen, skilfersteen, skis; ~ **ose**, ~ **ous**, lei= agtig, skisagtig; ~ *ose structure,* skisstruktuur, drukgelaagdheid.
schiz'oid, (n) gesplete persoonlikheid; skisoïde; (a) gesplete, skisoïed.
schizomycete', splytswam.
schizophren'ia, gespletenheid, skisofrenie.
schizophren'ic, (n) gesplete persoonlikheid; (a) ge= splete, skisofreen.
Schles'wig, Sleeswyk; ~ **-Holstein**, Sleeswyk-Hol= stein.
schnork'el, snuiwer, snorkel.
schol'ar, skolier, leerling, skoolkind; geleerde; beurs= houer; *a mere* ~, *a mere ass,* hoe geleerder hoe ver= keerder; ~ **ly**, geleerd, wetenskaplik; ~ **patrol**, sko= lierpatrollie; ~ **ship**, studiebeurs, stipendium; ge= leerdheid; kunde.
scholas'tic, (n) skolastikus; (a) skolastiek; skolasties, skools; akademies, universitêr; skool=; onderwys=; ~ **ism**, skolastiek.
schol'iast, kommentator, verklaarder, skolias.
schol'ium, (..lia), verklarende aantekening, kom= mentaar.
school[1], (n) skool (visse); ~ *of fish,* skool visse; (v) skole vorm (visse).
school[2], (n) skool; skoolgebou; oefenskool; groep, rigting; *in the* ~ *of ADVERSITY,* in die skool van beproewing; ~ *of AERONAUTICS,* lugvaart= skool; *AFTER* ~, na skooltyd; *of* ~ *(-going) AGE,* skoolpligtig; ~ *of ART,* kunsskool; *the ARTIST left no* ~ *behind him,* die kunstenaar het geen skool gestig nie; die kunstenaar het geen navolgers gehad nie; *AT* ~, op skool; ~ *of ENGINEERING,* inge= nieurskool; *DUAL-MEDIUM* ~, dubbelmedium= skool; *FROM* ~, uit die skool; *HIGH* ~, hoër= skool; *IN* ~, in die skool; *KEEP in after* ~, laat skoolsit, op skool laat bly; *LEAVE* ~, die skool verlaat; *the* ~ *of LIFE,* die leerskool v.d. lewe; ~ *of MINES,* mynbouskool; ~ *of MUSIC,* musiek= skool; *OUT of* ~, buite skooltyd; *PUT to* ~, in die skool sit; *STAY after* ~, skoolsit; *tell TALES out of* ~, uit die skool klik (klap); ~ *of THOUGHT,* denkrigting; *VISIT a* ~, 'n skool besoek; (v) on= derwys, leer, onderrig; oefen; bestraf, vermaan; ~ **administration**, skoolbestuur; ~ **age**, skoolgaande leeftyd; ~ **attendance**, skoolbesoek; ~ **-attendance officer**, skoolbesoekbeampte; ~ **badge**, skoolwa= pen; ~ **-bag**, skooltas; ~ **-bench**, skoolbank; ~ **board**, skoolraad; ~ **-book**, skoolboek; ~ **boy**, skoolseun; ~ **boyish**, skoolseunagtig; ~ **building**, skool(gebou); ~ **bus**, skoolbus; ~ **-caretaker**, skoolopsiener; S ~ **Certificate**, Skoolsertifikaat; ~ **child**, skoolkind; *treat someone like a* ~ *child,* iem. soos 'n skoolkind behandel; ~ **clothes**, skool= klere; ~ **case**, skooltas; ~ **colours**, skoolkleure; ~ **committee**, skoolkommissie; ~ **-day**, skooldag; ~ **-desk**, skoolbank; ~ **discipline**, skoolorde, skooltug; ~ **-doctor**, skooldokter; ~ **ed**, geskool; ~ **education**, skoolonderwys; ~ **exam**, ~ **examina= tion**, skooleksamen; ~ **excursion**, skooluitstappie; ~ **-farm**, skoolplaas; ~ **feeding**, skoolvoeding; ~ **fees**, skoolgeld; ~ **fellow**, skoolmaat; ~ **friend**, skoolmaat, skoolvriend; ~ **function**, skoolfees; ~ **fund**, skoolfonds; ~ **furniture**, skoolmeubels; ~ **gala**, skoolgala, ~ **-garden**, skooltuin; ~ **girl**, skooldogter, skoolmeisie; ~ **girlish**, skoolmeisieag= tig; ~ **-going**, skoolgaande; ~ **-going age**, skoolou= derdom; ~ **grounds**, skoolterrein; ~ **-holidays**, skoolvakansie; ~ **hostel**, skooltehuis, skoolkos= huis; ~ **hour**, skooluur; (pl) skooltyd; ~ **house**, skoolhuis; ~ **hygiene**, skoolhigiëne; ~ **ing**, opvoe= ding; onderwys; skool; *he has had little* ~ *ing,* hy het min onderwys geniet; maar skraal in die skrif wees; ~ **-inspection**, skoolinspeksie; ~ **-inspector**, skool= inspekteur; ~ **-instruction**, skoolonderrig; ~ **jour= ney**, skoolreis; ~ **-knowledge**, skoolse geleerdheid; ~ **language**, skooltaal; ~ **-leaver**, skoolverlater; ~ **-leaving examination**, skooleindeksamen; ~ **library**,

skoolbiblioteek; ~ **magazine**, skoolblad; ~ **man**, (..men), skoolse geleerde; opvoedkundige; ~ **mas= ter**, skoolmeester, onderwyser; ~ **mastering**, skool= houery; ~ **masterish**, skoolmeesteragtig, skoolvos= serig; ~ **masterism**, skoolmeesteragtigheid, skool= vossery; ~ **mate**, skoolmaat; ~ **material**, leermiddele; ~ **medical officer**, skoolarts; ~ **mis= tress**, skooljuffrou, onderwyseres; ~ **motto**, skool= leuse; ~ **premises**, skoolterrein; ~ **regulation**, skoolwet; ~ **report**, skoolrapport; ~ **requisites**, skoolbehoeftes; ~ **room**, klaskamer, skoolvertrek, skoolkamer, skoollokaal; ~ **s athletics**, skoleatle= tiek; ~ **session**, skoolsessie; ~ **song**, skoollied; ~ **subject**, skoolvak; ~ **-teacher**, onderwyser(es); on= nie (geselst.); ~ **-teaching**, (skool)onderwys; ~ **team**, skoolspan; skolespan; ~ **term**, skoolkwar= taal; ~ **time**, skooltyd; ~ **uniform**, skooluniform; skooldrag; ~ **-work**, skoolwerk; ~ **yard**, skool= grond, skoolterrein; ~ **year**, skooljaar.
schoon'er, skoener.
schottisch(e)', seties, Skotse polka.
sci'agram, X-straalfoto; skaduomtrek; skiagram.
sci'agraph, deursnee van 'n gebou; röntgenfoto, X-straalfoto; skiagrafie (bouk.).
sciag'raphy, röntgenfotografie; skaduweeprojeksie; skaduleer (tekenkuns).
sciam'archy, spieëlgeveg, geveg teen skaduwees (windmeulens), denkbeeldige stryd.
sciat'ic, heup=; ~ **a**, heupjig, iskias.
sci'ence, natuurwetenskap; wetenskap; kennis, kun= de; *APPLIED* ~, toegepaste wetenskap; *the DIS= MAL* ~, staathuishoudkunde; *LINGUISTIC* ~, taalwetenskap, linguistiek; *MAN of* ~, 'n weten= skaplike (man); ~ *of NUTRITION,* voedingsleer; *PHYSICAL* ~ *s,* natuurwetenskappe; *PURE* ~, suiwer wiskunde; ~ **building**, gebou vir natuur= wetenskappe; ~ **career**, wetenskaplike loopbaan; ~ **fiction**, wetenskapsfiksie; ~ **-master**, onderwyser in die natuurwetenskap.
scientif'ic, (natuur)wetenskaplik; ~ **organization**, wetenskaplike organisasie (liggaam).
sci'entist, geleerde, wetenskaplike; natuurkundige; navorser.
scientol'ogy, sciëntologie.
scil'icet, naamlik.
Scil'ly: *the* ~ *Islands,* die Sorlinge.
scim'itar, kromswaard (Oosters); ~ **-bill hoopoe**, swartbekkakelaar.
scintill'a, vonkie, sprankie; greintjie, sweempie; *not a* ~ *of evidence,* geen greintjie bewys nie.
scin'tillant, vonkelend.
scin'tillate, vonkel, flikker, tintel, skitter.
scintilla'tion, flikkering, skittering, vonkeling.
sci'olism, skyngeleerdheid.
sci'olist, halfgeleerde, skyngeleerde; ~ **'ic**, skynge= leerd.
sciom'achy, *kyk* **sciamachy**.
sci'on, spruit, kind, afstammeling; ent, steggie, stig= gie, twyg; ~ **cultivar**, bostamkultivar.
sci'rrhous, verhard.
sci'rrhus, bindweefselgewas, kankergewas.
sciss'el, metaalafknipsel, metaalafval.
sciss'ile, snybaar.
sciss'ion, snyding, (die) sny; splitsing.
sciss'or, (uit)knip; ~ **-bill**, skêrbek (voël); ~ **-grinder**, skêrslyper; boomsingertjie, sonbesie.
sciss'ors, skêr; *a PAIR of* ~, 'n skêr; ~ *and PASTE,* kompilasie; ~ **crossing**, dubbelkruising; ~ **-grin= der**, skêrslyper; sonbesie; ~ **lock**, skêrklem; ~ **movement**, skêrbeweging.
scis'sor-tooth, snytand.
sci'ssure, bars, kloof, skeuring.
sci'urine, eekhoringagtig.
sclaff, (n) ploeghou; (v) ploeg (gholf).
scler'a, buiteoogvlies, oogrok, sklera.
scleri'asis, weefselverharding.
scler'oderm, stuifswam.
sclerom'a, (-ta), **scleros'is**, (..ses), sieklike ver= harding, sklerose.
sclerose', verhard.
sclerot'ic, (n) verhardingsmiddel; oogrok; (a) (ver)= hard, skleroties.

sclerous 1211 *scourer*

scler'ous, (ver)hard.
scobs, saagsels, krulle, skaafsels, vylsel.
scoff¹, (n) kos, voedsel; (v) eet, weglê, inprop.
scoff², (n) bespotting, beskimping; voorwerp van bespotting; (v) spot, skimp, smaal, bespot; ~ *at,* bespot, beskimp; ~ **er,** spotter, skimper; ~ **ing,** (n) gespot, gesmaal, skimpery, skimptaal, spotsug; (a) spottend, skimpagtig, smalend.
scold, (n) feeks, geitjie, rissie (fig.); neulpot; (v) uitskel, beknor, uitbrander gee , berispe; bestraf, inklim, raas, skrobbeer; ~ **er,** bestrawwer, berisper; brompot.
scold'ing, (n) uitbrander, berisping, skrobbering; *get a* ~, raas kry; (a) berispend.
scolios'is, ruggraatverkromming, skoliose.
scoll'op, *kyk* **scallop.**
scolopen'dra, duisendpoot.
scom'ber, makriel.
sconce¹, (n) harspan, kop, skedel.
sconce², (n) bolwerk, skans; skerm.
sconce³, (n) armblaker, muurblaker.
sconce⁴, (n) boete; (v) beboet, straf.
scone, skon, botterbroodjie; *drop(ped)* ~, plaatkoekie.
scoop, (n) potlepel, skeplepel; skepgrafie; skepbak, skepding; skepper; skepemmer; skep; hoos; kaasboor; vangs; voordeel, wins; uitholling, holte; snip; nuussukses, groot slag, eerste mededeling, trefferberig; *MAKE a* ~, groot wins maak (gaps); groot nuus voor die ander koerante kry; *at ONE* ~, in een slag; (v) uitskep; skep (soort); uithol; 'n slag slaan; ander koerante voorspring; bymekaarskraap; ~ *OUT,* utskep; uithol, uitkap; ~ *UP,* optel, oplig; ~ **er,** uitskepper; uitholler; **-net,** skepnet; ~ **-wheel,** skeprat.
scoot, weghol, die spat neem, trap, die rieme bêre, spaander; ~ **er,** bromponie; ryplank, skopfiets, voetperd; ~ **erist,** bromponieryer.
scope, gesigskring; (speel)ruimte, geleentheid, kans; bestek; doel; omvang, trefwydte; vryheid van beweging, speling; *give AMPLE* ~, vry spel gee; *BEYOND the* ~ *of,* buitekant die plan (bestek) van; *HAVE* ~, vryheid hê; *offer a WIDE* ~, ruim veld bied; *a work of WIDE* ~, 'n werk van groot omvang.
scop'iform, besemvormig.
scop'ulite, skopuliet.
scorbut'ic, (n) skeurbuiklyer; (a) skeurbuik=, skorbutiek, aan skeurbuik lydend.
scorch, (n) (-es), skroeimerk; rit in vlieënde vaart; (v) brand, skroei, (ver)seng, blaker; braai (in son); woes jaag, wild ry; blaak; ~ *ed EARTH,* versengde (geskroeide) aarde; ~ *ed FLAVOUR,* brandsmaak; ~ **er,** iets wat skroei; snikwarm dag; mylvreter; doodhou; kopskoot; pragstuk; ~ **ing,** (n) senging; (a) verskroeiend, snikwarm, bloedig.
score, (n) keep, kerf (veral in hout); rekening, gelag; skraap, merk; twintigtal; stand, telling, aantal (behaalde) punte; partituur (musiek); lyn, streep; sukses: *BY* ~ *s,* by hope; *DEATH pays all* ~ *s,* die dood maak alles gelyk; *the* ~ *IS,* die telling is nou; *KEEP the* ~, die telling hou, aantekening hou; *tell LIES by the* ~, los en vas lieg, *LOSE the* ~, die telling kwytraak; *ON the* ~ *of,* weens, op grond van; *PAY one's* ~, betaal wat jy skuldig is; *PAY off old* ~ *s,* afreken met; *RAKE up old* ~ *s,* ou koeie uit die sloot haal; *RUN up a* ~, 'n rekening laat oploop; *SETTLE a* ~ *with someone,* met iem. afreken; *on THAT* ~, in daardie opsig; *THREE* ~, sestig; ~ *s of TIMES,* dikwels, baiemaal; *WHAT'S the* ~? hoe staan die spel? (v) kepies maak, inkerwe; sukses behaal; punte maak, 'n doel maak, punte behaal, punte aanteken (sport); skram, afskaaf; onderstreep; deurstreep (woorde); op musiek sit; tel, die telling hou, opteken; *that* ~ *s AGAINST you,* dit tel teen jou; *you will* ~ *BY it,* jy sal daardeur wen; ~ *a CENTURY,* 'n honderdtal behaal; *FAIL to* ~, geen punte behaal nie; ~ *a GOAL,* 'n doel behaal; ~ *a great HIT,* groot sukses behaal; *that IS where he* ~ *s,* dis waar hy die voorsprong het; ~ *OFF,* iem. oortroef; sukses behaal; ~ *a SUCCESS,* sukses behaal; ~ *a TRY,* 'n drie druk (aanteken);
~ *UNDER,* onderstreep; ~ *UP,* opskryf; aanteken; ~ **-board,** telbord; ~ **-book,** punteboek; ~ **-card,** telkaart, telblok, punteblok; ~ **less,** sonder punte; ~ *less draw,* nul-nulspel; ~ **r,** teller; ~ **-sheet,** puntelys.
scor'ia, metaalslak; lawabrok, vulkaniese slakke.
scoria'ceous, slakagtig, slakkerig.
scorifica'tion, metaalsuiwering.
scor'ing, puntetelling (sport); orkestrasie (musiek); kerwing; ~ *hits,* houe aanteken (speel); die teikens tref; ~ **-board,** puntebord, telbord; ~ **-card,** puntekaart, telkaart; ~ **-line,** doellyn; ~ **-surface,** telvlak.
scorn, (n) veragting, versmading, smaad, smadelikheid, skande, hoon; skamperheid; voorwerp van veragting; *HOLD up to* ~, aan die algemene veragting prysgee; *LAUGH to* ~, uitlag, bespot; *a* ~ *TO,* 'n voorwerp van veragting vir; (v) verag, versmaad, hoon, beskimp, smaad, minag; ~ *to work,* dit benede jou ag om te werk; ~ **er,** veragter; spotter, versmader.
scorn'ful, veragtend, versmadend, smadelik, skamper, minagtend; *BE* ~ *of,* verag; *SPEAK* ~ *ly of,* met veragting praat van; *THINK* ~ *ly of,* verag; ~ **ness,** smaad, minagting, veragting.
scorp'er, ctsnaald, graveeryster.
Scor'pio, die Skerpioen.
scorp'ioid, skerpioen.
scorpioid'al, skerpioenagtig.
scorp'ion, skerpioen; gesel; ~ **-grass,** vergeet-mynietjie.
scorzoner'a, skorsenier.
Scot¹, Skot; *great* ~! goeie genugtig!
scot², betaling, afrekening; belasting; *PAY* ~ *and lot,* bydra tot plaaslike belasting, *PAY someone* ~ *and lot,* met iem. afreken.
Scotch¹, (n) Skots (taal); whisky; *a SMALL* ~, 'n sopie (whisky); *THE* ~, die Skotte.
scotch², (n) (-es), kerf, insnyding; remblok, stopblok; wig; (v) kerwe; onskadelik maak; 'n blok voor 'n wiel sit; verydel; ~ *something,* 'n stokkie voor iets steek.
scotch'-block, keerblok.
Scotch: ~ **broth,** gort-en-groentesop; ~ **cart,** skotskar; ~ **cousin,** in ver bloedverwant; ~ **eggs,** eierfrikkadel; ~ **fillet,** rugfilet; ~ **light,** glimstrokies, glimplate, glimblokkies, ens.; ~ **man,** Skot; ~ **marriage,** huwelik van 'n weggelopte paar; ~ **mist,** misreën, vaarlandsdou; ~ **oath,** plegtige verklaring; ~ **rose,** duinroos; ~ **thistle,** Skotse distel; ~ **woman,** Skotse vrou.
scot'er, see-eend.
scot'-free, veilig, ongedeerd, onbeskadig; vry; belastingvry; *go* ~, sonder kleresskeur daarvan afkom; vrykom, loskom; ongedeerd uitkom.
Scot'ia, Skotland.
Scot'land, Skotland; ~ *Yard,* Scotland Yard, Londense speurdiens.
Scots, (n) Skots (taal); (a) Skots; ~ **man,** Skot(sman); ~ **woman,** Skotse vrou.
Scott: great ~! goeie genugtig!
Scott'icism, Skotse uitdrukking.
Scott'icize, verskots.
Scott'ish, (n) Skots (taal); *the* ~, die Skotte; (a) Skots; ~ **plaid,** Skotse geruit; ~ **terrier,** Skotse terriër.
scoun'drel, skelm, skurk, skobbejak, blikhouer, blikslaer, skelm, galgaas; *a THOROUGH* ~, 'n skobbejak; *an UNMITIGATED* ~, 'n deurtrapte skurk.
scour¹, (n) spoeling, afkabbeling; afskuring; maagwerking, buikloop; skittery (diere); (v) skuur, vrywe, afpoets; suiwer, reinig, skrop; uitspoel, wegvreet.
scour², (v) deurkruis; afsoek, rondsoek; rondtrek, swerf; (terrein) fynkam; deurloop; bevaar; onveilig maak; ~ *ABOUT,* rondswerf; ~ *the COASTS,* langs die kuste vaar (soek); ~ *the SEAS,* oral op die see soek.
scour'ed, gewas; geskuur, skoongemaak; ~ **basis,** skoon basis; ~ **fleece,** skoongewaste vag; ~ **wool,** gewaste wol; ~ **yield,** skoonopbrings.
scour'er, wasser; skoonmaker, skuurder; reiniger, reinigingstoestel; hardloper; landloper.

scourage, (n) gesel, geselroede; plaag, besoeking; kastyding; (v) kasty, teister; gesel; ~r, geselaar, kastyder.
scour'ing, (af)skuring, wrywing; spoeling; maagwerking (vee); afkabbeling; (pl) vuilgoed; afskuursel, skuursels; skuim, uitvaagsel, uitskot; ~ **agent**, skuurmiddel; ~-**awl**, kerfels; ~-**cloth**, skuurlap; ~-**mill**, wolwassery; ~ **pad**, skuurkussinkie; ~ **powder**, skuurpoeier; ~ **soap**, skuurseep; ~ **wool**, skuurwol.
scour' valve, spoelklep.
scout[1], (n) spioen, verkenner, verspieder; verkenning; verkenningsvaartuig; verkenningsvliegtuig; *on the* ~, op verkenning uit; (v) spioen(eer), verken, verspied, op verkenning uitgaan.
scout[2], (v) veragtelik afwys, met minagting verwerp; bespot.
scout: ~ **activities**, verkenningswerk; ~ **car**, verkenningspantserwa; ~ **corps**, verkenningskorps; ~**craft**, padvindery, verkennerskuns.
scout'ing, bespieding; verkenning, verkenningsdiens; ~ **activities**, verkenningswerk; ~ **flight**, verkenningsvlug; ~ **machine (plane)**, verkenningsvliegtuig.
scout: ~**master**, troeppleier (van Padvinders), Padvinderleier; ~ **patrol**, verkenningspatrollie.
scow, platboomskuit, praam.
scowl, (n) suur gesig, frons, misnoegde blik; (v) suur kyk, frons; ~ *at*, nors (kwaad) aankyk; frons; ~**ing**, suur, fronsend, kwaad.
scrabb'le, (n) gekrabbel, gekrap; (v) krabbel (skrif); vroetel; skarrel; klouter; skrop (hoenders).
scrag, (n) maer persoon of dier; dun, reepagtige plant; knoes; (v) (**-ged**), nek omdraai; ophang; aan die nek gryp, seer maak; ~-**end**, bonekstuk; ~-**giness**, maerte; dunheid; ~**gy**, maer, brandmaer, dun, vel en been.
scram, trap, vlug, weghol.
scram'ble, (n) gewoel; geklouter; gespook, gestoei; gegrabbel; *the* ~ *for GOLD*, die wedloop om goud; *MAKE a* ~ *for*, stoeiend losstorm op; (v) (af)klouter; grabbel, oormekaar val; stoei (sport); worstel, woel; roereiers bak; radbraak, verwar (boodskap); ~*d EGGS*, roereiers; ~ *a MESSAGE*, 'n boodskap verwar (radbraak); ~ *MONEY together*, geld bymekaarskraap; ~ *through one's WORK*, jou werk haastig afmaak; ~ **telephone**, grabbelteleffoon; ~**r**, klouteraar, grabbelaar; hutselaar (persoon), hutser (rekenaar).
scram'bling, klouterend, grypend, grabbelend; deurmekaar; slordig; haastig; ~ *plant*, klouterplant.
scran'nel, skraal; swak; dun, maer; pieperig.
scrap, (n) brok, stuk; oorskot, afval; greintjie; ou-yster, ysterafval; visafval; skroot; snipper, vodjie (papier); uitknipsel; bakleiery, vegparty; (pl) res; afvalvleis, afvalstukkies (vleis); afvalmateriaal; uitskraapsel, oorskietkos; *they had a BIT of a* ~, hulle het gehaak; *not CARE a* ~, geen flenter omgee nie; *EVERY* ~, elke stukkie en brokkie; *not a* ~ *of EVIDENCE*, nie 'n greintjie bewys nie; nie die minste bewys nie; *NOT a* ~, geen stukkie nie; *a* ~ *of PAPER*, 'n vodjie papier; *SELL as* ~, vir afbraak verkoop; (v) (**-ped**), skrap; afkeur; op die ashoop gooi; weggooi; afdank, verwerp; sloop (skip); baklei, rusie maak; ~-**book**, uitknipselboek, plakboek; ~-**dump**, afvalhoop, vuilgoedhoop.
scrape, (n) gekrap; gekras; verleentheid, moeilikheid; *BE in a* ~, in die knyp sit; *GET into a* ~, in moeilikheid beland; (v) skraap, krap; afvee (skoene); kras; skuur; ~ *ACQUAINTANCE with someone*, jou by iem. indring; ~ *AGAINST*, krap teen; ~ *AWAY*, afkrap; ~ *one's BOOTS*, jou skoene afskraap; ~ *one's CHIN*, skeer; ~ *DOWN*, afkrap; ~ *one's FEET*, met die voete skuif; ~ *HOME*, naelskraap wen; ~ *OFF*, afskraap; ~ *THROUGH*, deurskraap; net deurglip; net die paal haal; ~ *TOGETHER*, bymekaarskraap; *WORK and* ~ *as you may*, arbei en besuinig soveel as jy wil.
scrap'er, skrop; krapper, skrapper; skraper (gholf); krapyster; afstootmes (by slag); sieglem (hout).
scrap' heap, ashoop, vuilgoedhoop, afvalhoop, roeshoop; uitskothoop; *CONSIGN to the* ~, *THROW*

onto the ~, op die ashoop gooi, afdank, weggooi; *THROW a scheme on the* ~, 'n plan in die doofpot stop.
scrap'ing, (n) geskraap; geskuifel (voete); (pl) (boom)skraapsel; afval; sameskraapsel; (a) skraapagtig; skraperig.
scrap: ~-**iron**, ou-yster, ysterafval, skrootyster; ~-**leather**, leerafval; ~ **metal**, afvalmetaal; ~ **per**, vegter, bakleier, twissoeker, rusiemaker; ~ **pie**, oorskietpastei; ~**piness**, onsamehangendheid; ~**py**, onsamehangend, fragmentaries, in stukkies en brokkies; ~ **tray**, afvalbak; ~-**value**, afvalwaarde, rommelwaarde; ~-**wood**, afvalhout; ~ **yard**, afvalwerf, rommelwerf, roeswerf, skrootysterwerf, wrakwerf.
scratch, (n) wegspringlyn, gelykstaan (wedloop); nul (gholf); grif; (**-es**), krap, skrapie; skram; streep; *BRING someone up to* ~, iem. help om die vereiste peil te bereik; *COME off without a* ~, sonder 'n skraap daarvan afkom; *COME up to* ~, verwagtings vervul; jou plig nakom; *not FEELING up to* ~, nie lekker (fiks) voel nie; *FROM* ~, v.d. staanspoor af; v.d. begin af; *a* ~ *of the PEN*, 'n penstreep; *START from* ~, niks voorkry nie; by nul begin; (v) krap, skraap; skram; uitskraap; terugtrek (sport); bekrap (papier); trek (vuurhoutjie); ~ *ALONG*, aansukkel; *you* ~ *my BACK and I'll* ~ *yours*, krap jy my rug, dan krap ek joue; ~ *one's HEAD*, jou kop krap; ~ *a HORSE*, 'n perd terugtrek; ~ *OUT*, uitkrap; ~ *a RACE*, 'n wedloop (reisies) afstel; ~ *a RUSSIAN and you'll find a Tartar*, jy dink jy het 'n engel aan die kop en jy het 'n duiwel aan die stert; ~ *THROUGH*, doodtrek, deurhaal; (a) saamgeraap, bymekaargeskraap; optel; van die streep af; ~ **awl**, krasser; ~-**back**, rugkrapper; ~-**brush**, krapborsel; ~ **er**, krapper; krasser; ~-**gauge**, skryfblok (myn); kraspen; ~**ing**, (n) gekrap, gekrabbel; gekras; (pl) skraapsel; (a) krapperig; krassend; skraperig; ~ **majority**, toevallige meerderheid; ~ **man**, nulman; ~ **mark**, krapmerk; nulmerk, afsitstreep; ~ **pad**, kladblok; ~ **player**, nulspeler; ~-**proof**, krapbestand; ~ **race**, gelykstaanwedloop; ~ **side**, ~ **team**, saamgeraapte span, raap-en-skraapspan; ~ **vote**, onvoorhoedse stemming; ~-**wig**, pruikie; ~**y**, bymekaar geskraap; krassend; krapperig; krabbelrig, onduidelik; onafgewerk.
scrawl, (n) slordige skrif, gekrap, gekrabbel, kattebelletjie; (v) slordig skrywe, onleesbaar skrywe, krap, krabbel; ~ **er**, krapper.
scrawn'y, maer, dun, skraal, vel en been.
scray, visdief (voël); seeswael.
scream, (n) skreeu, gier, gil; ~ *s of LAUGHTER*, uitbundige geskater; *it's a PERFECT* ~, dis baie verspot; dis belaglik; dis genoeg om jou oor slap te lag; (v) skreeu, gil; ~ *with LAUGHTER*, skater v.d. lag; ~**er**, raasbek; doring, bobaas; malspul; watervoël.
scream'ing, (n) gegier, geskreeu, gegil; (a) skreeuend; rasend; ~ *COLOURS*, skreeuende kleure; *a* ~ *FARCE*, 'n verspotte klug.
scream'ingly, dol, uiters grappig; ~ **funny**, uiters gek, besonder grapperig, skreeusnaaks.
scream'y, skel, lawaaierig, skreeuerig.
scree, klippieshelling.
screech, (n) (**-es**), skreeu, gil; (v) skreeu, gil; kras; ~**ing**, gegil; gekras, gekrys; ~-**owl**, steenuil, naguil, kerkuil.
screed, (n) langdradige toespraak; lang klaagbrief, jeremiade; krasgeluid; gidspleister; profielgids (padbou); vlaklaag; (v) afvlak.
screen, (n) (projeksie)skerm; beskutting, masker; doek, film; sandsif; voorruit (motor); raster (drukkery); sif; *REVOLVING* ~, trommelsif; *THROW on the* ~, op die doek gooi (wys); *UNDER* ~ *of night*, onder bedekking van die nag; (v) beskerm; beskut; afskerm; masker; bedek; sif; keur, gradeer; deurlig (radiologie); noukeurig uitvra (uitpluis); afdraai; vertoon, aanplak; verfilm; ~ *off*, afskort; ~ **actor**, rolprentspeler; ~ **door**, gaasdeur, sifdeur; ~ **grid**, skermrooster; ~**ing**, (n) afskerming; vertoning (op doek); rasterwerk (drukw.);

screw, (n) skroef; woekeraar, vrek; ou knol, armsalige perd; salaris; krul, draaiorrel (tennis); trek (biljart); draaiskop (voetbal); *have a ~ LOOSE*, van lotjie getik wees; *he has a ~ LOOSE*, daar is 'n skroef los by hom; hy het 'n slag v.d. windmeul weg; sy bont varkie is weg; hy is van lotjie getik; *there is a ~ LOOSE*, daar is 'n speek los; *PUT the ~ on*, die duimskroewe aansit; (v) vasskroef; druk; draai, krul (tennis); draadsny; afpers; vertrek (gesig); afpers, uitsuig; gierig wees; *~ a BALL*, 'n bal laat krul; *~ up COURAGE*, moed bymekaarskraap; moed vat (skep); *~ up someone's DOOR*, iem. opsluit; *~ DOWN*, vasskroef; *~ up one's EYES*, jou oë op 'n skrefie trek; *his HEAD is ~ed on the right way*, hy weet wat hy doen; *~ HOME*, goed vasdraai, wegskroef; *~ IN*, vasskroef; *~ OFF*, afskroef; *~ ON*, aanskroef; *~ OUT of*, afpers; *~ UP one's face*, die gesig vertrek; *~ someone UP*, iem. druk; **~ anchor**, skroefanker; **~ bacterium**, skroefbakterie; **~ binding**, skroefband; **~ bolt**, skroefbout; **~-cap**, skroefdop; **~ coupling**, skroefkoppeling; **~ cup**, dopwaster; **~-cutter**, draadsnyer; **~-cutting**, draadsnywerk; **~ driver**, skroewedraaier.

screwed, verdraaid, saamgetrek; met skroefdraad (bout); besope, aangeklam; **~ bush**, skroefbos; **~ conduit**, skroefpyp; **~ nut**, skroefmoer; **~ plug**, skroefprop.

screw: ~-end, skroefent; **~ gear**, skroefrat; **~-hook**, skroefhaak; **~-jack**, domkrag, skroefdomkrag, hefbok; **~-key**, skroefsleutel; **~ kick**, draaiskop (rugby); **~-nut**, moer; **~-picket**, skroefpen; draaipen; **~ press**, skroefpers; **~-propeller**, skroef (skip); **~-rivet**, skroefnael, **~-shaft**, skroefas; **~-shaped**, skroefvorming; **~-spanner**, skroefsleutel; **~ steamer**, skroefboot; **~-stoppered**, (bottel) met skroefsluiting; **~-tap**, skroefboor; **~ thread**, skroefdraad; **~-top**, skroefdeksel; **~ vice**, bankskroef; **~-wrench**, skroefhamer, moersleutel; **~y**, kronkelend; skroefagtig; vrekkig, gierig; getik; dronkerig, aangeklam.

scrib'ble[1], (n) gekrap, gekrabbel; (v) krap, (af)krabbel; *~ down*, neerkrabbel.

scrib'ble[2], (v) grofkaard (wol).

scrib'bler, krapper; kladskrywer; prulskrywer, kladboek, kladskrif.

scribb'ling, gekrap; skrywery; **~-block**, kladskrif, kladboek; **~-book**, kladboek; **~-itch**, skryfjeukte, skryfsiekte; **~ paper**, kladpapier; **~-tablet**, kladblok(kie).

scribe, (n) skrywer; klerk; skrifgeleerde; sekretaris, skriba; kraspen; (v) skryf, merk, **~ r**, kraspen; **~-saw**, klein spansaag, profielsaag.

scrib'ing gouge, steekguts.

scrim, voeringlinne; toneellinne.

scrimm'age, stoeiery; los skrum; skermutseling, worsteling, bakleiery; *kyk ook* **scrum**.

scrimp, vrekkig wees; beknibbel; besuinig; afskeep; *~(i)ness*, suinigheid; gebrek(kigheid); **~y**, suinig, vrekkig.

scrim'shank, ontduik, versuim; **~er**, pligsversuimer; papbroek; bangbroek.

scrim'shaw, (n) knutselwerk (van matrose); (v) knutsel; skulpe verf, versier.

scrip[1], sakkie, tas.

scrip[2], briefie; stukkie papier; aandele(sertifikaat).

script, geskrif; skrif, handskrif; manuskrip; teks; skryfletter; antwoordboek (by 'n eksamen); draaiboek (rolprent); **~ letter**, skryfletter; **~ or'ium**, (..ria, -s), skryfvertrek.

script'ual, scrip'tural, skrifuurlik, Bybels; skrifmatig; skrif=; *~ doctrine*, Bybelleer.

script'ure, 'n heilige geskrif, skriftuur; *the S ~ s, Holy S ~*, die Heilige Skrif, die Bybel.

script'-writer, teksskrywer.

scrive, grif, graveer.

scriv'ener, makelaar, agent; notaris, skrywer; **~'s palsy**, skryfkramp.

scrof'ula, kliersiekte, skrofulose.

scrofulos'is, skrofulose.

scrof'ulous, klieragtig, skrofuleus; moreel besoedel; *~ness*, klieragtigheid.

scroll, (n) lys; krul; rol, perkamentrol; krullys; krulversiering; *his ~ is heavily CHARGED*, iem. het baie op sy boekie; iem. se boekie is vol; *~ of the LAW*, wetsrol; (v) oprol; met krulle versier; **~ ed**, met krulle; **~ end**, krulkant; **~-saw**, figuursaag, krulsaag; **~ work**, figuurwerk, krulwerk.

scroop, skarrel.

scrot'al, balsak=, skrotaal.

scrot'ocele, balbreuk.

scrot'um, (..ta), teelsak, balsak, skrotum.

scrounge, gaps, skaai, vaslê; bedel; *~ a cigarette from a friend*, 'n sigaret van 'n vriend bedel; **~ r**, vaslêer, gapser; bedelaar.

scrub, (n) pruldier; buk(sie); subsituutspeler; skrop; skropborsel; ruigte, struikgewas, kreupelhout; (v) **(-bed)**, skrop, skuur; swoeg; (a) dwergagtig; verpot (dier); afgeknot (plant); prul=, prullerig (dier); nietig; **~ ber**, skropper; krapborsel, draadborsel; gasreiniger; **~ bing**, (n) (die) skrop, geskuur; swoeg; (af)feil; (a) skrop=; **~ bing-brush**, skropborsel; **~ bing-cloth**, dweil(lap), skroplap; **~ bing day**, skropdag; **~-board**, spatlys; **~-oak**, dwergeik; **~-robin**, wipstertjie; **~ by**, armsalig; dwergagtig, klein; prullerig; ruig; **~-cattle**, prulbeeste, **~-plane**, skropskaaf; **~-tree**, dwergboom, kreupelbos.

scruff, agternek; *take by the ~ of the neck*, agter die nek beetkry.

scruff'y, slordig, vuil; verspot.

scrum, (n) skrum, oond (rugby); worsteling; *put the ball in the ~*, gooi die bal in die skrum; sit die brood in die oond; (v) **(-med)**, worstel; skrum; **~ cap**, skrumpet; **~ formation**, skrumformasie; **~ half**, skrumskakel; **~ mage = scrimmage; ~ mager**, skrummer; **~ maging**, skrumwerk.

scrump'tious, uitstekend, aangenaam; eersteklas; *be ~*, vorentoe (eersteklas) smaak.

scrunch, kraak, knars.

scru'ple, (n) beswaar; aarseling; gewetensbeswaar, skrupule; skroom; skrupel (20 grein); *HAVE ~ s about*, gemoedsbeswaar hê oor; *MAKE no ~*, geen beswaar maak nie; nie aarsel nie; *have NO ~ s*, niks ontsien nie; *have no ~ to SAY it*, nie aarsel om dit te sê nie; *a man WITHOUT ~*, 'n gewetenlose persoon; (v) swarigheid maak, aarsel; skroom; gewetensbeswaar hê.

scrupulos'ity = scrupulousness.

scru'pulous, nougeset, angsvallig, sorgvuldig, nouletttend, noukeurig, stip, skrupuleus; *~ honesty*, stipte eerlikheid; **~ ly**, nougeset, sorgvuldig, noukeurig, stip; *~ ly clean*, kraaksindelik, uiters skoon; **~ ness**, angsvalligheid, skroomvalligheid; stiptheid, nougesetheid, konsensieusheid.

scrutat'or, ondersoeker, navorser.

scrutineer', stemopnemer, nateller; ondersoeker.

scru'tinize, noukeurig ondersoek, napluis, nasnuffel; natel; navors; *~ r*, ondersoeker, navorser.

scru'tinous, ondersoekend.

scru'tiny, noukeurige ondersoek, betragting, navorsing; natelling (van stemme); *subject to ~*, onderworpe aan toesig; *be UNDER ~*, ondersoek word.

scry, (scried), die toekoms in 'n kristal lees.

scud, (n) vaart, vlug; verbygaande bui, drywende wolke; (v) **(-ded)**, hardloop, jaag, wegyl; drywe, vlieg (wolke).

scuff, sleepvoetend loop, skuur; skuifel.

scuff'le, (n) vegparty, stoeiery, worsteling, gespook, deurmekaar geveg; (v) stoei, veg, harwar, plukhaar, skermutsel, baklei, spook; skuifel; **~ r**, skoffelpik.

sculdugg'ery, *kyk* **skulduggery**.

scull, (n) (ligte) roeispaan; skulriem; skulboot; (v) roei met twee rieme, skifroei; **~er**, roeier, skuller; skulboot.

scull'ery, (..ries), wasplek, waskombuis, bykombuis, kleinkombuisie, washok, opwasplek, spoelkombuis; skottelgoedkamer; ~ **maid**, kombuishulp.

scull'ion, kombuisjong, skottelwasser; *make someone your* ~, iem. vir 'n vadoek gebruik.

sculp, beeldhou; ~ **tor**, beeldhouer; ~ **tress**, (-es), beeldhou(d)ster; ~ **tural**, beeldhou-, beeldhouers-; ~ **ture**, (n) beeldhoukuns; beeld(hou)werk; (v) beeldhou; uitsny; uitkap; graveer; ~ *tured frieze*, figuurfries; ~ **turesque**', asof dit gebeeldhou is, skultureel.

scum, (n) skuim; afval, uitvaagsel; *the* ~ *of the earth*, die laagste gespuis; (v) (-**med**,) afskuim; skuim.

scum'ble, (n) dekkleur, newelkleur; (v) 'n dekkleur aanbring; verdoesel.

scum: ~-**board**, skuimspaan; ~-**cock**, skuimkraan; ~ **mer**, skuimspaantjie; ~ **ming**, (af)skuiming; ~ **s**, afskuimsel; skuim; ~ **my**, skuimagtig, skuim-.

scunn'er, (n) teensin; *take a* ~ *at (against)*, walg van, met afkeer vervul word; (v) walg.

scupp'er, (n) spuigat; dwarsgeut (pad); (v) deur die spuigate loop; in die grond boor; tot sink bring; ~-**hole**, spuigat; ~-**hose**, ~-**shoot**, geut buitekant die spuigat.

scurf, roof; skurfte; roos; skilfer; kors, aanpaksel; ~ **iness**, roosagtigheid; skurftigheid; ~ **y**, met roos bedek; skilferagtig; skurftig.

scu'rrile, laag, gemeen, plat, vuil.

scurril'ity, laagheid, gemeenheid, platheid.

scu'rrilous, laag, gemeen, vuil; ~ **ness = scurrility**.

scu'rry, (n) geloop, gevlug; haas; (v) (**scurried, scurried**), weghardloop, heenskeer; wegtrippel.

scurv'iness, skurwigheid; veragtelikheid, smerigheid.

scurv'y, (n) skeurbuik; (a) aan skeurbuik lydend; gemeen, veragtelik, smerig; *play someone a* ~ *trick*, iem. 'n gemene poets bak.

scut, stompstert, haasstert.

scut'ate, skildvormig, skubbig (dierk.).

scutch, (n) pikhamer; (v) uitslaan; suiwer.

scutch'eon, wapenskild; sleutelskild, beslag; naambord, naamplaatjie.

scut'ellate, skildvormig; skottelvormig.

scutell'um, (..lla), skildjie, doppie, skutellum.

scut'iform, skildvormig.

scut'tle[1], (n) steenkoolbak, (steen)koolemmer.

scut'tle[2], (n) vlug, haastige ontruiming; hardloop; (v) vlug, op loop sit, weghardloop.

scut'tle[3], (n) luik; luikgat, valdeur; (v) die luike oopmaak, 'n skip self laat sink; gate in 'n skip boor; ~-**butt**, ~-**cask**, drinkfontein, watervat; ~-**port**, patryspoort.

scut'um, (..ta), skild; knieskyf; dop; skub (dierk.).

Scyl'la, Skilla; *between* ~ *and Charybdis*, tussen Skilla en Charybdis; tussen twee vure.

scythe, (n) sens, seis; (v) met 'n sens maai; sny.

Scyth'ian, (n) Skith; Skithies (taal); (a) Skithies.

sea, see; deining, golf, branding; oorvloed; menigte; *AT* ~, op see; *BE at* ~, op see wees; die kluts kwyt wees; in die middel van die wêreld wees; in die war wees; *BEYOND the* ~ *s*, in anderland; *BY* ~, oor see; *BY the* ~, aan die see; *the* ~ *can't CLEANSE him*, al die water v.d. see kan dit nie van hom afwas nie; *FOLLOW the* ~, op see gaan; *on the* ~ *FRONT*, by die see; *when the* ~ *GIVES up its dead*, by die opstanding; *GO to* ~, matroos word; *be HALF* ~ *s over*, hoenderkop wees; *there was a HIGH (heavy)* ~, die see was onstuimig; *on the HIGH* ~ *s*, op die oop see; *by LAND and* ~, te land en ter see; *embark on the* ~ *of MATRIMONY*, in die huweliksbootjie stap; *ON the* ~, op see; *PUT out to* ~, van wal steek; *a* ~ *of TROUBLES*, 'n oseaan van leed; ~ **acorn**, eendemossel; ~-**action**, seegeveg; ~ **aerodrome**, ~ **airport**, seevliegveld; ~ **air**, seelug; ~-**anchor**, seeanker; ~ **anemone**, seeanemoon, seeroos; ~ **attack**, seeaanval; ~-**bank**, seedyk; sandbank; ~ **bass**, seebaars; ~ **bear**, ysbeer; ~-**beaten**, deur die see geslaan, aan die see blootgestel; ~-**bed**, seebedding, seebodem; ~-**blue**, seeblou; ~-**board**, seekus, seegebied, kusstrook; ~-**boat**, seewaardige skip; seeboot; ~-**boot**, seelaars; ~-**born**, uit die see; op see gebore; ~-**borne**, oorsees; oor see aangevoer; see-; ~-**borne troops**, seetransporttroepe; ~-**breach**, deurbraak; ~-**bream**, seebrasem; ~-**breeze**, seewind; ~ **cadet**, seekadet; ~-**calf**, seehond, rob; ~ **canary**, wit dolfyn; ~ **captain**, skeepskaptein; ~-**carriage**, seetransport, seevervoer; ~ **chart**, seekaart; ~ **chest**, seemanskis; ~ **coast**, seekus; ~ **communication**, seeverbinding; ~ **cook**, skeepskok; ~-**cow**, walrus; ~ **crab**, seekrap; ~ **crow**, kokmeeu; ~ **damage**, seeskade; ~-**damaged**, deur seewater beskadig; ~-**devil**, seeduiwel; ~-**dog**, hondshaai; seehond, pikbroek; ~ **drome**, seevliegveld; ~ **eagle**, seearend; ~-**ear**, perlemoer; ~ **eel**, seepaling; ~ **egg**, seeegel; ~ **elephant**, seeolifant; ~ **farer**, seevaarder, skepeling, seeman; ~ **faring**, (n) seevaart; (a) seevarend; ~ **fennel**, seevinkel; ~-**fight**, seegeveg, seeslag; ~-**fire**, blinkwater; ~-**fish**, seevis; ~-**fishing**, seevissery; ~-**flea**, seevlooi; ~-**flower**, seeanemoon; ~-**foam**, seeskuim; ~ **fog**, seemis; ~ **food**, visgeregte, seekos; ~-**fowl**, seevoël; ~ **front**, seekant, strandgedeelte; ~-**gauge**, diepgang; peiltoestel, dieptemeter; ~-**gear**, seegerei; ~-**girt**, deur die see omring; ~-**god**, seegod; ~ **going**, seevarend; ~-**grass**, seegras; wier; ~-**green**, seegroen; ~-**gull**, seemeeu; ~ **hawk**, visarend; ~ **haze**, seenewel; ~-**head**, seehoof; ~-**hog**, bruinvis, seevark; ~ **holly**, seedistel; ~-**horse**, seeperdjie; walrus; ~-**kale**, seekool; ~-**king**, seekoning; ~-**kit**, seemansuitrusting.

seal[1], (n) seeleeu, rob; (v) robbe vang.

seal[2], (n) seël; stempel; beseëling; stempelafdruk; yk-merk; lak; *the GREAT S* ~, die Rykseël; *under his HAND and* ~, deur hom geteken en verseël; *LEADEN* ~, loodseël; ~ *of LOVE*, liefdespand; ~ *of OFFICE*, ampseël; *the PRIVY S* ~, die Geheimseël; *PUT one's* ~ *to*, jou seël heg aan; *under the* ~ *of SECRECY*, onder die seël van geheimhouding; *SET one's* ~ *to*, jou goedkeuring heg aan; *SET the* ~ *on something*, die seël op iets druk; *UNDER* ~, verseël; (v) beseël, bekragtig, bevestig; toelak, verseël; (af)dig; *a* ~ *ed BOOK*, 'n geslote boek; ~ *DOWN*, verseël; *a* ~ *ed ENVELOPE*, toegeplakte koevert; *his FATE is* ~ *ed*, sy vonnis is gevel; ~ *HERMETICALLY*, hermeties sluit; ~ *with a KISS*, met 'n soen beseël; *a* ~ *ed LETTER*, 'n verseëlde brief; *his LIPS are* ~ *ed*, hy mag niks sê nie; ~ *someone's LIPS*, iem. die mond snoer; iem. belet om iets te sê; ~ *ed ORDERS*, verseëlde bevele; ~ *up a TIN*, 'n blik toesoldeer; ~ *ed UP in ice*, ingevries; *the WINDOWS must be* ~ *ed up*, die vensters moet toegeplak word.

sea: ~ **lace**, seewier; ~ **lamprey**, seeprik; ~ **lane**, vaargeul; ~-**law**, seewet; seereg; ~ **lawyer**, vitterige persoon; korrelkop; ~-**legs**, seebene; *find (get) one's* ~-*legs*, jou seebene kry, leer om jou maklik op die dek te beweeg.

seal'er[1], robbejagter; robbeskip.

seal'er[2], verseëlaar; deklaag.

sea'-letter, seebrief.

sea'-level, seevlak, seespieël; *ABOVE* ~, bokant die seespieël (seevlak); *AT* ~, by die seevlak (seespieël).

seal'-fishery, robbevissery, robbevangs.

sea: ~ **life**, seelewe; ~-**line**, horison, kim; kus; lang vislyn.

seal'ing[1], robbejag.

seal'ing[2], bekragtiging, bevestiging; digting; ~ **agent**, digtingsmiddel; ~ **coat**, deklaag; afdiglaag; ~ **ring**, digtingsring.

seal'ing vessel, robbevaarder.

seal'ing wax, lak; ~ **tree**, kiaat *(Pterocarpus angolensis)*.

sea: ~-**lion**, seeleeu; *S* ~ *Lord*, lid van die admiraliteit in Engeland.

seal' ring, seëlring.

seal: ~-**rookery**, robbekolonie; ~ **skin**, robbevel.

seam, (n) soom, naat; aar, laag (kole); rimpel; *be BURSTING out of its* ~ *s*, uit sy klere groei; oor sy grense stroom; uit die nate bars; *CIRCULAR* ~, ringnaat; ~ *of COAL*, koollaag; *FRENCH* ~, rolnaat; *IN* ~ *s*, laagvormig; *LAPPED* ~, sluitnaat; *RUN and fell* ~, platnaat.

sea: ~ **man**, seeman, matroos; seevaarder, varensgesel; ~ **manship,** seemanskap, stuurmanskap; ~-**mark,** seebaken; ~ **men's institute,** seemanshuis; ~-**mew,** seemeeu; ~ **mile,** seemyl; ~ **mist,** seenewel; seemis.

sea'mer, naatbouler.

seam: ~ **bowler,** naatbouler; ~-**bowling,** naatboul; ~-**bowling attack,** naat(boul)aanval; ~-**lap,** naatrand; ~ **less,** sonder naat, naatloos.

sea' monster, seemonster.

seam: ~-**presser,** parsyster; ~ **stress, (-es),** naaister; ~-**weld,** naatsweislas; ~-**welding,** naatsweiswerk; ~ **y,** vol nate; ~ *y side,* verkeerde kant, keerkant; ongunstige (lelike) kant; *the* ~ *y side (of life),* die donker (lelike) kant v.d. lewe.

sé'ance, sitting, séance.

sea: ~ **needle,** geep; ~-**nymph,** seenimf; ~-**onion,** seeajuin; ~ **otter,** seeotter; ~-**ox,** walrus; ~-**pad,** seester; ~ **paper,** seebrief; ~ **parrot,** papegaaiduiker; ~-**pass,** seepas; ~-**piece,** seestuk, seegesig; ~-**pig,** seevark; dolfyn; ~-**pigeon,** seeduif; ~-**pike,** snoek; ~-**pink,** Engelse gras; papierkruid; ~ **plane,** seevliegtuig; ~ **plant,** seeplant; ~ **polyp,** seepoliep; ~ **port,** (see)hawe; ~ **port town,** haweplaas, haweplek; ~-**post,** seepos; ~ **power,** seemag; seemoondheid; ~ **quake,** seebewing.

sear¹, (n) tuimelaar (geweer).

sear², (v) brand, verskroei, uitbrand, toeskroei, digskroei; verhard; ~ *a wound,* 'n wond toeskroei; (a) droog, dor.

search, (n) ondersoek, soekery, soek; deursoeking, visentasie, huissoeking; *MAKE a* ~ *for,* soek na; (v) soek; ondersoek, naspeur, (na)snuffel, deursoek, vors; visenteer; peil; ~ *FOR,* soek na; ~ *someone FOR (weapons),* iem. visenteer (vir wapens); ~ *one's HEART,* jou hard deurgrond; *IN* ~ *of health,* op soek na gesondheid; ~ *a WOUND,* 'n wond peil; ~ **able,** te ondersoek; ~ **er,** soeker; deursoeker, huissoeker; visenteeryster; botterboor; visenteermes; sondeernaald, peilstif; ~ **ing, (n)** ondersoek, deursoeking, (a) deurdringend, ondersoekend, deurvorsend, grondig; noukeurig, diepgaande; ~**ing fire,** soekvuur; ~-**lamp,** soeklamp; ~ **light,** soeklig; *throw the* ~ *light onto something,* die soeklig op iets werp; ~-**party,** soekgeselskap; ~-**warrant,** visenteerbrief, lasbrief vir huissoeking.

sea' reed, helmgras.

sear'ing-iron, brandyster.

sea: ~-**risk,** seerisiko; ~ **rover,** seeskuimer, roofskip; swerwer op see; ~-**salt,** seesout; ~-**sand,** seesand; ~ **scape,** seegesig, seestuk; ~ **serpent,** seeslang; ~-**shanty,** matrooslied; ~ **shark,** withaai; ~-**shell,** seeskulp; ~ **shore,** seekus, seestrand; ~ **sick,** seesiek; ~ **sickness,** seesiekte.

sea'side, strand; seekant; *AT the* ~, aan die strand; *GO to the* ~, strand toe gaan; ~ **bungalow,** strandhuis; ~ **cottage,** strandhuisie; ~ **resort,** strandplek, strandoord; ~ **wear,** stranddrag.

sea: ~ **slug,** seeslak; tripang, seekomkommer; ~ **snail,** seeslak; ~ **snake,** seeslang.

seas'on, (n) seisoen, jaargety; geskikte tyd; tydperk; bronstyd; *at ALL* ~ *s,* altyd; *the DEAD (dull)* ~, die komkommertyd; *FOR a* ~, 'n tyd lank; *FRUIT in* ~, vrugte na die seisoen; *in GOOD* ~, op sy tyd; op sy plek; *at the HEIGHT of the* ~, in die drukste tyd v.d. seisoen; *IN* ~, tydig; gedurende die seisoen; *IN* ~ *and out of* ~, te pas en te onpas; *OUT of* ~, te onpas, ontydig; *the RAINY* ~, die reëntyd; *THE* ~ *s,* die jaargetye; *a WORD in* ~, 'n woord op sy tyd; *a WORD spoken in due* ~, *how good it is,* 'n pak op sy tyd is soos brood en konfyt; (v) geskik maak; smaaklik maak, geur, kruie; ontvars; ryp maak; laat droog word (hout); gewoon(d) word aan; akklimatiseer; temper, matig; ~ *a DISH of herbs,* 'n gereg kerrie; *let MERCY* ~ *justice,* laat geregtigheid deur barmhartigheid getemper word; ~ *MORTAR,* kalk insuur; ~ *oneself to hard WORK,* jou aan harde werk gewoond maak; ~ **able,** geskik, geleë, tydig; aktueel; passend by die seisoen.

seas'onal, seisoen(s)=, jaargetye=; ~ **greetings,** Kers= en Nuwejaarsgroete; ~ **valve,** weerklep, seisoens=

klep; ~ **industry,** seisoenbedryf; ~ **variation,** jaargetyeverskil; ~ **worker,** seisoenwerker.

seas'oned, gekruie, gesout, gepeper; beleë, droog (hout); ~ **food,** gekruide kos; ~ **iron,** getemperde yster; ~ **soldiers,** geharde soldate; ~ **wood,** gedroogde (beleë) hout.

seas'on: ~**ing,** toebereiding, klaarmaak; kruiesous, smaakmiddel, kruisel; geursel; ontvarsing; kruidery; droging (hout); ~ **less,** sonder jaargetye; ~-**ticket,** seisoenkaartjie.

sea' spray, bruiswater, seeskuim, brandersproei.

seat, (n) sitplek; stoel; gestoelte; sitting; setel; toneel; buiteplaas; landgoed; sitvlak, boom (van 'n broek); bril (van kleinhuisie); bedding; *take a BACK* ~, op die agtergrond raak; *have a* ~ *on a BOARD,* 'n setel in die raad hê; *BOOK* ~ *s,* plekke bespreek; *have a* ~ *on the COMMITTEE,* sitting in die komi= tee hê; *the DISEASE has its* ~ *in the liver,* die siekte het sy oorsprong in die lewer; *have a FIRM* ~, vas in die saal sit; *have a GOOD* ~, netjies op 'n perd sit; ~ *of GOVERNMENT,* regeringsetel; hoofstad; ~ *of HONOUR,* ereplaas; *KEEP one's* ~, bly sit; *LOSE one's* ~, jou sitplek verloor; jou setel verloor; nie herkies word nie; ~ *of the MIGHTY,* voorgestoelte; *all* ~ *s PLEASE!* inklim asb.! ~ *of the SCORNFUL,* kring v.d. spotters; *TAKE a* ~, gaan sit, plaasneem; *the* ~ *of the TROUBLE,* die eintlike moeilikheid; *the* ~ *of WAR,* die oorlogstoneel; (v) (laat) sit, plaas neem; van sitplekke voorsien; plek aanwys; mat (stoel); boom insit (broek); stel; *BE* ~ *ed,* gaan sit; ~ *a CANDIDATE,* 'n kandidaat 'n setel besorg; *be DEEPLY* ~ *ed,* diep gewortel wees; ~ *ONESELF,* gaan sit; *be able to* ~ *ten PERSONS,* sitplek vir tien mense hê; ~ *ed SHOE,* hellende hoefyster; ~ *ed STATUE,* sitbeeld.

sea' tangle, seewier.

seat: ~ **back,** rugleuning; ~ **belt,** sitplekgordel; veiligheidsgordel.

sea' term, seemansterm, vlootterm; ~ **inology,** vlootterminologie, seeterme, seeterminologie.

seat'ing, sitplek; onderstuk; fundasie; ~ **accommoda= tion,** sitplek; plaasruimte.

sea: ~-**toad,** seeduiwel; ~-**tossed,** deur die see geslinger; ~ **training,** seeopleiding; ~ **trout,** seeforel; ~ **trumpet,** trompetskulp; ~ **turtle,** seeskilpad; ~-**unicorn,** narwal; ~ **urchin,** see-egel; ~ **vegetation,** marineplantegroei; ~-**wall,** strandmuur, seewering, seedyk, seewal; ~ **ward,** seewaarts; ~ **ward de= fence,** kusverdediging, verdediging ter see; ~-**wa= ter,** seewater; ~-**wave,** seegolf; ~ **way,** seeroete, seeweg; ~ **weed,** seewier, seegras; ~-**wolf,** seewolf; kaper; ~-**worm,** seewurm; ~ **worthiness,** seewaardigheid; ~ **worthy,** seewaardig; ~-**wrack,** seegras.

seba'ceous, vetagtig, vet=; ~ **gland,** vetklier, smeerklier.

seba'cic, vet=; ~ **acid,** vetsuur.

sec'ant, (n) snylyn, sekans; (a) snydend, sny=.

sec'atur, snoeisker, tuinskêr; draadknipper.

secede', terugtrek; uittree, afskei; afskeur; ~ **r,** uittreder, afvallige; afskeier.

secern', skei, afskei, afsonder; ~ **ent, (n)** afskeidings= orgaan; afskeidingsmiddel; (a) afskeidend.

sece'ssion, afskeiding, terugtrekking, sesessie; ~ **ist, (n)** voorstander van afskeiding, afskeier; sesessionis; (a) afskeidend; afskeidingsgesind.

Sechuan'a, Setsjoeana (persoon); Tswana (taal).

seclude', afsluit; afsonder; uitsluit; ~ **d,** afgesonder, afgeslote, rustig, afgeleë.

seclu'sion, afsondering; eensaamheid, eensaamte; uitsluiting; afgeskeidenheid; afgelotenheid.

sec'ond, (n) tweede; ander; sekondant; nommer twee; tweede stem; sekonde (oorlosie); oomblik; (pl) ware van tweede kwaliteit; tweede porsie (kos); ~ *in COMMAND,* onderbevelhebber; ~ *of EX= CHANGE,* sekundawissel; ~ *from the FRONT,* naasvoor; *come a GOOD* ~, kort op nommer een kom; ~ *of REAR,* naasagter; *WAIT a* ~, wag 'n oomblikkie; *WITHIN* ~ *s,* binne enkele oomblik= ke; (v) sekondeer (mosie); ondersteun, bystaan, help; ter sy staan; *DEEDS must* ~ *words,* dade moet op woorde volg; die daad by die woord voeg;

secondary ~ *a MOTION*, 'n voorstel sekondeer; (a) tweede; ander; ondergeskik; *every* ~ *DAY*, al om die ander dag; *play* ~ *FIDDLE*, tweede viool speel; *HABIT is* ~ *nature*, gewoonte is tweede natuur; *at* ~ *HAND*, van hoorsê; *a* ~ *HELPING*, 'n tweede skeppie (porsie); ~ *LARGEST*, op een na die grootste; *be* ~ *to NONE*, vir niemand onderdoen nie; vir niemand agteruitstaan nie; *in the* ~ *PLACE*, in die tweede plek; ten tweede; *one's* ~ *SELF*, jou tweede ek; *on* ~ *THOUGHTS*, by nader insien; *have* ~ *THOUGHTS*, bedenkinge hê; ~ *THOUGHTS are best thoughts*, rype beraad is die beste beraad; (v) afstaan, leen (amptenaar); sekondeer (voorstel).

sec'ondary, (n) (..ries), afgevaardigde; ondergeskikte; satelliet; (a) sekondêr; ondergeskik; bykomend, bykomstig; ~ **battery,** akkumulator; ~ **cause,** byoorsaak; ~ **consideration,** oorweging van ondergeskikte belang; ~ **education,** middelbare onderwys; ~ **evidence,** getuienis uit die tweede hand, hoorsêgetuienis; ~ **importance,** van minder belang; ~ **industry,** fabrieksnywerheid; ~ **school,** middelbare skool.

sec'ond: ~ **ballot,** herstemming; ~ **base,** tweede rus (bofbal); ~ **-best,** op een na die beste, tweede beste, naasbeste; *come off* ~ *-best*, aan die kortste ent trek, uitoorlê word; die onderspit delf; ~ **birth,** wedergeboorte; ~ **bond,** tweede verband; ~ **-bond holder,** tweedeverbandhouer; ~ **childhood,** kindsheid, seniliteit; ~ **class,** tweede klas; ~ **cousin,** agterneef, kleinneef; ~ **er,** sekondant; ~ **floor,** tweede verdieping; ~ **hand,** helper, handlanger; onderskipper.

sec'ond-hand, (n) sekondewyser; (a) tweedehands; gedra; gebruik, halfslyt, geslete; antikwaries (boeke); *he has it AT* ~, hy het dit van hoorsê; *a* ~ *BOOKSELLER*, tweedehandse boekhandelaar, antikwaar; ~ **bookshop,** antikwariaat; ~ **clothes,** halfslyt klere.

sec'ond: ~ **-last,** voorlaaste; ~ **lieutenant,** tweede luitenant; ~ **ly,** in die tweed plaas, ten tweede; ~ **mate,** tweede stuurman; ~ **mourning,** ligte rou; ~ **officer,** tweede offisier; ~ **-rate,** tweederangs, tweedeklas; minderwaardig; ~ **reading,** tweede lesing; herlesing; *at a* ~ *reading*, by herlesing; ~ **-reading debate,** tweedelesingsdebat; ~ **running,** naloop (by distillasie); ~ **sight,** geestekykery, heldersiendheid; ~ **storey,** tweede verdieping; ~ **string,** tweede snaar; tweede keuse; ~ **tier,** tweede vlak; ~ **-tier government,** tweedevlakregering, tweedevlakbestuur; S~ **Volksraad,** Tweede Volksraad (hist.); ~ **wind,** tweede asem; ~ **-year student,** tweedejaarstudent.

sec'recy, geheimhouding; heimlikheid; verborgenheid; geheimdoenery; stilligheid, geheim; *IN* ~, heimlik, stilletjies; *IN the deepest* ~, in die diepste geheim; *PROMISE* ~, geheimhouding belowe; *RELY on one's* ~, op iem. se stilswye staatmaak.

sec'ret, (n) geheim; *BE in the* ~, ingewy wees; *GIVE away a* ~, 'n geheim verklap; *IN* ~, in die geheim, stilletjies; *KEEP a* ~, 'n geheim bewaar; *KEEP a thing* ~ *from a friend*, iets van hou vir 'n vriend; *LET a person into a* ~, iem. in 'n geheim inwy; *LET out a* ~, 'n geheim verklap; *MAKE a great* ~ *of*, onder stoele en banke versteek; *MAKE no* ~ *of something*, iets nie onder stoele en banke wegsteek nie; g'n geheim van iets maak nie; *an OPEN* ~, 'n openbare geheim; *be a TOP* ~, hoogs (uiters) geheim wees; (a) geheim, heimlik, bedek, verborge, verhole; stil; afgesonder, eensaam; *in one's* ~ *heart*, in jou binneste.

secretar'ial, sekretaris-, sekretarieel.
secretar'iat(e), sekretariaat; sekretarisskap.
sec'retary, (..ries), sekretaris; sekretaresse; geheimskrywer; *COLONIAL S*~, Koloniale Sekretaris; ~ *of EMBASSY*, ambassadesekretaris; *S*~ *for EXTERNAL Affairs*, Sekretaris van Buitelandse Sake; *HONORARY* ~, eresekretaris; *S*~ *of JUSTICE*, Sekretaris van Justisie; *S*~ *for LABOUR*, Sekretaris van Arbeid; ~ *of a LEGATION*, gesantskapsekretaris; *S*~ *of MINES*, Sekretaris van Mynwese; *PRIVATE* ~, privaatsekretaris, private sekretaris; privaatsekretaresse; geheimskrywer; *S*~ *of STATE*, Staatsekretaris; ~ *and TREASURER*, sekretaris-penningmeester; ~ **-bird,** sekretarisvoël, slangvanger; ~ **-general,** sekretaris-generaal; ~ **-treasurer,** sekretaris-penningmeester; ~ **ship,** sekretarisskap.

secrete', afsonder; afskei; wegsteek, verduister, verheimlik.

sec'ret: ~ **eye,** loervenstertjie; ~ **gutter,** versteekte geut; ~ **ink,** onsigbare ink; ~ **initiation,** geheime inlywing (inisiasie); ~ **initiation rite,** geheime inisiasieritus.

secre'tion, afskeiding, afskeisel; afsondering; verberging, verheimliking; ~ *of stolen goods*, verberging (heling) van gesteelde goed.

sec'retive, geheim, agterhoudend, terughoudend, geslote; geheimsinnig; ~ **ness,** geheimsinnigheid; terughoudendheid.

sec'ret life, verborge lewe.
sec'retly, stilletjies, in die stilligheid, in die geheim, sub rosa.
sec'retness, geheimhouding.
sec'ret organization, geheime organisasie, skuilorganisasie.
secret'ory, (n) afskeidingsklier; (a) afskeidend, afskeidings-.

sec'ret: ~ **parts,** skaamdele; ~ **police,** geheime polisie; ~ **service,** geheime diens, spioenasiediens; ~ **service agent,** agent, spioen; ~ **sin,** verborge sonde; ~ **society,** geheime vereniging; ~ **treaty,** geheime verdrag.

sect, sekte, gesindte.
sectar'ian, (n) sektaris, aanhanger van 'n sekte, sektariër; (a) sektaries; ~ **ism,** sektewese; sekteywer, soktegees.
sec'tary, sektaris, aanhanger van 'n sekte.
sec'tile, snybaar; gesplits.
sectil'ity, snybaarheid; gesplitsheid.
sec'tion, (n) afdeling; verdeling; deel; (deur)snee; skyfie, seksie; paragraaf; wetsartikel; trajek (spoorweg); groep, seksie; *CROSS* ~, dwarsdeursnee; *HORIZONTAL* ~, horisontale deursnee; *TRANSVERSE* ~, dwarsdeursnee; (v) in seksies verdeel; 'n deursnee maak.
sec'tional, ingedeel; plaaslik, distriks-, groeps-, wyks-, seksie-, seksioneel, afdelings-; ~ **sketch,** deursneetekening; ~ **view,** deursneeaansig; ~ **ism,** seksiegees; provinsialisme, partikularisme; ~ **ist,** (n) partikularis; (a) partikularisties; ~ **title,** deeltitel.
sec'tion-mark, paragraafteken.
sec'tor, sektor; groep; hoekmeter; tandboog; ~ *of a sphere*, bolsektor.
sector'ial, snydend, sektor-; ~ **tooth,** snytand, skeurtand.
sec'ular, (n) leek, wêreldlike priester, sekulier; (a) wêreldlik, tydelik, sekulêr; wêrelds; eeu-, honderdjarig; eeue-oud; blywend; ~ **arm,** wêreldlike mag; ~ **change,** gestadige verandering; ~ **clergy,** wêreldlike geestelikes; ~ **cooling,** langsame afkoeling; ~ **fame,** blywende roem; ~ **ism,** sekularisme, welsynsleer; ~ **ist,** (n) sekularis; (a) sekularisties; ~ **'ity,** wêreldlikheid, wêreldgesindheid; ~ **iza'tion,** sekularisasie, verwêreldliking; ~ **ize,** verwêreldlik, wêreldlik maak; ~ **music,** ongewyde musiek; ~ **power,** wêreldlike mag; ~ **struggle,** jarelange stryd.
secund'e, sekunde.
secun'dus, (..di), sekundus.
secur'able, versekerbaar; verkrybaar.
secure', (v) verseker, waarborg, beveilig, beskut, sekureer; versterk, vasmaak; aanskaf; in veiligheid bring; bereik, verkry; opsluit, vang; ~ *one's AIMS (ends, purpose)*, jou doel bereik; ~ *from (against) an ATTACK*, teen 'n aanval beveilig; ~ *a DEBT*, 'n skuld dek; sekuriteit gee vir 'n skuld; ~ *to someone his DUE*, iem. sy reg waarborg; ~ *someone's EXTRADITION*, iem. laat uitlewer; (a) seker, veilig; stellig; onbekommer, gerus; ~ *against burglars*, beveilig teen inbrekers; ~ **d,** gesluit; gewaarborg; verkry; veilig gemaak; ~ *d creditor*, preferente krediteur; ~ **foundation,** hegte fondament.
secur'iform, bylvormig.
secur'ing nut, borgmoer.

secur'ity, veiligheid, beveiliging; gerustheid, voorsorg; sekerheid; dekking, garansie; (..**ties**), waarborg, borg, pand; obligasie; sekuriteit; aandeel; (pl) aandele, effekte, obligasies, sekuriteite, waardepapiere; *COLLATERAL* ~, onderpand, bykomende sekuriteit, aanvullende sekuriteit; *ENTER into* ~, borg stel; *IN* ~ *for*, as borg vir; as waarborg vir; *LEND against* ~, op sekuriteit leen; *SOCIAL* ~, bestaansbeveiliging, maatskaplike beveiliging; veiligheidsregulasies; ~ *of TENURE*, sekerheid van ampsbehoud; ~ **bond**, borgakte; ~ **branch**, veiligheidstak, beveiligingsafdeling; **S**~ **Council**, Veiligheidsraad; ~ **door**, veiligheidsdeur; ~ **fence**, veiligheidsheining; ~ **guard**, veiligheidswag; ~ **measure(s)**, veiligheidsmaatreëls; ~ **officer**, veiligheidsoffisier; ~**-pact**, veiligheidsooreenkoms; ~ **police**, veiligheidspolisie; ~ **system**, veiligheidstelsel, sekuriteitstelsel.
sedan', draagstoel; koets; toemotor, sedan; ~ **chair**, draagstoel.
sedate', (v) stil, kalmeer; (a) kalm, besadig, besonne, ingetoë, stemmig, bedaard; ~**ly**, bedaard, kalm, stemmig, ingetoë; ~**ness**, kalmte, rus, besadigdheid, stemmigheid.
seda'tion, kalmering.
sed'ative, (n) stilmiddel, kalmeermiddel; (a) pynstillend; kalmerend.
sed'entariness, sittende lewenswyse.
sed'entary, (n) sittende; (a) sittend; ter plaatse gevorm (geol.), sedentêr; ~ **insects**, stilsitters; ~ **life**, sittende lewe(nswyse); ~ **population**, gesete bevolking; ~ **warfare**, stellingoorlog.
sedge, watergras, matjiesgoed, snygras.
sed'iment, besinksel, afsetting, sediment, afsaksel, droesem, grondsop, neerslag, moer; ~ **'ary**, afsettings-, besinkings-, sedimentêr; ~ **ary rock**, afsettingsgesteente, besinkingsgesteente; ~ **a'tion**, afsetting, besinking, sedimentasie; ~ **ation pit**, neerslagput.
sedi'tion, opruiing, ophitsing, opstand, sedisie, muitery; ~ **ary**, (n) opruier, ophitser, muiter; (a) oproerig; ophitsend.
sedi'tious, oproerig, opstandig, muitsiek, sedisieus; ~**ness**, oproerigheid, opstandigheid.
seduce', verlei, verlok; verkrag, defloreer; ~**ment**, verleiding, verlokking; ~**r**, verleier, verlokker, skaker.
sedu'cible, verleibaar.
sedu'cing, verleidelik, aanloklik.
seduc'tion, verleiding, seduksie.
seduc'tive, verleidelik, verloklik, verlokkend; ~**ness**, verleidelikheid, verloklikheid.
seduc'tress, (-es), verleister.
sedul'ity, naarstigheid, groot ywer.
sed'ulous, ywerig, fluks, volhardend; ~**ness** = **sedulity**.
see[1], (n) bisdom; biskopsetel; *the Holy S*~ *(of Rome)*, die Heilige Stoel.
see[2], (v) (saw, seen), sien; kyk; aanskou, begryp, insien, verstaan; besigtig; begelei; (be)sorg; omgaan; raadpleeg, spreek; besoek, kuier; ~ *ABOUT it*, daarvoor sorg; ingaan op; ~ *ACTION*, onder vuur kom (wees); ~ *AFTER*, kyk na, oppas; ~ *you AGAIN*, tot siens; *glad to* ~ *the BACK of somebody*, bly om van iem. ontslae te raak; ~ *to BED*, bed toe bring; ~ *somebody on BUSINESS*, met iem. oor sake praat; *as far as I CAN* ~, sover ek kan oordeel; ~ *to the CHILDREN*, kyk na die kinders; ~ *a CLIENT*, 'n kliënt ontvang; *have* ~*n better DAYS*, beter dae geken het; ~ *the DAY through*, die dag nog beleef; ~ *DAYLIGHT*, daglig sien; *oor die hond se stert wees*; ~ *a DOCTOR*, 'n dokter raadpleeg; ~ *a thing DONE*, sorg dat iets gedoen word; ~ *someone to the DOOR*, iem. deur toe bring; *unable to* ~ *either EARTH or sky*, geen hemel of aarde kan beken nie; ~ *EYE to eye*, dit eens wees; *as FAR as I can* ~, sover ek kan oordeel; *I* ~ *FROM the paper*, ek lees in die koerant; ~ *into the FUTURE*, die toekoms voorspel; *GO and* ~ *someone*, iem. gaan opsoek; ~ *HERE!* kyk hier! ~ *a person HOME*, iem. tuisbring; ~ *over a HOUSE*, 'n huis besigtig; *I* ~, ek verstaan; ~ *INTO some-*

thing, aandag aan iets skenk; iets ondersoek; ~ *you LATER*, tot siens! *LET me* ~, laat ek eers dink; ~ *LIFE*, die lewe leer ken; ~ *the LIGHT*, die eerste lewenslig aanskou; bekeer word; verstaan; *never to have* ~*n anything LIKE it*, nog nooit sowat belewe het nie; *MAY I* ~ *you?* mag ek met u praat? ~ *MUCH of a person*, baie met iem. in aanraking kom; *he does not* ~ *further than his NOSE*, hy sien nie verder as wat sy neus lank is nie; ~ *NOTHING but*, jou blind staar op; ~ *somebody OFF at the station*, iem. op die stasie gaan groet; iem. wegbring stasie toe; iem. wegsien; ~ *a person OUT*, iem. wegsien (uitlaat, deur toe bring); ~ *PAGE 10*, kyk (sien) bladsy 10; ~ *the POINT*, iets snap; ~ *through the PRESS*, die druk van 'n boek besorg; ~ *RED*, voel of 'n mens kan moor; woedend word; jou bloedig vererg; ~ *RIGHT*, weghelp; *we SHALL* ~ *what we shall* ~, die tyd sal leer; ~ *the SIGHTS*, die besienswaardighede besigtig; ~ *STARS*, jou ouma vir 'n eendvoël aansien; ~ *THINGS*, onder sinsbegogeling verkeer; in 'n dwaling wees; ~ *THROUGH it*, die saak deursien; sien wat agter die saak skuil; ~ *a matter THROUGH*, 'n saak tot 'n einde bring; tot die einde by 'n saak bly; *his friends will* ~ *him THROUGH*, sy vriende sal hom deurhelp; ~ *TO it that*, sorg daarvoor dat; *have too many things to* ~ *TO*, nie jou draai kan kry nie; ~ *OVER a house*, 'n woning besigtig; *I cannot* ~ *my WAY clear to*..., ek is nie in staat nie om...; *have enough coal to* ~ *the WINTER out*, genoeg steenkool hê om deur die winter te kom; ~ *the Old YEAR out, op Oujaarsnag opbly tot 12 uur*, (interj), sie(n) daar! sien jy nou!
seed, (n) saad; kiem; nakomelingskap, nageslag, afstammelinge; (v) saadskiet; saai; die saad (pitte) uithaal, ontpit; keur, rangskik (tennisspelers); *DE-LINTED* ~, saad sonder dons; *sow* ~ *s of DIS-CORD*, kwaad saad saai; *GO to* ~, *RUN to* ~, saadskiet; slorderig (slonsig) word; *RAISE up* ~, kinders verwek; *the* ~ *s of VICE*, die kiem v.d. kwaad; ~**-bearing**, saaddraend; ~**-bed**, saadbedding, saadakkertjie; broeines; ~**-box**, saaikas, saaipan; ~**-bud**, saadknop; ~**-cake**, anysoek; ~**-coat**, saadomhulsel; saadhuid, testa; ~**-coral**, klein stukkies koraal; ~**-corn**, saadkoring; ~**-cotton**, katoensaad; ~ **dispersal**, saadverspreiding; ~**-drill**, planter; ~**-eater**, saadeter.
seed'ed, saaddraend; besaai; sonder pitte, pitloos (dadels); gekeur, gerangskik (tennis); ~ **cloud**, bestrooide wolk; ~ **list**, keurlys; ~ **player**, gerangskikte (gekeurde) speler (tennis); ~ **raisins**, ontpitte rosyntjies.
seed: ~**er**, saaimasjien; ~ **head**, saadblom; ~**lness**, kaalheid; verwaarlosing; olikheid; ~**ing**, saadskiet; rangskikking (sport); ~**ing-plough**, planter; ~ **leaf**, kiemblad, kiemblaartjie, saadlob; ~**less**, sonder saad (pitte); ~**ling**, saaiplant, saailing; kiemplantjie; ~**-lobe**, saadlob; ~ **mealies**, saadmielies; ~**-pearls**, pêrelgruis; ~**-plant**, saailing; ~**-plot**, saaibed, saadakkertjie; broeines; ~**-pod**, saadpeul, saaddop; ~**-potato**, (aartappel)moer; saadaartappel; ~**-riddle**, saadskudder; ~**s'man**, saadhandelaar; ~**-store**, saadmagasyn, saadpakhuis; ~**-time**, saaityd; ~**-vessel**, saadhuisie; ~**y**, vol saad; armoedig, olik, siekerig, oes; toiingrig, slonsig; *feel* ~*y*, olik (oes, siekerig) voel.
see'ing, (n) (die) sien; gesigsvermoë; ~ *is BELIEV-ING*, sien is glo; *WORTH* ~, besienswaardig; (a) siende; (conj) aangesien; ~ *that he has gone*, aangesien hy weg is; ~**-eye dog**, leihond, gidshond (vir blindes).
seek, **(sought)**, soek; probeer; poog; begeer; ~ *AD-VICE*, raad vra; ~ *AFTER*, nastreef; *much sought AFTER*, gesog, sterk in aanvraag; ~ *one's BED*, jou bed opsoek; *not FAR to* ~, nie ver te soek na; ~ *and ye shall FIND*, soek en jy sal vind; ~ *OUT*, uitkies; opspoor; *the REASON is not far to* ~, die rede lê voor die hand; ~ *after TRUTH*, die waarheid soek; ~**er**, soeker.
seel, blinddoek, mislei.
seem, lyk, skyn; die skyn hê van; daar uitsien; *he* ~*s to be the FATHER*, hy is blykbaar die vader; *he* ~*s*

to be a good *FELLOW*, hy lyk 'n gawe kêrel; *it* ~*s as IF*, dit lyk asof; *it* ~*s to ME*, dit lyk (vir) my; *it* ~*s NOT*, dit lyk nie so nie; *it* ~*s SO*, so lyk dit, dit lyk so; *it* ~*s STRANGE*, dit lyk snaaks; *THINGS are not always what they* ~, skyn bedrieg; *it* ~*s to me THAT*..., dit lyk (vir) my of...; dit kom my voor of...; *he* ~*s to be TIRED*, hy lyk moeg; *I* ~ *TO*, dit lyk of ek, dit skyn of ek; *it WOULD* ~ *that*, dit lyk amper (half); ~**ing,** (n) skyn; (a) skynbaar, oënskynlik; ~**ingly,** oënskynlik, glo, in skyn, skynbaar; ~**liness,** betaamlikheid, geskiktheid, oorbaarheid; ~**ly,** betaamlik, geskik, welvoeglik, oorbaar, gepas, behoorlik.

seep, lek, deursyfer, sypel; ~**age,** lekkery, deursypeling, syfering; sypelwater, syferwater; ~**age water,** syferwater, sypelwater.

se'er, siener, profeet.

seer'sucker, sirsakar.

see'saw, (n) wipplank, wip; (v) wip, wipplank ry, op en neer ry; (a) op en neer gaande; (adv) op en neer, heen en weer.

seethe, kook, borrel, bruis, sied; ~**r,** kookketel.

seeth'ing, (n) bruising, borreling; (a) kokend, siedend; gloeiend warm; ~ *with discontent*, gistend van ontevredenheid.

seg'ment, (n) gedeelte, segment; geleding; lit; afdeling; (v) verdeel, in segmente deel; ~ '*ary,* segment=, segmentvormig; ~**a'tion,** verdeling (in segmente), splitsing.

seg'regate, (v) afsonder, afskei, segregeer; (a) afgesonder, afgeskei.

segrega'tion, afsondering, afskeiding; apartheid, segregasie; ~**ist,** afskeier.

seigneur', leenheer; *grand* ~, hoë meneer; groot kokkedoor.

seign'iorage, muntreg.

seign'iory, (..ries), heerlikheid; susereiniteit, leenheerskap; domein

seine, (n) sleepnet, treknet, seën; (v) met 'n treknet visvang.

seis'mal, seis'mic, aardbewings=, seismies.

seis'mograph, seismograaf, aardbewingsaanwyser, aardbewingsmeter.

seismog'raphy, seismografie.

seismol'ogy, aardbewingsleer, seismologie.

seismom'eter, seismometer.

seiz'able, grypbaar, neembaar, wat gevat kan word.

seize, gryp, vat, neem; aanpak; bemagtig, vasvat; beslag lê op, konfiskeer, buitmaak, verbeurd verklaar (goed); beset, oormeester (gebied); bevang (perd); vasbind, gevange neem; vasbrand (masjien); aanslaan (rem); ~ *d by APOPLEXY*, deur beroerte getref; ~ *upon a CHANCE*, die geleentheid aangryp; *be* ~ *d with FEAR*, deur vrees aangegryp wees; ~ *a FORTRESS*, 'n vesting inneem; ~ *HOLD of*, gryp; ~ *ON*, gryp, pak; ~ *an OPPORTUNITY*, 'n geleentheid aangryp; ~ *d with PANIC*, deur skrik bevange; ~ *somebody's PROPERTY*, op iem. se eiendom beslag lê.

seiz'er, gryper; beslaglêer.

seiz'ing, gryping; inbeslagneming; vasbranding (motor).

sei'zure, inbesitneming, beslaglegging; bevangenheid; aanval (van 'n siekte); oormeestering, oorrompeling, bemagtiging.

selach'ian, (n) haai; (a) haaiagtig.

sel'dom, selde, min; *it IS* ~ *that,* dit gebeur min dat; ~ *if EVER,* ~ *or NEVER,* selde of nooit.

select', (n) (die) uitverkorenes; (v) uitsoek, uitkies; uitvang; (a) uitgekies, keurig, selek; eksklusief, uitgesoek; ~ *AUDIENCE,* uitgelese gehoor; ~ *COMMITTEE,* gekose komitee; ~ *COMPANY,* uitgesoekte geselskap; ~ *NEIGHBOURHOOD,* uitsoekbuurt; ~ *ed TIMBER,* keurhout.

selec'tion, keuse, seleksie; uitkiesing; keuring; keur(spel) (mus.); versameling; *a* ~ *of goods*, 'n sortering goedere; ~ **board,** keurraad; ~ **committee,** keurkomitee; ~ **convener,** keurkomiteesameroeper.

select': ~**ive,** kiesend; ~**ive breeding,** teelkeuse; ~**iv'ity,** storingsvryheid; selektiwiteit; ~**ness,** keurigheid, uitgelesenheid; ~**or,** kieser; keurder; ~**or**

switch, kiesskakelaar; ~ **range,** keur; uitgesoekte verskeidenheid.

sel'enite, seleniet; maanbewoner.

selen'ium, selenium, seleen.

selen'ograph, maankaart; ~**er,** maanbeskrywer, selenograaf.

selenog'raphy, maanbeskrywing, selenografie.

self, (selves), eie-ek; eie persoon; self, ekheid, ego; ondergetekende (op tjek); *my BETTER* ~, my beter ek; *his BETTER* ~, sy beter inbors; *my FORMER* ~, wat ek was; *the LOVE of* ~, eieliefde; ~ *LOVES itself best*, jakkals prys sy eie stert; elke dassie prys sy kwassie; *my OTHER* ~, my tweede ek; *for* ~ *and PARTNERS*, namens myself en vennote; *my POOR* ~, arme ek; ~*-PRAISE is no praise*, eielof stink; eielof is uielof; ~**-abandonment,** selfversaking; ~**-abasement,** selfvernedering; ~**-abhorrence,** selfveragting; ~**-abnegation,** selfverloëning; ~**-absorption,** die opgaan in jouself; ~**-abuse,** selfbeskimping; selfbevlekking, masturbasie; ~**-accusation,** selfbeskuldiging; ~**-accusatory,** selfbeskuldigend; ~**-acting,** selfwerkend, outomaties; ~**-acting mine,** skokmyn; ~**-activity,** selfwerksaamheid; ~**-adjusting,** selfreëlend; ~**-admiration,** selfbewondering; ~**-advertisement,** eielof; ~**-aligning,** selfrigtend; ~**-appointed,** selfbenoem; ~**-approbation,** selfvoldoening; ~**-assertion,** aanmatiging; selfbewussyn; selfhandhawing; ~**-assertive,** aanmatigend; ~**-assertiveness,** aanmatiging; ~**-assumed,** aangematig; ~**-assurance,** selfvertroue, selfversekerdheid; ~**-assured,** vol selfvertroue; ~**-binder,** selfbinder; ~**-censure,** selfkritiek; ~ **censureship,** selfsensuur; ~**-centred,** in jouself opgaande; ekkerig, egosentries; ~**-centring,** selfsentrerend; ~**-chastisement,** selfkastyding; ~**-chosen,** selfgekose; ~**-closing,** selfsluitend; ~**-collected,** kalm, beheers; ~**-colour,** natuurlike kleur; egalige kleur; ~**-coloured,** eenkleurig, ewekleurig; ~**-command,** selfbeheersing; ~**-commitment,** selfblootstelling; ~**-complacency,** selfbehae, selfvoldoening, selfvoldaanheid, selftevredenheid, selfingenomenheid; ~**-complacent,** selfbehaaglik, selfingenome, selfvoldaan; ~**-composed,** vol selfvertroue, kalm, beheers; ~**-composure,** selfbeheersing, bedaardheid; ~**-conceit,** eiedunk, verwaandheid, ydelheid, eiewaan, alwetery, selfoorskatting, verbeelding; ~**-conceited,** verwaand; ~**-condemnation,** selfverwyt; ~**-condemned,** deur jouself veroordeel; ~**-confidence,** selfvertroue; ~**-confident,** vol selfvertroue, selfversekerd(e); ~**-conquest,** selfoorwinning; ~**-conscious,** selfbewus; verleë, skaam, onseker; ~**-consciousness,** selfbewussyn; selfbewustheid; selfgevoel; ~**-contained,** koel, stil; eenselwig, opsigselfstaande, onafhanklik; afgetrokke, teruggetrokke, afgesonder; kompleet, alles bevattend, in een stuk; ~**-contained flat,** volledig toegeruste woonstel; ~**-contempt,** selfveragting; ~**-contented,** selftevrede; ~**-control,** selfbeheersing, selfbedwang; ~**-conviction,** inwendige oortuiging; ~**-cooling,** selfkoelend; ~**-criticism,** selfkritiek; ~**-culture,** selfontwikkeling; ~**-deceit,** ~**-deception,** selfbedrog, selfverblinding; ~**-defeating,** selfverydelend; ~**-defence,** selfverdediging, noodweer; selfbehoud; noodweer (reg); *in* ~*-defence*, uit noodweer; ~**-delusion,** selfbegoëling; ~**-denial,** selfverloëning, onselfsugtig, selfloënend; ~**-denying,** onselfsugtig, selfloënend; ~**-dependence,** selfstandigheid; ~**-destroyer,** selfvernietiger, selfmoordenaar; ~**-destruction,** selfvernietiging; selfmoord; ~**-destructive,** selfvernietigend; selfmoordend; ~**-determination,** selfbeskikking; selfbestemming; eie keuse; *right of* ~*-determination*, selfbeskikkingsreg; ~**-devotion,** selfopoffering; ~**-discipline,** selftug; ~**-education,** selfopvoeding; ~**-effacement,** teruggetrokkenheid; ~**-effacing,** teruggetrokke; ~**-employed,** selfstandig; ~**-engrossed,** in jouself opgaande; ~**-enrichment,** selfverryking; ~**-esteem,** eiedunk; selfrespek; ~**-evident,** klaarblyklik, vanselfsprekend; *it is* ~*-evident*, dit spreek vanself; dit hoef geen betoog nie; ~**-examination,** selfondersoek; ~**-explanatory,** selfverduidelikend; ~**-expression,** uitdrukking van innerlike gevoe=

seligmanite   1219   semi

lens; selfontplooiing; seifuitlewing; ~-**exultation**, selfverheffing; ~-**feeder**, selfvoerder; ~-**feeding**, selfvoerend; ~-**fertilization**, selfbevrugting; ~-**filler**, selfvuller; ~-**glorification**, selfverheerliking; ~-**governed**, met eie regering; ~-**governing**, selfregerend; ~-**government**, selfbestuur, selfregering; ~-**help**, eiehulp; selfhelp; ~-*help store*, selfhelpwinkel; ~-**hood**, selfheid; ~-**humiliation**, selfvernedering; ~-**hypnosis**, selfhipnose; ~-**idolization**, selfvergoding; ~-**ignition**, selfontsteking; selfontbranding; ~-**immolation**, seifoffering; ~-**importance**, eiedunk, eiewaan, verwaandheid; ~-**important**, verwaand; ~-**imposed**, selfopgelê; ~-**indulgence**, selfbevrediging; ~-**indulgent**, selfbevredigend, genotsugtig; ~-**inflicted**, selftoegedien; ~-**interest**, eiebelang, eiebaat; baatsug; ~-**interested**, baatsugtig; ~-**ish**, selfsugtig, baatsugtig, egoïsties, ekkerig, eksugtig; ~-**ishness**, selfsug, egoïsme, eksug; ~-**knowledge**, selfkennis; ~-**less**, onbaatsugtig; ~-**loading rifle**, selflaaier; ~-**locking**, selfsluitend; ~-**love**, eieliefde, selfliefde; ~-**lubricating**, selfsmerend; ~-**lubrication**, selfsmering; ~-**made**, selfgemaak; deur eie inspanning vooruitgekom, outodidak; ~-*made man*, iem. wat deur eie inspanning vooruitgekom het; ~-**mastery**, selfbeheersing; ~-**mortification**, selfpyniging; ~-**murder**, selfmoord; ~-**murderer**, selfmoordenaar; ~-**oiling**, selfsmerend; ~-**opinion**, ingebeeldheid; eiewaan; ~-**opinionated**, eiewys, verwaand; ingebeeld; ~-**pity**, selfbejammering, selfbeklag; ~-**poisoning**, selfvergiftiging; ~-**pollination**, selfbestuiwing; ~-**pollution**, selfbevlekking; ~-**portrait**, selfportret; ~-**possessed**, kalm, bedaard, ~-**possession**, kalmte, selfbeheersing, selfversekerdheid; ~-**praise**, eielof; ~-*praise is no recommendation*, eielof stink; ~-**preservation**, selfbehoud; ~-**propelled**, motor-; selfaangedrewe; ~-**propelled scraper**, motorskrop; ~-**protection**, selfbeskerming; ~-**raising flour**, bruismeel; ~-**realization**, selfontplooiing; selfverwesenliking; ~-**recording**, selfregistrerend; ~-**regard**, selfagting; ~-**registering**, selfregistrerend; ~-**regulating**, selfreëlend; ~-**reliance**, selfvertroue, selfstandigheid; ~-**reliant**, selfstandig, vol selfvertroue; ~-**renunciation**, selfverloëning, onbaatsugtigheid; ~-**reproach**, selfverwyt, wroeging; ~-**respect**, selfrespek, eiewaarde; ~-**restraint**, selfbeheersing; ~-**reverence**, selfagting; ~-**ridicule**, selfspot; ~-**righteous**, eiegeregtig; ~-**rising**, selfrysend; ~-**rising flour**, bruismeel; ~-**rule**, selfbestuur; ~-**sacrifice**, selfopoffering; ~-**sacrificing**, selfopofferend; ~-**same**, einste, presies dieselfde; ~-**satisfaction**, selfvoldoening, selfingenomenheid; ~-**satisfied**, selftevrede, selfvoldaan; ~-**sealing**, selfdigtend; ~-**seeker**, baatsugtige, selfsugtige; ~-**seeking**, (n) selfsug, eiebaat; (a) selfsugtig; ~-**service**, selfbediening; ~-**service shop**, selfdienwinkel, selfbedieningswinkel, selfhelpwinkel; ~-**serving**, selfsugtig; ~-**set plants**, opslag; ~-**sown**, opslag-; ~-**sown seedling**, opslagplantjie; ~-**starter**, (self)aansitter; ~-**styled**, selfgenoemd, voorgewend; ~-**sufficiency**, selfgenoegsaamheid; selfvoldaanheid; selfvoorsiening; verwaandheid; ~-**sufficient**, selfgenoegsaam; verwaand; selfonderhoudend; ~-**suggestion**, outosuggestie; ~-**support**, selfversorging; ~-**supporting**, selfondersteunend, selfonderhoudend; ~-**surrender**, selfoorgawe; ~-**taught**, selfonderrig; outodidakties; ~-**taught man**, outodidak; ~-**torment**, selfkwelling; ~-**tormenting**, selfkwellend; ~-**torture**, selfkwelling; selfkastyding; ~-**treatment**, selfbehandeling; ~-**tuition**, selfonderrig; ~-**will**, eiesinnigheid, koppigheid; ~-**willed**, eiesinnig, koppig, eiewys; ~-**winding watch**, outomatiese oorlosie; ~-**worship**, selfaanbidding, selfvergoding.

selig'manite, seligmaniete.

sell, (n) bedrog, kullery; teleurstelling; (v) (**sold**), verkoop, van die hand sit; verhandel; aan die man bring; bedrieg; kul; verraai; ~ *by AUCTION*, by opbod (opslag) verkoop; laat opveil; ~ *like hot CAKES*, soos (soet)koek verkoop; *he will* ~ *his COUNTRY*, hy sal sy land verraai; ~ *an IDEA*, probeer om 'n idee te laat posvat; ~ *one's LIFE dearly*, jou lewe duur verkoop; ~ *OUT (OFF)*, uitverkoop, verkoop; ~ *the PASS*, jou eie mense verraai; ~ *one a PUP*, iem. toetrek (kul); ~ *someone down the RIVER*, iem. verraai; ~ *one's SOUL*, jou siel verkoop; ~ *someone UP*, iem. uitverkoop; ~ *ing like WILDFIRE*, soos (soet)koek verkoop.

sell'er, verkoper; *BEST* ~, treffer; suksesboek; *a SURE* ~, iets wat vanself 'n afsetgebied vind.

sell'ing, (die) verkoop; *art of* ~, verkoopkuns; ~-**off**, uitverkoop; ~-**out**, uitverkoping; ~-**price**, verkoopprys; ~-**value**, verkoopwaarde.

sell'er's market, verkopersmark.

sel'vage, sel'vedge, selfkant; aarkant, gangkant, kleiband (geol.); ~ **thread**, sterkdraad, skeringdraad, lengtedraad.

seman'tic, semanties, betekenis-; ~ **ist**, semantikus; ~ **s**, betekenisleer, semantiek.

sem'aphore, (n) semafoor (spoorweë); vlagseine, vlagseinwerk; (v) met vlae sein; per semafoor oorsein; ~ **code**, semafoorkode; ~ **flag**, seinvlag, semafoorvlag; ~ **message**, vlagberig; semafoorberig; ~ **signal**, vlagsein; semafoorsein; ~ **signaller**, vlagseiner; semafoorseiner.

semapho'ric, semafories.

semasiolog'ical, semasiologies.

semasiol'ogist, semasioloog.

semasiol'ogy, betekenisleer, semasiologie.

sem'blance, skyn, voorkome; glimp, sweem; aanvoelertjie; *put on the* ~ *of an ANGEL*, die voorkome van 'n engel aanneem; *HAVE the* ~ *of*, die skyn hê van; *PUT on a* ~ *of anger*, maak of jy kwaad is; *not a* ~ *of TRUTH*, geen skyn van waarheid nie.

sem'en, (**semina**), semen, saad, sperma.

semes'ter, semester, halfjaar.

sem'i-, half-; ~-**annual**, halfjaarliks; ~-**annular**, halfrond; ~-**arid**, halfdroog, halfdor; ~-**automatic**, halfoutomaties; ~-**barbarian**, (n) 'n halwe barbaar; (a) halfbarbaars; ~-**barbarous**, halfbarbaars; ~ **breve**, heelnoot; ~-**chord**, halwe koord; ~ **circle**, halfmaan, halwe sirkel; ~ **circular**, halfrond; ~-**civilized**, halfbeskaaf; ~ **colon**, kommapunt; ~-**conscious**, halfbewus; ~-**crystalline**, halfkristallyn; ~-**desert**, halfwoestyn; ~-**detached house**, skakelhuis, tweelinghuis, aanmekaarhuis, koppelhuis; ~ **diurnal**, halfdaagliks; ~ **final**, semifinale, halfeindwedstryd; voorlaaste (wedstryd); ~ **finalist**, halfeindeelnemer; ~ **final round**, halfeindronde; ~-**finished**, halfafgewerk; ~-**finished product**, halffabrikaat; ~ **fluid**, halfvloeibaar; taai; ~-**god**, halfgod; ~-**grand**, salonvleuel (klavier); ~-**invalid**, halfinvalide; ~-**lunar**, halfmaanvormig; ~-**lunar valve**, halfmaanklep; ~-**metal**, halfmetaal; ~-**monthly**, halfmaandeliks; ~-**mounted**, halfgemonteer; ~-**mute**, halfstom.

sem'inal, saad-, kiem-; *a* ~ *BOOK*, 'n gedagteryke boek; *in the* ~ *STATE*, rudimentêr, onontwikkel(d); ~ **discharge**, saadlosing; ~ **duct**, saadbuis; ~ **fluid**, saadvog; ~ **leaf**, kiemblaartjie, saadlob.

sem'inar, studiegroep; seminaar; besprekingsgroep.

sem'inarist, seminaris.

sem'inary, (..ries), kweekskool, seminarie.

semina'tion, saaiing; saadvorming; saaduitstorting, saadlosing, saaduitbarsting.

semini'ferous, saaddraend.

sem'i-official, halfamptelik; offisieus.

semiog'raphy, semiografie, voortekenbeskrywing.

semiol'ogy, semiologie, voortekenleer.

sem'i-: ~-**opaque**, halfdeurskynend; ~ **o'tics**, semiotiek, tekenleer; ~ **precious**, halfedel; ~ **precious stone**, siersteen, halfedelsteen; ~-**public service**, semistaatsdiens; ~ **quaver**, sestiende noot; ~ **rigid**, halfstyf; ~-**rough**, sukkelveld (gholf).

sem'is, halffabrikate.

sem'i-: ~-**savage**, halfbarbaars; ~-**skilled**, halfgeskoold (arbeid); ~-**sphere**, halfbolvormig; **semistate department**, semistaatsdepartement.

Sem'ite, Semiet.

Semit'ic, Semities.

Sem'itism, Semitisme.

sem'i: ~ **tone**, halwe toon; ~-**trailer**, leunwa; ~-**transparent**, halfdeursigtig, halfdeurskynend; ~-**urban**, halfstedelik; ~ **vowel**, halfklinker, halfvokaal.

semoli'na, griesmeel, gruismeel, semolina (geregistreerde handelsnaam).
sempitern'al, ewigdurend.
semp'stress, *kyk* **seamstress.**
sen, sen (Japanse muntstuk).
sen'ary, sestallig.
sen'ate, senaat; hoërhuis; ~ **house,** raadhuis, raadsaal.
sen'ator, senator; ~ '**ial,** senatoriaal, senaats=; ~ **ship,** senatorskap.
sen'atress, (-es), sen'atrix, (..trices), senatrise.
send, (sent), stuur, afstuur, wegstuur, versend, send; ~ *AFTER*, nastuur; ~ *ALONG*, oorstuur, deurstuur; ~ *AWAY*, wegstuur; ~ *BACK*, terugstuur; ~ *a ship to the BOTTOM*, 'n skip kelder; 'n skip in die grond boor; ~ *forth BUDS*, bot; ~ *someone about his BUSINESS*, van iem. ontslae raak; ~ *in one's CARD*, jou naamkaartjie instuur; ~ *(invitation) CARDS*, uitnodigingskaartjies stuur; ~ *one's COMPLIMENTS*, jou groete stuur; ~ *for the DOCTOR*, die dokter laat haal, stuur om die dokter; ~ *DOWN*, afstuur; wegja; verminder (koors); ~ *FLYING*, iem. onder stof loop; iem. onderstebo loop; ~ *FORTH*, uitstuur; laat hoor; afgee; uitskiet; ~ *IN*, instuur; ~ *a MESSAGE*, 'n boodskap stuur; ~ *in one's NAME*, jou laat aandien; jou laat inskryf; ~ *OFF*, wegstuur; laat uitskiet; uitstuur, uitgeleide doen; aan die slaap maak; ~ *ON*, deurstuur, aanstuur; ~ *OUT*, uitstuur; afgee; laat hoor; ~ *OVER*, oorstuur; ~ *someone PACKING*, iem. die bloupas gee; iem. wegbeorder; *be sent PACKING*, die bloupas kry; ~ *ROUND a notice*, 'n kennisgewing rondstuur, laat rondgaan, sirkuleer; ~ *to SLEEP*, aan die slaap laat raak; bewusteloos slaan; ~ *down from the UNIVERSITY*, uit die universiteit sit; ~ *someone on his WAY*, iem. weghelp; ~ *WORD*, laat weet, 'n boodskap stuur, berig stuur; ~**er,** (af)sender, stuurder; seintoestel; ~**ing,** (n) (die) afstuur, versending; (a) send=; ~**ing-key,** sendsleutel; ~**ing-station,** sendstasie; ~**-off,** vaarwel, uitgeleide; afskeidsfees; *give someone a* ~*-off*, iem. uitgeleide doen.
senec'io poisoning, sprinkaanbosvergiftiging; dunsiekte (by perde).
senecio'sis, dunsiekte.
Senegalese', (n) Senegalees; (a) Senegalees.
senes'cence, veroudering, gerontisme.
senes'cent, bejaard, ouerig; verouderend.
sen'eschal, rentmeester, hofmeester.
sen'green, prei.
sen'ile, ouderdoms=; hoogbejaard; kinds, seniel, afgeleef; ~ **decay,** ouderdomsverval.
senil'ity, ouderdomswakte, seniliteit.
sen'ior, (n) hoof; ouere; hoogste in rang; meerdere, senior; senior student; (a) ouer, senior; hoogste; oudste; hoër in rang; *she is my* ~, sy is ouer as ek; ~ **citizen,** senior burger; ~ **clerk,** senior klerk; ~ **counsel,** leidende advokaat, hoofadvokaat; S~ Counsel, Senior Advokaat; ~ **executive,** senior uitvoerende amptenaar; senior bestuurder; ~ **lecturer,** senior lektor; ~ **official,** senior amptenaar (beampte).
senior'ity, voorrang, senioriteit, hoër ouderdom; *promotion by* ~, verhoging volgens ranglys (diensjaar); ~ **list,** ranglys.
sen'ior: ~ **officer,** hoë offisier; ~ **partner,** oudste vennoot, hoofvennoot.
senn'a, seneblare; ~ **pods,** senepeule; ~ **tea,** seneafteksel.
senn'et, fanfare, trompetgeskal.
sensa'tion, gewaarwording, gevoel, aandoening; opskudding, sensasie; *cause a* ~, opskudding verwek; opsien baar.
sensa'tional, opsienbarend, sensasioneel, sensasiewekkend, gerugmakend; ~ *NEWS*, sensasienuus; *a* ~ *NOVEL*, 'n sensasieroman; ~ *STORY*, sensasieverhaal; ~**ism,** sensasielus, sensasiesug; sensuele kenleer; effekbejag.
sensa'tion: ~**-hunter,** sensasiesoeker; ~**-loving,** sensasiebelus; ~**monger,** sensasiewekker; ~ **play,** sensasiestuk; ~**-seeking,** sensasiesug.
sense, (n) sin, sintuig; gewaarwording, besinning; besef; gevoel; betekenis; oordeel, insig; redelikheid; begrip; verstand; ~ *of BEAUTY*, skoonheidsin; *BEREFT of one's* ~*s*, van jou sinne beroof; *BRING someone to his* ~*s*, iem. tot besinning bring; *when he CAME to his* ~*s*, toe hy hom kom kry; *in a CERTAIN* ~, in sekere sin (betekenis); ~ *of COLOUR*, kleurgevoel; *COME to one's* ~*s*, weer by jou sinne kom; *(plain) COMMON* ~, verstandigheid; gesonde verstand; ~ *of DIRECTION*, rigtingsin; *from a* ~ *of DUTY*, uit pligsgevoel; *in EVERY* ~, in alle opsigte; in elke opsig; *a FALSE* ~ *of security*, 'n ongegronde veiligheidsgevoel; *the FIVE* ~*s*, die vyf sintuie; *FRIGHTEN someone out of his* ~*s*, iem. hom lam laat skrik; *he had the GOOD* ~ *to*, hy was so verstandig om; *GRATIFY the* ~*s*, die sinne streel; ~ *of GUILT*, skuldgevoel; ~ *of HONOUR*, eergevoel; *have a keen* ~ *of HUMOUR*, 'n fyn sin vir die geestige hê; *IN a* ~, in sekere sin; ~ *of JUSTICE*, regsgevoel; *take LEAVE of one's* ~*s*, van jou verstand af raak; *LOSE one's* ~*s*, jou besinning verloor; *have LOST one's* ~*s*, buite kennis wees; buite weste wees; *it doesn't MAKE* ~, dis onverstaanbaar; dit het geen sin nie; *MAKE* ~, op pote staan; verstaanbaar wees; *I cannot MAKE* ~ *out of it*, ek kan daar geen tou aan vasknoop nie; vir my het dit geen sin nie; *a MAN of* ~, 'n verstandige man; *in the NARROW* ~, in die beperkte sin; *there is NO* ~ *in doing it*, dit sou onverstandig wees om dit te doen; *you are OUT of your* ~*s*, jy is van jou verstand af; *not to be in one's PROPER* ~*s*, van jou verstand af wees; *RECOVER one's* ~*s*, weer by kennis kom; *in his RIGHT* ~*s*, goed by sy verstand; by sy positiewe; *a* ~ *of SECURITY*, 'n gevoel van veiligheid; ~ *of SHAME*, skaamtegevoel; *the SIXTH* ~, die sesde sintuig; ~ *of SMELL*, reuksin; *in his SOUND and sober* ~*s*, by sy volle verstand; *in the STRICT* ~, in engere sin; ~ *of SUPERIORITY*, meerderheidsgevoel; *TALK* ~, praat verstandig; verstandig praat; *now you are TALKING* ~*!* nou praat jy (verstandig)! ~ *of TASTE*, smaaksin; ~ *of TOUCH*, tassin; *WHAT is the* ~ *of . . .?* wat help dit om . . .? *it's grand in every* ~ *of the WORD*, dis in elke betekenis v.d. woord groots; (v) voel, gewaarword, begryp, besef, bewus word van; ~ **danger,** gevaar aanvoel; ~**less,** bewusteloos; gevoelloos; sinneloos, onverstandig, dwaas; wesenloos; geesteloos; ~**lessness,** bewusteloosheid; onverstandigheid; sinneloosheid; gevoelloosheid; ~**-organ,** sintuig.
sensibil'ity, (..**ties**), gevoeligheid, vatbaarheid; ontvanklikheid; fyngevoeligheid, liggeraaktheid.
sen'sible, merkbaar; voelbaar; waarneembaar; verstandig; *be* ~ *ABOUT a matter*, 'n saak verstandig beskou; *be* ~ *OF the gravity of the situation*, die erns v.d. toestand besef; besef, bewus wees van die erns v.d. toestand; ~**ness,** gevoeligheid; verstandigheid.
sen'sibly, voelbaar; merkbaar; opmerklik; verstandig.
sen'sitive, (n) heldersiende; (a) heldersiende; fyngevoelig, liggeraak; eergevoelig; fyn, teergevoelig, aantreklik, fyngevat; ~ *TO*, gevoelig vir; *VERY* ~, fyn van nerf; ~**ness,** fyngevoeligheid; aantreklikheid; eergevoeligheid; teergevoeligheid; ~ **paper,** gevoelige papier; ~ **plant,** kruidjie-roer-my-nie, roerplantjie
sen'sitivism, sensitivisme.
sen'sitivist, sensitivis.
sensitiv'ity, gevoeligheid; liggeraaktheid; sensitiwiteit; ~ **training,** sensitiwiteitsopleiding.
sen'sitize, gevoelig maak.
sens'or, sensor.
sensor'ial, gevoels=, sintuiglik, sensories; ~ *impression*, sinsindruk.
sensor'ium, gevoelsetel, brein.
sen'sory, sintuiglik, sensories, gevoels=; ~ **cell,** sintuigsel; ~ **nerve,** gevoelsenuwee.
sen'sual, sinlik, wellustig, vleeslik, geil, sensueel; ~ *pleasure*, sinsgenot; ~**ism,** sinlikheid, wellustigheid; sensualisme; ~**ist,** wellusteling, sensualis; ~**'ity,** sinlikheid, wellus, wellustigheid, vleeslikheid, geilheid; ~**ize,** versinlik, sinlik maak; ~**ness** = **sensuality.**

sen'suous, sinstrelend; sinlik; ~**ness,** sinlikheid.
sent, *kyk* **send.**
sen'tence, (n) sin, volsin; uitspraak, vonnis (reg); ~ *of DEATH,* die doodvonnis; *PRONOUNCE* ~ *of DEATH,* die doodvonnis uitspreek; *PROVISIONAL* ~, handvulling, voorlopige vonnis; *SERVE a* ~, 'n vonnis uitdien; *UNDER* ~ *of death,* ter dood veroordeel; (v) vonnis, veroordeel; ~ *to death,* ter dood veroordeel.
senten'tious, bondig, kragtig; sinryk; diepsinnig; ~**ness,** bondigheid; sinrykheid.
sen'tience, gevoel, waarnemingsvermoë, waarneming.
sen'tient, waarnemend, voelend.
sen'timent, gevoel; gewaarwording; idee, gedagte; sentiment.
sentimen'tal, oorgevoelig, gevoelerig, sentimenteel; ~**ism,** oorgevoeligheid, sentimentaliteit; ~**ist,** sentimentele persoon, gevoelsmens; ~'**ity,** oorgevoeligheid, gevoelerigheid, sentimentaliteit; ~**ize,** sentimenteel wees; oorgevoelig wees.
sen'tinel, (n) brandwag, skildwag; *stand* ~, op wag staan; (v) bewaak; laat bewaak; op brandwag sit.
sen'try, (..tries), wag, skildwag, brandwag, *stand* ~, op wag staan; ~**-box,** (skild)waghuisie; ~**-go,** (skild)wagdiens; ~**-line,** (skild)waglyn; ~'**s beat,** (skild)wagronde; ~'**s post,** (skild)wagpos.
sep'al, kelkblaar, kelkieblaar; ~**oid,** kelkblaaragtig; ~**ous,** kelkblaar=.
separabil'ity, skeibaarheid.
sep'arable, skeibaar.
sep'arate, (n) afdruk, oordruk; (v) skei, afskei; verdeel, afsonder, afhok, uitmekaar gaan, ~ *CREAM,* melk afroom; ~ *pupils into CLASSES,* leerlinge in klasse verdeel; ~ *one thing FROM another,* een ding van 'n ander skei; (a) afsonderlik, apart, afgeskei, enkel; ~ *DEVELOPMENT,* eiesoortige (aparte) ontwikkeling; *send by* ~ *POST,* onder afsonderlike omslag stuur; ~ *TRIAL,* afsonderlike verhoor; ~**d,** uitmekaar, geskei; afgeroom; ~ **development,** afsonderlike ontwikkeling; ~**d milk,** afgeroomde melk; ~**ly,** afsonderlik; stuksgewyse; ~**ness,** verdeeldheid; afgesonderdheid; apartheid.
separa'tion, skeiding; afsondering; ~ *of GOODS,* boedelskeiding; *JUDICIAL* ~, skeiding tussen tafel en bed; ~ **allowance,** skeidingstoelae; ~ **order,** skeidingsbevel, egskeiding.
sep'aratism, sug tot afskeiding, separatisme.
sep'aratist, (n) voorstander van afskeiding, separatis; afgeskeidene; (a) separatisties, afskeidingsgesind.
sep'arative, skeidend.
sep'arator, skeier; afskeier; roomafskeier; ~**y,** afskeidings=.
separat'um, (..ta), afdruk, oordruk.
Sepe'di, Sepedi.
sep'ia, inkvis, seekat; sepia, bruin kleur, bruin waterverf.
sep'oy, (-s), sipoy.
sep'sis, besmetting, ettervergiftiging, bloedvergiftiging, sepsis.
sept, stam, sibbe.
septahed'ral, sewevlakkig.
septahed'ron, sewevlak.
sep'tal¹, (n) tussenskot.
sept'al², (a) stam=.
sep'tangle, sewehoek.
septang'ular, sewehoekig.
septar'ian, septaries.
sept'ate, met tussenskotte.
Septem'ber, September.
septen'ary, (n) sewetal; sewe; (a) sewetallig; sewejarig.
sep'tenate, sewedelig, sewetallig.
septenn'ate, sewejarige tydperk.
septenn'ial, sewejarig, sewejaarliks.
sept'foil, seweblad.
sep'tic, bederfveroorsakend, verrottend; septies; ~ *aem'ia,* septisemie, bloedvergiftiging; ~ **poisoning,** bloedvergiftiging; ~ **tank,** rottingsput, septiese tenk; ~ **virus,** lykgif.
septilat'eral, sewesydig.

septisyll'able, sewelettergrepige woord.
septuagenar'ian, (n) sewentigjarige, sewentiger; (a) sewentigjarig.
septuagen'ary, sewentigjarig.
Septuages'ima, Septuagesima, derde Sondag voor die Vaste.
Sep'tuagint, Septuagint.
sep'tum, (..ta), middelskorting, tussenwand, tussenskot, skeidingswand; septum.
sep'tuple, (n) sewevoud; (v) versewevoudig; (a) sewevoudig.
sepulch'ral, graf=; begrafnis=; ~ **customs,** begrafnisgebruike; ~ **rites,** begrafnisplegtighede; ~ **stone,** gedenksteen, grafsteen; ~ **urn** grafurn; ~ **voice,** grafstem.
sep'ulchre, (n) graf; *the HOLY S* ~, die Heilige Graf; *WHITED* ~, witgepleisterde graf; vrome bedrieër; (v) begrawe.
se'pulture, begrafnis.
sequa'cious, volgsaam, gedwee, slaafs; reëlmatig vloeiend (musiek); ~**ness, sequa'city,** volgsaamheid, gedweeheid, slaafsheid.
seq'uel, vervolg; gevolg; nasleep; naspel, nadraai, resultaat, vervolgbundel, vervolgdeel, vervolgwerk, *the* ~ *of an ACTION,* die nasleep van 'n daad; *IN the* ~, in die verdere verloop; hierna; *the* ~ *to a NOVEL,* die vervolg van 'n roman.
sequel'a, (-e), nawerking, gevolg; nasleep.
seq'uence, volgorde, opeenvolging, reeks; gevolg; ooreenstemming (gram.); sekwens (musiek); ~ *of CARDS,* volgkaarte; *the* ~ *of EVENTS,* die opeenvolging van gebeurtenisse; *HISTORICAL* ~, geskiedkundige volgorde; *a NATURAL* ~ *of,* 'n natuurlike gevolg van; ~ *of TENSES,* ooreenstemming van tye.
seq'uent, volgend.
sequen'tial, opvolgend; voortvloeiend.
seques'ter, (n) skeidsman; (v) afsonder; in beslag neem, sekwestreer; ~**ed,** eensaam, afgeleë; afgetrokke; ~**ed ESTATE,** gesekwestreerde boedel; ~**ed LIFE,** afgesonderde lewe.
seques'trate, sekwestreer, konfiskeer, beslag lê op.
sequestra'tion, sekwestrasie, beslaglegging, inbeslagneming, konfiskasie; afsondering; *compulsory* ~, gedwonge sekwestrasie.
seq'uestrator, sekwestreerder, beslaglêer, sekwester.
seq'uin, blinker; goue muntstuk (Venesië).
sequoi'a, (Amerikaanse) mammoetboom, sequoia.
sera'glio, (-s), vrouehuis, harem, serail.
se'raph, (-im, -s), seraf, engel; ~'**ic,** engelagtig, verhewe.
se'raphine, serfyn, harmonium, huisorrel.
Serb, (n) Serwiër; (a) Serwies; ~**ia,** Serwië; ~**ian,** (n) Serwiër; Serwies (taal); (a) Serwies.
sere, droog, verdor; *the* ~, *the yellow leaf,* die ouderdom.
serenade', (n) serenade; (v) 'n serenade bring, serenadeer; ~**r,** iem. wat 'n serenade bring, serenadesanger.
serena'ta, serenata.
serene', kalm; helder; bedaard; deurlugtig; *Your S* ~ *Highness,* U Deurlugtige Hoogheid. ~**ness, seren'ity,** helderheid; kalmte, deurlugtigheid.
serf, slaaf; lyfeiene, horige; ~**dom,** lyfeienskap; slawerny.
serge, sersje.
serge'ancy, sersantsrang, sersantskap.
serge'ant, sersant; ~**-at-arms,** stafdraer, seremoniemeester; ampswag (S.A.); ~**-major,** sersant-majoor; ~ **ship,** sersantskap, sersantsrang.
sergette', dun sersje.
ser'ial, (n) vervolgverhaal, vervolgstorie, feuilleton; tydskrif; (a) by gedeeltes; periodiek; in aflewerings, reeksgewyse; ~ **camera,** seriebeeldkamera; ~**ist,** feuilletonskrywer, feuilletonis; ~**iza'tion,** reeksgewyse plasing; ~**ize,** as vervolgwerk laat verskyn; ~ **letter,** reeksletter; ~**ly,** seriesgewyse; in aflewerringe; ~**ly numbered,** reeksgewyse genommer; ~ **number,** volgnommer; reeksnommer; ~ **photograph,** seriebeeld; ~ **publication,** vervolgwerk; ~ **rights,** serieregte; ~ **story,** vervolgverhaal; ~ **work,**

seriate   1222   **servility**

vervolgwerk; ~ **writer,** feuilletonskrywer, feuilletonis; vervolgverhaalskrywer.
ser'iate, (v) in 'n reeks rangskik.
ser'iate(d), (a) in 'n reeks gerangskik.
seriat'im, een na die ander; punt vir punt, puntsgewys(e), seriatim.
seri'ceous, syagtig.
se'riculture, sywurmteelt.
ser'ies, serie, reeks; opeenvolging; ~ **circuit,** seriebaan; ~ **coil,** seriespoel; ~ **motor,** seriemotor; ~ **winding,** seriewikkeling.
ser'igraph, serigraaf.
serig'raphy, serigrafie (kuns).
se'rin, sysie; Europese kanarie.
serinette', voëlorreltjie.
sering'a, sering; Brasiliaanse kaoetsjoekboom.
serio com'ic, halfernstig, ernstig-komies.
ser'ious, ernstig, serieus; plegtig, stemmig; gevaarlik; gewigtig, bedenklik; aansienlik; deeglik; *matters LOOK* ~, sake lyk sleg; *and NOW to be* ~, alle gekheid op 'n stokkie; *be QUITE* ~, dit in alle erns bedoel; ~**ly,** ernstig, in erns; *TAKE* ~*ly,* ernstig opneem; *TREAT* ~*ly,* erns maak met; ~ *TROUBLE,* ernstige moeilikheid (probleme); ~**ness,** erns(tigheid), bedenklikheid, serieusheid; *in all* ~*ness,* in alle erns.
ser'jeant, *kyk* **sergeant.**
serm'on, (n) preek, leerrede, predikasie; vermaning, strafpreek; sermoen; *the S*~ *on the MOUNT,* die Bergrede; ~*s in STONES,* natuurwaarhede; (v) preek; kapittel; ~**ize,** preek; sedelesse leer, vermaan; ~**izer,** preker; sedeleraar; ~**izing,** (n) gepreek, prekery; (a) preek=.
serolog'ic, serologies.
sero'logist, seroloog.
sero'logy, serologie, weikunde.
seros'ity, wateragtigheid, serum.
ser'ous, waterig, dun, serumagtig, weiagtig.
serp'ent, slang; serpent; slanghoring; musiek(instrument); voetsoeker (vuurwerk); *CHERISH a* ~ *in one's bosom,* 'n adder aan jou bors koester; *the OLD S*~, ou Satan; *THE S*~, die Slang (sterrek.); ~-**charmer,** slangbesweerder.
serp'entine, (n) serpentynsteen; kronkelpad; kronkellyn; kronkelrit; (v) kronkel, slinger, draai; (a) slangagtig; kronkelend; listig, slu; ~ **dance,** slangdans; ~ **pattern,** kronkelpatroon.
serpen'tinous, serpentynhoudend, serpentyn=.
serp'ent-like, slangagtig.
serp'ent's tail, slangstert.
serpi'ginous, voortkruipend; met herpes (blasiesuitslag).
se'rrate, getand; saagvormig; gekartel; ~**d,** getand, saagvormig; ~*d EDGE,* getande rand; ~*d PIN,* gleufkoppen.
serra'tion, saagvormige insnyding; getandheid, vertanding; riffeling.
se'rried, aaneengeslote, vas teen mekaar, kompak; ~ *ranks,* aaneengeslote geledere.
se'rrulate(d), fyngesaag.
serrula'tion, fyngetandheid, gesaagdheid.
ser'um, wei, serum, entstof.
serv'al, tierboskat, serval.
serv'ant, bediende, dienaar; hulp; kneg; diensbode, diensbare; beampte; amptenaar; *DOMESTIC* ~, tuishulp; *a GOOD* ~ *but a bad master,* 'n goeie bediende maar 'n slegte baas; *your HUMBLE* ~, u onderdanige dienaar; *your OBEDIENT* ~, u dienswillige dienaar; *PUBLIC* ~, staatsamptenaar; ~-**girl,** diensmeisie.
serve, (n) (die) afslaan (tennis); (v) dien, bedien; diens doen; help; voldoende wees vir; uitdien (tyd); opskep, voorsit, voordien, opdien (kos); verskaf; skink (drinkgoed); rondbring, rondgee; behandel; afslaan (tennis); gunstig wees; dek (diere); gooi (sport); ~ *one's APPRENTICESHIP,* as leerjong dien; ~ *AS,* diens doen as; ~ *a CAUSE,* 'n saak dien; ~ *on a COMMITTEE,* in (op) 'n komitee dien; ~ *a COW,* 'n koei dek; *DINNER is* ~*d,* die ete is opgeskep; ~ *one's own ENDS,* jou eie planne bevorder; *that EXCUSE will not* ~ *you,* daardie uitvlug sal jou nie help nie; ~ *with FOOD,* kos in=

skep vir; ~ *the GUNS,* die geskut bedien; ~ *on a JURY,* jurielid wees; ~ *MASS,* die mis bedien; ~ *two MASTERS,* twee here dien; ~ *NOTICE on,* kennis gee aan; ~ *an OFFICE,* 'n betrekking beklee; ~ *OUT,* uitdeel, uitgee; ~ *one's PROBATION,* 'n proeftyd uitdien; ~ *no useful PURPOSE,* geen nut hê nie; ondienstig wees; ~ *no earthly PURPOSE,* nêrens voor deug nie; ~ *its PURPOSE,* aan sy doel beantwoord; ~ *the PURPOSE of,* diens doen as; ~ *a useful PURPOSE,* van nut wees; *that* ~*s him RIGHT!* goed so! dis sy verdiende loon! ~ *ROUND,* uitdeel, rondgee; ~ *with the same SAUCE,* met gelyke munt terugbetaal; ~ *a SENTENCE,* straf uitdien; ~ *a SUMMONS on,* 'n dagvaarding bestel (beteken) aan; ~ *at TABLE,* by (die) tafel bedien; ~ *one's TIME,* jou tyd uitdien; jou straf uitsit; *this has* ~ *d it's TIME,* dit het sy tyd gehad; ~ *someone a TRICK,* iem. 'n poets bak; ~ *UP,* opdien, opskep, opdis; ~**r,** dienaar; bediende; diener, afslaner (tennis); koekspaan; skinkbord; tafelbediende; ~**ry,** (..**ries),** aanregkamer, opskepkamer.
Serv'ia, Serwië; ~**n,** (n) Serwiër; Serwies (taal); (a) Serwies.
serv'ice, (n) diens; kerkdiens; nut; diensverrigting; gereg; versiening (motor); afslaan (tennis); vervoermiddels; dekking (diere); voorsiening (bv. elektrisiteit); bestelling (dagvaarding); diening; stel, servies; betekenis; *the ARMED* ~*s,* die weermag; *AT your* ~, tot u diens; *BE in* ~, dien, in diens wees, werk; *the CIVIL* ~, die staatsdiens; ~ *of DEDICATION,* wydingsdiens; *DIVINE* ~, godsdiensoefening; kerkdiens; *DO someone a* ~, iem. 'n diens bewys; vir iem. 'n klip uit die pad rol; *GO into* ~, jou verhuur; *be called to HIGHER* ~, tot hoër diens opgeroep word; *HOLD a* ~, godsdiens hou; *IN* ~, in gebruik; *perform a KINDLY* ~, iem. 'n guns bewys; vir iem. 'n klip uit die pad rol; *LONG* ~, lang diensjare; *on His MAJESTY'S* ~, in Sy Majesteit se diens; *NAVAL* ~, seediens; *be OF* ~, van diens wees; *ON* ~, in diens; *PUT into* ~, in gebruik neem; *RELEASE from* ~, uit diens ontsethef; *RELIGIOUS* ~, godsdiensoefening; *RENDER a* ~, 'n diens bewys; *for* ~ *s RENDERED,* vir gelewerde dienste; *have SEEN* ~, as soldaat gedien het; *SHORT* ~, kort diening; *TAKE* ~ *with,* gaan werk by; *WITHDRAW from* ~, uit die gebruik neem; uit die vaart neem (skip); (v) diens gee, versien (motor); bedien; onderhou; ~ *a motor,* 'n motor bedien (versien, diens); ~**abil'ity,** diensbaarheid; dienstigheid; ~**able,** diensbaar, dienlik, nuttig, diensbaar, dienstig; ~**ableness,** diensbaarheid, bruikbaarheid; geskiktheid; ~ **benefit,** diensvoordeel; ~ **bonus,** diensbonus; ~-**book,** kerkboek; ~ **boot,** diensstewel; ~ **brake,** voetrem; ~ **card,** dienskaart; ~ **charge,** bedieningsgeld; dienshefting; dienslading; tafelgeld, dekgeld; ~ **colour,** weermagskleur, uniformkleur; ~ **connection,** verbruiksaansluiting; ~ **contract,** dienskontrak; ~ **corps,** intendans; ~ **door,** bedieningsdeur; ~ **extension,** diensverlenging; ~ **fee,** dekgeld; ~ **flat,** woonstel met bediening; ~ **flight,** diensvlug; ~ **fuse,** verbruiksekering; ~ **hatch,** diensluik; ~ **issue,** voorgeskrewe uitgifte; ~ **jacket,** jekker; ~ **kit,** velduitrusting; ~-**lift,** goederehyser; ~-**line,** afslaanlyn; ~ **load,** diensvrag; dienslading; ~ **mains,** verbruiksleiding; ~ **man,** weermagsman; herstelwerker; ~ **message,** diensberig; ~ **pay,** (soldate) soldy; ~ **record,** diensstaat, diensregister; werktuigkundige staat; ~-**record card,** dienskaart; ~ **revolver,** diensrewolwer; ~ **rifle,** diensgeweer; ~ **stairs,** dienstrap; ~ **stamp,** diensseël; ~ **station,** diensstasie, bedieningstasie, versienstasie; ~ **supervisor,** diensopsiener; ~ **switch,** hoofskakelaar; ~ **training,** militêre opleiding; ~-**utility body,** diensbak; ~ **women,** diensvroue.
serv'icing, bediening; instandhouding; onderhoud; versiening (motor).
serviette', servet.
serv'ile, slaafs; kruipend, kruiperig.
servil'ity, slaafsheid, onderworpenheid; kruiperigheid.

serv'ing, (die) dien; bediening; porsie (kos); ~-**dish**, opskepskottel; ~-**hatch**, bedienvenstertjie, dienluik; ~-**man**, dienskneg; ~-**spoon**, opskeplepel.

serv'itor, bediende, dienaar; vrye student.

serv'itude, diensbaarheid, verslaafdheid, slawerny; serwituut, beperking (op eiendom); ~ *OVER*, serwituut op; *PENAL* ~, gevangenisstraf.

ser'vo: ~ **motor** servomotor; ~-**rudder**, hulproer.

ses'ame, sesam; *open* ~, sesam, gaan oop.

Seso'tho, Sesotho (taal).

sesquicenten'nial, (n) anderhalfeeufees; (a) honderden-vyftigjarig.

sesquipedal'ian, anderhalf voet lank; veellettergrepig, eindeloos lank, ellelank; ~ **ism**, sesvoetigheid; gebruik van lang woorde.

ses'quiplane, anderhalfdekker.

sess'ile, steelloos, sonder steel, ongesteel(d).

se'ssion, sitting, sessie; vertoning (van film); byeenkoms; *CRIMINAL* ~, strafsitting; *PARLIAMENT is in* ~, die parlement sit; ~ **al**, sittings=; ~ **time**, sit(tings)tyd.

sestet', sekstet.

Sesut'o, Sesoeto, Sotho (taal).

set, (n) servies, stel (tafelgereedskap, ens.; tennis; kamers); versakking (grond); houding; neiging; ligging; broeisel; dekor (toneel); stel (film); rigting (gety); ondergang (son); steggie, stiggie, plantjie; spel (tennis); vrugknop; raam; stutsel (myn); snit (klere); span, ploeg, reeks; battery (ketels); kliek; kring, trop; toestel (radio); *a* ~ *of BOOKS*, 'n stel boeke; *make a DEAD* ~ *at*, 'n heftige aanval maak teen; *things are at a DEAD* ~, alles sit vas; ~ *of MIND*, neiging, aanleg; *not in OUR* ~, nie in ons groep (kliek) nie; *a* ~ *of ROOMS*, 'n stel kamers; *a* ~ *of TEETH*, 'n stel tande; (v) (~, ~), plaas; skik, afsit; plant; vasbyt (tande); bepaal; stel (ploeg; visier); verhard, hard word, droog, versteen (sement); aanstuur op, koers rig op; rig; skerp maak, aansit (saag); reël (granaat); inpeil (kompas); opgee; slyp (mes); aangee (toon); laat broei, eiers gee; saai; dek (tafel); klaarmaak; vasstel; bring; aanhits; spalk (been); beset (juwele); inlê, vrugte vorm; ondergaan (son); taan (roem); staan; set, golf (hare); styf word, bind (jellie); ~ *ABOUT a task*, aan 'n taak begin; ~ *off to ADVANTAGE*, voordelig laat uitkom; ~ *oneself AGAINST*, jou verset teen; ~ *ALIGHT*, aan die brand steek; ~ *APART*, apart sit; opsy sit, reserveer; ~ *ASIDE*, tersy lê; buite beskouing laat; wegsyfer; verwerp; vernietig; ~ *AT*, aanhits; ~ *BACK*, agteruitsit, terugsit, vertraag; laat inspring (drukker); ~ *the BALL rolling*, die eerste stap doen; iets aan die gang sit, ~ *bad BLOOD*, kwaad bloed set; ~ *BY*, bêre, spaar; ~ *one's CAP at someone*, na iem. vry; ~ *the COMPASS*, die kompas inpeil; ~ *(a) COURSE for*, stuur na; ten doel stel om; ~ *a COVER*, 'n plek dek; ~ *at DEFIANCE*, trotseer; uitdaag; ~ *with DIAMONDS*, met diamante beset; ~ *a DOG on*, 'n hond aanhits, sa sê vir 'n hond; ~ *DOWN*, neersit; opteken; ~ *DOWN at*, skat op; ~ *DOWN as*, beskou as; ~ *by the EARS*, onenigheid veroorsaak; ~ *at EASE*, gerus stel; tuis laat voel; ~ *an EXAMPLE*, 'n voorbeeld stel; ~ *EYES on*, te sien kry; ~ *one's FACE against*, sterk opponeer; ~ *the FASHION*, die toon aangee; ~ *FIRE to*, ~ *on FIRE*, aan die brand steek; ~ *on FOOT*, aan die gang sit; ~ *FORTH*, uiteensit; 'n reis begin, op reis gaan; ~ *FREE*, vrylaat; ~ *GOING*, aan die gang sit; ~ *in one's HABITS*, met vaste gewoontes; ~ *HAIR*, hare kartel; ~ *one's HEART on*, sterk begeer; jou sinne stel op; *a HEN*, 'n hen laat broei; ~ *up HOUSE*, 'n huishouding begin; ~ *IN*, intree, inval; begin, insit; inwerk; *jewels* ~ *IN gold*, juwele in goud gevat; ~ *aside a JUDGMENT*, 'n vonnis nietig verklaar; ~ *LAUGHING*, aan die lag maak; ~ *a LEG*, 'n been spalk; ~ *at LIBERTY*, in vryheid stel; ~ *at LOGGERHEADS*, in die harnas jaag; ~ *one's MIND on something*, vasbeslote wees om iets te kry; ~ *one's MIND to a task*, jou toelê op 'n taak; ~ *in MOTION*, aan die gang sit; ~ *to MUSIC*, toonset, op musiek sit; ~ *at NAUGHT*, verontagsaam, ignoreer, minag, bespot; ~ *OFF*, los=

laat; afsonder; verhoog; vertrek; aan die gang sit (masjien); versier; ~ *OFF against*, laat opweeg teen; stel teenoor; ~ *ON*, aanhits; verdryf; ~ *OUT*, uitsit; afbaken, aanlê; uiteensit; vermeld; wyd set (letters); vertrek; begin; ~ *the PACE*, die gang aangee; ~ *down PASSENGERS*, passasiers aflaai; *it* ~ *in to RAIN*, dit het begin reën; ~ *a RAZOR*, 'n skeermes aansit (skerp maak); *REACTION* ~ *in*, daar het 'n reaksie gekom; ~ *a RIDDLE*, 'n raaisel opgee; ~ *someone RIGHT*, iem. op sy plek sit; ~ *SAIL*, onder seil gaan; ~ *a SAW*, 'n saag skerp maak (aansit); ~ *up (a) SHOP*, 'n winkel begin; ~ *the SIGHT(S)*, die visier stel; *the STAGE is* ~, die toneel is gereed; ~ *a STONE*, 'n steen monteer; ~ *STORE by the neighbours' opinion*, waarde heg aan die bure se mening; ~ *the TABLE*, tafel dek; ~ *TALKING*, aan die praat bring; ~ *one's TEETH*, die tande op mekaar byt; ~ *THINKING*, jou laat nadink; iem. sy kop laat krap; ~ *in TRAIN*, aan die gang sit; ~ *a TRAP*, 'n lokval stel; ~ *UP*, oprig, instel, opsit; verhef; oopmaak; ~ *someone UP in business*, iem. die kapitaal verskaf vir 'n saak; ~ *UPON*, aanrand; *be* ~ *UPON*, daarop uit wees; van vaste voorneme wees; graag wil hê; ~ *a WATCH*, 'n oorlosie reg stel; *be* ~ *in one's WAYS*, in jou gewoontes vasgeroes wees; *all* ~ *to WIN*, oorgehaal om te wen; ~ *to WORK*, aan die werk spring; aan die gang sit; (a, adv) opgesit; styf, strak, onveranderlik, vas; voorgeskrewe (boeke); gereeld; geset; *dead* ~ *AGAINST*, sterk gekant teen; *all* ~ *FOR the journey*, reisvaardig; ~ *ON an idea*, vasbeslote; ~ *PHRASE*, stereotiepe uitdrukking; *his* ~ *PURPOSE*, sy vaste voorneme; *a* ~ *SPEECH*, 'n voorbereide toespraak; *at* ~ *TIMES*, op gesette tye; ~ *UP*, aan die gang bring; instel; *be* ~ *in one's WAYS*, in jou gewoontes vasgeroes wees.

seta'ceous, borselrig, borselagtig.

set: ~-**back**, terugsetting, terugslag, teenslag; insinking; inspringing (argit.); ~ **bolt**, klembout; ~ **book**, eksamenboek, voorgeskrewe boek; ~ **collar**, loskraag; ~ **design**, stelontwerp; stelinkleding; ~ **designer**, stelontwerper; ~-**down**, bestraffing, afjak, skrobbering, vermaning; ~ **face**, strak gesig; ~-**hammer**, sethamer.

setif'erous, seti'gerous, met hare, borselrig.

set: ~-**in**, begin; ~-**net**, stelnet; ~ **nut**, klemmoer; ~-**off**, versiersel; teenstelling; uitdelging; kompensasie, vergoeding; teë-eis; skuldvergelyking; versnyding (muur).

set'on, dreineerband.

set: ~-**out**, begin; uitrusting; vertoning; ~ **piece**, geykte (voorgeskrewe) stuk; ~ **phrase**, vaste (stereotiepe) uitdrukking; ~ **pin**, stelpen; ~ **rod**, maatstaf, maatstok; ~ **screw**, stelskroef; ~ **scrum**, vaste skrum; ~-**spanner**, oopbeksleutel; ~ **square**, tekendriehoek.

sett, kyk **set** (tennis).

settee', rusbank, sofa.

sett'er, steller, versteller; patryshond, jaghond; lokvoël; ~-**on**, (**setters-on**), aanhitser, opstoker.

set' theory, versamelingsleer (wisk.).

sett'ing, verharding (sement); raam, omlysting, montuur; toonsetting (musiek); inmesseling (ketel); toneelskikking; broeisel eiers; stand, aanwysing (instrument); rigting (kaart); inpeiling (kompas); reëling; lensopening (kamera); vrugvorming; agtergrond; omgewing; stolling (bloed); ~-**hammer**, sethamer; ~-**lotion**, setmiddel, (haar)kartelmiddel; ~ **out**, (pen) uitlê; vertrek; ~ **period**, bindtyd; ~-**pin**, stelpen; ~-**pole**, stootstok; ~ **property**, stolenskap; ~ **time**, verhardingstyd; ~-**tool**, setgereedskap.

set'tle, (n) sitbank, sofa; (v) (jou) vestig, domisilieer; besink, afsak (moer); neerslaan; bepaal, vasstel; laat bedaar; in orde bring, regmaak; vereffen, aansuiwer, verreken, afreken (skuld); afspreek; beklink; koloniseer; vassit (geld); gaan sit (voël); vassak (modder); stadig sink; skik, bylê (twis); ~ *an ACCOUNT*, 'n rekening vereffen (betaal); ~ *one's AFFAIRS*, jou sake regmaak; ~ *AMICABLY*, in der minne skik; ~ *a CASE out of court*, 'n saak

settled 1224 shabby

skik; ~ *a COUNTRY*, 'n land koloniseer; ~ *(on) the DAY*, die dag vasstel; ~ *a DEBT*, 'n skuld vereffen; ~ *DIFFERENCES*, geskille uit die weg ruim; ~ *DOWN*, jou vestig; bedaar; gaan trou; ~ *DOWN to work*, aan die werk gaan; *that is all we will* ~ *FOR*, net dit sal ons bevredig; net daarmee sal ons tevrede wees; dis ons minimumeis; ~ *one's HASH*, met iem. klaarspeel; 'n end maak aan sy grootpratery; ~ *for LESS*, minder aanneem (aanvaar); *that* ~ *s the MATTER*, daarmee is die saak opgelos (afgehandel); ~ *a PERSON*, hom onderdanig maak; hom verhinder om onaangenaamheid te veroorsaak; ~ *a QUARREL*, 'n geskil uit die weg ruim; ~ *a QUESTION*, 'n saak afhandel; ~ *one's foot in the STIRRUP*, die voete in die stiebeuels steek.

set'tled, vas, vasgestel; ingetrek (huis); afgehandel, afgedaan; gevestig; bestendig, bedaard; onveranderlik; betaal; uitgemaak; ~ *CONVICTION*, vaste oortuiging; ~ *GLOOM*, onveranderlike somberheid; ~ *LIFE*, bestendige lewe; *THAT is* ~ *then*, dis dan afgespreek (afgesproke).

set'tlement, vestiging; afbetaling, aansuiwering, afrekening; afdoening (sake); reëling, byegging, skikking; nedersetting, volksplanting, kolonie; oordrag, oormaking (geld); vasstelling; vergelyk; besinking; sakking (grond); verhandeling; vestiging; bemaking (erfenis); beslegting (saak); *COME to an amicable* ~ *with*, 'n minlike skikking tref met; *DEED of* ~, huwelikskontrak; akte van oordrag, skenking; *IN* ~ *of*, ter vereffening van; *MAKE a* ~ *on*, iets vassit op; iets bemaak aan; ~ **plan**, skikplan.

set'tler, nedersetter, setlaar, kolonis; beslissende daad (woord, argument); besinker, besinkbak; neerslagtoestel; *S~s' Day*, Setlaarsdag.

set'tling, betaling, verrekening; skikking; kolonisasie; (pl) afsaksel, moer, besinksel; ~-**day**, betaaldag; ~-**tank**, besinktenk.

set'-to, geveg, bakleiery; rusie; woordestryd.

set'-up, (n) inrigting, organisasie; oprigting; stelsel; opset; (a) ontwikkel, gevestig.

sev'en, sewe; ~ *of DIAMONDS*, ruitensewe; ~ *of HEARTS*, hartesewe; ~-**armed**, sewearmig; ~-**day**, sewedaags; ~-**fold**, sewevoudig; ~-**league boots**, sewemylslaarse; ~ **o'clock**, seweuur; ~-**teen**, sewentien; ~ **teenth**, sewentiende; *the* ~ *teenth century*, die sewentiende eeu; ~ **th**, sewende; *S* ~ *th day Adventist*, Sewendedagadventis; *S* ~ *th Day Adventist Church*, Sewendedagadventistekerk; ~ **th wicket**, sewende paaltjie (krieket); ~ **thly**, in die sewende plek; ~ **tieth**, sewentigste; ~ **ty**, sewentig; ~ **ty-five**, vyf-en-sewentig.

sev'enty-four¹, vier-en-sewentig.

sev'enty-four², streepvis.

sev'er, skei; afsonder; (los)skeur, afsny, afbreek; ~ *one's CONNECTIONS with*, as lid bedank; jou betrekking verbreek met; ~ *ONESELF from*, jou afskei van; ~ *RELATIONS with*, die betrekking verbreek met; ~ **able**, skeibaar.

sev'eral, (a) verskeie, verskillende; afsonderlike; etlike; respektief; eie; hoofdelik (regt.); ~ *OTHERS*, party (baie) ander; *their* ~ *WAYS*, hulle verskillende (eie) paaie; (pron) verskeie; ~**ly**, elkeen afsonderlik, elkeen op sy eie; *jointly and* ~*ly*, gesamentlik en afsonderlik.

sev'erance, skeiding, skeuring, afsondering, losmaking; afsnyding.

severe', streng, gestreng; fel, geweldig, ernstig; hard; strak; straf, afgedankste (pak); kwaai (aanval); *BE* ~ *on a person*, kwaai wees met 'n persoon; ~ *BIT*, strawwe stang; *a* ~ *BLOW*, 'n swaar slag; ~ *in one's JUDGMENT*, te fel in jou oordeel; ~ *REMARKS*, skerp aanmerkings; ~ *TEST*, swaar toets; ~ *TREATMENT*, streng(e) behandeling; *a* ~ *WINTER*, 'n strawwe winter.

sev'ered, afgeskei; afgesny.

severe'ly, erg, streng, hard; *leave* ~ *alone*, heeltemal links laat lê; ~ **mutilated**, ernstig geskend(e).

severe'ness, seve'rity, ernstigheid; hardheid, strengheid, felheid; strafheid.

Se'ville, Sevilla; ~ **orange**, bitterlemoen.

sew, (-ed, sewn), naai, werk (met naald en gare); ~ *IN*, innaai; ~ *ON*, aanwerk; ~ *UP*, toewerk.

sew'age, rioolvuil, rioolwater, rioolslyk; afvalstowwe; ~ **disposal**, wegdoen van rioolvuil; ~ **drain**, straatriool; ~ **ejector**, rioolpomp; ~ **farm**, rioolplaas; ~ **sludge**, rioolslyk; ~ **sump**, rioolput; ~ **water**, rioolwater.

sew'-and-fell seam, oorhandse naat.

sew'er¹, (n) kleremaker; naaier.

sew'er², (n) riool; geut; (v) rioleer; van riole voorsien; ~ **age**, rioolstelsel, riolering; ~ **age system**, rioolstelsel; ~-**gas**, rioolgas; ~-**pipe**, rioolpyp.

sew'ing, naaldwerk, naaigoed, naaiwerk; (die) naai; ~-**awl**, naaiels; ~-**basket**, werkmandjie; ~-**cotton**, naaigare; ~-**machine**, naaimasjien; ~-**needle**, naald; ~-**silk**, naaisy.

sewn, genaai; *kyk* sew.

sex, (n) (-es), geslag, sekse; seks, geslagsdrif, geslagtelikheid; *the FAIR* ~, die skone geslag; *the STERNER (STRONGER)* ~, die mansgeslag; *the WEAKER* ~, die Evasgeslag; (v) die geslag bepaal (van kuikens); ~ **act**, geslagsdaad, paringsdaad.

sexagenar'ian, (n) sestigjarige, sestiger; (a) sestigjarig.

sexagen'ary, sestigjarig.

Sexages'ima, Sexagesima, tweede Sondag voor die Vaste.

sexage'simal, sestigtallig.

sexang'ular, seshoekig.

sex' appeal, seksstraling, sinlike (liggaamlike) aantrekkingskrag; geslagsprikkeling.

sexcenten'ary, (n) (..ries), sesde eeufees; (a) seshonderdjarig.

sex' determination, geslagsbepaling.

sexed, geslags-; ~ **chicks**, kuikens wat volgens geslag verdeel is.

sex education, geslagsonderrig, seksonderrig; ~ **pioneer**, seksonderrigpionier.

sexenn'ial, sesjarig, sesjaarliks.

sex: ~**er**, geslagsbepaler; ~**iness**, wulpsheid; ~**ing**, geslagsbepaling; ~**ism**, seksisme; ~**ist**, seksis; ~ **law**, wet teen geslagsverkeer; ~**less**, geslagloos; ~-**linked**, geslagsgebonde; ~ **mania**, erotomanie; ~ **maniac**, geslagsmaniak, erotomaan; ~ **organ**, geslagsorgaan; ~ **perversion**, geslagsafwyking; ~ **pervert**, geslagtelik afwykende; ~-**ridden**, seksbehep; ~ **urge**, geslagsdrang.

sexolog'ical, seksuologies.

sexol'ogist, seksuoloog.

sexol'ogy, seksuologie.

sex'tain, sesreëlige versie.

sex'tan, sesdaags.

sex'tant, sekstant, hoogtemeter, meetskyf, sesde deel van 'n sirkel.

sextet(te)', sekstet.

sex'ton, koster; ~ **beetle**, miskruier; ~**ship**, kosterskap.

sex'tuple, (n) sesvoud; (v) versesvoudig; (a) sesvoudig.

sex'tuplet, sesling.

sex'ual, geslags-, geslagtelik, seksueel; ~ **abuse**, seksuele mishandeling; ~ **act**, geslagsdaad, paringsdaad; ~ **desire**, geslagsdrang, natuurdrif; ~ **fidelity**, seksuele trou; ~ **glands**, geslagskliere; ~ **harassment**, seksuele teistering; ~ **impotence**, geslagtelike onmag; impotensie; ~ **instinct**, teeldrif; ~ **intercourse**, geslagtelike gemeenskap, geslagsomgang; ~ **'ity**, seksualiteit, geslagsdrif; ~**ly transmitted disease**, seksueel oorgedraagde siekte; ~ **opening**, geslagsopening; ~ **organs**, geslagsdele, geslagsorgane; ~ **passion**, geslagsdrif; ~ **pervert**, geslagtelik afwykende; ~ **reproduction**, geslagtelike voortplanting; ~ **selection**, teelkeuse; ~ **urge**, geslagsdrif, geslagsdrang.

sex'y, wulps; seksbehep.

Seychelles', Seychelle.

shabb'ily, armoedig; gemeen; slordig; *treat someone* ~, iem. sleg behandel; iem. afskeep.

shabb'iness, armoedigheid, skamelheid; nietigheid; gemeenheid; kaalheid; slordigheid.

shab'by, kaal; toiingrig, haweloos, skamel; gemeen, laag; slordig, smerig; oes; torrerig; afgeslyt; afskeperig.

shab'rack, saalkleedjie, skabrak.
shack, pondok, krot, hut.
shac'kle, (n) skakel; koppel(ing); sluitring, boei, ketting; beuel; skommelstuk; harp (van ketting); (pl) boeie; hindernisse, belemmering; ~ *s of convention*, die keurslyf van vormlikheid; (v) boei; koppel; belemmer, beperk; ~ **bolt,** skakelbout, harpbout; ~ **joint,** harpsluiting.
shad, elf (vis).
shadd'ock, pampelmoes.
shade, (n) skadu(wee); koelte; gees, skim; (lamp)kap, glaskap, skerm; skakering, nuanse; tikkie, sweempie; ietsie; *a* ~ *BETTER,* 'n ietsie beter; ~ *of COLOUR,* kleurskakering; *DIFFERENT* ~ *s of,* verskillende skakerings van; ~ *s of MEANING,* betekenisverskille; betekenisnuanses; *the* ~ *s of NIGHT,* die duisternis; *PUT in the* ~, in die skadu stel; iem. ver oortref; *THE* ~ *s,* die skimmeryk; (v) beskadu; afskerm; beskut, beskerm; half bedek, aan die oog onttrek; oorskadu, verduister, versomber, donker kleur; arseer (skildery); ~ *in,* arseer; ~ **-card,** kleurekaart; ~ **-loving,** skaduweeliewend; ~ **tree,** koelteboom.
shad'iness, skadurykheid, lommerrykheid; verdagtheid, dubbelsinnigheid.
shad'ing, beskaduwing; arsering; skakering.
shad'ow, (n) skadu(wee); spook, gees, skim; beeld; skyn; afskaduwing, ewebeeld; sweem; spioen; beskerming; aanduiding, bewys; naloper; oorblyfsel; *AFRAID of one's own* ~, bang vir jou eie skaduwee; *CATCH at a* ~, die skyn vir werklikheid aansien; *the* ~ *of DEATH,* die doodskaduwee; *without a* ~ *of DOUBT,* sonder die minste twyfel; ~ *s under the EYES,* kringe onder die oë; *FIGHT with one's own* ~, teen skaduwees skerm; *FOLLOW someone like a* ~, iem. soos 'n skaduwee volg; *cast a* ~ *of GLOOM,* 'n skaduwee oor iets werp; *be as INSEPARABLE as one's* ~, iem. soos sy skaduwee volg; *may your* ~ *never grow LESS,* mag dit altyd met jou goed gaan; *PASS like a* ~, soos 'n skaduwee verbygaan; *SACRIFICE the substance for the* ~, die wese aan die skyn opoffer; *a* ~ *of one's former SELF,* net 'n skaduwee van wat jy was; *SOMEONE'S* ~, iem. se skaduwee; (v) beskadu, oorskadu; beskerm; volg soos 'n skaduwee, dophou; ~ **-boxing,** skynboks, skyngeveg; ~ **cabinet,** skimkabinet, beoogde ministerie; ~ **gram,** X-straalfoto, röntgenfoto, skiagram; ~ **graph,** skadubeeld; röntgenfoto; ~ **iness,** skaduweeagtigheid; vaagheid, duisterheid; ~ **less,** onbeskadu, skaduloos; ~ **minister,** skimminister; ~ **show,** skimmespel; ~ **y,** skaduweeagtig; skaduryk; onwesenlik; ontasbaar, skimagtig, vaag, duister.
shad'y, skaduryk, lommerryk; twyfelagtig, verdag, oneerlik; *a* ~ *CHARACTER,* 'n verdagte vent; ~ *SIDE,* skaduweekant; *on the* ~ *SIDE of fifty,* aan die verkeerde kant van vyftig.
shaft, pyl; as (masjien); disselboom (wa); skag (myn); steel (gholfstok); straal (lig); ~ **bottom,** skagbodem; ~ **-box,** skagkas; ~ **bush,** asbus; ~ **-head,** skagbek; pylspits; ~ **ing,** steierwerk; ~ **-key,** aansluitspy; skagspy; ~ **sinker,** skagdelwer, skaggrawer; ~ **-sinking,** skaggrawery; ~ **-timbering,** skagbetimmering; ~ **wall,** skagwand.
shag, boskasie, kroeshare; pluis; kerftabak; seeduiker (voël); ~ **giness,** harigheid; ~ **gy,** ruig, harig; ~ **dog,** harige hond; ~ **-dog story,** Armeense grap; ~ **(gy)-haired,** met ruie hare.
shagreen', ongelooide leer, sagryn(leer).
shah, sjah (vors van Persië).
shake, (n) (die) skud(ding); skok; bewing, trilling; handdruk, triller (mus.); *be ALL of a* ~, die bewarasie hê; *be no GREAT* ~ *s,* niks besonders (wafers) wees nie; *HAVE the* ~ *s,* die bewerasie hê; *THE* ~ *s,* koeekoors; *in two* ~ *s of a lamb's TAIL,* in 'n kits; (v) **(shook, -n)** skud; skok; bibber, bewe, tril, rittel; uitskud, uitslaan; wakker skud; wankel; wrik; dril; verswak; aantas; ~! vat so! ~ *with COLD,* rittel v.d. koue; ~ *DOWN,* afskud, uitsprei; ~ *the DUST from one's feet,* die stof van jou voete skud; *his FAITH was greatly* ~ *n,* sy vertroue is geskok; ~ *with FEAR,* van angs bewe; ~ *one's*

FIST at someone, jou vuis vir iem. wys; *his HAND* ~ *s,* sy hand bewe; ~ *HANDS,* die hand skud; ~ *HANDS with,* die hand gee aan; met die hand groet; ~ *one's HEAD,* die kop skud; ~ *OFF,* afskud; ontslae raak van; ~ *one's SIDES,* skater (v.d. lag); ~ *OUT,* uitskud; ~ *someone UP,* vuur onder iem. maak.
shake'down, kermisbed; *HAVE a* ~ *for the night,* onderdak vir die nag kry; *PREPARE a* ~, 'n kermisbed maak; ~ **cruise,** proefvaart; ~ **run,** looprit.
shak'en, geskok, ontdaan; geskud; *BADLY* ~, baie ontdaan; ~ *to the CORE,* hewig geskok; ~ *to its FOUNDATIONS,* tot sy grondveste geskud.
shake'-out, uitskudding; regskudding; peildaling.
shak'er, skudder; skudgeut.
Shakespear'ian, (n) Shakespearekenner; (a) Shakespeariaans.
shake'-up, wakkerskudding.
shak'iness, bouvalligheid; swakheid, bewerigheid.
shak'ing, skudding, (die) skud; bewing, gerittel; *give him a good* ~, skud hom goed deurmekaar; ~ **-up,** aansporing; opskudding.
shak'o, (-s), sjako (soort militêre hoed).
shak'y, bouvallig, trillerig, wikkelrig, bewerig; wankel, swak, onvas, onsolied; *FEEL* ~, skrikkerig voel; *a* ~ *HOUSE,* 'n bouvallige huis; *LOOK* ~, daar sleg uitsien; ~ *SECURITIES,* twyfelagtige aandele; ~ *in his SPELLING,* nie alte seker van sy spelling nie; *make a* ~ *START,* swak begin; ~ *VOTERS,* onbetroubare kiesers.
shale, skalie, leiaarde; ~ **-oil,** leiklipolie.
shall, (should), sal; moet; mag; *thou shalt not STEAL,* jy mag nie steel nie; *we* ~ *WIN,* ons sal (gaan) wen; *man* ~ *WORK to eat,* die mens moet werk om te eet.
shalloon', sjalon.
shall'op, sloep.
shallot', salot.
shall'ow, (n) ondiepte, vlak plek; (v) ondiep word, vlak word; vlak maak; (a) vlak, ondiep; oppervlakkig; ~ **-brained,** dom, onnosel; ~ **-hearted,** oppervlakkig; ~ **ing,** versanding; vlakwording; ~ **ness,** ondiepte; oppervlakkigheid.
shalt, *kyk* **shall.**
shal'y, skalieagtig, leiklipagtig.
sham, (n) bedrog; voorwendsel; skynvertoning; skyn, liemakery, aanstellery; namaaksel; fopspeen; (v) **(-med),** bedrieg, fop, kul; veins, jou aanstel, voorwend, fingeer; huigel; voorgee, maak asof, liemaak; ~ *DEATH,* maak of jy dood is; ~ *ILLNESS,* maak of jy siek is; ~ *SLEEP,* maak of 'n mens slaap; (a) geveins, gemaak, vals; kastig, voorgewend.
sha'man, sjamaan.
sham'anism, sjamanisme.
sham'ateur, kamma-amateur, skynamateur.
sham'ble, (n) slottende gang, slotgang, geslof; (v) slepend gaan, slof, skuifel; waggel.
sham'bles, slagplek, abattoir, slagpale; bloedbad, slagting, verwoesting; deurmekaarspul.
sham'bling, (n) geslof, slofgang; (a) sloffend; waggelend; onreëlmatig.
sham'door, blinde deur.
shame, (n) skande; skaamte; *BLUSH with* ~, bloos van (uit) skaamte; *BRING to* ~, *BRING* ~ *upon,* te skande maak; *CRY* ~ *upon,* skande roep oor; *DEAD to* ~, geen skaamte meer ken nie; *FOR* ~! foei! skaam jou! *LOST to* ~, skaamteloos; ~ *ON you!* foei! skaam jou! *PUT to* ~, in die skande steek, beskaam; *SENSE of* ~, skaamtegevoel; *TO his* ~, tot sy skande; *WHAT a* ~! hoe jammer tog! *be WITHOUT* ~, skaamteloos wees; (v) beskaam, skaam maak; skaam; onteer; ~ *someone into doing something,* iem. dwing om uit skaamte iets te doen; (interj) foei! ~ **-faced,** bedees, skaam, verleë, skamerig; ~ **-facedly,** skamerig, beskaamd, bedremmeld; ~ **-facedness,** skamerigheid, bedeesdheid; ~ **ful,** skandelik, hemeltergend; ~ **fully,** skandelik; ~ **fulness,** skandelikheid; ~ **less,** skaamteloos, onbeskaamd, goddeloos; ~ **lessly,** skaamteloos; ~ **lessness,** onbeskaamdheid, skaamteloosheid.
sham: ~ **excuse,** uitvlug; ~ **fight,** spieëlgeveg, skyn

geveg; ~**mer,** bedrieër; veinser, aansteller; ~**ming,** veinsing; *he is only* ~*ming*, hy hou hom maar so.
shamm'y, sham'oy, seemsleer, leerlap.
shampoo', (n) **(-s),** kopwassing; harewas(middel), sjampoe; (v) hare was, kop was; sjampoeneer; ~**powder,** haarwaspoeier.
sham'rock, klawer(blaar).
shan'dy, (..**dies),** limonadebier; ~**gaff,** bier-en-gemmerbier, bier-en-limonade.
Shan'gaan, Sjangaan (stam; stamlid); Sjangaans (taal).
shanghai', met geweld werf, pres, ronsel, ontvoer.
shank, (n) skenkel(been), lang been; been (pluimvee); steel, stingel; skoorsteenpyp; stif, angel (gereedskap); skag (boor, anker); skenkelhou, pyphou; skeen; hakskeenhou, steelhou (gholf); *have LONG* ~*s,* sekretarisbene hê; *ride S*~*s's MARE,* met dapper en stapper gaan; met stamper en stoter reis; te voet loop; *on S*~*s's PONY,* met dapper en stapper; met snaar en stramboel; ~ *and TROTTER,* skenkel en pootjie; (v) 'n hakskeenhou slaan (gholf); ~**-bone,** pypbeen, skeenbeen; ~**-end,** skenkelkant; agterkant.
shank'ings, pootjieswol.
shann'y, (shannies), slymvis.
shan't = **shall not.**
shan'tung, sjantoeng, Sjinese sy.
shan'ty¹, (..**ties),** liedjie; *kyk* **chanty.**
shan'ty², (..**ties),** pondok; skuur; hok; afdak; ~**town,** krotbuurt; blikkiesdorp.
shape, (n) vorm, fatsoen; toestand; gedaante, figuur; formaat; gestalte, gestaltenis; *in BAD* ~, in 'n slegte kondisie; *GIVE* ~ *to,* vorm gee aan; *in GOOD* ~, goed; op stryk; *BE in GOOD* ~, daar goed uitsien; *IN the* ~ *of,* in die gedaante van; *KNOCK into* ~, regmaak; regruk; brei, afrig; *LICK into* ~, fatsoeneer; *OUT of* ~, uit fatsoen; *PUT into* ~, fatsoeneer; *TAKE* ~, (vaste) vorm aanneem; *the* ~ *of THINGS to come,* die toekomstige toedrag van sake; (v) vorm, maak, bewerk, modelleer, fatsoeneer, formeer; uitdink, beraam; inrig; reël; ~ *BREAD,* brood opmaak; ~ *one's COURSE,* die koers rig; ~*d EDGE,* gefatsoeneerde rand; *see HOW things* ~, sien hoe sake ontwikkel; ~ *LOAVES,* brood opmaak; *the student is* ~*ing WELL,* dis 'n veelbelowende student; ~**less,** vormloos; mismaak, wanstaltig; ~**lessness,** wanstaltigheid; vormloosheid; ~**liness,** welgemaaktheid, welgeskapenheid; ~**ly,** welgeskape, goed gevorm, bevallig van vorm, mooi gevorm; ~**n,** vorm, fatsoeneer; ~**-pruning,** vormsnoei; ~**r,** fatsoeneerder; smidsaal; sterkarmmasjien (metaalw.); frees(masjien).
shap'ing, (n) formering; (a) vorm=; ~**-tool,** vormbeitel.
shard, potskerf; vlerkskild (insek).
share¹, (n) ploegskaar.
share², (n) deel, porsie, part; aandeel; (pl) aandele, effekte; *DEFERRED* ~, slapende aandeel; *DO one's* ~, jou deel doen; *that is your FAIR* ~, dit is jou regmatige aandeel; *FALL to someone's* ~, iem. ten deel val; *GO* ~*s with,* deel met; saam wins en verlies deel; *HAVE a* ~ *in,* deel hê in; *for MY* ~, wat my betref; ek vir my; *ORDINARY* ~, gewone aandeel; *REGISTERED* ~, aandeel op naam; *TAKE a* ~ *in,* deel hê in; deelneem aan; (v) deel; verdeel; uitdeel; deel hê in; sy aandeel hê; deelneem; ~ *and* ~ *ALIKE,* gelykop deel; ~*d BY* ~, gedeel deur; ~ *a FEELING,* jou in iets invoel; 'n gevoel onderskryf; *I* ~ *your OPINION,* ek stem met u saam; ek deel u mening; ~ *OUT,* uitdeel; ~ *a ROOM with,* saam in een kamer woon met; 'n kamer deel met; ~ *WINNINGS with,* die wins met ander deel.
share'-beam, balk (van ploeg).
share: ~**broker,** aandelemakelaar, effektemakelaar; ~**-capital,** aandelekapitaal; ~ **certificate,** aandeelsertifikaat; ~**-cropper,** deelsaaier, deelboer; ~**cropping,** deelboerdery; ~**d line,** deellyn; ~ **deal,** aandeletransaksie; ~**holder,** aandeelhouer; ~**holding,** aandeelhouding, aandelebesit; ~**holderportefeulje;** ~**-incentive scheme,** aandeleaansporingsplan; ~**-market,** aandelemark; ~**-out,** uitdelery;

uitdeling; ~**-pusher,** aandeelsmous; ~**-pushing,** aandelesmousery; ~**r,** deelgenoot, deelhebber; ~ **service,** deellyn.
shar'ing, verdeling; mededeling; belydenis.
shark, (n) haai; skurk, uitsuier; (v) van bedrog leef, uitsuig, swendel; insluk; ~**-like,** haaiagtig; ~**-net,** haainet; ~ **skin,** haaivelstof; ~ **spanner,** haaibeksleutel.
Shar'on, Saron.
sharp, (n) dur, kruis (musiek); bedrieër; (v) bedrieg, kul; skelm speel; met 'n kruis merk (mus.); (a, adv) puntig, skerp, skerpsnydend (voorwerp); hoogloopend, bitsig, snedig, venynig, vinnig (antwoord); spits; bytend; gepeper; gewiks; deurdringend; skerpsinnig (verstand); oorlams; gou; presies; slim, gevat, geslepe (persoon); vals (musiek); kruis (musiek); *a* ~ *ATTACK,* 'n hewige aanval; ~ *CONTRAST,* skerp teenstelling; *a* ~ *CONTEST,* hewige stryd; *a* ~ *CRY,* 'n deurdringende gil; ~ *CURVE,* skerp draai; *a* ~ *FALL,* 'n skielike daling; *a* ~ *FIGHT,* 'n hewige geveg; *at FIVE* ~, presies om vyfuur; *a* ~ *FROST,* 'n skerp ryp; *a* ~ *GALLOP,* 'n vinnige galop; ~ *INCLINE,* steil afdraande (opdraande); *KEEP a* ~ *look-out,* fyn oplet; *LOOK*~! roer jou (riete)! opskud! *be as* ~ *as a NEEDLE,* so slim soos die houtjie v.d. galg; ~ *PRACTICE,* slimstreke, kullery, knoeiery; *PULL up* ~, skielik inhou; *a* ~ *REBUKE,* 'n skerp (bytende) teregwysing; *SING* ~, te hoog sing; *a* ~ *TONGUE,* 'n skerp tong; 'n tong soos 'n skeermes; *TOO* ~ *for me,* te slim vir my; *a* ~ *TURN,* 'n kort draai; *a* ~ *VISAGE,* 'n spits gesig; ~*'s the WORD!* roer jou (riete)! ~**-cut,** skerp besnede; ~**-edged,** met skerp kant; ~**en,** skerp maak, (aan)slyp, wet, aanpunt (potlood); ~**er,** bedrieër, swendelaar, kuller; kaartknoeier; ~**-ground,** skerp geslyp; ~**ish,** taamlik skerp, skerperig; ~**ly,** skerp; ~**ness,** skerpheid; beeldskerpte; vinnigheid, vlugheid; ~ **practice,** oneerlike handelwyse, kullery, knoeiery; ~**-set,** uitgehonger; begerig; ~**-shooter,** skerpskutter; sluipskutter; ~**-sighted,** skerpsiende, skerpsinnig; ~**-tongued,** snipperig; ~**-witted,** geestig, skrander, gevat.
shatt'er, breek, verbrysel, verpletter; verstrooi, versplinter, fyn breek, verwoes, verbrokkel; die bodem inslaan, verydel; ruïneer; vernietig; skok; ~ *something to BITS,* verpletter; ~ *someone's HOPES,* iem. se verwagtings verydel; ~ **ed,** vergruis, verbrysel, versplinter, verbrokkel, verwoes; *his nerves were* ~*ed,* sy senuwees was klaar (kapot); ~**ing,** (n) verbryseling, verplettering; uitslaan (koring); (a) verpletterend; verwoestend; ~ **proof,** splintervry; ~**y,** splinterig.
shave, (n) (die) skeer; skaafmes; spaander; foppery, kullery; noue ontkoming; *a CLOSE* (narrow) ~, so hittete, naelskraap; *HAVE a* ~, jou laat skeer; (v) **(-d** or **-n),** skeer (baard); skawe (hout); afskeer (hare); verbyskram, verbyglip; afstroop; kort afsny; ~ *off,* afskeer; ~**ling,** monnik; ~**r,** skeerder; snuiter, knapie.
Shav'ian, (n) volgeling van G. B. Shaw; (a) van G. B. Shaw.
shav'ing, krul (hout); (die) skeer; skeerdery; (pl) krulle, skaafsels; ~**-basin,** ~**-bowl,** skeerbakkie; ~**-brush,** skeerkwas, skeerborsel; ~**-cream,** skeerpommade, skeerroom; ~**-glass,** skeerspieël; ~**-horse,** skaafbank; ~**-kit,** skeergereedskap; ~**-lotion,** skeerwasmiddel, skeerwatertjie; ~**-mirror,** skeerspieël; ~**-paper,** skeerpapier; ~**-powder,** skeerpoeier; ~**-saloon,** skeersalon; ~**-set,** skeergoed; ~**-soap,** skeerseep; ~**-stick,** skeerseep; ~**-strop,** skeerriem; ~**-tackle,** skeergoed; ~**-water,** skeerwater.
shawl, (n) tjalie, sjaal; (v) in 'n tjalie toedraai; 'n tjalie omhang; ~**-collar,** sjaalkraag.
she, sy; *A he or a* ~, 'n hy of 'n sy, 'n seun of 'n dogter; ~ *(train, ship) is COMING,* hy kom.
shea'-butter, galambotter.
sheaf, (n) **(sheaves),** gerf; ~ *of paper,* bondel papiere; *sheaves of CORN,* koringgerwe; ~ *of FLOWERS,* gerf blomme; (v) **(sheaved),** in gerwe bind.
shear, (n) helfte van 'n skêr; (die) skeer; afskuiwing;

shearing 1227 **shell**

skuifskeur; glyding; (pl) skaapskêr; tuinskêr; (v) **(-ed, shorn),** skeer; knip, sny; kaal maak, pluk; af= skuif; *be shorn of,* beroof word van; ~ **bill,** skêrbek (voël); ~**-blade,** kniplem; ~ **er,** skeerder; ~ **force,** skuifkrag.

shear'ing, (n) skeer (skape); (skuif)skeuring (geol.), dwarsafskuiwing, skuifwerking; knipwerk; (a) skeer=; ~ **board,** skeervloer; ~ **force,** afskuifkrag; ~**-fold,** ~**-pen,** skeerhok; ~ **machine,** skeerma= sjien; knipmasjien; ~ **season,** skeertyd; ~ **shed,** skeerhok, skeerhuis; ~ **strength,** skuifvastheid; ~ **stress,** skuifspanning; ~**-time,** skeertyd.

shear'ling, wissellam, tweetandskaap.

shear: ~ **mark,** skeermerk; ~ **plane,** skuifvlak; ~ **resistance,** skuifweerstand; ~ **rock,** wrywingsrots.

shears, skêr; skaapskêr; tuinskêr.

shear' strength, skeurvastheid.

shear'water, pylstormvoël.

she'-ass, (-es), donkiemerrie, eselmerrie.

sheath, skede; blaarskede; skild; koker, foedraal; vlerkskild (insek); mantel, dop (bom); ~ **dress,** ske= detabberd, skederok.

sheathe, in die skede steek; beklee, oortrek; ~*d CABLE,* omhulde kabel; *a metal ROD* ~*d in rub= ber,* 'n metaalstang met rubber beklee.

sheath'ing, dubbeling; bekleding, omhulsel; beman= teling; betimmering; bodembeslag; ~ **paper,** bou= papier.

sheath'-winged, skildvleuelig.

sheave, (n) skyf, blok, katrol; (v) (in gerwe) bind.

sheaves, *kyk* **sheaf,** (n).

She'ba, Skeba.

she'-bear, beerwyfie, berin.

shebeen', smokkelkroeg, smokkelhuis.

she'-cat, wyfiekat, katwyfie; katterige vroumens.

shed, (n) loods, skuur, afdak; werkwinkel; skeer= skuur, skeerhok; (v) (~, ~), stort; vergiet, uitgiet; pleng (bloed); skiet; werp; afgee, versprei; verloor (hare); laat val (blare); uitstraal (lig); wissel (tande); ~ *BLOOD,* bloed vergiet; *BLUEGUMS* ~ *their bark,* bloekombome laat hulle bas val; ~ *FEA= THERS,* verveer; ~ *FRAGRANCE,* geur versprei; *some trees* ~ *their LEAVES,* party bome verloor hulle blare; ~ *LIGHT upon,* lig werp op; ~ *a SKIN,* vervel; ~ *TEARS,* trane stort; ~ *TEETH,* tande wissel.

shedd'er, storter, vergieter; ~ *of blood,* bloedver= gieter.

shedd'ing, vergieting, plenging.

she: ~**-devil,** duiwelin; dierasie; ~**-dragon,** furie.

sheen, glans, skittering, luister; ~**y,** glinsterend, glansend.

sheep, (sing and pl) skaap; *the BLACK* ~, die swart skaap; *the BLACK* ~ *of the family,* die swart skaap v.d. familie; *there are BLACK* ~ *in every flock,* elke trop het sy swart skaap; *DIVIDE the* ~ *from the goats,* die bokke van die skape skei; *if one* ~ *leaps o'er the DYKE, the rest will follow,* as een skaap deur die hek is, volg al die ander; *separate the* ~ *from the GOATS,* die skape van die bokke skei; *as well be hanged for a* ~ *as for a LAMB,* doller as kop-af kan dit nie; *like LOST* ~, soos verdwaalde skape; *the SCABBED* ~ *infects the whole flock,* een brandsiek skaap steek die hele trop aan; *like* ~ *that have no SHEPHERD,* soos skape wat geen wagter (herder) het nie; soos verdwaalde skape; ~**-bree= der,** skaapteler; ~**-breeding,** skaapteelt; ~**-dip,** skaapdip; ~**-dipping,** skaapdippery; ~**-dog,** skaaphond; ~**-faced,** dom, onnosel; ~**-farmer,** skaapboer; ~**-farming,** skaapboerdery; ~**-fold,** skaapkraal; ~**-hook,** herderstaf, haakkierie; ~**-ish,** skaapagtig, onnosel, dom; *look* ~ *ish,* verleë lyk; lyk of die kraaie jou kos opgeëet het; ~**ishness,** ska= merigheid; onnoselheid; ~**-ked,** skaapluis; ~**-kraal,** skaapkraal; ~**like,** skaapagtig; gedwee, on= derdanig; ~**man,** skaapboer, skaapwagter; ~**-pen,** skaapkraal, hok; ~**-raising,** skaapboerdery; ~**-run,** skaapveld, skaapplaas; ~**'s brawn,** skaapsult; ~**-scab,** brandsiekte; ~**'s clothing,** skaapklere; *IN* ~ *'s clothing,* in skaapklere; *a WOLF in* ~ *'s clothing,* 'n wolf in skaapklere; ~**'s eye,** skaap=

ogie; *cast* ~ *'s eyes at,* verliefderig aankyk; ogies maak vir; ~**'s' shank,** skaapbeen; trompetsteek (touwerk); ~**'s' head,** skaapkop; ~**-shearer,** skaapskeerder; ~**-shearing,** skaapskeerdery; ~**-shears,** skaapskêr; ~ **skin,** skaapvel; bokjol, plaas= dans; ~ **sorrel,** steenboksuring; ~**-stealer,** skaap= steler, skaapslagter; ~**'s trotters,** skaappootjies; ~**-tick,** skaapluis; ~**'s' tongue,** skaaptong; ~**-walk,** skaapveld; ~**-wash,** skaapdip, dipgoed; ~**'s wool,** skaapwol.

sheer¹, (n) gier (skip); afwyking; (pl) maskraan (hawe); (v) afsak; uitwyk, swenk, 'n ander koers uitgaan; gier (skip); ~ *AWAY,* uitwyk; afwyk; ~ *OFF,* van koers verander; padgee.

sheer², (a) suiwer, rein, puur, louter; ragfyn, dun; fyn (materiaal); steil, loodreg (krans); *a* ~ *DROP,* 'n ononderbroke val; ~ *FALSEHOOD,* 'n groot leuen; *by* ~ *FORCE,* deur brute krag, deur ruwe geweld; ~ *NONSENSE,* pure (louter) onsin; *it is* ~ *PROPAGANDA,* dis pure propaganda; ~ *WASTE of time,* pure tydverspilling; (adv) steil, loodreg; meteens, heeltemal, reëlreg.

sheer' plane, afskuiwingsvlak.

sheet, (n) laken; vel (papier); oppervlakte; doods= kleed; koerantjie, blad; kaart; plaat; dek, lawadek (geol.); gordyn; seil; *BETWEEN the* ~*s,* onder die kombers; *start with a CLEAN* ~, met 'n skoon lei begin; *a* ~ *of FIRE,* 'n vuursee; *with FLOWING* ~*s,* met volle seile; *IN* ~*s,* in velle; in strome (reën); *a* ~ *of galvanised IRON,* 'n sinkplaat; ~ *of MUSIC,* musiekblad; *as PALE as a* ~, so bleek soos 'n laken; ~ *of PAPER,* vel papier; *the RAIN came down In* ~*s,* die reën het in strome geval; *a* ~ *of SNOW,* 'n sneeukleed; ~ *of STAMPS,* vel (blad) seëls; *a* ~ *of WATER,* 'n watervlakte; *three* ~*s in the WIND,* hoog in die takke; hoog veertien; aangeklam; (v) bedek; beklee (met 'n plaat); met 'n laken toemaak; die seile vasmaak; ~**-almanac,** muurkalender; ~**-anchor,** noodanker, pleganker; toeverlaat; ~ **copper,** plaatkoper, bladkoper; ~ **crosion,** bladerosie, oppervlakerosie; ~ **fire,** artille= rievuur, granaatvuur; ~ **gelatine,** plaatgelatien; ~ **glass,** vensterglas; ~ **ing,** lakenlinne, lakengoed; plaatbekleding; ~ **iron,** plaatyster; ~ **lead,** dek= lood, plaatlood; bladlood; ~ **lightning,** weerlig= (bundel); ~ **metal,** plaatmetaal; ~**-metal worker,** plaatmetaalwerker; ~ **tin,** bladtin; ~**-works,** plaatmeule; ~ **zinc,** bladsink.

she'-goat, bokooi.

sheikh, sjeik; ~**dom,** sjeikdom.

sheil'a, morrie.

shek'el, sikkel; (pl) geld, rykdom.

she'-lamb, ooilam.

shel'drake, kopereend (mannetjie).

shel'duck, kopereend (wyfie).

shelf, (shelves), rak; plank; vak; plaat; bank, rotslaag; sandplaat; venster (hooimied); plat (geol.); *CON= TINENTAL* ~, vastelandse plat; *ON the* ~, afge= dank, opsy gesit; *be ON the* ~, bokwagter word; op die bakoond sit; op die stoppelland wees; *PUT on the* ~, (fig.), aan die kapstok hang; ~ **life,** raklewe.

shell, (n) skil; skulp; peul, dop(pie), bolster, huls (okkerneut); huisie; skaal, skulp, omhulsel; romp (van gebou); binneste; doodkis; geraamte; granaat; tussenklas; buitenste, uitwendige; skyn; dop (skil= pad); oorskulp; *COME out of one's* ~, uit jou dop (skulp) kruip; *CREEP into one's* ~, in jou skulp kruip; *an EMPTY* ~, 'n leë dop; *(they)* ~ *ENE= MY positions,* (hulle) bombardeer die vyandelike stellings; *hardly OUT of the* ~, skaars uit die dop; *RETIRE into one's* ~, in jou dop (skulp) kruip; (v) skil; dop, afdop, uitdop; uitpeul; bombardeer, be= skiet; dors, afmaak (mielies); ~ *EGGS,* eiers afdop; ~ *NUTS,* neute afpel; ~ *OFF,* afskilfer; *have to* ~ *OUT,* moet opdok; ~ *OUT,* uitdop; ~ *PEAS,* er= tjies (uit)dop.

shellac', (n) skellak, skilferlak; (v) **(-ked),** vernis (met skellak).

shell: ~ **auger,** lepelboor; ~**back,** ou seerob, pik= broek; ~**-bit,** skulpboor; ~**-case,** granaatdop; ~**-crater,** granaatkrater, granaattregter; ~ **ed,** uitge=

dop; ~er, mielieafmaker; dopper; ~-fire, artillerievuur, granaatvuur; ~ fish, skulpvis; ~-gimlet, lepelboor; ~-gold, bronspoeier; ~-heap, afvalhoop; ~-hole, granaattregter; ~ing, bombardement, bombardering; afskilfering; uitdop; ~ing chisel, dopbeitel; ~ing plant, uitdopfabriek; ~less, doploos, sonder dop; ~ lime, skulpkalk; ~-mound = shell heap; ~-plate, rompplaat; ~ proof, granaatvry; bomvry; ~-proof shelter, granaatvrye (granaatvaste) skuilplek; ~-reamer, lepelruimer; ~-shock, bomskok; ~-snail, huisieslak; ~-splinter, bomskerf, granaatskerf; ~ tube, skulpbuisie; ~-work, skulpwerk; ~y, vol skulpe; skulp=, skulpagtig; skulperig.

shel'ter, (n) skuilplek, skuilkelder; beskutting, beskerming; skuiling, bedekking; onderkome; huisie, afdak, onderdak; dekmantel (fig.); *GIVE* ~, beskut; *TAKE* ~, skuil; *UNDER* ~, onder beskutting; onder dak; (v) beskut, beskerm; verskans (gholf); ~ *ONESELF*, skuil; ~ *from the RAIN*, beskerm teen die reën; ~ed, beskut, beskerm; verskans; skotvry; ~less, onbeskut; ~-tent, skuiltent, ligte veldtent; ~-trench, oordelde loopgraaf.

shel'tie, shel'ty, (..ties), Skotse ponie.

shelve, op die rak sit, bêre, weglê; rakke insit; uitstel, op die lange baan skuif, vir 'n onbepaalde tyd uitstel; skuins afhel; ~ *a matter*, 'n saak op die lange baan skuif; in die doofpot stop.

shelves, *kyk* shelf.

shel'ving, (n) rakke; (rak)planke; uitstel (saak); glooi; (a) skuins, hellend.

Shem, Sem.

shep'herd, (n) veewagter, skaapwagter, herder; *the Good S~*, die Goeie Herder; (v) oppas; ~ *boy*, wagtertjie; ~ *ess*, (-es), herderin; ~'s crook, herderstaf, haakkierie; ~'s pie, boerepastei, herderspastei; ~'s plaid, ~'s tartan, herdersgeruit; ~'s tree, witgatboom.

shepp'y, (sheppies), skaapkraal.

sherb'et, sorbet; vrugtedrank; suursuiker.

sherd, *kyk* shard.

she'riff, balju, skout; skepen; fiskaal; ~alty, ~dom, ~hood, ~ship, skoutamp, baljuamp; ~'s sale, baljuverkoping, baljuvendusie.

Sher'pa, Sjerpa.

she'rry, sjerrie.

Shet'land, (n) Shetland; (a) Shetlands; ~ pony, Shetlandse ponie.

shew, *kyk* show, (v).

shew'bread, toonbrood.

she'-wolf, (..wolves), wyfiewolf, wolvin.

shibb'oleth, wagwoord, sjibbolet.

shield, (n) skild; rondas; beskutting, beskerming; skut; *the other side of the* ~, die keersy v.d. medaljie; (v) beskerm, beskut; dek (persoon): ~-battery, skildbattery; ~-bearer, skildknaap, skilddraer; ~-helmet, sweishelm; ~ing, beskerming; afskerming; ~less, onbeskut; ~-like, skildagtig.

shift, (n) verandering, verwisseling; skof (werk); (werk)ploeg; verplasing; verskuiwing; uitvlug, lis, kunsgreep; hulpmiddel; *work DOUBLE* ~*s*, twee skofte werk; *an EIGHT-HOUR* ~, 'n werktyd van agt uur; ~*s and EVASIONS*, draaiery en uitvlugte; *MAKE* ~ *with*, met iets klaarkom; *MAKE* ~ *without*, sonder iets (moet) klaarkom; *MAKE* ~ *on a small pension*, met 'n karige pensioentjie aansukkel; (v) verskuiwe, versit, verplaas; verhuis; jou behelp; verander, verwissel; vervang; draai (wind); ver= spring; ~ *DOWN*, laer skakel (motor); verder wegskuif; ~ *FIRE*, die vuur verlê (mil.); ~ *FOR oneself*, vir jouself sorg; jou eie potjie krap; ~ *GEARS*, die rat wissel (verstel); ~ *one's GROUND*, van standpunt verander; dit oor 'n ander boeg gooi; ~ *OFF*, afskuif; ontduik; ~ *the SCENE*, die toneel verander; ~ *UP*, plek maak, opskuif; hoër skakel (motor); *the WIND is* ~*ing to the east*, die wind draai oos; ~able, verplaasbaar; ~ boss, skofbaas, ploegbaas; ~ crops, wisselgewasse; ~iness, sluheid; slimheid.

shift'ing, (n) verandering, verhuising; verskuiwing; uitvlug; (a) veranderend, veranderlik; skuiwend; (sand) ~ cultivation, wisselbou; ~-gauge, kruis=

hout; ~ sand, dryfsand; ~-spanner, skroefsleutel, verstelbare moersleutel.

shift: ~less, onbeholpe; onbekwaam, hulpeloos; nutteloos; radeloos; ~lessness, onbeholpenheids; onbekwaamheid; ~y, slu, onbetroubaar, skelm.

shikar', jag; ~ee, jagter.

shille'lagh, kierie, knopkierie.

shill'ing, (hist.), sjieling; *CUT off with a* ~, onterf; *TAKE the king's* ~, soldaat word; ~sworth, die waarde van 'n sjieling; 'n sjieling s'n.

shill'y-shally, (n) besluiteloosheid; weifeling; (v) (..llied), weifel; besluiteloos wees; aarsel; (a) weifelend, besluiteloos; ~er, weifelaar.

shi'ly, *kyk* shyly.

shim, (n) keil, wig; onderlegplaat; vulplaatjie; (v) (-med), keil.

shimm'er, (n) glans, glinstering; (v) glinster, glimmer.

shimm'y, (n) (shimmies), hempie; jakkalsdraf (dans); wielwaggeling; (v) jakkalsdraf dans; slinger.

shin, (n) skeen, maermerrie; skenkel (vleis); (v) (-ned), opklouter, beklim; die skene skop; ~-bone, skeenbeen.

shin'dig, (sl.), feestelikheid, fuif.

shin'dy, (..dies), bombarie, lawaai, rusie; *kick up a* ~, 'n bombarie opskop; lawaai maak.

shine, (n) skyn, glans; advertensie; *PUT a good* ~ *on the boots*, die stewels (skoene) mooi laat blink; *RAIN or* ~, reën of sonskyn; *TAKE a* ~ *to*, begin hou van; *TAKE the* ~ *out of someone*, iem. die loef afsteek; iem. van sy glans beroof; (v) (shone), skyn, glinster, blink; glans, straal; uitblink; laat straal; blink maak; ~r, blou oog; muntstuk; serpeling (vis).

shing'le¹, (n) spoelgruis, spoelklippies; (pl) grint.

shing'le², (n) dakspaan, dakplankie; skuinskniphaarstyl; (v) met dakspane toemaak; skuins knip (hare); ~r, dekker.

shin'gle road, spoelgruispad.

shin'gle roof, spaandak, plankiesdak.

shing'les, gordelroos (siekte).

shing'ly, vol spoelgruis.

shin'guard, skeenskut, skeendekker, beenskut.

shin'iness, skyn, glans, blinkheid.

shin'ing, (n) glans, skyn; (a) skitterend, blinkend, ligtend; *improve the* ~ *HOUR*, tyd op die beste wyse bestee; *be no* ~ *LIGHT*, geen groot gees wees nie.

Shin'toism, Sjintoïsme.

Shin'toist, (n) Sjintoïs; (a) Sjintoïs.

shin'y, blinkend, glansend.

ship, (n) skip; bodem, vaartuig; *ABANDON* ~, die skip verlaat; *on BOARD* ~, aan boord; *BY* ~, per skip; ~ *of the DESERT*, skip v.d. woestyn; kameel; *when my* ~ *comes HOME*, wanneer my skip met geld kom; ~ *of the LINE*, linieskip; ~*s that PASS in the night*, mense wat in die verbygaan vlugtig kennis maak met mekaar; *lose a* ~ *for a ha'porth o' TAR*, deur 'n stuiwer te bespaar groot skade ly; *TAKE* ~, skeepgaan; (v) (-ped), inskeep, verskeep, laai; aan boord neem; aanmonster (matroos); ~ *the OARS*, ophou met roei (werk); ~ *a SEA*, 'n groot golf aan boord kry; ~ *by TRAIN*, per spoor stuur; ~-biscuit, skeepsbeskuit; ~ board, skeepsdek; *on* ~board, aan boord; ~-breaker, skeepsloper; ~-breaking, skeepslopery; ~-breaking yard, skeepslopery; ~-broker, skeepsmakelaar; ~-builder, skeepsboumeester; ~-building, skeepsbou; ~building yard, skeepstimmerwerf; ~-canal, skeepvaartkanaal; ~-chandler, skeepsleweransier; ~-chandlery, skeepsleweransie; ~-channel, ~-geul; ~ load, skeepslading; skeepsvrag; ~ man, skipper; loods; ~ master, gesagvoerder, skeepskaptein; ~ mate, skeepsmaat; ~ ment, (skeeps)lading; verskeping; ~ money, vlootbelasting; ~ owner, skeepseienaar, reder; ~ per, verskeper, aflaaier; uitvoerder.

shipp'ing, inskeping; verskeping; skeepvaart; handelsvloot; skepe, skeepsmag; ~-agency, verskepingsdiens; ~-agent, verskeper, verskepingsondernemer; skeepsagent; ~-articles, skeepskontrak; ~ board, skeepvaartraad; ~-broker, skeepsmakelaar; ~-charges, verskepingskoste; ladingskoste; ~-clerk, verskepingsklerk, ekspedisieklerk; ~-com=

pany, skeepvaartmaatskappy; ~ **disaster**, skeepsramp; ~-**firm**, (skeeps)redery; ~-**house**, uitvoerfirma; ~ **intelligence**, skeepstyding; ~-**lane**, vaarwater; ~-**line**, skeepvaartlyn; ~-**office**, verskepingskantoor; ekspedisiekantoor; ~ **order**, reusebestelling; ~-**port**, handelshawe; ~-**ring**, skeepsring, skeepstrust; ~ **trade**, skeepvaarbedryf.

ship's: ~ **articles**, skeepskontrak; ~ **barnacle**, eendemossel; ~ **biscuit** skeepsbeskuit; ~ **boiler**, skeepsketel; ~ **boy**, skeepsjonge; ~ **bread**, klinkers, harde beskuit; ~ **captain**, skeepskaptein; ~ **carpenter**, skeepstimmerman; ~ **chandler**, skeepsleweransier; ~ **charges**, skeepsonkoste; ~ **company**, skeepsrol, monsterrol; ~ **cook**, skeepskok; ~ **doctor**, skeepsdokter.

ship'shape, in die haak, agtermekaar, in orde.

ship's: ~ **hold**, skeepsruim; ~ **hostess**, skeepswaardin; ~ **lantern**, skeepslantern; ~ **log**, seejoernaal; ~ **master**, skeepskaptein; ~ **officer**, skeepsoffisier; ~ **papers**, skeepspapiere; ~ **roll**, skeepsrol; ~ **surgeon**, skeepsdokter; ~ **tackle**, skeepstakel.

ship: ~-**way**, skeepshelling; skeepskanaal; ~-**worm**, paaiwurm; ~ **wreck**, (n) skipbreuk, stranding; (v) skipbreuk ly; *BE* ~ *wrecked*, skipbreuk ly; *THE* ~ *wrecked (crew)*, die skipbreukelinge; ~ **wright**, skeepstimmerman; ~ **yard**, skeepstimmerwerf, (skeeps)werf, marinewerf, skeepsbouwerf.

shire, graafskap.

shirk, (n) pligsversuimer, papbroek; (v) vermy, ontduik, versuim; ~ *work*, jou lyf spaar (bêre); ~ **er**, pligsversuimer; papbroek, lamsak.

shir(r), (n) rimpelwerk; (v) rimpel; ~*ed eggs*, spieëleiers; roomkrummelciers; ~**ring**, rimpelwerk, rimpelplooie.

shirt, hemp; *he has not a ~ to his BACK*, hy het nie 'n hemp om aan te trek nie; *BET one's* ~ *on a horse*, wed al wat jy het; *GIVE away the* ~ *off one's back*, jou hemp (baadjie) vir iem. uittrek; *put one's* ~ *on a HORSE*, al jou geld verwed; *IN one's* ~, in jou hemp; *KEEP your* ~ *on*, moenie kwaad word nie; moenie op jou perdjie klim nie; ~ *of MAIL*, maliekolder; *not to have a* ~ *to one's NAME*, geen draad aan die lyf hê nie; *near is my* ~, *but nearer is my SKIN*, die hemp is nader as die rok; elkeen is homself die allernaaste; ~ **blouse**, hempbloes(e); ~-**button**, hempsknoop; ~-**collar**, hempsboordjie; ~-**front**, borsie (van 'n hemp); ~**ing**, hemplinne, hemdegoed; ~-**pocket**, hempsak; ~-**sleeve**, hempsmou; ~-**stud**, boordjieknoop; ~-**tail**, hempslip.

shit, (vulgar), (n) stront, kak; (v) skyt, kak.

shiv'er[1], (n) splinter, stukkie, brokkie, spaander, stopklip; (v) verbrysel, in flenters breek; verpletter.

shiv'er[2], (n) rilling, siddering; *COLD* ~*s*, kouekoors; *THE* ~*s*, koue rillings, drilsiekte, dronksiekte, die bewerasie; (v) bewe, sidder, rittel, ril; huiwer.

shiv'ered, aan flenters.

shi'ver: ~**ing**, (n) bewerasie; (a) bewend, rittelend; ~**ing grass**, bewertjies, trilgras; ~**y**, bewerig; huiwerig.

shoal[1], (n) klomp, menigte, trop, skool (visse); *in* ~*s*, by hope; (v) skole vorm, wemel.

shoal[2], (n) vlak plek, vlak water; sandbank; (a) vlak; ~**y**, vol vlak plekke.

shock[1], (n) hopie gerwe; (v) hopies gerwe maak, gerwe opper.

shock[2], (n) boskasie, haarbos, kroeshare; ~ *of hair*, dik bos hare.

shock[3], (n) skok, botsing; (v) skok; aanstoot gee; vererg, teen die bors stuit; *be* ~*ed at*, geskok wees deur; aanstoot neem aan.

shock: ~ **absorber**, skokdemper, skokbreker; ~-**absorbing**, skokbrekend, verend; ~ **absorption**, skokbreking; ~ **action**, skokwerking; ~ **cord**, skokkoord; ~ **dog**, wolhaarhond.

shock'er, prul, sensasieroman; vuilgoed (persoon), smeerlap.

shock' head, kroeskop, bossiekop; ~**ed**, wolhaars, met 'n ruie bos hare, wolhaarkop=.

shock'ing, (n) (die) skok; (a) verskriklik, yslik; aanstootlik, ergerlik, stuitend; (adv) beroerd; ~**ly**, verskriklik, afskuwelik; ~ *ly pink*, fel (skerp) ligroos; ~**ness**, verskriklikheid; ergerlikheid.

shock: ~-**proof**, skokvas; ~ **tactics**, skoktaktiek; ~ **therapy**, ~ **treatment**, skokbehandeling; ~ **troops**, stormtroepe, skoktroepe; ~ **wave**, skokgolf; ~ **workers**, uitgesoekte werkspan.

shod, geskoei; *kyk* **shoe**, (v).

shodd'y, (n) (**shoddies**), lompewol, voddewol, prulwol; bog; (pl) afval; (a) sleg; nagemaak; prullerig; pretensieus; ~ **work**, knoeiwerk.

shoe, (n) skoen; hoefyster; hiel (lans); remskoen (wa); slytstuk (stamper); *that's ANOTHER pair of* ~*s*, dis 'n ander saak; *over* ~*s, over BOOTS*, as 'n mens A sê, moet jy ook B sê; *CAST an old* ~ *after a person*, iem. die beste toewens; *wait for DEAD men's* ~*s*, op 'n erfenis wag; *DIE in one's* ~*s*, aan die galg dans; *FEATHER-EDGED* ~, aanknyp= (hoef)yster; *be IN somebody's* ~*s*, in iem. se skoene staan; *do not throw away OLD* ~*s before you have new ones*, moenie vuil water weggooi voor jy skoon water het nie; *the* ~ *is on the OTHER foot*, dit is net mooi andersom; *PAIR of* ~*s*, paar skoene; *no one knows where the* ~ *PINCHES like the wearer*, elkeen weet die beste waar die skoen hom druk; *put the* ~ *on the RIGHT foot*, die kind by die naam noem; die spyker op die kop slaan; *SHAKE (quake) in one's* ~*s*, sidder en bewe; *not to wish to STAND in someone else's* ~, nie in iem. se skoene wil staan nie; *STEP into someone else's* ~*s*, iem. se plek inneem; (v) (**shod**), van skoene voorsien; beslaan (perd); ~ **black**, skoenpoetser; ~ **blacking**, skoenwaks, skoensmeer; ~-**box**, skoendoos; ~-**brush**, skoenborsel; ~-**buckle**, skoengespe; ~-**button**, skoenknoop; ~-**factory**, skoenmakery; ~ **horn**, skoenlepel, skoenhoring; ~**ing**, (n) beslaan; hoefbeslag; skoeisel, beskoeiing; (a) beslaan; ~**ing-hammer**, beslaanhamer; ~**ing-smith**, hoefsmid; ~-**lace**, skoenriem; skoenveter; ~-**last**, skoenlees, ysterlees; ~-**latchet**, skoenriem; ~-**leather**, skoenleer; ~**less**, kaalvoet; ~-**lift**, skoenhoring; ~ **maker**, skoenmaker; *who is worse shod than a* ~ *maker's wife*, skoenmaker se kinders loop kaalvoet; ~-**making**, skoenmakery; ~-**manufacture**, skoeiselvervaardiging, skoenmakery; ~-**nail**, skoenspyker; ~-**polish**, skoenwaks, skoensmeer; ~**r**, (perde)beslaner; ~ **rack**, skoenrak; ~ **shine**, skoensmeer; ~-**strap**, skoenband; wreefband; ~-**string**, skoenveter; *LIFT oneself up by one's* ~-*strings*, met min middele dit ver bring; *live ON a* ~-*string*, op die goedkoopste manier lewe; ~-**thread**, pikdraad; ~-**tree**, lees, skoenspanner.

sho'far, ramshoring.

Shon'a, Sjona.

shone, *kyk* **shine**, (v).

shoo, (v) jaag; (interj) sjuut!

shook[1], (n) duig; kisplank; (v) in stelle (duie) verpak.

shook[2], (v) *kyk* **shake**, (v).

shoot, (n) skeut, spruit, loot, uitloopsel, uitspruitsel; suiwer (tabak); jagtog, jagparty; skietwedstryd, skietoefening; stroomversnelling, waterstroom; oorloop; glyplank; glybaan; geut; stortkoker; aar (erts); strook; grondverskuiwing; (v) (**shot**), skiet; afskiet, doodskiet; uitbot, uitloop (boom); verskiet (ster); steek; afneem; vorm; uitgooi (anker); weggooi, stort (vuilgoed); trek, deurseok, deurtrek; kiek, afneem; ~ *AHEAD*, het naaste skrede voor= uitgaan; ~ *AT*, skiet na; *have shot one's BOLT*, jou rol uitgespeel hê; ~ *the BOLT (of a door)*, die grendel terugskuif; ~ *DOWN*, neerskiet; neerhaal (vliegtuig); ~ *EARS*, in die aar kom; ~ *a FILM*, 'n rolprent opneem; ~ *to KILL*, skiet om dood te maak; ~ *LEAVES*, blare kry; ~ *a MATCH*, aan 'n skietwedstryd deelneem; *it shot through my MIND*, dit het my te binne geskiet; dit het my skielik bygeval; ~ *OUT*, te voorskyn spring; ~ *it OUT*, dit met gewere (rewolwers) uitveg; *PRICES shot up*, pryse het skielik gestyg; ~ *a RAPID*, oor 'n stroomversnelling heenskiet; ~ *no RUBBISH*, moenie vuilgoed uitgooi nie; geen stortplek; ~ *STRAIGHT*, raak skiet; ~ *TENDRILS*, rank; ~ *TILLERS*, uitstoel; ~ *UP*, opskiet, uit die grond groei; vinnig grootword, opskiet (kind); ~**er**, skutter; skieter; blaasroertjie.

shoot'ing, (n) (die) skiet; jag; jagterrein; skietkuns; (a)

shop

skietend, skiet=; skietkuns=; ~ *the red,* uitkom van kam en belle (kalkoen); ~ **accident,** skietongeluk; ~ **affair,** skietery; ~**-board,** skaafplank; ~**-box,** jaghuis; skietplaas, jagplaas; ~ **competition,** skiet=wedstryd; ~ **expedition,** skiettog; ~**-gallery,** skiet=baan, skietkraam; ~**-ground,** jagveld, jaggebied; ~**-horse,** skietperd; ~ **incident,** skietvoorval; ~**-iron,** vuurwapen, geweer; ~ **lamp,** skietlamp; ~**-licence,** jaglisensie; ~ **match,** skietwedstryd; ~ **pain,** skietpyn; ~**-party,** skietparty; ~ **plane,** rei=skaaf; ~**-range,** skietbaan; ~ **season,** jagtyd, skiettyd; ~ **star,** vallende ster, verskietende ster; ~**-stick,** sitkierie; ~ **war,** skietoorlog.

shop, (n) winkel; werk(s)plek, werk(s)winkel; (v) **(-ped),** inkopies doen, winkel toe gaan; opsluit, ag=ter die tralies sit; verklik, in die hande bring; *ALL over the* ~, oral; hot en haar; *CLOSED* ~, geslote geledere; geslote werksorganisasie; *KEEP a* ~, 'n winkel hê; *SHUT up* ~, die winkel sluit; uittree; jou 'onttrek; tou opgooi; *SMELL of the* ~, geleerd klink; *don't TALK* ~, moenie oor jou werk praat nie; ~**-assistant,** winkelbediende, winkelklerk; ~**-boy,** loopjonge; ~**-breaking,** winkelinbraak; ~**-detective,** winkelspeurder; ~ **fitter,** winkelinrigter; ~ **fitting,** winkelinrigting; ~ **fittings,** (los) winkel=uitrusting; ~ **fixtures,** (vaste) winkeltoebehore; ~**-front,** winkelvenster; ~**-girl,** winkelmeisie; ~**-goods,** winkelware; ~**-hand,** winkelbediende; ~ **hours,** winkelure; ~ **inspector,** winkelinspekteur; ~ **keeper,** winkelier; ~**-lifter,** winkeldief; laailigter; ~**-lifting,** winkeldiefstal; ~**-man,** winkelier; winkel=klerk, verkoper; ~**per,** winkelbesoeker, klant.

shop'ping, inkopery, winkelbesoek; *go* ~, inkope gaan doen, winkels besoek; ~ **arcade,** winkelgang, winkelarkade; ~ **bag,** inkopiesak, inkooptas; win=kelsak; ~ **basket,** handmandjie; ~ **centre,** koop=sentrum, winkelsentrum; ~ **district,** ~ **quarter,** winkelwyk; ~ **voucher,** koopbewys; ~ **week,** win=kelweek.

shop: ~**-soiled,** gevlek, verkleur, verbleik, vuilerig; ~**-space,** winkelruimte; ~**-steward,** werkgesant, fabrieksmiddelaar, skakelman; ~**-talk,** vakpraat=jies, vakpratery; ~**walker,** klerkopsigter, winkel=opsigter; ~ **window,** winkelvenster; ~**-worn,** ge=vlek, verkleur, verbleik.

shore¹, (n) steun, balk, stutpaal, skoor; (v) steun, stut, dra, skoor.

shore², (n) kus, strand, oewer; *OFF* ~, naby die kus; *ON* ~, aan wal, aan land.

shore³, (v) *kyk* **shear,** (v).

shore: ~**-battery,** strandbattery; ~**-boat,** kussloep; ~**-end,** oewereinde (brug); landpunt (kabel); ~**-leave,** walverlof, landverlof; ~ **less,** sonder kus; on=begrens; ~**-line,** kuslyn; ~**-man,** kusbewoner; ~ **station,** kusstasie; ~ **ward,** landwaarts.

shorn, (v) *kyk* **shear;** *COME home* ~, met die kous oor die kop terugkom; kaal van iets afkom; ~ *OF,* ontdaan van; beroof van.

short, (n) kort begrip; kortsluiting (elektrisiteit); kort lettergreep; tekort; kort rolprent; kort skoot (pl) kort broek; sportbroek; ongesifte meel; *known as Jim FOR* ~, kortheidshalwe bekend as Koos; *IN* ~, kortliks, kortom, om kort te gaan; *the LONG and the* ~ *of it,* dit kom hierop neer; (a) kort; klein; beperk; kortaf; skraps, skaars; bros (koek); *put on* ~ *ALLOWANCE,* op klein rantsoen plaas; *give* ~ *CHANGE,* te min kleingeld teruggee; *take a* ~ *cut,* 'n kortpad kies; *at* ~ *DATE,* op kort sig; *a* ~ *DIS= TANCE,* 'n hanetreetjie; *by a* ~ *HEAD,* met 'n kort kop; ~ *LEAVE,* kleinverlof; *a* ~ *LIFE and a merry one,* 'n kort maar vrolike lewe; *give* ~ *MEA= SURE,* te kort doen; *have a* ~ *MEMORY,* kort van gedagte wees; gou vergeet; ~ *of MONEY,* kort van geld; *make* ~ *WORK of,* gou klaarspeel met; *meeting at* ~ *NOTICE,* spoedvergadering; ~ *of SIGHT,* bysiende; *be on* ~ *TIME,* onderure werk; *a* ~ *TURN,* 'n kort draai; *take* ~ *VIEWS,* kortsig=tig wees; (adv) skielik, opeens; *throw a BALL* ~, 'n bal nie ver genoeg gooi nie; *BE* ~ *of a thing,* iets kortkom; ~ *of BREATH,* kortasem; *be* ~ *of CASH,* verleë wees om geld; *COME* ~ *of,* nie die peil bereik nie; nie die paal haal nie; *CUT* ~, kort

1230

shot

afbreek; *CUT someone* ~, in die rede val; *FALL* ~ *of,* te kort skiet; minder wees as wat verwag is; ~ *by a FOOT,* 'n voet te kort; *GO* ~, kortkom; *KEEP* ~, korthou; *LITTLE* ~ *of,* bietjie minder as; am=per dieselfde as; *LITTLE* ~ *of miraculous,* byna wonderbaarlik; *he will do anything* ~ *OF murder,* hy sal alles doen behalwe (buiten) moord; *have a PLAYER* ~, 'n speler kortkom; *PULL up* ~, skielik inhou; *RUN* ~ *of,* 'n tekort hê aan iets, kortraak; *be RUNNING* ~, kortraak; *SELL* ~, op prysdaling verkoop; *STOP* ~, skielik bly staan; ~ *but SWEET,* kort maar kragtig; *TAKE someone* ~, iem. onverwags betrap; iem. skielik oorval; *TAKE someone up* ~, iem. in die rede val; iem. steur; *he was* ~ *WITH me,* hy het my baie kortaf behandel; ~ **age,** nood, skaarste, tekort; ~ *age of material,* materiaalgebrek; ~ **bill,** kortsigwissel; ~ **bread,** brosbrood, broskoek; krummelkoek; ~ **breathed,** kort van asem; ~ **circuit,** (n) kortsluiting; ~**-circuit,** (v) 'n kortsluiting veroorsaak; ~ **coming,** gebrek, tekortkoming; swakte; ~ **course,** kortkursus; ~**-crust,** broskors; ~ **cut,** kort paad=jie, napaadjie, reguit paadjie; ~**-dated bill,** kortsig=wissel; ~ **division,** kort deling; ~en, kort; korter word; bekort; verminder; bros maak; ~ **ening,** ver=korting; smeer; ~ **fall,** agterstand, tekort; ~ **game,** kortspel.

short'hand, snelskrif, stenografie; ~ **typist,** snelskrif=tikster, stenotipis; ~ **writer,** snelskrywer, steno=graaf.

short: ~**-headed,** kortskedelig; ~ **horn,** Korthoring= (bees); tweedekker; ~**ish,** korterig; ~ **leg,** kortby (kr.); ~**-length ball,** kort bal (kr.); ~**-lived,** kort=stondig, kort van duur; ~**ly,** netnou, binnekort, weldra, eersdaags, welhaas; kortliks; kortaf; ~ **measure,** skrapsmaat; ~**ness,** kortheid; ~*ness of breath,* aamborstigheid.

short'ometer, brosheidsmeter.

short: ~ **paper,** kortsigwissel; ~ **paste,** brostertdeeg; ~ **pastry,** broskors; ~ **rib,** vals ribbetjie; ~ **service,** kort bestelling (reg); ~**-set,** kort, inmekaar; ~**-sighted,** stiksienig, bysiende (let.); kortsigtig (fig.); ~**-sightedness,** bysiendheid; kortsigtigheid; ~ **sleeves,** kort moue; ~**-spoken,** kortaf; ~**-stapled,** kort van draad; ~**-stemmed,** laagstammig; ~ **stop,** kortby; ~ **story,** kortverhaal; ~ **temper,** op=vlieëndheid, kortgebondenheid; ~**-tempered,** kort=gebonde, opvlieënd, kortgebaker; ~ **term,** kort ter=myn; ~ **and medium term,** kort en medium termyn; ~**-term loan,** lening op kort termyn, korttermynle=ning; ~**-term policy,** beleid op kort termyn, korttermynbeleid; ~ **ton,** Kaapse of klein ton; ~ **wave,** kortgolf; ~**-wave transmitter,** kortgolfsen=der; ~ **weight,** ondergewig; ~**-winded,** kortasem; aamborstig, asmaties; ~**-windedness,** kortasemig=heid; ~**-witted,** dom; ~ **y,** (. . ties), kort man; kort kledingstuk, kortetjie.

shot¹, (n) rekening; *pay one's* ~, die gelag betaal.

shot², (n) skoot; skutter, skut (mens); hou; probeer=slag; dwarsdraad, inslag (sak); skootbereik; skiet=bereik, draagwydte; lopers, (skiet)hael, skroot; stoot (biljart); filmopname; gissing; inspuiting; weerskynsy; *a* ~ *in the ARM,* prikkeling, verster= king, aansporing; *a BIG* ~, 'n groot kanon, 'n grootbaas, groot kokkedoor; *CLOSE* ~, kortaf= standopname; *a CRACK* ~, 'n baasskut; *a* ~ *in the DARK,* 'n skoot in die donker; 'n raaiskoot; *a DEADLY* ~, 'n sekuur (knap) skut; *DROP with a* ~, neertrek; *EXCHANGE* ~*s,* na mekaar skiet; *do someone a* ~ *in the EYE,* iem. 'n poets bak; *FIRE with* ~, met koeëls skiet; *FULL* ~, geheelopname; *GOOD* ~!, mooi skoot!) skote Pretoors!; *a GOOD* ~, 'n goeie skut; 'n goeie probeerslag; *let him HAVE a* ~ *at it,* laat hom dit probeer; *LIKE a* ~, bliksemsnel, soos 'n koeël uit 'n geweer; onmiddel=lik; *a* ~ *in the LOCKER,* 'n appeltjie vir die dors; *have more than one* ~ *in one's LOCKER,* baie pyle in jou koker hê; *not by a LONG* ~, glad nie; *OUT of* ~, buite skoot, te ver; *a PARTHIAN* ~, 'n Par= tiese pyl; *a PARTING* ~, 'n afskeidsarsie; 'n laaste skoot; *PUTTING the* ~, gewig gooi, gewigstoot; ~ *and SHELL,* koeëls en granate; *SMALL* ~,

fynhael; *WITHIN* ~, onder skot (skoot); (v) *kyk*
shoot, (v); ~**-barrel,** haelloop; ~**-cartridge,** hael=
patroon; ~**-drill,** skrootboor, haelboor.
shot'-free, skotvry, ongestraf.
shot: ~**-gun,** haelgeweer; *a* ~*-gun wedding,* 'n ge=
dwonge (geforseerde) huwelik; ~**-hole,** koeëlgat;
~**-mould,** koeëlvorm; ~**proof,** koeëlvry, koeëlvas;
~**-putting,** gewigstoot; ~**-range,** skootsbereik; ~**-silk,** weerskynsy; ~**tist,** skut; ~**-tower,** haeltoring;
~**-woof,** onderslag; ~**-wound,** skietwond.
should, sou; moes; behoort; *his HORSE* ~ *win,* sy
perd moet wen (behoort te wen); *we* ~ *have
KNOWN,* ons moes dit geweet het; *I* ~ *LIKE to*
. . ., ek sou graag.
shoul'der, (n) skouer; skof; blad (diere); neus (berg);
padrand; *have BROAD* ~*s,* 'n breë rug hê; *have a
CHIP on the* ~, 'n ou grief hê; *give someone the
COLD* ~, iem. die rug toedraai (toekeer); iem.
links laat lê; *you can't put an old HEAD on young*
~*s,* verstand kom nie voor die jare nie; *an old
HEAD on young* ~*s,* 'n ou man se kop op 'n jong
man se lyf; ~ *of LAMB,* lamsblad; ~ *of MUT=
TON,* skaapblad; *take too much ON one's* ~*s,* te
veel op jou neem; *OPEN one's* ~*s,* met volle krag
moker, lostrek, *RUB* ~*s with,* in aanraking kom
met; *STAND* ~ *to* ~, skouer aan skouer staan;
SHRUG the ~*s,* die skouers ophaal; *STRAIGHT
from the* ~, op die man af; met volle krag; tromp=
op; ~ *of VENISON,* wildsblad; *put one's* ~ *to the
WHEEL,* die skouer teen (aan) die wiel sit; die han=
de uit die mou steek; (v) op die skouer neem; onder=
steun; verdring; wegstamp, wegstoot; (verantwoor=
delikheid) dra; ~ *ALONG,* vooruitstoot; *have to*
~ *the BLAME,* die verantwoordelikheid aanvaar;
~ *OUT,* wegstoot; ~**-belt,** draagband, bandelier;
~**-blade,** skouerblad (mens); bladbeen (vleis); ~**-bone,** skouerbeen; ~**-cartilage,** bladkraakbeen;
cloete-se-oor (skaap); ~ **ed,** met skouers, skouer-;
~ *ed mortise and tenon,* skouertap-en-gat; ~ **girdle,**
skouergordel; ~**-guard,** skouerskut; ~**-height,**
skouerhoogte; ~**-high,** skouerhoog; *carry* ~**-high,**
op die skouers dra; ~ **hole,** skouergat; ~ **-joint,**
skouergewrig; ~**-knot,** epoulet, skouerkwas; ~**-pegged,** boeglam, boomstyf; ~**-piece,** skouerstuk;
~**-plane,** skouerskaaf; ~**-point,** boeg; ~**-slip,**
skouerontwrigting; ~ **spray,** skouerruiker; ~**-strap,** skouerriem, skouerband; skouerlus; ~**-trim=
ming,** skouerbelegsel; ~**-width,** skouerbreedte.
shout, (n) skreeu; geroep; gejuig, kreet, gejubel; ~*s of
APPLAUSE,* toejuigings; *a* ~ *of TRIUMPH,* tri=
omfkreet; (v) skreeu, hard roep; juig, joel; ~ *AP=
PROBATION,* toejuig; ~ *someone DOWN,* iem
oorskreeu; ~ *FOR someone,* na iem. roep; iem.
toejuig; ~ *for JOY,* jubel van vreugde; ~ *with
LAUGHTER,* skaterlag; ~ *TO someone,* na of vir
iem. skree; ~ *at the TOP of one's voice,* skreeu so
hard 'n mens kan; ~ **distance,** roepafstand; ~**er,**
skreeuer; roeper.
shout'ing, gejoel; gejubel; geskreeu; geroep; *it is all
OVER bar (the)* ~, alles is feitlik verby; dis feitlik
klaarpraat; *not WORTH* ~ *about,* niks om van te
praat nie.
shove, (n) stoot, stamp; (v) skuiwe; stoot, stamp; du;
~ *ALONG,* vooruitdring; ~ *ASIDE,* opsy stoot;
~ *in one's OAR,* ook 'n duit in die armbeurs gooi;
~ *OFF,* afstoot; ~ *from SHORE,* van wal stoot;
~**-halfpennny,** sjoelbak (spel).
sho'vel, (n) skop, skopgraaf; (v) (**-led**), skep; ~ **board,**
sjoelbak; ~**ful,** graafvol; ~ **hat,** skuithoed; ~**ler,**
laaier; skepper; ~**ling,** laaiwerk.
show, (n) tentoonstelling, skou; eksposisie; vertoning;
vertoonkuns, optog, voorstelling; onderneming;
skyn, praal; skouspel; *it is ALL* ~, dis alles skyn;
dis pure spoggery; *ALL over the* ~, rond en bont;
DO something for ~, iets vir die naam doen; *make a
FINE* ~, 'n goeie vertoning maak; 'n goeie figuur
slaan, *be FOND of* ~, graag aandag trek; *graag
pronk; just FOR* ~, net vir die oog; vir die skyn; om
te pronk; *GIVE the* ~ *away,* die aap uit die mou
laat; *GIVE someone a fair* ~, iem. 'n billike kans
gee; *GOOD* ~!, mooi skoot!; *by* ~ *of HANDS,*
deur die hande op te steek; *MAKE a* ~ *of,* die skyn

aanneem van; met iets te pronk loop; *MAKE no* ~ *of,* nie te koop loop nie met; *MAKE a fine* ~ *of,* 'n
goeie vertoning maak; *MERE* ~, mooidoenery;
have NO ~ *at all,* nie die minste kans hê nie; *ON* ~,
te sien; ten toon gestel; *OUTWARD* ~, uiterlike
skyn; *make a POOR* ~, 'n treurige figuur slaan; *a
ROTTEN* ~, 'n oes affêre; *he RUNS the* ~, hy is
die baas; *STEAL the* ~, die meeste aandag trek; ~ *of STRENGTH,* magsvertoon; *the WHOLE* ~, die
hele boel; *WITHOUT much (any)* ~, sonder ver=
toon; (v) (**-ed, -n; -ed** or **shewn**), wys, toon, laat sien;
ten toon stel, skou; vertoon; optree; blyk gee van,
aan die dag lê; uitlê; laat uitkom; begelei; bewys
(respek); ~ *someone ABOUT,* iem. rondneem; ~ *to ADVANTAGE,* op sy voordeligste uitkom; ~ *CAUSE,* redes opgee; gronde aanvoer; ~ *the
DOOR,* iem. die deur wys; iem. uitskop; ~ *one's
FACE,* jou laat sien; ~ *a FAVOUR,* 'n guns bewys;
~ *FIGHT,* wil veg; veglustig wees; ~ *one's HAND,*
jou kaarte laat sien; ~ *IN,* laat binnekom; ~ *KINDNESS,* vriendelikheid betoon; ~ *a LEG,* uit
die bed klim; voortmaak; die been wys; ~ *MERCY,* genade betoon; ~ *OFF,* pronk, uitstal;
laat uitkom; aandag probeer trek; ~ *OUT,* uitlaat;
die deur wys; *TIME will* ~, die tyd sal leer; ~ *UP,*
duidelik laat blyk; aan die kaak stel, ontmasker; ~ *the WAY,* die weg wys; ~ *up WELL,* 'n goeie ver=
toning (indruk) maak; ~ *WILLING,* jou bereid=
willigheid toon; *that* ~*s YOU!,* daar het jy dit!; ~**-bill,** aanplakbiljet; ~**-box,** kykkas; ~ **business,**
vertoonkuns; ~**-card,** reklamekaart; ~**-case,**
toonkas, uitstalkas; ~**-down,** beslissende stryd,
kragmeting; uitdaging; ~**er,** uitstaller, vertoner.
show'er¹, (n) vertoner.
show'er², (n) reënbui; stortbad; stroom; *a* ~ *of BUL=
LETS,* koeëlreën; ~ *of RAIN,* reënvlaag; *like a
SUMMER* ~, soos 'n ou vrou se dans; (v) stort=
reën, neerstroom; begiet, besproei; oorstelp; ~ *blessings upon,* met seëninge oorlaai (oorstelp); ~**-bath,** stortbad; ~ **cubicle,** storthokkie; ~**-proof,**
waterdig; ~**y,** reënerig, buierig.
show: ~**-girl,** verhoogpop, verhoogmeisie; ~**-glass,**
uitstalkas; ~**-goat,** pronkbok; ~**-ground,** tentoon=
stellingsterrein; ~ **house,** vertoonhuis; ~**iness,**
pronksug, spoggerigheid; ~**ing,** voorstelling; ver=
toning; bewys, verklaring; voorkome; *on your
OWN* ~*ing,* volgens jou eie voorstelling; *make a
POOR* ~*ing,* sleg afsteek by; ~**-jumping,** spring=
vertoning (perde); ~ **man,** sirkusbaas; vertoner;
windmaker; ~**manship,** vertoonkuns; windma=
kery; ~**-off,** vertoon, vertoning; windmaker; ~ **people,** toneelmense; ~**-piece,** vertoonstuk, pronk=
stuk; ~**-place,** mooi plek, spogplek; ~**-rebate,** kor=
ting op tentoonstellings; ~**-room,** uitstalkamer,
toonlokaal, vertoonkamer; ~**-up,** ontmaskering;
~**-wether,** pronkhamel; ~**-window,** uitstalvenster,
vertoonvenster, winkelraam; ~**y,** pronkerig,
pronksiek, spoggerig, opsigtig, weids.
shrank, *kyk* **shrink,** (v).
shrap'nel, (granaat)kartets; ~ **helmet,** staalhelm; ~ **shell,** granaatkartets.
shred, (n) reep, stukkie, flenter, snipper (vrug); lap;
without a ~ *of CLOTHING,* sonder 'n draad klere
aan; *not a* ~ *of EVIDENCE,* nie 'n greintjie bewys
nie; *IN* ~*s,* in flenters, in toiings; *TORN to* ~*s,* in
flenters geskeur; (v) (**-ded**), (ver)snipper, stukkend
sny, repies sny; kerf; ~*ded MARMELADE,* re=
piesmarmelade; ~*ded MEAT,* snippervleis; ~*ded
WHEAT,* spinkoring; toutjiesmeel, draadjiesmeel;
~**der,** reepsnyer; kerwer; ~**dy,** in stukkies; gekerf.
shrew, feeks, helleveeg, heks, mannetjiesvrou, tang,
serpent, geitjie, kyfagtige vrou, wyf, spitsbekmuis,
skeerbekmuis.
shrewd, slu, listig, snugger, oorlams, uitgeslape;
skrander, skerpsinnig, snedig; bytend, skerp; *a* ~ *FELLOW,* 'n uitgeslape (skrander) vent; *make a* ~ *GUESS,* veilig raai; kan raai; *have a* ~ *IDEA,* vei=
lig raai; 'n spesmaas hê; *a* ~ *REPLY,* 'n snedige
(skerpsinnige) antwoord; *do one a* ~ *TURN,* iem.
se kanse bederf; ~**ness,** sluheid, lis, snuggerheid,
jakkalsstreke; uitgeslapenheid, skranderheid, ge=
wikstheid, snedigheid.

shrew'ish, lastig, twissiek, raserig, rissieagtig; ~**ness**, kyflus, kyfagtigheid; raserigheid.
shrew'-mouse, langsnoetmuis, spitsbekmuis, skeerbekmuis.
shriek, (n) skreeu, gil; ~ *with laughter*, gier van die lag, skaterlag; (v) skreeu, gil; ~**ing**, (n) geskreeu, gegil, gekras; (a) kras, skreeuerig; ~*ing headlines*, skreeuerige opskrif.
shriev'alty, (..ties), baljuskap.
shrift, bieg; *give short ~ to*, kort mette maak met; kort proses maak met.
shrike, janfiskaal, laksman.
shrill, (n) skel geluid; (v) uitgil, uitskree; (a) deurdringend, skril, skel, skelklinkend, snerpend; ~**ness**, skelheid; ~**-tongued**, met skel stem.
shrimp, (n) garnaal; dwergie; (v) garnale vang; ~**er**, garnaalvisser; ~**-net**, garnaalnet; ~ **pie**, garnaalpastei.
shrine, (n) altaar; graftombe; heilige plek; heiligdom; tempel; relikwieëkassie; (v) heilig bewaar.
shrink, (n) krimping; (v) (**shrank**, **shrunk**), krimp; inkrimp; opkrimp, slink; indroog, verskrompel; laat krimp; terugdeins, huiwerig wees; ~ *AT*, terugdeins vir; ~ *BACK*, terugdeins; ~ *FROM*, huiwer om; terugdeins vir; ~ *INTO oneself*, in jou dop kruip; ~ *UP*, inmekaarkrimp; ~ *in the WASH*, krimp by die was; ~**age**, krimping; slinking; opkrimping; vermindering; besuiniging; klink (grond); ~**er**, huiweraar; ~ **fit**, krimppassing; ~**ing**, (n) (die) krimp; ineenkrimping; vermindering; (a) terugtrekkend; krimperig; ~**-proof**, krimpvry; ~**-resistant**, krimptraag.
shrive, (-d or **shrove**, -d or **shriven**), die bieg afneem; absolusie gee; reinig van sonde, ontsondig.
shriv'el, (-led), rimpel, verskrompel, verlep, uitdroë.
shriv'en, gereinig van sonde.
shriv'ing, bieg; ontsondiging.
shroff, geldwisselaar.
shroud, (n) lykkleed, doodshemp, doodskleed; omhulsel, beskutting; (v) bedek; (om)hul; omfloers; beskut; in 'n doodskleed wikkel; ~*ed in mystery*, in geheimnisigheid gehul; ~**ing**, lykomhulsel; ~**-knot**, wantknop; ~**less**, onomhul, onbedek, sonder doodskleed.
Shrove Tues'day, Dinsdag voor Vastedag, Vasteaand.
shrub¹, vrugtedrank.
shrub², struik, bossie, heester; ~**bery**, (..ries), struikgewas, boskasie; struiktuin; ~**by**, vol bossies; ruig; struikagtig, ~**like**, struikagtig.
shrug, (n) skouerophaling; (v) (**-ged**), skouers optrek; ~ *off*, dit met 'n skouerophaling afmaak, verontagsaam.
shrunk'(en), vervalle; inmekaargekrimp, verrimpel; *kyk ook* **shrink**.
shuck, (n) dop, peul; (v) uitdop.
shudd'er, (n) huiwering, siddering, rilling, bewing, gril; *it gives one the ~s*, dit laat 'n mens gril; (v) huiwer, ril, beef, sidder, gril, ys; ~ *AWAY from*, terugdeins vir; *I ~ to THINK*, ek gril as ek daaraan dink; ~**ing**, (n) huiwering, rilling; (a) sidderend.
shuff'le, (n) geskuifel; geslof, slofgang; was, skommel (van kaarte); jakkalsstreek; omruiling van posisie; uitvlug, draai; *double ~*, horrelpypdans; (v) skuifel, slof; heen en weer skuiwe; meng; verwar; skommel (kaarte); uitvlugte soek, slim draaie maak; ~ *ALONG*, aanslof, aansukkel; ~ *AWAY*, wegslof; wegmoffel; ~ *the CARDS*, die kaarte was (skommel); ~ *on one's CLOTHES*, 'n mens se klere aanpluk; ~ *the FEET*, die voete heen en weer skuif; ~ *OFF*, wegdrentel; ~ *off RESPONSIBILITY*, die verantwoordelikheid afskuiwe; ~**r**, kaartskommelaar; bedrieër, uitvlugtesoeker; skuifelaar.
shuff'ling, (n) geskuifel; geslof; uitvlug, ontwyking; (a) skuifelend; sloffend; draaierig; listig, ontwykend.
Shu'lam(m)ite, Sunamitiese vrou.
shun, (**-ned**) vermy, ontwyk, sku.
'shun! *abbr. for* **attention**, gee ag!
shunt, (n) rangeerwerk; rangering; wisseling; newesluiting, aftakking (elek.); (v) rangeer, op 'n syspoor bring, regstoot; verspoor; uitstel, op die lange baan skuif; hom afmaak van; vertak; splits, aftak (elek.); ~**-coil**, aftakrol; ~**er**, rangeerder.
shunt'ing, rangering, rangeerwerk; aftakking (elek.); ~**-engine**, rangeerlokomotief; ~ **operations**, rangeerwerk(saamhede); ~**-switch**, rangeerwissel; ~**-yard**, rangeerwerf, rangeerterrein.
shut, (n) deksel, afsluiting; voeg, naat; (v) (~), sluit, toemaak; afsluit; toegaan; ~ *AWAY*, wegsluit; ~ *the DOOR against*, die deur sluit vir; *he ~ the DOOR on me*, hy het die deur in my gesig toegemaak; ~ *DOWN*, (vir goed) sluit, toemaak; ~ *one's EYES*, die oë toemaak; ~ *one's EYES to something*, jou oë vir iets sluit; ~ *IN by*, omring deur; ~ *IN*, opsluit, insluit; ~ *someone's MOUTH*, iem. die mond snoer; ~ *one's MOUTH*, jou mond hou; ~ *OFF*, afsluit; ~ *OFF from*, uitsluit; ~ *OUT*, buitesluit; ~ *up SHOP*, die winkel toemaak; tou opgooi; ~ *one's TEETH*, die tande op mekaar byt (klem); ~ *UP!* hou jou mond! bly stil! (a) toe, dig, gesluit; *bang ~*, toeklap; ~**-down**, stopsetting; sluiting; dienssluiting; werksluiting; ~**-off cock**, afsluitkraan.
shutt'er, (n) luik, blinding, hortjies; sluiter; skuif; sluis; valkleppie, (af)sluiter (kamera); (v) die luike toemaak; van hortjies voorsien; bekis; ~**ing**, bekisting; luike.
shut'tle, (n) spoeletjie, skoentjie (van 'n naaimasjien); weefspoel; letterplaatjie (tikmasjien); skuitanker; (v) heen en weer beweeg (skiet); *SPACE ~*, (ruimte)pendeltuig; ~**cock**, pluimbal; speelbal; ~*cock and battledore*, pluimbal en raket; ~ **release**, ontspanner *(fot.)*; ~ **service**, heen-en-weerdiens; ~ **system**, heen-en-weerstelsel.
shut'-off, afsluiting.
shy¹, (n) gooi; *have a ~ at*, iets waag; iets probeer raakgooi; bespot; (v) (**shied**), smyt, gooi, slinger.
shy², (n) sysprong; (v) (**shied**), wegspring, wegvlieg, skrik (dier); ~ *(away) from a task*, terugdeins van 'n taak; (a) skaam, verleë, beskroomd, eenkennig, inkennig, sku, verskimmeld, beskimmeld (persoon), skugter, huiwerig; afgesonder, afgeleë; swak (teler; draer); wantrouend, agterdogtig; skraal, sleg (grond); skrikagtig, skrikkerig (perd, dier); *BE ~ of*, skaam wees vir; *FIGHT ~ of*, probeer ontduik; padgee vir; *a ~ BEARER*, 'n skraal (slegte) draer; *a ~ BREEDER*, 'n swak (slegte) teler; *a ~ FELLOW*, 'n semelbroek; ~**er**, skrikkerige perd.
Shyl'ock, Shylock; afperser, woekeraar.
shy: ~**ly**, skaam, skamerig; ~**ness**, skaamheid, skaamte; verleentheid, skuwerigheid, skuheid; beskroomdheid; eenkennigheid, inkennigheid; skrikagtigheid, skigtigheid.
shys'ter, knoeier, konkelaar, slinkse persoon.
si, si (mus.).
Si'am, Siam; ~**ese'**, (n) Siamees; Siamees (taal); (a) Siamees; ~*ese CAT*, Siamese kat; ~*ese TWINS*, Siamese tweeling.
sib, (n) verwantskap; sibbe (antr.); (a) verwant.
Siber'ia, Siberië; ~**n**, (n) Siberiër; (a) Siberies.
sib'ilance, **sib'ilancy**, sissende geluid, sissing, gesis.
sib'ilant, (n) sisklank; (a) sissend.
sib'ilate, sis, 'n sisklank uitbring.
sibila'tion, gesis, sisgeluid.
sib'ling, broer of suster; bloedverwant; sibbelid.
sib' test, sibbetoets.
sib'yl, profetes, waarsegster, sibille; ~**line**, profeties, orakelagtig, sibillyns.
sic, sic, woordelik, net so.
sicca'tion, opdroging.
sicc'ative, (n) opdroënde middel, droogmiddel; (a) opdroënd.
sice¹, ses (by dobbelspel).
sice², staljong, stalkneg.
Sicil'ian, (n) Siciliaan; (a) Siciliaans.
Si'cily, Sicilië.
sick¹, (v) aanhits, sa sê.
sick², (n): *the ~*, die siekes; (a) siek, ongesteld; naar, mislik; sat; *BE ~*, ongesteld wees; opbring; *BE ~ of*, sat wees vir; dik wees vir; walging wek; *the one he has an aan; as ~ as a DOG*, so siek soos 'n hond; *FEEL ~*, naar (mislik) wees; *be ~ FOR*, smag na; *be ~ at HEART*, hartseer wees; treurig voel; *he*

MAKES me ~, hy gee my die piep (olel); ~ *in MIND and body*, geestelik en liggaamlik siek; *be* ~ *and TIRED of*, moeg en sat wees vir; ~ *of WAIT=ING*, sat van wag; ~**-bay**, siekelokaal, siekeboeg; ~**-bed**, siekbed; ~**-benefit**, siektetoelae, siekteby=stand, siektehulp; ~**-benefit fund**, siektebystands=fonds, siektehulpfonds; ~**-benefit society**, sieke=fonds; ~**-berth**, siekeboeg; ~**-call**, siekebesoek; siekesinjaal; ~**-club**, siekefonds; ~**-comfort**, sieke=troos; ~**-comforter**, sieketrooster.

sick'en, siek word; mislik word; naar maak; sat word; kwyn; ~ **ed**, siek gemaak, gewalg; ~**ing**, mislik, walglik; *be* ~*ing for MEASLES*, masels onder lede hê; *a* ~*ing SIGHT*, 'n walglike toneel.

sick: ~ **flag**, kwarantynvlag; ~**-fund**, siektefonds, siekefonds.

sic'kle, sekel; sekelveer.

sick' leave, siekteverlof.

sic'kle: ~ **man**, maaier; ~**-moon**, sekelmaan; ~**-sha=ped**, sekelvormig.

sick: ~**liness**, sieklikheid; ongesondheid; voosheid; ~**-list**, siekelys; ~**ly**, sieklik, ongesond, bekwaald; walglik; voos; ~**ness**, siekte, krankheid; mislik=heid; ~**-parade**, siekeparade, siekeappèl; ~**-pay**, siekeloon, siekesoldy, siekebesoldiging; ~**-report**, siekerapport; ~**-room**, siekekamer; ~**-visitor**, sie=ketrooster; ~**-ward**, siekesaal.

side, (n) sy, kant; flank; aanstellings, aanstellery; rand; helling; *from ALL* ~ *s*, van alkante; *there is ANOTHER* ~ *to every story*, alles het sy keersy; *AT his* ~, aan sy sy; *AT the* ~ *of*, langs; vergeleke met; *the BLIND* ~, die swak (skeel) kant; *on BOTH* ~ *s*, aan altwee kante (weerskante); *the RIGHT* ~, die ligkant; *see the BRIGHTER* ~ *of something*, iets v.d. blink kant bekyk; ~ *BY* ~, langs mekaar; *CHANGE* ~ *s*, plekke omruil; van standpunt verander; *the DARK* ~, die donker kant; *on EITHER* ~ *of*, weerskante van; *on EVERY* ~, aan elke kant; *on the FATHER'S* ~, van vaderskant; *prices were on the HIGH* ~, pryse was aan die hoë kant; dit was goedkoop; *the LIGHT* ~, die ligte kant; die ligkant; ~ *of a MOUNTAIN*, berghelling; *NO* ~, die spel is oor; *ON the* ~, in die geheim; as byverdienste; *ON my* ~, aan my kant; *ON one* ~, aan een kant; opsy; *ON this* ~, aan hierdie kant; duskant; *to ONE* ~, eenkant, opsy; *on the OTHER* ~, aan die ander kant; *the other* ~ *of the PICTURE (shield)*, die keersy (ander kant) van die medalje; *PUT on* ~, 'n aanstellerige houding aanneem; jou aanstel; aansit; *PUT on one* ~, opsy sit; *PUT to one* ~, wegstoot, geen ag op slaan nie; *on the RIGHT* ~ *of fifty*, onder vyftig; *it is always best to err on the SAFE* ~, 'n mens kan nooit te versigtig wees nie; *be on the SAFE* ~, aan die veilige kant wees; *the SEAMY* ~ *of life*, die lelike kant v.d. lewe; *on the SMALL* ~, kleinerig; *keep the SUNNY* ~ *up*, die blink kant bo hou; *SPLIT one's* ~ *s with laughter*, skud van die lag; *TAKE* ~ *s in a quarrel (on an issue)*, party kies in 'n rusie (oor 'n strydvraag); *there are two* ~ *s to every question (story)*, 'n wors het twee ente; *this* ~ *UP*, bo(kant); *get on a person's WEAK* ~, iem. in sy swak aantas; *show one's WORST* ~ *only*, net jou agterkant wys; *WRONG* ~ *out*, (die) binnenste buite; *get out of bed on the WRONG* ~, met die verkeerde voet uit die bed stap; *get on someone's WRONG* ~, iem. kwaad maak; (v) party kies, party trek; ~ *with someone*, iem. se kant kies; party kies vir; ~ **aisle**, sybeuk, syskip (kerk), ~**-altar**, syaltaar; ~ **ante-room**, sykamer; ~**-arms**, sygeweer; ~ **avenue**, sy=laan; ~**-bar**, sybalie (reg); ~**-bench**, sybank; ~ **board**, buffet; koskas; skinktafel; ~**-box**, sylosie; ~ **branch**, sytak; ~**-burns**, bakkebaard; ~**-canal**, sykanaal; ~**-car**, sywaentjie; syspanwa; ~**-centre**, middelvleuel; ~**-channel**, sykanaal; ~**-corridor**, sy=gang; ~**-cut**, sykanaal; ~ **dish**, bygereg; toekos; ~ **door**, sydeur; ~**-drain**, sygeut; ~**-drum**, klein trom=mel, tamboertjie; ~**-effect**, newe-effek, bykoms=tige gevolg; ~ **elevation**, syaansig; ~ **entrance**, sy=ingang; ~ **exit**, syuitgang; ~**-face**, profiel; ~ **fric-tion**, sywrywing; ~**-gable**, sygewel; ~**-gallery**, sy=galery; ~**-glance**, skuins blik; ~ **issue**, bysaak,

newevraagstuk; ~**-jump**, sysprong; ~ **ladder**, tou=leer; ~**-lamp**, sylamp; ~**-leap**, sysprong; ~ **light**, sylig; syraam; sydelingse lig; illustrerende eienaar=digheid; ~**-line**, sylyn; kantlyn (sport); byvak, by=baantjie, byverdienste; byeboerdery; bybedryf; ne=weartikel; *be on the* ~*-lines*, toeskouer wees; ~**-loading**, sylading; ~ **long**, sydelings; *steal* ~ *long glances*, onderdeur loer; skelm loer; ~ **mirror**, sy=spieël; ~**-note**, kanttekening; ~**-path**, sypaadjie; ~**-pavement**, sypaadjie; ~**-play**, syspeling; ~**-pocket**, sysak; ~ **purpose**, bybedoeling, byoog=merk; ~**-railing**, kantleuning.

sider'eal, sideries, sterre=; ~ **day**, sterredag; ~ **hour**, sterre-uur; ~ **month**, sterremaand; ~ **time**, ster=retyd; ~ **year**, sterrejaar.

sid'erite, ysterspaat, sideriet.

siderog'raphy, staalgraveerkuns, siderografie.

side: ~**-rope**, valreep; ~**-saddle**, meisiesaal, vroue=saal; ~**-scene**, coulisse, syskerm; ~**-screen**, sy=skerm; ~**-seam**, synaat; ~**-show**, kraampie, byver=toning; byonderneming; ~**-slip**, (n) gly; sygly, syslip (lugv.); loot, spruit; buite-egtelike kind; (v) laat slip (lugv.); uitgly; ~**s'man**, diaken; ~**-spit**, deurbrand; ~**-splitting**, om jou 'n boggel te lag; ~**-stay**, syanker; ~**-step**, (n) sysprong, systap, swenk; (v) (-**ped**), verbyspring, ontwyk, ontduik; ~ **street**, systraat; ~**-stroke**, syslag; kanthou; ~ **thrust**, steek van die kant; ~**-tipping**, kantelbak=; ~**-track**, (n) syspoor, wisselspoor; (v) op 'n syspoor bring; op die lange baan skuif; uitstel; ~*-track something*, iets op die lange baan skuiwe; ~ **valve**, syklep; ~**-view**, sygesig, syaansig, profiel; ~ **walk**, sypaadjie, voetstraat; ~ **wall**, symuur; sywal; ~ **ward(s)**, sywaarts, ~**-way**, syweg; ~ **ways**, syde=lings; ~**-winder**, kantskuiwer; ~**-whiskers**, bak=baard; ~ **wind**, sywind; *hear by a* ~ *wind*, 'n voël=tjie hoor fluit; ~ **window**, syvenster; syruit.

sid'ing, spoorweghalte; syspoor, wisselspoor; (die) party kies; *private* ~, privaat sylyn.

si'dle, (n) sywaartse beweging; (v) skeef loop, dwars loop; sluip.

Sidon'ian, (n) Sidoniër; (a) Sidonies.

siege, beleg, beleëring; *DECLARE a state of* ~, in staat van beleg verklaar; *LAY* ~ *to*, beleg slaan voor; *LAY* ~ *to a girl's heart*, by 'n nooi aanlê; *RAISE the* ~, die beleg opbreek; *in a STATE of* ~, in staat van beleg; ~**-artillery**, ~**-guns**, ~**-ord=nance**, beleëringsgeskut.

sienn'a, siënna; geelbruin (kleur).

sie'rra, siërra, bergketting; makriel.

sies'ta, middagslapie, siësta.

sieve, (n) sif; *try to carry water in a* ~, water in 'n mandjie probeer dra; sop met 'n vurk eet; (v) sif; ~**-brush**, sifborsel; ~**like**, sifagtig; ~**-plate**, sifplaat.

sift, sif; uitvra, uitpluis, navors, ondersoek; skif; ~ *out*, uitpluis, uitvors; uitsif; ~**ings**, sifsel.

sigh, (n) sug, versugting; *a* ~ *of relief*, 'n sug van verligting; (v) sug; suis (wind); ~ *for*, smag na, ver=lang na, versug; ~**ing**, sug, gesug.

sight, (n) gesig; (die) oë; (die) sien, sig; skouspel, spek=takel; vertoning; merkwaardigheid, besienswaar=digheid, gesigspunt; visier, korrel (geweer); uitsig; (-**s**) (ook) besienswaardighede; *play AT* ~, v.d. blad speel; *BACK* ~, visier; *CATCH* ~ *of*, te sien kry; *FAR* ~, versiendheid; *she found FAVOUR in his* ~, sy het genade gevind in sy oë; *at FIRST* ~, op die eerste gesig; *in the FOG the* ~ *was bad*, in die mis was die sig sleg; *FRONT* ~, korrel (van 'n ge=weer); *GET a* ~ *of*, te sien kry; *GET out of my* ~, gee pad voor my oë; *HATE the* ~ *of a person*, iem. nie kan uitstaan nie; *IN* ~, in sig, sigbaar; *IN* ~ *of all*, voor almal; *KNOW by* ~, van sien ken; *a LONG* ~ *better*, 'n hele ent beter; *LONG* ~, ver=siendheid; *LOOK a perfect* ~, soos 'n voëlver=skrikker lyk; *LOSE one's* ~, jou gesig verloor; *LOSE* ~ *of*, uit die oog verloor; oor die hoof sien; *LOST to* ~, uit die gesig verdwyn; *LOVE at first* ~, liefde op die eerste gesig; *MAKE a* ~ *of oneself*, jou belaglik maak; *out of* ~ *of MIND*, uit die oog, uit die hart; *NEAR* ~, bysiendheid; *ON* ~, op die eerste gesig; *OUT of* ~, uit die oog; *OUT of my* ~! trap! maak dat jy wegkom! *PAY at* ~, op sig betaal; *POINT of* ~, gesigspunt; *READ at* ~, voor die vuis lees; *have SECOND* ~, heldersiende wees; met die helm gebore wees; *a* ~ *to SEE*, pragtig om te sien; *SET one's* ~ *s at*, mik na (op); *SHOOT at* ~, dadelik skiet; *at SHORT* ~, op kort sig; *a* ~ *for SORE eyes*, 'n verruklike gesig; 'n lus vir die oë; dis om jou naar te maak; *WITHIN* ~, in sig; (v) te sien kry, waarneem; besigtig; presenteer; korrel aansit (geweer); mik, korrelvat (met geweer); aksepteer ('n wissel); ~ **bill**, sigwissel; ~-**defective**, gesigsgestremde; ~ **draft**, sigwissel; ~ **er**, proefskoot, peilskoot; ~ **exchange**, sigkoers; ~-**hole**, kykgaatjie; loergaatjie.

sight'ing, sig; korrelvat; waarneming; ~ **angle**, korrelhoek; bakenhoek; ~ **block**, peilblok; ~-**frame**, rigbok; ~ **shot**, proefskoot, rigskoot, peilskoot; ~-**setter**, visiersteller.

sight: ~ **less**, blind; ~ **lessness**, blindheid; ~ **liness**, fraaiheid, skoonheid; ~ **ly**, mooi, fraai; ~-**reading**, van die blad lees, bladlees; ~-**screen**, kolfskerm (krieket); ~ **seeing**, besigtiging van besienswaardighede; toerisme; ~ **seeing tour**, toeristereis, besigtigingsreis; kykrit, rondkyktoer; ~ **seer**, rondkyker; toeris; reisiger; skouspelkyker; ~-**telescope**, visierkyker; rigkyker; ~ **test**, oogtoets; ~ **value**, sigwaarde; ~-**vane**, diopter; ~ **worthy**, besienswaardig.

si'gillate, geblom.

sig'ma, sigma, Griekse s.

sig'moid, (n) sigmoïde; (a) sekelvormig, S-vormig; ~ **colon**, S-derm; ~ **curve**, groeikromme, groeikurwe.

sign, (n) teken, merk; bewysie; wenk; voorteken, sinnebeeld, simbool, kenteken; uithangbord; wagwoord; *AS a* ~ *of*, as teken van; as blyk van; ~ *s and COUNTERSIGNS*, geheime afgesproke tekens; *the* ~ *of the CROSS*, die teken v.d. kruis; ~ *of LIFE*, lewensteken; *show no* ~ *of LIFE*, geen teken van lewe toon nie; *MAKE a* ~, 'n teken gee; (v) teken; 'n teken gee; onderteken; ~ *AWAY*, skriftelik afstand doen van; ~ *one's NAME to*, onderteken; ~ *OFF*, afteken; ~ *ON*, aansluit; jou verbind; inskryf.

sig'nal, (n) sein; teken; sinjaal; ~ *of distress*, noodsein; (v) (-led), sein, oorsein, teken maak, sinjaleer; aankondig; (a) merkwaardig, skitterend; uitstekend, voortreflik, buitengewoon; *render* ~ *services*, buitengewone dienste bewys; ~-**arm**, seinarm, sinjaalarm; ~-**arrow**, sinjaalpyl; ~-**bell**, seinklok, sinjaalklok; ~-**book**, seinboek; ~ **buzzer**, (sein)gonser; ~-**box**, ~-**cabin**, seinhuisie, seinkamer, sinjaalhuisie; ~ **code**, seinregister; ~ **corps**, seinkorps; ~ **fire**, seinvuur; ~-**flag**, seinvlag; ~ **flare**, seinfakkel; ~ **gun**, seinskoot, seinkanon; ~ **horn**, seinhoring.

sig'nalize, onderskei; kenmerk; 'n sein gee, sinjaleer; aanwys; te kenne gee.

sig'nal: ~-**lamp**, seinlamp; ~-**language**, tekentaal; ~ **ler**, seiner; seinwagter; ~ **ler's key**, seinsleutel; ~-**letter**, seinletter; ~-**light**, seinlig.

sig'nalling, (n) sinjalering; seinwerk; (a) sein=, sinjaal=; ~-**apparatus**, seintoestel, sinjaaltoestel; ~-**code**, seinkode; ~-**disk**, seinskyf; ~ **flag**, seinvlag; ~ **instructor**, seininstrukteur; ~ **key**, seinsleutel; ~-**lamp**, seinlamp; ~-**lantern**, seinlantern; ~ **mirror**, seinspieël; ~ **officer**, seinoffisier; ~ **post**, seinpos; ~ **school**, seinskool; ~ **section**, seinafdeling.

sig'nal: ~ **ly**, opmerklik; swaar; merkwaardig; ~ **man**, (..men), vlagman, seiner, seinwagter; seingewer; ~-**master**, seinmeester; ~ **office**, seinkantoor; ~-**officer**, seinoffisier; ~ **pistol**, seinpistool; ~ **post**, seinpaal, seinmas; ~ **receiver**, seinontvanger; ~ **red**, sinjaalrooi; ~ **rocket**, seinvuurpyl; ~ **route**, seinweg; ~ **service**, seindiens; ~ **slit**, seingleuf; ~ **station**, seinpos, seinstasie; ~ **tower**, seintoring; ~ **traffic**, seinverkeer; ~ **unit**, sein(diens)eenheid; ~ **whistle**, seinfluit, sinjaalfluit.

sig'natory, (n) (..ries), ondertekenaar; (a) ondertekenend.

sig'nature, handtekening, ondertekening, naamtekening; teken; voortekening (mus.); sinjatuur; aanduiding; ~ **stamp**, naamstempel; ~ **tune**, kenwysie.

sign: ~-**board**, uithangbord; ~ **er**, ondertekenaar; merker.

sig'net, seël; kasjet, cachet; ~-**ring**, seëlring; ~-**seal**, handseël.

signif'icance, betekenis, belang, gewig; draagwydte.

signif'icant, betekenisvol; gewigtig; veelseggend; beduidend; betekenend; belangrik; belangwekkend; *a* ~ *LOOK*, 'n veelseggende blik; ~ *OF*, aanduidend (kenmerkend) van.

significa'tion, betekenis, aanduiding, beduidenis.

signif'icative, betekenend; betekenisvol; *be* ~ *of*, beteken, aandui.

sig'nify, (..fied), aandui; beteken; beduie, te kenne gee; inhou; *those in FAVOUR please* ~ *in the usual way*, dié wat daarvoor is, steek hande op, asseblief; *it does NOT* ~, dis van geen belang nie; dit maak geen saak nie.

sign'ing powers, tekenmagte, tekenbevoegdheid.

sign' manual, handtekening; seinhandboek.

sign'or, (It.), meneer; ~ *'a*, mevrou; ~ **in'a**, (me)juffrou.

sign: ~-**painter**, reklamedekorateur, sierverwer, bordjieskilder; ~-**painting**, sierverfwerk; ~ **post**, uithangbord; padwyser, wegwyser, predikant, handwyser; ~-**writer**, reklamedekorateur, letterskilder, opskrifskilder, naamskilder, bordjieskilder; ~-**writer's brush**, letterkwas; ~-**writing**, skilderskrif, reklamedekorasie, bordskildering, vensterskildering.

Sikh, Sikh.

sil'age, (n) inkuiling; kuilvoer; (v) inkuil; ~ **cutter** voerkerfmasjien; ~ **harvester**, kuilvoeroesmasjien.

sil'ence, (n) stilte; stilheid; stilswye; stilswy(g)endheid; vergetelheid; geheimhouding; *BREAK* ~, die stilswye verbreek; *a* ~ *FELL*, dit het stil geword; ~ *GIVES consent*, wie swyg, stem toe; ~ *is GOLD*, swye is goud; *IMPOSE* ~ *upon*, die swye oplê; iem. die mond snoer; *KEEP* ~, stilbly; *PASS into* ~, in vergetelheid geraak; *PASS over in* ~, stilswy(g)end verbygaan; *PUT someone to* ~, iem. stilmaak; (v) stilmaak, laat swyg, laat bedaar, die swye oplê, die mond snoer, dooddruk; ~ *someone*, iem. se mond snoer; ~ **box**, praatsel; ~ **cloth**, dempkleed; ~ **r**, knaldemper, geluiddemper, slagdemper, knalpot; magspreuk.

sil'encing, swyging; geluiddemping, knaldemping.

sil'ent, swygend, stil, geluidloos, geruisloos; stom; *BE* ~ *about*, nie praat van (oor) nie, swyg oor; *BECOME* ~, stil raak; *remain* ~ *as the GRAVE*, soos die graf swyg; *REMAIN* ~, swyg, stilbly; *a* ~ *VOLCANO*, 'n uitgewerkte vulkaan; ~ **film**, stil prent; ~ **ly**, stilletjies, in stilte, soetjies; ~ **partner**, stille (rustende) vennoot; ~ **reading**, stillees; ~ **sound**, geluidlose klank.

Sile'sia[1], Silesië.

sile'sia[2], Silesiese linne.

Sile'sian, (n) Silisiër; (a) Silesies.

sil'ex, vuurklip.

silhouette', (n) silhoeët, skadubeeld, afskaduwing; (v) afteken, afskadu, silhoeëtteer; *be* ~ *d against*, afgeteken staan teen.

sil'ica, kieselaarde, silika; ~ **glass**, silikaglas; ~ **rock**, kieselsteen.

sil'icate, silikaat; ~ **rock**, silikaatgesteente.

silica'tion, silikasie.

silic'eous, kieselhoudend, kiesel=, kieseldraend.

sili'cic, kiesel=, silisies; ~ **acid**, kieselsuur.

silifica'tion, verkieseling.

silic'ify, (..fied), verkiesel.

sil'icon, kiesel, silikon; ~ **chip**, silikonvlokkie.

silicos'is, silikose.

sil'iqua, silique', peul.

silk, (n) sy; systof; baard (van 'n mielie); senior advokaat; (pl) systowwe, syklere; *take* ~, senior advokaat word (Republiek van Suid-Afrika); koningsadvokaat (koninginsadvokaat) word, K.C. (Q.C.) word; (v) afbaard, afhaar; (a) sy=; *you cannot make a* ~ *purse out of a sow's ear*, alle hout is nie timmerhout nie; ~-**bark**, sybas; ~-**culture**, sywurmteelt, sykultuur; ~ **dress**, syrok; ~ **en**, sy=, van sy; syagtig; ~ **fabric**, systof; ~-**factory**, sywewery, syfabriek; ~ **fibre**, syvesel; ~ **gauze**, sygaas, ~-**gland**,

spinklier; ~ **handkerchief,** sysakdoek; ~ **hat,** pluis=
keil; ~ **industry,** syindustrie; ~**iness,** syagtigheid;
~**man,** (..**men**), syhandelaar; ~-**manufacturer,** sy=
fabrikant; ~-**mercer,** ~-**merchant,** syhandelaar;
~-**mill,** syfabriek; ~ **net,** synet; ~ **paper,** sypapier;
~ **shop,** sywinkel; ~ **stockings,** sykouse; ~ **thread,**
sydraad; ~-**thrower,** sywerker; ~ **trade,** syhandel;
~-**tree,** syboom; ~-**weaver,** sywewer; ~-**weaving,**
sywewery; ~-**winder,** syopdraaier; ~ **worm,** sy=
wurm.
silk'y, syerig, syagtig; stroperig; ~ **haired,** syharig; ~
wool, staalwol.
sill, drumpel; vensterbank; (intrusie)plaat (geol.);
dwarslêer, voetstuk (myn); voetbalk (van brug); ~
anchor, ankerbout; ~ **brick,** drumpelsteen; ~
height, vensterbankhoogte.
sill'abub, sillabub, stremmelk met wyn; *mere* ~, lou=
ter bombasme.
sill'iness, onnoselheid, dwaasheid; gekheid, verspot=
tigheid, geklikheid; meisieagtigheid; soutloosheid.
sill' plate, drumpelplaat.
sill'y, (n) (**sillies**), domkop; (a, adv) onnosel; gek,
dwaas, verspot, geklik, laf, meisieagtig, kinderag=
tig; *you ARE* ~! jy's laf! *DON'T be* ~! moenie ver=
spot wees nie! *KNOCK* ~, bewusteloos slaan;
LOOK ~, op jou neus kyk; *MAKE someone look*
~, iem. belaglik laat lyk; iem. 'n mal figuur laat
slaan; *the* ~ *SEASON,* komkommertyd; ~
THING, arme ding; onnosele ding.
sil'o, (n) (**-s**), silo, voerkuil, voertoring; opgaarkuil;
(v) inkuil.
silt, (n) afsaksel, slyk, slik, slib, modder, aanslibsel;
(v) versand, toeslik, toespoel, vol modder word; ~
up, verslik, tocspoel, verslib; ~ **a'tion,** aanslikking;
toeslikking; ~ **box,** slikvanger; ~ **deposit,** slikbe=
sinksel; ~**ing,** versanding; mynvulling; ~-**pit,** slik=
put; ~ **stone,** slikklip.
Silur'ian, (n) Siluriër; (a) Siluries.
sil'van, bosryk; *kyk* **sylvan.**
sil'ver, (n) silwer; silwergeld; tafelsilwer; silwergoed;
German ~, nieusilwer, argentaan; (v) versilwer; wit
(grys) word; (a) silwer=; *have a* ~ *tongue,* welspre=
kend wees; ~ **alloy,** silwerlegering; ~-**beater,** sil=
werpletter; ~ **brocade,** silwerbrokade; ~ **bromide,**
broomsilwer; ~ **chloride,** silwerchloride, silwer=
chloried; ~ **coin,** silwermunt; ~ **collection,** silwer=
kollekte; ~ **colour,** silwerkleur; ~ **dust,** silwer=
poeier; ~ **fir,** silwerden; ~ **fish,** silwervis; ~ **foil,**
bladsilwer; silwerpapier; ~ **fox,** silwervos; ~ **gilt,**
vergulde silwer; ~-**grey,** silwergrys; ~-**haired,** met
silwerhare; ~ **jackal,** silwerjakkals; ~ **jubilee,** sil=
werjubileum; ~ **leaf,** bladsilwer; ~ **leaf bitter ap=
ple,** satan(s)bos, silwerblaarbitterappel *(Solanum
eleagnifdium);* loodglans *(Steneum purpureum);*
~**ling,** silwerling; ~ **ly,** silwerig, silweragtig; ~
medal, silwermedalje; ~ **mine,** silwermyn; ~
money, silwergeld; ~-**moth,** silwermot, vismot; ~-
mounted, met silwerbeslag; ~ **nitrate,** helsteen, sil=
wernitraat; ~ **ore,** silwererts; ~ **pea,** silwerertjie
(Priestleya tomentosa); ~ **plate,** (n) silwerware,
silwergerei, silwergoed; silwerwerk; (v) versilwer;
~-**plated,** versilwer; ~-**plating,** versilwering; ~
screen, projeksieskerm, rolprentskerm, ~**side,** dy=
stuk, biltongvleis; ~**smith,** silwersmid; ~ **solder,**
silwersoldeersel; ~ **standard,** silwerstandaard; ~
thread, silwerdraad; ~-**tongued,** met welluidende
stem; welsprekend; ~-**tree,** witteboom, silwer=
boom *(Terminalia sericea,* Tvl., *Leucadendron ar=
genteum* K.P.); ~ **ware,** silwerwerk, silwergoed, ~
wattle, silwerbas; ~ **wedding,** silwerbruilof; ~
weed, ganserik; ~-**white,** silwerwit; ~ **wire,** silwer=
draad; ~ **y,** silweragtig, silwer=, silwerig, silwerwit;
met silwerglans; silwerhelder; silwerhoudend; ~*y
lustre,* silwerglans.
sil'viculture, bosbou.
sil'viculturist, bosbouer.
si'ma, sima.
sim'i, simi.
sim'ian, (n) aap; (a) aapagtig, aap=.
sim'ilar, (n) gelyke, ewekilik; (a) gelyksoortig, derge=
lik; eenders; ooreenkomstig; analoog; ~ *to,* gelyk=
vormig met; gelyk aan; ~ **figures,** gelykvormige fi=

gure; ~ **flexure,** gelykvormige buiging; ~ **frac=
tions,** gelykvormige breuke; ~**'ity,** (..**ties**), gelyk=
soortigheid, eendersheid, gelykheid, ooreenkoms;
~ **ly,** net so, op dieselfde manier, eweneens, insge=
lyks; ~ **terms,** gelyksoortige terme.
sim'ile, vergelyking.
simil'itude, gelykheid, ooreenkoms; ewebeeld;
gelyke.
sim'ilize, vergelykinge gebruik; deur vergelykinge
ophelder.
Sim'menthaler, Simmenthaler(bees).
simm'er, (n): *at a (on the)* ~, aan die pruttel (prut);
(v) saggies kook, pruttel, prut; sing (ketel); smeul;
borrel, borrelkook; ~ **heat,** prut(tel)hitte; ~**ing,**
geprut(tel); ~*ing tension,* broeiende spanning; ~-
oven, weloond.
sim'nel cake, simnelkoek.
Sim'on, Simon; ~ *PURE,* die ware Jakob; *a SIM=
PLE* ~, 'n uilskuiken, Dom Jan, Jan Swaap.
simon'iac, simonis; ..**ni'acal,** simonisties.
sim'ony, simonie.
simoon', samoem, (warm) woestynwind.
sim'ous, met 'n plat neus, platneus=.
sim'per, (n) gemaakte (aanstellerige) glimlag; (v) aan=
stellerig glimlag, meesmuil.
sim'ple, (n) geneeskragtige kruid; eenvoudige; (a)
eenvoudig, naïef, ongekunsteld; gewoon; louter;
homogeen (minerale); enkelvoudig, enkel; simpel,
onnosel; *it IS quite* ~, dit is heeltemal (baie) mak=
lik; *the* ~ *LIFE,* die eenvoudige lewenswyse; ~
SENTENCE, enkelvoudige sin; *tell the* ~
TRUTH, die eenvoudige waarheid vertel; ~ **addi=
tion,** eenvoudige optelling; ~ **equation,** eenvoudige
vergelyking; ~ **fraction,** enkelvoudige breuk; ~
fracture, eenvoudige beenbreuk; ~-**hearted,** een=
voudig, opreg; ~ **honours,** drie honneurs (erekaar=
te); ~ **interest,** enkelvoudige rente; ~ **life,** eenvou=
dige lewenswyse; ~ **majority,** gewone meerderheid;
~-**minded,** eenvoudig, onskuldig, argeloos; dom,
onnosel; ~**ness,** eenvoudigheid; eenvoud, onge=
kunsteldheid, natuurlikheid, naïwiteit, simplisiteit;
onnoselheid, simpelheid.
sim'pleton, dwaas, lummel, swaap, oliekoek, askoek,
jansalie, allemansgek; *a* ~, 'n japie, 'n swaap.
sim'ple weave, effe binding.
simpli'citer, sonder voorbehoud, absoluut.
simpli'city, eenvoud, ongekunsteldheid; onnoselheid,
simpelheid.
simplifica'tion, vereenvoudiging.
sim'plified, vereenvoudig.
sim'plify, (..**fied**), vereenvoudig.
sim'plism, gemaakte eenvoud.
simplis'tic, simplisties.
sim'ply, eenvoudig, gewoonweg, enkel, niks anders
as, net, puur, skoon, sommerso; sonder versiering;
you ~ *MUST wear a hat,* jy moet eenvoudig 'n
hoed opsit; *it's* ~ *NONSENSE,* dis pure kaf.
simulac'rum, (..**cra**), skynbeeld, namaaksel, naboot=
sing.
sim'ulant, (n) nabootser, simulant, (a) met die voor=
komste van, as nabootsing van, wat so lyk.
sim'ulate, veins, voorwend; simuleer; naboots, fin=
geer, namaak; voorgee; ~ **d,** gesimuleer(d); kastig
simula'tion, veinsing, skyn, nabootsing; voorwend=
sel; simulasie.
sim'ulator, nabootser; simulant.
simul'idae, kriewelmuggies.
simultane'ity, gelyktydigheid.
simultan'eous, gelyktydig, simultaan; ~ **ly,** tegelyker=
tyd.
sin, (n) sonde; oortreding; *his BESETTING* ~, sy
swak, sy grootste swakheid, sy gewoontesonde; ~
of COMMISSION, sonde van bedryf, daadsonde;
DEADLY ~, doodsonde; *FOR my* ~*s,* tot (vir)
my straf; *hate a person LIKE* ~, iem. soos die pes
haat; *LIVE in* ~, in sonde lewe; *MORTAL* ~,
doodsonde; *cover a MULTITUDE of* ~*s,* 'n me=
nigte foute (gebreke) bedek; ~ *of OMISSION,*
sonde van versuim; *ORIGINAL* ~, erfsonde; *the
SEVEN deadly* ~*s,* die sewe doodsondes; *it is a* ~
and a SHAME, dis 'n sonde en 'n skande; *as UGLY
as* ~, so lelik soos die nag; (v) (**-ned**), sonde doen,

sondig; *more* ~*ned against than* ~*ning*, meer gekrenk as krenkend.
Si'nai, Sinai; ~'**tic**, Sinaïties.
sin'apism, mosterdpleister, mosterdpap.
since, (adv) sinds, sedert, daarna, (de)wyl, vermits; waar; gelede, sindsdiens; van toe af; *EVER* ~, van toe af; *LONG* ~, lank gelede; (prep) sedert, sinds; ~ *yesterday*, van gister af; (conj) sedert, sinds, nadat; daar, omdat, aangesien; vandat; ~ *that is so*, omdat dit so is.
sincere', opreg, suiwer, eg, eerlik, innig, ongeveins, trouhartig; openhartig; ~ **ly**, opreg; *yours* ~ *ly*, opreg die uwe; geheel die uwe; jou toegeneë; u dienswillige; ~**ness** = sincerity.
since'rity, opregtheid, innigheid, ongeveinsdheid.
sincip'ital, voorkops, voorhoofs, bokop, kruin.
sin'ciput, kruin, voorkop, bokop.
Sind'hi, Sindhi.
sine[1], (n) sinus.
sin'e[2], (prep) sonder; ~ *die*, vir 'n onbepaalde tyd.
sin'ecure, amp sonder werk, erebaantjie, sinekuur.
sin'ew, sening, pees, spier; ~*s of war*, oorlogsmiddele; ~ **y**, gespierd, sterk, seningagtig, seningrig; ~*y meat*, seningrige vleis.
sin'ful, sondig, ~**ness**, sondigheid.
sing, (sang, sung), sing; besing; suis; fluit, tuit; ~ *to an AUDIENCE*, voor (vir) 'n gehoor sing; ~ *IN the new year*, met gesang die nuwe jaar ingaan; ~ *OUT*, uitsing; uitgalm, hard sing; ~ *to a PIANO*, by 'n klavier sing; ~ *someone's PRAISES*, iem. se lof verkondig; ~ *to SLEEP*, aan die slaap sing; ~ *SMALL*, 'n nootjie laer sing; mooi broodjies bak; ~ *another SONG (tune)*, 'n ander liedjie sing; 'n ander toon aanslaan; ~ *the same SONG*, elke dag dieselfde ou deuntjie sing; ander napraat; ~**able**, singbaar.
singe, seng, brand, skroei; ~ *your FINGERS*, jou vingers verbrand; ~ *HAIR*, hare skroei: ~ *your WINGS*, jou vingers verbrand; ~**ing**, (die) skroei, skroeiery, senging.
sing'er, sanger, sangeres.
Singhalese', (n) Singalees; Singalees (taal); (a) Singalees.
sing'ing, (n) sing; gesang; sangles; sangkuns; getuit, gesuis (in ore); (a) sangerig; singend; ~**-bird**, sangvoël; ~**-class**, sangklas; ~**-lesson**, sangles; ~**-master**, sangonderwyser; ~ **voice**, sangstem.
sing'le[1], (n) enkelspel; een; (pl) enkelspel; (a) enkelvoudig; enkel; eenmalig; eenlopend, ongetroud (persoon); enkelpersoons; alleen, afsonderlik; opreg; *in* ~ *COMBAT*, in 'n tweegeveg; *inspired with a* ~ *PURPOSE*, met net een doel voor oë.
sing'le[2], (v) uitsoek, uitkies; ~ *out*, uitsoek, uitkies.
sing'le: ~**-acting**, enkelwerkend; ~ **action**, eenslagwerking, enkelwerking; ~**-barrelled**, met een loop, eenloop; ~**-barrelled rifle**, enkelloopgeweer; ~ **bed**, enkelbed; ~ **bend**, wewersknoop, skootsteek; ~**-breasted**, met een ry knope, enkelbors; ~ **call**, enkelvoudige oproep; ~ **combat**, tweegeveg; ~**-day admission**, eendagtoelating; ~ **decker**, eendekker; ~**-decker bus**, eendekkerbus; ~ **court**, enkelbaan; ~ **crochet**, enkelsteek; ~ **employee**, ongetroude werknemer; ~**-engined**, eenmotorig; ~ **entry**, enkelboeking; ~**-eyed**, met een oog; eerlik, opreg, ondubbelsinnig; ~ **file**, agter mekaar, eeneen; *in* ~ *file*, een-een; ~ **furrow**, enkelvoor; ~**-furrow plough**, enkelvoorploeg; ~ **game**, enkelspel; ~**-handed**, alleen; met een hand; sonder hulp; ~ **harness**, eenperdtuig; ~**-hearted**, opreg, eerlik; ~**-heartedness**, opregtheid, heelhartigheid; ~ **life**, ongetroude lewe; ~**-line traffic**, eenstroomverkeer; ~ **man**, ongetroude man, vrygesel; ~**-masted vessel**, eenmaster; ~ **medium school**, enkelmediumskool; ~**-minded**, opreg; eerlik; ~**-mindedness**, eerlikheid; doelgerigtheid; ~**ness**, ongetroude staat; eenvoud, opregtheid, ~*ness of purpose*, doelbewustheid, doelgerigtheid, konsentrasie op een doel; ~**-phase**, eenfasig; ~**-pitch roof**, halfsaaldak, vlerkdak; ~**-plate clutch**, enkelskyfkoppelaar; ~ **pump**, eenslagpomp; ~ **quarters**, enkelkwartiere; ~ **room**, eenpersoonskamer; ~**-seater**, eenpersoonsmotor; eenpersoonsvliegtuig; ~ **sheet**, enkelbedlaken; ~**s**, ~**s match**, enkelspel; enkelwedstryd; ~**s champion**, enkelspelkampioen; ~**s play**, enkelspel; ~**s player**, enkelspeler; ~ **state**, ongetroude staat; ~**s tennis champion**, enkelspeltenniskampioen; ~**-storey**, ~**-story**, enkelverdieping.
sing'let, frokkie, onderhemp.
sing'le: ~ **ticket**, enkelkaartjie; ~ **ton**, enkeling; enetjie; ~ **track**, enkelspoor; ~ **width**, enkelbreedte.
sing'ly, alleen, afsonderlik; een vir een.
sing'song, (n) deuntjie, eenvoudige wysie, gedreun; jolsang, sangoefening; amateurskonsert; (v) (op)dreun, eentonig sing; (a) eentonig.
sing'ular, (n) enkelvoud; (a) enkelvoudig; eenvoudig, sonderling, eienaardig, singulier; seldsaam; vreemd, buitengewoon, sonderbaar, vreemdsoortig; *all and* ~, almal en elkeen in besonder; ~ **form**, enkelvoudsvorm.
singula'rity, (..ties), merkwaardigheid, sonderlingheid, sonderbaarheid, vreemdsoortigheid; enkelvoudigheid; eienaardigheid.
sin'gularly, besonder.
sin'ister, onheilspellend; noodlottig; sinister; links; oneerlik, laag, vals; *a* ~ *character*, 'n onsmaaklike karakter.
sinis'tral, (n) linkshandige; (a) linker, links; buiteegtelik; oneg; na links gedraai (skulp).
sink, (n) (op)wasbak, vuilwaterbak; spoelbak; riool; sinkput, sinkgat; (pl) besinksel; (v) (sank, sunk), sink; sak, daal; val; deursak; afgaan; agteruitgaan, swak word; verflou; laat sak; laat hang (kop); grawe, delf (put); delg (skuld) beswyk, sterf; kelder, tot sink bring (skip); ~ *BACK*, terugsink; *BE sinking*, al hoe swakker word; agteruitgaan; verflou; sterwe; ~ *a BOREHOLE*, 'n boorgat maak (sink); ~ *a DEBT*, 'n skuld delg; ~ *DIFFERENCES*, geskille laat rus; ~ *DOWN*, neersink; ~ *in someone's ESTIMATION*, in iem. se agting daal; ~ *a FACT*, 'n feit verswyg; ~ *one's HEAD*, die kop laat sak; *his HEART sank*, sy moed het hom begeef; ~ *IN*, deurdring, inwerk; *it does not fail to* ~ *IN*, dit gaan nie in 'n mens se klere sit nie; ~ *INTO*, insypel; ~ *MONEY in*, geld belê in; geld verloor in; ~ *one's NAME*, jou naam geheim hou; ~ *into OBLIVION*, in vergetelheid geraak; *the PATIENT is* ~*ing*, die sieke is sterwende; ~ *a SHAFT*, 'n skag grawe; ~ *a SHIP*, 'n skip laat sink (kelder); *his SPIRITS sank*, sy moed het hom begewe; *the STORM* ~*s*, die storm bedaar; *it's* ~ *or SWIM*, dis daarop of daaronder; ~ *a WELL*, 'n put grawe; *the WIND* ~*s*, die wind gaan lê; ~**able**, sinkbaar; ~**age**, sinking; inlaat; agteruitgang; ~**er**, skaggrawer; sinklood (aan vislyn); ~**-hole**, sinkgat; sinkput, afvoerput.
sink'ing, (n) (ver)sakking; (die) sink; naarheid; keldering (skip); daling; delging; afsakking; (a) sinkend; verminderend; *a* ~ *FEELING*, 'n nare gevoel; *the SUN is* ~, die son sak; ~**-fund**, amortisasiefonds, delgingsfonds; ~ **pump**, skagpomp; ~ **shaft**, delfskag.
sink: ~ **stone**, sinkklip.
sin: ~**less**, sondeloos, vlek(ke)loos; ~**lessness**, sondeloosheid; ~**ner**, sondaar.
Sinn Fein', Sinn Fein.
sin'net, *kyk* sennit.
sin'-offer(ing), soenoffer.
Sin'o-Japanese', Chinees-Japans.
sin'ologue, sinoloog.
sinol'ogy, sinologie.
sin'ter, (n, v) sinter; ~ **glass**, sinterglas.
sin'uate, gegolf, gekartel.
sinuos'ity, bogtigheid, kromming, bog; golwing, karteling; kronkeling.
sin'uous, bogtig, kronkelend, vol draaie; ingewikkeld; onbetroubaar; ~**ness**, *kyk* **sinuosity**.
sin'us, (~, -es), kromming; holte, boesem; sinus; fistel; baai, golf; *cavernous* ~, aarholte.
Si'on, Sion; ~**ite**, Sionis.
sip, (n) mondjievol, slukkie, teug, proefie; (v) (-ped), slurp, met klein slukkies (teugies) drink, proe-proe, nip.
siph'on, (n) sifon, hewel; spuitwaterbottel, spuitfles; (v) opsuig, hewel, oortap; ~ *out*, uithewel; ~ **age**,

siphuncle 1237 **skein**

hewelwerking; ~ **barometer**, hewelbarometer; ~ **bottle**, spuitwaterbottel; ~ **cock**, hewelkraan; ~ '**ic**, sifon=, hewel=; ~ **pipe**, hewelpyp.
siph'uncle, suigbuis.
sipp'er, iem. wat klein teugies drink, slurper.
sipp'et, geweekte brood; garneerroosterbrood.
sir, (n) heer, meneer; seur; sir (titel); (v) as meneer of sir aanspreek; *don't ~ me*, moenie my meneer noem nie.
sird'ar, opperbevelhebber, sirdar.
sire, (n) sire; vader; vaar (dier); teelhings; *top ~*, hoofvaar; (v) teel; verwek.
sir'en, sirene; verleister; mishoring; koe(t)stoeter; mo= tortoeter; waarskuwingsein; ~ **call**, lokroep; ~ **song**, sirenesang; ~ **voice**, lokstem.
siri'asis, sonsteek; sonbrand.
Si'rius, die Hondster.
sirl'oin, lendestuk, beeslende; ~ *of beef*, beeslende; ~ **steak**, lendeskyf.
sirocc'o, (-s), sirokko; droogmasjien.
si'rrah, kêrel, vent.
sis'al, sisal (hennep); sisalplant, garingboom.
sis'kin, sysie (Europa); pietjiekanarie.
sis(s), sies.
siss'y, (n) (**sissies**), papbroek, (a) meisieagtig, verwyf.
sis'ter, suster; verpleegster, hoofverpleegster; non; *BIG ~*, ousus; ~ *of CHARITY*, liefdesuster; *the FATAL S ~ s*, die Skikgodinne; *LITTLE ~*, kleinsus; ~ **hood**, susterskap; ~ -**in-charge**, hoof= verpleegster; ~ -**in-law, (sisters-in-law)**, skoonsus= ter; ~ **less**, susterloos; ~ **ly**, susterlik; teer.
Sis'tine, Sikstyns, Sixtyns.
Sisyphe'an: ~ *labour*, Sisufosarbeid.
sit, (sat), sit, gaan sit, plaas neem, sitting hê, poseer, broei (hen); pas; ~ *BACK in comfort*, in weelde lewe; ~ *heavily on another's CHEST*, op iem. se nek lê; ~ *on a COMMITTEE*, in 'n komitee dien (sitting hê); ~ *DOWN*, gaan sit; sit!; ~ *for an EXAMINATION*, 'n eksamen skryf (doen); ~ *on a FEELING*, 'n gevoel onderdruk; ~ *on the FENCE*, die kat uit die boom kyk; ~ *HEAVY on the stomach*, swaar lê op die maag; onverteerbaar wees; *the HEN wants to ~*, die hen is broeis; ~ *at HOME*, 'n huishen wees; ~ *on the JURY*, as jurie= lid dien; *MAKE someone ~ up*, iem. vreemd laat opkyk; iem. laat skrik; ~ *down to one's MEAL*, aan tafel gaan sit; ~ *ON someone*, iem. kortvat; iem. op sy plek hou; op iem. sit; ~ *OUT*, buitekant sit; uitsit ('n dans); die hele tyd bly sit; ~ *for one's PORTRAIT*, poseer; ~ *under a PREACHER*, in die gehoor van 'n prediker sit; *his PRINCIPLES ~ loosely on him*, hy is nie danig beginselvas nie; ~ *on a QUESTION*, oor 'n saak beraadslaag; ~ *STILL*, stilsit; bly sit; ~ *TIGHT*, hou wat jy het; nou aan die lyf sit (klere); vas in die saal sit; ~ *UP*, regop sit; opbly; ~ *UP with a sick person*, by 'n sieke waak; ~ *UP and take notice*, op en wakker wees; belang stel en oplet; *not to allow oneself to be sat UPON*, nie op jou kop laat sit nie; ~ *s the WIND there?*, waai die wind van daardie kant?
sit'atunga, waterkoedoe *(Tragelaphus spekei)*.
sit'-down, (n) sitplek; (a) sittend; ~ **lunch**, aansit= noenmaal; ~ **meal**, aansitete; ~ **strike**, sitstaking.
site, (n) ligging; bouterrein; ~ *and service scheme*, erf= en-diensplan; (v) terrein bepaal; plek kies; plaas, speel; ~ *a POSITION*, 'n plek aanwys; ~ *a ROAD*, 'n pad uitmeet; *the STORY is ~ d in Europe*, die verhaal speel in Europa; ~ **agent**, ter= reinagent; ~ -**map**, oorsigkaart; ~ **rating**, belasting volgens ligging; ~ -**rent**, terreinhuur; ~ **valuation**, grondwaardering; ~ **value**, liggingswaarde, ter= reinwaarde.
sit'-in, sitstaking.
sit'ing, plasing; aanleg.
sitiol'ogy, sitol'ogy, sitologie, voedingskunde, dieet= kunde.
sitophob'ia, sitofobie, voedselskuheid.
sitt'er, sitter; poseerder; broeivoël; model; maklike hou; *that was a ~*, dit was 'n maklike hou; *MISS a ~*, 'n presenthou (presentskoot) weier.
sitt'ing, (n) sitting; sessie; regsitting; vaste sitplek; broeisel eiers; broeityd; *GIVE a ~*, poseer; *at ONE ~*, agtereen, in een slag; ~ *PRETTY*, daar goed in sit; veilig wees; (a) sittend; *it is a ~ DUCK*, dis 'n doodmaklike teiken; *SHOOT a ~ bird*, 'n voël op die grond skiet; ~ -**hen**, broeihen; ~ -**room**, sitka= mer, voorkamer; sitplek.
sit'u: *in ~*, op die plek, in situ.
sit'uate, plaas; ~ **d**, geleë; *awkwardly ~ d*, in die knyp; ongerieflik geleë.
situa'tion, ligging; toestand, posisie; situasie; betrek= king, pos; *unable to find a ~*, geen werk kan kry nie.
sitz'-bath, sitbad.
six, ses; sestal; ~ *of the BEST*, ses goeie houe (met 'n rottang); *a COACH and ~*, 'n koets en ses perde; *it is ~ of the one and half a DOZEN of the other*, dis lood om ou yster; dis vinkel en koljander; dit is so lank as wat dit breed is; ~ *HOURS*, ses uur; ~ *HUNDRED*, seshonderd; ~ *O'CLOCK*, sesuur; *everything is at ~ es and SEVENS*, alles is holder= stebolder; alles is deurmekaar; ~ -**day week**, ses= dagweek; ~ **fold**, sesvoudig; ~ -**footer**, sesvoeter; ~ -**legged**, sesbenig.
six'pence, (hist.), sikspens; *not to HAVE a ~*, geen duit besit nie; *TURN every ~ over*, 'n oulap twee keer omdraai voor jy hom uitgee; ~ **worth**, vir 'n sikspens.
six'penny, sikspens werd; ~ **bit**, ~ **piece**, sespennie= stuk, sikspens.
six: ~ -**pounder**, sesponder; ~ -**shooter**, snelloopre= wolwer; ~ -**sided**, sessydig; ~ -**stringed**, sessnarig.
six: ~ **teen**', sestien; *sweet ~ teen*, 'n nooi(e)ntjie van sestien jaar; ~ **teenth'**, sestiende; ~ **teenth century**, sestiende-eeus; ~ **th**, sesde; ~ **th'ly**, ten sesde, in die sesde plek, ~ **tieth**, sestigste, ~ **ty**, sestig, sestigtal; ~ -**voiced**, sesstemmig.
siz'able, groot, taamlik dik; behoorlik.
size¹, (n) lymwater, gomwater, pap; planeersel; (v) lym, gom; pap.
size², (n) grootte; omvang; gestalte; maat, nommer; formaat; *that's ABOUT the ~ of it*, daarop kom dit neer; *a ~ too BIG*, 'n nommer te groot; *CUT down to ~*, op die ware grootte terugbring; ~ *of MESH*, maasgrootte; *MUCH of a ~*, min of meer van die= selfde grootte; *TRY it for ~*, kyk of dit pas; *of VAST ~*, ontsaglik groot; *he is YOUR ~*, hy is so groot soos jy; (v) sorteer, rangskik; van pas maak (klere); sif, skat, takseer; ~ *UP a situation*, sake deurkyk; ~ *UP a person*, iem. takseer (skat, beoor= deel).
sized, van 'n sekere grootte.
siz'er¹, papsmeerder, lymer, planeerder.
siz'er², sorteermasjien.
size: ~ -**roll**, lengtelys (soldate); maatlys (klere); ~ -**stick**, maatstok (van skoenmaker).
siz'iness, klewerigheid, taaiheid.
siz'ing¹, (die) lym, lymery, planering, planeersel; ~ **agent**, styfmiddel.
siz'ing², (die) afmeet (werk); lengteskikking.
siz'y, klewerig, taai.
siz'zle, (n) gesis, knettering, gespat; (v) sis, knetter, spat, braai.
siz'zling, gesputter, gespat, gesis; ~ *hot*, skroeiend warm.
sjam'bok, (n) sambok, aapstert; (v) met 'n sambok slaan, sambok inlê.
skald, skald, digter (Skandinawies).
skate¹, (n) rog (vis); *he is a cheap ~*, hy is sommer 'n twak.
skate², (n) skaats; (v) skaats, skaatsry, skaatse ry; ~ *over thin ICE*, op gladde (dun) ys skaats; jou op gevaarlike terrein waag; ~ *LIGHTLY on it*, lugtig daaroor gly; ~ **board**, skaatsplank; ~ **r**, skaatser, skaatsryer.
skat'ing, (die) skaatsry; ~ -**club**, skaatsklub; ~ -**rink**, skaatsbaan.
skean, dolk.
skedad'dle, (n) vlug; (v) trap, skoert, vlug.
skee, *kyk* ski.
skein, string; warboel; knoop; *a TANGLED ~*, ver= warring; 'n deurmekaarspul; ~ *of WOOL*, string wol; ~ **holder**, haspel; ~ **yarn**, stringgaring, string= gare.

skeletal 1238 *skivvy*

skel'etal, geraamte=, van 'n geraamte, skelet=.
skel'eton, geraamte, skelet, gebeente; kader; skets, eerste ontwerp; raamwerk; *A* ~ , 'n wandelende geraamte; *the S*~ *COAST,* die Seekus v.d. Dood; *a* ~ *in the CUPBOARD,* 'n geheime skande; 'n pynlike geheim; *there is a* ~ *in every CUPBOARD,* elke huis het sy kruis; *a FAMILY* ~ , 'n familieskande of -geheim; *a* ~ *at the FEAST,* stille kwelling, pretbederwer; ~ **army,** kernleer; ~ **construction,** raambou; ~ **crew,** kernbemanning; ~**ize,** tot 'n geraamte word, skeletteer; ~ **key,** diewesleutel, loper, passe-partout; ~ **map,** sketskaart; ~ **service,** nooddiens; ~ **staff,** kernpersoneel, kaderpersoneel, skadupersoneel; kernstaf (mil.).
skelp, (n) slag; (v) slaan; weghol; ~ **mark,** slagmerk.
skene = skean.
skep, mandjiebynes; rietmandjie.
skerr'y, (skerries), klip, rif.
sketch, (n) **(-es),** skets(tekening); omtrek; (v) skets; ~**-board,** tekenbord; ~**-book,** sketsboek; ~**er,** sketser, ontwerper; ~**iness,** onafgewerktheid, gebrek aan samehang; ~ **plan,** sketsplan; ~**y,** sketsmatig, onafgewerk, vlugtig geteken, onsamehangend; ~*y knowledge,* oppervlakkige kennis.
skew, (n) skuinste, helling; (a) skuins, skeef, windskeef; ~ **arch,** skewe boog; ~ **bald,** skilderbont (behalwe swart), bruinbont (perd); ~ **bridge,** skeef geboude brug; ~ **chisel,** skuinsbeitel.
skew'er, (n) vleispen; steekpen; rugpen; sosatiepen; (v) met 'n vleispen steek; inryg.
skew: ~**-eyed,** skeel; ~**ness,** skuinsheid, skeefheid; ~ **wheel,** skewetandrat.
skey, jukskei.
ski, (n) **(-s),** sneeuskaats, ski; (v) **(ski'd),** ski, met sneeuskaatse ry; ~ **boat,** skiboot; ~ **boot,** skistewel; ~ **cap,** skipet.
skid, (n) remblok, briekblok; remketting; (die) gly; laaiplek; (v) **(-ded),** gly, uitgly, rondskuiwe, rondglip; rem, briek; deurslaan (loko.); ~**-chain,** remketting; ~**ding,** (n) (die) sywaarts uitgly; glyding; (a) glyend; ~ **kid,** glyryer; ~ **mark,** glymerk; ~**-resistant,** glywerend.
skid row, boemelstraat, boemelbuurt; boemellewe; ~ **alcoholic,** boemel(straat)alkoholis; ~ **drinker,** boemel(straat)drinker.
ski'er, skiloper, skiër.
skiff, (n) skuitjie, bootjie; (v) skifroei.
ski'ing, skisport.
skil'ful, bekwaam, bedrewe, handig, knap.
skill, bekwaamheid, knapheid; deurtraptheid; bedrewenheid, handigheid; kunstigheid; verstand; ervarenheid; (pl) vaardighede; bekwaamhede; *game of* ~ , vaardigheidspel; vernufspel.
skilled, bekwaam, ervare, bedrewe, geskool(d), vaardig, geroetineerd; ~ *LABOUR,* vakarbeid, geskoolde arbeid; ~ *LABOURER,* geskoolde arbeider.
skill'et, driepootpot, vierpootpot, kookpotjie.
ski'lless, onbekwaam, onbedrewe.
skim, (v) **(-med),** afskuim, afskep; afstroop; sweef, voortgly, oorgly; skram, vlugtig deurkyk, gou deurlees, deursien, deurblaai; afskei, afroom (melk); ~ *ALONG,* stryk oor; gly langs; ~ *OVER,* vlugtig deurkyk; ~ *over the WATER,* oor die water sweef; (a) afgeroom; ~**med,** afgeroom; ~**mer,** skuimspaantjie; waterploeër (voël).
skim milk, afgeroomde melk; ~ **cheese,** weikaas; ~ **powder,** weipoeier; melkpoeier.
skim'ming, (n) glyery; swewing; afroming; afskepping; (pl) skuimaarde; (a) vlugtig; afskuimend.
skimp, suinig gee, afskeep; beknibbel, vrekkig wees; ~**iness,** skraalheid, skrapsheid; suinigheid, vrekkigheid; ~**y,** skraal, skraps.
skin, (n) vel, huid, skil (vrugte); vlies, kors; ~ *and ALL,* met huid en haar; huidjie en muidjie; *BATHE in one's* ~ , kaal (nakend) baai; *be* ~ *and BONE,* net vel en bene wees; daar uitsien soos die dood in Sluiters; *CURE* ~*s,* velle brei; *GET under someone's* ~ , iem. baie seermaak; *HAVE the* ~ *off someone,* iem. ooptrek; *JUMP out of one's* ~ , uiters bly wees; jou lam skrik; *NEXT to his* ~ , op sy kaal lyf; *his* ~ *is PEELING off,* hy gaan vel-af;

SAVE one's ~ , heelhuids daarvan afkom; *SOAKED to the* ~ , papnat; *by the* ~ *of one's TEETH,* net, ternouernood, broekskeur, hittete; *have a THICK* ~ , 'n dik vel hê; ongevoelig (onbeskaamd) wees; *THINK of one's* ~ , bang wees vir jou vel; *keep a WHOLE* ~ , heelhuids daarvan afkom; (v) **(-ned),** afslag; uitsuig; met 'n velletjie (rofie) bedek; toegroei, toegaan; *keep one's eyes* ~*ned,* goed dophou; ~ **cancer,** velkanker; ~ **cream,** velpommade; ~**-deep,** oppervlakkig; *beauty is but* ~*-deep,* mooi vergaan, maar deug bly staan; ~ **disease,** velaandoening; ~**-diver,** diepduiker, vryduiker, swemduiker, snorkelduiker; ~**-diving,** swemduik; ~**-dresser,** breier; ~ **flint,** vrek, inhalige mens; ~**-food,** velvoedsel; ~**ful,** besope; trommeldik; ~ **game,** bedrogspul, swendelary; ~**-gland,** huidklier; ~ **irritant,** huidprikkelstof; ~**less,** sonder vel; ~ **lotion,** velwater; ~**ned,** afgeslag; ~**ner,** afslagter; velhandelaar; pelshandelaar; bedrieër, afsetter; ~**iness,** maerheid; ~**ning,** (die) afslag; ~*ning knife,* slagmes; ~**ny,** maer, brandmaer, vel en been; vrekkig, gemeen; ~ **pouch,** velsak; ~ **rug,** velkaros, velkombers; ~ **specialist,** huidarts; ~**-stretcher,** borrievel; ~**-tight,** gespan, nousluitend, span=; ~**-tight trousers,** spanbroek; ~ **wool,** velwol, blootwol.
skip¹, (n) hysbak, mynhyser; vervoermandjie.
skip², (n) skipper (rolbal); kaptein (van 'n span).
skip³, (n) sprong; spring; heimlike vlug; (v) **(-ped),** spring, huppel, wip, riemspring; oorslaan, oorspring, uitlaat; ~ *the COUNTRY,* uit die land verdwyn; ~ *SCHOOL,* stokkiesdraai.
skip' box, valkas.
skip'jack, springkewer, kniptor; katonkel (vis).
skip'man, (..**men),** hysbakwagter.
skip'per¹, skipper (van skip); (v) ('n span) aanvoer; kaptein wees.
skip'per², springer; miet (in kaas); dikkoppie (skoenlapper).
skip: ~ **ping,** (n) gespring; riemspringery; (a) dartelend; springend; ~**ing-rope,** springtou; ~**py,** huppelrig.
skip'-way, hysbaan.
skirl, (n) gekrys, snerpende geluid; gedoedel (met doedelsak); (v) snerp, krys; doedel.
skirm'ish, (n) skermutseling; (v) skermutsel; ~**er,** skermutselaar.
ski'rett, suikerwortel.
skirt, (n) romp, heuprok, halfrok; slip, pant; kant, rand, soom; grens; saalklap; meisiemens, vroumens; (pl) afrandsels; oorstek (van dak); buitewyke (van stad); stiegriem; stiebeuelkleppe; *DIVIDED* ~ , rokbroek; *FLARED* ~ , wye romp, klokromp; (v) omboor; omsoom; langs die kus vaar; afrand (wol); ~*ed COMBINGS,* afgerande kamwol; ~*ed FLEECE,* afgerande vag; ~*ed WOOL,* afgerande wol; ~**-board,** strykplank; ~**-chaser,** meisiegek; ~**-front,** voorbaan; ~**-hanger,** heuprokhanger.
skirt'ing, (n) mantelvlies (vleis); rokgoed; afranding; (pl) afrandsels; ~ *a fleece,* 'n vag afrand; (a) afranding; ~**-board,** plint, vloerlys, spatlys; ~ **fillet,** vloerlyslat; ~**-table,** afrandtafel; afrandtafel.
skirt' placket, rokslip.
skit, parodie; spotskrif, burlesk, hekelskrif.
ski track, skibaan.
ski'-troops, skitroepe.
skitt'er, die water trap, gly, skeer; aas sleep (vir visse).
skitt'ish, skrikkerig, springerig, skigtig, sku (perde); wispelturig, ligsinnig, dartel, uitgelate; grillerig; opgewek; lewendig; vryerig; ~**ness,** skrikkerigheid, skuheid, skigtigheid; uitgelatenheid; lewendigheid.
skit'tle, (n) keël; (pl) keëlspel; *life is not all beer and* ~*s,* die lewe is nie net rosegeur en maneskyn nie; (v) keël speel; omgooi, verkwis; ~ *out,* uitknikker; ~**-alley,** keëlbaan; ~**-ball,** keëlbal; ~**-ground,** keëlbaan; ~**-pin,** keël; ~**-player,** keëlspeler; keëlspeelster.
skive, (n) diamantwerkerskyf; snyer; dun leer; leermes; (v) sny, splits (leer); afskaaf; slyp (edelsteen); ~**r,** dun leer; nerf; leermes.
skiv'ing, afskaaf.
skivv'y, (skivvies), diensmeisie.

skok'iaan, skokiaan.
skoll'y, (skollies), skollie.
sku'a, skua.
skuldugg'ery, verknoeiing, knoeiery, slenterstreek, swendelary, korrupsie; laagheid.
skulk, loer, skuil; ontwyk; jou plig versuim; ~ **er**, ontwyker, wegkruiper; pligsversuimer, lyfwegsteker.
skull, skedel, kopbeen; doodshoof, doodskop; ~ *and cross-bones*, seerowersvlag; ~**-cap**, kalotjie, mussie, skedelpet; kopbedekking.
skunk, muishond; stinkdier; stinkakkedis, stinkerd, smeerlap, vuilis, skobbejak.
sky, (skies), (n) lug, hemel, swerk, uitspansel; *drop out of a CLEAR* ~, soos 'n donderslag uit 'n onbewolkte hemel opdaag; *DROP from the skies*, uit die hemel val; *if the* ~ *FALLS we shall catch larks*, as die hemel val, is ons almal dood; *when the skies FALL and the oceans run dry*, wanneer die hingste vul en die perde horings kry; *IN the* ~, aan die hemel; *LAUD to the skies*, tot die hemel verhoog; hemelhoog prys; *the* ~ *is the LIMIT*, daar is geen grense nie; *REACH to the skies*, na die hemel reik; *RED* ~ *at night is the shepherd's delight*, aand rood, môre water in die sloot; *UNDER the open* ~, onder die blote hemel; (v) **(skied)**, hoog ophang; 'n lughou slaan; ~**-blue**, hemelsblou, ultramaryn; ~**-clad**, kaal, naak, nakend; ~**-coloured**, hemelsblou; ~**-diver**, lugduiker; valduiker; ~**-diving**, lugduik; ~ **er**, lugskoot, lughou (krieket); ~**-high**, hemelhoog, toringhoog; *fly* ~**-high**, die hoogte inskiet; hemelhoog vlieg; ~ **jacking**, lugkaping; ~ **lark**, (n) leeurik, lewerkie; (v) luidrugtig baljaar, streke uithaal, kaskenades maak, poetse bak; *go* ~ *larking*, vir kattekwaad rondloop; kattekwaad aanrig; ~ **less**, donker, bewolk, ~ **light**, dakvenster; bolig, daklig, skeplig; ~ **line**, horison, kim, gesigseinder; luglyn; silhoeët; stadsprofiel; ~ **pilot**, hemelloods, predikant; ~ **railway**, lugspoor; ~**-rocket**, vuurpyl; *to* ~**-rocket**, die hoogte inskiet; ~ **scape**, luggesig, luglandskap; ~ **scraper**, wolkekrabber, toringgebou; toringhuis; ~**-sign**, lugteken, lugadvertensie; ~ **ward**, hemelwaarts; ~ **way**, luglyn; lugroete, vliegroete; ~**-writing**, lugskrif, rookskrif.
slab¹, (n) blok, plat klip, steen, plaat; plat stuk, reep (lekkers); gedenksteen; ~ *of CHOCOLATE*, reep (plak) sjokolade; ~ *of MARBLE*, marmerblad.
slab², (a) taai.
slabb'er, *kyk* **slobber**.
slab: ~ **cake**, blokkoek; ~**-cork**, plaatkurk; ~**-like**, dik, plaatvormig; ~**-stone**, plat klip, plaatklip.
slack, (n) slap tyd, slapte; kommkommertyd; steenkoolgruis; metaalskuim; slap ent (van 'n tou); (v) vertraag, verslap, slabak; verminder, verflou; laat skiet; rus; ~ *OFF*, verslap; (a, adv) slap, los; traag, lui; laks, nalatig; stil; ~ *BATTER*, slap beslag; *BUSINESS is* ~, sake is slap; *GROW* ~, los word; laks word; *KEEP a* ~ *hand (rein)*, laks wees; sake hulle eie gang laat gaan; ~ *UP*, stadiger ry; 'n tou uitvier; *the WIRE is* ~, die draad hang slap; ~**-baked**, halfgaar, ongaar; ~ **coal**, koolgruis, gruiskole; ~ **en**, laat verslap, laat skiet; verflou; verslap, verminder; blus; ~ *en speed (pace)*, die vaart verminder; ~ **er**, luisak, luiaard, lamsak, jansalie, ~ **fit**, ruim passing; ~ **lime**, gebluste kalk; ~ **ness**, slapheid; traagheid, laksheid; lamlendigheid; ~ **pay**, slapteloon.
slacks, slenterbroek.
slack: ~ **season**, ~ **time**, komkommertyd, stil tyd; ~ **tyre**, pap band.
slag, (n) metaalskuim, smeltsel, slak; sintel; *basic* ~, basiese slak; slakmeel; (v) **(-ged)**, slak vorm; ~ **gy**, slakkerig; ~**-hole**, slakkig, slakgat; ~ **waste**, slakkeafval; ~**-wool**, slakkewol; klipwol.
slain, *kyk* **slay**; *BE* ~, sneuwel; *THE* ~, die gesneuweldes.
slake, les (dors); blus (kalk); ~ *d LIME*, gebluste kalk; ~ *one's THIRST*, jou dors les; ~ **less**, onlesbaar; onblusbaar.
slak'ing, lessing; blussing.
sla'lom, slalom.
slam, (n) harde slag; kap, slag (kaartspel); *GRAND* ~, groot kap, groot slag; *SMALL* ~, klein kap,

klein slag; (v) **(-med)**, diggooi, toegooi; toekap, toeslaan (deur); ~ *on the brake*, die rem aanslaan; ~**-lock**, klapslot.
sla'nder, (n) skinderpraatjies, laster, lastertaal, kwaadpratery, agterklap, eerrowing; (v) laster, skinder, beklad, beswadder, swartsmeer, belaag; ~ *someone*, iem. belaster; ~ **er**, lasteraar, skinderaar, skinderbek, skindertong, kwaadspreker; eerrower.
sla'nderous, eerrowend; skindersiek, lastersiek; lasterlik; ~ *TALK*, lasterpraatjies; ~ *TONGUE*, skindertong; ~ **ness**, lasterlikheid; lastersug.
slang, (n) slang; groeptaal; koeterwaals; jargon; maaktaal; (v) uitskel; ~ **ing**, uitskellery; ~ **ing match**, uitskellery; ~ **y**, plat, gemeensaam, groeptaal-.
slant, (n) skuinste, helling; neiging; *give it a MODERN* ~, 'n moderne kleur (aksent) daaraan gee; *ON the* ~, skuins; (v) skeef staan, afloop, afhel; kleur (nuus); (a) skuins, skeef; ~ **ed**, gekleur, partydig, skeef (nuus); ~ **ing**, (n) kromtrek(king); skewe voorstelling; (a) skuins, skeef; krom; ~ **surface**, hellingsvlak; ~ **wise**, skuins, skeef.
slap, (n) klap, slag, handslag; *give someone a* ~ *in the face*, iem. 'n klap in die gesig gee (lett.); iem. in die gesig vat (fig.); (v) **(-ped)**, 'n klap gee, slaan, wiks; (adv) reg; plotseling; pardoems; *he ran* ~ *into me*, hy het pardoems teen my vasgeloop; ~**-bang**, pardoems, met geweld; meteens, sommer; ~**-dash**, (n) afskeepwerk, opdonsery, gebrou; sorgeloosheid; (a) oorhaastig; halsoorkop, onverskillig; (adv) oorhaastig; sorgeloos, halsoorkop; ~**-happy**, verwese, benewel; uitgelate, uithundig; ~**-sided**, platsydig; ~ **stick**, (n) harlekynswepie; hansworstery, lawaai; growwe humor; (a) lawaaierig, kluitig; ~ **stick comedy**, spektakelstuk, dolle klug; ~**-up**, piekfyn, nuwerwets.
slash, (n) **(-es)**, sny; hou; split (in klere); (v) sny, raps; wild slaan, afransel; kap; kwaai kritiseer; kwaai besnoei; ~ *OPEN*, oopkloof; ~ *ed PRICES*, baie verlaagde pryse; ~ **er**, kapper; kapwapen; vegtersbaas; ~ **hammer**, mokerhamer; ~ **ing**, (n) (die) slaan; (a) skerp; kras; streng, sarkasties; vernietigend; ~ *ing reductions*, geweldige besnoeiings.
slat, (n) lat; windvlaag; hortjie; neusvlerk (vliegtuig); (v) **(-ted)**, van latte voorsien; hewig klap (seil).
slate¹, (n) lei; leiklip, leisteen; leikleur; daklei; *start with a CLEAN* ~, met 'n skoon lei begin; 'n nuwe blaadjie omslaan; *HAVE something on the* ~, iets op krediet koop; (v) met lei dek; *he is* ~ *d for president*, hy is as president benoem; (a) leikleurig, leiblou.
slate², (v) kritiseer, skrobbeer, hekel, inklim, roskam; uitskel.
slate: ~ **covering**, leibedekking; ~ **cutter**, leidekkersbyl; ~**-coloured**, leikleurig; ~ **miner**, leiklipbreker; ~**-pencil**, griffie, griffel; ~**-quarry**, leigroef; ~ **r**, leidekker; ~ **roof**, leidak; ~ **slab**, leiblad; ~**-work**, leiwerk.
slat' fence, skutting, latteheining.
sla'ting¹, uitbrander, skerp kritiek.
sla'ting², leimateriaal; leidekkerswerk.
slatt'ed, belat; ~ **blind**, hortjies, hortjieblinding; ~ **furniture**, lathoutmeubels; ~ **shelf**, latrak.
slatt'ern, slordige vrou, slodderkous, slet, flodderkous; ~ **liness**, slordigheid, slodderigheid; ~ **ly**, slordig, morsig, liederlik, slodderig.
slat'y, leiagtig; leiklipagtig.
slaught'er, (n) slagting; bloedbad; *like a lamb to the* ~, soos 'n lam ter slagting; (v) slag; vermoor; ~ **animal**, slagdier; ~**-cattle**, slagbeeste; ~ **er**, slagter; bloedvergieter; ~**-house**, slaghuis, slagplek; ~ **ous**, moorddadig; ~**-ox**, slagos; ~**-prices**, keelafsnypryse, erg mededingende pryse.
Slav, (n) Slaaf; (a) Slawies.
slave, (n) slaaf; slavin; werkesel; *a* ~ *to DRINK*, aan drank verslaaf; *LIBERATED* ~, vrygemaakte slaaf, apprentjie; *a* ~ *OF*, 'n slaaf van; *WHITE* ~, blanke slavin; *WORK like a* ~, jou afsloof; jou malle moer af werk; soos 'n esel werk; (v) sloof, slaaf, swoeg; ~**-bangle**, slaweband; ~**-bell**, slaweklok; ~**-born**, in slawerny gebore; ~**-chain**, slaweketting; ~**-child**, slawekind; ~**-dealer**, slawehan=

slaver — **sliminess**

delaar; ~-**driver**, slawedrywer; ~-**holder**, slawehouer, slawe-eienaar; ~-**hunt**, slawejag; ~ **lodge**, slawehuis; ~-**market**, slawemark; ~ **quarters**, slawekwartier.
slav'er¹, (n) slaweskip; slawehandelaar.
slav'er², (n) kwyl; (v) kwyl, bekwyl; ~ **er**, kwylbaard; ~ **ing chain**, skuimketting.
slav'ery¹, slawerny, slawelewe.
slav'ery², bekkwyl.
slave' trade, slawehandel; ~**r**, slawehandelaar; slaweskip.
slav'ey, diensmeisie.
Slav'ic, (n, a) Slawies.
slav'ish, slaafs; ~**ness**, slaafsheid.
Slav'ism, Slavisme.
Slavon'ia, Slawonië; ~**n**, (n) Slawoniër, Slaaf (ras); Slawonies (taal); (a) Slawonies; Slawies.
Slavon'ic, (n) Slawies (taal); (a) Slawonies; Slawies.
slaw, koolslaai.
slay, (slew, slain), doodmaak, doodslaan, vermoor; slag; ~ **er**, moordenaar.
slay'ing, (die) doodmaak, moord.
sleaz'y, slordig, liederlik, morsig; swak; flou.
sled, sledge, (n) slee; (v) met 'n slee ry; met 'n slee vervoer.
sledge'-hammer, voorhamer, smidshamer.
sleek, (n) gladhout; (v) glad maak; blink maak; (a) glad; sag; glansend, blink; geslepe, slu; vet (vee); ~-**haired**, ~-**headed**, met gladde (sluik) hare; ~**ness**, welgedaanheid; ~-**stick**, gladhout; ~ **stone**, gladsteen, polyssteen.
sleep, (n) slaap; vaak; *GO to ~*, inkruip, gaan slaap; aan die slaap raak; *HAVE a ~*, slaap; ~ *the ~ of the JUST*, rustig slaap; *PUT to ~*, aan die slaap maak; aan die slaap sus; *WALK in one's ~,* 'n slaapwandelaar wees; in jou slaap loop; (v) **(slept)**, slaap; rus; laat slaap; aan die slaap raak; ~ *AWAY,* verslaap; ~ *the hours AWAY,* die tyd verslaap; ~ *IN,* in die huis slaap; ~ *LATE,* 'n gat in die dag slaap; ~ *like a LOG,* soos 'n klip slaap; ~ *OFF his wine (debauch, dissipation),* sy roes uitslaap; ~ *ON something,* oor iets slaap; ~ *OUT,* uitslaap, by ander mense slaap; ~ *oneself SOBER,* jou roes uitslaap; ~ *like a TOP (log),* soos 'n klip slaap; ~ *WELL!,* lekker slaap! wel te ruste!; ~ **er**, slaper; (dwars)lêer (spoor); slaapvliegtuig; slaapwa; ~ **er crib**, hokstut; ~**ily**, slaperig, vaak; ~**iness**, slaperigheid; dooierigheid.
sleep'ing, (n) slaap; (a) slapend; ~ **accommodation**, slaapplek; ~-**bag**, slaapsak; ~-**car**, slaapwa; ~ **couch**, slaap(rus)bank; ~ **doll**, slaappop; ~-**draught**, slaapdrank; ~-**drug**, slaapmiddel; ~ **gown**, nagrok, nagkabaai; ~-**mat**, slaapmat; ~ **partner**, bedgenoot; rustende (stille) vennoot; ~-**pill**, slaappil; ~-**quarters**, slaapplek; nagkwartier; ~-**sickness**, slaapsiekte; ~-**suit**, slaappak, slaapklere; ~-**tablet**, slaappil.
sleep: ~**less**, slaaploos; ~**lessness**, slaaploosheid, slapeloosheid, insomnia; ~-**walker**, slaapwandelaar; ~-**walking**, slaapwandel; ~**y**, vaak, vakerig, sluimerig, gaperig; dooierig, vervelend; ~**y sickness**, vaaksiekte; ~**yhead**, slaapkous, slaapkop, jandooi.
sleet, (n) nat sneeu, ysreën; (v) sneeu en reën tegelyk; *it ~s,* dit ysreën.
sleeve, (n) mou (klere); huls; mof; sak; ring; silinder (granaat); skuif, buis; handvatsel (slinger); *HAVE something up one's ~,* iets in die mou hê; iets in die skild voer; *wear one's HEART (up)on one's ~,* die hart op die tong hê; *KEEP something up one's ~,* 'n slag om die arm hou; *LAUGH in one's ~,* in jou vuis lag; *ROLL up one's ~s,* jou moue oprol; jou klaarmaak; (v) van moue voorsien; voering insit; van 'n huls voorsien; ~-**bar**, sjevron; ~-**bearing**, hulslaer; ~-**board**, mouplank; ~-**coupling**, hulskoppeling, mofkoppeling; ~-**gear**, dubbelrat; ~-**hole**, mougat; ~**less**, moulóós, sonder moue; ~-**link**, mansjetknoop, mousknoop; ~-**valve**, hulsklep, mofklep, glyklep.
sleigh = **sled**.

sleight, handigheid, behendigheid; kunsgreep; ~ *of hand,* goëltoertjie, handigheid.
slen'der, skraal, maer, slank; rank; armsalig; tingerig, dun; gering, onbeduidend; min, swak; *on very ~ EVIDENCE,* op baie karige getuienis; ~ *MEANS,* karige middele; ~**ness**, skraalheid, slankheid; dunheid, tingerigheid; skraalte.
slept, *kyk* **sleep**, (v).
Sles'wick, Sleeswyk.
sleuth, speurder; speurhond; ~-**hound**, bloedhond, speurhond.
slew¹, (n) draai, swaai; (v) draai, verskuif; ~ *round,* omswaai.
slew², (v) *kyk* **slay**.
slew: ~ **ing bar**, swaaikoevoet; ~ **crane**, swaaikraan.
slice, (n) sny, skyf; strykmes (skilder); opskeptroffel; vislepel; vuurskop; skopgraaf; haaromhou, haarswenk(er) (gholf), uitswenkhou; snyhou, wegdraaihou (gholf); *a ~ of BREAD,* 'n sny brood; *quite a ~ out of my SALARY,* 'n hele hap uit my salaris; *a WHOLE ~ of bread,* omsny; (v) skywe sny, skyfies sny; versnipper; afsny; sny (gholf); klief; ~*d JAM,* skyfieskonfyt; ~*d SHOT,* haarswenker; ~**r**, snyer; skaaf; kerfmasjien.
slick, (n) streep (erts); olieopdrifsel, oliestreep; oliekombers, gladde kol; *an oil ~ on the sea,* 'n oliekol op die see; (v) glad maak; blink maak; poets; (a) handig, rats; skoon, puur; glad, blink, glansend (diere); geslepe; *give a ~ answer,* sommer dadelik antwoord; (adv) presies; glad, mooi, skoon, netjies; ~ **er**, oliejas; vormerstroffel; kuller, bedrieër; ~**ness**, gladheid, blinkheid; handigheid.
slide, (n) skuif; glybaan (geskut); speeltuig; afdraand; windklep; grondverskuiwing, aardverskuiwing, lawine; skyfie, plaatjie (vir projeksie); bloedsmeer; (die) gly; skuifplaatjie (masjien); *coloured ~s,* gekleurde skyfies (plaatjies); (v) **(slid)**, gly, glip, afgly, uitgly; skuiwe; laat gly; *LET things ~,* Gods water oor Gods akker laat loop; sake hulle eie gang laat gaan; ~ *OFF,* afgly; ~ *OVER a subject,* 'n onderwerp net effens aanroer; ~-**bar**, leibaan, leiyster; ~ **callipers**, skuifpasser; ~ **fastener**, skuifsluiter; ~-**knot**, skuifknoop; ~**r**, glyer; skuif; skuifblok; glyplank; ~ **rest**, beitelslee; ~ **rod**, skuifstang; ~-**rule**, rekenliniaal, skuifliniaal; ~ **valve**, skuifklep; ~ **viewer**, skyfiekyker.
slid'ing, (n) (die) skuif, skuiwing; (a) glydend; skuiwend; dalend; skuif=, wissel=; ~ **board**, skuifplank; ~ **bolt**, skuifbout, grendel; ~ **callipers**, skuifpasser; ~ **chute**, glybaan; ~ **die**, leiyster; ~ **door**, skuifdeur; ~ **friction**, skuifwrywing; ~ **gate**, skuifhek; ~ **gauge**, skuifpasser; ~ **fastener**, skuifsluiter; ~ **knot**, skuifknoop; ~ **joint**, skuifkoppeling; ~ **ladder**, inskuifleer; ~ **movement**, skuifbeweging; ~ **roof**, skuifdak; ~ **rule**, skuifliniaal, rekenliniaal; ~ **scale**, wisselskaal, veranderende loonskaal (arbeid), glyskaal; ~ **seat**, glybank; ~ **shute**, glybaan; ~ **sight**, skuifvisier; ~ **square**, swaaihaak; ~ **table**, skuiftafel; ~-**top desk**, skuifbladlessenaar; ~ **track**, glybaan; ~ **trumpet**, skuiftrompet; ~ **valve**, skuifklep.
slight, (n) minagting, geringskatting; veragting, versmading; (v) minag; veronagsaam; versmaad, geringskat, met weinig eerbied behandel; (a) gering, min, effentjies; oppervlakkig, onbetekenend; tingerig; *a ~ COLD,* 'n ligte verkoue; *NOT the ~est,* nie die minste nie; *PAY but ~ attention to,* min ag slaan op; *a ~ SLOPE,* 'n skotige afdraand; 'n skotige opdraande; ~ **er**, veragter, minagter; ~**ing**, (n) minagting, verontagsaming; (a) minagtend; veragtelik, smadelik; ~**ly**, effe(ntjies), 'n bietjie, enigsins, iets; ~ *ly more,* effens meer, 'n rapsie meer; ~**ness**, geringheid; oppervlakkigheid; tingerigheid.
sli'ly = **slyly**.
slim, (v) **(-med)**, verslank, 'n vermaeringskuur ondergaan; (a) slank, skraal, maer; dun, tinger(ig); geslepe, slim.
slime, (n) slyk, modder, slik, slib; fleim; (v) verslyk, verslib, slib; ~ *through,* deurglip, met jakkalsdraaie deurkom.
slim'iness, glipperigheid; glibberigheid; modderigheid.

slimm'ing, verslanking, vermaering(skuur); ~ **pills,** verslankingspille.
slim'ness, slankheid; tingerigheid; skraalheid; ~ *pills,* verslankingspille.
slim'y, slymerig; glyerig; glipperig; slibagtig, slibberig, modderig; inkruiperig, lekkerig.
sling, (n) slinger; doek; verband, band (arm), hangverband; swagtel; straalstrop, slingerstrop; draagband (geweer); *have one's arm in a* ~, jou arm in 'n verband dra; (v) **(slung),** slinger, swaai; smyt; ~ *INK,* baie skryf; ~ *MUD,* met modder gooi; ~ **dog,** gryphaak; ~**er,** slingeraar; gooier; ~ **stay,** slingeranker; ~ **stone,** slingerklip; ~ **thermometer,** slingertermometer.
slink¹, (n) vroeggebore kalf; (v) voor die tyd kalwe; 'n dooikalf afgooi (bees); 'n dooivul afgooi (perd).
slink², (v) **(slunk),** wegsluip, voortsluip.
slip, (n) uitglyding; vergissing, misstap, fout; steggie, stiggie; aardskuiwing; skeepshelling; hondeketting; miskraam; kussingsloop; onderrok; onderlyfie; voorskoot; baaibroekie; slip (lugv.); drukproef; strokie (papier); kennisgewing; bewys; vulstuk (trein); (die) gly; (die) glip; (pl) glippe (krieket); *there is many a* ~ *'twixt the CUP and the lip,* v.d. hand na die mond val die pap op die grond; tussen lip en beker lê 'n groot onseker, *a* ~ *of a GIRL,* 'n jong meisie(tjie); *GIVE someone the* ~, iem. ontglip; *MAKE a* ~, jou vergis, 'n fout maak; *a* ~ *of PAPER,* 'n strokie papier; *a* ~ *of the PEN,* 'n skryffout; *a* ~ *of the TONGUE,* 'n onbedagte woord, verspreking, misslag; *a* ~ *of a WOMAN,* 'n tingerige vroutjie; (v) **(-ped),** gly, glip, uitgly (oor skil); weggly; kruip; laat gly; loskom; laat slip (lugv., skeepsv.); laat val; ontval; voortskuiwe; 'n fout begaan, jou vergis, dooie vrug afwerp (dier); ~ *ACROSS to the butcher,* na die slagter oorwip; ~ *the ANCHOR,* die anker verloor; ~ *AWAY,* ontglip; ontsnap; ~ *ten CENT into the hand of the beggar,* 'n bedelaar tien sent in die hand stop; *the COW* ~*ed her calf,* die koei het 'n dooikalf afgegooi; ~*ped DISC,* skyfletsel; ~ *DOWN,* afgly, neergly, afsak, afseil; ~ *IN,* inglip; insluip; ~ *the LEASH,* losraak; uit 'n moeilikheid loswikkel; ~ *one's MEMORY,* jou geheue ontgaan; *the MONEY* ~*ped through his fingers,* die geld het deur sy vingers gegly; ~ *OFF,* wegkruip; afskuif; uitgooi; *the OPPORTUNITY* ~*ped through his fingers,* hy het die kans laat verbyglip; ~ *OUT,* uitgly, uitglip; ~ *a RING off one's finger,* 'n ring van jou vinger skuif; ~ *THROUGH,* deurglip; ~ *UP,* 'n fout begaan, jou vergis; *the YEARS* ~*ped away,* die jare het verbygevlieg; ~**-board,** skuifplank; ~**-bolt,** grendel; ~**-cover,** stoelkleed; oortreksel; ~**-dock,** hellende dok.
slipe, (n) reep, sny; slee; slag; (v) in repe sny; skil; stroop; ruim; ~ **wool,** blootwol.
slip: ~ **fibre,** skeelgaring; ~**-hook,** sliphaak; ~**-joint,** skuiflas; skuifskeurnaat (geol.); skuifkoppeling; ~**-knot,** skuifknoop, slipknoop; ~**-on,** oorrok, oorkleed; ~**-on cap,** skuifdop; ~**-over,** oortrektrui; ~ **page,** glip; gly.
slipp'er, (n) pantoffel, sloffie; remskoen; sluitblok (as); (v) onder die pantoffel laat deurloop, slaan; van pantoffels voorsien; ~**-bath,** leuningbad; ~**ed,** met pantoffels aan.
slipp'eriness, glipperigheid; bedrieglikheid; gladheid; geslepenheid.
slipp'ery, glipperig, glyerig, glad; listig, geslepe; wisselvallig, onseker; *as* ~ *as an EEL,* so glad soos 'n paling; *be on* ~ *GROUND,* op gladde ys wees.
slip: ~ **ping turn,** afglydraai; ~ **plane,** glipvlak; ~ **py** = **slippery;** *look* ~ *py!,* roer jou!; ~ **rail,** dwarsboom; ~**-resistant,** glipvry; ~**-ring,** sleepring; glyring; ~ **rope,** gliptou; ~**-scraper,** sleepskrop; ~**shod,** met afgeloopte (weggeslyte) hakke; slordig, onpresies (fig.); ~ **slop,** (n) soppies, waterige kos; sentimentele brousel; (a) prullerig, slordig; ~**socket,** skuifsok; ~**-stitch,** enkelbeentjie, glipsteek, enkelsteek; ~**-stream,** skroefwind (lugv.); warrelstroom; ~**-up,** flater, vergissing; ~**-surface,** glyvlak; ~ **way,** skeepshelling, glipweg; sleephelling.
slit, (n) slip (in baadjie); spleet; sny, skeur, bars; sponning, groef; kykgleuf (in tenk); (v) kloof; sny; aan stukke sny, repies sny; splits, bars (hout); inknip; ~**-eyed,** met oë op skrefies.
slith'er, gly, uitgly; swewend loop, gly-gly loop; kruip, seil (slang); ~ **y,** glad, glyerig.
slit: ~ **pocket,** ingesnyde sak, gleufsak, spleetsak; ~**-shirt,** spleetrok; ~ **ting,** klowing; sny; ~ **ting machine,** kloofmasjien; ~ **ting saw,** vylsaag; ~ **trench,** grip, skuilsloot.
slit'ter, klower; kloofmasjien.
sliv'er, (n) flenter, stukkie; splinter; reep; (v) stukkend sny; versplinter.
slob, modder, pappery; twak, ghwar, knoeier.
slobb'er, (n) kwyl; geteem; (v) kwyl, bekwyl; mors, slobber; knoei, afskeep; ~**er,** kwyler, kwylbaard; ~**ing,** gekwyl; ~ **y,** kwylend, kwylerig, slobberend, slobberig; slordig.
sloe, wildepruim (Amer.).
slog, (n) mokerhou; geswoeg; (v) **(-ged),** moker, hard slaan; swoeg, slaaf; ~ *away,* daarop los moker; opdruk.
slog'an, leuse, oorlogskreet, verkiesingskreet, (stryd)leuse, wagwoord, slagspreuk, verkoopsleuse.
slog'ger, mokeraar; swoeër; sukkelaar.
sloop, sloep.
slop¹, (n) (sl.), konstabel.
slop², (n) jas; oorbaadjie; (pl) wye broek; winkelklere, matroosklere.
slop³, (n) sentimentaliteit; morsery; (pl) pap kos; kasaterwater, slap drankies; skottelgoedwater; (v) **(-ped),** mors, vuil maak; ~ *overboard,* oorboord spoel; ~**-basin,** ~**-bowl,** spoelkom; ~ **brick,** ruwe baksteen; ~**-bucket,** toiletemmer, vuilwateremmer; ~**-builder,** knoeibouer; ~**-built,** swak gebou.
slope, (n) skuinste, hang, helling, steilte, glooiing; val, daling, afdraand; styging, opdraand; *gliding* ~, glyhelling; (v) skuins afloop, glooi, daal, afdraand loop; skuins hou; skuins sny; trap; ~ *ARMS,* die geweer oorbring; ~ *DOWN,* afgooi.
slop'ing, skuins; opdraand; afdraand; glooiend, ~ **grip,** gekromde greep; ~ **roof,** skuins dak.
slop: ~**-pail,** vuilwateremmer, toiletemmer; ~**piness,** slordigheid; sentimentaliteit; ~**-pish,** jansalieagtig; ~ **py,** morsig, slordig; sentimenteel, oordrewe; modderig, slykerig, slobberig; waterig, week, soppperig; ~ *py sentimentality,* stroperige sentimentaliteit; ~**-seller,** koopman in gemaakte klere; ~**-shop,** goedkoop (klere)winkel; ~**-sink,** vuilwaterbak, opwasbak; ~ **wag(g)on,** rioolwa; ~ **work,** slordige werk; goedkoop klerevervaardiging.
slosh, (n) pappery; pap kos; (v) slaan, moker; nat spat, plas; ~ **y,** modderig; papperig.
slot, (n) gleuf, opening; spleet, groef; uitsnyding; deurgang; sponning; spoor (takbok); valdeur; (v) **(-ted),** van 'n gleuf voorsien; ~**-borer,** langgatboor.
sloth, luiheid, vadsigheid, traagheid; luiaard (dier), luidier *(Bradypus choloepus);* ~ **ful,** lui, traag, vadsig.
slot'-hole, gleufgat.
slot'-machine, muntoutomaat; dobbelmasjien; ~ **stamp,** rolseël, outomaatseël.
slot: ~ **mortise,** dryftap; ~**-seam,** groefnaat.
slott'ed, gleuf-; gegleuf; gespleet; spleet-; gegroef; ingesink, uitgesny; ~ **aileron,** spleetroer; ~ **flap,** spleetklap; ~ **hole,** gleufgat; ~ **joint,** gleufkoppeling; ~ **nut,** gleufmoer; ~ **screw,** gleufkopskroef; ~ **wing,** spleetvlerk.
slott'ing, gleufwerk; ~**-machine,** gleufmasjien; ~**-saw,** gleufsaag; ~**-tool,** steekbeitel.
slouch, (n) geslof, slofgang; lummel; slofkous; slap houding; knoeier; hangrand; *he is no* ~, hy laat nie op hom wag nie; (v) slap hang, pap hang, afklap; in die oë trek (hoed); ~ **hat,** slaprandhoed, flaphoed, pap hoed; ~ **y,** slordig.
slough¹, (n) roof, kors; (afgegooide) slangvel; (v) vervel; weggooi; losgaan.
slough², (n) modderpoel, deurslag, moeras; *be in the S* ~ *of Despond,* op moedverloor se vlakte wees; ~ **y,** modderig, deurslagtig, moerassig.
Slov'ak, (n) Slowaak; (a) Slowakies, Slowaaks; ~ **ia,** Slowakye.

slo'ven, slordige mens, morser, slons.
Slovene', Sloven'ian, (n) Sloween; (a) Sloweens.
slo'ven: ~ **liness,** slordigheid, slonsigheid, slodderigheid; ~ **ly,** slordig, vieslik, liederlik, morsig, slonsig, verslons, slodderig; *a* ~ *ly woman,* 'n sloerie, slof.
slow, (v) vaart (snelheid) verminder, verlangsaam, stadiger gaan; ~ *down,* vertraag, stadiger laat werk; spoed verminder; (a) stadig, langsaam, dooierig, traag; vervelend; agter; slepend (siekte); lou, matig (oond); dood, slap (sake); drellerig; *a ~ AFFAIR,* 'n dooierige boel; *be ~ to ANGER,* nie gou kwaad word nie; *FIVE minutes ~,* vyf minute agter; ~ *to LEARN,* swaar van begrip; *in ~ MOTION,* in vertraagde tempo; toe; *NOT ~ to,* nie aarsel om, nie stadig om; ~ *to take OFFENCE,* nie gou beledig voel nie; *too ~ to catch a SNAIL,* te stadig vir jou eie begrafnis; ~ *of SPEECH,* swaar van tong; swaar ter tale; ~ *but SURE,* stadig maar seker; ~ *and SURE wins the race,* agteros kom ook in die kraal; ~ *in the UPTAKE,* traag van begrip; (adv) stadig, langsaam; *DEAD ~,* doodstadig; *GO ~,* stadig gaan; spoed verminder; ~ **coach,** drentelaar, draaier, draaikous, drel, trapsoetjies, harmansdrup, stadige mens; ~**-combustion stove,** smeulstoof; ~ **curve,** wye draai; ~**-down,** vertraging; ~**-footed,** stadig; ~ **ly,** stadig(ies), soetjies, langsaam, voetjie-voetjie; voetjie vir voetjie, op sy sloffies; ~ **march,** stadige mars; begrafnispas; ~**-match,** lont; ~ **motion,** vertraagde aksie; traaggang; ~**-motion picture,** vertraagde rolprent; ~ **movement,** stadige beweging; ~**-moving,** stadig, langsaam; ~**-moving stock,** trae voorraad; ~ **ness,** stadigheid; traagheid; ~**-paced,** stadig; ~**-setting,** stadig verhardend; ~ **train,** boemeltrein; ~**-witted,** stompsinnig, bot; ~**-worm,** blindewurm.
sloyd, slöjd, huisvlyt.
slub, (n) voorspinsel; (v) voorspin.
slubb'er, (n) voorspinmasjien, voorspinner; (v) knoei; bemors, mors.
slub: ~ **linen,** rulinne, voorspinlinne; ~ **yarn,** bultgaring.
slub'bing, afdunning, voorspinreep.
sludge, (n) modder; slyk, klei; boorslik, boorslyk; afsaksel, besinksel; (v) verslyk; ~ *off,* ontslyk; ~ **gas,** slykgas; ~ **hole,** slykgat; ~ **pump,** slykpomp; ~ **sump,** slykput; ~ **trap,** slykvanger.
sludg'y, modderig.
slue, draai, verskuif; *kyk ook* **slew** (n).
slug[1], (n) loper (vir geweer); koeël; loodstafie; prop; opstopper; (v) moker, geweldig slaan.
slug[2], (n) naakslak; luiaard; (v) **(-ged),** slakke uitroei; luier; stadig gaan; ~ **abed,** luiaard, laatslaper, luilak.
slug'gard, luiaard, 'n harmansdrup, leegloper, stoepsitter, jandooi; *the ~ is at his BEST when the sun goes to rest,* die son in die weste, die luiaard op sy beste; *the ~ makes his NIGHT till noon,* die luilak slaap 'n gat in die dag.
slug'gish, lui, traag, loom, vadsig, jansalieagtig, afkerig van inspanning; ~ **ness,** traagheid, stadigheid, luiheid.
sluice, (n) sluis; watervoor; (v) uitspoel, laat vol loop; laat uitstroom; spoel; vloei, 'n sluis insit; ~**-box,** sluistrog; ~**-chamber,** sluiskamer; ~**-gate,** sluisdeur; ~**-head,** sluishoof; ~**-keeper,** sluiswagter; ~ **room,** spoelkamer; ~**-valve,** sluisafsluiter; ~**-way,** sluiskanaal, watervoor; ~ **weir,** sluisoorloop.
sluic'ing, spoeling.
slum, (n) agterbuurt, armebuurt, krotbuurt, kroek; (v) **(-med)** die agterbuurte besoek; ~ **area,** krotstad; agterbuurt, gopse.
slum'ber, (n) sluimer, sluimering; slaap; (v) sluimer, slaap, indommel; ~ *away,* verslaap; ~ **ing,** (n) sluimering; (a) sluimerend, slapend.
slum'b(e)rous, sluimerig, slaperig; slaapwekkend.
slum: ~**-born,** in 'n agterbuurt gebore; ~**-child,** kind uit die agterbuurtes; ~ **clearance,** krotopruiming; ~ **dom,** die agterbuurte, gopse; ~**-dweller,** krotbewoner, flenterdorper; ~**-dwelling,** krotwoning, slopwoning; ~ **land,** die agterbuurtes; ~ **landlord,** krottemelker; ~ **landlordism,** krottemelkery; ~ **ming,** agterbuurtbesoek.
slump, (n) slapte, slap tyd; insinking; duikgang; plotselinge daling, ineenstorting, malaise; (v) insak; skielik daal, ineenstort.
slums, agterbuurt, gopse.
slung, *kyk* **sling,** (v).
slunk, *kyk* **slink.**
slur, (n) vlek, smet, klad, skandvlek; blaam, verwyt; slordige uitspraak; slegte skrif; verbindingsteken (musiek); *cast a ~ on,* 'n smet werp op, besoedel; (v) **(-red),** sleg, onduidelik, slordig uitspreek; bemors, besmeer, besoedel, beklad, besmet; sleep, trek (noot); ~ *over,* net aanroer; klanke insluk.
slu'rry, pap, flodder, slyk.
slush, slyk, modder; smeltende sneeu; ysmodder; sentimentaliteit; kletspraatjies, bogpraatjies; pappery; prulwerk; ~ **ice,** slobys; ~ **iness,** modderigheid, slykerigheid; stroperigheid, sentimentaliteit; ~ **snow,** slobsneeu; ~ **y,** modderig, slykerig; sentimenteel, stroperig.
slut, slons, sloerie, snol, vuil vrou; ~ **tish,** ~ **ty,** slordig, vuil, liederlik, morsig, slonserig; ontugtig; ~ **tishness,** slordigheid, vuilheid, morsigheid; ontugtigheid.
sly, (n): *do something on the ~,* iets agteraf doen; die kat in die donker knyp; iets om die hoekie doen; (a) slu, listig, agterbaks, uitgeslape, slim; oorlams, skelm, deurtrap, geslepe; skalks; *a ~ DOG,* 'n platjie, 'n slimmerd; *a ~ HIT,* 'n skimpskoot; *a ~ TRICK,* 'n slimmigheid; lis; ~ **boots,** slimmerd, karnallie; ~ **lodger,** sluipslaper; ~ **ly,** onderduims, op listige wyse; ~ **ness,** lis, sluheid; deurtraptheid, jakkalsstreke, slimheid, onderduimsheid, geslepenheid.
smack[1], (n) smak (bootjie).
smack[2], (n) tikkie; smakie; geurtjie, tintjie; (v) smaak na; laat dink aan; ~ *of,* laat dink aan; smaak na.
smack[3], (n) klap; hou, slag; pats; klapsoen; *have a ~ AT something,* iets probeer; *a ~ in the EYE,* 'n vernederende afjak; *a ~ in the FACE,* 'n klap in die gesig; *GIVE someone a resounding ~,* iem. 'n taai klap gee; (v) 'n klap gee, slaan, wiks; laat klap; ~ *with the lips,* smak met die lippe; (adv) pardoems, reg, vlak; *it went ~ through the window,* dit het reg deur die venster gegaan; ~ **er,** klaphou; klapsoen; ('n) uithaler.
small, (n) kruis (van rug); dun deel; klein advertensie; (pl) onderklere; soekertjies (advertensies); *the ~ of the back,* die kruis (v.d. rug); (a) klein; gering; weinig, min, luttel; petieterig; verpot, verboep (dier); onbeduidend; bekrompe, kleingeestig, fyn (druk); beknop (kamer); *think no ~ BEER of oneself,* 'n hoë dunk van jouself hê; *CHRONICLE ~ beer,* oor koeitjies en kalfies praat; *the ~ FRY,* die minder belangrikes; nietige mense; die jongspan, die kleinspan; *in the ~ HOURS,* in die vroeë oggendure; ~ *things amuse ~ MINDS,* flou grappe vermaak flou geeste; ~ *PROFITS quick returns,* klein winste, vinnige omset; *on a ~ SCALE,* op klein skaal; *indulge in ~ TALK,* oor koeitjies en kalfies praat; *of ~ VALUE,* van min waarde; *the still ~ VOICE,* die stem v.d. gewete; *in a ~ WAY,* op beskeie voet; ~ *WONDER!* geen wonder nie! (adv) fyn, klein; *FEEL ~,* klein voel; *make someone FEEL ~,* iem. klein laat voel; *LOOK ~,* beteuterd lyk, op jou neus kyk; *SING ~,* 'n toontjie laer sing; ~ **age,** wilde seldery; ~**-arms,** kleingewere; ~ **beer,** dunbier; beuselagtighede; ~ **bore,** klein kaliber; ~ **boy,** seuntjie; ~ **change,** kleingeld; ~ **coal,** gruiskole; ~ **craft,** klein vaartuie; ~ **farmer,** kleinboer; ~ **girl,** dogtertjie, meisietjie; ~ **holder,** kleinboer; ~ **holding,** kleinhoewe, boerderytjie; ~ **ish,** kleinerig; ~**-minded,** bekrompe, kleinsielig, benepe; ~**-mindedness,** bekrompenheid, kleinsieligheid, benepenheid; ~ **ness,** geringheid, nietigheid, kleinheid; ~ **pox,** pokkies; ~ **print,** fyn druk; ~**-scale map,** kleinskaalkaart; ~ **shot,** fyn hael, donshael; ~ **stock,** kleinvee; ~ **sword,** rapier; ~ **talk,** kafpraatjies, geklets; ~ **type,** klein druk; ~ **wares,** galanterieware.
smalt, kobaltglas, smalt.

smar'agdine, smarag=.
smar'my, inkruiperig, stroperig, flikflooierig.
smart, (n) pyn, smart; skrynerigheid; (v) smart ly; brand; pynig, seermaak; smart veroorsaak; *his FINGER* ~*s*, sy vinger brand; *you'll* ~ *FOR this*, jy sal daarvoor boet; ~ *UNDER a disappointment*, bitter voel deur 'n teleurstelling; (a) knap, skran= der, gevat, gewiks; aardig; vlug; fluks, oulik; lewen= dig, geestig, byderhand, snedig; wakker; netjies, sjiek, deftig, keurig, elegant, swierig, piekfyn, viets, modieus; *a* ~ *BLOW*, 'n harde slag; *a* ~ *PACE*, 'n vinnige pas; ~ *PEOPLE*, die hoëlui, die sjiek lui; *she is as* ~ *as a new PIN (as paint)*, sy is so netjies dat jy haar deur 'n ring kan trek; *a* ~ *RAP over the knuckles*, 'n taai raps oor die kneukels; *the* ~ *SET*, die hoëlui, die aansienlikes, die elite; die windma= kermense; *say* ~ *THINGS*, geestighede verkoop; ~ **alec(k),** wysneus, slimjan; ~ **dealing,** knoeiery; ~**en,** mooimaak, regmaak, opknap; ~**ing,** sner= pend, skrynend; ~**ly,** knap; fluks; oulik; wakker, netjies, keurig; piekfyn, viets; ~*ly dressed*, fyn uit= gevat; ~**-money,** roukoop, smartgeld; ~**ness,** knapheid, deftigheid, netheid; handigheid, gesle= penheid, gewiksheid, snedigheid; ~ **pace,** vinnige pas; ~ **retort,** gevatte (snediger) antwoord.
smash, (n) (-es), verbryseling; bankrotskap; breek= spul; doodhou, mokerhou (tennis); botsing, ramp; ineenstorting, debakel; moles, petalje; gemors; (v) verbrysel, stukkend slaan, verpletter, breek, stuk= kend gooi, ingooi (ruit); kapot slaan; moker (ten= nis); bankrot gaan; bots; ~ *to BITS*, in flenters slaan; ~ *DOWN*, afbreek; ~ *INTO*, bots met; ~ *UP*, verpletter, verniel; (adv) vierkant, direk; ~ **and-grab,** breek en gryp (inbraak); ~ **er,** breker; vernietigende slag; verpletterende antwoord, dood= hou; mokerhou (boks); aantreklike nooi; ~ **hit,** voltreffer; ~**ing,** (n) verpletterrng; (a) verplette= rend, vernietigend; uiters aantreklik; *they had a* ~*ing time*, hulle het baie pret gehad; ~**ing blow,** mokerhou, doodhou; ~**ing success,** reusesukses; ~**-up,** botsing, ongeluk; verbryseling, vernieling; ineenstorting.
smatt'er: ~**er,** halfweter, oppervlakkige kenner, skyngeleerde; ~**ing,** bietjie; mondjievol; opper= vlakkige kennis; *have a* ~*ing of Zulu*, 'n mondjie= vol Zoeloe ken.
smear, (n) vlek, kol; smeersel; (v) smeer, besmeer; be= soedel; beswadder, beklad; ~ **campaign,** smeer= kampanje, smeerveldtog, bekladdingsveldtog; ~ **letter,** smeerbrief; ~**y,** vetterig.
smegmat'ic, seepagtig; reinigend.
smell, (n) reuk, geur; snuf(fie); (v) (smelt), ruik; snuf= fel; ~ *ABOUT*, rondsnuffel; ~ *AT*, ruik aan; ~ *of the LAMP*, na die lamp ruik; dis middernagwerk; ~ *OUT*, uitvind, uitruik; ~ *of PETROL*, na petrol ruik; ~ *a RAT*, lont ruik, onraad merk; ~ *SWEET*, lekker ruik; ~ *one's WAY*, jou weg soek; ~**er,** ruiker; neus; spaansvlieg; ~**iness,** stank; ~**ing,** (n) (die) ruik; (a) stinkend; reuk=; ~**ing bottle,** reukbottel, reukflessie; ~**ing salts,** reuk= sout, vlugsout; ~**y,** stinkend, vieslik.
smelt[1], (n) spiering (vis).
smelt[2], (v) smelt (metaal); uitsmelt.
smelt[3], (v) *kyk* **smell,** (v).
smelt: ~ **er,** smelter; ~ **ery, (..ries),** gietery, smeltery; ~**-house,** smeltery.
smelt'ing, (n) (die) smelt; (a) smelt=; ~**-furnace,** smeltoond; ~**-house,** smeltery; ~**-pot,** smeltkroes; ~**-works,** smeltery.
smew, nonnetjie, saagbekeend.
smile, (n) glimlag; *be ALL* ~*s*, van oor tot oor glim= lag; *a BROAD* ~, 'n breë glimlag; *GIVE someone a* ~, vir iem. glimlag; (v) glimlag, toelag; ~ *AP= PROVAL*, glimlaggend goedkeur; ~ *AT some= thing*, oor iets glimlag; ~ *AWAY*, deur 'n glimlag verdryf; weglag; ~ *into one's BEARD*, in jou baard glimlag; ~ *BROADLY*, breed glimlag; *FORTUNE* ~*s on us*, die geluk lag ons toe; ~ *ON*, toelag; ~ *and look PLEASANT about something*, iets met 'n glimlag aanvaar; ~**r,** iem. wat glimlag.
smil'ing, vrolik, glimlaggend, laggend; *COME up* ~, goeie moed hou; *a* ~ *FACE*, 'n laggende gesig;

KEEP ~, hou die blink kant bo; *a* ~ *PROSPECT*, iets om na uit te sien, blye vooruitsig.
smirch, (n) (-es), klad, smet; kol, veeg; (v) beklad; be= smeer; bevuil; besoedel.
smirk, (n) gryns, grimlag; (v) meesmuil, grimlag.
smite, (n) hou, slag; (v) (**smote, smitten**) smyt; slaan; straf, kasty; tref, raak; verslaan; verontrus; *BE smitten with*, verlief wees op; *his CONSCIENCE smote him*, sy gewete het hom verontrus (gepla); ~ *one's HANDS together*, die hande saamslaan; ~ *HIP and thigh*, heup en skenkel slaan; 'n verplette= rende nederlaag toedien; *an IDEA smote him*, 'n gedagte het hom te binne geskiet; *be smitten with PLAGUE*, deur pes geteister; ~**r,** slaner; kastyder.
smith, smid, smit.
smithereens', smith'ers, flenters, stukkies; *IN* ~, fyn en flenters; *SMASH to* ~, fyn en flenters breek, kort en klein slaan.
smith'ery, smidswerk, smedery.
smith'ing, smidswerk, smeedwerk.
smith's: ~ **coal,** smidskole, smeekole; ~ **forge,** sme= dery; ~ **hammer,** smidshamer.
smith'sonite, sinkspaat.
smith's: ~ **tongs,** smeetang; ~ **work,** smidswerk.
smi'thy, (smithies), smidswinkel, smedery; ~ **coal,** smidskole.
smitt'en, *kyk* **smite,** (v).
smock, (n) smok; oorbroek; oorpak; oorrok; kraam= rok; (v) smok; ~**-frock,** oorpak, los tabberd; ~ **ing,** smok, smokwerk; smoksteek; frummelplooie.
smog, rookmis.
smok'able, rookbaar; ~**s,** rookgoed.
smoke, (n) rook; damp, walm; rookammunisie; rook= projektiel; *END in* ~, in rook opgaan; op niks uit= loop nie; *there is never* ~ *without a FIRE*, daar is nie 'n rokie nie of daar is 'n vuurtjie; waar 'n rook is, is 'n vuurtjie; *GO up in* ~, in rook vervlieg; op niks uitloop nie; *HAVE a* ~? wil jy rook? wil jy opsteek? *OUT of the* ~, uit die rook; *from the* ~ *into the SMOTHER*, v.d. wal in die sloot; *he WANTS a* ~, hy wil rook; (v) rook; uitrook; damp; ~ *AWAY*, geweldig rook; wegrook; ~ *like a CHIMNEY*, van sy mond 'n skoorsteen maak; ~ *HEAVILY*, straf (kwaai) rook; ~ *OUT*, uitrook; *put that in your PIPE and* ~ *it*, dit kan jy in jou sak steek; ~**-ball,** rookkoeël; ~**-black,** swartsel, roet= swart; ~**-blanket,** rookskerm; ~**-bomb,** rookbom; ~**-box,** rookkas; ~**-candle,** rookkers; ~**-cloud,** rookwolk; ~**-consumer,** rookverbrander; ~**-cur= tain,** rookgordyn.
smoked, rook=, gerook(te); ~ **bacon,** rookspek; ~ **glass,** berookte glas; ~ **glasses,** sonbril; ~ **ham,** gerookte ham; ~ **herring,** rookharing; ~ **meat,** rookvleis; ~ **sausage,** rookwors.
smoke: ~**-damper,** rookskuif; ~**-dried,** gerook; ~**-drum,** rooktrommel; ~**-dry, (..dried, ..dried),** in die rook hang; ~**-flue,** rookkanaal; ~ **fog,** rook= mis; ~**-grenade,** rookgranaat; ~**-helmet,** rook= hoed; ~**-house,** rookhok; ~**-less,** rookloos, rook= vry; ~**-less powder,** rooklose kruit; ~**-mortar,** rookmortier; ~**-pot,** rookpot; ~**r,** roker; rook= konsert; rookkoepee; *light (moderate)* ~*r*, matige roker; ~**-room,** rookkamer; ~**-screen,** rookskerm, rooksluier, rookgordyn; *throw a* ~ *screen over*, 'n rookskerm oor iets gooi; ~**r's requisities,** rookbe= nodigdhede, rookgoed; ~**r's throat,** tabakkeel; ~ **ry,** rookkamer; rookgerei; ~**s,** sigarette, rook= goed; ~**-stack,** skoorsteenpyp; ~**-tight,** rookvry, rookdig; ~ **tube,** rookkanaal; ~**-writing,** rook= skrif.
smok'iness, rokerigheid.
smok'ing, (n) rook; beroking; *no* ~ *allowed*, rook is verbied; *rook verbode*, (moe)nie rook nie; (a) rook=; rokend; dampend; ~**-cap,** kalotjie; ~**-car= riage,** rookwa; ~**-compartment,** rookkomparte= ment; ~**-concert,** rookkonsert; ~ **hot,** rokend warm (vet); ~**-jacket,** huisbaadjie; ~**-requisites,** rookgoed; ~**-room,** rookkamer; ~**-tobacco,** rook= tabak.
smok'y, rokerig; berook; rook=; vol rook; ~ **quartz,** rookkwarts.
smolt, jaaroudsalm.

smooth, (v) glad maak, gelykmaak, gelykstryk, effen; planeer; laat bedaar; versag, kalmeer, sus; plooi; ~ *AWAY*, glad stryk; uit die weg ruim; ~ *DOWN*, glad stryk; versag; ~ *OFF*, glad afwerk; ~ *OUT*, glad stryk; ~ *OUT differences*, verskille uitstryk; ~ *OVER*, effen, plooi; uit die weg ruim; bewimpel; ~ *something OVER*, iets bewimpel; ~ *the WAY*, die weg baan; wind sny; (a, adv) gelyk, glad, effe; egaal; sag; vriendelik; vleierig; vloeiend (styl); kalm, onbewoë; fyn (konfyt); *a* ~ *PASSAGE*, 'n kalm seereis; 'n voorspoedige verloop; *SAY* ~ *things*, heuning om die mond smeer; *a* ~ *TONGUE*, 'n gladde tong; ~ **barrel**, gladde loop; ~ **bore**, gladdeloop; ~ **-chinned**, met gladde ken; ~ **-faced**, baardloos, glad geskeer; huigelagtig; ~ **-file**, soetvyl.

smooth'ing, (n) (die) glad maak; effening; (a) stryk-; gelykmakend; ~ **-board**, strykbord; ~ **-iron**, strykyster; ~ **-plane**, soetskaaf; ~ **-trowel**, (vorm)stryktroffel.

smooth: ~ **jam**, fyn konfyt; ~ **ly**, sag; vloeiend; ~ *lyworking office*, goed georganiseerde kantoor; ~ **ness**, gladheid; egaligheid; ~ **-plane**, soetskaaf; ~ **-spoken**, ~ **-tongued**, vleiend, glad van tong; ~ **wine**, sagte wyn; ~ **words**, mooipratery.

smote, *kyk* **smite**, (v).

smother, (n) rook; stofwolk; smeuling; walm; (v) smoor, domp, doodsmoor, verstik; met 'n dik laag bedek; oorlaai, onderdruk; geheim hou; ~ *a BALL*, 'n bal dooddruk; ~ *FLAMES*, vlamme smoor; *FOOD* ~ *ed with sauce*, kos versuip in sous; ~ *with KINDNESS*, met vriendelikheid oorlaai; ~ *UP*, in die doofpot stop, stilhou; ~ **crop**, smoorgewas; ~ **tactics**, smoortaktiek (rugby); ~ **y**, verstikkend, smorend.

smoul'der, (n) smeulvuur; (v) smeul; glim; ~ **ing**, smeulend; broeiend, dreigend.

smudge, (n) vuil kol, vlek, smet; klad; dik rook; (v) bevlek, besmet, beklad, besmeer, besoedel; ~ **fire**, smeulvuur; ~ **-pot**, vuurpot.

smudg'iness, vuilheid, smerigheid.

smudg'y, vuil, smerig.

smug, (n) selfvoldane persoon, jansalie; blokker, boekwurm; (a) opgesmuk, keurig; burgerlik, fatsoenlik; bekrompe; selfvoldaan, selfgenoegsaam.

smug'gle, smokkel; ~ *IN*, insmokkel; ~ *OUT*, oor die grens smokkel; ~ **r**, smokkelaar; smokkelskip.

smugg'ling, smokkelary.

smug'ness, selfgenoegsaamheid, selfingenomenheid, selfvoldaanheid; bekrompenheid; huigelagtigheid.

smut, (n) roet; brand (in gesaaides); stuifbrand; vuil taal; vlek; *loose* ~, bedekte brand; (v) (-ted), vuil maak; bevuil; brand laat kry; ~ **-ball**, koringroes; ~ **-blight**, brandskimmel; ~ **-disease**, brand; ~ **tiness**, vuilheid, vieslikheid; ~ **ty**, besmet; vuil; vol roet; smerig; met stikbrand besmet (koring); skurf, skuins (grap).

Smyr'na, Smirna.

Smyr'niot, Smirnioot.

snack, porsie, deeltjie, happie, versnapering, peuselhappie, snoepgereg; tussenmaaltyd, ligte maaltyd; (pl) peuselgoedjies; southappies; ~ **-bar**, peuselkroeg; snelkafee; ~ **food**, peuselkos; snelkos; snoepkos.

snack'le iron, frituuryster.

snaf'fle, (n) trens, trenstoom; *ride someone on the* ~, mooi met iem. werk; (v) met 'n trens ry; beteuel; intoom; ~ **-bit**, trens; ~ **-bridle**, trenstoom; ~ **-ring**, trensring.

snag, (n) knoe(t)s, kwas; belemmering; uitsteeksel; stomp; hindernis, moeilikheid, haakplek, struikelblok; *be FULL of* ~ *s*, baie voete in die aarde hê; *THAT'S the* ~, daar is (sit) die haakplek; *THERE'S a* ~, daar's 'n kinkel in die kabel; *WHAT is the* ~ ? waar haper dit? (v) (-ged), stompe uithaal; knoeste wegkap; op die rotse stuur (skip); ~ **ged**, ~ **gy**, knoesterig, kwasterig, geduik, met duike; moeilik; ~ **-tooth**, uitsteektand, slagtand.

snail, (n) slak; snekrat; *DO something at a* ~ *'s pace*, iets op sy elf-en-dertigste doen; *GO at a* ~ *'s pace*, voetjie vir voetjie loop; die slakkegang gaan; (v) slakke doodmaak; ~ **-like**, slakagtig; stadig; ~

paced, doodstadig, so stadig soos 'n slak; ~ **-shell**, slakhuis, skulp; ~ **-slow**, so stadig soos 'n slak, doodstadig; ~ **-wheel**, snekrat; ~ **y**, slakagtig; vol slakke.

snake, (n) slang; *CHERISH a* ~ *in one's bosom*, 'n adder aan jou bors koester; *there is a* ~ *in the GRASS*, daar is 'n slang in die gras; *GREAT* ~ !, mapstieks!; ~ *s and LADDERS*, op-en-afspel; *SCOTCH the* ~, iets onskadelik maak; iets lam lê; *SEE* ~ *s*, die horries hê; *WAKE* ~ *s*, rusie veroorsaak; (v) kronkel, seil; ~ **-bird**, sekretarisvoël; slanghalsvoël; ~ **-bite**, slangbyt; ~ **-catcher**, slangvanger; ~ **-charmer**, slangbesweerder; ~ **-dance**, slangdans; ~ **-doctor**, slangdokter; ~ **-farm**, slangplaas; ~ **-fish**, slangetjie; ~ **-lizard**, pootjieslang; ~ **mungoose**, slangmuishond; ~ **-park**, slangpark, slangtuin; ~ **-pit**, slangkuil; ~ **-poison**, slanggif; ~ **'s root**, slangkruid, slangwortel, slanghoutjies; ~ **'s egg**, slangeier; ~ **'s-head**, slangkop; ~ **skin**, slangvel; ~ **-stone**, slangsteen; ~ **-weasel**, muishond; ~ **worship**, slangdiens; ~ **-worshipper**, slangaanbidder.

snak'ish, slangagtig.

snak'y, vol slange; slangagtig; ~ **rod**, slangstaf.

snap, (n) hap, byt; klap, knal, slag; kiekie; pit, gô, energie; knip; breuk; bars; *I don't CARE a* ~ *(of my fingers)*, ek gee geen flenter om nie; *a COLD* ~, 'n skielike koue; (v) (-ped), hap, gryp; kets (geweer); kraak; knal, klap; breek; spring; knip; toeslaan; kiek, afneem; (toe)snou; afknap; ~ *AT*, gryp na; toesnou; ~ *up a BARGAIN*, 'n kopie skraap; ~ *one's FINGERS*, met die vingers klap; ~ *one's FINGERS at*, verontsaam; *GO* ~, afbreek; ~ *someone's HEAD off*, iem. afsnou; ~ *someone's NOSE off*, iem. afsnou; iem. afjak; kortaf wees met iem.; ~ *OFF*, afbyt; afbreek; ~ *at an OFFER*, 'n aanbod gretig aanneem; ~ *SHUT*, toespring; ~ *TO*, toeklap; ~ *UP*, beetpak; opraap; (a) skielik, vinnig, blits-; verrassend, onverwag, onvoorbereid; *a* ~ *DEBATE*, 'n onverwagte debat; *a* ~ *DECISION*, 'n onoorwoë (onbedagte) besluit; *a* ~ *ELECTION*, 'n blitsverkiesing; *fire a* ~ *SHOT*, 'n knalskoot skiet (los); *a* ~ *VOTE*, 'n onverhoedse stemming; *pass by a* ~ *VOTE*, by verrassing aanneem.

snap: ~ **dragon**, leeubekkie; ~ **-fastener**, drukknoop; ~ **gauge**, bekkaliber; ~ **-happy**, skietlustig; ~ **-lock**, knipslot, springslot; ~ **per**, happer; klapper; ~ **pily**, bits, skerp; ~ **piness**, bitsheid; kortheid; ~ **pish**, bits, skerp, driftig, snipperig; ~ **pishness**, bitsigheid; snipperighoid, skerpheid, driftigheid; ~ **py**, knappend; vurig, opgewek; pittig; vinnig; gou, kort; swierig, keurig; *make it* ~ *py!* maak gou! roer jou! opskud! ~ **ring**, spanring; ~ **shoot**, op die aanslag skiet; ~ **-shooting**, knapskiet, knakvuur; ~ **shot**, (n) kiekie, (fotografiese) opname; (v) (**-ped**), kiek, afneem; ~ **switch**, snapskakelaar; ~ **tool**, snapper.

snare, (n) strik; wip; net; val; vanggat; valstrik; snaar (van trom); *lay a* ~, vir iem. 'n wip (strik) stel; (v) vang, verstrik.

snarl[1], (n) strik, knoop, kinkel, warboel, verwarring, verwikkeling; (v) verwar, verwikkel.

snarl[2], (n) knor; snou; (v) knor, grom, grou, toebyt; ~ *at*, toesnou.

snarl[3], (v) (metaal) uitklop.

snarl'er[1], klopyster; uitklopper.

snarl'er[2], brompot.

snarl'ing[1], (n) verwarring.

snarl'ing[2], (n) snouerigheid; (a) bits, nydig, snouerig.

snarl'ing iron, klopyster.

snatch, (n) (-es), ruk, greep; vlaag; stukkie, brokkie; diefstal; *BY* ~ *es*, met rukke; met tussenpose; *MAKE a* ~ *at*, gryp na; *a* ~ *of SONG*, 'n brokkie (stukkie) van 'n lied; (v) gryp, wegruk; steel; ~ *AT the present*, die teenswoordige aangryp; ~ *AWAY*, weggryp, wegruk; ~ *from DEATH*, aan die dood ontruk; ~ *FROM*, wegruk van; ~ *a KISS*, 'n soen steel; ~ *at an OFFER*, 'n aanbod aangryp; ~ *the OPPORTUNITY*, die geleentheid aangryp; ~ **-and-grab thief**, grypdief; ~ **er**, gryper; ~ **y**, ongereeld, onreëlmatig, met horte en stote.

sneak, (n) kruiper, gluiper; onderduimse persoon; verklikker; (v) sluip, stilletjies gaan, gluip, verklap, verklik; steel, snoep; ~ *ALONG*, voortsluip; ~ *AWAY*, wegsluip, heensluip; ~ *OFF*, stilletjies wegsluip, met die noorderson verdwyn; ~ *OUT*, uitsluip; ~ **ing**, (n) verklapping; gesluip; (a) kruiperig, gluiperig, druipstert; veragtelik; heimlik; *have a* ~*ing liking for him*, in die stilligheid van iem. hou; ~ **preview**, geheime voorvertoning; ~**-thief**, goudief, (in)sluipdief; ~**y**, gluiperig, kruiperig; verklapperig.

sneer, (n) spotlag, grynslag, hoonlag; (v) uitlag, meesmuil, grinnik; verag, bespot, hoon, die neus optrek vir; minagtend lag; ~ *at*, spot met; die neus optrek vir; ~**er**, smaler, spotter; ~**ing**, (n) beskimping; (a) spottend, honend; ~**ing laugh**, spotlag, hoonlag.

sneeze, (n) nies; niesbui; (v) nies; *not to be* ~ *d AT*, nie te versmaai nie; ~ *LOUDLY*, proes; ~**-wood**, nieshout; ~ **wort**, nieswortel.

sneez'ing, (n) nies, genies; (a) nies=; ~ **gas**, niesgas; ~ **powder**, niespoeier.

sneez'y, nieserig.

snib, (n) knip, grendel; (v) **(-bed)**, sluit, op slot sit.

snick, (n) kerf, keep; tikhou (kr.); (v) knip, sny, keep; laat wegskram; tik (kr.).

snick'er, (n) sagte runnik; gegiggel; (v) saggies runnik; giggel; ~ **snee'**, vegmes, steekmes.

snide, laag, bedrieglik, gemeen, vals.

sniff, (n) gesnuffel, ruik; (v) snuffel; snuiwe; ~ *ABOUT*, rondsnuffel; ~ *the AIR*, die lug opsnuif; ~ *AT a bottle*, aan 'n bottel ruik; ~ *AT an offer*, 'n aanbod met veragting afwys; ~ *OUT*, uitsnuffel; ~**er**, snuiwer.

sniff'le, (n) gesnuif; gesnuffel; (v) snuif; snuffel.

sniff'y, smalend, neusoptrekkerig, stinkerig.

snift, stoom afblaas; snuif; ~**er**, sopie, dop; bries; ~**ing-valve**, snuifklep.

snigg'er, (n) gegiggel, gegingegaap; (v) giggel, ginnegaap, onderdruk lag; ~**ing**, gegingegaap.

snip, (n) snip(pertjie); sny, knip; knipsel, stukkie, flenter; kleremaker; kopie; (pl) handskêr, blikskêr; (v) **(-ped)**, afsny, afknip, oopknip, sny.

snipe, (n) snip (voël); domkop; (v) snippe skiet; skiet, skuilskiet, sluipskiet, een vir een wegskiet; ~ *at*, uit 'n hinderlaag skiet; ~**r**, skerpskutter, sluipskutter; ~**r's nest**, skuttersnes; ~**-shooting**, snipjag.

snip'ing, sluipskiet(ery).

snipp'et, deel, stukkie, snippertjie; ~**y**, fragmentaries, snipperagtig; kort, hakkelrig.

snip'py, snipperig.

sniv'el, (n) snot; getjank, gesnuif; huigelary; (v) **(-led)**, snotter, huil, grens, femel; ~**ler**, snotteraar; tjanker; ~**ling**, (n) getjank; gesnotter; (a) snotterend, huilerig, tjankend.

snob, snob; ploert; ~ **appeal**, snobwaarde, spogbog; ~**bery**, ploertery, snobisme; ~**bish**, ploerterig, snobagtig; ~**bishness**, ~**bism**, snobisme, ploertsrigheid.

snock, (n) snock; (v) snoek vang; ~**er**, snoekboot; ~**ing**, snoekvangs.

snood, haarlint, haarband.

snook[1], (n) (Europese) snoek.

snook[2], (n) gebaar van minagting; *cock a* ~ *at*, die neus optrek vir; skewebek trek vir; 'n gebaar van minagting maak.

snook'er, snoeker, potspel; ~ **den**, snoekerspeelplek.

snoop, (n) snuffelaar; spioen; bemoeial; (v) rondloer, rondsnuffel; bespied; jou bemoei met; ~ *around*, rondspioeneer; ~**er**, snuffelaar; spioen; bemoeial; ~**y**, bemoeisiek, indringerig, nuuskierig.

snoot'y, verwaand, neusoptrekkerig.

snooze, (n) dutjie, slapie; (v) dut, visvang; leeglê.

snooz'y, slaperig.

snore, (n) gesnork; (v) snork; ~ *the roof off*, balke saag; planke saag; ~**r**, snorker.

snor'ing, gesnork; gesaag, houtsaery.

snork'el, snuiwer, snorkel.

snort, (n) gesnuif, geproes; snork; bries; snuiwer, snorkel (duikboot); (v) snuiwe (perd); proes, snork; ~ *out*, uitproes; ~**er**, snuiwer (duikboot); rukwind; mooi skoot (hou); kwaai skrobbering; ~**ing**, (n) gesnork, geproes; (a) briesend.

snot, snot; ~**tiness**, snotterigheid; ~**ty**, (n) **(..ties)**, snotneus; (a) snotterig, snot=.

snout, snuit, snoet; neus; ~**-beetle**, snuitkewer; ~**ed**, met 'n snoet; tuitvormig, snuitvormig; langneusig, langneus=.

snow, (n) kapok, sneeu; (pl) sneeuveld; *PERPETUAL* ~, ewigdurende sneeu; *as WHITE as* ~, sneeuwit, spierwit; (v) sneeu, kapok; *be* ~ *ed IN*, toegesneeu word; *be* ~ *ed UNDER with work*, toegegooi wees onder werk; meer werk hê as hare op jou kop; oorlaai word met werk; ~ *ed UP*, toegesneeu; oorlaai met werk; ~**ball**, (n) sneeubal; sneeuroos (plant); *not have a* ~ *ball's hope*, nie die geringste hoop hê nie; (v) met sneeuballe gooi; sneeubal; ~**ball effect** sneeubaleffek; ~**-bird**, sneeuvink; ~**-blind**, sneeublind; ~**-blindness**, sneeublindheid; ~**-blink**, sneeuglans; ~**-boot**, sneeustewel; ~**-bound**, ingesneeu, vasgesneeu; ~**-broth**, sneeuwater; ~**-capped**, met sneeu bedek; ~*capped mountain*, sneeuberg; ~**-clad**, besneeu; ~**-cloud**, sneeuwolk; ~**-crowned**, met sneeu bedek; ~**-crystal**, sneeukristal; ~**-drift**, sneeuval, sneeujag; sneeudrifsel; ~**drop**, sneeuvlokkie; ~ **fall**, sneeuval; ~**-field**, sneeuveld; ~**flake**, sneeuvlokkie; ~**-fox**, sneeuvos; ~**-goggles**, sneeubril; ~**-goose**, sneeugans; ~**-grouse**, sneeuhoender; ~**iness**, sneeuagtigheid; ~**like**, sneeuagtig; ~**-line**, sneeugrens, sneeulinie; ~**man**, sneeumens, sneeupop; *abominable* ~ *man*, afskuwelike sneeumens; ~**-pellet**, sneeukorrel; ~**-petrel**, sneeustormvoël; ~**-plough**, sneeuploeg, kapokploeg; ~**-shoe**, sneeuskoen; ~**-shove**, sneeuskop; ~**-shoveller**, sneeuopruimer; ~**-shower**, sneeubui, sneeuvlaag; ~**-slide**, ~**-slip**, sneeustorting, lawine; ~**storm**, sneeustorm; ~**-water**, sneeuwater; ~**-white**, sneeuwit, haelwit; *S* ~ *White*, Sneeuwitjie; ~**y**, sneeuagtig, besneeu, sneeu=; spierwit; ~**y sky**, sneeulug.

snub, (n) stompneus; wipneus; teregwysing, afjak; (v) **(-bed)**, afsnou, afjak; teregwys, bestraf; verwerp, verneder; (a) gewip; stomp; ~**ber**, afjakker; skokdemper (skeepst.); wiegdemper (motor); ~**-nosed**, stompneus=, platneus=, wipneus=.

snuff, (n) snuif; snuitsel; *LIKE a pinch of* ~, soos 'n handvol vlieë; *TAKE* ~, snuif; *TAKE in* ~, kwalik neem; *UP to* ~, ouer as twaalf; *not WORTH a pinch of* ~, nie 'n pyp twak werd nie; nie 'n knip voor die neus werd nie; (v) snuiwe; ruik aan, besnuffel; snuit (kers); ~ *a CANDLE with a pistol*, op 'n trippens skiet; *be* ~**-box**, snuifdoos; ~**-coloured**, snuifkleurig; ~**er**, (kers)snuiter; *pair of* ~ *ers*, kerssnuiter; ~**ertray**, snuiterbakkie.

snuff'le (n) snuiwende geluid, gesnuiwe; deur die neuspratery; (v) snuif; deur die neus praat.

snuff' mill, snuifmeul; snuifdoos.

snuff'y, soos snuif; snuifagtig; met snuif bemors; onaangenaam.

snug, (n) privaat kamertjie; (v) behaaglik maak; ~ *down*, gaan lê; (a, adv) gesellig, lekker, warm; beskut, gerieflik, knussig, snoesig, passend, sluitend; *be as* ~ *as a BUG in a rug*, lekker warm en gemaklik voel; *a* ~ *FORTUNE*, 'n redelike fortuin; *a* ~ *JOB*, 'n lekker baantjie; *LIE* ~, wegkruip; *MAKE* ~, jou lekker inrig; ~ **fit**, noupassing; presiese passing; ~**gery**, **(..ries)**, gesellige plek, privaathoekie, lekker hoekie; lêplek.

snugg'le, inkruip, jou warmpies nestel, lepellê; ~ *DOWN*, lekker gaan lê; ~ *UP against*, vasdruk teen.

snug'ly, behaaglik, lekker.

snug'ness, geselligheid, warmte; gerieflikheid.

so, so, sodanig; dus; *and* ~ *say ALL of us*, ons stem almal saam; ~ *AND* ~, dinges; dié en dit; ~ *ARE you!* jy ook! ~ *you are BACK again*, jy is dus weer terug; ~ *BE it*, laat dit so wees, dit sy so; *and* ~ *to BED*, daarmee is ons bed toe; *I DID* ~, ek het dit gedoen; ~ *DO I*, ek ook; *EVER* ~ *much better*, oneindig beter; ~ *FAR* ~ *good*, tot sover is alles agtermekaar; ~ *FAR*, tot sover; ~ *FAR as*, vir sover; *FIVE or* ~, omtrent vyf; *and* ~ *FORTH*, ensovoorts; *HOW* ~? hoe so? *HOW is your wife?* ~ ~, hoe gaan dit met jou vrou? Nie alte goed nie;

IF ~, as dit so is; *JUST* ~! net so! juis! ~ *LONG!* tot siens! *perhaps MORE* ~, miskien nog meer; ~ *much the MORE*, des te meer; ~ *MUCH better*, oneindig beter; ~ *MUCH for that*, dit is nou afgehandel; ~ *MUCH* ~ *that*, soseer, selfs dat, in so 'n mate dat; *he is talking* ~ *much NONSENSE*, hy praat pure kaf; *NOT* ~, glad nie; *and* ~ *ON*, ensovoorts; *QUITE* ~! presies! ~ *they SAY*, so word vertel; *you don't SAY* ~! ag nee! sowaar! ~ *THAT*, sodat; ~ *THAT'S that*, daarop kom dit nou neer; ~ *THEN*, so is dit dus; ~ *THERE!* wê! daar het jy dit nou! *I THINK* ~, ek dink so; *I THOUGHT* ~! dit kon ek dink! *I TOLD you* ~, ek het jou mos gesê; ~ *WHAT*? en wat daarvan?

soak, (n) (die) week, weking; suipparty; dronklap; *a* ~, 'n dronklap, 'n suiplap; (v) week, deurweek, intrek, drenk; drink; ~ *the GROUND with water*, deurdrenk die grond met water; ~ *IN*, intrek; deurdring; *PUT to* ~, laat week; *a RAG* ~*ed in (with) petrol*, 'n lap deurweek met petrol; ~ *the RICH*, laat die rykes betaal; ~ *UP*, opsuig; opslurp; ~ **age**, deursyfering; ~ **age pit**, sinkput; ~ **bath**, weekbad, dompelbad.

soaked, deurnat, deurweek, deurdrenk, druipnat; ~ *IN*, deurtrek van; deurdrenk van; ~ *TO the skin*, papnat; ~ *WITH rain*, papnat.

soak: ~**er**, drenker; suiplap; stortbui; ~**ing**, (n) deurweking; stortbui; *have a* ~*ing*, papnat word; (a) deurwekend, deurdringend.

so'-and-so, (n) dinges; vent; *if that is* ~, *I don't wish to speak with him*, as dit die vent is, wil ek nie met hom praat nie; (a) so-so, taamlik; *a* ~ *affair*, 'n treurige boel.

soap, (n) seep; *a BAR of* ~, 'n steen seep; *a CAKE of* ~, 'n koekie seep; *HOME-MADE* ~, boerseep; *LIQUID* ~, vloeistofseep; *SOFT* ~, sagte seep; vleiery, mooipraatjies; (v) inseep; seep smeer; met seep was; ~**-bag**, seepsakkie; ~**-boiler**, seepkoker, seepsieder; ~**-box**, seepkis; seepbak; ~**-box orator**, straatredenaar; ~**-bubble**, seepblaas, seepbel; ~**-copper**, seeppot; ~**-dish**, seepbakkie; ~**-ery**, (..**ries**), seepkokery; ~ **film**, seeplagie; ~**-flakes**, vlokseep, seepvlokkies; ~**-house**, seepkokery; ~**iness**, seperigheid; ~**less**, seeploos; ~ **opera**, sepie, seepopera, ligte vervolgverhaal (radio, TV); ~ **powder**, seeppoeier; ~ **saver**, seepspaarder; ~**stone**, seepklip, pypklip, seepsteen, talksteen; ~**-suds**, seepsop; ~**-works**, seepfabriek, seepsiedery; ~**y**, seperig, seepagtig, seep=; vleierig; salwend; ~*y water*, seepwater.

soar, hoog vlieg, opstyg, 'n hoë vlug neem, in die hoogte gaan; jou hoog verhef; swewe, staties sweef (vliegtuig); ~ *ABOVE*, uitstyg bo; *PRICES have* ~*ed*, pryse het die hoogte ingeskiet; ~**er**, sweefvlieër.

sob, (n) snik; (v) (**-bed**), snik; ~ *one's heart out*, bitter snik; lang trane huil; ~**bing**, (n) gesnik; (a) snikkend.

sob'er, (v) bedaar; laat bedaar; ernstig stem; ontnugter; nugter word; (a) matig; sober, nugter; verstandig; gematig, besadig, bedaard; stemmig; beskeie; *in* ~ *FACT*, sonder oordrywing; *as* ~ *as a JUDGE*, so stemmig soos 'n ouderling; ~**-headed**, ~**-minded**, bedaard, besadig; verstandig; nugter; ~**ness**, matigheid, soberheid; stemmigheid, bedaardheid; *what* ~*ness conceals, drunkenness reveals*, die mond van 'n dronk man praat die waarheid; ~**-sides**, bedaarde mens, Stil Jan; ~**-suited**, stemmig geklee(d).

sobri'ety = **soberness**.

sob'riquet, bynaam; spotnaam; aangenome naam.

sob: ~**-singer**, sniksanger; ~**-stuff**, sentimentele geklets, tranerigheid.

so'-called, sogenaamd; kastig.

socc'er, sokker, voetbal; ~ **ball**, sokkerbal; ~ **field**, sokkerveld; ~ **game**, sokkerspel; ~ **ite**, sokkerspeler; sokkerondersteuner; ~ **pool**, sokkerpot; ~ **team**, sokkerspan.

sociabil'ity, geselligheid.

so'ciable, (n) rytuig; driewieler; geselsbank; (a) gesellig, vriendelik; ~ **nature**, gesellige (vriendelike) aard; ~ **weaver**, versamelvoël, familievoël.

so'cial, (n) gesellighed, partytjie, gesellige byeenkoms; (a) sosiaal, maatskaplik; gesellig; *man is a* ~ *ANIMAL*, die mens is 'n sosiale wese; *a grave* ~ *ERROR*, 'n growwe sosiale flater; *be a* ~ *SUCCESS*, in die hoë kringe opgeneem word; *Minister of S* ~ *WELFARE*, Minister van Volkswelsyn; ~ **climber**, aansiensoeker, strewer, klimvoël; *S* ~ **Democrat**, Sosiaal-Demokraat; ~ **drinking**, gesellige drankgebruik; ~ **duties**, maatskaplike pligte; ~ **evil**, maatskaplike (sosiale) euwel; ~ **intercourse**, gesellige verkeer; ~**ism**, sosialisme; ~**ist**, (n) sosialis; (a) sosialisties; ~**is'tic**, sosialisties; ~**ite**, notabele; uitgaande persoon; uitganer; rinkinker; ~**'ity**, gesellighed, gemeenskapsin; ~**iza'tion**, sosialisasie; ~**ize**, sosialiseer; ~ **rank**, rang in die maatskappy; ~ **reformation**, maatskappyhervorming; ~ **science**, sosiologie; sosiale wetenskappe; ~ **security**, bestaansbeveiliging, maatskaplike beveiliging.

soci'ety, (..**ties**), maatskappy, gemeenskap; genootskap, vereniging; samelewing; (die) hoërskap, (die) vername wêreld, (die) deftige kringe; *FRIENDLY* ~, onderlinge hulpvereniging; *the S* ~ *of FRIENDS*, die Kwakers; *HIGH* ~, die hoêlui; *the S* ~ *of JESUS*, die Genootskap van Jesus, Jesuïeteorde; *LEARNED* ~, geleerde genootskap; ~ *of PARISH-LADIES*, sustersvereniging; ~ **lady**, sosiale vlinder.

Socin'ian, (n) Sociniaan; (a) Sociniaans; ~**ism**, Socianisme.

socio-cul'tural, sosiokultureel.

socio-econom'ic, sosiaal-ekonomies, sosio-ekonomies; ~ **upliftment**, sosiaal-ekonomiese (sosio-ekonomiese) opheffing.

sociog'raphy, sosiografie.

sociolog'ic(al), sosiologies.

sociol'ogist, sosioloog.

sociol'ogy, sosiologie.

sock[1], (n) lekkergoed, lekkers; (v) trakteer.

sock[2], (n) hou, slag; *a* ~ *in the eye*, 'n hou op die oog; (v) gooi, smyt; 'n hou toedien; (adv) reg, vierkant, vlak.

sock[3], (n) sok(kie); blyspel; ploegskaar; los binnesool; toneelskoen; *pull up your* ~ *s*, roer jou; ruk jou reg.

sock'er = **soccer**.

sock'et, sok, huls, koker; bus, pot; blok; deurboring, gat, buis; mof (pyp); potjie (heup); holte; kas (oog); pyp; ~ *of tooth*, tandkas; ~**-chisel**, sokbeitel; ~**-joint**, koeëlgewrig; sokverbinding; ~**-key**, soksleutel; ~ **outlet**, kontaksok (elek.); ~**-pipe**, sokpyp, insteekpyp; ~**-pole**, roeispaan.

sock' suspender, sokkie(op)houer, kous(op)houer.

so'cle, suilvoet, voetstuk (van 'n suil).

So'crates, Sokrates.

Socrat'ic, Sokraties.

sod[1], (n) smeerlap, vent.

sod[2], (n) sooi, kluit; *under the* ~, onder die kluite; in die graf; (v) (**-ded**), met sooie belê; onder die kluite steek.

sod'a, soda; spuitwater; *BICARBONATE of* ~, koeksoda; *CAUSTIC* ~, seepsoda; ~**-ash**, soda-as; ~**-fountain**, bruisbron, sodapomp, spuitwaterapparaat.

sodal'ity, vereniging, genootskap, broederskap.

so'da: ~**-lye**, sodaloog; ~**-water**, sodawater, spuitwater.

sodd'en, (v) deurweek; papnat maak; papnat word; (a) deurtrek, deurweek, papnat; kleierig, klouerig, wesenloos; opgeswel (van drank); ~ *with drink*, besope; deurtrek v.d. drank.

sod: ~ **ding**, sooibekleding; ~ **dy**, met sooie bedek, vol sooie; ~ **house**, sooihuis.

sod'ium, natrium; ~ **bicarbonate**, koeksoda; ~ **carbonate**, natron, wassoda; ~ **chloride**, tafelsout, natriumchloried; ~ **fluoride**, natriumfluoried; ~ **nitrate**, natronsalpeter.

So'dom, Sodom; ~ **apple**, sodomappel.

sod'omite, sodomieter, homoseksueel.

sodomit'ic, sodomities, homoseksueel.

sod'omy, sodomie.

sod' plough, braakploeg.

sof'a, sofa, rusbank, divan.

soff'it, binnewelwing, boog.
soft, (n) papbroek, stumper; (a, adv) sag (saf); mal; pap, week; soetsappig; teerhartig, gevoelig; onno= sel; verwyf; slap (boordjie); *a ~ ANSWER turneth away wrath,* 'n sagte antwoord keer die grimmig= heid af; *he is a BIT ~,* hy is dommerig; *he has a ~ JOB,* hy het 'n maklike baantjie; *he has a ~ SPOT for her,* hy het 'n warm hoekie in sy hart vir haar; hy het 'n swak vir haar; ~ **ball,** sagtebal; ~**-boiled,** sag gekook; ~ **cover,** slap band; ~**-cover book,** slap= band(boek); ~ **curb,** hakgal; ~ **currency,** sagte be= taalmiddele (valuta); ~ **drink,** alkoholvrye drank, koeldrank, mineraalwater; ~**en,** sag maak, week; versag; verminder, lenig; verweeklik, sagter stem, verteder; demp (kleure); matig; onthard (water); ~*en DOWN,* versag, temper; ~*en UP,* mak maak; week maak; ~**ener,** versagter, leniger; versag= middel.
soft'ening, (n) verweking, versagting; ontharding (water); (a) versagtend; ~ *of the BRAIN,* harsing= verweking; ~ *UP,* makmakery.
soft: ~ **furnishings,** gordynstowwe; meubelstowwe; ~ **goods,** wolstowwe, weefstowwe, katoenstowwe, tekstielgoedere; ~**-hearted,** teerhartig; ~**-hearted= ness,** teerhartigheid; ~ **iron,** smeyester, weekyster; ~ **job,** lekker (maklike) baantjie; ~ **landing,** sagte landing, seelanding (ruimtetuig); ~**ly,** saggies, suutjies; ~**ness,** sagtheid, weekheid; malsheid; ~**- nosed bullet,** dumdumkoeël, loodpuntkoeël; ~ **no= things,** verliefde praatjies; ~ **option,** maklike keuse; ~ **palate,** sagte verhemelte; ~ **pedal,** (n) sagte pe= daal, ~**-pedal,** (v) matig, lenig, minder belangrik laat voorkom; ~ **rot,** sagte vrot; ~ **sawder,** mooi= praatjies, heuningsmeerdery; ~ **soap,** (n) tuieseep, groen seep; vleiery; ~**-soap,** (v) vlei; ~-*soap some= one,* iem. na die mond praat; iem. heuning om die mond smeer; iem. met die stroopkwas bewerk; ~ **solder,** (n) tinsoldeersel, sagte soldeersel; (v) sagsol= deer; ~ **sore,** sagte (veneriese) sweer; ~**-spoken,** vriendelik, sag.
soft' spot, teer plek, swak; *attack someone's ~,* iem. in sy swak tas; *have a ~ for women,* 'n swak hê vir vroue.
soft: ~ **steel,** weekstaal; ~ **talk,** mooipraatjies; ~ **touch,** ligte aanslag; ~ **ware,** sagte ware; sagte goed, materiaalgoed; programme, programmatuur (rek.); ~ **ware package,** programpakket (rek.) ~ **water,** sagte water; ~**-wood,** greinhout; naaldhout; jong= hout; ~ **y,** (..**ties**), papbroek, stumper, sul; teer= hartige, goeierd.
sog'giness, papperigheid; deurweektheid.
sogg'y, deurweek, vogtig; kluitjierig; ~ *bread,* kluit= jiebrood, klererige brood.
soho'! so-nou, hanou!
soil[1]**,** (n) smet; vlek; vuilis, vuilgoed; (v) vuil maak, besoedel, bemors.
soil[2]**,** (n) grond, aarde; bodem; *fall on FERTILE ~,* in goeie aarde val; *on FOREIGN ~,* in die vreemde; *NATIVE ~,* geboortegrond; *SON of the ~,* kind van die land; (v) met groenvoer vetmaak; ~ **biol= ogy,** bodembiologie; ~ **chemist,** grondskeikun= dige; ~ **conservation,** grondbewaring; ~ **erosion** gronderosie.
soiled, vuil, besoedel; ~**-linen bag,** vuilgoedsak.
soil: ~ **expert,** bodemkundige; ~ **less,** sonder grond; smetloos; ~ **less, culture,** waterkultuur, die kweek sonder grond; ~ **moisture,** grondvog; ~**-moisture content,** grondvoggehalte.
soil' pipe, afvalvoerpyp, aftappyp.
soil: ~**-poisoning,** bodemvergiftiging; ~ **protection,** bodembeskerming; ~ **science,** grondkunde, bo= demkunde, ~ **survey,** bodemopname; ~ **test,** grondtoets; ~ **utilization,** (Amer.) grondbedryfs= leer; ~ **water,** bodemwater; ~ **yield,** bodemop= brengs.
soir'ee, aandparty.
soj'ourn, (n) verblyf; omwandeling; *Christ's ~ on earth,* die omwandeling van Jesus; (v) tydelik bly, vertoef, verwyl, jou ophou; ~**er,** vreemdeling, gas, reisiger; ~**ing,** omwandeling; verblyf; ~**ment,** ver= blyf.
sol[1]**,** sol (mus.).

sol[2]**,** oplossing
sol'a, sola(wissel); ~ *of exchange,* solawissel.
sol'ace, (n) troos, vertroosting; (v) (ver)troos, op= beur; ~**ment,** vertroosting, troos; ~**r,** vertrooster.
sol'anine, solanien, solanine.
solan'um, solanum.
sol'ar, son(s)=; ~ **climate,** sonklimaat; ~ **day,** son= dag; ~ **deity,** songod; ~ **eclipse,** sonsverduistering; ~ **energy,** sonkrag, sonenergie; ~ **heater,** sonver= warmer; ~ **heating,** solarisme; ~ **im'eter,** sonme= ter, solarimeter; ~ **'ium,** (..**ia**), sonkamer, solari= um; ~ **iza'tion,** sonbeligting, solarisasie; ~ **ize,** te lank belig; aan sonlig blootstel, solariseer; ~ **month,** sonmaand; ~ **myth,** sonmite; ~ **plexus,** sonnevleg, buikvleg, krop v.d. maag; ~ **radiation,** sonstraling; ~ **spot,** sonvlek; ~ **system,** sonstelsel; ~ **time,** sontyd; ~ **year,** sonjaar.
sola'tium, (..**tia**), skadeloosstelling; troosgeld.
sold, (v) *kyk* **sell,** (v); (a) verkoop; geplaas (aandele).
sol'der, (n) soldeersel; (v) soldeer.
sol'dering, (n) (die) soldeer; soldeerwerk; (a) soldeer=; ~**-bolt,** ~**-iron,** soldeerbout; ~ **flame,** soldeer= vlam; ~ **lamp,** soldeerlamp; ~ **tin,** soldeertin; ~ **tongs,** soldeertang.
sol'der stick soldeerstafie.
sol'dier, (n) soldaat; militêr, krygsman; *COME the old ~ over,* jou die wysheid v.d. jare aanmatig; an= der probeer iets wysmaak; ~ *of FORTUNE,* huur= soldaat, avonturier; (v) as soldaat dien, in krygs= diens wees; ~ *on,* aansukkel, vorentoe beur; ~ **ant,** rooimier, strydmier; ~ **crab,** hermietkreef; ~**ing,** soldatebcroep, krygadienu, uoldatoryl ~**ly, krygs= mans=,** krygshaftig; **'s box,** soldatekis; rommelkas; ~ **ship,** krygskuns; krygsmanskap; militêre eien= skappe; ~**y,** krygsvolk, die militêre, soldatevolk.
sole[1]**,** (n) tongvis.
sole[2]**,** (n) voetsool; sool; (v) versool.
sole[3]**,** (n) enkel, alleen; enigste; ~ *BILL of exchange,* solawissel; *on his ~ RESPONSIBILITY,* op sy eie verantwoordelikheid; ~ **agent,** alleenagent, enigste verteenwoordiger.
sol'ecism, taalfout; ongepastheid, onmanierlikheid, flater.
sole: ~ **distributor,** alleenversprelder; ~ **guardian= ship,** uitsluitende voogdy; ~**ly** alleenlik, enkel, en= kel en alleen.
sol'emn, plegtig, ernstig, statig, eerbiedwekkend, so= lemneel; ~**'ity,** (..**ties**), plegtigheid, statigheid; ~ **iza'tion,** viering, voltrekking; ~**ize,** vier, voltrek.
solen'oid, solenoïed, solenoïde, draadspoel.
sole piece, drumpel.
sole: ~ **possession,** alleenbesit; **- rights,** alleenreg.
sol'-fa, *kyk* **tonic solfa.**
solferi'no, persrooi.
soli'cit, ernstig vra; versoek; aanvra; inroep; aansoek doen om, sollisiteer; lok, aanklamp, aanlok, lastig val, aanspreek op straat, onsedelike voorstelle maak; ~ *an OFFICE,* na 'n betrekking vry; ~ *OR= DERS,* bestellings werf; ~ *in VAIN,* voor dooi(e)= mansdeur kom; ~**ant,** (n) versoeker, vraer, sollisi= tant; smekeling; (a) versoekend; vraend; ~**a'tion,** aansoek, sollisitasie, versoek; verlokking, (die) maak van onsedelike voorstelle; ~**ing,** (uit)lok= (king), aanklamping; ~**or,** prokureur; vraer; ~**or= general,** prokureur-generaal; ~**ous,** bekommerd, besorg; begerig, verlangend; ~**ress, (-es),** aansoek= ster, sollisitante; versoekster.
soli'citude, besorgdheid, bekommerdheid, sorg, be= kommering, ongerustheid.
sol'id, (n) vaste liggaam; (a) solied, massief; vas, stewig, ferm, bestendig, gedeë; deugdelik; trou; deeglik; gesond; eenparig; kubiek; *BE ~ for,* een= parig wees vir; *for five ~ HOURS,* vir vyf ronde ure; *a ~ VOTE,* eenparige stemme; ~ **angle,** lig= gaamshoek, drievalshoek; ~**a'rity,** gemeenskap= likheid, eenheid, solidariteit; ~ **contents,** kubieke inhoud; ~ **floor,** blokkiesvloer; soliede vloer; ~ **food,** vaste kos; ~ **fuel,** vaste brandstof; ~ **gas,** vaste gas; ~ **geometry,** stereometrie, ruimteleer, ruimtemeetkunde; ~ **ground,** vaste grond; ~**hoofed,** met vaste hoef; ~**if'iable,** verdigbaar; ~ **ifica'= tion,** verdigting, stolling, vaswording; ~ **ifica'tion**

point, stollingspunt; ~ **'ify,** (. . **fied),** verdig, vaste liggaam maak; verenig, konsolideer; ~ **'ity,** vastheid, stewigheid, fermheid; deeglikheid, deugdelikheid; soliditeit, massiwiteit; ~ **line,** volstreep; ~ **ly,** blokvas; *be ~ ly against,* daar eenparig teen wees; ~ **matter,** vaste stof; ~ **measure,** kubieke maat, inhoudsmaat; ~ **ness** = **solidity;** ~ **tyres,** massiewe bande.
solidung'ular, eenhoewig.
solil'oquize, 'n alleenspraak hou; met jouself praat.
soli'loquy (. .**quies),** alleenspraak, monoloog.
sol'iped, (n) eenhoewige dier; (a) eenhoewig.
sol'ipsism, solipsisme.
solip'sist, solipsis.
solitaire', solitêrsteen; solitêrspel, solitaire, patience; kluisenaar.
sol'itariness, verlatenheid, eensaamheid, eenselwigheid.
sol'itary, (n) (. .**ries),** kluisenaar; (a) eensaam, verlate, allenig, eenselwig; afgesonder(d); enigste, enkel; *one ~ exception,* een alleenstaande geval; ~ **bee,** malkopby; ~ **confinement,** afsonderlike opsluiting, selstraf.
sol'itude, eensaamheid, eensaamte, enigheid, verlatenheid; alleenheid; eensame plek.
sol'o, (soli, -s), solo; ~ **flight,** alleenvlug, solovlug; ~**ist,** solis, solosanger, solospeler.
Sol'omon, Salomo; *a judgement of ~,* Salomosoordeel.
Solomon'ian, Salomonies.
sol'o part, soloparty, solodeel.
so'lo seven, (-s), solussewe(plaat).
solpug'id, (-s), jagspinnekop, haarskeerder.
sol'stice, sonstilstand, solstitium, sonnewende, sonkeerpunt.
solsti'tial, sonstilstands=.
solubil'ity, oplosbaarheid.
sol'uble, oplosbaar; ~ **glass,** waterglas; ~**ness** = **solubility.**
sol'us, alleen; solus; solo.
solu'tion, (n) oplossing, ontbinding; rubberlym; *this may help in the ~ of the PROBLEM,* miskien help dit by die oplossing v.d. vraagstuk; *there is no ~ to the PROBLEM,* die vraagstuk is onoplosbaar; (v) met rubber lym.
solvabil'ity, oplosbaarheid.
sol'vable, oplosbaar.
solve, oplos; ontbind; deurhak; uitlê, verklaar.
sol'vency, betaalvermoë, gegoedheid, soliditeit; solventskap, solvensie.
sol'vent, (n) oplos(sings)middel; (a) in staat om te betaal, solvent, solied; ontbindend; oplossend.
sol'ver, oplosser.
som'a, soma, liggaam.
Somal'ia, Somalië.
somat'ic, liggaamlik, somaties.
somatol'ogy, liggaamsleer, somatologie.
som'atose, somatose.
som'bre, somber, duister, donker; swaarmoedig, swartgallig; ~ **bulbul,** willietiptol; ~**ness,** somberheid.
sombrer'o, (-s), breërandhoed, sombrero.
som'brous, somber, donker.
some, (pron) party, sommige; iets; bietjie; *GIVE him ~,* gee hom 'n bietjie; *KEEP ~ till more comes,* moenie al die aanbrandsel uit jou pot krap nie; ~ *SAY,* party sê; (a) enige, sommige, party, enkel, etlike; omtrent, sowat, ongeveer; een of ander; bietjie; *that's ~ APPLE,* dis darem 'n reuseappel; dis darem 'n appel! ~ *BOOK or other,* een of ander boek; ~ *DAY,* eendag, een of ander tyd; *DRINK ~ water,* drink 'n bietjie water; *to ~ EXTENT,* tot op 'n sekere hoogte; ~ *JOKE!* dis vir jou 'n grap! ~ *MONTHS ago,* enige maande gelede; ~ *MORE,* nog 'n bietjie; ~ *SUCH,* so een; *I must do it ~ TIME,* ek moet dit die een of ander tyd doen; ~ *TIME ago,* 'n hele ruk gelede; *WAIT ~ time,* 'n tydjie wag; (adv) erg, danig; ~ *two minutes,* sowat (omtrent) twee minute.
some'body, iemand, een of ander; *he thinks himself ~,* hy verbeel hom hy's wat wonders.
some'how, op een of ander manier; ~ *I could never get to like him,* om 'n onverstaanbare (onverklaarbare) rede kon ek hom nooit uitstaan (verdra) nie.
some'one, iemand, een.
so'mersault, (n) bolmakiesie, tuimeling, buiteling, duikeling; *turn a ~,* bolmakiesie slaan; (v) bolmakiesie slaan, agteroorslaan.
some' such, so een; so iets.
some'thing, iets; *an ACTOR or ~,* 'n toneelspeler of so iets; *it was ~ AWFUL,* dit was iets verskrikliks; *that will BE ~,* dit is ten minste iets; *this is ~ like a CAKE!* dis vir jou 'n koek dié! *it is ~ of a DISAPPOINTMENT,* dit is nogal teleurstellend; *a DROP of ~,* 'n snapsie; ~ *ELSE,* iets anders; ~ *of EVERYTHING,* van alles wat; *there is ~ FOR you,* dis nou weer te sê; daar is nou vir jou 'n ding; *a GLASS of ~,* 'n glas drinkgoed; *you HAVE ~ there,* nou sê jy iets; *HAVE ~ of another in one,* iets van 'n ander weghê; *there is ~ IN that,* dit beteken iets; daar is iets van waar; daar steek iets in; ~ *INDEFINABLE,* iets onbeskryfbaars; ~ *LIKE 200 pages,* naastenby 200 bladsye; *that's ~ LIKE a rose,* dis darem vir jou 'n roos; dis vir jou 'n bielie van 'n roos; *MAKE ~ of,* iets maak van; munt slaan uit; *it is ~ of a MIRACLE,* dit is soos 'n wonderwerk; ~ *NICE,* iets lekkers; ~ *or OTHER,* die een of ander; ~ *in the teaching PROFESSION,* een of ander betrekking as onderwyser; ~ *of a TEACHER,* so amper 'n onderwyser; ~ *like TEN,* omtrent tien; *THINK ~ of,* nogal iets dink van; ~ *like TWENTY,* so ongeveer twintig.
some: ~ **time,** (a) vroeër, vorige; (adv) soms, eertyds; ~ **times,** soms, somtyds, partymaal; ~ **way,** op een of ander manier; ~ **what,** iets, enigsins, enigermate, 'n bietjie, baster; ~ *what of a doctor,* 'n baster dokter.
some'where, êrens, iewers; ~ *or OTHER,* op een of ander plek; *I'll SEE you ~ first,* voor so iets gebeur, kan jy na die duiwel (josie) gaan.
somnam'bulate, in die slaap loop.
somnambula'tion, slaapwandeling.
somnam'bulator, slaapwandelaar.
somnam'bulism, slaapwandeling, somnambulisme.
somnam'bulist, slaapwandelaar, somnambuul.
somnifa'cient, (n) slaapmiddel; (a) slaapwekkend.
somnif'erous, vaakmakend, slaapwekkend.
somnil'oquence, somnil'oquism, slaappratery.
somnil'oquist, slaapprater.
som'nolence, som'nolency, slaperigheid, vaakheid, slaaplus.
som'nolent, vaak, slaperig; slaapwekkend.
som'nolism, hipnose.
son, seun; ~ *of BELIAL,* Belialskind; ~ *of a GUN,* (sl.), blikskottel; hierjy, swernoot; *the S ~ of MAN,* die Seun v.d. Mens, Christus; ~ *of MARS,* krygsman; ~ *of the SOIL,* boerseun.
son'ancy, klank, geluid.
son'ant, (n) stemhebbende klank; (a) stemhebbend, sonanties.
sona'ta, sonate.
sonati'na, sonatine.
song, lied, sangstuk; gesang; poësie; gedig; kleinigheid; *BREAK into ~,* 'n lied aanhef; *GIVE a ~,* iets sing; *MAKE a ~ (and dance) about it,* 'n ophef maak oor iets; *for a MERE ~,* vir 'n appel en 'n ei; vir 'n oulap en 'n bokstert; *make a ~ about NOTHING,* jou oor 'n dooie mossie verheug; *the SAME old ~,* die ou liedjie; *S ~ of SOLOMON,* die Hooglied van Salomo; *not WORTH a ~,* niks werd nie; ~**-bird,** sangvoël; ~**ful,** sangryk; ~**ster,** sanger; sangeres; sangvoël; ~ **stress, (-es),** sangeres; ~**-thrush,** sanglyster.
so'nic, sonies; ~ **barrier,** klankgrens.
sonif'erous, klankgewend, welluidend, klankgeleidend.
son'-in-law, (sons-in-law), skoonseun.
son'less, sonder seun, seunloos.
sonn'et, sonnet, klinkdig; ~ **cycle,** sonnettekrans; ~ **eer',** sonnetdigter.
so'nny, (sonnies), seuntjie, kêreltjie, boetie, jongie; ~, *where is your mother?* Boetie, waar is jou ma?
son'obuoy, klankboei.
sonom'eter, klankmeter, sonometer.

sonomet'ric, sonometries.
sonores'cent, knetterend.
sonorif'ic, klinkend, klankvoortbrengend.
sonor'ity, klankvolheid, welluidendheid, sonoriteit.
sonor'ous, welluidend, klankryk, klankvol, helderklinkend, sonoor; ~**ness,** welluidendheid, klankrykheid.
Son'qua reeds, sonkwasriet.
son'ship, seunskap.
soon, gou, spoedig, weldra, binnekort, eerlank, eersdaags, vroeg; ~ *AFTER,* kort daarna; ~ *AFTER midnight,* 'n rukkie na middernag; *AS* ~ *as,* so gou as, sodra; *SO* ~, al so gou; *he WOULD as* ~, hy sou liewer.
soon'er, vroeër; eerder; *the* ~ *the BETTER,* hoe eerder, hoe beter; *I would* ~ *DIE,* ek sou liewers doodgaan; ~ *or LATER,* vroeër of later, eendag; *he had NO* ~ *sat down than* . . ., hy het skaars gaan sit of; *no* ~ *SAID than done,* so gesê, so gedaan; ~ *said than DONE,* makliker gesê as gedaan; *no* ~ *THAN,* nouliks . . . of; *I'd* ~ *have THIS one,* ek sou hierdie een verkies.
soot, (n) roet; (v) met roet bedek; ~ *up,* verroet, vol roet pak; ~**-blower,** roetblaser; ~**-flake,** roetkorreltjie; ~ **flue,** roetgang; ~**-pocket,** roetvanger
sooth, waarheid, werklikheid.
soothe, versag; verlig, kalmeer, gerusstel, praat, sus, stil; bevredig; *that* ~ *d his wounded feelings,* dit was 'n pleister op sy wond; ~ **r,** verligter, versagter; fopspeen, foppertjie.
sooth'ing, kalmerend, stillend, gerusstellend.
sooth'say, (. .said), voorspel, waarsê; ~**er,** waarsêer, voorspeller.
soot: ~ **iness,** roetagtigheid; ~**y,** roeterig, roetagtig.
sop, (n) geweekte brood; paaimiddel, troosmiddel; omkoopmiddel; *a* ~ *to Cerberus,* 'n omkoopmiddel; 'n paaimiddel; (v) (**-ped**), insop, week, doop; papnat maak.
soph'ism, drogrede, strikrede, sofisme.
soph'ist, drogredenaar, sofis.
sophis'tic(al), bedrieglik, sofisties.
sophis'ticate, vervals; oulik maak, gekunsteld (onnatuurlik) maak; drogredes gebruik; ~**d,** gesofistikeerd, gekunsteld, gemaak, aanstellerig, onnatuurlik; vroegryp, vroegwys, wêreldwys, oulik, ouderwets (kind); ~*d machine,* presies (noukeurig) werkende masjien; presisiemasjien; ~*d electronics,* fyn elektronika, hoogontwikkelde elektronika; presisie-elektronika; ~*d person,* gesofistikeerde persoon (mens).
sophistica'tion, sofisme, drogredenering; vervalsing; bederf; oulikheid; gekunsteldheid; wêreldwysheid; swierigheid, sofistikasie.
soph'istry, (. .tries), vals redenering, sofistery, juristery.
Soph'ocles, Sophokles.
soph'omore, tweedejaarstudent.
soporif'erous, slaapwekkend.
soporif'ic, (n) slaapmiddel; (a) slaapwekkend, slaap=.
sop: ~**piness,** sopperigheid; sentimentaliteit; ~**ping,** papnat; ~*ping wet,* papnat; ~**py,** nat, papnat; sentimenteel; *be* ~*py about,* verlief wees op.
sopra'no, (. .ni, s), sopraan; eerste stem, diskant.
sorb, lysterbes, sorbe.
sorb'et, sorbet, vrugtedrank.
Sorb'ian, (n) Sorb; Wendies, Sorbies (taal); (a) Wendies, Sorbies.
sor'cerers, towenaar, toornaar, goëlaar, duiwelskunstenaar, heksemeester.
sor'ceress, (-es), heks, towenares.
sor'cery, towery, heksewerk, toordery, duiwelskunstenary, duiwelskunste.
sord'es, vuilgoed; koorsaanslag.
sord'id, laag, gemeen, vuig, vuil, walglik, smerig; inhalig, vrekkig, gierig, skraperig; vuilwit (biol.); *for* ~ *gain,* vir vuil gewin; ~**ness,** inhaligheid, gierigheid; laagheid, gemeenheid.
sord'ine, (toon)demper, geluiddemper, klankdemper, sordine.
sore, (n) seer, rou plek, wond; *REOPEN old* ~*s,* ou koeie uit die sloot haal; 'n ou wond oopkrap; (a, adv) seer, pynlik, rou; deerlik; gevoelig; bedroef;

swaar; *have a* ~ *BACK,* 'n seer rug hê; *he is like a BEAR with a* ~ *head,* hy is lelik uit sy humeur; *FEEL* ~ *about,* gevoelig wees oor; gekrenk voel oor; *it's a* ~ *POINT with him,* dis vir hom 'n teer plek; hy is daar sleg oor te spreek; *a SIGHT for* ~ *eyes,* 'n verruklike gesig; *TOUCH a* ~ *point,* 'n gevoelige snaar aanraak; *stick out like a* ~ *THUMB,* baie hinderlik wees; *a* ~ *TRIAL,* 'n swaar beproewing.
sore'ly, baie, besonder, skroomlik; *be* ~ *GRIEVED,* diep bedroef wees; *be* ~ *MISTAKEN,* jou deeglik misgis; ~ *TEMPTED,* erg (kwaai, baie) in die versoeking gebring.
sore'ness, pynlikheid, seerheid.
sor'ex, (sorrices), spitsbekmuis, skeerbekmuis.
sor'ghum, sorghum, graansorghum *(Andropogon).*
sor'icine, spitsbekmuisagtig.
sorit'es, kettingsluitrede, sorites.
sorn, klaploop; ~ *on someone,* op iem. se nek lê.
soro'ral, susterlik.
soro'ricide, sustermoord; sustermoordenaar.
soro'rity, (. .ties), susterskap; vroueverening, sustersvereniging, sororaat.
so'rrel¹, (n) skaapsuring.
so'rrel², (n) sweetvos, vosperd; rooibruinperd; (a) vos; rooibruin; bruingeel (perd).
so'rrow, (n) droefheid, sielesmart, droefenis, smart, leed, verdriet; *more in* ~ *than in ANGER,* meer jammer as kwaad; *EXPRESS* ~ *for a misdeed,* berou toon oor 'n misdaad; *the MAN of S*~*s,* die Man van Smarte; ~ *comes UNSENT for,* smart kom vanself; *WITH* ~ *I have to inform you,* met droefheid moet ek u meedeel; (v) treur, bedroef wees; ~**ful,** verdrietig, droewig, treurig; ~ **fulness,** verdrietigheid, droefheid, treurigheid; ~**ing,** (n) getreur, geklaag, geweeklaag; (a) treurig, hartseer, bedroef; ~**-stricken,** onder smart gebuk.
so'rry, treurig, armsalig; jammer; spyt; ~! ekskuus! verskoon my! *BE* ~, spyt wees; *a* ~ *EXCUSE,* 'n flou ekskuus; *FEEL* ~ *for oneself,* jou bejammer; jou aan selfbejammering oorgee; *a* ~ *FELLOW,* 'n treurige vent; *cut a* ~ *FIGURE,* 'n droewige figuur slaan; *I am* ~ *FOR him,* ek kry hom jammer; *a* ~ *LOT,* 'n armsalige spul (klomp); *in a* ~ *PLIGHT,* in 'n treurige toestand; *I am* ~ *to SAY,* tot my spyt moet ek sê; *a* ~ *SIGHT,* 'n treurige gesig; *I'm SO* ~! ekskuus! pardon!
sort, (n) soort; aard; klas; *after a* ~, op 'n manier; *ALL* ~*s of things,* allerhande soorte dinge; *it takes ALL* ~*s to make a world,* almal is nie eenders nie; *he is not a BAD* ~, hy is nie 'n slegte ou nie; *BE (feel) out of* ~*s,* siekerig (olik, oeserig) voel; van streek wees; uit jou humeur voel; *I* ~ *of EXPECTED it,* (sl.), ek het dit half (soort van) verwag; *a GOOD (DECENT)* ~, 'n gawe kêrel; *IN some* ~, in seker(e) mate; *he is MY* ~, hy is 'n man na my hart; *NOTHING of the* ~, niks daarvan nie; *a* ~ *OF,* 'n soort van; *he* ~ *OF glared at me,* hy het my woedend (soort van) aangegluur; *a PLAYER of* ~*s,* op sy manier 'n speler; *a POET of* ~*s,* 'n digter wat nie danig baie beteken nie; *a POOR* ~, ook 'n mens! *SOME* ~ *of,* 'n soort van; *SOMETHING of the* ~, so iets; *he is not THAT* ~, hy is nie daardie soort (tipe) mens nie; *and all that* ~ *of THINGS,* ensovoorts; *all* ~*s of THINGS,* alles en nog wat; (v) sorteer, gradeer; uitsoek, orden; ~ *out DIFFICULTIES,* moeilikhede uit die weg ruim; ~ *OUT,* uitsoek, skif; *I'll* ~ *him OUT,* ek sal met hom afreken; ek sal hom opdons; *THINGS will* ~ *themselves out,* dit sal vanself regkom; ~ *WITH,* in ooreenstemming wees met; bestaan; ~**able,** sorteerbaar; ~**er,** sorteerder.
sort'ie, uitval, uitvlug.
sort'ilege, waarsegging (deur lootjiestrekkery); lootjiestrekkery.
sort'ing, sortering, sorteer; uitsoek; skifting; rangskikking; ~ **belt,** sorteerband; ~ **gate,** inkeerhek; ~ **pen,** inkeerkraal; ~ **room,** sorteerkamer; ~ **table,** sorteertafel; ~ **tray,** sorteerbakkie.
sorti'tion, bepaling deur die lot.
SOS, noodsein, noodroep, SOS.
sosa'tie, sosatie.

so'-so, so-so, op 'n manier (plan), nie alte goed nie.
sot, (n) suiplap, dronkaard; (v) **(-ted),** suip.
soteriolog'ic, soteriologies.
soterio'logy, soteriologie.
So'tho, Sesoeto, Sotho.
sot: ~ **tish,** dronk, besope; ~ **tishness,** dronkenskap.
sotto vo'ce, sotto voce, op gedempte toon; binnensmonds.
sou, (-s), duit, sent; *he hasn't a* ~, hy besit geen bloue duit nie.
soubrette', (F), soubrette; koket.
soub'riquet, *kyk* **sobriquet.**
soufflé', soufflé.
Soudan', Soedan; ~ **ese,** Soedannees.
sough, (n) gesuis, sug; (v) sug, sis, soef, suisel.
sought, gesoek; gesog; *much* ~ *after,* gesog, in groot aanvraag; in trek; *kyk* **seek.**
soul, siel; wese; skepsel; *there wasn't a* ~ *ABSENT,* die laaste mens was daar; *with ALL my* ~, met my hele hart; *with FIFTY* ~*s on BOARD,* met vyftig siele aan boord; *keep BODY and* ~ *together,* siel en liggaam aanmekaarhou; *he cannot CALL his* ~ *his own,* hy kan nie boe of ba sê nie; *CARE of* ~*s,* sielesorg; *the* ~ *of the ENTERPRISE,* die siel v.d. onderneming; *a GOOD* ~, 'n goeie siel; *the* ~ *of HONOUR,* die eerlikheid self; *not a LIVING* ~, geen sterfling nie; *NOT a* ~, nie 'n lewende siel nie; *not dare to call one's* ~ *one's OWN,* geen seggenskap oor jouself hê nie; nie boe of ba durf sê nie; *POSSESS one's* ~ *in patience,* jou siel in lydsaamheid soek; *UPON my* ~! by my siel! *from his VERY* ~, uit die grond van sy hart; ~**-deadening,** sieldodend; ~**ful,** sielroerend, gevoelvol, sielverheffend; ~*ful eyes,* sprekende (gevoelvolle) oë; ~ **less,** sielloos; onbesield; ~ **lessness,** sielloosheid; onbesieldheid; ~**-mate,** sielsvriend; ~**-searching,** gewetensondersoek; selfondersoek; ~**-searing,** sieltergend; ~**-sick,** terneergeslae; ~**-stirring,** aangrypend, sielroerend.
sound¹, (n) see-engte.
sound², (n) (proef)sonde; wonderpeil; peilstif, sondeeryster; (v) peil; sondeer (wond).
sound³, (n) geluid, toon, klank; *not to utter a* ~, nie 'n geluid laat hoor nie; nie 'n kik gee nie; (v) klink, lui; laat klink; verkondig, uitbasuin; beklop, ondersoek; pols, uithoor, uitvra; ~ *an ALARM,* 'n alarm blaas; ~ *the ATTACK,* die aanvalsein blaas; ~ *someone's PRAISES,* iem. se lof uitbasuin; ~ *the RETREAT,* die aftog blaas; *that* ~*s all RIGHT,* dit klink heeltemal goed; ~ *SOMEONE,* iem. pols, aan die tand voel.
sound⁴, (a) gesond, gaaf, sterk; vas; deeglik, grondig, steekhoudend, gegrond; suiwer, solied; gedug; ~ *APPETITE,* gesonde eetlus; ~ *ARGUMENT,* gegronde argument; ~ *ASLEEP,* vas aan die slaap; *a* ~ *BEATING,* 'n gedugte pak slae; *as* ~ *as a BELL,* so gesond soos 'n vis; ~ *in BODY and mind,* gesond na liggaam en siel; *a* ~ *HIDING,* 'n gedugte pak slae; *a* ~ *MIND in a* ~ *body,* 'n gesonde gees in 'n gesonde liggaam; *of* ~ *MIND,* by jou volle verstand; *in his* ~ *and sober SENSES,* ten volle by sy sinne; ~ *in MIND and limb,* gesond van lyf en lede.
sound'able, peilbaar.
sound: ~ **amplification,** klankversterking; ~**-barrier,** klankgrens; klankversperring (in geboue); ~**-board,** klankbord; sangbodem; ~**-box,** klankbodem; klankkas; klankruimte (gram.); ~ **engineer,** klankingenieur; klanktegnikus.
sound'er¹, dieplood; peiler, proefsonde (vir 'n wond).
sound'er², klopper; (klank)ontvangtoestel; klankgeër.
sound'er³, trop (varke).
sound: ~**-deadening,** geluiddempend; ~ **effect,** byklank; klankeffek; ~**-film,** klankfilm, klankrolprent, geluidfilm; ~**-hole,** klankgat; ~ **impulse,** geluidsimpuls.
sound'ing¹ (n) geklink; (a) klinkend; gehorig (gebou).
sound'ing², (n) peiling; loding (skip); ondersoek, sondering (wond); (pl) peiling; diep ankergrond; *BE in* ~*s,* grond voel; *LOSE* ~*s,* nie grond voel nie; *TAKE* ~*s,* peil; (a) peilend.

sound'ing board, klankbord, galmbord.
sound'ing: ~ **balloon,** peilballon; ~ **device,** peiltoestel; ~ **lead,** dieplood, meetlood, paslood; ~ **line,** loodlyn, skietlood.
sound'less¹, geluidloos, stil, klankloos.
sound'less², onpeilbaar.
sound: ~ **lessness,** geluidloosheid; ~ **locator,** geluidsoeker, geluidvinder.
sound: ~**ly,** vas; gesond, flink; terdeë; ~**ness,** gaafheid, gesondheid, flinkheid.
sound: ~**-proof,** geluidvry, klankdig, geluiddig, geluiddempend; ~ **proofing,** klankdigting; ~ **radio,** klankradio; ~ **ranger,** klankmeter; ~ **relations,** goeie verhoudinge; ~ **reproduction,** geluidsweergewing; ~ **signal,** geluidsein, klanksein.
sound' test, gaafheidstoets.
sound: ~ **track,** klankbaan; ~ **wave,** geluidgolf, klankgolf.
sound wool, treksterk wol.
soup, so(e)p; *BE in the* ~, in die verknorsing wees; in die pekel wees; *LAND in the* ~, in die pekel beland; *THICKENED* ~, verdikte sop; ~**-bone,** sopbeen; ~**-bowl,** sopkom; ~**-cup,** sopkoppie.
soup' fin, vaalhaai.
soup: ~ **greens,** sopgroente; ~**-kettle,** sopketel; ~**-kitchen,** sopkombuis; ~**-ladle,** soplepel; ~**-meat,** sopvleis; ~**-plate,** sopbord, diepbord; ~**-pot,** soppot; ~**-powder,** soppoeier; ~**-spoon,** soplepel; ~**-stock,** vleissop; ~**-tablet,** soptablet; ~**-ticket,** sopkaartjie; ~ **tureen,** sopkom; ~ **y,** sopagtig; soppe- rig.
sour, (v) suur maak; versuur; verbitter; suur word; insuur; (a) suur; vrank; stuurs, nors; onaangenaam; *BE* ~, stuurs (nors) wees; *the JOKE has gone* ~, dit is nie meer 'n grap nie; *LOOK* ~, met 'n suur gesig loop; met 'n aalwynpil in jou kies loop; *he has a* ~ *OUTLOOK on life,* hy het 'n suur kyk op die lewe.
source, bron, oorsprong; haard; segsman; (pl) bronnemateriaal; ~ *of FOOD,* voedselbron; ~ *of INCOME,* bron van inkomste; ~ *of INFECTION,* besmettingsbron; ~ *of LAW,* regsbron; ~ *of LIGHT,* ligbron; ~ *of SUPPLY,* voorsieningsbron; ~**-book,** bronneversameling; ~ **rock,** brongesteente.
sour: ~ **dock,** (veld)suring; ~**dough,** suurdeeg; ~**dough bread,** suurdeegbrood; ~**-face,** suurpruim; ~ **fig,** suurvy; ghoena *(Carpobrotus);* ~ **grass,** suurgras; ~ **ing,** (die) versuur, versuring; suurdeeg; insuring; verbittering; ~**ish,** suurderig, rens (melk); ~**ly,** suur, gemelik; ~ **milk,** suurmelk; ~**ness,** suurheid, stuursheid; ~ **orange,** bitterlemoen; ~ **plum,** suurpruim; ~ **porridge,** suurpap; ~**-sweet,** suursoet, soetsuur.
sous¹, (n) pekelvleis; pekelsous; onderdompeling; (v) inpekel, insout; papnat maak; oorgooi.
souse², (adv) plotseling, pardoems.
sou'-sou, soe-soe *(Sechium edule).*
soutane', soutane, priesterkleed.
south, (n) suide; *the S* ~, die Suide; (a) suidelik, suid-; (adv) suidwaarts, in suidelike rigting; S ~ **Africa,** Suid-Afrika; S ~ **African,** (n) Suid-Afrikaner; (a) Suid-Afrikaans; S ~ **African-built,** Suid-Afrikaans vervaardig(de); S ~ **African War,** Tweede Vryheidsoorlog, Driejarige Oorlog, Engelse Oorlog; S ~ **America,** Suid-Amerika; S ~ **American,** Suid-Amerikaans; ~**-bound,** suidwaarts; S ~ **Atlantic,** Suid-Atlantiese Oseaan; S ~ **Brabant,** Suid-Brabant; ~ **coast,** suidkus; *S* ~ *Coast,* Suidkus (Natal); S ~ **Devon,** Suid-Devon(bees); S ~ **Dutch,** Suid-Hollands; ~**-east',** (n) suidooste; (a, adv) suidoos, suidoostelik; ~ **eas'ter,** suidooster; suidoostewind, Kaapse dokter; ~**-eas'terly,** suidoostelik; ~**erly,** suidelik.
southern, suidelik, oustraal; suider-, suid-; S ~ **Africa,** Suidelike Afrika, Suider-Afrika; S ~ **Cross,** Suiderkruis; ~ **er,** suiderling; S ~ **Hemisphere,** die Suidelike Halfrond; S ~ **Lights,** suiderlig; ~**most,** suidelikste; ~ **pochard,** bruineend.
south: ~**-facing,** met 'n suidelike uitsig; S ~ **Germany,** Suid-Duitsland; S ~ **Holland,** Suid-Holland; ~ **ing,** suidelike rigting, suideliking; ~ **land,** suider-

land, suidland; ~ **latitude,** suiderbreedte; ~**ly,** suidelik; S~ **Magnetic Pole,** Magnetiese Suidpool; ~**paw,** linksspeler; linksbokser, hotklou.
South: ~ **Pacific,** Stille Suidsee; ~ **Pole,** Suidpool; ~ **Seas,** Stille Suidsee; ~ **Sea Islander,** Suidseeeilander; ~ **Sotho,** Suid-Sotho.
south: ~-~-**east,** suidsuidoos; ~-~-**west,** suidsuidwes; ~ **ward,** suidwaarts; S~ **West,** Suidwes; ~-**west,** (n) suidweste; (a) suidwes; S~-**West African,** Suidwester; ~-**wes'ter,** suidwester; reënhoed, suidwester; ~-**wes'terly,** suidwestelik; ~-**western,** suidwestelik; S~ **westerner,** Suidwester; ~ **wind,** suidewind.
souv'enir, gedagtenis, soewenier, aandenking; ~ **envelope,** gedenkkoevert, herdenkingskoevert.
sou'wes'ter, suidwestewind; stormwind; reënhoed, suidwester, oliejas.
sov'ereign, (n) vors, heerser; opperheer, soewerein; pond (Britse geld); ~**ty,** (..**ties),** oppermag, soewereiniteit, oppergesag, ryksgesag; (a) oppermagtig, soewerein; uitnemend, probaat (middel); vernaamste.
sov'iet, sowjet; *the S~ Union, Union of S~ Socialist Republics,* die Sowjetunie, Unie van Sosialistiese Sowjetrepublieke.
sow¹, (n) sog; gietvoor (vir yster); ysterklont; *get (have, take) the wrong ~ by the ear,* aan die verkeerde adres wees.
sow², (v) **(-ed, sown** or **-ed),** saai, strooi; uitstrooi; versprei; ~ *BEANS in the wind,* vergeefse werk verrig; ~ *DISCORD,* kwaad saai, tweedrag veroorsaak; ~ *a FIELD with corn,* koring saai op 'n land; ~ *one's wild OATS,* jou jeugsondes begaan; *as you ~, so shall you REAP; REAP what one has ~n,* wat jy saai, sal jy maai; ~ *the WIND and reap the whirlwind,* die wind saai, maar die stormwind maai.
sow'back, sandwal.
sow' bag, saaisak.
sow'bread, varkbrood.
sow'er, saaier; verspreier; saaimasjien.
sow'ing, (die) saai, gesaaide; saaisel; ~ **drill,** saaimasjien; ~ **machine,** saaimasjien.
sow' thistle, melkdissel, sydissel.
soy, sojasous.
soy'(a), soja; ~ **bean,** sojaboontjie; ~-**bean meal,** sojameel; ~-**bean oil,** sojaolie.
soz'zled, besope, smoordronk.
spa, kruitbad; badplek, spa.
space, (n) ruimte, plek, uitgebreidheid, bestek, spasie; duur, tyd, ruk; toonafstand; *FOR a ~,* 'n tyd lank; *IN the ~ of an hour,* binne 'n uur; *LACK of ~,* ruimtegebrek; *LIMITATION of ~,* ruimtebeperking; ~ *does not PERMIT,* ruimte ontbreek; *it would TAKE up much~,* dit sou te veel ruimte in beslag neem; ~ *of TIME,* tydsbestek; *VANISH into ~,* in die lug verdwyn; (v) spasieer; ~ **agency,** ruimteagentskap; ~ **bar,** spasiebalk; ~ **charge,** ruimtelading; ~**craft,** ruimtevaartuig; ~**man** (..**men),** ruimtevaarder; ~ **science,** ruimtekunde; ~ **scientist,** ruimtekundige; ~ **ship** ruimteskip; ~ **shuttle,** (ruimte)pendeltuig; ~-**time,** ruimte-tyd; ~-**tracking,** ruimtenasporing, ~-**travel,** ruimtevaart, ruimtevlug; ~-**traveller,** ruimtevaarder, ruimtereisiger.
spa'cer, spasieerder; skeier; spasiebalk; ~ **bar,** spasiestaaf; ~ **ring,** skeiring.
spa'cial, ruimte-.
spa'cing, spasiëring, tussenruimte.
spa'cious, ruim, wyd, uitgestrek, groot; ~**ness,** ruimte, grootheid.
spade¹, (n) skoppens (kaarte); *ACE of ~s,* skoppensaas; *JACK of ~s,* skoppensboer; *KING of ~s,* skoppensheer; *QUEEN of ~s,* skoppensvrou.
spade², (n) graaf, spitgraaf; *CALL a ~ a ~,* die kind by sy naam noem; ~ **beard,** vierkantige baard; ~ **bone,** bladbeen (mens); ~'**ful,** graafvol; ~-**work,** graafwerk; pionierswerk, baanbrekerswerk, voorwerk, voorarbeid.
spadille' skoppenaas, spadille.
spad'ix, (spadices), (blom)kolf.
spaghett'i, spaghetti.
Spain, Spanje; *castles in ~,* lugkastele.

spall, (n) splinter, brokkie; (v) breek (gruis), fynmaak; afsplinter; ~**ing,** grofbreking; afsplintering; ~**ing hammer,** klipbrekershamer, splinterhamer; skroothamer.
spalpeen', skobbejak, skurk.
span, (n) span (diere); vak; kort tyd; spanning (brug); spanwydte; omvang; ~ *of life,* lewensduur; (v) **(-ned),** span, oorspan; afmeet; oorbrug; *kyk ook* **spin,** (v).
span'cel, spantou.
span'drel, hoekvlak; ~ **steps,** driehoektreetjies; ~ **wall,** booghoekmuur.
spang'le, (n) blinkgoed, blinkertjie; versiersel; galappel; (v) vonkel, skitter; versier (met glinsterende ornamente); ~ *d with stars,* met sterre besaai.
Span'iard, Spanjaard; Spaanse skip.
span'iel, Patryshond; kruiper, lekker.
Span'ish, (n, a) Spaans; *the ~ MAIN,* die Spaans-Wes-Indiese See; Karibiese See; *THE ~,* die Spanjaarde; ~ **castle,** Spaanse kasteel; lugkasteel; ~ **chalk,** Spaanse kryt, kleremakerskryt; ~ **fly,** spaansvlieg; ~ **grass,** espartogras; ~ **influenza,** Spaanse griep; ~ **juice,** drop; ~ **leather,** Spaanse leer; ~ **mackerel,** katonkel; ~ **reed,** spaansriet.
spank, (n) klap; (v) klap, slaan, pak gee, looi.
spank'er, besaan, vierde mas; trippelaar (perd); knewel, reus; opstopper; ~-**boom,** besaansboom.
spank'ing, (n) afranseling, loesing, pak slae; *give someone a ~,* iem. op sy tabernakel gee; iem. 'n loesing gee; (a) groot, kragtig, sterk; uitstekend, fyn, gaaf, lekker, eersteklas; *you've got a ~ car,* jy het 'n spoggerige motor; ~ **horse,** pronkperd; ~ **lie,** growwe leuen; ~ **pace,** vinnige draf.
span'less, onmeetlik.
spann'er, skroefhamer, (skroef)sleutel, moersleutel; *throw a ~ in the works,* 'n stok in die wiel steek; sake in die war stuur; ~ **jaw,** sleutelbek; ~-**pipe,** sleutelpyp.
spann'ing, oorbrugging.
span: ~ **roof,** staandak; ~-**saw,** spansaag.
spar¹, (n) spaat (mineraal).
spar², (n) spar, paal; ronde hout; mas (skip); dakspar.
spar³, (n) (die) skerm; vuisgeveg; hangeveg; (v) **(-red),** boks, skerm; op 'n speelse manier slaan; redetwis, kibbel.
spa'rable, skoenspykertjie.
sparax'is, fluweeltjie (blom).
spar'-deck, spardek, boonste dek.
spare, (n) ekstra; reserwestuk; (pl) onderdele, vervangstukke; (v) spaar, opspaar, bespaar; mis, klaarkom sonder; ontbeer; ontsien; *he cannot BE ~d,* hy kan nie gemis word nie; ~ *no EFFORT,* geen pogings ontsien laat nie; geen moeite ontsien nie; ~ *one's ENERGY,* jou kragte spaar; *have ENOUGH and to ~,* meer as genoeg hê; ~ *no EXPENSE,* geen koste ontsien nie; ~ *someone's FEELINGS,* iem. se gevoelens ontsien; *an HOUR to ~,* 'n uur vry (oor); *his LIFE was ~d,* sy lewe is gespaar; *can you ~ a MINUTE?* het jy 'n oomblik tyd? ~ *no PAINS,* geen moeite ontsien nie; *can you ~ me a RAND,* kan jy my 'n rand leen? ~ *the ROD and spoil the child,* wie die roede spaar, bederf sy kind; *no TIME to ~,* nie tyd oor nie; ~ *oneself the TROUBLE,* jou die moeite bespaar; (a) skraal, maer; reserwe-, orig; spaarsaam, matig; ~ **bedroom,** vrykamer; ~ **cash,** los geld; ~ **diet,** skraal kos; ryswater; *be on a ~ diet,* skraal kos kry; van ryswater leef; ~**ly,** maer, dun; suinig; ~**ness,** maerte; soberheid; armoedigheid; ~ **part,** onderdeel, reserwedeel, wisseldeel, vervangstuk; (pl) onderdele, reserwedele, wisseldele; ~ **room,** vrykamer; ~ **time,** vrye tyd; ~ **tyre,** reserweband, ekstra (orige) band; ~ **wheel,** wisselwiel, reserwewiel, noodwiel.
sparge, besprinkel; sproei; grintspat; ~**r,** sprinkeltoestel (fontein).
spar'ing, spaarsaam, karig; *be ~ of the TRUTH,* die waarheid geweld aandoen; ~ *of WORDS,* swygsaam; ~**ly,** min, smalletjies; ~**ness,** spaarsaamheid.
spark, (n) vonk; sprankie, greintjie; modejonker, vrolike Frans, windmaker; vryer; vonkreëlaar (motor); *ADVANCE the ~,* die vonk vervroeg; *have no*

~ *of FEELING*, geen greintjie gevoel hê nie; *make the ~ s fly*, die vonke laat spat; *the ~ s are beginning to FLY*, die poppe begin dans; ~ *of LIFE*, lewensvonk; *RETARD the ~*, die vonk, vertraag; *VITAL* ~, lewensvonk; (v) vonk, vonke afgee, sprankel, vonkel; vry, vlerksleep; ~ **advance**, vonkvervroeging; ~**-arrester**, vonkvanger; ~**-coil**, vonkspoel; ~**-control**, vonkbeheer, vonkreëling; ~**-distance**, slagwydte; ~**-gap**, slagwydte, vonkbrug; vonkgaping; ~**-ignition**, vonkontsteking; ~ **ing**, ontsteking; ~**ing-plug**, vonkprop, ontstekingsprop; ~**ish**, lewendig, vrolik; opgeskik.
spark'le, (n) vonk, vonkeling, glans, skittering, geflonker; tinteling; (v) vonkel, vonke skiet, vonk; sprankel, skitter, flonker; flikker; bruis, skuim (wyn); tintel; *her eyes ~ d with pleasure*, haar oë het van genoeë gevonkel; ~**r**, diamant; edelsteen; bruiswyn; ~**t**, vonkie; koolsuurkoeëltjie; sprankie.
spark' lever, vonksteller.
spark'ling, (n) geflonker, tinteling, geskitter, skittering, flonkering, getintel; (a) vonkelend, flikkerend, skitterend; ~ **light**, flonkerlig; ~ **wine**, vonkelwyn; skuimwyn; borrelwyn.
spark: ~**-plug**, vonkprop, ontstekingsprop; ~**-wave**, vonkgolf.
spar'ling, spiering.
spar'ring, skerm, boks; geredetwis; ~ **match**, boksoefening; ~ **partner**, skermmaat, oefenmaat (van 'n bokser).
spa'rrow, mossie; ~**-hawk**, sperwer, witvalk.
spar'ry, spaatagtig, spaat=.
sparse, dun, versprei; yl; ver uitmekaar; ~ *ly populated*, dun bevolk; ~**ness**, ylheid, dunheid.
Spart'a, Sparta; ~**n**, (n) Spartaan; (a) Spartaans.
spasm, kramp, trekking; stuiptrekking, spasme, spasmus; ~*s of coughing*, hoesbui.
spasmod'ic, krampagtig; met horte en stote, rukkerig; ~ *stricture*, krampvernouing.
spas'tic, (n) spastikus; (a) spasties; ~ *colon*, oorgevoelige grootderm.
spastic'ity, krampagtigheid, spastisiteit.
spat¹, (n) slobkous.
spat², (n) saad, kuit (van vis); (v) **(-ted)**, saadskiet, (vis)eiers lê.
spat³, (v) *kyk* **spit**, (v).
spatch'cock¹, (n) spithoender.
spatch'cock², (v) woorde haastig (bv. in telegram) invoeg; inlas.
spate, oorstroming, stroom, vloed; *the RIVER is in* ~, die rivier lê kant en wal; ~ *of WORDS*, woordevloed.
spathe, blomskede.
spath'ic, spaatagtig, spaat=.
spa'tial, ruimte=, ruimtelik.
spatt'ed, met slobkouse aan.
spattee', oorkous.
spatt'er, (n) gespat; spatsel; (v) spat, bespat, beklad; ~ **dash** (n) kamas; slobkous, oorkous; (v) grintspat, grofspat; ~ **finish**, grofspatafwerking.
spat'ula, strykmes; spatel; slaplemmes.
spat'ular, **spat'ulate**, lepelvormig, spatelvormig.
spav'in, beenspat.
spawn, (n) viseiertjies, kuit; gebroed; padda-eiers; (v) broei; eiers lê; kuitskiet; ~ **er**, kuitvis; ~ **ing ground**, ~ **ing place**, broeiplek; ~ **ing season**, broeityd.
spay, sny, steriliseer (tewe, sogge); ~ **ed bitch**, onvrugbaar gemaakte teef, gesteriliseerde teef.
speak, (**spoke**, **spoken**), spreek, praat, sê; ~ *ABOUT*, praat van (oor); ~ *by the BOOK*, (jou) noukeurig uitdruk; ~ *like a BOOK*, praat of dit gedruk is; soos 'n boek praat; ~ *to a BRIEF*, volgens opdrag praat; ~ *FOR someone*, namens iem. praat; ~ *FOR*, pleit vir; praat vir; ~ *out your HEART*, sê wat op jou hart lê; ~ *HIGHLY of someone*, iem. groot lof toeswaai; ~ *for ITSELF*, vanselfsprekend wees; *not to* ~ *the same LANGUAGE*, niks met mekaar gemeen hê nie; ~ *one's MIND*, rond= uit sê wat 'n mens dink; nie van jou hart 'n moordkuil maak nie; ~ *to a MOTION*, oor 'n mosie praat; *NOTHING to* ~ *of*, niks om van te praat nie; ~ *OUT*, harder praat; reguit praat; *we've had no RAIN to* ~ *of*, ons het geen reën gehad om van te praat nie; *SO to* ~, so te sê; ~ *on a SUBJECT*, oor 'n onderwerp praat; ~ *out on a SUBJECT*, jou mening oor 'n saak duidelik uitspreek; ~ *TO*, praat met; iem. vermaan; ~ *when you are spoken TO*, hou jou mond (bek)! ~ *out of TURN*, uit jou beurt praat; *it ~s VOLUMES*, dit spreek boekdele; ~ *WELL of*, gunstig praat van; *it ~s WELL for him*, dit sê baie vir hom; ~ **able**, noembaar; ~ **easy**, geheime kroeg, skelmkroeg; ~ **er**, spreker; luidspreker; voorsitter; *Mr. S~er*, mnr. die Speaker (Parlement); ~ **ership**, speakerskap; ~ **er system**, luidsprekerstelsel.
speak'ing, (n) (die) praat; (a) sprekend, pretend; *a* ~ *ACQUAINTANCE*, 'n oppervlakkige kennis; *COMPARATIVELY* ~, vergelykenderwyse; *within* ~ *DISTANCE*, binne praatafstand; *GENERALLY* ~, in (oor) die algemeen (gepraat); *LEGALLY* ~, van 'n regsoogpunt beskou; *a* ~ *LIKENESS*, 'n sprekende gelykenis; ~ *for MYSELF*, wat my betref; *ROUGHLY* ~, so min of meer; *STRICTLY* ~, streng gesproke; *we are not on* ~ *TERMS*, ons praat nie met mekaar nie; ons is kwaad vir mekaar; ~ **engagement**, spreekbeurt; ~ **trumpet**, skeepsroeper; spreekhoring, spreektrompet; ~ **tube**, praatbuis.
spear, (n) spies, speer, wig, spits; (v) met 'n speer deursteek; vinnig opskiet; ~**-fish**, speervis; ~ **fisherman**, visjagter; ~**-fishing**, visskietery, visjag; ~ **gun**, visgeweer; ~**-hand**, regterhand (van speerruiter); ~ **head**, speerpunt, spiespunt; wig; ~ **man**, spiesdraer, speerdraer; ~ **mint**, groenment, tuinment; ~**-point**, spiespunt; ~**-shaft**, lansskag, lanssteek; ~**-shaped**, spiesvormig; ~ **side**, swaardsy; vaderskant.
spec, *abbr. of* **speculation**, spekulasie; *on* ~, vir spekulasie; op goeie geluk; ~ **house**, spekulasiehuis.
spe'cial, (n) ekstratrein; spesiale uitgawe; spesiale pas; (a) spesiaal, besonder; *something* ~ *to that country*, iets eie aan daardie land; ~ **effect**, besondere effek; ~ **effects**, spesiale effekte (film); ~ **ism**, spesialisme; ~ **ist**, spesialis (persoon); spesialiteit (vak); ~ **ist company**, gespesialiseerde maatskappy; ~ **'ity**, (..**ties**), besonderheid; spesialiteit; ~ **iza'tion**, spesialisasie, verbesondering; ~ **ize**, spesialiseer; in besonderhede aangee, wysig; beperk; ~ *ize on*, jou toespits (toelê) op; ~ **licence**, spesiale lisensie; ~ **ly**, ekstra; veral; ~ **meeting**, buitengewone vergadering; ~ **relationship**, spesiale (besondere) verhouding; goeie vriendskap; ~ **train**, ekstratrein; ~ **ty**, *kyk* **speciality**.
spe'cie, (no pl) spesie, gemunte geld; *in* ~, in klinkende munt; ~ **escort**, spesiebewaker; ~ **point**, goudpunt.
spe'cies, (sing and pl) soort; spesie; geslag; gedaante; ~ *of ANIMAL*, diersoort; ~ *of BIRD*, voëlsoort; *a* ~ *OF*, 'n soort van; ~ **control**, soortbestryding; ~ **name**, soortnaam.
specif'ic, (n) spesifieke middel; (a) soortlik; spesifiek; eie aan die soort; bepaald, uitdruklik; *have no* ~ *AIM*, geen spesiale (bepaalde) doel hê nie; *for a* ~ *PURPOSE*, vir 'n bepaalde doel; ~ **ally**, uitdruklik, spesifiek, in die besonder; ~ **a'tion**, noukeurige verklaring, omskrywing, opnoeming; spesifikasie, bestek (bouwerk); ~ **gravity**, soortlike gewig; ~ **heat**, soortlike warmte; ~ **intent**, besondere opset; ~ **name**, soortnaam; ~ **performance**, spesifieke nakoming; reële eksekusie (reg).
spe'cify, (..**fied**), noukeurig vermeld; omskryf, spesifiseer; aanwys.
spe'cimen, monster, proef; voorbeeld, staaltjie; eksemplaar; *an OUTSTANDING* ~, 'n besondere eksemplaar; 'n uithaler (bv. perd); *a QUEER* ~, 'n snaakse entjie mens; *WHAT a ~!* ook 'n mens! wat 'n spektakel! ~ **answer**, modelantwoord; ~ **book**, monsterboek; ~ **copy**, proefeksemplaar; ~ **nommer**; ~ **page**, proefblad; ~ **signature**, proefhandtekening.
speciol'ogy, leer v.d. ontstaan van soorte, spesiologie.
specios'ity, skoonklinkendheid; bevalligheid; bevalligheid; skoonskynendheid.
spe'cious, bevallig; mooilykend; skoonklinkend;

speck

skoonskynend; ~**ness**, bevalligheid; mooiskynendheid.
speck¹, (n) vet vleis; walvisspek; seekoeispek.
speck², (n) vlek, smet, stip; stukkie, deeltjie; vlekkie; spatsel; ~ *of DUST*, stoffie; *a MERE* ~, soos die swart van 'n mens se nael; (v) spikkel, vlek, sprikkel.
speck'le, (n) spikkel, vlekkie, stippel, stippie; (v) bespikkel, bestip, sprikkel; ~**d**, bont, gespikkel(d). gevlek, skilder=; ~**d bean**, skilderboontjie; ~**d pigeon**, kransduif, bosduif; ~**less**, vlekloos.
specs, *abbr. for* **spectacles**, bril.
spec'tacle, skouspel, vertoning; toneel, gesig, aanblik; (pl) bril; *MAKE a* ~ *of oneself*, jou verspot maak (gedra); *a PAIR of* ~*s*, 'n bril; *see everything through ROSE-COLOURED* ~*s*, deur 'n rooskleurige bril kyk; *see things through TINTED* ~*s*, deur 'n gekleurde bril kyk; *WEAR* ~*s*, bril, bril dra; ~-**case**, brilhuisie, brildosie; ~**d**, gebril, met 'n bril; ~-**frame**, brilraam; ~-**glass**, brilglas; ~-**maker**, brilmaker; ~ **play**, kykstuk, spektakelstuk; ~ **weaver**, brilwewer.
spectac'ular, skitterend, pragtig; skouspelagtig, aanskoulik, toneelmatig; op effek bereken, belus op vertoon; *a* ~ *play*, 'n kykstuk.
spectat'or, toeskouer, aanskouer, aankyker; ~ **behaviour**, toeskouergedrag; ~ **total**, toeskouersgetal.
spec'tral, spookagtig, spook=; spektraal; ~ **analysis**, spektrale analise, spektrumanalise; ~ **tarsier**, spookdier.
spec'tre, spook, verskyning, skim, spookbeeld, spookgestalte; ~-**ship**, spookskip.
spectrochem'Istry, spektrochemie.
spec'trogram, spektrogram.
spec'trograph, spektrograaf; ..**graph'ic**, spektrografies.
spectrog'raphy, spektrografie.
spectrol'ogy, spektrologie.
spectrom'eter, spektrometer.
spectromet'ric, spektrometries.
spectrom'etry, spektrometrie.
spec'trophone, spektrofoon.
spec'troscope, spektroskoop.
spectroscop'ic(al), spektroskopies.
spectros'copy, spektroskopie.
spec'trum, (..**tra**), spektrum; ~ **analysis**, spektrumanalise.
spec'ula, kroonglasbol.
spec'ular, spieëlend, spieël=; ~ **iron**, ysterglans.
spec'ularite, spekulariet.
spec'ulate, bespiegel, bepeins, jou verdiep in bespieëlinge, teoretiseer; spekuleer; ~ *on one's CHANCES*, gissinge maak oor jou kanse; ~ *in SHARES*, met aandele spekuleer.
specula'tion, spekulasie, handelsonderneming; oorpeinsing, bespieëling; beskouing; teorie.
spec'ulative, gewaag, spekulatief, onseker; bespieëlend, teoreties; riskant.
spec'ulator, spekulant, bespieëlaar, bespieëlende wysgeer, teoretikus.
spe'culum, (..**la**) speculum, spieëltjie.
sped, *kyk* **speed**, (v).
speech, (-es), redevoering, rede, toespraak; gesprek; taal, spraak; *AFTER-DINNER* ~, tafelrede; ~ *of the DAY*, feesrede; *DIRECT* ~, direkte rede; *FREE* ~, vryheid van spraak; *INDIRECT* ~, indirekte rede; *MAKE a* ~, 'n toespraak hou; *PARTS of* ~, woordsoorte, rededele; ~ *is SILVER, silence is golden*, spraak is silwer, swye is goud; ~ *of THANKS*, dankwoord; *from the THRONE*, troonrede; *have* ~ *WITH*, praat met; ~ **chorus**, spreekkoor; ~-**craft**, spraakleer; ~-**day**, prysuitdelingsdag; ~-**defective**, spraakgestremde, iem. met 'n spraakgebrek; ~**ifica'tion**, redevoering, toespraak; ~**ify**, (..**fied**), oreer, praat; babbel; ~**less**, spraakeloos; stom; ~**lessness**, spraakloosheid; stomheid, verstomming, spraakloosheid; ~-**reading**, liplees; ~ **therapist**, spraakterapeut; ~ **therapy**, spraakterapie, spraakheelkunde; ~-**training**, spraakoefening, spraakopleiding.
speed, (n) snelheid, vaart; haas, spoed; gang (van ratkas); versnelling; *full* ~ *AHEAD*, volle stoom vorentoe; *full* ~ *ASTERN*, volle stoom agtertoe; *travel AT* ~, teen 'n hoë snelheid reis; *AT a* ~ *of 75 km per hour*, met 'n snelheid van 75 km per uur; *at FULL* ~, in volle vaart; uit alle mag; *GOOD* ~, voorspoed; alle heil; *more HASTE less* ~, hoe meer haas hoe minder spoed; *SINKING* ~, daalsnelheid; *have a good TURN of* ~, vaart hê; (v) (**sped**), spoed, haastig (gou) maak; snel; jaag; vriendelik sien vertrek ('n gas); (**-ed**), verstel (motor); snelheid reguleer; ~ *an ARROW*, 'n pyl afskiet; *GOD* ~, God sy met u; ~ *the parting GUEST*, die vertrekkende gas wegsien; ~ *ON*, voortsnel; ~ *up PRODUCTION*, die produksie opvoer (versnel); ~ *UP*, versnel, verhaas, die snelheid verhoog; ~ *on one's WAY*, haastig verder gaan; ~ *up the WORK*, die werk bespoedig; ~-**boat**, snelboot, jaagboot; ~-**box**, ratkas; ~-**cop**, jaagkonstabel, verkeerskonstabel; ~-**craze**, snelheidsmanie; ~ **er**, jaer; ~ **gear**, spoedrat; ~-**hump**, spoedbreker, vaartbreker; ~**ily**, spoedig, gou, haastig; ~**ing**, jaag; vinnig ry; versnelling; ~ **ing fine**, jaagboete; ~ **ing motorist**, jaende (motor)bestuurder; ~ **ing up**, versnelling, voortgang; *the work needs* ~ *ing up*, die werk moet versnel word; ~-**limit**, spoedgrens; spoedbeperking; snelheidsgrens; ~ **limitation**, snelheidsbeperking; ~ **maniac**, ~ **merchant**, jaagduiwel, kilometervreter; ~**om'eter**, spoedmeter, snelheidsmeter, kilometermeter, kilometerteller, odometer; ~ **range**, snelheidsgebied; ~ **restriction**, snelperk, snelheidsbeperking; ~**ster**, jaagmotor, resiesmotor, ~ **track**, jaagbaan; ~-**trap**, spoedstrik; snelstrik, jaagstrik; ~-**trapper**, jaagvanger; ~-**trial**, snelheidstoets, snelheidsrit; ~-**up**, versnelling, bespoediging; ~**way**, reisiesbaan; jaagbaan; snelweg, snelbaan; deurpad; ~ **wobble**, voortwaggeling, vaartrukking.
speed'well, veronika, ereprys.
speed'y, gou; haastig; vinnig; geswind, spoedig.
spel(a)eolog'ical, spelcologics, spelonkkundig.
spel(a)eol'ogist, spelonkkundige, speleoloog.
spel(a)eol'ogy, spelonkkunde, speleologie.
speen, afloop (druiwe).
spell¹, (n) beurt; tyd, rukkie; *a COLD* ~, skielike kou(e); *FOR a* ~, 'n tyd lank; *a long* ~ *of SERVICE*, 'n lang diensty; *TAKE a long* ~ *in the sickroom*, 'n lang tyd in die siekekamer aflos; (v) (**-ed**), aflos, beurte neem.
spell², (n) betowering, begoëling, aantrekkingskrag; towerspreuk; towerkrag; paljas; *BREAK the* ~ *of*, onder die bekoring uitkom van; *CAST a* ~ *on (over)*, begoël; *FALL under the* ~ *of*, onder die bekoring kom van; *LAY under a* ~, betower.
spell³, (v) (**-ed** or **spelt**), spel (van woorde); beteken; uitloop op; ~ *OUT*, uitspel; *these changes* ~ *RUIN*, hierdie veranderings beteken ondergang.
spell: ~ **bind**, (..**bound**), betower; fassineer; ~ **binder**, betoweraar; boeiende spreker; ~ **bound**, betower(d), in ekstase, verruk.
spell'er, speller; spelboek.
spell'ing, spelling; skryfwyse, spelwyse; ortografie; ~-**bee**, spelwedstryd; **book**, spelbock; ~ **error**, spelfout; ~ **list**, spellys; ~ **mistake**, spelfout; ~ **pronunciation**, spellinguitspraak; ~ **reform**, spellinghervorming.
spelt¹, (n) spelt, emmerkoring.
spelt², (v) *kyk* **spell³**. (v).
spel'ter, sink; handelsink; harde soldeersel.
spen'cer, onderlyfie (met lang moue); jakkie.
spend, (**spent**), uitgee; bestee; spandeer; deurbring, verkwis, ~ *a DAY*, 'n dag deurbring; ~ *all she has on DRESS*, alles aan haar lyf hang; ~ *FREELY*, kwistig wees met jou geld; ~ *MONEY on entertaining*, geld uitgee vir onthale; ~ *the NIGHT*, oornag; ~ *ONESELF*, jou afmat; ~ *SPARE time in studying*, vrye tyd aan studie bestee; *the STORM has spent itself*, die storm het uitgeraas; ~ *one's STRENGTH*, jou kragte uitput; ~-**all**, verkwister, deurbringer; ~ **er**, verkwister, deurbringer; ~ **ing**, (n) besteding, (die) uitgee; spandeerdery; deurbringing; (a) koop=, deurbringerig; ~ **ing money**, sakgeld; ~ **ing power**, koopkrag; ~ **thrift**, (n) deurbrin=

ger, deurtrekker, verspiller, verkwister; (a) verkwistend, deurbringerig.
spent, (v) *kyk* **spend;** (a) uitgeput; flou (koeël); gebruik; geslete; ~ **bullet,** flou koeël; ~ **cartridge,** leë patroondop.
sperm, saad, sperma; oorsprong.
spermacet'i, spermaceti; ~ **candle,** spermacetikers; ~**-oil,** walvistraan, visolie, spermaceti-olie.
spermat'ic, saad=.
spermatozo'on, (. . **zoa**), saaddiertjie, saadsel.
spermatozo'id, spermatosoïed, spermatosoïde.
sperm: ~**-oil,** walvistraan, visolie, spermaceti-olie; ~**-whale,** potvis, cachalot.
spew, spoeg, spu; uitbraak, opbring; ~**er,** spoeger, spuwer; braker.
spha'celate, kouevuur laat kry.
sphenog'raphy, wigskrif.
sphen'oid, (n) wigbeen; kambeen (vleis); (a) wigvormig.
sphe'ral, kring=, sfeer=.
sphere, (n) kring; sfeer, gebied, terrein, werkkring; omvang; bol, globe; hemelliggaam; *HARMONY of* ~ *s,* harmonie v.d. sfere; ~ *of INFLUENCE,* invloedsfeer; ~ *of INTEREST,* belangesfeer; ~ *of LIFE,* lewensterrein; *a wider* ~ *of WORK,* 'n uitgebreider arbeidsveld; (v) rond, bolvormig maak.
sphe'ric, hemels (poëties); sferies.
sphe'rical, bolvormig, bolrond, sferies, bol=; ~ **bearing,** bollaer; ~ **cover,** boldop; ~ **seat,** bolbedding; ~ **surface,** bolvlak; ~ **triangle,** boldriehoek; ~ **trigono'metry,** boldriehoeksmeting.
spheri'city, bolvormigheid.
sphe'rics, radiosteurings.
sphe'roid, afgeplatte bol, sferoïed, sferoïde; ~**al,** sferoïdaal, korrel=; ~*al graphite,* korrelgrafiet.
spherom'eter, rondingsmeter.
sphe'rule, klein bolletjie.
sphinc'ter, sluitspier, ringspier, poortspier.
sphinx, (-es), sfinks; *as silent as the* ~, swyg soos die graf; ~**-like,** sfinksagtig; enigmaties.
sphyg'mus, pols(slag), pulsasie.
sphygmoman'ometer, bloeddrukmeter.
sphygmom'eter, polsmeter.
spi'ca, koringaarverband.
spic'ate, aarvormig.
spice, (n) spesery, kruie; sweempie, tikkie; smakie; *the* ~ *of LIFE,* die pikante in die lewe; *MIXED* ~, gemengde speserye; (v) kruie; ~*d BEEF,* gekruide beesvleis; ~*d CAKE,* kruiekoek; ~*d WINE,* gekruide wyn; ~**r,** spesery; speserykas, kruiekas.
spi'ciness, gekruidheid; geurigheid; gewaagdheid; pikantheid.
spick' and span', piekfyn, agtermekaar; (spik)splinternuut; silwerskoon.
spic'ular, skerp, puntig.
spic'ulate, bedek met fyn punte, stekerig.
spic'ule, aartjie; skerp punt, naaldjie (plantk.).
spi'cy, speseryagtig, gekrui, kruierig, smaaklik, geurig; pikant; gewaag, onbetaamlik; *a* ~ *story,* 'n pikante (skurwe, onbetaamlike) verhaal(tjie).
spid'er, spinnekop; spaider (vierwielige rytuig); ~**-crab,** seespinnekop; ~**-fly,** soos 'n spinnekop; **spinnekopagtig;** ~**-line,** kruisdraad (verkyker); ~**-monkey,** slingeraap; ~**'s web,** spinnerak; ~**y,** spinnekopagtig.
spif(f)'licate, afransel, toetakel, kafdraf.
spig'ot, spy, spie; tap (kraan); swik (vat); spytap; prop, spons.
spike, (n) aar (gras); lang spyker; briefpriem; priem, tand; spykerskoen, naelskoen (sport); (v) vasspyker, spykers inslaan; vernael, vasnael; ~ *a GUN,* 'n kanon vernael; ~ *someone's GUNS,* iem. droogsit; ~*d HELMET,* punthelmet; ~ *a RUMOUR,* 'n gerug dooddruk; ~*d SHOE,* naelskoen, spykerskoen; ~ **file,** penlias; ~**-hammer,** spoorspykerhamer; ~ **heel,** spykerhak; ~**-heeled lark,** vlaktelewerkie; ~ **nail,** lang spyker.
spike'let, aartjie.
spike'nard, nardus.
spike: ~ **oil,** laventelolie; ~**-rush,** waterbiesie.
spik'iness, skerpheid, spitsheid, puntigheid.
spik'ing, vernaeling (kanon); vaspenning.

spik'y, spits, puntig, spigtig, skerp.
spile, (n) spil, pen; paal; swik, gat; (v) van 'n swik (gat) voorsien; ~**-hole,** swikgat.
spi'ling, paalwerk; paalstutting, staakwerk.
spill¹, (n) brandstokkie, opsteekstokkie, opsteekpapiertjie.
spill², (n) val (van ryding); *have a nasty* ~, lelik val; (v) **(spilt** or **-ed),** uitgooi, mors, uitstort, verspil; ~ *the beans,* die aap uit die mou laat; ~ **age,** oorloop; uitloopwater; storting; stortsel; ~ **er,** storter, morser, vergieter; ~**ikin,** spaander, splinter; ~**proof,** stortvas; ~*proof hob,* stortvaste stoofblad; ~ **way,** uitloop, oorloop; afvoergeut.
spilt, vermors, gestort; *kyk* **spill,** (v); *it is no use crying over* ~ *milk,* gedane sake het geen keer nie.
spin, (n) draai; tolvlug (vliegtuig); toertjie, ritjie, rytoer; krul; skop; draaiing (biljart); wenteling; *GO for a* ~, gaan ry, 'n ritjie maak; *GO into a* ~, begin tol; (v) **(spun** or **span, spun),** spin; ronddraai; krul (gholf); laat afrol; laat sak (eksamen); vertel; 'n tolvlug maak, tolvlieg (vliegtuig); ~ *the BALL,* draaiballe boul; ~ *a COIN,* 'n munt opgooi; *my HEAD* ~ *s,* ek is duiselig; my kop draai; *make the MONEY* ~, die geld laat rol; *we shall have to make our MONEY* ~ *out,* ons sal suinig met ons geldjies moet werk; ~ *ROUND,* in die rondte draai; ~ *out a short STORY into a novel,* 'n kortverhaal tot 'n roman uitrek; ~ *like a TOP,* soos 'n tol draai; ~ *a YARN,* 'n storie vertel, 'n verhaal opdis.
spin'ach, spin'age, spinasie.
spin'al, ruggraat=; ~ **column,** werwelkolom, rugstring, ruggraat; ~ **consumption,** rugmurgtering; ~ **cord,** rugmurg; ~ **curvature,** ruggraatverkromming; ~ **meningitis,** rugmurgvliesontsteking.
spin'ate, doringvormig.
spin'dle, (n) spil; spoel, as; (v) lank en skraal groei; ~ **bearing,** spillaer; ~**-legged,** met speekbene; ~**-legs,** speekbene, rietbene; ~ **machine,** freesmasjien; ~ **oil,** masjienolie; ~**-shanked,** speekbeen=; ~**-shanks,** speekbene, speekbeentjies, skarminkel; ~**-shaped,** spilvormig; ~ **side,** spil(le)sy, moederskant.
spin'dly, lank en skraal.
spin'-drier, wenteldroër, toldroër.
spin'drift, waaiskuim.
spine, ruggraat, rugstring, werwelkolom; doring, stekel; rug (van boek); ~**-chiller,** rilverhaal; rilprent; ~**-chilling,** skrikaanjaend, gruwel=.
spine'less, sonder ruggraat; papbroek(er)ig, pap; doringloos; *be* ~, sonder murg (pit) wees; sonder ruggraat wees; ~ **cactus,** doringlose turksvy, kaalblaarturksvy; ~ **ness,** papbroek(er)igheid, papheid.
spinet', spinet.
spinif'erous, doringrig, stekelrig.
spin'iform, doringvormig, stekelvormig.
spin'naker, spinnaker.
spinn'ate, spinvormig.
spinn'er, spinner, spinster; spinmasjien; naafkap (lugskroef); draaibord, draaier, draaibouler (krieket); ~ **et,** spinklier, spinorgaan, spintepel.
spinn'ing, (n) (die) spin; tolvlieëry (vliegtuig); ronddraaiing; (a) spin=; ronddraaiend; ~ **count,** spintelling; ~ **frame,** spinfabriek; ~**-machine,** spinmasjien; ~**-mill,** spinfabriek, spinmasjien; wewery; ~**-mule,** spinmasjien; ~ **quality,** spintelling, spingehalte; ~ **top,** draaitol; ~**-wheel,** spinwiel.
spin'-off, newe-effek; nasleep; byvoordeel.
spin'ose, doringagtig, skerp.
spinos'ity, doringagtigheid, stekel(r)igheid; neteligheid.
spin'ous, doringagtig, skerp, stekel(r)ig; doringrig.
spin'ster, spinster; oujongnooi, ongetroude dame; vryster; ~ **hood,** oujongnooiskap.
spin'ule, (klein) dorinkie.
spin'y, doringagtig, stekel(r)ig; netelig, lastig.
spir'acle, luggat, spuitgat (walvis), spirakel.
spiraea'a, spiraea, sierstruik (*Astilbe japonica*).
spir'al, (n) skroefvorm, spiraal; (v) **(-led),** kronkel, draai, spiraalsgewyse loop; (a) spiraalvormig, skroefvormig; ~ **bandage,** spiraalverband; ~ **bit,** spiraalboor; ~ **chute,** wentelgeut; ~ **dive,** spiraaldaling, spiraalduik; ~ **drill,** grondboor, spiraalboor; ~ **gear,** spiraalrat; ~**'ity,** spiraalvorm; ~

line, spiraallyn; ~ **ly**, spiraalsgewyse; ~ **spring**, spiraalveer, springveer; ~ **staircase**, draaitrap; wenteltrap; ~ **vault**, tregtergewelf; ~ **wheel**, spiraalrat.
spir'ant, spirant, skuringsgeluid, frikatief; glyer.
spire¹, (n) kronkeling, spiraal.
spire², (n) spits, top, bergtop; toringpunt, toringspits; ~ *of steeple*, toringnaald; (v) spruit, ontkiem; puntig opskiet; ~**d**, spits, van torings voorsien.
spirill'um, (..la), skroefbakterie, spiril.
spi'rit, (n) gees; geeskrag, durf; opgewektheid; vuur; lewe; asem; moed, besieling; gevoel, sin; skim; gesindheid; (pl) sterk drank; brandewyn; brandspiritus; lewendigheid; ~ *of the AGE*, tydgees; *ANIMAL* ~ *s*, lewenslus; *in the BEST of* ~ *s*, in die beste stemming; *CHOICE* ~ *s*, groot geeste; *ENTER into the* ~ *of the occasion*, jou aanpas by die stemming van die geleentheid; *in GOOD* ~ *s*, in goeie (opgewekte) luim; *be in HIGH* ~ *s*, opgeruimd wees; *the HOLY S* ~, die Heilige Gees; *IMMERSE in* ~ *s*, in versterkwater sit; *IN a* ~ *of mockery*, aangevuur deur spotlus; in die gees; *LACK of* ~, lamlendigheid; *in LOW* ~ *s*, neerslagtig; *a MASTER* ~, 'n groot gees; *in a* ~ *of MISCHIEF*, uit baldadigheid; *when the* ~ *MOVES*, wanneer die gees in jou vaar; *the MOVING* ~ *of an undertaking*, die siel van 'n onderneming; *OUT of* ~ *s*, neerslagtig; *RECOVER one's* ~ *s*, jou opgeruimdheid terugkry; *the* ~ *of REVOLT*, die gees van opstandigheid; ~ *s of SALT*, soutsuur, soutgees; *THAT'S the* ~, so moet dit wees; dit is die regte gees; ~ *s of TURPENTINE*, terpentynolie; *the* ~ *is WILLING but the flesh is weak*, die gees is gewillig, maar die vlees is swak; ~ *s of WINE*, wyngees; *WITH* ~, opgewek, vol vuur; *take something in the WRONG* ~, iets verkeerd opneem; (v) aanwakker, besiel, aanvuur, moed gee; ~ *away*, wegtoor, gou laat verdwyn; ~**ed**, lewendig, flink; opgeruimd, vurig, moedig; *mean* ~ *ed*, laag van gees; ~**edness**, lewendigheid; vurigheid; ~**ism**, spiritisme; ~**ist**, spiritis; ~**-lamp**, spirituslamp; ~**less**, geesteloos, leweloos, sonder besieling, slap, papbroek(er)ig, futloos, lewendig dood; ~**-level**, waterpas; ~**-rapper**, klopmedium, geesteklopper; ~**-rapping**, geestekloppery, ~**-stove**, spiritusstoof; pompstofie; ~**-trade**, handel in spiritualieë (geesryke dranke)
spi'ritual, (n): *Negro* ~, Negerlied; (a) geestelik, onstoflik, stoffeloos, geestes-, spiritueel; ~ **adviser**, sielversorger; ~ **comfort**, sieletroos; ~ **healing**, geloofsgenesing; ~**ism**, spiritisme; spiritualisme (wysb.); ~**ist**, spiritis; spiritualis (wysb.); ~**is'tic**, spiritualisties; spiritisties; ~**'ity**, onstoflikheid, geestelike lewe; ~**iza'tion**, vergeesteliking; ~**ize**, vergeestelik; verinnerlik; 'n geestelike betekenis gee; besiel; ~ **life**, geestelike lewe; ~**ly**, geestelik; ~**-minded**, geestelik gesind; ~**-mindedness**, geestelike gesondheid (aanleg); ~ **struggle**, sielestryd.
spirituel(le)', verfynd, eteries, rein.
spi'rituous, geesryk, sterk, alkoholies; ~ **liquor**, geesryke (sterk) drank; ~**ness**, geesrykheid.
spi'rit world, geestewêreld.
spirochaet'e, spirocheet.
spirom'eter, asemmeter, spirometer.
spirt, (n) uitspuiting, uitbarsting; (v) spuit, uitbars.
spir'y¹, puntig, spits.
spir'y², spiraalvormig.
spit¹, (n) braaispit; landtong, uitham; (v) **(-ted)**, aan 'n spit steek; deursteek, deurboor.
spit², (n) speeksel, spoeg, spuug; *the very* ~ *of his FATHER*, uitgeknip sy pa; ~ *and POLISH*, poetswerk; (v) **(spat)**, spoeg, spuug; afspat (rots); ~ *OUT*, uitspoeg; ~ *it OUT*, dit uitspoeg; dit reguit sê.
spitch'cock, (n) speetjiespaling, gebraaide paling; (v) in mootjies sny en braai.
spit' curl, plakkrul.
spite, (n) wrok, nyd, boosaardigheid, wrewel; *HAVE a* ~ *against*, 'n wrok koester teen; *IN* ~ *of*, ten spyte van; in weerwil van; ondanks; *IN* ~ *of this*, met dit al; *OUT of* ~, uit wrok; (v) krenk, kwaad maak, vermaak; dwarsboom; vererg, pla; *CUT off one's nose to* ~ *one's face*, wie sy neus skend, skend sy aangesig; *you WON'T* ~ *me*, ek is nie Vermaak se kind nie; ek laat my nie vermaak nie; ~**ful**, kwaadaardig, nydig, boosaardig, spytig, wrewelig, haatlik; ~**fulness**, haatlikheid, kwaadaardigheid, boosaardigheid, spytigheid.
spit: ~ **fire**, vuurvreter, drifkop, heethoof; rissie; ~**ter**, spoeger, spuwer.
spit'ting, spoeg; afspatting; ~ **image**, ewebeeld; ~ **snake**, spoegslang.
spit'tle, speeksel; ~ **bug**, skuimbesie.
spittoon', spoegbakkie, kwispedoor.
Spitz'bergen, Spitsberge.
spiv, vertrouenswendelaar, afsetter, bedrieër, kuller, opligter; sluikhandelaar.
splanch'nic, ingewands-.
splash, (n) **(-es)**, plas, plons; spatsel, gespat; *a* ~ *of COLOUR*, 'n kleurspatsel; *MAKE a* ~, opsien baar; baie vertoon maak; *MAKE a* ~ *of*, in groot letters druk; (v) bespat, plas, nat spat, bemodder; prominent plaas, vet druk; 'n ophef maak van; ~ *NEWS*, nuus in groot letters druk; ~ *OUT*, uitspat; ~ *through WATER*, deur water plas; ~**back**, spatplaat; ~**-board**, spatbord, spatskerm, modderskerm (perdekar); ~ **cover**, spatdeksel; ~**er**, plasser; modderskerm, spatbord; ~**ing**, (n) geplas; (a) spattend; opsienbarend; ~ **mark**, spatsel; ~**-proof**, spatbestand, spatvas, spatdig; ~**y**, modderig, bemodder, bespat; windmakerig; opsienbarend.
splat, dekstrook, ruglat.
splatt'er, plas, spat; mompel; ~**dash**, lawaai; ~**dashes**, slobkouse, oorkouse.
splay, (n) skuinste, skuinsvlak; uitskuinsing; (v) verswik, verstuit; skuins afloop; uitskuins, skuins bou; oopsprei; ~**ed BRICK**, skuinssteen; ~**ed WORK**, geskuinste werk; (a) plat; skeef; na buite gekeer; ~**-ear**, skuinsoor (skaap); oopgesprei; lomp; ~**-foot**, platvoet, ganspoot; ~**-footed**, platvoet; ~**ing**, oopspreiding; ronding (hoek); ~**-knot**, kloofkwas; ~**-mouthed**, met skewe mond; ~**-toes**, weglêtone.
spleen, milt; miltsug; gemeliktheid, swaarmoedigheid, wrewel, slegte humeur, swartgalligheid; *a FIT of* ~, 'n slegte bui; *VENT one's* ~, jou gal kwytraak; jou ergernis lug; ~**ful**, ergerlik, brommerig, swaarmoedig; ~ **index**, miltsyfer; ~**ish** = **spleenful**; ~**-sick**, miltsugtig; ~ **wort**, miltkruid; ~**y** = **spleenful**.
splenal'gia, miltsteek, miltpyn.
splen'dent, skitterend, pragtig.
splen'did, (a) pragtig, kostelik, luisterryk, glansryk, skitterend, manjifiek, glorieryk, uitstekend; (interj) ryperd! mooi skoot!
splen'didness, **splen'dour**, prag, glans, grootsheid, luisterrykheid, praal, majesteit, heerlikheid, glansrykheid, skittering, weidsheid.
splenet'ic, (n) brompot; lyer aan 'n miltkwaal; middel teen miltkwaal; (a) miltsugtig; milt-; gemelik, brommerig.
splen'ic, milt-; ~ **fever**, miltkoors, miltsiekte, miltvuur; ~ **vein**, miltaar.
splenit'is, miltontsteking.
splice, (n) splitslas; splitsing; spalklas (houtw.); (v) splits; las, verbind; trou; ~ *the main BRACE*, 'n dop steek; *to BE* ~ *d*, hulle skapies bymekaargejaag hê; ~**r**, splitslas; splitser; lasser; lastoestel; ~ **rod**, spalkstang.
spline, gleuf; groef; glyspy; ~**d**, gegroef; ~**d gear**, groefrat; ~**d shaft**, groefas.
splint, (n) spalk; splinter; skuifelbeentjie (perd); splytpen; knop; breukspalk; *put in* ~ *s*, spalk; (v) spalk; ~**-bone**, kuitbeen, fibula; griffelbeen (van perd); ~**coal**, matkool, dowwe steenkool.
splin'ter, (n) splinter, skerf, spaan, spaander, spleetveer (van wa); (v) splinter, versplinter; ~**-bar**, swingel; ~**-bomb**, skerfbom; ~ **group**, splintergroep; ~**less glass**, skerfvry (skerfvaste) glas; ~ **party**, splinterparty; ~**-proof**, splintervry, skerfvry; ~**y**, splinterig; skilferig.
splint'ing, spalking.
split, (n) skeuring, onenigheid, tweespalt; spleet, skeur, bars; verdeeldheid; klowing; half-om-half (drank); (v) (~), skeur; splits; verdeel; kloof; deurkap; bars; verklik, verklap; ~ *a DIAMOND*, 'n

splitting   1256   *sporting*

diamant kloof; ~ *the DIFFERENCE*, die verskil deel; ~ *the FEE*, die koste verdeel; ~ *HAIRS*, haarkloof; ~ *ON someone*, iem. verklap, verklik; ~ *OPEN*, oopsplits, oopkloof; ~ *one's SIDES with laughter*, uitbundig lag; ~ *UP*, ontbind; uitmekaar gaan; ~ *the VOTE*, die stemme verdeel; (a) gesplits, verdeel; verpletter; gesplete; *in a ~ second*, in 'n kits; blitsvinnig; ~ **bearing**, splitlaer; ~ **bullet**, spleetkoeël; ~ **eagle**, dubbele adelaar; ~ **infinitive**, geskeie infinitief; ~ **nut**, splitmoer; ~ **peas**, split= ertjies; ~ **personality**, gesplete persoonlikheid; ~ **pin**, splytpen; ~ **pole**, gekloofde paal, kloofpaal; ~**-pole fence**, paaltjiesheining; ~ **ring**, splitring; ~ **rivet**, splitnael; ~ **roof**, kloofstaandak; ~**-second**, breukdeel van 'n sekonde, ondeelbare oomblik; ~ **skirt**, spleetrok; ~**ter**, splitser; klower.

splitt'ing, (n) klowing; splitsing; splyting (atoom); (a) klowend; barstend; *his HAIR is ~*, sy hare splits; *a ~ HEADACHE*, 'n barstende hoofpyn; ~**-fee**, verdelingskoste; ~**-wedge**, kloofyster.

splodge, splotch, (n) vlek, klad; (v) beklad, vol smeer.
splotch'y, vlekkerig, beklad.
splurge, (n) bohaai, drukte; (v) bohaai maak, vertoon maak.
splutt'er, hoes (vliegtuig); spat; brabbel; *kyk ook* **sputter**.
spode, spodeporselein.
spoff'ish, bemoeisiek, lawaaierig.
spoil, (n) buit, roof; voordeel; oorskietgrond; uitge= graafde grond; ~*s of war*, buit; (v) **(-t** or **-ed)**, be= derwe; vertroetel; verbrou, bederwe, opdons; vergal; verslons (klere); beduiwel (dier); *BE ~ing for*, baie verlang na; ~ *one's CHANCE(S)*, jou kans(e) be= derf; ~ *the FUN*, die pret bederf; ~ *someone's GAME*, iem. se pret bederwe; roet in iem. se kos gooi; *be ~ing for a QUARREL*, skoor soek; rusie soek; ~*ing TACTICS*, afbrekende taktiek; ~ **able**, bederfbaar; ~**age**, bederfproses, bederwing; be= derf; bedorwe goed; ~**ed**, bedorwe, gepiep; ~**er**, bederwer; verstoorder; plunderaar; ~**-sport**, spel= bederwer, pretbederwer; ~**s system**, buitstelsel; baantjies-vir-boeties-stelsel; ~**t = spoiled**; ~*t CHILD*, bedorwe kind; ~*t voting PAPER*, bedor= we stembrief; ~**-trade**, onderkruiper, markbeder= wer, prysbederwer; spelbederwer.

spoke[1], (n) (wiel)speek; *put a ~ in someone's wheel*, 'n stok in iem. se wiel steek; iem. dwarsboom; (v) spe= ke insit; 'n speek steek in.
spoke[2], (v) *kyk* **speak**.
spoke: ~**-gauge**, speekmaat; ~ **shave**, speekskaaf; trekmes.
spok'en, gesproke; *the ~ LANGUAGE*, spreektaal; *the ~ WORD*, die gesproke woord.
spokes'man, (..men), woordvoerder; spreekbuis (fig.).
spokes'woman, (..men), woordvoerster.
spoke: ~**-tightener**, speeksleutel; ~**-wood**, speek= hout.
spol'iate, (uit)plunder, verniel, roof.
spolia'tion, (uit)plundering, verwoesting; afpersing; knoeiery (met 'n dokument).
spol'iator, rower, plunderaar; ~**y**, plunder=, roof=.
spondai'c(al), spondeïes.
spon'dee, spondee.
spon'dyl(e), werwel(been).
sponge, (n) spons; afsponsing; dronkaard, dronklap; opskeploerder, klaploper; parasiet; deeg; *PASS the ~ over*, iets uit die wêreld maak; iets vergeet; *THROW up the ~*, 'n saak gewonne gee; tou op= gooi; (v) afspons, spons; uitvee; opsuig; klaploop; ~ *DOWN*, afspons, met 'n spons afwas; ~ *ON someone*, op iem. teer; opskeploer; *SOMEONE on whom one can ~*, 'n melkkoeitjie; ~**-bag**, spons= sakkie; ~**-bath**, sponsbad; afsponsing; ~**-cake**, suikerbrood; sponskoek; ~ **cloth**, sponsdoek, sponslap; ~**-diver**, sponsvisser; ~**-down**, afspon= sing; ~**-finger**, sponskoekie; ~ **flagellum**, spons= pen; ~**-hanger**, sponshanger; ~ **like**, sponsagtig; ~**ous**, sponsagtig; ~ **pudding**, sponspoeding; ~**r**, klaploper; parasiet; panlekker, opskeploerder; skuimer; ~ **rubber**, sponsrubber; ~ **spicule**, spons= naald.

spo'ngiform, sponsvormig.
spo'nginess, sponsagtigheid; voosheid.
spo'ngite, sponssteen.
spo'ngy, sponsagtig; voos; swamagtig; ~ **gold**, spons= goud; ~ **silver**, sponssilwer.
spon'sion, borgtog.
spon'sor, (n) borg (van bv. sportspan); doopgetuie, peet; bevorderaar; uitsaaiadverteerder, ondersteu= ner, onderskrywer; *stand ~*, getuie wees; (v) borg, beskerm, bevorder; jou naam leen aan; waarborg, borg staan vir; ~**ed**, geborg; ~*ed ADVERTISE= MENT*, ondersteunde (geborgde) advertensie; ~*ed BY*, geborg deur; onder beskerming van; ~**'ial**, peet=; ~ **ship**, borgskap.
spontane'ity, spontaniteit, ongedwongenheid, na= tuurlike aandrang.
spontan'eous, uit eie beweging, vrywillig, ongesog, spontaan; ongedwonge, ongekunsteld, natuurlik; wild groeiend, veld= (van plante); self=; ~ **combus= tion**, selfverbranding; selfontbranding; ~ **genera= tion**, selfontstaan, selfvoortbrenging; ~ **ignition**, selfontsteking; ~**ly**, uit eie beweging, spontaan, vanself; ~**ness = spontaneity**.
spoof, (n) (sl.), foppery, kullery; (v) fop, kul, verneuk; ~**er**, verneuker (plat).
spook, spook; ~**ish**, ~**y**, spookagtig.
spool, (n) spoeletjie; tolletjie; klos; (v) opdraai.
spoon, (n) lepel; lepelvormige roeispaan; sukkelaar; smoorverliefde; *BE ~s on*, smoorverlief wees op; *LIE like ~s*, lepellê; *he should have a LONG ~ who sups with the devil*, wie hom met die bose inmeng, moet op sy hoede wees; sorg dat jy altyd 'n slag om die arm hou; *born with a SILVER ~ in one's mouth*, met 'n goue lepel gebore wees; in gelukskind wees; *get the WOODEN ~*, laagste op die ranglys kom; (v) vry, opsit; lepel, met 'n lepel skep; 'n paphou slaan (kr.); ~ **out**, uitskep, uitlepel; ~ **beak**, ~ **bill**, lepelgans, lepelaar; ~**-bit**, lepelboor; ~**-brake**, le= pelrem; ~**-chisel**, lepelbeitel; ~**-dish**, lepelbak; ~**-drift**, waaiskuim; ~**-drill**, lepelboor.
spoon'erism, toevallige omsetting, spoonerisme.
spoon: ~**-feed**, (..**fed**), met die lepel voer; voorkou (fig.); ~**-feeding**, kunsmatige instandhouding; ~**ful**, lepelvol, skeppie; ~**-meat**, lepelkos; ~**-net**, skepnet; ~**-shaped**, lepelvormig; ~ **wood**, smalblad *(Hartogia capensis)*; ~**y**, (n) (..**nies**), domkop; sentimentele persoon; (a) sentimenteel, verlief; dwaas.
spoor, (n) spoor; (v) opspoor, die spoor volg, die spoor sny.
sporad'ic(al), verspreid, sporadies, af en toe voorko= mend; ..**dically**, kol-kol, verspreid, sporadies.
spora'tion, spoorvorming.
spore, spoor (saadjie), kiem; ~**-bearing**, spoor= draend; ~ **formation**, spoorvorming; ~**less**, spoor= loos; ~ **ling**, spoorkiemplant.
sporif'erous, spoordraend.
sporifica'tion, spoorvorming.
sporogen'esis, spoorvorming.
spor'ophore, spoordraer.
spor'ophyll, sporofil.
spor'ophyte, spoorplant, sporofiet.
sporophyt'ic, sporofities.
sporozo'an, (n) sporosoön; (a) sporosoïes.
spo'rran, sakkie, tassie (Skots).
sport, (n) sport; grap, korswel, pret, vermaak; sport= man; tydverdryf, speletjie; afwyking (plant, dier); speelbal; grapmaker, gawe kêrel; *do BE a ~*, wees nou so gaaf (lief) om; ~ *for the DEAF*, dowesport; sport vir dowes; *IN ~*, vir die grap; vir die aardig= heid; *the ~ of KINGS*, perdewedrenne; *MAKE ~ of*, gekskeer met; vir die gek hou; *OLD ~*, ou kêrel; ~ *for the PHYSICALLY DISABLED*, sport vir liggaamlik gestremdes; *a REAL ~*, 'n gawe kêrel; (v) speel, jou vermaak, ontspan; spog met, te koop loop met; ~ *a gold watch*, met 'n goue oorlosie pronk; ~ **conference**, sportvergadering; ~**ful**, vro= lik, speels.
sport'ing, sportief, sport=; sportliewend; spelend; *a ~ CHANCE*, 'n onsekere (twyfelagtige) kans; *a ~ FELLOW*, 'n sportiewe kêrel; *a ~ OFFER*, 'n gawe aanbod; *for ~ PURPOSES*, vir sportdoel=

eindes; *TAKE a* ~ *chance*, dit waag; ~ **circles**, sportkringe; ~ **column**, sportrubriek; ~ **editor**, sportredakteur; ~ **fellow**, sportiewe kêrel; ~ **ly**, gekskerend; skalks, speels; sportief; ~ **news**, sportnuus, sportberigte; ~ **offer**, gulle aanbod; ~ **requisites**, sportbenodigdhede; ~ **rifle**, jaggeweer; ~ **shorts**, sportbroek; ~ **spirit**, sportgees, sportiwiteit; ~ **term**, sportterm; ~ **wear**, sportdrag; ~ **world**, sportwêreld; ~ **writer**, sportskrywer.

sport'ive, vrolik, opgeruimd, spelerig, speels, dartel, sportief; ~**ness**, opgeruimdheid, dartelheid, speelsheid.

sports, sport; atletiek; ~ **association**, sportvereniging; ~ **blouse**, sportbloese; ~ **car**, sportmotor; ~ **clothes**, sportdrag; ~ **club**, sportklub, sportvereniging; ~ **coat**, sportbaadjie; ~ **column**, sportrubriek; ~ **complex**, sportinrigting; sportgebou(e); ~ **coupé**, sportkoepee; ~ **department**, sportafdeling; ~ **dress**, sportkostuum; ~ **editor**, sportredakteur; ~ **field**, ~ **ground**, sportterrein; ~ **lover**, sportliefhebber; ~**man**, sportman; ~**manlike**, edelmoedig, gaaf, sportief, eerlik; ~**manship**, sportmanskap; ~ **master**, sportonderwyser; ~ **meeting**, sportbyeenkoms; ~ **outfit**, sporttoerusting; ~ **paper**, sportblad; ~ **results**, sportuitslae; ~ **shirt**, sporthemp; ~ **shop**, sportwinkel.

sport'ster, sportvlieëtuig.

sports: ~ **suit**, sportpak; ~ **wear**, sportdrag; ~**woman**, sportvrou; ~ **writer**, sportskrywer.

spor'ulate, spore vorm.

sporula'tion, spoorvorming.

spo'rule, spoortjie.

spot, (n) kol, merk, smet, vlek; plek; punt; stip, stippie, stippel; kleinigheid; moedervlek; moesie; sopie; slukkie; mondjievol; (pl) kolligte (teater); *BLIND* ~, blindevlek; *it was a* ~ *of BOTHER to him*, dit was roet in sy kos; dit was vir hom 'n las; *without a* ~ *on his CHARACTER*, vlek(ke)loos van karakter; *see* ~*s before one's EYES*, duiselig word; *have a* ~ *of food*, 'n stukkie te ete hê; *HAVE a* ~, 'n kleintjie maak; 'n sopie drink; *IN* ~*s*, hier en daar; plek-plek; *KNOCK* ~*s off a person*, iem. ver oortref; *be ON the* ~, op stryk wees (in 'n spel); dadelik aanpak, fluks wees; op die plek wees; onmiddellik daar wees; *ON* ~, ter plaatse; *be killed ON the* ~, op slag dood wees; *come OUT in* ~*s*, 'n (huid)uitslag kry; *to be PUT on the* ~, in die pekel sit; in lewensgevaar verkeer; *there are* ~*s even on the SUN*, daar is nie koring sonder kaf nie; *TAKE a* ~, 'n sopie drink; 'n snapsie maak; *TOUCH a tender* ~, 'n tere snaar aanroer; *touch a person's WEAK* ~, iem. in sy swak tas; (v) **(-ted)**, bevlek, besoedel; spikkel; sprinkel; bespikkel, merk; uitsoek; uitken, raaksien, opsoek (teiken); (raak) raai, vooruitsien (eksamenvraag); waarneem; ~ *someone in a CROWD*, iem. in 'n skare uitken; ~ *the WINNER*, die wenner kies (uitsoek); ~-**apparatus**, skiettoestel; ~ **cash**, kontant; ~ **check**, steekproef; ~ **fine**, afkoopboete; boete; ~-**landing**, puntlanding; ~**less**, vlekloos, onbevlek, smet(te)loos, silwerskoon, bloedskoon; ~**lessly**, sonder vlek, smetloos; (n) ~ **light**, soeklig, draailamp, stippellig; skietlig; *in the* ~ *light*, op die voorgrond; (v) laat uitkom, beklemtoon; na vore bring; ~-**projector**, skietlig; ~ **sale**, onmiddellike verkoop; ~ **sample**, grypmonster, steekmonster; ~-**sight**, skietvisier; ~-**stitch**, matrassteek; ~ **ted**, bont, skilder (bees); gespikkel(d), gekol, gevlek; uitgeken, raakgesien; ~**ted hyena**, tierwolf, gevlekte hiëna; ~**ted lily**, bontlelie; ~ **ter**, lugspioen, waarnemingsvlieëtuig; soeker, waarnemer, opspoorder; ~**tiness**, kollerigheid; onreëlmatigheid; ~**ty**, gespikkel(d), vlekkerig; kollerig; kol-kol; onreëlmatig; ~-**weld**, puntsweis; ~-**welder**, puntsweiser; ~-**welding**, puntsweis, stiksweis.

spous'al, (n) huwelik, bruilof; (a) huweliks=, bruilofs=.

spouse, eggenoot, eggenote, gade, gemaal, gemalin.

spout, (n) tuit; geut; spuit, pyp; waterstraal (van walvis); tregter; *BE up the* ~, in die verknorsing wees; *PUT up the* ~, verpand; (v) spuit; guts; oreer, deklameer, hoogdrawend voordra; *blood* ~*s from the wound*, bloed guts uit die wond; ~-**adze**, geutdissel;

~**er**, spuiter; volksredenaar; walvis; ~-**hole**, spuitgat.

sprag, (n) remblok, briekblok; stut (in myn); (v) **(-ged)**, rem; stut.

sprain, (n) verstuiting, verswikking; (v) verrek; verstuit, verswik.

sprang, *kyk* **spring**, (v).

sprat, spiering, sprot; *throw a* ~ *to catch a mackerel (whale)*, 'n spiering uitgooi om 'n kabeljou te vang.

sprawl, (n) lomp houding; gespartel; (v) spartel; jou uitstrek; versprei wees; lomp uitrek; wyd uitmekaar skryf; *send someone* ~*ing*, iem. platslaan.

spray[1], (n) skeutjie, takkie, spruitjie; streepruiker; ruiker; loot.

spray[2], (n) skuim; sproeireën, stuifwater; spuitjie, sproeier, verstuiwer; verstuiwing; stofreën; spuitstof, spuitmiddel; (v) (be)spuit, sproei; verstuiwe; bestuif; ~-**aircraft**, spuitvliegtuig; ~-**attack**, sproeiaanval; ~**er**, spuiter; sproeier, verstuiwer; ~**er valve**, sproeiklep; ~-**gun**, sproeispuit.

spray'ing, (die) sproei; bestuiwing; spuitwerk; ~ **apparatus**, sproeitoestel; ~ **flight**, sproeivlug; ~ **machine**, sproeier, sproeimasjien; ~ **nozzle**, sproeikop, sproeier.

spray: ~ **irrigation**, sprinkelbesproeiing; ~-**nozzle**, sproeikop, sproeier; ~-**paint**, sproeiverf, spuitverf; ~-**painter**, spuitskilder, spuitverwer; ~-**painting**, spuitverf; spuitverfwerk; ~-**plane**, spuitvliegtuig; ~-**pump**, verstuiwer, spuitpomp; ~-**race**, spuitdip.

spread, (n) verspreiding, verbreiding, uitgebreidheid; uitgestrektheid, omvang; breedte van vertakking; rekbaarheid; seilwerk; ontplooiing; spreiwydte; spanning (boog); dis, maaltyd; fees; *LIKE a* ~, van 'n goeie tafel hou; *PREPARE a* ~ *for someone*, 'n feestelike ete vir iem. voorberei; *the* ~ *of a bird's WINGS*, die spanwydte van 'n voël se vlerke; (v) **(spread)**, versprei, uitbrei; ontplooi; uitstrooi, rondstrooi, strooi (mis); span (seil); uitslaan (vlerke); smeer (brood); dek (tafel); oopslaan (waaier); verdeel (oor 'n tydperk); voortplant; ~ *BUTTER on bread*, botter op brood smeer; ~ *ONESELF*, die groot meneer uithang; breed sit; ~ *out a RUG*, 'n mat oopgooi; ~ *a RUMOUR*, 'n gerug rondstrooi; ~ *the TABLE*, die tafel dek; ~ *out on the TABLE*, op die tafel ooplê; *the bird* ~*s its TAIL*, die voël pronk met sy stert; ~-**eagle**, (n) adelaar met uitgespreide vlerke; misdadiger; pronker; (v) oopspalk; uitsprei; (a) blufferig, grootpraterig; ~-**eagleism**, bluffery, grootpratery; ~**er**, sproeier; verspreier; uitstrooier, rondstrooier; ooprekker; spreimiddel; ~**ing**, (n) verspreiding; (a) weglê(horings); wydsprelend, wydstrekkend; ~**ing horns**, weglehorings; ~**ing tree**, boom met wydspreiende takke; ~-**over**, spreiding; ~**s**, kontrakspreiding, brugspreiding (ekon.).

spree, (n) fuif, jool; drinkpartytjie; *on the* ~, aan die swier; aan die jol; (v) fuif, boemel; aan die drink wees, gloria hou.

sprig, (n) takkie, lootjie, twygie; spruit, punt, spriet, skeut; uitgroeisel; skotspyker; penkop, snuiter (seun); *a royal* ~, persoon van adellike afkoms; (v) **(-ged)**, met penne vassit; met blaartjies versier; ~ **ged**, met takkies, met twygies versier; ~ **ged muslin**, geblomde neteldoek; ~**gy**, vol takkies.

spright'liness, lewendigheid, opgewektheid, vrolikheid, beweeglikheid.

spright'ly, (spring)lewendig, vrolik, dartel, fleurig.

spring[1], (n) lente, voorjaar, voorsomer; *in* ~, in die lente.

spring[2], (n) bron, fontein.

spring[3], (n) spring, sprong, veer, veerkrag, motief, dryfveer, oorsprong, elastisiteit, vering, strik, valstrik, wip; (v) **(sprang, sprung)**, spring, voortkom, ontstaan, ontspring, afkomstig wees van; kromtrek, bars (hout); opjaag, verras (wild); ~ *an ARCH*, 'n boog bou; ~ *to the ASSISTANCE of someone*, iem. te hulp snel; ~ *AT*, spring na; ~ *to ATTENTION*, flink op aandag kom; ~ *AWAY*, wegspring; ~ *BACK*, terugspring; *a BREEZE sprang up*, 'n windjie het opgesteek; ~ *into FAME*, skielik beroemd word; ~ *to one's FEET*, opspring; ~ *a LEAK*, 'n lek kry; ~ *to LIFE*, in die lewe kom;

spring 1258 squadron

opduik; ~ *to MIND,* te binne skiet; ~ *a MINE,* 'n myn laat ontplof; ~ *a QUESTION on someone,* skielik met 'n vraag op iem. afkom; ~ *a SURPRISE on someone,* iem. verras; ~ *at somebody's THROAT,* iem. na die keel spring; ~ *UP,* opspring; ontstaan; opkom (wind); verrys; *a WELLsprung car,* 'n goed geveerde motor; ~ **action,** veerwerking; ~ **assembly,** veersamestel; ~ **balance,** veerskaal, veerbalans, trekskaal; ~**-beam,** veerbalk; ~ **bed,** springmatras; binneveermatras; ~**binding,** klembinding; ~**-blade,** veerblad; ~**-board,** springplank, duikplank; ~ **bok,** springbok; ~**-bolt,** veerbout; ~**-bow,** boogveer; ~**-bows,** nulpasser; ~**-box,** veerkoker; ~**-bracket,** veerbeuel; ~**-cap,** veerdop; ~**-carriage,** geveerde rytuig; ~**-cart,** veerkar, geveerde kar.
spring: ~ **chicken,** jong hoender; gansie, piepkuiken; ~**-clean,** deeglik skoonmaak; ~**-cleaning,** voorjaarskoonmaak; groot huisskoonmaak; ~ **clearance,** lenteopruiming.
spring: ~**-clip,** veerknip, veerklamp, veerlas; ~**-collar,** veerring; ~**-compressor,** veerdrukker; ~**-contact,** veerkontak; ~ **cup,** veerdop; ~**-divider,** veerpasser.
spring: ~ **er,** springer; jaghond; dolfyn; veerwerker; ~**-eye,** veeroog; bron, oog (van fontein); ~**-gaiter,** veerkous; ~ **gun,** geweerval, stelgeweer; ~**-halt,** hanespat (by perde); ~**-hare,** springhaas.
spring'-head, bron; oorsprong.
spring: ~**-heeled,** veerkragtig; ~ **hook,** optelhaak, veerhaak; ~**iness,** elastisiteit; veerkragtigheid; ~**ing,** vering; groei; ~ **iron,** veertang.
spring lamb, lentelam, voorjaarlam.
spring: ~ **latch,** veerklink; ~**-leaf,** veerblad; ~ **less,** veerloos, sonder vere; ~ **less cart,** skotskar; ~ **less waggon,** stampwa.
spring'let, klein fonteintjie.
spring'like¹, voorjaars=, lente=, lenteagtig.
spring'like², elasties, veeragtig.
spring: ~ **lock,** veerslot; ~ **mattress,** veermatras, binneveermatras.
spring: ~ **onion,** inmaakuitjie, stingelui, jong uitjie; ~ **rain,** voorjaarsreën, lentereën.
spring: ~ **saddle,** veersaal; ~ **seat,** veerstoel.
spring' song, lentelied.
spring' steel, veerstaal.
spring: ~ **tide,** hoogwater, springvloed, springgety; lente; ~ **time,** lente; jeug.
spring: ~ **trap,** slagyster; ~**-trolley,** ~**-wagon,** veerwa; ~**-washer,** veerring.
spring' water, fonteinwater.
spring' weather, lenteweer.
spring'y, veerkragtig; elasties.
spri'nkle, (n) motreën; sprinkeling; (v) sprinkel, begiet; inklam; besproei; bestrooi, strooi; motreën, stofreën; ~ **irrigation,** sprinkelbesproeiing; besprinkeling; ~ **r,** bestrooier; strooibus; sproeier; sprinkelspuit; sprinkelaar; sproeiwa; sprinkelblusser; ~ **r installation,** sprinkelblusstelsel.
sprink'ling, besprinkeling; klein hoeveelheid (getal), stuk of wat; *a* ~ *of people,* 'n handjievol mense.
sprint, (n) nael(wed)loop; *100 m* ~ , 100 m-naelloop; (v) nael, sny, hardloop; ~ **er,** naelloper; hardloper.
sprit, spriet, boegspriet.
sprite, gees, spook; kabouter, fee.
sprit' sail, sprietseil.
sprock'et, tandrat; kettingrat; getande ketting; wipstuk (van dakrand); ~ **chain,** staafketting, skarnierketting; ~ **wheel,** kettingrat.
sprout, (n) spruit, loot, uitloopsel, uitspruitsel, suier; *Brussels* ~ *s,* spruitkool, Brusselse spruitjies; (v) uitspruit, uitloop, uitbot, groei, laat groei, uitskiet; suiwer (tabak); opskiet; ~ *ed oats,* uitgeloopte hawer.
spruce¹, (n) denneboom, sparden.
spruce², (v) mooimaak, netjies aantrek, opskik; ~ *UP,* opknap; ~ *oneself UP,* jou fyn uitvat; jou regruk; (a) netjies, keurig, piekfyn, viets, vief.
spruce: ~**-beer,** dennebier; ~ **fir,** spar(boom).
spruce'ness, netheid, keurigheid.
sprue¹, sproei (siekte).
sprue², gietgat, gietopening; gegote vulsel (vulling).

sprung, geveer; *kyk* **spring³,** (v); ~ **floor,** geveerde vloer; ~ **seat,** veermat.
spry, lewendig, rats, wakker, vief; ~**ness,** ratsheid, lewendigheid.
spud, (n) grafie; slangkoppelaar; diksak; ertappel, aartappel; (v) **(-ded),** skoffel; aartappels uithaal.
spue, uitbraak; spoeg, spu.
spume, (n, v) skuim.
spumes'cence, skuiming, skuimerigheid.
spumes'cent, skuimerig, skuimend.
spum'iness, skuimerigheid, skuimagtigheid.
spum'ous, spum'y, skuimend, skuimagtig; swammig.
spun, (n) gespinde sy; (a) gespin, gesponne; ~ **concrete,** slingerbeton; ~ **glass,** glaswol; ~ **gold,** gouddraad.
spunk, moed, durf, fut; toorn, drif; vonk; *have no* ~ , sonder fut wees; sonder murg wees; ~ **less,** futloos, sonder durf; ~ **y,** dapper, flink, vurig.
spun: ~ **rayon,** gespinde rayon; ~ **silk,** gespinde sy; sygaring; ~ **silver,** silwerdraad; ~ **sugar,** garingsuiker; ~ **yarn,** skiemansgaring.
spur, (n) spoor; spoorslag, aansporing, prikkel; uitloper (van 'n berg); stut; blinde spoor (spoorw.); *GILT* ~ *s,* goue spore; *on the* ~ *of the MOMENT,* sonder om na te dink, dadelik, op die ingewing van die oomblik; *PUT* ~ *s to,* die spore gee; *WIN one's* ~ *s,* jou spore verdien; (v) **(-red),** aanspoor, die spore gee; van spore voorsien; *do not* ~ *a free HORSE,* moenie 'n gewillige persoon aanjaag nie; ~ *ON,* por, aanspoor; ~ **box,** spoorsok.
spurge, melkbos, wolfsmelk (plant).
spur' gear', reguit tandrat.
spur'ious, oneg, vals, nagemaak, vervals; ~ **argument,** vals argument; ~ **edition,** onwettige nadruk; ~ **ness,** onegtheid, valsheid.
spur'less, sonder spore.
spurn, (n) veragting, versmading, verwerping; (v) verag, versmaad, wegskop, verstoot, verskop; ~ **er,** veragter.
spur' pinion, rondsel.
spurred, met spore, gespoor.
spu'rr(e)y, spurrie (plant).
spu'rrier, spoormaker.
spurt, (n) uitspuiting; uitbarsting; vaart, plotselinge versnelling; vlaag; aandrang; kragtige poging; *BY* ~ *s,* met rukke; *MAKE a* ~ , alle kragte inspan; (v) uitspuit; spat; weglê; laat nael; ~ *out,* uitspat.
spur'-toed frog, platanna.
spur' wheel, tandrat, kamwiel.
spur'-winged, met spoorvlerke; ~ **goose,** wildemakou.
sput'nik, spoetnik.
sputt'er, (n) gesputter; geratel; (v) knetter, pruttel; borrel; sputter; hoes; hakkel; rammel, brabbel; ~ **er,** brabbelkous.
sput'um, (sputa), speeksel, sputum, fluim.
spy, (n) **(spies),** spioen, bespieder; (v) **(spied),** spioeneer, bespied, verken, verspied, uitvis; afloer, gluur, afkyk; bemerk, ontdek; ~ *AT,* bespied; ~ *ON,* bespied, nagaan, afloer; ~ *OUT,* uitvors, uitvis; ~ *OUT the land,* die terrein verken; ~ *into a SECRET,* 'n geheim probeer ontrafel; ~**-boat,** spioenskip; ~ **er,** verspieder; ~ **glass,** verkyker; ~ **hole,** kykgat, loergat; ~**ing,** spioenasie, bespieding; geloer; ~**-ring,** spioenasienet; ~ **system,** spioenstelsel.
squab, (n) jong duif; kussing; vetsak, diksak (kind); rusbank, sofa, ottoman; (a) dik, lywig; (interj) woeps.
squab'ble, (n) rusie, twis, kibbelary, relletjie; (v) twis, rusie maak, skoor, dwarstrek; ~ **r,** rusiesoeker, dwarstrekker.
squabb'ling, gekyf, geharwar.
squab: ~ **by,** kort en dik; ~**-chick,** piepkuiken; ~ **pie,** duiwepastei; vleispastei.
squad, afdeling (militêr); klomp; seksie; span, ploeg (werkers); *AWKWARD* ~ , rou span; *FLYING* ~ , blitspatrollie; ~ **car,** blitsmotor; vangwa; ~ **ganger,** spanbaas, ploegbaas.
squad'ron, eskadron (ruiters); smaldeel, eskader (ske

pe); eskadrielje (vliegtuie); ~ **commander,** eskader=
kommandant; ~ **leader,** eskaderleier.
squa'lid, vuil, morsig, smerig; ~ **'ity,** ~ **ness,** vuilheid,
smerigheid, goorheid; ellende.
squall, (n) gil, geskreeu; windvlaag, stormbui, ruk=
wind; *LOOK out for* ~ *s, be PREPARED for* ~ *s,*
op jou hoede wees vir gevare; (v) skreeu, gil; ~ **er,**
skreeuer; ~ **y,** stormagtig, onstuimig; buierig, win=
derig.
squal'oid, haai=, haaiagtig.
squa'lor, morsigheid, vuilis, vuilheid, liederlikheid.
squam'a, (-e), skub.
squam'ate, geskub.
squam'iform, skubvormig.
squam'ose, squam'ous, geskub, skubbig; skubvor=
mig.
squan'der, verkwis, verspil, deurbring, verbras, ver=
boemel; ~ *AWAY,* vermors, deurbring; ~
MONEY, met geld smyt; ~ **er,** deurbringer, ver=
kwister; ~ **ing,** verspilling, vermorsing; ~ **mania,**
spilsug.
square, (n) vierkant; kwadraat, tweede mag; ruit, vak
(dambord); plein; winkelhaak; vierkantige blok
(huise, ens.); domkop; 'n ou vrome, 'n remskoen,
ou knol, 'n ouderwetse suurknol; *BRING to a* ~, in
die kwadraat verhef; *do things ON the* ~, eerlik
sake doen; *a meeting ON the* ~, 'n vergadering op
die plein; *OUT of* ~, nie haaks nie; (v) vierkantig
maak; reghoekig maak; haaks maak; tot die tweede
mag verhef, kwadreer (wisk.); vereffen, reël, om=
koop; klop, ooreenstem (syfers); aanpas by; ~ *AC=
COUNTS with,* afreken met; *try to* ~ *the CIRCLE,*
daarsie aan sy stert probeer optel; die onmoontlike
probeer doen; *these FACTS do not* ~ *with your
evidence,* hierdie feite kan nie met jou getuienis ver=
soen word nie; ~ *SOMEONE,* iem. omkoop; ~
UP to someone, iem. met gebalde vuiste trotseer; ~
UP, in orde bring; afbetaal, afreken; ~ *UP to,* reg=
staan om te baklei; (a, adv) vierkantig, kwadraat,
reghoekig; in die haak, haaks, in orde, kiets, afgere=
ken, niks skuldig nie; eerlik, regskape; *ALL* ~, ge=
lykop; sonder verlies; *BE* ~ *with someone,* kiets
wees; iem. niks skuld nie; met iem. gelyk wees
(gholf); *DO the* ~ *thing by someone,* iem. eerlik
behandel; *EVERYTHING is fair and* ~, alles is
eerlik; *GET* ~, werk tot op datum bring; *GET
things* ~, sake in die haak kry; sake agtermekaar
kry; *GET* ~ *with,* afreken met; inhaal; *a* ~ *PEG in
a round hole,* die verkeerde man op die verkeerde
plek; *meet with a* ~ *REFUSAL,* iets botweg ge=
weier word; ~ **bar,** vierkantstaaf; ~ **-bashing,** dril=
lery; ~ **bend,** haaks buigstuk; ~ **bit,** kruisboor; ~
bracket, vierkanthakie; ~ **-built,** vierkant; breedge=
skouer(d); ~ **d,** geruit; sterk gebou; ~ **dance,** ka=
driel; ~ **deal,** eerlike transaksie; ~ **-dealing,** eerlik=
heid, eerlike behandeling; ~ **d stone,** haaks klip;
~ **d timber,** gekantregte hout; ~ **degree,** graadvier=
kant; ~ **d paper,** ruitjiespapier; ~ **file,** blokvyl,
vierkantvyl; **S** ~ **head,** Duitser (spotnaam); ~ **-
headed,** met 'n vierkantige kop; ~ **inch,** vierkant=
duim; ~ **-jawed,** met 'n sterk ken; ~ **knot,** plat=
knoop, kruisknoop; ~ **leg,** rugby (kr.); ~ **-lipped
rhinoceros,** witrenoster; ~ **ly,** rondùit, eerlik; *treat*
~ *ly,* eerlik behandel; ~ **meal,** ('n) stewige maal; ~
measure, (opper)vlaktemaat, vierkantsmaat; ~
mouth, plat bek; ~ **ness,** eerlikheid; vierkantigheid;
~ **number,** kwadraatgetal; ~ **-rigged,** met raseile;
~ **root,** vierkantswortel, ~ **sail,** raseil; ~ **-
shouldered,** breed geskouer(d); ~ **stance,** lynstand;
reghoekige stand; ~ **-toed,** met vierkantige neus
(van 'n skoen); styf, vormlik; ~ **-toed shoe,** stomp=
neusskoen.
squa'ring, (die) haaks maak; kwadrering; vlakte=
maatberekening; ~ *ing of the circle,* kwadratuur
v.d. sirkel.
squash¹, (n) **(-es),** skorsie (groente); murg-van-groen=
te, vroeëpampoen.
squash², (n) sap, vrugtesap; kwas, suurlemoensap; ge=
drang; muurbal (sport); (v) kneus; platdruk, fyn=
maak; dooddruk, verbrysel; 'n kopskoot gee, die
mond snoer; ~ *someone,* iem. se mond snoer; iem.
'n kopskoot gee; ~ **court,** muurbalbaan; ~ **hat,**

pap hoed; ~ **iness,** papperigheid; ~ **rackets,** muur=
bal; ~ **y,** sag, papperig; platgedruk.
squat, (n) gehurkte houding; dikkerd, potjierol, vaat=
jie; (v) **(-ted),** neerhurk; neerlaat; ~ *down,* gaan sit
(op die hurke), neerhurk; (a) kort, kort en dik;
~ **closet,** hurkkloset; ~ **ter,** neerhurker; plakker;
kolonis; ~ **ter camp,** plakkerkamp; ~ **ter leader,**
plakkerleier; ~ **ter township,** plakkerbuurt; ~ **ting,**
(n) (die) hurk; plakkery; (a) gehurk.
squaw, (Indiaanse) vrou.
squawk, (n) gekrys, skreeu; (v) krys, skreeu, knars.
squeak, (n) gepiep, gegil; *it was a narrow* ~, dit was so
hittete; (v) knars; piep; gil; verklik; ~ **er,** pieper;
skreeuer; jong voël; verklikker; ~ **ing,** gepiep; ~ **y,**
pieperig; krakend; ~ *y voice,* piepstemmetjie.
squeal, (n) skreeu, gil; (v) tjank, gil; verklik, verkla;
~ **er,** skreeuer; jong voël; vark; verklikker, ver=
raaier; kermer, kermkous, klaer; ~ **ing,** geskreeu,
gegil; verklikkery; klaery, klaaglied.
squeam'ish, mislik; liggeraak; kieskeurig, puntenerig;
preuts; sedig; ~ **ness,** mislikheid; sedigheid; ligge=
raaktheid; puntenerigheid.
squee'gee, gomlastiekroller, aanstryker; gomlastiek=
spaan; waterbesem.
squeez'able, omarmbaar; uitdrukbaar.
squeeze, (n) druk(king); afpersing; kneusing; ge=
drang; afdruk; omarming; beperking, inkorting; *a*
~ *of the HAND,* 'n handdruk; *it was a TIGHT* ~,
dit was 'n groot gedrang; dit het knap gepas; (v)
druk; pers; vasdruk; uitpers, uitdruk; omhels; druk
uitoefen op; afdruk; ~ *to DEATH,* dooddruk; ~
someone DRY, iem. uitmelk; ~ *somebody's
HAND,* iem. se hand druk; ~ *MONEY out of* ~
MONEY from, geld losslaan van; geld pers uit; *a*
~ *d ORANGE,* 'n uitgedrukte lemoen; ~ *OUT,*
uitdruk; uitwring; ~ **r,** drukker; pers.
squelch, (n) slag; onaangename verrassing; kleitrap=
pery; doodhou; geklots; (v) verpletter; onderdruk;
tot swye bring, van stuk bring; smoor; deur modder
trap; kleitrap.
squib, (n) voetsoeker; sisser; klapper; skotskrif, paro=
die; *a damp* ~, 'n flou grap; (v) **(-bed),** 'n skotskrif
skrywe, hekel.
squid, pylinkvis.
squiff'y, (sl.) aangeklam, besope.
squil'gee = **squeegee.**
squill, seehiasint, sterhiasint; seeajuin.
squinch, (-es), hoekboog.
squint, (n) skeelheid; skeelkykery, kykie; *HAVE a* ~,
skeel kyk; *TAKE a* ~ *at,* kyk na, effentjies loer na;
(v) skeel kyk; oormekaar kyk; skeel wees; loer; (a)
skeel; ~ **er,** skeelkyker; ~ **-eyed,** skeeloog=, skeel=
kwaadaardig; *slightly* ~ *-eyed,* soetskeel; ~ **ing,** (n)
skeelkykery; (a) skeelkykend, skeel; boosaardig; ~
window, dakvenstertjie.
squire, (n) landedelman; skildknaap; (v) begelei;
~ **'archy,** landadel.
squirm, (n) kronkeling, gekronkel; (v) kruip, kriewel,
inmekaarkrimp, kronkel, wurm.
squi'rrel, eekhoring, eekhorinkie.
squirt, (n) spuitjie; straal(tjie); windmaker, windbuks,
grootprater; (v) (be)spuit; uitspuit; ~ **er,** spuit;
grootprater; ~ **ing,** gespuit.
stab, (n) steek, dolksteek; dodelike slag, belediging;
belastering; *a* ~ *in the back,* 'n steek in die rug, 'n
verraderlike aanval; (v) **(-bed),** steek, deursteek,
doodsteek; prik; wond, bitter seermaak; ~ *some=
one in the BACK,* iem. in die rug steek; ~ *to
DEATH,* doodsteek; ~ *to the HEART,* 'n dolk in
die hart stoot; in die diepste van die siel tref; ~ **-awl,**
steekels; ~ **ber,** steker; messteker; sluipmoorde=
naar; dolk; ~ **bing,** stekery; ~ **bing stitch,** deur=
druksteek.
stabil'ity, vastheid, vastigheid, standvastigheid, sta=
biliteit, bestendigheid.
stabiliza'tion, stabilisasie, stabielmaking, bestendi=
ging.
stab'ilize, bestendig, stabiliseer; ~ **r,** stabilisator; rol=
demper (motor); stabilisasievlak (vliegtuig).
stab'ilizing, stabiliserend.
sta'ble¹, (n) stal; renperde; (pl) staldiens; stalparade
(v) op stal hou (sit); op stal staan.

sta'ble², (a) duursaam; standvastig, vasberade, stabiel; bestendig (skeik.); ~ **market**, bestendige mark.

sta'ble: ~-**bar**, stalboom; ~-**boy**, staljong, stalkneg; ~-**broom**, stalbesem; ~-**bucket**, stalemmer; ~-**companion**, stalmaat; kamermaat; klubmaat; ~-**door**, bo-en-onderdeur; staldeur; *lock the ~-door after the horse has been stolen,* die put demp nadat die kalf verdrink het; ~ **duties**, staldiens; ~-**guard**, stalwag; ~-**hand**, ~-**help**, staljong; ~-**horse**, stalperd; ~-**keeper**, stalkneg; ~-**lantern**, stallantern; ~ **man**, stalkneg, staljong; ~-**manure**, stalmis; ~ **odour**, stallug, stalruik; ~-**pail**, stalemmer; ~-**prong**, stalvurk; ~ **rent**, stalhuur; ~-**yard**, stalwerf.

stab'ling, stalle, stalgeleentheid, stalling.

stab' stitch, deurdruksteek.

stacca'to, staccato.

stack, (n) mied; groep skoorstene; massa; stapel, hoop; ~ *of corn,* koringmied; (v) mied pak; opstapel; op 'n hoop dra; ophoop; ~ *ARMS,* gewere koppel; ~ *AWAY,* wegbêre; ~-**burn**, miedbrand; ~**ed**, gestapel(de); ~ **er**, miedpakker; ~ **gas**, skoorsteengas; ~**ing**, (die) pak (mied); stapeling; ~-**stand**, miedstellasie; ~-**yard**, hooikamp.

stad'ium, (..dia), stadion.

stad(t)'holder, stadhouer; ~'**s**, stadhouerlik; ~ **ship**, stadhouerskap.

staff, (n) staf (mil.); personeel (skool, kantoor); kierie, stok; (note)balk (musiek); steun, stut; *the ~ of someone's old AGE,* die steun in iem. se ouderdom; *EDITORIAL* ~, redaksie; *GENERAL* ~, generale staf; *INCREASE of* ~, personeeluitbreiding; *bread is the ~ of LIFE,* brood is 'n onontbeerlike voedsel; *ON the* ~, op die personeel (skool, kantoor); *REDUCTION of* ~, personeelverminde= ring; *SOMEONE'S* ~, iem. se stut en steun; (v) van personeel voorsien; van 'n staf voorsien (mil.); beman; ~ **captain**, stafkaptein; ~ **car**, personeelmotor; ~ **clerk**, personeelklerk; ~ **college**, hoër krygskool, stafkollege; ~ **corps**, stafkorps; ~ **cutback**, personeelvermindering; ~ **discount**, personeelafslag; ~ **expenses**, personeeluitgawes, uitgawes aan personeel; ~ **ing**, personeelvoorsiening; ~-**like**, stafvormig; ~ **method**, noteskrif; ~ **notation**, notebalkskrif; ~ **nurse**, stafverpleegster; ~ **office**, personeelkantoor; ~ **officer**, stafoffisier; ~ **room**, personeelkamer; ~ **sergeant**, stafsersant; ~ **writer**, vaste medewerker (aan 'n blad).

stag, takbok, hert; bulos; kalkoenmannetjie; ramhamel; voorspekulant; (v) spekuleer; ~-**beetle**, vlieënde hert.

stage, (n) toneel; verhoog; steier, stellasie, stadium; fase; trap, graad; trek, skof, trajek; halte; *APPEAR on the* ~, op die planke optree; *AT that* ~, op daardie tydstip; *BRING upon the* ~, opvoer, op die planke bring; *hold the CENTRE of the* ~, alle aandag trek; *(travel) by EASY* ~ *s,* met kort dagreise, rus-rus; *this is the FIRST* ~, dit is die eerste trek; *GO off the* ~, die planke verlaat; *GO on the* ~, op die toneel gaan; toneelspeler word; *IN* ~ *s,* geleidelik; *OFF* ~, af; agter die skerms; *ON* ~, op; *PUT on the* ~, op die planke bring; *QUIT the* ~, van die toneel verdwyn; die toneel verlaat; *SET the* ~, die toneel inrig; *THE* ~, die toneelwese; (v) opvoer; op die planke (toneel) bring; ensceneer; in trekke ry; op tou sit, aan die gang sit; ~ *a STRIKE,* 'n staking begin; ~ *a WALK-OUT,* uitstap; ~-**box**, loge; ~ **career**, toneelloopbaan; ~-**coach**, poskoets; poswa; ~-**craft**, toneelkuns; ~ **critic**, toneelbeoordelaar; ~ **curtain**, toneelskerm; ~ **decoration**, toneelversiering; ~ **direction**, toneelaanwysing; ~ **director**, verhoogdirekteur; ~ **door**, toneelingang, artieste-ingang; ~ **dress**, toneelkostuum; ~ **driver**, posryer, poskoetsdrywer; ~ **fever**, toneelmanie, toneelkoors; plankekoors, verhoogvrees; ~ **fright**, plankevrees, verhoogvrees; ~-**hand**, toneelhelper; ~ **hero**, teaterheld; ~-**manage**, ensceneer; ~ **management**, regie, toneelleiding; verhoogbestuur; ~ **manager**, toneeldirekteur; verhoogbestuurder; ~ **name**, toneelnaam; ~ **painter**, toneelskilder; ~ **play**, toneelspel; ~ **player**, toneelspeler; ~ **properties**, toneelbenodigdhede; ~**r**, ervare toneelspeler; monteur; *old* ~**r**, veteraan; ~ **right**, reg van opvoering; ~**ry**, toneelvertoning; ~ **setting**, toneelinkleding; ~ **star**, toneelster; ~ **set**, dekor; stel; ~-**struck**, toneelmal; versot op die toneel; ~ **version**, bewerking vir die toneel.

stag' evil, klem in die kake (by perde).

stage: ~ **whisper**, hoorbare gefluister; ~ **writer**, dramaturg; toneelskrywer; ~**y**, teatraal, toneelmatig.

stagfla'tion, stagflasie.

stagg'er, (n) wankeling, waggeling; waggelende gang; verspringing; *the* ~ *s,* duiseligheid; (v) waggel, wankel; weifel, aarsel; dronkslaan, versteld laat staan, verbluf; verspring (plante); versprei (vakansies); ~ *ALONG,* aansteier; ~ *INTO,* inslinger; ~ *the SCHOOL HOLIDAYS,* skoolvakansies versprei; ~**ed**, versteld, verstom; trapsgewyse; gesprei; verspringend; ~**ed holidays**, verspreide vakansies; ~**ed rows**, verspringde (skuins) rye; ~**ing**, (n) waggeling, verspringing; (ver)spreiding; wisseltyd; slingering; (a) waggelend; wankelend; verbluffend, skokkend, verbysterend; *a ~ ing blow,* 'n geweldige slag; ~**s**, dronksiekte, malkopsiekte, draaisiekte.

stagg'ing, spekulasie.

stag: ~-**headed**, met 'n kaal kop; ~-**horn**, herthoring; ~**hound**, windhond; herthond; ~-**hunting**, hertejag.

sta'ging, opvoering; montering; stellasie, steier.

stag' knees, bokkneë.

stag'nant, stilstaande (water); stagnant; lusteloos, traag; ~ **air**, dooie lug.

stag'nate, stilstaan, stagneer; traag word.

stagna'tion, stilstand, gebrek aan bedrywigheid, stagnasie.

stag' party, ramparty; kool sonder spek.

sta'gy, teatraal, toneelmatig.

staid, besadig, ernstig, bedaard, stemmig; nugter; ~**ness**, besadigdheid, bedaardheid, stemmigheid; nugterheid.

stain, (n) vlek; klad, spat(sel), smet; kleur, tint, verf; blaam, skandvlek; *without a ~ on one's character,* met 'n onbevlekte karakter; (v) vlek, besmet, verf; bemors, smeer, besoedel, beklad; beits (hout); brandskilder (glas); ~**ed**, besoedel, besmet, gevlek; gekleur, gebrand (glas); gebeits (hout); ~**ed GLASS**, gebrandskilderde glas; ~**ed WOOD**, gebeitste hout; ~ **er**, verwer; besoedelaar; brandskilder; beitser; kleurder; ~**ing**, kleuring, brandskilder; beitsing (hout); brandskildering; ~**less**, rein, skoon, vlekloos; onbesoedeld, smetloos, roesvry, vlekvry (staal); ~*less steel,* vlekvrye staal; ~-**removal**, vlekverwydering; ~-**remover**, vlekverwyderaar, ontvlekkingsmiddel; ~-**resistant**, vlekbestand.

stair, trap, tree; (pl) trap; *BELOW* ~ *s,* ondertoe; onder; *DOWN* ~ *s,* onder; *a FLIGHT of* ~ *s,* 'n trap; *UP* ~ *s,* bo; op die solder; ~-**carpet**, traploper; ~-**case**, trap; ~-**flight**, traparm; ~-**hall**, trapportaal; ~-**head**, trapkop; ~-**landing**, oorloop; ~-**railing**, trapleuning; ~-**rod**, traproede, trapkleedstafie; ~-**rug**, traploper; ~-**step**, trappie; ~ **way**, trap.

stake, (n) paal, staak; brandstapel; handaambeeld; plaat, wedgeld, inset, pot, prys; aandeel; (pl) speelgeld; potgeld, inleggelde, inset; *have everything AT* ~, alles veil hê; *be CONDEMNED to the* ~, tot die brandstapel veroordeel word; *have a ~ in a COUNTRY,* eiendom in 'n land besit; *DIE at the* ~, op die brandstapel sterf; *our FREEDOM is at* ~, ons vryheid is op die spel; *HAVE a ~ in,* belange hê in; geïnteresseer wees in; *your LIFE is at* ~, jou lewe is op die spel; jou lewe hang daarvan af; *there is MUCH at* ~, daar is baie op die spel; (v) afpaal, ompaal, afbaken; stut; waag; vaspen; aan 'n paal vasbind; wed; ~ *out a CLAIM,* 'n kleim afpen; ~ *EVERYTHING,* alles waag; ~ *EVERYTHING on one throw,* alles op een kaart waag; ~-**boat**, vasleënde boot; ~**holder**, deelhebber; insethouer, pothouer; ~-**net**, staaknet.

stak'ing chisel, stuikyster.

stal'actite, (hangende) druipsteen, stalaktiet; ~ **cave**, druipkelder.

stal'agmite, (staande) druipsteen, stalagmiet.

stale¹, (n) lokvoël; voorwerp van bespotting.

stale², (v) verslyt; muf word; uitgeput raak; uitput; water (dier); (a) oud, vermuf (brood); verslete, afgesaag (grap); verswak, verskaal (bier); suf, oorspeel (persoon); bevange (perd); verjaar (tjek); *that is* ~ *NEWS*, dis ou nuus; *TURN* ~, verslaan, verskaal (bier); ~ **bread,** ou brood; ~ **cheque,** verjaarde tjek; ~ **joke,** afgesaagde grap.
stale'mate, (n) pat (skaak); dooie punt; skaakmat; (v) pat sit; in die knyp bring, vaskeer, op 'n dooie punt bring.
stale'ness, vermuftheid, oudheid.
stale' news, ou nuus.
Stal'inism, Stalinisme.
stalk¹, (n) steel, halm, stingel (plant); skag (van veer).
stalk², (n) deftigte stap; (die) bekruip, bekruiping; bekruipery; (v) deftig stap; wild bekruip (betrek).
stalk'-borer, stronkboorder, stronkruspe(r).
stalk: ~ **er,** sluipjagter; ~ **ing,** (n) bekruiping; statige (stywe) stap; (a) bekruip=; ~ **ing-cap,** bekruipmus, jagmus; ~ **ing-horse,** jagperd, skietperd; voorwendsel; *be made a* ~ *-horse*, as sondebok gebruik word; as skuifmeul gebruik word.
stalk: ~ **less,** steelloos; stingelloos; ~ **like,** stingelvormig; ~ **y,** steelagtig; stingelrig.
stall¹, (n) handlanger, sakkerollersmaat.
stall², (n) stalletjie, kraam; kiosk; uitstalplank; toonbank; stal, hok; staking (motor); vertraging; koorbank; koorstoel; werkplek (myn); (pl) stalles (in teater); (v) op stal sit; vaslê, vassit; staak, gaan staan (motor); deursak, oortrek (vliegtuig); *the engine* ~ *ed*, die enjin het gaan staan (doodgeraak, gestaak); ~ **age,** stalgeld; staangeld, staanplek; ~ **fed,** in die stal gevoer, stal=; ~ **-feed, (, , fed),** vetvoer; ~ **ing,** (n) (die) stilstaan, doodgaan, staking (enjin); stalling; (a) deursak=; ~ **ing-point,** deursakpunt; ~ **ing-speed,** deursaksnelheid, staakspoed.
stall'ion, hings.
stall'-keeper, houer van 'n stalletjie.
stal'wart, (n) staatmaker, getroue; ringkop; (a) kragtig, stoer, swaar gebou; fris; flink, stoutmoedig; vasberade, standvastig.
stam'en, meeldraad, stamen.
stam'ina, stamina, uithouvermoë, weerstandsvermoë, volhardingsvermoë, aanhouvermoë.
stam'inate, met meeldrade, bemeeldraad.
staminif'erous, meeldraad=, met meeldrade.
stamm'er, (n) gehakkel, gestotter; (v) stamel, hakkel, stotter; ~ **er,** hakkelaar, stotteraar, stamelaar; ~ **ing,** (n) gehakkel, gestamel; (a) hakkelrig, stotterend, stamelend.
stamp, (n) stempel, seël; merk; yk, ykmerk; stempelafdruk; waarmerk; posseël; prent; soort, karakter, stamper (meul); *BEAR the* ~ *of*, die stempel dra van; *MEN of that* ~, manne van dié soort; *SET one's* ~ *upon*, jou stempel druk op; (v) stamp; fyn stamp; stempel, merk, waarmerk; opdruk; 'n posseël plak op, frankeer; ~ *as a COWARD*, as 'n lafaard brandmerk; ~ *one's FOOT*, met die voet stamp; ~ *ON*, plat trap; ~ *OUT*, uittrap, uittrap, doodtrap (vuur); ~ **-act,** seëlwet; ~ **-album,** posseëlalbum; ~ **-battery,** stampbattery; stampery; ~ **-booklet,** posseëlboekie; ~ **-cancelling machine,** rojeermasjien; ~ **-case,** posseëldosie, posseëlsakkie; ~ **-collecting,** (die) versamel van posseëls, filatelie; ~ **collection,** posseëlversameling, ~ **-collector,** posseëlversamelaar, filatelis; ~ **-cutter,** stempelsnyer; ~ **-damper,** posseëlbevogtiger, seëllekker; ~ **-dealer,** posseëlhandelaar; ~ **-duty,** seëlreg; ~ **ed,** gefrankeer; gestempel, gedruk; ~ *ed leather*, goudleer; ~ *ed paper*, geseëlde papier.
stampede', (n) paniek, skielike vlug, wilde vlug; stormloop, toeloop; (v) in 'n paniek vlug (dierc); wanordelik vlug; op loop sit, weghol; ~ *the police*, die polisie platloop.
stamp: ~ **er,** stamper; stempel; ~ **-hinge,** seëllakker.
stamp'ing, gestamp; stempeling; ~ **-ground,** rolplek, houplek; ~ **-machine,** stempelmasjien; rojeermasjien; ~ **-mill,** stampmeule.
stamp: ~ **mill,** stampmeule, stampery; ~ **-mount,** plakstrokie; ~ **-office,** seëlkantoor; ~ **-pad,** stempelkussing; ~ **-paper,** geseëlde papier; posseëlpapier; ~ **tax,** seëlbelasting.

stance, houding, posisie, stand; staanposisie (gholf).
stanch, (n) stelping, stolling; stuiting; stelpmiddel; (v) stelp, laat stol, laat ophou met vloei.
sta'nchion, (n) steunpaal; steunbeuel; styl; paal; stut; (v) stut, van stutte voorsien; aan 'n paal bind.
stanch: ~ **less,** nie te help nie; ~ **ness,** beginselvastheid; trou, gehegtheid; *kyk* **staunch.**
stand, (n) stand, posisie; staanplek; erf, standplaas; stilstand; standpunt; stelling; weerstand; standertjie; staander; tribune; pawiljoen; verhoog; kraampie, stalletjie; onderstel, raamwerk; rak; voetstuk; dikte (van gesaaides); ~ *of ARMS*, stel wapens; volledige bewapening; *BRING to a* ~, tot stilstand bring; *COME to a* ~, tot stilstand kom; *MAKE a* ~ *against*, weerstand bied, vasskop, vastrap; *a fine* ~ *of MEALIES*, 'n mooi lap mielies; *TAKE one's* ~ *on*, 'n standpunt inneem oor; stelling inneem teen; *TAKE a firm* ~, sterk stelling inneem; 'n standpunt inneem; *I take my* ~ *on the WORDING of the act*, ek gaan uit v.d. bewoording v.d. wet; (v) **(stood),** staan; gaan staan; bly stilstaan; laat staan; van krag wees; bestand wees teen; weerstaan; opstel; veel, uithou, verdra; deurstaan; kandidaat wees, jou kandidaat stel; trakteer, betaal; toelaat; ~ *ABOUT*, rondstaan; ~ *AGAINST*, weerstaan; bestand wees teen; jou kandidaat stel teen; staan teen; ~ *ALOOF*, jou op 'n afstand hou; ~ *under ARMS*, onder die wapen wees; ~ *ASIDE*, opsy staan; ~ *to ATTENTION*, op aandag staan; ~ *in AWE of somebody*, vir iem. bang wees (ontsag hê); ~ *BACK for no one*, vir niemand agteruitstaan nie; ~ *in the BREACH*, in die bres staan; *BUY as it* ~ *s*, voetstoots koop; ~ *BY someone*, iem bystaan; lojaal wees teenoor; ~ *BY*, daarby staan; opsy gaan; jou gereedmaak om te help; bystaan, tersy staan; vashou aan; klaar wees om te help; ~ *on CEREMONY*, op formaliteite gesteld wees; ~ *a good CHANCE*, 'n goeie kans hê; ~ *CLEAR*, opsy staan; *these CONDITIONS still* ~, hierdie voorwaardes bly nog van krag; ~ *in DANGER*, gevaar loop; ~ *on one's DEFENCE*, jou kragtig weer; ~ *in DOUBT*, twyfel, ~ *DOWN*, ondertoe loop; gaan sit, nie meer saamspeel nie; jou kandidatuur intrek, terugstaan; ~ *DRINKS*, op drank trakteer; ~ *at EASE*, op die plek rus; ~ *EASY!* rus! ~ *or FALL by*, staan of val met; ~ *FAST*, vasstaan, bly staan, standhou; *I can't* ~ *the FELLOW*, ek kan die vent nie verdra (veel) nie; ~ *FIRM*, vastrap, pal staan; ~ *FIRST*, eerste wees; ~ *FOR*, verteenwoordig; 'n voorstander wees van; ~ *FORTH*, vorentoe kom; ~ *to GAIN by*, kans hê om wins te maak; ~ *one's GROUND*, jou man staan; ~ *to one's GUNS*, standhou, voet by stuk hou; ~ *HIGH with*, baie in die guns wees by; ~ *IN for someone*, vir iem. as plaasvervanger optree; ~ *a JOKE*, 'n grap verdra; *as the MATTER now* ~ *s*, soos die saak nou is, *he* ~ *s two METERS*, hy is twee meter lank; *he won't* ~ *any NONSENSE*, hy sal nie nonsies verdra nie; ~ *under heavy OBLIGATIONS*, swaar verpligtinge hê, ~ *OFF*, opsy staan; op 'n afstand bly; ~ *for OFFICE*, kandidaat wees; ~ *ON*, staan op; herus op; ~ *OUT*, uitpuil (oë); nie meedoen nie; volhou; vorentoe kom; ~ *OUT in relief*, skerp afgeteken wees; ~ *OUT against*, vasstaan teen; ~ *OUT above others*, onder ander uitblink; ~ *OUT for*, ywer vir; ~ *OVER*, oorstaan, uitgestel word, voorlopig wag; ~ *for PARLIAMENT*, kandidaat vir die Parlement wees; ~ *PAT upon*, van niks wil weet nie as; ~ *by a POLICY*, 'n beleid handhaaf; *the PROMISE* ~ *s*, die belofte bly van krag; ~ *by a PROMISE*, jou belofte gestand doen; *it* ~ *s to REASON*, dit spreek vanself; ~ *on one's RIGHTS*, vir jou regte opkom; *unable to* ~ *the SIGHT of somebody*, iem. nie voor jou oë kan verdra nie; ~ *in good STEAD*, goed te pas kom; ~ *the moral TEST*, die toets van sedelikheid deurstaan; ~ *TOGETHER*, bymekaarstaan; ~ *a TREAT*, trakteer; ~ *one's TRIAL*, teregstaan; *be UNABLE to* ~ *someone*, iem. nie kan veel nie; iem. nie kan verdra nie; ~ *UP*, opstaan; ~ *UP for*, verdedig; opkom vir; jou inspan vir; ~ *UP to someone*, jou handhaaf teen iem.; jou man staan; ~ *UP to hard wear*,

kwaai slytasie weerstaan; ~ *UP for oneself*, jou regte eis; jou handhaaf teenoor ander; ~ *it against the WALL*, sit dit teen die muur; ~ *in someone's WAY*, in iem. se pad staan; *let nothing* ~ *in one's WAY*, niks in jou pad laat staan nie; ~ *WELL with*, goed aangeskrewe staan by; *to wish to know WHERE one* ~ *s*, wil weet waar jy aan of af is; *show WHERE one* ~ *s*, kleur beken.

stan'dard, (n) standerd (skool); standaard, norm, vereiste, peil, maatstaf, gehalte; banier, vaan; kolom; ysterpaal; stander; staanpaal; rong (wa); *BELOW* ~, benede peil; ~ *of COMPARISON*, vergelykingsnorm; ~ *of LIFE*, lewenstandaard; ~ *of LIVING*, lewenstandaard, lewenspeil; *his work was of a LOW* ~, sy werk was van 'n lae gehalte; *RAISE the* ~, die peil verhoog; *he is in* ~ *SIX*, hy is in standerd ses; *UP to* ~, op peil; (a) standaard-; vas, onveranderlik; stam-, hoogstammig; ~**-bearer,** vaandeldraer; ~ **boiler,** standaardketel; ~ **brick,** standaardsteen; ~ **deviation,** standaardafwyking; ~ **gauge,** standaardkaliber, standaardmaat; ~**-gauge railway,** standaardspoor; ~ **grade,** standaardgraad; ~**iza'tion,** vasstelling, normalisering, standaardisering; ~**ize,** normaliseer, standaardiseer; yk; ~ **lamp,** staanlamp; ~ **practice,** standaardpraktyk, algemene praktyk; ~ **price,** standaardprys; ~ **pronunciation,** standaarduitspraak; ~ **publication,** standaarduitgawe; ~ **rose,** stamroos; ~ **size,** standaardgrootte; ~ **time,** standaardtyd; ~ **wage,** standaardloon; ~ **weight,** standaardgewig; ~ **width,** standaardwydte, normale wydte; ~ **work,** standaardwerk.
stand'-by, steun, stut, bystand; gereedheid; staatmaker; reserwe; noodhulp; ~ **time,** gereeddiens.
stand'-in, invaller, plaasvervanger, dubbelganger.
stan'ding, (n) uithouding; rang, stand; standaard; duur; (die) staan; posisie, naam; staanplek; *in GOOD* ~, van goeie naam; *a man of HIGH* ~, 'n persoon van aansien; *of LONG* ~, lank gevestig, baie oud; (a) staande, stilstaande; duursaam; stereotiep; erken, vasgestel, vas, bepaald; *do something* ~ *on one's HEAD*, iets fluit-fluit (baie maklik) doen; *a* ~ *JOKE*, 'n ou grap; *place a* ~ *ORDER*, 'n vaste bestelling plaas; *a* ~ *PHRASE*, 'n geykte uitdrukking; *a* ~ *RULE*, 'n vaste (staande) reël; ~ **army,** staande leër; ~ **committee,** vaste (staande) komitee; ~ **jib,** kluiwer; ~ **ladder,** staanleer, trapleer; ~ **offer,** vaste aanbod; ~ **orders,** reglement van orde; ~**-place,** staanplek; ~**-room,** staanplek, staanruimte; ~ **vice,** bankskroef; ~ **water,** staande water.
stand'-off, eenkant; ~ **half,** losskakel; ~**ish,** gereserveerd(d), uit die hoogte, ongenaakbaar, terughoudend, hoogmoedig; *be* ~*ish with someone*, terughoudend wees; iem. op 'n afstand hou.
stand: ~ **owner,** erfeienaar; stalletjiehouer; ~**-pipe,** standpyp; ~**point,** standpunt, gesigspunt.
stand'still, stilstand; *BRING to a* ~, laat stilstaan, tot stilstand bring; *COME to a* ~, tot stilstand kom; halt; *WORK oneself to a* ~, werk dat jy die kromme note haal; jou oorhoeks werk.
stand'-to, oggendparade.
stand'-up, regop; hewig, kwaai; *a* ~ *fight*, 'n kwaai geveg; ~ **bar,** staankroeg; ~ **meal,** ~ **supper,** buffetete.
stan'iel, toringvalk.
stank, *kyk* **stink** (v).
stann'ery, (n) (..ries), tinmyn; tinfabriek; (a) tin-.
stann'ic, tinagtig, tin-; ~ **acid,** tinsuur.
stannif'erous, tinhoudend.
stann'iol, stanniool.
stan'nite, tinkies, stanniet.
stann'ous, tinhoudend; tin-.
stan'za, stansa, vers.
stapes, stiebeuel (in oor).
sta'ple¹, (n) kram; *HASP and* ~, kram en oorslag; ~ *and HOOK*, kram en haak; (v) vaskram, met 'n kram vassit.
sta'ple², (n) stapel, wollengte; hoofproduk, hoofbestanddeel, hoofskottel; mark; draad; *wool of fine* ~, wol van 'n fyn draad; (v) sorteer, klassifiseer; (a) vernaamste, hoof-; ~ **commodity,** stapelartikel; ~ **fibre,** houtwolvesel; ~ **food,** volksvoedsel, hoofvoedsel; ~ **length,** stapellengte.
sta'pler¹, krammasjien; kramtang; kramdrukker; kramskieter.
sta'pler², wolsorteerder.
stap'ling machine, krammasjien; kramtang.
star, (n) ster; sterretjie, asterisk; filmster, toneelster; beroemdheid, beroemde kunstenaar, hooffiguur; kol (op dier se voorkop); *the* ~*s were AGAINST it*, die noodlot wou dit nie hê nie; *his* ~ *is in the ASCENDANT*, dit gaan voor die wind met hom; hy maak opgang; ~ *of BETHLEHEM*, die ster van Betlehem; voëlmelk, môrester (plant); *BORN under an unlucky* ~, onder 'n ongelukkige gesternte gebore; *FIXED* ~ *s*, vaste sterre; *I SAW* ~ *s*, ek het sterretjies gesien; *make someone SEE* ~ *s*, iem. sterretjies laat sien; iem. slaan dat hy sy ouma vir 'n eendvoël aansien; *SHOOTING* ~, vallende ster; *the S* ~ *s and STRIPES*, die Amerikaanse vlag; *you may THANK your* ~ *s*, jy kan van geluk praat; jy kan dankie sê; *UNLUCKY* ~, ongelukster; (v) (-red), met sterre tooi; van 'n sterretjie voorsien; as vernaamste speler (speelster) optree; die hoofrol speel; ~ **attraction,** hoofaantrekkingskrag; glansitem; ~**-blind,** bysiende.
star'board, stuurboord; *on the* ~ *side*, aan stuurboord.
star' burr, sterklits.
star: ~**-chart,** sterrekaart; ~**-coral,** sterkoraal; ~**dom,** sterstatus; ~ **dust,** sterregewemel.
starch, (n) stysel; setmeel; styfheid; vormlikheid; (v) stywe.
starch: ~**ed,** gestyf; ~ **factory,** styselfabriek; ~ **grain,** styselkorrel; ~**iness,** styselagtigheid, setmeelagtigheid; styfheid; ~ **paste,** plakstysel; ~ **sugar,** dekstrose; ~ **water,** styselwater; ~**y,** vol stysel; styselagtig; styf; ~**y food,** styselkos.
stare, (n) starende blik; (v) staar, aanstaar, aangaap; staroog; ~ *AT*, aanstaar; ~ *AT something with fixed intensity*, iets strak aankyk; ~ *someone out of COUNTENANCE*, iem. so aanstaar dat hy verleë word; ~ *a person DOWN*, iem. aanstaar totdat hy verleë word; iem. die oë laat neerslaan; ~ *someone in the FACE*, iem. aanstaar; *FAMINE* ~ *d them in the face*, hongersnood was hulle voorland; ~**r,** aanstaarder; kyker.
star: ~**-finch,** rooistertjie; ~**fish,** seester; ~**-flower,** sewester; ~**-gazer,** sterrekyker; dromer; ~**-gazing,** (n) sterrekykery; dromery; verstrooidheid; (a) dromerig; ~ **globe,** sterrebol.
star'ing, aangapend, starend; skel, opsigtig (kleure); ~ **coat,** deurmekaar haarkleed; ~ **hair,** kroeshare; ~ **mad,** stapelgek; ~ **red,** opsigtig rooi, knalrooi.
stark, styf, strak, stram; volslae; star, onbuigsaam; *and stiff*, stokstyf; (adv) heeltemal, gans; louter; ~ **blind,** stokblind; ~ **dead,** morsdood; ~ **facts,** naakte feite; ~ **mad,** stapelgek; ~ **madness,** totale kranksinnigheid; ~**-naked,** moedernaak, sonder 'n draad aan, poedelnakend.
star: ~**less,** sterloos, sonder sterre; ~**let,** sterretjie; jong (beginnende) aktrise; ~**light,** sterlig; ~**like,** soos 'n ster, ster-.
starl'ing¹, spreeu.
starl'ing², stroombreker (brug).
star: ~**lit,** sterverlig; ~ **pistol,** ligpistool; ~**red,** gester; ~ **runner,** steratleet; sterhardloper.
star'ry, met sterre besaai, sterre-; ~**-eyed,** te idealisties; ~ **heavens,** sterrehemel; ~ **host,** sterreheer; ~ **light,** sterlig; ~**-lit,** sterverlig; ~ **splendour,** sterreprag.
star: ~**-shaped,** stervormig; ~ **shell,** liggranaat; ~**-shine,** sterrelig; ~**-shower,** sterrereën; ~**-spangled,** met sterre besaai; *the* ~**-spangled banner,** die Amerikaanse vlag; ~**-stone,** stersaffier.
start, (n) begin, aanvang, staanspoor; voorsprong; ruk, skielike beweging, skrikbeweging; (die) wegspring; wegspringplek, beginpaal, beginstreep; *AT the* ~, in die begin; *a BAD* ~, 'n slegte begin; *be at the* ~ *of one's CAREER*, aan die begin van jou loopbaan wees; *make an EARLY* ~, vroeg begin; *a FALSE* ~, 'n verkeerde begin; *from* ~ *to FINISH*, v.d. begin tot die end; *by FITS and* ~ *s*, met rukke

en stote; *give a* ~ *in LIFE*, aan die gang (op die been) help; *be off to a FLYING* ~, dadelik 'n voorsprong hê; *FOR a* ~, om mee te begin; *FOR a* ~ *I wish to say*, om mee te begin, wil ek opmerk; *make a FRESH* ~, opnuut begin; *FROM the* ~, v.d. begin; uit die staanspoor (uit); *GIVE a* ~, laat skrik; *GIVE a* ~ *to*, in beweging (aan die gang) sit; *GIVE someone a* ~ *(in a race)*, iem. voorgee (in 'n wedloop); *HAVE the* ~ *of a person*, iem. voor wees, 'n voorsprong hê op iem.; *MAKE a* ~, begin; aanstaltes maak; *MAKE a good* ~, goed begin; *get the* ~ *of one's RIVALS*, 'n voorsprong op jou mededingers hê; *get off to a SLOW* ~, stadig begin (wegspring); *WITH a* ~, met 'n ruk; *give someone fifteen YARDS* ~, iem. vyftien tree voorgee; (v) begin, vertrek; lanseer; skrik; opspring; wegspring, hardloop; oprig; opper, opwerp; opjaag (wild); aansit, aanskakel (motor); aan die gang sit, op tou sit; ~ *BACK*, terugskrik: ~ *BUSINESS*, 'n saak begin; ~ *a COMPANY*, 'n maatskappy oprig; ~ *CRYING*, aan die huil gaan; ~ *from a DREAM*, uit 'n droom wakker skrik; ~ *a FIRE*, vuur maak; brand stig; ~ *on a JOURNEY*, 'n reis begin; ~ *LAUGHING*, aan die lag gaan; ~ *something OFF*, iets aan die gang sit; ~ *ON*, begin met; ~ *READING*, begin lees; *RIVALS* ~ *ed up*, mededingers het op die toneel verskyn; ~ *with a clean SHEET*, met 'n skoon lei begin; ~ *from one's SLEEP*, wakker skrik; ~ *UP*, skrik; opspring; *to* ~ *WITH*, om mee te begin; ~ *WORK on*, begin werk aan; ~ *WORKING*, begin werk; ~ *off on the WRONG foot*, verkeerd begin; ~ **button**, aansitknoppie.
start'er, aanjaer; aansitter (motor); afsetter (sport); seingeër, tekengeër; deelnemer; trapaansitter; plantjie, suursel; beginnermeel; *doubtful* ~, onsekere beginner; ~ **button**, aansitknop; ~ **motor**, aansitmotor; ~**'s pistol**, afsetpistool; ~ **switch**, aansitskakelaar.
start'ing, skrik; vertrek, begin; wegspring; ~**-cable**, aansitkabel; trekkabel, ~ **clutch**, aansitkoppelaar; ~**-crank**, slinger; ~**-gate**, wegspringhek; ~**-gear**, aansitwerk; ~**-handle**, ~**-lever**, aansitslinger; ~ **motor**, aansitmotor, aansitter; ~**-pen**, wegspringhok; ~**-place**, beginplek, wegspringplek; ~**-point**, staanspoor; uitgangspunt, wegspringplek, afspringplek; ~**-post**, wegspringpaal; ~ **power**, aansitvermoë; ~ **price**, insetprys; baanweddenskap; ~ **salary**, beginsalaris; ~**-signal**, vertreksein; wegspringsein; ~ **switch**, aansitskakelaar; ~**-valve**, aansitklep.
star'tle, skrikmaak, ontstel, verbaas, laat skrik, verras, verbluf; ~**r**, verrassing; iets verbasingwekkends; skrikmaker.
start'ling, ontstellend, skrikwekkend, sensasioneel, opsienbarend, verrassend.
star: ~ **trap**, stervormige valluik; ~ **tube**, sterbuisie; ~ **turn**, glansnommer; hoofrol.
starva'tion, uithongering; gebrek; hongersnood; uitgehongerdheid; *die of* ~, van honger sterf; ~**-diet**, hongerdieet; ~ **wages**, hongerloon.
starve, uithonger, laat gebrek ly; van honger omkom, verhonger, laat wegkwyn (uitteer); - *to DEATH*, van honger (laat) omkom; ~ *for KNOWLEDGE*, hunker na kennis; ~ *into SURRENDER*, deur honger tot oorgawe dwing; ~**d**, uitgehonger, verhonger; ~ **ling**, (n) uitgehongerde mens (dier), hongerlyer; (a) kwynend, armoedig, maer.
starv'ing, doodhonger; *be* ~, verhonger, so honger dat jy 'n spyker se kop kan afeet (afbyt).
star: ~ **watch**, stuurboordwag; ~ **wheel**, sterrat; ~**-worship**, sterrediens, astrolatrie; ~**-worshipper**, sterredienaar; ~ **wort**, sterroos.
state¹, (n) staat, land; toestand, gesteldheid; luister, prag, statigheid, staatsie; staatsmag, ryk; afdruk (ets); rang; *AFFAIRS of* ~, staatsake; *the* ~ *of AFFAIRS*, die toedrag van sake; *on BEHALF of the* ~, van staatsweë; *in a* ~ *of DEFENCE*, in staat van verdediging; ~ *of DISEASE*, siektetoestand; ~ *of EMERGENCY*, noodtoestand; *HEAD of* ~, staatshoof; *IN* ~, in gala, in staatsie; op groot voet; offisieel; *LIE in* ~, op 'n praalbed lê; *LIVE in great* ~, op groot voet lewe; *in a MANNER fitting his* ~, soos dit by sy stand pas; *the MARRIED* ~, die gehude staat; ~ *of MIND*, gemoedstoestand; ~ *of PARTIES*, stand v.d. partye; *PRISONER of* ~, staatsgevangene; *ROBES of* ~, galakleding; *SECRETS of* ~, staatsgeheime; *in a* ~ *of SIEGE*, in staat van beleg; *UNITED S*~*s of America*, die Verenigde State van Amerika; *in a* ~ *of WAR*, in staat van oorlog.
state², (v) vermeld; berig; opgee; te kenne gee; sê; konstateer, vasstel; ~ *a CASE*, 'n saak uiteensit; ~ *in EVIDENCE*, getuig; ~ *FACTS*, feite aanvoer; ~ *a PRICE*, 'n prys opgee.
state: (a) staats-; parade-; gala-; praal-; ~ **affair**, staatsaak; ~ **aid**, staatshulp; ~**-aided**, met subsidie v.d. staat, met staatsondersteuning; ~**-aided schemes**, staatsondersteunde ondernemings; ~ **attorney**, staatsprokureur; ~ **ball**, staatsbal; ~ **bank**, staatsbank; ~ **bed**, praalbed; staatsiebed; ~ **call**, offisiële (amptelike) besoek; ~ **carriage**, staatsierytuig; ~ **ceremonial**, staatsplegtigheid; ~ **church**, staatskerk; ~ **coach**, staatskoets; ~ **craft**, diplomasie, staatkunde; ~ **criminal**, staatsmisdadiger; ~ **document**, staatstuk; (pl) staatspapiere; ~ **dress**, pronkgewaad.
sta'ted, aangegee; vermeld, bepaald; ~ *AMOUNT*, gegewe bedrag; ~ *CASE*, spesiale saak; *on the* ~ *DAY*, op die bepaalde dag; *at* ~ *INTERVALS*, op gesette tye; *unless OTHERWISE* ~, tensy anders vermeld; *the TIME was not* ~, die tyd is nie vermeld nie; *at* ~ *TIMES*, op vaste ure.
state: ~ **demesne**, staatsgronde; ~ **exploitation**, staatsekploitasie; ~ **funeral**, staatsbegrafnis; ~**-hood**, nasieskap; ~ **less**, staatloos; ~ **librarian**, staatsbibliotekaris; ~ **library**, staatsbiblioteek; ~ **liness**, statigheid, deftighid, luister; ~**ly**, statig, plegstatig, weids, groots; pragtig; ~ **loan**, staatslening; ~ **lottery**, staatslotery.
state'ment, opgawe, mededeling, verklaring, verslag, berig; stelling; staat; rekening; tabel; *ANNUAL* ~, jaarstaat; *MONTHLY* ~, maandstaat; ~ *of SERVICE*, diensstaat; *WEEKLY* ~, weekstaat.
state: ~ **money**, staatsgeld; ~ **monopoly**, staatsmonopolie; ~ **occasion**, staats(aan)geleentheid; ~**-owned**, van die staat; staats-; ~ **paper**, staatsdokument, offisiële stuk; ~ **president**, staatspresident; ~ **prison**, staatsgevangenis; ~ **prisoner**, staatsgevangene; ~ **property**, staatseiendom.
stat'er, verklaarder.
state: ~ **room**, praalkamer, pronkkamer, staatsaal; luukse kajuit; ~ **secret**, staatsgeheim; ~ **security**, staatsveiligheid; *S*~*s General*, State-Generaal.
states'man, (..men), staatsman; staatkundige; ~**like**, soos 'n staatsman, 'n staatsman waardig, takties, diplomaties; ~ **ship**, staatkunde; staatsmanswysheid; staatsbeleid.
state: ~ **subsidy**, staatstoelae; staatssubsidie; ~**-tested**, deur die staat gekeur; ~ **treaty**, staatsverdrag, ~ **trial**, staatsverhoor; ~ **unity**, staatseenheid; ~ **visit**, staatsbesock; ~ **witness**, staatsgetuie.
stat'ic, stilstaande, staties; ewewigs-; vas; ~ **electricity**, statiese elektrisiteit; ~ **energy**, arbeidsvermoë van plek; ~ **line**, treklyn (lugv); ~ **warfare**, stellingoorlog.
stat'ical, staties; ewewigs-; ~**ly**, staties; staties.
stat'ice, papierblom; strandroos *(Limonium)*.
stat'ics, statika, ewewigsleer.
sta'tion, (n) stasie; standplaas; stand, posisie, rang; pos; sentrale (elek.); ~ *in LIFE*, rang in die maatskappy; *a MAN of* ~, iem. van stand; *NAVAL* ~, vlootbasis; *TAKE one's* ~, jou plek inneem; (v) stasioneer, (op)stel, plaas.
sta'tionaries, besettingstroepe.
sta'tionary, stilstaande, vas, blywend, onbeweeglik, stand-; ~ **boiler**, vaste ketel; ~ **crane**, standhyskraan; ~ **engine**, landbouketel; standmasjien; standmotor; ~ **plant**, vaste masjinerie; ~ **troops**, vaste troepe; ~ **warfare**, stellingsoorlog.
sta'tion bookstall, spoorwegboekstalletjie, spoorwegboekwinkel.
sta'tioner, handelaar in skryfbehoeftes, boekhandelaar.
sta'tionery, skryfbehoeftes, skryfware, skryfgerei;

continuous ~, kettingvorms; ~ **invoice,** faktuur vir skryfbehoeftes; *continuous* ~ *invoices,* ketting=fakture.
sta'tion: ~-**house,** stasiehuis; ~-**master,** stasiemees=ter; ~-**wagon,** busmotor; stasiewa.
stat'ism, staatsbemoeiing.
stat'ist, statistikus; staatsman; voorstander van staatsbeheer.
statis'tic, (n) statistiek; (a) statisties.
statis'tical, statisties; ~ **processing,** statistiese ver=werking; ~ **return,** statistiese opgawe; ~ **service,** statistiekdiens.
statisti'cian, statistikus.
statis'tics, statistiek.
stat'olith, ewewigsteentjie, statoliet.
stat'oscope, statoskoop.
stat'uary, (n) beeldhoukuns; beeldhouwerk; (..ries), beeldhouer; beeldegroep; (a) beeldhou=.
stat'ue, standbeeld; ~**d,** van standbeelde voorsien; ~-**foundry,** beeldgietery.
statuesque', soos 'n standbeeld, standbeeldagtig; statig.
statuette', (stand)beeldjie.
stat'ure, lengte, gestalte, grootte; liggaamsbou, lig=gaamsgrootte; statuur; *short in* ~, klein van ge=stalte (postuur), kort.
stat'us, stand, rang, posisie, staat, status; *of social* ~, van goeie stand; ~ **quo,** status quo, bestaande toestand.
stat'utable, wettig, wetlik.
stat'ute, wet, instelling, statuut, verordening; *BY* ~, deur wetsbepaling; *S~ of LIMITATIONS,* Verja=ringswet; *S~ of Westminster,* Statuut van West=minster; ~-**book,** wetboek, statuteboek; *place on the* ~-*book,* tot wet verhef, in die wetboek opneem; ~ **labour,** dwangarbeid; ~ **law,** geskrewe (afge=kondigde) wet; ~ **mile,** landmyl.
stat'utory, wetlik voorgeskrewe, wetsregtelik, statu=têr; ~ **declaration,** wetsregtelike verklaring; ~ **duty,** wetsregtelike plig; ~ **offence,** statutêre oor=treding; ~ **powers,** wetlike bevoegdhede (mag).
staunch¹, (v) *kyk* **stanch.**
staunch², (a) sterk, stewig, stoer, onwankelbaar, be=proef; trou, staatmaker=; waterdig; ~**ness,** trou, gehegtheid, stoerheid, beginselvastheid.
stave, (n) duig (vat); staaf; strofe, stansa (poësie); no=tebalk (musiek); sport (van leer); (v) **(-d** or **stove),** in duie slaan, verbrysel, 'n gat slaan in, stukkend slaan; duie insit (vat); kalfater (nate); ~ *IN,* in=slaan, breek; ~ *something OFF,* iets afwend; iets voorkom; ~-**rhyme,** stafrym; ~-**wood,** duighout.
stay, (n) verblyf; versterking, steunstut, steunsel, stut; anker (meg.); stilstand, oponthoud; uitstel, opskor=ting; stuiting; uithouvermoë; stag, mastou (skip); (pl) korset, borsrok; *the sole* ~ *of the family,* die enigste steun v.d. gesin; (v) bly, woon; loseer; vertoef, stut, steun; uitstel, opskort (vonnis); skors ('n aksie); uithou, volhou; oorstag gooi (skip); ver=anker; teëhou, stuit; in bedwang hou; ~ *AWAY,* wegbly; ~ *BEHIND,* agterbly; *it has COME to* ~, dit het 'n blywende plek gekry; ~ *for DINNER,* vir ete bly; ~ *the EXECUTION of a judgment,* die uit=voering van 'n vonnis opskort; ~ *one's HAND,* op=trede terughou; *it is HERE to* ~, dit is blywend hier; ~ *at HOME,* tuis bly; met Jan Tuisbly se kar=retjie ry; ~ *at the HOTEL,* by die hotel tuis wees; ~ *IN,* tuis bly; skoolsit; ~ *the NIGHT,* oornag, die nag oorbly; ~ *ON,* in diens bly, aanbly; ~ *OUT,* uitbly; ~ *the PACE,* bybly, byhou; ~ *up with a PATIENT,* by 'n pasiënt waak; ~ *PUT,* onbe=weeglik bly; ~ *after SCHOOL,* skoolsit, inbly; ~ *one's STOMACH,* die ergste honger stil; ~ *UP,* opbly; ~ *WITH,* bly by; loseer by; ~-**at-home,** (n) huishen; tuisblyer; (a) huisvas, tuissittend; ~-**away,** tuisblyer; wegblyer; ~-**bolt,** ankerbout; ~**er,** blyer; uithouer (perd); ~ **hole,** ankergat; ~**ing,** opskorting (vonnis); verankering; ~ **ing power,** uithouvermoë; ~-**in strike,** sitstaking; ~-**lace,** korsetveter, borsrokveter; ~ **less,** sonder steun; sonder borsrok; sonder baleine; onkeerbaar; onophoudelik; veranderlik; ~-**maker,** borsrokma=ker, korsetmaker; ~-**nut,** ankermoer; ~-**peg,** an=

kerpen; ~-**pin,** dam; ~ **pole,** ankerpaal; ~-**rod,** steunstang; ankerstang; ~-**sail,** stagseil; ~-**tube,** steunpyp; ~-**wire,** ankerdraad.
stead, stede, plaas, plek; nut, diens; *IN his* ~, in sy plek; *IN* ~ *of,* in plaas van; *STAND one in good* ~, goed te pas kom; ~ **fast,** standvastig; onwrikbaar; ~ **fastness,** vastheid; onwrikbaarheid; ~ **ily,** voort=durend; besadig; gelykmatig; ~ **iness,** gereeldheid, deeglikheid, onwankelbaarheid, stewigheid; ~ *iness in flight,* vliegvastheid.
stead'y, (n) steun, stut, teenhouer; vaste kêrel; (v) **(steadied),** vastheid gee aan; tot bedaring bring; nie laat beef (skud) nie; gelykmatig maak; koers laat hou; tot ordelikheid bring; besadig maak; ~ *DOWN,* besadig word; ~ *the HELM,* die helm reghou; ~ *himself to KICK,* hom reghou om te skop; (a) vas, onwankelbaar, standvastig, gestadig, gelykmatig; gereeld; deeglik, oppassend; besadig; ~ *ATTENDANCE,* gereelde bywoning; *a* ~ *DE=CLINE,* ('n) gestadige agteruitgang; *a* ~ *DRIVER,* 'n veilige bestuurder; *GO* ~, 'n vaste nooi (kêrel) hê; ~ *INCREASE,* geleidelike vermeerdering; *KEEP her* ~, hou koers; *not* ~ *on his LEGS,* nie vas op sy bene nie; ~ *NOW!* stadig oor die klippe! *travel at a* ~ *PACE,* teen 'n egalige spoed ry; ~ *STATE,* ewewigstoestand; (interj) so nou! ~-**go=ing,** kalm, bedaard; *a* ~-*going sort of person,* 'n soliede persoon; ~**ing spring,** ewewigsveer; ~**ing strap,** hangband.
steak, skyf (vleis); biefstuk; moot (vis); ~-**and-kidney pie,** bief(stuk)-en-niertjie-pastei; ~ **burger,** bief=burger; ~**house,** braaieetplek, braairestourant.
steal, (stole, stolen), steel, vaslê; gap(s), skaai; sluip, kruip; ~ *AWAY,* wegsluip; soos 'n groot speld ver=dwyn; ~ *FROM someone,* iem. besteel; ~ *a GLANCE at,* skelmpies kyk na; ~ *a person's HEART,* iem. se liefde wen; ~ *IN,* insluip; inglip; ~ *a MARCH on somebody,* iem. voor wees; iem. voorspring; ~ *OUT,* uitsluip; ~ *a RIDE,* stilletjies saamry; ~ *the SHOW,* die meeste aandag trek; ~ *someone's THUNDER,* met iem. anders se kalf ploeg; ~ *one's WAY into,* binnesluip; ~**ing,** ste=lery, diefstal; gesluip.
stealth, heimlikheid; geheime handeling; onder=duimsheid; *by* ~, stilletjies; ~ **ily,** ~ **y,** steelsgewys; heimlik, onderduims, skelmpies; tersluiks; ver=sigtig.
steam, (n) stoom; (water)damp, wasem; *full* ~ *AHEAD,* volle stoom (krag) vorentoe; *full* ~ *A=STERN,* volle stoom agtertoe; *BLOW off* ~, stoom afblaas; *at FULL* ~, met volle stoom; *GET* ~ *up,* stoom maak; vaart kry; onthuts raak; *GO on* ~, begin produseer; *LET off* ~, stoom afblaas; uitraas; *under one's OWN* ~, op eie krag; *UNDER* ~, met stoom op; (v) stoom; damp; uitstoom; gaar stoom (kos); vaar; *become (get)* ~*ed UP,* ontstoke raak; ~-**bath,** stoombad; ~ **boat,** stoomboot; ~-**boiler,** stoomketel; ~ **brake,** stoomrem; ~-**chest,** stoomkas; ~ **clean,** stoomskoonmaak; ~-**clean=ing,** stoomskoonmaak; stoomskoonmakery; ~-**coal,** stoomkole; ~-**cock,** stoomkraan; ~-**con=sumption,** stoomverbruik; ~ **crane,** stoomkraan; ~-**cylinder,** stoomsilinder; ~ **disinfection,** stoom=ontsmetting; ~-**dredger,** stoombaggermasjien; ~ **drier,** stoomdroër; ~-**drill,** stoomboor; ~-**driven,** met stoomkrag; ~ **ed,** gestoom; ~*ed to the gills,* smoordronk; ~ **ed pudding,** stoompoeding; ~-**en=gine,** stoomasjien, stoomwerktuig; ~ **er,** stoom=skip; stoomkoker; stoomketel; stoombrandspuit; ~-**gauge,** stoomdrukmeter, manometer; ~-**gener=ation,** stoomopwekking; ~ **generator,** stoomketel; ~ **hammer,** stoomhamer; ~-**heat,** stoomhitte; ~-**heating,** stoomverwarming; ~ **ing hot meal,** dam=pende maaltyd; ~ **iron,** parsyster; ~-**jacket,** stoommantel; ~-**launch,** stoomsloep, stoombar=kas; ~-**laundry,** stoomwassery; ~ **line,** stoomlei=ding; ~ **locomotive,** stoomlokomotief; ~-**mill,** stoommeule; ~-**navigation,** stoomvaart; ~-**pipe,** stoompyp; ~-**piston,** stoomsuier; ~ **plough,** stoomploeg; ~-**power,** stoomkrag; ~-**press,** (n) stoompers; roller; (v) rol; ~-**pressure,** stoom=druk; ~-**proof,** stoomdig; ~-**pump,** stoompomp;

steamship 1265 *step*

~-roller, (n) stoomwals, stoomroller; (v) die stoomwals gebruik; stootskraap; deurjaag, deurdruk, deurdryf.
steam'ship, stoomboot, stoomskip; ~ communication, stoomvaartverbinding; ~ company, stoomvaartmaatskappy; ~ line, stoomvaartlyn.
steam: ~-shovel, stoomgrawer; ~-tight, stoomdig; ~-tractor, stoomtrekker; ~-tram, stoomtrem; ~-trap, kondenseerpot; ~ tug, stoomsleepboot; ~-valve, stoomklep; ~-wagon, stoomwa; ~ whistle, stoomfluit; ~ winch, stoomwindas; ~ y, vol stoom; dampend, stomend; ~-yacht, stoomjag.
ste'arate, stearaat.
stea'ric, vet=, stearine=; ~ acid, vetsuur.
ste'atite, speksteen, seepklip, steatiet.
steatit'ic, speksteenagtig, speksteen=.
steatocele', vetbreuk.
steatopy'gia, steatopigie.
steed, (stryd)ros, perd.
steel, (n) staal; slypstaal; swaard; vuurslag; *COLD* ~, dolk, bajonet, swaard; *as TRUE as* ~, onkreukbaar eerlik, (v) staal, hard maak, pantser; ~ *one's heart*, jou hart verhard; (a) staal=, van staal; gehard; ~ angle, hoekstaal, ~-armoured, gepantser; ~ bath, staalbad; ~ beam, staalbalk; ~ blue, staalblou; ~-casting, staalgietsel; ~-clad, gepantser; ~-coloured, staalkleurig; ~ concrete, staalbeton; ~-engraver, staalgraveur; ~ engraving, staalgravure; graveerkuns; ~ facing, staalbekleding; ~ factory, staalsmedery; ~-foundry, staalgietery; ~ frame, staalraam; ~ girder, staalbalk; ~ grey, staalgrys; ~ hammer, staalhamer, ~-hearted, moedig, onverskrokke; hardvogtig; ~ helmet, staalhelm; ~ify, (..fied), verstaal; ~ industry, staalbedryf; ~ medicine, staalmiddel; ~-mill, staalwalsery; ~ pen, staalpen; ~ plate, staalplaat, ~-plated, gepantser; ~ reinforcement, staalwapening; ~ rope, staalkabel; ~ scraper, skraper; ~ sleeper, staaldwarslêer; ~ tape, staalband; ~ trap, slagyster, ~ wire, staaldraad; ~ wool, staalwol; ~ works, staalfabriek; ~ y, staal=, staalagtig; staalhard; ~ yard, unster, Romeinse weegskaal.
steen'bok, steenbok.
steen'bras, steenbras.
steep¹, (n) steilte, hoogte; afgrond; remhoogte; (a) steil; hoog, kras, kwaai (pryse); *that's a BIT* ~, dis kwaai! sak, Sarel! *a* ~ *PRICE*, 'n hoë prys; *a* ~ *ROOF*, 'n spits dak; *SEEM a bit* ~, lyk of dit 'n bietjie kwaai is; lyk of dit te veel gevra is; ~ *TURN*, steil draai.
steep², (n) indoping; vloeistof; (die) week; (v) indoop, indompel, week; ~ *in*, drenk in.
steeped, deurtrek, deurweek; verstok; deurknee; ~ *in ALCOHOL*, deurtrek van (sterk) drank; ~ *in CRIME*, verhard in misdadigheid; ~ *in FRENCH*, gekonfyt in Frans; *be* ~ *in MISERY*, in die diepste ellende gedompel wees.
steep'en, steil word.
steep'er, loogkuip.
stee'ple, (klok)toring, toringspits; ~ chase, hinderniswedren (perde); hinderniswedloop (mense); ~d, getoring, met torings; ~ hat, tuithoed, punthoed, toering; ~ jack, skoorsteenwerker; toringwerker.
steep: ~ly, steil; ~ness, steilte; ~y, steilerig.
steer¹, (n) bul; jong os, tollie.
steer², (v) stuur, rig, koers vat; lei; ~ *CLEAR of*, omseil, vermy, buite bereik bly van; ~ *CLEAR of someone*, uit icm. se pad bly; ~ *FOR*, koers vat na; ~ *an HONEST course*, padlangs loop; ~ *a MIDDLE course*, 'n middeweg kies; ~ *by the STARS*, op die sterre stuur; ~ *a STRAIGHT course*, 'n reguit pad loop, reg deur see gaan; ~ *clear of TROUBLE*, moeilikheid vermy; tussen die klippe deur seil; ~ *clear of WORK*, jou lyf spaar (bêre); ~ able, bestuurbaar; ~ age, stuur, roer; tussendek; ~ age passenger, tussendekpassasier; ~er, stuurman; lokvoël.
steer'ing, stuur, besturing; ~-arm, stuurhefboom; ~-column, stuurkolom; ~-committee, reëlingskomitee; ~-control, stuurbeheer; ~-gear, stuurtoestel; roertoestel; ~-handle, stuur; ~-house, stuurhuis; ~-oar, stuurriem; ~ orders, roerbevele.

~-rod, stuurstang; ~-wheel, stuurrat, stuurwiel; ~-worm, stuurskroefrat.
steers'man, (..men), stuurman; ~ship, stuurmanskap.
steeve, (n) helling; (v) oorhel; laat oorhel.
stegnos'is, verstopping.
stel'e, (-ae), grafsuil.
stell'ar, sterre=, van die sterre, stellêr; ~ month, sterremaand.
stell'ate(d), stervormig; bester.
Stell'enbosch¹, (n) Stellenbosch; *a* ~ *professor*, 'n Stellenbosse professor.
stell'enbosch² (v): ~ *somebody*, iem. in rang verlaag.
stellif'erous, vol sterre; met stervormige figure.
stell'iform, stervormig.
stell'ular, stervormig.
stem¹, (n) keerwal; keerder; (v) (-med), stuit, teenhou; opdam; stelp (bloed); stroom-op roei (vaar, seil); *try to* ~ *the tide*, die stroom probeer stuit; probeer wal gooi teen iets.
stem², (n) stam, stingel; geslag; voorstewe, boeg (skip); skag (van veer); steel (van pyp); as; bout; stam(woord); *from* ~ *to stern*, van voor-tot agterstewe; (v) (-med), afstroop (tabak); saampers (springstof); (die) steel afhaal; stingels verwyder; ~ *from*, voortspruit (ontstaan) uit; ~ leaf, stingelblad; ~less, stingelloos; ~ let, stammetjie; stingeltjie.
stemm'a, (-ta), stamboom, afstamming; fasetoog, oog (van insekte).
stem: ~-pitting, stamgleuf, gleufsiekte; ~-shoe, boegskoen; ~ stitch, stamnotsock; ~ ware, (wyn)kelkies.
stench, stank; ~-expelling, stankverdrywend; ~-preventing, stankwerend; ~-trap, stankafsluiter, stanksperder.
sten'cil, (n) patroonplaat, sjabloon; sjabloneerwerk; wasplaat; tekenpatroon; (v) (-led), met 'n sjabloon verf; sjabloneer; ~ brush, sjabloonkwas; ~ cutter, patroonsnyer; ~ler, patroonsnyer; ~ling, sjabloonwerk; sjabloondruk; ~ paper, wasvel; ~-plate, merkplaat, patroonplaat; ~ printing, sjabloondruk; ~-sheet, sjabloonplaat.
Sten (gun), Stengeweer.
stenoch'romy, stenochromie.
sten'ogram, stenogram.
sten'ograph, snelskrifletter, stenograaf.
stenog'rapher, snelskrywer, snelskryfster, stenograaf.
stenograph'ic, snelskrif=, stenografies.
stenog'raphy, snelskrif, stenografie.
stenoph'yllous, smalbladig.
stenoteleg'raphy, stenotelegrafic.
sten'tor, stentor; donderaar, bulderaar.
stentor'ian, hard, luid, bulderend, stentor=; *in a* ~ *voice*, met 'n bulderende (stentor=) stem.
sten'torphone, stentorfoon, baasluidspreker.
step¹, (n) stap, tree; voetstap; optrede; sport (van leer); trappie; drumpel; maatreël; (pl) trapleer; *BREAK* ~, uit die pas loop, ~ *BY* ~, stap vir stap; *CHANGE* ~, die pas verander; *a FALSE* ~, 'n misstap; *it is only a FEW* ~*s to my house*, dis maar 'n hanetreetjie na my huis; *take the FIRST* ~, die eerste stappe doen; *FOLDING* ~*s*, touleer; *FOLLOW in someone's* ~*s*, in iem. se voetspoor volg; *take a* ~ *FORWARD*, 'n tree vorentoe gee; *GO a* ~ *further*, 'n stap verder gaan; *keep IN* ~, in die pas bly; *KEEP* ~ *with*, byhou met; gelyke tred hou met; in die pas bly; *take the NECESSARY* ~*s*, die nodige stappe doen; *take ONE* ~ *at a time*, voetjie vir voetjie loop; *OUT of* ~ *with the times*, heeltemal verouderd; uit voeling met die moderne opvattings; *a* ~ *in the RIGHT direction*, 'n stap in die regte rigting; *WALK in* ~, in die pas loop; *WATCH one's* ~, in jou spoor trap; in jou pasoppens bly; op jou telle pas; (v) (-ped), stap, tree, loop; betree, skry; vorder; trap; ~ *ACROSS*, oorstap; ~ *ALONG*, aanstap; ~ *ASIDE*, opsy tree (staan); ~ *BACK*, terugtree, terugstaan; ~ *into the BREACH*, in die bres tree; ~ *DOWN*, afklim; afstaan; ~ *FORWARD*, vorentoe kom (stap); ~ *HIGH*, die voete hoog optel; ~ *IN*, binnetree; ~

OFF, afstap; ~ *ON*, trap op; ~ *ON it*, vet gee; ~ *OUT*, na buite gaan; vinnig stap; die pas verleng; ~ *it OUT*, met treë meet, aftree; ~ *on someone's TOES*, op iem. se tone trap; ~ *UP to*, nader; ~ *it UP*, dit versnel; ~ *UP the tax*, die belasting verhoog; ~ *this WAY*, kom hiernatoe.
step-² (pref): ~ **brother**, stiefbroer; ~ **child**, stiefkind.
step'dance, stapdans.
step: ~ **daughter**, stiefdogter; ~ **father**, stiefvader.
step: ~**-in**, inklimgordel, inglipper; ~**-ladder**, trapleer, staanleer.
step'mother, stiefmoeder; ~ **ly**, stiefmoederlik; *treat someone in a ~ly manner*, iem. stiefmoederlik behandel, iem. hond maak.
step'-parents, stiefouers.
steppe, steppe, hoogvlakte, grasvlakte; ~ **buzzard**, bruinvalk; ~ **region**, steppestreek.
stepped, trapvormig; ~ **gable**, trapgewel.
stepp'ing-stone, oorspringklip; vastrapplek; stapklip, stapsteen; middel, hulpmiddel.
step: ~**-plate**, treeplaat; ~**-pulley**, trapkatrol; ~**-sight**, trapvisier.
step: ~ **sister**, stiefsuster; ~ **son**, stiefseun.
step: ~**-up**, versterking, verhoging; ~ **wise**, trapsgewyse.
stercora'ceous, mis-, misagtig, drek-.
stere, stere, kubieke meter.
ster'eo, (-s), stereo; stereoklank; stereotipe; stereofoto; stereofotografie; ~ **blanket**, matryskombers.
stereochem'ical, stereochemies.
stereochem'istry, stereochemie.
stereoch'romy, stereochromie.
stereognos'tic, stereognosties.
ster'eogram, stereogram.
ster'eograph, stereograaf.
stereog'raphy, stereografie.
ste'reo headphones, stereokopstuk.
stereom'eter, stereometer.
stereomet'ric(al), stereometries.
stereom'etry, stereometrie.
stereophon'ic, stereofonies.
stereo'phony, stereofonie.
stereo phot'ograph, stereofoto.
stereophotog'raphy, stereofotografie.
ste'reoradio, stereoradio.
ste'reoscope, stereoskoop.
stereoscop'ic, stereoskopies; ~ **photograph**, stereofoto.
stereos'copy, stereoskopie.
ste'reo sound, stereo(klank).
ste'reotype, (n) stereotipe, stereotipedruk; stereotiepplaat; (v) stereotipeer; (a) afgeslyt, afgeslete; ~ **d**, stereotipies, onveranderlik, vervelend; ~ **r**, stereotipeur.
ster'eotypy, stereotiepdruk, stereotipie.
ste'rile, onvrugbaar, steriel, gus (dier); dor, maer (grond); gesteriliseer; geestelik arm; ~ **ewe**, gusooi.
steril'ity, onvrugbaarheid, steriliteit; geestelike armoede; *infectious* ~, besmetlike onvrugbaarheid.
steriliza'tion, sterilisasie, onvrugbaarmaking.
ste'rilize, onvrugbaar maak; steriliseer, kiemvry maak; ~ **r**, sterilisator, steriliseerder; ontsmettingsmiddel; ontsmetter.
sterl'et, sterlet.
sterl'ing, (n) sterling; *pound* ~, pond sterling; (a) sterling; eg. suiwer, onvervals, voortreflik gaaf, deeglik; *a* ~ *FELLOW*, 'n gawe kêrel; 'n staatmaker; *a work of* ~ *MERIT*, 'n baie waardevolle werk; ~ **area**, sterlinggebied.
stern¹, (n) hek; agterstewe (skip); stert, agterste; spieël; *sit at the* ~, aan die roer wees.
stern², (a) ernstig, stug, stroef, bars, onbuigsaam, hardvogtig; hard (feit); ~ *necessity*, harde noodsaaklikheid.
stern'al, stert-; agterste.
stern: ~**-boss**, skroefnaaf; ~**-chaser**, jaagkanon; ~**-fast**, vasmaaktou, meertou, ~ **hold**, agterruim, agteronder; ~ **light**, agterlig; ~**most**, agterste.
stern'ness, strengheid, stroefheid, hardheid.
stern: ~**-post**, agterstewe; ~ **sheets**, stuurstoel.
stern'um, (..na), sternum, borsbeen; borsplaat.
sternuta'tion, (die) nies.

sternut'ative, sternu'tatory, (n) niesmiddel; niesgas; (a) nies-, niesveroorsakend.
stern'utator, niesmiddel.
stern'-wheel, hekwiel; ~ **er**, ~ **steamer**, hekwieler, hekwielboot.
stert'orous, snorkend.
steth'oscope, stetoskoop, gehoorpyp.
stethoscop'ic, stetoskopies.
stethos'copy, ondersoek met die gehoorpyp, stetoskopie.
steve'dore, stuwadoor, dokwerker.
stew, (n) gestoofde vleis (gereg); bredie; visdam; (pl) bordeel; *BE in a* ~, in die knyp sit; woedend wees; *IRISH* ~, ertappelbredie; (v) stowe, smoor; ~ *ed CABBAGE*, gestoofde kool; *let him* ~ *in his own JUICE*, laat hom in sy eie vet (sop) gaar kook.
stew'ard, rentmeester; beampte (sport); hofmeester; opsigter; seremoniemeester; tafelbediende, bottelier, kelner; ~ **ess, (-es)**, kelnerin; hofmeesteres; ~ **ship**, rentmeesterskap; hofmeesterskap.
stew'ing, (die) stowe; ~ **apples**, stoofappels; ~ **meat**, stoofvleis; ~ **steak**, stoofbiefstuk.
stew: ~**-meat**, stowevleis; ~**-pan**, stoofkastrol.
stick, (n) (stuur)stok; lat; wandelstok; kierie; kolf; keu (biljart); mas; stronk; strykstok (musiek); sukkelaar, remskoen (fig.); stut (myn); *the BIG* ~, magsvertoon; ~ *of BOMBS*, string bomme; *be in a CLEFT* ~, in die knyp wees; nie hot of haar weet nie; jou in 'n hoekie bevind; *CUT one's* ~, jou hoed vat; *a* ~ *is quickly found to beat a DOG with*, as 'n mens 'n hond wil slaan, kan jy maklik 'n stok kry; *a* ~ *of DYNAMITE*, dinamietkers; *a DRY* ~, 'n droë bokkem; *a few* ~ *s of FURNITURE*, 'n paar stukkies meubels; *GATHER* ~ *s*, hout optel; *GET the wrong end of the* ~, aan die kortste end trek; dit verkeerd hê; *GIVE someone the* ~, iem. onder die lat kry; *IN the* ~ *s*, in die gramadoelas; *a POOR old* ~, 'n arme drommel, 'n sukkelaar; *a QUEER old* ~, 'n snaakse ou, 'n sonderling; *the THIN end of a* ~, aan die korste kant; *he WANTS the* ~, hy moet slae kry; (v) **(stuck)**, steek; klewe, vassit; aanhou; deursteek; aanplak (biljette); verdra; trou bly; ~ *AROUND*, rondhang; ~ *AT nothing*, jou deur niks laat stuit nie; ~ *no BILLS*, aanplak verbied; ~ *like a BURR*, klou soos 'n klits; *I CAN'T* ~ *him*, ek kan hom nie verdra nie; ~ *FAST*, vassit; *a great deal* ~ *s to the FINGERS*, daar bly baie aan die strykstok hang; ~ *by a FRIEND*, 'n vriend bystaan; *it* ~ *s in my GIZZARD*, dit steek my in die krop; ~ *to one's GUNS*, voet by stuk hou; ~ *your HAT on*, sit jou hoed op; ~ *IT*, volhou; *he cannot* ~ *it any LONGER*, hy kan dit nie langer uithou nie; ~ *out a MILE*, baie duidelik wees; glashelder wees; ~ *in the MUD*, vasval; stadig, onprogressief; *the NAME has stuck to this day*, hy behou vandag nog die naam; ~ *out your NECK*, jou blootstel (blootgee); *he* ~ *s at NOTHING*, hy stuit vir niks nie; ~ *it ON*, dit dik aanmaak; ~ *it OUT*, tot aan die end uithou; ~ *out for better PAY*, sterk aandring op 'n hoër loon; ~ *it in your POCKET*, steek dit in jou sak; *it* ~ *s in one's THROAT*, dit steek mens in die krop; ~ *TO*, vashou aan; kleef aan; trou bly aan; iets in jou besit hou; ~ *TO it*, aanhou; ~ *TO one's opinion*, by jou mening bly; ~ *TOGETHER*, aanmekaar plak; mekaar trou bly; ~ *UP for someone*, vir iem. opkom; *be stuck (saddled) WITH someone or something*, opgeskeep sit met iets of iem.; ~ *to one's WORD*, jou aan jou woord hou; ~ **cinnamon**, pypkaneel; ~ **er**, steker; aanhouer; plakker; plakadvertensie; aanplakbiljet; reklameseël; plakstrook; ~ **iness**, klewerigheid, taai(ig)heid; ~ **ing**, plak, kleef; deursteek; ~ **ing place**, vasvalplek; vassitplek; ~ **ing plaster**, kleefpleister, hegpleister; ~**ing-tape**, kleefband, plakband; ~**-in-sect**, stokinsek, stokkiesduiwel; ~**-in-the-mud**, onprogressiewe mens; sukkelaar, remskoen, ambraal, jansalie.
stic'kle, weifel; onbetroubaar wees, uit twee monde praat; ~ **back**, stekelbaars; ~ **r**, beswaarmaker; voorvegter, ywerraar; aanhouer; *be a* ~ *r for ETIQUETTE*, erg gesteld wees op etiket; *a REAL* ~ *r*, 'n puntenerige mens; 'n ywerraar.

stick'-up, (n) aanhouding; (a) staande, regop.
stick'water, afvalwater.
stick'y, klewerig, taai; lastig; *a* ~ *BUSINESS*, 'n moeilike (onaangename) saak; *come to a* ~ *END*, 'n nare uiteinde hê; *strike a* ~ *PATCH*, 'n onaangename stadium beleef; met 'n moeilike probleem te doen kry; ~-**fingered**, langvingerig.
stiff, (n) rondloper, niksnuts; kadawer (plat); geld; wissel; dokument, papier; *a big* ~, 'n hopelose knop; (a, adv) styf, stram, stewig, onbuigsaam; stokkerig; verstyf, star; strak; hoogmoedig; onvriendelik, stroef; swaar, moeilik; koppig; *BORE a person* ~, iem. dodelik verveel; *a fairly* ~ *CLIMB*, dis taamlik steil; *face* ~ *COMPETITION*, sterk mededinging hê; *meet it with a* ~ *DENIAL*, dit beslis ontken; *a* ~ *EXAMINATION*, 'n moeilike eksamen; *KEEP a* ~ *upper lip*, dapper wees; jou taai hou; *have a* ~ *NECK*, 'n stywe nek hê; koppig wees; *a* ~ *PACE*, 'n vinnige pas; *a* ~ *PRICE*, 'n hoë prys; *SCARED* ~, doodgeskrik; *lie* ~ *and STARK*, stokstyf lê; vier stewels in die lug lê; ~-**backed**, styf; ~ **brush**, harde borsel; ~ **collar**, stywe boordjie; ~ **cover**, hardeband (boek); ~**en**, styf maak, stywe; moed inpraat; koppig word; styg, hoër word (pryse); verstram; ~**ener**, verstywer; regmakertjie, versterker; ~**ening**, verstywing, versterking; ~ **exercise**, strawwe oefening; ~ **fight**, hewige geveg; ~**ish**, stywerig; nogal moeilik; ~**ishness**; stywerigheid; ~ **law**, streng wet; ~-**necked**, hardnekkig, koppig, halsstarrig; hoogmoedig; *be* ~-*necked*, verwaand wees; ~**ness**, styfheid, stramheid, strammigheid, stywigheid, styfte, starheid; stroefheid; ~-**sickness**, stywesiekte.
sti'fle¹, (n) kniegewrig.
sti'fle², (v) verstik, versmoor, doodsmoor, onderdruk; ~ *something at birth*, iets in die kiem smoor.
sti'fle: ~-**bone**, kniegewrigsbeen (van perd); ~-**joint**, kniegewrig (van perd).
stif'ling, verstikkend; drukkend, versmorend, benoud, snikheet; ~*ly hot*, smoorwarm, smoorheet.
stig'ma, (-s, -ta), stigma; litteken, brandmerk, skandvlek, skandmerk, skandteken; stempel (plantk.); ~**t'ic**, gebrandmerk; ~**tiza'tion**, brandmerk, skandvlek, stigmatisasie; ~**tize**, brandmerk, skandvlek, skandmerk, stigmatiseer; ~**tized**, gebrandmerk, geskandvlek, gestigmatiseer.
stile, oorstap, oorklimtrap, steg; styl (bouk.); *help a lame dog over a* ~, iem. oor die klippe help; iem. uit die nood help.
stilett'o, (n) (-(e)s), stilet, priem; (v) doodsteek, deurboor; ~ **heel**, spykerhak.
still¹, (n) distilleerketel, stookketel; (v) distilleer, stook (drank).
still², (n) stilte; stilfoto; *the* ~ *of the night*, die stilte v.d. nag; (v) stilmaak, bedaar, kalmeer; (a) stil; kalm; *be as* ~ *as the GRAVE*, doodstil wees; soos die graf swyg; *a* ~ *small VOICE*, die sagte stem v.d. gewete; ~ *WATERS run deep*, stille waters, diepe grond; (adv) nog steeds, nog altyd; nogtans, tog, ewenwel, nietemin; ~ *ANOTHER*, nog een; ~ *MORE*, nog meer; altyd meer.
still'age, onderstel, stellasie.
still: ~ **birth**, doodgeboorte; ~-**born**, doodgebore; ~-*born lamb*, dooi(e)lam.
still: ~ **camera**, stilkamera; ~ **life**, stillewe; ~**ness**, stilte, stilheid, rus, kalmte; ~ **photograph**, stilfoto; ~ **picture**, stilfoto; stilprent.
still'-room, distilleerkamer.
stilt, (n) stelt; rooipootelsie (voël); *on* ~*s*, op stelte; (v) op stelte loop; ~-**bird**, steltloper.
stilt'ed, op stelte, bombasties, hoogdrawend, geswolle; onnatuurlik; ~ *ARCH*, steltboog; ~ *GAIT*, steltgang; ~ *SPEECH*, geykte spraak; ~**ness**, hoogdrawendheid, bombasme.
stilt: ~**er**, steltloper; ~-**walker**, steltloper.
stim'ulant, (n) prikkel, stimulant, stimulans; versterkende middel, stimuleermiddel; (a) prikkelend, opwekkend.
stim'ulate, aanspoor, opwek, aanvuur, verlewendig; stimuleer, prikkel; ~ *one to activity*, iem. tot handeling aanspoor.
stim'ulating, opwekkend; prikkelend; stimulerend.

stimula'tion, aansporing, aanporring, aanvuring; prikkeling.
stim'ulative, (n) prikkelmiddel; (a) prikkelend, opwekkend.
stim'ulator, aansporing, prikkel; aanporder, aanvuurder, stimuleerder.
stim'ulus, (..li), prikkel; aansporing; opwekkende middel, stimulant, stimulans, stimulus.
stim'y, *kyk* **stymie**.
sting, (n) angel (by); prikkel; stekel; steek; knaging, wroeging; die pynlike; afpersing; *the BOWLING lacks* ~, die boulwerk is futloos; ~*s of CONSCIENCE*, gewetenswroeging; *the* ~ *is in the TAIL*, die steek sal aan die end kom; die agterste draai kom met rok en kabaai; die hinkende perd kom agter aan; *TAKE the* ~ *out of something*, die angel uit iets haal; (v) **(stung)**, steek, zits (by); prik; brand; leed veroorsaak; ~ *someone into ACTION*, iem. tot handeling aanspoor; ~ *a CLIENT*, 'n kliënt die vel oor die ore trek; ~ *him FOR ten rand*, hom tien rand laat betaal; hom uit tien rand bedrieg; *IT* ~*s*, dit maak seer; ~ *to the QUICK*, diep in die hart tref; *stung by REMORSE*, vol gewetenswroeging; *the SMOKE stung his eyes*, die rook het sy oë laat brand.
sting'er, angel, steker; steekinsek; steekplant; taal klap; bytende antwoord.
sting'-fly, blindevlieg.
stin'giness, vrekk(er)igheid, suinigheid, skraapsug.
sting'ing, stekend, brandend, vlymend; *what is* ~ *you?*, wat makeer jou?, het jy dit of kry jy dit?; ~ **blow**, taai klap; ~ **criticism**, bytende kritiek; ~-**nettle**, brandnekel, brandnetel.
sting'-ray, pylstertvis.
sting'less, angelloos, sonder angel; goedaardig.
stin'gy, suinig, inhalig, gierig, vrekkig, skraapagtig, skraapsugtig, krenterig.
stink, (n) stank; *there'll be a* ~ *about this*, dit sal 'n herrie afgee; (v) **(stank** or **stunk)**, stink, sleg ruik; 'n slegte naam hê; *it* ~*s to high HEAVEN*, dit skrei ten hemel; *it* ~*s in his NOSTRILS*, dit walg 'n mens; ~ *OUT*, deur stank verdryf; *the place stank of TOBACCO smoke*, die plek het van tabakswalms gestink; ~**ard**, stinkerd; stinkdier; ~-**ball**, stinkkoeël; stinkbol; ~-**bomb**, stinkbom; ~-**beetle**, stinkkewer; ~-**bug**, stinkgogga, stinkbesie; ~-**bush**, stinkbos; ~ **er**, stinkstok; stinkerd; stinkdier; vrotterd; nare vent; smerige eksamenvraag; kwaai brief, brander; ~-**fly**, (..**flies)**, stinkvlieg; ~-**gland**, stinklier; ~-**horn**, stinkswam.
stink'ing, stinkend; walglik; *cry* ~ *fish*, afbrekend kritiseer; ~ **badger**, stinkdas; ~ **camomile**, stinkblom.
stink: ~-**shell**, stinkbom; ~-**stone**, stinksteen; --**trap**, stankvanger; ~ **weed**, stinkblaar; ~ **wood**, stinkhout; ~ **wood tree**, stinkhout(boom).
stint, (n) beperking, bekrimping; karigheid; vasgestelde skof (werk); taak; rantsoen; *LABOUR without* ~, werk sonder om op moeite te sien; *WITHOUT* ~, rojaal, onbekrompe; (v) spaarsaam wees; skraal toemeet; jouself bekrimp (afskeep), beknibbel; beperk; ~ *MONEY*, op geld sien; ~ *ONESELF*, jouself te kort doen (afskeep); ~ *less*, onbeperk, rojaal.
stip'ate, dig op mekaar (staande).
stipe, stronk; stingel; steel.
stip'end, salaris, loon, besoldiging; stipendium (as beurs).
stipen'diary, (n) (..ries), loontrekker, gesalarieerde; stipendiumhouer, beurshouer; (a) loontrekkend, gesalarieer; ~ **steward**, besoldigde opsiener.
stip'iform, steelvormig.
stip'ple, (n) stippel; stippelwerk; (v) stippel, punteer; ~ **printing**, stippeldruk; ~**r**, punt(eer)penseel, punt(eer)naald, punteerder.
stip'pling, stippeling; stippelwerk.
stip'ular, met steunblare.
stip'ulate, bepaal, voorwaarde maak, beding, stipuleer, vaslê; ~**d**, bepaal, gestipuleer.
stipula'tion, voorwaarde, stipulasie, beding(ing), bepaling.
stip'ulator, bepaler.

stip'ulate, blaarstingel, steunblad.
stir, (n) beweging; geraas; drukte, bedrywigheid; sensasie, opskudding; ontroering, gemoedsbeweging; *CAUSE a* ~, opskudding veroorsaak; *IN a* ~, in beroering; (v) **(-red),** roer; verroer; omroer; beweeg; geraas maak; aanpor; opstaan; opwek, verwek; wek; ~ *one's BLOOD,* opgewondenheid veroorsaak; ~ *up the COUNTRY,* die land in beroering bring; ~ *up DISCONTENT,* ontevredenheid veroorsaak; *not* ~ *a FINGER,* nie 'n vinger verroer nie; ~ *a FIRE,* in 'n vuur krap (aanpor); *without* ~ *ing a FOOT,* sonder om 'n voet te verroer; ~ *the IMAGINATION,* die verbeelding aangryp; ~ *up MUD,* onaangename feite opsnuffel; *not to* ~ *OUT of the house,* nie 'n voet buite die deur sit nie; ~ *one's STUMPS,* jou knieë dra; jou lyf roer; ~ *UP,* omroer; aanhits, oprui; verwek; ~ *UP the anger of others,* ander aanhits (oprui); ander oprorig maak; ~ *up a person's WRATH,* iem. kwaad maak; ~**-about,** hawermeelpap; hotom.
stirp'iculture, rasveredeling.
stirps, stamvader.
stir'rer, roerder, roerlepel; opruier.
stir'ring, (n) beweging; aandrang; roering; *he wants* ~ *UP,* hy moet wakker geskud word; (a) roerend, pakkend, aangrypend; bedrywig; ~ *MUSIC,* opwekkende (vrolike) musiek; *a* ~ *POEM,* 'n roerende gedig; *a* ~ *TALE,* 'n spannende (aangrypende) verhaal; ~**-up,** verwekking.
sti'rrup, stiebeuel; beuel; ~**-bar,** stiebeuelknip; ~**-cup,** afskeidsglasie; 'n glasie op die valreep; ~**-iron,** stiebeuel; ~**-leather,** ~**-strap,** stiegriem.
stitch, (n) (-es), steek; pyn; *without a* ~ *of CLOTHING,* sonder 'n draad klere; *the DOCTOR put a* ~ *in,* die dokter het die wond geheg; *DROP a* ~, 'n steek laat val; *not a DRY* ~ *on one's body,* nie 'n droë draad aan jou lyf nie; *have one IN* ~*es,* iem. laat skaterlag; *LOSE a* ~, 'n steek laat val; *a* ~ *in TIME saves nine,* voorsorg bespaar baie kommer; betyds keer is 'n goeie geweer; werk op tyd maak welbereid; (v) stik; naai; ~*ed BOOK,* ingenaaide boek; ~*ed SEAM,* gestikte naat; ~*ed UP,* toegewerk; geheg (wond); ~**er,** stikker, stikmasjien; draadhegter; ~**ery,** naaiwerk; ~**ing,** stiksel, naaisel, naaiwerk, stik.
stiv'er, stuiwer; *not a* ~, geen bloue duit nie.
St. John's' wort, Sint Janskruid.
stoat, hermelyn, wesel.
stock, (n) stomp; voorraad; kapitaal; stam, wortelstok; geslag, ras; veestapel, hawe; vleisekstrak; aftreksel; slot; vilet (blom); stok (bouk.); stel, handvatsel; houtgedeelte; laai (geweer); greep, kolf (pistool); (pl) effekte, aandele, staatspapiere; voetblok; vilette (blom); *BE in* ~, in voorraad wees; *BE on the* ~*s,* op stapel wees; in bewerking wees; *DELIVER from* ~, uit die voorraad lewer; ~*s and DIES,* skroefsnygereedskap; snytuig, ringsnyer; *of GOOD* ~, van goeie familie (afkoms); ~ *on HAND,* inventarisvoorraad; *HAVE in* ~, in voorraad hê; *HOLD* ~, aandele hê; *take* ~ *IN,* jou bemoei met; *KEEP in* ~, in voorraad hou; *LARGE* ~, grootvee; *LAY in a* ~ *of,* 'n voorraad daarvan insamel; jou voorsien van; *LOCK,* ~ *and barrel,* romp en stomp; soos dit reil en seil; *put something ON the* ~*s,* iets op stapel sit; *OUT of* ~, nie in voorraad nie; *put a PRISONER in the* ~*s,* 'n gevangene in die blok sit; *ROLLING* ~, rollende materiaal; *SMALL* ~, kleinvee; ~*s and SHARES,* aandele en effekte; *TAKE* ~, die inventaris opmaak, die voorraad opneem; *TAKE* ~ *of somebody,* iem. opsom; iem. deurkyk; *TAKE no* ~ *in someone's words,* geen geloof heg aan iem. se woorde nie; *TAKE* ~ *of something,* iets betrag; iets goed deurkyk; iets in oënskou neem; (v) voorsien van, van voorrade voorsien; in voorraad hê, daarop nahou; aankoop; ~ *a FARM,* 'n plaas uitrus; 'n plaas van vee voorsien; ~ *a POND,* 'n dam van vis voorsien; (a) stereotiep, oud, afgesaag, gebruiklik; *a* ~ *jest,* 'n staande (ou) grap; ~**-account,** voorraadrekening.
stockade', (n) paalwerk, palissade; verskansing; (v) met paalwerk versterk, verskans.

stock: ~**-blind,** stokblind; ~**-bolt,** kolfbout; ~**-book,** inventarisboek, voorraadboek; ~**-breeder,** veeboer, veeteler; ~**-breeding,** veeteelt, veetelery; ~**-brick,** pleistersteen; ~ **broker,** effektemakelaar, beursmakelaar, beursagent; ~ **broking,** effektehandel; ~**-buckle,** stropgespe; ~**-car,** stampmotor; ~**-car race,** stampmotorwedren; ~**-car racing,** stampmotorwedrenne; ~ **commodity,** stapelartikel; ~**-deaf,** stokdoof; ~**dove,** klein bosduif; ~ **exchange,** (effekte)beurs, aandelebeurs; ~**-fair,** veevendusie; ~**-farm,** veeplaas; ~**-farmer,** veeboer; ~**-farming,** veeboerdery; veebedryf; ~**-feeding,** (die) voer van vee; ~ **fish,** stokvis; ~ **holder,** effektehouer; ~**iness,** gesetheid, blokkerigheid.
stock'inet, stokkinet.
stock'ing, kous; windkous (lughawe); bevoorrading; *one METER eighty in his* ~*s,* een meter tagtig op sy kouse; *(horse with a) WHITE* ~, witvoet (perd); ~**ed,** gekous; *in his* ~*ed feet,* met kouse; sonder skoene; ~**-loom,** breimasjien; ~**-stitch,** koussteek; ~**-weaver,** kouswewer; ~**-yarn,** breiwol.
stock: ~**-inspector,** vee-inspekteur; ~**-in-trade,** handelsvoorraad, winkelvoorraad; smousgoed; uitrusting; gereedskap; geestelike kapitaal; ~**ist,** handelaar; voorraadhouer; ~**jobber,** effektehandelaar; beursspekulant; ~ **jobbing,** effektehandel, spekulasie in effekte, agiotasie; ~**-keeper,** veeboer; magasynmeester; ~ **list,** beursnotering; ~ **man,** veeboer; ~**-market,** veemark; effektebeurs, effektemark; ~**-owner,** effektebesitter; veeboer; ~ **pattern,** vaste handelspatroon; ~ **pile,** (n) voorraadstapel, noodvoorraad; opberging; (v) opberg, opstapel, opberg; ~ **piling,** opberging, opbergprogram, voorraadvorming, opstapeling van voorrade; ~**-pot,** soppot; ~**-raiser,** veeboer; ~**-raising,** veeboerdery; ~**-room,** pakhuis, magasyn; monsterkamer; ~ **size,** standaardgrootte; voorraadmaat; ~**-still,** doodstil, botstil; ~**-taker,** voorraadopnemer; ~**-taking,** voorraadopname, inventarisasie; terugblik; ~**-taking sale,** opruimingsverkoping; inventarisuitverkoping; ~**-theft,** veediewery, veediefstal; ~**-thief,** veedief; ~**-whip,** karwats.
stock'y, vet en dik; ~ *person,* stompie.
stock'yard, veekraal.
stodge, (n) vulsel, stopsel; swaar kos; vraat; (v) volprop, gulsig eet.
stod'giness, onverteerbaarheid; dooierigheid.
stodg'y, swaar; onverteerbaar; dooierig (mens); volgeprop.
stoep, stoep; ~**-bench,** stoepbank; ~**-plant,** stoepplant; ~**-room,** stoepkamer.
Sto'ic, (n) Stoïsyn; (a) Stoïsyns.
sto'ic, (n) stoïsyn; (a) stoïsyns; ~ **al,** stoïsyns; ~ **ism,** stoïsisme, gelatenheid.
Sto'icism, Stoïsynse leer, Stoïsisme.
stoke, stook; volstop; ~ **hold,** ~ **hole,** stookplek, stookgat; ~**r,** stoker.
stole[1], (n) stool, stola, mantel.
stole[2], (v) *kyk* **steal.**
stol'en, gesteel.
stol'id, dom; bot; dof, gevoelloos; onaandoenlik; koppig; flegmaties; ~**'ity,** onaandoenlikheid, ongevoeligheid; styfheid; flegma.
stol'on, spruit, loot, uitloper.
stom'a, (-ta), huidmondjie, stoma.
sto'mach, (n) maag; buik; pens (van diere); eetlus; geaardheid; *a fellow with a BIG* ~, 'n kêrel met 'n halfaampie; *on an EMPTY* ~, op die nugter maag; *he had no* ~ *for the FIGHT,* hy het nie lus gehad vir die geveg nie; *HIGH* ~, verwaandheid, trotsheid; *MAKE a god of one's* ~, van sy maag 'n afgod maak; *I have NO* ~ *for it,* dit stuit my teen die bors; *PROUD* ~, verwaandheid, hoogharigheid; *my* ~ *TURNS at it,* dit maak my mislik; (v) sluk, verkrop; *BE UNABLE to* ~ *something,* iets nie kan verkrop nie; *I CANNOT* ~ *that,* ek kan dit nie sluk nie; ~**-ache,** maagpyn; ~**-cavity,** maagholte; ~**complaint,** maagkwaal; ~**-disease,** maagsiekte; ~ **er,** keurslyf; ~**'ic,** (n) maagversterkende middel, maagmiddel; (a) maag-; ~**-lining,** maagvlies; ~**poison,** maaggif; ~**-pump,** maagpomp; ~**-worm,** maagwurm; ~**-ulcer,** maagseer.

stomatit'is, ontsteking v.d. mondslymvlies, stomatitis.
stomato'logy, mondwetenskap, stomatologie.
stomat'oscope, mondkyker, stomatoskoop.
stone, (n) klip; pit (van vrug); haelsteen; niersteen; graweel; gewigsmaat (14 pond); *give someone ~s for BREAD,* iem. klippe vir brood gee; *CAST the first ~,* die eerste klip gooi; *the ~s will CRY out,* die klippe sal dit uitroep; *have a HEART of ~,* 'n hart van steen hê; *KILL two birds with one ~,* twee vlieë met een klap slaan; *LEAVE no ~ standing,* nie twee klippe opmekaar laat staan nie; alles op hare en snare sit; *LEAVE no ~ unturned,* hemel en aarde beweeg; niks onbeproef laat nie; *LEAVE no ~ standing,* geen steen op die ander laat nie; *~ of OFFENCE,* steen des aanstoots; *PILE of ~s,* klipstapel; *a ROLLING ~ gathers no moss,* 'n swerwer bly 'n derwer; *SINK like a ~,* soos 'n baksteen (klip) sink; *THROW ~s at someone,* iem. met klippe gooi; iem. beswadder (belaster); (v) stenig; die pitte uithaal; plavei, met stene belê, uitstraat; (a) klip=, steen=; **S ~ Age,** Steentydperk; **~-bass,** biskop; **~ beacon,** klipbaken; **~-blind,** stokblind; **~-borer,** boormossel; **~ bottle,** kruik; **~-breaker,** klipbreker; **~-breaking,** klipbrekery; **~-bream,** bastergaljoen; **~-broke,** platsak; **~chat,** bontrokwagter, bontrokkie; **~-chisel,** klipbeitel; **~-coal,** antrasiet; **~-colour,** klipgrys; **~-coloured,** klipgrys; **~-crusher,** klipbreker, vergruiser, klipbreekmasjien; **~-crushing,** klipbrekery; **~-cutter,** klipkapper, klipbeitelaar; **~-cutter's chisel,** klipbeitel; **~ cutting,** klipbrekery; **~ d,** met klippe gegooi; pitloos; *~ d dates,* pitlose dadels; **~-dead,** morsdood; **~-deaf,** stokdoof, potdoof; **~-dresser,** klipkapper; **~ drill,** klipboor; **~ facing,** klipvoorwerk; **~ floor,** klipvloer; **~-fruit,** pitvrug; **~ hammer,** kliphamer; **~ implement,** klipwerktuig; **~ jug,** kruik; **~-laying,** steenlegging; **~ mason,** klipmesselaar; **~ pavement,** klipplaveisel; klipsypaadjie; **~-pit,** steengroef; **~ pitching,** klipbestrating; **~-quarry,** steengroef, klipgat; **~ saw,** klipsaag; **~'s cast,** **~'s throw,** hanetreetjie, klipgooi, **~-thrower,** klipgooier; **~ throwing,** klipgooiery; **~ wall,** (n) klipmuur; obstruksie (in die parlement); **~ wall,** (v) verdedigend speel; obstruksie voer; **~-wall,** (a) doodveilig (sport); **~-waller,** muurstapelaar, obstruksievoerder; **~-walling,** klipmuurwerk, klipstapeling; obstruksie; **~ ware,** klipware, erdewerk; **~ work,** klipwerk; **~ worker,** klipkapper, klipwerker.
ston'iness, klipperigheid; hardheid.
ston'ing, steniging; klipgooiery; ontpitting.
ston'y, klipperig, klip=; strak; hard, hardvogtig, ongevoelig, *give him a ~ stare,* icm. strak (sonder herkenning) aankyk; **~-broke,** platsak; **~-hearted,** hardvogtig; **~ ridge,** kliprant; **~ silence,** kille stilswye.
stood, *kyk* **stand,** (v).
stooge, (n) figurant, strooipop; ondergeskikte, werktuig; (v) dool; *~ (a)round,* ronddool.
stook, (n) tuithoop, gerfhoop, (v) hoopdra.
stool, (n) stoel (sonder leuning), bankie; kruk; ontlasting, stoelgang; vensterbank; *FALL between two ~s,* tussen twee stoele val; *GO to ~,* jou ontlas; *sit on the ~ of REPENTANCE,* op die sondaarsbankie sit; *between TWO ~s one falls on the ground,* as jy op twee stoele tegelyk wil sit, kom jy op die grond te lande; (v) stoel; ontlasting hê; **~-pigeon,** lokduif, lokvoël, lokvink.
stoop¹, (n) stoep; *kyk ook* **stoep.**
stoop², (n) kruik, bak.
stoop³, (n) krom houding; (v) buk, buig; krom loop vooroor loop, vooroor staan, vooroor buig; jou verlaag (verwerdig); *~ to a mean ACTION,* jou verlaag tot gemeenheid; *~ to CONQUER,* jou verlaag om jou doel te bereik; **~ing,** gebukkend, krom, inmekaar; **~-shouldered,** met krom rug.
stop, (n) halte (spoorweg); stilhouplek, stilstand; register (orrel); klep, toets; ploffer, klapper (taalklank); toon, wysie, melodie; einde, end; leesteken; stuiter (elektr.); *BRING to a ~,* tot stilstand bring; *COME to a ~,* gaan staan; ophou; *FULL ~,* punt; *PULL out all the ~s,* niks agterweë laat nie; *PUT a ~ to something,* 'n end maak aan; daar 'n stokkie voor steek; *WITHOUT a ~,* sonder om op te hou; (v) **(-ped),** stop, toestop, digmaak; 'n einde maak aan; ophou; uitskei; stuit, keer, teenhou; stelp (bloed); vul, stop (tand); laat stilstaan, gaan staan, stilhou, halt maak; voorkeer; oorbly, loseer; tot staan bring; stopsit; inhou (loon); staak (by werk); *~ BLOOD,* bloed stelp; *~ a CHEQUE,* 'n tjek keer; *~ one's EARS,* jou ore toestop; *~ a FIRE from spreading,* keer dat 'n brand versprei; *this has GOT to ~,* dit moet end kry; *~ a HOLE,* 'n gat toestop; *~ a HORSE,* 'n perd keer; *~ IT!* skei nou uit! hou op!; *the MATTER will not ~ there,* dit sal nie daarby bly nie; *~ someone's MOUTH,* iem. se mond snoer; *~ at NOTHING,* vir niks stuit nie; *~ PAYMENT,* betaling staak; *~ SHORT,* skielik vasstees; *~ a TOOTH,* 'n tand stop; *the TRAIN ~s there,* die trein hou daar stil; *the WATCH has ~ped,* die oorlosie het gaan staan; *~ WORK,* ophou (werk); staak; *~ a WOUND,* die bloed stelp; (interj) hanou! hou stil! hou op! **~-axle,** astap, kortas; **~ bead,** skeistrook; **~-block,** stootblok, keerblok; **~ brick,** vloeisteen; **~-butt,** koeëlvanger; **~-cleat,** stootklamp; **~ cock,** afsluitkraan.
stope, (n) delfplek, afbouplek; (v) delf, afbou; **~ box,** kokersluis; **~ face,** afboufront; **~r,** afbouer; houer, breker.
stop: **~-face,** stuitvlak; **~ gap,** stoplap; stopmiddel; noodhulp; stopwoord.
stop'ing, frontwerk, afbou.
stop: **~-light,** stoplig; **~-nut,** sluitmoer, borgmoer; **~ order,** aftrekorder; **~-order deduction,** aftrekmagtiging; **~-over,** oornagting; stilhouplek.
stop'page, (die) ophou, staking, stopsetting, uitskeiding; oponthoud; stilstand; skorsing; aanhouding; inhouding; **~ account,** inhou(dings)rekening; **~ clerk,** inhou(dings)klerk.
stopped, gekeer; gestop; gestuit; gestelp (bloed); **~ end,** doodloopent.
stop'per, prop, kurk; *put a ~ on something,* 'n end aan iets maak.
stop: **~-pin,** stuitpen; **~ ping,** (die) ophou, stilstand, afsluiting; (tand)stopsel, (tand)vulling, vulsel; **~ping fire,** keervuur, stuitvuur; **~ping place,** halte, rusplek.
stop'ple, (n) prop, kurk; (v) toeprop, toekurk
stop: **~ plug,** stopprop; **~-press,** laat berigte; **~ rack,** keerbalk; **~ ring,** stuitring; **~ screw,** stuitskroef; **~ sign,** stopteken; **~ signal,** stopsein; **~ street,** stopstraat; **~ valve,** afsluitklep; **~ watch,** stopoorlosie.
stor'age, opsameling, ophoping; opgaring; opberging, bewaring; pakhuisgeld, bewaargeld, bergloon; bêreplek, pakplek; pakhuisruimte; *COLD ~,* koelkamer; *IN ~,* weggepak, weggebêre; **~ accommodation,** opslagruimte; **~ battery,** akkumulator; **~-bin,** opslagbak, opgaarkis; **~-chamber,** opslagkamer; **~ charges,** berg(ings)koste; opslagkoste; **~-dam,** bewaardam, opgaardam; **~ fee,** bewaargeld; bergloon, pakhuisgeld; **~ loft,** paksolder; **~ pit,** opbergingsplek; bewaarplek; **~ reservoir,** opgaardam; **~ room,** pakkamer; **~ space,** bergruimte; pakplek; **~ tank,** opgaartenk; **~ yard,** opslagwerf.
stor'ax, storaks (boom).
store, (n) voorraad; oorvloed; pakhuis, magasyn, opslagplek, stoor; winkel; vetmaakbees; (pl) voorraad; benodigdhede; *there is something IN ~ for one,* iets staan jou te wagte; dis jou voorland; daar wag iets vir jou; *KEEP in ~,* in voorraad hou; *a ~ of KNOWLEDGE,* 'n skat van kennis; *SET great ~ by,* op prys stel; baie waarde heg aan; *do not SET too much ~ by that,* moenie daarop staatmaak nie; moenie te veel waarde daaraan heg nie; *~s and SUPPLIES,* magasyn en voorrade; *there is a SURPRISE in ~ for you,* daar wag 'n verrassing vir jou; *what has TOMORROW in ~ for us?,* wat gaan môre vir ons oplewer? (v) bêre; opstapel, wegpak; voorsien van; versamel, opgaar; *~ AWAY,* wegpak, bêre; *~ UP,* opgaar, versamel; **~-breaker,** winkelinbreker; **~-breaking,** winkelinbraak; **~ cattle,** voerbeeste, vetmaakbeeste; **~-detective,** winkelspeurder; **~ house,** voorraadskuur, pakhuis,

bewaarplaas; stoor; skatkamer; ~**keeper,** winkelier; magasynmeester; pakhuisbaas; ~**man,** (..**men),** magasynmeester, pakhuisman; ~**-ox,** (-en), vetmaakos, voeros; ~**-room,** bêreplek, pakkamer; ~**-ship,** proviandskip; ~**s clerk,** pakhuisklerk; ~**s list,** voorraadlys.

stor'ey, (-s), verdieping; *the FIRST* ~, die eerste verdieping; *LOWER* ~, onderverdieping; *the SECOND* ~, die tweede verdieping; *be a little wrong in the UPPER* ~, van lotjie getik; *he is weak in the UPPER* ~, nie al sy varkies is in die hok nie.

stor'ied[1]**,** met verdiepings.

stor'ied[2]**,** histories; vermaard, in die geskiedenis vermeld; kleurig; *the* ~ *past,* die historiese verlede.

stork, ooievaar; sprinkaanvoël; *BLACK* ~, groot swart sprinkaanvoël; *WHITE* ~, groot wit sprinkaanvoël; ~**-party,** ooievaarspartytjie.

storm, (n) storm; stortbui; vlaag, beroering, uitbarsting; bestorming; ~ *of APPLAUSE,* stormagtige toejuiging; *a* ~ *of BULLETS,* 'n koeëlreën; blase *BY* ~, stormenderhand verower; *CAPE of S~s,* Stormkaap; *MAGNETIC* ~, magnetiese storm; *and STRESS,* storm en drang; *a* ~ *in a TEACUP,* 'n storm in 'n glas water; (v) storm; stormjaag; bestorm; woed, bulder, tier; uitvaar; te keer gaan; ~ *AT a person about something,* uitvaar teen iem. oor iets; ~ *INTO a room,* 'n kamer binnestorm; ~**-area,** stormgebied; ~**-beaten,** deur storms geteister; ~**-belt,** stormstreek; ~**-bird,** stormvoël; ~**bound,** deur storms opgehou (vasgekeer); ~**cloud,** onweerswolk; ~ **damage,** stormskade; ~ **drain,** stormpyp, stormriool; ~ **drum,** stormtrom; ~**-finch,** stormvoël; ~**iness,** stormagtigheid; ~**ing,** (n) bestorming; (a) aanvallend; ~**ing-party,** aanvallende party; ~**-lamp,** stormlamp; ~**-lantern,** stormlantern; ~**-petrel,** stormvoël; ~ **sail,** stormseil; ~**-signal,** stormteken, stormsein; ~**-tide,** stormgety; ~**-tossed,** deur storms geslinger; ~**-troops,** stormtroepe; ~**-warning,** stormwaarskuwing.

storm'-water, vloedwater, stormwater; ~ **drain,** noodvoor; ~ **drainage,** vloedwaterafvoer; ~ **pipe,** vloedwaterpyp; ~ **sewer,** vloedwaterriool.

storm'y, stormagtig; onstuimig; ~ **night,** stormnag; ~ **petrel,** stormvoël; ~ **weather,** stormweer.

story[1]**,** (..**ries),** *kyk* **storey.**

story[2]**,** (..**ries),** verhaal, vertelling, geskiedenis, historie; vertelsel; storie; verslag, berig; verklaring; *but that is ANOTHER* ~, maar dit is 'n ander ding (saak); *the* ~ *GOES that,* dit word vertel dat; *I have HEARD that* ~ *before,* dit weet ek al; *that is HIS* ~, dis wat hy sê; dit weet hy te vertel; *make a LONG* ~ *short,* om kort te gaan; *that is an OLD* ~, dis 'n ou storie; ek ken daardie rympie; *there is a* ~ *doing the ROUNDS,* die gerug doen die ronde; *the SAME old* ~, die ou liedjie; *SERIAL* ~, vervolgverhaal; *SHORT* ~, kortverhaal; *tell someone a TALL* ~, iem. 'n ongelooflike verhaal vertel; *tell TALL stories,* wolhaarstories vertel; spekskiet; *TELL stories,* verhale vertel; jok, spekskiet (fig.); *you are TELLING me a* ~, jy speel met my; jy jok; jy skiet spek; ~**-book,** storieboek; ~**-teller,** verhaler, verteller; leuenaar; ~**-telling,** vertellery, vertelkuns; spekskietery, gejok.

stoup, wywatervaatjie; kruik.

stout, (n) donker bier, swartbier; (a) fris, fors, sterk, stoer; dapper, onversetlik; swaarlywig, dik, swaar, korpulent; *I* ~ *and thou* ~, *who will bear the ASHES out?,* ek meneer en jy meneer, wie sal dan die wa moet smeer?; ~ *FELLOW!,* ou bees!, ou perd! ryperd!; *have a* ~ *HEART,* onverstrokke (dapper) wees; *put up a* ~ *RESISTANCE,* taai weerstand bied; ~**-hearted,** moedig, dapper; *be* ~**-hearted,** moedig (dapper) wees; 'n groot hart hê; ~**-heartedness,** onverskrokkenheid, dapperheid; ~**ish,** dikkerig, taamlik geset; ~**ness,** gesetheid; moed; sterkte, stoerheid.

stove[1]**,** (n) stoof; droogoond; voetstofie; kaggel.

stove[2]**,** (v) *kyk* **stave,** (v).

stove: ~**-blacking,** stoofpolitoer; ~**-brush,** stoofborsel; ~ **grate,** stoofrooster; ~**-pipe,** kaggelpyp;

stoofpyp; hoë hoed, keil; ~**-pipe trousers,** noupypbroek; ~**-plate,** stoofplaat; ~**-polish,** stoofwaks.

stov'er, mieliestronke, veevoer.

stow, bêre, wegsit; bewaar; stu; laai; verstop; ~ *AWAY,* bêre, wegpak; ~ *IT!,* hou nou op!; bly stil!; ~**age,** bêreplek; laairuimte; laaivermoë; pakhuisgeld, bergloon; lading; inlaai, berging; stuwasie; ~**away,** (n) verstekeling, blindepassasier, wegkruiper; ~ **away,** (v) jou versteek (op 'n skip), wegkruip; ~ **expenses,** stuwasiegeld; ~**ing,** rotsopvulling.

strabis'mus, skeelkykery, skeelheid, strabisme.

strabot'omy, skeelkykoperasie, strabotomie.

strad'dle, wydsbeen loop (staan, sit); op twee gedagtes hink; ~ *a target,* 'n doelwit invurk; ~**s,** kontrakspreiding, brugspreiding (ekon.); ~**-trench,** hurksloot; ~**-truck,** buidelwa.

strafe, (sl.), beskiet; hewig aanval; opdons.

strag'gle, dwaal, swerwe, verdwaal; agterbly, verstrooid raak, streep-streep loop; lank uitskiet (plant); verstrooid raak; ~**r,** agterblyer; afdwaler; sukkelaar; swerfvoël; wilde loot.

stragg'ling, verstrooid, verspreid, uitgestrek; agterblywend; ongereeld; slordig; ~ **gait,** onreëlmatige gang.

stragg'ly, verstrooid, verspreid; yl (baard); ongelyk.

straight, (n) reguit ent; reguit stuk; vyf opeenvolgende kaarte, volgkaarte; pylvak (sport); peilvlak (waterpas); *out of the* ~, nie reguit nie, krom, skeef; (a) reguit, direk, ronduit, op die man af; ruiterlik, opreg, eerlik; in orde, aan die kant; orent; sluik (hare); skoon (in tennis); *the ACCOUNTS are* ~, die rekeninge is in orde; *as* ~ *as an ARROW,* pylreguit; so reguit soos 'n kers; *as* ~ *as a DIE,* so reguit soos 'n roer; *keep a* ~ *FACE,* jou gesig in die plooi hou; jou lag inhou; *keep to the* ~ *and NARROW path,* die smal pad bewandel; *ask a* ~ *QUESTION,* iets op die man af vra; *two* ~ *SETS,* twee agtereenvolgende skoon stelle; *give a* ~ *TALK,* openhartig praat; (adv) onmiddellik; reguit; ~ *ACROSS,* regoor; ~ *AWAY,* op staande voet, reëlreg, voetstoots; ~ *in the EYES,* reg in die oë; ~ *in the FACE,* reguit in die gesig; *GET* ~ *with,* sake in orde maak met; *GIVE it to him* ~, hom reguit die waarheid vertel; ~ *from the HORSE'S mouth,* uit die allerbeste bron; *KEEP (go)* ~, op die regte pad bly; in orde hou; *MAKE* ~ *for a place,* na 'n plek pyl; ~ *OFF,* dadelik; sonder meer; ~ *ON,* reguit; ~ *OUT,* ronduit, prontuit; *PUT* ~, reguit, in orde bring; aan kant maak; sake regsit; ~ *OUT,* ronduit, prontuit; *be QUITE* ~, eerlik wees; ~ *SETS,* skoon stelle; *let someone have it* ~ *from the SHOULDER,* iem. kaalkop jou mening gee; *TALK* ~ *out,* reguit praat; *THINK* ~, logies dink; ~ *THROUGH,* dwarsdeur; ~ *UP,* penorent; ~ **angle,** gestrekte hoek; ~ **arch,** plat boog; ~ **brandy,** skoon (onvermengde) brandwyn; ~ **comedy,** blyspel (sonder sang, ens.); ~**-edge,** metaalduimstok; reihout; ~**-eight,** agt op 'n ry; agt-in-lyn (motor); ~**en,** reguit maak; regmaak, opknap; regtrek; ~*en things out,* die saak weer regmaak; ~**ening bar,** trekkoevoet; ~ **faggoting,** leersteek; ~ **fight,** tweekandidaatverkiesing; ~ **flush,** vyf opeenvolgende kaarte van een kleur; ~ **forward,** reguit, sonder omweë, rondborstig; padlangs; ~**streeks;** ~**forwardness,** opregtheid, rondborstigheid; ~**-grained wood,** langsdradige hout; ~ **hair,** steil hare; ~ **hand,** vyf volgkaarte; ~ **jacket,** *kyk* **strait jacket;** ~**-laced,** *kyk* **strait-laced;** ~ **line,** reguit lyn; ~**-lined,** reglynig; ~ **lock,** opêslot; ~**ness,** direktheid; orde; sluikheid (van hare); opregtheid; engte, noute; ~ **set,** skoon stel; ~ **shooting,** raakskiet; ~ **talk,** openhartige gesprek; ~ **thinking,** logiese denke; ~**way,** dadelik, onmiddellik.

strain, (n) inspanning, uiterste poging; verrekking; verstuiting; trant, manier; toon, wysie; druk; spanning; trekspanning; oorspanning; drukspanning; vormverandering (geol.); inslag; verdraaiing; karakter, aanleg, trek; tikkie, element; geslag, lyn, bloed, ras, bloedlyn (vee); stam (hoenders bv.); *BE under a* ~, onder spanning verkeer; *their FRIEND-SHIP stood the* ~, hulle vriendskap was hierteen

straining bestand; *from a GOOD* ~, van goeie familie; *there is a* ~ *of INSANITY in the family*, daar is kranksinnigheid in die familie; *of NOBLE* ~, van goeie familie; *it is a* ~ *ON him*, dit eis baie van hom; *RELIEVE* ~, spanning verlig; *in the SAME* ~, in dieselfde trant; (v) verrek, verstuit; verlê; ooreis, forseer; pers; filtreer, deurgiet, deurgooi, deursyfer, (deur)syg, (deur)sif (vloeistof); span (draad); styf trek; uitrek; verdraai (waarheid); ~ *AT*, hard trek, beur; alte nougeset wees; ~ *one's EARS*, die ore spits; ~ *after EFFECT*, op effek jagmaak; ~ *one's EYES*, die oë ooreis; ~ *at a GNAT*, alte nougeset wees; jou kop oor kleinighede breek; ~ *at a GNAT and swallow a camel,* 'n muggie uitsif en 'n kameel insluk; ~ *the LAW*, die wet verdraai; ~ *every NERVE*, jou tot die uiterste inspan; ~ *OUT*, uitsyg; ~ *a POINT*, oordryf; let ver gaan; ~ *the VOICE*, die stem forseer; ~-**burst**, spanningsbreuk; ~**ed**, gespanne; gemaak, onnatuurlik, geforseer(d); verdraaid, verwronge; ~*ed NERVES*, oorspanne senuwees; ~*ed RELATIONS*, 'n gespanne verhouding; ~**er**, melkdoek, sygdoek; deursyger, siffie, vergiettes, gaatjiesbak; draadtrekker; ~-**gauge**, rekmeter.

strain'ing: ~ **arch**, steunboog; ~ **beam**, spanbalk; ~ **bolt**, spanbout; ~ **post (pole)**, trekpaal, ankerpaal, spanpaal; ~ **trestle**, rekbok.

strait, (n) seestraat; engte; moeilikheid; bergpas; *be in DIRE* ~ *s*, in die verknorsing wees; erg verleë wees; (a) nou, eng; beperk; bekrompe; *the* ~ *gate*, die enge poort; ~**en**, beperk; styf span; in die knyp bring, in ~ened circumstances, in armoedige omstandighede; dit nie breed hê nie; ~ **jacket**, dwangbaadjie, dwangbuis; *in a* ~ *jacket*, gestrem; ~-**laced**, styf geryg; gedwonge; kleingeestig, preuts; ~ **waistcoat**, dwangbuis.

stramin'eous, strooi=, strooiagtig; strooikleurig, liggeel; waardeloos.

stramon'ium, stinkblaar, stinkolie.

strand[1], (n) string, draad; koord; vesel (tou); (v) afbreek (van 'n draad); vleg.

strand[2], (n) strand, kus; (v) laat strand, strand; ~**ed**, gestrand, vergaan; verleë; geskore; in die moeilikheid; *BE* ~ *ed*, op die strand loop; skipbreuk ly (fig.); bly sit; vassteek, nie verder kan kom nie; ~*ed GOODS*, strandgoed; ~*ed without any MONEY*, geskore wees, sonder geld.

strand'ed: ~ **cable**, stringkabel; ~ **cotton**, stringgaring; ~**ed steel**, veselstaal; ~ **wire**, draadtou.

strand'ing[1], vlegting; breking.
strand'ing[2], stranding.

strange, vreemd, onbekend; sonderling, snaaks, eksentriek, ongewoon, aardig, raar, sonderbaar; wonderlik, opvallend; *FEEL* ~, nie lekker voel nie; ontuis voel; ~ *to SAY*, dis snaaks, maar; *I am* ~ *to the WORK*, ek is onbekend met (onbedrewe in) die werk; ~**ness**, vreemdheid, onbekendheid; eienaardigheid, wonderlikheid, ongewoonte, sonderlikheid, rarigheid.

strang'er, vreemdeling, vreemde, onbekende, buitelander, uitlander; *BE a* ~, onbekend wees; *BE a* ~ *in Jerusalem*, 'n vreemdeling in Jerusalem wees; *be a* ~ *to all DISCIPLINE*, niks van dissipline weet nie; *you are QUITE a* ~, 'n mens sien jou so min.

stra'ngle, (ver)wurg; versmoor; onderdruk; ~ **d**, verwurg; gesmoor; ~**hold**, wurggreep; *have a* ~ *hold on someone*, 'n wurggreep op iem. hê; ~ **r**, verwurger; smoorklep (motor); ~**s**, nuwesiekte; droes.

stra'ngling, (ver)wurging.

strang'ulate, toetrek, vasbind; (ver)wurg; ~ **d**, ingesnoer, verwurg.

strangula'tion, (ver)wurging; beklemming (breuk); afbind, afsnoering.

strang'ury, pynlike waterlating, stranguurie.

strap, (n) platriem; riem; band; strop; skeerriem; lis (lus); *APPLY the* ~, met die platriem gee, die platriem inlê; *GIVE someone a taste of the* ~, iem. onder die platriem (strop) laat deurloop; (v) (**-ped**), met riem vasmaak; vasgord; skerp maak; uitlooi, afransel; ~ *on*, aangespe; ~ **hanger**, luspassasier, lushanger, staanpassasier; ~-**hinge**, tongskarnier; ~**less**, sonder band; ~**less gown**, skouerlose tab-

berd; ~**less sandal**, plakkie, oop sandaal; ~-**oil**, rottangolie, streepsuiker.

strappad'o, wipgalg.

strap: ~ **per**, lang sterk man; leuen; slaner; ~ **ping**, (n) pak slae, loesing; vasmaak; belatting; (a) sterk, groot, frisgebou, stewig; ~ **ping machine**, bindmasjien; ~ **saw**, bandsaag.

strat'agem, krygslis; streek.

strate'gic(al), strategies; krygskundig; ~ *arms limitation talks (SALT)*, kernsperverdragonderhandelinge; ~ **goal**, strategiese doelwit; ~ **interest**, strategiese belang.

strat'egist, strateeg; krygskundige.

strat'egy, krygskunde; strategie.

stratic'ulate, in dun lae, gelaag.

stratifica'tion, laagsgewyse ligging, laagvorming, gelaagdheid, stratifikasie.

strat'ified, in lae, gelaag, laagvormig, meerlaag=.

strat'iform, laagvormig, gelaag.

strat'ify, (..**fied**), in lae vorm, stratifiseer.

stratigraph'ic, stratigrafies.

stratig'raphy, leer v.d. aardlae, stratigrafie.

stratoc'racy, soldateregering, militaristiese bewind, stratokrasie.

strat'osphere, stratosfeer.

stratospher'ic, stratosferies.

strat'um, (..**ta**), laag, stratum; aardlaag.

strat'us, (..**ti**), laag; wolklaag, stratus, wolkbank; ~ *of coal*, steenkoollaag, steenkoolbed.

straw, (n) strooi, strooitjie; drinkstrooitjie; kleinigheid; *the last* ~ *BREAKS the camel's back*, die laaste loodjies weeg die swaarste; *not CARE a* ~, niks omgee nie; maling aan iets hê; *CATCH at a* ~, aan 'n strooihalm vasklou; *DRAW* ~ *s*, lootjies trek; *HAVE a* ~ *to break with someone,* 'n appeltjie met iem. te skil hê; *that was the LAST* ~, dit was die laaste druppel wat die emmer laat oorloop het; *a MAN of* ~, 'n strooipop; 'n man van toet; *STUMBLE over a* ~ *and leap over a block,* 'n muggie uitsif en 'n kameel insluk; *THROW* ~ *s against the wind,* water in 'n mandjie dra; *a* ~ *in the WIND,* 'n aanduiding; *a* ~ *shows which way the WIND blows,* 'n klein aanduidinkie kan baie sê; *not WORTH a* ~, niks werd nie; (a) strooi=; van strooi.

straw'berry, (..**rries**), aarbei; *..berries and cream*, aarbeie en room; ~ **bush**, aarbeistoel; ~ **cake**, aarbeikoek; ~ **essence**, aarbeigeursel; ~ **leaf**, aarbeiblaar; ~ **mark**, moedervlek; ~ **roan**, vosskimmel.

straw: ~-**bottomed**, met 'n strooisitplek; ~-**built**, van strooi; ~-**colour**, liggeel, strooikleur; vaalbruin; ~-**coloured**, strooikleurig; ~-**cutter**, strooisnyer, strooikerwer; ~ **flower**, sewejaartjie, strooiblom; ~ **hat**, strooihoed; ~ **hut**, strooihuis; ~ **mattress**, strooimatras; ~ **needle**, hoedenaald; ~ **vote**, proefstemming; ~**y**, strooiagtig, strooierig.

stray, (n) verdwaalde dier; verwaarloosde dier; verwaarloosde kind; swerwer; swerweling, afgedwaalde enkeling; (v) verdwaal, swerf, dool; kronkel; die verkeerde pad gaan, afdwaal; wegloop (dier); ~ *from the point*, van die punt afdwaal; (a) afgedwaal; verdwaal; dakloos; verspreid; toevallig; sporadies; *a* ~ *BULLET*, 'n verdwaalde koeël; ~ *CURRENT*, swerfstroom (elek.); *a* ~ *CUSTOMER,* 'n toevallige klant; ~ *NOTES*, los aantekeninge; ~ *THOUGHTS*, los gedagtes; ~**ed**, verdwaal; ~**er**, dwaler; afgedwaalde.

streak, (n) streep; sliert; straal; laag; strook; streepsiekte (suikerriet); *have a CRUEL* ~ *in his character,* 'n wrede trek in sy geaardheid hê; *a* ~ *of HUMOUR,* 'n tikkie humor; ~ *of LIGHT*, ligstreep; ~ *of LIGHTNING*, bliksemstraal; *have a* ~ *of MADNESS,* 'n streep hê; *a SUPERSTITIOUS* ~, 'n bygelowige streep; (v) strepe maak; streep; jaag, nael; kaalnael, kaalhol; ~**ed**, gestreep; ~ **er**, kaalbasloper, kaalnaeler, kaalholler; ~**iness**, gestreeptheid; ~**like**, sliert(er)ig; ~**y**, gestreep, geaar, streperig, deurwas; ~*y pork (bacon)*, deurwaste varkvleis (varkspek).

stream, (n) stroom; spruit, rivier, waterstroom; vloed; *row AGAINST the* ~, teen die stroom op roei; *COME on* ~, begin produseer; *DOWN* ~, stroom af; *UP* ~, stroom op; *a* ~ *of VISITORS,* 'n stroom besoekers; *go (swim) WITH the* ~, met die stroom saamgaan; *SWIM against the* ~, stroomop gaan; (v) stroom, loop; waai, wapper; laat uitloop; ~**-anchor**, werpanker; ~**-bed**, stroombedding; ~**er**, wimpel; vlag; windsak (lugv.); papierlint; spandoek; noorderlig; ~ **flow**, stroomvloei; ~**ing**, stromend; ~*ing eyes*, betraande oë; ~**let**, stroompie, lopie; ~**line**, (n) stroomlyn, vaartlyn, vaartbelyning; (v) stroomlyn, vaartbelyn; rasionaliseer, vereenvoudig; ~**lined**, stroombelyn, vaartbelyn, gestroomlyn; ~**lining**, stroombelyning, vaartbelyning; rasionalisering; ~ **tin**, spoeltinerts; ~**y**, stromend.

street, straat; *be ~ s AHEAD*, 'n hele ent voor wees; *GO on the ~s*, op straat gaan; 'n straatvrou word; *IN the* ~, op straat; *LIVE in the ~s*, op straat boer; *the MAN in the ~*, die groot publiek; die gewone man; Jan Publiek; *ON the ~s*, op straat; *not be in the SAME ~*, ver agter staan; glad nie van dieselfde gehalte wees nie; nie by 'n ander se stof kom nie; nie by iem. se hakke kom nie; *be UP someone's ~*, net so in iem. se kraal wees; binne iem. se gebied; *a WOMAN of the ~s*, 'n straatvrou; ~ **arab**, straatkind, skollie; ~ **car**, bus; ~**-cleansing**, straatreiniging; ~ **collection**, straatkollekte; ~ **corner**, straathoek; ~ **door**, voordeur; ~**-fight**, straatgeveg, straatbakleiery; ~**-fighter**, straatvegter, straatbakleier; ~**-fighting**, straatgevegte; ~ **floor**, grondverdieping; ~**-lamp**, straatlamp; ~**-light**, straatlig; ~**-lighting**, straatverligting; ~ **main**, hoofleiding; ~ **name**, straatnaam; ~**-orderly**, straatreiniger; ~**-paver**, straatwerker; ~**-performer**, straatkunstenaar; ~**-robber**, straatrower; ~**-robbery**, straatroof; ~ **scene**, straattoneel; straatgesig (skildery, tekening); ~**-singer**, straatsanger; ~**-sweeper**, straatveër; ~**-trader**, straathandelaar; ~ **traffic**, straatverkeer; ~ **tune**, straatwysie; ~ **walker**, straatloper, straatmeisie, straatvlinder, slegte vrou.

strelitz'ia, piesangblom, kraanvoëlblom, strelitzia, paradysblom.

strength, sterkte, krag; forsheid, getalsterkte; swaarte (tabak); frisheid, gehalte (alkohol); treksterkte (wol); *~ of the ARMY*, leërsterkte; *BELOW ~*, nie voltallig nie; *his ~ FAILS him*, sy kragte begeef hom; *FROM ~ to ~*, van krag tot krag; *be in FULL ~*, op volle sterkte wees; *GO from ~ to ~*, van krag tot krag gaan; *IN ~*, in groot getalle; *~ of MIND*, geesteskrag; *ON the ~ of*, op grond van, kragtens; *~ of the PARTIES*, die stand v.d. partye; *RECOVER one's ~*, jou kragte herwin; weer sterk word; *SHOW of ~*, magsvertoon; *TRY each other's ~*, kragte met mekaar meet; *UP to ~*, op sterkte; ~**en**, sterk maak, versterk, stywe; ~**ened**, gerugsteun; versterk; ~**ener**, versterker; versterking; ~**ening**, stywing, versterking; ~**less**, kragteloos, swak.

strenuos'ity = **strenuousness**.

stren'uous, ywerig, kragtig, volhardend, onvermoeid, energiek; ingespanne, veeleisend, swaar; ~ *days*, moeisame (vermoeiende) dae; ~**ness**, ywer, krag; inspanning.

streptococ'cal, streptokokke-.

streptococ'cus, (..**cocci**), streptokokkus.

streptomy'cin, streptomisien, streptomisine.

stress, (n) nadruk, klem; klemtoon; inspanning; drukspanning; (trek)spanning (elektr.); krag; drang; benardheid; druk; spanningsdruk; *under ~ of CIRCUMSTANCES*, deur omstandighede gedwing; *LAY ~ on*, nadruk lê op; *~es of LIFE*, storm en drang v.d. lewe; *~ and STRAIN*, druk en spanning; *the ~ is on the second SYLLABLE*, die aksent (klem) kom op die tweede lettergreep; *owing to ~ of WEATHER*, as gevolg van slegte weer; (v) beklemtoon, nadruk lê op, aksentueer; ~**ed**, beklemtoon; onder spanningsdruk; ~ **mark**, klemteken.

stretch, (n) (**-es**), uitgestrektheid; streek; vlakte; rekking, rek; spanning; geweldaandoening; oorskryding; oordrywing; ruk, tydperk; ent, trajek (spoor); *work six hours AT a ~*, ses uur aanmekaar (sonder onderbreking) werk; *AT a ~ we can accommodate two more*, as dit moet, kan ons nog twee huisves; *DO a ~; be in FOR a ~*, tronkstraf uitdien; *~ of IMAGINATION*, verbeeldingskrag; *not by a LONG ~*, lank nie, glad nie; *ON the ~*, gespanne; *a long ~ of ROAD*, 'n lang ent pad; *be SERVING a ~*, op regeringskoste loseer; *after a ~ of YEARS*, na verloop van jare; (v) rek; uitrek; uitstrek; inspan; oordryf; 'n ruim uitleg gee aan; geweld aandoen; *~ one's AUTHORITY*, jou gesag oorskry; *~ DOWN*, reik tot; *~ yourself FORWARD*, jou uitstrek; *~ one's LEGS*, jou bene rek; jou litte los maak; *~ OUT*, uitrek; uitstrek; *~ a POINT*, oordrywe, te ver gaan; 'n toegewing maak, een oog toemaak; *~ the TRUTH*, die waarheid geweld aandoen; ~**ed**, gerek; gevlek (vel).

stretch'er, voukateltjie, veldkatel, veldbed, voubed; draagbaar (vir sieke); rekker; rekyster (sport); dwarsbalkie, sport; oordrywing; spanstuk; strekseen; voetbankie (in skuit); ~**-bearer**, baardraer, siekedraer; ~ **frame**, spanraam; ~ **plate**, spanplaat; ~ **rod**, spanstaaf, spanstang.

stretch'ing, rekking; oorskryding; ~ **bond**, strykverband; ~ **course**, stryklaag; ~ **force**, spankrag.

stretch'y, rekkerig.

strew, (**-ed**, **-ed** or **-n**), strooi, bestrooi, besaai.

stri'a, (**-e**), groef, streep; draad; skrapie; fyn aar (in marmer); ribbetjie; skeirib (in 'n suil).

stri'ate, (v) groef, skraap; (a) gegroef, gestreep; geaar.

stria'tion, streping; streep; groefie; gestreeptheid; groewing.

strick'en, gepla, siek; geslaan, getref; swaar beproef; *with a ~ FACE*, met 'n verslae gesig; *~ with FEVER*, lydend aan koors, deur koors aangetas; *a ~ HEART*, 'n gebroke hart; *~ with REMORSE*, berouvol; *~ with TERROR*, met vrees bevange; *in a ~ VOICE*, met diepbedroefde stem; *~ in YEARS*, oud van dae.

strict, streng; stip, nougeset; strik; noukeurig, presies; eng; *BE very ~ with her children*, baie streng wees teenoor haar kinders; *~ on PUNCTUALITY*, nougeset oor stiptheid; *~ RULES*, enge reëls; *in the ~ SENSE*, in die eng(er) betekenis; *a ~ WATCH*, streng toesig.

strict'ly, stip; streng; ~ **confidential**, streng vertroulik; ~ **speaking**, streng geneem (gesproke).

strict'ness, strengheid; noukeurigheid; striktheid.

stric'ture, sametrekking, verenging; kritiese opmerking, afkeurende kritiek, afkeuring.

stride, (n) tree, stap, skrede; *AT a ~*, met een stap; *GET into one's ~*, op dreef kom; op stryk kom; *with RAPID ~s*, met rasse skrede; *TAKE something in one's ~*, iets fluit-fluit doen; sonder buitengewone inspanning verrig; *THROW someone out of his ~*, iem. van stryk bring; iem van sy wysie af bring; (v) (**strode**, **stridden** or **strid**), groot stappe maak, lang treë gee, skry; oor iets heenstap; *~ out*, vinnig aanstap.

strid'ent, krassend, skel, skerp.

strid'ulant, krassend, piepend.

strid'ulate, kras, piep.

stridula'tion, gekras, gepiep.

strife, twis, tweedrag, onenigheid, stryd; *be at ~ with*, twis met; ~**-torn**, verdeeld, twistend.

strike, (n) (werk)staking, strekking, (rif)rigting (geol.); klap; slag; vonds; aanboring (olie); byt (vis); *GO on ~*, staak; *GO-SLOW ~*, sloerstaking; *the men ON ~*, die stakers; *SIT-DOWN ~*, sitstaking; (v) (**struck**, **struck** or **stricken**), slaan; blaker, raps; foeter; aanslaan (toon); stoot, stamp, bots, tref; lyk, voorkom, skyn; stryk (vlag); trek (vuurhoutjie); inboesem (vrees); byt (vis); raak, vat; wortelskiet (plant); staak (werkers); strek (geol.); munt, stempel (geld); *~ AT*, slaan na; *~ an ATTITUDE*, 'n gemaakte houding aanneem, poseer; *~ an AVERAGE*, die gemiddelde neem; *~ BACK*, terugslaan; *~ a BALANCE*, 'n balans opmaak; *the BAND struck up*, die orkes het begin speel; *~ a BARGAIN*, 'n kopie maak; 'n slag slaan; *BE struck on*, verlief wees op; *~ BLIND*, met blindheid slaan; *~ a BLOW*, 'n slag slaan; *~ a BLOW for freedom*, vir die vryheid veg; *~ CAMP*, die kamp opbreek; *the CLOCK ~s*, die klok slaan; *~ COINS*, munte slaan; *~ one's COLOURS*, die vlag stryk; *~ up a*

CONVERSATION with, 'n praatjie aanknoop met; ~ DEAD, doodslaan; ~ me DEAD! mag ek doodval! ~ out in another DIRECTION, 'n ander koers inslaan; 'n nuwe rigting inslaan; ~ DOWN, platslaan; ~ the DRUM, die trom roer; ~ someone's FANCY, in iem. se smaak val; ~ the FLAG, die vlag stryk; ~ at the FOUNDATIONS, die grondveste ondermyn; iets rysmier; ~ into a GALLOP, begin galop, op 'n galop trek; struck on a GIRL, been-af oor 'n meisie; the argument struck HOME, die argument het getref; die argument was 'n raakskoot; ~ out for HOME, op die huis afpyl; the HOUR has struck, die uur het aangebreek; ~ upon an IDEA, op 'n gedagte kom; ~ while the IRON is hot, die yster slaan (smee) terwyl dit warm is; ~ a LIGHT, lig maak; ~ out a new LINE, 'n nuwe weg inslaan; ~ off the LIST, van die lys skrap; ~ it LUCKY, 'n geluk kry; ~ a MATCH, 'n vuurhoutjie trek; it ~ s ME, dit tref my; dit kom my voor; ~ the right NOTE, die regte toon aanslaan; ~ the OARS, die roeispane uitslaan; ~ OFF, afslaan; druk; deurtrek; aftik; ~ OIL, olie raakboor; geluk hê met 'n onderneming; ~ OUT, deurtrek, skrap; 'n uitval maak; 'n mokerhou slaan; ~ OUT for oneself, jou eie weg baan; ~ down an OPPONENT, 'n teenstander platslaan; struck down by the PLAGUE, neergetrek deur die pes; ~ it RICH, 'n ryk vonds doen; 'n slag slaan; ~ from the ROLL, van die rol skrap; ~ ROOT, wortelskiet; ~ at the ROOT of, die wortel tref van; ~ into a SONG, 'n lied aanhef; ~ SPARKS from, vonke slaan uit; ~ a TENT, 'n tent afbreek; ~ TENTS, die kamp opbreek; ~ TERROR into someone's heart, iem. met skrik vervul; ~ for higher WAGES, om 'n hoër loon staak; ~ aircraft, aanvalsvliegtuig; ~-a-light, vuurslag; ~-breaker onderkruiper; ~ committee, stakingskomitee; ~ fault, strekverskuiwing; ~ fund, stakingsfonds, stakingskas; ~ leader, stakingsleier; ~ pay, stakingstoelaag, stakingsuitkering; ~ r, staker; slaner; treffer; slaande klok; voorslaner (smid); hamer (geskut); naald (geweer); slagpen; stoter (biljart); kolwer (bofbal).
strik'ing, treffend, opvallend, pakkend, ooglopend, in-die-oog-lopend, frappant, geprononseer, markant; ~ distance, trefafstand; slagwydte; ~ force, aanvalsmag; ~-pin, slagpen; ~-plate, aanslagplaat; ~ power, slaankrag (leër); trefkrag (koeël); ~ price, trefbasis, trefprys.
string, (n) lyn, tou; sliert; seilgare; riempie, veter; uitloper (aar); rits, snoer, string (krale); reeks, ry; aaneenskakeling; snaar (musiekinstrument); ~ of BEADS, kralesnoer; BIT of ~, stukkie lyn (tou); have many ~ s to one's BOW, baie snare op jou boog hê; the FIRST ~, die beste, (music) FOR ~ s, (musiek) vir strykorkes; HARP on the same ~, altyd op dieselfde aambeeld slaan; a ~ of HORSES, 'n stoet perde; KEEP someone on a ~, iem. aan 'n lyntjie hou; a ~ of LIES, 'n rits leuens; with NO ~ s attached, sonder enige voorwaardes of beperkings; ~ of PEARLS, pêrelsnoer; PULL ~ s, drade trek; PLUCK the ~ s, die snare tokkel; the SECOND ~, die tweede beste, die handperd; the ~, always STRAINED, snaps at last, die boog kan nie altyd gespan wees nie; THE ~ s, die strykinstrumente; TOUCH a ~, 'n snaar aanraak; WITHOUT ~ s, sonder voorwaardes of beperkings; (v) (strung), inryg, insnoer (krale); besnaar; snare insit; vasbind; drade afhaal, afhaar, afdraad (boontjies); HIGHLY strung, hooggespanne, fynbesnaarde, oorgevoelig; HIGHLY strung person, senuweeorrel; ~ a LINE, 'n lyn span; ~ OUT, uitrek, uitsprei; ~ TOGETHER, inryg; ~ UP, ophang; to be strung up, opgehang word; ~ bean, snyboon; rankboon; ~ board, trapskort; ~ course, bandlaag; ~ development, lintbebouing, ~-drill, lynoefening; ~ ed, besnaar(d), snaar-; ~ ed instrument, snaarinstrument.
strin'gency, strengheid; benardheid; dringendheid; skaarste.
strin'gent, streng; drukkend, knellend; bindend; skaars, skraps.
string'er, uitlopertjie, aartjie, strepie, strokie, snoer-

tjie; dwarsbalk, verbindingsbalk; hulpkorrespondent, bykorrespondent.
string'iness, draderigheid; seningrigheid (vleis).
string'ing, snaarwerk; besnaring.
string' instrument, strykinstrument.
string'less, sonder snare, snaarloos; veselloos; sonder drade, draadloos; haarloos; ~ bean, haarlose boontjie.
string: ~ orchestra, strykorkes; ~ quartet, strykkwartet.
string'y, veselagtig, stokkerig, draderig; seningrig, taai.
strip, (n) streep, strook, reep; beleglat; TEAR to ~ s, aan flenters skeur; TEAR a ~ off someone, iem. oor die kole haal; (v) (-ped), afstroop; plunder, berowe; afslag; uitklee, ontklee, uitskud, uittrek (klere); onttakel (skip); droog melk (koei); ontneem; afskilder; afdruk; doldraai, afdraai (draad van skroef); afhaal (bed); in repies sny (vrugte); aftakel (skip); ~ BARE, iem. kaal uitskud; iem. rot en kaal steel; ~ a COW, 'n koei droogmelk; ~ ped of his DIGNITY, ontdaan van sy waardigheid; ~ DOWN, stroop; ~ GEARS, tandratte stroop; ~ OFF, afdruk, afstroop; ~ a SHIP, 'n skip onttakel; ~ cartoon, strokiesprent; ~ development, lintbou, lintbebouing.
stripe, (n) streep; striem, hou; chevron (mil.); streepsiekte; GET one's ~ s, jou strepe kry; tot 'n hoër rang bevorder word; (militêre) verhoging kry; LOSE one's ~ s, gedegradeer wees; tot laer rang verlaag word; (v) streep; bestreep; ~ d, gestreep, streep-; ~ d material, strepiesgoed.
strip: ~ floor, strookvloer, strookplanke; ~ iron, bandyster; ~ leaf, gestroopte tabak; ~ light, streeplig.
strip'ling, jongeling, jongman; opgeskote seun, penkop.
stripped, geblaar (tabak).
stripp'er, afslagter; skilmasjien; stroper; ontkleedanseres.
stripp'ing, afstroping; ontkleding; aftuiging, aftakeling (skip); ontbloting; ~ chisel, stroopbeitel; ~ container, plukkis; ~ film, aftrekfilm.
strip: ~ pings, laaste melk; ~ road, strookpad; ~-steel, bandstaal; ~-tease, ontkleedans, lokdans, verleidans, tergdans; ~-teaser, ontkleemeisie, ontkleedanseres; ~ wise, strooksgewys.
strip'y, gestreep, met strepe, streperig.
strive, (strove, striven), probeer, poog, trag, strewe; worstel; jou bes doen, jou inspan; wedywer; ~ for PEACE, streef na vrede; ~ against TEMPTATION, veg teen die versoeking; ~ r, strewer.
striv'ing, (n) wedywer; inspanning; (a) wedywerend.
strob'oscope, stroboskoop.
stroboscop'ical, stroboskopies.
strode, kyk stride, (v).
stroke, (n) skoot; hou, raps; haal; slaglengte (motor); strook, beroerte, liefkosing, streling, streep, trek; stoot (biljart); ~ of APOPLEXY, beroerte; AT a ~, met een slag; a ~ of a BRUSH, 'n penseelstreep; do a good ~ of BUSINESS, 'n goeie slag slaan; a CLEVER ~, 'n slim set; little ~ s FELL great oaks, klein oorsake het groot gevolge; klein begin, aanhou win; the FINISHING ~, die genadeslag; a ~ of GENIUS, 'n geniale idee; GET eight ~ s, tot agt houe veroordeel word; a ~ of LIGHTNING, 'n bliksemslag; a ~ of LUCK, 'n gelukslag (gelukskoot); met jou neus in die botter val; be OFF one's ~, van slag wees; ON the ~ of one, op die kop eenuur; klokslag eenuur; ~ of PARALYSIS, verlamming; at one ~ of the PEN, met een pennestreep; a ~ of POLICY, 'n politieke set; PUT someone off his ~, iem. van stryk bring; ROW ~, slagroei; die slag aangee; a ~ of WIT, 'n geestige set; not a ~ of WORK, nie 'n steek werk nie; (v) streel, liefkoos, paai; aai; 'n streep trek; slagroei; stryk oor; ~ someone DOWN, iem. laat afkoel; iem. tot bedaring bring; ~ someone's HAIR the wrong way, iem. vererg; ~ someone the WRONG way, iem. verkeerd aanpak; iem. omkrap; ~ batsman, stylkolwer; ~ oar, slagriem, slagspaan; ~ play, houespel (gholf); stylkolfwerk (krieket).

stroll, (n) wandeling; *go for a* ~, gaan loop; (v) wandel, loop, slenter, drentel, rondswier, flenter, flankeer, flaneer; rondswerwe; ~ **er**, wandelaar; drentelaar, slenteraar; ~**ing**, wandeling; flankeerdery, slentery.

strom'a, (**-ta**), steunweefsel, stroma.

strong, sterk, kragtig; fors; ferm; fiks, fris; heg; vurig, dugtig, versterk; swaar, magtig; kras, skerp; galsterig (botter); *by the* ~ *ARM*, met geweld; ~ *CHALLENGE*, sterk (groot) uitdaging; *we are GOING* ~, ons het baie sukses; ons gaan nog een stryk vorentoe; *use* ~ *LANGUAGE*, kras taal gebruik; *the MARKET is* ~, die mark is vas; *thirty MEN* ~, dertig man sterk; *you have a* ~ *POINT there*, daar het jy 'n goeie argument; *his maths is not his* ~ *POINT*, sy krag lê nie in die wiskunde nie; *that's PRETTY* ~, dis nogal kras; *a* ~ *REPUBLICAN*, 'n oortuigde (vurige) republikein; ~ *SUIT*, sterk kleur (kaarte); sterkpunt; krag; ~-**arm**, uitsmyter; ~-**arm methods**, geweld; hardhandige metodes; ~-**backed**, sterk van rug; ~-**box**, brandkas; brandtrommel; ~ **butter**, galsterige botter; ~ **drink**, sterk drank, alkohol; hardehout; ~-**headed**, koppig; kragtig; knap; ~**hold**, sterkte, bolwerk, vesting; ~**ish**, nogal sterk; ~ **language**, kras taal; gekruide woorde; ~-**limbed**, sterk (van lede).

strong'ly, sterk; kragtig; ~ *BUILT*, sterk gebou; *FEEL* ~ *about*, sterk voel oor.

strong: ~**man**, sterk man; kragmens; leier; ~-**minded**, kragtig, sterk, vasberade; ~ **point**, steunpunt; sterktepunt (mil.); ~-**room**, brandkamer, kluis; brandkelder; ~-**willed**, hardnekkig; doelgerig.

stron'tia, stronsiaan.

stron'tium, stronsium.

strop, (n) skeerriem, strykriem; (v) (**-ped**), slyp, skerp maak; ~ *a razor*, 'n skeermes skerp maak (slyp, aansit).

stroph'e, strofe.

stroph'ic, strofies.

stropp'er, skeermesslyper.

strove, *kyk* **strive**.

struck, *kyk* **strike**, (v); ~ *from the roll*, van die rol geskrap.

struc'tural, bou-, boukundig; struktureel, struktuur-; ~ **alteration**, struktuurverandering; verbouing; ~ **design**, struktuurontwerp; ~ **draughtsman**, boutekenaar; ~ **engineer**, boukundige; bou-ingenieur; ~ **engineering**, bou-ingenieurswese; ~ **formula**, struktuurformule; ~ **steel**, boustaal; ~ **steelwork**, boustaalwerk.

struc'ture, bou, struktuur; samestelling; bousel; gewrog; bouwerk; samestel.

strug'gle, (n) worsteling, geveg, stryd, gespook; gesukkel; *the* ~ *to DEATH*, die stryd op lewe en dood; *the* ~ *for EXISTENCE*, lewenstryd; die stryd om die bestaan; *the* ~ *for LIFE*, lewenstryd; die stryd om die bestaan; (v) worstel, baklei; spartel, swoeg, strewe, stribbel, noustrop trek, (dood)sukkel; ~ *ALONG*, voortworstel, met moeite vooruitkom, aansukkel; ~ *with DIFFICULTIES*, met moeilikhede te kampe hê; ~ *INTO one's clothes*, jou klere aansukkel; ~ *THROUGH*, deurworstel, deursukkel; ~**r**, worstelaar, stryder.

strugg'ling, (n) gespartel; (a) worstelend.

strum, (n) gekras; getrommel; getjingel; (v) (**-med**), trommel; tjingel; kras.

strum'a, (**-e**), kropgeswel, krop, skildkliervergroting, struma.

strumm'ing, getrommel; getjingel.

strum'ose, **strum'ous**, klieragtig, klier-.

strum'pet, hoer, slet, ligtekooi.

strung, *kyk* **string**, (v).

strut, (n) deftige stap; stut, skoorpaal (myn); styl; (v) (**-ted**), trots loop, pronk; stut.

struth'ious, volstruis-, volstruisagtig.

strutt'er, pronker.

strych'nine, strignien, strignine, wolwegif.

stub, (n) stompie (sigaret); blok; teenblad; domkop; entjie; (v) (**-bed**), skoonkap, uitkap; dooddruk (sigaret); ~-**axle**, krinkas, stompas; ~**biness**, stompheid, stoetsheid, gesetheid.

stub'ble, stoppel; stoppelland; ~**d**, stoppel(r)ig; ~ **field**, stoppelland; ~-**goose**, stoppelgans.

stubb'ly, stoppel-, stoppelrig, stoppelig; ~ **beard**, stoppelbaard; ~ **hair**, stoppelhare.

stubb'orn, hardnekkig, koppig, weerspannig, halsstarrig, stug, obstinaat; ~ *person*, 'n hardekop; ~**ness**, koppigheid, hardnekkigheid, obstinaatheid, halsstarrigheid, stugheid; ~**ly**, koppig, halsstarrig, weerspannig.

stubb'y, kort en dik; stomp; stoppel(r)ig.

stub: ~-**file**, kolfvyl, vlakvyl; ~ **mortise**, stomp tapgat; ~ **nail**, buksspyker.

stucc'o, (n) (**-es**), stukadoorpleister, stukadoorkalk, stukadoorgips; (v) pleister, stukadoor; ~-**worker**, stukadoor.

stuck, vasgeraak, vasgeval; *kyk ook* **stick**, (v); *BE* ~, vassit; *GET* ~, vasval, vassit; *squeal like a* ~ *PIG*, soos 'n maer vark skreeu; ~ **moulding**, oplêlys; ~-**up**, trots, hovaardig, verwaand, wipperig.

stud[1], (n) stoetery (vee); *the horse is at* ~, die perd (hings) is vir teeldoeleindes beskikbaar.

stud[2], (n) halsknopie, boordjieknoop; nok; knoppie; klinknael, omklinkspyker; stut, stuitpennetjie; draagknop (bajonet); tapbout; beslagspyker; skyfie, soolknop (voetbalskoen); (v) (**-ded**), met knoppies versier; beslaan, spykers inslaan; beset, bedek; versprei; besaai (met sterre); ~-**bolt**, tapbout.

stud: ~-**book**, stamboek; ~-**cattle**, stamboekvee.

stud'ded, besaai (met sterre); beslaan.

stud'ding sail, lyseil.

stud'ent, student (van 'n universiteit); leerling, skolier; navorser; ~ **centre**, studentesentrum; ~ **days**, studentetyd; ~ **instructor**, leerlinginstrukteur; ~ **interpreter**, leerlingtolk; ~ **life**, studentelewe; ~**like**, studentikoos; ~ **movement**, studentebeweging; ~ **newspaper**, studentekoerant; ~ **nurse**, leerlingverpleegster; ~ **officer**, studentoffisier; ~ **pilot**, leerlingvlieënier, leerlingvlieër; ~**s' almanac**, studentealmanak; ~**s' corporation**, studentekorps; ~**ship**, studentskap; studiebeurs; ~**s' jargon**, studentetaal; ~**s' magazine**, studenteblad; ~**s' prank**, studentegrap, studentestreek; ~**s' rag**, studentejool; ~**s' representative council**, verteenwoordigende studenteraad; ~**s' society**, studentevereniging; ~**s' song**, studentelied; ~**s' union**, studentebond.

stud: ~-**ewe**, stoetooi; ~-**farm**, stoetery; stoetplaas; ~-**farming**, stoetboerdery; ~-**fee**, dekgeld; ~-**horse**, dekhings; volbloedhings, stamboekperd.

stud'ied, geleerd; bestudeer(d); deurwrog; gekunsteld; opsetlik; ~**ly**, opsetlik.

stud'io, (**-s**), ateljee; werkkamer; klanksaal (radio); ~ **orchestra**, ateljeeorkes.

stud'ious, fluks, ywerig, vlytig, leergraag, leergierig, studieus; angsvallig, sorgsaam; opsetlik; *with* ~ *CARE*, met stipte sorgvuldigheid; *with* ~ *POLITENESS*, met opsetlike hoflikheid; ~**ness**, leerlus, leergierigheid; angsvalligheid, ywer(igheid).

stud: ~-**mare**, stoetmerrie, aanteelmerrie; ~-**ram**, stoetram, volbloedram; teelram; ~-**stock**, stoetvee; ~ **thorn**, elandsdoring; duwweltjie.

stud'y, (**studies**), (n) studie; studeerkamer; skets; (pl) leerwerk; *in a BROWN* ~, in gepeins versink; *a* ~ *of a CHILD*, 'n kindersketse; *DEVOTE much* ~ *to*, 'n ernstige studie maak van; *her FACE was a* ~, dit was die moeite werd om haar gesig te bestudeer; haar gelaatsuitdrukking was interessant; *MAKE a* ~ *of*, 'n studie maak van; *PURSUE one's studies*, jou studie voortsit; *SUBJECT of one's* ~, studievak; (v) (**studied**), studeer; bestudeer; strewe na; instudeer (toneelrol); rekening hou met; ~ *the CONVENIENCE of others*, met die gerief van ander rekening hou; ~ *for a DEGREE*, vir 'n graad studeer; ~ *his own INTERESTS*, na sy eie belange kyk; ~ *LAW*, in die regte studeer; ~ *MEDICINE*, in die medisyne studeer; ~ *a MATTER*, studie maak van 'n saak; ~ *for the MINISTRY*, vir predikant studeer; ~ *MUSIC*, musiek studeer; ~ *something OUT*, iets ontwerp (naspeur); ~ *UNDER someone*, onder iem. studeer; ~ *UP*, inpomp, blok; ~-**circle**, studiekring; ~ **group**, studiegroep; ~ **hour**, studieuur; ~ **leave**, studieverlof; ~ **loan**, studielening; ~-**room**, studiesaal; ~-**tour**, studiereis.

stuff, (n) stof; goed, materiaal; goedere; lading; bog; afval (myne); *DO your* ~, laat ons sien wat jy kan doen; voer jou taak uit; *that's the* ~ *to GIVE them!* dons hulle op! *this is GOOD* ~, dis iets goeds; *HOT* ~! mooi so! mooi skoot! *he is really HOT* ~, hy is inderdaad iets besonders; *he KNOWS his* ~, (sl.), hy ken sy werk; *it's all* ~ *and NONSENSE*, dis pure kaf; *POOR (SORRY)* ~, bog; kaf; snert; *THAT'S the* ~! dis die ware Jakob! (v) (vol)stop, volprop, instop, inprop; (op)vul; opstop, stoffeer; voorlieg; wysmaak.
stuffed, gestop; gevul; ~ *ANIMAL*, opgestopte dier; ~ *APPLE*, gevulde appel; *stand like a* ~ *DUMMY*, soos 'n houtpop staan; ~ *with FACTS*, vol feite geprop; ~ *TURKEY*, gestopte kalkoen.
stuff: ~ *one's EARS with wool*, wol in die ore stop; *don't IMAGINE you can* ~ *me*, jy moet jou nie verbeel jy kan my alles wysmaak nie; ~ *ONESELF*, jou dik eet; ~-**er**, opvuller; opstopper; ~**iness**, bedompigheid, dufheid, benoudheid; aanmatiging; ~**ing**, opstopsel, vulsel, vulling; opstopwerk; *knock the* ~*ing out of someone*, iem. opdons; met iem. afreken; ~**y**, benoud, bedompig, muf, duf, onfris; nors, vies; konvensioneel, skynsedig, preuts; aanmatigend, ~*y nose*, verstopte neus.
stultifica'tion, verdwasing; verydeling.
stul'tify, (..**fied**), gek maak, dwaas maak; verydel, kragteloos maak; belaglik maak.
stum, (n) ongegiste wyn, mos; (v) (**-med**), nie laat gis nie.
stum'ble, (n) misstap, struikeling; (v) struikel; strompel, swik; hakkel; ~ *AGAINST (across, upon) someone*, iem. op die lyf loop; toevallig raakloop; ~ *ALONG*, voortstrompel; ~ *OVER*, val oor; ~ *THROUGH a recitation*, hakkel-hakkel opsê; ~**r**, struikelaar, strompelaar.
stum'bling, (n) struikeling, strompeling, gestrompel; (a) struikelend, strompelend; ~**-block**, struikelblok, hinderpaal; ~**-stone**, hinderpaal.
stum'er, (sl.), vals tjek; vals munt; namaaksel.
stump, (n) stomp; stompie, entjie; pen, paaltjie (kr.); been (fig.); *BE (go) on the* ~, politieke toesprake hou; op die bokwa wees; *DRAW* ~*s*, ophou speel (krieket); *GO on the* ~*s*, politieke toesprake hou; op die bokwa wees; *MOVE one's* ~*s*, jou riete roer; *STIR one's* ~*s*, jou riete roer; *TAKE the* ~*s*, politieke toesprake hou; op die bokwa wees; (v) afstomp; omslaan; strompel; stamp, stonk (krieket); toesprake hou; vasvra, verleë maak; ~ *AWAY*, wegstamp; ~ *the COUNTRYSIDE*, die platteland platry; ~ *FOR someone*, vir iem. propaganda maak; *this QUESTION* ~*s me*, hierdie vraag is bo kant my vuurmaakplek; ~ *UP*, betaal, opdok.
stumped, raad-op; gedoesel; *BE* ~, raad-op wees; dronkgeslaan wees; *BE* ~ *for an answer*, nie weet wat om te doen nie.
stump: ~**-foot**, horrelvoet; ~**iness**, stompheid; stoetsheid; gesetheid; ~**nose**, stompneus; ~**nosed**, stompneus-; ~ *orator*, verkiesingsredenaar; ~**oratory**, ~ *speech*, verkiesingsredevoering, bokwa toespraak; ~**-tailed**, stompstert-; ~**y**, met stompe; afgestomp, geset, dik, vet; gedronge (gestalte).
stun, (**-ned**), verdowe; bedwelm; katswink slaan, bewusteloos slaan; dronkslaan; ~**ned**, verbyster, verstom.
stung, *kyk* **sting**, (v).
stunk, *kyk* **stink**, (v).
stun: ~**ner**, mokerhou; prageksemplaar; doodgooier; ramkat, bulperd, doring; ~**ning**, bedwelmend; manjifiek, verbluffend, uitstekend, pragtig; ~**ning-box**, doodmaakhok, verdowingshok.
stun' sail, lyseil.
stunt[1], (n) dwerg; belemmering, agterlikheid; (v) in die groei belemmer; verpot; teëhou; klein bly.
stunt[2], (n) kunsie, foefie; waagtoer(tjie); toer, laai, kordaatstuk, kragproef; kunsvlug; waagstuk; aardigheid, nuwigheid; tweejarige walvis; *DO* ~*s*, toere uithaal; *PUBLICITY* ~, reklamestreek; (v) kunsvlieg, kunsvlugte uitvoer; toere uithaal; ~**ed**, klein, dwergagtig, verboep, verpot (dier); afgeknot (plant); ~**-flyer**, fratsvlieër, kunsvlieër; ~**-flying**,

kunsvlieëry; ~**man**, waagkunstenaar, waaghals; ~ **pilot**, kunsvlieënier.
stupe[1], (n) uilskuiken, swaap.
stupe[2], (n) warm kompres; (v) warm omslae omsit, fomenteer.
stupefa'cient, (n) verdowingsmiddel; (a) verdowend.
stupefac'tion, bedwelming, verdowing.
stupefac'tive, verdowend, bedwelmend.
stup'efier, verdower; bedwelmende middel, verdowingsmiddel.
stup'efy, (..**fied**), bedwelm, verdowe; verstomp; verstom; benewel, dronkslaan; versuf.
stupen'dous, verbasend groot, kolossaal, ontsaglik, verbasingwekkend; ~**ness**, ontsaglikheid, verbasingwekkende grootte.
stup'id, (n) domkop, esel, dommerik; (a) dom, onnosel, eselagtig, onsinnig, stompsinnig, suf, stom, dikkoppig; wesenloos; vervelend; *he is not as* ~ *as he LOOKS*, hy is nie onder 'n uil uitgebroei nie; *what a* ~ *THING*, wat 'n stommiteit; ~'**ity**, ~**ness**, domheid, dwaasheid, onnoselheid, eselagtigheid, stompsinnigheid.
stup'or, versuftheid; loomheid, bedwelming, koma, verdowing.
stur'dily, op 'n kragtige manier.
sturd'iness, krag, stoerheid, forsheid.
sturd'y[1], (n) dronksiekte (skape).
sturd'y[2], (a) kragtig, stoer, fors.
stur'geon, steur (vis).
stutt'er, (n) gehakkel, gestamel, gestotter; (v) hakkel, stotter, stamel; ~**er**, hakkelaar, stotteraar; ~**ing**, (n) gehakkel, gestotter; (a) hakkelrig, hakkelend.
St. Vi'tus's dance, senuweetrekkings, Sint Vitus dans.
sty[1], (n) (**sties**), varkhok; *have grown up in a* ~, in 'n varkhok grootgeword het; (v) op hok sit.
sty[2], (**sties**), **stye**, (-**s**), karkatjie.
Sty'gian, Stigies; pikdonker, hels.
style, (n) styl; mode; manier; skryfstif; skryftrant; sonwysernaald; tydrekening; houtstyl; model (rok); smaak; deftigheid; firmanaam; betiteling, naam; *built in the CAPE Dutch* ~, in die Kaaps-Hollandse styl gebou; *DO things in* ~, alles deftig doen; *ELEVATED* ~, verhewe styl; *FAULT of* ~, stylgebrek; *be in GOOD* ~, van goeie smaak getuig; *live in GRAND* ~, op groot voet lewe; *LIVE in* ~, op groot voet lewe; *NEW* ~ *(calendar)*, Gregoriaanse tydrekening; *OLD* ~ *(calendar)*, Juliaanse tydrekening; *in PROPER* ~, behoorlik, soos dit hoort; *PURITY of* ~, stylsuiwerheid; *SKILL in* ~, stylvaardigheid; *THAT'S the* ~! so moet dit wees! mooi so! *UNDER the* ~ *of*, onder die (firma)naam van; (v) noem, betitel, bestempel; stileer; ~**less**, stylloos; ~**lessness**, stylloosheid.
styl'et, stilet, naaldjie; priem.
styl'iform, stifvormig.
styl'ing, vormgewing, stilering.
styl'ish, na die mode, nuwerwets, swierig, elegant, agtermekaar, stylvol; ~**ness**, swierigheid, stylvolheid, nuwerwetsheid.
styl'ist, stilis, bekwame skrywer; ~'**ic**, stilisties; ~*ic error*, stylfout; ~'**ics**, stilistiek.
styl'ite, pilaarheilige.
styliza'tion, stilering.
styl'ize, stileer.
styl'ograph, stilograaf; ~'**ic**, stilografies; ..**og'raphy**, stilografie.
styl'oid, priemvormig, stifvormig.
styl'us, stilus, skryfstif; borsel (dierk.); naald (fonograaf); styl (bot.).
stym'ie, (n) blinde bal, stuiter (gholf); (v) stuit; vaskeer; *be* ~*d by a question*, vasgevra word.
styp'tic, (n) bloedstelpende middel, bloedstelpingsmiddel, bloedstolmiddel, bindmiddel; (a) bloedstelpend, saamtrekkend, stolmiddel-.
Styr'ia, Stiermarke; ~**n**, (n) Stiermarker; (a) Stiermarks.
Styx, Styx, Stuuks.
suabil'ity, vervolgbaarheid.
su'able, vervolgbaar.
sua'sion, oorreding.
suas'ive, oorredend; ~ *power*, oorredingskrag.

suave, vriendelik, goedig, lief, minsaam, sag, urbaan; vleiend; tegemoetkomend.
suav'ity, vriendelikheid, lieflikheid, minsaamheid, tegemoetkomendheid, urbaniteit; vleiendheid.
sub¹, (n) (abbr.), subredakteur; ledegeld; tweede hoofartikel; duikboot; luitenant (leër); onderluitenant (vloot); (v) bydrae betaal; redigeer.
sub², (prep) onder; ~ *JUDICE*, sub judice, onbeslis, onafgehandel; ~ *ROSA*, sub rosa, vertroulik, in die geheim; ~ *VOCE*, onder die woord, sub voce.
suba'cid, suuragtig, suurderig.
subacid'ity, suuragtigheid.
subaer'ial, oppervlakte-.
suba'gent, subagent, onderagent.
sub'altern, (n) ondergeskikte, junior offisier, luitenant; (a) ondergeskik.
subaltern'ate, ondergeskik; opeenvolgend.
subaquat'ic, suba'queous, onderwater-.
sub'area, wyk.
sub'article, tweede hoofartikel.
subaudi'tion, die lees tussen die reëls.
sub'calibre, spaarkaliber.
sub'camp, onderkamp.
sub'chief, onderhoof.
subcir'cuit, subkring, subbaan.
sub'class, (-es), onderafdeling, onderklas.
sub'clause, subartikel.
subclav'ian, onder die sleutelbeen.
subclav'icle, eerste rib.
subcommitt'ee, subkomitee, onderkomitee.
subcon'scious, halfbewus, onderbewus; ~ *mind*, die onderbewussyn, die onderbewuste; ~ *ness*, onderbewustheid.
subcon'tinent, subkontinent.
subcon'tract, (n) onderkontrak.
subcontract', (v) onderkontrakteer.
subcontrac'tor, onderkontraktant, onderaannemer.
subcord'ate, byna hartvormig.
subcos'tal, onder die ribbes.
subcran'ial, onder die kopbeen.
sub'culture, afwyking; subkultuur.
subcutan'eous, onder die vel, onderhuids.
subdeac'on, hulpdiaken.
subdean', onderdeken; adjunk-dekaan.
subdeve'loped, onderontwikkel(de); ~ *country*, onderontwikkelde land.
subdivide', onderverdeel.
subdivis'ible, onderverdeelbaar.
subdivi'sion, onderverdeling; gedeelte.
subdu'al, onderwerping.
subdue', onderwerp, ten onder bring, oorwin, bedwing, beheers, oormeester, baasraak, vermeester; tem, mak maak (dier); versag, demp, temper (lig, kleur); ~ *d*, onderworpe, gekneg; gematig; gedemp; mat; ingehoue (krag); ~ *d lighting*, getemperde lig; ~ *r*, onderwerper.
sub-econom'ic, subekonomies; ~ *housing*, subekonomiese behuising.
sub-e'dit, persklaar maak, redigeer; ~ *ing*, (die) persklaarmaak, nasienwerk, redigering.
sub-ed'itor, onderredakteur, subredakteur.
suber'eous, sube'ric, sub'erose, kurkagtig, kurk-; *suberic acid*, kurksuur.
sub'family, (..lies), onderfamilie.
sub'fuce, donker, somber.
sub'genus, ondergeslag.
subglobose', subglob'ular, effens (ietwat) bolvormig.
sub'grade, ondergraad.
sub'group, ondergroep.
sub'head, onderhoof; tussenhofie; ~ *ing*, onderdeel, ondertitel.
subhum'an, (n) diermens, beesmens; (a) minder as menslik.
subhum'id: ~ *climate*, hoëveldklimaat.
subinoc'ulate, afent.
sub'inspector, onderinspekteur.
subja'cent, onderlêend; laer geleë, onderliggend.
sub'ject¹, (n) onderdaan; vak, tema; voorwerp (studie); onderwerp (gram.); persoon, indiwidu; liggaam, lyk; proefpersoon, proefdier; pasiënt, behandelde; *a DELICATE (difficult)* ~, 'n netelige onderwerp (saak); ~ *for DISSECTION*, lyk (liggaam, voorwerp) vir ontleding; ~ *of DISCUSSION*, onderwerp van bespreking; ~ *and OBJECT*, onderwerp en voorwerp; *ON the* ~ *of*, omtrent, in verband met; ~ *and PREDICATE*, onderwerp en gesegde (predikaat); ~ *of STUDY*, leervak; (a) onderworpe, onderhorig; onderhewig; afhanklik; blootgestel(d); vatbaar; ~ *to his APPROVAL*, onderworpe aan sy goedkeuring; ~ *to such CONDITIONS as*, onder sodanige voorwaardes as; ~ *to your CONFIRMATION*, onderworpe aan u goedkeuring; ~ *to FITS*, onderhewig aan toevalle; las hê van toevalle; ~ *to RATIFICATION*, onderworpe aan bekragtiging; ~ *to prior SALE*, behoudens voorverkoop; ~ *TO*, onderworpe aan (verandering); onderhewig aan (storms); vatbaar vir.
subject'², (v) onderwerp; ondergeskik maak; blootstel (aan); ~ *to an EXPERIMENT*, proewe neem met, eksperimenteer met; ~ *TO*, blootstel aan; ondergeskik maak aan.
sub'ject heading, opskrif.
subject': ~ *ion*, onderwerping, oormeestering; bedwang, onderworpenheid; afhanklikheid; ~ *ive*, onderwerplik, subjektief; ~ *ive case*, eerste naamval, nominatief; ~ *iveness*, ~ *iv'ity*, subjektiwiteit.
sub'ject: ~ *matter*, onderwerp, stof, leerstof; inhoud; ~ *meeting*, vakvergadering; ~ *picture*, genrestuk.
subjoin', byvoeg, toevoeg, agtervoeg.
sub jud'ice, nog hangende, aanhangig, onbeslis, sub judice.
sub'jugate, onderwerp, onder die juk bring, ten onder bring.
subjuga'tion, onderwerping.
sub'jugator, onderwerper.
subjunc'tion, toevoeging.
subjunc'tive, (n) subjunktief, aanvoegende wyse; (a) toevoegend, aanvoegend, subjunktief; ~ *mood*, aanvoegende wys(e).
sub'leader, tweede hoofartikel.
sub'lease, (n) onderkontrak; onderverhuur, onderverpagting.
sublease', (v) onderverhuur.
sublessee', onderhuurder.
subless'or, onderverhuurder, tussenverhuurder.
sublet', (~, ~), onderverhuur, weer verhuur, afverhuur; ~ *ting*, onderverhuring, tussenverhuring, weerverhuring.
sub-lieuten'ant, onderluitenant (vloot); vaandrig (leër).
sub'limate, (n) sublimaat; (v) sublimeer, verfyn, ver(e)del; (a) gesublimeer(d).
sublima'tion, sublimasie, verfyning, veredeling.
sublime', (n) die verhewene, sublieme; *from the* ~ *to the ridiculous*, v.d. verhewene tot die belaglike; (v) verhef, veredel, sublimeer, verfyn; (a) verhewe, voortreflik, goddelik, skoon, geesverheffend; subliem; ~ *ness*, verhewenheid.
sublim'inal, (n) onderbewussyn; (a) onderbewus; ~ *consciousness*, die onderbewussyn.
sublim'ity, verhewenheid, die sublieme, sublimiteit; toppunt.
sublinea'tion, onderstreping.
sublin'gual, ondertong-.
sublun'ar(y), ondermaans, sublunêr.
sub'-machine-gun, submasjiengeweer.
sub'man, (..men), minderwaardige mens, ondermens.
subman'ager, onderbestuurder.
submarine', (n) duikboot, onderseeboot; (a) ondersees, onderseese-; ~ *base*, duikbootbasis; ~ *boat*, duikboot; ~ *bomb*, dieptebom; ~ *cable*, onderseese kabel; ~ *destroyer*, duikbootjaer, duikbootjagter.
sub'marine: ~ *mine*, onderwatermyn; ~ *tender*, duikbootmoederskip; ~ *war*, ~ *warfare*, duikbootoorlog.
subma'riner, duikbootvaarder.
submaxil'la, onderkaak; ~ *ry*, onderkaaks-.
submerge', onderdompel; oorstroom; onder water sit; wegsink; onderduik.
submerged', ondergedompel; oorstroom; beskut; ~ *BENEATH several feet of water*, onder 'n hele

submergence 	*subtend*

paar voet water; *REMAIN* ~, onder water bly; ~ **rock**, blinde rots.
submer'gence, wegsakking, wegsinking; onderdompeling; oorstroming.
submersed', ondergedompel.
submers'ible, duik=, dompel=; ~ **pump**, dompelpomp.
submer'sion, onderdompeling; oorstroming.
submicroscop'ic, submikroskopies.
submi'ssion, onderwerping; gehoorsaamheid, onderdanigheid; submissie; voorlegging; ootmoed; ~ **clause**, onderwerpingsbepaling.
submiss'ive, onderdanig, nederig, volgsaam, gedwee, ootmoedig, berustend, deemoedig, gelate; ~ **ness**, deemoed, onderworpenheid.
submit', (-ted), onderwerp, die hoof in die skoot lê, getroos; oorlaat; voorlê; indien; beweer; ~ *a DOCUMENT*, 'n stuk voorlê; *I* ~ *that*, ek meen dat; ek hou vol dat; ~ *to God's WILL*, jou aan die wil van God onderwerp.
submul'tiple, faktor, onderdeel.
subnorm'al, ondernormaal.
sub'office, bykantoor.
sub'order, suborde, onderorde.
subord'inance, onderworpenheid.
subord'inate, (n) onderhorige, ondergeskikte; (v) ondergeskik maak aan, subordineer; (a) ondergeskik, onderhorig; ~ **clause**, bysin.
subordina'tion, onderhorigheid, ondergeskiktheid, subordinasie.
subor'dinative, onderskikkend.
suborn', omkoop; oorhaal; ~ *a'tion*, omkoping, omkopery; ~ **er**, omkoper.
sub'outcrop, bedekte dagsoom.
subov'ate, byna eiervormig.
sub'paragraph, subparagraaf.
sub'plough, dolploeg, panbreker, diepbreker.
subpoen'a, (n) dagvaarding, subpoena; (v) dagvaar; ~ **money**, getuiegeld.
subpol'ar, onderpools.
subrep'tion, verheling, verkryging deur misleidende voorstelling, subrepsie.
subrepti'tious, onderduims, deur slinkse middele verkry.
sub'rogate, in die plaas stel.
subroga'tion, subrogasie.
sub ros'a, onder ons meisies; sub rosa, vertroulik.
subsat'urated, byna versadig, byna deurdrenk.
subscrib'able, onderskryfbaar.
subscribe', inteken; bydra; onderteken; op die lys sit; onderskrywe; *I CANNOT* ~ *to that*, daarmee stem ek nie saam nie; ~ *d CAPITAL*, geplaaste kapitaal; ~ *to a FUND*, tot 'n fonds bydra; *the LOAN was fully* ~ *d*, die lening is volteken; ~ *one's NAME to*, jou instemming betuig met; ~ *to a NEWSPAPER*, op 'n nuusblad inteken; ~ *for SHARES*, aandele opneem; ~ *TO that*, dit onderskryf.
subscrib'er, intekenaar, inskrywer, abonnee; ondertekenaar; huurder (telef.); ~ *to a DOCTRINE*, aanhanger van 'n leer; ~ *to a FUND*, bydraer tot 'n fonds; ~ *to a PAPER*, intekenaar op 'n blad; ~ *for SHARES*, inskrywer op aandele.
subscrip'tion, subskripsie, intekengeld; intekening; kontribusie; bydrae; ledegeld; abonnement; onderskrif; huur; ondertekening; huur (van telefoon); ~ **list**, subskripsielys, intekenlys; ~ **price**, intekenprys; ~ **rate**, intekengeld; inskrywingskoers (aandele); ~ **rights**, inskrywingsregte; ~ **share**, inskrywingsaandeel, subskripsieaandeel; ~ **ticket**, intekenbiljet.
sub'section, onderafdeling, onderartikel, subartikel.
sub'sequence, opvolging.
sub'sequent, volgende, opvolgende; later, naderhand; ~ *conditions*, ontbindende voorwaardes; ~ **ly**, daarna, naderhand; ~ *ly to that*, daarna.
subserve', dien, behorderlik wees.
subserv'ience, **subserv'iency**, onderdanigheid, gedienstigheid; gedweeheid; diensigheid; kruiperigheid.
subserv'ient, diensig; diensbaar; bevorderlik; kruiperig; onderdanig.
subside', sak; bedaar, kalm word, tot rus kom, uitwoed, gaan lê; daal; insak, versak, insink, wegsak, besink; ~ *into a CHAIR*, op 'n stoel neersak; ~ *INTO*, verval tot, oorgaan tot; *the RIVER* ~ *d*, die rivier het gesak; *the STORM* ~ *d*, die storm het bedaar.
sub'sidence, invalling, insakking, instorting; (grond)= versakking; wegsakking; insinking, sakplek, daling.
subsid'iary, (n) (..ries), noodhulp, plaasvervanger; dogtermaatskappy, filiaal; hulpmiddel; (pl) hulptroepe; (a) behulpsaam; hulp=; subsidiêr; bykomstig, aanvullend; ~ **account**, hulprekening, byrekening; ~ **books**, hulpboeke, byboeke, steundokumente; ~ **company**, filiaalmaatskappy, dogtermaatskappy; ~ **industry**, newebedryf; ~ **record**, byregister; ~ **troops**, hulptroepe.
subsidiza'tion, subsidiëring.
sub'sidize, geldelik steun, subsidieer, hulp verleen.
sub'sidizing, subsidiëring.
sub'sidy, (..dies), geldelike steun, subsidie, toelae, bydrae; onderstandsgeld.
subsist', bestaan, lewe, voortbestaan; onderhou.
subsist'ence, bestaan; broodwinning, leeftog; lewensonderhoud; ~ *and transport (travelling) allowance*, reis-en-verblyftoelae, ~ **agriculture**, bestaanslandbou; ~ **allowance**, onderhoudstoelae; ~ **economy**, bestaansekonomie; ~ **farming**, selfversorgende boerdery, bestaansboerdery.
subsist'ent, bestaande; inherent.
sub'soil, (n) onderlaag, ondergrond; (v) diepploeg, woelploeg; ~ **er**, ~ **plough**, dolploeg, panbreker, grondbreker, diepbreker, skeurploeg; ~ **water**, grondwater.
subson'ic, subsonies.
sub'species, ondersoort, subspesie.
sub'stance, selfstandigheid; stof, werklikheid; vermoë; wesenlikheid, substansie; die essensiële, pit, kern; hoofinhoud; bestanddeel; *GIVE the* ~ *of*, gee die inhoud van; *IN* ~, in hoofsaak; *have LITTLE* ~, nie veel om die lyf hê nie; *MAN of* ~, 'n vermoënde man; *the* ~ *for the SHADOW*, die wese aan die skyn opoffer; ~ *and SHADOW*, skyn en wese; *WASTE one's* ~, jou goed deurbring.
sub'standard¹, (n) substanderd.
substand'ard², (n) minderwaardig, substandaard=.
substan'tial, selfstandig; wesenlik, werklik; aansienlik, welgesteld; stewig, deeglik, solied, lywig; beduidend; stoflik; substansieel; ~ **amount**, aansienlike bedrag.
substantial'ity, werklikheid; vastheid; deeglikheid; aansienlikheid.
substan'tially, aansienlik; in wese, in hoë mate.
substan'tiate, verwesenlik; bewys, staaf; bevestig.
substantia'tion, waarmaking, stawing, bewys; bevestiging.
substantiv'al, selfstandig, substantiwies.
sub'stantive, (n) selfstandige naamwoord, substantief; (a) selfstandig; onafhanklik; ~ **appointment**, vaste aanstelling; ~ **law**, materiële reg; ~ **ly**, in wese, wesenlik; ~ **pay**, substantiewe besoldiging; ~ **rank**, vaste rang, effektiewe rang.
sub'station, substasie.
sub'stitute, (n) plaasvervanger, plaasbekleër, waarnemer; vervangingsmiddel, substituut, surrogaat; (v) vervang, in die plek stel; as plaasvervanger optree, substitueer; ~ *fraudulently*, onderskuif; skelm vervang.
substitu'tion, vervanging, substitusie; *surreptitious* ~, onderskuiwing; ~ **al**, plaasvervangend.
sub'stitutive, vervangend.
sub'strate, **substrat'um**, (..ta), onderlaag, substraat; grondslag; grondlaag; *it has a* ~ *of truth*, daar sit 'n kiem van waarheid in.
struc'tion, **sub'structure**, fondament, onderbou.
subsume', insluit (in 'n klas); opneem (onder 'n reël).
subsump'tion, insluiting, opneming, subsumpsie; minor (sluitrede).
sub'surface, (n) boonste ondergrond; (a) onder die oppervlak; ~ **water**, grondwater.
subten'ancy, onderhuur.
sub'tenant, onderhuurder.
subtend', onderspan, teenoorstaan.

subtense', (n) koorde; (a) onderspanne.
sub'terfuge, uitvlug, voorwendsel.
subterran'ean, onderaards, ondergronds; ~ **cable**, ondergrondse kabel; ~ **water**, grondwater, sakwater.
subterran'eous, ondergronds, onderaards; heimlik.
sub'til(e), (veroud.) = **subtle**.
subt'ilize, vlugtig maak; fyn uitspin; haarklowe.
sub'title, (n) ondertitel, tweede titel; deeltitel; (v) byskrifte (ondertitels) aanbring.
sub'tle, slim; listig, slu, geslepe, spitsvondig, subtiel; fyn, teer; skerpsinnig, vernuftig; haarfyn; ~**ness**, ~**ty**, slimheid, listigheid, geslepenheid; subtiliteit; spitsvondigheid; fyn onderskeidingsvermoë; ~**-witted**, skerpsinnig.
sub'tly, op subtiele wyse, subtiel.
sub'total, subtotaal.
subtract', aftrek, verminder; ~ *one amount from another*, een bedrag van 'n ander aftrek; ~**ion**, aftrekking, vermindering.
sub'trahend, aftrektal, aftrekker.
subtrop'ical, subtropies.
sub'ulate, sub'uliform, elsvormig.
sub'union, subunie.
sub'unit, onderdeel, subeenheid.
sub'urb, voorstad, voordorpie.
suburb'an, voorstedelik; kleinsteeds; ~**ite**, voorstadsbewoner.
suburb'ia, die voorstede.
sub'variety, ondervariëteit, subvariëteit.
subvene', byspring.
subven'tion, bystand, hulp, subsidie; ondersteuning.
subver'sion, omkering; omwerping; ondermyning, ondergrawing.
subvers'ive, ondermynend, opruiend, omverwerpend; *be* ~ *of*, omvergooi, ondermyn, ondergrawe.
subvert', omwerp, omkeer, omgooi; ondermyn, ondergrawe; ~**er**, ondergrawer, omverwerper; ~**ible**, omgooibaar.
sub'way, duikweg, onderaardse deurgang; ondergrondse spoorweg, moltrein.
subzer'o, onder vriespunt.
succades', sukade, gesuikerde vrugte.
succedan'eous, plaasvervangend.
succedan'eum, (..**nea**), plaasvervanger; surrogaat.
succeed', opvolg; volg op, kom na; slaag, sukses hê, meeval; vlot; *he* ~ *ed IN*, dit het hom geluk om; hy het daarin geslaag om; ~ *to a POST*, in 'n amp opvolg; *nothing* ~ *s like SUCCESS*, alles loop die voorspoedige mee; ~ *as a TEACHER*, slaag as 'n onderwyser; ~ *to a TITLE*, 'n titel erf; ~ *to the THRONE*, die troon bestyg; ~**ing**, volgende, opvolgende.
success', sukses, goeie uitslag, gunstige afloop; welslae, voorspoed; *meet with GREAT* ~, baie sukses hê; *INQUIRE without* ~, tevergeefs navraag doen; *be MAKING a* ~ *of things*, welslae met iets behaal; met iets slaag; *he PROVED a* ~, hy het uitstekend gevaar; hy was 'n sukses; *WITHOUT* ~, onverrigtersake, tevergeefs; onsuksesvol; ~**ful**, voorspoedig, geslaag, welgeslaag, gelukkig, suksesvol; ~**ful candidate**, geslaagde kandidaat; ~**fully**, suksesvol, met welslae; ~**fulness**, voorspoed; sukses; geslaagdheid.
succe'ssion, opvolging, troonopvolging; erfopvolging; suksessie, aanbesterwing; opeenvolging; reeks, ry, volgorde; nakomelingskap; *BY* ~, volgens erfreg; *IN* ~, agtereen; *IN* ~ *to*, as opvolger van; *LAW of* ~, suksessiereg; *hold PROPERTY in* ~, eiendom volgens erfreg in besit hê; *in RAPID* ~, vinnig na mekaar; *TITLE by* ~, geërfde titel; ~ **act**, suksessiewet; ~ **al**, erflik; agtereenvolgend; ~ **duty**, suksessiereg.
success'ive, agtereenvolgend, na mekaar, suksessief; *each* ~ *day*, elke volgende dag; ~**ly**, agtereenvolgens, agtervolgens, na mekaar.
success'or, opvolger; erfgenaam, erfopvolging; ~ *in title*, regsopvolger.
succinct', bondig, beknop, kernagtig, saaklik, pittig; ~**ness**, bondigheid, beknoptheid, pittigheid, kernagtigheid.
succ'our, (n) steun, hulp(betoon), bystand; ontset; (v) steun, bystaan, ondersteun, help; ontset; ~**er**, helper, steuner.
succ'uba, (-e), succ'ubus, (..bi), nagspook, sukkubus.
succ'ulence, succ'ulency, sappigheid.
succ'ulent, (n) vetplant; (a) sappig, sopperig; sapryk; vetplantagtig; ~ **plant**, vetplant, sukkulent.
succumb', beswyk; swig, val; wyk; toegee; die stryd gewonne gee; ~ *to temptation*, toegee aan versoeking.
succurs'al, (n) hulpkerk; bykantoor, filiaal; (a) hulp=, by=.
such, (pron) sulkes, sulke mense, sulke dinge; *ALL* ~, al sulkes; ~ *AS*, hulle wat; *AS* ~, sodanig; *NONE* ~, sonder gelyke; ~ *a ONE*, so een; (a) sulke, sodanig, dusdanig, so; van so 'n aard; ~ *A*, so 'n; *on* ~ *a DATE*, op sodanige datum; ~ *is LIFE*, so gaan dit in die lewe; *in* ~ *a MANNER*, op so 'n manier; ~ *and* ~ *a PERSON*, dié en daardie; *in* ~ *and* ~ *a PLACE*, op dié en dié plek; *it is* ~ *a PLEASURE*, dit is regtig aangenaam; *I have no PREJUDICE against foreigners as* ~, ek het geen vooroordeel teen vreemdelinge net omdat hulle vreemdelinge is nie; ~ *a THING*, iets dergeliks; so iets; *until* ~ *TIME as*, tot tyd en wyl; ~**like**, dergelike; ~**wise**, in dié voeë, sodanig.
suck, (n) suiging; (die) suig, gesuig; *GIVE* ~, laat drink; *a* ~ *OF*, 'n mondjievol van; *TAKE a* ~ *at*, suig aan; (v) suig, (uit)suie, insuig; drink; ~ *DRY*, droog suig; beroof; ~ *IN*, opsuig; verswelg, indrink; ~ *ed in with one's mother's MILK*, met die moedermelk ingedrink; ~ *OUT*, uitsuig; ~ *something from one's THUMB*, iets uit die duim suig; ~ *UP to someone*, iem. lek.
suck'er, pypkan; uitloper, suier (plant); suigpyp; jong walvis; steggie, stiggie, spruit (plant); speenvark; suiglekker, suigstokkie; stokkielekker; suigbal (gholf); dwaas, domkop, bobbejaan; *remove* ~*s*, plante suiwer; ~**-fish**, loodsman; ~ **lamb**, suiplam.
suck'ing, (n) gesuig, suiging; (a) suigend; ~**-bottle**, suigbottel, pypkan; ~ **calf**, suipkalf; ~**-disk**, suigorgaan; suigleer; ~**-fish**, suigvis; ~ **lamb**, suiplam; ~**-pig**, speenvark; ~ **pipe**, suigbuis; ~ **pump**, suigpomp; ~ **tube**, suigbuis.
suc'kle, soog; die bors gee; laat drink.
suck'ling, suiging; suigkind; suiplam; suipkalf; suipdier.
suc'rose, rietsuiker, sukrose.
suc'tion, suiging; ~ **brush**, suigborsel; ~ **cleaner**, stofsuier; ~**-cup**, suigglas; ~ **dredger**, suigbagger; ~**-fan**, (suig)waaier; ~**-flask**, suigfles; ~**-gas**, suiggas; ~ **gauge**, suigmeter; ~**-glass**, suigbottel, suigfles; ~**-hose**, suigslang; ~**-oil**, suigolie; ~**-pipe**, suigpyp, suigbuis; ~ **power**, suigkrag; ~ **pump**, suigpomp; ~ **ram**, pompsuier; ~ **stroke**, suigslag; ~**-sweeper**, stofsuier; ~ **tube**, suigbuis; ~ **valve**, suigklep.
suctor'ial, suig=; ~ **antenna**, suigspriet; ~ **insect**, suiginsek; ~ **mouth**, suigmond; ~ **organ**, suigorgaan; ~ **pump**, suigpomp.
Sudan', Soedan; ~**ese'**, (n, a) Soedannees.
sudar'ium, (..**ria**), sud'ary, (..**ries**), sweetdoek.
suda'tion, sweting, sweet.
sudator'ium, (..**ria**), sweetbad; sweetkamer.
sud'atory, (n) (..**ries**), sweetbad; sweetmiddel, sweetdrank; (a) swetend.
sudd, opdrifsels.
sudd'en, (n) skielikheid; *(all) of a* ~, skielik, eensklaps, meteens; (a) plotseling, skielik, ineens, onverwags; subiet; ~ *death*, (gholf), valbyl; blitsbeslissing; ~**ly**, skielik, eensklaps, meteens, onverwags, plotseling; ~**ness**, skielikheid, onverwagtheid.
sudorif'erous, sweet=, sweetverwekkend.
sudorif'ic, (n) sweetmiddel, sweetdrank; (a) sweetdrywend, sweet=; ~ **cure**, sweetkuur.
suds, seepsop, seepwater; ~**y**, skuimerig, vol seepskuim.
sue, vervolg (geregtelik), aanspreek, dagvaar, aanskrywe, eis; ding na (die hand van); ~ *for DAMAGES*, 'n eis om skadevergoeding instel; ~ *someone for DEBT*, iem. weens skuld laat vervolg; ~ *for DESERTION*, dagvaar weens verlating; ~ *for*

suède   1279   *sulk*

DIVORCE, egskeiding aanvra; ~ *for her HAND*, om haar hand ding; ~ *out a PARDON*, genade vra en verkry.
suède, Sweedse (handskoen)leer.
su'er, eiser.
su'et, harde vet, niervet; ~ **dumpling**, vetkoek; ~ **pudding**, niervetpoeding.
suff'er, ly; ondergaan, verduur; besuur; uitstaan, deurstaan; uithou; toelaat, gedoog, duld; ~ *the children to COME*, laat die kindertjies kom; ~ *DEATH*, sterf; ~ *DEFEAT*, die neerlaag ly; *he does not* ~ *FOOLS gladly*, hy kan 'n dwaas nie verdra nie; onnoseles nie kan verdra nie; ~ *FOR it*, daarvoor boet; ~ *FROM*, ly aan; las hê van; ~ *from HALLUCINATIONS*, aan hallusinasies ly; onder sinsbegogeling verkeer; ~ *in MIND and BODY*, geestelik en liggaamlik ly; ~ **able**, draagbaar, draaglik; toelaatbaar, duldbaar; ~ **ance**, toelating, dulding; pyn, smart; lydsaamheid; *on* ~ *ance*, uit genade; met vergunning (reg); ~ **ed**, gely, verduur; ~ **er**, lyer, pasiënt; dulder; lydende party; ~ **ing**, (n) lyding; (a) lydend.
suffice', genoeg wees, voldoende wees, uitkom; *that* ~ *s to PROVE it*, dit is voldoende bewys; ~ *it to SAY that*, dit is genoeg om te sê dat; ~ *it for me to SAY*, ek kan volstaan deur te sê; *that WILL* ~ *for us*, ons sal daarmee uitkom.
suffi'ciency, genoegsaamheid, voldoendheid, toereikendheid; voldoende voorraad (aantal); geskiktheid.
suffi'cient, (n) genoeg; (a) genoeg, genoegsaam, voldoende, toereikend; *BE* ~, genoeg wees; ~ *unto the DAY is the evil thereof*, elke dag het genoeg aan sy eie kwaad; ~ *in LAW*, regsgeldig, van krag; ~ **ly**, voldoende, genoeg.
suff'ix, (n) (-es), agtervoegsel, suffiks.
suffix', (v) agtervoeg, suffigeer.
suff'ocate, verstik, versmoor.
suff'ocating, verstikkend, benoud; broeiwarm; ~ **ly**, stikkend; ~ *ly hot*, smoorwarm; ~ **gas**, stikgas.
suffoca'tion, versmoring, verstikking.
suff'ragan, (n) hulpbiskop, suffragaan; (a) hulp=, onderhorig.
suff'rage, stem, stemreg.
suffragette', suffragette, stemregvrou, stemjuffer.
suff'ragist, voorstander van (vroue)stemreg.
suffumiga'tion, beroking.
suffuse', oorgiet, oorsprei, oordek; vloei oor, loop oor; *her face was* ~ *d with tears*, haar gesig was vol trane.
suffu'sion, oorgieting, oordekking, onderloping; deurtrekking; weefselbloeding; blos, tint.
Suf'ism, Soefisme.
su'gar, (n) suiker; vleitaal, mooipraatjies, soet woordjies, heuning om die mond; *ACID of* ~, oksaalsuur; ~ *of LEAD*, loodasetaat; *LUMPS of* ~, suikerklontjies; *he is not MADE of* ~ *or salt*, hy sal nie smelt nie; ~ *of MILK*, melksuiker, laktose; ~ *and WATER*, suikerwater; (v) oorsuiker, suiker bygooi, versuiker, versoet, soet maak; luier, jou nie inspan nic; verbloem; ~ *the PILL*, die pil verguld; ~ *ed WATER*, suikerwater; ~ *ed WORDS*, heuningsoet woordjies, mooipraatjies; ~ **-bag**, suikersak; ~ **-basin**, suikerpot; ~ **-bean**, suikerboontjie; ~ **-beet**, suikerbeet; ~ **-bird**, suikerbekkie, jangroentjie, suikervoël; ~ **-boiling**, suikerkokery; ~ **-bounty**, suikerpremie; ~ **-bowl**, suikerpot; ~ **-bush**, suikerbos, protea; ~ **candy**, kandysuiker; suiker=klontjie, teesuiker; ~ **-cane**, suikerriet; ~ **-cask**, suikerkerkis; ~ **-castor**, suikerstrooier; ~ **-coat**, (n) suikerlagie; (v) smaaklik maak; versuiker, verguld (fig.); ~ **content**, suikergehalte; ~ **crop**, suikeroes; ~ **-daddy**, suikeroompie, paaipappie, vroetelpappie; ~ **-doll**, suikerpop; ~ **-dredger**, suikerstrooier; ~ **er**, luilak, lamsak; ~ **estate**, suikerplantasie; ~ **excise**, suikeraksyns; ~ **field**, suikerland; ~ **-grower**, suikerkweker, suikerboer; ~ **-growing**, suikerkultuur, suikerkwekery; ~ **-house**, suikerraffinadery, suikerfabriek; ~ **icing**, suikerglasuur; ~ **industry**, suikernywerheid, suikerbedryf, suikerindustrie; ~ **iness**, suikeragtigheid; ~ **ing**, versuikering; ~ **-loaf**, suikerbrood; ~ **-loaf hat**, punthoed;

~ **lozenge**, suikerkoekie; ~ **-mill**, suikerfabriek, suikermeul; ~ **-mite**, suikermiet, suikerwurm; ~ **-pea**, suikerertjie; ~ **-pine**, suikerden(nehout); ~ **plantation**, suikerplantasie; ~ **-planter**, suikerkweker, suikerprodusent; ~ **-refiner**, suikerraffinadeur, suikerfabrikant; ~ **-refinery**, suikerraffinadery; ~ **-scoop**, suikerskoppie; ~ **-spoon**, suikerlepel; ~ **-stick**, langlekkergoed, borssuiker; ~ **-tongs**, suikertangetjie; ~ **trade**, suikerhandel; ~ **-water**, suikerwater; ~ **y**, suikeragtig, suikerig, soet; vleierig.
suggest', opper, aan die hand doen, inblaas, influister, suggereer, voorstel, aanraai, dui op; te kenne gee; voorstaan; laat dink aan, voor die gees roep; *the IDEA* ~ *s itself*, die gedagte kom vanself op; *I* ~ *THAT*, ek beweer dat; ek doen aan die hand dat; ~ **er**, ingewer, opperaar; ~ **ibil'ity**, ontvanklikheid, vatbaarheid vir suggestie; ~ **ible**, ontvanklik, vatbaar (vir suggestie).
sugges'tion, ingewing; influistering, inblasing; suggestie, voorslag; voorstel; wenk; aanduiding, sweempie; *AT my* ~, op my voorstel; *OFFER a* ~, iets aan die hand doen; *ON the* ~ *of*, op voorstel van.
sugges'tive, suggestief; veelseggend, veelbetekenend; leerryk; wat nuwe gesigspunte gee; *BE* ~ *of*, laat dink aan; ~ *TALK*, dubbelsinnige gesprek; ~ **ness**, suggestiwiteit.
suicid'al, selfmoord=, selfmoordend; ~ *tendencies*, selfmoordneigings.
sui'cide, selfmoord; selfmoordenaar; *commit* ~, selfmoord pleeg; ~ **pact**, selfmoordooreenkoms; ~ **troops**, selfmoordsoldate.
suit, (n) proses, regsgeding; pak (klere); versoek, aansoek; kleur (kaarte); uitrusting; opeenvolging; stel; ~ *of ARMOUR*, wapenrusting; *with COSTS of* ~, met die koste v.d. geding; *FOLLOW* ~, kleur beken (kaartspel); ook so maak, dieselfde doen; ~ *to MEASURE*, snyerspak; ~ *of MOURNING*, roupak, roukleed; *PRESS a* ~, 'n pak klere stryk (pars); *PRESS one's* ~, jou saak yweiig bevorder; *one's STRONG* ~, jou krag; jou sterkte; *acting is not his STRONG* ~, hy is nie uitgeknip vir 'n toneelspeler nie; (v) pas, geleë kom; voldoen; weg; geskik wees; bevredig; aanstaan; dien; ~ *the ACTION to the word*, die daad by die woord voeg; ~ *one ADMIRABLY*, 'n mooi lyf daarvoor hê; jou uitstekend geval; reg in jou smaak val; *it* ~ *s my BOOK*, dit kom in my kraam te pas; *COFFEE does not* ~ *me*, koffie akkordeer nie met my nie; ~ *one's COMPLEXION*, by 'n mens se gelaatskleur pas; *that* ~ *s him down to the GROUND*, dit kon hom nie beter pas nie; *he is HARD to* ~, dis moeilik om hom tevrede te stel; ~ *someone to a T*, iem. volkome pas; *it does not* ~ *all TASTES*, dit is nie na iedereen se smaak nie; *WILL Tuesday* ~ *you?* is Dinsdag 'n geskikte dag vir jou? *WILL that* ~ *you?* sal dit vir jou gerieflik wees? *when it* ~ *s YOU*, wanneer dit vir jou geleë is; ~ *YOURSELF*, soos jy verkies; nes jy wil, ~ **abil'ity**, geskiktheid, doelmatigheid, voeglikheid, voegsaamheid; gepastheid; bruikbaarheid; ~ **able**, geskik, voegsaam, passend, voeglik, gepas; behoorlik; *not* ~ *able for CHILDREN*, nie geskik vir kinders nie; ~ *able to the OCCASION*, paslik vir die geleentheid; ~ **ableness** = **suitability**; ~ **ably**, gepas; na behore; ~ **ably qualified**, (korrek) gekwalifiseer(de); ~ **case**, handkoffer, reistas, valies.
suite, reeks, stel; suite; gevolg, entourage; groep; *EN* ~, en suite; *a* ~ *of FURNITURE*, 'n stel meubels; *a* ~ *of ROOMS*, 'n stel vertrekke (kamers).
suit'ed, geskik, gepas; met 'n pak (klere) aan.
suit'ing, pakstof.
suit' length, paklengte.
suit'or, versoeker; vryer, galant; eiser, party (in 'n hofsaak).
sul'cate, met vore, gegroef.
sulk, (n) slegte bui, nukkerigheid, pruilery; *BE in the* ~ *s*; *HAVE the* ~ *s*, in 'n slegte luim wees; nukkerig (dikmond) wees; (v) suur kyk, pruil, dikmond wees, nors wees; ~ **ily**, nors, nukkerig; ~ **iness**, norsheid, pruilery, humeurigheid, stuurrigheid.

sulk'y¹, (n) (..kies), drafkarretjie, tweedisselboomkarretjie.
sulk'y², (a) pruilerig, suur, nors, diklip, hanglip, humeurig, stuurs.
sul'lage, vuilgoed, afval, vuilis; rioolvuil; besoedeling, vuiligheid; ~ **pit**, slikput.
sull'en, gemelik, nors, somber, ongesellig; stuurs, stug, koppig, weerbarstig, weerspannig; ~ **ly**, op 'n stuurs manier; ~**ness**, norsheid, somberheid, stuursheid.
sull'y, (sullied), bemors, besmet, besoedel; beklad; *refuse to* ~ *one's HANDS*, jou hande nie aan iets vuil wil maak nie; ~ *someone's good NAME*, iem. in sy eer aantas.
sul'phate, sulfaat; swa(w)elsuursout; ~ *of LIME*, swa(w)elsuurkalk; ~ *of POTASH*, kaliumsulfaat.
sul'phide, sulfied, sulfide, swa(w)elverbinding.
sul'phite, sulfiet.
sul'phonal, sulfonaal.
sul'phur, (n) swa(w)el, sulfer; *FLOWERS of* ~, swa(w)elblom, fyn swa(w)el; (v) swa(w)el; ~ **ate**, swa(w)el; blomswa(w)el; ~ **bath**, swa(w)elbad; ~ **cement**, swa(w)elsement; ~ **content**, swa(w)elgehalte; ~ **dioxide**, swa(w)eldiokside, swa(w)eldioksied; ~**'eous**, swa(w)elagtig, swa(w)el-; satanies, hels; ~**ett'ed hydrogen**, swa(w)elwaterstof.
sulphur'ic, swa(w)el-; ~ **acid**, swa(w)elsuur.
sul'phurize, swa(w)el; met swa(w)el berook.
sul'phurizing, beroking, (behandeling) met swa(w)el.
sul'phur: ~-**match**, swa(w)elvuurhoutjie; ~-**ore**, swa(w)elerts.
sul'phurous, swa(w)el-; swa(w)elagtig, sulfereus; ~ **odour**, swa(w)ellug; ~ **vapour**, swa(w)eldamp.
sul'phur: ~-**pan**, swa(w)elbakkie; ~-**pit**, swa(w)elgat; ~-**rain**, swa(w)elreën; ~-**shy**, swa(w)elgevoelig; ~-**spring**, swa(w)elbron; ~ **wort**, swa(w)elwortel; ~-**yellow**, swa(w)elgeel.
sul'tan, sultan.
sulta'na, sultana(rosyntjie); sultane (koningin).
sul'tan: ~ **ate**, sultanaat; ~**ess, (-es)**, sultane.
sultan'ic, sultanies.
sul'triness, bedompigheid, swoelheid, drukkende hitte, soelte, broeierigheid.
sul'try, drukkend, swoel, smoorwarm, smoorheet, broeierig, bedompig, benoud.
sum, (n) som; totaal; inhoud; bedrag; oormaat, hoeveelheid; totaalbedrag; groottotaal; *the boy is GOOD at* ~ *s*, die seun kan goed somme maak; *IN* ~, kortweg, kortom; *IN the* ~ *of*, ten bedrae van; *a LUMP* ~, 'n ronde som; *the* ~ *of his OBJECTIONS is this*, sy besware kom hierop neer; *the* ~ *and SUBSTANCE*, die kern; ~ *TOTAL*, totaalbedrag; (v) **(-med)**, optel; somme maak; ~ *UP*, opsom, saamvat, resumeer; optel; ~ *UP a person*, iem. in 'n paar woorde beskryf.
sum'ac(h), sumak, looiersboom; pruimbas.
Sumat'ra, Sumatra; ~**n**, (n) Sumatraan; (a) Sumatraans.
summ'arily, kortweg, summier, sonder veel omslag, op staande voet; ~ *ARRESTED*, op staande voet gearresteer; *DEAL* ~ *with*, kort mette maak met.
summ'arize, opsom, saamvat, resumeer.
summ'ary, (n) **(..ries)**, opsomming, kort samevatting, uittreksel, ekstrak, afkooksel; (a) summier; kort, beknop, sonder omweë; kortaf; *put to* ~ *USE*, dadelik gebruik; ~ *DISMISSAL*, ontslag op staande voet; ~ *execution*, onmiddellike teregstelling; ~ *judgement*, summiere (dadelike) vonnis; ~ *justice*, standreg; ~ *trial*, summiere verhoor.
summa'tion, optelling; opsomming; totaal.
summ'er¹, (n) lêerlatei; dwarsbalk.
summ'er², (n) opteller.
summ'er³, (n) somer; *a (* ~ *'s) DAY*, 'n somerdag; *INDIAN* ~, opslagsomer; *in the* ~ *of his LIFE*, in die somer v.d. lewe; *have seen MANY* ~ *s*, baie somers gesien het; (v) oorsomer, die somer deurbring; ~ **afternoon**, somermiddag; ~ **air**, somerlug; ~ **attire**, somerklere; ~ **breeze**, somerkoelte; ~ **capital**, somerhoofstad; ~ **clearance**, someropruiming, ~ **cloud**, somerwolk; ~ **crop**, somergewas; ~ **dress**, somerrok; somerdrag; ~ **evening**, someraand; ~ **freckles**, somersproete; ~ **frock**, somerjurkie; ~

fruits, somervrugte; ~ **game**, somerspel; somersport; ~ **hat**, somerhoed; ~ **heat**, somerhitte; ~ **holidays**, somervakansie; ~ **house**, somerhuis; tuinhuis; prieel; ~-**like**, someragtig, somers; ~ **month**, somermaand; ~ **morning**, somermôre; ~ **night**, somernag; ~ **palace**, somerpaleis; ~ **pruning**, somersnoei; ~ **rain**, somerreën; ~ **rash**, hittepuisies, hitteuitslag; ~ **residence**, somerverblyf; ~ **resort**, someroord; ~ **sale**, someropruiming, someruitverkoping.
summ'ersault, *kyk* **somersault**.
summ'er: ~ **season**, somerseisoen; ~ **sleep**, somerslaap; ~ **solstice**, somersonstilstand; ~ **suite**, somerpak; ~ **sun**, somerson; ~ **term**, somerkwartaal; ~**time**, somer(tyd); ~ **underwear**, someronderklere; ~ **wear**, somerklere, somerdrag; ~-**weather**, somerweer; ~**y**, somers, someragtig.
summ'ing-up, samevatting, opsomming.
summ'it, toppunt, top, kruin; ~ **conference**, ~ **meeting**, leierskonferensie, spitsberaad; ~ **talks**, spitsberaad, leiersberaad.
summ'on, dagvaar; oproep, ontbied, sommeer; opeis; ~ *into BEING*, in die lewe roep; ~ *up COURAGE*, moed bymekaarskraap; ~ *PARLIAMENT*, die parlement byeenroep; ~**er**, dagvaarder, eiser.
summ'ons, (n) **(-es)**, dagvaarding, lasbrief; sommasie, aanskrywing; oproep; *serve a* ~, 'n dagvaarding beteken (dien) aan; (v) dagvaar.
sump, oliebak; sinkput; mynput (geol.); ~ **case**, krukkas, krukbak; ~ **pump**, dreineerpomp.
sump'ter, pakdier, lasdier; ~-**horse**, pakperd; ~-**mule**, pakmuil, pakesel; ~-**saddle**, paksaal.
sump'tuary, onkostebeperkend, weeldebeperkend, weelde-; ~ **duty**, weeldebelasting; ~ **edict**, ~ **law**, weeldewet.
sumptuos'ity, weelde; weelderigheid; kosbaarheid.
sump'tuous, weelderig, kosbaar, ryk, pragtig, sumptueus; ~**ness**, weelderigheid.
sun, (n) son; sonskyn; sonlig; *nothing NEW under the* ~, niks nuuts onder die son nie; *a PLACE in the* ~, 'n plek in die son; *RISE with the* ~, teen dagbreek opstaan; *his* ~ *SET while it was still day*, sy son het ondergegaan terwyl dit nog dag was; *the* ~ *SHINES on all alike*, die son skyn op slegtes en goeies; *the* ~ *puts all the STARS to flight*, as meerderman kom, moet minderman wyk; *TAKE the* ~, in die son sit; *WITH the* ~, in die rigting v.d. son; *WORSHIP the rising* ~, die opkomende son aanbid; *let not the* ~ *go down upon your WRATH*, laat die son nie oor jou toorn ondergaan nie; (v) **(-ned)**, *oneself*, aan die son blootstel; in die son lê (sit); ~ **bath**, sonbad; ~-**bathe**, 'n sonbad neem; ~-**bather**, sonbaaier; ~ **beam**, sonstraal; ~-**bird**, suikervoëltjie, suikerbekkie, kolibrie; ~-**blind**, sonskerm, rolblinding; ~-**bonnet**, kappie; ~ **burn**, sonbrand; ~ **burnt**, gebruin; (deur son) verbrand; ~ **canopy**, sontent:
sun'dae, vrugteroomys.
Sun'day, Sondag; *his* ~ *BEST*; *his* ~-*go-to-meeting CLOTHES*, sy Sondagsklere, sy kisklere; *a* ~ *'s CHILD*, 'n gelukskind; ~ **observance**, Sondagheiliging; ~ **paper**, Sondagblad; ~ **school**, Sondagskool; ~-**school teacher**, Sondagskoolonderwyser(es); ~ **suit**, Sondagspak.
sun: ~-**cured**, in die son gedroog; ~-**deck**, sondek.
sun'der, skei, vaneenskeur, uitmekaarruk, verbreek.
sun: ~ **dew**, doublom, sondou (plant); ~-**dial**, sonwyser; ~-**down**, sonsondergang; ~ **downer**, skemerkelkie, aandsopie; ~ **downer party**, skemerpartytjie; ~-**dried**, in die son gedroog, songedroog; ~-**dried hides**, droë velle (huide); ~-**dried brick**, rou steen.
sun'dries, diverse, allerhande dinge, kleinighede.
sun'dry, diverse, allerhande, verskeie; *ALL and* ~, elkeen en almal; ~ *EXPENSES*, diverse uitgawes.
sun: ~-**dry**, (v) **(..dried)**, in die son droog; (a) sondroog; ~ **fish**, sonvis; ~ **flower**, sonneblom.
sung, gesing; gesonge; *kyk* **sing**.
sun: ~-**gazer**, sonnekyker; skurwejantjie, ouvolk; ~-**glass**, brandglas; ~-**glasses**, donker bril; ~-**glow**, sonkring; songloed; ~-**god**, songod; ~-**hat**, sonhoed; ~-**helmet**, sonhelm.

sunk, versonke; versink; ingelaat; gesonke; *kyk* **sink,** (v).
sunk'en, ingeval, hol; ondergegaan (son); hangend (kop); ~ **bath,** versonke bad; ~ **cheeks,** hol wange; ~ **eyes,** oë agter in die kop; ~ **garden,** uitgegraafde tuin, dieptuin; ~ **road,** hol pad; ~ **rock,** blinde klip.
sun: ~ **less,** sonder son, sonloos; somber; ~ **light,** sonlig; ~ **like,** sonagtig; ~ **lit,** sonnig, deur die son beskyn; ~ **-myth,** sonmite.
sunn' hemp, sunnhennep.
sun'niness, sonnigheid; opgewektheid, vrolikheid.
sun'ny, sonnig; opgewek, vrolik; *the* ~ *side of LIFE,* die helder (sonnige) kant van die lewe; *the* ~ *SIDE,* die sonkant; *the* ~ *side of SIXTY,* nog nie sestig jaar nie.
sun: ~ **-porch,** glasstoep, sonportaal; ~ **proof,** bestand teen die son; ~ **-ray,** sonstraal; ~ **rise,** sonop, sonsopgang; ~ **-roof,** sondak; ~ **'s altitude,** sonstand, sonshoogte; ~ **set,** sononder, sonsondergang; *the* ~ *set of life,* die lewensaand; ~ **-shade,** sambreel; sonskerm; ~ **-shield,** sonskerm.
sun'shine, sonskyn; ~ *comes after RAIN,* na reën kom sonskyn; *no* ~ *but has some SHADOW,* "'n druppel gal in die soetste wyn"; daar is 'n bitter druppel in die soetste kelk; ~ **roof,** skuifdak (motor).
sun: ~ **shiny,** sonnig; ~ **'s' orbit,** sonweg; ~ **spot,** sonvlek; ~ **stroke,** sonsteek, sonstraal; ~ **struck,** met sonsteek; ~ **-suit,** sonpak; ~ **-tan,** bruining; ~ **-tanned,** gebruin; ~ **-tanning,** sonbrand; ~ **-tan oil,** sonbrandolie; ~ **-time,** sontyd; ~ **-visor,** sonskerm; ~ **ward,** sonwaarts; ~ **-worship,** sondiens; ~ **-worshipper,** sonaanbidder.
sup, (n) slukkie, teugie, happie, mondjievol; *neither bite nor* ~, nòg nat nòg droog oor die lippe; (v) **(-ped),** die aandete gebruik, soepeer.
su'per, (n) opsiener; heuningkas; figurant (op verhoog); (a) superfyn, eersteklas, kostelik, heerlik.
sup'erable, oorkombaar, oorkoomlik, oorwinbaar; ~ **ness,** oorkoomlikheid.
superabound', in oorvloed aanwesig wees, volop wees.
superabun'dance, oorvloed, oordaad, oormaat.
superabun'dant, oorvloedig, volop.
superacid'ity, oorsuurheid.
superadd', nog byvoeg; ~ **i'tion,** verdere byvoeging (byvoegsel).
superann'uate, pensioeneer, afdank weens ouderdom; verjaar; *become* ~ *d,* verjaar.
superannua'tion, pensioenering; emeritaat (predikant); verslyting; verjaring; pensioen; *term of* ~, verjaringstermyn; ~ **act,** pensioenwet; ~ **fund,** pensioenfonds.
superb', voortreflik, pragtig, skitterend, groots; ~ **ity,** trots; ~ **ness,** voortreflikheid.
sup'ercargo, (-es), ladingsbestuurder, skeepskoopman.
sup'er cement, edelsement.
supercharge', aanjaag (motor); oorversadig; oorverhit; ~ **d cabin,** drukkajuit; ~ **d engine,** aangejaagde enjin; ~ **r,** (druk)aanjaer, kompressieverhogingspomp; ~ **valve,** aanja(ag)klep.
supercharg'ing, aanjaging.
supercil'iary, winkbrou=.
supercil'ious, trots, hoogmoedig, verwaand, uit die hoogte; ~ **ness,** verwaandheid, trots, hoogmoed.
supercool', oorafkoel; ~ **ed,** oorafgekoel; ~ **ing,** oorafkoeling.
superdread'nought, superslagskip, superdreadnought.
supere'go, superego.
superem'inence, uitmuntendheid, voortreflikheid.
superem'inent, buitengewoon voortreflik.
supereroga'tion, oordrewe pligsvervulling; *a work of* ~, oorbodige (goeie) werk; oorbodigheid, oortolligheid.
supererog'atory, oortollig, oorbodig.
superexalt', oormatig verhef (verhoog).
superex'cellence, besondere uitmuntendheid.
superex'cellent, allesoortreffend, buitengewoon voortreflik.
superfecun'dity, oordadige vrugbaarheid.

superfi'cial, oppervlakkig; vlak; superfisieel, onbekook, bo-op; oppervlak=; *become* ~, vervlak; ~ **expansion,** oppervlakuitsetting; ~ **foot,** vierkantvoet; ~ **'ity,** (..ties), oppervlakkigheid; ~ **iza'tion,** vervlakking; veruitwendiging; ~ **ize,** vervlak; veruitwendig; ~ **ly,** bolangs; oppervlakkig; oortollig; ~ **measure,** vlaktemaat; ~ **scald,** skilbrand; ~ **work,** afskeepwerk; ~ **wound,** skraapwond, vlak wond.
superfi'cies, (sing and pl), oppervlak.
sup'erfine, allerfynste, eersteklas, haarfyn, superfyn (wol).
superflu'ity, oortolligheid; oorvloed.
super'fluous, oortollig; oorbodig; ~ **ness,** oortolligheid; oorbodigheid.
superfuse', oorgiet; oorafkoel.
superfu'sion, oorgieting; oorafkoeling.
superheat', (n) oorhitte; (v) oorverhit; ~ **er,** oorverhitter; ~ **ing,** oorverhitting.
su'perhive, heuningkas.
superhum'an, bo(we)menslik.
superimpose', bo-op lê; nog bo-op sit; superponeer; ~ **d,** oorheenliggend; opgelê; gesuperponeer.
superimposi'tion, oplegging.
superincum'bent, bo-opliggend, boliggend.
superinduce', toevoeg, byvoeg.
superinduc'tion, toevoeging, byvoeging.
superintend', toesig hou; ~ **ence,** toesig; ~ **ent,** (n) superintendent, opsiener; (a) toesiende; ~ **ent-general,** superintendent-generaal.
super'ior, (n) meerdere; superieur; owerste; moesoek; *have no* ~ *in COURAGE,* almal in moed oortref; *MOTHER* ~, moederowerste; (a) hoër; beter; meerderwaardig; oormagtig; opper=, groter; superieur, voortreflik; verhewe (bo); hooghartig; bo= standig (plantk.); *with a* ~ *AIR,* uit die hoogte; *BE* ~, hooghartig wees; *BE* ~ *to,* oortref; verhewe wees bo; ~ *in NUMBERS,* in groter getalsterkte; *a* ~ *PERSON,* iem. wat alles weet; 'n hoogmoedige mens; ~ **authority,** hoër gesag; ~ **court,** hoër hof; ~ **force,** oormag; ~ **'ity,** hoër rang; meerderheid, voortreflikheid, voorrang, superioriteit; ~ **knowledge,** meerdere kennis, ~ **letter,** hooggedrukte letter(teken) (bv. x²); ~ **numbers,** oormag; ~ **officer,** meerdere, hoër offisier; ~ **planets,** buitenste planete; ~ **rank,** hoër rang.
superja'cent, bo-opliggend, boliggend.
super'lative, (n) oortreffende trap, superlatief; (a) oortreffend; onoortroffe, hoogste, grootste, superlatief; ~ **degree,** oortreffende trap, superlatief; ~ **ness,** onoortreffendheid, onoortreflikheid.
superlun'ar(y), bomaans, boweaards, boaards.
sup'erman, (..men), oppermens.
sup'ermarket, supermark; selfhelpwinkel; alleswinkel.
supermun'dane, boweaards, boaards.
supernac'ulum, uitsoekwyn; *drink* ~, tot op die laaste druppel drink.
supern'al, (poet.), hemels, boweaards, boaards, goddelik.
supernat'ant, drywend, ~ **liquor,** bovloeistof, bowater.
superna'tural, bo(we)natuurlik, boaards; ~ **ism,** supernaturalisme; ~ **ist,** ~ **ness,** bo(we)natuurlikheid.
supernorm'al, bonormaal.
supernum'erary, (n) **(..ries),** ekstra amptenaar, ekstra offisier; ergie juksker; supernumerêr; figurant, ekstra bediende; (a) ekstra, oortollig, botallig, reserwe=.
supernutri'tion, oorvoeding.
superphos'phate, superfosfaat.
superpose', bo-op sit, bo-op lê.
superposi'tion, openplasing, opmekaarplasing, superposisie.
su'perpower, supermoondheid.
su'per race, opperras, heersersras.
supersat'urate, oorversadig.
supersatura'tion, oorversadiging.
sup'erscribe, die opskrif skryf, van 'n opskrif voorsien; jou naam sit bo; adresseer.
superscrip'tion, opskrif; adres.

supersede', skors; vervang; verdring; verbygaan; afskaf, afsit; die plek inneem van; agteruitdring; ~*d BY*, vervang deur; *be* ~ *d in COMMAND*, van die bevel onthef word.
supersen'sible, bo(we)sinlik.
supersen'sitive, oorgevoelig; ~**ness**, oorgevoeligheid.
supersen'sual, supersen'suous, bo(we)sinlik.
superse'ssion, vervanging; afskaffing, afdanking.
superson'ic, supersonies; ~ **flight**, supersoniese vlug; ~ **shock-wave**, supersoniese skokgolf.
supersti'tion, bygeloof, bygelowigheid, waangeloof.
supersti'tious, bygelowig; ~**ness**, bygelowigheid.
superstrat'um, (..ta), boonste laag, bolaag.
sup'erstructure, bo(we)bou, bouwerk.
sup'ertax, (-es), ekstrabelasting, superbelasting.
superterran'ean, bo(we)gronds.
supervene', bykom, oorkom; tussenkom.
superven'ient, bykomend, nuut.
superven'ing, opvolgend, nakomend.
superven'tion, optrede, onverwagte tussenkoms.
supervise', opsig hou, toesig hou (oor), kyk na.
supervis'ing, toesighoudend.
supervis'ion, opsig, toesig.
supervis'or, opsigter, opsiener; ~**y**, toesighoudend, toesiende.
sup'ine, (n) supinum; (a) op die naat van die rug, agteroor; agtelosig, onverskillig; laks; traag; ~**ness**, laksheid; traagheid; lusteloosheid.
supp'er, (n) aandete, soepee; *HAVE* ~, die aandete gebruik; *the LORD'S S*~, die Awendmaal, Nagmaal; (v) die aandete gebruik; ~**less**, sonder aandete; ~**-time**, tyd vir aandete; etenstyd.
supplant', vervang, ondermyn, verdring, onderkruip; ~**er**, verdringer, onderkruiper.
sup'ple, (v) buigsaam maak; (a) lenig, buigsaam, buigbaar, soepel, smedig; rekbaar; plooibaar; slap (ledemate); gedwee, meegaande, kruipend; ~**-jack**, slap kierie; kweperkierie.
supp'lement, (n) aanhangsel, byvoegsel, aanvulling, byblad, bylae, supplement.
supplement', (v) aanvul, byvoeg, toevoeg; aansuiwer; ~**al**, aanvullend; ~*al to*, ter aanvulling van; aanvullend by; ~**al angle**, byhoek, supplementshoek.
supplement'ary, aanvullend, aanvullings=, supplementêr; ~ **angle**, supplementshoek, byhoek; ~ **examination**, aanvullende eksamen; ~ **payment**, nabetaling, agterskot.
sup'pleness, lenigheid, buigsaamheid; slapheid; kruiperigheid.
supp'liant, (n) smekeling, smeker; (a) smekend, smeek=.
supp'licant, smekeling, versoeker.
supp'licate, versoek, soebat, bid, smeek.
supp'licating, smekend.
supplica'tion, versoek, (af)smeking, smeekgebed, smeekbede, gesmeek.
supp'licator, bidder, vraer; ~**y**, smekend, smeek=.
suppli'er, leveransier, verskaffer.
supply', (n) (..plies), voorraad, kommissariaat; aanbod, verskaffing; lewering, leweransie; toevoer; (pl) benodigdhede, proviand, lewensmiddele, mondprovisie, eetware, mondbehoeftes, (mond)voorraad; toegestane gelde (op die begroting); *COMMITTEE of* ~, begrotingskomitee; ~ *and DEMAND*, vraag en aanbod; ~ *of LIGHT*, ligvoorsiening; *SOURCE of* ~, toevoerbron; *VOTE supplies*, gelde toestaan; (v) (..plied), (ver)skaf, voorsien; lewer; aanvul, voldoen aan; sorg vir; ~ *a DEMAND*, aan die vraag voldoen; ~ *a LOSS*, 'n verlies vergoed; ~ *a NEED*, in 'n behoefte voorsien; *in SHORT* ~, skaars; ~ *the TRADE*, aan die handel lewer; ~ **cable**, toevoerkabel; ~ **chain**, aanvoerketting; ~ **cistern**, toevoerbak; ~ **column**, kommissariaatkolonne; ~ **council**, leweringsraad; ~ **department**, leweringsdiens; ~**-dump**, opslagplek; ~ **line**, toevoerlyn; ~**-main**, hoofftoevoerleiding; ~ **meter**, verbruiksmeter; ~**-net**, toevoernet, aanvoerstelsel; ~ **note**, verskaffingsbewys; ~**-pipe**, aanvoerbuis; toevoerpyp; ~ **route**, toevoerroete; ~**-ship**, voorraadskip; ~ **system**, toevoerstelsel; ~ **voltage**, voerspanning.

support', (n) ondersteuning, onderskraging, steun, bystand, hulp; toeverlaat; onderhoud; bestaan; stut, steunsel, steunstuk; styl; staf, versterking; onderstel; *the CHIEF* ~ *of our side*, die steunpilaar van ons kant; *GIVE* ~ *to*, steun verleen aan; *IN* ~ *of*, ten bate van, tot steun van; *without MEANS of* ~, sonder bestaansmiddele; *speak in* ~ *of a MOTION*, ten gunste van 'n voorstel praat; *POINT of* ~, steunpunt; *REQUIRE* ~, hulp (steun) nodig hê; *the* ~ *of his SISTER*, die steun van sy suster; *TROOPS in* ~, steuntroepe; (v) steun, ondersteun; (onder)skraag, help; onderhou; uithou, verdra, volhou; die middele verskaf vir; van voedsel voorsien; bewys, staaf, stut, dra; versterk, aanmoedig; *too little FOOD to* ~ *life*, te min kos om aan die lewe te bly; ~ *a FAMILY*, 'n gesin onderhou; ~ *a MOTION*, 'n voorstel steun; ~ *a ROLE*, 'n rol speel; ~ *a SPEAKER*, 'n spreker steun; saam met 'n spreker op die verhoog verskyn; ~**able**, draaglik, houdbaar, duldbaar; verdedigbaar; ~ **end**, draent; ~**er**, volgeling, ondersteuner, helper, steunpilaar, versorger; voorstander; steun, stut; kampvegter; donateur; skildhouer (her.).
support'ing, bykomend, aanvullend; steun=, steunend; ~ **actor**, byspeler; ~ **aircraft**, steunvliegtuig; ~ **beam**, steunbalk; ~ **board**, steunplank; ~ **cast**, byspelers; ~ **document**, stawende stuk; ~ **film**, voorfilm; ~ **programme**, voorprogram; ~ **troops**, steuntroepe; ~ **wall**, stutmuur, steunmuur.
support' rail, steunreling.
suppos'able, denkbaar, veronderstelbaar.
suppose', veronderstel, aanneem; vermoed, glo, meen, dink; ~ *you GO to bed*, hoe sal dit wees as jy bed toe gaan? *LET us* ~, laat ons aanneem; *what do you* ~ *he MEANT?* wat dink jy het hy bedoel? ~ *you are RIGHT*, gestel (veronderstel) dat jy reg is (gelyk het); *I* ~ *SO*, waarskynlik wel; *I do not* ~ *you will be THERE*, jy sal seker nie daar wees nie; ~ *we go for a WALK?* hoe sal dit wees as ons gaan stap?
supposed', vermeen, gewaand, veronderstel(d); *you are not* ~ *to CRY*, jy mag nie huil nie; *she is not* ~ *to KNOW*, sy mag nie weet nie; *his* ~ *PARENTAGE*, sy vermeende afkoms; *he is* ~ *to be RICH*, hy is glo ryk; hy is kamma ryk; *his* ~ *SISTER*, sy vermeende suster; *he is* ~ *to WORK*, hy is veronderstel om te werk.
suppos'ing, aangeneem, veronderstel (dat), gestel.
supposi'tion, veronderstelling, vermoede, mening; *on the* ~ *that*, in die veronderstelling dat; ~**al**, vermoedelik, veronderstel(d), hipoteties.
supposi'tious, denkbeeldig.
supposti'tious, ingebeeld, vals, gewaand, oneg; ~**ness**, onegtheid.
suppos'itory, (..ries), steekpil, setpil.
suppress', onderdruk; bedwing; demp (opstand); inhou; dooddruk, smoor; stilhou, verswyg; agterhou; weglaat; verbied (boek); ~ *evidence*, getuienis smoor; ~**ible**, bedwingbaar, onderdrukbaar; ~**ion**, onderdrukking; weglating, verswyging; opheffing; geheimhouding; smoring; ~**ive**, onderdrukkend; ~**or**, onderdrukker, demper.
supp'urate, etter, dra, sweer, versweer.
suppura'tion, ettering, verswering, ettervorming.
supp'urative, (n) ettervormende middel; (a) ettervormend, etterend.
su'pra, hierbo, supra.
supraclavic'ular, bokant die sleutelbeen.
supramaxill'ary, bokakebeen=.
supramun'dane, boaards.
supraren'al gland, bynier.
suprem'acy, oppermag, oppergesag, (opper)heerskappy; oormag, oorwig, supremasie.
supreme', (n) die hoogste; (a, adv) hoogste, opperste, allerhoogste; oppermagtig; vernaamste; *BE* ~, oppermagtig wees; *with* ~ *CONTEMPT*, met die grootste minagting; *at the* ~ *HOUR*, op die laaste oomblik; *the* ~ *MOMENT*, die laaste uur; *at the* ~ *MOMENT*, op die kritieke oomblik; *PAY the* ~ *sacrifice*, jou lewe opoffer, sterf; *pay the* ~ *PENALTY*, die doodstraf ondergaan; *RULE* ~, oppermagtig wees; *the* ~ *SACRIFICE*, die hoogste of-

surah fer; *STAND* ~, almal oortref; *the* ~ *TEST,* die hoogste toets; ~ **authority,** oppergesag; S~ **Being,** die Opperwese; ~ **command,** opperbevel; S~ **Court,** Hooggeregshof; ~ **folly,** die toppunt van dwaasheid; ~ **head,** opperhoof.

sur'ah, soerasy.

sur'al, kuit-; ~ **muscle,** kuitspier.

sur'base arch, korfboog.

surcease', (n) skorsing, staking; einde; (v) ophou, staak; eindig.

surcharge', (n) oorlaaiing, oorlading, bobelasting; oorgewigkoste, oorbetaling; ekstraport, strafport; strafgelde; toeslag, byslag; boete; oordruk, by= druk (op posseël); (v) te veel laat betaal; ekstra laat betaal; oorlaai; oorversadig; opdruk (pos= seël).

sur'cingle, oorgord.

surc'oat, opperkleed, bokleed.

surc'ulose, surc'ulous, met suiers, suier=.

surd, (n) stemlose medeklinker; onmeetbare getal; wortelvorm, wortelgetal; (a) stemloos, dof; on= meetbaar (getal).

sure, (a) seker, gewis; onfeilbaar, stellig; veilig; *send by a* ~ *HAND,* met 'n betroubare bode stuur; *put in a* ~ *PLACE,* op 'n veilige plek bêre; *a* ~ *SHOT,* 'n raakskieter, 'n sekuur (fyn) skut; ~ *THING!* alte seker! *that is a* ~ *WINNER,* dit kan nie verkeerd loop nie; dit behoort maklik te wen; (adv) seker, waarlik, wis, ja-nee; *BE* ~ *about it; BE* ~ *of,* seker wees van; *BE* ~ *to come,* kom tog seker; *you CAN be* ~ *of that!* dit moet jy weet! *he will COME* ~ *enough,* hy sal ongetwyfeld kom; *he is* ~ *to be a CREDIT to his country,* hy sal ongetwyfeld 'n bate vir sy land wees; *as* ~ *as DEATH,* so seker as twee maal twee vier is, so seker as wat; *be* ~ *to DO it,* doen dit seker; *as* ~ *as EGGS are eggs,* so seker as twee maal twee vier is; ~ *ENOUGH,* waarlik, werklik, seker; *be* ~ *of one's FACTS,* seker van jou saak wees; *as* ~ *as FATE,* so seker as twee maal twee vier is; *FOR* ~, stellig, seker; *as* ~ *as GOD made little apples,* so seker as wat; *as* ~ *as a GUN,* so seker as wat, so waar as padda manel dra; dis nie altemit nie; *I am* ~ *I don't KNOW,* ek is seker dat ek nie weet nie; *MAKE* ~ *that,* jou verseker van; jou oortuig dat; sorg dra dat; *MAKE* ~ *that you come,* kom tog seker; ~ *of YOURSELF,* seker van jou saak; (interj) bepaald! ja, seker! ~**-footed,** vas op die voete; onfeilbaar; betroubaar; ~ **ly,** seker, stellig, sonder twyfel, warempel, voorwaar, wrag= gies, darem, tog, vervas, sweerlik; ~ **ness,** seker= heid.

sure'ty, (..**ties**), borg, waarborg, pand; sekerheid, ge= wisheid; *OF a* ~, stellig, seker; *STAND* ~ *for,* borg staan vir; ~ **ship,** borgtog; borgstelling; *deed of* ~ *ship,* akte van borgstelling.

surf, (n) branders, branding; (v) branderplank ry, branders ry, gier.

surf'ace, (n) oppervlak; vlak(te); bodem; blad (pad); buitekant; *BREAK* ~, bo die water kom; bo kom; *ON the* ~, aan die oppervlak; *a PLANE* ~, 'n plat vlak; *SQUARE* ~, vlaktemaat; (v) glad skuur, ska= we, polys; opduik, opkom, bokom; bedek; verhard (pad); 'n blad gee; planeer (papier); (a) oppervlak= kig; bogronds; uiterlik; geveins; ~ **coat,** bladlaag (pad) deklaag (verf); ~ **crack,** windbars; ~ **craft,** bowatervaartuig; ~ **current,** oppervlakstroom; ~ **drain,** grondgeut; ~ **erosion,** oppervlakerosie; ~ **layer,** bolaag; ~ **mail,** landpos; seepos; ~**man,** spoorwerker; ~**-measure,** vlaktemaat; ~ **noise,** plaatgekrap (radio); ~ **plane,** vlakskawer, gladma= ker; onderlaag; vlakblok; vlakslyper; ~ **raider,** bo= waterkaper; ~**-right,** oppervlakreg; ~ **soil,** bo= grond; ~ **temperature,** oppervlaktemperatuur; ~ **wind,** grondwind; ~ **wiring,** bogrondse geleiding; ~ **workings,** dagbouwerkplekke.

sur'facing, opduiking; gladmaking; planering; ver= harding.

surf: ~**-bathing,** (die) baai in die branding, branders ry; ~**-board,** branderplank, ryplank, swemplank, gierplank; ~**-boat,** platboomskuit; reddingsboot; brandingsboot.

surf'eit, (n) oorlaaiing, oorversadiging; walging; (v) ooreet, die maag oorlaai; (jou) oorversadig; ~ *one= self with,* jou teë-eet aan.

surf: ~**er,** golfryer; ~**ing,** golfry, branderplank ry, gier; ~**-riding,** branderplank ry.

surge, (n) golf; stortsee; drukgolf; branding, golwing, deining; stuwing (elek.); (v) hoog gaan; golf, dein, aanswel; ~ *BY,* verbyrol; ~ *IN,* binnestroom.

sur'geon, snydokter, chirurg; arts; *DENTAL* ~, tandarts; *be subjected to the* ~ *'s KNIFE,* onder die mes kom.

sur'gery, heelkunde, snykuns, chirurgie; (..**ries**), spreekkamer; *plastic* ~, plastiese snykunde (chi= rurgie).

sur'gical, heelkundig, chirurgies; ~ **case,** instrument= kissie; operasieveval; ~ **fever,** wondkoors; ~ **knife,** opereermes; ~ **shock,** operasieskok.

surg'ing, (n) opwelling; golwing; (a) golwend, brui= send.

sur'icate, graatjiemeerkat, stokstertmeerkat.

surl'iness, norsheid, stugheid, stuursheid, knorrig= heid, onbeleefdheid.

surl'y, nors, stuurs, suur, stug, stroef, stoets, iese= grimmig, somber, dreigend; ~ *fellow,* 'n iesegrim, 'n suurknol, 'n suurpruim.

surmis'able, vermoedbaar.

surmise', (n) vermoede, gissing; (v) vermoed, gis, raai, (ver)onderstel.

surmount', te bowe kom, oorwin, oorkom; ~*ed by a weathercock,* met 'n weerhaan bo-op; ~**able,** oor= koomlik, oorkombaar.

surn'ame, (n) van, familienaam; (v) 'n van gee; ~**d,** met die van.

surpass', oortref; oorskry, te bowe gaan; ~**able,** oor= trefbaar; ~**ing,** bo alles uitstekend, ongeëwenaard, volprese, weergaloos; *of* ~*ing beauty,* uiters mooi.

surp'lice, koorkleed, koorhemp; ~**d,** met 'n koor= hemp aan.

surp'lus, (n) (**-es**), teveel, oorskot, surplus, opgeld; (a) oortollig, orig, oorbodig; ~ **age,** surplus, oorskot; ~ **energy,** oortollige energie; ~ **oil,** oorskietolie; ~ **population,** oorbevolking; ~ **production,** oorpro= duksie; ~ **value,** oorwaarde, meerwaarde.

surpris'al, verrassing; oorrompeling.

surprise', (n) verrassing; verbasing; bevreemding; oorrompeling; *CAUSE* ~, verbasing wek; *COME as a* ~, verras; *be TAKEN by* ~, verras (oorrom= pel) word; *TO the* ~ *of,* tot verbasing van; (v) ver= ras; verbaas; oorrompel, oorval; betrap; ~ *in the ACT,* op heter daad betrap; *BE* ~*d at,* verwonderd wees oor; *LOOK* ~*d,* verwonderd kyk (lyk); (a) onverwag, verrassend; onvoorbereid; verrassings; ~ **attack,** verrassingsaanval; ~ **packet,** verrassin= kie, verrassingspakket; ~ **party,** verrassingsparty, invalparty, skrikpartytjie; ~ **visit,** onverwagte be= soek.

surpris'ing, verrassend, verbasend; ~**ly,** verrassend.

surre'alism, surrealisme.

surre'alist, (n) surrealis; (a) surrealisties.

surrebut', (**-ted**), die derde maal verweer, tweede tri= pliek lewer; ~ **tal,** ~ **ter,** derde repliek.

surrejoin', die tweede maal antwoord, tripliseer; ~ **der,** tweede repliek, tripliek.

surren'der, (n) oorgawe; uitlewering; afstand; afkoop (polis); (v) oorgee; jou gevange gee; hensop; uitle= wer; afstaan; afstand doen van; laat vaar; ~ *to the ENEMY,* jou aan die vyand oorgee; ~ *one's ES= TATE,* boedel oorgee; sterf; ~ *ONESELF,* jou oorgee; ~ *an insurance POLICY,* 'n assuransiepo= lis afkoop; ~ **value,** afkoopwaarde.

surrepti'tious, bedrieglik, onderduims; heimlik, steels; oneg; ~ **edition,** onwettige nadruk; ~**ly,** on= derduims, stilletjies, agteraf; in die geheim, heimlik; ~**ness,** heimlikheid; onderduimsheid.

su'rrogate, plaasvervanger, surrogaat.

surroga'tion, surrogasie.

surround', (n) omsingeling; (v) omring, om= singel, insluit; ~**ing,** (n) insluiting, o= (pl) omgewing; (a) omringend, omgeleë de; omgewings=.

surt'ax, (n) (**-es**), ekstra belasting, byhe lasting; (v) ekstra belas.

surveill'ance, toesig, opsig; bewaking; *under* ~, onder bewaking; ~ **unit,** waakeenheid.

surveill'ant, toesighoudend, bewakend.

surv'ey¹, (n) opmeting (grond); besigtiging; oorsig, beskouing; landmetersdepartement; landmeterskaart; opname; *geological* ~, geologiese opname.

survey'², (v) bekyk, beskou, besigtig, in oënskou neem; opneem; landmeet, opmeet (grond); toesig hou; ondersoek.

surv'ey, ~ **flight,** opmetingsvlug; ~ **group,** opmetingsgroep.

survey'ing, (n) landmeting, opmeting; opneming; opname; landmeetkuns; (a) landmeetkundig; ~ **chain,** landmetersketting, meetketting; ~ **party,** opnemingsbrigade; ~ **ship,** ~ **vessel,** opmetingskip.

surv'ey map, oorsigkaart.

survey'or, inspekteur, opsigter; landmeter; ~**-general, (surveyors-general),** landmetergeneraal; ~**- peg,** landmeterspen; ~**'s chain,** landmetersketting, meetketting; ~**ship,** opsigterskap; landmeterspos, amp van landmeter; ~**'s level,** landmeetwaterpas; ~**'s rod,** meetroede, maatstok; ~**'s wheel,** meetrat.

surviv'al, oorlewing, voortbestaan; oorblyfsel; ~ *of the fittest,* oorlewing (behoud) v.d. sterkste; ~ **kit,** noodpakkie, oorlewingspakkie.

survive', oorlewe; in lewe bly, voortlewe, deurleef, deurkom, voortbestaan; agterbly, langer lewe as, lewendig oorbly; ~ *d BY,* oorlewe deur; ~ *one's CONTEMPORARIES,* jou tydgenote oorlewe; ~ *all PERILS,* alle gevare deurlewe.

surviv'ing, oorlewend, langslewend; ~ **spouse,** langslewende gade.

surviv'or, langslewende, oorlewende, agtergeblewene, agterblywende; opvarende (van gestrande skip); ~ **ship,** oorlewing.

susceptibil'ity, vatbaarheid, gevoeligheid; liggeraaktheid; *wound (offend) a person's susceptibilities,* iem. se gevoeligheid kwes.

suscep'tible, (teer)gevoelig, vatbaar, ontvanklik; emosioneel; ~ *to FEMALE charms,* nie bestand teen die bekoring van die vrou nie; ~ *to FLATTERY,* gevoelig vir vleiery; ~ *of PROOF,* vatbaar vir bewys; ~ *TO,* ontvanklik vir; ~ **ness** = **susceptibility.**

suscep'tive, vatbaar, ontvanklik.

sus'pect¹, (n) gewantroude; verdagte persoon; (a) verdag.

suspect'², (v) verdink, wantrou, agterdog koester; vermoed; *a* ~ *ed CASE of,* 'n vermoedelike geval van; ~ *ONE of lying,* vermoed dat iem. lieg.

suspend', ophang; opskort; skors, suspendeer; staak, intrek; ~ *ed ANIMATION,* skyndood; ~ *ed FLOOR,* hangvloer; ~ *ed HOSTILITIES,* vyandelikhede staak; ~ *ed IMPURITIES,* swewende onreinhede (vuiligheid); ~ *one's JUDGMENT,* jou oordeel opskort; ~ *a LICENCE,* 'n lisensie intrek; ~ *a driving LICENCE,* 'n rybewys intrek; *five MEMBERS were* ~ *ed,* vyf lede is geskors; ~ *from OFFICE,* uit sy amp skors; ~ *PAYMENT,* betaling staak; ~ *ed SENTENCE,* opgeskorte vonnis; ~ *ed WATER,* gesuspendeerde water.

suspend'er, kousophouer, sokkieophouer; ~ **belt,** kousgordel; ~ **pantie,** hegbroekie.

suspense', onsekerheid, twyfel, spanning, angs; opskorting; uitstel; *in* ~, in spanning; ~ **account,** afwagrekening, voorlopige rekening.

suspensibil'ity, sweefvermoë.

suspen'sible, hangbaar; swewend; blywend.

suspen'sion, staking; skorsing; opskorting; suspensie; ophanging; vering; suspensie (in vloeistowwe); ~ *of ARMS,* wapenstilstand; *IN* ~, in swewende toestand; *HOLD in* ~, in opgeloste toestand bevat; ~ *of HOSTILITIES,* wapenskorsing, wapenstilstand; ~ *of LICENCE,* intrekking van 'n lisensie; ~ *of PAYMENT,* staking van betaling; ~ *of SENTENCE,* opskorting van vonnis; *SOLUTION in* ~, sweefmengsel; ~ **arm,** steunarm; ~ **bolt,** hanghout; ~ **bridge,** swaaibrug, sweefbrug, hangbrug; ~ **cable,** hangkabel; ~ **decree,** skorsingsbesluit; ~ **joint,** veringkoppeling; ~ **lamp,** hanglamp; ~ **rail-**

way, sweefbaan, hangspoor; ~ **system,** veringstelsel; ~ **wire,** ophangdraad; lugdraad.

suspen'sive, opskortend; onseker; twyfelagtig; ~ **power,** skorsingsreg.

suspen'soid, suspensoïde, suspensoïed.

suspen'sor, draagband; (kiem)draer; ~ **y,** (n) (**..ries**), draagband; (a) draend; hangend; opskortend; ~ **y bandage,** hangverband, draagverband.

suspi'cion, agterdog, verdenking, vermoede, mistroue, suspisie, argwaan; wantroue; sweem, ietsie, tikkie; spesmaas; *ABOVE* ~, bokant alle verdenking; *have a* ~ *AGAINST,* agterdog koester teen; *CAST* ~ *on,* iem. verdag maak; *I HAVE a* ~ *that,* ek vermoed dat; *on MERE* ~, bloot op vermoede; *on* ~ *of MURDER,* onder verdenking van moord; *NOT a* ~ *of,* nie die minste bewys nie; *arrest a person ON* ~, 'n verdagte arresteer; *be UNDER* ~ *of,* onder verdenking staan van.

suspi'cious, verdag; wantrouig, wantrouend, suspisieus, agterdogtig, argwanend, nagaande; *BE* ~ *of,* wantrou; *under* ~ *CIRCUMSTANCES,* in verdagte omstandighede; ~**-looking,** verdag lykend; ~**ness,** agterdog, wantrouigheid; verdagtheid.

suspira'tion, sug, asemhaling.

suspire', sug.

Sus'sex, Sussex; ~ **cattle,** Sussexbeeste.

sustain', steun; verdra; help, aanmoedig; aanhou (noot); volhou; hooghou; ly, deurstaan, verduur, uithou; oploop (wond); handhaaf; staaf; *it will not* ~ *COMPARISON,* dit kan geen vergelyking deurstaan nie; ~ *DAMAGE,* skade kry; ~ *a DEFEAT,* 'n nederlaag ly; ~ *an INJURY,* beseer word; ~ *a LOSS,* 'n verlies ly; ~ *a NOTE,* 'n noot rek (aanhou); ~ *an OBJECTION,* 'n beswaar handhaaf; ~ *a VIEW,* 'n standpunt stel; ~**able,** vol te hou; verdedigbaar.

sustained', volgehou, onverminderd, aanhoudend; gedrae; ~ *DEFENCE,* volgehoue verdediging; ~ *EFFORT,* onafgebroke inspanning; ~ *EXPERIENCE,* langdurige ondervinding; ~ *STYLE,* gedrae styl; ~ *YIELD,* aanhoudende opbrings.

sustain': ~ **er,** ondersteuner; ~ **ing,** (n) gedraenheid; (a) steunend; ~ *ing food,* voedsame ete; ~ *ing power,* uithouvermoë; ~ **ment,** steun, ondersteuning, bystand, hulp; (die) volhou.

sus'tenance, (lewens)onderhoud; lewensmiddele, voedsel, voeding, kos.

sustenta'tion, steun, hulp, onderhoud, sustentasie; ~ **fund,** steunfonds, sustentasiefonds.

susten'tion, gedraenheid.

susurra'tion, gefluister, fluistering; geruis, gegons.

susu'rrous, fluisterend, ruisend; ritselend; murmelend.

sut'ler, laersmous, soetelaar.

su'tra, soetra.

suttee', weduweeverbranding, sati, sutti.

su'tural, naat=; aaneengelas.

su'ture, (n) naat; wondnaat; hegting, sutuur, sutura; aaneenlassing; (v) toenaai, toewerk, vasheg.

suz'erain, suserein, leenheer; opperheer; ~ **state,** sureine staat; ~ **ty,** opperheerskappy, sesereiniteit.

svelte, slank, lenig.

swab, (n) swabber; pluisie, depper, wattetjie, watteprop; suiglap; dweil; skropbesem; lomperd; (v) **(-bed),** dep, skoonmaak, was, met 'n doek afwas; opvee; skrop, dweil; ~ **ber,** skropper; swabber; skropsoldaat, skropmatroos.

Swab'ia, Swabe; ~ **n,** (n) Swaab (persoon); Swabies (taal); (a) Swabies.

swad'dle, toedraai, in 'n verband wikkel, toewikkel, omswagtel; ~ **up,** toebaker.

swadd'ling: ~**-band,** ~**-cloth,** luier, doek, bande, belemmering; keurslyf; windsel; ~**-clothes,** babakleertjies, kinderklere; *no longer in* ~**-clothes,** die kinderskoene ontgroei wees.

swag, buit, roof; bondel; ~**-belly,** boepens, dikpens; vetsak, dikkerd.

swage, (n) smee(saal) (van smid); staalvorm; stempel; tandsetter (saag); (v) saalsmee, vormsmee; stempel; ~ **block,** saalaambeeld; matrysblok; ~ **r,** saalsmeder; smeesaal; tandsteller (vir saag); ~ **tool,** staalsmeevorm.

swagg'er, (n) gebluf; aanstellings, windmakery, blaaskakery, spoggerigheid; slingerstap; (v) spog, grootpraat, bluf; windmakerig stap; ~ *about*, die groot meneer uithang; (a) spoggerig, windmakerig; ~-**cane**, spogkierie(tjie); ~ **drill**, stokdril; ~-**stick**, spogkierie(tjie); ~ **er**, grootprater, spogter, spogger, grootdoener, poghans; ~ **ing**, (n) grootdoenery, pralery; (a) pronkend, windmakerig, pralerig; ~ **parade**, pronkparade.
swag'ing, saalwerk, saalsmeding; ~ **machine**, saalsmeemasjien.
swag'man, (..**men**), smous, landloper.
Swahil'i, Swahili (taal); (~, -s), Swahili (lid v.d. volk).
swain, boerkneg, boerneef; kêrel, vryer.
swa'llow[1], (n) swa(w)el(tjie); *one* ~ *does not make a summer*, een swa(w)eltjie maak nie die somer (lente) nie.
swa'llow[2], (n) sluk; keel; (v) sluk, insluk; verswelg; wegslaan, inslaan; ~ *EVERYTHING hook, line and sinker*, alles vir soetkoek opeet; *have to* ~ *all the INSULTS*, al die beledigings moet sluk; ~ *one's PRIDE*, jou trots moet sluk; ~ *one's WORDS*, jou woorde terugtrek.
swa'llow dive, swaelduik.
swa'llower, slukker.
swa'llow fish, seeswaeltjie.
swa'llowing, (die) sluk; verkropping.
swa'llow-tail, swaelstert; ~ **ed**, met 'n swaelstert; gevurk; ~ **ed coat**, swaelstertmanel, puntbaadjie.
swa'llowwort, skelkruid.
swam, *kyk* **swim**, (v)
swamp, (n) moeras, vlei, drasland; (v) vasval, vassit; oorstroom; oorstelp, versink, oorweldig, verswelg, opsluk; ~ *SOMEONE*, iem. oorweldig; iem. toesak; ~ *ed with WORK*, toe onder die werk; ~ **fever**, moeraskoors; ~ **ness**, moerassigheid, vleierigheid; ~ **y**, deurslagtig, moerassig, vleiagtig, drassig; ~ **y ground**, moeras; vleigrond.
swan, swaan; *a black* ~, 'n swart swaan; ~-**herd**, swaanoppasser.
swank, (n) spoggerigheid, windmakery, opskeppery, opsnyery, mooidoenery, pralery, windmakerigheid; spogter, windmaker; (v) spog, windmaak, pronk, jou aanstel; ~ *on horseback*, knipmes ry; ~ **y**, spoggerig, pralerig, uithaler=.
swan: ~ **like**, soos 'n swaan; ~-**mussel**, eendemossel; ~-**neck**, swaannek; ~ **nery**, (..**ries**), swaanboerdery; ~ **ny**, swaan=; vol swane; ~ **s' down**, swaandons; ~ **song**, swanesang.
swap, *kyk* **swop**.
swaraj', selfbestuur; ~ **ist**, voorstander van selfbestuur (in Indië).
sward, grasveld.
swarm, (n) swerm; menigte; (v) swerm; wemel, krioel, wriemel; ~ *up a ladder*, 'n leer opklouter (opklim); ~ **er**, trekby; swermkorf; ~ **ing**, (n) geswerm, gewriemel; (a) wemelend, swerm=; *be* ~ *ing with ants*, krioel van miere; ~ **ing season**, swermtyd.
swart, swart, donker, bruin, blas; somber.
swar'thiness, donkerheid, blasheid, swartheid; somberheid.
swar'thy, donker, blas, bruin; somber.
swash, (n) gekabbel, geklots; (v) plas, klots, kletter, plons; slaan; ~ **buckler**, vuurvreter; baasspeler, grootprater, rusiemaker; bluffer; ~ **buckling**, (n) baasspelerigheid, pronkery; (a) pronkerig, grootpraterig, blufferig.
swas'tika, hakekruis, swastika.
swat, (**-ted**), (dood)slaan.
swatch, monster, stofmonster, staaltjie, voorbeeld.
swath, strook; ry; afgemaaide gras; snywydte.
swathe, (n) verband, windsel; (v) baker, toedraai; verbind; vasbind, omswagtel; beswagtel.
swath'er, platsnyer.
swath'ing cloth, swagtel.
swatt'er, vlieëplak, vlieëslaner.
sway, (n) swaai; heerskappy, gesag, beheersing; lyfswaai (gholf); (v) slinger, swaai; beheers, oorhel; heers, regeer, bestuur; hys; ~ *ed BY*, gelei deur; ~ *ed by PREJUDICE*, deur vooroordeel beheers; ~ *the SCEPTRE*, die septer swaai; ~-**back**, lamkruis (siekte); ~-**backed**, holrug=; ~ **rod**, swaaistang.
Swaz'i, Swazi (bevolkingslid en taal); ~ **land**, Swaziland; ~ **lander**, Swazilander.
swear, (n) vloekery; (v) (**swore, sworn**), vloek, swets, knoop; beëdig, onder eed verklaar, sweer; ~ *AT somebody*, iem. vloek; ~ *on the BIBLE*, op die Bybel sweer; ~ *BY a remedy*, groot waarde heg aan 'n middel; ~ *BY someone or something*, by iets of iem. sweer; ~ *IN*, beëdig; ~ *by everything that's HOLY*, by jou siel en saligheid sweer; ~ *away a person's LIFE*, iem. onder eed die lewe beroof; ~ *an OATH*, 'n eed aflê; ~ *OFF*, afsweer; ~ *the PEACE against*, sweer dat jou lewe bedreig word; ~ *by all that one holds SACRED*, hoog en laag sweer; ~ *a person to SECRECY*, iem. geheimhouding onder 'n eed oplê; ~ *TO something*, op iets sweer; *be unable to* ~ *TO it*, dit nie onder eed kan bevestig nie; nie heeltemal seker daarvan wees nie; ~ *TREASON against a person*, iem. onder eed van verraad beskuldig; ~ *like a TROOPER*, soos 'n matroos vloek; ~ *a WITNESS*, 'n getuie die eed afneem; ~ **er**, vloeker, vloekbek; swetser; eedsweerder; ~ **ing**, vloekery, swetsery, vloektaal; ~ **ing-in**, eedaflegging, beëdiging; ~-**word**, vloekwoord.
sweat, (n) sweet; geswoeg; uitsweting, verdamping; *by (in) the* ~ *of one's BROW*, in die sweet van jou aanskyn; *in a COLD* ~, paniekerig; *DRIPPING with* ~, nat van die sweet; *IN a* ~, natgesweet; in die benoudheid; *an OLD* ~, 'n veteraan, 'n oudstryder, 'n ou soldaat; (v) sweet; swoeg, hard werk; suig, eksploiteer; uitslaan, uitwasem; ~ *FOR it*, daarvoor boet; ~ *ed LABOUR*, arbeid vir 'n hongerloon; *MAKE others* ~, ander laat sweet; ~ *OUT*, uitsweet; ~-**band**, sweetband (om kop, of in hoed); ~-**chamber**, sweetkamertjie; ~-**cloth**, sweetdoek; ~-**duct**, sweetkanaaltjie; ~ **er**, oortrektrui, woloorhemp; sweetmiddel; uitsuier; ~-**gland**, sweetklier; ~-**lness**, swetertgheid.
sweat'ing, sweting, sweet; ~-**bath**, sweetbad; ~ **feet**, sweetvoete; ~-**fever**, sweetkoors; ~ **hands**, sweethande; ~-**iron**, roskam; ~-**room**, sweetkamer; ~-**sickness**, sweetsiekte; ~ **system**, hongerloonstelsel, uitbuitstelsel.
sweat: ~-**locks**, sweetklosse; ~-**nose**, sweetneus; ~-**pore**, sweetporie; ~ **secretion**, sweetafskeiding; ~ **shop**, werkplek wat hongerlone betaal.
sweat'y, swetrig, natgesweet; sweet=; ~ **smell**, sweetlug; ~ **wool**, sweetwol.
Swede[1], Sweed.
swede[2], koolraap.
Swed'en, Swede.
Swed'ish, (n, a) Sweeds; ~ **safety matches**, Sweedse vuurhoutjies.
sween'y, spierverswakking, spieratrofie (by perde).
sweep, (n) veeg; swaai, draai; slag; woop; vaart; verspreiding (van 'n siekte); skoorsteenveër; golwing, deining; dakboogstuk; lang roeispaan; veeglood (kr.); *a* ~ *of the ARM*, 'n armswaai; *BEYOND the* ~ *of*, buite die bereik van; *a* ~ *of the BRUSH*, 'n kwasveeg; *make a CLEAN* ~, skoonskip maak; *a wide* ~ *of the PLAIN*, 'n wydgestrekte vlakte; *the RIVER makes a great* ~ *to the right*, die rivier maak 'n elmboogswaai na die regterkant; (v) (**swept**), vee, wegvee, skoonvee; verbyvlieg; wegskuif; afsoek (rivier); stryk oor; die oë laat gaan oor; bestryk (kanon); meesleep, wegswaai; swenk; beloop (skip); ~ *ALONG*, aanstryk, voortsnel; ~ *ASIDE*, wegvee; ~ *AWAY*, wegvee; ~ *the BOARDS*, skoonskip maak; ~ *before your own DOOR*, vee voor jou eie deur; ~ *the HORIZON*, die gesigseinder bespied; ~ *INTO a room*, 'n kamer instorm; ~ *MINES*, myne opruim; *he* ~ *s every= thing into his NET*, alles is van sy gading; ~ *all OBSTACLES from one's path*, alle struikelblokke uit jou weg ruim; ~ *OFF*, wegvee; ~ *someone OFF his feet*, iem. se voete onder hom uitslaan; ~ *ON*, voortyl; ~ *OUT*, uitvee; ~ *PAST*, verbyvlieg; verbyseil; ~ *ROUND*, omswaai; *the SEARCH= LIGHT* ~ *s the sky*, die soeklig bestryk die lug; ~

the SEAS, die see skoonvee; die see deurkruis; ~ UP, opvee; opjaag; ~**er**, veër; baanveër (masjien).
sweep'ing, (n) gevee; gestryk; veegsel; (a) veënd; wyduitgestrek; veelomvattend; ingrypend, deurtastend (ondersoek); groot, ontsaglik, verregaande, oorweldigend, verreikend; *a* ~ *GENERALIZATION*, 'n omvattende veralgemening; *a* ~ *MAJORITY*, 'n verpletterende meerderheid; ~ **reduction,** groot vermindering; ~ **statement,** veralgemening, gewaagde bewering; ~**s,** vuilis; veegsels; vloerwol, vlegsels; uitvaagsel.
sweep: ~**-net,** sleepnet; ~ **rake,** laaihark; ~ **saw,** spansaag.
sweep'stake, wedrenprys; insetgeld; wedlootjie; wedrenne.
sweet, (n) soet; lekker; soetigheid; liefling, skat; (pl) lekkers, lekkergoed; nagereg, dessert; *take the* ~ *with the BITTER*, die soet met die suur aanneem; *the* ~*s and the BITTERS of life*, die soet en die suur v.d. lewe; *the* ~*s of LIFE*, die genietinge v.d. lewe; *MY* ~, *MY* ~*est*, liefste; *the* ~*s OF*, die genot van; *STOLEN* ~*s are always* ~*er*, gesteelde vrugte smaak die lekkerste; *no* ~ *without SWEAT*, wie heuning wil eet, moet steke verdra; (a, adv) soet; lieflik; snoesig, beminlik, bevallig (persoon); aangenaam; gelief, dierbaar; lekker, vars; *BE* ~ *on*, verlief wees op; *a* ~ *GIRL*, 'n liewe meisie; *a* ~ *NATURE*, 'n liewe geaardheid; *NICE and* ~, lekker soet; *whisper* ~ *NOTHINGS*, liefdespraatjies fluister; ~ *ONE*, skat, liefie; *for your* ~ *SAKE*, vir (om) jou ontwil; ~ *SEVENTEEN*, nooi(en)tjie van sewentien jaar, oulike sewentienjarige; *it SMELLS* ~, dit ruik lekker; *have a* ~ *TOOTH*, lekkerbekkig wees; lief wees vir soetigheid; *one's own* ~ *WILL*, eie goeddunke; ~ **bread,** alvleis, soetvleis; skildklier; sweserik; stertjies en peertjies; ~**-briar,** eglantier; ~ **broom,** heidekruid; ~ **cane,** soetriet; ~ **clover,** heuningklawer, stinkklawer; ~ **corn,** suikermielie(s); ~**-dish,** lekkergoedbakkie; ~**en,** soet maak; suiker bygooi; veraangenaam, liefliker maak; ~ **factory,** lekkergoedfabriek; ~ **flag,** kalmoes; ~ **grass,** soetgras; ~ **heart,** (n) soetlief, beminde, hartjie, vryster, uitverkorene; knapsekerwel, duiwelskerwel (onkruid); kêrel, nooi, vryer; (v) vry; *go* ~*hearting*, gaan vry; ~**ish,** soeterig, soetagtig; ~**ly,** beminlik, liefies; glad, byna vanself; ~ **manufacturer,** lekkergoedfabrikant; ~**manufacturing industry,** lekkergoed(vervaardigings)nywerheid; ~ **meat,** lekker, lekkergoed; (pl) suikergoed; ~ **melon,** spanspek; ~ **milk,** soetmelk, vars melk; ~**-milk cheese,** soetmelkkaas; ~**-natured,** saggeaard, vriendelik; ~**ness,** soetheid; frisheid, geurigheid; lieflikheid; ~ **oil,** soetolie; ~ **pea,** pronkertjie, siertertjie, blomertjie; ~ **potato,** patat(ta); ~ **reasonableness,** gematigdheid, meegaandheid; ~**-root,** soethout; ~**-scented,** welriekend, geurig; ~**-shop,** lekkergoedwinkel; ~**-smelling,** geurig, welriekend; ~**-sour sauce,** soetsuur sous; ~**-spoken,** vriendelik; ~**-stuff,** lekkergoed; suikergoed; soetigheid; ~**-tempered,** saggeaard, sagsinnig; ~ **tooth,** lekkerbek, snoeper; ~**-toothed,** lekkerbekkig; ~**-thorn,** soetdoring; ~ **water,** vars water; ~**-william,** duisendskoon, baardangelier; ~ **wine,** soet wyn; ~ **willow,** lourierwilger; ~ **wort,** soetkruid; ~**y,** (..ties), liefling; lekkertjie.
swell, (n) (die) swel; swelsel, swelling, geswel; deining (see); aanswelling; aanswellende klanke; groot meneer; windmaker; ~ *of the BUTTOCKS*, dikte van die boud (perd); *WHAT a* ~ *you are!* maar jy is fyn uitgevat! (v) (**-ed, swollen** or **-ed**), swel, opswel; uitdy; toeneem, groei; opblaas; verhoog, vergroot; dikker word; verwaand wees; ~ *into a big AMOUNT*, oploop tot 'n groot bedrag; ~ *the FUNDS*, die fondse styf; ~ *with INDIGNATION*, van verontwaardiging wil bars; *his heart* ~*ed with PRIDE*, sy hart het van trots geswel; ~ *into a ROAR*, tot 'n gebrul aangroei; *the winds* ~ *the SAILS*, die winde vul die seile; *the SOUNDS* ~ *into a roar*, die geluide gloei aan tot 'n gebrul; (a) ryk, deftig, piekfyn, vernaam; ~ *CLOTHES*, spoggerige klere; *a* ~*ed HEAD*, verwaandheid; *they had a* ~ *TIME*, hulle het dit uitermate geniet;
~ **coal,** swelsteenkool; ~ **dom,** die hoëlui; ~**-fish,** egelvis; ~**ing,** (n) geswel, opswelling, swelsel; (a) aanswellend; ~**-organ,** swelregister.
swel'ter, (n) smoorhitte, bedompigheid; (v) verdroë, verskroei; smoor, stik, bedompig wees; uitsweet.
swel'tering, snikheet; broeiend, smorend; *a* ~ *DAY*, 'n snikwarm dag; ~ *HEAT*, smoorhitte; *it is* ~ *HOT*, dis broeiend warm; die kraaie gaap; *under the* ~ *SKY*, onder die skroeiend warme lug.
swept, (v) gevee(g); *kyk* **sweep;** ~**-back hair,** agteroorgekamde hare; ~**-back wing,** pylvlerk.
swerve, (n) swaai; swenking, sysprong; (v) afdwaal, afwyk; uitwyk; verbyspring, opyspring; wegswaai, swenk, padgee; ~ *FROM one's purpose*, van jou spoor afdwaal (afwyk); ~ *IN*, inswenk; ~ *OUT*, uitswenk; ~ *TO(WARDS)*, afwyk na, swaai na; ~**r,** swaaibal.
swift, (n) windswa(w)eltjie, toringswa(w)eltjie; skoelapper; draairaam (vir gare); houthamer; akkedis; (a) vinnig, rats, gou, snel, vlug, geswind; *be* ~ *to anger*, gou kwaad word; (adv) gou, vinnig; ~**er,** boomtou; ~**-flowing,** snelstromend; ~**-footed,** snelvoetig, gou, vinnig; ~**-handed,** rats met die hande; ~**let,** windswa(w)eltjie; ~**ness,** snelheid; ratsheid; ~**-winged,** snelvlieënd.
swig, (n) sluk; (v) (**-ged**), wegsluk, met groot slukke drink.
swill, (n) varkkos, draf, spoeling; skottelgoedwater, vuil water; lawaaiwater; (v) suip, slurp; (uit)spoel, afspoel; ~**er,** suiplap, dronkaard; spoeling; ~**-tub,** varkbak.
swim, (n) swem; *BE in the* ~, goed op hoogte van sake wees; in die mode wees; *GO for a* ~, *HAVE a* ~, gaan swem; *in the* ~ *WITH*, rondgaan met; (v) (**swam, swum**) swem; drywe; oorswem; draai; duiselig wees; ~ *in BUTTER*, in botter dryf; *my HEAD* ~*s*, ek word duiselig; ~ *a HORSE*, 'n perd laat swem; ~ *in LUXURY*, in weelde baai; ~ *like a STONE*, soos 'n klip swem; ~ *against the STREAM*, stroom-op swem; ~ *with the TIDE*, met die stroom saamgaan; ~ **mer,** swemmer; swemvoël.
swimm'ing, (n) swem, geswem, swemmery; swemsport; duiseligheid; *GO* ~, gaan swem; *his eyes are* ~ *in TEARS*, sy oë swem in trane; (a) swem=, drywend; ~**-apparatus,** swemtoestel; ~**-bath,** swembad; ~**-belt,** swemgordel; ~ **bird,** swemvoël; ~**-bladder,** swemblaas; ~**-competition,** swemwedstryd; ~**-costume,** swemkostuum, baaipak, swempak; ~**-drawers,** swembroek; ~ **eyes,** betraande oë; ~**ly,** vlot, fluks, lekker; ~**-pool,** swemgat; swembad; ~**-practice,** swemoefening; ~**-school,** swemskool; ~**-suit,** swempak, swemkostuum; ~**-teacher,** swemonderwyser(es).
swin'dle, (n) bedrieëry, skelmstuk, bedrog, verneukery, swendelary, afset; (v) swendel, bedrieg, vastrek, verneuk, toetrap; ~ *a person out of money*, iem. verneuk met 'n som geld; ~**r,** bedrieër, swendelaar, verneuker, afsetter, opligter.
swin'dling, (n) opligtery, bedrieëry, swendelary, boerebedrog; (a) bedrieglik, swendelagtig.
swine, swyn, vark; smeerlap, vuilgoed, luns; **erysipelas,** vleksiekte; ~**-fever,** varkpes, varkkoors; ~ **herd,** varkoppasser; ~**-plague,** varkpes; ~**-pox,** varkpokke; waterpokkies (by mense); ~**ry,** (..ries), varkhok; trop varke.
swing, (n) swaai; skoppelmaai, skommel; draai; kring; gang; slingering; swingel; swenking; swaaislag; *be in FULL* ~, in volle gang wees; *GET into the* ~ *of*, op stryk kom; *GO with a* ~, voor die wind gaan; *let him HAVE his* ~, gee hom die vrye teuels; *what you LOSE on the* ~*s, you make up on the roundabouts*, die verliese word deur die winste goedgemaak; jy kom niks verder nie; *the* ~ *of the PENDULUM*, die swaai van die slinger; die terugslag (reaksie); *TAKE a* ~ *at someone*, iem. bydam; (v) (**swung** or **swang, swung**), slinger, swaai; skommel; lui, bengel (klok); hang; draai; bewerkstellig; ~ *into ACTION*, tot die aanval oorgaan; ~ *at ANCHOR*, voor anker lê; ~ *a DEAL*, 'n koop beklink; *the DOOR swung to*, die deur het toegeswaai;

he'll ~ *FOR it,* hy sal daarvoor hang; ~ *from the GALLOWS,* aan die galg hang; *HAVE to* ~ *for murder,* die strop kry weens moord; ~ *the LEAD,* siekte voorwend; spekskiet; ~ *into LINE,* in die gelid (slagorde) kom; ~ *OVER,* omswaai; *there wasn't ROOM to* ~ *a cat,* 'n mens kon jou nie draai nie; ~ *ROUND,* omdraai, omswenk; ~ *TO,* oorswaai na; ~ *VOTES,* stemme beïnvloed; ~**-bar,** rekstok; ~**-bearing,** standaardpeiling; ~**-boat,** skoppelmaaiskuit, skommelbootjie; ~ **bolt,** swaaibout; ~ **bridge,** draaibrug; ~ **door,** draaideur, swaaideur.
swinge, gesel, kasty, straf, afransel.
swing(e)'ing: ~ *BLOW,* kwaai hou; ~ *LIE,* yslike leuen; ~ *MAJORITY,* oorweldigende meerderheid; *a* ~ *PROFIT,* 'n reuseprofyt.
swing'er, swaaier; swaaibal (kr.).
swing' gate, swaaihek; slagboom, sluitboom; valpoort.
swing'ing, (n) geswaai; skommeling; (a) swaai=; skommel=; draaiend; swaaierig; ~ **blow,** swaaislag, trekhou; ~**-room,** swaairuimte; beweegruimte; ~ **screen,** skommelsif.
swi'ngle, (n) swingel; vlaskierie; (v) swingel, slaan; ~**-bar,** swingel; ~ **strap,** swingelriem; ~ **tree,** swingel, swingelhout.
swing: ~ **link,** skamelhanger; ~ **mirror,** draaispieël; ~ **music,** swing, skommelmusiek, swaaimusiek; ~**-over,** omswaai; ~ **plough,** wipploeg; ~**-saw,** hangsaag; ~ **sign,** uithangbord; ~ **tree,** swingel; ~**-up door,** opswaaideur; ~**-wheel,** dryfrat.
swin'ish, varkagtig, swynagtig; vuil, liederlik; ~ **ness,** smerigheid, vuilheid, liederlikheid, swynagtigheid.
swipe, (n) wip; harde slag, mokerhou; veeghou; (v) slaan, moker; veeg (tennis); steel.
swipes, dun bier, slegte bier.
swirl, (n) gewarrel, warreling, gewirwar; draaikolk; (v) draai, warrel.
swish, (n) geruis, ritseling; (-es), hou, slag; (v) swiep, suis, ruis; afransel; looi; (a) spoggerig; ~ **y,** ruisend, ritselend, swiepend.
Swiss, (n) Switser(s); *BROWN* ~, Switserse bees, Bruin Switser; *THE* ~, die Switsers; (a) Switsers; ~ **chard,** blaarbeet, beetspinasie; ~ **cottage,** chalet; ~ **guard,** Switserse lyfwag; ~ **roll,** rolkoek, konfytrol.
switch, (n) (-es), wissel (spoorw.); wisselstroom; skakelaar, (lig)knoppie, aandraaiknoppie (elek.); omruiling; omswaai; loot, lat; vals haarvlegsel; kwas (bees); rysweep, karwats; roede; (v) uitklop, slaan, afransel; (in)skakel, omskakel, aanknip, aandraai (elek.); wissel, rangeer, op 'n ander spoor bring; verplaas, verskuif; omswaai; oorslaan na; ~ *to one's FAVOURITE subject,* oorgaan na 'n mens se geliefkoosde onderwerp; ~ *OFF,* afdraai, afskakel; ~ *ON,* inskakel, aandraai, aanskakel, aanknip; ~ *OUT,* uitskakel, afknip; ~ *OVER,* omskakel; ~ *PLACES,* plekke ruil; ~ *(over) TO,* oorgaan na; ~**-back,** hobbelbaan; ~**-blade knife,** veerknipmes; ~ **board,** skakelbord; ~ **board operator,** skakelbordoperateur; ~ **board panel,** skakelpaneel; ~**-box,** skakelkas; ~ **er,** wisselwagter; ~**-gear,** skakelwerk, skakeltuig; ~**-indicator dial,** wyserplaat; ~**-key,** skakelsleutel; ~**-lever,** skakelhefboom; wisselhefboom (spoor); ~**-lock,** skakelaarslot; ~ **man,** wisselwagter; ~**-over,** oorskakeling, omskakeling; oorgang; ~**-shutter,** skakelaarskild; ~ **tower,** seintoring.
Swit'zerland, Switserland.
swiv'el, (n) spil, draaiskyf, werwel; (v) (-led), op 'n spil draai; krink; ~**-arm,** krinkas; ~ **block,** draaiblok; ~ **bridge,** draaibrug; ~ **castor,** swaaipootrollertjie; ~ **chair,** draaistoel; ~**-eye,** skeeloog; ~**-eyed,** skeel; ~ **fork,** draaivurk; ~**-gun,** swaaikanon; ~ **hook,** draaihaak; ~**-joint,** spillas, werwelskarnier; ~ **lamp,** draailamp; ~ **nozzle,** swaaimondstuk; ~ **plate,** draaiskyf; krink (wa).
swizz'le stick, roerstokkie, mengstokkie.
swob, *kyk* **swab.**
swoll'en, geswel; *kyk* **swell,** (v); ~ **ness,** dikte; swelsel; ~ **river,** vol rivier.

swoon, (n) beswyming, floute; *go off in a* ~, flou val; (v) flou word, (be)swym; verswak, wegsterwe.
swoop, (n) oorval, verrassingsaanval; *AT a* ~; *with one FELL* ~, met een slag; *COME down with a* ~, neerskiet; (v) neerskiet; onverwags aanval; jou stort op; oorval; ~ *DOWN upon the enemy,* op die vyand toesak; ~ *UPON,* neerskiet op.
swop, (n) ruil; (v) **(-ped),** omruil, ruil; *never* ~ *HORSES while crossing the stream (in midstream),* moenie op die kritieke oomblik van plan verander nie; ~ *PLACES,* plekke ruil; ~ *STORIES (yarns),* mekaar stories (grappies) vertel; ~ **arrangement,** ruilooreenkoms.
sword, swaard; sabel; *BUCKLE one's* ~, die swaard aangord; *CROSS* ~ *s with someone,* die swaard met iem. kruis; kragte meet met; *the* ~ *of DAMOCLES,* die swaard van Damokles; *DRAW the* ~, die swaard trek; *with DRAWN* ~, met getrekke swaard; *GRASP the* ~, die swaard gryp; ~ *of HONOUR,* eresabel; *who LIVES by the* ~ *shall perish by the* ~, almal wat die swaard neem, sal deur die swaard vergaan; *MEASURE* ~ *s,* die swaard kruis; kragte meet (met); *PUT to the* ~, platkap, neersabel, oor die kling jaag; *SHEATHE the* ~, die swaard in die skede steek; ~**-arm,** regterarm; ~**-bearer,** swaarddraer, wapendraer; ~**-belt,** sabelkoppel, sabelriem; ~**-blade,** swaardlem, sabellem; ~**-cane,** degenstok; ~**-cut,** sabelhou, sabelkap, ~**-cutler,** swaardveër; ~**-dance,** swaarddans; ~**-fish,** swaardvis; ~**-frog,** sabellus; ~**-grass,** rietgras; ~**-hand,** regterhand; ~**-hilt,** geves, sabelgreep; ~**-knot,** sabelkwas; ~**-law,** swaardreg; ~**-lily,** swaardlelie; ~**-play,** skerm(kuns); skermutseling; ~**-player,** swaardvegter; ~**-shaped,** swaardvormig; ~**-sheath,** sabelskede; ~**-side,** vaderskant; ~**-sling,** sabelband; ~**'s man,** swaardvegter; skermer; ~**'s manship,** skermkuns; ~**-stick,** degenstok; ~**-swallower,** swaardslukker; ~**-thrust,** sabelstoot.
swore, *kyk* **swear,** (v).
sworn, beëdig; geswore; kwaai; ~ **enemies,** geswore vyande; ~ **friends,** geswore vriende; ~ **statement,** beëdigde verklaring; ~ **translator,** beëdigde vertaler.
swot, (n) blokker; blokwerk; (v) **(-ted),** hard werk, blok, inpomp; ~ *AT a subject,* 'n vak blok; ~ *LATIN,* Latyn blok; ~ *UP a question,* 'n vraag blok; ~ **ter,** blokker; ~ **ting,** geblok.
swum, *kyk* **swim,** (v).
swung, *kyk* **swing,** (v).
syb'arite, sibariet; wellustelinrg.
sybarit'ic(al), sibarities; wulps, wellustig.
syc'amine, swartmoerbeiboom.
syc'amore, wildevyeboom; - **maple,** esdoring.
syce, staljong.
syc'ophancy, lae vleiery, kruiperigheid, lekkery.
syc'ophant, lekker; kruiper, vleier, sikofant; ~**'ic,** vleiend, kruiperig.
sycos'is, baardskurfte, huiduitslag, baardwurm, sikose.
sy'enite, siëniet.
syllab'ic, lettergrepig, sillabies.
syllab'icate, syllab'ify, (..fied), **syll'abize,** (-d), in lettergrepe verdeel (uitspreek).
syllabi(fi)ca'tion, lettergreepvorming; lettergreepverdeling.
syll'able, (n) lettergreep; (v) in lettergrepe uitspreek.
syll'abub = **sillabub.**
syll'abus, (-es, ..bi), leerplan, sillabus.
syll'ogism, sluitrede, sillogisme.
syllogis'tic, sillogisties.
syll'ogize, sillogiseer, sillogisties redeneer.
sylph, luggees, silfe; fee; slank meisie; - **id,** silfide; ~**-ish,** silfagtig; slank.
syl'van, lommerryk, bosryk; bosbewonend.
sylvicult'ural, bosboukundig, bosbou=.
syl'viculture, houtteelt, bosbou, boskultuur.
sylvicult'urist, bosboukundige.
symbio'sis, saamlewing, simbiose.
symbio'tic, saamlewend, simbioties.
sym'bol, sinnebeeld; simbool; teken.
symbol'ic(al), simbolies, sinnebeeldig.

sym'bolism, simboliek, simbolisme.
sym'bolist, simbolis.
symboliza'tion, sinnebeeldige voorstelling; simbolisering.
sym'bolize, sinnebeeldig voorstel, simboliseer.
symmet'ric(al), simmetries, eweredig, harmonies.
symm'etrize, simmetries maak.
symm'etry, eweredigheid, simmetrie; *plane of* ~, simmetrievlak.
sympathet'ic, medelydend, deelnemend, goedgesind, meewarig, simpatiekgesind; simpatiek; simpateties; welwillend (oorweging); *be* ~ *to*, saamvoel (meevoel) met; ~ **ink**, simpatetiese ink; ~ **nerve**, simpatetiese senuwee; ~ **pain**, weerpyn, simpatetiese pyn; ~ **strike**, staking uit simpatie, solidariteitstaking, simpatiestaking.
sym'pathize, medelye hê; deelneming voel, simpatiseer; ~ *with a person*, met iem. meeleef (saamvoel); iem. sy deelneming betuig, kondoleer met iem.; ~ **r**, simpatiseerder; deelnemer.
sym'pathy, (..thies), medelye, meegevoel, deelneming, meewarigheid, simpatie; *FEEL* ~ *for*, meegevoel koester met; *HAVE* ~ *with*, met iem. saamvoel (meevoel); *VOTE of* ~, mosie van deelneming.
symphon'ic, simfonies.
symphon'ious, harmonies, welluidend.
sym'phonist, komponis van simfonieë.
sym'phony, (..nies), simfonie; ~ **concert**, simfoniekonsert; ~ **orchestra**, simfonieorkes.
sympos'ium, (..sia), drinkgelag, feesgelag, gasmaal; simposium, samespreking.
symp'tom, (siekte)verskynsel, (ken)teken, voorteken, simptoom; (pl) siektebeeld; siektetekens; ~ **at'ic(al)**, simptomaties; *be* ~ *atic of*, 'n aanduiding wees van, wys op; ~ **atol'ogy**, simptomeleer, siekteverskynselleer.
synaer'esis, sametrekking, sinerese.
synaesthes'ia, sinestesie.
synagog'ical, sinagogies.
syn'agogue, sinagoge.
synallagmat'ic, wederkerig; ~ **contract**, wederkerige kontrak.
syn'chromesh, sinchroskakelend.
synchron'ic, sinchronies.
syn'chronism, gelyktydigheid, sinchronisme.
synchronist'ic, sinchronisties.
synchroniza'tion, saamvalling, regulering, sinchronisasie.
syn'chronize, gelyktydig wees (gebeur); laat saamval; reël, sinchroniseer, gelykstel, reguleer; ~ **r**, sinchroniseerder.
syn'chronous, gelyktydig, sinchroon.
syn'chrony, sinchromie.
synclin'al, sinklinies.
syn'cline, trog, plooidal, sinklien; *pitching* ~, duikende sinklien.
syn'copate, saamtrek, verkort; sinkopeer.
syncopa'tion, sinkopering; sametrekking.
syn'cope, sametrekking; sinkopee; floute.
syncret'ic, sinkreties.
syn'cretism, sinkretisme.
syncretist'ic, sinkretisties.
syn'dic, beampte, sindikus; ~ **alism**, sindikalisme; ~ **alist**, sindikalis; ~ **alis'tic**, sindikalisties.
syn'dicate, (n) sindikaat, kartel; (v) tot 'n kartel vorm.
syn'drome, sindroom; siektebeeld.
synec'doche, sinekdogee.

syn'ergism, sinergisme.
synergis'tic, saamwerkend, saamwerking=, sinergisties.
syngenet'ic, singeneties.
syn'od, sinode, kerkvergadering; ~ **al**, sinodaal; ~ **'ic(al)**, sinodaal.
syn'onym, sinoniem.
synonym'ic, sinonimies.
synonym'ity, sinsverwantskap, sinonimie.
synon'ymous, gelykbetekenend, met dieselfde betekenis, sinverwant, sinoniem.
synon'ymy, sinonimie, sinsverwantskap, gelykbeduidenis.
synop'sis, (..ses), kort begrip, samevatting, sinopsis.
synop'tic, sinopties, oorsigtelik; *the S* ~ *Gospels*, die Evangelies van Matteus, Markus, Lukas; ~ **table**, oorsigstafel.
synov'ia, gewrigsvog, litwater, ledewater.
synov'ial, gewrigs=; ~ **fluid**, gewrigsvog, ledewater; ~ **membrane**, gewrigsvlies.
synovit'is, gewrigsontsteking, sinovitis.
syntac'tic, sintakties.
syn'tax, sintaksis.
syntec'tic, sintekties.
syntex'is, sinteksis (geol.).
syn'thesis, (**syntheses**), samevoeging, samestelling, sintese.
synthet'ic, samestellend, sinteties; ~ **butter**, kunsbotter; ~ **detergent**, seeplose wasmiddel; ~ **fibre**, kunsvesel; ~ **honey**, kunsheuning; ~ **resin**, kunshars; ~ **rubber**, kunsrubber; ~ **silk**, kunssy; ~ **wool**, kunswol.
syn'thetize, saamvoeg, sintetiseer.
synton'ic, afgestem.
syn'tonize, afstem.
syn'tony, afstemming.
syph'ilis, geslagsiekte, vuilsiekte, sifilis.
syphilit'ic, (n) sifilislyer; (a) sifilities.
syph'on, spuitwaterfles; sifon, hewel.
sy'ren, *kyk* **siren**.
Sy'ria, Sirië; ~ **n**, (n) Siriër; Siries (taal); (a) Siries.
syri'nga, sering (boom).
sy'ringe, (n) spuit; *hypodermic* ~, onderhuidse spuit; (v) spuit, inspuit; uitspuit.
sy'rinx, (-es, ..nges), stemorgaan (voël); buis.
syr'tis, (syrtes), welstand.
sy'rup, stroop; *golden* ~, gouestroop; ~ **cake**, stroopkoek; ~ **ing**, verandering in stroop, verstroping; ~ **y**, stroperig, stroopagtig.
systal'tic, saamtrekkend.
sys'tem, stelsel, sisteem; gestel, konstitusie; leerstelsel (godsdienstig); inrigting, samestel; net (spoorweg); metode; formasie; ~ *of CONTROL*, beheerstelsel, kontrolestelsel; ~ *of GOVERNMENT*, regeringstelsel; *the SOLAR* ~, die sonnestelsel; ~ *of WORKING on the decimal*, staffelmetode; ~ **at'ic**, stelselmatig, sistematies; ~ **at'ics**, sistematiek; ~ **atist**, vormer van 'n stelsel; sistematikus; ~ **atiza'tion**, vorming van 'n stelsel; sistematisering; ~ **atize**, sistematiseer; ~ **atizer** = **systematist**; ~ **less**, stelselloos; ~ **manager**, afdelingsbestuurder; ~ **planning**, stelselbeplanning; ~ **s analyst**, stelselontleder; ~ **switch**, netskakelaar.
sys'tole, sametrekking, krimping (van die hartspiere); sistolie.
systol'ic, sistolies.
sys'tyle, met 'n suilery.
syzygi, samestand; sisigie; dipodie.

T

t, (ts, t's), t; *the CLOTHES fit to a T*, die klere is nommer pas; *DOT one's i's and cross one's* ~ *'s*, die puntjies op die i's sit; nadruk lê op; *it SUITS me to a T*, dit pas my volkome; *TO a T*, op 'n haar; op 'n druppel water.

ta, daai, dankie.
Taal, (hist.), Patriot-Afrikaans; Afrikaans.
tab, lus (skoen); skouerlussie; tongetjie; oorklap; veterpunt; strokie; sluitwaster.
tab'anid, blindevlieg, steekvlieg.

tab'ard, tabberd; wapenrok.
tab'aret, gestreepte meubelstof; sybekleding.
tabb'y, (n) gewaterde sy, tabyn; **(tabbies),** gestreepte kat; oujongnooi; kwaadspreekster; beton; (v) **(tab= bied),** streep, water (stof), moireer; (a) gestreep; ge= vlam; ~ **cat,** wyfiekat, katwyfie.
tabefac'tion, uittering, wegkwyning.
tab'ernacle, (n) tabernakel; tent; menslike liggaam; *the FEAST of T~s,* die Loofhuttefees; *this FLESHY* ~, hierdie aardse tabernakel; (v) bly; beskut.
tab'es, uittering, wegkwyning; *dorsal* ~, rugmurg= uittering.
tabet'ic, (n) teringlyer; (a) teringagtig.
tab'id, teringagtig, uitterend; uitgeteer.
tab'inet, gewaterde stof, tabinet.
tab'lature, tablatuur (mus.); tekening, muurskilde= ring; beeld.
ta'ble, (n) tafel; dis; tabel, lys; plato, tafelland; tafe= reel, tablo; *AT* ~, aan tafel sit; *BE at* ~, aan tafel sit; *CLEAR a* ~, die tafel afdek (afneem); *the matter will COME on the* ~, ter sprake kom; ter tafel kom; ~ *of CONTENTS,* inhoudsopgawe; *DRINK someone under the* ~, iem. onder die tafel drink; *keep a GOOD* ~, 'n welvoorsiene tafel hê; goeie kos voorsit; ~ *of INTEREST,* rentetafel; *LAY something on the* ~, iets ter tafel lê; *LEAVE the* ~, van tafel opstaan; *the LORD'S* ~, die tafel v.d. Here; ~ *of MORTALITY,* sterftetabel; *keep OPEN* ~, gasvry wees; oop tafel hou; ~ *of PRE= CEDENCE,* voorranglys; *RISE from* ~, van tafel opstaan; *SPREAD a* ~, 'n tafel dek; *TURN the* ~*s on someone,* wraak neem; die bordjies verhang; *the ~s are TURNED,* die rolle is omgekeer; die bord= jies is verhang; *WAIT at* ~, aan tafel bedien; (v) tabelleer, rangskik; ter tafel lê, op die tafel lê; voor= stel, indien (verslag); ~ *a MOTION,* kennis van 'n voorstel gee; ~ *a REPORT,* 'n verslag ter tafel lê.
tab'leau, tableau', (-x), tablo.
ta'ble: ~ **allowance,** tafelgeld; ~ **appointments,** tafel= uitrusting, ~**-bell,** tafelklokkie; ~**-boarder,** daglo= seerder; ~**-boarding,** daglosies; ~**-centre,** tafellap, tafelloper; ~**-cloth,** tafelkleedjie; tafeldoek, tafella= ken; ~**-companion,** tafelgenoot, disgenoot; ~**-co= ver,** tafelkleedjie; ~ **decoration,** tafelversiering; ~ **d'= hôte,** oop tafel; ~ **grand,** vleuelklavier; ~**-grapes,** eetdruiwe; ~ **guest,** tafelgas; ~ **hand,** tafelwerker; ~**-knife,** tafelmes; ~**-lamp,** staanlamp, tafellamp; ~ **land,** plato, hoogvlakte, tafelland; ~**-laying,** ta= feldek; ~**-leaf,** tafelblad; ~**-leg,** tafelpoot; ~**-lift= ing,** tafeldans; ~**-linen,** tafelgoed, tafellinne; ~**-manners,** tafelmaniere; ~**-mat,** tafelmatjie; ~**-money,** tafelgeld; **I** ~ **Mountain,** Tafelberg; ~**-moving,** tafeldans; ~ **music,** tafelmusiek; ~**-nap= kin,** servet; ~**-plate,** tafelsilwer; ~**-potato,** eeter= tappel, eetaartappel; ~**-poultry,** slagpluimvee; ~**-rapping,** tafeldans; ~**-runner,** tafelloper; ~**-salt,** tafelsout; ~ **silver,** mesware; tafelsilwer; ~ **spoon,** eetlepel; paplepel; ~ **spoonful,** eetlepelvol.
tab'let, tablet; pil; steentjie; *MEMORIAL* ~, ge= denkplaat; *a* ~ *of SOAP,* 'n koekie seep.
ta'ble: ~**-talk,** tafelgesprek; ~ **tennis,** tafeltennis; ~**-tilting,** tafeldans; ~ **top,** tafelblad; ~**-turning,** ta= feldans; ~**-vice,** bankskroef; ~ **ware,** tafelgereed= skap, tafelgoed; eetgerei; ~ **wine,** tafelwyn.
tab'loid, tablet, pilletjie; kompakte koerant, ponie= koerant; ~**-newspaper,** minikoerant; poniekoerant.
taboo', (n) verbod; taboe; ban; heiligverklaring; (v) verbied, taboe verklaar, in die ban doen; (a) taboe, verbode; heilig, onaantasbaar.
tab'or, tamboeryn, handtrom.
tab'ouret, stoeltjie, sitbankie, taboeret, borduur= raam; naaldekussing.
tab'o(u)rine, tamboeryn, handtrom.
tab'ular, tabellaries; tafelvormig, tafel=; afgeplat; *in* ~ *form,* tabellaries, gegroepeer.
tab'ulate, (v) tabelleer, 'n tabel maak van, tabuleer; plat maak; gelykmaak; (a) plat, tafelvormig; ~**d,** in tabelle, getabelleer, tabellaries; plat.
tabula'tion, tabellering.
tab'ulator, tabuleermasjien, tabelleermasjien.
tab' washer, sluitwaster.

tac'amahac, gomhars, takamahak.
tache¹, sproet, vlek.
tache², gespe, haak.
tach'inid, sluipvlieg.
tachis'toscope, tagistoskoop.
tach'ograph, toereteller, tagograaf.
tachom'eter, toereteller, tagometer; spoedmeter, snelheidsmeter.
tachyblas'tic, tagiblasties.
tach'ygraph, tagigraaf, snelskrywer; snelskrif; ~**er,** snelskrywer.
tachygraph'ic(al), snelskrif=, stenografies.
tachy'graphist, snelskrywer.
tachyg'raphy, tagigrafie, snelskrif.
tachym'eter, tagimeter.
ta'cit, versweë, stilswy(g)end, swygsaam; vanselfspre= kend.
ta'citurn, (stil)swy(g)end, swygsaam, stil.
taciturn'ity, swygsaamheid, stilswy(g)endheid.
tack, (n) platkopspyker; stif; rygsteek (naaldwerk); wending; klewerigheid; hals (van 'n seil); koers, gang; kos; *get down to BRASS* ~*s,* tot die kern v.d. saak gaan; *CHANGE one's* ~, dit oor 'n ander boeg gooi; *GET onto a NEW* ~, 'n nuwe rigting inslaan; *on the RIGHT* ~, op die regte spoor; *SHIFT one's* ~, dit oor 'n ander boeg gooi; 'n an= der koers inslaan; *be on the WRONG* ~, op die verkeerde spoor wees; (v) keer, laveer; (vas)ryg, in= ryg (klere); opryg; vasspyker; vasmaak; van rigting verander; ~ *together,* aanmekaarryg.
tack'et, skoenspyker; platkopspyker.
tack'ey, *kyk* **tacky.**
tack'iness, klewerigheid.
tack'ing, rygwerk; (die) vasspyker; ~**-hole,** heggat; ~**-stitch,** rygsteek; ~**-thread,** rygdraad.
tac'kle, (n) wapentuig; toestel, gereedskap; takelasie, takelwerk, takel; doodvat, duik (rugby); (v) vang, pak, iem. plant, neertrek, lak, duik, platloop (voet= bal); inspan, optuig (diere); aanpak, bydam, aan= val; ~ *low!,* vat laag!; ~**-block,** katrol, hysblok; ~**r,** doodvatter.
tack'ling, tuig; gerei; gereedskap; lakwerk, doodvat (voetbal).
tack'y, (n) **(tackies),** seilskoen; (a) klewerig.
tact, beleid, deursig, slag, takt; maatslag; ~**ful,** be= leidvol, taktvol; ~**fullness,** takt; ~**ic,** takties, be= hendig; ~**ical,** takties, meesterlik; ~**i'cian,** krygs= kundige, taktikus; ~**ics,** taktiek, krygskunde.
tac'tile, voelbaar; tasbaar; gevoels=; tas=; ~ **hair,** tas= hare; ~ **organ,** tasorgaan; ~ **sense,** tassin, gevoel.
tactil'ity, tasbaarheid, voelbaarheid.
tact'less, taktloos, lomp; ~**ness,** taktloosheid.
tac'tual, tas=, van die tassin, tasbaar.
tad'pole, paddavis.
taen'ia, (-e), lintwurm; rolverband; kroonlys (argi= tektuur); haarband.
taff'eta, taf.
taff'rail, agterreling.
taf'ia, Wes-Indiese rum, tafia.
tag, (n) stif; lissie; veterpunt; skoenriempunt; rafel; uiteinde; aanhangsel; brokstuk; leuse; refrein; adreskaart, etiket; afgesaagde aanhaling, stereo= tiepe gesegde; slotwoorde; blok; hegplaatjie; tong, metaalpunt, bandjie; (V) **(-ged),** aanheg; verbind; naloop; voorsien van 'n punt, voorsien van 'n eti= ket; as slot toevoeg; frot speel; tik (by kinderspel); ~ *AFTER,* agternadraf; ~ *ALONG with,* saam= draf; ~ *oneself ON to someone,* jou opdring aan iem.; ~**-end,** die laaste stuk, stert, oorskiet; ~**ger,** naloper; ~ **rag:** ~ *rag and bobtail,* Jan Rap en sy maat, skorriemorrie, Jan en alleman; ~**-tail,** wurm, inkruiper, naloperljie.
Tag'us, Taag.
Tahi'ti, Tahiti; ~ **an,** (n) Tahitiaan; Tahitiaans (taal); (a) Tahitiaans.
tail¹, (n) beperkte eiendom.
tail², (n) stert; stuitjie; keersy (muntstuk); pant; sleep (van rok); aanhang, tou, gevolg; onderkant; pant= baadjie; agterste gedeelte; buitehoek (v.d. oog); roei (van komeet); streep (in mynwese); bodem (van koeël); (pl) pantbaadjie, swaelstertpak; *the* ~ *is wagging the DOG,* Klaas is baas; *the* ~ *of the*

EYE, die hoek van die oog; ~ *FIRST*, agterstevoor; *HEADS or* ~ *s*, kruis of munt; jantjie of waentjie; *KEEP your* ~ *up*, hou maar moed; *SNEAK away with one's* ~ *between one's LEGS*, stert tussen die bene vlug; druipstert wegloop; *TURN* ~, ysterklou in die grond slaan; die hasepad kies; op loop sit; *TWIST someone's* ~, met iem. afreken, hom op sy plek sit; (v) 'n stert vorm; 'n stert aansit; tou; soos 'n skaduwee volg; dophou; ~ *AFTER*, agterna tou; ~ *OFF*, agterbly, uitsak; opraak; verminder (in aantal, gehalte); ~ *to the TIDE*, met die gety saam swaai; ~ **beam**, kruppelbalk; ~-**board**, agterskot, agterklap, karet; ~-**bone**, stuitjie; ~**coat**, swaelstert(manel); ~ **comb**, steelkam; ~-**drive**, draaiduik (vliegtuig); ~**ed**, met 'n stert, stert=; ~ **end**, laaste ent, stert, agterste punt; ~-**ender**, nakomer; ~-**fat**, stertvet; ~-**feather**, stertveer; ~-**fin**, stertvin; ~ **gun**, agterkanon; ~ **gunner**, agterkanonnier; ~-**head**, stertwortel; ~**ing**, binnekop (baksteen); ~ **ings**, uitskot; oorskiet, gewaste grond; ~-**lamp**, agterlamp; ~ **less**, sonder stert, stompstert=; ~-**light**, agterste lig, agterlig.

tail'or, (n) kleremaker, snyer; *the* ~ *makes the MAN*, die klere maak die man; die vere maak die voël; *RIDE like a* ~, soos 'n matroos perdry; (v) klere maak; ~-**bird**, kwê-kwê; ~**ed** gesny; ~**ed** *SKIRT*, snyershalfpak; *WELL* ~**ed**, goed gesny; goed gekleed; ~**ess**, (-**es**), kleremaakster; ~**ing**, snyerswerk; kleremakery; snit; ~-**made**, deur 'n snyer gemaak, snyers=, aangemeet; ~-**made suit**, snyerspak; ~ **'s canvas**, stywe seildoek; ~ **'s chalk**, snyerskryt, platkryt; ~ **'s dummy**, paspop; ~ **'s table**, skavot.

tail: ~ **piece**, stertstuk; slotvinjet (boek); ~ **pipe**, suigbuis; ~-**pocket**, pantsak, agtersak; ~ **quill**, stertveer; ~-**race**, benedeloop; ~-**rod**, leistang; ~-**root**, stertwortel; ~-**rope**, balanstou; ~-**skid**, stertsteun; ~-**slide**, agteruitgly; ~-**spin**, tolvlug (vliegtuig); ~ **stick**, loskop (werkbank); ~-**water**, afloopwater; ~-**wheel**, stertwiel; ~ **wind**, meewind, wind van agter.

tain, bladtin.

taint, (n) kleur, tint; vlek, blaam, skandvlek; smet, wansmaak; erflike kwaal, spoor (van erflike siekte); bysmaak (politiek); (v) bederf; 'n smet (wansmaak) veroorsaak; besmet, bevlek, besoedel, aansteek; *the air was* ~**ed** *with smoke*, die lug was besoedel met rookwalms; ~**ed**, onrein, besoedel; ~**ed meat**, vleis met 'n krakie, smetterige vleis; ~ **less**, onbevlek, smetloos; ~ **worm**, miet.

take, (n) ontvangste; vangs; beurt; (v) (**took, -n**), neem; vat, pak, gryp; bemagtig, vang; aanneem, oorneem; bring, besorg; raak, tref; trou; in besit neem, verower (land); huur; aanpak; jou toevlug neem tot; aangaan by; besiel; trek; gebruik (voedsel, medisyne); boei; verstaan; doen, aflê (eed); *we were* ~**n** *ABACK by the news*, die nuus het ons dronkgeslaan; ~ *ACCOUNT of*, rekening hou met; ~ *ACROSS*, na die ander kant bring, oorsit; ~ *in the ACT*, op heter daad betrap; ~ *ACTION*, stappe doen; 'n aksie instel; ~ *ADVANTAGE of*, gebruik (misbruik) maak van; voordeel trek uit; ~ *someone's ADVICE*, iem. se raad aanneem; ~ *legal ADVICE*, regskundige advies inwin; ~ *AFTER*, aard na; ~ *AIM*, korrelvat, aanlê; rig; ~ *AMISS*, kwalik neem; ~ *APART*, uitmekaar haal; ~ *up ARMS*, na die wapen gryp; ~ *up an ATTITUDE*, 'n houding aanneem; ~ *AWAY*, wegneem; ~ *BACK*, terugneem; ~ *it BADLY*, jou dit baie aantrek; ~ *BEARINGS*, peil; ~ *to one's BED*, gaan lê; ~ *in BOARDERS*, kosgangers hou; ~ *to the BOATS*, in die bote gaan; ~ *to one's BOSOM*, liefkry, vriende word met; ~ *BREATH*, asemhaal; ~ *a BUS*, per bus gaan; *that* ~ *s the CAKE*, dit span die kroon; *we CAN* ~ *it*, ons kan ons man staan; ~ *CARE*, oppas; ~ *CARE of my dog*, sorg vir my hond; ~ *a CHANCE*, dit waag; ~ *one's CHANCE*, jou kans afwag; dit waag; ~ *CHARGE*, die leisels in hande neem; die beheer oorneem; ~ *CHARGE of*, sorg vir; ~ *a COLD*, koue vat; ~ *on all COMERS*, almal uitdaag; *I* ~ *it as a COM=*

PLIMENT, ek beskou dit as 'n kompliment; ~ *into one's CONFIDENCE*, in jou vertroue neem; ~ *into CONSIDERATION*, in aanmerking neem; *he took a lot of CONVINCING*, dit het moeilik gegaan om hom te oortuig; ~ *COUNSEL with*, raadpleeg; ~ *COVER*, skuil; ~ *the CUP*, die beker wen; ~ *a CUP of coffee*, koffie drink; ~ *into CUSTODY*, gevange neem; in bewaring neem; ~ *a DEGREE*, 'n graad behaal; ~ *DELIGHT in*, behae skep in; *it* ~ *s some DOING*, dit is nie elke man se werk nie; *it* ~ *s a lot of DOING*, dit is nie elke man se werk nie; dis nie maklik nie; *DON'T* ~ *long over it*, jy moet dit maar gou afmaak; ~ *DOWN*, opteken, opskryf; afhaal ('n boek); verneder (ander mense); ~ *DOWN (a peg or two)*, op sy plek sit; 'n toontjie laer laat sing; ~ *DOWN a building*, 'n gebou afbreek (sloop); ~ *a DRAW*, 'n skuifie neem; ~ *to DRINK*, aan die drink raak; ~ *a DRIVE*, gaan ry; ~ *to EARTH*, in 'n gat kruip; ~ *it EASY*, dit maklik opneem; jou nie oorinspan nie; ~ *it EASY!*, stadig oor die klippe!; ~ *EFFECT*, in werking tree, van krag word; ~ *EVIDENCE*, getuienis afneem; ~ *the EYE*, die aandag trek; ~ *a FALL*, val; ~ *a FANCY to*, behae skep in, liefkry; *the horse will not* ~ *the FENCE*, die perd wil nie oor die heining spring nie; ~ *the FIELD*, uittrek; op kommando gaan; veldwerk doen (krieket); ~ *things as you FIND them*, sake vir lief neem; vat soos jy dit kry; ~ *FIRE*, aan die brand raak; vlam vat; *do you* ~ *me for a FOOL?*, dink jy dat ek gek is?; *what do you* ~ *me FOR*, wat dink jy van my?; ~ *it FROM me*, ek verseker jou, ek sê vir jou; *that does not* ~ *FROM his achievement as poet*, dit doen geen afbreuk aan sy verdienste as digter nie; ~ *for GRANTED*, as vanselfsprekend beskou; ~ *to bad HABITS*, slegte gewoontes aankweek; ~ *a HAND*, saammaak, help; ~ *in HAND*, onderneem; ter hand neem; in toom hou; *HAVE what it* ~ *s*, aan die vereistes voldoen; ~ *into one's head*, in jou kop kry; ~ *to HEART*, ter harte neem; ~ *HEART*, moed skep; ~ *HEED*, oppas; ~ *to one's HEELS*, vlug, die hakke lig; ~ *to the HILLS*, die berge in vlug; ~ *a HOLIDAY*, vakansie neem; met vakansie gaan; ~ *someone HOME*, iem. huis toe bring; *I* ~ *it that*, ek veronderstel dat; ~ *ILL*, skielik siek word; ~ *something ILL*, dit kwalik neem; ~ *an ILLNESS*, 'n siekte kry (opdoen); ~ *IN*, inlei; ontvang; inneem (kennis); ~ *someone IN*, iem. lelik toetrap; iem. 'n rat voor die oë draai; iem. koudlei; iem. knolle vir sitroene verkoop; opvang; begryp; glo, sluk; aanneem (wasgoed); vernou (klere); ~ *IN everything*, alles wat gesê word, inneem; alles noukeurig volg; ~ *INTO account*, meereken; in aanmerking neem; *be a man and show that you can* ~ *IT*, wees dapper en staan jou man; *I* ~ *IT that you will be coming*, ek neem aan dat jy kom; *he can't* ~ *IT*, hy is kleinserig (pieperig); ~ *a JOKE*, 'n grap verdra; ~ *a JOURNEY*, 'n reis onderneem; ~ *a KNOCK*, 'n klap kry; ~ *the LEAD*, leiding gee; ~ *a LEAP*, spring, 'n sprong doen; ~ *LEAVE*, afskeid neem; verlof neem; ~ *it or LEAVE it*, kies of deel; ~ *LEGAL advice*, regsadvies inwin; ~ *one's LIFE into one's hands*, jou lewe in die gevaar stel; ~ *a LIFE*, iem. om die lewe bring; ~ *a LINE*, 'n rigting volg; 'n gedragslyn slaan; *it will not* ~ *you LONG*, jy kan dit gou klaar hê; ~ *a good LOOK*, goed kyk; ~ *a LOOK at that!*, kyk net daarna!; ~ *an insult LYING down*, 'n belediging gedwee verdra; ~ *someone's MEASURE*, iem. se maat neem; iem. takseer; ~ *MEASURES*, maatreëls tref; *it* ~ *s 30 MINUTES to town*, ons ry 30 minute dorp toe; ~ *MINUTES*, notule hou (opstel); ~ *in MOISTURE*, vog opneem; ~ *God's NAME in vain*, die naam van God ydel(lik) gebruik; ~ *a NAP*, 'n uiltjie knip; ~ *out NATURALIZATION papers*, jou laat naturaliseer; ~ *in NEEDLEWORK*, naaldwerk vir ander doen; *can I* ~ *the NEWS to be official?* mag ek die berig as amptelik beskou?; ~ *in a NEWSPAPER*, op 'n koerant inteken; ~ *NOTES*, aantekeninge maak; ~ *NOTICE*, kennis neem; ontslaan word, jou ontslag kry; ~ *an OATH*, sweer, 'n eed aflê; ~

taken   1291   *talking*

OFF, wegtrek; uittrek; aftrek (van 'n prys); in beweging kom; aanloop; opstyg (vliegtuig); wegvlieg (voël); wegneem; ontlas van; ~ *someone OFF*, iem. komieklik voorstel; ~ *OFFENCE*, aanstoot neem; ~ *the OFFENSIVE*, tot die aanval oorgaan; ~ *OFFICE*, minister word; in diens tree; ~ *ON*, aan boord neem; kans sien vir; uitdaag; aanneem; op jou neem; aanpak; onderneem; *if the idea* ~ *s ON*, as die idee inslaan; as die idee populêr word; ~ *ON more than you can do*, meer onderneem as wat jy kan doen; ~ *ON workers*, arbeiders in diens neem; ~ *it OUT of someone*, iem. dit laat ontgeld; iem. se krag verswak, bv. 'n siekte; ~ *OUT*, uitneem, verwyder ('n vlek); uitgaan met; ~ *the OPPORTUNITY*, v.d. geleentheid gebruik maak; ~ *OVER*, oorneem; ~ *PAINS*, moeite doen; *PAINT will not* ~ *on a greasy surface*, verf sal nie vassit op 'n vetterige oppervlak nie; ~ *PART*, deelneem; ~ *up PASSENGERS*, passasiers oplaai; ~ *out a PATENT for*, 'n patent neem op; ~ *to PIECES*, uitmekaarhaal, uitmekaarneem; ~ *PLACE*, gebeur, plaasvind; ~ *the PLUNGE*, die stoute skoene aantrek; ~ *a POINT*, 'n punt stel; 'n argument aanvoer; ~ *POSITION*, stelling neem; ~ *PRISONER*, gevange neem; ~ *a PORTRAIT*, fotografeer, afneem; ~ *a PRIZE*, 'n prys wen (verwerf); ~ *up a PROFESSION*, 'n beroep kies; ~ *PUNISHMENT*, gekasty word (fig.); *it* ~ *s two to make a QUARREL*, twee is nodig om rusie te maak; ~ *as READ*, gelees beskou; ~ *for a RIDE*, vir 'n ritjie neem; bedrieg, kul; ~ *ROOT*, wortelskiet, groei; ~ *in SAIL*, seil verminder; ~ *the SALUTE*, die saluut beantwoord; ~ *a SEAT*, gaan sit, plaasneem; ~ *a SERVICE*, 'n godsdiensoefening lei; ~ *SHIP*, aan boord gaan, ~ *off one's SHOES*, jou skoene uittrek; ~ *SIDES*, party kies; ~ *STEPS*, maatreëls neem; stappe doen; ~ *a STEP*, 'n tree gee; ~ *to SOMEONE*, tot iem. aangetrokke voel; ~ *STOCK*, inventarieer, inventaris opmaak; *he* ~ *s a lot of STOPPING*, dis moeilik om hom te keer; ~ *in one's STRIDE*, maklik afhandel; *do you* ~ *SUGAR with your tea?*, gebruik jy suiker by jou tee?; ~ *THINGS as they come*, sake aanvaar soos hulle kom; koffie drink soos die kan hom skink; ~ *SUGAR*, suiker gebruik; ~ *out a SUMMONS against*, iem. laat dagvaar; ~ *THOUGHT*, ernstig oorweeg; ~ *one's TIME*, jou nie haas nie; *these things* ~ *TIME*, hierdie dinge vereis tyd; hiervoor het 'n mens tyd nodig; ~ *TO drinking*, aan die drink raak; ~ *TO crime*, 'n misdadiger word; ~ *TO gambling*, aan die dobbel raak; ~ *TO someone*, van iem. begin hou; ~ *a TRAIN*, per trein gaan; ~ *TROUBLE*, moeite doen; ~ *UNAWARES*, verras; ~ *UP*, in beslag neem; ~ *UP a matter with someone*, 'n saak met iem. bespreek; ~ *UP room*, ruimte inneem; ~ *UP a new post*, 'n nuwe betrekking aanvaar; ~ *UP a matter*, 'n saak aanpak; ~ *UP journalism*, joernalis word; ~ *UP a collection*, 'n kollekte opneem; *I'll* ~ *you UP on that*, ek daag jou daaroor uit; ~ *a WALK*, wandel, gaan loop; ~ *to the WATER*, van stapel loop; in die water spring; ~ *the WATERS*, die baaie gebruik; ~ *in WATER*, lek; ~ *up WITH*, begin omgaan met; *think you can* ~ *it WITH you*, dink jy kan 'n biltong saamneem; ~ *someone at his WORD*, iem. letterlik opneem; iem. glo; ~**-away food**, koop-en-loopkos, meeneemkos; ~**-away restaurant**, meeneemrestourant, saamneemrestourant, koop-en-looprestourant; ~**-away service**, saamneemdiens, wegneemdiens; ~**-away-snacks**, koop-en-loophappies; ~**-down**, vernedering; ~**-in**, bedrog, kullery.

tak'en, geneem; ~ *in ADULTERY*, in egbreuk betrap; *be* ~ *ABACK by something*, uit die veld geslaan wees deur iets; *be* ~ *ILL*, siek word; *NOT to be* ~, vir uitwendige gebruik; *the POINT is well* ~, die argument hou steek; *be* ~ *UP with*, ingenome wees met; baie belang stel in; in beslag neem (tyd); *be* ~ *WITH someone*, ingenome wees met iem.

tak'e-off, karikatuur; vermindering; wegspring; wegspringplek; opstyging; opstyg (vliegtuig); ~ **point**, opstygplek; ~ **run**, aanloop; ~ **speed**, opstygsnelheid.

take'-over, oorneming, oorname.

tak'er, nemer; aannemer (van 'n weddenskap); veroweraar; ontvanger; *there were no* ~ *s*, niemand wou dit hê nie; niemand wou byt nie.

tak'ing, (n) (die) neem; ontvangs; verowering; (pl) ontvangste; (a) innemend, bekoorlik; aansteeklik; ~**-off**, opstyging.

talc, talk, talkaarde, speksteen; ~**ite**, talkiet; ~**ose**, ~**ous**, talkagtig, speksteenagtig.

tale, storie, vertelling, verhaal; sprokie; getal, aantal; *DEAD men tell no* ~ *s*, die dooies swyg; *OLD wives'* ~ *s*, ouvrouepraatjies; *I PREFER to tell my own* ~, ek verkies om my eie verklaring te gee; *tell* ~ *s out of SCHOOL*, uit die skool klap; *all SORTS of* ~ *s will get about*, allerhande stories sal rondvertel word; *the* ~ *runs as it pleases the TELLER*, van hoor en sê, lieg 'n mens baie; ~**-bearer**, nuusdraer, kwaadspreker, verklikker, klikspaan; ~**-bearing**, (n) verklikkery, nuusdraery; (a) verklikkerig.

tal'ent, talent, gawe, begaafdheid, aanleg; talent (gewig, munt); ~**ed**, begaaf, talentvol.

tal'es, jurielys.

tale: ~**-teller**, verteller, verklikker, klikspaan; ~**-telling**, geklik.

tal'ion, weervergelding, vergeldingsreg.

tal'iped, (n) horrelvoet; (a) met 'n horrelvoet; horrelvoet-.

tal'ipes, horrelvoet.

tal'ipot, tal'iput, waaierpalm.

tal'isman, (-s), talisman; towermiddel, gelukbringer.

talk, (n) gesprek; gerug; gepraat, pratery; praatjies; onderhoud, bespreking; *it is ALL* ~, dis net grootpratery (bluf, windlawaai); ~ *is CHEAP, but money buys the whisky*, praatjies vul geen gaatjies; *it is EMPTY* ~, dis sommer praatjies, dis ydel gepraat; *IDLE* ~, praatjies vir die vaak, kletspraatjies; sommer praatjies; *INFLAMMATORY* ~, opruiende taal; ~ *is* ~, *but 'tis MONEY buys lands*, praatjies vul geen gaatjies; *there is* ~ *OF*, daar is sprake van; *SMALL* ~, kletspraatjies, praatjies oor koeitjies en kalfies; peuterpraatjies; *SILLY* ~, kafpraatjies, gebasel; *the* ~ *of the TOWN*, iets waarvan almal die mond vol het; (v) praat, gesels, gedagtes wissel, spreek; ~ *ABOUT*, praat van; bespreek; ~ *AT*, beknor, beskimp; ~ *AWAY*, daarop los praat; ~ *BACK*, brutaal antwoord; ~ *BIG*, grootpraat; ~ *the hind leg off a DONKEY*, land en sand aanmekaar praat; 'n perd se stert afpraat; ~ *someone DOWN*, iem. doodpraat; iem. tot swye bring; ~ *DOWN to someone*, iem. se begripsvermoë onderskat; ~ *nineteen to the DOZEN*, land en sand aanmekaar praat; ~ *through one's HAT*, kaf praat; ~ *one's HEAD off*, jou flou praat; ~ *oneself HOARSE*, jou hees praat; ~ *HORSES*, oor perde en wedrenne gesels; ~ *someone INTO something*, iem. 'n gat in die kop praat; iem. iets aanpraat; ~ *NONSENSE*, kaf praat; raaskal; ~ *of NOTHING else*, die mond vol hê van iets; ~ *OF*, praat van; ~ *someone OUT of something*, iem. iets uit die hoof praat; ~ *OUT a motion*, 'n voorstel doodpraat; ~ *OVER*, bespreek; ompraat; ~ *the matter OVER*, die saak bepraat; oor die saak gesels; ~ *someone OVER*, iem. oorhaal; iem. ompraat; ~ *things OVER thoroughly*, sake deeglik bespreek; kruis en dwars bespreek; ~ *things OVER with someone*, sake met iem. bespreek; ~ *a person ROUND*, iem. ompraat; *he* ~ *s for the SAKE of* ~ *ing*, hy praat net omdat praat praat is; sy praat is op; ~ *SHOP*, oor jou vak (werk) praat; ~ *SPORT*, oor sport gesels; ~ *about THIS and that*, oor koeitjies en kalfies praat; konsistorie hou; ~ *TO*, praat met; iem. die kop was (die waarheid sê); ~ *out of one's TURN*, die aap uit die mou laat kom; jou mond verbypraat; ~**ative**, spraaksaam, praatsiek; praterig, babbelagtig; ~**ative person**, babbelbek; praatgraag; ~**ativeness**, spraaksaamheid, praterigheid; ~**ee-~ee**, brabbeltaal, koeterwaals; ~**er**, prater, spreker; ~**ie(s)**, klankrolprent, klankfilm, praatfilm.

talk'ing, (n) gepraat, pratery, praat; *do the* ~, die praatwerk doen; (a) pratend, praat-; ~ **machine**, praatmasjien; ~ **point**, onderwerp van gesprek; ~**to**, skrobbering; *give someone a* ~ *-to*, iem. die leviete (krionieke) voorlees; iem. skrobbeer.

tall, groot; lang (lank), hoog; spoggerig; onbillik; kras; *a* ~ *HAT*, 'n pluiskeil; *a* ~ *ORDER*, geen kleinigheid nie; 'n onuitvoerbare onderneming; *tell* ~ *STORIES*, kluitjies verkoop, spekskiet; *that's a* ~ *STORY*, sak, Sarel!; *a* ~ *SUM*, 'n groot som; ~ *TALK*, grootpratery, bluffery; ~**boy**, hoë laaikas; ~**ness**, lengte, grootte.
tall'ow, (n) talk; kersvet; harde vet; (v) met vet in= smeer; vet smeer; vet maak; vet vorm; ~ **candle**, vetkers; ~**-chandlery**, kersmakery; ~**-dip**, vetkers; ~**-faced**, bleek; ~**ish**, ~**y**, talkagtig; vetagtig; vet= terig; ~ **soap**, dierlike seep.
tall'y, (n) **(tallies)**, kerfstok; keep, kerf; aantal; reke= ning; bordjie, plaatjie, naamhoutjie, etiket; dupli= kaat; *BUY by the* ~, by die getal koop; *TAKE* ~ *of*, tel; (v) **(tallied)**, inkerf, natel; klop, ooreenstem; pas; op die kerfstok sit; strook; ~ *with*, strook met, klop met; ~**-board**, kontrolebord; voorraadbord; ~ **card**, kontrolekaart; ~ **clerk**, telklerk; laai= meester.
tally-ho', (n) jagterskreet; vierperdewa; dwarsskop; (v) sa skreeu; (interj) sa!
tall'y: ~**-keeper**, kontroleur; ~**man**, (..**men**), kre= dietwinkelier, kerfstokwinkelier; ~**-shop**, kerf= stokwinkel; ~ **system**, getuiestelsel; afbetaling= stelsel.
Tal'mud, Talmoed; ..**mud'ic**, Talmoed=, Talmoedies; ~**ist**, Talmoedis.
tal'on, klou; stok, oorskietkaarte (kaartspel); ojieflys (arg.); hiel, nok (gebou); ~**ed**, met kloue.
tal'us, **(tali)**, puin, glooiingspuin (geol.); helling; en= kelbeen; ~ **cone**, puinkeël; ~ **slope**, puinhelling; ~ **wall**, keermuur.
tamabil'ity, tembaarheid.
tam'able, tembaar; ~**ness**, tembaarheid.
taman'dua, **tam'anoir**, klein miereter.
tam'arin, grootooraap.
tam'arind, tamarinde, suurdadelboom.
tam'arisk, dawee, tamarisk(boom), abikwageel= hout.
tambook'ie, tamboekie; ~**-grass**, tamboekiegras; ~**- thorn**, tamboekiedoring.
tambot'i, tambotie *(Spirostachys africanus)*; ~**- grass**, tambotiegras.
tam'bour, (n) tamboer, trom; borduurraam, tamboe= reerraam; borduurwerk; (v) tamboereer, borduur; ~ **frame**, tamboereerraam, tamboeryn; ~**ine'**, tamboeryn.
tame, (v) mak maak, tem; (a) mak, gedwee, onderda= nig; geskik (perd); flou, vervelend; slap, suf; ~**less**, ontembaar; ~**ness**, makheid, gedweeheid; verve= ling; ~**r**, temmer, makmaker.
Ta'mil, (n) Tamil; (a) Tamil=.
tam'ing, temming; (die) mak maak; (die) leer.
tam'is, sygdoek, sifdoek.
Tamm'any Hall, politieke knoeiery.
tamm'y, **(tammies)**, **tam-o'-shan'ter**, (Skotse) wol= mus.
tamp, opvul, vasslaan, vasstamp; opstop.
tam'pan, hoenderbosluis, tampan.
tam'per, (n) stamper; (v): ~ *with*, knoei aan (met); peuter aan (met); omkoop; in die geheim bewerk; vervals, omrokkel; ~**er**, vervalser; ~**ing**, bemoei= ing, inlating; vervalsing.
tamp'ing, opvulling, prop; stopsel; vasstamping; ~ **machine**, instampmasjien; onderstopmasjien; ~**- rod**, laaistok; stampstok, stokyster.
tam'pion, geweerprop, prop.
tam'pon, (n) tampon, prop (vir wonde); *plug with a* ~, tamponneer; (v) toestop, tamponneer.
tam'tam, *kyk* **tomtom**.
tan[1], (n) *kyk* **tangent**.
tan[2], (n) taankleur; bronskleur; looibas; (v) **(-ned)**, looi; bruin brand, brons, bruin, verbrand, bruin word, afransel, vel; (a) geelbruin, taankleurig; ~**- coloured**, geelbruin, taankleurig.
tan'dem, (n) tweelingfiets, tandem; (a) die een agter die ander, tandem=.
tang[1], (n) seebamboes.
tang[2], (n) metaalklank; (v) klink.
tang[3], (n) tong (gespe); angel (gereedskap); tand (vurk); arend (van sens); doring (van mes, beitel);

hefpunt; stert (geweer); bysmaak, skerp nasmaak; luggie; eienaardigheid; tikkie.
tan'ga, tanga, riembikini.
Tanganyi'ka, Tanganjika.
tang'elo, **(-es)**, tangelo, pomelonartjie.
tan'gency, raking; *point of* ~, raakpunt.
tan'gent, raaklyn, tangens; *fly (go) off at a* ~, skielik van koers verander; van die os op die esel spring; ..**n'tial**, (n) tangensiaal; (a) tangensieel; ~ **line**, raaklyn; ~ **point**, raakpunt; ~ **sight**, visier, klap= visier.
tangerine', (n) nartjie, nartjiekleur; (a) nartjierooi, nartjiekleurig.
tangibil'ity, voelbaarheid, tasbaarheid.
tan'gible, tasbaar, voelbaar.
ta'ngle, (n) verwikkeling, wirwar, knoop, verwarring, warboel; *be in a* ~, in die war wees, deurmekaar wees; (v) ingewikkeld maak, verwar, verwikkel; deurmekaar maak; *a* ~ *d AFFAIR* 'n warboel; ~ *d VEGETATION*, struikgewas; ~**foot**, lymvel; sterk drank.
ta'ngly, verwikkel(d), deurmekaar, in die war.
ta'ngo, **(-s)**, (n) tango; (v) die tango dans.
tang'y, met 'n sterk smaak of geur, pikant.
tank, (n) tenk; waterbak; vergaarbak; vegwa; (v) in 'n tenk bewaar (behandel); in 'n tenk laat loop; ~ *up*, brandstof inneem; suip; ~**a**, tanka, 5-reëlige (stem= mings)gedig; ~ **age**, tenkinhoud; tenkgeld; diere= meel, vleismeel; ~**ard**, drinkkan, skinkkan, flap= kan; ~ **division**, tenkafdeling, tenkdivisie; ~**-dozer**, stotertenk; ~ **engine**, tenkmotor; ~**er**, tenkskip; tenkwa; ~ **farming**, waterwekery; ~ **landing craft**, tenklandingsvaartuig; ~**-shelter**, tenkskuiling; ~**-steamer**, tenkskip; ~**-trap**, tenk= kuil, tenkgat; ~ **troops**, tenktroepe.
tan: ~**-mill**, basmeule; looiery; ~ **nage**, (die) looi; ~**ned**, gelooi; gebruin, gebrons (gesig), songe= bruin, songebrand.
tan'ner, looier; ~**'s trade**, looiery; ~**'s vat**, looikuip; ~**'s work (yard)**, looiery.
tan: ~ **nery**, (..**ries**), looiery; ~ **nic**, looi=; ~ **nic acid**, looisuur; ~ **nin**, tannien, tannine, looistof, looi= suur.
tan'ning, bruining, bronsing, bruinbrand; tannien, tannine; (die) looi; *give someone a* ~, iem. uitlooi; iem. 'n pak slae gee; ~ **bark**, looibas; ~ **extract**, looiekstrak; ~ **oil**, sonbrandolie; ~ **pit**, looikuip.
tan'talite, tantaliet.
tantaliza'tion, tantalisasie, temptering, streling met bedrieglike hoop.
tan'talize, met ydel hoop streel, liemaak, tempteer, tantaliseer; ~**r**, kweller.
tan'talus[1], drankkassie (met slot).
Tan'talus[2], Tantalus; ~ **cup**, Tantalusbeker.
tan'tamount, gelykwaardig, gelykgeldend, gelyk= staande met; *BE* ~ *to*, gelykstaan met; neerkom op; *BE* ~ *to treason*, gelykstaan met verraad.
tan'trum, slegte bui, slegte humeur; *BE in a* ~, die kwaai mus ophê; *GET into a* ~, kwaad word.
tan: ~**-vat**, looikuip; ~**-works**, ~**-yard**, looiery.
Tanzan'ia, Tanzanië.
tap[1], klop; tikkie; (v) tik (biljart); klop.
tap[2], (n) kraan; kantien, drinkplek; tap (in 'n vat); aansluitklem; ~ *and DIE*, snytap en snymoer; *EXCELLENT* ~, baie goeie drank; *ON* ~, met 'n kraan; altyd beskikbaar; (v) **(-ped)**, aftap (vloei= stof); uittap; 'n kraan (tap) inslaan; aanvoor, eks= ploiteer; 'n moerdraad sny; aftak (elek.); onder= skep, afluister; meeluister; uitvra; uithoor; ~ *a PERSON*, iem. pols; ~ *SOMEONE of something*, iem. pols; iem. uithoor; iets by iem. afrokkel; ~ *a SOURCE*, uit 'n bron put; ~ *a SUBJECT*, 'n on= derwerp ter sprake bring; ~ *the WIRES*, die tele= graafdraad tap (melk); ~ **beer**, vatbier, vaatjiebier; ~ **bolt**, tapskroef; ~**-borer**, sluitgatboor.
tap'-dance, klopdans; ~**-dancing**, klopdans(ery).
tap'-drill, tapgatboor.
tape, (n) band; lint; snoer; maatband; telegram= strook; telegrafiese koersberig; papierstrook; *BREAST the* ~, die lint breek (in 'n wedloop); *RED* ~, amptelike omslagtigheid, rompslomp; (v) vasbind (met 'n band); met band omwikkel; lint

taper   1293   **taste**

insteek; 'n bandopname maak van; *HAVE some~ one* ~ *d*, 'n opinie gevorm hê oor iem.; ~ *OFF*, afbind, afsnoer; *the SPEECHES were* ~ *d*, daar is 'n bandopname v.d. toesprake gemaak; ~ *UP*, met lint verbind; ~ **-factory,** bandwewery; ~ **-library,** bandoteek; ~ **-line,** ~ **-measure,** meetlint, rolmaat, maatlint, maatband.
tap'er, (n) waskers; toespitsing; keëlvorming; keël≈ vorm; (v) spits toeloop; afdun; dun loop; spits word; ~ *OFF*, geleidelik verminder; afdun; gelei= delik vernou; ~ *OFF into*, in 'n punt uitloop; (a) spits.
tape: ~ **recorder,** bandopnemer; ~ **recording,** band≈ opname.
tap'er: ~ **hole,** taps gat; ~ **tap,** voorsnytap.
tap'ering, (n) spitsheid, puntigheid; tapsheid; afdun= ning; (a) spits, puntig; taps.
tap'estried, behang.
tap'estry, (..**tries**), behangsel, muurtapyt, wand= tapyt; tapytwerk; tapisserie.
tape: ~ **-weaver,** bandwewer; ~ **worm,** lintwurm.
tap'-hole, tapgat.
tapioc'a, tapioka.
tap'ir, tapir.
tap'is, tapyt; *BRING on the* ~, ter sprake bring; op die lappe bring; *COME on the* ~, op die lappe kom.
tap' loan, deurlopende lening.
tap'per, tapper.
tapp'et, klepligter; ~ **clearance,** klepspeling; ~ **dog,** klepligterklou; ~ **shaft,** klepligteras.
tapp'ing¹, klopdans; geklop, getik.
tapp'ing², tappery.
tapp'ing: ~ **har,** tapyster (gietery); ruimyster; ~ **beetle,** ghannaghoentjie; ~ **hammer,** toetshamer; ~ **screw,** draadsnyskroef.
tap-'room, drinkplek, tappery.
tap'-root, penwortel.
tap'ster, kantienman, skinker.
tar, (n) teer; matroos; *BEAT the* ~ *out of someone*, icm. uitlooi; *JACK t* ~, pikbrock, matroos; (v) **(-red),** teer, beteer, met teer smeer; ~ *red all with the same BRUSH*, almal met dieselfde gebreke; ~ *and FEATHER*, teer en veer; ~ *OVER*, teer.
ta'radiddle, (colloq.) leuentjie.
ta'radiddle, tarantella.
ta'rantism, danswoede.
taran'tula, (-s), tarantula, bobbejaanspinnekop.
tar'-barrel, teervat.
tarboosh', (-es), fes.
tar-brush, (-es), teerkwas; *have a touch of the* ~, (derog.), gekleurde bloed in die are hê.
tar'-bucket, teerputs.
tard'igrade, (n) luidier, traagloper (dier); (a) traaglo≈ pend; traag, lui.
tard'ily, stadig, langsaam.
tard'iness, traagheid, onwilligheid.
tard'y, traag, stadig, dralend, langsaam; onwillig; laat(bloeiend); ~ **riser,** laatslaper.
tare¹, (n) onkruid, wilde ertjie, wiek.
tare², (n) tarra, eiegewig; (v) die tarra bereken.
targ'et, skyf, teiken; mikpunt; doelwit; *disappearing* ~, valskyf; ~ **amount,** teikenbedrag; ~ **area,** skyf= gebied; ~ **audience,** teikengehoor; ~ **date,** teiken= datum; ~ **pit,** skyfgat; skyfkuil; ~ **practice,** (die) skyfskiet; ~ **quantity,** teikenhoeveelheid; ~ **-seeking missile,** teikenjagprojektiel; ~ **shooting,** skyfskiet.
ta'riff, (n) tarief; ~ *of charges (fees)*, kostetarief; (v) 'n tarief vasstel; ~ **duty,** uitvoerreg, invoerreg, doe= anereg; ~ **premium,** tariefpremie; ~ **rate,** toltarief; ~ **reform,** tariefhersiening; ~ **union,** tolunie, tol= verbond; ~ **wall,** tariewemuur; ~ **war,** tariewoor= log.
tarl'atan, dun moeselien (neteldoek), tarlatan.
tarm'ac, tar macad'am, teermacadam, teerpad; teer= blad, teerbaan; aansitblad.
tar'-melter, teerketel.
tarn¹, bergmeertjie.
tarn², *kyk* **tern,** (n).
tarn'ish, (n) vlek, verkleuring; verbleking; dofheid; aanslag (op metaal); (v) besoedel, bevlek, beswalk; aanslaan, verbleek, die glans verloor, dof maak.

ta'ro, taro.
ta'roc, tarokspel (kaartspel).
tar'-oil, teerolie.
ta'rot = **taroc.**
tarpaul'in, (geteerde) bokseil, (teer)seil; matroos= hoed; seerob.
Tarpei'an, Tarpeïes.
tar'-pot, teerpot.
tar'radiddle, leuentjie.
tar'ragon, dragon; ~ **vinegar,** dragonasyn.
tarred, geteer; ~ **pole,** teerpaal; ~ **road,** teerpad; ~ **rope,** geteerde tou, teertou; ~ **whipcord,** geteerde ribkoord.
tar'ring, teerwerk.
ta'rry¹, (v) **(tarried),** draal, talm, draai, vertoef, uit= bly, versuim.
tar'ry², (a) teeragtig, teer=.
tars'al, (n) voetwortelbeentjie; (a) voetwortel=, hot= notjie=; tarsaal; ~ **joint,** hakgewrig.
tars'ia, houtinlegwerk.
tar'sier, nagaap.
tar: ~ **soap,** teerseep; ~ **stain,** teervlek.
tars'us, (..**si**), voetwortel, tarsus; kraakbeen, plaat (van die ooglede).
tart, (n) tert (gebak); flerrie, vryerige vroumens, snol, ligtekooi; (a) vrank, suur; bitsig, skerp.
tart'an¹, (n) tartaan (boot).
tart'an², (n) Skotse ruitjiesgoed, tartan; Skotse doek; Hooglander; (a) tartan=; ~ **track,** tartanbaan.
Tart'ar¹, (n) Tartaar; drifkop, woesteling, kwaaikop; *catch a* ~, jou moses teëkom; met 'n drifkop te doen kry; (a) Tartaars.
tart'ar², (n) wynsteen; aanpaksel op tande; *CREAM of* ~, kremetart; ~ *EMETIC,* braakwynsteen.
tartare': ~ *sauce*, Tartaarse sous, tartaresous.
Tart'arean, Tartarus=; hels.
Tart'arian, Tartaars.
tarta'ric, wynsteen=; ~ **acid,** wynsteensuur.
Tart'arus, Tartarus; die onderwêreld, hel.
Tart'ary, Tartarye.
tart: ~ **-filling,** tertvulsel; ~ **let,** tertjie.
tart'ness, suurheid, vrankheid; skerpheid, bitsigheid.
tart'rate, wynsteensuursout, tartraat.
task, (n) taak, werk, skof, vak, arbeid; *TAKE to* ~, op die vingers tik; die leviete voorlees; oor die kole haal; voor stok kry; *be TAKEN to* ~, knor kry; les opsê; (v) werk opgee; hard laat werk; baie verg van; op die proef stel; ~ **force,** taakmag; ~ **master,** werkgewer, baas, taakgewer, leermeester; ~ **sys= tem,** stelsel van stukwerk; ~ **-work,** taakwerk; stukwerk.
Tasman'ia, Tasmanië; ~ **n,** (n) Tasmaniër; (a) Tasmanies.
tass, sopie, slukkie.
tass'al, tasal.
tass'el, (n) kwas, klossie; fraiing; *come into* ~, in die saad kom; (v) van 'n klossie voorsien, 'n kwassie aansit; ~ **led,** met kwassies versier.
tast'able, proebaar, smaaklik.
taste, (n) smaak; proet, slukkie; voorsmaak; na= smaak; bysmaak; styl, trant; voorkeur, voorliefde; *there is no ACCOUNTING for* ~ *s,* smaak verskil; oor die smaak kan 'n mens nie twis nie; *in BAD* ~, in slegte geur; getuigend van slegte smaak; onkies; smaakloos; *like a BAD* ~ *in the mouth*, soos 'n sleg= te nasmaak; soos as in die mond; ~ *s DIFFER*, smaak verskil; *EVERYONE to his* ~, elkeen na sy smaak; *GIVE a* ~, laat proe; *in GOOD* ~, smaak= vol; *show GOOD* ~, van goeie smaak getuig; *HAVE a* ~ *for,* 'n liefhebber wees van; *LEAVE a bad* ~, 'n slegte nasmaak hê; *LEAVE a nasty* ~ *in the mouth,* 'n slegte nasmaak(tuig); hê; *a MAN of* ~, iem. met smaak; *SENSE of* ~, smaaksin(tuig); *TO my* ~, na my smaak; *TO* ~, na smaak; *be TO one's* ~, in die smaak val; *something TO one's* ~, iets na jou smaak; iets van jou gading; *be given a* ~ *of the WHIP,* onder die kweperlat deurloop; met die kweperlat kry; (v) proe; smaak; eet; nuttig; be= proef; ondervind; *it* ~ *s GOOD*, dit smaak lekker; dit smaak na meer; ~ *OF,* smaak na; ~ **ful,** smaak= vol; ~ **fulness,** smaakvolheid; goeie smaak; ~ **less,**

laf, smaakloos; ~**lessness**, smaakloosheid, lafheid; ~**r**, proeër; proefglasie; kaasboor; botterboor; ~-**remover**, smaakoplosser.
tast'ily, smaakvol.
tas'tiness, smaaklikheid.
tas'ting: ~-**knife**, kaasboor; ~-**order**, magtiging om wyn te proe.
tas'ty, lekker, smaaklik.
tat, (-ted), knoopwerk maak, knoop.
ta-ta', tot siens.
Ta'tar, *kyk* **Tartar**.
tatt'er, vod, flenter, toiing, flard; *in* ~*s*, in toiings (pluiens); ~**demal'ian**, (n) voëlverskrikker, verflenterde kêrel; (a) verflenter; ~**ed**, in toiings, toiingrig, verflenter, haweloos; ~*ed and torn*, lyk of die aasvoëls jou beetgehad het; in flenters wees.
Tatt'ersalls, Tattersalls, reisiesweddery, wedkantoor.
tatt'ing, spoelwerk, knoopwerk; macramé.
tat'tle, (n) geklets, gebabbel; (v) babbel, kekkel, skinder; ~**r**, babbelaar, praatkous, kekkelbek, uitsaaistasie, praatjiesmaker; *a* ~*r*, Kaatjie Kekkelbek, 'n uitsaaistasie.
tattoo'¹, (n) taptoe; *beat the devil's* ~, met die vingers trommel.
tattoo'², (n) tatoeëring; (v) tatoeëer; ~**er**, tatoeëerder; ~**ing**, tatoeëring, tatoeëermerke; ~-**ink**, tatoeëerink; ~-**marks**, tatoeëermerke.
tatt'y, (tatties), skerm, mat; (a), toiinging, vuil.
taught, *kyk* **teach**.
taunt, (n) skimp, hoon, smaad; skimprede, skimpskeut, skimpskoot, aanfluiting, haatlikheid; spot; verwyt; (v) beskimp, hoon, terg; verwyt; (a) buitengewoon hoog (mas); ~**er**, honer, skimper; ~**ing**, (n) beskimping, tergery, veragting; (a) honend, beledigend, tergend; ~**ingly**, honend, spottend.
taur'ine, bul=.
Taur'us, die Stier (diereriem).
taut, strak, gespanne, styf; in goeie orde (van 'n skip); ~**en**, styf trek, styf span, aanhaal.
tautolog'ic(al), toutologies, herhalend.
tautol'ogism, toutologie, herhaling, woordherhaling.
tautol'ogize, herhaal.
tautol'ogy = **tautologism**.
tautoph'ony, klankherhaling.
tav'ern, tappery, drinkplek, kroeg, kantien, oog, wynhuis; herberg, taverne; *frequent the* ~, aldag oog toe gaan; ~**er**, ~-**keeper**, kroegbaas, kantienhouer.
taw¹, (n) albaster; albasterspeletjie; ghoen.
taw², (v) witlooi, tou.
tawd'riness, opgesmuktheid; opsigtigheid.
tawd'ry, (n) (..dries), goedkoop opskik; (a) opgesmuk, opsigtig, skynskoon, prullerig; goedkoop.
taw'er, witlooier; ~**y**, (..ries), witlooiery, aluinlooiery.
taw'ing, aluinlooiery, witlooiery.
tawn'iness, taankleurigheid.
tawn'ish, valerig.
tawn'y, donkergeel, bruingeel, geelbruin; vaal; taankleurig, tanig; ~ **eagle**, grootbruinarend.
taws(e), plak.
tax, (n) (-es), belasting; las, tribuut; eis, swaar proef; *AFTER* ~, na aftrek van belasting; *it will be a HEAVY* ~ *upon him*, dit sal hom swaar op die proef stel; *be a* ~ *ON*, tot las wees vir; (v) belas; takseer, veel verg van, op die proef stel; betig; beskuldig; ~ *one's MEMORY*, jou geheue inspan (toets); goed nadink; ~ *one's PATIENCE*, jou geduld op die proef stel; *do not* ~ *your STRENGTH too much*, eis nie te veel van jou krag nie; ~ *WITH dishonesty*, beskuldig van oneerlikheid; ~**abil'ity**, belasbaarheid; ~**able**, belasbaar, skatbaar, skatpligtig, synsbaar.
taxa'tion, belasting; ~ *of COSTS*, taksering van koste; *DIRECT* ~, direkte belasting.
tax: ~ **burden**, belastingdruk; ~ **collector**, belastinggaarder, ontvanger van belasting (inkomste); ~ **consultant**, belastingkonsultant; ~ **dodger**, belastingontduiker; ~-**dodging**, belastingontduiking; ~**ed**, aangeslaan, getakseer; ~*ed costs*, getakseerde koste; ~**er**, skatter, waardeerder; ~ **evader**, belastingontduiker; ~-**exempt**, belastingvry; ~ **form**,

belastingvorm; ~-**free**, vry van belasting, belastingvry; ~ **gatherer**, ontvanger van belasting (inkomste), belastinggaarder.
tax'i, (n) huurmotor, taxi; *call a* ~, 'n taxi (huurmotor) ontbied; (v) in 'n huurmotor (taxi) ry (vervoer); (met 'n vliegtuig) op die aanloopbaan ry; ~ **cab**, huurmotor, taxi.
tax'idermist, diereopstopper, taksidermis.
tax'idermy, opstopkuns, taksidermie.
tax'i: ~-**driver**, ~-**man**, huurmotorbestuurder, taxibestuurder; ~ **meter**, tariefmeter, taximeter.
ta'xing, (n) oplegging van belasting; (a) moeilik, veeleisend; ~ **master**, ~ **officer**, waardeerder, vassteller (van belasting).
tax'i: ~ **plane**, passasiersvliegtuig; ~ **rank**, staanplek vir huurmotors (taxi's); ~ **strip**, rolbaan.
tax'iway, rybaan, rolbaan.
taxo'nomer, taxo'nomist, taksonoom.
taxo'nomy, sistematiek, taksonomie.
tax' payer, belastingbetaler.
T'-bar, T-yster.
T'-bone steak, T-beenskyf.
tchick, met die tong klap, tjiek.
tea, (n) tee; ligte ete; *not for al the* ~ *in CHINA*, vir geen geld ter wêreld nie; *it is not my CUP of* ~, dis nie my smaak nie; *HIGH* ~, (Eng.), ligte teemaaltyd; aandete; *KIND of* ~, teesoort; *MAKE* ~, tee maak; *TAKE* ~, tee drink; (v) op tee onthaal, tee drink; ~-**bag**, teesakkie; *stringless* ~*bag*, toutjielose teesakkie; ~-**break**, teepouse, teetyd; ~-**bush**, teestruik; ~-**caddy**, ~-**canister**, teeblik.
teach, (**taught**), onderwys gee; onderrig; skoolhou; leer, les gee; doseer; *I'll* ~ *you to be CHEEKY*, ek sal jou leer om brutaal te wees; ~ *one's GRANDMOTHER to suck eggs*, die eier wil wyser wees as die hen; *she* ~*es HISTORY*, sy gee les in geskiedenis; ~ *someone a LESSON*, iem. 'n les leer; iem. wys waar Dawid die wortels gegrawe het; *this will* ~ *you to SPEAK the truth*, dit sal jou leer om die waarheid te praat; *to* ~ *someone a THING or two*, iem. 'n les leer; iem. wys waar Dawid die wortels gegrawe het; ~**abil'ity**, leergierigheid, bevatlikheid; leersaamheid; ~ **able**, leerbaar; bevatlik, leergierig; aanneemlik.
teach'er, onderwyser(es), onnie (geselst.), skoolmeester, dosent(e); ~**s' association**, onderwysersvereniging; ~**'s certificate**, onderwysersertifikaat, onderwysakte; ~**'s examination**, onderwyserseksamen; ~**'s residence**, onderwyserswoning; ~-**student**, kwekeling.
tea'-chest, teekis.
teach'ing, (n) onderwys; onderrig; leer; (a) onderwys=, onderwysend; ~ **aids**, leermiddele; ~ **experience**, onderwysondervinding; ~ **guide**, studiegids; ~ **post**, onderwysbetrekking; ~ **profession**, onderwysberoep, onderwysersamp; ~ **staff**, onderwyspersoneel, onderwysers, leerkragte.
tea: ~-**cloth**, teekleedjie; ~-**cosy**, teemus; teebeurs; ~ **cup**, teekoppie; *a storm in a* ~ *cup*, 'n storm in 'n glas water; 'n groot geraas oor niks; ~-**dealer**, teehandelaar; ~-**fight**, teeparty (geselst.); ~-**garden**, teetuin; ~-**gown**, namiddagjapon; ~-**house**, teehuis, kafee; ~ **interval**, elfuur, teepouse.
teak, Indiese kiaathout, djatihout *(Tectona grandis)*; *African* ~, Transvaalse kiaat *(Pterocarpus angolensis)*.
tea'-kettle, teeketel.
teak'-oil, meubelolie.
teal, rooibekeendjie; gevlekte eendjie; teeleendjie.
tea: ~-**lead**, teelood; ~-**leaf**, teeblaar.
team, (n) span; ploeg; bediening (kanon); (v) inspan; werk uitbestee, laat aanneem; ~-**event**, spannommer; ~ **spirit**, spangees; ~ **ster**, voerman, drywer; ~-**work**, samewerking, spanwerk; samespel.
tea: ~-**party**, teeparty(tjie); ~ **pot**, teepot; ~ **poy**, teetafeltjie.
tear¹, (n) traan, waterlander; *BATHED in* ~*s*, in trane swem; *BURST into* ~*s*, in trane uitbars; *IN* ~*s*, in trane; *it MOVES one to* ~*s*, dit beweeg mens tot trane; *shed* ~*s of REMORSE*, trane van berou stort; *SWIMMING in* ~*s*, betraan; *a TORRENT of* ~*s*, 'n tranevloed; *a VALE of* ~*s*, 'n tranedal;

tear², (n) skeur; *wear and* ~, slytasie; (v) **(tore, torn)**, skeur, verflenter; losruk; pluk, trek; jaag, storm; ~ *ALONG*, nael; ~ *AT*, ruk aan; ~ *oneself AWAY*, jou losskeur; *unable to* ~ *oneself AWAY*, nie kan wegkom nie; ~ *DOWN*, afskeur; ~ *FROM*, wegruk van; ~ *FROM the room*, uit die kamer jaag; ~ *oneself FROM*, jou losskeur van; ~ *one's HAIR*, jou hare uittrek; ~ *in HALF*, middeldeur skeur; ~ *OFF*, afskeur; wegnael; ~ *OPEN*, oopskeur; ~ *OUT*, uitskeur; ~ *out a PAGE*, 'n blad uitskeur; ~ *to PIECES*, stukkend skeur; ~ *into a ROOM*, die kamer instorm (binnestorm); ~ *up by the ROOTS*, met wortel en tak uittrek; *THAT'S torn it*, dit het die saak verbrou; ~ *down the STREET*, die straat afjaag.
tear: ~ **-bag**, traanklier; ~ **-bomb**, traanbom; ~ **-drop**, traan.
tear'er, skeurder.
tear: ~ **ful**, vol trane, tranerig, huilerig, treurig, betraan; ~ **-gas**, traangas, traanrook.
tear'ing, (n) skeur, skeuring; (a) heftig; wild; rasend; skeurend; *in a* ~ *RAGE*, rasend van woede; *at a* ~ *RATE*, in vlieënde vaart; ~ **machine**, rafelmasjien; ~ **pace**, vlieënde vaart; ~ **strength**, skeursterkte.
tear: **-jerker**, tranetrekker; ~ **less**, sonder trane; ~ **like**, tranerig.
tea: ~ **-room**, teekamer, kafee, koffiehuis; ~ **-rose**, teeroos.
tear: ~ **-shaped**, traanvormig; ~ **-shell**, traangranaat, traanbom; ~ **-stained**, betraan.
tea'-sales, teeverkopings, teeveilings.
tease, (n) kwelgees, terggees; (v) terg, pla; liemaak; kwel, versondig, sar, treiter, moveer; wolkam, pluis; pluiskam (hare); ~ *HAIR*, hare pluiskam, hare terugkam; ~ *the LIFE out of someone*, iem. se siel uittrek.
teas'el, pluisdistel; kammasjien, wolkam; ~ **er**, kaardster.
teas'er, plaer, treiteraar, plaaggees, koggelaar; kogelram, speelram; lastigheid; probleem; ~ **mail**, prikkelpos.
tea: ~ **-service**, ~ **-set**, teeservies; ~ **-ship**, teeskip; ~ **-shop**, kafee, koffiekamer, ~ **-shower**, teesprei, teesluier, teedoekie; ~ **-shrub**, teestruik.
teas'ing, kam (van wol); plaery, gejil, gesar, getorring; gefoeter; *FOND of* ~, plaagsiek, plaerig; *FONDNESS of* ~, plaagsug.
tea: ~ **spoon**, teelepel; ~ **spoonful**, teelepelvol; ~ **stain**, teevlek; ~ **-stall**, ~ **-stand**, teestalletjie ~ **-strainer**, teesiffie; ~ **-supply**, teevoorraad.
teat, tepel (mens); speen (dier); pram, tet (plat).
tea: ~ **-table**, teetafel; ~ **-taster**, teeproeër; ~ **-things**, teegoed; ~ **-time**, teetyd; ~ **-tray**, skinkbord; ~ **-trolley**, teewaentjie, ~ **-urn**, teekan; ~ **-wagon**, verdiepingtafeltjie, teewaentjie.
teaz'el, tea'zle = **teasel**.
tec, *abbr. of* **detective**, speurder.
tech'nical, tegnies; vak; ~ **dictionary**, tegniese woordeboek, vakwoordeboek; ~ **difficulty**, tegniese beswaar; ~ **hitch**, masjiensteurnis; ~ **'ity**, (..**ties**), tegniese onderskeiding, vakterm, ~ **journal**, vakblad; ~ **school**, ambagskool, vakskool; ~ **staff**, tegniese personeel; ~ **term**, vakterm; ~ **terminology**, vaktaal, vakterminologie.
techni'cian, tech'nicist, tegnikus.
tech'nicolour, kunskleur.
tech'nics, tegniek, tegnika.
technique', tegniek; *flying* ~, vliegstyl.
technoc'racy, tegnokrasie.
tech'nocrat, tegnokraat.
technocrat'ic, tegnokraties.
technolog'ical, tegnologies.
technol'ogy, tegnologie.
tecton'ic, boukundig; tektonies (geol.); ~ **s**, boukuns; tektoniek.
tec'tonite, tektoniet.
tector'ial, dek=, bedekkend.
tec'tric, (**tectri'ces**), dekveer.
ted, (-**ded**), oopkrap en omdraai, oopsprei, omkeer (hooi); ~ **der**, keerder, keermasjien.
tedd'ybear, speelbeertjie, kunsbeertjie, teddiebeer.
Tedd'y: ~ **boy**, skorrie; ~ **girl**, morrie.

Te De'um, Te Deum, danklied.
ted'ious, vervelig, lastig, langdradig, saai, seurderig, eentonig; gerek, vermoeiend, langwylig; ~ **ness**, verveligheid, vervelendheid, eentonigheid; ~ **person**, seurkous; ~ **voice**, seurstem.
ted'ium, verveligheid, verveling, vermoeienis, gerektheid, eentonigheid, saaiheid.
tee¹, (n) letter t; T-vormige voorwerp.
tee², (n) pen (platring); bof (gholf); doel; (v) pen, oppen; bof; ~ **off**, afslaan.
tee'-bolt, T-bout.
tee'-box, sandkissie, sandbakkie.
tee'ing: ~ **-disc**, bofskyfie; ~ **-ground**, bof(perk).
tee: ~ **-iron**, T-yster; ~ **-joint**, T-las.
teem¹, ledig, uitgooi (gesmelte staal).
teem², swanger wees; ter wêreld bring, baar; wemel, krioel; ~ *with*, wemel van; ~ **ing**, (n) gewemel; (a) swanger, dragtig (dier); vrugbaar; wemelend, krioelend; ~ *ing with*, wemel van, vergewe van.
teen¹, (n) verdriet, smart.
teen², (n) tien; ~ **-age (years)**, tiendeijare; ~ **-aged**, tienderjarig; *teenage party*, tienerparty..
teen'ager, tienderjarige, tiener.
teens, tienderjare (ouderdomsjare tussen 13 en 19); *in one's* ~, tussen dertien en negentien (jaar oud), in jou tienderjare.
teen'y, klein; ~ **-weeny**, baie klein.
teeth, *kyk* **tooth**.
teethe, tande kry.
tee'thing, (die) tande kry; ~ **-powder**, tandekrypoeier; ~ **-ring**, bytring; ~ **troubles**, aanvangsprobleme.
teetot'al, geheelonthouers=, afskaffers=; ~ **ism**, geheelonthouding; ~ **ler**, afskaffer, geheelonthouer, blouknoop.
teetot'um, dobbeltolletjie.
teff, tef.
teg, tweetandskaap.
teg'ular, dakpanagtig, teëlagtig; dakpanvormig, teëlvormig.
teg'ument, bedekking, deksel, vlies, huid, vel; ~ **ary**, vlies=, vel=.
tehee', (n) gegiggel; (v) giggel.
telearch'ics, teleargi, afstandsbeheer.
tel'ecast, (n) televisieuitsending, beeldsending; (v) (~), televiseer, beeldsend; ~ **er**, beeldsender, televisiesender.
telecommunica'tion, telekommunikasie.
tel'econtrol, afstandsbediening.
tel'egram, telegram, draadberig; *exchange of* ~ *s*, telegramwisseling; ~ **boy**, telegrambode; ~ **-carrier**, telegrambesteller; ~ **form**, telegramvorm.
tel'egraph, (n) telegraaf; *Minister of Posts and T* ~ *s*, Minister van Pos= en Telegraafwese; (v) telegrafeer, sein; **-apparatus**, telegraaftoestel; ~ **-cable**, telegraafkabel; ~ **company**, telegraafmaatskappy.
teleg'rapher, telegrafis; telegrafeerder.
telegraphese', telegramstyl.
telegraph'ic, telegrafies; ~ **address**, telegramadres.
teleg'raphist, telegrafis.
tel'egraph: ~ **line**, telegraaflyn; ~ **message**, telegram; ~ **messenger**, telegrambode, telegrambesteller; ~ **office**, telegraafkantoor; ~ **operator**, telegrafis; ~ **pole**, telegraafpaal; ~ **rates**, telegraaftarief; ~ **service**, telegraafdiens; ~ **system**, telegraafnet; telegraafstelsel; ~ **wire**, telegraafdraad.
teleg'raphy, telegrafie.
telemechan'ics, telemeganika.
telem'eter, afstandsmeter, telemeter.
telemet'ric, telemetries.
telem'etry, telemetrie.
teleolog'ic(al), teleologies.
teleol'ogy, teleologie.
telepath'ic, telepaties.
telep'athist, telepatis, telepaat.
telep'athy, telepatie.
tel'ephone, (n) telefoon; *ANSWER the* ~, die telefoon beantwoord; *BE on the* ~, 'n telefoon hê; telefonies verbind (aangesluit) wees; *BY* ~, oor die telefoon; *ON the* ~, telefonies; (v) telefoneer, (op)bel, skakel; ~ **(address) book**, telefoonboek, telefoongids; ~ **booth**, telefoonhokkie; ~ **box**, telefoonhokkie; ~ **cable**, telefoonkabel; ~ **call**, tele=

telephonic — **temporary**

foonoproep; ~ **connection,** telefoonverbinding, te=lefoonaansluiting; ~ **conversation,** telefoonge=sprek; ~ **directory,** telefoongids; ~ **exchange,** tele=foonsentrale; ~ **extension,** telefoonuitbreiding, by=lyn; ~ **girl,** telefoniste, telefoonjuffrou; ~ **mess=age,** telefoonberig; ~ **office,** telefoonkantoor; ~ **operator,** telefonis; ~ **pole,** telefoonpaal; ~ **re=ceiver,** telefoonhoring (-ontvanger); ~ **service,** te=lefoondiens; ~ **set,** telefoontoestel; ~ **staff,** tele=foonpersoneel; ~ **system,** telefoonnet; ~ **user,** tele=foongebruiker; ~ **wire,** telefoondraad.

telephon'ic, telefonies, telefoon=.
teleph'onist, telefonis; telefoonjuffrou.
teleph'ony, telefonie.
telephot'o, (-s), telefoto; ~ **lens,** telefotolens.
telephot'ograph, (n) telefoto; (v) telefotografeer.
telephotograph'ic, telefotografies.
telephotog'raphy telefotografie.
telepoint'er calculator, afstandsigrekenaar.
tel'eprinter, telekstoestel, druktelegraaf; ~ **ex=change,** telekssentrale; ~ **message,** teleksberig; ~ **operator,** teleksbediener.
tel'escope, (n) verkyker, teleskoop; (v) inmekaar=skuif, konsertina; ~ **table,** uittrektafel, inskuif=tafel.
telescop'ic, teleskopies; inskuifbaar; ~ **gate,** tele=skoophek; ~ **ladder,** teleskoopleer; ~ **rifle,** geweer met verkykervisier; ~ **sight,** visierkyker; ~ **star,** teleskopiese ster; ~ **wing,** uittrekvlerk, teleskopiese vlerk.
tel'escoping, ineenskuiwing; ~ *of gut,* knoopderm.
teletype': ~ **machine,** druktelegraaf; ~ **setter,** tele=drukker.
tel'eviewer, televisiekyker, TV-kyker, kassiekyker.
tel'evise, televiseer, beeldsend, beeldsaai.
televi'sion, televisie, beeldradio, kassie; *on* ~, oor te=levisie, oor die beeldradio, op die kassie; ~ **picture,** televisiebeeld; ~ **receiver,** televisieontvanger; ~ **re=ception,** beeldradio-ontvangs, televisieontvangs; ~ **set,** beeldradiotoestel, televisietoestel, kassie; ~ **transmitter,** televisiesender, beeldsender.
tele'writer, teleskrywer.
tel'ex, (n) (-es), teleks; (v) per teleks stuur; ~ **message,** teleksboodskap.
tell, (told), sê; vertel, meedeel, verhaal; meld, berig; onderrig; beveel; tel; onderskei; sien; verklik; uit=werking hê; indruk maak; *20 ALL told,* 20 alte=saam; *who CAN* ~? wie kan sê? wie weet? *DON'T* ~ *me that,* moenie my dit wysmaak nie! *I told him FLAT,* ek het hom definitief gesê; ~ *someone's FORTUNE,* iem. se toekoms voorspel; iem. skrob=beer; ~ *that to the MARINES,* maak dit aan die swape wys; *nobody can* ~ *ME that,* dit laat ek my nie vertel nie; dit laat ek my nie wysmaak nie; *you're* ~*ing ME,* weet ek dit nie! ek sou so dink! nou praat jy! net so; juis; ja, dis waar; *you NEVER can* ~, 'n mens kan nooit weet nie; 'n koei kan moontlik 'n haas vang; ~ *OFF,* berispe; tel; aan=wys; ~ *ON a person,* verklik; iem. aantas; jou uit=put; *every SHOT told,* elke skoot was raak; *I told you SO!* daar het jy dit! *I* ~ *you STRAIGHT,* ek sê jou reguit; *the STRAIN is beginning to* ~ *on him,* die spanning begin hom aantas; ~ *the TALE,* dit navertel; ~ *TALES,* uit die skool klap, verklik; ~ *someone a THING or two,* iem. roskam; iem. die leviete voorlees; *be able to* ~ *the TIME,* op die oor=losie kan kyk; *TIME will* ~, die tyd sal leer; ~ *the TRUTH,* die waarheid vertel; *be UNABLE to* ~ *the twins apart,* nie die tweeling uitmekaar ken nie; ~ *someone by his WALK,* iem. aan sy gang (manier van loop) herken; *WHAT dit I* ~ *you?* het ek jou nie gesê nie? daar het jy dit! ~ *someone WHAT you think of him,* iem. slegsê; iem. oor die kole haal; *he WON'T be told a thing,* hy laat hom niks wysmaak nie; ~ *the WORLD,* alles uitblaker; ~**er,** verteller, mededeler; kassier (bank); stempnemer; teller.
tell'ing, (n) (die) vertel; vertelling; *there is no* ~, nie=mand kan raai nie; **(a)** indrukwekkend, boeiend, treffend, pakkend; veeleisend; kragtig; raak (skote).
tell'ing-off, uitbrander, skrobbering; *give someone a* ~, iem. slegsê; iem. skrobbeer; iem. oor die kole haal.

tell'tale, (n) verklikker, nuusaandraer, klikspaan; toermeter (enjin); **(a)** verraderlik; verklikkend.
tellur'ian, (n) aardbewoner; **(a)** aards, aard=.
tellur'ic, telluries, aards.
tellur'ion, tellurium (instrument).
tellur'ium, telluur, tellurium (delfstof).
telluro'meter, tellurometer.
tel'pher, sweefbaan; lugkabelwaentjie; ~ **age,** lugka=belvervoer; ~ **line** lugkabellyn, sweefbaan; ~ **way,** sweefbaan.
Tem'bu, Temboe; ~ **land,** Temboeland.
temerar'ious, roekeloos, vermetel, astrant.
teme'rity, vermetelheid, astrantheid, roekeloosheid.
tem'per, (n) aard, temperament, gemoedsgesteldheid; stemming, humeur; opvlieëndheid, slegte luim; mengsel; hardheid; gaarheid (van metale); *be in a BAD* ~, in 'n slegte bui wees; *BE in a* ~, uit jou humeur wees; *HAVE a* ~, gou kwaad word, gou op jou perdjie wees; *he did it IN* ~, hy het dit in sy woede gedoen; *KEEP one's* ~, bedaard bly; *LOSE one's* ~, uit jou humeur raak; kwaad word; ~ *of MIND,* geestesgesteldheid; *OUT of* ~, uit jou hu=meur; kwaad; (v) vermeng; versag, matig; temper, hard maak (metaal); laat bedaar; aanmaak, brei (klei); tempereer (musiek); ~ *JUSTICE with mercy,* reg met genade versag; *God* ~*s the WIND to the shorn lamb,* God gee krag na kruis.
tem'pera, tempera.
tem'perament, gemoedsgesteldheid, temperament, aard.
temperamen'tal, temperamenteel; aangebore; onbe=heers, buierig; ~**ly,** van nature, van temperament.
tem'perance, matigheid; gematigdheid, soberheid; onthouding; ~ **drink,** alkoholvrye drank; ~ **hotel,** afskaffershotel; ~ **movement,** drankbestryding; matigheidsbeweging; ~ **society,** matigheidsge=nootskap; afskaffersbond.
tem'perate, matig, gematig, sober, getemper; bedaard; ~**ness,** gematigdheid; ~ **zone,** gematigde lugstreek.
tem'perature, warmtegraad, temperatuur; *AT a* ~ *of,* by 'n temperatuur van; *CHANGE of* ~, tempe=ratuurverandering; *DIFFERENCE in* ~, tempera=tuurverskil; *FALL in* ~, temperatuurverminde=ring; *FLUCTUATION in* ~, temperatuurskom=meling; *HAVE a* ~, koorsig wees; *MAINTAIN the* ~ *of,* op temperatuur hou; *RISE in* ~, tempera=tuurverhoging; *he is RUNNING a* ~, hy is koorsig; *TAKE the* ~ *of,* die koors meet van; ~ **chart,** tem=peratuurkaart; ~ **graph,** temperatuurkromme.
tem'pered, getemper, gehard; geaard, gehumeur(d); ~ **steel,** geharde (getemperde) staal.
tem'pest, onweer, storm, orkaan; uitbarsting; ~-**beaten,** deur storms gebeuk; ~-**tossed,** deur storms geteister.
tempes'tuous, stormagtig, onstuimig; ~**ness,** storm=agtigheid, onstuimigheid; ~ **weather,** stormweer.
Tem'plar[1]**,** Tempelier; *Good* ~, geheelonthouer.
tem'plar[2]**,** advokaat; student in die regte.
tem'plate, *kyk* **templet.**
tem'ple[1]**,** slaap (van kop).
tem'ple[2]**,** tempel; *BUILDING of a* ~, tempelbou; *CONSECRATION of a* ~, tempelwyding; *VIO=LATOR of a* ~, tempelskender; ~ **dancer,** tempel=danseres; ~ **flower,** frangipani; ~ **gate,** tempel=poort; ~ **service,** tempeldiens.
tem'plet, patroon, vormhout; maatplaat; kielwig; draagstuk (bouk.).
tem'po, (tempi), maat, tempo.
tem'poral[1]**, (n)** slaapbeen; **(a)** slaap=.
tem'poral[2]**, (a)** tyd=; tydelik, wêreldlik, sekulêr.
tem'poral: ~ **artery,** slaapslagaar; ~ **bone,** slaap=been.
tem'poral conjunction, voegwoord van tyd.
temporal'ity, (..ties), tydelikheid; (pl) wêreldse goed, temporalieë.
tem'poral power, wêreldlike mag.
tem'poralty, lekedom, wêreldlike stand.
tem'porarily, tydelik, voorlopig.
tem'porariness, tydelikheid.
tem'porary, tydelik, voorlopig, waarnemend; onbe=storwe; ~ **bridge,** noodbrug; voorlopige brug; ~

temporization 1297 **tenuity**

employment, tydelike werk; ~ **job,** tydelike pos; ~ **receipt,** voorlopige kwitansie; ~ **tooth,** wisseltand, melktand; ~ **unfitness,** tydelike ongeskiktheid.

temporiza'tion, gedaal, geskipper, uitstel; draadsittery.

tem'porize, die mantel na die wind hang; jou na die tydsomstandighede skik; sake tydelik skik; draal, uitstel, probeer tyd wen; skipper, 'n afwagtende houding aanneem; ~ **r,** tydwinner, draaier; weifelaar; weerhaan, draadsitter, manteldraaier.

te'mporizing, tydwins, geskipper, temporisasie.

tempt, in versoeking bring, verlei, uitlok, versoek, verlok; beproef; trotseer; ~ *the APPETITE,* die eetlus prikkel (wek); ~ *FATE,* die noodlot (gevaar) trotseer; ~ **able,** verleidelik; ~ **a'tion,** versoeking, verlokking, aanvegting, temptasie; *lead us not into* ~ *ation,* lei ons nie in versoeking nie; ~ **er,** verleier, versoeker, verlokker; ~ **ing,** (n) uitlokking, verleiding; (a) verleidelik, aanloklik; verloklik; ~ **ress, (-es),** verlokster, bekoorster.

temse, sif, gaatjiesbak.

tem'ulence, dronkenskap.

tem'ulent, dronk; dranksugtig.

ten, tien; *BY* ~ *s,* by tiene, in tientalle; *the* ~ *COMMANDMENTS,* die Tien Gebooie; ~ *to ONE,* tien teen een; *it is* ~ *to ONE that he will do it,* dit is hoogs (baie) waarskynlik dat hy dit sal doen; *the* ~ *TRIBES,* die tien stamme van Israel; *the UPPER* ~ , die elite, die hoëlui.

tenabil'ity, houbaarheid.

ten'able, houbaar; verdedigbaar; benutbaar (beurs); *the post is* ~ *for five years,* die dienstyd strek oor vyf jaar.

tena'cious, taai; hardnekkig, onversetlik, vashoudend; klewerig; *BE* ~ *of,* vashou aan; ~ *of LIFE,* vasklou aan die lewe; *have a* ~ *MEMORY,* 'n sterk geheue hê; ~ **ness, tena'city,** taaiheid; klewerigheid; volharding; hardnekkigheid.

ten'ancy, (..cies), huur, huurbesetting; pag; *period of* ~ , huurtermyn.

ten'ant, (n) huurder; pagter; bewoner; ~ *at will,* huurder sonder kontrak; (v) huur; in pag hê; bewoon; beset; ~ **able,** verhuurbaar; bewoonbaar (huis); ~ **farmer,** pagter, pagboer; ~ **less,** onverhuurd, leegstaande, onbewoon(d); ~ **ry,** huurders; gesamentlike pagters.

tench, seelt (vis).

tend¹, oppas, versorg, verpleeg, hoed; bedien (masjien); ~ *the sick and the wounded,* die siekes en gewondes verpleeg.

tend², geneig wees, 'n neiging toon; lei; strek, strewe; beweeg, gaan; bydra; ~ *to,* bydra tot; die neiging hê om.

ten'dency, (..cies), strekking, neiging; tendens, tendensie; aanleg; gesteldheid, stemming (van die mark); inslag; *have a* ~ *to,* oorhel na.

tenden'tious, strekkings=, tendensieus; doelgerig.

ten'der¹, (n) aanbod; inskrywing, tender, offerte; *GIVE out to* ~ , aanbestee; *INVITE* ~ *s,* inskrywings vra (afwag); *PUT up for* ~ , inskrywings vra; *SEND in a* ~ *for,* inskryf op; *a* ~ *in full SETTLEMENT,* 'n aanbod in volle betaling; *extend the VALIDITY of a* ~ , die geldigheid van 'n inskrywing verleng; (v) (aan)bied; inskrywe, 'n tender indien; ~ *and CONTRACT for,* tender en kontrakteer vir, aanbestee, aanneem; ~ *EVIDENCE,* getuienis aangebied; ~ *FOR,* inskryf op; tender vir; ~ *one's RESIGNATION,* jou bedanking indien; ~ *one's SERVICES,* jou dienste aanbied; ~ *THANKS,* dank uitspreek.

ten'der², (n) voorraadskip, geleiskip; kolewa (trein); sleepwa, aanhaakwa; moederskip (vliegtuie); landingsboot; adviesboot; betaalmiddel (finansies).

ten'der³, (a) sag, teer; gevoelig; tingerig, teergevoelig, week, fyn; pynlik; jonk; delikaat; mals, sag (vleis); *a* ~ *CONSCIENCE,* 'n teer gewete; *a* ~ *HEART,* 'n teer hart; ~ *MEAT,* sagte vleis; *the SKIN was* ~ , die vel was gevoelig; *a* ~ *SUBJECT,* 'n teer saak.

Ten'der Board, Tenderraad.

ten'derer, tenderaar, inskrywer.

ten'derfoot, nuweling, groentjie, rou riem.

ten'der: ~ **-hearted,** teerhartig, gevoelig, weekhartig;

~ **-heartedness,** teerhartigheid; ~ **ize,** sag maak; klop, beuk; ~ **izer,** sagmaakmiddel; vleisbeuker; ~ **ling,** troetelkind; ~ **loin,** lendestuk; beesfilet; ~ **-minded,** teerhartig; ~ **ness,** sagtheid, malsheid (van vleis); teerheid, teervoeligheid, weekheid.

ten'dinous, seningagtig.

ten'don, sening, pees.

ten'dril, (heg)rank; ~ **led,** met ranke.

Ten'ebrae, donker mette (R.K.).

tenebrif'ic, duistermakend, verdonkerend.

ten'ebrose, ten'ebrous, duister, donker.

ten'ement, paggoed; woning, woonhuis, verblyf; huurkamerhuis, huurkamers; huurgrond; erf; ~ **-house,** skakelhuis; deelhuis, versamelhuis.

ten'et, (leer)stelling, leerstuk; leer; beginsel ~ *of faith* leerstelsel.

ten: ~ **fold,** tienvoudig; ~ **ner,** tienrandnoot; tienpondnoot (hist.).

tenn'iquoit, ringtennis, dwergtennis.

tenn'is, tennis; *game of* ~ , tennisspel; ~ **-ball,** tennisbal; ~ **club,** tennisklub; ~ **-court,** tennisbaan.

tennisette', dwergtennis, minitennis, tenniset.

tenn'is: ~ **match,** tenniswedstryd; ~ **-partner,** tennismaat; ~ **-racquet,** tennisraket; ~ **-shoe,** tennisskoen; ~ **tournament,** tennistoernooi; ~ **wear,** tennisklere.

ten'on, (n) pen, tap; haak; (v) 'n tap maak; met 'n pen voeg; ~ **-joint,** tapvoeg; ~ **-saw,** tapsaag, rugsaag, voegsaag.

ten'or, gang, loop, rigting, inhoud; gees, strekking; afskrif; altviool; tenoor (stem); *the even* ~ *of one's life (days),* die kalme verloop van jou lewe (dae); ~ **clef,** tenoorsleutel.

ten'orite, tenoriet.

ten'or violin, altviool.

ten'-pounder, tienponder.

tense¹, (n) tyd (gram.); *future, past, present* ~ , toekomende, verlede, teenwoordige tyd.

tense², (v) span; (a) strak, styf; gespanne, gelaai; *become* ~ , verstrak; ~ **ly,** gespanne, gelaai; ~ **moment,** oomblik van spanning; ~ **ness,** strakheid, gespannenheid, geladenheid.

tensibil'ity, rekbaarheid, spanbaarheid.

ten'sible, rekbaar, spanbaar.

ten'sile, rekbaar; ~ **force,** spankrag; ~ **strength,** breekkrag, trekvastheid; ~ **stress,** trekspanning; ~ **test,** trektoets.

ten'sion, (n) spanning, rekking; spankrag; gespannenheid; opgewondenheid; inspanning; *LOW* ~ , laagspanning; *HIGH* ~ , hoogspanning; (v) span; ~ **-bar,** spanstaaf; ~ **-rod,** spanstang; ~ **-spring,** spanveer; ~ **stress,** trekspanning; pool, klem; ~ **test,** trektoets.

ten'sity, strakheid, gespannenheid.

ten'sive, spannend.

tensom'eter, spanningsmeter.

ten'sor, trekspier.

tent¹, (n) rooi wyn.

tent², (n) pluksel; (v) 'n wond met pluksel oophou.

tent³, (n) tent; kap (kar); (v) (in tente) kampeer; *DEVERMINIZING* ~ , ontduisingstent; *PITCH a* ~ , 'n tent opslaan; *STRIKE* ~ , die kamp afbreek; *STRIKE a* ~ , 'n tent afslaan.

ten'tacle, voelorgaan, tasorgaan, voelhoring, vangarm, voeler, tentakel.

tentac'ulate(d), met voelorgane.

ten'tative, (n) proefneming, poging; (a) voorlopig; by wyse van proef; tentatief; weifelend; versigtig.

tent: ~ **-bed,** veldbed; ~ **camp,** tentekamp; ~ **-cloth,** seil; ~ **-dweller,** tentbewoner; ~ **ed,** in tente.

ten'ter¹, (n) opsigter (van masjien).

ten'ter², (n) spanraam; spanhaak; (v) styf span, trek; ~ **er,** spanner; ~ **hook,** spanhaak; *be on* ~ *hooks,* op hete kole sit; ~ **ing,** spanproses.

tent' fly, tentklap; tentseil.

tenth, (n, a) tiende; ~ **ly,** in die tiende plek.

tent: ~ **-maker,** tentmaker; ~ **-peg,** tentpen; ~ **-pegging,** pensteek (ruiteroefening); ~ **-pin,** tentpen; ~ **-pole,** tentpaal; ~ **-shaped,** tentvormig; ~ **tortoise,** knoppiesdopskilpad.

ten'uis, (-es), tenuis.

tenu'ity, fynheid, ylheid, dunheid; eenvoud; tingerheid.

ten'uous, dun, tingerig, yl, swak; ~ **ness,** *kyk* **tenuity.**
ten'ure, eiendomsreg, besit; genot, bekleding; looptyd (van 'n lening); ~ *of LEASE,* looptyd van huur (bruikhuur); ~ *of LIFE,* lewensduur; ~ *of OFFICE,* diensttyd; ~ *at WILL,* huur sonder kontrak.
tepefac'tion, (die) loumaak; louwording.
tep'efy, (..**fied**), lou maak; lou word.
tep'id, lou; ~ '**ity,** ~ **ness,** louheid.
te'raphim, terafim, huisgode.
teratol'ogy, leer van wonders; studie van monstrositeite, teratologie.
terce, *kyk* **tierce.**
ter'cel, mannetjiesvalk.
tercen'tenary, (n) (..**ries**), derde eeufees, drie-eeuefees; (a) driehonderdjarig.
ter'cet, terset (in sonnet); tersine (in lang gedig).
te'rebinth, terpentynboom; *oil of* ~, terpentynolie; ~ '**ine,** terpentynagtig, terpentyn=.
tered'o, (-s), paalwurm.
terg'al, rug=.
ter'giversate, draai, uitvlugte soek, afvallig word.
tergiversa'tion, draaiery, uitvlugte, jakkalsdraaie, afvalligheid.
ter'giversator, afvallige; bontspringer.
term, (n) termyn, diensttyd; straftyd; sitting; term; duur; kwartaal; woord; uitdrukking; bepaling, voorwaarde; perk, grens; lid; (pl) voorwaardes; verstandhouding; *in* ~ *s of the ACT,* kragtens (ooreenkomstig, ingevolge) die wet; *not on ANY* ~ *s,* onder geen voorwaardes nie; glad nie; *BRING someone to* ~ *s,* iem. dwing om voorwaardes aan te neem; *BUY on* ~ *s,* op afbetaling koop; *COME to* ~ *s,* dit eens word; tot 'n vergelyk kom; *on* ~ *s and CONDITIONS,* onder (op) bepalings en voorwaardes; ~ *of COURT,* hoftermyn; *DURING* ~, in die sittingstyd; *DURING the* ~, gedurende die kwartaal; *on EASY* ~ *s,* op maklike betalingsvoorwaardes; *on EQUAL* ~ *s,* op voet van gelykheid; op gelyke voet; *be on EVEN* ~ *s,* niks op mekaar voorhê nie; *in the most FLATTERING* ~ *s,* in die vleiendste bewoording; *in GENERAL* ~ *s,* in algemene bewoording; *on GOOD* ~ *s,* op goeie voet; *be on GOOD* ~ *s with someone,* op goeie voet met iem wees; *speak in the HIGHEST* ~ *s of,* met die hoogste lof praat van; ~ *of IMPRISONMENT,* straftyd; gevangenistermyn; *IN* ~ *s of,* ooreenkomstig, luidens; *on* ~ *s of INTIMACY,* op vertroulike voet; ~ *s of LEASE,* verhuurvoorwaardes; ~ *of LIFE,* lewensduur; *MAKE* ~ *s,* tot 'n vergelyk kom; ~ *s of MONTHLY,* maandeliks betaalbaar; ~ *of OFFICE,* diensttyd; ~ *s of PAYMENT,* betalingsvoorwaardes; *in PLAIN* ~ *s,* ronduit; *REDUCE to the lowest* ~ *s,* ('n breuk) verklein; soveel moontlik vereenvoudig; ~ *s of REFERENCE,* opdrag; perke van ondersoek; *REMAIN on good* ~ *s with someone,* op goeie voet met iem. bly; iem. tot vriend hou; *SERVE one's* ~, jou tyd uitdien; *not on SPEAKING* ~ *s,* nie met mekaar praat nie; *in the STRONGEST* ~ *s,* in die kragtigste bewoording; *TECHNICAL* ~ *s,* vakterm, tegniese term; *for a* ~ *of YEARS,* vir 'n bepaalde aantal jare; (v) noem, benoem.
term'agancy, twissug, kyfagtigheid.
term'agant, (n) feeks, rusiemaakster, helleveeg, rissie, heks, kat, geitjie; (a) kyfagtig, rusiemakerig, raserig.
term'inable, begrensbaar, bepaalbaar; aflosbaar (verband); opsegbaar (kontrak); aflopend (jaargeld).
term'inal, (n) uiterste, einde, eindpunt; end; endvlak; endstasie; terminaal; pool, klem (elek.); (a) grens=; slot=, end=; uiterste; kwartaals; termyn=; ~ **account,** termynrekening; ~ **aerodrome,** endvliegveld; ~ **bud,** eindknop; ~ **dive,** endduik; ~ **leaflet,** eindblaartjie; ~ **pressure,** enddrukking; ~ **rhyme,** endrym; ~ **speed,** endsnelheid; ~ **station,** endstasie; ~ **statue,** grensbeeld; ~ **subscription,** periodieke betaling; termynbetaling; ~ **syllable,** eindsillabe; slotlettergreep; ~ **value,** eenvoudigste vorm; eindwaarde; ~ **velocity,** eindsnelheid; ~ **voltage,** klemspanning.

term'inate, begrens; end, eindig, afloop; beëindig, 'n end maak aan, opsê (kontrak); ~ *a CONTRACT,* 'n kontrak opsê; ~ *IN,* eindig op, uitloop op.
termina'tion, (end)begrensing; slot, end, einde; beëindiging; afbreking; uitgang; *BRING to a* ~, ten einde laat loop; *PUT a* ~ *to,* 'n end maak aan.
term'inating decimal, eindigende desimaal.
term'inator, beëindiger, opsêer; beligtingsgrens.
terminolog'ical, terminologies; ~ *inexactitude,* onjuistheid, onnoukeurigheid, afwyking v.d. waarheid.
terminol'ogy, (vak)terminologie; *technical* ~, vakterminologie, vaktaal.
ter'minus, (-es, ..**ni**), eindpunt, eindhalte, endstasie, terminus.
term'ite, rysmier, termiet.
term'less, grensloos, eindeloos.
tern[1], (n) sterretjie.
tern[2], (n) terne (lotery); (a) drietallig, drievoudig.
tern'ary, (n) (..**ries**), drietal; (a) drietallig.
tern'ate, driedelig, drie-drie.
Terpsichore'an, van Terpsichore, dans=; ~ **art,** danskuns.
te'rra, aarde; ~ *FIRMA,* terra firma, vaste grond; *set foot on* ~ *FIRMA,* weer op vaste grond wees; ~ *INCOGNITA,* terra incognita, onbekende land.
te'rrace, (n) terras; (v) terrasse maak, terrasseer; ~ **d,** terrasvormig; ~ *d garden,* terrastuin.
te'rracing grad'er, terrasgooier.
terra-cott'a, terra-cotta.
terrain', terrein.
terran'eous, land=.
te'rrapin, varswaterskilpad.
terra'queous, uit land en water bestaande.
terrar'ium, (..**ria**), terrarium.
terraz'zo, terrazzo.
terrene', aards, van die grond.
terres'trial, (n) aardbewoner; (a) aards, land=, ondermaans; ~ **animal,** landdier; ~ **deposit,** landafsetting; ~ **globe,** die aardbol, die globe; ~ **magnetism,** aardmagnetisme.
te'rret, leiselring.
te'rrible, verskriklik, yslik, vreeslik, skrikbarend; ~ **ness,** verskriklikheid, vreeslikheid.
te'rribly, vreeslik, verskriklik, ontsettend, geweldig.
ter'ricole, (n) grondbewoner; (a) grondbewonend.
terri'colous, grondbewonend.
te'rrier, Terriër.
terrif'ic, verskriklik, skrikwekkend; ontsettend.
te'rrified, bang, verskrik; ~ *AT the thought of,* verskrik deur die gedagte aan; ~ *BY threats,* bang wees vir dreigemente; ~ *OF a fierce dog,* bang vir 'n kwaai hond.
te'rrify, (..**fied**), verskrik, skok, bang maak, laat skrik; ~ *to DEATH,* doodbang maak; ~ *INTO,* deur skrikaanjaging bring tot; ~ **ing,** skrikwekkend, skrikbarend, skrikaanjaend.
terri'genous, aard=, grond=.
te'rrit = **terret.**
territor'ial, (n) landweersoldaat, landweerman; (a) territoriaal; grond=; landweer=; ~ **army,** gebiedsmag; landweer; ~ **authority,** gebiedsowerheid; ~ **expansion,** gebiedsuitbreiding; ~ **force,** landweer.
territorial'ity, territorialiteit.
territor'ial: ~ **ize,** territoriaal maak, die grense uitbrei; ~ **right,** territoriale reg; ~ **separation,** gebiedskeiding; ~ **waters,** territoriale waters, gebiedswaters.
te'rritory, (..**ries**), gebied, grondgebied; bodem; landstreek; *SURRENDER of* ~, gebiedsafstand; *VIOLATION of* ~, gebiedskending.
te'rror, skrik, ontsteltenis, angs, verskrikking, skrikbeeld; lastige persoon, onnut; *FLY in* ~ *of the earthquake,* vlug uit vrees vir die aardbewing; *the KING of T* ~ *s,* die koning van verskrikkinge, die dood; *the* ~ *of the NEIGHBOURHOOD,* die skrik v.d. buurt; *REIGN of* ~, skrikbewind; *the REIGN of T* ~, die skrikbewind; *TO the* ~ *of,* tot skrik van; *a* ~ *for WORK,* 'n regte werkesel; ~ **ism,** skrikbewind; terrorisme; ~ **ist,** terroris; ~ **iza'tion,** skrikaanjaging; terrorisering; ~ **ize,** skrik aanjaag, bang

maak; terroriseer; ~-**smitten**, ~-**stricken**, ~-**struck**, met skrik vervul, paniekerig, doodbang.
te'rry, handdoekgoed.
terse, beknop, bondig, kernagtig, gedronge, sinryk; ~**ly**, beknop; ~**ness**, beknoptheid, kortheid, sinrykheid.
ter'tian, (n) derdedaagse koors; (a) anderdaags, derdedaags; ~ **fever**, derdedaagse koors.
ter'tiary, (n) (..ries), tersiêre formasie; (a) van die derde orde, tersiêr; ~ **education**, tersiêre onderwys.
ter'tius, derde (van 'n bepaalde naam), tertius.
terza rim'a, tersine.
terzett'o, terset, driesang.
tessel'la, mosaïekblokkie, mosaïeksteentjie.
tess'ellar, geruit; ingelê, mosaïekagtig.
tess'ellated, geruit; mosaïek=.
tessella'tion, ingelegde werk, mosaïek.
tess'era, (-e), mosaïekblokkie, teëltjie, steentjie.
test¹, (n) dop, skaal (skilpad).
test², (n) toetssteen; toets, proef; smeltkroes; reagens (chem.); meting; toets(wedstryd); skulp; saadhuid; *the ACID* ~, die vuurproef; *CARRY out a* ~, toets; *PUT to the* ~, op die proef stel; ~ *of SKILL*, vaardigheidstoets; *STAND the* ~, die proef (toets) deurstaan; *SUBJECT to a severe* ~, aan 'n streng toets onderwerp; (v) toets, beproef, ondersoek, keur; probeer; op die proef stel; invlieg (vliegtuig); ~ *a pupil in HISTORY*, 'n leerling in geskiedenis toets; ~ *a pupil on his KNOWLEDGE of the Bible*, 'n leerling se Bybelkennis toets; ~**able**, toetsbaar; bemaakbaar.
testa'cea, skaaldiere; ~**n**, (n) skaaldier; (a) skaaldier=.
testa'ceous, met 'n harde dop, skaal-; skulp=; rooibruin, geelbruin.
tes'tacy, nalating van 'n testament.
test' aeroplane, proefvliegtuig, toetsvliegtuig.
test'ament, testament, wilsbeskikking; ~**'ary**, testamentêr.
testam'ur, getuigskrif; sertifikaat.
tes'tate, wat 'n testament nalaat.
testa'tion, erflating.
testat'or, erflater, testateur.
testat'rix, (..trices), testatrise, erflaatster.
test: ~ **case**, toetssaak; ~-**check**, steekproef; ~-**cock**, toetskraan; ~**ed**, beproef; probaat; *a* ~ *ed remedy*, 'n probate (beproefde) middel; ~-**field**, proefveld, toetsveld; ~ **flight**, proefvlug, toetsvlug; ~-**glass**, reageerbuis.
tes'ter¹, toetser.
tes'ter², baldakyn, (ledekant)hemel; klankbord.
tes'ticle, teelbal, saadbal, knater, peer.
testic'ular, **testic'ulate**, balvormig.
testifica'tion, betuiging; getuienis.
tes'tifier, getuie.
tes'tify, (..fied), getuig; plegtig verklaar; getuienis aflê; ~ *AGAINST a person*, getuienis aflê teen 'n persoon; ~ *TO*, getuig van.
test'ily, knorrig, prikkelbaar.
testimon'ial, getuigskrif, huldeblyk; attestaat, attes, attestasie; ~**ize**, 'n huldeblyk aanbied; 'n getuigskrif gee.
tes'timony, (..nies), getuienis, betuiging, verklaring; die Tien Gebooie; bewys; *BEAR* ~ *to*, getuig van; *CALL in* ~, tot getuie roep; *ON the* ~ *of*, volgens die verklaring van; *PRODUCE* ~ *of*, bewys lewer van; *the TABLES of the* ~, die Tien Gebooie.
test'iness, knorrigheid, prikkelbaarheid.
test'ing, toets(ing), meting, keuring; beproewing; (die) probeer; ~-**bench**, proefbank; ~-**instrument**, proefinstrument; ~-**range**, proefskietbaan; ~ **right**, toetsingsreg.
test: ~-**lesson**, proefles; ~ **match**, toets(wedstryd); ~-**message**, proefberig; ~ **paper**, reageerpapier; proefwerk; ~ **pilot**, invlieër, proefvlieër, toetsvlieënier; ~-**point**, proefpunt; ~ **team**, toetsspan, landspan; ~-**trip**, proefrit; ~-**tube**, reageerbuisie, proefglasie, proefbuisie; ~-**tube baby**, proefbuisbaba; ~-**type**, toetsletters, letters om gesigskerpte te toets.
testud'inal, skilpad=.

testudinar'ious, **testudin'eous**, skilpadagtig; skilpaddopvormig; skilpaddopagtig.
testud'o, (-s, **testudines**), skilpad; stormdak, skilddak, testudo.
tes'ty, gemelik, prikkelbaar, liggeraak, kortgebonde, wrewelig.
tetan'ic, klem=, kramp=, tetanus=.
tet'anus, kramp, wondkramp, tetanus, kaakklem, klem-in-die-kaak, styfkramp.
tetch'iness, knorrigheid, gemelikheid, liggeraaktheid.
tetch'y, knorrig, gemelik, liggeraak.
tête'-à-tête', (n) gesprek onder vier oë, privaat gesprek, tête-à-tête; tweepersoonsrusbank; (a, adv) onder vier oë, privaat, tête-à-tête.
teth'er, (n) spantou; looptou; speelruimte; *it is BEYOND his* ~, dis bokant sy vuurmaakplek; *be at the END of one's* ~, gedaan wees; jou rieme styfgeloop hê; ten einde raad wees; *have COME to the end of one's* ~, jou rieme styfloop; wurg; (v) span; op tou slaan, lynslaan; kniehalter.
tet'ra: ~ **chord**, viersnarige instrument; ~**d**, viertal; ~**dac'tyle**, viervingerig; met vier tone; ~**gon**, vierhoek; ~**g'onal**, vierhoekig; ~**gram**, vierletterwoord; vierhoek; ~**hed'ral**, viersydig, viervlakkig; ~**hed'ron**, viervlak, tetraëder.
tetral'ogy, (..gies), tetralogie.
tetram'erous, vierdelig.
tetram'eter, viervoetige versreël.
tetrapet'alous, vierkroonbladig.
tet'rapod, (n) vierpotige (insek); (a) vierpotig.
tetrapod'ic, viervoetig (vers).
tetrap'odous, vierpotig.
tetrap'terous, viervlerkig.
tet'rarch, viervors; ~**y**, (..chies), viervorstedom.
tetrasperm'ous, viersadig.
tet'rastich, vierreëlig; met vier versies.
tetrasyllab'ic, vierlettergrepig.
tetrasyll'able, vierlettergrepige woord.
tett'er, douwurm, omloop, roos.
Teut'on, Teutoon; Germaan; ~**'ic**, Teutoons; Germaans; ~**ism**, Germanisme; Duitse gees; ~**ize**, germaniseer, verduits.
text, teks; skriftuurplaas; onderwerp; *stick to one's* ~, nie afdwaal nie; jou by jou teks hou; ~**book**, handboek, handleiding, leerboek; ~-**hand**, grootskrif.
tex'tile, (n) weefstof, tekstielstof; (pl) tekstielware; (a) geweef, tekstiel=, weef=; ~ **fibre**, tekstielvesel; ~ **mill**, wewery.
text'ual, teks=, tekstueel; woordelik; ~ **criticism**, tekskritiek; ~**ist**, teksgeleerde, skrifgeleerde, Bybelkenner.
tex'ture, weefsel; tekstuur; struktuur; samestelling, bou.
thal'amus, (..mi), vrouekamer, binnekamer; blombodem; talamus (anat.).
thall'ium, tallium.
thallo'phyte, loofplant, tallofiet.
Thames, Teems; *he won't SET the* ~ *on fire*, hy sal nie baie uitrig nie; hy het nie die buskruit uitgevind nie; *SET the* ~ *on fire*, opslen baar.
than, as, dan; *she is a BETTER housewife* ~ *a singer*, sy blink meer uit as huisvrou dan as sanger; *it is better to use HOT water* ~ *cold*, dit is beter om warm as koue water te gebruik; *a MAN* ~ *whom no one is better able to judge*, 'n man wat die beste bevoeg is om te oordeel; *you are TALLER* ~ *he*, jy is langer as hy; *you TRUST him more* ~ *me*, jy vertrou hom meer as vir my.
than'age, rang, amp.
than'atoid, skynbaar dood, doods; dodelik.
thanatophob'ia, doodsvrees.
thane, leenman, edelman.
thank, dank, bedank, dankie sê; ~ *GOD*, God sy dank; ~ *the LORD*, dank sy die Heer; ~ *you very MUCH*, baie dankie; ~ *you for NOTHING!* dank jou die duiwel; ~ *one's STARS*, dankiebly wees; van geluk kan praat; ~ *YOU*, dankie; *I got SMALL* ~ *s*, ek het stank vir dank gekry; ~**ful**, dankbaar; erkentlik; ~**fulness**, dankbaarheid, erkentlikheid; ~**ing**, dankende, met dank; ~*ing you in anticipation*, by voorbaat hartlik dank; ~**less**,

ondankbaar; onerkentlik; ~ **lessness**, ondankbaarheid; onerkentlikheid; ~**-offering**, dankoffer.

thanks, dankie; dankbetuiging, dankwoord; ~ *AWFULLY*, baie dankie; ~ *to your EFFORTS*, danksy jou pogings; *HEARTY* ~, hartlik dank; *LETTER of* ~, skriftelike dankbetuiging; *MANY* ~, baie dankie; ~ *so MUCH*, dankie tog; ~ *very MUCH*, baie dankie; *NO* ~, nee dankie; ~ *for NOTHING!* dank jou die duiwel; ~ *to your OBSTINACY*, danksy jou koppigheid; *RECEIVED with my* ~, met dank ontvang; *RENDER* ~, dank betuig; *RETURN* ~, dank; *with my SINCERE* ~, met my opregte dank; *I got SMALL* ~, ek het stank vir dank gekry; ~ *TO*, te danke aan; *VOTE of* ~, mosie van dank; ~ *to YOU*, deur jou toedoen.

thanks'giving, danksegging; ~ **day**, dankdag; ~ **service**, dankdiens.

thank: ~**-offering**, dankoffer; ~**worthy**, dankenswaardig.

that, (pron) (**those**), dit; dié, daardie; wat; *AFTER* ~, daarna; *AGAINST* ~, daarteenoor; *AS to* ~, wat dit betref; *AT* ~, daarop; *he is not as BAD as all* ~, so sleg is hy nie; ~ *which has BEEN*, dit wat verby is; *BEFORE* ~, voor die tyd; *FOOL* ~ *I was*, dwaas wat ek was; ~ *IS*, dit wil sê; ~ *IS* ~, dis tot daarnatoe; genoeg daarvan; daar is verder niks op te sê nie; *who is* ~ *LAUGHING?* wie lag daar? *LIKE* ~, so; *a shoemaker and a POOR one at* ~, 'n skoenmaker en nogal 'n slegte een; *PUT this and* ~ *together*, bring die dinge met mekaar in verband; ~ *'s RIGHT*, so is dit; *SO* ~ *'s* ~, nou is die saak in orde; *THIS*, ~ *and the other*, alles en nog wat; *UPON* ~, daarop; *Mrs. A (Miss C* ~ *WAS)*, mev. A, gebore mej. C.; ~ *WHICH has been*, wat gewees het; wat was; *WITH* ~, daarmee; (a, adv) soveel, sodanig; so; *my hands were* ~ *COLD*, my hande was so erg koud; *he has* ~ *CONFIDENCE in his brother*, hy het soveel vertroue in sy broer; *in* ~ *DIRECTION*, soontoe; *in* ~ *WAY*, op daardie manier; (conj) dat, sodat, opdat; *not* ~ *I don't CARE*, nie dat ek nie omgee nie; *not* ~ *I KNOW of*, nie sover ek weet nie; *I'm not all* ~ *OLD*, ek is darem nog nie so oud nie.

thatch, (n) dekgras, dekstrooi, dekriet; grasdak, strooidak, rietdak; (v) dek; ~*ed HOUSE*, strooidakhuis, grasdakhuis, rietdakhuis; ~*ed ROOF*, grasdak, strooidak, rietdak; ~**er**, dekker; ~**-grass**, dekgras.

thatch'ing, dek; dekstrooi; ~ **grass**, dekgras; ~ **lath**, deklat; ~ **needle**, deknaald; ~ **spade**, dekspaan; ~ **straw**, dekstrooi.

thatch: ~ **roof**, grasdak, strooidak, rietdak, matjiesdak; ~ **spade**, dekspaan.

thaum'atrope, draaiende skyf, wonderwiel.

thaum'aturge, wonderdoener; towenaar; ..**tur'gic**, wonderdoenend; ..**tur'gist**, wonderdoener; ..**tur'gy**, wonderdoenery; towerkuns.

thaw, (n) ontdooiing; dooi, dooiweer; (v) smelt, dooi (sneeu); ontdooi, hartliker word.

the, die; ~ *more so BECAUSE*, des te meer omdat; ~ *more* ~ *MERRIER*, hoe meer siele hoe meer vreugde; *all* ~ *MORE reason why you should*, soveel meer rede waarom u behoort; ~ *MORE so as*, te meer daar; *we are* ~ *POORER for his departure*, sy vertrek maak ons armer; ~ *SOONER* ~ *better*, hoe eerder hoe beter.

the'archy, teokrasie, godsregering.

the'atre, teater, skouburg; toneel; saal, operasiekamer; ~ *of OPERATIONS*, die operasieterrein; ~ *of WAR*, die oorlogstoneel; ~**-goer**, skouburgbesoeker, teaterbesoeker; ~**-going**, teaterbesoek, skouburgbesoek; skouburgbesoekende; *the* ~*-going public*, die skouburgpubliek; die teaterpubliek; ~**-land**, teaterwêreld, toneelwêreld, skouburgwêreld; ~**-mad**, skouburgmal; ~ **manager**, skouburgdirekteur; teaterbestuurder; ~ **sister**, teatersuster, operasiesuster.

theat'rical, (n) toneelvoorstelling, opvoering; (pl) die toneel; (a) toneel=; toneelagtig, teater=; teatraal; aanstellerig; *private (amateur)* ~*s*, amateurtoneel, liefhebberytoneel; ~ **company**, toneelgeselskap,

skouburggeselskap; ~**'ity**, toneelaangeleentheid; aanstellerigheid; teatrale vertoon; ~ **world**, teaterwêreld, toneelwêreld, skouburgwêreld.

Theb'an, (n) Thebaan; (a) Thebaans.

thee, u.

theft, diefstal; stelery, diewery.

the'ic, teesuiper; ~**ism**, teesuipery.

the'ine, teïen, teïne.

their, hulle, hul; ~**s**, hulle s'n.

the'ism, teïsme.

the'ist, teïs; ~ **'ic(al)**, teïsties.

them, hulle.

themat'ic, tematies.

theme, onderwerp, tema; opstel; oefening; woordstam.

themselves', hul(le)self; hul(le) self; hulle self; *they know it* ~, hulle weet dit self.

then, (a) destyds, toenmalig; *the* ~ *administrator*, die toenmalige administrateur; (adv) dan, toe, toentertyd, toenmaals, daarna, vervolgens; *BEFORE* ~, voor daardie tyd; *BY* ~, dan, teen daardie tyd; *FROM* ~, van toe af; *NOW and* ~, af en toe, nou en dan; *every NOW and* ~, so af en toe; *and ONLY* ~, en slegs dan; *SINCE* ~, sedert (van) dié tyd; *it must* ~ *SOAK for one hour*, daarna moet dit een uur week; ~ *and THERE*, op staande voet, onmiddellik; *TILL* ~, tot dan, tot dié tyd; *not UNTIL* ~, toe (dan) eers; (conj) dus, dan; ~ *it is no use your going*, dan het dit geen sin dat jy gaan nie.

then'al, handpalm=; voetsool=.

then'ar, handpalm; voetsool; duimbal, duimkussinkie.

thence, daarvandaan, van toe af, vandaar; heen; daaruit, daardeur; *(from)* ~ *we went to L.*, van daar het ons na L. gegaan; ~**forth**, ~**forward**, van dié tyd af, sedert dié tyd.

theocent'ric, teosentries.

theoc'racy, (..**cies**), teokrasie, godsregering, godsbestuur.

theocrat'ic, teokraties.

theod'icy, (..**cies**), teodisee.

theod'olite, teodoliet.

theog'ony, (..**nies**), geslagsregister van die gode, teogonie.

theolo'gian, godgeleerde, teoloog.

theolo'gical, godgeleerd, teologies.

theol'ogize, teologiseer.

theol'ogy, (..**gies**), godgeleerdheid, teologie.

theoph'any, teofanie.

theorb'o, (**-s**), teorbe, basluit.

the'orem, stelling, teorema.

theoret'ic, teoreties; ~ **al**, teoreties; ~ **al examination**, ~ **test**, teoretiese eksamen (toets); ~ **ally**, teoreties, in teorie; ~ **s**, teorie.

the'orist, teoretikus.

the'orize, teoretiseer; bespiegelinge maak.

the'ory, (..**ries**), teorie; boekwysheid; ~ *of CHANCES*, kansrekening; ~ *of EVOLUTION*, evolusieteorie; *IN* ~, in teorie; ~ *of MUSIC*, musiekteorie; ~ *of RADIATION*, stralingsteorie.

theos'opher, teosoof.

theosoph'ic(al), teosofies.

theos'ophist, teosoof.

theos'ophy, teosofie.

therapeut'ic, genesend; geneeskundig, terapeuties; ~**s**, geneeskuns, geneeswyse, geneeskunde, terapie.

therapeut'ist, geneeskundige, terapeut.

ther'apist, terapeut.

the'rapy, geneeskuns, geneeswyse, terapie; *occupational* ~, beroepsterapie.

there, daar, daarso; daarheen, daarnatoe, soheen, soontoe; aldaar; *he is ALL* ~, hy is nie onder 'n kalkoen uitgebroei nie; *he is not ALL* ~, hy het nie al sy varkies in die hok nie; *I AGREE with you* ~, op daardie punt is ek dit met jou eens; ~ *AND* ~, daar en daar; ~ *you ARE*, daar is dit; daar het jy dit; ~ *and BACK*, heen en terug; uit en tuis; *FROM* ~, daarvandaan; ~ *is GLORY for you*, dit noem ek nou roem; *you have me* ~, daar het jy my vas; *HERE and* ~, hier en daar; *but* ~ *it IS*, dis nou eenmaal so; *he LEFT* ~ *last night*, hy het gister=

aand daarvandaan (van daar) vertrek; *NEAR* ~, daar naby; *OVER* ~, daar oorkant; *SO* ~! en nou weet jy dit! ~ *and THEN*, op staande voet, op die plek, op die daad, onmiddellik, dadelik; *UP* ~, daar bo; ~ **about'**, omtrent daardie tyd; ~ **abouts'**, daar iewers, daaromtrent; so naasteby, omtrent; ~ **af'ter**, daarna; daarvolgens; ~ **among'**, daartussen, daaronder; ~ **anent'**, wat dit betref, daaromtrent; ~ **at'**, daar.

there'by, daardeur, op dié manier; ~ *hangs a tale*, in verband hiermee is daar 'n hele geskiedenis.

there: ~ **fore**, daarom, dus, gevolglik, bygevolg, derhalwe, mitsdien, ergo; ~ **from'**, daarvandaan; ~ **in'**, daarin; ~ **inaf'ter**, daarna; ~ **inbefore'**, daarvoor; ~ **of'**, daarvan; hiervan; ~ **on'**, daarop; ~ **to'**, daartoe, daaraan; daarby, boonop; ~ **tofore'**, tevore, vroeër; ~ **un'der**, daaronder; ~ **un'to**, daartoe, daarby; ~ **upon'**, daarop, daarna; ~ **with'**, daarmee; ~ **withal'**, daarby, bowendien, buitendien.

ther'iac, teëgif.

theriomorph'ic, teriomorfies, diervormig.

therm, warmte-eenheid, term; ~ **ae**, warmbronne; warmwaterbaaie.

therm'al, termaal, warm, warmte=, termies; ~ *ANALYSIS*, termiese ontleding; ~ *BATHS*, warmwaterbaaie, warmbronne; ~ *CAPACITY*, soortlike warmte, warmtekapasiteit; ~ *CONDUCTION*, warmtegeleiding; ~ *CONDUCTIVITY*, warmtegeleidingsvermoë; ~ *EFFICIENCY*, termiese nuttige effek; ~ *EXPANSION*, warmteuitsetting; ~ *RADIATION*, warmtebestraling; ~ *SPRING*, warmbron; ~ *STRESS*, hittespanning; ~ *UNIT*, warmte-eenheid.

therman'tidote, waaier.

therm'ic, warmte=, termies.

thermobarom'eter, termobarometer.

thermocau'tery, hittechirurgie.

thermochem'ical, termochemies.

thermochem'ist, termochemikus.

thermochem'istry, termochemie.

thermodynam'ic, termodinamies.

thermodynam'ics, termodinamika.

thermoelec'trical, termo-elekties.

thermoelectric'ity, warmte-elektrisiteit, termo-elektrisiteit.

thermogen'esis, warmteverwekking, termogenese.

thermogenet'ic, warmteverwekkend, termogeen.

therm'ograph, termograaf.

thermog'raphy, termografie.

thermom'eter, termometer; warmtemeter; koorspennetjie; ~ **reading**, termometerstand.

thermomet'ric(al), termometries.

thermom'etry, termometrie.

thermophil'ic, hitteliefhebbend, termofiel.

thermoplas'tic, termoplasties; ~ **s,** termoplastika.

therm'oscope, termoskoop.

therm'ostat, termostaat; ..**stat'ic,** termostaties.

thermothe'rapy, termoterapie, warmtebehandeling.

thermot'ropism, termotropisme.

ther'oid, dieragtig, dier=.

thesaur'us, tesourus, woordeboek; skatkamer.

these, hierdie, dié; *kyk* **this;** ~ *ten years and more*, al meer as tien jaar.

thes'is, (theses), stelling; tesis; proefskrif; verhandeling; dissertasie.

Thes'pian, (n) toneelspeler, toneelspeelster; (a) T(h)espies; dramaties, tragies; ~ *art*, dramatiese kuns.

theur'gist, towenaar.

the'urgy, wonderwerk, wonderkrag; towerkuns.

thew, (**d**), gespier(d), sterk; ~ **less**, sonder spiere; ~**s,** krag, spiere; geeskrag; *be all* ~ *s and sinews*, murg in jou pype hê; van yster en staal wees; ~ **y,** gespier(d), sterk.

they, hulle, hul; ~ *SAY*, dit (daar) word gesê; ~ *WHO*, dié wat; die mense wat.

thick, (n) dikte; dikste, digste gedeelte; hewigste; *the* ~ *of the FIGHTING*, die hewigste v.d. geveg; *in the* ~ *of THINGS*, in die middel van, in die hartjie van; *through* ~ *and THIN*, deur dik en dun; (a) dik; dig; mistig, troebel, onduidelik; diep, hees (van klanke); dom; maats, kop in een mus; gewaag, kras; *that is a BIT* ~, dis 'n bietjie kras; dis 'n bietjie dik vir 'n daalder; *as* ~ *as HOPS*, soos hare op 'n hond; *as* ~ *as PEAS*, soos sand aan die see; *his SPEECH is* ~, sy tong is swaar; *be as* ~ *as THIEVES*, dik vriende wees; kop in een mus wees; onder een sambreel boer; *his TONGUE is* ~, sy tong is swaar; *the floor was* ~ *WITH dust*, daar was 'n dik laag stof op die vloer; *be* ~ *WITH a person*, intiem met iem. wees; (adv) dig; dik; *the BLOWS came* ~ *and fast*, dit het houe gereën; *LAY* (spread) *it on* ~, met die heuningkwas bewerk; *SPREAD it on* ~, met die heuningkwas bewerk; dit dik aanmaak; dit dik oplê; ~-**blooded,** dikbloedig; ~-**bodied,** swaarlywig; ~-**coated,** dik van vel; ~**en,** dik maak, verdik, bind (sop); dik word; talryker word, toeneem; ingewikkeld word; ~**ener,** verdikker; bindmiddel; ~**ening,** diksel; verdikking; bindmiddel, verdikmiddel, verdikkend.

thick'et, lap bossies, ruigte.

thick: ~ **flank**, diklies; ~-**growing,** dig(groeiend); ~ **head**, domkop, dikkop; ~ **headed,** dom, onnosel, dikhoofdig; ~ **ish,** dikkerig, dikagtig; ~-**leaved,** met digte blare; dikblad=; ~-**lipped,** dik van lippe, diklippig; ~ **ly,** dik, dig; ~ *ly sown*, dig gesaai; ~-**necked,** diknekkig; (n) ~ **ness,** dikte; digtheid; (v) ewe dik maak; ~ **nesser,** dikteskaafmasjien; ~ **rib,** dikrib; ~ **set,** geset, dik, stewig, bonkig; dig begroei; ineengedronge (gestalte); ~-**skinned,** dik van vel, dikhuidig, dikvellig; botvellig, ongevoelig; ~-**skulled,** dikkoppig; dom, onbevatlik; ~-**tongued,** swaar van tong; ~-**witted,** dom, bot.

thief, (thieves), dief; *DEN of thieves*, diewehol; *when thieves FALL out honest men come to their own*, as kok en koksmaat rusie kry, dan hoor jy waar die sopvleis (spek) bly; *like a* ~ *in the NIGHT*, soos 'n dief in die nag; *SET a* ~ *to catch a* ~, met diewe moet 'n mens diewe vang; *SMALL thieves are hanged, big ones go free*, klein diewe het ysterkettings, groot diewe goue kettings; klein misdadigers hang ons op, die grotes val deur die strop; *it TAKES a* ~ *to catch a* ~, jy moet 'n dief met 'n dief vang; *they're as THICK as thieves*, hulle is kop in een mus; ~-**proof,** ~-**resisting,** diefvry, inbraakvry, diefwerend, steelvry.

thieve, steel; ~**ry,** diefstal, diewery.

thieves" Latin, diewetaal, bargoens.

thiev'ing, (n) diewery, stelery; (a) stelend; diefagtig; steel=.

thiev'ish, diefagtig, langvingerig; ~**ness,** diefagtigheid.

thigh, dy, bobeen; ~ **bone** dybeen, femur; ~-**boot,** kapstewel; ~ **measurement,** dymaat.

thill, disselboom

thim'ble, vingerhoed; oogring (in tou); kous (in touwerk); lusring; toukram; *hiding the* ~, warmpatat speel; ~-**case,** vingerhoeddosie; ~ **ful,** vingerhoedvol.

thin, (v) (-ned), dun maak; verdun; maer word; slink; verminder; uitdun (plante); ~ *out*, uitdun; (a) dun; skraal, maer; yl; flou; deursigtig; swak; ~ *AT= MOSPHERE*, yl atmosfeer; *a* ~ *AUDIENCE*, 'n klein gehoor; *a* ~ *DISGUISE*, 'n skrale vermomming; *a* ~ *EXCUSE*, 'n flou ekskuus; *as* ~ *as a LATH*, so maer soos 'n kraai; ~ *POPULATION*, skraal bevolking; *SKATE on* ~ *ice*, jou op gevaarlike terrein waag.

thine, u, van u, u s'n, die uwe, dyn.

thin: ~-**faced,** maer van gesig; ~ **flank,** dunlies.

thing, ding; goed; saak; voorwerp; spulletjie; dinges; iets; (pl) goed, goeters; voorwerpe; dinge; *ABOVE all* ~ *s*, bo alles; *in ALL* ~ *s*, in elke opsig; *ALL* ~ *s taken together*, alles bymekaargeneem; *ANO= THER* ~, iets anders; *as* ~ *s ARE*, soos sake nou staan; ~ *s are looking BAD*, sake lyk sleg; *a* ~ *of BEAUTY*, iets moois; *DEAR little* ~, skattige mensie; *all* ~ *s being EQUAL*, as alles gelyk is; onder origens gelyke omstandighede; *the FIRST* ~, die eerste van alles; *it was a FOOLISH* ~ *to do*, dit was dom om so iets te doen; dit was 'n dom ding om te doen; ~ *s FOREIGN*, uitheemse voorwerpe; *a GOOD* ~, 'n voordelige iets; *and a GOOD* ~ *too!* dit is maar goed; *make a GOOD* ~ *of*, munt slaan uit; *the GREAT ~ is*, die vernaamste is; die ding waar dit op aankom, is; *do the HANDSOME ~ by a person*, iem. rojaal behandel; *JUST the ~*, net die regte ding; die ware Jakob; *the LATEST ~ in hats*, die allernuutste hoedemode; *it doesn't MEAN a ~*, dit beteken hoegenaamd niks; *make a MESS of ~s*, alles verbrou; *NOT a ~*, niks nie; *NOT the ~*, onvanpas; ongeskik; *OLD ~*, ou skat; *ONE ~ at a time!* elke ding apart! *for ONE ~*, in die eerste plek; om maar iets te noem; *that is ONE good ~*, dit is een troos; *PACK up all your ~s*, pak al jou goed in; *POOR ~*, arme drommel; *not QUITE the ~*, nie heeltemal soos dit hoort nie; *you STUPID ~*, jou domkop! *no SUCH ~*, glad nie so iets nie; *TAKE ~s too seriously*, sake te ernstig beskou; *it is just one of THOSE ~s*, dis iets wat soms maar so gebeur; *he knows a ~ or TWO*, hy is nie 'n pampoenkop nie; hy is ouer as twaalf; *an UNUSUAL ~*, iets buitengewoons; *the VERY ~*, net die regte ding; *the VERY ~ I want*, net wat ek wil hê; *~s are going WRONG*, sake loop skeef.

thing'amy, thing'umajig, thing'umbob, thing'ummy, dinges, watsenaam, hoe sê 'n mens nou weer, watsegoed, goeters.

think, (n) denke, (die) dink; mening; gepeins; (v) **(thought),** dink; nadink, bedink; vind, waan; glo, meen, ag; oorweeg, prakseer; van plan wees; 'n denkbeeld vorm van; *~ ABOUT*, dink oor; oorweeg; *give someone something to ~ ABOUT*, iem. sy kop laat krap; *~ ALIKE*, eenders dink; *~ ALOUD*, hardop dink; *~ BETTER of something*, van gedagte verander; *~ BETTER of someone*, 'n hoër dunk van iem. hê; *I wouldn't ~ of DOING such a thing*, om so iets te doen, sou nooit in my gedagte opkom nie; *I don't care what other people ~ about me*, dit kan my nie skeel wat ander mense van my dink nie; *I DON'T ~ so*, ek dink nie so nie; *I DON'T ~!* moenie glo nie! *if you ~ it FIT*, as jy dit goedvind; *~ no HARM*, geen kwaad vermoed nie; *JUST ~!* verbeel jou! *~ LITTLE of*, min dink van; nie 'n hoë dunk hê nie van; *I could not ~ of the MEANING*, die betekenis kon my nie byval nie; *~ MUCH of*, baie dink van; hoë agting hê vir; *I thought as MUCH!* dit kon ek dink! *I can't ~ of his NAME*, ek kan my sy naam nie herinner nie, sy naam wil my nie te binne skiet nie; *I didn't ~ to NOTE down the number of the car*, ek het nie daaraan gedink om die motor se nommer op te skryf nie; *he ~s NOTHING of R2,000*, R2,000 is vir hom niks; *~ OF*, dink aan; *~ OF it!* dink net daaraan! *ONLY ~!* dink maar net! *~ OUT*, uitdink; *~ OVER*, nadink; bepeins; 'n plan hê; in ag neem; *~ it OVER*, daaroor nadink; *~ things OVER*, goed oor sake nadink; *~ it PROBABLE*, dit waarskynlik ag; *~ it PROPER*, dit geskik ag; *I thought SO*, dit kon ek dink; *I should ~ TWICE*, ek sou dit nogeens oorweeg; ek sou huiwerig wees om dadelik te handel; ek sou eers die kat uit die boom kyk; *that's WHAT you ~!* dit dink jy maar! *what do YOU ~ you're doing?* en toe, wat doen jy nou? my heiden, wat makeer jy! *~ able*, denkbaar; *~ er*, denker, dinker, peinser; filosoof; *~-tank*, dinkskrum.

think'ing, (n) mening; dink, denke; gedagte; *~ is very far from KNOWING*, dink is iets anders as weet; *WAY of ~*, denkwyse; *to my WAY of ~*, volgens my mening; myns insiens; (a) denkend, redelik, dink=; *every ~ man and woman*, elkeen wat sy verstand gebruik; *~-cap: put on one's ~-cap*, begin planne maak; jou gedagtes laat gaan; *~ faculty*, dinkvermoë.

thin: *~-lipped*, dunlippig, met dun lippe; *~ly*, dunnerig, dunnetjies, dun; *~ly disguised as*, skraal verbloem as; *~ ner*, *~ners*, (n) verdunmiddel, verdunner; (a) dunner, maerder; *~ness*, dunheid, skraalte, maerte; ylheid; *~ning*, (die) uitdun, uitdunning; *~nish*, dunnerig, taamlik dun; *~skinned*, dunhuidig, dunvellig; fyngevoelig, liggeraak; teer; prikkelbaar; *be ~-skinned*, liggeraak wees; fyn van nerf wees.

third, (n) derde deel; terts (mus.); eensestigste van 'n sekonde; *~ of EXCHANGE*, tertia; *LESSER ~*,
kleinterts; (a) derde; *~ time lucky*, drie maal is skeepsreg; alle goeie dinge bestaan uit drie; *~-best*, op twee na die beste; derdebeste; *~ class*, (n) derde klas; derderangs; (a) minderwaardig, sleg; *~ degree*, afdreiging van bekentenis; *~ estate*, derde stand; *~-hand*, uit die derde hand; derdehands; *~ly*, ten derde, in die derde plek; derdens; *~ party*, derde party (persoon); *~-party insurance*, derde(party)versekering, derdedekking; *~-party risk*, derdepersoonsrisiko; *~-rate*, derderangs, minderwaardig; *~-rate business*, snertsaak; vrot besigheid; *~ reading*, derde lesing; *~ root*, derdemagswortel.

thirst, (n) dors; begeerte; *HAVE a ~*, 'n droë keel hê; *a ~ for KNOWLEDGE*, 'n dors na kennis; (v) dors hê; dors; *~ after*, vurig verlang na; *~ er*, dorstige; *~ er after knowledge*, leergierige; *~ iness*, dorstigheid; *~-quenching*, dorsstillend; *~y*, dorstig, dors; *MAKE ~y*, uitdors; *~y WORK*, dit laat 'n mens dors kry.

thir'teen, dertien; *~th*, dertiende.

thirt'ieth, dertigste.

thir'ty, dertig; *the thirties*, die dertigerjare.

this, (these), dit; hierdie, dié; *AFTER ~*, hierna; in die vervolg; *~ AFTERNOON*, vanmiddag; *over AGAINST ~*, hierteenoor; *ALL ~*, dit alles; *for ALL ~*, tog; nogtans, darem, nietemin; *AS to ~*, wat dit betref; *BEFORE ~*, vantevore; *BY ~*, hiermee; *~ DAY*, vandag; *to ~ DAY*, tot vandag toe; *in these DAYS*, deesdae, in ons dae; *~ EVENING*, vanaand; *FOR ~*, hiervoor; *FROM ~*, hiervan; hiervandaan; *LIKE ~*, op dié manier; *~ is the MAN*, dis hy, dis hy dié; *~ MORNING*, vanmôre; *~ MUCH I can tell you*, dit kan ek jou sê; *~ ONCE*, hierdie een keer; *for ~ and that REASON*, hieroor en daaroor; hierom en daarom; *~, THAT and the other*, alles en nog wat; *~ and THAT*, dit en dat; *by ~ TIME*, teen hierdie tyd, nou al; *~ WAY*, hierheen; *~ day WEEK*, vandag oor 'n week; *these four WEEKS*, die afgelope vier weke; *WITHOUT ~*, hiersonder; *~ WORLD*, die ondermaanse.

thi'stle, distel; doring; sydissel; *~-down*, distelwol; *~-finch*, distelvink; *~ funnel*, langbeentregter, tregterbuis.

thi'stly, vol distels, distelagtig.

thi'ther, daarnatoe, daarheen, soontoe, soheen.

tho', abbr. of **though.**

thole¹, (n) roeipen, dol(pen).

thole², (arch.), (v) verdra, verduur, uitstaan.

thole'-pin, roeipen, dolpen.

Thom'as, Thomas; *doubting ~*, ongelowige Thomas.

Thom'ism, Thomisme.

Thom'ist, (n) Thomis; (a) Thomisties.

thong, (n) voorslag; agterslag (sweep); riem; *cut LARGE ~s of other men's leather*, van 'n ander man se vel breë rieme sny; *men cut LARGE ~s of other men's leather*, van anderman se leer word breë rieme gesny; *cut ONE'S ~ according to one's leather*, die tering na die nering sit; (v) met 'n riem slaan; 'n riem aansit; *~ing*, stropnaaiwerk.

Thor, Thor, dondergod.

thora'cic, bors=; *~ artery*, borsslagaar; *~ cavity*, borsholte; *~ region*, borsstreek; *~ skeleton*, ribbekas; *~ vertebra*, borskaswerwel.

thor'al, huweliks=.

thor'ax, (..races), borskas; borsstuk; *~ surgeon*, borskassnydokter, torakschirurg.

thor'ite, toriet.

thor'ium, torium.

thorn, doring; doringbos; *a ~ in one's FLESH*, 'n doring in die vlees; *a ~ among ROSES*, maljan onder die hoenders; *SIT on ~s*, op hete kole sit; *one's path is STREWN with ~s*, jou pad is vol dorings; *~-apple*, stinkblaar, stinkolie; steekappel; *~-back*, stekelrog; *~-bush*, doringstruik; *~ hedge*, doringheining; *~iness*, doringagtigheid; netelig= heid; *~ scrub*, doringveld; *~-set*, vol dorings; *~ shrub*, doringbos; *~-tree*, doringboom; *~y*, doringrig, doringagtig, vol dorings; lastig, netelig; *a ~y matter*, 'n netelige saak.

tho'rough, deur en deur, grondig, deeglik; diepgaande, deurtastend; fiks, flink, volledig, volkome, dug=

tig, eg; deurtrap; *a* ~ *GENTLEMAN*, 'n pure wit≠man; *a* ~ *SCOUNDREL*, 'n deurtrapte skurk; ~-**bass**, generale bas; ~**bred**, (n) reisiesperd, vol≠bloedperd; rassuiwer mens; (a) volbloed, opregge≠teel, ras≠, raseg; beskaaf; ~**bred horse**, volbloedperd, stamboekperd; ~**fare**, deurgang, straat; *NO* ~*fare*, deurgang verbied, geen deur≠gang; *RIGHT of* ~*fare*, deurgangsreg; ~**going**, deurtastend, radikaal, afdoende; ~**ly**, deur en deur, deeglik; terdeë; van hawer tot gort; flink; ~**ness**, deeglikheid, flinkheid, volkomenheid; ~-**paced**, volmaak; deurtrap, volleerd, bedrewe; ~-**pin**, waaigal.
thorp(e), dorpie, gehuggie.
those, daardie, diegene, dié; ~ *PEOPLE*, daardie mense; ~ *of YOU*, dié van julle.
thou, (v) met u aanspreek; (pron) u.
though, hoewel, alhoewel; al; ofskoon, immers, tog; *AS* ~, asof; *EVEN* ~, al, selfs al; ~ *the LOAD be heavy*, al is die vrag ook swaar; *what* ~ *the WAY is long*, al is die pad ook hoe lank; *I WISH you had told me* ~, ek wens tog dat jy my gesê het.
thought, (n) gedagte; mening, gevoel; dinkvermoë; gepeins; oorweging; verdigsel; nadenking; plan, idee, inval; tikkie, bietjie; *AT the* ~, by die gedagte; *DEEP in* ~, diep in gedagte; ingedagte; ~ *is FREE*, gedagtes is tolvry; elkeen kan dink wat hy wil; *take* ~ *for the FUTURE*, sorg vir die toekoms; *a HAPPY* ~, 'n gelukkige inval; *absorbed IN* ~, diep in gedagte; *LOST in* ~, in gedagtes verdiep; *without a MOMENT'S* ~, sonder om 'n oomblik na te dink; *take no* ~ *of the MORROW*, bekommer jou nie oor die dag van môre nie; *have NO* ~ *for others*, niks vir 'n ander oorhê nie, selfsugtig wees, *I had NO* ~ *of going*, ek het geen plan gehad om te gaan nie; *I had no* ~ *of OFFENDING him*, ek was nie van plan om hom te beledig nie; *his ONE* ~ *was how to escape*, al waar hy aan gedink het, was hoe om te ontsnap; *QUICK as* ~, bliksemsnel; *on SECOND* ~*s*, by nader insien; by ryper nadink; na rype beraad; *after SERIOUS* ~, na rype beraad; *TAKE* ~, jou goed bedink; *I'll TELL you my* ~*s*, ek sal jou sê wat ek dink; *give a bit OF* ~ *to the problem*, dink 'n bietjie na oor die vraagstuk; (v) *kyk* **think**; *I* ~ *of resigning*, ek het daaraan gedink om te bedank.
thought'ful, bedagsaam, sorgsaam; taktvol; sugges≠tief; vol gedagtes; *BE* ~ *of others*, oor ander mense ook dink; bedagsaam wees; *HOW* ~ *of you*, hoe vriendelik van jou om daaraan te dink; ~**ness**, sorgsaamheid, bedagsaamheid.
thought'less, onbesadig, sorgloos, gedagteloos, onbesonne, onnadenkend; ~**ness**, onbedagsaam≠heid; onbesonnenheid; onberedeneerdheid; lig≠vaardigheid; ylhoofdigheid.
thought: ~-**out**, goed deurgedink (uitgedink); deur≠dag; deurwrog; ~-**provoking**, gedagteprikkelend, gedagteryk; ~-**reader**, gedagteleser; ~-**reading**, (die) lees van iem. se gedagtes; ~-**transfer(ence)**, gedagteoorbrenging, telepatie.
thous'and, duisend; ~*s AND* ~*s*, derduisende; *BY* ~*s*, by duisende; *make a* ~ *and one EXCUSES*, allerhande verontskuldiginge (verskonings) hê; *IN their* ~*s*, by duisende; *a MAN in a* ~, 'n man dui≠send; *ONE in a* ~, een uit 'n duisend; *a* ~ *and ONE*, honderd-en-een; ~*s of PEOPLE*, duisende mense; *it is a* ~ *PITIES*, dis tog alte jammer; *a* ~ *THANKS*, 'n duisend maal dank; *a* ~ *TIMES*, duisend maal; ~*s UPON* ~*s*, duisende der duisen≠de; ~ **fold**, (n) duisendvoud; (a) duisendvoudig; ~-**headed**, duisendhoofdig; ~**s**, versierlekkertjies; ~ **th**, duisendste.
Thrace, T(h)rasië.
Thra'cian, (n) Trasiër; (a) Trasies.
thra'ldom, slawerny, lyfeienskap, slawejuk, diens≠baarheid.
thrall, (n) knegskap, lyfeienskap, diensbaarheid; slaaf; *have in* ~, gevange hou; (v) tot slaaf maak, verslaaf, diensbaar maak; (a) verslaaf.
thrash, dors (graan); slaan, afransel, afros, uitklop, uitlooi, uitpiets, uitransel, uitwiks, afstof, uitkwint, raps; uitfoeter; oortref, klop, verslaan; ~ *out a*

matter, 'n saak uitvors; agter die waarheid kom; ~**er**, slaner; dorser; dorsmasjien; seevos (haai).
thrash'ing, dorsery, (die) dors; loesing, pak slae, siep≠sop-en-braaiboud, streepsuiker; *GIVE someone a severe* ~, iem. 'n afgedankste loesing gee; *be GIVEN a* ~, op jou herrie kry, 'n pak slae kry; *you are IN for a* ~, 'n pak slae is jou voorland (naam); jy kan jou lyf vetsmeer; ~ **floor**, dorsvloer; ~ **ma≠chine**, dorsmasjien, trapmasjien.
thrason'ical, grootpraterig, blufferig.
thread, (n) draad; garing, gare; seilgaring, seilgare; samehang; skroefdraad; *not a DRY* ~, nie 'n droë draad nie; *FEMALE* ~, moerdraad; *GATHER up the* ~*s*, die drade saamvat; *HANG by a* ~, aan 'n draadjie hang; *LEFT-hand* ~, linksdraad; *the* ~ *of LIFE*, die lewensdraad; *LOSE the* ~, die draad (kluts) kwytraak; *have LOST the* ~, die kluts (draad) kwyt wees; *a* ~ *RUNS through*, daar loop 'n draad deur; *it is* ~ *and THRUM*, dis vinkel en koljander; *WORN to a* ~, gaar gedra; (v) 'n draad deursteek; aan 'n draad ryg; deurboor, deurdring; inryg, drade span; van 'n draad voorsien; ~ *BEADS*, krale inryg; ~ *a NEEDLE*, 'n draad deur 'n naald steek; ~ *a SCREW*, 'n (skroef)draad in≠sny; ~ *one's WAY through*, jou weg baan deur (vleg deur); ~*ed WITH*, deurweef met.
thread'bare, kaal, verslyt; goor, afgesaag; ~ *ARGU≠MENT*, afgesaagde argument; *WEAR something* ~, iets gaar (heeltemal stukkend) dra; ~**ness**, kaal≠heid; afgesaagdheid.
thread: ~**ed**, ingeryg; van 'n draad voorsien; ~*ed pipe*, pyp met skroefdraad; ~ **gauge**, skroefdraad≠kaliber; ~**iness**, draderigheid; ~ **lace**, garingkant; ~ **paper**, papier om gare in te bewaar; ~ **worm**, haarwurm; ~**y**, draderig.
threat, (be)dreiging, dreigement; ~ *of REVENGE*, 'n wraakdreigement; *UNDER* ~ *to*, onder bedreiging met (van).
threat'en, dreig, bedreig; *IMPRISONMENT* ~ *s him*, gevangenisstraf hang oor sy kop; ~ *to LEAVE*, dreig om weg te gaan; ~ *WITH*, dreig met; ~**ed**, bedreig; ~**er**, dreiger.
threat'ening, (n) dreigement, bedreiging; (a) dreig≠dreigend; *a* ~ *letter*, 'n dreigbrief; ~**ly**, dreigend.
three, drie; ~ *CHEERS*, drie hoera's; *IN* ~ *s*, drie-drie; *T* ~ *in ONE*, die Drie-eenheid; *the* ~ *R'S*, lees-, skryf- en rekenkuns; *RULE of* ~, verhou≠dingswet; *when* ~ *SUNDAYS (Thursdays) come together*, wanneer die perde horings kry; ~ *TI≠MES* ~, drie maal drie; ~ *WOMEN (and a goose) make a market*, vroue het altyd iets te ruil; ~-**act play**, driebedryftoneelstuk, drieakter; ~-**ball match**, driespel; ~-**banded plover**, strandlopertjie; ~-**barrelled**, drieloop≠; ~-**burner stove**, driepit≠stoof, drievlamstoof; ~-**colour printing**, drie≠kleuredruk.
three'-cornered, driehoekig, driehoeks≠; ~ **contest**, driehoeksverkiesing; driehoekige geveg; ~ **hat**, driekanthoed, steek; ~ **stamp**, driehoek-, driehoe≠kige seël.
three: ~-**course dinner**, eetmaal met drie gange; ~-**day sickness**, driedaesiekte; ~-**decker**, driedekker; ~-**dimensional**, driedimensionaal, ~-**dimensional film**, dieptefilm; ~-**edged**, driekantig; ~ **eights**, drieaks, drieag(t)stes; ~ **fold**, drievoudig, drieduб≠bel(d); drieledig; ~-**forked**, drietand≠; ~-**four time**, driekwartmaat; ~-**handed**, met drie hande, drie≠hand≠; driemans≠; ~-**handed bridge**, driemansbrug; ~-**hoofed**, driehoewig; ~-**legged race**, driebeen≠wedloop; ~-**lobed**, drielobbig; ~-**master**, driemas≠ter; ~-**part**, driestemmig; ~ **pence**, trippens (vero); ~ **penny bit**, ~ **penny-piece**, trippens; ~ **penny≠worth**, vir 'n trippens; 'n trippens s'n; ~-**phase**, driefasig; ~-**piece**, driestuk; ~-**pin plug**, driepen≠prop; ~-**ply wood**, tripleks, drielaag(hout); ~-**ply wool**, driedraadwol; ~-**pointed**, driepuntig; ~-**pronged**, met drie tande, drietand≠; ~-**prong plug**, driepensteker, driepenprop.
three'-quarter, (n) driekwart; agterspeler; (a) drie≠kwart≠; ~ **bed**, driekwartbed; twyfelaar; ~ **sleeve**, driekwartmou; ~ **trousers**, halfmasbroek.
three: ~-**roomed house**, driekamerhuis; ~ **score**, ses≠

thremmatology 1304 *throw*

tig; ~ *score (years) and ten*, sewentig jaar; ~-**seater**, driepersoons=; ~-**sided**, driesydig, driekantig; ~**some**, drie persone; driespan, driespel (gholf); drietal; ~-**speed gearbox**, driegangratkas; ~-**stringed**, driesnarig; ~-**way**, drierigtings=; drietak=; drieweg=; driegat=; ~-**way socket**, driegatkontak; ~-**way switch**, driewegskakelaar; ~-**year old**, drie= jaaroud.
thremmatol'ogy, vee- en planteteelt.
thren'ode, (-s), thren'ody, (..dies), klaaglied, lyksang.
thresh, dors; *kyk* **thrash**; ~**er**, dorser; dorsmasjien, trapmasjien.
thresh'ing, (n) dorsery, (die) dors; (a) dors=; trap=; ~-**flail**, dorsvleël; ~-**floor**, trapvloer, dorsvloer; ~-**machine**, dorsmasjien, dorser, trapmasjien.
thresh'old, drumpel; drempel (fig.); aanvang, begin, ingang, vooraand; ~ *OF consciousness*, bewus= synsdrempel; *ON the* ~ *of*, aan die vooraand van.
threw, *kyk* **throw**, (v).
thrice, drie maal, driekeer; ~ *done is well done*, drie maal is skeepsreg; ~-**blessed**, werklik geseën; ~-**told**, afgesaag.
thrift, suinigheid; spaarsaamheid, spaarsin; voor= spoed; grasangelier; ~ *is good revenue*, om te spaar, is om te vergaar; ~ **club**, spaarklub; ~**iness**, spaarsaamheid; suinigheid; ~**less**, verkwistend; ~**lessness**, kwistigheid; spilsug; ~ **movement**, spaarbeweging; ~ **society**, spaarvereniging; ~**y**, spaarsaam; suinig; voorspoedig.
thrill, (n) trilling; huiwering; tinteling; siddering; sen= sasie, opwinding; ontroering; sensasieverhaal; *a* ~ *of joy*, 'n tinteling van vreugde (blydskap); (v) deur= dring; ontroer, laat ril, deurtintel, deurhuiwer, aan= gryp; 'n ontroering veroorsaak; ril; deurtril; ~**ed**, ontroer; opgewonde; in ekstase; aangegryp; gegril; gehuiwer; *his story* ~ *ed listeners*, sy verhaal het die gehoor aangegryp; ~**er**, sensasieverhaal; griesel= stuk, gruwelstuk; sensasieroman; spanningstuk; rilprent; riller; ~**ing**, deurdringend; opwindend, aangrypend, pakkend, sensasioneel, huiwering= wekkend; trillend; ontroerend; spannend; ~-**seek**= **er**, sensasiesoeker; ~-**seeking**, (n) sensasiesug; sen= sasielus; (a) sensasiebelus.
thrips, blaaspootjie.
thrive, (throve or **-d, thriven** or **-d),** bloei, vooruitkom, gedy; akkordeer; voorspoedig gaan; aard, geil groei, floreer; *sheep* ~ *in this district*, skape aard goed in hierdie distrik; ~**r**, gelukskind.
thriv'ing, gelukkig, voorspoedig, welvarend, flore= rend.
thro', abbr. *of* **through**.
throat, keel; hals; gorrel, strot; nou ingang; uitgang; monding; klouhoring; *be AT one another's* ~ *s*, me= kaar aan die keel vlieg; mekaar invlieg; *CLEAR one's* ~, keel skoonmaak; *CUT someone's* ~, iem. se keel afsny; *CUT one's own* ~, jou eie keel afsny; *CUT each other's* ~ *s*, mekaar se keel afsny; *FLY at one another's* ~ *s*, mekaar aan die keel vlieg; *FORCE it down someone's* ~, dit iem. opdring; *be FULL to the* ~, buikvol wees; *GIVE someone the lie in his* ~, iem. vir 'n leuenaar uitmaak; *JUMP down someone's* ~, iem. invlieg; *LIE in his* ~, op 'n streep lieg; *POUR everything down one's* ~, alles deur jou keelgat jaag; *PUSH something down some= one's* ~, iets aan iem. opdring; *SEIZE by the* ~, by (aan) die keel gryp; *STICK in one's* ~, jou dwars in die krop steek; *TAKE by the* ~, aan die keel gryp; *the WORDS stuck in his* ~, die woorde het in sy keel bly steek; *go down the WRONG* ~, by die ver= keerde keelgat ingaan; ~ **bolt**, halsbout; ~-**cut**= **ting**, (n) keelafsny; (a) moorddadig; moordend; ~-**lash**, keelband; ~ **plate**, broekplaat; ~**y**, keel= gutturaal, skor; met los strotvel.
throb, (n) klop, klopping; gehyg; (v) **(-bed)**, klop, bons; hyg; tril, pols; ~ **bing**, (n) klop, geklop, ge= bons; (a) kloppend.
throe(s), hewige pyn, wee, doodsangs; barenswee.
thrombos'is, trombose; aarverstopping, bloedprop; *coronary* ~, kroonaarverstopping, kroonaartrom= bose, koronêr.
thrombot'ic, tromboties.
thromb'us, bloedklont, trombus.

throne, (n) troon; podium; pronksetel; *ACCESSION to the* ~, troonsbestyging; *COME to the* ~, die troon bestyg; aan die regering kom; *DRIVE from the* ~, onttroon; *SUCCESSION to the* ~, troons= opvolging; *no* ~ *without a THORN*, elke huis het sy kruis; (v) troon, setel; tot die troon verhef; ~**less**, troonloos, sonder troon; ~-**room**, troon= saal.
throng, (n) gedrang, menigte, toeloop, gewoel; saamswerm; (v) dring, opdring, verdring; toe= stroom, drom; *the streets were* ~ *ed with people*, die strate het gewemel van mense.
thro'stle, lyster; ~**(-frame)**, spinmasjien.
throt'tle, (n) (keel)gorrel, strot, lugpyp; strotklep; handversneller; versnelklep; afsluitklep, smoorklep (motor); gaskraan; *at full* ~, in volle vaart; (v) (ver)wurg, versmoor; laat stik, die gorrel toeknyp; die motor vertraag, petroltoevoer smoor (enjin); ~-**valve**, stoomklep; smoorklep (motor).
throt'tling, verwurging; versmoring; smoring (motor).
through, (a) deurgaande, deur=, deurlopend (diens); (adv) deur en deur; deur, heeltemal deur, tot die einde toe; *ALL* ~, die hele tyd deur; ~ *AND* ~, deur en deur, heeltemal, in alle opsigte; *FALL* ~, deurval; *the plan FELL* ~, die plan het misluk; *GO* ~ *with*, voortgaan met; *he is* ~ *with that JOB*, hy het daardie werk klaar; *LOOK* ~ *and* ~, van kop tot tone beskou; *you have PUT me* ~ *to the wrong number*, jy het my die verkeerde nommer gegee; jy het my met die verkeerde nommer verbind; *READ* ~ *and* ~, weer en weer lees; *RIGHT* ~, dwars= deur; *SEE* ~ *someone*, *SEE someone* ~, iem. deur= help; iem. deurgrond; *be* ~ *with SOMEONE*, klaar met iem. wees; niks meer met iem. te doen wil hê nie; *TRAVEL* ~, deurreis; (prep) uit; langs; deur middel van; gedurende; ten gevolge van; ~ *DIP= LOMATIC channels*, langs diplomatieke weg; ~ *no FAULT of one's own*, sonder eie toedoen; *I wished I should have fallen* ~ *the FLOOR*, ek het gewens dat die aarde my kon verswelg het; ~ *rose= coloured GLASSES*, deur 'n rooskleurige bril; ~ *LIFE*, gedurende die hele lewe; *get* ~ *the WORK*, die werk klaarkry; *she waited* ~ *twenty long YEARS*, sy het twintig lange jare gewag; ~ **bolt**, skroefbout, deurloopbout; ~ **carriage**, deurgaan= de wa; ~ **connection**, deurverbinding, ~ **freight**, deurvrag; ~ **journey**, deurreis; ~**out'**, dwarsdeur, deur, deur en deur, heeltemal; deurgaans; ~ *out the year*, die hele jaar deur; ~ **passenger**, deurgaande passasier; ~ **pipe**, deurlooppyp; ~**put**, toevoer; ertsproduksie; ~ **rate**, deurvrag; ~ **road**, deur= looppad; ~-**stone**, kopsteen; ~ **street**, deurloop= straat; ~ **ticket**, deurgaande kaartjie; ~ **traffic**, deurverkeer, deurgaande verkeer; ~ **train**, deur= gaande trein; ~ **way**, deurweg, deurpad; ~**way valve**, eenwegklep.
throw, (n) worp, gooi; valhoogte, spronghoogte (geol.); draai (sy); *stake all on a SINGLE* ~, alles op een kaart verwed; *a STONE'S* ~, 'n klipgooi; so ver 'n mens met 'n klip kan gooi; (v) **(threw, -n)**, gooi, werp; uitgooi, stort; afgooi; smyt, duiwel; on= dergooi; voortbring (kleintjies); (in 'n toestand) bring; draai, twyn (van sy); ~ *ABOUT*, rondgooi; ~ *one's ARMS about*, met die arms swaai; ~ *AS= IDE*, opsy gooi; ~ *oneself AT a man*, agter 'n man aanloop; ~ *oneself AWAY on*, jou verslinger aan; ~ *AWAY*, weggooi; *be* ~ *n BACK upon*, jou toevlug moet neem na (tot); ~ *BACK*, agteroor gooi (kop); terugwerp (leër); ~ *into the BARGAIN*, op die koop toe (by)gee; *BE* ~ *n*, afval; afgegooi word; ~ *a BRIDGE over a river*, 'n brug oor 'n rivier slaan; ~ *away a CHANCE*, 'n kans laat verbygaan; ~ *out one's CHEST*, die bors uit= stoot; ~ *on your CLOTHES*, jou klere gou-gou aanpluk; ~ *into CONFUSION*, verwar; ~ *the DOOR open*, die deur oopgooi; die weg voorberei; ~ *DOWN*, neergooi, omgooi, platgooi; ~ *out of EMPLOYMENT*, ontslaan, werkloos maak, op straat gooi; ~ *FEATHERS*, verveer; ~ *a FIT*, die stuipe kry; 'n toeval kry; ~ *a FOAL*, vul; ~ *up the GAME*, ingee; die spel prysgee; ~ *the HAMMER*,

hamergooi; ~ *in one's HAND*, tou opgooi; gewone gee; die saak opgee; ~ *up one's HANDS*, die hande opsteek, hensop; ~ *the helve after the HATCHET*, die kindjie met die badwater weggooi; ~ *out a HINT*, 'n wenk gee; ~ *IN*, op die koop toegee; opgooi (kaartspel); ingooi (bal); ~ *something IN*, op die koop toegee; ~ *oneself INTO*, met hart en siel aanpak; ~ *everything INTO one's work*, alle aandag aan jou werk wy; ~ *a KISS*, 'n soen(tjie) waai; 'n kushandjie gee; ~ *LIGHT on*, lig werp op; ~ *in one's LOT with*, lief en leed deel met; ~ *oneself on someone's MERCY*, jou op iem. se genade werp; ~ *one's MONEY about*, met geld smyt, geld verkwis; ~ *OFF*, afgooi, afwerp; uitgooi; oplewer; verwerp; kwytraak; ~ *OFF bad friends*, slegte geselskap los; ~ *OFF a cold*, 'n verkoue kwytraak; ~ *OPEN*, oopsit; oopstel; ~ *the doors (gates) OPEN wide*, die deure wawyd oopgooi; ~ *OUT*, uitgooi; uitsend (hitte); versprei; verwerp; ~ *OUT a hint*, 'n wenk gee; *my calculation was* ~*n OUT*, my berekening was verkeerd; ~ *OUT of a bar*, uit 'n kroeg smyt; ~ *OUT of work*, werkloos maak; ~ *OVER*, omgooi, omvergooi; afsê; ~ *OVER old friends*, ou vriende ignoreer (versaak); ~ *OVERBOARD*, oorboord gooi; ~ *a PARTY*, 'n partytjie gee; ~ *POINTS*, 'n wissel oorhaal; ~ *into PRISON*, in die tronk smyt; ~ *a PUNCH*, 'n vuishou slaan; ~ *into SHAPE*, vorm gee aan; ~ *the SKIN*, vervel; ~ *up the SPONGE*, oorgee, hendsop; tou opgooi; ~ *STONES*, met klippe gooi; ~ *a TANTRUM*, te kere gaan; ~ *it in his TEETH*, dit voor sy kop gooi; ~ *TOGETHER*, bymekaargooi; ~ *into TOUCH*, oor die kantlyn gooi; ~ *in the TOWEL*, tou opgooi; ~ *oneself UPON*, jou op genade verlaat; ~ *in one's WEIGHT*, jou inspan, jou steun gee; jou gewig in die skaal werp; ~ *one's WEIGHT against*, jou gewig inwerp (in die skaal lê) teen; ~ *one's WEIGHT about*, bemoeisiek (indringerig) wees; grootmeneer speel; astrant optree; ~-**away**, weggooiing, -goed; ~-**back**, agteruitsetting, terugslag; agteroorwerping; terugaarding, atavistiese neiging; ~ **er**, gooier; ~-**er-in**, ingooier (rugby); ~-**forward**, vorentoegooi; ~**ing**, gooi, gooiery; opgooi (wol); ~*ing the javelin*, spiesgooi; ~**ing-stick**, knopkierie; ~**ing wheel**, pottebakkerskyf; ~-**off**, staanspoor, begin; ~-**outs**, uitskot; ~**ster**, sydraaier, sytwynder.

thrum[1], (n) fraiing, draad, growwe garing; (v) fraiings maak.

thrum[2], (n) getokkel, getrommel; (v) (**-med**), trommel, tokkel, tjingel; ~**ming**, getokkel.

thrush[1], (**-es**), lyster (voël).

thrush[2], spru, sproei; vrotstraal (perd).

thrust, (n) stoot; steek; stamp; skermstoot; druk; opskuiwingskrag (geol.); slaankrag; trekkrag (lugskroef); stootkrag; dryfkrag (van persoon); (v) (~, ~), stoot; steek; du; ~ *ASIDE*, opsy stoot; ~ *AWAY*, wegstoot; ~ *FORTH*, uitstoot; uitsteek; ~ *FROM his rights*, uit sy regte gestoot; *give someone a few HOME* ~ *s*, iem. 'n paar kopskote gee; ~ *IN*, indring; ~ *oneself INTO*, jou êrens inwerk; ~ *oneself ON a person*, jou aan iem. opdring; ~ *OUT one's hand*, jou hand uitsteek; ~ *into PRISON*, in die tronk stop; ~ *THROUGH*, deursteek; ~ **bearing**, druklaer; ~ **block**, drukblok, stublok; ~-**cap**, drukdop; ~-**er**, stoter; deurdrukker; oorambisieuse persoon; ~-**fault**, opskuiwing; oorskuiwing; ~**ing**, stotend; stekend; deurdrywend, ~**ing person**, deurdrywer; ~-**plane**, oorskuiwingsvlak; ~ **plate**, drukplaat; ~-**screw**, drukskroef; ~-**washer**, drukwaster; ~-**weapon**, steekwapen.

thud, (n) dowwe slag, smak, bons, plof; (v) (**-ded**), neerbons, neerplof.

thug, wurger, sluipmoordenaar; skurk, boef; ~ **gee**, wurgstelsel; ~**gery**, boef-, skurkagtigheid, boewery, skurkery; ~**gish**, skurkagtig, boefagtig.

Thul'e, Thule; *ultima* ~, die hoogste goed; die verste punt.

thumb, (n) duim; *be ALL* ~ *s*, lomp (onhandig) wees; *BITE one's* ~ *at*, jou tong uitsteek vir; *turn DOWN the* ~, veroordeel, verwerp; *his FINGERS are all* ~*s*, hy het twee linkerhande; is onhandig;

HAVE under one's ~, onder die duim hê; *HOLD* ~*s for a person*, vir iem. duim vashou; *HOLD somebody under your* ~, iem. onder die duim hou; *KEEP under one's* ~, onder die duim hou; *the RULE of* ~, die praktiese metode; *by RULE of* ~, volgens die praktyk; *SUCK something from one's* ~, iets uit jou duim suig; *keep one's* ~ *on someone's THROAT*, die voet op iem. se nek hou; *TOM T*~, Klein Duimpie; *be UNDER the* ~ *of*, onder die plak sit van; ~*s UP!*, hou moed! tien uit die kant bo!; (v) beduimel; hanteer, betas; deurblaai; aftrommel, onhandig speel; duimgooi; ~ *a lift*, duimry, duimgooi, bedelry; ~ **button**, drukknop; ~-**gauge**, boerekruishout; ~-**index**, duimgreep; ~-**latch**, (deur)werwel; deurknip; ~ **less**, sonder duim; onhandig; ~-**lock**, drukslot; duimskroef; ~-**mark**, vingervlek; ~-**marked**, beduimel; ~-**nail**, duimnael; ~-**nail sketch**, klein tekeninkie; kort skets (prosa); ~-**nut**, spanmoer, handmoer; ~-**piece**, drukblad; ~-**print**, duimafdruk; ~-**screw**, duimskroef; vleuelskroef; ~-**stall**, duimeling, duimskut; ~-**sucking**, duimsuig; duimsuiery; ~-**tack**, duimspykertjie, drukspykertjie.

thump, (n) stoot, slag, stamp; (v) moker, stamp; plof, bons, bonk, slaan; ~ **er**, stamper; yslike ding (persoon), knewel (dier), bul; ~**ing**, (n) gestamp; gebons; (a) buitengewoon groot, reusagtig, kolossaal; *a* ~*ing lie*, 'n yslike leuen.

thun'der, (n) donder, donderweer, swaarweer, onweer; gedreun, gerommel; (ban)bliksem; ~ *of APPLAUSE*, dawerende toejuiging; *a FACE like* ~, 'n woedende gesig; ~ *and LIGHTNING*, donder en blits; *LOOK black as* ~, baie kwaad lyk; *STEAL someone's* ~, iem. voorspring; die wind uit iem. se seile haal; met 'n ander man se kalwers ploeg; *in a VOICE of* ~, met donderende stem; (v) donder; bulder, dawer, fulmineer; ~-**and-lightning**, (n) donkergrys stof; (a) peper-en-soutkleurig; ~ **bolt**, donderslag, blits, bliksem, bliksemskig; ~ **clap**, donderslag, bliksemslag; ~-**cloud**, donderwolk; ~ **er**, donderaar; dondergod; ~-**flash**, donderslag; ~**ing**, (n) gedawer; (a) donderend; oorverdowend; (adv) verbasend, verduiwels; ~-**ous**, donderend, dawerend; ~ **peal**, donderslag; ~ **storm**, donderstorm, onweersbui, swaarweer; ~-**struck**, deur die bliksem getref; verbaas, verstom; *be* ~ *struck*, oorbluf wees; stomverbaas wees; ~**y**, donderagtig, donder-.

thur'ible, wierookvat.

thur'ifer, wierookdraer, wierookwaaier.

thurif'erous, wierookvoortbrengend, wierook-.

thurifica'tion, bewieroking; wierookbranding.

Thurin'gian March, Thuringse Mark.

Thurs'day, Donderdag.

thus, dus; so, aldus, op dié manier; ~ *FAR*, tot sover, tot dusver; ~ *MUCH I can tell you*, soveel kan ek jou wel sê.

thwack, (n) slag, hou, mokerhou; (v) moker, klop, afransel.

thwart, (n) roeibankie; (v) dwarsboom, teenwerk, teëgaan, teengaan; kruis; in die wiele ry; dwarstrek, (a) dwars; skuins; ~ **er**, dwarstrekker; ~**ing**, dwarstrekkerig, belemmerend; ~ **ships**, dwarsskeeps.

thy, u, van u.

thyme, tiemie.

thym'us, (..**mi**), timusklier, groeiklier.

thym'y, tiemieagtig.

thyr'oid, (n) skildklier, tiroïed, tiroïde; (a) skildvormig; ~ **cartilage**, skildvormige kraakbeen; ~ **gland**, skildklier.

thyrs'us, (..**si**), Bacchusstaf.

thyself', u(self).

tiar'a, tiara, kroon, driekroon.

Tib'er, Tiber.

Tibet', Tibet; ~ **an**, (n) Tibetaan; Tibetaans (taal); (a) Tibetaans.

tibet', tibet, Tibetaanse stof.

tib'ia, (**-e**), skeenbeen; ~ **l**, skeenbeen-; ~ **l artery**, skeenslagaar.

tic, spiertrekking, senuweetrekking; ~ **douloureux**, (aan)gesigspyn.

tick[1], (n) tyk (materiaal); kussingoortreksel.

tick², (n) bosluis; skaapluis; luis.

tick³, (n) krediet; *buy on ~*, op krediet koop; (v) krediet gee, laat opskryf.

tick⁴, (n) tik; regmerkie; strepie; *in a FEW ~s*, in 'n kits, in 'n japtrap; *TO the ~*, op die sekonde; *in TWO ~s*, in 'n kits, in twee telle, in 'n japtrap; (v) tik; aanstreep, merk; *MAKE something ~*, iets aan die gang hou; *~ OFF*, aanstip; merk; aftik; *~ someone OFF*, iem. op die vingers tik; iem. goed die waarheid sê; *the engine ~ed OVER*, die enjin het geluier.

tick'-bird, bosluisvoël.

tick'er, tikker(tjie); oorlosie; telegraaftoestel, druktelegraaf; hart; *~-service*, druktelegraafdiens; *~-tape*, telegraafstrook, druk=, teleksstrook.

tick'et, (n) kaartjie; toegangskaartjie; reiskaartjie, intreebiljet; lootjie; paspoort; kandidatelys; pryskaartjie; sertifikaat; partyprogram; verkiesingsprogram; etiket; *that's the ~!*, mooi so! dis net reg! dis die ware Jakob!; (v) van 'n kaartjie voorsien; 'n pryskaartjie opsit, merk; *~-box*, loket; *~-collector*, kaartjiesondersoeker; *~ed*, met 'n kaartjie; *~-examiner*, kaartjiesondersoeker; kaartjieknipper; *~-gate*, kaartjiehek; *~-holder*, kaartjiehouer; *~-office*, kaartjieskantoor; *~-of-leave man*, voorwaardelik vrygestelde; *~-punch*, kaartjieknipper; *~ window*, loket.

tick'ey, (-s), (hist.) trippens; *~ social*, tiekieaand.

tick'-fever, bosluiskoors (mense); ooskuskoors (beeste).

tick'ing¹, matrasgoed, tyk (materiaal).

tick'ing², getik; gerikketik; *~-off*, skrobbering; *give someone a ~-off*, iem. 'n skrobbering gee.

tic'kle, (n) gekielie; kielierige gevoel; krieweling; (v) kielie; prikkel, streel; *BE ~d*, geamuseer(d) wees; *~d to DEATH*, uiters geamuseer(d); *~ someone's FANCY*, op iem. se lagspiere werk; amuseer; vermaak; die smaak prikkel; *I was ~d at the IDEA*, die idee het my vermaak; *~ the PALATE*, die eetlus opwek; die smaak prikkel; *~d PINK*, uiters geamuseer(d); *~ UP*, aanspoor; *~r*, iem. of iets wat kielie; netelige vraag, raaisel; vlotterpen, prikkelaar (motor).

tick'ling, gekielie, gekittel; krieweling, gekriewel, gekriebel; *what is ~ you?*, het jy dit of kry jy dit?

tick'lish, kielierig; liggeraak; netelig, lastig, gevaarlik, delikaat; *a ~ POSITION*, 'n netelige posisie; *a ~ QUESTION*, 'n netelige kwessie; *~ness*, kielierigheid; liggeraaktheid; neteligheid.

tick' paralysis, bosluisverlamming.

tick'-tack', tiktak.

tick'-tock, tiktak; toktokkie (speletjie).

tid'al, gety=; *~ air*, getylug; *~ basin*, getyhawe; *~ kom*; *~ current*, getystroom; *~ flow*, getystroming; *~ harbour*, getyhawe; *~ range*, getyverloop; *~ river*, getyrivier, vloedmonding; *~ stream*, getystroom; *~ wave*, vloedgolf, getygolf.

tid'bit, *kyk* titbit.

tidd'ly-winks, skyfiespel; ringgooi(spel).

tide, (n) (ge)ty, eb en vloed; tyd; stroom; stroming; *AGAINST the ~*, teen die stroom in; *work DOUBLE ~s*, dag- en nagskofte werk, dag en nag werk; *the ~ of EVENTS*, die loop van gebeurtenisse; *take the ~ at the FLOOD*, die geleentheid aangryp; *FULL ~*, hoogwater; *GO with the ~*, met die stroom saamgaan; *HIGH ~*, hoogwater; *the ~ is IN*, dis hoogwater; *LOW ~*, laagwater; *NEAP ~*, dooie gety; *the ~ is OUT*, dis laagwater; *STEM the ~*, die stroom keer; *STOP the ~*, die gety keer; *SWIM with the ~*, met die stroom saamgaan; (v) met die stroom vaar (dryf); *~ someone over a difficulty*, iem. 'n moeilikheid te bowe help kom; iem. uithelp; *~-free*, getyvry; *~-gate*, sluisdeur; *~-gauge*, getymeter; *~ less*, getyvry; *~-lock*, skutsluis, getysluis; *~-mark*, hoogwaterlyn; laagwaterlyn; hoogwatermerk, laagwatermerk, lyn; *~-stream*, getystroom; *~-table*, getytafel; *~-waiter*, doeanebeampte; *~ water*, getywater; *~ wave*, vloedgolf, getygolf.

tid'ily, netjies, sindelik.

tid'iness, netheid.

tid'ings, berig, tyding, nuus, mare.

tidol'ogy, leer van die getye.

tid'y, (n) (..dies), kindervoorskoot; antimakassar, kleedjie; rommelsakkie; werksakkie, werkmandjie; vuilbak; (v) (..died), opknap; aan die kant maak, opruim; *~ ONESELF*, jou regmaak; *~ UP*, opredder, opruim; aan die kant maak; (a) netjies, sindelik, aan kant, ordelik; mooi; ordentlik; *a ~ DAY'S work*, 'n goeie dag se werk; *a ~ PENNY*, 'n mooi sommetjie; *a ~ PERSON*, 'n netjiese mens; *a ~ SUM (of money)*, 'n mooi (aardige) sommetjie.

tie, (n) band, knoop; strik; das; gelykopspel; verbindingsteken; verbindingsbalk; boog (musiek); verpligting; ankerbout; dwarslêer (myn); bint (in dak); *~s of BLOOD*, bloedverwantskap; *~s of FRIENDSHIP*, vriendskapsbande; *MATRIMONIAL (nuptial) ~*, huweliksband; *PLAY (shoot) off a ~*, 'n beslissende wedstryd speel; *the VOTING is a ~*, die stemme staak; (v) ewe veel punte behaal, gelykop speel, gelykspeel; bind, vasbind, vasknoop, snoer; strik; verbind; aan bande lê, beperk; *~ it in a BOW*, strik dit; *~ DOWN*, verplig; bind aan; *~ someone DOWN to something*, iem. aan iets bind; *~ a person's HANDS*, iem. se hande vasbind; iem. bind (beperk); *~ the connubial KNOT*, die huwelik sluit; *~ OFF*, vasbind; *two PLAYERS ~ for the prize*, twee spelers wen die prys saam; *~ someone's TONGUE*, iem. se mond snoer; *~ UP*, vasbind; opbind; verbind (wond); vassit, vas belê (geld); *it all ~s UP*, dit kom ooreen; *~ YOUR ~*, knoop jou das; *~ WITH*, gelykstaan met; gelykop speel met; *~-anchor*, bindanker; *~-bar*, spanstaaf, koppelstaaf, bindstaaf; *~-beam*, bindbalk; dwarslêer; trekstang; *~-bolt*, ankerbout; bindbout.

tied, gebonde; vasgebind, vasgeknoop; gelyk, gelykop; *a ~ HOUSE*, 'n gebonde dranksaak (-huis); *~ to his MOTHER'S apron strings*, aan mamma se roksbande vas wees; nog mamma se babatjie; *the two TEAMS ~*, die twee spanne het gelykop gespeel.

tie: *~-knot*, dasknoop; *~-pin*, daspeld.

tier, (n) ry, reeks; binder; laag; verdieping (koek); (v) in rye rangskik; opstapel.

tierce, terts (mus.); drie volgkaarte, driekaart; vaatjie.

tier'cel, **tier'celet**, mannetjiesvalk.

tier'cet, terset (sonnet); tersine (langer gedig).

tie: *~-rod*, koggelstok; trekstang, stuurstang; spoorstang, koppelstang; bindstang; spanstaaf; baanstang; *~-stitch*, hoedeknoopsteek; *~-up*, verwikkeling; staking, verbinding; *~-wig*, pruik met strik; *~-wire*, binddraad.

tiff, (n) rusie, standjie; slegte bui; sluk, teug; *BE in a ~*, kwaad wees; *HAVE a ~*, rusie kry; (v) woorde kry; kwaad wees; met teugies drink, nip.

tiff'in, (n) ligte middagmaal; (v) 'n ligte ete gebruik.

tig'er, (Indiese) tier; gedugte teenstander; rusiemaker; *like a ~*, soos 'n tier; wreed en woes; *~-beetle*, sandkewer; *~-cat*, tier(bos)kat; *~-fig*, streepvy; *~-fish*, tiervis; *~-ish*, tieragtig; wreed; *~-like*, tieragtig; *~-lily*, tierlelie; *~('s)-eye*, tieroog (halfedelsteen); *~-shark*, tierhaai; skaamhaai; *~-spotted*, soos 'n tier gestreep; met kolle soos 'n tier; *~-wolf*, tierwolf *(Hyena corcuta)*.

tight, (n) vaste spel, vas (rugby); (a) nou, eng, spannend; vas, strak; netjies; styf, skaars (van geld); gierig; geswael, dronk, aangeskote; *be in a ~ CORNER*, in die knyp (noute) wees; *a ~ FIT*, baie nousluitend (klere); *MONEY is ~*, geld is skaars; *a ~ ROPE*, 'n stywe tou; (adv) styf, vas; *HOLD on ~*, hou styf vas; *SIT ~*, vas (in die saal) sit.

tight'en, nouer maak, vaster maak; stywer span; aandraai (skroef); *~ one's BELT*, die maag ingord; *~ up CONTROL*, die beheer verskerp; *~ one's GRIP*, vaster vat; *~ up the REGULATIONS*, die regulasies verskerp; *~er*, spanner (draad).

tight: *~-fisted*, gierig, vrekkig; *~-fitting*, noupassend, nousluitend; *~ forward*, vaste voorspeler; *~ head*, vaskop(man); *~head lock*, vaskopslot; *~ head loose*, vaste los(spel); *~ knot*, stywe knoop; *~-laced*, styf geryg; preuts, bekrompe; *~ lass*, agtermekaar nooientjie; *~-lipped*, met styfgeperste lippe; geslote; *~ly*, styf; *~ match*, taai (kwaai) wedstryd; ~**ness**, engheid, nouheid; strakheid; skaarsheid (geld); ~ **play**, vaste spel; ~**rope**, gespanne koord; ~**-rope dancer**, koorddanser, draadloper; ~**-rope dancing**, koorddansery; ~**s**, spanbroek, spanpak; kaalpak; ~ **scrum**, vaste skrum; ~ **spot**, gevaarpunt; knyp; noute.

tig'on, tierleeu.

tig'ress, (-es), tierwyfie; *as fierce as a* ~, so kwaai soos 'n tierwyfie.

tigrid'ia, daglelie.

tig'rish, *kyk* **tigerish**.

tike, *kyk* **tyke**.

tila'pia, tilapia, kurper.

til'de, tilda, tilde (~).

tile, (n) dakpan, teël; pluiskeil; *GO on the* ~*s*, pierewaai; *have a* ~ *LOOSE*, nie al die varkies in die hok hê nie; van lotjie getik; (v) beteël, met panne dek; met teëls uitlê; geheimhouding oplê; ~ **batten**, panlat; ~**-burner**, panbakker; teëlbakker.

tiled, met panne gedek, geteël; ingelê; ~ **bath**, teëlbad; ~ **floor**, teëlvloer; ~ **roof**, pandak; ~ **wall**, teëlmuur.

tile: ~**-field**, teëlbakkery; ~ **floor**, teëlvloer; ~**-kiln**, teëloond; ~**-layer**, teëldekker; teëllaag; ~**-maker**, teëlmaker, teëlbakker; ~**r**, pandekker, teëldekker, dakdekker; ~ **roof**, pandak, teëldak; ~**-works**, panbakkery, teëlbakkery.

til'ing, teëlwerk; beteëling; teëlbekleding; dakpanne.

till[1], (n) geldlaai; geldkis.

till[2], (n) kleigrond; (v) bebou, ploeg, bewerk.

till[3], (prep) tot; *you can call* ~ *the COWS come home*, al jou roepery sal niks help nie; *true* ~ *DEATH*, getrou tot die dood; *not* ~ *MIDNIGHT*, nie voor middernag nie; ~ *THEN*, tot dan; (conj) tot, totdat.

till: ~ **able**, ploegbaar, beboubaar, bewerkbaar; ~ **age**, landbebouing, akkerbou; grondbewerking.

till'er[1], (n) landbouer; bewerker; korsbreker.

till'er[2], (n) helmstok, stuurstok, roerpen.

till'er[3], (n) loot, uitloopsel, waterloot, suier; (v) uitloop.

till'er: ~**-chain**, ~**-rope**, stuurreep, stuurtou.

till'ing, (die) ploeg, bebouing, grondbewerking.

till: ~**-lifting**, laaibesteling; ~**-money**, kasgeld; ~**-robber**, ~**-sneak**, ~**-tapper**, laaidief, laailigter.

tilt[1], (n) tent, kap, seil; (v) met 'n seil toemaak.

tilt[2], (n) toernooi, steekspel; woordestryd; skuinsheid, skuinste, helling; smeehamer; *at FULL* ~, in volle vaart; *GIVE it a* ~, te lyf gaan; *RIDE full* ~ *at*, in volle vaart afstorm op; (v) steek; omstamp, omgooi; skuins staan; kantel, wip, laat oorhel; smee; ~ *AT*, steek na, lostrek op, aanval (fig.); ~ *one's CHAIR*, jou stoel laat agteroorleun; ~ *one's HAT*, jou hoed skuins dra; ~ *OVER*, skeef staan; omkantel; ~ *at the RING*, ringsteek; ~ *UP*, kantel; omwip; ~ *at WINDMILLS*, teen windmeules (denkbeeldige euwels) veg, ~ **er**, kampvegter; ringsteker; kantelaar, omgooier.

tilth, bebouing; akkerbou; ploegland.

tilt' hammer, smeehamer, sterthamer.

tilt'ing, (n) toernooi, lansvegtery; kanteling; (a) gekantel; toernooi-; ~ **car**, stortkar, wipkar; ~**-lance**, toernooilans; ~**-place**, toernooiveld.

tilt' roof, tentdak, geboë saaldak.

tilt' yard, toernooiveld.

tim'bal, keteltrom.

tim'ber, (n) timmerhout, hout; bos; balk, kromhout; kniehout (skip); (v) stut; beskoei (mynskag); ~**-cart**, houtwa; ~**-headed**, dom, bot; ~**-hitch**, timmersteek; ~ **ing**, betimmering, timmerwerk; houtbeskutting, bekisting (myn); ~ **line**, boomgrens; ~ **man**, houtkapper; houthandelaar; ~**-merchant**, houthandelaar; ~**-mill**, saagmeule; ~ **rot**, houtverrotting; ~**-seasoning**, houtdroging; ~**-trade**, houthandel; ~**-tree**, timmerhoutboom; ~**-work**, houtwerk; ~**-yard**, timmerwerf; paaltjies (krieket); *there was a row in his* ~*-yard*, sy paaltjies het gespat.

tim'bre, timbre, toonkleur, toonskakering.

tim'brel, tamboeryn.

time, (n) tyd; stonde; maat; keer, maal, skoot, slag; tempo; pas; ~ *AFTER* ~, keer op keer; *AFTER a* ~, na 'n rukkie; *AFTER* ~, later as die bepaalde tyd, laat; ~ *and AGAIN*, herhaaldelik, telkemale; *work AGAINST* ~, alle kragte inspan om betyds klaar te kry; *be AHEAD of one's* ~, jou tyd vooruit wees; *for ALL* ~, vir altyd; *ALL the* ~, die hele tyd; gedurig; *at ALL* ~*s*, altyd; te alle tye; *of ALL* ~, van alle tye; *at ONE* ~, te eniger tyd; enige tyd; *ARRIVE before* ~, te vroeg aankom; *ASK the* ~, vra hoe laat dit is; *AT all* ~*s*, te(n) alle tye; *AT the* ~, toe, destyds; *AT* ~*s*, so nou en dan; somtyds; by tye; *BEAT* ~, die maat slaan; *be BEFORE one's* ~, jou tyd vooruit wees; *BEG* ~, uitstel vra; *BEHIND the* ~*s*, uit die tyd; met verouderde idees; *for the* ~ *BEING*, intussen, tydelik; *BIDE one's* ~, jou tyd afwag; *BY the* ~ *that*, wanneer; *COME up to* ~, op die regte tyd kom; *in* ~ *to COME*, in die toekoms; *his* ~ *has COME*, sy uurtjie het geslaan; sy laaste uur het geslaan; *in COURSE of* ~, met verloop van tyd, mettertyd; *at this* ~ *of the DAY*, teen hierdie tyd v.d. dag; nou nog; *so that's the* ~ *of DAY!*, staan sake so!; *the* ~ *of DAY*, die uur; *be DOING* ~, jou straf uitdien; *his* ~ *is DRAWING near*, sy tydjie word kort; *in DUE* ~, ter geleëner tyd; op die gesette tyd; vroeër of later; *EVERY* ~, elke keer; *there is* ~ *for EVERYTHING*, alles het sy tyd; daar is tyd vir alles; *have a TINE* ~, iets besonder geniet; ~ *FLIES*, die tyd vlieg; *chairman FOR the* ~ *being*, fungerende (dienende) voorsitter; *FOR a* ~, 'n rukkie, 'n tyd lank; *take (seize)* ~ *by the FORELOCK*, die geleentheid aangryp; die kans waarneem; as dit pap reën, moet jy skep; *FREE* ~, vrye tyd; ~ *of FRET and fury*, die stormen-drangperiode; *FROM* ~ *to* ~, af en toe, van tyd tot tyd; goeie ou tyd; *make GOOD* ~, vinnig reis; *In GOOD* ~, goed op tyd; *be having a GOOD* ~, 'n heerlike dag hê; *all in GOOD* ~, op 'n geleë tydstip; *have a HARD* ~ *of it*, dit moeilik hê; harde bene kou; *HAVE no* ~ *for someone*, iem. nie kan verdra nie; ~ *HEALS all wounds*, die tyd is die beste heelmeester; *it is HIGH* ~, dis hoog tyd; *have a HOT* ~, lelik bontstaan; *from* ~ *IMMEMORIAL*, sedert onheuglike tye; van toeka se dae; *IN* ~, betyds (vir ete); uiteindelik; *JUNCTURE of* ~, tydsgewrig; *KEEP* ~, die maat hou; *KEEP good* ~, goed tydhou; *KEEP up with the* ~*s*, met die tyd saamgaan; *KILL* ~, die tyd verdryf; *LACK of* ~, tydsgebrek; *LAPSE of* ~, tydsverloop; *it will LAST my* ~, dit sal hou so lank ek leef; *LENGTH of* ~, tydsduur; ~ *LIES heavy on one's hands*, jy kan die tyd nie omkry nie; *have the* ~ *of one's LIFE*, dit besonder geniet; *at my* ~ *of LIFE*, op my leeftyd; *be given the* ~ *of one's LIFE*, dit hotagter kry; les moet opsê; *not for a LONG* ~, selde indien ooit; *MANY* ~*s*, dikwels, baie; *it is only a MATTER of* ~, dis net 'n kwessie van tyd; *Greenwich MEAN* ~, middelbare Greenwichtyd; ~ *out of MIND*, sedert onheuglike tye; ~ *is MONEY*, tyd is geld; *MOST of the* ~, gewoonlik, meestal; *make the MOST of the* ~, die tyd uitkoop; ~ *and MOTION study*, tyd-en bewegingstudie; *in the NICK of* ~, net betyds; *have NO* ~ *for something*, geen belang in iets stel nie; *have NO* ~ *for someone*, iem. nie kan duld nie; *in NO* ~, in 'n kits; *in next to NO* ~, byna onmiddellik; *at NO* ~, in geen stadium nie; nooit nie; ~ *s out of NUMBER*, baie maal, tallose kere; *NOW is your* ~, nou is jou kans; *for OLD* ~ *'s sake*, ter wille v.d. verlede; *OLDEN* ~*s*, die ou tyd; *ON* ~, op die bepaalde tyd; volgens rooster; *arrive ON* ~, betyds aankom; *ONCE upon a* ~, vanmelewe se dae; eenmaal; *at ONE* ~, eenmaal; *ONE at a* ~, een-een; *OTHER* ~*s, other manners*, ander tye, ander sedes; *OUT of* ~, uit die tyd; uit die pas; *my* ~ *is my OWN*, ek beskik oor my tyd; *let me have the information in your OWN* ~, gee my die inligting wanneer dit jou pas; *PASS the* ~ *of day*, groet; 'n rukkie gesels; *PLAY for* ~, tyd probeer wen; sake probeer vertraag; *POINT of* ~, tydstip; *PRECISELY on* ~, presies op tyd; klokslag; *there is no* ~ *like the PRESENT*, die geskikste tyd is nou; *at the* ~ *of going to PRESS*, by die ter perse gaan; met druktyd; *it is only a QUESTION of* ~, dit is net 'n kwessie van tyd; *a RACE AGAINST* ~, 'n wed-

timeous 1308 **tiny**

loop teen die tyd; *at the RIGHT* ~, op die regte tyd; *the* ~ *is RIPE*, dit is hoog tyd; *RUN against* ~, meer te doen hê as wat jy tyd voor het; *at the SAME* ~, terselfdertyd; tegelykertyd; *SAVING of* ~, tydsbesparing; ~*s and SEASONS*, gesette tye; *SERVE* ~, tronkstraf uitdien, jou tyd uitsit (in die tronk); *SERVE one's* ~, as leerjonge dien; *be on SHORT* ~, deeltyds werk; *the SIGN of the* ~*s*, die teken v.d. tyd; *SPACE of* ~, tydsbestek; *SPARE* ~, vrye tyd; *SPEND* ~, die tyd deurbring (slyt); *TAKE* ~, tyd neem; ~ *will TELL*, die tyd sal leer; *TELL the* ~, op die oorlosie kyk; sê hoe laat dit is; *TEN* ~*s five*, tien maal vyf; *by THAT* ~, dan, teen daardie tyd; *by the* ~ *THAT income tax is deducted*, nadat inkomstebelasting afgetrek is; *there is a* ~ *for all THINGS*, alles het sy tyd; ~ *and TIDE wait for no man*, 'n mens moet die geleentheid aangryp; smee die yster solank dit warm is; *the trains run TO* ~, die treine loop presies op tyd; *from* ~ *TO* ~, van tyd tot tyd; af en toe; *TWO at a* ~, twee tegelyk; *UNTIL such* ~ *as*, tot tyd en wyl; *UNIT of* ~, tydeenheid; ~ *is UP*, die tyd is om (verstreke); ~ *WAS when*, daar was 'n tyd toe; *WASTE of* ~, tydverkwisting; *WHAT is the* ~?, hoe laat is dit?; *the* ~ *of the YEAR*, die tyd v.d. jaar; *the* ~ *is not YET (come)*, die tyd het nog nie gekom nie; (v) regsit; die maat aangee; maat hou; die juiste tydstip kies, die tyd reël; die tyd bepaal; die tyd opneem; klok; ~ *your BLOWS*, sorg dat elke hou op die regte oomblik geplant word; ~ *a FUSE*, 'n lont stel; ~ *ONESELF*, vasstel hoe gou jy iets kan doen; vasstel hoe lank dit jou neem om iets te doen; ~ *a THING well*, iets reël om op die regte tyd te gebeur; *not WELL* ~*d*, ongeleë, nie op die geskikte tyd nie; ~**-bargain**, termyntransaksie; ~ **bomb**, tydbom; ~**-book**, tydboek; ~**-card**, uurkaart, rooster; ~**-clock**, kontroleklok, stempelklok; ~**-exposure**, tydopname; ~ **factor**, tydfaktor; ~**-fuse**, tydontsteker; tydbuis; ~**-glass**, sandlopertjie; ~**-honoured**, eerbiedwaardig, tradisioneel, eeue-oud; ~**-ignition**, tydontsteking; ~ **keeper**, oorlosie; tydopnemer, tydbeampte; tydreëlaar, tydaangeër; ~**-killer**, tydverkorter; niksdoener; tydkorting; ~**-lag**, vertraging; ~ **less**, oneindig; tydeloos; ontydig; ~**lessness**, oneindigheid; tydeloosheid; ~**-limit**, tydgrens; termyn; ~ **liness**, tydigheid; ~**-lock**, klokslot; ~ **ly**, tydig, vroeg, instyds, betyds.

time'ous, tydig; ~**ously**, betyds.

time: ~**-payment**, termynbetaling; ~**piece**, uurwerk, klok; ~ **r**, tydopnemer; tydhouer; ~**-rate**, tydloon; ~**-recorder**, tydopnemer; ~**-saving**, (n) tydbesparing; (a) tydbesparend; ~**-scale**, tydskaal; ~**-serving**, (n) manteldraaiery, draadsittery; (a) veranderlik; onbestendig; ~**-sheet**, tydstaat; werklys, uurstaat; ~**-shell**, tydgranaat; ~**-signal**, tydsein; ~ **switch**, tydskakelaar; ~ **table**, (diens)rooster, diensreëling; lesrooster; werkplan; treinrooster; vliegtuig-, vlugrooster; ~**-thief**, dagdief; ~**-wasting**, tydrowend; ~**-work**, werk by die uur, uurloonwerk; ~**-worker**, uurloner; ~**-worn**, oud, verslete; verouder(d), afgesaag.

tim'id, skaam, skamerig, skroomvallig, beskroomd, huiwerig, bangerig, angsvallig, bedees, vreesagtig; verleë, eenkennig, inkennig, sku(erig), skugter; *as* ~ *as a fawn*, so bang soos 'n bok vir 'n skoot hael; ~**ity**, ~**ness**, skamerigheid, skroomvalligheid, vreesagtigheid; eenkennigheid, timiditeit, inkennigheid, skuheid, skroom, skrikagtigheid, skaamheid.

tim'ing, tydreëling, regulering, vonkstelling (motor); tydsberekening; tydmeting; ~ **gear**, reguleertoestel; tydrat, reëlrat; ~ **mark**, reguleermerk.

timoc'racy, timokrasie.

timocrat'ic, timokraties.

tim'orous, bangerig, skrikkerig, huiwerig, skrikagtig, skimmel; beskroomd, skroomvallig, vreesagtig, angsvallig, skroomagtig; ~**ness**, skrikkerigheid, skroomvalligheid, beskroomdheid; bangerigheid.

Tim'othy, Timoteüs.

tim'panist, poukenis.

tim'pano, (..**pani**), pouk, keteltrom.

tin, (n) tin; blik; blikkie (houer); geld; (v) (**-ned**), vertin; inlê, verduursaam; inmaak, inblik; (a) tin=; blik=; ~ **box**, blik.

tinc'al, tinkal, natuurlike boraks.

tin' can, blik; blikkantien.

tinctor'ial, kleur=, verf=.

tinc'ture, (n) tinktuur; kleur, tint; tikkie, sweempie; ~ *of iodine*, jodiumtinktuur, joodtinktuur; (v) kleur, verf; 'n smaak gee.

tin'der, tonteldoek; *as dry as* ~, so droog soos strooi; ~**-box**, tonteldoos; kruitvat; ~**-bush**, tontelbossie; ~ **y**, tonteldoekagtig; maklik ontvlambaar.

tine, tand (van eg, vurk); punt (van takbokhoring).

tin'ea, omloop.

tined, getand.

tin' foil, (n) bladtin; foelie(sel), stanniool, blinkpapier; (v) verfoelie, met bladtin bedek.

ting, (n) tingeling, geklingel; (v) klink, klingel.

tinge, (n) tint, kleur; tikkie; smakie, bysmaak; (v) tint, kleur, verf; 'n smakie (geurtjie) gee aan; *hair* ~ *d with grey*, hare met grys gespikkel.

ti'ngle, (n) tinteling, prikkeling; getingel; tingeling; getuit; (v) klink; tintel; suis; tuit.

ti'ngling, (n) tinteling, getuit, geruis, suising, suiseling; prikkeling; ~ *in the ears*, getuit in die ore; (a) brandend.

tin: ~ **god**, afgodjie; *he thinks himself a little* ~ *god*, hy dink hy is die baas van die plaas; ~ **hat**, staalhelm; *put the* ~ *hat on something*, 'n end daaraan maak; ~**-hat target**, halfkolskyf.

tink'al = **tincal**.

tink'er, (n) ketellapper, blikslaer; knoeier; gelap, geknoei; *I don't care a* ~ *'s curse (cuss)*, ek gee nie 'n flenter om nie; (v) heelmaak, lap; knoei, konkel, prutsel; ~ *it UP*, daaraan knoei; *he spent much time* ~ *ing WITH his motor bike*, hy bestee baie tyd met knutsel aan sy motorfiets; ~ **er**, lapper; knoeier.

tin'kering, prutsel(a)ry; lapwerk; ~ **with**, geliefhebber met; prutseling met; gewerskaf; ~ **measures**, lapmiddels.

tin'kle, (n) getjingel, geklingel; getokkel; gerinkel; (v) klink, rinkel; tokkel; ~ **r**, klokkie.

tink'ling, geklingel, getjingel; rinkeling.

tin: ~ **liquor**, tinoplossing; **T~ Lizzie**, Tin Lizzi; (hist.); rammelkas, tjorrie; ~ **man**, tingieter, blikslaer; ~ **man's mallet**, blikslaershamer; ~ **man's shears**, blikskêr; ~ **mine**, tinmyn; ~**-mining**, tinontginning; ~ **mug**, blikbeker.

tinned, ingelê, blikkies=; ~ **foods**, blikkieskos; ~ **meat**, blikkiesvleis.

tin: ~ **ner**, tingrawer; vertinner; blikslaer; ~ **ning**, vertinning; inmaak, inlê.

tinnit'us, oorsuising, gesuis, tuiting.

tin: ~ **ny**, tinhoudend; tingtig; blikkerig; ~ **opener**, bliksnyer; ~ **ore**, tinerts; ~ **pail**, blikemmer; ~ **plate**, (n) blik; blikbord; ~**-plate**, (v) vertin; ~**-plater**, blikwerker; ~ **pot**, (n) blikpot; ~ **pot**, (a) prullerig; *it was a* ~*pot affair*, dit was 'n treurige spulletjie; ~ **roof**, sinkdak, blikdak.

tin'sel, (n) skynskoon, verguldsel, klatergoud; opskik; (v) (**-led**), met klatergoud versier; verguld (a) skoonskynend; oppervlakkig; skyn=.

tin: ~ **shanty**, blikpondok; ~**smith**, blikslaer; ~ **snips**, blikskêr; ~ **solder**, soldeertin, tinsoldeersel; ~ **soldier**, bliksoldaatjie; ~**stone**, tinerts, tinoksied, tinokside.

tint, (n) tint, kleur; (v) tint, kleur.

tint'ed, gekleur, geverf; ~ **glass**, getinte glas; ~ **glasses**, gekleurde bril.

tint'ing, tinting, kleuring.

tintinnab'ular, rinkelend, klingelend.

tintinna'bulate, klingel.

tintinnabula'tion, gerinkel, geklink, getjingel.

tintinnab'ulous, klingelend; klokluiers=.

tintinnab'ulum, (..**la**), klokkie.

tin'to, tintwyn.

tintom'eter, kleurmeter.

tin' town, blikkiesdorp.

tin'ty, bont gekleur.

tin: ~ **type**, metaalfoto; ~ **ware**, blikwerk, blikgoed; blikslaerswerk.

tin'y, klein, nietig, gering, petieterig.

tip¹, (n) tip, top; bolpunt; spits, punt; *to the ~s of his FINGERS*, in hart en niere; *FROM ~ to ~*, van punt tot punt; *the ~ of the NOSE*, die punt v.d. neus; *from ~ to TOE*, van kop tot tone; *it is on the ~ of my TONGUE*, dis op die punt van my tong; (v) **(-ped)**, 'n punt aansit.
tip², (n) skuinste, kanteling; vuilgoedhoop, ashoop; stortkar, wipkar; stompie; wenk; geheime inligting; fooi, duimkruid, drinkgeld; beslag; *BACK a ~*, op 'n perd wed waarop jy 'n wenk gekry het; *a GOOD ~*, 'n goeie wenk; 'n goeie fooi; *MISS one's ~*, die bal mis slaan; *a STRAIGHT ~*, 'n wenk uit die eerste hand; *TAKE the ~*, die wenk aanneem; (v) **(-ped)**, beslaan; omrand; skuins hou, wip, stort; gooi; tik; top (biljart); 'n fooi gee; 'n wenk gee; *be ~ped AS the next president*, as die volgende president genoem word; *~ the BALANCE*, die skaal laat oorslaan; die deurslag gee; *~ someone OFF*, iem. 'n wenk gee; *~ OVER*, omgooi, kantel; *~ UP*, skuins hou; skuins stoot; *~ the WAITER*, die kelner 'n fooi gee; *~ a WINK*, 'n wenk gee.
tip: *~ cart*, stortkar, wipkar, tuimelkar; *~ cat*, kennetjie(spel); *~ chute*, stortgeut; *~ lorry*, stortwa, wipwa; *~ mound*, afvalhoop, storthoop; *~-off*, wenk.
tipp'er, fooigeër; wipper; storttoestel.
tipp'et, mantelkraag, pelskraag.
tipp'ing, fooigeëry; storting; *~ bridge*, wipbrug; *~ bucket*, wipemmer; *~ chute*, stortgeut; *~ furnace*, kanteloond; *~ gear*, wiptoestel; *~ gears*, wipper; *~ plant*, storttoestel; *~ site*, stortterrein (vuilgoed); *~ system*, fooistelsel; *~ truck*, storttrok.
tip'ple, (n) sterk drank; glasie; ertshoop; koolhoop; (v) 'n dop steek, drink.
tipp'ler¹, dronklap, slampamper, drinkebroer, brandewynsak, drinker, wynsak, nathals.
tipp'ler², wipper (voertuig), omkippelaar; tippelaarduif.
tipp'ling¹, suipery; drankgebruik.
tipp'ling², omkanteling; *~ gear*, omkippelaar.
tip' shoe, halfmaanyster.
tip'siness, besopenheid.
tip'staff, geregsdienaar.
tip'ster, wenkgewer.
tip'sy, dronk, besope, hoenderkop, nat, aangeskote, aangebrand, aangekap, getik, gerook, halfdronk, gebier, gekoring, gebraai, gedop, lekker, gedrink; *BE ~*, die straat meet; *HALF ~*, lekkerlyf; *~ cake*, aanklamkoek; *~ tart*, aanklamtert.
tip'-tilted, opwip=; *~ nose*, wipneus.
tip'toe, (n); *ON ~*, op die tone; *ON ~ with expectation*, in gespanne verwagting, (v) op die tone loop; (adv) suutjies, op die tone.
tip'-top, (n) die beste, hoogste; hoogtepunt; (a, adv) eersteklas, prima, allerbeste; *everything's ~*, dis eersteklas, piekfyn.
tip' truck, stortwa.
tip'-up, wip=, opklap=, klap=; *~ bed*, opklapbed; *~ seat*, klapstoel.
tirade', tirade, uitval.
tirailleur', skerpskutter.
tire¹, (n) buiteband); (v) 'n buiteband aansit; *kyk* **tyre**.
tire², (n) hooftooisel; opskik.
tire³, (v) moeg word; verveel; moeg maak, vermoei; *~ to DEATH*, dodelik verveel; *~ OF something*, moeg word vir iets; *~ OUT*, afmat; *~ WITH*, moeg maak van; *~d*, moeg, tam, mat; *BE ~d of something*, tee vir iets wees; moeg wees vir (van) iets; *~d OUT*, doodmoeg, pê, kapot; *~d'ness*, tamheid, moegheid; matheid; *~less*, onvermoeid; rusteloos; *~some*, vermoeiend; langdradig afmattend; verveland; *~someness*, langdradigheid; ver= velendheid.
tire'woman, (arch.), kamerjuffrou, kamenier.
tir'ing, vermoeiend; verveland.
tir'ing-room, kleedkamer (skouburg).
tir'o, (-s), beginner, groentjie, nuweling.
tirocin'ium, leertyd; eerste beginsels.
tir'o verse, sukkelvers.
tir'wit, kiewiet, klap-klappie.
'tis, dis.
tiss'ue, weefsel; goudlaken; reeks, aaneenskakeling;
sneespapier; *CONNECTIVE ~*, bindweefsel; *a ~ of LIES*, 'n aaneenskakeling (sameweefsel) van leuens; *MUSCULAR ~*, spierweefsel; *~ paper*, sneesdoekie, snesie, sneespapier(tjie).
tit¹, tepel, tet (plat).
tit², mees; kapokvoëltjie; piet-tjou-tjou.
tit³, tik; *~ for tat*, leer om leer.
Tit'an¹, *the ~s*, die Titane.
tit'an², reus, hemelbestormer; songod; *~ate*, tita= naat.
titan'ic, reusagtig, tamaai groot, titaan=, titanies.
titanif'erous, titaanhoudend.
titan'ium, titaan.
tit'bit, lekkerny, lekker happie, lekker brokkie, versnapering, keurhappie.
tith, tiendepligtig, skatpligtig.
tith'able, tiendepligtig, skatpligtig.
tithe, (n) tiende, tiende gedeelte; (v) skatting hef; *~-gatherer*, tiendegaarder, tiendeheffer.
tith'ing, tiendereg; tiendeheffing.
Ti'tian, Titiaan, Tiziano.
tit'illate, streel; prikkel; kielie.
titilla'tion, streling; prikkeling; gekittel.
tit'ivate, optooi, mooimaak, opknap, opskik.
titiva'tion, optooiing, opknapping, opskikking.
tit'lark, koester(tjie).
ti'tle, (n) naam; titel, opskrif, betiteling; goudgehalte; aanspraak; eiendomsreg; (pl) titulatuur; *CONFER a ~ on someone*, 'n titel toeken aan iem.; *HAVE a ~ to*, geregtig wees op; *~ of LAND*, grondbrief; *~ to PROPERTY*, eiendomsbewys; *under the STYLE and ~ of*, onder die (firma)naam; *SUC= CESSOR to a ~*, regsopvolger; (v) betitel, noem, tituleer; *~d*, getitel, met 'n titel; *~-deed*, transportakte, titelbewys, grondbrief, eiendomsbrief, eiendomsbewys, kaart en transport; *~-holder*, titelhouer; *~-leaf*, titelblad; *~less*, naamloos; titelloos, sonder titel; *~ mania*, titelsug; *~-page*, titelblad; *~-part*, *~-role*, titelrol.
tit'ling¹, titeldruk.
tit'ling², mees.
tit'mouse, (.. mice), mees.
Ti'toism, Titoïsme.
Ti'toist, (n) Titoïs; (a) Titoïsties.
tit'rate, die gehalte bepaal, titreer.
titra'tion, titrasie, titrering.
titt'er, (n) gegiggel; (v) giggel, lag, ginnegaap; *~ing*, gegiggel, gelag.
titt'ivate, *kyk* **titivate**.
tit'tle, tittel, puntjie, jota, stippel; *not one jot or ~*, geen jota of tittel nie; *~-tattle*, (n) geklets, gebabbel, gekekkel; onwyse verhale; (v) klets, babbel; skinder.
titt'up, (n) huppeling; (v) huppel, bokspring; *~(p)y*, wankel, onvas; springerig.
ti'tubate, struikel; waggel.
tituba'tion, krieweliguid; verleentheid; waggeling.
tit'ular, (n) titularis; (a) titulêr, in naam; *~ saint*, beskermheilige; *~y*, titulêr.
'T'-joint, T-las.
to, (adv) toe; *COME ~*, bykom; *pull the DOOR ~*, trek die deur toe; *~ and FRO*, heen en weer; (prep); tot, na, na . . . toe, vir, jeens; voor; (plus inf.) te, om te; *~ ACCOUNT rendered*, aan gelewerde rekening; *APPLY ~*, aansoek doen by (om); het betrekking op; *~ ARMS!* te wapen! *~ his ASTON= ISHMENT*, tot sy verbasing; *AVAILABLE ~*, beskikbaar vir; *~ the BEST of one's ability*, so goed as jy kan; *it ADDS up ~ R10*, alles saam is R10; *bring ~ someone's ATTENTION*, onder iem. se aandag bring; *BACK ~ back*, rug aan rug; *~ the BEST of your ability*, na jou beste vermoë; so goed as wat jy kan; *~ a hair's BREADTH*, op 'n haar na; *true ~ CHARACTER*, in ooreenstemming met sy karakter; *CHEER ~ the echo*, dawerend toejuig, toejuig dat dit dreun; *a CHILD ~ him*, 'n kind in vergelyking met hom; soos 'n kind vir hom; *COM= PARED ~*, in vergelyking met; *~ this DAY*, tot op die huidige dag; *~ a certain DEGREE*, in sekere mate; *they DIED ~ a man*, die laaste een is dood; *next DOOR ~ us*, langsaan ons; *DRINK oneself ~ death*, jou dooddrink; *EASY ~ explain*, maklik om

te verklaar; *ELECT* ~ *the council*, in die raad benoem (verkies); *there is no END* ~ *his ingenuity*, daar is geen end aan sy vernuftigheid nie; *there is no END* ~ *his patience*, sy geduld is eindeloos; ~ *that END*, met die doel; *FACE* ~ *face*, van aangesig tot aangesig; *I told him* ~ *his FACE*, ek het hom in sy gesig gesê; ~ *his FANCY*, na sy smaak; *FIVE* ~ *six*, vyf minute voor ses; *GO* ~ *bed*, gaan slaap, bed toe gaan; ~ *GOODS*, aan bestelling; *be R10* ~ *the GOOD*, R10 maak (wen); *drink* ~ *your HEALTH*, op jou gesondheid drink; *HUNDRED* ~ *one*, 'n honderd teen een; *there is more* ~ *IT than that*, daar sit meer agter; dit het groter betekenis; *KIND* ~, vriendelik teenoor; goed vir; *we want* ~ *KNOW*, ons wil weet; ~ *the best of my KNOWLEDGE*, sover ek weet; ~ *the LAST man*, tot die laaste man (toe); almal; ~ *the LEFT of*, links van; ~ *LET*, te huur; *true* ~ *LIFE*, lewensgetrou; ~ *my LIKING*, na my smaak (sin); *a MEANS* ~ *an end*, 'n middel tot 'n doel; *made* ~ *MEASURE*, na maat gemaak; ~ *my MIND*, volgens my mening; *speak* ~ *a MOTION*, oor 'n voorstel praat; *I haven't a cent* ~ *my NAME*, ek is platsak; *NOMINATE* ~ *the council*, in die raad benoem; ~ *PAY*, verskuldig; *pull* ~ *PIECES*, in flenters skeur; ~ *which PLACE?* waarheen? *PLY* ~ *S.A.*, op S.A. vaar; ~ *the POINT*, ter sake; *POINT* ~, wys na iets; *he PROMISED* ~, hy het beloof om; ~ *the PURPOSE*, ter sake, toepaslik; ~ *good PURPOSE*, met sukses; *all* ~ *no PURPOSE*, alles tevergeefs; *READ* ~ *someone*, vir iem. (voor)lees; *go* ~ *SCHOOL*, skool toe gaan; *go* ~ *the SCHOOL*, na die skoolgebou gaan; *wet* ~ *the SKIN*, nat tot op jou vel; *put a child* ~ *SLEEP*, 'n kind aan die slaap maak; ~ *my TASTE*, volgens (na) my smaak; ~ *TASTE*, na smaak; *food with a TASTE* ~ *it*, smaaklike kos; *TEN* ~ *one it is true*, dit is tien teen een waar; *bring* ~ *TRIAL*, voor die hof bring; in verhoor neem; *on the WAY* ~ *school*, op pad skool toe; ~ *the WEST of*, wes van; *WHAT is that* ~ *you?* wat het jy daarmee te doen? wat kan dit jou skeel? wat beteken dit vir jou? ~ *WHICH*, waartoe; waaraan; *take* ~ *WIFE*, tot vrou neem; *WRITE* ~ *someone*, aan iem. skryf.

toad, padda; walglike persoon, pes; *clawed* ~, platanna; ~**-eater**, inkruiper; vleier; ~**-eating**, (n) inkruiperigheid, lekkery; (a) inkruiperig, lekkerig, witvoetjiesoekerig; ~**-fish**, seeduiwel; ~ **flax**, vlas(leeu)bekkie; ~**-in-the-hole**, ouvrou-onder-die kombers; ~ **ling**, paddatjie; ~ **spit**, paddaskuim; ~**stone**, paddaklip; ~ **stool**, paddastoel, slangkos, duiwelsbrood; ~**y**, (n) **(toadies)**, pluimstryker, lekker, inkruiper, witvoetjiesoeker, strooplekker (v) (..**died**), pluimstryk, witvoetjie soek, inkruiperig wees; ~**ying**, inkruiping, lekkery; ~**yish**, lekkerig, witvoetjiesoekerig; ~**yism**, pluimstrykery, kruipery, lekkery, witvoetjiesoekery, gelek.

toast, (n) roosterbrood, kraakbrood; heildronk, feesdronk; gevierde persoon, gehuldigde; *be the* ~ *of one's DAY*, gevierd wees; *the* ~ *was DRUNK in champagne*, die heildronk is in sjampanje gedrink; *HAVE someone on* ~, met iem. kan maak wat jy wil; *she was the* ~ *of every PARTY*, sy was gevierd; *PROPOSE a* ~, 'n heildronk instel; *WARM as* ~, lekker warm; (v) braai, rooster; 'n heildronk instel/die gesondheid drink van; ~**ed sandwich**, geroosterde toebroodjie; ~**er**, roostervurk; broodrooster; insteller van 'n heildronk; ~**ing**, roostering; heildronk drink; ~**ing-fork**, roostervurk; ~**master**, seremoniemeester; ~**-rack**, broodstandertjie.

tobacc'o, (-s), tabak, twak; ~ **ashes**, tabakas; ~**-box**, tabakdoos; ~ **chlorosis**, tabakchlorose; ~ **company**, tabakmaatskappy; ~ **culture**, tabakbou, tabakverbouing; ~**-curing**, tabakdroging; ~ **cutter**, tabakkerwer, kerfmasjien; ~ **dust**, tabakstof; ~ **extract**, tabakekstrak; ~ **factory**, tabakfabriek; ~ **fumes**, tabakdamp; ~ **heart**, rokershart; ~**-jar**, tabakpot; ~ **juice**, tabaksop; ~ **leaf**, tabakblaar; ~**nist**, tabakhandelaar, tabakwinkel; ~**-pipe**, (tabak)pyp; ~**-plant**, tabakplant; ~**-pot**, tabakpot; ~**-pouch**, tabaksak, twaksak; ~ **shed**, tabakskuur; ~**-shop**, tabakwinkel; ~ **smell**, tabaklug; ~

smoke, tabakrook; tabakwalm; ~**-stopper**, pypstoppertjie; ~**-twister**, tabakdraaier; ~ **wrapper**, dekblad.

to-be', toekomstig; *the BRIDE* ~, die aanstaande bruid; *THE* ~, die toekoms.

tobogg'an, (n) toboggan, (rodel)slee; (v) toboggan ry, sleetjie ry; rodel; 'n afdraand afgly.

tob'y (tobies), blaasop (vis); ~ **jug**, oumannetjieskruik.

Toc' H, Toc H.

toc'o, straf, pak slae, loesing.

tocol'ogy, verloskunde.

toc'sin, brandklok, alarmklok, stormklok; *sound the* ~, die alarmklok lui.

today', vandag, hede; teenswoordig; *one* ~ *is worth two tomorrows*, een voël in die hand is beter as tien in die lug.

tod'dle, (n) waggelgang, trippelgang; kleuter; (v) waggel, trippel; ~ **round**, rondkuier; ~**r**, strompelaartjie, waggelaartjie.

todd'y, (toddies), grok, sopie, regmakertjie.

to-do', drukte, konsternasie, ophef; *CAUSE a* ~, 'n bohaai veroorsaak; *it was a PRETTY* ~, dit was 'n hele affère (gedoente).

toe, (n) toon, onderent; neus (van voorwerpe); *BIG* ~, grootoon; *DIG in one's* ~*s*, vasskop; ysterklou in die grond slaan; *LITTLE* ~, kleintoontjie; *be ON one's* ~*s*, wakker (slaggereed) wees; op en wakker; *you will have to be ON your* ~*s*, jy sal wakker moet loop; jy sal vroeg moet opstaan; jy sal slaggereed moet wees; *from TOP to* ~, van kop tot tone; *TREAD on somebody's* ~*s*, op iem se tone trap; iem. te na kom; iem. aanstoot gee; *TURN up one's* ~*s*, bokveld toe gaan; (iv) die toon (van kous) heelmaak; skop; ~ *IN*, met die voete na binne loop; ~ *the LINE*, op die streep staan; gehoorsaam wees; in jou spoor trap; jou skik (voeg) na; *MAKE someone* ~ *the line*, iem. in sy spoor laat trap; iem. tot gehoorsaamheid dring; ~ *OUT*, uitstaan; ~**-bone**, kootjie; ~**-cap**, neus (van skoen); ~**-catch**, stoot; ~**-clip**, toonlip; ~**d**, met tone; ~**-dancer**, toondanser(es); ~**-drop**, voetverlamming; ~**-nail**, toonnael; ~**-nailed**, oorhoeks bespyker; ~**-piece**, toonstuk.

toff, grootmeneer, pronker, windmaker.

toff'ee, toff'y, (toffies), toffie; tameletjie.

toft, opstal, werf.

tog, (n) kleding(stuk), mondering; (pl) sportklere; voetbalklere; (v) **(-ged)**, aantrek.

tog'a, toga.

tog'bag, kleresak, sportsak.

togeth'er, saam, bymekaar; gelyk, gelykweg; gesamentlik; deurmekaar; *ALL of us* ~, almal saam; *BELONG* ~, bymekaar hoort; *CLOSE* ~, digby mekaar; *COME* ~, vergader, saamkom; *for DAYS* ~, dae aanmekaar; *MULTIPLY* ~, met mekaar vermenigvuldig; ~ *WITH*, saam met; mitsgaders; ~**ness**, (die) saam wees.

togg'ery, pluiens, plunje.

tog'gle, dwarspen; dwarsstuk; ~ **block**, pasblok; ~ **bolt**, haakveerbout; ~**-harpoon**, ~**-iron**, dwarspenharpoen; ~**-joint**, kniegewrig; elmbooggewrig; ~ **lever**, skarnierhefboom; ~ **switch**, knikskakelaar.

toil¹, (n) (in pl. only), net, strik; *in someone's* ~, in iem. se strikke.

toil², (n) swaar arbeid; geswoeg; geslaaf; (v) swaar werk, swoeg, (af)sloof, slaaf, ploeter, sjou, omswoeg; ~ *ALONG*, voortswoeg; aanpiekel; ~ *AT*, werk (slaaf) aan; ~ *and MOIL*, werk en swoeg, swoeg en sweet, swoeë; *they* ~ *NOT, neither do they spin*, hulle arbei en hulle spin nie; ~ *THROUGH*, deurworstel; ~ *UP the hill*, teen die opdraande uitbeur; ~**er**, swoeër, werkesel.

toil'et, toilet; toiletbord; toiletkamer; kleinhuisie, kasteeltjie, privaat, klooster; *make one's* ~, jou toilet maak; ~**-basin**, waskom; ~**-cover**, toiletkleedjie; ~ **glass**, toiletspieël, kleedspieël; ~**-paper**, toiletpapier; ~**-powder**, toiletpoeier; ~ **requisites**, ~**ries**, toiletbenodigdhede, toiletartikels; ~ **roll**, toiletrol; ~**-room**, waskamer, toiletkamer; ~ **seat**, bril; ~**-set**, wasstel, toiletstel; ~ **soap**, toiletseep;

~ **table,** kleedtafel; ~**-tissue,** toiletpapier; ~**-trained,** sindelik.
toil: ~**ing,** geploeter, geswoeg, gesjou; ~*ing and moiling,* gesloof; ~**some,** swaar, vermoeiend, afmattend; ~**someness,** moeisaamheid; ~**worn,** afgemat, afgewerk, vermoeid.
Tokay', Tokaidruiwe; Tokaiwyn.
tok'en, teken; kenteken; bewys; gedagtenis, aandenking; *IN* ~ *of,* as teken van; *by the SAME* ~, op dieselfde manier; om dieselfde rede; ~ **coin,** ruilmunt; tekenmunt; ~ **coinage,** tekengeld; ruilgeld; ~ **force,** simboliese mag, erkenningsmag; ~ **payment,** erkenningsbetaling, simboliese betaling; ~ **resistance,** weerstand bloot as gebaar; ~ **strike,** betoogstaking.
To'kyo, Tokio.
told, *kyk* **tell.**
tolerabil'ity, draaglikheid, duldbaarheid, uitstaanbaarheid.
tol'erable, draaglik, uitstaanbaar; taamlik; duldbaar, passabel, skaflik; ~**ness,** draaglikheid, duldbaarheid, uitstaanbaarheid.
tol'erably, redelik, taamlik, skaflik, vry, nogal, so-so.
tol'erance, verdraagsaamheid; toelating, toleransie; dulding; speelruimte, speling.
tol'erant, verdraagsaam.
tol'erate, verdra, duld, uitstaan, (ge)doog; aansien.
tolera'tion, verdraagsaamheid; dulding, toelating.
toll'¹, (n) klokgelui, geklep; (v) klepper, tamp, lui (klok); die doodsklok lui; ~ *the bell for the death of,* die doodsklok lui vir.
toll², (n) tol, tolgeld, skatting; *take a HEAVY* ~, swaar verliese toebring; *TAKE* ~, 'n tol hef; verg, eis; (v) tol betaal; tolgeld eis; ~ **able,** tolpligtig; ~ **age,** tolgeld; ~**-bar,** slagboom, tolhek; ~**-booth,** tolhuis; ~**-bridge,** tolbrug; ~**-collector,** tolgaarder; ~**-free,** tolvry; ~ **gate,** tolhek; ~**-gatherer,** tolgaarder; ~**-house,** tolhuis.
toll'ing, gelui.
toll: ~ **man,** tolgaarder; tollenaar; ~**-money,** tolgeld; ~**-road,** tolpad; ~**-union,** tolverbond.
toll'y¹, (tollies,) jongossie, tollie.
toll'y², (slang), kers.
Tom¹, *abbr. for* **Thomas,** Thomas; Tom; ~ *DICK and Harry,* Jan Rap en sy maat; Jan, Piet en Klaas; Piet, Paul en Klaas; *there's more knows* ~ *FOOL than* ~ *FOOL knows,* 'n gek se bekendheid strek verder as sy kennis; *LONG* ~, skeepskanon, Long Tom; ~ *THUMB,* Klein Duimpie.
tom², mannetjieskat, kater.
tom'ahawk, (n) strydbyl; (v) met 'n strydbyl kap.
toma'to, (-es), tamatie; ~ **chutney,** tamatieblatjang; ~ **cocktail,** tamatiekelkie; ~ **cream soup,** tamatieroomsop; ~ **jam,** tamatiekonfyt; ~ **juice,** tamatiesap; tamatiesous; ~ **puree,** tamatiepuree; ~**-red,** tamatierooi; ~ **salad,** tamatieslaai; ~ **sauce,** tamatiesous; ~ **soup,** tamatiesop; ~ **stew,** tamatiebredie.
tomb, (n) graftombe, graf; grafkelder; (v) begrawe.
tom'hac, tombak, rooi messing.
tomb'less, sonder gratsteen.
tom'bola, lotery, tombola.
tom'boy, rabbedoe(s), wilde meisie, maltrap.
tomb'stone, grafsteen, serk.
tom'-cat, mannetjieskat, kater.
tome, lywige boekdeel, foliant.
tom'entose, tomen'tous, donserig, harig.
tomen'tum, dons; viltlaag.
tomfool', (n) gek, dwaas; (v) gekheid uithaal, gekskeer; ~**ery,** gekheid, gekskeerdery, lawwigheid, sotterny, apespel.
tomm'y, (tommies,) tommie (soldaat); broodjie; (pl.) lewensmiddele; *soft (white)* ~, vars brood; ~**-bar,** knewel; handkoevoet; ~**-gun,** submasjiengeweer, handmasjiengeweer; ~**-rot,** bog, kaf, onsin, lawwigheid; ~**-screw,** knewelskroef; ~**-shop,** koswinkel; hakkery.
tomnodd'y, (..ddies,) uilskuiken, domkop.
tomo'rrow, môre, more; *the day AFTER* ~, oormôre; ~ *is ANOTHER day,* môre is nog 'n dag; ~ *never COMES,* die dag van môre kom nooit; ~ *MORNING,* môrevroeg, môreoggend; ~ *or the NEXT day,* môre-oormôre.

tom'tit, winterkoninkie; mees.
tom'-tom, (n) tomtom, trom; (v) op die tomtom slaan, trommel.
ton, ton; *LONG* ~, groot of Engelse ton, 2 240 lb.; *METRIC* ~, 1 000 kilogram (2 204,6 lb.); ~*s of MONEY,* geld soos bossies; ~*s of PEOPLE,* hope mense, 'n magdom mense; *SHORT* ~, klein of Kaapse ton, 2 000 lb.
ton'al, toon-, klank-, tonaal.
ton'alite, tonaliet (geol.).
ton'alist, tonalis.
tonal'ity, toonaard, klankgehalte, tonaliteit, toonhoogte, toonskakering; kleurskakering.
to'-name, bynaam.
tone, (n) toon, klank; klem; aard; kleurskakering, kleurdiepte, kleur; gees, stemming; deftigheid; *ADOPT a* ~, 'n toon aanslaan; *ENGAGED* ~, besetsein (telef.); *LOWER the* ~, die toon verlaag; *PURITY of* ~, toonsuiwerheid; *SET a high* ~, 'n hoë toon aangee; *SPEAK in a low* ~, op sagte toon praat; *TAKE a high* ~, 'n hoë toon aanslaan; *TRUE in* ~, toonvas; *the* ~ *of the UNIVERSITY,* die gees v.d. universiteit; (v) stem; harmonieer; die toon aangee; kleur; tint; 'n tint aanneem; ~ *DOWN,* bedaar; temper; versag, laer stem; *her HAT* ~*s with her dress,* haar hoed pas by haar rok; ~ *UP,* krag gee, besiel; hoër stem; op hoër peil bring; trek, aanhaal (kabel); ~**-colour,** toonkleur; ~**-control,** toonknop; toonreëling; ~**-deaf,** musikaal doof, toondoof; ~ **exercise,** klankoefening; ~**less,** toonloos; klankloos; ~**lessness,** toonloosheid; ~**-painter,** toonskilder; ~**-painting,** toonskildering; ~**-picture,** ~**-poem,** toondig; ~**-poet,** toondigter; ~ **range,** toonomvang; ~ **scale,** toonleer, toonladder; ~ **syllable,** beklemtoonde lettergreep; ~ **value,** toonwaarde; ~ **volume,** toonsterkte.
tongs, tang; *not to touch something with a pair of* ~, iets nie met 'n tang wil aanraak nie.
tongue, (n) tong; taal, spraak; skoenleertjie, tongetjie (van skoen, ens.); angel (geweer); ewenaar, naald (skaal); klepel (klok), uitloper (geol.); *give someone a BIT of one's* ~, iem. onder die tong laat deurloop; iem. goed slegsê; iem. 'n uitbrander gee; *I could have BITTEN off my* ~, ek kon my tong afbyt; *with one's* ~ *in one's CHEEK,* op spottende wyse; *keep a CIVIL* ~ *in one's head,* beleef bly; *CONFUSION of* ~*s,* spraakverwarring; *give* ~ *to DOUBT,* twyfel uitspreek; *it FELL from his* ~, dit het hom ontglip; *FIND one's* ~, begin praat; *GIFT of* ~*s,* begaafdheid in tale; *GIVE* ~, sê, uitspreek; blaf; *HOLD one's* ~, jou mond hou; *a* ~ *as KEEN as a razor,* 'n tong so skerp soos 'n skeermes; *give someone the LENGTH of one's* ~, iem. onder die tong laat deurloop; *have a LONG* ~, baie praat; *have a LOOSE* ~ *(in one's head),* loslippig wees; *LOSE one's* ~, geen stomme woord sê nie; *have LOST one's* ~, jou tong verloor het; *have you LOST your* ~? het jy geen mond nie? *the MOTHER* ~, die moedertaal; *be ON the* ~*s of men,* almal het die mond vol daarvan; *a* ~ *like a RAZOR,* 'n tong soos 'n skeermes; *have a READY* ~, gevat wees; nie op jou mond geval wees nie; 'n draad vir elke naald hê; *give someone a lick with the ROUGH side of one's* ~, iem. skrobbeer; *a SLIP of the* ~, 'n onbedagsame woord; *the* ~ *TALKS at the head's cost,* ydel gepraat beskaam die verstand; *speak with a THICK* ~, swaar van tong wees; *his* ~ *is TIED,* hy mag nie praat nie; *have something on the TIP of one's* ~, iets op die punt van die tong hê; *WAG one's* ~, praatsiek wees; *have the* ~*s WAGGING,* die tafel oor iem. dek; die tonge oor iem. roer; *set people's* ~*s WAGGING,* die tonge los maak; skinderpraatjies veroorsaak; *a WELL-OILED* ~, 'n gladde tong; (v) die tong gebruik; oor die tong laat gaan; praat; ~**-bone,** tongbeen; ~**d,** getong, tong-; ~**-file,** tongvyl; ~**-fish,** tongvis; ~**less,** spraakloos; sonder tong; ~ **let,** tongetjie; ~**-shaped,** tongvormig; ~**-tie,** tongbeklemming, spraakgebrek; ~**-tied,** swaar van tong; spraakloos, gebonde, gemuilband; *be* ~**-tied,** met die mond vol tande staan; ~**-twister,** tongknoper; swaar woord, snelsêer; ~**-wagging,** geklets; ~**-worm,** tongwurm.

tong'uing plane, groefskaaf, ploegskaaf; tongbeitel.
ton'ic, (n) versterkmiddel, tonikum; grondtoon; toni=
ka (musiek); *be a* ~, die vrolikheid vanself wees; (a) spannend, versterkend; toon=, tonies; ~ **accent,** sil=
labiese aksent.
toni'city, tonisiteit, toon; veerkrag; spierwerking.
ton'ic: ~ **sol-fa',** solfanotering, solfaskrif; ~ **spasm,** toniese kramp.
tonight', vanaand, vannag.
ton'ish, modieus.
ton'ite, toniet, skietkatoen.
tonk'a: ~ **bean,** tonkaboontjie; ~ **tree,** tonkaboom.
to'nnage, tonmaat; skeepsruimte, laairuimte, tonne=
inhoud; tonnegeld; ~ **deck,** meetdek; ~ **displace=
ment,** waterverplasing.
tonolog'ical, tonologies.
tonol'ogy, toonleer; tonologie.
tonom'eter, toonmeter; spanningsmeter; drukmeter.
ton'sil, mangel, keelklier; ~ **lec'tomy,** mangelopera=
sie; ~ **lit'is,** ontsteking v.d. mangels, mangelontste=
king, tonsilitis.
tonsor'ial, barbiers=, skeer=; ~ **art,** skeerkuns.
ton'sure, (n) kruinskering, tonsuur; (v) die kruin skeer.
tontine', lyfrente, tontine.
too, te, alte; ook, eweneens; ~ *CHARMING,* allerbe=
minliks; ~ *MUCH of a good thing,* te veel van 'n goeie ding; moenie die ding oordryf nie; *only* ~ *TRUE,* maar alte waar; ~ ~ *will in TWO,* as die pap te dik is, brand dit aan; *not* ~ *bad a WINTER,* 'n taamlik goeie winter.
took, *kyk* **take,** (v).
tool, (n) werktuig, stuk gereedskap; artefak; handlan=
ger; (v) bewerk; glad maak; stempel (boek); ~*ed* **binding,** gedrewe boekband; ~**-bag,** gereedskap=
sak; ~**-box,** ~**-case,** ~**-chest,** gereedskapskis;
~ **er,** bewerker; klipbeitel; ~**-fitter,** gereedskap=
bankwerker; ~**-holder,** gereedskaphouer; ~**-
handle,** handvatsel; ~**-house,** gereedskapskuur;
~ **ing,** bewerking; kliphouwerk; regkapping, bebei=
teling; stempelversiering, omslagversiering, be=
stempeling; geperste sierdruk; ~**-kit,** stel gereed=
skap; gereedskapstel; gereedskaphouer; ~**-maker,** gereedskapmaker; ~**-room,** gereedskapkamer; ~**-
set,** stel gereedskap; gereedskapstel; ~**-sharpener,** gereedskapslyper; ~**-shed,** werkswinkel; gereed=
skapskuur; ~**-shop,** gereedskapwinkel; ~**-smith,** gereedskapsmid; ~**-store,** gereedskapwinkel; ge=
reedskapkamer.
toot, (n) getoeter, geblaas; (v) blaas, toeter; ~**er,** blaashoring, toeter.
tooth, (n) **(teeth),** tand; byter; kam (van masjien); ver=
tanding (ratte); *ARMED to the teeth,* tot die tande gewapen; *he would give his BACK teeth,* hy sou wat wou gee; *ARTIFICIAL* ~, vals tand, kunstand; *CAST a thing in a person's teeth,* iets voor iem. se kop gooi; *CLENCH one's teeth,* op die tande byt; *in the teeth of CRITICISM,* trots baie kritiek; *CUT one's teeth,* tande kry; *in the teeth of DANGER,* in die bek van gevaar; *DRAW someone's teeth,* iem. se mag aan bande lê; *set the teeth on EDGE,* laat gril; met walging vervul; *FIGHT* ~ *and nail,* met hand en tand beveg; *in the teeth of the GALE,* in die bek v.d. storm in; *GET long in the* ~, oud word; *IN the teeth of,* ten spyte van; *LIE in one's teeth,* soos 'n tandetrekker lieg; *LONG in the* ~, na die ou kant toe; met afgeslyte tande; *be LONG in the* ~, al vol=
bek wees; *DEFEND with* ~ *and NAIL,* met hand en tand verdedig; *SHOW one's teeth,* jou tande wys; *by the SKIN of the teeth,* naelskraap, so hitte=
te; *have a SWEET* ~, 'n lekkerbek wees; baie van soetigheid hou; *in the teeth of his WARNINGS,* ten spyte van sy waarskuwings; (v) van tande voorsien; tande aansit; inmekaarsluit; ~**ache,** tandpyn; ~**-
billed,** met getande snawel; ~**-brush,** tandeborsel;
~ **caries,** tandbederf, tandkaries; ~**-comb,** fyn=
kam; ~**-decay,** tandbederf, tandverrotting.
toothed, getand; ~ *WHALE,* tandwalvis; ~ *WHEEL,* kamrat, slagrat.
tooth: ~ **enamel,** tandglasuur; ~**ful,** slukkie, bietjie;
~**ing,** vertanding; tandvorming; ~**less,** sonder tande, tandeloos; ~ **let,** tandjie; ~ **paste,** tandepas=
ta; ~ **pick,** tandeskoonmaker, tandekrapper, tan=
destokkie; ~**-powder,** tandepoeier; ~ **socket,** tand=
kas; ~ **some,** smaaklik, lekker; ~**someness,** smaak=
likheid; ~**y,** met groot tande; getand.
too'tle, toeter, blaas.
toot'ling, getoeter, geblaas.
toot'sy(-woot'sy), voetjie, pootjie.
top¹, (n) tol (speelding); *as DRUNK as a* ~, so dronk soos 'n matroos; *SLEEP like a* ~, soos 'n klip slaap.
top², (n) top, toppunt, kruin, spits; bokant; mars (aan mas); kap; deksel; vors (dak); boleer (skoen); bo=
vlak; blad (tafel); bo-ent, koppenent; bostuk (kle=
re); eerste (in klas); kamwol; bolaag; (pl) beste; bo=
steenkool; lowwe (van groente); *on* ~ *of it ALL,* tot oormaat van ramp; *AT the* ~, bo-aan; *BE on* ~, bobaas wees; *BLOW one's* ~, woedend word; *the* ~ *of his BENT,* die toppunt van sy neigings; *from* ~ *to BOTTOM,* van bo tot onder; ~*s of CAR= ROTS,* wortellowwe; ~ *of one's CLASS,* eerste in die klas; *COME out on* ~, wen; *COME* ~, bo-aan staan; eerste kom; *COME out* ~ *dog,* bobaas wees; bobaas uit die stryd kom; *be at the* ~ *of one's FORM,* reg op jou stukke wees; *GO over the* ~, bo-
oor gaan; *the* ~ *of the MORNING to you,* goeie=
môre; *ON* ~ *of this,* boonop; *RISE to the* ~, na bo kom; *at the* ~ *of the TABLE,* aan die hoof (bo-ent) v.d. tafel; *eye someone from* ~ *to TOE,* iem. van kop tot tone beskou; *have got to the* ~ *of the TREE,* bo in die boom wees; die hoogste sport be=
reik het; *shout at the* ~ *of one's VOICE,* so hard skree as 'n mens kan; *on* ~ *of the WORLD,* hoog in jou skik; (a) boonste, hoogste, hoogstaande, voor=
aanstaande, beste, voorste, eerste; bo=, top=; *the* ~ *DOG,* die bobaas; *at* ~ *SPEED,* so vinnig moont=
lik.
top³, (v) top, aftop, snoei (boom); 'n kap opsit; oor=
tref; hoër wees as; uitmunt bo; jou verhef; ~ *a BALL,* 'n kophou slaan; 'n bal op die kop slaan; ~ *the LIST,* bo-aan staan; ~ *the POLL,* die meeste stemme kry; ~ *all RIVALS,* alle mededingers uit=
stof; ~ *UP,* byvul, volmaak; versterk; optop (bote); oplaai.
top'az, topaas; ~**ine,** topaasagtig; ~**'olite,** topaso=
liet.
top: ~ **beam,** hanebalk; ~**-boot,** kapstewel; ~ **boy,** seun wat eerste (in die klas) staan; ~ **class,** topklas;
~ **coat,** oorjas; ~ **dog,** baas, bobaas, boperd, nom=
mer een; ~ **door,** bodeur; ~ **drawer,** boonste laai;
~**-dress,** bobemes; ~**-dressing,** bobemesting, kop=
bemesting.
tope¹, (n) ruwe haai.
tope², (n) mangobos.
tope³, (n) Boeddhistiese monument.
tope⁴, (v) suip, baie drink.
topee', kurkhoed.
top'-end, bo-ent.
top'er, dopsteker, drinkebroer, nathals, suiper, drin=
ker, brandewynvlieg, suiplap, slampamper.
top: ~**-flight,** eersterangs; bobaas(speler); ~ **floor,** boonste verdieping; ~**ful,** propvol; ~ **gallant mast,** bramsteng; ~ **gallant sail,** bramseil; ~ **gear,** hoog=
ste versnelling; bokerf; ~ **grade,** hoogste kwaliteit.
toph, tandsteen; jigknobbel; graweel.
top: ~ **hat,** (pluis)keil; ~**-heaviness,** topswaarte; ~**-
heavy,** topswaar, bowigtig; ~**-hole,** uitstekend, eer=
steklas.
toph'us, (..phi) = **toph.**
top'i, kurkhoed.
topiar'ian, snoei=.
top'iarist, snoeikunstenaar, kunssnoeier.
to'piary, (n) snoeikuns; vormbome; (a) snoei=; ~ **art,** snoeikuns, siersnoeikuns, vormsnoeikuns.
top'ic, onderwerp, tema; *the* ~ *of the day,* die onder=
werp van gesprek.
top'ical, plaaslik; geleentheids=, aktueel; ~ *ALLU= SION,* toespeling op plaaslike omstandighede; *of* ~ *INTEREST,* van aktuele belang; *a* ~ *SONG,* 'n aktuele lied; *a* ~ *SUBJECT,* 'n aktuele onderwerp;
~**'ity,** aktualiteit.
top: ~**knot,** kuif; kuifwol; haarbondel; ~**-lantern,** maslantern; ~ **layer,** bolaag; ~**less,** bostukloos;

topographer 1313 *toss*

~ **less dress**, bostuklose rok; ~ **-level**, hooggeplaaste, leiers=; ~ **-level talks**, leierberaad, spitsberaad; ~ **-light**, toplig; ~ **-lighting**, boverligting; ~ **line**, boonste reël; bolyn; ~ **-line**, van die hoogste kwaliteit; uit die boonste rakke; ~ **management**, topbestuur; ~ **mast**, marssteng; ~ **most**, boonste, hoogste; ~ **notch**, (n) toppunt; bokerf; ~ **-notch**, (a) hoogste, beste; ~ **-notcher**, doring, haan, bobaas; ~ **note**, hoogste noot.
topog'rapher, plekbeskrywer, topograaf.
topograph'ic(al), plekbeskrywend, topografies.
topog'raphy, plekbeskrywing, topografie.
top'onym, pleknaam, toponiem.
toponym'ic, toponimies.
toponym'ics, pleknaamkunde, toponimie.
topon'ymy, pleknaamkunde, toponimie.
topp'er, (n) ramkat, doring; boonste laag; (pluis)keil; (sigaret)stompie; heupjas.
top'pie, tiptol, kluitjiekorrel, geelgat.
top' piece, bostuk.
topp'iness, oppervlakkige bysmaak (botter).
topp'ing[1], (n) (die) top van bome; (pl) afgesnoeide takke.
topp'ing[2], (a) boonste; uitstekend, piekfyn, puik; heerlik; *a* ~ *MORNING*, 'n lieflike oggend; *a* ~ *PLAY*, 'n eersteklas toneelstuk.
top' plate, boplaat.
top'ple, topswaar wees; omval, omtuimel, omkantel, onderstebo gooi; ~ *over (down)*, omval, omkantel, omtuimel, ombuitel.
top: ~ **price**, hoogste prys, topprys; ~ **rail**, marsleuning; ~ **sail**, marsseil, ~ **-sawyer**, bosaer; bobaas; scorer, speler wat die hoogste punte behaal; ~ **secret**, hoogs geheim; ~ **-sewing**, oorhandsteek, ~ **side**, bokant; binneboudvleis; ~ **sides**, skeepskante bokant die waterlyn; ~ **soil**, bogrond; ~ **speed**, hoogste snelheid, topsnelheid; ~ **spin**, tol; ~ **stitching**, bostiksel; ~ **-stone**, sluitsteen, dekklip; ~ **storey**, ~ **story**, boonste verdieping; ~ **surface**, bovlak.
topsy-turv'ey, (a) onderstebo; skots en skeef; (adv) onderstebo, op sy kop, deurmekaar, agterstevoor; *TURN everything* ~, alles onderstebo keer; alles op stelte sit; *the world has turned* ~, die wêreld staan op sy kop; *everything WAS* ~, alles was deurmekaar; ~ **dom**, verkeerde wêreld, chaos, deurmekaarboel.
top' wool, kamwol.
top' yield, kamwolopbrengs; hoogste opbrengs.
toque, toque, mussiehoed; makaakaap.
tor, klipkop, rotsheuwel.
torb'anite, torbaniet.
torc, gedraaide metaalhalsband.
torch, (-es) flitslig, toorts, fakkel, flambou; *ELECTRIC* ~, toorts, flitslig; *HAND on the* ~, die vuur aan die lewe hou; *PUT to the* ~, aan die brand steek; ~ **-bearer**, fakkeldraer; ~ **-commando**, fakkelkommando; ~ **light**, toortslig, fakkellig; ~ **light procession**, fakkeloptog.
tor'chon: ~ **lace**, torchonkant, ~ **paper**, korrelpapier.
torch: ~ **race**, fakkelwedloop; ~ **run**, fakkelloop.
tore, *kyk* **tear**[2], (v).
to'reador, berede bulvegter, toreador.
tore'ro, bulvegter te voet, torero.
toreut'ic, beeldhouwerk=.
torfa'ceous, moeras=.
torm'ent[1], (n) foltering, kwelling, marteling, tormentasie.
torment'[2], (v) folter, pyning, kwel, deurknaag, tormenteer; ~ *someone*, iem. se siel uittrek; ~ **ed**, gepla, gekwel, gefolter; ~ **ing**, (n) tormentasie, foltering; (a) kwellend, folterend; ~ **or**, kwelgees, folteraar, plaaggees; ~ **ress**, (-es), kwelster, pynigster, plaagster.
torm'ina, koliek.
torn, (v) *kyk* **tear**[2], (v); (a) geskeur, flenterig.
tornad'ic, orkaan=, tornado=.
tornad'o, (-es), werwelstorm, windhoos, tornado; ~ **cloud**, tregterwolk, tornadowolk.
torose', **tor'ous**, vol knobbels; gespier(d); bulterig.
torped'o, (n) (-es), torpedo; torpedovis; (v) torpedeer;

~ **attack**, torpedoaanval; ~ **-boat**, torpedoboot; ~ **bomber**, torpedobomwerper; ~ **carrier**, torpedovliegtuig; ~ **-catcher**, torpedojaer; ~ **destroyer**, torpedojaer; ~ **fish**, torpedovis, drilvis; ~ **man**, torpedis; ~ **-net**, torpedonet; ~ **plane**, torpedovliegtuig; ~ **-scissors**, netskêr; ~ **-tube**, torpedobuis.
torp'id, styf, bewegingloos; lusteloos, loom; stadig, traag; ongevoelig; ~ *'ity*, styfheid; traagheid; loomheid; ongevoeligheid.
torp'ify, (..fied), ongevoelig maak; verstyf.
torp'or, styfheid, verstywing; traagheid; gevoelloosheid; geesverdowing; ~ **if'ic**, verdowend.
torq'uate(d), ringnek=.
torque, koppel, torsie, draaimoment; wringkrag; gedraaide metaalhalsband; ~ **tighten**, wringdraai; ~ **tube**, wringbuis; ~ **wrench**, wringsleutel.
torrefac'tion, uitdroging; roostering.
to'rrefy, (..fied), verseng; brand, rooster; uitdroog.
to'rrent, sterk stroom; (stort)vloed; *IN* ~ *s*, in strome; *a* ~ *of WORDS*, 'n woordevloed.
torren'tial, in strome, stromend; onstuimig; ~ **downpour**, stortreën.
Torricell'ian, Torricelliaans; ~ **tube**, Torricellibuis.
to'rrid, dor, verskroeiend, heet; ~ *'ity*, ~ **ness**, brandende hitte, versenging; ~ **zone**, tropiese (skroeiende) lugstreek, trope.
tors'el, krul.
tor'sion, draaiing, kronkeling, wringing, torsie; gedraaidheid; *MOMENT of* ~, wringmoment; *RADIUS of* ~, torsiestraal.
tor'sional, torsie=, draai=, wring=; spiraalvormig; ~ **moment**, torsiemoment; ~ **scale**, torsieskaal; ~ **spring**, wringveer; ~ **strain**, wringing, verwringing; ~ **stress**, wringspanning.
tor'sion: ~ **balance**, torsieskaal; ~ **spring**, torsieveer; ~ **stress**, wringspanning; ~ **wrench**, wringsleutel.
tors'ive, spiraalvormig, gedraai.
torsk, kabeljou.
tors'o, (-s), romp (van standbeeld), torso; bolyf.
tort, onreg, nadeel; onregmatige daad, delik; *law of* ~ *s*, deliktereg.
torticoll'is, stywe nek, skewe nek.
tort'ile, gedraai, kronkelend.
tor'tious, onregverdig, onregmatig, benadelend.
tort'oise, skilpad; ~ **-shell**, skilpaddop; ~ **-shell spectacles**, skilpaddopbril.
tortuos'ity, (..ties), bogtigheid, kronkeling, kromming; jakkalsdraaie, skelmstreke.
tort'uous, bogtig, gekronkel, gedraai, krom; slinks, skelm; gewronge (styl); ingewikkeld; ~ **ness** = **tortuosity**.
tor'ture, (n) foltering, marteling; martelary; *DEATH by* ~, marteldood; *INSTRUMENT of* ~, marteltuig; *PUT to the* ~, martel, op die pynbank lê; (v) folter, martel; verdraai (betekenis); deurknaag; ~ *words*, woorde verdraai; ~ **-chamber**, folterkamer; ~ **r**, folteraar, pyniger; ~ **-room**, folterkamer.
tor'turing, (n) foltering; (a) folterend, martelend.
tor'us, (tori), blombodem, torus, vrugwenhoid.
Tor'y, (n) (Tories), Tory, Konserwatief; (a) Tory=, Konserwatief; ~ **ism**, politieke konserwatisme, behoudsug, Toryisme.
tor'yism, konserwatisme.
tosh, kaf, onsin, bog, geswam, twak.
toss, (n) (-es), gooi, worp; opgooi (van munt); loot; slingering; *TAKE a* ~, bakensteek, sandruiter word, van 'n perd afval; *WIN the* ~, die lootjie wen; (v) gooi; opgooi; rondsmyt; rondrol, woel (in die bed); skud; loot (sport); ~ *ABOUT*, heen en weer slinger; ~ *ASIDE*, opsy gooi; ~ *AWAY*, weggooi; ~ *off a BEER*, 'n glas bier wegslaan; ~ *a person in a BLANKET*, iem. beesvel laat ry; ~ *DOWN*, neersmyt; ~ *FOR something*, oor iets loot; ~ *one's HEAD*, die kop agteroor gooi; ~ *INTO*, na binne gooi (slaan); ~ *OFF one's work*, gou-gou klaarmaak; ~ *a PANCAKE*, 'n pannekoek opgooi; ~ *for SIDES*, vir kante loot; ~ *UP*, opgooi; ~ *ed by the WAVES*, deur die golwe heen en weer geslinger; ~ **er**, opgooier; smyter; ~ **ing**, slingering, hewige beweging; ~ **pot**, suiplap, dronk=

lap; ~-**up**, (die) opgooi; onsekerheid; *it's a* ~ *-up,* dis twyfelagtig; dis 'n dubbeltjie op sy kant.
tot[1], (n) optelsom, optelling; (v) **(-ted)**, optel; ~ *UP,* opstel; opsom; ~ *UP to,* beloop.
tot[2], (n) kleutertjie, snuitertjie; snaps, sopie, hartver= sterkinkie, drankie, doppie, skrikmakertjie, regma= kertjie, aitsatjie, bokhaelskoot, blymakertjie (klein); *take a STIFF* ~, 'n stywe dop steek; ~ *SYSTEM,* dopstelsel; *TINY* ~, snuiter, kleuter, kleintjie.
tot'al, (n) volle som, som, totaal; (v) **(-led)**, optel; by= mekaartel; bedra, beloop; (a) volkome; totaal, ge= heel; finaal; ~ **abstainer**, geheelonthouer, afskaf= fer; ~ **abstinence**, geheelonthouding, afskaffing; ~ **amount**, totaal, volle bedrag; ~ **eclipse**, algehele verduistering; ~**itar'ian**, (n) totalitaris; (a) totali= têr; ~**ita'rianism**, totalitarisme; ~**ity**, totaal, tota= liteit, algeheelheid; *in its* ~*ity,* in sy geheel; ~**iza= tor**, totalisator, toto; ~*izator jackpot,* woekerpot; ~**ize**, optel, saamtel, die totaal bereken; die totali= sator gebruik; ~**izer**, totalisator, toto; optelma= sjien; ~**ly**, heeltemal, geheel en al, totaal, volslae; ~ *war,* totale oorlog.
tote[1], (n) *abbr. for* **totalizator**, toto; *DOUBLE* ~, koppeltoto; *EACH way* ~, gewone totogeriewe.
tote[2], (v) vervoer; dra.
tot'em, totem, stamteken; ~**'ic**, totem=; ~**ism**, tote= misme; ~**ist**, totemis; ~**ist'ic**, totemisties; ~**-pole**, ~**-post**, totempaal.
tot' system, dopstelsel.
tott'er, waggel, wankel, strompel; ~**er**, waggelaar, wankelaar; ~**-grass**, bewertjies; ~**ing**, (n) wanke= ling, strompeling, waggeling; (a) waggelend, onvas, wankelend, wankelbaar; bouvallig.
tou'can, toekan.
touch, (n) (**-es**), aanraking; voeling; tassing; gevoel; tik; ietsie, bietjie, sweem; buitelyn; grens (voetbal); ligte aanval; aanslag (mus.); trek; toets; aan= slaanspeletjie, frot (speletjie); kleurvegie; *GOLD to the* ~, koud om aan te voel; *a* ~ *of COLOUR,* 'n bietjie kleur; 'n kleurvegie; 'n bietjie gekleurde bloed; *FIND* ~, voeling kry; uitskop (rugby); op slag kom; *put on the FINISHING* ~*es to some= thing,* die laaste hand aan iets lê; *GAME of* ~, aan= aan; *GET in* ~ *with,* in aanraking kom met; ~ *and GO,* op die nerf af; so hittete; *it was* ~ *and GO,* dit het geen haar geskeel nie; dit was so naelskraap; dit het broekskeur gegaan; *he is GOOD for a* ~, hy sal jou seker met geld help; *a* ~ *of GOUT,* 'n ligte jigaanval; *a* ~ *of ILLNESS,* 'n aandoening; *be IN* ~ *with,* in voeling wees met; *a* ~ *of IRONY,* 'n tikkie ironie; *KEEP in* ~ *with,* in voeling bly met; *LOSE* ~ *with,* kontak verloor met; *have LOST one's* ~, van slag wees; jou slag verloor het; *KICK into* ~, uitskop; oor die kantlyn skop; *a* ~ *of NATURE,* 'n natuurlike kenmerk; *a NEAR* ~, 'n noue ontkoming; *a* ~ *OF,* 'n ietsie; *be OUT of* ~ *with,* uit voeling wees met; *the PERSONAL* ~, die persoonlike stempel; *the PIANO has a splendid* ~, die klavier het 'n besonder goeie aanslag; *PLAY* ~, aan-aan speel; *a* ~ *of SALT,* 'n knypie sout; *SOFT to the* ~, sag voel; (v) voel, tas, vat aan; bevoel; aanraak; tref; aanroer; tik; roer; aanslaan, speel; aangaan, aandoen (skepe); bykom; aanstoot (gla= se); ~ *AT,* aangaan by; *I wouldn't* ~ *him with a BARGE POLE,* ek sou nie met 'n tang aan hom raak nie; ~ *the BELL,* op die knop druk; ~ *BOT= TOM,* grond voel; *no one CAN* ~ *him,* sy maters is dood; *DON'T* ~ *me,* hou jou hande tuis; bly van my lyf af; ~ *someone FOR something,* iets uit iem. kry; ~ *GLASSES,* (glase) klink; *not a HAIR of your head shall be* ~*ed,* nie 'n haar van jou hoof sal gekrenk word nie; ~ *one's HAT,* die hoed lig; *there is NO one to* ~ *him,* sy moses is dood; sy maters is dood; ~ *OFF,* afvuur; laat ontplof; veroorsaak (rusie); ~ *ON something,* 'n oomblikkie by iets stil= staan; iets aanroer, aanraak; ~ *PITCH,* met pik omgaan; ~ *ed with PITY,* deur medelye aangegryp; ~ *to the QUICK,* diep raak; ~ *someone on the RAW,* 'n tere snaar aanroer; *REFUSE to* ~ *drink,* weier om jou mond aan drank te sit; *SENSE of* ~, tassin(tuig); ~ *the SPOT,* die seerplek aanraak; ~

on (upon) a SUBJECT, 'n onderwerp aanroer; ~ *UP,* opknap; bywerk; retoesjeer (foto); ~ *WOOD,* hou duim vas; aftik; 'n ongeluk kastig afweer; ~**able**, aan te raak, voelbaar; ~**-and-go**, onseker; gevaarlik; nerf-nerf, ampertjies, so hittete, byna, tussen lewe en dood; *it was* ~ *-and-go,* dit het nael= skraap gegaan; ~**-back**, dooddruk (bal); ~**-down**, ('n) drie (rugby); landing (vliegtuig); landing; ~ **down**, (v) druk (rugby); land (vliegtuig); ~**er**, aan= raker, treffer; raakbal (rolbal); ~**-hole**, laaigat, sundgat; ~ **iness**, liggeraaktheid, eergevoeligheid, kleinserigheid, gevoeligheid; ~**ing**, (a) roerend, hartroerend, sielroerend, aandoenlik; (prep) aan= gaande, betreffende; ~**-judge**, grensregter; ~**-kick**, kantskop, buiteskop; ~**-line**, buitelyn, sylyn; *sit on the* ~ *-line(s),* maar net 'n toeskouer wees; ~**-me= not**, kruidjie-roer-my-nie; ~**needle**, toetsnaald; ~**-pan**, kruitpan; ~ **paper**, salpeterpapier; ~ **stone**, toetssteen; bassaniet; ~**-typing**, blindtik; ~**-typist**, blindtikster; ~**-up**, opknapping; aanvuring, opfris= sing; ~ **wood**, swam, glimhout.
touch'y, gevoelig, gevoelerig, liggeraak, prikkelbaar, kortgebaker(d), aangebrand, aantreklik; ontvlam= baar; teer, delikaat; *BE* ~, jou op jou perdjie wees; liggeraak wees; kortgebaker(d) wees; fynbesnaard wees; *a* ~ *FELLOW,* 'n kruidjie-roer-my-nie.
tough, (n) ruwe vent, skurk, boef; breker; (a) taai (vleis, persoon); hard, styf; moeilik, lastig (vraag= stuk); onversetlik, koppig; kwaai; streng; *a* ~ *CUSTOMER,* 'n lastige klant; 'n moeilike vent; *a* ~ *FELLOW,* 'n harde koejawel; *GET* ~ *with,* hard aanpak; *a* ~ *JOB,* 'n moeilike werk; *as* ~ *as LEATHER,* so taai soos leer; *have* ~ *LUCK,* teen= spoed hê; *as* ~ *as NAILS,* so taai soos 'n ratel; ~**en**, taai maak; ~**ening**, verharding; verhard; ~**ish**, taaierig; ~**ness**, taaiheid, hardheid.
toupee', pruik(ie).
tour, (n) toer; (rond)reis; *EDUCATIONAL* ~, skool= reis; ~ *de FORCE,* kragtoer; ~ *of INSPECTION,* inspeksiereis; *MAKE a* ~ *of the town,* 'n kykrit deur die stad doen; *ON* ~, op reis; (v) (rond)reis, 'n reis maak; besoek, bereis; op toer gaan; ~ *the country,* die land bereis; ~**er**, toeris; toermotor; ~ **guide**, toergids.
tour'ing, (n) (die) reis, gereis, getoer; (a) toer=; ~**-car**, toermotor; ~**-speed**, togsnelheid; ~ **team**, toer= span.
tour'ism, toerisme.
tour'ist, reisiger, toeris; plesierreisiger; ~ **agency**, reisagentskap; reisburo, toeristeagentskap; ~ **class**, toeristeklas; ~ **industry**, toeristebedryf, toe= risme; ~ **party**, reisgeselskap; ~ **traffic**, toeriste= verkeer.
tour'malin(e), toermalyn.
tour'nament, toernooi, wedstrydreeks.
Tour'nay, Doornik.
tourn'ey, (n) toernooi, steekspel; (v) aan 'n toernooi deelneem.
tourn'iquet, skroefverband, aarpers, knelverband, toerniket; draaikruis.
tournure', vorm, wending, ronding; busseltjie, tournure.
tou'sle, in wanorde bring; verfrommel, verfomfaai, rondpluk; ~**d**, verward, deurmekaar.
tout, (n) klantelokker; werwer; perdespioen; (v) spioeneer, beloer; aanlok, klante lok; werf (klante) aanprys; koopware opdring aan; perde beloer; ~ **er**, spioen (veral van perde); klantelokker; ~**ing**, werwery.
tow[1], (n) growwe vlas; touwerk; tougaring.
tow[2], (n) (die) sleep; sleeptou; *HAVE in* ~, op sleep= tou hê; *the damaged car is IN* ~, die beskadigde motor word gesleep; *TAKE in* ~, op sleeptou neem; (v) sleep, treil, voorttrek, op sleeptou neem; boegseer (boot); ~*ed FLIGHT,* sleepvlug; ~*ed TARGET,* sleepteiken; ~**age**, sleepwerk, slepery; sleeploon; sleepkoste.
to'ward, (a) gewillig, leergierig, gehoorsaam; (adv) op hande; aan die gang; ~**ness**, gewilligheid, leer= saamheid.
to'wards, (prep) na . . . toe, na; tot, teen; jeens; in= sake, met betrekking tot; teenoor; *his ATTITUDE*

tow-boat 1315 *traction*

~ **me**, sy houding teenoor my; ~ *MORNING*, teen die môre; ~ *TOWN*, dorp se kant toe.
tow'-boat, sleepboot.
tow'el, (n) handdoek; *OAKEN* ~, kierie; *THROW in the* ~, die saak opgee; tou opgooi; ingee; (v) (-**led**), afdroog (met 'n handdoek); ransel, uitlooi, klop; ~-**bracket**, handdoekroller; ~-**gourd**, va= doekkalbas; ~-**horse**, handdoekrak; ~**ling**, hand= doekgoed; afdroging; *give someone a* ~ *ling*, iem. onder die skaapstert laat deurloop; ~-**rack**, ~- **rail**, handdoeklat; ~-**roller**, handdoekroller.
tow'er[1], (n) sleper, trekker.
tow'er[2], (n) toring; burg, vesting; toevlug; ~ *of strength*, toeverlaat; staatmaker; steunpilaar; (v) hoog uitsteek; hoog vlieg; ~ *over*, uitrys bo; ~ **bell**, toringklok; ~-**bolt**, skuifgrendel; ~-**clock**, toring= klok; ~**ed**, getoring, met torings; ~**ing**, baie hoog; geweldig; ~ *ing AMBITION*, sterk eersug; *in a* ~*ing RAGE*, woedend; ~**y**, getoring; hoog ver= hewe.
tow'ing, (n) gesleep; (a) sleep=; ~-**aeroplane**, sleep= vliegtuig; ~-**cable**, sleeptou; ~-**flight**, sleep(tou)= vlug; ~-**hawser**, sleeptros; ~-**line**, treklyn; sleep= tou; ~-**loop**, sleeplus; ~-**net**, sleepnet, treknet; ~-**path**, treilpad, jaagpad; ~-**rope**, sleeptou, treil= lyn; ~-**vessel**, sleepboot; ~-**wire**, sleepdraad.
tow' line, boegseerlyn, treil, sleeptros, sleeptou.
town, (n) stad; dorp; *ABOUT* ~, in die stad; *IN* ~, in die stad; *MAN about* ~, windmakerige niksdoe= ner; wêreldwyse persoon; losbol, ligmis; *OUT of* ~, uit die stad; *PAINT the* ~ *red*, die dorp op horings neem; *the TALK of the* ~, die hele dorp het die mond daarvan vol; *WOMAN of the* ~, vrou van los sedes, ligtekooi; (a) steeds; ~-**born**, in 'n stad gebore; ~ **boundary**, dorpsgrens; stadsgrens; ~-**bred**, in die stad opgegroei; ~ **clerk**, stadsklerk; ~ **clock**, stadsklok; ~ **council**, stadsraad; ~ **coun= cillor**, stadsraadslid; ~ **crier**, stadsomroeper; ~- **dweller**, stadsbewoner; ~ **ee'**, dorpsgas; stedeling.
tow'-net, sleepnet, treknet.
town: ~ **girl**, stadsdogter, dorpsdogter; ~**guard**, stadswag, dorpswag; ~ **hall**, stadhuis; stadsaal; ~ **house**, dorpshuis, stadswoning; ~-**house**, tuinhuis; ~**ish**, stadagtig, steeds; ~**lands**, meent; dorps= grond; ~**let**, dorpie; ~ **life**, dorpslewe; stadslewe; ~ **miss**, stadsjuffie; ~-**mouse**, dorpsgas; ~ **news**, stadsnuus; ~ **planner**, stadsontwerper; ~ **planning**, stadsbeplanning; dorpsaanleg, stadsbou; ~ **prison**, stadsgevangenis; ~ **quarter**, stadswyk; ~ **ranger**, dorpsveldwagter; ~ **scape**, stadsgesig; ~ **school**, dorpskool, stadskool; ~**s'folk**, stadsmense; ~**ship**, dorp(sgedeelte), stadsgebied; stadswyk, ~**ship board**, dorpsraad; ~**s'man**, stedeling, dorpenaar, stadsbewoner, stadsgenoot; ~**s'people**, stadsmen= se, dorpsmense, stedelinge, dorpelinge, dorpsgaste; ~ **talk**, dorpspraatjies; ~**ward(s)**, stadwaarts; ~-**wear**, stadsdrag.
tow: ~-**path**, jaagpad, sleeppad; ~-**rope**, sleeptou; **wire**, sleepdraad; ~**y**, toutjiesagtig.
toxaem'ia, bloedvergiftiging, toksemie.
tox'ic, giftig, toksies; gif=; ~ **ant**, (n) gif; (a) giftig.
toxi'city, giftigheid.
toxicolog'ical, toksikologies.
toxicol'ogist, gifkenner, toksikoloog.
tox'icol'ogy, toksikologie, (ver)gifteleer.
toxic: ~ **smoke**, gifrook; ~ **substance**, gifstof; ~ **symptoms**, tekens van vergiftiging.
tox'in, toksien, gifstof.
toxo'philite, boogskutter.
toxophilit'ic, boogskutters=.
toxo'phily, boogskietery.
toxophob'ia, vrees vir gif.
toy, (n) speelgoed, snuistery; speelding; prul; speel= bal; (pl) speelgoed; *a* ~ *in the hands of*, 'n speelbal in die hande van; (v) speel; ~ *with one's FOOD*, aan jou kos peusel; ~ *with the IDEA of*, daaraan dink om; ~ *with a SUBJECT*, in 'n vak liefhebber; ~ *WITH*, street; speel met; (a) speelgoed=; dwerg=, miniatuur=; ~-**box**, speelgoedkis; ~ **dog**, skoot= hondjie, dwerghondjie, miniatuurhondjie; ~ **horse**, (speelgoed=) perdjie; ~**ingly**, speel-speel; ~ **man**, (..**men**), speelgoedverkoper; ~ **pram**, pop=

waentjie; ~**shop**, speelgoedwinkel; ~ **soldier**, speelgoedsoldaatjie.
T'-piece, kruisbalkie; T-stuk.
trace[1], (n) string (van tuig); *IN the* ~, aan die werk; *KICK over the* ~*s*, onklaar trap; onregeerbaar word.
trace[2], (n) spoor; voetspoor; bewys, teken, sweem; skets; ligspoor (koeël); *DISAPPEAR without a* ~, spoorloos verdwyn; *KEEP* ~ *of*, in die oog hou; *no* ~ *REMAINS*, geen spoor bly oor nie; *a* ~ *of SU= GAR*, 'n tikkie suiker; (v) opspoor, naspeur, op= diep; ontwerp; oortrek, natrek, traseer; skets, te= ken; die spoor volg; ~ *BACK to*, nagaan tot; ~ *a LINE*, 'n lyn trek; ~ *a MAP*, 'n kaart natrek; ~ *OUT*, uitstippel, aandui; ~ *a PLAN*, 'n plan ont= werp; ~ *a SIGNATURE*, 'n handtekening nate= ken; ~ **able**, naspeurbaar; opspoorbaar; ~ **ele= ments**, spoorelemente; ~**less**, spoorloos; ~**r**, opspoorder; naspeurder; kalkeerder; natrekker; aanwyser; afsteker; ligspoor; ~**r bullet**, ligspoor= koeël, vuurkoeël; ~**r cartridge**, ligspoorpatroon; ~**ry**, loofwerk (klip); netwerk; Gotiese (venster)or= namentiek; dekoratiewe patroon; trasering.
trache'a, (**-e**), lugpyp; tragea; lugbuis (insek); ~**l**, lug= pyp=, trageaal.
tracheot'omy, lugpypinsnyding, trageotomie.
trachit'is, lugpypontsteking, tragitis.
trachom'a, tragoom, oogbindvliesontsteking.
trach'yte, tragiet.
tra'cing, (n) natrekwerk; natrektekening; nasporing, naspeuring; oordruk; omtrek; (a) natrek=; ~-**cloth**, natreklinne, kalkeerlinne; ~-**cord**, randkoord; ~- **paper**, deurtrekpapier, aftrekpapier, natrekpapier, kalkeerpapier; ~-**pen**, trekpen; ~-**wheel**, aftrek= wieletjie.
track, (n) spoor; getrapte pad; sypad; plaaspad; vee= paadjie, voetpaadjie, baan (lugvaart, hemelligga= me); spoorlyn, spoor(baan); renbaan; atletiekbaan; rusperband; *BE on someone's* ~, op iem. se spoor wees; *the BEATEN* ~, die platgetrapte pad, die gebaande weg; *COVER up one's* ~*s*, jou spoor uit= wis; *DOUBLE* ~, dubbelspoor; *FOLLOW in his* ~*s*, in sy voetspore volg; *GET onto someone's* ~*s*, op iem. se spoor kom; *KEEP* ~ *of*, op die spoor bly van; op hoogte bly met die gang (verloop) van sake; *LEAVE the* ~, ontspoor; *LOSE* ~ *of*, uit die oog verloor; *MAKE* ~*s*, die knieë bêre (dra), die rieme neerlê; *MAKE* ~*s for*, afpyl op; jaag na; *with a one-* ~ *MIND*, met net een doelwit; *a MOUNTAIN* ~, 'n bergpad; *OFF the* ~, die spoor kwyt, van die spoor; *ON his* ~, op sy spoor; *put someone on the RIGHT* ~, iem. op die regte spoor bring; *not on the RIGHT* ~, v.d spoor af; die spoor byster, *SINGLE* ~, enkelspoor; *STOP in one's* ~*s*, in jou vier spore vassteek; *keep* ~ *of (the) TIME*, die tyd dophou; *be on the WRONG* ~, die verkeerde pad betree; die spoor byster wees; in die oupad (ougras) wees; (v) opspoor; naspeur, die spoor volg; sleep; ~ *DOWN*, opspoor; ~ *a FAULT in a cable*, 'n fout in 'n kabel opspoor; ~ **age**, sleep; spoorweg; spoorlyne; ~-**clearer**, baanskuiwer, baanruimer; ~-**cycle**, spoorrywiel; ~ **ed**, met rusper= of kruip= bande; ~ *ed vehicle*, kruipbandvoertuig; ~ **er**, ver= volger; speurhond; spoorsnyer; ~ **event**, baannom= mer; ~ **gauge**, spoormaat; ~**ing**, opsporing, spoorsny; ~**ing battery**, opsporingsbattery; ~**ing device**, volgtoestel; ~ **layer**, spoorlêer; ~**less**, onbe= gaan, ongebaan, spoorloos; ~ **less tram**, trembus; ~ **lessness**, ongebaandheid; spoorloosheid; ~ **road**, grootpad; jagpad; ~ **suit**, sweetpak; ~ **way**, voetpad; ~-**worker**, baanwerker.
tract, streek; verloop; verhandeling; traktaatjie; ~**abil'ity**, buigsaamheid, gewilligheid, geseglik= heid; ~ **able**, buigsaam, gedwee, handelbaar, volg= saam, geseglik, mak, meegaande; ~**ness** = **tract= ability**.
trac'tate, verhandeling.
trac'tile, smee(d)baar.
trac'tion, trek(king), sleuring, traksie; trekkrag; strekking; saamtrekking; *electric* ~, elektriese krag; ~ **al**, trek=; ~-**engine**, straatlokomotief, stoomtrekker; ~-**wheel**, dryfrat;

trac'tive, trekkend, trek=; ~ **power**, trekkrag.
trac'tor, trekker; trekmotor; stoomwa; ~**-scraper**, skraaptrekker; ~ **set paper**, vouperforasiepapier.
trade, (n) handel; sake; beroep, bedryf; vak, ambag; bedryfswese; (pl) passaatwinde; *two of a ~ never AGREE*, vakmense stem nooit saam nie; *BE in the ~*, in die handel wees; *BRANCH of ~*, handelstak; *a chemist BY ~*, apteker van beroep; *DOMAIN of ~*, handelsgebied; *FREE ~*, vryhandel; *FREEDOM of ~*, handelsvryheid; *JACK of all ~s, master of none*, 'n man van twaalf ambagte en dertien ongelukke; *a KNOWLEDGE of the ~*, sakekennis, vakkennis; *a ROARING ~*, 'n bloeiende handel; *THE ~*, die handel; *each man TO his own ~*, skoenmaker, hou jou by jou lees; *the TRICK of the ~*, die geheim v.d. ambag; (v) handel drywe, handel, sake doen; ~ *IN*, inruil; ~ *in KIND*, uitruil; ~ *ON*, voordeel trek uit; eksploiteer, uitbuit; ~ *a WATCH for a camera*, 'n oorlosie vir 'n kamera verruil; ~ *WITH someone*, met iem. handel drywe; ~ **account**, bedryfsrekening; ~ **agreement**, handelsooreenkoms; ~ **allowance**, handelsafslag; ~ **balance**, handelsbalans; ~ **bill**, handelswissel; ~ **card**, adreskaart; ~ **commissioner**, handelskommissaris; ~ **council**, arbeidsraad; ~ **cycle**, handelsiklus; ~ **depression**, handelslapte, -depressie; ~ **discount**, handelskorting, handelsrabat; ~ **dispute**, arbeidsgeskil; ~ **explosive**, handelspringstof; ~ **goods**, negosiegoed; ~ **guild**, handelsgilde.
trade'-in, inruil(ing); ~ **price**, inruilprys; ~ **value**, inruilwaarde.
trade: ~ **journal**, vakblad; handelsblad; ~ **legislation**, handelswetgewing; ~ **list**, pryslys; ~ **mark**, handelsmerk; fabrieksmerk; ~ **monopoly**, alleenhandel; ~ **name**, handelsnaam; *registered ~ name*, geregistreerde handelsnaam; ~ **partnership**, handelsvennootskap; ~ **price**, groothandelprys; ~ **profit**, handelswins; ~ **prospects**, handelsvooruitsigte; ~**r**, handelaar; koopman, negosiant; koopvaarder, handelskip; ~ **recession**, resessie, handelslapte; ~ **reciprocity**, wederkerigheid in die handel; ~ **risk**, bedryfsrisiko; handelsrisiko; ~ **route**, handelsroete, handelsweg; ~ **sample**, monster; ~ **school**, handelskool; vakskool; ~ **secret**, vakgeheim, fabrieksgeheim; ~**s'-hall**, vakverenigingsaal; ~**s'man**, (..**men**, **tradespeople**), handelaar, koopman; winkelier; werksman; *skilled ~sman*, vakman; ~**s'men's entrance**, leweransiersingang, diensingang; ~**speople**, handelaars, winkeliers; ~ **statistics**, handelstatistiek; ~ **test**, vaktoets; ~ **union**, vakbond, vakvereniging, werkersbond; ~ **union congress**, vakuniekongres; ~**-unionism**, vakuniestelsel, vakverenigingswese; ~**-unionist**, vakbondlid; voorstander v.d. vakbondstelsel; ~ **usage**, handelsgebruik; ~ **wind**, passaat(wind).
trad'ing, (n) handel; (a) handeldrywend, handels=; ~ **account**, handelsrekening, eksploitasierekening, omsetrekening; ~ **association**, handelsvereniging; ~ **capital**, bedryfskapitaal; ~ **centre**, handelstad, handelsentrum; ~ **company**, handelsmaatskappy; ~ **house**, handelsfirma; ~ **port**, handelshawe; ~ **post**, handelstasie, handelsnedersetting; ~ **profit**, handelswins; ~ **site**, handelsperseel; ~ **station**, handelstasie; ~ **vessel**, handelsvaartuig, koopvaarder.
tradi'tion, oorlewering, tradisie; *ACCORDING to ~*, volgens (die) oorlewering; *a SLAVE to ~*, verslaaf aan tradisies; ~**al**, tradisioneel, oorgelewer; ~**alism**, gehegtheid aan tradisie, tradisionalisme; ~**alist**, tradisionalis, tradisievolger; ~**ally**, tradisioneel, volgens tradisie; ~**-bound**, tradisievas.
traduce', belaster, beskinder, wanvoorstellings maak; ~**ment**, belastering, bekladding; ~**r**, lastertong, bekladder.
traff'ic, (n) handel; vervoer; verkeer; *have no ~ with someone*, geen omgang met iem. wil hê nie; niks te doen wil hê met iem. nie; (v) (**-ked**), handel drywe, handel, smous; ~ *in*, handel dryf in; ~**able**, verhandelbaar; rybaar; ~ **arrangements**, verkeersreëlings; ~ **artery**, verkeersweg; ~ **block**, verkeersversperring; ~ **circle**, verkeersirkel; ~ **circuit**, verkeersirkel, verkeerseiland; ~ **congestion**, verkeersophoping, ~**-control**, verkeerskontrole; ~**-control car**, verkeersmotor; ~ **cop**, verkeersbeampte; ~ **density**, verkeersdigtheid; ~ **guide**, verkeersgids; ~ **indicator**, rigtingwyser; ~ **inspector**, verkeersinspekteur; ~ **interchange**, verkeerwisselaar, wisselkruising; ~ **island**, verkeerseiland; ~ **jam**, verkeersknoop, verkeersophoping, verkeerstremming, verkeersversperring; ~**ker**, handelaar; ~*ker in drugs*, smokkelaar met dwelmmiddels; ~ **lamp**, verkeerslamp; ~ **lane**, verkeersbaan; ~ **law**, verkeerswet; ~ **light**, verkeerslig; ~ **line**, verkeerstreep; ~ **manager**, verkeersbestuurder; ~ **map**, verkeerskaart; ~ **obstruction**, verkeersbelemmering; ~ **officer**, verkeersbeampte; ~ **police**, verkeerspolisie; ~ **regulation**, verkeersregulasie; verkeersreëling; ~**-return**, verkeerstaat, verkeersverslag; ~ **route**, verkeersroete; ~ **rules**, verkeersreëls; ~ **service**, verkeersdiens; ~ **sign**, padteken; ~**-signal**, verkeersteken; ~ **trade**, ruilverkeer; ~ **volume**, verkeersvolume.
trag'acanth, dragantgom.
traged'ian, treurspeldigter; treur(spel)speler.
traged'ienne, treurspelspeelster, tragedienne.
tra'gedy, (..**dies**), treurspel, tragedie; droewige gebeurtenis.
tra'gic, tragies; treurig; ~**al**, tragies.
tragicom'edy, tragikomedie.
tragicom'ic, tragikomies.
trag'ic scene, treurtoneel.
trail, (n) sleep (van rok); spoor; sleepsel (van slang); rank; stert (komeet); pad; *swords AT the ~*, sabel in die hand; *FOLLOW the ~*, spoorsny; *he has LOST the ~*, hy is die spoor kwyt; *OFF the ~*, van die spoor af; *ON the ~*, op die spoor; (v) sleep, sleur; agtervolg, agternasit; agterloop; plat trap; rank; die spoor volg, opspoor; loshang; saamstoot (rolbal); ~ *ALONG with him*, met hom voortsleep; ~ *ARMS*, geweer in die hand neem (dra); ~ *ARMS!* in die hand geweer! ~ *BEHIND*, agter aansukkel; ~ *one's COAT*, uitdaag; uittart; ~ *OFF*, wegsterf; ~ *a PIKE*, in die leër dien; ~ *SOMEONE*, op iem. se hakke volg; ~**-blazer**, baanbreker, wegbaner, spoormaker; ~**er**, rankplant; sleepwaentjie, aanhangwaentjie; sleepwiel; aanhanger; filmbrokkies, lokprent, voorloper (as advertensie).
trail'ing, (n) (die) sleep, gesleep; agtervolging, opsporing; (a) sleep=, trek=; ~ **aerial**, sleeplugdraad; ~ **axle**, agteras; ~ **cable**, sleepkabel; ~ **net**, sleepnet, heknet; ~ **points**, uitrywissel; ~ **wheel**, agterwiel; sleepwiel.
trail'-net, treknet.
train, (n) trein; stoet, optog (mense); nasleep; aanhang, gevolg; stert; streep, reeks, aaneenskakeling (mil.); ~ *ARMOURED ~*, pantsertrein; *BRING in its ~*, saamsleep; meebring; *BY ~*, per spoor, per trein; ~ *of CAMELS*, karavaan kamele; *CATCH a ~*, 'n trein haal; ~ *of EVENTS*, reeks gebeurtenisse; ~ *of GEARS*, rattestel; *GOWN with a ~*, sleepjapon; ~ *of GUNPOWDER*, loopvuur; *MISS a ~*, 'n trein mis; 'n trein nie haal nie; *ON the ~*, in die trein; *PRIORITY of ~s*, voorrang van treine; ~ *of THOUGHT*, gedagtegang; ~ *of WHEELS*, ratwerk; (v) oefen; brei; dril; skool; oplei; sleep; afrig; dresseer (dier); rig (geweer); per spoor reis; lei, snoei (plant); ~ *a GUN (up)on*, 'n kanon rig op; *TAKE a ~*, 'n trein haal; met die trein ry; ~ *as (for) a TEACHER*, opgelei word as onderwyser; ~**able**, oefenbaar, leersaam; gedwee; ~**-bearer**, sleepdraer; ~ **crash**, treinbotsing.
train'ed, geoefen; opgelei; ervare, geskool; gedresseer; *a ~ DOG*, 'n geleerde (gedresseerde) hond; *a ~ ELEPHANT*, 'n gedresseerde olifant; ~ *HORSE*, geleerde (mak) perd; ~ *NURSE*, opgeleide verpleegster; *a ~ TEACHER*, 'n opgeleide onderwyser.
trainee', kwekeling, opleideling; vakleerling; ~**-settler**, leerlingnedersetter.
train'er, instrukteur, opleier; breier, afrigter; temmer, menner (diere).
train: ~ **fare**, reisgeld, treingeld; ~ **ferry**, spoorpont.
train'ing, oefening; opvoeding; opleiding; onderrig;

afrigting, skoling, (die) brei; dressering (dier); *AU-RAL* ~, oorskerping; *BE in* ~, geoefen wees; opgelei (gebrei) word; *GO into* ~, begin oefen; ~ **aeroplane,** ~ **aircraft,** opleidingsvliegtuig; ~ **aid,** opleimiddel; ~ **ambulance,** instruksieambulans; ~ **area,** opleidingsgebied; ~ **batallion,** instruksiebataljon; ~**-battery,** instruksiebattery; ~**-cadre,** instruksiekader; ~**-camp,** oefenkamp; ~**-centre,** opleidingsinrigting, opleisentrum; ~**-college,** opleidingskool; normaalskool; opleidingskollege; ~**-corps,** instruksiekorps; ~**-course,** opleidingskursus; ~**-depot,** opleidepot; ~**-establishment,** opleidingskollege; ~**-ground,** oefenterrein, oefengrond; ~**-officer,** opleidingoffisier; ~**-programme,** oefenprogram, opleiprogram; ~**-quarters,** oefenkwartiere; ~**-regulations,** opleivoorskrifte; ~ **ring,** oefenkryt; ~**-ship,** opleidingskip; oefenskip; ~**-squadron,** instruksie-eskader; ~**-unit,** opleieenheid; instruksieeenheid.
train: ~ **journey,** treinreis; ~**-load,** treinlading, treinvrag; ~**-marker,** agterskyf; ~**-mile,** treinmyl.
train'-oil, traanolie; ~ **factory,** traankokery.
train: ~ **service,** treindiens; ~**-sick,** naar, mislik, treinsiek, ~**-sickness,** treinsiekte, naarheid, misliklieid; ~ **staff,** treinpersoneel; ~ **traffic,** treinverkeer, spoorverkeer.
traipse, (n) slofkous; slofgang; (v) slenter, strompel; ~ *ABOUT,* 'n plek platloop; ~ *AFTER someone,* agter iem. aanloop (aandrentel).
trait, trek, karaktertrek, eienskap; streek; toets.
trait'or, verraaier; ~ **ous,** verraderlik; ~ **ousness,** verraderlikheid.
trait'ress, (-es), verraaister.
trajec'tory, (..ries), baan; koeëlbaan, trajek.
tram¹, (n) inslagsy.
tram², (n) trem; kolewa; koekepan; *trackless* ~, trembus; (v) **(-med),** trem ry; per trem vervoer; ~**-car,** trem, tremwa; ~ **conductor,** tremkondukteur, trembestuurder; ~ **connection,** tremverbinding; ~**-driver,** trembestuurder; ~ **line,** tremspoor.
tramm'el, (n) boei; hinderpaal; ellipspasser; stangpasser; (ketel)haak; net; (pl) belemmeringe; kluisters, boeie; (v) **(-led),** belemmer, bind; vang; kniehalter; ~**-net,** voëlnet, skakelnet.
tram: ~**mer,** koekepanopsigter, =werker; ~ **ming,** koekepanvervoer.
tramon'tane, (n) uitlander, vreemdeling; (a) transalpyns; vreemd, barbaars.
tramp, (n) omswerwing; gestamp; voetstap; hoefslag; landloper, rondloper, straatloper; swerfling, padloper; voetreis, wandeltog; mars; vragskip, vragsoeker (skip); *on the* ~, aan die rondloop; aan die werk soek; (v) trap; rondloop, skooi; aftrap; stamp, voetslaan, loop; *we had to* ~ *it,* ons moes voetslaan; ~ **ing,** landlopery, rondloop.
tram'ple, (n) getrap, getrappel, gestamp; vertrapping; (v) trap, vertrap; ~ *to DEATH,* doodtrap; ~ *DOWN,* plattrap; ~ *someone in the DUST,* iem. in die stof verneder; ~ *under FOOT,* met die voete vertrap; ~ *ON,* omtrap; ~**r,** trapper, vertrapper.
tramp'ling, getrappel.
tramp'oline, wipmat, trampolien, springmat; ~ **jumping,** trampolienspring.
tram'polinist, trampolienspringer.
tramp: ~ **service,** vragdiens; ~ **steamer,** vragsoeker.
tram: ~**-rail(s),** tremspoor; ~ **service,** tremdiens; ~**-shed,** tremskuur, remise; ~ **shelter,** tremhuisie; ~ **staff,** trempersoneel; ~ **stop,** tremhalte; ~ **terminus,** tremterminus; ~ **ticket,** tremkaartjie.
tram'way, tremspoor; ~ **company,** tremmaatskappy; ~ **staff,** trempersoneel; ~ **traffic,** tremverkeer; ~ **man,** tremwerker; ~**s,** tremspoor.
trance, (gees)verrukking, geesvervoering; beswyming, skyndood; hipnotiese toestand, droomtoestand.
tranq'uil, rustig, kalm, bedaard, trankiel; ~ **l'ity,** rus, stilte, kalmte, bedaardheid, sielsrus; ~ *lity of mind,* gemoedsrus; ~ **liza'tion,** bedaring, gerusstelling; ~ **lize,** gerusstel, sus, kalmeer, laat bedaar; stil; ~ **lizer,** kalmeermiddel, bedaarmiddel, depressant.
transact', onderhandel; verhandel; verrig, afhandel; behartig; ~ *business,* sake verrig; ~ **ion,** onderhandeling; handeling; verhandeling, verrigting, transaksie; vergelyk, skikking; ~ **or,** onderhandelaar; bewerker, uitvoerder, verhandelaar.
transal'pine, (n) transalpinis; (a) transalpyns, anderkant die Alpe.
transatlan'tic, transatlanties.
transcend', te bo gaan, oortref; ~ **ence,** ~ **ency,** oortreffing, voortreflikheid; ~ **ent,** voortreflik, uitstekend; bonatuurlik, transendentaal; ~ **en'tal,** bonatuurlik, transendentaal; ~ **en'talism,** transendentalisme; ~ **entalist,** (n) transendentalis; (a) transendentalisties.
transcontinen'tal, transkontinentaal.
transcribe', oorskrywe, afskryf; omset (mus.); kopieer, transkribeer; ~ **r,** oorskrywer, kopiis.
tran'script, afskrif, kopie.
transcrip'tion, oorskrywing; afskrif, transkripsie; afskrywing.
transcur'rent, kruis=.
transdu'cer, oordraer; oorvormer.
transect', dwars deursny; ~ **ion,** deursnee.
tran'sept, transep, kruisbeuk, dwarsbeuk, skip (van kerk).
trans'fer, (n) oordrag, transport; afstandoorbringing, oorplasing, verplasing; afdruk; oorskrywing, oorboeking; afstrykpatroon; oordrukpatroon; verplaaste soldaat; verplaasbriefie (skool); *deed of* ~, transportakte.
transfer', (v) **(-red),** oordra, transporteer; oorboek; verplaas; oorbring, oorplaas; oordruk, afdruk; ~ *to,* oordra op (rekening); oordra aan (persoon); ~ **abil'ity,** oordraagbaarheid.
trans'ferable, oordraagbaar; verplaasbaar, *not* ~, nie-oordraagbaar, nie oordraagbaar nie, onverhandelbaar (op tjeks).
trans'fer: ~**-book,** oordragboek; ~ **deed,** transportakte; ~ **dues,** hereregte; ~ **duty,** hereregte.
transferee', persoon aan wie oorgedra word, transportnemer; sessionaris, ontvanger; oorgeplaaste.
trans'fer: ~ **ence,** oordrag, oordraging, oorsetting; verplasing; ~**-ink,** oordrukink, ~ **or,** oordraer, transportgewer; ~**-paper,** oordrukpapier; ~**-picture,** aftrekprent; ~ **platform,** oorstapplatform; ~ **secretary,** oordragsekretaris; ~**-ticket,** oorstapkaartjie; ~ **voucher,** oordragbewys.
transfigura'tion, omskepping; gedaanteverwisseling, verheerliking (van Christus op die berg).
transfig'ure, verheerlik, van gedaante verander; omtower, omskep.
transfix', deurboor, deursteek; ~ **ed,** deursteek, deurstoke; deurboor; aan die grond genael; ~ **ion,** deursteking, deurboring.
transform', vervorm, van vorm verander; omskep, omvorm; van gedaante laat verwissel; herlei (wisk.); transformeer; ~ *one thing INTO another,* een ding in iets anders verander; *the old TENNIS COURT has been* ~ *ed to a garden,* die ou tennisbaan is in 'n tuin omgeskep; ~ **able,** veranderbaar, vervormbaar; ~ **a'tion,** (gedaante)verandering; vervorming; gedaanteverwisseling; herskepping; transformasie (elek.); ~ *ation of matter,* stofomsetting; ~ **a'tive,** herskeppend, transformerend; ~ **er,** vervormer; omsetter, transformator (elek.); ~ **er oil,** omsetolie; ~ **ism,** ontwikkelingsleer.
transfuse', oorstort, oorgiet; oorbring; oortap; ~ *BLOOD,* bloed oortap; ~ *INTO,* ingiet; inprent; aansteek; laat deurtrek van.
transfus'ible, oorgietbaar.
transfu'sion, oorgieting, transfusie; deurtrekking; oortapping (bloed); deurdringing, inprenting; *give a blood* ~, 'n bloedoortapping gee.
transgress', oortree; oorskry; sondig; skend; ~ **ion,** oortreding; oorskryding, vergryp, sonde; ~ **ive,** oorskrydend, oortredend; ~ **or,** oortreder, sondaar.
tranship', *kyk* **trans-ship.**
trans'ience, trans'iency, verganklikheid, kortstondigheid.
trans'ient, verganklik, kortstondig, verbygaande; oorgangs=; ~ **chord,** oorgangsakkoord; ~ **condition,** oorgangstoestand; ~ **note,** oorgangsnoot.
transis'tor, transistor; ~ **radio,** transistorradio.

trans'it, deurgang; vervoer; deurtog, deurvaart, deurvoer; verkeersweg; oorgang; *IN* ~, deurtrekkend; onderweg, in transito; *GOODS in* ~, deurvoergoedere; *the* ~ *of VENUS,* die oorgang van Venus; ~ **camp,** deurgangskamp; ~ **charge,** deurgangskoste; ~ **dues,** ~ **duties,** deurvoerregte, deurvoerbelasting; ~ **goods,** deurvoergoedere.
transi'tion, oorgang; verandering; ~ **al,** ~ **ary,** oorgangs-; ~ **point,** oorgangspunt; ~ **stage,** oorgangstydperk, oorgangstadium.
trans'itive, oorganklik, transitief.
trans'itoriness, kortstondigheid, verganklikheid.
trans'itory, verganklik, kortstondig, verbygaand; vlugtig; ~ **clause,** oorgangsbepaling.
trans'it: ~ **port,** deurvoerhawe; ~ **stage,** oorgangstadium; ~ **state,** oorgangstoestand; ~ **trade,** deurvoerhandel, transitohandel.
Transjord'an, Transjordan'ia, Transjordanië.
Transkei': *the* ~, die Transkei.
translat'able, vertaalbaar; ~ **ness,** vertaalbaarheid.
translate', vertaal, oorsit, oorbring; vertolk; omsit; verplaas, oorplaas (biskop); wegneem; deursien; verander, vervorm; opknap, oplap; ten hemel voer; ~ *a BISHOP,* 'n biskop oorplaas; ~ *d FROM Afrikaans,* uit Afrikaans vertaal; ~ *INTO Afrikaans,* in Afrikaans vertaal; ~ *WORDS into deeds,* woorde in dade omsit.
transla'tion, vertaling, oorsetting; oordrag; oorplasing (biskop); verplasing; oorseining; *a close* ~, 'n getroue vertaling; ~ **bureau,** vertaalburo.
translat'or, vertaler, oorsitter; oorbringer, herleier (teleg.); *sworn* ~, beëdigde vertaler.
translit'erate, oorskryf, transkribeer; translitereer.
translitera'tion, transkripsie; transliterasie.
translu'cence, translu'cency, deursigtigheid, deurskynendheid.
translu'cent, deurskynend.
translun'ar(y), bowemaans; boweaards.
transmarine', oorsees, oorsee geleë.
trans'meate, deurgaan, deurtrek.
trans'migrant, landverhuiser.
trans'migrate, verhuis, wegtrek.
transmigra'tion, oorgang, verhuising; deurgang; ~ *of the soul,* sielsverhuising.
transmig'ratory, oorgaande, verhuisend.
transmissibil'ity, oordraagbaarheid; oorerflikheid.
transmiss'ible, oordraagbaar; oorsendbaar; oorerflik.
transmi'ssion, oorsending, oorseining; versending; deurlating (lig); oorerwing; oorlewering, oorhandiging, oordrag; transmissie; dryfwerk (motor); voortplanting (geluid); uitsending (radio); oorbrenging (elek.); ratkas; gangwissel; ~ *of heat,* oorbrenging van warmte; ~ **box,** senderkas; ~ **interval,** sendpouse; ~ **key,** sendsleutel; ~ **line,** hoogspanningsleiding; ~ **-shaft,** dryfas; oorbringas; ~ **time,** stuurtyd, sendduur; ~ **-wire,** transmissieleiding.
transmit', (-ted), oorsend; oorstuur; oorsein (berig); uitsend (radio); deurstuur; oorlewer; oorplant; oorbring; nalaat; deurlaat, gelei; oordra; voortplant (geluid); ~ *a DISEASE,* 'n siekte oordra; ~ *LIGHT,* lig deurlaat; ~ *a PARCEL,* 'n pakkie deurstuur; ~ *SOUND,* geluid voortplant; ~ **tal,** *kyk* **transmission;** ~ **ter,** versender; deurseiner; spreekbuis; oorsender, seintoestel; seingewer; sleutel.
transmit'ting, (uit)sending; ~ **-aerial,** sendantenne; ~ **-agent,** oorplanter (siekte); ~ **-key,** seinsleutel; ~ **set,** sender, sendtoestel; ~ **station,** sender, omroep, sendstasie; ~ **wave,** sendgolf; ~ **wave length,** sendgolflengte; ~ **wire,** senddraad.
transmog'rify, (..fied), wonderlik verander, omtower, metamorfoseer.
transmutabil'ity, veranderbaarheid, verwisselbaarheid.
transmut'able, veranderbaar, verwisselbaar.
transmuta'tion, verandering, verwisseling, transmutasie.
transmute', verander, omsit, omwissel.
transnorm'al, abnormaal, buitengewoon.
transocean'ic, oorsees; anderkant die oseaan; ~

flight, oseaanvlug; *the first* ~ *FLIGHT by aeroplane,* die eerste vlug oor die see.
tran'som, dwarsbalk, dwarslêer, draagbalk (brug); skamel; hekbalk; dwarslat; kalf (bouk.).
transpar'ency, deursigtigheid, helderheid; transparant.
transpar'ent, deurskynend; deursigtig; klaarblyklik; opreg; ~ **ly,** klaarblyklik.
transpic'uous, deurskynend.
transpierce', deurboor, deursteek.
transpira'tion, uitwaseming (plante); uitdamping, sweet, uitsweting; (die) uitlek; transpirasie.
transpire', uitwasem (plante); uitsweet; uitlek, rugbaar word (nuus); gebeur, plaasvind.
transpirom'eter, verdampingsmeter, transpirometer.
trans'plant¹, (n) oorplanting; verplanting; oorgeplante iets; transplantaat.
transplant'², (v) verplant, oorplant; verplaas; ~ *a heart,* 'n hart oorplant; ~ **able,** verplantbaar; ~ **a'tion,** verplanting, oorplanting oorbrenging; ~ **er,** verplanter, oorplanter; ~ *er of a heart,* hartoorplanter.
trans'port, (n) transport; vervoer(wese); vervoering; (sins)verrukking; vlaag; transportskip; vervoermiddels; gedeporteerde; *MINISTER of T* ~, Minister van Vervoer; *MINISTRY of T* ~, Ministerie van Vervoer.
transport', (v) vervoer, transporteer; verplaas, oorbring; deporteer; in vervoering bring, meesleep, verruk; ~ *ed with ANGER,* blind van woede; ~ *ed with JOY,* verruk van vreugde; ~ **abil'ity,** vervoerbaarheid; ~ **able,** vervoerbaar.
trans'port: ~ **-aeroplane,** transportvliegtuig; verkeersvliegtuig; troepevliegtuig; ~ **allowance,** reistoelae; vervoertoelae; ~ **-animal,** transportdier; ~ **a'tion,** vervoer, transport; oorbrenging; ~ **a'tion service,** vervoerdiens; ~ **-case,** swaargewonde; ~ **difficulties,** vervoermoeilikhede; ~ **'er,** vervoerder; transportryer; vervoerwa; ~ **-rider,** transportryer, togganger; ~ **-riding,** transportry; ~ **-ship,** transportskip; troepeskip; ~ **strike,** vervoerstaking; ~ **undertaking,** vervoeronderneming; ~ **-wagon,** transportwa, togwa; ~ **-work,** transportwerk.
transpos'able, omsetbaar, verplaasbaar.
transpos'al, omsetting, verplasing, wisseling.
transpose', verplaas, omsit, omwissel; oorbring (algebra); transponeer (mus.).
transposi'tion, verplasing, omsetting; transposisie (mus.); woordomsetting; (die) oorbring, oorbrenging (algebra); ~ **cypher,** letterwisseling.
trans-ship', (-ped), oorskeep, verskeep; oorlaai; ~ **ment,** oorskeping (mense); oorlaai (goedere); ~ **ment charges,** oorlaaikoste.
transubstan'tiate, in 'n ander wese verander, van vorm verander.
transubstantia'tion, gedaanteverandering, selfstandigheidsverandering, transsubstansiasie.
transuda'tion, deursweting, uitsweting; deursyfering.
transud'atory, deurswetend.
transude', deursweet, uitsweet; deursypel.
Transvaal', (n) Transvaal; *Eastern, Northern, Southern, Western* ~, Oos-, Noord-, Suid-, Wes-Transvaal; (a) Transvaals; ~ **er,** Transvaler.
transval'ue, hersien, 'n ander waarde toeken aan.
transverb'erate, deurslaan.
transvers'al, (n) dwarslyn, snylyn; (a) dwarslopend, transversaal.
transverse', (n) dwarsspier; dwarsstuk; (v) omkeer; (a) dwars, dwarslopend; transversaal; ~ **axis,** breedteas; ~ **dyke,** dwarsgang; ~ **flute,** dwarsfluit; ~ **river,** dwarsrivier; ~ **section,** dwarsdeursnee; ~ **shaft,** dwarsas; ~ **spring,** dwarsveer; ~ **strap,** dwarsband.
Transylvan'ia, Seweburge, Transsilvanië; ~ **n,** (n) Seweburger; (a) Transsilvanies, Seweburgs.
trant'er, smous, venter.
trap¹, (n) kleed, klerasie; (pl) goeters, bagasie; *pack your* ~ *s,* vat jou goed; rol jou mat op; (v) versier, optooi.
trap², (n) val, strik, wip, vanggat, lokval; slagyster; hinderlaag, valstrik; valdeur, luik; listige bedrog; eenperdkarretjie, lokbeampte, lokvoël; stankaf-

trapan

sluiter, sinkputjie; sperder; *be CAUGHT in a* ~, in 'n val sit; gevang wees; *FALL into a* ~, in 'n val loop; *FALL into someone's* ~, in iem. se strik loop; in iem. se net val; *LEAD someone into a* ~, iem. in 'n val laat loop; *SET a* ~, 'n val stel; *SET a* ~ *for someone*, vir iem. 'n wip (val) stel; vir iem. lae lê; *SHUT your* ~*!* hou jou bek! *WALK straight into the* ~, reg in die val loop; *WALK into a* ~ *one has set for another*, 'n gat vir iem. grawe en self daarin val; (v) **(-ped)**, vang; in die val laat loop, vaskeer; betrap.
trapan', *kyk* **trepan.**
trap: ~**-cellar**, ruimte onder die toneel; ~**-cover**, luik; ~**-cut**, liplas; ~ **door**, luik, valdeur.
trapes, (n) slons; (v) rondflenter, slenter; *pack up one's* ~, jou matte oprol; jou goed vat.
trapeze', sweefstok, sweefrek, trapesium.
trapez'ium, (-s, ..zia), trapesium.
trapezohed'ron, trapesoëder.
trap'ezoid, (n) trapesoïed, trapesoïde; (a) trapesoï= daal.
trap: ~**-fall**, ~**-hole**, valkuil, valgat; ~ **flower**, fuik= blom; ~ **gun**, stelgeweer; ~ **mine**, verneukmyn, fopmyn; ~**-nest**, valnes; ~ **per**, strikspanner, wild= vanger, pelsjagter; ~ **ping**, verlokking; betrapping; pelsjag.
trapp'ings, opskik, sieraad.
trap: ~ **ping system**, lokvalstelsel; ~ **trench**, vanggrip; ~**-valve**, valklep.
Trap'pist, Trappis; ~ **monk**, Trappistemonnik.
trash, (n) afval, vuilgoed, oorskiet; bog, twak, kaf; droë blare, bogpraatjies, twakpraatjies, wildewol= haarpraatjies; (v) blare (van suikerriet) afstroop; snoei; weggooi, verwerp; ~**iness**, bogterigheid, niksbeduidendheid; snert; ~**y**, prullerig, sleg, on= bruikbaar, bog=, bogterig; ~**y novel**, snertroman.
trass, tras.
trauma, (-s, -ta), wond, verwonding, besering; trau= ma; ~**t'ic**, (n) wondmiddel; (a) wond=; traumaties; ~ **tism**, verwonding.
trav'ail, (n) werk, moeite, trawal; barensnood, ba= renswee; (v) moeg maak, vermoei, afmat; in ba= rensnood verkeer.
trav'el, (n) reis; reisverhaal; beweging, loop; slag (van masjiendele); beweegkrag; vlug (van hyskraan); hefhoogte (domkrag); (pl) reisbeskrywing, reisver= haal; (v) **(-led)**, reis, bereis, toer; gaan, trek, aflê; (hom) voortplant (geluid, ens.); loop; ~ *BACK= WARDS and forwards*, heen en weer gaan (reis); *LIGHT* ~*s extremely fast*, lig word baie vinnig voortgeplant; *his MIND* ~*s over the events*, in sy gees het hy die gebeurtenisse opgeroep; ~ *off the POINT*, van die onderwerp afdwaal; ~ *in SOAP*, met seep smous; *ON his* ~*s in Europe*, op reis in Europa; ~ *THROUGH*, deurreis; *change the* ~ *of the VALVES*, die slag v.d. kleppe verander; ~ **agency**, reisburo; ~ **agent**, reisagent; ~**-book**, reis= verhaal; ~ **bureau**, reisburo; ~ **led**, bereis, berese.
trav'eller, reisiger; bandroller, rolpasser (wamakery); loopkat; ~**-crane**, loopkraan; **'s cheque**, reistjek, reisigerstjek; ~**'s guide**, reisgids; ~**'s joy**, diewe= kruid; ~**'s tale**, 'n ongelooflike storie, 'n kluitjie.
trav'elling, (n) reis; (a) reisend, reis=; ~**-allowance**, reistoelae; ~**-companion**, reisgenoot, reismaat; ~**-costume**, reiskostuum; ~**-crane**, loopkraan; loop= kat; ~ **dune**, trekduin; ~**-expense**, reiskoste; ~**-kitchen**, kombuiswa; ~ **library**, reisbiblioteek; ~**-party**, reisende geselskap; ~**-requisites**, reisbe= nodigdhede; ~**-rug**, reisdeken; ~ **scholarship**, reis= beurs; ~ **stage**, loopsteier; ~ **stairs**, roltrap; ~**-trunk**, reiskoffer.
trav'elogue, reispraatjie; reisrolprent.
trav'el: ~ **shower**, reisgeskenkparty; ~ **sickness**, treinsiekte, reissiekte, naarheid; ~**-soiled**, ~**-stain= ed**, vuil v.d. reis; ~ **time**, reistyd; ~**-worn**, vuil, verslyt.
trav'erse, (n) dwarshout, dwarsstuk; roete; opname; dwarsbeweging; teenspoed; ontkenning (reg); breedtespreiding; breedteriggveld; breedteverstel= ling; dwarswal, syweer (vesting); dwarsstyl (draag= baar); trekmeting; dwarsgalery; waarnemingslyn; (v) dwars draai; deurkruis; opneem; dwarsboom;

treat

reis, deurreis, deurloop, aflê; ontken, ekspsies op= werp (reg); dwars loop; deursny; ~ *a vast distance*, 'n groot afstand aflê; (a) dwars, oorkruis; roete=; ~ **flute**, dwarsfluit; ~**-map**, roetekaart; ~ **r**, rolbrug; draaiskyf; ~ **survey**, roetepeiling; ~ **table**, draai= skyf; ~ **wheel**, meetwiel.
trav'ertin(e), travertyn.
trav'esty, (n) (..ties), vermomming, verkleding; kari= katuur, parodie; travestie; *a* ~ *of justice*, 'n bespot= ting v.d. gereg; (v) (..tied), parodieer; travesteer; vermom.
travois', Rooihuidslee.
trawl, (n) treilnet, sleepnet, dregnet, treknet; (v) treil, met 'n sleepnet visvang; ~**er**, visboot, treiler; treil= visser; ~**erman**, sleepnettrekker, treilvisser; ~**-net**, sleepnet.
trawl'ing, treilvissery.
trax'cavator, ruspergraaf.
tray, skinkbord, presenteerblad; bak, laai; platkissie (vrugte); droogstellasie; pan; ~ **agriculture**, wa= terkweking; ~**-cloth**, skinkbordkleedjie.
trea'cherous, verraderlik, vals, trouelos, slinks; *a* ~ *CROSSING*, 'n gevaarlike oorgang; ~ *LAUGH*, judaslag; *a ROAD* ~ *with rain*, 'n gevaarlike pad as dit nat is; ~ **ness**, verraderlikheid, valsheid, slinks= heid.
trea'chery, valsheid, trouelosheid, verraaiery; ver= raad; judasstreek.
trea'cle, beesstroop, swartstroop, melasse.
trea'cly, stroperig.
tread, (n) tree; voetstap, tred, skrede; loopvlak (mo= torband); betrapping (perd); *with measured* ~, met afgemete stap; (v) **(trod, trodden)**, tree, stap, loop; betree; bewandel, vervolg; skoei (band); ~ *on AIR*, in die wolke wees; ~ *the BOARDS*, toneelspeler wees; ~ *the DECK*, seeman wees; ~ *DOWN*, ver= trap; ~ *on EGGS*, versigtig wees; ~ *in someone's FOOTSTEPS*, in iem. se voetspore stap; ~ *GRAPES*, druiwe trap; ~ *on someone's HEELS*, iem. op die hakke volg; ~ *on thin ICE*, op gevaarli= ke terrein wees; ~ *LIGHTLY*, versigtig te werk gaan; saggies loop; ~ *MEASURE*, passies maak; voete warm maak; dans; ~ *on a person's NECK*, jou voet op iem. se nek sit; ~ *ON*, trap op; ~ *OUT*, uittrap, blus (vuur), demp; ~ *on the STAGE*, to= neel speel, toneelspeler wees; ~ *on a person's TOES*, op iem. se tone trap; iem. te na kom; ~ *UNDERFOOT*, vertrap; ~ *UPON*, vertrap; ~ *WARILY*, lig loop, versigtig wees; ~ *WATER*, watertrap; ~**er**, loper, trapper.
trea'dle, trap(per), pedaal; ~**-bar**, trapstang; ~**-ma= chine**, trapmasjien.
tread'mill, trapmeule; sleurwerk; *be at the* ~, sleur= werk doen.
treas'on, verraad; *an ACT of* ~, verraad; *HIGH* ~, hoogverraad; ~**able**, verraderlik; skuldig aan ver= raad; ~**ableness**, verraderlikheid.
trea'sure, (n) skat; rykdom; (v) versamel, as 'n skat bewaar; opgaar, versamel, vergaar; ~**-chamber**, skatkamer; ~**-chest**, skatkis; ~ **d**, kosbaar; ge= waardeer; ~**-house**, skatkamer; ~**-hunt**, skat(te)= jag; ~**-hunter**, skatgrawer; fortuinsoeker; ~**r**, skatbewaarder; tesourier; penningmeester; ~**r-general**, (..s-general), tesourier-generaal; ~ **rship**, tesourierskap; penningmeesterskap; ~**-seeker**, skatgrawer; fortuinsoeker; ~ **trove**, vonds, gevon= de skat.
trea'sury, (..ries), skatkamer; skatkis; tesourie; fis= kus; departement van finansies; ~**-bench**, minis= tersbank; ~ **bill**, skatkiswissel; ~ **bond**, skatkis= obligasie; ~ **note**, skatkisnoot; ~ **office**, tesourie; ~ **warrant**, skatkismagbrief, skatkisbewys.
treat, (n) onthaal, fees; genot; *GIVE someone a* ~, iem. onthaal (trakteer); *it was a REAL* ~, dit was 'n hele aardigheid; dit was baie genotvol; *it was QUITE a* ~, dit was 'n plesier; dit was 'n hele aar= digheid; *STAND a* ~, trakteer; (v) behandel; be= werk (erts); onthaal, vergas, trakteer; ~ *as a JOKE*, as 'n grap beskou; ~ *OF an important sub= ject*, dit gaan oor 'n belangrike saak; dit behandel 'n belangrike onderwerp; ~ *ONESELF to*, jou die weelde veroorloof van; jou trakteer op; ~ *a*

treatise 1320 *trial*

PATIENT, 'n pasiënt behandel; ~ *TO a meal,* vergas op 'n maal; ~ *WITH,* onderhandel met ('n persoon); behandel met (medisyne); ~**able,** geseglik, handelbaar; ~**er,** onthaler, trakteerder; bewerker (erts).
treat'ise, verhandeling, vertoog.
treat'ment, behandeling; *medical* ~, mediese behandeling.
treat'y, (treaties), verdrag, traktaat; verbond; ooreenkoms; *BE in* ~ *for,* in onderhandeling wees oor; *ENTER upon a* ~, 'n verdrag sluit; *by PRIVATE* ~, uit die hand; ~ **port,** verdraghawe; ~ **provision,** verdragbepaling.
tre'ble, (n) eerste stem, sopraan(stem); (die) drievoudige; diskant; drie maal soveel; *HALF* ~, halflangbeen; *TRIPLE* ~, drieslagsteek; (v) verdrievoudig; verdriedubbel; (a) drievoudig, driedubbeld; sopraan=, hoog (sang); drie maal; ~ **clef,** solsleutel, G-sleutel; ~ **crochet,** langbeentjie; ~ **play,** driekuns (bofbal); ~ **stitch,** langbeen(steek); *double* ~ *stitch,* dubbelslagsteek, dubbellangbeentjie.
treb'ly, driedubbel, drie maal.
tree, (n) boom; as; lees (skoene); saalboom; swingelhout; geslagsboom, geslag, stam; (pl) geboomte; *you cannot judge a* ~ *by its BARK,* moenie 'n man op sy baadjie takseer nie; *know a* ~ *by its FRUIT,* 'n boom aan sy vrugte ken; *a* ~ *is known by its FRUIT,* aan die vrugte ken 'n mens die boom; ~ *of HEAVEN,* hemelboom *(Ailanthus altissima); the* ~ *of the KNOWLEDGE of good and evil,* die boom v.d. kennis van goed en kwaad; ~ *of LIBERTY,* vryheidsboom; ~ *of LIFE,* boom v.d. lewe; *remove the OLD* ~ *and it will wither to death,* 'n ou boom word nie maklik verplant nie; *at the TOP of the* ~, op die boonste sport; *be UP a* ~, in die knyp wees; in die verknorsing wees; met die hand in die hare sit; *a* ~ *must be bent while it is still YOUNG,* buig die boompie solank hy jonk is; (v) in 'n boom jaag; iem. laat vlug; op die lees sit (skoen); ~ **agate,** boomagaat; ~ **aloe,** boomaalwyn; ~**-creeper,** boomklimop; ~**-cricket,** donderbesie; ~**-dozer,** boomstoter; ~**-feller,** houtkapper; ~**-felling,** boomkappery; ~**-fern,** boomvaring; ~**-frog,** boompadda; ~**-fungus,** boomswam; ~ **less,** boomloos, sonder bome; ~**-line,** boomgrens; ~**-lizard,** boomkoggelmander; ~ **lore,** boomkunde; ~**-nail,** houtpen; ~ **nursery,** boomkwekery; ~**-nymph,** boomnimf; ~**-planter,** boomplanter; ~**-planting,** boomplantery; ~**-snake,** boomslang; ~**-top,** boomtop; ~**-worship,** boomverering.
tre'foil, klawer; klawerblad; drieblaar; ~**ed,** klawervormig.
trek, (n) trek; (v) **(-ked),** trek; ~**-chain,** trekketting; ~ **ker,** trekker; ~**-ox,** trekos; ~ **wagon,** trekwa.
trell'is, (n) (-es), latwerk, prieel; traliewerk; (v) van traliewerk voorsien; oplei; ~ **ed,** getralie; opgelei; ~**-fence,** staketsel, tralieheining; ~**-gate,** traliehek; ~ **ing,** latwerk; traliewerk; ~**-window,** tralievenster; ~**-work,** latwerk; traliewerk.
trem'atode, suigwurm, trematode.
trem'ble, (n) bewing, siddering, trilling; bewerasie; (pl) trekkings; *be ALL of a* ~, die bewerasie hê; *THE* ~ *s,* bewerasie; (v) bewe, sidder; huiwer; skud; gril; ~ *AT the sight of,* beef by die aanskou van; *his life* ~ *s in the BALANCE,* sy lewe hang aan 'n sydraadjie; ~ *with FEAR,* beef van angs; *HEAR and* ~! hoor en beef! ~ *for someone's SAFETY,* vrees vir iem. se veiligheid; ~ *in one's SHOES,* staan en beef; ~ *at the THOUGHT,* sidder by die gedagte; ~**ment,** bewing; triller; ~ **r,** bewer; bangkat, bangbroek; trillerveer; alarmklok; elektriese klokkie.
trem'bling, (n) bewing; gerittel, siddering; trilling; (a) bewend, bewerig, rittelend; ~ **fit,** bewerasie; ~ **poplar,** trilpopulier.
trem'bly, bewerig.
trem'ellose, drillerig, trillend.
tremen'dous, verskriklik, gedug, vreeslik; yslik; ~ **ness,** vreeslikheid, verskriklikheid; yslikheid.
trem'olant, triller, trilregister, tremulant.
trem'olo, (-s), trilling, triller, tremulant, tremolo (mus.).

trem'or, bewing, siddering; huiwering; getril; aardbewing, skudding.
trem'ulant = **tremolant.**
trem'ulous, bewend, bewerig, trillend; bevrees, huiwerend; ~ **ness,** bewerigheid, gebeef; aarseling.
trench, (n) (-es), loopgraaf, prospekteersloot; sloot; grippie, greppel; riool; (v) uitgrawe; loopgrawe maak; diep omspit; ~ *DOWN,* inkuil; ~ *(UP)ON,* inbreuk maak op; grens aan; betrekking hê op.
trench'ancy, skerpheid, snydendheid, bytendheid; deurtastendheid.
trench'ant, snydend, skerp, bytend; beslis, deurtastend.
trench' coat, soldatejas.
trench'er, houtbord, broodbord; dolwevoer; grawer; ~ **companion,** tafelmaat; ~ **friend,** klaploper; ~**-valiant:** *be a* ~*-valiant,* stadig by die vak, gou by die bak wees; fluks by die bak wees.
trench: ~ **erman,** goeie eter; *a good* ~ **erman,** 'n smulpaap; goed kan weglê; 'n goeie mondslag slaan; ~**-excavator,** loopgraafbagger; ~ **fever,** loopgraafkoors; ~**-fighter,** frontvegter; ~ **foot,** boetson; slootvoet; ~ **garrison,** loopgraafbesetting; ~ **mortar,** mynwerper, loopgraafmortier; ~ **picket,** loopgraafwag; ~**-plough,** (n) diepploeg, woelploeg; (v) diep ploeg; ~ **shelter,** loopgraafskuiling; ~ **system,** loopgraafnet; ~ **warfare,** loopgraafoorlog, stellingoorlog.
trend, (n) neiging, rigting, koers, strekking, stroming, tendens; gang; loop; *a DOWNWARD* ~, 'n daling; 'n neiging om te daal; ~ *of EVENTS,* loop van sake; ~ *of THOUGHT,* gedagtegang; *a* ~ *TOWARDS a simpler style,* 'n neiging in die rigting van eenvoud; *an UPWARD* ~, 'n styging; 'n neiging om te styg; (v) loop, uitstrek; 'n neiging hê in 'n sekere rigting; ~ **seam,** rolnaat; ~**-setter,** rigtingaanduier, rigtinggewer, tendenssteller.
tren'tal, lyksang, elegie.
trepan'¹, (n) skedelboor, harsingpanboor, trepaan; (v) **(-ned),** trepaneer, die skedel deurboor.
trepan'², (n) bedrieër, kuller; (v) **(-ned),** in 'n strik lok.
trepan': ~ **a'tion,** skedelboring, panboring; ~ **ner,** panboorder; ~ **ning,** *kyk* **trepanation.**
trephine', (n) skedelsaag, trefien; (v) met die skedelsaag (trefien) opereer; ~ **r,** skedelsaer.
trep'id, siddernd; ontsteld; ~ **a'tion,** siddering, huiwering; ontsteltenis; bewing, bewerasie, angs.
tres'pass, (n) (-es), oortreding; vergryp, sonde; inbreukmaking; *forgive us our* ~ *es,* vergeef ons ons skulde; (v) oortree; vergryp, sondig; misbruik maak van; inbreuk maak op; beslag lê op; ~ *AGAINST,* sondig teen; ~ *on a person's HOSPITALITY,* van iem. se gasvryheid misbruik maak; ~ *against the LAW,* die wet oortree; ~ *on someone's TIME,* beslag lê op iem. se tyd; ~ **er,** oortreder; ~ *ers will be prosecuted,* oortreders sal vervolg word; ~ **ing,** oortreding; *no* ~ *ing allowed,* oortreders sal vervolg word; ~**-offering,** soenoffer.
tress, (n) (-es), haarlok, haarstring, vlegsel; (v) krul; vleg; ~ **y,** lokkig, krullend.
tre'stle, stellasie, bok; vormbank, stut, skraag; ~ **board,** tekenbord; ~**-bridge,** bokbrug; ~ **legs,** bokpote; ~ **table,** boktafel; ~**-work,** skraagwerk, stutwerk.
tret, oorgewig; vervoerslytasie; refaksie.
Treves, Trier.
trews, (Skotse) Hooglanderbroek.
trey, drie (van kaarte); ~ *of diamonds,* ruiten(s)drie.
tri'able, probeerbaar, beproefbaar; verhoorbaar.
tri'ad, drieklank; drietal; tritis; driebeen.
tri'al, besoeking, beproewing; proef, eksperiment, proefneming, ondersoek, verhoor; proefdruk (seëls); *old AGE has many* ~ *s,* die ouderdom kom met baie gebreke; *BE on one's* ~, teregstaan; ~ *by BATTLE,* vuurproef; *BRING up for* ~, voor die hof bring; *COME up for* ~, onder verhoor kom, voorkom; *COMMIT for* ~, ter strafsitting verwys; *by* ~ *and ERROR,* deur die probeer-en-trefmetode; *without the FORM of a* ~, sonder vorm van proses; *GIVE a* ~, probeer; *GO on* ~, teregstaan, voorkom; *MAKE a* ~, 'n proef neem; 'n eksperi=

ment uitvoer; op die proef stel; *PUT on* ~, verhoor; *REMAND for* ~, ter strafsitting verwys; *STAND* ~ *for murder*, weens moord teregstaan; *a* ~ *of STRENGTH*, 'n kragproef, 'n kragmeting; *SUBJECT to* ~, aan 'n toets onderwerp; ~ *by SWORD*, oordeel by tweegeveg; *UNDERGO* ~, verhoor word; ~ *for WITCHCRAFT*, hekseproses; ~ **and error**, probeer en fouteer; ~**-and-error method**, probeermetode, eksperimentele metode; ~ **ascent**, proefvlug; ~ **balance**, proefbalans; ~ **balloon**, proefballon; ~ **case**, verhoorsaak; ~ **consignment**, proefsending; ~ **exposure**, proefbeligting; ~ **flight**, proefvlug; ~ **judge**, verhoorregter; ~ **load**, proeflas; ~ **marriage**, proefhuwelik; ~ **match**, proefwedstryd; ~ **month**, proefmaand; ~ **order**, proefbestelling; ~ **pit**, proefskag; ~ **plant**, proefaanleg; ~ **ride**, proefrit; ~ **run**, proefloop; proefrit; ~ **shipment**, proefsending; ~ **trip**, proefvaart; proefrit.
tri'angle, driehoek; triangel (mus.); driepoot; *the eternal* ~, die ewige driehoek.
tria'ngular, driehoekig; ~ **bandage**, driehoekverband; ~ **contest**, driehoekverkiesing; driehoekwedstryd; ~ **cross**, drieaskruising; ~ **file**, driekantvyl; ~ **gusset**, driehoekstuk; ~ **stamp**, driehoekseël; ~ **treaty**, drievoudige verdrag.
tria'ngulate, trianguleer.
triangula'tion, driehoeks(op)meting, triangulasie.
tri'arch, (n) drievors; (a) driestralig; ~**y**, triargie; driemanskap.
Triass'ic, Trias-.
triba'dism, trib'ady, Lesbiese liefde, tribadie.
trib'al, stam-; ~ **authority**, stamowerheid; ~ **chief**, stamhoof; ~ **feud**, stamrusie, stamtwis; ~ **fight**, stamgeveg; ~ **god**, stamgod; ~ **ism**, stamorganisasie; stamskap; ~ **marriage**, stamhuwelik; ~ **system**, stamstelsel.
tribe, stam, volkstam; familie, ras, geslag; nasie (fig.); ~ **s'man**, stamgenoot, lid van 'n stam.
trib'rach, tribrag.
tribula'tion, beproewing, verdrukking, wederwaardigheid, bekommering, rampspoed.
tribulo'sis (ovium), geeldikkopsiekte (by skape).
tribun'al, regbank, geregshof, gereg, regterstoel, vierskaar.
trib'une, volksverteenwoordiger, tribuun (persoon); spreekgestoelte, tribune, verhoog; ~ **ship**, tribunaat.
trib'utary, (n) (..ries), syrivier, sytak, bystroom; uitloopsel; skatpligtige; (a) skatpligtig, synsbaar; sy-, tak-.
trib'ute, skatting; syns, skatpligtigheid; hulde(blyk); bydrae; omkoopsom; *FLORAL* ~ *s*, blom(me)hulde; *pay the LAST* ~ *to*, die laaste eer bewys aan; *LAY a* ~ *on*, 'n skatting lê op; *PAY the* ~ *of nature*, die tol v.d. natuur betaal; *PAY* ~ *to his genius*, hulde aan sy begaafdheid bring; *lay UNDER* ~, 'n skatting oplê; ~ **-money**, skatting; ~ **r**, skatpligtige.
tri'car, driewieler(motor).
trice[1], (n) oomblik, oogwink; *IN a* ~, een-twee-drie, in 'n kits, gou-gou, in 'n ommesientjie; *he gives TWICE who gives in a* ~, wie gou gee, gee dubbel.
trice[2], (v) ophys; vaskoppel, vasmaak.
tricen'tenary, *kyk* **tercentenary**.
tri'ceps, (n) driekopspier; (a) driehoofdig, driekoppig.
trichi'asis, trigiase.
trich'ina, (-e), haarwurm, trigine.
trichinos'is, triginose.
tri'chinous, triginous.
tricholog'ical, haarkundig, trigologies.
trichol'ogist, haarkundige, trigoloog.
trichol'ogy, haarkunde, trigologie.
tri'chord, (n) driesnarige instrument; (a) driesnarig.
trichos'is, haarsiekte, trichose.
trick, (n) lis, (skelm)streek; toer; behendigheid; kunsie, kunsgreep, foefie; kultoertjie, slenterslag; trek, pakkie, slag (kaartspel); gewoonte; aanwensel; poets, grap, petalje, hebbelikheid, jilletjie, laai; *BE up to all kinds of* ~ *s*, vol streke wees; *be played a DIRTY* ~, 'n lelike streep getrek word; 'n lelike poets gebak word; *this ought to DO the* ~, dit behoort te werk; *a* ~ *of FORTUNE*, 'n gril v.d. noodlot; *he soon LEARNED the* ~, hy het gou die slag gekry; *there is NO* ~ *to it*, dis geen heksekuns nie; *an OLD* ~, 'n ou laai; *he was up to his OLD* ~ *s again*, hy was weer met sy ou streke besig; *PLAY* ~ *s*, kunste maak; poetse bak; *PLAY a* ~ *on someone*, iem. 'n kool stowe; iem. 'n knop draai; iem. 'n poets bak; iem. 'n streep trek; *SHOW* ~ *s*, kunsies vertoon; *know the* ~ *s of the TRADE*, die geheime v.d. vak ken; al die knope ken; al die kunsies ken; *know a* ~ *worth TWO of that*, 'n baie beter plan hê; *be UP to many* ~ *s*, baie laaie (streke) hê; *that* ~ *won't WORK*, daardie kunsie sal nie werk nie; (v) bedrieg, knoei, fop, kul; betrek; streke uithaal; ~ *someone INTO*, iem. deur lis (skelmstreke) beweeg om; ~ *ed OUT in all her finery*, uitgedos in haar kisklere; ~ *OUT of*, afhandig maak; deur skelmstreke iets kry; ~ **er**, bedrieër, kuller; verneuker; fopper; ~ **ery**, kullery, bedottery; verneukery; foppery, gefop; ~ **iness**, bedrieglikheid; ~ **ish**, bedrieglik.
tric'kle, (n) gedruppel, sypeling; stroompie, syferplek; *a mere* ~, 'n karige toevoer (voorraad); (v) druppel, aftap; biggel, rol; uitlek; sypel; ~ *DOWN*, neerbiggel; neerdrup; *tears* ~ *DOWN her cheeks*, trane biggel (rol) oor haar wange; *the news* ~ *d OUT*, die nuus het uitgelek.
trick'ling, (n) drup, syfering; druppeling; (a) druppend.
trick: ~ **question**, slinkse vraag; strikvraag; ~ **rider**, kunsruiter; ~ **riding**, rykunsies; ~ **ster**, bedrieër, bedriegster; skelm; ~ **sy**, speels, uitgelate; snaaks; ~ **-track**, triktrak(spel); ~ **y**, bedrieglik, vol streke, listig; oulik, oorlams; lastig, netelig; gewaag.
tri'colour, (n) driekleur; (a) driekleurig; *T'* ~, Driekleur; ~ **ed**, driekleurig.
tric'ot, tricot, breigoed; ~ **stitch**, hekelsteek.
tricotyled'onous, driesaadlobbig.
tricus'pid, driepuntig, drieknobbelig.
tri'cycle, (n) driewiel(er); (v) op 'n driewiel ry.
tridac'tylous, drievingerig; met drie tone.
trid'ent, drietand; drietandvurk; ~ **ate**, met drie tande.
tridimen'sional, met drie afmetings.
tried, beproef, getoets; geslaag; *kyk* **try**, (v).
trienn'ial, (n) driejarige plant; driejaarlikse herdenking; (a) driejarig; driejaarliks.
tri'er, ondersoeker; regter; proef; volharder, aanhouer; verhoorder van reg(saak).
trifar'ious, drieledig; in drie rye.
trif'id, driedelig, driespletig.
tri'fle, (n) kleinigheid, bakatel, ietsie, skyntjie, beuselagtigheid, datjie, dingesie, prutsding, wiesewasie; brokkiespoeding, koek(vla)poeding, kockstruif; *for EVERY* ~, om die hawerklap; vir elke kleinigheid; *waste one's TIME on* ~ *s*, jou tyd met kleinighede mors; *a* ~ *VAGUE*, 'n bietjie vaag; (v) beusel, verspeel, futsel; korswel, gekskeer, spot, skerts; ~ *AWAY*, verspil, vermors, vertreusel; *he is NOT to be* ~ *d with*, hy laat nie met hom speel nie; ~ *WITH*, gekskeer met; peuter met; ~ **r**, beuselaar; spotter; futselaar.
trif'ling, (n) gepeuter, onbeduidendheid, niksbeduidendheid; (a) niksbeduidend, onbenullig, kinderagtig, beuselagtig; miniem, nietig.
trifol'iate, drieblad(er)ig, drieblaar-, met drie blare.
tri'form, drievormig.
trifurc'ate, met drie takke, drieledig.
trig[1], *abbr. for* **trigonometry**.
trig[2], (n) remblok; (v) (-ged), opknap, versier; rem; (a) netjies agtermekaar.
trig'amous, drie maal getroud.
trig'amy, driewywery, trigamie.
trigem'inous, drieling-; drievoudig.
trigg'er, (n) sneller, trekker; (v) aftrek; veroorsaak; ~ *off*, aan die gang sit, veroorsaak; ~ **-catch**, snellerknip; ~ **-finger**, aftrekvinger, wysvinger, voorvinger; ~ **-fish**, varkvis; ~ **-guard**, geweerbeuel, snellerbeuel; ~ **-hand**, snellerhand; ~ **-happy**, snellermal, skietlustig; ~ **-lever**, sneller; ~ **-screw**, snellerskroef; ~ **-spring**, snellerveer.
trig'on, driehoek; ~ **al**, driehoekig.

trigonomet'ric(al), trigonometries; ~ **beacon**, driehoeksbaken; ~ **survey**, driehoeksmeting; topografiese inrigting.
trigonom'etry, driehoeksmeting, trigonometrie.
trig'ram, drieklank, triftong.
trihed'ral, driekants=, drievlakkig, met drie kante; ~ **angle**, drievlakshoek, driekantshoek.
trihed'ron, drievlak, triëder.
trike, *abbr. for* **tricycle**.
trilat'eral, (n) driehoek; (a) driehoekig, driesydig, driekantig.
trilin'ear, van drie lyne.
trili'ngual, drietalig.
trilit'eral, van drie letters, drieletter=.
trill, (n) triller; trilling; trilklank; (v) tril, met trillende geluid praat (sing), vibreer; ~**ing**, (een van 'n) drielingkristal; trilling, trillende geluid.
trill'ion, triljoen.
trilob'ate, drielobbig.
triloc'ular, driehokkig.
tril'ogy, trilogie.
trim, (n) opskik, tooisel, garneersel; toestand, orde; verdeling (vrag); stelling; stuurlas, koplas (skeepv., lugv.); *in FIGHTING* ~, slagvaardig; *IN* ~, in goeie staat; in keurige orde; *OUT of* ~, ongelyk verdeel; ongebalanseer; onklaar; uit die haak; *in PERFECT* ~, in die haak; gereed en oorgehaal; (v) **(-med)**, tooi, versier; snoei, knip, reg sny, skoonknip, mooi sny; bysny; skoonmaak; stou; afwerk, bewerk; byknip (hare); beklee; belê (rok), garneer; in orde bring; snuit (kers); skipper, die mantel na die wind hang; by geen party aansluit nie; verdeel (vrag); stel; bestraf; opmaak; afrand (spekvleis); ~ *someone's JACKET*, iem. op sy baadjie gee; ~ *with LACE*, met kant opmaak; ~ *the SAILS*, die seile na die wind span; ~ *UP*, netjies afwerk; ~ *WELL*, goed balanseer; ~ *one's sails according to the WIND*, die seile na die wind span; (a) netjies, viets, fyn; in orde, goed uitgerus; ~**-ballast**, balanseerballas.
tri'maran, drierompskuit, trimaran.
tri'mer, drievoud, trimeer (chem.).
trim'erous, drietallig; driedelig.
trimes'ter, kwartaal, trimester, derde deel v.d. akademiese jaar.
trimes'tr(i)al, driemaandeliks.
trim'eter, drievoetige versreël, trimeter.
trim: ~**mer**, optooier, opmaker, versierder; afwerker; snoeier; opstopper; knipper, snoeiskêr; draagbalk; politieke weerhaan, draaier, skipperaar; stouer (op skip); loesing, afranseling; tremmer (skip, myn); raveelbalk.
trim'ming, oplegsel, garneersel, versiersel, opmaaksel; afranseling, loesing; afwerking; bekleding, bekleewerk; toebehoorsels; opsmuk; fraaiing; randafwerking; belegwerk; draaiery, geskipper; (pl) oortollighede; toebehore; afrandstukkies; afsnysels, afknipsels; ~ **axe**, snoeibyl; ~ **comb**, knipkam; ~ **joist**, raveelsybalk; ~ **lever**, stelhefboom; ~ **machine**, afwerkmasjien; stelvlak; ~ **rafter**, raveelspar; ~ **tank**, balanstenk, ewewigstenk.
trim'ness, netheid, ordelikheid.
tri'morph, trimorf; ~**'ic**, drievormig, trimorf; ~**'ism**, trimorfisme, drievormigheid.
trim'park, trimpark.
trin'al, drievoudig.
trine, (n) drietal; (a) drievoudig.
tri'ngle, gordynpaal; kroonlys; staander; smal skeilys.
Trinitar'ian, (n) Trinitariër, (a) Trinitaries; ~**ism**, Drie-eenheidsleer, leer v.d. Drie-eenheid.
trin'ity, (..ties), drie-eenheid; drietal; *Holy T*~, Heilige Drie-eenheid.
trink'et, sieraad, kleinood, snuistery; ~**-box**, juweelkissie.
trino'mial, (n) drieterm; (a) drietermig; drienamig, drietallig.
tri'o, (-s), drietal, trits; trio, driesang.
tri'ole, triool.
tri'olet, triolet.
trip, (n) uitstappie, toggie, rit, toertjie; trippelpassie; misstap, struikeling; klink (elektr.); slaankant (hamer); (v) **(-ped)**, struikel, val; pootjie; 'n uitstappie maak; 'n misstap begaan; trippel, huppel; betrap; klink (elektr.); uithaak (anker); ~ *OVER difficult words*, oor moeilike woorde struikel; ~ *UP*, pootjie; op 'n fout betrap.
tripart'ite, driedelig, drieledig; ~ *treaty*, driesydige verdrag.
triparti'tion, driedeling, verdeling in drie.
tripe, ingewande; pens, afval; bog, kaf; ~, *HEAD and trotters*, afval; ~ *and ONIONS*, pens met uie; *TALK* ~, kaf verkoop; ~ *and TROTTERS*, pens en pootjies.
tripet'alous, drieblarig.
trip'-hammer, smeehamer, smidshamer.
triph'thong, drieklank, triftong.
tri'plane, driedekker (vliegtuig).
tri'ple, (n) drievoud; drietal; (v) verdrievoudig; (a) drievoudig, driedubbeld; *T*~ **Alliance**, Drievoudige Verbond; ~ **crown**, pouslike kroon; ~**-headed**, driehoofdig; ~ **pole**, driepolig; ~ **rhythm**, trippelmaat.
trip'let, drietal; terset, tersine; driereëlige versie; drieling; trits; triool (mus.); (pl) drieling.
tri'ple: ~ **time**, tripelmaat, drieslagsmaat; ~ **treble**, drieslagsteek.
trip'lex, drievoudig, driedubbel; tripleks.
trip'licate, (n) drievoud, triplikaat; *in* ~, in triplo, in drievoud; (v) in triplo uitgee; verdrievoudig, tripleer; (a) drievoudig; driedubbel.
triplica'tion, verdrievoudiging.
tripli'city, (..ties), drievoudigheid.
trip'lite, tripliet.
trip'od, drievoet, driepoot, driebeen; ~**al**, drievoetig; ~ **rest**, drievoetbok.
Tripolitan, (n) Tripolitaan; (a) Tripolitaans.
tripp'er, plesierreisiger, plesierganger.
trip'ple, (n, v) trippel (perd); ~**r**, trippelaar.
trip'terous, met drie vlerke.
triptique', triptiek (drieledige motorpas).
trip'tych, triptiek, drieluik.
trique'trous, driehoekig.
trir'eme, drieriemgalei, trireem.
trisect', driedeel, in drie gelyke dele verdeel; in derdes verdeel; ~**ion**, verdeling in drie gelyke dele, driedeling; ~**or**, driedeler.
tris'mus, kaakkramp, trismus, mondklem, klem in die kake.
trisperm'ous, driesadig.
trist'ful, treurig, droewig.
trisyllab'ic, drielettergrepig.
trisyll'able, drielettergrepige woord.
trite, alledaags; afgesaag, laag-by-die-grond, verslyt, banaal, triviaal, afgeslyt; ~**ness**, alledaagsheid; afgesaagdheid, trivialiteit.
trit'icale, korog.
Trit'on, Triton, seegod; meerman; *a* ~ *among the minnows*, 'n eenoog onder die blindes, 'n reus onder die dwerge.
trit'urate, vermaal, vergruis, verpoeier.
tritura'tion, vermaling, verpoeiering.
tri'umph, (n) triomf, seëpraal, sege; oorwinningsvreugde; segetog; *in* ~, triomferend; (v) triomfeer, seëvier, koning kraai; ~ *over all difficulties*, alle moeilikhede glansryk oorwin.
trium'phal, triomferend, seëvierend, seë=; ~ **arch**, triomfboog, ereboog, segepoort; ~ **car**, ~ **chariot**, segewa; ~ **march**, segetog; ~ **procession**, segetog, triomftog; ~ **wreath**, segekrans.
trium'phant, triomfantlik, seëvierend, seëpralend; ~ *over one's enemies*, triomferend oor jou vyande.
trium'vir, (-i, -s), drieman, triumvir; ~**ate**, driemanskap, triargie, triumviraat.
tri'une, drie-enig; *the* ~ *Godhead*, die Drie-eenheid.
triun'ity, drie-enigheid.
trival'ent, driewaardig.
trival'vular, driekleppig.
triv'et, drievoet, driebeen; *as right as a* ~, so reg soos 'n roer; ~ **table**, driepoottafeltjie.
triv'ia, kleinighede, nietighede.
triv'ial, vervelig; alledaags; beuselagtig, triviaal, onbeduidend, onbelangrik; plat; ~ *MATTERS*, kleinighede, nietighede; ~ *NAME*, volksnaam; ~ *'ity*,

trivium 1323 *trousseau*

(..**ties**), onbeduidendheid, kleinigheid, beuselary, beuselagtigheid; platheid.
triv'ium, trivium.
tri-week'ly, drieweekliks; drie maal per week.
troat, (n) geskreeu, geblêr; (v) skreeu, blêr.
tro'car, driehoekige naald, trokar.
trocha'ic, trogeïes.
troch'al, wielvormig.
troche, tablet.
troch'ee, trogee.
tro'chlea, katrol; rolvormige deel.
trochom'eter, afstandsmeter, trogometer.
trod'(den), *kyk* **tread**, (v).
trog'lodyte, grotbewoner, spelonkbewoner; kluisenaar; troglodiet; mensaap.
troglodyt'ic, grotbewoners=; kluisenaars=; troglodities.
troik'a, troika; driespan.
Troj'an, (n) Trojaan; *a REAL ~*, 'n staatmaker; *WORK like a ~*, jou nie spaar nie; uiters hard werk; (a) Trojaans; *allow the ~ horse within one's walls*, die Trojaanse perd inbring.
troll¹, (n) reus; dwerg, aardmannetjie.
troll², (n) rondsang; visstokkatrol; rol, gerol; (v) laat rondgaan; ('n) rondsang sing; rondbeweeg; visvang.
troll'ey, (-s), trollie, molwa; kontakrol, rolkontak (trem); loopkat; dienwaentjie; *~-bus*, trembus, elektriese bus; *~ head*, kontakrol; *~ jack*, roldomkrag.
troll'op, slegte vrou, slet, straatvrou, slons; *~ish*, *~y*, slonserig, ontugtig.
troll'y, (trollies) = **trolley**.
trom'ba, trompet.
trom'bone, tromboon, skuiftrompet; basuin.
trom'bonist, trombonis; basuinblaser.
tromm'el, trommelsif, draaiende ertssif; wasvat (myn).
troop, (n) trop, klomp, hoop, menigte, drom; troep; (pl) troepe, soldate; *~ of BABOONS*, trop bobbejane; *CONCENTRATION of ~ s*, troepesametrekking; *~ s of the LINE*, linietroepe; (v) bymekaarkom; in troppe loop; troepsgewyse formeer; *~ AWAY*, op 'n streep weggaan; *~ing the COLOURS*, vaandelparade hou; *~ TOGETHER*, bymekaarskool; *~-carrier*, troepewa; transportskip; troepevliegtuig; troepeskip; *~ er*, ruiter, kavalleris, kavalleriesoldaat; pantsersoldaat; troepevliegtuig; transportskip; kavallerieperd; *swear like a ~ er*, soos 'n matroos vloek; *~-horse*, kavallerieperd; *~ing*, samedromming; *~ing the colours*, vaandelparade; *~ leader*, troepleier, spanleier; *~ movement*, troepebeweging; *~ sergeant*, troepsersant; *~ sergeant-major*, wagmeester; *~ ship*, transportskip, troepeskip; *~-train*, troepetrein; *~ transport*, troepevervoer; troepevliegtuig; troepeskip, transportskip.
trope, troop; styIfiguur.
troph'ic, voedings=, trofies.
trop'hied, met trofeë versier.
troph'y, (trophies), trofee; beker; *floating ~*, wisseltrofee, wisselbeker.
trop'ic, (n) keerkring; (pl) trope; *T~ of CANCER*, Kreefskeerkring; *T~ of CAPRICORN*, Steenbokskeerkring; *THE ~ s*, die keerkringslande, die trope; (a) tropies.
trop'ical, tropies; keerkrings=; hartstogtelik; *~ disease*, tropiese siekte.
tropicaliza'tion, aanpassing by die trope.
trop'ically: *~ suit*, tropepak; *~ year*, sonjaar.
trop'icalize, vir die trope inrig; by die trope aanpas; *~ d*, tropevas.
tropicopol'itan, (n) tropiese plant (dier); (a) tropies.
trop'ism, tropisme (groeirigting); tropie (beweging).
tropolog'ical, oordragtelik, figuurlik.
tropol'ogy, beeldspraak, tropologie.
trop'osphere, troposfeer.
tropospher'ic, troposferies.
trot, (n) draf; kleuter; *AT a ~*, op 'n draf; *BREAK into a ~*, in 'n draf oorgaan; *in FULL ~*, in volle (gestrekte) draf; *GO for a ~*, gaan ry; *KEEP someone on the ~*, iem. geen rus laat nie; iem. aan die gang hou; *WIN at a ~*, speel-speel (fluit-fluit) wen; (v)(-ted), draf, op 'n draf ry; saalboom ry; laat draf; *~ AFTER*, nadraf, nadrentel; *~ ALONG*, aandraf; *~ AWAY*, wegdraf; *~ someone off his LEGS*, iem. boeglam maak; iem. poot-uit laat werk; *~ OUT*, laat draf; pronk met; *~ OUT an excuse*, met 'n verskoning voor die dag kom.
troth, trou, waarheid; *BY my ~*, regtig, waarlik, op my woord; *IN ~*, op my woord; *PLIGHT one's ~*, jou woord verpand; troubelofte doen.
trott'er, (hard)drawwer; reisiger; poot (dier).
trott'ing, (n) draf; (a) drawwend; *~-horse*, drawwer; *~-match*, drafwedstryd, harddrawwery.
trottoir', sypaadjie.
troub'adour, troebadoer, minnesanger.
trou'ble, (n) moeite; onrus; sorg, kwelling; las, sonde, beslommernis, ongerief, torment; storing; verknorsing; geneuk; penarie, moeilikheid; struweling; twis; kwaal (siekte); onenigheid, geskil; opontboud, teëspoed; storing; *no ~ at ALL*, geen moeite nie; nie te danke nie; *ASK for ~*, moeilikheid soek; *BE in ~*, in die moeilikheid (knyp) sit; *there is ~ BETWEEN them*, hulle het moeilikheid met mekaar; *CAUSE ~*, moeilikheid veroorsaak; moles maak; *GET into ~*, in ongeleentheid raak; vasbrand; *get a GIRL into ~*, 'n meisie in die ander tyd laat kom; *GIVE ~*, las veroorsaak; *GO to all this ~*, al hierdie moeite doen; *meet ~ s HALFWAY*, moeilikhede vooruitloop; die bobbejaan agter die bult gaan haal; *HAVE ~ with*, las hê van; *LOOK for ~*, moeilikheid soek; *MAKE ~*, twis stook; *his OLD ~*, sy ou kwaal; *get someone OUT of ~*, iem. uit 'n moeilikheid help; *PUT someone to a lot of ~*, iem. baie las veroorsaak; *~ s never come SINGLY*, 'n ongeluk kom nooit alleen nie; *TAKE the ~*, die moeite doen; jou die moeite getroos; *THAT is the ~*, die moeilikheid sit daarin; *never ~ s TILL ~ s you*, moenie die bobbejaan agter die bult gaan haal nie; moenie moeilikhede tegemoetloop nie; *WHAT is the ~?* waar skort dit? wat is die skorting? (v) moeite veroorsaak; kwel; lastig val, pla; foeter, beslommer, neul, tormenteer; beroer; *~ oneself ABOUT*, jou kwel oor; *I didn't ~ to ANSWER*, ek het nie moeite gedoen om te antwoord nie; *may I ~ you for a CUP of coffee?* mag ek asb. 'n koppie koffie kry? *DON'T let it ~ you*, bekommer jou nie daaroor nie; *I did not ~ to GO*, ek het dit nie die moeite werd geag om te gaan nie; *~ ONESELF to*, moeite doen om; *the PAINS in my side ~ me a great deal*, die pyne in my sy pla my baie; *I am SORRY to ~ you about this*, dit spyt my om jou (u) hieroor lastig te val.
trou'bled, gestoor, verontrus; gekwel; onrustig; veelbewoë; *BE ~ with*, las hê van; gepla(ag) wees met; *FISH in ~ waters*, in troebel water visvang; *a ~ REIGN*, 'n veelbewoë regering; *~ SLEEP*, onrustige slaap; *a ~ WORLD*, 'n wêreld vol beroeringe.
trou'ble: *~-free*, moeitevry; *~-maker*, rusiemaker, oproerer, opstoker, twissoeker; *~-making*, opstokery, twissoekery, onrussoekery; *~ r*, woelwater, rusverstoorder; *~-seeker*, sondesoeker; *~-shooter*, foutspeurder, opspoorder, regmaker; *~-shooting*, foutspeurdery.
trou'blesome, lastig, neulerig, vervelig; *a ~ person*, 'n laspos, 'n lolpot; *~ ness*, lastigheid, neulerigheid.
trou'blous, onrustig, lastig, moeilik; *~ times*, tye van beroering; veelbewoë tyd.
trough, trog, bak; seesog; dal; slenk (geol.); *~ of the sea*, golfdal; *~ compass*, trogkompas; *~ conveyer*, vervoertrog; *~ gutter*, bakgeut.
trounce, afransel, uitlooi, 'n groot pak gee, kafloop.
trounc'ing, afranseling, loesing.
troupe, troep, geselskap; *~ r*, toneelspeler, toneelspeelster.
trous'er: *~-button*, broeksknoop; *~ clip*, broekknyper; *~ ed*, met 'n broek aan; *~ ing*, broekstof, broekgoed; *~-leg*, broekspyp; *~-pocket*, broeksak; *~-press*, broekpers.
trous'ers, broek; *a PAIR of ~*, 'n broek; *WIDE ~*, sambalbroek.
trouss'eau, (-s, -x), (bruids)uitset, trousseau, (bruids)uitrusting.

trout, (n) forel; (v) forelle vang; ~-**coloured**, skimmel, appelblou (perd); ~-**farm**, forelplaas; ~-**fishing**, forelvangs; ~**let**, forelletjie; ~-**stream**, forelloop, forelwaterstroom; ~-**tackle**, visgereedksap; ~**y**, vol forel.
trouvère, minnesanger, troebadoer.
trove, vonds; *kyk* **treasure**, (n).
trov'er, hofsaak weens wederregtelike toe-eiening, terugvorderingsproses.
trow, glo, meen.
trow'el, (n) troffel; *lay it on with a* ~, dit dik opsmeer; (v) (**-led**), pleister; ~ **board**, pleisterplank; ~**ling**, troffelwerk.
Troy, Troje.
troy' weight, troygewig, juweliersgewig, trooisgewig.
tru'ancy, stokkiesdraaiery, skoolversuim; werkversuim.
tru'ant, (n) stokkiesdraaier, skoolversuimer; werkversuimer; *play* ~, stokkiesdraai; (v) stokkiesdraai; (a) pligversakend, stokkiesdraaierig, lui; dwalend; ~-**school**, tugskool.
truce, wapenstilstand, bestand; verposing; *FLAG of* ~, wit vlag; ~ *of GOD*, Godsvrede.
tru'cial, verdrags=.
truck[1], (n) ruilhandel; smousware, negosiegoed; bog, kaf; *have no* ~ *with another*, niks met iem. te doen hê nie; niks met mekaar uit te waai hê nie; (v) ruilhandel drywe; handel, smous, verkwansel; ~ *one's soul for gold*, jou siel vir geld verkoop.
truck[2], (n) stootwaentjie, rolwa; transportwa; onderstel (voertuig); vragmotor, lorrie; wa, goederewa, trok; *light* ~, bakkie; (v) in goederewaens wegstuur; in 'n trok laai; ~ **age**, trokkoste; trokvoorraad; ~-**buster**, troksmid; ~-**driver**, lorrie-, vragwabestuurder.
truck'le, (n) ratjie, wieletjie; (v) kruip, jou slaafs onderwerp; ~ *to*, kruip voor; witvoetjie soek by; ~-**bed**, rolbed; ~**r**, kruiper, lekker.
truck'ling, (n) kruipery; (a) slaafs, kruiperig.
truck: ~ **shop**, dwangwinkel; ~ **system**, dwangkoopstelsel.
truc'ulence, **truc'ulency**, woestheid, wreedheid, barbaarsheid; veglus.
truc'ulent, woes, wreed, barbaars; kwaai.
trudge, (n) sukkelgang, sukkeldraf; sukkelaar; (v) aansukkel, strompel.
trudg'en (stroke), loopslag (swem).
true, (n): *IN* ~, waterpas; haaks; *OUT of* ~, nie suiwer reg nie; nie haaks nie; (v) suiwer, haaks of reg maak; in die regte posisie bring; stel, laat spoor (wiele); afwerk; suiwer laat loop; waterpas maak; (a) waar, waaragtig; werklik; gelykluidend; eg; opreg; getrou; trou; juis, suiwer, reg, in die haak; bestendig; *her words have COME* ~, haar woorde is bewaarheid; *as* ~ *as FAITH*, so waar as padda manel dra; so waar as vet; ~ *to one's FRIENDS*, getrou aan jou vriende; *as* ~ *as GOSPEL*, so waar as 'n boek; *a* ~ *JUDGMENT*, 'n suiwer oordeel; ~ *to LIFE*, getrou na die lewe; lewensgetrou; ~ *to NATURE*, natuurgetrou; ~ *OF most people*, waar v.d. meeste mense; *if the REPORT is* ~, as die gerug waarheid bevat; *as* ~ *as STEEL*, so eerlik soos goud; *a* ~ *STORY*, 'n waar (ware) verhaal; *that is only TOO* ~, dit is maar alte waar; ~ *to TYPE*, raseg; tipies; ~ *VALUE*, egte waarde; *her VOICE is very* ~, haar stem is suiwer; *many a* ~ *WORD is spoken in jest*, agter gekskeerdery skuil dikwels die waarheid; met gekskeerdery word dikwels die waarheid bedoel; (adv) waar; eg; suiwer; regtig; *BREED* ~, suiwer teel; *COME* ~, bewaarheid word; *as* ~ *as GOD*, so waar as ek leef; *HOLD* ~, geld vir; *SING* ~, suiwer sing; ~-**bearing**, geografiese (ware) peiling; ~ **believer**, streng regsinnige, egte gelowige; ~-**blue**, (n) beginselvaste persoon, opregte man; man uit een stuk; ~-**born**, eg, volbloed; ~-**breed**, raseg; ~ **copy**, noukeurige (ware) afskrif; ~ **course**, ware koers; ~-**hearted**, trouhartig; ~-**love**, soetlief, geliefde; ~ **millet**, voëlsaad, trosgras; ~ **ness**, waarheid; getrouheid; egtheid; ~ **north**, geografiese noorde; (ware) pool; ~ **penny**, eerlike kêrel; ~ **pole**, geografiese (ware) pool; ~ **time**, sontyd.

truf'fle, knolswam, truffel.
tru'ing, (die) regmaak, laat pas, pasmaak; ~ **tool**, pastoestel.
tru'ism, onmiskenbare waarheid; banaliteit, gemeenplaas, waarheid soos 'n koei.
truis'tic, vanselfsprekend.
tru'ly, regtig, opreg, getrou; waarlik; feitlik, sowaar, rêrig, reg-reg, inderdaad, voorwaar, wraggies, wraggieswaar, wragtie, waaragtig, wrintig; *BE* ~ *thankful*, werklik dankbaar wees; *it has* ~ *been SAID*, dit is tereg gesê; *WELL and* ~ *laid*, goed en behoorlik gelê; *YOURS* ~, hoogagtend (steeds) die uwe.
trump[1], (n) basuin, trompet; *the* ~ *of DOOM, the LAST* ~, die basuin v.d. laaste oordeel; (v) op 'n trompet (basuin) blaas.
trump[2], (n) troefkaart; staatmaker; *A* ~, 'n agtermekaar kêrel; 'n staatmaker; *BE a* ~, trou bystaan; *DRAW* ~*s*, die troewe uitspeel; *FORCE someone to play* ~*s*, iem. dwing om sy troefkaarte te speel; iem. tot die uiterste dryf; *HOLD all the* ~*s*, al die troefkaarte in die hand hê; *PUT someone to his* ~*s*, iem. tot die uiterste dryf; iem. raad-op maak; *TURN up* ~*s*, goed uitval; meeval; alle verwagtinge oortref; (v) troef; öortroef; ~ *up a story*, iets uit jou duim suig; iets versin; iets uit die lug gryp; ~ **card**, troefkaart.
trumped'-up, vals, versonne, deurgestoke; *a* ~ *AFFAIR*, 'n deurgestoke kaart; *a* ~ *CHARGE*, 'n versonne (valse) aanklag.
trump'ery, (n) (..**ries**), ydelheid, ydele praal, skyn; bog, kaf; (a) ydel, nietig; skoonskynend; prullerig, waardeloos.
trump'et, (n) trompet; loftuiter; spreekhoring; trompetgeskal; *BLOW one's own* ~, jou eie basuin blaas; jou eie lof verkondig; die loftrompet blaas; *he BLOWS his own* ~, jakkals prys sy eie stert; Boel prys sy eie stert; elke dassie prys sy kwassie; *the LAST* ~, die basuin v.d. laaste oordeel; (v) trompet, uitbasuin; trompetter; ~ *forth someone's praise*, die loftrompet blaas oor iem.; ~ **blast**, trompetstoot; basuingeskal; ~-**call**, trompetsinjaal; trompetgeskal; ~ **er**, trompetblaser; trompettervoël; *be one's own* ~*er*, jou eie basuin blaas; ~ **er hornbill**, boskraai; ~-**fish**, trompetvis; ~-**flower**, trompetterblom; ~-**major**, trompetmajoor; ~**ry**, trompetgeskal; ~-**shaped**, trompetvormig; ~-**shell**, trompetskulp.
trump' suit, troefkleur.
trunc'al, stam=, romp=.
trunc'ate, (v) afknot, afsny, afstomp, top.
trunc'ate, **trunca'ted**, (a) afgeknot, afgesny, getop; ~ *d cone*, afgeknotte keël.
trunca'tion, afkapping, afknotting; verminking.
trun'cheon, (n) knots, gummistok, knuppel, mokerstok, wapenstok, kierie; baton; kommandostaf; (v) slaan, moker.
trun'dle, (n) rolletjie, wieletjie; rolwa; rolbed; (v) rol; ~-**bed**, rolbed; ~-**head**, lanternrat; ~**r**, stadige bouler.
trunk, (boom)stam, stomp; romp; stronk, trommel, koffer, kis; slurp (olifant); skag, koker; hooflyn (telefoon); (pl) kort onderbroek; swembroekie, baaibroekie; ~-**call**, hooflynoproep; ~ **drawers**, kort onderbroek; ~-**fish**, sonvis, plaatvis; ~-**line**, hooflyn; ~ **main**, hoofpyp; ~-**maker**, koffermaker; ~-**road**, hoofverkeerspad, hoofweg; ~-**root**, penwortel; ~-**route**, hoofroete, hooflyn; ~ **sleeve**, pofmou; ~-**target**, rompskyf.
trun'nel, houtpen.
trunn'ion, spil; astap; dratap; jukbout; ~ **bridge**, vakwerkbrug; ~ **frame**, draagtapraam; ~-**nut**, penmoer; draagtapmoer; ~-**pin**, draagtapper; ~ **rod**, ankerstang; ~ **roof**, vakwerkdak.
truss, (n) (-es), tros; bondel; hangwerk; breukband; dakstoel; stut(balk) draagsteen; kap (van dak); (v) bind, opbind, vasmaak; veranker; stut; *like a* ~ *ed FOWL*, vasgebind; ~ *UP*, opbind; ~ **beam**, vakwerkbalk; ~-**bolt**, ankerbout; ~-**bridge**, vakwerkbrug; ~ *ed girder*, vakwerklêer; ~ *ed roof*, vakwerkdak.
truss'ing, vakwerk (bouk.); versterking; ~ **needle**, opbindnaald, vleisnaald.

truss: ~-**post**, hangstyl; ~ **rod**, ankerstang.
trust, (n) vertroue; geloof; bewaring; krediet; pand; kartel, trust; *ACCEPT on* ~, op goeie geloof aan= neem; *BREACH of* ~, troubreuk; *HOLD in* ~, in bewaring hê; *MUTUAL* ~, effektetrust; *supply with goods ON* ~, krediet gee; *a POSITION of* ~, 'n vertrouenspos; *PUT* ~ *in*, vertroue stel in; *PUT not your* ~ *in princes*, vertrou nie op prinse nie; *TAKE on* ~, op goeie vertroue aanneem; (v) ver= trou, glo; toevertrou; krediet gee; ~ *to someone FOR*, op iem. staatmaak vir; ~ *IN*, vertrou op; ~ *IN God*, vertrou op God; *let's* ~ *to LUCK*, laat ons hoop dat alles sal regkom; ~ *to one's LUCK*, hoop dat alles sal regkom; ~ *one's MEMORY*, op jou geheue staatmaak; *he did NOT* ~ *himself to*, hy kon nie op homself vertrou nie om; *you can* ~ *him to do SOMETHING foolish*, jy kan seker wees dat hy 'n dwaasheid sal begaan; *I* ~ *THAT* . . ., ek hoop dat . . .; ~ *TO*, toevertrou aan; ~ *someone WITH something*, aan iem. iets toevertrou; ~ **ac= count**, trustrekening; ~ **bank**, trustbank; ~ **com= pany**, trustmaatskappy; ~ **deed**, trustakte; ~**ed**, vertroud.
trustee', trustee; beheerder; kurator; *BOARD of* ~ *s*, kuratorium; ~ *of an ESTATE*, kurator van 'n boe= del; ~ **ship**, kuratorskap; voogdyskap.
trust: ~ **er**, gelower, gelower, vertrouer; ~ **estate**, trust= boedel; ~**ful**, vertrouend, vol vertroue; ~ **fulness**, goeie vertroue; ~ **fund**, trustfonds; ~ **ifica'tion**, trustvorming; ~**ify**, (..**fied**), tot 'n trust vorm; ~**iness**, eerlikheid, trou, vertroubaarheid; ~ **less**, sonder vertroue; onbetroubaar, onvertroubaar; ~ **money**, trustgeld, toevertroude geld; ~ **territory**, voogdygebied; ~**worthiness**, betroubaarheid, ver= troubaarheid; ~**worthy**, vertroubaar, betroubaar, vertroud, trou, vertrouenswaardig; ~**y**, (n) (..**ties**), bevoorregte gevangene; handlanger, ver= trouensman; (a) eerlik, vertroubaar, getrou, be= proef.
truth, waarheid; opregtheid, trou; eerlikheid, egtheid; juistheid; *CLOUD the* ~, die waarheid bewimpel; *the COLD* ~, die harde waarheid; ~ *seeks no CORNERS*, die waarheid wil nie verberg word nie; ~ *is stranger than FICTION*, die waarheid klink soms na 'n fabel; die waarheid klink dikwels na 'n onwaarheid; ~ *finds FOES where it makes none*, die waarheid wil nie gesê wees nie; *FOLLOW not* ~ *too near the heels, lest it dash out thy teeth; he who FOLLOWS* ~ *too closely will have dirt kicked in his face*, moenie te naarstig strewe om agter die waarheid te kom nie; *GET at the* ~, agter die waar= heid kom; *tell someone a few HOME* ~ *s*, iem. goed die waarheid vertel; *that was a HOME* ~, dit was 'n raakskoot; *the* ~ *HURTS*, die waarheid maak seer; *IN* ~, waarlik, inderdaad; ~ *IS the* ~, hot is hot en haar is haar; *the greater the* ~, *the greater the LIBEL*, hoe nader aan die waarheid, hoe erger die laster; *LOVE of* ~, waarheidsliefde; *the* ~ *will OUT*, al is 'n leuen nog so snel, die waarheid agter= haal hom wel; *in PLAIN* ~, om die volle waarheid te sê, ~ *is* ~ *to the end of RECKONING*, die waar= heid bly die waarheid; *there is SOME* ~ *in it*, daar is nogal iets waars daarin; *be SPARING of the* ~, die waarheid spaar; ~ *to TELL*, om die waarheid te sê; *TELL (speak) the* ~ *and shame the devil*, sê die waarheid bo alles; *to TELL you the* ~, om die waarheid te sê; *the UNVARNISHED* ~, die naak= te waarheid; *tell someone the UNVARNISHED* ~, iem. onbewimpeld die waarheid vertel; *VIOLATE the* ~, die waarheid gewold aandoen; ~ *needs not many WORDS*, die waarheid het min woorde no= dig; ~ **drug**, waarheidsmiddel; ~**ful**, waarheidlie= wend; betroubaar; waar; ~ **fulness**, betroubaar= heid; waarheid; *depend on his* ~ *fulness*, op sy eer= likheid staatmaak; ~ **legion**, waarheidsleër; ~ **legionnaire**, waarheidsridder; ~**less**, vals, ontrou; ~**loving**, waarheidliewend; ~ **serum**, waarheidse= rum.
try, (n) (**tries**), poging, probeerslag; proef; drie (rug= by); druk(doel); *CONVERT a* ~, 'n drie vervyf; *HAVE a* ~ *at something*, iets 'n slag probeer; *SCORE a* ~, 'n drie druk; (v) (**tried**), probeer, trag,

poog; beproef, op die proef stel; terg; besoek; ding aanpak; ondersoek; verhoor; jou bes doen, jou in= span, jou vermoei; uitbraai, uitkook (vet); suiwer (metaal); ~ *ALL things*, beproef alle dinge; *BE tried for*, onder verhoor kom weens; ~ *one's BEST*, jou bes doen; ~ *out a CAR*, 'n motor toets; ~ *to COME*, probeer kom; ~ *CONCLUSIONS with*, jou kragte meet met; ~ *a DOOR*, kyk of die deur goed gesluit is; ~ *on a DRESS*, 'n rok aanpas; ~ *FOR*, streef na; ~ *FOR a post*, probeer om 'n betrekking te kry; skiet na 'n pos; ~ *one's HAND at*, probeer; ~ *HARD to*, jou uiterste bes doen om; ~ *JOINTLY*, gesamentlik verhoor; ~ *one's LUCK*, jou geluk beproef; *don't* ~ *it ON (with) me*, moenie streke by my kom uithaal nie; probeer dit maar nie met my nie; ~ *OUT*, suiwer; uitkook, uitbraai; toets; ~ *one's PATIENCE*, jou geduld op die proef stel; ~ *SEPARATELY*, afsonderlik ver= hoor; ~ *before you TRUST*, vertrou net wat op die proef gestel is; *it's no USE to* ~ *it on me*, moenie probeer om jou streke op my uit te haal nie; ~ *for WHITE*, probeer om vir blank deur te gaan; pro= beer deurgaan vir wit; ~-**cock**, proefkraan; ~- **house**, traankokery.
try'ing, (n) probeerslag; probeer; *there is NOTHING like* ~, probeer is die beste geweer; *it's no USE* ~ *it on*, moenie probeer om jou streke uit te haal nie; (a) vermoeiend, lastig; inspannend, smartlik, pynlik; haglik; ~-**on room**, paskamer; ~-**plane**, roffel= skaaf, reiskaaf; ~-**cock**, proefkraan; ~-**house**, traankokery.
try: ~-**line**, doellyn; ~-**on**, probeerslag; aanpassing; verskalking, lis; ~-**out**, proef, toets; proefslag; proefrit; probeerslag; ~-**plane**, reiskaaf; ~-**sail**, gaffelseil; ~-**square**, winkelhaak; ~-**works**, traan= kokery.
tryst, (n) afspraak; samekoms; bymekaarkomplek; (v) afspreek, 'n afspraak maak met; ~ **ing-place**, bymekaarkomplek; versamelplek.
tsar, tsaar; ~**dom**, tsaredom; ~ **'evitch**, tsarewitsj; ~ **ev'na**, tsarewna; ~ **in'a**, tsarina.
Tsar'ism, Tsarisme.
Tsar'ist, (n) Tsaris; (a) Tsaristies.
T'-section, T-profiel.
tses'sebe, basterhartbees, tsessebe.
tset'se(-fly), tsetsevlieg.
tsot'si, (-**s**), tsotsi.
T'-square, tekenhaak.
tub, (n) bad; balie, kuip; sponsbad; koekepan, myn= trok; oefenboot; *have (take) a COLD* ~, 'n koue bad neem; *every* ~ *must STAND on its own bottom*, elkeen moet sy eie potjie krap; laat elkeen op sy eie pote staan; *THROW a* ~ *to the whale*, deur aflei= ding gevaar afwend; (v) (-**bed**), bad; in 'n kuip (vat) plant; roei (in 'n oefenboot).
tub'a, tuba; ~**l**, basuin=; buis=, pyp=.
tubb'y, rond soos 'n vaatjie, swaarlywig; dof (musie= kinstrument); ~ **person**, stompie, proppie.
tube, (n) pyp; buis; band, binneband (motor), laai= buis; moltrein, ondergrondse spoorweg, (v) van 'n pyp (buis) voorsien; in 'n pyp sluit; met 'n moltrein ry; ~-**blower**, roetblaser; ~-**brush**, pypborsel; ~- **cleaner**, pypborsel, pypskraper; ~ **colours**, buis= verf; ~-**cutter**, pypsnyer; ~ **flap**, vellingvoering; ~ **hole**, pypgat.
tube'less, buisloos; ~ **tyre**, lugbuiteband, pomp= buiteband.
tube'-mill, silindermeul; ~ **pan**, koekvorm.
tub'er, geswel; bol, knol; pypsetter.
tube rail'way, ondergrondse (elektriese) spoorweg, moltrein.
tub'ercle, knoppie, puisie; knolletjie, knobbeltjie.
tuberc'ular, teringagtig, tuberkuleus; knobbelagtig, bolagtig; knoetserig, knoppiesrig; ~ **consumption**, longtering.
tuber'culize, tuberkuleus (teringagtig) maak (word).
tuber'culated, knobbelrig; vratterig.
tuberc'ulin, tuberkulien.
tuberculos'is, tuberkulose, tering; *pulmonary* ~, longtering.
tuberculot'ic, (n) tuberkuloselyer, teringlyer; (a) tu= berkuleus, teringagtig.

tuberculous

tuberc'ulous, teringagtig.
tu'ber: ~ **if'erous,** boldraend, knoldraend; ~ **ose,** (n) soetemaling; (a) knolvormig; knoldraend; ~ **os'ity,** uitwas; knop, knobbel; knopperigheid; ~ **ous,** knobbel(r)ig, bolvormig, bolagtig, knolagtig.
tube: ~ **-shaft,** holas; ~ **-shaped,** buisagtig; ~ **-valve,** ventiel, bandklep; ~ **vice,** pypskroef.
tub'ing, pyplengte; stuk buis, buiswerk; (gomlastiek)slang; ~ **-machine,** buismasjien.
tub: ~ **-shaped,** balievormig; ~ **-thumper,** seepkisprediker; seepkispolitikus; heftige redenaar; ~ **-thumping,** (n) seepkispolitiek; seepkisrede; skreeuery, lawaai; (a) lawaaierig; seepkis-.
tub'ular, buisvormig; pyp-, pypvormig; ~ **boiler,** vlampypketel; ~ **bone,** pypbeen; ~ **bridge,** kokerbrug, pypbrug; ~ **drill,** holboor; ~ **flower,** tuitblom; ~ **frame,** pypraam; ~ **gate,** pyphek; ~ **girder,** kokerlêer; ~ **lock,** kokerslot; ~ **pole,** pyppaal; ~ **post,** lugdrukpos; ~ **power,** pypkruit; ~ **railway,** ondergrondse spoorweg, molspoorweg; ~ **scaffolding,** pypsteier; ~ **sock,** windkous; ~ **spanner,** pypsleutel, kokersleutel; ~ **steel,** staalpyp, buisstaal; ~ **strut,** pypstut.
tub'ulate, (v) tot buise vorm; van 'n buis voorsien; (a) buisvormig; met 'n pyp (buis).
tub'ule, pypie, buisie.
tub'ulose, tub'ulous, buisvormig.
tub' wheel, bakkiespomp.
tuck¹, (n) trompetgeskal.
tuck², (n) opnaaisel, oprygsel; plooi, vou; eetgoed, snoepgoed; (v) inslaan, plooi; vou, omslaan; opnaaisels maak; intrek; lekker warm toemaak; oprol; inrol; ~ *AWAY,* wegsteek; ~ *IN,* invou; toemaak (met komberse); toestop, inbaker, toedek; inneem; lekker wegslaan (kos); ~ *up SLEEVES,* die moue oprol; ~ *UNDER,* onder insteek; ~ *UP,* invou; opstroop (moue); ~ *someone UP,* iem. met 'n kombers toemaak; ~ **-away chair,** inskuifstoel; ~ **-box,** snoepdoos; ~ **er,** kantkraag; kos; *best bib and* ~ *er,* beste klere, kisklere.
tuck'et, trompetgeskal.
tuck: ~ **-in,** smulparty, stewige maaltyd; insteeksel; ~ **-marker,** opnaaiselvoetjie; ~ **-net,** klein netjie; ~ **-out** = **tuck-in;** ~ **-shop,** snoepwinkel.
Tud'or, (n) Tudor; (a) Tudor=.
Tues'day, Dinsdag.
tuf'a, tufkryt.
tufa'ceous, tufkrytagtig.
tuff, tufsteen; ~ **a'ceous,** tuf=, tufagtig; ~ **cone,** tufkeël.
tuft, (n) bos; kuif; kwas, pluim; tros, graspol; volk; (v) met pluime versier; klossies aansit; in klompies groei; 'n matras deurnaai; ~ *of grass,* (gras)pol.
tuft'ed, gepluim, gekuif; gekwas; ~ *CARPET,* pluistapyt; ~ *GRASS,* polgras; ~ *RUG,* pluistapyt.
tuft: ~ **rug,** pluismat; ~ **y,** gekuif, gepluim; klossieagtig, met klossies.
tug, (n) trek, ruk; sleepboot, sleper; inspanning; lus, lissie, oog; *I felt a great* ~ *at PARTING,* ek het bitter swaar afskeid geneem; ~ *of WAR,* toutrek; (v) (-ged), trek, ruk; sleep; ~ *at,* ruk aan, pluk aan; ~ **boat,** sleepboot; ~ **ger,** trekker; rukker; ~ **man,** sleper.
Tui'leries, die Tuilerieë.
tui'tion, onderwys, onderrig; skoolgeld; ~ **al,** ~ **ary,** onderwys=, leer=; ~ **-fee,** skoolgeld, opleidingsgeld, studiegeld.
Tukkie, Tukkie, student v.d. Universiteit van Pretoria.
tul'a(-work), niëllowerk.
tul'ip, tulp; *wild* ~ *s,* bobbejaantjies; ~ **-bed,** tulpbedding, tulpperk; ~ **-bulb,** tulpbol; ~ **-grower,** tulpweker; ~ **-growing,** tulpkwekery; ~ **oman'ia,** tulpmanie; ~ **-trade,** tulphandel; ~ **-tree,** tulpboom; ~ **-wood,** tulphout.
tulle, tulle, sluiersy, netsy.
tum'ble, (n) val, tuimeling, duikeling; bolmakiesie; warboel; *have a NASTY* ~, lelik val; *TAKE a* ~, bolmakiesie slaan; buitel, tuimel; rol; woel; kunste maak; rondgooi; rondsmyt; duiwel; val-val loop, struikel, gooi, smyt; foeter; verfrommel, omkrap; ~ *ABOUT,*

tungstite

rondwoel; rol; tuimel; ~ *ACROSS someone,* iem. op die lyf loop; ~ *ALONG,* aantuimel; ~ *DOWN,* instort; afrol; omval, omtuimel, ombuitel; ~ *about one's EARS,* inmekaarval, ineenstort; ~ *IN,* intuimel; ~ *INTO,* aanskiet (klere); intuimel, inval; inkruip (bed); ~ *OFF,* aftuimel, afval, afduiwel; ~ *OUT,* uitval; uitgooi; ~ *OVER,* omrol; ~ *OVER a mat,* oor 'n mat struikel; ~ *to PIECES,* in stukke val; ~ *TO something,* agterkom hoe sake inmekaar sit, iets snap; ~ *up the STAIRS,* val-val die trap opgaan; ~ **-bug,** miskruier, rolkewer; ~ **down,** bouvallig, vervalle; ~ **-drier,** tuimeldroër.
tum'bler, (drink)glas; duikelaar; tuimelaar(duif); akrobaat; ~ **-lock,** tuimelaarslot; ~ **-switch,** tuimelskakelaar.
tum'ble-weed, tolbossie.
tum'bly, bouvallig; hobbelagtig, ongelyk.
tum'brel, tum'bril, miskar; ammunisiewa; stortkar, skotskar.
tumefac'tion, opswelling; geswel; galvorming (bot).
tum'efy, (..fied), laat swel; opswel.
tumes'cence, swelling; geswel.
tumes'cent, opswellend; geswel.
tum'id, bombasties, geswolle, hoogdrawend; opgeswel; ~ **'ity,** ~ **ness,** opswelling; geswollenheid, hoogdrawendheid.
tumm'y, (tummies), magie, maag, pens(ie); boepens(ie); ~ **-ache,** maagpyn.
tum'our, geswel, gewas; tumor; *BENIGN* ~, goedaardige gewas; *MALIGNANT* ~, kwaadaardige gewas.
tump¹, (n) maag, pens(ie), magie.
tump², (n) getokkel, getrommel.
tump³, (n) karretjie.
tump⁴, (n) bultjie; hoop (miershoop, molshoop); (v) operd, aanerd; ~ **ing-plough,** operdploeg.
tump'-line, draagriem.
tum'tum, piesanggereg.
tum'ular, grafheuwelagtig.
tum'ult, opskudding, rumoer, lawaai, roesemoes, spektakel, oploop, oproer; *in a* ~, in beroering.
tumul'tuous, rumoerig, oproerig, onstuimig, stormagtig; ~ **ness,** oproerigheid, onstuimigheid.
tum'ulus, (..li), grafheuwel.
tun, (n) vat; skag (van skoorsteen); (v) (~ **ned**), in vate gooi.
tun'a, tuna (vis) *(Thunnus thynnus).*
tun'able, stembaar.
tun'dra, toendra, moeraswêreld.
tune, (n) toon; klank; deuntjie; melodie; (sang)wysie, sang; stemming; *BE in* ~, goed ooreenstem; gestem wees; *BE in* ~ *with,* harmonieer met; *CALL the* ~, die toon aangee; *CHANGE one's* ~, 'n ander toon aanslaan; 'n ander deuntjie sing; uit 'n ander vaatjie tap; *DANCE to another's* ~, na iem. se pype dans; *find the* ~ *FAMILIAR,* die deuntjie al goed ken; *GIVE us a* ~, speel (sing) vir ons iets; *IN* ~ *with,* in harmonie met; harmonieer met; *OUT of* ~, ontstem; vals; *he who pays the PIPER calls the* ~, wie die geld het, het die mag; *SING another* ~, 'n ander toon aanslaan; 'n ander deuntjie sing; uit 'n ander vaatjie tap; *SING in* ~, harmonies (gelykluidend) sing; *TO the* ~ *of,* op die wysie van; tot die bedrag van; (v) stem; instem; instel; die toon aangee; klink; sing, aanhef; (laat) saamstem; ~ *IN,* afstem, inskakel, instem; ~ *d to the same PITCH,* eenders gestem; ~ *UP,* stem; instel (motor); ~ **ful,** sangerig, melodieus, welluidend; ~ **fulness,** sangerigheid, welluidendheid; ~ **less,** toonloos, klankloos; stom; onwelluidend; stil; ~ **lessness,** toonloosheid; onwelluidendheid; ~ **r,** stemmer; instemmer; afstemmer (radio); stemvurk; steller.
tung, tung; ~ **-estate,** tungplaas; ~ **-oil,** tungolie; ~ **-oil industry,** tungolienywerheid; ~ **plantation,** tungplantasie.
tung'state, wolframaat, tungstaat.
tung'sten, tungsten, wolfram; ~ **steel,** tungsten-, wolframstaal.
tung'stic: ~ **acid,** wolframsuur; ~ **ochre,** wolframoker.
tung'stite, wolframiet.

tung'-tree, tungboom.
tun'ic, soldatebaadjie; tuniek, tunika; boestroentjie; uniform; vlies, omhulsel, vel.
tun'icate, manteldier.
tun'icle, tuniek; (oog)vlies, vliesie.
tun'ing, (n) (die) stem, stemming, gestem; instemming (radio); (a) stemmend; ~ **call,** instemproep; ~**-cone,** stemhoring; ~**-fork,** stemvurk; ~ **hammer,** stemhamer; ~**-key,** stemsleutel; ~**-peg,** ~ **pin,** stemskroef.
Tunis'ia, Tunisië; ~ **n,** (n) Tunisiër; (a) Tunisies.
tunn'age, *kyk* **tonnage.**
tunn'el, (n) tonnel; deurgrawing; gang; skag; pyp; (v) (-led), tonnel; deurgrawe; uithol; ondergrawe; ~**-borer,** tonnelboorder; ~ **culture,** tonnelteelt; ~ **ling,** tonnelwerk, graafwerk; ~**-net,** fuik, patrysnet; ~**-pit,** ~**-shaft,** tonnelbek, skag; ~**-vault,** tongewelf.
tunn'y, (tunnies), *kyk* **tuna.**
tun'y, welluidend; pakkend (van melodie), mooi.
tup, (n) ram; slaankant (van hamer); (v) **(-ped),** ('n ooi) dek.
tup'pence, twee pennies; *not worth* ~, nie 'n flenter werd nie.
turb'an, (n) tulband; (v) 'n tulband opsit; ~ **ed,** getulband.
turb'id, troebel, modderig; verward, deurmekaar; ~ **'ity,** ~ **ness,** troebelheid, modderigheid.
turb'inate, tolvormig; spiraalvormig; ronddraaiend.
turbina'tion, tolbeweging.
turb'ine, turbine; bont, turbineboot; ~ **dynamo, (-s),** turbodinamo; ~ **jet,** turbinestraal; turbinestraler; ~ **steamer,** turbineboot.
turbin'iform, tolvormig.
turb'it, platkopduif.
turb'o: ~ **alternator,** turbowisselstroomgenerator; ~ **generator,** turbogenerator; ~ **jet,** turbinespuitvliegtuig, turbinestraler, turbinestraalvliegtuig; ~ **prop,** ~ **propellor,** skroefturbinemotor; turbineskroefvliegtuig.
turb'ot, tarbot (vis).
turb'ulence, turb'ulency, woelerigheid, woelsug, woeligheid, woeling; onstuimigheid; oproerigheid, onrustigheid, bandeloosheid.
turb'ulent, woelerig; onstuimig; oproerig, woelsiek, rumoerig; onrustig.
Turc'o, (-s), Trans-Algerynse soldaat; ~ **phobe,** Turkehater; *kyk ook* **Turk.**
turd, miskoek; drek; drol, keutel.
tureen', sopkom.
turf, (n) turf; turfgrond; sooi; kweek, grasveld; renbaan, resiesbaan; *he is on the* ~, hy bestaan v.d. wedrenne; hy is besig met renbaansport; (v) met sooie dek; met kweek beplant; ~**-clad,** turfbedek; ~ **club,** wedrenklub, reisiesklub; ~ **ite,** ~**man,** liefhebber v.d. renbaansport, renbaanliefhebber; ~ **seat,** sooibank; ~ **wicket,** grasbaanblad; ~**y,** vol sooie, turfagtig; sportliewend.
tur'gency, opswelling, verdikking; hoogdrawendheid.
tur'gent, swellend, geswel.
turges'cence = **turgency.**
turges'cent, swellend, geswel; hoogdrawend.
tur'gid, opgeswel; geswolle, opgeblase, trots; bombasties; ~ **'ity,** ~ **ness,** opswelling; bombas, hoogdrawendheid; geswollenheid, opgeblasenheid.
Tur'in, Turyn
Turk, Turk; woesteling; hardekop; *TURN* ~, van aard verander, ontaard; *a YOUNG* ~, 'n jong Turk; ~ **estan,** Turkestan.
Turk'ey¹, (n) Turkye; (a) Turks.
turk'ey², (-s), kalkoen; ~ **buzzard,** bromvoël; ~ **cock,** kalkoenmannetjie; *as red as a* ~ *cock,* so rooi soos 'n kalkoen; ~ **corn,** mielies; ~ **hen,** kalkoenwyfie; **T** ~ **leather,** Turkse leer; **T** ~ **oak,** moseik; ~**-poult,** jong kalkoen; **T** ~ **red,** rooidoek, turksrooi; ~**'s egg,** kalkoeneier; ~ **trot,** kalkoenpas; modedans; **T** ~ **twill,** rooidoek; ~ **wattles,** kalkoenbelle.
Turk'ish, (n, a), Turks; ~ **bath,** Turkse bad; ~ **coffee,** Turkse koffie; ~ **delight,** Turkse lekkers; ~ **millet,** graansorghum; ~ **tobacco,** Turkse tabak; ~ **towel,** growwe handdoek.

Turk: ~ **'(o)man,** (n) Turkomaan; Turkmeens (taal); (a) Turkmeens; ~ **'ophil(e),** Turksgesinde; ~ **'ophobe,** anti-Turksgesinde; Turkehater.
tur'lington, monnikebalsem.
turm'alin(e), *kyk* **tourmalin(e).**
turm'eric, borrie; koerkoemawortel; ~ **paper,** koerkoemapapier.
turm'oil, (n) onrus, gewoel, verwarring, gejaagdheid, ontsteltenis; *throw into a* ~, in beroering bring; (v) verontrus, ontstel, kwel.
turn, (n) draai, wending, swenk(ing); omkeer; omwenteling (wiel); keerpunt, kentering; kromming, bog; slag (tou); helling (geweer); draaibank; toertjie; wandeling; beurt, kans (sport); streek; diens; aanleg, aard; dubbelslag (mus.); nommer (op program); ~ *and* ~ *ABOUT,* beurtelings, om die beurt, beurt-beurt; *AT every* ~, gereeld; *he led AT the* ~, hy was voor by die draai (na nege putjies) (gholf); *do someone a BAD* ~, iem. 'n ondiens bewys; *do nobody a BAD* ~, niemand 'n strooitjie in die pad lê nie; niemand enige kwaad aandoen nie; *BE on the* ~, op die keerpunt staan; *a* ~ *for the BETTER,* 'n gunstige wending; *BY* ~ *s,* om die beurt, beurtelings; *everything depends on the* ~ *of a CARD,* alles hang af van hoe die kaarte val; *DO someone a good* ~, iem. 'n diens bewys; *DONE to a* ~, net mooi gaar; ~ *of DUTY,* diensyd; *at EVERY* ~, oral; *a* ~ *of FORTUNE'S wheel,* 'n wending van die noodlot; *take a* ~ *in the GARDEN,* 'n draaitjie in die tuin gaan loop; *it GAVE me quite a* ~, dit het my heelwat geskok; *GIVE someone quite a* ~, iem. laat skrik; *GIVE a new* ~ *to,* 'n nuwe wending gee aan; *one GOOD* ~ *deserves another,* die een diens is die ander werd; as twee hande mekaar was, word albei skoon; *HAVE a* ~, 'n beurt kry; *be of a HUMOROUS* ~ *of mind,* humoristies aangelê wees; *do someone an ILL* ~, iem. 'n ondiens bewys; *IN* ~, beurt-beurt, om die beurt; na mekaar; *IN his* ~, op sy beurt; *take a* ~ *to the LEFT,* draai links; *the* ~ *of LIFE,* die lewensverandering; *the MILK is on the* ~, die melk word suur; ~ *of MIND,* geestesrigting; *a practical* ~ *of MIND,* prakties aangelê; *ON the* ~, suur word (melk); aan die keer (gety); *OUT of* ~, uit sy beurt; *a man with a PHILOSOPHICAL* ~ *of mind,* iem. wat wysgerig van aard is; *PLAY out of* ~, uit jou beurt speel; *a* ~ *for POLITICS,* 'n liefhebbery vir die politiek; *SERVE its* ~, aan sy doel beantwoord; *a SHARP* ~, 'n Kaapse draai; *don't SPEAK out of your* ~, moenie uit jou beurt praat nie; *a good* ~ *of SPEED,* 'n goeie snelheid; *TAKE a* ~, draai; 'n beurt waarneem; *TAKE* ~ *s,* mekaar aflos, ~ *of the TIDE,* kentering v.d. gety; *a* ~ *of over R1000 a WEEK,* 'n omset van R1000 per week; *a* ~ *of WIT,* 'n geestige set; *at the* ~ *of the YEAR,* by die wisseling v.d. jaar; (v) draai; laat draai; omkeer, verander; wend; wegjaag; torring; omslaan (blad); omtrek; maak; keer; omspit, omwoel (grond); omploeg; duiselig word; suur word, bederf (melk); vertaal; verander word; ~ *ABOUT,* omdraai; ~ *to ACCOUNT,* voordeel trek uit; tot voordeel aanwend; ~ *ADRIFT,* aan sy lot oorlaat; ~ *into AFRIKAANS,* in Afrikaans vertaal; ~ *AGAINST,* draai teen; *a finely* ~ *ed ANKLE,* 'n mooi gevormde enkel; ~ *ASIDE,* afwend; ~ *one's ATTENTION to,* jou aandag wy aan; ~ *someone AWAY,* iem. wegstuur (wegjaag); ~ *AWAY,* weggaan; ~ *BACK,* terugdraai; laat omdraai; ~ *one's BACK on someone,* iem. die rug toekeer; ~ *the BALANCE,* die deurslag gee; ~ *a BLIND eye to,* oogluikend toelaat; iets kastig nie sien nie; *my BRAIN* ~ *s,* ek wil gek word; ~ *out CARS,* motors fabriseer; ~ *COLOUR,* bloos; van kleur verander; ~ *a COMPLIMENT,* 'n kompliment maak; ~ *the CORNER,* die hoek omgaan, die ergste moeilikheid oorwin; ~ *DOWN,* omvou (bladsy); oopslaan; afwys (kandidaat); verwerp ('n versoek); *be* ~ *ed DOWN,* afgewys word; die neewoord kry; verwerp word; ~ *a deaf EAR to,* dood wees vir; Oos-Indies doof wees; ~ *the EDGE of something,* iets stomp maak; iets laat omlê; ~ *the FLANK of an army,* 'n leër omtrek; ~ *FROM,* jou afkeer van;

not ~ a *HAIR*, geen spier vertrek nie; ~ *one's HAND to*, jou toelê op, aanpak; *his success has ~ed his HEAD*, sy sukses het sy kop op hol gebring; ~ *on his HEELS*, op die plek omdraai; ~ *a HUNDRED*, honderd jaar oud word; *time to ~ IN*, slaaptyd; ~ *IN*, kooi toe gaan, gaan slaap; invou; inlewer; ~ *INSIDE out*, binnestebuite keer; ~ *INTO*, verander in; indraai (pad); ~ *a KEY*, 'n sleutel omdraai; *this LAD will not ~ out well*, daar sal niks van hierdie seun word nie; ~ *LOOSE*, losmaak, loslaat, die halter afhaal; *the MATTER ~ed out well*, die saak het goed afgeloop; ~ *over in one's MIND*, nadink oor; ~ *up one's NOSE*, die neus optrek (veragtelik); ~ *OFF*, toedraai (kraan); afdraai; afwend; in die pad steek; ~ *ON*, afhang van; oopdraai; aandraai; ~ *ON the tap*, draai die kraan oop; *a friendly dog may ~ ON you if you tease it*, 'n vriendelike hond sal hom omdraai en jou aanval as jy hom terg; ~ *OUT*, opdaag; vervaardig; leegmaak; op straat sit; ~ *the renters OUT at the end of the month*, die huurders aan die einde v.d. maand op straat sit; *the boy ~ed OUT a rogue*, die seun het 'n skurk geword; ~ *OUT well*, goed uitval (uitdraai); ~ *OVER*, omdraai; omslaan; omgooi; oormaak; ~ *OVER a new leaf*, 'n nuwe begin maak; ~ *something OVER in one's mind*, 'n saak herkou; daar goed oor nadink; *OVERWORK has ~ed his brain*, van te veel werk is sy brein aangetas; ~ *over a PAGE*, 'n blad omblaai; ~ *PALE*, bleek word; ~ *an honest PENNY*, 'n eerlike stukkie brood verdien; ~ *out your POCKETS*, keer jou sakke om; ~ *out for PRACTICE*, opdaag vir oefening; ~ *to PROFIT*, wingsgewend maak; ~ *into RIDICULE*, belaglik maak; ~ *out this ROOM*, haal die meubels uit hierdie kamer (vir skoonmaak); ~ *ROUND*, omdraai; van mening verander; ~ *the SCALE*, die deurslag gee; die balans laat oorslaan; ~ *SHORT*, skielik omdraai; ~ *SOLDIER*, soldaat word; ~ *the STOMACH* mislik maak; laat walg; ~ *the TABLES*, die bordjies verhang; ~ *TAIL*, op loop sit; weghol; ~ *the TIDE*, die deurslag gee; ~ *TO*, verander in; aanpak; aanstaltes maak; jou wend tot; *the water ~d TO ice*, die water het verys; *as he ~ed TO me I recognized him*, toe hy hom na my kant omdraai, het ek hom herken; ~ *TO someone for advice*, jou tot iem. wend om raad; ~ *TO page 20*, kyk op bl. 20; ~ *out one's TOES*, die tone na buite draai; ~ *TOPSY-TURVY*, onderstebo draai, omkeer; ~ *TRAITOR*, verraaier word; *it ~ed out to be TRUE*, dit het waar geblyk; ~ *TURTLE*, omslaan, omkantel (boot); ~ *UP*, omdraai (sooi); te voorskyn kom; opslaan, opdraai; omslaan (broekspyp); uitploeg, uitspit; ~ *something UP*, laat vaar; ophou; ~ *it UP!* basta! hou op! ~ *someone UP*, iem. laat opgooi; ~ *UP unexpectedly*, êrens aangewaai kom; onverwags aankom; *the lost document ~ed UP*, die verlore dokument het te voorskyn gekom; ~ *UPON*, aanval; invlieg; *the interpretation of the sentence ~s UPON the precise meaning of one phrase*, die vertolking v.d. sin hang af v.d. presiese betekenis van een sinsnede; ~ *UPSIDE DOWN*, omdraai, omkeer; onderstebo keer; omvergooi; in verwarring bring; ~ *on the WATERWORKS*, begin huil; *not to know which WAY to ~*, nie weet hoe jy jou moet draai nie; kleitrap; *he did not know which WAY to ~*, hy het nie geweet hoe hy hom moet draai nie; die wêreld het toe te nou geword; ~**-about,** omkeer; draai, omkering; omdraaiing; mallemeule; ~**-back,** omslag; ~**-back collar,** omslaankraag; lêkraag; ~**bench,** draaibank; ~**-bridge,** draaibrug; ~**-buckle,** skroefslot; spanmoer; draadspanner; ~**-button,** werwel; ~**-cap,** (draaier), verkleurmannetjie, weerhaan, oorloper, tweegatjakkals; ~**-cock,** afsluitkraan; ~ **down,** omslaan; ~**-down collar,** omslaanboordjie; omslaankraag; ~ **er,** (kuns)draaier; tuimelaar(duif); ~**er's chisel,** houtdraaibeitel; ~**ery,** kunsdraaiery, draaiwerk.

turn'ing, (n) draai, draaiing; kunsdraai; bog; kromming, kronkeling; kentering; plooi, vou; afdraaisel (metaal); (pl) afdraaisels, boorsels, metaalkrulle (staalfabriek); skaafsel(s) houtskaafsel(s); (a) draaiend, draaierig, draai=; ~ **basin,** draaikom, draaidok; ~**-bay,** draaiplek; ~**-bridge,** draaibrug, ~**-crane,** draaikraan; swaaikraan; ~**-lathe,** draaibank; ~**-loom,** draaibank; ~**-moment,** draaimoment; ~**-point,** keerpunt; draaiplek; draaipunt; ~**-points,** draaiwissel; ~ **radius,** draaistraal; ~ **saw,** spansaag; ~**-shop,** draaiery; ~**-tool,** draaibeitel; ~**-turret,** draaitoring.

turn'ip, raap; ~**-cabbage,** koolraap; ~ **seed,** raapsaad; ~ **tops,** raaplowwe.

turn: ~ **key,** sipier, tronkbewaarder; ~**-off,** uitdraaiplek; ~**-out,** opkoms; produksie; voorkoms; knap vertoning; perd en rytuig; uitrusting; staking; wisselspoor; verbreding; ~ **over,** omset, produksie en verkoop (handel); omkering; omslaan, omkanteling; klep; toetertjie; ~**-over table,** klaptafel; ~ **pike,** draaihek; tolhek; tolpad; slagboom, draaiboom; ~ **pike road,** tolpad; ~**-plough,** skaarploeg; ~**-round,** omdraaiing; heen-en-weertyd; ~**-screw,** skroewedraaier; ~ **side,** dronksiekte (honde); ~ **sole,** sonneblom; heliotroop; ~ **spit,** spitdraaier; ~ **stile,** draaihek, draaiboom; ~**-table,** draaiskryf (loko); draaibrug; skamel (w); draaitafel (grammofoon); ~**-up,** opstaande kant; omslag; worp (dobbel); toeval, onverwagte verskynsel; opkoms (by vergadering); lawaai.

turp'entine, (n) terpentyn; *oil of ~*, terpentynolie; (v) terpentyn aansmeer; ~**-grass,** terpentyngras; ~**-tree,** terpentynboom.

turpentin'ic, terpentynagtig; terpentyn=.

turp'itude, skandelikheid, skanddaad, laagheid, verdorwenheid.

turps, *abbr. of* **turpentine,** terpentyn.

turq'oise, (n) turkoois; turkooiskleur; (a) turkoois=, turkooisblou, turkooiskleurig; ~ **blue,** turkooisblou.

tu'rrel, trekhaak.

tu'rret, torinkie; skiettoring, geskuttoring; ~**ed,** van torings voorsien, met torinkies, getoring, toringvormig; ~ **cloud,** toringwolk; ~ **gun,** toringkanon.

tur'tle¹, (n) seeskilpad; *turn ~*, omslaan, omkantel; (v) skilpaaie vang.

tur'tle², (n) tortelduif; ~**-dove,** tortelduif.

tur'tle: ~**-shell,** (n) skilpaddop; (a) skilpaddop=; ~ **soup,** skilpadsop.

Tus'can, (n) Toskaner; Toskaans (taal); (a) Toskaans; ~**y,** Toskane.

tush¹, (n) (-es), slagtand, hoektand (perd).

tush², (interj) sjt! foei!

tusk, (n) slagtand, hoektand; olifantstand; braaktand (perd); (v) met die slagtande stoot, oopskeur; ~**ed,** met slagtande; ~**er,** groot olifant (met slagtande); uitgegroeide bosvark; ~**y,** met slagtande.

tuss'er, sywurm; tussorsy.

tuss'ive, hoes=.

tus'sle, (n) worsteling, gestoei; (v) worstel, stoei, plukhaar; veg.

tuss'ock, bossie; graspol; veerbos; ~**-grass,** stoelgras, polgras; ~**-moth,** grashuisie.

tuss'ore(-silk), tuss'ur, tussorsy.

tut¹, (n) stuk(werk); (v) (-ted), stukwerk doen.

tut², (interj) still! st! bog! toe nou!

tut'elage, voogdy(skap); onmondigheid, minderjarigheid.

tut'elar(y), beskermend, beskerm=; ~ **angel,** beskermengel; ~ **deity,** beskermgodheid; ~ **god,** beskermgod; ~ **saint,** beskermheilige; ~ **spirit,** beskermgees.

tut'enag, Berlynse silwer; Indiese sink.

tut'or, (n) privaat onderwyser, huisonderwyser; studieleier; afrigter, breier; tutor (aan Britse universiteite); (v) onderwys, privaat les gee, leer; regeer; ~ **aircraft,** lesvliegtuig; ~**ess, (-es),** goewernante.

tutor'ial, (n) studieklas, breiklas; (a) groeps=; ~ **class,** breiklas; ~ **system,** groepsonderrig, tutoriale stelsel.

tut'or: ~ **ship,** leermeesterskap; dosentskap; voogdyskap; ~ **sister,** susterdosente.

tutt'i, tutti (mus.), almal; ~**-frutti,** vrugteallegaartjie, tutti-frutti, vrugteroomys.

tutt'y, onsuiwer sinkoksied.

tut'-work, stukwerk.

tu-whit' tu-whoo', hoe-hoe (van 'n uil).
tuxed'o, (wit) aandbaadjie, tuxedo.
tuyere', blaaspyp, blaasmond.
twad'dle, (n) gebabbel, gebasel, geklets; bogpraatjies; *talk* ~, twakpraatjies (bogpraatjies) verkoop; (v) babbel, klets; ~ **r**, babbelaar, kletser.
twadd'ly, kletserig, babbelagtig.
twain, twee; *in* ~, in twee.
twang, (n) getjingel, getweng; skerp geluid; neusklank; (v) tingel, tokkel, bespeel; deur die neus praat.
'twas, dit was.
tweak, (n) knyp; ruk; (v) knyp; trek, ruk.
tweed, tweed.
twee'dle, vioolklank; ~ *dum and* ~ *dee*, vinkel en kol= jander, die een is soos die ander.
'tween, *abbr. of* **between**, tussen; ~ *decks*, tussendeks.
tween'y, hulpbediende.
tweet, (n) getjilp; (v) tjilp.
tweez'er, met 'n tangetjie uittrek.
tweez'ers, tangetjie, haartang, doringtangetjie; pinset; *pair of* ~, krultang, haartangetjie.
twelfth, twaalfde; T ~ **-day**, Driekoningedag; ~ **man**, reserwespeler, twaalfde man (krieket); T ~ **-night**, Driekoningeaand.
twelve, twaalf; ~ **fold**, twaalfvoudig; ~ **month**, jaar; *this day* ~ *month*, vandag oor 'n jaar; ~ **o'clock**, twaalfuur.
twen'tieth, twintigste.
twen'ty, twintig, twintigtal; *in the TWENTIES*, in die twintigerjare, in die jare twintig; *twenty-four hours SERVICE*, dag-en-nagdiens, etmaaldiens; ~ **-first**, een-en-twintigste; ~ **-five line**, kwartlyn (voetbal); ~ **fold**, twintigvoudig; ~ **-pounder**, twintigponder.
twi'bill, hellebaard, dubbelbyl.
twice, twee maal, twee keer, dubbel; ~ **-born**, wedergebore; ~ **r**, tweemaaldoener; setter-drukker; ~ **running**, twee keer na mekaar; ~ **-told**, twee maal vertel, welbekend.
twid'dle, (n) krul, draai; (v) draai, speel; ~ *one's thumbs*, met jou duime staan en speel; tyd verkwis.
twig, (n) takkie, twygie; waterwysstokkie; *best to BEND while 'tis a* ~, buig die boompie solank hy nog jonk is; *as the* ~ *'s BENT, the tree is inclined*, jonk gewend, oud gedoen (gekend); buig die boompie terwyl hy nog jonk is; *HOP the* ~, bokveld toe gaan; *WORK the* ~, met die wiggelroede werk; (v) (**-ged**), snap, begryp; *do you* ~ *it?* snap jy dit? ~ **gy**, takkiesrig, vol takkies; ~ **insect**, stokinsek, wandelende tak; ~ **snake**, stokslang, voëlslang; ~ **-wilter**, verwelkbesie.
twil'ight, (n) skemering, skemer(lig), skemerdonker, skemeraand, aandgrou; *AT* ~, in die skemering; ~ *of the GODS*, godeskemering; *in the* ~ *of early HISTORY*, in die aandskemering v.d. vroeë geskiedenis; (v) dof (swak) verlig; ~ **hour**, skemeruur; ~ **sleep**, pynlose bevalling (kindergeboorte).
twill, (n) keper (stof); gekeperde stof; (v) keper; ~ **ed**, gekeper.
twin, (n) een van 'n tweeling; dubbelganger; teenhanger; (pl) 'n tweeling; (v) (**-ned**), koppel, pare vorm; 'n tweeling kry; (a) tweeling=; dubbel=; paar-paar; ~ **bed(stead)s**, twee enkelbeddens; tweelingbedde; ~ **birth**, tweelinggeboorte; ~ **-born**, as tweeling gebore; ~ **brother**, tweelingbroer; *the T* ~ *Brothers*, die Tweeling (sterre).
twine, (n) tou; seilgare; draai, kronkeling; strengeling; warboel; (v) vleg, inmekaardraai, strengel; ~ *round*, omvleg.
twin-en'gined, tweemotorig.
twinge, (n) steek, steekpyn; kwelling, wroeging; ~ *of CONSCIENCE*, gewetenswroeging; ~ *of RE= MORSE*, wroeging; (v) steek; knaag.
twin igni'tion, dubbelontsteking.
twin'ing, slingerend; vlegtou; gevlegte tou.
twin'kle, (n) oogknip; blik, oogwink; vonkeling, flikkering, tinteling; *a* ~ *in one's eye*, 'n ondeunde blik; (v) knipoog; vonkel, flonker, flikker.
twi'nkling, (n) flikkering, flonkering, geflikker, vonkeling; *IN a* ~, *IN the* ~ *of an eye*, in 'n oogwink; (a) tintelend, flikkerend.

twin: ~ **ning**, verdubbeling; ~ **-screw**, dubbelskroef (skip); ~ **set**, tweelingstel; paarstel; ~ **ship**, tweelingskap; ~ **sister**, tweelingsuster.
twirl, (n) draai; krul; (v) dwarrel, draai; ~ *one's MOUSTACHE*, met jou snor speel; jou snor draai; ~ *ROUND*, omkronkel; ~ *one's THUMBS*, met jou duime speel; ~ **er**, ronddraaier; ~ **y**, draaiend.
twist, (n) verdraaiing; draai; kronkel; katoengaring; vleg; tou; gril; verrekking; kink (in kabel); wringing; lok; vlegsel (hare); roltabak; drankmengsel, half-om-half; eetlus; twist, rinkhals(dans); ineendraaiing; neiging, aanleg; *GIVE a* ~ *to a word*, 'n woord verdraai; *GIVE it a* ~, 'n krul maak aan; dit draai; *a MORAL* ~, 'n sedelike afwyking; ~ *of TOBACCO*, roltabak, ~ *-'n-TURN*, draaiskommel (delwerye); ~ *s and TWIRLS*, bogte en kronkelinge; *a* ~ *of the WRIST*, 'n (ver)draaiing v.d. gewrig; 'n handigheid (slag); (v) draai; verdraai; verrek, verwring; strengel, vleg (hare); vertrek; ~ *an ANKLE*, 'n enkel verstuit; ~ *someone's ARM*, druk op iem. uitoefen; ~ *EVIDENCE*, getuienis verdraai; ~ *someone round one's FINGER*, iem. om jou pinkie draai; ~ *ed SEAM*, verdraaide naat; ~ **dance**, twist, rinkhalsdans; ~ **-drill**, spiraalboor; ~ **ed**, gedraai, verrek; gekronkel; gekinkel; ~ **er**, vlegter; draadtang; wurghout, opwenstok (bloedstelping); draaier; uitvlugtesoeker, manteldraaier; draaibal, trekbal (krieket); dwarsbalk; ~ **ing**, (n) strengeling; verdraaiing; draaiing; draaiery; (a) draaiend; ~ **ing moment**, wringmoment, torsiemoment; ~ **y**, draaiend, kronkel(r)ig.
twit, (**-ted**), pla, verwyt, berispe.
twitch, (n) (**-es**), ruk; senuweetrekking; steek; (v) ruk; pluk, trek; krampagtig trek, spartel, stuiptrek, vertrek; ~ **ing**, (n) sparteling, stuiptrekking; (a) stuiptrekkend, rukkerig; ~ **grass**, kweekgras.
twite, vink.
twitt'er, (n) gekwetter, gekweel, getjirp; gegiggel; trilling; (v) kweel, sing, kwetter, tjilp; giggel; ~ **a'tion**, opgewondenheid.
two, (**-s**), twee; ~ *BY* ~, twee-twee, in pare; ~ *is COMPANY, three is none*, twee is 'n paar, drie onpaar; *CUT in* ~, middeldeur sny; *in a DAY or* ~, oor 'n dag of wat; *when* ~ *FRIDAYS (Sundays) come together*, in die jaar nul; wanneer die perde horings kry; ~ *HEADS are better than one*, twee koppe is beter as een, al is een 'n skaapkop; *be IN* ~ *minds*, onseker, onbeslis wees, *IN* ~ *'s*, tweetwee; in groepe van twee; *cut INTO* ~, in twee stukke sny; *KNOW a thing or* ~, ouer as twaalf wees; ~ *O'CLOCK*, tweeuur; ~ *to ONE*, twee teen een; *ONE or* ~ *people*, 'n paar mense; ~ *can PLAY at that game*, slaan is niks nie, maar die oor en weer slanery; *slaan is twee man se werk*; dit kan ek ook doen; ek is mans genoeg vir jou; *PUT* ~ *and* ~ *together*, jou gesonde verstand gebruik; jou eie gevoeltrekking maak; *it takes* ~ *to make a QUARREL*, slaan is niks nie, maar die oor en weer slanery; *be READY in* ~ *s*, in 'n kits klaar wees, *T* ~ *SICILIES*, Koninkryk van Napels en Sicilië; ~ *-THIRD'S majority*, tweederdemeerderheid; ~ *in a TRADE never agree*, vaklui is dit selde eens; ~ **ball**, tweespel (gholf); ~ **-coloured**, tweekleurig; ~ **-cycle engine**, tweeslagmotor; ~ **-decker**, tweedekker; ~ **deep**, in twee rye; *stand* ~ *deep*, in twee rye staan; ~ **-dimensional**, tweedimensionaal; ~ **-edged**, tweesnydend; ~ **-engined**, tweemotorig; ~ **-faced**, met twee gesigte; onopreg, vals, dubbelhartig, geveins; ~ **fold**, tweevoudig; dubbel; ~ **-furrow plough**, tweevoorploeg; ~ **-handed**, tweehandig; tweepersoons=; ~ **-handed saw**, tweemansaag; ~ **handled**, met twee handvatsels; ~ **-headed**, tweehoofdig; ~ **-leaved**, tweeblarig, met twee blare; ~ **legged**, tweebeen=, tweebenig; ~ **-man school**, tweemanskool; ~ **-monthly**, tweemaandeliks; ~ **ness**, tweeheid, dualiteit; ~ **-part**, tweestemmig; tweedelig; ~ **-party system**, tweepartystelsel; ~ **pence**, twee pennies; twee oulap; *not care* ~ *pence*, niks omgee nie; ~ **penny-halfpenny**, veragtelik; nikswerd, onbeduidend; ~ **-piece**, twee-stuk; ~ **-pin plug**, tweepuntsteker; ~ **-pin socket**, tweepensok; ~ **-ply**, tweedraads; tweelaag=; ~ **-ply wool**, twee=

draadswol; ~-pounder, tweeponder; ~-roomed flat, tweekamerwoonstel; enkelwoonstel; ~-row cultivator, tweeryskoffelploeg; ~-row engine, dubbelgelidmotor; ~-row planter, tweeryplanter; ~-seater, tweepersoonsmotor, tweesitplek(motor); tweepersoonsvliegtuig; ~-sided, tweesydig; met twee kante; ~some, tweespel; dubbelspel; dans vir twee mense; paar; ~-speed, met twee versnellings; ~-step, tweestapdans; ~-stream policy, tweestroombeleid; ~-stroke engine, tweeslagmotor; ~-third's majority, tweederdemeerderheid; ~-timer, huigelaar, veinser, tweegatjakkals; ~-toned, tweekleurig; ~-tongued, dubbeltongig, vals; ~-toothed, tweetand=.

two'-way, tweerigtings=; tweetak=; tweegat=; ~ communication, heen-en-weerverbinding; ~ girdle, rek-en-trek; ~ joint, dolosskarnier; ~ reinforcement, roosterwapening; ~ road, tweerigtingspad; ~ set, sendontvanger; ~-socket, tweegatkontak; ~ switch, dubbelskakelaar; ~ traffic, tweerigtingsverkeer.

two: ~-wheeled, tweewiel=; ~-year old, tweejarige (kind, dier).

twy'er, blaaspyp.

tycoon', geldbaas, magnaat.

ty'ing, (die) vasbind.

tyke, ploert, gemene vent; brakkie; tjokker(tjie).

tym'pan, timpaan, persraam; vlies.

tympan'ic, trommel=; ~ cavity, trommelholte; ~ membrane, trommelvlies; ~ nerve, trommelsenuwee.

tympanit'es, trommelsug, opblaassiekte, windsug.

tympanit'is, trommelvliesontsteking, timpanitis.

tym'panum, (..na), trommelvlies; trommelholte, middeloor; timpaan (bouk.).

type, (n) tipe, soort; voorbeeld; toonbeeld; stempel; grondvorm; (druk)letter; setsel (drukkery); *IN* ~, geset; *in LARGE* ~, in groot letters geset; *PUPILS of that* ~, daardie soort leerlinge, leerlinge van daardie tipe; *in SMALL* ~, in klein letter geset; *TRUE to* ~, raseg; tipies; (v) afbeeld; tipeer, sinnebeeldig voorstel; met 'n tikmasjien skrywe, tik; druk; ~-area, setspieël; ~-box, ~-case, letterkas; ~-correcting fluid, flaterwater, korreksievloeistof; ~-face, lettertipe; ~-founder, lettergieter; ~-foundry, lettergietery; ~ letter, drukletter; ~-metal, lettermetaal; ~-page, setspieël, bladspieël, drukspieël; ~ script, tikskrif; drukskrif; ~ setter, lettersetter; setmasjien; ~ setting, (die) set, setwerk;

~ setting machine, setmasjien; ~ write, (..wrote, ..written), tik; ~ writer, skryfmasjien, tikmasjien; ~ writer-ribbon, tikmasjienband, tikmasjienlint; ~ writing, (die) tik, tikwerk; tikskrif, masjienskrif; ~ written, getik.

typ'ex machine, kodemasjien.

typhlit'is, blindedermontsteking.

typh'oid, (n) tifoïedkoors, ingewandskoors; (a) tifeus; ~ fever, ingewandskoors, maagkoors.

typhoman'ia, ylhoofdigheid.

typhon'ic, tifonies.

typhoon', tifoon, stormwind.

typh'us, vlektifus, tifuskoors, luiskoors.

typ'ical, tipies, tiperend; sinnebeeldig; kenmerkend, kensketsend; *be* ~ *of*, tipies wees van, kenmerkend wees vir.

typifica'tion, tipering, tipifikasie; afbeelding; sinnebeeld.

typ'ify, (..fied), afbeeld; tipeer; sinnebeeldig voorstel.

typ'ing, tik, tikwerk; ~ pool, tikpoel.

typ'ist, tikster, tipiste.

typ'ograph, setmasjien.

typog'rapher, drukker, tipograaf.

typograph'ic(al), tipografies, druk=; ~ *al ERROR*, drukfout; ~ *al UNION*, drukkersvakbond, tipograwebond.

typog'raphy, drukkuns, tipografie.

typolo'gic, tipologies.

typol'ogy, tipologie.

tyrann'ic(al), tiranniek, tirannies.

tyrann'icide, tirannemoord; tirannemoordenaar.

ty'rannize, tiranniseer, despoties regeer; wreed wees; ~ *over a people*, 'n volk tiranniseer.

ty'rannous, tirannies.

ty'ranny, (tyrannies), tirannie, dwingelandy, wreedheid; geweldenary.

ty'rant, tiran, geweldenaar, dwingeland, despoot.

Tyre¹, Tirus.

tyre², (n) buiteband; (v) 'n buiteband aansit; ~ lever, bandligter; ~ wall, buitebandwand.

Tyr'ian, (n) Tiriër; (a) Tiries.

ty'ro, *kyk* tiro.

Ty'rol, Tirol; ~ ean, ~ ese', (n) Tiroler; (a) Tiroler=, Tirools.

ty'rotoxin, melkgif.

Tyrrhen'ian, Tirrheens.

tzar, *kyk* tsar.

Tzigane', (n) Hongaarse Sigeuner; (a) Sigeuns, Sigeuner=.

U

u, (u's), u; *little* ~, u'tjie.

U'-beam, U-balk.

ubi'ety, plaaslikheid; die ligging.

ubiquitar'ian, (n) ubikwitariër, gelower in die alomteenwoordigheid (van die liggaam van Christus); (a) alomteenwoordig.

ubiq'uitous, alomteenwoordig.

ubiq'uity, alomteenwoordigheid, ubikwiteit.

U'-boat, U-boot, (Duitse) duikboot.

U'-bolt, krambout.

udd'er, uier.

udom'eter, reënmeter, udometer.

Ugan'da, Uganda, Oeganda.

ugh! ba! foei! ga! poe!

uglifica'tion, verleliking.

ug'lify, (..fied), verlelik, lelik maak.

ug'liness, lelikheid, afsigtelikheid; haatlikheid.

ug'ly, (n) (uglies), oogskerm; voëlverskrikker, lelikerd; (a) lelik, afsigtelik; skandelik; gemeen; gevaarlik; haatlik; *an* ~ *CUSTOMER*, 'n gevaarlike vent; *an* ~ *DUCKLING*, 'n lelike eendjie; *an* ~ *SILENCE*, 'n dreigende stilte; *as* ~ *as SIN*, so lelik soos die nag; *an* ~ *SITUATION*, 'n gevaarlike toestand; ~ *WEATHER*, onaangename (stormagtige) weer.

Ug'rian, Ug'ric, (n) Oegriër; (a) Oegries.

uh'lan, ulaan, lansier.

U'-iron, U-yster.

ukase', oekase, dekreet, bevelskrif.

Ukraine', Oekraïne.

Ukrain'ian, (n) Oekraïner; Oekraïns (taal); (a) Oekraïns.

ukule'le, ukelele.

ul'cer, sweer, geswel, ettergeswel, abses; kanker (fig.); *duodenal (gastric)* ~. maags(w)eer; ~ ate, sweer, versweer, etter; laat sweer; ~ a'tion, swering, ettering; ~ ative, swerend; ~ ed, swerend, etterend; ~ ous, vol swere.

uli'ginal, uli'ginose, wateragtig; moerassig, moeras=, klam, vleierig.

ull'age, ontbrekende hoeveelheid, kortkoms (aan 'n byna vol vat); lek; uitsettingruimte; oorskiet.

ul'min, humus.

ul'mus, olm (boom).

ul'na, (-e), elmboogbeen, ellepyp; ~ r, ellepyp=.

ulo'trichan, wolharig.

ul'ster, jas, oorjas; ulster.

ulter'ior, verder, later; aan die ander kant; verborge, geheim; ~ *MOTIVE*, bybedoeling, newebedoeling; *an* ~ *OBJECT*, 'n bybedoeling

ultima 1331 *unaltered*

ul'tima, laaste; verste; ~ *RATIO,* laaste uitweg; geweld; ~ *THULE,* ultima thule, end van die wêreld, uithoek van die aarde.
ul'timate, laaste, allerlaaste, uiterste, slot-; beslissend, finaal; fundamenteel, grond-; eventueel; ~ **analysis,** elementêre analise, kenanalise, volledige analise; ~ **load,** breekbelasting; ~**ly,** eindelik, uiteindelik, ten laaste, per slot van rekening; ~ **object,** einddoel; ~ **principles,** grondbeginsels; ~ **resistance,** breekweerstand; ~ **result,** einduitslag; uiteindelike gevolg; ~ **strength,** breekvastheid; ~ **stress,** breekspanning.
ultimat'um, (-s, ..ta), ultimatum; eindbesluit; grondbeginsel; laaste eis; *deliver an* ~, 'n ultimatum stel.
ul'timo, laaslede, v.d. vorige maand, jongslede.
ultimogen'iture, opvolgingsreg van die jongste seun, minoraat.
ul'tra, (n) ekstremis, heethoof; (a) ultra-, ekstremisties, heethoofdig; (prep) anderkant; ~ **conservative, (n)** aartskonserwatiewe, verkrampte; (a) verkramp, aartskonserwatief; ~**-high,** ultrahoog; ~**ist,** ekstremis, ultra; ~**-liberal, (n)** verligte, aartsliberalis; (a) verlig, aartsliberaal; ~ **marine', (n)** ultramaryn, donkerblou; (a) oorsees; ultramaryn, ~**-modern,** ultramoderm, hipermodern; ~ **montane, (n)** vreemdeling; pousgesinde; (a) van die anderkant van die berg, ultramontaans; Italiaans (R.K.); ~**mon'tanism,** ultramontanisme, oordrewe pousgesindheid; ~**mon'tanist,** ultramontaan, pousgesinde; ~**mun'dane,** bowenaards; van die hiernamaals; ~**-polite,** oorbeleef; ~ **sonic,** ultrasonies; ~**-sonorous,** ultrasonoor; ~ **vi'olet,** ultraviolet; ~**-violet rays,** ultraviolet strale; ~ **vir'es,** ultra vires, buite die bevoegdheid van; ~ **visible,** onsigbaar.
ultron'eous, vrywillig, spontaan, uit eie beweging.
ul'ulate, huileer.
ulula'tion, ululasie.
U'-magnet, hoefmagneet.
umaram'ba, (-s), oemaramba.
um'bel, (blom)skerm; ~**late,** skermvormig, blomskerm-; ~**lif'erous,** skermdraend; ~ *liferous plant,* moerwortel; ~**liform,** skermvormig; ~**l'ule,** skermpie.
um'ber, (n) omber, bergbruin, donkerbruin verf; ombervoël; ombervis; (v) beskadu; donkerbruin verf; (a) omberkleurig, donkerbruin, bergbruin; ~ **ed,** gebruin; bruin geverf.
umbil'ical, na(w)el-; ~ **bandage,** naelband; ~ **cord,** na(w)elstring; ~ **pyaemia,** na(w)elbesmetting; ~ **region,** na(w)elstreek.
umbil'icate, na(w)elvormig.
umbili'ciform, umbi'liform, na(w)elvormig.
umbilic'us, (..ci), na(w)el.
um'bles, binnegoed; ingewande van wild.
um'bo, (-nes, -s), (skild)knop; ~**nate,** knopvormig; getepel.
um'bra, (-e), kernskaduwee, skaduweekeël; ongenooide gas.
um'brage, skaduwee, koelte, lommer; ergernis, aanstoot; *GIVE* ~ *to,* aanstoot gee aan, vererg; *TAKE* ~, aanstoot neem; jou aan iets stoot.
umbra'geous, skaduryk; beskadu, lommerryk; liggeraak.
umbrell'a, sambreel; *under the* ~ *of,* onder die vaandel (seggenskap bewind) van; ~**-case,** sambreelsak; ~**'d,** met 'n sambreel; beskut, beskerm; ~**-frame,** sambreelraam; ~**-holder,** sambreelstander; ~ **roof,** sambreeldak; ~**-runner,** skuifring (van 'n sambreel); ~**-shaped,** sambreelvormig; ~**-stand,** sambreelstander; ~**-thorn,** sambreelboom, haaken-steek; ~**-tree,** kiepersol(boom), nooiensboom.
umbrette', hamerkop(voël).
um'brose, skaduryk, lommerryk.
um'laut, umlaut.
umph! hm!
um'pire, (n) skeidsregter (sport); arbiter, beoordelaar; (v) as skeidsregter optree; ~ **ship,** skeidsregterskap.
um'piring, skeidsregterskap; beoordeling.
ump'teen, baie, verskeie, ek weet nie hoeveel nie; ~**th,** hoeveelste, soveelste.

unabashed', onbeskaamd; nie uit die veld geslaan nie, nie verleë nie.
unabat'ed, onverminderd, onverswak.
unabbrev'iated, onafgekort, onverkort.
una'ble, onbekwaam, nie in staat nie.
unabol'ished, onafgeskaf.
unabridged', onverkort, volledig.
unab'rogated, nie afgeskaf nie.
unabsorbed', ongeabsorbeer.
unaccent'ed, toonloos, sonder klemtoon.
unacceptabil'ity, onaanneemlikheid.
unaccept'able, onaanneemlik, verwerplik, onaanvaarbaar, onwelkom; ~**ness,** onaanneemlikheid, onaanvaarbaarheid.
unaccept'ed, onaangenome.
unaccess'ible, ongenaakbaar, ontoeganklik; onbereikbaar.
unaccomm'odating, onvriendelik, ontoegeeflik, oninskiklik, ontoeskietlik.
unaccom'panied, onvergesel, sonder begeleiding, alleen.
unaccom'plished, onvoltooi(d), onuitgevoer; sonder talente.
unaccountabil'ity, onverantwoordelikheid; onverklaarbaarheid.
unaccount'able, onverantwoordelik; onverklaarbaar; ~**ness,** onverantwoordelikheid; onverklaarbaarheid.
unaccount'ably, op onverklaarbare wyse.
unaccount'ed, onverantwoord; vermis (soldaat).
unaccred'ited, ongemagtig.
unaccus'tomed, ongewoon; ~ *to,* ongewoon(d) (ongewend) aan; ~**ness,** ongewoondheid, ongewoonte.
unachiev'able, onuitvoerbaar, onbereikbaar.
unacknowl'edged, nie erken nie; oorgeneem sonder erkenning; onbeantwoord (brief).
unacquaint'ed, onbekend (met); onkundig.
unacquired', onverkry; natuurlik, aangebore.
unact'able, onopvoerbaar, onspeelbaar.
unact'ed, nie opgevoer nie.
unac'tuated, nie gedryf nie.
unadaptabil'ity, onaanpasbaarheid.
unadapt'able, nie aanpasbaar nie, onaanpasbaar.
unaddict'ed, nie verslaaf nie.
unadjust'ed, onvereffen; ongereël; onaangepas.
unadmin'istered, onbcheer(d)
unadmired', onbewonderd.
unadmitt'ed, nie toelaatbaar nie; nie toegelaat nie; onaanneemlik.
unadmon'ished, onvermaand, ongewaarsku.
unadored', onbemin; ongeëer.
unadorned', onversier, onopgesmuk; eenvoudig.
unadul'terated, onvervals, suiwer, skoon.
unadvisabil'ity, onraadsaamheid; ongeseglikheid.
unadvis'able, onraadsaam, ongerade, ongeseglik.
unadvised', onbedagsaam, onverstandig, onberade, onverslgtig, ~**ly,** onbedagsaam, onverstandig, onversigtig.
unaesthet'ic, onesteties; lelik.
unaffect'ed, natuurlik, ongekunsteld, opreg, sonder aanstellery; onaangedaan, onaangetas, nie betrokke nie, onbeïnvloed; ~**ness,** natuurlikheid, ongekunsteldheid.
unaffil'iated, nie aangesluit nie, ongeaffilieer.
unaffirmed', nie bevestig nie, onbevestig.
unafraid', onbevrees, nie bang nie.
unaid'ed, sonder hulp, alleen, selfstandig.
unaimed', ongerig (geweer); toevallig; ~ *fire,* verdwaalde koeëls.
unalarmed', onbevrees, nie verontrus nie, gerus.
unal'ienable, onvervreemdbaar.
unal'ienated, onvervreemd.
unaligned', afsydig, onverbonde.
unallev'iated, nie verlig (versag) nie.
unallied', nie verwant nie; sonder bondgenote.
unallott'ed, nie toegeken nie.
unallow'able, ontoelaatbaar, ongeoorloof.
unalloyed', onvermeng, suiwer.
unalterabil'ity, onveranderlikheid.
unal'terable, onveranderlik, vas; ~**ness,** onveranderlikheid, vastheid.
unal'tered, onverander(d), ongewysig.

unambig'uous, ondubbelsinnig, duidelik.
unambi'tious, nie eersugtig nie, beskeie; traag; ~ness, gebrek aan ambisie; traagheid.
unamiabil'ity, stroefheid, stuursheid, onbeminlikheid.
unamen'able, nie verantwoordelik nie; onvatbaar.
unamend'ed, nie verbeter nie, ongeamendeer.
unam'iable, onbeminlik, stuurs, stroef.
unamus'ing, onvermaaklik, onprettig, vervelend.
unan'alysed, onopgelos; onontleed.
unan'imated, onbesiel(d); leweloos.
unanim'ity, eenstemmigheid, eensgesindheid, eenparigheid, gelykgesindheid, eenheid, enigheid.
unan'imous, eenstemming, unaniem, eenparig, eensgesind, eendragtig, eendragtiglik, eens; ~ly, eenparig, eensgesind, soos een man, uit een mond.
unannealed', ongetemper.
unannounced', onaangedien, onaangemeld, onverwag.
unanoint'ed, ongesalf.
unan'swerable, onweerlegbaar; onweersspreeklik; an ~ argument, 'n onweerlegbare argument (redenering).
unan'swered, onbeantwoord; onweerlê.
unanti'cipated, onverwag, onvoorbedrag.
unappalled', onverskrokke, onvervaard.
unappa'relled, ongekleed.
unappeal'able, waarteen nie in hoër beroep gegaan kan word nie.
unappeas'able, onversoenlik; onbevredigbaar.
unappeased', onversoen; onbevredig, ongestil.
unap'petising, onaantreklik.
unapplied', onaangewend; doelloos.
unappre'ciated, ongewaardeer; miskend.
unappre'ciative, nie-waarderend; ~ness, gebrek aan waardering.
unapprehend'ed, nie verstaan nie; nie gearresteer nie.
unapproachabil'ity, ongenaakbaarheid; ontoeganklikheid.
unapproach'able, ontoeganklik, ongenaakbaar.
unapprop'riated, sonder baas; nog ter beskikking; nie vir 'n bepaalde doel bestem nie; ~ profits, onaangewende wins (boekhou).
unapproved', nie goedgekeur nie, verwerp.
unapt', onbekwaam; ongeskik; ongeneig; onvanpas; sonder aanleg; ~ness, onbekwaamheid; ongeskiktheid; ongeneigdheid.
unar'guable, onbetwisbaar, onweersspreeklik.
unarm', ontwapen; ~ed, ongewapen; ontwapen; onbeman.
unar'moured, ongepantser.
unarranged', ongerangskik, ongeorden, nie gereël nie.
unarrayed', ongeklee; ongeordineer.
unarrest'ed, nie gearresteer nie; onbelemmer(d).
unartic'ulated, ongeleerd; onduidelik.
unartifi'cial, nie kunsmatig nie, natuurlik.
unartis'tic, onartistiek, sonder kunssin, nie kunssinnig nie.
u'nary, eenledig, eensheids=.
unascertain'able, onbepaalbaar.
unascertained', onseker, onuitgemaak.
unashamed', onbeskaam(d), onbeskof, sonder skaamte; ~ly, onbeskaamd; skaamteloos; ~ness, onbeskaamdheid; skaamteloosheid.
unasked', ongevra, ongenooi; uit eie beweging, op eie houtjie.
unaspir'ing, oneersugtig, sonder pretensie.
unassailabil'ity, onaantasbaarheid.
unassail'able, onaantasbaar, onbetwisbaar, onweerlegbaar.
unassailed', onbetwis.
unassert'ive, beskeie.
unassim'ilable, onassimileerbaar, onaanpasbaar.
unassist'ed, alleen, sonder hulp.
unasso'ciated, nie verenig nie; nie verwant nie.
unassort'ed, ongesorteer.
unassum'ing, beskeie, sonder pretensies, pretensieloos, platweg.
unassured', onverseker.
unattached', los; alleenstaande, nie verbonde nie; nie verloof nie; be ~, alleenlopend wees; los wees.

unattain'able, onbereikbaar.
unattemp'ted, onbeproef.
unattend'ed, alleen, onvergesel, sonder gevolg; onbewaak.
unattest'ed, onbetuig; nie-ingesweer.
unattrac'tive, onaantreklik, onaanloklik.
unauthen'tic, nie outentiek nie, oneg, vals; ~ated, nie gewettig nie; nie bekragtig nie.
unauth'orized, ongemagtig; onwettig; onbevoeg, ongeregtig; ~ persons prohibited, geen toegang sonder verlof.
unavailabil'ity, onverkrygbaarheid.
unavail'able, onverkrygbaar, nie beskikbaar nie, vergeefs; nutteloos.
unavail'ing, tevergeefs, van geen waarde nie, nutteloos, onbegonne.
unavenged', ongewreek.
unavoid'able, onvermydelik, onafwendbaar; ~ness, onafwendbaarheid.
unaware', onwetend, onbewus; be BLISSFULLY ~ of the whole affair, v.d. hele saak niks weet nie; I was ~ of the FACT, ek was onbewus van die feit; ~ness, onwetendheid, onbewustheid.
unawares', onverwags, onverhoeds; plotseling, onwetend; sonder om daarop bedag te wees; CATCH someone ~, iem. oorval; they were TAKEN ~ by his action, sy gedrag het hulle oorrompel (verras).
unawed', nie bang nie, onbeskroomd, sonder ontsag, onverskrokke.
unbacked', ongeleer, nie touwys nie; onberede; nie gesteun nie; sonder leuning; ~ horse, 'n perd waarop nie gewed is nie.
unbag', (-ged), uit die sak skud; uitskud.
unbaked', nie gebak nie; ongebak; onbekook; ~ brick, rou steen.
unbal'ance, die ewewig verstoor; van stryk bring; getik raak; mallerig raak; ~d, uit die ewewig, ongebalanseer(d), onewewigtig; getik, nie by sy volle verstand nie.
unball'ast, ballas verwyder.
unban'dage, die verband afneem, ontswagtel.
unbap'tized, ongedoop.
unbar', (-red), ontgrendel, oopmaak.
unbear'able, ondraaglik, onuitho(u)baar, onuitstaanbaar; ~ness, onuitstaanbaarheid, ondraaglikheid, onuitho(u)baarheid.
unbeat'able, onverslaanbaar, onoorwinlik, onoortreflik, onoortrefbaar.
unbeat'en, nie verslaan nie, onoortroffe, onoorwonne; ongebaan; ongeklits (eier).
unbeaut'eous, unbeaut'iful, lelik, onskoon, onooglik.
unbecom'ing, ongepas, ongevoeglik, onvoegsaam; onwelvoeglik, onbetaamlik, onordelik.
unbefit'ting, onbetaamlik, onvoegsaam.
unbefriend'ed, onbevriend; nie begunstig nie.
unbegot'(ten), ongebore; ewig.
unbeknown', onbekend; sonder die medewete van.
unbelief', ongeloof.
unbeliev'able, ongelooflik.
unbeliev'er, ongelowige.
unbeliev'ing, ongelowig.
unbeloved', onbemin(d).
unbend', (..bent), ontspan; losmaak; loskom; iem. laat gaan; vriendeliker word, ontdooi, minder stroef wees; ~able, onbuigbaar; onbuigsaam (fig.); ~ableness, onbuigsaamheid; ~ing, onbuigsaam, hardnekkig; styf; ontoegeeflik; afsydig, stroef; ~ingness, stugheid; strengheid.
unbeseem'ing, onbetaamlik, onvoegsaam, onwelvoeglik, ongepas.
unbesought', onafgesmeek.
unbewailed', onbeween.
unbi'as(s)ed, onbevooroordeeld, onpartydig, onbevange.
unbib'lical, onbybels.
unbid'able, ongeseglik, onhandelbaar.
unbidd'en, ongenooi, ongevraag; vanself; ~ GUESTS are often welcomest when they are gone; an ~ GUEST knows not where to sit, ongenooide gaste hoort agter deure en kaste; ongenooide gaste hoort agter die deur.
unbig'oted, nie dweepsiek nie, gematig, besadig.

unbind', (..bound), losbind, ontbind.
unblam'able, onberispelik, onskuldig.
unbleached', ongebleik.
unblem'ished, rein, onbevlek, onbesoedeld, vlekloos, onbesmet; *an ~ reputation*, 'n onaantasbare naam.
unblend'ed, ongemeng.
unblest', ongeseën(d).
unblink'ing, sonder om 'n oog te knip, starend, strak.
unblind'ed, overblind.
unblood'ed, nie opreg nie (perde).
unblood'y, onbloedig; *~ sacrifice*, bloedlose offerande.
unblown', nie gewaai nie; nog nie oop nie (blom).
unblush'ing, skaamteloos, onbeskaamd; *~ ly*, sonder skaamteblos, sonder blik of bloos; *~ ness*, skaamteloosheid, onbeskaamdheid.
unboiled', ongekook; rou.
unbolt', oopmaak, ontsluit, ontgrendel, losskroef.
unbone', die bene uithaal, ontbeen; *~ d'*, ontbeen.
unbooked', onbespreek, ongereserveer(d).
unboot'ed, ongestewel(d).
unbord'ered, sonder rand.
unborn', ongebore.
unbos'om, ontboesem, lug gee aan, die hart uitstort; *~ oneself*, jou hart uitpraat; alles uitpak.
unbot'tle, uitgiet; lug gee aan.
unbought', ongekoop.
unbound', oningebind (boek); loshangend (hare); losgemaak; *~ ed*, onbegrens, onbeperk, grensloos.
unbowed', ongeboë; ongebroke.
unbo'wel, die ingewande uithaal; ontwei, openbaar; oopmaak.
unbrace', losmaak, losgespe; ontspan.
unbrand'ed, ongebrand, sonder eiendomsmerk (vee).
unbreak'able, onbreekbaar; onverbreeklik.
unbred', onopgevoed, ongemanierd.
unbrib'able, onomkoopbaar.
unbridge'able, onoorbrugbaar.
unbridged', sonder brug, brugloos.
unbri'dle, die toom afhaal, aftoom; vrylaat; *~ d*, ongetoom; losbandig, toomloos, ongebreidel, uitgelate, onbeteueld.
unbrok'en, ononderbroke, onafgebroke, onverbroke, heel; ongeleerd, ongetem; wys; *~ journey*, ononderbroke reis.
unbroth'erly, onbroederlik.
unbruised', ongekneus.
unbrushed', ongeborsel; *~ goods*, ongepluisde stowwe.
unbuc'kle, losgespe, afgord.
unbuilt', ongebou; *~ upon*, onbebou.
unburd'en, ontlas, ontboesem; *~ one's HEART, ~ ONESELF*, jou hart uitstort; alles uitpak; lug gee aan jou gevoelens.
unbu'ried, onbegrawe.
unburned', **unburnt'**, onverbrand; ongebak, rou (stene); *~ brick*, rou steen.
unbus'inesslike, onprakties; onsaaklik; onsaakkundig.
unbutt'on, losknoop.
uncage', uit die kooi laat, vrylaat.
uncall'ed, ongeroep; ongestort, nie ingevorder nie (geld); astrant; ongevra(ag); ongelos (goed); *~ -for*, ongeroep, ongevra(ag); onvanpas; onafgehaal (goed); ongewens, onnodig, ongewettig.
uncan'celled, nie deurgehaal (ingetrek, herroep) nie.
uncann'y, geheimsinnig, spookagtig, onheilspellend, grillerig, angswekkend.
uncap', (-ped), ontseël (heuningkoek).
uncared'-for, verontagsaam; verwaarloos, onversorg.
uncar'ing, onbesorg(d); verwaarlosend; onverskillig.
uncarp'eted, sonder tapyt, kaal.
uncase', uit die kassie neem; blootlê, uithaal.
uncashed', ongewissel; *~ cheque*, ongewisselde tjek; *~ draft*, onverdiskonteerde wissel.
unceas'ing, onophoudelik, eindeloos, voortdurend, onafgebroke.
uncen'sored, ongesensor, nie deur die sensor nagesien nie.
unceremon'ious, familiêr, sonder pligpleging; onbeleef, ongegeneerd; *~ ly*, sonder pligpleginge, som‑

mer kaalkop, tromp-op, kortaf; *~ ness*, informaliteit; onbeleefdheid.
uncert'ain, onseker, ongewis; besluiteloos; onbepaald, onduidelik; wisselvallig, ongestadig, wankel, veranderlik; wispelturig, onbetroubaar; *be ~ ABOUT somebody*, onseker omtrent iem. wees; *I am ~ OF going*, ek weet nie of ek kan gaan nie; *~ WEATHER*, ongestadige weer; *~ ty*, onsekerheid, twyfelagtigheid; veranderlikheid; besluiteloosheid; wispelturigheid.
uncertif'icated, ongesertifiseer(d).
uncert'ified, ongesertifiseer(d).
unchain', ontketen, losmaak, ontboei.
unchall'engeable, onwraakbaar; onuitdaagbaar.
unchall'enged, ongehinder(d); onbetwis, onbestrede; ongewraak; onuitgedaag; *suffer it to pass ~*, sonder opmerking laat verbygaan.
unchange'able, onveranderlik.
unchanged', onverander(d); ongewissel(d).
uncharacteris'tic, nie karakteristiek van . . . nie, nie eie aan . . . nie.
uncha'ritable, liefdeloos, onbarmhartig, onchristelik, onmenslik, hard; *~ ness*, liefdeloosheid, onmenslikheid, hardheid.
unchart'ed, ongekaart; onbevare (see); onbekend.
unchart'ered, ongeoorloof; sonder oktrooi.
unchaste', onkuis.
uncha'stened, ongestraf; ongekuis.
unchas'tity, onkuisheid.
unchecked', los, vry, ongedwonge, ongehinderd; onbeteuel(d).
uncheer'ful, onvrolik, troosteloos, onopgeruimd, somber, bedruk, neerslagtig.
unchiv'alrous, onridderlik.
unchri'sten, die doop ontneem; *~ ed*, ongedoop, ongekersten.
unchris'tian, onchristelik; *~ like*, onchristelik; *~ ly*, onchristelik.
unchron'icled, onvermeld.
unchurch', in die kerklike ban doen, uit die kerk stoot; *~ ed*, nie tot 'n kerk behorende nie; nie deur die kerk geseën nie.
un'cial, (n) unsiaal, Romeinse letter, hoofletter; (a) unsiaal.
un'ciform, haakvormig.
uncirc'umcised, onbesnede.
uncirc'umscribed, nie omskryf nie; onbeperk.
unciv'ic, onburgerlik.
unciv'il, onbeleef(d), ongemanierd; *~ ized*, onbeskaaf(d), barbaars, baar.
unclad', ongekleed, kaal.
unclaimed', onopgeëis, onafgehaal; onbeheer(d), sonder baas; *~ GOODS*, onopgeëiste goedere; *~ PAY*, onopgeëiste loon.
unclamp', die klem losmaak.
unclasp', losgespe; losmaak; (hande) los.
unclassed', **unclass'ified**, oningedeel(d), ongeklassifiseer(d).
un'cle, oom; pandjiesbaas, pandjieshouer, lommerdhouer; *speak to someone like a DUTCH ~*, iem. 'n vaderlike skrobbering gee; *U~ SAM*, Broer Jonatan, die Verenigde State van Amerika.
unclean', onrein; onkuis, vuil; *~ liness*, *~ ness*, onreinheid, onsuiwerheid.
uncleansed', ongesuiwer(d).
unclear', onduidelik; onhelder, dof.
uncleared', onvereffen; oningeklaar; onuitgeklaar (deur doeane).
un'cle-in-law, **(uncles-in-law)**, aangetroude oom.
uncle'rical, nie van 'n geestelike nie, onklerikaal.
unclimb'able, on(be)klimbaar.
unclipped', ongesnoei(d); onafgeknip.
uncloak', die mantel afhaal; ontmasker.
unclog', (-ged), vrymaak; bevry, oopmaak.
unclose', ontsluit, oopmaak.
unclosed', oop, ontsluit.
unclothe', uittrek, ontklee.
uncloud'ed, onbewolk.
unclutt'er, skoonmaak, bevry, *~ ed*, onbevange (gees); netjies, sonder rommel.
unc'o, (n) (-s), vreemdeling; (a) onbekend, vreemd; (adv) buitengewoon, erg, vreemd.

uncock', in rus bring (geweer); ontspan; die (hoed)rand afslaan; ~ *your wrist*, maak jou pols weer reguit (gholf).
uncoff'ined, ongekis, sonder kis.
uncoil', afrol, losdraai.
uncoined', ongemunt.
uncollect'ed, nie versamel nie; nie in ontvangs geneem nie; nie ingevorder nie; verward.
uncol'oured, ongekleur(d); onopgesmuk.
uncombed', ongekam, deurmekaar.
uncombin'able, onverenigbaar.
uncombined', vry, onverbind.
uncome-at'-able, onbereikbaar, ongenaakbaar.
uncome'ly, onbevallig, onaantreklik.
uncom'fortable, ongemaklik, ongerieflik, nie op jou gemak nie; ~ **ness**, ongerieflikheid, ongemaklikheid.
uncom'forted, ongetroos.
uncommand'ed, sonder opdrag, sonder bevel.
uncommen'dable, nie aan te beveel nie.
uncommer'cial, sonder handelsgees, in stryd met handelsgewoontes.
uncommis'erated, onbetreur(d).
uncommitt'ed, nie bedrewe nie, ongedaan; nie toevertrou nie; vry, ongebonde.
uncomm'on, ongewoon, seldsaam, buitengewoon; ~ **ly**, buitengewoon, verbasend; ~ **ness**, ongewoonheid.
uncommun'icable, nie mededeelbaar nie; onkommunikeerbaar.
uncommun'icative, stil, teruggetrokke, swygsaam, onmededeelsaam, terughoudend; ~ **ness**, terughoudendheid, swygsaamheid.
uncompan'ionable, ongesellig.
uncomplain'ing, berustend, gelate; nie klaerig nie; ~ **ly**, gelate, berustend; ~ **ness**, gelatenheid, berusting.
uncomplet'ed, onvoltooi(d), onafgewerk.
uncom'plicated, eenvoudig, nie ingewikkeld nie.
uncomplimen'tary, sonder komplimente, onvriendelik.
uncomply'ing, oninskiklik, onhandelbaar.
uncompound'ed, enkelvoudig, nie samegestel(d) nie.
uncomprehending, nie-begrypend, onbegrypend.
uncom'promising, onplooibaar, onbuigsaam, onversetlik; ontoegeeflik, oninskiklik; beginselvas.
unconcealed', nie verberg nie, onverborge, oop, openlik.
unconcern', onverskilligheid, kalmte, bedaardheid, traak-my-nieagtigheid, louheid, onbekommerdheid.
unconcern'ed, doodgerus, perdgerus, houtgerus, onbevange; onverskillig, onbekommerd, traak-my-nieagtig; *be* ~ *about*, jou dit niks aantrek nie; houtgerus (ongeërg, traak-my-nieagtig) wees; ~ **ly**, losweg, ongeërg.
unconcil'iatory, onversoenlik.
uncondemned', onveroordeel(d).
uncondi'tional, onvoorwaardelik.
unconfessed', nie bely nie, onbelede; nie gebieg nie.
unconfined', op vrye voet; onbeperk.
unconfirmed', onbevestig, ongestaaf; nie (as lidmaat) aangeneem nie.
unconform'able, onkonformeerbaar; ongelykvormig; onooreenkomstig, strydig; onreëlmatig, diskordant.
unconform'ity, ongelykvormigheid; onbestaanbaarheid.
uncongealed', ongestol, nie verstyf nie.
uncongen'ial, ongelyksoortig; onsimpatiek; ongepas, strydig met.
unconnect'ed, onverbonde; onsamehangend; in geen verband nie; alleenstaande, sonder verwante of betrekkinge; ~ **ness**, onsamehangendheid.
unconq'uerable, onoorwinklik, onoorwinbaar.
unconq'uered, onoorwonne.
unconscien'tious, gewetenloos; nie nougeset nie, traag, slap.
uncon'scionable, gewetenloos; onredelik, onbillik, onregverdig, buitensporig.
uncon'scious, (n): *the* ~, die onbewuste; (a) onbewus, gevoelloos; bewusteloos, katswink, flou, buite wete; ~ **ly**, onbewus; onopsetlik, onwetend; ~ **ness**, onbewustheid; bewusteloosheid.
uncon'secrated, ongewy.
unconsid'ered, nie in aanmerking geneem nie; buite beskouing gelaat; ondeurdag; onbelangrik.
unconsoled', ongetroos.
unconstitu'tional, onkonstitusioneel, ongrondwettig; ~ **'ity**, ongrondwetlikheid.
unconstrained', ongedwonge, los, vry; natuurlik, onbevange.
unconstraint', losheid, ongedwongenheid; onbevangenheid.
unconsumed', onverteer(d), onverbrand.
uncon'summated, onvoltooi(d), onvolvoer(d).
uncontam'inated, onbesmet, onbesoedel(d), rein.
uncon'templated, onvoorsien; onverwag; onbedink, onbedag.
uncontest'ed, onbetwis; onbestrede; ~ *election*, onbestrede verkiesing.
uncontradict'ed, onweerlê; onweersproke.
uncontrollabil'ity, onbeheerbaarheid, onbedwingbaarheid; onbestuurbaarheid.
uncontroll'able, onbedwingbaar, onbeheerbaar, onbedaarlik; onbestuurbaar (motor).
uncontrolled', onbedwonge; onbeheers; onbeteuel(d); onbelemmer(d); bandeloos; onbeheer, beheerloos.
uncontrover'sial, onomstrede.
uncon'troverted, onbetwis.
unconven'tional, sonder pligpleginge, informeel, natuurlik, onkonvensioneel, vry, ongewoon.
unconvers'able, ongesellig, ongeskik vir die omgang.
unconvert'ed, onbekeerd; onvervyf (rugby).
unconvert'ible, nie omsetbaar nie.
unconvict'ed, onveroordeeld.
unconvinced', onoortuig.
unconvinc'ing, onoortuigend.
uncooked', ongekook, rou.
uncoop'erative, nie tegemoetkomend nie, ontoeskietlik.
uncoor'dinated, ongekoördineer(d).
uncork', ontkurk, die prop uittrek; lug gee aan.
uncorrect'ed, nie nagesien nie, onverbeter(d).
uncorrob'orated, onbevestig, ongestaaf.
uncorrup'ted, onbedorwe.
uncount'able, ontelbaar.
uncount'ed, ongetel; talloos.
uncou'ple, afhaak; losmaak; afkoppel, ontkoppel.
uncourt'eous, onbeleef, onhoflik.
uncourt'ly, lomp, onbeleef, baar, onbeskaaf.
uncouth', onbehoue; onbeleef; ru, grof, onbeskaaf, ongeskik, onhandig, japierig, japieagtig, torrerig; ~ **ness**, ongeskiktheid, ongepoetsheid.
uncov'er, ontdek, oopmaak; die deksel wegneem; kaal maak; ontbloot; ~ **ed**, oop, bloot; ongedek (dier); ~ *ed wire*, kaal draad.
uncov'eted, ongevra(ag); onbegeer(d); nie verlang nie.
uncreas'able, kreukelvas, kreukelvry.
uncreat'ed, ongeskape.
uncrit'ical, onkrities; goedgelowig.
uncrossed', ongekruis; ongedwarsboom, onbelemmer(d); *an* ~ *cheque*, 'n ongekruiste tjek.
uncrown', van die kroon beroof, die kroon ontneem; ~ **ed**, ongekroon; ontkroon.
uncrush'able, onbreekbaar; kreukelvry.
unc'tion, salwing; smeersel, oliesel; salwende vleitaal; geveinsde geesdrif; *administer EXTREME* ~, die laaste oliesel toedien; *this is* ~ *to his SOUL*, dit is salf op sy wonde.
unc'tuous, salfagtig, vetterig; salwend; *BE* ~, salwend (skynvroom) wees; ~ *OILS*, vetolies; ~ *RECTITUDE*, salwende vroomheid; ~ **ly**, glad, salwend; ~ **ness**, selfvoldaanheid, salwing.
unculled', ongesorteer(d); nie uitgesoek nie.
uncult'ivable, onbewerkbaar; onbeskaafbaar.
uncul'tivated, onbebou; onbewerk; onontwikkel(d); nie aangekweek nie; onbeskaaf(d).
uncul'tured, onbeskaaf(d); onbebou; kultuurloos.
uncurbed', ongebreidel, ongetem.
uncurl', ontkrul, die krul uithaal; reguit maak.
uncurtailed', onverkort; nie ingekort nie.

uncus'tomary, ongewoon, ongebruiklik.
uncus'tomed, belastingvry, doeanevry.
uncut', ongekerf (tabak); ongesny; onoopgesny (boek); ongeslyp (glas); ongeslyp (diamant).
undam'aged, onbeskadig; ongeskonde; heel, ongehawend.
undamped', ongedemp; onverminder(d).
undat'ed, ongedagteken, ongedateer; onbeperk.
undaunt'ed, onversaag, onverskrokke, onvervaard, stoutmoedig, onbeskroomd, onbevrees; nie afgeskrik nie; ~ *by difficulties*, nie afgeskrik deur moeilikhede nie; ~ **ness**, onbevreesdheid, onverskrokkenheid, onversaagdheid.
undebauched', onbedorwe.
undec'agon, elfhoek; ..ca'gonal, elfhoekig.
undecahed'ral, elfvlakkig.
undecahed'ron, elfvlak.
undecayed', onverwelk; nie vergaan nie.
undecay'ing, onverganklik, ewigdurend, onsterflik.
undeceive', uit 'n droom help, uit 'n dwaling help, beter inlig, ontgogel, ontnugter.
undecep'tion, ontnugtering, ontgogeling.
undecid'ed, onbeslis; weifelend, besluiteloos; *leave the matter* ~, iets in die midde laat.
undeciph'erable, onontsyferbaar, onleesbaar.
undecked', onversier(d); sonder dek, oop.
undeclared', onverklaar(d); onuitgesproke; versweë.
undeclin'able, onverbuigbaar.
underlined', overboë.
undec'orated, onversier(d).
undecort'icated, ongeskil; nie ontbas nie.
undefeat'ed, onverslaan.
undefend'ed, onverdedig, weerloos; ~ *action*, versteksaak.
undefiled', onbesmet, onbevlek, onbesoedel(d).
undefin'able, onbepaalbaar, onomskryfbaar; ~ **ness**, onomskryfbaarheid.
undefined', onbepaal(d), onbestem(d), vaag.
undeliv'erable, onbestelbaar, nie aflewerbaar nie.
undelivered', onafgelewer, onbesorg; nie verlos nie.
undemand'ing, beskeie.
undemocrat'ic, ondemokraties.
undemon'strable, onbewysbaar.
undemon'strative, gereserveer(d), geslote, toe, terughoudend.
undeni'able, onloënbaar, onteenseglik, onweerlegbaar, onmiskenbaar.
undenomina'tional, nie-sektaries; neutraal.
undepend'able, onbetroubaar, onberekenbaar, geen staat op te maak nie.
undeplored', onbetreur(d).
undepraved', onbedorwe.
un'der, (a) onder=, onderste; (adv) onder, onderkant; (prep) onder; benede; kragtens; ~ *ARMS*, onder die wapens, gewapen; ~ *ARREST*, in hegtenis; ~ *one's BREATH*, fluisterend; ~ *the CIRCUMSTANCES*, in die omstandighede; ~ *CONSTRUCTION*, in aanbou, ~ *COVER*, onder dekking; in die geheim; *land* ~ *CULTIVATION*, bewerkte land; *DOWN* ~, aan die ander kant van die wêreld; Australië; ~ *DURESS*, onder dwang; ~ *FIRE*, in 'n geveg, onder vuur; ~ *one's HAND*, onder jou hand; geteken, verseël; ~ *my HAND and seal*, onder my hand en seël; ~ *an HOUR*, binne 'n uur; ~ *the INFLUENCE (of drink)*, dronk; ~ *LOCK and key*, agter slot en grendel; ~ *MAIZE*, beplant met mielies; ~ *PENALTY of*, op straf van; *land* ~ *the PLOUGH*, grond onder die ploeg; ~ *his own POWER*, op eie krag; ~ *REPAIR*, besig om herstel te word; ~ *the ROSE*, in die geheim; ~ *SAIL*, onder seil; in beweging; ~ *SENTENCE of death*, ter dood veroordeel; ~ *SEVENTEEN*, onder sewentien; ~ *WATER*, onder water; ~ *WAY*, op pad; op koms; aan die gang; ~ *his father's WILL*, volgens sy vader se testament.
underachieve', onderpresteer.
underachieve'ment, lae prestasie, onderprestasie.
underact', swak speel (toneel), onderspeel.
un'deractivity, verslapping.
underage', onmondig, minderjarig; te jonk.
un'deragent, onderagent, subagent.
un'derarm, onder die arm; onderlangs.

underbaked', rou, nie deurgebak nie.
un'derbelly, (..bellies), onderpens.
underbid', (~ or ..bad(e), ~ or -den), minder bie; te min bie; onderbie; ~ **ding**, onderbieding.
un'derblanket, onderkombers.
un'derboil, onderkook, nie genoeg kook nie (stroop).
un'derbodice, onderlyfie.
underbred', onopgevoed; nie volbloed nie.
un'derbrowned, nie bruin genoeg nie.
un'derbrush = **undergrowth**.
un'dercarriage, onderstel; landingstoestel.
un'dercast, korttelling.
un'dercharge, (n) te lae prys; te swak lading; (v) te min vra, te min laat betaal; te swak laai (battery).
un'dercloth, onderkleed.
underclothed', nie voldoende geklee nie.
un'derclothes, **un'derclothing**, onderklere.
un'derclub', (-bed), die afstand onderskat (gholf).
un'dercoat, onderlaag; onderbaadjie.
un'dercoating, grondverf, onderlaag.
un'derconsumption, onderonsumpsie, onderverbruik.
un'der-cook[1], (n) onderkok.
undercook'[2], (v) te min kook; ~**ed**, ongaar, rou.
undercool'ing, onderkoeling.
un'dercurrent, onderstroom; verborge strekking, neiging.
un'dercut[1], (n) lendestuk.
un'dercut[2], (n) optrekhou, opskepskoot (gholf).
undercut'[3], (v) (~), 'n lughou slaan, opskep (gholf).
undercut'[4], (v) (~), ondergrawe; onderkruip; verdring (deur laer pryse); te min vra (pryse); groef (swels), ~**ting**, uitkalwing; onderbieding; onderkruipery.
un'derdeck, benededek, onderdek.
un'derdevel'oped, onderontwikkel(d); swak ontwikkel(d), agterlik; ~ *country*, ontwikkelingsland.
un'derdevel'opment, onderontwikkeling.
underdo', (..did, ..done), halfgaar maak; oorbeklemtoon.
un'derdog, die lydende party, die onderdrukte, *be the* ~, die lydende party wees.
un'derdone[1], (n) te klein dosis.
underdone'[2], (a) halfgaar, rouerig, bloederig, bloedrou.
underdone'[3], (a) oorbeklemtoon.
un'derdose[1], (n) te klein dosis, te min.
underdose'[2], (v) 'n te klein dosis gee.
un'derdrain[1], (n) sugsloot.
underdrain'[2], (v) onder die grond dreineer.
un'derdress[1], (n) onderklere.
underdress'[2], (v) te dun aantrek; te min aantrek.
underem'phasis, onderbeklemtoning.
underem'phasize, onderbeklemtoon.
underemploy'ment, werkskaarste.
underes'timate, (n) onderskatting; geringskatting; (v) geringskat; te laag skat, ~ *something*, te lig oor iets dink; iets onderskat.
underestima'tion, onderskatting; geringskatting.
underex'ercised, sonder genoeg oefening.
underexpose', onderbelig, te kort belig.
underexpo'sure, onderbeligting.
underfed', ondervoed.
underfeed', (..fed), ondervoed, te min kos gee; ~ **ing**, ondervoeding.
underfoot', onder die voet; *TRAMPLE* ~, (onder die voete) vertrap; *be TRAMPLED* ~, onder die voete raak; vertrap word.
un'derframe, onderstel.
un'dergarment, stuk onderklere; onderkleed.
undergo', (..went, ..gone), ondergaan; ly, deurstaan, verduur, ervaar.
un'dergrade, ondergraads, minderwaardig.
un'dergrad'uate, (n) ongegradueerde; (a) voorgraads.
undergraduette', vroulike ongegradueerde.
un'derground, (n) ondergrond; ondergrondse trein, moltrein; *go* ~, onderduik, wegkruip; afgaan (in myn); (a) ondergronds, onderaards; in die geheim; ~ **engineering**, diepbou; ~ **ice**, grondys; ~ **movement**, geheime beweging; ~ **railway**, ondergrondse spoorweg, molspoorweg; ~ **water**, grondwater.

undergrown', nie volgroei nie, onuitgegroei, verpot.
un'dergrowth, ruigte, kreupelhout, struikgewas, fyn= ruigte; verpotheid.
un'derhand, (a) agterbaks; heimlik; geniepsig, onder= langs, onderduims; onderhands; (adv) stilletjies, agteraf; *serve* ~, onderlangs afslaan; ~ **bowling**, onderhandse boulwerk; ~ **contract**, onderhandse kontrak; ~ **ed**, onderduims, agterbaks; met te min kragte; ~ **service**, onderhandse afslaan.
underhung', vooruitstekend, uitsteek=.
underinflat'ed, te pap.
underinsur'ance, onderversekering.
underinsure', onderverseker.
underinsured', te laag verseker.
un'derjaw, onderkakebeen, onderkaak.
un'derking, onderkoning.
un'derlay¹, (n) onderlegsel; helling; onderlêer.
underlay'², (v) (..laid), onderlê, stut, steun.
un'derlayer, onderlaag.
underlet', (~), onder die waarde verhuur; onderver= huur.
underlie', (..lay, ..lain), tot grondslag hê; onder lê.
un'derline¹, (n) buiklyn.
underline'², (v) onderstreep; aanstreep.
un'derlinen, ondergoed; onderlinne.
un'derling, ondergeskikte, handlanger.
un'derlip, onderlip.
underly'ing, daaronder geleë, onderliggend; grond=, dieperliggend; ~ **cause**, grondoorsaak; ~ **idea**, grondgedagte; ~ **principle**, grondbeginsel; ~ **rock**, grondgesteente.
un'derman¹, (n) (..men), iem. laer in rang.
underman'², (v) (-ned), te swak beman; ~ **ned**, nie vol= doende beman nie.
un'der-master, ondermeester.
undermen'tioned, ondergenoemde, onderstaande.
undermine', ondermyn; ondergrawe; inkalf; in die ge= heim werk; sloop; ~ **r**, ondermyner, ondergrawer.
un'dermost, onderste, benedenste.
un'dernamed, ondergenoemd(e).
underneath', (n) onderkant; (a) onderste; benede=; (adv) onder; (prep) benede, onder, onderkant.
un'dernote, gedempte toon.
undernour'ish, ondervoed; ~ **ed**, ondervoed; ~ **ment**, ondervoeding.
un'derofficer, onderoffisier.
underpaid', sleg betaal, te min betaal.
un'derpants, onderbroek.
un'derpart, onderdeel.
un'derpass, (-es), duikweg.
underpay', (..paid), te min betaal; onvoldoende fran= keer; ~ **ment**, onderbetaling, onvoldoende beta= ling.
underpeo'pled, *kyk* **underpopulated**.
un'derpillow, onderkussing; peul, bolster.
underpin', (-ned), stut; ~ **ning**, onderstutting.
un'derplot, ondergeskikte intrige, byhandeling.
underpoliced', met onvoldoende polisie.
underpop'ulated, nie voldoende bevolk nie.
underprice', 'n te lae prys bied; 'n laer prys vra (as).
underpriv'ileged, minderbevoorreg, onderbevoorreg.
underprize', te laag waardeer.
underproduc'tion, geringe produksie, onderproduk= sie.
un'derproof, onder normale sterkte (alkohol).
underprop', (-ped), onderstut, steun.
underquote', laer noteer as, 'n laer prys opgee.
underrate', onderskat; minag; te laag waardeer.
underripe', nie heeltemal ryp nie, halfryp.
underrun'¹, (n) onderopbrengs.
underrun'², (v) (..ran, ~), onderdeur loop.
undersat'urated, onversadig.
undersatura'tion, onderversadiging.
underscore', onderstreep.
un'dersea, ondersees; ~ **s**, onder die see.
un'der-secretary, (..ries), ondersekretaris.
undersell', (..sold), goedkoper verkoop; onderkruip, onder die markprys verkoop; ~ **er**, prysbederwer; ~ **ing**, onderkruiping.
un'derset¹, (n) onderstroom.
underset'², (v) (~), steun, onderstut.
undersexed', seksueel ontwikkeld(d).

un'dersheet, onderlaken.
un'der-sheriff, onderbalju.
un'dershirt, onderhemp.
undershoot', (..**shot**), te kort land; te kort skiet; ~ *the mark*, te gou grondvat, te kort land.
undershot', te kort; terugdalend; ~ **jaw**, swak ken, visbek; ~ **wheel**, onderslagrat.
un'derside, onderkant.
undersigned', ondergetekende.
undersized', onder die middelbare grootte, onder die maat.
un'derskirt, onderrok.
underslung', hang=, onder aangebring; ~ **cabin**, hangkajuit; ~ **motor**, hangmotor; ~ **radiator**, hangverkoeler.
undersold', goedkoper verkoop; *kyk* **undersell**.
understaffed', met te min personeel.
understamped', met te min seëls.
understand', (..**stood**), verstaan, deurgrond, snap, begryp, vat; hoor, verneem, die indruk kry; meen, veronderstel, stilswygend aanneem, opvat; ~ *ABOUT*, verstaan; *AM I to* ~ *that* ...?, moet ek daaruit aflei dat ...?; *what do you* ~ *BY?*, wat verstaan jy onder?; *I was GIVEN to* ~, my is te verstaan gegee; ek is onder die indruk gebring; *it IS to be understood*, dis te begrype; *NOW* ~ *me*, ver= staan my nou goed; ~ **able**, begryplik, verstaan= baar; ~ **ably**, begryplikerwys.
understand'ing, (n) verstandhouding, afspraak; skik= king; verstand, begrip, kennis; ooreenkoms; *COME to an* ~, tot 'n skikking kom; *MEN of* ~, verstandi= ge manne; ~ *OF*, insig in; *ON the* ~ *that*, met dien verstande dat; *it PASSES my* ~, dis bo my vuur= maakplek; dit gaan my verstand te bowe; *PEOPLE without* ~, mense sonder verstand; *SLOW of* ~, toe, bot; *SLOWNESS of* ~, hardleersheid; stadige begrip; *on THIS* ~, op dié voorwaarde; (a) verstan= dig, skrander; simpatiek, begrypend.
understate', versag, verklein; nie die volle waarheid meedeel nie; te laag opgee; onderbeklemtoon; ~ **ment**, onderskatting, verkleining; te lae opgawe; onderbeklemtoning; *that IS an* ~ *ment*, dit sê ver te min; *the* ~ *ment of the YEAR*, die onderskatting v.d. jaar.
understock', te min voorraad hê; te min vee hê; ~ **ed**, onderbewei.
understood', verstaan; vanselfsprekend; *that IS* ~, dit spreek vanself; *it IS* ~, daar word verneem dat; *MAKE oneself* ~, jou verstaanbaar maak; *it MUST be clearly* ~, dit moet duidelik verstaan word; *the NOUN is* ~, die selfstandige naam= woord is verswyg; *I* ~ *you to SAY*, my indruk was dat jy gesê het; *an* ~ *THING*, iets vanselfspre= kends.
un'derstrapper, handlanger, ondergeskikte.
un'derstratum, onderlaag.
understrung', te slap gespan.
un'derstudy, (n) (..dies), dubbelspeler, plaasvervan= ger; (v) (..died), 'n rol instudeer (as plaasvervan= ger); vervang.
undersubscribed', onvolteken.
un'dersurface, (n) onderkant; (a) ondergronds.
undertake', (..**took, -n**), onderneem; aanvat, aanpak; waarborg; jou verbind, vas belowe.
un'dertaker, lykbesorger, begrafnisondernemer; on= dernemer, aannemer.
undertak'ing, onderneming; verpligting, verbintenis; lykbesorging; ~ **business**, begrafnisonderneming; ~ **parlour**, roukamer.
un'dertenancy, onderhuur.
un'dertenant, onderhuurder.
un'derthings, onderklere, ondergoed.
undertimed', onderbelig (foto); te kort gekook.
un'dertone, (n) gedempte toon, gesmoorde toon, fluistertoon, fluisterstem; getemperde kleur; onder= toon (aandelemark); *in an* ~, met gedempte stem, met fluisterstem.
undertone', (v) te swak fikseer; fluister.
undertrump', laer troef, ondertroef.
undervalua'tion, onderskatting, te lae waardering.
underval'ue, onderskat; minag; te laag waardeer; ~ **r**, onderskatter; minagter.

un'dervest, onderhempie, frokkie.
un'derwater, (n) grondwater; (a) onder water; onder=water=; ondersees.
un'derwear, onderklere, ondergoed.
un'derweight, (n) ondergewig; (a) onder die gewig.
un'derwood, kreupelhout, ruigte, struikgewas, fyn=ruigte.
un'derworld, onderwêreld; teëvoeters, antipode; skorriemorrie.
underwrite', (..wrote, ..written), onderskryf, onder=teken; assureer, verseker.
un'derwriter, ondertekenaar; versekeraar, assura=deur; garandeerder, garant.
un'derwriting, onderskrywing; versekering; garande=ring, waarborg.
undescribed', onbeskryf.
undescried', onontdek.
undeserved', onverdiend.
undeserv'ing, onverdienstelik, onwaardig; *be ~ of praise*, geen lof verdien nie.
undesigned', onopsetlik, nie voorbedag nie; ~ ly, on=opsetlik, ongeërg, onbedoel(d).
undesign'ing, opreg, argeloos.
undesirabil'ity, ongewensheid; onwenslikheid.
undesir'able, (n) ongewenste persoon; (a) onwenslik; ongewens, onbegeerlik.
undesired', ongewens, ongevra(ag).
undesir'ous, nie verlangend nie, onverskillig.
undetach'able, onafneembaar.
undetect'ed, verborge, onontdek.
undeterm'ined, onbeslis, onbepaald, onbeslund, on=uitgemaak; onseker.
undeterred', onverskrokke, nie afgeskrik nie; *be ~ by*, jou nie laat afskrik nie deur.
undevel'oped, onontwikkel(d); onontgonne, onont=gin (land); dof (vrugte); agterlik.
undev'iating, reguit; onwankelbaar, onversetlik, on=wrikbaar; gereeld, konstant.
un'dies, onderklere, ondergoed.
undigest'ed, onverteer(d); onverwerk; onryp; onbe=kook.
undigestibil'ity, onverteerbaarheid.
undigest'ible, onverteerbaar.
undig'nified, onwaardig, sonder waardigheid.
undilut'ed, onverdun; onvermeng.
undimin'ished, onverminder(d); onverswak.
undimmed', onverduister(d), helder.
undine', waternimf.
undiplomat'ic, ondiplomaties, taktloos, nie taktvol nie.
undirect'ed, sonder leiding; rigtingloos, koersloos; sonder adres.
undirig'ible, onbestuurbaar.
undisband'ed, onafgedank.
undiscerned', onopgemerk.
undiscern'ible, onsigbaar, onwaarneembaar.
undiscern'ing, nie skerpsiende nie; kortsigtig; sonder onderskeidingsvermoë.
undischarged', nie ontslaan nie; onafbetaal(d); nie af=geskiet nie; onafgelaai.
undis'ciplined, ongeoefend; sonder tug, tugteloos, ongedissiplineer(d).
undisclosed', versweë, onvermeld.
undiscov'erable, onontdekbaar.
undiscov'ered, onontdek.
undiscrim'inating, nie onderskeidend nie, nie skerp=sinnig nie; ~ ly, voor die voet.
undiscussed', onbesproke, onbehandel(d), onbe=spreek.
undisguised', onbewimpel(d), oop; onvermom; op=reg, openhartig; onverbloem(d).
undismayed', onverskrokke, onversaag.
undisposed', ongeneë; onaangewend, sonder dat daaroor beskik is; ~ *of*, onverkoop.
undispu'table, onbetwisbaar.
undisput'ed, onbetwis, onbestrede, ongewraak.
undissem'bled, ongeveins, opreg, eerlik.
undissolv'able, onoplosbaar.
undissolved', onopgelos; nie ontbind nie; onge=smelt.
undisting'uishable, onherkenbaar; nie te onderskei nie; eenders.

undisting'uished, onduidelik; nie beroemd nie, onver=maard; onaansienlik.
undistrib'uted, onuitgekeer, onverdeel(d); ~ *PRO*=*FITS*, onuitgekeerde (onverdeelde, onaangewen=de) winste; ~ *-profits TAX*, belasting op onuitge=keerde winste.
undisturbed', kalm, bedaard; ongehinder(d); effe; on=gesteurd; ~ *use*, ongestoorde gebruik.
undivers'ified, eentonig; eenvormig; eenders.
undivid'able, onverdeelbaar.
undivid'ed, onverdeeld, geheel; ~ *attention*, onver=deelde aandag.
undivorced', ongeskei.
undivulged', geheim, nie bekend nie, versweë; onont=sluier(d).
undo', (..did, ..done), oopmaak, losmaak, losbind, losknoop; ongedaan maak; tot niet maak, te niet doen; in die ongeluk stort, te gronde rig; herstel, weer goedmaak; ~ *past actions*, die verlede onge=daan maak.
undock', uit die dok bring.
undocked'[1], uit die dok gebring.
undocked'[2], nie stompstert nie.
undo'er: ~ er, verwoester; verleier; ~ ing, verderf, onge=luk, ondergang; (dier) losmaak; tenietdoening.
undomes'tic, onhuislik; ~ ated, ongetem, wild.
undone', ongedaan; los; verlore, geruïneer; *BE* ~, ge=ruïneer wees; *BECOME* ~, losraak; *what is DONE, cannot be* ~ , gedane sake het geen keer nie; *a TASK* ~ , 'n onuitgevoerde taak.
undoubt'ed, ongetwyfeld, ontwyfelbaar, stellig, se=ker; ~ ly, ongetwyfeld, ontwyfelbaar, stellig; seker, sonder twyfel.
undrain'able, onuitputlik; nie droog te maak nie.
undramat'ic, ondramaties.
undraped', ongekleed, ongedrapeer(d); naak.
undrawn', nie geteken nie; nie getap nie; nie getrek nie.
undread'ed, ongevrees.
undreamed', undreamt', ongedroom, nooit verwag nie; ongehoord.
un'dress[1], (n) môrekleed; négligé; huisklere, eenvou=dige klere; ~ *uniform*, klein tenue.
undress'[2], (v) uittrek, ontklee; ontswagtel; ~ ed, on=gekleed, uitgetrek, onaangetrek; onverbind; onbe=werk; ongekap (klip); ~ ing cubicle, ontkleehokkie, kleedkamertjie.
undried', ongedroog, nat.
undrilled', ongeoefen(d).
undrink'able, ondrinkbaar.
undue', onbehoorlik; buitensporig, oordrewe, oor=matig, onbetaamlik; nog nie vervul nie; ~ *haste*, buitensporige haas.
un'dulant, golwend; ~ **fever**, maltakoors.
un'dulate, (v) golf, onduleer; laat tril; (a) gegolf, golwend.
un'dulating, (n) gegolf, (a) golwend, golfvormig, wegdeinend.
undula'tion, golwing, golfbeweging, ondulasie.
un'dulatory, golwend; golf=; golfvormig; ~ *MO*=*TION*, golfbeweging; ~ *THEORY*, golwingste=orie, golfteorie.
undul'y, oormatig, meer as nodig, oordrewe, te veel; ten onregte.
undut'iful, ongehoorsaam; oneerbiedig; nalatig, plig=vergete; ~ ness, ongehoorsaamheid; oneerbiedig=heid.
undyed', ongeverf, ongekleur(d).
undy'ing, ewig, onverganklik, onsterflik.
unearned', onverdien(d); ~ *income*, stille inkomste.
unearth', opgrawe; openbaar, blootlê; (wild) uit 'n lê=plek jaag; opdiep, aan die lig bring; ~ ly, bo(we)na=tuurlik, spookagtig, grieselig; skrikwekkend; *at an* ~ *ly hour*, onmenslik vroeg.
uneas'iness, besorgdheid; ongemak; ongerustheid.
uneas'y, ongemaklik; onrustig; ongerus; nie op jou gemak nie; besorg; lastig; woelig; onvas (skip); *feel* ~ *ABOUT the children*, ongerus voel oor die kin=ders; *I felt* ~ *AT the thought of . . .*, ek het onrustig gevoel by die gedagte dat . . . ; ~ *LIES the head that wears the crown*, vir regeerders is daar min rus; 'n regeerder is sy rus kwyt.

uneatable 1338 *unfinished*

uneat'able, oneetbaar.
uneat'en, ongeëet.
uneclipsed', nie verduister nie; nie oortref nie.
uneconom'ic, onekonomies; ~ **al**, onekonomies, ver= kwistend.
uned'ifying, onstigtelik.
une'ducable, onopvoedbaar.
uned'ucated, onopgevoed, ongeletterd.
uneffaced', onuitgewis.
unelu'cidated, nie toegelig nie, onopgehelder.
unembar'rassed, ongedwonge, nie verleë nie, on= geërg, onbelemmer(d); onbeswaard, sonder skuld.
unembell'ished, nie verfraai nie, onversier(d).
unembroid'ered, ongeborduur(d).
unemo'tional, sonder gevoel, nie emosioneel nie, on= aandoenlik; onbewoë.
unemphat'ic, sonder nadruk; flou, swak.
unemploy'able, (n) iem. aan wie geen werk gegee kan word nie; (a) ongeskik vir werk; onbruikbaar; ~ **ness**, ongeskiktheid vir werk; onbruikbaarheid.
unemployed', (n) werklose; (a) werkloos, arbeidloos; ongebruik.
unemploy'ment, werkloosheid; ~ **benefit**, werkloos= heidsuitkering; ~ **fund**, werkloosheidsfonds; ~ **in**= **surance**, werkloosheidsversekcring.
unencum'bered, onbelas, onbeswaar(d), sonder ver= band; vry, los.
unend'ing, eindeloos, oneindig.
unendorsed', nie-geëndosseer.
unendowed', nie begiftig nie; onbegaaf.
unendur'able, ondraaglik.
unenforce'able, onuitvoerbaar; onafdwingbaar.
unenforced', onuitgevoer; nie afgedwing nie.
unenforcibil'ity, onuitvoerbaarheid; onafdwingbaar= heid.
unenfran'chised, sonder stemreg, nie stemgeregtig nie.
unengaged', vry, ongebonde; nie besig nie, onbeset; nie verloof nie; onbespreek.
un-Eng'lish, onengels.
unenlight'ened, dom, oningelig, onkundig.
unenliv'ened, onopgewek.
unentailed', onvervreemdbaar, vry.
unen'terprising, sonder ondernemingsgees, sonder inisiatief.
unentertain'ing, onvermaaklik; vervelend, droog.
unenthusiast'ic, onentoesiasties, sonder geesdrif, flou, lou.
unentombed', onbegrawe.
unen'viable, onbenydenswaardig.
unen'vied, onbenyd.
uneq'uable, onegalig, onegaal, oneffe; veranderlik.
uneq'ual, ongelyk, verskillend; oneffe; ongelykmatig; ~ **to the task**, nie bereken vir die taak nie; nie opge= wasse vir die taak nie; ~ **led**, ongeëwenaard, sonder weerga, onvergelyklik.
unequiv'ocal, ondubbelsinnig, ontwyfelbaar, onom= wonde; ~ **ly**, ondubbelsinnig; ~ **ness**, ondubbel= sinnigheid.
une'rring, seker, onfeilbaar; nooit mis nie; raak.
unescap'able, onontwykbaar, nie te ontgaan nie; on= vermydelik.
unessayed', onbeproef.
unessen'tial, (n) bysaak, bykomstigheid; (a) nie wens= lik nie, onbelangrik, onessensieel.
unestab'lished, ongevestig; nie in vaste diens nie; onbewese.
unesteemed', ongeag.
unes'timable, onskatbaar, onberekenbaar.
unes'timated, onbereken(d).
uneth'ical, oneties.
unevangel'ical, onevangelies.
unevap'orated, onverdamp.
une'ven, ongelyk, oneffe, hobbelagtig; skurf; onge= lykmatig; onewe (getal); hakerig, onegaal; ~ **ness**, oneffenheid, hobbelagtigheid; ~ **number**, ongelyke getal.
unevent'ful, onbelangrik; rustig, onbewoë; *an* ~ *week,* 'n week waarin niks belangriks gebeur het nie.
unexac'ting, nie veeleisend nie.
unexam'ined, nie nagesien nie; nie geëksamineer nie.

unexam'pled, voorbeeldeloos, weergaloos, ongeëwe= naard.
unexcelled', onoortroffe.
unexcep'tionable, sonder fout, onberispelik, onaan= vegbaar, onaantasbaar.
unexcep'tional, nie buitengewoon nie; doodgewoon.
unexcit'ing, nie opwindend nie, vervelend.
unex'ecuted, onuitgevoer, onverrig.
unex'ercised, ongeoefen(d).
unexhaust'ed, onuitgeput.
unexpect'ed, onverwag, onvoorsien, skielik, plotse= ling; ~ **ly**, onverwags, eensklaps, skielik; ~ **ness**, onverwagtheid.
unexpend'ed, onbestede.
unexpen'sive, goedkoop, nie duur nie.
unexper'ienced, nie ondervind nie; onervare.
unexpired', onafgeloop, onverstreke, nie om nie.
unexplained', onverklaar(d).
unexplod'ed, onontplof.
unexplored', onbekend, nie ondersoek nie.
unexposed', nie blootgestel nie, beskut; onbelig.
unexpressed', onuitgesproke, versweë.
unex'purgated, ongesuiwer, ongekuis.
unexting'uished, ongeblus, onuitgedoof.
unexting'uishable, onblusbaar.
unfaced', ongevlak (muur).
unfad'able, onverbleikbaar, kleurvas; onverwelk= baar; onverganklik; onverwelklik.
unfad'ed, onverwelk; onverbleik.
unfad'ing, onverwelkbaar; kleurvas.
unfail'ing, onfeilbaar; onuitputlik; seker.
unfair', oneerlik, onopreg, skelm; partydig; onbillik, onredelik, onregmatig, ongunstig; *by* ~ *means,* op oneerlike wyse; ~ **ness**, oneerlikheid; partydigheid; onbillikheid, onregmatigheid, ongunstigheid.
unfaith'ful, ontrou, troueloos, vals; ongelowig; ~ *to his FRIENDS,* ontrou teenoor sy vriende; ~ *in LOVE,* onstandvastig in liefde; ~ **ness**, ontrouheid, troueloosheid, valsheid.
unfal'tering, standvastig, onwrikbaar, vas; nie weife= lend nie; glad, sonder vassteek.
unfamed', onberoemd.
unfamil'iar, vreemd, ongewoon, onbekend; *a person* ~ *with our customs,* 'n persoon wat onbekend is met ons gewoontes; ~ '**ity**, onbekendheid; onge= woonheid; ongewoonte.
unfa'shionable, ouderwets, nie na die mode nie, ou= modies, oud-modies.
unfash'ioned, ongevorm(d), ongefatsoeneer(d).
unfa'sten, losmaak.
unfa'thered, sonder (erkende) vader; vaderloos.
unfa'therly, onvaderlik.
unfath'omable, onpeilbaar, grondeloos, ondeurgron= delik; ~ **ness**, onpeilbaarheid, ondeurgrondelik= heid.
unfath'omed, ongepeil, onmeetlik; ondeurgrond.
unfav'ourable, ongunstig; ~ **ness**, ongunstigheid.
unfav'ourably, ongunstig.
unfeared', ongevrees.
unfear'ing, onbevrees.
unfeasibil'ity, ondoenlikheid, onpraktiesheid.
unfeas'ible, ondoenlik, onprakties, onuitvoerbaar.
unfeath'ered, ongeveerd.
unfed', ongevoed; ongevoer.
unfeel'ing, ongevoelig, hardvogtig, gevoelloos, dikvellig.
unfeigned', ongeveins, opreg; ~ **ness**, ongeveinsd= heid, opregtheid.
unfelt', ongevoel, ondeurvoel(d).
unfem'inine, onvroulik.
unfenced', onomhein, nie omhein nie; onbeskerm(d).
unferment'ed, ongegis; ~ *wine,* ongegiste wyn.
unfert'ile, onvrugbaar.
unfert'ilized, onvrugbaar; onbevrug, geil (eier).
unfett'er, bevry, losmaak; van boeie bevry, ontboei; ontketen; ~ **ed**, ongeboei(d), ongebonde, vry.
unfil'ial, onkinderlik.
un'filled, ongevul; leeg; ~ *need,* steeds gevoelde behoefte.
unfind'able, onkrybaar, onvindbaar.
unfi'ngered, ongevinger(d), onaangeraak.
unfin'ished, onvoltooi, nie klaar nie; onafgewerk,

onaf, onafgedaan; onafgemaak; ~ *worsted*, pluis=kamstof; ~**ness**, onafgewerktheid, onafgerond=heid.
unfit', (v) **(-ted)**, ongeskik maak; (a) onbekwaam, on=geskik; ongepas; nie gesond nie; ~ *for (human) CONSUMPTION*, oneetbaar; *he is* ~ *to be a PARSON*, hy deug nie vi. predikant nie; ~**ness**, ongeskiktheid; ongesondheid; ~**ted**, ongeskik; nie toegerus nie.
unfitt'ing, onvanpas; nie passend nie; onbetaamlik; ongeskik; *it is* ~, dit pas nie.
unfix', losmaak; ~**ed**, onbepaald; los.
unflagg'ing, onverslap, onverdrote, onverflou; ~ *zeal*, onverdrote ywer.
unflapped', sonder klap.
unflatt'ering, onvleiend.
unfledged', sonder vere; onervare; jonk; onbedrewe.
unflex'ible, onbuigsaam.
unflinch'ing, onverskrokke; onversetlik, onwrikbaar.
unfold', ontvou, ontplooi; uitsprei; uitlê; openbaar, onthul; ~**ing**, blootlegging; verklaring; openba=ring.
unforbear'ing, onverdraagsaam.
unforbidd'en, nie verbied nie.
unforc'ed, ongedwonge, vrywillig; natuurlik.
unford'able, nie deurwaadbaar nie, sonder 'n drif.
unforsee'able, nie te voorsien nie, onvoorspelbaar.
unforeseen', onvoorsien.
unforewarned', ongewaarsku.
unforgett'able, onvergeetlik.
unforgiv'able, onvergeeflik.
unforgiv'en, onvergewe.
unforgiv'ing, onversoenlik.
unforgott'en, onvergete; onvergeetlik.
unformed', ongevorm; vormloos.
unfort'ified, onversterk; weerloos.
unfort'unate, (n) ongelukkige; (a) ongelukkig, ramp=spoedig, onfortuinlik; ~**ly**, ongelukkig; ~**ness**, rampspoedigheid, ongelukkigheid.
unfound'ed, ongegrond; vals; ongevestig; *utterly* ~, uit die lug gegryp; heeltemal ongegrond.
unframed', ongevorm(d); onomlys, ongeraam(d).
unfran'chise, ontkieser; ~**d**, sonder stem, stemloos.
unfrater'nal, onbroederlik.
unfray', uitrafel, losdraai.
unfreeze', ontvries.
unfreez'ing, ontvriesing.
unfrequent'ed, eensaam, onbesog, verlate; onbereis.
unfriend'ed, sonder vriende.
unfriend'liness, onvriendelikheid, onhartlikheid.
unfriend'ly, onvriendelik, stug, onhartlik; ~ *with people*, onvriendelik teenoor mense.
unfrock', as predikant afsit, van die herdersamp onthef.
unfroz'en, onbevrore; ontvries.
unfruit'ful, onvrugbaar; vrugteloos; ~**ness**, onvrug=baarheid; nutteloosheid, vrugteloosheid.
unfulfilled', onvervul(d), onvolvoer(d); onbevredig.
unfund'ed: ~ *debt*, vlottende (ongefundeerde) skuld.
unfurl', uitsprei, ontplooi, oopmaak, ontvou; ~ *co=lours*, 'n vaandel ontplooi.
unfurn'ished, ongemeubileer(d).
unfused'¹, ongesmelt.
unfused'², met die lont uitgehaal.
ungain'liness, onhandigheid, lompheid, slungelagtig=heid.
ungain'ly, lomp, onhandig, onbehoue, onhandel=baar, slungelagtig.
ungall'ant, onhoflik; lafhartig.
ungarn'ished, ongestoffeer(d); onopgesmuk, onver=sier.
unga'rrisoned, sonder garnisoen.
ungath'ered, nie versamel nie; ongepluk.
ungear', ontkoppel, losmaak.
ungen'erous, onedelmoedig; suinig, inhalig.
ungen'ial, onvriendelik, ongesellig, onaangenaam; ongunstig.
ungenteel', onbeleef, onbeskof; nie deftig nie.
ungen'tle, onhoflik, ongemanierd; onwellewend, on=ridderlik; onsag, onvriendelik.
ungen'tlemanly, onwellewend, onfatsoenlik, onge=manierd.

ungen'tly, op ruwe wyse, onsag; onhoflik.
unget-at'-able, onbereikbaar, onbekombaar, ontoe=ganklik.
ungift'ed, sonder talente, talentloos.
ungird', losgord, losmaak.
ungirth', die buikgord losmaak.
unglazed', onverglaas; sonder ruite.
unglove', die handskoene uittrek; sonder handskoene.
unglue', afweek; ontgom.
ungod'liness, goddeloosheid, sondigheid.
ungod'ly, goddeloos, sondig, godvergete.
ungov'ernable, toomloos, onregeerbaar, onbeheers=baar, onbetoombaar, onhandelbaar, woes; ~**ness**, toomloosheid, onhandelbaarheid, onregeerbaar=heid, woestheid.
ungov'erned, regeringloos; toomloos, onbeteueld.
ungrace'ful, onbevallig, lomp, onsierlik, lelik.
ungra'cious, stuitend, onhoflik; onvriendelik; onaan=genaam; onwillig; ~**ness**, onwilligheid; onhoflik=heid; onbeleefdheid.
ungraft'ed, ongeënt.
ungrammat'ical, ongrammatikaal.
ungrate'ful, ondankbaar, onerkentlik; ~**ness**, on=dankbaarheid, onerkentlikheid.
ungrat'ified, onvoldaan, onbevredig.
unground', ongemaal.
unground'ed, ongegrond; ongeaard.
ungrudg'ing, gewillig, gul, van harte gegun; ~**ly**, van harte, gul, sonder voorbehoud; ~**ness**, gulheid, gewilligheid.
u'ngual, nael=; klou=; klouvormig.
unguard'ed, onbewaak, onbeskerm(d); onversigtig, onbedagsaam; ~**ly**, onverhoeds, onbedag; ~**ness**, onbewaakte toestand.
ung'uent, salf, smeersel; olie; strykaol.
ungue'ssed, ongeraai.
ungui'culate, met naels (kloue).
unguid'ed, sonder gids, sonder geleide.
ung'uiform, klouvormig; naelvormig.
ung'ula, (-e), hoef; klou; nael.
ung'ulate, (n) hoefdier; (a) hoefvormig; gehoef, een=hoewig.
ungum', **(-med)**, ontgom; ~**med'**, ongelym.
unhack'neyed, nie afgesaag nie, fris.
unhair', haar-af maak; onthaar, afhaar.
unhal'low, ontheilig; ~**ed**, ongeheilig, goddeloos, onrein.
unham'pered, ongebonde, onbelemmer(d), ongehin=der(d).
unhand', los, loslaat, vrylaat.
unhand'iness, onhandigheid, lompheid.
unhand'some, lelik, onooglik; nie rojaal nie; ongepas.
unhand'y, onhandig, lomp; onhanteerbaar; lastig, moeilik.
unhanged', onopgehang.
unhapp'iness, ongeluk, ellende, hartseer; ongelukkig=heid.
unhapp'y, ongelukkig, hartseer.
unharmed', onbeskadig, onbenadeel(d), veilig, onge=deerd.
unharmo'nious, onwelluidend, onharmonies.
unharn'ess, uitspan, aftuig.
unhatched', onuitgebroei.
unhatt'ed, sonder hoed, hoedloos.
unheal'able, ongeneeslik, onheelbaar.
unhealth'iness, ongesondheid.
unhealth'y, ongesond; onveilig.
unheard', onverhoord; ongehoord, verregaande; ~ *of*, ongehoord, verregaande.
unheat'ed, onverhit, onverwarm.
unheed'ed, onopgemerk, veronagsaam, verwaarloos.
unheed'ful, agteloos, sorgeloos.
unheed'ing, agtelosig, onbekommerd.
unhelp'ful, onbehulpsaam.
unhero'ic, onheroïes.
unhes'itating, vasberade, sonder aarseling, beslis; ~**ly**, volmondig, sonder aarseling.
unhewn', ongekap; ru.
unhidd'en, nie verberg nie, openlik.
unhind'ered, ongehinder(d), onbelemmerd.
unhinge', uit die hingsels lig; krenk; verwar, van stryk bring.

unhinged', van die skarniere af; in die war; kranksin= nig; *his MIND is* ~, sy verstand is gekrenk; *be QUITE* ~, skoon van jou wysie af wees.
unhisto'ric(al), onhistories.
unhitch', afhaak, uitspan; losmaak (toue); uitspan (diere).
unhol'iness, onheiligheid.
unhol'y, onheilig, goddeloos; *an* ~ *mess,* 'n vreeslike gemors.
unhome'ly, onhuislik.
unhon'oured, ongeëer(d).
unhood', die kap afhaal.
unhook', losmaak, afhaak.
unhoped', ongehoop, onverwag; ~ **for**, onverhoop, onverwag.
unhorse', afgooi, uit die saal gooi.
unhoused', sonder huis, dakloos.
unhulled', ongedop; ongeskil.
unhur'ried, langsaam, stadig, bedaard; ~ **ly**, stadig.
unhurt', ongedeerd, onbeseer(d), ongekwes, behoue.
unhusked', ongedop.
unhydrat'ed, ongeblus, ongehidrateer; ~ *lime,* onge= bluste kalk.
unhygien'ic, onhigiënies, ongesond.
Un'iate, Uniaat.
uniax'ial, eenassig.
unicam'eral, met een wetgewende kamer, eenkamer=.
unicap'sular, eenhokkig.
unicell'ular, eensellig.
un'icoloured, effekleurig; eenkleurig.
un'icorn, eenhoring; ~-**fish**, horingvis *(Monoceros)*.
un'icycle, eenwieler.
uniden'tate, eentandig.
unident'ifiable, onherkenbaar; onidentifiseerbaar.
uniden'tified, onherken, nie geïdentifiseer nie.
unidiomat'ic, nie idiomaties nie.
unifi'able, verenigbaar.
unifica'tion, vereniging, eenwording, unifikasie.
uniflor'ous, eenblommig.
unifol'iate, eenbladig.
un'iform¹, (n) uniform; tenue; *in FULL* ~, in groot tenue; *in UNDRESS* ~, in klein tenue; (v) in uni= form steek.
un'iform², (v) eenvormig maak; (a) eenvormig, een= ders, gelykvormig; egalig; onveranderlik, konstant; *a volume* ~ *with the others in the series,* 'n boekdeel wat eenvormig met die ander in die reeks is.
un'iform: ~ **allowance**, uniformtoelae; ~ **cloth**, uniformstof.
un'iform: ~ **'ity**, eenvormigheid, uniformiteit, gelyk= vormigheid, eenheid; egaligheid; ~ **load**, gelyk= matige las; ~ **ly**, deurgaans, onveranderlik; ~ **mix**= **ture**, egalige mengsel; ~ **pressure**, gelykmatige druk.
un'ify, (..fied), verenig, tot een maak, eenheid bring in.
unijug'ate, eenjukkig.
unilat'eral, eensydig; slegs een kant bindend; ~ **ism**, eensydigheid; ~ **'ity**, eensydigheid.
unili'ngual, eentalig; ~ **ism**, eentaligheid.
unillum'inated, onverlig.
unill'ustrated, ongeïllustreer(d).
uniloc'ular, eensellig; eenhokkig.
unima'ginable, ondenkbaar; onbegryplik.
unima'ginative, arm aan fantasie, sonder verbeel= dingskrag, nugter, verbeeldingloos.
unima'gined, ongedink; ondenkbaar.
unimpaired', ongeskaad, onverminder(d), onver= swak, intak, onbeskadig.
unimpa'ssioned, koel, bedaard, nugter.
unimpeach'able, onberispelik, onkreukbaar; onaan= tasbaar, onbetwisbaar, onwraakbaar.
unimpeached', onbeskuldig; onaangetas.
unimped'ed, onbelemmer(d), onverhinder(d); ~ **ness**, onbelemmerdheid.
unimport'ant, onbelangrik.
unimpos'ing, onindrukwekkend.
unimpregnat'ed, onbevrug.
unimpressed', nie beïndruk nie, nie geïmponeer nie; ongestempel(d).
unimpress'ible, onoorreedbaar.
unimpre'ssionable, onvatbaar vir indrukke, onont= vanklik.

unimpress'ive, onindrukwekkend, onbeduidend; ~ **ness**, onbeduidendheid.
unimpro'vable, onverbeterlik.
unimproved', onverbeter(d), onbewerk; nie produk= tief gemaak nie (van land).
unimpugn'able, onaanvegbaar.
unincorp'orated, oningelyf.
uninfest'ed, onbesmet.
unimflamm'able, nie ontvlambaar nie, onbrandbaar.
uninflect'ed, onverboë.
unin'fluenced, onbeïnvloed, onbevooroordeeld, on= partydig.
uninformed', nie op hoogte nie, oningelig.
uninhab'itable, onbewoonbaar.
uninhab'ited, onbewoon(d).
uninhib'ited, uitgelate, onbekommerd; ongebonde.
unini'tiated, (n) oningewyde; (a) oningewyd; onge= sout.
unin'jured, onbeskadig, ongedeerd, onbenadeel(d), ongeskonde.
uninspect'ed, onbesien(s).
uninspired', onbesield.
uninspir'ing, saai, vervelend.
uninstruct'ed, onwetend; ongeletterd; oningelig.
unin'sulated, ongeïsoleer.
uninsurabil'ity, onversekerbaarheid.
uninsur'able, onversekerbaar.
uninsured', onverseker(d), ongedek.
unintell'igent, onbevatlik, dom, onintelligent.
unintelligibil'ity, onverstaanbaarheid.
unintell'igible, onverstaanbaar, onduidelik; ~ *to the audience,* onverstaanbaar vir die gehoor.
unintend'ed, onopsetlik, nie bedoel nie.
uninten'tional, onopsetlik, ongewild, nie opsetlik nie; ~ **ly**, onopsetlik, nie moedswillig nie, per ongeluk.
unin'terested, ongeïnteresseerd, onverskillig; ~ **ness**, onverskilligheid.
unin'teresting, oninteressant, vervelend, droog.
unintermitt'ent, onafgebroke, onverpoos.
uninterred', onbegrawe.
uninterrup'ted, onafgebroke, onbelemmerd; onge= steur(d), ongestoor; onverpoos; ononderbroke; deurlopend (kommentaar); ~ **ness**, onafgebroken= heid; ongestoordheid.
uninves'tigable, onnaspeurlik.
uninvit'ed, ongenooi, ongevra(ag).
uninvit'ing, afstotend, onaanloklik, onaantreklik.
un'ion, unie; vereniging; samestelling; huwelik; ver= binding; verbond, verbintenis, band; eendrag, har= monie, eensgesindheid; aaneenvoeging, koppeling; aansluiting; *U* ~ *coat of ARMS* (hist), Uniewapen; *POSTAL* ~, Posunie; ~ *and PROVINCIAL mat= ters,* uniale en provinsiale sake; ~ *is STRENGTH,* eendrag maak mag; U ~ **Buildings**, Uniegebou; U ~ **Day**, (hist.) Uniedag; ~ **hook**, verbindings= hoek; ~ **ism**, vakbondwese; ~ **ist**, lid van 'n vak= bond; unionis; ~ **ize**, in 'n vakunie organiseer; U ~ **Jack**, Union Jack, Britse vlag; ~ **nut**, koppelmoer; ~ **socket**, koppelsok; ~ **screw**, trekskroef.
unip'arous, wat een kleintjie op 'n keer baar; eentak= kig (plantk.).
unipart'ite, onverdeel(d).
un'iped, eenvoetig.
unipet'alous, eenmantelig.
uniplan'ar, eenvlakkig.
unipol'ar, eenpolig; ~ **'ity**, eenpoligheid.
unique', (n) unikum; (a) enig, ongeëwenaard, uniek, enig in sy soort, eenmalig; ~ **ness**, enigheid.
uni'roned, ongeboei (gevangene); ongestryk (klere).
un'isex, uniseks; ~ **ual**, eenslagtig.
un'ison, harmonie, ooreenstemming; gelykluidend= heid, eenklank; eensgesindheid; *in* ~, in harmonie, eenstemmig, eensgesind.
unis'onance, eenstemmigheid, harmonie.
unis'onant, unis'onous, harmonies, eenstemmig.
uniss'ued, ongeplaas, onuitgegee.
un'it, eenheid; ~ *of ELECTRICITY,* elektriese een= heid; ~ *of FORCE,* krageenheid; ~ *of HEAT,* warmte-eenheid; ~ *of LENGTH,* lengte-eenheid; ~ *of LIGHT,* ligeenheid; ~ *of MEASURE,* maat= eenheid; ~ *of POWER,* krageenheid; *THERMAL* ~, warmte-eenheid; ~ *of TIME,* tydeenheid; ~ *of*

unitable 1341 *unmarketable*

VOLUME, inhoudsmaat; ~ *of WEIGHT*, gewigseenheid; ~ *of WORK*, arbeidseenheid.
unit'able, verenigbaar.
unitar'ian, (n) unitariër; (a) unitaries.
Unitar'ianism, Unitarisme.
un'itary, eenheids=, wat 'n eenheid vorm.
unite', verenig; aaneenvoeg; verbind, saamspan, saamsmelt, byeenvoeg, saamvoeg; vereen, saambind.
unit'ed, verenig, byeen, verbonde, gesamentlik; eendragtig, eendragtiglik; *U~ BRETHREN*, Morawiese Broers, Herrnhutters; ~ *we stand, DIVIDED we fall*, eendrag maak mag; *a ~ FRONT*, 'n aaneengeslote (verenigde) front; *the U~ KINGDOM*, die Verenigde Koninkryk; *U~ NATIONS*, Verenigde Volke; *the U~ PROVINCES of Holland*, die Verenigde Provinsies van Holland; *U ~ STATES of AMERICA*, Verenigde State van Amerika.
un'it trust, eenheidtrust.
unitiza'tion, eenheidsverpakking; vrageenheidsvorming.
un'ity, (unities), eenheid; eendrag, ooreenstemming, verbond, eensgesindheid; *AT ~*, eensgesind; *the DRAMATIC unities*, die drie eenhede (tyd, plek en handeling); ~ *is STRENGTH*, eendrag maak mag.
univ'alence, eenwaardigheid.
univ'alent, eenwaardig.
un'ivalve, eenkleppig.
univa'lvular, eenkleppig; eenskulpig.
univers'al, (n) algemeenheid; universeel, universalium; kruiskoppelaar; (a) algemeen, universeel; algemeen versprei; wêreld=; veelsydig; *sole and ~ heir*, enigste en universele erfgenaam; ~ **approval**, algemene byval; ~ **conscription**, algemene diensplig; ~ **coupling**, kruiskoppeling; ~ **dividers**, universeelpasser; ~ **franchise**, algemene stemreg; ~ **heir**, enigste erfgenaam; ~**ist**, universalis; ~'**ity**, universaliteit, algemeenheid; alomvattendheid; ~**ize**, algemeen maak; ~ **joint**, kruiskoppeling; ~ **language**, wêreldtaal; ~ **legatee**, enigste erfgenaam; ~**ly**, algemeen, oral en altyd; ~ **provider**, algemene leweransier; ~ **suffrage**, algemene stemreg.
un'iverse, heelal, wêreld.
univer'sity, (n) (..**ties**), universiteit; (a) universiteits=, universitêr; ~-**bred**, akademies gevorm; ~ **building**, universiteitsgebou; ~ **college**, universiteitskollege; ~ **extension classes**, universiteitsuitbreidingsklasse; ~**man**, akademikus; ~ **professor**, universiteitsprofessor, hoogleraar; ~**team**, universiteitspan; ~ **training**, universiteitsopleiding.
unjust', onregverdig, onbillik; *be ~*, met twee mate meet, onregverdig wees.
unjustifi'able, onverdedigbaar, ongeregverdig; onverantwoordelik.
unjus'tified, ongeregverdig, ongeregtig, ongegrond.
unjust'ly, ten onregte, onbillik.
unkempt', ongekam; slordig, verwaarloos, torrerig.
unkenn'el, (-led), opjaag (jakkals); uit die hondehok laat.
unkept', onbewaar(d); nie onderhou nie, verwaarloos.
unkind', onvriendelik; ~**ly**, onvriendelik; hard; ~**ness**, onvriendelikheid; hard.
unking', onttroon.
unking'ly, onkoninklik.
unknight'ly, onridderlik.
unknit', (-ted), lostrek, lostorring.
unknot', (-ted), losmaak; ontknoop.
unknow'able, ondeurgrondelik, onnaspeurbaar, onkenbaar; ~**ness**, onkenbaarheid, onnaspeurbaarheid.
unknow'ing, onbewus, onwetend; ~**ly**, sonder om dit te weet, onwetend, onbewus.
unknown', (n) onbekende; *TWO ~ s*, twee onbekendes; *THE ~*, die onbekende; (a) onbekend; *the U~ SOLDIER*, die onbekende soldaat; ~, *UNKISSED*, onbekend maak onbemind; ~, *UNLOVED*, onbekend maak onbemind.
unlab'oured, onbewerk; ongedwonge, natuurlik.
unlace', losryg, losmaak.

unlad'en, ongelaai, onbelas.
unlad'ylike, nie soos 'n dame nie, onvroulik, onfyn.
unlament'ed, onbeklaag, onbetreur(d).
unlatch', oopmaak, die knip afhaal.
unlaw'ful, onwettig; buite-egtelik (kind); ongeoorloof; onregmatig; ~ **detention**, wederregtelike aanhouding; ~**ness**, onwettigheid; onegtheid; onregmatigheid; ongeoorloofdheid.
unlearn', afleer, verleer; ~**ed**, ongeleerd, onwetend; ~**ing**, afwenning; ~**t**, nie geleer nie, ongeleer.
unleash', losmaak; loslaat.
unleav'ened, ongesuur(d), ongegis.
unless', tensy, so nie, behalwe, indien nie.
unlett'able, onverhuurbaar.
unlett'ered, nie gemerk nie; ongeletterd.
unli'censed, sonder lisensie, ongeoorloof, onbevoeg.
unlicked', ongelek; onverslaan, onoorwonne; onuitgelooi; rou, baar, ongemanierd.
unlight'ed, nie verlig nie; nie aangesteek nie (bv. sigaar).
unlik'able, onbeminlik, onaantreklik.
unlike', anders; ongelyk; verskillend; *the brothers ARE ~*, die broers lyk nie na mekaar nie; *that IS too ~ him*, dit is heeltemal in teenstelling met sy geaardheid; so iets sal hy nooit doen nie; ~**d**, onbemind; ~ **fractions**, ongelyknamige breuke; ~**lihood**, onwaarskynlikheid; ~**ly**, onwaarskynlik; ~ **poles**, ongelyknamige pole (elek.); ~ **signs**, teenoorgestelde tekens.
unlim'ber, afhaak.
unlim'ited, onbegrens, onbeperk; geweldig baie.
unlined'[1], sonder lyne, ongelinieer(d) (papier); sonder plooie (gesig), glad, plooiloos.
unlined'[2], sonder voering, onuitgevoer.
unlink', losmaak; uithaak.
unli'quidated, ongelikwideer(d).
unlist'ed, nie-genoteer, ongenoteer; ongelys; ~ **shares**, ongenoteerde aandele.
unload', aflaai, afpak; ontlaai, uitlaai; los (skepe); (aandele) verkoop; die patroon uithaal; lug gee aan, verlig; ~**ed**, afgelaai, ongelaai (wapen); onbelas; ~**er**, ontlaaier; aflaaier; ~**ing berth**, losplek.
unlock', oopsluit, ontsluit, oopmaak; openbaar, onthul.
unlooked'-for, onverwag, onvoorsien.
unloose', losmaak.
unlov(e)'able, onbeminlik.
unloved', ongelief, onbemind.
unlove'ly, onbeminlik; onaantreklik, lelik.
unlov'ing, liefdeloos.
unluck'iness, onvoorspoedigheid, ongelukkigheid.
unluck'y, ongelukkig, onvoorspoedig, rampspoedig, onfortuinlik; ~ *in CARDS, lucky in love*, ongelukkig in die spel, gelukkig in die liefde; ~ *DAY*, ongeluksdag; *this is rather ~ FOR you*, jy tref dit nogal ongelukkig; ~ *NUMBER*, ongeluksgetal.
unmade', ongemaak; onopgemaak (bed); ongeskape.
unmaid'enly, onjonkvroulik, onvroulik.
unmaimed', onvermink, ongeskonde.
unmake', (..**made**), vernietig; afbreek, ongedaan maak.
unmall'eable, onsmeebaar.
unman', (-ned), ontman; verwyf maak, van manlike eienskappe beroof; ontmoedig; van manskappe beroof.
unman'ageable, onhandelbaar, onregeerbaar, lastig; onbestuurbaar; ~**ness**, onhandelbaarheid.
unman'like, vrouagtig, onmanlik; onmenslik.
unman'liness, onmanlikheid.
unman'ly, onmanlik; lafhartig; onmenslik.
unmanned', ontman, onbeset; ontmoedig; lafhartig; ontman; *this loss has ~ him completely*, hierdie verlies het hom al sy moed ontneem.
unmann'ered, ongemanierd, onbeskof.
unmann'erliness, ongemanierdheid, onmanierlikheid, onhebbelikheid, onbeskoftheid.
unmann'erly, onmanierlik, onhebbelik, ongepoets.
unmanured', onbemes.
unmapped', nie in kaart gebring nie, ongekarteer.
unmarked', ongemerk; nie nagesien nie; onopgemerk; ~ *by*, nie onderskei deur.
unmark'etable, onbemarkbaar, onverkoopbaar.

unmarred', onbeskadig.
unmar'riageable, ontroubaar.
unma'rried, ongetroud, ongehuud, egteloos; ~ *state*, ongehude staat.
unmar'tial, vredeliewend, onkrygshaftig.
unmas'culine, onmanlik.
unmask', ontmasker, demaskeer, die masker afhaal; die bedekking wegneem; die sterkte verraai; ~ *ONESELF*, jou in jou ware gedaante toon; ~ *a PERSON*, iem. se masker afruk; ~ **ed**, ontmasker.
unmast'ered, onvermeester; onbedwonge.
unmatch'able, onvergelyklik.
unmatched', ongeëwenaard, enig, weergaloos; on= paar (diere); nie by mekaar passend nie.
unmat'ed, sonder maat; ongepaar.
unmatured', ongeryp, onryp.
unmean'ing, niksbetekenend, onbeduidend, niksseg= gend.
unmeant', onopsetlik, nie bedoel nie.
unmea'surable, onmeetlik, onbegrens; grensloos; on= meetbaar; *kyk ook* **immeasureable**.
unmea'sured, ongemeet; onmeetlik.
unmed'itated, onoordag.
unmelod'ious, onwelluidend, wanklinkend.
unmelt'ed, ongesmelt.
unmen'tionable, onnoembaar; ~ **s**, onnoembare din= ge; onderklere; (onder)broek.
unmen'tioned, onvermeld, ongerep.
unmerch'antable, onverkoopbaar.
unmer'ciful, ongenadig, onbarmhartig, wreed, mee= doënloos, onmenslik; ~ **ness**, onbarmhartigheid, onmenslikheid.
unme'rited, onverdien(d).
unmeritor'ious, onverdienstelik.
unmethod'ical, onmetodies; onstelselmatig.
unmil'itary, onmilitêr, onkrygshaftig.
unmind'ful, onagsaam, onverskillig; ~ *of*, sonder om te dink aan, sonder om jou te steur aan.
unmi'ngled, ongemeng.
unmistak'able, onmiskenbaar, seker.
unmit'igated, onvervals, nie verminder nie; deurtrap (skelm); *an* ~ *scoundrel*, 'n deurtrapte skurk.
unmix', ontmeng; ~ **ed**, onvermeng, ongemeng, sui= wer; gelyksoortig.
unmod'ified, ongewysig.
unmolest'ed, ongestoord, ongehinderd, ongemoeid, ongemolesteer.
unmoor', losmaak, die anker lig, losgooi (skip).
unmor'al, amoreel, sonder sedelikheid, onsedelik.
unmortg'aged, nie onder verband nie, onbeswaard, vry, los.
unmor'tified, onverneder, onverswak; onboetvaar= dig.
unmo'therly, onmoederlik, stiefmoederlik.
unmot'ivated, ongemotiveer(d).
unmould', die fatsoen verloor; uitkeer (poeding).
unmount', uitmekaar neem, demonteer; afklim (van perd); ~ **ed**, onberede; ongemonteer, onopgeplak (portret).
unmourned', nie betreur nie, onbeween, onbe= treur(d).
unmov'able, onbeweegbaar; onaandoenlik.
unmoved', onbewoë, koel, ongeroer; roerloos; nie verplaas nie.
unmov'ing, beweginglos.
unmus'ical, onmusikaal; onwelluidend; ~ **'ity**, ~ **ness**, onmusikaliteit; onwelluidendheid.
unmut'ilated, onvermink, ongeskonde.
unmuz'zle, die muilband afhaal; ~ **d**, ongemuilband.
unnail', die spyker uithaal; oopmaak.
unnam(e)'able, onnoemlik, onnoembaar.
unnamed', ongenoem(d); naamloos.
unna'tional, onnasionaal.
unna'tural, onnatuurlik; gedwonge, ontaard; kuns= matig; ~ **ness**, onnatuurlikheid; gedwongenheid.
unnav'igable, onbevaarbaar.
unne'cessarily, onnodig, verniet.
unne'cessary, onnodig, oorbodig, verniet.
unnego'tiable, onverhandelbaar; onrybaar (pad); ~ **ness**, onverhandelbaarheid; onrybaarheid.
unneigh'bourly, onbuurskaplik, onvriendskaplik.
unnerve', verswak, ontsenu, verlam, ontstel.
unnerv'ing, ontsenu(w)end, verswakkend; skrikwek= kend, angswekkend.
unnot'ed, ongemerk; onbekend.
unnot'iceable, onmerkbaar.
unnot'iced, onopgemerk, onbemerk, soetjies.
unnou'rished, nie gevoed nie.
unnum'bered, ongeteld, talloos; ongenommer(d).
unobjec'tionable, onberispelik; onaanstootlik; ~ **ness**, onaanstootlikheid.
unobli'ging, nie tegemoetkomend nie, onvriendelik, ontoeskietlik.
unobscured', onverduister(d); helder.
unobserv'able, nie waarneembaar nie, onmerkbaar.
unobserv'ant, onopmerksaam, onoplettend; ~ **ness**, onoplettendheid.
unobserved', onopgemerk, skelmpies; ongesien(s).
unobstruct'ed, onbelemmer(d), ongehinder(d); vry, oop.
unobtain'able, onverkry(g)baar, onbereikbaar.
unobtrus'ive, beskeie, nie indringerig nie; onopval= lend, onopsigtig; ~ **ness**, beskeidenheid; onopsig= tigheid.
unocc'upied, leeg, onbewoon(d); nie besig nie, onbe= set, vry.
unoffend'ing, onskuldig, onskadelik; nie aanstootlik nie.
unoffi'cial, nie-amptelik, onoffisieel; ~ *strike*, wilde (onwettige) staking.
unoffi'cious, nie opdringerig nie.
unop'ened, ongeopen.
unopposed', onbestrede, sonder opposisie; onverhin= der; ~ *ELECTION*, onbestrede (onbetwiste) ver= kiesing; ~ *MOTION*, onbestrede mosie.
unordained', ongeorden.
unorgan'ic, onorganies.
unorg'anized, ongeorganiseer(d), deurmekaar, onor= delik.
unor'iented, ongeoriënteer(d).
unori'ginal, onoorspronklik, afgelei.
unornament'al, onsierlik.
unorth'odox, ketters, onortodoks; afwykend; ~ *Jew*, onortodokse Jood.
unostenta'tious, eenvoudig, beskeie, sonder vertoon; ~ **ly**, sonder dat dit opval.
unowned', sonder eienaar; nie erken nie.
unpack', uitpak, aflaai, afpak.
unpaid', onbetaald; ongesalarieer; ongestort; onge= frankeer(d); ~ *CAPITAL*, onopgevraagde kapi= taal; ~ *LEAVE*, onbesoldigde (onbetaalde) verlof.
unpaired', ongepaar(d).
unpal'atable, onsmaaklik, sleg, laf, onverkwiklik, on= aangenaam, ongenietbaar; *an* ~ *STORY*, 'n on= smaaklike verhaal; *an* ~ *TRUTH*, 'n onaange= name waarheid.
unpap'ered, ongeplak, onbehang.
unpa'ralleled, ongeëwenaard, weergaloos, voorbeel= deloos, uniek.
unpard'onable, onvergeeflik.
unpard'oned, onvergewe.
unparliamen'tary, onparlementêr; ongeoorloof.
unpart'ed, ongeskei.
unpat'ented, ongepatenteer(d).
unpatriot'ic, onpatrioties, onvaderlandsliewend.
unpat'ronized, ondersterm(d); nie ondersteun nie.
unpaved', ongeplavei, ongestraat; ongebaan (fig.).
unpay'able, onbetaalbaar, nie-winsgewend.
unpedagog'ic, onpedagogies.
unpeeled', ongeskil.
unpeg', (-ged), die penne uithaal; die beperkings op= hef.
unpen'sioned, sonder pensioen, ongepensioeneer(d).
unpeo'ple, ontvolk; ~ **d**, onbevolk; sonder mense, eensaam.
unperceiv'able, onmerkbaar.
unperceived', ongemerk, onopgemerk, onbemerk; ~ *by (of) anyone*, ongemerk deur iem.
unperf'orated, ongetand, ongeperforeer.
unperformed', onuitgevoer; ongedaan, onvolvoer, onverrig.
unpe'rishable, onverganklik.
unpermitt'ed, ongeoorloof, nie toegelaat nie.
unperplexed', nie verleë nie.

unperturbed 1343 *unrefined*

unperturbed', onverstoor(d), (hout)gerus, ongeërg.
unphilosoph'ic(al), onfilosofies, onwysgerig.
unpick', lostorring, lostrek; uithaal (steke); oopsteek (slot); ~ **ed**, nog nie gekies nie; ongepluk; losgetorring.
unpin', **(-ned)**, losspeld, die spelde uithaal.
unpit'ied, onbeklaag, onbejammer.
unpit'ying, onbarmhartig; meedoënloos, wreed.
unplaced', ongeplaas; nie 'n plek verkry nie; sonder betrekking.
unplant'ed, onbeplant; ongeplant.
unplay'able, onspeelbaar (stuk); onmoontlik; onopvoerbaar (toneelstuk); ~ **ness**, onspeelbaarheid; onopvoerbaarheid.
unpleas'ant, onaangenaam, onaardig, suur, wrang; *make* ~, veronaangenaam; ~ **ness**, onaangenaamheid.
unpleas'ing, onbehaaglik, onaangenaam.
unpli'able, onbuigsaam.
unploughed', ongeploeg.
unplug', (-ged), die prop uittrek.
unplumbed', ongepeil.
unpoet'ic, ondigterlik.
unpoint'ed, sonder punt; sonder leestekens; ongevoeg (muur).
unpoised', onewewigtig.
unpol'ished, ongepolys, nie blink gevryf nie; onbeskaaf, onverfyn, onbeholpe; onversorg (styl).
unpollut'ed, onbesoedel(d), onbesmet.
unpop'ular, onpopulêr, ongewild; ~ *AMONGST (with) people*, ongewild onder mense; ~ *BECAUSE (on account) of*, onpopulêr weens; ~ **'ity**, onpopulariteit, ongewildheid.
unpop'ulated, onbevolk.
unprac'tical, onuitvoerbaar; onprakties.
unprac'tised, ongeskool(d), onervare, ongeoefen(d); ongebruik.
unprecedent'ed, ongehoord, ongekend, weergaloos; sonder presedent, sonder voorbeeld.
unpredict'able, onvoorspelbaar (sake); onberekenbaar (mense).
unprej'udiced, onbevooroordeel(d), onbevange, onpartydig.
unpremed'itated, onvoorbedag, nie vooraf beraam nie; nie opsetlik nie; onvoorberei(d)
unprepared', onvoorberei(d), ongereed; ongewapen; onklaar; ~ *FOR the drought*, onvoorberei(d) vir die droogte; ~ *WITH an excuse*, ongereed met 'n verskoning; ~ **ness**, onvoorbereidheid.
unprepossessed', onbevooroordeeld.
unpossess'ing, ongunstig; nie innemend nie.
unpresent'able, ontoonbaar; onvertoonbaar.
unpressed', ongestryk.
unpresum'ing, beskeie, nie aanmatigend nie.
unpretend'ing, ongeveins; nie aanmatigend nie, beskeie; ~ **ness**, beskeidenheid.
unpreten'tious, onopvallend, pretensieloos.
unprevail'ing, nutteloos.
unpriced', ongeprys.
unpriest', as priester afsit.
unprime', ontstook.
unprin'cipled, beginselloos; gewetenloos, ~ **ness**, beginselloosheid; gewetenloosheid.
unprint'able, ondrukbaar, nie geskik om gedruk te word nie.
unprint'ed, ongedruk (boeke); onbedruk (stowwe).
unpriv'ileged, onbevoorreg.
unprocur'able, onverkrygbaar.
unproduc'tive, onvrugbaar, onproduktief; nie winsgewend nie, renteloos; ~ **ness**, onvrugbaarheid, onproduktiwiteit.
unprofaned', ongeskonde.
unprofe'ssional, onprofessioneel; in stryd met jou beroep; leke=, nie-vakkundig; *an* ~ *opinion*, die mening van 'n leek.
unprof'itable, onvoordelig, vrugteloos, nie betalend nie, nie-winsgewend, onwinsgewend.
unprogress'ive, ouderwets, konserwatief.
unprohib'ited, toegelaat, wettig.
unprolif'ic, onvrugbaar.
unprom'ising, min belowend; ongunstig.
unprompt'ed, spontaan, vanself gegee.

unpronounce'able, nie uit te spreek nie, onuitspreekbaar.
unprop'ertied, nie-besittend; besittingloos.
unpropi'tious, onvoorspoedig, ongunstig; ~ **ness**, ongunstigheid.
unpropor'tional, oneweredig; *kyk* **disproportionate**.
unpros'perous, onvoorspoedig.
unprotect'ed, onbeskerm(d), onbeskut.
unprotest'ing, gelate, lydelik.
unprov'able, onbewysbaar.
unproved', nie bewys nie, onbewese; onbeproef.
unprov'en, onbewese.
unprovid'ed, onvoorsien; onversorg; misdeeld.
unprovoked', sonder aanleiding, nie uitgelok nie, moedswillig; ~ **ly**, goedsmoeds.
unpublish'able, onpubliseerbaar.
unpub'lished, ongepubliseer(d), onuitgegee; onbekend; ongedruk.
unpunc'tual, nie presies op tyd nie, ongereeld, laat; ~ **'ity**, ongereeldheid.
unpun'ished, ongestraf; *go* ~, ongestraf bly.
unpurch'asable, onkoopbaar.
unpu'rified, ongelouter, ongesuiwer(d).
unqual'ified, onbevoeg, ongekwalifiseer(d), onbeperk, onverdeeld; onomwonde; onvermeng; onversaag; ~ *FOR a post*, onbevoeg vir 'n betrekking; ~ *IN history*, ongekwalifiseer(d) in geskiedenis.
unquelled', onbedwonge, ongedemp (opstand).
unquench'able, onversadigbaar, onlesbaar; onblusbaar.
unquenched', onuitgeblus, ongedoof (vuur); ongeles (dors); ongestil (honger).
unques'tionable, onbetwisbaar, ontwyfelbaar; onaanvegbaar; *it is* ~, dit staan soos 'n paal bo water.
unques'tionably, onbetwisbaar, onteensoglik.
unques'tioned, nie ondervra nie; ongevra; onbetwis, nie weerspreek nie, bo alle twyfel verhewe; *it goes* ~, dit word nie in twyfel getrek nie.
unques'tioning, sonder om vrae te stel; onvoorwaardelik, blind.
unqui'et, (n) onrus; (a) onrustig, rusteloos; ~ *times*, bewoë tye.
unquot'able, nie geskik om aangehaal te word nie, onsiteerbaar.
unquot'ed: ~ *share*, nie-genoteerde (ongenoteerde) aandeel.
unram'ified, onvertak.
unrat'ified, onbekragtig.
unrav'el, (-led), ontwar, uitrafel, ontplooi; ophelder; ontsyfer, uitpluis, ontraadsel; ~ **ling**, ontknoping, ontraadseling.
unraz'ored, ongeskeer.
unreach'able, onbereikbaar.
unread', ongelees (boek); onbelese (persoon).
unread'able, onleesbaar.
unread'iness, ongereedheid; onwilligheid.
unread'y, nie gereed nie; onvoorbereid; aarselend, traag, talmend.
unre'al, onwesenlik; onwerklik; irreëel, denkbeeldig; ~ **is'tic**, onrealisties; ~ **'ity**, onwesenlikheid.
unreas'on, onverstandigheid, onsin, dwaasheid; ~ **able**, onredelik, onbillik, onskaplik; verkeerd; onverstandig; ~ **ed**, redeloos; onheredeneerd; ~ **ing**, onnadenkend.
unrebuk'ed, onberisp, onbestraf.
unrecip'rocated, onbeantwoord.
unreck'oned, ongetel, nie bereken nie.
unreclaimed', onopgeëis; onontgin (land).
unrec'ognizable, onherkenbaar, onkenbaar.
unrec'ognized, nie herken nie.
unrecommend'ed, nie aanbeveel nie.
unrec'ompensed, onbeloon, nie vergoed nie.
unreconciled', onversoen(d).
unreconcil'able, onversoenlik; onverenigbaar.
unrecord'ed, onvermeld, nie opgeskryf nie.
unredeem'able, onaflosbaar.
unredeemed', nie vrygekoop nie, nie gelos nie; onverlos; nie vrygemaak nie; onvervul(d) (belofte); onaflgelos (pand); *an* ~ *promise*, 'n onvervulde belofte.
unredressed', nie vergoed nie; nie herstel nie.
unreel', afdraai, afrol.
unrefined', onverfyn(d), onbeskaaf, niksgewend; on-

gesuiwer(d), ongeraffineer; ~ **ore,** ongesuiwerde erts; ~ **silver,** ongeaffineerde silwer; ~ **sugar,** ruwe suiker.
unreflect'ing, onnadenkend, gedagteloos; onweerkaatsend.
unreform'able, onverbeterlik.
unreformed', onbekeerd; onverbeter(d).
unrefreshed', onverkwik.
unrefut'ed, onweerlê, onbestrede.
unregard'ed, verontagsaam, verwaarloos.
unregen'eracy, onverbeterlikheid.
unregen'erate, onwedergebore; sondig, verdorwe; ~ **d,** onwedergebore.
unre'gistered, oningeskrewe; nie-aangeteken, onaangeteken, ongeregistreer(d) (brief).
unrehearsed', onvoorbereid; ongerepeteer.
unrelat'ed, onverwant, nie-verwant; nie in verband met mekaar staande nie; nie vertel nie.
unrelaxed', onvermoeid, onverslap.
unrelent'ing, onbarmhartig, onvermurfbaar, onbuigsaam, onverbiddelik; sonder ophou, sonder verslapping; ~ **ly,** onverbiddelik.
unreliabil'ity, onbetroubaarheid; ongeloofwaardigheid.
unreli'able, onbetroubaar; ongeloofwaardig.
unrelieved', eentonig, onafgewissel; vervelend; onafgelos.
unreli'gious, ongodsdienstig.
unremark'able, onmerkwaardig; onopmerklik, onopvallend.
unrem'edied, onverhelp.
unremem'bered, vergete.
unremitt'ing, onverpoos, onverflou, gedurig, onophoudelik, aanhoudend.
unremun'erative, nie lonend nie, nie winsgewend nie, onvoordelig.
unrenewed', nie hernuwe nie; nie wedergebore nie.
unrepaid', nie terugbetaal nie; nie vergeld nie.
unrepair', toestand van verval, bouvalligheid; *kyk ook* **disrepair;** ~ **ed,** vervalle, verwaarloos.
unrepeal'able, onherroeplik; onherroepbaar.
unrepealed', onherroep.
unrepeat'able, onherhaalbaar.
unrepent'ant, onboetvaardig, verstok.
unrepent'ing, sonder berou, onboetvaardig.
unrepent'ing, geduldig, gelate, stil.
unreplace'able, onvervangbaar.
unreplen'ished, onaangevul(d).
unreport'ed, onvermeld, nie berig nie.
unrepresent'ed, onverteenwoordig.
unreproached', onberispe, ongelaak.
unreproved', onberispe, ongelaak.
unrequest'ed, ongevra.
unrequit'ed, onvergeld, onbeloon, onbeantwoord; ~ *love,* onbeantwoorde liefde.
unres'cued, ongered, onverlos.
unresent'ing, sonder wrok, sonder om iem. kwalik te neem.
unreserved', openhartig, rondborstig, onvoorwaardelik, onbeperk; onbespreek, ongereserveer; ~ **ly,** onvoorwaardelik, sonder voorbehoud; ~ **ness,** vrymoedigheid, openhartigheid.
unresigned', nie gelate nie.
unresist'ed, nie weerstaan nie; sonder teenstand.
unresist'ing, lydelik, sonder om weerstand te bied.
unresolved', onopgelos; besluiteloos, weifelend.
unrespect'ed, ongeag.
unrespon'sive, stil, nie antwoordend nie; onverskillig, onsimpatiek, terughoudend, stug.
unrest', onrus, angs; beroering, woeligheid; ~ **ful,** onrustig, rusteloos.
unrestored', nie herstel nie; nie teruggegee nie.
unrestrain'able, onbedwingbaar, onbedaarlik; ~ **ness,** onbedwingbaarheid.
unrestrained', oningehou, onbeperk, onbeteueld, onbeheers, onbedwonge, teuelloos, vry, ongedwonge; bandeloos; ~ **ness,** teuelloosheid, onbeteueldheid.
unrestrict'ed, onbeperk, vry, onbelemmer(d).
unretard'ed, onvertraag.
unreten'tive, nie vashoudend nie; swak (geheue).
unretract'ed, onherroep.
unreturned', nie terug nie; onbeantwoord; onverkies nie.

unrevealed', ongeopenbaar.
unrevenged', ongewreek.
unrevers'able, onomkeerbaar; ~ **ness,** onomkeerbaarheid.
unrevised', onhersien; *an* ~ *edition,* 'n onhersiene uitgawe.
unrevoked', onherroep.
unreward'ed, onbeloon.
unreward'ing, van min nut; ondankbaar.
unrhymed', rymloos (verse); onberym.
unrhyth'mical, onritmies.
unridd'en, onberede.
unrid'dle, oplos, ontsyfer, ontraadsel.
unrid(e)'able, onrybaar.
unri'fled, glad, ongetrokke (geweerloop).
unrig', (**-ged),** aftakel (skip).
unright'eous, onregverdig, ongeregtig, sondig; ~ **ness,** ongeregtigheid; goddeloosheid; onregverdigheid.
unrip', (**-ped),** oopsny, lostorring.
unripe', groen, onryp; onvolwasse; ~ **ness,** onrypheid; onvolwassenheid.
unriv'alled, ongeëwenaard, weergaloos, sonder mededinger, onvergelyklik.
unriv'eted, nie met naels vasgeklink nie.
unroad'worthy, onpadwaardig.
unroast'ed, ongebrand (koffie); ongebraai, ongerooster (vleis).
unrobe', uittrek, uitklee; die mantel (toga) afhaal.
unroll', afrol, afwikkel; uitrol; ontplooi.
unroman'tic, onromanties, alledaags.
unroof', die dak afbreek; ~ **ed,** sonder dak, dakloos.
unroot', ontwortel, uitroei; *kyk ook* **uproot.**
unround', ontrond (vokaal).
unruf'fled, kalm, stil, onverstoord, onbewoë, onbekommerd; glad.
unruled'¹, nie geregeer nie.
unruled'², ongelinieer(d) (papier).
unrul'iness, weerbarstigheid, wildheid, onhandelbaarheid, balsturigheid.
unrul'y, wild, losbandig, onhandelbaar, onordelik; woes, onstuimig; balsturig, omgekrap, balhorig; weerbarstig, weerspannig.
unsad'dle, afsaal; afgooi.
unsafe', onveilig, gevaarlik, gewaag; onbetroubaar.
unsaid', ongesê, onuitgespreek, versweë; ~ *words,* versweë woorde.
unsal'aried, onbesoldig, ongesalarieer(d).
unsale'able, onverkoopbaar.
unsalt', ontsout.
unsalt'ed, ongesout; vars; *an* ~ *horse,* 'n ongesoute perd.
unsalub'rious, ongesond.
unsanc'tified, ongeheilig, ongewyd.
unsanc'tioned, onbekragtig; ongeoorloof; nie goedgekeur nie.
unsan'itary, onhigiënies, ongesond.
unsapon'ifiable, onverseepbaar.
unsat'ed, onversadig.
unsa'tiable, onversadigbaar.
unsatisfac'tory, onbevredigend, onvoldoende; ~ *FOR a senior student,* onbevredigend vir 'n senior student; *an explanation* ~ *TO the teacher,* 'n verklaring onbevredigend vir die onderwyser.
unsat'isfied, ontevrede, onbevredig, onvoldaan.
unsat'isfying, onbevredigend.
unsat'urated, onversadig, nie deurtrek nie; ~ **ness,** onversadigdheid.
unsaved', ongered, nie verlos nie, verlore.
unsav'ouriness, onsmaaklikheid, onverkwiklikheid, aanstootlikheid.
unsav'oury, onsmaaklik, onaangenaam, onverkwiklik, aanstootlik.
unsay', (..said), herroep, terugtrek, terugneem.
unscal'able, onbestygbaar; on(be)klimbaar (berg); ~ **ness,** on(be)klimbaarheid.
unscaled'¹, nie beklim (bestyg) nie.
unscaled'², sonder skubbe, skubloos.
unscann'able¹, onskandeerbaar.
unscann'able², onmeetbaar.
unscared', nie afgeskrik nie, onverskrokke.
unscarred', sonder littekens.

unscathed', ongedeerd, ongeskaad, sonder letsel.
unschooled', ongeskool(d), ongeleerd, onkundig; ongekunsteld.
unscientif'ic, onwetenskaplik.
unscoured', ongewas; nie geskrop nie; ~ **wool**, ongewaste wol.
unscram'ble, weer skei; ontrafel; *you cannot* ~ *eggs*, gedane skade kan nie ongedaan gemaak word nie.
unscreened'[1], onbeskut.
unscreened'[2], ongesif (kole).
unscrew', losskroef, uitskroef, losdraai.
unscrip'tural, onbybels, onskriftuurlik.
unscrup'ulous, gewetenloos, beginselloos; sonder beswaar; ~ **ness**, gewetenloosheid, beginselloosheid.
unseal', oopmaak; die seël verbreek; ~ **ed**, onverseël(d), oop; ondig (fles).
unsearch'able, ondeurgrondelik, onnaspeurlik; onpeilbaar.
unseas'onable, ontydig, ongeleë, ongeskik; buiteseisoens.
unseas'oned, sonder kruie, ongekruie (kos); nat, onuitgedroog (hout); nie gewoond (aan klimaat) nie; onervare, onverhard.
unseat', ontsetel (verteenwoordiger); afgooi (deur perd); uitgooi; uitwip; van die troon stoot; ~ **ed**, afgegooi; ontsetel.
unsea'worthiness, onseewaardigheid.
unsea'worthy, onseewaardig.
unsec'onded, ongesekondeer.
unsectar'ian, neutraal; non-sektaries, nie-sektaries.
unsecured', onbeveilig; ~ **claim**, uitstaande vordering; ~ **creditor**, konkurrente krediteur; ~ **debt**, ongedekte skuld.
unsee'ing, onsiende; blind; sonder om te sien, onoplettend.
unseem'liness, onbetaamlikheid, onwelvoeglikheid, ongepastheid, wanvoeglikheid.
unseem'ly, onbetaamlik, onvoegsaam, onwelvoeglik, onbehoorlik, ongepas, onvanpas, wanvoeglik, onordentlik.
unseen', (n) (die) ongesiende; ~ **translation**, onvoorbereide vertaling (oefening); (a) ongesien, onsigbaar.
unse'gregated, ongeskei, ongesegregeer.
unseiz'able, ongrypbaar; onverbeurbaar.
unselect'ed, onuitgesoek, deurmekaar.
unselfcon'scious, vrymoedig, ongeërg, natuurlik; ~ **ness**, natuurlikheid, vrymoedigheid.
unself'ish, onselfsugtig, onbaatsugtig; ~ **ness**, onselfsugtigheid, belangeloosheid.
unsensa'tional, alledaags, gewoon.
unsent', ongestuur(d); nie aangestuur nie.
unsent'enced, nie gevonnis nie.
unsentiment'al, nugter, onsentimenteel.
unsep'arable, onskeibaar; onafskeibaar.
unsep'arated, ongeskei.
unserved', onopgedien; nie afgelewer nie (dagvaarding); ongedek (dier).
unservi'ceable, ondienstig, ongeskik, onbruikbaar; ~ **ness**, ondienstigheid.
unset', stomp (mes); nie ondergegaan nie (son); slap; ongemonteer (diamante); onbeplant; ongeorden(d); ongestel (slagyster); ~ **saw**, slap saag.
unset'tle, verwar, van stryk bring; in onsekerheid bring; krenk (verstand).
unsett'led, onseker, verwar(d), deurmekaar, onbepaald; rusteloos; onvas, ongedurig, onbestendig (weer); besluiteloos, ontsteld, onbetaal(d) (rekening); hangende, onafgehandel, onuitgemaak (vraagstuk); ongevestig, sonder vaste woonplek; onbewoon(d); ~ *DEBT*, uitstaande skuld; ~ *QUESTION*, onuitgemaakte saak; ~ *WEATHER*, ongestadige (onbestendige) weer.
unsett'lement, onvastheid; verwarring.
unsev'ered, ongeskei.
unsew', lostorring; ~ **n**, ongenaai, ongestik.
unsex', geslagloos maak; ~ **ed**, nie (volgens geslag) uitgesoek nie; ~ **ual**, geslagloos; sonder geslagsdrif.
unshac'kle, bevry, die boeie losmaak; uitskakel.
unshad'ed, onbeskadu; sonder kap.
unshad'owed, onbeskadu; onverduister(d).
unshake'able, onwrikbaar, onomstootlik.

unshak'en, vas, onwrikbaar, ongeskok, onverswak, wankelloos, onbesweke, kalm.
unshamed', nie beskaamd nie.
unshape'ly, wanstaltig, misvorm.
unshap'en, vormloos, wanskape.
unshav'en, ongeskeer.
unsheathe', uit die skede haal; ~ *the sword*, die swaard trek.
unshed', nie gestort nie; ~ *tears*, ingehoue trane.
unshelled', onafgemaak; ongedop (bone); nie beskiet nie.
unshel'tered, onbeskut.
unshiel'ded, onbeskerm(d).
unshif'ting, onveranderlik, bewegingloos.
unship', **(-ped)**, ontskeep, aflaai; (roeispane) los; wegneem, afhaal, uithaal.
unshocked', ongeskok.
unshod', onbeslaan (perd); ongeskoei(d), sonder skoene, skoenloos.
unshoe', (..**shod**), die hoefysters aftrek; ontskoei.
unshorn', ongeskeer; ongeknip.
unshrink'able, krimpvry, krimpvas.
unshrink'ing, onvervaard, onversaag, onbevrees.
unshroud', die doodskleed verwyder; ontbloot.
unsif'ted, ongesif.
unsight'ed, nie in sig nie; sonder visier; blind.
unsight'liness, onooglikheid, lelikheid, afsigtelikheid.
unsight'ly, onooglik, lelik, afsigtelik.
unsigned', ongeteken.
unsink'able, onsinkbaar; ondelgbaar (skuld).
unsized'[1], nie volgens grootte gerangskik nie.
unsized'[2], ongegom, ongelym; ~ **paper**, vloeipapier.
unskil'ful, onbekwaam, onbedrewe, onhandig.
unskilled', onbedrewe, onervare; ongeskool(d), baar; ~ **labour**, ongeskoolde arbeid; ~ **labourer**, ongeskoolde arbeider.
unslaked', ongeblus (kalk); ongeles (dors).
unsleep'ing, altyd waaksaam.
unsmil'ing, sonder 'n glimlag, doodernstig.
unsmirched', onbesoedel(d), onbevlek.
unsmoked', onberook.
unsnare', uit 'n strik bevry.
unsob'er, nie sober nie; onmatig.
unsociabil'ity, ongeselligheid, mensskuheid.
unso'ciable, ongesellig; menssku, sku; onhuislik; ~ **ness**, mensskuheid, ongeselligheid.
unso'cial, antimaatskaplik; ongesellig.
unsoiled', onbesoedel(d), onbevlek, skoon.
unsold', onverkoop.
unsol'der, die soldeersel losmaak.
unsol'dierly, onmilitêr, onkrygshaftig; 'n soldaat onwaardig.
unsoli'cited, ongevra(ag).
unsoli'citous, onbekommerd, onbesorg; ongeërg.
unsol'vable, onoplosbaar.
unsolved', onopgelos.
unsophis'ticated, onvervals, onbederf; ongekunsteld, natuurlik, eenvoudig, eg
unsort'ed, ongesorteer(d), ongeorden(d).
unsought', ongesoek; ongesog (fig.).
unsound', ongesond, bederf; swak, gebrekkig; sieklik; onbetroubaar; ondeugdelik; onjuis; ongegrond; onsuiwer; onvas; *of* ~ *mind*, met gekrenkte geestesvermoëns; nie by jou volle verstand nie; ~ **ed**, ongemeet, ongepeil; ~ **ness**, ongesondheid, ondeeglikheid.
unsown', ongesaai.
unspar'ing, onverdrote, onvermoeid; mild, kwistig; ~ *efforts*, onvermoeide pogings.
unspeak'able, onuitspreeklik; onnoembaar, nameloos; onbeskryflik; ~ *AGONY*, namelose lyding; *an* ~ *BORE*, 'n uiters vervelende vent.
unspe'cified, ongespesifiseer(d), nie vermeld nie, onbepaald.
unspent', onuitgegee, onbesteed, ongespandeer, onverbruik; onuitgeput; onafgeskiet; ~ *bullet*, onafgeskiete koeël.
unspilt', ongestort, nie gemors nie.
unsplin'terable, onsplinterbaar.
unsplit', ongekloof, onverdeeld.
unspoiled', **unspoilt'**, onbedorwe.

unspok'en, onuitgesproke, ongeuit, ongesê.
unspontan'eous, onnatuurlik, gemaak, geforseer(d), nie spontaan nie.
unsport'ing, unsports'manlike, onsportief.
unspott'ed, ongevlek, rein, ongespikkel(d); onopgemerk.
unsprung', sonder vere (rytuig); nie afgeklap (afgegaan) nie (val).
unsta'ble, onvas, veranderlik; wankelend, wankel, onbestendig, wrikbaar, wankelbaar; labiel; ~ness, onvastheid; onbestendigheid.
unstained', ongeverf; ongekleur(d); onbesmet, onbeklad.
unstamped', ongestempel; ongeseël, ongefrankeer(d).
unstarched', ongestyf; slap.
unstar'tled, doodgerus, nie verskrik nie.
unstates'manlike, ontaktvol, kortsigtig; nie passend by 'n staatsman nie.
unstat'utable, unstat'utory, onwetlik, onwettig.
unstead'fast, onstandvastig, ongestadig, wispelturig.
unstead'iness, veranderlikheid, onbestendigheid, wispelturigheid, wankelbaarheid.
unstead'y, veranderlik, wankelend, onvas, onbestendig, wispelturig, ongereeld, wisselvallig; *be ~ on one's FEET,* die straat meet; *hoog trap; an ~ LIGHT,* 'n flikkerende lig; *be ~ on one's OPINIONS,* veranderlik van opvatting wees; *~ of PURPOSE,* met wisselvallige doelstelling.
unsteer'able, on(be)stuurbaar.
unstint'ed, onbekrompe; ruim, onbeperk.
unstirred', ongeroer(d).
unstitch', lostorring, uittorring, lostrek.
unstop', (-ped), oopmaak; ooptrek; uittrek (orrelregister); ~**pable,** onkeerbaar; ~**per,** ontkurk.
unstrained', ongefiltreer; nie deurgesyg nie; nie gespan nie; natuurlik, ongedwonge, ongeforseer(d).
unstrap', (-ped), losgespe; die riem (band) afhaal.
unstrat'ified, ongelaag.
unstrength'ened, onversterk.
unstressed', onbetoon(d), onbeklemtoon(d).
unstring', (..strung), afspan; ontspan; afryg; verslap; van stryk bring.
unstriped', ongestreep.
unstrung', ontspan, verslap, verlam, van stryk.
unstud'ied, onbestudeer(d); ondeurdag;' ongekunsteld, spontaan, natuurlik.
unstuffed', nie volgestop (opgestop) nie, sonder opstopsel.
unsubdued', nie oorwin nie, onbeteuel(d), ononderdruk, onbedwonge.
unsubmiss'ive, ongehoorsaam, weerspannig, ongeseglik.
unsubscribed', waarop (waarvoor) nie ingeteken is nie.
unsub'sidized, ongesubsidieer.
unsubstan'tial, onstoflik; onliggaamlik, onwerklik; onwenslik; sleg, onvoedsaam; ~ '**ity,** ~**ness,** onstoflikheid; onwerklikheid; onwesenlikheid.
unsubstan'tiated, onbevestig, onbewys, ongestaaf.
unsub'tle, voor die hand liggend, onsubtiel.
unsuccess', mislukking.
unsuccess'ful, onsuksesvol; nie geslaag nie; misluk, vergeefs; *BE ~,* nie slaag nie; ~ *CANDIDATE,* gesakte kandidaat, druipeling; verslane kandidaat; *RETURN ~,* onverrigter sake terugkom; ~ **ly,** tevergeefs; ~**ness,** onvoorspoedigheid.
unsuitabil'ity, ondoelmatigheid, ongeskiktheid.
unsuit'able, ongeskik, onvanpas; ongunstig; ondoelmatig; ~ *FOR winter,* ongeskik vir die winter; ~ *TO the occasion,* onvanpas vir die geleentheid.
unsuit'ed, ongeskik, nie passend nie.
unsull'ied, onbevlek, onbeklad, onbesmet, rein.
unsung', ongesing; onbesing.
unsupplied', nie voorsien nie; nie gelewer nie.
unsupport'ed, nie gesteun (ondersteun) nie; ~ *assertion,* 'n ongestaafde bewering.
unsure', onseker, onvas, onbetroubaar; ~**ness,** onsekerheid, onvastheid.
unsurmount'able, onoorkoomlik.
unsurpass'able, onoortrefbaar, onoortreflik.
unsurpassed', onoortroffe, ongeëwenaar(d), onvolprese.

unsurveyed', onopgemeet; onbekyk, ongesien.
unsuscep'tible, onvatbaar, onontvanklik.
unsuspec'ted, onverdag.
unsuspec'ting, doodgerus, perdgerus, houtgerus; argeloos, onskuldig, sonder agterdog, sonder om kwaad te vermoed.
unsuspi'cious, nie agterdogtig nie, argeloos, regdenkend, niks vermoedend nie; ~**ness,** argeloosheid, regdenkendheid.
unsustained', nie volgehou nie.
unswad'dle, ontswagtel.
unswayed', onbeïnvloed; standvastig.
unsweet', onsoet; ~**ened,** onversoet, sonder suiker; ~*ened chocolate,* onversoete sjokolade.
unswept', ongevee.
unswerv'ing, onwrikbaar, trou, onwankelbaar; koersvas, doelgerig; ~**ly,** padlangs, doelgerig.
unsworn', onbeëdig.
unsymmet'rical, onsimmetries, skeef.
unsympathet'ic, onsimpatiek.
unsystemat'ic, onsistematies, ongereeld, stelselloos; onmetodies.
untack', losmaak, losryg.
untact'ful, ontaktvol, taktloos.
untaint'ed, onbesmet, vlekloos, sonder blaam; onbedorwe.
untal'ented, onbegaaf, talentloos.
untam'able, ontembaar; ~**ness,** ontembaarheid.
untamed', ongetem, wild, woes.
untamped', ongestamp.
unta'ngle, ontwar, losmaak.
untanned', ongelooi (leer); onuitgelooi; ongebruin (mens).
untapped', onafgetap.
untarn'ished, onbesoedel(d), onbevlek, vlekkeloos; onverbleek, onaangeslaan (metale).
untarred', ongeteer.
untast'ed, ongeproe; onaangeraak.
untaught', ongeleer(d), onwetend; nie aangeleer nie, spontaan.
untaxed', onbelas; onbeskuldig.
unteach'; afleer; ~**able,** onleerbaar, hardleers.
untear'able, onskeurbaar.
untech'nical, ontegnies.
untem'pered, ongehard; onversag, ongetemper.
untemp'ted, nie verlei nie, nie versoek nie.
unten'able, onhoudbaar, onmoontlik.
unten'antable, onbewoonbaar.
unten'anted, onbewoon(d).
untend'ed, onversorg, onopgepas.
unte'rrified, onverskrokke, nie bang nie.
untest'ed, onbeproef, ongetoets.
unteth'er, losmaak (dier).
unthanked', onbedank.
unthank'ful, ondankbaar, onerkentlik; ~**ness,** ondankbaarheid, ondank.
unthatched', ongedek (dak).
unthaw', ontdooi.
unthink'able, ondenkbaar.
unthink'ing, onnadenkend, onbesonne, gedagteloos; ~**ly,** sonder om te dink, onnadenkend; ~**ness,** onbedagsaamheid, onnadenkendheid.
unthought'-of, onverwag, onbedag, ongehoord.
unthrashed', ongeslaan.
unthreshed', ongedors, ongetrap.
unthread', die draad uittrek.
unthrif'tiness, verkwisting, spandabelrigheid.
unthrif'ty, spandabelrig, verkwistend, nie spaarsaam nie.
unthriv'ing, onvoorspoedig, ondankbaar; sleg groeiend.
unthrone', onttroon.
untid'iness, onordelikheid, slordigheid, morsigheid, slonsigheid.
untid'y, slordig, onsindelik, deurmekaar, slonsig; onordelik; ~ *GIRL,* slodderkous; ~ *PERSON,* slordige mens, slodderjoggem.
untie', losmaak, losbind, losknoop.
until', tot, totdat; *NOT ~ then,* tot dan; *NOT ~,* nie voordat nie; ~ *THEN,* dan eers.
untill'able, onbeboubaar.
untilled', onbebou, onbewerk.

untimeliness 1347 *unwounded*

untime'liness, ontydigheid.
untime'ly, (a) ontydig, ongeleë, voorbarig; (adv) ontydig, te vroeg.
untinged', ongekleur(d), ongetint; onbesmet.
untinted', ongekleur(d), ongetint.
untired', onvermoeid.
untir'ing, onvermoeid, onverdrote.
unti'tled, sonder titel.
un'to, tot; vir; ~ *death,* tot die dood toe.
untold', talloos; onvermeld; onnoemlik; onberekenbaar; ~ *MISERY,* namelose ellende; ~ *WEALTH,* onmeetlike rykdom.
untomb', opgrawe.
untorn', ongeskeur(d), heel.
untouchabil'ity, onaantasbaarheid, onaanraakbaarheid; onreinheid (Hindoes).
untouch'able, (n) Hindoeparia, onaantasbare; (a) onaantasbaar; onherkenbaar, ongeëwenaar(d); ~ **ness,** onaantasbaarheid, onaanraakbaarheid.
untouched', onaangeroer(d), onaangeraak, ongerep; ongedeerd; onbewoë, onaangedaan.
unto'ward, ongunstig, teenspoedig; eiewys, koppig, lastig; onbetaamlik; ~ **ness,** ongunstigheid; onbetaamlikheid.
untrace'able, onopspoorbaar; onnaspeurlik; ondeurgrondelik.
untracked', ongebaan(d); onopgespoor(d).
untract'able, onhandelbaar.
untrained', ongeoefen(d), baar, ongebrei; ongedresseer(d) (diere); onopgelei (mense).
untramm'elled, onbelemmer(d).
untrans'ferable, onoordra(ag)baar.
untranslat'able, onvertaalbaar; ~ **ness,** onvertaalbaarheid.
untranspar'ent, ondeursigtig.
untrav'elled, onbereis.
untreat'ed, onbehandel(d).
untried', ongetoets, onbeproef; onverhoor; onervare.
untrimmed', onversier, eenvoudig, onopgeskik; ongeknip (hare); ongesnoei (bome).
untrodd'en, onbetree, ongebaan(d), onbegaan.
untrou'bled, ongestoord, onbewoë, kalm, rustig.
untrue', onwaar, vals; ontrou.
untrust'worthiness, onbetroubaarheid; ongeloofwaardigheid.
untrust'worthy, onbetroubaar; ongeloofwaardig.
untruth', onwaarheid, leuen; ontrou; ~ **ful,** onopreg, oneerlik, vals; leuenagtig; ~ **fulness,** onwaarheid; onopregtheid, valsheid.
untun'able, onstembaar.
untune', ontstem; in die war bring; ~ **d',** ongestem.
unturned', onomgekeer, onomgedraai; onomgespit.
untut'ored, onbeskaaf, ru; ongeleerd; ongeletterd; ongevorm, baar.
untwine', losdraai, losmaak; ~ **d',** ongetwyn.
untwist', losdraai.
untyp'ical, nie tipies nie, ontipies, atipies.
unurged', onaangespoor.
unus'able, onbruikbaar; ~ **ness,** onbruikbaarheid.
unused', ongebruik, onbestee; ~ *to,* ongewoond, nie gewend aan nie.
unus'ual, ongewoon, buitengewoon, merkwaardig, ongebruiklik, ~ **ness,** buitengewoonheid, ongewoonheid, merkwaardigheid.
unutt'erable, onuitspreeklik; onbeskryflik; *an ~ FOUL,* 'n opperste gek; ~ *JOY,* onuitspreeklike blydskap; ~ *THINGS,* onnoembare dinge.
unuttered', onuitgesproke.
unvac'cinated, ongeënt.
unval'ued, ongeskat; ongewaardeer.
unvanq'uished, onoorwonne.
unvar'iable, onveranderlik.
unvar'ied, onveranderd, eentonig, met weinig variasie, sonder afwisseling.
unvarn'ished, nie vernis nie; onopgesmuk, eenvoudig; onverbloem(d); *the* ~ *truth,* die reine (onverbloemde) waarheid.
unva'rying, onveranderlik, sonder afwisseling.
unveil', ontsluier, onthul (monument); aan die lig bring; ~ **ed,** ongesluier.
unven'tilated, ongeventileer, sonder vars lug.
unver'ifiable, onbewysbaar; kan nie getoets word nie.

unver'ified, ongekontroleer(d); onbewese; nie nagesien nie.
unversed', onervare, onbedrewe.
unvi'ctualled, sonder voedsel.
unvi'olated, ongeskonde, ongeskend; ongekrenk, onverkrag.
unvis'ited, onbesog.
unvit'rified, onverglaas.
unvoiced', onuitgesproke, nie geuit nie; stemloos.
unvouched' (-for), onbevestig; ongewaarborg.
unwalled', onbemuur(d).
unwant'ed, nie verlang nie; ongewens.
unwar'iness, onversigtigheid.
unwar'like, onkrygshaftig, vredeliewend.
unwarmed', onverwarm(d).
unwarned', ongewaarsku.
unwarped', reguit, nie krom nie, nie skeefgetrek nie; billik, onpartydig; suiwer.
unwa'rrantable, onverantwoordelik, onverdedigbaar; ongeoorloof, onbehoorlik.
unwa'rranted, ongewettig; ongeoorloof, ongeregverdig; ongemotiveer(d); ongemagtig; ongewaarborg.
unwar'y, onversigtig, onbesonne, onbedag.
unwashed', ongewas; *the GREAT* ~, die gepeupel; ~ *WOOL,* ongewaste wol.
unwatched', onbewaak; onbespied.
unwa'tered, onbesproei, nie natgelei (natgemaak) nie; nie met water verdun nie; onverdun; onverwater (kapitaal).
unwav'ering, vas; onwrikbaar, standvastig.
unweak'ened, onverswak.
unweaned', ongespeen.
unwear'able, kan nie gedra word nie, nie drabaar nie.
unwear'ied, onvermoeid, onverdrote.
unwear'ying, onvermoeid, onvermoeibaar, aanhoudend, onverdrote.
unwea'thered, onverweer.
unweave', ontrafel.
unwedd'ed, ongetroud.
unweed'ed, ongeskoffel; vol onkruid.
unwel'come, onwelkom.
unweight'ed, onverswaar.
unwell', onwel, siek, kroeserig, kaduks, onfris, ongesteld.
unwept', onbeween, onbeklaag, onbetreur.
unwhit'ened, ongewit.
unwhite'washed, ongewit.
unwhole'some, ongesond; skadelik; ~ **ness,** skadelikheid; ongesondheid.
unwiel'diness, swaarte, onhandelbaarheid, logheid.
unwiel'dy, swaar, onhandelbaar, log.
unwill'ing, onwillig; ongeneig; teësinnig, ongeneë; ~ *FOR her name to appear,* ongeneë om haar naam te laat verskyn; *he* ~ *TO,* geen lus (sin) hê nie om; nie geneig wees nie om; ~ **ly,** met teësin, ongraag; ~ **ness,** onwilligheid, teensin.
unwind', (..wound), afrol, afwikkel, loswikkel, afdraai, afwen, afwoel, loswind, losgaan.
unwink'ing, sonder om 'n oog te knip; waaksaam; *an* ~ *stare,* 'n starende blik.
unwis'dom, onverstandigheid, onwysheid, dwaasheid.
unwise', onverstandig, dom.
unwished', ongewens.
unwith'ered, onverwelk.
unwitt'ing(ly), onwetend, onbewus, onbedoeld.
unwom'anly, onvroulik.
unwont'ed, ongewoon, buitengewoon.
unwood'ed, onbebos, sonder bome.
unwooed', sonder minnaar (vryer).
unwork'able, onprakties, onuitvoerbaar; onbewerkbaar.
unwork'manlike, onhandig, onprakties; gebrekkig; onsaaklik.
unworld'ly, nie-wêrelds, onwêrelds; geestelik.
unworn', ongedra, nuut; nie geslyt nie.
unwo'rried, nie gekwel nie, onbekommerd.
unworth'iness, onwaardigheid; ongepastheid.
unworth'y, onwaardig; onbetaamlik, ongepas; *conduct* ~ *of you,* gedrag wat jou onwaardig is.
unwound', afgerol, losgedraai.
unwound'ed, ongewond, ongedeerd.

unwov'en, ongeweef.
unwrap', (-ped), ontvou, oopmaak, loswikkel.
unwreaked', ongewreek.
unwreathe', losmaak.
unwri'nkled, sonder rimpels (plooie).
unwritt'en, ongeskrewe; ~ *law,* gewoontereg, ongeskrewe wet.
unwrought', onbewerk, ru.
unyield'ing, onversetlik, standvastig, onwrikbaar; onbuigsaam; koppig, eiesinnig; onbesweke; onelasties; ~ **ness,** onbuigsaamheid; koppigheid.
unyoke', uitspan, die juk afhaal; ophou; bevry.
up, (n): ~ *s and downs,* voor- en teenspoed; wisselvallighede; (v) oplig, aanlê; styg, hoër gaan; *he* ~ *s and says,* hy spring op en sê; (adv) op, bo, na bo, boontoe; *be* ~ *and ABOUT,* besig wees; werskaf; (weer) op die been wees; *be* ~ *and ABOUT early,* vroeg uit die vere wees; *be* ~ *AGAINST,* te doen hê met; *it's ALL* ~ *with him,* dis klaar met hom; *BE* ~ *to,* in die mou hê; *what have you BEEN* ~ *to?,* wat het jy aangevang? wat het jy uitgevoer?; *CHEER* ~ , op= vrolik; wees vrolik! *COLOUR* ~ , bloos; *COME* ~ *with someone,* iem. inhaal; *COME* ~ *with a suggestion (solution),* 'n voorstel (oplossing) aan die hand doen; ~ *to DATE,* op hoogte van die tyd; tot (op) datum; *be* ~ *and DOING,* in die weer wees; *have to be* ~ *and DOING,* moet uitkruip; moet uitspring; ~ *one day and DOWN the next,* op en af; ~ *and DOWN,* op en af; ~ *to the EYES in work,* toegegooi onder die werk; *five FLOORS* ~ , vyf verdiepings hoër op; *FULL* ~ , heeltemal vol (beset); *FURTHER* ~ , hoër op; *the GAME is* ~ , die saak is verlore, dis klaar; *be* ~ *to no GOOD,* bose planne hê; *she has put her HAIR* ~ , sy dra nou bolla; sy het haar hare opgesit; *the HUNT is* ~ , die jag het begin; *HURRY* ~ , maak gou; *it IS* ~ *to him,* dit is sy saak; dit berus by hom; *KEEP* ~ *with things,* op hoogte van sake bly; *KEEP* ~ *with the Joneses,* bybly met die bure; *LOOK him* ~ *and down,* hom van kop tot tone bekyk; *LOOK him* ~ , hom opsoek (besoek); *MAIZE is* ~ , die prys van mielies het gestyg; ~ *to the MARK,* v.d. vereiste gehalte; *be* ~ *to MISCHIEF,* kwaad doen; *not* ~ *to MUCH,* niks besonders nie; nie te waffers nie; *dressed* ~ *to the NINES,* fyn uitgevat; ~ *to NOW,* tot nou toe; *his NUMBER is* ~ , dis klaar met hom; *the ROAD is* ~ , die pad is opgebreek; ~ *for SALE,* te koop; *SAVE* ~ , spaar; *his work is* ~ *to SCRATCH,* sy werk is v.d. vereiste gehalte; *SPEAK* ~ , harder praat; *STAND* ~ , opstaan; *with STEAM* ~ , onder stoom; *his TEMPER is* ~ , hy is kwaad; ~ *THERE,* daarso (bo); *he was THREE* ~ , hy was drie (punte) voor; *TIME is* ~ , die tyd is om (verstreke); ~ *TO,* tot aan; *it is* ~ *TO you,* dit rus op jou; dit is jou verantwoordelikheid; *be* ~ *TO something,* iets aanvang; besig wees met; ogewasse wees; in staat wees; *WHAT is* ~ *?,* wat makeer? wat is aan die gang? wat is gaande? wat gaan aan? *the WIND is* ~ , die wind het opgesteek; ~ *WITH you!,* staan op!; *from YOUTH* ~ , van jongs af; (prep) op; ~ *in ARMS,* onder die wapens; in opstand; in verset; verontwaardig; ~ *HILL and down dale,* berg op en berg af; ~ *the POLE (spout),* in die knyp; ~ *STREAM,* stroom op; ~ *TOWN,* in die stad; ~ *a TREE,* in 'n boom; in 'n penarie; in die war.
up as, oepas(boom); verderflike invloed; gif; ~ **-tree,** oepasboom.
upbear', (..**bore,** ..**borne),** steun, ophef, oplig.
up'beat, opslag, opmaat (mus.).
upbraid', berispe, verwyt, roskam.
up'bringing, opvoeding.
up'cast, (n) (die) opgooi; ventilasieskag; (v) (~), opgooi; (a) na bo gegooi; opgeslaan; ~ **-shaft,** lugskag, uittrekskag.
up'-country, (n) binneland; (a) binnelands; (adv) na (in) die binneland; na (in) die onderveld.
up'-current, stygwind; stygstroom.
up'-draft, stygwind; stygstroom.
up-end', regop plaas (sit).
up'grade¹, opdraand, helling; *on the* ~ , stygend; aan die beter word; (a, adv) opdraande.

upgrade'², (v) bevorder; veredel.
up'growth, groei, ontwikkeling; opslag.
upheav'al, opstand, oproer, omwenteling; opstoting, rysing, opheffing.
upheave', (-d or ..**hove),** ophef.
uphill', opdraand; swaar, moeilik, bars; *an* ~ *STRUGGLE,* 'n opdraande stryd; *an* ~ *TASK,* 'n moeilike taak; *it was* ~ *WORK,* dit het smoor gegaan.
uphold', (..**held),** handhaaf; staande hou; hooghou; ~ *a decision,* 'n uitspraak bekragtig; ~ **er,** ophoueer; ondersteuner; verdediger, handhawer.
uphol'ster, beklee, behang, oortrek, stoffeer; ~ **er,** bekleër, stoffeerder; ~ **ing,** stoffering; ~ **y,** bekleeding, stoffering, bekleedsel; stoffeerdery, stoffeerwerk; stoffeerkuns.
up'keep, onderhoud, onderhoudskoste, instandhouding.
up'land, (n) hoogland; (a) hooglands.
up'lift, (n) verheffing, opheffing.
uplift', (v) oplig; ophef; ~ **ing,** hartversterkend, sielverheffend; ~ **ment,** opheffing.
up'most, boonste, hoogste.
upon', op, bo-op, by; aan; *he piled BOOK* ~ *book,* hy het die boek na boek opmekaar gestapel; *I CAME* ~ *the missing document,* ek het op die vermiste dokument afgekom; *they FELL* ~ *him,* hulle het hom aangeval; ~ *my HONOUR,* op my eer, regtig; *I LOOK* ~ *him as an authority,* ek beskou hom as 'n deskundige; ~ *my SOUL!,* op my woord! by my siel!; ~ *THAT,* daarop; ~ *THIS,* hierop; *once* ~ *a TIME,* eendag, eenmaal; *THOUSANDS* ~ *thousands,* duisende en duisende; ~ *WHAT?,* waarop?; ~ *WHICH?,* waarop; ~ *my WORD,* op my woord! by my siel!
upp'er, (n) boleer; (pl) slobkouse; boleer, oorleer; *be down on one's* ~ *s,* brandarm wees; (a) boonste, bo=, hoër; ~ **air,** boand; bolug; ~ **arm,** boarm; ~ **band,** boband (om geweer); ~ **case,** bokas, hooflet= ters; ~ **class,** hoër stand; ~ **crust,** bokors; die elite (fig.); ~ **-cut,** opstopper, gesighou (boks); skephou (tennis); ~ **deck,** bodek; ~ **denture,** bostel; U ~ **Egypt,** Bo-Egipte; ~ **floor,** boverdieping; ~ **gallery,** engelebak.
upp'er hand, oorhand; *GET the* ~ , die oorhand kry; *HAVE the* ~ , die oorhand hê.
Upp'er House, Hoërhuis.
up'per: ~ **jaw,** bokaak; ~ **layer,** bolaag; ~ **leather,** boleer; ~ **limb,** boonste lit; ~ **limit,** boonste grens; ~ **lip,** bolip; *keep a stiff* ~ *lip,* moed hou, nie ingee nie.
upp'ermost, (a) hoogste, boonste, belangrikste; (adv) eerste, bo-op; *BE* ~ , die oorhand hê; die botoon voer; bo drywe; *SAY whatever comes* ~ , sommer enige ding uitblaker.
upp'er: ~ **room,** oppersaal; ~ **stor(e)y,** boonste ver= dieping; *have something wrong in one's* ~ *stor(e)y,* nie al jou varkies in die hok hê nie; ~ **ten:** *the* ~ *ten,* die hoogste kringe; die elite; ~ **topgallant sail,** bobramseil; ~ **topsail,** bomarsseil; ~ **wind,** hoogtewind, bowind.
upp'ish, trots, verwaand, uit die hoogte; vrypostig; ~ **ness,** vrypostigheid; verwaandheid.
upraise', oprig, oplig.
up'right, (n) paal; pilaar, styl, stutpaal, staander; regop paal (voetbal); (a) regop, orent; opreg, braaf, eerlik; ~ **collar,** staankraag; ~ **course,** staanlaag (stene); ~ **grand,** staanklavier; ~ **ness,** opregtheid, regskapenheid; ~ **piano,** staanklavier; ~ **sights,** staanvisier.
upris'ing, rebellie, opstand; (die) opstaan.
up'roar, oproer, geraas, lawaai, herrie, spektakel.
uproar'ious, lawaaierig, rumoerig, stormagtig; uitbundig; ~ **ly,** met lawaai; ~ **ness,** lawaaierigheid, stormagtigheid; uitbundigheid.
uproot', uitroei; ontwortel.
up'saddle, opsaal.
upset'¹, (n) verwarring, ontsteltenis; omkanteling, omkering, (die) omval; ommekeer; omwenteling, onverwerping; *EMOTIONAL* ~ , emosionele steuring; *MENTAL* ~ , geestelike steurnis; (v) (~, ~), omverwerp; omgooi, omstamp, omstoot; laat om=

slaan; verydel, in die war stuur; ontstel, van stryk bring, omkrap, verstoor; ~ *someone's APPLE-CART*, iem. se planne verydel; *BE* ~, van stryk wees; ontsteld wees; omlê; *a CAR was* ~, 'n motor het omgeslaan; *she was* ~ *by the NEWS*, die nuus het haar ontstel; ~ *his PLANS*, sy planne in die war stuur; ~ *a WILL*, 'n testament ongeldig verklaar; (a) ontsteld.

up'set², inset-; ~ **price**, inset, eerste bod, reserweprys.

upsett'ing, steurend.

up'shot, uitslag, uitkoms, resultaat, slotsom.

up'side-down, onderstebo, deurmekaar, in verwarring; *turn the house* ~, die huis op horings neem.

up'slope, helling, opdraande.

up'stage, hoogmoedig, verwaand.

upstairs', (a) bo-, boonste; (adv) op die boonste verdieping; boontoe; ~ **room**, bokamer.

upstand'ing, regop; agtermekaar, fluks.

up'start, (n) parvenu; verwaande persoon, snip; (a) verwaand, vrypostig, astrant.

up'stream, stroomopwaarts, stroom op.

up'stroke, ophaal, opwaartse beweging; stygslag; opstryk (mus.).

up'surge, opwelling; styging; oplewing.

up'sweep, steil helling; opswaai; oplewing.

up'swing, opswaai; oplewing.

up'take, begrip, verstand; (die) oplig; *QUICK in the* ~, vlug van begrip; *SLOW in the* ~, traag van begrip.

up'throw, opgooi; opligting; opskuiwing.

up'thrust, opwaartse stoot; opstoting.

up-to-date', nuwerwets, op hoogte, tot (op) datum, by; *BE* ~, op hoogte van die tyd wees; by wees; ~ *BOOKS*, bygeskrewe rekeninge; *BRING someone* ~, iem. op hoogte van sake bring; *KEEP oneself* ~, jou op hoogte stel; bybly; ~ *RECORDS*, bygewerkte stukke.

up'town, (n) bostad; bowyk; (a) in die bodorp, bodorps-.

up'turn¹, (n) opswaai; kentering, oplewing; omgekeerde stuk.

up'turn², (v) omgooi, omkeer; opslaan; omploeg; opswaai, oplig, ophef.

up'ward, opwaarts; *an* ~ *tendency*, neiging om te styg; opwaartse neiging.

up'wards, opwaarts, na bo, boontoe; ~ *of 1 000 PEOPLE*, meer as 1 000 mense; *PUPILS of seven and* ~, leerlinge van sewe jaar en daarbo.

up'wash, stygstroom.

up'wind, (n) opwaartse wind; (adv) teen die wind, wind op.

uraem'ia, uremie.

Ur'al, Oeral(gebergte).

uran'ic, uraan-; ~ **acid**, uraansuur; ~ **oxide**, uraanoksied, uraanokside.

uran'ium, uraan.

uranog'raphy, hemelbeskrywing, uranografie.

uranol'ogy, sterrekunde, uranologie.

uranom'etry, uranometrie.

Uran'us, Uranus.

urb'an, stedelik, steeds, stads-; ~ *AREA*, stadsgebied; ~ *MOTORWAY*, stedelike motorweg.

urbane', wellewend, hoflik, welgemanierd.

urb'anism, verstedeliking.

urb'anite, stedeling.

urban'ity, hoflikheid, beleefdheid, wellewendheid.

urbaniza'tion, verstedeliking.

urb'anize, verstedelik, steeds maak.

urch'in, seuntjie, knapie; bloedjie, kleuter; deugniet, skelm, boefie; straatseun, joggie.

Ur'du, Oerdoe.

ur'ea, ureum.

uret'er, urineleier, ureter.

ureth'ra, urinebuis, uretra, pisbuis.

uret'ic, urinebevorderend, ureties.

urge, (n) drang, aandrang, aandrywing; *the* ~ *of LIFE*, die lewensdrang; *SEX (SEXUAL)* ~, geslagsdrang; (v) aandring, aanspoor; aanpor, aandryf; dringend versoek; nadruk lê op; prikkel; opwek; voortdrywe; bespoedig; ~ *to ACTION*, tot dade aanspoor; *to* ~ *someone ON*, iem. aanspoor;

~ *the OXEN on*, die osse aandruk; met die osse praat; ~ *someone TO*, by iem. aandring om.

ur'gency, dringendheid, drang, spoed, dringende noodsaaklikheid; *there is no* ~, daar is geen haas by nie; ~ **signal**, spoedsein; noodsein.

ur'gent, dringend, spoedeisend; ernstig; *BE in* ~ *need of*, dringend behoefte hê aan; *an* ~ *MATTER*, 'n dringende saak; ~ *NEED*, dringende behoefte; nooddwang; ~**ly**, dringend.

ur'ger, aanporder.

ur'ic, urine-, pis-; ~ **acid**, urinesuur.

ur'im: ~ *and thummim*, urim en tummim.

ur'inal, urineglas; urinaal, waterplek, fluitplek; urineproefbuisie; urienhouer.

ur'inary, (n) (..ries), urinebak; (a) urine-; ~ **bladder**, waterblaas, urineblaas, pisblaas; ~ **organ**, urineorgaan; ~ **system**, urinestelsel; ~ **tract**, urinekanaal.

u'rinate, urineer, water, fluit.

urina'tion, urinering, watering.

ur'ine, water, urine, pis; ~ **stain**, urinevlek; ~ **trough**, urinekrip.

urinif'erous, urineleidend.

urinol'ogy, urinologie.

urn, (n) vaas, kruik, urn; lykbus; pot, kan; ketel; (v) in 'n urn (kruik) bewaar; ~**'iform**, kruikvormig, urnvormig; ~**-shaped**, kruikvormig.

ur'ocyst, blaas.

ur'olith, blaassteen.

urolog'ic, urologies.

urol'ogist, uroloog.

urol'ogy, urineleer, urologie.

uros'copy, urineondersoek, uroskopie.

Urs'a, die Beer; ~ *Major*, die Groot Beer; ~ *Minor*, die Klein Beer.

urs'ine, beer-, beeragtig.

urticar'ia, netelroos, galbulte, bort, urtikaria.

urt'icate, steek, brand (soos brandnetels); prikkel.

u'rubu, swart aasvoël (Amer.).

U'ruguay, Uruguay; ~ **an**, (n) Uruguaan; (a) Uruguaans.

us, ons; *ALL of* ~, ons almal; *ALL of* ~ *say so*, ons sê almal so.

usabil'ity, bruikbaarheid.

us'able, bruikbaar.

us'age, gebruik, gewoonte, usansie; behandeling; *CUSTOMARY* ~, gebruiklikheid; ~ *s of the SERVICE*, weermagsgebruike.

us'ance, gebruik; wisselgebruik, uso; rente; *bill (payable) at* ~, usowissel.

use, (n) gebruik, besteding; nut; gewoonte; aanwending; doeleinde; nuttigheid; voordeel; *COME into* ~, in swang kom; *in COMMON* ~, in algemene swang; algemeen gebruiklik; *once a* ~ *and ever a CUSTOM*, jong gewend, oud gedoen; *in DAILY* ~, in daaglikse gebruik; *be of no EARTHLY* ~, hoegenaamd van geen nut wees nie; *HAVE no* ~ *for*, nie kan gebruik nie; nie kan duld (veel) nie; *IN* ~, in gebruik; ~ *your LOAF*, gebruik jou verstand (kop); *MAKE good* ~ *of*, goeie gebruik maak van; *it is not MUCH* ~, dit baat (help) nie veel nie; *of NO* ~, van geen nut nie; *it is NO* ~, dit help tog nie; *OF* ~, nuttig; *be OUT of* ~, in onbruik wees; nie gebruik word nie; *PUT to good* ~, goeie gebruik maak van; *it is no* ~ *TALKING*, praat help tog nie; *WHAT is the* ~*?*, wat help dit?; ~ *and WONT*, vaste gewoonte; (v) gebruik, aanwend; behandel; gebruik maak van, jou bedien van; verbruik; nuttig; gewoonlik doen; ~ *BAD language*, vloek; ~ *every OPPORTUNITY*, van elke geleentheid gebruik maak; ~ *UP*, verbruik, opgebruik; (die voorraad) uitput.

used, gewoond; gebruik; halfslyt (klere); *he* ~ *to COME here*, dit was sy gewoonte om hier te kom; *he has* ~ *me like a DOG*, hy het my sleg behandel; *GET* ~ *to*, gewoond raak aan; *he has* ~ *me ILL*; *he ILL-* ~ *me*, hy het my sleg behandel; *he* ~ *to SAY*, hy het dikwels gesê; ~ *UP*, opgebruik; uitgeput; ~ **car**, tweedehandse (gebruikte) motor.

use'ful, nuttig, dienstig; *COME in* ~, goed te pas kom; handig inkom; nuttig wees; *MAKE oneself generally* ~, oraal help waar jy kan; *be PRETTY* ~ *at*, nogal vaardig wees met; nogal knap wees;

SERVE no ~ *purpose,* van geen nut wees nie; niks help nie; nutteloos wees; ~**ness,** nut(tigheid), bruikbaarheid.

use: ~ **less,** nutteloos; ydel; onbruikbaar, ondienstig; vergeefs; nikswerd; ~ **lessness,** nutteloosheid, ondienstigheid; ~**r,** gebruiker; verbruiker; *right of* ~ *r,* gebruiksreg.

ush'er, (n) deurwagter; inleier; seremoniemeester; hulponderwyser; geregsbode; *U* ~ *of the Black Rod,* Draer van die Swart Roede; (v) aandien, binnelei, aankondig; ~ *in a new ERA,* 'n nuwe tydperk inlui; *not* ~ *ed IN,* onaangemeld; ~ *OUT,* na buite lei, uitlei; wegsien; ~ *into the WORLD,* die wêreld instuur; ~ **ette',** plekaanwyser; geleidster; ~ **ship,** deurwagterskap; seremoniemeesterskap.

us'quebaugh, whisky.

ustilag'o, stuifbrand.

ustula'tion, brand(ing).

u'sual, gewoon, gebruiklik; *as* ~, soos gewoonlik; in die reël; deurgaans; op die ou trant; ~**ly,** gewoonlik, in die reël, deurgaans; ~**ness,** alledaagsheid, gewoonheid.

us'uary, gebruiker.

usucap'tion, besitreg.

us'ufruct, (n) vruggebruik, genotreg, lyftog, usufructus; (v) die vruggebruik hê van.

usufruc'tuary, (n) (..ries), vruggebruik; (a) vruggebruiks=, vruggebruikers=.

u'surer, woekeraar.

usur'ious, woekerend, woeker=; ~ **interest,** woekerrente; ~ **profit,** woekerwins; ~**ness,** inhaligheid.

usurp', wederregtelik toe-eien; jou aanmatig; onregmatig in besit neem; oorweldig; ~**a'tion,** oorweldiging, toe-eiening, verdringing; inbreuk; ~**atory,** aanmatigend, oorweldigend; ~**er,** verdringer, oorweldiger, geweldenaar; aanmatiger.

u'sury, woeker; woekerwins; woekerrente.

us'us, gebruik, usus.

ut, ut (mus.).

uten'sil, werktuig, gereedskap; houer; *kitchen (cooking)* ~*s,* kombuisgereedskap, kombuisbenodigdhede, kombuisgerei.

ut'erine, baarmoeder=; ~ **brother,** halfbroer (van moederskant); ~ **sister,** halfsuster (van moederskant).

ut'erus, (uteri), baarmoeder; moer (dier).

utilitar'ian, (n) utilitaris, aanhanger v.d. nutsgedagte; (a) nuttigheids=, utiliteits=; utilitaristies; ~ *view= point,* nuttigheidsoogpunt; ~**ism,** utilitarisme, nuttigheidsleer.

util'ity, nut, nuttigheid, bruikbaarheid, utiliteit; ~ **clothes,** draklere; ~ **company,** nutsmaatskappy; ~ **horse,** werksperd; ~**man,** handlanger, faktotum, nutsman; hulptoneelspeler, figurant.

utiliza'tion, benutting, nuttige aanwending, gebruikmaking.

ut'ilize, benut, gebruik, gebruik maak van, bestee, aanwend; besig.

ut'most, (n) uiterste; *AT the* ~, op (die) sy meeste (hoogste); *DO one's* ~, jou uiterste (bes) doen; *TO the* ~, tot die uiterste; (a) uiterste, verste; grootste; hoogste, beste; *the* ~ *KINDNESS,* die innigste vriendelikheid; *the* ~ *LIMITS,* die uiterste grense.

Utop'ia, Utopia.

utop'ia, utopie; hersenskim; gelukstaat.

utop'ian, (n) utopis; (a) utopies, idealisties; ~**ism,** utopisme.

ut'ricle, sel; liggaamsholte; sakkie, blasie (plantk.).

u'triform, sakvormig.

utt'er, (v) uiter, uit, sê, uitspreek; uitdruk, uitbring, uitstoot, slaak; in omloop bring, uitgee; ~ *a forged CERTIFICATE,* 'n vervalste sertifikaat uitgee; ~ *a CRY,* skreeu; *FORGE and* ~, vervals en uitgee; *not* ~ *a single WORD,* met 'n mond vol tande; nie 'n enkele woord sê nie; (a) volkome, totaal, volslae, algeheel, volstrek, uiterste; ~ *DARKNESS,* volslae duisternis; ~ *FOOL,* opperste dwaas; ~ *MISERY,* die diepste ellende; ~ *RUIN,* volslae ondergang; ~**able,** wat geuit kan word; uitspreekbaar; ~**ance,** uiting, uitlating; uitspraak; uitdrukking; voordrag, spreektrant; *give* ~ *ance to,* uiting gee aan; ~**er,** uitspreker; uitreiker (reg); ~**ing,** uiting; uitgifte; *forgery and* ~ *ing,* vervalsing en uitgifte; ~**ly,** volkome, heeltemal; totaal, absoluut.

utt'ermost, verste; uitterste; *to the* ~, heeltemal tot die uiterste.

U' tube, U-buis.

U' turn, U-draai.

uv'ula, (-e), kleintongetjie, huig, uvula; ~**r,** van die kleintongetjie, uvulêr, huig=.

uxor'ious, slaafs aan sy vrou onderworpe, wyfsgehoorsaam; te versot op sy vrou, vrousiek; verwyf; ~**ness,** verwyfdheid.

V

v, (vs, v's, vees), v; *little* ~, v'tjie; V, V-keep.

vac'ancy, (..cies), vakature, oopgevalle (vakante) betrekking; gaping, lakune; oop plek; leë ruimte; ledigheid; wesenloosheid; *FILL a* ~, 'n vakature vul; *a* ~ *FOR,* vakature vir; plek vir; *GAZE into* ~, wesenloos staar; *LIST of vacancies,* vakaturelys; *there is a* ~ *on his STAFF,* daar is 'n vakature in (op) sy personeel.

vac'ant, vakant; leeg; onbebou; onbeset, oop; ledig; leeghoofdig, gedagteloos, wesenloos, uitdrukkingloos, dom; *BECOME* ~, oopval; *a* ~ *CHAIR,* 'n leë stoel; *a* ~ *HOUSE,* 'n leë huis; ~ *LAND,* onbeboude (oop) grond; ~ *POSSESSION,* onmiddellike woonreg; *a* ~ *POST,* 'n vakante pos; *a* ~ *STARE,* 'n wesenlose blik.

vacate', afstand doen van (pos); uittrek, ontruim (huis); leegmaak; nietig verklaar.

vaca'tion, vakansie; vrye tyd; afstand; ontruiming; *on* ~, met (op) vakansie; ~ **course,** vakansiekursus; ~ **leave,** vakansieverlof.

vac'cinal, vaksine=, inentings=.

vac'cinate, inent, ent, vaksineer.

vaccina'tion, inenting, enting, vaksinasie; ~ **mark,** entmerk; ~ **pad,** entkussing.

vac'cinator, inenter.

vac'cine, (n) entstof, vaksine; *oral* ~, slukentstof; (a) inentings=, vaksine=; ~ **lymph,** entlimf.

vaccin'ia, koeipokkies.

va'cillate, weifel, besluiteloos wees, hink, hengel; wankel; kleitrap; skommel; slinger.

va'cillating, weifelend, aarselend, twyfelmoedig, wankelmoedig, weifelmoedig.

vacilla'tion, weifeling, aarseling; twyfelmoedigheid, weifelmoedigheid, besluiteloosheid, wankeling; slingering.

va'cillator, weifelaar; ~**y,** wankelend, weifelend.

vacu'ity, (..ties), leë ruimte, leegheid; wesenloosheid, leeghoofdigheid.

vac'uole, vakuool, selholtetjie.

vac'uous, leeg; wesenloos, uitdrukkingloos, onnosel, dom.

vac'uum, (..cua, -s), leegte, luglee ruimte, vakuum, lugleegte; ~ **box,** vakuumkas; ~ **brake,** lugrem; ~ **cleaner,** stofsuier; ~ **desiccator,** lugleë droogtoestel; ~ **distillation,** lugleë distillasie; ~ **extractor,** suigdroeër; ~ **flask,** vakuumfles; ~**-gauge,** vakuummeter; drukmeter, verklikker; ~ **pipe,** vakuumpyp; ~ **pump,** vakuumpomp; ~ **tank,** suigtenk, vakuumtenk; lugleë tenk; ~ **tube,** lugleë buis; ~ **valve,** lugklep.

vademec'um, handboek, vraagboek, vademekum.

vag'abond, (n) rondloper, swerwer, skobbejak, straatloper, padloper; (v) swerf, rondloop; ~ **age,**

vagary 1351 *vanish*

rondlopery; landlopery; ~**ism,** geswerf, landlopery; ~**ize,** swerf, rondloop.
vagar'y, (..ries), gril, nuk, luim, gier.
va'gina, vagina, skede.
va'ginal, van die skede, skede=.
vaginit'is, skedeontsteking, vaginitis.
vagin'oscope, vaginoskoop.
vag'rancy, rondlopery, landlopery, geswerf.
vag'rant, (n) rondloper, landloper, swerwer; (a) swerwend, rondtrekkend; onsamehangend; ~ **current,** swerfstroom, werwelstroom.
vague, vaag, onduidelik; onbestemd, onbepaald, onseker; droomagtig; *not the* ~*st NOTION,* nie die vaagste benul nie; *his PLANS are still* ~, sy planne het nog nie vaste vorm aangeneem nie; *a* ~ *RUMOUR,* 'n los (vae) gerug; ~**ly,** vaagweg; ~**ness,** onsekerheid; vaagheid.
vain, ydel, verwaand; vrugteloos, vergeefs; beuselagtig, sinloos; *BE in* ~, tevergeefs; *DO something in* ~ *iets* tevergeefs doen; ~ *HOPE,* ydele hoop; *IN* ~, tevergeefs, verniet; *take the NAME of God in* ~, die naam van God ydellik gebruik; *all RESISTANCE was in* ~, alle weerstand was vergeefs; ~ **glor'ious,** verwaand, pronkend, grootpraterig, blufferig, ydel, roemsugtig; ~ **glor'iousness,** verwaandheid, grootpraterigheid; ~**glor'y,** ydelheid, grootpratery, bluf, roemsug; ~**ly,** vergeefs; ~**ness,** ydelheid, nutteloosheid.
val'ance, (n) valletjie, draperie; damas; skerm; (v) drapeer.
vale¹, (n) vallei, dal; sloot; ~ *of tears,* tranedal.
vale², (n, interj) vaarwel.
valedic'tion, afskeid, vaarwel, afskeidsgroet.
valedic'tory, afskeids=; ~ **address,** afskeidsrede.
val'ence, val'ency, valensie; *kyk ook* **valance.**
Valen'cia, Valencia; ~ **orange,** Valencialemoen.
Val'entine, Valentyn; liefie, geliefde; minnebrief; (pl) minnelekkers; *St.* ~ *'s day,* Valentynsdag (14 Febr.).
valer'ian, duiwelsklou, balderjan, valeriaan.
val'et, (n) lyfbediende, dienaar, lyfkneg, kamenier; (v) bedien, as bediende optree.
valetudinar'ian, (n) sukkelaar; sieke; (a) siek, sieklik; sukkelend; ~**ism,** sieklikheid.
valetud'inary, (n) sieklikheid; (a) sieklik; sukkelend.
Valhall'a, Walhalla, paradys.
val'iance, onverskrokkenheid, dapperheid.
val'iant, dapper, moedig, kloekmoedig, manhaftig.
val'id, geldig, van krag; gangbaar; deugdelik, grondig, gegrond; regsgeldig; *a* ~ *EXCUSE,* 'n geldige verskoning; ~ *in LAW,* regsgeldig; ~**ate,** geldig maak, legaliseer, valideer, bekragtig; ~**a'tion,** geldigverklaring, bekragtiging.
valid'ity, krag, geldigheid, gangbaarheid, deugdelikheid, validiteit; ~ *of a CLAIM,* gegrondheid van 'n eis; *PERIOD of* ~, geldigheidsduur.
valise', reissak, handsak, handtas; ransel.
Val'kyr, (-s), Valkyr'ia, (-s), Valky'rie, (-s), Walkure.
Valkyr'ian, Walkure=.
vall'ey, (-s), vallei, dal; laagte; kloof; kiel (dak); ~ *of the shadow of DEATH,* die vallei v.d. skaduwee v.d. dood; ~ *of TEARS,* die aardse tranedal; ~ **board,** kielplank; ~ **gutter,** kielgeut; ~ **hour,** slap uur; ~ **line,** dallyn; ~ **period,** slap tyd; ~ **rafter,** kielspar; ~ **roof,** kieldak; ~ **tile,** kielpan.
valon'ia, akkerdoppe.
valoriza'tion, valorisasie.
val'orize, valoriseer, stabiliseer.
val'orous, dapper, moedig, heldhaftig.
val'our, moed, dapperheid, onverskrokkenheid.
valse, wals.
val'uable, kosbaar, waardevol; (pl) kosbaarhede; ~ *consideration,* geldwaardige teenprestasie.
valua'tion, waardering, skatting, valuasie; waardebepaling; *AT a* ~, teen taksasie; *DISPOSE of at a low* ~, teen 'n lae prys afstand doen van; *SET (put) too high a* ~ *on,* te hoog aanslaan; *TAKE him at his own* ~, sy eie skatting van homself aanvaar; ~ **court,** waarderingshof; ~ **roll,** waarderingslys, waardasielys, skattingslys.
val'uator, skatter, waardeerder, taksateur, taksateur.

val'ue, (n) waarde, prys; betekenis; ~ *in EXCHANGE; EXCHANGE* ~, ruilwaarde; *GET good* ~ *for one's MONEY,* goeie waarde vir 'n mens se geld kry; *know the* ~ *of MONEY,* die waarde van geld ken; *of NO* ~, van geen waarde nie; *OF* ~, waardevol, kosbaar; *OUT of* ~, te lig of te donker (skildery); *PRESENT* ~, toonwaarde, kontantwaarde; *for* ~ *RECEIVED,* vir waarde ontvang; *SET a high* ~ *on,* baie waarde heg aan; hoog waardeer; *TO the* ~ *of,* ter waarde van; *UNDER* ~, onder die waarde; (v) waardeer, skat, takseer, valueer; op prys stel, waarde heg aan; ~ *AT,* skat (waardeer) op; *he does not* ~ *that at a BRASS FARTHING,* hy heg nie die minste waarde daaraan nie; *he* ~ *s himself ON his business acumen,* hy beroem hom op sy sakevernuf; ~**d,** geskat; gewaardeer; ~ **judgment,** waardeoordeel; ~**less,** waardeloos, nikswerd, niksbeduidend; ~**r,** skatter, takseerder, waardeerder, taksateur.
val'vate, klep=; klepvormig.
valve, klep; skuif, afsluiter; radiolamp, radiobuis; ventiel (aan motorband); *GRIND* ~*s,* kleppe inslyp; ~ *of the HEART,* hartklep; ~ **adjustment,** klepstelling; ~-**body,** klephuis; ~ **box,** klepkas; ~-**cap,** klepdop; ~-**chamber,** ~-**chest,** klepkas, klepkamer; ~ **clearance,** klepspeling; ~ **cock,** klepkraan; ~-**cover,** klepdeksel; ~**d,** met kleppies; ~ **engine,** klepmotor; ~-**file,** baanvyl; ~-**gasket,** kleppakking; ~ **gearing,** kleppratwerk; ~-**grinder,** klepslyper; ~-**grinding,** klepslyping; ~-**head,** klepkop; ~ **less,** kleploos, sonder kleppe; ~-**lift,** kleplighoogte; ~-**lifter,** klepligter, klepstoter, ~ **lock,** klepsluiter; ~ **mechanism,** klepmeganisme; ~ **packing,** kleppakking; ~ **plunger,** klepdompelaar; ~-**push rod,** klepstoter; ~-**seat,** klepbedding; ~ **shaft,** klepsteel; ~ **spindle,** klepspil; ~-**spring,** klepveer; ~-**stem,** klepsteel; ~ **stroke,** kleplighoogte; ~-**tappet,** klepligter, klepstoter; ~-**timing,** klepreëling; ~ **transmitter,** lampsender; ~-**vane,** klepvleuel; ~-**wings,** kleppote.
valv'iform, klepvormig.
val'vular, klepvormig, klep=.
val'vule, kleppie.
vam'brace, onderarmskut, voorarmskut.
vamoos(e)', vamose', trap, skoert, spaander, laat vat.
vamp¹, (n) verleidster, gewetenlose koket; (v) koketteer met, vry na, verlok.
vamp², (n) oorleer, boleer; lap; geïmproviseerde begeleiding; (v) heelmaak, lap; versin; improviseer, op die gehoor begelei (mus.); ~ *up,* oplap; saamflans; uit die vuis lewer; ~ **er,** lapper; improviseerder van 'n begeleiding.
vam'pire, bloedsuier, uitsuier, bladneus *(Rhinolophus);* vampier; woekeraar; ~ **bat,** vampier, bloedsuiervlermuis.
vampi'ric, vampieragtig, vampier=.
vam'pirism, vampirisme, uitsuiery; afpersing.
vam'plate, stootplaat, handskut.
van¹, (n) wasmasjien; (v) **(-ned),** (erts) was.
van², (n) voorhoede, voorpunt, spits; leiers; *BE in the* ~, op die voorpunt wees; *the* ~ *of CIVILIZATION,* die spits (voorpunt) v.d. beskawing.
van³, (n) vervoerwa, goederewa, bagasiewa, verhuiswa, agterwa; konkteurswa; toemotorwa, afleweringswa, wa; (v) **(-ned),** vervoer, aanry.
vanad'ium, vanadium.
Van'dal, Vandaal; (a) Vandaal=, Vandaals=.
van'dal, vandaal, verwoester, vernielsugtige; ~**ism,** vandalisme, vernielsug; ~**is'tic,** vandalisties, vernielsugtig.
Van der Hum', Van der Hum(likeur).
Vandyke', puntkraag; punt; Van Dyckskildery, ~ **beard,** bokbaardjie; ~ **brown,** rooibruin(kleur).
vane, weerhaan; vaan, vaandel, wiek, vlerk (van meule); spreier (masjinerie); ~**d,** gewiek; ~ **sight,** windvisier.
van'guard, voorhoede; voorpunt, spits.
vanill'a, vanielje; ~ **essence,** vanielje-essens; ~ **filling,** vanieljevulsel; ~ **sauce,** vanieljesous.
vanill'ism, vanieljesiekte, jeuksiekte.
van'ish, verdwyn, wegraak; verswind; vervlieg; vergaan, wegsterwe; ~ *into thin AIR,* soos 'n groot

vanity   1352   *vector*

speld verdwyn; ~ *into NOTHING*, in rook vergaan; ~**ed**, verdwyn, verdwene; ~**ing cream**, smeltpommade; ~**ing point**, verdwynpunt; ~**ing target**, valskyf, duikskyf.

van'ity, verwaandheid, ydelheid; onwerklikheid, skyn; nietigheid; vrugteloosheid; waardeloosheid; leegheid; *ALL is* ~, alles is ydelheid; *V* ~ *FAIR*, ydelheidskermis; ~ *OF vanities*, ydelheid der ydelhede; ~ **bag**, tooisakkie, jesebelsakkie; ~ **case**, jesebeltassie, smuktassie, grimeertassie, tooitassie; ~ **mirror**, smukspieëltjie.

van'man, (..**men**), afleweraar.

vanq'uish, oorwin, verslaan; ~**er**, oorwinnaar, veroweraaar.

Van Rieb'eeck Day, Van Riebeeckdag.

van'tage, voordeel (tennis); wins; ~ **ground**, voordelige ligging; gunstige posisie; ~ **point**, gunstige posisie; uitkykplek.

vap'id, flou, laf, smaakloos; sinloos; ~ **'ity**, flouheid, lafheid; sinloosheid.

vap'orable, verdampbaar.

vaporif'ic, verdampings=, damp=, verdampend.

vap'oriform, dampvormig.

vaporim'eter, dampmeter, vaporimeter.

vaporiza'tion, uitwaseming, verdamping, dampvorming.

vap'orize, (laat) verdamp; verstuif; ~**r**, verdamper; verstuiwer; vergasser; vaporisator.

va'porizing carburett'or, vergasser.

vap'orous, dampig, vol damp; vlugtig.

vap'our, (n) damp, wasem; stoom; walm; rook; mis; (v) wasem, damp; rook; spog, grootpraat; ~ **bath**, stoombad; ~**er**, windsak, grootprater; ~**ish**, damperig, newelig; neerslagtig; spoggerig, grootpraterig; ~ **lock**, gasprop; lugsluiting; ~ **pressure**, dampdruk; gasdruk; ~**-proof**, dampdig; ~**y**, dampend, wasig; vaag.

vapula'tion, afranseling, kastyding, loesing.

variabil'ity, variabiliteit, veranderlikheid; wispelturigheid.

var'iable, (n) veranderlike grootheid; variant; veranderlike, variabele; (pl) veranderlike winde; (a) veranderlik, onbestendig; wisselvallig, ongedurig; veranderbaar, wisselbaar; verstelbaar; ~ **gear**, wisselrat; ~**ness**, veranderlikheid; wispelturigheid; ~ **star**, veranderlike ster; ~ **wind**, veranderlike wind.

var'iance, verandering; afwyking, wisseling; teëspraak; stryd, geskil, meningsverskil; onenigheid; strydigheid; *BE at* ~, dit nie eens wees nie; dit oneens wees; in stryd wees (met); *SET at* ~, in onmin bring; in die harnas jaag.

var'iant, (n) wisselvorm; variant; (a) veranderlik; verskillend; variërend.

varia'tion, verandering; afwyking; skommeling, afwisseling; verskeidenheid; variasie; ~ *in COURSE*, koersafwyking; ~ *of RESISTANCE*, weerstandsverandering; ~ *of TONE*, toonskakering; ~ *of VOLUME*, volumevariasie; *by WAY of* ~, vir die verandering, ter afwisseling.

varicell'a, waterpokkies.

va'ricocele, spataarbreuk.

var'icoloured, veelkleurig, bont.

va'ricose, geswel, vergroot; spataar=, varikeus; ~ **stocking**, spataarkous; ~ **vein**, spataar.

var'ied, verskeie, verskillend; afwisselend, gevarieerd; veelkleurig, bont.

var'iegate, bont maak; afwissel; skakeer; ~**d**, (kakel)bont, geskakeer(d), veelkleurig; ~**d tick**, bontbosluis.

variega'tion, afwisseling; skakering; veelkleurigheid.

vari'ety, (..**ties**), verskeidenheid, afwisseling; veelsydigheid; afwyking; variëteit; ~ *of COLOURS*, kleuremengeling; *a* ~ *of GOODS*, 'n verskeidenheid ware; *for a* ~ *of REASONS*, om verskillende redes; *for the SAKE of* ~, vir verandering; ter afwisseling; ~ *is the SPICE of life*, verandering van spys laat eet; *by WAY of* ~, vir afwisseling; ~ **artist**, variétéarties; ~ **company**, variétégeselskap; ~ **concert**, variakonsert, verskeidenheidskonsert; ~ **entertainment**, ~ **show**, variététeater.

var'iform, van verskillende vorme, veelvormig.

vari'ola, (regte) pokkies.

variola'tion, inenting.

var'iole, holtetjie, putjie, gaatjie; ~ **vaccine**, pokstof.

var'iolite, poksteen, varioliet.

var'ioloid, (n) ligte (gewysigde) pokkies; (a) pokkiesagtig.

variom'eter, variometer, stygmeter.

var'ious, verskillend, verskeie, velerhande, velerlei.

var'ix, (**varices**), spataar; aarswelling, aarspat.

varl'et, kneg; skelm; vabond; *an* ~ *'s an* ~, *though they be dressed in gold and scarlet*, al dra 'n aap 'n goue ring, hy is en bly 'n lelike ding.

varm'int, ongedierte; duiwelskind, swernoot; skelm.

varn'ish, (n) vernis; glans; verbloeming, skyn; (v) vernis; verlak; aanstryk; 'n glimp gee aan, verbloem, opsmuk; ~**ed tinfoil**, verniste bladtin; ~**er**, vernisser, (ver)lakker, verglanser; ~**ing**, verlakking.

vars'ity, (n) (..**ties**), universiteit; (a) universiteits=; *kyk* **university**.

var'us, horrelvoet; krombeenmens; huidvin.

var'y, (**varied**), verander, afwissel, varieer; verskil; afwyk, variasies maak op (mus.); *OPINIONS* ~ *on this matter*, oor hierdie saak is daar verskil van mening; *TASTES* ~, smaak verskil.

va'rying, afwisselend, veranderlik; *in* ~ *DEGREES*, in meerdere of mindere mate; *with* ~ *SUCCESS*, met wisselende geluk; ~ **current**, onbestendige stroom.

vas, (**-a**), (bloed)vat; buisie, geleier.

vas'cular, vaat=; van die bloedvate; vaskulêr; vaatryk; ~ **bundle**, vaatbundel; ~ **'ity**, vatevoorsiening; ~ **ray**, vaatstraal; ~ **system**, bloedvatstelsel; vaatstelsel; ~ **tissue**, vaatweefsel; ~ **wall**, vaatwand.

vas'culum, (..**la**), botaniseertrommel.

vase, vaas, blompot.

vasec'tomy, vaatuitsnyding, vasektomie.

vas'iform, buisvormig; (bloed)vatvormig.

vasoconstric'tion, vaatvernouing.

vasoconstrict'or, vaatvernouer.

vasomot'or, (n) vasomotoriese senuwee; (a) vasomotories.

vas'ospasm, vaatkramp.

vass'al, (n) ondergeskikte, leenman, vasal; kneg, slaaf; (a) ondergeskik; ~**age**, leenmanskap; leendiens; diensbaarheid, onderworpenheid; slawerny; ~**ry**, leenmanskap; diensbaarheid; knegskap.

vast, (n) eindeloosheid; uitgestrektheid; *the* ~ *ocean*, die eindelose see; (a) ontsaglik, onmeetlik; kolossaal, groot, (wyd)uitgestrek, grensloos; veelomvattend; erg, baie; ~ **multitude**, ontsaglike menigte; ~**ly**, ontsaglik, geweldig, kolossaal; ~**ness**, uitgestrektheid; oneindigheid; ontsaglikheid.

vat, (n) vat, vaatjie; kuip, bak, stukvat; (v) in 'n vat gooi.

Vat'ican, Vatikaan; ~ *CITY*, die Vatikaanstad; *the* ~ *STATE*, die Vatikaanstaat.

vati'cinate, voorspel, profeteer.

vaticina'tion, voorspelling, profesie.

vati'cinator, voorspeller.

vaud'eville, vaudeville, variétévoorstelling.

Vaudois', (n) Waldenser, Waadtlander; Waadtlands (dialek); (a) Waldenser=, Waadtlands.

vault, (n) verwulf, gewelf, welf, welfsel, welwing, kelder, grafkelder, sprong, spring; *CRANIAL* ~, skedeldak; *the* ~ *of HEAVEN*, die hemelgewelf; (v) oorwelf; van 'n gewelf voorsien; spring; ~ *into the saddle*, in die saal spring; ~**ed**, gewelf; ~**ed roof**, gewelfde dak; ~**er**, springer; akrobaat.

vault'ing, (n) gewelf; oorwelwing; paalspring; (die) oorspring; (a) spring=; ~ **exercise**, springoefening; ~ **horse**, bok, springperd, breedteperd, perd (gimnastiek); ~ **pole**, springstok, polsstok.

vault'y, gewelfagtig.

vaunt, (n) gepronk, grootpratery, gespog; (v) grootpraat, bluf, spog, roem op; ~**er**, pronker, grootprater.

V: ~ **beam**, V-straal; ~ **belt**, V-band; ~ **block**, V-blok.

veal, kalfsvleis; ~ **chop**, kalfskarmenaadjie; ~ **cutlet**, kalfskotelet; ~ **loaf**, kalfsvleisbrood; ~ **rib chop**, kalfsribkarmenaadjie; ~ **steak**, kalfskyf.

vec'tion, oordraging.

vec'tor, vektor (mat.); oordraer (van siekte).

Ved'a, Veda.
vedette', vedette, brandwag, ruiterwag.
Ve'dic, Vedies.
veer, draai, van rigting verander; skiet gee, vier, uittol (tou); van mening verander; ~ *and HAUL,* laat skiet en weer trek; ~ *ROUND,* omslaan; van koers verander.
ve'getable, (n) plant; groente; (pl) groente, moeskruid, toekos; (a) plantaardig, plante=; groente=; ~ **black,** plantswartsel; ~ **charcoal,** natuurlike houtskool; ~ **brimstone,** bliksempoeier; ~-**cutter,** groentesnyer; ~ **diet,** plantvoedsel, groentedieet; ~ **dish,** groenteskottel (-bak); groentegereg; ~ **dye,** plantkleurstof; ~ **earth,** teelaarde; ~ **farmer,** groenteboer; ~ **farming,** groenteboerdery; tuinery; ~ **fat,** plantvet; ~ **fibre,** plantvesel; ~ **garden,** groentetuin; ~ **kingdom,** planteryk; ~ **market,** groentemark; ~ **marrow,** murgpampoen, murgvan-groente; ~ **matter,** plantaardige stof; ~ **mould,** teelaarde; ~ **oil,** kookolie, slaaiolie, plantolie; ~ **oyster,** oesterplant, hawerwortel; ~ **parchment,** perkamentpapier; ~-**parer,** groenteskiller; ~ **pest,** groenteplaag; ~ **purée,** groentepuree; ~ **rack,** groenterak; ~ **soup,** groentesop; ~ **stew,** stoofgroente; ~ **tallow,** plantvet; ~ **tar,** houtteer; ~ **wax,** plantwas.
ve'getal, (n) plant; groente; (a) vegetatief, groei=; plantaardig.
vegetar'ian, vegetariër, groente-eter; (a) vegetaries; ~**ism,** vegetarisme.
ve'getate, groei; 'n plantlewe lei, vegeteer.
vegeta'tion, plantegroei; wasdom; plantwêreld, vegetasie; uitwas, woekering.
ve'getative, groeiend, groei=; plant=; vegetatief.
ve'hemence, hewigheid, heftigheid, drif, onstuimigheid, geweld.
ve'hement, vurig, heftig, driftig, onstuimig, geweldig, hewig.
ve'hicle, rytuig, vervoermiddel, voertuig; middel; oplosmiddel, verdunningsmiddel (vir verf, medisyne); draer; geleier; ~ **park,** voertuigpark.
vehic'ular, vervoer=; voertuig=, rytuig=, ~ **traffic,** voertuigverkeer.
veil, (n) sluier, floers; skerm, masker; voorhang(sel); dekmantel; mom; *BEYOND the* ~, aan die ander kant v.d. graf; *DRAW the* ~ *over,* die sluier trek oor; *RAISE (lift) the* ~, die sluier oplig; *TAKE the* ~, non word; *UNDER the* ~ *of,* onder die sluier (dekmantel) van; (v) sluier, befloers; maskeer, omsluier; bewimpel, verbloem; vermom; 'n sluier dra.
veiled, gesluier(d), bedek; *a* ~ *FIGURE,* 'n gesluierde gedaante; ~ *in MYSTERY,* in 'n waas van geheimsinnigheid gehul; *a* ~ *THREAT,* 'n bedekte dreigement.
veil'ing, bedekking, omsluiering; sluierstof.
vein, (n) aar; vlam (in marmer); laag (kole); nerf (plantk.); luim, stemming, gees; bron; gawe; aanleg, neiging; trant; *enough to FREEZE the blood in one's* ~*s,* genoeg om die bloed in jou are te laat stol; *in LIGHTER* ~, in ligter luim; *POETIC(AL)* ~, digaar; *in (a) REMINISCENT* ~, in 'n herinneringstemming; *in the SAME* ~, in dieselfde gees; *in SERIOUS* ~, in ernstige luim; (v) aar; ~ **ed,** vol are; geaar(d), deuraar; aarryk; aaragtig; generf (plantk.); ~**ing,** bearing; ~**let,** aartjie; nerfie; ~**like,** aaragtig; ~ **quartz,** aarkwarts; ~ **stone,** gangerts; ~**y,** vol are.
vel'ar, (n) velêre klank; (a) velêr, sagteverhemelte=.
velariza'tion, velarisering.
vel'arize, velariseer.
veld, veld, ~ **food,** veldkos, ~ **management,** veldbestuur; veldbeheer; ~**shoe,** ~ **schoen,** velskoen; ~ **sore,** brandseer.
velle'ity, swak wil, wilswakte.
vel'licate, (krampagtig) trek.
vellica'tion, (senuwee)trekking, (gesigs)vertrekking.
vell'um, vel, perkament, velyn, kalfsperkament; perkamenthandskrif; ~ **paper,** velynpapier.
velocim'eter, snelheidsmeter.
velo'cipede, rywiel, fiets.
velo'city, (..ties), snelheid, vinnigheid, gang; omloopsnelheid; *ARIAL* ~, vlaktesnelheid; *STRIKING* ~, trefsnelheid.
vel'odrome, fietsrybaan.
vel'omat, velomat.
velour(s)', fluweel; fluweelborsel; veloer.
vel'um, (vela), sagte verhemelte; velum; sluier.
velut'inous, fluweelagtig.
vel'vet, (n) fluweel; *be on* ~, in gunstige omstandighede verkeer; die beste daaraan toe wees; dit koninklik hê; (a) fluweel=; van fluweel; *the* ~ *glove,* bedrieglike uiterlike (sagtheid); ~ **bean,** fluweelboontjie; ~ **brush,** fluweelborsel; ~**een',** katoenfluweel; ~**ing,** fluweelstof; pluis; ~**like,** fluweelagtig; ~ **monkey, (-s),** blouaap; ~ **tree,** fluweelboom; ~**y,** fluweelagtig, fluwelig, fluweelsag; ferweelagtig; fluweel.
ven'al, omkoopbaar, te koop, veil.
venal'ity, omkoopbaarheid, veilheid, venaliteit.
ven'ate, geaar; generf.
vena'tion, nerwatuur; aarstelsel.
vend, verkoop, vent.
Ven'da, Venda.
vend: ~**ee',** koper; ~**er,** verkoper, venter.
vendett'a, bloedwraak, vendetta; vete.
vendibil'ity, verkoopbaarheid.
vend'ible, verkoopbaar.
vend'ing machine, muntoutomaat, verkoopmasjien.
ven'dor, verkoper; muntoutomaat; ~**'s shares,** inbringersaandele, verkopersaandele.
veneer', (n) fineerhout, ingelegde houtwerk, inlegwerk; vernis; oplegsel; (v) inlê, fineer, vernis; verbloem.
veneered, fineer=; glasuur=; ople=; ~ **brick,** glasuursteen; ~ **door,** fineerdeur; ~ **work,** fineerwerk.
veneer'ing, fineerwerk; finering; oplêwerk; ~-**hammer,** fineerhamer; ~-**plane,** fineerskaaf.
veneer' saw, fineersaag.
venerabil'ity, eerbiedwaardigheid, agbaarheid.
ven'erable, eerwaardig, eerbiedwaardig, hoogwaardig, agbaar; ~**ness,** eerwaardigheid.
ven'erate, eerbiedig, vereer.
venera'tion, eerbied, verering, eerbetoon; *hold in* ~, hoog vereer.
ven'erator, vereerder.
vener'eal, veneries, geslags=; ~ **disease,** veneriese siekte, vuilsiekte, geslagsiekte.
ven'ery[1]**,** wellus, mingenot.
ven'ery[2]**,** jag.
ven'esect, bloedlaat.
venesec'tion, bloedlating.
Vene'tian, (n) Venesiaans; (a) Venesiaans; ~ **blind,** hortjiesblinding, skuifblinding, sonblinding; ~ **chalk,** kleremakerskryt; ~ **glass,** Venesiaanse glas; ~ **lace,** Venesiaanse kant; ~ **mosaic,** terrazzo; ~ **pearl,** vals pêrel, glaspêrel; ~ **shutter,** hortjie, hortjiesluik.
Venezue'la, Venezuela; ~**n,** (n) Venezolaan; (a) Venezolaans.
ven'geance, wraak; *EXACT* ~, wraak neem; *TAKE* ~ *on,* wraak neem op; *WITH a* ~, erg, kwaai, dat dit so kraak.
venge'ful, wraaksugtig; ~**ness,** wraaksug.
ven'ial, vergeeflik, geoorloof; ~'**ity,** vergeeflikheid.
Ven'ice, Venesië; ~ **glass,** Venesiaanse glas.
ven'ison, wildbraad, wildsvleis; *HAUNCH of* ~, wildsboud; *JERKED* ~, biltong; *ROAST* ~, wildbraad.
ven'om, gif; venyn; *spit* ~ *at,* venyn (gif) spoeg teen; ~ **duct,** gifbuis; ~ **fang,** giftand; ~**ous,** giftig, venynig; ~**ousness,** giftigheid; venynigheid.
ven'ous, aar=, geaar; ~ **haemorrhage,** aarbloeding; ~ **pressure,** aardruk; ~ **pulse,** aarpols.
vent, (n) luggat, opening; spleet; uitlaat; uiting; ventiel, uitweg, split, slip; swikgat; sundgat, laaigat; gat, anus, aars (hoender); *give* ~ *to,* lug (uiting) gee aan; (v) lug, uiting gee aan; 'n opening maak in; ontlug; asem skep; ~ *one's SPLEEN,* lug gee aan jou ergernis; ~ *one's WRATH,* uitdrukking gee aan jou toorn; ~ **age,** vingergaatjie.
ven'ter[1]**,** spierknoppie.
ven'ter[2]**,** buik, onderlyf, abdomen; baarmoeder; *of ONE (the same)* ~, van dieselfde moeder; *by*

vent' hole | 1354 | *vernacular*

TWO *(several)* ~s, van twee verskillende moeders.
vent' hole, luggat, trekgat.
vent'iduct, lugkanaal, lugkoker, lugpyp.
ven'til, ventiel, klep.
ven'tilate, lug gee, (uit)lug, deurlug, ventileer; bespreek, wêreldkundig maak; ~ *a grievance,* 'n grief lug.
vent'ilating, lug=, ventileer=; ~ **brick,** lugsteen; ~ **eyebrow,** dakvenster; ~ **flue,** ventilasiekanaal; ~ **shaft,** lugskag; ~ **tissue,** sponsweefsel.
ventila'tion, lugvervarsing, lugtoevoer, verlugting, belugting, ventilasie; openbare bespreking; ~ **cowl,** ventilasiekap; ~ **fan,** waaierventilator; ~ **shaft,** ventilasieskag.
ven'tilator, luggat, lugvervarser, lugkoker, lugvenster, ventilator; ~ **hatch,** ventilatorluik; ~ **window,** trekvenster.
vent: ~ **peg,** swik; ~ **pipe,** rioollugpyp; ~ **plug,** ontlugprop.
ven'tral, buik=, ventraal; ~ **fin,** buikvin; ~ **laughter,** diep lag; ~ **side,** onderkant; ~ **sucker,** buiksuier; ~ **wall,** buikwand.
ven'tricle, ventrikel, holte; hartkamer.
ven'tricose, ven'tricous, met 'n groot maag, buikig, boepens=; geswel.
ventril'oquism, buikspreek.
ventril'oquist, buikspreker.
ventril'oquize, buikspreek.
ventril'oquy, buiksprekery.
ventros'ity, swaarlywigheid.
vent' shaft, ontlugskag.
ven'ture, (n) onderneming; waagstuk; waagspel, spekulasie; *AT a* ~, op goeie geluk; *DECLINE the* ~, weier om te waag; (v) waag, riskeer; op die spel sit; so vry wees, die vryheid neem, durf; *I* ~ *to ASK,* ek wil so vry wees om te vra; *I* ~ *to DIFFER from you,* ek wil so vry wees om van u te verskil; *nothing* ~, *nothing HAVE,* wie nie waag nie, sal nie wen nie; ~ *one's LIFE,* jou lewe waag; *I will not* ~ *an OPINION,* ek sal dit nie waag om 'n mening uit te spreek nie; ek sal my nie verstout om 'n mening uit te spreek nie; *I* ~ *to SAY,* ek durf sê; ~ *on a TASK,* 'n taak (durf) aanpak; ~**r,** waaghals; ~**some,** vermetel, waaghals(er)ig, gewaag; ~**someness,** vermetelheid, waaghals(er)igheid, gewaagdheid.
ven'turous, *kyk* **venturesome.**
vent' window, trekvenster.
ven'ue, plek van geregtelike verhoor; bymekaarkomplek, byeenkomplek, vergaderplek; *change the* ~, die plek van verhoor verander; op 'n ander plek vergader.
Ven'us, Venus; die Aandster; *MOUNTAIN of* ~, skaamheuwel, venusheuwel; *MOUNTS of* ~, vroulike borste; ~**'s girdle,** Venusgordel; venusgordel (dierk.); ~**'s hair,** venushaarvaring.
Venus'ian, Venusiaan (denkbeeldige inwoner van Venus).
Ven'us shell, venusskulp.
vera'cious, waar; waaragtig, getrou, waarheidliewend; ~**ness,** waarheid; waarheidsliefde.
vera'city, geloofwaardigheid, betroubaarheid; waarheidsliefde; waaragtigheid; waarheid.
veran'da(h), veranda, stoep.
verb, werkwoord, verbum.
verb'al, (n) werkwoordelike (verbale) selfstandige naamwoord; (a) woordelik; werkwoordelik; mondeling; woord(e)=; letterlik; ~ *CRITICISM,* mondelinge kritiek; ~ *DISPUTE,* woord(e)stryd; ~ *EVIDENCE,* mondelinge getuienis; ~ *MESSAGE,* mondelinge boodskap; ~ *NOUN,* werkwoordelike (verbale) selfstandige naamwoord; ~ *ORDER,* mondelinge bevel; ~ *PLAY,* woordspel; ~ *TRANSLATION,* letterlike vertaling; ~ *WAR,* woordoorlog; ~**ism,** letterknegtery, woordsiftery, verbalisme; ~**ist,** letterkneg, woordsiffer, woordvitter; ~**'ity,** letterlikheid; ~**ize,** tot 'n werkwoord maak; omslagtig wees.
verbat'im, (a) woordelik; (adv) woord vir woord, woordelik.
verben'a, verbena, ysterkruid.

verb'iage, woordevloed, bombas(me), omhaal van woorde.
verb'icide, woodverknoeier; woordverknoeiing.
verb'ose, woordryk, breedsprakig, omslagtig, wydlopig.
verbos'ity, woord(e)rykdom, woordevloed, wydlopigheid, langdradigheid, omslagtigheid, breedsprakigheid, groot omhaal van woorde.
verd'ancy, groenheid; groenigheid; baarheid.
verd'ant, groen, fris; baar, onervare.
verd-antique', groen marmer, groen serpentyn; kopergroen; groen aanpaksel, groenspaan, patina (op ou brons).
verd'ict, uitspraak; beslissing, vonnis; *CONSIDER your* ~, dink na oor jou uitspraak; *GIVE a* ~, uitspraak doen; *OPEN* ~, onbesliste uitspraak; *RETURN a* ~, uitspraak lewer.
verd'igris, groenroes, kopergroen, groenspaan.
verd'ite, verdiet (geol.).
verd'ure, groenheid, groenigheid; frisheid, bloei.
verd'urous, groen.
verge, (n) rand, kant, soom; grens; staf, roede; *BE on the* ~ *of,* op die punt wees om; *on the* ~ *of DEATH,* op die rand van die dood; *on the* ~ *of TEARS,* klaar om te huil; (v) naby kom, grens aan; neig; *it* ~*s on IMPUDENCE,* dit grens aan onbeskaamdheid; ~ *ON,* naby kom aan; grens.
ver'ger, stafdraer; koster; ~**ship,** kosterskap; stafdraersamp.
Ver'gil, Vergilius; ~**'ian,** Vergiliaans.
verid'ical, waarheidsprekend; waar.
verifiabil'ity, bewysbaarheid; kontroleerbaarheid.
ve'rifiable, bewysbaar, toetsbaar, verifieerbaar; kontroleerbaar.
verifica'tion, bewys; waarmaking; stawing; bevestiging; toetsing, bewyslewering; bekragtiging, verifikasie; *in* ~ *of,* as bewys van, ter stawing van.
ve'rifier, bekragtiger; kontroleerder, nakyker.
ve'rify, (..fied), bewys; bekragtig; bevestig; ondersoek, nasien, nasyfer, nagaan, nakyk, toets, kontroleer; verifieer; ~ *his figures,* die juistheid van sy syfers toets.
ve'rily, voorwaar, inderdaad, waarlik.
verisim'ilar, waarskynlik.
verisimil'itude, waarskynlikheid; skynwaarheid.
ve'ritable, waaragtig; eg, opreg; *a* ~ *rogue,* 'n egte skurk.
ve'ritably, waaragtig.
ve'rity, waarheid; egtheid.
ver'juice, groenvrugtesap.
verm'eil, (n) vergulde silwer; goudvernis; vermiljoen; (a) vermiljoen.
verm'ian, wurmagtig, wurm=.
vermicell'i, vermicelli.
verm'icide, wurmmiddel, wurmgif, wurmdoder.
vermic'ular, wurmvormig, wurmagtig.
vermic'ulate, (v) wurmvormig versier (merk); (a) wurmvormig, kronkelend, soos 'n wurm; deur wurms gevreet; vol wurms, wurmstekig.
vermicula'tion, wurmgang, wurmvormige beweging; wurmagtige versiering (merk); beskadiging deur wurms.
verm'icule, wurmpie.
vermic'ulite, vermikuliet.
vermic'ulose, vermic'ulous, vol wurms; wurmagtig; wurm=.
verm'iform, wurmvormig.
vermif'ugal, wurmdrywend.
verm'ifuge, wurmmiddel.
verm'igrade, voortkruipend, voortkronkelend.
vermil'lion, (n) vermiljoen; (v) vermiljoen kleur; (a) vermiljoen, vermiljoenkleurig.
verm'in, ongedierte, goggas; skorriemorrie, gespuis; ~**ate,** vol ongediertes word; goggas laat vermeerder; ~**a'tion,** vemeerdering van goggas; wurmsiekte; ~ **destroyer,** ~ **killer,** insektepoeier; ~**o'sis,** wurmbesmetting; ~**ous,** vol ongedierte, vol goggas; ~**-proof,** ongediertevry; ~**-proofing,** rotgaas; rotdigting.
vermiv'orous, wurmvretend.
verm'outh, vermoet.
vernac'ular, (n) landstaal, moedertaal, volkstaal; om=

vernal — **vestry**

vern'al, gangstaal; tongval, dialek; (a) inheems, inlands, vaderlands; van die landstaal; ~ism, idiomatiese uitdrukking (van die volkstaal); volksidioom; ~ize, in die landstaal oorbring (oorgaan).
vern'al, lente-, voorjaars-; ~ equinox, lente-dag-ennagewening; ~ fever, lentekoors; ~ flower, lenteblom; ~ grass, soetgras.
vern'ant, lentebloeiend.
verna'tion, bladligging in knop.
vern'ier, vernier, nonius; ~ callipers, vernierpasser; ~ coupling, vernierkoppeling; ~ gauge, skuifpasser; ~ scale, noniusskaal; ~ screw, vernierskroef, noniusskroef.
ve'ronal, veronal (geregistreerde handelsnaam).
Veronese', (n) Veronees; (a) Veronees.
veron'ica, ereprys (blom), veronika.
ve'rricule, haarbossie.
verruc'a, (-e), vratjie.
ve'rrucose, ve'rrucous, vol vratjies; vratagtig, vrat-.
vers'ant, hang (van 'n berg), helling, skuinste, afdraand.
vers'atile, veranderlik, beweegbaar; onstandvastig, alkantig.
versatil'ity, veranderlikheid, veelsydigheid, alsydigheid; beweeglikheid van gees.
verse, (n) vers; versreël; poësie, gedig; sang; koeplet, strofe; *BLANK* ~, rymlose verse; *the FIRST and second* ~ *of*, die eerste en tweede vers van; *IN* ~, op rym; in digmaat; (v) dig, berym, verse maak; op rym sit; ~ *oneself in*, jou bedrewe maak in.
versed, bedrewe, ervare; *well* ~ *in*, goed bedrewe in; goed onderlê in; gekonfyt wees in.
verse: ~-let, versie; ~-monger, rymelaar, pruldigter; ~-mongering, rymelary; ~r, rymelaar, pruldigter.
vers'et, voorspel; tussenspel.
vers'icle, versie.
vers'icoloured, veelkleurig, bont; wisselend van kleur.
versic'ular, verse-; ~ division, verdeling in verse.
versifica'tion, versbou; verskuns; beryming.
vers'ifier, rymelaar, versiemaker.
vers'ify, (..fied), berym, dig, verse maak.
ver'sion, weergawe; lesing; vertaling, oorsetting; draaiing, wending; bewerking, vorm; voorstelling, verklaring, vertolking; *his* ~ *of the quarrel*, sy weergawe v.d. rusie.
vers'o, (-s), linkerbladsy; keersy (medalje); verso.
verst, werst (1 067 m, Russiese maat).
vers'us, teen, versus.
vert¹, (n) bekeerling; (v) oorgaan (tot 'n ander kerk).
vert², (n) groenigheid; groen; reg om groen hout te kap.
vert'ebra, (-e), werwel(been).
vert'ebral, werwel-, ruggraats-; ~ column, werwelkolom, ruggraat, rugstring; ~ ribs, vals ribbes.
vertebrat'a, gewerwelde diere.
vert'ebrate, (n) gewerwelde dier; (a) gewerwel; kragtig.
vertebra'tion, werwelbou, werwelverdeling.
vert'ex, (vertices), toppunt, top; spits; boogtop; kruin; ~ *of angle*, hoekpunt.
ver'tical, (n) loodlyn; tophoek; loodregte stand, vertikale vlak; sirkel; *out of the* ~, uit die lood, nie loodreg nie, skuins; (a) loodreg, vertikaal; regop, staande; ~ angle, tophoek, hoogtehoek; teenoorstaande hoek; ~ axis, vertikale as; ~ boiler, staanketel; ~ engine, vertikale enjin; ~ interval, hoogteverskil; ~'ity, regstandigheid; ~ line, loodlyn; ~ly, loodreg, regop, vertikaal; ~*ly opposite angles*, teenoorstaande hoeke; ~ plane, vertikale vlak; ~ tiling, muurbeteëling.
vert'ical, krans.
verti'cillate(d), kransstandig.
verti'ginous, draaierig, duiselingwekkend.
vert'igo, (-s), duiseling, duiseligheid.
vertu', *kyk* virtu.
verv'ain, ysterkruid.
verve, besieling, geesdrif, vuur, gloed.
verv'et, blouaap.
ve'ry, (a) waar, eg, opreg; werklik; einste; *that* ~ *DAY*, daardie selfde dag; dieselfde dag nog; *the veriest FOOL knows this*, die grootste swaap weet dit; *he is the* ~ *IMAGE of his father*, hy is sy pa uitgeknip; ~ *IMPORTANT person (VIP)*, baie belangrike persoon (BBP); 'n hooggeplaaste; groot kokkedoor; *for* ~ *JOY*, uit louter vreugde; *the* ~ *LAST*, die allerlaaste; *the* ~ *MAN*, net die regte man; *the* ~ *MENTION of the matter was enough*, die blote vermelding v.d. saak was al genoeg; *he said it this* ~ *MINUTE*, hy het dit nou net gesê; *for that* ~ *REASON*, juis om dié rede; *this is the* ~ *SPOT*, dis die presiese (einste) plek; *the* ~ *THING*, net die regte ding; *the* ~ *THOUGHT of it*, net die gedagte daaraan; *the* ~ *TRUTH*, die opregte waarheid; *his* ~ *WORDS*, sy eie woorde; (adv) baie, danig, seer, regtig; erg, heel, uiters; *it's ALL* ~ *well for you to say so*, jy kan maklik so sê; *the* ~ *BEST*, die allerbeste; *the* ~ *FIRST*, die heel eerste; ~ *GOOD!* mooi so!; ~ *MANY*, regtig baie; *thank you* ~ *MUCH*, baie dankie; *for your* ~ *OWN*, vir jou alleen; *he looked* ~ *PLEASED*, hy het hoog in sy skik gelyk; ~ *PROBABLY*, hoogs waarskynlik; ~ *WELL*, baie goed; nou goed.
Ve'ry: ~ cartridge, Verypatroon; ~ light, ligkoeël; ~ pistol, ligpistool; ~ signal, ligkoeëlsein.
vesic'a, blaas, blaar.
ves'ical, blaas-, blaar-.
ves'icant, (n) trekpleister, blaartrekker; (a) blaartrekkend.
ves'icate, blare trek.
ves'icating, blaartrekkend.
vesica'tion, blaartrekking.
ves'icatory, (n) (..ries), blaartrekkende middel; trekpleister; (a) blaartrekkend.
ves'icle, gasblasie, gasbel; sel; holtetjie; stoomgaatjie.
vesic'ular, gasblaas-, gasbel-, blaasagtig; vol blasies, blasierig.
vesic'ulate, blasies vorm; ~d, vol blasies, blaasagtig.
vesicula'tion, blaasvorming.
vesic'ulose, vesic'ulous = **vesicular**.
Vespa'sian, Vespasianus.
ves'per, aand; aandster; aanddiens, vesper; ~-bell, vesperklok, aandklok; ~ tide, aanduur.
ves'pertine, aand-.
ves'piary, (..ries), wespenes.
ves'pine, wespe-, perdeby-, perdebyagtig.
vess'el, vat; kruik, fles, kan; houer; kom; vaartuig, skip; bloedvat; (pl) vaatwerk; *a CHOSEN* ~, 'n uitverkore vat; *EMPTY* ~*s make the most sound*, leë vate maak die meeste lawaai; groot lawaai, maar weinig wol; *the WEAKER* ~, die swakkere vat.
vest¹, (n) onderbaadjie; frokkie, onderhemd.
vest², (v) klee; beklee (pos), oorgaan op; berus by; toevertrou; verleen aan; ~ *IN*, berus by, ~ *with POWER*, met mag beklee; *the PROPERTY* ~*s in the heir*, die eiendom gaan oor op die erfgenaam; ~ *UPON*, oorgaan op.
Ves'ta¹, Vesta.
ves'ta², wasvuurhoutjie.
ves'tal, (n) Vestaalse maagd; non; kuise vrou; (a) kuis, eerbaar; Vestaals; V~ virgin, Vestaalse maagd.
vest'ed, gevestig; bestaande, verleende, verkreë; ~ *INTERESTS*, bestaande (gevestigde) belange; *under the POWERS* ~ *in me*, kragtens die bevoegdhede aan my verleen; ~ *RIGHTS*, gevestigde regte.
ves'tibule, portaal, vestibule (gebou); mondholte.
ves'tige, spoor, voetspoor; oorblyfsel; teken; sweem; greintjie; rudiment; *without a* ~ *of CLOTHING*, sonder 'n draad klere; *not a* ~ *of EVIDENCE*, geen greintjie bewys nie; *not a* ~ *of TRUTH*, geen greintjie waarheid nie.
vesti'gial, rudimentêr, onontwikkel(d).
ves'ting, vestiging; bekleding; onderhempmateriaal.
ves'titure, bekleding; hare; skubbe; kors.
vest'ment, gewaad, kleding; altaardoek; (pl) priestergewaad.
vest' pocket, onderbaadjiesak; ~ dictionary, sakwoordeboekie.
ves'try, (..ries), kerkraad; konsistorie(kamer); sakristie; ~ clerk, kassier (van kerkraad); ~ man, kerkraadslid.

ves'ture, (n) kleding, kledingstuk, gewaad; (v) (be)= klee; ~ r, koster, sakristein.
vesuv'ian, (n) windvuurhoutjie; (a) vulkanies.
Vesuv'ian, (a) Vesuviaans.
Vesuv'ius, Vesuvius.
vet, *abbr. of* veterinary surgeon, veearts, dierearts.
vetch, (-es), wilde-ertjie; wiek; ~ y, vol wieke; wiek= agtig.
vet'eran, (n) veteraan, oud-stryder, oud-gediende; ringkop; (a) oud; beproef, ervare; ~ car, veteraan= motor, veteraankar.
veterina'rian, (n) veearts, (a) veeartsenykundig, vete= rinerêr.
vet'erinary, (n) (.. ries), veearts, dierearts; (a) veeart= senykundig, veearts=; ~ college, veeartsenykollege; ~ faculty, veeartsenyfakulteit; ~ school, veeartse= nyskool; ~ science, veeartsenykunde; ~ surgeon, veearts, dierearts.
vet'o, (-es), (n) verbod; veto; *PUT (place) a ~ on,* die veto uitspreek oor; *RIGHT of ~ ,* reg van veto, ve= toreg; (v) verbied; afkeur; veto, die veto uitspreek oor, verwerp.
vex, terg, pla, kwel, vererg; tempteer, sar, prikkel; verstoor, versteur; *be ~ ed at,* vererg wees oor; ~ a'tion, ergernis; kwelling, gekweldheid, ergerlik= heid, temptasie; plaag; verdriet, verdrietlikheid.
vexa'tious, ergerlik, hinderlik, lastig; verdrietlik; kwelsiek; tergend; ~ person, sondesoeker; ~ ness, ergerlikheid; las; verdriet.
vexed, geërger, geraak, gegrief, gepla(ag), ergerlik, vies, verstoor; *a ~ question,* 'n netelige kwessie.
vexillo'logy, vlagkunde.
vexill'um, (vexilla), vlag, vaandel, banier.
vex'ing, ergerlik, sarrend, tergend.
V' formation, V-formasie.
vi'a¹, (n) pad, weg; *V ~ APPIA,* die Appiese weg; *V ~ DOLOROSA,* Via Dolorosa, die Lydensweg; *V ~ LACTEA,* die Melkweg; *~ MEDIA,* die midde(l)= weg.
vi'a², (prep) oor, via.
viabil'ity, lewensvatbaarheid; kiemkrag (bot.).
vi'able, lewensvatbaar, ekonomies uitvoerbaar.
vi'aduct, (n) viaduk; boogbrug.
vi'al, flessie; fiool; *LEYDEN ~ ,* Leidse fles; *pour out the ~ s of WRATH upon,* fiole van toorn uitgiet oor.
viam'eter, afstandsmeter, meetwiel.
vi'and(s), geregte, kos, lewensmiddel(e), spyse.
viat'icum, padkos, teerspyse; reisgeld; viaticum; laas= te oliesel (R.K.); draagbare altaar.
vib'rant, trillend; bewend.
vibrate', tril, vibreer; slinger, skommel; beef, sidder.
vib'ratile, trillend.
vibrat'ing, trillend, vibrerend; ~ screen, trilsif, vi= breersif.
vibra'tion, trilling, vibrering, slingering; *amplitude of ~ ,* trillingswydte; ~ less, trillingvry; ~ waves, skuddingsgolwe.
vibra'tor, vibrator, vibreerder; trillerveer.
vib'ratory, trillend, tril=; *a ~ voice,* 'n bewende (tril= lende) stem; ~ motion, trilbeweging; ~ test, tril= toets.
vib'rio, (-nes), trildiertjie.
vibriss'a, (-e), neushaar; trilhaar; trilveer.
vib'roscope, trillingsmeter, vibroskoop.
viburn'um, viburnum, sneeubal.
vic'ar, vikaris; ~ age, vikariaat; pastorie, vikariswo= ning; ~ apostolic, apostoliese vikaris; ~ -general, vikaris-generaal; ~ 'ial, vikaris=; ~ 'iate, vikariaat.
vicar'ious, plaasvervangend; tweedehands; middel= lik; *suffer ~ punishment,* 'n ander se straf onder= gaan; ~ authority, plaasvervangende mag; ~ suf= fering, lyding in die plek van 'n ander.
vic'arship, vikarisskap.
vice¹, (n) skroef; (v) in 'n skroef vasdraai; vasklem.
vice², (n) ondeug; fout, gebrek; onsedelikheid; ~ *pun= ishes itself,* die kwaad loon die meester.
vice-³, (prep) in die plek van, vise-, onder=; ~ -ad'mi= ral, vise-admiraal; ~ -cap'tain, onderkaptein; ~ - cap'tainship, onderkapteinskap; ~ -chair'man, vise-voorsitter, ondervoorsitter; ~ -chair'manship, ondervoorsitterskap; ~ -chan'cellor, onderkanse=
lier, vise-kanselier; ~ -chan'cellorship, vise-kanse= lierskap.
vice'-clamp, handklou.
vice: ~ -con'sul, vise-konsul; ~ -con'sular, vise-kon= sulêr; ~ -consulate, vise-konsulaat; ~ -con'sulship, vise-konsulskap; ~ ge'rent, (n) plaasvervanger; (a) plaasvervangend.
vice' lever, skroefslinger.
vi'cenary, vicenn'ial, twintigjarig; twintigjaarliks.
vice: ~ -pre'sidency, vise-presidentskap; ~ -pre'si= dent, vise-president; ondervoorsitter; ~ -prin'cipal, vise-prinsipaal, onderhoof; ~ reg'al, onderkonink= lik; ~ re'gal train, goewerneurstrein; ~ -reg'ency, vise-regentskap; ~ -reg'ent, vise-regent; ~ 'reine, onderkoningin; ~ 'roy, onderkoning; ~ roy'al, on= derkoninklik; ~ roy'alty, onderkoningskap.
vice vers'a, vice versa, omgekeerd, andersom.
vi'cinage, nabyheid; buurskap; omgewing.
vicin'ity, (.. ties), buurt, buurskap, nabuurskap; na= byheid, omgewing, omstreke; *IN the ~ of,* in die omgewing van; omstreeks; *in the ~ of R100,* so om en by R100.
vi'cious, sleg, bedorwe; boosaardig; foutief, verkeerd; venynig; geniepsig, kwaadaardig; wys (diere); kwaad; skerp, visieus; *a ~ ATTACK,* 'n venynige aanval; *~ CIRCLE,* bose (ergerlike, noodlottige) kringloop; duiwelskringloop; *~ CRITICISM,* venynige kritiek; *~ TENDENCIES,* slegte nei= gings; ~ ness, slegtheid, bedorwenheid; boosaar= digheid, kwaaiheid; geniepsigheid.
viciss'itude, wisselvalligheid; lotswisseling, weder= waardigheid; verandering, wisseling; *the ~ s of life,* die wederwaardighede v.d. lewe.
vic'tim, slagoffer, prooi; dupe; *fall a ~ to,* die slagof= fer word van; ~ iza'tion, kullery, afsettery, tekort= doening, weerwraak, viktimisasie (na 'n staking bv.); ~ ize, viktimiseer, 'n slagoffer maak; offer; verniel; bedrieg, te kort doen; afset; weerwraak neem op.
vic'tor, oorwinnaar; *to the ~ the spoils,* aan die oor= winnaar die buit.
victor'ia, victoria (rytuig); victoria regina (waterle= lie); kroonduif.
Victor'ia: ~ Cross, Victoriakruis; ~ Falls, Victoria= waterval; ~ n, (n) Victoriaan; (a) Victoriaans.
victorine', damespelskraag.
victor'ious, oorwinnend, seëvierend; *be ~ over,* seë= vier oor.
vic'tory, (.. ries), oorwinning, sege, seëpraal, vikto= rie; *GAIN the ~ over,* die oorwinning behaal oor; *a MORAL ~ ,* 'n morele oorwinning; *a PYRRHIC ~ ,* 'n Pyrrhusoorwinning (Pirrusoorwinning).
vic'tual, (n) mondvoorraad, proviand; (pl) kos, voed= sel, mondbehoeftes, mondvoorraad, mondprovi= sie, spys(e), eetware, lewensmiddele, leeftog; (v) (-led), proviandeer, van lewensmiddele voorsien; ~ ler, proviandmeester; proviandskip; *licensed ~ ler,* drankhandelaar; ~ ling, (n) voedselvoorsie= ning, proviandering, voedselverskaffing; (a) voed= selvoorsienend, provianderend; ~ ling house, eet= huis, herberg; ~ ling officer, proviandoffisier; ~ ing ship, voorradeskip; ~ ing yard, proviandwerf.
vicu'gna, vicu'na, vikoenja, vikoena; ~ wool, vikoen= jawol.
vid'e, kyk, sien, vide.
videl'icet, naamlik, dit wil sê.
video, (-s), video; ~ cassette, videokasset; ~ cassette recorder, videokassetopnemer; ~ film, videofilm; ~ tape, videoband; ~ tape recorder, videobandop= nemer.
vid'imus, (-es), outentieke afskrif, verslag; ondersoek.
vid'uage, weduweeskap.
vid'uous, weduwee=.
vie, meeding, wedywer; ~ *with,* iem. na die kroon steek; meeding met; ~ r, mededinger.
Viennese', (n) inwoner van Wenen, Wener; Weense (vrou); (a) Weens.
Viet'nam, Viëtnam.
view, (n) uitsig, gesig, vergesig, blik; stand, verskiet; opinie, mening, sienswyse, gevoel, denkbeeld; doel= wit, doel; kykie; beskouing; oënskou; aansig; besig= tiging; *on a CLOSER ~ ,* op die keper beskou; by 'n

vigesimal   1357   *violin*

nadere beskouing; *COME in* ~, in sig kom; *EXPOSE to* ~, aan die oog vertoon, ontbloot; *take a DIFFERENT* ~ *of*, 'n ander mening toegedaan wees; 'n ander standpunt inneem; *hold DIFFERENT* ~*s*, ander menings daarop nahou; van mening verskil; *take a DIM* ~ *of*, maar min dink van; *at FIRST* ~, op die eerste gesig; *FRONT* ~, vooraansig; *in FULL* ~ *of*, in die lig van; met die oog op; *a GRAND* ~, 'n pragtige uitsig; *HAVE in* ~, beoog; op die oog hê; *HAVE* ~*s upon*, beskouings hê omtrent; *HOLD a* ~, meen, van mening wees; *IN* ~, te sien; in sig; *IN* ~ *of*, in die lig van; met die oog op; *with that IN* ~, met die oog daarop, te dien einde, ten einde; *KEEP in* ~, in die oog hou; ~ *s on LIFE*, lewensbeskouing, lewensopvatting; *LOST TO* ~, uit die oog; *ON* ~, te sien, uitgestal; blootgelê; *PASS from* ~, uit die gesig verdwyn; *POINT of* ~, gesigspunt; *from my POINT of* ~, myns insiens; *take a POOR* ~ *of something*, nie baie van iets dink nie; *SIDE* ~, syaansig; *his* ~ *s on the SUBJECT*, sy beskouings oor die saak; *TAKE the* ~, die mening huldig; *TAKE a different* ~, 'n ander mening toegedaan wees; *TAKE the long* ~, ver vooruit dink; versigtig wees; *WITH a* ~ *to*, met die oog op; met die bedoeling om; ten einde; (v) besien, bekyk, besigtig, beskou; in oënskou neem; aanskou; sien; ~ *with SORROW*, met lede oë aanskou (aansien); ~ *a proposal UNFAVOURABLY*, 'n voorstel as onwenslik beskou; ~ **er**, opsigter; toeskouer; besigtiger; aanskouer; beeldsoeker; prentekyker (toestel); ~**-finder**, soeker, loervenstertjie, beeldsoeker; ~**ing**, besigtiging; ~ **less**, sonder uitsig; ~ **point**, gesigspunt, standpunt, oogpunt; uitkykplek; ~ **window**, uitkykvenster; ~**y**, onprakties, eksentriek; vol fiemies.
viges'imal, twintigste.
vi'gil, (die) waak; vieraand, heilige aand; nagwag; (pl) nagtelike gebede; nagwaak; *keep* ~*s*, waak.
vi'gilance, waaksaamheid; versigtigheid; slaaploosheid; ~ **committee**, werdakomitee, waaksaamheidskomitee.
vi'gilant, waaksaam, wakend, noulettend, wakker; **..an'te**, lid van waaksaamheidskomitee; nagwag.
vignette', (n) krulle; karakterskets; vinjet; (v) 'n vinjet maak van.
vig'orous, kragtig, sterk, fors; deurtastend, flink, energiek; gespierd; ~ **ly**, flink; ~ **ness**, krag, forsheid; energie.
vig'our, krag, sterkte, energie, fermheid; gespierdheid; fluksheid, flinkheid; ~ **less**, kragteloos.
Vik'ing, Wiking.
vile, laag(hartig), snood, gemeen, vuig; skandelik, veragtelik, afskuwelik; beroerd, miserabel, ellendig; ~ **ly**, op 'n gemene manier; ~ **ness**, laagheid, gemeenheid, vuigheid.
vilifica'tion, smaad, laster, slegmakery.
vil'ifier, lasteraar, swartsmeerder, bekladder.
vil'ify, (..fied), beskinder, belaster, smaad, van sy eer beroof.
vil'ipend, minag, deur die modder sleur, verkleineer.
vill'a, villa; landhuis.
vill'age, dorp; dorpie; ~ **clerk**, dorpsklerk; ~ **council**, dorpsraad; ~ **ground**, dorpsgrond; ~ **management board**, dorpsbestuur; ~ **r**, dorpeling, dorpsbewoner, dorpenaar; dorpsgas; ~ **school**, dorpskool.
vill'ain, skurk, onnut, booswig, boef, onverlaat, snoodaard, verraaier; lyfeiene; *the* ~ *of the PIECE*, die skurk; *PLAY the* ~, die sondebok (die skurk) speel; ~ **age**, lyfeienskap; ~ **ous**, sleg, skurkagtig, verfoeilik; ~ **ousness**, ~**y**, (..**nies**), boosheid, laagheid, slegtheid; boewery, boewestreek, boefagtigheid, skurkagtigheid, skurkery, skurkestreek.
vilanelle', villanelle (gedig).
vill'ein, lyfeiene, horige, dorper; ~ **age**, lyfeienskap.
vill'ose, harig, harerig.
villos'ity, harigheid; behaarde plek.
vill'ous, harig.
vill'us, (**villi**), haar; vlokkie.
vim, energie, fut, gô, pit.
vim'inal, tak-, takvormig.
vina'ceous, wyn-; wynrooi.

vinaigrette', reukflessie.
vin'cible, oorwinlik.
vin'culum, (..**cula**), boei; band; verbindingstreep.
vin'dicable, verdedigbaar; bewysbaar.
vin'dicate, regverdig; handhaaf; suiwer; verdedig; *he has been completely* ~ *d*, hy is (van die beskuldiging) heeltemal gesuiwer.
vindica'tion, regverdiging; verdediging; handhawing; terugvordering.
vin'dicative, verdedigend, wrekend, straffend.
vin'dicator, verdediger, voorspraak.
vin'dicatory, verdedigend, regverdigend, straffend; ~ *of*, ter verdediging van; ~ **laws**, strafwette.
vindic'tive, wraakgierig, wraaksugtig, uit wraak, haatdraend; ~ **ness**, wraaksug.
vine, wingerdstok, druiwestok, wynstok; rankplant, klimop; *under one's* ~ *and FIG-TREE*, onder eie dak; onder jou eie vyeboom; *a FRUITFUL* ~, 'n vrugbare vrou; ~**-bower**, druiweprieel; ~**-clad**, met wingerde begroei; ~**-culture**, wynbou; ~**-cutting**, druiwestiggie, druiwesteggie; ~**-disease**, wingerdsiekte; ~**-dresser**, wingerdsnoeier; ~**-fretter**, filloksera.
vin'egar, (n) asyn; (v) asyn bygooi, versuur; (a) asyn-, asynsuur-; ~ **ish**, ~ **y**, asyn-, asynagtig, suur.
vine: ~**-grower**, wynboer; ~**-growing**, wynbou; ~**-leaf**, wingerdblad, druiweblaar; ~**-louse**, druiweluis; ~**-peach**, lemoenspanspek; ~**-pergola**, druiweprieel; ~ **ry**, (..**ries**), druiwekwekery; ~**-shoot**, wingerdrank; ~**-snake**, voëlslang, stokslang; ~**-stake**, wingerdpaal; ~ **-tendril**, druiwerank; ~ **yard**, wingerd; ~ **yard tractor**, wingerdtrekker.
vi'niculture, wynbou.
vinicul'turist, wynbouer.
vinif'erous, wynproduserend.
vin'ificator, wynmaaktoestel.
vinom'eter, wynmeter.
vin'ous, wynagtig; wyn-; wynrooi; ~ **fermentation**, alkoholiese gisting; ~ **flavour**, wynsmaak; ~ **inspiration**, dronkmanswysheid, besieling wat deur drank verkry word.
vint, wyn maak.
vin'tage, (n) wynoes; druiweoes; druiwetyd; wynjaar; soort wyn; *a bottle of the 1950* ~, 'n bottel v.d. 1950-wynoes; (a) uitstekend; oud; ~ **car**, noagmotor; ~ **festival**, wingerdfees; ~ **r**, druiweplukker; ~ **time**, parstyd; ~ **wine**, kwaliteitswyn; ~ **year**, buitengewone wynjaar.
vint'ner, wynhandelaar.
vin'y, wynstok-.
vi'ol, **vio'la**, altviool.
vi'ola[1], viola.
vi'ola[2], (klein) gesiggie.
vi'olable, skendbaar.
viola'ceous, violetkleurig.
vi'olate, skend, oortree; verkrag; skoffeer, onteer (persoon); inbreuk maak op, geweld aandoen; ontheilig, verbreek.
viola'tion, skending, skennis, verbreking, oortreding; verkragting; inbreuk; ontheiliging; ~ *of the air*, skending v.d. lugruim.
vi'olator, skender, oortreder, vroueskender, verkragter.
vi'olence, geweld; gewelddpleging; gewelddadigheid, geweldenary; handtastelikheid; felheid, hewigheid; heftigheid; verkragting; *BY* ~, met geweld; *DIE by* ~, 'n gewelddadige dood sterf; *DO* ~ *to*, aanrand, geweld aandoen; *PERSONAL* ~, lyfsgeweld; *PUBLIC* ~, openbare geweld; *ROBBERY with* ~, roof met geweld; *USE* ~, geweld gebruik.
vi'olent, geweldig, hewig, ongenadig, heftig, fel; onstuimig; gewelddadig; onsag; ~ *CONDUCT*, gewelddadigheid; *a* ~ *DEATH*, 'n gewelddadige dood; *lay* ~ *HANDS on*, gewelddadig optree teen; jou vergryp aan; *be in a* ~ *TEMPER*, in 'n verskriklike humeur wees; ~ **ly**, met geweld.
vi'olet, (n) viooltjie; pers; (a) perskleurig, violet.
violin, viool; ~**-bow**, strykstok; ~**-case**, vioolkis; ~ **clef**, vioolsleutel; ~ **ist**, violis, vioolspeler; ~**-maker**, vioolmaker; ~**-player**, vioolspeler; ~**-playing**, vioolspel; ~ **recital**, vioolkonsert; ~ -

shaped, vioolvormig; ~ **solo,** vioolsolo; vioolstuk; ~ **string,** vioolsnaar.
vi'olist, altspeler, altviolis.
violoncell'ist, tjellis, tjellospeler.
violoncell'o, (-s), violonsel, tjello.
vip'er, adder, slang; *nourish a ~ in one's bosom,* 'n adder aan die bors koester; ~ **ine,** ~ **ish,** ~ **ous,** slangagtig; venynig; ~ **'s bugloss,** slangkruid.
virag'o, (-s), mannetjiesvrou, manwyf, helleveeg, rissie, feeks, tang, geitjie (fig); *a ~,* 'n hen met spore; 'n rissie; 'n mannetjiesvrou.
vires'cence, groenheid; groenwording.
vires'cent, groenwordend; groen.
virg'ate¹, (n) landmaat (12,1 hektaar).
virg'ate², (a) dun; regop.
Vir'gil, Vergilius; ~ **'ian,** Vergiliaans.
vir'gin, (n) maagd; (a) maagdelik; ongerep, onbevlek, suiwer; *the Blessed V ~, the V ~ Mother,* die Heilige Maagd; ~ **al,** maagdelik; rein; ~ **al milk,** maagdemelk; ~ **-born,** uit die Heilige Maagd gebore; ~ **chorus,** maagderei; ~ **forest,** ongerepte oerwoud, oerbos; ~ **gold,** gedeë goud, maagdegoud; ~ **honey,** stroopheuning.
Virgin'ia, Virginië (V.S.A.); ~ **creeper,** wildewingerd; ~ **n, (n)** Virginiër; (a) Virginies; ~ **tobacco,** Virginiëtabak, Virginiese tabak.
vir'gin: ~ **'ity,** maagdom, maagdelikheid; reinheid, ongereptheid; ~ **'s bower,** klematis; ~ **snow,** skoon sneeu; ~ **soil,** rou grond, ongebraakte grond; ~ **wool,** nuwe wol, nuutwool.
Virg'o, die Maagd (sterrebeeld).
vir'gule, latjie, takkie; komma.
virides'cence, groenagtigheid; groenerigheid; groenwording.
virides'cent, groenagtig; groenwordend.
virid'ity, groenheid; groen kleur.
vi'rile, manlik, manhaftig, manmoedig; fors, gespierd, sterk, kragtig, lewenskragtig.
viril'ity, manlikheid, manhaftigheid; manbaarheid; gespierdheid.
virolog'ical, virologies.
virol'ogist, viroloog.
virol'ogy, virologie.
vir'ose, vir'ous, giftig.
virtu', kunsliefde; kunskennis; *articles of ~,* kuriositeite, kunsvoorwerpe.
virt'ual, feitlik, eintlik, wesenlik, werklik, virtueel, skynbaar; *he is the ~ principal,* hy is feitlik die hoof; ~ **focus,** denkbeeldige brandpunt; ~ **ly,** in werklikheid; feitlik; ~ **value,** middelbare waarde.
virt'ue, deug, deugsaamheid; krag; eerbaarheid; kuisheid; doeltreffendheid; *BY ~ of,* op grond van; uit hoofde van; uit krag van; kragtens; *a woman of EASY ~,* 'n vrou van los sedes; 'n onkuise vrou; *HAVE the ~ of,* die deug (doeltreffendheid) hê; *MAKE a ~ of necessity,* van die nood 'n deug maak; *by ~ of his OFFICE,* uit hoofde van sy amp; *~ is its own REWARD,* deug bring sy eie beloning; *WOMANLY ~,* vrouedeug; ~ **less,** sonder deug; kragteloos.
virtuos'ity, vaardigheid, virtuositeit.
virtuos'o, (..tuosi), virtuoos; kunsliefhebber.
virt'uous, deugsaam, deugliewend; rein, kuis, eerbaar; ~ **ness,** deugsaamheid; kuisheid, eerbaarheid.
vi'rulence, kwaadaardigheid; boosaardigheid, venynigheid; hewigheid.
vi'rulent, kwaadaardig; boosaardig, venynig; heftig, bitter, skerp.
vir'us, virus, gif, smetstof.
vis'a, (n) visum; ondertekening; stempel; (v) viseer, stempel.
vis'age, aangesig, gelaat.
vis'ard, *kyk* **visor.**
vis-à-vis', (n) vis-à-vis; rytuig (rusbank) waar twee persone reg teenoor mekaar sit; (adv) regoor mekaar, teenoor, vis-à-vis; (prep) teenoor, regoor.
viscar'a, reënboogdruppel (blom).
vis'cera, ingewande, binnegoed; ~ **l,** ingewands-; ~ **te,** die ingewande uithaal; ontwei.
vis'cid, taai, klewerig; ~ **'ity,** taaiheid, klewerigheid, viskositeit.

viscom'eter, viskometer.
viscosim'eter, *kyk* **viscometer.**
viscos'ity, taaiheid, viskositeit.
vis'count, burggraaf; ~ **cy,** (..**cies),** burggraafskap; ~ **ess',** (-es), burggravin.
vis'cous, klewerig, taai, skaars vloeibaar, taaivloeibaar, dikvloeibaar; ~ **ness** = **viscosity.**
vis'é, (n) visum; ondertekening; stempel (v) viseer, stempel.
visibil'ity, sigbaarheid; helderheid; sig; *~ was very good,* die lig (sigbaarheid, sig) was baie goed; ~ **meter,** sigmeter.
vis'ible, sigbaar, te sien, waarneembaar; duidelik; aanskoulik; *~ horizon,* gesigseinder.
vis'ibly, sienderoë, sigbaar.
Vis'igoth, Wes-Goot; ~ **ic,** Wes-Goties.
vi'sion, (n) (die) sien; gesigskerpte; gesig, visioen, droombeeld, droomgesig; verskyning; blik; siening; verbeeldingskrag, visie; beskouing; versiendheid, deursig; *BEYOND our ~,* verder as ons kan sien; *BREADTH of ~,* ruimhartigheid, ruimheid van blik; *FIELD of ~,* gesigsveld; *HAVE a ~ of something,* iets in jou verbeelding sien; (v) in 'n droom sien; jou voor oë tower; ~ **al,** gegrond op 'n visioen; gesigs=; ingebeeld; ~ **ary, (n)** (..**ries),** dweper, dromer, geestesiener, fantas, plannemaker; (a) hersenskimmig, ingebeeld, fantasies, dromerig, onprakties; *~ary eye,* sienersoog; ~ **ist,** siener; dromer; ~ **less,** sonder visie.
vis'it, (n) besoek, kuier, visite; *COME on a ~,* kom kuier; *be ON a ~,* met besoek wees; *PAY a ~,* besoek aflê; *RETURN a ~,* 'n teenbesoek bring; (v) besoek, kuier; 'n besoek aflê, 'n visite maak; beproef; teister, straf; inspekteer; *~ the INIQUITY of the fathers upon the children,* die misdaad van die vaders aan die kinders besoek; *~ UPON,* besoek aan; as straf oplê; ~ **ant, (n)** besoeker, kuiergas; trekvoël; (a) besoekend, kuier=; ~ **a'tion,** beproewing, besoeking; ondersoek, inspeksie, deursoeking; huisbesoek; Mariaboodskap; ~ **(at)or'ial,** besoekend, besoekers=.
vis'iting, (die) kuier, besoek, kuiery; *have a ~ ACQUAINTANCE, be on ~ TERMS,* vir mekaar kuier; ~ **book,** visiteboek; ~ **card,** naamkaartjie; visitekaartjie; ~ **day,** besoekdag, ontvangdag; ~ **hours,** besoekure; ~ **place,** aanloopplek; ~ **room,** besoekerskamer.
vis'itor, kuiergas, besoeker; (pl) besoekers, kuiergaste; ~ **'ial,** inspeksie=, visitasie=; *~ial address,* 'n toespraak by 'n visitasie; ~ **s' book,** vreemdelingeboek; hotelregister; ~ **s' bureau,** besoekersburo; ~ **'s room,** vrykamer, besoekerskamer.
vis'or, visier; masker; klep; kykgleuf; ~ **ed,** gemasker(d); met 'n visier.
vis'ta, uitsig, verskiet, vergesig, deurkyk, vista.
Vis'tula: *the ~,* die Weichsel.
vis'ual, gesigs=; opties; visueel; ~ **acuity,** gesigskerpte; ~ **aids,** aanskouingsmiddele; ~ **angle,** gesigshoek; ~ **education,** aanskouingsonderwys; ~ **flight,** sigvlug; ~ **horizon,** sigbare horison; ~ **instruction,** aanskouingsonderwys; ~ **instrument,** optiese instrument; *~iza'tion,* aanskoulikmaking, veraanskouliking, voorstelling; visualisering; ~ **ize,** aanskoulik maak, veraanskoulik; 'n beeld vorm van, in voorstelling maak; visualiseer, jou voor die gees roep; ~ **line,** gesigslyn; ~ **nerve,** gesigsenuwee; ~ **point,** oogpunt; ~ **purple,** gesigspurper; ~ **range,** gesigsveld, gesigsbereik; ~ **training,** oogskerping.
vit'al, lewens=, lewensvatbaar, kragtig, vitaal; essensieel, deurslaggewend, beslissend; lewensbelangrik; lewensgevaarlik; noodlottig; besield; *BE ~ to,* van die allerhoogste belang wees vir; *of ~ IMPORTANCE,* v.d. allerhoogste belang; van lewensbelang; *not of ~ IMPORTANCE,* nie lewensbelangrik nie; dis nie moord of doodslag nie; *of ~ INTEREST,* van lewendige belang; *~ to one's PURPOSE,* onontbeerlik vir jou doel; *a ~ WOUND,* 'n dodelike wond; ~ **condition,** lewensvoorwaarde; ~ **error,** noodlottige fout; ~ **fact,** deurslaggewende feit; ~ **fluid,** lewensap; ~ **force,** lewenskrag; ~ **function,** lewensbelangrike funksie;

lewensverrigting; ~ **ism,** vitalisme; ~ **ist,** (n) vitalis; (a) vitalisties; ~ **'ity,** lewenskrag, vitaliteit, lewens= duur; kiemkrag, lewensvatbaarheid; ~ **ize,** lewe gee; lewenskrag gee, inspireer; ~ **juice,** lewensap; ~ **ly,** essensieel, noodsaaklik; ~ **necessity,** lewens= belang; ~ **parts,** lewensdele, edele dele; ~ **power,** lewenskrag; ~ **principle,** lewensbeginsel; ~ **ques**= **tion,** lewensvraag; ~ **s,** vernaamste lewensorgane; (die) essensiële; ~ **spirit,** lewensgees; ~ **statistics,** bevolkingstatistiek; mate van bors, middel, heupe; bors-, middel-, heupmaat; ~ **warmth,** lewens= warmte.

vit'amin, vitamine, vitamien; *rich in* ~ *s,* vitamineryk; ~ **content,** vitaminegehalte; ~ **ize,** vitamineer; ~ **tablet,** vitaminetablet.

vitell'us, (..**telli),** dooier, eiergeel; vitellus.

vi'tiate, besmet, bederf, vervals; ongeldig maak, ver= nietig; ~ *the language,* die taal bederf.

vi'tiated, bederf, besmet, verpes; ~ **air,** verpeste lug; ~ **judgment,** gebrekkige oordeel; ~ **mind,** onrein gemoed.

vitia'tion, bederf, verontreiniging, besoedeling, be= smetting; ongeldigmaking.

vit'iculture, wingerdbou.

viticult'ural, wingerdbou=.

viticul'turist, wynbouer, wingerdboer.

vitol'philist, vitolfilis, sigaarbandversamelaar.

vitreos'ity, glasagtigheid.

vit'reous, glas=, glasagtig, glasig; ~ **body (humour),** glasvog; ~ **electricity,** glaselektrisiteit; ~ **enamel,** brandemalje; ~ **porcelain,** glasporselein; ~ **silica,** silikaglas; ~ **ness** = **vitreosity.**

vitres'cence, verglasing.

vitres'cent, verglasend.

vit'ric, glasagtig, glas=; ~ **s,** glaswerk, glasgoed.

vitrifac'tion, verglasing.

vit'rifiable, vergla(a)sbaar.

vitrifica'tion, verglasing.

vit'rified, verglaas; ~ **brick,** verglaasde teël of steen; ~ **enamel,** brandemalje; ~ **tile,** verglaasde dakpan.

vit'riform, glasagtig.

vit'rify, (..**fied),** tot glas maak, verglaas, in glas verander.

vit'riol, vitrioel; *BLUE* ~, blouvitrioel, kopervitri= oel; *GREEN* ~, ystervitrioel; *OIL of* ~, vitrioel= olie, swawelsuur; ~ **ate,** met vitrioel behandel; ~ **'ic,** vitrioelagtig, vitrioelhoudend; venynig, bit= sig; ~ **-throwing,** vitrioelgooiery.

Vitru'vian, Vitruviaans.

vitt'a, (-e), kleurband; kraus.

vit'ular, vit'uline, kalfagtig, kalf=.

vitup'erate, uitskel, beskimp, berispe, laak.

vitupera'tion, (die) uitskel; geskimp; smaadrede.

vitup'erative, skellend, skimpend, skimp=, slegmaak=.

vi'va! lewe! lank sal hy lewe!

viva'cious, lewendig; beweeglik; vrolik, opgewek; standhoudend, oorblywend (plante); ~ **ness,** le= wendigheid; opgewektheid.

viva'city, lewendigheid, opgewektheid, lewenslustig= heid, élan.

vivar'ium, (..**ria),** visdam, akwarium; vivarium, die= retuin.

viv'at! lewe! vivat! lank mag hy lewe!

viva vo'ce, (n) mondelinge eksamen; (a) viva voce, mondeling.

vives, oorsiekte (by jong perde).

viv'id, duidelik, helder, lewendig; skitterend; tekenag= tig; ~ *COLOURS,* helder kleure; *a* ~ *DESCRIP*= *TION,* 'n lewendige beskrywing; ~ *IMAGIN*= *ATION,* sterk verbeeldingskrag; *have a* ~ *RECOLLECTION of,* nog baie duidelik onthou; ~ **ness,** duidelikheid, helderheid, aanskoulikheid.

vivifica'tion, opwekking tot nuwe lewe; besieling, verlewendiging.

viv'ify, (..**fied),** verlewendig; besiel, laat herleef.

vivip'arous, vivipaar, lewendbarend.

viv'isect, lewendig ontleed (oopsny).

vivisec'tion, viviseksie, (die) oopsny van lewende die= re; ~ **ist,** beoefenaar van viviseksie; voorstander van viviseksie.

viv'isector, beoefenaar van viviseksie, viviseksor.

vix'en, wyfiejakkals; feeks, serpent, geitjie, dierasie,
heks, duiwelin, kwaai wyf, kwaai vroumens, regte kat; ~ **ish,** feeksagtig, duiwelagtig, heksagtig.

viz'ard, *kyk* **visor.**

vizier', visier; ~ **ate,** visierskap.

V: ~ **joint,** V-las; ~ **neck,** V-nek, kloofhals; ~ **notch,** V-keep.

voc'able, woord; woordklank.

vocab'ulary, (..**ries),** woordelys; woordeskat; naam= lys.

voc'al, (n) vokaal, klinker; (a) mondeling; stemheb= bend; vokaal, stem=; *become* ~, jou stem laat hoor; ~ **chord,** stemband; ~ **ism,** gebruik v.d. stemorga= ne; klinkerstelsel, vokaalstelsel, vokalisme; ~ **ist,** sanger, sangeres; ~ **'ity,** stemvermoë; klankryk= heid; ~ **iza'tion,** vokalisasie; ~ **ize,** uitspreek; stem= hebbend maak; laat hoor, praat; sing; vokaliseer; ~ **music,** sang, vokale musiek; ~ **organ,** stemor= gaan; ~ **part,** sangparty; ~ **performer,** sanger, sangeres.

voca'tion, beroep; professie; ambag; roeping; geroe= penheid; *FEEL a* ~ *for,* 'n roeping voel vir; *MISS one's* ~, jou roeping mis; *MISTAKE one's* ~, 'n verkeerde beroep kies.

voca'tional, beroeps=; vak=; ~ **education,** beroepson= derwys; ~ **guidance,** beroepsvoorligting; ~ **guide,** beroepsvoorligter; ~ **school,** vakskool; ~ **training,** beroepsopleiding; vakopleiding.

voc'ative, (n) vokatief; (a) roepend, aansprekend, vo= katief.

vocif'erant, (n) skreeuer; (a) skreeuend, lawaaierig.

vocif'erate, uitroep, raas, uithulder.

vocifera'tion, geskreeu, gebulder, geraas.

vocif'erous, skreeuend, lawaaierig, luidrugtig, uit= bundig; ~ **ness,** luidrugtigheid, uitbundigheid, la= waaierigheid.

vod'ka, wodka.

voe, baaitjie, inham.

vogue, swang, mode; populariteit; *BRING into* ~, in swang bring; *COME into* ~, in swang kom; op= gang maak; *HAVE a great* ~, baie in die mode wees; 'n groot aanhang hê; *IN* ~, in die mode; *OUT of* ~, uit die mode; ~ **word,** modewoord.

voice, (n) stem; spraak; uiting, uitdrukking; stemheb= bende klank; seggenskap, reg om te praat; vorm; geluid; *ACTIVE* ~, bedrywende vorm; *in a CLEAR* ~, hardop; *COMPASS of the* ~, stem= omvang; *FIND* ~ *in song,* jou in sang uit; *FOR* ~ *s,* meerstemmig; *GIVE* ~ *to,* uiting gee aan, vertolk; *she has a GOLDEN* ~, sy het 'n suiwer (goue, prag= tige) stem; *be IN good* ~, goed by stem wees; *HAVE a* ~ *in,* seggenskap hê in; *give* ~ *to his IN*= *DIGNATION,* uiting (uitdrukking) gee aan sy ver= ontwaardiging; *LOSE one's* ~, jou stem verloor; *in a LOUD* ~, hardop; met luide stem; *in a LOW* ~, saggies; *have NO* ~ *in,* geen seggenskap hê nie in; *with ONE* ~, met algemene stemme, eenstemmig, eenparig; *PASSIVE* ~, lydende (passiewe) vorm; ~ *of the PEOPLE,* volkstem; *the POPULAR* ~, die volkstem; *RAISE one's* ~, jou stem verhef; *a STILL, small* ~, die gesuis van 'n sagte stiltе; die stem v.d. gewete; *at the TOP of one's* ~, luidkeels, hardop; *speak with TWO* ~ *s,* met twee monde praat; *like the* ~ *of one crying in the WILDER*= *NESS,* soos die stem van 'n roepende in die woes= tyn; (v) uitdrukking gee aan, vertolk, verkondig; stem (orrel); stemhebbend maak; van 'n klankbaan voorsien (film); ~ **artist,** stemkunstenaar; ~ **d,** stemhebbend; ~ **-box,** strottehoof; ~ **less,** sonder stem; spraakloos, stom, stemloos, onuitgesproke; sonder seggenskap; ~ **lessness,** spraakloosheid; stemloosheid; ~ **part,** sangparty; ~ **pipe,** spreek= buis; ~ **production,** stemoefening; stemvorming; ~ **-training,** stemoefening; ~ **tube,** spreekbuis.

void, (n) ruimte; leegte, gaping; lugruimte; leemte; (die) niet; (v) ontlas; vernietig, ongeldig maak, nie= tig verklaar; uit die weg ruim; ontruim; (a) leeg; nietig; kragteloos; ongeldig; vakant; onbloot van, vry van, sonder; *DECLARE* ~, nietig verklaar; *FALL* ~, vakant word; *NULL and* ~, van nul en gener waarde; ~ *OF,* sonder, vry van; ~ **able,** ver= nietigbaar; opsegbaar; ~ **ance,** lediging; ontrui= ming; ontslag; ~ **ness,** vernietigbaarheid, opseg=

voile   1360   vouchsafe

baarheid; ontruimbaarheid; onwaarde; leegheid; kragteloosheid; ongeldigheid.
voile, voile.
vol'ant, vlieënd; gou, vinnig, rats; gevleuel(d).
Vol'apuk, Vol'apük, Volapük.
vol'ar, handpalm=; voetsool=.
vol'atile, vlugtig; ongedurig; wuf, wispelturig; ~ **acid,** vlugtige suur; ~ **fuel,** vlugtige brandstof; ~ **oil,** vlugtige olie; ~ **salt,** vlugsout.
volatil'ity, vlugtigheid; onbestendigheid.
volatiliza'tion, vervlugtiging; vlugtigmaking; verdamping.
volat'ilize, vlugtig maak, vervlugtig; vervlieg, volatiliseer, verdamp.
volcan'ic, vulkanies, vulkaan=; ~ **ash,** vulkaanas; ~ **cone,** vulkaankeël; ~ **dome,** lawakoepel; ~ **dust,** vulkaanstof; ~ **eruption,** vulkaniese uitbarsting; ~ **pipe,** kraterpyp; ~ **rock,** effusiegesteente; ~ **slag,** vulkaniese slak; ~ **vent,** kraterpyp.
vol'canism, vulkanisme.
volcan'o, (-es), vulkaan, vuurspuwende berg; *extinct* ~, uitgedoofde vulkaan.
volcanol'ogy, vulkanologie, studie van vulkane.
vole[1]**,** (n) vole (kaartspel); (v) al die trekke wen.
vole[2]**,** (n) woelmuis; waterrot.
vol'et, triptiekvleuel.
Vol'ga, Wolga.
vol'itant, fladderend, vlieënd.
voli'tion, wil; wilskrag, wilsuiting, wilsinspanning; *of one's own* ~, uit eie beweging; ~ **al,** wils=, van die wil.
vol'itive, van die wil, wils=.
voll'ey, (n) (-s), sarsie, salvo; vlughou (tennis); stortvloed; *a* ~ *of CURSES,* 'n stortvloed (stroom) vloeke; *DISCHARGE a* ~, 'n salvo afvuur; (v) uitbraak, uitbars, losbrand; 'n salvo skiet; in die vlug slaan; ~ **ball,** vlugbal; ~**-firing,** salvovuur.
vol'plane, (n) sweefvlug; (v) sweef.
vol'planist, sweefvlieër.
volt[1]**,** volt.
volt[2]**,** swenking, wending.
vol'tage, stroomspanning; *low* ~, swak (lae) spanning; ~ **coil,** spanningspoel; ~ **divider,** spanningsdeler; ~ **drop,** spanningsval; ~ **indicator,** spanningsverklikker, spanningswyser; ~ **regulator,** spanningsreëlaar.
volta'ic, voltaïes, galvanies; ~ **battery,** galvaniese battery; ~ **cell,** galvaniese element.
vol'taism, galvanisme.
voltam'eter, voltameter.
volte, swenking.
volte-face', (n) volte-face, frontverandering, omswaai, omkeer; (v) regsomkeer maak, omswaai.
volt'meter, voltmeter, spanningsmeter.
volubil'ity, gladheid, woordrykheid, woordrykdom.
vol'uble, woordryk, vlot (van tong); slingerend, klimmend (bot.); ~ **ness,** woordrykheid; gladheid.
vol'ume, boekdeel; band; grootte; omvang, kubieke inhoud, volume; bakmaat (dam) sterkte; massa; papirusrol; geluidsterkte; *BY* ~, volgens inhoud; *in FIVE* ~ *s,* in vyf dele; *GATHER* ~, in omvang toeneem; *SPEAK* ~ *s,* boekdele spreek; *the* ~ *of his VOICE,* die omvang van sy stem; ~ **control,** sterktereëlaar; sterktereëling, volumereëling; ~ **ratio,** volumeverhouding.
volumet'ric, volumetries; ~ **analysis,** maatanalise; ~ **change,** volumeverandering; ~ **efficiency,** vullingsgraad; ~ **flask,** meetfles.
volum'inous, lywig, dik, omvangryk, volumineus; veelskrywend, produktief; woordryk, uitgebreid; ~ **ness,** lywigheid; woordrykheid.
vol'untarily, gewillig, uit eie beweging.
vol'untariness, vrywilligheid.
vol'untarism, voluntarisme.
vo'luntarist, vrywilliger, volontêr.
vol'untary, (n) (..ries), vrywilliger; orrelstuk, tussenspel; vrywillige bydrae; (a) vrywillig; ongedwonge, onverplig; spontaan, vry; willekeurig, moedswillig; ~ **plants,** opslag; ~ **school,** vrye skool; ~ **training,** vrywillige opleiding.
volunteer', (n) vrywilliger, volontêr; *serve as a* ~, as vrywilliger diens doen; (v) vrywillig onderneem;

vrywillig diens doen; aanpresenteer; (a) vrywilligers=, vrywillig; ~ **corps,** vrywilligerseenheid; ~ **plants,** opslag; ~ **reserve,** vrywilligersreserwe.
volup'tuary, (n) (..ries), wellusteling; (a) wellustig.
volup'tuous, wellustig, sinlik, voluptueus; ~ **ness,** wellus, wellustigheid, sinlikheid.
volute', (n) krul, voluut; spiraal; krullys; rolslak; (a) gekrul; spiraalvormig; opgerol; ~ **d,** spiraalvormig; gekronkel(d); ~ **spring,** skroefveer, keëlveer.
volu'tion, rollende beweging; kronkeling; draai.
vol'vulus, dermkronkel.
vom'er, ploegbeen (in neus).
vom'it, (n) braaksel, vomeersel; vomitief, braakmiddel; (v) braak, vermeer, vomeer, kots, opgooi, jongosse inspan; ~ **ing,** braking, gebraak, opgooiery, gekots; (die) opgooi; ~ **ive, (n)** braakmiddel, vomitief; (a) braak=; ~ **-nut,** braakneut.
vom'itory, (n) (..ries), braakmiddel; toegang, uitgang; vomitorium; (a) braakwekkend.
vomituri'tion, vergeefse braakpogings, mislikheid, gekokhals.
voo'doo, (n) voedoe, toorkuns, toordery; (v) toor; ~ **ism,** toorkuns.
vora'cious, gulsig, vraatsugtig, verslindend.
vora'ciousness, vora'city, vraatsug, gulsigheid.
vort'ex, (-es, ..tices), maalstroom; draaikolk, dwarreling; ~ **motion,** werwelbeweging; ~ **wheel,** turbine.
vort'ical, draaiend, draai=.
vorti'ginous, dwarrelend, draaiend.
Vosges: *the* ~, die Vogese.
vot'aress, (-es), aanhangster; vereerster, bewonderaarster.
vot'ary, (..ries), aanhanger, volgeling; beoefenaar; ordebroeder; vereerder, bewonderaar; aartsliefhebber.
vote, (n) stem; stemming; stemreg; stembriefie; mosie; begrotingspos; *CARRIED by 20* ~ *s,* aangeneem met 'n meerderheid van 20 stemme; *CASTING* ~, beslissende stem; ~ *of CENSURE,* mosie (voorstel) van afkeuring; *CHOSEN by popular* ~, by algemene stemming gekies; ~ *of CONDOLENCE,* mosie van roubeklag; ~ *of CONFIDENCE,* mosie van vertroue; *without a DISSENTIENT* ~, sonder 'n teenstem; *the* ~ *for EDUCATION,* die bedrag vir onderwys gestem; *the FLOATING* ~, die vlottende stem; *HAVE a* ~, stemgeregtig wees; *a* ~ *of NO CONFIDENCE,* 'n mosie van wantroue; *PROCEED to the* ~, tot stemming oorgaan; *PUT to the* ~, tot stemming bring; *RECORD one's* ~, jou stem uitbring, stem; *RETURN a* ~, 'n stem uitbring; *a* ~ *of SYMPATHY,* 'n mosie van deelneming; *TAKE a* ~, laat stem; ~ *of THANKS,* mosie van dank; *WITHOUT a* ~, sonder stem; (v) stem, 'n stem uitbring; toestaan, goedkeur, bewillig; verklaar; voorstel aan die hand doen; ~ *AGAINST,* stem teen; ~ *by BALLOT,* met geslote briefies stem; *I* ~ *we go to BED,* ek stel voor dat ons bed toe gaan; ~ *a person into the CHAIR,* iem. tot voorsitter verkies; ~ *DOWN,* afstem; ~ *FOR,* stem vir; ~ *IN,* verkies; ~ *by SHOW of hands,* stem deur die hand op te steek; ~ **-catcher,** stemjagter, stemvanger; ~ **-catching,** stemvangery; ~ **less,** nie-stemgeregtig, sonder stemreg, stemloos; ~ **lessness,** stemloosheid.
vot'er, kieser, stemgeregtigde; ~ **s' roll,** kieserslys; *put on the* ~ *s' roll,* op die kieserslys sit.
vo'ting, stem, stemming, stemmery; ~ *by ballot,* stemming met geslote briefies; ~ **age,** stemgeregtigde leeftyd; ~ **cattle,** stemvee; ~ **paper,** stembriefie.
vot'ive, gelofte=, volgens gelofte, votief; ~ **altar,** dankaltaar; ~ **bowl,** offerskaal; ~ **mass,** votiefmis; ~ **offering,** dankoffer; ~ **tablet,** geloftetafel, votiefplaat.
vouch, getuig, bevestig; instaan (vir), goedstaan, borg staan; staaf, afdoende bewys; *we can* ~ *FOR,* ons kan daarvoor instaan; ~ *FOR someone,* vir iem. instaan; ~ *for the TRUTH of,* instaan vir die waarheid van; ~ **er,** kwitansie, bewys; teenblad; borg.
vouchsafe', vergun, toestaan, verwerdig, inwillig; *he* ~ *d no reply to the charge,* hy het hom nie verwerdig

vow

om op die beskuldiging te antwoord nie; ~**ment**, inwilliging, vergunning.
vow, (n) eed, gelofte, plegtige belofte; *REGISTER a* ~ *to do it,* 'n gelofte aflê om dit te doen; *TAKE the* ~*s,* die kloostergelofte aflê; 'n kloosterling word; (v) 'n gelofte doen; sweer, plegtig belowe; toewy (aan).
vow'el, klinker, vokaal; ~ **chart**, vokaalkaart; ~ **gradation**, klankwisseling, vokaalwisseling, ablaut; ~**ize**, die klinkers invoeg (aanbring); ~ **mutation**, klankwysiging, vokaalwisseling, umlaut; ~ **point**, vokaalteken; ~ **rhyme**, klinkerrym; ~ **system**, vokaalstelsel.
voy'age, (n) seereis, vaart; (v) 'n seereis maak, vaar; reis; bereis; ~ **policy**, reispolis; ~**r**, seereisiger.
V'-shaped, V-vormig.
vug(g), vugh, ertsholte.
Vul'can, Vulkanus, Vulcanus.
Vulcan'ian, Vulcan'ic, van Vulcanus (Vulkanus).
vulcan'ic, vulkanies.
vulcanic'ity, vulkanisme.
vul'canism, vulkanisme.
vul'canite, eboniet, vulkaniet.
vulcaniza'tion, vulkanisering.
vul'canize, vulkaniseer; ~*d rubber,* gevulkaniseerde rubber; ~**r**, vulkaniseerder.
vul'canizing cement, vulkaniseergom.
vul'gar, (n) (die) ordinêre mense; gespuis; massa; (a) plat; ordinêr, laag, gemeen, banaal, vulgêr; ongepoets; grof; algemeen, volks=, algemeen in swang; *her tastes are* ~, haar smaak is grof; ~ **abuse**, skeltaal; ~ **era**, Christelike tydvak; ~ **expression**, plat uitdrukking; ~ **fraction**, gewone breuk; ~ **'ian**, ordinêre persoon; ryk buffel; ~**ism**, platheid, plat uitdrukking; ~**ist**, voorstander van platheid; ~ **'iter**, gemeenlik; ~ **'ity**, (..ties), laagheid, gemeenheid; banaliteit, ordinêrheid, vulgariteit, onbeskoftheid, vulgêrheid; ~**iza'tion**, vulgarisasie; ~**ize**, vulgariseer, verlaag, plat (gemeen) maak; ~ **speech**, plat taal; ~ **superstition**, volksbygeloof; ~ **tongue**, volkstaal.
Vul'gate: *the* ~, die Vulgata (Vulgaat).
vulnerabil'ity, vul'nerableness, kwesbaarheid, wondbaarheid; trefbaarheid.
vul'nerable, kwesbaar, wondbaar; trefbaar.
vul'nerary, (n) wondkruid; (a) helend, genesend.
vul'picide, jakkalsuitroeier; jakkalsuitroeiing.
vul'pine, jakkalsagtig; listig, slim, skelm, slu.
vul'ture, aasvoël; gier; grypvoël, uitsuier.
vul'turine, vul'turish, vul'turous, aasvoëlagtig; hebsugtig, roofsugtig.
vul'turine guinea-fowl, aasvoëltarentaal.
vul'va, (-e), vulva, skaamspleet; ~**l**, ~**r**, skaamspleet=.
vulvit'is, vulvitis, ontsteking v.d. vulva.
vy'ing, meedingend; *kyk* **vie**.

W

w, (ws, w's), w; *little* ~, w'tjie.
wad, (n) vulsel, prop, stopsel, pluisie; watte; rol (banknote); *a* ~ *of banknotes,* 'n rol banknote; (v) (-**ded**), 'n prop (pluisie) maak; toestop, 'n prop insteek; watteer, met watte uitvoer; ~*ded with conceit,* opgeblase van waandheid.
wad'able, deurwaadbaar.
wa'dding, watte; verbandwatte; kapok; vulsel.
wa'ddle, (n) skommelgang, gewaggel, skommelende gang; (v) waggel, skommel.
wa'ddy, (waddies), (Australiese) knopkierie.
wade, (n) (die) loop deur; gesukkel; (v) deurgaan, deurwaad; deurworstel, deursukkel; ~ *through a BOOK,* 'n boek deurworstel; ~ *IN,* heftig aanval; ~ *INTO someone,* iem. lelik inklim; ~ *INTO one's food,* lekker weglê aan die kos.
wad'er, wader; waadvoël; steltloper; (pl) waterlaarse, kapstewels.
wad'hook, koeëltrekker; proptrekker.
wa'di, (-s), (droë) rivierbedding (sloot), oemaramba; donga, sloot.
wad'ing, (die) waad, deurloop; ~ **bird**, steltloper, waadvoël.
wa'dy, (wadies), *kyk* **wadi**.
Wafd, (hist.), Wafd (Egiptiese nasionale party).
waf'er, (n) wafel (koek); hostie (R.K.); ouel; oblietjie; (v) toeplak; met 'n ouel bevestig; ~**-cake**, wafel= (koek); ~**-iron**, wafelyster, wafelpan.
wa'ffle¹, (n) keuwelary, gesels; (v) klets, babbel, gorrel (eksamen).
wa'ffle², (n) wafel; ~**-iron**, wafelyster, wafelpan; ~**-pan**, wafelpan.
waff'ling, keuwelary, geklets, (ge)gorrel (eksamen).
waft, (n) noodsein; windjie, luggie; vleugie; vleuelslag; (v) drywe; wuif; aanwaai; meevoer.
wag, (n) swaai; skud; kwispeling (van stert); terggees, spotvoël; uilspieël; grapmaker; *have a good old CHIN* ~, lekker (met mekaar) gesels; *PLAY* ~, stokkiesdraai; *a* ~ *of the TAIL,* 'n swaai v.d. stert; (v) (-**ged**), kwispel, swaai; skud; *the DOG* ~*s its tail,* die hond swaai sy stert; ~ *one's FINGER,* die vinger dreigend ophou; ~ *one's HEAD,* jou kop skud; *the TAIL* ~*s the dog,* Klaas is baas; ~ *the TONGUE,* die tong roer; *her TONGUE* ~*s continually,* haar mond is nooit stil nie; *how* ~*s the WORLD?,* hoe gaan dit in die (buite)wêreld?

wage¹, (n) loon; besoldiging, verdienste; (pl) (werk)= loon, verdienste, gasie; *a DAY'S* ~ *for a day's work,* loon volgens werk; *EARN scanty* ~*s,* 'n karige besoldiging (loon) trek; *the* ~*s of SIN is death,* die loon v.d. sonde is die dood.
wage², (v) voer, maak; ~ *BATTLE*, slag lewer; ~ *a STRUGGLE,* 'n stryd voer; ~ *WAR,* oorlog voer; **W**~ **Act**, Loonwet; ~ **agreement**, loonooreenkoms; ~**-bill**, loonlys; **W**~ **Board**, Loonraad; **W**~**-Board determination**, Loonraadvasstelling; ~ **determination**, loonvasstelling; ~ **dispute**, loongeskil; ~**-earner**, loonarbeider, loontrekker; broodwinner, koswinner; ~**-fund**, loonfonds; ~**ling**, huurling.
wa'ger, (n) weddenskap; *lay a* ~, 'n weddenskap aangaan; wed; (v) verwed, wed.
wage: ~**-rate**, loonstandaard, loontarief; ~ **regulation**, loonreëling; ~ **scale**, loonskaal.
wa'gerer, wedder.
wage: ~**s'-fund**, loonfonds; ~ **sheet**, loonlys; ~ **slave**, loonslaaf; ~ **strike**, loonstaking; ~ **war**, loonstryd; ~ **work**, loonarbeid; ~ **worker**, loonarbeider.
wagg'er, seiner; ~**y**, korswel, streke, tergery, grapmakery, skalksheid.
wagg'ing, (n) (die) kwispel, kwispeling, roering; (a) roerend; los.
wagg'ish, ondeund, vol streke, skalks.
wag'gle, wikkel, swaai, kwispel; wiggel (met gholfstok).
wag(g)'on, wa, bokwa; trok, goederewa, vragwa; *HITCH one's* ~ *to a star,* hoog mik; jou doelwit hoog stel; *small LOW* ~, molwa; ~ **age**, vraggeld; ~**-bed**, wakatel; ~**-boiler**, kofferketel; ~**-box**, wakis; ~**-brake**, warem, wabriek; ~**-builder**, wamaker; ~**-builder's apprentice**, leerlingwamaker; ~**-driver**, wadrywer; ~**er**, wadrywer; *the W*~*er,* die Voerman (ster); ~**ette'**, ligte waentjie, trollie; ~**ful**, wavol, wavrag; ~**-house**, waenhuis; ~**-load**, wavrag; ~**-maker**, wamaker; ~**-road**, wapad; ~ **roof**, tonneldak; ~ **shop**, trokwerkplaas; ~**-train**, walinie; konvooi; ~**-tree**, waboom; ~**-vault**, tonnelgewelf; ~**-wheel**, wawiel; ~ **wright**, wamaker.
Wagner'ian, (n) Wagneriaan; (a) Wagneriaans.
Wag'nerite, Wagneriaan.
wagon-lit', slaapwa.

wag'tail, kwikstertjie, kwikkie, akkermannetjie.
waif, swerwer, daklose, uitgestotene; verwaarloosde kind; wegloopdier; optelgoed; opdrifsel, strandgoed; goed sonder baas; ~s and strays, stukkies en brokkies; verwaarloosde kinders.
wail, (n) weeklag, gehuil, gekerm, gejammer; (v) weeklaag, kerm; ~**ful,** klaaglik, jammervol; ~**fulness,** klaaglikheid.
wail'ing, weeklag, gejammer, geweeklaag, gejeremieer; a ~ and gnashing of teeth, wening en knersing van die tande; **W**~ **Wall,** Klaagmuur.
wain, wa; CHARLES's W~, die Groot Beer; LESSER W~, die Klein Beer.
wain'scot, (n) paneelwerk, lambrisering, beskot; (v) beklee, lambriseer; ~**ing,** paneelwerk, beskot, lambrisering.
wain'wright, wamaker.
waist, middel; lees; lyfie; middeldek, kuil (skip); ~**-band,** gordel, lyfband; ~**-belt,** gordel, lyfband; ~**-cloth,** lendedoek; ~**coat,** onderbaadjie; sleeved ~coat, onderbaadjie met moue; ~**-deep,** ~**-high,** tot aan die middel; pensdiep (diere); ~**-line,** middellyn; ~**-measure,** middelmaat; ~**-pin,** skarnierbout.
wait, (n) (die) wag, wagtery, tussenpose, wagtyd; oponthoud; hinderlaag, loer; (pl) Kers(fees)sangers, Kers(fees)musikante; LIE in ~, in hinderlaag lê; voorlê; we had a LONG ~, ons moes lank wag; (v) wag, afwag; versuim; vertoef; oppas; bedien (by tafel); jou opwagting maak (by minister); ~ DINNER for a person, met die ete vir 'n persoon wag; ~ FOR, wag op (vir); JUST you ~!, wag maar!; ~ a MINUTE, wag 'n bietjie; ~ ON, bedien; ~ one's OPPORTUNITY, jou kans afwag; I will ~ your PLEASURE, ek is tot u diens; ~ and SEE, die loop van sake afwag; 'n afwagtende houding aanneem; ~ before SPEAKING, wag met praat; ~ one's TIME, jou tyd afwag; ~ one's TURN, jou beurt afwag; ~ UPON, bedien (aan tafel); ~**er,** tafelbediende, diener, kelner; afwagter; skinkbord.
wait'ing, (n) (die) wag; wagtery; bediening; opwagting; BE in ~, byderhand wees; IN ~, wagtend; bedienend; KEEP someone ~, iem. laat wag; NO ~, geen wagtery nie; (a) (af)wagtend; bedienend; play a ~ game, die kat uit die boom kyk; ~**-list,** waglys; ~**-maid,** binnehulp; ~**-room,** wagkamer; ~**-woman,** kamerbediende, kamenier.
wait'ress, (-es), bediende, kelnerin, kafeemeisie.
waive, opgee, afstand doen van, prysgee; laat vaar; ~ payment, betaling kwytskeld; ~**r,** kwytskelding; afstand.
wake¹, (n) (see)sog, sogwater, kielwater; volgstroom (vliegtuig); spoor; IN the ~ of, in die voetspore van; in die sog van; SAIL in someone's ~, in iem. se sog (kielwater, kielsog) vaar.
wake², (n) kermis; gedenkfees; nagwaak (by lyk).
wake³, (n) (die) waak; (v) **(woke** or **-d, -d** or **woke(n)),** ontwaak; wakker word; wek, wakker maak; wakker wees; bewus word van; opwek; wakker roep, aanvuur, aanwakker; ~ up to, bewus word van; ~**ful,** waaksaam; wakker, slaaploos, wakend; ~**fulness,** waaksaamheid; slaaploosheid.
wak'en, wakker maak, wek; wakker word.
wak'er, wekker.
wake'-robin, aronsklek, varkblom.
wak'ing, (n) (die) waak; (a) wakker, waaksaam, wakend; ~ hours, die ure wat 'n mens wakker is.
Walden'ses, Waldensers.
Walden'sian, (n) Waldenser; (a) Waldensies.
wale, (n) haal, streep, striem, merk; (v) striem, blou slaan.
Wales, Wallis; NEW South ~, Nieu-Suid-Wallis; PRINCE of ~, Prins van Wallis.
Walhall'a, kyk **Valhalla.**
walk, (n) wandeling; stap, pas, gang; wandelplek, laan, loopplek; weiveld; wandel; werkkring; sfeer; gebied; wandelpad, promenade; wyk; rondte; stand, posisie; AT a ~, op 'n stap; GO for a ~, 'n entjie gaan loop, gaan wandel; HAVE a ~**-over,** platloop; fluit-fluit wen; geen mededinging hê nie; KNOW someone by his ~, iem. aan sy loop ken; ~ in LIFE, werkkring; lewensloop; all ~s of LIFE,

alle werkkringe; alle lewenslope; TAKE a ~, 'n entjie gaan loop; gaan wandel; (v) loop, wandel, stap, gaan; stryk; voetslaan; betree, bewandel; spook, rondwaar; ~ ABOUT, rondloop, rondgaan, rondwaar; ~ upon AIR, baie bly wees; ~ ALONG, aanloop; ~ the ANCHOR up, die anker optrek; ~ AWAY, wegstap; ~ AWAY with something, iets steel; ~ the BOARDS, toneelspeler wees; ~ BY, verbystap, verbygaan; ~ the CHALK, langs 'n krytstreep loop (om te wys dat 'n mens nugter is); ~ the DECK, heen en weer op die dek loop; ~ a DOG, met 'n hond gaan stap; ~ DOWN, afkom, afloop; ~ with GOD, met God wandel; godvrugtig lewe; ~ a HORSE, 'n perd op 'n stappie ry; ~ the HOSPITALS, in die medisyne studeer; ~ IN, inkom, binnekom; ~ INTO someone, iem. op die lyf loop; iem. inklim (invlieg); ~ one's LEGS off, loop tot jy van moegheid omslaan; ~ OFF, wegstap; weggaan; weglei; ~ OFF with, iets vaslê; iets fluit-fluit verower; ~ ON, aanloop; ~ OUT, uitloop; ~ OUT with someone, iem. die hof maak, na iem. vry; ~ OUT on someone, iem. in die steek laat; ~ OVER, oorgaan, oor 'n seker(e) plek gaan; maklik oorwin, fluit-fluit wen; ~ the PLANK, uitgeskop word; oor die plank loop; make someone ~ the PLANK, iem. se voete spoel; ~ the ROUNDS, die rondte doen; you must learn to ~ before you RUN, eers kruip, dan loop; ~ in one's SLEEP, slaapwandel; ~ the STREETS, op straat loop (in ongunstige betekenis); ~ UP, boontoe loop; ingaan; ~ WITH a person, met iem. saamloop; iem. die hof maak; ~**er,** voetganger, loper, wandelaar, stapper; loopvoël; ~**ie-lookie,** draagbare televisiesender; ~**ie-talkie,** tweerigtingradio, geselsradio, loopgeselser; praat-en-looppop.
walk'ing, (n) (die) loop, lopery, stappery; (a) lopend, loop=, wandel=; a ~ FASHION-PLATE, 'n modepop; a ~ SHADOW, 'n wandelende geraamte; ~ **bird,** loopvoël; ~**-chair,** loopwaentjie; stootstoeltjie; ~ **dictionary,** wandelende woordeboek; alweter; ~ **doll,** looppop; ~**-dress,** wandelkostuum, looprok; ~ **encyclop(a)edia,** wandelende ensiklopedie; alweter; ~ **gentleman,** figurant; ~ **leaf,** wandelende blaar; ~ **library,** wandelende biblioteek; ~**-orders,** ~**-papers,** afdanking, ontslag; ~**-race,** stapwedloop; ~**-shoe,** stapskoen; ~**-stick,** kierie, wandelstok; ~**-stick-insect,** stokinsek, wandelende tak, spooksprinkaan; ~**-ticket** = **walking-orders;** ~**-tour,** wandeltog, looptoer.
walk'-out, staking.
walk'-over, maklike oorwinning; oorwinning sonder spel; onbestrede verkiesing; it WAS a ~ for them, hulle het fluit-fluit gewen; it WAS a ~, die wedstryd is prysgegee; die wedstryd sonder spel wen.
Walky'rie, kyk **Valkyrie.**
wall, (n) muur; wand; wal; BLANK ~, kaal muur; blinde muur; with one's BACK to the ~, in die nou gedryf; ~s have EARS, die mure het ore; daar is te veel dak op die huis; GO to the ~, die onderspit delf; HANGING ~, dak (in myntonnel); run one's HEAD against a ~, met jou kop teen 'n muur loop; ~ of PARTITION, skeidsmuur; PUSHED to the ~, in die nou gedryf; in die moeilikheid gebring; SEE through a brick ~, gewiks wees; groot deursig hê; TURN one's face to the ~, jou end voel nader kom; the WEAKEST goes to the ~, die swakste delf die onderspit; a WHITE ~ is a fool's paper, gekke en dwase skryf hulle name op deure en glase; (v) ommuur, 'n muur bou om; ~ IN, ommuur; ~ OFF, afhok; ~ UP, toemessel.
wa'llaby, (..bies), klein kangaroe, wallaby; Australiër.
Wal(l)ach'ia, Walagye; ~**n,** (n) Walagyer; (a) Walagys.
wall' advertisement, muurreklame.
wall'a(h), bediende; vent; baas.
wall'-anchor, muuranker.
wallaroo', groot kangaroesoort, wallaroo.
wall: ~ **beam,** muurbalk; ~ **bed,** klapbed; ~ **bench,** muurbank; ~ **bracket,** muurarm; ~ **chisel,** steenbeitel; ~ **clamp,** verbandstuk; ~ **clip,** muurklem; ~ **clock,** hangklok; ~**-creeper,** muurklimmer

(voël); klimop (ranker); ~-**cress**, skeefkelk; ~ **cup-board**, blinde kas; muurkas.

walled, met mure; ~ **IN**, ommuur; ~ **TOWN**, ommuurde stad; ~ **UP**, toegemessel.

wa'llet, sakkie; notetassie, portefeulje, geldboekie; sakboek, briewetas; knapsakkie, kossakkie.

wall: ~-**eye**, skeeloog; glasoog, witoog (perd); ~-**eyed**, skeel; glasoog-, witoog-; ~-**face**, muurvlak; ~-**flower**, muurblom (ook fig.); randeier; ~-**fruit**, vrugte van opgeleide bome; ~ **hanging**, muurbehangsel; ~ **ing**, muurwerk; bergstutting; ~-**iron**, muursteun; ~-**knot**, duiwelsklou; ~ **lamp**, muurlamp; ~ **less**, sonder mure; ~ **lining**, muurbekleding; ~ **map**, muurkaart.

Wallon'ia, Waleland.

Walloon', (n) Waal; (a) Waals.

wa'llop, (n) klap, opstopper; (v) afransel, looi, afros.

wa'lloping, (n) loesing, afgedankste pak; *give some- one a* ~, iem. 'n loesing gee; iem. slaan dat hy opslae maak; (a) yslik, kolossaal, tamaai.

wall'ow, (n) rolplek; (v) rol, woel, vroetel, wentel; swelg; versink wees in; ~ *in money*, in geld (weelde) swem.

wall: ~-**painting**, muurskildering; ~ **paper**, plakpapier; ~-**pin**, muurpen; ~-**plate**, muurplaat; langbalk (skag); ~ **plug**, muurkontak, muursteker, muurprop; ~ **pocket**, skuiwergat; ~-**post**, muurstyl; ~-**rue**, klipvaring; ~ **slab**, muurblad; ~ **socket**, muursok; ~ **space**, muurruimte.

Wall' Street, Wall Street, New Yorkse geldmark (beurs).

wall: ~ **tile**, muurteël; ~-**to**-~ **carpet**, volvloertapyt; ~-**tree**, leiboom.

wal'nut, okkerneut (vrug); okkerneutboom; okkerneuthout; *over the* ~ *s and the wine*, by die nagereg.

wal'rus, (-es), walrus.

waltz, (n) (-es), wals; (v) wals; huppel, ronddans.

wam'pum, skulpkrale.

wan, flets, bleek, asvaal; afgemat; somber.

wand, (tower)staf; *magic* ~, towerstaf.

wan'der, dwaal, omswerwe; (rond)dool, drentel, (rond)waar; afdwaal; yl; ~ *ABOUT*, rondswerf; *his MIND* ~ *s*, hy yl; ~ *ON*, verder swerf; ~ *OUT of the room*, uit die kamer dwaal; ~ *from the POINT*, van die onderwerp afdwaal; ~ **er**, swerwer, swerfling, swerfster; rondloper.

wan'dering, (n) swerwery, ronddoling, divagasie, gedwaal; afdwaling; ylhoofdigheid; (pl) swerftogte, omswerwings; ylhoofdigheid; (a) swerwend, ronddwalend, wandelend; afdwalend; *the* ~ *Jew*, die wandelende Jood; ~ **abscess**, kruipsweer; ~ **heart**, swerfhart; ~ **kidney**, los niertjie, wandelende nier; ~ **light**, dwaallig; ~ **spirit**, dwaalgees.

wan'derlust, trekgees, wanderlust.

wanderoo', baardaap.

wane, (n) afneming, verswakking, verbleking; verval; wankant (hout); *on the* ~, aan die taan, in verval, aan die verminder; (v) verbleek, taan; verminder, verswak, afneem, verflou.

wan'gle, losslaan, loskry (geld); konkel, bekook; vervals, skelm verkry; ~ **r**, knoeier, kuller; vervalser.

wan'ing, (n) afneming, verbleking; verkleining; (a) afnemend; tanend; ~ *moon*, afnemende maan.

want, (n) gebrek; behoefte, gemis, broodsgebrek; derwing, armoede, ontbering; skaarste; benodigdheid; *BE in* ~, gebrek ly; *in* ~ *of a CLERK*, 'n klerk nodig hê; *be in* ~ *of EMPLOYMENT*, werk soek; *FALL into* ~, tot (in) armoede verval; *a man of FEW* ~ *s*, 'n man van min behoeftes; *FOR* ~ *of*, by gebrek aan; *IN* ~ *of*, gebrek ly aan; *be in* ~ *of MONEY*, geldgebrek hê; *NO* ~ *of*, 'n oorvloed van; ~ *of SPACE*, gebrek aan ruimte; *SUPPLY the* ~ *s of*, in die behoeftes voorsien van; *it was not for* ~ *of TRYING*, dit was nie omdat ons nie probeer het nie; (v) nodig hê, behoef, derwe; skeel; wens, verlang; mis, te kort kom, gebrek ly; ontbreek, begeer; *it* ~ *s DOING*, *it s to be DONE*, dit moet gedoen word; *he* ~ *s EXPERIENCE*, hy kom ondervinding kort; *I* ~ *to GO*, ek wil gaan; *his HAIR* ~ *s cutting*, sy hare moet geknip word; *this* ~ *s careful HANDLING*, dit moet versigtig aangepak word; *he* ~ *s to KNOW*, hy wil weet; *he does not*

~ *for MONEY*, hy het geen gebrek aan geld nie; *you don't* ~ *MUCH!*, dis 'n mooi grap! is dit al! nog iets?; ~ *for NOTHING*, aan niks gebrek hê nie; *TELL Piet I* ~ *him*, sê vir Piet ek roep hom; *WHAT do you* ~ *with me?*, wat wil jy van my hê?

wan'ted, gevra, benodig, verlang; *the* ~ *PERSON*, die persoon na wie gesoek word; *BE* ~; ~ *by the POLICE*, gesoek word (deur die polisie); ~ *to PURCHASE*, te koop gevra.

wan'ting, behoeftig, gebrekkig, sonder, ontbrekend; *BE* ~, ontbreek, uitbly, te kort kom, te kort skiet; *he is not* ~ *in COURAGE*, dit ontbreek hom nie aan moed nie; *FOUND* ~, in gebreke wees; te lig bevind word; *be* ~ *IN*, te kort skiet in.

wan'ton, (n) ligmis, ligtekooi, wellusteling; robbedoe; *play the* ~, onverantwoordelik wees; losbandig wees; (v) dartel wees, baljaar, jakker; (a) speels, ligsinnig, dartel, baldadig, brooddronk, stoeisiek, uitgelate; vol fiemies (nukke), veranderlik; woes, wild; onverantwoordelik; moedswillig; wellustig, losbandig, wulps; *that is* ~ *destruction*, dit is moedswillige vernieling; ~ **ly**, moedswillig, roekeloos; ~ **ness**, dartelheid, ligsinnigheid, broodronkenheid, euwelmoed, baldadigheid; wulpsheid.

wap, *kyk* **whop**.

wa'pentake, distrik, wyk, afdeling.

wa'piti, wapiti, (Kanadese) takbok.

war, (n) oorlog, kryg; stryd; oorlogvoering; ~ *of AGGRESSION*, aanvalsoorlog; *the ART of* ~, krygskuns; *be AT* ~ *with*, in oorlog wees met; ~ *of ATTRITION*, uitputtingsoorlog; *CARRY the* ~ *into the enemy's country (into enemy territory)*, tot die aanval oorgaan; aanvallend optree; *CIVIL* ~, burgeroorlog; *COLD* ~, koue oorlog; *COUNCIL of* ~, krygsraad; *DECLARE* ~ *on a country*, oorlog verklaar teen 'n land; *ENTER into* ~, besluit om oorlog te voer; ~ *of EXTERMINATION*, uitdelgingsoorlog; vernietigingsoorlog; *all's FAIR in love and* ~, in liefdesake en oorlog is alles geoorloof; *be on a* ~ *FOOTING*, op voet van oorlog verkeer; *GO to* ~, oorlog maak; oorlog toe gaan; *HOT* ~, skietoorlog; *IN* ~, in die oorlog; *have been IN the* ~ *s*, gehawend lyk; ~ *to the KNIFE*, 'n oorlog om lewe en dood; *MAKE* ~, oorlog voer; ~ *of MOVEMENT*, bewegingsoorlog; ~ *of NERVES*, senuweeoorlog; *there is a* ~ *ON*, dit is oorlog; *a PRIVATE* ~, 'n persoonlike vete; *be in a STATE of* ~, in staat van oorlog verkeer; *WAGE* ~ *against*, oorlog voer teen; (v) (**-red**), oorlog voer, stryd voer; ~-**axe**, strydbyl; ~ **baby**, (buite-egtelike) oorlogskindjie.

war'ble¹, (n) gekweel, lied; (v) kweel, sing.

war'ble², (n) rugseer; geswel, knop; ~-**fly**, osvlieg, beesvlieg.

war'bler, tinktinkie; sangvoël, fluiter; singer.

war'bling, (n) gefluit, gekweel; (a) trillend.

war: ~-**bond**, oorlogsobligasie; ~-**bonus**, oorlogstoelae; ~ **book**, oorlogsboek; ~-**bound**, deur die oorlog vasgekeer; ~ **budget**, oorlogsbegroting; ~-**chariot**, strydwa; ~-**chest**, krygskas; strydkas; ~-**cloud**, oorlogswolk; ~ **contribution**, brandskatting; ~ **correspondent**, oorlogskorrespondent, oorlogsverslaggewer, oorlogsberiggewer; ~ **council**, oorlogsraad; ~-**craft**, krygskuns; oorlogsvaartuig; ~-**cry**, oorlogskreet; oorlogslied.

ward, (n) stadswyk, wyk; siekesaal, afdeling (hospitaal); oppasser; wag, baskerming; voogdyskap; bevoogde; pleegkind, beskerming; besetting, bewaking; vesting; tronk; baard (van sleutel); (pl) sleutelkepies; *KEEP watch and* ~, die wag hou; *UNDER* ~, onder voogdyskap; (v) bewaak, beskerm, beskut; ~ *something off*, iets afweer; iets keer.

war: ~-**dance**, krygsdans, oorlogsdans; ~-**debt**, oorlogskuld.

ward' duty, (..ties), siekesaaldiens.

war'den, opsigter; hoof, bestuurder; voog; bewaarder; direkteur.

war'der, bewaarder, sipier; wagter.

ward'ing-file, slotvyl.

ward'-mote, wykvergadering.

war'-dog, oorlogshond; vuurvreter.

war'dress, (-es), tronkbewaarster.
ward'robe, klerekas; garderobe; klere; ~ **dealer**, handelaar in tweedehandse klere; ~ **mistress**, kostumier; ~ **trunk**, hangkoffer.
ward: ~ **room**, offisierskamer; ~**ship**, voogdyskap, beskerming; ~**-sister**, hoofverpleegster, saalsuster.
ware, (n) ware, goed; (pl) koopware; (v) oppas vir; (interj) pas op!
war: ~ **effort**, oorlogspoging; ~ **experience**, oorlogsondervinding.
ware'house, (n) pakhuis, bêreplek, warehuis, loods; (v) in 'n pakhuis bêre, wegpak; ~ **charges**, pakhuiskoste; ~**-keeper**, pakhuiseienaar; magasynmeester; ~**-loft**, paksolder; ~ **man**, pakhuiseienaar; magasynmeester; ~**-room**, pakplek.
war: ~ **ensign**, oorlogsvlag; ~ **establishment**, oorlogsterkte; ~**fare**, krygskuns; oorlog; *aerial* ~*fare*, lugoorlog; ~**faring**, (n) oorlogvoering, stryd, vegtery; (a) oorlogvoerend, strydend; ~**-game**, oorlogspel; ~ **grave**, oorlogsgraf; ~**-guilt**, oorlogskuld; skuld aan die oorlog; ~ **head**, torpedokop; bomkop; knaldop; ~**-horse**, oorlogsperd; vuurvreter; *like an old* ~*-horse*, soos 'n oorlogsperd; soos 'n vuurvreter.
war'ily, versigtig; *tread* ~, op jou hoede wees, opletloop.
war' indemnity, oorlogskadeloosstelling.
war'iness, versigtigheid, behoedsaamheid.
war: ~ **like**, oorlogsugtig, krygshaftig, strydbaar; militêr, oorlogs-, krygs-; ~ **likeness**, oorlogsugtigheid, krygshaftigheid, strydbaarheid; ~**-loan**, oorlogslening.
war'lock, towe(r)naar, toornaar.
war' lord, opperste krygsheer.
warm, (n) warm plek; warmte; *I'll stay here in the* ~, ek sal hier bly waar dit warm is; (v) warm maak (word), verwarm; *my HEART* ~*s to him*, my hart begin warm klop vir hom; ~ *somebody's JACKET*, iem. uitlooi; ~ *ONESELF at the fire*, jou by die vuur warm maak; ~ *UP*, opwarm (kos); verwarm (kamer); voorverwarm, warm draai (motor); warm word; ~*ed UP food*, opgewarmde kos; ~ *to the WORK*, algaande lus vir die werk kry; (a, adv) warm; ywerig, driftig; innig, hartlik, vurig, gloeiend; vars (van 'n spoor); welgesteld; *you are GETTING* ~, jy word warm (speletjie); *GROW* ~, warm word; *KEEP a place* ~, vir iem. plek hou; *MAKE things* ~ *for someone*, die wêreld vir iem. benoud maak; *he is a* ~ *MAN*, hy sit daar goed in; *be* ~ *in OFFICE*, heeltemal tuis in die werk voel; *have a* ~ *PLACE for*, 'n teer plekkie hê vir; *a* ~ *RECEPTION*, 'n warm ontvangs; ~ *THANKS*, innige dank; *it was* ~ *WORK*, dit het daar warm toegegaan.
war' map, oorlogskaart.
warm: ~**-blooded**, warmbloedig; ~ **coat**, warmjas; ~**-hearted**, hartlik, goedhartig; ~**-heartedness**, hartlikheid, goedhartigheid; ~ **house**, broeikas.
warm'ing, (n) verwarming; afranseling; afdroging; (a) verwarmend, verwarmings-; ~ **device**, verwarmer, verwarmingstoestel; ~ **oven**, louoond; ~ **pan**, bedverwarmer; plaasvervanger; ~**-up**, opwarming.
warm: ~**ish**, warmerig; ~**ly**, warmpies, warm; met vuur.
war'monger, oorlogsaanblaser, oorlogs(op)stoker; ~**ing**, oorlogstokery.
warm' spring, warm bron.
warmth, warmte; geesdrif, gloed; hartlikheid.
warn, waarsku, vermaan; verwittig, in kennis stel; aanmaan; onder die oog bring; ~ *AGAINST*, waarsku teen; *you HAVE been* ~*ed*, wees gewaarsku; ~ **er**, waarskuwer, vermaner.
war'ning, (n) waarskuwing, vermaning; kennisgewing; aankondiging; opsê (diens); aanmaning; *let it BE a* ~, laat dit as waarskuwing dien; *GIVE* ~, diens opsê; waarsku; *at a MOMENT'S* ~, oombliklik; *TAKE* ~, wees gewaarsku; *TAKE* ~ *from him*, spieël jou aan hom; (a) waarskuwend, vermanend; ~ **board**, waarskuwingsbord; ~ **broadcast**, waarskuwingsomroep; ~ **cross**, waarskuwingskruis; ~ **device**, waarskuwingstoestel; ~ **letter**, vermaanbrief; aanmaning; ~ **light**, waarskuwings-

lig; ~ **sign**, waarskuwingsteken; ~ **signal**, waarskuwingsein, waarskuwingsteken.
War' Office, Ministerie van Oorlog (Engeland).
warp, (n) skering (drade), lengtedraad; (die) skeeftrek, kromtrek(king) (hout); kettingdraad (van 'n wal); afwyking, ontaarding; vooroordeel; slyk, slib; sleeptou, werptros; *MENTAL* ~, geestesafwyking; ~ *and WOOF*, skering en inslag; (v) (krom)trek, skeeftrek; optrek; skeef voorstel, verdraai; skeer (weefgetou); laat toespoel deur slyk; op 'n dwaalspoor bring, laat afdwaal van; *poverty will* ~ *his DISPOSITION*, armoede sal hom laat ontaard; ~ *one's JUDGMENT*, jou oordeel benewel.
warped, skeef; krom; bedorwe, ontaard; verdraai; ~ *MIND*, verdorwe gees; *he has a* ~ *OUTLOOK*, hy het 'n skewe (verwronge) kyk op die lewe; ~ *PERSONALITY*, verdorwe (verwronge) persoonlikheid.
war: ~**-paint**, oorlogsverf; oorlogsmondering; grimering; ~**-path**, oorlogspad; *be on the* ~*-path*, ten stryde trek; in die weer wees; strydlustig wees; ~**-pay**, oorlogsoldy; ~**-pilot**, oorlogsvlieër.
warp'ing, kromtrekking; skering; verbuiging (geol.); ~ **machine**, skeringmasjien.
war: ~**-plane**, oorlogsvliegtuig; ~ **profit**, oorlogswins; ~ **profiteer**, oorlogswinsmaker.
wa'rrant, (n) volmag; lasbrief, magsbrief, magtiging, bevelskrif, dwangbevel; grond, regverdiging; waarborg; uitbetalingsmandaat; ~ *of APPREHENSION*, lasbrief vir inhegtenisneming (aanhouding); ~ *of ATTORNEY*, volmag, prokurasie; ~ *of ARREST*, bevelskrif tot aanhouding; ~ *of DISTRESS*, bevelskrif tot beslaglegging; *a* ~ *is OUT against him*, 'n lasbrief is teen hom uitgereik; *ROYAL* ~, koninklike bevelskrif; (v) vrywaar, waarborg, instaan vir, garandeer; regverdig, wettig; bekragtig; magtig; *I'LL* ~ *you*, dit kan ek jou verseker; *they* ~ *the QUALITY of their goods*, hulle staan in vir die gehalte van hulle ware; ~ **able**, gewettig, verdedigbaar, geoorloof; ~**ed**, gewaarborg, gegarandeer; gewettig; gemagtig; ~**ee'**, gevolmagtigde; ~**er**, volmaggewer; waarborger; borg; verkoper; ~ **officer**, adjudant-offisier; ~ **or** = **warranter**; ~**-order**, lasbrief; ~**-voucher**, skatkisbiljet; skatkisorder; ~**y**, (..**ties**), waarborg, sekerheid; volmag, garansie(bewys).
war' records, oorlogsargief; oorlogsgedenkskrifte; oorlogsverslae.
wa'rren, konynkamp; boerplek van konyne; krotbuurt.
wa'rring, (n) stryd; (a) strydend, mededingend; inkonsekwent.
wa'rrior, (n) krygsman, vegsman, soldaat; *the unknown* ~, die onbekende soldaat; (a) krygsmans-, krygshaftig; ~ **ant**, amasonemier.
war' risk, oorlogsrisiko.
War'saw, Warschau.
war: ~ **ship**, oorlogskip; ~**-song**, krygslied; ~**-steed**, oorlogsperd; ~ **strength**, oorlogsterkte.
wart, vrat(jie); knoe(t)s, kwas; vrotpootjie (ertappels); *paint someone with his* ~*s*, nie iem. se foute probeer wegsteek nie.
war: ~ **talk**, oorlogspraatjies; ~**-tank**, oorlogstenk.
war: ~ **time**, (n) oorlogstyd; (a) oorlogs-; ~ **veteran**, oud-gediende, oud-stryder; ~**-weary**, oorlogsmoeg; ~ **whoop**, krygsgeskreeu, strydkreet; ~ **widow**, oorlogsweduwee; ~**-worn**, uitgeput, behoedsaam; ~**-worker**, oorlogswerker
wart: ~**-disease**, vrotpootjie (ertappels); ~ **hog**, vlakvark; ~**y**, vol vratte, vratterig.
wa'ry, behoedsaam, versigtig; *be* ~, op jou hoede wees; versigtig wees.
was, was; *kyk* **be**.
wash, (n) was; wasgoed; wassing; kielwater (boot); vloeistof, wasmiddel; skottelgoedwater; plas; slyk; flou drank; waterverf; vernissie; afspoelsel, spoelgrond, aanspoelsel; golfslag; spoelsel; *have a* ~ *and BRUSH-UP*, jou opknap; *it will COME out in the* ~, dit sal agterna regkom; dit sal uiteindelik tog regkom; ~ *one's DIRTY linen in public*, onenigheid in die openbaar uitmaak; private onsmaaklikhede in die openbaar lug; *HANG out the* ~, wasgoed

washing

uithang; *PUT it in the* ~, gooi dit in die was; (v) was; uitwas; spoel, uitspoel; afspoel; bespoel; reinig; ~ *ABOUT*, omspoel; ~ *ASHORE*, aan land spoel; ~ *AWAY*, uitwas; wegspoel; ~ *and BRUSH up*, jou opknap; ~ *the DISHES*, die skottelgoed was; ~ *DOWN*, afspoel; ~ *down FOOD*, kos afspoel; ~ *one's HANDS of someone*, jou hande in onskuld was; jou hand van iem. aftrek; ~ *one's dirty LINEN in public*, onenigheid in die openbaar uitmaak; *you should* ~ *(out) your MOUTH*, jy moet jou mond gaan uitspoel; ~ *OFF*, afwas; ~ *OUT*, uitspoel; uitwas; ~ *ed OUT*, verkleur, verbleik; bleek; flou, poot-uit, gedaan; *feel* ~ *ed OUT*, pap (poot-uit, gedaan) voel; *the competition was* ~ *ed OUT*, die wedstryd het doodgereën (verreën); ~ *OVER*, omspoel, oorspoel; ~ *OVERBOARD*, oorboord spoel; ~ *UP*, was; skottelgoed was; uitspoel; *this WON'T* ~, dit sal nie gewas kan word nie; dié vlieër gaan nie op nie; dit hou geen steek nie; ~ **able**, wasbaar, waseg; ~**-ableness**, wasbaarheid; ~**-away**, verspoeling; ~**-basin**, waskom, lampetkom; ~**-board**, wasplank, wasbord; ~**-bottle**, wasfles; ~**-bowl**, waskom; ~**-cloth**, waslap; ~**-day**, wasdag; ~**-deck**, spoeldek; ~**-drawing**, waterverftekening; ~**-er**, waster, moerplaatjie, sluitring; wasser, wasmasjien; ~**-er-up**, bordewasser; ~**-erwoman**, wasvrou; washulp; ~**-ery**, wassery; wastoestel; ~**-girl**, washulp; wasvrou; ~**-hand-basin**, waskom; ~**-hand-stand**, wastafel; ~**-house**, washuis; ~**-iness**, flouheid; waterigheid; bleekheid; swakheid.

wash'ing, (n) wasgoed; (die) was; spoelsel; (a) wassend; ~ **agent**, wasmiddel; ~ **basin**, waskom; ~ **bear**, raccoon, wasbeer *(Procyoninus)*; ~ **day**, wasdag; ~**-girl**, washulp; wasvrou; ~**-line**, wasgoedtou, drooglyn; ~**-machine**, wasmasjien; ~ **place**, wasplek; ~**-plant**, wassery, wastoestel; ~**-powder**, waspoeier; ~**-rag**, waslap; ~**-room**, waskamer; ~**-silk**, wasbare sy; ~ **soda**, wassoda, kristalsoda; ~**-stand**, wastafel; ~**-stone**, wasklip; ~**-tub**, wasbalie, wasvat.

wash: ~**-leather**, seemsleer; ~**-out**, afwassing; uitspoeling; weggespoelde plek; verspoeling; mislukking, misoes, gemors, fiasko, hardekoejawel, nikswerd; *BE a* ~*-out*, 'n misoes (mislukking) wees; *he IS a* ~*-out as a preacher*, as prediker is hy 'n mislukking; ~**-rag**, waslap; ~**-room**, waskamer; ~**-stand**, wastafel; ~**-stand-basin**, lampetkom; ~**-trough**, wastrog; ~**-tub**, wasbalie, wasvat; ~**-up**, (die) was; ~**y**, waterig, dun; flou; sonder pit; bleek; verbleik (kleure).

wasp, perdeby, wesp; ~**ish**, wespagtig; stekerig; opvlieënd, liggeraak, kort van draad, bitsig; *be* ~*ish*, gou op jou perdjie wees; kort van draad (opvlieënd) wees; ~ **like**, wespagtig; ~**'s nest**, perdebynes; ~**'s sting**, perdebyangel; ~**-waisted**, met 'n perdebymiddeltjie.

wa'ssail, (n) drinkparty, fuif; (v) fuif, 'n drinkparty hou; toedrink.

wast'age, verkwisting, vermorsing, verspilling; slytasie; troepeverbruik; getalsvermindering; ~ *of LABOUR*, arbeidsverlies; verlies van werkkragte; ~ *in STAFF*, personeelverliese.

waste, (n) verkwisting, verspilling, vermorsing; afval, rommel; verweringsmateriaal, verweringspuin; slytasie, afneming; verbruik; verval, verwaarlosing; oorskiet; woestyn, woesteny; afvoerpyp; poetskatoen; *ATOMIC* ~, kernafval; *HASTE makes* ~, haastige spoed is selde goed; *NUCLEAR* ~, kernafval; *RUN (go) to* ~, verlore gaan, ongebruik wegloop; ~ *of TIME*, tydverspilling; *a* ~ *of WATERS*, 'n eindelose see; *WILLFUL* ~ *makes woeful want*, vandag verteer, môre ontbeer; vandag vermorsing, môre verknorsing; (v) verwoes, verniel; versnipper; (ver)mors, verspil, verkwis, weggooi; verknoei; verbruik; opraak; verlore raak; wegkwyn, uitteer; afslyt (masjien); ~ *AWAY*, wegkwyn, wegteer; ~ *one's BREATH*, tevergeefs praat; woorde vermors; ~ *MONEY on*, geld verkwis op; ~ *an OPPORTUNITY*, 'n geleentheid laat verbygaan; ~ *TIME*, tyd verspil; ~ *not, WANT not*, wie spaar, vergaar; vandag vermor-

water

sing, môre verknorsing; wie spaar, dié het; ~ *one's WORDS*, jou woorde vermors; *kind WORDS are simply* ~ *d on him*, vriendelike woorde word aan hom net verspil; (a) verlate, woes; ongebruik, woestynagtig; onbewerk, onbebou(d); oortollig; vermors; afval; *LAY* ~, verwoes; *LIE* ~, onbewerk lê; ~**-basket**, prulmandjie, snippermandjie; ~**-book**, kladboek; ~**d**, verwoes; tevergeefs; ~**-drain**, vuilwaterriool; ~**-dump**, afvalhoop; ~**ful**, verkwistend, deurbringering, (ver)spilsugtig, spandabel; durabel; skadelik; verwoestend, vernielend; ~ **fulness**, (ver)spilsug, deurbringerigheid, spandabelheid; vernielsug; ~**-gate**, afvoersluis; ~ **land**, onbeboude (onbewerkte) grond; ~ **less**, onuitputlik; ~ **material**, afval; ~**-mining**, afvalafbou; ~**-pack**, rotsopvulling; ~ **paper**, skeurpapier, snipperpapier; ~ **paper basket**, snippermandjie; ~**-pipe**, afvoerpyp; ~ **products**, afvalprodukte; ~ **r**, verkwister, vermorser, deurbringer, geldmorser, verspiller; niksnuts; afval; ~**-receiver**, afvalhouer; ~ **space**, verlore ruimte; ~ **water**, afloopwater; vuilwater; ~**-weir**, uitloop.

wast'ing, (n) vermorsing, verkwisting, verspilling; kwyning; (a) verkwistend; uitterend, verterend, verswakkend; kwynend; ~ **asset**, verdwynende bate; ~ **disease**, uitterende siekte.

wast'rel, mislukte artikel; misbaksel; swerwer; straatkind, verwaarloosde kind; verkwister, deurbringer.

watch, (n) (-es), oorlosie, horlosie; wag, wagdiens; waaksaamheid; *BE on the* ~ *for*, oppas vir; op die loer wees na; uitkyk na; *FIRST* ~, eerste wag; *KEEP* ~, wag hou, *KEEP a good* ~, goed uitkyk; *KEEP* ~ *and ward*, goed die wag hou; *MIDDLE* ~, hondewag; *set a* ~ *before my MOUTH*, sit 'n wag voor my mond; *the* ~ *es of the NIGHT*, die nagwaak; die slaaplose ure v.d. nag; *ON THE* ~, op wag; *RELIEVE the* ~, die wag aflos; *SET a* ~ *upon someone*, iem. laat bewaak; ~ *and WARD*, groot waaksaamheid; (v) waak; wag hou; oplet, dophou, bespied, beloer, gadeslaan, bewaak; *be* ~ *ed BY*, bewaak word deur; *hold a* ~*ing BRIEF*, opdrag hê om sake dop te hou; ~ *a CASE*, 'n pasiënt dophou; 'n saak dophou; 'n regsaak volg; ~ *ed by DETECTIVES*, deur speurders dopgehou; *if you DON'T* ~ *it*, as jy nie oppas nie; ~ *a FLOCK*, 'n trop oppas; ~ *FOR*, op die uitkyk wees na; ~ *IT!*, pas op!; ~ *for an OPPORTUNITY*, 'n geleentheid afwag; *you had better* ~ *OUT*, jy moet in jou pasoppens bly; ~ *OVER*, 'n wakende oog hou oor; ~ *and PRAY*, waak en bid; *a* ~ *ed POT (kettle) never boils*, niks word deur ongeduldige afwagting bespoedig nie; ~ *(mind) your STEP*, baie versigtig wees; in jou pasoppens bly; opletloop; ~ *THROUGH*, deurwaak; ~**-box**, waghuisie; ~**-boy**, bewaker, wagjong; ~**-bracelet**, oorlosiearmband; ~**-case**, oorlosiekas; ~**-chain**, oorlosieketting; ~ **committee**, waaksaamheidskomitee; ~ **dial**, wyserplaat; ~**-dog**, waghond; ~ **er**, waker; waarnemer; spioen; ~**-fire**, wagvuur, kampvuur; ~ **ful**, oplettend, waaksaam, wakend; ~ **fulness**, waaksaamheid; ~**-glass**, oorlosieglas; lunet; ~**-guard**, oorlosieskut; oorlosieketting; ~**-hand**, oorlosiewyser; ~**-house**, waghuis; ~**-key**, oorlosiesleutel; ~**-light**, naglig; ~**-maker**, oorlosiemaker; ~**-making**, oorlosiebedryf; ~ **man**, bewaker, wagter; ~ *man, what of the NIGHT?*, wagter, wat is daar van die nag?; ~ *man on the TOWER*, toringwagter; ~**-pocket**, oorlosiesakkie; ~**-spring**, oorlosieveer; ~**-stand**, oorlosiestaandertjie; ~**-tower**, wagtoring; ~**-turret**, wagtorinkie; ~ **word**, wagwoord; leuse; **works**, ratwerk van 'n oorlosie.

wa'ter, (n) water; spoelsel; *be for ALL* ~ *s*, van alle markte tuis wees; ~ *on the BRAIN*, waterhoof; *much* ~ *will flow under the BRIDGES*, daar sal nog baie water in die see loop; *CAST one's bread on the* ~ *s*, jou brood op die water uitwerp; *pour COLD* ~ *on someone's plans*, koue water op iem. se planne gooi; *dit dwarsboom*; *DEAD* ~, stil water; *be in DEEP* ~ *s*, in groot moeilikhede verkeer; *like* ~ *off a DUCK'S back*, soos water op 'n eend se rug; so goed as vet op 'n warm klip; *through FIRE and* ~, deur alle gevare; *of the FIRST* ~, v.d. eerste water;

uitstekend; *FISH in troubled ~s*, in troebel water visvang; *like a FISH out of ~*, soos 'n vis op droë grond; soos iem. wat uit sy element is; *HARD ~*, harde water; *HEAVY ~*, swaarwater; *keep one's HEAD above ~*, die kop bo water hou; *come HELL or high ~*, buig of bars; *HIGH ~*, hoogwater; *HOLD ~*, water bevat; steekhou (fig.); geldig wees; opgaan; *that does not HOLD ~*, dit hou nie steek nie; *get into HOT ~*, in die moeilikheid kom; *be in HOT ~*, in die knyp (pekel) wees; in die verknorsing wees; jou vasloop; *~ on the KNEE*, water op die knie; *LEAD ~*, waterlei; *at LOW ~*, by laagwater; *in LOW ~*, in geldelike moeilikheid; *MAKE ~*, water inkry; *pour OIL on troubled ~s*, (fig.), olie op die golwe giet (gooi); *ON the ~*, op see; *OVER the ~*, oor die water; *PASS ~*, fluit; water afslaan; *POOR in ~*, waterarm; *cast ~ into the SEA*, water in die see dra; *carry ~ in a SIEVE*, water in 'n mandjie dra; *be in SMOOTH ~*, weer vry kan asemhaal; *SPEND money like ~*, geld rondgooi (verspil); *STILL ~s run deep*, stille waters diepe grond, onder draai die duiwel rond; *TAKE to the ~*, van stapel loop; te water gaan; *TREAD ~*, watertrap; *we never miss the ~ until the WELL runs dry*, 'n mens waardeer die skat eers as hy verlore is; *if ~ cannot be had, we must make shift with WINE*, by gebrek aan brood eet 'n mens korsies van pastei; *WRITTEN in ~*, van korte duur; (v) water gee, natmaak, bewater, natlei, benat, begiet; van water voorsien; water laat inneem (loko); met water verdun; traan (oë, mond); laat suip (diere); moireer (sy); water, urineer; *~ DOWN*, verwater; met water verdun (verflou); *~ DOWN one's demands*, water in jou wyn gooi; *his EYES ~*, sy oë water; *make one's MOUTH ~*, jou laat watertand; *~ one's WINE*, water in jou wyn gooi; ~-**bag**, watersak; ~-**bailiff**, waterfiskaal; ~-**bar**, waterkeerder; ~-**barrel**, watervaatjie; ~-**bearer**, waterdraer; ~-**bearing**, (n) waterdraery; waterlaer (meg.); (a) waterhoudend; water=; ~-**bed**, waterlaag; ~-**berry**, waterbessie; ~-**bird**, watervoël; ~-**blast**, watersproeiing; drukwaterspuit; ~-**blister**, waterblaas; W~-**Board**, Waterraad; ~ **borne**, oor die see vervoer; skeeps=; drywend; water; see=; spoel=; ~ **borne diseases**, siektes deur drinkwater veroorsaak; ~ **borne sewerage**, rioolstelsel, spoelriolering; ~ **borne traffic**, waterverkeer; ~-**bottle**, waterfles, waterbottel; kraffie; ~-**bound**, deur water opgehou; ~-**brash**, sooibrand; ~-**bubble**, waterblasie; ~ **buck**, waterbok; ~-**buffalo**, waterbuffel; ~-**bug**, waterkewer; ~-**butt**, watervaatjie; ~-**carrier**, waterdraer; ~-**cart**, waterkar; *on the ~-cart*, nie sterk drank gebruik nie; ~-**case**, watersaak; ~-**cask**, watervat; ~-**chute**, afglyplank, glygeut; ~-**clock**, waterklok, wateruurwerk; ~-**closet**, spoellatrine, spoelsekreet; ~-**cloud**, waterwolk; ~-**cock**, waterkraan; ~-**colour**, waterverf, waterverftekening, akwarel; *a box of ~-colours*, 'n verfdoos; ~-**colour painter**, waterverfskilder, akwarellis; ~ **column**, waterkolom; ~-**cooled**, met waterverkoeling; ~-**cooling**, waterverkoeling; ~ **course**, waterloop; W ~-**Court**, Waterhof; ~ **craft**, swemkuns; vaartuie; ~-**crane**, waterpomp; waterkraan; ~ **cress**, bronkors, bronslaai; ~ **culture**, waterkultuur; ~-**cure**, waterkuur; ~-**diviner**, waterwyser; ~-**dog**, waterhond; ou matroos; ~-**drain**, dreineersloot, dreineervoor; ~-**drawer**, putter; ~-**dressing**, waterverband; ~-**drill**, waterboor; ~-**drip**, drup; ~-**drop**, (water)druppel; ~-**duties**, waterbelasting, ~-**ed**, gewater; verwater; ~ **ed silk**, weerskynsy, moirésy; ~-**engine**, brandspuit; ~ **er**, natmaker; natspuiter; ~ **erf**, watererf; ~-**fall**, waterval; ~-**famine**, watergebrek, waternood; ~-**finder**, waterwyser, watersoeker; ~-**fly**, watervlieg; ~ **fowl**, watervoël; ~-**front**, waterkant; ~-**furrow**, watervoor; ~-**gas**, watergas; ~-**gate**, sluis; vloeddeur; ~-**gauge**, watermeter; waterdrukmeter; ~-**glass**, waterglas; wateruurwerk; waterglas (chem.); ~-**grass**, uintjie; ~-**hammer**, waterslag; ~-**hazard**, waterhindernis (gholf); ~-**head**, bron; waterdrukhoogte; ~-**heater**, waterverwarmer; ~-**heating**, waterverwarming; ~-**hen**, watervoël; ~-**hole**,

drinkgat; watergat; ~-**hose**, waterslang; ~ **hydrant**, brandkraan; ~-**iness**, waterigheid.

wa'tering, (n) (die) natgooi, begieting, bewatering; watervoorsiening (aan diere); water (oë, mond); (a) suip=; water=, drink=; waterleidend; betraand; ~-**bag**, suipsak; ~-**bucket**, suipemmer; ~-**can**, gieter; ~-**cart**, waterkar; ~-**hose**, waterslang; ~-**place**, badplek, strand; suipplek; ~-**trough**, waterbak, drinkbak.

wa'ter: ~ **intake**, wateropneming; ~-**ish**, waterig; wateragtig; ~-**jacket**, watermantel, koelmantel; ~-**jet**, waterstraal; ~ **law**, waterreg; waterwet; ~ **less**, sonder water; waterloos; ~ **less cooker**, stoompot, stoomkastrol; ~-**level**, waterhoogte; waterstand; waterpas (instrument); ~-**lily**, waterlelie; ~-**line**, watermerk; draaglyn, waterlyn (skip); waterafskeiding; waterlinie (vestingbou); ~-**lined paper**, waterlynpapier; ~-**logged**, moerassig, deurslagtig, drassig; versuip (grond); deurweek, vol water getrek (hout).

Waterloo', Waterloo; *meet one's ~*, jou moses kry (teëkom).

wa'ter: ~ **loss**, waterverlies; ~-**main**, hoofwaterpyp; ~ **man**, veerman, roeier; skuitvoerder; brandweerman; ~ **manship**, roeikuns; ~ **mark**, (n) watermerk (in papier); waterlyn, waterpeil, waterstand; (v) van 'n watermerk voorsien; ~-**melon**, waatlemoen, waterlemoen; ~-**meter**, watermeter; ~-**mill**, watermeule; ~-**mole**, watermol; eendbekdier, voëlbekdier; waterbobbejaan; ~-**mongoose**, kommetjiesgatmuishond; ~-**monkey**, waterkruik; ~-**newt**, watersalamander; ~-**nymph**, waternimf, najade; ~-**ordeal**, waterbesoeking, waterproef; ~-**outlet**, wateruitlaat; ~ **paint**, waterverf; ~-**pipe**, waterpyp; ~-**plane**, watervliegtuig; ~-**plant**, waterplant; ~-**plate**, warmwaterbord; ~-**pocket**, ondergrondse waterpoel; waterholte; ~-**poise**, vogmeter; ~-**polo**, waterpolo; ~ **pore**, waterporie; ~-**power**, waterkrag; ~-**pressure**, waterdruk; ~ **proof**, (n) reënjas; waterdigte stof; (v) waterdig maak; (a) waterdig; ~-**proofing**, waterdigting; ~ **proof sheet**, rubberlaken; ~ **proof sheeting**, hospitaallinne; ~-**pump**, waterpomp; ~-**ram**, hidrouliese pers; ~ **rat**, waterrot; ~-**rate**, waterbelasting; ~-**resistant**, watervas; ~-**resources**, watervoorrade; waterhulpbronne; ~ **reticulation**, waternet; ~-**run**, waterloop; waterkering; ~ **scape**, waterskap, watergesig; ~ **shed**, waterskeiding, opvanggebied; kentering, keerpunt; ~-**shoot**, waterloot; waterpyp; ~ **side**, waterkant; ~-**ski**, waterski; ~ **skiing**, waterski(sport); ~-**skin**, watersak; ~-**snake**, waterslang; ~-**soaked**, deurweek (deurtrek) van water; ~-**softener**, waterversagter; ~-**softening**, waterontharding; ~-**spaniel**, Waterhond; ~-**spider**, waterspinnekop; ~ **spout**, waterstraal; waterhoos; ~ **sprinkler**, sproeier; sprinkelaar; sprinkelwa; ~-**sprite**, watergees; ~ **stain**, watervlek; ~-**superintendent**, fiskaal; ~ **supply**, watervoorraad; wateraanvoer, drinkwatervoorsiening; suiping (diere); ~ **surface**, wateroppervlak; ~ **system**, waterleiding; ~-**table**, grondwaterstand, grondwatervlak; ~-**tank**, watertenk; ~-**tap**, (water)kraan; ~ **tight**, waterdig; ~ **tightness**, waterdigtheid; ~ **tissue**, waterweefsel; ~-**tortoise**, waterskilpad; ~-**tower**, watertoring; ~ **transport**, watervervoer; vaartuie; ~ **trough**, drinkbak, waterbak; ~ **valve**, waterklep; ~ **vapour**, waterdamp, ~-**vein**, wateraar; ~-**vole**, waterrot; ~-**wag(g)on**, waterwa; *be on the ~-wag(g)on*, nie sterk drank gebruik nie; ~-**wave**, waterkartel (hare); ~ **way**, waterweg; bevaarbare rivier; watergang; ~-**wheel**, skeprat, waterrat; ~-**witch**, waterheks.

wa'terworks, waterwerke; *TURN on the ~*, begin huil; *then the ~ were TURNED on*, daar kom die waterlanders.

wa'ter: ~-**worn**, deur water afgeslyt; ~ **y**, pap, wateragtig, waterig, dun, sopperig, verdun, vogtig; smaakloos; bleek; *a ~y grave (death)*, 'n watergraf; 'n graf in die golwe.

watson'ia, suurknol, rooipypie, waspypie, watsonia.

watt, watt; ~ **age**, wattverbruik.

wa'ttle[1], (n) bel, lel (van pluimvee); (v) van belle voor=

wattle

sien; ~d *CRANE*, lelkraan(voël); ~d *STAR=LING*, lelspreeu.

wa'ttle², (n) (looi)basboom, wattel(boom), Australie=se akasia; vlegwerk; lat; (v) met latwerk toemaak; ~-**and-daub hut**, huisie van klei en latte, hartbees=huisie, mandjiehut; ~-**work**, latwerk, paalwerk; vlegwerk.

watt'meter, wattmeter.

waul, miaau, tjank.

wave, (n) golf; brander, baar; golflyn; (die) waai, wuif; golwing; opwelling; kartel; ~ *of CRIME*, vlaag van misdade; *a* ~ *of ENTHUSIASM*, 'n op=welling van geesdrif; *a* ~ *of the HAND*, 'n (hand)=wuif; 'n handgebaar; *PERMANENT* ~, vaste haargolf (kartel); (v) golf; wiegel; wapper, wuif, swaai; kartel, golf (hare); water (sy); vlam; ~ *ASIDE*, van die hand wys; opsy wink; ~ *AWAY*, beduie om weg te gaan; ~ *someone NEARER*, iem. wink om nader te kom; ~ *TO*, waai vir; ~ **action**, golfwerking; ~ **band**, golfband; ~-**bread**, beweeg=brood; ~-**crest**, golftop; ~ **length**, golflengte; ~**less**, sonder golwe, kalm, glad; ~**let**, golfie; ~**like**, golwend, golf=; ~ *like motion*, golfbewe=ging; ~-**line**, golflyn; ~ **loaf**, beweegbrood; ~-**mark**, golfriffel; ~-**meter**, golfmeter; ~-**motion**, golfbeweging; ~ **moulding**, golflys; ~-**offering**, be=weegoffer; ~ **trough**, golfdal.

wav'er, weifel, aarsel; besluiteloos wees; slinger; wan=kel; wyk; bewe, flikker (vlam).

wave' range, golfomvang; golfveld.

wav'er, ~**cr**, weifelaar; ~**ing**, (n) geweifel, weifeling; (a) wankelend, wankelmoedig, besluiteloos; ~**y**, onvas, weifelend.

wave' stitch, kartelsteek.

wav'ey, (-s), sneeugans.

wav'iness, gegolfdheid; golwing.

wav'ing, (n) gegolf; gewuif; (a) golwend.

wav'y¹, (**wavies**), sneeugans.

wav'y², (a) golwend, gekartel.

wawl, *kyk* **waul**.

wax¹, (n) woede, drifbui; *be in a* ~, woedend wees.

wax², (n) was; byewas; lak; oorwas; *BLEACHED* ~, wit was; *like* ~ *in one's HANDS*, soos klei in jou hande; iem. se speelbal wees; *MINERAL* ~, aard=was; *MOULD someone like* ~, iem. na jou pype laat dans; (v) met was opvryf; ~**ed paper**, was=papier.

wax³, (v) was, toeneem; groei (maan); word; ~ *MERRY*, vrolik word; ~ *and WANE*, toeneem en afneem.

wax: ~**bill**, sysie; ~ **candle**, waskers; ~-**chandler**, waskersmaker; ~-**cloth**, wasdoek; ~ **coating**, was=laag; ~ **doll**, waspop; ~**en**, was=, van was; ~**en tablet**, wastafeltjie; ~-**flower**, wasblom; ~ **heath**, washeide; ~-**light**, waskers; ~**like**, wasagtig; ~-**modelling**, wasmodellering, wasboetseerkuns; ~-**moth**, wasmot; ~-**painting**, wasskildery; wasskil=derkuns; ~-**palm**, waspalm; ~-**paper**, waspapier; ~-**plant**, wasplant; ~-**pocket**, waskliertjie (van by); ~ **tablet**, wastafel(tjie); ~ **taper**, waskers; ~-**tree**, wasboom; ~ **work**, wasbeeld; wasmodelle=ring; ~ **worker**, wasboetseerder, waswerker; ~ **works**, wasbeeldmuseum..

wax'y¹, (a) boos, boosaardig.

wax'y², (a) wasagtig.

way, pad, weg; rigting; manier, gewoonte, gebruik, wyse; geleentheid; gang, snelheid; tak (elektr.); *know one's* ~ *ABOUT*, jou wêreld ken; *not to know one's* ~ *ABOUT*, geen benul van steg ken nie; *stand in the ANCIENT* ~, jou by die oue hou, op die ou paaie bly; *ANY* ~, in elk geval; op enige manier; *by* ~ *of APOLOGY*, ter verontskuldiging; *on their* ~ *BACK*, op hulle terugreis; *he is in a BAD* ~, dit gaan sleg met hom; *things are in a BAD* ~, dit gaan sleg; *BAR the* ~, die weg versper; *BE in the* ~, in die pad wees; *you cannot have it BOTH* ~*s*, jy moet die een of die ander doen; *have it BOTH* ~*s*, jou mes na albei kante wil laat sny; *BY the* ~, langs die pad; terloops, tussen hakies; *BY* ~ *of*, by wyse van; *BY* ~ *of Kimberley*, oor Kimberley; *I CANNOT see my* ~ *to alter it*, ek sien geen kans om dit te verander nie; *there are more* ~*s of killing a CAT*

way

than choking it with cream, daar is meer as een ma=nier om 'n kat dood te maak; *CLEAR the* ~, opsy staan; die pad skoonmaak; *COME the* ~ *of some=one*, iem. te beurt val; *COME in someone's* ~, bin=ne iem. se bereik kom; deur iem. ervaar word; *the W* ~ *of the CROSS*, die Kruisweg; *DEVISE* ~*s and means*, middele beraam; planne aan die hand doen; *that's the* ~ *to DO it*, só moet dit gedoen word; *that is not the* ~ *to DO things*, dis nie die regte manier nie; dis geen manier nie; *there are more* ~*s to kill a DOG than by hanging*, daar is meer as een manier om 'n kat dood te maak; *DOWN our* ~, hier in ons buurt (geweste); *EVERY* ~, in elke op=sig; *fall into EVIL* ~*s*, op die verkeerde weg raak; *in the FAMILY* ~, swanger, in die ander tyd; *FEEL one's* ~, voel-voel gaan; tastend jou pad soek; *FIGHT one's* ~, veg-veg jou weg baan; *FIND the* ~, die pad kry; *FIND a* ~ *out*, 'n uitweg vind; *the* ~ *of all FLESH*, die weg van alle vlees; *the FURTHEST* ~ *about is the nearest* ~ *home*, 'n ompad is dikwels die kortste pad; *GATHER* ~, vaart kry; *in a GENERAL* ~, in die algemeen; *GET out of my* ~! gee pad voor! *GET one's* ~, jou sin kry; *GET out of the* ~, padgee; *GET under* ~, in beweging kom; *GET into the* ~ *of*, in die ge=woonte verval om; *GIVE* ~, wyk, padgee; *GIVE* ~ *to temptation*, aan die versoeking toegee; *GO one's* ~, jou gang gaan; vertrek; *GO one's own* ~, jou nie aan ander steur nie; *GO the right* ~ *about a thing*, iets op die regte manier aanpak; *he HAS a* ~ *with him*, hy is innemend; *HAVE things all one's own* ~, jou eie kop kan volg; jou sin kry; *HAVE a* ~ *of*, 'n neiging (slag) hê om; *let someone HAVE his* ~, sy sin gee; iem. sy gang laat gaan; *IN a* ~, in sekere opsig; *be IN the* ~, in die pad staan; *let us KEEP it that* ~, laat ons dit so hou; *LEAD the* ~, die pad wys; die weg baan; ~ *of LIFE*, lewenswyse; lewensvorm; *a LITTLE goes a long* ~, 'n bietjie kan 'n mens lank gebruik; 'n mens hoef baie min daarvan te gebruik; ~ *of LIVING*, lewenswyse; *a LONG* ~ *off*, ver; *not by a LONG* ~, lank nie, glad nie; *the LONGER* ~ *round is the nearest* ~ *home*, die kortste pad neem dikwels die langste; die kort=ste pad is dikwels die verste; *LOOK the other* ~, wegkyk; maak of jy iem. nie sien nie; in die ander rigting kyk; *LOSE the* ~, verdwaal; *MAKE* ~, plek maak; uit die pad gaan; opskiet; *MAKE one's* ~, jou weg baan; vooruitkom; *in all MANNER of* ~*s*, op allerhande maniere; ~*s and MEANS*, (geld)middele; *the NARROW* ~, die smal (enge) pad; *in NO* ~, glad nie; *in NO* ~ *inferior to*, in geen opsig minder nie as; *in the same OLD* ~, op die ou trant; *foresake the OLD* ~*s (customs)*, die ou paaie verlaat; *ON the* ~, op pad, aan die kom; *ONCE in a* ~, by wyse van uitsondering; *ONE* ~ *or another*, op die een of ander manier; *ONE* ~ *and another*, alles bymekaar geneem; *there is no other* ~ *OPEN to me*, daar staan vir my geen ander weg oop nie; *go OUT of one's* ~ *for*, die moeite (opoffering) getroos vir; *OUT of the* ~, uit die pad; afgeleë; ongewoon; *OUT-OF-THE-* ~ *place*, 'n afgeleë plek; 'n uithoek; *get something OUT of the* ~, van iets ontslae raak; *it is nothing OUT of the* ~, dit is niks besonders nie; *go OUT of one's* ~, jou die moeite getroos; die moeite doen; *OVER the* ~, aan die oorkant; *go one's OWN* ~, jou eie gang gaan; *let him go his OWN sweet* ~, laat hom maar sy twak op sy eie manier kerwe; *have one's OWN* ~, jou sin kry; jou eie kop volg; *the PARTING of the* ~*s*, die skeiding v.d. weë; *PAVE the* ~, die weg baan; *PAY one's* ~, jou onkoste dek; *PERMA=NENT* ~, spoorbaan; *PREPARE the* ~ *for die* weg voorberei; *PUT someone out of the* ~, iem. uit die weg ruim; *PUT someone in the* ~ *of*, iem. in die geleentheid stel; *PUT (lay, throw) something in someone's* ~, iem. tot iets in staat stel; dit vir iem. moontlik maak om te verkry (bereik); *RIGHT of* ~, ryreg; deurgangsreg; voorrangsweg; *It is a long* ~ *ROUND*, dit is 'n ompad; *SHOW the* ~, die pad (weg) wys; *in a SMALL* ~, op klein skaal; *in SOME* ~, op een of ander manier; *SQUEEZE one's* ~ *in*, binnedring; *STAND in the* ~, in die pad staan; *that's the* ~ *to TALK,* so moet 'n mond (bek) praat; *THAT* ~, diékant uit; op dié manier; *THAT'S the* ~, dis die regte manier; *get into the* ~ *of THINGS,* mooi op stryk kom; *to my* ~ *of THINKING,* volgens my mening; soos ek dink; *in THIS* ~, op hierdie manier; *it's THIS* ~, die saak is so; dit is hierlangs (daarlangs); *THIS* ~ *or that,* sus of so; hiernatoe of daarnatoe; *not to know which* ~ *to TURN,* nie vorentoe of agtertoe weet nie; *there are no TWO* ~*s about it,* daar is geen alternatief nie; *UNDER* ~, aan die gang; onderweg; op pad; onder seil; *be UNDER* ~, in beweging wees; onderweg wees; aan die kom wees; *in WHAT* ~? op watter manier? *there are more* ~*s to the WOOD than one,* daar is meer as een manier om 'n kat dood te maak; *the* ~ *of the WORLD,* die wêreld se beloop; *go the WRONG* ~ *about it,* iets verkeerd aanpak; (adv) ver; ~ *BACK,* daar ver; lank gelede; ~ *BEHIND,* ver agter; ~ *DOWN south,* daar ver in die suide; ~ *OFF,* ver weg; ~ *OUT,* ver buite; ~-**bill,** vragbrief, geleibrief, vraglys; laaibrief; ~**farer,** voetganger; reisiger; ~ **faring,** (n) rondreis; trekkery; (a) reisend, rondtrekkend; ~ **lay',** (..**laid),** belaag, beloer; voorlê, in hinderlaag lê; oorval; ~ **lay'er,** belaer; ~-**leave,** oorwegreg, deurgangsreg; ~**less,** sonder pad; ~-**maker,** wegbereider; ~ **mark,** wegwyser; ~-**shaft,** omsetas; ~ **side,** (n) die kant v.d. pad; *fall by the* ~ *side,* uitsak; (a) langs die pad; ~ **side station,** tussenstasie; ~ **ward,** eiewys; verkeerd, eiesinnig, vol nukke; ~ **wardness,** eiewysheid; verkeerdheid, eiesinnigheid; ~-**worn,** vermoeid.

wayz'goose, perspiekniek, drukkersfees, joernalistefees.

we, ons; *EDITORIAL* ~, redaksionele meervoud; *the ROYAL* ~, die koninklike meervoud; die deftigheidsmeervoud; die beskeidenheidsmeervoud.

weak, swak; flou, pap, kragteloos, lamlendig; slap(perig); sieklik; tingerig; pieperig; luttel; toonloos, onbeklemtoon; *a* ~ *DEMAND for,* 'n geringe aanvraag na; *the* ~*est GOES to the wall,* die swakste delf die onderspit; *a* ~ *HAND,* slegte kaarte; *in a* ~ *MOMENT,* in 'n swak oomblik; *his* ~ *POINT,* sy swak kant; *the* ~*er SEX,* die swak geslag; die swakkere vat; *the* ~ *SPOT,* die swak kant; die wondbare plek; *the* ~*er VESSEL,* die swakkere vat; ~ **attendance,** slegte (swak) opkoms; ~-**brained,** swakhoofdig; ~ **current,** swakstroom (elek.); ~ **demand,** klein (geringe) aanvraag; ~**en,** verswak; verslap; aanleng, verwater, verflou; slapper maak, verdun; ~**ening,** verflouing; verswakking; verwatering; ~-**eyed,** swak van gesig; ~-**headed,** swakhoofdig; ~-**hearted,** weekhartig; ~**ish,** swakkerig, voos; ~-**kneed,** swak in die knieë; papbroekerig; ~**ling,** swakkeling lamsak, jabroer; papbroek; ~**ly,** swak, sieklik, swakkies; ~-**minded,** verstandelik swak; besluiteloos; ~ **mixture,** flou mengsel; ~**ness,** swakheid; swakte, swak; slegtigheid, lamlendigheid; weekheid; *have a* ~ *ness for,* 'n swak hê vir; baie hou van iets; ~-**sighted,** swaksiende, slegsiende, swak van oë, sleg van gesig; ~ **solution,** flou oplossing; ~-**spirited,** kleinmoedig, flouhartig; ~ **tea,** flou tee; ~-**willed,** sonder wilskrag; swak van karakter.

weal¹, (n) striem, streep, litteken, swelsel; (v) striem, slaan.

weal², (n) geluk, welvaart, welsyn; heil; wel; *the PUBLIC (common)* ~, die algemene welsyn; *in* ~ *and WOE,* in lief en leed; *the* ~ *and the WOE,* die wel en wee.

wealth, rykdom; welstand, vermoë; fortuin, weelde; oorvloed; skat; *a* ~ *of FRUIT,* vrugte in oorvloed; *a* ~ *of pretty GIRLS,* 'n magdom van mooi meisies; *a* ~ *of INFORMATION,* 'n skat van kennis; *a MAN of* ~, 'n (skat)ryk man; *MARRY* ~, ryk trou; *MUCH* ~ *makes wits waver,* sterk bene kan alleen die weelde dra; *be ROLLING in* ~, in goud swem; ~**iness,** rykdom; ~**y,** welgesteld, bemiddeld, ryk, gefortuneer; *a* ~ *y man,* 'n (skat)ryk man, 'n nabob.

wean, speen; afwen, losmaak van, afleer; *have been* ~*ed,* van iets gespeen wees; ~**er,** speendoppie;

speenvarkie; speenkalf; speendier; ~**ing,** speen, spening; ~**ling,** gespeende kind (dier).

wea'pon, wapen; strydmiddel; ~**ed,** gewapen(d); ~**less,** ongewapen.

wear¹, (v) wend, draai (skip).

wear², (n) gebruik; mode; (die) dra; drag; klerasie; slytasie; slyting; *a COAT the worse for* ~, 'n baadjie wat baie gedra is; *for their OWN* ~, vir eie gebruik; *for SUMMER* ~, vir somerdrag; ~ *and TEAR,* slytasie; *fair* ~ *and TEAR,* billike slytasie; *the WORSE for* ~, gehawend, baie geslyt; (v) **(wore, worn),** dra; verslyt, wegslyt; aanhê; slyt; gedra word; hê, vertoon; uitput, moeg maak; ~ *AWAY,* wegslyt, uitskuur; *the wife* ~*s the BREECHES,* die vrou dra die broek; *the DAY wore on,* die dag het stadig verbygegaan; ~ *DOWN,* slyt; afmat; ~ *GLASSES,* bril dra; ~ *one's HEART on one's sleeve,* die hart op die tong hê; *the INSCRIPTION has worn away,* die opskrif is afgeslyt; *this MATERIAL* ~*s twice as well,* hierdie stof dra twee maal so goed; ~ *OFF the pattern of the linoleum,* die patroon v.d. linoleum afslyt; *the years* ~ *ON,* die jare gaan verby; ~ *down the OPPOSITION,* die teenstand geleidelik uitput; ~ *OUT,* uitslyt; uithol, uitskuur, uitloop; *the work* ~*s me OUT,* die werk maak my doodmoeg; ~ *shoes OUT quickly,* skoene gou opdra; *after 40 years of teaching he was completely worn OUT,* nadat hy 40 jaar onderwys gegee het, was hy 'n senuweewrak; *his PATIENCE was worn out at last,* uiteindelik het sy geduld opgeraak; ~ *to RAGS (tatters),* aan flenters dra; *better* ~ *out than RUST out,* liewer wegslyt as wegroes; ~ *a SCAR,* 'n litteken hê; *the SHOES* ~ *well,* die skoene dra goed; ~ *one's SHOES down on one side,* die skoene skeef afloop; ~ *THIN,* dun word; *that excuse has worn a little THIN,* daardie verontskuldiging is nou taamlik afgeslyt; ~ *THREADBARE,* kaal slyt; ~ *out one's WELCOME,* te lank by iem. kuier; die honde mak maak; ~ *one's YEARS well,* jou jare goed dra; ~**able,** draagbaar; ~**er,** draer.

wear'ied, vermoeid, afgemat.

wear'iless, onvermoeid.

wear'iness, moegheid, afmatting, uitgeputheid, tamheid, vermoeidheid; verveling.

wear'ing, (n) (die) dra; verwering; slytasie; (a) vermoeiend, uitputtend; ~ **apparel,** klere; ~ **face,** slytvlak.

wear'isome, vervelig, vermoeiend, afmattend; ~**ness,** verveligheid, vermoeienis, afmatting.

wear: ~ **resistance,** slytbestandheid; ~ **test,** dratoets.

wear'y, (v) (..**ried),** moeg word van; vermoei, afmat; verveel; ~ *FOR,* verlang na; ~ *OF,* moeg word van; (a) moeg, vermoeid, afgemat, tam, afgetob, uitgeput; sat; vervelend; afmattend; ~ *of LIFE,* lewensmoeg; ~ *WILLY,* Moeë Jan; rondloper, bondeldraer; ~ *and WORN,* moeg en afgemat.

weas'and, lugpyp, gorrelpyp; *slit someone's* ~, iem. keel-af sny.

weas'el, wesel; muishond; *catch a* ~ *asleep,* 'n skrander persoon uitoorlê; ~-**faced,** met skerp (gelaats)trekke.

wea'ther, (n) weer; weersgesteldheid; *in ALL* ~*s,* in mooi of slegte weer; *APRIL* ~, reën en sonskyn tegelyk; *BAD* ~, slegte weer; *make BAD* ~, slegte weer tref; *make HEAVY* ~ *of,* dit opdraand kry; ~ *PERMITTING,* as die weer goed is; *be UNDER the* ~, mismoedig wees; siekerig wees; van stryk wees; (v) deurstaan, braveer; verkrummel, verweer (rotse); lug, aan die lug blootstel; loefwaarts seil; die loef afsteek; ~ *a CRISIS,* jou gedurende 'n krisis staande hou; ~ *a STORM,* 'n storm deurstaan; ~-**beaten,** verweer(d); deur slegte weer geteister; ~-**board,** waterslagplank; ~-**bound,** deur slegte weer opgehou; ~-**box,** weerhuisie; ~-**bureau,** weerstasie, weerburo; ~-**chart,** weerkaart; ~-**coat,** reënjas; ~ **cock,** weerhaan, windwyser, vaantjie; verkleurmannetjie; *be a* ~*cock,* jou mantel na die wind draai; 'n verkleurmannetjie wees; ~ **conditions,** weersgesteldheid; ~-**deck,** oop dek; ~-**drip,** druplys.

wea'thered, verweer(d); ~ **joint**, drupvoeg; ~ **wool**, verweerde wol.

wea'ther: ~ **eye**, *keep one's* ~ *eye open*, op jou hoede wees; goed oppas; ~ **forecast**, weervoorspelling, weersverwagting; ~ **forecaster**, weervoorspeller; ~ **gauge**, reënmeter; ~**-glass**, weerglas, barometer; ~ **ing**, verwering; ~ **ing agent**, verweringsmiddel; ~**-line**, stormtou; ~ **lore**, weergelofies; weerkennis; ~**-map**, weerkaart; ~**-message**, weerberig; ~ **most**, meer na die loefsy; ~**proof**, teen die weer bestand, weerdig; weervas (kleur); ~**-prophet**, weerprofeet; weerkundige; ~**-quarter**, windkant; ~**-report**, weerberig; ~**-screen**, windskerm; ~**-service**, weerkundige diens; ~**-ship**, weerskip; ~**-shore** loefwal; ~**-side**, loefsy, weerkant; ~**-stained**, verweer(d); ~**-station**, weerstasie; weerburo; ~**-vane**, weerhaan, windwyser; ~**-wise**, weerkundig; ~**-worn**, verweer(d).

weave, (n) weefsel; weeftrant; (v) (**wove**, **woven**), wewe, weef, vleg; ~ *all pieces on the same loom*, almal oor een kam skeer; kiep-kiep roep; ~ **pattern**, weeftrant; weefpatroon.

weav'er, wewer; wewervoël; vink; ~**-bird**, vink, wewervoël; ~**'s beam**, kettingroller; ~**s' guild**, wewersgilde; ~**'s knot**, wewersknoop.

weav'ing, (die) weef; weefwerk, weefkuns; ~ **loom**, weefspoel.

weaz'en, *kyk* **wizened**.

web, web, (spinne)rak; weefsel, spinsel; swemvlies (watervoël); groot rol papier, spantuk (myn); arm (hoetyster), scil; middelrib (balk); wang; liggaam; rib (spoorstaaf); baard (sleutel); *a ~ of lies (and deceit)*, 'n weefsel van leuens (en bedrog); ~ **bed**, met swemvliese; geweb; ~ **belt**, seillyfband; ~ **bing**, touweefsel; omboorsel; seil; seildoek; ~ **by**, soos 'n web; webagtig; met swemvliese; ~**-eye**, vlies op die oog; ~**-fingered**, met vliese tussen die vingers; ~**-foot**, swempoot; ~**-footed**, met swempote; ~ **girth**, seilbuikgord; ~ **leggings**, seilkamaste; ~**-toed**, met vliese tussen die tone; ~**-wheel**, blokwiel

wed, (**-ded**), trou, in die eg verbind, hu, in die huwelik tree.

wedd'ed, getroud, gehuud; *BE ~ to*, getroud wees met; verknog wees aan; ~ *HAPPINESS*, huweliksgeluk; ~*'s hand*, huwelikslewe; ~ *LOVE*, egtelike liefde; ~ *PAIR*, egpaar; ~ *to his PIPE*, onafskei(d)baar van sy pyp.

wedd'ing, bruilof, trouparty, trouery, huwelik; *silver, golden, diamond* ~, silwer bruilof, goue bruilof, diamantbruilof; ~ **anniversary**, huweliksherdenking; troudag; ~**-bell**, huweliksklok; ~ **breakfast**, bruilofsontbyt; ~**-cake**, bruidskoek; ~**-card**, troukaartjie; ~ **celebration**, bruilof, troufees, huweliksfees; ~ **ceremony**, huwelikseremonie, trouplegtigheid; ~ **clothes**, troukiere, ~ **day**, troudag; ~ **dress**, trourok; ~**-favour**, bruilofstrik; ~ **feast**, bruilof, troufees; ~ **garment**, trourok; bruilofskleed; ~**-guest**, bruilofsgas; ~ **journey**, huweliksreis; ~ **march**, troumars, bruilofsmars; ~ **party**, trougeselskap, trouparty; ~**-present**, trougeskenk; huweliksgeskenk; ~**-ring**, trouring, troupand; ~ **trip**, huweliksreis.

wedge, (n) wig, keil; spie; punt; remyster, ligyster (gholf); *a ~ of CAKE*, 'n stuk (sny) koek; *the thin END of the ~*, die skerp kant van die wig; die eerste toegewing; (v) 'n wig inslaan; oopkloof; opmekaar pak; ~*d BETWEEN*, tussenin gedruk; ~ *it INTO the suitcase*, dit in die reistas indruk; ~ *OFF*, wegdruk; ~ *OUT*, uitwig; ~ *UP*, opkeil; ~**-bolt**, wigbout; ~ **heel**, wighak; ~**-shaped**, wigvormig; ~**-tailed**, met 'n wigvormige stert.

wed'lock, huwelik, huweliksstaat, eg; *born IN ~*, eg, wettig; *born OUT of ~*, buite-egtelik.

Wednesday, Woensdag; *on ~s*, Woensdae.

wee, baie klein; *a ~ BIT*, 'n baie klein bietjie (stukkie); *the ~ FOLK*, die feë; die kleintjies.

weed, (n) onkruid, vuilgoed; sigaar; tabak; knol; lang lummel; nikswerd dier; (pl) weduweedrag, rougewaad; onkruid; *ill ~s GROW apace*, onkruid vergaan nie; *be a LOVER of the ~*, graag rook; *get RID of the ~s*, die onkruid uitroei; ~*s want no SOWING*, onkruid vergaan nie; (v) skoffel, skoonmaak, onkruid uittrek; ~ *out*, uitskoffel, uitroei; verwyder, suiwer; ~**er**, skoffelaar, wieder; skoffel= (masjien); ~**-grown**, vervuil, vol gras; ~ **iness**, vervuiling, vervuildheid; ~**ing**, geskoffel, (die) skoffel; skoonmaak; skoffelwerk; ~**ing-fork**, tuinvurk; ~**ing-hoe**, skoffelpik; ~**-killer**, onkruidgif, onkruidmiddel; onkruiddoder; ~**y**, vol onkruid, vervuil; lummelagtig; skraal en lank; niksbeduidend.

week, week; ~ *and ~ ABOUT*, al om die ander week; *not FOR ~s*, nie in (vir) weke nie; *FRIDAY ~*, Vrydag oor agt dae; ~ *IN*, ~ *out*, week na week; *KNOCK someone into the middle of next ~*, iem. opdons; iem. slaan dat hy opslae maak; *a ~ at the OUTSIDE*, 'n week op sy (die) langste; *PER ~*, per week; *a ~ of SUNDAYS*, sewe weke; *THIS day ~*, vandag oor 'n week; *TODAY ~*, vandag oor agt dae; *a ~ or TWO*, 'n paar weke; ~**day**, werkdag, weeksdag; *on ~days*, in die week; ~ **end**, (n) naweek; *spend a ~end*, 'n naweek deurbring; (v) die naweek deurbring; ~**ender**, naweekgas; ~ **end excursion**, naweekekskursie.

week'ly, (n) (..**lies**), weekblad; (a) week=, wekliks; ~ **cleaning**, weeklikse skoonmaak; ~ **magazine**, weekblad; ~ **statement**, weekstaat; ~ **wage**, weekloon.

ween, (poet.), dink, meen.

weep, (**wept**), huil; ween; treur, betreur; skrei; uitvloei, sweet; lek; *it's no use ~ing ABOUT it*, dit help niks om daaroor te huil nie; *they wept AT the sight of the accident*, hulle het gewen by die aanskoue van die ongeluk; ~ *FOR someone in distress*, ween uit meegevoel vir iem. in nood; ~ *FOR one's sins*, ween oor jou sondes; ~ *FOR a dear friend*, 'n dierbare vriend beween; ~ *FOR*, beween; *for JOY*, huil van vreugde; ~ *one's heart OUT*, bitterlik huil; ~ *TEARS of joy*, vreugdetrane stort; ~**er**, klaer, wener, huiler, huilebak; rouband; rousluier; ~**ers**, handboordjies; roumansjette.

weeping, (n) gehuil, geween, geskrei, gesnik; (a) huilend, wenend; ~ **cypress**, treursipres; ~ **oak**, treureik; ~ **willow**, treurwilg(er).

weep'y, huilerig, tranerig; tjankerig.

weev'er, pieterman (vis).

weev'il, kalander; ~**y**, vol kalanders.

wee'-wee, water, plassie maak, piepie (kindertaal).

weft, inslag(draad); *kyk ook* **waft**; ~ **yarn**, inslaggaring.

weigh, (n) weeg; (v) weeg; oorweeg, bedink, wik, in oorweging neem; lig (anker); ~ *AGAINST*, opweeg teen; in die skaal kom (plaas) teen; ~ *ANCHOR*, die anker lig; *this ARGUMENT does not ~ with him*, hierdie argument tel nie by hom nie; *one good ARGUMENT ~s down six bad ones*, een gegronde argument weeg op teen ses swakkes; ~ *the CONSEQUENCES*, die gevolge oorweeg; ~ *DOWN*, neerdruk; laat hang; laat oorslaan; ~*ed DOWN with*, neergedruk deur; belas with met; ~*ed and FOUND wanting*, geweeg en te lig bevind; ~ *IN with*, vorendag kom met; ~ *in a JOCKEY*, 'n jokkie weeg (voor die wedren); ~ *out a JOCKEY*, 'n jokkie weeg (na die wedren); ~ *OUT*, afweeg; *this POINT ~s with me*, hierdie punt weeg swaar by my; ~ *the PROS and cons*, die voor- en nadele in oorweging neem; ~ *UP*, skat, takseer; optig, ophys; ~ *heavily UPON*, druk op; swaar rus op; ~ *one's WORDS*, jou woorde weeg; ~**able**, weegbaar; ~ **age**, weegloon; ~**-beam**, weeghaak, Romeinse balans, unster; ~**-bridge**, weegbrug; ~**er**, weër; ~**-in**, inweging.

weigh'ing, (n) geweeg, weëry; (a) weeg=; ~**-chair**, weegstoel; ~**-house**, weegplek; ~**-machine**, weegbrug, weegtoestel; ~**-room**, weegkamer.

weight, (n) gewig, swaarte; las; druk, drukking; nadruk; *ATTACH much ~ to*, die klem lê op; *sell BY ~*, by (volgens) gewig verkoop; *CARRY ~*, gewig dra; invloed hê, gewig dra; *CARRY little ~*, min invloed hê; van min belang wees; *the ~ of EVIDENCE*, die oorwig v.d. getuienis; *GIVE ~ to*, nadruk lê op; krag verleen aan; *light IN ~*, lig van gewig; *INSPECTOR of ~s and measures*, yker; *LAY ~ upon*, gewig heg aan; nadruk lê op; *LEND ~ to*, krag verleen aan; *LIFT ~s*, gewigte optel;

LOSE ~, ligter (maerder) word; ~s *and MEA=SURES*, mate en gewigte; *MEN of* ~, manne van invloed; *a* ~ *off one's MIND*, 'n pak (las) v.d. hart; *the* ~ *of OPINION is . . .*, die meeste mense meen dat . . .; *OVER* ~, oorgewig, te swaar; *PICK up* ~, vet word; toeneem in gewig; *the* ~ *of PROBA=BILITIES*, die waarskynlikste; *PULL one's* ~, jou plek vol staan; jou plig nakom; *not to PULL one's* ~, nie jou plig vervul nie; nie jou plek vol staan nie; jou lyf wegsteek (spaar); slabak; *a* ~ *from one's SHOULDERS*, 'n berg van jou skouers af; *THROW one's* ~ *about*, baasspeel; grootmeneer wees; *THROW in one's* ~ *with*, jou gewig in die skaal werp; jou invloed gebruik; *THROW in one's* ~ *against*, jou invloed gebruik teen; jou gewig in die skaal lê teen; *UNDER* ~, onder die gewig, te lig; *WORTH its* ~ *in gold*, sy gewig in goud werd; (v) swaarder maak; belas, beswaar; ~ **distribution,** gewigsverdeling; ~**ed**, beswaar, gelaai; ~**ed mean,** beswaarde gemiddelde; ~**ed vote**, gelaaide stem; ~**iness,** belangrikheid; ~**less,** sonder gewig; gewig=loos; ~**lessness,** gewigloosheid; ~**-lifter,** gewigop=teller; ~**-lifting,** gewig optel; ~ **limit,** gewigsgrens; ~ **reduction,** vermaering; gewigsvermindering, ge=wigsverlies; ~**y,** gewigtig, belangrik; van groot in=vloed; *a* ~ *y matter*, 'n belangrike (gewigtige) saak.

weir, waterkering, wal, dwarswal, dwarsmuur, beer, studam.

weird, (n) noodlot; begoëling; (a) onheilspellend, aak=lig, naar; eienaardig, sonderling; bo(we)natuurlik, spookagtig; *the W*~ *sisters*, die Skikgodinne.

welch, *kyk* **welsh.**

wel'come, (n) welkom, verwelkoming; *ADDRESS of* ~, verwelkomingsadres; *BID someone* ~, iem. welkom heet; ~ *is the best CHEER*, 'n hartlike ont=vangs is meer as die vrolikheid werd; *OUTSTAY one's* ~, langer bly as wat jou gasheer van hou; *be given a WARM* ~, hartlik ontvang word; (v) ver=welkom, welkom heet; ~ *a PERSON to one's home*, iem. verwelkom in jou woning; ~ *someone into the RANKS*, iem. in die geledere verwelkom; ~ *a THING*, iets toejuig; (a) welkom; *BE* ~ *to it*, dis tot jou diens; nie te danke nie; *as a* ~ *CHANGE*, vir 'n prettige verandering; *as (the) FLOWERS in MAY*, hartlik welkom; *he MADE me* ~, hy het my vriendelik ontvang; ~ *as SNOW in the harvest*, alles behalwe welkom; *you are* ~ *to take STEPS*, dit staan jou vry om stappe te doen; *YOU'RE* ~ *!* tot u diens! nie te danke; (interj) ~ *home*, welkom tuis; ~**r,** verwelkomer.

weld[1], (n) reseda (blomsoort).

weld[2], (n) las, welnaat, sweisnaat; smeeplek; (v) sweis, aanmekaarsmee, (aanmekaar)las; wel, gaslas; ver=bind, saamsmelt; ~ **abil'ity,** sweisbaarheid; ~ **able,** sweisbaar; lasbaar; ~**ed,** gesweis; gelas; ~ **er,** swei=ser.

weld'ing, (n) sweising; sweiswerk; (a) sweis=; verbin=dend; ~ **heat,** sweishitte; ~ **iron,** smeeyster; ~ **joint,** sweislas; ~ **machine,** sweismasjien; ~ **rod,** sweisstaaf; ~ **shop,** sweiswinkel; ~ **tack,** hegswei=sing; ~ **wire,** sweisdraad; ~ **works,** sweiswerk=plaas.

weld: ~**less,** sonder las; ~**metal,** sweismetaal.

wel'fare, welvaart, voorspoed; welsyn; *Department of Social W*~, Departement van Volkswelsyn; ~ **centre,** maatskaplike sentrum; ~ **duties,** welsyns=diens; ~ **fund,** welsynsfonds; ~ **officer,** welsynsbe=ampte; proefbeampte; ~ **organization,** welsynsor=ganisasie; ~ **service,** welsynsdiens; ~ **state,** welsynstaat; ~ **work,** maatskaplike werk; ~**-work=er,** maatskaplike werker (werkster).

welk, verwelk, verdor.

wel'kin, (poet.), swerk, wolkehemel, uitspansel; *make the* ~ *ring*, die lug laat weergalm.

well[1], (n) put, bron; fontein; traphuis, diep ruimte; inkpot; koker; *the* ~ *of the COURT*, die vloer v.d. hofsaal; *the* ~ *ran DRY*, die put het opgedroog; *a* ~ *of SILENCE*, 'n diep stilte; *SINK a* ~, 'n put grawe; (v) opwel, ontspring, opborrel; ~ *up*, op=wel.

well[2], (n) die goeie; *let* ~ *ALONE*, moenie slapende honde wakker maak nie; *WISH someone* ~, iem. die beste toewens; *the SICK and the* ~, die siekes en die gesondes; (a) **(better, best)**, wel; goed; gesond; *carry one's AGE* ~, jou jare goed dra; *it is ALL very* ~, dit is alles goed en wel; *ALL is not* ~, dis nie alles pluis nie; *all's* ~ *that ENDS* ~, end goed, alles goed; ~ *ENOUGH*, goed genoeg; ~ *over the FAST*, mag die vas u wel bekom; *GET* ~, beter word; *that is* ~ *and GOOD*, dit is goed en wel; *that is JUST as* ~, dit is net so goed; *that is all VERY* ~, dit is alles goed en wel; (adv) **(better, best)**, goed; deeglik; terdeë; ~ *in ADVANCE*, ver vooruit; *AS* ~ *as*, net so goed as; sowel as; *that one AS* ~, daardie een ook; *you may* ~ *ASK*, jy kan wel vra; ~ *AWAY*, goed op pad; *be* ~ *AWARE*, ten volle bewus wees; *it may* ~ *BE*, dit kan so wees; ~ *BE=GUN is half done*, 'n goeie begin is halfpad gewin; ~ *BELOW*, ver onder; *you did* ~ *to COME*, jy het reg gehandel deur te kom; *he may* ~ *be DEAD*, heel moontlik is hy dood; *DO someone* ~, iem. regtig goed behandel; *DO yourself* ~, jou te goed doen, jou nie afskeep nie; ~ *DONE!* goed so! mooi skoot! *the steak is* ~ *DONE*, die biefstuk is goed gaar; ~ *DOWN*, baie minder; *the clothes FIT* ~, die klere pas goed; ~ *and GOOD*, nou goed dan; *LOOK* ~, goed kyk; mooi (goed) lyk; *you MIGHT as* ~, jy kan gerus (so maak); *be* ~ *OFF*, welgesteld wees; *you are* ~ *OUT of it*, gelukkig dat jy daaruit is; *you may* ~ *SAY that*, dit mag jy gerus sê; *SPEAK* ~ *of*, met lof praat van; *it SPEAKS* ~ *for him*, dit strek hom tot eer; *STAND* ~ *with someone*, in die goeie boekie van iem. staan; *you may as* ~ *STAY*, jy mag (kan) net so goed bly; *the STONE is* ~ *and truly laid*, die steen is heg en deeglik gelê; ~ *THEN*, nou ja; *THINK* ~ *of*, 'n hoë dunk hê van; ~ *in TIME*, ruim (goed) betyds; *TURN out* ~, goed afloop; *he is* ~ *UP in history*, hy is goed onderlê in geskie=denis; ~ *OVER an hour*, 'n goeie (ronde) uur; ruim 'n uur; *VERY* ~, baie goed; nou goed; toe maar; *it is all VERY* ~, dis alles goed en wel; (interj) wel; ~ *I NEVER!* goeie genugtig! nou toe nou! ~ *THEN!* nou toe! ~**-advised,** verstandig, welbedag; ~**-ap=pointed,** goed ingerig, volledig uitgerus, van alle ge=makke voorsien; ~**-arranged,** goed ingerig, welin=gerig; ~**-attended,** goed bygewoon, ~**-baked,** deurgebak; ~**-balanced,** presies in ewewig; verstan=dig, ewewigtig; besadig; ~**-behaved,** goed opge=voed, soet, gehoorsaam; oppassend, fatsoenlik; ~**-being,** welsyn; welstand, welvaart; ~**-beloved,** dierbaar, welbemind, beminde; ~**-born,** hoogge=bore, van goeie familie; ~**-bred,** goed opgevoed, welopgevoed, welgemanierd, wellewend, goedge=manierd; volbloed (perd); ~**-built,** fris gebou, sterk gebou, welgemaak; gedamasseer; ~ **chosen,** goed gekies; ~**-conditioned,** goedaardig; in goeie staat; ~**-conducted,** goed beheer; van uitnemende ge=drag; oppassend; goed gedirigeer (musiek); ~**-con=nected,** van goeie familie; goed inmekaar gesit; met goeie kontakte; ~ **considered,** weldeurdag, beson=ne, weloorwoë; ~ **cut,** welbesnede; ~**-defined,** goed omskrewe; welomskrewe; omlyn; ~**-descen=ded,** van goeie afkoms; ~**-deserved,** welverdiend.

well' digger, putgrawer.

well: ~ **directed,** goed gelei; ~**-disposed,** welgesind, goedgesind, welmenend; ~**-doer,** weldoener; ~**-doing,** regskapenheid; pligsbetragting; ~ **done,** goed gedoen; heeltemal gaar (vleis); ~ **earned,** eer=lik verdien; ~ **educated,** welopgevoed, geletterd; ~**-established,** goed gevestig; ~**-favoured,** mooi, aanvallig; ~**-fed,** welgedaan; deurvoed, goed ge=voed; ~ **filled,** goed vol; ~**-fitting,** presies passend; ~**-fleshed,** in goeie kondisie; ~**-formed,** welgeska=pe, welgevorm(d); ~**-found,** goed uitgerus (toege=rus); ~ **founded,** gegrond; ~ **governed,** goed be=heer(d); welgeordend; ~**-groomed,** goed versorg; ~**-grown,** fris; goed uitgegroei.

well: ~ **head,** bron; oorsprong; ~ **hole,** put; ~ **house,** puthuisie.

well'-informed, goed ingelig, goed op hoogte; ont=wikkeld.

well'ing, opwelling.

well'ington (boot), kapstewel, kniestewel.

well: ~**-intentioned,** goed bedoel, welmenend; ~-

judged, goed geoordeel; goed gemik (bal); ~ **kept**, welversorg; ~-**knit**, gespierd, stewig, sterk; ~-**known**, (wel)bekend; ~-**looking**, knap van uiterlik, aanvallig; ~ **made**, goed gemaak, welgemaak; welgeskape; ~-**mannered**, goedgemanierd, welgemanierd, wellewend; fatsoenlik; ~-**meaning**, welmenend, goed bedoel; ~-**meant**, goed bedoel, welgemeen; ~ **nigh**, byna, welhaas, vrywel, nagenoeg; ~-**off**, welgesteld, ryk; ~-**oiled**, goed geolie, goed gesmeer; ~-**ordered**, goed gereël; ordelik; ~-**patronized**, goed beklant; ~-**pitched**, goed geplant (bal); ~-**planned**, goed beplan; ~-**pleased**, weltevrede, hoog(s) in sy skik; ~-**posted**, op hoogte; ~-**prepared**, welbereid; ~-**preserved**, welversorg; ~-**proportioned**, goedgevorm; ~-**proven**, beproef; ~-**provided**, goed voorsien, welvoorsien; ~-**read**, belese; deurknee; ~ **regulated**, goed gereël, welgeordend, ordelik; ~-**reputed**, van goeie naam; ~-**risen**, goedgerys; ~-**rounded**, gerond; ~ **satisfied**, weltevrede; ~-**seasoned**, goed gekruie; beleë, goed gedroog; ~ **set**, stewig, gespierd; ~-**shaped**, ~-**shapen**, goed gevorm; welgeskape.
well: ~ **sinker**, putgrawer; ~ **sinking**, putgrawery.
well: ~ **spent**, welbestee(d), goed bestee; ~-**spoken**, beskaaf; welbespraak.
well'-spring, bronwel, oorsprong.
well'-sprung, met goeie vere.
well' staircase, trappehuis.
well: ~-**stocked**, welvoorsien, ruim (goed) voorsien; ~ **supplied**, goed voorsien, welvoorsien; ~ **tended**, goed versorg, welversorg; ~-**timbered**, met bale hout; bosryk; met goeie hout gebou; ~ **timed**, betyds, net op tyd, juis op die regte tyd; tydig; goed gemik; ~-**to-do**, ~-**to-do**, welgesteld *be* ~-**to-do**, welgesteld wees; jou skapies op die droë hê; ~-**trained**, goed geoefen, goed geleer; geskik (dier); ~-**tried**, beproef; ~-**trodden**, dikwels gebruik, baie besoek; ~-**turned**, mooi gevorm; mooi uitgedruk, mooi gesê; ~ **understood**, welbegrepe; ~ **versed**, goed onderlê; gekonfyt.
well' water, putwater; bronwater.
well: ~-**watered**, waterryk; ~-**wisher**, vriend, goedgesinde, begunstiger; ~-**wooded**, bosryk, bosagtig; ~-**worded**, goed opgestel (verwoord); ~-**worked**, deurwrog; ~-**worn**, verslyt, slyterig; afgesaag; ~-**written**, goed geskryf.
Welsh¹, (n) Wallies (taal); Walliser; (a) van Wallis, Wallies.
welsh², (v) laat spat, met die noordeson vertrek, verdwyn (sonder om te betaal); wegraak; ~ **er**, weglooper, skuldontduiker.
Welsh: ~ **rabbit**, ~ **rarebit**, roosterbrood met kaassous; ~ **man**, Walliser.
welt, (n) rand; omboorsel; strookkant; striem, hou; afranseling; fels (by metaal); (v) omboor, belê; soom; van rande voorsien; looi, afransel; fels (by metaal).
welt'ed, gefels, met 'n rand; ~ **edge**, felsrand; ~ **joint**, felsnaat; ~ **pocket**, ingesitte sak; ~ **shoe**, buitenaatskoen, randgenaaide skoen.
wel'ter, (n) warboel, chaos, mengelmoes; (dic) woel, rol; mokerhou; ~ *of war*, oorlogsberoering; (v) slinger, rol, wentel; (a) swaargewig-; ~-**weight**, weltergewig (boks); swaarruiter.
wen, mol, vetgewas; keelgeswel; grootstad.
wench, (n) (-es), (boere)meisie, meisiemens; slet; *a buxom* ~, 'n frisgeboude nooi; (v) ontug pleeg; meisies naloop; ~ **er**, hoereerder; ~ **ing**, ontug, hoerery.
wend, gaan, jou begeef; ~ *one's way*, jou begeef.
Wend, Wend; ~ **ic**, ~ **ish**, (n) Wendies (taal); (a) Wendies.
went, *kyk* **go** (v).
wen'tletrap, wenteltrap (skulpvis).
wept, *kyk* **weep**.
were, was; *kyk* **be**.
wer(e)'wolf, (..**wolves**), weerwolf.
Werther'ian, Werteriaans.
Wer'therism, Werteriaanse oorgevoeligheid.
Wes'leyan, (n) Wesleyaan; (a) Wesleyaans; ~ **Church**, Wesleyaanse Kerk.

west, (n) die weste; *the Far W* ~, die Verre Weste; (a) wes-, weste-, westelik; (adv) wes, na die weste; *go* ~, na die weste gaan; bokveld toe gaan; ~-**bound**, weswaarts; ~ **coast**, weskus; ~ **corner**, westehoek; ~ **end**, weseinde; ~ **er**, (n) westewind; (v) wes draai; sak (son); ~ **ering**, na die weste toe; ondergaande, dalend (son); **W**~**erling**, Westerling; ~ **erly**, westelik.
West'ern, (n) Westerling; (a) Westers; *the* ~ *DESERT*, die Westelike Woestyn; *the* ~ *HEMISPHERE*, die Westelike Halfrond; *the* ~ *POWERS*, die Westerse Moonthede; *the* ~ *PROVINCE*, die Westelike Provinsie, Boland.
west'ern, (a) westelik, wes-; ~ *COAST*, weskus; ~ *FRONT*, westerfront; ~ *LONGITUDE*, westerlengte; *the* ~ *WIND*, die westewind.
West'ern: ~ **Cape**, Wes-Kaapland; ~ **er**, Westerling; ~ **Germany**, Wes-Duitsland.
westerniza'tion, verwestersing.
west'ernize, verwesters.
west'er(n)most, westelikste.
West'ern Transvaal, Wes-Transvaal.
West: ~-**Indian**, (n) Wes-Indiër; (a) Wes-Indies; ~-**Indies**, Wes-Indië.
west'ing, westering, die vaar in westelike rigting; westelike deklinasie.
Westphal'ia, Wesfale; ~ **n**, (n) Wesfaler; (a) Wesfaals.
west: ~ **side**, westekant; ~ **ward**, weswaarts, westelik; ~ **wind**, westewind.
wet, (n) nattigheid, vogtigheid, vog; nat weer; regmakertjie, snapsie, sopie, (v) (-**ted**), natmaak; bevogtig; nat word; ~ *a BARGAIN*, op 'n (wins)kopie drink; ~ *the BED*, die bed natmaak; ~ *the other EYE*, nog 'n doppie steek; ~ *one's LINE*, gaan visvang; ~ *one's WHISTLE*, 'n dop steek; *he likes to* ~ *his WHISTLE*, hy hou van sy doppie (sopie, snapsie); sy lewer is nat; (a) nat, vogtig; klam; reënagtig; ~ *BLANKET*, spelbederwer, pretbederwer; remskoen; *DRIPPING* ~, papnat; ~ *or FINE*, mooiweer of nie; ~ *from the PRESS*, net gedruk; *as* ~ *as a RAT*, papnat, sopnat; ~ *to the SKIN*, papnat; ~ *with TEARS*, nat van trane; ~ **bridge**, laagwaterbrug; ~ **canteen**, kantien; ~ **cell**, nat sel; ~ **concrete**, slap beton; ~ **dock**, drywende dok; ~ **ewe**, lammerooi; ~ **goods**, wyn en drank.
weth'er, hamel.
wet: ~ **ness**, natheid, vogtigheid; ~-**nurse**, (n) min, soogvrou; (v) soog; ~ **pack**, skeergoedtas; ~ **paint**, nat verf; ~-**rot**, verrotting; ~ **table**, benatbaar; ~ **ting agent**, bevogtigingsmiddel; ~ **tish**, klam, natterig; **W** ~ **Triangle**, Noordsee.
whack, (n) slag; deel, aandeel; (v) beuk, moker, slaan, afransel; saam deel, verdeel; ~ **er**, reus, knewel, ~ **ing**, (n) pak slae, loesing; *give someone a* ~ *ing*, iem. afransel; iem. beuk; iem. 'n loesing gee; iem. 'n pak gee; (a) kolossaal, tamaai.
whale, (n) walvis; *a* ~ *of a CATCH*, 'n groot vangs; *it's very LIKE a* ~, dit kan maklik waar wees (spottend); *a* ~ *of a TALE*, 'n oordrywing, spekskietery; *have a* ~ *of a TIME*, dit uiters geniet; (v) op walvisvangs gaan (vaar); ~-**boat**, walvisboot; ~ **bone**, balein; ~-**calf**, walviskalf; ~-**catcher**, walvisvanger; ~-**catching**, walvisvangs; ~ **fin**, balein; walvisvin; ~-**fishing**, ~-**hunting**, walvisvangs; ~-**hunter**, walvisjagter; ~ **man**, walvisvanger; walvisvaarder; ~-**meal**, walvismeel; ~-**meat**, walvisvleis; ~-**oil**, walvistraan; ~ **r**, walvisvaarder (skip); walvisvanger; ~ **ry**, walvisvangs; walvisfabriek; ~-**shark**, walvishaai.
whal'ing, walvisvangs; ~-**gun**, harpoenkanon; ~-**master**, kaptein van 'n walvisvaarder; walvisbaas; ~ **ship**, walvisvaarder; ~-**station**, walvisstasie; ~-**trade**, walvisvangshandel.
whang, (n) mokerhou; (v) moker.
wharf, (n) (-**s**, **wharves**), landingsplek, kaai; (v) meer, vasmeer; ~ **age**, kaaigeld, hawegeld; ~ **inger**, ~-**master**, ~-**owner**, kaaimeester.
what, (pron) wat; hoe; hê? ~ *ABOUT John?* wat van Jan? het jy nuus van Jan? ~ *ABOUT something to eat?* hoe lyk dit met 'n happie kos? ~ *do I CARE?* wat traak dit my? *COME* ~ *may*, wat ook al ge-

beur; ~ *is the DATE?* die hoeveelste is dit? ~-*D'YE-CALL-HIM*, dinges, hoe's sy naam ook weer? *FINE day* ~? 'n mooi dag, nê? ~ *FOR?* waarvoor? waarom? met watter doel? om watter rede? *give someone* ~ *FOR*, iem. opdons; iem. straf; *and* ~ *HAVE you?* en wat nie al nie? ~ *HO!* haai, kyk hier! *not to KNOW* ~ *'s* ~, nie weet wat hot of haar is nie; nie weet wat is wat nie; *she KNOWS* ~*'s* ~, sy weet hoe die vurk in die hef steek; sy weet waar Dawid die wortels gegrawe het; sy weet hoe sake staan; sy weet dat twee maal twee vier is; *LEND me* ~ *you can*, leen my soveel as wat jy kan; ~ *is he LIKE?* hoe sien hy daar uit? hoe lyk hy? *and* ~ *'s MORE*, en wat meer is; ~ *is your NAME?* wat is jou naam? ~ *NEXT?* wat nou weer? nou word dit nog mooier! kan jy dit glo! *and* ~ *NOT*, en wat nie al nie; ~ *OF it?* wat daarvan? ~ *if he REFUSES?* sê nou maar hy weier? *SO* ~ ? en wat daarvan? *I'll TELL you* ~, ek sal jou sê; ~ *did I TELL you!* daar het jy dit nou! dis net wat ek gesê het! ~ *THEN?* wat dan? en nou? ~ *THOUGH they are rich?* watter saak maak dit of hulle ryk is? ~ *is the TIME?* hoe laat is dit? ~ *'s UP?* wat skort (skeel)? *WELL*, ~ *of that?* nou wat daarvan? ~ *is YOURS?* wat neem jy? wat is joune? (a) watter; wat; *I know* ~ *DIFFICULTIES there are*, ek ken die moeilikhede; ~ *a DIN there was!* was dit nie vir jou 'n lawaai nie! ~ *a FOOL you are!* hoe 'n gek is jy tog! *give* ~ *HELP one can*, alle moontlike hulp verleen; ~ *a MAN!* dis vir jou 'n man! ~ *MANNER of man is he?* watter soort man is hy? ~ *MATTER?* watter verskil maak dit? ~ *NEWS?* wat is die nuus? enige nuus? ~ *a PITY*, dis alte jammer; hoe jammer tog! ~ *little REMAINED*, die bietjie wat nog oor was; ~ *a thing to SAY!* hoe kan 'n man so iets sê! ~ *TIME is it?* hoe laat is dit? ~ *WITH rates, repairs, doctor's bills, we have saved very little*, as gevolg van belastings, onderhoudskoste en doktersrekeninge het ons baie min gespaar; ~ *WONDER if . . .?* is dit 'n wonder as . . .?

whate'er', (digterlik vir) wat ook (al).

whatev'er, wat ook (al); al wat; ~ *it may BE*, wat dit ook al mag wees; *is there any CHANCE* ~? bestaan daar die geringste moontlikheid? *there is no DOUBT* ~, daar is nie die geringste twyfel nie; ~ *FOR?* waarvoor dan tog? ~ *HAPPENS*, wat ook al mag gebeur; ~ *HAVE you got there?* wat op aarde het jy daar? *do* ~ *you LIKE*, maak net wat jy wil; ~ *MEASURES*, watter maatreëls ook al; *NOTHING* ~, niks hoegenaamd nie; *for* ~ *REASON*, om watter rede ook al; ~ *was THAT*, wat was dit nou weer?

what: ~*not*, snuisterykak(kie), standertjie; iets; ~*so(ever)* = **whatever**.

what's-his-name, dinges; jy weet mos nie; hoe's sy naam, hoesenaam.

wheal¹, striem, haal, hou.

wheal², galbult.

wheal³, tinmyn.

wheat, koring, duiskoring; *BEARDED* ~, baardkoring; *SEPARATE the* ~ *from the chaff*, die kaf van die koring skei; ~ **aphis**, koringluis; ~ **belt**, koringstreek; ~-**bran**, koringsemels; ~-**bread**, koringbrood; ~-**corn**, koringkorrel; ~-**crop**, koringoes; ~-**drill**, koringplanter.

wheat'ear¹, koringaar.

wheat'ear², bontrokkie (voël).

wheat'en, koring~; ~ **bran**, koringsemels; ~ **meal**, koringmeel, tarwemeel.

wheat: ~-**field**, koringland; ~-**flour**, meelblom; ~-**germ**, koringkiem; ~-**flake**, koringvlok(kie); ~**ings**, koringafval; ~-**land**, koringland; ~-**meal**, koringmeel; ~-**rust**, koringroes; ~-**straw**, koringstrooi.

whee'dle, flikflooi, vlei, pamperlang; lek, soebat; ~ *somebody INTO doing something*, iem. 'n gat in die kop praat; ~ *MONEY from someone's pocket*, geld uit iem. losslaan; ~**r**, flikflooier, vleier, pluimstryker.

whee'dling, geflikflooi, pluimstrykery.

wheel, (n) wiel, rat; rolletjie; swenking; fiets; pottebakkerskyf; spinwiel; draaibeweging, wenteling;

AT the ~, aan die stuurwiel; ~ *and AXLE*, windas; *BREAK on the* ~, radbraak; *a CHAIR on* ~*s*, 'n rolstoel; *the* ~ *has turned full CIRCLE*, ons is weer waar ons begin het; *the FIFTH* ~ *of a coach*, die vyfde wiel aan die wa; *break a FLY on the* ~, 'n vlieg met 'n voorhamer doodslaan; *FORTUNE'S* ~, die rat van die fortuin; *GO on* ~*s*, op wieltjies gaan; so glad soos seep gaan; *the* ~*s of LIFE*, die lewensgang; *ON the* ~, besig om gemaak te word; *run on OILED* ~*s*, op geoliede rollertjies loop (fig.); so glad soos seep gaan; *put a SPOKE in someone's* ~, iem. dwarsboom; 'n stok in die wiel steek; *TOOTHED* ~, tandwiel; ~*s WITHIN* ~*s*, 'n ingewikkelde saak; konkelry; (v) draai; rol; swaai; krink (wa); (laat) swenk; stoot; fiets; omkeer, omdraai; in 'n kring beweeg; ~ *ABOUT*, keerswenk; *LEFT* ~, links swenk; ~ *into LINE*, inswenk; *RIGHT* ~, regs swenk; ~ *ROUND*, omswenk, omdraai; ~ **alignment**, wielsporing; ~-**and-axle joint**, draaigewrig; ~-**axle**, wielas; ~ **barrow**, kruiwa; ~ **base**, asafstand; ~ **boss**, wielnaaf; ~ **brace**, wielomslag; ~-**brake**, wielrem; ~-**chain**, stuurketting; ~ **chair**, rolstoel, siekestoel; ~-**control**, wielbesturing; ~-**drag**, remskoen; ~-**ed**, met wiele; ~**er**, kruier, ryer; agterdier, agterperd, agteros; wielmaker, wamaker; ~-**flange**, wielflens; ~-**harness**, agtertuig; agtertuie; ~-**horse**, agterperd; staatmaker; ~-**house**, stuurhuis; ~-**hub**, wielnaaf; ~**ing**, swenking; draaiing; ~-**landing**, wiellanding; ~-**lock**, wielslot; ~ **man**, fietser, fietsryer; ~-**nave**, wielnaaf; ~-**nut**, wielmoer; ~ **rein**, agterleisel; ~-**rim**, wielvelling; ~-**rope**, stuurreep; ~-**scraper**, wielskrop; ~-**spanner**, wielsleutel; ~-**stop**, wielrem; ~-**stud**, wieltapbout; ~ **suspension**, wielvering; ~-**tapper**, wielproewer; ~-**tapping**, wielproef; ~-**trace**, agterstring; ~-**track**, spoorwydte; ~-**turner**, wieldraaier; ~-**work**, ratwerk; ~ **wright**, wielmaker; wamaker.

wheeze, (n) gehyg, aamborstigheid; gefluit (in keel); speletjie; afgesaagde segswyse; grap, anekdote; (v) hyg, moeilik asemhaal; fluit (keel).

wheez'iness, aamborstigheid.

wheez'ing, gefluit.

wheez'y, hygend, aamborstig, kortasem.

whelk¹, puisie.

whelk², wulk (slak).

whelm, oorstelp; verswelg; oorrompel.

whelp, (n) welp; kleintjie; kwajong, rakker, niksnut; (v) kleintjies kry; uitbroei ('n skelm plan).

when, (n), wanneer; *as to the* ~ *and the why*, wat betref die vraag wanneer en waarom; (pron) wanneer; *FROM* ~? van wanneer af? *SINCE* ~ *things have been better*, en van toe af gaan dit beter; (adv) wanneer, toe, as; terwyl; ~ *COLD*, wanneer dit koud is; ~ *DUE*, op die vervaltyd; ~ *FINE*, by mooi weer, as dit mooi weer is; *FROM* ~? van wanneer af? *at that MOMENT* ~, metdat; ~ *he SAW me, he approached*, toe hy my sien, kom hy nader; *SAY* ~, sê wanneer dit genoeg is; ~ *it SNOWS the mountains are white*, wanneer dit kapok, is die berge wit; *TILL* ~? tot wanneer? *there are TIMES* ~ . . ., daar is tye waarop . . .; *he WALKS* ~ *he might ride*, hy loop terwyl hy kan ry.

whence, (n) waarvandaan; *we know neither our* ~ *nor our whither*, ons weet nie waarvandaan ons kom of waarheen ons gaan nie; (adv) waarvandaan, van waar; *I take it* ~ *it COMES*, van 'n esel kan jy 'n skop verwag; ~ *the NAME?* vanwaar die naam? ~**soever**, waarvandaan ook.

whene'er', whenev'er, whensoev'er, wanneer ook al; elke maal as, telkens as.

where, (pron) waarheen, waarvandaan; ~ *do you COME from?* waar kom jy vandaan? ~ *on EARTH?* waar op aarde? ~ *TO?* waarheen? (adv) waar; waarheen, waarnatoe, waarso; ~ *are you GOING?* waarheen gaan jy? *I shall KNOW* ~ *I am*, ek sal weet hoe sake staan; *KNOW* ~ *you are with someone*, weet wat jy aan iem. het; ~ *is the SENSE of it?* van watter betekenis is dit? watter nut het dit? *THAT'S* ~ *it is*, daar lê die knoop; dis waar dit is; ~ *WAS I?* waar was ek nou weer?

whereabout(s)', (n) verblyfplek; lêplek, boerplek

adres; ~ *unknown*, verblyf onbekend; (adv) waar êrens, waar omtrent.
where: ~**as'**, nademaal, vermits, aangesien, daar; ~**at'**, waarop; ~**by'**, waardeur, waarby; **'er'** = **wherever;** ~**fore**, dus, daarom, waar, vermits, weshalwe; waarom; ~**in'**, waarin, waarby; ~**in'to**, waarin; ~**of'**, waarvan; ~**on'**, waarop; ~**soev'er**, waar ook al; ~**to'**, waarvan; waarnatoe; ~**upon'**, waarop; ~**v'er**, waar ook al; oral waar; ~**with**, waarmee.
where'withal, middele; *the* ~ *to pay*, die (geld)middele om te betaal.
whe'rry, (wherries), veerskuit; roeibootjie; ~**man**, veerman.
whet, (n) (die) skerp maak, wet, slyp, aanslyp; (v) **(-ted)**, slyp, skerp maak, aanslyp, aansit; prikkel; opwek, lus maak; ~ *the appetite without satisfying it*, iem. liemaak.
wheth'er, (pron, a) watter van twee; (conj) hetsy, of; *DOUBT* ~, twyfel of; ~ *we GO or not*, of ons gaan of nie.
whet'stone, slypsteen, stryksteen.
whett'er, slyper, slypsteen.
whew! soe! allawêreld!
whey, wei, dikmelkwater; ~**-face**, bleekgesig; ~**ish**, weiagtig.
which, (pron) watter, wie, wat; *BY* ~, waarby; *who was to HAVE* ~? wie moet die een, wie die ander hê? *one can't TELL* ~ *is* ~, 'n mens kan die twee nie onderskei nie; (a) watter; ~ *way shall we go?* watter kant toe sal ons gaan? ~ **e'er'**, ~**ev'er**, ~**soev'er**, wat(ter) ook al.
whiff[1], (n) platvis.
whiff[2], (n) asemtog; trek; luggie, snuffie, reuk, ruikie; sigaartjie; skif (bootjie); *a* ~ *of CHLOROFORM*, 'n snuifie chloroform; *I want a* ~ *of FRESH air*, ek wil 'n luggie gaan skep; *a* ~ *of GRAPE-SHOT*, 'n skoot hael; (v) uitblaas.
whif'fle, (n) suggie, windvlagie; (v) stoot, saggies waai; weifel; flikker; ~**tree**, *kyk* **whippletree.**
Whig, Whig, Liberaal.
while[1], (n) rukkie, wyle, pose, poos; *AFTER a* ~, na 'n rukkie; kort daarop; *ALL this* ~, al die tyd; *BETWEEN* ~ *s*, tussendeur, nou en dan; *FOR a* ~, 'n tydjie; *in a LITTLE* ~, binnekort; *for a LONG* ~, 'n lang tyd; *ONCE in a* ~, af en toe; so nou en dan; *THE* ~, ondertussen; *I will make it WORTH his* ~, ek sal sorg dat dit hom sal betaal; (v) (die tyd) verdrywe; ~ *away the time*, die tyd verdryf.
while[2], (conj) terwyl, onderwyl, solank as.
whilst, terwyl.
whim, gril, nuk, gier, frats; streek, bevlieging, bui, wiesewasie; windas (masj.); (pl) hipokonders; *be FULL of* ~*s (and fancies)*, vol fiemies (kwinte, snare) wees; *have a SUDDEN* ~ *or fancy*, 'n gier kry.
whim'brel, reenfluiter (voël).
whim'per, (n) gehuil, gegrens, getjank; gekreun; (v) kerm, kreun; grens; huilerig praat, drein; huil, tjank; ~**er**, huiler, tjanker; ~**ing**, klaerig, grenserig.
whim'sical, wispelturig, vol nukke, buierig, vol fiemies; koddig, sonderling, vreemd, raar; ~**'ity**, (..**ties**), ~**ness**, gril, nuk, wispelturigheid; grilligheid.
whim'sy[1], (..**sies**), nuk, gier, gril.
whim'sy[2], (..**sies**), windas.
whim'-wham, speeldingetjie; nuk; prul.
whin'[1], doringbos, doringstruik.
whin[2], harde klip; basalt.
whine, (n) gekerm, gehuil, getjank; (v) kerm, tjank, huil, teem, drein, grens; ~**r**, tjanker, grensbalie, huilbak.
whing'er, dolk, lang mes.
whin'ing, (n) gekla, getjank, huilery, temery, gegrens; (a) huilerig.
whinn'y, (n) gerunnik; (v) **(whinnied)**, runnik; ~**ing**, gerunnik.
whin'(sill), whin'stone, harde sandklip, doleriet, basalt.
whip, (n) sweep; peits; karwats; sambok; koetsier; aanmaning; katrol; sweep (parlement); *APPLY the* ~, onder die sweep laat deurloop; iem. onder die sweep kry; *CRACK the* ~, die sweep laat klap; *a GOOD* ~, 'n goeie koetsier; *the LASH of a* ~, 'n sweepslag (sweepklap); ~ *and SPUR*, in vlieënde haas; (v) **(-ped)**, slaan, piets, wiks, raps; oorhands naai, kriel; klop, klits (eiers); dors; wip; afgeransel word; ~ *CREATION*, alles (almal) kafloop; ~ *EGGS*, eiers klits; ~ *up a HORSE*, 'n perd aandruk; ~ *OFF*, afpluk; wegraap; ~ *OUT*, uitpluk; uitwip; bitsig uiting gee aan; ~ *OUT a dagger*, 'n dolk uitpluk; ~ *it out of SIGHT*, iets vinnig wegsteek; ~ *into SHAPE*, in orde bring; ~ *UP*, opsweep; gou bymekaar maak; opraap; haastig saamflans (voorberei); ~ *UP voters*, kiesers bymekaartrommel; ~ *UP a meal*, 'n eetmaal in 'n kits berei; ~**cord**, geribde stof, duiwelsterk, ribkoord; voorslag; ~**-gin**, hysblik; ~ **hand**, regterhand; *hold (have) the* ~ *hand*, baas wees; die hef in die hande hê; ~**-handle**, sweepstok; ~**-holder**, sweepkoker; ~**lash**, voorslag(riempie).
whipped: ~ **cream**, slagroom; ~ **edge**, krielsoom.
whip'per, slaner, kastyder; voorman; ~**-snapper**, kindjie, japsnoet; indringer.
whipp'et, windhond, renhond; klein oorlogstenk, snelvegwa; ~**-race**, hondereisies.
whipp'ing, omslaan; omslaansteek; geslaan, pak slae, loesing, drag slae; *give someone a* ~, iem. laat riemspring; iem. rottangolie gee; ~**-boy**, sondebok; ~**-post**, geselpaal, skavotpaal; ~**-top**, draaitol, dryftol, sweeptol.
whip'pletree, swingel(hout).
whip'poorwill, bokmelker (Amerikaanse voël).
whip: ~**-round**, kollekte, beroep; ~**-saw**, kuilsaag, treksaag; spansaag; ~**-snake**, sweepslang; ~**-socket**, sweepkoker; ~**-staff**, roerstok; sweepstok; ~**ster**, kêreltjie, japsnoet; ~**-stitch**, (n) oorhandse steek, kriel; (v) oorhands werk, kriel; ~**-top**, dryftol.
whirl, (n) draaikolk, drukte, dwarreling, warreling, draai; verwardheid, verbystering; *be in a* ~, verward wees; (v) dwarrel, warrel, draai, vinnig ronddraai; (laat) duisel; maal (water); ~ *round*, rondomtalie draai, rondtol.
whirl'igig, kringloop, dwaling, draaitol, woer-woer; mallemeule; waterhondjie; *the* ~ *of time*, die wirwar v.d. lewe; die kringloop v.d. tyd.
whirl: ~**ing**, (n) dwarreling, maling; (a) draaiend; ~**ing-platform**, rondomtalie; ~**pool**, draaikolk, maalstroom, wieling; ~**wind**, (d)warrelwind, draaiwind, windhoos; *sow the wind and reap the* ~*wind*, wie wind saai, sal stormwind maai; ~**y**, (rond)draaiend.
whir(r), (n) gegons, gebrom, geruis, gesnor; (v) gons, brom, snor, ruis; ~**ing**, gesnor.
whisk, (n) besempie; stoffer; eierklitser; roomklopper; swaai; vee(g); (v) afstof, afborsel; rondfladder; klop, klits; wip, gryp; ~ *AWAY*, wegloer, sommer laat verdwyn; vinnig verdwyn; ~ *OFF*, wegvoer, afruk; ~ *ROUND*, jou vinnig omdraai; ~ **broom**, grasbesempie.
whis'ker, snor (van katsoorte); (pl) baard; bakbaard; wangbaard; *BY a* ~, so littete; *that JOKE has got* ~*s*, dis 'n stokou grap; ~**ed**, met 'n bakbaard; bebaard; met 'n snor.
whis'ky[1], **(whiskies)**, whisky.
whis'ky[2], **(whiskies)**, ligte karretjie.
whisper, (n) fluister, gefluister; geritsel, geruis; *GIVE the* ~, die wenk gee; *IN* ~*s*, fluisterend; (v) fluister, suutjies praat; influister, toefluister; ritsel, ruis; ~ *something into someone's EAR*, iem. iets in die oor fluister; *HEAR it* ~ *ed that*, 'n voëltjie hoor fluit dat; *it IS* ~ *ed*, die gerug doen die ronde, daar word gefluister; ~**er**, fluisteraar; nuusdraer, verklikker.
whis'pering, (n) gefluister, fluistering; *where there is* ~, *there is lying*, suutjies (saggies) praat, is duiwels raad; (a) fluisterend; ~ **campaign**, fluisterveldtog; ~**-dome**, ~**-gallery**, fluistergewelf; ~ **tube**, spreekbuis.
whist[1], (n) whist (kaartspel).
whist[2], (interj) sjuut! sjt!
whist'-drive, whistparty.

whi'stle, (n) gefluit; fluitjie; *AT his* ~, op sy wenk; *the ~ of a BULLET,* die gefluit van 'n koeël; *as CLEAN as a ~,* skerp omlyn; *as DRY as a ~,* kurkdroog; *GIVE a ~,* fluit; *PAY for one's ~,* duur betaal vir 'n gril; *WET one's ~,* jou keel smeer (natmaak); (v) fluit; klap, verklik; ~ *in the DARK,* by die kerkhof fluit; jou pure man hou; *you may ~ FOR it,* jy kan dit op jou maag skrywe; dis neusie verby; ~ *FOR the wind,* na die wind fluit; *have to ~ FOR something,* na iets fluit; op jou duim fluit vir iets; *let someone GO ~,* jou glad nie aan iem. steur nie; ~ *down the WIND,* laat vaar; opgee; verniet praat; beskinder; *when I need you I'll ~ for YOU,* as ek jou nodig het, sal ek vir jou fluit; ~**r,** fluiter; ~ **stop,** fluitsein.

whi'stling, (n) fluitery, gefluit; fluittoon; (a) fluitend; *a ~ woman, a crowing hen, is neither fit for God nor men,* meisies wat fluit, word die deur uitgesmyt (en hennetjies wat kraai, word die nek omgedraai); ~ **buoy,** brulboei; ~ **kettle,** fluitketel.

whit¹, kriesel, siertjie, bakatel, kleinigheid, ietsie, snars; *EVERY ~,* in alle opsigte; *NEVER a ~; in NO ~,* nie die minste nie; glad nie.

Whit², Pinkster.

white, (n) wit; witheid; blank; Blanke; *the ~ of an EGG,* die wit van 'n eier; *the ~ of the EYE,* die wit v.d. oog; *the W~ House,* die Wit Huis; *IN ~s,* in wit klere; *POOR ~,* armblanke; (v) wit maak; wit; afwit; ~ *out,* uitwit; (a) wit; blanje (vlag); bleek; blank; grys (hare); rein, suiwer, onskuldig; *BLEED someone ~,* iem. uitsuig; iem. kaal maak; *show the ~ FEATHER,* lafhartig wees; *a ~ LIE,* 'n noodleuen; 'n leuentjie om beswil; *a ~ MAN,* 'n gawe kêrel; 'n witman; *the ~ RACE,* die blanke ras; *turn ~ as a SHEET,* jou vaal skrik; *stand in ~ STREET,* opregte berou hê; ~ **alkali,** witbrak; ~ **alloy,** namaaksilwer; ~ **ant,** (n) termiet, rysmier; ~**-ant,** (v) ondergrawe, rysmier, ondermyn; ~**-backed vulture,** witrugaasvoël; ~**-bait,** witvis; ~ **bear,** ysbeer; ~**-beard,** witbaard, ou man; ~ **blood corpuscle,** wit bloedliggaampie; ~**-blooded,** witbloedig; ~ **book,** witskrif, witboek; ~ **bread,** fynbrood, witbrood; ~ **cleaner,** witsel; ~ **death,** tering; ~ **clover,** stinkklawer; witklawer; ~ **coffee,** koffie met melk, koffie verkeerd; ~**-collar,** kantoorwerker; intellektueel; ~**-collar worker,** salaristrekker, gesalarieerde, kantoorwerker; ~ **coronet,** wit hoefkroon; ~**-crested,** witkuif-; ~ **elephant,** wit olifant; *a ~ elephant,* 'n kosbare oortolligheid; 'n wit olifant; ~ **eye,** glasogie; ~ **face,** wit gesig; ~**-faced duck,** nonnetjie-eend; ~ **fetlock,** wit muis; ~**-fish,** baardman, witvis; ~ **foot,** witvoet: W ~ **Friar,** Karmeliet; ~ **frost,** ryp; ~**-glazed,** witglans-; ~ **gold,** witgoud; ~ **grub,** miswurm; ~**-handed,** met onbesoedelde hande; ~**-headed,** met grys hare; ~ **heat,** gloeihitte; gloeiende toorn; ~ **heel,** witvoet; ~ **horses,** witgekuifde golwe; golfkoppe, wit koppe; ~**-hot,** witgloeiend; ~ **iron,** blik; ~ **lead,** witlood; ~ **leather,** seemsleer; ~ **leg,** kraambeen; ~ **lie,** noodleuen; ~ **light,** gewone lig; ~ **lime,** (n) witsel; ~**-lime,** (v) afwit; ~ **line,** wit streep; blanko reël; ~**-lipped,** met bleek lippe; ~**-livered,** lafhartig; ~ **maize,** wit mielies; ~ **man,** witman, witmens, blanke; man honderd; ~ **matter,** witstof; ~ **mealy-bug,** wolluis; ~ **meat,** wit vleis; ~ **metal,** witmetaal; ~ **mouse,** wit muis; ~ **muzzle,** melkbek, witsnoet; ~**n,** wit maak; bleek (wit) word; ~**ner,** bleikmiddel; ~**ness,** witheid, blankheid; ~**ning,** (die) bleek word; wit; witsel; ~**-out,** witsig; ~ **opal,** melkopaal; ~ **paper,** witboek, witskrif, regeringsrapport; ~**-paper heath,** lemoenbloeisels *(Erica papyracea);* ~ **pastern,** wit koot; ~ **pear,** witpeer; ~ **pepper,** witpeper; ~ **poplar,** silwerpopulier; ~ **rhinoceros,** witrenoster; ~ **rope,** ongeteerde tou; ~ **rust,** witroes; ~ **sale,** verkoop van wit goed; ~ **sauce,** witsous; ~ **scourge,** tering; ~ **shark,** blouhaai; ~ **slave,** blanke slavin; ~ **slaver,** handelaar in blanke slavinne; ~**-slave traffic,** handel in blanke slavinne; ~ **slavery,** blanke slawerny; ~ **smith,** blikslaer; ~ **smut,** witbrand; ~ **stinkwood,** witstinkhout; ~ **stork,** wit ooievaar, groot wit sprinkaanvoël; ~**-tailed gnu,** swartwildebees; ~ **thorn,**

witdoring(boom); ~ **vitriol,** sinksulfaat, witvitrioel; ~ **wash,** (n) witkalk, witsel; vernissie, skyn; (v) skoon was, van blaam suiwer, goedpraat; wit, afwit; ~ **washer,** witter; goedprater; ~ **wine,** witwyn; ~**-winged,** witvlerk-.

whith'er, waarheen, waarnatoe; ~**soev'er,** waarheen ook al.

White' Russia, Wit-Rusland.

whit'ing¹, wyting (vis).

whit'ing², witkalk, witsel; kryt.

whit'ish, witagtig, witterig.

whit'leather, witleer.

whit'low, fyt.

Whit' Monday, Pinkstermaandag.

Whit'sun, Pinkster; ~ **day,** Pinkstersondag.

Whit' Sunday, Pinkstersondag.

Whit'sun: ~ **holiday,** Pinkstervakansie; ~ **tide,** Pinksterdae, Pinkster; ~ **week,** Pinksterweek.

whit'tle, (n) slagtersmes, lang mes; (v) afsny, snipper, besnoei, inkort; ~ *AWAY,* wegsny; versnipper; ~ *DOWN,* besnoei, afbrokkel, versnipper; verklein; ~ *OFF,* wegsny; ~ *UP,* opkerf.

whit'y, witterig, witagtig.

whiz(z), (n) gegons, gefluit; (v) sis, gons, fluit, suis, snor, zits; (interj) woerts! zoem! ~**ing,** gesnor.

who, wie, wat; *A ~ 's ~,* biografiese jaarboek, personeregister; ~ *AND ~,* wie almal; ~ *GOES there?* wie is daar? werda! *KNOW ~'s ~,* almal ken.

who'a! hook! hokaai! hanou!

whoev'er, wie ook al.

whole, (n) geheel, hele; totaal; alles; *AS a ~,* in sy geheel; *the ~ of FRANCE,* die hele Frankryk; *NATURE is a ~,* die natuur is 'n eenheid; *ON the ~,* oor (in) die algemeen; *the ~ of his SALARY,* sy hele salaris; *THE ~,* alles, die geheel; (a) heel, geheel, gans; gaaf; gesond; onbeskadig; vol; volkome; *ten ~ DAYS,* tien volle dae; *with one's ~ HEART,* met hart en siel; *go the ~ HOG,* tot die uiterste gaan; *considered IN ~ or in part,* in sy geheel of in sy dele beskou; *the ~ LOT,* die hele boel, die hele sitsewinkel; *the ~ PLACE,* die hele plek; *with a ~ SKIN,* heelhuids; *the ~ TIME,* die hele tyd, heeltyd; *the ~ TRUTH,* die hele (volle) waarheid; ~**-bound,** heeltemal in leer gebind; ~**-coloured,** effekleurig, eenkleurig; ~**-fruit jam,** heelvrugtekonfyt; ~**-hearted,** hartlik, opreg, van ganser harte; volmondig; onverdeeld; ~**-heartedly,** met hart en siel; volmondig; opreg; *promise ~-heartedly,* met hart en mond belowe; ~**-heartedness,** hartlikheid, opregtheid; ~**-hogger,** deurdrywer, deurvoerder, deurdrukker; ~**-hoofed,** eenhoewig; ~**-length,** in volle lengte; van die kop tot die voete; ~ **meal,** ongesifte (growwe) meel; ~ **meal bread,** growwe brood, volkoringbrood; ~ **milk,** volmelk; ~**ness,** heelheid, geheelheid; onverdeeldheid; ongeskondenheid.

whole'sale, (n) groothandel; *sell ~,* by die groot maat verkoop; (a) groothandel-; grootskeeps, algemeen, massaal; (adv) op groot skaal, by die groot maat; ~ **dealer,** groothandelaar; ~ **price,** groothandelsprys; ~**r,** groothandelaar; ~ **slaughter,** algemene slagting; ~ **trade,** groothandel.

whole'some, gesond, voedsaam, heilsaam; ~**ness,** heilsaamheid, gesondheid.

whole'-time, voltyds; heeltyds; ~ **service,** voltydse diens.

wholl'y, heeltemal, geheel, volkome, geheel en al; ~ *OWNED,* in volle besit; ~ *OWNED subsidiary,* volle filiaal.

whom, wat; vir wie, aan wie; *BY ~,* deur wie; *the MAN ~ you saw,* die man wat jy gesien het; *TO ~,* aan wie; ~ **e'er,** ~ **ev'er,** ~ **soev'er,** wie ook, aan wie ook al.

whoop, (n) skreeu, roep; (v) roep, skreeu; optrek (kinkhoes).

whoop'ee, pret; *make ~,* luidrugtig juig; fuif.

whoop'ing-cough, kinkhoes.

whop, (-ped), ransel, kafloop; oorwin, verslaan; ~ **per,** groot pak; 'n groot leuen; bakbees, knewel; bielie, bul; ~ **ping,** (n) afranseling, pak; neerlaag; (a) tamaai, yslik, ('n) knewel van 'n ...

whore, (n) hoer; (v) hoereer; ~ **dom**, hoerery; ~ **master**, ~ **monger**, hoereerder; souteneur.
whor'ish, hoeragtig, ontugtig.
whorl, kronkel, draai (van 'n skulp); blomkrans (in hout); ~ **ed**, kransvormig; gedraai; ~ **ing**, draai.
whor'tleberry, (..rries), bloubessie.
whose, wie s'n, wie se, van wie.
whosoev'er, wie ook al.
why, (n) waarom; *want to know all the* ~ *s and wherefores*, alle besonderhede wil weet; die naatjie v.d. kous wil weet; (adv) hoekom, waarom; *you are AFRAID, that's* ~, jy is bang, dis dié; ~ *SO?* hoe so? *THAT's* ~, daarom; (interj) mos, tog, wel; ~, *that's mother!* maar sowaar dis mos moeder!
wich'elm, *kyk* **wych-elm**.
wick¹, pit (lamp).
wick², dorpie.
wicked¹, met 'n pit.
wick'ed², (n) (die) goddeloses; die kwaad (bose); *the* ~ *know no REST*, vir die goddelose is daar geen vrede nie; *THE* ~, die goddeloses; (a) goddeloos, sondig, sleg; ondeund, onnutsig (kind); kwaai, wys (dier); ~**ness**, boosheid, sonde, slegtheid; onnutsigheid, stoutheid.
wick'er, (n) biesie, matjiesgoed; riet, wilgerloot; rottang; mandjiewerk; mandjie; (a) gevleg; riet=; ~ **basket**, rietmandjie, biesiemandjie; ~**-bottle**, mandjieflès, ~ **chair**, rietstoel, gevlegte stoel; rottangstoel; ~ **cradle**, mandjiewieg, biesiewieg; ~ **ware**, ~ **work**, vlegwerk; mandjiewerk; rottanggoed; ~ **work carriage**, mandjiewa; ~ **work cradle**, mandjiewieg.
wick'et, draaihek; onderdeur; deurtjie; baan, kolfblad (kr.); paaltjie (by kr.); *be on a GOOD* ~, goed af wees; in 'n voordelige posisie wees; *be on a STICKY* ~, in die verknorsing wees; ~**-gate**, paaltjieshek; ~**-keeper**, paaltjiewagter.
wide, (n) wydloper (krieket); bakbal; *to the* ~, geheel en al; totaal; (a, adv) wyd; breed; ruim, uitgebreid, veelomvattend; ver; hemelsbreed; mis; *over a* ~ *AREA*, oor 'n uitgestrekte gebied; ~ *AWAKE*, nie aan die slaap nie; *give someone a* ~ *BERTH*, uit iem. se pad bly; *a* ~ *CIRCLE of friends*, 'n breë vriendekring; *a* ~ *DIFFERENCE*, 'n hemelsbreë verskil; *FAR and* ~, wyd en syd; *from FAR and* ~, van heinde en ver; ~ *FLUCTUATIONS*, groot skommelinge; ~ *HORIZONS*, verre horisonne; ~ *of the MARK*, heeltemal mis; ver verkeerd; ~ *OF*, ver van; *SHOOT* ~, misskiet; ~ *of the TRUTH*, heeltemal onwaar; *the* ~ *WORLD*, die wye wêreld; ~**-angled lens**, wyehoeklens; ~**-awake**, (n) breërandhoed; (a) helder wakker; op en wakker; op jou hoede; uitgeslape, geslepe; ~ **band**, breë band; ~**-brimmed**, breërand=; ~**-brimmed hat**, breërandhoed; ~**-eyed**, met groot oë; verbaas; ~ **gauge**, groot spoorwydte, breë spoor; ~ **knowledge**, breë kennis.
wide'ly, wyd; breed; algemeen; ~ *ADVERTIZED*, oral geadverteer; *it is* ~ *BELIEVED*, baie mense glo dit; ~ *DISCUSSED*, veelbesproke; ~ *KNOWN*, algemeen bekend; ~ *READ*, belese (persoon); algemeen gelees (boek).
wide'-mouthed, met 'n oop mond, oopmond.
wid'en, wyer maak (word); verbreed; verruim, uitsit; ~**ed**, verbreed; verruim, uitsit; ~**er**, ruimer.
wide'ness, wydte, breedte, ruimte, uitgestrektheid.
wi'dening, verwyding, verbreding, verruiming.
wide: ~ **open**, wyd oop; baie onseker; ~ **reading**, belesenheid; ~**-skirted**, wyeromp=; met breë rok, breërok=; ~**-spread**, algemeen verbrei, uitgebrei(d); wyd versprei; ~**-spreading**, uitgestrek, breedgetak; verreikend.
wi'dgeon, fluiteend.
wid'ow, (n) weduwee, weduvrou; flap (voël); *the* ~ *'s CRUSE*, die weduwee se kruik; *a GRASS* ~, 'n grasweduwee; 'n onbestorwe weduwee; (v) tot weduwee of wewenaar maak; ~**-bird**, flap; ~**ed**, (n) agtergeblewene, agterblywende; (a) tot weduwee gemaak, beroof van jou lewensgesel(lin); ~**er**, wewenaar; ~ **hood**, weduweeskap, weduweestaat; ~ **lady**, weduwee.

wid'ow's: ~ **cap**, weduweemussie; ~ **cruse**, weduwee se kruik; ~ **mite**, weduwee se penning; ~ **peak**, gepunte haarlyn; ~ **pension**, weduweepensioen.
wid'ow: ~**-spider**, knopiespinnekop; ~**'s veil**, rousluier; ~**'s weeds**, rougewaad; ~ **woman**, weduwee.
width, wydte; breedte (van iets); breedheid, uitgestrektheid; ruimheid; ~ *of mesh*, maaswydte; ~ **wise**, in die breedte.
wield, hanteer; swaai; uitoefen, voer; bestuur; ~ *AUTHORITY*, gesag uitoefen; ~ *the PEN*, die pen voer; ~ *POWER*, mag uitoefen; ~ *the SCEPTRE*, die septer swaai; ~**able**, hanteerbaar; ~**er**, hanteerder; ~**y**, handelbaar, hanteerbaar.
wife, (**wives**), vrou, eggenote, gemalin, gade; *OLD wives' tales*, ouwypraatjies, ouvroupraatjies; *TAKE to* ~, tot vrou neem; *all the WORLD and his* ~, die hele wêreld; ~**-beater**, vroueslaner; ~ **hood**, staat van gehude vrou; vroulike staat; ~ **less**, ongetroud; vrouloos; ~**like**, ~**ly**, vroulik; ~**-ridden**, onder die pantoffel.
wif'ie, vroutjie.
wig, (n) pruik; (v) (**-ged**), 'n pruik opsit, van 'n pruik voorsien; 'n uitbrander gee, iem. se kop was, roskam; ~ **block**, pruikbol; ~**ged**, gepruik, met 'n pruik; ~**ging**, skrobbering, uitbrander.
wig'gle, (n) geskommel; kronkeling; (v) skommel; kronkel.
wight, wese, kêrel, mens, skepsel.
wig'maker, pruikmaker.
wig'wam, wigwam, Indiaanse hut, pondok.
wild, (n) wildernis, woesteny; die natuur; *the CALL of the* ~, die roepstem v.d. natuur; *IN the* ~ *s*, in die gramadoelas; (a) wild; woes; smoorkwaad, skungdekwaad; verwilderd; onregeerbaar; losbandig; dwaas; fantasies; bang, sku; stormagtig; ongeleer(d); *BE* ~ *about something*, met iets dweep; *a* ~ *COAST*, 'n stormagtige (woeste) kus; *not in his* ~ *est DREAMS*, nie in sy stoutste drome nie; *in the* ~ *est DISORDER*, in die grootste wanorde; *DRIVE someone* ~, iem. dol maak; ~ *with EXCITEMENT*, dol van opwinding; *GO* ~, woedend word; *a* ~ *-GOOSE chase*, 'n sinelose tog; 'n dwase onderneming; *GROW* ~, wild groei; *beyond one's* ~ *est HOPES*, bokant 'n mens se stoutste verwagtings; ~ *with JOY*, dol van vreugde; *MAKE a* ~ *guess*, blindweg raai; *a* ~ *NIGHT*, 'n stormagtige (onstuimige) nag; *a* ~ *RUMOUR*, 'n los gerug; *RUN* ~, wild rondloop; wild groei; *let children RUN* ~, kinders vir weer en wind laat rondloop; *a* ~ *STATEMENT*, 'n ongegronde verklaring; *a* ~ *TALE*, 'n fantastiese verhaal; *be* ~ *WITH someone about something*, kwaad vir iem. wees oor iets; ~ *and WOOLLY*, onbeskaaf, ru; ~ *and whirling WORDS*, wilde wolhaarwoorde; onverantwoordelike praatjies; (adv) blindweg, halsoorkop; los en vas; ~ **animal**, wilde dier; ~ **ass**, wilde-esel; ~ **beast**, wilde dier; ~ **boar**, wildevark; ~ **born**, wild gebore; wild; ~ **cat**, (n) wildekat; rissie; swendelaar; swendelfirma; (v) olie soek (in 'n min belowende streek); (a) onbesonne, onprakties; *a* ~ *SCHEME*, 'n onbesonne onderneming; ~ *STRIKE*, 'n onwettige staking.
wild: ~ **catter**, swendelaar; ~ **catting**, swendelary (by oliesoekery); ~ **chestnut**, wildekastaiing; ~ **dog**, wildehond; ~ **duck**, wilde-eend.
wil'debeest, wildebees.
wil'derness, (**-es**), wildernis, woestyn, woesteny; *IN the* ~, in die wildernis; *the VOICE of one crying in the* ~, 'n stem roepende in die woestyn.
wild: ~**-eyed**, met verwilderde oë; ~ **fig**, wildevy; ~ **fire**, dwaalliggie; Griekse vuur; roos; wildvuur (tabaksiekte); *spread like* ~ *fire*, soos 'n lopende vuurtjie versprei; van mond tot mond gaan; ~ **flower**, veldblom; ~ **fowl**, voëlwild; watervoëls; ~ **goose**, wildegans; *a* ~ *-goose chase*, 'n sinlose tog; 'n dwase onderneming; ~ **guess**, blinde raaiskoot; ~ **horse**, wildeperd; ongeleerde perd; ~ *horses would not drag him there*, hy is nie met 'n stok daar te kry nie; ~ **ing**, wilde plant; wildeappel; ~ **life**, wild; diereêreld; natuurlewe; wilde lewe; ~ **man**, barbaar, wilde; heethoof; ~ **ness**, woestheid; ~ **oats**, wildehawer; *sow one's* ~ *oats*, jou uitleef; ~ **olive**, olien=

hout(boom); ~ **orange**, botterklapper; ~ **pear**, dikbas, blompeer, drolpeer *(Dombeya rotundifolia)*; ~ **pepper-tree**, bergsering; ~ **plum**, suurpruim; ~ **seringa**, wildesering; ~ **sheep**, wilde skaap; ~ **spark**, swierbol; ~ **talk**, wolhaarstories; ~ **watermelon**, kafferwaatlemoen, makataan.

wile, (n) streek, lis, kunsgreep, bedrog; (v) verlok, verskalk.

wil'ful, moedswillig, opsetlik; eiesinnig, eiewys; ~ **KILLING**, opsetlike doodslag; ~ **MISCONDUCT**, opsetlike wangedrag; ~ **MURDER**, moord met voorbedagte rade; ~ **ly**, opsetlik; moedswillig; ~*ly deaf*, horende doof; Oos-Indies doof; ~ **ness**, eiesinnigheid, opsetlikheid; moedswilligheid.

wil'iness, slimheid, sluheid, listigheid.

will¹, (n) wil; wens; sin; wilskrag; willekeur; testament; *AFTER one's* ~, na eie begeerte; *AGAINST one's* ~, teen wil en dank; teen jou sin; teen heug en meug; *AT* ~, na eie goedvinde; *with the BEST* ~ *in the world*, met die beste wil ter (in die) wêreld; *take the* ~ *for the DEED*, die goeie wil vir die daad neem; *DISPOSE by* ~, by testament beskik; *Thy* ~ *be DONE*, U wil geskied; *of one's own FREE* ~, uit vrye beweging; *men of GOOD* ~, manne van goeie wil; *HAVE one's* ~, jou sin kry; *his* ~ *is LAW*, sy wil is wet; *MAKE one's* ~, jou testament maak, testeer; *have a* ~ *of one's OWN*, 'n eie wil hê; *the POPULAR* ~, die volkswil; *STRENGTH of* ~, wilskrag; *according to his own SWEET* ~, na eie goeddunke; na willekeur; *last* ~ *and TESTAMENT*, uiterste wil (en testament); *where there's a* ~ *there's a WAY*, waar daar 'n wil is, is 'n weg; wie wil, kan; *do something WITH a* ~, iets met lus doen; *WORK with a* ~, met lus (uit alle mag) werk; (v) wil, begeer, wens; deur wilskrag dwing; bemaak (in testament).

will², (aux. v) (**would**), sal; *ACCIDENTS* ~ *happen*, ongelukke gebeur altyd; ~ *AWAY*, bemaak, nalaat, vermaak; *BOYS* ~ *be boys*, seuns is nou eenmaal seuns; ~ *MONEY to a school*, geld aan 'n skool bemaak (nalaat); *MURDER* ~ *out*, 'n moord kom altyd uit; *she* ~ *have NONE of me*, sy wil niks met my te doen hê nie; *he* ~ *SIT like this for hours*, so sit hy ure aanmekaar; *this* ~ *be Pretoria, I SUPPOSE?* dit is nou seker Pretoria, nè? *WHAT wilt thou?* wat wil u hê? *the WOUND would not heal*, die wond wou nie gesond word nie; ~**er**, erflater.

Will'iam, Willem.

Will'ie, Willie; *WEARY* ~, Moeë Jan; *WEE* ~ *Winkie*, Klaas Vakie.

will'ing, gewillig, willig, bereidwillig, bereid; *I AM* ~ *to*, ek is bereid om; *GOD* ~, as dit die wil van God is; ~**ly**, goedskiks, gewillig, bereidwillig, graag; ~**ness**, gewilligheid, willigheid, bereidwilligheid.

will-o'-the-wisp', dwaallig; blinkwater, swerwer; glibberige mens; *he is a* ~, hy is soos 'n voël op 'n tak.

will'ow¹, (n) wolf, pluismasjien; (v) uitpluis; uitslaan.

will'ow², (n) wilger(boom); kolf (kr.); *WEAR the* ~, die laagste plek inneem; treur oor 'n geliefde; *WIELD the* ~, die kriekketkolf hanteer; ~**-herb**, wilgerrosie; ~**-pattern**, wilgerpatroon; ~**-tree**, wilgerboom, wilkerboom; ~**-warbler**, ~**-wren**, hofsanger (voël); ~**y**, vol wilgers; wilgeragtig; slank, skraal; slap.

will'-power, wilskrag.

will'y-nill'y, teen wil en dank, noodgedwonge, of jy wil of nie, goedskiks of kwaadskiks, nolens volens.

wilt¹, (n) verwelksiekte; (v) kwyn, verwelk, verlep; verslap, slap hang; ~*ed vegetables*, verlepte groente.

wilt², (v) *kyk* **will**, (v).

wil'y, listig, slim, geslepe, slu; *a* ~ *fox*, 'n uitgeslape karnallie.

wim'ble, (n) houtboor; swikboor; (v) boor; ~ **brace**, booromslag.

wim'ple, sluier; wimpel; swart kappie; (v) omsluier; omvou, kronkel.

win, (n) oorwinning, sukses; wen(slag), winslag (v) (**won**), wen, win; verdien; behaal; berei; dop (albasters); ~ *APPROVAL*, goedkeuring wegdra; ~ *one's BREAD*, jou brood verdien; ~ *somebody's CONSENT*, iem. oorhaal om toestemming te gee; ~ *the DAY*, die oorwinning behaal; ~ *EASILY*, loshande wen; ~ *the FIELD*, die slag wen; ~ *FRIENDS*, vriende maak; ~ *HOME*, die huis haal; ~ *or LOSE*, of jy wen of verloor; daarop of daaronder; ~ *MINERALS*, delfstowwe ontgin; ~ *against great ODDS*, teen sterk weerstand wen; ~ *someone OVER*, iem. oorhaal; ~ *the PORT*, die hawe bereik; ~ *a PRIZE*, 'n prys wen; ~ *ROUND*, oorhaal; ~ *one's SPURS*, jou spore verdien; ~ *THROUGH*, alle moeilikhede oorwin; ~ *the TOSS*, die opgooi (lootjie) wen; ~ *a VICTORY*, 'n oorwinning behaal; ~ *one's WAY*, jou weg baan; vorentoe beur.

wince, (n) immekaarkrimping; huiwering, rilling; terugdeinsing; (v) terugdeins; huiwer; inmekaarkrimp; ~ *under pain*, inmekaarkrimp van pyn.

win'cey, wolkatoen.

winceyette', winceyette.

winch, (n) (**-es**), windas, wen, wenas; lier; hystoestel; slinger; (v) hys; ~**-drum**, wentol; ~**-launching**, lierlansering.

win'cing, krimping; rilling; terugdeinsing; *without* ~, sonder om 'n spier te vertrek.

wind¹, (n) draai, bog; hysing; (v) (**wound**), draai, 'n draai maak; (om)kronkel; wend; wikkel, hys, slinger; opwen; draai (tou); ~ *a BLANKET round someone*, iem. in 'n kombers toedraai; ~ *someone round one's FINGER*, iem. om jou vinger draai; ~ *OFF*, afdraai; *wound up to the last PITCH of expectation*, in gespanne verwagting; ~ *UP*, opdraai (gare); beëindig; vereffen; likwideer (saak); opwen (oorlosie); *he wound UP by declaring*, hy het geëindig deur te verklaar.

wind², (n) wind; snuf, reuk; lug, lugstroom; blaasinstrument; asem; suiging; opgeblasenheid; *AGAINST the* ~, wind op; *BEFORE the* ~, wind af; met die stroom; *BETWEEN* ~ *and water*, tussen twee vure; in die knyp; *what* ~ *has BLOWN you hither?* van waar, Gehasi? wat voer jou hierheen? *BREAK* ~, 'n wind opbreek; 'n wind laat; *CAST to the* ~*s*, oorboord gooi; in die wind slaan; *FIND out how the* ~ *blows*, kyk uit watter hoek die wind waai; *come from the FOUR* ~*s*, uit alle oorde kom; *scatter to the FOUR* ~*s*, in alle rigtings verstrooi (verdrywe); *GAIN the* ~, die loef afsteek; *GET* ~ *of*, iets uitvind; 'n snuf (iets) in die neus kry; *GET the* ~ *up*, in die knyp raak; *GET* ~ *of something*, 'n voeltjie hoor fluit; *GO like the* ~, so vinnig soos die wind gaan; *have a GOOD* ~, 'n lang asem hê; *GUST of* ~, rukwind, windvlug; *HIGH* ~*s blow on high hills*, die hoogste bome vang die meeste wind; *it's an ILL* ~ *that blows nobody good*, daar is altyd in geluk by 'n ongeluk; geen kwaad sonder baat; daar waai geen wind nie of dit is vir iem. van nut; *something IN the* ~, iets aan die broei; *is that how the* ~ *LIES?* waai die wind uit daardie hoekie? *go LIKE the* ~, soos 'n blits wees; *OFFSHORE* ~, landwind; *PUT the* ~ *up someone*, iem. bang maak; *does the* ~ *blow from that QUARTER?* waai die wind uit daardie hoekie? *RAISE the* ~, die nodige geld in die hande kry; *RECOVER one's* ~, op asem kom; *SAIL close to the* ~, skerp by die wind seil; twyfelagtige dinge doen; op die kantjie af wees; *trim one's SAILS to every* ~, jou huik (seil) na die wind hang; *get one's SECOND* ~, jou tweede asem kry; *TAKE* ~, uitlek; rugbaar word; *TAKE the* ~ *out of someone's sails*, iem. die loef afsteek; *in the TEETH of the* ~, reg teen die wind op; *the* ~ *is TEMPERED to the shorn lamb*, kruis na krag en krag na kruis; *THROW to the* ~*s*, laat vaar; oorboord gooi; *as VARIABLE as the* ~, soos die wind waai; *between* ~ *and WATER*, op 'n gevaarlike pad; *sow the* ~ *and reap the WHIRLWIND*, die wind saai en die stormwind maai; *WHISTLE down the* ~, laat vaar, opgee; *WITH the* ~, wind af; met die stroom; (v) blaas, toeter; die lug kry van, ruik; asem skep; uitasem raak; laat blaas; wind-uit slaan; ~ *a HORSE*, 'n perd se litte losmaak; *the HOUNDS* ~ *the fox*, die honde kry die reuk van die vos.

windage 1377 **winning**

win'dage, speelruimte, speling.
wind: ~ **bag,** windsak, grootprater, windlawaai, windbuks, snoeshaan, windmaker, praatjiesmaker, praatkous, raasbek; ~ **band,** blaasorkes; ~**-blown,** verwaaid; ~ **bound,** deur teenwinde opgehou; ~ **break,** windskerm; windskut; ~ **breaker,** leerbaadjie; windjekker; ~**-charger,** windlaaier; ~**-cheater,** windsnyer; windboorder (gholf); ~**-chest,** blaasbalk; ~**-colic,** windkoliek; ~**-cone,** windkeël; ~ **direction,** windrigting; ~**-dried,** winddroog; ~**-drying,** winddroging; ~ **ed,** uitasem; ~**-egg,** windeier.
wind'er, opdraaier; spoeletjie; haspelaar; slinger; hysmasjien; rankplant.
wind: ~ **fall,** afgewaaide vrugte; buitekans, meevallertjie; ~ **fall timber,** omgewaaide hout; ~**-flower,** anemoon; ~ **furnace,** droogoond; ~**-gall,** swelsel; ~**-gauge,** windskuif (van geweer); windmeter; ~**-gust,** windvlaag; ~**-hover,** toringvalk; ~**-indicator,** windwyser; windkous; ~ **iness,** winderigheid; lugtigheid, bangerigheid.
wind'ing, (n) kronkeling, draai; winding, wikkeling (elek.); hysing; opwenning; (a) kronkelend, bogtig, kronkel-, draai-; ~ **drum,** toutrommel, hystrommel; ~ **engine,** hysmasjien; ~**-engine driver,** hysmasjinis; ~ **gear,** hystoestel; optrekker; ~ **path,** kronkelpad, slingerpad; ~ **rope,** hystou; ~ **sheet,** lykkleed, doodshemp, doodlaken; ~ **staircase,** draaitrap, wenteltrap; ~ **tackle,** hystakel; ~**-up,** likwidasie; afwikkeling
wind: ~ **instrument,** blaasinstrument, intensity, windsterkte; ~**-jammer,** seilskip.
wind'lass, (n) (-es), wen(as), windas; (v) ophys, optrek, opwen.
wind'less, windstil; ~ **ness,** windstilte.
wind'mill, windpomp; windmeule; *HAVE ~s in one's head,* vol krulle (flemies) wees; *THROW one's cap over the ~,* roekeloos handel; *TILT against ~s,* teen windmeulens veg.
wind' orchestra, blaasorkes.
win'dow, venster; opening; *DRESS one's ~,* met jou deugde te koop loop; *have all one's GOODS in the ~,* alles net vir die skyn vertoon; *FRENCH ~,* oopslaande raam; ~ **arch,** vensterboog; ~ **bay,** vensteruitbou, erker; ~**-blind,** blinding, rolgordyn; ~**-box,** vensterkassie; ~**-catch,** vensterknip; ~ **cleaner,** vensterskoonmaker; ~**-curtain,** venstergordyn; ~**-dresser,** uitstaller; ~**-dressing,** uitstalling, uitstalkuns; spoggery, misleidende vertoon; ~**-drip,** waterlys; ~ **ed,** met vensters; ~ **envelope,** ruitkoevert, vensterkoevert; ~**-fastener,** vensterknip; werwel; ~**-frame,** raamkosyn; ~ **garden,** venstertuin; ~**-gazing,** vensterkykery; ~**-glass,** vensterglas; ~**-grate,** ~**-grating,** venstertralie; ~**-ledge,** vensterbank; ~ **less,** sonder vensters; ~ **pane,** vensterruit; ~**-peeper,** afloerder; ~**-sash,** vensterraam, skuifraam; ~**-seat,** vensterbank; ~ **shop,** winkels kyk, loerkoop; ~**-shopping,** vensterkykery, loerkopery, kuierkoop; ~**-shutter,** vensterluik, hortjie; ~**-sill,** vensterbank.
wind: ~ **pipe,** lugpyp; ~**-pocket,** lugkolk; ~**-pollinated,** windbestuif; ~ **pressure,** winddruk; ~ **proof,** winddig; ~ **resistance,** windweerstand; ~ **rose,** kompasroos; ~**-row,** windry, lang hoop (hooi); ~ **screen,** windskerm; voorruit; ~ **screen wiper,** ruitveër, windskermveër; ~**-sorted,** deur die wind gesorteer; ~**-speed,** windsnelheid; ~**-spout,** tornado, dwarrelwind, windhoos; ~ **strength,** windsterkte; ~**-swept,** winderig; verwaaid; ~ **table,** windtabel; ~**-tunnel,** windtonnel.
wind'-up, end; besluit; afwikkeling.
wind: ~**-vane,** weerhaan; ~ **velocity,** windsnelheid.
wind'ward, (n) loefsy, windkant; *get to ~ of,* bo die wind kom; die loef afsteek; (a) na die wind; *to ~,* loefwaarts; ~ **side,** loefsy; ~**-side anchor,** loefanker.
wind'y, winderig; opgeblase, windmakerig, grootpraterig; ydel; bangerig, lugtig; *on the ~ side of the law,* buite gevaar v.d. wet.
wine, (n) wyn; donkerrooi; *ADAM'S ~,* pompwater; *you cannot know ~ by the BARREL,* moenie 'n man op sy baadjie takseer nie; skyn bedrieg; *new ~*

in old BOTTLES, nuwe wyn in ou sakke; *good ~ needs no BUSH,* goeie wyn het nie 'n kans nodig nie; goeie wyn prys homself; *DRY ~,* droëwyn; *FOND of ~ and women,* van Wyntjie en Tryntjie hou; lief vir wyn en vroumense; *IN ~,* lekker, aangeklam; *when ~ is IN, wit is out,* wyn in die man, wysheid in die kan; *NOBLE ~,* edelwyn; *RED ~,* rooiwyn; *SPIRITS of ~,* wyngees; *SWEET ~,* soetwyn; *WHITE ~,* witwyn; (v) wyn drink; op wyn onthaal; ~ *and dine,* eet en drink; ~ **bag,** wynsak; ~ **bibber,** wynsuiper, wynsak; ~ **bibbing,** wynsuipery; ~ **bottle,** wynbottel; ~ **bowl,** wynbeker; ~ **cabinet,** drank-, wynkabinet; ~**-cask,** wynvat; ~ **cellar,** wynkelder; ~ **chemist,** wynchemikus; ~ **cooler,** koelvat; ~**-cradle,** flesmandjie; ~ **cup,** wynbeker; ~ **decanter,** wynkraffie; ~**-farm,** wynplaas; ~**-farmer,** wynboer; ~**-farming,** wynboerdery; ~**-fly,** wynvlieg; ~ **frappé,** yswyn, verkoelde wyn; ~ **glass,** wynkelkie, wynglas; ~**-grower,** wynboer; ~**-growing,** wynbou, wynboerdery; ~**-house,** wynwinkel, wynhandelshuis; drankwinkel; ~ **lees,** wynmoer; ~**-list,** wynlys; wynkaart; ~**-maker,** wynmaker; ~**-making,** wynbereiding; ~ **marc,** wynmoer; ~**-merchant,** wynhandelaar; ~**-pit,** stikgat; ~ **press,** parsbalie, wynpers, trapbalie; ~**-red,** wynrooi; ~ **ry,** wynmakery; ~ **sap,** winterappel; ~ **skin,** wynsak; ~ **steward,** wynkelner; ~**-stone,** wynsteen; ~**-taster,** wynproewer; ~**-tasting,** wynproef; ~**-trade,** wynhandel; ~**-treader,** druiwetrapper; ~**-tub,** kuipbalie; ~**-vat,** wynvat; ~ **vault,** wynkelder; ~ **vinegar,** druiweasyn.
wing, (n) vlerk (voël), wiek, vlerk (windmeul); vleuel (leër); modderskerm, sygeboi; vleuel (gebou, rugby); buitespeler (sokker); boog (van passer); vlug; skerm (toneel); *CLIP someone's ~s,* iem. kortwiek; *his ~s have been CLIPPED,* sy vlerke is geknip; *FEAR lent ~s to her feet,* die vrees het haar vleuels gegee; *GET one ~s,* jou vleuels kry; *IN the ~s,* agter die skerms; *LEND ~s to,* verhaas; *MONEY takes to itself ~s,* geld rol, *ON the ~,* in die vlug; in die weer; in beweging; *PLAY left ~,* op die linkervleuel speel; *SPREAD one's ~s,* jou vleuels uitslaan; *he is SPROUTING ~s,* hy is te goed vir hierdie wêreld; *TAKE ~,* wegvlieg; *TAKE under one's ~,* onder jou beskerming neem; *TAKE ~s to itself,* voete kry; wegraak; (v) van vleuels voorsien; vlieg, deurklief (voël); aanspoor; vleuellam skiet; ~ *AWAY,* wegvlieg; ~ *its way HOME,* huis toe vlieg; ~**-beat,** vleuelslag; ~**-canopy,** baldakyn; ~**-case,** vlerkskild; ~ **collar,** wegstaanboordjie; ~**-commander,** vleuelkommandeur; ~ **compasses,** kwadrantpasser; ~**-control,** vlerkbesturing; ~**-cover,** dekvere.
winged, gevleueld(e); ~ *NUT,* vleuelmoer, vlerkmoer; ~ *WORDS,* gevleuelde woorde.
wing: ~ **er,** vleuel; ~**-footed,** snelvoetig, snel; ~ **forward,** kantvoorspeler; ~ **less,** sonder vlerke; ~ **less locust,** voetganger(sprinkaan); ~ **let,** vlerkie; ~**-nut,** vleuelmoer; ~**-play,** buitespel, vleuelspel; ~ **rib,** voorrib; ~**-screw,** vleuelskroef; ~**-sheath,** vlerkskild; ~**-span,** vlerkspan; ~**-spread,** vlerkspan; vleuelafstand, vlug; ~**-stroke,** vleuelslag; ~ **surface,** vlerkopperviak; ~ **three-quarter,** vleuel (rugby); ~**-tip,** vlerkpunt.
wink, (n) knipogie; wink, oogwink; *in the ~ of an EYE,* in 'n oogwink; *take FORTY ~s,* 'n uiltjie knip; *a NOD is as good as a ~ to a blind horse,* dit help nie om 'n blinde iets met die hand te beduie nie; *QUICK as a ~,* in 'n oogwink; *he did not get a ~ of SLEEP,* hy het nie 'n oog toegemaak nie; *TIP someone the ~,* iem. die wenk gee; (v) wink; knipoog, luik; flikker; ~ *at something,* iets deur die vingers sien; ~ **er,** knikker; oogklappie.
wink'ing, (n) oogknip; *as EASY as ~,* doodmaklik; *in the ~ of an EYE,* in 'n oogwink; *LIKE ~,* soos 'n gedagte; (a) knip-; knippend.
wi'nkle, arikreukel, alikreukel.
wink'le-picker, skerppuntskoen.
winn'er, wenner; pryswenner; oorwinnaar.
winn'ing, (n) (die) wen, oorwinning; winning (minerale); verowering; (pl) wins; (a) wen-; innemend, voorkomend, aantreklik; bekoord; *the ~ CANDI=*

DATE, die gekose kandidaat; *the* ~ *HIT*, die beslissende hou; ~ *MANNERS*, innemende maniere; *the* ~ *SIDE*, die wenkant (wenspan); ~-**post**, wenpaal, eindpaal.

winn'ow, (n) (die) uitwaai, wan; (v) wan, uitkaf, uitwaai, waai; sif; ~-**er**, wanner; wanmasjien.

winn'owing, (die) uitwan; uitsifting; ~ **basket**, wanmandjie, uitwaaimandjie; ~ **fan**, jaagbesem; ~ **machine**, wanmasjien.

win'some, innemend, bekoorlik, aantreklik, vriendelik; ~ **ness**, innemendheid, vriendelikheid, bekoorlikheid.

win'ter, (n) winter; *HARD* ~, kwaai (strawwe) winter; *IN* ~, in die winter; *a MAN of 60* ~ *s,* 'n man van 60 jaar; *latter PART of* ~, nawinter; (v) oorwinter; deur die winter voer; (a) winter=; ~ **apple**, winterappel; ~ **cherry**, lampionvrug, jodekers; ~ **clothing**, winterklere; ~ **coat**, winterhare; winterjas; ~ **crop**, winteroes; ~ **crops**, wintergewasse; ~ **dress**, winterrok; ~ **garden**, wintertuin; ~ **green**, wintergroen; ~ **ing**, oorwintering; ~ **palace**, winterpaleis; ~ **quarters**, winterverblyf; ~ **rainfall area**, winterreënstreek; ~ **relief**, winterhulp; ~ **residence**, winterverblyf; ~ **sale**, winteruitverkoop, winteruitverkoping; ~ **season**, winterseisoen; ~ **solstice**, wintersonstilstand; ~ **sports**, wintersport.

win'try, winteragtig, winter=; koud; ~ **weather**, winterweer.

win'y, wynagtig, wyn=; aangeklam.

winze, (n) daling, daalgang (myn); (v) aftonnel.

wipe, (n) veeg; klap; sakdoek; *take a* ~ *at a person*, iem. met die plat hand byloop; (v) afvee, afdroë; uitvee; ~ *out an ACCOUNT*, 'n skuld delg; *the whole ARMY has been* ~ *d out*, die hele leër is totaal uitgewis; ~ *AWAY*, afvee; uitwis; uitdelg; ~ *one's BOOTS on a person*, iem. met die grootste minagting behandel; ~ *out a DEBT*, 'n skuld delg; ~ *out a DEFICIT*, 'n tekort goedmaak; ~ *out a DISGRACE*, 'n skande uitwis; ~ *DISHES*, skottelgoed afdroog; ~ *someone's EYE*, iem. die loef afsteek; ~ *your EYES*, jou oë uitvee; ~ *one's FACE*, jou gesig afvee; ~ *the FLOOR with someone*, van iem. kleingeld maak; iem. verneder; ~ *off a LOSS*, 'n verlies afskryf; ~ *OFF*, afvee, wegvee; ~ *OUT*, uitvee, uitwis, vernietig; ~ *off a SCORE*, 'n skuld vereffen; ~ *UP*, opvee, skoonvrywe; ~**r**, doek; afveër; kontakarm (elek.).

wip'ing, (die) afvee.

wire, (n) draad; telegram, draadberig; staaltou; telegraafdraad; *BARBED* ~, doringdraad; *BY* ~, telegrafies; *LIVE* ~, gelaaide draad; ondernemende mens; *OVER the* ~ *s*, per telefoon; *PULL* ~ *s*, agter die skerms sit; die drade trek; (v) sein, telegrafeer; met draad vasmaak; aan 'n draad ryg; in 'n strik vang (wild); drade insit; van drade voorsien (gebou), bedraad; inryg; met draad versterk; draadhindernisse aanlê; ~*d for ELECTRICITY*, met elektriese geleiding; ~ *IN*, omhein; ~ *ME*, stuur my 'n telegram; ~ **anchor**, draadanker; ~ **balloon**, bolrooster; ~-**bender**, draadbuier; ~ **brad**, skoenspyker; ~ **bridge**, hangbrug; ~ **brush**, draadborsel; ~ **cable**, draadkabel, staalkabel; ~ **cage**, draadkooi; ~-**clipper**, draadknipper; ~ **coil**, rol draad; ~-**cutter**, draadskêr, draadknipper, draadtang; ~-**dancer**, koorddanser; ~-**die**, draadvormer; ~ **draw**, (..drew, -n), draadtrek, rek; verdraai; haarkloof, spitsvondig redeneer; ~ **drawer**, draadtrekker; ~ **drawn**, tot draad getrek; spitsvondig, subtiel; ~ **dropper**, draadhangertjie; ~-**edge**, braam (van beitel); ~ **entanglement**, draadversperring; ~ **fence**, draadheining; ~ **fuse**, draadsekering; ~ **gauge**, draaddikte, draadmaat; ~ **gauze**, draadgaas, metaalgaas; ~ **glass**, draadglas; ~ **grate**, draadrooster; ~-**gun**, staaldraadkanon; ~ **hairbrush**, draadhaarborsel; ~-**haired**, steekhaar=; ~ **hawser**, staalkabel.

wire'less, (n) draadloos (vero.), radio; draadlose toestel; draadlose telegrafie; (v) uitsaai; 'n draadlose berig stuur; (a) radio=; ~ **aerial**, antenne; ~ **call**, radio-oproep; ~ **control**, radiobesturing; ~ **licence**, radiolisensie, luistergeld; ~ **mast**, lugdraadmas; ~ **mechanic**, radiowerktuigkundige; ~ **message**, radioberig; draadlose berig; ~ **operator**, radiobediener; ~ **repairer**, radiohersteller; ~ **set**, radiotoestel; ~ **station**, uitsaaistasie, radiostasie, radio-omroep; ~ **telegraphist**, radiotelegrafis, marconis; ~ **telegraphy**, draadlose telegrafie; ~ **telephony**, draadlose telefonie; ~ **tender**, radiowa; ~ **transmission**, radio-oorseining.

wire: ~ **man**, telegraafarbeider, draadmonteur; draadspanner; ~ **mesh**, draadmaas; ~-**nail**, draadspyker; ~ **netting**, sifdraad, ogiesdraad; ~-**nippers**, draadtang, draadskêr; ~ **pliers**, draadtang; ~ **puller**, draadtrekker; konkelaar, leier, (politieke) intrigant; ~ **pulley**, kabelkatrol; ~-**pulling**, draadtrekkery, politieke intriges, geknoei, gekonkel, toutrekkery; ~ **recorder**, draadopnemer; ~ **rod**, draadstang; ~ **roll**, draadrol; ~ **rope**, draadtou, staal(draad)tou; ~ **ropeway**, sweefspoor, kabelspoor; ~-**shears**, draadskêr; ~ **staple**, kram; ~-**stitch**, (n) hoededraadsteek; (v) draadheg, met staaldraad werk; ~-**stitcher**, draadhegter; ~-**stitching**, draadhegwerk; ~-**strainer**, draadtrekker; draadspanner; ~-**straining**, draadspan; ~-**tapper**, draadtapper; ~-**tapping**, draadtappery; ~-**walker**, koorddanser; ~-**walking**, koorddansery; ~-**way**, sweefbaan; ~ **wheel**, speekwiel; ~ **wool**, draadwol; ~-**work**, draadwerk; ~-**worker**, draadwerker; ~-**works**, draadfabriek; ~-**worm**, haarwurm; draadwurm; ~-**wound**, met draadwikkeling; ~-**wove**, velyn(papier).

wir'iness, draadagtigheid; taaiheid, gespierdheid.

wir'ing, draadvlegwerk; draad; draadwerk, draadspanwerk; draadleiding, bedrading; draadnet; geleiding(snet); (die) insit van drade, verspanning; ~ **diagram**, draadskema, aansluitskema; ~ **machine**, draadhegmasjien; ~ **post**, trekpaal; ~ **shed**, verspanningswinkel.

wir'y, draad=, draadagtig; taai, gespierd.

wis'dom, wysheid; verstand; *no* ~ *like silence*, swye is goud; die wysste is hy wat stilbly; ~ **tooth**, verstandtand, verstandskies; *he hasn't cut his* ~ *teeth yet*, hy is nog 'n uilskuiken; hy is nog nat agter die ore.

wise[1], (n) manier, wyse; *in ANY* ~, op die een of ander manier; *IN this* ~, op hierdie manier; *in NO* ~, glad nie, hoegenaamd nie.

wise[2], (a) verstandig, wys, slim, vroed; raadsaam; *who is ANY the* ~ *r?* wie is nou dom Jan en wie slim Jan? *BE* ~ *to something*, goed op hoogte wees met; deeglik bewus wees van; *be* ~ *after the EVENT*, agterna slim wees; *where IGNORANCE is bliss, 'tis folly to be* ~, waar onkunde geluk bring, is wysheid dwaasheid; *NONE the* ~ *r*, niks te wete gekom het nie; ~ *and OTHERWISE*, slim en nie slim nie; *PUT someone* ~, iem. inlig (reghelp); *a SADDER* ~ *r man*, iem. wat al baie harde bene gekou het; *nobody will be THE* ~ *r*, daar sal geen haan na kraai nie; ~ **acre**, wysneus, waanwyse, beterweter, japsnoet; ~ **crack**, (n) kwinkslag; snedige gesegde; epigram; (v) (spottende) aanmerkings maak; ~ **ly**, verstandig; ~ **ness**, wysheid; raadsaamheid; ~ **woman**, verstandige vrou; waarsegster; vroedvrou; towenares.

wish, (n) (-es), wens, verlange, begeerte; wil; *AGAINST one's* ~, teen heug en meug; *the* ~ *is FATHER to the thought*, die wens is vader v.d. gedagte; *GET one's* ~, jou wens vervul sien; *GOOD* ~ *es*, beste wense; *his* ~ *was not GRANTED*, sy versoek is nie toegestaan nie; *if* ~ *es were HORSES beggars might ride*, as is verbeelding het moet wense rig 'n mens maar min uit; *by his SPECIAL* ~, op sy uitdruklike verlange; (v) wens; verlang, begeer; wil; *he could not* ~ *it BETTER*, hy kon dit nie beter verlang het nie; ~ *someone at the BOTTOM of the sea*, iem. na die maan wens; ~ *FOR*, verlang na; *I* ~ *to GO*, ek wil graag gaan; *I* ~ *he were GONE*, ek wens dat hy al weg is; ~ *someone JOY of something*, iem. die geluk gun; ~ *someone SUCCESS*, iem. voorspoed (sukses) toewens; ~ **bone**, geluksbeentjie, vurkbeentjie; ~ **ful**, verlangend; ~ *ful thinking*, wensdinkery; ~ **ing**, wens; ~ *ing bone* = **wishbone**; ~ **ing-well**, wensfontein(tjie).

wish'-wash, damwater; kasaterwater, flou drinkgoed; kletspraatjies, kaf.

wishy-washy / wizened

wish'y-washy, flou, onbenullig, laf; waterig, sopperig.

wisp, bondel, bossie, hopie; toutjie (hare); *a ~ of smoke,* 'n yl rokie; *~y,* yl; kollerig (hare), toutjiesagtig; toutjiesrig; tingerig.

wistar'ia, wiste'ria, wistaria, bloureën.

wist'ful, peinsend, droefgeestig; verlangend, weemoedig; smagtend; *~ ness,* droefgeestige verlange; weemoed.

wit¹, (n) geestigheid, vernuf; verstand; wysheid; geestige persoon; *not to have ALL one's ~s about one,* nie al jou varkies in die hok hê nie; *have all one's ~s ABOUT one,* jou sinne bymekaar hê; nie aan die slaap wees nie; *DRIVE someone out of his ~s,* iem. van sy verstand laat raak; *be at one's ~s' END,* heeltemal raadop wees; nie hot of haar weet nie; ten einde raad wees; *he has more ~ in his FINGER than you in your whole body,* hy het meer verstand in sy pinkie as jy in jou hele lyf; *the FIVE ~s,* die vyf sinne; *FRIGHTEN someone out of his ~s,* iem. die skrik op die lyf ja; *LIVE by one's ~s,* deur bedrog probeer bestaan; 'n boereverneuker wees; *be OUT of one's ~s,* jou verstand kwyt wees; geestelik gekrenk wees; *be PAST the ~s of man,* die mens se verstand te bowe gaan; *have QUICK ~s,* vlug van begrip wees; *READY ~,* gevatheid; *in one's RIGHT ~s,* by jou volle verstand; *SET one's ~s to work,* jou verstand gebruik; *have SLOW ~s,* bot wees; *keep one's ~s TOGETHER,* kop hou, nie van stryk raak nie.

wit², (v) (arch.) (wot) weet; *to ~,* te wete, naamlik.

witch, (n) (-es), heks, towenares; towenaar; verleidster; platvis; (v) toor, beheks, bekoor, verlei; *~craft,* toordery, towery, toorkuns, duiwelskunstenary, duiwelskunste; *~-doctor,* toordokter; *~-elm, kyk* **wych-elm;** *~ery,* toordery, heksery; betowering.

witch'es': *~ broom,* heksebesem; *~ cauldron,* hekseketel; *~ dance,* heksedans; *~ sabbath,* heksesabbat; *~ trial,* hekseproses.

witch: *~-grass,* kweek(gras); *~-hunt,* heksejag; ketterjag; *~-hunter,* heksejagter, ketterjagter; *~ing hour,* toweruur; spookuur; *~like,* heksagtig; *~weed,* rooiblom, mieliegif, rooibossie.

witenagemot', witenagemot, wetgewende vergadering v.d. Angelsaksers.

with, met; saam met; mee; by; van; *AWAY ~ it,* weg daarmee; *BE ~ someone,* met iem. wees; *blessed ~ BEAUTY,* bedeel met skoonheid; *~ CHILD,* in die ander tyd, swanger; *DOWN ~ fever,* aan die koors lê; *tremble ~ FEAR,* bewe van angs; *FIGHT ~ courage,* moedig veg; *~ GOD,* met God wees; in die hemel wees; *~-IT,* bydertyds, eietyds; *~ all his LEARNINGS,* he is the simplest of men, ten spyte van al sy geleerdheid het hy die eenvoudigste mens gebly; *I have no change ~ ME,* ek het nie kleingeld nie; *who is NOT ~ us, is against us,* wie nie vir ons is nie, is teen ons; *PUT up ~,* verdra; *it RESTS ~ you,* dit hang van jou af; *STIFF ~ cold,* styf v.d. koue; *TEN ~ the children,* tien met die kinders ingesluit; *~ THAT,* daarmee; daarop; *~ TIME,* met verloop van tyd, mettertyd; *it VARIES ~ the individual,* dit wissel van persoon tot persoon; *what do you WANT ~ me?* wat wil jy van my hê? *no knife ~ WHICH to cut it,* geen mes om dit mee te sny nie; *geen mes waarmee dit gesny kan word nie; he WON ~ ease,* hy het maklik (fluit-fluit) gewen; *~ YOUNG,* dragtig, beset (diere).

withal', (adv) bowendien; verder, tewens; (prep) met, mee.

withdraw', (..drew, -n), terugtrek (troepe); wyk; herroep (ambassadeur); terugneem; uitneem; jou onttrek van, (jou) verwyder; uittree; afneem; wegtrek; ophou; *~ a BILL,* 'n wetsontwerp terugtrek; *~ a BOOK from circulation,* 'n boek intrek; *the CANDIDATE withdrew from the election,* die kandidaat het teruggestaan; *~ from CIRCULATION,* uit omloop neem; *~ yourself FROM,* jou onttrek aan; *~ a LAW,* 'n wet herroep; *~ MONEY from circulation,* geld aan die omloop onttrek; *~ into ONESELF,* in jou skulp kruip; *~ a SHIP from service,* 'n skip uit die vaart neem; *~ one's SUPPORT,* jou verdere steun terugtrek; *~ one's WORDS,* jou woorde terugtrek; *~able,* opsegbaar; intrekbaar.

withdraw'al, terugtrekking; opvraging; terugname, terugvordering; herroeping, intrekking; verwydering; afsegging, uittreding; *~ of capital,* afvloei (onttrekking) van kapitaal; *~ slip,* opvrastrokie.

withdraw': *~er,* terugtrekker; *~n,* teruggetrek; ingetrek; afgesonder.

with'e, takkie, lat, loot.

with'er, (ver)welk, verlep; verflens; verdor, verskrompel, wegkwyn, uitdor, uitdroog; laat verwelk; *~ed,* verwelk, verlep; verskrompel(d), verdor; uitgedroog; *~ing,* (n) wegkwyning; uitdroging; verwelking; verskrompeling; (a) verdorrend; vernietigend; *a ~ing look,* 'n vernietigende blik.

with'ers, skof (van 'n perd); *our ~ are unwrung,* dit raak ons nie; dit kan ons nie skeel nie.

withhold', (..held), terughou, agterhou (geld); weerhou, afhou; onttrek; weier; *~ one's hand,* geen stappe doen nie.

within', (n) die binnekant; *seen from ~,* soos van binne gesien; (adv) binne-in, daarbinne, binne; *GO ~,* binnegaan; *STAY ~,* in die huis (binne) bly; (prep) binne, in; *~ an ACE,* dit het min geskeel, dit was so hittete; *~ BOUNDS,* binne die perke (grense); *~ the last DAY or two,* sedert 'n dag of wat; *~ a few DAYS,* binne 'n paar dae; *~ DOORS,* binnenshuis; *FROM ~,* van binne; *beaten ~ an INCH of his life,* so amper doodgeslaan; *~ INCHES,* binne enkele duime; binne 'n paar duim; *he was RUNNING ~ himself,* hy het gehardloop sonder om al sy kragte in te span; *live ~ one's INCOME,* die tering na die nering sit; *KEEP ~ the law,* binne die perke van die wet bly; *~ LIMITS,* binne (sekere) perke; *NOT ~ a mile of...,* nie binne 'n myl van ...nie; *~ RANGE,* binne trefafstand; *~ REACH,* binne bereik; *~ REASON,* redelikerwys; *~ SECONDS,* binne enkele sekondes; *a TASK well ~ his powers,* 'n taak waartoe hy goed in staat is; *~ a WEEK of his return,* binne 'n week na sy tuiskoms.

with-it, bydertyds, eietyds.

without', (n) die buitekant, uitwendige; (adv) buitekant, van buite; *DO ~,* ontbeer, sonder klaarkom; *GO ~ him,* sonder hom gaan; (prep) sonder; buite, buitekant; *~ DOUBT,* ongetwyfeld; *~ FAIL,* seker, onfeilbaar; *FROM ~,* van die buitekant; *GO ~ something,* sonder iets bly; *~ a JACKET,* sonder baadjie; *~ NUMBER,* talloos; *~ OBLIGATION,* sonder enige verpligting; *it goes ~ SAYING,* dit spreek vanself; *WITHIN and ~,* inwendig en uitwendig; (conj) tensy.

withstand', (..stood), weerstaan, weerstrewe, weerstand bied teen, bekamp; uitstaan; jou versit teen.

with'y, (withies) = withe.

wit'less, onnosel; onverstandig, laf; *~ness,* onnoselheid; lafheid.

wit'ling, lawwe grapmaker.

wit'ness, (n) (-es), getuie; omstander; getuienis; *BEAR ~,* getuig; *BROWBEAT a ~,* 'n getuie intimideer; *CALL a ~,* 'n getuie oproep; *CALL to ~,* tot getuie roep; *~ for the CROWN,* staatsgetuie, kroongetuie; *~ for the DEFENCE,* getuie vir die verdediging; *his LIFE was a ~ to his honesty,* sy lewe het bewys gelewer van sy eerlikheid; *~ for the PROSECUTION,* getuie vir die vervolging; (v) getuig; getuienis aflê; as getuie onderteken; bywoon, sien; *~ AGAINST,* getuienis aflê teen; *~ a SIGNATURE,* 'n handtekening waarmerk; *~-box,* getuiebank; *~-fee,* getuiegeld.

witt'icism, kwinkslag, geestige gesegde, boutade.

witt'iness, geestigheid, sinrykheid.

witt'ingly, opsetlik, met voorbedagte rade.

witt'y, geestig, gevat, geesryk; snedig; sinryk; *a ~ rejoinder,* 'n gevatte antwoord.

wive, trou, tot vrou neem; 'n vrou gee.

wiv'ern, *kyk* **wyvern.**

wives, *kyk* **wife.**

wiz'ard, towenaar; dolosgooier; duisendkunstenaar; *~ry,* towenary, towery.

wiz'ened, gerimpel(d), dor, droog, verskrompel.

wo! hokaai! hook! hanou!

woad, wede (plant).

wobb'le, (n) waggeling, slingering; aarseling; onvast=heid; (v) waggelend loop; laat waggel; skommel, slinger, wiebel, wikkel, wiegel; weifel, aarsel; wip; swak staan; ~ **r,** waggelaar; weifelaar.

wob'bliness, onvastheid, wikkelrigheid, wankelheid.

wob'bling, wiegeling, wikkeling, gewiegel.

wob'bly, bewerig; onvas, mankoliekig, lendelam, wikkelrig, wankel.

woe, wee(dom), ellende, ramp; (pl) rampe, ellende, moeilikhede; ~ *BE to him,* mag hy vervloek word; ~ *BETIDE you,* wee jou gebeente; ~ *the DAY,* wee die dag; ~ *is ME!* wee my! *WEAL and* ~, wel en wee; lief en leed; ~ **begone,** armsalig, ongeluk=kig, treurig; ~ **ful,** treurig, jammerlik, droewig.

wold, vlakte, veld.

wolf, (n) **(wolves),** wolf; vrouejagter, meisiegek; huid=siekte, lupus; wanklank, wolfnoot (mus.); vraat, haai; *CRY* ~, alarm maak; *CRY* ~ *too often,* een keer te veel alarm maak; *have a* ~ *by the EARS,* nie hot of haar kan nie; *KEEP the* ~ *from the door,* hongersnood uit die huis hou; *a LONE* ~, eens=paaier, ronkedoor; *be as RAVENOUS as a* ~, so honger soos 'n wolf wees; soos 'n wolf vreet; *a* ~ *in SHEEP'S clothing,* 'n wolf in skaapsklere; 'n hui=gelaar; *THROW someone to the wolves,* iem. aan die wolwe oorgee (vir die wolwe gooi); *feel as if a* ~ *were gnawing at one's VITALS,* 'n skreeuende hon=ger hê; *give the* ~ *the WETHER to keep,* wolf skaapwagter maak; (v) vraterig eet, verslind; ~ **-call,** roepfluit; ~ **-cub,** klein wolfie; leerlingpadvin=der; ~ **-dog,** ~ **-hound,** Wolfhond; ~ **-fish,** seewolf; ~ **ish,** wolfagtig, wreed; gulsig; ~ **-moth,** koring=mot; ~ **-pack,** trop wolwe; ~ **-pit,** wolfkuil.

wo'lfram, wolfram, tungsten; ~ **ite,** wolframiet; ~ **steel,** wolframstaal.

wolf: ~ **'s-bane,** wolfswortel; ~ **'s-claw,** ~ **'s-foot,** wolfsklou; ~ **skin,** wolfsvel; ~ **spider,** jagspinne=kop; ~ **-trap,** wolwehok; ~ **-whistle,** roepfluit.

wo'lverine, veelvraat (dier).

wo'man, (n) **(women),** vrou; vroumens; maitresse, by=sit; diensmeisie; *a* ~ *'s ADVICE is a poor thing, but he is a fool who does not take it,* vroueraad is goeie raad; *tied to a* ~ *'s APRON STRINGS,* nie sonder 'n vrou kan klaarkom nie; *there is a* ~ *in the CASE,* daar sit 'n vrou agter; *women's COUNSELS oft are cold,* brandewyn en vroueraad is goeie dinge, maar jy moet dit bietjies-bietjies gebruik; *a* ~, *a dog (an ass) and a walnut tree, the more you beat them the better they be,* 'n vrou moet slae kry; *women are necessary EVILS,* die vrou is 'n onmisbare ergernis; *he made an HONEST* ~ *of her,* hy het haar tot sy wettige vrou gemaak; *IMAGE of a* ~, vrouebeeld; *there's a* ~ *IN it,* daar sit 'n vrou agter; *a KEPT* ~, 'n maitresse (bywyf, bysit), houvrou; *OLD* ~, ou vrou; *my OLD* ~, my ou beste; ~ *with a PAST,* 'n vrou wat iets op haar kerfstok het; *PLAY the* ~, papbroekig wees; 'n meid wees; 'n ou meid; *a* ~ *of the TOWN,* 'n straatvrou; *women change as often as the WIND,* 'n vrou is soos 'n môrereën; *a* ~ *'s WIT,* vroulike intuïsie; ~ *of the WORLD,* vrou v.d. wê=reld; *a* ~ *'s WORK is never done,* aan 'n vrou se werk kom daar geen einde nie; (v) jou soos 'n vrou gedra; laat huil; as vroumens aanspreek; (a) vroue=, vroulik; ~ **-born,** uit 'n vrou gebore; ~ **doctor,** vroulike dokter; ~ **farmer,** boerin; ~ **friend,** vrien=din; ~ **-hater,** vrouehater; ~ **hood,** vroulike staat; ~ **ish,** verwyf; vroulik; ~ **ishness,** vroulikheid; ver=wyfdheid; ~ **ize,** verwyf maak; agter die vroue aan=loop; onsedelik lewe; ~ **izer,** hoereerder; ~ **kind,** die vroulike geslag, vroumense; vroulikheid; ~ **less,** sonder vrou(e); ~ **librarian,** bibliotekaresse; ~ **like,** soos 'n vrou, vroulik; ~ **liness,** vroulikheid; ~ **ly,** vroulik, swak; ~ **ly guile,** vrouelis; ~ **pilot,** vliegster.

wo'man's: ~ **lib,** vrouelib, vrouebevryding; ~ **name,** vrouenaam; ~ **size,** vrouegrootte; ~ **wit,** vroulike intuïsie (instink).

woman: ~ **-stealing,** vroueroof; ~ **student,** damestu=dent; ~ **suffrage,** vrouestemreg; ~ **worker,** werk=ster; ~ **writer,** skryfster.

womb, baarmoeder, (moeder)skoot, uterus; moer (diere); *in the* ~ *of time,* in die skoot v.d. tyd.

wom'bat, wombat, buidelmuis.

wo'men, vroue, vroumense; ~ **folk,** vroumense; ~ **kind,** dames, vrouens; ~ **police,** vrouepolisie.

wo'men's: ~ **champion,** vrouekampioen; ~ **club,** vroueklub; ~ **disease,** vrouesiekte; ~ **home** vroue=tehuis; ~ **hostel,** dameskoshuis, damestehuis; ~ **league,** vrouebond; ~ **lib,** vrouelib, vrouegelykstel=ling, vrouevryheidsbeweging; vroueregte; ~ **move=ment,** vrouebeweging; ~ **rights,** vroueregte; ~ **so=ciety,** vrouegeselskap; ~ **suffrage,** vrouestemreg; ~ **team,** vrouespan; ~ **ward,** vrouesaal.

won, *kyk* **win,** (v); gewen, gewin.

wo'nder, (n) wonder; wonderwerk, mirakel; verba=sing; verwondering; *is it ANY* ~ *that?* is dit te ver=wonder dat? *CAUSE* ~, verwondering veroor=saak; ~ *s will never CEASE,* die tyd van wonders is nog nie verby nie; wonders is nog nie uit die wêreld nie; *this CHILD is a* ~, dis 'n wonderkind; *DO* ~ *s,* wonders verrig; *FOR a* ~, wonder bo wonder; wonderlik genoeg; *a NINE-DAYS* ~, 'n agtste wonder; *NO* ~ *that,* geen wonder nie dat; dit is glad nie verbasend nie; ~ *OF* ~ *s,* wonder bo won=der; *PROMISE* ~ *s,* goue berge beloof; *the SEVEN* ~ *s of the world,* die sewe wêreldwonders; *in SILENT* ~, met stomme verbasing; *it is SMALL* ~ *that,* dit is nie verbasend nie dat; *it is a* ~ *THAT,* dit is 'n wonder dat; *WORK* ~ *s,* won=ders verrig; 'n wonderlike uitwerking hê; *a* ~ *of the WORLD,* 'n wêreldwonder; (v) wonder; jou ver=wonder; verbaas wees; verlang om te weet; nuus=kierig wees; jou afvra; *I am BEGINNING to* ~, ek vra my af; ek begin wonder oor . . .; *CAN you* ~ *at it?* kan jy jou daaroor verwonder? *I* ~ *he wasn't KILLED,* dit verbaas my dat hy nie dood is nie; ~ **ful,** wonderlik, wonderbaarlik; verbasend; prag=tig, heerlik, wonderskoon; lieflik; ~ **fulness,** won=derlikheid; ~ **ingly,** met verbasing; ~ **land,** tower=land, wonderland; ~ **ment,** verwondering, be=vreemding; ~ **-struck,** verbaas; ~ **-worker,** wonder=doener; ~ **-working,** wonderdadig.

wo'ndrous, wonderlik, wonderbaar; wonderskoon; ~ **ness,** wonderbaarheid; wonderskoonheid.

wonk'y, (sl.), bewerig, duiselig; ontroubaar.

wont[1]**,** (n) gewoonte; *according to his* ~, volgens sy gewoonte; (a) gewoond, gewend; *be* ~ *to,* gewoond wees.

won't[2]**,** *contr. of* **will not;** sal nie, wil nie.

wont'ed, gewoon(d), gewend.

woo, vry na, die hof maak, opsit; probeer oorhaal; verlok, pamperlang, flikflooi.

wood, bos, woud; hout(stok) (gholf); rolbal; (pl) rol=bal(le); bosse, houtsoorte; *CUT* ~, hout kap; *DRAWN from the* ~, uit die vat getap; *IN the* ~, in die vat; *do not HALLOO till you are out of the* ~, moenie die dag voor die aand prys nie; *be OUT of the* ~, buite gevaar wees; oor die hond se rug wees; *not to be OUT of the* ~ *yet,* nog nie in die verleentheid wees; nog nie buite gevaar wees nie; ~ *in the ROUND,* saaghout; *go through a* ~ *and pick up a crooked STICK,* beter soek en slegter kry; *TOUCH* ~, (die ongeluk) aftik; *not able to see the* ~ *for the TREES,* vanweë die bome die bos nie sien nie; *there are more WAYS out of the* ~ *than one,* 'n ding kan op meer as een manier gedoen word; daar is baie maniere om 'n ding te doen; *WINE in the* ~, vat=wyn; ~ **alcohol,** houtgees; ~ **anemone,** wildewin=blom; ~ **-ant,** bosmier; ~ **ashes,** houtas; ~ **-beetle,** houtkewer; ~ **bind,** ~ **bine,** wildekanferfoelie; ~ **-block,** houtblok; ~ **-borer,** boorkewer; ~ **-bound,** toe van bosse; ~ **-carver,** houtsnyer; ~ **-carving,** houtsnykuns; houtsneewerk; ~ **charcoal,** hout=skool; ~ **chat,** steenvalk; ~ **-chopper,** houtkapper; ~ **-chuck,** groen speg; ~ **cock,** houtsnip; ~ **craft,** boskennis; houtbewerking; ~ **-culver,** ringduif; ~ **cut,** houtsnee, houtsneegravure, houtgravure, ~ **cutter,** houtkapper; houtgraveur; ~ **cutting,** houtkappery; houtsneekuns; ~ **-dust,** houtpoeier, ~ **ed,** bosryk; bosagtig.

wood'en, van hout, hout=; styf, houterig; dom; ~ **doll,**

wood: ~-**engraver**, houtgraveur; ~-**engraving**, houtsnee, houtgravure; houtsnykuns; ~-**fibre**, houtvesel(s); ~-**file**, houtvyl; ~-**fretter**, houtwurm; ~-**fungus**, houtswam; ~-**gas**, houtgas; ~-**god**, houtgod, sater; ~-**hoopoe**, kakelaar; ~-**horse**, saagbok; ~-**house**, houtskuur; ~ **industry**, houtnywerheid; ~ **iness**, bosagtigheid; stokkerigheid; ~ **land**, boswêreld, bosland; ~-**loft**, houtsolder; ~-**lot**, (plaas)plantasie; ~-**louse**, houtluis; ~-**machinist**, houtmasjienwerker; ~ **man**, boswagter; houtkapper; ~ **miller**, saagmeulenaar; ~-**mite**, houtmiet; ~-**notes**, ongekunstelde poësie; wildsang; ~-**nymph**, bosgodin, bosnimf; ~-**opal**, versteende hout; ~-**owl**, katuil; ~ **pecker**, houtkapper (voël); speg; aambeeldvoël; ~ **pie**, bont houtkapper; ~-**pigeon**, bosduif; houtduif; ~ **pile**, houthoop; ~-**pulp**, houtpap; houtstof; ~-**right**, kapreg; ~-**rot**, vermolming; ~-**saw**, houtsaag, boksaag; ~-**scape**, boslandskap; ~-**screw**, houtskroef; ~-**shed**, houtloods; ~ **s'man**, bosbewoner; ~ **sorrel**, bossuring; ~-**stack**, houtstapel; ~ **stain**, houtbeits; ~ **stork**, geelbekkooievaar, nimmersat; ~-**sugar**, houtsuiker; ~ **tar**, houtteer; ~ **technology**, houttegnologie; ~-**tissue**, houtweefsel; ~-**turner**, houtdraaier; ~-**turning**, houtdraaiwerk; ~-**ward**, boswagter; ~-**wind**, houtblaasinstrument; houtblaser; ~-**wool**, skaafsels, houtwol, boomwol; ~ **work**, houtwerk; ~ **worker**, houtwerker; ~ **worm**, houtwurm; ~-**y**, bosryk; bosagtig; hout-, houtagtig; stokkerig; ~**y ridge**, bosrant; ~-**yard**, houtwerf.

woo'er, vryer, kêrel, geliefde, minnaar.

woof¹, (n) dwarsdraad, inslag; *warp and* ~, skering en inslag.

woof!² (interj) woef!

woo'ing, hofmakery, vryery.

wool, wol; dons(hare); kroeshare, wolhare; wolgoed; *DYED in the* ~, in die wol ingeverf; deurtrap; *GO for* ~ *and come home shorn*, met die kous oor die kop terugkom; ~ *in die GREASE*, vetwol; *KEEP your* ~ *on*, moenie so kwaad word nie; *much cry and LITTLE* ~, veel geskreeu en weinig wol; *LOSE one's* ~, kwaad word; *PULL the* ~ *over someone's eyes*, sand in iem. se oë strooi; iem. vet om die oë smeer; *there is no* ~ *so WHITE but a dyer can make it black*, daar is geen koei so bont of sy het 'n vlekkie aan nie; ~ **auction**, wolveiling; ~-**bale**, wolbaal; ~-**ball**, wolbal; haarbol (in dier); ~-**bearing sheep**, wolskaap; ~-**blade**, wolkruid; ~-**broker**, wolmakelaar; ~-**buyer**, wolkoper; ~-**card**, wolkaard; ~-**carder**, wolkaarder; ~-**carding**, (die) uitkam van wol; wolkaardery; ~ **cheque**, woltjek; ~-**classer**, wolklasseerder, wolklasser; ~-**classing**, wolklassering, wolklas(sing); ~ **clip**, (wol)skeersel; ~-**comber**, wolkammer; ~-**combing**, wolkammery; ~-**dealer**, wolhandelaar; ~-**district**, woldistrik; ~-**dyed**, in die wol geverf; ~ **exchange**, wolbeurs; ~ **expert**, woldeskundige; ~ **fat**, wolvet, lanolien; ~ **fabric**, wolstof; ~-**farmer**, wolboer; ~-**farming**, wolboerdery; ~-**fell**, langwolvel.

wool'-gathering, (n) bymekaarmaak van wol; gesuf, verstrooidheid; (a) verstrooid, dromerig; *BE* ~ *in the* kop vol muisnotte hê; sit en droom; verstrooid wees; *his WITS are* ~, hy sit en suf.

wool: ~-**grader**, wolklasseerder, wolklasser; ~-**grading**, wolklassering; wolklas(sing); ~-**grower**, skaapboer, wolboer; ~-**growing**, (n) wolkwekery, wolproduksie; (a) wolproduserend; ~ **industry**, wolbedryf; ~ **lace**, wolkant; ~ **led**, wolriaend, wol-.

wool'len, (n) wolgoed, wolstof; (a) wol-, van wol; ~ *BLANKET*, wolkombers; ~ *CARD*, wolkaard; ~ *DRAPER*, verkoper van wolgoedere; ~ *FABRIC*, kaardstof; ~ *INDUSTRY*, wolbedryf; kaardstofnywerheid; ~ *MILL*, kaardstoffabriek; wolfabriek; ~ *WASTE*, wolafval; poetswol; ~ *YARN*, kaardgaring.

wool: ~ **levy**, wolheffing; ~**liness**, wollerigheid; wolkerigheid.

wool'ly, wollerig, gekroes (hare) wolhaar-, wol-; hees (stem); voos (groente); dof; verward; suf; vaag; ~ **aphis**, bloedluis; ~ **head**, wolkop-, kroeskop; ~-**headed**, kroesharig, wolkop-; ~-**witted**, suf.

wool: ~ **man**, wolkoper; ~-**manufacturer**, wolfabrikant; ~ **market**, wolmark; ~-**merchant**, wolhandelaar; ~-**mill**, wolmeul, wolfabriek; ~-**mixer**, wolmenger; ~ **monger**, wolhandelaar; ~ **moth**, kleremot; ~-**oil**, wololie; ~-**pack**, wolbaal; skaapwolkie; ~ **pieces**, stukkies wol; ~ **press**, wolpers; ~-**producer**, wolprodusent; ~ **production**, wolproduksie; ~ **sack**, wolsak, wolbaal; setel v.d. Lord Kanselier in die Engelse Hoërhuis; *reach the* ~ *sack*, op die kussing kom; ~ **sale**, wolveiling; ~ **scouring**, wolwassery.

wool'sey, *kyk* **linsey-woolsey**.

wool: ~-**shears**, skaapskêr; ~-**shed**, wolskuur; ~-**sorter**, wolsorteerder; ~-**sorters' disease**, miltvuur; ~-**sorting**, wolsortering; ~-**staple**, woldraad, wolstapel; ~-**stapler**, wolhandelaar; ~ **store**, wolpakhuis; ~ **suit**, wolpak; ~ **table**, woltafel, sorteertafel; ~ **trade**, wolhandel; ~ **washery**, wolwassery; ~ **wax**, wolwas; ~ **yarn**, wolgaring; ~ **yolk**, wololie, vetsweet.

woom, bewerbont.

wootz, Indiese gietstaal.

Wop¹, (derog.), Italianer.

wop², *kyk* **whop**.

Worc'ester(shire) sauce, worcestersous.

word, (n) woord; berig, tyding; bevel; wagwoord, parool; *in A* ~, kortom; *not to say a* ~ *ABOUT something*, geen woord oor iets rep nie; *suit the ACTION to the* ~, die daad by die woord voeg; *ADDRESS one's* ~ *to*, die woord rig tot; *AT his* ~, op sy woord; *go BACK on one's* ~, jou woord nie gestand doen nie; *BEG leave to say a few* ~*s*, die woord vra; *I don't BELIEVE a* ~ *he says*, ek glo niks wat hy sê nie; *BEYOND* ~*s*, onuitspreeklik; *BIG* ~*s*, grootpratery; *proceed from* ~*s to BLOWS*, van woorde tot dade oorgaan; *his* ~ *is as good as his BOND*, jy kan op sy woord reken; *make one's* ~ *one's BOND*, jou woord vir iets verpand; jy kan op hom staatmaak; ~*s break no BONES*, woorde maak nie seer nie; *BREAK one's* ~, jou woord nie hou nie; *BRING* ~, berig bring; *CHOOSE one's* ~*s*, jou woorde tel; *COME to* ~*s*, rusie kry; woorde kry; ~ *of COMMAND*, bevel; ~*s are wise men's COUNTERS*, the money of fools, met woorde voer 'n slim man sy planne uit en 'n dom man net 'n bestaan; ~*s CUT more than swords*, woorde maak seerder as swaarde; *assist someone with* ~*s and DEEDS*, iem. met raad en daad bystaan; *not to have a* ~ *to throw to a DOG*, nie boe of ba sê nie; *his DYING* ~*s*, sy sterfbedwoorde, sy laaste woorde; *a* ~ *in one's EAR*, 'n vertroulike mededeling; *EAT one's* ~*s*, jou woorde terugtrek; *not to be able to get a* ~ *in EDGEWAYS*, geen kans kry om iets te sê nie; ~*s FAIL me*, ek weet nie wat om te sê nie; *man of FEW* ~*s*, iem. wat nie boe of ba sê nie; iem. wat min praat; *many* ~*s will not FILL a bushel*, praatjies vul geen gaatjies nie; ~ *FOR* ~, woord vir woord; *too FUNNY for* ~*s*, baie snaaks; *GIVE the* ~ *to attack*, die bevel gee om aan te val; *I GIVE you my* ~ *to*, ek verseker jou; *GIVE one's solemn* ~, met hand en mond belowe; *your* ~*s GIVE you away*, jou woorde verraai jou; *GOD'S* ~, Gods Woord, die Heilige Skrif; *be as GOOD as one's* ~, jou woord gestand doen; *not to have a GOOD* ~ *for someone*, iem. vir al wat sleg is, uitmaak; *HAVE a* ~ *with*, praat met; *HAVE* ~*s with*, woorde hê met; rusie maak met; *HAVE the last* ~, die laaste woord hê; *HIGH* ~*s*, kwaai woorde; *an HONEST man's* ~ *is as good as his bond*, 'n man se woord, 'n man se eer; ~ *of HONOUR*, erewoord; *a HOUSEHOLD* ~, 'n bekende naam of spreuk; *IN a* ~, kortom; *KEEP one's* ~, jou woord hou; *to want to have the LAST* ~ *always*, altyd die laaste woord wil hê; *the LAST* ~ *has not yet been heard about the matter*, die muisie sal 'n stertjie hê; *the LAST* ~ *on (in)*, die finale uitspraak; die allernuutste; die allerbeste; *his* ~ *is LAW*, sy woord is ja en amen; *he is too LAZY for* ~*s*, hy is so lui dat hy iets kan oorkom; *one* ~

LEADS to another, die een woord lok die ander uit; *LEAVE* ~, 'n boodskap agteriaat; *the LIVING* ~, die lewende woord; *the W* ~ *of the LORD*, die Woord v.d. Here; *be at a LOSS for* ~*s*, woorde kortkom (soek); *he is never at a LOSS for* ~*s*, hy kan sy woord goed doen; ~*s of LOVE*, liefdeswoorde; *a MAN of his* ~, 'n waarmaker van sy woord; *in so MANY* ~*s*, met soveel woorde; *by* ~ *of MOUTH*, mondeling; *MUM'S the* ~, sjt! hou jou mond! moenie 'n woord rep nie! bly stil! *(upon) MY* ~*!* op my woord! mapstieks! maggies! *say NE'ER a* ~, geen stomme woord sê nie; *have NO* ~ *of someone*, geen taal of tyding van iem. ontvang nie; *that is NOT the* ~ *for it*, dit is nie die regte woord daarvoor nie; dit is nie eintlik juis nie; dit is nog baie erger; *have NO* ~*s to*, nie in woorde kan sê nie; *in OTHER* ~*s*, met ander woorde; *fine* ~*s butter no PARSNIPS*, praatjies vul geen gaatjies nie; *PLEDGE one's* ~, jou woord gee; *PUT in a* ~ *for*, 'n goeie woord doen vir; *PUT something into* ~*s*, iets onder woorde bring; verwoord; *PUT* ~*s into someone's mouth*, iem. woorde in die mond lê; ~ *got ROUND that*, dit word gesê dat; *have a* ~ *to SAY*, 'n woord op die hart hê; *ask someone to SAY a* ~ *or two*, iem. vra om iets te sê; *have a* ~ *to SAY*, 'n woordjie op die hart hê; *a* ~ *in SEASON*, 'n woord op sy tyd; *a* ~ *out of SEASON*, 'n woord op 'n ongeleë tyd; *SEND* ~, laat weet; 'n boodskap stuur; *in every SENSE of the* ~, in alle opsigte; *SHARP'S the* ~, roer jou riete; *not a SINGLE* ~, geen Spaanse woord nie; geen stomme woord nie; *not to say a SINGLE* ~, geen stomme woord sê nie; *SPEAK a good* ~ *for*, 'n goeie woordjie doen vir; *a* ~ *SPOKEN is past recalling*, 'n gesproke woord kan nie herroep word nie; *SUIT the deed to the* ~, die daad by die woord voeg; *you may TAKE my* ~ *for it*, jy kan my glo; jy kan daarop reken; *TAKE the* ~*s out of a person's mouth*, die woorde uit iem. se mond neem; *TAKE someone at his* ~, iem. op sy woord glo; presies doen soos iem. sê; *say THE* ~, ja sê; *he hasn't a* ~ *to THROW at a dog*, hy kan nie boe of ba sê nie; *THROW in a* ~, 'n woordjie tussenin sê; *TRIP someone up with his own* ~*s*, iem. met sy eie woorde vang; *there is not a* ~ *of TRUTH in it*, daar is niks van waar nie; *have a* ~ *or TWO to say*, 'n woord op die hart hê; *UPON my* ~*!* nou toe nou! goeie genugtig! *WASTE* ~*s*, woorde verspil; ~*s are but WIND*, woorde is soos die wind; *a* ~ *to the WISE*, 'n goeie begryper het maar 'n halwe woord nodig; (v) onder woorde bring; bewoord, inklee, formuleer; **~age**, woordgebruik; **~-blind**, woordblind; **~-blindness**, woordblindheid; **~-building**, woordvorming; **~-couple**, woordpaar; **~craft**, woordkuns; **~-deaf**, woorddoof; **~-deafness**, woorddoofheid; **~-ending**, woorduitgang; **~form**, woordvorm; **~-heading**, trefwoord; **~ily**, langdradig; **~iness**, woordrykheid, langdradigheid; **~ing**, bewoording, inkleding; **~less**, spraakloos; onuitgesproke; sonder woorde; **~-list**, woordelys; **~lore**, woordkennis; woordvorming; **~monger**, woordkramer; **~-painter**, woordkunstenaar; **~-painting**, woordsildering; **~-perfect**, rolvas; lettervas; **~-picture**, woordsildery; **~-play**, woordspeling; **~-splitter**, woordsifter, haarklower; **~y**, woordryk, langdradig, omslagtig.

wore, kyk **wear**, (v).

work, (n) werk, arbeid, werksaamheid, uitwerking; *ALL* ~ *and no play makes Jack a dull boy*, die boog kan nie altyd gespan bly (wees) nie; *a* ~ *of ART*, 'n kunswerk; *AT* ~, aan die werk; by die werk; *is your husband AT* ~ *today?* het jou man vandag gaan werk? *CLERK of* ~*s*, werkeklerk; bouopsigter; *have one's* ~ *CUT out for one*, jou hande vol hê; *a good DAY'S* ~, 'n goeie dag se werk; *do GOOD* ~, jou tyd nuttig bestee; goed werk; *GOOD* ~*s*, liefdadigheid; *many HANDS make light* ~, baie hande is 'n haas se dood; *HARD* ~, swaar werk; *LIGHT* ~, ligte werk; *MAKE short* ~ *of*, gou speel met; baie hande maak ligte werk; *MIGHTY* ~*s*, wonderwerke; *OFF* ~, met siekteverlof; werkloos; *OUT of* ~, sonder werk; *PUBLIC* ~*s*, openbare werke; *PUT to* ~, aan die werk sit, aan die gang sit;

make SAD ~ *of*, verknoei; *SET to* ~, aan die gang sit, aan die werk sit; *UP to his eyes in* ~, toegegooi met werk; *the* ~*s of a WATCH*, die ratwerk van 'n oorlosie; *it is not* ~ *that kills but WORRY*, werk maak nie gedaan nie, maar kommer wel; (v) (**-ed** or **wrought**), werk, arbei; uitwerking hê (op iets); bewerk, bearbei ('n persoon); verwerk; uitvoer; maak, doen; oplos; bereken, uitreken, uitsyfer; verrig; tot stand bring, teweegbring; veroorsaak; knie (deeg); hanteer, laat werk; eksploiteer (myn); gis, rys (suurdeeg); ~ *AGAINST*, teëwerk; ~ *AT*, werk aan; ~*ing at full BLAST*, in volle gang; ~ *AWAY*, voortwerk; ~ *a CHANGE*, 'n verandering teweegbring; ~ *against a CAUSE*, 'n saak teëwerk; ~ *for a DEAD horse*, sonder vergoeding werk; ~ *the men to DEATH*, die manne hulle dood laat werk; ~ *for a DEGREE*, vir 'n graad werk; ~ *DOWN*, afsak; *he that will not* ~ *shall not EAT*, wie nie werk nie, sal nie eet nie; *the EXPENSES* ~ *out at R2*, die onkoste bedra (kom te staan op) R2; ~ *on someone's FEELINGS*, op iem. se gevoel werk; ~ *FOR a cause*, vir 'n saak werk; ~ *like a HORSE*, soos 'n esel (os) werk; ~ *IN with*, goed inpas by; *the clerks* ~*ed IN with one another*, die klerke het mooi saamgewerk; *some INFLUENCES* ~ *downwards*, party invloede werk nadelig; ~ *LOOSE*, loswerk, losdraai; ~ *MISCHIEF*, onheil stig; ~ *out a MINE*, 'n myn uitput; ~ *OFF*, losraak; uitdelg; van die hand sit; *the stiffness in my leg gradually* ~*ed OFF*, die styfheid in my been het gaandeweg verdwyn; *one cannot* ~ *OFF a toothache*, tandpyn gaan nie oor van werk nie; ~ *ON*, aanhou werk; besig wees aan; werk vir; ~ *OUT*, uitwerk, uitreken, bereken (onkoste); uitkom; uitput; oplos; beraam; teweegbring; *something will not* ~ *OUT*, dit kan nie opgelos word nie; ~ *OUT at*, te staan kom op; ~ *one's PASSAGE*, jou passasie verdien; jou sout verdien; ~ *oneself up into a PASSION*, jou deur drif laat meesleep; ~ *through a PROGRAMME*, 'n program afwerk; ~ *in a QUOTATION*, 'n aanhaling te pas bring (invleg); ~ *ROUND to*, met 'n ompad bereik; ~ *to RULE*, volgens die handboek werk; baie stadig werk; ~ *out one's own SALVATION*, jou eie saligheid uitwerk; ~ *out a SCHEME*, 'n plan ontwerp (uitwerk); *that SCHEME* ~*s well*, die skema is heeltemal goed in die praktyk; ~ *the SCENT*, die reuk volg; ~ *up a SKETCH*, 'n skets uitwerk; *make SHORT* ~ *of*, gou klaarspeel met, korte mette maak met; ~ *off STEAM*, oordadige werkkrag (uitgelatenheid) afwerk; ~*ed by STEAM*, gedryf deur stoom; ~ *up a SUBJECT*, jou in 'n onderwerp inwerk; ~ *against TIME*, uit alle mag werk om binne 'n sekere tyd klaar te kry; ~ *TOGETHER*, saamwerk; ~ *TOWARDS something (some aim)*, iets bevorder; ~ *a TYPEWRITER*, op 'n tikmasjien werk; ~ *UP*, opwerk; vooruithelp; aanhits, opsweep; deurwerk; ~ *UP his history*, hom in geskiedenis inwerk; *to be* ~*ed UP*, in 'n senuweetoestand wees; ~ *UP a business*, 'n saak opbou; ~ *saam laat floreer*; *be* ~*ing UP for something*, jou klaarmaak vir iets; aan die broei wees; ~ *UPON*, invloed hê op; ~ *one's WAY*, jou weg baan; vooruitkom, vorentoe beur; *the WHEELS* ~ *on an axle*, die wiele draai om 'n as; ~ *one's WILL*, jou sin deurvoer; *the WIND* ~*s round*, die wind draai; ~ *in WITH*, pas by; ~ *WONDERS*, wonders verrig; *it WON'T* ~, dit sal nie gaan (werk) nie; **~abil′ity**, uitvoerbaarheid; bewerkbaarheid; **~able**, uitvoerbaar; bewerkbaar; ~*able knowledge*, gangbare kennis; **~ableness**, uitvoerbaarheid; bewerkbaarheid; **~aday**, gewoon, alledaags, werk=; ~*aday clothes*, werkklere; **~-bag**, werksak; **~-basket**, werkmandjie; **~-bench**, werkbank; **~-box**, naaikissie, werkkissie; **~day**, werk(s)dag; **~er**, werker, werkkrag, arbeider; werkster; werkby; ~ **face**, werkvlak; **~-fellow**, werkmaat; **~-girl**, werkmeisie; **~-hand**, werker, handlanger; **~ horse**, trekperd; gewillige werker; **~house**, werkhuis, armhuis.

work′ing, (n) (die) werk; behandeling; bewerking; hantering; winning, eksploitasie (van 'n myn); uit=

voering; vervaardiging; bedryf; werking; gisting; myn; trekking (van gesig); werskaffery; (pl) delfplekke, ertsuitgrawings; roersels (v.d. siel); *the ~ s of CONSCIENCE*, die stem v.d. gewete; *an OLD ~*, 'n uitgewerkte myn; (a) werkend; gangbaar; bruikbaar; werk=; bedryfs=; *~ CONDITIONS*, werkstoestande; *have a ~ KNOWLEDGE of a language*, 'n gangbare kennis van 'n taal hê; *be in ~ ORDER*, in orde wees; gereed vir gebruik wees; *~ account*, eksploitasierekening, bedryfsrekening; *~ cap*, werkpet; *~ capacity*, werkvermoë; *~ capital*, bedryfskapitaal; *~ class*, werkersklas, arbeidersklas; *~ classes*, werkerstand; *~ condition*, werkende toestand; *~ conditions*, arbeidsvoorwaardes; werksomstandighede; *~ costs*, bedryfskoste; *~ day*, (n) werkdag; (a) werk=, gewoon; *~ depth*, werkdiepte; *~ drawing*, konstruksietekening; *~ dress*, werkrok; werkklere; *~ expenses*, bedryfskoste, eksploitasiekoste; *~ face*, werkfront; *~ foreman*, werkende voorman; *~ group*, werksgroep; studiegroep; werkgeselskap; *~ head*, kragkop; *~ horse*, werkperd; *~ hour*, werkuur; *~ hours*, diensure, werktyd; *~ life*, werksame lewe; werklewe; *~ light*, werklig; *~ load*, werklas; werkvrag; *~ majority*, effektiewe meerderheid; groot genoeg meerderheid; *~-man*, arbeider, werk(s)=man; *~ model*, werkende model; *~-out*, raming, spesifikasie, berekening; *~ part*, bewegende deel (masjien); *~ party*, werkploeg; studiegroep; werkgemeenskap; *~ place*, werkplek; *~ plan*, werksplan; *~ plant*, bedryfsinstallasie; *~ profit*, bedryfswins; *~ stock*, bedryfsmateriaal; *~ stress*, werkspanning, toelaatbare spanning; *~ surface*, wrywingsvlak, draagvlak; *~ time*, werktyd; *~ voltage*, bedryfspanning; *~-woman*, werksvrou, werkster.

work: *~-less*, sonder werk, werkloos; *~-maid*, werkmeisie; *~ man*, werk(s)man; (pl) werkvolk, werk(s)=mense, werkliede; *it is a poor ~ man who quarrels with his tools*, 'n slegte ambagsman gee sy gereedskap die skuld; *~ men's compensation*, skadeloosstelling vir werk(s)mense; **W~ men's Compensation Act**, Skadeloosstellingswet; *~ men's compensation commissioner*, ongevallekommissaris; *~ men's insurance*, werkluiversekering; *~ manlike*, handig, deeglik afgewerk, knap, goed uitgevoer; vakkundig, saakkundig; *~ manship*, maaksel; vakmanskap, vakkennis; knapheid, handigheid; bewerking, afwerking, uitvoering, bekwaamheid, vaardigheid; *~ master*, voorman, opsigter; *~ mate*, werkmaat; *~-out*, oefening; *~ people*, werk(s)mense; *~-place*, werkplek; *~ reservation*, werkafbakening; *~-room*, werkkamer, werkplaas, werkplek, werksaal.

works, fabriek; werkplek; bedryf; aanleg (spoorweg; telefoon), bedrywigheid; ratwerk, masjinerie, installasie; binnegoed, werke (van skrywer); vestingwerke; *CLERK of ~*, werkeklerk, bouopsigter; *PUBLIC ~*, openbare werke; *~ account*, bedryfsrekening; *~ accountant*, bedryfsrekenmeester, bedryfsrekenaar; *~ chemist*, fabriekskeikundige; *~ clerk*, bouopsigter.

work: *~-seeker*, werksoeker; *~-seeking*, werksoekery; *~ engineer*, bedryfsingenieur; *~-sheet*, werkstaat; *~-shop*, werkplek, werkplaas, werkswinkel; *~-shy*, lui, werksku, arbeidsku, arbeidsonwillig; *~-shyness*, werkskuheid; *~ s' manager*, bedryfsleier; fabrieksbestuurder; *~-table*, werktafel; *~-ticket*, tydkaart, werkkaart; *~-woman*, werkster, werkvrou.

world, wêreld; die wêreldse lewe; die mensdom, mense; *ALL the ~*, die hele wêreld; *he was ALL the ~ to her*, hy was vir haar alles; *ALL the ~ over*, oor die hele wêreld; *ALONE in the ~*, alleen op die wêreld; *the ANIMAL ~*, die dierewêreld; *the ~ of ART*, die kunswêreld; *have the best of BOTH ~ s*, voordeel uit teenoorgestelde omstandighede trek; uiterstes probeer versoen; *BRING into the ~*, in die wêreld bring; *CARRY the ~ before one*, vinnig vooruitgaan; *~ of CHESS*, skaakwêreld; *a CITIZEN of the ~*, 'n wêreldburger; *in ~ CLASS*, van wêreldformaat; *the ~ to COME*, die hiernamaals; *it is a CRUEL ~*, die wêreld is wreed; *a ~ of DIFFERENCE*, 'n hemelsbreë verskil; *go DOWN in the ~*, agteruitgaan; *the ~ of DREAMS*, die droomwêreld; *to the ~'s END*, tot aan die end van die wêreld; *~ without END*, tot in ewigheid; *the ~ of FASHION*, die modekringe; *take the ~ as one FINDS it*, sake aanvaar soos hulle is; *the ~, the FLESH and the devil*, al die versoekings op aarde; *not FOR all the ~*, vir niks ter wêreld nie; *be prepared to GIVE the ~*, die wêreld wil gee; *GO out into the ~*, die wye wêreld ingaan; *it will do you a ~ of GOOD*, dit sal jou baie goed doen; *the GREAT ~*, die groot wêreld; *the ~ of IDEAS*, die ideëwêreld; *KNOW the ~*, jou wêreld ken; *all the ~ KNOWS*, almal weet; *for all the ~ LIKE*, presies soos (asof); *the LEARNED ~*, die geleerde wêreld; *the ~ of LITERATURE*, die letterkundige (literêre) wêreld; *LIVE out of the ~*, teruggetrokke leef; *LOOK for all the ~ like*, daar presies uitsien soos; *the LOWER ~*, die onderwêreld; *a MAN of the ~*, 'n man v.d. wêreld; *the NETHER ~*, die onderwêreld; *the NEXT ~*, die hiernamaals; *make a NOISE in the ~*, groot opspraak verwek; *NOT for the ~*, vir geen geld ter wêreld nie; *live OUT of the ~*, soos 'n kluisenaar lewe; *all's RIGHT with the ~*, dit gaan voor die wind; alles is reg; *what will the ~ SAY?* wat sal die mense daarvan sê? *let the ~ SLIDE*, sake hulle gang laat gaan; *it is a SMALL ~*, die wêreld is klein; berge en dale ontmoet mekaar; *the ~ of SPORT*, die sportwêreld; *all the ~'s a STAGE*, die wêreld is 'n speeltoneel; die wêreld is 'n pypkaneel, elk suig daaraan en kry sy deel; *they THINK the ~ of*, hulle dink wat wonders van; hulle het 'n besonder hoë dunk van; *THIRD ~*, derde wêreld; *out of THIS ~*, hemels, manjifiek; *be on the TOP of the ~*, in jou glorie wees; *he is on TOP of the ~*, die wêreld is syne; *the ~ seems TOPSY-TURVY*, die wêreld lyk onderstebo; *the WAY of the ~*, die wêreld se beloop; *know the WAYS of the ~*, weet wat daar in die wêreld te koop is (aangaan); *a ~ too WIDE*, ver (veels) te wyd; *all the ~ and his WIFE*, almal; Jan Rap en sy maat; *~-beater*, wêreldkampioen; *~ dominion*, wêreldheerskappy; *~-famous*, wêreldberoemd; *~ language*, wêreldtaal; *~ liness*, wêreldsgesindheid, wêreldsheid, aardsgesindheid; *~ ling*, wêreldling.

wor'ldly, wêreldsgesind, wêrelds, aards; *~-minded*, wêreldsgesind; *~-wise*, wêreldwys, ervare.

world: *~-old*, so oud soos die wêreld; so oud soos die Kaapse wapad; oeroud; *~ power*, wêreldryk; *~ record*, wêreldrekord; *~ scarcity*, wêreldskaarste; *~ state*, wêreldmoondheid; *~ supply*, wêreldvoorraad; *~ war*, wêreldoorlog; *~-weary*, lewensmoeg; *~-wide*, wêreldwyd, wêreld=.

worm, (n) wurm; ruspe(r); koelslang (stokery); koeëltrekker; krasser; skroefdraad (bout); nietige wurm, nieteling (mens); wroeging; *~ of CONSCIENCE*, gewetenswroeging; *I am a ~ TODAY*, ek is vandag geen pyp tabak werd nie; *even a ~ will TURN*, selfs die minste versit hom; (v) kruip; kronkel; wurm; wurms uitroei, van wurms suiwer (bevry); 'n skroefdraad sny in; wriemel; jou stilletjies inwerk, inkruip; (inligting) uitvis; *he ~ ed his ARM clear*, hy het sy arm losgewurm; *~ oneself into someone's CONFIDENCE*, jou in iem. se vertroue langs kronkelweë indring; *try to ~ a SECRET (information) out of*, met slimmigheid 'n geheim probeer agterkom; *~ one's WAY in*, jou êrens inwoel; *~-bearing*, wurmlaer; *~-bit*, skroefboor; *~-cast*, wurmhope, *~ drive*, wurmaandrywing; *~-eaten*, deur wurms gevreet, wurmstekig; verouderd; **fishing** visvang met wurmaas; *~-gear*, skroefrat; *~-hole*, wurmgat; *~-holed*, vol wurmgate; *~-killer*, wurmmiddel, wurmgif; *~-like*, wurmagtig; *~ powder*, wurmpoeier; *~'s-eye view*, wurmperspektief; *~-shaft*, wurmas; *~-shaped*, wurmvormig; *~-wheel*, wurmrat, skroefrat; *~ wood*, wildeals; absint; alsem; *~ y*, vol wurms; wurmagtig; laag, kruiperig.

worn, afgeleef, verslyt, gaar; afgesaag; uitgeput, moeg; *kyk* **wear**, (v); *~ with AGE*, afgeleef; *a ~ JOKE*, 'n ou grap; *be ~ OUT*, uitgeput wees; poot-

uit wees; uitgedien wees; ~-**out,** verslyt; verslete; vermoeid; verouderd; dol (draad van moer).
wo'rried, afgemat; gepla; bekommerd.
wo'rrier, kwelgees; kweller.
wo'rriment, verdriet, las, kwelling.
wo'rry, (n) **(worries),** kwelling, bekommernis, las, moeite; swaarte, gesanik, gekweldheid, sorg; gelol, getorring; gepluk, geskud; byt; (v) **(worried),** jou bekommer, jou kwel; pla, terg, seur; lastig val, verpes; peuter, lol, hinder, drein; afmartel, bekreun; pieker; tob; ruk aan, aan die gorrel pak; ~ *oneself ABOUT,* jou kwel oor; *don't* ~ *ABOUT the matter,* moenie oor die saak tob nie; moet jou nie daaroor bekommer nie; ~ *ALONG,* voortsukkel; *the dog worries a BONE,* die hond ruk en pluk aan 'n been; *I CAN'T* ~, ek gee geen flenter om nie; ~ *to DEATH,* tot die dood toe kwel; *DON'T let that* ~ *you,* maak jou nie sorge daaroor nie; laat dit jou nie kwel nie; ~ *a person INTO,* iem. verpes totdat; *we can* ~ *about that LATER,* dis vir later sorg; ~ *the LIFE out of someone,* iem. verpes; iem. gedurig lastig val; *do not* ~ *about the MORROW,* jou nie oor die dag van môre bekommer nie; ~ *OVER,* jou kwel om (oor); ~ *a PROBLEM out,* 'n vraagstuk sukkel-sukkel oplos; ~ *with QUESTIONS,* met vrae lastig val; ~ *a SECRET out,* 'n geheim uit iem. wurg (wurm); *WHY* ~*?* môre is ook 'n dag.
worse, (n) iets ergers (slegters); *from BAD to* ~, van kwaad tot erger; *a CHANGE (turn) for the* ~, 'n ongunstige wending; verslegting; *but* ~ *FOLLOWS,* die ergste kom nog; *HAVE the* ~ *of it,* die onderspit delf; die slegste daaraan toe wees; (a, adv) erger; slegter; *for BETTER, for* ~, in voor- en teëspoed; in lief en leed; *be the* ~ *for DRINK,* besope wees; *be the* ~ *FOR,* gely hê onder; *it is GETTING* ~, dit word slegter; *to MAKE matters* ~, tot oormaat van ramp; *it MIGHT have been* ~, dit kon nog erger gewees het; *he is NONE the* ~ *for it,* dit het hom geen kwaad gedoen nie; hy het geen nadeel daarvan ondervind nie; niks slegter daaraan toe wees nie; ~ *OFF,* in 'n ongunstiger (slegter) posisie; armer; *STILL* ~, tot oormaat van ramp; *the* ~ *for WEAR,* geslyt, verslete, toiingrig; *come out of something the* ~ *for WEAR,* kaal van iets afkom.
wors'en, vererger, erger word; agteruitgaan.
wor'ship, (n) aanbidding, verering; godsdiens, erediens; vergoding; edelheid; *HIS* ~, Sy Edelagbare; *PLACE of* ~, kerk; *PUBLIC* ~, erediens; *YOUR* ~, U Edelagbare; (v) **(-ped),** aanbid, vereer; veraf= go(o)d; kerk toe gaan; ~ *the golden CALF,* die goue kalf aanbid; ~ *the GROUND someone treads on,* iem. aanbid; ~ *the LORD,* die Here aanbid; ~**ful,** gesien, agbaar, edelagbaar, eerwaardig; ~**per,** aanbidder; vereerder; kerkganger.
worst, (n) ergste; slegste; *AT the* ~, in die allerergste geval; *AT his* ~, op sy slegste; *the* ~ *is still to COME,* „hef aan" lê nog voor; *if the* ~ *COMES to the* ~, in die ergste geval; as alles misloop; as die nood aan die man kom; *DO your* ~, doen wat jy wil, doen die ergste wat jy kan doen; *even though you may DO your* ~, al maak jy dit so erg moontlik; *HAVE (get) the* ~ *of,* die onderspit delf; aan die kortste end trek; daar die slegste van afkom; *things at their* ~ *will MEND,* dis die donkerste net voor dagbreek; dis die droogste net voor die reën; wanneer die toestand op die ergste is, kom daar verbetering; *the* ~ *of it is THAT . . .,* die ergste daarvan is dat . . .; (v) oorwin, verslaan, wen, uit= stof; (a) ergste; slegste.
wor'sted[1], (n) kamstof; (a) kam=, kamstof=.
wor'sted[2], (a) verslaan, oorwin; *BE* ~, die onderspit delf; ~ *BY,* uitgestof deur, verslaan deur.
wor'sted: ~ **cloth,** ~ **fabric,** ~ **material,** kamstof; ~ **mill,** kamstoffabriek; ~ **web,** kamgaringseil; ~ **yarn,** kamdraad, kamgaring.
wort, kruid; mout.
worth, (n) waarde; prys; verdienstelikheid, voortreflikheid; (a) werd; *for ALL he was* ~, uit alle mag; so vinnig as hy kon; *not* ~ *a BEAN,* geen bloue duit werd nie; *it is* ~ *a great DEAL of money,* dit is baie geld werd; *what is* ~ *DOING, is* ~ *doing well,* werk wat die moeite werd is, is die moeite werd; wat die moeite werd is, moet goed gedoen word; *he is* ~ *a FORTUNE,* hy besit 'n fortuin, hy is skatryk; *it is* ~ *HEARING,* dis die moeite werd om te hoor; ~ *KNOWING,* wetenswaardig; *not* ~ *MUCH,* min werd; nie veel om die lyf hê nie; *NOT* ~ *a rap,* geen bloue duit werd nie; ~ *NOTHING,* niks werd nie; *he is not* ~ *POWDER and shot,* 'n koeël is te goed vir hom; *RETAIL something for what it is* ~, iets vir dieselfde prys verkoop as dié waarvoor jy dit gekry het; *not* ~ *his SALT,* nie sy sout werd nie; ~ *SEEING,* besienswaardig; *SHOW one's* ~, wys van watter stoffasie jy gemaak is; *SELL something for what it is* ~, iets verkoop waarvoor dit werd is; iets vir dieselfde prys verkoop; *TAKE this for what it is* ~, nie vir die waarheid daarvan instaan nie; ~ *the TROUBLE,* die moeite werd; ~ *WHILE,* die moeite werd; ~**ily,** waardig; ~**iness,** waardigheid; ~**less,** waardeloos, vrotsig, uitgedien(d), nikswerd; ~*less shares,* waardelose aandele, snertaandele; ~**lessness,** waardeloosheid; vrotsigheid.
wor'thy, (n) *(.. thies),* verdienstelike persoon, agtens= waardige mens; beroemdheid; (a) waardig; agtens= waardig; werd; *a CAUSE* ~ *of support,* 'n saak wat ondersteuning verdien; *the LABOURER is* ~ *of his hire,* die arbeider is sy loon werd; *a* ~ *MAN,* 'n agtenswaardige man; *NOT* ~, onwaardig; *NOT* ~ *of,* nie werd nie om.
worth'while, verdienstelik, waardevol.
wot, weet; *God* ~, God weet; *kyk* **wit**[2].
would, wou; *kyk* **will,** (v); *DO what he* ~ *. . .,* wat hy ook al gedoen het; ~ *to GOD that . . .,* mag God gee dat . . .; ~ *to HEAVEN I were gone,* was ek maar liewer weg; ~ *it were OTHERWISE,* was dit tog maar anders; *the WOUND* ~ *not heal,* die wond wou nie gesond word nie; ~-**be,** kastig, sogenaamd; in-die-dop, aanstaande; aspirant; ~-*be leaders,* aspirant-leiers.
wound[1], (v) *kyk* **wind**[1].
wound[2], (n) wond, kwetsuur, besering, seerplek; *reopen old* ~*s,* ou wonde oopkrap; (v) wond, kwes; krenk, seermaak; ~ *to the QUICK,* diep wonde slaan; ~ *someone's SELF-RESPECT,* iem. in sy eer krenk; ~**able,** wondbaar, kwesbaar; ~-**dresser,** wondverbinder; ~**ed,** gekwes, gewond; *the* ~*ed,* die gewondes; ~-**fever,** wondkoors; ~ **wort,** wondkruid, betonie.
wov'en, geweef; (v); *kyk* ~ **fabric,** weefstof.
wove' paper, velynpapier.
wow, (n) suksesstuk; treffer; (interj) wat!
wrack, seewier; aanspoelsel, wrakgoed.
wraith, gees, skim; dubbelganger.
wra'ngle, (n) twis, rusie, stryery; struweling; (v) twis, rusie maak, haspel, stry, redetwis; ~ *over (about) small points,* twis oor nietighede; ~**r,** rusiemaker, twissoeker; geslaagde in die eerste klas (Cambridge).
wra'ngling, geharwar, gekrakeel, gerusie, (gerede)= twis, gestry, stryery.
wrap, (n) omhulsel; reisdeken; halsdoek, serp; om= slag, mantel; tjalie; (v) **(-ped),** (in)wikkel, toedraai; hul; inrol; toemaak; ~*ped in PAPER,* in papier toegedraai; ~ *ROUND,* toedraai; toemaak; ~ *UP,* verpak; toerol, omwikkel.
wrapped, toegedraai; toegemaak; ingerol; ~ *in DARKNESS,* in duisternis gehul; ~ *in MIST,* toe v.d. mis; ~ *in OBSCURITY,* in duisternis gehul; ~ *in SLEEP,* vas aan die slaap; ~ *in THOUGHT,* in gepeins versink; verdiep in gedagte; *be* ~ *UP in,* verdiep in; besete deur; versink in.
wrap: ~**page,** omhulsel, omslag; ~**per,** omslag; pak= papier; omwindsel; dekblad (sigaar); huisjas, ja= pon; reisdeken; inpakker; ~**per-plate,** mantelplaat; ~**ping,** (n) omslag; pakpapier; (die) inpak; (die) toedraai; verpakking; wikkeling; (a) toemaak=, pak=, toedraaiend; ~**ping material,** toemaakgoed; pakgoed; ~**ping paper,** pakpapier.
wrasse, lipvis.
wrath, gramskap, toorn, toornigheid, grimmigheid, verbolgenheid, vergramdheid; ~**ful,** boos, kwaad, toornig, vergramd, woedend, verbolge; ~**fulness,** boosheid, gramskap.

wreak, wreek; lug gee aan, koel; ~ *vengeance on*, jou wraak koel op; ~**er**, wreker.

wreath, krans; blomkrans, guirlande; kring, ring; vlegsel, wrong (hare).

wreathe, bekrans, omkrans; (be)strengel; 'n krans vleg, krul; kronkel; verwring; ~ *one's ARMS round someone*, jou arms om iem. strengel; ~*d IN smiles*, die ene glimlag.

wreath'y, gedraai, gekronkel; bekrans.

wreck, (n) wrak; skipbreuk, die vergaan (van 'n skip); verwoesting, ondergang; armsalige oorblyfsel, ruïne; strandgoed, wrakgoed; *he is a nervous* ~, hy is 'n senuweewrak; (v) vernietig, te gronde rig; skipbreuk laat ly; strand, vergaan; laat misluk; demonteer; afbreek, aftakel; ~ *someone's LIFE*, iem. se lewe verwoes; ~ *a TRAIN*, 'n trein laat verongeluk; ~ *age*, wrak; wrakgoed, wrakhout; oorblyfsels, bouvalle; ~ **buoy**, wrakboei.

wrecked, gestrand, vergaan; verongeluk; geknak; ~ *GOODS*, wrakgoed; ~ *HOPES*, vernietigde hoop (verwagtinge); ~ *SAILORS*, skipbreukelinge.

wreck: ~**er**, verwoester; vernieler; sloper (gebou); stranddief; berger (van wrakgoed); ~**ing**, verongelukking; vernieling, verwoesting; berging; aftakeling; ~**ing association**, bergingsmaatskappy; ~**ing-bar**, breekyster; ~ **master**, strandvoog.

wren, winterkoninkie.

wrench, (n) (-es), skroefsleutel, moersleutel; verrekking, verwringing; verstuiting; ruk, draai; moeilike skeiding; woordverdraaiing; *a GREAT* ~, 'n smartlike verlies; *NOT without a* ~, nie sonder smart nie; *PARTING was a hard* ~, die afskeid was pynlik; (v) verdraai, verwring, verrek; ruk; verstuit; wring, draai; ~ *AWAY*, wegruk; ~ *from the CONTEXT*, uit die verband ruk; ~ *FROM*, ontruk, afneem; ~ *OPEN*, oopbreek, oopruk; ~**ing**, wringing.

wrest, (n) draai, ruk; stemsleutel; (v) uitruk; draai, wring; ~ *FROM*, ontruk, ontworstel; afpers; afdwing; ~ *a SECRET from someone*, 'n geheim van iem. afdwing; ~ *a WORD*, die betekenis van 'n woord verdraai.

wre'stle, (n) worstelstryd, worsteling; geworstel, stoeiery; stoeiwedstryd, worstelwedstryd; (v) worstel, stoei; ~ *with GOD*, met die Here worstel; ~ *in PRAYER*, vurig bid; ~ *with TEMPTATION*, teen die versoeking stry; ~ **r**, worstelaar, stoeier.

wre'stling, (n) (die) stoei, stoeiery; worsteling; *ALL-IN* ~, rofstoei; *PROFESSIONAL* ~, beroepstoei; (a) stoei-, stoeiend, worstelend, worstel-; ~ **arena**, stoeikryt; ~ **match**, stoeiwedstryd; ~ **place**, worstelplek, worstelperk; ~ **ring**, stoeikryt.

wretch, (-es), ellendeling, skurk, onverlaat, snoodaard; sukkelaar, ongelukkige drommel; ~ **ed**, ellendig, jammerlik, lamlendig, miserabel, erbarmlik, beroerd; stom, ongelukkig; veragtelik; vervlakste; ~**edness**, ellende, armoede, erbarmlikheid, ellendigheid; rampsaligheid, misère.

wrick, (n) verrekking; *a* ~ *in the neck*, 'n stywe nek; (v) verrek, verdraai; *kyk* **rick**.

wrig'gle, (n) kronkeling; gewriemel; gekronkel; (v) woel, vroetel; kronkel, kriewel; (in)wikkel; wring; ~ *into one's CLOTHES*, jou in jou klere inwikkel; ~ *out of a DIFFICULTY*, deur uitvlugte jou uit 'n moeilikheid loswikkel; ~ *OUT*, uitdraai; ~ *OUT of something*, jou uit iets uitdraai; loskom, loswurm; ~**r**, draaier; wriemelaar; muskietlarwe; flikflooier.

wright, bouer; maker; vakman

wring, (n) druk, draai; wringing; (v) *out* (**wrung**), wring, uitdraai; verdraai; pers, druk; ~ *out CLOTHES*, klere uitdraai (uitdroog); ~ *a CONFESSION from*, 'n bekentenis afdwing van; ~ *FROM*, afvorder van; ~ *someone's HAND*, iem. 'n stywe handdruk gee; ~ *one's HANDS*, jou hande wring; *it* ~ *s my HEART*, dit folter (pynig) my; ~ *MONEY out of*, geld afpers van; ~ *someone's NECK*, iem. se nek omdraai; *his SOUL was wrung with agony*, hy het in hewige sielsangs verkeer; ~ *TEARS from*, trane pers uit; ~**er**, verdrukker; afperser; draaimasjien.

wring'ing, wringing; ~ **machine**, wringmasjien; ~**wet**, papnat.

wri'nkle, (n) rimpel, plooi; riffel; riffeling; kreukel; plannetjie; (v) rimpel, plooi; riffel; kreukel; ~ *the forehead*, die voorkop op 'n plooi trek; ~**d**, gerimpel(d); ~*d with age*, gerimpel deur die ouderdom.

wri'nkly, vol kreukels; vol rimpels; gerimpel; opgekrimp.

wrist, handgewrig, pols(gewrig); ~ **action**, polswerk; ~**-ball**, polsbal; ~**band**, mansjet; armband; ~**-drop**, neerhangende pols, polsverlamming; ~**-glove**, polsmoffie; ~**-guard**, polsskerm, polsskut; ~**let**, armband; polsskerm, polsband; ~**-roll**, draai van die arm (gewrig); ~(**let**) **watch**, polsoorlosie; ~**-strap**, polsband.

writ, (n) skrif; bevel; bevelskrif; geskrif; dagvaarding, lasbrief; aanskrywing; sommasie, dwangbevel; ~ *of EXPULSION*, uitsettingsbevel, uitsettingsdekreet; *HOLY W*~, die Heilige Skrif; *SERVE a* ~ *on someone*, 'n dagvaarding aan (op) iem. bestel; (v) *kyk* **write**; *COUNTRY COUSIN* ~ *large on him*, dis duidelik dat hy 'n plaasjapie is.

write, (**wrote**, **written**), skrywe, skryf; skriftelik uitdruk; neerskryf; opskryf; ~ *AWAY*, sommer skryf; aanhou skrywe; ~ *BACK*, terugskrywe; ~ *a CHEQUE*, 'n tjek uitskryf; ~ *DOWN*, opskryf, opteken; afskryf; afkam, afmaak; skriftelik weerlê; neerhalend skryf van; ~ *him off as a FOOL*, hom as 'n dwaas beskou (afskryf); *he* ~*s a good HAND*, hy skryf mooi, hy het 'n mooi handskrif; *nothing to* ~ *HOME about*, niks besonders nie; ~ *in INK*, skryf met ink; ~ *INTO*, inskryf; *writ LARGE*, aan alles merkbaar; ~ *OFF*, afskryf; *when a car is 2 years old you can* ~ *R400 OFF its initial value*, as 'n motor 2 jaar oud is, kan jy R400 aftrek van sy oorspronklike koopprys; ~ *ON*, skryf op; aanhou skryf; ~ *OUT*, uitskryf (rekeninge); oorskryf; ~ *oneself OUT*, niks meer hê om oor te skryf nie; ~ *for the PAPERS*, in (vir) die koerante skryf; ~ *to the SECRETARY*, skryf aan die sekretaris; ~ *UP*, neerskryf, uitwerk; bywerk; byhou, byskryf (boekhou); in besonderhede beskrywe; ophemel; opvysel; ~**-off**, afskrywing; kwytskelding.

writ'er, skrywer, outeur; klerk; versekeraar; skryfster; ~ *for the press*, joernalis, persman; ~**'s cramp**, skryfkramp; ~ **ship**, skrywerskap.

write'-up, ophemeling, opvyseling; breedvoerige beskrywing; verwatering van 'n bate.

writhe, draai; wring; (inmekaar)krimp; ~ *AT*, ineenkrimp by; ~ *with PAIN*, krimp van pyn; ~ *with SHAME*, ineenkrimp van skaamte.

writh'ing, wringing.

writ'ing, skrif; geskrif; skrywe, skrywery; beskrywing; opskrif; styl; (pl) werke, geskrifte; *COMMIT to* ~, neerskrywe; op skrif bring; swart op wit sit; *IN* ~, skriftelik; op skrif; *MANIA for* ~, skryfwoede; *MANNER (style) of* ~, skryfwyse; *PASSION for* ~, skryflus; *PUT something in* ~, iets op skrif stel; ~ *on the WALL*, skrif aan die muur; ernstige waarskuwing; *the* ~ *is on the WALL*, die skrif is aan die muur; ~**-book**, skryfboek; ~**-case**, skryftassie; skryfkissie; ~**-desk**, lessenaar, skryftafel, skryfburo; ~**-ink**, skryfink; ~**-materials**, skryfbehoeftes, skryfgereedskap; ~**-pad**, skryfblok; ~**-paper**, skryfpapier; ~**-room**, skryfkamer; ~**-saloon**, skryfsalon; ~**-table**, skryftafel, lessenaar.

writt'en, geskrewe; skriftelik; op skrif; *a* ~ *CONSTITUTION*, 'n geskrewe konstitusie; ~ *EXAMINATION*, skriftelike eksamen; *it IS* ~ *that*, daar staan geskrywe dat; *the* ~ *LANGUAGE*, die skryftaal; ~ *in WATER*, kortstondig.

wrong, (n) onreg; oortreding; kwaad, ongelyk, *BOTH are in the* ~, hulle is albei verkeerd; *DO* ~ *to*, veronreg, onreg aandoen; *IN the* ~, ongelyk hê; verkeerd wees; *the KING can do no* ~, die koning is onskendbaar; *PUT someone in the* ~, iem. die skuld gee; iem. in die ongelyk stel; *TWO* ~*s don't make a right*, 'n tweede fout maak nie die eerste reg nie; twee maal swart is nie wit nie; (v) kwaad doen; onreg aandoen, onbillik behandel; te kort doen, verongelyk, veronreg; ~ *a person*, iem. 'n onreg aandoen; (a) verkeerd; foutief; onjuis; abuis; nie in orde nie, nie in die haak nie; *give the* ~ *ANSWER*, die verkeerde antwoord gee; *BE* ~, verkeerd wees; ongelyk hê; *get out of BED on the* ~ *side*, met die verkeerde voet uit die bed stap; *in the* ~ *BOX*, in die verknorsing; in die moeilikheid; by die verkeerde adres; *DO something* ~, 'n misstap begaan; *get hold of the* ~ *END of the stick*, iets aan die verkeerde ent beetkry; *catch on the* ~ *FOOT*, onverhoeds betrap; ~ *in the HEAD*, getik; *there is NOTHING* ~ *with that*, daar is niks verkeerd daarmee nie; ~ *SIDE out*, binneste buitekant; *on the* ~ *SIDE of the blanket*, buite-egtelik (gebore); *on the* ~ *SIDE of fifty*, oor die vyftig; ~ *SIDE up*, onderstebo; *it went down the* ~ *WAY*, dit het in 'die verkeerde keelgat gekom; *set about something in the* ~ *WAY*, sake agterstevoor aanpak; agterstevoor te werk gaan; *WHAT is* ~? wat makeer? (adv) mis, verkeerd; *DO* ~, verkeerd handel, kwaad doen; *GO* ~, 'n fout begaan (maak); spaak loop; verkeerd doen; verdwaal; die verkeerde weg opgaan; misloop; *everything WENT* ~, alles het verkeerd geloop; ~ **doer**, kwaaddoener; oortreder; ~ **doing**, (die) kwaad doen; oortreding; sonde.

wrong'ful, onregverdig, onbillik; wederregtelik, verkeerd; ~ *ACT*, onregmatige daad; ~ *ARREST*, wederregtelike inhegtenisneming; ~ *DISMISSAL*, ongegronde ontslag; ~**ly**, verkeerdelik;

~*ly and unlawfully*, wederregtelik; ~**ness**, onregverdigheid, onbillikheid; wederregtelikheid.

wrong: ~-**headed**, dwars, verkeerd, eiewys, eiesinnig; ~**ly**, verkeerdelik; ten onregte; ~**ness**, verkeerdheid.

wrote, *kyk* **write**.

wroth, toornig, gramstorig; *be* ~ *with someone*, boos wees vir iem.

wrought, gevorm; bewerk; gesmee; verwerk; geskaaf; *kyk* **work**, (v); *become* ~ *up about something*, iets jou in jou siel laat versondig; ~ **copper**, smeekoper; ~ **iron**, smeeyster; werkyster; ~ **silver**, gedrewe silwer; ~ **steel**, smeestaal; ~-**up**, opgewonde, hooggespanne, histeries, oorprikkel.

wrung, *kyk* **wring**, (v)

wry, skeef, windskeef; verdraai; knorrig; *make a* ~ *FACE*, 'n suur gesig trek; *give someone a* ~ *LOOK*, iem. skeef aankyk; ~-**legged**, met gedraaide bene; ~**ly**, suur; skeef; *REMARK* ~ *ly*, ewe knorrig (suur) opmerk; *SMILE* ~ *ly*, suur glimlag; ~ **mouth**, skeefbek (vis); ~-**mouthed**, skewemond=; ~ **neck**, draaihals (voël); skewe nek; skeefnek; ~-**necked**, met 'n skewe nek; ~**ness**, skeefheid; knorrigheid.

Wy'andotte, Wyandotte(hoender).

wych'-elm, bergiep.

wye, Y; Y-vormige ding; Y-stuk; Y-pyp.

wynd, straatjie, stegie, gangetjie.

wyv'ern, gevleuelde draak.

X

x, (**xs**, **x's**), x; *little* ~, x'ie.

xan'thene, xanteen.

xanth'in(e), xantine, xantien.

Xanthipp'e, Xantippe; boosaardige vrou.

xan'thophyll, blaargeel, bladgeel, xantofiel.

xan'thous, geel; Mongools.

xab'ec, driemaster, sjebek.

xen'oblast, xenoblas.

xen'ocryst, xenokrist.

xenog'amy, kruisbevrugting, xenogamie.

xen'olite, xenoliet.

xen'olith, xenoliet.

xenoman'ia, voorliefde vir die buiteland, xenomanie.

xen'omorph, xenomorf.

xenomorph'ic, vreemdvormig, nie-eievormig.

xenophob'ia, vreemdelingevrees, xenofobie.

xeroph'agy, dieet van droë kos; xerofagie.

xeroph'ilous, teen droogte bestand.

xer'ophyte, dorslandplant, woestynplant, xerofiet.

xerophy'tic, dorsland=, woestyn=, xerofities.

xero'sis, uitdroging, xerose.

Xho'sa, Xhosa, Kōsa.

xiph'ias, swaardvis.

xiph'oid, swaardvormig.

X'mas, *abbr. for* **Christmas**, Kersfees.

X'-ray, (n) (-s), X-straal, röntgenstraal; (v) bestraal, met X-strale behandel; onder die ligte kom; ~ **machine**, röntgenmasjien; ~ **radiation**, röntgenstraling; ~ **treatment**, X-straalbehandeling; ~ **tube**, röntgenbuis.

xyl'em, houtweefsel, xileem.

xyl'ograph, houtsnee, houtgravure, xilografie.

xylog'rapher, houtgraveur, xilograaf.

xylograph'ic, xilografies.

xylog'raphy, houtsnykuns, houtgraveerkuns, xilografie.

xyl'oid, houtagtig.

xylol'ogy, houtkunde.

xyl'onite, selluloïed, selluloïde.

xyloph'agous, houtvretend.

xyl'ophone, xilofoon.

xyl'ose, houtsuiker, xilose.

xys'ter, beenskraper, krapystertjie.

xys'tus, (..ti), laan; oordekte suilegang; xistus.

Y

y, (**ys**, **y's**), y; *little* ~, y'tjie; ~ *is a crooked letter and you can't make it straight*, sommer het nie rede nie (skilpad het nie vere nie, jakkals dra nie klere nie); omdat hoekom 'n draai is.

yacht, (n) (seil)jag; (v) in 'n jag seil; ~-**club**, jagklub, seilbootklub; ~**er**, (seil)jagvaarder; ~**ing**, (die) seil met 'n jag; seiljagsport; ~**ing basin**, jagbassin, (seil)jaghawe; ~**s'man**, (seil)jagvaarder; ~**s'manship**, (seil)jagkuns; ~**s'woman**, (seil)jagvaarster.

yaff'il, **yaf'fle**, groen houtkapper (voël).

yah! ba! boe! wê!

yahoo', bees, verdierlikte mens.

Yahveh', Jahwe(h), Jehova.

yak, knoros, brulos, jak.

yam, broodwortel.

Yank[1], *abbr. of* **Yankee**.

yank[2], (n) ruk; (v) ruk, pluk, trek.

Yank'ee, (n) Amerikaner, Yankee; (a) Amerikaans, Amerikaner=, Yankee=; ~ *Doodle (Dandy)*, Amerikaanse volksliedjie; ~ **dom**, die Amerikaners; Amerikanerdom; ~**fied**, veramerikaans; ~**fy**, (..fied), veramerikaans; ~**ism**, Amerikanisme, Yankeeïsme.

yap, (n) geblaf; (v) (**-ped**), blaf, kef; babbel.

yapp, slap boekband; lipomslag, lipband.

yapp: ~**er**, keffer, hakskeenbyter; ~**ing**, geblaf; geklets, gebabbel.

yard[1], (n) werf, agterplaas, erf; (v) kraal; bewaar.

yard[2], (n) jaart, tree; ra (seil); *BY the* ~, by die el; tot in die oneindige; *THE Y* ~, Scotland Yard.

yard'age[1], bewaargeld, werfgeld.

yard'age[2], jaartmaat.

yard'-arm, nok v.d. ra.
yard'-master, rangeermeester.
yard'-measure, maatstok, duimstok.
yard: ~ **s'man,** werfwagter; ~ **sneaker,** ~ **snoozer,** sluipslaper.
yard'stick, maatstok; *measure things by the SAME* ~, almal oor dieselfde kam skeer; met dieselfde mate meet; *have TWO different* ~ *s*, met twee mate meet.
yarn, (n) storie; grap; draad, gare, garing; *spin a LONG* ~, lank van draad (stof) wees; *SPIN a good* ~, 'n goeie storie vertel; *SPIN someone a* ~, iem. 'n storie vertel; *SPINNER of* ~ *s*, grapverteller; *SWOP* ~ *s*, mekaar stories vertel.
ya'rrow, duisendblad.
yash'mak, sluier (van Mohammedaanse vroue).
ya'taghan, Turkse sabel, kromswaard.
yaw, (n) slingering, afwyking; gier; (v) skuins loop, slinger, skud; gier; ~ **-axis,** gieras; ~ **angle,** gierhoek; ~ **-indicator,** gieraanwyser; ~ **ing angle,** gierhoek; ~ **ing plane,** giervlak.
yawl¹, (n) klein seiljag; jol.
yawl², (n) skreeu; (v) skreeu, tjank, joel
yawn, (n) gaap; *smother a* ~, 'n gaap smoor; (v) gaap; ~ **er,** gaper; ~ **ing,** gegaap; ~ **y,** gaperig.
yaws, framboesia, frambesia, buba.
yclept', (spottend vir) genoem, genaamd.
ye, u; julle, jul; *how d'* ~ *DO?* aangenaam! bly u te ken(ne)! hoe gaan dit? ~ *GODS and little fishes!* goeie genade!
yea, ja; *LET your* ~ *be* ~ *and your nay nay*, laat jou ja ja wees en jou nee nee; *not to SAY* ~ *or nay*, ja-nee sê.
yean, (v) lam; ~ **ling,** lammetjie.
year, jaar, jaartal; ~ *s and* ~ *s AGO*, jare der jare gelede; ~ *s AND* ~ *s*, jare der jare; ~ *of ASSESSMENT*, aanslagjaar; *have many* ~ *s BEHIND one*, baie jare agter die rug hê; ~ *s know more than BOOKS*, die verstand kom met die jare; ~ *BY* ~, jaar na jaar; *CALENDAR* ~, kalenderjaar; *he CARRIES his* ~ *s well*, hy dra sy jare goed; *in the COURSE of the* ~ *s*, in die loop v.d. jare; met die jare; *the CURRENT* ~, die lopende jaar; *this DAY* ~, vandag oor 'n jaar; *for DONKEY'S* ~ *s*, vir baie jare; *in the* ~ *'S DOT (one)*, in die jaar nul; *FINANCIAL* ~, boekjaar; *FOR* ~ *s and* ~ *s*, jare der jare; *FROM* ~ *'s end to* ~ *'s end; FROM one* ~ *'s end to another*, v.d. een jaar na die ander; van jaar tot jaar; *FULL of* ~ *s*, sat van dae; ~ *of GRACE*, jaar (in die Christelike jaartelling); ~ *IN,* ~ *out*, jaar in, jaar uit; *getting on IN* ~ *s*, begin oud word; *the* ~ *before LAST*, voorverlede jaar; *the* ~ *s that the LOCUSTS have eaten*, die sprinkaanjare; *this time NEXT* ~, hierdie tyd volgende jaar; *NEXT* ~, volgende (aanstaande) jaar; *NOT for many* ~ *s*, nie vir baie jare nie; *ONCE a* ~, een maal per jaar; *PER* ~, per jaar; *the whole* ~ *ROUND*, die hele jaar deur, ~ *of SERVICE*, diensjaar; *THIS* ~, vanjaar; *in a* ~ *'S TIME*, oor 'n jaar; *he is YOUNG for his* ~ *s*, hy is jonk vir sy jare; hy dra sy jare goed; *THREE or more* ~ *s*, drie jaar of langer; *be WELL on in* ~ *s*, na die ou kant toe staan; ~ **-book,** jaarboek; ~ **-end,** jaareinde; ~ **ling,** (n) jaaroud dier (perd, ens.); (a) jaaroud, eenjarig; ~ **ly,** jaarliks.
yearn, sterk verlang, smag, hunker, snak, reikhals; medelye voel; ~ *for (after) love*, smag na liefde; ~ **ing,** (n) vurige verlange, hunkering, reikhalsing; (a) verlangend, smagtend.
year' old, jaaroud, een jaar oud.
yeast, suurdeeg; gis; skuim; ~ **bread,** suurdeegbrood; ~ **iness,** skuimerigheid; gisting; oppervlakkigheid; voosheid; ~ **plant,** gisplantjie; ~ **powder,** bakpoeier, gispoeier; ~ **starter,** suurdeegplantjie; ~ **vitamine,** gisvitamine; ~ **y,** suurdeegagtig; gistend, skuimend; oppervlakkig.
yegg, (-s), **yegg'man,** (..men), inbreker, brandkasdief.
yelk, *kyk* **yolk.**
yell, (n) gil, skreeu, angskreet; (v) gil, skreeu, (uit)gier; ~ *with*, dit uitskreeu van; ~ **ing,** (n) geskreeu, gegier, gegil; gehuil; (a) skreeuend.
yell'ow, (n) geel; *the* ~ *s*, geelsug; jaloesie; (v) geel word; geel maak; vergeel; (a) geel; jaloers, afgunstig; agterdogtig; lafhartig; ~ **back,** goedkoop roman; ~ **-bill,** geelbek; ~ **-bill duck,** geelbekeend; ~ **boy,** geelvink; goudstuk; ~ **brass,** geelkoper; ~ **cross,** mosterdgas; ~ **-dun,** geel; ~ **fever,** geelkoors; ~ **flag,** geel vlag, kwarantynvlag; geel iris; ~ **-grey,** geelskimmel (perd); ~ **-gum,** suiglinggeelsug; ~ **hammer,** vlasvink; ~ **ing,** vergeling, geelwording; ~ **ish,** gelerig; **Y** ~ **Jack,** geelkoors; ~ **jack,** kwarantynvlag, geel vlag; ~ **maize,** geelmielies; ~ **ness,** geelheid; ~ **peach,** geelperske; ~ **peril,** die geel gevaar; ~ **press,** sensasiepers; ~ **rice,** vandisierys, begrafnisrys, geelrys (met rosyntjies); ~ **sickness,** geelsug; ~ **-skinned,** geelvellig; ~ **soap,** geel seep; ~ **spot,** geel kolletjie (in oog); ~ **sugar,** geel suiker; ~ **tail,** halfkoord, albakoor; ~ **-wood,** geelhout; ~ **y,** gelerig, geelagtig.
yelp, (n) getjank, gekef; (v) tjank, kef; ~ **er,** keffer, tjanker.
yen¹, jen (Japanse muntstuk).
yen², (sl.), hewige begeerte, verlange, hunkering, drang (*kyk* **yearn(ing)**).
yeo'man, (..men), grondeienaar; lyfwag (Engeland); *hofbediende*; berede soldaat; vry boer; ~ *of the GUARD*, soldaat v.d. lyfwag; *RENDER* ~ *('s) service*, onskatbare hulp verleen (in tyd van nood); ~ **ry,** landmilisie, berede milisie; grondbesitters.
yes, (-es), ja; jawel; *say* ~, toestem, ja sê; ~ **-man,** jaseer; sikofant.
yes'terday, gister; ~ *AFTERNOON*, gistermiddag; *the DAY before* ~, eergister; ~ *MORNING*, gistermôre.
yes'ter-eve, (digterlik vir) gisteraand.
yes'termorn, (digterlik vir) gisteroggend.
yes'teryear, (digterlik vir) verlede jaar; die onlangs verlede.
yet, (adv) nog; egter, edog (vero.), maar nogtans, ewenwel; al; tog; tot nog toe; immers; ~ *AGAIN*, telkens weer; *AS* ~, voorlopig; tot nog toe; ~ *AWHILE*, vereers; *he is not DEAD* ~, hy is nog nie dood nie; ~ *to be DONE*, nog te doen; *not JUST* ~, nie nou al nie; *I have* ~ *to LEARN*..., ek het nog nooit gehoor...; *NEVER* ~, nog nooit; ~ *NEVERTHELESS*, maar nietemin; *NOR* ~, en ook nie; *NOT* ~, nog nie; *there is* ~ *TIME*, daar is nog tyd; *and* ~ *TRUE*, en tog waar; (conj) en tog, maar; *strange* ~ *true*, vreemd maar tog waar.
yet'i, jeti, afskuwelike sneeumens.
yew, taksusboom.
Yidd'ish, Jiddisj, Jodeduits, Jodetaal; ~ **er,** (n) Jood; (a) Joods.
yield, (n) opbrengs, produksie (myn); rendement; vloei (fontein); oes; (v) oplewer, opbring, afwerp, voortbring, inbring, produseer; ingee; toestaan, swig; gelok; oorgee; afstaan, opgee; wyk; verleen; meegee; toegee, voorrang gee (by pad); ~ *CONSENT*, toestemming gee; ~ *to DESPAIR*, jou aan wanhoop oorgee; ~ *to superior FORCE*, vir die oormag swig; ~ *up the GHOST*, die gees gee; *not* ~ *an INCH*, nie 'n duim wyk nie; ~ *the PALM to someone*, die veld ruim; vir iem. onderdoen; ~ *a POINT*, iets toegee; iets gewonne gee; ~ *PRECEDENCE to*, voorrang gee aan; ~ *oneself PRISONER*, jou gevange gee; ~ *PROFIT*, wins oplewer; voordeel afwerp; ~ *to a REQUEST*, 'n versoek toestaan; *the TAX will* ~ *the required revenue*, die belasting sal die verlangde som opbring; ~ *to TEMPTATION*, vir die verleiding swig; ~ *to the TIMES*, jou skik na tydsomstandighede; ~ *to TREATMENT*, met welslae behandel word; ~ *UP*, uitlewer; ~ *WELL*, goed dra; ~ **ing,** (n) oorhandiging; oplewering; toegewing; produktiwiteit; (a) produktief; toegewend, buigsaam, meegewend; ~ **point,** elastisiteitsgrens; ~ **-road,** toegepad; ~ **sign,** toegeeteken, voorrangteken.
yod'el, (n) gejodel; (v) **(-led),** jodel.
yog'a, joga, Hindoeaskese.
yog'hurt, jogurt (dikmelk), bakteriedikmelk, kunsmatige dikmelk.
yog'i, Indiese wysgeer, kluisenaar, jogi.
yo'-heave-ho', vat! (los) vat! trek! (skiet) trek!
yoho'! joho!

yoke, (n) juk; dwarsstuk, skouerstrook, skouerstuk (naaldwerk); (huweliks)band; *BEAR the* ~ *in one's youth,* die juk in jou jeug dra; *IN the* ~, in die juk; *bend his NECK to the* ~, sy nek onder die juk buig; *a* ~ *of OXEN,* twee osse (onder die juk); *PASS under the* ~, onder die juk kom; *PUT the* ~ *upon,* in die eg verbind; *SEND under the* ~, die juk oplê; *SUBMIT (yield) to the* ~, onder die juk buig; *THROW off the* ~, die juk afgooi; (v) inspan, die juk oplê; koppel; verenig, saamvoeg; saamtrek; ~-**bone,** jukbeen; ~**fellow,** eggenoot, eggenote; maat.
yolk, eiergeel, dooier; wolvet; *double* ~, dubbeldoor; ~-**bag,** ~-**sac,** geelsakkie, dooiersak; ~**y,** vetterig.
yok'el, takhaar, agtervelder, plaasjapie, lummel.
yoke: ~ **mate,** eggenoot, eggenote; maat; ~-**piece,** bostuk (van hemp); ~-**pin,** jukskei.
Yom Kip'pur, Joom Kippoer, Groot Versoendag.
yon, daardie, ginds.
yon'der, (a) daardie, ginds, gene; (adv) gunter, daar, daarso, daar ginds, daar gunter; *over* ~, daar oorkant; daar gunter.
yore, die ou tyd, vanmelewe; *in DAYS of* ~, in toeka se dae; vanmelewe; in vroeër dae; in die dae van olim; *OF* ~, van ouds.
york'er, duikbal, streepbal (kr.).
York'shire, Yorkshire; *come* ~ *over,* iem. fop (kul); ~ **pudding,** deegtoespys, Yorkshirepoeding.
you, jy, jou; julle; u (beleef); ~ *IDIOT,* jou swaap; ~ *NEVER can tell,* 'n mens weet nooit nie; ~ *soon get USED to it,* 'n mens raak gou daaraan gewoon(d).
young, (n) kleintjie; ~ *and OLD,* jonk en oud; *THE* ~, die jongmense; *WITH* ~, dragtig; (a) jong, jeugdig; baar, onervare; klein; *a* ~ *BLOOD,* 'n jong bog; 'n swierbol; *in one's* ~ *DAYS,* in jou jonger jare; ~ *FOR his age,* jonk vir sy jare; *the* ~ *in HEART,* die jeugdiges van gees; ~ *JONES,* die jong Jones; ~ *MAN,* jong man; *her* ~ *MAN,* haar kêrel; *the NIGHT is yet* ~, dis nog vroeg; *one is only* ~ *ONCE,* 'n mens is net een maal jonk; *the* ~ *ONES,* die jongspan; ~ *PEOPLE,* jongmense; ~ *SAINT, old devil,* jonk vroom, oud boos; *not as* ~ *as one USED to be,* nie meer so danig jonk nie; ~ *in YEARS,* jonk van dae.

young'berry, (..**berries),** youngbessie.
young: ~**er,** jonger; jongste (van twee); *the* ~**er set,** die jongspan; ~**ish,** nog jonk, jongerig, jeugdig; ~**ling,** (digterlik vir) jongeling, jeugdige; jong dier, jong plant; ~**ster,** jongeling, kind, snuiter, tjokker, penkop.
your, u (beleef); julle; jou.
yours, joue; julle s'n; u s'n, van u; ~ *AFFECTIONATELY,* jou liefhebbende; ~ *FAITHFULLY,* u dienswillige; *I LIKE* ~ *better,* ek hou meer van joue; ~ *OF the 1st,* u brief van die 1ᵉ; ~ *RESPECTFULLY,* hoogagtend die uwe; ~ *SINCERELY,* geheel die uwe; ~ *TRULY,* hoogagtend, u dienswillige (die uwe); *WHAT'S* ~? wat sal jy drink? wat is joune? ~ *of YESTERDAY,* u brief van gister; *YOU and* ~, jy en jou gesin; jy en al wat jy het, jy en joune.
yourself, jouself; uself; self; *BE* ~, wees jouself (natuurlik); ruk jou reg; *you cannot go BY* ~, jy kan nie alleen gaan nie; *DO it* ~, doen dit self; *did you HURT* ~? het jy seer gekry? *PULL* ~ *together,* ruk jou reg; *you are not QUITE* ~, jy is nie op jou stukke nie; *you* ~ *SAID so,* jy het dit self gesê; *you are SITTING by* ~, jy sit alleen; jy sit op jou eentjie.
youth, jonkheid, jeug; jeugdigheid; jongmense, jongspan; jong kêrel, jongeling; ~ *and AGE will never agree,* oud en jonk is dit nooit eens nie; ~ *will have its COURSE,* die jeug moet uitraas; *in his EARLY* ~, in sy prille jeug; *FROM* ~ *onwards,* van kindsbeen af; ~**ful,** jeugdig, jonk; ~**fulness,** jeugdigheid; ~ **hostel,** jeugherberg; ~ **movement,** jeugbeweging.
yowl, (n) gehuil, geskree, gekerm; (v) tjank, huil, kerm.
yo'-yo, (-s), klimtol.
Y'pres, Ieper.
Y'ssel Lake, Ysselmeer, Suidersee.
ytterb'ium, ytterbium.
ytt'rium, yttrium.
yucc'a, jukka, adamsnaald.
Yugosla'via, Joego-Slawië; ~**n,** Joego-Slawies.
Yule, Kersfees; Kerstyd; ~-**log,** Kersblok: ~**tide,** Kers(fees)tyd, Kersgety.

Z

z, (zs, z's, zeds), z; *little* ~, z'tjie.
zaff'er, zaff're, kobalterts, saffloer.
Zambe'si, Zambezi.
Zambia, Zambië; ~**n,** (n) Zambiër; (a) Zambies.
zan'y, (zanies), grapmaker, hanswors.
Zan'zibar, Zanzibar.
zareb'a, zari'ba, takkraal, takheining, doringkraal, verskansing.
zeal, ywer, geesdrif, toewyding, werkgees, beywering.
Zea'land, (n) Seeland; (a) Seeus; ~**er,** Seeu, Seelander.
zeal'ot, yweraar, drywer; dweper; ~**'ical,** dweperig, fanatiek; ~**ry,** dweepsug, heethoofdigheid; fanatisme.
Zeal'ots, Selote.
zeal'ous, (vol)ywerig, vurig, geesdriftig, ~ *in the pursuit of the truth,* ywerig in die najaag v.d. waarheid; ~**ness,** vuur, geesdrif, ywer(igheid).
zeb'ra, sebra, kwagga, streepesel; ~ **crossing,** sebraoorgang; ~-**wolf,** buidelwolf.
zeb'rine, sebraägtig, sebra=.
zeb'u, Seboe, Indiese bees.
Zeb'ulon, Sebulon.
zed, die letter z.
Zee'land, Seeland; ~ **language,** Seeus; ~**er,** Seeu, Seelander.
zena'na, harem, vroueverblyf; ~ **mission,** sending onder die Indiese vroue.
zen'ith, toppunt, hoogtepunt, senit; *at the* ~ *of his career,* op die hoogte (top) van sy loopbaan.
ze'olite, seoliet.

zeph'yr, sefier, luggie, windjie; sefierstof, damesgeruit; ~ **yarn,** borduurwol.
zepp'elin, zeppelin, lugskip.
ze'ro, (-s), nul, zero, sero; nulpunt; vriespunt; *ABSOLUTE* ~, absolute nulpunt; *BE (stand) at* ~, op nul staan; *FLY at* ~, laer as 300 m vlieg; (v) op nul bring; die aanvalsuur vasstel; geweer op skoot bring; ~ *in,* op nul bring; ~ **day,** zerodag; ~ **hour,** (geheime) aanvalsuur; ~ **line,** nullyn; ~ **mark,** nulstreep; ~ **meridian,** nulmeridiaan; ~ **point,** nulpunt; ~ **reading,** nulstand.
zest, smaak; genot; lus, gretigheid; geesdrif; *ADD to,* die genot verhoog van; iets pikants voeg by; pittig maak; *DO something with* ~, iets geesdriftig aanpak; ~ *for LIFE,* lewensvreugde.
zetet'ic, heuristies, ondersoekend.
zeug'ma, seugma, sillepsis.
Zeus, Zeus (Griekse oppergod).
zi'beline, sibelien, sibeline.
zig'zag, (n) sigsag(lyn); slingerpad, sigsagpad; (v) **(-ged),** sigsagsgewyse gaan; slinger, slinger-slinger loop; (a) sigsag=, slingerend, kronkelend, kwingkwang; *in a* ~ *line,* (adv) sigsagvormig; sigsagsgewys(e), met kronkelinge, draai-draai; ~ **braid,** kartelband, tandjiekoord; ~ **line,** sigsaglyn, slingerlyn; ~ **path,** ~ **road,** sigsagpad, slingerpad; ~ **worm,** kartelwurm.
Zimbab'we, Zimbabwe.
zinc, (n) sink; (v) met sink beklee, versink, galvaniseer; ~ **alloy,** sinklegering; ~-**blende,** sinkblende; ~ **box,** sinkkas; ~ **chills,** kouekoors (sinksweis=

werk); ~ **coat**, sinklaag; ~ **covering**, sinkbedeking; ~**if'erous**, sinkhoudend; ~ **foil**, sinkfoelie.
zinc'ode, positiewe pool.
zinc'ograph, (n) sinklugdruk, sinkografie; (v) sinkografies reproduseer.
zincog'rapher, sinkgraveur.
zincog'raphy, sinkdruk, sinkografie.
zinc: ~ **ointment**, sinksalf; ~ **ore**, sinkerts.
zinc'ous, sinkagtig, sink=.
zinc: ~ **oxide**, sinkoksied; ~ **rod**, sinkstaaf; ~ **spar**, sinkspaat.
zink'y, sinkhoudend, sink=.
zinn'ia, jakobregop, besoetjie.
Zi'on, Sion; ~**ism**, Sionisme; ~**ist**, (n) Sionis; (a) Sionisties.
zip, (n) gefluit, gegons, gerits; pit, fut; rits, ritssluiter; (v) **(-ped)**, zits; fluit; sis; *the BULLET* ~*ped past*, die koeël het verbygefluit; ~ *UP*, met 'n rits sluit; ~**-fastener**, ~ **per**, rits(sluiter), ritssluiting, tjorsluiting, treksluiter.
zirc'on, sirkoon.
zith'er(n), siter; ~**ist**, siterspeler.
zith'ori ~-player, siterspeler; ~**-playing**, siterspel.
zlot'y, zloty (Poolse muntstuk).
zod'iac, diereriem, sodiak.
zodi'acal, van die diereriem, sodiakaal; ~ **light**, sodiakale lig.
zo'etrope, soötroop, lewensrat.
zo'ic, diere=, soïes; fossielhoudend.
Zol'aism, Zolaïsme, naturalisme.
zom'bi(e), zombie, lewende lyk.
zon'al, gordel=, sone=, gordelvormig.
zon'ar(y), sonaal.
zone, (n) lugstreek, sone, gebied, songordel, kring; streek, landstreek; aardgordel; strook; *TEMPERATE* ~, gematigde streek; *the TORRID* ~, die heet lugstreek; (v) soneer, (in streke) verdeel; ~ **fire**, strookvuur; ~ **time**, streektyd.
zon'ing, sonering; streekbou, sonebou; streekverdeling, streekindeling.
zon'ure, ouvolk, skurwejantjie.
zoo, *abbr.* for **zoological garden**, dieretuin.
zoochem'istry, dierlike skeikunde, soöchemie.
zoog'amy, geslagtelike voortplanting.
zoogeog'raphy, dieregeografie, soögeografie.
zoog'rapher, dierebeskrywer, soögraaf.
zoograph'ic, dierebeskrywend, soögrafies.
zoog'raphy, dierebeskrywing, soögrafie.
zool'ater, diereaanbidder.
zool'atry, diereaanbidding.
zo'olite, dierlike verstening, dierefossiel, soöliet.
zoolog'ical, dierkundig, soölogies; ~ **garden**, dieretuin.
zool'ogist, dierkundige, soöloog.
zool'ogy, dierkunde, soölogie.
zoom, (n) zoemvlug; gezoem; (v) zoem; die hoogte inskiet (vliegtuig).
zoomag'netism, diermagnetisme, soömagnetisme.
zo'omorph, dierafbeelding; ~'**ic**, in dierevorm.
zooph'agous, vleisetend.
zoophob'ia, vrees vir diere, soöfobie.
zo'ophyte, soöfiet, plantdier.
zoophyt'ic, soöfities.
zoophytol'ogy, soöfitologie.
zooplas'tic, soöplasties.
zooplas'tics, soöplastiek.
zo'ospore, soöspoor, swermspoor.
zootax'y, diere-indeling.
zoothe'rapy, soöterapie.
zoot'omist, dierontleder.
zoot'omy, dierontleding, soötomie.
Zoras'ter, Zoroaster, Zarathustra.
Zoroas'trianism, Zoroastrisme.
Zoroas'trian, (n) Zoroastris; (a) Zoroastristies.
zou'ave, soeaaf.
zounds! duiwels! drommels!
Zui'der Zee', Suidersee.
Zul'u, Zoeloe; Zoeloetaal; ~ **land**, Zoeloeland.
Zwing'lian, (n) Zwingliaan; (a) Zwingliaans.
zygodac'tyl, (n) klimvoël; (a) met klimvoete.
zygom'a, **(-ta)**, jukbeen, wangbeen.
zygomat'ic, jukbeen=, wangbeen=; ~ **bone**, wangbeen, jukbeen.
zygomorph'ic, **zygomorph'ous**, sigomorf.
zy'gote, sigoot.
zym'ochemistry, gistingskeikunde, fermentasiekeikunde, simochemie.
zymos'is, gisting; infeksiesiekte.
zymot'ic, gistings=; aansteeklik; besmetlik.

1. ABBREVIATIONS

A

English		Afrikaans
a.	adjective	b.nw.
a.	active	bedr.
A.	ampere	amp., A
Å.	angström	Å
AA	Automobile Association	AA
AA	Alcoholics Anonymous	AA
AAA	Amateur Athletic Association	—
a.a.r.	against all risks	t.a.r.
A.B.	able-bodied	gesond; sterk
abbr.	abbreviation	afk.
A B C	the alphabet	A B C
ab init.	*ab initio* (from the beginning)	ab init.
abl.	ablative; ablaut	abl.
abr.	abridged	verkort
abs.	absolutely	abs.
a/c	account	rek.
A/C	account current	R/K.
a.c.	alternating current	ws.
Acad.	Academy	Akad.
acc.	accused	bekl.; besk.
acc.	accusative	akk.
acc.	account	rek.
A.C.F.	Active Citizen Force	A.B.M.
act.	active	bedr.
a.d.	*ante diem* (before the day)	n.d.
a.d.	*a dato* (from date)	a.d.
ad.	advertisement	advt.
a/d	after date	n/d
A.D.	*Anno Domini* (in the year of our Lord)	A.d.; n.C.
ADC	Aide-de-camp	ADC.; adj.
add.	addressed	geadr.
ad fin.	*ad finem* (to the end)	ad fin.
ad inf.	*ad infintum* (to the infinte)	ad inf.
ad int.	*ad interim* (meanwhile)	a.i.
adj.	adjective; adjectival	adj.; b.nw.; byv.
adj.	adjunct	adjk.
Adj.	Adjudant	adjt.
ad lib.	*ad libitum* (at pleasure)	ad lib.
Adm.	Admiral	adml.
Admin.	Administration; Administrator	admin.
Adv.	adverb	adv.; bw.
Adv.	Advocate	adv.
ad val.	*ad valorem* (according to value)	ad val.
advt.	advertisement	advt.
aet(at).	*aetatis* (of age)	aet.
Afr.	Afrikaans; Afrikaner	Afr.
A.G.	Adjutant-General	A.G.
agric.	agriculture	landb.
agt.	agent	agent
A.I.	artificial insemination	K B; K.I.; A.I.
al.	alias	al.
Alg.	Algebra	Alg.; Stelk.
alt.	altitude	hoogte
a.m.	*ante meridiem* (before noon)	vm.
A.M.D.G.	*ad majorem Dei gloriam* (for the greater glory of God)	A.M.D.G.
Amer.	America(n)	Am.
A.M.I.C.E.	Associate Member of the Institution of Civil Engineers	A.M.I.C.E.
A.M.I.E.E.	Associate Member of the Institution of Electrical Engineers	A.M.I.E.E.
amp.	ampere	amp.
amt.	amount	bedr.
anal.	analysis; analytic(al)	ontl.
Anat.	Anatomy	Anat.
A.N.C.	African National Congress	A.N.C.
Angl.	Anglican; Anglicism	Angl.
ann.	annals	annale
anon.	anonymous	anon.
ans.	answer	antw.
antiq.	antiquarian	oudhk.
a/o	account of	rek. van.
app.	appellant	app.

English		Afrikaans
app.	appendix	aanh.
appl.	applause	appl.; toej.
appro.	approval	op sig
Apr.	April	Apr.
aq.	*aqua* (water)	water
Arab.	Arabian; Arabic	Arab.
arch.	archaic	arg.
Arch.	Architecture	Argit., Bouk.
Archaeol.	Archaeology	Argeol., Oudhk.
A.R.C.M.	Associate of the Royal College of Music	A.R.C.M.
Arith.	Arithmetic	Rek.
arr.	arrives (train); arrival	aank.
art.	article	art.; lw.
a/s	after sight	n/s
A/S	Account Sales	V/R
A.S.	Anglo-Saxon	As.
ass.	association	ver.
asst.	assistant	asst.
ass(ur).	assurance	ass.
Astrol.	Astrology	Astrol.
Astr(on).	Astronomy	Astr.; Sterrek.
at.	atomic	atomies
atmos.	atmosphere	atm.
Att.-Genl.	Attorney-General	prok.-genl.
attrib.	attribute; attributive	attr.
atty.	attorney	prok.
Aud.-Gen.	Auditor-General	oud.-genl.
Aug.	August	Aug.
auth.	author	skr.
aux.	auxiliary verb	hulpww.
av.	average	gem.
avdp.	avoirdupois	avdp.
ave.	avenue	laan

B

b.	bowled	geb.
b.	born	geb.
B.A.	*Baccalaureus Artium* (Bachelor of Arts)	B.A.
B.Agr.	*Baccalaureus Agriculturae* (Bachelor of Agriculture)	B.Agric.
bal.	balance	bal.; s.
B. Arch.	*Baccalaureus Architecturae* (Bachelor of Architecture)	B. Arch.
bar.	barometer	bar.
Bart.	Baronet	baron
batn.	battalion	bat.
batt.	battery	batt.
B.B.	Bill Book	W/B
B.B.C.	British Broadcasting Corporation	—
B.C.	before Christ	v.C.
B.Ch.	*Baccalaureus Chirurgiae* (Bachelor of Surgery)	B.Ch.
B.C.L.	*Baccalaureus Civilis Legis* (Bachelor of Civil Law)	B.C.L.
B.Com.	*Baccalaureus Commercii* (Bachelor of Commerce)	B.Com.
Bd.	boulevard	bd.
B.D.	*Baccalaureus Divinitatis* (Bachelor of Divinity)	B.D.
b/d	brought down	o/b
B.D.C.	bottom dead centre	O.D.P.
B/E	Bill of Exchange	wissel
B.Econ.	*Baccalaureus Economiae* (Bachelor of Economics)	B.Econ.
B.Ed.	*Baccalaureus Educationis* (Bachelor of Education)	B.Ed.
B.Eng.	Bachelor of Engineering	B.Ing.
B/F, b.f.	brought forward	o/b
B.F.B.S.	British and Foreign Bible Society	B.B.B.G.
b.h.p.	brake horse power	apk.; rpk.
Bib.	Bible; Biblical	Byb.
Biol.	Biology	Biol.
bk.	book	bk.
Bkk.	Bookkeeping	Boekh.
B/L	Bill of Lading	L/B
bldg(s).	building(s)	geb.
B.Litt.	*Baccalaureus Litterarum* (Bachelor of Literature)	B.Litt.
B.Med.	Bachelor of Medicine	B.Med.
B.Mil.	*Baccalaureus Militaris* (Bachelor of Military Science)	B.Mil.
B.Mus.	*Baccalaureus Musicae* (Bachelor of Music)	B.Mus.
B.N.	bank-note	banknoot
B.O.	Branch Office	bykantoor; filiaal
b.o.	buyer's option	kk.
Bot.	Botany	Bot.; Plantk.
BP.	Bishop	biskop

English		Afrikaans
B/P	Bills Payable	B/W
Br.	Britain; British	Br.
B/R	Bills Receivable	O/W
Brig.-Gen.	Brigadier-General	brig.-genl.
Bro.	Brother	br.
Bro. in X.	Brother in Christ	Br. in X.
Bros.	Brothers	brs.; gebr.
b.s.	balance sheet	bs.
B.Sc.	*Baccalaureus Scientiae* (Bachelor of Science)	B.Sc.
B.Sc. Agric.	Bachelor of Agricultural Science	B.Sc. Agric.
bt.	bought	gekoop
Bt.	Baronet	baron; jhr.
bush.	bushel	boe.
B.V.Sc.	*Baccalaureus Veterinariae Scientiae* (Bachelor of Veterinary Science)	B.V.Sc.

C

c.	*circa* (about)	ca.; ong.
c	cent; centime	c
C.	*caput* (chapter)	cap., hfst.
C	centigrade (Celsius)	C
C.A.	Chartered Accoutant	G.R.
C.A.E.	Council of Atomic Energy	R.A.K.
cal.	calendar	kal.
cal.	calorie	cal., kal.
Can.	Canada	Kan.
c. and b.	caught and bowled	gev. en geb.
Cant.	Canticles	Hoogl.
Cantab.	*Cantabrigienses* (of Cambridge)	—
cap.	*caput* (chapter)	cap.; hfst.
CAPAB	Cape Performing Arts Board	KRUIK
cap(s).	capital letter(s)	kap.; hfl.
Capt.	Captain	kapt.
car.	carat	kar.; kt.
carr. pd.	carriage paid	v.v.
C.A.(S.A.)	Chartered Accountant (South Africa)	G.R.(S.A.)
cat.	catalogue	kat.
C.B.	Cash Book	K.B.
C.B.	Companion of the Bath	C.B.
C/B	Credit Balance	k.s.
C.B.C.	Christian Brothers' College	C.B.C.
C.B.E.	Commander of the British Empire	C.B.E.
C.C.	Cricket Club	krieketklub
C.C.	Chamber of Commerce	K.v.K.
c.d.	cum dividend	cum div.
c/d	carried down	a/b
C.D.	*Corps Diplomatique* (Diplomatic Corps)	C.D.
Cdr.	Commander	kmdr.
cent.	*centum* (hundred)	honderd
cert.	certificate	sert.
cet. par.	*ceteris paribus* (other things being equal)	cet. par.
c. ex.	*cum expenses* (with costs)	c. ex.; m. k.
cf.	*confer* (compare)	cf.; vgl.
C.G.S.	Chief of the General Staff	H.G.S.
ch.	chestnut (horse)	vos
C.H.	Companion of Honour (Brit.)	—
chap.	chapter	cap., hfst.
Ch. B.	*Chirurgiae Baccalaureus* (Bachelor of Surgery)	Ch.B.
Chem.	Chemistry	Chem.; Skeik.
Ch.M.	*Chirurgiae Magister* (Master of Surgery)	Ch. M.
chq.	cheque	tjek
Chr.	Christ; Christian	Chr.
Chron.	Chronicles	Kron.
C.I.D.	Criminal Investigation Department	speurdepartement
c.i.f.	cost, insurance, freight	k.a.v.
C.-in-C.	Commander-in-Chief	K.G.
circ.	*circa, circiter* (about)	ca.
cit.	citation	sit.
C.J.	Chief Justice	hoofregter
cl	centilitre	cl
class.	classic(al)	klass.
Class.	classics	Klass.
C.M.G.	Companion of St. Michael and St. George (Brit)	
C.N.A.	Central News Agency	C.N.A.
C/N	Credit Note	K/B
Co.	Company	Kie.; My.
C.O.	Commanding Officer	B.O.
c/o	care of	o/s; p.a.
c/o	corner of	h/v
C. of C.	Chamber of Commerce	K.v.K.
co-ed.	co-educational	—
col.	coloured	gekleur(d)

English		Afrikaans
Col.	Colonel	kol.
Col.	Colossians	Kol.
coll.	collective	koll.
Coll.	College	Koll.
colloq.	colloquial	geselst., omgangst.
Comdt.	Commandant	kmdt.
Comdt.-Genl.	Commandant-General	K.G.
comm.	commission	komm.
comm.	committee	kom.
Comm.	Commodore	kmdoor.
comp.	comparative	komp.; verg. tr.
con.	*contra* (against)	teen; vs.
conj.	conjunction; conjunctive	konj.; voegw.
cons.	consignment	bes.
cons.	consonant	kons., medekl.
Cons.-Gen.	Consul-General	kons.-genl.
cons. note	consignment note	V/B
contd.	continued	voortgesit
contr.	contract	kontrak
co-op.	co-operative (society)	koöp.
cor.	corner	h/v
Cor.	Corinthians	Kor.
Corp.	Corporal	kpl.
corr.	correspondence; correspondent	korr.
cos	cosine	cos
cosec	cosecant	cosec
cot	cotangent	cot
cp.	compare	cf.; vgl.
C.P.	Cape Province	K.P.
Cpl.	Corporal	kpl.
cr.	corner	h/v, hk.
Cr.	Creditor	kr.
Cr.	credit	kt.
cresc.	*crescendo* (with increasing volume)	cresc.
c.s.	*cum suis* (with his own)	c.s.
c/s	cases	kissies
C.S.A.	Christian Students' Association	C.S.V.
C.S.I.R.	Council for Scientific and Industrial Research	W.N.N.R.
C.S.M.B.A.	Civil Service Medical Benefit Association	M.H.V.S.
C.T.	Cape Town	Kaapstad
cu(b).	cubic	kub.
cum div.	*cum dividendo* (with dividend)	cum div.
cur.	current	des.
curt. a/c	current account	l.r.
c.w.o.	cash with order	k.m.b.
cwt.	hundredweight	cwt.; sentenaar

D

d.	*dele* (delete)	del.
d.	*denarius* (penny)	d.
d.	died	gest., oorl.
D/A	Documents against Acceptance	D/A
Dan.	Daniel	Dan.
dat.	dative	dat.
d.b.	day-book	dagboek
D.C.	*da capo* (from the beginning)	D.C.
d.c.	direct current	gs.
D.C.L.	Doctor of Civil Law	D.C.L.
D.Com.	*Doctor Commercii* (Doctor of Commerce)	D.Com.
dd.	delivered	afgelewer
d/d.	days after date	d.d.
D.D.	*Doctor Divinitatis* (Doctor of Divinity)	D.D.
d.d.	*de dato* (dated)	d.d.; ged.
D.D.S.	Doctor of Dental Surgery	D.D.S.
DDT	dichloro-diphenyltrichloro-ethane	DDT
D.E.	Director of Education	D.O.
Dec.	December	Des.
decl.	declination	dekl.
D.Econ.	Doctor of Economics	D.Econ.
D.Ed.	Doctor of Education	D.Ed.
def.	definition	bep.; def.
deg.	degree	gr.
D.E.I.C.	Dutch East India Company	H.O.I.K.; N.O.I.K.
del.	*deleatur* (delete)	del.
del.	*delineavit* (he drew this)	del.
delv.	delivery	afl.
Dem.	Democrat	Dem.
demob.	demobilisation	demob.
D.Eng.	Doctor of Engineering	D.Ing.
dep.	departs (train)	vert.
dep.	deputy	adjk.
dept.	department	dept.

English		Afrikaans
der.	derivation	afl.; ontl.
Deut.	Deuteronomy	Deut.
D.F.B.	Deciduous Fruit Board	SVR.
D.F.C.	Distinguished Flying Cross	D.F.C.
D.F.M.	Distinguished Flying Medal	D.F.M.
D.G.	*Dei gratia* (by the grace of God); *Deo gratias* (thanks be to God)	D.G.
D.G.	Director-General	D.G.
dial.	dialect	dial.
dict.	dictionary	wdb.
dif.	difference; different	versk.
dim.	diminutive	verklw.
dim.	*diminuendo* (getting softer)	dim.
dipl.	diploma	dipl.
Dir.	Director	Dir.
dis.	discount	disk., rab.
dist.	district	dist.
div.	dividend	div.
div.	division	afd.
D. Litt.	*Doctor Litterarum* (Doctor of Literature)	D. Litt.
D.Lit. et Phil.	*Doctor Litterarum et Philosophiae* (Doctor of Literature and Philosophy)	D. Litt. et Phil.
D.M.	*Doctor Medicinae* (Doctor of Medicine)	D.M.; Dr. Med.; M.D.
DM	Deutsche Mark	DM
D.Med.Vet.	*Doctor Medicinae Veterinariae* (Doctor of Veterinary Medicine)	D.Med.Vet.
DMS	Decoration for Meritorious Service	DVD
D.Mus.	*Doctor Musicae* (Doctor of Music)	D.Mus.; Mus.D (oc).
D/N	Debit Note	D/b
D/O	Delivery Order	A/B
do.	*ditto* (the same)	do.
Dom.Sc.	*Domestica Scientiae* (Domestic Science)	Dom. Sc.
doz.	dozen	dos.
D/P	Documents against Payment	D/B
D.Phil.	*Doctor Philosophiae* (Doctor of Philosophy)	D.Phil.; Ph.D.
Dr.	Doctor	dr.
Dr.	debtor	dr.; versk.
D.R.	Dutch Reformed	N(ed). G(eref).; N(ed). H(erv).; Geref.
dr.	drachma	dr.
D.R.A.; D.R.C.	Defence Rifle Association; Defence Rifle Club	V.S.V.
D.R.C.	Dutch Reformed Church	N.G.K.
Dr. Med.	Doctor of Medicine	Dr. Med.
Dr. Phil.	Doctor of Philosophy	Dr. Phil.
d/s	days after sight	d/s
D.Sc.	*Doctor Scientiae* (Doctor of Science)	D.Sc.
D.S.C.	Distinguished Service Cross	D.S.C.
D.S.M.	Distinguished Service Medal	D.S.M.
D.S.O.	Distinguished Service Order	D.S.O.
Dt.	Debit	Dt.
d.t.	*delirium tremens*	d.t.
Dr. Th(eol).	*Doctor Theologiae* (Doctor of Theology)	Dr. Theol.; Th(eol). D(r).
Du.	Dutch	Ndl.
dup.	duplicate	dup.
D.V.	*Deo Volente* (God being willing)	D.V.
D.V.Sc.	*Doctor Veterinariae Scientiae* (Doctor of Veterinary Science)	D.V.Sc.
dwt.	pennyweight	dwt.
dyn.	dynamics	Din.

E

E.	East	O.
E.	second-class (ship)	tweede klas
ea.	each	elk
E.&O.E.	errors and omissions excepted	B.F.&W.
E.C.	Executive Committee	U.K.; U.R.
E.C.	earth-closet	privaat
Eccles.	Ecclesiastes	Pred
E.C.M.	European Common Market	E.G.M.
Econ.	Economics	Ekon.
Ed.	editor	red.
ed.	edition	dr.; ed.
E.D.	Education Diploma	O.D.
E.E.C.	European Economic Community	E.E.G.
e.g.	*exempli gratia* (for example)	bv.; e.g.
e.h.p.	electrical horse-power	epk.
E.I.	East Indies	O.I.
e.l.	electric light	e.l.
E.L.	East London	O.L.

English		Afrikaans
E.long.	Eastern longitude	O.L.
elec.	electrical; electricity	elektr.
encl.	enclosure	byl.
ency.	encyclopaedia	ensiklopedie
ENE.	east-north-east	O.N.O.
Eng.	England; English	Eng.
eng.	engineer	ir.
Entom.	Entomology	Entom.
e.o.	*ex officio* (officially)	e.o.
Ep.	Epistle	*Sendbrief*
E.P.	Eastern Province	O.P.
Eph.	Ephesians	*Ef.*
E.P.N.S.	electroplate on nickel silver	versilwer
erron.	erroneous(ly)	verkeerd
ESCOM	Electrical Supply Commission	E.V.K., Evkom, EVKOM
ESE.	east-south-east	O.S.O.
esp.	especially	ins.; veral
Esq.	Esquire	mnr.
est.	established	opgerig
et al.	*et alibi* (and elsewhere)	e.a.
etc.	*et cetera* (and so forth)	e.a.; e.d.; ens.; e.s.m.; etc.
et seq.	*et sequentes* (and the following, sing.)	e.v.
Ethnol.	Ethnology	Etnol.
et sqq.	*et sequentes* (and the following, pl.)	e.vv.
etym.	etymology	etim.
Eur.	Europe; European	Eur.
ex.	exercise	oef.
exam.	examination	eksamen
exc.	except	behalwe
Exc.	Excellency	Eks.
Ex. Co.	Executive Committee	U.K.; U.R.
Exod.	Exodus	Ex.
ex off.	*ex officio* (officially)	ex off.; e.o.
exor.	executor	eksekuteur
exp.	export(ation)	uitvoer
expr.	expression	uitdr.
ext.	extension	uitbr.
Ezek.	Ezekiel	*Eseg.*

F

f.	foot	vt.
f.	feminine	v(r).
f	*forte* (loud)	f
f.	frank	fr.
F	Fahrenheit	F
F.	Friday	Vr.
fam.	family	fam.
far.	farad	f.
f.a.s.	free alongside ship	v.l.s.
F.B.A.	Fellow of the British Academy	—
F.B.I.	Federal Bureau of Investigation	—
F.B.S.	Fellow of the Botanical Society	—
F.C.	Field Cornet	vk.
F.C.	Football Club	VK
F.C.I.	Federated Chamber of Industries	—
fcp.	foolscap	fol.
F.C.S.	Fellow of the Chemical Society	—
F.D.	*fidei defensor* (Defender of the Faith)	fid. def.
Feb.	February	Febr.
fec.	*fecerunt* (they made this); *fecit* (he made this)	*fec.*
f(em).	feminine	v(r).
ff	*fortissimo* (very loud)	ff
f.f.d.	free from damage	v.v.b.
fff	*fortisissimo* (as loud as possible)	fff
F.G.S.	Fellow of the Geological Society	—
f.i.	for instance	bv.
F.I.A.	Fellow of the Institute of Actuaries	—
Fid. Def.	*fidei defensor* (Defender of the Faith)	fid. def.
fig.	figure	fig.
fig.	figurative	fig.; oordr.
fl.	florin	fl.
Fl.	Flemish	Vl.
(f.)l. to r.	from left to right	v.l.n.r.
FM	frequency modulation	FM
F.M.	Field-Marshal	veldm.
F.M.	full moon	V.M.
fm.	fathom	vadem
f.o.b.	free on board	v.a.b.; v.o.s.
f.o.c.	free of charge	franko
fo.	folio	deel

English		Afrikaans
fol.	following	vlg.; ost.
f.o.r.	free on rail	v.o.s.
f.o.s.	free on station	v.o.s.
FOSKOR	Fosfaatontwikkelingskorporasie	FOSKOR
f.o.w.	first on water	e.o.w.
f.p.	foot-pound	voetpond
F.P.S.	Fellow of the Philosophical Society	—
fr.	franc	fr.
Fr.	France; French	Fr.
F(ri).	Friday	Vr.
fr. above	from above	v.b.
F.R.A.M.	Fellow of the Royal Academy of Music	—
F.R.A.S.	Fellow of the Royal Astronomical Society	—
F.R.C.M.	Fellow of the Royal College of Music	—
F.R.C.O.	Fellow of the Royal College of Organists	—
F.R.C.P.	Fellow of the Royal College of Physicians	—
F.R.C.S.	Fellow of the Royal College of Surgeons	—
freq.	frequently	dikwels
F.R.G.S.	Fellow of the Royal Geographical Society	—
F.R.H.S.	Fellow of the Royal Horticultural Society	—
Fri.	Friday	Vr.
F.R.I.B.A.	Fellow of the Royal Institute of British Architects	—
F.R.S.	Fellow of the Royal Society	—
F.R.S.L.	Fellow of the Royal Society of Literature	—
F.S.A.	Fellow of the Society of Antiquarians	—
F.S.E.	Fellow of the Society of Engineers	—
F.T.	Free Trade	v.h.
ft.	foot; feet	vt.
fur.	furlong	fur.
fut	future	toek.
F.Z.S.	Fellow of the Zoological Society	—

G

g.	guinea	ghn.
Gael.	Gaelic	Gael.
gal.	gallon	gall.; gell.; g.
Gal.	Galatians	Gal.
galv.	galvanic	galvanies
GATT	General Agreement on Trade and Tariffs	GATT
G.B.	Great Britain	G.B.
G.B.E.	Grand Cross of the British Empire	G.B.E.
G.C.	George Cross	G.C.
G.C.B.	Grand Cross of the Bath	G.C.B.
G.C.D.	greatest common divisor	G.G.D.
G.C.F.	greatest common factor	G.G.D.
G.C.M.	greatest common measure	G.G.D.
G.C.M.G.	Grand Cross of St. Michael and St. George	—
gen.	general	alg.
gen.	genitive	gen.
Gen.	Genesis	Gen.
gend.	gender	geslag
Gen.	General	genl.
Geogr.	Geography	Aardr.; Geogr.
Geol.	Geology	Aardk.; Geol.
geom.	geometry	meetk.
Ger.	Germany	Duitsl.
G.G.	Governor-General	G.G.
G.G.	Government Garage	G.G.
G.H.Q.	General Headquarters	G.H.K.
G.H.S.	Girls' High School	H.M.S.
gloss.	glossary	glos.
G.M.T.	Greenwich Mean Time	G.T.
Gosp.	Gospel	Ev.
Goth.	Gothic	Got.
G(ov).-G(en).	Governor-General	G(oew).-G(enl).
govt.	government	goewt.; reg.
G.P.	General Practitioner	dr.
G.P.O.	General Post Office	H.P.K.
gr.	grain	gr.
Gr.	Greek	Gr.
gram.	grammar	gram.
gro.	gross	gros
G.S.	General Staff	G.S.
G.T.	Greenwich time	G.T.
guar.	guarantee	garansie
G.U.C.	Grey University College	G.U.K.
gym.	gymnasium; gymnastics	gimn.

H

h.	hour	u.
Hab.	Habakkuk	*Hab.*
Hag.	Haggai	*Hag.*

English		Afrikaans
h. & c.	hot and cold (water)	w. & k.
h.c.	*honoris causa* (mark of honour)	h.c.
H.C.F.	Highest Common Factor	G.G.D.
hdbk.	handbook	hdbk.
H.E.	Higher Education	H.O.
H.E.	His Excellency	S. Eks.
H.E.	Her Excellency	H. Eks.
Heb.	Hebraic; Hebrews	*Hebr.*
H.E.D.	Higher Education Diploma	H.O.D.
H.Em.	His Eminence	S. Em.
her.	heraldic; heraldry	her.
hf.-bd.	half-bound	in halfleerband
hf.-cf.	half-calf	in half(kalf)leerband
H.G.	High German	Hd.
H.H.	Her (His) Highness	H. (S.) H.
H.H.	His Holiness	S.H.
H.I.H.	His Imperial Highness	S.K.H.
His Hon.	His Honour	S.Ed.; S. Ed. Agb.
His Rev.	His Reverence	S.Eerw.
hist.	history	Gesk.
H.M.	His (Her) Majesty	S. (H). M.
H.M.C.	Historical Monuments Commission	H.M.K.
H.M.S.	His (Her) Majesty's Ship	—
H.N.P.	Herstigte Nasionale Party	H.N.P.
hoc loc.	*hoc loco* (in this place)	h.l.
H.O.D.	Hebrew Order of David	—
Hon.	Honourable	Agb.; Ed.; Ed. Agb.; WelEd.
Hon. Sec.	Honorary Secretary	ere-sekr.
Hort.	Horticulture	Tuinb.
Hos.	Hosea	*Hos.*
hosp.	hospital	hosp.
h.p.	horse power	pk.
h.p.	hire purchase	huurkoop
H.Q.	Headquarters	HK
H.R.H.	His (Her) Royal Highness	S. (H.)K.H.
H.S.H.	His Serene Highness	S.D.; S.D.H.
H.S.R.C.	Human Sciences Research Council	R.G.N.
hypoth.	hypothesis	hipotese

I

ib(id).	*ibidem* (in the same place)	ib(id).
i.c.	*in casu* (in this case)	i.c.
id.	*idem* (the same)	id.
I.D.B.	Illicit Diamond Buying	O.D.H.
I.D.C.	Industrial Development Corporation of S.A., Ltd.	N.O.K.
I.E.	Indo-European	Ide.
i.e.	*id est* (that is)	d.i.; i.e.
i.f.o.	in favour of	t.g.v.
I.G.B.	Illicit Gold Buying	O.G.H.
I.G.Y.	International Geophysical Year	I.G.J.
i.h.p.	indicated horse power	a.pk.
I.L.H.	Imperial Light House	I.L.H.
illus.	illustrated	afb.; geïll.
I.L.O.	International Labour Organization	I.A.O.
imp.	imperative	geb. wys.; imp.
imperf.	imperfect	impf.; onvolm. tyd; onvolt.
impers.	impersonal	onpers.
impr.	*imprimatur* (imprint)	impr.
in.	inch	dm.
inc.	incorporated	geïnk.
incl.	inclusive	inkl.; insl.
incog.	*incognito* (unknown)	incog.
incor.	incorporated	ingelyf
Ind.	India(n)	Ind.
I.N.D.	*In Nomine Dei* (in the name of God)	I.N.D.
indecl.	indeclinable	onverbuigbaar
indef.	indefinite	onbep.
indic.	indicative	ind.
Indon.	Indonesia	Indon.
inf.	infinitive	inf.
inf.	infantry	inf.
infra dig.	*infra dignitatem* (beneath his dignity)	infra dig.
(in) loc. cit.	*(in) loco citato* (in the passage already quoted)	(in) loc. cit; t.a.p.
inorg.	inorganic	anorg.
I.N.R.I.	*Iesus Nazarenus, Rex Iudaeorum* (Jesus of Nazareth, King of the Jews)	I.N.R.I.
ins.	insurance	ass(ur).
Insp.	Inspector	insp.
insp.	inspection	insp.
inst.	*instant* (this month)	deser

English		Afrikaans
instr.	instrument	instr.
int.	interest	int.
int. al.	*inter alia* (among other things)	o.a.
interj.	interjection	tw.
interm.	intermediate	intermediêr
internat.	international	internasionaal
intr(ans).	intransitive	intr.; onoorg.
intro.	introduction	inl.
inv.	invoice	fakt.
I.O.G.T.	Independent Order of Good Templars	—
IOU	I owe you	skuldbewys
I.Q.	intelligence quotient	I.K.
I.R.C.	International Red Cross	I.R.K.
irreg.	irregular(ly)	onreëlmatig
Is.	Isaiah	Jes.
Iscor	South African Iron and Steel Corporation	Yskor
Isr.	Israel; Israelite	Isr.
It.	Italian; Italy	It.
ital.	italics	kurs.

J

Jam.	James	*Jak.*
Jan.	January	Jan.
Jap.	Japan(ese)	Jap.
J.C.	Jesus Christ	J.C.
J.C.	Junior Certificate	J.S.
Jer.	Jeremiah	*Jer.*
Jhb.; Jo(h)burg.	Johannesburg	Johburg.
Jno.	John	*Joh.*
Josh.	Joshua	*Jos.*
J.P.	Justice of the Peace	V.R.
jr	junior	jr.
Judg.	Judges	*Rigt.*
Jul.	July	Jul.
jun.	*junior* (the younger)	jr.
Jun.	June	Jun.
junc.	junction	aansl.
jurisp.	jurisprudence	jur.; regs.
Just.	Justinian	Just.

K

K.B.E.	Knight Commander of the British Empire	K.B.E.
K.C.	King's Counsel	K.C.
k.p.b.	kitchen, pantry, bathroom	k.s.b.

L

l.	latitude	—
l.	left	l.
l.	length	l.
l.	lira	l.
L.	Licentiate	Lis.
£	*libra(e)* (pound)	£
lab.	laboratory	lab.
Lab.	Labour	Arb.
Lam.	Lamentations (Book of)	Klaagl.
lang.	language	taal
lat.	latitude	breedtegraad
Lat.	Latin	Lat.
lb(s).	*libra(e)* (pound weight)	lb(s).; pd(e).
l.b.w.	leg before wicket	b.v.p.
L/C	letter of credit	K/B
l.c.	lower case	o.k.
L.C.M.	least common multiple	K.G.V.
L/Cpl.	Lance-Corporal	o. korp.
L.D.	*Laus Deo* (glory to God)	L.D.
L.D.S.	Licentiate of Dental Surgery	—
leg.	legal	jur.
Lev.	Leviticus	*Lev.*
lex.	lexicon	wdb.
l.h.	left hand	lh.
Lib.	Liberal	Lib
lib.	library	bibl.
Lieut.	Lieutenant	luit.
L(ieu)t.-Col.	Lieutenant-Colonel	luit.-kol.
L(ieu)t.-Genl.	Lieutenant-General	luit.-genl.
Lit.	Literature	Lettk.
lit.	literally	lett.
Litt.D.	*Literarum Doctor* (Doctor of Literature)	Litt.D.
LL.B.	*Legum Baccalaureus* (Bachelor of Laws)	LL.B.
LL.D.	*Legum Doctor* (Doctor of Laws)	LL.D.
LL.M.	*Legum Magister* (Master of Laws)	LL.M.
loc. cit.	*loco citato* (at the place quoted)	l(oc). c(it).; t.a.p.

English		Afrikaans
log.	logarithm	log.
long.	longitude	lengtegraad
l.p.	low pressure	LD
L.P.	Liberal Party	L.P.
L.Q.	Last Quarter	L.K.
L.R.A.M.	Licentiate of the Royal Academy of Music	L.R.A.M.
L.R.C.M.	Licentiate of the Royal College of Music	L.R.C.M.
l.s.	*locum sigilli* (the place of the seal)	l.s.
L.S.	*Lectori Salutem* (hail to the reader)	H.d.L.; L.S.
L.s.d.	*librae, solidi, denarii* (pounds, shillings, pence)	L.s.d.
Lt.	Lieutenant	luit.
Ltd.	Limited	Bpk.
l. to r.	left to right	l.n.r.
Luth.	Lutheran	Luth.
LXX	The Septuagint	LXX

M

m.	masculine	m.
m.	mile	m.
m.	month	md.
M	mark	M
M.	Monday	Ma.
M	Monsieur	M.
M.A.	*Magister Artium* (Master of Arts)	M.A.
mag.	magistrate	mag.; land.
Maj.	Major	maj.
Maj.-Gen.	Major-General	genl.-maj.
Mal.	Malachi	Mal.
Mar.	March	Mrt.
m(asc).	masculine	m(l).
Maths.	Mathematics	Mat.; Wisk.
matric.	matriculation	matriek.
Matt.	Matthew	Matt.
max.	maximum	maks.
M.B.	*Medicinae Baccalaureus* (Bachelor of Medicine)	B.M.; M.B.
M.B.E.	Member of the Order of the British Empire	M.B.E.
M.C.	Master of Ceremonies	seremoniemeester
M.C.	Military Cross	M.C.
M.C.C.	Marylebone Cricket Club	M.C.C.
M.Com.	*Magister Commercii* (Master of Commerce)	M.Com.
M.C.P.	Member of the College of Preceptors	—
m/d	months after date	m/d
M.D.	Middle Dutch	Mnl.
M.D.	*Medicinae Doctor* (Doctor of Medicine)	D.M.; Dr. Med.; M.D.
M.Div.	*Magister Divinitatis* (Master of Divinity)	M.Div.
M.E.	Middle English	Me.
M.E.C.	Member of the Executive Committee	L.U.K.
mech.	mechanics	werkt.
M.Econ.	*Magister Economiae* (Master of Economics)	M.Econ.
M.Ed.	*Magister Educationis* (Master of Education)	M.Ed.
med.	medical; medicine	geneesk.; med.
med.	(study of) medicine	med.; geneesk.
memo.	memorandum	mem(o).
Messrs.	*Messieurs* (gentlemen)	hh.; mnre.
metaph.	metaphysics	metaf.
meteor.	meteorology	meteor.
meton.	metonymy	meton.
mf	*mezzo forte* (moderately loud)	mf
Mgr.	Monseigneur	mgr.
MHD	Middle High Dutch	Mnl.
M.H.G.	Middle High German	Mhd.
Mic.	Micha	Miga
M.I.C.E.	Member of the Institution of Civil Engineers	M.I.C.E.
mil.	military	mil.
min.	minute	min.
min.	mining	mynw.
min.	minimum	min.
Min.	Minister	min.
mineral.	mineralogy	miner.
M.L.A.(C.)	Member Legislative Assembly (Council)	L.V.
Mlle.	Mademoiselle	mej.
m.m.	*mutatis mutandis* (with the necessary changes)	m.m.
MM.	*Messieurs* (gentlemen)	hh.; mnre.
M.M.	Military Medal	M.M.
M.Med.	Master of Medicine	M.Med.
Mme(s).	Mesdame(s)	mev(v).
M.O.	money order	G.W., P.W.
mod.	modern	mod.
M.O.H.	Medical Officer of Health	gesondheidsbeampte
M(on).	Monday	Ma.
mo(s).	month(s)	md(e).

English		Afrikaans
M.O.T.H.	Memorable Order of Tin Hats	M.O.T.H.
mp	*mezzo piano* (moderately soft)	mp
M.P.	Member of Parliament	L.P.
M.P.	Military Police	M.P.
M.P.C.	Member of the Provincial Council	L.P.R.
m.p.g.	miles per gallon	m.p.g.
m.p.h.	miles per hour	m.p.u.
M.P.S.	Member of the Pharmaceutical Society	L.A.V.
Mr.	Mister	mnr.
M.R.A.	Moral Rearmament	M.H.
Mrs.	Mistress	mev.
m/s	months after sight	m/s
M.Sc.	*Magister Scientiae* (Master of Science)	M.Sc.
MS(S).	manuscript(s)	hs(s).; ms(s).
Mt.	Mount	berg
M.Th.	Master of Theology	M.Th.
mus.	music	mus.
Mus. B(ac).	*Musicae Baccalaureus* (Bachelor of Music)	B. Mus.; Mus. B(ac).
Mus. D(oc).	*Musicae Doctor* (Doctor of Music)	D. Mus.; Mus. D(oc).
M.V.	motor vessel	ms.
myth.	mythology	mit.

N

n	neuter	neut., ons.
n.	noun	(s.)nw.
n.	*natus* (born)	geb.
N.	North	N.
N.A.	North Africa; North America	N.A.
Nah.	Nahum	Nah.
NAPAC	Natal Performing Arts Council	NARUK
Nat.	National; Nationalist	Nat.
N.A.T.O.	North Atlantic Treaty Orgnisation	N.A.V.O.
N.A.U.	Natal Agricultural Union	N.L.U.
n.b.	no ball	g.b.
N.B.	*Nota Bene* (take notice)	L.W.; N.B.
N.C.O.	non-commissioned officer	onderoffisier
N.C.W.	National Council of Women	N.V.R.
n.d.	no date	s.d.
N.D.	Nature Doctor	N.D.
NE.	North-east	N.O.
N.E.D.	Natal Education Department	N.O.D.
N.E.F.	New Education Fellowship	N.O.B.
neg.	negative	neg.
Neh.	Nehemiah	Neh.
N.E.I.C.	Netherlands East India Company	N.O.I.K.
nem. con.	*nemine contradicente* (no one contradicting)	nem. con.
nem. dis(s).	*nemine dissentiente* (no one dissenting)	nem. dis(s).
Neth.	Netherlands	Ndl.
n(cut).	neuter	ons.
N.F.	Newfoundland	N.F.
NHG.	New High German	Nhd.
n.l.	new line	n.r.
N.lat.	North(ern) latitude	NBr.
N.long.	North longitude	N.L.
N.M.	National Mark	N.M.
N.M.	New Moon	N.M.
N.N.	*nomen nescio* (name unknown)	N.N.
NNE.	North-north-east	N.N.O.
NNW.	North-north-west	N.N.W.
No.	*numero* (number)	no.; nr.
n.o.	not out	n.u.n
nol. pros.	*nolle prosequi* (be unwilling to prosecute)	nol. pros.
nom.	nominative	nom.
nom. cap.	nominal capital	nom. kap.
non-com.	non-commissioned officer	onderoffisier
Nos.	numbers	nos.; nrs.
Nov.	November	Nov.
N.P.	National Party	N.P.
N.P.	Notary Public	prok.
n.p. (new par.)	new paragraph	n.p. (nuwe par.)
nr.	near	naby
N.S.W.	New South Wales	N.S.W.
N.T.	New Testament	N.T.
N.T.A.	Natal Teachers' Association	N.T.A.
nth	to the nth (any required) power	nste
N.T.O.	National Theatre Organisation	N.T.O.
n.u.	name unknown	n.o.
N.U.	Natal University	N.U.; U.N.
num.	numeral	telw.
Num.	Numbers	Num.
N.U.S.A.S.	National Union of South African Students	N.U.S.A.S.

English		Afrikaans
NW.	North-west	N.W.
N.Y.	New York	N.Y.
N.Z.	New Zealand	N.S.

O

o/a	on account	o.r.
OAU	Organisation of African Unity	OAE
OB	Ossewa-Brandwag	OB
ob.	*obiit* (died)	gest.; ob.
o.b.	on board	a.b.
Obad,	Obadiah	Obad.
obdt.	obedient	d(iens)w.
OBE	Order of the British Empire	OBE
obj.	object	obj.; voorw.
Obstet.	Obstetrics	Verlosk.
O.C.	Officer Commanding	B.O.
Oct.	October	Okt.
O/D	overdraft	O/R.
O.E.	Old English	Oe.
O.E.D.	Oxford English Dictionary	O.E.D.
O.F.	Old French	Ofr.
off.	official	off.
O.F.S.	Orange Free State	O.V.S.
O.F.S.A.U.	Orange Free State Agricultural Union	O.V.S.L.U.
O.F.S.T.A.	Orange Free State Teachers' Association	O.V.S.O.V.
O.F.S.U.	Orange Free State University	U.O.V.S.
O. Ger.	Old Germanic	Ogerm.
O.H.G.	Old High German	Ohd.
O.H.M.S.	in his (her) majesty's service	I.D.H.M.
O.K.	all correct	goed; in goeie orde
Ol.	Olympiad	Olimpiade
O.M.	Order of Merit	—
ON.	Old Norse	On.
on a/c	on account	o.r.
op.	*opus* (work)	op.
O.P.	out of print	uit druk
op. cit.	*opere citato* (in the work quoted)	a.w.; op. cit.
opt.	optative	opt.
O.R.	owner's risk	er.
Ord.	Ordinance	Ord.
orig.	original	oorspr.
o/s	out of stock	uitverkoop
O.S.	Old Saxon	Os.
O.T.	Old Testament	O.T.
Oxon.	*Oxoniensis* (of Oxford)	—
oz.	ounce(s)	ons

P

p.	page	bl., p.
p.	*per* (for)	p.
p	*piano* (soft) (mus.)	p
p.a.	*per annum* (per year)	p.a.; p.j.
P/A	Power of Attorney	prokurasie
P.A.C.	Pan-African Congress	P.A.C.
PACOFS	Performing Arts Council O.F.S.	SUKOVS
PACT	Performing Arts Council Transvaal	TRUK
par.	paragraph	par.
Parl.	Parliament	parl.
part.,	participle	dw.
pass.	passive	lydende vorm
path.	pathology	patol.
P.A.Y.E.	pay as you earn	L.B.S.
P.B.	private bag	ps.
p. bag	postal bag	ps.
p.c.	postal(card)	poskaart
p.c.	petty cash	kleinkas
p.c.	per cent	p.s.
P.C.	Privy Counsellor	geheime raadgewer
P.C.	Police Constable	konst.
P.C.	Provincial Council	P.R.
pcl.	parcel	pakket
pd.	paid	bet., btd.
p.d.	*per diem* (per day)	p.d.
P.D.	*Pro Deo* (gratis, free)	P.D.
P.E.	Port Elizabeth	P.E.
P.E.N.	Poets, Playwrights, Essayists, Editors, Novelists	P.E.N.
perf.	perfect	perf.; volm.
per pro.	*per procurationem* (by proxy)	per pro.; p.p.
pers.	personal	pers.
pers. pron.	personal pronoun	pers. vnw.
per yd.	per yard	p. jt.
P.F.	Permanent Force	B.M.

English		Afrikaans
p. ft.	per foot	p. vt.
p.h.	per hour	p.u.
Ph.D.	*Philosophiae Doctor* (Doctor of Philosophy)	D.Phil.; Ph.D.
Phil.	Philology	Filol.
Phil.	Phillippians	Filip.
Philem.	Philemon	Fil.
Philol.	Philology	Filol.
phon.	phonetics	fonet.
phot.	photograph (etc.)	fot.
Phys.	Physics	Fis., Nat.
Physiol.	Physiology	Fisiol.
pl.	plural	mv., pl.
plup.	pluperfect	pqpf.
p.m.	*post meridiem* (afternoon)	nm.
p.m.	per month	p.m.
p.m.	per minute	p.m.
P.M.	Prime Minister	E.M.
P.M.	Post Master	P.M.
P.M.G.	Postmaster-General	P.M.G.
P/N	promissory note	prom.
P.O.	Post Office	Pk.
P.O.	postal order	P.O.
Pol.	Politics	Pol., Staatsl.
pop.	population	bevolking
Port.	Portuguese; Portugal	Port.
poss. pron.	possessive pronoun	bes. vnw.
Potch.	Potchefstroom	Potch.
P.O.W.	Prisoner(s) of War	krygsgevangene(s)
pp.	pages	bll., pp.
pp	*pianissimo* (very soft)	pp
p.p.	*per procurationem* (by proxy)	per pro.; p.p.
p.p.	past particle	verl. dw.
P.P.	Parcel Post	P.P.
P.P.	Progressive Party	P.P.
p.p.c.	*pour prendre congé* (to take leave)	p.p.c.
ppp	*pianisissimo* (as softly as possible)	ppp
pr.	pair	paar
pred.	predicate	gesegde
pref.	preface	voorwoord
pref.	prefix	voorv.
prep.	preposition	voors.
pres.	present	pres.; teenw.
Pres.	President	pres., voors.
pret.	preterite	pret.; verl. t.
prim.	primary	prim.
Prin.	Principal	prin.
pro.	professional	pro.
P.R.O.	public relations officer	skakelbeampte
Prof.	Professor	prof.
Proff.	Professors	proff.
Prog.	Progressive	Prog.
pron.	pronoun	vnw.
Prot.	Protestant	Prot.
pro tem.	*pro tempore* (for the time being)	pro tem.
Prov.	Proverbs	Spr.
Prov.	Province; Provincial	Prov., prov.
prox.	*proximo* (next)	a.s.; e.k.; prox.
P.S.	*postscriptum* (postscript)	Ns.; PS
Ps.	Psalm	Ps.
ps(eud).	pseudonym	ps.
Psychol.	Psychology	Psig.; Sielk.
pt.	part	dl.; ged.
pt.	pint	pt.
pt.	point	pt.
Pte.	Private (soldier)	wm.
P.T.O.	please turn over	b.o.; S.O.S.
Pty.	Proprietary	Edms.; Eiens.
P.U. for C.H.E.	Potchefstroom University for Christian Higher Education	P.U. vir C.H.O.
pub.	public	openb.; pub.
p.w.	per week	p.w.
P.W.D.	Public Works Department	D.O.W.; D.P.W.
p. yd.	per yard	p. jt.

Q

q.	query	vraag
Q	quarter	kwartier
q.a.	*quod attestor* (to which I witness)	q.a.
Q.C.	Queen's Counsel	Q.C.
q.e.	*quod est* (which is)	d.i.; i.e.; q.e.
Q.E.D.	*quod erat demonstrandum* (that which had to be demonstrated)	q.e.d.

English		Afrikaans
Q.E.F.	*quod erat faciendum* (that which had to be done)	q.e.f.
qlty.	quality	kwal.
Q.M.	Quartermaster	kwartiermeester
Q.M.G.	Quartermaster-General	KMG
q.q.	*qualitate qua* (in the capacity of)	q.q.
qr.	quarter	kw.
q.s.	*quantum sufficit* (sufficient quantity)	q.s.
qt.	quart	kwart gelling
qt.	quantity	kwant.
qt.	quietly, secretly	skelmpies; stilletjies
q.v.	*quod vide* (which see)	q.v.

R

r.	right	regs
r.	radius	r.
r.	rule	reël
R	Rand	R
R	Réaumur	R
R.	railway	spoorweg
R.A.	Royal Academy	—
R.A.F.	Royal Air Force	R.A.F.
rall.	*rallentando* (with decreasing pace)	rall.
R.A.M.	Royal Academy of Music	R.A.M.
R.A.U.	Rand Afrikaans University	R.A.U.
R.C.	Roman Catholic	R.K.
R.C.C.	Roman Catholic Church	R.K.K.
R.D.	refer to drawer	v/t
rd.	road	weg
Rd.	Rixdollar	Rd.
Rds.	Rixdollars	Rds.
reb.	rebate	rab.
rec.	receipt	kwitansie
recd.	received	ontv.
redup(l).	reduplicate	redupl.
ref.	reference	ref.; verw.
ref.	referee	skeidsregter
Ref.	Reformed	Geref.; Herv.
refl.	reflexive	refl., wederk.
regd.	registered	aanget.
regt.	regiment	regt.
rel.	relative	betr., rel.
rel. pron.	relative pronoun	betr. vnw.
rem.	remark	opm.
Rep.	Republic	Rep.
Resp.	respectively	resp.
ret.	retired	gep.
retd.	returned	teruggestuur
Rev.	Reverend	ds.; eerw.; pred.; V.D.M.
Rev.	Revelations	Openb.
revs.	revolutions	o.
R.F.C.	Rugby Football Club	R.V.K.
r.h.	right hand	rh.
R.H.A.	Royal Horse Artillery	—
rhet.	rhetoric(al)	retorika
R.I.	*Rex Imperator* (King and Emporor)	R.I.
R.I.P.	*requiescat in pace* (may he rest in peace)	R.I.P.; R.I.V.
rit.	*ritardando* (slower)	rit.
R(iv).	River	riv.
R.M.	Resident Magistrate	R.M.; land.
RM	Reichsmark	RM
rm.	ream	riem
R.M.S.	Road Motor Service	PMD.
R.N.	Royal Navy	—
rom.	roman type	rom.
Rom.	Romans	Rom.
R.P.	reply paid	antw. bet.
r.p.m.	revolutions per minute	o.p.m.
R.R.	Right Reverend	H.Eerw.
r.r.	*reservatis reservandis* (with the necessary reservations)	r.r.
R.S.A.	Republic of South Africa	R.S.A.
R.S.A.	Radio South Africa	R.S.A.
R.S.V.P.	*répondez, s'il vous plaît* (please reply)	A.A.U.B.; R.S.V.P.
Rt. Hon.	Right Honourable	H.Ed.
r. to l.	right to left	v.r.n.l.
Rt. Rev.	Right Reverend	WelEerw.
R.U.	Rugby Union	R.U.
R.U.	Rhodes University	R.U.
Russ.	Russia	Rusl.
Russ.	Russian	Rus.
R(y).	Railway	spoorweg

S

English		Afrikaans
s.	*solidus* (shilling)	s.
S.	Sunday	So.
S.	South	S.
S.A.	South Africa	S.A.
S.A.	South America	S.A.
S.A.	senior advocate	S.A.
s.a.	*sine anno* (without date)	s.a.; s.j.
S.A.A.	South African Airways	S.A.L.
S.A.A.F.	South African Air Force	S.A.L.M.
S.A.A.U.	South African Agricultural Union	S.A.L.U.
Sab.	Sabbath	So.
S.A.B.C.	South African Broadcasting Corporation	S.A.U.K.
SABRA	South African Bureau of Race Affairs	SABRA
S.A.B.S.	South African Bureau of Standards	S.A.B.S.
S.A.C.S	South African College School	S.A.K.S.
S.A.L.A.	South African Library Association	S.A.B.V.
Sam.	Samuel	Sam.
SAMPI	South African Maize Producers' Institute	SAMPI
S.A.M.R.	South African Mounted Rifles	—
S.A.M.W.U.	South African Mine Workers' Union	S.A.M.W.U.
S.A.N.	South African Navy	S.A.V.
SANTA	South African National Tuberculosis Association	SANTA
S.A.P.	South African Police	S.A.P.
SAPA	South African Press Association	SAPA
S.A.P.F.	South African Permanent Force	S.A.S.Mag.
S.A.R.	South African Republic	Z.A.R.
S.A.R.&H.	South African Railways and Harbours	S.A.S. & H.
S.A.S.	South African Ship	S.A.S.
SASOL	Suid-Afrikaanse Steenkool-, Olie- en Gaskorporasie, Bpk.	SASOL
Sat.	Saturday	Sa.
S.A.T.A.	South African Teacher's Association	S.A.T.A.
Satour	South African Tourist Corporation	Satoer
S.A.T.S.	South African Transport Services	S.A.V.
sc.	*scilicet* (to wit, namely)	sc.; t.w.
S.C.	*Senior Consultus* (Senior Counsel)	S.C.
S.C.A.	Students' Christian Association	C.S.V.
s. caps	small capitals	klein hoofl.
Scand.	Scandinavia(n)	Skand.
scil.	*scilicet* (to wit, namely)	sc.
Script.	Scripture	H.S.
s.d.	*sine die* (indefinitely)	s.d.
S.D.G.	*Soli Deo Gloria* (glory be to God alone)	S.D.G.
SE.	South-east	S.O.
S.(E.)A.T.O.	South (Eastern) Asian Treaty Organisation	SAVO
sec.	second	sek.
sec	secant	sec
Sec.	Secretary	sekr.
sec(y).	secretary	sekr., sekre.
Sel. Com.	Select Committee	G.K.
Sen.	Senate; Senator	sen.
sen.	*senior* (the elder)	sr.
Sept.	September	Sept.
seq.	*sequens* (the following, sing.)	d.a.v., seq., vlg.
seqq.	*sequentes* (following, pl).	vv., seqq.
sfz	*sforzando* (with sudden emphasis)	sfz
Sgt.	Sergeant	sers.
Sgt.-maj.	Sergeant-Major	sers.-maj.
s.g.	specific gravity	s.g.
sgd.	signed	get.; w.g.
S.G.E.	Superintendent-General of Education	S.G.O.
sh.	shilling	s.
sin	sine	sin
sing.	singular	ekv.
S.J.	*Societatis Jesu* (Society of Jesus)	S.J.
S.J.P.	Special Justice of the Peace	S.V.R.
Skt.	Sanskrit	Skt.
S.lat.	South latitude	SBr.
S.long.	Southern longitude	S.L.
S.M.	station-master	SM
S.M.	Southern Cross Medal	S.M.
s.o.	seller's option	vo.
soc.	society	ver.
S.O.D.	Shorter Oxford Dictionary	S.O.D.
S.O.E.	Sons of England	S.O.E.
SOEKOR	Southern Oil Exploration Corporation	SOEKOR
SOS	wireless code-signal of extreme distress	SOS
S.P.	State President	S.P.
sov.	sovereign	pd.
Sp.	Spain; Spanish	Sp.
S.P.C.A.	Society for the Prevention of Cruelty to Animals	D.B.V.

English			Afrikaans
spec.	special		spes.
sp. gr.	specific gravity		s.g.
S.P.Q.R.	*Senatus Populusque Romanus* (the senate and people of Rome)		S.P.Q.R.
sq.	square		vk.
sqn.	squadron		esk.
sq(q).	*sequentes; sequentia* (the following)		d.a.v.; s(e)q. vlg.
S.R.C.	Students' Representative Council		S.R.; V.S.R.
SS.	steamship		ss.
S.S.B.	Special Service Batallion		S.D.B.
SSE.	South-south-east		S.S.O.
SSW.	South-south-west		S.S.W.
st.	stone		14 pd.
St.	Street		str.
St.	Saint		H.; St.
stat.	statute		wetb.
sta.	station		sta.
Std.	Standard		st.
stg.	sterling		stg.
stud.	student		stud.
subj.	subject		onderw.; subj.
subj.	subjunctive		subj.
subst.	substantive		substantief
S(un).	Sunday		So.
sup.	*supra* (above)		sup.
sup(erl).	superlative		oortr.; sup.
suppl.	supplement		sup.
Supt.	Superintendent		supt.
s.v.	*sub voce* (under the voice)		s.v.
s.v.p.	*s'il vous plaît* (please)		asb.; s.v.p.
SW.	South-west		S.W.
S.W.A.	South West Africa		S.W.A.
SWAPAC	South West African Performing Arts Council		SWARUK
S.W.G.	standard wire gauge		SDN
syl.	syllable		letg.; sill.
syn.	synonym		sin.

T

t.	tome		Tom.
t.	ton		t.
T.	temperature		T.
T1, T2, T3	Teacher's Certificate 1st, 2nd, 3rd Class		O1, O2, O3
tab.	table		tab.
tan	tangent		tan
tar.	tariff		tar.
T.A.U.	Transvaal Agricultural Union		T.L.U.
T.B.	tuberculosis		t.b.c., tbc
tech.	technical		tegn.
technol.	technology		tegnol.
T.E.D.	Transvaal Education Department		T.O.D.
tel.	telegraph; telegraphic		tel., telegr.
tel. add.	telegraphic address		tel. ad.
temp.	temperature		temp.
T.E.P.A.	Teachers' Educational and Professional Association		T.E.P.A.
test.	testament		test.
T.H.	Their Highnesses		HH. KK. HH.
Th.	Thursday		Do.
Th.D.	*Theologiae Doctor* (Doctor of Theology)		Dr. Theol; Th(eol) D(r).
theol.	theology		teol.
The Rt. Hon.	The Right Honourable		S. Ed. Gestr.; S. H. Ed.
The Rt. Rev.	The Right Reverend		S. H. Eerw.
Thess.	Thessalonians		*Thess.*
Thos.	Thomas		*Tom.*
T.H.S.T.A.	Transvaal High School Teachers' Association		V.O.T.M.S.
Tim.	Timothy		*Tim.*
Tit.	Titus		*Tit.*
TNT	trinitrotoluene		TNT
Toc H.	Talbot House		—
trans.	transitive		oorg.
transl.	translation		vert.
Treas.	treasurer		penm.; tes.
T.R.H.	Their Royal Highness		HH. KK. HH.
Trig(on).	Trigonometry		Trig.
trs.	transpose		tr.
T.T.	telegraphic transfer		t.o.
T.T.A.	Transvaal Teachers' Association		—
T.U.	Trade Union		vakbond
T.U.C.	Trade Union Congress		—
T(ues).	Tuesday		Di.
Tvl.	Transvaal		Tvl.

English		Afrikaans
typ.	typographer; typographic(al)	tip.

U

u.c.	upper case	b.k.
U.C.O.F.S.	University College of the Orange Free State	U.K.O.V.S.
U.C.T.	University of Cape Town	U.K.
U.D.F.	Union Defence Force	U.V.M.
U.E.I.C.	United East India Company	V.O.I.K
U.D.I.	unilateral declaration of independence	—
U.F.	University of the Orange Free State	U.O.
u.f.o.	unknown flying object	o.v.v.
U.G.	Union Government	U.R.
UHF	ultra-high frequency	UHF
u.i.	*ut infra* (as below)	u.i.
U.K.	United Kingdom	V.K.
ult.	*ultimo* (last)	jl.; l.l.; ult.
U.N.	University of Natal	N.U.; U.N.
UNESCO	United Nations Educational, Scientific and Cultural Organisation	UNESCO
UNISA	University of South Africa	UNISA
Univ.	University	univ.
U.N.(O.)	United Nations (Organisation)	V.V.(O.)
U.O.	University of the Orange Free State	U.O.
U.O.F.S.	University of the Orange Free State	U.O.V.S.
u.p.	under proof	o.p.
U.P.	University of Pretoria	U.P.
U.P.	United Party	V.P.
U.P.E.	University of Port Elizabeth	U.P.E.
u.s.	*ut supra* (as above)	u.s.
U.S.	University of Stellenbosch	U.S.
U.S.A.	United States of America	V.S.A.
U.S.S.R.	Union of Socialistic Soviet Republics	U.S.S.R.
usu.	usually	gew.
U.W.	University of the Witwatersrand	U.W.; Wits.
ux.	*uxor* (wife)	v(r).

V

v.	verse	v., vs.
v.	*vide* (see)	kyk; sien
v.	*versus* (against)	vs.
v.	verb	v.; ww.
V	volt	v.
val.	valuta	val.
v(b).	verb	v.; ww.
V.C.	Victoria Cross	—
V.C.	Vice Chancellor	V.K.
V.D.M.	*Verbi Dei (Divini) Minister* (Minister of the Word of God)	V.D.M.
Ven.	Venerable	H. Eerw.
vet.	veterinary surgeon	veearts
v.f.	very fair	taamlik goed
v.g.	very good	baie goed
v.i.	verb intransitive	onoorg. ww.
vid.	*vide* (see, look)	kyk; sien
V.I.P.	very important person	B.B.P.
Vis.	Viscount	burggraaf
viz.	*videlicet* (namely)	d.w.s.; nl.; m.n.; t.w.
voc.	vocative	vok.
vocab.	vocabulary	woordelys
vol.	volume	dl.; ged.; jg.; vol.
V.P.	Vice-President	V.P.
vs.	*versus* (against)	vs.
Vulg.	Vulgata	Vulg.
v.v.	*vice versa* (the opposite)	v.v.; omgekeerd

W

W.	West	W.
W.	Wednesday	Wo.
w.	week	w
w.	weak	sw.
w.	wicket	p.
W.A.U.	Women's Agricultural Union	V.L.U
W.B.	way-bill	laaibrief
w.c.	water-closet	privaat
wd.	word	wd.
W(ed).	Wednesday	Wo.
W.G.A.	Wool Growers' Association	W.G.A.
W.I.	West Indies	W.I.
Wits.	University of the Witwatersrand	U.W.; Wits.
w(k).	week	w(k).
W. long.	Western longitude	W.L.
Wm.	William	Willem, William

English		Afrikaans
W.N.W.	West-north-west	W.N.W.
W./O.	Warrant Officer	adj.-off.
w.o.	walk over	p.g.
Wor.	Worship	Ed. Agb.
W.P.	Western Province	W.P.
wt.	weight	gew.
w/v	weight/volume	gew./v.

X

Xmas	Christmas	Kersfees

Y

yd.	yard	jt.
Y.M.C.A.	Young Men's Christian Association	C.J.M.V.
Your Hon.	Your honour	U Ed.
y(r).	year	j.
yrs.	yours	U dw.
Y.W.C.A.	Young Women's Christian Association	C.J.V.V.

Z

ZANU	Zimbabwe African National Union	ZANU
ZAPU	Zimbabwe African People's Union	ZAPU
Zech	Zechariah	Sag.
Zeph	Zephaniah	Sef.
Zool.	Zoology	Soöl.

2. SI- AND METRIC UNITS

English		Afrikaans
A	ampere	A
C	1. centigrade, Celsius	C
	2. coulomb	
°C	degree Celsius	°C
cc, cm³	cubic centimetre	cc, cm³
cal.	calory	kal.
cg	centigram	cg
cl	centilitre	cl
cm	centimetre	cm
cumec, m³/s	cubic metre per second	kumek, m³/s
db	decibel	db
Dg	decagram	Dg
dg	decigram	dg
Dl	decalitre	Dl
dl	decilitre	dl
Dm	decametre	Dm
dm	decimetre	dm
g	gram	g
gcm	gram centimetre	gcm
gcs	gram centimetre per second	gcs
gm	gramme	gm
H	henry	H
h	hour	h
ha	hectare	ha
Hg(m)	hectogram	Hg
Hl	hectolitre	Hl
Hm	hectometre	Hm
Hz	hertz	Hz
J	joule	J
K	kelvin	K
kg	kilogram	kg
kl	kilolitre	kl
km	kilometre	km
km/h	kilometres per hour	km/h
kV	kilovolt	kV
kVa	kilovolt ampere	kVa
kW	kilowatt	kW
kW.h	kilowatt hour	kW.h
l	litre	l
m	metre	m
mbar	millibar	mbar
mg	milligram	mg
ml	millilitre	ml
mm	millimetre	mm
MVA	megavolt ampere	MVA
N	newton	N
N.m	newton meter	N.m
Pa	pascal	Pa
S	siemens	S
V	volt	V
V.A	volt ampere	V.A
W	watt	W
Wb	weber	Wb

3. SYMBOLS

&	ampersand	ampersand
@	at	teen
A1	first class; the best	eersteklas; die beste

English		Afrikaans
B	black (pencil)	swart (potlood)
2B	double black (pencil)	dubbel swart (potlood)
3B	treble black (pencil)	driedubbel swart (potlood)
C	1. Roman 100	Romeinse 100
	2. Celsius, centigrade	Celsius
D	Roman 500	Romeinse 500
$	dollar	dollar
=	equals	is gelyk aan
H	hard (pencil)	hard (potlood)
HB	hard and black (pencil)	hard en swart (potlood)
2H	double hard (pencil)	dubbel hard (potlood)
3H	treble hard (pencil)	driedubbel hard (potlood)
L	Roman 50	Romeinse 50
£	pound (money)	pond (geld)
M	Roman 1 000	Romeinse 1 000
V	Roman 5	Romeinse 5
×	multiplication sign	vermenigvuldigingsteken
X	Roman 10	Romeinse 10